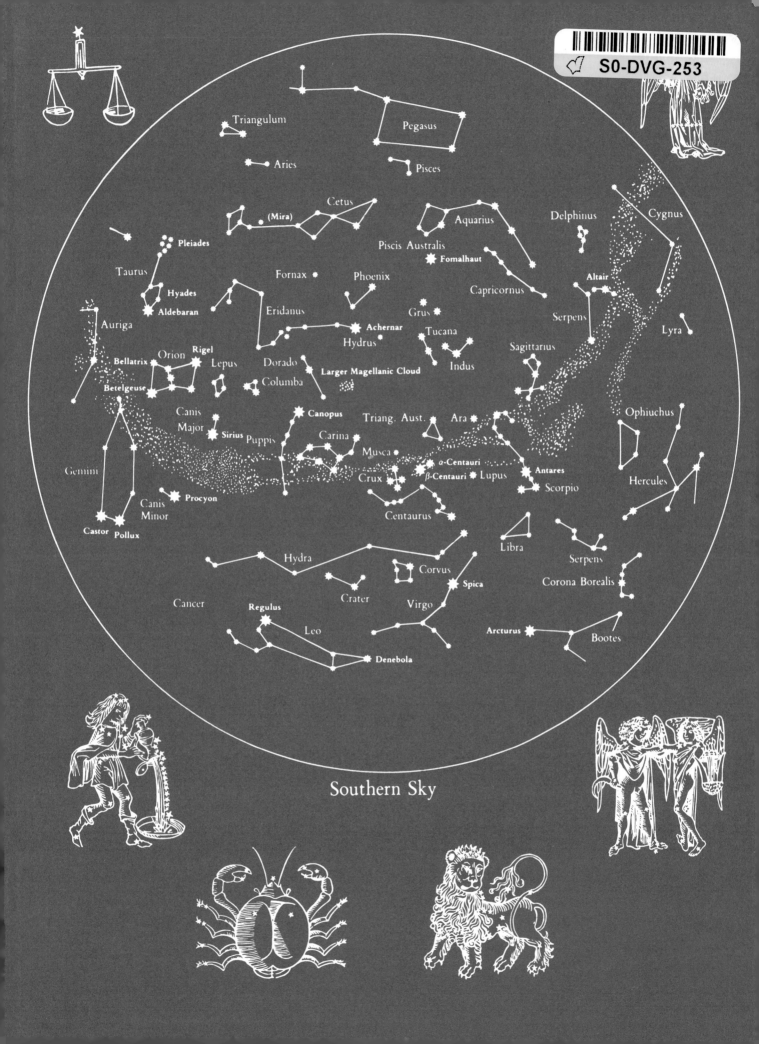

Southern Sky

THE NEW UNIVERSAL FAMILY ENCYCLOPEDIA

THE NEW UNIVERSAL FAMILY ENCYCLOPEDIA

RANDOM HOUSE

Copyright © 1981 Laurence Urdang Associates Ltd, Aylesbury
Copyright © 1985 Ottenheimer Publishers, Inc.
Jacket copyright © 1985 Random House, Inc.

All rights reserved. No part of this publication
may be reproduced or transmitted, in any form
or by any means, without permission.

Printed in the United States of America

International Standard Book Number: 394-53934-6
Library of Congress Catalog Card Number: 85-42711

PICTURE CREDITS

Black and white

The names of the agencies appear first, followed by the relevant page numbers. Where applicable the photographers' names follow immediately after the page number.

Heather Angel: 216, 235, 303, 760, 872, 904, 922; Ardea London: 1/P. Morris, 448/J. B. and S. Bottomley, 478/Dennis Avon and Tony Tilford, 483/K. Fink, 654/B. N. Douetil, 671/Pat Morris, 807/David and Katie Urry, 998/Dennis Avon and Tony Tilford, 1042 (right)/Acans Weaving; Ashmolean Museum, Oxford: 50, 1005; Australian Information Service, London: 60 (bottom left), 194, 666, 710, 713, 950; Clive Barda: 97; Barnaby's Picture Library: 60 (top left, center left, and bottom right), 84 (top left), 96, 156, 169, 184, 443, 472 (bottom right), 526, 821, 980, 982, 1050; BBC Hulton Picture Library: 220, 232, 260, 283, 294, 306, 319, 391, 465 (right), 537, 574, 594, 632, 684, 727, 816, 835, 847, 876, 910, 974, 1034, 1069; Courtesy of the British Library; 735; Courtesy of the Trustees, The British Museum: 455, 947; Courtesy of the British Tourist Authority: 2, 593, 861, 971 (bottom right), 1047; Camera Press: 27 (bottom right) 29, 34, 53, 64, 74, 84 (bottom right), 105, 112, 115, 132 (left), 146, 147, 152, 186, 190, 203 (left and right), 217, 256, 269, 291, 295, 313, 352, 360, 376 (right), 392, 407, 437, 480, 520, 524 (left), 536, 539, 555, 577, 607, 608, 624, 633, 638, 640, 645, 667, 670, 677, 693, 695 (left), 738, 749, 756, 762, 767, 773, 862, 903, 925, 934, 955, 970, 981, 984, 1013, 1020, 1033, 1042 (left), 1068; Bruce Coleman Ltd.: 10/Peter Jackson, 37/John Markham, 82/Udo Hirsch, 233/Cyril Laubscher, 225/Bill Wood, 405, 604/Graham Pizzey, 658/Jane Burton; The Danish Tourist Board: 39; Mary Evans Picture Library: 87, 174, 205, 286, 380/Sigmund Freud Collection, 423, 474/Harry Price Collection, University of London, 518, 522, 597, 708, 819, 959, 971 (top left and top right), 1074, 1077; Eric and David Hosking: 22 (top left), 102, 136 (left), 176, 199, 251, 355, 401, 445, 485, 490, 585, 702, 746, 814, 824 (left), 874, 897, 1052, 1059; Courtesy of the Imperial War Museum: 211, 589 (right); Reproduced by permission of the Director of the India Office Library and Records: 1028; Courtesy of the Italian State Tourist Office: 867, 899; Japan National Tourist Organization: 202; Crown Copyright, Reproduced with the permission of the Controller of Her Majesty's Stationery Office and of the Director, Royal Botanic Gardens, Kew: 4; Keystone: 326, 363, 412, 462, 595, 656, 936; Frank W. Lane: 201/Yves Temple, 308/Arthur Christiansen 725/R. van Nostrand; Mansell Collection: 22 (top right), 25, 27 (top right), 73, 78, 79, 106, 108, 110, 132 (top), 188, 192, 207, 227, 266, 275, 309, 312, 394, 408, 424, 488, 495, 496, 530, 552, 553, 589 (left), 623, 689, 706, 728, 736, 739, 744, 833, 841, 846, 879, 930, 940, 985, 1008, 1010, 1032, 1045 (left and right); Merseyside County Museums, Liverpool: 196; Tony and Marion Morrison: 7, 158, 564; Courtesy of the Trustees, The National Gallery, London: 388, 643, 793, 830, 852, The National Portrait Gallery, London: 153, 163, 166, 245, 290, 569, 695 (right), 837, 889, 1024, 1037 (bottom); The Natural History Photographic Agency: 142, 310/Stephen Dalton (top and bottom); Courtesy of the High Commissioner for New Zealand: 404, 919; Popperfoto: 41, 141, 281, 293, 311, 346, 472 (bottom center), 533, 544, 573,

621, 685, 718, 772, 797, 902, 926, 929, 1016 (left); Reproduced by gracious permission of Her Majesty the Queen: 204, 300, 576, 1022; Royal Greenwich Observatory: 237 (right), 694, 913, 945; The Salvation Army: 864; SATOUR photograph: 179; The Scottish National Portrait Gallery: 790; Smith Collection: 14, 168 (top and bottom), 278, 470 (right), 493, 908; Sperry New Holland: 237 (left); Sport and General Press Agency: 528, 534, 551; Sporting Pictures (UK) Ltd.: 138, 705, 757; The Tate Gallery, London: 464, 1001; Thomas Photos, Oxford: 158; John Topham Picture Library: 94, 124, 164 (right), 181, 213, 325, 429, 472 (bottom left), 571, 631, 680, 730, 753, 822; U.S. Army: 605, 995; U.S. Library of Congress: 8 (right), 187 (left), 302, 306 (bottom), 320, 349, 368, 376 (left), 403, 415, 440, 456, 465 (right), 470 (left), 513, 538, 572, 584 (left), 584 (right), 709, 729, 905, 938, 975, 1002, 1037 (top), 1051, 1054, 1071; U.S. Military Academy Archives: 420; U.S. National Portrait Gallery: 8 (left); U.S. Office of the Vice President: 164; U.S. Office of War Information, National Archives: 136 (right), 453; U.S. The White House: 524 (right), 824 (right); Victoria and Albert Museum, Crown Copyright: 116, 127, 157, 215, 489, 507, 516, 557, 562, 568, 614, 663, 678, 687, 826, 971 (bottom left); Vision International: 60/Angelo Hornak (top right), 60/Paolo Koch (center right), 472/Elizabeth Weiland (top right, top center, and top left); Reproduced by permission of the Trustees. The Wallace Collection, London: 374, 430; Peter Warren: 58 (bottom left, center and right); Windsor Safari Park: 543; The Zoological Society of London: 122, 1016 (right).

Color

Maps Macmillan Education Limited. World, Political copyright © 1980, 1984 Macmillan Publishers; World, Physical copyright © 1980, 1984 Macmillan Publishers; World, Population copyright © 1980, 1985 Macmillan Publishers; World, Economic Development copyright © 1980, 1984 Macmillan Publishers; World, Climatic Regions copyright © 1980, 1984 MacMillan Publishers; World, Vegetation copyright © 1980, 1984 Macmillan Publishers; World, Geology copyright © 1980, 1984 Macmillan Pubishers; North America, Physical and Political copyright © 1980, 1984 Macmillan Publishers; USA, Political copyright © 1980, 1985 Macmillan Publishers; South America, Physical and Political copyright © 1980, 1984 Macmillan Publishers; Europe, Physical and Political copyright © 1980, 1984 Macmillan Publishers; Western Europe, Physical and Political copyright © 1980, 1984 Macmillan Publishers; Soviet Union, Physical and Political copyright © 1980, 1984 Macmillan Publishers; Africa, Physical and Political copyright © 1980, 1984 Macmillan Publishers; Asia, Physical and Political copyright © 1980, 1984 Macmillan Publishers; Australasia, Physical and Political copyright © 1980, 1984 Macmillan Publishers.

Endpapers *Artwork:* Berry/Fallon Design, *Prints:* Ann Ronan Picture Library.

Preface

In some 25,000 articles and almost 1,500,000 words, the contributors and editors of this encyclopedia have attempted to cover the whole range of human activity—history, sciences, the arts, geography, biography, ideas, and beliefs, as well as sports, hobbies, and pastimes. To reach this goal, extensive use has been made of a computerized system specifically designed to assist in the compilation and typesetting of a very large body of research and manuscript. This system permitted the creation of a data base that could be quickly and easily kept up to date and that automatically checked for cross referencing. More important, it allowed the compilation of the book by subject areas before the final editing into an alphabetical arrangement, thus ensuring consistent coverage of each subject and all subject areas. The text is supported by more than 1200 photographs, drawings, and diagrams, and in addition, a 16-page, full-color atlas of the world is bound into the center of the book.

In order to cover such a wide range of subjects in one relatively compact volume, contributors and editors were instructed to provide the maximum amount of information in the available space and to confine themselves to facts rather than speculation and opinions. They had to meet the challenge of making often complex and sophisticated concepts intelligible in a limited space to general readers who might have no specialized knowledge of many of the subjects. To make this volume as useful as possible, all those who contributed to it were guided by three principles: to write in simple but precise non-technical language comprehensible to the general reader; to present all material concisely without oversimplification; and to make sure that all articles would be informative and of value to the modern reader, including all levels of students.

We believe that the contributors and writers have succeeded admirably and produced a truly up-to-date encyclopedia that everyone can use for quick, easy, and accurate reference and that everyone can browse through for instruction and increased awareness and knowledge in almost every field. Who was *Thomas Jefferson* and what did he accomplish? What is a *capybara* and what does it look like? When did *Martin Luther King* die and who killed him? Where is *Samarkand* and how many people live there? What is the theory of *relativity* about and what are its practical applications? What is the *theater of the absurd* and who are its chief exponents? *The New Universal Family Encyclopedia* will answer thousands upon thousands of such questions with precise, intelligible answers and lead many readers to explore such topics and related ones more fully.

The editors would like to thank all of the many contributors, special advisers, researchers, writers, and others whose work and diligence have contributed so much to the scope, accuracy, and readability of this volume.

Notes on using this encyclopedia
1. All articles are in alphabetical order.
2. The extensive use of cross references makes this encyclopedia virtually self-indexing. Two cross-reference symbols are used: an asterisk (*) preceding a term in the text indicates that the term has its own article in this encyclopedia and that further or related information will be found there; a raised square (□) preceding a term indicates that an illustration relevant to the article being read will be found at or near the term so marked; the term itself may also contain pertinent information.
3. The population figures given for cities and towns refer, wherever possible, to the actual cities and towns themselves, rather than to the larger urban areas of which they may be a part.
4. Except for a small number of the most familiar Chinese names (as Canton, Chiang Kai-shek, China, Chou En-lai, Inner Mongolia, Mao Tse-tung, Peking, Sun Yat-sen, Tibet, Yangtze River, and Yellow River), this encyclopedia follows official Chinese practice in using the pinyin system of transliterating Chinese names. When pinyin is used, however, the names will also be found in the older Wade-Giles system in their alphabetical place, so that the reader who is looking up a Chinese name in its older spelling will be referred to the modern pinyin name under which the article appears (the Wade-Giles equivalent and any other conventional western name is then also given in parentheses following the pinyin name at the main article).

EDITORIAL STAFF

Revised Edition
Editors
Stephen P. Elliott
Alan Isaacs

Assistant Editors
Suzanne Stone Burke
Carol B. Dudley
Susan Carter Elliott
Alexander Hellemans
Elizabeth J. Jewell
Rebecca Lyon
Jennifer Monk
David Pickering
Neil Asher Silberman
Anne Skagen
Diane Bell Surprenant
Dinah Verman

First Edition
Editor
Alan Isaacs

Subject Editors
Barbara Barrett
John Daintith
Thomas Hill Long
Elizabeth Martin
Judith Ravenscroft
Michael Scott Rohan
Jennifer Speake

Assistant Editors
Robert Hine
Jonathan Hunt
Nada Lyons
Martin Manser
Susan O'Neill
Carol Russell
Mary Shields
Jacqueline Smith
Elizabeth Tootill
Maurice Waite
Rosalind Williams

Illustration and Design
Barbara Barrett
Juliet Brightmore (consultant)
Jennifer Speake
Robert Updegraff

Picture Research
Jacqueline Smith
Valerie Walker

Artwork
Oxford Illustrators Ltd.

Contributors
J.E. Abbott
Francis Absalom
Joan Ashley
Howard H. R. Bailes
Jill Bailey
Helen Banks

Antoinette Bates
Alison Bideleux
T. J. Boardman
Charles Boyle
O.M.C. Buchan
W.P. Cass
Kathleen Clarke
P.B. Clarke
J.A. Cudden
S.R. Elliot
Martin Elliott
Jane A. Freeman
B.J. Golding
Chris Gray
M.B. Hamilton
P.W. Hanks
G.R. Hawting
Vincent Hetreed
Anne Holloway
Glyn Alyn Hughes
Valerie Illingworth
Yvonne Jacobs
J.B. Katz
Helen Kearsley
Susan Laker
N.R.M. de Lange
David Langford
Marise Larkin
Richard Latham
Bridget Loney
Michael MacCarthy-Morrogh
Iseabail Macleod
Martin Meggs
Denise Mitchell
J.S. Morris
Sa'id Mosteshar-Gharai
Jocelyn Murray
H.M. Nahmad
Ruth D. Newell
Pastor Stuart Olyott
John Oram
Stephanie L. Pain
Ann Palmer

Christopher D. Parker
Kathleen A. Pavelko
I.G. Pears
Volodimir Pechenuk
David A. Ramsay
Elfrida Savigear
Michael Scherk
Kenneth Scholes
Nigel Seller
J.H. Shaw
N. Shiel
Adrian Shubert
Laurel Thomas Silantien
R.L. Sims
Richard Smith
Jane Southern
Stella Stiegeler
B.R. Stratton
Stephanie Stuart
Eric A. Taylor
Ivan Vince
Margaret Wallis
C.S.P. Wolstenholme
Rebecca Woodell
R. Wrigley

Advisers
Stephen Brooks
Jacqueline Bruce
Richard Elms
Clive Farahar
A.M. Genton
Lawrence Hills
Michael Naish
Sally Naish
Michael D. Robson
J.T.R. Sharrock
Margaret Spencer
Mike Torbe
Basil Wright

Computerization
Barry Evans
Sarah Mitchell

A

Aachen (French name: Aix-la-Chapelle)   50 46N 06 06E A spa city in W West Germany, in North Rhine-Westphalia near the Belgian and Dutch borders. It is an important industrial center with iron and steel and textile industries. Its technical university was established in 1870. *History*: it was the N capital of Charlemagne's empire and many Holy Roman Emperors were crowned in the cathedral (founded in 796 AD). It was annexed by France in 1801 and passed to Prussia (1815). Extensively damaged during World War II, it was the first major German city captured by the Allies (1944). Population (1980 est): 242,700.

Aalborg. *See* Ålborg.

Aalst (French name: Alost)   50 47N 05 12E A city in N central Belgium, on the Dender River. It possesses the country's oldest town hall (begun 1200). Industries include textiles and brewing. Population (1981 est): 78,860.

Aalto, Alvar   (1898–1976) Finnish architect and furniture designer. Aalto established a distinctive "Finnish" style, with his use of timber and high pitched roofs. After World War II he became increasingly individualistic and his hall of residence at the Massachusetts Institute of Technology and the Helsinki Hall of Culture (1958) are among his best work.

Aaltonen, Wäinö   (1894–1966) Finnish sculptor. He is known for the portrait sculptures of the Finnish Olympic runner Paavo Nurmi (1924) and of Sibelius (1928).

AARDVARK   *This strange animal feeds entirely on termites and ants. It has very few teeth, which are weak and peg-shaped and specialized to cope with its diet.*

aardvark (Afrikaans: earth pig)   A nocturnal African mammal, *Orycteropus afer*, also called ant bear. It is about 5 ft (1.5 m) long, lives in grassland, and has a long snout, large ears, and a thick tail. Its strong claws are used to dig burrows and tear open the mounds of termites, which are picked up with its long sticky tongue. The aardvark is the only member of its order (*Tubulidentata*).

aardwolf   A nocturnal mammal, *Proteles cristatus*, that lives in open and bushy regions of southern and eastern Africa. It resembles a small striped hyena, about 20 in (50 cm) high at the shoulder, but has small simple teeth suitable for feeding on termites (which form the main part of its diet). It spends the day in burrows, often those deserted by other animals. Family: *Hyaenidae* (hyenas); order: *Carnivora*.

Aarhus. *See* Århus.

Aaron, Hank   (Henry Louis A.; 1934–   ) US baseball player. He played for the Milwaukee (later Atlanta) Braves (1954–74) and for the Milwaukee Brewers (1975–76). An outfielder, he was best known for his consistent hitting and was credited with a record career total of 755 home runs. He became a member of the Baseball Hall of Fame in 1982.

Aaron   In the Old Testament, the elder brother of Moses, whom he assisted as leader of the Israelites in their journey from Egypt to the Promised Land (Canaan). Although he yielded to the people's demand to build the *golden calf as an idol, he and his descendants were confirmed by Jehovah as priests of the Hebrew nation.

abaca (*or* Manila hemp)   A fiber obtained from the leafstalks of a palmlike plant, *Musa textilis* of the Philippines, related to the banana. It is used for ships' ropes and similar objects as it is buoyant and resistant to the action of sea water.

abacus   A calculating device consisting of balls strung on wires or rods set in a frame. It is probably of Babylonian origin but its use declined in Europe with the introduction of *Arabic numerals in about the 10th century AD. Until recently it was still in use in the Middle East and Japan.

Abadan   30 20N 48 15E A city in SW Iran, on an island in the Shatt (river) al-Arab. Much of Iran's oil is brought here by pipeline for refining or exporting. Population (1976): 296,081.

Abakan   53 43N 91 25E A city in the Soviet Union, the capital of the Khakass autonomous region (*oblast*) in the RSFSR at the confluence of the Abakan and Yenisei Rivers. It is the center of a coalmining district. Population (1980 est): 123,000.

abalone   A marine *gastropod mollusk belonging to the widely distributed family *Haliotidae*, of rocky coasts, also called ear shell or ormer. Up to 12 in (30 cm) long, their dishlike □shells have a row of holes along the outer edge through which deoxygenated water and waste products are expelled from the body. The large foot is considered a delicacy and the shells are used as mother-of-pearl for ornaments.

abandonment   In law, the voluntary relinquishment of property or rights without passing them on to another. For example, when a ship is left crewless and adrift, notice of abandonment can be issued to the insurers and a claim made for a constructive total loss (as opposed to an actual total loss if it sinks).

Abbadids   A Muslim dynasty in Andalusia (1023–91). Abbad I (reigned 1023–42) declared Seville's independence from Córdoba (1023) and by war and intrigue enlarged his territory. Abbad II (reigned 1042–69) continued this expansion, but failed to capture Córdoba. He is remembered for his delight in a flower garden planted over his enemies' skulls. Abbad III (d. 1095; reigned 1069–91), poet and king, made Seville an important cultural center. The hostility of Spanish Christians forced him into an alliance with the *Almoravids, who later deposed him (1091) and exiled him to N Africa, where he died.

'Abbasids   A powerful dynasty of *caliphs, which ruled Islam from 750 AD to 1258. They were descended from Mohammed's uncle al-Abbas (566–652). In 750 they seized power from the Umayyads in Damascus and moved their capital to Baghdad. The 'Abbasids were known for their imposition of strict religious orthodoxy and their patronage of scholarship. Under *Harun ar-Rashid (786–809) the dynasty was at its peak. By the 10th century its powers were declining as provincial governors asserted their independence of Baghdad, which was still, however, an important commercial, cultural, and intellectual center. Baghdad fell to the Mongols in 1258 and a branch of the 'Abbasids was installed in Cairo until that city fell to the *Ottomans in 1517. The last of the line died in 1538.

Abbas (I) the Great   (1557–1628) Shah of Persia (1588–1628) of the Safavid dynasty, who greatly extended Persian territory by defeating the Uzbeks (near Herat, 1598) and the Ottomans (1605, 1618). He created a standing army, established the Persian capital of Isfahan, and was an effective patron of the arts.

Abbas II   (1874–1944) The last Khedive of Egypt (1892–1914), who supported nationalist opposition to British influence and was deposed when Britain declared a protectorate over Egypt in 1914.

Abbeville   50 06N 1 57E A city in N France, in the Somme department situated near the mouth of the Somme River. It was here that Louis XII married Mary, sister of Henry VIII of England. Notable buildings include a gothic church (15th–17th centuries) and there are brewing, sugar-refining, and carpet industries. Population (1975): 26,581.

Abbevillian   A culture of the Lower *Paleolithic in Europe. It is characterized by crude stone hand axes made by hammering flakes off a flint with another stone. Named for *Abbeville in France, the Abbevillian also appears in Britain but in Africa similar early hand axes are designated *Acheulian.

Abbey Theatre   A Dublin theater opened in 1904 and closely associated with the *Irish Literary Renaissance. The Abbey Theatre produced plays by Yeats, Lady Gregory, Synge, George Russell (pseudonym AE) Shaw, and O'Casey and gained an international reputation as a repertory theater dedicated to performing mainly plays by Irish playwrights on Irish subjects. The original playhouse burned down in 1951, but a new theater opened in 1966.

Abbott, Berenice (1898–) US photographer. As an assistant to Man *Ray in Paris during the 1920s, she photographed well-known artists and writers. From 1929 her work included a photographic documentation of New York City and, later, of phenomena in the world of science.

ABC Mediation (1915) An unsuccessful attempt by Argentina, Brazil, and Chile to mediate differences between the US and Mexico after the US had sent troops to Vera Cruz, Mexico.

Abd Allah (1846–99) Sudanese leader, known as the Khalifa (caliph). In 1885 he succeeded Muhammad Ahmad (*see* Mahdi, al-) as leader of the uprising against the Egyptian government of the Sudan. He was defeated by *Kitchener in 1898 and was killed in subsequent mopping-up operations.

'Abd al-Malik ibn Marwan (c. 646–705 AD) Fifth *caliph (685–705) of the Umayyad dynasty, who subdued opposition to Umayyad rule of Islam. He defeated the northern Arab tribes in 691 and, with the help of his general al-Hajjaj, overcame resistance in Iraq (692). In 697 he captured Carthage. During his reign, Arabic became the administrative language of the empire and a new Muslim currency was coined.

'Abd ar-Rahman III an-Nasir (891–961 AD) Emir (912–29) and first caliph (929–61) of the Umayyad Arab dynasty of Córdoba. He conquered Muslim Spain and also campaigned against the Christian north: in 924 he took Pampalona, the capital of Navarre, but was defeated by the King of León in 939. Under his rule, Córdoba became a noted center of learning and the arts.

Abdelkader (c. 1807–83) Algerian nationalist, who resisted the French invasion. He became Emir of Mascara in 1832 and gained control of the Oran region. Victories against the French (1835–37) facilitated a further extension of his territories. Defeated in 1841, he withdrew to Morocco and finally surrendered to the French in 1847.

abdomen In mammals (including man), the region of the body extending from the lower surface of the diaphragm to the pelvis. The abdomen contains the intestines, liver, pancreas, kidneys, gall bladder, and—in females—the ovaries and womb. In arthropods, the abdomen is the posterior section of the body, which is usually segmented.

Abdulhamid II (1842–1918) Sultan of the Ottoman Empire (1876–1909), notorious for the Armenian massacres (1894–96). Following defeat by Russia (1877), he dismissed parliament and suspended the constitution. Thereafter he ruled autocratically, instituting many administrative reforms, especially in education, and opposing western interference in Ottoman affairs. The revolt of the *Young Turks in 1908 brought about his deposition.

Abdul-Jabbar, Kareem (b. Ferdinand Lewis Alcindor; 1947–) US basketball player. At 7 ft 2 in in height, he played college basketball (1965–69) at the University of California at Los Angeles (UCLA), during which time the school won three National Collegiate Athletic Association (NCAA) titles. With the Milwaukee Bucks (1969–75) and the Los Angeles Lakers (1975–), he was named the National Basketball Association (NBA) regular season most valuable player (MVP) six times.

Abdullah (1882–1951) Emir of Transjordan (1921–46) and first King of Jordan (1946–51). He fought with T. E. *Lawrence in the Arab revolt against Turkish rule during World War I. He was assassinated in 1951.

Abdul Rahman, Tunku (1903–73) Malaysian statesman. He was the first prime minister of independent Malaya (1957–63) and of Malaysia (1963–70). He led the Alliance Party to electoral victory in 1955, becoming chief minister and negotiating Malayan independence from Britain (1957) and the formation of Malaysia (1963).

Abel. *See* Cain.

Abelard, Peter (1079–1142) French philosopher. His ill-fated marriage with Heloïse, niece of a canon of Paris, ended when Abelard was castrated by thugs hired by the canon (1118). He retired to a monastery and she became a nun. Abelard turned his formidable powers as a logician to establishing a coherent relationship between faith and reason (*see* scholasticism). A quarrelsome disputant, Abelard was perpetually in trouble with the church authorities; his *Sic et Non* (*For and Against*), for example, outraged opponents by listing points on which acknowledged authorities differed.

abelmosk A flowering plant, *Hibiscus moschatus* (*H. abelmoschus*), native to India. It has large flowers with yellow petals and red centers and grows to a height of 24–71 in (60–180 cm). Abelmosk is cultivated for its

seeds, which yield musk used in perfumes, and for its young fruits, which are used as vegetables. Family: *Malvaceae* (mallow family).

Abeokuta 7 10N 3 26E A city in SW Nigeria. It is an important quarrying and agricultural center but manufacturing is limited. Population (1975 est): 253,000.

ABERDEEN *Provost Skene's House, dating from the 16th century. Saved from demolition in the early 1950s, it has since been extensively restored.*

Aberdeen 57 10N 2 04W A city, port, and former county of NE Scotland, the administrative center of Grampian Region situated on the North Sea coast between the mouths of the Rivers Don and Dee. Aberdeen is an old cathedral city with a university dating from 1494 (King's College). Fishing has always been important, as has the working of local granite; the "Granite City" provided stone for London's cobbled streets in the 18th century. Other industries include shipbuilding, paper making, textiles, chemicals, and engineering. Aberdeen's proximity to North Sea oil has transformed it into an important service center for the oil industry. Aberdeen has well-known research institutes for fisheries, soils, and animal nutrition. Population (1981): 190,200.

Aberdeen, George Hamilton-Gordon, 4th Earl of (1784–1860) British statesman; prime minister (1852–55). He was foreign secretary in Sir Robert *Peel's Conservative government (1841–46). Aberdeen succeeded Peel as leader of the "Peelites" (1850) and became prime minister of a coalition government of Whigs and Peelites.

Aberdeen Angus A breed of polled (naturally hornless) beef cattle, originating from NE Scotland. Short, stocky, and usually black (some have red coats), they are hardy and adapt well to different climates. Angus bulls are commonly mated with dairy breeds to produce a polled beef cross.

Aberdeen terrier. *See* Scottish terrier.

aberration **1.** A defect in a lens or mirror that causes blurring or distortion of the image. The three most important types are spherical aberration, chromatic aberration, and *astigmatism. Spherical aberration is caused by rays from the outside of the lens or mirror being brought to a focus at a different point from those nearer to the center. In chromatic aberration, different colors are focused at different points, since the refractive index of glass varies with the wavelength (*see* achromatic lens). **2.** An apparent displacement in the position of a star or other heavenly body resulting from the motion of the observer with the earth in its orbit round the sun.

Abidjan 5 19N 4 00W The capital of the Ivory Coast, off the Gulf of Guinea. A small village until developed by the French in the 1920s, it became the capital in 1934. It is now an important port, linked to the sea by the Vridi Canal. The National University was founded in 1964. Population (1976 est): 850,000.

Abilene 38 55N 97 13W A city in N central Kansas. Situated on the Smoky Hill River, it was founded in 1856 and quickly became a distribution hub for cattle from Texas. It is now a major shipping center for the area's grain and livestock and houses the memorabilia of Dwight D. Eisenhower. Population (1980): 6572.

Abilene 32 27N 99 45W A city in central Texas. A major trading center for cotton, grain, and livestock, it has timber mills as well as clothing and food-processing industries. Population (1980): 98,231.

Abjuration, Act of (1581) The declaration of independence by the United Provinces. The Dutch thus renounced their allegiance to *Philip II of Spain. *See also* Revolt of the Netherlands.

Abkhaz Autonomous Soviet Socialist Republic (*or* Abkhazia) An administrative division in the S Soviet Union, in the Georgian SSR between the Black Sea and the Caucasus Mountains. Most of the population is Abkhazian or Georgian and lives along the narrow subtropical coastal lowland. The region is predominantly agricultural, producing tobacco, tea, and citrus fruits, and the chief mineral is coal. There are several health resorts. *History*: invaded by the Romans, it later gained independence before coming under the Ottoman Turks in the 16th century. It became a Russian protectorate in 1810 and an autonomous republic in 1921. Area: 3320 sq mi (8600 sq km). Population (1981 est): 509,000. Capital: Sukhumi.

abnormal psychology That branch of *psychology that deals with the basic theory involving psychotic or behavioral disorders, such as *schizophrenia and *phobias and abnormalities due to brain damage and retardation.

Åbo. *See* Turku.

Abolition Movement The 19th century political and moral campaign to abolish *slavery in the US. Soon after the Revolutionary War, opponents of the institution of slavery began to pressure the national government to restrict its legality. In 1787 slavery was prohibited in the Northwest Territory and in 1808 Congress enacted a law that ended the importation of slaves into the US. By the terms of the *Missouri Compromise of 1820, slavery was prohibited in the area of the Louisiana Purchase north of the 36°30′ line. Among the early leaders of the Abolition Movement were William Lloyd *Garrison, publisher of the *Liberator* and one of the founders of the New England Anti-Slavery Society; Frederick *Douglass, a prominent orator and publisher; and James Birney, who ran for President as the candidate of the abolitionist Liberty Party in 1840 and 1844. Another abolitionist party, the Free Soil Party, sponsored the candidacy of former President William Van Buren in 1848. During the 1850s, Harriet *Tubman actively aided fugitive slaves to escape to freedom by means of the secret *Underground Railroad route. Perhaps the most influential work of anti-slavery literature was the novel *Uncle Tom's Cabin* written by Harriet Beecher *Stowe. The issue of slavery was finally settled by the *Civil War and the adoption of the 13th Amendment in 1865.

Abomey 7 14N 2 00E A city in S Benin. It was the capital of the Yoruba kingdom of Dahomey until captured by the French (1893). Population (1979 est): 41,000.

Abominable Snowman A creature, also called Yeti (Tibetan: Bearman), that is believed to live at high altitudes in the Himalayas. There have been no authenticated sightings, but gigantic footprints in the snow have been photographed (which may have other natural causes).

Aborigines 1. The dark-skinned hunters and gatherers who inhabited Australia before European settlement. There were about 500 Aboriginal tribes, which were linguistic groups having no social or political unity. The main social units were seminomadic bands. They were a diverse people culturally but, in general, material culture was rudimentary, while kinship organization and terminology were complex. Political affairs were conducted by older men. Male initiation and circumcision were commonly practiced. Aboriginal mythology was generally rich and elaborate and included accounts of creation during the primordial dawn, which they call "Dream Time." There are roughly 136,000 people of Aboriginal descent in Australia. The small proportion who maintain a nomadic way of life are threatened by encroachments upon their lands as these are opened up for mineral exploitation. A movement to protect Aborigines' rights has gathered momentum and in 1971 the first Aborigine MP was elected. **2.** Any indigenous people inhabiting a country, especially as contrasted with invaders or colonizers.

abortion The expulsion or removal of a fetus from the womb before it is capable of independent survival. Abortion may be natural (a miscarriage) or medically induced. Clinical methods for induced abortions include dilatation and curettage, suction by a vacuum aspirator, and the administration of certain drugs. Until 1973 many states severely restricted the use of induced abortion, but the US Supreme Court ruled in the case of *Roe* v. *Wade* that the decision of whether to have an abortion during the first three months of pregnancy should be left to the woman concerned and her physician. States may, however, restrict induced abortions after the third month. The moral question of abortion continues to be an issue of debate between the opponents of legalized abortion, the "Pro-Life" movement, and the supporters of the present policy, the "Pro-Choice" movement.

Aboukir Bay, Battle of (July 25, 1799) The battle in which Napoleon defeated the Ottoman Turks during his occupation of Egypt. The 7000-strong French army defeated the unruly Turkish force of 18,000.

Abraham In the Old Testament, patriarch and founder of the Hebrew nation, whose story as given in Genesis (11–25) appears to refer to events before 2000 BC. Born at Ur in Chaldaea, he followed a divine command and went first to Haran in N Mesopotamia and then to Canaan, accompanied by Sarah, his wife, and his nephew Lot. After being forced to withdraw to Egypt because of a famine, he returned to Canaan, where God promised him that the land would belong to his descendants. He had eight sons. God tested his obedience by commanding him to sacrifice his son Isaac; when he was about to obey, a ram was substituted and God reaffirmed the promises regarding Abraham's posterity.

Abraham, Plains of A plateau in E Canada, on the W edge of Quebec citadel. Here Gen James Wolfe defeated the French under Gen Montcalm (September 13, 1759), leading to British control over Canada.

abrasives Hard rough substances used to wear down the surfaces of less resistant materials. They are widely used in both industry and the home for polishing, grinding, cleaning, and shaping. Abrasives are either natural, such as sandpaper, emery, and pumice, or synthetic, such as silicon carbide and carborundum.

abraxas A mystic word, the Greek letters of which make 365 when read as numbers. Such words are found engraved and sometimes personified as a half-animal half-human deity on gemstones used as charms until the 13th century AD. It is particularly associated with *Gnosticism.

Abruzzi (*or* Abruzzo) A region in E central Italy. It consists of the Apennines in the W and a coastal region in the E. Agriculture is limited, producing mainly cereals. Manufacturing industry is primarily for local needs but there is a large fishing fleet. Area: 4167 sq mi (10 794 sq km). Population (1980 est): 1,245,112. Capital: L'Aquila.

abscess A pus-filled cavity surrounded by inflamed tissue, usually caused by bacterial infection. Abscesses may form anywhere in the body, including the skin, gums, and internal organs. They may heal without treatment, but usually they require draining and sometimes also antibiotics.

abscission The separation of a plant organ, such as a fruit or a leaf, from its stem. Individual cells at the base of the organ weaken by losing calcium from their cell walls and a sealant layer of cells protects the newly exposed surface. Abscission is controlled by plant hormones (*see* auxin).

absinthe A highly alcoholic drink made from spirits infused with herbs, including aniseed and wormwood. Absinthe has been banned in many countries because of the harmful effects of wormwood, and substitutes, known by different names (e.g. anis, pastis), are drunk instead. Absinthe is pale green and becomes cloudy when diluted with water.

absolute magnitude. *See* magnitude.

absolute zero The lowest temperature that can theoretically be attained. It is equal to –273.15°C or 0 K. In practice, absolute zero can never be reached, although temperatures of a few thousandths of a degree above absolute zero have been achieved. *See* cryogenics.

absolutism A political system, characteristic of European monarchies between the 16th and 18th centuries, in which the sovereign attempted (with limited practical success) to centralize power in his own person. *Louis XIV of France is often regarded as the typical absolute monarch. Justified by the theory of the *divine right of kings, absolutism was associated in the 18th century with enlightened despotism (*see* Enlightenment) but was challenged by the ideals of the *American and *French Revolutions.

absorption The assimilation of a substance by a solid or liquid, with or without chemical reaction. Moisture, for instance, can be absorbed from air by dehydrating agents, such as sulfuric acid. Certain porous solids, such as charcoal and zeolites, are able to absorb large quantities of gas. The process is distinguished from *adsorption in that the absorbed substance is held in the bulk of the solid rather than on a surface.

abstract art A nonobjective and nonrepresentational form of art. Tendencies to abstraction can be found in almost any age or school of art, particularly oriental and decorative art. However, the widespread use of *photography in the 20th century to create a permanent visual record of people, places, events, etc., made the strictly representational function of painting much less important. This shift of emphasis released artists from the confines of realism, enabling them to explore the wider fields of abstraction. In about 1910 *Kandinsky produced the first abstract watercolor, heralding the free expression of such artists as Jackson *Pollock; in contrast, *cubism led to the geometric abstract style of such painters as Piet *Mondrian and Kasimir *Malevich. A particular characteristic of abstract sculpture is the use of new materials, such as plastic, glass, and steel. *See also* action painting; constructivism; minimal art; op art; orphism; Stijl, de; suprematism.

abstract expressionism. *See* action painting.

Abstraction-Création An international group of abstract geometric artists, active from 1931 to 1936 and based in France under Georges Vantongerloo (1886–1965) and Auguste Herbin (1882–1960). It was also the name of their annual journal and exhibition.

Abu al-Wafa (940–98 AD) Persian mathematician and astronomer, who made notable contributions to *trigonometry. He invented the secant and cosecant functions (the inverse of the sine and cosine), drawing up accurate tables for them and for the sine and tangent functions.

Abu Bakar (c. 1843–95) Sultan of Johore (now in Malaysia) from 1885 to 1895. He became ruler of Johore in 1862, a year after Britain gained control of the state's foreign affairs, and contributed greatly to the maintenance of internal stability, fostering trade and agricultural development.

Abu Bakr (c. 573–634 AD) The first *caliph (632–34), known as as-Siddiq (the righteous). One of the earliest Muslims, Abu Bakr accompanied Mohammed to Medina and became caliph on his death. As caliph he defeated the rebellious tribes and began the invasion of Syria and Iraq.

Abu Dhabi. *See* United Arab Emirates.

Abu Hanifah (700–67 AD) Influential Muslim theologian and teacher of jurisprudence. Of Persian origin, he lived in Kufa (now in Iraq), where he died, perhaps in prison, after refusing to accept a post under the ruling dynasty. He left virtually no writings, but was known as a champion of the use of reason and analogy in law. His teachings form the basis of one of the two orthodox schools of the *Sunnites.

Abuja 9 10N 7 06E A town in central Nigeria. Agriculture is the most important activity with some local manufacturing. It became Nigeria's federal capital in 1982. Population (1972 est): 14,476.

Abu Nuwas (c. 762–c. 813 AD) Arab poet. Although he learned his craft from older poets and from the Bedouins, he abandoned traditional poetic forms and became popular for sophisticated lyrics celebrating the pleasures of wine and erotic affairs with women and boys. A favorite at the Abbasid court of *Harun ar-Rashid at Baghdad, he is portrayed in the *Arabian Nights* as a free-thinking pleasure-seeker.

Abu Simbel A monumental rock-cut temple complex constructed about 1250 BC by Pharaoh Ramses II in *Nubia. Four colossal statues of Ramses, each 66 ft (20 m) high, at the entrance were raised to escape inundation by Lake Nasser (1968).

Abutilon A genus of tropical and subtropical perennial herbs and shrubs (over 100 species). The plants reach a height of 12–60 in (30–150 cm) and have drooping stems with bell-shaped flowers. Some species are grown as ornamental plants. *A. avicennae* is cultivated in China for fiber (China jute). Family: *Malvaceae* (mallow family).

Abydos An ancient city in Upper Egypt, founded before 3000 BC and continuously occupied until Roman times. It was a principal center of *Osiris worship. The most impressive remaining structure is Seti I's Great Temple (c. 1300 BC), with shrines for six deities and the god pharaoh. The Table of Abydos, a king list carved on its walls, provides information about earlier pharaohs.

abyssal zone The ocean depths lying below 1000 m. It is the zone of greatest ocean depth, lying seaward of the continental slope (*see* continental shelf). Since no light penetrates to these depths, they contain relatively little marine life and the temperature never rises above 34°F (4°C). The ocean depths below 19,500 ft (6000 m), the deep-sea trenches, are sometimes classified separately as the **hadal zone.**

Abyssinian cat A breed of short-haired cat, many individuals of which are descendants of one exported to the UK from Abyssinia in the 19th century. They have slender bodies and wedge-shaped heads with large ears. The reddish-brown coat has black or brown markings and the eyes are green, yellow, or hazel. The Red Abyssinian is a rich copper-red.

Acacia A genus of tropical and subtropical trees and shrubs (over 700 species), particularly abundant in Australia (*see* wattle). Acacias have clusters of yellow or white flowers, produce long flattened pods, and usually have compound leaves consisting of many small leaflets. In some species

the leaflets do not develop and the leafstalks assume their function, being broad and flattened. These species are often very spiny. Acacias yield a number of useful products: gums (including *gum arabic), tannins, dyes, and woods suitable for furniture. Many are grown as ornamental plants. Family: *Leguminosae.*

Académie Française The French literary academy founded by Cardinal de Richelieu in 1634 (incorporated 1635) to preserve the French literary heritage. Its membership is limited at any one time to 40 "immortals," who have included Corneille, Racine, and Voltaire. It is continuously engaged in the revision of the official French dictionary.

Academy, Greek The college founded (c. 385 BC) near Athens by Plato, which continued in various guises until its dissolution by Justinian in 529 AD. It is famed mainly for contributions to philosophy and science. At first metaphysics and mathematics predominated but in the mid 3rd century BC philosophical skepticism became the overriding tendency.

Academy of Motion Picture Arts and Sciences An organization founded in Hollywood in 1927 to raise the artistic and technical standards of the film industry. It is responsible for the annual presentation of the Academy Awards, popularly known as Oscars, for excellence in acting, writing, directing, and other aspects of film production.

Acadia A former French colony in E Canada centered on present-day Novia Scotia. The original French settlement was destroyed by the British in 1613. Conflict over Acadia between French and British continued until 1763, when it fell finally to the British. Many Acadians were deported by the British and resettled in Louisiana, where their descendants, called Cajuns, still live. Longfellow's poem *Evangeline* tells their story.

Acadia National Park A national park on Mount Desert Island and part of Isle au Haut and the mainland along the N Atlantic coast of Maine. Established in 1919 as Layfayette and in 1929 as Acadia, it includes Cadillac Mountain 1530 ft (465 m). Area: 116.5 acres (47.2 hectares).

Acanthus A genus of perennial herbaceous plants (about 50 species), mostly native to the Mediterranean region: *A. mollis* and *A. spinosus* are the species most commonly planted in temperate gardens. Growing to a height of 40–60 in (1–1.5 m), they have tough leaves, often spiny and with deeply cut margins, and spikes of purple and white flowers. The fruit—a capsule—explodes to disperse the seeds. Family: *Acanthaceae.*

ACANTHUS *The spiky leaf of Acanthus spinosus inspired the decorative architectural motif used on Corinthian and Composite columns.*

acanthus A decorative element of classical architecture. It is mainly found on the capitals of Corinthian and Composite columns, and normally comprises heavy carvings of stylized leaves.

a cappella (Italian: in the church style) A marking on a piece of music for several voices, indicating that it is to be sung unaccompanied.

Acapulco 16 51N 99 56W A seaside resort in S Mexico, on the Pacific Ocean. Known as the Riviera of Mexico, it has fine sandy beaches and many hotels. Population (1978 est): 421,088.

Accademia The principal art gallery in Venice, opened in 1756 to display work by Venetian artists. Formerly a monastery, it houses masterpieces by such painters as Bellini, Titian, and Canaletto in a collection with items dating from the 13th century.

acceleration The rate of change of a body's velocity. Linear acceleration is the rate of change of linear velocity. It is measured in such units as meters per second per second. Angular acceleration is the rate of change of angular velocity and is measured in such units as radians per second per second.

acceleration of free fall (*g*) Formerly called acceleration due to gravity; the acceleration of a falling body when air resistance is neglected. Caused by gravitational attraction between the body and the earth, it varies slightly at different points on the earth's surface. Its standard value is 32 ft (9.806 m) per second.

accelerator principle The economic principle that investment will accentuate economic booms and *depressions. As income rises, businesses gain confidence in the expected future level of demand and increase their investment in plant and equipment; this pushes up employment in the capital-goods industries and heightens the boom. The converse applies to a slump.

accelerators Large machines used for accelerating beams of charged particles (electrons, protons, neutrons, etc.) to very high speeds primarily for research in *particle physics. The particles are accelerated by electric fields either in a straight line, as in the *linear accelerator, or in a circle, as in the *cyclotron, *synchrotron, and *synchrocyclotron. The beam is confined to its path by magnetic fields. The energies of the particles are measured in millions of electronvolts (MeV) or giga-electronvolts (1000 MeV = 1 GeV), some modern accelerators attaining several hundred GeV. Particle accelerators are used by directing a beam of particles at a stationary target or, for greater energy, by colliding two beams of particles together. Accelerators are also used to create artificial isotopes and in *radiotherapy. The first accelerator was a linear accelerator, produced in 1932 by *Cockcroft and *Watson.

accentor A small sparrow-like songbird belonging to an Old World family (*Prunellidae*; 12 species), usually restricted to northern and mountain regions. It has a red or brownish-gray plumage with gray underparts, often streaked or striped. Accentors feed on insects or—in winter—seeds and berries. The family includes the *dunnock (hedge sparrow).

accessory In criminal law, a person who incites another to commit a crime but is not present when the crime is committed is an accessory before the fact. (An abettor is distinguished from an accessory before the fact by being present at the commission of a crime.) A person who assists another whom he knows has committed a crime is an accessory after the fact.

Accius, Lucius (170–c. 85 BC) Roman tragic dramatist, admired for his melodramatic plots and lively rhetorical style. About 700 lines survive from over 40 of his plays, mainly on Greek mythological themes. He also wrote treatises on poetry and grammar.

accomplice In law, a person concerned with one or more other persons in committing a crime, either as a principal or an *accessory.

accordion A portable musical instrument invented in Berlin in 1822. A member of the reed-organ family, the accordion is a boxlike instrument in which bellows operated by the left arm force air through reeds mounted in end panels. In the modern **piano accordion** a small piano-like keyboard played by the right hand supplies the melody, while buttons operated by the left hand produce chords. The instrument is supported in front of the player's body by straps.

accountancy The profession of preparing, verifying, and interpreting the accounts of a business. The main branches are bookkeeping, auditing, financial accounting, and cost accounting. Bookkeeping is concerned with the preparation of records of all the financial transactions undertaken by a firm or a self-employed person, usually on a day-to-day basis. The books of account kept by a firm usually include a cash book to record all payments and receipts, a nominal ledger in which all transactions with named clients, suppliers, etc., are recorded, a purchase and a sales ledger, and sometimes purchase and sales day books. Auditing is the process of verifying that the bookkeeping and the preparation of accounts have been carried out accurately and truthfully. In most countries, including the UK and the US, auditing is carried out by an independent firm of accountants, which is required to certify that a company's accounts are a true record of its transactions during the past year. Financial accounting consists of analyzing a firm's transactions and summarizing them in the firm's annual accounts. These will normally consist of a profit and loss account and a balance sheet. The former lists the total sales, total purchases, opening and closing value of the inventory (or work in progress), and the expenses, enabling the profit or loss in the period to be calculated. The balance sheet lists the firm's assets and liabilities. Cost accounting identifies the costs of production at all stages of a manufacturing process. Unlike financial accounting it can be used to measure economic performance and the relative efficiency of the constituent parts of a business.

Accra 5 32N 0 12W The capital of Ghana, a port on the Gulf of Guinea. It is built on the site of three 17th-century trading fortresses founded by the English, Dutch, and Danish. It became the capital of the Gold Coast in 1877. Following the opening of a railway to the agricultural hinterland (1923) it developed rapidly into the commercial center of Ghana. The University of Ghana was founded in 1948 at Legon, just outside Accra. Population (1970): 564,194.

acetaldehyde (CH_3CHO) A colorless liquid *aldehyde with a pungent smell, formed by the oxidation of *ethanol. On further oxidation it becomes acetic acid.

acetic acid (CH_3COOH) The *acid contained (3% to 6%) in vinegar. It can be made from alcohol but for industrial purposes is commonly made from *acetaldehyde and is used in the manufacture of plastics.

acetone (*or* dimethyl ketone; CH_3COCH_3) A colorless inflammable liquid used as a solvent, for example in nail-polish remover and in the manufacture of rayon.

acetylcholine A chemical that transmits impulses between the ends of two adjacent nerves and is confined largely to the parasympathetic nervous system. Acetylcholine is released on stimulation of the nerve and diffuses across the gap of the *synapse to stimulate the adjacent nerve. It is rapidly converted to an inactive form by the enzyme cholinesterase, permitting the passage of a further impulse.

acetylene (*or* ethyne; C_2H_2) A colorless toxic inflammable gas. The two carbon atoms are joined by a triple bond and it forms the basis of a series of compounds called *alkynes. Acetylene is made by the action of water on calcium carbide and is widely used as a starting material for many organic compounds. Because of its high flame temperature (about 1864°F [3300°C]) it is used in oxy-acetylene welding.

Achaea A region of ancient Greece occupying the N coast of the Peloponnesus and SE Thessaly. The 12 towns of the region formed the **Achaean League** in the 4th century BC. Dissolved in the late 4th century, it was revived by the ten surviving cities in 280 BC and included non-Achaean cities, such as Sicyon. The League finally disintegrated when Achaea was annexed by Rome in 146 BC. Its NW part approximates the modern department of Achaea.

Achaeans An ancient Greek people mentioned by Homer as being among the besiegers of *Troy. They were probably related to the *Dorian Greeks but also seem to have had associations with *Mycenaean culture.

Achaemenians An ancient Persian dynasty founded by Achaemenes in the 7th century BC. Cyrus I (reigned c. 645–602 BC), Cambyses I (c. 602–559 BC), *Cyrus the Great (559–530 BC), who founded the Achaemenian (or Persian) Empire, and *Cambyses II (529–521 BC) belonged to the senior branch of the family. *Darius I (522–486 BC) headed the junior line, which included *Xerxes I (486–465 BC). The Achaemenian dynasty ended in 330 BC, when Alexander the Great defeated Darius III (336–330 BC).

Achebe, Chinua (1930–) Nigerian novelist of the Ibo tribe. His first novel, *Things Fall Apart* (1958), deals with the arrival of missionaries and colonial government in the Ibo homeland. The conflict between traditional African society and western values is a central theme in all his work. *A Man of the People* (1966) is a satirical attack on corrupt politics in modern Africa. His other works include a collection of short stories and a book of poems, *Beware Soul Brother* (1971).

achene A small dry *fruit having a single seed that is attached to the fruit wall at one point only. The fruit does not open at maturity (i.e. the fruit is indehiscent) and the seed is thus retained until germination. Lettuce fruits are examples of achenes.

Achernar A conspicuous blue star, apparent magnitude 0.5 and 114 light years distant, that is the brightest star in the constellation Eridanus.

Acheron A river in N Greece, in Greek mythology the chief river of the underworld. In Dante, it is the river across which the souls of the dead are ferried to hell by *Charon.

Acheson, Dean (Gooderham) (1893–1971) US lawyer and statesman. Serving in a variety of government posts including leading delegate to the Bretton Woods Conference (1944) and undersecretary of state (1945–47), he became influential in shaping foreign policy. As secretary of state in *Truman's cabinet (1949–53), his foreign policy aimed at the containment of Soviet communism. This led him to play a leading role in developing the Truman Doctrine, the *Marshall Plan, and the *North Atlantic Treaty Organization. After 1953 he continued advising American presidents. His memoir, *Present at the Creation*, was awarded the 1970 Pulitzer Prize.

Acheulian A culture of the Lower *Paleolithic. It is characterized by hand axes made by hammering flakes off a flint with a hammer of wood, antler, or bone, thus producing a more regular and effective tool than the

*Abbevillian hand axe. Named after St Acheul near Amiens (N France) the Acheulian occurs widely in Eurasia and also in Africa where it apparently originated and survived longest (until about 58,000 years ago). Acheulian sites provide the earliest evidence of man's use of fire and are often associated with *Homo erectus* remains (*see* Homo).

Achilles In Greek mythology, the greatest Greek warrior in the Trojan War. The son of Peleus, King of Thessaly, and Thetis, a sea nymph, he was dipped by his mother in the River Styx as a child, which made his whole body invulnerable except for the heel by which she had held him. After a quarrel with *Agamemnon he ceased fighting until the death of his friend *Patroclus at the hand of *Hector. Achilles then slew Hector and was himself later killed by Paris, who shot a poisoned arrow into his heel.

achromatic lens A combination of lenses used to eliminate chromatic *aberration in an optical system. The simplest type has two lenses of different powers made from different kinds of glass. The chromatic aberration of one lens is cancelled by the chromatic aberration of the other lens.

acids and bases Acids are chemical compounds containing hydrogen that can be replaced by a metal atom to produce a *salt. They have a sour taste and turn litmus red. When dissolved in water they dissociate into ions. Hydrochloric acid (HCl), for instance, gives chloride ions and hydrogen ions: $HCl + H_2O \rightarrow Cl^- + H^+ + H_2O$. The hydrogen ion is associated with a water molecule, a combination referred to as a hydroxonium ion (H_3O^+).

Strong acids dissociate completely in water; hydrochloric acid, sulfuric acid (H_2SO_4), and nitric acid (HNO_3) are common examples. Such compounds are extremely corrosive, sulfuric and nitric acids being particularly so because they are also powerful oxidizing agents. **Weak acids** do not dissociate completely. Many of these are organic compounds, usually carboxylic acids, which contain the carboxylate group –CO.OH. A large number occur naturally: for example, acetic acid (CH_3COOH) in vinegar, citric acid ($C_3H_4(OH)(COOH)_3$) in citrus fruits, and lactic acid ($C_2H_4(OH)COOH$) in milk.

Bases are compounds that react with acids to form salts and water. Bases that dissolve in water, known as **alkalis**, produce hydroxide ions (OH⁻). Many are metal hydroxides, such as sodium hydroxide (NaOH) and potassium hydroxide (KOH). Ammonia is also a base, reacting with water molecules to form ammonium ions and hydroxide ions: $NH_3 + H_2O \rightarrow NH_4^+ + OH^-$. The neutralization of an acid by a base in solution is a reaction in which hydrogen and hydroxide ions combine to give water. In chemistry the simple concept of acids and bases has been extended to include the concept of an acid as any compound that can donate a proton and a base as a proton acceptor. This (the Brönsted-Lowry theory) can be applied to reactions in nonaqueous solvents. A further extension of the terms (Lewis theory) defines an acid as an acceptor of an unshared electron pair and a base as a pair donor. *See also* pH.

acmeism A movement in Russian poetry in the 1910s and 1920s that asserted the value of precision against what was seen as the abstract vagueness of the symbolist movement. Because it was apolitical it met with official hostility, and several of its members, including *Akhmatova and *Mandelstan, were persecuted.

acne A skin condition, common in adolescence, affecting the face, chest, and back. Acne is caused by overactivity and inflammation of the sebaceous glands: oily sebum accumulates in the hair follicles, producing pustules and

MOUNT ACONCAGUA

blackheads. Acne usually disappears by the late twenties; severe cases can be treated with antibiotics.

Aconcagua, Mount (Spanish name: Cerro Aconcagua) 32 40S 70 02W A mountain in W Argentina, in the Andes, regarded as being the highest point in the W hemisphere. It is of volcanic origin. Height: 22,835 ft (6960 m).

aconite A European herbaceous plant, *Aconitum napellus*, also known as monkshood. Growing to a height of 40 in (1 m), its flowers are usually purplish-blue and hood-shaped; the bulbous roots yield poisonous *alkaloids, including aconitine, which have been used in medicine as *narcotics and analgesics. The genus, which is restricted to N temperate regions, also includes wolfsbane (*A. lycotonum*). Family: *Ranunculaceae* (buttercup family).

acornworm A wormlike marine invertebrate animal, 2–71 in (5–180 cm) long, that burrows in soft sand or mud. Its front end is acorn-shaped, with the mouth at the base. It filters food particles from sea water, which enters the mouth and passes out through gill slits along the length of the body. Chief genera: *Balanoglossus, Saccoglossus*; phylum: *Hemichordata*.

acouchi (*or* acushi) A small long-legged *rodent belonging to the genus *Myoprocta* (about 5 species). Acouchis have the same habits and lifestyle as the closely related agoutis but are smaller, measuring up to 18 in (45 cm) long. They have a thin white-tipped tail and lack the colored rump hairs of agoutis.

acoustics The branch of physics concerned with the production, propagation, reception, properties, and uses of sound. It has several subdivisions. The most important, architectural acoustics, is concerned with the design of public auditoriums so that sounds can be heard in all parts of them with the maximum clarity and the minimum distortion. *Ultrasonics is the study of very high frequency sound, especially as it is used in the investigation of matter and in industrial processes. The structure and function of sound sources, such as the voice, loudspeakers, etc., and sound receptors, such as the ear, microphones, etc., also form part of the study of acoustics. Other fields include speech communication and the design of machines that can understand spoken instructions.

acquired character. *See* Lamarckism.

acquired immune deficiency syndrome (AIDS) A sexually transmitted but slightly contagious disease of viral origin. The disorder is characterized by a marked decrease of helper-induced T-lymphocyte cells, resulting in a general breakdown of the immune system. AIDS manifests itself by the occurrence of opportunistic infections, such as persistent Herpes simplex, diffuse pneumonitis, mycobacterial tuberculosis, or by Kaposi's syndrome (tumors involving the skin and mucous membranes). Other sarcomas and a host of persistent disorders occur also. About 6000 cases (1984) are reported world-wide, and approximately half of these were fatal. The disease is found most frequently in homosexual males, intravenous drug users, and Haitians. The etiological agent, which can be transmitted by blood, and possibly by sperm or saliva, is the human T-cell leukemia virus type III (HTLV-III). The virus has been found in AIDS patients, but also in healthy individuals.

acquittal In criminal law, the clearing of an accused person of the charge against him, usually by court verdict. Acquittal prevents a person from being prosecuted for the same offense again. Anyone charged as an *accessory to a crime is automatically acquitted if the principal is acquitted.

Acre (Arabic name: 'Akko) 32 58N 35 06E A city in N Israel, on the Mediterranean coast. Acre was held by the Crusaders for many years and was in Turkish hands for several centuries. Allocated to the Arabs under the UN plan for *Palestine, it fell to the Jews in May, 1948, and became part of Israel. Its notable structures include walls and a mosque from the 18th century, and caravanserais. It is a fishing port and a center for light industry. Population (1970): 215,299.

acrolith A statue made, especially in ancient Greece, of marble for the flesh and gilded wood for the clothing. This method was a cheaper substitute for chryselephantine (gold and ivory) statuary. The acrolith's purpose was usually religious or monumental.

acromegaly A rare disease in which a noncancerous tumor of the pituitary gland secretes abnormally large amounts of *growth hormone. This causes enlargement of the face, hands, feet, and heart. The tumor can be destroyed by X-rays or surgically removed.

acropolis (Greek: high town) In ancient Greek towns, the isolated rocky plateau on which stood the religious and administrative nucleus of the town and which served as a citadel in time of war. *Mycenae and *Corinth have imposing examples, but the most famous is the Acropolis of

Athens, which is still adorned by remains of buildings erected by *Cimon, *Themistocles, and *Pericles after the sack of Athens by the Persians (480 BC). These buildings include the *Propylaea, *Parthenon, Erectheum, and the reconstructed temple of Athena Nike.

acrylic painting A method of painting using acrylic paint. An opaque bright smooth easily applied mixture, it has been used by many pop artists, notably David *Hockney.

acrylics Synthetic materials produced by *polymerization of acrylonitrile (vinyl cyanide; $CH_2:CHCN$). Acrylic resins are used in paints and plastics, a common one being Perspex. Acrylic fiber is widely used in textiles, mainly for knitwear, furnishing fabrics, and carpets. The fibers are strong, absorb little water, and resist most substances encountered in use, although they become plastic in hot water or steam. Modacrylic is acrylic fabric or yarn with more than 15% of other fibers added.

Acta The ancient Roman *Acta Senatus* (*Senate Business*) were official records of *Senate proceedings compiled by a senator chosen by the emperor. The *Acta Diurna* (*Daily News*) constituted a popular gazette of political and social news, instituted by Julius Caesar in 59 BC and continuing until 300 AD. The emperor's official enactments were also known as *Acta*.

Actaeon A mythological Greek hunter, son of the god Aristaeus and Autonoe, daughter of Cadmus, King of Thebes. Ovid, in his *Metamorphoses*, relates how Actaeon accidentally caught sight of the goddess Artemis bathing naked and was turned by her into a stag and killed by his own hounds.

ACTH (adrenocorticotrophic hormone) A peptide hormone, secreted by the anterior lobe of the pituitary gland, that stimulates the cortex of the adrenal glands to produce three types of *corticosteroid hormones. Secretion of ACTH is stimulated by physical stress and is regulated by secretions of the *hypothalamus of the brain.

actinides A group of related chemical elements in the periodic table ranging from actinium (atomic number 89) to lawrencium (atomic number 103). They are all radioactive and include a number of *transuranic elements. Chemically, they resemble the *lanthanides, having unfilled inner electron shells.

actinium (Ac) A highly radioactive metal that occurs naturally in uranium minerals. It is the first of the actinide series of elements and is chemically similar to the lanthanide elements. It was discovered in 1899 by A. L. Debierne (1874–1949). At no 89; at wt (227); mp 615°F (1050°C); half-life of ^{227}Ac 21.6 yrs.

actinium series One of three naturally occurring series of radioactive decays. The actinium series is headed by uranium-235 (known as actinouranium), which undergoes a series of alpha and beta decays ending with the stable isotope lead-207. See also thorium series; uranium series.

actinomycetes Bacteria belonging to the order *Actinomycetales*. They have rigid cell walls and often form branching filamentous moldlike colonies. Some may cause diseases in plants and animals, particularly *Mycobacterium tuberculosis*, which causes tuberculosis, and *M. leprae*, which causes leprosy; others are relatively harmless parasites inhabiting the gastrointestinal tract. Many are found in soil, where they decompose organic matter. Certain species produce valuable *antibiotics.

action painting A modern style, also called abstract expressionism, in which paint is sprayed, splashed, or dribbled over a large canvas to form an unpremeditated and usually abstract design. Jackson *Pollock invented it in 1947 to give free rein to his own emotions. It was later also used by Willem *de Kooning to produce figurative pictures. Together with color-field painting (see Rothko, Mark), action painting was the dominant style in the US in the 1950s and made New York, for the first time, the most advanced center of modern art.

action potential The change in electric potential on the surface of a nerve cell that occurs when the cell is stimulated. It results from sodium and potassium ions moving across the cell membrane. The electrochemical impulse travels along the nerve fiber, and in this way information is transmitted through the *nervous system. See also neuron; synapse.

Actium, Battle of (31 BC) The decisive land and sea battle that ended the civil war in ancient Rome. Octavian, later *Augustus (the first Roman emperor), defeated the forces of *Mark Antony and *Cleopatra.

activated charcoal Charcoal that has been processed to increase its power of absorption by heating it to drive off absorbed gas. It then has a high capacity for further absorption of gas in its pores. Uses of activated charcoal include removing impurities from gases and liquids and as filters in gas masks.

active galaxy Any galaxy, including *Seyfert galaxies, certain *radio galaxies, and *quasars, in which there is an unusually large release of energy, often from the center of the object. It has been suggested that the source of such violent activity is a supermassive *black hole.

act of God In law, an occurrence due to a sudden violent natural cause, such as a storm, which could not reasonably have been guarded against and loss from which could not have been avoided or predicted.

Acton, John Emerich Edward Dalberg-Acton, 1st Baron (1834–1902) British historian, born in Naples. As a Whig MP (1859–66) he formed a close friendship with Gladstone. Acton mobilized liberal Roman Catholic opinion against the doctrine of papal infallibility promulgated in 1870. Appointed professor of modern history at Cambridge (1895) he planned the *Cambridge Modern History*.

Actors' Studio An actors' workshop founded in New York in 1947 by Elia *Kazan and others. Under its director Lee Strasberg (1901–82), who joined it in 1950, it became famous for its emphasis on "method" acting, which was developed from the theories of *Stanislavsky. Film actors influenced by it include Marlon *Brando, Rod Steiger (1925–), and James *Dean.

Acts of the Apostles The fifth book of the New Testament, written by Luke about 63 AD as a sequel to his Gospel. Starting with the ascension of Christ, it deals with the rise and spread of the Christian Church from a single Jewish congregation at Jerusalem, where Peter is prominent, to Paul's first missionary journey and his eventual imprisonment at Rome.

actuary A mathematician employed by an *insurance company to calculate the premiums payable on policies. The calculations are based on statistically determined risks and eventualities (e.g. sickness, life expectancy).

acupuncture A traditional Chinese system of healing in which thin metal needles are inserted into selected points in the body. The needles are stimulated either by manual rotation or electrically. Acupuncture is used in the Far East to relieve pain and in China as an anesthetic for surgical operations. The traditional explanation of its effectiveness, dating back to 2500 BC, relates to balancing the opposing life forces *yin and yang. Recent research in the West suggests that the needles may activate deep sensory nerves, which cause the pituitary and midbrain to release endorphins (natural pain killers; see encephalins).

Adad A Babylonian and Assyrian weather god. He was worshiped as both creator and destroyer of life: his summer rains ensured a good harvest but his storms and floods brought terror and death. His father was Anu, god of the heavens.

Adalbert (c. 1000–72) German churchman, Archbishop of Bremen. From a noble Saxon family, he became a trusted and powerful adviser to Emperor Henry III. He was active in the evangelization of Scandinavia, the Orkneys, Iceland, and Greenland until his exile from Henry IV's court in 1066.

Adam, Adolphe-Charles (1803–56) French composer. He composed over 60 operas but is primarily remembered for his romantic ballet *Giselle* (1841), the earliest full-length ballet in the traditional repertoire.

Adam and Eve In the Old Testament, the first human beings. According to Genesis (2.7–3.24), Jehovah (or Yahweh) created Adam from dust in his own image and put him in the Garden of Eden. His wife Eve was created from one of his ribs. Tempted by the serpent (the devil) to eat the forbidden fruit of the Tree of Knowledge of Good and Evil, Eve succumbed to the temptation and induced Adam to eat the fruit also. They became aware of their guilt and were expelled from Eden. Their sons included *Cain and Abel.

Adam de la Halle (c. 1240–1290) French poet and musician. He traveled with his patron Robert II of Artois and became famous at the court of Charles of Anjou in Naples, where he died. His *Jeu de la feuillée* and *Jeu de Robin et Marion*, the first comic opera, combined popular songs with a sequence of realistic narrative scenes.

adamellite A variety of *granite consisting of roughly equal proportions of potassium feldspar and sodic plagioclase feldspar, with one or more ferromagnesian minerals.

Adamov, Arthur (1908–70) French dramatist of the *Theater of the Absurd. Born in Russia, Adamov went to Paris in 1924. The experimental forms of his plays owe much to the images and logic of dreams, which include *La Parodie* (1947) and *Le Ping Pong* (1955). His later, more political, work included anti-Gaullist sketches. He committed suicide in Paris.

ABIGAIL ADAMS *First lady, wife of President John Adams, mother of President John Quincy Adams, and recorder of her times.*

Adams, Abigail (1744–1818) US first lady; wife of John *Adams, 2nd president and mother of John Quincy Adams, 6th president. She married John Adams at the age of 20 and bore him five children. A strong supporter of her husband's political career, she was an advocate of women's rights and a chronicler of the customs of her day.

Adams, Brooks (1848–1927) US historian, brother of Henry *Adams. He held that the success of a civilization is closely allied with its economics, and he applied Darwin's theory of survival of the fittest to the development of societies. His notable works include *The Law of Civilization and Decay* (1895) and *America's Economic Supremacy* (1900).

Adams, Charles Francis (1807–86) US diplomat; ambassador to Britain (1861–68). He was the grandson of John Adams and the son of John Quincy Adams. He was influential in keeping Britain neutral during the US Civil War and attempted to prevent British-built ships from joining the Confederate fleet, protesting against the dispatch of the *Alabama* (1862). He represented the US in the subsequent *Alabama* claims for compensation against Britain (1871).

Adams, Henry (1838–1918) US historian. After completing Harvard, he served as secretary to his father, Charles Francis Adams, in Washington and Britain. He returned to Harvard in 1870 to teach and edit the *North American Review*. After working as a radical political journalist, he became disillusioned with active politics and turned to fiction and history, writing a long history of early democracy in America (1889–91). His most influential works were *Mont Saint Michel and Chartres* (1913), a study of the unity of art and religion in the middle ages, and his autobiography, *The Education of Henry Adams* (1918).

Adams, James Truslow (1878–1949) US historian. A conservative, he extolled oldtime values and believed in interpreting facts and their interrelations. *The Founding of New England* (1921) earned him a Pulitzer Prize. Other works include *The Epic of America* (1931) and *The Living Jefferson* (1936).

Adams, John (1735–1826) US statesman; first vice president (1789–97) and second president of the US (1797–1801). A graduate of Harvard College and a lawyer in his native Massachusetts, he early became prominent in opposing British rule, attacking the Stamp Act and serving on patriot committees. As a delegate to the first and second Continental Congresses (1774–78), he supported George *Washington as commander of the army and the passage of the Declaration of Independence. He was the main author (1780) of the Massachusetts constitution. With Benjamin *Franklin and John *Jay, he represented the US in the peace negotiations

JOHN ADAMS *Second president (1797–1801) who also served his country as its first vice president.*

with Britain that ended the Revolutionary War (1783) and was subsequently US minister to Britain (1785–88). As vice president he played a pivotal role in the Senate, breaking the many tie votes of the era. Succeeding Washington as president, his disputes with Alexander *Hamilton, unpopular legislation, and conflicts with Vice President Thomas *Jefferson over US policy toward Revolutionary France all contributed to the loss of his personal popularity and that of his Federalist party. Adams was defeated by Jefferson in the election of 1800 and retired to his home in Quincy, Mass.

Adams, John Quincy (1767–1848) US statesman; sixth president of the US (1825–29), son of John *Adams. Educated in Europe (1778–80), he returned to the US, where he followed his father's example, attending Harvard and becoming a lawyer. A diplomat under Washington and his father, he was elected (1803) to the Senate, from which he resigned in 1808. His expertise in diplomacy was subsequently used as minister to Russia (1809–14), in negotiating the Treaty of Ghent to end the War of 1812, as minister to Britain (1815–17) and as Pres. *Monroe's secretary of State (1817–25). At the State Department he obtained Florida (1819) and helped promulgate the *Monroe Doctrine. In the disputed election of 1824, in which Andrew *Jackson had more electoral votes, Adams was elected president by the House of Representatives, thanks to the support of Henry *Clay. During his term Adams concentrated on internal improvement projects, but neglected politics. As a result he lost the election of 1828 to Jackson. Adams reentered politics as a representative in the House (1831–48), where he adamantly opposed the extension of slavery.

Adams, Richard (1920–) British novelist. He worked in the civil service from 1948 to 1974. His children's book *Watership Down* (1972), an epic treatment of the adventures of a community of rabbits, became an international bestseller. His later novels include *Shardik* (1974), *The Plague Dogs* (1977), and *The Girl in a Swing* (1980).

Adams, Samuel (1722–1803) US politician. A propagandist of revolution against Britain, he led the *Stamp Act agitation of 1765. His protests against British troops in Boston led to the Boston Massacre (1770) and he helped to plan the *Boston Tea Party (1773). He signed the Declaration of

Independence (1776), served in the *Continental Congress until 1781, and was then governor of Massachusetts (1794–97).

Adams-Onis Treaty (or Transcontinental Treaty; 1819) An agreement between the United States and Spain that, in essence, gave Florida and the Oregon Territory to the US and Texas to Spain. Formulated by Secretary of State John Quincy Adams and Spain's Luis de Onís, the treaty erased any Spanish claims to land east of the Mississippi River in return for possession of Texas.

Adana 37 00N 35 19E A city in S Turkey, the fourth largest in the country. The prosperity of this important agricultural and industrial center comes from the surrounding fertile valleys, where much cotton is grown, and its position on the Anatolian-Arabian trade routes. It has a university (1973). Population (1973 est): 383,046.

adaptive radiation The process by which a uniform population of animals or plants evolves into a number of different forms over a period of time. The original population increases in size and spreads to occupy different habitats. It forms several subpopulations, each adapted to the particular conditions of its habitat. In time—and if the subpopulations differ sufficiently—a number of new species will be formed from the original stock. The Australian marsupials evolved in this way into burrowers, fliers, carnivores, herbivores, and many other different forms.

Addams, Jane (1860–1935) US social worker and reformer. She cofounded Hull House, a settlement house, in Chicago in 1889 and led the nation in attempts to improve living conditions in the slums and to reform child labor laws. She led pacifist and women's rights groups and shared the Nobel Peace Prize in 1931. Among her notable works is *Twenty Years at Hull House* (1910).

addax A rare African antelope, *Addax nasomaculatus*, about 40 in (1 m) high at the shoulder, that lives in small herds in the Sahara Desert. It has a grayish hide with a white patch on the face, long spirally twisted horns, and broad hooves suitable for running over loose sand. □mammal.

adder A widely distributed European *viper, *Vipera berus*, about 31 in (80 cm) long, common in heathland areas. It is usually grayish with a broad black zigzag line along its back and black spots on its sides. Although venomous, its bite is rarely fatal. It is one of the three species of snakes found in Britain. The name adder is also given to a highly venomous Australian snake (death adder) of the cobra family and to some harmless North American snakes. □reptile. *See also* puff adder.

addiction. *See* drug dependence.

Addington, Henry, 1st Viscount Sidmouth (1757–1844) British statesman; prime minister (1801–04), replacing Pitt the Younger. Addington was attacked for his management of the Napoleonic Wars and resigned. As home secretary (1812–21) he introduced stern measures against radical and working-class movements and he has been held responsible for the *Peterloo Massacre.

Addis Ababa 9 02N 38 43E The capital of Ethiopia, on a central plateau 8000 ft (2440 m) above sea level. It became the new capital of Ethiopia in 1889 and was capital of Italian East Africa (1936–41). Growth in the 20th century has been rapid. It is the country's administrative center and chief market place. Its major industries produce cement, tobacco, textiles, and shoes. A railroad line links the city with the port of Djibouti on the Gulf of Aden. It is also an important pan-African center with the headquarters of the Organization of African Unity and the UN Economic Commission for Africa. The National University was established in 1961. Population (1978 est): 1,125,340.

Addison, Joseph (1672–1719) British essayist and poet. In 1703 he published "The Campaign" (1705), a poem to celebrate Marlborough's victory at Blenheim. He began to contribute to Richard *Steele's journal, the *Tatler*, and in 1711 Addison and Steele founded the *Spectator*, for which Addison wrote essays famous for their clarity, wit, and elegance. He is also remembered for the tragedy *Cato* (1713).

Addison's disease A rare disease of the adrenal glands, first described by Thomas *Addison, characterized by a reduced secretion of corticosteroid hormones. This leads to weakness, intestinal upsets, darkening of the skin, low blood pressure, and collapse. Formerly fatal, Addison's disease can now be readily treated with synthetic steroids.

addition reaction A chemical reaction in which atoms or molecules combine to form a single molecule. It is frequently encountered in organic *chemistry, since many substances readily add to the double or triple bonds in alkenes, alkynes, aldehydes, etc. *Aromatic compounds are less susceptible, while *alkanes do not undergo addition. *See also* polymerization; substitution reaction.

additive process. *See* color.

Adelaide 34 56S 138 36E The capital of South Australia, on the Torrens River. Founded in 1837, the city was laid out in wide straight streets with extensive parklands separating the city from its suburbs. The University of Adelaide was founded in 1874. It is an important commercial and industrial center with harbor facilities at Port Adelaide. Industries include the manufacture of cars and textiles, oil refining, and electronics. Population (1980 est): 934,200.

Adélie Land. *See* Terre Adélie.

Aden 12 50N 45 03E The capital of South Yemen, on the **Gulf of Aden**, an arm of the Indian Ocean connecting the main body with the Red Sea. Taken by the British in 1839, Aden was an important coaling station on the route to India through the Suez Canal (opened 1869). It became part of the Federation of Saudi Arabia in 1963 and was the scene of fighting between rival nationalist groups until 1968, when it became the capital of the independent republic of South Yemen. Economic activity centers on the port, which suffered from the closure of the Suez Canal (1967–75), and an oil refinery. Population (1977 est): 285,373.

Adenauer, Konrad (1876–1967) German statesman. He was a successful Rhineland politician until the Nazi government forced him out of public life (1934) and imprisoned him (1934, 1944). In 1946 Adenauer reemerged as chairman of the Christian Democratic Union (CDU) and became the first chancellor of the Federal Republic of Germany (1949–63). He presided over the German economic miracle but was personally more concerned with foreign policy. He established that West Germany was part of W Europe, did much to restore its international prestige, and built up Franco-German friendship.

adenoids Two masses of tissue situated at the back of the nose. They consist of lymphatic tissue, which destroys disease-causing microbes in the throat. In children they are normally large, and when associated with recurrent throat infections or persistent breathing through the mouth are usually removed surgically. This operation is often combined with tonsillectomy (removal of the tonsils) as the tonsils tend to be infected at the same time.

adenosine triphosphate. *See* ATP.

adhesives Substances used for bonding materials together. Adhesives are usually colloidal solutions that set to a hard film adhering to the surfaces of the materials. There are many different types. Animal glues are forms of collagen (a protein) produced by boiling bones, hides, horns, etc., and drying the resulting jelly. They are water soluble and usually contain additives to preserve them. Vegetable glues (mucilages) are also water-soluble substances, such as starch, or gums, such as gum arabic or tragacanth. Other natural adhesives include waterglass, pitch, and rubber latex. In addition many synthetic resins are used as adhesives. **Thermoplastic adhesives** (polymers, such as polystyrene, asphalt, and polyvinyl compounds) remain soluble after setting and melt when heated; these are used where flexible bonding is needed, for example in attaching the soles of shoes, safety glass, sticky tape, etc. **Thermosetting adhesives** (condensation polymers, such as *epoxy resins) are insoluble, chemically inert, and will not melt. They are set by heat or by an added catalyst (hardener). They are used for bonding wood, paper, textiles, plastics, etc.

adiabatic process Any process in which heat neither enters nor leaves a system. Usually, such a process changes the temperature of the system. An example is the sudden compression of a gas, causing its temperature to rise. The compression is assumed to take place so quickly that the gas loses none of its acquired heat.

Adige River A river in Italy, rising in the N and flowing mainly SE, entering the Adriatic Sea near Po. Navigation is difficult because of its rapid current. Length: 220 mi (354 km).

Ádi Granth The sacred canonical scriptures of *Sikhism, compiled in 1604 by Arjun Mal (1581–1606). It consists of about 6000 hymns, mostly the work of the first five *gurus, together with the writings of some Bhakta saints and Muslim Sufis (*see* Sufism). The Sikhs do not venerate images but the *Ádi Granth* has itself become the object of worship.

Adirondack Mountains A mountain range in N New York state. It consists of a glaciated plateau rising to 5344 ft (1629 m) at Mount Marcy. Its scenic gorges, waterfalls, and many lakes make it a popular tourist area.

ADJUTANT STORK *Standing about 5 ft (1.5m) tall, these grotesque birds congregate with vultures around animal carcasses, which provide their food.*

adjutant stork A large carrion-eating *stork, *Leptotilos dubius*, occurring in Asia and similar to the related *marabou. It has a white plumage with dark-gray back, wings, and tail, a short neck, and a heavy pointed bill. Its head and neck are naked and a bald pouch hangs from the throat. Order: *Ciconiiformes*.

Adler, Alfred (1870–1937) Austrian psychiatrist, whose theories concerning the psychology of the individual introduced the concept of the inferiority complex. Initially an associate of Sigmund *Freud, Adler's views diverged from Freud's and by 1911 he had founded his own school of thought. Adler viewed each individual as a unique entity striving to compensate for feelings of inferiority resulting from physical or social disabilities (*The Neurotic Constitution*, 1912) and regarded sex as simply an opportunity to express dominance. Adler emphasized the importance of education and, in 1921, opened the first of his child-guidance clinics in Vienna.

Adler, Felix (1851–1933) German-born US educator, who founded the Society for Ethical Culture (1876). Through the resulting ethical movement and in books, such as *An Ethical Philosophy of Life* (1918), he proclaimed the importance of morality in human affairs and advanced the view that moral considerations arose independently of any religious creeds. He instigated many educational and social reforms.

administrative law The law regulating the organization, responsibilities, and powers of a country's administrative bodies, such as the civil service, customs and excise, and social services. Many countries enforce this law through special courts, but in *common law countries it is dealt with in the ordinary courts.

Admiralty Court. *See* maritime law.

Admiralty Islands A group of about 40 islands in the SW Pacific Ocean, in Papua New Guinea in the Bismarck Archipelago. Copra and pearls are exported. The main island is Manus with the chief town, Lorengau. Area: about 800 sq mi (2000 sq km) Population (1970): 22,447.

Adonis In Greek mythology, a youth from Cyprus, loved by *Aphrodite for his great beauty. *Zeus decreed that his time should be divided between Aphrodite on earth, Persephone, queen of the underworld, and himself. He was celebrated in many festivals as a vegetation god, his death and resurrection representing the seasonal decay and regeneration of nature.

adoption In law, the process whereby the natural parent's legal rights and obligations toward an unmarried *minor are transferred to another adult. The need for a male heir has traditionally been one of the prime motives for adoption and the welfare of the adopted child was not the main consideration. This was reflected in Roman Civil law, which subsequently influenced the adoption laws of a number of European and Latin-American countries. The increased effectiveness of birth control, the legalization of abortion, and the social acceptance of one-parent families has decreased the number of children available for adoption in recent years. However, greater emphasis, including publicity on television, has been given to finding adoptive homes for children with special needs, e.g. older children, children of mixed race, and the physically or mentally handicapped.

Adowa (Adwa *or* Aduwa) 14 02N 38 58E A city in N Ethiopia. Emperor Menelik II defeated the Italians nearby in 1896, halting their expansion into Ethiopia until 1935. It is a market center for agricultural produce including grains, honey, and coffee. Population (1971 est): 16,430.

adrenal glands Two small pyramid-shaped *endocrine glands in man and other mammals, one at the upper end of each of the kidneys. Each gland has an outer cortex, controlled by hormones secreted by the pituitary gland, and an inner medulla, controlled directly by the nervous system. The cortex secretes three classes of steroid hormones that regulate the balance of salts and water, the use of carbohydrates, and the activity of the sex glands (*see* corticosteroid). The medulla produces the hormones *adrenaline and *noradrenaline. *See also* Addison's disease; Cushing's syndrome.

adrenaline (*or* epinephrine) A hormone secreted by the central core (medulla) of the adrenal glands. A *catecholamine derived from the amino acid tyrosine, adrenaline increases heart rate, raises blood pressure, and increases the level of blood glucose. Its release is triggered by stress in preparation by the body for "fight or flight." Adrenaline is also secreted by nerve endings of the sympathetic nervous system. *See also* noradrenaline.

adrenocorticotrophic hormone. *See* ACTH.

Adrian, Edgar Douglas, 1st Baron (1889–1977) British physiologist, whose work was largely concerned with the electrical properties of the nervous system. He developed techniques for recording nerve impulses from single nerve fibers and later studied the electrical activity of the brain. He shared a Nobel Prize (1932) with Sir Charles *Sherrington.

Adrian IV (Nicholas Breakspear; c. 1100–59) Pope (1154–59). The only English pope, also known as Hadrian IV, he was unanimously elected after a career of papal service, leading the mission to the Scandinavian churches (1152). His claim that the Holy Roman Empire was held by papal grant occasioned a major quarrel with Emperor *Frederick Barbarossa, whom he refused to crown until Frederick had done homage for his office. Adrian also intervened in the internal politics of France and Sicily.

Adrianople, Battle of (378 AD) The battle in which the Eastern Roman emperor *Valens was defeated and killed defending Adrianople (now Edirne, Turkey) against the Visigoths. The Huns had driven the Visigoths across the Danube in 376 AD, prompting them to attack the Romans at Adrianople.

Adriatic Sea A northern arm of the Mediterranean Sea, extending between Italy and Yugoslavia for about 466 mi (750 km). Its principal ports are Brindisi, Bari, Venice, Trieste, and Rijeka. The Italian and Yugoslav coasts are strikingly different: the one flat and sandy, the other rocky and irregular with many offshore islands.

adsorption The production of a layer of atoms or molecules of a substance on a solid or liquid surface. The adsorbed atoms or molecules may be strongly held by chemical bonds (**chemisorption**), in which case the adsorbed layer is usually only one molecule thick. Adsorption may also occur through weaker physical forces (**physisorption**), often giving rise to several molecular layers.

adult education Education of all kinds for adults, but usually the various forms of education provided for adults once their formal education has ceased. Adult education may be specifically vocational or assist in general cultural development.

adultery Voluntary sexual relations between a married person and someone who is not that person's husband or wife. In some jurisdictions, also, a distinction is made between double and single adultery, the former being committed when both parties are married to other persons, the latter where only one is so married. In some states, adultery is a crime. Adultery is rarely relied on as a grounds for divorce since no-fault divorce became popular.

Aduwa. *See* Adowa.

advaita (Sanskrit: nondualism) The Hindu philosophical view, derived from the *Upanishads, that the individual soul and ultimate reality are indivisibly one; the apparent separation of subject and object, or spirit and matter, is only illusion. Realization of this truth leads to liberation. Some thinkers see all phenomena, including the self, as altogether unreal; others maintain that the existence of the soul is qualified by, or dependent upon, *Brahman, who alone is fully real. Chief among the proponents of *advaita* is the 8th-century philosopher *Shankara.

Advent (from Latin: *adventus*, coming) The first season of the *church year, leading up to *Christmas. It begins on the Sunday nearest St Andrew's Day (Nov 30). From the 6th century it has been observed as a solemn preparation for celebrating Christ's birth and for his Second Coming.

adventists Several Protestant Christian denominations that stress a belief in the imminent Second Coming of Christ. In the US adventism began in 1831 with the millenarian preaching of William Miller (1782–1849), who predicted the Second Coming for 1843–44, but postponed the date when his prediction proved false. In the UK a similar movement was founded in 1832 as the Catholic Apostolic Church. There have been numerous adventist movements, the Seventh-Day Adventists being the principal church today.

advertising The publicizing of a product or service, usually in order to increase sales. In some cases it is used to discourage sales (e.g. of cigarettes) or to promote noncommercial activities (e.g. highway safety). Although some 3% of the U.S. *gross national product is spent on advertising, there is no evidence to show that advertising actually persuades people to buy things they do not want. Consumer advertising seeks to sell one branded product at the expense of others (e.g. toothpaste), to publicize a manufacturer's name when his product is the same as everyone else's (e.g. gasoline), or to persuade people that a category of products (e.g. wool) should be bought in preference to some other category (e.g. man-made fibers). Trade advertising is restricted to specific sections of the public (e.g. doctors or caterers). Advertisements may be informative, assisting purchasers to make a choice between products, or persuasive, in which case it may exaggerate some aspect of a product by appealing to the purchaser's image of himself. Advertising is carried by newspapers, by television and radio, by public transportation, and at the point of sale. The industry is largely in the hands of advertising agencies, which work closely with their clients researching, copywriting, and producing the advertisements as well as reserving space in the press and time for broadcasting.

Adwa. *See* Adowa.

Adygei An autonomous region (*oblast*) in the SW Soviet Union, in the RSFSR. It was formed in 1922 for the Muslim Adyghian people. It has valuable forests and oil and natural-gas deposits. Area: 2934 sq mi (7600 sq km). Population (1980 est): 405,300. Capital: Maikop.

Adzhar Autonomous Soviet Socialist Republic (*or* Adzharia) An administrative division in the S Soviet Union, in the Georgian SSR on the Black Sea. It is mainly mountainous with a subtropical coastal plain. A popular holiday region, it is also the country's main producer of tea and citrus fruits. Industries include shipyards and oil refining. Area: 1160 sq mi (3000 sq km). Population (1981 est): 362,000. Capital: Batumi.

Aechmea A genus of herbaceous plants (over 140 species), native to South America, where they grow upon the branches of trees (but are not parasitic). From the center of a rosette of spiny-toothed leaves, 12–24 in (30–60 cm) long, grow flower stalks bearing showy red or yellow flowers, often with blue tips. Some species, for example *A. fulgens* and *A. fasciata*, are cultivated as ornamental greenhouse plants. Family: *Bromeliaceae* (pineapples, etc.).

Aedes A genus of mosquitoes, widespread in the tropics and subtropics, that are important as vectors of diseases of man and livestock including yellow fever and dengue (transmitted by *A. aegypti*) and Rift Valley fever (transmitted by *A. cabalus*).

Aegae (modern name: Vergina) The capital, with *Pella, of ancient Macedon (*see* Macedonia). During the 1970s archeological work on a nearby mound revealed tombs believed to be those of *Philip II of Macedon and his immediate family. Treasures found here include magnificent wall paintings, golden jewelry, and silver vases.

Aegean civilizations The prehistoric settlements on the islands of the Aegean Sea (between mainland Greece and Asia Minor). At the beginning of the Bronze Age (c. 3000 BC) an influx of immigrants to the *Cyclades islands (S Aegean) brought a high level of sophistication and prosperity, which can be seen from the excavations on Thera (*or* Santorini). The subsequent civilization of *Minoan Crete was at its greatest between the 17th and 15th centuries BC. At the end of the 15th century the related *Mycenaean civilization of mainland Greece began to assert its supremacy, lasting until about 1200.

Aegean Sea A section of the NE Mediterranean Sea, lying between Greece and Turkey and containing many islands, including the Cyclades, Dodecanese, and N Sporades.

Aegina (Modern Greek name: Aíyina) A Greek island in the Aegean Sea, one of the largest in the Saronic group lying SSW of Piraeus. It achieved its greatest prosperity in the 5th century BC but fell to Athens (458), which later expelled all its inhabitants. Today it serves as a holiday resort for Athenians. Area: 33 sq mi (85 sq km).

Aegina, Gulf of. *See* Saronic Gulf.

Aegis In Greek mythology, a breastplate worn by Zeus and his daughter Athena. At its center was an image of *Medusa, which petrified enemies.

Aelfric (c. 955–c. 1020) Anglo-Saxon prose writer and Abbot of Eynsham from 1005. His *Catholic Homilies* (990–92), collections of sermons, and his *Lives of the Saints* (996–97) were important contributions to the

spread of learning in the 10th century. He also wrote a Latin grammar, thus acquiring his nickname, Grammaticus.

Aeneas A legendary Trojan leader, son of *Anchises and *Aphrodite, and hero of Virgil's *Aeneid*. After the Greek victory in the Trojan War, he sailed away from burning Troy with his family and other survivors and was shipwrecked near Carthage. He fell in love with *Dido but abandoned her to continue his divinely ordained voyage to Italy, where he founded what was to become Rome.

Aeneas Silvius. *See* Pius II.

Aeolian harp A musical instrument named for the Greek wind god *Aeolus, consisting of a wooden resonating box strung with gut strings of varying thicknesses. When hung in the open air it produces chordal sounds that vary according to the wind pressure.

Aeolus The Greek god of the winds and ruler of Aeolia. In Homer's *Odyssey* he gave Odysseus a bag containing contrary winds; Odysseus' companions untied it, causing his ship to be blown back to Aeolia.

Aepyornis A genus of extinct flightless birds (ratites), also called elephant birds because of their huge size and bulk. They are known only from fossil bones and eggs found in Madagascar.

aerobe An organism that requires free oxygen for oxidation of foodstuffs to release chemical energy in the process of *respiration. Most living organisms are aerobes; exceptions include certain yeasts and bacteria. These organisms, called **anaerobes**, produce chemical energy by a series of reactions in which free oxygen is not required. **Obligate anaerobes** never use oxygen for respiration, while **facultative anaerobes** normally use oxygen but are able to switch to anaerobic respiration when free oxygen is deficient.

aerodynamics The study of the behavior and flow of air around objects. As air is a viscous fluid any object moving through it experiences a drag. Aerodynamics is important in the design of vehicles traveling at more than 31 mph (50 kph), buildings and bridges, engines, furnaces, as well as aircraft (*see* aeronautics) and missiles. Proposed cross-sections of models of such objects are often tested in wind tunnels or in water, smoke or colored dyes being used to trace the flow of the fluid around the surface and to measure the lift and drag forces. This enables the best streamlined shapes to be found in order to avoid *turbulence.

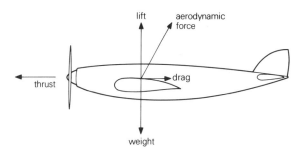

forces acting on aircraft

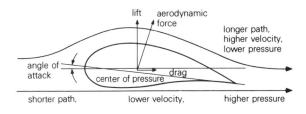

cross-section of airfoil

AERONAUTICS *The forces acting on an aircraft. The airfoil cross-section shows how the lift, which keeps it in the air, results from the passage of the airfoil through the air, causing a lower pressure above it and a higher pressure below it.*

aeronautics The science and history (*see also* aircraft) of flight. An object flying through air is subject to four basic forces: its own weight (vertically downward as a result of gravity), lift (to counterbalance its weight and keep it in the air), thrust (to force it through the air), and drag (resulting from friction between the body and the air). Birds and insects use their wings to provide both lift and thrust; man, in his heavier-than-air fixed-wing craft, uses an airfoil to provide the lift and an *internal-combustion engine (propeller or jet) to provide the thrust (see also gliders). *Helicopters use rotating airfoils to provide lift, while *rockets use no lift surfaces, the jet of expanding gas providing both lift and thrust. Man's lighter-than-air craft (see airships; balloons) use helium or hydrogen to reduce the craft's weight in relation to the volume of air it displaces to such an extent that the lift is provided by buoyancy. The use of airfoils as lift surfaces depends on *Bernoulli's theorem, according to which the total energy of a flowing fluid remains constant; thus, if the velocity of the fluid increases, its pressure decreases in proportion. An airfoil is a wing so shaped that (at subsonic speeds) air is accelerated over its rounded leading edge and curved upper surface, causing a reduced pressure above it. A smaller reduction in air velocity on its underside causes a slightly increased pressure below it. The combination of these pressure differences provides the lift. The design of practical aircraft wings has to take into account a number of complex factors, including suitable streamlining to avoid *turbulence in the airflow, stability over different angles of attack, the provision of suitable control surfaces (flaps, ailerons, etc.), and adequate strength and rigidity. At supersonic speeds these forces are somewhat altered (see sound barrier) and the airfoil has to be more sweptback and more streamlined. At hypersonic speeds (i.e. in excess of five times the speed of sound) the *aerodynamics changes again and blunter noses and even smaller wings are needed.

aerosol A colloidal suspension of particles of liquid or solid in a gaseous medium. Fog, mist, and smoke are common natural examples. By means of pressurized packages, aerosols can be produced from a huge range of substances, including insecticides, paints, hairsprays, etc. In these, the substance is mixed with an easily liquefied gas (often a fluorinated or chlorinated hydrocarbon), which acts as a propellant when the pressure is released. Fears have been expressed that fluorinated hydrocarbons, being lighter than air, could cause chain reactions in the upper atmosphere, which could destroy the *ozone layer. As this layer protects life on earth from the sun's ultraviolet radiation, measures have been encouraged to ban the use of fluorinated hydrocarbons in aerosols. See colloids.

Aeschines (c. 397–c. 322 BC) Athenian orator, who was an opponent of *Demosthenes. He was part of the Greek embassy to Philip of Macedon that in 350 negotiated peace, for which Demosthenes tried unsuccessfully in 343 to convict him of treason. In 330 Aeschines was defeated in his attempt to prevent Demosthenes being awarded a crown for his services to Athens and he retired to Rhodes.

Aeschylus (c. 525–456 BC) Greek tragic dramatist, the first of the great trio of Athenian tragedians that included Sophocles and Euripides. He wrote over 80 plays, of which only 7 survive: *The Persians* (472), *Seven against Thebes* (467), the *Oresteia* trilogy (*Agamemnon, Libation Bearers, and Eumenides*; 458), *Suppliant Women* and *Prometheus Bound*. His introduction of a second actor, allowing dialogue and action independent of the chorus, and his innovations in costume and scenery, transformed the conventions of drama. His deeply religious plays dramatize the perpetual conflict between human passions and divine will.

Aesculapius The Greek god of medicine, son of Apollo and Coronis. He was taught medicine by the centaur Chiron. The sick, believing in Aesculapius' power to cure them through dreams, came to sleep in his temples, the chief of which were at Epidaurus and on the island of Cos.

Aesop The supposed author of a collection of Greek fables, said by Herodotus to be a slave from Samos who lived in the 6th century BC. Originating in popular folklore, the fables are anecdotal stories whose animal characters are used to illustrate a moral point. The Roman poet Phaedrus popularized them in the 1st century AD, and the French poet La Fontaine wrote more sophisticated versions in the 17th century.

Aesthetic movement A British literary and artistic movement of the late 19th century, summarized in the slogan "art for art's sake." Reacting against the ugliness of industrialism and against contemporary utilitarian social philosophies, its followers sought to create beauty for its own sake, self-consciously divorcing art from life. Their artistic precursors were the *Pre-Raphaelite Brotherhood, formed in 1848, whose emphasis on pure aesthetics was continued by Swinburne, William Morris, and others, culminating in the work of Oscar Wilde, Aubrey Beardsley, and the other contributors to the periodical *The Yellow Book* (1894–97).

aesthetics The philosophical study of art and critical judgments about art. It includes questions concerning the nature of beauty and general questions about ascribing value—what we mean when we say that a work of art is good and how we arrive at standards of judgment. Objective views hold that beauty or value is in the object and that aesthetic judgments are true or false. Subjective views see value as something an observer brings to the

work of art—it may be purely a matter of personal preference or, as *Kant held, something that can be universally agreed on. There are also various approaches to evaluation, including analytical views that discuss the standards and logic of evaluation, and those that consider the social or moral significance of art.

Aeth–. For names beginning Aeth see Eth–.

Aetius, Flavius (d. 454 AD) Roman general. After a checkered early career, he became virtual ruler of the western Empire, dominating the emperor, Valentian III (reigned 425–55). Aetius defeated the Huns under Attila at the *Catalaunian Plains (451) but was powerless to halt their invasion of Italy. He was subsequently murdered by Valentian.

Aetolia A region of ancient Greece N of the Gulf of Corinth. In 326 BC the tribes of Aetolia formed the **Aetolian League**, a federation that became a leading military power in Greece. In 27 BC Aetolia was included in the Roman province of Achaea. It forms part of the modern department of Aetolia and Acarnania.

Afars A Cushitic-speaking people of the Horn of Africa, also known as Danakils. They are mainly nomads, herding goats and camels. Their social organization is complicated, with patrilineal kinship groups, age sets each under the authority of a chief, and a class division between the Asaimara (red men) nobles and the Adoimara (white men) lower class. Afars are nominally Muslim but the influence of earlier Cushitic beliefs persists.

Afars and the Issas, French territory of the. See Djibouti, Republic of.

Affenpinscher A breed of toy dog, also called monkey terrier. Small but sturdy, it has small erect ears, a short tail, and a short usually black coat with long hair on the legs and face. Height: 9–11 in (23.5–28 cm).

Afghan hound A breed of large dog having long legs, large drooping ears, and a very long silky coat, which may be of any color. The Afghan probably originated in ancient Egypt and was later used in Afghanistan to hunt leopards and gazelles. Height: 27–29 in (68–73 cm) (dogs); 24–26 in (61–66 cm) (bitches).

Afghani, Jamal ad-Din al- (1838–97) Muslim religious and political reformer. Of obscure origins, al-Afghani lived at various times in Istanbul, Egypt, Paris, India, and Persia. He argued for the unity of all Muslims and resistance to European interference in the Muslim countries. He has been seen as a forerunner of Arab nationalists.

Afghanistan, Democratic Republic of A state in central Asia. The country is mountainous, the Hindu Kush range rising over 20 000 ft (6000 m). The only lower-lying areas are along the Amu Darya (ancient name: Oxus) River in the N and the delta of the Helmand River in the SW. The population consists of mixed ethnic groups, the largest being the *Pathans and the Tadzhiks. *Economy*: largely agricultural, with stock raising (especially of fat-tailed sheep) having particular importance. There has been industrial development in recent years, especially since the discovery of natural gas in the N. The first natural-gas power station was opened in 1972. Textiles are important, especially carpet making, and attempts are being made to develop the considerable mineral resources and improve communications. Building of asphalt roads has been carried out in recent years with US and Soviet help. There are still no railroads, although plans have been investigated for a line connecting Kabul with Iran. Main exports include Persian lambskins, fruit, cotton, wool, carpets, and natural gas (to the Soviet Union). *History*: before the opening up of international sea routes in the 15th century Afghanistan was an important center on the overland routes across central Asia. For centuries under the rule of different powers, including the Mongol Genghis Khan in the 13th century, it became an independent kingdom in 1747. During the 19th century Afghanistan became involved in the struggle between Britain and Russia for influence in central Asia. Following two wars with Britain (1839–42 and 1878–80) it became a buffer state between British India and Russia, with Britain controlling its foreign policy. In 1919, under the leadership of *Amanollah Khan, Afghanistan attempted to free itself of British influence, which led to further fighting between the two countries. This third Afghan War led to the recognition of Afghanistan as an independent state in 1921. In 1926 Amanollah declared himself king. He was deposed in 1929 by a brigand chief, Habibullah, who was in turn defeated by Nader Khan. When the latter was assassinated in 1933 he was succeeded by his son, King Zahir. During the years following World War II there has been considerable friction with Pakistan over the question of an independent Pathan state in Pakistan. In 1973 the monarchy was overthrown by Mohammed Daud, a cousin of King Zahir, and in 1977 a constitution was approved setting up a republic with Daud as president. In 1978 he was killed in a military coup and a new government under Nur Mohammed Taraki was set up by members of the Marxist People's Democratic Party. Two further coups occurred in 1979; in the second Babrak Karmal was brought to power with Soviet aid. Soviet military occupation of Afghanistan provoked worldwide condemnation and US withdrawal from the 1980 Olympic Games in Moscow, which prejudiced the success of the games. The US, which all along had officially supported a political solution, nonetheless increased its covert supply of arms to the Afghan freedom fighters.

By the mid 1980s the total Soviet military and economic investment in Afghanistan over the course of the conflict was high and continued to mount. In 1984 the USSR boycotted the Los Angeles Olympics, despite US efforts to urge Soviet participation. Resistance in Afghanistan to the Soviet Union and Babrak Karmal's puppet government continued, and by the mid 1980s the military situation was stalemated. The flood of millions of Afghan refugees into neighboring Pakistan created a growing social and political problem for that nation. Joint official languages: Pushtu and Dari Persian. Official currency: afghani of 100 puls. Area: 657,500 sq km (250,000 sq mi). Population (1983 est): 14,177,000. Capital: Kabul.

aflatoxin. *See* Aspergillus.

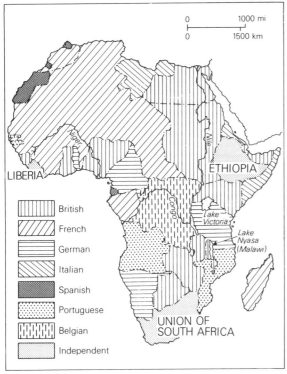

AFRICA *In the scramble for Africa the European powers annexed most of the continent. The map shows the positions in 1914.*

Africa The second largest continent in the world. Linked to SW Asia by the Isthmus of Suez, it is of irregular triangular shape with more than two thirds of its area lying to the N of the equator, which runs across the center of the continent. Except for Australia, its relief is the most uniform of all the continents, consisting principally of two well-defined physical regions: a S tableland and a lower but still elevated plain in the N. A notable feature of the NE is the *Great Rift Valley, which contains the most extensive system of freshwater lakes in the world after North America, as well as the continent's highest point, Mount *Kilimanjaro. Madagascar, the fourth largest island in the world, lies off the SE coast but there are few island groups. The principal rivers are the Nile, Niger, Zaïre, and Zambezi. Africa's climate and vegetation vary considerably from the arid desert of the Sahara to the tropical rainforest of the Congo basin. The inhabitants of Africa are principally of Negroid origin, although the originators of the Berber language group remain dominant in N Africa and the Sahara and there are a few Cushite-speaking peoples in the NE. *History*: Africa's long history has been substantiated by Louis *Leakey's finds of hominoid man at Olduvai Gorge. The earliest African civilization was established in Egypt in about 3400 BC. Also in N Africa the Phoenicians founded Carthage (9th century BC), later conquered by the Romans (146 BC). From the 7th century AD Arab influence was strong and Islam spread with the trans-Sahar-

an and East African coastal trade. Several African kingdoms and empires emerged during this period, notably the Sudanese empires of Ghana, Mali, and Songhai. From the 15th century European exploration and exploitation began, initiated by the Portuguese. Slaves, ivory, and gold were exported from Africa from the 17th to the late 19th centuries, during which time the Atlantic slave trade was active, over 10 million slaves being shipped to the plantations of America and the West Indies. This enforced migration considerably changed the composition of the American and West Indian populations. From 1880 to 1912 most of Africa was partitioned by the European powers, which imposed political boundaries upon the continent that bore no relationship to former political and social organizations; this resulted in long-standing problems. In the 1950s there was movement toward independence and Africa now consists chiefly of independent nations. Famine and political and social unrest have characterized modern Africa. In 1983 the worst drought in 100 years caused severe crop loss and consequent shortages of food and consumer and industrial goods. A declining balance of trade, resulting from poor exports and the oil glut, forced many African nations to borrow from the International Monetary Fund (IMF) and from Western lenders. In the 1980s Africa saw the worst fiscal crisis since the beginning of its independence movement. Under pressure from the IMF and the lending nations, governments of many African states imposed austere economic measures on their people. Area: about 30,300,000 sq km (11,700,000 sq mi). Population (1981 est): 486,000,000.

African art The traditional art of the peoples of sub-Saharan or Black Africa. Among these peoples the visual or plastic arts were not distinguished one from another or from the religious and cultural life of the community. Artists, however, were professionals who enjoyed a respected and sometimes priestly and hereditary status, working on commission or with royal patronage. They produced ceremonial masks, figures for use in the ancestor cults, weapons, furnishings, and everyday utensils. Carving and sculpture in wood, ivory, copper alloys, terracotta, and clay were the dominant art forms, but artistic skills extended to textiles, basketry, leatherwork, and wall and body painting; they also included the mastery of sophisticated techniques, such as the *cire perdue process of bronze-casting. Most of the extant examples of traditional art are less than 200 years old, but these are often representative of much earlier developments. Art flourished in the area of West Africa roughly extending from Senegal and Mali in the N, through the countries bordering the Atlantic, to N Angola and Zambia and E to the chain of great lakes. Within this area a large number of styles are evident. The Dogon of Mali are noted for their stylized rectangular wooden masks. The Yoruba of Nigeria and Dahomey (now Benin) made naturalistic human heads and figures, and similar figures in brass and terracotta were produced at the Yoruba center, Ife, in Nigeria, as early as the 12th century. The skill in casting metal passed from Ife to Dahomey, where the Edo people produced brass reliefs and sculpture. The Baule of the Ivory Coast made finely polished masks and figures; they and the Ashanti of Ghana are the only African people to have used gold leaf to cover sculptures and other carved wooden objects. In the Congo region, ancestral figures, masks, fetishes, and other decorated objects were made in great profusion, chiefly in human and animal forms that were rendered not naturalistically but symbolically, as part of a magical or religious view of reality. It was this quality in African art that perhaps most appealed to many 20th-century western artists, including Picasso, Modigliani, and Epstein, upon whom it has had a profound effect.

African hunting dog A large long-legged wild dog, *Lycaon pictus*, also called the Cape hunting dog, that is widespread south of the Sahara. It is about 24 in (60 cm) high at the shoulder and has a heavy head, large ears, and a short coat mottled in black, yellow, and white. These dogs hunt in packs, chasing their prey (usually gazelle and young wildebeest) until it tires and can be pulled down.

African languages A geographical classification of the heterogeneous languages spoken in the African continent. The *Hamito-Semitic group extends across N Africa from Mauretania to Somalia. The *Nilo-Saharan group is spoken in many dialects in central Africa, and the *Niger-Congo languages, many of them *Bantu languages, cover most of the area S of the Sahara. In S Africa the *Khoisan languages survive. There are up to a thousand indigenous languages of the continent as well as the European languages (*English, *Afrikaans, *French, *Portuguese) imported by colonizers. *Malagasy, a language of *Austronesian origin, is spoken in Madagascar. *Swahili is an important lingua franca in East Africa. Certain African languages are unique in using click sounds in their phonology; predominance of certain consonantal groups (kp, gb, mb, nd) is also common in Africa.

African violet A flowering plant, *Saintpaulia ionantha*, native to tropical East Africa. The plants have rosettes of hairy, often deeply ridged, leaves, bear clusters of pink, blue, purple, or white flowers, and grow to a height of

4–6 in (10–15 cm). Many varieties and hybrids have been developed as ornamentals. Family: *Gesneriaceae*.

Afrikaans. *See* Afrikaner.

Afrikaner A South African of Dutch or *Huguenot descent. The Afrikaners comprise about 60% of the Republic's white population. Formerly called "Boers" (farmers), they have undergone considerable urbanization since the 1930s. In the 18th and 19th centuries they led a seminomadic life, resisting governmental control from Cape Town. Their two independent states, the South African Republic and the Orange Free State, came under British rule after the second *Boer War. Their language, Afrikaans, derives, but is distinct, from Dutch and together with English has been an official language of South Africa since 1925. *See also* Great Trek.

Afro-Asiatic languages. *See* Hamito-Semitic languages.

Agade. *See* Akkad.

Agadir 30 30N 9 40W A port in SW Morocco, on the Atlantic coast. Its growth has followed the development of the port and inland resources. An earthquake in 1960 destroyed much of the town and killed about 12,000 people. Population (1971): 61,192.

Aga Khan IV (1936–) Imam (leader) of the *Ismaili sect of Muslims (1957–), succeeding his grandfather Aga Khan III.

agama A common African broad-headed lizard belonging to the family *Agamidae* (50 species). 12–18 in (30–45 cm) long, agamas have a thick body and a tapering tail and feed on insects. The common agama (*Agama agama*) is variously colored: dominant males have a brick-red head, blue body and legs, and banded tail; other males are duller colored, like the females.

Agamemnon King of Mycenae and commander of the Greek army in the Trojan War. His quarrel with Achilles is the main theme of Homer's *Iliad*. After his return from Troy with Cassandra, the captured daughter of King Priam, he was murdered by his wife Clytemnestra and her lover Aegisthus. The subsequent vengeance of his son Orestes is the central theme of *Aeschylus' *Oresteia* trilogy.

Agana 13 28N 144 45E The capital of Guam in the W Pacific Ocean, in the Mariana Islands. The University of Guam was established here in 1952. Population (1970): 2119.

Agapanthus A genus of herbaceous plants native to South Africa and cultivated for ornament in greenhouses and tropical gardens. *A. africanus* (African lily) has long strap-shaped leaves and large clusters of blue funnel-shaped flowers borne on a tall stalk. There are many cultivated varieties and hybrids. Family: *Amaryllidaceae*.

agar-agar A gelatinous substance obtained from seaweed. A solution in water sets to a firm jelly, which is used for growing bacteria.

agaric A fungus belonging to a large family (*Agaricaceae*) found throughout the world. The group includes many edible mushrooms, such as the white mushroom (*Agaricus bisporus*) and field mushroom (*A. campestris*), as well as the poisonous death cap (*see* Amanita). The visible part of the fungus consists of a stipe (stalk) bearing a cap with gills on the undersurface. Class: *Basidiomycetes*. *See also* fly agaric; mushroom.

Agassiz, Jean Louis Rodolphe (1807–73) Swiss natural historian. Agassiz's early work centered on the study of extinct species, fossilization, and glaciation. His later theories on animal species were contrary to those of Charles Darwin. In his *Essay on Classification* (1859) he argued that organisms were immutable and independent of each other and that there was no possibility of evolution from one source. As professor of zoology at Harvard University, his innovative teaching methods revolutionized the study of natural science in the US. His son **Alexander Agassiz** (1835–1910) was a marine zoologist and mining engineer. His copper mine became noted for its modern and enlightened management. He was a benefactor to various biological institutions and founded his own research station, from which he mounted expeditions to study marine fauna and the sea bed.

agate A banded or concentrically patterned form of *chalcedony. The banding is due to intermittent deposition in rock cavities and the colors, ranging from white, milky blue, yellow, and brown to red, are due to traces of mineral or organic coloring matter. Being hard, it is used for mortars for grinding. It is also used for ornamental purposes, for which the stone may be artificially dyed.

Agathocles (361–289 BC) Tyrant (317–304) and King (304–289) of Syracuse. After seizing power he gained control of E Sicily but fled to Africa after his defeat (311) by the Carthaginians. By 304 he had brutally pacified the Sicilian opposition and took the title of king. He died without establishing a dynasty.

AGAVE *The leaves of this plant are coated with wax. Only 2–3 grow per year and they store large reserves of food materials.*

Agave A genus of plants (about 300 species) of the S US and tropical America, many of which are widely grown for ornament. Agaves have a basal tuft of thick fleshy, sometimes toothed, leaves and a cluster of flowers that—in some species—grows on a tall stalk (up to 40 ft [12 m] high). Growth is slow—it may be 60 or more years before flowers are produced; after flowering the plant dies. Several species are commercially important as a source of fiber, especially *sisal; the fermented juice of others is used as an alcoholic drink (pulque) or distilled to produce spirits (*see* tequila). Family: *Agavaceae* (or *Amaryllidaceae*). *See also* century plant.

Agee, James (1909–55) US poet, novelist, and film critic. After graduating from Harvard he published a book of poems, *Permit Me Voyage* (1934), and wrote influential film reviews for various magazines. *Let Us Now Praise Famous Men* (1941), in collaboration with the photographer Walker Evans, is a bitter account of the lives of Alabama sharecroppers. He also produced two autobiographical novels, *The Morning Watch* (1951) and *A Death in the Family* (1957, Pulitzer Prize), and several filmscripts.

Agency for International Development (AID) US government agency that carries out economic assistance programs to developing countries to help develop resources, increase productivity, increase quality of life, and promote economic and political stability. Established by the Foreign Assistance Act of 1961.

Age of Reason. *See* Enlightenment.

age set A recognized group of persons, usually males initiated at the same time, that is an important feature of the organization of many primitive societies. Each age set may pass through a series of stages (age grades) to which are assigned various functions requiring abilities dependent upon age, such as physical strength, experience, and wisdom. Typically there will be one or more grades of warriors and of elders who exercise political and often ritual authority. *See also* initiation rites.

Agesilaus II (444–360 BC) King of Sparta (c. 399–360). A noted general, he achieved some success against the Persians in Asia Minor (396–395) and against the Boeotians at Coronea (394). His subsequent diplomatic activities contributed to Sparta's disastrous defeat by the Thebans at Leuctra (371). Xenophon wrote a memoir of Agesilaus.

agglomerate A rock composed of a mixture of coarse angular fragments and finer-grained material formed by volcanic explosions; it is usually found in or near the volcanic vent.

Agha Mohammad Khan (1742–97) Shah of Persia (1796–97), who founded the Qajar dynasty (1796–1925). The chief (1758) of one of the clans of the Qajar tribe, he made himself ruler of the whole of Persia and was crowned in 1796. He was the first ruler to make Tehran his capital.

Agincourt, Battle of (October 25, 1415) The battle that took place during the *Hundred Years' War at Agincourt (now in the Pas-de-Calais), in which the French were defeated by an English army led by Henry V. The decisive English victory, which owed much to their outstanding archers, was achieved with not more than 1600 dead; the French may have lost as many as 6000 men.

aging (*or* senescence) The degenerative process in an organism that precedes death. In man aging is characterized by a gradual decline in the efficiency of the repair mechanisms of the body tissues, leading to increased susceptibility to disease; it is also associated with a reduction and then loss of fertility. In some elderly people there is marked physical and mental deterioration (senility). There are several theories to account for the aging process. Some maintain that it is due to the accumulation of errors in metabolism brought about by faulty protein synthesis in the cells; others that aging—particularly in plants after flowering and some animals after reproduction—is a genetically programmed event.

Agnes, St (4th century AD) Roman virgin and martyr. Nothing certain is known about her life, but according to legend she was martyred under Diocletian for refusing to marry and subsequently resisting plans to make her a prostitute. Feast day: Jan 21. Emblem: a lamb.

Agnesi, Maria Gaetana (1718–99) Italian mathematician and philosopher. A child prodigy, Agnesi became the first woman to occupy a chair of mathematics when she was appointed to that at Bologna University in 1750. On the death of her father in 1752, she devoted herself to religion and charitable work. The curve $x^2y = a^2 (a - y)$ is known as the "Witch of Agnesi" because she called it a *versiera* (Latin: turning), a word also meaning witch in colloquial Italian.

Agnew, Spiro T(heodore) (1918–) US Republican politician; vice president (1969–73), who gained notoriety for his attacks on the critics of President Nixon. A lawyer, he was elected governor of Maryland in 1966 before becoming Nixon's running mate. He was accused of taking bribes as governor and vice president, and in 1973 a federal tax case forced him to resign his office. He was given a suspended prison sentence and fined $10,000.

Agnon, Shmuel Yosef (Samuel Josef Czaczkes; 1888–1970) Jewish novelist, born in Galicia, who settled in Palestine in 1907. His treatment of contemporary Jewish themes in *The Day Before Yesterday* (1945) and other works was influenced by folklore and traditional religious literature. In 1966 he shared the Nobel Prize.

agnosticism The philosophical view that doubts the existence of God and other spiritual phenomena and claims that even if they do exist it is impossible to know anything about them. Although this position occurs sporadically throughout history, the term was apparently coined by T. H. *Huxley in 1869. Agnosticism was subsequently enthusiastically embraced by rationalists, who hesitated on philosophical or social grounds to adopt outright *atheism. Agnosticism is now frequently loosely used to mean neither knowing nor caring about the supernatural world.

Agora A central feature of ancient Greek town planning. Similar to the Roman *forum, the primary function of the agora was as the town market. In addition, however, it also became the main social and political meeting place. Together with the acropolis, it normally contained the most important buildings of the town.

agoraphobia. *See* phobia.

agouti A rabbit-sized rodent belonging to a genus (*Dasyprocta*; 13 species) of Central and South American forests. Agoutis have long legs, small ears, and a very short hairless tail. The hair on the rump is often long and brightly colored and can be erected when the animal is alarmed. Agoutis feed on leaves, roots, and berries and are commonly eaten by the Indians. Family: *Dasyproctidae* (agoutis and pacas); suborder: *Hystricomorpha*.

Agra 27 09N 78 00E A city in India, in Uttar Pradesh on the River Jumna. Former capital of the Mogul Empire (1566–69 and 1601–58), it fell to the British in 1803 and from 1835 until 1862 was capital of the North-West Provinces. Notable buildings include the celebrated *Taj Mahal and a fine 16th-century fort. Its university was established in 1927. A major commercial, industrial, and communications center, it produces carpets. Population (1971): 591,917.

agranulocytosis The condition resulting from a deficiency or absence of certain white blood cells (called granulocytes). Agranulocytosis may be caused by an allergic reaction to drugs, cytotoxic drugs (which damage the bone marrow), and severe infection. Symptoms include weakness, fever, and a sore throat; treatment includes withdrawal of the suspect drug, fresh-blood transfusions, and antibiotics.

Agricola, Georgius (George Bauer; 1494–1555) German physician and mineralogist. Working as a physician in several mining towns, he carried out a systematic study of mining and minerals; this study consistently discounted the traditional "magical" attributes of minerals, describing instead their observable physical properties. His publications concerning these properties culminated in his *De re metallica* (1556), which for two centuries was the standard text on mining and metallurgy.

Agricola, Gnaeus Julius (40–93 AD) Roman governor of Britain and father-in-law of his biographer Tacitus. Sent to govern Britain in 78, after holding previous legionary posts there, he followed a policy of romaniza-

tion, exploration, and expansion. He circumnavigated the mainland and advanced the Roman frontiers in annual campaigns, reaching the Scottish Highlands before his recall in 84.

Agricultural Adjustment Act (1933) A law that established the Agricultural Adjustment Administration, an agency to promote recovery from the Depression among US farmers; part of the New Deal. By controlling farm production and therefore surplus products, prices could be fixed and farmers' incomes increased. This was done by fixing quotas, rewarding underproduction, and penalizing, through taxation, overproduction. The law was declared unconstitutional by the Supreme Court in 1936.

Agricultural Research Service (ARS) US government agency that administers research programs in animal and plant protection and production; soil, air, and water use and improvement; farm product processing, storage, and distribution; and human nutrition. Its headquarters are in Beltsville, Md.

agricultural revolution The name given to the changes in agriculture in Britain that took place mainly in the 18th century. The open-field system of strip farming was replaced by larger enclosed fields, hedged and ditched, in which improved agricultural methods and new implements could be used; the quality of cattle and sheep was improved by scientific stock breeding. This resulted in a greater production of food for the growing industrial population (*see* industrial revolution), although it meant hardship for those farmers who were displaced by *enclosure.

agriculture The study of farming. Settled farming probably dates back to the 10th millennium BC, when in many regions of the world it began to replace man's activities as a hunter and gatherer of food. The domestication of cattle, goats, sheep, and pigs together with the cropping of wheat, barley, rice, etc., enabled settled communities to evolve and primitive civilizations to flourish in such regions as the fertile river basins of the Tigris, Euphrates, and Nile.

Farming has developed in various ways in different parts of the world, depending largely on climatic conditions, the type of land, and the local system of land tenure. Many areas are suitable only for *livestock farming whereas in many others large-scale *arable farming is possible. In some cases the most economically successful farms are mixed arable and livestock.

Until the end of the 19th century farming was based on energy derived from man and his draft animals. Some parts of the world still use such traditional methods; however, during the 20th century, especially in developed countries, the *tractor has become the primary energy source. In this century, too, there has been great success in improving breeds of plants and animals, improving soil fertility (*see* fertilizers), increasing mechanization, and control of plant and animal pests, measures that have enormously increased the quantity and quality of food produced. These measures are now being applied in the developing world, where they are bringing about the Green Revolution that is needed to feed the world's growing population.

However, misuse of modern intensive farming methods can cause such problems as soil erosion, while pollution by excessive use of fertilizers, weedkillers, insecticides, etc., can seriously damage the environment. The reconciliation of optimum food production with conservation of the environment is one of the principal tasks of the UN *Food and Agriculture Organization.

Agriculture, Department of (USDA) US executive department, headed by the Secretary of Agriculture, a cabinet position. It oversees farm income; develops foreign markets; combats hunger and malnutrition; directs environment, conservation, and rural development projects; conducts agricultural research; and ensures standards of quality in the daily food supply. Established in 1862, the department includes the Farmers Home Administration, the Agricultural Cooperative Service, the Food and Nutrition Service, *Agricultural Research Service, and the Forest Service.

Agrigento 37 19N 13 35E A seaport in Italy, in S Sicily. Founded about 580 BC, it has famous ancient temples and is the birthplace of the philosopher Empedocles. Sulfur mining is the main occupation. Population (1971): 49,213.

agrimony A herbaceous perennial plant of the genus *Agrimonia* (especially *A. eupatoria*), native to Europe but grown in most temperate regions. Up to 40 in (1 m) tall, it has a spike of small yellow flowers and toothed oval leaves that yield a yellow dye. Family: *Rosaceae*.

Agrippa, Marcus Vipsanius (?63–12 BC) Roman general and close associate of Emperor *Augustus, whose daughter Julia was his third wife. After military successes in Gaul (38 BC) Agrippa became consul (37 BC).

He played an important part in the defeat of Mark Antony at *Actium (31 BC) and greatly contributed to the military successes of Augustus.

Agrippina the Elder (?13 BC–33 AD) The daughter of *Agrippa, wife of *Germanicus Caesar, and mother of Emperor *Caligula. A courageous and high-minded woman, she accompanied her husband on his campaigns. After his death she incurred the hostility of Tiberius, who exiled her to Pandataria, where she died in suspicious circumstances. Her daughter, **Agrippina the Younger** (15–59 AD), was notorious for her political intrigues. She probably murdered her uncle, Emperor Claudius, who was also her third husband, to make way for the succession of her son, Nero. She exerted considerable political influence early in Nero's reign, but after they had quarreled he had her murdered.

agronomy The management of land, especially for the production of arable crops. Agronomy involves the determination of the nature of a soil and how its fertility may be improved by such processes as drainage, irrigation, the application of natural and artificial fertilizers, and husbandry techniques (e.g. *crop rotation). Equally important is the breeding of crop plants that are better suited to a particular soil.

Aguascalientes 21 51N 102 18W A city in central Mexico. The commercial center for a region producing fruit and vegetables, its industries include ceramics production, tanning, and railroad engineering. There are medicinal hot springs nearby. Population (1978 est): 247,764.

Agulhas, Cape 34 50S 20 00E A cape in South Africa, in W Cape Province. It is the most southerly point of the African continent and has a lighthouse (1849).

Ahad Ha'am (Asher Ginsberg; 1856–1927) Hebrew essayist and an influential Zionist thinker. Born in Russia, he moved to London in 1908 and participated in negotiations leading to the *Balfour Declaration. In 1922 he settled in Palestine. Critical of political *Zionism, he looked to nationalism to achieve the moral and cultural regeneration of the Jewish people. His adopted name means "One of the People."

Ahaggar Mountains (or Hoggar Mts) A plateau area in S Algeria, in the central Sahara. It averages about 2950 ft (900 m) but reaches 9573 ft (2918 m) at Mount Tahat and consists chiefly of rocky desert.

ahimsa (Sanskrit: noninjury) The ethical practice, strictly observed in *Jainism but also of fundamental importance in *Hinduism and *Buddhism, of not causing harm to any living thing. Because of the belief in reincarnation, these religions respect all forms of life as being parts of the cycle of rebirth. Vegetarianism is consequently widespread in Asia. The doctrine of nonviolence (see satyagraha) as applied by Mohandas *Gandhi to political conflicts was derived from the principle of ahimsa.

Ahmadabad (or Ahmedabad) 23 03N 72 40E A city in central India, in Gujarat. Founded in 1411, it is one of India's leading industrial centers; it is a major rail center and its textile industry (established 1859–61) is one of the largest in the country. Its university was established in 1949. Population (1971): 1,585,544.

Ahmadiya A religious sect founded in the Punjab by Mirza Ghulam Ahmad of Qadiyan (1839–1908), who was of Muslim background. His teaching combined elements of Islam, Christianity, and Hinduism. He taught that Jesus was buried in Srinigar and that he himself was the messiah and *Mahdi. In 1918 the Ahmadiya split into two groups, the larger regarding Mirza Ahmad as a prophet, the smaller regarding him only as a reformer, and so remaining closer to orthodox Islam. Both groups are based in Pakistan, but have communities elsewhere.

Ahmad Shah Durrani (c. 1723–73) Afghan ruler (1747–73), who founded the Durrani dynasty. Ahmad was commander in India for the Persian *Nader Shah. When Nader died (1747), Ahmad succeeded him as shah and built an empire that was bordered by the Oxus River, Tibet, the Indus River, and Persia. After his death, the empire collapsed.

Ahmed III (1673–1736) Sultan of the Ottoman Empire (1703–30). After a successful war against Russia (1711–13) Ahmed suffered defeat at the hands of Austria and by the Peace of Passarowitz (1718) the Ottomans lost Hungary and parts of Serbia. In 1730 he was deposed and died in captivity. His reign is often known as the Tulip Age because of the flower's contemporary popularity.

Ahmose I King of Egypt (c. 1570–1546 BC), who founded the 18th dynasty. He liberated Egypt from the *Hyksos, retaking Memphis, and reasserted Egyptian power in Nubia and Palestine. After more than a century of alien domination, he reorganized the administration of his reunited country, and encouraged trade and commerce.

Ahmose II King of Egypt (570–526 BC) of the 26th dynasty, who was described by the Greek historian Herodotus. He came to power in a military coup but ruled for 44 years in peace and prosperity.

Ahriman In *Zoroastrianism, the evil spirit created, and ultimately to be overcome, by *Ahura Mazda. According to Zoroastrian dualism he is the essence of untruth, greed, anger, and jealousy and hence the cause of suffering in the world.

Ahura Mazda The supreme deity of *Zoroastrianism, creator of all things good and just. He represents the creative principle, living in eternal light, and is opposed to Ahriman, the destructive principle, living in darkness.

Ahvaz 31 17N 48 43E A city in SW Iran, the capital of Khuzestan province. On the site of an ancient city it is a communications and administrative center for the nearby oilfields. Population (1976): 329,006.

Ahvenanmaa Islands. See Åland Islands.

ai. See sloth.

Aid to Families with Dependent Children (AFDC) US government welfare program that provides supplemental funds for low-income families with dependent children.

Aiken, Conrad (1899–1973) US writer and critic. Influenced by T. S. *Eliot, whom he knew at Harvard, he was a prolific writer of poetry including *Selected Poems* (1929), which was awarded a Pulitzer Prize and "Preludes to Definition," contained in *Collected Poems* (1953). His fiction includes both short stories and novels, among which are the novels *Blue Voyage* (1927) and *Great Circle* (1933) in which he dealt with his parents' deaths. His critical writings comprise *Collected Criticism* (1958). An autobiography, *Ushant*, appeared in 1952.

Aiken, Howard Hathaway (1900–73) US mathematician, who pioneered the construction of electronic computers. His Mark I, built in 1944 and later used by the US navy, anticipated the modern digital computer.

aikido A Japanese form of unarmed combat, primarily for self-defense by means of dodging an attacker and leading him in the direction in which his momentum takes him before subduing him without injury. Like other *martial arts it emphasizes the need for a calm frame of mind and total physical control. It has developed into a competitive sport in which two people fight in one or two one-minute rounds. See also judo; jujitsu.

Ailanthus. See tree of heaven.

Ailey, Alvin (1931–) US dancer and choreographer. He formed his own modern dance group, the Alvin Ailey Dance Theatre, in 1958 after studying with such dancers as Martha Graham, Hanya Holm, and Lester Horton. His best-known works include *Revelations* (1960), *Creation of the World* (1960), *Roots of the Blues* (1961), *Labyrinth* (1963), *Pas de Duke* (1976), and *Phases* (1980).

Ain River A river in E France, flowing SSW from the Jura Mountains to join the River Rhône 18 mi (29 km) above Lyons. Length: 118 mi (190 km).

Ainu A Caucasoid people living on certain islands of Japan and the Soviet Union (Hokkaido, Sakhalin, Kurile Islands). Traditionally a hunting and food-gathering people, distinct from the surrounding Mongoloid peoples, they are now few in number and much changed in both appearance and culture. They were once noted for their profusion of body hair, but intermixture has made them resemble the Japanese and their traditional culture has largely disappeared. They speak a language that is not related to any other known language.

air. See atmosphere.

aircraft Any machine capable of flying. Man's attempts to fly fall into two categories: those using lighter-than-air machines (see airships; balloons) and those using heavier-than-air machines. The latter include wing-flapping birdlike devices, rotating wing machines (see helicopters), and fixed-wing aircraft, first *gliders and then powered airplanes. By the end of the 19th century it was clear to all but the most eccentric that man was both too weak and too heavy to emulate birds. Flapping wings combine both thrust and lift (see aeronautics) in one device; man needs to separate these two components, obtaining lift from a fixed wing and thrust from an engine. 19th-century experience of gliding, especially by Otto *Lilienthal, provided the Wright Brothers with the information they needed to build their first powered aircraft. The power source was provided by the Otto-Daimler *internal-combustion engine. By 1907 the Wrights were able to remain airborne for 45 minutes; in 1909 the Frenchman Louis *Blériot flew across the English Channel, and in the same year the French rotary Gnome engine revolutionized aircraft-engine design (this engine and its derivatives powered many early aircraft, including several used in World War I). By the beginning of the war aircraft were sufficiently advanced to be used for reconnaissance and their usefulness as bombers soon became evident. Fast maneuverable fighters to shoot down the slower heavily laden bombers

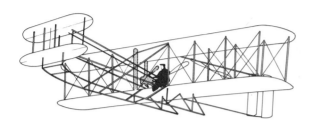

Wright Brothers' Flyer *The first powered flight at Kitty Hawk, North Carolina, on December 17, 1903 lasted 12 seconds.*

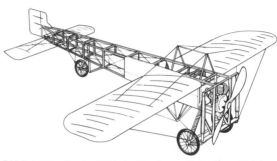

Blériot XI. *Louis Blériot's 30-minute flight from Calais to Dover on July 25, 1909 was the first cross-channel flight.*

Handley Page 42E Hannibal *In 1928 the British airline, Imperial Airways, bought eight HP42 aircraft. The 24-seater Hannibal had a top speed of 100 mph (160 km/hr).*

Douglas DC3 *Introduced in 1936, it was widely used in World War II as the Dakota transport. Its Pratt and Whitney 1200 hp engines gave it a maximum speed of 200 mph (320 km/hr).*

Vickers Viscount *Introduced into service in 1950, it was the first successful turboprop airliner. Powered by four engines, it carried 60 passengers.*

De Havilland Comet I *The first jet airliner, it went into service in 1952. Crashes due to metal fatigue caused its withdrawal and in 1958 it was replaced by the Comet IV.*

Boeing 747 *Nicknamed the "jumbo jet" this wide-bodied jetliner, which can carry up to 500 passengers, has been in service with many airlines since 1970.*

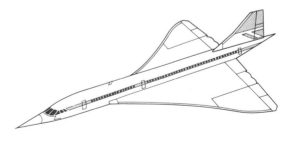

Concorde *The first supersonic airliner, it was built by the French and British in cooperation. Powered by four engines, it came into service in 1976.*

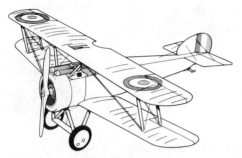

Sopwith Camel *A highly maneuverable fighter, first delivered in 1917. Its 130 hp Clerget engine gave it a top speed of 113 mph (181 km/hr).*

Fokker Eindecker E111 *German fighter, in service from 1915. It had a top speed of 83 mph (133 km/hr) and the first machine gun synchronized to fire through the propeller.*

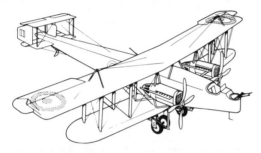

Handley Page 0/400 *The largest World War I bomber. Its twin 360 hp engines enabled it to carry 2000 lbs (907 kg) of bombs.*

Supermarine Spitfire *British fighter. Originally powered by a Rolls-Royce Merlin engine, it later had the Griffon engine, giving it a top speed of 450 mph (724 km/hr).*

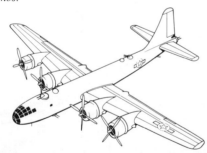

Boeing B-29 Superfortress *This enormous US bomber entered the war in 1943 and was used to drop the atom bombs on Japan.*

Messerschmitt 109 *German fighter, designed in 1935. The latest version (the 109G) had an 1800 hp engine enabling it to fly at 430 mph (692 km/hr).*

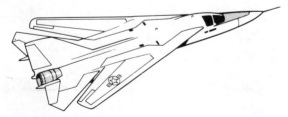

General Dynamics F-111 *US fighter and fighter-bomber, the first warplane to have swing wings (1967). It is powered by a Pratt and Whitney TF30 turbo fan.*

Hawker Siddeley Harrier *British VTOL aircraft developed in 1969. Two movable nozzles direct the thrust of its engine downwards for vertical take-off.*

were an obvious subsequent development. By the end of the war aerial combat was established as an integral part of modern warfare, both sides being equipped with a range of fighters, bombers, and reconnaissance aircraft.

After the war and during the 1920s, air shows and flying clubs run by ex-wartime pilots using World War I aircraft sprang up all over the world, popularizing the concept of flying and heralding the age of civil aviation. Private airlines were founded in the 1920s, and during the 1930s a worldwide network of commercial routes developed. The Atlantic was first flown nonstop from New York to Paris in 1927 by Charles *Lindberg and by 1939 there was a transatlantic flying-boat service, using Class C Short flying boats with in-flight refueling.

Between the wars all the main countries of the world were also building up their air forces, those with expansionist aspirations more quickly than the others. By the outbreak of World War II aircraft of all kinds were poised for aerial combat. During the war the main US bombing force consisted of 12,700 Boeing B17s, 18,000 Consolidated B24 Liberators, and toward the end of the war, a fleet of Boeing B29 Superfortresses. Germany entered the war with 370 Dornier Do 17s and the Heinkel He 111, some 7300 of which had been made by the end of the war. The Junkers 88 entered service in 1940 and at the end of the war (1945) the Arado Ar 234 jet bomber was used for the first time.

The US fighter pilots had some 10,000 Lockheed P38 Lightnings and 15,000 P51 Mustangs during the war. Dominant British fighters were the Supermarine Spitfire and the Hawker Hurricane, the latter being slightly slower than the main German fighter, the Messerschmitt Me Bf109. Later British fighters included the De Havilland Mosquito. The British jet-powered Gloster Meteor entered service in 1944, as did the German Messerschmitt Me 262 jet.

By the end of war the practicality of the *jet engine had been established and it has dominated aircraft design ever since. However, the first postwar generation of civil aircraft used the jet engine to drive propellers. The highly successful Boeing 707 (with its four engines in pods suspended below the wings) followed in 1954 and the French Caravelle (with two rear-mounted engines) in 1959.

The first aircraft to break the *sound barrier were military and nearly all modern warplanes are supersonic and armed with missiles. Examples include the US McDonnell Douglas Phantom, Convair Hustler, and General Dynamics Swingwing F111; the British Hawker Hunter and Avro Vulcan; the French Mirage; and the Soviet MiGs. The first supersonic passenger aircraft (SST) to fly was the Soviet Tupolev Tu-144 in 1968. This was followed a year later by the Anglo-French Concorde, which despite opposition from conservationists, is now in service. However, long- and medium-range passenger services are likely to be dominated for most of the remainder of this century by the wide-bodied (jumbo) jets, such as the Boeing 747 and the European Airbus.

aircraft carrier A naval vessel with a large flat deck for launching and landing warplanes. The first flight from the deck of a ship was made in 1910, and the first true aircraft carrier, *Argus*, was completed for Britain's navy in 1918, too late for action in World War I. Carriers played a dominant role in World War II, despite early predictions that *battleships would be the most important warships. Carriers were especially effective in the war against the Japanese, where they were instrumental in destroying the Japanese fleet. After World War II carriers came to be regarded chiefly as tactical units, although they saw considerable action in the Korean and Vietnam Wars. The USS *Enterprise*, the first nuclear-powered carrier (1961), displaced 76,000 tons and steamed more than 270,000 mi (432,000 km) before requiring refueling. The introduction of larger and heavier aircraft required the refitting of carriers. Because of the increased range of aircraft, the enormous cost of carriers, and the development of sophisticated missiles, there have been few aircraft carriers built in the 1970s, and indications are that their size, cost, low speed, and vulnerability will preclude their extensive use in the future.

air-cushion vehicle. See Hovercraft.

Airedale terrier The largest breed of terrier, originating in Yorkshire, England. It has a long squarish muzzle, a short tail, and a tan-colored wiry coat with a black saddle region. A powerful and intelligent dog, the Airedale has been used as a guard dog, for hunting, and as a police dog. Height: 23–25 in (58–61 cm) (dogs); 22–23 in (56–58 cm) (bitches). □dog.

airfoil. See aeronautics.

Air Force, Department of the US government military department within the Department of *Defense. Directed by the Secretary of Defense, it consists of the Air Staff, which furnishes professional assistance to the Secretary and Chief of Staff, and the field organization, which consists of

the major commands, separate operating agencies, and direct reporting units. It was established by the National Security Act of 1947.

Air Force, United States (USAF) US branch of military service. Part of the Department of *Defense since 1947, it is directed by the Secretary of the Air Force and supervised by a professional staff under the chief of staff. Beginning as the Aeronautical Division of the Army Signal Corps in 1907, it evolved into the Army's Air Service division by 1918. By 1926 it was known as the Air Corps and, during World War II, as Army Air Forces. In 1956 the Air Force was given responsibility for land-based missile systems and, in 1965, satellite development.

air sac In zoology, a thin-walled air-filled sac that functions in the breathing mechanism of birds, some insects, and some lizards. In birds there are five pairs in the spaces between the internal organs and around or in some bones. They are connected with the air passages and enable a constant supply of air to the lungs during flight.

airships See dirigibles.

air space In international law, the space above a country over which that country is sovereign. Under the Outer Space Treaty (1967), outer space is not subject to national appropriation.

Aisne River A river in N France. Rising in the Argonne Forest, it flows mainly NW joining the Oise River near Compiègne. It was a major battleground of *World War I. Length: 175 mi (282 km).

Aistulf (d. 756) King of the Lombards (749–56). Aistulf captured Ravenna (751) and then threatened Rome. The pope sought the aid of *Pepin, King of the Franks, who twice defeated Aistulf at Pavia (755, 756).

Aix-en-Provence (Latin name: Aquae Sextiae) 43 31N 5 27E A city in S France, in the Bouches-du-Rhône department. The capital of Provence in the middle ages, it has a gothic cathedral and a university (1409). The artist Cézanne was born here. An agricultural center, it trades in olive oil and fruit. Population (1975): 117,119.

Aix-la-Chapelle. See Aachen.

Aix-la-Chapelle, Congress of (1818) Meeting of the Quadruple Alliance (Great Britain, Austria, Prussia, and Russia) and France at Aix-la-Chapelle (now Aachen). The Alliance reaffirmed the political reorganization of Europe established by the Congress of *Vienna (1814–15) and restored France's status as an independent power: it withdrew its occupying forces and admitted France into what thus became the Quintuple Alliance.

Aix-les-Bains (Latin name: Aquae Gratiane) 45 41N 5 55E A spa and resort in E France, in the Savoie department. Situated in a picturesque valley, it is noted for its hot sulfurous springs. Population (1975): 22,293.

Ajaccio 41 51N 8 43E The capital of Corsica, a port on the Gulf of Ajaccio. Napoleon I was born here and his home is now preserved as a museum. Tourism is the principal industry. Population (1968): 42,300.

Ajanta 20 30N 75 48E A village in W India, in Maharashtra. It is renowned for its Buddhist caves hewn out of the granite cliffs. Dating from the 1st century BC to the 7th century AD, they consist of monasteries and temples, some of which contain remarkable paintings illustrating the life of the times.

Ajax A legendary Greek hero, son of Telamon, King of Salamis. Described in Homer's *Iliad* as great in stature and in courage, he fought *Hector in single combat. He became insane with rage after being defeated by Odysseus in the contest for the armor of the dead *Achilles. *Sophocles' play *Ajax* depicts the hero recovering his sanity, only to be driven by shame to suicide.

Ajmer (Ajmere or Ajmir) 26 29N 74 40E A city in India, in Rajasthan. It contains the white marble tomb of a Muslim saint and a Mogul palace. A focal point of road and rail routes, it is a commercial and industrial center. Population (1971): 262,851.

Akashic records The "pictures" of all past events, emotions, and thoughts, believed by occultists to be retained in supersensory fluid called Akasha. Clairvoyants and mediums claim to have access to these records.

Akbar (I) the Great (1542–1605) The third Mogul emperor (1556–1605). After establishing his authority, Akbar embarked on the extension of his rule over all N India by a series of military campaigns in Punjab, Rajput, Gujarat, Bengal, Kashmir, and Sind. Late in his reign he conquered the Deccan, further to the south. As ruler he was noted for his able administration, the development of trade, reforms of taxation, the abolition of extortion, and his tolerance toward non-Muslims. *See also* Mogul art.

Akhenaton (or Ikhnaton)   King of Egypt (1379–1362 BC) of the 18th dynasty, one of whose wives was *Nefertiti. He replaced the traditional *Amon cult with the monotheistic worship of the sun god, *Aton, and built a new capital Akhetaton (see Tell el-Amarna). Internal disorder during his reign enabled the Hittite king, *Suppiluliumas, to remove N Syria from Egyptian control.

Akhmatova, Anna   (Anna Andreevna Gorenko; 1889–1966) Russian poet. Her first books, *Evening* (1912) and *Beads* (1914), consisting chiefly of short, intensely lyrical, love poems, were immediately successful. She was married to Nikolai Gumiliov (1886–1921), founder of *acmeism, from 1910 until 1918. After the Revolution she wrote on public as well as personal themes, but her essential style remained unchanged. Her works were banned from 1922 until 1940, and she was again denounced in 1946. In the 1960s, however, her work was restored to favor.

Akiba ben Joseph   (died c. 135 AD) One of the outstanding teachers of early rabbinic Judaism. He came to scholarship late in life, but became a master of biblical interpretation and law. He supported the revolt of *Bar Kokhba and was martyred by the Romans.

Akkad   The capital city and dynastic name of a S Mesopotamian kingdom established about 2300 BC, N of *Sumer. Akkad, the site of which is still unidentified, was founded by *Sargon, who extended his rule over most of Mesopotamia. The Semitic language of Akkad, Old Akkadian, spread to much of the Middle East, developing later into the languages of both *Babylonia and *Assyria. About 2150 BC, barbarian invasions brought about Akkad's decline and the short-lived reascendancy of *Ur.

Akola   20 40N 77 05E A city in W India, in Maharashtra. It is an educational and commercial center. Population (1971): 168,438.

Akron   41 04N 81 31W A city in Ohio. It is the main center of the US rubber industry, specializing in tires; other industries include plastics and chemicals. Its university was established in 1870. Population (1980): 231,177.

aksak   A type of musical meter, found in the vigorous asymmetrical dance rhythms of the E Mediterranean, deriving from Turkish sources. *Bartók recorded examples of these rhythms in Bulgaria and named them Bulgarian rhythms.

Aksum (or Axum)   14 05N 38 40E An ancient town in N Ethiopia. It was capital of the Christian Aksumite Empire (1st–6th centuries AD). According to tradition, the *Ark of the Covenant was brought here from Jerusalem. The old town is now a popular tourist attraction.

Aktyubinsk   53 43N 91 25E A city in the S Soviet Union, in the Kazakh SSR on the Ilek River. Founded (1869) as a Russian fort, it is now an important industrial center. Population (1981 est): 205,000.

Alabama   A state in the SE, on the Gulf of Mexico. Alabama borders Tennessee on the N, Georgia on the E, Florida on the S, and Mississippi on the W. A small portion of S Alabama flanks the Gulf of Mexico, where an inlet forms the important port of Mobile. Except for the forested uplands in the NE it consists of an undulating plain, drained by the Alabama and Tombigbee Rivers. The iron and steel industry, based on deposits of iron ore, coal, and limestone around the state's largest city, Birmingham, is the most important industry. Other industries include the production of oil, metal goods, chemicals, plastics, and defense and space projects. Cotton production in the central Black Belt has decreased since the boll weevil blight (1915) but remains a principal crop along with peanuts, soybeans, and corn; the raising of cattle and poultry is also important. Industry, however, supplies the greatest portion of the state's revenue. Diversification of agriculture and increased industrialization have helped to improve Alabama's standard of living, although it remains economically one of the poorest states. It has, nonetheless, a rich rural culture, particularly among its large black community. *History*: first explored by the Spanish in the 16th century. Settlement, however, was begun by the French. It passed to the British (1763) after the French and Indian Wars. In 1783 it came under US control and with an area to the S added in the Louisiana Purchase (1803) became a state in 1819. Following the War of 1812 and statehood, the demand for cotton brought a wave of settlement from neighboring states. The wealthier settlers established slave-based plantations in the fertile bottomlands. Because of the dominance of "King Cotton," the slave-owning planters were a crucial influence in firing anti-Union sentiments before the Civil War. Following secession from the Union (1861), the state sent most of its white male population to fight against the North. The period since its readmittance (1868) has been marked by troubled race relations between the white and black communities. A 1954 Supreme Court decision declaring school segregation unconstitutional, resulted in increased racial tension and violence. Montgomery, the capital, became the scene of numerous outbreaks of unrest, including a year-long boycott of public buses by blacks. The Alabama Freedom March in 1965 marked a milestone in the social protest movement of the late 1950s and 1960s. An indication of change in the area of race relations was reflected in the 1982 gubernatorial race, in which former governor George Wallace received 80 percent of the black vote. Area: 133,677 sq km (51,609 sq mi). Population (1980): 3,890,061.

Alabama claims   Compensation claimed by the US government from Britain for damage caused by the *Alabama* and other warships of the *Confederate states in the Civil War (1861–65). Britain was accused of violating its neutrality by allowing these ships to be built or equipped in its shipyards. In 1871 the dispute was referred to arbitration by Italy, Switzerland, and Brazil. Britain was found liable and ordered to pay more than $15 million. This was the first major settlement of an international dispute by arbitration.

alabaster   A pure fine-grained form of *gypsum. It is white or delicately shaded and often translucent and attractively veined. It has long been worked ornamentally, for carvings, etc., but weathers too easily for external use. The alabaster of Volterra, Tuscany, is well known.

Alain-Fournier   (Henri-Alban Fournier; 1886–1914) French novelist. The son of a country schoolmaster, he became a literary journalist in Paris and was killed in World War I. The mood of his one completed novel, *Le Grand Meaulnes* (1913), is nostalgic and almost mystical; set in the French countryside of his childhood, it describes a young man's search for a girl he has glimpsed only briefly.

Alamogordo   32 54N 105 57W A city in S New Mexico. The first atom bomb was exploded in a test near here on July 16, 1945. Population (1970): 23,000.

Alamo, the   A mission in San Antonio, Texas. During the Texas revolution it was defended from Feb 24 until March 6, 1836, by fewer than 200 Texan volunteers (including Davy Crockett), who were all massacred during the onslaught of 4000 Mexican troops led by Santa Anna. Six weeks later a victory at San Jacinto secured Texan independence.

Alanbrooke, Alan Francis Brooke, 1st Viscount   (1883– 1963) British field marshal. He joined the Royal Field Artillery in 1902, serving as a staff officer in World War I. In World War II, after service in France, he became commander in chief of the home forces. Appointed Chief of the Imperial General Staff in 1941, he advised Churchill at all his conferences with Roosevelt and Stalin.

Åland Islands   (Finnish name: Ahvenanmaa Islands)   A group of over 6000 islands and islets under Finnish administration, at the entrance to the Gulf of Bothnia. Population (1977 est): 22,455. Capital: Mariehamn.

Alarcón, Pedro Antonio de   (1833–91) Spanish novelist. He began his career as a poet and journalist, but his literary reputation is based on his later novels, especially *The Three-Cornered Hat* (1874), which was used by Manuel de *Falla as the basis for a ballet.

Alarcón y Mendoza, Juan Ruiz de   (1581–1639) Spanish dramatist. Born in Mexico, he became one of the leading dramatists of the Golden Age of Spanish drama. His best-known play is *La verdad sospechosa* (?1619), a satirical comedy. He apparently ceased to write after being appointed to the Council for the Indies in 1626.

Alaric I   (c. 370–410 AD) King of the *Visigoths. Alaric served in the Roman army as the commander of the Gothic auxiliary forces before his election as King of the Visigoths. After failing to reach a peaceful agreement with the Roman imperial administration, he invaded Greece and Italy. Alaric died shortly after his forces sacked Rome (410).

Alaska   The largest state in the US, occupying the extreme NW corner of the North American continent. Alaska juts out into the sea, which surrounds it on three sides. The Pacific Ocean lies to the S, the Bering Sea, the Bering Strait, and the Chukchi Sea to the W, and the Arctic Ocean to the N. Alaska borders Canada on the E (the Yukon Territory and British Columbia), which separates it from the coterminous "lower 48" states. It is a mountainous volcanic area; from the coast extend the Seward Peninsula in the S and the Alaska Penninsula further north. Alaska has roughly four physiographical regions. The Pacific mountain system, including the Coast Ranges and the Alaska Range (where Mt McKinley, the highest peak in North America, rises to over 20,000 ft (6100 m), dominates the S. The central region consists of uplands and lowlands. The Rocky Mountains extend into Alaska toward the N, forming the Brooks Range. The North Slope reaches down from the Brooks Range to the Arctic Ocean. There are numerous rivers, chief of which is the Yukon flowing W into the Bering Sea. It has an indented coastline with many islands. One third of the state lies within the Arctic Circle. The economy is based principally on the state's rich mineral wealth. The discovery of oil (1950) and subsequent finds (1968) have made oil production a major industry and there are abundant supplies of natural gas. Coal, gold, and copper are all mined. Fishing, especially salmon, and forestry are also major industries. Agricultural development is hindered by the short growing season and severe climate. Fur trapping has declined in importance although sealskins (from the offshore Pribilof Islands) remain an important export. Conflict between further development and the preservation of the natural landscape has become a major problem. *History*: first settled by Russians following voyages by the Dane Vitus Bering (1728, 1741), it was under the trade control of the Russian American company until 1867 when it was purchased by the US (it became known as Seward's Folly after the secretary of state who had led the negotiations). A number of gold rushes in the late 19th century helped to swell the sparse population. It became the 49th state in 1959. Environmental issues are under continuous debate in Alaska. The most famous was that of the Alaska Pipeline, an oil pipeline running 789 mi (1270 km) through the state. Opposed because of the supposed detrimental effect it would have on the state's ecology, the pipeline was eventually approved and was completed in 1977. Area: 586,412 sq mi (1,518,800 sq km). Population (1980): 400,481. Capital: Juneau.

Alaska Highway A road from Dawson Creek, Canada to Fairbanks, Alaska, built for defense against Japan (1942). Open throughout the year, it now serves tourism and economic development. Length: 1523 mi (2437 km).

Alaskan Boundary Dispute (1898–1903) A disagreement between the US and Canada over access from the Pacific Ocean across US-owned Alaska, to the Klondike gold fields in Yukon Territory, Canada. Canada claimed possession of the inlets and strip of land along the coast; the US claimed the same area as part of its purchase of Alaska from Russia in 1867. Due to inadequate surveying, both sides felt they had legitimate claims. An international panel of six settled the question in favor of the US.

Alaskan malamute. *See* husky.

Alaskan North Slope A low-lying plain in N Alaska, from the Arctic Ocean S to Brooks Range. It is a main source of oil, discovered during the 1960s, in Alaska.

Alaska Purchase (1867) The sale of Alaska Territory by Russia to the US for $7,200,000. Negotiated by Secretary of State William H. *Seward at the urging of settlers in the California-Washington territories, the purchase of this unsurveyed land was often referred to as "Seward's Folly" or "Seward's Ice Box."

Alaska Range A mountain range in S Alaska, arcing NE from the N end of the Aleutian Range at the base of the Alaska Peninsula and then SE to the SW Yukon Territory, Canada, border. Mt. McKinley, 20,320 ft (6194 m), the highest point in North America, is here.

Alastor In Greek legend, the son of Neleus and brother of Nestor, killed by Heracles on the island of Pylos. The name was also applied to the personified spirit of vengeance that could possess a man.

Alba, Fernando Alvarez de Toledo, Duke of (*or* Alva; 1507–83) Spanish general, who successfully commanded Habsburg forces against Protestants in Germany and the French in Italy. Philip II of Spain placed him in command of the Netherlands (1567–73), where his ruthless attempts to subdue the Dutch Protestants made him very unpopular, both in Spain and the Netherlands, and led to his recall. He led the successful expedition against Portugal (1580–81). *See also* Revolt of the Netherlands.

Albacete 39 00N 1 52W A city in SE central Spain, in Murcia. A market center, it is famous for the manufacture of cutlery and daggers. Its notable buildings include the 16th-century cathedral. Population (1974 est): 100,545.

albacore A fast-swimming *tuna fish, *Thunnus alalunga*, found in warm seas. It has very long pectoral fins and reaches up to 40 in (1 m) in length. It is the chief source of tuna for canning.

Alba-Iulia (German name: Karlsburg) 46 04N 23 33E A city in W central Romania, on the River Mureş. A former capital of Transylvania, its manufactures include leather goods and wine. Population (1979 est): 46,020.

Alban, St (3rd century AD) The first English martyr. A pagan soldier, he protected a Christian priest and was converted by him. On admitting this to the Roman authorities, he was scourged and beheaded on a site subsequently dedicated to him as the Abbey of St Albans in the city of St Albans in Hertfordshire, England. Feast day: June 22 or 17. Emblem: a stag.

Albania, Socialist People's Republic of (Albanian name: Shqiperia) A country in SE Europe, occupying part of the Balkan Peninsula on the Adriatic Sea. It consists of a mountainous interior, rising to

over 9000 ft (2700 m), with extensive forests and fertile coastal lowlands. The people, of whose origins little is known, belong to two main groups, the *Ghegs (N of the River Shkumbi) and the *Tosks (S). *Economy*: mainly agricultural, organized into state farms and collectives, although industrial development is increasing (the principal industries being agricultural processing, textiles, oil products, and cement). There have been recent attempts to develop the rich mineral resources, especially oil, lignite, copper, chromium, limestone, salt, and bauxite, as well as the rich natural-gas deposits. Main exports include crude oil, bitumen, chrome ore, copper wire, tobacco, fruit, and vegetables. *History*: became independent in 1912 after more than four centuries of Turkish rule. Following a civil war, in which Italy intervened, Albania became a republic in 1925 and a monarchy in 1928, when its president, Ahmed Beg Zogu (1895–1961), was proclaimed as King Zog. After occupation by Italy and Germany during World War II, another republic was set up in 1946, with a communist-controlled assembly. It aligned itself with the Soviet Union but after the death of Stalin relations between the two countries weakened and in 1961 diplomatic relations were broken off. Meanwhile Albania, alone among the other East European communist states, maintained close relations with China. In recent years, however, the alliance has cooled, and in 1978 Albania suspended commercial relations with China; a trade agreement signed in 1983 suggested an easing of tensions between the two countries. Fiercely communist, Albania maintains a hostile stance toward both the USSR and the US, denouncing the arms race and US-Soviet domination of Third World countries. Albania expressed enthusiastic support for the Argentines during the Falkland Islands crisis of 1982. Population (1983) est: 2,846,000. Capital: Tirana. Main port: Durrës. Enver *Hoxha, as first party secretary, has been executive leader since 1946. Official language: Albanian. Currency: lek of 100 qintars. Area: 11,101 sq mi (28,748 sq km). Population (1983): 2,846,000. Capital: Tirana. Main port: Durrës.

Albanian An Indo-European language, the only modern representative of a distinct branch of this linguistic group, spoken by two million Albanians and known by them as Shqiptar. It is divided into two main dialects, *Gheg and *Tosk.

Albany 42 40N 73 49W The capital of New York state, located on the Hudson River. Founded in 1614 by the Dutch, it is one of North America's oldest cities and has several notable public buildings, including the state capitol (1879). Economic growth accelerated with the building of the Erie Canal (1825) and today its main industries are brewing, the manufacture of electrical goods and textiles, and printing and publishing. Population (1980): 101,727.

Albany Congress (1754) A meeting of representatives from the American colonies to form a common defense and to discuss Indian affairs. Delegates from New Hampshire, Massachusetts, Rhode Island, Connecticut, New York, Pennsylvania, and Maryland worked to gain the loyalty of the Iroquois Indian tribes, previously allied with the French. Agreements reached were short-lived. Benjamin Franklin's resultant Albany Plan of Union, although not ratified by any of the colonies, was a model draft of the future US Articles of Confederation and US Constitution.

albatross A large seabird belonging to a family (*Diomedeidae*; 14 species) that occurs mainly in southern oceans. It has a stout hooked bill; usually a white or brown plumage, often with darker markings on the back, wings, or tail; and very long narrow wings (the wandering albatross, *Diomedea exulans*, has the largest wingspan of any bird, reaching up to 12 ft (3.5 m). Albatrosses can glide for hours over the open sea, feeding on squid and cuttlefish; they come ashore only to breed. Order: *Procellariiformes* (*see* petrels).

albedo A measure of the reflecting power of a nonluminous object, such as a planet or natural satellite or a surface feature on such a body. It is the ratio of the amount of light reflected in all directions from the object to the amount of incident light. Clouds, snow, and ice have high albedos while volcanic rocks have very low albedos.

Albee, Edward (1928–) US dramatist. His early one-act plays, notably *Zoo Story* (1958) and *The Death of Bessie Smith* (1960), analyze contemporary social tensions using techniques of the *Theater of the Absurd. His first three-act play, *Who's Afraid of Virginia Woolf?* (1962), which dramatizes the love-hate relationship of an academic couple, was very successful. Later plays include *A Delicate Balance* (1967, Pulitzer Prize) and *Seascape* (1975).

Alberoni, Giulio (1664–1752) Spanish-Italian cardinal and statesman, who rose to prominence during the War of the Spanish succession. In 1713 he was appointed consular agent for Parma at the court of Philip IV of Spain and in 1715 became prime minister of Spain and a cardinal. An ambitious foreign policy, which angered England, France, and Holland, resulted in his banishment to Italy (1719).

ALBATROSS *The waved albatross (Diomedea irrorata) breeds on the Galapagos Islands.*

Albers, Josef (1888–1976) German abstract painter, designer, and poet. His successful career as an influential art teacher and theoretician began at the *Bauhaus school of design and after 1933 continued in the US, where he painted a famous series of abstract paintings entitled *Homage to the Square*.

Albert I (1875–1934) King of the Belgians (1909–34). As commander in chief of the Belgian army, Albert led his country's heroic but unsuccessful resistance to the German invasion (1914) and contributed to the Allied victory in World War I. After the war he did much to encourage industrial reconstruction and currency reform.

Albert (I) the Bear (?1100–70) The first Margrave of Brandenburg (1150–70), who took the title following conquests that brought him Havelland in E Europe. Further campaigns extended his territories, in which he sponsored land-reclamation schemes and missionary work.

Albert II Alcibiades (1522–57) Margrave of Brandenburg, prominent in the conflict between Emperor Charles V and the German Protestants. A Protestant, he nevertheless supported Charles until 1551, when he turned his coat and joined Maurice of Saxony and the French. Defeated by Charles' brother Ferdinand, in 1553, he was outlawed and fled to France.

Albert III (1443–1500) Duke of Saxony jointly with his brother Ernest (1441–86) from 1464 until 1485, when the Saxon lands were divided between them. He campaigned for the Holy Roman Emperor and in 1488–89 restored imperial authority in Holland, Flanders, and Brabant. He died while repressing a rebellion in Friesland, where he was governor (1498–1500).

Albert, Lake. *See* Mobutu, Lake.

Albert, Prince (1819–61) Prince Consort of the United Kingdom and younger son of Ernest I, Duke of Saxe-Coburg-Gotha. In 1840 he married his cousin Queen Victoria and became her chief adviser. Although he was initially unpopular, his devotion to duty and his active patronage of the arts, science, and industry eventually won him respect. He is perhaps best remembered for his organization of the *Great Exhibition (1851). He died of typhoid.

Alberta A province of W Canada, mostly on the Great Plains. It consists mainly of a plateau, rising to the foothills of the *Rocky Mountains in the SW. The undulating S prairie and parkland further N support profitable ranches and grain farms. Alberta is Canada's largest oil and gas producer, possesses vast coalfields, and includes the Athabasca tar sands, one of the world's largest oil reserves (at present untapped). Manufacturing is based on agriculture and mineral resources. Lumbering, construction, and tourism are also important. *History*: first explored in the 18th century, Alberta became Canadian territory in 1869. The arrival of the railroad from E Canada (1883) facilitated agricultural settlement, and Alberta grew rapidly (especially 1900–14), becoming a province in 1905. Alberta's government tends to be controlled by one party for long periods, notably by the

Social Credit Party (1935–71). Area: 248,799 sq mi (644,389 sq km). Population (1981): 2,237,724. Capital: Edmonton.

Albert Canal A canal in Belgium, completed in 1939. It links the Meuse River at Liège with the Scheldt River at Antwerp. Length: 80 mi (130 km).

LEON BATTISTA ALBERTI *The west front of Sta Maria Novella (Florence).*

Alberti, Leon Battista (1404–72) Italian Renaissance architect. Alberti, who was also a painter, writer, musician, and scientist, is known mainly for being among the first Renaissance architects fully to grasp the principles of classical architecture. As his innovative façade of Sta Maria Novella in Florence demonstrates, he adapted these rules to 15th-century requirements. He built relatively little, his most significant buildings being the churches of S Sebastiano and S Andrea in Mantua and the incomplete Tempio Malatestiano in Rimini. His abiding influence upon architecture was through his treatise *De re aedificatoria* (*On Architecture*; 1452), which was translated into several European languages in the 16th century.

Albert of Brandenburg (1490–1545) German churchman, Cardinal Archbishop and Elector of Mainz. Although a religious liberal, a patron of the arts, and a friend of *Erasmus, he is chiefly remembered as the object of Luther's attacks for his sale of indulgences. In later life he supported the *Counter-Reformation.

Albertsville. *See* Kalemie.

Albertus Magnus, St (c. 1200–80) German bishop, philosopher, and Doctor of the Church. Provincial of the German Dominicans (1254–57) and for a short time Bishop of Regensburg, he taught constantly throughout his life. His best-known pupil was *Aquinas. An outstanding scholar, he wrote extensively on logic, natural and moral sciences, scripture, and theology. Feast day: Nov 15.

Albi 43 56N 2 08E A city in S France, the capital of the Tarn department on the Tarn River. A center of Catharism, it gave its name to the Albigensian heresy (*see* Albigenses). Notable buildings include the gothic cathedral and the 13th-century archbishop's palace, which is now a museum housing works by Toulouse-Lautrec (a native of Albi). An agricultural market, it has textile, glass, and cement industries. Population (1975): 49,456.

Albigenses Followers of the Christian heresy of Catharism (*see* Cathari), who flourished in southern France in the 12th and 13th centuries. The Albigenses, named for the town of Albi in Languedoc, were the object of the Albigensian Crusade, launched in 1208 and led by Simon de *Montfort. They were finally suppressed by the Inquisition, which operated in the area from 1233.

albinism An inherited disorder in which tyrosinase, one of the enzymes required for the formation of the pigment *melanin, is absent. Albinos have abnormally pale skin, fair hair, and pink or light-blue irises. The condition can be eased by the use of spectacles to treat the lens abnormalities common in albinos and by protection of the skin and eyes from direct sunlight.

Albinism, which can affect all human races, is also seen in wild and domestic animals.

Albino horse A horse exhibiting the characteristics of albinism and bred to maintain the color type. Albinos have pinkish sensitive skin, pure-white hair, and blue eyes. Defective eyesight is common, lessening its usefulness as a riding horse.

Albinoni, Tomaso (1671–1750) Italian composer and court musician to the Duke of Mantua. His works, which influenced J. S. Bach, include 50 operas, a violin concerto, and two oboe concertos. The *Adagio* for organ and strings often attributed to Albinoni was in fact composed by his Italian biographer Remo Giazotto.

Alboin (died c. 573) King of the Lombards (c. 565–c. 573). He succeeded to lands in central Europe and then conquered N Italy, establishing the kingdom of Lombardy (572), with his capital at Pavia.

Ålborg (or Aalborg) 57 03N 09 56E A city and seaport in Denmark, in N Jutland. Founded in 1342 AD, it has a gothic cathedral and a 16th-century castle. A university was established in 1974. Its industries include shipbuilding and textiles. Population (1981 est): 154,385.

albumins A class of proteins that are soluble in both water and dilute aqueous salt solutions. Serum albumins are constituents of blood; α-lactalbumin is found in milk; and ovalbumin is part of egg white. Preparations of albumins are used in therapeutic transfusions.

Albuquerque 35 05N 106 38W A city in New Mexico, on the Rio Grande. The state's largest city, it is situated in a rich agricultural area and food canning and the manufacture of livestock products are its principal industries. It is the home of the University of New Mexico (1892). Population (1980): 331,767.

Albuquerque, Alfonso de (1453–1515) Portuguese governor in India (1509–15). He was already a veteran soldier when he led his first expedition to India (1503). By a series of conquests he established Portuguese influence in the Indian Ocean based on three strongholds—Goa, Ceylon, and Malacca. He led the first European fleet to sail into the Red Sea and took Hormuz in 1515. Private enemies at the Portuguese court sought to discredit him and he was recalled, dying at sea.

Al Bu Sa'id The ruling dynasty of Oman since 1749 and of Zanzibar from 1749 to 1964. In 1749 Ahmad ibn Sa'id, the dynasty's founder, seized power over Oman and Zanzibar. In 1856 Oman and Zanzibar were divided. Zanzibar continued under Bu Sa'idi rule under the British protectorate (1890–1963) but the dynasty was overthrown when Zanzibar was incorporated into Tanzania (1964). The present ruler of Oman is Qaboos ibn Sa'id.

Alcaeus (6th century BC) Greek lyric poet. A member of the aristocracy of the island of Lesbos and a friend of *Sappho, he went into exile when the tyrant Pittacus gained power and wandered for many years in Thrace and Egypt. His work, only fragments of which survive, was greatly admired by *Horace.

Alcántara 39 44N 6 53W A town in W Spain in Estremadura. A magnificent Roman bridge (105 AD) spans the Tagus River here. Population (1970): 4636.

Alcatraz An island, in W California in San Francisco Bay. It was the site of a notorious maximum security prison from 1934 until 1962.

alcázar (Arabic *al-qasr*: castle, palace) A Spanish fortress built during the conflicts between Moors and Christians in the 14th and 15th centuries. The most renowned is the Alcázar of *Seville, built by King *Pedro the Cruel. The word remains an element in certain placenames, e.g. Alcázar de San Juan.

Alcázar de San Juan 39 42N 3 12W A city in S central Spain, in New Castile on La Mancha plain. It is associated with Cervantes' *Don Quixote*. Population (1970): 26,963.

alchemy A pseudoscience combining practical *chemistry with magical or mystical views of man and his relationship to the universe. Originating independently in China and Egypt, probably before the 3rd century BC, alchemy remained a legitimate branch of science and philosophy in Asia, Europe, and the Islamic lands for over 1500 years and is the ancestor of modern chemistry. It had three principal goals, the emphasis on which varied from place to place: the elixir of life (to ensure immortality), the panacea (or universal medicine), and the means of transmuting base metals into gold (see philosopher's stone). In China, *Taoism, which highly esteemed long life, fostered alchemical experimentation in search of the elixir. In Europe, concentration upon gold-making brought alchemy into disrepute.

Alcibiades (c. 450–404 BC) Athenian general and politician. Brought up by *Pericles, he was the pupil and lover of *Socrates. Alcibiades encour-

aged Athenian imperialism during the *Peloponnesian War (431–404) until, accused of desecrating monuments in Athens, he defected to Sparta (415). He regained Athenian favor (410) and was a successful commander until defeat, the fault of a subordinate, forced him into exile (406). He was murdered in Phrygia.

Alcmeon (c. 500 BC) Greek pioneer in medical science, from Croton (S Italy). Following *Pythagoras' experimental tradition, Alcmeon used dissection and vivisection to investigate human sense organs. He discovered the optic nerve and located the center of sensation in the brain.

Alcmaeon In Greek mythology, the son of Amphiarus, one of the *Seven Against Thebes, and Eriphyle. He killed his mother to avenge the death of Amphiarus, and was pursued by the Furies. His first wife was Arsinoë, daughter of King Pegeus of Psophis, but on his wanderings he married the daughter of the river god Achelous, and was pursued and killed by Pegeus and his sons. His own sons later avenged his death by killing Pegeus.

Alcmaeonids An aristocratic family prominent in virtually all ancient Athenian political crises, usually on the radical side. In 632 BC Megacles (an Alcmaeonid) violated the sanctuary of Athena by having a political opponent treacherously murdered there. The oracle of Delphi placed a hereditary curse on the family, banishing it from Athens. The Alcmaeonids returned under Solon, withdrew under Pisistratus, and returned again after the expulsion of Hippias (511/510 BC). *Cleisthenes was an Alcmaeonid; *Pericles and *Alcibiades had Alcmaeonid mothers.

Alcock, Sir John (William) (1892–1919) British aviator. He served with the Royal Naval Air Service in World War I and in 1919, accompanied by (Sir) Arthur Brown (1886–1948), was the first to fly the Atlantic Ocean. They flew from Newfoundland to Ireland, in 16 hours 27 minutes.

Alcoholics Anonymous A voluntary organization started in the US in 1934 to help alcoholics to help themselves. Members, who must have an honest desire to stop drinking, help one another on the basis of group therapy by sharing their experiences of alcoholism. There are local autonomous groups in over 90 countries. An associated organization, **AL-ANON**, provides support for the close relatives of alcoholics.

alcoholism An illness caused by physical and psychological dependence on alcohol (*see also* drug dependence). The incidence of alcoholism varies between different societies: it is most common in countries where alcohol is readily available and where heavy drinking is socially acceptable. Alcoholism causes mood changes, deterioration in personal standards and habits, and periods of memory loss. Continued heavy consumption will eventually lead to cirrhosis of the liver, heart disease, and damage to the nerves. Sudden withdrawal may produce specific symptoms: tremor, delusions, and hallucinations. Treatment, which is lengthy and difficult, includes initial alcohol withdrawal (with appropriate sedation) accompanied and followed by adequate psychological support. Drugs such as disulfiram (Antabuse), which cause vomiting after drinking alcohol, may assist the treatment. Nonmedical solutions to problems of alcoholism include group therapy in the company of other alcoholics (see Alcoholics Anonymous).

alcohols The class of organic compounds that includes *ethanol (ethyl alcohol; C_2H_5OH) and *methanol (methyl alcohol; CH_3OH). Ethanol is the common alcohol found in intoxicating drinks and is often called simply "alcohol." Alcohols contain at least one hydroxyl group and have the general formula ROH, where R is a *hydrocarbon group. They react with *acids to give *esters and water. Primary alcohols oxidize to form *aldehydes and secondary alcohols to form *ketones.

alcohol strength The measurement of the percentage volume of *ethanol (ethyl alcohol) in alcoholic drinks in order to calculate government duty on them. In the US, 100° proof is 50% alcohol by volume. Until 1980, the UK used a similar system for spirits, but with 57.06%, measured at 59°F (15°C), as the standard (100° proof), pure alcohol being 175° proof. France and Italy formerly used the Gay-Lussac scale, which simply states the percentage volume of alcohol, measured at 59°F (15°C). The OMIL (International Organization of Legal meterology) system, now used throughout the European Economic Community (EEC), is based on percentage volume of alcohol at 68°F (20°C). Thus a bottle of liquor labeled in the EEC "35% vol" is approximately equivalent to 61° proof in the former UK system or 70° proof in the US system.

Alcott, Amos Bronson (1799–1888) US philosopher, educator, reformer, and writer; father of Louisa May Alcott. He had several schools in Connecticut, Boston, and Philadelphia, before founding the Temple School (1834) in Boston. Here he attempted to develop the well-rounded student, intellectually, emotionally, and physically. He also founded Fruitlands (1843), an experimental community in Harvard, Mass., and advocated transcendentalism throughout his later life. Among his works are *Ralph Waldo Emerson* (1865) and *Concord Days* (1872).

Alcott, Louisa May (1832–88) US novelist. Daughter of the social theorist Bronson Alcott, her education was supplemented by instruction from *Thoreau, *Emerson, and her neighbor Nathaniel *Hawthorne. Her first book, *Flower Fables* (1854), was written when she was 16 to raise money for her family. *Hospital Sketches* (1863) recounted her experiences as a nurse in the Civil War. *Little Women* (1868–69), her most famous book, was, like her subsequent children's books, largely autobiographical. Other works include *An Old Fashioned Girl* (1870), *Little Men* (1871), and *Jo's Boys* (1886).

Alcuin (c. 735–804 AD) English theologian and educator, who inspired the Carolingian renaissance. He became the religious and educational adviser to Charlemagne after meeting him in 781. He established important libraries and developed a method of teaching based on *Boethius, St *Augustine, and the study of grammar. Among his pupils was Rabanus Maurus (c. 780–856). He compiled numerous educational manuals and was also a poet. His letters are important sources for the study of Carolingian society.

Aldanov, Mark (M. Aleksandrovich Landau; 1886–1957) Russian novelist. He emigrated to France in 1919 and to the US in 1941. His best-known work is a trilogy about Revolutionary France, comprising *Saint Helena* (1924), *The Ninth Thermidor* (1926), and *The Devil's Bridge* (1928). *The Fifth Seal* (1936) was an anti-Soviet satire and *The Tenth Symphony* (1931), a portrait of Beethoven's Vienna.

Aldebaran A conspicuous *red giant, apparent magnitude 0.9 and 68 light years distant, that is the brightest star in the constellation Taurus. It is both a visual *binary star and an irregular *variable star.

aldehydes A class of organic chemicals that contain the -CHO group. They are prepared by the oxidation of alcohols and are themselves oxidized to form carboxylic acids. Most are liquids; common aldehydes are *formaldehyde and *acetaldehyde.

Alden, John (1599–1637) English colonist in America. He sailed to America on the *Mayflower* in 1620 and is said to have been the first Pilgrim to set foot in the new land at Plymouth, Mass. He was a signer of the *Mayflower Compact*, cofounded Duxbury, Mass., and served as deputy governor of Massachusetts twice (1623–41; 1650–86). He is immortalized in Henry Wadsworth Longfellow's poem "The Courtship of Miles Standish" (1858) for courting Priscilla Mullins (whom he did in fact marry) for his friend Miles Standish.

alder A tree or shrub belonging to a genus (*Alnus*; about 30 species) of the N hemisphere. The leaves are roundish and toothed; the flowers grow as separate male and female catkins on the same tree. The fruit is a woody cone containing small winged nuts. The black alder (*A. glutinosa*), about 65ft (20 m) high, is found in wet places throughout Europe and Asia and in N Africa. Its timber is used in general woodworking. Family: *Betulaceae* (birch family).

alderfly An insect, also known as a fish fly, having two pairs of delicate finely veined wings and long antennae. Up to 2in (50 mm) long (including the wings), alderflies live near fresh water, feeding on smaller insects and laying their eggs on reeds. The larvae, which are also carnivorous, live in the water and crawl out to pupate in burrows in the soil. Family: *Sialidae*; order: *Neuroptera* (lacewings, etc.).

Alderney (French name: Aurigny) 49 43N 2 12W The third largest of the Channel Islands, separated from the French coast by the dangerous Race of Alderney channel. Its economy is based on dairy farming and tourism. Area: 3 sq mi (8 sq km). Population (1980 est): 2000. Chief town: St Anne.

Aldhelm, St (c. 640–709 AD) English abbot and bishop. Abbot of Malmesbury from about 675, he became Bishop of Sherborne about 705. He founded several churches and monasteries. His Latin writings include various treatises, a work on saints, and religious poems. Feast day: May 25.

Aldington, Richard (1892–1962) British poet, novelist, and biographer. In 1913 he married his fellow Imagist poet Hilda *Doolittle. He suffered shell shock in World War I; *Death of a Hero* (1929) and *The Colonel's Daughter* (1931) are his best-known novels. Among his frequently controversial biographies are studies of D. H. Lawrence (1950) and T. E. Lawrence (1955).

Aldiss, Brian W(ilson) (1925–) British novelist. Most of his novels and short stories are science fiction and he has written a history of the genre, *Billion Year Spree* (1975). He edited many science-fiction anthologies, and his individual collections include *The Saliva Tree* (1966) and *Last Orders* (1977).

aldol An organic compound that contains a *hydroxyl group (OH) and an *aldehyde group (CHO) bound to adjacent carbon atoms. A common aldol is **acetaldol** ($CH_3CHOHCH_2CHO$), which is used as a sedative and hypnotic drug.

aldosterone A steroid hormone that acts on the kidney tubules to regulate the content of salts and water in the body. Derived from cholesterol, aldosterone is produced by the cortex of the adrenal glands in response to changing blood volume, changing levels of sodium and potassium, and the presence of the pituitary hormone *ACTH.

Aldrich, Thomas Bailey (1836–1907) US novelist and poet. He left school at 13 and began writing for magazines while working in New York as a clerk. He is known for his light verse and short stories and his autobiography, *The Story of a Bad Boy* (1870).

Aldrich-Vreeland Currency Act (1908) US law that created the National Monetary Commission and paved the way for the Federal Reserve Act of 1913. Aimed at alleviating the bank failures and currency shortages of 1907, the bill provided for relief in such cases by authorizing temporary emergency currency issuance by organized bank groups. Meanwhile, the commission was to study banking conditions and recommend reforms.

Aldridge, Ira Frederick (1804–67) US actor. The first great black tragedian, he made his debut as Othello in London in 1826 and made several successful European tours in Shakespearean roles.

Aldrin, Buzz (Edwin Eugene A., Jr.; 1930–) US astronaut. A graduate of West Point (1951), he served in Korea as an Air Force pilot before entering the astronaut program at the National Aeronautics and Space Administration (NASA) in 1963. He was part of the two-man crew on the Gemini XII flight in 1966 and was the second man to walk on the moon during the 1969 flight of Apollo 11.

ale. *See* beer.

aleatoric music Music that incorporates elements of chance in its structure. The term from Latin *alea*, a game of dice, was first used in the 1950s to describe John *Cage's experiments in determining compositional procedures of pitch, rhythm, structure, and dynamics by the use of the *I Ching.

Alegría, Ciro (1909–61) Peruvian novelist, imprisoned and finally exiled to Chile and the US from 1934 until 1948 for his political activities. His works embody his deep knowledge of, and sympathy for, the Peruvian Indians: his best-known novel, *Broad and Alien Is the World* (1941), deals with the resistance of an Indian tribe to the usurping white man.

Alekhine, Alexander (1892–1946) French chess player, born in Russia. He became world champion by defeating *Capablanca (1927), losing the championship in 1935, but holding it again from 1937 until his death. He regarded chess as an art, the aesthetic merits of which were more important to him than winning.

Alemán, Mateo (1547–?1614) Spanish writer, famous for his picaresque novel *Guzman de Alfarache* (1599–1604), the scurrilous adventures of a youth who runs away from home and is finally condemned to the galleys, where he repents. The book became popular throughout Europe. Alemán himself was often imprisoned for debt and emigrated to Mexico in 1607.

Alençon 48 25N 0 05E A city in NW France, the capital of the Orne department situated at the confluence of the Sarthe and Briant Rivers. The former capital of the duchy of Alençon, it is famed for its lace (especially point d'Alençon). It serves an agricultural area. Population (1975): 34,666.

Aleppo (Arabic name: Halab) 36 14N 37 10E A city in NW Syria. The Crusaders tried in vain to capture it, and from 1516 to 1919 Aleppo was part of the Ottoman Empire. After World War II, it was incorporated into independent Syria. It is now an industrial center and the terminus of a pipeline from Iraq; its university was founded in 1960. Population (1975 est): 778,523.

Alessandria 44 55N 8 37E A city in N Italy, in Piedmont on the Tanaro River. It is a railroad center and has an important engineering industry. The surrounding district is agricultural. Population (1980 est): 101,075.

Ålesund (*or* Aalesund) 62 28N 6 11E A seaport in W Norway. Founded in the 9th century AD, it is an important trading center, especially for fishing in northern waters. Population (1981 est): 34,630.

Aletsch Glacier The largest glacier in Europe, in Switzerland in the Bernese Oberland lying SE of the Aletschhorn mountain. Length: 16 mi (26 km).

Aleut A native of the Aleutian Islands and W Alaska, similar to the *Eskimo in culture. Aleuts hunted seals, whales, and walrus, using skin-covered boats called bidarkas, which were like *kayaks but often two-manned. They also fished for salmon and in some areas hunted caribou and bear. They produced fine basketry and worked stone, bone, and ivory. Their population was considerably reduced during the Russian administration of the area and today their culture has been much changed by the impact of the modern world. Their language is closely related to Eskimo. It has three dialects, the two principal ones being Attuan and Unalaskan.

Aleutian Islands A chain of volcanic Alaskan islands lying between the Bering Sea and the Pacific Ocean, divided politically between the Soviet Union and the US. The chief settlements are on Unalaska. Russian exploitation of supplies after 1741 greatly reduced the population, but fishing and seal, otter, and fox hunting are now regulated. There are strategic US military stations on the islands and underground nuclear tests have been made.

alewife A small silvery fish, *Pandopus pseudoharengus*, up to 12in (30 cm) long. It occurs chiefly in the Atlantic coastal waters of North America but has recently become established in the Great Lakes. It is an important food fish and is also used in the manufacture of fertilizers. Family: *Clupeidae* (herrings).

Alexander (1876–1903) King of Serbia (1889–1903); the last of the *Obrenović dynasty. Alexander's arbitrary rule, including the abolition of the liberal constitution in 1894, and his unpopular marriage in 1900 led to his assassination, and that of his wife, by a group of army officers.

Alexander I (c. 1077–1124) King of the Scots (1107–24), who ruled the highlands of Scotland while his brother and successor David ruled the lowlands. He was noted for his reform of the Scottish church and his foundation of the monastery of Scone (1114). He aided Henry I of England's campaign against Wales (1114).

Alexander I (1777–1825) Emperor of Russia (1801–25), succeeding his unstable father Paul I. Alexander made some educational and administrative reforms but was more concerned with foreign policy. France's defeat of Russia at *Friedland in 1807 forced Alexander to agree to the Treaty of *Tilsit, which lasted until Napoleon's unsuccessful invasion of Russia in 1812. After Napoleon's defeat, Russia controlled the *Congress Kingdom of Poland. Alexander turned to religious mysticism, hoping to establish a new Christian order in Europe by means of the Holy Alliance (1815) with Austria and Prussia. Toward the end of his life he withdrew into seclusion.

Alexander II (1198–1249) King of the Scots (1214–49). Hoping to regain the northern counties of England, he supported the unsuccessful *Barons' War (1215–17) against King John. In 1221 he married Joan, the sister of Henry III of England, and gave up his claims to English territory in 1237, when the present border between England and Scotland was fixed.

Alexander II (1818–81) Emperor of Russia (1855–81). After the conclusion of the *Crimean War (1856) Alexander embarked upon a program of modernization. He emancipated the serfs (1861) and reorganized administration, the army, the judicial system, local government, and education. These reforms were not wholly successful because Alexander lacked personnel able to implement them. He presided over Russian expansion into Central Asia and the victorious war against Turkey (1877–78). The end of his reign saw the growth of radical opposition and he was killed by a bomb thrown into his coach.

ALEXANDER (III) THE GREAT *A detail of a mosaic at Pompeii, which shows Alexander on his horse Bucephalus pursuing the fleeing Darius III (d. 330) of Persia. Alexander's decisive victory was fought at Gaugamela in 331.*

Alexander (III) the Great (356–323 BC) King of Macedon (336–323), who between 334 and his death conquered most of the world known to antiquity. Alexander, who was a pupil of Aristotle, inherited a plan to invade Persia from his father Philip II; having secured his position in Macedon and Greece, he put this plan into action. In 333 he defeated the Persian king *Darius III at Issus; in 332 he reduced Tyre in his greatest victory. Alexander then proceeded to conquer Egypt and Babylon (331). Moving on to Media and then east into central Asia, he finally embarked on the Indian expedition (327–325). He crossed the Indus River and conquered the Punjab. Forced to turn back by his reluctant army, he died at Babylon shortly after the marathon return journey. In the administration of his empire Alexander adopted a novel policy of appointing subject races to posts of responsibility, which some historians have called idealism and others, opportunism. His outstanding gifts as a general, however, are indisputable.

Alexander III (Rolando Bandinelli; c. 1105–81) Italian pope. Elected in 1159, he was immediately challenged by the antipope Victor IV, who was supported by *Frederick Barbarossa. He eventually forced Frederick to reconcile himself with the Church at the Peace of Venice in 1177. He imposed penance on *Henry II of England for the murder of Thomas *Becket. He called and presided at the third *Lateran Council, which conferred the exclusive right of papal elections on the cardinals.

Alexander III (1241–86) King of the Scots (1249–86). He married (1251) Margaret, daughter of Henry III of England. Under his leadership, the Scots defeated the Norwegians at the battle of Largs (1263) and by the Treaty of Perth (1266) gained the Isle of Man and the Hebrides from Norway.

Alexander III (1845–94) Emperor of Russia (1881–94). Owing to the assassination of his father Alexander II and the influence of the lawyer K. P. Pobedonostsev (1827–1907), Alexander's reign showed extreme conservatism. He increased police powers, persecuted revolutionaries, permitted education to decline, and encouraged the russification of subject races. Under him, Russia made its last conquests in Central Asia and the Middle East.

Alexander VI (Rodrigo Borgia; c. 1431–1503) Pope (1492–1503), notorious for his immorality, nepotism, and extravagance. Father of four illegitimate children, he used papal wealth to further the career of his son, Cesare *Borgia, who pursued Alexander's territorial ambitions in Italy. He was a generous patron of artists and was responsible for demarcating the respective areas of influence of Spain and Portugal in the New World.

Alexander Archipelago A chain of islands in the US, off the SE coast of Alaska. They consist of the summits of a submerged mountain chain and their rugged densely forested terrain supports an abundance of wildlife.

Alexander Nevsky (c. 1220–63) Prince of Novgorod (1236–63) and Grand Prince of Vladimir (1252–63). Alexander's fame rests on his defeat of the Swedes (1240) near the Neva River (thus acquiring his name Nevsky) and of the Teutonic Knights (1242) on Lake Peipus. Despite the opposition of many Russians, he accepted the overlordship of the invading Mongols, thereby saving N Russia from certain devastation.

Alexander of Hales (c. 1170–1245) English scholastic philosopher, born at Hales (Gloucestershire). He became professor of theology in Paris and in 1236 a Franciscan. He is renowned for his efforts to combine the newly rediscovered *Aristotelianism, as mediated by the Arabic thinkers, such as *Averroes, with the Platonist tradition mediated by St *Augustine of Hippo.

Alexander of Tunis, Harold, 1st Earl (1891–1969) British field marshal. In World War II he commanded the evacuation of British forces from Dunkirk. He became commander in chief in the Middle East (1942) and directed the offensive that defeated the Germans in N Africa (1943). He ended the war as Allied supreme commander in the Mediterranean and was subsequently governor general of Canada (1946–52).

Alexander Severus. See Severus Alexander.

Alexandria (Arabic name: al-Iskandariyah) 31 13N 22 55E The chief seaport and second largest city in Egypt, between Lake Mareotis and the Mediterranean Sea. It handles most of Egypt's trade and the chief export is cotton; industries include oil refining and cotton ginning. The University of Alexandria was established in 1942. *History*: founded in 332 BC by Alexander the Great, partly on the island of Pharos, which was linked to the mainland by a breakwater, it remained the Egyptian capital for over a thousand years. It was a Greek and Jewish cultural center with a famous library (see Alexandria, Library of) and in 30 BC fell to the Romans, becoming their most important regional capital. It declined following the discovery of the Cape of Good Hope passage and the removal of the capital to Cairo. It was bombarded by the British in 1882, Pompey's Pillar being one of the few ancient monuments to escape destruction. Two obelisks that also survived, *Cleopatra's Needles, were removed and one is now in London, the other in New York. During World War II the city suffered many air raids but since then has seen rapid expansion. Population (1976): 2,319,000.

Alexandria 38 48N 77 03W A city and port in E Virginia on the Potomac River, S of Washington, D.C. Established in 1749, Alexandria's historic sites include Christ Church. The *Alexandria Gazette* (1784), the oldest daily newspaper in the United States, is still published here. Manufactures include wood products and chemicals. Population (1980): 103,217.

Alexandria, Catechetical School of A Christian theological school at Alexandria from the late 2nd to the 4th century AD. Its early teachers, *Clement and *Origen, dominated the School's approach, which was a Platonic mystical philosophy that stressed divine transcendence, the deity of Christ, and a Trinitarianism that was almost tritheism. Athanasius was typically Alexandrian in opposing the Arian and related heresies.

Alexandria, Library of The greatest library of the ancient world, which in its heyday may have contained more than 700 000 items. A composite library, museum, and school, it was founded in the 3rd century BC by Ptolemy I Soter and his son, Ptolemy II Philadelphus. Large parts were destroyed in fires, notably in 97 BC, and it was finally destroyed by the Arabs in 696 AD. The survival of much of classical Greek literature is due to the work of its scholars.

alexandrine A verse meter consisting of a line of 12 syllables usually with major stresses on the sixth and final syllables. The name is derived from 12th-century French poems about Alexander the Great. It was the dominant verse form in 17th-century French poetry and was used by *Racine and *Corneille.

Alexis (1690–1718) The son and heir of *Peter the Great of Russia. Alexis' unhappy relations with his father progressively worsened and in 1716 Alexis fled to Vienna. Peter lured him back and condemned him to death for treason. He died before his execution.

Alexius I Comnenus (1048–1118) Byzantine emperor (1081–1118), who founded the Comnenian dynasty. Seizing the throne in a coup, Alexius revived the weakened Byzantine state, defeating the Normans and Seljuq Turks, who were encroaching on Byzantine territory, and introducing administrative reforms. However, in the second half of his reign, the Empire was threatened by the advance of the Crusaders. His achievements were celebrated in the *Alexiad* of his daughter *Anna Comnena.

alfalfa A perennial flowering plant, *Medicago sativa*, also called lucerne. Growing to a height of 40in (1 m), it resembles clover, having clusters of small purple flowers. Native to Europe, it is widely grown as forage for cattle and because of its ability to fix nitrogen. Family: *Leguminosae*.

al-Farabi, Mohammed ibn Tarkhan (d. 950) Muslim philosopher, physician, mathematician, and musician, of Central Asian origin. He is acknowledged to be one of the greatest Muslim thinkers and his works on medicine and music became standard treatises. But it was his contribution to Arabic philosophy that earned him renown. A staunch believer in the truth of Islam, Al-Farabi strove to bring the whole of Greek philosophy into conformity with its doctrines.

Alfieri, Vittorio, Count (1749–1803) Italian poet and dramatist. He abandoned a military career in order to travel widely throughout Europe (1767–72). After the success of his first play, *Cleopatra* (1775), he devoted himself entirely to literature. He wrote 28 plays, of which his 19 tragedies, among them *Saul* and *Mirra*, depict romantic heroes struggling against tyranny and oppression. He also wrote poetry and an autobiography, *La vita* (1804).

Alfonsin, Raúl (1926–) Argentine statesman; president (1983–). A lawyer, he was a member of the Radical Party, serving as president of the party from 1965. His election to the presidency ended the almost-40-year reign of the Peronist Party. An advocate of civil and human rights, Alfonsín fought corruption in the government and military and attempted to ease Argentina's economic distress and stormy relations with other countries in the aftermath of Argentina's unsuccessful attempt to occupy the Falkland Islands.

Alfonso (V) the Magnanimous (1385–1458) King of Aragon (1416–58) and, as Alfonso I, of Sicily (1416–58) and Naples (1443–58). During the 1420s he helped Queen Joanna II of Naples (1371–1435; reigned 1414–35) to resist the claims of Louis III of Anjou (1403–34) to the Neapolitan throne. After her death he seized the throne himself and his court at Naples became a brilliant center of Renaissance culture.

Alfonso VI (d. 1109) King of León (1065–1109) and of Castile (1072–1109). In 1085 Alfonso took Toledo from the Muslims but in the following year suffered defeat by the Almoravids of N Africa, with whom conflict continued until 1108. Alfonso's marriage to Constance of Burgundy brought cultural ties with France and he supported the introduction of Cluniac monasticism to León. His reign is also notable for the exploits of El Cid.

Alfonso VIII (d. 1214) King of Castile (1158–1214), famous for his defeat of the Moors at Navas de Tolosa (1212). He married Eleanor, a daughter of Henry II of England; their daughter was *Blanche of Castile.

Alfonso (X) the Wise (c. 1221–84) King of Castile and León (1252–84). He made his court at Toledo a center of learning and a haven for Arab and Jewish, as well as Christian, scholars. He compiled a legal code, the Seven Divisions of the Law, but it never came into effective use. He also failed in an attempt (1257) to become the first Spanish Holy Roman Emperor.

Alfonso XIII (1886–1941) King of Spain from birth until 1931. Alfonso, who came of age in 1902, ruled during a turbulent period of social unrest and political instability and several attempts were made on his life. The dictatorship (1923–30) of Miguel *Primo de Rivera undermined his reign and he abdicated in 1931 following Republican victories in municipal elections.

Alfred the Great (849–99) King of Wessex (871–99). He prevented the Danish conquest of England, defeating them at Edington (878) after a campaign of guerrilla warfare. After his victory he allowed the Danes to keep their conquests in Mercia and East Anglia provided that Guthrum, their king, was converted to Christianity. Alfred built a navy of warships to defend the south coast against further Danish invasions (885–86; 892–96) and protected Wessex with a chain of fortifications. He took London (886), thus gaining control of all England except the Danish areas. Alfred did much to revive learning, translating important Latin works into English. He also devised a legal code.

Alfvén, Hannes Olof Gösta (1908–) Swedish astrophysicist. A specialist in *plasma physics, his original work includes studies of sunspots, cosmic rays, and the aurora. His work on the interaction of plasma with magnetic fields (magnetohydrodynamics) forms the basis of several proposed systems for harnessing nuclear fusion power; he shared the 1970 Nobel Prize for this work.

algae A vast group of simple plants (about 25,000 species) that contain the green pigment chlorophyll (and can therefore carry out photosynthesis) but have no true stems, roots, or leaves (see Thallophyta). They range from single-celled organisms to the giant seaweeds. Most algae are aquatic, although some live in damp places on land—on rocks, trees, or in soils. A few are parasitic or associate with other organisms (see lichen). Reproduction is extremely variable and may involve asexual means, such as cell division, fragmentation, or spore production, and/or sexual means by gamete production. The more advanced algae often alternate between sexual and asexual phases. Algae provide a valuable food source for aquatic herbivorous animals and many are used as fertilizers and in industry. There are generally considered to be seven divisions of algae (see red algae). Some of the unicellular forms are alternatively classed as *Protozoa.

Algarve The most southerly province of Portugal, bordering on Spain and the Atlantic Ocean. It became a Moorish kingdom in 1140 and was the last stronghold of the Moors in Portugal, being reconquered in 1249. Sparsely populated inland, its fertile coastal belt is densely populated and produces chiefly grain, figs, almonds, and olives; fishing is also important. Tourism is a flourishing industry. Area: 1957 sq mi (5071 sq km). Population (1979 est): 308,800. Chief town: Faro.

algebra The branch of mathematics that uses symbols to represent unknown quantities. The first treatise on the subject was written by Diophantus of Alexandria in the 3rd century AD and the name derives from the Arabic *al-jabr*, a term used by the mathematician al-Khwarizmi to denote the addition of equal quantities to both sides of an equation and later adopted as the name for the whole subject. Algebra was used in ancient Babylon, Egypt, and India and brought to Europe by the Arabs. In classical algebra symbols, such as x and y, represent ordinary numbers and the central part of the subject is the study of algebraic equations. Modern, or abstract, algebra is concerned with any system of quantities that obey a particular set of general rules and relationships. Such systems may or may not obey the *commutative laws or even the *associative laws that hold in arithmetic.

Algeciras 36 08N 5 27W A port in S Spain, in Andalusia on the Bay of Gibraltar. Founded in 713 AD, it was destroyed by Alfonso XI of Castile (1311–50; reigned 1312–50) in 1344. The present town was rebuilt in 1760. In 1906 it was the site of the Algeciras Conference, a meeting of European powers to solve their dispute over Morocco. Its exports include oranges and cork. Population (1970): 81,662.

Alger, Horatio (1832–99) US novelist and churchman, known for his stories of the rise from "rags to riches." Born in Massachusetts and educated for the ministry, Alger wrote his first novel in 1864 and followed with more than 135 others, all with the theme of riches achieved by virtuous, hard-working young men. His works include *Ragged Dick* (1867), *Tattered Tom* (1871), and *The Young Miner* (1879).

Algeria, Democratic and Popular Republic of A country in N Africa, on the Mediterranean Sea. It consists chiefly of the N Sahara Desert, with the Atlas Mountains in the N and small fertile areas near the coast. The inhabitants, who live almost entirely in the N, are mainly Arabs and Berbers. *Economy*: mainly agricultural although industrialization has proceeded rapidly since independence, financed by the discovery of oil (the main export) and natural gas in the desert areas. *History*: a former province of the Roman Empire, Algeria was subjugated in the 7th century by the Arabs, who introduced Islam. Overrun by Turks in the 16th century, it became a pirate state in the 18th century under the domination of *deys*, independent rulers who preyed on Mediterranean shipping. Algeria was annexed by the French in the 19th century and in 1881 the N section became part of Metropolitan France. A war of independence, waged by the *Front de Libération nationale (FLN), lasted from 1954 to 1962 when independence was granted by de Gaulle, following referenda held in both Algeria and France. A republic was set up under Ahmed *Ben Bella but was overthrown in 1965 by a Council of Revolution. Col Houari *Boumédienne became president and in 1976 was elected for a further six years in office. In the same year a new constitution was adopted in which the one-party principle was reaffirmed, the FLN being the only political party permitted in Algeria. Following Boumédienne's death in December, 1978, Colonel Benjedid Chadli (1929–   ) became the new president. Official language: Arabic; French is also widely spoken. Official religion: Islam. Currency: dinar of 100 centimes. Area: 919,595 sq mi (2,381,745 sq km). Population (1979 est): 18,250,000. Capital and main port: Algiers.

Algiers (Arabic name: al-Jaza'ir; French name: Alger) 36 45N 3 05E The capital of Algeria, an important port in the N of the Mediterranean Sea. Its main exports include wine, citrus fruits, and iron ore. The University of Algiers was founded in 1879 and the University of Science and Technology in 1974. *History*: originally founded by the Phoenicians, it was re-established by the Arabs in the 10th century. Overrun by Turks in the 16th century, it became a base for Barbary pirates until taken by the French in 1830. During World War II it was the headquarters of the Allied forces in N Africa and for a time the seat of the French government-in-exile. It was the scene of several uprisings during the Algerian struggle for independence from France (1954–62). Population (1974 est): 1,503,720.

algin (sodium alginate) A slimy substance extracted from seaweed. It is used as a thickener in such foods as ice cream and in industrial compounds.

Algirdas (or Olgierd; d. 1377) Grand Duke of Lithuania (1345–77). A pagan ruler, Algirdas was nevertheless tolerant of the Orthodox Church. He fought the Poles, Mongols, and Teutonic Knights and extended Lithuania eastward.

Algol (or Winking Demon) A white 2nd-magnitude star in the constellation Perseus. Its regular variations in brightness have been known for centuries. It is the prototype of the **Algol variables**, a class of eclipsing *binary stars: Algol revolves around its fainter companion in 2.87 days.

ALGOL (*algo*rithmic *l*anguage) A computer-programming language. It is used to express mathematical and scientific problems in a way that can be processed by computer. ALGOL is a high-level language, i.e. statements made in it resemble English and algebraic formulae rather than a computer notation. *See* program.

Algonkian A group of North American Indian languages, including *Cree, *Cheyenne, *Blackfoot, and others spoken by tribes living to the S and E of Hudson Bay and in the eastern woodland zone. The Algonkian peoples lived by hunting and fishing and roamed widely in small family groups. They moved their possessions by means of toboggans and crafted their clothing from the hides of animals, such as deer, caribou, and moose. Their religion involved a belief in a single creator god, and they relied on the protective and curative powers of medicine men, who possessed considerable authority within Algonkian society. The Algonkians were eventually driven from their original homelands in the middle of the 17th century by the neighbouring *Iroquois.

Algonkin The language and name of a North American Indian people of Quebec and Ottawa in Canada. The *Algonkian language group was named for it. Algonkin culture was similar to that of other Algonkin-speaking tribes of the area.

Algren, Nelson (1909–81) US novelist. He trained as a journalist in Chicago, where most of his fiction is set, and briefly became a migrant worker during the Depression. In his novels, such as *Never Come Morning* (1942), he portrayed the underworld of American city life in an intense naturalistic style. *The Man with the Golden Arm* (1949), about drug addiction, brought him international fame.

ALHAMBRA *The arcade around the Court of the Lions features the horseshoe arches characteristic of Moorish architecture.*

Alhambra A castle on a hilly terrace outside *Granada (Spain), built between 1238 and 1358. It was the last stronghold of the Muslim kings of Granada. Combining citadel and palace, it is an outstanding example of Moorish architecture, with magnificent courts and gardens. The name derives from Arabic *al-hamra*, the red, an allusion to the red stucco used on the walls.

Al Hudaydah. *See* Hodeida.

Ali (c. 600–67) The cousin of *Mohammed and his son-in-law by marriage to *Fatimah. Born at Mecca, he was the second, or perhaps the first, person to embrace Islam. He became the fourth caliph in 656, but faced much opposition and was murdered in 661 at Kufa, Iraq. His tomb is venerated at Najaf. According to *Shiite Muslims, Ali was the only legitimate successor of Mohammed and only his descendants are recognized as *imams.

MUHAMMAD ALI *A familiar display of clowning amuses a Philippine official (right) before Ali's defeat of Joe Frazier in Manila, 1975.*

Ali, Muhammad (Cassius Marcellus Clay; 1942–   ) US boxer. A gold medalist in the 1960 Olympic Games, he became professional world heavyweight champion (1964). On becoming a Black Muslim he changed his name and was soon afterward stripped of his title for three years because of his refusal to be inducted into the army. Defeated (1971) by Joe *Frazier, he again became champion in 1974 by defeating George Foreman (1949–   ), losing the title briefly in 1978 to Leon Spinks. His defeat of Spinks later that year made him the only boxer to become champion three times. In 1980 he was defeated by Larry Holmes in his bid to regain the world title. He is renowned for his extroverted personality.

Alicante 38 21N 0 29W A port in SE Spain, in Valencia on the Mediterranean Sea. Exports include wine, olive oil, and fruits and it serves as an outlet for Madrid. Industries include oil refining, textiles, chemicals, soap, and tobacco. It is a popular tourist resort. Population (1974 est): 213,143.

Alice Springs 23 42S 133 52E A city in central Australia, in S Northern Territory. It is a major center for beef cattle and mineral transportation, linked by air, road, and rail with Adelaide and by air and the Stuart Highway with Darwin. It is also a base for tourism. Population (1979 est): 16,500.

alien A person born in a foreign country who has not qualified as a US citizen.

Alien and Sedition Acts (1798) Four laws enacted ostensibly to prevent domestic subversion but actually to check the threat posed to the *Federalist Party by Thomas Jefferson's Republican Party. The Naturalization Act delayed voting rights for the immigrants upon whom the Republicans depended for support. The Alien Act and Alien Enemies Act authorized deportation of aliens suspected of threatening the government and the Sedition Act prohibited criticism of the government, thereby nullifying the First Amendment. The Alien Act expired in 1800 and the Sedition Act in 1801. The Alien Enemies Act was never enforced. The Naturalization Act was repealed in 1802.

alienation A pathological feeling of self-estrangement and loss of moral purpose. Hegel used the term to refer to a condition in which an individual's freedom of choice and action appears to him to have become an independent force constraining him. Marx made special use of the concept of alienated labor, believing that when men are forced to sell their labor to employers they are alienated from their own productive abilities. In contemporary common usage the term is applied loosely to situations in which people feel alienated from society, considering themselves to be "outsiders" with no sense of belonging to a community. In this meaning it overlaps the concept of *anomie.

Aligarh 27 42N 78 25E A city in N India, in Uttar Pradesh. An agricultural trading center, it is the site of the notable Aligarh Muslim University (founded as a college in 1875). Population (1971): 252,314.

alimony In law, a money allowance that a court may order a husband to pay to his wife for her support and that of any children, if, through separation or divorce, he is no longer living with her. Only occasionally are such payments awarded against the wife, because in general she has no legal obligation to maintain her husband. With easier and earlier divorces now granted, the courts have tended to lower alimony in cases where the wife is earning or is able to earn the same income as the husband.

Ali Pasa, Mehmed Emin (1815–71) Grand Vizier (chief minister) of the Ottoman Empire five times between 1852 and 1871. He represented the Ottomans at the Congress of Paris (1856) following the Crimean War and was an advocate of Ottoman friendship with France and Britain. He was one of the architects of the period (1839–76) of Ottoman reform known as the Tanzimat (Reorganization).

aliphatic compounds Organic chemical compounds that are not *aromatic. They include the *alkanes, *alkenes, and *alkynes as well as some cyclic compounds (cycloalkanes).

Aliutor. See Paleo-Siberian languages.

alizarin (1,2 dihydroxy-anthraquinone; $C_{14}H_6O_2(OH)_2$) An orange-red crystalline solid, formerly extracted from madder root and used in dyeing. It is almost insoluble in water but dissolves in alcohol. Alizarin is now made from *anthracene and yields a wide variety of dyes.

alkali. See acids and bases.

alkali metals The elements forming group I of the *periodic table: lithium, sodium, potassium, rubidium, cesium, and francium. All are soft, silvery-white *metals with low densities, melting points, and boiling points. In chemical reactions they tend to form positive ions and have a valence of 1. They are highly reactive, form soluble salts with nonmetals, generally release hydrogen on contact with water, and react with air to form oxides. The oxides and hydroxides are alkalis.

alkaline-earth metals The elements forming group II of the *periodic table: beryllium, magnesium, calcium, strontium, barium, and radium. They are similar to the *alkali metals in appearance and chemistry, but are harder, have higher melting and boiling points, and are somewhat less reactive. They have a valence of 2. The **alkaline earths** are the oxides of these metals.

alkaloids A group of nitrogen-containing basic compounds that are produced by plants and have diverse effects on the body. Many alkaloids are used as medicinal drugs, including quinine, reserpine, morphine, scopolamine, and atropine. Others, such as strychnine and coniine (from hemlock) are poisons. Caffeine, nicotine, and LSD are also alkaloids.

alkanes (or paraffins) A series of hydrocarbons, which contain only single bonds between the carbon atoms. They have the general formula C_nH_{2n+2}. The first four members of the series methane (CH_4), ethane (C_2H_6), propane (C_3H_8), and butane (C_4H_{10}) are gases, higher members are liquids or waxes. They are obtained from natural gas or oil and they and their substitution products have many uses.

alkanet A herbaceous plant of the genus *Anchusa*, native to Eurasia but widely grown for ornament (*A. azurea* is a common garden plant). It may reach a height of 20–48 in (50–120 cm), with clusters of small blue or white flowers and narrow or oval leaves. Family: *Boraginaceae*.

A similar and related plant, *Pentaglottis sempervirens*, is also called alkanet.

alkenes (or olefins) Hydrocarbons that contain at least one carbon–carbon double bond in their molecules. The simplest types, with one double bond, have the general formula C_nH_{2n}; ethylene (or ethene, C_2H_4) is the first member of this series. The alkenes are more reactive than the *alkanes, undergoing addition and polymerization reactions. They are obtained by cracking petroleum and their main use is as starting materials in industrial chemistry.

Al Khalil. See Hebron.

al-Khwarizmi, Muhammed ibn Musa (c. 780–c. 850 AD) Arabic mathematician, who introduced the Hindu decimal system and the use of zero into Arabic mathematics. He also extended the work of Diophantus on algebraic equations in a book the title of which included the word *al-jabr* ("transposition"), from which the modern word "algebra" is derived.

Al-Kindi, Abu Yusuf Ya'qub ibn Ishaq (died c. 870) Muslim Arab philosopher, born in al-Kufa (now in Iraq). He was dubbed "philosopher of the Arabs" as he was the only Arabic philosopher of pure Arab stock. He made the whole field of Greek science his own and was among the first Arabic scholars to interest himself in philosophy from a scientific rather than a theological viewpoint.

alkynes (or acetylenes) Hydrocarbons that contain at least one carbon–carbon triple bond in their molecules. The simplest types, with one triple bond, have the general formula C_nH_{2n-2}; acetylene (or ethyne, C_2H_2) is the first member of this series. The alkynes, like the *alkenes, undergo addition and polymerization reactions. They are extremely reactive, tending to explode under pressure, and are difficult to use in large quantities.

Allah (Arabic, probably from *al-ilah*: the god) The Islamic name of God. Allah was worshiped in pre-Islamic Arabia as early as the 3rd century BC. In Mecca he was given special rank as "the god," but lesser tribal gods continued to be worshiped alongside him until *Mohammed proclaimed the rigorous monotheism of Islam. As formulated by Mohammed, Allah is the one omnipotent and omniscient God, the same God as worshiped by Jews and Christians. He is eternal, the creator of the universe, the judge of men, merciful and compassionate. His word is embodied in the *Koran.

Allahabad 25 57N 81 50E A city in N India, in Uttar Pradesh at the confluence of the Ganges and Jumna Rivers. It is principally an administrative and educational center; its university was established in 1887. There is an annual religious festival and a much larger one every 12 years. A former center of the independence movement, it was the home of the Nehru family. Population (1971): 490,622.

Allegheny Mountains A mountain range extending from North Carolina to Pennsylvania. Part of the Appalachian Mountains, it consists of well-rounded uplands rising to 4860 ft (1480 m) at Spruce Knob. It forms the watershed between the Atlantic Ocean and the Mississippi River and was for many years a frontier zone between French settlers in the Mississippi Basin and English colonists along the coast.

Allegheny River A river rising in N Pennsylvania, flowing NW through New York and SW through Pennsylvania before joining the Monongahela River at Pittsburgh to become the Ohio River. Length: 235 mi (524 km).

allegory A verse or prose narrative in which characters and events in the plot refer to a deeper, usually moral, meaning. It is an ancient and universal form, similar to but usually longer than the *fable and the parable. Examples of allegory include the French *Roman de la rose* (13th century), Bunyan's *The Pilgrim's Progress* (1678), Swift's *Gulliver's Travels* (1726), and Orwell's *Animal Farm* (1945).

Allegri, Gregorio (1582–1652) Italian composer. He was appointed a singer in Pope *Urban VIII's chapel in 1629. An important composer of church music, his works include a *Miserere* for nine voices, two volumes of concertinos, and two volumes of motets.

allele Any one of the various alternative forms of a *gene that can occur at the same site on a *chromosome. In *Drosophila* fruit flies, for example, several alternative eye colors are possible depending on which of the various alleles of the gene for eye color is present in the individual.

allemande A 16th-century processional dance in 4/4 time originating in Germany. Popular in France and in England under the name almand or almain, it reappeared in the 18th century as an elaborate figure dance for couples, in 2/4 time. A stylized version of the early dance was frequently used by Bach, Couperin, and other contemporary composers to open a suite. The name is also applied to a lively German-Swiss folk dance resembling the *Ländler*.

Allen, Bog of (Irish name: Moin Almkaine) An area of peat bogs in the Republic of Ireland, covering much of the central plain. The peat is used for fueling power stations and for domestic use. Area: 370 sq mi (958 sq km).

Allen, Ethan (1739–89) American soldier, who pursued the independence from New York of the Green Mountain region (now Vermont), which was claimed by both New York and New Hampshire. Between 1770 and 1775 he commanded the *Green Mountain Boys, which with Benedict *Arnold's forces captured Fort Ticonderoga (1775), the first American victory in the American Revolution. He was held captive by the British (1775–78). Vermont declared its independence but was not recognized by the Continental Congress. Allen did much to ensure Vermont's independence but died before it achieved statehood in 1789.

WOODY ALLEN *He is an enthusiastic amateur jazz clarinetist.*

Allen, Woody (Allen Stewart Konigsberg; 1935–) US film actor and director. His performances are witty portrayals of social inadequacy and embarrassment. His films include *Play It Again, Sam* (1972) and *Annie Hall* (1977); he also directed *Interiors* (1978), *Manhattan* (1979), *Zelig* (1983), and *Broadway Danny Rose* (1984).

Allenby, Edmund Henry Hynman, 1st Viscount (1861–1936) British field marshal. After experience in the Boer War, he commanded the Third Army in France in World War I. In 1917, appointed commander in chief of the Egyptian Expeditionary Force against the Turks in Palestine, he captured (Dec. 9) Jerusalem (as a "Christmas present" for the British people) and then went on to devastate the Turks at Megiddo (1918). He ended his career as high commissioner in Egypt (1919–25).

Allende (Gossens), Salvador (1908–73) Chilean statesman; president of Chile (1970–73), the first Marxist to come to power through free elections. A founder of the Chilean Socialist Party, Allende governed a coalition of left-wing parties. His nationalization policies created much opposition and he was overthrown and killed by a military coup.

Allentown 40 37N 75 30W A city in the US, in Pennsylvania. It has important steel and machinery industries. Population (1980): 103,758.

allergy An abnormal reaction by the body that is provoked by certain substances, including pollen, dust, certain foods and drugs, fur, molds, etc. Normally all foreign substances (antigens) entering the body are destroyed by *antibodies without further trouble. Allergic people, however, become hypersensitive to certain antigens (called allergens), so that whenever they are subsequently encountered they stimulate not only the normal antibody reaction but also the specific symptoms of the allergy. Allergic conditions include *hay fever, some forms of *asthma and *dermatitis, and *urticaria. Treatment includes the use of *antihistamines, corticosteroids, and *desensitization.

Alliance for Progress A program initiated in 1961 by Pres. John F. Kennedy to maintain democracy, improve economic conditions, and further social development in 22 Latin American countries. Largely financed by the US, the program has had disappointing results.

Allied Powers The nations united in opposition to the *Central Powers in World War I and to the *Axis Powers in World War II. In World War I the Allies were initially Britain, France, and Russia, bound by the Treaty of London (1914), and later included Italy, Japan, and Portugal; the US was an associated power from 1917. In World War II the chief Allies were Britain, France (1939–40, 1944–45), the Soviet Union (from June, 1941), the US (from December, 1941), and China.

Allier River A river in central France. Rising in the Cévennes, it flows NNW through the fertile Limagne area, joining the Loire River near Nevers. Length: 250 mi (403 km).

alligator A large broad-snouted ☐reptile belonging to the genus *Alligator* (2 species). Each side of the jaw contains 17–22 teeth, which are all covered when the mouth is closed. The American alligator (*A. mississippiensis*) is mainly black and lives in rivers of the SE US, reaching a length of 16–20 ft (5–6 m); the rare Chinese alligator (*A. sinensis*) of the Yangtze River is smaller. They dig burrows in which they hibernate during cold weather. Order: *Crocodilia* (*see* crocodile).

Allingham, Margery (1904–66) British detective-story writer. Her mild-mannered likable detective Albert Campion appeared in a popular series of novels begun in the 1920s and ending with *Cargo of Eagles* (1968). *Tiger in the Smoke* (1952), *The China Governess* (1963), and *The Mind Readers* (1965) are among her most acclaimed books.

Allium A genus of herbaceous plants (about 450 species), including the *onion, *shallot, *garlic, *leek, *chive, etc. They have bulbs, those of several species being widely used in temperate regions for food and flavoring, and in many the flowers are replaced by small bulbs (bulbils), by means of which the plants can be propagated. Family: *Liliaceae* (or *Alliaceae* according to some authorities).

allopathy Literally, the use of drugs or other means to induce a reaction in the body that will counteract—and therefore relieve—the symptoms of a disease. The term is used by practitioners of *homeopathy to describe the orthodox system of medicine.

Allosaurus A large bipedal dinosaur of the Jurassic and Cretaceous periods (200–65 million years ago). Up to 34 ft (11 m) long, it had large strong hind limbs, a well-developed tail, small forelegs, and thick protective knobs of bone over the eyes. Although fairly slow, it hunted prey, possibly in groups, and was equipped with sharp claws, powerful jaws, and sharp pointed teeth. Order: *Saurischia*.

allotropes Two or more different physical forms of the same element or compound. Allotropes have different arrangements of atoms in their crystals or molecules and occasionally quite different chemical behavior. Diamond and graphite, for example, are allotropes of carbon.

alloy A blend of a metal with other metals or nonmetals, formed by mixing the molten substances and allowing the mixture to cool and solidify. An alloy is usually harder than any of its constituents. The first alloy was probably *bronze, which was used in Europe in about 2000 BC. *Steel and *brass are the most widely used alloys. Alloys of aluminum are also widely used, especially in the aircraft industry. Some metals, such as lead and aluminum, will not mix when they are melted together because their different densities make them separate into two layers. However, many metals do combine to form alloys, which may consist of intermetallic compounds, solid solutions, heterogenous mixtures, or any combination of these forms. In general, intermetallic compounds tend to be hard and brittle: iron carbide, which strengthens iron to form *steel is an example. Solid solutions, on the other hand, are usually soft and ductile: cartridge-case *brass is a typical example.

Most alloys melt over a range of temperatures unlike a pure metal, which has a specific melting point. **Eutectic alloys** are an exception to this rule, they consist of solid solutions having the lowest melting point of all the possible mixtures of the components. They are used in fuses and other safety mechanisms.

All Saints' Day A Christian feast commemorating all saints, whether known or unknown. In the Eastern Churches it has always been observed on the first Sunday after Pentecost. In the West its date varied until fixed as Nov. 1 by Gregory III. *See also* Hallowe'en.

All Souls' Day A Christian feast in the Western Church commemorating all Christians who have died (the "faithful departed"). It is observed on Nov. 2. Requiem masses, containing the *Dies Irae*, are celebrated.

allspice (*or* pimento) A widely used aromatic spice, so named because it combines the flavors of several different spices. It is derived from the powdered dried unripe berries of an evergreen tree, *Pimenta dioca*, which is native to Central America and the West Indies and grows to a height of 30 ft (9 m). Family: *Myrtaceae*.

Allston, Washington (1779–1843) The earliest US Romantic painter. He studied at Harvard University before training at the Royal Academy (1801–03) in England. He finally settled in Boston in 1818. The drama of his early landscapes and biblical subjects was replaced by a quieter mood in such later works as *Moonlight Landscape* (Boston). He also wrote poetry and one novel.

Alma Ata 43 19N 76 55E (name until 1921: Verny) A city in the S Soviet Union, the capital of the Kazakh SSR. Situated in the foothills of the Trans-Alay Alatau (mountains), it is one of the Soviet Union's most beautiful cities. Industries include food and tobacco processing, and it has a thriving film industry. Its museum is housed in the former Russian Orthodox cathedral, the world's second highest wooden building. It has many educational institutions. *History*: founded in 1854 as a fort, it soon became a trade center. The completion of the Turkistan-Siberian railroad in 1930, on which it is situated, resulted in its rapid growth. Population (1981 est): 975,000.

Almagest. *See* Ptolemy.

almanac A calendar of the months and days of the year containing astronomical and other miscellaneous data. It usually includes information about eclipses, phases of the moon, positions of the planets, times of sunset and sunrise and of high and low tides, as well as religious and secular holidays. A well-known example is *The Old Farmer's Almanac*. Modern almanacs include official government publications listing national statistics.

al-Mansurah. *See* Mansura, El.

Almeida, Francisco de (c. 1450–1510) Portuguese colonialist. The first viceroy of Portuguese India (1505–09), Almeida consolidated Portuguese rule there and expanded its power in the Indian Ocean. He organized further voyages of discovery that reached Madagascar and fought the Arabs on the African coast.

Almería 36 50N 2 26W A port in S Spain, in Andalusia on the Gulf of Almería. It was a thriving town under the Moors (8th–15th centuries) and has a fine 16th-century cathedral. Exports include grapes and oranges. Population (1974 est): 125,738.

Almohads A fundamentalist reforming Muslim movement that ruled much of N Africa and Spain (1130–1269). Comprising the Masmudah Berber tribe, the Almohads recognized Ibn Tumart (d. 1130) as their leader in 1121 and he directed them against the ruling *Almoravids, taking the title of mahdi. On his death he was succeeded by Abd al-Mu'min (d. 1163), who completed the conquest of N Africa and Spain from the Almoravids. The Almohads regarded Muslims who did not follow them as unbelievers and Abd al-Mu'min became their *caliph. His descendants ruled the state until the fall of Marrakech to the Marinid Berber dynasty in 1269.

almond A tree, *Prunus amygdalus*, native to SW Asia but widely grown in warm regions for its nuts. The edible nuts are produced by a variety called sweet almond; the nuts of the bitter almond yield aromatic almond oil, used as a flavoring. Almond trees grow to a height of 23 ft (7 m); they have attractive pink flowers and are grown for ornament in cooler regions. Family: *Rosaceae*. *See also* Prunus.

Almoravids A military Muslim missionary movement that ruled much of N Africa and Spain in the 11th and 12th centuries. The Almoravids were founded by Ibn Yasin (d. 1059) and after his death Yusuf ibn Tashufin (d. 1107) conquered NW Africa and invaded Spain. At the battle of Zallaqah (1086) he defeated the rising Christian power of León and Castile and Muslim Spain now came under Almoravid control. After Yusuf's death in Marrakech, the Almoravid capital that he had founded, his state was ruled by his descendants until 1147, when it fell to the *Almohads.

Alnico An *alloy of aluminum, nickel, and cobalt. It is a ferromagnetic material and is used to make permanent magnets.

Aloe A genus of succulent herbaceous plants (about 200 species), all native to Africa. A stem is usually absent, the toothed fleshy leaves forming a basal rosette, up to 16 in (40 cm) in diameter. The flowers are red or yellow and some species are ornamental (e.g. *A. variegata*); the juice of some species, especially *A. vera*, is used as a purgative (bitter aloes). Family: *Liliaceae*.

Aloysius, St (Luigi Gonzaga; 1568–91) Italian patron of youth. A noble, he entered the Society of Jesus against his father's wishes in 1585 and studied philosophy and theology. Famous for his simple piety and charity, he died while tending plague victims in Rome. Feast day: June 21.

alpaca A shaggy-coated hoofed mammal, *Lama pacos*, traditionally domesticated and bred in the South American Andes. Its dark fine high-quality fleece reaches nearly to the ground from its shoulder height of 35 in (90 cm) and is shorn every two years, each animal yielding about 7 lb (3 kg). Alpacas thrive at high altitudes, keeping to damp grassy plateaus. Family: *Camelidae* (camels).

Alp Arslan (c. 1029–1072) Sultan of Turkey (1063–72) of the Seljuq dynasty. He succeeded his uncle *Toghril Beg. His victory over the Byzantines at Manzikert in 1071 opened Asia Minor to Muslim penetration for the first time.

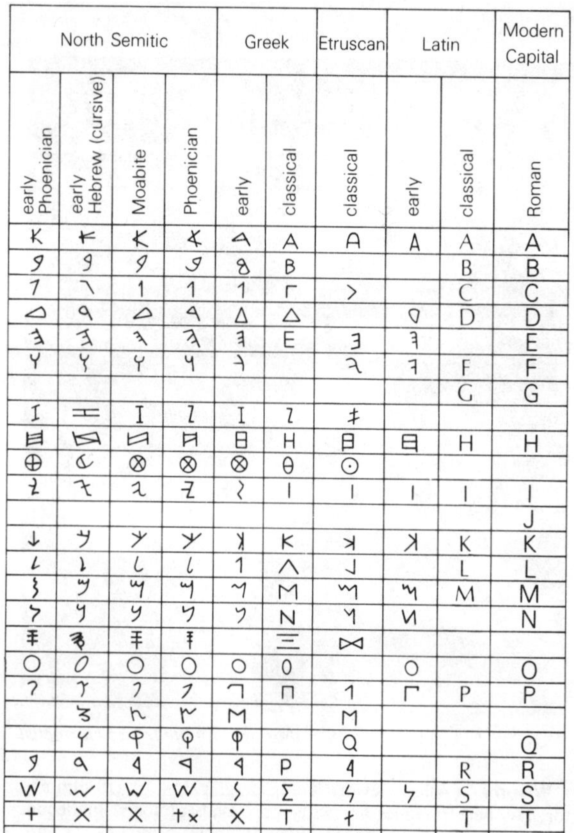

North Semitic				Greek		Etruscan	Latin		Modern Capital
early Phoenician	early Hebrew (cursive)	Moabite	Phoenician	early	classical	classical	early	classical	Roman
⪫	⪪	K	⪫	⪤	A	A	A	A	A
⫟	⫟	⫟	⫟	𐌁	B			B	B
7	�7	1	1	1	Γ	⟩		C	C
◁	ⵕ	◁	◁	Δ	△	◖		D	D
⪥	⪥	⪥	⪥	⪥	E	Ⴈ	⪫	E	E
Ⴘ	Ⴘ	Ⴘ	ⴼ	⪣		⪫	F		F
								G	G
I	ⵓ	I	ⵌ	I	ⵌ	ⵣ		H	H
⊞	ⵙ	ⵌ	ⴰ	𐌇	H	𐌇	𐌇		
⊕	⵨	⊗	⊗	⊗	θ	☉			
ⵖ	ⵖ	ⵖ	ⵌ	ⵌ	I	I	I	I	I
									J
↓	ⵕ	ⵢ	ⵢ	ⵖ	K	ⵕ	ⵕ	K	K
ⵔ	ⵔ	�	ⵌ	ⵌ	∧	ⵕ		L	L
ⵌ	ⵌ	ⵌ	ⵍ	ⵌ	M	ⵍ	ⵜ	M	M
ⵕ	ⵢ	ⵌ	ⵌ	ⵌ	N	ⵍ	ⵒ		N
ⵌ	ⵌ	ⵌ	ⵌ	𐌎	Ξ	ⵝ			
O	0	O	O	0	0		O		O
ⵒ	ⵢ	ⵒ	ⵒ	ⵌ	Π	ⵌ	Γ	P	P
	ⵌ	ⵌ	M		M				
	ⵞ	ⵖ	ⵖ	ⵖ		Q			Q
ⵖ	ⵌ	ⵌ	ⵌ	ⵌ	P	ⵌ	ⵌ	R	R
W	ⵌ	W	W	ⵌ	Σ	ⵌ	ⵌ	S	S
+	×	×	+×	×	T	ⵌ		T	T
					Y	∨	∨		U
									V
									W
						×		X	X
								Y	Y
								Z	Z

ALPHABETS *The letters of the modern Roman alphabet have developed from the ancient North Semitic script. This script in its Aramaic form was also the ultimate source of the Arabic alphabet and probably of the Brahmi alphabet, from which the numerous scripts of modern India are derived.*

alphabets Writing systems in which each symbol represents a speech sound (*see* phonetics). Many *pictographic writing systems developed as far as ideography and even *syllabaries, but the breakthrough to true alphabetic phonetic writing took place, it seems, only on the E shores of the Mediterranean around 2000 BC. From this *Semitic alphabet all the major alphabets in use today—Roman, Greek, *Cyrillic, Hebrew, Arabic, and *Devanagari—are ultimately derived.

It is hard now to appreciate the achievement of identifying speech sounds separately from meaning and of analyzing syllables into vowels and consonants. It meant that the number of symbols required to record a language was reduced from many thousands to between 20 and 40. Moreover, it became possible to write down unfamiliar or foreign words without reference to their sense.

Correspondence between conventional *spelling and speech sounds is rarely exact. Speech sounds change continually over the centuries, while spelling forms tend to become conventionalized and static. In Greek, for example, where the alphabet has been used to represent the language for almost 3000 years, the letters ι, η, υ, $\epsilon\iota$, and $o\iota$, which originally represented different sounds, now all represent the sound /i:/; by contrast, γ, which used to represent a single sound, now represents four quite distinct sounds, depending on the letters adjoining it. On the other hand, Czech and Turkish, both of which have adopted or revised a modified version of the Roman alphabet within the last hundred years, display great regularity between sound and spelling. These two and many other languages that have taken over the Roman alphabet use accents and other diacritics to indicate sounds for which there is no standard Roman alphabet symbol. With the passage of time, however, the use of diacritics itself becomes conventionalized and unsystematic.

From time to time, attempts have been made to develop alphabets that record speech sounds absolutely regularly and systematically. The most important of these is the *International Phonetic Alphabet.

Alpha Centauri A conspicuous nearby *multiple star in the constellation Centaurus. The two brightest components form a yellow visual *binary star that is seen as the third brightest star in the sky, magnitude –0.27. The much fainter third component, **Proxima Centauri**, is the nearest known star, lying 4.3 light years away.

alpha decay A spontaneous radioactive disintegration in which a nucleus ejects an *alpha particle. This process reduces the mass number of the nucleus by four and its atomic number by two. An example is the decay of uranium-238 into thorium-234.

alpha particle The nucleus of a helium-4 atom, consisting of two protons and two neutrons. It is extremely stable and is emitted by some radioactive nuclei in the process known as *alpha decay.

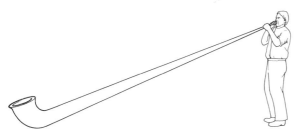

ALPHORN *The instrument is constructed from long wooden staves bound together with birch bark. Instruments similar to the alphorn are used in Poland and Scandinavia as well as in Switzerland.*

alphorn A musical instrument used in Switzerland for calling cattle. Made of wood, it is commonly 6.5 ft (2 m) long or more. Its mouthpiece is similar to that of a cornet. Being valveless, it plays only harmonics.

Alpine orogeny The period of mountain building that occurred mainly during the Tertiary period, beginning about 65 million years ago. The regions most affected extend from S Europe and N Africa across S Asia to Indonesia, resulting in the formation of the Alps, Atlas Mountains, and Himalayas, and across a belt bordering on the Pacific Ocean. It is the most recent *orogeny and is probably still continuing in some parts of the world.

Alps The highest mountain range in Europe. It extends some 500 mi (800 km) in an arc roughly E–W through France, Switzerland, Italy, and Austria, and rises to 15,771 ft (4807 m) at Mont Blanc near the W end. Several major rivers rise here, including the Rhône, Rhine, Drava, and Po. The snowline varies between 7874 ft and 9843 ft (2400 m and 3000 m) and many of the lower slopes are used as pasture in summer, while in winter the Alps are Europe's major skiing area. There are several road and rail routes across the chain, including a number of tunnels. *See also* Maritime Alps.

Alsace (German name: Elsass) A planning region and former province in NE France, separated from West Germany by the Rhine River. It is a fertile agricultural area and has important potassium deposits. *History*: it was often a scene of conflict between France and Germany. Under Roman occupation from the 1st century AD, it became a Frankish duchy in the 5th century and was part of the Holy Roman Empire from the 10th to the 17th centuries. Its cities, which became effectively independent in the middle ages, were important centers of the Reformation in the 16th century. The French gained control of Alsace in 1648, after the Thirty Years' War, but it was lost to Germany in 1871, after the Franco-Prussian War, and linked with *Lorraine to form the German imperial territory of **Alsace-Lorraine**. This existed until it reverted to France in 1919. It came under German control again in World War II and was restored to France in 1945. Area: 3208 sq mi (8310 sq km). Population (1981 est): 1,570,500.

Alsatian dog. *See* German shepherd dog.

alsike A perennial Eurasian *clover, *Trifolium hybridum*, also called Swedish or Alsatian clover, with typically three-lobed leaves and a pink flower head about 0.4 in (1 cm) in diameter. Capable of fixing atmospheric nitrogen, it is often used to improve the nitrate level in soil. Family: *Leguminosae*.

Altaic languages A family of languages comprising languages of the *Turkic, *Mongolian, and *Manchu-Tungus groups. Named for the Central Asian Altai Mountains, languages of this family are spoken in N China, the Mongolian People's Republic, the Soviet Union, Afghanistan, Iran, and Turkey. The genetic relationship between the various Altaic languages is debatable, but certain common features are discernible, notably sound harmony. The connection of *Japanese and *Korean with this family is questionable.

Altai Mountains A mountain system in Asia, extending from Siberia, Soviet Union, into China and Mongolia. It rises to 14,783 ft (4506 m) at Belukha in the Soviet Union and has important lead, silver, and zinc reserves.

Altair A conspicuous white star, apparent magnitude 0.77 and 16.5 light years distant, that is the brightest star in the constellation Aquila.

Altamira Upper *Paleolithic cave site in N Spain, recognized in 1879. Doubts as to the authenticity of the 150 magnificent polychrome paintings of animals on the cave's ceiling were eventually settled by Henri *Breuil in 1901. Bison, painted in red ocher with black manganese manes, tails, and hooves, are the chief species depicted. *See also* Magdalenian.

Altdorf 46 53N 8 38E The town in central Switzerland where William Tell engaged in his legendary exploits. Population (1971 est): 8647.

Altdorfer, Albrecht (c. 1480–1538) German artist, who was one of the first European painters to paint landscapes for their own sake. His masterpieces, few of which survive, show his love of forested mountains, depicted in minute detail, and include *The Battle of Issus* and *St George* (both Alte Pinakothek, Munich). He worked in Regensburg, where he became city architect and a member of the council.

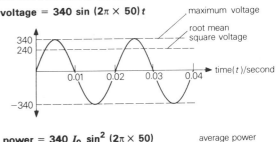

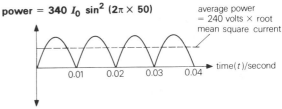

ALTERNATING CURRENT *The voltage and power waveforms in a 240-volt, 50-hertz supply. The current ($I = I_0 \sin (2\pi \times 50) t$) has a similar waveform to the voltage.*

alternating current (ac) Electrical current that periodically reverses its direction. It is the form of current that is produced when a coil of wire rotates in a magnetic field and, as this is the way in which current is produced in *power stations by *electric generators, it is the form of current most widely used. The electromotive force (emf), E, produced by a generator is equal to $E^1\sin \omega t$, where E^1 is the maximum emf, ω is the angular velocity of rotation, and t is the time. Thus the current has the form of a sine wave, with a frequency $\omega/2\pi$.

The chief advantage of ac is that the voltage can be stepped up with a transformer before transmission to minimize energy losses in the lines and then reduced to a safer level by another transformer for domestic use. In most European countries the ac supply has a frequency of 50 hertz, is transmitted at several hundreds of kilovolts, and is used at 220 volts. In the US the supply frequency is 60 hertz and the voltage is 110 volts.

alternation of generations A phenomenon occurring in the *life cycles of many plants and some animals (particularly *coelenterates) in which there is an alternation between two distinct forms (generations), which differ from each other in structure, reproduction, and also often in habit. In plants the generation reproducing sexually is the gametophyte and the asexual generation is the sporophyte. Either phase may be predominant in a particular species; for example, the gametophyte is dominant in mosses and the sporophyte in flowering plants. In coelenterates sedentary asexual polyps alternate with free-living sexual medusae.

alternative energy The investigation and use of new sources of power, based on natural energy flows in the environment. Most countries now rely heavily on *fossil fuels (oil, coal, and natural gas) and nuclear power for their energy needs. However, reserves of fossil fuels are declining and, although dates for their total exhaustion vary, their price must rise as they become increasingly scarce. The estimates of reserves of recoverable uranium are also uncertain and there is opposition to the development of nuclear breeder reactors, mainly on the grounds of safety and environmental hazard from waste disposal. Fusion reactors are still in the experimental stage. Although nuclear power is still regarded as the main option, it is also necessary to explore the alternatives. Renewable energy sources are those that do not use up finite mineral resources. Of these *solar power, *wind power, and *wave power are being most seriously investigated in several countries. *Hydroelectric power is already in use and has limited potential for further expansion. A number of other alternatives are of interest. Tidal power is the use of water raised by the tide and collected behind a barrage to generate electricity in a similar way to hydroelectric generation. There are few sites where the tidal rise makes this a feasible project. The Severn estuary in Britain, which has an average tidal rise of 29 ft (8.8 m), is said to form the best site in Europe.

Geothermal power comes from the heat beneath the earth's crust. In Iceland naturally heated water is taken from rocks near the surface, but in most places geothermal power is not feasible.

Biomass energy, methane generated from sewage, refuse, or specially cultivated organisms, has also been considered. As with many of the other alternative energy sources it is most suitable for small-scale specialized uses. Governments all over the world are examining alternative energy sources in order to reduce their dependence on fossil fuels.

Althing The parliament of Iceland, the oldest in the world, founded in about 930 AD. Since independence in 1944 it has been the country's sovereign legislature. It has 60 members in two houses of equal power.

Althusius, Johannes (1557–1638) German political philosopher. He became professor of law at Herborn Calvinist college (1594), where he wrote his most famous work, *Politics Methodically Arranged and Illustrated by Holy and Profane Examples* (1603). Althusius attempted a systematic approach to political science, based on the concept of contracts between different groupings in society.

Altichiero (c. 1330–c. 1390) Italian painter. Influenced by *Giotto, Altichiero is credited with the foundation of the Veronese school. His only surviving works are the late frescoes in S Anastasia but there are also cycles in the Basilica of S Antonio and the Oratorio di S Giorgio in Padua.

altimeter A device for measuring altitude in one of two ways. A **pressure altimeter** consists of an aneroid *barometer calibrated in meters (or feet) above sea level. A **radio altimeter** consists of a device that measures the time taken for a radio or radar signal to reach the ground and return.

altitude The angular distance of an astronomical body above or below an observer's horizon. It reaches a maximum of 90° when the body is directly overhead. It is used with the angular distance **azimuth**, which is measured eastward along the horizon from the direction of N, to specify the position of an astronomical body on the *celestial sphere.

alto A high adult male singing voice produced by falsetto. Range: that of the *countertenor and *contralto.

altocumulus cloud (Ac) A medium type of *cloud appearing as globular masses in bands across the sky.

altostratus cloud (As) A medium type of *cloud appearing as a grayish sheet, sometimes thin enough for the sun to be seen through it. It usually heralds rain.

altruism. *See* egoism.

aluminum (Al) A light silvery-white metal first isolated by Wöhler in 1827. Although it is the most abundant metal in the earth's crust, its extraction is difficult and energy consuming. The main source is *bauxite, an impure hydrated oxide. The metal is extracted by electrolysis of the oxide dissolved in a flux of low melting point with the mineral cryolite. Its most important uses depend on its lightness (relative density 2.70), ductility, and good electrical conductivity. It is used in electrical power cables, kitchen utensils, and many industrial applications. Pure aluminum is soft, but its alloys with copper, magnesium, and other elements have considerable strength. This combined with their low densities makes such alloys important in aircraft construction. Compounds include alum $(K_2SO_4Al_2(SO_4)_3.24H_2O)$ and the oxide (Al_2O_3), which occurs naturally as corundum and *ruby and is used as an abrasive, a gem, and in *lasers. The hydroxide $(Al(OH)_3)$ is used in glass manufacture and as an antacid in medicine. At no 13; at wt 26.9815; mp 399°F (660.4°C); bp 1001°F (1800°C).

alums Crystalline hydrated double sulfates of monovalent and trivalent metals. The typical example is potash alum (often called simply alum; $K_2SO_4.Al_2(SO_4)_3.24H_2O$), which is used as a mordant, size for paper, styptic, and astringent. Other related substances exist in which the potassium and aluminum ions are replaced by other monovalent or trivalent ions respectively. For example, **chrome alum** is $K_2SO_4.Cr_2(SO_4)_3$. It is a dark-purple substance used in dyes, printing, and tanning.

alunite (*or* alumstone) A mineral consisting of potassium and aluminum sulfate and aluminum hydroxide, $K_2SO_4.Al_2(SO_4)_3.4Al(OH)_3$. It is a source of alum and a potential source of potash. It is usually found associated with volcanic rocks altered by sulfurous gases.

Alvarado, Pedro de (c. 1485–1541) Spanish conquistador, who accompanied Hernán Cortés in his conquest of Mexico, becoming governor of Tenochtitlán (Mexico City). He conquered parts of Guatemala (1523–24) and El Salvador (1524). In 1534 he embarked on an expedition to take Ecuador but was bought off by a rival.

Alvarez, Luis Walter (1911–) US physicist, who works at the University of California. Working with F. *Bloch he made the first measurement of the neutron's magnetic moment and won the Nobel Prize (1968) for research on short-lived fundamental particles. During World War II, he worked on the development of the atom bomb.

Alvárez Quintero brothers Spanish dramatists, Serafin (1871–1938) and Joaquin (1873–1944) Alvárez Quintero. In collaboration, they wrote nearly 200 popular plays, set mainly in their native Andalusia. Simple entertainment was their chief aim, although *El Amor que pasa* (1904) and *Malvaloca* (1912) were more serious works.

Alvars A group of wandering poets and mystics, fervently devoted to Vishnu, which flourished in S India in the 7th–10th centuries AD. Almost exclusively male, they worshiped ecstatically, with song and dance. Their 4000 hymns in the Tamil language, collected in the 10th century, sing the praises of Vishnu and his various incarnations.

alveolus. *See* lung.

Alyattes (d. 560 BC) Fourth King of Lydia (c. 617–560), which he made a major power. Alyattes extended his kingdom as far as the Halys River (585) following a war against Media that was ended by the combatants' fear at the sight of the sun's eclipse. Alyattes, who was buried in a huge round tomb near Sardis, was succeeded by his son Croesus.

Alypius (4th century AD) Greek writer, from Alexandria in Egypt. His *Introduction to Music* is the chief surviving guide to classical Greek music, preserving its notation and complex scale system.

Alyssum A genus of low-growing herbaceous plants (about 150 species), mostly native to S Europe but widely grown in gardens. Alyssums have small flowers grouped in terminal clusters. Varieties of sweet alyssum (*A. maritimum*), 4–6 in (10–15 cm) high, have white or pink flowers and are grown as annuals. Perennial alyssums include *A. saxatile*, which grows to a height of 12 in (30 cm) and has yellow flowers. Family: *Cruciferae*.

Alzheimer's disease (*or* presenile dementia) A degenerative disease that affects nerve cells of the brain. It causes speech disturbances, progressive loss of mental faculties, and other symptoms of senility although it may occur in middle age. Its cause is unknown and there is no cure. Named for the German neurologist Alois Alzheimer (1864–1915).

Amadeus (VIII) the Peaceful (1383–1451) Count of Savoy (1391–1434). Amadeus became duke in 1416, when Savoy was made a duchy by Emperor Sigismund. Amadeus abdicated in 1434 and in 1439 was elected antipope as Felix V by the schismatic Council of *Basle. He resigned in 1449.

Amagasaki 34 42N 135 23E A port in Japan, in S Honshu on Osaka Bay. An industrial center, it has metal, chemical, and textile industries. Population (1980): 524,000.

Amalasuntha (or Amalasuentha; 498–535 AD) The daughter of Theodoric, King of the Ostrogoths, and regent (526–34) for her son Athalaric (516–34). After Athalaric's death she shared the throne with her cousin and second husband, Theodahad (d. 536), who, having banished her, was party to her murder.

Amalekites In the Old Testament, a nomadic tribe living in SW Palestine and the Sinai, who were descended from Esau. They attacked the Israelites on their journey out of Egypt and remained their enemies until finally suppressed during the reign of Hezekiah.

Amalfi 40 37N 14 36E A seaport and resort in Italy in Campania on the Gulf of Salerno. A major port in the 10th century, its maritime code of law was recognized in the Mediterranean area until the latter half of the 18th century.

Amana Society Residents of seven villages in E central Iowa, on the N shore of the Iowa River, SW of Cedar Rapids. Founded as the Amana Church Society in 1855, it was a communistic cooperative society run by elders of the Community of True Inspiration, a sect founded in Germany in 1714. Reorganized as the Amana Society, a cooperative stock company, in 1932, its members share in profits from its industries, mainly agricultural, and are given medical care benefits.

Amanita A genus of widely distributed mushroom fungi (about 100 species). Several species are extremely poisonous, including the deadly destroying angels (*A. vena* and *A. virosa*), the *death cap, and the *fly agaric. Some species are harmless and sometimes eaten, for example panther cap (*A. pantherina*). Family: *Agaricaceae* (see agaric).

Amanollah Khan (1892–1960) Emir (1919–26) and King (1926–29) of Afghanistan. Amanollah obtained Afghan independence from Britain in 1919. He introduced a policy of westernization and declared Afghanistan a kingdom in 1926. In 1929 a revolt forced him into exile in Switzerland.

Amaranthus A genus of herbaceous plants (50–60 species) native to tropical and subtropical regions but now widely distributed (see pigweed). The small petal-less flowers grow in long drooping spikes. Several species are grown for ornament, including *A. caudatus* (love-lies-bleeding), 24–40 in (60–100 cm) tall with dark-red flowers, *A. tricolor* (Joseph's coat), with purple flowers and red, yellow, and green leaves. Family: *Amaranthaceae*.

Amaravati school A style of Indian religious sculpture that originated in Amaravati in S India in the 2nd century BC and flourished until the 3rd century AD. A series of bas-reliefs of the life of Buddha have survived from Amaravati, showing the school's fusion of naturalism with elegance. The style spread through Ceylon to SE Asia.

Amarillo 35 14N 101 50W A city in N Texas. Expansion followed the arrival of the railroad (1887) and the discovery of gas (1918) and oil (1921). Today Amarillo has meat-packing, flour-milling, oil-refining, and rubber industries. Population (1980): 149,230.

Amarna Tablets *Cuneiform inscriptions found at Tell el-Amarna (Middle Egypt) in 1887. Most of the tablets were written about 1350 BC. They record administrative correspondence between the pharaoh and his vassal kings in Palestine and Syria.

Amaryllis A perennial herbaceous plant, *Amaryllis belladonna*, also called belladonna lily, native to South Africa but widely cultivated for ornament. Growing from bulbs, it has strap-shaped leaves and a 18 in (45 cm) long stem bearing a cluster of 5–12 funnel-shaped sweet-scented flowers, usually rose-pink and often veined. Family: *Amaryllidaceae*.

Amaterasu In Japanese mythology, the sun goddess, supreme among the *kami* (spirits). She was the daughter of *Izanagi, born either from his eye or from a mirror held by him. She was symbolized by a mirror, which she gave to her grandson Ninigi, forerunner of the Japanese emperors, as part of the imperial regalia. It is still preserved at the Shinto shrine at Ise (S Honshu).

Amati A family of violin makers in Cremona, Italy. **Andrea Amati** (c. 1520–c. 1578) developed the design that became the standard modern violin. His sons **Antonio Amati** (?1550–1638) and **Girolamo Amati** (1551–1635) worked as a team. Girolamo's son **Niccolò Amati** (1596–1684) was the family's greatest craftsman and taught Andrea *Guarneri and *Stradivari. They also made violas and cellos.

Amazon River (Portuguese name: Rio Amazônas) The largest river system and the second longest river in the world, it is the chief river of South America. Rising as the Río Marañón in the Andes, in Peru, it flows generally W–E to enter the Atlantic Ocean in NE Brazil. Its drainage basin extends over much of Brazil, and parts of Venezuela, Colombia, Ecuador, Peru, and Bolivia. It is covered by a mantle of tropical rain forest (selva) and provides valuable forest products including rubber, quinine, and nuts. Navigable to oceangoing vessels as far as Iquitos, 2300 mi (3700 km) upstream, the river and its tributaries provide an essential communications system. New roads, including the Trans-Amazonian Highway, are now opening up the hinterland. Length: 4000 mi (6440 km). Drainage basin area: about 2,250,000 sq mi (5,827,500 sq km).

Amazon ant A *slave-making ant of the genus *Polyergus* (especially *P. rufescens* or *P. lucidus*). Amazon ants, which have long sharp sickle-shaped mandibles, raid nests of *Formica* ants to steal eggs and larvae that hatch to become workers in their own colony. Amazon ants cannot feed or brood without slave workers.

Amazons (Greek: breastless ones) A mythical nation of female warriors who were believed by the ancient Greeks to live in Pontus, near the Black Sea. Trained for war and hunting, the Amazons got their name from their habit of removing the right breast to facilitate the drawing of bows. They intervened in the *Trojan War against the Greeks, but Achilles killed their queen, Penthesilea. The Athenians said that at one time they invaded Attica but were defeated by *Theseus, who took their queen Hippolyte captive.

Ambartsumian, Viktor A(mazaspovich) (1908–) Soviet astrophysicist, who taught at the University of Leningrad before becoming director of the Byurakan Observatory. He wrote the first classic Russian textbook of theoretical astrophysics. His most notable work was the description of radio sources as explosions in the core of galaxies.

amber A translucent or opaque yellow fossil resin exuded by coniferous trees; insects and leaves are often preserved in the mineral, having been trapped on the sticky surface prior to hardening. It is found predominantly in Tertiary deposits around the S Baltic coast. It is used for beads, ornaments, and amber varnish.

ambergris A waxy substance found in the intestines of sperm whales. It contains mainly cholesterol, with fatty oils and steroids and has a musky scent. It is used in making perfumes.

Ambler, Eric (1909–) British novelist. He began writing suspense novels in the 1930s, skillfully creating an atmosphere of fear and tension appropriate to the times. These novels, which include *The Dark Frontier* (1936), *The Mark of Dmitrios* (1939), and *Journey into Fear* (1940), were set mostly in W Europe; in later novels, such as *A Passage of Arms* (1959), he used more exotic settings. Other works include *The Nightcomers* (1956), *The Light of the Day* (1965), and *In Care of Time* (1981).

ambo A raised platform in early churches with a reading stand for the reading of the Bible during services. It was most popular in Italy, although even there it began to be replaced by the pulpit during the 14th century.

Amboise 47 25N 1 00E A town in France, in the Indre-et-Loire department on the Loire River. Its fine gothic chateau was damaged during World War II but has since been restored. Population (1975): 11,116.

Ambon (or Amboina) 03 41S 128 10E An Indonesian island off SW Ceram. Produce includes cloves, nutmegs, and copra. Area: 386 sq mi (1000 sq km). Chief town: Ambon.

amboyna A tropical Asian tree, *Pterocarpus indicus*, that reaches a height of about 30 ft (9 m) and yields reddish beautifully grained wood used for furniture. Family: *Leguminosae*.

Ambrose, St (c. 339–97 AD) Italian bishop of Milan and Doctor of the Church. Born at Trier, he was appointed a provincial governor in 370 with his headquarters at Milan. After becoming a priest, he was made Bishop of Milan in 374 and was famous as a preacher and for his breadth of scholarship. He championed orthodoxy and the rights of the church against the civil power. Feast day: Dec. 7.

ambrosia beetle A wood-boring beetle, *Trypodendron lineatum*, that tunnels the wood of dying and fallen trees. It carries its food supply—a type of fungus—with it into the tunnels, and this produces black spores that color infected wood distinctively. Family: *Scolytidae* (bark beetles).

Amenemhet III King of Egypt (c. 1842–1797 BC) of the 12th dynasty. He regulated the lake of El *Faiyum to irrigate S Egypt, and built the Labyrinth (later described by the Greek historian Herodotus) nearby as an administrative center.

Amenhotep III King of Egypt (c. 1417–1379 BC) of the 18th dynasty. He controlled Palestine and Syria through vassal kings and maintained good relations with *Babylon. Many of the monumental buildings at *Karnak, *Luxor, and elsewhere in Egypt were erected by him. He was the father of *Akhenaton.

America. *See* United States of America.

American Academy and Institute of Arts and Letters US honorary association devoted to fostering art, literature, and music. Originally, the institute (1898) and the academy (1904) were separate, but merged in 1977 to include a total elected membership of 250, with 75 from other countries admitted as honorary members. Awards are given annually, the most prestigious and highest honor being the Gold Medal.

American Bar Association US association of attorneys. Membership is voluntary, but only members of state bars are admitted. Founded in 1878, the organization promotes uniformity of the law, coordinates state and local activities, and promotes constant education in the law through maintenance of a library and the work of special committees.

American Civil Liberties Union (ACLU) A US organization that protects and promotes civil rights and liberties. Founded in 1920 by a group headed by Roger Baldwin, it sponsors protests, public declarations, test cases in law courts, and other measures against what it believes are violations of civil liberties.

American eagle. *See* bald eagle.

American Expeditionary Force (AEF) US troops under Gen. John J. Pershing sent to Europe during World War I. Following a presidential directive, the AEF kept its identity as a separate unit and was not integrated into the Allied forces, but played a key part in the defeat of Germany.

American Federation of Labor (AFL) US labor organization founded by Samuel Gompers in 1886. Organized to oversee and coordinate the specialized craft and trade (skilled worker) unions, it advocated better working conditions and higher wages through strikes and collective bargaining. In 1955 it merged with the Congress of Industrial Organizations (CIO).

American Federation of Labor-Congress of Industrial Organizations (AFL-CIO) A federation of US labor unions formed by the amalgamation in 1955 of the two major US unions—the AFL and CIO. It is currently composed of about 110 national and international unions giving a US membership of about 13.5 million and an affiliated membership of 55,000. Delegates from the member unions attend a biennial convention to decide policy. Committees contribute recommendations on subjects ranging from civil rights to safety and occupational health. Affiliated members must conform to requirements laid down by the AFL-CIO but remain autonomous within these limits.

American Fur Company US fur trading company established by John Jacob Astor in 1808. The company soon monopolized the fur market across America and by 1810 had established the Pacific Fur Company at Ft. Astoria, Oregon, to compete with Canada for the China fur trade. Although Astoria was lost during the War of 1812, Astor's American Fur Company had grown, by 1834, into the largest US fur company. Company explorations eased the way for settlers.

American Import Duties Act. *See* Townshend Acts.

American Indian Movement (AIM) A militant movement, organized in 1968 to promote civil rights for Indians in the US and Canada. Its objectives are the reformation of the Bureau of Indian Affairs and the observance of past treaties. The dramatization of these goals was carried out in 1972, when members took over the Washington, DC headquarters of the Bureau of Indian Affairs and in 1973, when they occupied the historic site of an Indian massacre (1890) at Wounded Knee, South Dakota.

American Indians A diverse group of peoples of North, Central, and South America and the Caribbean Islands. In many respects they resemble the Mongoloid peoples of Asia, which has led to their classification as a subtype of the *Mongoloid race. However, their physical diversity, and the possession of certain features not common among Mongoloids, suggest other origins. Their ancestors probably migrated to the Americas from Asia via Alaska between 10,000 and 20,000 years ago. They have coarse dark and usually straight hair, a skin coloration ranging from copper-brown to a yellowish-brown, dark eyes, and sparse body hair. They speak a great variety of languages and their traditional cultures range from that of primitive hunters and gatherers to the elaborate and complex civilizations of the *Aztecs, *Mayas, and *Incas.

American Library Association (ALA) US organization that promotes universal library services. Established in 1876, its open membership, numbering about 35,000, is responsible for standardization of library systems, library education, and accreditation of library schools.

AMERICAN INDIANS *These South American Indians in Xingu (Brazil) cover their bodies with elaborate paintings.*

American literature The literature in English of the British colonies of North America and, after 1776, of the United States. The earliest colonial literature consisted mainly of religious and political tracts. The first notable poets were Anne Bradstreet (1612–72) and Edward Taylor (1642–1729), both of Massachusetts. The intellectual dominance of New England was continued into the early 18th century by the theologian and metaphysician Jonathan Edwards (1703–58). The period of the American Revolution was dominated by political writers, such as Benjamin Franklin and Thomas Paine. Influential writers of the early 19th century included Washington Irving, James Fenimore Cooper, and Edgar Allen Poe and American literature came to its full maturity in the works of the New England writers Nathaniel Hawthorne, Ralph Waldo Emerson, and Herman Melville, the poets Walt Whitman and Emily Dickinson, and the humorist Mark Twain. The influence of English literature on the early development of American literature was now reciprocated, notably in the works of the novelist Henry James and the poets T. S. Eliot and Ezra Pound, all of whom went to live in Europe. They were followed in the 1920s by Ernest Hemingway and F. Scott Fitzgerald. The tradition of portraying American life has transcended changes in style and has included such important writers as Edith Wharton, Willa Cather, Stephen Crane, Theodore Dreiser, Sinclair Lewis, and John Dos Passos. Other writers who achieved a transatlantic reputation include the dramatists Eugene O'Neill, Tennessee Williams, and Arthur Miller and the poets Robert Frost, Robert Lowell, and John Berryman. The vitality of 20th-century American literature is most evident in the novel, the later practitioners of which include such writers as William Faulkner, John Steinbeck, Henry Miller, Thomas Wolfe, Norman Mailer, Saul Bellow, John Updike, and Thomas Pynchon.

American Medical Association (AMA) US federation of state medical associations that promotes educational and ethical standards in the medical profession. Established in 1847, with a current membership of over 200,000, it coordinates and disseminates scientific information to the profession and health information to the public.

American Revolution (1775–83) The conflict in which the 13 colonies of North America gained independence from Britain. American resentment at Britain's authoritative rule focused in the mid 18th century on taxation. Protests against such legislation as the *Stamp Act (1765) and *Townshend Acts (1767) culminated in the *Boston Tea Party (1773), to which Britain responded with the punitive *Intolerable Acts (1774). The First *Continental Congress was summoned at Philadelphia and, after attempts by both sides at negotiation had failed, the first shots of the war were fired at *Lexington and Concord (April, 1775). In the autumn the Americans invaded Canada, taking Montreal and besieging Quebec until forced to withdraw to Ticonderoga in Spring, 1776. On July 4 the Second Continental Congress issued the *Declaration of Independence. Gen Howe landed on Long Island in August and defeated the newly appointed American commander in chief, Washington, near White Plains. At the beginning of

January, 1777, however, Washington dealt a counterblow at Princeton before settling in winter quarters at Valley Forge. Britain's strategy in 1777 was based on a plan for Burgoyne to march S from Canada and join forces with Howe at the Hudson River. Burgoyne duly arrived at the Hudson (Aug) but Howe had left New York by sea, landed at Chesapeake Bay, and defeated Washington at the Brandywine, taking Philadelphia (Sept). Burgoyne, meanwhile, was forced to surrender his army at *Saratoga, a defeat that proved a turning point by bringing France into the war on the American side. In 1778 the British began an offensive in the S that resulted in several American defeats. Howe's successor, Clinton, took Charleston, South Carolina, and Cornwallis defeated Gates at Camden (1780). In early 1781 the Americans won decisively at Cowpens (Jan. 17) but lost the battle of Guilford Court House (March 15). Cornwallis now moved into Virginia, establishing a base at Yorktown. There besieged by an American-French force under the Comte de Rochambeau (1725–1807) and Washington, on October 19 Cornwallis surrendered. Ultimate American victory was now assured although conflict continued, chiefly at sea. The British navy had been threatened throughout by American privateers and the activities of such commanders as John Paul *Jones, but the main threat at sea came from America's European allies—the French, Spanish (from 1779), and Dutch (from 1780), who gained control of the English Channel and threatened invasion. In 1783 Britain acknowledged American independence in the Treaty of *Paris.

American River A river rising in the Sierra Nevada Mountains in NE California, flowing SW to join the Sacramento River at Sacramento. The California Gold Rush (1849) was precipitated by John A. Sutter's discovery of gold (1948) at one of the river's head streams. Length: 30 mi (49 km).

American Samoa. *See* Samoa.

American Tobacco Case (1911) US Supreme Court case (*US* v. *American Tobacco Co.*) decided against the American Tobacco Company. The company was ordered to reorganize to allow for fairer competition in the tobacco industry. The decision did not break the tobacco monopoly completely and thus weakened current antitrust laws.

America's Cup A sailing race held periodically off Newport, Rhode Island, in which US yachts are challenged for a cup won by the US *America* off the Isle of Wight in 1851. The US retained the cup until 1983, when it was won by the Australian entry *Australia II.*

americium (Am) The fourth transuranic element, synthesized (1944) by G. T. Seaborg and others by addition of neutrons to plutonium followed by β-decay. It forms the oxide (AmO_2) and such trihalides as $AmCl_3$; it is strongly radioactive. At no 95; at wt (243); mp 584°F (994°C).

amethyst A gemstone comprising a purple variety of *quartz. Its color is due to impurities, particularly iron oxide. The best crystals are found in Brazil and the Urals. It is used for jewelry. Birthstone for February.

Amhara A descendant of the invading Semitic conquerors of the Cushitic peoples of Ethiopia. They occupy the southern area of the central highlands of Ethiopia over which, with the Tigré, they have exercised political dominance until the present day. Their society is hierarchical and largely feudal. The emperors were believed to be descended from the biblical king *Solomon. They are a Christian people, who belong to the Coptic Church. Amharic is the language of the Amharas and the principal and official language of Ethiopia. It is derived from a language related to Ethiopic or Ge'ez, the liturgical language of the Ethiopian Church, and is written in Ge'ez characters. It is similar to *Semitic languages in grammar but its vocabulary is largely *Cushitic.

Amherst, Jeffrey, Baron (1717–97) British soldier prominent in the French and Indian War (1754–63) in North America. In 1758 he took the fortress of Louisburg and became commander in chief in America. He captured Crown Point and Ticonderoga in 1759. By 1760 he had conquered Montreal. He was governor general of British North America from 1760 to 1763.

Amici, Giovanni Battista (1786–1863) Italian astronomer, microscopist, and optical instrument maker. He is best known as the inventor of the *achromatic lens. With his own microscopes he discovered many details of orchid pollination and seed development; in astronomy, he studied double stars and Jupiter's moons, as well as designing improved mirrors for reflecting telescopes.

Amiens 49 54N 2 18E A city in NE France, the capital of the Somme department situated on the Somme River. Known as Samarobriva in pre-Roman times, it was the ancient capital of Picardy. The Peace of Amiens (1802), which marked a respite in the Revolutionary and Napoleonic Wars, was signed here. Its fine gothic cathedral survived the damage of both World Wars. An important railroad junction, Amiens' industries include textiles, tires, and chemicals. Population (1975): 135,992.

Amin Dada, Idi (c. 1925–) Ugandan politician; president (1971–79). He rose rapidly in the army, becoming commander in 1966. He overthrew Milton *Obote to become president and in 1972 ordered the expulsion of 80,000 non-Ugandan Asians. In 1975 he became president of the Organization of African Unity. A flamboyant and unpredictable personality, his prestige was severely damaged by the successful Israeli commando raid (1976) on Entebbe airport to rescue passengers hijacked by Palestinian terrorists. He and his government were notorious for their brutality; Amin was overthrown in a Tanzanian-backed coup after which he went into exile.

Amindivi Islands. *See* Lakshadweep.

amines A class of basic organic compounds derived from ammonia (NH_3), in which one (primary amines), two (secondary amines), or three (tertiary amines) of the hydrogen atoms are replaced by organic radicals or groups. *See also* amino acids.

amino acids A group of organic acids characterized by having at least one carboxyl group (–COOH) and at least one amino group (–NH$_2$). About 20 different amino acids comprise the basic constituents of *proteins, the arrangement and types of amino acids determining the structure and hence the function of the protein molecule. Certain essential amino acids cannot be manufactured by the body and must be supplied in the diet. In man these are: arginine, histidine, isoleucine, leucine, lysine, methionine, phenylalanine, threonine, tryptophan, and valine.

Amirante Islands An archipelago of sparsely populated coral islands in the W Indian Ocean, belonging to the Seychelles. They are leased to private companies, usually for coconut plantations.

Amis, Kingsley (1922–) British novelist and poet, one of the *Angry Young Men of the 1950s. Educated at Oxford, he taught at Swansea and Cambridge universities and in the US. His first novel, *Lucky Jim* (1954), a comic satire on middle-class academic life, was a popular success. In later novels, such as *I Want It Now* (1968), *Ending Up* (1974), and *Jake's Thing* (1979), his humor became progressively darker. He published several volumes of poetry, contributed to the important verse anthology *New Lines* (1956), and edited the *Oxford Book of Light Verse* (1978).

Amish US and Canadian Protestant sect, a conservative faction of the *Mennonites. The Amish disagreed with certain Mennonite beliefs on conformity, or lack of it, broke away, and settled in North America, mainly Pennsylvania and Ontario, Canada. Jakob Ammann, a Mennonite bishop in Switzerland, made the initial break in the 1690s, and by 1727 his followers had begun to settle in Pennsylvania. The Amish live conservatively, dress uniformly, and are self-sufficient, depending on farming as a livelihood and, usually, avoiding modern conveniences.

Amistad Case A US Supreme Court case (1840) that ruled that a slave who escapes illegal bondage is considered free. In 1839 illegally enslaved Africans being transported to the Caribbean on the Spanish ship *Amistad* mutinied, killing two crew members. A US ship then seized the *Amistad* off Long Island and imprisoned the slaves until sympathetic supporters insisted that the case be brought to trial. John Quincy Adams defended them in 1840 before the Supreme Court, which declared them free.

Amman 31 57N 35 56E The capital of Jordan. Amman was the capital of the biblical Ammonites, and there are some Greek and Roman remains. Under the British mandate in Palestine, the town grew from a small village, and in 1946 it became the capital of independent Jordan. The city has had large influxes of refugees following fighting in the Arab-Israeli Wars (1948, 1967, and 1973); in 1970 tension resulting from the refugee presence led to fighting on the streets of Amman between Jordanian forces and Palestinians. The university was founded in 1962. Amman is now an important communications center, with some manufacturing industry. Population (1980 est): 1,232,600.

Ammanati, Bartolommeo (1511–92) Florentine mannerist architect and sculptor. Beginning as an assistant of *Sansovino in Venice, Ammanati later worked with *Vasari in Rome on the Villa Giulia. In Florence he was responsible for the Ponte Sta Trinità and the garden façade of the Palazzo Pitti; as a sculptor he is best known for the Neptune fountain in the Piazza della Signoria.

ammeter An instrument for measuring electric current. The two most common types are the moving-coil and the moving-iron ammeters. The moving-coil ammeter is more sensitive but will measure only alternating current. The moving-iron ammeter will measure both alternating and direct current but is less sensitive and its scale is nonlinear. Some modern instruments are electronic and have a digital display.

ammonia (NH_3) A colorless toxic gas used for the manufacture of fertilizers, nitric acid, explosives, and synthetic fibers. When dissolved in water, ammonia produces an alkaline solution of ammonium hydroxide (NH_4OH), an unstable compound that cannot be isolated from solution.

ammonite A *cephalopod mollusk belonging to the subclass *Ammonoidea* (over 600 genera), abundant during the late Paleozoic and Mesozoic eras, becoming extinct 100 million years ago. Their fossilized remains have either straight or coiled shells, some up to 80 in (200 cm) in diameter, containing many chambers, which provided buoyancy for the free-swimming animal. □fossil.

Ammonites An ancient Semitic tribe who were descended from Benammi, the son of Lot, and lived E of Jordan. They worshiped the god Moloch and often warred against the Israelites.

amnesia Loss of memory resulting from such causes as head injuries, drugs, hysteria, senility, or psychological illness. The memory loss may be for events before the injury or disease (retrograde amnesia) or for events after it (anterograde amnesia). In some cases specific areas of the brain show pathological changes. Treatment is related to the cause.

Amnesty International An organization, founded by Peter Benenson in the UK in 1961, aiming to defend freedom of speech, opinion, and religion in all parts of the world. Its work consists of campaigns for the release of "prisoners of conscience," against torture, and for human rights and it is concerned for the welfare of refugees. It has some 100,000 members in 75 countries and is funded by voluntary contributions.

amniocentesis The removal for examination of a small quantity of the fluid (amniotic fluid) that surrounds an unborn baby in the mother's womb. The specimen may be taken by needle through the abdominal wall or, later in pregnancy, the opening of the womb. Tests on the amniotic fluid may reveal the presence of certain diseases or congenital disorders in the baby (e.g. Down's syndrome or spina bifida). If serious abnormality is detected, the possibility of abortion at an early and safe stage can be considered. Amniocentesis is particularly useful when there is a family history of serious congenital disease. *See also* prenatal diagnosis.

Amoeba A genus of free-living microscopic animals (□*Protozoa*). They occur widely in soil, fresh water, and salt water and their flexible cells assume various shapes. The common amoeba (*A. proteus*) may be up to 0.02 in (0.5 mm) long. Amoebas move by extending their cytoplasm into broad lobes (pseudopodia), which are also used to engulf food particles (e.g. bacteria and other protozoans) and liquids. They reproduce by binary *fission and under adverse conditions form cysts with a thick protective wall surrounding the cell. Some related forms are parasitic, including *Entamoeba histolytica*, which causes amoebic dysentery in man. Class: *Sarcodina*.

Amon The supreme Egyptian deity. Originally a local god of Thebes, he acquired major status in the ascendancy of the 18th (Theban) dynasty in about 1570 BC. He became associated with the rival god *Ra and as Amon-Ra became the national god. Great temples were built to him at Luxor and Karnak (c. 1400 BC). Except during the brief reign of *Akhenaton, Amon-Ra remained supreme god until the Assyrians captured Thebes in 663 BC.

Amorites Semitic nomads of Palestine and Syria, who invaded the centers of civilization of Mesopotamia during the late 3rd millennium and 2nd millennium BC. They occupied *Babylonia, assimilated its culture and established numerous small kingdoms. Many Babylonian kings, including *Hammurabi, were of Amorite stock. *Mari and *Aleppo were important centers under Amorite control.

amortization 1. The discharging of a debt (e.g. a mortgage) through (usually equal) periodic payments of principal and interest. 2. The depreciation of an asset through wear or obsolescence. The value of a fixed asset purchased by a company is not charged in full to its profit and loss account in the year in which it is purchased. Instead it is amortized over its useful life in the accounts, i.e. only a certain portion of its cost is charged to the profit and loss account each year.

Amos (early 8th century BC) An Old Testament prophet of Judah. **The Book of Amos** contains his prophecies delivered in Israel. He denounces the luxury and injustice of the privileged nation and predicts God's judgment by means of an Assyrian invasion and natural calamities.

amount of substance A quantity proportional to the number of particles, such as atoms or ions, in a substance. The constant of proportionality is *Avogadro's number. Amount of substance is measured in *moles.

Amoy. *See* Xiamen.

ampere (A) The *SI unit of electric current equal to the current that when passed through two parallel infinitely long conductors placed 1 meter apart in a vacuum produces a force between them of 2×10^{-7} newton per meter of length. This 1948 definition replaced all former definitions including that of the international ampere based on the rate of deposition of silver from a solution of silver nitrate. Named for A. M. *Ampère.

Ampère, André Marie (1775–1836) French physicist, who was a professor at Bourg and later in Paris. He is remembered for his fundamental work on the physics and mathematics of electricity and electromagnetism. He introduced the important distinctions between electrostatics and electric currents and between current and voltage, demonstrated that current-carrying wires exert a force on each other, and gave an explanation of magnetism in terms of electric currents. The unit of electric current is named for him.

Ampère's law The strength of the magnetic field at any point produced by a current (I) flowing through a conductor of length l is proportional to Il/d^2 where d is the distance between the point and the conductor. Named for A. M. *Ampère.

amphetamine A stimulant drug that produces a feeling of alertness and well-being, increases muscular activity, and reduces fatigue and appetite. Because of the risk of addiction, particularly when combined with barbiturates ("purple hearts"), amphetamine is now rarely prescribed. It is occasionally used to treat obesity and narcolepsy (a tendency to fall asleep at any time). Trade name: Benzedrine. *See also* drug dependence.

amphibian An animal belonging to the class *Amphibia*, which contains over 2500 species of frogs, toads, newts, salamanders, and caecilians. Adult amphibians breathe through lungs and have adapted to a wide range of habitats; however they require damp surroundings in order to minimize loss of body fluids through their thin, moist, and usually scaleless skin. Generally amphibians lay their eggs in ponds or rivers, often migrating long distances to do so. The eggs hatch into aquatic tadpole larvae that breathe using gills and develop into adults by a complete bodily transformation known as *metamorphosis.

amphiboles A group of rock-forming minerals, mostly complex hydrous ferromagnesian silicates. The anthophyllite-cummingtonite subgroup contains anthophyllite, gedrite, cummingtonite, and grunerite; the hornblende subgroup contains tremolite, actinolite, hornblende, edenite, hastingsite, and kaersutite; the alkali amphibole subgroup contains glaucophane, nebeckite, richterite, and katophorite. Amphiboles are common in igneous and metamorphic rocks and often occur in fibrous or acicular forms, including some forms of *asbestos.

amphioxus A small slender fishlike animal, also caled lancelet, belonging to the subphylum *Cephalochordata* (about 30 species). Up to 2 in (5 cm) long, they occur in shallow coastal waters, living mostly in burrows with the front end protruding. Food particles are filtered from the water, which enters the mouth and leaves through gill slits; there is a supportive rodlike *notochord and a nerve cord running the length of the body. Amphioxus is thought to resemble the primitive ancestors of other chordate animals, including vertebrates. Genera: *Branchiostoma*; *Asymmetron*. *See also* Chordata.

amphisbaena A wormlike lizard, also called worm lizard, belonging to the family *Amphisbaenidae* (120 species) occurring in tropical and subtropical America and Africa and the Mediterranean region. Up to 24 in (60 cm) long, amphisbaenas are specialized for burrowing having reduced eyes, a small head with thick skull bones, and, except for one genus (*Bipes*), no legs. They feed on insects and larvae.

amphitheater An elliptical or circular building with tiers of seats surrounding an arena, designed by the Romans as a setting for gladiatorial and wild-beast shows, mock sea battles, etc. Small wooden amphitheaters were built throughout the Roman world. The earliest stone amphitheater is that at Pompeii (c. 70 BC). The largest is the *Colosseum in Rome but there are also impressive remains of amphitheaters in Arles, Nîmes, Capua, Verona, and in Sicily and N Africa.

Amphitrite The Greek goddess of the sea. Poseidon chose her to be his wife when he saw her dancing with her sister Nereids. She rejected him and fled to the island of Naxos, but he sent a dolphin to reclaim her. She bore him three sons, Triton, Rhodos, and Benthesicyma.

Amphitryon In Greek mythology, a grandson of Perseus who was betrothed to Alcmene, daughter of the King of Mycene. While he was away at war, Zeus assumed his appearance and seduced Alcmene, who conceived *Heracles from the union.

amphora An ancient Greek two-handled vase used as a container for liquids and fruit, and sometimes as an urn for holding ashes of the dead or for prize awards. The most important are the Black Figure vases (600–480 BC) of black-painted red earthenware, depicting mythological scenes. Other undecorated types, sometimes tapering to a pointed base, were in general use for transporting oil and wine until Roman times.

AMPHORA *A Greek form of the 6th century* BC.

amplifier A device for increasing the magnitude of some quantity by using power from an external source. The term usually refers to an electronic device for intensifying an electrical signal in an alternating-current circuit, with an external steady voltage supply. Originally built with *thermionic valves, but now almost exclusively with *transistors, amplifiers are designed to multiply the input (current, voltage, or power) by a specific factor, known as the gain. Often an amplifier consists of several stages, the output from one stage becoming the input to the next stage. This method is used in the more complex and specialized type of amplifier used in sound-reproduction systems.

amplitude modulation. *See* modulation.

Amr ibn al-As (d. 663 AD) Arab soldier, who led the Muslim conquest of Egypt. Following the conquest of Syria he led the invasion of Egypt; Alexandria fell in 642. Having helped *Mu'awiyah I secure the caliphate (661), he governed Egypt until his death.

Amritsar 31 35N 74 56E A city in NW India, in Punjab. Founded in 1577 by the fourth guru of the Sikhs, Ram Das, it has become the center of the Sikh faith. It was the scene of a massacre (1919), in which hundreds of Indian nationalists were killed when fired upon by troops under British control. In June 1984 about 1000 people died when the Sikh shrine, the Golden Temple, was fortified by Sikh extremists and stormed by the army. The dead included the Sikh extremist leader Sant Jarnail Bhindranwale. The subsequent assassination of Mrs Indira Gandhi later in the year was a reprisal for this event. A commercial, cultural, and communications center, it manufactures textiles and silk. Population (1971): 407,628.

Amsterdam 52 21N 4 54E The official capital of the Netherlands, in North Holland province on the Amstel and IJ Rivers. The government seat is at The Hague. Linked to the North Sea by canal (1876), it is a major seaport. It is also an important financial and industrial center, possessing a renowned diamond cutting and polishing trade. Industries include shipbuilding, dairy produce, tobacco, and brewing. The city is mostly built on piles and linked with a radial system of canals and approximately 1000 bridges. Notable buildings include the 13th-century Oude Kerk (Old Church), the 15th-century Nieuwe Kerk (New Church), and a royal palace (1665). It possesses two universities, the Rijksmuseum, containing a superb collection of Dutch and Flemish paintings, and the Stedelijk Museum with its leading modern-art collection. *History*: chartered in 1300, it joined the Hanseatic League in 1369. During the 17th century it prospered as a seaport; it gained significantly through Antwerp's loss of trade following the closure of the Scheldt River under the Treaty of Westphalia (1648). It became the capital in 1808. Population (1981 est): 712,294.

Amu Darya River A river in central Asia. Rising in the Pamirs, it flows mainly NW through the Hindu Kush and the Turkmen and Uzbek SSRs to join the Aral Sea through a large delta. It forms part of the border between Afghanistan and the Soviet Union and it is important for irrigation. It is navigable for over 800 mi (1450 km). Length: 1500 mi (2400 km).

Amundsen, Roald (1872–1928) Norwegian explorer, the first person to reach the South Pole. In 1897 he became first mate on the *Belgica*, which was engaged in Antarctic exploration. After sailing the *Northwest Passage in the *Gjöa* (1903–06) he abandoned his plan to reach the North Pole on hearing of *Peary's success (1909). He himself beat *Scott to the South Pole in 1911. In 1926 he flew a dirigible over the North Pole with Umberto *Nobile. Amundsen died while searching for Nobile following the latter's dirigible crash in the Arctic Ocean.

Amundsen Sea A small section of the S Pacific Ocean, bordering on Ellsworth Land in Antarctica.

Amur River (Chinese name: Heilong Jiang *or* Hei-Lung Chiang) A river in NE Asia. Rising in N Mongolia, it flows generally SE and NE through Mongolia, the Soviet Union, and China, to the Sea of Okhotsk. It forms the border between the Soviet Union and Manchuria and has been the scene of much Sino-Soviet friction since the 1960s. Length: 2700 mi (4350 km).

amyl alcohol ($C_5H_{11}OH$) A colorless oily liquid *alcohol that has eight *isomers: pentan-1-ol, pentan-2-ol, etc. It is obtained from *fusel oil and is used as a solvent.

amylase A digestive enzyme that breaks down starch and glycogen into maltose. It is present in saliva (as ptyalin) and in pancreatic juice.

Anabaptists (from Greek: rebaptizers) Any of various radical religious groups originating in several continental countries during the *Reformation. They were called Anabaptists because they rejected infant baptism in favor of baptizing adults when they professed their faith. Persecuted by Roman Catholics and Protestants, they were accused of fanaticism, heresy, and immorality. Modern research has shown them in a somewhat more favorable light. They believed in pacifism, common ownership of goods, millenarianism, and held radical political views. Prominent leaders were the German Thomas Münzer (c. 1490–1525), killed after the Peasants' Revolt, and *John of Leiden. Their modern descendants, such as the *Mennonites, number more than 500,000 in all.

anabolism. *See* metabolism.

ANACONDA *This enormous snake spends most of the time in water, although it may climb trees to bask or search for prey. Like other boas, it bears live young.*

anaconda A nonvenomous South American *constrictor snake, *Eunectes murinus*. Up to 33 ft (10 m) long, it is typically dark green with oval black spots and lives in swamps and rivers, feeding on fish and small caymans and also hunting deer, peccaries, and birds along the water's edge.

Anacreon (6th century BC) Greek lyric poet. He fled from his native island of Teos before the Persian invasion, and lived at Samos and then Athens, under the patronage of Hipparchus. His work, only fragments of which survive, consisted chiefly of love lyrics and drinking songs, written in a formal and restrained style.

anaerobe. *See* aerobe.

anagnoresis (Greek: recognition) A literary term referring to the moment of recognition of a previously unsuspected truth. The concept was defined in Aristotle's *Poetics*. It is considered an essential part of the plot of tragedy, in which the protagonist's recognition of his tragic flaw occurs at the climax and leads to his downfall. The best-known example occurs in Sophocles' *Oedipus Rex* when Oedipus discovers that he has unknowingly killed his father and married his mother.

Anaheim 33 50N 117 56W A city in S California near Los Angeles. It is a major tourist center, containing the famous Disneyland opened in 1955. Population (1980): 221,847.

analgesics A class of drugs that relieve pain. **Narcotic analgesics**, such as *morphine, are powerful pain killers that act directly on the brain. Some anesthetics also have analgesic properties. *Aspirin and paracetemol are examples of **antipyretic analgesics**, which also reduce fever. These drugs are not addictive but are less potent than the narcotics. *See also* drug dependence; narcotics.

analog computer. *See* computer.

analytic geometry The study of geometrical relations by algebraic methods. Geometrical figures are placed in a *coordinate system, each point in the figure being represented by its coordinates, which satisfy an algebraic equation. Also known as coordinate geometry or Cartesian geometry, after its inventor, René *Descartes.

anamorphosis A perspective technique used in painting and drawing to distort an image or object seen from a normal viewpoint. The image's true form is only recreated when viewed from an angle or through a special device, such as a peephole. A famous example is the elongated skull in Hans Holbein's *Ambassadors* (1533; National Gallery, London).

Ananda (5th century BC) The first cousin, favorite disciple, and personal attendant of the Buddha. At his insistence a Buddhist order was founded to admit women.

anaphylaxis A form of *allergy that follows the interaction of the foreign substance (allergen) with antibody that is bound to the surface of certain cells (mast cells). This leads to the release of bradykinin, *histamine, and other chemicals, which cause the symptoms. Symptoms are either local (such as asthma) or general (shock and collapse). The latter usually follows injection of the allergen (such as penicillin) and is a medical emergency; it is treated with injections of corticosteroids and adrenaline.

anarchism A political theory advocating abolition of the state and all governmental authority. Most anarchists believe that voluntary cooperation between individuals and groups is not only a fairer and more moral way of organizing society but is also more effective and orderly. Anarchism aims at maximizing personal freedom and holds that societies in which freedom is limited by coercion and authority are inherently unstable. *Proudhon thought that anarchism could be achieved by peaceful change, but *Bakunin believed that violent means were necessary. As an influential political force, anarchism was defeated in Russia by communism but persisted in Europe, especially in Spain until the end of the Civil War (1939).

Anastasia (1901–?1918) The youngest daughter of *Nicholas II of Russia. Although she was believed to have been executed after the Russian Revolution, a Mrs Anna Anderson claimed from 1920 that she was Anastasia. In 1961 her claim was officially rejected.

Anasatasius I (c.430–518 AD) Byzantine emperor (491–518). Anastasius instituted thorough financial and administrative reforms and built a defensive wall to protect Constantinople. His adherence to the heretical *Monophysite doctrine was unpopular.

Anatolia. *See* Asia Minor.

Anatolian languages An extinct subgroup of the *Indo-European language family, which included Palaic, Luwian, Lydian, and Lycian. Originally spoken in Asia Minor, some date back to 2000 BC. The classification is sometimes used in a geographical sense to include all the languages of ancient Asia Minor, some of non-Indo-European origin. There is some confusion about the relation of the Anatolian languages to *Hittite and a precise classification of the relations between these and Indo-European has not been achieved. *See also* Indo-Hittite languages.

anatomy The study of the structure of living organisms. Early studies of human anatomy were made by the Greek physician Galen, in the 2nd century AD, but it was not until the 16th century that the prejudice against dissecting human cadavers was overcome and anatomists—notably *Vesalius—made valuable contributions to the science. In the 17th century William *Harvey discovered the circulation of blood and the development of the microscope enabled advances in the detailed structure of the body to be made by such microscopists as *Malpighi, *Leeuwenhoek, and *Swammerdam. In the 20th century anatomy received a valuable tool with the development of the electron microscope, which greatly extended the investigation of microscopic structure. Today anatomy explores structure within the context of function (*see* physiology). Specialized branches of anatomy include embryology (the study of development), *histology (tissues), and *cytology (cells).

Anaxagoras (c.500–428 BC) Greek philosopher, born at Clazomenae (Asia Minor). In about 480 he moved to Athens, but because of his influence on *Pericles, he was eventually (450) banished on a trumped-up charge of impiety. He diverged from some other early Greek philosophers by stating that the physical universe was made up of an infinite number of substances and that matter was infinitely divisible. He was also the first to explain solar eclipses.

Anaximander (c.610–c.546 BC) Greek philosopher, born in Miletus (Asia Minor). He was one of the earliest thinkers to develop a systematic philosophical view of the physical universe. He held that it came from something unlimited, not just one particular kind of matter, and maintained that the earth lay unsupported at the center of the universe. He also had an evolutionary view of the origin of life, holding that it arose in the sea, and that man evolved from some more primitive species.

Anaximenes (died c.528 BC) Greek philosopher, who lived in Miletus (Asia Minor). He believed that the universe fundamentally consisted of air or vapor; different degrees of condensation correspond to different degrees of density in matter. He held that air, being constantly in motion, possessed life and that its motion accounted for changes in physical objects.

ancestor worship In many primitive societies, the propitiation of the spirits of dead forebears, usually with the object of persuading them to exert their powers on behalf of their descendants in hunting, warfare, etc. Ancestor cults can also be socially important in reinforcing the authority of living elders, who, as guardians of the ancestral shrines, are the spirits' mouthpieces. Festivals for the dead involving visits to the tombs, food offerings, and sacrifices were features of ancient Greek and Roman religion. An ancestor cult formed an important part of traditional Chinese religion and also survives in the Buddhist family altar (*butsudan*) in Japanese households.

Anchieta, José de (1534–97) Portuguese poet and scholar. He became a Jesuit in 1551, and in 1553 joined a mission in Brazil. He helped protect the Indians from slavery and was one of the founders of the city of São Paulo. As well as his chiefly religious poetry and historical works he wrote a grammar of the Indian language, Tupí, and descriptions of the Indian culture.

Anchises In Greek mythology, a Trojan nobleman, father of *Aeneas by *Aphrodite. He was blinded for boasting of his relationship with the goddess. Carried from burning *Troy on Aeneas' back, he died in Sicily.

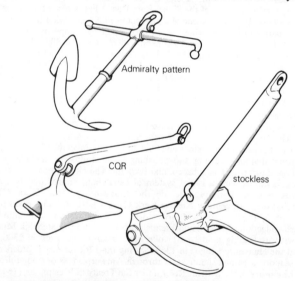

Admiralty pattern

CQR

stockless

ANCHOR *Three common forms of anchor.*

anchor Any device used for mooring a vessel to the bottom of a body of water. In ancient times a heavy stone was used, attached to the vessel by a rope. Today various patent anchors are in use. They are designed for different kinds of bottom—sandy, rocky, muddy, etc.—and usually dig into the bottom with their bladelike flukes. Depending on the size of the vessel, the anchor rode, or attachment to the vessel, may be entirely of heavy chain, as in the case of larger boats and ships, or of a short length of chain to which a rope, usually of nylon, is attached.

Anchorage 61 10N 150 00E A city and major port in S Alaska at the head of Cook Inlet. Founded in 1914 as the terminus of the Alaska Railroad, its main industries are defense projects and the development of natural resources, especially coal and gold. Population (1980): 174,430.

anchovy A small herring-like fish belonging to the tropical and warm-temperate family *Engraulidae* (100 species). 4–10 in (10–25 cm) long, anchovies have a large mouth extending behind the eye, a small lower jaw, and a pointed snout. They live in large shoals, chiefly in coastal waters, and are widely fished for food, bait, and animal feeds. □oceans.

Anchusa. *See alkanet.*

ancien régime The social and political system of France prior to the *French Revolution.

Ancona 43 37N 13 31E A seaport in central Italy, the capital of Marche on the Adriatic Sea. It dates from 1500 BC, when it was founded by the Dorians. Its industries are connected with shipbuilding, engineering, and sugar refining. Population (1980 est): 107,796.

Andalusia (Spanish name: Andalucia) The southernmost region of Spain, bordering on the Atlantic Ocean and Mediterranean Sea. It occupies chiefly the river basin of the Guadalquivir and is one of Spain's most fertile regions producing citrus fruits, olives, and wine. Under Roman control after the 2nd century BC, the region was named Andalusia (after its 5th-century Vandal settlers) by the Muslims, who invaded the region in the early 8th century; much evidence of the Muslim occupation remains. In the 15th century Castile finally recovered Andalusia from the Muslims. After the *Moriscos (Christians of Moorish descent) were expelled in 1609 the region's prosperity diminished. It is now popular with tourists, who are attracted by the great Moorish buildings found especially in Córdoba, Seville, and Granada.

Andalusian horse A breed of large strong horse developed in Spain in the 15th century. Andalusian horses are usually gray (but sometimes bay or black), with a long silky mane and tail and a high stepping movement. Docile and attractive, they are often used in parades and bullfighting. Height: 15.75–16.75 hands (1.60–1.70 m).

Andaman and Nicobar Islands A Union Territory of India, comprising two island groups in the E Bay of Bengal. The Andaman forests support plywood and match industries. Coconuts, rubber, and coffee are also important. The Nicobar Islands 75 mi (120 km) S of the Andaman Islands, produce coconuts, arecanuts, and fish. *History*: the Andaman Islands were an Indian penal colony until 1945. Both groups were occupied by Japan (1942–45) and transferred to India (1947). Area: 3215 sq mi (8293 sq km). Population (1981): 188,254. Capital: Port Blair.

Andamanese The indigenous inhabitants of the Andaman and Nicobar Islands in the Bay of Bengal. They are of negrito racial type. Their traditional culture, surviving only in southern areas among the Jarawa and Onge tribes, was based upon gathering shellfish, fishing, and hunting, using single outrigger canoes, nets, lines, and bows and arrows. Tools and weapons were often made from large shells. There was no method known to them of making fire. Social organization was simple. Tribes were divided into hunting bands, several of which might acknowledge a common chief. Trading between coastal and inland bands was extensive. Ritual initiation was important and various taboos were a prominent feature of their ritual life. Their language, Andamanese, is almost extinct and has no known relations.

Andersen, Hans Christian (1805–75) Danish author, famous for his fairy tales. The son of a shoemaker, he attempted to become an actor in Copenhagen. A benefactor enabled him to attend the university there in 1828; he subsequently traveled widely in Europe and wrote novels, plays, and travel books. His international reputation, however, was earned by the 168 fairy tales that he wrote between 1835 and 1872. These include such classics as "The Snow Queen," "The Little Mermaid," and "The Ugly Duckling."

Anderson, Carl David (1905–) US physicist, who works at the California Institute of Technology. He shared the 1936 Nobel Prize for showing (1932) that cloud-chamber tracks were made by *positrons, whose existence had been predicted by Dirac. In 1935 Anderson discovered the first *meson, thinking it was the particle predicted by *Yukawa. In fact Anderson's meson is now known as the muon, whereas Yukawa's particle is known as the pion (discovered by *Powell).

Anderson, John B(ayard) (1922–) US politician and lawyer. After law school he was in the foreign service (1952–55) in Germany before running for Congress in 1960. He served in the House of Representatives as a Republican from Illinois (1961–81) and chaired the House Republican Conference (1969–80). He ran for president on an independent ticket in 1980 and, although unsuccessful, received 7% of the popular vote. After 1983, he concentrated on promoting the National Unity Party, which he founded.

Anderson, Marian (1902–) US singer. Having established a reputation as a contralto abroad, she was refused permission by the Daughters of the American Revolution (DAR) to use Washington, D.C.'s Constitution

Hall for a recital in 1939 and was later sponsored by Eleanor Roosevelt in a concert at the Lincoln Memorial. In 1955 she became the first black to sing a leading role with the Metropolitan Opera. She was awarded the Presidential Medal of Freedom (1963) and a Congress-authorized gold medal for her contribution to the arts (1978).

HANS CHRISTIAN ANDERSEN

Anderson, Maxwell (1888–1959) US playwright. A journalist, he had his first play, *White Desert*, produced on Broadway in 1923. He wrote about war, corruption, and injustice. *What Price Glory?* (1924) and, later, *Key Largo* (1939) and *Storm Operation* (1944) dealt with the disillusionment of war. *Both Your Houses* (1933), a satire on Congress, won the Pulitzer Prize. Other works include *Saturday's Children* (1927), *Winterset* (1935), *High Tor* (1937), *Knickerbocker Holiday* (1938; with Kurt *Weill), and *The Eve of St. Mark* (1942).

Anderson, Robert (1805–71) US Union soldier in the Civil War. In charge of Ft. Sumter, South Carolina, he, with inadequate supplies, withstood a 2-day attack (1861) by the Confederates before surrendering the fort. This was the first battle of the Civil War.

Anderson, Sherwood (1876–1941) US author. Born in a small town in Ohio, he held a variety of jobs before abandoning job and family in 1906 to become a writer. He was encouraged by Theodore *Dreiser, Carl *Sandburg, and other Chicago writers and by Gertrude *Stein in Paris. He finally settled in Virginia as a newspaper owner; there he in turn encouraged *Faulkner and *Hemingway. *Winesburg, Ohio* (1919), his best-known book, is a series of tales about the stunted lives of a small-town community. His novels included *Poor White* (1920), *Many Marriages* (1923), *Dark Laughter* (1925), and *Beyond Desire* (1933). Other works include story collections, *The Triumph of the Egg* (1921) and *Death in the Woods* (1933), and the autobiographical *Story Teller's Story* (1924).

Andes (Spanish name: Cordillera de los Andes) A mountain system in W South America. It extends N for about 4500 mi (7250 km) from Cape Horn to the Isthmus of Panama, reaching 22,835 ft (6960 m) at Mount Aconcagua and separating a narrow coastal belt from the rest of the continent. Comprising a series of parallel mountain ranges, it is chiefly of volcanic origin and contains several active volcanoes, including *Cotopaxi; earthquakes are common phenomena. It is rich in mineral wealth; the chief metals extracted include gold, silver, platinum, mercury, copper, and lead.

andesite A group of volcanic rocks comprising the fine-grained equivalent of *diorite. They consist mainly of plagioclase-feldspar and one or more ferromagnesian minerals, and many andesites are porphyritic. They are found associated with basalts and rhyolites in island arcs and orogenic regions. The Andesite Line is the geographic boundary between continental andesitic rocks and oceanic basalts, traced through the Pacific.

Andhra Pradesh A state in E central India, on the Bay of Bengal. The coastal plain rises westward over the Eastern *Ghats into the *Deccan plateau. Rice, sugar cane, cotton, tobacco, and pulses are farmed. Large forests provide teak, bamboo, and fruit trees. Manganese, iron ore, mica, and coal are mined. A few industries exist, such as textile, machinery, and shipbuilding, which has been developed with cheap hydroelectricity. *History*: the Andhra people and culture have flourished since the 1st century BC. From 1700 local rulers gradually lost control to France and Britain. A center of 20th-century Indian nationalism, the Telegu-speaking area of *Madras became Andhra Pradesh state in 1953. Further boundary adjustments were made in 1956 and 1960. Area: 106,258 sq mi (275,281 sq km). Population (1981): 53,403,619. Capital: Hyderabad. Chief seaport: Vishakhapatnam.

Andizhan 40 40N 72 12E A city in the SW Soviet Union, in the Uzbek SSR on the River Andizhan-Say. Situated in the fertile *Fergana Valley, Andizhan has always been the region's main trade center. Its industries include engineering. Population (1981 est): 238,000.

Andong (or An-tung) 40 06N 124 25E A port in NE China, in Liaoning province on the Yalu estuary and on the border with North Korea. It was opened to foreign trade in 1907. Its industries, developed under the Japanese occupation (1931–45), include paper, silk, cotton, and chemicals. Population (1953): 360,000.

Andorra, Coprincipality of (Catalan name: Valls d'Andorra; French name: Les Vallées d'Andorre) A small principality in the E Pyrenees, between France and Spain. It is mountainous with peaks reaching heights of about 9500 ft (almost 3000 m). *Economy*: tourism is an important source of revenue supplementing the primarily agrarian economy (wheat, potatoes, livestock raising, and tobacco). *History*: records of Andorra's existence as a state date from 1278, when it was placed under the joint overlordship of the Bishop of Urgel in Spain and the Comte de Foix in France. The latter's rights passed in the 16th century to the French crown and are now held by the president. Andorra pays dues in alternate years of 960 francs to France and 460 pesetas to the bishopric respectively. Executive and legislative powers lie with the coprinces' permanent delegates in Andorra while a Council General of the Valleys holds responsibility for administration. Andorra is a tax haven and immigration has been substantial in recent years. Official language: Catalan; French and Spanish are also spoken. Official currencies: French and Spanish currencies are both in use. Area: 179 sq mi (465 sq km). Population (1981): 35,460. Capital: Andorra la Vella.

Andrássy, Gyula, Count (1823–90) Hungarian revolutionary and statesman. In the *Revolution of 1848 Andrássy supported Lajos *Kossuth. With Ferenc *Deák he negotiated the Dual Monarchy of *Austria-Hungary (1867) and was Hungary's first constitutional prime minister (1867–71). From 1871 to 1879 he was the Austro-Hungarian foreign minister and strove to halt Russian expansion into the Balkans.

André, John (1751–80) British soldier. While serving as adjutant to the commander in chief of British troops in the American Revolution, he negotiated with the treacherous Benedict *Arnold, the commander of West Point, for its surrender. He was captured by Washington's army and tried and executed as a spy.

Andrea del Sarto (Andrea d'Agnolo; 1486–1530) A leading Florentine Renaissance painter, whose work, through its influence on his pupils *Pontormo, Giovanni Battista Rosso (1494–1540), and *Vasari, became a starting point for Tuscan *mannerism. He was able to combine Florentine draftsmanship with a Venetian feeling for color and atmosphere and his compositions resemble relief scupture. Andrea spent most of his life in Florence, producing a series of frescoes in the cloister of the Scalzi and the SS Annunziata. Among his most important paintings are several representing the Holy Family, some portraits, and the *Madonna of the Harpes* (1517; Uffizi).

Andrew, St In the New Testament, one of the 12 Apostles. Originally a fisherman in partnership with his brother Simon Peter, he was a disciple of John the Baptist before following Jesus. Apparently crucified, he is the patron saint of Scotland and Russia. Feast day: Nov. 30.

Andrew II (1175–1235) King of Hungary (1205–35). Andrew was forced by his recalcitrant barons to accept the *Golden Bull in 1222, which limited royal powers. He participated in the fifth Crusade (1218).

Andrić, Ivo (1892–1975) Serbian writer. He wrote his first major book, *Ex Ponto* (1918), while imprisoned by the Austrians as a Yugoslav nationalist. He later served abroad in the Yugoslav diplomatic service, but his native Bosnia provided the settings and themes for his novels, notably *Bosnian Story* (1945) and *The Bridge on the Drina* (1945). He was awarded the Nobel Prize in 1961.

Androcles The hero of a story by Aulus Gellius (?125–?165 AD). Androcles was an escaped slave who removed a thorn from the paw of a lion. The lion later recognized the recaptured slave in the arena and spared him; both were freed. The story was satirized in the play, *Androcles and the Lion*, by G. B. *Shaw.

androgens A group of steroid hormones that influence the development and function of the male reproductive system and determine male secondary sexual characteristics, such as the growth of body hair and deepening of the voice at puberty. The major androgens are *testosterone and androsterone, produced by the testes in higher animals and man and also in small amounts by the adrenal glands and ovaries in mammals. Natural and synthetic androgens are used in medicine to treat conditions caused by androgen deficiency. Some androgens promote the growth of muscle and bone. These—the anabolic steroids—have been used for their body-building effects in debilitated patients and in athletes.

Andromache In Greek mythology, the wife of Hector, the chief Trojan warrior. She appears in Homer's *Iliad*. After the fall of Troy she became the slave of Neoptolemus, son of Achilles, and bore him three sons. After his death she married Helenus, brother of Hector.

Andromeda A constellation in the N sky near Cassiopeia. The brightest star is the 2nd-magnitude Alpheratz. The constellation contains the spiral **Andromeda galaxy**, which is the largest of the nearby galaxies in the *Local Group.

Andropov, Yuri Vladimirovich (1914–84) Soviet statesman and general secretary of the Soviet Communist Party (1982–84) and president of the Soviet Union (1983–84). He was ambassador to Hungary (1953–57) during the 1956 uprising and headed the KGB (1967–82).

Andros, Sir Edmund (1637–1714) British colonial governor of Dominion of New England. Appointed by the Duke of York (later James II) as governor of New York in 1674, he was recalled in 1681, but returned in 1686 to govern the consolidated Dominion of New England, which by 1688 included the New England colonies, New York, and New Jersey. Although he carried out his duties for England admirably, the colonists were disgruntled and rebelled in 1689 when James II was dethroned in England. Sent back to England for trial, Andros was acquitted and later returned to govern Virginia (1692–97).

androsterone. *See* androgens.

anechoic chamber A room used in acoustical experiments that is designed to absorb nearly all the sounds produced in it. Its walls, floor, and ceiling are constructed from insulating and absorbent materials.

Aneirin (6th century AD) Welsh poet. His poem "Y Gododdin," preserved in the manuscript *Book of Aneirin* (c. 1250), celebrates the heroes of an expedition sent from Edinburgh to recapture Catterick from the Saxons. Out of 300 warriors only one survived.

anemia A reduction in the number of red cells or the quantity of red pigment (*see* hemoglobin) in the blood. It may be due to loss of blood, for example after an accident or operation or from chronic bleeding of a peptic ulcer, or lack of iron, which is necessary for the production of hemoglobin. **Hemolytic anemias** are caused by increased destruction of the red blood cells, as may occur in certain blood diseases (e.g. *sickle-cell disease and *thalassemia) and malaria or because of the presence of toxic chemicals. Anemia can also result from the defective production of red cells, such as occurs in **pernicious anemia** (when it is due to deficiency of *vitamin B_{12}).

The main symptoms of anemia are extreme tiredness and fatiguability, breathlessness, pallor, palpitations, and poor resistance to infection. The treatment depends on the cause.

anemometer An instrument for measuring the velocity of a fluid, often the velocity of the wind. In one type, the fluid drives a small windmill or set of cups, the rate of rotation of which is a measure of the velocity of the fluid. Two other common types of anemometer are the *Pitot tube and the *Venturi tube.

Anemone A genus of herbaceous perennial plants (about 150 species) mostly native to N temperate regions. The leaves are segmented and the flowers lack true petals (the sepals function as petals). The Eurasian wood anemone (*A. nemorosa*), 10–15 cm high, has white flowers. Many species are cultivated as ornamentals for their brightly colored flowers, including the poppy and Japanese anemones (*A. coronaria* and *A. japonica*). Family: *Ranunculaceae*.

aneroid barometer. *See* barometer.

anesthesia A state of insensitivity to pain. Anesthesia occurs in certain diseases of the nervous system, but the term usually refers to the state induced artificially for surgical operations. It may be produced by anesthetic drugs or other means, including *hypnosis and *acupuncture. Alcohol and opium derivatives have been used as anesthetics for centuries, but it was not until the 1840s that the first anesthetic gases—ether, nitrous oxide, and chloroform—were used to induce **general anesthesia** (total unconsciousness). This procedure now involves premedication (including administration of sedatives) to prepare the patient for surgery, followed by induction of anesthesia by injecting a short-acting barbiturate (usually sodium thiopentone). Anesthesia is maintained by inhalation of an anesthetic gas. **Local anesthesia** is usually used for dental surgery and also for other operations when the medical state of the patient makes general anesthesia unadvisable. Procaine and lignocaine are widely used local anesthetics. **Spinal anesthesia** (epidural or subarachnoid) produces loss of sensation in a particular part of the body by injecting a local anesthetic into the space around the spinal cord. It may be used, for example, during a difficult childbirth.

aneurysm A swelling in the wall of an artery, due to a weakness in the wall. The most common cause in the western world is now *atherosclerosis. Aneurysms may rupture, causing fatal hemorrhage. Treatment consists of surgical removal of the aneurysm and its replacement with a graft.

Angara River A river in the Soviet Union, in SE Siberia. It flows mainly NNW from Lake Baikal to the Yenisei River. Length: 1150 mi (1840 km).

Angarsk 52 31N 103 55E A city in the Soviet Union, in the SE central RSFSR on the Trans-Siberian Railway. An oil-refining center, it is connected by pipeline to the Volga-Urals field. Population (1981 est): 245,000.

Angel Falls (Spanish name: Salto Angel) The highest cataract in the world, in SE Venezuela on a tributary of the Río Caroní. Height: 3211 ft (979 m).

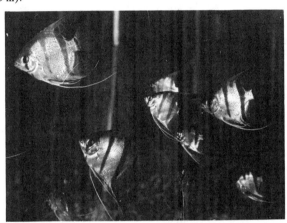

ANGELFISH *The Amazonian angelfish (Pterophyllum scalare) is a favorite aquarium fish. After an elaborate courtship, eggs are deposited and stick to water plants. They hatch in about 48 hours.*

angelfish 1. A fish of the tropical marine family *Chaetodontidae*, having a narrow oval laterally compressed body, a small mouth, and often an elongated snout. Up to 28 in (70 cm) long, angelfish are solitary, living around coral reefs and feeding on small invertebrates. They are usually patterned in a variety of brilliant colors. 2. A South American *cichlid fish of the genus *Pterophyllum*, especially *P. scalare*, which is valued as an aquarium fish.

Angelica A genus of tall perennial herbs (about 70 species) distributed in the N hemisphere and New Zealand. They grow up to 7 ft (2 m) tall and have umbrella-like clusters of white or greenish flowers. The Eurasian species *A. archangelica* yields an oil used in liqueur and perfume making, and its stems are candied to make the confectionary angelica. *A. sylvestris* (wild angelica) is native to Europe and Asia and introduced in Canada. Family: *Umbelliferae*.

Angelico, Fra (Guido di Pietro; c. 1400–55) Italian painter of the early *Renaissance, born in Vicchio (Tuscany). In the early 1420s he became a Dominican monk in Fiesole. His order transferred in 1436 to St Mark's Convent, Florence, where he painted several frescoes, including a famous *Annunciation*. From 1445 to about 1450 he painted fresco cycles in the Vatican but only the *Scenes from the Lives of SS Stephen and Lawrence* has survived. His other major work is *The Coronation of the Virgin* (Uffizi). He was an exclusively religious painter, whose spiritual serenity is reflected both in his art and his "angelic" nature (hence his popular name).

Angell, Sir Norman (1874–1967) British author, economist, and Labor politician. He received the Nobel Peace Prize in 1933 for his opposition to totalitarianism and his influential antiwar book *The Great Illusion* (1910).

angels (Greek: messengers) In Christianity, Judaism, and Islam, supernatural beings who were created at the same time as the material universe and whose primary role was to praise and serve God. Many, however, followed *Lucifer in his rebellion, becoming devils in *hell. In both Old and New Testaments angels appear as emissaries from God to man. *Dionysius the Areopagite systematized angelology into nine orders in the celestial hierarchy, the rank of angel being the lowest of these. Later medieval theologians debated such questions as the nature of angels' bodies, but since the 17th century angelology has been generally ignored. In art, angels are usually depicted as winged human figures. *See also* archangels.

Angers 47 29N 0 32W A city in W France, the capital of the Maine-et-Loire department on the Maine River. The former capital of Anjou, it has many fine buildings, including a 13th-century moated chateau, a cathedral (12th–13th centuries), and the 15th-century Logis Barrault (Barrault House). Its varied manufactures include wine, textiles, and agricultural machinery. Population (1975): 142,966.

Angevins Two dynasties descended from the rulers of the medieval French duchy of *Anjou. Founded by Fulk I (d. 938), his successors as Counts of Anjou, notably Fulk III Nerra (972–1040) and *Geoffrey Martel, expanded the county in France during the 10th and 11th centuries. The marriage in 1128 of Geoffrey Plantagenet, Count of Anjou, to *Matilda, daughter of Henry I of England, gave rise to the accession to the English throne in 1154 of their son as Henry II, the first *Plantagenet King of England. The so-called Angevin empire, which stretched from the River Tweed to the Pyrenees, was broken up by *Philip II Augustus of France in the early 13th century and in 1246 Louis VIII's brother Charles became Count of Anjou. Charles conquered Naples and Sicily, where as *Charles I he founded a second Angevin dynasty. The Angevin claim to Naples and Sicily passed to the French crown in 1486.

angina pectoris Chest pain caused by a reduction in the supply of blood to the heart due to narrowing of the coronary blood vessels supplying the heart. It is usually associated with *atherosclerosis, is brought on by exercise, and can herald a heart attack. Treatment includes rest and administration of glyceryl trinitrate and drugs to reduce blood pressure.

angiosperm Any flowering plant. Angiosperms comprise a vast group of diverse leafy green plants (about 250,000 species) in which the seeds are formed within an ovary, which becomes the *fruit. They are thought to have evolved from the cone-bearing *gymnosperms in the Jurassic period (about 180 million years ago), rapidly radiating and becoming the dominant plants in the mid-Cretaceous (about 100 million years ago). They include many trees and shrubs but most are herbaceous. The 300 families are grouped into two classes: the *monocotyledons and *dicotyledons.

Angkor A ruined city in Kampuchea, founded about 880 AD as capital of the *Khmer empire. It was rediscovered, covered by jungle, in 1860. Angkor was the center of a sophisticated irrigation system, with huge reservoirs (barays) for controlling water supplies to the surrounding rice fields. Its temples, decorated with extensive relief sculpture, were intended to emulate mountains in dressed stone; chief of these are the Angkor Wat (early 12th century) and Bayon (c. 1200).

anglerfish A marine fish, also called goosefish, belonging to the order *Lophiiformes*. Anglerfish are generally small and have flat bodies, large heads, and wide mouths. The first ray of the spiny dorsal fin is modified to form a "fishing line" ending with a fleshy flap of skin—the "bait," which is often luminous in deepsea species. Fish, invertebrates, and even seabirds are lured and snapped up by the huge mouth. In some deepsea species, the male is parasitic on the female, becoming permanently anchored by the mouth and dependent upon her for nourishment. □oceans.

Angles A Germanic tribe originating from the Angeln district of Schleswig, which together with the *Saxons and *Jutes invaded and conquered most of England during the 5th century AD. They settled in *Northumbria, *Mercia, and *East Anglia. England is named for them.

Anglesey (Welsh name: Ynys Môn; Latin name: Mona) A low-lying island off the NW coast of Wales, linked to the mainland by road and rail bridges over the Menai Strait. The chief agricultural activity is sheep rearing. Tourism, especially along the coast, is developing in importance. Recent industrial developments include the building of an aluminum smelter. Area: 272 sq mi (705 sq km). Population (1977 est): 63,200. Chief town: Beaumaris.

Anglican Communion The fellowship of episcopal Churches in communion with the see of Canterbury. Until 1786, when the consecration of bishops for foreign sees was legalized, it consisted of the Churches of England, Ireland, and Wales and the Episcopal Church of Scotland. In 1787 the Protestant Episcopal Church of the US was founded and thereafter

Anglican dioceses were formed in all parts of the British Empire and elsewhere. Total membership is estimated at 65 million.

Anglo-Burmese Wars The wars that resulted in the British annexation of Burma. In the first Anglo-Burmese War (1824–26) Burmese forces provoked the British-Indian forces into war by crossing into Bengal to attack Arakanese refugees and Britain captured, and kept, Rangoon. The aggressive action of a British naval officer provoked the second war (1852), which resulted in the annexation of Lower Burma. In the third war (1885), which occurred when the French, encouraged by the Burmese king, threatened British interests in Burma, Britain gained Upper Burma.

Anglo-Egyptian Treaty (1936) The treaty between Britain and Egypt whereby Egypt gained independence after 50 years of British occupation. Britain maintained a military alliance with Egypt and a naval base at Alexandria.

Anglo-Japanese Alliance (1902–23) The alliance between Britain and Japan contracted to maintain their interests in China and Korea respectively against Russian encroachment. The alliance brought Japan into World War I but subsequently lapsed as Britain sought friendship with the US, Japan's rival in the Pacific.

Anglo-Saxons The Germanic conquerors of Britain during the 5th century AD (*see* Angles; Saxons; Jutes). They first established a number of separate kingdoms, principally *Northumbria, *Mercia, and *Wessex, but eventually England was unified under an Anglo-Saxon dynasty. Kings ruled with the assistance of a *witan or council of wise men. Popular government and justice at the local level took the form of *hundred courts. They were eventually converted to Christianity. The Anglo-Saxons developed a rich art and literature. Their language is also known as Old English. *See also* English.

Angola, People's Republic of A country in SW Africa, on the Atlantic Ocean situated mainly to the S of the Congo River. The Cabinda district, however, lies to the N of the Congo and is separated from the rest of the country by a section of Zaïre. The country consists of a narrow coastal plain and a broad dissected plateau that reaches heights of over 6500 ft (2000 m). The inhabitants are almost all Negroes (mainly of Bantu origin) with small numbers of mixed race and a rapidly decreasing white population. *Economy*: agriculture is now being reorganized on a state-run and cooperative basis and the main crops are sugar cane and coffee. Angola is rich in mineral resources and diamonds have long been an important source of revenue. There is considerable oil production, especially offshore from Cabinda, and this has opened up new possibilities for industrial development. Hydroelectricity is being harnessed from the short steep river systems descending to the coastal plains and these schemes will provide irrigation as well as power. Main exports include oil, coffee, diamonds, and iron ore. The economy was severely disturbed by the civil wars (1974–76) and one effect was the withdrawal of Portuguese technicians, but these are being replaced to some extent by Cubans. *History*: discovered and settled by the Portuguese in the late 15th century, the area remained a Portuguese colony (apart from a brief period of Dutch occupation from 1641 to 1648) until 1951 when it became an overseas province of Portugal. During the 1950s and 1960s there was a rise in nationalism and three main independence movements emerged: the MPLA (Popular Movement for the Liberation of Angola), the FNLA (National Front for the Liberation of Angola), and UNITA (National Union for the Total Independence of Angola). After its own change of government in 1974 Portugal agreed in principle to independence for Angola but, owing to lack of internal unity and opposition from the remaining white population, civil war broke out. The various groups took over different parts of the country and in November, 1975, Portugal granted independence to the "Angolan people" rather than to any one group. The People's Republic of Angola was declared by the MPLA, with its capital in Luanda, and a coalition of the FNLA and UNITA formed a People's Democratic Republic of Angola, based on Huambo. The MPLA was supported by the Soviet Union and Cuba and the FNLA by the US and certain W European countries. Eventually, with further help from Cuba, the MPLA gained control in 1976 but opposition continues. In 1979 Dr José Eduardo dos Santos was elected president following the death of Dr Antonio Agostinho Neto (1922–79). Official language: Portuguese. Official currency: kwanza of 100 lwei. Area: 481,351 sq mi (1,246,700 sq km). Population (1981 est): 6,920,000. Capital and main port: Luanda.

Angora goat A breed of goat, originating in Turkey, whose long silky hair is regularly sheared and used commercially to make *mohair. Mohair is now also obtained from several other goat breeds derived from the Angora.

Angora rabbit A breed of domesticated rabbit, originating in France in the 17th century, of which there are now both English and French varieties. The long wool, which is usually white but can be black or blue, is periodically shorn and spun for use in clothing manufacture (**Angora wool**).

angostura A bitters made from distilled herbs and plants. Angostura bitters originated in Ciudad Bolívar (formerly Angostura) in Venezuela as a tonic and febrifuge but its manufacture was transferred to Trinidad in 1975.

Angoulême 45 40N 0 10E A city in SW France, the capital of the Charente department on the Charente River. The site of a 12th-century cathedral, its varied manufactures include paper, refrigerators, felt, and iron. Population (1975): 50,500.

Angoulême, Charles de Valois, Duc d' (1573–1650) French soldier. An illegitimate son of Charles IX, he was imprisoned (1605–16) for conspiring against Henry IV. He subsequently rose through the influence of Richelieu and then Mazarin to several important military commands, including that of the siege of Huguenot-held La Rochelle (1627).

Angry Young Men A group of British novelists and dramatists in the 1950s whose attitudes included dissatisfaction with postwar British society and disrespect for the so-called "Establishment" and its traditional institutions. Many of them came from working-class or lower-middle-class backgrounds. The phrase "angry young man" was first applied to the dramatist John *Osborne. Among other writers associated with this group were the novelists Kinglsey *Amis, John *Wain, Alan Sillitoe, and John *Braine.

Ångström, Anders Jonas (1814–74) Swedish physicist and astronomer. He was a founder of spectroscopy, his work on solar spectra leading to the discovery (1862) of hydrogen in the sun. He also studied geomagnetism. The **angstrom**, a unit of wavelength equal to 10^{-10} m (one tenth of a nanometer), is named for him.

Anguilla 18 14N 63 05W A West Indian island in the E Caribbean Sea, in the Leeward Islands. Formerly part of the UK Associated State of St Kitts-Nevis-Anguilla, it became a separate British dependency in December, 1980. Its economy is based chiefly on stock raising, salt production, boatbuilding, and fishing. Area: 35 sq mi (90 sq km). Population (1980 est): 6500. *See also* St Kitts-Nevis.

angular momentum The product of the *moment of inertia of a body and its angular velocity about an axis. It is an important quantity in physics since the total angular momentum of a closed system is conserved.

angular velocity. *See* velocity.

angwantibo A small rare nocturnal prosimian primate, *Arctocebus calabarensis*, also called the golden potto, found in West African forests. It is 9–12 in (23–30 cm) long, has pale-brown fur and large eyes, and moves through the trees, feeding chiefly on insects. Family: *Lorisidae*.

Anhui (*or* Anhwei) A province in E China. The Yangtze River in the S and the Huai River in the N are linked by ancient waterways, which provide transport and irrigation. Main products are tea, rice, soybeans, silk, and steel. Area: 54,000 sq mi (13,986 sq km). Population (1980 est): 48,030,000. Capital: Hefei.

Anhwei. *See* Anhui.

anil A small shrub, *Indigofera anil*, native to India and the original source of the blue dye *indigo, which is now produced synthetically. Family: *Leguminosae*.

aniline (*or* phenylamine; $C_6H_5NH_2$) A colorless oily nonflammable liquid *amine. It is used to make dyes, plastics, and drugs and is made by the reduction of nitrobenzene obtained from *coal tar.

animal A living organism belonging to the kingdom *Animalia*. Animals are typically mobile and feed on *plants, other animals, or their remains. Their body *cells lack the rigid cellulose wall of plant cells and they require specialized tissues, such as bone, for protection and support. Because of their activity, animals have specialized organs for sensing the nature of their environment; information from the sense organs is transmitted and coordinated by means of a nervous system. Individuals of the same species have a consistent body form; growth occurs in all regions of the body and ceases at a certain stage of development, usually when sexual maturity has been attained.

There are over one million species of animals, grouped into about 30 phyla (authorities differ in their classification of the lesser phyla). *See also* life; taxonomy.

animal behavior. *See* ethology.

animal worship. *See* totemism.

animism 1. The belief that the physical world is permeated by a spirit or a vital principle sometimes called the *anima mundi*. Georg Ernst *Stahl

phylum (approx. no. species)	important classes	representative members	phylum (approx. no. species)	important classes	representative members
Protozoa (30 000)	Sarcodina Ciliata Flagellata Sporozoa	*Amoeba* *Stentor* *Trypanosoma* *Plasmodium*	Annelida (9000)	Oligochaeta Polychaeta Hirudinea	earthworms lugworms leeches
Porifera (5000)		sponges	Arthropoda (>1 000 000)	Arachnida Crustacea Insecta	spiders, scorpions lobsters, crabs, woodlice beetles, wasps, ants, flies, bugs
Coelenterata (9000)	Hydrozoa Scyphozoa Anthozoa	*Hydra*, Portuguese man-of-war jellyfish sea anemones, corals	Echinodermata (6000)	Myriapoda Asteroidea Echinoidea Holothuroidea	centipedes, millipedes starfish sea urchins sea cucumbers
Platyhelminthes (9000)	Turbellaria Trematoda Cestoda	planarians flukes tapeworms	Chordata (55 000)	Chondrichthyes Osteichthyes	sharks, rays bony fish (salmon, carp, eels, perch, etc.)
Nematoda (10 000)		roundworms		Amphibia	frogs, toads, newts, salamanders
Mollusca (100 000)	Gastropoda Bivalvia Cephalopoda	snails, slugs mussels, oysters, cockles squids, octopus		Reptilia Aves Mammalia	lizards, snakes, crocodiles, turtles birds mammals, including man

ANIMAL   *A simplified classification of the animal kingdom (major phyla only are listed).*

was its leading proponent. **2.** In anthropology, all forms of belief in spiritual agencies. Two main classes of such beings are distinguished: the souls of the dead (*see* ancestor worship) and other personalized supernatural entities.

anise   An annual Egyptian herb, *Pimpinella anisum*, growing to a height of up to 30 in (75 cm) and having umbrella-like clusters of small yellow-white flowers. It is extensively cultivated in subtropical areas for the licorice-flavored oil (principally anthole) extracted from its small seeds, which is widely used in certain foods, beverages, and liqueurs. Family: *Umbelliferae.*

Anjou   A former province in W central France, approximating to the present-day Maine-et-Loire department. Anjou was inherited by the future Henry II of England in 1151 and remained under English rule until the early 13th century, when it was lost to France. Permanently annexed to the French crown in 1480, it ceased to exist as a province in 1790. *See also* Angevins.

Ankara   39 55N 32 50E The capital of Turkey, in the W central region of the country. There is evidence of human settlement from very early times, and it has long been an important trading town. Conquered by Alexander the Great in the 4th century BC, it later came within the Roman and Byzantine Empires. It was attacked by Persians and Arabs, and in the 11th century it was defeated by the Turks. It became the capital of modern Turkey in 1923 and since then has expanded considerably; it has three universities including the Middle East Technical University (1956). Population (1980): 1,877,755.

ankylosaur   A heavily armored dinosaur of the late Cretaceous period, which ended 65 million years ago. Ankylosaurs were low and flat and their backs were covered with hard protective bony plates. *Euoplocephalus* (or *Ankylosaurus*) reached a length of 16 ft (5 m), weighed 3 tons, and its plated tail ended in a large bony knob. Order: *Ornithischia.*

An Lu Shan   (703–57 AD) Chinese military governor, who in 756 declared himself emperor of a new Yan dynasty. Tang imperial troops opposed him but An Lu Shan seized the capital Chang An and the emperor was forced to flee. An Lu Shan was murdered shortly afterward but only in 763 did the imperial army succeed in putting down the rebellion.

Annaba   (former name: Bône)   36 57N 7 39E A large port in E Algeria, on the Mediterranean Sea. An early center of Christianity, it held the bishopric of St Augustine (396–430 AD). In 1832 it was captured by the French. Mineral exports are important, particularly phosphates and iron ore. Industries include flour milling and iron and steel processing. Population (1974 est): 313,174.

Anna Comnena   (1083–?1148 AD) Byzantine historian. The daughter of Emperor *Alexius I Comnenus, Anna married (1097) Nicephorus Bryennius (?1062–1137) and conspired (1118) to depose her brother John II (1088–1143; reigned 1118–43) in favor of her husband. She was banished to a convent, where she wrote the *Alexiad*, an account of her father's achievements and of the early Crusades from a Byzantine point of view.

Anna Ivanovna   (1693–1740) Empress of Russia (1730–40). A niece of *Peter the Great, Anna married (1710) Frederick William, Duke of Courland (d. 1710). She was elected by the Supreme Privy Council to become empress on the condition that she accept a number of provisions curtailing her powers. In practice, however, she became an autocrat, whose administration was run by her German advisers. In the Russo-Turkish War (1736–39) she regained Azov.

Annam   A region in central Vietnam, long ruled from Hue. The Chinese, who had occupied it in 111 BC, were driven out in 939 AD, and it was a powerful independent state until becoming a French protectorate in 1884. In 1949 it became part of independent Vietnam.

Annapolis   38 59N 76 30W The capital of Maryland, on the Severn River. Founded in 1648, it was here that Congress received George Washington's resignation as commander in chief of the Continental Army and ratified the peace treaty ending the American Revolution (1783). The US Naval Academy was established here in 1845 and the many historic buildings and riverside setting make it a popular tourist resort. It is also a minor seaport and has seafood industries. Population (1978 est): 29,592.

Annapolis Convention   (1786) A meeting at Annapolis, Md., to discuss interstate commerce. Although 13 states had been asked to attend, only representatives from Virginia, Delaware, Pennsylvania, New Jersey,and New York were there. It was decided to reconvene in Philadelphia the next year to discuss, on a broader scale, the revisions needed in the Articles of Confederation. Thus, the Annapolis Convention paved the way for the Constitutional Convention (1787).

Annapolis Royal   44 44N 65 32W A town and port in E Canada, in Nova Scotia. One of the first settlements in Canada (1632), it was Nova Scotia's capital until 1749. A market town, it attracts many tourists. Population (1976): 738.

Annapurna, Mount   28 34N 83 50E A massif in NW central Nepal, in the Himalayas. Its highest peak **Annapurna I**, at 26,504 ft (8078 m), was first climbed in 1950 by a French team.

Ann Arbor   42 18N 83 43W A city in Michigan. A research and educational center, it is the site of the University of Michigan (1817) and its manufactures include chemicals and precision instruments. Population (1980): 107,316.

Ann, Cape A peninsula in NE Massachusetts jutting into the Atlantic Ocean, NE of Gloucester and N of Massachusetts Bay. Gloucester, on the S shore is the main town on the cape. Fishing, boating, and tourism are important to the economy.

Anne (1665–1714) Queen of England and Scotland (Great Britain from 1707) and Ireland (1702–14). Anne, the last Stuart monarch, was the daughter of the Roman Catholic James II but was herself brought up as a Protestant. Following the overthrow (1688) of James, she supported the accession of her Protestant brother-in-law, William III, whose heiress she became. She married (1683) Prince George of Denmark (1653–1708); none of her children survived childhood. Anne therefore agreed to the Act of *Settlement (1701), which provided for the Hanoverian succession after her death.

Anne was greatly influenced by the Duke and Duchess of *Marlborough. In 1710, however, having quarreled with the Marlboroughs and faced with a country dissatisfied with the leadership, Anne returned to her earlier principles.

Anne (Elizabeth Alice Louise) (1950–) Princess of the United Kingdom, sixth in line of succession to the throne, the only daughter of *Elizabeth II and Prince Philip. An accomplished horsewoman, in 1973 she married Lieutenant Mark Phillips (1948–), a gold medalist in the equestrian events in the 1972 Olympic Games. Their son Peter was born in 1977 and daughter Zara in 1981.

annealing. *See* heat treatment.

Annecy 45 54N 6 07E A city in SE France, the capital of the Haute-Savoie department. Its situation on Lake Annecy and pleasant climate have made it a popular tourist center. Population (1975): 54,594.

annelid worm An invertebrate animal belonging to a phylum (*Annelida*) of about 9000 species, widely distributed in salt water, fresh water, and on land. The body is characteristically a muscular cylinder divided into many fluid-filled segments. Annelids vary greatly in form and habit and are divided into three classes: the Polychaeta, or bristleworms (*see* ragworm; lugworm; fanworm); the Oligochaeta (*see* earthworm; tubifex), and the Hirudinea (*see* leech).

Anne of Austria (1601–66) The wife (1615–43) of Louis XIII of France, whose antipathy toward her was aggravated by that of his chief minister Cardinal de Richelieu. After her husband's death she was regent (1643–51) for her son Louis XIV and chose her lover *Mazarin to succeed Richelieu.

Anne of Bohemia (1366–94) The first wife (from 1382) of Richard II of England and daughter of Emperor Charles IV. Her household extravagance was a cause of dissension between Richard and parliament. She died of the plague.

Anne of Brittany (1477–1514) Duchess of Brittany (1488–1514), succeeding her father Francis I (1435–88; ruled 1458–88). Her marriages to Charles VIII of France (1491) and to his successor Louis XII (1499) initiated the union of Brittany with France, in spite of Anne's desire to preserve Breton autonomy.

Anne of Cleves (1515–57) The fourth wife of Henry VIII of England. The marriage (January, 1540) was arranged to effect an alliance with German Protestant rulers but Henry found Anne unattractive and quickly divorced her (July, 1540).

Annigoni, Pietro (1910–) Italian painter. One of the most famous 20th-century artists to use the techniques of the Old Masters, Annigoni has worked chiefly in *tempera and *fresco. He is best known for his portraits of President Kennedy (1961) and Queen Elizabeth II (1955 and 1970). In recent years he has devoted himself to a fresco cycle of the life of Christ in the Church of S Michele Arcangelo, in Ponte Buggianese, near Florence.

annihilation The conversion of a particle and its antiparticle into electromagnetic radiation (annihilation radiation) as a result of a collision. The energy of the radiation is equivalent to the combined mass of the two particles. *See also* antimatter.

annual rings (*or* growth rings) A pattern of rings visible in a cross section of a tree trunk, produced by different rates of wood growth corresponding to the seasonal fluctuations in climate in temperate regions. Each year the wood produced in spring consists of large cells corresponding to vigorous growth; autumn wood has small cells as growth slows down, and in winter growth ceases. The number of rings gives an estimate of the age of the tree. *See also* dendrochronology.

annuals Plants that complete their life cycle—from germination, flowering, and seed production to death—within one year. Many annuals are used for bedding plants (e.g. marigolds) and flower extensively in the summer months. *Compare* perennials.

annuity A form of pension in which an institution, such as an *insurance company, makes a series of periodic payments to a person (annuitant) or his or her dependents over a number of years (term), in return for money paid to the institution either in a lump sum or in installments. An immediate annuity begins at once and a deferred annuity after a fixed period. An annuity certain is for a specific number of years. A life annuity is paid from a certain age until death.

annulment The process establishing that a marriage is not legally valid, as opposed to *divorce, which ends a valid marriage. An invalid marriage is considered void, never to have existed. A marriage is usually void if there is a serious defect, for example if the husband or wife is insane, too young, or already married. In less serious cases, for example when the husband or wife is unable or unwilling to consummate the marriage, the marriage may be declared void if either partner wishes it.

Annunciation In the Bible, the announcement by the angel Gabriel to the Virgin Mary of her conception of Christ (Luke 1.26–38). The feast, in full called the Annunciation of the Blessed Virgin Mary, or Lady Day, is celebrated on March 25.

anoa A rare black hoofed mammal, *Anoa depressicornis*, standing 40 in (1 m) high at the shoulder. Anoas occur in thick tropical forests of Sulawesi (Indonesia) and nearby islands and are hunted for their hides, horns, and meat. Family: *Bovidae*.

anode The positive electrode of an electrolytic cell, valve, etc. It is the electrode by which the electrons leave the system. *Compare* cathode.

anodizing A process in which a light metal or alloy, usually aluminum, is covered with a protective layer by oxidation in an electrolytic cell. Usually the cell contains chromic acid; the metal treated is the anode of the cell. A porous layer of oxide is formed, which can be dyed to give a colored finish.

anole A small arboreal New World lizard belonging to the genus *Anolis* (165 species). 5–18 in (12–45 cm) long, anoles have a triangular head and pads on their fingers and toes covered with minute hooks for grip. Their skin changes color from brown to green in response to changes in temperature, light, or danger. Males have an expansible red or yellow throat fan (dewlap). Family: *Iguanidae*.

anomie A condition of a society or of individuals in which social standards or goals are unclear, in conflict, or absent. Anomic individuals reject or are unable to find meaningful social norms by which to interpret or organize their lives. Losing their sense of social belonging, they may turn to crime, the selfish pursuit of power, or even suicide. The term was first introduced into sociology in a systematic form by *Durkheim in his *Suicide* (1897).

Anopheles A widespread genus of *mosquitoes (about 350 species), the females of which are important as vectors of the malarial parasite *Plasmodium*. The best-known malaria carrier is *A. maculipennis*. Some species transmit filariasis and encephalitis. Unlike other mosquitoes the larvae lack a siphon and lie flat on the surface of the water.

anorexia nervosa A psychological illness in which the patient, usually an adolescent girl, refuses food over a long period. It often starts with dieting to lose weight, which becomes obsessional: the patient becomes emaciated and may—without treatment—starve to death. The psychological causes are complex, often involving disturbances in family relationships. Hospitalization may be required for the treatment, which involves intensive nursing, sedation, and *psychotherapy.

Anouilh, Jean (1910–) French dramatist. His commitment to the theater was early and total; his first play, *The Ermine*, was performed in 1932. He achieved his first success in 1937 with *Traveller without Luggage*. His plays include reworkings of Greek myths (*Antigone*, 1944), social comedies (*Ring Round the Moon*, 1950), and historical dramas (*Becket*, 1962). A skilled craftsman, he exploits the most basic dramatic conventions, such as coincidences and flashbacks. His work, although often considered old-fashioned, remains popular both in France and abroad.

Anschluss (German: union; 1938) The union of Austria with Germany. Following the forced resignation of the Austrian chancellor *Schuschnigg, Nazi forces entered Austria and Schuschnigg was imprisoned. *Anschluss* was declared and ratified by a plebiscite.

Anselm of Canterbury, St (c. 1033–1109) Italian theologian and philosopher, Archbishop of Canterbury, and Doctor of the Church. Appointed to the see of Canterbury in 1093, Anselm defended church rights against

William II Rufus until he went into exile to Rome in 1097. Recalled by
*Henry I in 1100, he eventually reached an uneasy compromise with him.
He is the leading early scholastic philosopher and is perhaps best known for
his formulation of the ontological argument for the existence of God. Feast
day: April 21. Emblem: a ship.

Ansermet, Ernest (1883–1969) Swiss conductor. Briefly a mathematics
teacher, he studied composition with *Bloch and conducting with *Nikisch. After touring with *Diaghilev's ballet company he founded the Suisse
Romande Orchestra in 1918, remaining its director until 1967. He was
famous for his interpretations of *Stravinsky and other 20th-century
composers.

Anshan (*or* An-shan) 41 05N 122 58E A city in NE China, in Liaoning
province. Its steel complex, the largest in China, was developed under Japanese occupation (1931–45), when its population grew rapidly. It also has
engineering, chemical, and cement industries. Population (1957 est):
805,000.

ant An insect belonging to the family *Formicidae* (over 10,000 species).
Ants occur in almost all terrestrial habitats, are .02–10 in (0.05–25 cm)
long, and show a high degree of social organization. A colony consists of
wingless sterile female workers and a smaller number of fertile males and
females that are generally the progeny of a single queen. The young males
and females fly from the nest to mate, after which the males die and the
young queens found new colonies. Ant societies range from simple groups
of a few individuals to large complex nests comprising millions of ants and
sometimes involving a second species taken as slaves to work in the colony
(*see* slave-making ant).

Some ants have stings; others secrete burning acids (such as formic acid)
as a defense. Feeding habits vary from rapacious predators (*see* army ant)
to harmless scavengers; others milk honeydew from aphids and certain
species cultivate fungi as a food supply within the nest. Order:
Hymenoptera. □insect.

Antakya. *See* Antioch.

Antalya 36 53N 30 42E A city in SW Turkey, on the Gulf of Antalya.
Founded in the 2nd century BC, it flourished particularly under the Seljuqs
in the 13th century, and it is now an important coastal resort. Nearby are
two Roman amphitheaters and the ruins of Perga. Population (1980):
173,501.

Antananarivo (former name: Tananarive) 18 52S 47 30E The capital of
Madagascar. It was occupied by the French in 1895. A cultural center, it
has a university (1961) and two cathedrals. Industries include tobacco and
leather goods. Population (1978): 400,000.

Antar (6th century AD) Arab poet and warrior, celebrated in the 10th-
century *Romance of Antar* as the model of desert chivalry. The son of a
Bedouin chieftain and a slave girl, Antar was said to have proved his courage in numerous battles and adventures before being allowed to marry his
beloved Abla.

Antarctica The most southerly continent, surrounding the South Pole.
Almost circular in shape, it is indented by the Weddell and Ross Seas. It
consists chiefly of a vast ice-covered plateau and contains about 90% of the
world's ice. Calculations suggest that should this ice melt sea levels would
rise by about 200 ft (60 m). The continent's climate is the severest in the
world; in 1960 the world's lowest recorded temperature—of −126°F
(−87.8°C)—was made at the Soviet station of Vostok. Although lacking in
vegetation it has abundant wildlife including whales, seals, and penguins.
Scientific stations were established during the International Geophysical
Year (1957–58). Some nations (*see* Australian Antarctic Territory; British
Antarctic Territory; Norwegian Antarctic Territory; Ross Dependency;
Terre Adélie) have political claims to territory in Antarctica. Argentina
and Chile have also laid claims, as yet unrecognized, to portions of British
Antarctic Territory (*see also* Antarctic Treaty). *History*: in his voyage of
1772–75 Capt James Cook reached 71°10′S. Many discoveries and explorations took place during the 19th century culminating in the famous race
for the South Pole. This was reached first by Roald *Amundsen of the
Norwegian Antarctic Expedition on December 14, 1911, and a month later
by *Scott of the British Antarctic Terra Nova Expedition. Scott and his
team perished on the return journey. Area: about 5,500 000 sq mi
(14,200,000 sq km).

Antarctic Ocean The sections of the S Atlantic, Pacific, and Indian
Oceans around Antarctica. Except in the height of summer (late Feb to
early March), it is covered by drifting pack ice.

Antarctic Peninsula A peninsula extending 1200 mi (1930 km) N from
Antarctica toward South America, claimed by the UK. The first part of
Antarctica to be sighted (1820), it has volcanic mountains in the S.

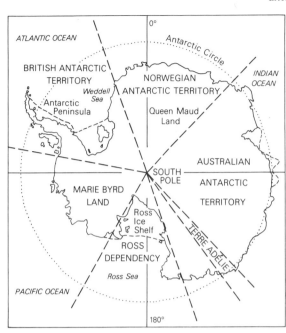

ANTARCTICA *Under the Antarctic Treaty (1959) all political
claims were halted and freedom of scientific research in the
continent was ensured.*

Antarctic Treaty (1959) An agreement, signed by Argentina, Australia,
Belgium, Chile, France, Japan, New Zealand, Norway, South Africa, the
Soviet Union, the UK, and the US, to maintain the Antarctic as a demilita-
rized zone for 30 years.

Antares An immense remote yet conspicuous red supergiant, apparent
magnitude 0.94 and about 400 light years distant, that is the brightest star
in the constellation Scorpius. It is a visual *binary star.

ant bear. *See* aardvark.

antbird A passerine bird belonging to a large family (*Formicariidae*; 223
species) occurring in the forest undergrowth of Central and South America. About 3–14 in (8–35 cm) long, antbirds have shrill voices and hooked
bills and feed chiefly on insects (although the larger species may eat small
lizards, snakes, and young birds). The female is dull brown but the male
usually has a brightly patterned plumage.

anteater A long-tailed animal belonging to a family (*Myrmecophagidae*;
3 species) occurring in tropical South America. It is toothless and has a
narrow snout with a long sticky tongue used to pick up ants and termites
after tearing open their nests with its powerful claws. The giant anteater
(*Myrmecophaga tridactyla*) reaches 6 ft (1.8 m) in length and has gray and
black fur and a bushy tail (□mammal). The other species are smaller
arboreal animals with prehensile tails (*see* tamandua). Order: *Edentata*.

The name anteater is given to several other unrelated animals that feed on
ants or termites: the *pangolins (scaly anteaters), *echidnas (spiny anteaters), and *aardvark.

Antelami, Benedetto (active 1177–1233) Italian sculptor. The most
famous Italian sculptor of the medieval period, Antelami developed a style
that marked the transition between the *romanesque and the *gothic. His
best-known works are the reliefs on the doors of the baptistry at Parma, of
which he was probably also the architect.

antelope A hoofed mammal belonging to the family *Bovidae* and occurring chiefly in Africa but occasionally in Asia. Antelopes are typically
fast-running and graceful, grazing or browsing in large herds on open
grasslands, although some are more solitary and live in bush and woodland.
The shoulder height varies from 10 in (25 cm) in the *royal antelope to
71 in (180 cm) in the *eland. All male antelopes and some females have
horns. *See also* dik-dik; duiker; gazelle; gnu; kudu; waterbuck.

antenna (*or* aerial) An electrical conductor that transmits and receives
radio or other electromagnetic waves. An oscillating *electromagnetic field,
caused by waves from a distant source, induces an oscillating current in the
receiving antenna. A transmitting antenna works by the same process in
reverse, creating waves from an electrical signal. A modern antenna for

UHF (ultra-high frequency) and VHF (very high frequency) consists of a dipole formed from two metal rods, each approximately one-quarter of the operating wavelength. In the Yagi antenna a reflector rod is set behind the dipole and several director rods are placed in front of it. This provides a considerably more directional array than the simple dipole and is widely used as both a receiving and transmitting antenna for television.

antenna (zoology) The sensory feeler of insects, crustaceans, and many other arthropods, one or two pairs of which are attached to the head. They are usually jointed threadlike structures containing receptors of sound, smell, touch, and temperature.

Antenor (late 6th century BC) Athenian sculptor. His signature appears on the base of a marble *kore on the Athenian Acropolis. He sculpted the Harmodios and Aristogeiton group, looted by Xerxes (480 BC) and restored after Alexander the Great's Persian expedition.

Antheil, George (1900–59) US composer. He studied with Ernest *Bloch and in 1922 moved to Europe, where his avant-garde work *Le Ballet méchanique* (1924) for bells, motor horns, airplane propellers, etc., caused a furor. His later works are more traditional in style and include several film scores.

anthelminthics Drugs used to treat infections of the intestines caused by parasitic worms. Piperazine is commonly used to expel roundworms and threadworms. Tapeworm infections are treated with niclosamide or dichlorophen.

anther. *See* stamen.

antheridium The reproductive organ producing the male cells (gametes) in ferns, mosses, algae, and fungi. It is usually a club-shaped structure, the rounded head containing the gametes.

Anthony, Susan B(rownell) (1820–1906) US reformer and suffragette. A lifelong advocate of equal rights for women, she was instrumental in the passage, 14 years after her death, of the 19th Amendment to the Constitution, which granted full voting rights to women. She worked for the American Anti-slavery Society (1856–61) and the National Woman Suffrage Association (1869–90), led the National American Woman Suffrage Association (1890–1906), and was a co-author of the 4-volume *History of Woman Suffrage* (1881–1900).

Anthony of Egypt, St (c. 251–356 AD) Egyptian hermit and founder of Christian monasticism. An ascetic from the age of 20, he withdrew until 305 into complete isolation, emerging to organize followers into a monastic community living according to a rule. When he was about a hundred years old, he preached against *Arianism. His combat with temptation in the desert is described in Athanasius' *Life of Saint Anthony*; it became a frequent subject in Christian art. Feast day: Jan. 17. Emblem: a pig and a bell.

Anthony of Padua, St (1195–1231) Portuguese friar and Doctor of the Church. Famous for his preaching, he devoted his efforts to converting heretics in N Italy and the Albigenses in S France until his appointment as professor of theology to the Franciscan Order in 1223. He is often invoked as a finder of lost property. Feast day: June 13.

anthracene ($C_{14}H_{10}$) A colorless crystalline *aromatic compound. It is obtained from coal tar and is used in making dyes.

anthracite. *See* coal.

anthrax A contagious disease of many animals, including farm livestock, that can be transmitted to man. Caused by the bacterium *Bacillus anthracis*, it is usually contracted by eating contaminated food. Onset is often sudden with a rise in body temperature, staggering, respiratory distress, convulsions, and death. In horses and pigs a subacute form may occur, with progressive swelling of the throat and neck resulting in labored breathing and choking. In many countries the authorities must be notified of any outbreaks. Treatment is with antibiotics and prevention is by vaccination of herds in areas where the disease is endemic. Man may develop localized swellings after handling infected carcasses or acquire a pneumonia from inhaling the bacterial spores.

anthropoid ape A tailless *primate belonging to the family *Pongidae*, includes the gibbons, chimpanzees, orang-utans, and gorillas. *See* ape.

anthropology The scientific study of man in his physical and social aspects. In the widest meaning of the term it includes *archeology, *linguistics, cultural or social anthropology, and physical anthropology. It is particularly concerned with the systematic and comparative study of human diversity. Physical anthropology is concerned with the origins and evolution of man through the examination of his fossil remains, and the study and classification of the races of man through comparison of anatomical and physiological characteristics (*see also* anthropometry). Cultural anthropology is concerned with the evolution of human society and culture, including language, and with the systematic comparison of social, linguistic, technical, and behavioral diversity. Social anthropology has a more restricted meaning and is the comparative study of social behavior, social organization, social forms and institutions, custom, culture, and belief, and has traditionally confined itself to the study of "primitive" societies.

anthropometry The science concerned with the measurement of the human body, particularly with respect to the variation that exists between different populations and races. Anthropometry ranges from the measurement of structural characteristics, such as height, cranial capacity, etc., to the analysis of chemical constituents of the body, such as blood groups. By comparing fossil and present-day measurements anthropometry has also helped to reveal the sequence of events that has occurred during the evolution of man.

anthropomorphism Mankind's tendency to ascribe to nonhuman creatures the motives, feelings, etc., of human beings. This is particularly evident in the concept of God. The anthropomorphism of ancient Greek religion was ridiculed by *Xenophanes of Colophon (6th century BC) but Christian discussions of the divine personality, will, etc., have still not escaped from an implicit anthropomorphism. Religious art can scarcely avoid being anthropomorphic.

Anthurium A genus of tropical American plants (550 species), some of which are cultivated as greenhouse or pot plants for their ornamental flowers or foliage. The flower heads consist of a cylindrical cluster (spadix) of tiny flowers surrounded by a large petal-like part (spathe), which is often brightly colored (e.g. in *A. scherzerianum* it is red). Family: *Araceae* (arum family).

anti-aircraft gun Any gun capable of rapid fire, high elevation, and speedy adjustment. Calibers are 0.8 in to 5.5 in (20–140 mm) but most common pieces are 3–4 in (87–100 mm). Upper range limit is about 40,000 ft (12,000 m) and targets may be engaged at a few hundred feet. Guns are aimed visually or electronically so that the aircraft flies into the round or shellburst. The role of anti-aircraft guns has largely been replaced by ground-to-air guided missiles.

antiballistic missiles High-speed nuclear weapons used to attack hostile *ballistic missiles. Operated by ground-based radar and computers, they rely for their final attack on their own guidance systems, destroying the target by radiation from their warheads. Short-range versions with low-yield warheads (e.g. US *Sprint*) are designed to seek and destroy targets within the earth's atmosphere; long-range missiles with high-yield warheads operate in space (e.g. US *Spartan*, Soviet *Galosh*).

Antibes 43 35N 7 07E A city in France, in the Alpes-Maritimes department. A tourist resort and a port for pleasure craft on the Côte d'Azur, it produces flowers, perfumes, and chocolates. Population (1975): 56,309.

antibiotics Drugs derived from microorganisms and used to treat infections caused by bacteria or fungi. Synthetic drugs with similar properties are also known as antibiotics. Bacteriocidal antibiotics, such as *penicillin, actually kill bacteria, whereas bacteriostatic antibiotics, such as *tetracycline and *chloramphenicol, simply halt their growth. Examples of antifungal antibiotics are nystatin and griseofulvin. Possible adverse effects of antibiotic treatment include allergic reactions and the development of resistant strains of bacteria, which may set up a secondary infection. In spite of side effects, however, the widespread use of antibiotics since World War II has virtually eliminated the scourge of bacterial and fungal infectious diseases.

antibody A protein produced by certain white blood cells (lymphocytes) that reacts specifically with and neutralizes a foreign protein (e.g. a bacterium), which is known as the **antigen**. Antibody production is stimulated by contact with the antigen: subsequent exposure to the antigen produces a greater antibody response, which provides the basis of *immunity. Antibodies contribute to the body's resistance to infection and are responsible for the rejection of foreign tissue or organ transplants.

Antichrist In the New Testament, a person or institution opposed to Christ, whose appearance will precede His second coming (John 2.18–22). Some Christians believed *Nero to be the Antichrist; many reformers, for example Wycliffe and Luther, saw the pope or the papacy in this role.

anticline An arch-shaped *fold or upfold in folded rock strata, the oldest rocks occurring at the core. In areas of complex folding an upfold may have its youngest rocks at the core, the resulting structure being termed an antiform. *Compare* syncline.

anticoagulants Drugs, such as heparin and warfarin, that interfere with blood clotting. They are used when there has been, or there is a risk of, clots forming in the blood vessels, as after *thrombosis of the leg veins.

Anti-Comintern Pact An agreement among the Axis powers in opposition to the Comintern (*or* Third *International). Germany and Japan signed the Pact in 1936 to protect themselves against communism and they were later joined by Italy (1937) and Spain (1939).

Anti-Corn Law League   A British organization formed in 1839 to work for the repeal of the *Corn Laws. Under the able leadership of Richard *Cobden and John *Bright, the League gained widespread support from manufacturers as well as workers and achieved its objective in 1846.

anticyclone (or high)   An area of atmospheric pressure higher than the surrounding air with one or more isobars of approximately circular form around its center. Winds, generally light, circulate around the high pressure center in a clockwise direction in the N hemisphere and anticlockwise in the S hemisphere. Calm settled weather is usually synonymous with anticyclones in temperate latitudes.

antidepressants   A class of drugs used to relieve depression. The most widely used are the tricyclic antidepressants, which include amitriptyline and imipramine, and the tetracyclic antidepressants. They provide a wide range of drugs to treat a variety of depressive symptoms. The MAO inhibitors prevent the action of the enzyme monoamine oxidase in breaking down adrenaline and related compounds that affect mood. These antidepressants may have serious side effects and are therefore restricted to the treatment of severe psychological disorders.

Antietam, Battle of   (September 17, 1862) A decisive engagement in the US *Civil War, which prevented the Confederate capture of Washington, DC. In the last of a series of battles, the advance of the Confederate general Robert E. *Lee was checked at Antietam by the Union general George B. *McClellan. The South lost about 10,000 men but McClellan allowed Lee to withdraw into Virginia.

Anti-Federalist Party   US political party, advocating states' rights. Under the leadership of Thomas Jefferson and James Madison, a coalition formed to oppose the ratification of the US Constitution (1787–88). The addition of the Bill of Rights to the Constitution was largely an appeasement for the Anti-Federalists, who felt that a central government would wield too much authority. By 1793 the party was absorbed into the Jeffersonian Republican Party, which became the Democratic-Republican Party and then the Democratic Party.

antiferromagnetism   The magnetic property of a material that has its microscopic magnetic *moments lined up in domains, as in *ferromagnetism, except that in these materials the antiparallel arrays oppose each other. The lower the temperature, the greater this alignment; up to a certain temperature, known as the Néel temperature, the relative magnetic *permeability is slightly greater than one and increases with temperature. Above this temperature the material is paramagnetic (see paramagnetism).

antifreeze   A substance added to water in cooling systems to lower the freezing point and thus prevent damage in cold weather from freezing. Glycols and methanol, together with a corrosion inhibitor, are commonly used.

antigen. See antibody.

Antigone   In Greek mythology, the daughter of *Oedipus and Jocasta, whose story forms the basis of Sophocles' tragedy *Antigone*. When her father was banished from Thebes she accompanied him into exile in Colonus. Her brothers Eteocles and *Polyneices had agreed to reign alternately in Thebes, but Eteocles' refusal to yield the crown led to their killing each other in single combat. Despite the Theban senate's decree prohibiting the burial of Polyneices, Antigone performed the funeral rites for her brother. She was consequently ordered to be buried alive by Creon, ruler of Thebes, and hanged herself.

Antigonus I   (c. 382–301 BC) Macedonian general, nicknamed Monophthalmus or Cyclops (One-eye). After the death of his patron *Antipater, Antigonus became ruler of Asia Minor. He declared himself king in 306 but his ambition to rule a reunited Macedonian empire was opposed. His rivals combined forces, after Antigonus' successes against them individually, and defeated and killed him in battle at Ipsus.

Antigonus II Gonatas   (c. 320–239 BC) King of Macedon (276–239), who re-established Macedonian hegemony in Greece. He defeated Athens and Sparta in the Chremonidean War (c. 267–c. 262) and Ptolemy II of Egypt in the naval battle of Cos. During his reign the Macedonian court became a center of culture.

Antigua and Barbuda   A West Indian country in the E Caribbean Sea, comprising the islands of Antigua, Barbuda, and Redonda (uninhabited). Tourism is the chief source of revenue; sugar and cotton production are also important. *History* Antigua was discovered by Columbus (1493) and colonized by British settlers in 1632. It formed an associated state within the British Commonwealth from 1967 until gaining independence in 1981.

It is a member of CARICOM. Area: 170 sq mi (440 sq km). Population (1983): 78,000. Capital: St John's.

antihistamines   Drugs that interfere with the action of *histamine, a chemical produced by the body that is responsible for the symptoms of an allergic reaction. Antihistamines are therefore used to treat hay fever, nettle rash, and other allergies. Some antihistamines (e.g. dramamine) are used to prevent travel sickness and others are effective sedatives (drowsiness is a common side effect of many antihistamines).

Anti-Lebanon Mountains   A mountain range running NE–SW for 93 mi (150 km) along the Lebanese-Syrian border and rising to 9232 ft (2814 m) at Mount Hermon.

Antilles   The islands of the West Indies, excluding the Bahamas. The group is divided into the *Greater Antilles and the *Lesser Antilles.

Anti-Masonic Party   A minority US political party that arose after the disappearance of a former freemason in 1826. The widely held belief that the man had been murdered by freemasons for revealing their secrets led to the formation of the party to oppose Masonic candidates for office in the New York Assembly. Effective on the state level, the party held the first national nominating convention in US politics (1831), a system later adopted by the major parties. The Anti-Masons merged with the Whigs (who opposed the policies of Andrew Jackson) in 1838.

antimatter   Hypothetical matter in which the constituent atoms consist of antiparticles. For every elementary particle (see particle physics) there exists an antiparticle that is identical except for certain of its properties, such as electric charge and isospin number, which are of equal magnitude but opposite in sign. The photon and the neutral pion are their own antiparticles. An atom of antimatter would contain a nucleus of antiprotons and antineutrons surrounded by positrons (antielectrons). If matter were to meet antimatter, they would annihilate each other in a burst of radiation. See also annihilation.

antimony (Sb)   A metallic element, probably known in antiquity. It occurs in nature as the element and more commonly in the sulfide *stibnite (Sb_2S_3). The element exists in two forms: the normal metallic form, which is brittle bluish-white and flaky, and an amorphous gray form. Antimony is a poor conductor of heat and electricity. It forms the oxide (Sb_2O_3) by burning in air and the volatile hydride, stibine (SbH_3), which like many antimony compounds is toxic. Pure antimony is used in making *semiconductors; other uses include addition to lead to increase its hardness in battery plates, in type metal, and as oxides or sulfides in paints, glasses, and ceramics. At no 51; at wt 121.75); mp 382°F (630.7°C); bp 1003°F (1750°C).

anti-novel. See nouveau roman.

Antioch   (modern Turkish name: Antakya) 36 12N 36 10E A city in central S Turkey, near the coast and the Syrian border. Founded in 301 BC, it had a large early Christian community, and there are notable Roman mosaics in the Archeological Museum. Population (1970): 66,550.

Antiochus I Soter   (324–261 BC) King of Syria (281–261) of the Seleucid dynasty. Antiochus lost some Seleucid territory to Egypt but achieved peace with Macedon (278) and repulsed a Gallic invasion, which earned him the title Soter (Saviour). He founded many cities.

Antiochus II   (c. 287–246 BC) King of Syria (261–246) of the Seleucid dynasty. Little is known of his reign apart from his reconquest (260–253) of some of the territory in Asia Minor lost by his father *Antiochus I Soter and his political marriage (252) to the Egyptian princess Berenice.

Antiochus (III) the Great   (c. 242–187 BC) King of Syria (223–187) of the Seleucid dynasty. After crushing separatist revolts at home, Antiochus initiated a policy of expansion. His incursions on Egyptian territory were temporarily halted by his defeat at Raphia (217) but his great campaign (212–206) through Armenia, Parthia, and Bactria to the Indus River paralleled that of Alexander the Great. He finally defeated the Egyptians in 198. Antiochus then became involved in hostile diplomacy with Rome and in 192 invaded Greece. Driven out by the Romans (190), his defeat destroyed Seleucid power in the Mediterranean.

Antiochus IV Epiphanes   (c. 215–163 BC) King of Syria (175–163) of the Seleucid dynasty. Antiochus maintained the empire, campaigning successfully against the Egyptians until forced by the Romans to withdraw (168). He promoted Greek culture throughout the empire but met with resistance from the *Maccabees (167–160) when he ruthlessly imposed Greek religion on the Jews.

Antiochus VII Sidetes   (c. 159–129 BC) The last Seleucid King of Syria (139–129). Following early military successes, including the reconquest of Jerusalem (134), he attempted to postpone the Parthian conquest of the Seleucid empire and died in battle.

anti-oxidants Substances that inhibit oxidation of such products as foods, paints, plastics, fuels, etc. Natural anti-oxidants include ascorbic acid (vitamin C). Additives are usually phenol derivatives.

antiparticle. *See* antimatter.

Antipater (397–319 BC) Macedonian general. Antipater was chief military and diplomatic aide to Philip of Macedon and then to Alexander the Great, becoming regent after Alexander's departure for the East. To maintain this position after Alexander's death, he suppressed internal rebellions and crushed the imperial ambitions of Alexander's second-in-command Perdiccas (d. 321). After Antipater's death Alexander's empire began to disintegrate.

Antipater (d. 4 BC) The son of *Herod the Great. Disowned in infancy, but restored to favor in about 17 BC, he struggled ruthlessly to succeed his father. He had his half-brothers executed in about 7 BC but was himself executed shortly before Herod's own death.

Antipater the Idumaean (d. 43 BC) Procurator (governor) of Judea (47–43). His adroit manipulation of successive Roman backers, including *Caesar, who appointed him procurator, brought privileges for Judea and financial advantages for himself. He was assassinated and his son *Herod the Great subsequently succeeded to his position.

Antiphon (c. 480–411 BC) Athenian orator, important in the development of a vigorous and precise Greek prose style. Antiphon conspired to establish oligarchic rule at Athens (411) but a more moderate democratic government prevailed and he was tried and executed despite a brilliant self-defense.

Antipodes Islands 49 42S 178 50E A small group of rocky uninhabited islands in the S Pacific Ocean, belonging to New Zealand. Their fur seal population has been greatly reduced by hunting. Area: 24 sq mi (62 sq km).

antipope Those raised to the papacy in opposition to a lawfully elected pope. There have been about 40 antipopes. The first, Hippolitus, was created in the early 3rd century. During the later Roman Empire and during the middle ages most antipopes represented rival factions supporting different political or doctrinal claims. In the 11th and 12th centuries some 14 antipopes were chosen by the Holy Roman Emperors, who had had until 1059 a considerable voice in papal elections and who resented the Church's growing independence from lay control. From 1378 another group of antipopes was elected following the *Great Schism, when a group of cardinals left Avignon (*see* Avignon papacy) to return to Rome; the popes remaining at Avignon and under French control were styled antipopes thereafter. The Council of Pisa (1409) elected a new pope to end the Schism, but he too was regarded as an antipope until unity was restored at the Council of *Constance (1515). There have been no antipopes since the mid-14th century.

antique An artifact of aesthetic and historical or sociological significance, now not in general use or manufacture. The term does not include painting and sculpture. Until recently an antique was required to predate about 1830, when factory production increased, but today import and export laws of most countries require an age of a hundred years for antiques. Antique collecting was a pastime of the wealthy until the 20th century, when its increasing popularity has widened the scope of collectable objects to include all kinds of domestic items.

Antirrhinum A genus of chiefly Mediterranean and W North American herbaceous plants (about 40 species). The most widely cultivated species is the ornamental snapdragon (*A. majus*), 12–31 in (30–80 cm) high with brightly colored two-lipped tubular flowers adapted to pollination by large bees. It grows naturally as a perennial but is usually treated as an annual and grown from seed. Family: *Scrophulariaceae*.

Anti-Saloon League (1895–1950) US temperance organization. The league worked for the prohibition of liquor in the US prior to the ratification of the 18th (Prohibition) Amendment in 1919 and afterwards for enforcement of the amendment. In 1950 it became part of the National Temperance League.

antisemitism Hostility toward the *Jews, which has characterized their existence since the *Diaspora (6th century BC). Its origins perhaps go back to the distrust invariably felt for a coherent minority held together by strong religious and cultural ties, which are themselves strengthened as the hostility intensifies. The early history of the Jews did nothing to dispel this inherent mistrust: represented as God's chosen people in the Old Testament and the betrayers of Christ in the New Testament, their unpopularity in medieval Europe was reflected in totally unfounded beliefs that they used Christian children as human sacrifices. Encouraged and, in some cases, forced to become moneylenders (an activity forbidden to Christians by

canon law; *see* usury), they were by the 13th century persecuted throughout Europe. Expulsion (England, 1290; France, 1306; Spain, 1492), massacre (Germany, 1348; Spain, 1391), the Inquisition (1478), and papal bull (1555) deprived medieval Europe of large numbers of its Jews, many of whom enriched the Muslim countries of N Africa and Turkey. It was not until the 18th-century *Enlightenment had introduced a degree of religious freedom that they came back in any numbers. However, in the 19th century antisemitism gained new impetus from nationalist sentiments, especially in Germany. In France, it became public in the *Dreyfus affair. In Russia, government-tolerated (and sometimes government-inspired) *pogroms were common in the late 19th and early 20th centuries but antisemitism reached its peak in Hitler's final solution, which cost the Jews between five and six million lives (*see* holocaust). In the postwar years, since the establishment of the state of Israel, antisemitism has to some extent been replaced by Arab anti-Zionism, but it continues to be active in E Europe, especially the Soviet Union. Social discrimination, such as the exclusion of Jews from private clubs, still exists in even apparently tolerant western countries that have legislation against racial discrimination.

antiseptic A substance that kills bacteria and other dangerous microorganisms and can be applied to the skin (to cleanse wounds, before surgery, etc.) or taken internally. Antiseptics are generally distinguished from *disinfectants, which are too toxic to be used on or within the body.

Antisthenes (c. 445–c. 360 BC) Greek philosopher and disciple of *Socrates. Antisthenes was a critic of society and is regarded as a formative influence on cynicism (*see* Cynics). Principally a moral philosopher, he argued for a simple and virtuous way of life that would lead to happiness.

antitank gun Any flat-trajectory *gun using ammunition suitable for destroying *tanks. Guns in tanks themselves are the most common examples. Artillery weapons are light low-silhouette easily deployed pieces. Short-range specialized missiles are replacing the lighter antitank guns.

antitoxin An *antibody produced against a toxin. Antitoxins can be isolated from inoculated healthy animals and used to treat or prevent specific infections; for example, an antitoxin against tetanus is obtained from the plasma of animals inoculated against tetanus.

antitrust acts Federal and state legislation to protect trade and commerce from unlawful restraints, price discrimination, price fixing, and monopolies. In the 19th century some businessmen fixed prices and destroyed rival businesses by manipulating raw materials and access to transport. The Sherman Antitrust Act (1890), the first of several measures, prohibited contracts "in restraint of trade." Interpreted narrowly at first, these laws were strengthened by successive legislation (including the Clayton Act 1914, Federal Trade Commission Act 1914, and the Robinson-Patman Act 1936).

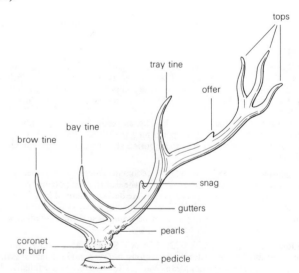

ANTLERS *The number of branches increases with the age of the stag. This antler has 6 branches; a stag with a head of 12 branches is called a royal.*

antlers The paired bony structures growing from the heads of deer, generally confined to males. In temperate regions the antlers begin to grow in early summer: they are at first covered with velvety skin, which is later shed. Used for fighting and display, the antlers are shed each year at the end of the mating season. Deer grow their first set of antlers, which are usually straight spikes, at the age of 1–2 years. The number of points is increased in successive years.

antlion An insect belonging to a family (*Myrmeleontidae*) in which the adults resemble dragonflies and live only long enough to mate and lay eggs. The predatory larva lives 1–3 years, generally at the bottom of a conical pit in loose sand: any insect that falls into the pit is snapped up with its large jaws, which protrude from the sand. Order: *Neuroptera*.

Antofagasta 21 51S 102 18W A city in NW Chile, a port on the Pacific Ocean. It is a commercial and industrial center. The chief industries are metal refining and founding; exports include nitrates and copper. The University of the North was established here in 1956. Population (1976 est): 159,980.

Antonello da Messina (c. 1430–c. 1479) Italian painter, born in Messina (Sicily). He trained in Naples, where he probably learned the Flemish technique of oil painting; this he introduced to Venice during a visit in 1475. The realism of Flemish art also deeply influenced his style, particulary in *St Jerome in His Study* and *Portrait of a Man* (both National Gallery, London).

Antonescu, Ion (1882–1946) Romanian general and politician. A pro-Nazi, he became prime minister (1940), replacing *Carol II's government with a totalitarian regime. In 1941 he commanded the army in Bessarabia. He was executed for war crimes.

Antoninus Pius (86–161 AD) Roman emperor (138–61). Antoninus was admitted by Emperor Hadrian to his advisory council and adopted as his successor in 138. His reign was peaceful and generally prosperous. Only minor campaigns were fought abroad and noted legal reforms were introduced; the *Antonine Wall was built during his reign. He was deified after his death.

Antonioni, Michelangelo (1912–) Italian film maker. Born into a bourgeois provincial family and interested in film making as a student, in 1939 he moved to Rome to work for the magazine *Cinema*. His first films were *Gente del Po* (1943–47) and *Cronaca di un amore* (1950). Later films include *L'avventura* (1959), *La notte* (1961), *Blow-Up* (1966), *Zabriskie Point* (1970), and *The Passenger* (1975).

Antony, Mark. *See* Mark Antony.

Antrim A county in NE Northern Ireland, bordering on the Atlantic Ocean and the Irish Sea. It consists mainly of a basalt plateau sloping inland to lough Neagh in the SW. On the N coast is the famous *Giant's Causeway. The county is predominantly agricultural producing oats, potatoes, flax, and livestock. Industry includes the manufacture of man-made fibers, which has largely replaced traditional linen production. Area: 1200 sq mi (3100 sq km). Population (1971 est): 355,716. County town: Belfast.

An-tung. *See* Andong.

Antwerp (Flemish name: Antwerpen; French name: Anvers) 51 13N 4 25E A city in Belgium, on the Scheldt River. Antwerp is one of the largest seaports in the world and has important shipbuilding and ship-repairing industries. Other industries include oil refining, diamond cutting, textiles, and electronics. It possesses many fine buildings, including the 14th-century gothic cathedral, the printer Christopher Plantin's house (now a museum), and the 16th-century Butchers' Hall. It is the birthplace of Rubens and Van Dyck and some of their paintings form part of a fine collection housed in the Royal Gallery of Fine Arts. There is a large Flemish-speaking population. *History*: it was the leading commercial center of western Europe in the 16th century but religious strife and its sacking by Spaniards (1576) led to its decline, further hastened by the closure of the Scheldt River (1648). The revival of its economy began when Belgium purchased the shipping rights of the river from the Netherlands. Antwerp was occupied and damaged in both World Wars. Population (1981 est): 190,652.

Anu The Mesopotamian god of the heavens and father of all the gods. He represented the infinite and all-embracing sky and was worshiped as the source of all order and rule.

Anubis Egyptian god of the dead, usually represented as a crouching jackal or a jackal-headed man. He supervised the weighing of the souls of the dead, and also the embalming of the body. He was reputed to have invented this process to preserve the body of *Osiris.

Anura An order of amphibians (over 2000 species) comprising the *frogs and *toads. Anurans are specialized for jumping, having a short backbone, no tail, and large muscular hind legs. The eggs hatch into tadpoles, which undergo *metamorphosis into adults. This order is also called the *Salientia*.

Anuradhapura 8 20N 80 25E A city in Sri Lanka. The ancient capital of the island (5th century BC to 8th century AD), it is the site of the sacred bo tree descended from the original at *Buddh Gaya and the first Buddhist temple in Ceylon. Population (1981): 36,248.

anus. *See* intestine.

Anvers. *See* Antwerp.

Anville, Jean-Baptiste Bourguignon d' (1697–1782) French geographer and cartographer, specializing chiefly in ancient and medieval geography. As geographer to the French king from 1719, he greatly improved the accuracy of maps of Italy, Asia, and Africa.

anxiety Generalized pervasive fear. Anxiety is partly the feeling of apprehension, partly the behavior of avoiding frightening situations, and partly the associated bodily changes, such as sweating, a fast pulse, and tense muscles. It is normal to feel anxiety when some danger is present or expected. However, when severe anxiety is out of all proportion to any real threats it can be a sign of mental illness. Tranquilizing drugs, *psychotherapy, *behavior therapy, and *autosuggestion are used as treatments. *See also* neurosis; phobia.

Anyang 36 04N 114 20E A city in E China, in Henan province. It was the last capital (1384–1111 BC) of the Shang dynasty and splendid archeological remains have been unearthed here. Industries include cotton and steel. Population (1953): 124,900.

ANZAC The *A*ustralian and *N*ew Zealand *A*rmy *C*orps, which served in World War I in Europe and the Middle East. On ANZAC Day, April 25 (the day of the ANZAC landing in Gallipoli in 1915), in Australia and New Zealand the dead of both World Wars are remembered.

Anzengruber, Ludwig (1839–89) Austrian dramatist and novelist. Originally an actor, he wrote a successful series of realistic plays about rural life, many of them in local dialect. They include the tragedy *Der Meineidbauer* (1871) and the comedy *Die Kreuzelschreiber* (1872). He also wrote short stories and two novels.

Anzio 41 27N 12 38E A seaport and resort in Italy, in Lazio on the Tyrrhenian Sea. It is the birthplace of Nero. During World War II it was the scene of Allied landings in Italy. There is an important fishing industry. Population (1971): 22,927.

ANZUS A security treaty concluded in 1951 by *A*ustralia, *N*ew Zealand, and the *US*, requiring members to provide mutual aid in the event of aggression by foreign powers.

Aomori 40 50N 140 43E A city in Japan, in N Honshu on Mutsu Bay. One of Japan's major ports, it exports rice, fish, and timber. Population (1980): 288,000.

aorta. *See* artery; heart.

Aosta 45 43N 7 19E A city in Italy, capital of Valle d'Aosta on the Dora Baltea River. Situated amid impressive mountain scenery, it has important Roman remains and a cathedral (12th–19th centuries). Tourism and steel are the main industries. Population (1971): 36,906.

aoudad A tawny-colored sheep, *Ammotragus lervia*, also called Barbary sheep, that is the only wild sheep in Africa. Aoudads live in dry rocky northern regions and obtain water mainly from vegetation and dew. They stand 41 in (102 cm) at the shoulder and have outward-curving horns and a long fringe of hair hanging from the neck and chest.

Apache A North American Indian people inhabiting areas of Arizona, New Mexico, and Oklahoma. Their main divisions are the Jicarillos, Mescaleros, Chiricahuas, Western Apache, Lipan, and Kiowa-Apache and their language is of the *Athabascan type. The Apaches migrated from the Northwest to their present area of settlement around 1000 AD and preserved a semi-nomadic way of life. In addition to hunting, some groups practiced farming and handicrafts. Their raids on the villages of the Pueblo Indians and the Spanish settlements of the Southwest earned the Apaches a warlike reputation. Although the various Apache groups were usually independent, they sometimes formed alliances under the leadership of national chiefs such as *Cochise and *Geronimo, who led Apache warriors in continuing warfare against the US Army until 1886. The Apache population today is approximately 15,000.

Apache Wars (1860–86) US frontier battles between the Apache Indians and the US Army in the Southwest. The refusal of the Apache and other Indian tribes to give up their lands to the whites led to a series of fierce battles, mainly in Arizona, New Mexico, Texas, and Oklahoma. Apache chief Cochise made peace in 1872, but renegade chief Geronimo resisted until 1886, when he and his followers were settled at Fort Sill, Oklahoma.

apartheid (Afrikaans: apartness) The policy of separate development of the white and non-white populations in South Africa. Apartheid, which was introduced by the Afrikaner National Party in 1948, aims to divide South Africa into separate regions for whites and blacks. The white minority that governs South Africa has been criticized for this policy and in 1961 South Africa was forced to withdraw from the British Commonwealth.

apatite The commonest phosphorous mineral, of composition $Ca_5(PO_4)_3(OH,F,Cl)$. It is found as an accessory mineral in many igneous rocks, especially pegmatites, as well as metamorphosed limestones. It is used in the production of fertilizers. The enamel of teeth is composed almost entirely of apatite (*see also* fluoridation) and the chief inorganic constituent of bone is hydroxyapatite, $Ca_{10}(PO_4)_6(OH)_2$. *See* Plate III.

Apatosaurus *See* Brontosaurus.

ape A highly intelligent tailless *primate belonging to the family *Pongidae* (11 species), found in central Africa and S Asia. There are two subfamilies: the arboreal *Hylobatinae* (*see* gibbons; siamang) and the ground-dwelling *Ponginae* (*see* chimpanzees; orang-utans; gorillas), also called great apes. Forest apes are often solitary but ground-dwelling apes live in complex societies and all have highly developed means of communication.

Some tailless primates of other families are also called apes.

Apeldoorn 52 13N 5 57E A city in the E central Netherlands, in Gelderland province. The 17th-century Castle Loo, a royal summer residence, is nearby. Its industries include blanket, cloth, and paper production. Population (1981 est): 140,769.

Apelles (4th century BC) The court painter of Alexander the Great. He seems to have specialized in portraits and allegories aiming, like many contemporary artists, at *trompe l'oeil* realism. His most famous pictures included *Aphrodite Rising from the Waves* and *Alexander as Zeus*. His style of portraiture influenced fashions in painting for more than two centuries.

Apennines (Italian name: Appennino) A mountain range in Italy. It extends about 652 mi (1050 km) down the Italian peninsula from the Maritime Alps in the NW to the Strait of Messina in the S. The range is not generally very high but it affords few easy crossing points; the highest peak is Monte Corno at 9560 ft (2914 m). The Apennines are volcanic in the S (*see* Vesuvius).

aphelion The point in the orbit of a body around the sun at which the body is furthest from the sun. The earth is at aphelion on about July 3. *Compare* perihelion.

aphid An □insect, also called a plant louse, belonging to a family (*Aphidae*) of important plant pests. Small, soft, and often wingless, aphids have long thin antennae and weak legs and are usually green (greenfly), red, or brown. There are two thin tubes projecting from the abdomen from which honeydew is secreted. Aphids feed on plant sap, piercing plant tissues with sharp beaklike mouthparts, causing leaf curl, retardation of growth, and often forming galls. The aphid's great fecundity and the ability of the female to reproduce by *parthenogenesis results in frequent outbreaks of the pest. Order: *Hemiptera*.

Aphraates (4th century AD) The first Father of the Syrian Church. He lived a monastic life and may also have been a bishop. He wrote numerous tractates summarizing the Christian faith.

aphrodisiac A drug that increases sexual desire or sexual performance. No true aphrodiasic has yet been discovered and most preparations act (if at all) by suggestion. Some drugs (such as *alcohol and *morphine) produce a general euphoria and reduce inhibitions but usually have an adverse effect on sexual performance. Local irritants, such as cantharides (Spanish fly), can prolong an erection at the cost of considerable discomfort.

Aphrodite In Greek mythology, the goddess of love, called *Venus by the Romans. According to Homer she was the daughter of Dione and Zeus; Hesiod says that she was born from the foam after *Uranus had been castrated and his genitals thrown into the sea. She was said to have emerged from the sea at Paphos in Cyprus or at the island of Cythera. She was the wife of Hephaestus but was unfaithful to him and had an affair with Ares. She is portrayed by later writers as the mother of Eros. Paris' choice of her as the most beautiful of the three goddesses at the wedding feast of Peleus and Thetis (the others were Hera and Athena) caused the *Trojan War. She was revered throughout Greece as the personification of spiritual love but she also embodied sensual lust.

Apia 13 48S 171 45W The capital and chief port of Western Samoa, in N Upolu on the S Pacific Ocean. The head of state's residence was formerly the home of Robert Louis Stevenson. Copra, bananas, and cocoa are exported. Population (1976 est): 30,000.

APIS *The sacred bull of Memphis was associated with the solar cult and was often depicted with its emblem, the sun disc, between its horns.*

Apis The Egyptian bull god. Originally a minor fertility god, he became associated with *Ptah and later *Osiris, at which point he became known as Serapis. A bull sacred to him was kept until another with appropriate markings was found; it was then ritually drowned in the Nile and its body mummified in the Serapeum vault at Saqqarah.

apocalypse (Greek: revelation) In the New Testament, the Revelation of St John the Divine. The term is also used of various noncanonical writings, such as the *Book of Enoch*, and of parts of the Old Testament books of *Isaiah*, *Ezekiel*, and *Daniel*. These are all examples of "apocalyptic literature." Full of symbolism and imagery, they describe visions of a great new era that will suddenly supersede the present age of suffering.

Apocrypha (Greek: hidden things) Twelve books taken over by the early Christian Church from the Greek version of the Old Testament but not forming part of the Hebrew Bible. They originated in the Hellenistic Judaism of Alexandria but were not accepted as canonical by orthodox Jews and were treated in various ways in Christian Bibles. In the *Vulgate, most of them are printed with the Old Testament but they are omitted or printed as a separate section in Protestant versions of the Bible. They are: I Esdras, Tobit, Judith, the Rest of Esther, the Wisdom of Solomon, Ecclesiasticus, Baruch with the Epistle of Jeremy, the Song of the Three Holy Children, the History of Susanna, Bel and the Dragon, the Prayer of Manasses, and I and II Maccabees.

apogee The point in the orbit of the moon or of an artificial satellite around the earth at which the body is furthest from the earth. *Compare* perigee.

Apollinaire, Guillaume (Wilhelm de Kostrowitzky; 1880–1918) French poet. Born in Italy, he settled in Paris in 1900. A champion of *cubism and other avant-garde movements, he blended lyricism with experiment in his poetry, first collected in *Alcools* (1913). While recovering from a head wound sustained in World War I, he wrote a surrealist play, *Les Mamelles de Tirésias* (1917), and a modernist manifesto, *L'Esprit nouveau et les poètes*. The poems in *Calligrammes* (1918) included daring typographical experiments. He died in the 1918 flu epidemic.

Apollo A Greek god of many aspects, symbol of light, of reason, and of male beauty. He is also associated with medicine, prophecy, music and poetry, the care of animals and crops, morality, and the maintenance of society. He and his sister *Artemis were the children of *Zeus by *Leda. He established his oracle at Delphi after killing Python, its dragon guardian.

craft	astronauts	launch date	comments
Apollo 7	W. Schirra W. Cunningham D. Eisele	October 11, 1968	first manned flight of Apollo spacecraft
Apollo 8	F. Borman J. Lovell W. Anders	December 21, 1968	first manned flight around moon
Apollo 9	J. McDivitt D. Scott R. Schweickart	March 3, 1969	complete Apollo craft tested in earth orbit
Apollo 10	T. Stafford J. Young E. Cernan	May 18, 1969	rehearsal of moon landing
Apollo 11	N. Armstrong E. Aldrin M. Collins	July 16, 1969	first manned moon landing July 20
Apollo 12	C. Conrad A. Bean R. Gordon	November 14, 1969	second moon landing
Apollo 13	J. Lovell F. Haise J. Swigert	April 11, 1970	mission aborted after in-flight explosion in service module
Apollo 14	A. Shepard E. Mitchell S. Roosa	January 31, 1971	third moon landing
Apollo 15	D. Scott J. Irwin A. Worden	July 26, 1971	fourth moon landing
Apollo 16	J. Young C. Duke T. Mattingly	April 16, 1972	fifth moon landing
Apollo 17	E. Cernan H. Schmitt R. Evans	December 7, 1972	last moon landing

APOLLO MOON PROGRAM

Apollo moon program The US program to land men on the moon by 1970, announced by President Kennedy in 1961. The program was directed by *NASA. The preliminary manned Mercury (1961–63) and Gemini (1965–66) projects provided valuable information and experience. The method selected for the landing was for a Saturn V rocket to launch the Apollo spacecraft toward the moon and, once the craft was in lunar orbit, for a capsule—the lunar module—to descend to the moon's surface carrying two astronauts. The third astronaut remained in the orbiting craft. At the end of the surface mission the lunar module's descent stage was left on the moon while its ascent stage was shot into lunar orbit and docked with the orbiting craft. Following the transfer of the two astronauts, the ascent stage was jettisoned and the spacecraft put in a flight path toward earth. The astronauts traveled to and from the moon in the command module, the rocket engines for in-flight maneuvers, fuel cells, etc., being carried in the separate service module. The latter was jettisoned prior to re-entering the earth's atmosphere; the command module finally splashed down in the ocean.

The first six Apollo missions were unmanned test flights, the next four being manned. Apollo 11 made the first manned lunar landing in July, 1969. Of the six ensuing missions, all, except Apollo 13, were highly successful, the scientific content of the information obtained increasing with each lunar landing.

Apollonius (2nd century AD) Greek grammarian, nicknamed Dyskolos (Bad-tempered). Of his 29 works on grammar, 4 survive. He introduced critical methods into grammar, seeking explanations rather than descriptions of sentence structure.

Apollonius of Perga (c. 261–c. 190 BC) Greek mathematician, who studied under *Archimedes. In a series of eight books, he described a family of curves known as *conic sections, comprising the circle, ellipse, parabola, and hyperbola.

Apollonius of Rhodes (3rd century BC) Greek epic poet. He was sometime head of the Library of Alexandria and was the chief rival of the poet *Callimachus. His four-volume *Argonautica*, in the style of *Homer, tells the story of the quest for the *Golden Fleece and is notable for its treatment of Medea's love for Jason, showing a sympathy to the woman's viewpoint unusual at this time. He also wrote epigrams, and commentaries on other Greek poets.

Apollonius of Tyana (1st century AD) Pythagorean philosopher and reputed miracle worker, from Tyana in Cappadocia. He was the subject of a biography by the Roman Flavius Philostratus in about 200 AD, possibly commissioned as anti-Christian propaganda by the empress Julia Domna.

apologetics In Christianity, the defense of the faith by theologians using intellectual and philosophical arguments. The name apologists refers especially to 2nd-century writers, such as *Justin Martyr and *Tertullian, who argued for Christianity against paganism. Later apologists defended orthodox Christian doctrines against heretical ones. In the 20th century one of the main apologetic tasks has been to explain how orthodox Christian belief is still reasonable in a scientific age.

apomixis The formation and development of an embryo without the fusion of male and female sex cells. This can occur in both plants and animals. The embryo is usually formed from the unfertilized egg (see parthenogenesis). In certain cases apomixis is triggered by a male sex cell that enters the egg but does not fuse with it.

apoplexy. *See* stroke.

Apostles In the New Testament, the 12 men chosen by Jesus as his disciples who, after his death, were to spread his teaching throughout the Roman world. Originally they were: Andrew, Bartholomew (*or* Nathaniel), James son of Alphaeus, James son of Zebedee, John, Jude (*or* Thaddeus), Judas Iscariot, Matthew (*or* Levi), Philip, Simon Peter, Simon the Zealot, and Thomas. After his suicide Judas Iscariot was replaced by Matthias. St Paul is also included among the Apostles because of his claim to having seen Jesus after the resurrection. *See also* Acts of the Apostles.

Apostles' Creed A Christian profession of faith in three sections concerning God the Father, Jesus Christ, and the Holy Spirit. Widely used in the Western Churches, it is of uncertain date but its present title first occurs in a letter of St Ambrose of about 390 AD.

Apostolic Constitutions A collection of Christian ecclesiastical administrative regulations and instructions for worship. Although its full title is "Ordinances of the Holy Apostles through Clement," and it ends with the 85 "Apostolic Canons," it probably originated in late 4th-century Syria and not from the Apostles. Its eight books contain much that is derived from the 3rd-century *Didascalia Apostolorum* and the 2nd-century *Didache*, which are significant sources of information about the early Church.

apostolic succession A Christian doctrine held by the Roman Catholic and Orthodox Churches and by some Anglicans. Its upholders claim that the Apostles appointed the first bishops and that there is thus a continuous line of succession from the Apostles to the present ministries of these Churches along which the power and authority given by Christ to the former have passed to the latter.

Appalachian Mountains A mountain range that extends NE–SW from the Mohawk River to Alabama, separating the Mississippi-Missouri lowlands from the Atlantic coastal plain. It consists of a series of mountain ranges and plateaus, including the *Allegheny Mountains, the *Catskill Mountains, and the White Mountains of New Hampshire. Its highest point is Mount Mitchell, at 6684 ft (2038 m). Coalmining is important, providing anthracite and bitumen; iron ore is also extracted. Poor communications and lack of employment have contributed to the establishment of a regional assistance program within the area. It also contains the **Appalachian Trail**, the longest continuous footpath in the world.

Appaloosa An American breed of spotted riding horse with a wispy mane and tail. The white Appaloosa is completely white with dark spots over the whole body but other types may be of any color as long as the hindquarters are white with spots of the color of the rest of the coat. Height: 14½–15⅓ hands (1.47–1.60 m).

appeal In law, the review of a court decision by a higher court, usually at the request of one of the parties to the case. The decisions of some administrative or professional bodies may also be appealed against in the courts. Appeals in *common law systems are usually based on alleged errors of law in the original trial, but may sometimes also be based on errors of fact. *See also* courts of law.

appeasement The policy implemented by the British prime minister, Neville *Chamberlain, of giving way to the demands of Hitler and Mussolini in the hope of maintaining peace. It culminated in the *Munich Agreement (1938) and was finally shown to be futile in March, 1939, when Hitler seized Czechoslovakia.

appendicitis Inflammation of the *appendix. Appendicitis is most common in childhood and adolescence. It usually starts with a vague pain around the navel that becomes localized in the right lower region of the abdomen. Diarrhea may also occur. Surgical removal to prevent rupture of the appendix and subsequent *peritonitis is usually required.

appendix (*or* vermiform appendix) A thin blind-ended tube, 3–4 in (7–10 cm) long, that opens from the end of the large intestine. It has no known function in man and is prone to infection (*see* appendicitis). In herbivorous animals (e.g. rabbits and cows) the appendix is large and plays an important part in the digestion of vegetable matter.

Appert, Nicolas (1750–1841) French inventor, who discovered that food can be preserved by boiling it in sealed containers. In 1812 he opened the world's first commercial canning factory.

Appian Way The road, built about 312 BC by the statesman Appius Claudius, between Rome and Capua. It was the first in the strategic network of Roman roads. A short stretch is still visible near Rome.

apple A deciduous tree or shrub of the genus *Malus* (about 35 species), native to N temperate regions and widely cultivated for their rounded fleshy □fruits (pomes). Several species have been cultivated, especially *M. pumila* of W Asia, with the development of numerous varieties of dessert, cooking, and *cider apples. Shoots of the required variety are grafted onto selected rootstocks. Some varieties are ornamental. Apples are also used for soft drinks and as a source of pectin. Family: *Rosaceae. See also* crab apple.

Appleseed, Johnny (John Chapman; 1774–1845) US nurseryman and folk hero. He acquired the name of Johnny Appleseed and became a legend in his own time by walking throughout the Midwest, planting, selling, or giving away apple seeds to the settlers. His eccentricity and bizarre appearance and his pious gentleness with people and animals contributed to the myth.

Appleton layer. *See* ionosphere.

Appomattox 37 21N 78 51W A town in central Virginia. The Confederate leader, Robert E. Lee, surrendered here to Ulysses Grant on April 9, 1865, effectively ending the US Civil War.

Appomattox River A river rising near Appomattox in central Virginia and flowing E to its junction with the James River at Hopewell. Length: 137 mi (221 km).

apricot A tree, *Prunus armenica*, native to China and widely grown in warm temperate countries, especially Spain, for its fruits. It is 20–30 ft (6–9 m) tall and has white five-petaled flowers and toothed heart-shaped leaves. The hairy-skinned orange-yellow fruits have sweet flesh and smooth stones. Family: *Rosaceae*.

April Fourth month of the year. Derivations of the name vary; it may be from *aperire* (Latin: to open), *aper* (Latin: wild boar), *aphros* (Greek: Aphrodite), or *áparas* (Vedic: following). It has 30 days. The zodiac signs for April are Aries and Taurus; the flowers are sweet pea and daisy, and the birthstone is the diamond.

April Theses The *Bolshevik party program devised by *Lenin during the *Russian Revolution (1917). Its demands included the cessation of Bolshevik support for the Provisional Government, Russia's withdrawal from World War I, and the redistribution of land among the peasants.

a priori knowledge Any kind of knowledge that is in no way derived from sense exerience, observation, or experiment. Many philosophers therefore hold that a priori knowledge is impossible. However, those attracted to *intuitionism have defended its possibility, especially with regard to theological problems. Kant insisted on the reality of a priori knowledge in the form of the necessary conditions of our having any experience at all, e.g. the notions of causality, space, and time.

apse A semicircular or polygonal eastern end of a church, characteristic of the *basilica and *romanesque and *Norman architecture. Seats for the clergy ran around the apse walls behind the centrally placed altar.

Apuleius, Lucius (2nd century AD) Roman writer and rhetorician. Educated at Carthage and Athens, he traveled in the East before returning to Africa to marry Pudentilla, a rich widow. His *Apologia* is his defense against a charge that he had won her by magic. *The Golden Ass*, the only surviving complete Latin novel, describes the misadventures of one Lucius, who is accidentally turned into an ass; he is finally restored to human form by Isis.

Apulia (*or* Puglia) A region in SE Italy, on the Adriatic Sea. It consists of lowlands in the N and S (the "heel" of Italy) and a hilly central area. Wheat is the main agricultural crop; tobacco, vegetables, olives, figs, vines, and almonds are also produced. Manufacturing industry is mainly related to agriculture although modern industries are being developed, particularly at Taranto. Area: 7470 sq mi (19,347 sq km). Population (1980 est): 3,943,333. Capital: Bari.

Aqaba 29 32N 35 00E A port in Jordan, on the **Gulf of Aqaba**, a narrow inlet at the NE end of the Red Sea. Aqaba was the Roman stronghold of Aelana. Being Jordan's only port, it has been considerably expanded, despite difficult navigation and an exposed site, to handle the export of phosphates. Population (1964 est): 10,000.

aquamarine A pale blue or green variety of *beryl. Many fine specimens of this gemstone come from Brazil, Madagascar, and California.

aqua regia A fuming yellow corrosive mixture of one part *nitric acid to three or four parts *hydrochloric acid. It dissolves all metals, even gold, and is used in *metallurgy.

aquarium A receptacle containing fresh or salt water for maintaining aquatic plants or animals (particularly fish) or a building in which such receptacles are kept or displayed. To duplicate natural conditions, modifications including the use of a water heater (for tropical species), aerator, and filter may be necessary. The first public aquarium was opened at the London Zoo in Regent's Park, London, in 1853.

Aquarius (Latin: Water Bearer) A large constellation in the S sky, lying on the *zodiac between Pisces and Capricornus.

aquatint An etching technique that produces a tonal effect similar to that of wash drawing. A satisfactory method was invented in the 1760s by a Frenchman, Jean Baptiste Le Prince (1733–81). Sharply defined areas of tone are employed, usually in conjunction with etched lines. A printing plate is sprinkled with powdered asphaltum or resin, which is then fixed to the plate by heating. Stopping-out varnish is used to mask different areas as the plate is immersed for varying lengths of time in an acid bath. *Goya, *Picasso, and *Miró have used the technique with outstanding effect.

aquavit A *spirit distilled from grains and flavored with caraway seeds. It is best served ice cold. Aquavit is drunk predominantly in Scandinavia.

Aquaviva, Claudio (1543–1615) Italian churchman, the fifth general of the Society of Jesus, elected in 1581. The son of a nobleman, he saw Jesuit numbers increase from 5000 to 13 000 during his office and laid down definitive educational guidelines for the order in *Ratio studiorum* (1599).

AQUEDUCT *The Pont du Gard built by the Romans in 19* BC *across the River Gard in Provence (France).*

aqueduct A narrow bridge, channel, or conduit designed to enable water to flow at a steady rate over an irregular natural terrain, such as a valley. Aqueducts were built by the Greeks, but the technique was developed to its highest level of sophistication by the Romans. Impressive Roman examples still survive at Nîmes, Segovia, and Rome. Much the same principles are still used in modern irrigation systems throughout the world.

Aquila (Latin: eagle) An equatorial constellation lying in the Milky Way near Cygnus. The brightest star is *Altair.

Aquilegia A genus of perennial herbaceous plants (100 species) of temperate regions, commonly known as columbines. Their showy flowers have petals with long honey-secreting spurs. A favorite garden flower, aquilegias have been cultivated since the 16th century. Many modern garden hybrids, which have large long-spurred flowers, are derived from the European columbine (*A. vulgaris*), 16–40 in (40–100 cm) high with purple to white flowers. Family: *Ranunculaceae*.

Aquilèia 45 47N 13 22E A town in N Italy, at the head of the Adriatic Sea. Founded by the Romans in 181 BC, it was of great strategic and military importance but failed to regain its former prominence following its destruction by Attila in 452 AD. Population (1971): 3041.

Aquinas, St Thomas (c. 1225–74) Italian Dominican theologian, scholastic philosopher, and Doctor of the Church, known as *Doctor Angelicus*. Born near Naples, the son of Count Landulf of Aquino, he was educated at the Benedictine school at Monte Cassino and at the University of Naples. Joining the Dominican Order in 1244 in spite of parental opposition, he became a pupil of *Albertus Magnus in Paris (1245) and followed him to Cologne in 1248. He returned to Paris as a lecturer in 1252, becoming a leading defender of the Dominicans against their critics at the University of Paris. He was a lecturer and theological adviser to the papal Curia between 1259 and 1269 and then taught at Paris until 1272, when he was appointed a professor at Naples. He died at Fossanova on his way to the Council of Lyons and was canonized in 1323. His prolific writings include commentaries on the Scriptures, on Aristotle and other philosophers, and academic disputations. His two most influential works are the *Summa contra gentiles* (1259–64), written for the use of missionaries, and the uncompleted *Summa theologica* (1266–73), the first systematic work on Latin theology. In opposition to the Averroists (*see* Averroes) and Augustinians he attempted to reconcile Christian faith and human reason. His arguments to prove the existence of God have been very influential and the Roman Catholic Church recognizes him as one of its most important theologians. Feast day: March 7.

Aquitaine (Latin name: Aquitania) A planning region in SW France, bordering on the Bay of Biscay. Formerly an administrative region in Roman Gaul, it extended from the Pyrenees N to the River Loire. It became an independent duchy under the Merovingians (7th century). The marriages of Eleanor of Aquitaine to Louis VII of France and then to Henry II of England resulted in rival French-English claims to the territory (*see* Hundred Years' War). Area: 15,984 sq mi (41,408 sq km). Population (1981 est): 2,584,400.

arabesque A type of decorative design employing intricate geometrical patterns on a flat surface. The term (meaning "Arabian") was first used in England in the mid-17th century to describe panels of scrollwork ornamentation that were thought to resemble the Arab style. Historically, however, arabesque decoration is Greco-Roman in origin.

Arab horse An ancient breed of horse originally bred by the Bedouins in Arabia. It is usually gray, chestnut, or bay with a long silky mane and tail, a wedge-shaped head, and an arched neck. The Arab is prized as a riding horse because of its speed, hardiness, and docile temperament. Height: 14–15 hands (1.42–1.52 m).

Arabia A peninsula in the Middle East, forming the SW tip of Asia and bordered by the Red Sea, the Gulf of Aden, the Gulf of Oman, and the Persian Gulf. It consists of Saudi Arabia, North and South Yemen, Oman, the United Arab Emirates, Qatar, Bahrain, and Kuwait. Mountains in the W (most fertile in the S) slope downward to steppe and desert in the E. Agriculture is still the main occupation, despite flourishing modern oil industries. *History*: as remains of irrigation systems show, S Arabia was the site of technologically advanced ancient civilizations. Arabia was often conquered in part, but its total conquest was long prevented by its deserts. It was conquered briefly by the Persians in 575 AD and later unified from Mecca by Islam in the 7th century, when the previously warring Arab tribes turned their attention to the conquest of N Africa, SW Asia, and S Europe. Arabia quickly became disunited again, however. From the 16th century until World War I the Ottoman Turks held nominal control over much of the peninsula, challenged chiefly by the *Wahhabiyah, a Muslim sect that was led by the Saud family, which conquered Arabia (except for the SW) and finally established Saudi Arabia (1932). From the mid-19th century until the late 1960s the UK was the chief foreign presence.

Arabian Desert 1. A desert chiefly in Saudi Arabia, covering most of *Arabia. Area: about 887,844 sq mi (2,300,000 sq km) 2. A desert in E Egypt between the River Nile and the Red Sea.

Arabian Sea A section of the NW Indian Ocean between Arabia and India. Connected to the Mediterranean Sea by the Red Sea and the Suez Canal, it forms a major shipping route.

Arabic A member of the *Semitic group of languages. It is written from right to left. Arabic is the mother-tongue of some 110 million people inhabiting SW Asia (the Middle East) and the countries of N Africa. Arabic can be roughly classified into three parts: (a) Classical Arabic, the language of the *Koran and the great Arab writers and poets; (b) Modern Literary, or Standard, Arabic, the language of the press and broadcasting; and (c) the colloquial dialects (vernaculars), which differ in a greater or lesser degree from country to country. Categories (a) and (b) are known as "Written Arabic," the vernaculars are almost entirely spoken forms.

Arabic literature The literature of the Arabic-speaking peoples, the majority of whom live in N Africa and the Middle East. Most Arabic writing is scholarly, consisting of works on religion, philosophy, grammar, history, translations from the Greek, etc. Literature strictly speaking may be divided into two periods, the classical (6th–16th centuries) and the modern literary revival in the Middle East, which started in the 19th century and reflected a heavy indebtedness to the West. The earliest example of classical literature was a pre-Islamic poetic form, the *qasidah* (6th century), which continued to dominate Arabic verse for generations. An ode of 60 to 100 lines, it was written in praise of the poet himself, his tribe, or his patron. Its main interest for modern readers lies in the dramatic descriptions of early Bedouin desert life; the most important collection is the *Mu'allaqat* (8th century). During the Umayyad period (661–750) there arose a second important poetic genre, the *ghazal*, a short love poem. The golden age of classical Arabic literature developed during the 'Abbasid period (750–1055) with the assimilation of many Greek and Roman authors and the growth of a cosmopolitan urban culture, of which *Abu Nuwas was the outstanding poet. The traditional verse continued to flourish, however, its most famous practitioner being al-*Mutanabbi, who brought a new rhetorical sophistication to the *qasidah*. Sufi mysticism influenced some Arabic writers in the 11th–12th centuries, but its main effect was on Persian and Turkish writers. Literary prose also developed during the 'Abbasid period; among the most influential writers were the essayist al-Jahiz (d. 869) and the critic and philologist Ibn Qutaybah (d. 899). Because of the authority of the Koran, Arabic was maintained as the language of religion and scholarship, but declined as a literary medium under the *Mamelukes (1250–1517) and in the Ottoman Empire (16th–19th centuries). Nationalist movements especially in Egypt and Syria beginning in the late 19th century largely account for the modern literary renaissance in these countries, where writers have adopted such western forms as the novel and drama.

Arabic numerals The number symbols 0, 1, 2, 3, 4, 5, 6, 7, 8, 9. They are believed to have originated in India and were introduced into Europe by the Arabs in about the 10th century AD. *Compare* Roman numerals.

Arab-Israeli Wars. *See* Israel, State of.

Arab League An organization formed to promote unity and cooperation among Arab nations. Formed in Cairo in 1945, it consisted of those Arab countries that were then independent; others joined on attaining independence. The current members are Algeria, Bahrein, Democratic Republic of Yemen, Djibouti, Egypt, Iraq, Jordan, Kuwait, Lebanon, Libya, Mauritania, Morocco, Oman, Qatar, Saudi Arabia, Somalia, Sudan, Syria, Tunisia, United Arab Emirates, and Yemen Arab republic. The League has had some success in the economic, scientific, and cultural fields, but in political affairs, unified action has been hindered by ideological conflicts between its moderate and radical members. In 1975 the Arab League recognized the *Palestine Liberation Organization as the official representative of the Palestinian people and admitted it to full membership in the League. Following the Egyptian-Israeli peace treaty in 1979, Egypt was temporarily expelled from the organization and the headquarters of the Arab League was transferred to Tunis.

arable farming The cultivation of plants for food, fibers, vegetable oils, etc., especially on a field scale. Fruit and vegetable production is usually considered as a specialized farming activity (*see* horticulture). The methods employed in arable farming depend on the crop being grown, the climate and soil type of the region, farming traditions, and the economic state of the farmer and his market. Arable farming is often carried out in conjunction with livestock farming, enabling the farmer to grow his own animal feeds and to make use of animal manures as *fertilizers. Grass is the chief feed for *ruminant livestock and a major arable crop. Special seed mixtures are sown to produce either permanent pasture or a temporary grass meadow lasting only a few years, often as part of a system of *crop rotation. Apart from grazing, grass is cut and conserved for winter food as either hay (dried grass) or *silage.

Cereal crops are a principal source of food for man and are important animal feed. The major cereals are wheat, barley, rice, and corn with oats, millet, sorghum, and rye cultivated to a lesser extent. Wheat may be sown either in autumn or spring, according to the variety, and is harvested in late summer when the grain is hard, yielding between 0.6 and 1.5 tons of grain per acre. Cereals are harvested using a *combine harvester and the grain is often dried to ensure safe storage.

Beans are grown as a major source of vegetable protein, the most important being soybeans, produced chiefly in China and the US. They are harvested mechanically using a specially adapted combine harvester that separates the beans from the rest of the crop. Harvesting root crops, such as potatoes and sugar beets, requires specialized machines that excavate the crop and remove soil. Turnips and rutabagas are root crops grown mainly for animal fodder. Crops grown for their oil content include sunflower, peanut, linseed, cottonseed, and rape; cotton, flax, and jute are important sources of textile fibers. Many other crops, including tea, coffee, and tobacco, are of major economic importance and each requires specialized husbandry techniques to give maximum yields. Modern scientific investigation of arable crops (*see* agronomy) and their requirements together with innovations in mechanization, fertilizers, pesticides, *irrigation, and plant breeding have resulted in dramatic increases in crop yields and productivity, bringing about a Green Revolution in western countries and, more recently, in developing countries.

Arabs A Semitic people originally inhabiting the Arabian peninsula. They are roughly divided into two cultural groups: the nomadic *Bedouin tribes and the settled communities of the towns and oases. Wealth from oil has recently led to industrialization and westernization in the towns, but Islam remains a strong conservative force in social customs, particularly in the restrictions it places upon women's role in society. The Arabs were known in antiquity to the Greeks, Romans, and Jews and are mentioned by name in the later Old Testament books. They appeared as a power in world history early in the 7th century AD, with the rise of Islam, and they carried their language (*see* Arabic), religion, and culture as far as Spain in the W and Indonesia in the E. In modern usage "Arab" designates Arabic-speaking peoples of SW Asia, Egypt, N Africa, and parts of sub-Saharan Africa, whether or not they are of Arab descent.

Aracajú 10 54S 37 07W A city and port in NE Brazil, the capital of Sergipe state near the mouth of the Rio Continguiba. It is a commercial and industrial center; the chief industries are sugar refining, cotton milling, and tanning. Its university was founded in 1967. Population (1975 est): 226,248.

Arachne In Greek mythology, a girl from Lydia who defeated Athena in a tapestry-weaving contest. The jealous goddess destroyed all Arachne's work; she attempted to hang herself, but Athena changed her into a spider.

arachnid An invertebrate animal belonging to an order (*Arachnida*; 65,000 species) of chiefly terrestrial *arthropods, including the *spiders, *scorpions, *harvestmen (daddy-longlegs), *ticks, and *mites. An arachnid's body is divided into two parts: a combined head and thorax (cephalothorax) and an abdomen. The cephalothorax bears four pairs of legs and two pairs of head appendages, one of which consists of strong pincer-like claws. Arachnids are mostly carnivorous, feeding on the body juices of insects and other small animals; many secrete poison from specialized glands to kill prey or enemies. Others are parasites, some of which are carriers of disease. Arachnids usually lay eggs, which hatch into immature adults.

Arad 46 10N 21 19E An industrial city in W Romania, on the Mureş River. It was Austro-Hungarian until 1919 and has a large Hungarian community. Population (1979 est): 172,669.

Arafat, Yasser (1929–) Palestinian leader. Committed to military confrontation with *Israel as a means of restoring the territory and rights of the Palestinians, Arafat was one of the founders of al-Fatah, also known as the Palestinian National Liberation Movement, which began guerrilla warfare and terrorism against Israel in the late 1950s. Arafat became the president in 1968 of the *Palestine Liberation Organization, which was recognized in 1974 by the *Arab League as the sole legitimate representative of the Palestinian people. Arafat's flamboyant style and personal charisma helped the PLO to survive expulsion from Jordan in 1970 and evacuation from Beirut in 1982.

Arafura Sea A shallow section of the W Pacific Ocean between Australia and New Guinea. It contains uncharted rocks, which make navigation dangerous.

Arago, (Dominique) François (Jean) (1786–1853) French astronomer and physicist, who was professor of physics at the École Polytechnique in Paris. He did important work in astronomy, electricity, magnetism, meteorology, and optics (particularly polarized light). He was an advocate of the wave theory of light and worked with *Fresnel to obtain experimental evidence to support it.

Aragon A region and medieval kingdom in NE Spain, of which Ramoir I (d. 1063) was the first king (1035–63). A series of conquests during the 11th and 12th centuries brought the Aragonese rule over much of N Spain. Union with Catalonia was secured by marriage in 1140. Later expansion gave the Aragonese Sicily (1282) and Sardinia (1320) and culminated in the conquest by *Alfonso the Magnanimous of the kingdom of Naples (1442). In 1469 *Ferdinand the Catholic, heir to the Aragonese throne, married *Isabella the Catholic of Castile and on his accession in 1479 the two kingdoms were united.

Aragon, Louis (1897–1982) French poet, novelist, and journalist. In 1919 he and André *Breton founded the surrealist journal *Littérature*; his first books of poetry, *Feu de joie* (1920) and *Le Mouvement perpétuel* (1925), and his novel, *Le Paysan de Paris* (1926), are vigorously surrealist. He committed himself to communism and turned to Marxist-oriented social realism, especially in novels, such as *Holy Week* (1958) and the series entitled *Le Monde réél* (1933–51). He was editor of the left-wing weekly *Les Lettres françaises*.

aragonite A white or grayish mineral consisting of calcium carbonate, usually with sharp orthorhombic crystals that are often twinned. With age, heat, or pressure aragonite changes into calcite and is therefore generally found in relatively young rocks. Many shells consist of aragonite.

Araguaia, Rio A river in central Brazil, rising in the Brazilian Highlands and flowing generally NE to join the Rio Tocantins. Length: over 1100 mi (1771 km).

Arakan A state in W Burma, extending along the Bay of Bengal and flanked by the Arakan Yoma, a mountain range rising over 1000 ft (3000 m). The principal economic activity is the cultivation of rice. The majority of the inhabitants are of Burmese descent but there is a large minority of Bengali Muslims in the N. *History*: a powerful kingdom in the 15th century, it was absorbed into Burma (1783) before passing to Britain (1826–1948). The activities of secessionist movements led to its change of status (from a division to a state) in 1975. Area: 14 191 sq mi (36,762 sq km). Population (1973): 1,710,506. Capital: Sittwe.

Arakcheev, Aleksei Andreevich, Count (1769–1834) Russian soldier and statesman. From 1796 to 1798 Arakcheev reorganized the Russian army but his brutality led to his dismissal. He was recalled by Alexander I in 1808 and became war minister. After Napoleon's defeat (1815) he served as minister of internal affairs, establishing many military-agricultural communities, in which Russia's army lived in times of peace. On the accession of Nicholas I in 1826 he resigned.

Aral Sea The fourth largest lake in the world, in the SW Soviet Union in the Kazakh and Uzbek SSRs. It receives the Amu Darya and Syr Darya Rivers and has no outlets. Its maximum depth varies by 10%. Area: about 25,477 sq mi (66,000 sq km).

Aramaic A western branch of the Semitic group of languages. Its 22-character alphabet is the ancestor of both Hebrew and Arabic alphabets. Aramaic became extensively used during the late Babylonian empire and was the official language of the Persian Empire under *Darius I. It replaced Hebrew as the language of the Jews from about the time of the Exile in 605 BC until after the rise of Islam.

Aran Islands (Irish name: Arainn) A group of islands in Galway Bay, off the W coast of the Republic of Ireland, comprising Inishmore (the largest), Inishmaan, and Inisheer. Their harsh environment was portrayed in J. M. Synge's *Riders to the Sea*. Area: 18 sq mi (46 sq km). Chief town: Kilronan.

Aranjuez 40 02N 3 37W A city in central Spain, in New Castile on the Tagus River. Its fine palace (1778) was used by the Spanish court until 1890. It is a tourist resort and market town. Population (1970): 29,548.

Arany, János (1817–82) Hungarian poet. Born into a poor peasant family, he became a teacher, editor, and notary. His poem *Toldi* (1847), the adventures of a peasant youth at the 14th-century Hungarian court, was acclaimed as a national epic; he added two sequels, the romantic *Toldi szerelme* (1848) and the comic *Toldi estége* (1854). His powerful but melancholy ballads are perhaps his finest works.

Arapaho Group of North American Indians, of the Algonkian language. They were found in the Red River Valley in N Minnesota. Migration to the plains split up the group; the Northern Arapaho lived in Wyoming and the Southern Arapaho were found in Colorado. The Atsina or Gros Ventre Indians were also part of the Arapaho group. Closely related to the *Cheyenne and *Blackfoot Indians, the Arapaho's main ceremony was the sun dance. Presently, the Northern Arapaho are found on the Wind River Reservation, Wyo., the Southern in Oklahoma; and the Atsina on Fort Belknap Reservation in Montana.

Ararat, Mount (Turkish name: Ağrı Daği) 39 44N 44 15E A mountain in E Turkey, near the Soviet and Iranian borders. It is volcanic in origin and isolated but for a secondary peak 7 mi (12 km) away. Traditionally, Noah's ark came to rest here after the flood (Genesis 8.4). Height: 16,946 ft (5165 m).

Araucanians Indians of central Chile, divided into three major groups, the Picunche, Mapuche, and Huilliche. They were farmers and herders of llamas, living in small autonomous hamlets of patrilineal kin. They could build in stone but lacked the elaborate culture of other Andean peoples, such as the *Inca. The Mapuche resisted Chilean rule until late in the 19th century. There are now about 200,000 living on reservations. The Araucanian language has been comparatively resistant to Spanish influence.

Araucaria A genus of coniferous trees (about 15 species), native to Australasia and South America (it is named for a district of Chile). They have whorled horizontal branches covered with scale leaves, and male and female flowers usually grow on separate trees. The genus includes the ornamental *monkey puzzle and several trees yielding useful timber, including the Norfolk Island pine (*A. heterophylla*); the hoop pine (*A. cunninghamii*)

mii) and the bunya bunya (*A. bidwillii*), both from E Australia; and the parana pine (*A. angustifolia*), of Brazil. Family: *Araucariaceae*.

Arawak Indians of the Greater Antilles and northern and western areas of the Amazon basin. Their languages are the most widespread of the South American Indian languages and include Goajiro in Colombia, Campa and Machiguenga in Peru, and Mojo and Bauré in Bolivia. They are sedentary farmers growing manioc and corn. Prior to the Spanish conquests they were divided into numerous hereditary chiefdoms. They were never a warlike people and in the Caribbean area *Carib tribes frequently raided Arawak groups and enslaved Arawak women. Their religion involved belief in personal guardian spirits. The tribal gods were the spirits of chiefs represented by a hierarchy of idols called zemis, which were housed in temples.

Arbil. *See* Irbil.

arbitration 1. A method of settling a commercial dispute in which each party presents his case to a disinterested third party (arbitrator). The disinterested third party is chosen by the disputing parties. The disputing parties agree beforehand to abide by the third party's decision. This method of settling disputes is widely used in commerce because it is quicker and cheaper than litigation. 2. An attempt to settle an industrial dispute by submitting the case to an arbitrator, such as a government conciliation service. In this case the award is usually accepted as morally binding on both sides, but usually it is an issue, such as wage rates, that cannot be settled by law.

arborvitae A coniferous tree of the genus *Thuja* (6 species), native to North America and E Asia. They have scalelike leaves, which densely cover the flattened stems, and small scaly cones, 0.4–0.7 in (1–1.8 cm) long. The Chinese arborvitae or cedar (*T. orientalis*), which grows to a height of 98 ft (30 m), is a popular ornamental tree; the giant arborvitae, or western red cedar (*T. plicata*), of W North America, grows to a height of 130 ft (40 m) and yields a valuable timber. Family: *Cupressaceae*.

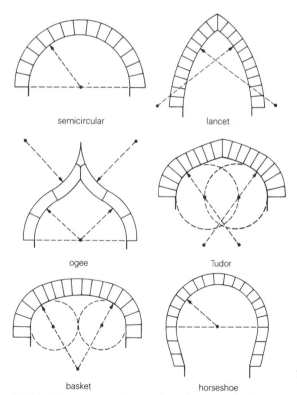

semicircular   lancet

ogee   Tudor

basket   horseshoe

ARCH *The semicircular arch characterized Roman, Romanesque, and Norman architecture; the lancet, ogee, Tudor, and basket arches were gothic and later medieval developments; the horseshoe arch is typical of Islamic architecture.*

Arbutus A genus of evergreen trees and shrubs (about 20 species) distributed in Central and North America and W Europe. The small white or pinkish flowers are borne in terminal clusters and the berries are fleshy and reddish. The leaves are tough, dark green, toothed, and shiny above. The strawberry tree (*A. unedo*) of SW Europe is widely grown as an ornamental, reaching a height of 30 ft (9 m). Family: *Ericaceae*.

Arcadia A mountainous region of ancient Greece, in the central Peloponnesus, that was identified in the literature of Greece, Rome, and the Renaissance (e.g. in Sidney's *Arcadia*) as an earthly paradise. It is a modern department.

Arc de Triomphe A ceremonial arch standing at the center of the Étoile at the top of the Champs Elysées in Paris. It was commissioned to celebrate the victories of *Napoleon I and built between 1806 and 1836 to the designs of Jean Chalgrin (1739–1811).

arch In architecture, a structure spanning a horizontal space. The development of the arch was one of the greatest Roman contributions to building technology. By using interlocking and mutually supporting pieces of stone it is possible to span greater distances than can be achieved with single megaliths; also arches can be employed to provide a more even distribution of pressure throughout the building. The basic forms of arch are the pointed, or gothic, arch, and the rounded, or classical, arch.

Archangel (Russian name: Arkhangelsk) 64 32N 40 40E A port in the NW Soviet Union, in the RSFSR on the Dvina River, 30 mi (50 km) from the White Sea. Founded in 1584, it was Russia's leading port until the early 18th century. The Soviet Union's largest timber-exporting port, it has timber-processing and shipbuilding industries and also supports a fishing fleet. Population (1981 est): 391,000.

archangels In Christian belief, supernatural beings ranked immediately above *angels in the celestial hierarchy. Michael is the only archangel mentioned in the New Testament (Jude); in Revelation 12 he is the leader of the angels who cast out the dragon from heaven. Gabriel, as the angel of the annunciation, is traditionally included among the archangels, as is Raphael, the helper of Tobias in the apocryphal Book of Tobit. Another archangel, Uriel, is named in II Esdras.

archbishop A chief bishop who has some jurisdiction over the other bishops in an ecclesiastical province, i.e. a group of dioceses, as well as having authority in his own diocese. Until the 8th or 9th century such men were called "metropolitans," a title still used by Orthodox Christians whose archbishops are of lower rank. Some Roman Catholic archbishops have no provincial authority, their titles being merely honorary. The Church of England has only the Archbishops of Canterbury and of York.

archegonium The reproductive organ producing the female cells (gametes) in ferns, mosses, algae, fungi, and some gymnosperms. It is flask-shaped, the swollen base containing the egg cell and the neck providing an entrance for the male gametes.

archeology The scientific study that is concerned with the recovery and interpretation of the material remains of man's past. Archeology may be supplemented by written records, where they exist, but its techniques are principally concerned with nonliterary evidence for man's social and cultural development. Modern archeology has numerous specialized branches—classical, industrial, underwater, etc. Before the 19th century, digging was carried out to plunder precious objects from ruins. Scientific excavation followed the realization that often more could be learned from the surroundings in which objects are discovered than from the objects themselves. Essential techniques include stratigraphy, based on the principle that in any sequence of deposits the uppermost is latest and the lowest earliest, and typology, the study of changes in forms (e.g. of pottery). New methods of dating constantly evolve: *radiometric dating, *paleomagnetism, *thermoluminescence, *varve dating, and *dendrochronology are all valuable with different types of material.

Archeopteryx A genus of extinct primitive birds, fossils of which date from the Jurassic period (160–120 million years ago). It had many reptilian features, such as numerous teeth, a long bony tail, and claws on the hand, but was fully feathered and is believed to be the ancestor of modern birds. *Archeopteryx* lived in dense forests, climbing trees using its claws and gliding down in search of food.

archer fish A small fish of the genus *Toxotes*, especially *T. jaculatrix*, which occurs in coastal and estuarine waters of SE Asia and Australia. Up to 7 in (18 cm) long, archer fish capture flying insects by firing a stream of water droplets through the mouth and are able to shoot down prey over distances of more than 40 in (1 m). Family: *Toxotidae*.

archery A sport in which generally a specified number of arrows are shot at a target over a prescribed distance. The modern bow developed from the medieval longbow, but the skill of shooting arrows from a bow dates back 30 millenniums. **Target archery** consists of shooting at a target of standard size marked with five or ten scoring zones. Different competitions require different permutations of distances and numbers of arrows. **Field archery**

consists of shooting at large animal figures with superimposed scoring rings. In **clout shooting** arrows are shot into the air to fall on a target marked on the ground, while in **flight shooting** the purpose is to achieve the maximum distance. Archery is an amateur sport, governed internationally by the Fédération internationale de Tir à l'Arc (founded 1931).

Arches National Park A national park in SE Utah. Established as a national monument in 1929 and as a national park in 1971, it features wind-eroded rock formations of giant arches. Area: 130 sq mi (336 sq km).

Archilochus (c. 680–c. 640 BC) Greek poet. Probably the bastard son of an aristocrat of Paros and a slave woman, he was forbidden to marry Neobule by her father Lycambes, who became the target of viciously satirical poems. Archilochus became a mercenary soldier and probably died in battle. His poems, only fragments of which survive, range from the lyrical to the biting, and are frequently colloquial in style.

Archimedes (c. 287–c. 212 BC) Greek mathematician and inventor, regarded as the greatest scientist of classical times. Archimedes was born in Syracuse, Sicily, and studied in Alexandria, afterward returning to Syracuse, where he remained for the rest of his life. He is best known for his discovery of *Archimedes' principle, supposedly in response to the King of Syracuse asking him to determine whether a gold crown had been adulterated with silver. Legend has it that he made his discovery while taking a bath and ran through the streets of Syracuse shouting "Eureka!" He is also credited with the invention of *Archimedes' screw, although the device was probably already known to the Egyptians. He was killed by a soldier during the Roman invasion of Syracuse.

Archimedes' principle The principle that when a body is partly or wholly immersed in a fluid its apparent loss of weight is equal to the weight of the liquid displaced. Named for *Archimedes.

Archimedes' screw A device for raising water, reputed to have been invented by *Archimedes. It consists of an inclined helical screw rotated about a central axis in a trough of water.

archipelago A group of islands within close proximity to each other. The term was formerly used for the sea in which the islands are scattered, originally being applied to the Aegean Sea.

Archipenko, Alexander (1887–1964) Russian-born sculptor and painter. From 1908 he worked in Paris, where he was associated with *cubism. He introduced the use of the hole as an elemental part of sculpture and created the first works of art combining sculpture and painting. His sculptures of moving figures, which were abstracted into geometrical shapes, declined in quality after his move to New York (1923).

architecture The art of designing and constructing buildings that are both functionally and aesthetically satisfying. Factors principally influencing an architect are: the use to which the building will be put; the materials obtainable; the resources available in money and labor; and contemporary artistic taste. The earliest civilizations built on a monumental scale for their gods or the deified dead (*see* pyramids; ziggurat). Secular architecture reflected the needs of local rulers for security, comfort, and—very important—display. The Greeks were the first to develop the concepts of proportion and harmony that still influence western architectural theory. Roman engineers greatly extended flexibility of design by their use of arches and domes. Medieval European architecture reached its zenith in the gothic *cathedral but the Renaissance brought a resurgence of interest in all types of building; the rediscovered principles of classical architecture dominated theory and practice until the *gothic revival at the beginning of the 19th century. In the 20th century technical advances in the use of prestressed concrete opened the way to modern architecture; while the necessities of engineering increasingly determine a building's appearance, the best modern architects demonstrate that architecture can still survive as an art form.

archons The supreme magistrates in most ancient Greek city states. At Athens there were nine archons, including an eponymous archon, who was the chief archon and gave his name to the year, a king-archon (responsible for religion), and a polemarch (responsible for military affairs). In origin the Athenian archons were a ruling aristocracy, which had replaced the earlier monarchy. After 487 BC they were chosen by lot and their authority declined, their role becoming chiefly judicial.

Archytas (early 4th century BC) Greek mathematician, from Tarentum (S Italy). Famous in antiquity as an innovator in many fields of mathematics, he distinguished between geometrical, arithmetical, and harmonic progressions, worked out the numerical relations between notes of different musical scales, and found a geometrical construction to double the cube.

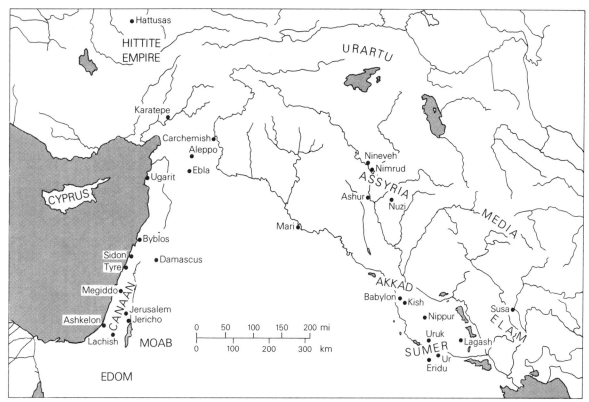

Mesopotamia and the Levant *Kingdoms and towns* (c. 2000–700 BC).

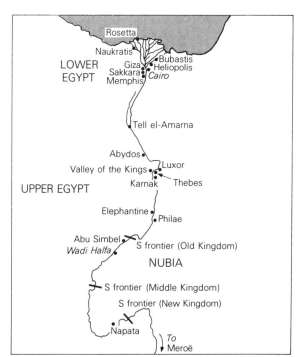

Ancient Egypt *Civilization grew up in the narrow fertile strip along the banks of the Nile* (c. 4500–343 BC).

Pre-Columbian Mesoamerica *The homelands of the principal ancient Mesoamerican peoples and the sites of their towns* (c. 1000 BC–1500 AD).

ARCHEOLOGY

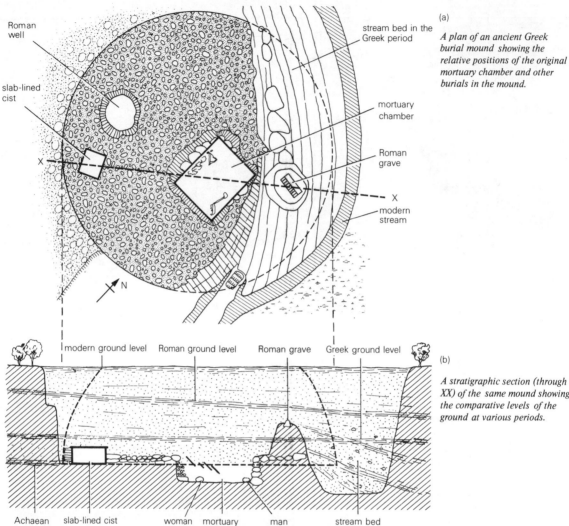

A plan of an ancient Greek burial mound showing the relative positions of the original mortuary chamber and other burials in the mound.

(b)

A stratigraphic section (through XX) of the same mound showing the comparative levels of the ground at various periods.

The discovery and subsequent restoration of an Early Bronze Age jar, which was excavated at Myrtos (Crete) in 1968 (see below).

the orders of classical architecture

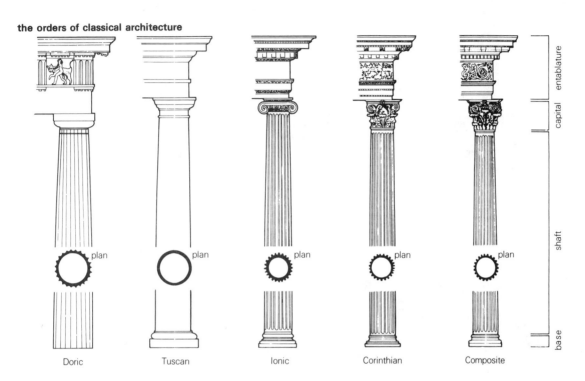

| Doric | Tuscan | Ionic | Corinthian | Composite |

plan · plan · plan · plan · plan

entablature · capital · shaft · base

some terms in classical architecture

pediment · acroterion · tympanum · cornice · cornice · frieze · architrave · capital · triglyph · metope · echinus · abacus · entablature · column · shaft · flutes · entasis (curvature of shaft) · drum · stylobate

some terms in gothic architecture

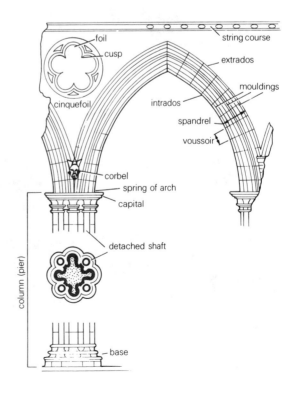

string course · foil · cusp · extrados · mouldings · cinquefoil · intrados · spandrel · voussoir · corbel · spring of arch · capital · detached shaft · column (pier) · base

Sagrada Familia (1903-26; Barcelona) *By Antonio Gaudi y Cornet.*

The Seagram Building (1956-58; New York) *By Mies van der Rohe and Philip Johnson (1906-   ).*

Guggenheim Museum (1956-59; New York) *By Frank Lloyd Wright.*

Chapel Notre-Dame-du-Haut (1950-55; Ronchamp) *By Le Corbusier.*

Sydney Opera House (1957-73) *By Jφern Utzon (1918-   ).*

Georges Pompidou Center (1972-77; Paris) *By Richard Rogers (1933–   ) and Renzo Piano (1937–   ).*

ARCHITECTURE *The early 20th century, just before World War I, saw the birth of the modern movement in architecture. The use of steel and the introduction of reinforced concrete (first used in France), together with the extensive use of glass, enabled new architectural concepts, such as the skyscraper, to be developed. Modern architecture has been characterized by a functional approach and a greater freedom in design.*

Arcimboldo, Giuseppe (1527–93) Mannerist painter, born in Milan. He moved to Prague in 1562, becoming painter and designer of court pageants to successive Habsburg emperors. Contemporaries praised his ingenious symbolism and he is remembered for his grotesque portraits, such as the head of a cook composed of pots and pans, fish and meat.

Arctic Circle The area around the North Pole enclosed by the parallel of latitude 66°32′N. It includes parts of Greenland, the Soviet Union, the US, Canada, and Scandinavia and extensive areas of ice-covered ocean, notably the Arctic Ocean. Within the Arctic Circle the sun remains below the level of the horizon for a period of time in winter and remains above it in summer; the length of time for which this occurs increases poleward. The population consists mainly of Eskimos, who live by hunting. *History*: during the 16th century exploration of the Arctic by the Dutch and English began in the search for a Northeast or Northwest Passage to the Far East. In 1725–42 the Russian Imperial Navy carried out exploration under the direction of Peter the Great and Russia became the most active of the Arctic explorers. In 1879 a US expedition under G. W. De Long (1844–81) became trapped in the ice while attempting to reach the North Pole and its ship was crushed. Wreckage found off the coast of Greenland having drifted across the Arctic Ocean suggested that a sea route through the ice was possible. The Norwegian Fridtjof *Nansen in the *Fram* drifted for nearly two years (1893–95) through the ice and proved that the North Pole was within an ice-covered sea. Robert E. *Peary was the first to reach the North Pole (1909). Since then extensive exploration has been carried out with mapping and geological and meteorological studies; the Soviet Union has been particularly active and, like the US, has established several drifting scientific stations.

Arctic fox A small fox, *Alopex lagopus*, found throughout tundra regions. It feeds on birds and small □mammals, especially lemmings and Arctic hares, and grows a dense woolly coat of fur in winter. There are two color varieties: the white fox, which has a white winter coat and a brown summer coat; and the blue fox, which is dark gray in summer and pale gray in winter. Arctic foxes have been farmed commercially for their fur.

Arctic Ocean The world's smallest ocean, almost completely enclosed by North America, Eurasia, and Greenland. Explored since the 17th century, it is covered by ice.

Arctic tern A slender red-billed *tern, *Sterna paradisaea*, up to 15 in (38 cm) long and having a white plumage with gray wings and a black crown. It breeds in coastal regions from N Britain to the Arctic and migrates to Antarctic seas in winter.

Arcturus A conspicuous *red giant in the constellation Boötes that is the brightest star in the N sky. It has an apparent magnitude of –0.05 and is 36 light years distant. The three stars in the handle of the *Plow curve in its direction.

Ardashir I Shah of Persia (224–41 AD), who founded the Sasanian dynasty. In 224 Ardashir defeated and killed the last Parthian ruler at the battle of Hormizdagan. He made *Zoroastrianism the state religion and is honored in Zoroastrian tradition.

Ardebil 38 15N 48 18E A city in NW Iran, close to the border with the Soviet Union and to the Caspian Sea. It has a carpet- and rug-making industry. Population (1976): 147,404.

Ardennes A chain of hills in W Europe. It extends through N Luxembourg, S Belgium, and NE France at an average height of about 1640 ft (500 m), forming the watershed between the Meuse and Moselle Rivers. Chiefly wooded, agriculture is limited to pastoralism. There was heavy fighting here in both World Wars.

are (a) A unit of area in the *metric system equal to 100 square meters. The *hectare is more frequently used than the are.

Areca. *See* betel.

Arendt, Hannah (1906–75) US political theorist and author; born in Germany. She fled Nazi Germany and came to the United States in 1941. After *The Origins of Totalitarianism* (1951) was published, she taught at several universities. Her works include *The Human Condition* (1958), *Eichmann in Jerusalem* (1963), *Crises of the Republic* (1972), and the unfinished 3-volume *The Life of the Mind* (1978).

Areopagus A hill in Athens, Greece, NW of the Acropolis and the name of the ancient Athenian court that met there. Originally an aristocratic council, the Areopagus became primarily a homicide court after about 462 BC, when its political authority was transferred to the democratic assembly.

Arequipa 16 25S 71 32W A city in S Peru. Originally an Inca city, it was refounded by the Spanish (1540). Notable buildings include the cathedral (1612) and two universities. It is an important commercial center and the wool-processing center of Peru. Population (1972): 302,316.

Ares The Greek god of war, identified by the Romans with *Mars. Son of Zeus and Hera, his popularity never rivaled that of the other Olympian gods. He loved *Aphrodite, by whom he had three offspring, Deimos, Phobos, and Harmonia.

Aretino, Pietro (1492–1556) Italian satirist. Son of a shoemaker, he claimed to be the bastard son of a nobleman. He lived in Rome (1517–27), patronized by Pope Leo X and becoming famous for his vicious satires and bawdy lyrics. He then settled in Venice, where he made a fortune by writing scurrilous satires on people or by being bribed not to do so. His letters, published in six volumes (1537–57), provide a vivid portrait both of Aretino and of his times. The earthy *Ragionamenti* (1534–36) portrayed the underworld of prostitutes. He also wrote five comedies.

Arezzo 43 28N 11 53E A city in central Italy, in Tuscany. Originally an Etruscan settlement, it has many fine medieval buildings. Petrarch was born here. A market town, it has various industries. Population (1971): 87,128.

argali A race of mountain-dwelling sheep, *Ovis ammon ammon*, of central Asia. Argalis are the largest Eurasian wild sheep, reaching a weight of 375 lb (170 kg) and having massive deeply ridged curved horns. They live in herds and graze at very high altitudes during the summer.

Argenteuil 48 52N 2 20E A city in France, a NW suburb of Paris on the Seine River. An industrial center, it developed around the 7th-century convent of which Héloïse was abbess. Population (1975): 103,141.

Argentina, Republic of The second largest country in South America, occupying almost all the land S of the Tropic of Capricorn and E of the Andes. It includes the E part of the island of Tierra del Fuego and has claims to the *Falkland Islands and their dependencies in the Antarctic. It consists chiefly of subtropical plains and forests (the Gran Chaco) in the N, the fertile temperate pampas in the center, the Andes in the W, and the semidesert Patagonian plateau in the S. The inhabitants are almost entirely European in origin, mainly Italian and Spanish, with a very small and dwindling Indian population. *Economy*: chiefly agricultural with stock rearing, especially cattle, having overwhelming importance. The main industries have traditionally been meat processing and packing but there has been recent growth in a variety of areas, including oil refining, plastics, textiles, and chemicals. Natural-gas deposits have been intensively explored and developed and Argentina is practically self-sufficient in oil, the most notable oilfields being around Comodoro Rivadavia. There are plans to increase the use of hydroelectric power and nuclear energy is also being developed. Main exports include meat and meat products (badly affected by the EEC ban on meat imports in 1974), wool, cereals, minerals, and metals. *History*: colonized by the Spanish from 1515 onward. During this period the native Indian inhabitants, who had previously had to defend themselves against the Incas, put up a fierce resistance but by the 19th century they had almost been wiped out. The country gained its independence in 1816, under José de San Martín, and a new constitution in 1853 marked the end of a period of civil war and unrest. Since the late 19th century Argentina has been ruled for most of the time by a series of military dictatorships. Most prominent among the rulers since World War II has been Lt Gen Juán *Perón, who came to power in 1946. Following the death (1952) of his very popular wife, Eva, his power was weakened and in 1955 he was overthrown in a military revolution. The Perónist movement, however, continued to attract strong popular support and in 1973, following the election of one of his supporters, Dr Hector Campóra, he returned to power but died the following year. He was succeeded by his second wife, Isabel, but as the economic situation continued to deteriorate and political violence and industrial unrest increased, many allegations of corruption were made against her government. In 1976 Lt Gen Jorge Rafael Videla came to power at the head of a three-man junta and strong measures were introduced to combat the violence and unrest and to steady the economy. Lt Gen Roberto Viola succeeded Videla as president in 1981 but was later removed from office by the military junta, led by Gen Leopoldo Galtieri, who subsequently became president in December, 1981. On April 2, 1982, Argentina launched an invasion of the Falkland Islands (which it calls the Islas Malvinas) but following armed conflict with a task force sent by the UK was forced to surrender on June 14, 1982. This defeat forced Galtieri's resignation and he was succeeded as president by Reynaldo Bignone. In 1983 the junta under Bignone was forced to call a popular election. After eight years of military rule, which was characterized by "death squads," left-wing terrorist reprisals, and a ruined economy, Raul Alfonsín was elected president in an unexpected victory over the Perónist Party candidate. Pledging to bring democratic government to Argentina and to the right-wing Perónist labor party, Alfonsín brought exiled Isabel Perón back into political life in an attempt to unify the country.

In the 1980s Argentina faced the worst economic crisis of its history. Staggering international debt that threatened to precipitate a world banking crisis brought demands for economic austerity measures from the International Monetary Fund, one of its chief lending agents. This, combined with an inflation rate over 600%, all-time high prices, and ongoing general strikes, placed the country in a severe economic and social position. The Falkland Islands sovereignty issue continued to be debated in the United Nations. Official language: Spanish. Official religion: Roman Catholic. Official currency: new peso of 100 centavos. Area: 1,072,515 sq mi (2,777,815 sq km). Population (1983 est): 29,627,000. Capital and main port: Buenos Aires.

argentite An important ore of silver, sometimes called silver glance. It is a sulfide of silver, found in association with other sulfide ores, such as lead, zinc, and copper.

argon (Ar) A noble gas that occurs in the atmosphere (0.94%). Although previously observed in the solar spectrum, it was first isolated in 1894 by Rayleigh and Ramsay, by the distillation of liquid air. Because it is chemically inert, it is used to fill fluorescent lamps and as an inert gas blanket for welding reactive metals. At no 18; at wt 39.948; mp −308.6°F (−189.2°C); bp −302.3°F (−185.7°C).

Argonauts In Greek mythology, the 50-man crew of *Jason's ship *Argo*, on the quest of the *Golden Fleece. Accounts of its composition vary, but all agree that it included the shipbuilder Argo, the tireless helmsman Tiphys, the keen-sighted Lynceus, *Heracles and his follower Hylas, and even *Orpheus and the Dioscuri, *Castor and Pollux. During the voyage the Argonauts encountered such perils as the *Sirens, the *Harpies, the Symplegades (moving rocks that crushed ships) and the bronze giant Talos.

Argonne A hilly forested area in NE France. It was the scene of heavy fighting during both World Wars.

Argos 37 38N 22 43E A town in the NE Peloponnese (S Greece). Belonging in Homeric times to a follower of *Agamemnon, Argos gave its name to the surrounding district (the Argolid). Eclipsed by nearby Sparta after the 6th century BC, Argos remained neutral or the ineffective ally of Athens during the 5th-century struggles between Sparta and Athens. Considerable remains of the city survive.

Århus (*or* Aarhus) 56 10N 10 13E A seaport in Denmark, in E Jutland. One of the oldest cities in Denmark, it has a gothic cathedral and a university (1928). Its industries include oil refining, machinery, and textiles. Population (1981 est): 245,565.

aria (Italian: air) A solo song with instrumental accompaniment, usually in an opera or oratorio. The name was originally also used of separate instrumental pieces but its meaning became restricted with the development of the three part *aria da capo* in the works of Monteverdi, Scarlatti, and Handel. Attacked as undramatic by reformers, such as Gluck and Wagner, the aria form is little used in modern opera.

Ariadne In Greek legend, the daughter of *Minos, King of Crete, and Pasiphaë. She helped *Theseus to kill the Minotaur and escape from its labyrinth. He abandoned her on the island of Naxos, where she was found by *Dionysus, who married her.

Ariane. *See* European Space Agency.

Arianism A Christian heresy started by *Arius, which held that the Son of God, Jesus Christ, was not truly divine. In 325 AD the Council of Nicaea banished the Arians, who included some influential bishops, and affirmed that the Father and the Son were coequal, coeternal, and "of one substance." Although the Arians were soon restored and a version of the heresy was officially accepted for a time, Arianism was finally defeated at the Council of Constantinople in 381 AD.

Arica 18 30S 70 20W An oasis city and port in N Chile, on the Pacific Ocean. A railroad line connects it with La Paz in Bolivia and it handles about half Bolivia's trade. Population (1976 est): 121,740.

Aries (Latin: Ram) A constellation in the N sky, lying on the *zodiac between Taurus and Pisces. The brightest star, Hamal, is of 2nd magnitude.

Arikara An Indian people of North America who lived along the Missouri River in what are now North and South Dakota. They were related to the *Pawnee in their language, which belongs to the Caddoan group, and in culture, which was of Plains Indian type. They were expert corn growers and their farming villages were often trade centers visited by the nomadic hunting tribes. They practiced the sun-dance cult involving self-torture. There are today approximately 700 living on the Fort Berthold Reservation.

Ariosto, Ludovico (1474–1533) Italian poet. He spent most of his life in the active service of the Este, the ducal family of Ferrara. He wrote several plays and much lyric verse but is best known for his long epic poem, *Orlando furioso* (1516). One of the greatest works of the Italian Renaissance, it recounts the adventures of the paladin Roland (*see* Charlemagne) and the wars between the Franks and Saracens. It was published in its final revised form in 1532. Its precursor was the *Orlando innamorato* (1483) of *Boiardo.

Aristaeus In Greek legend, the son of *Apollo and the nymph Cyrene. He was the patron of bee keepers, and was credited with the introduction of the vine and the olive. According to Virgil, he caused the death of *Eurydice.

Aristagoras (5th century BC) Tyrant of *Miletus (Asia Minor). Aristagoras persuaded the Greek cities of *Ionia to rebel against Persian rule (499) but despite Athenian assistance the rebellion failed (494). He died fighting in Thrace.

Aristarchus of Samos (c. 310–230 BC) Greek astronomer, who maintained that the earth rotates upon its axis and orbits the sun. He made the first attempts to estimate trigonometrically the size and distance from the earth of the sun and the moon.

Aristarchus of Samothrace (c. 217–145 BC) Greek critic and grammarian. He was head of the great Library of Alexandria from about 180 to 145, and later retired to Cyprus. He edited important editions of *Homer and wrote commentaries on *Aeschylus, *Sophocles, *Herodotus, and many other writers.

Aristides the Just (c. 520–c. 468 BC) Athenian statesman and noted commander in the *Greek-Persian Wars. Ostracized (c. 485) because of his opposition to Themistocles' naval policy, Aristides returned in 480 and offered his services against the Persians, commanding land forces at Salamis. In 477 he was chosen to assess the tribute required from each member of the *Delian League.

Aristippus (c. 435–c. 356 BC) Greek philosopher and a pupil of *Socrates. Aristippus founded the Cyrenaic school of *hedonism and was exclusively concerned with practical morality (*see* Cyrenaics). He equated the highest good with pleasure, virtue he equated with the rationally controlled pursuit of enjoyment.

Aristophanes (c. 450–c. 385 BC) Greek comic dramatist. He wrote about 40 plays, of which 11 survive: *The Acharnians* (425), *The Knights* (424), *The Clouds* (423), *The Wasps* (422), *The Peace* (421), *The Birds* (414), *Lysistrata* (411), *Thesmosphoriazusae* (410), *The Frogs* (405), *Women in Parliament* (393), and *Plutus* (388). His plots were satirical fantasies on contemporary topics, such as literature, *Socrates, social manners, and militaristic Athenian foreign policy; this led to his unsuccessful prosecution by the politician *Cleon.

Aristotelianism Tendencies in philosophical thought that originated with *Aristotle. Interpretations of his work appeared until the eclipse of ancient philosophy in the 6th century AD. Texts were preserved by Arab scholars, their work culminating in the 12th-century commentaries of *Averroes. *Aquinas in the 13th century made Aristotle the metaphysical basis of Christian theology but the Latin Averroists produced their own conflicting theories, holding, for instance, that a proposition can be philosophically true although theologically false. In the Renaissance the term Aristotelianism became synonymous with obscurantist opposition to new learning and science.

Aristotle (384–322 BC) Greek philosopher and scientist. His father was court physician in Macedonia. Aristotle joined *Plato's Academy at Athens (367–347) but, failing to become head of the Academy at Plato's death, he accepted the protection of Hermeias, ruler of Atarneus in Asia Minor, and married his patron's niece. About 343 *Philip of Macedon appointed Aristotle tutor to his son *Alexander, then aged 13. After Alexander's accession in 336, Aristotle founded, with generous assistance from Alexander, a research community complete with library and museum at Athens (the *Lyceum). There *Theophrastus studied botany and Aristoxenus (born c. 370) music, and Aristotle, among other projects, organized a comparative study of 158 constitutions of Greek states. When Alexander died in 323 BC, anti-Macedonian reaction at Athens forced Aristotle to withdraw to *Chalcis, where he died. Aristotle wrote over 400 books on every branch of learning, including logic, ethics, politics, metaphysics, biology, physics, psychology, poetry, and rhetoric. Ironically, those that survive (about one-quarter), edited by Andronicus of Rhodes about 40 BC, are apparently memoranda for his students' use, not intended for general publication. *See also* Aristotelianism.

arithmetic The branch of mathematics that deals with elementary theories of numbers, measurement, and computation. The fundamental operations of arithmetic are addition, subtraction, multiplication, and division. Addition and multiplication are assumed to obey the *associative law, the *commutative law, and the *distributive law. Other operations in arithmetic include extracting roots, raising a number to a power, and taking *logarithms. Arithmetic is also concerned with fractions and the various number systems, such as the *decimal system and the *binary system.

arithmetic progression (or arithmetic sequence)   A sequence of numbers in which successive terms have a constant difference, for example, 1, 4, 7, 10, 13 . . . .

Arius   (c. 250–336) Libyan theologian, who initiated the heresy *Arianism. He was a priest at Alexandria until excommunicated for his views in 321. However, by enlisting the support of such prominent churchmen as *Eusebius, Arius developed his cause into a major controversy. At the first Council of *Nicaea (325) he was condemned through the influence of *Athanasius. Recalled from exile (c. 334), he died a few days before he was to be received back into the Church.

Arizona   A state in the SW US. Utah lies to the N, New Mexico to the E, where the Colorado River forms the border; Mexico lies to the S and California and Nevada to the SW and NW. It falls into two natural regions: in the NE lies part of the Colorado Plateau, an area of dry plains and escarpments, and in the S and W is an area of desert basins and gentle valleys, drained by the Gila and Salt Rivers. The Colorado River flows through the Grand Canyon in the NW of the state. In such an arid region inadequate water supplies have long been a problem and a number of major irrigation projects have been built since the beginning of 20th century. Most of the population lives in urban settlements in the S and W. Manufacturing (electrical, communications, aeronautical, and aluminum products) is the major industry. The state produces over half of the US's copper as well as gold, silver, oil, and timber. Tourism is an important source of revenue. The main crops are cotton, vegetables, and citrus fruits; livestock is also important. It is traditionally a center for Indian folk arts and crafts, having the largest Indian population in the US; the main tribes are the Navajo, Hopi, and Apache. History: inhabited by Indians as early as 25,000 BC, the area was explored by the Spanish in the 16th century. Following the Mexican War, Arizona, then part of New Mexico, was ceded to the US (1848). Prospectors heading for California during the 1849 gold rush discovered copper in Arizona. Within 20 years the industry was flourishing; Arizona became known as the Copper State. Arizona was part of the Confederacy during the Civil War. When Confederate troops were routed, many of the settlers fled the state leaving an almost entirely Indian population. Legislation such as the Homestead Act, giving land to settlers with the requirement that they worked it, encouraged resettlement. It was in Tombstone, famous for its lawlessness, that Wyatt Earp participated in the notorious gunfight at the O.K. Corral. Intermittent warfare with the Apaches made ranching and cattle raising precarious. The defeat of Geronimo, the Apache chief, in 1886, freed Arizona from the Indian threat, and ranching prospered. When Arizona received statehood in 1912, it was still a rugged and undeveloped territory. The Roosevelt Dam and subsequent federal irrigation projects marked the beginnings of its transformation into a thriving state. A desert region, with low precipitation, Arizona has had continual problems with the threat of water shortage. The water problem took another form in 1983 when early melting snows led to overflowing dams and a water release that caused the most severe flooding of the Colorado River in the state's history. Area: 113,909 sq mi (295,023 sq km). Population (1980): 2,717,866. Capital Phoenix.

Arkansas   A S central state, lying W of the Mississippi River. Missouri lies to the N, Tennessee and Mississippi to the E, with the Mississippi River forming the E border; Louisiana lies to the S and Texas and Oklahoma to the W. It consists chiefly of the largely forested uplands of the N and W, descending to the Mississippi alluvial plain in the E and the West Gulf coastal plain in the S. The Arkansas River bisects the state from W to E. The state is no longer primarily agricultural although the Mississippi Plain provides rich fertile agricultural land; soybeans and rice have replaced cotton as the major crop. Oil production began in 1921; there are major lumbering, petroleum, and gas developments around Smackover and El Dorado and coal deposits in the Arkansas River Valley. The state produces 90% of US bauxite from an area to the N and SW of Little Rock. Manufacturing is chiefly of consumer goods. Arkansas remains, however, one of the poorest US states. History: explored by the Spanish and French in the 16th and 17th centuries, it formed part of the *Louisiana Purchase by the US in 1803. It became a state in 1836, seceded from the Union in 1861. The cotton-based economy suffered after the break-up of the plantation holdings, and a shift to sharecropping followed the Civil War. Arkansas farmers were subject to severe control by money and transportation interests. The Democratic Party, which has dominated the state since Reconstruction, gradually adopted legislative reforms that favored agriculture. However,

the subsistence farming, poverty, and poor education that characterized the farmers of the Ozark Mountains has remained little changed. Their unique culture has been romanticized in American song and literature. Racial issues have often been central in Arkansas' history. Orville Faubus, governor of Arkansas, brought worldwide attention to Little Rock in 1957, when he called in the National Guard to prevent integration of the public schools, thereby defying a federal court order to integrate. Federal troops were sent to Little Rock to enforce the integration order. In 1983, West Memphis voters elected the first black mayor of a major Arkansas city. Area: 153,104 sq mi (137,539 sq km). Population (1980): 2,285,513. Capital: Little Rock.

Arkansas River   A river in the S central US, rising in central Colorado and flowing E and SE to join the Mississippi in Arkansas. Length: 1450 mi (2335 km).

Arkhangelsk.   See Archangel.

Ark of the Covenant   In the Old Testament, the sacred chest of the Israelites that contained the tablets of the law (see Ten Commandments) and was symbolic of God's presence and the *covenant made between God and Israel. Made of acacia wood, inlaid, and covered with gold, it was eventually placed in the Temple of Jerusalem. It probably disappeared during the *Babylonian exile. The shrine in a synagogue where the encased scrolls of the *Torah are kept is also called an ark or "holy ark" (aron kodesh).

ark shell   A *bivalve mollusk belonging to a chiefly tropical family (Arcidae). Ark shells are boat-shaped and are attached to rocks by means of strong threads. The Noah's ark shell (Arca tetragona) occurs in rock crevices along the S coast of Britain and is about 1.8 in (4.5 cm) long.

Arkwright, Sir Richard   (1732–92) British inventor and industrialist, who invented a spinning frame powered by water, the so-called water frame (patented in 1769). Arkwright subsequently mechanized other spinning processes and his mills were vandalized by spinners put out of work by the incipient factory system.

Arlberg Pass   A mountain pass in W Austria, in the Alps, linking Vorarlberg with the Tirol by road. A railroad tunnel (completed 1884) cuts through the mountain for a distance of over 6 mi (10 km). Height: 5910 ft (1802 m).

Arles   43 41N 4 38E A town in SE France, in the Bouches-du-Rhône department on the Rhône delta. An important Roman settlement, it became the capital of Gaul in the 4th century AD and the capital of the kingdom of Arles (formed from the kingdoms of Burgundy and Provence) in the 10th century. It has many Roman remains, including an amphitheater. Other notable buildings include the 11th-century cathedral and the museum of arts and crafts founded by the poet Mistral. Several painters have lived and worked here, including Van Gogh and Gauguin. An agricultural market, it manufactures chemicals, machinery, and food products. Population (1975): 50,345.

Arlington National Cemetery   The largest cemetery in the US, comprising 420 acres (170 hectares). Since 1864 it has been the burial ground of Americans killed in action and of eminent public servants.

arm   In human anatomy, the upper limb, which extends from the shoulder to the wrist. The bone of the upper arm (the humerus) is connected by a ball-and-socket joint to the shoulder bone, permitting a wide range of movements. It forms a hinge joint at the elbow with the bones of the forearm (the ulna and radius), permitting movement in one plane only. The radius can be twisted across the ulna, enabling the palm of the hand to be turned upward.

Armada, Spanish   The fleet of 130 ships sent by Philip II of Spain in 1588 to invade England. After indecisive encounters with the English fleet the Armada anchored off Calais only to be dispersed by English fireships during the night of July 28. A major engagement off Gravelines followed, in which the Armada was defeated. It suffered further losses in storms as it escaped around Scotland and Ireland, arriving in Spain with 86 ships. The defeat was a major psychological blow to Spain, which had claimed divine authority for its crusade against Protestant England.

armadillo   A mammal belonging to the family Dasypodidae (12 species), widespread in open country in the southern US and South America. Armadillos have a covering of jointed bands or horny plates that enables them to roll themselves into a ball for protection. They have long-clawed toes for burrowing, simple peglike teeth, and feed on insects and other invertebrates. Armadillos range in size from the giant armadillo (Priodontes giganteus), about 48 in (120 cm) long, to the rare pink fairy armadillo (Chlamyphorus truncatus), 5 in (12 cm) long. Order: Edentata.

Armageddon.   See Megiddo.

Armagh An inland county in S Northern Ireland, bordering on the Republic of Ireland. It consists of lowlands in the N adjoining lough Neagh and low hills in the S. It is predominantly agricultural; produce includes potatoes, flax, and apples. There are few industries, the manufacture of linen having declined in importance. Area: 512 sq mi (1326 sq km). Population (1971 est): 133,969. County town: Armagh.

Armenian Church The Church founded by St Gregory the Illuminator (c. 240–332) about 300 AD. Armenia was the first nation to adopt Christianity as a state religion. Its Church is the second largest of the Eastern Christian Churches and has much in common with the others as regards dogma and liturgy, although it has also absorbed some Western influences. The head of the Church is the Patriarch of Etchmiadzin, called the Catholicos. There are Armenian churches in several parts of the world.

Armenians A people of NE Turkey and SW Russia speaking an Indo-European language. Approximately 1.5 million live in Turkey, Europe, and America and 4 million in the Armenian Soviet Socialist Republic, with smaller numbers in the Georgian and Azerbaidzhan SSRs. Their culture is ancient and highly developed, with a literature written in an alphabet derived from Greek and Syriac script. Their language is the only representative of a distinct branch of the Indo-European family. Herodotus claimed they were related to the ancient Phrygians. They call themselves Hay and their land Hayastan. They are mainly Monophysite Christians and belong to the *Armenian Church. During the 19th and 20th centuries they suffered massacres at the hands of the Ottoman Turks, their rulers since the 16th century, who feared the growing influence of nationalism among them.

Armenian Soviet Socialist Republic A constituent republic in the S Soviet Union. It is a densely populated and mountainous region, with no navigable rivers. Industry is developing rapidly and includes food processing, metallurgy, and chemicals. The rich mineral deposits include copper, lead, and zinc. The raising of livestock is the chief agricultural activity. *History*: the region formed the E part of the historic area inhabited by the *Armenians. It was acquired by Russia in 1828. The Russian province declared its independence in 1918 but it subsequently formed part of the Transcaucasian Soviet Federated Republic (*see* Transcaucasia). It became a separate republic in 1936. Area: 11,490 sq mi (29,800 sq km). Population (1981 est): 3,100,000. Capital: Yerevan.

Armentières 50 41N 2 53E A city in N France, in the Nord department on the Lys River. Its complete destruction in World War I was commemorated in the song "Mademoiselle from Armentières." Its manufactures include linen and hosiery. Population (1975): 27,473.

Arminius (c. 18 BC–17 AD) Leader of the Germanic tribe of the Cherusci, famous as a master of the surprise attack. He organized a revolt against the Romans (9 AD), destroying three Roman legions. Defeated (16 AD) by Germanicus, Arminius nevertheless thwarted the Roman conquest of Germany. He was killed by a pro-Roman German tribesman.

Arminius, Jacobus (1560–1609) Dutch Protestant theologian and reformer. A pupil of *Beza, he was a professor of theology at Leiden. Current Calvinist theology taught that God preordained some men to salvation and others to destruction. Arminius, however, emphasized God's grace and man's freedom to accept or reject salvation. This controversial doctrine later came to be known as Arminianism.

armor Defensive equipment used as a protection in warfare. Body armor (helmet, breastplate, greaves) was used in Bronze Age Greece. The Romans evolved heavier armor for both men and horses. In the early Middle Ages *chainmail was widely used but after about 1300 plate armor, often sumptuously decorated and encasing the whole body, was worn by knights on horseback. Gunpowder gradually rendered body armor obsolete, although in World War I metal helmets were revived as a protection from shrapnel.

Armor is also used to protect modern war vehicles and their occupants against projectiles or fragments. Armor plate includes hardened metal alloys cast in varying thicknesses and designed to be mounted with sloping surfaces to give protection against armor-piercing projectiles. Its considerable weight has prompted experiments in light alloys and plastics, using multiple skins to inhibit projectile penetration. Most recent is the "Chobham" armor, produced by the Military Vehicle and Engineering Establishment at Chobham, Surrey.

armored car A wheeled armored patrol vehicle, first used in combat in Libya (1912). Early types were commercial vehicles and converted trucks with inadequate protection, armament, and cross-country performance. They now have independent suspension, all-wheel drive, better armor, carry machine guns or a light gun, and may be amphibious. They use speed, concealment, and skillful tactical handling to perform their role.

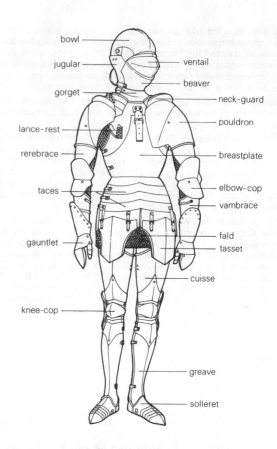

ARMOR *The skill of the European armorer reached its height in the late 15th and early 16th centuries when suits of plate armor were made to cover the entire body.*

Armory show The first exhibition of European avant-garde art organized in the US. It was held by a group of New York artists in the 69th regiment armory in New York in 1913. *Picasso, *Braque, *Matisse, and the entire cubist school were given great prominence.

Armstrong, Edwin Howard (1890–1954) US electrical engineer, who in 1939 introduced frequency *modulation as a method of broadcasting radio signals to eliminate much of the static associated with amplitude modulation. He had earlier invented the *superheterodyne receiver, which made radio reception much better and greatly increased the popularity of radio sets. A contentious and litigious man, he committed suicide.

LOUIS ARMSTRONG

Armstrong, Louis (1900–71) US jazz trumpeter and singer, known as "Satchmo." Born in New Orleans, he learned to play the cornet in his youth. His career took him to Chicago, where he made many recordings (some of them with Earl Hines), which earned him a worldwide reputation. He played with several large orchestras as a soloist but most frequently led his own group. His gravelly singing voice and superb trumpet playing were featured in many films. His infectious enthusiasm made many jazz converts and generated good will on several world tours, during some of which he represented the US for the government.

Armstrong, Neil Alden (1930–) US astronaut, the first man to walk on the moon. A Navy pilot during the Korean War, he began working for the National Aeronautics and Space Administration (NASA) (1955–71) and became an astronaut in 1962. He flew Gemini 7 (1966) and was commander of Apollo 11 (1969). As he stepped onto the moon he said "That's one small step for a man, one giant leap for mankind."

army An organized force of soldiers, which may be composed of full-time professionals, *militia reserves, conscripts, or mercenaries or of a combination of these. Armies exist for combat and to enhance a nation's prestige; they may also exert domestic political power and provide manpower for such activities as roadbuilding and land development.

Armies were raised throughout the ancient world, where mercenaries were usually relied upon to supplement a militia (as in the Greek city states) or a standing army (as in Rome). The medieval armies of Europe depended upon the mounted feudal knight, who was obliged to undertake short-term military service for his lord. As campaigns became longer, mercenaries were increasingly relied upon and with the introduction of firearms in the 15th century the foot soldier became important. Early modern standing armies reached their zenith with those of the 17th- and 18th-century absolute monarchs, especially Louis XIV of France and Frederick the Great of Prussia. By comparison the standing army maintained since 1661 in England was small, Cromwell's *New Model Army having left a lasting distrust of militarism. The 19th century saw a growing emphasis on the mass armies that resulted from *conscription—a measure widely adopted in Continental Europe. During World Wars I and II nations relied heavily on conscription and trained reserve troops to meet manpower needs. Postwar trends have included the combination of national armies into allied forces, such as those of NATO and the Warsaw Pact states, and the growing specialization of armies in response to technological advances.

army ant A New World *ant of the genus *Eciton* or related genera that does not build a permanent nest but has alternating nomadic and static phases synchronized to the egg-laying of the wingless queen. The wasplike males are large and winged and the soldier ants have large hooked jaws and hunt in vast "armies," killing other insects, young birds, reptiles, and small mammals. Subfamily: *Dorylinae. See also* driver ant.

Army, Department of US government military department within the Department of *Defense. Directed by the Secretary of Defense and the Secretary of the Army, it is charged with organizing, training, and equipping active duty and reserve forces. It also administers environmental improvement programs. Originally the Department of War (1789–1947), it became the Department of the Army by the passage of the *National Security Act of 1947.

Army, United States Ground forces of the military. Its programs ensure the readiness of land forces, both active duty and reserve troops. It also administers environmental protection, waterway navigation, flood and beach erosion control, and water resource development programs. The Army provides assistance at all levels in times of natural disaster. Established as the American Continental Army in 1775, the US Army has fought in all major conflicts since the War of 1812. The draft has been implemented from time to time, but since 1973 it has been a volunteer army with a 1980 stipulation that all men between 18 and 20 must register for the draft. The US Military Academy at West Point, administered by the Army, educates and trains men and women to be Army officers.

army worm The *caterpillar of a widely distributed moth, *Leucania unipunctata*. Army worms periodically swarm in large numbers, eating crops in their path and causing severe damage, especially in North America.

Arnauld, Antoine (1612–94) French theologian, philosopher, and logician; member of a prominent Jansenist family closely connected with the Abbey of Port-Royal. His attacks on the Jesuits, especially *De la fréquente communion* (1643), eventually forced him into exile in Brussels. He presented important objections to *Descartes' *Meditations* and, in collaboration with *Pascal and Pierre Nicole (1625–95), wrote the influential *La Logique ou l'art de penser* (1662), known as the *Port-Royal Logic*.

Arnhem 52 00N 5 53E A city in the E Netherlands, the capital of Gelderland province. In World War II a large airborne landing of British troops attempted to secure a bridgehead over the Rhine River here to facilitate an Allied invasion of Germany. The attempt failed with heavy casualties (September 1944). A railroad junction, its industries include engineering and pharmaceuticals. Population (1981 est): 128,717.

Arnhem Land A plateau in Australia, in N Northern Territory. It is primarily an Aboriginal reserve. Bauxite deposits are worked at Gove. Area: about 60,000 sq mi (150,000 sq km).

Arno River A river in central Italy. Rising in the Apennines, it flows mainly W through Florence and Pisa to the Ligurian Sea. It burst its banks in 1966 causing disastrous floods in Florence. Length: 150 mi (240 km).

*The conventional formula of benzene devised by F. A. Kekulé von Stradonitz (1829–96). With alternating double bonds it would be unsaturated and have properties similar to the *alkenes.*

In the benzene molecule the bonds are actually intermediate between single and double bonds. This is often represented as a resonance hybrid between the two conventional structures.

often represented as

The modern explanation of the bonding involves a delocalized orbital above and below the ring. The six valence electrons (one from each carbon atom) are free to move in this orbital. This explains the properties of benzene and the fact that all C-C bonds are equal.

AROMATIC COMPOUND

Arnold, Benedict (1741–1801) American general in the American Revolution. Brilliant but erratic, he served with distinction at Fort Ticonderoga and Quebec (1775), commanded a fleet on Lake Champlain (1776), and fought in Connecticut, the Mohawk Valley, and Saratoga (1777). In 1780 he treacherously planned to surrender the vital West Point position. The plot miscarried and he fled to the British for whom he led raids in Virginia and Connecticut. From 1781 he lived in England.

Arnold, Henry Harley ("Hap"; 1886–1950) US Air Force general. A West Point graduate (1907) who trained for flying under the *Wright brothers, he served in World War I as head of an air squadron and, afterwards, as department air service officer (1919–22). He commanded the US Army Air Forces (1942–46) and became the first five-star general in the Air Force (1949).

Arnold, Thomas (1795–1842) British educator. Appointed headmaster of Rugby (1828), Arnold reformed the school and instituted the form and prefectorial systems, which came to characterize English public schools. Arnold's piety was infectious, and Rugby became noted for "muscular Christianity." *Tom Brown's Schooldays* (see Hughes, Thomas) provides a eulogistic record of Arnold's achievement.

Arnold, Matthew (1822–88) British poet and critic, son of Thomas Arnold. He worked as a government inspector of schools from 1851 to 1886. His critical works include *Essays in Criticism* (1865; 1888) and *Culture and Anarchy* (1869), in which he asserted literary and cultural values as an antidote to the progressive materialism of Victorian society. His moral beliefs and doubts were given more personal expression in his poetry, which included "Dover Beach" (1867) and the narrative poems "The Scholar Gypsy" (1853) and "Sohrab and Rustum" (1853).

Arnold of Brescia (d. 1155) Italian religious reformer. He studied at Paris, perhaps under *Abelard, and became an Augustinian canon after returning to Italy, where he immediately condemned the worldliness prevalent in the Church. He argued, among other things, that the papacy should not have secular power. He was excommunicated in 1148 and was eventually captured by Emperor Frederick Barbarossa, condemned, and hanged at Rome.

aromatic compound A type of cyclic organic chemical compound that includes *benzene and its derivatives. On conventional theories of valence these compounds appear to be unsaturated (i.e. contain double bonds). However, benzene and similar compounds are much less reactive than the *alkenes, tending to undergo substitution reactions rather than addition reactions. The explanation for the stability of the benzene ring lies in a model in which the carbon atoms are joined by single bonds and the extra six valence electrons are free to move around the ring in a delocalized orbital. The phenomenon also occurs in some other compounds having an unsaturated ring, for example ferrocene ($Fe(C_5H_5)_2$). Aromatic compounds were originally distinguished from *aliphatic compounds because of the distinctive properties of benzene compounds, many of which have a fragrant odor.

Aroostook River A river rising in N central Maine and flowing NE into Canada to join the St John River in New Brunswick. A boundary dispute in 1839, which was settled by the Webster-Ashburton Treaty (1842) which set Maine's boundaries, was known as the Aroostook War. Length: 140 mi (226 km).

Aroostook War (1839) US-British border dispute in Maine and New Brunswick, Canada. When Maine became a state in 1820, the boundaries were never officially charted. The Aroostook River Valley area was claimed by both countries and skirmishes over the land resulted. A preliminary boundary agreement was effected in 1839 and fighting was averted, but it was not until 1842 that the Webster-Ashburton Treaty fixed the boundaries.

Arp, Jean (Hans) (1887–1966) French sculptor and poet. He was one of the founders of the *dada movement (1916) and later associated with the surrealist movement in Paris. Arp experimented with collages of torn colored papers, designed according to chance, and produced numerous painted wood reliefs. In about 1930 he began his abstract sculptures suggesting organic rather than geometric forms. His wife and occasional collaborator was the artist Sophie Tauber (1889–1943).

Árpád (died c. 907 AD) Magyar chieftain. In 875 Árpád led the Magyars from the Caucasus region into present-day Hungary in search of a new homeland after their defeat by the Pechenegs. He founded the first Hungarian royal dynasty, the Árpád, which ruled Hungary until 1301.

arquebus. See musket.

Arrabal, Fernando (1932–) Spanish playwright and novelist, who writes in French and lives in France. His plays, which have some of the characteristics of the *Theater of the Absurd, deal chiefly with themes of terror and violence; they include Le Cimitière des voitures (1958), Le Grand Cérémonial (1966), and And They Put Handcuffs on the Flowers (1973).

Arras 50 17N 2 46E A city in N France, the capital of the Pas-de-Calais department on the Scarpe River. The former capital of Artois, it passed to France in 1640. It had a famous medieval tapestry trade and the tapestry called "arras" is named for it. Robespierre was born here. The 18th-century cathedral and fine 16th-century town hall were badly damaged during World War I. An agricultural market, its industries include agricultural machinery and hosiery. Population (1975): 50,396.

Arrau, Claudio (1903–) Chilean pianist. He gave his first recital at the age of five and studied in Berlin under Martin Krause (1853–1918), a pupil of Liszt. He returned to Chile in 1940 to found a piano school. He is famous particularly for his interpretations of Beethoven and Brahms.

arrest The forcible detention of a person to compel obedience to the law. A person is taken into custody for the purpose of holding or detaining him to answer a criminal or civil charge. Arrest involves the authority to arrest, the assertion of that authority, and the restraint of that person to be arrested. In theory any citizen can make an arrest and is bound to do so if a felony or breach of the peace is committed in his presence, but in practice most valid arrests are made by the police or other law-enforcement officers, who are empowered to make arrests without warrants.

Arrhenius, Svante August (1859–1927) Swedish physicist and chemist, who became professor of the University of Stockholm in 1895. He won

the 1903 Nobel Prize for Chemistry for his theory of electrolytic dissociation. He later worked on the application of physical chemistry to living processes. His theory of universal life-diffusion involved "spores" emitted by habitable worlds and driven by light-pressure across space.

arrhythmia An abnormal rhythm of the heart beat. Sometimes this may produce symptoms, such as palpitation, breathlessness, and chest pain. Arrhythmias may be associated with heart disease but may occur without any obvious cause.

Arrian (Flavius Arrianus; 2nd century AD) Roman historian. As governor of *Cappadocia, he defeated a barbarian invasion (134 AD). He wrote several works on Asian history; his Anabasis is our most important source of information about *Alexander the Great.

arrow-poison frog A small generally brightly colored terrestrial frog belonging to a family (Dendrobatidae) occurring in Central and South American forests. Poisons produced by skin glands protect the frogs from predators and were used by Indians to poison arrow tips. In many species the young are incubated on the back of the male. Chief genera: Dendrobates, Phyllobates.

arrowroot A herbaceous perennial plant, Maranta arundinacea, native to Guyana but widely cultivated in the West Indies for the edible and very pure fine starch that is extracted from its underground fleshy tubers and used in cooking. The plant is about 5 ft (1.5 m) high and has short-stalked white flowers and broad-bladed leaves with long narrow sheaths. Several other species yield a similar starch. Family: Marantaceae.

Arrowsmith (1925) Novel about early 20th-century American medicine by Sinclair *Lewis; winner of a Pulitzer Prize (declined by Lewis) in 1926. It tells of Dr. Martin Arrowsmith and his experiences in rural and urban medicine and in research. It also shows his efforts to avoid the commercialism that had crept into American medicine.

Arrow War. See Opium Wars.

arrow worm A small planktonic invertebrate animal belonging to a phylum (Chaetognatha; 50 species) occurring chiefly in tropical seas. Arrow worms have an elongated arrow-shaped body divided into a head, trunk, and tail, with fins on the sides and tail. They feed on crustaceans, larvae, etc.

ars antiqua (Latin: old art) A style of European music of the 13th century. It was particularly associated with composers of the Parisian school, such as *Pérotin and Léonin (late 12th century), and characterized by the use of complex forms of *organum. It was succeeded by *ars nova.

arsenic (As) A brittle semimetal that occurs in nature in a variety of forms: native, as the sulfides realgar (As_2S_2) and orpiment (As_2S_3), as sulfarsenides, such as arsenopyrite (FeSAs), and as arsenates. The element occurs in several forms and was known to the ancients. Pure arsenic has important uses as a dopant in the semiconductor industry. Arsenic and its common compounds are extremely poisonous; tests for its presence need to be accurate and reliable. Compounds include the white oxide (As_2O_3), the gaseous hydride arsine (AsH_3), and arsenates, some of which are used as insecticides. At no 33; at wt 74.9216; mp 485°F 817°C) (28 atm); sublimes 372°F (613°C).

arsine (or hydrogen arsenide; AsH_3) A colorless poisonous gas that smells like garlic. It is an unstable compound and decomposes into *arsenic and hydrogen.

Arsinoe II (c. 316–270 BC) The daughter of *Ptolemy I Soter of Egypt. After two dynastic marriages she became the wife of and coruler with her brother *Ptolemy II Philadelphus (c. 276). Ambitious, forceful, and capable, she was an active participant in war, politics, and administration.

Arsinoe III (c. 235–c. 204 BC) The sister and wife of Ptolemy IV Philopator (reigned 221–203 BC) of Egypt. She participated energetically in the power politics surrounding her lethargic husband. News of her murder, suppressed until Ptolemy's death, caused rioting, which overthrew her former rivals.

ars nova (Latin: new art) A style of European music of the 14th century, which succeeded *ars antiqua. The name was taken from the title of a treatise by Philippe de Vitry (1291–1361), which set out new principles for the composition of *motets and for the notation of complex rhythms. Its greatest French exponents were *Machaut and *Dufay.

arson In common law, maliciously setting fire to something, originally someone else's house. This definition, however, has been broadened by state statutes and criminal codes. In several states, this crime is divided into arson in the first, second, and third degrees. The first degree includes the burning of an inhabited dwelling-house in the nighttime; the second degree, the burning (at night) of a building other than a dwelling-house, but so situated with reference to a dwelling house to endanger it; the third degree, the burning of any building or structure not the subject of arson in the first or second degree, or the burning of property with intent to defraud or prejudice an insurer.

Artaud, Antonin (1896–1948) French actor, poet, producer, and theoretician of the theater. In the 1920s he was involved with *surrealism and cofounded, with the poet and playwright Roger Vitrac (1899–1952), the Théâtre Alfred Jarry, where surrealist-inspired plays were produced that were forerunners of the *Theater of the Absurd. Impressed by the symbolism, gesture, and other nonlinguistic elements of oriental theater, he developed the theory of a *Theater of Cruelty in essays later collected in *Le Théâtre et son double* (1938).

Artaxerxes II (c. 436–358 BC) King of Persia (404–358). He defended his position against his brother *Cyrus the Younger, who was defeated and killed at *Cunaxa (401), and against a revolt of the provincial governors, the Satraps (366–358). Persia nevertheless declined under his rule.

Art Deco The style of design predominant in the decorative arts of the 1920s and 1930s. The name derives from the 1925 Exposition Internationale des Arts Décoratifs et Industriels Modernes in Paris. In deliberate contrast to *Art Nouveau, Art Deco was characterized by emphatic geometrical lines and shapes, vibrant color schemes, and the use of modern man-made substances, such as plastic. Influenced by the *Bauhaus, Art Deco included among its practitioners *Lalique and *Erté. It was debased by shoddy mass production, but interest in it rekindled late in the 1960s. □cinema.

Artemis In Greek mythology, the daughter of Zeus and Leto and twin sister of Apollo. Settled in *Arcadia, she and her band of Oceanids and nymphs spent their time hunting. Love was banned, and Artemis rigorously punished all transgressors. *Actaeon was killed for watching her bathe and *Orion for touching her. Despite this severity, her help was invoked during childbirth, and she was protectress of both animal and human young. Ephesus was the most famous center of her worship. She was associated with the moon and identified by the Romans with *Diana. *Compare* Hecate.

Artemis, Temple of One of the Seven Wonders of the World, built at *Ephesus in 356 BC. The deity worshiped here was the many-breasted fertility goddess called Diana of the Ephesians in Acts 19.28, rather than the classical *Artemis.

Artemisia (5th century BC) Queen of Halicarnassus. She accompanied Xerxes I on his invasion of Greece, despite her prophecy that the mission would fail, and fought bravely at Salamis (480).

Artemisia (died c. 350 BC) Queen of Caria (c. 353–c. 350), who succeeded her brother and husband Mausolus. Artemisia initiated the construction of his famous tomb, the *Mausoleum. In 350 she subjugated Rhodes and nearby islands.

arteriosclerosis The loss of elasticity in the walls of arteries. This somewhat vague term is used to cover various conditions of the arteries and arterioles (small arteries) associated with the aging process. It is also used loosely as a synonym for *atherosclerosis.

artery A thick-walled blood vessel that carries oxygen-rich blood away from the *heart to supply all the tissues and organs of the body. The largest is the aorta, which leads directly from the heart and descends into the abdomen, giving rise to all the other arteries (*see* Plate IV). In middle age the lining of the arteries commonly becomes thickened by *atherosclerosis, which may lead to various diseases caused by obstruction of blood flow (e.g. strokes, heart attacks). *See also* blood pressure.

artesian well A well sunk into an aquifer (a water-saturated rock stratum) that is confined between two layers of impermeable rock and through which water flows upward under pressure. The aquifer reaches the surface and receives rainfall where the water table is higher than the place at which the well is sunk, resulting in a head of pressure.

Artevelde, Jacob van (c. 1290–1345) Flemish statesman. In the 1330s he established the alliance of Flemish towns with those of Brabant, Hainault, and Holland to protect the Low Countries from the economic repercussions of the war between France and England. His dictatorial policies in Ghent, his home town, led to his assassination in 1345.

arthritis Inflammation of one or more joints, causing pain, swelling, and restriction of movement. Many different diseases can cause arthritis, the most important of which are *osteoarthritis, rheumatoid arthritis, and *gout. **Rheumatoid arthritis**, which is more common in women, usually affects the hands and feet and often also the hips, knees, and shoulders. The synovial membrane lining the joint becomes inflamed, resulting in damage to the cartilage over the joint with consequent pain and deformity. Rheumatoid arthritis is an autoimmune disease (*see* autoimmunity) and is diag-

nosed by a blood test (the blood contains the characteristic rheumatoid factor) and X-rays. Treatment is usually based on drugs to reduce the pain and inflammation (*see* analgesic); some patients benefit from treatment with gold salts and steroids, while severe cases may require surgical replacement of the affected joint(s).

arthropod An invertebrate animal belonging to the largest and most diverse phylum (*Arthropoda*) of the animal kingdom, containing about a million species (i.e. 75% of all known species). There are about 12 classes, the most important of which are the *arachnids, *crustaceans, *insects, *centipedes, and *millipedes. An arthropod has a segmented body with a hard outer skeleton (cuticle) made of *chitin, which is shed periodically to allow the body to grow. Jointed appendages are modified for swimming, walking, feeding, respiration, reproduction, etc. Young arthropods are often very different from the adults and go through a series of changes (*see* metamorphosis) to reach the adult form. Arthropods are found in fresh and salt water, air, and land and have exploited every food source. Many are harmful—as pests, parasites, or vectors of disease—but others are beneficial to man, as pollinators, food sources, predators of pests, and decomposers of organic wastes.

Arthur, Chester Alan (1830–86) US political leader; 21st President of the United States (1881–85). Born in Vermont and educated at Union College, Arthur became a lawyer active in the Abolition movement before the Civil War. During the war he served in the Union army and was appointed quartermaster general of New York. In 1871 President Grant named him collector of customs at the Post of New York. Throughout his career, Arthur was an active member of the Republican Party and he was elected as the party's candidate for vice president in 1880. Following the assassination of Pres. James *Garfield in 1881, Arthur succeeded to the presidency himself. The most notable achievement of his single term in office was a reform of the government bureaucracy through the Pendleton Civil Service Act of 1883. Because of political differences with the leaders of the Republican Party, Arthur was denied renomination for president in 1884. After leaving office, he returned to private life and died in New York City in 1886.

Arthurian legend The body of medieval *romances concerning the legendary British king Arthur and his knights; also known as the Matter of Britain. Arthur first emerges as a figure of romance in the *Historia Regum Britanniae* of *Geoffrey of Monmouth, although a 6th-century military leader of the Welsh may have been a historical model. In the legend, he is the son of Uther Pendragon, was born at Tintagel in Cornwall, became king of Britain at 15, and won a number of famous victories. He married Guinevere and held court at Caerleon in Wales (or, in some versions, at □Camelot, which may have been near South Cadbury, Somerset). Involved in a war at Rome, he left his kingdom in the charge of his nephew Modred, who betrayed him and abducted Guinevere. Arthur returned to Britain and defeated Modred but was himself mortally wounded. He was taken away to the Isle of Avalon (the Celtic paradise, associated with Glastonbury) to be healed. Succeeding writers added a wealth of detail to this story, developing new characters, themes, and episodes. *Wace introduced the knightly fellowship of the Round Table and also mentioned the ancient tradition that one day Arthur would return from Avalon to rule Britain again. *Layamon added magical elements to the story, and French and other writers from the 12th century onward, starting with *Chrétien de Troyes, took up the exploits of individual knights, such as Lancelot, Perceval, Gawain, and Galahad. Arthur himself gradually became a background figure, interest centering on the quest of the *Holy Grail, the adulterous affair of Guinevere and Lancelot, and other characters. Other well-known characters were the magician Merlin and the sorceress Morgan le Fay (Arthur's sister). Sir Thomas *Malory's *Morte d'Arthur* (c. 1470) was the culmination of the medieval tradition, although the material has continued to inspire such versions as Tennyson's *Idylls of the King* (from 1842) and T. H. White's *The Once and Future King* (1958).

artichoke A perennial thistle-like herbaceous plant, *Cynara scolemus*, also known as globe artichoke, native to central and W Mediterranean regions and widely grown in warm temperate areas for its nutty-tasting immature flower heads, which are considered a great delicacy. The hairy indented straplike leaves, 1 m long, arise each year from the base of the short annual stems, which carry branched flower stalks bearing purplish flowers. Family: *Compositae. *See also* Jerusalem artichoke.

Articles of Confederation The first national constitution of the United States. First proposed by Richard Henry *Lee of Virginia in 1776 and formulated by a committee headed by John *Dickinson of Delaware, the Articles of Confederation granted each of the states one vote in Congress and apportioned federal taxes according to the value of the surveyed land in each state. By its terms, Congress could wage war and borrow and issue money. After considerable debate in the *Continental Congress, the Articles were passed in 1777, but it was not until 1781 that they were ratified by all the states. The most serious weakness of the federal system under the Articles of Confederation was the inability of Congress to compel the states to obey federal laws, to levy new taxes, and to regulate interstate trade. Because of these shortcomings, a stronger federal system was needed and in 1789 the Articles of Confederation were replaced by the US *Constitution.

artificial insemination The artificial introduction of semen into the vagina of a female at a stage in the menstrual or estrous cycle when the chances of conception are high (i.e. at ovulation). Although practiced as early as the 14th century by Arab horse breeders, the techniques of artificial insemination used in the livestock industry were developed largely in the Soviet Union during the early 20th century. Semen collected from a single well-bred male can be stored at low temperatures for months before being used to fertilize many females. This has resulted in dramatic breed improvements and the control of venereal disease. Artificial insemination is occasionally used in human medicine. In cases when the husband is infertile semen is obtained from an anonymous donor (artificial insemination donor—AID). Semen may be provided by the husband in cases of impotence (artificial insemination husband—AIH). *See also* test-tube baby.

artificial kidney. *See* dialysis.

artificial respiration The restoration of the flow of air into and out of the lungs when the patient's own breathing movements have ceased, for example after drowning, poisoning, etc. Mouth-to-mouth respiration—the "kiss of life"—involves a person breathing out into the patient's mouth: carbon dioxide in this exhaled air acts as a stimulus for the natural breathing reflexes. In hospitals artificial respiration is provided by a *respirator, which may be required during surgery, severe pneumonias, and after head injuries.

Artigas, José Gervasio (1764–1850) The national hero of Uruguay. He fought for the independence of his country from Argentina until he was driven into exile in Paraguay in 1820.

artillery *Firearms with a caliber in excess of 20 mm, used to bombard enemy positions, disrupt communications, destroy enemy artillery, and provide cover and support for friendly troop deployments. Early guns were classed by projectile weight, e.g. 12-pounder. Modern weapons are identified by caliber: light (below 120 mm), medium (121–160 mm), heavy (161–210 mm), and super or very heavy (above 211 mm). *Gun projectiles have flat trajectories, while *mortars and *howitzers have high trajectories, with correspondingly short ranges. Artillery rockets (excluding antitank missiles) deliver more explosive further, without needing heavy launchers. Some artillery projectiles have nuclear warheads, but most are high explosive. Modern electronic equipment enables artillery fire to score a direct hit with near certainty on any visible target; as this also applies to the guns themselves (as targets) the tendency is now for artillery to be fired by remote control.

Artiodactyla An order of hoofed mammals (150 species), distributed worldwide except for Australasia and Antarctica. Artiodactyls are terrestrial herbivores having two or four toes on each foot and often bearing horns. They range in size from the smallest *chevrotains to the *giraffe. The group is divided into three suborders: *Suiformes* (pigs, peccaries, and hippopotamuses); *Tylopoda* (camels and llamas); and *Ruminantia* (see ruminant), which comprises deer, cattle, antelopes, giraffes, pronghorns, and chevrotains. *Compare* Perissodactyla.

Art Nouveau A decorative style pervading all visual art forms in Britain, France, Germany (see Jugendstil), Austria (Sezessionstil), Belgium, Spain, and the US in the 1890s and early 1900s. It is characterized by designs of naturalistic foliage and biomorphic shapes linked by undulating lines. In Britain it is associated with the *Arts and Crafts movement of William *Morris, the architectural and interior designs of C. R. *Mackintosh, and the graphic work of Aubrey *Beardsley. Louis Comfort Tiffany (1848–1933), influenced by the arts and crafts movement, popularized Art Nouveau in the US with his interior designs and glass creations. On the Continent leading examples of Art Nouveau are the Parisian metro designs of Hector Guimard (1867–1942), the extravagant Barcelona flats and hotels designed by Antonio *Gaudí, and the Belgian stores and houses of Victor *Horta, all of which use sinuous lines and exposed ironwork. A parallel effect in glassware of tinted glass and lead solder was achieved by René *Lalique and Emile *Gallé.

Artois A former province of NW France approximating to the present-day Pas-de-Calais. It belonged from the 9th century until 1180 to the Counts of *Flanders, after which it passed to *Philip II Augustus of France. It was acquired from the French crown by the Counts of *Burgun-

dy in 1329, passing to the *Habsburgs in 1500 until regained by France during the *Thirty Years' War (1618–48).

Arts and Crafts movement An English 19th-century aesthetic movement derived from William *Morris and his Pre-Raphaelite associates, whose firm was founded (1861) to produce handmade furnishings. In opposing contemporary mass production the movement revived the principles of medieval craftsmanship and respect for materials; it also promoted the ideal of the artist as craftsman-designer. It culminated in the establishment of the Century Guild for Craftsmen (1882) and the Arts and Crafts Exhibition Society (1888). The preference for curvilinear patterns helped to create the emerging *Art Nouveau style.

Aruba 12 30N 70 00W A West Indian island, in the Netherlands Antilles. Oil refining is important. Area: 75 sq mi (193 sq km). Population (1979 est): 62,288. Chief town: Oranjestad.

arum (or arum lily) A plant of the tropical African genus *Zantedeschia* (8 species), especially *Z. aethiopica*, widely grown as an ornamental. It has arrow-shaped leaves and the flower head consists of a cylindrical cluster of tiny yellow flowers surrounded by a white funnel-shaped bract (spathe), resembling a petal. Family: *Araceae*.

The European genus *Arum*, of the same family, contains the *cuckoopint. The related bog arum, or wild calla (*Calla palustris*), grows in swamps of N temperate and subarctic regions. It has heart-shaped leaves and small flowers enveloped in a white spathe.

Arunachal Pradesh (name until 1972: North-East Frontier Agency) A state in NE India, stretching N from the Brahmaputra Valley to the Himalayas. There it shares a disputed border with Tibet, from which Chinese troops have twice invaded since 1945. Mostly rainforest, Arunachal Pradesh is inhabited by hill tribes. Area: 31,430 sq mi (81,426 sq km). Population (1981): 628,050. Capital: Ziro.

Arundel 50 51N 0 34W A market town in SE England, in West Sussex on the River Arun. Its 11th-century castle (mainly rebuilt in the 19th century) is the seat of the Dukes of Norfolk. Other notable buildings include the 19th-century Roman Catholic cathedral. Population (1981): 2235.

Arval Brethren (Latin: *Fratres Arvales*, Brothers of the Field) In ancient Rome, a college of 12 priests, who organized a festival every May dedicated to the corn goddess Dea Dia. The priests were chosen from high-ranking officials and included the emperor.

Aryans Peoples speaking *Indo-European, *Indo-Iranian, or *Indo-Aryan languages. It has been claimed that all the Indo-European peoples originated from an Aryan people who dispersed from a common homeland into Europe and N India. Indo-Aryan-speaking peoples certainly invaded and settled in N India in the second millennium BC. They were tribal herdsmen who later became farmers. The earliest literature of India, the Vedas, written in *Sanskrit, contains hymns, spells, and details of the ritual practices of the Aryans.

Arya Samaj A controversial Hindu theosophical movement, founded in 1875 at Bombay by Swami Dayananda Saraswali (1824–83). It denounced popular idolatry and advocated a return to the oldest Vedic authorities. It also supported the emancipation of women and untouchables, because the old authorities neither justified nor assumed their lower status. Unlike many contemporary movements, Arya Samaj made no attempt to convert non-Indians.

ASA rating The American Standards Association measure of the sensitivity or speed of photographic *film. A film rated at 200 is twice as fast (i.e. needs half the exposure time) as 100 ASA film. General-purpose films have speeds between 50 and 160 ASA. High-speed films for indoor photography and poor light are rated between 200 and 500 ASA.

asbestos A fibrous form of certain silicate minerals, particularly the *amphiboles anthophyllite, tremolite, riebeckite, and actinolite, or a fibrous form of *serpentine, called chrysotile. Blue asbestos is crocidolite, a fibrous riebeckite. Asbestos is heat-resistant, chemically inert, and has a high electrical resistance; it has therefore a wide industrial application. The fibers are spun and woven or made into blocks. The main producers are Canada, the Soviet Union, and Brazil. *See also* asbestosis.

asbestosis A lung disease caused by the inhalation of asbestos fibers. It is an occupational disease to which those exposed to large amounts of the mineral are particularly prone: tighter factory health controls have greatly reduced its incidence. It affects the air sacs of the lungs, which become thickened and scarred, causing breathlessness: patients are liable to develop lung cancer.

Ascaris A genus of *nematode worms with a worldwide distribution, important as parasites of livestocks and man. Adult worms are smooth and cylindrical, 6–12 in (15-30 cm) in length, and can live in the intestines of their hosts for up to a year. After mating, eggs pass out in the host's feces and infection occurs when food contaminated with eggs is eaten.

Ascension 7 57S 14 22W A British island in the S Atlantic Ocean, a dependency of St Helena. It is rocky, has little vegetation, and was uninhabited until 1815. A British telecommunications center, it is also a US air base and space research station. Area: 35 sq mi (88 sq km). Population (1981): 971. Chief settlement: Georgetown.

Ascension In the Christian calendar, the day on which it is believed Christ ascended into Heaven (see Acts 1.4–11). Since the 4th century it has been celebrated 40 days after Easter.

asceticism Systematic self-discipline for spiritual ends, usually involving fasting, vigils, sexual abstinence, and renunciation of worldly goods and pleasures. *Stoicism advocated ascetic practices in order to subdue unruly passions. Christian asceticism is based on the theory of identifying with Christ's sufferings and is viewed not as an end in itself but as a means to contemplation of and spiritual union with the divine. It became an important element in certain monastic orders and in Christian *mysticism. In Islam, asceticism is particularly associated with *sufism and there is also a strong tradition of asceticism in Buddhism and Hinduism (see fakir).

Asch, Sholem (1880–1957) Jewish novelist, born in Poland, who wrote chiefly in Yiddish. He traveled in Europe, Israel, and the US, becoming a US citizen in 1920. In his controversial later novels, which include *The Nazarene* (1929) and *The Apostle* (1943), he expressed his belief in the essential unity of Judaism and Christianity.

Aschaffenburg 49 58N 9 10E A city in S central West Germany, in Bavaria on the Main River. It contains the 17th-century Johannisburg Castle, a former residence of the Archbishops of Mainz. Its varied manufactures include clothing and precision instruments. Population (1971 est): 55,300.

Asclepius In Greek mythology, a son of *Apollo and the god of medicine. He was instructed by the centaur *Chiron in hunting and medicine and learned to effect many miraculous cures. When he restored *Hippolytus to life as a favor for Artemis, Zeus became angry and struck him dead with a thunderbolt. It was believed that those suffering from illness or disease could be cured by sleeping all night in one of his temples.

Ascoli Piceno 42 52N 13 35E A city in central Italy, in Marche. An ancient settlement, it has many Roman and medieval remains. Its manufactures include glass, chemicals, and textiles. Population (1971): 55,053.

Ascomycetes A large class of fungi (about 15,000 species), known as sac fungi because their spores are formed in a saclike structure (called an ascus). The nonreproductive part of these fungi is often a microscopic meshwork of cells. The group includes the *truffles, *yeasts, *Penicillium, and *Aspergillus.

ascorbic acid. See vitamin C.

Ascot 51 25N 0 41W A village in S England, in Berkshire. The construction of its famous racetrack was ordered by Queen Anne in 1711. Traditionally the sovereign opens the Royal Ascot meeting in June.

ASDIC. See echo sounding.

ASEAN. See Association of South-East Asian Nations.

asepsis The condition in which material is uncontaminated by bacteria, fungi, and other disease-causing microorganisms. Surgical operations, the packaging of surgical supplies, and the preparation of intravenous drugs are carried out under aseptic conditions, which are produced by using *antiseptics, heat, or radiation.

Asgard In Norse mythology, the home of the gods and of heroes killed in battle, comprising over 12 kingdoms and palaces, as well as *Valhalla. From earth it was reached by the bridge Bifrost (the rainbow).

ash A tree of the genus *Fraxinus* (about 50 species), native to the N hemisphere. Many species yield a pale-yellow wood of commercial importance and others are widely grown as ornamentals. Reaching a height of 98 ft (30 m), ashes have compound leaves made up of pairs of oval or lance-shaped leaflets, small inconspicuous flowers, and winged fruits ("ash keys"). Most species are deciduous, including the European ash (*F. excelsior*). Family: *Oleaceae* (olive family). See also mountain ash.

Ashanti A people of the S part of Ghana, who speak the Twi language. They are an agricultural people producing crops for local markets and cocoa for export. Their social organization is based upon matrilineal kin groups living in villages governed by headmen. The Ashanti established an empire in S Ghana during the 18th and 19th centuries, ruled by a paramount chief with military and religious functions. They worship a pantheon of gods and practice an ancestor cult.

Ashanti A former kingdom in West Africa, now comprising S Ghana. During the 18th century it was active in the slave trade, supplying slaves to British and Dutch traders. Following several wars it became a British colony in 1902. The modern region of Ashanti now occupies part of its area.

Ashcan School A group of artists who, in the early 20th century, portrayed life in New York City realistically. Known as "The Eight," their paintings depicted everyday, common, living conditions, complete with the ashcans and garbage cans on streets and in backyards. The group included Robert Henri (1865–1929), William Glackens (1870–1938), George Luks (1867–1933), and Maurice Prendergast (1861–1923).

Ashdod 31 48N 34 38S A city in central Israel, on the Mediterranean coast. It was an important city in the ancient Philistine Empire, and an artificial harbor (started 1961) has now made it into one of Israel's major ports. There is also textile manufacturing. Population (1971 est): 39,700.

Ashe, Arthur (Robert) (1943–) US tennis player, the first black player to win the US singles title (1968) and winner of the 1975 singles title at Wimbledon. South Africa's refusal to allow him to play there in 1970 led to its exclusion from the *Davis Cup. In 1980 he retired from tournament play following heart surgery, but subsequently served as the captain of US Davis Cup team.

Asher, tribe of One of the 12 *tribes of Israel. It claimed descent from Asher, the son of Jacob and Jacob's concubine Zilpah. Its original territory was to the W and NW of the Sea of Galilee, adjoining Phoenicia.

Ashkelon (or Ashqelon) 31 40N 34 35E A seaport 12 mi (19 km) N of Gaza (Israel), known from the biblical story of Samson as a *Philistine stronghold. In Hellenistic times it was a cultural center. The Arabs captured it in 636 AD. During the Crusades it changed hands several times before being destroyed by Sultan *Baybars (1270). The modern Israeli settlement was established in 1948.

Ashkenazim Jews of German or Eastern European origin, as opposed to *Sephardim. They have a distinct tradition of pronouncing Hebrew, as well as other customs, and until this century they mostly spoke *Yiddish. The first Ashkenazy synagogue in London was founded in 1690. Ashkenazim now form some 85% of world Jewry.

Ashkenazy, Vladimir (1937–) Russian pianist and conductor, famous for his interpretations of Mozart and Chopin, among others. He won the 1955 Warsaw Chopin Competition and was joint winner of the 1962 Tchaikovsky Competition. In 1973 he settled in Iceland.

Ashkhabad 37 58N 58 24E A city in the SW Soviet Union, the capital of the Turkmen SSR. It is near the Iranian border in an oasis in the *Kara Kum desert. Although virtually destroyed in 1948 by an earthquake, it has been rebuilt and is now an administrative, industrial, and transportation center, producing food, carpets, glass, and machinery. Population (1981 est): 325,000.

Ashley Cooper, Anthony. See Shaftesbury, Anthony Ashley Cooper, 1st Earl of.

Ashmolean Museum A museum in Oxford, England, housing paintings and archeological collections. The collection was donated to Oxford University in 1675 by Elias Ashmole (1617–92) and put on public display in 1683. Its highlights include Italian Renaissance paintings and English 19th-century works.

ashrama In *Brahmanism, the *ashramas* are the four ideal stages of life through which Hindus of the upper three castes should pass. First comes the celibate student of religion, then the married householder, the forest hermit, and finally the wandering ascetic. Only in later life, therefore, can spiritual release be sought.

Ashton, Sir Frederick (William Mallandaine) (1904–) British ballet dancer and choreographer, born in Ecuador. He joined the Sadler's Wells Ballet in 1935, became an associate director in 1952, and was director of Britain's Royal Ballet from 1963 to 1970. His works include *Cinderella* (1948), *Ondine* (1958), *La Fille mal gardée*, and many ballets choreographed for Margot Fonteyn.

Ashur The oldest Assyrian capital (modern Qalat Sharqat) on the Tigris River 60 mi (96 km) S of Mosul in Iraq. Ashur was already an important trading city in the heyday of *Sumer and *Akkad. Named for its guardian sun-god, Ashur became capital of the rising *Assyrian empire (14th century BC) to which it gave its name. With its later cocapitals *Nimrud and *Nineveh it was destroyed in 612 BC. First excavated in 1903, Ashur's ruins include major temples and a *ziggurat.

Ashurbanipal King of Assyria (668–?627 BC), son of Esarhaddon. He suppressed two serious revolts during his reign and conquered the city of Tyre, but is best known as the founder of a remarkable library at Nineveh, some of the items in which are now in the British Museum.

Ashurnasirpal II King of Assyria (883–859 BC), who continued the restoration of the *Assyrian Empire by efficient administration, an invincible army, and brutality in punishing rebellion. He used deported captives to rebuild Kalhu (now *Nimrud, Iraq).

Ashwander v. Tennessee Valley Authority (1936) US Supreme Court case that ruled that the government may dispose of its property as it wishes. The Tennessee Valley Authority (TVA) contracted to sell excess power to private companies. The suit filed in federal court maintained that the TVA had acted unconstitutionally and, therefore, the government contracts were invalid. The Supreme Court ruled in the government's favor.

Ash Wednesday In the Christian calendar, the first day of *Lent, which is so named from the custom, probably dating from the 8th century, of marking the foreheads of the congregation with ashes as a sign of penitence.

Asia The largest continent in the world, it occupies about one-third of the dry land in the world. Asia is generally accepted as extending W to the Ural Mountains in the Soviet Union, although physically Europe is a peninsula of Asia. It is separated from the continent of Africa by the Red Sea and bounded on the N by the Arctic Ocean. Its S and E limits are less distinct and it includes the islands of Indonesia, Japan, the Philippines, and Taiwan. Asia is a continent of great diversity. Topographically it is the highest of the continents and has the greatest relief. It contains the world's highest point (Mount *Everest) and also its lowest (the *Dead Sea). Its great central mass of mountains and plateaus, which include the Himalayas, has historically formed a major barrier between N and S Asia. Vast alluvial plains border the major rivers, including the Ganges, Mekong, and Ob and the Yangtze and Yellow Rivers. Containing about half of the world's total population, it is the most populous continent, the highest concentrations being in the SE (China, India, and Japan). There are three main population groups: Negroid (in the Philippines), Mongoloid (including the Chinese, Japanese, and Koreans), and Caucasoid (including the Arabs, Afghans, and Pakistanis). Other groups, including the Malays, are a mixture of these main races. All the world's major religions originated in Asia, only Christianity spreading W to any great extent. Others include Hinduism (with the largest following), Buddhism, Islam, Confucianism (in China), and Shintoism (in Japan). Agriculture is the chief occupation, employing about two-thirds of the total population. Asia also has important mineral resources, notably the oil and natural-gas deposits of the Arab states. Area: 17,139,445 sq mi (44,391,162 sq km). Population (1968 est): 2,052,000,000.

Asia Minor (*or* Anatolia) The westernmost part of Asia between the Black Sea in the N, the Mediterranean Sea in the S, and the Aegean Sea in the W; it approximates present-day Turkey in Asia. For much of the second millennium BC, Asia Minor was the center of the *Hittite empire. After the Hittites' collapse (12th century BC) central and W Asia Minor were dominated by *Phrygia, which reached its zenith in the 8th century, when the Assyrian Empire conquered SE Asia Minor. Phrygia fell to *Lydia in the 6th century but in 546 Cyrus the Great established Achaemenian control over Asia Minor. In 333 it was conquered by Alexander the Great of Macedon and after his death, during the *Hellenistic age, the S was contested by the *Seleucids and *Ptolemies, while small kingdoms, such as *Pergamum, *Cappadocia, *Bithynia, and *Pontus, established themselves elsewhere. Asia Minor came under Roman control in the 2nd and 1st centuries BC, forming part of the *Roman Empire and then the *Eastern Roman (subsequently Byzantine) Empire. Conquered by the Seljuq Turks in the 11th century AD and overrun by the Mongols in the 13th, Asia Minor was incorporated in the Ottoman Empire during the 14th and 15th centuries.

Asian Games An athletics meeting for all Asian countries affiliated to the International Amateur Athletic Federation. Quadrennial from 1954, they were first held in New Delhi in 1951.

asiento de negros A contract between the Spanish Crown and a private contractor, in which the Crown sold the exclusive rights to import slaves into its American colonies. The *asiento* began in 1595 and was held successively by Portuguese, Genoese, French, English, and Spanish contractors before it was suppressed in 1778.

Asimov, Isaac (1920–) US science-fiction writer and biochemist, born in Russia. He began writing science-fiction stories in 1939, and his many books include the *Foundation* Trilogy (1951–53; sequel 1982) and collections of short stories, notably *I, Robot* (1950) and *Nightfall* (1969). His books popularizing scientific topics include *Inside the Atom* (1956), *The Human Brain* (1964), and *The Stars in their Courses* (1971).

Aske, Robert. *See* Pilgrimage of Grace.

Asmara (*or* Asmera) 15 20N 38 49E A city in N Ethiopia, the capital of Eritrea province. The population still includes many Italians, Eritrea having been an Italian colony from 1890 until Allied occupation (1941). Notable buildings include the cathedral (1922) and Grand Mosque (1937); it has a university (1958). Industries include meat processing, distilling, and clothes manufacture. Population (1978 est): 373,827.

Aso, Mount 32 55N 131 02E A volcano in Japan, on central Kyushu. It has five cones, one with the longest active crater in the world, 71 mi (114 km) in circumference. Height: 5223 ft (1592 m).

Asoka (died c. 232 BC) Emperor of India (c. 270–c. 232 BC) of the Maurya dynasty (c. 321–c. 185 BC). His dominion extended over the whole of N India and most of the S. After his conquests he adopted the Buddhist faith and had his edicts carved on rock and stone pillars throughout the empire, telling the story of his conversion and issuing orders to comply with the morality of the new faith.

asp An aggressive European *viper, *Vipera aspis*, that lives in dry habitats. About 24 in (60 cm) long, it is gray-brown to coppery brown with dark bars or zigzags, gray, yellowish, or blackish underparts, and a yellow patch under the tail tip. The snout is upturned into a small spike.

The asp that killed Cleopatra was probably the Egyptian cobra (*Naja haje*).

Asparagus A genus of herbaceous plants (about 300 species), with creeping underground stems (rhizomes), found throughout the Old World. *A. officinalis* is widely cultivated in temperate and subtropical regions for its young edible shoots, which are considered a delicacy. Several African species are ornamental: *A. plumosus*, known as **asparagus fern**, produces attractive feathery sprays of branchlets. Family: *Liliaceae*.

Aspen 39 11N 106 49W A city, 7800 ft (2378 m) above sea level in the Rocky Mountains, in W central Colorado. Chiefly a resort, Aspen began as a silver mine camp in 1879 and flourished until 1893, when silver was devalued. Population (1980): 3678.

aspen One of several *poplar trees having slender flattened leafstalks, so that the leaves tremble in the faintest breeze. The European aspen (*Populus tremula*), which grows to a height of 80 ft (25 m) has rounded toothed leaves. Its soft white wood is used for matches and paper pulp.

Aspergillus A genus of fungi that includes many common molds, often found on rotting food. Some species, especially *A. fumigatus*, can cause disease in man (aspergillosis), the most severe form of which affects the lungs producing tuberculosis-like symptoms. *A. flavus*, a mold that infects peanuts, produces the poison aflatoxin, which may be responsible for certain cancers. Class: *Ascomycetes*.

asphalt A black highly viscous or solid hydrocarbon compound, used in road construction and the manufacture of roofing materials. It is obtained from the distillation of certain crude oils and from surface deposits (asphalt lakes), which occur naturally after the lighter fractions of a crude oil reservoir have evaporated.

asphodel A white- or yellow-flowered lily-like plant of the mostly Mediterranean genera *Asphodelus* and *Asphodeline*. In Greek mythology, the asphodel associated with the dead and said to grow in the Elysian fields was *Asphodeline lutea*, which has yellow flowers. The asphodel of the early English and French poets was probably the daffodil. The bog asphodel (*Narthecium ossifragum*), of NW Europe, grows in swampy regions. It grows to a height of 30 cm and has a head of small yellow flowers. Family: *Liliaceae*.

asphyxia Suffocation: obstruction to the supply of oxygen to the tissues. This is a life-threatening condition since the brain cannot survive for longer than about four minutes without oxygen. It can result from any condition that prevents air from reaching the lungs, including drowning and choking. Breathing poisonous gas (e.g. carbon monoxide) also causes asphyxia.

Aspidistra A genus of herbaceous plants (8 species) native to E Asia. *A. elatior* is commonly grown as a hardy pot plant in western countries for its ornamental leaves, which are long, stiff, dark green (sometimes striped), and grow in sheaves from the reduced stem. It may occasionally produce small purple bell-shaped flowers. Family: *Liliaceae*.

aspirin Acetylsalicylic acid: a drug widely used in the form of tablets to treat mild pain, such as headache and toothache. It also relieves inflammation and is therefore helpful in the treatment of rheumatoid arthritis, and it reduces fever. In some people aspirin may cause bleeding from the stomach. *See also* analgesics.

Asquith, Herbert Henry, 1st Earl of Oxford and (1852–1928) British statesman and Liberal prime minister (1908–16). Asquith's government introduced important social reforms, including noncontributory old-age pensions (1908) and the National Insurance Act (1911); it ended the veto power of the House of Lords with the 1911 Parliament Act. After the outbreak of World War I Asquith headed a Liberal-Conservative coalition government (1915–16). He remained leader of the Liberal Party until 1926. His second wife **Margot Asquith** (1865–1945) wrote an outspoken *Autobiography* (1922).

ass A small fast-running mammal belonging to the genus *Equus* (horses), native to Africa and Asia. Asses are about 80 in (200 cm) long, weighing up to 55 lb (250 kg), and have characteristically long ears. The Asiatic wild ass (*E. hemionus*) has a gray or tan hide, a dark bristly mane, and a dark stripe along the back. The African wild ass (*E. asinus*) is the ancestor of the domestic donkey. Asses have long been used as pack animals. *See also* mule.

Assad, Hafiz al- (1928–) Syrian statesman; president (1971–). In 1966, following the coup in Syria by the radical Ba'athists, he became minister of defense. In 1970 he led a coup by the military wing of the *Ba'ath party and was elected president the following year.

Assam A state in NE India, mostly in the Brahmaputra Valley beyond Bangladesh. High rainfall supports tea, Assam's economic mainstay. Rice, jute, sugar cane, and cotton are also grown. Other than forest products and crafts there is little manufacturing. Assam produces half of India's oil, as well as coal. *History:* a flourishing region by 1000 BC, Assam received later migrants from China and Burma. Burmese invasions led Britain to assume control (1826). In World War II Assam played a strategic role in the Allied advance into Burma. Area: 30,310 sq mi (78,523 sq km). Population (1981): 19,902,826. Capital: Dispur.

assassin bug An insect belonging to a widely distributed family (*Reduviidae*; 4000 species), usually black or brown with a long beak used to pierce the skin and suck blood or body fluids from its prey. Assassin bugs generally prey on other insects but some attack mammals, including man. As well as inflicting a painful bite, they may transmit diseases, such as kala-azar and Chagas' disease. Suborder: *Heteroptera*; order: *Hemiptera*.

Assassins (Arabic: hashish eaters) A sect of the Ismaili. In Persia and Syria in the 12th and 13th centuries they were notorious for their practice of stabbing opponents to further their political and religious aims. It was commonly believed that the stabbings were carried out while they were under the influence of hashish, hence their name. They killed mainly Muslims, but also some Crusaders.

Assateague Island 38 05N 75 10W An island, separating Chincoteague Bay from the Atlantic Ocean, off the coasts of and part of Maryland and Virginia. The home of wild ponies and a Coast Guard station, Assateague became a National Seashore preserve in 1965. Length: 32 mi (52 km).

assault and battery In law, battery is the unlawful use of any physical force on someone else. Assault is an attempt to commit a battery or any other unlawful act that makes someone reasonably fear battery, whether or not there is any real intention to harm him. The offender is likely to face criminal charges and may also be sued for damages by his victim. Some "aggravated" assaults, as for example with a deadly weapon, carry higher penalties.

assemblage A work of art in which random objects and materials are integrated on a panel or in a free-standing construction, often to produce a satirical or surrealist effect. Early examples, from around 1915, include the *ready-mades of *Duchamp and the collages of Picasso. More recent assemblages are those of the *pop art movement, using everyday objects, such as clothing, furniture, and household utensils.

assembler A computer *program that makes up part of the *software of a computer. It converts instructions in a programing language into a form that the machine can follow directly.

assignats Paper money issued (1789–96) during the *French Revolution in order to pay off the government's debts. Initially they stimulated the economy and solved the problem of money shortage but ultimately they caused inflation, which reached a peak in 1795, when assignats with a face value of 45,500 million francs but virtually no real value were in circulation.

Assiniboine River A river in W Canada, rising in SE Saskatchewan and flowing generally SE through wheat-growing country to join the Red River at Winnipeg. Length: 590 mi (950 km).

Assisi 43 04N 12 37E A city in central Italy, in Umbria. It is the birthplace of St *Francis of Assisi, who founded the Franciscan Order in 1209, and is the site of a Franciscan convent, which has two gothic churches containing frescoes by Giotto. Population (1971): 24,002.

Associated Press. *See* news agency.

association In psychology, the linking of one idea to another. Similarity of meaning, physical similarity, and contrast can all cause an idea to call forth several others. When two mental events occur together an association forms between them: this is the basis of one kind of learning. According to

the associationist school of psychology, the association of ideas is the basic process underlying human behavior. **Free association** is the chief method of *psychoanalysis: a patient speaks aloud his stream of consciousness, from which the analyst obtains clues to the underlying unconscious thought processes.

Association of South-East Asian Nations (ASEAN) An international organization, founded in 1967, to assist the cultural, economic, and social development of its member states (Indonesia, Malaysia, the Philippines, Singapore, and Thailand). It aims to eliminate trade barriers, promote cultural exchanges, facilitate communications between members, and improve technology, commerce, and industry.

associative law The mathematical rule, obeyed by addition and multiplication in ordinary *arithmetic, that the order in which successive identical operations are performed does not affect the result: for addition $a + (b + c) = (a + b) + c$; for multiplication $a(bc) = (ab)c$

Assyrian Empire An ancient kingdom on the Upper Tigris (now N Iraq), where the Assyrians (named for their god Ashur) settled in about 2500 BC, forming a dependency of Babylon. Ashur-uballit I (c. 1365–c. 1330) laid the foundations of the Empire, which after a period of decline was extended by *Tiglath-pileser I (1120–1074), who conquered the city of Babylon. A new era of aggressive expansion was initiated by *Ashurnasirpal II (883–859). The Assyrian domain was extended to Syria and Palestine under Shalmaneser III (858–824) and Assyrian ascendancy reached its zenith under *Tiglath-pileser III (745–727). *Sargon II (722–705), *Sennacherib (704–681), and *Esarhaddon (680–669) maintained the Empire but *Nineveh, the capital, fell to Media and Babylon in 612. The Assyrians built magnificent palaces with friezes that reflected their warlike character.

Astaire, Fred (Frederick Austerlitz; 1899–) US dancer and film star. He began his career as a music-hall dancer with his sister, Adele, a frequent partner. His best-known films are the 1930s musicals in which he was teamed with Ginger Rogers. These include *Top Hat* (1935), *Follow the Fleet* (1936), and *Shall We Dance* (1937). His later costars included Judy Garland, Leslie Caron, and Audrey Hepburn.

Astarte The Phoenician goddess of love and fertility, equivalent to the Babylonian *Ishtar and sometimes regarded as the counterpart of *Aphrodite. She was associated with the moon and often represented by a crescent.

astatine (At) A short-lived radioactive *halogen. Its longest-lived isotope, ^{210}At, has a half-life of 8.3 hours. Small amounts exist in nature as a result of uranium and thorium decay. At no 85; at wt (210); mp 200°F (302°C); bp 219°F (337°C).

Aster A genus of perennial herbaceous plants (about 500 species), many species of which are commonly known as Michaelmas daisies. Native to N temperate regions, they are widely grown as garden plants. Usually 24–40 in (60–100 cm) tall, they have flowers with blue, red, or white rays and a central yellow disc. *A. amellus* and *A. aeris* are common ornamental species. Family: *Compositae.

asteroid A small nonluminous rocky body that orbits a star. Over 100,000 orbit the sun, mostly (probably 95%) in a main belt between the orbits of Mars and Jupiter, 2.17–3.3 astronomical units from the sun. Of the remainder, some, such as *Icarus, have highly elliptical orbits that bring them close to the sun while others, including the *Trojan group, lie far beyond the main belt. The smallest asteroids are less than 0.6 mi (1 km) across with only about 200 exceeding 60 mi (100 km): the largest is *Ceres (623 mi (1003 km)). They are probably debris from collisions of bodies that formed between Mars and Jupiter. In turn, most meteorites (*see* meteor) are considered fragments of asteroids.

asthma A disorder in which breathlessness and wheezing are aggravated by certain stimuli, which cause the bronchi (which conduct air to the lungs) to become constricted. Bronchial asthma may be stimulated by a wide range of conditions and substances: it may be an allergic reaction (*see* allergy), it may occur secondarily to respiratory infection, or it may be brought on by exertion, certain drugs, or strong emotion. Treatment is by means of drugs that dilate the bronchi and—in the case of allergic asthma—by removing the allergen or by *desensitization. Severe asthmatic attacks require injections of corticosteroids. Cardiac asthma is associated with some forms of heart disease and requires a different treatment.

Asti 44 54N 8 13E A town in NW Italy, in Piedmont. It is famous for its sparkling wine (Asti Spumante). Population (1971): 76,048.

astigmatism A form of *aberration that can occur in mirrors and lenses (including the eye). It results when the curvature is different in two mutually perpendicular planes; rays in one plane may then be in focus while rays in the other are out of focus. It is corrected in the eye by the use of cylindrical lenses.

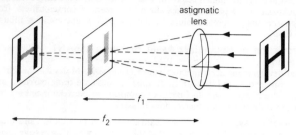

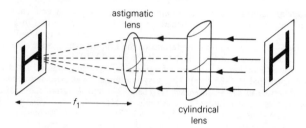

ASTIGMATISM *An astigmatic lens cannot focus vertical and horizontal lines at the same time. Here the vertical focal length f_1 is shorter than the horizontal focal length f_2. In the human eye this would be corrected by glasses with cylindrical lenses, reducing the overall focal length in the horizontal plane only, so that both vertical and horizontal lines are in sharp focus at distance f_1.*

Astilbe A genus of perennial herbaceous flowering plants (about 25 species), native to E Asia and North America and commonly cultivated for ornament in temperate regions. The flowers (usually pink or red) grow in branching plumelike clusters; the plants may reach a height of 5 ft (1.5 m). Family: *Saxifragaceae.*

Aston, Francis William (1877–1945) British chemist, who developed the mass spectrometer for separating ions according to their atomic weight. His discovery of the isotopes of many nonradioactive elements, and of the whole-number rule governing their masses, won him the 1922 Nobel Prize for Chemistry.

Astor, John Jacob (1763–1848) American businessman and financier. Born in Germany, Astor arrived in New York in 1783 and became active in the fur trade. With the opening of the American West, he quickly expanded his business to include shipping to the Far East and international agreements with Canadian traders and merchants. In 1811 he established his first Northwestern outpost, called Astoria, at the mouth of the Columbia River, and in later years he established many more fur trading stations throughout the Far West. In addition to amassing vast wealth through shipping and the fur trade, Astor also invested heavily in New York real estate. At the time of his death, he was reportedly one of the wealthiest men in America, leaving an estate estimated at more than $20,000,000.

Astoria 46 11N 123 50W A city and port in NW Oregon, near the mouth of the Columbia River. It was first explored by Meriwether Lewis and William Clark in 1805–06, and John Jacob Astor established the Pacific Fur Company here in 1811. Population (1980): 9998.

Astrakhan 46 22N 48 04E A port in the Soviet Union, in the SE RSFSR on the Volga River. The city was an important trading center with the East until the Russian Revolution, after which its importance declined. Astrakhan fur, from the Karakul lamb of central Asia, was first brought to Russia by Astrakhan traders. More than half the population is employed in fishing or allied occupations. Population (1981 est): 470,000.

astrolabe An instrument for observing the altitude of celestial bodies and for solving other astronomical problems. Dating back to antiquity, it was used by mariners to determine latitude from the 15th century until the invention of the *sextant. The simple medieval astrolabe consisted of a graduated brass disc suspended in a vertical plane, with a movable sighting arm (the alidade) pivoted at its center. The modern prismatic astrolabe is used to measure the time taken for a celestial body to reach a predetermined altitude. It consists of an artificial horizon, such as a pool of mercury, and a prism placed in front of a telescope. Starlight enters the telescope directly by reflection from the prism and also indirectly after reflection by the artificial horizon. The two images thus formed move diagonally across the field of view of the telescope as a result of diurnal motion. At the altitude defined by the angle of the prism (usually 60°) the two images coincide.

astrology The study of the movements and positions of the heavenly bodies in relation to their presumed influence upon human affairs. Astrology originated in *Babylonia and then passed to Greece, India, China, and the Islamic lands. In medieval Europe astrologers had a respected role in public and personal life. Astrology is based upon an elaborate system of putative correspondences between celestial and mundane phenomena: each "house" (*see* zodiac), for instance, imparts a particular character to those born under its influence and the sun, moon, and principal planets in various positions relative to the houses and to each other predispose people to good or ill. The two branches of astrology are "natural" (concerned mainly with observations and theory) and "judicial" (foretelling events in individual lives by means of a horoscope). *See also* birthstone.

astronomical unit (AU) A unit of length equal to the mean distance between the earth and the sun 92.9 × 10^6 miles (1.495× 10^{11} meters).

astronomy The study of celestial bodies and the universe of which they form part. One of the most ancient of the sciences, naked-eye astronomy flourished in China, Babylonia, Egypt, and classical Greece (*see* Aristarchus of Samos; Hipparchus; Ptolemaic system). After the decline of ancient Greek culture, interest in astronomy was the preserve of the Arabs for many centuries and it was they who developed the *astrolabe. European interest in the heavens, transmitted from the Arabs through Spain, reawakened in the 16th century with the work of *Copernicus and Tycho *Brahe, who were able to separate the science of astronomy from *astrology. But it was not until 1609 that Galileo's refracting *telescope (invented in Holland in 1608) enabled the sky to be investigated in any detail; in 1671 Newton devised the more effective reflecting telescope. These devices provided the means for the development of **descriptive astronomy**, **astrometry** (the measurement of the position of celestial bodies), and *celestial mechanics. In the 19th century, the use of spectroscopy (*see* spectrum) to study the physical and chemical composition of the universe provided the basis for the new sciences of *astrophysics and astrochemistry.

Until the 1940s all observations of the heavens were made by observing the light that passed through the "optical window" in the atmosphere. *Jansky's discovery (1932) that radio waves are emitted by celestial bodies, enabled the "radio window" in the atmosphere to be opened; with *radio astronomy a whole new dimension was added to the investigation of the universe.

With the use of rockets, artificial satellites, space probes, and space observatories all restrictions on observation imposed by the atmosphere were removed, enabling investigations to be made over the whole electromagnetic spectrum. But dependence on electromagnetic radiation as the source of information for astronomical investigations ended with the first moon landings and the unmanned *planetary probes.

This gradual evolution of astronomical instruments has been parallelled by far-reaching changes in *cosmology.

astrophysics The study of the physical and chemical processes and characteristics associated with celestial objects. It is based on theories developed in astronomy, physics, and chemistry and on observations of the radiation emitted by the objects. Originally only studies at optical and then at radio and infrared wavelengths were made, but with the recent advent of rockets and artificial satellites, sources of X-rays, gamma rays, and ultraviolet radiation can also be observed. *See also* cosmology.

Asturias A coastal region in NW Spain corresponding to the present-day province of Oviedo. When the Muslims invaded Spain in 718, the Visigoths withdrew to Asturias, where, protected by the Cantabrian Mountains in the S, they established a new kingdom, preserving Visigothic and Christian traditions. During the next two centuries, Asturias, the sole surviving Christian Spanish kingdom and the center of resistance to the Muslim advance, expanded into León and Galicia, especially under Alfonso III (reigned 866–c. 910). After his death the kingdom was divided between León, Castile, and Navarre.

Asturias, Miguel Ángel (1899–1974) Guatemalan novelist and poet. His novel *El Señor Presidente* (1946) is a study of political dictatorship; many of his other works, such as *Hombres de Maíz* (1949) and *Mulata de tal* (1960), reflect his interest in Mayan mythology and culture. He was awarded the Nobel Prize in 1967.

Asunción 25 15S 57 40W The capital of Paraguay, an important port in the S on the Paraguay River. Founded in 1536, it was for a time the center of the Spanish settlements in the area. The National University was founded in 1890 and the Catholic University in 1960. Industries include flour milling, food processing, and textiles. Population (1979 est): 481,706.

Aswan (or Assuan; Greek name: Syene)   24 05N 32 56E A city in S Egypt, on the Nile River. Some ruins of the ancient city of Syene remain. The city is a popular tourist center and winter resort. Nearby quarries supplied granite for many Egyptian monuments. The *Aswan High Dam and earlier Aswan Dam are also nearby and have stimulated growth within the city. Population (1976): 144,000.

Aswan High Dam   A major dam in Egypt, on the Nile River near Aswan. Begun in 1960 and financed by the Soviet Union, it was completed in 1970. It is about 3 mi (5 km) long and 328 ft (100 m) high; its reservoir, **Lake Nasser**, extends for about 350 mi (560 km) behind the dam. Since its construction the famous annual Nile floods have been controlled and water is available for irrigation, for domestic and industrial purposes, and for hydroelectric power. Ancient Nubian monuments (notably the *Abu Simbel and □Philae temples) that were threatened with permanent flooding were moved to new sites. About 4 mi (7 km) downstream is the earlier **Aswan Dam** (completed 1902); 1.2 mi (2 km) long and 177 ft (54 m) high, this provides irrigation water.

asymptote   A straight line that a two-dimensional curve approaches but never meets as the curve is extended infinitely.

Asyut (or Assiut; ancient name: Lycopolis)   27 14N 31 07S The largest city in Upper Egypt, on the Nile River. It is an important commercial center and is renowned for its handicrafts, such as ivory carvings and tulle shawls, and its textile industries. Below the city the Asyut barrage provides water for irrigation. It has a university (1957). Population (1976): 214,000.

Atacama Desert (Spanish name: Desierto de Atacama)   A cool arid area in N central Chile, extending for about 700 mi (1100 km) S from the Peruvian border. It consists chiefly of a series of salt basins and is one of the driest areas in the world; in some parts no rain has ever been recorded. There are valuable deposits of copper and it is a major source of nitrates. Area: about 31,000 sq mi (80,290 sq km).

Atahuallpa (or Atahualpa; d. 1533)   The last King of the Inca Empire (1532–33). On the death of his father Huayna Capac (1525) the Empire was divided between Atahuallpa and his brother Huascar. Atahuallpa overthrew his brother and declared himself king but was then captured by the Spanish conquistador Pizarro and, in spite of agreeing to the payment of a ransom, was executed.

Atalanta   A swift-footed huntress of Greek mythology. Hippomenes (or Meilanion), on her promise to marry any man who could outrun her, raced with her. Furnished with three of the Hesperides' golden apples by *Aphrodite, which he dropped to distract her, he won the race and married her.

Atatürk, Kemal (Mustafa Kemal; 1881–1938)   Turkish statesman, who was the chief founder of modern Turkey; president (1922–38). Born in Salonika, he entered the army and distinguished himself in World War I. After the war he opposed the humiliating Treaty of *Versailles and as president of the provisional government organized the defeat of the Greek invasion of Asia Minor (1920). In 1922 the Ottoman sultan was deposed and Mustafa Kemal became the first president of Turkey. From then until his death he worked to make Turkey a modern secular state. He took the surname Atatürk (Father of the Turks) in 1934.

ataxia   Loss of muscular coordination, often caused by disease of the part of the brain (the cerebellum) that controls movement. Ataxia may accompany severe vitamin B_{12} and folic acid deficiencies or follow a brain hemorrhage.

Atget, (Jean) Eugène (Auguste) (1856–1927)   French photographer. He turned to photography in 1898 after a career first at sea and later on the stage. He specialized in scenes of Parisian life, including a notable series on brothels (commissioned 1921). Apart from Man *Ray's interest in the surrealist effect of his shop-window series, he received recognition only after his death.

Athabasca, Lake   A lake in W Canada, in NW Saskatchewan and NE Alberta, drained by the Slave River. Uranium ores were discovered on the N shore (1950s). Area: 3120 sq mi (8080 sq km).

Athabascan   A group of North American Indian languages spoken by tribes living to the west of Hudson Bay in Alaska and Canada, and by some tribes of the SW US. The northern group includes Koyukon, Tanana, *Chippewa, Slave, and Yellowknife, and the southern group includes *Apache and *Navajo.

Athabasca River   A river in W Canada, in N Alberta flowing from the Rocky Mountains to Lake Athabasca through tar sands estimated to contain half the world's known oil reserves. Length: 765 mi (1230 km).

KEMAL ATATÜRK   *In the center, photographed in 1922.*

Athanasian Creed   A Christian profession of faith traditionally attributed to St *Athanasius but probably dating from the 5th century. Its central statements concern the doctrines of the *Trinity and of the *Incarnation. Once popular in the Western Churches, it is now little used.

Athanasius, St (296–373 AD)   Egyptian churchman, Bishop of Alexandria. After attending the Council of *Nicaea in 325, he was appointed Bishop of Alexandria in 328 and remained primate of Egypt for 43 years. During this time he led the opposition to the powerful *Arianism that flourished in the East under the emperors Constantine and Constantius. He was expelled from his see four times, but his orthodox teaching regarding the divinity of Jesus Christ was ultimately affirmed by the Council of Constantinople (381). Feast day: May 2.

atheism   The denial of the existence of God (or gods). Historically atheism has taken many different forms. In theocratic societies charges of atheism were frequently made against individuals or groups suspected of antisocial behavior or of dissent from the prevailing orthodoxy. Philosophical materialists, such as *Hobbes, were also attacked as atheists but the spread of *rationalism in the 18th century created a climate sympathetic to atheism. In the 19th century, scientific advances challenged the old arguments for the existence of God, making atheism respectable philosophically, if not socially. Today rigorous atheists hold either that the concept of God, being untestable, is simply meaningless (see logical positivism) or that all we know by scientific means about the universe suggests that God is a false notion (see humanism). *Compare* agnosticism.

Athelstan (d. 939)   King of England (925–39), succeeding his father Edward the Elder; he was crowned King of Mercia in 924. He defeated a Scottish invasion force in 937 and is also known for six extant legal codes.

Athena (or Pallas Athena)   The Greek goddess of war and of wisdom, the protectress of Athens. Born from the head of Zeus, fully armed with a javelin, she was his favorite child. In the Trojan War she constantly aided the Greeks. She also helped Heracles in his labors and guided Perseus on his expedition against the Gorgons. Odysseus voyaged home from Troy under her protection. A virgin goddess, in peacetime she was a patroness of the arts and industry. Athens is named for her, and the Parthenon was the center of her worship. She is identified with the Roman *Minerva.

Athenagoras (2nd century AD)   Greek Christian apologist, who taught in Athens and Alexandria. His *Apology* or *Legatio pro Christianis* (177) addressed to *Marcus Aurelius, defended Christianity against charges of cannibalism and licentiousness arising from misunderstandings of the doctrines of the Eucharist and universal love.

Athens   33 57N 83 23W A city in NE Georgia, on the Oconee River. The University of Georgia was established here in 1801. Industries include textiles, lumber, dairy products, and electrical appliances. Population (1980): 42,549.

ATHENS *The Parthenon.*

Athens (Modern Greek name: Athínai) 37 59N 23 42E The capital of Greece, situated on a plain in the SE of the country near the Saronic Gulf. It is the administrative, cultural, and economic center of the country and is administratively joined to its port and main industrial sector, *Piraeus. Tourism is an important source of revenue. Athens is a city that combines the ancient and the modern, with only one or two small Byzantine and neo-Byzantine churches surviving to testify to the period between Roman times and the early 19th century. The many remains of ancient Athens are focused on the Acropolis. Crowned by the *Parthenon, it contains the Ionic Erechtheum, the Propylaea (a gateway), and the tiny temple of Athena Nike. To the NW, the recently restored Agora (market), contains the Theseum (5th century BC), probably the best-preserved ancient temple. To the N and E lies modern Athens, which includes the university, founded in 1837. *History*: there is evidence of settlements dating back to the 3rd millennium BC. Athens probably enjoyed its first rise to fame under Pisistratus and his sons in the 6th century BC. Around the year 506 Cleisthenes established a democracy for the free men of Athens. During the following century it became the leading Greek city state, defeating the Persians with the aid of its powerful navy (see Greek-Persian Wars). The Long Walls, connecting the city to Piraeus, and the Parthenon date from this period. Under Pericles, it reached a peak of intellectual brilliance with the philosophy of Socrates and the drama of Aeschylus, Sophocles, and Euripides. Defeated by Sparta in the *Peloponnesian War (431–404), it recovered slowly, regaining its intellectual supremacy with such figures as Plato, Aristotle, and Aristophanes. Its role as a major political power, however, was finally lost when defeated by Philip of Macedon in 338 BC, and in the 2nd century BC it came under the rule of Rome. Owing to the influence of Hellenic culture on the Romans it continued to prosper and, despite being overrun by Germanic tribes in the 4th century AD, maintained its academic standing until the closure of the schools of philosophy by Justinian in 529. The city fell to the Crusaders in 1204 and was under Turkish occupation from 1456 until 1833, when it became the capital of the newly independent kingdom of Greece. Since then it has grown from almost nothing to a busy modern city. It has been the scene of frequent revolts and civil wars and was occupied by the Germans in World War II. Population (1981): 885,136.

atherosclerosis (*or* atheroma) Patchy thickening of the lining of arteries caused by the deposition of fatty material and fibrous tissue. This tends to obstruct the blood flow and predisposes to *thrombosis, which may lead to a heart attack or a stroke. In the western world atherosclerosis is common in adults: its underlying cause remains a controversial issue but is believed to be associated with a diet high in animal fats (see cholesterol) and refined sugar, cigarette smoking, and obesity. Its incidence increases with age and it is exacerbated by high blood pressure. The extent of the condition can be reduced by treatment of any underlying illness.

athlete's foot. *See* ringworm.

athletics Sports that involve running, walking, throwing, and jumping competitions. They are divided into track and field events. At international level the track events include races over 100 m, 200 m, 400 m, 800 m, 1500 m, 5000 m, and 10 000 m; the 110 m and 400 m hurdles (see hurdling); the 4 × 100 and 4 × 400 m relay races; the 3000 m steeplechase; the *marathon; and the 20 km walk (see walking). The standard field events are *high jump, *long jump, *triple jump, *pole vault, *shot put, *discus throw, *hammer throw, and *javelin throw. In addition there are the *decathlon (for men), the modern pentathlon, and the *pentathlon (for women). The governing body is the International Amateur Athletic Federation.

Athos, Mount 1. 40 10N 24 19E A mountain in NE Greece, at the end of Aktí, the easternmost of the three promontories of Chalcidice. Height: 6670 ft (2033 m). 2. An autonomous Greek Orthodox monastic republic occupying the mountain. Area: 31 sq mi (80 sq km). Population (1971 est): 1713.

Atlanta 33 45N 84 23W The capital of Georgia, situated at the foot of the Appalachian Mountains. Founded in 1837 and partly destroyed by Gen Sherman in 1864, it is now the industrial, administrative, transportation, and cultural center of the whole of the SE of the US. Its major industries include aircraft, machinery, cottonseed oil, textiles, clothing, and chemicals. Population (1980): 425,022.

Atlantic, Battle of the. *See* World War II.

Atlantic Charter (1941) An agreement between President Franklin D. Roosevelt and British prime minister Winston Churchill that stated common national policies. Freedom of choice of government, improved worldwide economic and social conditions, freedom of the seas, and freedom from unwanted territorial takeovers and changes were some of the main points, as well as an end to Nazism and the use of force.

Atlantic City 39 23N 74 27W A city in the US, in New Jersey on Absecon Beach (an island on the Atlantic coast). A major pleasure resort, it has five piers and a multitude of amusements, shops, hotels, and parks; gambling casinos were introduced in the late 1970s. A popular conference center, it is the site of the annual Miss America Pageant (first held in 1921). Its industries include glassware, china, and confectionery. Population (1980): 40,199.

Atlantic Intracoastal Waterway A shipping route along the Atlantic coast. It serves the ports between Cape Cod and Florida Bay. Length: 1550 mi (2495 km).

Atlantic Ocean The world's second largest ocean, extending between Antarctica, America, Europe, and Africa. It is the world's most heavily traveled seaway, although floating ice is a hazard. Its major currents include the *Gulf Stream crossing it W–E. Its floor is rich in minerals, oil and gas now being exploited. The Mid-Atlantic Ridge has peaks rising above sea level as islands, such as the Azores. The youngest of the oceans, the Atlantic was formed when the continents now surrounding it first split apart about 200 million years ago.

Atlantic Wall The extensive fortifications built by the Germans in *World War II along the Atlantic coast. They failed to prevent *D-day Normandy landings by US and British troops (June 6, 1944).

Atlantis In Greek legend, a large island civilization in the Atlantic beyond the Pillars of Hercules (Straits of Gibraltar), which, according to Plato's dialogues the *Timaeus* and *Critias*, was destroyed by earthquake. The story, transmitted to the Greeks by the Egyptians, may refer to a cataclysmic volcanic eruption (c. 1450 BC) on the island of *Thera in the Cyclades N of Crete.

Atlas In Greek mythology, the brother of Prometheus and son of the Titan Iapetus and the nymph Clymene. As a punishment for his part in the revolt of the Titans against the Olympians he was forced to hold up the pillars separating heaven from earth. From the 16th century this was commonly depicted in the frontispieces of books of maps, which thus came to be called atlases.

Atlas Mountains A mountain system in NW Africa, extending generally NE from the Atlantic coast of Morocco to Tunisia. It consists of several mountain chains and plateaus and rises to 13 664 ft (4165 m) at Mount Toubkal in the Moroccan Great Atlas range.

atman (Sanskrit: breath, soul) A fundamental concept of Hinduism, signifying the individual soul or the eternal essential self. When the body dies the *atman* is continuously reincarnated until final spiritual release is achieved. In the later *Upanishads, and in the Hindu philosophical schools of Samkhya and orthodox Vedanta, the function of *atman* and its relation to *Brahman is the central issue. Some thinkers regard these two as analogous principles only; for others they are essentially identical.

atmosphere (meteorology) The gaseous envelope surrounding the earth or any other celestial body. The earth's atmosphere is composed of nitrogen (78.08%), oxygen (20.95%), argon (0.93%), and carbon dioxide (0.03%), together with small proportions of other gases and variable amounts of water vapor. In the lowest layer of the earth's atmosphere, the **troposphere**, air temperature decreases as height increases. The thickness of this layer varies from about 4.5 mi (7 km) to about 10 mi (16 km) at the equator. It is here that most meteorological phenomena occur. In the **stratosphere**, which goes up to about 31 mi (50 km), temperature is fairly constant because the sun's radiation counteracts the effect of decreasing density. Above the stratosphere lie the **mesosphere**, extending up to about

50 mi (80 km), in which temperatures decrease with height, and the **thermosphere**, in which temperatures increase with height; these fall within the *ionosphere. The outermost layer, from about 248 mi (400 km), is called the **exosphere**. From 62 mi (100 km) upward the oxygen dissociates into atoms. There is little nitrogen above 93 mi (150 km). The atmosphere protects the earth from excessive radiation and cosmic particles and is important in maintaining the heat balance of the earth. *See also* ozone.

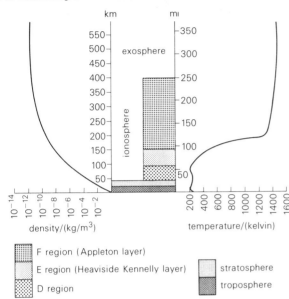

ATMOSPHERE *The density of the atmosphere falls off sharply with height above the earth's surface. The more complicated temperature variation is shown in the graph, which also illustrates the regions of the ionosphere.*

atmosphere (unit)   A unit of pressure equal to 101,325 pascals or 760 millimeters of mercury.

atmospheric pressure   The pressure exerted by the atmosphere. It decreases with altitude and, at ground level, varies around 760 millimeters of mercury, 101,325 pascals, or 1013.25 millibars.

atom.   *See* atomic theory.

atomic bomb.   *See* nuclear weapons.

atomic clock   A highly accurate clock based on the frequency at which certain atoms or molecules vibrate between two states. For example, the nitrogen atom in the ammonia molecule vibrates through the plane of the three hydrogen atoms and back again with a frequency of 23,870 hertz. In the ammonia clock, a quartz-crystal oscillator feeds energy into ammonia gas at this frequency. The ammonia only absorbs energy at this frequency, enabling a feedback circuit to control the frequency of the oscillator. *See also* cesium clock.

atomic energy.   *See* nuclear energy.

Atomic Energy Commission   *See* Nuclear Regulatory Commission.

atomic mass unit (amu)   A unit of mass equal to one-twelfth of the mass of an atom of carbon-12 ($1.660,33 \times 10^{-27}$ kg). Atomic weights (relative atomic masses) are based on this unit. The unit is also called the dalton (after John *Dalton).

atomic number (Z)   The number of protons in a nucleus of an atom. It determines the position of the element in the *periodic table and, in a neutral atom, is equal to the number of electrons surrounding the nucleus. It is also known as proton number.

atomic theory   The theory that an atom is the smallest particle of an element that can take part in a chemical reaction. *Democritus is credited with first conceiving the idea, which was, however, vigorously attacked by *Aristotle since Democritus's atoms existed in a vacuum, an idea repugnant to Aristotle. The atomic concept fell from favor until the early 19th century, when John *Dalton used the idea to explain the fact that elements combined together in simple proportions. The structure of the atom was first investigated by Lord *Rutherford, who discovered that it consisted of a heavy positively charged core (the *nucleus) surrounded by *electrons. Niels Bohr elaborated on this model (*see* Bohr atom) but the modern

concept of the atom was not finally elucidated until the advent of Schrödinger's *wave mechanics.

Almost all of the atom's mass is concentrated in the nucleus, which consists of positively charged *protons and neutral *neutrons of almost equal mass (the mass of the electron is only 1/1836 that of the proton). The number of electrons in a neutral atom is equal to the number of protons in the nucleus, as the charge on the proton is equal but opposite to that of the electron. The electrons can be thought of as existing in a series of shells around the nucleus, each shell corresponding to a particular energy level. According to the *Pauli exclusion principle each shell may only hold a certain number of electrons. The chemical behavior of an atom is largely determined by the number of electrons in its outermost shell, as atoms are most stable when they have no partly filled shells, a state often achieved by chemical combination. In combining, atoms may either share electrons to form covalent bonds or gain (or lose) electrons to form electrovalent (ionic) bonds (*see* chemical bond).

All the nuclei of an element contain the same number of protons (p) but not always the same number of neutrons (n). Atoms with the same value of p but a different value of n are called isotopes of that element. The value of ($n + p$) is called the mass number. Isotopes are referred to in several ways, e.g. uranium-235, U-235, ^{235}U, $^{235}_{92}$U (the subscript in this case being the *atomic number, the value 235 being the mass number of a particular uranium isotope). *See also* particle physics.

atomic weight   The ratio of the average mass of the atoms in a given sample to one-twelfth the mass of a carbon-12 atom. The modern, more correct, name is relative atomic mass.

atomism   The philosophical attitude that seeks irreducible elements, whether of matter or thought, to account for the (compound) phenomena that we actually experience. The Greek *Democritus believed that the world is composed of qualitatively similar atoms of different shapes. In this view, atoms may be either completely independent of one another or related in contingent or necessary ways. *Lucretius was an influential proponent of atomism, and *Gassendi, *Boyle, and *Locke revived it in the 17th century. Logical atomism, held temporarily by both *Russell and *Wittgenstein, assumed that there were unanalyzable specks of meaning that could be articulated in atomic propositions, from which no subordinate proposition could be derived.

Aton   In Egyptian religion, the one supreme god proclaimed by *Akhenaton and symbolized by a solar disk with arms.

atonality   The use in music of all 12 notes of the scale in such a way as to avoid *tonality. Atonality arose from the increasing *chromaticism of the music of the late 19th century. Schoenberg's second string quartet (1907–08), for example, begins in the key of F sharp minor but has an atonal final movement. *See also* serialism.

atonement   In religious belief, the idea of reconciliation between God and man or, literally, at-one-ment with God. The idea implies that the relationship between God and mankind has been interrupted or damaged by human failing or sin. In Judaism, *Yom Kippur or the Day of Atonement is the holiest day of the year. In Christianity, the crucifixion of Christ is traditionally interpreted as a sacrifice for men's sins that effects a reconciliation with God and brings to an end the estrangement started by Adam's sin.

Atonement, Day of.   *See* Yom Kippur.

ATP (adenosine triphosphate)   An energy-rich compound (a nucleotide) with an important role in the metabolism of living organisms. On its formation from ADP (adenosine diphosphate) in the mitochondria of cells, ATP incorporates a large amount of energy that, on release, is used by cells to manufacture proteins, carbohydrates, fats, etc., and to provide the energy for muscle contraction and other dynamic processes.

Atreus   In Greek mythology, King of Mycenae, the son of Pelops and father of Agamemnon and Menelaus. His house was cursed as a result of a feud between him and his brother Thyestes over the throne of Mycenae. After Thyestes had seduced his wife, Atreus killed Thyestes' sons and served them at a feast. Another son of Thyestes, Aegisthus, later killed Atreus.

atrium (anatomy).   *See* heart.

atrium (architecture)   **1.** Originally an important part of a Roman house, a central, partly covered court, frequently colonnaded, which often contained the shrine to the household god. Around it were the entrances to the main rooms. Later it became the main reception room of the house. **2.** An open area or courtyard in front of early Christian churches.

There is no simple way to illustrate an atom:

 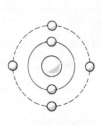 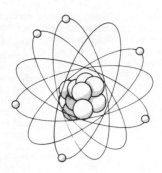 

by the 19th century it was regarded as a minute solid billiard ball;

with the work of Rutherford between 1906 and 1914 and Bohr in 1913 it was depicted as a miniature solar system with a central nucleus and orbiting electron;

Sommerfeld's refinements of quantum theory in 1916 led to a model with precessing elliptical orbits and spinning electrons;

by 1926 Schrödinger's wave mechanics had been published, based on de Broglie's dual wave – particle concept of electrons. The atom is now regarded as a nucleus surrounded by a "haze" of probabilities that electrons will occur in certain positions.

The main characteristic of an atom, as the smallest particle of matter, is not what our models of it look like but the way it absorbs and emits energy.

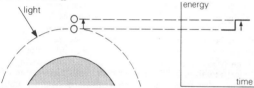 

When an atom absorbs energy (e.g. when light of the right wavelength falls on it) its electrons jump to a higher energy level.

When these electrons fall back to their original (ground) state they emit energy (as light, ultraviolet, etc.).

All matter and therefore all atoms, according to modern physics, consists of two kinds of particles: leptons and quarks. Electrons are leptons; the particles of the nucleus (protons and neutrons) are each made up of different arrangements of three quarks.

The simplest atomic nucleus is the hydrogen nucleus consisting of one proton.

An isotope of hydrogen, deuterium, has a nucleus consisting of one proton and one neutron.

All other nuclei consist of arrangements of protons and neutrons. The carbon nucleus consists of six protons and six neutrons.

ATOMIC THEORY

atropine An alkaloid, extracted from deadly nightshade, that acts on certain nerves of the autonomic nervous system. It is used during anesthesia to decrease secretions of the lungs, which lowers the risk of postoperative chest infections. It also dilates the pupil of the eye and speeds up the heart rate.

Atropos. *See* Fates.

Attalus I Soter (269–197 BC) Ruler of *Pergamum (241–197), who took the title of king after a victory over the Galatians (before 230). By his conquests in Asia Minor and his support of Roman opposition to Philip V of Macedon (237–179; reigned 220–179), he made Pergamum a significant power.

attar of roses (otto of rose *or* essence of rose) A fragrant colorless or pale-yellow oil distilled from fresh rose petals. It is produced in Bulgaria, S France, Morocco, and Turkey. About 1 gram of attar is extracted from 4 kilograms of roses. Rosewater is a by-product of the distillation. It is used to make perfumes and in flavorings.

Attenborough, Sir Richard (1923–) British film actor, director, and producer. After numerous appearances in British war films and comedies he developed into a versatile character actor in such films as *Loot* (1969) and *10 Rillington Place* (1971). As director, his films include *Young Winston* (1974), *A Bridge Too Far* (1977), and *Gandhi* (1982).

attenuation The reduction in amplitude of an electromagnetic wave or an electric current during transmission. In electric circuits attenuation is often introduced to reduce unwanted components of a signal. Broadcast electromagnetic radiation is attenuated as it passes through buildings, etc., and to a lesser extent by its passage through the atmosphere. In space, however, the attenuation is negligible.

Attica A region of ancient E central Greece. According to Greek legend the 12 towns of Attica were united by Theseus into a single state, which was dominated by Athens by the 5th century BC.

Attila (c. 406–53) King of the Huns (434–53), known as the Scourge of God. After murdering his brother and coruler, Bleda, he extended his possessions in central Europe and attacked (441–43) the eastern frontier of the Roman Empire. In 451 he invaded Gaul and suffered his only defeat, at the battle of the *Catalaunian Plains. His campaigns in Italy (452) caused much destruction. The pope paid him to spare Rome and Attila died shortly afterward.

Attlee, Clement (Richard), 1st Earl (1883–1967) British statesman; Labor prime minister (1945–51). A lawyer by profession, Attlee taught at the London School of Economics (1913–23). He was elected to Parliament in 1922 and was leader of the Labor Party (1935–55). As the first postwar prime minister he presided over the establishment of the welfare state, nationalizing major industries and introducing the National Health Service. His government also granted independence within the Commonwealth to India.

attorney general As head of the Department of Justice and chief law officer of the federal government, the attorney general represents the US in legal matters generally and gives advice and opinions to the president and to the heads of the executive departments of the government when so requested. The attorney general appears in person to represent the government in the US Supreme Court in cases of exceptional importance. Each state also has an attorney general, who is the chief law officer of the state. He gives advice and opinions to the governor and to executive and administrative departments or agencies.

Attorney General of the United States Chief law officer of the US. Appointed by the president and a member of his cabinet, the attorney general administers the Department of *Justice, directs the penal system, advises the president and executive department heads on legal matters, oversees US marshals, and represents the United States in legal matters. The Judiciary Act of 1789 provided for the office of attorney general.

Attucks, Crispus (?1723–70) US black slave and sailor, the first American victim of the American Revolution. An escaped slave, Attucks was a merchant seaman for twenty years. While in Boston in 1770, he was part of a group of protesters against excessive colonial taxation that was fired upon by the British and was the first to die.

Aube River A river in N central France, rising on the Plateau de Langres and flowing NW to the Seine River. Length: 140 mi (225 km).

Auber, Daniel François Esprit (1782–1871) French composer. He is remembered for his 48 operas, chiefly light works to librettos by the playwright A. E. Scribe (1791–1861), written for the Paris Opéra-Comique. Of these only *La Muette de Portici* (1828) and *Fra Diavolo* (1830) are performed with any frequency.

aubergine A spiny herbaceous plant, *Solanum melongena*, native to S Asia and also known as eggplant. It is commonly grown in warmer regions for its fruit, a large white, yellow, or purple berry that is eaten as a vegetable. The plant grows to a height of 24–40 in (60–100 cm). Family: *Solanaceae*.

Aubrietia (*or* Aubrieta) A genus of trailing perennial flowering plants (about 15 species), native to mountainous areas of E Europe and W Asia. *A. deltoidea* is commonly grown in rock gardens, bearing small purple, red, or pink flowers. Family: *Cruciferae*.

Auburn 32 36N 85 29W A city in E Alabama. The site of Auburn University (1856), it also has textile and lumber mills. Population (1980): 28,471.

Aubusson 45 58N 2 10E A town in central France, in the Creuse department on the Creuse River. It has been renowned for its carpets and tapestries since the 16th century. Population (1968): 5641.

Aubusson, Pierre d' (1423–1503) French cardinal and grand master of the Knights *Hospitallers. Remembered chiefly for his defense of Rhodes against the Turks in 1480, he secured a long-term truce in 1481 by agreeing to imprison the Ottoman sultan's enemy and brother.

Auch 43 40N 0 36E A city in SW France, the capital of the Gers department on the Gers River. The former capital of Armagnac and Gascony, it has a gothic cathedral with a magnificent 17th-century organ. Population (1975): 25,070.

Auckland 36 55S 174 47E The largest city and port in New Zealand, on North Island occupying an isthmus between Waitemata Harbor and Manukau Harbor. Founded in 1840, it was the capital of New Zealand until 1865. The University of Auckland was established in 1882 and there are two cathedrals (Roman Catholic and Anglican). The city is connected with the mainly residential North Shore by the Auckland Harbor Bridge (1959). Auckland is a major industrial center with engineering, food processing, shipbuilding, and chemical industries. The chief exports are iron and steel, dairy products, and meat. Population (1977 est): 150,100.

Auckland Islands 50 35S 166 00E A group of six uninhabited islands in the S Pacific Ocean, belonging to New Zealand. An attempt to introduce cattle and sheep was unsuccessful (1852). Area: 234 sq mi (611 sq km).

auction A method of selling goods publicly, in which many prospective buyers compete with each other, the sale being made to the highest bidder. If bidding does not reach a reserve price specified by the vendor, then the auctioneer withdraws the goods. Rules vary from trade to trade, but the auctioneer usually acts as the seller's agent, charging him a commission on goods sold. Antiques, works of art, houses, and some commercial commodities are sold by auction. In a **Dutch auction**, the sale is offered first at an unrealistically high price, which is lowered gradually until a bid is made.

Auden, W(ystan) H(ugh) (1907–73) British poet. His early volumes, beginning with *Poems* (1930) and *Look, Stranger!* (1936), established him as the leading figure of a group of left-wing poets of the 1930s, that included Stephen *Spender, Louis *MacNeice, and C. *Day Lewis. He also wrote verse dramas in collaboration with Christopher *Isherwood, with whom he went to the US in 1939. He became a US citizen in 1946. He wrote several opera libretti, notably for Stravinsky's *The Rake's Progress* (1951), and his later poetry was characterized by a form of Christian existentialism that replaced his earlier Marxism.

Audenarde. *See* Oudenaarde.

audio frequency A frequency in the range 20 to 20,000 hertz, i.e. the range of frequencies to which the human ear is sensitive.

audiovisual education Education carried out with the help of audio (sound) or visual techniques. There are a whole range of audiovisual aids, including television, tape and video recorders, teaching machines, and overhead projectors and the long-established wallcharts and blackboards. Although audiovisual education has been used throughout history, its systematic application developed in the 20th century. Research into the method has shown that, when properly used, it increases both the student's interest and his recall of the material presented. Since 1958 the US Congress has provided aid for educational broadcasting.

auditing. *See* accountancy.

Audubon, John James (1785–1851) US naturalist and artist noted for his lifelike drawings and paintings of birds. Educated in France, Audubon emigrated to the US, where he developed an interest in bird migration and began painting birds and other animals. *The Birds of America* (4 vols, 1827–38) established his reputation as an illustrator. The National Audubon Society, founded in his honor in 1886, is dedicated to the conservation of birds throughout the US.

Auger effect The spontaneous ejection of an electron from an excited, singly charged, positive ion to form a doubly charged ion. The ion may be excited by a gamma ray from its nucleus or by bombarding it with particles, such as photons or electrons. It is named for the French physicist Pierre Auger.

Augsburg 48 21N 10 54E A city in S West Germany, in Bavaria at the confluence of the Wertach and Lech Rivers. It is a major industrial center; its manufactures include textiles, chemicals, cars, aircraft, and printing machinery. Many of its historic buildings, including the 10th-century cathedral, survived the bombardment of World War II. *History:* founded by the Romans in 15 BC, it became an important banking and commercial center in the 15th and 16th centuries mainly with the aid of the Fugger and Welsen merchant families. An imperial free city from 1276, it was the seat of the notable diets of 1530 (*see* Augsburg Confession) and 1555 (*see* Augsburg, Peace of). It is the birthplace of Holbein and Brecht. Population (1980 est): 246,600.

Augsburg, League of (1686) An alliance originally consisting of the Holy Roman Empire, Spain, Sweden, and several German states. In 1689 they were joined by England, Holland, and Savoy, thus forming the *Grand Alliance, which waged war on Louis XIV of France from 1689 to 1697.

Augsburg, Peace of (1555) A religious compromise issued by an imperial diet at Augsburg, over which the future Emperor *Ferdinand I presided, which established the coexistence of Roman Catholicism and Lutheranism in Germany. Each prince was to determine the denomination of his territory, which was to be either Catholicism or Lutheranism. In order to safeguard Catholic property, any prince who became a Protestant was to renounce his land and revenues. The settlement gave Germany 50 years of peace.

Augsburg Confession The main and distinctive confession of faith of the Lutheran Churches. Drawn up in its original form by Melancthon and approved by Luther, it was presented to the imperial diet that Emperor Charles V had summoned at Augsburg in 1530 to judge Luther's controversial preaching.

augury Ritual divination practiced in ancient Rome by augurs, priests skilled in the auspices, or interpretation of certain natural occurrences. The word "auspice" derives from the Latin for "bird" + "observation"; the commonest means of augury were the flight and song of birds, but thunder, lightning, movements of animals, and the appetites of tame chickens were also studied. Signs on the augur's left were propitious, those on his right unpropitious. Augury accompanied every major undertaking, to ascertain through the auspices whether the gods were favorably inclined.

August Eighth month of the year. Its name is derived from *Augustus* in honor of Augustus Caesar, the first Roman emperor. It has 31 days. August's zodiac signs are Leo and Virgo; its flower is the poppy, and its birthstones are the sardonyx and the peridot.

Augusta 33 29N 82 00W A town in Georgia on the Savannah River. It is a medical and service center for the many government installations nearby. Population (1970): 59,864.

Augusta 44 17N 69 50W The capital of Maine, on the Kennebec River. Established as a trading post in 1628, it has a large timber industry. Population (1980): 21,819.

Austin, Stephen F(uller) (1793–1836) US settler leader in Texas. In 1821 he paved the way for an Anglo-American colony in then-Spanish Texas on a land grant left to him by his father. He negotiated with Mexican President Santa Anna and when he saw no future for Texas as a part of Mexico, fought valiantly for Texas's independence (1836). He served briefly, before his death, as the first secretary of state for Texas.

Augustine of Hippo, St (354–430 AD) North African theologian; Father and Doctor of the Church, born at Tagaste. His mother was a Christian but, after studying at Carthage, he became a Manichaean. He taught rhetoric in Rome and in Milan, where he was attracted to *Neoplatonism. However, under the influence of St *Ambrose, Bishop of Milan, he was finally converted to Christianity in 386. On his return to Africa, he lived as a monk until he was ordained at Hippo in 391. He became Bishop of Hippo in 396 and died there during a Vandal siege. His works are the most important and influential of those written by the early Fathers, especially *The City of God*, a defense of Christianity in 22 books, and his spiritual autobiography, *The Confessions*. His other writings include commentaries on the scriptures, sermons, letters, and treatises against the heresies *Manichaeism, Donatism (see Donatists), and Pelagianism (see Pelagius). He was most actively involved in the Pelagian controversy, in which he upheld the doctrines of original sin and divine grace. Feast day: Aug 28.

Augustinians A term sometimes used generally to refer to all the Roman Catholic religious orders that follow the Rule of St Augustine, a program for the religious life drawn up by *Augustine of Hippo. More specifically it refers to the orders of the Augustinian (or Austin) Canons, founded in the 11th century, and the Augustinian Hermits (or Austin Friars), founded in the 13th century, both of which have corresponding orders for women.

AUGUSTUS *During his reign the coinage was restored to the control of the Senate and coins were marked S.C. (senatus consulto, by decree of the Senate); the emperor's head is shown on the obverse.*

Augustus (or Octavian; 63 BC–14 AD) The first Roman emperor, who restored the greatness of the Roman world following the disintegration of the Republic. Augustus, who was born Gaius Octavius, was the great-nephew and adopted son of Julius Caesar. After Caesar's assassination in 44, Augustus (now Gaius Julius Caesar Octavianus; or Octavian) came to an agreement with *Mark Antony and in 43 they formed the second *Triumvirate with *Lepidus. Lepidus was forced to retire in 36 and Augustus' relations with Mark Antony failed to withstand Antony's abandonment of his wife Octavia (Augustus' sister) for *Cleopatra. Antony's defeat at Actium in 31 allowed Augustus to establish his personal supremacy at the head of an autocratic government known as the principate. In 27 he was proclaimed Augustus (sacred).

Augustus was an outstanding administrator and consolidated the so-called Pax Romana (Roman Peace) that he had established with a durable administrative and financial system. The patronage of his close adviser *Maecenas fostered a literary renaissance and with the military assistance of *Agrippa, and later of his own stepson *Tiberius, he secured and then expanded the Empire. In 4 AD he named Tiberius, the son of his third wife *Livia Drusilla, his heir. Augustus was deified after his death.

Augustus I (1526–86) Elector of Saxony (1553–86). A moderate Protestant, he was a follower of Lutheranism and a harsh opponent of Calvinism. His economic, administrative, and social reforms made Saxony one of the most prosperous German states.

Augustus (II) the Strong (1670–1733) King of Poland (1697–1706, 1710–33). Augustus' invasion of Livonia (1700) began the Great *Northern War, in which he was defeated by Charles XII of Sweden (1702). Augustus was deposed by the Polish diet (1704), formally abdicating in 1706, but was restored by Russia in 1710. His malgovernment precipitated Poland's decline.

auk A stout-bodied seabird belonging to a family (*Alcidae*; 22 species) occurring in the N hemisphere and having a black and white plumage and short pointed wings. The family includes *puffins, *razorbills, *guillemots, the little auk (*Plautus alle*), and the extinct flightless great auk (*Pinguinus impennis*). Order: *Charadriiformes* (gulls, plovers, etc.).

Aung San (c. 1914–47) Burmese statesman; leader of the independence movement. Committed to radical politics from his student days at Rangoon University, Aung San founded the Anti-Fascist People's Freedom League in 1944. He played a crucial role in the negotiations that led to Burmese independence from Britain but was assassinated before it was fully attained.

Aurangzeb (1618–1707) The last Mogul emperor of India (1658–1707); the youngest son of *Shah Jahan. When Shah Jahan fell ill in 1657 Aurangzeb fought a war of succession against his older brother Dara Shikoh. Easily winning, he ascended the throne of Delhi with the title Alamgir ("world-seizer"). A ruthless ruler, he augmented the empire to its greatest extent but in his fervent Muslim orthodoxy he made enemies of his Hindu subjects and in effect weakened Mogul power.

Aurelian(us), Lucius Domitius (c. 215–275 AD) Roman emperor (270–75). Aurelian was of humble birth and owed his accession to the army. He restored imperial unity by his victories over the Vandals, *Zenobia of Palmyra, and the Gallic Empire at Châlons. He was murdered near Byzantium.

auricula A *primula, *P. auricula*, or any of the hybrids derived from it. Native to the Alps, it is widely grown as a garden plant, having showy yellow flowers.

Auriga (Latin: charioteer) A conspicuous constellation in the N sky near Orion, lying in the Milky Way. The brightest star is *Capella.

Aurignacian A culture of the Upper *Paleolithic marked by the use of thick scrapers and heavy blades of stone and flint, flat bone points, and polished bone or antler pins. First recognized at Aurignac (SW France) in 1860 the industry dates back to about 34,000 BC. Since it differs, especially in bonework, from earlier and later (*Gravettian) toolkits, Aurignacian culture may have come from outside Europe. These people hunted mammoth and horse; they also engraved symbols and pictures on rocks (see Lascaux).

auroch An extinct European wild ox, *Bos primigenius*, that survived in Poland until the early 17th century. Standing 6 ft (1.8 m) at the shoulder, aurochs were black with long curved horns and are believed to be ancestors of modern domestic cattle.

Aurora In Roman mythology, the goddess of the dawn. She was called Eos by the Greeks.

aurora A display of diffuse changing colored light seen high in the earth's atmosphere, often taking the form of streamers or drapery and usually green or red. Aurorae occur predominantly in polar regions when energetic charged particles from the sun become trapped in the earth's magnetic field. The rapidly moving particles interact with atoms and molecules in the upper atmosphere and cause them to emit light.

Auschwitz. See Oświęcim.

auscultation The use of a *stethoscope to listen to sounds produced within the body, which forms an essential part of a medical examination. Auscultation of lungs, heart, and intestines are the most useful for reaching a diagnosis.

Ausgleich (German: compromise; 1867) The constitutional settlement that established the Dual Monarchy of *Austria–Hungary (1867–1918).

Ausonius, Decimus Magnus (died c. 395 AD) Roman poet, born at Burdigala (Bordeaux). The tutor of *Gratian, Emperor Valentinian's son, Ausonius became governor of Gaul. *Mosella*, his most famous poem, was written in hexameters and described the Moselle River and its surrounding countryside.

JANE AUSTEN *The only portrait of her from life, which was done by her sister Cassandra.*

Austen, Jane (1775–1817) British novelist. She was the daughter of a clergyman and lived an outwardly uneventful life with her family in the south of England, settling in Chawton in Hampshire in 1809. Her six major novels are *Sense and Sensibility* (1811), *Pride and Prejudice* (1813), *Mansfield Park* (1814), *Emma* (1815–16), *Northanger Abbey* (1818), and *Persuasion* (1818). Their heroines are drawn from the rural landed gentry, and their plots trace the development of relationships that generally culminate in marriage. Her novels are distinguished by her delicate and often ironic wit and her sensitive insight into personal and social tensions.

austenite A form of *steel that exists when the metal is heated to about 587°F (1000°C), in which the carbon exists as a solid solution in the iron. Austenitic steels retain this structure at room temperature because of the presence of an alloying element, such as manganese. Austenite is nonmagnetic and has a high ductility. Named for Sir William C. Roberts-Austen (1843–1902).

Austerlitz, Battle of (December 2, 1805) The battle in which Napoleon's 68,000-strong army outmaneuvered and defeated almost 90,000 Russians and Austrians led by *Kutuzov. It took place near Austerlitz (now Slavkov u Brna, Czechoslovakia). Napoleon's great victory forced the Austrians to make peace with France by the Treaty of Pressburg and the Russian army to return to Russia.

Austin 30 18N 97 47W A city in the US, the capital of Texas on the Colorado River. The site of the University of Texas (1883), its industries include food processing. Population (1980): 345,496.

Australasia A term applied loosely to encompass the islands of the S Pacific: Australia, New Zealand, New Guinea, and their associated islands. The Malay Archipelago and the Philippines are also sometimes included. *See also* Oceania.

Australia, Commonwealth of A country in the S Pacific comprising the smallest continent. The nation of Australia is a federation of states (including Tasmania, an offshore island state to the SE). There are five mainland states (Queensland, New South Wales, Victoria, South Australia, and Western Australia) and two territories (the Northern Territory and the Australian Capital Territory, an enclave within New South Wales where Canberra, the federal capital, is located). External territories include *Norfolk Island, *Christmas Island, the *Cocos (Keeling) Islands, and the *Australian Antarctic Territories. Much of the country has a hot dry climate and a large part of the vast central plains, the Australian Shield, is desert or semidesert. The Great Barrier Reef, the world's most extensive

coral reef, lies off the tropical NE coast, and the highest mountains, reaching 7,000 ft (2,000 m), are in the Great Dividing Range, which runs parallel to the E coast. The Murray River and its tributaries form the main river system. The inhabitants are very largely of European, especially British, origin, but there are about 125,000 Aborigines (45,000 of pure stock and 80,000 of mixed stock). Constituting the native people, the Aborigines were detribalized and placed on reservations with the arrival of the whites in the 18th and 19th centuries. Most have now been assimilated into rural and urban areas, but race relations remains a problem. Efforts have been made toward equalization of treatment of the aborigines, including the enfranchisment of aborigines of pure stock in 1962, but economic and social barriers persist.

Australia is noted for its unique flora and fauna, including the koala bear, the kangaroo, the wallaby, the dingo, and the distinctive gum tree, or eucalyptus. Since World War II the population has increased dramatically, largely as a result of immigration. *Economy*: agriculture continues to make a substantial contribution to the economy, the main crops being wheat and other cereals, sugar cane, and fruit. Livestock, particularly sheep and cattle, is also important. Since the 1960s, however, growth in the industrial sector has been especially marked, the leading manufactures being iron and steel products, transportation equipment, and machinery. Mining is now of vital importance, especially the extraction of coal, iron, bauxite, uranium, copper, lead, and zinc. There have been significant discoveries of oil and natural gas and about 70% of oil for home consumption is now produced in Australia. The main exports are wool, meat, cereals, sugar, iron ore, and nonferrous ores. *History*: the country was inhabited by the Aborigines, immigrants from SE Asia, for approximately 20,000 years before the arrival of the Europeans, beginning with the Portuguese in the 16th century and the Dutch in the early 17th century. In 1770 Captain Cook claimed the fertile E coast for Britain and the area, known as New South Wales, was at first used mainly as a penal colony. The introduction of the merino sheep, however, encouraged expansion of civilian settlements, and Australia gradually became a British dependency. The discovery of gold in Victoria in 1851 attracted large numbers of immigrants, and from this period the colonies struggled for greater independence, developing broadly similar structures and policies. In 1901 the six colonies were federated to form the Commonwealth, becoming an independent dominion of the British Empire. In 1911 the site for the federal capital, under the title of the Australian Capital Territory, and the Northern Territory were added to the Commonwealth. Strong measures were introduced in the late 19th century to prevent immigration by non-whites and these had a continuing influence on immigration policy. In 1974, however, Gough *Whitlam abolished the "white Australia" policy and a new immigration scheme was introduced in 1979, which was aimed at extending the country's nondiscriminatory image. Australia played a significant part in both World Wars, taking an important role in the Gallipoli campaign in World War I and cooperating closely with the US in World War II. Since the war closer ties have been developed with Asia, especially with Japan, which now takes a third of Australia's exports. In 1978 the Northern Territory achieved self-government although the federal government retained control over uranium. Australia is a member of the British Commonwealth. Prime minister: Robert J. Hawke. Official language: English. Official currency: Australian dollar of 100 cents. Area: 2,967,283 sq mi (7,686,884 sq km). Population (1983 est): 13,265,000. Capital: Canberra. Main port: Sydney.

Australian Alps A mountain range in SE Australia. Part of the *Great Dividing Range, it extends from E Victoria into SE New South Wales and contains the *Snowy Mountains and Mount *Kosciusko, Australia's highest mountain. It is a popular winter-sports area.

Australian Antarctic Territory The area of Antarctica claimed by Australia. It includes all the land lying S of latitude 60°S and between longitudes 45°E and 160°E, excluding *Terre Adélie. Several research stations are sited here.

Australian Capital Territory An administrative division of SE Australia. It was created in 1911 from the Limestone Plains region of New South Wales as a site for *Canberra, the capital of Australia. Jervis Bay was transferred to the territory in 1915 for development as a seaport. It is the site of several important institutions, including the Australian Academy of Science, the Royal Military College, and the Royal Australian Naval College (at Jervis Bay). Area: 939 sq mi (2432 sq km). Population (1980 est): 226,600.

Australian Rules. *See* football.

Austral Islands. *See* Tubuai Islands.

Australopithecus A genus of fossil manlike higher primates of the late Pliocene and Pleistocene eras of S and E Africa. Although small in brain size, their cranial and skeletal structures were more like those of modern man than of apes. They walked erect and probably hunted and used primitive tools. They may have been the direct ancestors of modern man, but opinion differs on this. The question is complicated by the fact that there were two basic types of australopithecine, a more robust apelike form called *Paranthropus* and the more manlike form of *Australopithecus*. One branch of the latter may have evolved into *Homo erectus* (□*Homo*). The creature discovered by Louis *Leakey at *Olduvai in 1959 and given by him the generic name of *Zinjanthropus* has now been included with the other australopithecines as *Australopithecus boisei*.

Austrasia The eastern Frankish kingdom created together with *Neustria by the partition in 511 of the Merovingian kingdom by *Clovis. Occupying an area that is now NE France and West Germany, its capital from 629 was at Metz. Austrasia was increasingly dominated by the mayors of the palace (viceroys), the last of which, *Pepin the Short, deposed the Merovingians in 751 and reunited the Frankish territories into what became the Carolingian empire. *See also* Franks.

Austria, Republic of (German name: Österreich) A country in central Europe, on the N side of the Alps. A large part of the country is mountainous but the E area consists of lower hills and plains, with the Danube River flowing through the NE. Most of the inhabitants are German but there are minorities of Croats, Slovenes, and others. *Economy*: although agriculture and forestry are important, there is considerable heavy industry, based particularly on iron and steel. Hydroelectric power is a valuable source of energy. Tourism has grown in recent years, both summer and winter. Main exports include iron and steel, machinery, paper and paper products, wood, and textiles. *History*: Austria has a long history of human habitation, going back to the Celtic settlements of the early Iron Age. The area was part of the Roman Empire from 15 BC until the 5th century AD when it was overrun by Germanic tribes. In succeeding centuries it was occupied in turn by Slavs and Magyars from whom it was taken in 955 by the Holy Roman Emperor *Otto I. He conferred it upon Leopold of Babenberg, who founded the first Austrian dynasty. In 1282 the *Habsburgs acquired Austria, which was to become the core of their vast empire. In 1526 Bohemia and Hungary were united under the Austrian crown. The Austrian Empire continued to hold a predominant position in Europe until the middle of the 19th century when its power was lessened by successive defeats, especially in the *Austro-Prussian War. In 1867 the Habsburgs were forced to acknowledge the nationalist aspirations of Hungary and formed the Dual Monarchy of *Austria-Hungary, under the Emperor *Francis Joseph. During his reign there was considerable unrest, especially among the Slav peoples of the very diverse Empire; the assassination of the Archduke Francis Ferdinand by Serbian nationalists in 1914 was the immediate cause of World War I. In 1918 Austria became a republic. In spite of efforts on the part of the chancellor *Schuschnigg to maintain independence, it was annexed by Nazi Germany in 1938 (*see* Anschluss). After World War II it was occupied jointly by the Allies, regaining its independence as a republic in 1955. Chancellor Bruno *Kreisky, who came to power in 1970 as head of Austria's first all-socialist government. In the 1983 elections, in which debate focused on economic issues, the Social Democrats (Kreisky's party), who favored government-sponsored work programs, lost their absolute majority in the legislature (held since 1971) to the Christian Democrats, who supported aid to private industry. Chancellor Kreisky promptly announced his resignation and was replaced by Fred Sinowatz, who formed a coalition cabinet composed of Social Democrats and members of the Freedom party. President: Dr Rudolf Kirchschläger. Official language: German. Currency: schilling of 100 groschen. Area: 32,375 sq mi (85,853 sq km). Population (1983 est): 7,574,000.

Austria-Hungary, Dual Monarchy of The Habsburg monarchy from 1867 to 1918. It was established by the *Ausgleich* (compromise) in response to the militant demands of Hungarian nationalism. The empire of Austria and the kingdom of Hungary each had its own laws, parliament, and ministries but were united by the monarch (Emperors *Francis Joseph and then *Charles), minister for foreign affairs and minister for war, and by the biannual meetings of delegations of representatives of each parliament. The Dual Monarchy was weakened by resurgent nationalism in the early 20th century and disappeared in 1918 with the proclamation of an Austrian republic.

Austrian Succession, War of the (1740–48) The war between Austria and Prussia, in which Britain supported Austria and France and Spain were allied to Prussia. It was brought about by the disputed succession of *Maria Theresa to the Austrian lands. Hostilities were begun by *Frederick the Great of Prussia, who annexed the Austrian province of Silesia in 1740. Unstable alliances were formed between European powers on the Continent and hostilities overseas, especially between France and Britain, were exacerbated. The war was ended by the Treaty of *Aix-la-Chapelle, at which Prussia obtained the greater share of Silesia.

Austro-Asiatic languages A family of about 150 languages and dialects spoken in SE Asia. They include Vietnamese, *Khmer, Nicobarese in the Nicobar Islands, and the *Munda languages of India. In fact there is little superficial resemblance among languages of the family, and their common ancestors and date of separation are difficult to establish. There have, accordingly, been attempts to link them to other language families, as was done in the Austro-Tai hypothesis (first proposed in 1906), which postulated a super-family to include the Austro-Asiatic languages, the *Austronesian languages, and certain languages of Indochina.

Austronesian languages A large language family, also caled Malayo-Polynesian, spoken in the Malay peninsula, Taiwan, Madagascar, and the islands of the Pacific Ocean. There are two subgroups: the Western branch, which has up to 200 member languages and includes Malay, Indonesian, Malagasy, Javanese, and Tagalog; and the Eastern or Oceanic branch, which has up to 300 members and includes the languages of the islands in the S and central Pacific, such as Samoa, Tahiti, Tonga, Fiji, New Guinea, and Hawaii. There is some doubt as to whether the languages of Taiwan form a separate group or are part of the Western branch.

Austro-Prussian War (*or* Seven Weeks' War; 1866) A war between German states led respectively by Austria and Prussia. The Prussian victory was an important landmark in Bismarck's strategy for uniting Germany under Prussian leadership.

auteur theory In film criticism, emphasis on the dominant role of the director. It was developed in the 1950s by several writers for the French magazine *Cahiers du Cinéma* who later became directors themselves, notably Truffaut, Godard, Rohmer, and Chabrol. Their method of evaluation, which was based on a consideration of the director's technique, intentions, and personal style, influenced several British and US film critics during the 1960s.

autism A rare and severe mental illness that starts in early childhood. Autistic children are aloof and do not form normal personal relationships but they can become emotionally attached to things. They do not communicate normally, often cannot form abstract concepts, and they are very upset by tiny changes in their familiar surroundings. Most, but not all, are mentally retarded. Autism can be caused by brain damage and can also be inherited. Lengthy specialized education is usually necessary for autistic children.

auto-da-fé (Portuguese: act of faith) The public ceremony at which persons convicted of crimes by the *Inquisition in Portugal, Spain, and their colonies were sentenced. Punishment of victims, including the burning of heretics, was the responsibility of the secular authorities. The first *auto-da-fé* was held in Seville in 1481 and the last, in Mexico in 1815.

autogiro An aircraft with large horizontal freely rotating blades to obtain lift. It differs from the *helicopter in that a propeller provides forward motion, which in turn causes the rotation of the unmotorized horizontal blades.

autoimmunity A condition in which the body produces antibodies (called autoantibodies) that damage or destroy its own tissues. This produces symptoms of various **autoimmune diseases**, the majority of which are poorly understood. Rheumatoid *arthritis is caused by the production of autoantibodies against joint tissue; the disease can be diagnosed by the detection of these antibodies in the serum. A more general production of autoantibodies causes systemic *lupus erythematosis, which can affect most tissues in the body.

automatic pilot A device utilizing a gyroscope for keeping an aircraft on a given course. When the aircraft goes off course, the gyro axis rotates, operating electrical contacts, which make the necessary adjustments to the control surfaces.

automation The use of electronic devices controlled by a computer in mechanical processes that would otherwise be controlled by human operators. It has made considerable impact on production engineering in such fields as steel and chemical manufacture. Telecommunications (automatic telephone exchanges), transport (navigation, railroad signals), and mining also employ automated systems.

automobile A self-propelled road vehicle. The search for a means of replacing the horse as a means of transport began seriously at the beginning of the 18th century, when *Newcomen and *Watt had shown that steam could be harnessed to produce power. Joseph Cugnot (1725–1804) in 1770 used a steam engine to drive a gun tractor and in 1808 Richard *Trevithick built a working steam carriage. But neither these vehicles nor the many other steam carriages of the first half of the 19th century were more than cumbersome novelties. An effective horseless carriage needed a smaller, more efficient power source. This was eventually provided by two German engineers, Nikolaus *Otto and Gottlieb *Daimler, who in 1876 patented

Benz 8hp *1600 of these "horseless carriages" were sold between 1898 and 1900. Described as the first reliable car offered to the public, its twin-cylinder 1570 cc engine gave it a top speed of 18 mph (29 km/hr).*

Rolls-Royce Silver Ghost *First built in 1907 (and continuing in production until 1927) it quickly established itself as "the best car in the world." Its 7-liter 6-cylinder engine gave it a top speed of 65 mph (105 km/hr).*

Ford Model T *15 million of this first mass-produced car (nicknamed the "Tin Lizzie") were made between 1908 and 1927. Its 4-cylinder, 2898 cc engine gave it a top speed of 40 mph (64 km/hr).*

Bugatti Royale *Made to compete with the Rolls-Royce, this magnificent 13-liter 8-cylinder automobile cost about $25,000 in 1927 – a price even outside the range of its intended customers - the crowned heads of Europe. Seven were sold.*

Volkswagen *Nicknamed "the Beetle," this 1937 German design by Ferdinand Porsche was still selling in the 1970s, making it the best selling car ever made. Its air-cooled slow-revving rear engine increased from 1131 to 1600 cc over the years.*

MG TC *This post-war British sports car (1946–55) was little changed from the TA model first built in 1937. The TC had a 1250 cc engine.*

Buick *This 1949 US car represented a release from wartime restrictions and set the trend for a generation of large American cars.*

Mini *The best selling British car ever made. Designed by Alec Issigonis, the Mini was introduced in 1959 and is still selling. Its frontwheel drive, transverse engine, and 10-inch wheels make it an extremely roomy car for its size.*

Citroën GS *This 1970 French car features Citroën's highly successful self-leveling hydropneumatic suspension. Its 1-liter engine drives the front wheels.*

the Otto-cycle *internal-combustion engine. In 1885, another German, Karl *Benz, used a 3 hp version of this engine to power a tricycle capable of 15 mph (20 km per hour). By 1890 both Daimler and Benz were selling the motorized dog carts that were the forerunners of the modern car. In France, during the closing decade of the 19th century, Panhard, Comte Albert de Dion, Georges Bouton, and Peugeot were all producing and selling cars. In the US, Henry Ford built his car in 1896. In the UK, Henry *Royce, dissatisfied with the quality of foreign cars decided to build his own. In partnership with C. S. *Rolls, he sold his first Rolls-Royce Silver Ghost in 1907.

By the start of World War I, automobiles were in common use; by this time they were much the same in basic shape and design as they are today. Propeller shafts had replaced chains and belts, pneumatic tires had ousted solid tires, and open carriage bodies had given way to closed sedans. Although World War I was the last of the "horse" wars, by 1918 more and more motorized vehicles (including *tanks) were in military use. Nevertheless, motoring was still the preserve of the affluent. It was not until 1925, when Ford brought the price of his Model T down to $290 that motoring became accessible to ordinary people. During the 1930s the price of cars steadily declined, but the real mass market did not develop until after World War II. Before the war it was rare for a model to sell a million vehicles, now a popular car has to do so to be a commercial success.

The future of the private car is uncertain: diminishing world reserves of oil make fuel increasingly expensive, the cost of the cars themselves has risen sharply, and the pollution and noise they create makes them the enemy of conservationists and urban planners. It may be that the gasoline supplies will hold out until an economic alternative is found (*see* electric car) or it may be that once again the private car will become the privilege of the rich.

automobile racing Racing in cars, from stockcars to highly specialized Grand Prix vehicles, one of the most popular US spectator sports. Early races, such as the 1895 race from Paris to Bordeaux and back, were held on public roads, but since the early 1900s they have usually been held on closed-circuit courses. The most prestigious form of racing is Grand Prix (Formula One) racing, for which specially built single-seater vehicles are raced by professional drivers for manufacturers or private owners. The Drivers World Championship (instituted in 1950) is awarded according to points won in certain Formula One races. Formula One cars must weigh at least 530 kg, must not have more than 12 cylinders, and must not have an engine capacity in excess of 3000 cc (or 1500 cc if they are supercharged). Formulas Two (minimum weight 450 kg for 4 cylinders, 475 kg for 6 cylinders, or 500 kg in excess of 6; engine capacity less than 2000 cc) and Three (maximum of 4 cylinders and 1600 cc) function largely as training grounds for Formula One drivers. **Sports-car racing** is for production-type modified sports cars; the most famous sports-car race is the Le Mans 24 Hours. *See also* drag racing; karting; rally; stock-car racing.

autopsy (necropsy *or* postmortem) The dissection and examination of a dead body. An autopsy is performed when the cause of death is uncertain: it may provide further information on a poorly understood disease or evidence of criminal involvement. Except for sudden death or death due to obscure causes, permission for autopsy must be granted by the relatives.

autoradiography The use of photography to examine the distribution of a *radioisotope in a thin specimen. The specimen is placed on a photographic plate, which after development shows the distribution of the radioisotope.

autosuggestion A way of changing one's behavior by firmly repeating ideas to oneself. It can be used to control undesirable habits or to cope with anxiety and is sometimes taught to psychiatric patients. *See also* hypnosis.

autumnal equinox. *See* equinox.

autumn crocus A herbaceous perennial European plant, *Colchicum autumnale*, also called meadow saffron. It has narrow strap-shaped leaves, up to 12 in (30 cm) long, and a single purple-blue crocus-like flower, which appears in autumn after the leaves have died. The drug colchicine, extracted from the corms, is used in the treatment of gout and in genetic research. Some plants of the genus are cultivated for ornament. Family: *Liliaceae*. *Compare* Crocus.

Autun 46 58N 4 18E A city in central France, in the Saône-et-Loire department on the Arroux River. Famous for its school of rhetoric during Roman times, it has several Roman remains. Its manufactures include furniture and leather. Population (1975): 22,949.

Auvergne A planning region and former province in S central France. Its name derives from the Averni, who strongly resisted Roman control of the area. Crossed by the volcanic Auvergne Mountains that rise to over 6000 ft (1800 m), it has many mineral springs and some level fertile districts. It is predominantly agricultural and is noted for the growing of

wheat and grapes and the rearing of cattle; cheese and wine are also produced. Area: 10,032 sq mi (25,988 sq km). Population (1981 est): 1,320,000.

Auxerre 47 48N 3 35W A city in central France, the capital of the Yonne department on the Yonne River. Its gothic cathedral has exceptional 13th-century stained glass windows. Wine and metal goods are produced here. Population (1975): 39,955.

auxin An organic substance, produced within a plant, that stimulates, inhibits, or modifies growth of the plant. Auxins are sometimes known as plant hormones. The main auxin is indoleacetic acid (IAA). Auxins are responsible for a variety of effects, for example shoot curvature, leaf fall, and fruit growth. Synthetic auxins, such as 2,4-dichlorophenoxyacetic acid (2,4-D), are used as weedkillers for broad-leaved weeds (*see* herbicide).

avadavat A small plump songbird, *Estrilda amandava*, also called red munia. Occurring in meadows and marshes of Asia, it is the only *waxbill found outside Africa. In the breeding season the male plumage is bright red with mottled brown patches and white speckling.

avalanche A rapid movement of snow and ice, and sometimes rock debris, down steep slopes. They may occur in winter, when fresh snow slides off an older compacted snow surface, and in spring, when thaws cause the mass to slip. Avalanches can cause severe damage with loss of life and property and in populous mountain areas steel avalanche-sheds are used to protect roads and railroads.

Avalon The paradise of Celtic mythology to which King Arthur (*see* Arthurian legend) was taken after his final battle. It was ruled by *Morgan le Fay, famous for her magical powers, and has been identified with Glastonbury, England.

Avebury 51 27N 1 51W A village in S England, in Wiltshire, on the site of a large complex of Neolithic and early Bronze Age stone circles, banks, and ditches. The principal circle, with its ditch and outer bank, encloses over 30 acres (12 hectares); within it are two smaller ones. Nearby is *Silbury Hill.

Aveiro 40 38N 8 40W A port in NW Portugal, on an inlet of the Atlantic Ocean. Its museum contains medieval art treasures. It has agricultural industries. Population (1970): 51,709.

Avellaneda 34 40S 58 20W A city in Argentina, a suburb of Buenos Aires on the Río de la Plata. It is highly industrialized with meat processing, oil refining, and tanning. Population (1970): 337,538.

AVENS *Water avens* (Geum rivale) *is widely distributed in damp shady places of the N hemisphere. Its flowers have purple sepals and orange-pink petals.*

avens A perennial herbaceous plant of the genus *Geum* (about 40 species), native to temperate and Arctic regions. Most species rarely exceed 24 in (60 cm) in height. Their flowers, 8–12 in (2–3 cm) long, are white, yellow, orange, or red, either solitary or in clusters. *G. coccineum* is a common ornamental. Family: *Rosaceae*.

average 1. (mathematics) A representative or middle value of a set of quantities. The arithmetical average (*or* arithmetical mean) is found by adding the quantities in a set and dividing the total by the number of quantities: the arithmetical average of 7, 8, 13, and 20 is 12 (48 divided by 4). The geometric average (*or* geometric mean) is found by multiplying together the numbers in a set and extracting a root equal to the number of quantities: the geometric average of 2, 9, and 12 is 6 ($\sqrt[3]{216}$). 2. (insurance) Loss or damage to property. In *marine insurance it refers to a partial loss. A **particular average** affects only one interest, whereas a **general average** is shared among all the parties concerned (e.g. if a deck cargo has to be jettisoned to save a ship in a storm, all the cargo owners have to contribute to the loss). In fire insurance, average is used to combat underinsurance. For example, if an insurer has only insured his goods for a proportion of their total value, he will only be paid that proportion of any claim for a partial loss.

Avernus, Lake A small crater lake near Naples and Cumae (the earliest Greek colony in Italy). In ancient times it was believed to be the entrance to the infernal regions, and *Avernus* was often used by writers as a synonym for the underworld. In Virgil's *Aeneid*, Aeneas descends to the infernal regions through a cave near the lake.

Averroes (Ibn Rushd; 1126–98) Muslim philosopher and a judge in Córdoba and Seville. Averroes' main works were his commentaries on Aristotle, which greatly influenced the philosophy of medieval Christianity. He defended philosophy as the highest form of inquiry, holding that faith and reason are not necessarily in conflict but are separate ways of arriving at the truth.

aversion therapy A form of *conditioning used to treat some kinds of undesirable behavior, such as sexual deviation, alcoholism, and drug addiction. An unpleasant stimulus (e.g. an electric shock) is associated with a stimulus related to the problem behavior (e.g. the taste of alcohol). *See also* behavior therapy.

Avesta The sacred scriptures of *Zoroastrianism. Written in Old Iranian, the five books of the *Avesta* contain prayers (probably by Zoroaster himself) hymns, ritual and liturgical instruction, and the main body of Zoroastrian law. Its surviving form dates from about the 6th century AD.

Avicenna (980–1037) Persian philosopher and physician. Avicenna received extensive education in science and philosophy and served various rulers during his life, as government official and physician. His encyclopedia of philosophy, *Ash-Shifa* (*The Recovery*), encompasses logic, psychology, metaphysics, and natural sciences and parts were subsequently translated into Latin. Avicenna's *Canon of Medicine*, based on Roman and Arabic medicine and his own medical knowledge, became a popular text throughout the Middle East and Europe.

Avignon 43 56N 4 48E A city in SE France, the capital of the Vaucluse department on the Rhône River. The papacy, under French control, was removed to Avignon (1309–77; *see* Avignon papacy) and there were subsequently rival popes at Rome and Avignon until 1417 (*see* Great Schism). Famous landmarks include the 14th-century papal palace and the 12th-century bridge, of which only four arches remain. A popular tourist center, Avignon trades in wine and has chemical, soap, and cement industries. Population (1975): 93,024.

Avignon papacy (1309–77) The period during which the popes resided in Avignon (France) rather than Rome. It is sometimes called the Babylonian Captivity (in reference to the *Babylonian exile in Jewish history). The papal court was established in Avignon, a papal fief, by *Clement V, who, like his six successors in Avignon, was French. English and German criticism of French dominance over the papacy eventually forced its return to Rome under Gregory XI. Shortly afterward the division in the Church known as the *Great Schism occurred, largely in response to the increased power acquired by the cardinals during the Avignon papacy.

Avignon school A school of painting established when Clement V moved the papal court from Rome to Avignon in 1309 and imported Italian 14th-century masters, notably Simone *Martini, to decorate the papal palace. After the pope's return to Rome (1377) painters remaining in Avignon developed a unique style, fusing Italian and Flemish influences. The artists of the school include Nicholas Froment (active 1450–90) and its most celebrated work is the anonymous *Villeneuve Pietà* (c. 1460; Louvre).

Avila 40 39N 4 42W A city in central Spain, in Old Castile on the Adaja River. A popular tourist center, the old part of the town is enclosed by 12th-century walls and has a notable gothic cathedral (11th–15th centuries). St Teresa was born here. Population (1970): 30,983.

avocado A tree, *Persia americana*, up to 59 ft (18 m) tall, native to Mexico and Central America but now extensively cultivated in Florida, California, and South Africa for its fruit. These fruits—**avocado pears**— may reach a weight of 4lb (2kg): they have a green to dark-purple skin, a fatty flesh rich in fat, protein, and vitamins A and B, and a single hard seed.

avocet A wading bird of the genus *Recurvirostra*, having long slender legs and a long thin upcurved bill used to skim the surface of mud or water in search of small invertebrates. The Eurasian avocet (*R. avosetta*), 20 in (50 cm) long, has a black-and-white plumage and gray-blue legs and is protected in Britain. Family: *Recurvirostridae*; order: *Charadriiformes* (gulls, plovers, etc.).

Avogadro, Amedeo, Conte di Quaregna e Ceretto (1776–1856) Italian physicist, who became professor of physics at the University of Turin. He developed *Gay-Lussac's hypothesis that equal volumes of gases contain equal numbers of particles, establishing the difference between atoms and molecules. Because he made this vital distinction the theory is now known as Avogadro's hypothesis. His name is also commemorated in **Avogadro's number** (*or* the Avogadro constant), the number of molecules in one mole of substance (it has the value $6.022,52 \times 10^{23}$). Avogadro's work was largely neglected during his life and was not acknowledged until *Cannizzaro brought it to public notice in 1854.

Avon, 1st Earl of. *See* Eden, Anthony.

Avon River The name of several rivers in the UK, including: 1. A river in central England, flowing SW from Northamptonshire to the Severn River at Tewkesbury. Length: 96 mi (154 km). 2. A river in SW England, flowing S and W from Gloucestershire to the Severn estuary at Avonmouth. Length: 75 mi (120 km). 3. A river in S England, flowing S from Wiltshire to the English Channel. Length: 60 mi (96 km).

axiology The theory of values in ethics and aesthetics, particularly the search for the good and its nature. Axiology investigates basic principles governing moral judgment, types of value, and the place of values (or norms) within the frameworks of philosophical systems. *Plato, for instance, held to an absolute theory of the Idea of the Good, while *Hume and others believed that values were relative, depending on degrees of approval felt by persons making value judgments. *Kant found the source of value in practical reason, while in *utilitarianism it lay in the principle of the greatest happiness for the greatest number.

axiom An assumption or principle, used to prove a theorem, that is itself accepted as true without proof. Some mathematicians reserve the term for an assumption in logic, using postulate for an assumption made in other fields.

axis deer A slender deer, *Axis axis*, also called chital, that usually lives in small herds near rivers in India and Sri Lanka. Axis deer measure up to 40 in (100 cm) at the shoulder and are reddish with white spots and pale underparts.

Axis Powers The coalition of Germany, Italy, and Japan that opposed the *Allied Powers in *World War II. It originated in agreements going back to 1936 and it culminated in the Tripartite Pact (1940).

axolotl A salamander, *Ambystoma mexicanum*, occurring in Mexican lakes. It reaches a length of 10 in (25 cm), has a long tail and weak limbs, and is typically dark brown. Axolotls retain their larval characteristics permanently, reproducing in this state, although under certain conditions they may develop into adults. Family: *Ambystomatidae*.

axon. *See* neuron.

Axum. *See* Aksum.

Ayacucho 13 10S 74 15W A city in S central Peru. The battle of Ayacucho (1824) was fought nearby, resulting in Peru gaining independence from Spain. An agricultural center, tourism is also important. It has a university (founded 1677 and reopened 1957). Population (1970 est): 24,374.

Ayatollah Ruholla Khomeini. *See* Khomeini, Ayatollah Ruholla.

aye-aye A rare arboreal *prosimian primate, *Daubentonia madagascariensis*, occurring only in the coastal forests of N Madagascar. It is 34–46 in (86–104 cm) long including the tail (20–24 in [50–60 cm]) and has dark shaggy fur and large ears used to detect wood-boring insects, extracting them with its incisor teeth and narrow elongated third finger. The aye-aye is the only member of its family (*Daubentoniidae*).

Ayer, Sir Alfred (Jules) (1910–) British philosopher. Ayer's major contribution to British philosophy was his bringing to England the teachings of the *Vienna Circle, in particular the doctrine of *logical positivism. This he expounded in *Language, Truth and Logic* (1936). His later books include *The Foundations of Empirical Knowledge* (1940), *The Problem of Knowledge* (1956), and an autobiography *Part of My Life* (1977).

AYERS ROCK

Ayers Rock The largest monolith in the world, in Australia, in SW Northern Territory. It consists of a vast red rock rising 1099 ft (335 m) above the surrounding plain with a circumference of 6.25 mi (10 km). Its color varies according to atmospheric changes and the position of the sun.

Ayesha (c. 613–78) The third and favorite wife of *Mohammed and daughter of *Abu Bakr. She married at the age of nine. She led a revolt against *Ali but was defeated (656) and ended her life in exile in Medina. She is known as "the mother of believers."

Aymara A people of the Peruvian and Bolivian highlands. They grow potatoes and other crops and herd llamas and alpacas. Their costume is characterized by the woolen poncho and conical headwear with earflaps. They live in small extended-family settlements in which elders, who are also ritual shamans (*see* shamanism), have authority. In the 15th century the Aymara were incorporated into the Inca empire under Viracocha. Later Spanish influence made them nominally Catholic but earlier beliefs persist. Today there are approximately 1,360,000 Aymaras and their language, Aymaran, is one of the strongest surviving native Indian languages.

Ayrshire cattle A breed of red or brown and white cattle originating in Ayrshire, SW Scotland. A hardy breed, Ayrshires are primarily producers of good quality milk, used especially in cheese making. Many herds have been replaced by the higher yielding *Friesians.

Ayub Khan, Mohammad (1907–74) Pakistani statesman; president (1958–69). After a distinguished military career he became defense minister in 1954. Following President Iskander Mirza's coup d'état in 1958 Ayub Khan became chief martial law administrator and then ousted Mirza to become president. He negotiated (1966) the ceasefire agreement with *Shastri following the India-Pakistan war of 1965. He was forced to resign following civil unrest in East Pakistan.

Ayutthaya (*or* Ayuthi) 14 20N 100 35E A city in central Thailand. The former capital of the country (1350–1767), it is noted for its exceptional architecture, which survived a sacking by the Burmese. Population (1970 est): 39,291.

azalea A deciduous shrub of the genus *Rhododendron. (Most horticulturalists prefer to restrict the term rhododendron to the large evergreen species.) Growing to a height of up to 6.5 ft (2 m), azaleas are all native to the uplands of North America and S Asia but are now widely cultivated as ornamentals. The attractive flowers are large, fragrant, and funnel-shaped (about 2.4 in [6 cm] in diameter) and of various colors. Family: *Ericaceae*.

Azaña, Manuel (1880–1940) Spanish statesman, who was prominent in the Second Republic (1931–39). His premiership (1931–33) introduced internal reforms but was unpopular for its repression of opposition. He was president (1936–39) during the Spanish Civil War and fled to France after Gen Franco's Nationalist victory.

Azande An African people speaking a Sudanic language who live in areas of the Sudan, Zaïre, and the Central African Republic. They are an ethnically mixed people, who practice agriculture, hunting, and various crafts, including ironwork. They were traditionally divided into a number of warring kingdoms. They live in scattered homesteads and are organized into a number of dispersed patrilineal clans. Their religion takes the form of an ancestor cult. Belief in witchcraft is a central aspect of their lives, most misfortunes being attributed to it.

Azerbaidzhan Soviet Socialist Republic A constituent republic in the S Soviet Union, on the Caspian Sea. It consists mainly of the hot dry plain of the Kura and Araks Rivers, surrounded by the Caucasus Mountains. The Azerbaidzhani, who comprise most of the population, are a

Turkic-speaking Shiite Muslim people renowned for their carpet weaving. The region was acquired by Russia from Persia in the early 19th century, proclaimed its independence in 1918, but subsequently formed part of the Transcaucasian Soviet Federated Socialist Republic (*see* Transcaucasia), becoming a separate republic in 1936. Azerbaidzhan is one of the oldest oil-producing areas of the world and its most important industries are oil and gas, with a developing chemical industry. Agriculture is diversified and expansion is planned. The main crops are cotton, tobacco, and fruit, including grapes for wine. Area: 33,430 sq mi (86,600 sq km) Population (1981 est): 6,200,000. Capital: Baku.

Azhar, al- A mosque and center of traditional Muslim studies in Cairo. Inaugurated in 972 AD following the Fatimid conquest of Egypt, al-Azhar was originally controlled by the *Ismaili. It became a *Sunnite institution under Saladin but it was not until after the Ottoman conquest (1517) that it gained its present preeminence. It is now regarded as the most authoritative center of Islam and receives students from the whole Muslim world. In Egypt it has university status.

azimuth. *See* altitude.

azo dyes A class of synthetic dyes containing the **azo group** (–N = N–). First produced in 1858, they now outsell all other dyes combined. This success is due to exceptional color-fastness and versatility in application, including the ability to dye natural and synthetic fibers direct, i.e. without a mordant. Virtually any color may be obtained; examples are methyl orange, Bismarck brown, and Congo red.

Azores (Portuguese name: Açôres) 38 30N 28 00W Three groups of volcanic islands in the N Atlantic Ocean, in Portugal. The chief islands include São Miguel, Terceira, Faial, and Flores. Settled by the Portuguese in the 15th century, they were previously uninhabited. Naval fighting between the English and Spanish took place here in the 16th and 17th centuries. The site of US air bases, they produce fruit, tobacco, and wine. Area: 888 sq mi (2300 sq km). Population (1970): 336,100. Capital: Ponta Delgada, on São Miguel.

Azorín (José Martinéz Ruíz; 1874–1967) Spanish novelist, essayist, and critic. His works include the autobiographical novels *La voluntad* (1902) and *Antonio Azorín* (1903), as well as the collection of essays *Los pueblos* (1905), inspired by the history and landscape of Castile.

Azov, Sea of A NE arm of the Black Sea, to the main body of which it is connected by the narrow Kerch Strait. Area: 14,668 sq mi (38,000 sq km).

AZTECS *The calendar stone in the National Museum of Anthropology, Mexico City. The inner circle contains the 20 day signs of the Aztec calendar, while the central panel depicts the day on which the Aztecs believed the world would be destroyed by earthquake.*

Aztecs A *Nahuatl-speaking people who ruled an empire in central and S Mexico before their defeat by Hernán Cortés in the 16th century. They had an advanced, elaborate, and rich civilization centered on their capital Tenochtitlán and other cities. They were expert builders and constructed large palaces and temples in which they worshiped many gods, especially Huitzilopochtli to whom they sacrificed human victims, captives of warfare, by ripping out their hearts while they still lived. Their social organization was hierarchical with authority and influence vested in a class of chiefs and priests and in the kings, the last of whom was *Montezuma.

Aztec-Tanoan languages An American Indian language group, spoken in the SW US and central America. It has two branches: Uto-Aztecan and Kiowa-Tanoan. Uto-Aztecan is the larger; its most widely used language, Nahua, is spoken by the *Nahuatl people of central and W Mexico. Other Uto-Aztecan languages include those of the Paiute Indians in California and Utah, the *Hopi in Arizona, and the *Comanche in Texas. The Kiowa-Tanoan branch has only four members and is spoken in New Mexico and by the *Kiowa of Oklahoma.

Azuela, Mariano (1873–1952) Mexican novelist. He practiced medicine in Mexico City before joining Pancho Villa's forces during the Mexican revolution. *The Underdogs* (1916) described the suffering it caused. Later novels, such as *Los caciques* (1917) and the posthumous *Esa sangre*, express disgust with Mexican society both before and after the revolution.

B

Baal An ancient fertility god worshiped throughout the Near East, especially in Canaan. As champion of the divine order against chaos he defeated the sea god Yamm. The myth of his conflict with Mot, god of death and sterility, is closely linked to the natural processes of vegetation: his defeat and descent into the underworld represents famine and drought, and his resurrection and victory over Mot symbolizes rain and fertility.

Baalbek 34 00N 36 12E A town in E Lebanon, originally commanding Phoenician trade routes. The Roman colony here, called Heliopolis, has left extensive and imposing remains, including temples dedicated to Jupiter and Venus (1st–3rd centuries AD).

Ba'al Shem Tov (Israel ben Eliezer; c. 1700–60) Charismatic Jewish leader and mystic, the founder of *Hasidism. He lived in Podolia (then part of Poland) and attracted an enormous following by his powerful personality and his teaching, a blend of popular pietism and mystical Judaism. He is the subject of many colorful legends. His name means "Master of the Good Name."

Ba'ath Party An Arab political party, influential in many Middle Eastern countries, notably Syria and Iraq, that urges the creation of a united socialist Arab nation. The Ba'athists supported the formation of the *United Arab Republic (1958–61) and rose to power in Iraq and Syria in 1963.

Babbage, Charles (1792–1871) British mathematician and inventor. In an attempt to produce more accurate mathematical tables, Babbage conceived the idea of a mechanical computer that could store information. Although never completed, it was the forerunner of the modern computer.

Babbitt, Irving (1865–1933) US scholar and critic. While professor of French at Harvard (1894–1935), he wrote extensive works on literature and social questions, including *Rousseau and Romanticism* (1919) and *Democracy and Leadership* (1924). He was a leader of the "neohumanist" thinkers, who opposed Romanticism and advocated the classical values of restraint and moderation.

Babbitt, Milton (1916–) US composer. He taught music and mathematics at Princeton University. His compositions employ *serialism, which uses all 12 tones of the chromatic scale equally, and include music for synthesizers. His works include *Philomel* (1963–64) and *A Solo Requiem* (1976–77).

babbler A small songbird belonging to a family (Timaliidae; 280 species) occurring in Old World regions, particularly in SE Asia. Babblers have short rounded wings, a long tail, strong legs and bill, and a noisy babbling cry. The plumage is often brightly colored, although some species are plain brown. Babblers live in wooded regions, searching the undergrowth in groups for insects and berries.

Babel, Isaac Emmanuilovich (1894–1941) Russian short-story writer. Of Jewish descent, he served in the imperial army, but fought for the Bolsheviks in 1917. His *Odessa Tales* were published in 1916 in a journal edited by *Gorki. *Red Cavalry* (1926) was a series of sketches based on his experience in the war against Poland. He died in a Siberian prison camp, a victim of Stalin's purges, but was posthumously rehabilitated in the 1950s.

Babel, Tower of In the Bible (Genesis 2.1–9), a tower intended to reach heaven. Angered by the presumption of the building, Jehovah caused the builders to speak different languages, so that they were incomprehensible to each other and were forced in confusion to abandon the work. The legend attempts to account for the diversification of languages. It also probably alludes to the Babylonian ziggurats, which for the Israelites were examples of Gentile pride.

Bab el-Mandeb A strait between Africa and the SW Arabian Peninsula, connecting the Red Sea with the Gulf of Aden. It is 20 mi (32 km) wide and at one point is divided by Perim Island.

Babeuf, François-Noël (1760–97) French revolutionary. Propagator of extreme egalitarian ideas, he plotted to overthrow the *Directory. His "conspiracy of equals" was exposed and Babeuf was executed. Secret societies perpetuated his doctrines, known as Babouvism.

Babi faith A religion founded in 1844 by Mirza 'Ali Mohammed (1819–50), who became known as the Bab (the Gate). He proclaimed himself the 12th and last imam of certain *Shiite sects, which had prophesied his reappearance. He was imprisoned and later shot on government orders, and his followers were subsequently persecuted. Babism centered on the belief that God reveals himself to man through prophets who would continue to appear until the end of the world. It was the immediate precursor of the *Baha'i faith.

babirusa A hairless wild pig, *Babyrousa babyrussa*, of Sulawesi (Indonesia). About 40 in (100 cm) long, babirusas live in damp forests and are good swimmers, feeding on water plants, fruit, and tubers. Males have two pairs of curved tusks; the tuskless females have only one pair of teats.

baboon A large *Old World monkey belonging to the genus *Papio* (5 species), of African and Asian grassland. Baboons are 37–73 in (95–185 cm) long including the tail (18–28 in [45–70 cm]) and have a shaggy mane and a long doglike face with large teeth. They feed on insects, small vertebrates, and vegetable matter. They live in well-organized troops containing 40–150 individuals arranged in a social hierarchy according to age and sex. *See also* hamadryas. □mammal.

Babur (Baber *or* Babar; 1483–1530) Emperor of India (1526–30), who founded the *Mogul dynasty. Descended from Genghis Khan and Timur, Zahir-ud-din Muhammad (nicknamed Babur) became ruler of Fergana (1495) in Uzbekistan but failed to reconquer his ancestors' kingdom of Samarkand. Capturing Kabul, he invaded India from Afghanistan in 1525. In 1526 he defeated and killed Ibrahim Lodhi, Sultan of Delhi (1517–26), and rapidly subjugated all of N India. His story is related in his famous memoirs, the *Babur-Nameh*.

Babylon The capital of ancient Babylonia, strategically positioned on the *Euphrates River S of modern Baghdad. Its first period of prominence was about 2150 to 1740 BC, under a dynasty of which *Hammurabi was the most illustrious member. Subsequently, rising *Assyrian power threatened Babylonian independence, although some Babylonians, such as Nebuchadnezzar I (reigned c. 1146–1123), temporarily reversed the trend. Sacked by *Sennacherib (689 BC), Babylon was rebuilt from 625 BC onward, especially during the reign (c. 605–562) of *Nebuchadnezzar II. It was the remains of this city that were excavated by *Koldewey and from which the famous Ishtar Gate was recovered. In 539 BC Babylon surrendered to *Cyrus the Great of Persia. By 275 BC it was virtually depopulated. *See also* Babel, Tower of; Hanging Gardens; ziggurat.

Babylonia The area of *Mesopotamia on the alluvial plain along the lower reaches of the Euphrates River, which was controlled by ancient *Babylon. Before about 2000 BC approximately the same area was known as *Sumer. The Babylonians were a blend of Semitic peoples, like their rivals, the *Assyrians, to the NW. Apart from Babylon, the former Sumerian capital of *Ur and the port of *Eridu were major cities.

Babylonian exile The period from the destruction of the Jerusalem *Temple by *Nebuchadnezzar (586 BC) to the Jews' return under *Cyrus the Great (538 BC), during which time most of the Jews lived in exile in *Babylonia. It was here that parts of the Hebrew Bible were written, and that certain characteristic Jewish attitudes and institutions (e.g. the *synagogue) developed. This exile established the beginnings of the *diaspora; many Jews remained in Babylonia, and in late antiquity and the middle ages it had one of the largest and most important Jewish communities in the world.

Bacău 46 32N 26 59E A city in E Romania, on the Bistriřa River. An important road and rail junction, its industries include oil refining, textiles, and paper manufacture. Population (1979): 141,981.

baccarat games Various related card games, the object of which is to hold cards totaling nine, counting only the final digit of a total of ten or over (thus 10 equals 0). **Chemin de fer** was formerly popular in casinos. In this game the players take turns to be banker, against whom the other players make their bets. The banker then deals two cards to another player and two to himself. If the cards of either total nine, or failing that eight, this total wins and bets are settled accordingly. Otherwise a third card is taken or refused as necessary (taken if the total is four or under, refused if six or over). The highest total wins. **Punto banco** is identical to chemin de fer except that bets are placed against the casino on either the banker or his opponent.

Bacchanalia The Roman form of the Hellenistic mystery rites in honor of Bacchus (*see* Dionysus). The cult reached Rome from S Italy in the 2nd century BC. Originally involving only women, Bacchic worship included ecstatic rituals and secret orgies. In 186 BC a decree of the Senate prohibited Bacchanalia in Rome.

Bacchus. *See* Dionysus.

Bacchylides (c. 516–c. 450 BC) Greek lyric poet, nephew of Simonides and a rival of Pindar. Born on the island of Ceos, he lived at the court of Syracuse until the death of his patron Hiero in 467. Egyptian papyrus fragments discovered in 1896 contain parts of 14 odes and 6 dithyrambs (choral songs).

JOHANN SEBASTIAN BACH

Bach, Johann Sebastian (1685–1750) German composer and keyboard player, the greatest member of a large musical family. An orphan from the age of nine, he was brought up and taught by his brother Johann Christoph Bach (1671–1721). He subsequently became a chorister in Lüneburg and in 1703 a violinist at the Weimar court. In 1707 he married his cousin Maria Barbara Bach (1684–1720); after her death he married Anna Magdalena Wilcken (1701–60). In 1708 he rejoined the Weimar court as organist, remaining there for nine years. He became kapellmeister at the court of Prince Leopold of Anhalt at Köthen in 1717 and finally cantor of St Thomas' Church, Leipzig, in 1723. During his lifetime Bach achieved greater recognition as an organist than as a composer; he composed much organ music and was a skilled improviser on keyboard instruments. Among his greatest works are the *St John Passion* (1723), the *St Matthew Passion* (1729), and the *Mass in B minor* (1733–38), as well as over 200 cantatas. His compositions for orchestra include violin and harpsichord concertos and the *Brandenburg Concertos* (1721). For the harpsichord and clavichord he composed a collection of 48 preludes and fugues entitled the *Well-Tempered Clavier* (Part I, 1722; Part II, 1744) and the *Goldberg Variations* (1742); he also wrote music for the violin, cello, and lute. Bach's music did not become widely known until Mendelssohn revived it, giving the first performance of the *St Matthew Passion* since Bach's time in 1829.

Of Bach's 20 children, 3 sons became famous musicians. His eldest son **Wilhelm Friedemann Bach** (1710–84) studied in Leipzig and became church organist in Dresden (1733–46) and subsequently in Halle (1746–64). He ended his life in poverty, leaving cantatas, concertos, and symphonies.

His third son **Karl Philipp Emanuel Bach** (1714–88) studied law and philosophy but later turned to music, becoming musician to Frederick the Great in Berlin and subsequently becoming director of the principal church in Hamburg in succession to Telemann. In his works, which were highly regarded by Haydn and Mozart, he developed a new monophonic style of composition that became the basis of the classical style. His works include symphonies, concertos, and much keyboard music.

J. S. Bach's 11th son **Johann Christian Bach** (1735–82), called the English (or London) Bach, studied in Berlin and after holding posts in Italy became music master to the British royal family. He composed 13 operas, as well as concertos, church music, and piano pieces.

bacillus Any rod-shaped bacterium. The term is used specifically for bacteria of the genus *Bacillus*: spore-forming species including parasites of plants and animals. *B. anthracis* was first shown to cause anthrax in livestock by Robert *Koch.

backgammon A board game for two players that was known in ancient Mesopotamia, Greece, and Rome and in medieval England (as "the tables"). Each player has 15 pieces, which are moved around the 24 chevrons (points) marked on the board, the number of points moved being indicated by the throws of two dice. From their prescribed starting positions the players move in opposite directions. Each tries to bring all his pieces into the last quarter (his home board or inner table), after which he can remove them from the board (bear them off). Simultaneously he must block his opponent's moves. A chevron is occupied (point is made) when a player has two or more pieces on it, i.e. his opponent cannot land on it. A single piece on a point is a blot, i.e. vulnerable to the opponent's taking it and forcing it to travel around the board again.

background radiation Low-intensity radiation naturally present on the earth. It results either from the bombardment of the earth by *cosmic rays or from naturally occurring radioactive substances in the earth's crust.

backswimmer A *water bug, belonging to the worldwide family *Notonectidae* (nearly 200 species), that swims on its back, using a pair of oarlike legs for propulsion. Backswimmers can fly but are normally found in fresh water, preying voraciously on insects, tadpoles, and small fish. They must return to the surface periodically to replenish their air store.

Bacolod 10 38N 122 58E A port in the central Philippines, in NW Negros. It is a sugar-refining center serving the Philippines' most important sugar-growing area. Population (1980): 266,604.

Bacon, Francis (1909–) British painter. He was self-taught and began painting in the 1930s. His mature style is evident in his *Three Studies* (of figures for the base of a *Crucifixion* [1945]). Another of his well-known paintings is *Study after Velázquez* (1951), a version of Velázquez's portrait of pope Innocent X. His paintings are characterized by strong rich colors, a sinister blurring or erasure of human features, and an often violent dramatic quality.

Bacon, Francis, 1st Baron Verulam, Viscount St Albans (1561–1626) English lawyer and philosopher. He became a lawyer in 1582 and was elected to Parliament in 1584. During the 1590s, in the hope of political advancement, he cultivated the friendship of the 2nd Earl of *Essex but in 1601 assisted the prosecution for treason of his former patron. Under James I (reigned 1603–25) Bacon's career advanced more smoothly: he became a commissioner for the union of Scotland and England (1604), attorney general (1613), and Lord Chancellor (1618). In 1621, found guilty of bribery and corruption he was fined and banished from office and parliament.

Bacon's fame rests more securely on his philosophical and literary output and his influence on scientific thought in the later 17th century was considerable. In 1597 he published his first group of *Essays* on truth, death, friendship, etc. *The Advancement of Learning* (1605) presented a new classification of sciences and was expanded in the *De augmentis scientiarum* of 1623. In *Novum organum scientiarum* (1620) he argued that knowledge can be derived only from experience, advocating the scientific method of *induction. His other works include a *History of Henry VII* (1622) and the *New Atlantis* (1626), which describes his ideal state.

Bacon, Roger (c. 1214–c. 1292) English monk, scholar, and scientist, called Doctor Mirabilis for his diverse skills and learning. In three books written for Pope Clement IV he attempted to systematize the current state of knowledge; other works prophesied airplanes, microscopes, around-the-world voyages, steam engines, and telescopes. His astronomical knowledge enabled him to detect errors in the Julian *calendar. He has also been credited with the invention of *gunpowder and of the magnifying glass.

Bacon's Rebellion (1676) An uprising in Virginia that protested excessive taxation on tobacco crops and lack of defense against Indian raids. Nathaniel Bacon (1647–76), asked by the colonists to lead an army against the Indians, received little support from Virginia Gov William *Berkeley. Bacon, with a large following, drove the governor out of Jamestown, burned the city, and asked the people of Virginia to make an oath of allegiance to him. Even after his death from a fever shortly thereafter, Bacon's Rebellion continued under new leadership until it was subdued by the governor.

bacteria Microscopic single-celled organisms found wherever life is possible. Generally 0.000004–0.0002 in (0.0001–0.005 mm) long, they may be spherical (*see* coccus), rodlike (*see* bacillus), or spiral-shaped (spirillum) and often occur in chains or clusters of cells. The so-called true bacteria have a rigid cell wall, which may be surrounded by a slimy capsule, and they often have long whiplike flagella for locomotion and short hairlike pili used in a form of sexual reproduction. A few bacteria are autotrophic, i.e. they can grow on simple inorganic substrates using carbon dioxide gas from the atmosphere to manufacture their own nutrients, but the majority are heterotrophic, requiring a source of organic carbon and a variety of other nutrients for growth. A single bacterium reproduces by dividing into two new cells; some species can do so every 15 minutes leading to rapid population growth. Some form resistant spores, which can survive for several years in adverse conditions.

The most important role of bacteria is in decomposing dead plant and animal tissues and releasing their constituents to the soil (*see* carbon cycle). Nitrogen-fixing bacteria in the soil or sea convert atmospheric nitrogen gas to nitrites and nitrates, which can then be used by plants (*see* nitrogen cycle). Many industrial processes are dependent on bacteria, including cheese making and *fermentation reactions. Bacteria inhabit the digestive systems of animals and play an important part in digestion, especially in *ruminants. However, certain (pathogenic) species may infect body tissues and cause disease while others, such as *Salmonella*, can cause *food poisoning.

bacteriophage (*or* phage) A *virus that infects a bacterium. 25–800 nanometers in size, phages may be spherical, filamentous, or tadpole-shaped with a head and tail. They consist of a protein coat surrounding a core of nucleic acid (either DNA or RNA) that is inserted into the bacterium. The viral genes then use the protein-synthesis apparatus of the bacterium to produce new phages, which are released from the cell, usually causing its destruction.

Bactria An ancient region of central Asia, SE of the Aral Sea. An Achemenian province from about 600 BC, it was conquered, despite fierce resistance, by Alexander the Great and subsequently passed to the Seleucids. In the mid-3rd century BC Diodotus I (died c. 239) established an independent Bactrian-Greek kingdom that later encompassed present-day Soviet Central Asia, Afghanistan, and Pakistan. From the 1st century AD the nomadic Kushan tribe occupied Bactria, introducing Buddhism and artistic styles influenced by Buddhist, Iranian, and Greek-Roman sources. Until about 600 AD Bactria was the hub of overland trade between east and west and a center for the interchange of religious and artistic ideas.

Badajoz 38 53N 6 58W A city in SW Spain, in Estremadura on the Guadiana River. Attacked on numerous occasions, it was pillaged by Wellington's troops (1812) during the Peninsular War. It has a 13th-century cathedral. Population (1974 est): 103,317.

Badalona 41 27N 2 15E A port in NE Spain, in Catalonia, forming an industrial suburb of Barcelona. Industries include glass, shipbuilding, and textiles. Population (1970): 162,888.

Baden 47 28N 8 19E A spa city in N Switzerland. The diet (assembly) of the Swiss Confederation met here (1424–1712). Its hot sulfur springs have been visited since Roman times. Population (1974 est): 67,300.

Baden-Baden 48 45N 8 15E A spa in SW West Germany, in Baden-Württemberg in the Black Forest. The hot springs have been used since Roman times. Population (1971 est): 36,900.

Baden-Powell, Robert Stephenson Smyth, 1st Baron (1857–1941) British general and founder of the Boy Scouts. After service in India and various parts of Africa, he achieved fame through his defense of Mafeking in the *Boer War (1899–1900). Utilizing the experience of character training he had gained overseas, he founded the Boy Scouts in 1908 and, with his sister Agnes, the Girl Guides in 1910. *See also* Scouting.

Baden-Württemberg A *Land* in SW West Germany, bordering on France and Switzerland, formed by an amalgamation of three former *Länder* (1952). It contains the Black Forest, several spas, and fertile agricultural land. Its population and economy have expanded greatly since World War II, when many refugees from further E settled here. A large proportion of Germany's watches, jewelry, and musical and medical instruments are made in Baden-Württemberg and there are also textile, chemical, and car industries. Area: 13,800 sq mi (35,751 sq km). Population (1980 est): 9,235,600.

badger A nocturnal burrowing mammal of the *weasel family (*Mustelidae*). The largest of the eight species is the gregarious Eurasian badger (*Meles meles*), about 90 cm long, with short strong legs, long coarse grayish hair on the body, and a black and white striped head. It lives in a complex of burrows (a set) and feeds on insects, rodents, worms, berries, etc. The American badger (*Taxidea taxus*) is smaller and lives alone when not breeding. The remaining badgers are found in S and SE Asia and include the smallest species—the ferret badgers (genus *Melogale*), about 60 cm long.

Bad Godesberg. *See* Godesberg.

badlands An elevated area dissected by gullies and deep valleys. This type of landscape is typical of arid and semiarid areas, where rainfall is intermittent and an adequate vegetation cover is prevented from forming or is destroyed through, for example, overgrazing; severe soil erosion may occur. The name was originally applied to the Badlands of South Dakota.

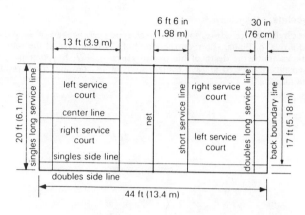

BADMINTON *The dimensions of the court. The top of the net at the center is 5 ft. (1.5 m) above the floor.*

badminton An indoor court game for two or four players, played with rackets and a shuttlecock or bird of nylon or cork and feathers. It originated in India and is the national sport of several Asian countries. Badminton was introduced in England and the US in the 1870s. It is a volleying game (the shuttles do not bounce) and points are scored only by the serving side. If the serving side fails to make a good return the service changes (in doubles games both partners serve before their opponents). A game is usually played to 15 points (women's singles go to 11 points).

Badoglio, Pietro (1871–1956) Italian general, who rose to prominence during World War I. He directed Mussolini's conquest of Ethiopia (1935–36) but in 1940 resigned during the disastrous Italian campaign in Greece. After Mussolini's fall (1943), he became prime minister and negotiated the armistice with the Allies. He resigned in 1944.

Baeck, Leo (1873–1956) German Jewish theologian. Under the *Nazis, he became the spiritual leader of German Jewry, continuing to teach in Theresienstadt concentration camp (1943–45). After the war he settled in London. In his major work, *The Essence of Judaism* (1905), Baeck argued for the superiority of Judaism to Christianity.

Baedeker, Karl (1801–59) German publisher of guidebooks. His first guide, to Coblenz (1829), was followed by a series that became internationally famous.

Baekeland, Leo Hendrik (1863–1944) US industrial chemist, born in Belgium. He invented Bakelite (*see* urea-formaldehyde resins), the first synthetic thermosetting plastic. The discovery was made while Baekeland was searching for a synthetic substitute for *shellac.

Baer, Karl Ernest von (1792–1876) Russian embryologist. He showed that mammalian eggs were not the follicles of the ovary but microscopic particles inside the follicles. He described the development of the embryo from layers of tissue, which he called *germ layers*, and demonstrated similarities in the embryos of different species of vertebrates.

Baeyer, (Johann Friedrich Wilhelm) Adolf von (1835–1917) German chemist, who became professor at the University of Strasbourg and then at Munich. He discovered barbituric acid (1865), synthesized indigo (1878), and developed several organic dyes. Baeyer also calculated the angles between the carbon atoms in organic compounds, showing (1885) how strained bonds affect chemical reactivity in closed carbon chains. He was awarded the 1905 Nobel Prize for his synthesis of indigo.

Baez, Joan (1941–) US folksinger, whose performance at the 1959 Newport Festival led to a series of successful recordings of folksongs and later of contemporary protest songs. An active pacifist, she opposed the Vietnam War and worked to relieve suffering and famine in Cambodia.

Baffin, William (c. 1584–1622) English navigator. In two voyages (1615, 1616) with Capt Robert Bylot he attempted in the *Discovery* to find the *Northwest Passage. He eventually despaired of its existence but explored the Hudson Strait, giving his name to Baffin Bay and Baffin Island.

Baffin Island The largest island of the Canadian Arctic, in Franklin district lying N of Hudson Strait. It is separated from Greenland by a Strait forming **Baffin Bay** (in the N) and Davis Strait. Mountainous with many glaciers and snowfields, its sparse population is concentrated in Frobisher Bay. Area: 476,068 sq km (183,810 sq mi).

Bagehot, Walter (1826–77) British economist, political theorist, literary critic, and journalist. He first worked as a banker, his interest in banking theories being reflected in his *Lombard Street* (1873). While editor of the *Economist* magazine (1860–77), he wrote his major political works, *The English Constitution* (1867), which analyzes the comparative powers of the British organs of government, and *Physics and Politics* (1872), applying Darwin's principles of natural selection to political society.

Baghdad 33 20N 44 26E The capital of Iraq, on the Tigris River near the center of the country. Built by the caliph (Islamic leader) Mansur in the 8th century, it was a center of commerce, learning, and religion until sacked by the Mongols in 1258. Modern Baghdad grew after becoming the capital of independent Iraq (1927) and is now an important administrative, communications, and manufacturing center with three universities (1947, 1957, and 1963). Population (1977): 3,205,645.

Baghdad Pact A treaty between Turkey, Iraq, Iran, Pakistan, and the UK. Signed in 1955, its goals were military, economic, and social cooperation in the Middle East. When Iraq withdrew from it in 1959, its headquarters moved to Ankara from Baghdad and it was renamed the *Central Treaty Organization.

Baghdad Railroad A rail link between Europe and Asia Minor, running from Turkey to Iraq. Its construction, begun in the late 19th century with German backing, was seen by the British as a threat to their position in India and it was a point of contention in World War I.

Baglioni A family that dominated Perugia (Italy) from 1425 until 1534. Its leading members were **Malatesta Baglioni** (1389–1437), who established the family's position in Perugia; **Giampaolo Baglioni** (c. 1470–1520), who came to power in 1500 following a family feud that resulted in the assassination of many of his relatives; and **Malatesta Baglioni** (1491–1531), a *condottiere who served both Venice and Florence, betraying the latter to the pope in 1530. The Baglioni were banished from Perugia in 1534.

bagpipes A reed-pipe instrument of ancient origin, found in many countries. Air is forced into a windbag either by the mouth (Scottish bagpipes) or by a bellows (Northumbrian pipes). By pressing the bag under his arm the player pushes air into the sounding pipes, which consist of one to three drones and a single chanter pipe. Drone pipes each sound one continuous note. The chanter pipe is fitted with holes, which are covered by the player's fingers. Bagpipes are regarded as the national instrument of Scotland, having been introduced to the British Isles in the 13th century.

Baguio 16 25N 120 37E A city in the N Philippines, in W Luzon. It is a popular summer resort and the site of the national military academy. Gold and copper are mined. Population (1975 est): 100,209.

bagworm moth A moth belonging to the widely distributed family *Psychidae* (800 species). The larvae live in cases made of silk covered with leaves, twigs, grass, etc., with only the head and forelegs projecting. Males emerge after pupation, flying in search of the wingless females, which remain in their cases.

Baha'i faith A religion founded in Persia in 1863 by Mirza Husain 'Ali (1817–92), who was known as Baha' Allah (Glory of God). He proclaimed himself to be the Promised One whose coming was foretold by the Bab (*see* Babi faith). His eldest son and then his great-grandson led the Baha'is after his death until 1957. Since 1963 the faith has been governed by the Universal House of Justice, a council at Haifa, Israel, elected by national spiritual assemblies. The basic tenet of the faith is that God reveals himself to man through prophets who appear at various stages in history and the most recent of these is Baha' Allah. Baha'is advocate a universal faith, world peace, an international language, the equality of men and women, and the abolition of all prejudices. During the 20th century the faith has spread to the West.

Bahamas, Commonwealth of the A state consisting of about 700 islands and innumerable cays in the West Indies, off the SE coast of Florida. The principal islands, which are mainly low lying, include New Providence (with the capital Nassau), Grand Bahama, Abaco, Eleuthera, Andros, and Watling Island (San Salvador). The majority of the population is of African descent. *Economy*: with its mild subtropical climate and beautiful beaches, the main industry of the Bahamas is tourism, which accounts for over 50% of revenue and employment. Efforts are now being made to develop agriculture and fisheries, finance, and industry (especially oil refining). Foreign investment is encouraged by the tax position, 90% of companies being foreign-owned. Main exports include cement, petroleum and petroleum products, chemicals, and fish. *History*: in 1492 Columbus made his first landing in the W hemisphere on the island of San Salvador. The first European occupation comprised an English religious settlement in the mid-17th century, and the islands became a British crown colony in 1717.

From 1964 the country had increasing control over its own affairs and in 1973 it attained full independence within the Commonwealth. In the 1980s high unemployment and its effects on the populace brought concern that standards of service in tourism were declining. An increase in crime, drugs, and unrest among the youth was also seen as related to unemployment, which in 1983 had reached 25%. Bahamian disaffection with the US government over provisions of the Caribbean Basin initiative requiring the Bahamas to divulge banking secrets, became public. Prime Minister Pindling also claimed unequal tax treatment by the US, regarding business tourism as compared with other Caribbean nations. The Bahamas is a member of CARICOM. Prime Minister: Lynden Oscar Pindling. Offical language: English. Official currency: Bahamian dollar of 100 cents. Area: 5353 sq mi (13,864 sq km). Population (1983 est.): 223,000. Capital and main port: Nassau.

Bahawalpur 29 24N 71 47E A city in Pakistan, situated on the railroad between Karachi and Lahore. It is an expanding industrial center producing cotton and soap. Population (1972): 133,956.

Bahia. *See* Salvador.

Bahía Blanca 38 45S 62 15W A port in Argentina. It is a major distribution center; exports include grain, meat, and wool. The National University of the South was founded here in 1956. Population (1970): 182,158.

Bahrain, State of An independent sheikdom in the Arabian Gulf, occupying a low-lying archipelago between Saudi Arabia and the Qatar Peninsula. The two main islands, Bahrain and Al-Muharraq, are connected by a causeway and there are also plans for a causeway to Saudi Arabia. The inhabitants are mainly Arabs. *Economy*: almost totally dependent upon oil. A large refinery on Bahrain Island processes not only the relatively small amounts of local oil, first discovered in 1931, but also much larger amounts coming from Saudi Arabia by pipeline. Efforts are being made to develop other industry with some success. An aluminum smelter on Bahrain is the largest non-oil industrial plant in the Gulf. The formerly important pearl-fishing industry is now in decline. Bahrain is important as a transport center in the Gulf and the modern harbor of Mina Salman has extensive shipping facilities and a free transport area. In 1975 the government licensed the setting up of Offshore Banking Units, a move that increased Bahrain's commercial importance. By the early 1980s Bahrain had become the most important money center between Europe and Singapore. *History*: the islands were under Portuguese rule from 1521 until 1602, and during parts of the 17th century Iran had control, eventually being expelled by the Khalifa family, who have ruled the area for most of the time since. It was a British protected state from 1861 until 1971 when full independence was declared by the emir, Sheik Isa ibn Sulman al-Khalifa (1933–). In 1975 political unrest led to the dissolution of the National Assembly. Bahrain became a member of OPEC in 1970. In 1975 political unrest led to the dissolution of the National Assembly. Bahrain became a member of OPEC in 1970. The majority of the population are Arab Muslims, equally divided between Sunni and Shiah sects. Differences between the two groups remained political and social tensions. In 1981 plans for a coup by Shiah Muslims who were part of an Iranian-backed underground group, were exposed. Causing widespread disruption in the government, the fomenting of the plot underscored the rift between Sunni and Shiah, which some observers had thought was healing. Official language: Arabic; English is also widely spoken. Official religion: Islam. Official currency: Bahrain dinar of 1000 fils. Area: 255 sq mi (660 sq km). Population (1983 est): 383,000. Capital and main port: Manama.

Baikal, Lake A lake in the SE central Soviet Union, in the Buryat ASSR. It is the largest freshwater lake in Asia and at 5316 ft (1620 m) the deepest in the world. It is fed by over 300 streams but drained by only one, the Angara River. Area: 12,160 sq mi (31,500 sq km).

bail The release by a court of an imprisoned person, usually while awaiting trial, into the keeping of people who agree to ensure his reappearance at a particular date and time. If these people, called "sureties," then fail to produce him, they forfeit whatever sum of money the court has set for bail. The person bailed must also stand as surety for himself; if thought trustworthy, he may be bailed without other sureties, "in his own recognizance." Judges have wide discretion as to whether bail should be granted and for what amount.

Bailey bridge A type of military bridge invented by Britain's Sir Donald Bailey during World War II. Consisting of light strong standardized interlocking truss sections, it can be easily assembled in the field. Pontoons can be provided for longer spans, the longest of which was that of the 4000 ft (1200 m) bridge built across the Maas River in Holland.

Baja California. *See* Lower California.

Bakelite. *See* urea-formaldehyde resins.

Baker, Howard (Henry, Jr.) (1925–) US politician. A Republican from Tennessee, he served in the US Senate (1966–85). He headed the Senate committee that probed the Watergate scandal (1973) and was Senate minority (1977–81) and majority leader (1981–85). He ran unsuccessfully for the Republican presidential nomination in 1980 and did not seek reelection to the Senate in 1984.

Baker, Josephine (1906–75) US singer and dancer. She danced in *La Revue Nègre* (1925) in Paris and then went on to a leading role in the *Folies-Bergère*. A blues singer, she spent most of her life in France, entertaining and running her own nightclub there and touring internationally; eventually, she became a French citizen (1937). She was awarded the French Legion of Honor for her World War II work in the resistance; she supported the US civil rights movement during the 1960s and worked closely with international adoption agencies.

Bakhtyari A major tribe of W Iran of some 400,000 members speaking the Luri dialect of Persian. About one-third are still nomadic herdsman living in tents. They make an annual grueling migration of 150 miles (240 km) from their winter pastures on the plains to the summer pastures in the mountains. Authority is vested in hereditary chiefs, who have often played an influential role in Iranian politics. The Bakhtyari are of the Islamic faith, but their women have a greater degree of freedom than is usual among Muslims.

baking powder A mixture, usually of *sodium bicarbonate and *tartaric acid or *cream of tartar, used in baking. It generates carbon dioxide on heating or wetting, thus making the dough rise.

Bakst, Léon (Lev Samoilovich Rosenberg; 1866–1924) Russian artist, who modernized theater design. He was born in St Petersburg, where he trained in the Imperial Academy of Arts and became court painter, before turning to scenery design in 1900. His greatest achievements were for ballets produced by Sergei *Diaghilev in Paris, where he later settled.

Baku 40 22N 49 53E A port in the S Soviet Union, the capital of Azerbaidzhan SSR on the Caspian Sea. The old town is a maze of narrow streets and ancient buildings, including mosques and a 17th-century palace. It is the oldest center of Soviet oil production, and oil is still the basis of its economy. Population (1981 est): 1,046,000.

Bakunin, Mikhail Aleksandrovich (1814–76) Russian anarchist. An interest in dialectics led Bakunin to study German philosophy at Berlin University, where he became exposed to socialist philosophy. He participated in the Revolutions of 1848 and in 1849 he was arrested in Dresden, handed over to Russian officials, and exiled to Siberia. In 1861 he escaped to London. He participated in the First *International but came into conflict with Marx and was expelled. He had many followers in Italy, Spain, Russia, and elsewhere.

Bakwanga. *See* Mbuji-Mayi.

Balaclava, Battle of (October 25, 1854) An indecisive battle between Russian and British-Turkish forces in the *Crimean War. It is notorious for the heavy British casualties caused by misunderstanding between Lord *Raglan, the British commander in chief, and Lord Lucan (1800–88), the cavalry commander. The courageous Light Brigade charged Russian artillery at the end of a narrow valley and of its 673 men, 113 were killed and 134 wounded.

Balakirev, Mili Alekseevich (1837–1910) Russian composer, one of the *Five. He was the founder of the Free School of Music in St Petersburg (1862). His works, such as the tone poem *Tamara* (1867–82) and the piano fantasy *Islamey* (1869), reflect his romanticism and Russian musical nationalism.

balalaika A Russian plucked instrument of the guitar family, played singly or in a balalaika orchestra. It has a long fretted fingerboard, a triangular body, and three wire strings that are plucked with a plectrum. It is made in different sizes, the smaller being held like a guitar and the larger balanced on the floor like a double bass.

balance A sensitive device for comparing two masses, consisting of a beam pivoted at its center (usually on an agate knife edge) with pans hanging from each of its ends. The material of unknown mass is placed in one pan and standard weights are placed in the other. A pointer indicates when the beam is horizontal and the whole device is enclosed in a glass case to avoid drafts and temperature changes. The accuracy of a balance is increased by using a rider—a small weight hung on a calibrated scale on the balance arm itself. A standard balance will weigh to the nearest 0.0001 g, while extremely sensitive **microbalances** can be used to weigh objects with a mass of only 1 microgram. *See also* spring balance.

balance of payments The difference between a country's income and its expenditure abroad. It is usually divided into a current account and a capital account. The current account records the country's *balance-of-trade earnings or deficit on visible goods and its invisible earnings or deficit on such items as insurance, transport, tourism, and some kinds of government spending. The capital account records all long- and short-term capital flows, both in the public and private sectors. If the sum of the current and capital accounts shows a deficit there will be a net loss of foreign exchange, which the government must take steps to remedy. Measures include deflation by *monetary or *fiscal policy to reduce imports, the imposition of *tariffs or import *quotas, incentives to increase exports, the introduction of stringent *exchange control regulations, and ultimately *devaluation of the currency. If the balance of payments shows a persistent surplus a revaluation of the currency may be required.

balance of power The principle seeking to ensure that no nation or group of nations becomes too dominant. Practiced by Greek city states, which formed intercity alliances, the principle was adopted in Europe in the alliance system of 15th-century Italy. In 1815 at the Congress of *Vienna, Prussia, Russia, Britain, France, and Austria realigned European frontiers to establish themselves as equal powers and to ensure peace. Tensions remained, however, and rival alliances led to further wars to prevent or restore national dominance. In the 20th century the League of Nations and the UN have both tried to establish international harmony, but the development of nuclear weapons acts as the greatest deterrent to any state sufficiently ambitious to threaten international equilibrium.

balance of trade The difference in money between the value of a country's imports and its exports. The balance of trade is sometimes known as the visibles account because it refers only to actual goods. Together with the invisibles account and capital transfers it makes up the *balance of payments. The invisibles account includes such earnings as selling insurance abroad and spending by foreign tourists. Thus the balance of trade can be in deficit without necessarily meaning that the balance of payments will also be in deficit.

Balanchine, George (Georgy Melitonovich Balanchivadze; 1904–83) US ballet dancer and choreographer, born in Russia. He worked for Diaghilev's Ballets Russes in Europe from 1924 and went to the US in 1933. In 1948 he became first artistic director of the New York City Ballet (1948–83). His ballets include *Firebird* (1950) and *Don Quixote* (1965), and he also choreographed for films and stage musicals.

Balaton, Lake A lake in W Hungary, the largest in central Europe. There are vineyards and holiday resorts on its shore and its outlet is a canal leading to a tributary of the Danube River. Area: 231 sq mi (598 sq km).

Balboa 8 57N 79 33W A port in the Panama Canal Zone, at the Pacific end of the Panama Canal. It was named for the explorer Vasco Núñez de *Balboa. It has extensive harbor facilities. Population (1970): 2569.

Balboa, Vasco Núñez de (c. 1475–1517) Spanish explorer. Having settled in Hispaniola, he became a stowaway on an expedition to present-day Colombia (1510), moved on to Panama, and founded a settlement at Darién (1511). In 1513 he set off across the Isthmus in search of gold. Sighting the Pacific, which he called the South Sea, after 25 grueling days, he claimed it for Spain. He was subsequently accused, unjustly, of treason and beheaded by the governor of Darién, Pedrarias (d. 1531).

bald eagle A large sea *eagle, *Haliaetus leukocephalus*, also called the American eagle; it is the national emblem of the US and an endangered species. It is dark brown with a white head and tail and has a prominent curved beak and unfeathered legs. It feeds on carrion and fish and has rough skin on the toes for grasping slippery prey.

Baldwin, James Arthur (1924–) US novelist, essayist, and dramatist. His first novel, *Go Tell It on the Mountain* (1953), is based on his experience of poverty and religion in Harlem, New York City, where he was born. He lived in Paris from 1948 to 1957, when he returned to the US as an active civil-rights campaigner. His works include novels, such as *Giovanni's Room* (1956) and *Tell Me How Long the Train's Been Gone* (1968), two plays, and several collections of essays, notably *Notes of a Native Son* (1955), *The Fire Next Time* (1963), and *Just Above My Head* (1979).

Baldwin, Stanley, 1st Earl (1867–1947) British statesman, who was Conservative prime minister (1923–24, 1924–29, 1935–37). As chancellor of the exchequer (1922–23), Baldwin negotiated the British World War I debt to the US. He dealt as prime minister with the *General Strike (1926). Baldwin was much criticized for condoning Italy's conquest of Ethiopia and his apparent reluctance to rearm in the face of Germany's military build-up. His management of the events leading to Edward VIII's abdication complied with public opinion.

Baldwin I (c. 1058–1118) King of Jerusalem (1100– 18). Baldwin succeeded his brother Godfrey of Bouillon, whom he had accompanied on the first Crusade, taking Edessa in 1098. Baldwin considerably expanded the territory of Jerusalem.

Balearic Islands An archipelago in the W Mediterranean Sea comprising a Spanish province. It includes the chief islands of *Majorca, *Minorca, *Ibiza, and Formentera, together with several islets. The islands were taken by Aragon from the Moors in the 14th century. Area: 1936 sq mi (5014 sq km). Population (1970): 558,287. Capital: Palma, on Majorca.

baleen (or whalebone) The horny material that forms the food-sieving plates in whalebone *whales. Baleen was formerly used to manufacture stays in corsets, but has now largely been replaced by synthetic materials.

Balenciaga, Cristóbal (1895–1972) Spanish fashion designer, who moved to Paris in 1937. He built up an elite clientele, which was attracted by his starkly elegant styles, especially his tailored suits.

Balfour, Arthur James, 1st Earl of (1848–1930) British statesman and Conservative prime minister (1902–05). His government passed an *Education Act (1902), the Irish Land Purchase Act (1903; see Land Acts, Irish), and concluded the Anglo-French entente (1904). In World War I Balfour, as foreign secretary (1916–19), issued his famous *Balfour Declaration.

Balfour Declaration (1917) The decision of the British government, made known in a letter of Nov 2 from the British foreign secretary, Arthur *Balfour, to the chairman of the British Zionist Federation, to support the establishment of a national Jewish home in Palestine. The letter promised British aid to Zionist efforts to establish such a home, providing that the interests of existing non-Jewish communities in Palestine be maintained as well as the rights and political status of Jews in any other country. Arab aspirations in Palestine, however, prevented the British government from fulfilling the promise of the Declaration, which was abandoned in 1939.

Bali An Indonesian island off E Java. Mountainous and volcanic, it has southern fertile plains that produce chiefly rice. The Balinese are famed for their arts and handicrafts, and it is a popular tourist resort. *History*: Hindu since the 7th century AD, Bali resisted the 16th–17th century spread of Islam through Indonesia and became an enclave of Hindu culture. Dutch rule became complete only in 1908, although trade began in the 17th century. In the 1965–67 Indonesian purge of communists 40,000 people were killed. Area: 2146 sq mi (5558 sq km). Population (1980): 2,469,930. Chief town: Denpasar.

Balikpapan 1 15S 116 50E A port in Indonesia, in SE Kalimantan on the Makassar Strait. Its refinery processes local and imported oil. Population (1971): 137,340.

Balkan Mountains (Bulgarian name: Stara Planina) A mountain range extending 311 mi (500 km) E–W for the entire width of central Bulgaria. It rises to 7795 ft (2376 m) at Botev Peak.

Balkans An area in SE Europe consisting of present-day Greece, Albania, Yugoslavia, Bulgaria, part of Romania, and the European part of Turkey. Part of the Roman empire from the 2nd century BC and of the Eastern Roman (Byzantine) Empire from the 5th century AD, the Balkans were ruled by the Ottoman Turks from the 15th to the 19th and 20th centuries, when independence was granted to Greece (1829), Serbia (1878), Romania (1878), Bulgaria (1908), and Albania (1912). The competition between European powers for control of the Balkans, coupled with integral rivalries, contributed to the outbreak of World War I, after which Yugoslavia was created out of Serbia. All the Balkan states, except Greece, became communist after *World War II.

Balkan Wars (1912–13) Two military confrontations that preceded World War I. In the first (1912–13) the Balkan League (Bulgaria, Serbia, Greece, and Montenegro) defeated Turkey. In the concluding Treaty of London, Turkey lost all its European possessions except E Thrace. In the second Balkan War (1913) the victors fought over their acquisitions in Macedonia, from most of which Bulgaria was excluded by the Treaty of *Bucharest; Turkey regained Thrace.

Balkhash, Lake A lake in the S central Soviet Union, in the E Kazakh SSR. Since it has no outlet, it fluctuates in size, and it is generally shrinking. Area: about 20,000 sq km (7720 sq mi).

Balla, Giacomo (1871–1958) Italian futurist painter, born in Turin. He was influenced by *pointillism before he became associated with *futurism (1910) and painted many dynamic studies of light and movement, notably birds in flight, and the humorous *Dog on a Leash* (1912; Buffalo).

ballad A form of popular narrative poetry. Originally intended for singing or recitation, ballads have a simple basic stanza form (four lines rhyming *abcb*); repetition and direct speech are characteristic devices. Subject matter includes love, family feuds, war, magic, biblical tales, the deeds of Robin Hood and the knights of the Round Table (see Arthurian legend),

the exploits of cowboys and outlaws. The ballad dates back many centuries. Some of the finest examples of the form were composed in the 15th century in N England and Scotland; debased versions were later printed on single sheets of paper (broadside ballads) for sale by peddlers. Later still a tradition of literary ballads grew up (e.g. Kipling's "Danny Deever"). Notable ballad collections are Bishop *Percy's *Reliques* (1765) and F. J. Child's *English and Scottish Popular Ballads* (1883–98).

ballade A form of medieval French lyric poetry or song. It consists of three stanzas and a final *envoi* (address); each stanza has the same rhyme scheme and final line, which serves as a refrain. It was used for formal and commemorative songs. Guillaume de *Machaut pioneered this form in the 14th century, and in the 15th century it was used by Charles d'*Orléans and François *Villon, among others.

ballet A dramatic art in which dancing and mime, accompanied by music, combine to tell a story or evoke a mood. Ballet originated in the formal dances of French court entertainments, notably under Louis XIV (see Lully). In the 18th century ballet established itself in the public theater but still as an adjunct to *opera or other forms of drama. Idolized ballerinas such as Sallé (1707–56) and Carmargo (1710–70) introduced less constricting dress and Jean-Georges Noverre (1727–1810) extended ballet's dramatic range. Dancing on the tips of the toes (*sur les pointes*) was introduced early in the 19th century, possibly by Taglioni (1804–84). This period saw the heyday of romantic ballet, epitomized in Coralli's *Giselle* (1841).

Modern ballet arose in the early 20th century when *Fokine and subsequently *Diaghilev (see also Ballets Russes) combined the polished technique of the imperial Russian dancers with the naturalism advocated by the American Isadora *Duncan. Their reforms gave scope to the talents of such dancers as *Nijinsky and *Pavlova, the composers *Stravinsky and *Ravel, the choreographers *Massine and *Balanchine, and the designer *Bakst. Independent ballet companies grew up all over Europe and the US during the 1930s. England had two such groups, one led by Marie *Rambert (now the Ballet Rambert) and the other by Ninette de *Valois and Frederick *Ashton (now the *Royal Ballet). Other notable companies are the *Bolshoi and *Kirov from the Soviet Union and George *Balanchine's New York City Ballet. Since World War II innovative choreographers such as *Cranko, *Béjart, Merce Cunningham, Alvin Ailey, and Twyla Tharpe have created new ballets inspired by folk dance, jazz, and even gymnastics.

Ballets Russes A Russian ballet company (1909–29) founded in Paris by *Diaghilev. It gave the West its first opportunity to see Russian imperial dancers and through its world tours brought ballet to a wider public. In attempting to fuse dance, mime, music, and scenery into a harmonious unity, it fostered the most avant-garde talents of the period and greatly influenced the subsequent development of ballet. Its choreographers included *Fokine, *Massine, *Balanchine, and *Nijinsky, who was also one of its principal dancers. *Ravel and *Stravinsky composed music for several of its ballets. Among its scene designers were *Bakst and the painters *Picasso, *Matisse, and *Miró.

Ballinger-Pinchot Controversy (1909–11) A disagreement over the public rights to western water lands. Richard Ballinger (1858–1922), President William H. Taft's secretary of the interior, made public again lands that had been closed by the government. Gifford Pinchot (1865–1946), chief of the forestry division of the Department of Agriculture, accused Ballinger of catering to private enterprise. Ballinger was cleared by a congressional committee and Pinchot was fired by President Taft.

ballistic missiles Rocket-powered nuclear missiles without wings or other lift surfaces that are propelled to desired altitudes and velocities and then follow an unpowered trajectory similar to that of a projectile fired from a gun. Their accuracy requires careful thrust calculations and onboard preset or inertial guidance systems and is calculated as a probability (e.g. 45–60%) of landing within a stated radius about their target (*Circular Error of Probability*). Intercontinental ballistic missiles (ICBMs) are capable of reaching any point on the surface of the earth. Both the US and the Soviet Union possess large numbers of these, some of which (MIRVs—multiple independently targeted re-entry vehicles) have up to ten separate warheads. See also antiballistic missiles; V-2 rocket.

ballistics The study of projectiles and the extent to which their trajectories are affected by shape, propulsion systems, gravity, temperature, wind, etc. There are three branches: interior, dealing with all aspects of propulsion within a gun barrel or at launch; exterior, concerned with the trajectory of the projectile in flight; and terminal, relating to the effects of the missile on the target.

ball lightning A luminous moving sphere, several centimeters in diameter, occurring just above the ground on rare occasions during thunder-

BALLET

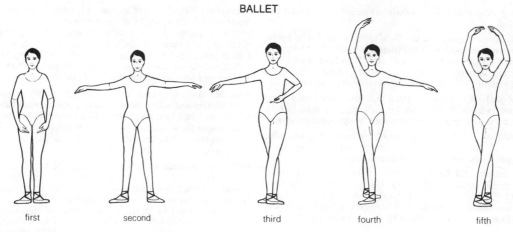

first second third fourth fifth

the five ballet positions

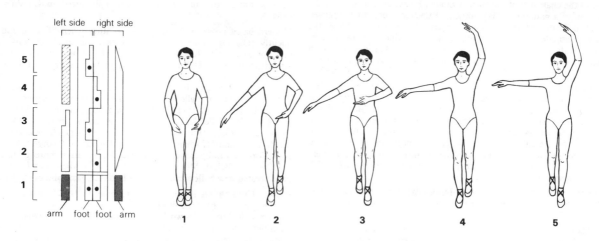

left side right side

5 4 3 2 1

arm foot foot arm

1 2 3 4 5

Labanotation *Since Rudolph Laban (1879–1958) published his system for recording dance movements in 1928 it has gained widespread acceptance. In this simple example, the initial positions of the legs and arms are indicated at (1). Subsequent positions (2–5) are seen by reading upwards from the bottom. The dancer, starting with feet together and arms at her sides, takes four even steps forward, beginning with the right foot, and moves her arms upwards and outwards (the different shadings representing low, middle, and high positions).*

storms. It hisses, has a distinct odor, and may be either red, orange, or yellow. It lasts for only a few seconds and then either dies away or explodes. The phenomenon is not fully understood but one theory suggests that it consists of *plasma.

balloons Lighter-than-air craft, consisting of a bag of gas that displaces a volume of air of greater mass than the total mass of the balloon and its contents. The first successful balloon flight, indeed man's first aerial voyage, was made in 1783 by the *Montgolfier brothers' hot-air balloon; it flew 2 mi (9 km) across Paris. Two years later a *Charlière* hydrogen balloon (designed by J. A. C. Charles, the formulator of *Charles's Law) flew across the English Channel. In 1821 coal gas was used for the first time as a cheap alternative to hydrogen. This opened the way for many exploits by showmen, scientists, and explorers. Balloons must be tethered (for parachuting, scientific experiments, etc.) or they will fly where the wind blows them; *dirigible balloons first appeared in the middle of the 19th century. However, by the end of the century interest in flying was centered on heavier-than-air machines (*see* aircraft).

The use of balloons in war began with Napoleon's observation balloons in 1794, after which they continued to play a sporadic but largely ineffectual part, until their extensive use in both World Wars in the form of barrage balloons.

The sport of **ballooning** has enjoyed a revival in recent years, the preferred vehicle being a hot-air balloon carrying its own propane air heater. The

height record for a manned balloon is 30,480 m (1957). A solo balloon crossing of the Atlantic Ocean was made in 1984.

balm A fragrant-leaved herbaceous plant of, or related to, the genus *Melissa*, native to the Old World. Lemon balm, or balm gentle (*M. officinalis*), is widely grown in temperate regions and used for flavoring foods or beverages and scenting perfumes. The European bastard balm (*Melittis melissophylum*) is more strongly scented. Others species include bee balm (*Monarda didyma*) and horse balm (*Collinsonia canadensis*). Family: *Labiatae*.

balsa An evergreen tree, *Ochroma pyramidale*, native to Central and South America, also called corkwood. About 40 ft (12 m) tall, it is the source of an extremely light pale-colored wood, which is widely used for corks, canoes, floats, etc. Although easily crushed, it is technically a hardwood. Family: *Bombacaceae*.

balsam An aromatic resinous substance of plant origin, used in medicine for its soothing and healing properties and in perfumery. Balsam of Peru is derived from the Central American leguminous tree *Myroxylon peneirae*, grown in El Salvador.

The name is also given to many plants of the family *Balsaminaceae*. The garden balsam (*Impatiens balsamina*), native to India, is widely cultivated for its showy red flowers, which have a tubular spur and five unequal petals. The balsam apple (*Momardica balsamina*) is an ornamental vine.

Baltic languages A group of Indo-European languages closely related to the Slavonic languages and spoken on the E shores of the Baltic Sea.

*Lithuanian and *Latvian (Lettish) are still extant: Old Prussian has been extinct since the 17th century. Deriving from northern Proto-Indo-European, the Baltic, Slavonic, and Germanic languages share important morphological and word-formation features.

Baltic Sea A section of the Atlantic Ocean in N Europe, bounded by Denmark, Sweden, Finland, the Soviet Union, Poland, and East Germany. To the W, it leads into the Little Belt, the Great Belt, and the Sound, and to the E, the Gulfs of Bothnia, Finland, and Riga. It has very low salinity since it receives rivers draining almost one-fifth of Europe and it can freeze sufficiently to hinder navigation.

Baltic Shield. *See* shield.

Baltic states The territories on the SE coast of the Baltic Sea that comprise the present-day Latvian, Lithuanian, and Estonian SSRs of the Soviet Union. The Danes conquered N Estonia in the 13th century while S Estonia with Latvia (then comprising Livonia) fell to the Teutonic Knights. Lithuania formed an independent state until united with Poland in 1569 in the Union of *Lublin. The region came under Russian rule in the 18th century but briefly, between World Wars I and II, formed the independent states of Latvia, Lithuania, and Estonia.

Baltimore 39 25N 76 40W The largest city in Maryland, at the mouth of the Patapsco River. Established in 1729, it was named for— the Barons Baltimore, the first of whom, George Calvert (c. 1580–1632), founded Maryland. It was the starting point of the first US railroad (1827). It is the site of many historical buildings, including the US's first Roman Catholic cathedral (1806–21) and the Edgar Allan Poe House (1830). Baltimore is a major educational and cultural center and contains a number of universities; in the 1980s considerable rebuilding around the port area has revitalized the city. It has been a busy seaport and shipbuilding center since the late 18th century (Baltimore clippers were renowned throughout the world); other important industries include the manufacture of steel, sugar and food processing, oil refining, and chemicals. Population (1980): 786,775.

Baltimore oriole An American *oriole, *Icterus galbula*, of North America, so named because the black and orange plumage of the male resembles the colors of the Barons Baltimore (*see* Baltimore). It feeds on insects, has an attractive song, and builds a woven pouchlike nest.

Baluchistan A province in W Pakistan, on the Arabian Sea and the Iranian and Afghani borders. Mostly rough arid highlands, it is inhabited by pastoral Pathans, Baluchs, and other peoples. The NW deserts are practically uninhabited but the coastal plain and E lowlands support wheat, barley, maize, and herbs. There is little industry other than crafts, textiles, and food processing. Baluchistan has extensive mineral resources. *History*: on the trade routes from India to the Middle East, Baluchistan has flourished since ancient times. Nominally part of larger empires, it usually enjoyed autonomy until Britain won control (19th century). In 1947 it became part of Pakistan. Area: 134,050 sq mi (347,190 sq km). Population (1972 est): 2,409,000. Capital: Quetta.

Baluchitherium An extinct hornless rhinoceros that lived in the Oligocene epoch (between 30 million and 20 million years ago). Fossilized remains found in central Asia show that it was over 16 ft (5 m) high, with a heavy giraffe-like body, and was probably the largest terrestrial mammal ever to have lived.

Balzac, Honoré de (1799–1850) French novelist. Educated at Vendôme, he became a lawyer's clerk in Paris. He wrote popular novels under pseudonyms, and then attempted to become a businessman; in 1828, however, bankruptcy forced him to turn to writing again. *Les Chouans* (1829), a historical novel about Breton peasants, was his first successful novel, and in the next 20 years he added over 40 novels to his life's work, the cycle *La Comédie humaine*. In these novels, which included *Eugénie Grandet* (1833), *Le Père Goriot* (1834), and *La Cousine Bette* (1846), he developed new techniques of realism to explore human behavior. Balzac lived extravagantly in Parisian society, constantly in debt and in love, and married his last mistress, Eveline Hanska, during his fatal illness in 1850.

Bamako 12 40N 7 59W The capital of Mali, a port in the S on the Niger River. A center of Muslim learning under the medieval Mali Empire, it had dwindled to a small village by the end of the 19th century when it was occupied by the French. It became the capital of the French Sudan in 1905. Population (1976): 404,022.

Bamberg 49 54N 10 54E A city in SE West Germany, in Bavaria on the Regnitz River. The romanesque cathedral was founded in 1004 and its bishops were princes of the Holy Roman Empire until 1803. Its varied industries include engineering and textiles. Population (1971 est): 69,900.

bamboo A treelike plant of the tribe *Bambuseae*, native to tropical and subtropical regions, particularly SE Asia. From an underground stem (rhizome) arise hollow woody jointed stems, which may reach a height of 130 ft (40 m) in some species. These are used for building and a variety of other purposes, while the young shoots are eaten as a vegetable. Some bamboos are cultivated in temperate gardens for their graceful foliage. Family: *Gramineae* (grasses).

Bana (7th century AD) Sanskrit writer. He traveled widely in India before becoming court poet of the Buddhist emperor *Harsa. The *Harsacarita* is a prose chronicle written to celebrate his patron's accession to the throne. The prose romance *Kadambari* exploits sophisticated narrative techniques to describe a complex love intrigue.

Banaba. *See* Ocean Island.

banana A palmlike plant of the Old World tropical genus *Musa*, especially *M. paradisiaca sapientum*, cultivated throughout the tropics from prehistoric times for its edible fruit. The "trunk," up to 30 ft (9 m) high, is composed of the overlapping bases of the leaves, which are often 10 ft (3 m) or more long. The tip of the flowering stem bears male flowers and hangs down; clusters of female flowers, further up the stem, develop into seedless fruits, up to 12 in (30 cm) long, without being fertilized. (All cultivated bananas are sterile hybrids: the plants are propagated from suckers arising from the underground rhizome.) Most bananas are eaten fresh, but varieties called plantains are cooked and eaten when still green, forming a staple food in East and West Africa and the Caribbean. Family: *Musaceae*.

Bancroft, George (1800–91) US historian, diplomat, and educator. Originally a teacher and city official in Boston, he was appointed secretary of the navy (1845) under President James Polk. During this time, Bancroft was responsible for the founding of the Naval Academy at Annapolis, Md. Although he served as minister to England (1846–49) and to Prussia and the German empire (1867–74), he is best known for his *History of the United States*, a 10-volume work (1834–74) that earned him the title "Father of American History." Other works include *History of the Formation of the Constitution of the United States of America* (1882).

Banda, Hastings Kamuzu (1905–) Malawi statesman; president (1964–). A physician, he worked in the UK and the US before returning home (then Nyasaland) in 1958 to lead the fight against federation with Rhodesia and for independence. On independence (1964) he became president and in 1971, life president.

Bandar Abbas 27 12N 56 15E A town in S Iran, on the Strait of Hormuz. It is a naval base important to the security of the Persian Gulf.

Bandaranaike, S(olomon) W(est) R(idgeway) D(ias) (1899–1959) Sri Lankan statesman; prime minister (1956–59). In 1951 he founded the Sri Lanka Freedom Party (SLFP) and became prime minister as head of an alliance of socialist and nationalist parties—the People's United Front, which pursued a neutral foreign policy and nationalist domestic policies (including the substitution of English with Sinhalese as the official language). He was assassinated by a Buddhist monk and was succeeded as head of the SLFP by his wife **Sirimavo Ratwatte Dias Bandaranaike** (1916–), the world's first woman prime minister (1960–65, 1970–77). Her socialist coalition with the Marxist party was defeated in 1965 but returned to power in 1970.

Bandar-e Bushehr. *See* Bushire.

Bandar Seri Begawan (former name: Brunei Town) 4 56N 114 58E The capital of Brunei, a port in the NE near the mouth of the Brunei River. Population (1971): 36,987.

Bandeira, Manuel Carneiró de Sousa (1886–1968) Brazilian poet. He was forced by tuberculosis to give up his architectural studies in São Paulo. After meeting the French poet Paul *Eluard while in a Swiss sanatorium, he decided to try a literary career. The originality of his first book, *A cinza das horas* (1917), was immediately recognized; his modernist style developed more fully in *Libertinagem* (1930) and *Estrêla da Manhã* (1936). He was also an influential critic, translator, and university professor.

bandicoot A ratlike *marsupial mammal of a family (*Peramelidae*; 20 species) occurring in Australia (including Tasmania) and New Guinea. About the size of rabbits, bandicoots are mainly carnivorous, eating insects, worms, and grubs. They are shy creatures and build nests of grass and leaves among thick vegetation.

Bandjermasin. *See* Banjarmasin.

Bandung 6 57S 107 34E A city in Indonesia, in W Java. A cultural and industrial center and tourist resort, it was formerly the administrative center of the Netherlands East Indies. Its chief industries are chemicals, quinine, plastics, metal processing, and textiles. It has two universities, established in 1957 and 1959, and a nuclear research center (1964). At the **Bandung Conference** of 1955 representatives of 29 African and Asian countries met to oppose colonialism. Population (1971): 1,201,730.

BANDICOOT *A short-nosed bandicoot (genus Thylacis or Isoodon), which is 14-16 in (35-40 cm) long (excluding the tail). As in other bandicoots, the pouch opens towards the rear.*

Banff 57 40N 2 31W A town in NE Scotland, in Grampian Region on the Moray Firth, at the mouth of the River Deveron. It is a resort with fishing and distilling industries, and was the county town of the former county of Banff, covering 630 sq mi (1632 sq km) from the Moray Firth to the Cairngorm Mountains.

Bangalore 12 58N 77 35E A city in S India, the capital of Karnataka. Founded in the 16th century, it fell to the British in 1791. The Institute of Science was established in 1909 and Bangalore University in 1964. An expanding industrial center, Bangalore's many modern industries include aircraft assembly, machine tools, and electronics. Population (1971): 1,540,741.

Bangka (*or* Banka) An Indonesian island in the Java Sea, off SE Sumatra. Its government-owned tin mines are among the world's most productive; other mineral deposits include gold, manganese, and iron. The population is largely Chinese. Area: 4600 sq mi (11,914 sq km). Chief town: Pangkalpinang.

Bangkok (Thai name: Krung Threp) 13 44N 100 30E The capital and main port of Thailand, in the SW near the mouth of the Chao Phraya River. It became a royal city and the capital in 1782. Distinctive features of the city are its canal system and the many Buddhist temples. There has been considerable expansion since World War II. Most of the country's industry and commerce is centered on Bangkok and it has eight universities. Population (1979 est): 4,870,509.

Bangladesh, People's Republic of A country in the Indian subcontinent, lying between the Himalayas and the Bay of Bengal, in the delta of the Ganges and Brahmaputra Rivers. Bangladesh is the most densely populated country, and one of the poorest regions, in the world, beset continually by famine and floods. The land, which is generally low lying, is on the whole fertile but it has to support a very large population, most of whom are Bengalis. *Economy*: about three-quarters of the inhabitants are occupied in agriculture, rice being by far the most important food crop. Bangladesh produces 50% of the world's raw jute, its main export. Fishing, both freshwater and saltwater, is important not only as a valuable food source, but also for oil and other fish products. Traditional industries include jute milling and textile manufacture but plans for further industrial development are hindered by the comparative lack of mineral resources. Most industry is now nationalized. Communications are greatly aided by the many natural shipping channels that the country's rivers provide. *History*: the area formed part of the kingdom of Bengal, and its conquest by the Afghans in the 12th century led to the growth of the Islamic religion. It was part of British India from 1857 until 1947 when it became independent as a province of Pakistan (East Pakistan). In 1974 floods and famine led to political unrest and terrorism and in 1975 Mujib assumed absolute power on a one-party basis but shortly afterward he and his family were assassinated in a military coup. After several more coups and countercoups, General *Ziaur Rahman assumed power in 1976 and was elected president in 1978 in the

first presidential election on a basis of adult suffrage. In 1977 amendments to the constitution established Bangladesh as an Islamic state. General Ziaur was assassinated in an unsuccessful insurrection in 1981. His successor, Abdus Sattar (1906–), was ousted in a military coup (1982) and replaced by Justice Choudhury. Choudhury, however, was a figurehead president backed by the military regime under General Hossain Mohannad Ershad. In late 1983, Ershad announced that he was assuming the presidency and Choudhury was subsequently phased out of government office. Balgladesh became a member of the Commonwealth of Nations in 1972. Official language: Bengali. Official religion: Islam. Official currency: taka of 100 paisa. Area: 142,797 sq km (55,126 sq mi). Population (1983 est): 96,539,000. Capital: Dacca. Main port: Chittagong.

Bangui 4 23N 19 20E The capital of the Central African Republic, a port in the SW on the Ubangi River. Founded in 1889, the port handles goods for both the Central African Republic and Chad; its main exports are cotton and coffee. Its university was established in 1969. Population (1975 est): 301,793.

Bangweulu, Lake 11 15S 29 45E A lake in E Zambia. Discovered by Livingstone (1868), it is shallow and bordered by swamps. During the rainy season its waters cover an area of up to 3783 sq mi (9800 sq km).

Banja Luka 44 47N 17 11E A city in W Yugoslavia, in Bosnia and Hercegovina on the Vrbas River. It has several mosques, a university (1975), and diverse industries. Population (1971): 91,000.

Banjarmasin *or* Bandjermasin 3 22S 114 33E0 A port in Indonesia, in S Kalimantan on the Barito delta. Its exports include rubber and timber. Its university was established in 1960. Population (1971): 281,673.

banjo A plucked string instrument of US origin, originally played by plantation slaves. The banjo became popular in minstrel shows, vaudeville, jazz, and folk music. The body of the banjo is a round metal hoop covered with parchment on one side; the fretted fingerboard has five or six strings, which are plucked with the fingers or with a plectrum.

Banjul (name until 1973: Bathurst) 13 20N 16 38W The capital of The Gambia, a port in the W at the mouth of the Gambia River, founded by the British in 1816. Population (1977 est): 43,890.

Banka. See Bangka.

Bank for International Settlements (BIS) A bank in Basle, Switzerland, which acts as a bank for *central banks (mostly European and American) and is governed by representatives of several of them. It was set up in 1930 to coordinate reparations after World War I. Although most of its functions are now performed by the *International Monetary Fund, it has important duties as a trustee.

Bankhead, Tallulah (1903–68) US actress. She won critical acclaim as a stage actress in such plays as Lillian Hellman's *Little Foxes* (1939) and Thornton Wilder's *The Skin of Our Teeth* (1942), but her popularity as a film star owed more to her extravagant lifestyle than to the quality of her performances.

Bankhead, William Brockman (1874–1940) US politician, speaker of the House of Representatives (1936–40). From a family of legislators, he became a lawyer and then was elected to the Congress as a representative from Alabama in 1916. He served the House of Representatives in various capacities until his election as speaker, an office he held until his death. He was the father of actress Tallulah Bankhead.

Bank of the United States Two successive financial institutions established to regulate the economic transactions of the federal government. The First Bank of the US was founded by Secretary of the Treasury Alexander *Hamilton in Philadelphia in 1791. Opposition by state banks led to its dissolution in 1811. After the War of 1812, the finances of the federal government needed reorganization, and the Second Bank of the US was created by Congress in 1816. By the terms of its twenty-year charter, it held all federal assets and was empowered to establish branches in all states. The constitutionality of its activities was upheld by the Supreme Court in the case of *McCulloch* v. *Maryland* in 1819. Pres. Andrew *Jackson opposed the power of the Bank of the US and withdrew all federal deposits in 1833. Jackson later vetoed a plan to recharter the Bank and it ended operations in 1836. *See also* Federal Reserve System.

bank rate. See minimum lending rate.

bankruptcy proceedings The legal process by which the property of a person who cannot pay his debts is distributed among his creditors. Bankruptcy is either voluntary or involuntary. A **voluntary** proceeding is initiated by the debtor's own petition to be adjudged a bankrupt and have the benefit of the law. In **involuntary** bankruptcy, the debtor is forced into bankruptcy on the petition of a sufficient number of his creditors.

banks. *See* Bank for International Settlements; Bank of England; Bank of the United States; central bank; commercial bank; International Bank for Reconstruction and Development; merchant bank.

Banks, Sir Joseph (1743–1820) British botanist and explorer. During his most famous expedition, around the world with James *Cook (1768–71), he showed that the marsupial mammals of Australia were more primitive than the placental mammals of other continents and he also discovered many new species of plants. Banks promoted the introduction of economic plants from their native regions to other countries and he was known as a patron of young scientists. He was president of Britain's Royal Society from 1778 until his death.

Banksia A genus of shrubs and trees (about 50 species) all native to dry areas of Australia; some are known as Australian honeysuckles. The flowers are borne in dense spikes and give rise to hard winged seeds. Family: *Proteaceae*.

Banks Island The westernmost island of Canada's Arctic Archipelago, in Franklin district. Mostly hilly plateau, it supports numerous Arctic animals. Area: 23,230 sq mi (60,166 sq km).

Banneker, Benjamin (1731–1806) US surveyor and scientist. The son of a slave, he was for the most part self-educated. He became the first black ever appointed to an official position by a president when George Washington asked him to assist in surveying the Territory of Columbia, the site for a new national capital. He was also known for his almanacs, the first of which was published in 1792.

Banner System A system of military organization adopted by the Manchu tribes and used by the *Qing dynasty to rule China. It was initiated in 1601 by *Nurhachi, who enrolled his warriors under yellow, white, blue, or red banners. Later four bordered banners were added and all tribesmen were enrolled. Each banner formed an administrative unit, which contributed a quota of men when it became necessary to raise an army and also facilitated taxation. In return bannermen were allocated land. After the Manchu conquest of China and the establishment of the Qing, eight Chinese and eight Mongol banners were added.

Bannister, Sir Roger (Gilbert) (1929–   ) British doctor and middle-distance runner, who on May 6, 1954, was the first man to run a mile in under 4 minutes (3 minutes 59.4 seconds). In 1975 he was knighted.

Bannockburn 56 06N 3 55W A village in Scotland, near Stirling on the Bannock Burn (a tributary of the River Forth). 1 mi (1.5 km) NW is Scotland's most famous battlefield, where in 1314 the Scots defeated the English, who had come to relieve the besieged Stirling Castle. Population (1973 est): 4759.

banshee (Irish *bean-sidhe*: woman of the fairies) In Irish folklore, a female specter whose weeping announced the imminent death of a person.

bantam One of many breeds of dwarf fowl, possibly named for the district of Bantam in Indonesia, from where they were formerly exported to the West. Bantams generally weigh about 1 lb (450 g).

Banten A region in W Java (Indonesia), which was the center of a Muslim sultanate until 1683 when it became part of the Dutch East Indies. The town of Banten was a flourishing port for the European spice trade from the 16th to the 18th centuries, after which the harbor silted up.

banteng A wild ox, *Bos banteng*, of forests in SE Asia. About 60 in (150 cm) high at the shoulder, bantengs are brown with white socks and a white rump patch and have relatively small horns. They feed on young grass and bamboo shoots.

Banting, Sir Frederick Grant (1891–1941) Canadian physiologist, who, with C. H. *Best, discovered a technique for the successful isolation of the hormone *insulin from pancreatic tissue in 1921. This enabled the successful treatment of patients suffering from *diabetes (caused by lack of insulin). Banting was awarded a Nobel Prize (1923) with J. J. R.*Macleod but he divided his share with Best in recognition of his colleague's achievement.

Bantu A large subgroup of African languages of the *Niger-Congo group spoken over the whole of the S half of Africa by about 60 million people. It includes Zulu, Xhosa, and Kongo; perhaps the most widely known representative is *Swahili, the language of Tanzania and lingua franca of E Africa. The Bantu languages are tonal, with the exception of Swahili, and make extensive use of suffixes and prefixes. Many use a number of click sounds. The Bantu people are very diverse in culture and social organization and include herdsmen, farmers, hunter-gatherers, and fishers. They probably migrated southward from an area near the Cameroon-Nigeria border, displacing small pygmy and Bushmen tribes, approximately 2000 years ago.

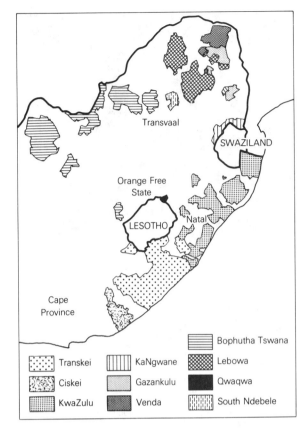

BANTU HOMELANDS *The areas designated as black African territories in South Africa are dispersed over the E and N parts of the country.*

Bantu Homelands (or Bantustans) The areas of South Africa designated for the black populations, comprising just over 13% of the land area. Acts of parliament in 1913 and 1936 controlled the extent of African lands and prohibited blacks from holding land in white areas. The Bantu Authorities Act (1951) gave limited administrative and legislative powers to the Bantu authorities, and the Bantu Self-Government Act (1959) divided the black populations into national units, most of them with homelands in several separate areas. Limited self-government was to be granted to these areas; the *Transkei was the first to receive this (1963). The Bantu Homelands Constitution Act (1971) aimed at similar self-government for other areas. Full independence has been granted to Transkei (1976), *Bophutha Tswana (1977), Gazankulu, KaNgwane, *Venda (1979), and Ciskei (1981). Other Bantu Homelands include KwaZulu, Lebowa, and Qwaqwa. The Bantustan policy has been constantly opposed by African leaders (in particular Chief Gatsha Buthelezi of KwaZulu), and many of the territories have resisted moves toward— self-government and independence, regarding it as a poor substitute for majority rule in South Africa as a whole.

Banville, Théodore Faullain de (1823–89) French poet. He wrote a technical treatise on French poetry and revived old forms, such as the *ballade and the *rondeau. His best-known collection is *Odes funambulesques* (1857). He helped many younger writers, including *Rimbaud.

banyan A tropical Asian tree, *Ficus benghalensis*, related to the fig and reaching a height of 98 ft (30 m). Individual trees commonly grow into impenetrable thickets as the branches produce supporting aerial roots, which grow down to penetrate the soil and subsequently give rise to thorny branches of their own. Family: *Moraceae*.

baobab A tropical African tree, *Adansonia digitata*, with a tapering conical trunk (the base of which may exceed 33 ft [10 m] in diameter) reaching a height of 59 ft (18 m) and bearing branches at its apex. The drab bat-pollinated flowers give rise to fruits that contain a succulent edible pulp surrounded by a tough woody capsule. The bark yields a fiber of local importance, and the trees are grown as ornamentals in some subtropical areas. Family: *Bombacaceae*.

BANYAN   *In India it is regarded as a sacred tree and is carefully tended.*

Baotou (*or* Pao-t'ou)   40 38N 109 59E A city in N China, in the Inner Mongolia AR on the Yellow River. It is a major industrial center, with a nuclear power station. Industries include iron and steel, aluminum, sugar, and textiles. Population (1953): 149,400.

baptism   A ceremony of initiation, occurring in many religions, involving the use of water as a symbol of purification from sin. In the Christian Church, where it is a *sacrament and is done in the name of the Father, the Son, and the Holy Spirit, it involves the candidate's total or partial immersion in water or the mere wetting of his head. Both the *Baptists and the modern descendants of the *Anabaptists practice adult baptism, but most other Churches prefer infant baptism.

Baptists   Protestant Christians who baptize, by immersion, only those old enough consciously to accept the Christian faith. Each Baptist Church is autonomous. The sect was an outgrowth of the Anabaptists of the Reformation period who fled England for Holland. In Britain there were two main types, "General Baptist" Churches, owing their origin in 1612 to John Smyth (c. 1554–1612) and Thomas Helwys (c. 1550–c. 1616), and "Particular Baptist" Churches, founded in 1633 by Calvinists who believed that salvation was only for a particular few. The latter had modified its doctrines by 1891, when both movements merged into the Baptist Union. The first Baptist Church in America was established at Providence, Rhode Island, by Roger Williams in 1639. The majority of Baptists, of whom there are over 30 million worldwide, live in the US and most of them are associated with the Baptist World Alliance.

Baqqarah   A cattle-herding Arab people of Chad and the Sudan. As a result of contact and intermixture with other local peoples they have dark skins and speak a distinct dialect of Arabic. They migrate seasonally between northern wet-season grazing lands and southern dry-season river areas.

bar   A unit of pressure equal to 10^5 pascals (0.987 atmosphere). The commonly used unit is the millibar (one-thousandth of a bar).

Baranof Island   A US island, off the coast of SE Alaska in the Alexander Archipelago. Area: 1607 sq mi (4162 sq km). Chief town: Sitka.

Barbados, State of   An island state in the West Indies, E of the Windward Islands. It is generally low lying except for a district in the NE and is subject to hurricanes. Most of the population is of African descent. *Economy*: high-density agriculture, with sugar cane as the main crop, and tourism are important. The policy of encouraging some small industries has been helped by the discovery of offshore oil and natural gas. Main exports include sugar and sugar products (including rum), petroleum and petroleum products, clothing, and electrical goods. *History*: occupied by the British in 1627, it remained a British colony until 1966, when it became a fully independent state within the Commonwealth of Nations. Prime Minister: J. M. G. M. Adams (1931–). Official language: English. Official currency: Barbados dollar of 100 cents. Area: 166 sq mi (430 sq km). Population (1983 est): 251,000. Capital and main port: Bridgetown.

Barbarossa   (Khayr ad-Din; d. 1546) Turkish pirate. Barbarossa (Italian: Redbeard) entered the service of the Ottoman Sultan of Turkey to protect his possessions on the Barbary coast of N Africa against Spanish and Portuguese attack. He captured Algiers in 1529 and Tunisia in 1534 and his defeat of Emperor Charles V's fleet in 1538 gave the Turks control of the E Mediterranean.

Barbary   A region in N Africa stretching from Egypt to the Atlantic Ocean and from the Mediterranean Sea to the Sahara. It is named for its oldest inhabitants, the *Berbers. In antiquity it consisted of Mauritania, Numidia, Africa, Propria, and Cyrenaica. It was successively conquered by the Romans, Vandals, Arabs, Turks, Spaniards (parts of Morocco), French (Algeria, Tunisia, and Morocco), and Italians (Tripoli). Between the 16th and 18th centuries, Barbary was notorious for its pirates, who caused havoc in the Mediterranean.

Barbary ape   A large monkey, *Macaca sylvana*, also called magot, the only *macaque found in N Africa. Barbary apes are tailless and roam in bands over the forest floor, feeding on seeds, leaves, insects, and small animals. The colony of Barbary apes in Gibraltar was probably introduced by man.

barbastelle   A large-eared insect-eating bat, *Barbastella barbastella*, of Europe, S Asia, and NE Africa. About 5 cm long, slender, and long-legged, barbastelles fly early in the evening. Family: *Vespertilionidae*.

barbel   A long slender freshwater fish, belonging to the genus *Barbus*, that is related to *carp and occurs in clear fresh waters of Asia, Africa, and Europe. It has four fleshy threadlike appendages (barbels) near its mouth, which detect prey, mainly invertebrates, while exploring the river bed. *B. barbus* of Europe is usually 12–20 in (30–50 cm) long.

Barber, Samuel   (1910–81) US composer. Two of his works, the opera *Vanessa* (1958) and the piano concerto (1963), won Pulitzer Prizes. His style, although basically lyrical, became increasingly dissonant in his later works. His output includes chamber music, choral works, symphonies, and concertos. His best-known work is the *Adagio for Strings*, an arrangement of the slow movement of his string quartet (1936).

barberry.   *See* Berberis.

barbet   A small brightly colored forest bird belonging to a tropical family (*Capitonidae*; 76 species) most commonly found in Africa. 3–12 in (8–30 cm) long, barbets have large heavy bills with bristles around the chin and beak and a monotonously repeated call. They feed mainly on fruit but also take insects, lizards, and birds' eggs. Order: *Piciformes* (woodpeckers, etc.).

Barbirolli, Sir John   (1899–1970) British conductor of Franco-Italian parents. Originally a cellist, he organized his own string orchestra, and subsequently became conductor of several major opera companies and orchestras in Britain and the US. From 1949 until his death he was principal conductor of the Hallé Orchestra, Manchester.

barbiturates   A class of drugs that act by depressing the activity of the brain. Short-acting barbiturates, such as thiopental, are used for inducing *anesthesia. Medium-acting barbiturates, such as pentobarbital, are used as sleeping tablets. Small doses of long-acting barbiturates, such as phenobarbital, are used for day-time sedation and to control epilepsy. As barbiturates are habit-forming and may cause true addiction, with serious effects on the mind and body, their use is now severely limited. They have been shown to be associated with the increased incidence of falls and fractures in elderly patients. Overdosage is a medical emergency and can cause death by inhibiting the breathing center in the brain.

Barbizon school   A group of French landscape painters who worked in the village of Barbizon, near the Forest of Fontainebleau, in the 1840s. Truth to nature combined with romantic settings typify the works of the school's founder Theodore *Rousseau, *Daubigny, Narcisse-Virgile Diaz de la Pena (c. 1807–76), and others. Dark trees and ponds betray their debt to Dutch landscape painting but their constant practice of open-air oil sketching to capture light effects inspired the impressionists to paint finished works outside. Fringe members of the school included *Corot and *Millet.

Barbor, John   (1316–95) Scottish poet. He became archdeacon of Aberdeen in 1357, studied at Oxford and Paris, and received a royal pension in 1388. In *The Bruce*, a Scottish national epic, he celebrated Scotland's fight for independence under *Robert (I) the Bruce and James Douglas.

Barbusse, Henri   (1873–1935) French novelist. His novel *Under Fire* (1916), based on his experiences in World War I, expresses the disillusion that led him first to pacifism and later to communism. *Clarté* (1919) lent its name to a short-lived international movement. Barbusse died in the Soviet Union.

barcarolle   A piece of music in imitation of the songs of Venetian gondoliers. It is usually in 6/8 or 12/8 time and has a gentle rocking movement.

Examples include Offenbach's *Barcarolle* from *The Tales of Hoffman* and Chopin's *Barcarolle* for the piano.

Barcelona   41 25N 2 10E A city in NE Spain, in Catalonia on the Mediterranean Sea. It is Spain's second largest city, its largest port and leading commercial and industrial center. Manufactures include locomotives, aircraft, textiles, and electrical equipment. The country's cultural center and the focus of Catalan art and literature, it has many educational establishments, libraries, and museums; the University of Barcelona was founded in 1430. The city's numerous fine buildings include the palace of the Aragón kings, a cathedral (14th–15th centuries), and a 14th-century monastery. It has several Art Nouveau buildings designed by Antonio Gaudí, notably the Sagrada Familia church (1903–26). *History*: founded by the Carthaginians, it was taken by the Moors in 713 AD and by Charlemagne in 801 AD. In 1137 Catalonia and Aragón united and Barcelona became the capital, rivaling Genoa and Venice as a leading European port. During the 19th century it became important industrially through its cotton industry. The center of the Catalan separatist government, it was the seat of the Catalan autonomous government and later of the Republican government, during the Spanish Civil War (1936–39). In 1939 Barcelona fell to Gen Franco and the Republican government finally surrendered. Population (1974 est): 1,809,722.

Barclay de Tolly, Mikhail Bogdanovich, Prince   (1761–1818) Russian field marshal. In 1810, after brilliant campaigns against Napoleon, he became minister of war. Promoted to field marshal (1814), he commanded the army that invaded France in 1815.

Barcoo River.   *See* Cooper Creek.

bard   In ancient Celtic societies, a poet whose duty was to eulogize heroes and to celebrate notable events, such as victories, and the laws and traditions of the community. Bards constituted a distinct social class with hereditary rights and privileges. The class was at one time subdivided according to functions. In 10th-century Wales the three bardic ranks were *pencerdd* (chief of song), *bardd teulu* (household bard), and *cerddor* (minstrel); an earlier Irish classification was *druid*, *filid*, and *baird*. Bards ceased to exist in Gaul at an early date, but they survived in Scotland and Ireland to the 18th century and, in a somewhat artificial and diminished role, continue to exist in Wales to the present. Today the term is used to describe any type of poet. *See also* eisteddfod; Welsh literature.

Bardeen, John   (1908–) US physicist, who became professor at the University of Illinois in 1951. He shared the 1956 Nobel Prize for his part in the invention of the transistor (with W. B. *Shockley and W. H. *Brattain) while working at the Bell Telephone Laboratories in 1948. He also shared the 1972 Nobel Prize for his work on the theory of superconductivity (with L. N. Cooper and J. R. Schrieffer). This theory is known as the BCS theory after the initials of its authors.

Bardot, Brigitte   (1934–) French film actress. Her films include *And God Created Woman* (1956), *Vie privée* (1961), *Viva Maria* (1965), and *Shalako* (1968). She became probably the best-known sex symbol of the 1960s.

Barebones Parliament   The assembly, also known as the parliament of saints, called by Oliver *Cromwell in July, 1653. It consisted mainly of merchants and lesser gentry, nominated by the congregations. In Dec the moderates among them resigned their power to Cromwell.

Bareilly   28 20N 79 24E A city in India, in Uttar Pradesh. Founded in 1537, it was a center of the Indian Mutiny. The Indian Veterinary Research Institute was established nearby in 1889. Manufactures include sugar, rope, and furniture. Population (1971): 296,248.

Barenboim, Daniel   (1942–) Israeli pianist and conductor, who studied in Salzburg, Paris, and Rome. He made his debut in London in 1955. In 1967 he married the cellist Jacqueline *du Pré, with whom he gave recitals. Increasingly active as a conductor in the 1970s, Barenboim has conducted the Orchestre de Paris since 1975.

Barents, Willem   (c. 1550–97) Dutch navigator. He led three expeditions (1594, 1595, 1596) to discover a *Northeast Passage, reaching the Novaya Zemlya islands and discovering Spitsbergen (1596). On his last voyage he was forced to winter at Icehaven, where his camp was found in 1871. He died at sea on his return journey. The Barents Sea is named for him.

Barents Sea   A section of the Arctic Ocean between Eurasia and Svalbard, Franz Josef Land, and Novaya Zemlya. It covers part of the Eurasian continental shelf, which before the Pleistocene Ice Age was land. It is rich in fish.

Barère, Bertrand   (1755–1841) French revolutionary. Initially a moderate in the National Convention, he subsequently became a member of the

Committee of *Public Safety during the *Reign of Terror. Imprisoned after the fall of Robespierre (July, 1794), he escaped into exile, returning to France in 1830.

DANIEL BARENBOIM   *Conducting the Orchestre de Paris.*

Bar Harbor   44 23N 68 13W A resort town in SE Maine. It is located on Mount Desert Island and is known for its palatial summer homes. Population (1980): 4124.

Bar Hebraeus   (1226–86) Syrian bishop and scholar. Bar Hebraeus studied medicine at Antioch and Tripoli. He was consecrated bishop in 1246 and became Primate of the East in 1264. His writings, in Syriac and Arabic, include the *Granary of Mysteries* and the *Chronicle*.

Bari   41 07N 16 52E A seaport in Italy, the capital of Apulia on the Adriatic Sea. It has a cathedral (12th–15th centuries) and a university (1924). Industries include chemicals, textiles, and oil refining. Population (1980 est): 387,710.

barite (*or* barytes)   A barium ore consisting of barium sulfate, sometimes called heavy spar. It is colorless when pure, but often white, yellow, or brown, due to impurities. It is used in the manufacture of paint and heavy paper, as a mineral filler in rubber and linoleum manufacture, and in concrete and glassmaking. The chief producers are the US, West Germany, and Ireland.

baritone   A deep adult male singing voice, lower than tenor and higher than bass. Range: G at the bottom of the bass stave to G two octaves above.

barium (Ba)   A silvery reactive metal that resembles calcium in its behavior. It was discovered in 1808 by Sir Humphry Davy and occurs naturally as barytes ($BaSO_4$) and witherite ($BaCO_3$). The sulfate is used as a white pigment in paint and, because of its opacity to X-rays, is used in X-ray diagnosis. All soluble barium compounds are toxic, the carbonate being used as rat poison. At no 56; at wt 137.34; mp 725°C.

bark   The dead outer layer of the stems and roots of woody plants, which protects the inner tissues from desiccation, extremes of temperature, pests and diseases, and physical damage. Antiseptic deposits, such as tannins, give the color. Bark may include layers of insulating *cork, which is responsible for the characteristic ridges and patterns on some tree trunks. Small breathing pores (caled lenticels) in the bark are conspicuous in many of the smooth-barked trees (such as *Prunus* species) but are hidden in the cracks of rough-barked species. The bark of some trees is of commercial importance, being a source of cinnamon, quinine, and various other products.

bark   A sailing vessel with three or more masts. Square sails are set on all masts except the aftermast, which carries fore-and-aft sails. In a **barkentine** only the foremast has square-rigged sails.

bark beetle   A hard cylindrical beetle, also called an engraver beetle, belonging to a family (*Scolytidae*; 7000 species) of wood borers. It is usually less than 6 mm long, colored red-brown or black, and causes considerable damage to trees. It burrows underneath the bark to lay eggs that develop into burrowing larvae: the elaborate patterns of tunnels produced are generally characteristic of the species. Certain species also transmit diseases (*see* bark beetle) and can be serious economic pests.

Barker, Harley Granville. *See* Granville-Barker, Harley.

Barkhausen, Heinrich (1881–1956) German physicist, who became professor of electrical engineering at the University of Dresden. He discovered (1919) the effect in which ferromagnetic materials placed in an increasing magnetic field become magnetized in small jumps (Barkhausen effect).

barking deer. *See* muntjac.

Barkley, Alben William (1877–1956) US politician, vice president (1949–53). Born and educated in Kentucky, he went to law schools in Georgia and Virginia. A Democrat, he served in the House of Representatives from 1912 until being elected to the Senate in 1927. While a senator he was minority and then majority leader and was a chief supporter of President Roosevelt's New Deal and President Truman's Fair Deal. As vice president, under Truman, he had a more active role than previous vice presidents.

Barkly Tableland An area of Australia, extending SE of the Gulf of Carpentaria, in Northern Territory, into Queensland. It consists of undulating uplands on which beef cattle are raised. Area: about 50,000 sq mi (130,000 sq km).

Bar Kokhba (Simeon bar Kosiba; d. 135 AD) Jewish freedom fighter. In 132 he launched a revolt against Roman rule and attempted to set up an independent Jewish state. He was hailed as Messiah by *Akiba, but did not enjoy widespread support and was killed when his last stronghold, Betar, fell. Some of his correspondence has been recovered from caves in the Judean desert.

Barlach, Ernst (1870–1938) German expressionist sculptor and playwright. First influenced by *Jugendstil*, he only found his mature style after visiting Russia (1906). His bulky figures, usually in wood, with their expressive faces and angular and rigid outlines were inspired both by his studies of Russian peasants and by *gothic sculpture. The Nazis destroyed much of his work.

Bar-le-Duc 48 46N 5 10E A city in NE France, the capital of the Meuse department on the Ornain River. Its manufactures include metal goods, textiles, and jams. Population (1975): 20,516.

Barletta 41 20N 16 17E A seaport in Italy, in Apulia on the Adriatic coast. It possesses a romanesque cathedral and a castle. An agricultural center, it has an important wine trade; chemicals and cement are also manufactured. Population (1971): 75,728.

barley A *cereal grass of the genus *Hordeum*, especially *H. vulgare*, which produces its grain in four rows and can be grown as far north as N Norway; *H. distichon* (two-rowed barley); and *H. hexadistichon* (six-rowed barley). Over 165 million tons of grain are harvested annually in temperate, subtropical, and subarctic regions from the various strains of barley. It is malted and used in the brewing industry, made into food for cattle and pigs, milled to produce pearl and pot barley (used in soups and stews), and used in breadmaking.

Bar Mitzvah (Hebrew: son of the commandment) The ceremony marking the initiation of a Jewish boy into the adult community at the age of 13. At this age he assumes his full religious responsibilities and it is customary for him to read publicly from the *Torah in the synagogue for the first time. In some communities a parallel ceremony (Bat Mitzvah) exists for girls.

Barnabas, St In the New Testament (Acts), a Christian Apostle of the 1st century. After going with St Paul to evangelize Cyprus (his birthplace) and the European mainland, he clashed with him and they parted company. He is traditionally regarded as the founder of the Cypriot Church. Feast day: June 11.

barnacle A marine *crustacean belonging to the subclass *Cirripedia* (1000 species). Some members of the group are parasites, but the typical (nonparasitic) barnacles live attached—head downward—to rocks, ships' hulls, etc., and filter food particles from the water with long feathery appendages, which protrude from the calcareous shell. Goose barnacles (e.g. *Lepas anatifera*)—so called because they were believed in the middle ages to be an immature form of the barnacle goose—are attached by means of a stalk; others, including the acorn barnacle (*Balanus*), are unstalked. Barnacles are hermaphrodite; their larvae are free-swimming, but later settle and become fixed to a surface by means of a cement-like substance secreted by their antennae.

barnacle goose A European *goose, *Branta leukopsis*, which is a regular winter visitor to Britain. It has a distinctive cream face, dark crown and breast, and a white chevron on the tail and grazes on coastal meadows and salt marshes. They were once believed to hatch from barnacles!

Barnard, Christiaan Neethling (1922–) South African surgeon, who (in 1967 at the Groote Schuur Hospital in Cape Town) performed the world's first successful heart transplant operation. His patient, Louis Washkansky, received the heart of a road-accident victim but died 18 days later from pneumonia. In another patient (1974) he implanted a second heart, connecting the circulatory systems to perform as one.

Barnard, Edward Emerson (1857–1923) US astronomer, who became professor at the University of Chicago (1895). He discovered Jupiter's fifth satellite (1892), a total of 16 comets, and **Barnard's Star** (1916) in the constellation Ophiuchus, the star with the most rapid proper motion.

Barnaul 53 21N 83 45E A city in the S Soviet Union, in the RSFSR on the Ob River. The center of an industrial and mining area, its industries include engineering, textiles, chemicals, and timber. Population (1981 est): 549,000.

Barnave, Antoine Pierre (1761–93) French revolutionary. A chief spokesman of the *Jacobins, he developed royalist sympathies in 1791 through personal contact with Louis XVI. Advocating a constitutional monarchy, he became leader of the *Feuillants and was executed.

Barnburners A nickname for the radical part of the New York Democratic Party from the early 1840s to the early 1850s. Opposed to the extension of slavery into the territories, they merged with the Free Soil Party, which supported presidential candidate Martin Van Buren. Their opponents, within the Democratic Party, were nicknamed Hunkers.

Barnegat Bay 39 52N 74 07W A bay on the E central coast of New Jersey, sheltered from the Atlantic Ocean by Long Beach Island and Island Beach. It is part of the inland-waterway for small craft. Length: 30 mi (49 km).

barn owl An *owl belonging to a family (*Tytonidae*; 9 species) with a worldwide distribution. Barn owls have heart-shaped faces, long feathered legs, and usually a reddish plumage with pale underparts. The common barn owl (*Tyto alba*), 12–18 in (30–45 cm) long, nests in old barns and belfries and hunts for small rodents.

Barnum, Phineas Taylor (1810–91) US showman. His presentation of such novel exhibits as human "freaks," including the dwarf Tom Thumb, and natural curiosities at the American Museum from 1842 attracted unprecedented crowds. In 1850 he organized the successful US tour of the Swedish singer Jenny Lind. His circus, which he called "The Greatest Show on Earth," established in 1871, merged with that of his rival, J. A. Bailey (1847–1906), to become the Barnum and Bailey Circus in 1881.

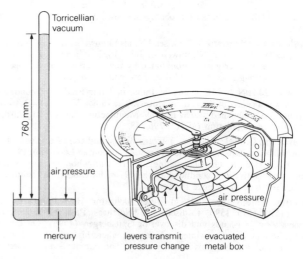

BAROMETER *In the mercury barometer the height of the mercury column is directly proportional to the air pressure and is independent of the diameter of the tube. In the aneroid barometer movements of the lid of the evacuated metal box are transmitted to the pointer by the levers.*

Baroda 22 19N 73 14E A city in India, in Gujarat. The siting of an oil refinery at nearby Kouali has helped to promote Baroda's industrial growth and its chief products include petrochemicals, cotton textiles, wood, and tobacco. Population (1971): 467,422.

Baroja, Pío (1872–1956) Spanish novelist. He abandoned a career as a doctor to manage a family bakery in Madrid. His first book of short stories, *Vida sombrías* (1900), was followed by nearly a hundred novels. His early heroes were rebels or reformers embodying his own desire to inspire political action, but the tone of later books—especially *Laura, o la soledad sin remedio* (1939)—was more skeptical and pessimistic.

barometer An instrument for measuring atmospheric pressure. There are two main types: the mercury barometer and the aneroid barometer. In the mercury barometer, atmospheric pressure forces mercury from a reservoir into a vertical evacuated glass tube marked with a scale. The height of the mercury column is directly proportional to the atmospheric pressure. In the aneroid barometer, variations in the atmospheric pressure on the lid of an evacuated metal box cause a pointer to move around a dial. The aneroid barometer is less sensitive than the mercury barometer but it is smaller, more portable, and more convenient to use.

Barons' Wars 1. (1215–17) The civil war between King John of England and his barons. John's failure to honor the *Magna Carta led the barons to offer the English crown to the future Louis VIII of France, who invaded England. John's death and the reissue of Magna Carta (1216) removed many baronial grievances but war continued until 1217 when peace was established and the Magna Carta again reissued. 2. (1264–67) The civil war between Henry III of England and his barons led by Simon de *Montfort. War broke out following Henry's repudiation of the Provisions of Oxford, which gave the barons much power. Henry was captured at the battle of *Lewes (1264) and England was controlled by de Montfort until his death (1265). Hostilities continued until 1267.

baroque In architecture, a style dominant in European Roman Catholic countries during the 17th and early 18th centuries. The name probably derives from the Spanish *barrueco*, an irregularly shaped pearl. The baroque began in Italy as a reaction against *classicism. It was characterized by curved and broken lines, ornate decoration (which led to the *rococo), and elaborate spatial effects.

In art, the baroque was a style that developed from Italian *mannerism, complementing baroque architecture. Both art and architecture were used to popularize Catholic beliefs during the *Counter-Reformation. Baroque art was characterized by the vivid presentation of stories of saints, miracles, and the crucifixion. Leading exponents of the baroque were the sculptor and architect *Bernini, the architect *Borromini, and the painters *Caravaggio and *Rubens.

In music, the compositions of the 17th and early 18th centuries, from Monteverdi to Bach, are frequently called baroque music. A variety of styles and forms flourished during this period, the use of the term referring to the period rather than a particular style. This period saw the development of *opera, *oratorio, the concerto grosso (*see* Corelli, Arcangelo), and the trio sonata.

Barossa Valley. *See* South Australia.

Barotse. *See* Lozi.

Barotseland A former kingdom in central Africa, now comprising Western Province in Zambia. Inhabited by the *Lozi people, it was put under British protection through two treaties (1890, 1900) by the Lozi chief, Lewanika (d. 1916). The area attempted to break away as a separate kingdom on Zambian independence (1964).

Barquisimeto 10 03N 69 18W A city in NW Venezuela. It is the commercial center of a coffee-growing area and has a university (1963). Population (1976 est): 430,000.

barracuda A shoaling fish of the family *Sphyraenidae* (about 20 species), found in all tropical seas and caught for food and sport. Its body is up to 6 ft (1.8 m) long and bears two dorsal fins. Barracudas feed voraciously on other fish and the larger species are considered dangerous to man. Order: *Perciformes*.

Barranquilla 11 00N 74 50W An important port in NW Colombia, on the Río Magdalena near its mouth on the Caribbean Sea. Its manufactures include textiles, vegetable oils, and chemicals. It has two universities (1941, 1967). Population (1978 est): 825,487.

Barras, Paul François Jean Nicolas, Vicomte de (1755–1829) French revolutionary. Although he joined the National Convention as a Jacobin, Barras turned against Robespierre and helped to secure his downfall in 1794. As commander of Paris, Barras suppressed a royalist uprising in 1795 by allowing Napoleon Bonaparte to turn his guns on the agitators.

A member of the Directory from 1795 to 1799, Barras resigned during Napoleon's coup d'état (1799).

Barrault, Jean-Louis (1910–   ) French actor and director. He has directed influential productions of both classical and avant-garde plays and was director of the Théâtre de France from 1959 to 1968. He is also renowned for his mime, especially in the film *Les Enfants du paradis* (1944).

barrel organ 1. A musical instrument popular in the 18th and 19th centuries, much used in churches. It consists of a simple organ mechanism operated by a wooden cylinder (or barrel) set with brass pins and turned by a handle, which also works a bellows. 2. A musical instrument of the 19th century more properly called **barrel piano** and often confused with the barrel organ. A popular street instrument, its barrel and pin mechanism causes leather-covered hammers to strike strings.

Barren Grounds (*or* Lands) The largely uninhabited permafrost plain of N Canada, stretching from about 59°N to the Arctic Ocean and from Hudson Bay to the Mackenzie Valley. Caribou and other animals live on the short grasses and other flowering plants.

Barrès, Maurice (1862–1923) French writer and politician. In the trilogy *La Culte de moi* (1888–91) he described a searching period of self-analysis resulting in his entry into politics. His rigid nationalism was expounded in another trilogy, *Le Roman de l'énergie nationale* (1897–1902), and linked with Catholicism in *La Colline inspirée* (1913). His memoirs, *Mes cahiers* (14 vols, 1929–57), were published posthumously.

Barrie, Sir James (Matthew) (1860–1937) British dramatist and novelist. The son of a Scots weaver, he came to London as a freelance writer in 1885. After two successful novels about Scottish rural life he wrote mostly for the theater. His best-known plays are *The Admirable Crichton* (1902), *Peter Pan* (1904), which has also remained a popular children's book, and *Dear Brutus* (1917).

barrier reef. *See* reef.

Barrow 71 17N 156 47W A village in N Alaska, just SW of Point Barrow, which is the northernmost point in the United States. An Eskimo village, Barrow is mainly a whaling center and serves as a base for the US Navy's Arctic Research Laboratory nearby. Population (1980): 2207.

barrow A prehistoric burial mound, also called a tumulus or cairn. From about 2000 BC earth barrows, concealing stone or timber passages and burial chambers, were built all over Europe for the interment of warrior chiefs. Long (i.e. rectangular or trapezoidal) barrows, such as at West Kennet (S England), were used for Neolithic multiple burials. Round barrows were more usual in Bronze Age cultures. Barrows continued in use in Iron Age Europe, for example the *Hallstatt barrow cemetery at Hohmichele (Germany) on the Upper Danube (6th century BC), and as late as the 7th century AD, for example the *Sutton Hoo ship burial.

Barrymore, Lionel (1878–1954) US actor. After studying art in Paris and achieving success as a stage actor he became known primarily as a film actor. He is remembered for his performances in the first series of *Dr Kildare* films. His sister **Ethel Barrymore** (1879–1959) acted with Sir Henry Irving in London, and later became a leading actress in the US with performances in both classical and modern plays. A theater in New York was named for her in 1928. Their brother **John Barrymore** (1882–1942) was also an actor. His greatest stage success was his performance of Hamlet in 1922. As a film star during his later career he was famous for such films as *Grand Hotel* (1932) and *Moby Dick* (1930). He was also renowned for his good looks and his tempestuous private life.

Barth, Heinrich (1821–65) German explorer and geographer. He traveled widely in the Mediterranean (1845–47) and in 1850 joined, as scientific observer, a British expedition to West Africa. His record of this expedition is contained in *Travels and Discoveries in North and Central Africa* (5 vols, 1857–58).

Barth, John (1930–   ) US novelist and academic. His novels, which combine philosophical seriousness with bawdy humor, include *The Sotweed Factor* (1960), *The End of the Road* (1961), *Giles Goat-Boy* (1966), *Chimera* (1974), *Letters* (1979), and *Sabbatical, A Romance* (1982). He often emphasizes the artificiality of fiction by parodying literary conventions.

Barth, Karl (1886–1968) Swiss Protestant theologian. As a pastor during World War I, he became disillusioned with modern liberal theology in the face of extreme suffering. In such influential works as *Epistle to the Romans* (1919) and the four-volume *Church Dogmatics* (1932–67) he returned to the principles of the Reformation and the teachings of the Bible, emphasizing God's sovereignty and man's sinfulness, which necessitates grace. He held professorships at several German universities (1921–35) and at Basle (1935–62).

Bartholdi, Frédéric August (1834–1904) French sculptor, famous for his patriotic monuments. Best known are the Lion of Belfort, commemorating the gallant defense of Belfort during the Franco-Prussian War (1870–71), and the *Statue of Liberty.

Bartholomew, St Christian Apostle. Although mentioned in lists of the Apostles, his name is never connected with any incident from the New Testament. He is sometimes identified with the Nathanel mentioned by John (1.45–51; 21.2). The historian Eusebius tells of his taking the Gospel to India. Feast day: Aug 24.

Bartlett, Josiah (1729–95) US signer of the Declaration of Independence, public official, and physician. He served as a delegate to the Continental Congress (1775), in various court positions in New Hampshire (1779–90), and as governor of the state (1793–94).

Bartók, Béla (1881–1945) Hungarian composer. Bartók studied and taught at the Budapest Academy of Music, where he and *Kodály undertook research into Hungarian folksong. In 1940 he went to live in the US, where he died in poverty. His music blends elements of E European folk music with dissonant harmonies into an astringent and often percussive style. A virtuoso pianist, he composed three piano concertos, a set of progressive pieces for students, entitled *Mikrokosmos* (1926–37), and other piano works. His stage works include the opera *Duke Bluebeard's Castle* (1911) and the ballet *The Miraculous Mandarin* (1919). In his six string quartets and *Music for Strings, Percussion, and Celesta* (1936) he explored unusual sonorities. His most popular work is the *Concerto for Orchestra* (1943).

Bartolommeo, Fra (Baccio della Porta; c. 1472–1517) Florentine Renaissance painter. After training under Cosimo Rosselli (1439–1507), he became a supporter of *Savonarola, whose death moved him to join the Dominican monastery of S Marco (1500) and abandon painting until 1504. His exclusively religious works were close to *Raphael and *Leonardo in style; they include *St Mark* and the *Pietà* (both Palazzo Pitti, Florence).

Barton, Clara (1821–1912) US schoolteacher, who founded the American Red Cross. During the Civil War (1861–65) she helped obtain supplies for wounded soldiers. She later worked for the International Red Cross in the Franco-Prussian War (1870–71) and then established its American branch, serving as its first president (1881–1904).

Barton, Sir Edmund (1849–1920) Australian statesman; Australia's first prime minister (1901–03). He was leader of the Federal Convention in 1897 that drafted the bill to unite the separate states of Australia.

Baruch, Bernard (1870–1965) US economist and adviser to Presidents Wilson, F. D. Roosevelt, and Truman. He helped to coordinate industries during World War I and to draft the economic items of the Treaty of Versailles. He served on the UN Atomic Energy Commission (1946), recommending control of atomic energy production.

baryon A collective term for *nucleons and other elementary particles that have a proton or neutron in their decay products. All baryons have a *quantum number called the baryon number, which is equal to +1. Their antiparticles have a baryon number equal to –1. The baryon number is always conserved in an interaction. *See* particle physics.

Baryshnikov, Mikhail (Nikolayevich) (1948–) International ballet dancer; born in USSR. A leading dancer with Russia's Kirov Ballet, he felt a need for fewer artistic restrictions and defected to the West in 1974, while on tour in Canada. After appearing in several productions in Canada and the US, he joined the American Ballet Theatre (ABT) (1974–78) and danced briefly with the New York City Ballet (1978–79) before becoming artistic director of ABT (1980–). He has appeared in movies and had an award-winning television special.

barytes. *See* barite.

baryton A musical instrument of the *viol family popular in the 18th century. Held between the knees, it had six gut strings and a number of sympathetic wire strings, which could be plucked. Haydn, whose patron Prince Esterhazy was a keen player, wrote many pieces for it.

basalt A volcanic rock of basic composition, typically dark, heavy, and fine textured. It consists essentially of calcic plagioclase feldspar and pyroxene, with magnetite, apatite, and often olivine as accessory minerals. Three broad groups of basalt are recognized: alkali basalt, high-alumina basalt, and tholeiite. The basalts constituting the ocean floor, generated at midoceanic ridges, are tholeiites. Many volcanoes and huge lava plateaus consist of basalt, which constitutes over 90% of volcanic rocks.

baseball A nine-a-side bat-and-ball game that evolved from *rounders, played mainly in the US, Japan, and Latin America. The object for each team while batting is to score as many runs as possible and while fielding to prevent the other team from doing so; the team with the highest score wins.

A team bats until three players are out; one turn at bat for both teams constitutes an inning, of which there are usually nine in a game. The pitcher, standing at the pitcher's mound, throws the ball to the batter, standing at home plate, who tries to hit it into fair territory and run. He scores a home run by making a complete circuit of the bases (first, second, third, and home). A player may strike out (if he misses the ball in each of three attempts), be caught out, tagged out (if he or the base he is running toward is touched by a player with the ball before the runner reaches the base), or be put out by being hit by a batted ball while running.

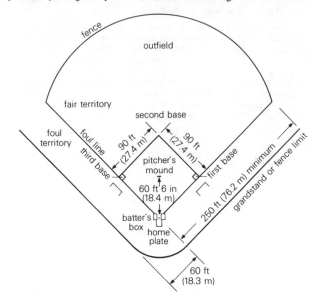

BASEBALL *The dimensions of the field.*

Basel. *See* Basle.

basenji A breed of dog originating in central Africa. It is lightly built and has a wrinkled forehead, pricked ears, and tightly curled tail. The short glossy coat is usually chestnut with white markings but can be black and white. Height: 40–43 cm.

bases. *See* acids and bases.

Bashkir A Turkic language and people of the Bashkir ASSR in the Soviet Union. The language is related to Tatar and Kazakh. The Bashkirs, originally nomads herding mainly horses and sheep, settled in their present territory under Mongol rule (13th–15th centuries). Russian domination of the area after 1551 led to the encouragement of agriculture and village life. Collectivization has obliterated the traditional tribal and clan organization. The Bashkir are either Muslims or Eastern Orthodox Christians by faith.

Bashkir Autonomous Soviet Socialist Republic (*or* Bashkiria) An administrative division in the E central Soviet Union, in the RSFSR. The Turkic-speaking Bashkirs comprise some 25% of the population. Bashkiria has large oil and natural-gas deposits, as well as coal, iron ore, and copper and has expanding chemical, coal, steel, and timber industries. Grains are the chief agricultural product. It was the first autonomous Soviet republic (1919). Area: 55,430 sq mi (143,600 sq km). Population (1981 est): 3,860,000. Capital: Ufa.

Basho. *See* Matsuo Basho.

Basic English A simplified form of the English language, which uses a vocabulary of 850 common English words. It was developed in the late 1920s by the linguist C. K. *Ogden, who intended it to be a simply learned method of international communication and a rival to *Esperanto. The vocabulary divides into 600 nouns, 150 adjectives, and 100 operations, which include verbs. These building blocks are used to form complex ideas without the necessity of complex vocabulary items; for instance the concept "prepare" would be expressed as "get ready," and such combinations can replace 4000 standard English verbs.

Basidiomycetes A large class of fungi (about 13,000 species) that includes many *mushrooms, the *bracket fungi, *puffballs, etc., as well as important microscopic forms, such as the parasitic *rusts and *smuts of crops. They all have the same kind of reproductive organ—a basidium, which is typically club-shaped and produces spores at the tips of stalklike projections.

Basie, Count (William B.; 1904–84) US jazz pianist and band leader. He was influenced by Harlem ragtime pianists, played in vaudeville shows, and formed his own band in 1935. He became famous for his distinctive "big band" style and his piano playing. He recorded many albums, including *Blues by Basie* and *Swingin' Count*.

basil An annual herbaceous plant of the Indian genus *Ocimum*, cultivated as a pot herb. Sweet basil (*O. basilicum*), up to 12 in (30 cm) high, has toothed leaves and small white or bluish flowers. The dried clove-scented leaves are used to flavor various dishes. Family: **Labiatae*.

Basil (I) the Macedonian (d. 886 AD) Byzantine emperor (876–86), who founded the Macedonian dynasty. Of humble origin, Basil became coemperor (867) with Michael III (reigned 842–68) but murdered him in 868. He strengthened Byzantine power in Asia Minor and in S Italy and revived Roman law in a legal text known as the Basilica.

Basil II Buigaroctonus (c. 958–1025 AD) Byzantine emperor (976–1025). He secured Byzantine conquests in Syria and extended his empire by conquering territory in Georgia and Armenia. He was named Bulgaroctonus (slayer of the Bulgars) after defeating the Bulgarians at Ochrida (1014): he blinded their entire army except for every 100th man, who was left with one eye with which to lead his comrades back to their ruler; the Bulgarian khan died of shock.

basilica 1. A Roman public meeting hall. In imperial times, many had a layout similar to the Basilica of Maxentius in Rome: rectangular ground plan, colonnaded aisles, entrance porch (narthex), and windows in the upper story (clerestory). 2. A Christian church based on a similar plan (e.g. S Giovanni in Laterano in Rome). The influence of the plan can still be seen in western church architecture.

Basilicata A mountainous region in S Italy. A poor region economically, it is almost entirely dependent upon agriculture producing wheat, olives, vines, potatoes, sheep, and goats. Area: 9987 sq km 3856 sq mi . Population (1976 est):0 617,257. Capital: Potenza.

basilisk 1. An arboreal lizard belonging to the tropical American genus *Basiliscus*. Up to 24 in (60 cm) long, it has a narrow body, a whiplike tail, and a flat lobe protruding from the back of its head. It has long hind legs with lobed toes fringed with scales, enabling it to run over the surface of water. Family: *Iguanidae*. 2. A legendary snakelike serpent of ancient Greece and Rome whose glance was believed to be fatal to all living things except the weasel, and later the cock, which both had the power to destroy it.

Basil the Great, St (c. 330–79 AD) Bishop of Caesarea in Cappadocia. His name is usually linked with St *Gregory of Nazianzus and St *Gregory of Nyssa (his brother). Known as the Cappadocian Fathers, they were the chief defenders of orthodox Christian philosophy against *Arianism in the 4th century. Thoroughly educated in both classical pagan and Christian culture, he adopted a monastic life and then lived as a hermit before becoming Bishop of Caesarea in 370. He developed a rule that formed the basis of monasticism in the Eastern Church. He is traditionally considered the author of the liturgy of St Basil, still used on certain days in the Orthodox Church. He wrote many theological works. Feast day: June 14.

basketball A five-a-side court game invented in the US (1891) by James Naismith (1861–1939). The object is to toss or put an inflated ball into the opponents' basket, a net mounted 10 ft (3.05 m) above the floor on a backboard. Players use only their hands, passing the ball or dribbling it by bouncing, and they may not run with it. A professional game has 4 12-minute quarters. The Americans have dominated all Olympic competition, which began in 1936. The premier professional basketball league is the National Basketball Association in the US (founded in 1949) but European professional leagues have grown in popularity. *See also* Harlem Globetrotters.

basking shark A large *shark belonging to the family *Cetorhinidae*. Up to 49 ft (15 m) long, they are gray-brown or blackish and inhabit cold and temperate regions of the Atlantic, Pacific, and Indian Oceans. Basking sharks usually occur in shoals near the surface and float or swim slowly, feeding on plankton.

Basle (French name: Bâle; German name: Basel) 47 33N 7 36E The second largest city in Switzerland, on the Rhine River where the French, German, and Swiss borders meet. A Roman fort originally occupied the site. During the Reformation it became a major literary center and the scholar Erasmus taught at the university (founded 1460). Its notable features include the medieval city gates and the cathedral. Basle is a major commercial and industrial center, strategically positioned in the European railroad system and the chief riverport in Switzerland. Industries include chemicals, pharmaceuticals, and engineering. The Bank for International Settlements was established here in 1929. Population (1980 est): 182,143.

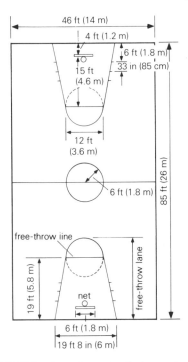

BASKETBALL *Court dimensions for international play.*

Basle, Council of A general council of the Roman Catholic Church summoned by Pope Martin V in 1431 to consider the heretical *Hussites and the nature of papal power. The council, having reaffirmed the principle that general councils are answerable only to God, grew increasingly antipapal and in 1437 Eugenius IV, Martin's successor, moved it to Ferrara. However, a minority of councillors remained at Basle, electing the antipope, Felix V, in 1439. He resigned in 1449 and the council was brought to an end.

Basque A non-Indo-European language spoken by the Basque people of the W Pyrenean areas of Spain and France. Basque is a very ancient language, apparently unrelated to any other and called Euskara by the Basques themselves. It is still spoken by about 500,000 people. The Basques, predominantly farmers and seafarers, are descended from a people known to the Romans as the Vascones. Today there are about 750,000 Basques in Spain and 170,000 in France. They are strongly Roman Catholic and traditionally enjoyed a degree of regional autonomy, forming an independent government (1936–37) at the time of the Spanish Civil War. Nationalism remains a significant force among them in many areas today.

Basra 30 30N 47 50E A city in SE Iraq, on the Shatt (river) al-Arab. It is linked by rail and river steamer to Baghdad; the modern port (Al Ma'qil) was constructed by the British during World War I. Population (1970 est): 333,684.

Bass, Sam (1851–78) US outlaw. He led a gang of bank, stagecoach, and train robbers in the west and was known for giving what he robbed to the poor. He was killed by a Texas ranger at Round Rock, Texas, in 1878.

bass (fish) One of several perchlike *bony fish of the order *Perciformes*, often valued as food and game fish. The majority belong to the family *Serranidae* (*see* sea bass), which includes the common European bass (*Dicentrarchus labrax*). This can grow up to 40 in (1 m) long and has a gray or blue back with a white or yellowish belly and silvery flanks. North American freshwater bass belong to the family *Centrarchidae*.

bass (music) 1. The deepest adult male singing voice. Range: E below the bass stave to E two octaves above. 2. The lowest voice or instrumental part of a piece of music.

Bassano, Jacopo (Jacopo *or* Giacomo da Ponte; c. 1517–92) Italian painter of the Venetian school, born in Bassano, the son of a painter. In Venice he was influenced by Titian before adopting the elongated figure style of *Parmigianino. He was one of the earliest painters of rustic life, in both secular, e.g. *Pastoral* (Lugano), and religious scenes, e.g. *Adoration of the Kings* (National Gallery, Edinburgh).

Bassein 16 46N 94 45E A port in Lower Burma, on the River Bassein. Situated at the terminus of a railroad to Rangoon, it is the country's second port exporting chiefly rice, coal, and salt. Population (1973 est): 126,045.

basset horn A woodwind instrument, the tenor member of the *clarinet family. It has a rich velvety tone but lacks the brilliance of the upper range of the A or B flat clarinet. Mozart wrote for it.

basset hound A breed of □dog originating in France. It has a long body with very short legs and a narrow face with drooping ears and a mournful expression. The short smooth coat ranges from black to light brown in color with white patches. Basset hounds have a keen sense of smell and were formerly popular hunting dogs. Height: 13–15 in (33–38 cm).

bassoon A musical instrument of the woodwind family. Its conically bored tube is about 8 ft (2.5 m) long and is bent back on itself. It has a metal crook into which a double reed is inserted. Its extensive compass (about three and a half octaves above B flat below the bass stave) allows it a melodic as well as a bass role. Composers have made much use of its humorous staccato quality.

Bass Strait A channel separating the mainland of Australia from Tasmania. It has valuable oil and natural-gas deposits. Length: 180 mi (290 km). Maximum width: 240 km (150 mi).

basswood A *lime tree, *Tilia americana*, also called American lime or linden, sometimes exceeding 80 ft (25 m) in height. It yields commercially important timber that is especially prized for carving, and a tough fiber derived from the bark is of local importance.

bast fibers Fibers, such as *flax, *hemp, and *jute, that are obtained from the stems of certain plants. The fibers are freed from the stalk by retting (soaking) or mechanical peeling and are used for textiles, sacking, twines, and ropes.

Bastia 42 41N 9 26E A port in Corsica, on the NE coast. Founded by the Genoese in the 14th century, it was the former capital of Corsica and is the island's largest city. Fishing and the manufacture of tobacco and wine are the principal economic activities. Population (1968): 50,100.

Bastille A fortress in Paris, which was a state prison in the 17th and 18th centuries and a symbol of the corrupt and despotic Bourbon monarchy. It was built in about 1370 to protect the wall around Paris against English attack and became a state prison under Cardinal de *Richelieu. The storming of the Bastille on July 14, 1789, is regarded as the beginning of the *French Revolution.

Basutoland. *See* Lesotho, Kingdom of.

bat A flying mammal belonging to the order *Chiroptera* (981 species), distributed in most temperate and tropical regions. There are two suborders: the *fruit bats (*Megachiroptera*; 150 species) and the insect-eating bats (*Microchiroptera*; 831 species). Bats may also feed on pollen, nectar, blood, and small animals. The wings are extensions of skin that are supported between the forelimb, with its very long fingers, the hind limbs, and the tail. Most bats use *echolocation for navigation: this is highly developed in insectivorous bats, which catch prey on the wing whereas fruit bats have large eyes adapted for night vision. Bats can be found roosting in caves and buildings during daytime.

Bataan A mountainous forested peninsula in the Philippines, in W Luzon W of Manila Bay. In a famous action during World War II, US-Filipino forces resisted the Japanese invasion for almost three months here (1942). After their capture, thousands of US and Filipino troops died on the notorious forced Bataan Death March. Length: about 30 mi (48 km).

bateleur An African snake *eagle, *Terathopius ecaudatus*, having very long wings and a short tail. It is highly maneuverable and flies vast distances, preying on snakes, other reptiles, mammals, and carrion, which it seizes with its short rough powerful toes.

Bateson, William (1861–1926) British biologist, whose experiments on inheritance helped found the science of genetics, a term that he first proposed. Bateson investigated the way in which certain traits, such as comb shape in fowl, are transmitted from one generation to the next. His results (1905–08) corroborated the findings of Gregor *Mendel published in 1865. He also found that certain characteristics were inherited together (a phenomenon now known as linkage, due to the occurrence of the controlling genes on the same chromosome), but he refused to accept the chromosome theory proposed by T. H. *Morgan to account for this.

batfish A carnivorous fish, belonging to a family (*Ogcocephalidae*; about 60 species) of *anglerfish, found in tropical and temperate seas. It has a slender lumpy-skinned body up to 14 in (36 cm) long and a broad flat head with an elongated upturned snout. Using thickened limblike pectoral and pelvic fins, it crawls on the bottom searching for prey.

BATELEUR *This African eagle has exceptionally long wings and may fly up to 200 mi (300 km) a day in search of prey.*

Bath 51 23N 2 22W A city in SW England, on the River Avon. A spa town of great architectural interest, it was an early Roman center known as Aquae Sulis because of its hot natural springs. The elaborate Roman baths have survived. Bath became fashionable as an elegant spa town in the 18th century when many of the finest buildings were built. Bath Abbey, mainly 16th-century, lies in the town center. Bath University dates from 1966. Population (1981): 79,965.

Bath, Order of the A British order of knighthood, formed by George I in 1725 as a successor to the Knights of the Bath. It comprises the sovereign and three classes of knights companions: knights and dames grand cross (GCB), knights and dames commanders (KCB), and companions (CB). Women have been admitted since 1971.

batholith A large mass of intrusive igneous rock of unknown depth and often occupying many thousands of square kilometers. They are composed mainly of granite and occur in association with mountain belts. They are often surrounded by a zone of mineralized rocks (metamorphic aureole).

Bathurst. *See* Banjul.

batik Cloth, traditionally cotton, dyed by a special method. An ancient Indonesian craft, developed especially in Java, batik work involves the application of melted wax, later removed, to protect parts of the material from the dye; repeating the process using different wax patterns and several dyeings produces intricate multicolored geometric patterns, symbolic motifs, or stylized pictures of birds, animals, or flowers. Some designs have been passed on in families for a thousand years.

Batista y Zaldívar, Fulgencio (1901–73) Cuban statesman, who was president from 1940 to 1944 and, after returning to power in 1952 by means of a military coup, from 1954 to 1958. His authoritarian government generated opposition, notably from Castro's guerrilla movement, by which Batista was ousted.

Baton Rouge 30 30N 91 10W The capital of Louisiana situated on the Mississippi River at the head of oceangoing navigation. It is a major deepwater port with oil and sugar refineries. It has several state institutions, including the Louisiana State University (1860). Population (1970): 165,921.

Battani, al- (Latin name: Albatenius; c. 858–929) Islamic astronomer, born in Haran (Turkey) and noted for his book on stellar motions. Using trigonometric methods, he improved the accuracy of many astronomical measurements, including the length of the year, the precession of the equinoxes, and the inclination of the ecliptic.

battery A cell that can be recharged by passing a current through it in the direction opposite to that of the discharge current, thus reversing the chemical changes occurring during discharge at the electrodes. The most common example is the lead-acid battery used in motor vehicles. This consists, when charged, of a positive lead dioxide electrode and a negative spongy lead electrode, both immersed in sulfuric acid with a relative density of 1.20–1.28. During discharge lead sulfate forms on the electrodes and the acid density falls.

Nickel-iron (NiFe) batteries with an electrolyte of 20% potassium hydroxide are also used. Interest in *electric cars has stimulated battery development in recent years. While lead batteries will deliver up 8×10^4 joules per kilogram, the newer zinc-air battery can produce five times this energy density.

battleship A heavily armored naval vessel designed to combine large size, maneuverability, and extensive cruising range with the most powerful armament. Larger than a *cruiser and smaller than an *aircraft carrier, the battleship was the flagship vessel of a fleet. There have been no new battleships built since World War II, as they have been largely replaced by other more versatile and less expensive vessels.

Batumi 41 37N 41 36E A port in the S Soviet Union, in the Georgian SSR on the Black Sea. It has an oil refinery, shipping oil piped from Baku, a range of light industries, and there are tea plantations on the city's outskirts. Population (1981 est): 124,000.

Baudelaire, Charles (1821–67) French poet. He inherited his father's fortune in 1842 and lived extravagantly until what was left of the capital was placed in trust by his family (1844). Forced to earn a living, he began to publish art criticism and poetry and wrote the autobiographical novel *La Fanfarlo* (1847). In 1852 he discovered Edgar Allan *Poe, publishing several translations of his works (1856–65). His only volume of poetry, *Les Fleurs du mal* (1857, revised 1861), contained several erotic poems, which led to his being convicted for obscenity. He became increasingly disillusioned; while in Belgium in 1866 he became paralyzed as a result of venereal disease and died in Paris soon after.

Baudouin I (1930–   ) King of the Belgians (1951–   ), succeeding his father Leopold III. He was interned by the Nazis in World War II. In 1960 he married Fabiola de Mora y Aragón (1928–   ).

Bauhaus A German school of design. One of the most important influences on 20th-century art, the Bauhaus enjoyed a short life. Founded in 1919 at Weimar and was closed by the Nazis in 1933. From 1925 to 1932 it was housed at Dessau in a building designed by *Gropius (its director until 1928), itself a work of great influence. Connected with some of the best designers of the age, the Bauhaus sought to produce a practical synthesis of all the arts, from furniture design to architecture, and to develop a coherent style appropriate for the industrial 20th century. The functional style the Bauhaus helped to evolve still has considerable influence in the arts, from the international style of architecture to tubular steel furniture. *See also* Kandinsky; Klee; Mies van der Rohe; Moholy-Nagy.

Baum, L(yman) Frank (1856–1919) US novelist. After working as a journalist, he created in *The Wonderful Wizard of Oz* (1900) a classic children's fantasy land that provided material for 13 sequels and was made into a movie in 1938. In all, he wrote about 60 books, mostly for children.

Baumgarten, Alexander Gottlieb (1714–62) German philosopher, a follower of Christian Wolff (1679–1754) and *Leibniz. In 1740, he became professor of philosophy at Frankfurt-am-Oder. He invented the term *aesthetics and his *Aesthetica* (1750) is a pioneering work on that subject.

Baur, Ferdinand Christian (1792–1860) German Protestant theologian. Baur's early work was concerned with the gnostic background of Christianity. He was much influenced by *Hegel. In 1826, he became professor of theology at Tübingen University, and his later work on St Paul led him to question the authenticity of the New Testament and marked the beginnings of radical biblical criticism.

Bautzen 51 14N 14 23E A city in SE East Germany, on the Spree River. A battle was fought here in 1813, in which Napoleon's army defeated an allied army of Russians and Prussians. Its industries include the manufacture of vehicles and machinery. Population (1973 est): 44,395.

bauxite The chief ore of aluminum. It is a residual deposit formed by the weathering of aluminum-rich rocks (mainly syenites) under tropical conditions and consists mainly of hydrated aluminum oxide. The main producers are Australia, Jamaica, Surinam, Guyana, Guinea, Sierra Leone, and Yugoslavia.

Bavaria (German name: Bayern) The largest *Land* of West Germany, bordering on Austria, Czechoslovakia, and East Germany. A third is forested, providing valuable timber resources. Predominantly agricultural, the main crops are rye, wheat, and barley; hops are grown around Munich. Bavaria is a popular tourist area. *History*: a duchy and later a kingdom

ruled by the Wittelsbachs from 1180 to 1918, it then became a republic. From the ensuing political unrest Hitler drew much of his early support. Area: 29,232 sq mi (70,547 sq km). Population (1980 est): 10,896,900. Capital: Munich.

bay A Mediterranean evergreen tree, *Laurus nobilis*, also known as sweet bay and bay laurel, widely grown as an ornamental shrub or pot plant. It can reach a height of 65 ft (20 m), has aromatic dark-green lance-shaped leaves, small yellowish flowers, and blackish berries. The leaves are used to season food. Family: *Lauraceae* (see laurel).

Bayard, Pierre Terrail, Seigneur de (c. 1473–1524) French soldier, known as "le bon chevalier sans peur et sans reproche" (the good knight without fear and without reproach). He served in the Italian wars of Charles VIII, Louis XII, and Francis I, gaining particular distinction at Fornovo (1495) and Marignano (1515). Pope Julius II sought unsuccessfully to hire him.

Baybars I (1223–77) Sultan of Egypt and Syria (1260–77) of the *Mameluke dynasty. Brought to Egypt as a slave, he rose in the army and in 1260 he was prominent at the decisive victory over the Mongols at Ayn Jalut. Between 1263 and 1271 he severely reduced the power of the Crusaders in Syria. He became the subject of a popular folk biography.

bayberry A deciduous shrub, *Myrica pensilvanica*, rarely exceeding 10 ft (3 m) in height, bearing flowers in catkins and oblong 4 in (10 cm)-long leaves. It is native to E North America and sometimes cultivated in other temperate areas. Family: *Myricaceae*.

The name is also given to the purple-blue berries of the *bay tree.

Bayeux 49 16N 0 42W A city in NW France, in the Calvados department on the Aure River. Its museum houses the famous *Bayeux tapestry and there is a fine 13th-century cathedral. It was the first French town to be liberated by the Allies in World War II (June 7, 1944). Industries include dairy foods and plastics. Population (1975): 14,528.

Bayeux tapestry An 11th-century embroidered linen strip, 231 ft (69 m) long, which depicts the Norman conquest of England (1066). The tapestry, which starts with King Harold's visit to Normandy and ends with the battle of Hastings, is of great historical value. It was probably commissioned for Bayeux cathedral by its bishop, Odo, the half-brother of William the Conqueror, whose wife Matilda is traditionally, though improbably, credited with its making. The tapestry now hangs in the museum at Bayeux (France).

Bayezid II (c. 1447–1512) Ottoman Sultan of Turkey (1481–1512). During his reign Turkish dominions in the Balkans and the Crimea were extended; war with Venice (1499–1503) brought territory in Greece and the Adriatic. Warfare with Egypt and the Safavid dynasty of Persia occupied the last decade of his reign. In 1512 Bayezid abdicated, dying soon afterward.

Bayle, Pierre (1647–1706) French Protestant critic and controversialist. He taught philosophy at Sedan from 1675 until forced into exile in Rotterdam. There he was professor of philosophy from 1781 to 1793, when his contentious religious tracts and determined opponents lost him the chair. Undeterred, he began publication of his masterwork, the *Dictionnaire historique et critique* (1796), a model of scholarship, style, and philosophical skepticism, which was both influential and successful.

Bay of Pigs (Spanish name: Bahia de los Cochinos) A bay on the SW coast of Cuba where on April 17, 1961, about 1200 Cuban exiles attempted to invade the country. Hoping to overthrow the Marxist regime of Fidel *Castro, and supported by the US *Central Intelligence Agency, the invasion was unsuccessful and the US was criticized for its involvement.

bayonet A blade that may be attached to the muzzle of a firearm. The bayonet, which is thought to have originated in the early 17th century in Bayonne (France), replaced the pike. Early bayonets were inserted into the gun, which could not then be fired, a drawback resolved in the 1680s by the development of the socket bayonet. This was attached to a tube that was placed over the muzzle. Bayonets were used in both World Wars.

Bayonne 43 30N 1 28W A city in SW France, in the Pyrénées–Atlantiques department at the confluence of the Ador and Nive Rivers. The chief port of the Basque country, it was formerly famous for its swords and knives; the bayonet was developed here in the early 17th century. Its varied industries include aircraft, distilling, and leather. Population (1975): 44,706.

Bay Psalm Book Probably the first book printed in America, which contained the Psalms in metrical form. It was published in 1640 in Cambridge, Massachusetts, by a group of Congregationalists.

Bayreuth 49 27N 11 35E A city in SE West Germany, in Bavaria. It is famous as the home and burial place of Richard Wagner, who designed its

Festival Theater (1872–76), where his operas are performed annually. Its industries include the manufacture of textiles and machinery. Population (1971 est): 64,000.

Bazaine, Achille François (1811–88) French marshal, who served in the Crimean War (1854–56), in Italy against Austria (1859), and in Mexico (1863). He was commander in chief in the Franco-Prussian War (1870–71), when he surrendered after being besieged at Metz. For this he was condemned for treason but escaped to exile in Spain.

bazooka Originally a 2.36 inch (60 mm) antitank rocket launcher fired from the shoulder and used by the US army in World War II. It consisted of a 54 inch (1.4 m) breech-loaded tube, open at both ends, firing a 3½ lb (1.6 kg) rocket to an effective range of about 135 m (150 yd). The term was later applied to all similar weapons. The name came from a tubular wind instrument made famous by Bob Burns, an American comedian.

BCG (bacille Calmette Guérin) A vaccine consisting of a weakened form of the tuberculosis bacterium, which is injected to give partial protection against tuberculosis. It acts by stimulating the body's defense system without causing the disease. A successful vaccination produces a lump at the injection site.

Beaconsfield, Benjamin Disraeli, 1st Earl of. See Disraeli, Benjamin.

Beadle, George Wells (1903–) US geneticist, who provided fundamental evidence for the nature of gene function. Working with molds, he proposed the theory that each gene was responsible for the production of a single enzyme, which itself controlled a particular chemical reaction in the cell. He shared a Nobel Prize (1958) with *Tatum and *Lederberg.

beagle A long-established breed of dog originating in England. It has a deep chest, strong shoulders, and drooping ears. The short smooth coat is usually dark brown to light tan with white patches. With their keen sense of smell, beagles have long been used as hunting hounds; more recently, they have become popular household pets. Height: 13–16 in (33–40 cm).

Bean,Roy (c. 1825–1903) US frontier justice of the peace. A saloon keeper in Vinegaroon, Texas (now Langtry), in 1882, he was appointed and then elected justice of the peace and held court in his saloon, making outrageous but shrewd judgments and dispensing appropriate sentences.

bean The seed or fruit of certain herbs, shrubs, or trees of the family *Leguminosae. They are widely cultivated and not only form a good source of protein for man and livestock but also provide raw material for a wide range of derived products. See broad bean; carob bean; French bean; haricot bean; lablab; lima bean; mung bean; runner bean; soybean; tonka bean.

bear A large heavy mammal belonging to a family (*Ursidae*; 7 species) found in Europe, Asia, and America. Bears have a shaggy coat and a short tail and walk flat on the soles of their broad feet. They can stand erect and make good use of their powerful limbs and long curved claws. Eyesight and hearing are poor but bears have an excellent sense of smell; they can exist on any kind of food but most of them are vegetarian. Newly born bears are very small (about the size of rats), blind, and toothless. The female stays in the den suckling her young until they can accompany her outside. Order: *Carnivora. See black bear; brown bear; polar bear; sloth bear; spectacled bear; sun bear.

bearberry A prostrate evergreen shrub of the genus *Arctostaphylos*, native to North and Central America, especially *A. uva-ursi*, which is also widespread in Europe and Asia. The woody stems may reach 7 ft (2 m) in length, sending out roots at intervals. The flowers are white to pink and bell-shaped, and the berries are red. The plant is an important colonist. Family: *Ericaceae*.

bearded lizard An Australian lizard, *Amphibolurus barbatus*, occurring in scrub and desert regions. Up to 24 in (60 cm) long, it has a long head, a whiplike tail, a gray to yellowish spiny skin, and a bright-yellow mouth; a throat pouch swells to resemble a spiny beard during aggressive or courtship displays. It feeds on insects, small lizards, and snakes.

bearded tit. See reedling.

bearded vulture. See lammergeier.

Beardsley, Aubrey Vincent (1872–98) British illustrator. Virtually self-taught, he achieved notoriety with his grotesque and erotic imagery in periodicals and several books, including Oscar Wilde's *Salome* and Alexander Pope's *Rape of the Lock*. His designs are composed of curved lines, characteristic of *Art Nouveau, which contrast with dense areas of black ink. He died of tuberculosis in France.

beardworm A deep-sea wormlike animal, up to 12 in (30 cm) long, belonging to the invertebrate phylum *Pogonophora* (20 species). Beardworms live in tubes built in the mud of the ocean floor. Their head ends are crowned with tentacles, which protrude from the tubes and are believed to function in respiration and feeding (beardworms lack a digestive system).

Bear Flag Revolt (1846) A revolt of US settlers in California against Mexican rule. A group of American settlers in the Sacramento Valley seized some horses from the Mexican government and raised the "bear" flag over the "Republic of California." It remained until replacement by the US flag a few months later during the *Mexican War.

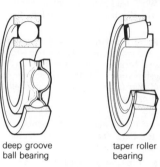

deep groove
ball bearing

taper roller
bearing

BEARINGS *Common examples of ball bearings and roller bearings.*

bearings A support for a rotating shaft or the interface between a crank and a reciprocating part. Bearings are designed to reduce friction and wear to a minimum and to dissipate the heat generated. In plain bearings, lubrication is achieved by maintaining a film of lubricant between the faces either as a result of their relative motion or by pumping it through channels into the interface. Some small bearings, made of powdered copper or bronze impregnated with oil or graphite, are self-lubricating, while some low-friction plastics (e.g. polytetrafluoroethylene) do not require lubrication. Bearing surfaces or shells are usually made of softer materials (e.g. brass or white metal) than is the shaft.

In **ball and roller bearings** friction between the faces is reduced by replacing the sliding action of a plain bearing by a rolling action. The balls or rollers are usually made from chromium (0.5–2.0%) steels.

bear market A stock or commodity market in which there is a continuing downward movement in prices. An initial fall in prices, caused by adverse economic factors, is often magnified by consequent selling by investors. *Compare* bull market.

Bear River A river that rises in NE Utah in the Uinta Mountains and loops north through SW Colorado and S Idaho before flowing S into NW Utah to empty into the Great Salt Lake near Brigham City. The land at its mouth serves as a waterfowl sanctuary. Length: 350 mi (565 km).

Beas River A river in NW India, flowing mainly W from the Himalayas to the Sutlej River. It forms part of the Punjab irrigation scheme. Length: 290 mi (470 km).

Beatitudes In the New Testatment, the eight blessings with which Jesus opened the Sermon on the Mount (Matthew 5.3–12). They describe such Christian virtues as meekness, mercy, and purity of heart (e.g. "Blessed are the meek: for they shall inherit the earth."). The word derives from the Latin of the *Vulgate, *beati sunt* (blessed are).

Beatles A British rock group, which achieved worldwide popularity during the 1960s. The Beatles appeared at the Cavern Club in Liverpool in 1962 and subsequently recorded "Love Me Do" and "She Loves You," which became top of the Hit Parade in 1963. By this time the group consisted of George *Harrison, John *Lennon, Paul *McCartney, and Ringo *Starr; they toured the US successfully, made two films, and were awarded MBEs in 1965. The most original of the group's subsequent albums were *Sergeant Pepper's Lonely Hearts Club Band* (1967), which reflected the Beatles' experience of drugs and eastern mysticism, and the double *White Album* (1968). In 1970 they disbanded to pursue separate careers. In 1980, John Lennon was murdered.

Beat movement American literary and social movement of the 1950s that opposed the values of conventional society through art, poetry, and permissive attitudes towards sex and the use of drugs. The movement originated in Greenwich Village in New York City and later centered in San Francisco. Among the most prominent leaders of the Beat movement were the novelists Jack *Kerouac and William *Burroughs and the poets Allen *Ginsburg, Lawrence *Ferlinghetti, and Gregory Corso (1930–). Ferlinghetti's City Lights Press in San Francisco became noted for its publication of the works of many writers of the Beat movement.

BEATLES *(From left) Ringo Starr, Paul McCartney, John Lennon, and George Harrison (with bugle).*

Beatrix (1938–) Queen of the Netherlands since the abdication (1980) of her mother Queen Juliana. Her marriage (1966) to the West German Claus von Amsberg (1926–) caused some controversy.

beats Variations in the intensity of sound when two tones of nearly equal frequency are heard. The effect is similar to that of *interference. At certain times, the amplitudes of the waves reinforce each other and, at intermediate times, they tend to cancel each other out. The frequency of the beats is equal to the difference in the frequencies of the two notes.

Beauce An area in central France, in the Paris Basin. Consisting of a fertile plain, it is an important wheat-growing area and is known as the "granary of France."

Beaufort scale A scale of wind speed. It is based on easily observable indicators, such as smoke, tree movement, and damage incurred, and was devised in 1805 by Admiral Sir Francis Beaufort (1774–1857).

Beaufort Sea The section of the Arctic Ocean N of North America, between the Chukchi Sea and the Canadian archipelago. It is often covered by floating ice.

Beauharnais, Alexandre, Vicomte de (1760–94) French general, who served in the American Revolution and then became involved in French Revolutionary politics. He commanded in the Rhine (1793) but was guillotined (1794) for failing to relieve Metz. His widow *Joséphine married Napoleon, whom his son **Eugène de Beauharnais** (1781–1824) served in Italy and Egypt. In 1805 he became viceroy of Italy and in 1812 commanded in Napoleon's Russian campaign. He lived in exile after Napoleon's fall. His sister **Hortense de Beauharnais** (1783–1837) married (1802) Napoleon's brother Louis *Bonaparte, King of Holland. Their son was the future Napoleon III.

Beaulieu 50 49N 1 27W A village in S England, in Hampshire. The parish church was formerly the refectory of a Cistercian abbey founded here in 1204 by King John. In the grounds of the Palace House, home of Lord Montague, is the National Motor Museum. Population (1973 est): 1165.

Beaumarchais, Pierre-Augustin Caron de (1732–99) French dramatist. Son of a watchmaker, he became rich and famous with *The Barber of Seville* (1775) and *The Marriage of Figaro* (1778), his comedies about the busybodying intrigues of a cunning valet; they inspired operas by *Rossini and *Mozart. He undertook secret missions abroad for Louis XV and Louis XVI, supplied arms to the American revolutionaries, and sponsored the first complete edition of *Voltaire's works. Constantly involved in lawsuits, he wrote *Mémoires* (1773–75) in self-defense.

Beaumont 30 05N 94 06W A city and port in E Texas, on the Naches River. A distribution center since 1835, Beaumont became a center of the oil industry when the famous Spindletop oil fields were opened in 1901. Linked to the Gulf of Mexico by the Sabine-Neches Canal, it is a major shipping center for its petroleum, rice, livestock, sulfur, chemical, rubber, and timber industries. Population (1980): 118,102.

Beaumont, Francis (1584–1616) British dramatist. He studied law at Oxford. From about 1607, he collaborated with John *Fletcher in writing about 12 plays, including *Philaster* (1610) and *The Maides Tragedy* (1611). He was probably sole author of *The Knight of the Burning Pestle* (1607). In 1613 he married and retired from the theater.

Beaumont, William (1785–1853) US physician, who investigated digestion in the human stomach. As an army surgeon in 1822, he treated a trapper named Alexis St Martin for shotgun injuries. These left a permanent opening in his patient's stomach wall and abdomen through which Beaumont sampled the stomach contents. He recognized the chemical nature of digestion, including the importance of hydrochloric acid. His patient lived to the age of 82.

Beaune 47 02N 4 50E A city in E central France, in the Côte-d'Or department. The center for the wine trade of Burgundy, it has a wine museum and its manufactures include casks, oil, and mustard. Population (1975): 19,972.

Beaufort number	description of wind	wind speed	
		knots	meters per second
0	calm	<1	0.0– 0.2
1	light air	1– 3	0.3– 1.5
2	light breeze	4– 6	1.6– 3.3
3	gentle breeze	7–10	3.4– 5.4
4	moderate breeze	11–16	5.5– 7.9
5	fresh breeze	17–21	8.0–10.7
6	strong breeze	22–27	10.8–13.8
7	near gale	28–33	13.9–17.1
8	gale	34–40	17.2–20.7
9	strong gale	41–47	20.8–24.4
10	storm	48–55	24.5–28.4
11	violent storm	56–63	28.5–32.6
12	hurricane	≥64	≥32.7

BEAUFORT SCALE

Beauregard, Pierre Gustave Toutant de (1818–93) US Confederate general. A West Point graduate (1838) who remained loyal to the South and his native state of Louisiana when the Civil War began, he was appointed brigadier general in the Confederate army in 1861. He was responsible for the bombardment and surrender of Fort Sumter (1861), the first battle of the war, for victory at the first battle of *Bull Run, and for holding back Union troops at Shiloh, Tenn. (1862), Charleston, S.C. (1862–64), and Richmond, Va. (1864).

Beauvais 49 26N 2 05E A city in N France, in the Oise department. Its fine cathedral (begun 1227) was damaged during World War II and the factory in which the famous Gobelin tapestries had been made since the 17th century was completely destroyed (the industry was subsequently moved to Paris). Beauvais is a market town, trading in dairy produce, fruit, and cereals. Population (1975): 56,725.

Beauvais tapestry Tapestry produced by the state-subsidized Beauvais factory, in France, established in 1664. The court painter François *Boucher designed pastoral, Italian, and Chinese scenes for the workshops, which specialized in furniture and screen tapestries. Production declined in the 19th century.

Beauvoir, Simone de (1908–) French novelist and essayist. The constant companion of Jean-Paul *Sartre from their meeting at the Sorbonne in 1929, her writings have explored the implications of *existentialism. Her novels include *The Blood of Others* (1948) and *The Mandarins* (1956). *The Second Sex* (1953) argued for the liberation of women from their traditional roles in a male-dominated society. Other works include *The Coming of Age* (1973) and *All Said and Done* (1975).

beaver A large aquatic *rodent, *Castor fiber*, of Europe, Asia, and North America. Over 40 in (1 m) long and weighing up to 88 lb (40 kg), beavers have a dark sleek waterproof coat and a broad flat tail used for balance and swimming. They live in family groups, building a "lodge" of sticks and mud with underwater entrances and dams above and below. They use their large incisor teeth to cut wood for building and bark for a winter food. During the summer they feed on vegetation. Family: *Castoridae*. □mammal.

Beaverbrook, Max(well) Aitken, 1st Baron (1879–1964) British newspaper proprietor and politician, born in Canada. In 1919 he bought a majority interest in the *Daily Express*. In 1921 he founded the *Sunday Express* and in 1929 bought the *Evening Standard* (London). He served in Lloyd George's World War I cabinet and in Churchill's World War II cabinet.

Bebel, August (1840–1913) German socialist leader. Bebel became interested in the labor movement while living in Leipzig, where in 1865 he came under the influence of Wilhelm *Liebknecht. In 1869 he helped to found the German Social Democratic Party, for which he became a leading spokesman in the Reichstag.

bebop. *See* bop.

Beccaria, Cesare Bonesana, Marchese de (1738–94) Italian legal theorist and political economist. He achieved international fame with the publication of his *Crimes and Punishments* (1764), the first comprehensive account of the principles behind criminal law. In attacking legal corruption, torture, capital punishment, etc., it was responsible for the reform of penal codes in many countries. Beccaria became a professor of political philosophy at Milan in 1768 and held several important public offices in the Austrian government.

bêche-de-mer. *See* trepang.

Bechet, Sidney (1897–1959) US jazz clarinetist and soprano saxophone player. He achieved wide recognition after a tour of Europe in 1919, subsequently worked with Duke Ellington, and after World War II lived in Paris. He is one of the few jazz musicians to have popularized the soprano saxophone.

Bechuanaland. *See* Botswana, Republic of.

Becket, St Thomas (c. 1118–70) English churchman. Becket entered the household of Theobald (d. 1161), Archbishop of Canterbury, and in 1154 became *Henry II's chancellor. Succeeding Theobald as archbishop in 1162, Becket resigned the chancellorship and quarreled with Henry. Becket's refusal to swear allegiance to the Constitutions of *Clarendon forced his resignation and exile in France (1164–70). Subsequent attempts to resolve the quarrel failed and on December 29, 1170, he was murdered in Canterbury Cathedral at Henry's instigation. Canonized in 1173, his shrine at Canterbury became one of the most important pilgrimage centers in medieval Europe.

Beckett, Samuel (1906–) Irish novelist, dramatist, and poet. After studying at Trinity College, Dublin, and traveling for several years in Eu-

rope, he settled finally in Paris in 1937. He writes in both French and English. His plays, which include *Waiting for Godot* (1954), and his prose works, such as *Malone Dies* (1956) and *How It Is* (1964), treat human existence with a nihilism tempered by desperate humor. His later works, such as *Breath* (1972) and *Not I* (1973), are notably brief and concentrated. He won the Nobel Prize in 1969.

THOMAS BECKET *This drawing from a 13th-century manuscript shows the archbishop arguing with Henry II of England (above) and Louis VII of France (below).*

Beckmann, Max (1884–1950) German expressionist painter, born in Leipzig. His experiences of World War I inspired his grotesque paintings of distorted sometimes mutilated bodies, often indicting German social evils, as in *Night* (1919; Düsseldorf). In later years in Amsterdam and the US he painted a series of triptychs influenced partly by *Bosch.

becquerel (Bq) The *SI unit of activity (radioactivity) equal to the number of atoms of a radioactive substance that disintegrate in one second. Named for Antoine Henri *Becquerel.

Becquerel, (Antoine) Henri (1852–1908) French physicist, who was professor at the Conservatoire des Arts et Métiers in Paris. He discovered radioactivity (1896) by chance, on finding that invisible rays from uranium salts could affect a photographic plate even through a light-proof wrapper. For his fundamental research on these radiations, Becquerel shared the Nobel Prize (1903) with his associates Pierre and Marie *Curie. He also performed research in magnetism and in optics, particularly polarization and absorption in crystals. His grandfather **Antoine César Becquerel** (1788–1878) left the army to join *Ampère in his study of electricity, becoming one of the founders of electrochemistry.

bedbug A flat wingless insect, about 0.2 in (5 mm) long, belonging to a family (*Cimicidae*; 30 species) of blood-sucking parasites. In temperate regions *Cimex lectularius* is the species that most commonly attacks man, hiding by day in bedding, furniture, etc., and becoming active at night. It inflicts a painful bite but does not transmit disease. Bedbugs can be easily eradicated by insecticide sprays or fumigation. Order: *Hemiptera* (bugs).

Bede, St (c. 673–735 AD) English historian, known as the Venerable Bede. After 682 he lived at the monastery of Jarrow in Northumberland. His *Ecclesiastical History of the English People* (c. 731), written in Latin and later translated into English under King Alfred, is a great historical work and remains an important source for Anglo-Saxon history from 54 BC to 597 AD. He also wrote poems in English, but only one is extant, his "Death Song." He was the author of many grammatical, scientific, and historical works. Feast day: May 27.

Bedford, John, Duke of (1389–1435) The third son of Henry IV; known as John of Lancaster. He was protector of England and regent of France (1422–35) during the minority of his nephew Henry VI. He pursued the *Hundred Years' War and procured the execution of Joan of Arc (1431).

Bedfordshire A county in the South Midlands of England. It is chiefly low lying, rising to the Chiltern Hills in the SW, and is drained by the Great Ouse River. Agricultural products include wheat and vegetables. The chief industries, centered on Luton, Dunstable, and Bedford, are motor vehicles, agricultural engineering, and electrical manufactures. Area: 477 sq mi (1235 sq km). Population (1981): 504,986. Administrative center: Bedford.

Bedlam The popular name for the Bethlehem Royal Hospital, a mental hospital located from 1815 until 1931 in London. Founded in 1247, it was transferred to Beckenham, in Kent in 1931. "Bedlam" has passed into the English language as a synonym for "madhouse."

Bedlington terrier A breed of dog originating in Bedlington, N England, in the early 19th century. It has long legs and a long narrow face and is a sporting dog. The thick coat may be blue, blue and tan, liver, or sandy. Height: about 16 in (40 cm).

Bedouin The nomadic *Arab tribes of the Syrian and Arabian deserts and other desert regions of the Arab world. Their economy is based on camels, sheep, and goats. At present they are found within the political boundaries of Saudi Arabia, Yemen, the United Arab Emirates, Kuwait, Iraq, Jordan, Israel, Egypt, and the *Maghrib states. The policies of these countries are to restrict the movements of the nomadic population and induce them to take up a settled existence. Courageous fighters, the Bedouin played an active role in the early Arab conquests.

bedsore An ulcer that develops in areas of skin subject to continuous pressure, such as may occur in elderly or other bedridden patients who are unable to change their position frequently. The pressure reduces the blood supply to the affected part. Patients at risk require careful nursing, with frequent changes of position and massage to prevent bedsores from developing.

bedstraw A weak, often climbing, plant of the widely distributed genus *Galium* (300 species), common in damp places. Lady's bedstraw (*G. verum*), native to Europe, is a weedy perennial, up to 30 in (75 cm) tall, with small yellow flowers. Its name derives from the legend that Mary rested on a bed of these plants while giving birth to Christ. Family: *Rubiaceae* (madder family). *See also* cleavers.

Bedworth 52 28N 1 29W A market city in central England, in Warwickshire. It has coalmining, brick-making, and light engineering industries. Population (1981): 41,991.

bee A four-winged insect (0.4–1.2 in [10–30 mm] long) belonging to the superfamily *Apoidea* (about 12,000 species), of worldwide distribution. Bees feed on pollen and nectar from flowering plants using well-developed tongues and are important pollinators, transferring pollen on their hairy bodies and broad back legs. The ovipositor is used to sting attackers and in some species is barbed, remaining in the wound.

Most solitary bees nest in soil, hollow trees, or wall cavities. Some, however, tunnel into wood (*see* carpenter bee) or construct nests using earth (*see* mason bee) or leaves (*see* leafcutter bee). The female lays one or more eggs in a nest that is then sealed, leaving the larvae to develop. The social bees (families *Apidae* and *Halictidae*) live in communities organized into castes—workers (infertile females), drones (males, developed from unfertilized eggs), and a queen (a fertile female). Colonies are established in trees, walls, or cliffs (*see also* honeybee). Order: *Hymenoptera*.

Beebe, Charles William (1877–1962) US explorer and naturalist. As head of tropical research for the New York Zoological Society (1916–52) he conducted numerous expeditions and, in 1934, made a record undersea descent of 3028 ft (923 m) in a bathysphere. He wrote many books describing his observations and adventures, including *Monograph of the Pheasants* (1918–22) and *Galapagos* (1923).

beech A tree of the genus *Fagus* (10 species), native to N temperate regions. Beeches have smooth gray bark and a broad dense crown, occasionally reaching a height of 130 ft (40 m). The leaves are oval, pointed, and toothed, the flowers are unisexual and inconspicuous, and the fruits are nutlike seeds enclosed in husks (beechnuts or mast). The common beech of Europe and Asia is *Fagus sylvatica*, the timber of which is used for furniture and flooring, while that of North America is *F. grandiflora*. Family: *Fagaceae*.

In the S hemisphere beeches are represented by a related genus (*Notofagus*; 14 species) and differ in being evergreen and having separate trees bearing male or female flowers. Some are of importance for their durable timber, edible nuts, or ornamental value.

Beecham, Sir Thomas (1879–1961) British conductor. He used his inherited fortune for the advancement of English musical life. He was a memorable interpreter of Haydn and Mozart and championed the works of

Richard Strauss, Sibelius, and particularly Delius, whose friend and biographer he became. He founded the London Philharmonic Orchestra (1932) and the Royal Philharmonic Orchestra (1947).

Beecher, Henry Ward (1813–87) US Congregational preacher and author. He was the son of a distinguished preacher, and brother of Harriet Beecher *Stowe. He was a pastor first in Indianapolis and then for 40 years in Brooklyn, New York, where his sermons and his writings, in which he advocated the abolition of slavery and women's suffrage, were widely influential.

Beecher, Lyman (1775–1863) US preacher educator, and father of Henry Ward *Beecher and Harriet Beecher *Stowe. He became well known for his sermons while minister of Congregational churches in Litchfield, Conn., (1810–26) and Boston (1826–32) and president of Lane Theological Seminary (1832–50) in Cincinnati. An advocate of Calvinism, he made speeches against dueling, slavery, and the use of alcohol that were widely circulated.

bee-eater A brightly colored bird belonging to a family (*Meropidae*; 24 species) occurring mainly in tropical Old World regions. Bee-eaters have pointed wings, long central tail feathers, a slender curved bill, and, commonly, a black eye stripe. They nest in burrows and feed in flight, chiefly on bees and wasps. Order: *Coraciiformes* (hornbills, kingfishers, etc.).

beefwood. *See* Casuarina.

beekeeping (*or* apiculture) The rearing of colonies of *honeybees in hives either for their *honey or *beeswax or for pollinating flowers. Sheets of wax in wooden frames (starter combs) are hung vertically inside the hive. Onto these the bees build wax cells that they fill with honey and seal. When a frame is full it is removed, the honey is extracted, and the comb is reused. A colony makes about 71 lb (32 kg) of honey in a summer, but 31 lb (14 kg) of this is needed by the bees for food during the winter; following a bad summer they must be fed sugar syrup. About 10,000–20,000 bees survive the winter; during the spring, when a colony has increased to over 50,000, a large group is likely to leave the hive (i.e. it swarms). The beekeeper collects the swarm and puts it into an empty hive.

beer and brewing Beer is an alcoholic drink made from fermented malt flavored with hops. Brewing is the process of making beer. Barley, or other grain, is first malted by being allowed to germinate, the resulting malt being dried (kilned), ground, and heated with water (mashed). Starch in the grain is converted into soluble carbohydrates by enzymes in the malt. The resulting liquid wort is boiled with hops to concentrate the wort and utilize the bitter flavor of the hops. The wort is then filtered and cooled ready for fermentation. Yeast is added and the carbohydrates in the wort are converted into alchohol. The liquid is drained and stored. Different brewing methods and types of ingredients produce different varieties of beer. Beer was drunk in ancient Egypt and has been enjoyed in a great many countries ever since. **Ale** was originally a stronger drink than beer, brewed without hops. The terms are now interchangeable, although ale is sometimes reserved for stronger brews fermented at higher temperatures. **Mild** beer is made with fewer hops than **bitter** and a darker malt is used to impart color. **Lager** is traditionally a light beer matured over a long period at low temperature. **Stout** is made from a blend of roasted barley and malts.

Beerbohm, Sir Max (1872–1956) British caricaturist and writer. He published several collections of essays, caricatures, and brilliant parodies during the 1890s. His only novel, *Zuleika Dobson* (1911), is an ironic romance set at Oxford University.

Beersheba 31 15N 34 47E A city in S Israel, the largest in the Negev. In World War I it was the scene of a British victory over the Turks. Beersheba has a university (1965) and manufactures chemicals and glass. Population (1979 est): 107,000.

beeswax A substance produced by bees to build honeycombs. It is collected by heating the honeycomb in water (after removing the honey) so that the floating wax can be separated after solidification on cooling. Beeswax (melting point 66–70°C [61–69°C]) is used in high-quality polishes, etc.

beet A herbaceous plant, *Beta vulgaris*, native to Europe and the Mediterranean region, stemless but sometimes exceeding 40 in (1 m) in height. Several varieties are widely cultivated in temperate areas, the most important of which is the *sugar beet. The taproot of the red or garden beet is eaten as a vegetable, while the mangel-wurzel (*B. vulgaris vulgaris*) is an important fodder variety. The spinach beet is grown for its leaves, used as a vegetable. Family: *Chenopodiaceae*.

Beethoven, Ludwig van (1770–1827) German composer, born in Bonn. His father, a court musician, attempted to exploit him as a child prodigy. Often boorish and temperamental, he nevertheless won a consider-

LUDWIG VAN BEETHOVEN *This portrait of Beethoven as a young man is considered to be one of the best likenesses of him.*

able following for his piano playing and compositions in Vienna, where he settled in 1792 after studying there with Haydn. At the age of 30 he began to go deaf, an experience that increased his loneliness and eccentricity, but did not stop him composing. His later years were plagued by illness and by his adoption of his troublesome nephew Karl. About 600 of Beethoven's works survive, among them 9 symphonies, 5 piano concertos, 1 violin concerto, 16 string quartets, 10 violin and piano sonatas, 32 piano sonatas, 2 ballets, 2 masses, 1 opera, and about 200 song settings. His early masterpieces, influenced by Mozart and Haydn, include much chamber music, piano works, and the first and second symphonies. During his middle years he produced the *Emperor* piano concerto (1809), the *Kreutzer* sonata (1803), the opera *Fidelio* (1805–14), and the rest of the symphonies, up to the eighth. His last most intense works include the *Missa Solemnis* (1818–23), the ninth symphony (1817–23), and the innovative late string quartets.

beetle An insect belonging to the largest order (*Coleoptera*; about 278,000 species) of the animal kingdom. The forewings are specialized as hard structures (called elytra), which cover the functional hindwings when these are not in use. The elytra and the thick cuticle provide protection against predation and desiccation and enable aquatic species to trap a store of air. Beetles occupy a wide range of habitats and have exploited all possible food sources—many feed on plants or animals or scavenge their remains and a few are parasitic.

Many beetles are of great economic importance: some species are serious pests of crops, timber, textiles, and stored grains and cereals; others are useful by preying on insect pests or by speeding up the process of *decomposition. See also* weevil.

Begin, Menachem (1913–) Israeli statesman; prime minister (1977–83). Born in Poland, he led the Polish Zionist youth movement until the outbreak of World War II and from 1942 commanded the militant *Irgun Zvai Leumi* in Palestine. After the establishment of the State of Israel in 1948, he founded the Freedom (Herut) Movement and became the leader of the parliamentary opposition. In 1973 he became joint chairman of the Likud coalition and then prime minister with the victory of Likud in the 1977 elections. Under the auspices of Pres. Jimmy *Carter, Begin held negotiations with Egyptian President Anwar *Sadat that led to the Camp David Accords and the signing of a peace treaty between Egypt and Israel in 1979. Begin and Sadat were jointly awarded the Nobel Peace Prize in 1978. In the aftermath of Israel's invasion of Lebanon in 1982, Begin resigned from office and retired to private life.

Begonia A genus of generally succulent herbaceous plants (about 1000 species) native to the tropics. They are widely grown as ornamental pot or garden plants for their attractive, often brightly colored, flowers with pink, yellow, or white "petals" in two unequal pairs (as in *B. semperflorens*) or for their variegated leaves (as in *B. rex*). The underground parts are long lived and may be tuberous, fibrous, or rhizomatous. Family: *Begoniaceae.*

Behan, Brendan (1923–64) Irish playwright. His first play, *The Quare Fellow* (1954), and his autobiography, *Borstal Boy* (1958), were based on his years of detention and imprisonment for Irish Republican Army (IRA) activities. His best-known play, *The Hostage* (1956), treated a basically tragic situation with characteristic liveliness and boisterous comedy.

behaviorism A school of psychology, founded in the US by J. B. *Watson in the early 20th century, in which the emphasis is on describing and predicting observable behavior: unconscious ideas, feelings, and the process of thinking are regarded as unimportant. The behaviorist concentrates on understanding the laws relating a stimulus to a response, how responses are built up into complex behaviors, and how *conditioning affects behavior. The approach was successful in describing how animals learned tasks in the laboratory but has been limited in its ability to account for such complex processes as emotion, language, and interpersonal relationships. *Behavior therapy was developed from behaviorism and is an established psychiatric treatment.

behavior therapy A method of treating mental disorders that is based on the view that psychological problems are the result of faulty learning. It was developed mainly by H. *Eyzenck. Sometimes *conditioning is used to teach new behavior, such as better ways of relating to other people, or to eliminate undesirable behavior, such as excessive drinking (*see* aversion therapy). It includes treatment for *phobias, in which repeated exposure to the feared object or situation gradually reduces the subject's fear of it. *See also* behaviorism.

Behrens, Peter (1868–1940) German architect. Coming to architecture from the *Arts and Crafts movement, he erected his most influential buildings before World War I. He occupies a transitional period in architectural development, evolving a modernistic style that echoed a functional classicism and was notable for its complete lack of ornamentation in design. His most important building was the AEG turbine works in Berlin (1909–11), which was one of the first industrial buildings to be evaluated as a work of architecture.

Behring, Emil Adolf von (1854–1917) German bacteriologist, who produced an antitoxin that conferred passive immunity against tetanus. By 1882 Behring and Paul *Ehrlich had developed a serum that provided effective immunity against diphtheria and also aided its treatment in established cases. He was awarded a Nobel Prize in 1901.

Behrman, S(amuel) N(athaniel) (1893–1973) US dramatist, noted for his comedies. His first, *The Second Man*, was produced on Broadway in 1927, and was followed by *Serena Blandish* (1928), *End of Summer* (1936), *Wine of Choice* (1938), and *No Time for Comedy* (1939). Other works include *Meteor* (1929), *Brief Moment* (1931), and *Fanny* (in collaboration with Joshua Logan; 1954).

Behzad (c. 1455–c. 1536) Persian painter, regarded as one of the greatest of Islamic miniaturists. As director of the academy at Herat he was an influential teacher and the many imitators of his richly colored and dramatic style have made his works—few of which are signed—difficult to identify.

Beibu Gulf. *See* Tonkin, Gulf of.

Beida. *See* Zawiyat al-Bayda'.

Beiderbecke, Bix (Leon Bismarck B.; 1903–31) US jazz cornetist and pianist, famous for the purity of his cornet tone and such songs as "Singin' the Blues." Toward the end of his short life he played with Louis Armstrong and in the band of Paul Whiteman (1891–1967). The originality of his own compositions is evident in "In a Mist" (1927) for piano.

Beijing. *See* Peking.

Beira 19 49S 34 52E A port in E Mozambique, on the Mozambique Channel. Founded in 1891 by the Portuguese, it became a major port serving central S Africa. It was the main export outlet of Rhodesia (now Zimbabwe) until Mozambique's independence (1975). Exports include ores, cotton, and food products. Population (1970); 113,770.

Beirut 33 52N 35 30E The capital of the Lebanon, situated on the E Mediterranean Sea. After centuries of Turkish domination, it was held by the French from World War I until 1941, when it became the capital of the newly independent Lebanon. Much was badly damaged in the civil war (1975–76) and in 1982 when Israeli forces besieged the city and forced the

Palestine Liberation Organization to leave. It has four universities. Population (1978 est): 702,000.

Béjart, Maurice (Maurice-Jean de Berger; 1928–) French ballet dancer and choreographer. His works are characterized by such diverse influences as jazz and Indian mysticism. In 1954 he founded his own company, which was renamed Le Ballet du XXme Siècle when it became based in Brussels in 1960.

bel. *See* decibel.

Belasco, David (1853–1931) US theater manager and dramatist. Most of his plays were adaptations and collaborations. He is best remembered for his spectacular productions involving experimental scenic and lighting effects, and for his promotion of young actors.

Belau (formerly Palau) A group of islands in the W Pacific Ocean, within the UN Trust Territory of the *Pacific Islands. Self-government was achieved in 1981 and the islands became the Republic of Belau. Area: 184 sq mi (476 sq km). Population (1977 est): 13,519.

bel canto (Italian: fine singing) A delicate and lyrical style of singing that was developed in Italian opera during the 17th and 18th centuries. Notable singers included Farinelli (1705–82) and Jenny *Lind. During the 19th century, the enlargement of orchestras resulted in the development of a more declamatory style of singing.

Belém 1 27S 48 29W A port in N Brazil, the capital of Pará state on the Rio do Pará. It exports products from the Amazon basin including nuts, jute, and rubber. Its university was founded in 1957. Population (1980 est): 758,117.

belemnite The fossilized shell of an extinct *cuttlefish, sometimes called a thunderbolt. Cylindrical and pointed at one end, they are most commonly found in deposits of the Jurassic and Cretaceous periods (150–65 million years ago).

Belfast 54 40N 5 50W The capital of Northern Ireland, a seaport situated where the Lagan River enters Belfast Low on the border between Co Antrim and Co Down. It is the province's commercial and administrative center and its industries include shipbuilding, electronics, and engineering. The principal buildings, including the City Hall (1906) and Parliament Buildings (1932) at Stormont, were built in the late 19th and early 20th centuries. Queen's University received a royal charter in 1909. *History*: large-scale growth of Belfast came with the expansion of the linen-making and shipbuilding industries in the 19th century; it became a city in 1888. The Parliament of Northern Ireland sat in the city from 1921 to 1972. Its recent history has been marked by the conflict between Protestant and Roman Catholic communities; each has become increasingly concentrated in ghettoes. This has led to an exacerbation of the housing problem, which is now one of the worst in Europe. The British army has maintained a presence on the streets of Belfast since August, 1969. Population (1971): 360,150.

Belfort 44 17N 1 32E A city in E France, the capital of the Territoire de Belfort. Strategically situated between the Vosges and Jura mountains, it has been besieged many times. Industries include wine. Population (1975): 57,317.

Belgae The Germanic tribes occupying NE *Gaul in ancient Roman times. Julius Caesar named them and considered them the most warlike of the Gauls. He defeated them in 57 BC but they continued their opposition to the Romans from SE Britain, to which area they had been migrating from about 100 BC.

Belgaum 15 54N 74 36E A city in India, in Karnataka. Manufactures include cotton, furniture, and leather. Population (1971): 213,830.

Belgian Congo. *See* Zaïre, Republic of.

Belgium, Kingdom of (French name: Belgique; Flemish name: België) A country in NW Europe, on the North Sea. It is generally low lying except for the Ardennes in the SE. The main rivers are the Scheldt and the Meuse and these and others are linked by canals to form an extensive network of inland waterways. The population is divided between the French and the Flemish, with small minorities of Germans and others. *Economy*: highly industrialized, with coal and iron resources supporting considerable heavy industry. Food processing and textiles are also important. Agriculture is highly intensive, the main cash crop being sugar beet. Belgium is an important center for trade and has been since the middle ages. It still has one of the highest proportions of export revenue to total income in the world. In 1921 a customs union was formed with Luxembourg and in 1948 both joined with the Netherlands to form the *Benelux Economic Union. Belgium is also a member of the EEC and almost two-thirds of its trade is with other members. Main exports include iron and steel, chemicals, machinery, and motor vehicles. *History*: the name Belgium

comes from the *Belgae, a Celtic tribe named by Caesar, and the area was part of the Roman Empire until about the end of the 2nd century AD, when it was invaded by Germanic tribes. In medieval times it was divided into several counties, duchies, and the bishopric of Liège, during which time the cities of Ghent, Bruges, and Ypres rose to virtual independence and economic prosperity through the wool industry. Particularly in view of its strategic position, Belgium had considerable importance in the balance of power in Europe over the centuries and from the middle ages onward— it was ruled by several European nations in turn, including Austria, Spain, and France. After being occupied by France during the Napoleonic Wars, it was joined to the Netherlands in 1815. Following an uprising, it became independent in 1830, and the National Congress elected Prince Leopold of Saxe-Coburg as King of the Belgians (*see* Leopold I) in 1831. The country was eventually recognized by all of Europe in 1839. In spite of efforts to remain neutral it was attacked and occupied by Germany in both World Wars. When the Germans invaded in 1940, King *Leopold III surrendered immediately but the government struggled on in exile in London. In 1950, after a political crisis, the king was persuaded to abdicate in favor of his son, *Baudouin. The main political problem since World War II has been tension between the French-speaking Walloons in the S and the Flemish-speaking community in the N. Efforts are being made to create a federal structure of government under which the Flemish, French-speaking, and bilingual Brussels regions would obtain a large measure of regional autonomy. The loss in 1960 of the Belgian Congo, now Zaïre, had an adverse effect on Belgium's economy. Dr Wilfried Martens, who led a series of coalition governments from 1979, resigned in March, 1981, and was succeeded by Mark Eyskens. Dr Martens was re-appointed as prime minister of a fresh coalition government in December, 1981. Official languages: French, Flemish, Dutch, and German. Official currency: Belgian franc of 100 centimes. Area: 11,778 sq mi (30,513 sq km). Population (1983 est): 9,865,000. Capital: Brussels. Main port: Antwerp.

Belgorod-Dnestrovski (Romanian name: Cetatea Alba) 46 10N 30 19E A port in the Soviet Union, in the SW Ukrainian SSR on the Dnestr estuary. A commercial center, it has fishing, fish-processing, and winemaking industries. *History*: founded by Greek colonists in the 6th century BC, it subsequently passed to the Romans and then the Byzantines. Turkish from 1484, it was acquired by Russia in the 19th century. It was under Romanian rule from 1918 to 1940. Population (1981 est): 255,000.

Belgrade (Serbo-Croat name: Beograd) 44 50N 20 30E The capital of Yugoslavia and of Serbia, situated in the NE at the confluence of the Rivers Danube and Sava. A settlement and route center from very early times, it became the Serbian capital in the early 15th century. It later suffered Turkish and Austrian occupations but again became capital of Serbia in the late 19th century and of Yugoslavia after World War I. It was occupied by the Germans in World War II and has expanded considerably in the years since then. The University of Belgrade was founded in 1863 and the Arts University in 1973. Population (1971): 746,000.

Belinsky, Vissarion (1811–48) Russian literary critic, an influential advocate of social realism and naturalism. He championed *Pushkin, *Lermontov, and *Gogol, whom he later denounced as a betrayer of naturalism.

Belisarius (c. 505–65 AD) Byzantine general of *Justinian I's reign. After successfully checking Persian invasions on the empire's eastern frontier and overthrowing the African Vandal kingdom (534), Belisarius began his conquest of the Ostrogoths of Italy, and captured Rome, Naples, and Ravenna (540) before being recalled to Constantinople. In 546 he returned to Italy to quell the resurgent Ostrogoths but was again recalled, his command being given to *Narses.

Belitung (*or* Billiton) An Indonesian island in the Java Sea. Its tin mines, now government owned, have attracted a large Chinese community. Area: 1866 sq mi (4833 sq km). Chief town: Tanjungpandan.

Belize (name until 1973: British Honduras) A country in Central America, on the Caribbean Sea between Mexico and Guatemala. The country is generally low lying, rising to the Maya Mountains in the SW. It is subject to hurricanes, one of which severely damaged the former capital, Belize City, in 1961. The population is of African, Spanish-American, and Mayan Indian descent, with small minorities of E Indians, Syrians, and Chinese. *Economy*: mainly agricultural; although almost half the country is forested, the combined value of sugar and citrus exports have exceeded that of timber since the early 1960s. *History*: archeological evidence suggests that the area was once an important Mayan settlement. The coast was discovered by Columbus in 1502 but the first European occupation was an independent settlement of British woodcutters, which held out against the Spanish throughout the 17th century. From the late 18th century more control was exercised by the British government and in 1862 it became a colony under Jamaica. It became an independent colony in 1884 and attained internal self-government in 1964. Claims, based on early Spanish treaties, were made to it by Guatemala but despite disputes Belize achieved full independence in 1981, becoming the last Commonwealth country on the American mainland to obtain self-government. An ongoing border dispute with Guatemala had delayed Belize's complete independence, and in the early 1980s the conflict had not yet been resolved. Despite its small size geographically and its lack of political strength, Belize has been able to maintain a relatively steady economic and social equilibrium in comparison with its Latin American neighbors. Prime minister: George C. Price. Official language: English; Spanish is also widely spoken. Official currency: Belize dollar of 100 cents. Area: 8867 sq mi (22,963 sq km). Population (1983 est): 154,000. Capital: Belmopan.

Belize City 17 29N 88 10W The chief port of Belize, on the Caribbean coast. It was formerly capital of Belize but following a severe hurricane (1961), Belmopan, which became capital in 1970, was constructed inland. The main exports are timber, coconuts, and corn. Population (1980): 39,887

ALEXANDER GRAHAM BELL *Inaugurating the New York-Chicago telephone line in 1892.*

Bell, Alexander Graham (1847–1922) Scottish-born US scientist and inventor. He went to Canada in 1870 and to the US in 1873, where he became professor of vocal physiology at Boston University. Bell's work in telegraphy and telephony led to the invention of the telephone, which he patented in 1876, demonstrated at American exhibitions, and had formed the Bell Telephone Co. by 1877. He also performed basic work in sound recording, electro-optical communication, and aerodynamics.

belladonna. *See* deadly nightshade.

belladonna lily. *See* Amaryllis.

Bellarmine, St Robert (1542–1621) Italian Jesuit theologian, cardinal (from 1549), and archbishop of Capua (1602–05): canonized in 1930. An influential counter-Reformation theologian, he held Galileo in high esteem and privately advised him to regard the Copernican system as hypothetical, although he formally pronounced the system "false and erroneous". His writings include *Disputationes de controversiis Christianae fidei* (1586–93), a statement of Catholic doctrine, and he played an important part in the revised edition of the Vulgate published in 1592. Stoneware wine jugs with a bearded face made in the Rhineland between about 1550 and 1700 became known as Bellarmines, on the grounds that they were Protestant caricatures of the cardinal.

Bellay, Joachim de (1522–60) French poet. In 1549 he published *Défense et illustration de la langue française*, the manifesto of the *Pléiade, and *Olive*, the first book of love sonnets in French. While accompanying his cousin Cardinal Jean du Bellay on a mission to Rome, he wrote *Antiquités de Rome* (1558) and *Regrets* (1558).

Belle Fourche River A river rising in NE Wyoming and flowing E to South Dakota where it joins the Cheyenne River. The Belle Fourche Reservoir is formed by a dam just over the South Dakota border and is connected to the river by a canal. Length: 350 mi (564 km).

Belle-Isle, Charles Fouquet de, Duc de (1684–1761) French marshal, who rose to prominence during the Wars of the Spanish (1701–14) and Polish (1733) Successions. His influence at court led to France's opposition to Maria Theresa in the War of Austrian Succession (1740–48). As minister of war (1758–60), he implemented a series of army reforms.

Bellerophon In Greek mythology, the grandson of Sisyphus and son of Glaucus, King of Corinth. Sent by Iobates, King of Lycia, to kill the *Chimera, he was able to carry out his task by flying above the dragon on Pegasus, a winged horse he had previously captured and tamed with the aid of Athena.

Bellingshausen, Fabian Gottlieb, Baron von (1778–1852) Russian explorer. In 1819 he led an expedition to the Antarctic, surveying the South Georgia and South Sandwich Islands and discovering the islands Peter I and Alexander I. The Bellingshausen Sea was named for him.

Bellingshausen Sea A section of the S Pacific Ocean bordering on Antarctica, extending between the Antarctic Peninsula and Ellsworth Land. It always contains pack ice.

Bellini, Jacopo (c. 1400–c. 1470) Venetian painter, who was a pupil of *Gentile da Fabriano. In the early 1420s he probably visited Florence, where he became familiar with the artistic developments of the Renaissance. Although his few surviving paintings retain the decorative conventions of Byzantine and Gothic art, his two sketchbooks (British Museum and Louvre) reveal a remarkable understanding of perspective. They influenced his son-in-law Andrea *Mantegna and his two sons, who both trained under him. The eldest, **Gentile Bellini** (c. 1429–1507), is best known for his portraits and procession scenes. *The Procession in St Mark's Square* (Accademia, Venice) depicts his native city with a realism that anticipates Canaletto. In 1479 he accompanied the Doge to Constantinople, where he painted Sultan Mehmed II (National Gallery, London). Gentile's brother **Giovanni Bellini** (c. 1430–1516) was an important influence on Venetian art, especially through his pupils *Titian and *Giorgione. His early work is indebted to Mantegna. From about 1475 his use of the Flemish technique of oil painting, introduced to him by *Antonello da Messina, led to his richer use of color and softer treatment of form. His paintings included several altarpieces, such as *Madonna and Saints* (S Zaccaria, Venice) in which he gave great importance to the landscape, and portraits, such as *Doge Loredano* (National Gallery, London).

Bellini, Vincenzo (1801–35) Italian opera composer. Of his 11 operas, *La somnambula* and *Norma* (both 1831) and *I Puritani* (1835) remain popular, although they require singers of outstanding ability to meet the demands of the *coloratura style.

Bellinzona 46 12N 9 02E A city in S Switzerland, on the Ticino River. It is dominated by three 15th-century castles. A tourist center, it also has small industries. Population (1970): 16,979.

Bello, Andrés (1781–1865) Venezuelan scholar and poet. He accompanied Simón Bolívar on a revolutionary mission to London in 1810 and stayed there until 1829. The pastoral poems of *Silvas americanas* (1826–27) are influenced by Virgil. He founded the University of Chile (1843), drafted the country's legal code, and wrote books on many subjects, including a definitive Spanish grammar (1847).

Belloc, (Joseph-Pierre) Hilaire (1870–1953) British poet and essayist. Born in France, he was educated at Oxford and served as a Liberal in Parliament from 1906 to 1910. His works include essays, historical biographies, and satirical novels, often illustrated by his friend G. K. *Chesterton. A devout Roman Catholic, he vigorously opposed the socialism of G. B. *Shaw and H. G. *Wells. His most popular works are light verse, such as *Cautionary Tales* (1907).

Bellow, Saul (1915–) Canadian-born US novelist, the son of poor Russian Jewish immigrants. His first novel, *Dangling Man* (1944), influenced by *existentialism, was followed by *The Adventures of Augie March* (1953) and *Henderson the Rain King* (1959). His later novels, such as *Mr Sammler's Planet* (1970), *Humboldt's Gift* (1975), and *The Dean's December* (1982), are more ironic and reflective studies of harassed Jewish intellectuals in a bewildering urban chaos. He won the Nobel Prize in 1976.

Bellows, George (Wesley) (1882–1925) US painter. One of the eight members of *Ashcan School, he painted realistic scenes, primarily of New York City and environs. His well-known works include *Stag at Sharkey's* (1907), *Up the Hudson* (1908), *Men of the Docks* (1912), *The Cliff Dwellers* (1913), and *Dempsey Through the Ropes* (1924).

Belmonte y García, Juan (1892–1962) Spanish matador, who was active from 1913 until 1934 and was regarded as one of the greatest of all time. His technique of working very close to bulls, using his cape to induce them to move around him, revolutionized bullfighting.

Belmopan 17 12N 88 00W The capital of Belize, on the Belize River about 50 mi (80 km) inland from Belize City, which it succeeded as capital in 1970 after the latter was damaged by a hurricane in 1961. Population (1980): 2932.

Belo Horizonte 19 54S 43 54W A city in SE Brazil, in Minas Gerais state. Founded in 1897, it was Brazil's first planned city. Distinctive architecture includes Oscar Niemayer's Chapel of São Francisco. The chief industries include cotton textiles, meat processing, and iron and steel. It is the site of two universities. Population (1980 est): 1,442,483.

Belorussian Soviet Socialist Republic (Belorussia *or* White Russia) A constituent republic in the W central Soviet Union. The majority of its inhabitants are Belorussians, an Eastern *Slav people. Belorussia has an important engineering industry and the largest petrochemical complex in Europe. Cereals are the basis of agriculture, and dairy farming and pig breeding are expanding. Belorussia (formed in 1919) was badly devastated in World War II. It has a separate seat in the UN. Area: 80,134 sq mi (207,600 sq km). Population (1981 est): 9,700,000. Capital: Minsk.

Belshazzar In the Old Testament, the son of *Nebuchadnezzar and the last King of Babylon. At a feast given by him, the prophet Daniel interpreted the supernatural handwriting that appeared on the wall—*Mene, Mene, Tekel, Upharsin*—as foretelling the destruction of Babylon and Belshazzar's downfall (Daniel 5.25).

beluga 1. A giant *sturgeon, *Huso huso*, up to 28 ft (8.4 m) long, that occurs in the Caspian and Black Seas and the Volga River of E Europe. It is a highly prolific egg producer and the source of the best caviar. 2. *See* white whale.

Belyi, Andrei (Boris Nikolaevich Bugaev; 1880–1934) Russian symbolist poet and critic. He studied mathematics and philosophy at Moscow University, but his interest in mysticism led him into symbolism. In 1901 he published *Simfoniya*, an attempted synthesis of all the arts around a prose poem, and several volumes of poetry and criticism. Disillusioned with the aftermath of the Revolution, he lived abroad from 1921 to 1923.

Bemba A Central *Bantu people of NE Zambia and neighboring areas of Zaïre and Rhodesia whose language has become widely spoken in Zambia. They were traditionally ruled by members of the matrilineal royal clan from which the supreme chief, or Chitimukulu, came.

Bembo, Pietro (1470–1547) Italian scholar. He was secretary to Pope Leo X from 1513 to 1521 and was made cardinal in 1539. His most important work, *Prose della volgar lingua* (1525), set out to develop Italian into a literary language equal to Latin. *Rime* (1530) is a collection of his Italian poetry.

Benares. *See* Varanasi.

Ben Bella, Ahmed (1919–) Algerian statesman; president (1963–65). A leading figure in the struggle for the independence of Algeria, after service in the French army during World War II he helped to form the *Front de Libération nationale (FLN) in 1954. Imprisoned by the French for six years, he was released at independence in 1962 and elected prime minister (1962–63) and then president. He was overthrown in 1965 by *Boumédienne and imprisoned until 1980.

Benchley, Robert Charles (1889–1945) US humorist. He edited *Vanity Fair* and worked as drama critic for *Life* and the *New Yorker*. He published 15 volumes of his collected humorous essays, including *My Ten Years in a Quandary* (1936). Other works include *Of All Things* (1921), *The Treasurer's Report* (1930), *Inside Benchley* (1941) and *Benchley Beside Himself* (1943). He acted in several films and himself made 46 short comic films. His grandson **Peter Benchley** (1940–) is also a popular novelist. He is the author of *Jaws* (1974), *The Deep* (1976), *The Island* (1979), and *The Girl of the Sea of Cortez* (1982).

Benda, Julien (1867–1956) French novelist and philosopher. An advocate of the classical ideals of reason and order, he wrote several books attacking the philosophy of *Bergson. His most famous work, *La Trahison des clercs* (1927), demanded that the intellectual's commitment to truth should not be compromised by political or emotional involvements.

Bendigo 36 48S 144 21E A city in Australia, in central Victoria. It grew rapidly following a gold discovery in 1851 and is now a commercial center with the third largest livestock market in Australia. Population (1976 est): 50,169.

bends. *See* decompression sickness.

Benedict XV (Giacomo della Chiesa; 1854–1922) Pope (1914–22). A papal diplomat, he was elected shortly after the outbreak of World War I, in which he maintained a strict neutrality while attempting to negotiate peace and to curb atrocities. Thereafter he reformed papal administration and diplomacy and was a notable supporter of missionary activity.

Benedictines The monks and nuns belonging to the Roman Catholic Order of St Benedict (OSB), a union of independent abbeys all of which follow the Rule of St *Benedict of Nursia. They have always acted as scholars and educators and were responsible for preserving the learning of antiquity after the fall of the Roman Empire. They have also exercised a great influence in maintaining high standards for the sacred art and music used in the liturgy. The liqueur Bénédictine is named for the order and is made at Fécamp, France.

Benedict of Nursia, St (c. 480–c. 550) Italian saint, the father of western monasticism. Educated at Rome, he withdrew from society about 500 and lived for a time as a hermit near Rome. He eventually established 12 monasteries with 12 monks each. About 525 he and a few monks established themselves at Monte Cassino, where he drew up his monastic rule, which provided for government by an elected abbot, residence in one place, obedience, observance of prayers at fixed hours (the Divine Office), common ownership of property, and a life of work, prayer, and study. The Rule was originally intended for laymen, and Benedict himself was apparently not ordained. He was buried at Monte Cassino. Feast day: March 21. Emblems: a broken cup and a raven.

benefit of clergy The development in England of the 12th-century canon law that criminous clerks (criminal clerics) should not be tried by both ecclesiastical and secular courts. Henry II's acceptance of this principle gave all clerics the right to be tried solely in ecclesiastical courts. These could not inflict capital punishment, from which clergy were thus immune. Much abused in the later middle ages, the privilege was increasingly limited during and after the Reformation although it was not finally abolished until the early 19th century.

Bene Israel (Hebrew: Children of Israel) Indian Jewish community of uncertain origin, now concentrated mainly in Bombay.

Benelux The customs union formed by *Be*lgium, the *Ne*therlands, and *Lux*emborg in 1948. It was the first free-trade market in Europe. The three countries standardized prices, welfare benefits, wages, and taxes and allowed free immigration and movement of labor and capital between them. All three countries are now members of the *EEC, which has similar aims.

Beneš, Edvard (1884–1948) Czechoslovak statesman. In 1918 Beneš helped Tomáš *Masaryk to found Czechoslovakia and became foreign minister, playing an important role in the League of Nations. In 1935 he became president but went into exile when he was forced to cede the *Sudetenland to Germany (1938). He spent World War II as president of a provisional government in London, returning to Czechoslovakia in 1945. He resigned the presidency in 1948, when Czechoslovakia became a communist state.

Benét, Stephen Vincent (1898–1943) US poet and novelist. Son of an army officer, he wrote chiefly on themes of American history and myth. His best-known works are the epic poems *John Brown's Body* (1928), about the Civil War, which won a pulitzer Prize (1929), and *Western Star*, which was awarded the same prize in 1944. He also wrote the short story *The Devil and Daniel Webster* (1937).

Benevento 41 08N 14 46E A town in S Italy, in Campania. It has Roman remains and a 9th-century cathedral. Its manufactures include leather goods, agricultural machinery, confectionery, and Strega liqueur. Population (1971): 59,016.

Bengal A region of the Indian subcontinent, in the NE on the Bay of Bengal around the vast Ganges and Brahmaputra deltas. Divided between India and Bangladesh, it has a flourishing culture. *History*: on the fringe of early Indian civilization, Bengal became the center of Buddhist (8th–12th centuries), Hindu (11th–13th centuries), and finally Islamic dynasties. The base for British expansion through India, it was partitioned between India and Pakistan at independence (1947). *See also* West Bengal.

Bengal, Bay of The shallow NE limb of the Indian Ocean, between the Indian subcontinent on the W and Burma and the Andaman and Nicobar Islands on the E. Shipping and coastal life are dominated by the NE winter monsoon and the SW summer monsoon.

Bengali An Indo-Aryan language spoken by 80 million people in Bangladesh and West Bengal (India). The literary form of the language uses many *Sanskrit words. It was the first Indian language to imitate western literary modes in fiction, drama, and poetry. There is a distinct colloquial form.

Benghazi (or Banghazi; Italian name: Bengasi) 32 07N 20 05E The second largest city in Libya, on the Gulf of Sidra. Severely damaged during World War II, it has experienced recent growth with the development of local oilfields; other industries include light engineering. Population (1973): 282,192.

Benguela (or Benguella) 12 34S 13 24E A town in W Angola, on the Atlantic Ocean. It is overshadowed as a port by Lobito; industries include fish drying and soap production. Population (1970): 40,996.

DAVID BEN-GURION *The father of the Israeli nation, noted for his informality, had a magnetic personality that caused him to be revered throughout the world.*

Ben-Gurion, David (1886–1973) Israeli statesman, known as the Father of the Nation. He was Israel's first prime minister (1948–53, 1955–63). Born David Gruen in Poland, he adopted the Hebrew name Ben-Gurion after arriving in Palestine in 1906. In 1917 he joined the British Army's Jewish Legion to free Palestine from Ottoman control (achieved in 1918) and after the establishment of British rule worked to establish a Jewish home in Palestine, promised in the *Balfour Declaration. In 1920 he founded the General Federation of Labor (the Histadrut) and in 1930, the Israeli Workers' Party (Mapai). Becoming chairman of the Zionist Executive in 1935, he led the Zionist effort to establish a Jewish state, finally achieved in 1948. As prime minister he formed an Israeli army from the varous guerrilla groups and adopted a tough line against Arab attack. After resigning the prime ministership in 1963, he was leader of the opposition party, the Rafi, until his retirement in 1970.

Beni, Río A river in Bolivia. Rising near La Paz, it flows generally NE to join the Río Mamoré. Length: over 1000 mi (1600 km).

Benin, People's Republic of (name until 1975: Dahomey) A country in West Africa, on the Gulf of Guinea. Flat forests and swamps in the S rise to plateaus in the center and to mountains in the N. The population is mainly Fon and Yoruba in the N and Somba and Bariba in the S. *Economy*: chiefly agricultural, the main crops being corn, cassava, rice, and vegetables. Cotton has been introduced in the N and coffee in the S, and these provide the main exports. Forests produce palm oil and kernels, and there is some freshwater fishing. Offshore oil has been found and hydroelectric schemes are being planned in conjunction with Togo. Most industry has been nationalized. *History*: the powerful Aja kingdom of Dahomey was a center of the slave trade in the 17th century but was conquered by the French in 1893 and became part of French West Africa. Dahomey attained

self-government in 1958 and became an independent republic within the French Community in 1960. Since then the country has been shaken by a series of military coups. In the last (1972) Lt Col Ahmed (Malthieu) Kerékou seized power. In 1974 he established a Marxist-Leninist state. In 1983 the expulsion from Nigeria of 2,000,000 illegal aliens, mostly from Ghana, brought a mass exodus of homeless people through Benin as they made their way back to their native countries. Causing a crisis situation in Benin, it was expected that the refugee problem would lead to long-term serious disruptions since it was likely that many of the stranded would remain in that country. Official language: French. Official currency: CFA (Communauté financière africaine) franc of 100 centimes. Area: 43,464 sq mi (112,600 sq km). Population (1983 est): 3,754,000. Capital: Porto Novo. Main port: Cotonou.

Benin City 6 19N 5 41E A city in Nigeria. It is an important center for the rubber industry and also exports palm oil. Population (1975 est): 136,000.

Benjamin In the Old Testament, the youngest son of Jacob by Rachel, who died during childbirth. He was named Ben-oni (son of ill luck) by Rachel before she died but called Benjamin (son of good luck) by Jacob. He became his father's favorite after Joseph was sold into slavery in Egypt. Figuratively he represents the especially loved younger son. His descendants formed one of the 12 *tribes of Israel and later, with the tribe of Judah, formed the southern kingdom of Judah.

Benjamin, Judah Philip (1811–84) US statesman and lawyer. A lawyer by profession, he served in the Louisiana legislature and the US Senate (1852–61) before becoming attorney general (1861) of the Confederacy at the beginning of the Civil War. He then served as secretary of war (1861–62) and secretary of state (1862–65) until the collapse of the Confederacy, at which time he went to England and practiced law.

Benn, Gottfried (1886–1956) German poet. He worked as a doctor in Berlin and, during both World Wars, in the army. His early expressionist style, evident in *Morgue* (1912) and *Fleisch* (1917), gave way to the more precise intellectual style evident in *Statische Gedichte* (1948). His theories of poetry, contained in *Probleme der Lyrik* (1951), attracted T. S. *Eliot.

Bennett, (Enoch) Arnold (1837–1931) British novelist. A magazine editor in London, he published his first novel, *A Man from the North*, in 1898 and lived in Paris from 1902 to 1912. His best-known novels are about life in Staffordshire, where he grew up. They include *Anna of the Five Towns* (1902), *The Old Wives' Tale* (1908), and *Clayhanger* (1910).

Bennett, James Gordon (1795–1872) US newspaper editor, born in Scotland. After writing for several newspapers, he distinguished himself as Washington correspondent for the *New York Enquirer*. In 1835, he founded the *New York Herald* (1835), in which he pioneered many of the techniques of modern journalism, including the use of the telegraph to speed news gathering. His son **James Gordon Bennett** (1841–1918) became editor of the *Herald* in 1867. He financed several explorers, including Stanley in his quest for Livingstone, an Arctic expedition, and the quest for the Northwest Passage.

Bennett, Richard Bedford, Viscount (1870–1947) Canadian statesman; Conservative prime minister (1930–35). A lawyer and businessman, he was a champion of protective tariffs. In 1932 he presided over the Imperial Economic Conference in Ottawa, which established bilateral trade agreements between countries in the British Commonwealth.

Ben Nevis 56 48N 5 00W The highest mountain in the British Isles, in the Highland Region of Scotland, in the Grampians. Height: 4406 ft (1343 m).

Bennington, Battle of (1777) A Revolutionary War battle in which colonial troops were victorious over the British at Bennington, Vt. British and Loyalist troops, commanded by a German colonel, Friedrich Baume, planned to raid Bennington's supply stores, but they were stopped by American troops. This battle marked the beginning of the decling of Gen. John *Burgoyne's N campaign in America.

Benny, Jack (Benjamin Kubelsky; 1894–1974) US entertainer. A comedian in vaudeville from an early age, he began making motion pictures in 1929. His act was centered around comic playing of the violin, delayed doubletake, meanness, and, from 1933, always being 39 years old. He had his own radio (1932–55) and television shows (1950–65).

Benoit de Sainte-Maure (12th century AD) French poet. His long epic poem, *Roman de Troie*, is loosely based on the legends of *Troy. He is possibly also the author of a verse history of the Dukes of Normandy, commissioned by Henry II in 1174.

Benoni 26 12S 28 18E A city in South Africa, in the S Transvaal on the Witwatersrand. Founded in 1903 as a gold-mining center, it is an important industrial city, especially for engineering. Population (1980 est): 206,810.

Bent, William (1809–69) US pioneer and fur trader. He established Bent's Fort (1832), a trading post in Colorado, becoming the territory's first while settler.

Bentham, Jeremy (1748–1832) British philosopher, pioneer of *utilitarianism. From a wealthy middle-class background, he began his law studies at 15. He preferred legal theory to practice and in 1776 published *A Fragment on Government*. In 1789 *Principles of Morals and Legislation* presented utilitarianism to the world. He retired to the country in 1814, a hero to republicans across Europe, and wrote copiously on politics and ethics until his death. He founded the *Westminster Review* (1823) to promote philosophical radicalism.

Bentinck, Lord William (Henry Cavendish). *See* Portland, William Henry Cavendish Bentinck, 3rd Duke of.

Bentivoglio An aristocratic family that ruled Bologna (Italy) from 1447 until 1506. **Sante Bentivoglio** (1424–63) established his family's supremacy in Bologna. He and his son **Giovanni Bentivoglio** (1443–1508) were notable patrons of the arts. Increasingly autocratic, and unpopular, Giovanni and his family were expelled from Bologna in 1506 with the support of Pope *Julius II. Subsequent members of the family, notably **Guido Bentivoglio** (1579–1644), were famous diplomats and authors, but the family never regained its former political power.

Benton, Thomas Hart (1889–1975) US painter of rural life. As the leader and spokesman of the American Regionalist painters of the 1930s, Benton advocated the need to free US painting from the overwhelming influence of French abstract art and to create an indigenous artistic tradition. He is also known for his murals for such public institutions as the New School of Social Research, New York, and the Missouri State Capitol in Jefferson City.

bentwood furniture Furniture constructed by a mass-production process invented by a Viennese designer Michael Thonet (1796–1871). It involved steaming beechwood rods and laminated board until they could be bent into the desired shapes. The shaped sections were transported unassembled and screwed together at the destination. Typical chairs, coat stands, etc., are curved in rococo style. The technique has been exploited by modern designers, such as Marcel *Breuer and many Scandinavian designers.

Benue, River A river in West Africa. Rising in N Cameroon, it flows W across Nigeria to join the Niger River at Lokoja. Length: 870 mi (1400 km).

Benxi (*or* Pen-ki) 41 21N 123 45E A city in NE China, in Liaoning province. It is a center of iron and steel production. Population (1953): 449,000.

Benz, Karl (Friedrich) (1844–1929) German engineer and □automobile manufacturer. In 1885 he built the first automobile to be driven by an internal-combustion engine. The Benz Company merged with Daimler in 1926 to form Daimler-Benz, the makers of Mercedes-Benz automobiles.

Benzedrine. *See* amphetamine.

benzene (*or* benzol; C_6H_6) A colorless highly flammable liquid. It is the simplest □aromatic compound, its molecules consisting of a ring of six carbon atoms each with a hydrogen atom attached. Benzene is obtained from *oil and from *coal tar. It is widely used in the chemical industry, for example in making *detergents, *nylon, and *insecticides.

benzodiazepines A class of tranquilizing drugs that act by depressing specific areas of the brain. Despite this, overdosage of these drugs is rarely dangerous. Benzodiazepines, such as diazepam (Valium) and chlordiazepoxide (Librium), are used as *sedatives. Diazepam is also used to control epileptic seizures and chlordiazepoxide is helpful in the treatment of alcohol-withdrawal symptoms. Nitrazepam (Mogadon) is used as a sleeping pill (*see* hypnotics). Both nitrazepam and diazepam are habit forming.

benzoic acid (C_6H_5COOH) A white crystalline powder, the simplest of the carboxylic acids (*see* fatty acids). It occurs naturally in many plants and is used in preserving food.

benzoin 1. ($C_6H_5CHOHCOC_6H_5$) A white or yellowish crystalline substance used to make other organic compounds. 2. (*or* gum benjamin) A fragrant gum resin obtained from the trunk of a SE Asian tree, *Styrax benzoin*. It is used in medicine (as a constituent of friar's balsam), in cosmetics, and in perfumery.

Ben-Zvi, Itzhak (1884–1963) Israeli statesman; president (1952–63). Born in Russia, where he was an active Zionist, he went to Palestine in 1907. With David *Ben-Gurion, Ben-Zvi helped to found the state of Israel (1947). He was also a noted archeologist.

Beowulf An Anglo-Saxon epic poem preserved in a late 10th-century manuscript. Probably composed or at least reworked in the 8th century by a Christian poet sympathetic to pagan ideals of honor and courage, it alludes to historical events of early 6th-century Scandinavia. In the first part the hero, Beowulf, kills the marauding monster, Grendel, and when Grendel's mother attempts vengeance he tracks her to her underwater cave and kills her. In the second part, Beowulf, now king of the Swedish tribe of Geats, slays a dragon and seizes its hoard of treasure, but is mortally wounded.

Bérain the Elder, Jean (1637–1711) French designer, engraver, and painter; royal designer to Louis XIV of France. He designed festival decorations, furniture, tapestries, and opera costumes for the court, often decorated with immense detail, which influenced the later rococo style. He used many Chinese motifs in his designs to satisfy the king's fondness for oriental art.

Beranger, Pierre Jean de (1780–1857) French poet and songwriter. His satirical verse and republican sentiments led to his imprisonment under the Bourbon monarchy.

Berbera 10 30N 45 25E A port in N Somalia, on the Gulf of Aden. It has a deepwater harbor and exports sheep, leather, ghee, frankincense, and myrrh. Population (1980 est): 65,000.

Berberis A genus of deciduous or evergreen spiny shrubs (over 400 species), commonly known as barberry, mostly native to Central and E Asia and South America but also occurring in parts of Europe, Africa, and North America. The small yellow or orange flowers usually grow in clusters and the fruits are bright-red berries. Several species are widely grown as ornamentals for their flowers, fruits, or attractive autumn foliage. Berberis is implicated in a rust disease of wheat and is therefore outlawed in some areas. Family: *Berberidaceae*.

Berbers A Muslim people occupying parts of N Africa (Morocco, Algeria, Tunisia, and adjacent regions) and speaking a non-Semitic language. Prior to the Arab conquests of the 7th century AD and the establishment of Arabic speech, Berber languages were spoken over the whole of the area from Egypt to the Atlantic. Though Arabic has long been the dominant language it has not entirely ousted Berber, which is spoken by an estimated ten million people, and Morocco is still predominantly Berber in population. The Berbers played an important role in the Islamic conquest of the Iberian peninsula in the 8th century and in the subsequent occupation of Spain. The Berbers are largely agriculturalists, although some still follow a nomadic way of life.

Berchtesgaden 47 38N 13 00E A resort in SE West Germany, in the Bavarian Alps. It is the site of Hitler's fortified mountain retreat, the Berghof. Salt has been mined here since the 12th century. Population (1970 est): 39,800.

Berdyaev, Nikolai (1874–1948) Russian mystical philosopher. He was expelled from Russia (1922) for teaching religion and until World War II his academy near Paris and his journal *The Path* spread his ideas in Europe. He saw communism as an ungodly manifestation of Russia's messianic destiny. *Dreams and Reality* (1950) summarizes his ideas.

Berdyansk (name from 1939 until 1958: Osipenko) 46 45N 36 47E A port in the SW Soviet Union, in the Ukrainian SSR on the Sea of Azov. It is a seaside resort and its most important economic activities relate to fishing. Flour milling and oil refining are also carried out. Population (1977 est): 119,000.

Berenson, Bernard (1865–1959) US art historian, whose works set new standards of criticism. Inspired by the beauty of Italy, where he spent most of his life, he wrote the definitive *Italian Painters of the Renaissance* (1894–1907). His aesthetic delight is captured in *Drawings of the Florentine Painters* (1903).

Berezniki 59 26N 56 49E A port in the E Soviet Union, in the RSFSR on the Kama River. Founded in 1883, it is now one of the largest centers for the chemical industry in the Soviet Union. Population (1981 est): 188,000.

Berg, Alban (1885–1935) Austrian composer. A friend and pupil of *Schoenberg, he adopted *atonality and used *serialism, though in a highly personal and original fashion. His greatest works are the operas *Wozzeck* (1915–21) from the play by *Büchner and *Lulu* (1928–35) from plays by *Wedekind, the intensely personal *Lyric Suite* (for string quartet; 1925–26), and a violin concerto (1935).

Bergamo 45 42N 9 40E A city in Italy, in Lombardy in the foothills of the Alps. It has a 12th-century romanesque cathedral. Machinery, textiles, and cement are manufactured. Population (1980 est): 124,150.

bergamot A tree, *Citrus bergamia*, closely related to the orange. An essence (oil of bergamot) extracted from the rind of its fruit is used in perfumery, for which the tree is cultivated in S Italy and Sicily. *See* Citrus.

The name is also given to two plants of the mint family (*Labiatae*): *Mentha citrata*, which yields an extract similar to oil of bergamot, and *Monarda citriodora* (lemon bergamot) sometimes used in a tealike beverage.

Bergen 60 23N 5 20E A seaport and second largest city in Norway, situated in the SW. Founded about 1070 AD, it became the chief commercial city and the country's capital (12th–13th centuries). It had important connections with Hanseatic merchants (14th–18th centuries). It was rebuilt after damage by fire in 1702, 1855, and 1916 and by bombing during World War II. It is a cultural center with a university (1948), several museums, and an art gallery. Other notable buildings include the 12th-century Maria-kirke (a stone-built church) and the 13th-century Håkonshall (a royal palace). Its industries include shipbuilding and oil refining. It exports fish products and base metals. Population (1981 est): 207,799.

Bergenia A genus of herbaceous perennial plants (6 species), native to central and E Asia but often cultivated as ornamentals for their attractive foliage and early-blooming pink or white flowers. Family: *Saxifragaceae*.

Bergen op Zoom 51 30N 4 17E A port in the SW Netherlands, in North Brabant province. An important 15th-century cloth and fishing center, its industries now include oyster fisheries and iron and steel processing. Population (1981 est): 44,422.

Bergius, Friedrich (1884–1949) German chemist, who shared the 1931 Nobel Prize with C. Bosch for research in high-pressure chemical techniques. He manufactured light motor fuels from either coal or heavy petroleum residues by treating them with hydrogen under high pressure and temperature (1913). This process was used extensively by Germany in World War II. After Germany's defeat he emigrated to Spain and then to Argentina.

Bergman, Ingmar (1918–) Swedish film and stage director. His films, which express his austere human vision with great intensity, include *The Seventh Seal* (1956), *Wild Strawberries* (1957), *Persona* (1966), *Scenes from a Marriage* (1974), *Autumn Sonata* (1978), and *Fanny and Alexander* (1982). He was director of the Royal Dramatic Theater, Stockholm, from 1963 to 1966.

Bergman, Ingrid (1915–82) Swedish actress. She went to Hollywood in 1939 and became an international film star, appearing in such films as *Casablanca* (1942), *For Whom the Bell Tolls* (1943), *Notorious* (1946), and numerous other major films, her last being *Autumn Sonata* (1978). She also played in several notable stage productions. She received Academy Awards as best actress for *Gaslight* (1944) and *Anastasia* (1956).

Bergson, Henri (1859–1941) French philosopher and psychologist, one of the greatest thinkers of his time. To reconcile free will and *determinism, Bergson distinguishes between consciousness, an indivisible flow of cumulative states in which (free) will operates, and the external physical world where causality reigns and objects and events are fixed and discrete. He championed creative against analytic thinking in stylish and penetrating works that include *Matière et mémoire* (1896) and *L'Évolution créatrice* (1907). He won the Nobel Prize for Literature in 1927.

Beria, Lavrenti Pavlovich (1899–1953) Soviet politician. Head of the Soviet secret police from 1938, Beria became a member of the politburo (now the presidium) in 1946. After Stalin's death in March, 1953, he was involved in a power struggle with Malenkov and Khrushchev. He was accused of conspiracy in July, tried secretly, and executed in December.

beriberi A disease caused by deficiency of *vitamin B$_1$ (thiamine), common in areas where the staple diet is polished rice (thiamine occurs mainly in the rice husks). Dry beriberi affects the peripheral nerves, causing muscular weakness and pain. Wet beriberi is probably the result of combined protein malnutrition and thiamine deficiency: it causes accumulation of fluid and swelling of the limbs, leading eventually to heart failure. Treatment consists of providing a diet with adequate thiamine and vitamin supplements.

Bering, Vitus Jonassen (*or* V. J. Behring; 1681–1741) Danish navigator. In 1724 he was commissioned by the Russians to explore the area between Siberia and America. He made several voyages from Kamchatka on the last of which (1741) he sighted Alaska from the strait named for him. On his way back, suffering from scurvy, he was wrecked off Bering Island, where he died. The Bering Sea is also named for him.

Bering Sea A section of the N Pacific Ocean between the Soviet Union, Alaska, and the Aleutian Islands. Navigation is difficult, with storms and a partial ice covering in winter. The NE continental shelf contains oil and gas, as yet unexploited.

Bering Strait A narrow shallow channel between Asia and North America, connecting the Bering Sea with the Arctic Ocean. During the Ice Age it bridged the continents when the sea level fell.

Berkeley 37 53N 122 17W A city in California on San Francisco Bay. It is the headquarters of the University of California, where *berkelium was discovered. Its manufactures include soap, paint, and chemicals. Population (1980): 103,328.

Berkeley, Busby (William Berkeley Enos; 1895–1976) US dance director. He is best known for his elaborate choreography for Hollywood film musicals in the 1930s and 1940s. These include *42nd Street* (1933), the *Gold Diggers* series (1933–37), and *Babes in Arms* (1939).

Berkeley, George (1685–1753) Irish bishop and idealist philosopher. In *A New Theory of Vision* (1709), *Principles of Human Knowledge* (1710), and *Three Dialogues between Hylas and Philonous* (1713), he argued that the material world exists only in being perceived by the mind, a view that influenced *Hume and, indirectly, *Kant. Berkeley's later works, such as *Siris* (1744) are interesting but increasingly eccentric.

Berkeley, Sir William (1606–77) English colonist; governor of Virginia (1641–49, 1660–77). His attempts to foster trade relations with the Indians were thwarted by Nathaniel Bacon (1647–76), who led a force against the Indians that was defeated by Berkeley's troops (Bacon's Rebellion). Berkeley is also noted as the author of a play, *The Lost Lady* (1638).

berkelium (Bk) A synthetic transuranic element synthesized by Seaborg and others in 1949 by bombarding americium with helium ions. The longest-lived isotope (^{249}Bk) has a half-life of 314 days; visible amounts of the chloride (BkCl$_3$) have been produced. At no 97; at wt (247).

Berkshire A county of S England. Under local government reorganization in 1974 it lost a substantial part of the NW to Oxfordshire, while gaining part of SW Buckinghamshire, including Slough. It consists mainly of lowlands rising to the Berkshire Downs in the N. It is bordered by the River Thames in the NE and crossed by the River Kennet. It is predominantly agricultural; chief products are barley, dairy produce, pigs, and poultry. Industries include paints, plastics, and pharmaceutical goods at Slough and light engineering and horticulture at Reading; the Atomic Research Establishment is at Aldermaston. Area: 485 sq mi (1256 sq km). Population (1981): 675,153. Administrative center: Reading.

Berle, Adolf Augustus, Jr. (1895–1971) US lawyer and statesman. A member of Pres. Franklin D. *Roosevelt's "Brain Trust," he was a planner for both the federal government and New York State from 1934 until 1937. He was US assistant secretary of state for Latin American affairs (1938–44), ambassador to Brazil (1945–46), and special adviser on Latin America during Pres. John F. Kennedy's administration.

Berlichingen, Götz von (1480–1562) German knight and mercenary. A professional adventurer, he was already famous for his exploits, in which he lost his right hand, when he became a rebel leader in the *Peasants' War (1525). After a period of imprisonment he continued his career, serving Emperor Charles V against the Turks in the 1540s. His exploits inspired Goethe's *Götz von Berlichingen* (1773).

Berlin 52 31N 13 20E A city in N Germany, on the Spree River, divided since 1948 into East Berlin, now capital of the German Democratic Republic (East Germany), and West Berlin, part of the Federal Republic of Germany (West Germany). *History*: founded in the 13th century, it was an important strategic and commercial center and a member of the Hanseatic League. Its independence was reduced by the *Hohenzollern Electors of Brandenburg from the 15th century, but it became their capital and grew in importance with their increasing power, becoming the capital of Prussia in the 18th century and of the German Empire in 1871. Badly damaged in World War II, it was occupied by the four major powers after the defeat of Germany. In 1948 Berlin became two separate administrative units: Soviet-controlled East Berlin and West Berlin, formed from the US, UK, and French zones. The Soviet Union blockaded the city for almost a year but it failed to extend its influence to West Berlin (*see* Berlin airlift). In 1961 a dividing wall was built to curb the flow of refugees from E to W.

East Berlin The capital of East Germany. Postwar recovery has been slower than in West Berlin. Industrial products include electrical goods, chemicals, machinery, and clothing. At the border with West Berlin stands the *Brandenburg Gate, E of which runs the Unter den Linden (the famous tree-lined avenue), carefully restored in the 1960s. But the Wilhelmstrasse, where Hitler had his chancellery, has failed to regain its former impor-

BERLIN   *King Edward VII and Queen Alexandra of Great Britain entering Berlin through the Brandenburg Gate on a state visit to the Emperor William II in 1906.*

tance. East Berlin is the site of Humboldt University, formerly Frederick William University (1810), where famous scholars such as Humboldt, Fichte, Hegel, and Ranke worked. Area: 156 sq mi (403 sq km). Population (1980 est): 1,145,743.

West Berlin The largest city and a *Land* of West Germany, forming an enclave within East Germany. Despite difficulties in communications it is an active industrial and commercial center, subsidized by West Germany. Its numerous industries include the manufacture of electrical equipment, clothing, and chemicals as well as publishing and printing. A major landmark is the Kaiser Wilhelm Church, the ruins of which have been preserved as a reminder of the World Wars. The Free University of Berlin was established in 1948. Area: 188 sq mi (480 sq km). Population (1980 est): 1,898,900.

Berlin, Congress of   (1878) A meeting of European powers, which revised the Treaty of *San Stefano that had ended the 1877–78 Russo-Turkish War. The Congress, which was dominated by the German chancellor, *Bismarck, limited Russian naval expansion, permitted Austria-Hungary to occupy Bosnia-Herzegovina, and gained Turkish recognition of the independence of Serbia, Romania, and Montenegro and of Bulgarian autonomy under Turkish suzerainty.

Berlin, Irving   (Israel Baline; 1888–   ) US composer of musical comedies and film scores, born in Russia. He emigrated with his family to the US in 1893. He wrote "Alexander's Ragtime Band" while working as a singing waiter and subsequently composed the music for many musicals, including *Annie Get Your Gun* (1946), *Call Me Madam* (1950), and *Mr President* (1962). His songs include "God Bless America," "White Christmas," and "Blue Skies."

Berlin, Sir Isaiah   (1909–   ) British philosopher and historian. Although based mostly in Oxford, he was also a diplomat in Washington and Moscow. His works include *The Inevitability of History* (1954), *The Age of Enlightenment* (1956), and *Two Concepts of Liberty* (1959).

Berlin airlift   (1948–49)   An operation by the Allies after World War II to supply isolated West Berlin with the necessities of life. In 1948 the Soviet Union cut off all rail, road, and water links with the city in an attempt to force the Allies to abandon their rights there. The airlift continued until the blockade was lifted as a result of an embargo on exports from the E European states.

Berliner Ensemble   A theater company founded by Bertolt *Brecht in East Berlin in 1949. It became fully independent after its move to the Theater am Schiffbauerdamm in 1945 and was directed after Brecht's death in 1956 by his widow, Helene Weigel (1900–71). The company devoted itself exclusively to works written or adapted by Brecht, and its several European tours won international acclaim for his work.

Berlin West Africa Conference   (1884–85) A series of meetings held at Berlin under the chairmanship of *Bismarck to settle the dispute over possession of the Congo Basin (Central Africa). Among the powers that attended were France, Germany, the UK, Belgium, and Portugal. The Conference declared that the Congo Basin should be neutral with free trade and shipping and that an independent Congo Free State be established; it forbade slave trading.

Berlioz, (Louis) Hector   (1803–69) French Romantic composer and conductor. Against family opposition he abandoned medicine for music. His first successful work, the *Symphonie Fantastique* (1830–31), was influenced by his love for an Irish actress, Harriet Smithson (1800–54). As winner of the Prix de Rome he went to Italy to study; on his return in 1833 he married Harriet. His dramatic symphony *Harold in Italy* (1834) and choral symphony *Romeo and Juliet* (1839) were popular successes, but the cantata *The Damnation of Faust* (1846) and the opera *Benvenuto Cellini* (1834–38) failed. The oratorio *The Childhood of Christ* (1850–54) was his last major success, for his two-part opera *The Trojans* (1856–59) was not performed complete in his lifetime. Other orchestral works include the overture *Le Corsair* (1851–52) and *Le Carnaval romain* (1844). He was the author of a famous treatise on orchestration and a volume of memoirs.

Bermejo, Río   A river of S central South America. Rising in S Bolivia, it flows SE into Argentina to join the Paraguay River. Length: 650 mi (1046 km).

Bermuda   A British crown colony, comprising some 300 coral islands (of which 20 are inhabited), in the W Atlantic Ocean. The largest island is Bermuda (or Great Bermuda), while smaller ones include Somerset, Ireland, and St George. *Economy:* the subtropical climate with its mild winters has contributed to tourism, which forms the basis of the islands' economy. Agricultural products include vegetables and bananas; onions, potatoes, and lily bulbs are exported to the US. *History:* visited by the Spanish navigator Juan de Bermudez, they were first settled in 1609. They became self-governing in 1968 but demands for independence have grown; the governor was assassinated in 1973 and there was serious rioting in December, 1977. The island's governor, Sir Richard Posnett, resigned in 1983 after accusations of irregularities in his expense account. Governor: Viscount Dunrossil. Official language: English. Official currency: Bermuda dollar of 100 cents. Area: 20 sq mi (53 sq km). Population (1983 est): 58,000. Capital: Hamilton.

Bermuda Triangle The most notorious of several geographic regions, all lying roughly between 30° and 40° of latitude, in which numerous ships and aircraft have vanished without trace. The Triangle covers about 1,500,000 sq mi (3,900,000 sq km) between Bermuda, Florida, and Puerto Rico. No generally satisfactory explanation of these disappearances has been advanced, but the great depth of the sea and powerful currents may explain the lack of wreckage.

Bern (French name: Berne) 46 57N 95 58W The capital of Switzerland, on the Aare River. Founded as a military post in the 12th century, it joined the Swiss Confederation in 1353 and became the capital in 1848. Its many notable buildings include the gothic cathedral (15th century). Since the 16th century it has had a bear pit, now maintained as a tourist attraction. The university was founded in 1834. It has considerable industry and contains the headquarters of several international organizations. Population (1980 est): 145,254.

Bernadette of Lourdes, St (1844–79) French peasant girl, who in 1858 claimed to have had 18 visions of the Virgin Mary at a grotto near Lourdes. At 20 she became a nun. She was canonized in 1933. The shrine built at the spot is a place of international pilgrimage where miraculous cures are claimed to have occurred. Feast day: Feb 18 or April 16.

Bernadotte, Folke, Count (1895–1948) The nephew of Gustavus V of Sweden (1858–1950; reigned 1907–50). He became president of the Swedish Red Cross in 1946. In 1948 he was appointed mediator in Palestine but was assassinated by Jewish terrorists.

Bernadotte, Jean Baptiste Jules (c. 1763–1844) French marshal, who was King of Sweden (1818–44) as Charles XIV John, founding the present Swedish royal house. Rising from the ranks, he became famous under Napoleon with whose support in 1810 Bernadotte was adopted as heir by the dying Charles XIII of Sweden. Turning against Napoleon, Bernadotte contributed to his defeat at Leipzig (1813). In 1814 he forced Denmark to cede Norway to the Swedish monarchy.

Bernanos, Georges (1888–1948) French novelist and Catholic polemicist. His constant theme was the war between good and evil, characteristically portrayed in his best-known book, *The Diary of a Country Priest* (1936). Disturbed by European political trends, he lived in exile in Brazil from 1938 to 1945.

Bernard, Claude (1813–78) French physiologist, who helped establish the experimental principles used in modern research. A student of François *Magendie, Bernard discovered that a secretion of the pancreas breaks down fat into its constituents and that the liver is able to synthesize glucose from glycogen. He also showed how blood flow through capillaries is regulated by contraction of their walls, controlled by vasoconstrictor nerves. Bernard developed the concept of the internal environment (*milieu intérieur*) of the body, the regulation of which is a basic physiological function.

Bernardin de Saint-Pierre, Jacques Henri (1737–1814) French naturalist and writer. He was a disciple of Rousseau, whose ideas influenced the didactic romance for which he is chiefly remembered, *Paul et Virginie* (1787), which is set on the island of Mauritius.

Bernard of Chartres (died c. 1130) French scholastic philosopher, who taught at Chartres (1114–24). A Platonist, he held a realist theory of universals (*see* realism) but tried to reconcile Platonic and Aristotelian metaphysics. His only extant work is a treatise on Neoplatonism.

Bernard of Clairvaux, St (1090–1153) French theologian and Doctor of the Church. A Cistercian, he established in 1115 a monastery at Clairvaux that became a model of reform and influenced other monasteries in France and elsewhere. He was chosen by Pope Eugenius III to preach the second Crusade in 1146. His faith was based on an exalted mysticism, which is the subject of many of his Latin writings. Feast day: Aug 20. Emblem: a beehive.

Bernard of Menthon, St (923–1008) Italian churchman and vicar general of the diocese of Aosta. A native of Savoy, he established hospices on two Alpine passes, which are named for— him, as are the dogs that were kept by the monks and trained to aid travelers. Feast day: May 28.

Berne Convention An international *copyright agreement of 1866. Its main provision guarantees copyright in all signatory countries of any work copyrighted in any one of them. The US is still not a signatory.

Bernese Oberland (*or* Bernese Alps) A section of the Alps in SW Switzerland, 65 mi (105 km) long, between the Rhône and Aare Rivers. Its mountain peaks include the Eiger and the Finsteraarhorn and it is a popular area for mountain climbing.

Bernhard of Saxe-Weimar, Duke (1604–39) German general, who fought for the Protestants in the *Thirty Years' War. He took command of

the forces of Gustavus Adolphus on Gustavus' death in 1632 and campaigned successfully in S Germany. After losing at Nördlingen (1634) he held command for the French in SW Germany.

SARAH BERNHARDT *In the role of Hamlet at a London theater (1889).*

Bernhardt, Sarah (Sarah Henriette Rosine Bernard; 1844–1923) French actress. Her voice and emotional power were especially suited to tragic roles. Plays in which she gave notable performances include *Phèdre* (1879), *La Dame aux camélias*, and *L'Aiglon* by Edmond Rostand. Her worldwide tours gained her international acclaim. She was also manager of several theaters in Paris and opened the old Théâtre des Nations as the Théâtre Sarah Bernhardt.

Bernina, Piz 46 23N 9 54E A mountain in SE Switzerland, in the Alps near St Moritz. Height: 13,284 ft (4049 m).

Bernini, Gian Lorenzo (1598–1680) Italian *baroque sculptor and architect, born in Naples, the son of a sculptor. Precociously talented, he worked chiefly in □Rome under papal patronage. His first major sculptures were for Cardinal Scipione Borghese and included *Apollo and Daphne* (1622–24; Borghese Gallery, Rome). Encouraged by Urban VIII, he extended his talents into the fields of painting and, more successfully, architecture, major works being the baldachin over the tomb of St Peter (1624–33) and the piazza and colonnade (1656–67) of St Peter's, Rome. Later sculptures included fountains for Roman piazzas, *The Ecstasy of St Teresa* (1645–52; Cornaro Chapel, Sta Maria della Vittoria, Rome), and such portrait busts as *Louis XIV* (1665; Versailles).

Bernoulli A family of notable Swiss mathematicians and physicists, who, as Flemish Protestants, were driven out of the Netherlands in the 1580s. The most famous was **Daniel Bernoulli** (1700–82), who made important contributions to fluid dynamics, especially his discovery in 1738 of *Bernoulli's principle concerning the speed and pressure of fluid flow. He also attempted to explain the properties of gases at varying temperatures and pressures by regarding the gas as consisting of many tiny particles. His father **Jean Bernoulli** (1667–1748) and uncle **Jacques Bernoulli** (1654–1705) were both eminent mathematicians, who often worked together and jointly developed the calculus of variations. Jean also made discoveries in *probability theory and Jacques in *complex numbers. Daniel's brother **Nicolas Bernoulli** (1695–1726) also contributed to the theory of probability.

Bernoulli's principle The principle of conservation of energy applied to fluid flow. If the effects of friction are neglected the total energy of the flow at any point in a pipe is equal to the sum of the kinetic energy due to the flow velocity, the gravitational potential energy due to height, and the energy of pressure in the fluid itself. Bernoulli's theorem states that the sum of these three components is constant throughout a flow system. Named for Daniel *Bernoulli.

Bernstein, Eduard (1850–1932) German politician. A journalist, Bernstein joined the Socialist Democratic Party in 1872. In 1878 he was exiled from Germany on account of his political beliefs. He returned to Berlin in 1901, becoming the leader of the revisionist movement. He was elected to the Reichstag in 1902. As a protest against his party's support of World War I, he joined the Independent Social Democrats. His most important book, *Evolutionary Socialism* (1898), contains his criticisms of Marxist theory.

Bernstein, Leonard (1918–) US conductor, composer, and pianist. From 1958 to 1969 he was musical director and conductor of the New York Philharmonic Orchestra (1958–69) and became famous for his concerts and recordings. He composed symphonies, choral works, and songs, often containing jazz and folk elements, including *Jeremiah* (1944), *Fancy Free* (1944), and *Chichester Psalms* (1965). His musicals, such as *On the Town* (1944) and *West Side Story* (1957), have been widely popular. □Stern, Isaac.

Berre, Étang de 43 27N 5 05E A saltwater lagoon in S France, in the Bouches-du-Rhône department. Connected by canal to the Mediterranean Sea (through the Rove tunnel) and the Gulf of Fos, it has important oil refineries and saltworks situated around its shores. Area: 60 sq mi (155 sq km).

Berruguete, Pedro (c. 1450–c. 1504) Castillian Renaissance painter. In the 1470s he worked in Italy at the court of Urbino, where he painted *Federigo da Montefeltro and his Son* (Urbino). On returning to Spain (1482), he painted frescoes for Toledo cathedral and altarpieces for the Dominican order in Avila. His son **Alonso Berruguete** (c. 1489–1561) was a mannerist painter and sculptor, who worked in Italy (c. 1504–c. 1517) and became court painter to Emperor Charles V (1518). He combined his talents in his masterpiece the San Benito altarpiece (now dismantled) in Valladolid.

berry Loosely, any small succulent *fruit. Botanically, a berry is a simple fruit with a thin skin and pulpy flesh containing many loose seeds: the tomato and grape are examples. Blackberries and raspberries are not strictly berries, but collections of small *drupes.

Berry A French province that was sold to the crown by the Viscount of Bourges in 1101 and was absorbed by the departments of Cher and Indre in 1790.

Berry, Chuck (Charles Edward B.; 1926–) US singer and songwriter, who was one of the first musicians to popularize rock and roll. His songs, such as "Maybellene," "Johnny B. Goode," and "Roll Over, Beethoven" influenced the Beatles, the Rolling Stones, and others.

Berry, Jean de France, Duc de (1340–1416) The third son of John II of France, who was appointed (1358) governor of Auvergne, Languedoc, Périgord, and Poitou, where his repressive policies caused a peasants' revolt (1381–84). He was coregent during the minority (1380–88) of his nephew Charles VI.

Berry, Marie-Caroline de Bourbon-Sicile, Duchesse de (1798–1870) The wife of Charles, Duc de Berry (1778–1820), the son of Charles X of France. After Charles X's death, she conspired to obtain the French throne for her son Henri, Comte de Chambord (1820–83), instigating an unsuccessful revolt in the Vendée (1832).

Berryman, John (1914–72) US poet. On the University of Minnesota faculty from 1955, his poetry is collected in *Poems* (1942), *The Dispossessed* (1948), *Homage to Mistress Bradstreet* (1956), *Berryman's Sonnets* (1967), *Love and Fame* (1971), and *Delusions* (1972; posthumously). *The Dream Songs* (1969) includes *77 Dream Songs* (1964; Pulitzer Prize) and *His Toy, His Dream, His Rest* (1968). He also wrote a critical biography, *Stephen Crane* (1950); a novel, *Recovery* (1973), was published after his suicide in 1972.

berserkers (Old Norse: bear-shirts) In Scandinavian mythology, savage warriors whose frenzy in battle transformed them from men into wolves or bears and made them immune from being harmed by the sword or fire. In the frenzy of battle they would howl and foam at the mouth—hence the phrase "to go berserk." They were devotees of *Odin and, in early Scandi-navian history, warriors called berserkers were often employed as bodyguards to nobles.

Berthelot, (Pierre Eugène) Marcelin (1827–1907) French chemist and politician, who became professor at the Collège de France (1865). A pioneer of organic chemical synthesis, he demolished the theory that organic compounds contained a "vital force." As a student of chemical thermodynamics he distinguished between endothermic and exothermic reactions, but wrongly concluded that the heat of a reaction was its driving force. He became a senator in 1881 and foreign secretary in 1895.

Berthollet, Claude Louis, Comte (1748–1822) French chemist and physician. He discovered potassium chlorate and introduced bleaching by chlorine; he also showed that ammonia consists of hydrogen and nitrogen. Berthollet helped to clarify the concept of chemical affinity and, working with *Lavoisier, developed a new chemical nomenclature. He traveled to Egypt as scientific adviser to Napoleon, who made him a senator and a count.

Bertillon, Alphonse (1853–1914) French criminal investigator, who developed a system for identifying criminals based on the description and measurement of physical characteristics. The system, also known as anthropometry, was eventually superseded by fingerprinting techniques. His brother **Jacques Bertillon** (1851–1922) was a statistician. As head of the Paris bureau of social statistics, he developed new systems of data analysis. He was particularly interested in the high incidence of alcoholism in France and the decline of the French population in comparison with rates in other countries.

Bertolucci, Bernardo (1940–) Italian film director. Many of his films are strongly influenced by Marxist ideology, notably *Before the Revolution* (1965) and the epic *1900* (1977). He achieved his greatest commercial success with the controversial *Last Tango in Paris* (1972).

Bertrand, Henri Gratien, Comte (1773–1844) French marshal, who in 1804 became an aide de camp to Napoleon, whose complete trust he won. He accompanied Napoleon into exile, both to Elba and St Helena, where he kept a diary that is an important historical source.

Bertran de Born (?1140–?1215) French knight and troubador poet. He composed lyrics glorifying love, ambition, and especially war. His castle at Hautefort was besieged and captured by Richard Lionheart, whose loyal officer he became.

Berwick, James Fitzjames, Duke of (1670–1734) Marshal of France, who was the illegitimate son of James II of England. He was educated in France and gained military experience in Europe. On the deposition of James (1688), Berwick supported his attempts to regain the throne and played a prominent part in the battle of the *Boyne. His victory in the employ of France at Almansa (1707) established Philip V on the Spanish throne. He was killed besieging Philippsburg in the War of the Polish Succession.

beryl A mineral consisting of beryllium alumino-silicate, found principally in granites and granite pegmatites. It occurs as crystals up to one meter in length and is white, pale blue, or green. It is the chief source of beryllium. *Aquamarine and *emerald are gem varieties. *See* Plate III.

beryllium (Be) A light (relative density 2.34) alkaline-earth metal that was discovered in 1828 by F. Wöhler and A. Bussy (1794–1882) independently. Its salts are highly toxic and require careful handling. It occurs in nature in such minerals as *beryl and phenacite (Be_2SiO_4). It is transparent to X-rays and is used as windows on X-ray tubes. Alloys with copper are extensively used and the oxide (BeO), having a high melting point (4590°F [2530°C]), is used as a ceramic. At no 4; at wt 9.0122; mp 741°F (1278°C); bp 1392°F (2450°C).

Berzelius, Jöns Jakob, Baron (1779–1848) Swedish chemist, whose main work was the discovery of atomic compositions of chemical compounds. He discovered the elements selenium (1817), silicon (1824), and thorium (1828) and determined the atomic and molecular weights of more than 2000 elements and compounds. He introduced the current notation for chemical formulae and the use of oxygen as a reference standard for atomic weights. Following the invention of electric cells, Berzelius experimented on electrolysis and developed a theory of electrostatic bonding in compounds. He published a standard textbook of chemistry in 1830.

Bes The Egyptian god of recreation, also associated with children and childbirth. Images of the god, represented as a grotesque dwarf with a tail, were kept in homes as protection against evil.

Besançon 47 14N 6 02E A city in E France, the capital of the Doubs department on the Doubs River. It has a cathedral (11th–13th centuries) and a university (1691). Victor Hugo was born here. It is the French watchmaking center and produces automobiles and textiles. Population (1975): 126,187.

Bessarabia A region in the SW Soviet Union, largely in the Moldavian and Ukrainian SSRs and with a predominantly Moldavian population. Bessarabia is very fertile, the main crops being wine grapes, fruit, wheat, and tobacco; cattle and sheep are raised. The chief industry is agricultural processing. *History*: the region was colonized by the Greeks and later fell successively to the Romans, Huns, Magyars, Mongols, and Turks, passing to Russia in 1812. In 1918 Bessarabia declared its independence, later voting for union with Romania. In 1940 Romania ceded Bessarabia to the Soviet Union. Area: about 17,100 sq mi (44,300 sq km).

Bessarion, John (c. 1400–72) Greek scholar and cardinal. As Archbishop of Nicaea, he attempted to unite the Byzantine and Western Churches, eventually joining the latter and settling in Italy, where he became a cardinal in 1439. He was an outstanding scholar and exercised an important influence in introducing the study of Greek in the Renaissance. His large library of Greek manuscripts is preserved in Venice.

Bessemer, Sir Henry (1813–98) British engineer and inventor, who patented (1855) a process for manufacturing cheap steel (*see* Bessemer process). His Sheffield steelworks, built in 1859, are still producing steel. Bessemer was a prolific inventor, patenting some 114 inventions.

Bessemer process A steelmaking process invented by Sir Henry *Bessemer in 1855. A long cylindrical vessel (Bessemer converter) is charged with molten pig iron; air, introduced through holes in the bottom of the converter, is blown through the iron to oxidize the carbon, silicon, and manganese impurities. Phosphorus is removed by reaction with the converter's basic refractory lining. Carbon, in the form of spiegel, is then added to give steel of the required carbon content. In the modern VLN (very low nitrogen) process, a mixture of oxygen and steam is blown through the iron instead of air, to avoid absorption of nitrogen by the steel.

Best, Charles Herbert (1899–1978) US physiologist, who, as an undergraduate research assistant to *Banting, helped discover the technique for isolating the hormone insulin from pancreatic tissue in 1921. Best also discovered choline, a B vitamin. The Banting and Best department of medical research was created at Toronto University in 1923.

bestiary A medieval treatise containing short accounts of different species of animal, both real and imaginary. Based on ancient Greek and Latin sources, bestiaries were very popular and were often fancifully illustrated. They were generally wildly inaccurate in their natural history, as their compilers were more interested in the morals to be drawn from each beast's real or supposed attributes than in scientific fact.

Bestuzhev-Riumin, Aleksei Petrovich, Count (1693–1766) Russian statesman. Bestuzhev served as a diplomat abroad until 1740. In the reign of the empress *Elizabeth he directed foreign policy and was Russia's chancellor from 1744 to 1758. He allied Russia with Austria and Britain against France and Prussia, a policy made obsolete by the realignment of European alliances on the eve of the *Seven Years' War. He was dismissed in 1758 and banished to his estate.

Beta Centauri A remote yet conspicuous blue giant, apparent magnitude 0.63 and about 425 light years distant, that is the second brightest star in the constellation Centaurus.

beta decay A radioactive process in which a neutron within a nucleus decays by the *weak interaction into a proton, an electron (beta particle), and an antineutrino; alternatively, a proton may decay into a neutron, a positron, and a neutrino. Since the nuclear charge changes by one in both cases, the nucleus is converted into the nucleus of another element.

betatron A type of particle *accelerator used for producing very high energy electrons. The electrons are accelerated around a circular path in an evacuated torus-shaped chamber, by means of a large pulsed magnetic field. Electron energies up to 300 MeV have been produced.

betel A mixture of the boiled dried seeds (**betel nuts**) of the areca, or betel palm (*Areca catechu*), and the leaves of the betel pepper (*Piper betle*), which produces copious salivation when chewed with lime—a practice common among the populations of S Asia and the East Indies. Betel nuts contain an alkaloid of some value in expelling intestinal worms, and the mild stimulation resulting from chewing the mixture has led to its use in some religious ceremonies.

Betelgeuse An immense remote yet conspicuous red supergiant, over 500 light years distant, that is the second brightest star in the constellation *Orion. It is a *variable star with its magnitude ranging, usually, from 0.3 to 0.9 over a period of about 5.8 years.

Bethany (present-day name: Al-'Ayzariyah) 31 46N 35 15E A village on the *West Bank of the Jordan River, near Jerusalem. It is now named for Lazarus, whom Christ resurrected here (John 11.1–44).

Bethe, Hans Albrecht (1906–) US physicist, born in Germany. After studying under *Rutherford he returned to Germany but left when Hitler came to power. After two years in England he finally settled in the US, working on the atom bomb during World War II. His earlier researches in quantum electrodynamics proved valuable in working out the details of the nuclear fusion process that occurs in stars. For this work he received the 1967 Nobel Prize.

Bethlehem 31 42N 35 12E A city on the *West Bank of the Jordan River, near Jerusalem. The Church of the Nativity was built in 326 over the grotto that is the presumed birthplace of Jesus Christ. A university was founded here in 1973. Population (1975 est): 30,000.

Bethlehem 40 36N 75 22W A city in the US, in Pennsylvania. A major steel center, it also has cement, textile, and electrical-equipment industries. Population (1980): 70,419.

Bethlen, Gábor (1580–1629) Prince of Transylvania (1613–29), a Protestant, who opposed Emperor Ferdinand II during the Thirty Years' War. Bethlen, after seizing northern Hungary, was elected King in 1620 but renounced the crown (1621) in exchange for Ferdinand's agreement to allow Hungarian Protestants to worship freely. Bethlen again took up arms against Ferdinand in 1623 and 1626 but then withdrew from the war.

Bethmann-Hollweg, Theobald von (1856–1921) German statesman. As minister of the interior, secretary of state, and chancellor (1909–17) successively, he instituted a number of electoral and legal reforms. In 1914, attempting to justify aggressive German foreign policy, he described the treaty guaranteeing Belgian neutrality as a "scrap of paper." In 1917 his efforts to secure a negotiated peace led to his overthrow by *Ludendorff and *Hindenburg.

Bethune, Mary McLeod (1875–1955) US educator and public official. Born in South Carolina of former slaves, she founded the Daytona Normal and Industrial Institute for Girls (Bethune-Cookman College since 1923) in Florida in 1904 and was the college's president (1923–42). She was also founder of the National Council of Negro Women in 1935 and was active in government affairs for minority groups.

Béthune 50 32N 2 38E A city in France, in the Pas-de-Calais department. An important coalmining center, it also produces beet sugar and textiles. Population (1975): 28,279.

Betjeman, Sir John (1906–84) British poet. He published his first book of poetry in 1933. His verse autobiography, *Summoned by Bells* (1960), reflected the nostalgia and gentle social satire characteristic of his other poems. He also revived and fostered interest in Victorian and Edwardian architecture. He became England's poet laureate in 1972 and served until his death.

betony A perennial herb, *Stachys officinalis* (or *Betonica officinalis*), up to 12 in (30 cm) high. It has round-toothed leaves and a dense head of reddish-purple tubular flowers arising from a square stem. Betony is found on open grassland, heaths, and hedgerows from Eurasia to N Africa. The leaves may be used for tea and for herbal tobacco. Family: *Labiatae*.

Bettelheim, Bruno (1903–) US psychologist; born in Austria. After spending a year in German concentration camps, he came to the US (1939). From 1944, he taught educational psychology at the University of Chicago. His article "Individual and Mass Behavior in Extreme Situations" (1943) examined the human mind and stresses in the concentration camps. His theories about and work with disturbed children are documented in *Love is Not Enough* (1950) and *Truants From Life* (1954). Other works include *Dynamics of Prejudice* (1950), *The Empty Fortress* (1967), and *The Uses of Enchantment* (1976).

Betti, Ugo (1892–1953) Italian dramatist. He studied law and became a magistrate and, after 1944, librarian at the Ministry of Justice. The themes of many of his 26 plays, notably *Corruption in the Palace of Justice* (1944) and *The Fugitive* (1953), concern justice and social responsibility.

Beust, Friedrich Ferdinand, Count von (1809–86) German statesman; the chief opponent of *Bismarck. As prime minister of Saxony (1853–66) he allied Saxony with Austria in the Austro-Prussian War of 1866. He became chancellor of the Austrian Empire in 1867 and negotiated the *Augsleich* that established the Dual Monarchy of *Austria-Hungary. In domestic policy he was a liberal constitutionalist.

Bevan, Aneurin (1897–1960) British politician. A brilliant orator, Bevan clashed with the Labour Party in 1939 over its ambivalence toward Hitler. As minister of health (1945–51), he was the architect of the *National Health Service.

bevatron A type of *synchrotron used for accelerating protons at Berkeley, California. It can produce protons with energies up to 6 GeV.

Beverly Hills A city in California. A residential suburb of Los Angeles, it is the home of many film and television celebrities. Population (1970): 33,400.

Bevin, Ernest (1881–1951) British politician and labor leader. Bevin formed, and was general secretary (1921–40) of, the Transport and General Workers' Union and in 1937 became chairman of the TUC. In 1940 he became minister of labor, serving in Churchill's war cabinet. He was foreign secretary (1945–51) in the postwar Labour government, when he contributed to the formation of NATO.

Beza, Theodore (1519–1605) French Calvinist theologian. Trained as a lawyer, he went to Geneva in 1548, having formally renounced the Roman Catholic faith. He became professor of Greek at Lausanne University and first rector of the Geneva Academy (1559), which Calvin had just founded for the education of Protestant theologians. He is remembered both as a Bible translator and a defender of Protestantism. After Calvin's death (1564) Beza succeeded to his leadership of the Swiss Calvinists.

Béziers 43 21N 3 13E A city in S France, in the Hérault department. In 1209 many of the inhabitants were massacred by Simon de Montfort during the crusade against the Albigenses. It is a commercial center for wines and spirits and its manufactures include chemicals and textiles. Population (1975): 85,677.

bezique A card game, usually for two players, that became popular in France about 1860. Two packs of 32 cards are used (standard packs with the cards from two to six removed). Each player is dealt eight cards; the next card indicates the trump suit and the rest form the stockpile. The object is to score points by collecting melds (certain combinations of cards) and to take tricks containing brisques (aces and tens). Play continues until one player's score reaches 1000 or 1500.

Bhagalpur 25 14N 86 59E A city in India, in Bihar. An agricultural trading center, its manufactures include textiles (especially silk). Its university was established in 1960. Population (1971): 172,202.

Bhagavadgita (Sanskrit: Song of the Lord) Hindu poem probably composed about 300 BC, forming part of the epic *Mahabharata*. It blends and reconciles a number of Hindu philosophies. Arjuna, one of the five Pandava brothers, is compelled to battle with his kinsmen, the Kauravas; he is persuaded by *Krishna, acting as his charioteer, of the virtue of selflessly performing the duties of caste. Krishna enumerates the ways by which one can attain liberation from the limitations of matter: by virtuous actions, by devotion to God, by philosophical speculation, by asceticism, or by meditation.

Bhamo 24 15N 97 15E A town in Burma, on the Irrawaddy River near the border with China. Principally a trading center, it has a government sugar factory.

Bharhut A Buddhist stupa (shrine) complex in Nagod state (N India), excavated in 1874. It provided evidence for the earliest phases of Buddhist architecture; carvings on the stone railings are the earliest representational reliefs from India (2nd century BC). Nothing now remains at the site.

Bhatpara 22 51N 88 31E A city in India, in West Bengal. It is an ancient seat of Sanskrit learning. Jute processing is the principal industry. Population (1971): 204,750.

Bhavachakra (Sanskrit: wheel of becoming) In Buddhism, an image of the cyclical nature of earthly existence, in the form of a wheel held by the demon of impermanence. Its segments represent the six possible states into which beings are reborn: the realms of gods, titans, hungry ghosts, humans, animals, and demons. At the center, turning the wheel, are greed, hatred, and delusion, depicted as a cockerel, snake, and pig, biting each other's tails. Around the rim, the 12 stages in the cycle of life are symbolically expressed.

Bhavnagar 21 59N 72 19E A port in India, in Gujarat on the Gulf of Cambay. An important industrial and commercial center, its manufactures include textiles, bricks, and tiles. Population (1971): 225,358.

Bhopal 23 17N 77 28E A city in India, the capital of Madhya Pradesh. Notable buildings include the unfinished Taj-ul-Masjid, the largest mosque in India. Its university was established in 1970. Bhopal's varied manufactures include vehicle parts and cotton textiles. In 1984 over 2000 people died after poisonous isocyanate gas escaped from the American-owned Union Carbide factory in the city. Population (1971): 298,022.

Bhoskhara II (1114–c. 1185) Indian mathematician, who introduced a new notation. He was the first to use the decimal system in a written work, invented the + and − convention, and used letters to represent unknown quantities as in modern algebra.

Bhubaneswar 20 13N 85 50E A city in India, the capital of Orissa. An ancient city dating back to 500 AD, it is famous for its many temples. Utkal University (founded in 1943) was moved here in 1962. Population (1971): 105,491.

Bhutan, Kingdom of (Bhutanese name: Druk-yul) A small country in the E Himalayas, strategically positioned between India and Tibet. It is entirely mountainous, rising over 7300 m (21,900 ft) in the N. Over half the population are of Tibetan origin, known as Bhutias, with minorities of Nepalese in the S and Indians in the E. *Economy*: mainly agricultural; forests cover almost 70% of the land and there are plans for further planting. As well as traditional industries, such as bamboo and lacquer woodwork, other small industries are being encouraged and hydroelectricity is being developed. A new postal system was inaugurated in 1972 and since then postage stamps have been a valuable source of foreign currency, together with tourism, which has only recently been developed. *History*: although the early history of Bhutan is obscure it does appear to have existed as a political entity for many centuries. In 1865 part of S Bhutan was annexed by the British, following various border disputes, and a treaty was concluded in which Britain agreed to pay an annual subsidy. By a further treaty in 1910 Britain agreed not to interfere in Bhutan's internal affairs and in 1949 this was replaced by a similar treaty concluded with India. In 1910 Sir Ugyen Wangchuk was elected the first hereditary maharaja (now referred to as king). In 1969 the absolute monarchy was replaced by a "democratic monarchy" and power is now divided between the king, the Council of Ministers, the National Assembly, and the monastic head of Bhutan's lamas. Head of state: King Jigme Singye Wangchuk (1955–). Official language: Dzongkha Bhutanese. Official currency: ngultrum of 100 chetrums. Area: 18,000 sq mi (46,600 sq km). Population (1983 est): 1,386,000. Capital: Thimphu.

Bhutto, Zulfikar Ali (1928–79) Pakistani statesman; president (1971–73) and then prime minister (1973–77). He formed the Pakistan People's Party in 1967 and became president after the secession of East Pakistan (Bangladesh). Ousted by a military coup, he was defeated in the subsequent election and sentenced to death (1978) for conspiring to murder a political opponent. He was executed a year later in spite of worldwide pleas to Gen *Zia for clemency.

Biafra The Ibo secessionist eastern region of the Federal Republic of Nigeria (1967–70). In an attempt to protect the interests of the *Ibo people against the dominant *Hausa, a unilateral declaration of independence was made under the leadership of Lieut Col Odumegwu Ojukwu (1933–). The federal government under Gen *Gowon refused to recognize the new state and took up arms against it. The decimated Ibo surrendered on January 15, 1970.

Biafra, Bight of. *See* Bonny, Bight of.

Bialik, Chaim Nachman (1873–1934) Jewish poet and translator, born in the Ukraine. The success of his major poem *The Talmud Student* (1894) established his reputation as the leading Hebrew poet of his time. His poetry is often lyrical and visionary but also condemns Jewish passivity in the face of oppression. He left the Soviet Union in 1921 and settled in Palestine in 1924.

Bialystok 53 09N 23 10E A city in NE Poland. It grew mainly under the Branicki family in the 18th century. In World War II the Germans killed half the population and destroyed the industry but cloth manufacture has been revived. Population (1979 est): 218,000.

Biarritz 43 29N 1 33W A city in SW France, in the Pyrénées-Atlantiques department on the Bay of Biscay. It became a fashionable resort under the patronage of the Empress Eugénie in the mid-19th century. Population (1975): 27,653.

biathlon An athletic event consisting of combined shooting and cross-country *skiing, first included in the Winter Olympic Games in 1960; competitors ski 12.5 mi (20 km) with rifles and ammunition and at each of four points along the course take five shots at 150 m (164 yd).

Bible (Greek *biblia*, books) The collected books of the *Old Testament, the *New Testament, and the *Apocrypha. *Canon*: the canon of the Hebrew Old Testament was definitively established by the rabbinical council of Jamnia (90–100 AD), although most of the books had acquired authority much earlier. The council rejected a number of books that formed part of the Greek version of the Old Testament, the *Septuagint, and these constitute most of the Apocrypha, accepted in varying degrees as sacred scripture by some Christian Churches and rejected by others. The New Testament canon was also established gradually but had essentially its present form by the 3rd century AD. To Christians it represented the complete fulfillment of the prophecies of the Old Testament. *Divine inspiration and biblical criticism*: both Jews and Christians originally regarded their scriptures as divinely inspired, hence correct in every particular. Although Roman Catholics and Protestants differed as to whether the Bible was the sole source of revealed truth, all Christians agreed, until relatively recently, on the literal truth of the contents, a belief slowly eroded by the development of science from the 17th century onward. Despite the attempts to condemn scientific findings when these appeared to conflict with scripture, as in the case of *Galileo, scientific method was soon applied to the study of the Bible itself and the procedures of historical scholarship, textual criticism, archeology, etc., were brought to bear on all aspects of the text. *Texts*: the oldest extant complete manuscript of the Old Testament dates from the 11th century AD, but there are much earlier versions of parts of the text, for example the Pentateuch (*see also* Dead Sea Scrolls). The fact that there is almost no variation among the many manuscripts of the Old Testament attests to the care with which the Jewish scribes, known as the Masoretes, preserved the text from the 6th century AD onward. The earliest fragments of the New Testament date from the 2nd century AD; thereafter there are an extremely large number of manuscripts of quite early date.

Bible Societies Various Protestant organizations formed to promote and distribute Bibles to all peoples. One of the first societies, the Society for Promoting Christian Knowledge, was founded in England in 1698. The American Bible Society distributes several million Bibles annually. In 1946 some 20 international societies combined to form the United Bible Societies.

Bibliothèque Nationale The national *library of France in Paris, containing around seven million volumes. It is based on the royal libraries of Charles the Wise (1364–80) and his successors, notably those of Louis XI, Charles VIII, and Francis I. From 1537 it received a copy of every book published in France. It was given its present name in 1795.

bicycles Light two-wheeled vehicles, the wheels of which are moved by cranks attached to pedals operated by the rider. Bicycles developed in the 19th century from a two-wheeled hobby-horse type of conveyance known as the dandy-horse or celeripede. Around 1840 a Scotsman, Kirkpatrick Macmillan, applied the dandy-horse principle to models with pedals. The first true bicycles, with rotary cranks on their front wheels, went into production in Paris in 1865. Known as velocipedes, these heavy-framed wooden-wheeled devices were nicknamed "boneshakers," but nevertheless popularized cycling as a pastime. To increase efficiency the front wheel was gradually made larger, resulting in the 20-year vogue of the ordinary (*or pennyfarthing*) bicycle. This was superseded by the so-called safety bicycle, which had a chain and sprocket drive to the rear wheel and was essentially the same as the modern bicycle. Invented by 1876, it went into production in 1885. Pneumatic rubber tires (1889), a freewheeling mechanism (1894), and variable gears (1899) were later refinements.

An inexpensive means of transport and recreation, bicycles have enjoyed a revival in developed countries since the fuel crises of the 1970s. Cycling is also a form of competitive sport. Racing first became popular in France, where the earliest race was held (1868) and now has a wide following throughout Europe (*see* Tour de France). Road races take place on public roads, sometimes through normal traffic, using lightweight bicycles with sophisticated gears. Track races are run on special steeply banked tracks and cyclo-cross races are held across country.

Bidault, Georges (1899–1983) French statesman; prime minister (1946, 1949–50). A leader of the French resistance during World War II, Bidault served as president of the Resistance Council in 1944 and foreign minister and president in de Gaulle's first (provisional) government. He broke with the Gaullists over their policy toward Algerian independence, becoming head of the Organisation de l'Armée secrète, and from 1962 to 1968 lived in exile.

Biddle, John (1615–62) English religious leader, founder of Unitarianism (*see* Unitarians). While a schoolmaster he wrote his *Twelve Arguments* against the deity of the Holy Ghost, for which he was imprisoned in 1645. Although his adherents began to meet openly from 1652, he was arrested and banished under Cromwell and finally died in prison in London.

Biddle, Nicholas (1786–1844) US banker and financier. After serving in several government embassies abroad and in the Pennsylvania legislature, he became the president of the Second Bank of the United States in 1823. He advocated a strong national bank and ran it well. In 1832, when Biddle attempted to have the charter renewed, Pres. Andrew Jackson and his Democratic Party objected to the strong national influence of the bank, and by 1836 it had become a state bank of Pennsylvania. Biddle served as president of the bank until 1839.

Biedermeier style A style of furniture and painting that flourished under bourgeois patronage in Austria, Germany, and Scandinavia from about 1816 to about 1848. It was satirically named for the fictional character Gottlieb Biedermeier, who was created by the poet Ludwig Eichrocht (1827–92) to characterize bourgeois bad taste. Biedermeier furniture, which was the first to be mass produced, utilized French *Empire style design for modern functional purposes. Biedermeier paintings aimed at extreme naturalism in outdoor scenes and intimacy in interiors and portraits.

Biel (French name: Bienne) 47 09N 7 16E A city in NW Switzerland, on Lake Biel. It is the only official bilingual Swiss town (French and German). A watchmaking center, it also manufactures machinery. Population (1980 est): 53,793.

Biela's comet A comet, period 6.6 years, that was discovered in 1826 and was observed on its 1846 return to split in two. Although seen in 1852 the portions subsequently disintegrated. The resulting stream of meteoroids (*see* meteor) produced spectacular meteor storms in November, 1872 and 1885. It was named for the Austrian astronomer Wilhelm von Biela (1782–1856).

Bielefeld 52 02N 8 32E A city in N West Germany, in North Rhine-Westphalia. Its linen mills were the first in Germany to be mechanized (1851). Silks, clothing, and machinery are also manufactured here. Population (1980 est): 312,600.

Bielsko-Biala 49 50N 19 00E A city in S Poland. It was formed in 1951 from two separate towns on the Biala River. It has an important textile industry. Population (1979 est): 160,000.

Bien Hoa 10 58N 106 50E An ancient city in S Vietnam, on the Dong Nai River. Known for its pottery, it also has paper, steel, and chemical industries, supplied by hydroelectric power. Population (1971): 177,513.

Bienne. *See* Biel.

Bierce, Ambrose Gwinnett (1842–?1914) US writer. After service in the Civil War, he became a journalist in California and London (1872–75). His story collections, *In the mid of Life* (1891), *Can Such Things Be?* (1893), and *The Devil's Dictionary* (1906), reflect his preoccupation with death and its aftermath. Not inappropriately, he disappeared in Mexico during *Villa's revolt.

bigamy The criminal offense of willfully and knowingly marrying a person while being married to another. Defenses to a charge of bigamy include an honest and reasonable belief in the death of the original marriage partner, especially if absent for seven years or more, and an honest and reasonable belief that the first marriage was invalid or has been dissolved. Although a person would not be guilty of bigamy if he can prove these defenses, the second marriage will still be invalid in such cases.

big-bang theory A cosmological theory (*see* cosmology), first proposed in the 1920s, that all the matter and radiation in the universe originated in an immense explosion that began the expansion of the universe, which still continues. The explosion occurred about 10 to 20 thousand million years ago. As the initially high temperature of the early constituents decreased, hydrogen and helium were able to form: the observed cosmic abundance of helium agrees very well with the predicted value. This matter eventually interacted to form galaxies. The theory also predicts that the radiation formed shortly after the explosion should by now have cooled to about three kelvin. This is indeed the temperature of the isotropic microwave background radiation, detected in 1965 and now considered strong evidence for the big-bang theory.

Big Bend National Park A national park in SW Texas, along the large bend of the Rio Grande on the Mexican border. Within the park are the Chisos Mountains, as well as desertland and numerous canyons. Established as a national park in 1944, Big Bend contains Indian fossils and ruins and many species of wildlife. Area: c. 1000 sq mi (c. 2600 sq km).

Bighorn Mountains A chain of mountains in N Wyoming arcing NW into S Montana, part of the Rocky Mountains. The highest point is Cloud Peak (13,165 ft; 4013 m). Bighorn Basin, to the W, is important for its oilfields.

bighorn A mountain sheep, *Ovis canadensis*, of North America. There is considerable variation within the species, ranging from the small Nelson's bighorn to the largest Rocky Mountain bighorns, which stand 40 in (100 cm) at the shoulder. Bighorns have transversely ribbed horns that grow in a spiral up to 40 in (100 cm) long.

Bihar A state in N India, bordering on Nepal. The densely populated rural Ganges plain in the N produces rice, other grains, sugar cane, pulses, and vegetables. The S Chota Nagpur plateau yields minerals, including much of the world's mica, and supports iron and steel and engineering works. *History*: the center of N Indian civilization from 1500 BC, Bihar was part of numerous empires and witnessed the early development of Buddhism and Jainism. It was a center of 19th-century Indian nationalism.

Area: 67,116 sq mi (173,876 sq km). Population (1981): 69,823,154. Capital: Patna.

Bihari An Indo-Aryan language spoken in Bihar (India) and in Nepal by about 40 million people. It is related to *Bengali and less closely to *Hindi. There are three main dialects; only one, Maithili, has any significant literature.

Bijapur 16 52N 75 47E A city in India, in Karnataka. The ancient capital of a powerful Islamic kingdom (1489–1686), it has many fine Islamic buildings. Population (1971): 103,931.

Bikaner 28 01N 73 22E A city in India, in Rajasthan. The former center of a princely state, its fort (1571–1611) houses a fine collection of Sanskrit and Persian manuscripts. Bikaner is famous for the manufacture of carpets, shawls, and blankets. Population (1971): 188,518.

Bikini Atoll 11 35N 165 20E An atoll in the central Pacific Ocean in the *Marshall Islands. It was the site of US atomic and hydrogen bomb tests (some underwater) from 1946 to 1958.

Bilbao 43 15N 2 56W A port in N Spain, the largest city in the Basque Provinces on the Nervión River. One of Spain's chief ports, its exports include iron ore, lead, and wine. Metallurgical industries are especially important; others include chemicals, fishing, and shipbuilding. Its university was founded in 1968. Population (1974 est): 457,655.

bilberry A deciduous shrub, *Vaccinium myrtillus*, 30–60 cm high, also known as blaeberry, huckleberry, and whortleberry. It is found on acid moors and mountains in N Europe and N Asia. The green angular stems bear small pointed leaves that turn red in autumn. The globular pink flowers, which droop like tiny bells, develop into blue berries. These may be eaten raw or cooked, used in preserves, or used to make wine and spirits. Family: *Ericaceae* (heath family).

Bilbo, Theodore Gilmore (1877–1947) US politician, senator from Mississippi (1935–47). After graduation from Vanderbilt University law school in 1907, he served in Mississippi in the state senate (1908–12), as lieutenant governor (1912–16), and as governor (1916–20; 1928–32) before being elected to the US Senate as a Democrat. He was in favor of states' rights and advocated white supremacy.

Bilderdijk, Willem (1756–1831) Dutch poet and dramatist. He was a precursor of Romanticism in Dutch literature. Of his many poetic works, the most memorable is an unfinished epic poem on biblical themes entitled *De ondergang der eerste wareld* (*The Destruction of the First World*; 1810).

bile A yellow, green, or brown alkaline fluid secreted by the liver and stored in the *gall bladder. Contraction of the gall bladder, which is triggered by a hormone that is released from the duodenum in the presence of food, causes the bile to be expelled through the common bile duct into the intestine. Bile is composed of a mixture of bile salts (which emulsifies fatty foods for digestion) and bilirubin (a breakdown product of the blood pigment *hemoglobin).

bilharziasis. See schistosomiasis.

bill, parliamentary. See parliament.

billiards A game for two players or pairs of players, using cues and balls on a table. There are various forms but the table usually measures 10 × 5 ft (3 × 1.5 m) and a carom table has no pockets (holes around the edges of the table). Points are scored using three balls 2 in (5.2 cm) in diameter, which are white, white with a spot, and red. The white and the white-with-a-spot balls are cue balls, one for each player. The cue ball must strike both the other balls to score a carom. A player continues to shoot until he fails to make a carom. In three-cushion billiards the cue ball must hit the cushion (the interior ridge of the table) three times before striking the second object ball. See also pool; snooker.

Billiton. See Belitung.

bill of exchange (or bank draft) A written order signed by one person (drawer) requiring a second person (drawee) to pay on demand or at a stated date an amount of money to, or to the order of, a specified person or the bearer (payee). A check is a bill of exchange payable on demand and drawn on a banker. Bills of exchange are used in foreign trade and can be discounted (sold for cash before their maturity date at less than their face value).

Bill of Rights 1. (1791) The first ten amendments to the US Constitution, adopted as a whole in 1791 and described by Jefferson as "what the people are entitled to against every government on earth." They are (1) freedom of press, speech, and religion; (2) the right to bear arms; (3) prohibition of quartering of troops; (4) protection against unlawful search and seizure; (5) the right of due process of law; (6) the right to a fair and public trial; (7) the right to a trial by jury; (8) prohibition of cruel punishments; (9) protection of nonenumerated rights; and (10) reservation of powers, i.e. powers not reserved for the federal government reside in the states. 2. (1689) The document that set out the conditions on which the British throne had been offered to William and Mary in 1688 (see Glorious Revolution). It incorporated the Declaration of Rights and declared that the monarch must rule according to the law and with parliamentary consent. MPs were to be freely elected and guaranteed freedom of speech. The Roman Catholic Stuart claim to the throne was terminated.

Billroth, Christian Albert Theodor (1829–94) Prussian-born surgeon. Billroth joined Vienna University in 1867 and—with the aid of antiseptic techniques—pioneered several important surgical operations on the stomach and intestine.

Billy the Kid (William H. Bonney/Henry McCarty; 1859–81) US outlaw. Born in New York City, he was raised in the west and is said to have killed his first man at the age of 12. He took part in the New Mexico cattle war of 1878, in which he killed a sheriff. By 1881, when he was gunned down by Sheriff Patrick Garrett, 21 deaths had been attributed to him.

bimetalism A monetary system in which currency was convertible into either of two metals (usually gold and silver) in a fixed ratio. When adopted by many countries at the beginning of the 19th century it proved unstable, as one metal was always undervalued and one overvalued. *Compare* gold standard.

binary star Two stars moving around each other under mutual gravitational attraction. The components of a **visual binary** can be distinguished by telescope whereas a **spectroscopic binary** can only be detected by spectroscope measurements, the components usually being very close. In an **eclipsing binary** the orbital plane is so orientated that one component passes alternately in front of and then behind the other, causing the combined brightness to fluctuate.

binary system A number system that uses only two digits 0 and 1. Numbers are expressed in powers of 2 instead of powers of 10, as in the decimal system. In binary notation, 2 is written as 10, 3 as 11, 4 as 100, 5 as 101, and so on. *Computers calculate in binary notation, the two digits corresponding to two switching positions (e.g. on or off) in the individual electronic devices in the logic circuits.

binding energy The energy released when protons and neutrons bind together to form an atomic nucleus. The mass of a nucleus is always less than the sum of the masses of the constituent protons and neutrons. The missing mass is converted into the binding energy according to *Einstein's law $E = mc^2$.

bindweed A widely distributed climbing plant of the temperate and subtropical genera *Convolvulus* and *Calystegia*. Bindweeds twine their stems around other plants for support and can be persistent weeds. The leaves are large and arrow-shaped and the conspicuous white, pink, or yellow flowers are funnel-shaped. Family: *Convolvulaceae*.

Black bindweed and copse bindweed (genus *Bilderdykia*; 3 species) lack the conspicuous flowers of the other bindweeds. Family: *Polygonaceae* (dock family).

Binet, Alfred (1857–1911) French psychologist, who pioneered the principles used in intelligence tests. Binet observed how his two young daughters responded to his tests using simple objects and pictures to assess their character and intelligence (*Experimental Study of Intelligence*, 1903). He later applied his techniques to measure the educational achievements of schoolchildren.

Bing, Sir Rudolf (1902–) British opera administrator, born in Austria. He was a founder (1933) and general manager of the Glyndebourne Festival Opera for more than a decade. He helped found the Edinburgh Festival and was its artistic manager (1947–49). He managed the Metropolitan Opera, New York, from 1950 until 1972.

Bingen 49 58N 7 55E A city in W West Germany, in Rhineland-Palatinate at the confluence of the Rhine and Nahe Rivers. According to legend Archbishop Hatto II was devoured (c. 970) by mice on a nearby rock in the Rhine for maltreating his subjects. It is a center of the wine and tourist trades. Population (1971 est): 23,700.

Bingham, George Caleb (1811–79) US genre painter. With little formal training, he painted scenes of life along the Mississippi and Missouri Rivers and portraits in Washington, D.C. (1840–44). From 1844 his works were mostly river scenes and political events, an interest acquired from his time as a state legislator. Well-known works include *Fur Traders Descending the Missouri* (1845), *Shooting for the Beef* (1850), *The Trapper's Return* (1851), *Canvassing for a Vote* (1851), and *Stump Speaking* (1854).

Bingham, Hiram (1875–1956) US archeologist, explorer, educator, and politician. A teacher at Yale, he led expeditions to South America

(1906–15), where he uncovered Vitcos and Machu Picchu, ancient Inca cities. He was a lieutenant governor of Connecticut (1923–24) and a US senator (1925–33). His works include *Inca Land* (1922) and *Lost City of the Incas* (1948).

bingo (former names: tombola; housy-housy) A gambling game that developed in the 1880s from the children's game of lotto. Each player buys a card containing lines of random numbers from 1 to 75, usually. The five vertical columns of numbers on the card are headed by the letters B-I-N-G-O. Balls, or slips or disks of cardboard or plastic, each with a letter and a number, are drawn and as they are called out, the players cover corresponding squares on their cards with counters; the first person to complete a line either vertically, horizontally, or diagonally, on the card wins.

binoculars A portable optical instrument used for magnifying distant objects. It consists of two telescopes fixed side by side, one for each eye, inside which there are a number of lenses for magnifying and focusing the image and usually prisms for altering the direction of the light and thus increasing the effective length of the telescope.

binomial nomenclature A system devised by *Linnaeus in the 18th century for the scientific naming of plants and animals, each species being identified by two internationally recognized Latin names—the name of the genus (written with an initial capital letter) followed by the name of the species. The names are usually written in italics and the specific name may be followed by the author's name, usually abbreviated. Thus the wolf is *Canis lupus* L (for Linnaeus).

binomial theorem The theorem, discovered by *Newton in 1676, that the quantity $(a + n)^n$, where n is an integer, can be expanded in a series: $(a + b)^n = a^n + na^{n-1}b + [n(n-1)\ a^{n-2}b^2]\ /\ 2! + [n(n-1)(n-2)\ a^{n-3}b^3]\ /\ 3! + \ldots + b^n$ where, for example, 3! (called factorial three) is $3 \times 2 \times 1$.

BINTURONG *This carnivore can be tamed and reputedly makes an affectionate pet.*

binturong A mammal, *Arctictis binturong*, of SE Asia, closely related to the *palm civets. It has a dark-gray shaggy coat, tufted ears, short legs, and a bushy prehensile tail (24 in [60 cm] long): the animal measures up to 5 ft (1.5 m) long from head to tail. Binturongs live in trees and feed mainly on fruit and other vegetation; they are more vocal than civets, often growling or hissing.

bioassay A test of the strength or quantity of a biologically active substance by a comparison of its effect upon animals, isolated tissues, or microorganisms with that of a standard preparation.

Bio-Bio River A river in Chile. Rising in the Andes, it flows generally NW to enter the Pacific Ocean and forms the S boundary of middle Chile. Length: about 240 mi (390 km).

biochemistry The scientific study of the chemical composition and reactions of living organisms. Development of the appropriate analytical techniques has enabled great advances in modern biochemistry, which dates from the 1900s. Central to biochemistry is *metabolism and the determination of the complex sequence of reactions involved in the digestion of food, the utilization of energy, the manufacture of new tissues, the breakdown of old tissues, and the formation of excretory products. Biochemists are also concerned with the role of *genes, *hormones, and *enzymes in initiating and controlling metabolic reactions. This understanding is necessary to determine the requirements of a balanced diet as well as the causes and possible treatment of many diseases.

biodegradable substances Materials that can be broken down by biological processes—such as decomposition by fungi and bacteria—and can therefore be reused by living organisms (*see* recycling). Substances that are **nonbiodegradable**, such as plastics, can persist in the environment, causing pollution.

bioengineering (*or* biomechanics) The application of biological and engineering principles to the design and manufacture of equipment for use in conjunction with biological systems. Examples include artificial limbs, heart pacemakers, heart-lung machines, and life-support systems for astronauts and deepsea divers, etc.

biogenetic law (*or* recapitulation theory) A theory postulated by Ernst *Haeckel in 1866 stating that the development of an animal in its lifetime (*see* ontogeny) tends to recapitulate the evolutionary development of its ancestors (*see* phylogeny).

biological control The control of pests by the use of living organisms. The controlling agent is usually a predator, parasite, or disease of the pest organism. For example, the virus disease myxomatosis was introduced to Australia and Britain to control the rabbit population. Recent methods of controlling insect pests include the release of sterile males to mate among the population, so reducing the numbers of eggs laid. Biological control avoids the indiscriminate action and environmental pollution of chemical pesticides.

biological sciences The scientific disciplines concerned with the study of life. The earliest recorded biological observations come from ancient Egypt but it was Greek and Roman scholars, such as *Aristotle, *Hippocrates, and *Galen, who made the first detailed anatomical descriptions of living things. Not until the 16th and 17th centuries were further advances made by such anatomists as *Vesalius and William *Harvey. The introduction of the microscope in the 17th century enabled microorganisms, tissues, and individual cells (*see* cytology) to be observed for the first time.

By the 18th century a wealth of descriptions of individual organisms had been produced and attempts were made to arrange them into related groups (*see* taxonomy), notably by *Linnaeus, whose system is still in use today, and Georges *Cuvier, whose studies of fossilized animal remains founded the science of paleontology. Various theories of *evolution culminated in the publication of Charles *Darwin's theory of the origin of species in 1858. Six years later, Gregor *Mendel reported his findings on the principles of inheritance, which are fundamental to *genetics, although it was not until 1953 that James *Watson and Francis *Crick determined the molecular structure of *DNA—the genetic material.

During the 20th century progress in *biochemistry, *physiology, *cell biology, and *biophysics has been made possible by innovations in microscopical and analytical techniques, such as electron microscopy, chromatography, and the use of *radioactive tracers. Biological discoveries have revolutionized both medicine and agriculture. *See also* botany; ecology; ethology; zoology.

biological warfare The use of disease-causing microorganisms as weapons. In World War I, the Germans infected Allied cavalry horses with bacteria causing *glanders. Although biological warfare is now officially banned by the major powers, research continues in developing new strains of such organisms as the plague bacterium (*Pasteurella pestis*) and the smallpox virus. The organisms are required to be highly virulent (but not necessarily lethal) and would be deployed probably in an aerosol package dropped by bombers or delivered in the warhead of a missile. Alternatively, they could be added to water or food supplies in a covert operation.

bioluminescence The production of light by living organisms, including certain bacteria, fungi, and various animals (e.g. fireflies and glowworms, protozoans, and bony fishes). In some the *luminescence is due to symbiotic light-producing bacteria. The light is emitted by the compound luciferin when it is oxidized: the reaction is catalyzed by an enzyme, luciferase. The emission of light may be continuous, as in bacteria, or intermittent, as in the flash of fireflies. The significance of bioluminescence is unknown in most species, but in some it serves to attract mates or lure prey.

biomass The total weight (mass) of all living organisms (or of all members of a particular species) found in a given area. Biomass is expressed as mass per unit area.

biomass energy. *See* alternative energy.

biome A geographical region that is characterized by a predominant type of vegetation and associated fauna. Examples include grassland, desert, tropical forest, etc.

bionics The study of living systems in order to design man-made systems based on similar principles. It assumes that most living creatures have adapted in the best possible way to their environments. The applications of bionics include the design of a ship's propeller modeled on a fish's tail and the use of knowledge of nerve physiology in data-processing systems.

bionomics. See ecology.

biophysics The scientific discipline concerned with the explanation of biological phenomena in terms of the laws of physics. Biophysics emerged in the 1940s with the work of such scientists as Max *Perutz and John *Kendrew, who applied the phenomenon of *X-ray diffraction to determine the structure of biological molecules; this was followed by Maurice *Wilkins' work on DNA. More recent topics include the nature of the nervous impulse, the properties of biological membranes, the mechanism of muscle contraction, and the operation of sense organs, showing how aspects of chemistry, physiology, and other biological disciplines are necessarily involved in biophysics.

biopsy The removal of a sample of living tissue from the body for microscopic examination. Biopsies are used to assist in the diagnosis of diseases, including cancer (from biopsies of tumors in the breast, lymphatic system, etc.), jaundice (from a liver biopsy), and anemia (from a bone-marrow biopsy).

biosphere The zone of the earth and its atmosphere that is occupied by living organisms. The most heavily populated regions of the biosphere are the surfaces of land and sea.

biotin. see vitamin B complex.

birch A deciduous tree or shrub of the genus *Betula* (40 species), of the N hemisphere. Birches grow to a height of up to 80 ft (25 m) and have thin smooth bark, pale gray or yellowish-brown, that peels off in strips. The glossy leaves are usually triangular, with toothed edges. The flowers are male and female catkins producing tiny winged nuts. Birch wood, especially that of the Eurasian silver birch (*B. pendula*), is used for furniture. Birch bark is used for tanning and roofing, and the bark of the paper birch (*B. papyrifera*) was used by Indians to make birch-bark canoes. Family: *Betulaceae.*

bird A warm-blooded animal belonging to the class *Aves* (about 8600 species), adapted for flight by having forelimbs modified as wings and a body covering of *feathers. Other adaptations include a light skeleton with hollow bones and a large keel-shaped breastbone providing attachment for the powerful flight muscles. The jaws are elongated into a horny bill (teeth are absent or reduced). Birds have good eyesight and color vision and most are active by day, feeding on a wide variety of plant and animal material. Through flight, they have managed to colonize almost every available terrestrial, freshwater, and marine habitat.

Social behavior plays an important part in the life of birds, which show complex patterns of behavior in territorial and courtship displays, *nest building, egg incubation, and care of the young. Many communicate by means of song (*see* songbird) and some undergo long seasonal *migrations.

Birds are of great economic importance to man. The eggs and flesh of many provide food, several species being domesticated and bred for this purpose (*see* poultry). Wildfowl and game birds are hunted for sport, and the feathers of some birds provide ornamental plumes, pillow and duvet stuffings, etc. Other species are pests, for example by damaging crops (particularly cereals) or by fouling buildings in cities. Certain diseases, notably psittacosis, are transmitted to man by birds. Modern birds include both flying and flightless species (*see* ratite); they are grouped into 28 orders, the largest of which is the *Passeriformes* (*see* passerine bird). *See also* ornithology.

bird cherry A small tree, *Prunus padus*, of upland Europe, up to 50 ft (15 m) high with dark bark and pale-green oval leaves, finely serrated around the margins. The sweet-scented white flowers are grouped in loose clusters. The small black bitter-tasting fruits are fermented to make alcoholic drinks. Family: *Rosaceae. See also* cherry.

bird of paradise A bird, 12–25 in (30–65 cm) long, belonging to a family (*Paradisaeidae*; 40 species) occurring in New Guinea and neighboring islands. The male is usually brightly colored, with long tail feathers and ornamental plumes, and performs an acrobatic display to attract the dull-colored female. Their feathers are much prized and were formerly exported for use in ladies' hats. See Plate V.

bird-of-paradise flower A herbaceous perennial plant, *Strelitzia reginae*, native to South Africa and cultivated under glass in temperate regions and as a bedding plant in the tropics. The flower cluster, 8 in (20 cm) long, is orange, scarlet, and blue and resembles a bird's head. The oblong leaves rise to a height of 35 in (90 cm) from the rootstock. Family: *Musaceae* (banana family).

bird of prey A bird that hunts other animals for food, also called raptor. Birds of prey are divided into the nocturnal hunters, comprising the owls (order *Strigiformes*), and those that hunt by day, comprising the eagles, falcons, hawks, secretary bird, and the vultures (order *Falconiformes*). Live prey is normally taken but the vultures specialize in feeding on carrion. Birds of prey are characterized by their strong hooked bills for tearing flesh, clawed talons, and powerful flight with a high-speed dive onto prey.

Birdseye, Clarence (1886–1956) US inventor and industrialist. He worked on a method of fast-freezing food and packaging it and, by 1924, had founded a company that eventually became General Foods. Continuing to work on better methods of freezing, he accumulated over 300 patents and greatly reduced the amount of time needed for freezing.

bird's nest fern An Old World tropical *fern, *Asplenium nidus*, that has a dense rosette of upward-pointing leaves, 24–48 in (60–120 cm) long, with a central hollow forming a nest in which humus collects. The roots branch into this to obtain water and nutrients. The plant is grown for ornament. Family: *Aspleniaceae.*

bird's nest orchid A widely distributed saprophytic *orchid, *Neottia nidus-avis*, most commonly growing in beech woodlands. Named from the dense round cluster of roots at the stem base, it reaches a height of 10–16 in (25–40 cm) and produces spikes of brown flowers in early summer.

bird spider Any of the large *tarantula spiders that may catch and eat small birds.

bireme. See ships.

Birendra Bir Bikram Shah Dev (1945–) King of Nepal (1972–), following the death of his father Mahendra, whose policies he undertook to follow. He married (1970) Aishwarya Rajya Laxmi Devi Rana.

Birkenhead 53 24N 3 02W A port in NW England, in Merseyside on the Wirral Peninsula, linked with Liverpool across the River Mersey by road and rail tunnels and ferry. An important industrial center, it has shipbuilding, engineering, and flour-milling industries. Population (1981): 123,907.

Birkhoff, George David (1864–1944) US mathematician, who gave the Maxwell-Boltzmann theory of gases a rigorous mathematical basis. He also produced a mathematical theory of aesthetics and a theory of gravitation. *See also* statistical mechanics.

Birmingham 52 30N 1 50W A city in central England, in the West Midlands. Britain's second largest city, it is a center of the motor-vehicles industry and besides general engineering and metalworking also produces bicycles, firearms, chemicals, plastics, tires, chocolate, and jewelry. A cultural center, it possesses two universities, Aston University (1966) and Birmingham University (1900). Originally an Anglo-Saxon settlement, its development dates largely from the industrial revolution although its metalworking tradition is much older. It was severely damaged by bombing during World War II. Population (1981): 920,389.

Birmingham 33 30N 86 55W A city in Alabama. Settled in 1813, it is the state's largest city and the main industrial center of the South. It has an important iron and steel industry, which uses local iron ore deposits; other industries include chemicals, cement, and cotton. Population (1980): 284,413.

Biró, Laszlo (1900–) Hungarian inventor, who in 1938 patented the ballpoint pen containing quick-drying ink.

Birobidzhan. See Jewish autonomous region.

birthmark A blemish that is present on the skin at birth. Known medically as a nevus, it is usually harmless and may disappear with age. Birthmarks are caused by a defect in the skin cells or by an abnormality of the underlying blood vessels.

birthstone In *astrology, a gemstone associated with a particular date of birth. The wearing of one's birthstone as a lucky charm originated in the ancient belief that certain gems had supernatural powers. The modern list of birthstones is usually as follows: January—garnet; February—amethyst; March—bloodstone; April—diamond; May—emerald; June—pearl; July—ruby; August—sardonyx; September—sapphire; October—opal; November—topaz; December—turquoise.

Biscay, Bay of (French name: Golfe de Gascogne; Spanish name: Golfo de Vizcaya) An inlet of the Atlantic Ocean, off the coast of W France and N Spain. It is comparatively deep and subject to gales and rough seas. The fish caught here include anchovies, cod, sardines, and tuna. Width: about 199 mi (320 km).

Biscayne Bay   An inlet of the Atlantic Ocean in SE Florida. Miami is on its N shores and part of the Florida Keys form a buffer between the bay and ocean on the S end. Length: 40 mi (65 km); width: 2–10 mi (3.5–16 km).

bisexuality.   *See* homosexuality.

Bishops' Wars   (1639, 1640) The wars fought between the Scots and Charles I of Great Britain following his attempts to enforce the Anglican Prayer Book and government of the Church by bishops on the Presbyterian Scots.

Biskra   34 50N 5 45E An oasis city in N Algeria, on the N edge of the Sahara. It is an important center for the date trade. Population (1966): 59,052.

Bismarck   46 50N 100 48W The capital of North Dakota on the Missouri River. Named for Otto von Bismarck (1873) to entice German investment, it is an agricultural market center. Population (1980): 44,485.

BISMARCK   *An English cartoon in Punch (1890) satirizes his resignation following disagreements with the emperor.*

Bismarck, Otto Eduard Leopold, Prince von   (1815–98) Prussian statesman; first chancellor of the German Empire (1871–90). A conservative, known as the Iron Chancellor, Bismarck came to prominence after the collapse of the *Revolution of 1848. As Prussian foreign minister (1862–71) he was determined to establish Prussian hegemony in Germany and to undermine Austrian dominance there. He embroiled Austria in war over Schleswig-Holstein and following its defeat in the Austro-Prussian War of 1866 *William I of Prussia became president of the North German Confederation. After victory in the *Franco-Prussian War (1870–71) William accepted the imperial crown and Bismarck became chancellor of the new German Empire. Bismarck's domestic policy in succeeding years was concerned chiefly with keeping liberalism at bay. He also came into conflict with the Roman Catholic Church (*see* Kulturkampf) and, abroad, presided over the Congress of *Berlin (1878) and formed the *Triple Alliance with Austria and Italy. Losing the support of William II, Bismarck resigned in 1890 over the abolition of antisocialist laws.

Bismarck Archipelago   A group of volcanic islands in the SW Pacific Ocean, in Papua New Guinea. It includes New Britain, New Ireland, and the Admiralty Islands. Area: 19,173 sq mi (49,658 sq km). Population (1966): 218,265.

bismuth (Bi)   A dense white brittle metal, similar in properties to tin and lead. It was first distinguished by C. Geoffroy in 1753. It is obtained as a by-product of lead, copper, tin, silver, and gold refining and also occurs naturally as the pure metal, the sulfide (Bi_2S_3), and the oxide (Bi_2O_3). It has unusual properties for a metal, having low thermal and electrical conductivity, and decreasing in volume on melting. With tin and cadmium it is used to make low-melting alloys in *fire prevention systems. At no 83; at wt 208.9808; mp 271.3°C; bp 1560°C.

bison   A massive hoofed ☐mammal belonging to the genus *Bison* (2 species). The North American bison (*B. bison*) was once abundant on the plains but is now found only on reserves. Over 60 in (150 cm) at the shoulder and weighing up to 2200 lb (1000 kg), it has a shaggy mane and low-slung head with incurved horns. The smaller European bison (*B. bonasus*), also called wisent, is now found only in zoos. Family: *Bovidae*.

Bissau   11 50N 15 37N The capital and chief port of Guinea-Bissau, on the Geba estuary. Founded by the Portuguese in 1687, it became capital of Portuguese Guinea in 1941. In 1974 Madina do Boe was chosen as the site of a planned new capital. Population (1979): 109,486.

bistort   A perennial herb, *Polygonum bistorta*, of temperate Europe, also called snake-root or Easter-ledges. The upper leaves are triangular, with sheathing bases, and there is a dense terminal spike of tiny pink flowers. Family: *Polygonaceae* (dock family).

bit   A *bi*nary digi*t*. The basic unit of information in information theory and computer memory stores. It is the amount of information needed to specify one of two alternatives, i.e. to distinguish between 1 and 0 in the *binary notation.

Bithynia   An ancient region of Asia Minor, S of the Black Sea. Of Thracian origin, the Bithynians long remained independent, resisting the aggression of the Achaemenians, Alexander the Great, and the Seleucids. By the 3rd century BC it had become a kingdom and expanded territorially and commercially. Conflict with Pergamum and later Pontus brought Roman involvement. Bequeathed by Nicomedes IV (reigned 91–74 BC) to Rome, Bithynia became an increasingly important province as Rome's frontiers expanded E.

Bitola   (Turkish name: Monastir)   41 01N 21 21E A city in S Yugoslavia, in Macedonia. After five centuries of Turkish rule, it was taken by the Serbs in 1912. Its products include sugar, carpets, and textiles. Population (1971): 65,851.

bittern   A bird belonging to the subfamily *Botaurinae*, occurring throughout the world in swamps and reedbeds. The European bittern (*Botaurus stellaris*) is a solitary bird, about 28 in (70 cm) long, with a yellow-brown dark-streaked plumage that provides excellent camouflage. The male produces a "booming" call. The little bittern (*Ixobrychus minutus*) is only 14 in (34 cm) long with buffish-white wing patches. Family: *Ardeidae* (herons, etc.).

Bitterroot Range   A mountain chain in W Montana and E Idaho, part of the Rocky Mountains. It forms most of the border between the two states and includes the Beaverhead Mountains. The highest point is Scott Peak (11,393 ft; 3473 m); the Continental Divide runs through the S portion of the range.

bittersweet   A perennial plant, the woody *nightshade.

bitumen   The tarry residue left after *distillation of oil, lignite, or coal, consisting almost entirely of a mixture of carbon with large *hydrocarbon molecules. Its principal uses are in roadmaking, waterproofing buildings, and binding cement. Bitumen sometimes occurs naturally in asphalt lakes.

bivalve   A *mollusk belonging to the class *Bivalvia* (also called *Lamellibranchia* and *Pelecypoda*; about 10,000 species). Bivalves are characterized by having two hinged shell plates (valves) and include *clams, *mussels, *oysters, and *scallops. Bivalves inhabit both salt and fresh water: some are free swimming; others burrow in sand, mud, or rock. They draw water between the shell valves using their ciliated gills and inner surfaces (mantle) to extract oxygen and food particles from it. Most bivalves are of separate sexes but some are hermaphrodite. Some hermaphrodite bivalves, including *Ostrea* oysters, incubate the fertilized eggs.

Bizerte (*or* Bizerta)   37 18N 9 52E A port in N Tunisia, on the Mediterranean Sea. It dates back to Phoenician times as a port and was known as Hippo Zarytus or Diarrhytus. Retained by the French as a naval base following Tunisian independence (1956), fighting broke out before France surrendered the base in 1963. Population (1976 est): 62,000.

Bizet, Georges   (Alexandre César Léopold B.; 1838–75) French composer. He studied under *Gounod and *Halévy and in 1855 produced his first major work, the symphony in C major. He won the Prix de Rome in 1857. Among his best-known works are the incidental music to *Daudet's play *L'Arlésienne* (1872) and the opera *Carmen* (1873–74), which was at first disliked by the public and attacked by the critics. This censure hastened Bizet's death, three months after the premiere; it is now one of the world's most popular operas.

Bjerknes, Vilhelm Friman Koren (1862–1951) Norwegian meteorologist and physicist. A pioneer of weather forecasting, his 1897 mathematical models of atmospheric and oceanic motions led to his full-scale meteorological predictions (1904). His son **Jakob Bjerknes** (1897–), also a meteorologist, initiated the use of high-altitude photography in weather surveys and forecasting (1952).

Björling, Jussi (Johann Jonaton B.; 1911–60) Swedish tenor. Trained at the Royal Opera School, Stockholm, he made his debut there in 1930. He sang in all the world's major opera houses.

Bjørnson, Bjørnstjerne (Martinius) (1832–1910) Norwegian novelist, poet, and playwright, who was also active in politics and worked as a theater director and newspaper editor. His works, based on the sagas and his knowledge of rural life, include the novel *På Guds veje* (*In God's Way*; 1889) and the plays *En fallit* (*The Bankrupt*; 1875) and *Det ny system* (*The New System*; 1879). He is also remembered as the author of the Norwegian national anthem. He was awarded the Nobel Prize in 1903.

Black, Hugo (LaFayette) (1886–1971) US jurist, politician, associate justice of the Supreme Court (1937–71). After holding several local government jobs in Alabama, he served in the US Senate as a Democrat (1927–37) where he supported the establishment of the Tennessee Valley Authority and the Wages and Hours bill of 1937. Appointed to the Supreme Court by President Franklin D. Roosevelt in 1937, he was generally known as a liberal and advocated a broad interpretation of the Constitution, especially of the rights guaranteed in the First Amendment.

Black, Joseph (1728–99) Scottish physician and chemist, born in Bordeaux, who became professor at Glasgow University and later at Edinburgh University. He independently discovered carbon dioxide, deduced its presence in air, and discovered the bicarbonate compounds. His work on heat led him to introduce the concepts caloric, heat of fusion, latent heat, specific heat, and thermal capacity. He was also the first to distinguish between heat and temperature.

Black and Tans The soldiers recruited by the British Government to fight the IRA in Ireland in 1920–21. Their name derives from their uniform, khaki with black caps and belts. They acted with great severity and were hated by the Irish.

black bear The native bear of North American forests, *Ursus* (or *Euarctos*) *americanus*. American black bears grow to a weight of 330 lb (150 kg); they climb well and eat berries, pine cones, and grass as well as small animals.

The name is also used for the Himalayan black, or moon, bear, *Selenarctos thibetanus*, which inhabits forests of central and E Asia and has a white V-shaped mark on its chest.

Blackbeard. *See* Teach, Edward.

black beetle. *See* cockroach.

blackberry (*or* bramble) A prickly scrambling shrub, *Rubus fruticosus* (an aggregate species), occurring worldwide. The stems, up to 16 ft (5 m) long, root wherever they touch the ground. The dark-green leaves usually consist of five oval toothed leaflets and the pinkish-white flowers are borne in terminal clusters. The fruits, each of which consists of an aggregate of several small berries, are eaten raw or made into pies, jellies, preserves, etc. Family: *Rosaceae*.

blackbird A songbird, *Turdus merula*, that is one of the commonest European birds, particularly in urban areas. The male, about 10 in (25 cm) long, is black with a bright-yellow bill and eye ring; the larger female is dark brown with a dark bill. Blackbirds feed chiefly on worms and other invertebrates but will also eat scraps. Family: *Turdidae* (thrushes).

blackbirding The kidnapping of Polynesians to provide slave labor for the sugar and cotton plantations of Australia and the South Pacific islands. Legislation against it was passed in Australia (1868) but was not effective, and it was not until the beginning of the 20th century that the practice died out.

black body A theoretical body that absorbs all the electromagnetic radiation falling upon it. When heated it emits radiation (black-body radiation) having a continuous distribution of wavelengths with a maximum at a particular wavelength, which depends only on the temperature of the body.

blackbuck A common antelope, *Antilope cervicapra*, of Indian grasslands. Blackbucks are about 31 in (80 cm) high; females are yellowish brown and males darker, both with white underparts. Males have ridged

spiral horns up to 26 in (65 cm) long. They live in herds of 10–30 animals, grazing at dawn and dusk.

Blackburn 53 45N 2 29W A city in NW England, in Lancashire on the Leeds-Liverpool Canal. Traditionally a cotton-weaving town, its chief industry now is engineering (including carpet machinery); textiles, electronics, paper, and paint are also important. Population (1981): 88,236.

blackcap A European *warbler, *Sylvia atricapillus*. About 6 in (14 cm) long, it has an olive-brown plumage with paler underparts and a darker cap (black in the male and reddish-brown in the female). Blackcaps feed chiefly on insects but—before migrating—they eat fruit to build up energy reserves.

Black Codes (1865–66) Laws enacted by Southern states regarding the rights of the free blacks. Interracial marriages were prohibited, public facilities were segregated, and work and court rights were restricted. The Civil Rights Act (1866) and the Fourteenth Amendment to the Constitution (1868) forced the states to repeal these laws.

Black Consciousness The recognition by minority black communities throughout the world of their identity, history, and culture, as distinct from that of whites. Political and social movements contributing to the development of black consciousness in the US have included the Universal Negro Improvement Association in the 1920s, the National Association for the Advancement of Colored People, the National Urban League (1911), the activities of civil rights leaders such as Martin Luther *King and Jesse *Jackson and the *Black Muslims.

blackcurrant A shrub, *Ribes nigrum*, native to most of Europe and N Asia and widely cultivated. The stems and three-lobed leaves emit a characteristic smell. The drooping clusters of greenish bell-shaped flowers develop into edible black berries, used in preserves, wine, beverages, and as a source of vitamin C. Family: *Grossulariaceae* (gooseberry family).

Black Death The worst outbreak of *plague, principally bubonic but also pneumonic and septicemic, of the medieval period. Orginating in the Far East, it spread through Europe and England in May, 1348. Estimates of mortality rates vary from 20% to more than 50%. The outbreak had a profound effect not only on demographic trends but also upon rural society and the economy as a whole. Further outbreaks followed in the 1350s and 1370s.

black earth. *See* chernozem.

Blackett, Patrick Maynard Stuart, Baron (1897–1974) British physicist. He made the first cloud-chamber photographs showing nuclear disintegrations as a result of bombardment (1925) and identified the distintegration products. He improved the Wilson cloud-chamber detector and used it in the study of cosmic radiation, for which work he received the Nobel Prize (1948).

black-eyed Susan A North American perennial herb of the genus *Rudbeckia* (19 species) with showy flower heads, the rays generally yellow, darker at the base and disk flowers blackish and prominent. The plants grow to a height of 24 in (60 cm) and have rough narrow leaves. Also called coneflowers, many species (e.g. *R. fulgida* var *speciosa*) are cultivated in gardens. Family: *Compositae*.

blackfly Any black *aphid, especially the bean aphid (*Aphis fabae*). Bean aphids occur in masses on beans, spinach, dock, etc., in summer months. They overwinter as fertilized eggs in *Euonymus*, *Viburnum*, and *Philadelphus* trees.

black fly A small humpbacked fly, also called buffalo gnat and turkey gnat, belonging to a family (*Simuliidae*; about 300 species) of worldwide distribution. The bloodsucking females attack man and domestic animals and some are vectors of disease. In Africa, for example, *Simulium damnosum* and *S. neavei* transmit a filarial worm that causes "river blindness."

Blackfoot A North American Indian people inhabiting areas of Saskatchewan and Alberta in Canada and Montana in the US. The Blackfoot nation is actually a confederacy of three main sub-groups: the Siksikas, the Piegans (Pikuni), and the Bloods (Kainah). The language of all three groups is *Algonkian. In the 19th century, the Blackfoot were known as nomadic buffalo hunters and skilled horsemen who resisted the encroachment of settlers into their territory. The total Blackfoot population today is approximately 10,000.

Black Forest (German name: Schwarzwald) An extensively forested mountainous area in SW West Germany, in Baden-Württemberg E of the Rhine Valley. Covered chiefly with coniferous forests, the timber industry is important with associated cuckoo-clock making and woodcrafts; it is also a popular tourist area.

black grouse A Eurasian *grouse, *Lyrurus tetrix*, of moorlands. The male (also called blackcock), 20 in (50 cm) long, has a glossy black plumage and a lyre-shaped tail; the female is reddish brown. Both have conspicuous red wattles above the eyes. In the breeding season the males perform an elaborate courtship display (lek) on a communal display ground.

Black Hand A Serbian secret society pledged to the liberation of Serbs from Habsburg and Ottoman rule. On June 28, 1914, they were responsible for the assassination of the Austrian archduke, Francis Ferdinand, an event contributing to the outbreak of World War I.

Black Hawk War (1832) A conflict between the US and the Sauk and Fox Indians. The Indian chief Black Hawk (1767–1838) resisted attempts to force his people W of the Mississippi River and near La Crosse, Wisconsin, nearly a thousand Indians were massacred by the US army despite a flag of surrender.

Black Hills Mountains in SW South Dakota and NE Wyoming between the Belle Fourche River on the N and the Cheyenne River on the S. The highest point is Harney Peak (7242 ft; 2208 m). Its features include the Black Hills National Forest, Wind Cave National Park, Mount Rushmore National Memorial, and Devil's Tower National Monument.

black hole A celestial "object" that has undergone such total *gravitational collapse that no light can escape from it: its *escape velocity exceeds the speed of light (*see* velocity of light). Once a collapsing object's radius has shrunk below a critical value (the Schwarzschild radius) it becomes a black hole; for a star, this radius is about 6 mi (10 km) or less. The surface having this radius is called the event horizon of the black hole. The object will continue to contract until compressed to an infinite density at a single central point—a singularity. A black hole is thus a region of greatly distorted space (and time) the size of which increases with the mass of the contracting material.

No black hole has as yet been unambiguously detected. The collapsed core remaining from the *supernova explosions of massive stars are, however, promising candidates, especially if they are components of a *binary star and thus more easy to detect. The X-ray binary Cygnus X-1 has a probable black-hole component. It has been suggested that black holes of immense size and mass (10^6 to 10^9 solar masses) may exist at the centers of certain galaxies and be powerful sources of energy.

Black Hole of Calcutta A small cell 18 ft × 12 ft (5.5 m × 4.5 m) in which over one hundred British soldiers were allegedly confined overnight in 1756. According to their commander John Holwell fewer than 25 men survived. The outrage was perpetrated by the Nawab of Bengal, who, objecting to the fortification of Calcutta by the East India Company, attacked and defeated the British garrison.

blackmail In law, the criminal offense of making any unreasonable demand with a view to gain, backed up by a threat of violence or injury to the person involved or to his property or by a threat of exposing his immorality or misconduct.

black mass An obscene and blasphemous parody of the Roman Catholic mass, celebrated by satanists in honor of the devil. A naked woman is usually present at or on the altar and participants take hallucinatory drugs or other potions. *See* satanism.

Blackmore, R(ichard) D(oddridge) (1825–1900) British historical novelist, famous chiefly for *Lorna Doone* (1869), a romance set on Exmoor during the Restoration.

Blackmun, Harry Andrew (1908–) US jurist, lawyer, and teacher; Supreme Court associate justice (1970–). After graduation from Harvard Law School (1932), he entered private practice in Minneapolis (1934), taught law at the University of Minnesota (1945–47), and was judge of the US 8th circuit court of appeals. He was appointed to the Supreme Court in 1970 by Pres. *Nixon. He was conservative in his opinions on criminal matters, but was a moderate liberal regarding civil rights, maintaining in *Roe* v. *Wade* (1973) that abortion is the private choice of a woman.

Black Muslims Members of the Nation of Islam movement founded in Detroit in 1930 by W. D. Fard, known also as Walli Farrad and Wallace Fard Muhammad, and believed by Black Muslims to be the Mahdi or Savior. After the disappearance of Fard in 1933, the movement was led by Elijah Muhammad (1897–1975) and won support among blacks in northern industrial cities. One of the movement's most well-known leaders, Malcolm X (1925–65) was assassinated. Restricted to blacks, it aims to establish a new Islamic state and follows many Muslim practices, although some of its beliefs are unorthodox. After his father's death, Wallace Muhammad assumed leadership, bringing the sect closer to orthodox Islam.

Blackpool 53 50N 3 03W A resort in NW England, on the Lancashire coast. It is an entertainments center famous for its Tower (modeled on the Eiffel Tower), Pleasure Beach, and illuminations; it is also a conference center. Population (1981): 147,854

Black Prince, Edward the. *See* Edward, the Black Prince.

Black Sea An inland sea bounded by Bulgaria, Romania, the Soviet Union, and Turkey; it is connected to the Mediterranean Sea via the Bosporus in the SW and to the sea of Azov in the N. The principal towns on its coast are Burgas and Varna in Bulgaria, Constanţa in Romania, Odessa and Sevastopol in the Soviet Union, and Trabzon in Turkey. Its salinity is kept low principally by the influx of fresh water from the Danube and Dnepr Rivers.

Blackshirts The colloquial name for the Fasci di Combattimento, founded by Mussolini in 1919 and forming the backbone of Italian *fascism. They wore distinctive black shirts; their name is also used in reference to the *SS.

black snake A small-headed venomous snake, *Pseudechis porphyriacus*, of Australian wetlands. About 5 ft (1.5 m) long, it is blue-black with a red belly. Family: *Elapidae* (cobras, mambas, coral snakes). In North America the name is given to a nonvenomous snake, *Zamenis constrictor*.

Blackstone, Sir William (1723–80) British jurist. His fame rests largely on his *Commentaries on the Laws of England* (1765–69), a series of lectures delivered at Oxford. Highly influential in legal education, they presented the first comprehensive account of English law. Blackstone became a member of Parliament in 1791 and a judge in 1770.

black swan The only Australian *swan, *Cygnus atratus*. Almost 40 in (1 m) in length, both sexes have a pure black plumage, red bill, and a trumpeting call.

blackthorn (*or* sloe) A thorny shrub, *Prunus spinos*, forming dense thickets, up to 13 ft (4 m) high, in many parts of Europe and Asia. The clusters of white flowers usually appear before the leaves, which are oval and toothed. The bitter-tasting blue-black stone fruits are used to flavor sloe gin; the hard wood is used for walking sticks and tool handles. Family: *Rosaceae*.

blackwater fever A serious complication of malaria in which the malarial parasite causes widespread destruction of red blood cells, leading to the excretion of blood pigments in the urine (which becomes dark brown—hence the name). The patient has a high fever and jaundice and requires careful nursing, with blood transfusions if necessary.

Blackwell, Elizabeth (1821–1910) US physician, first woman doctor in the US. Born in England, she came to the US (1932) with her family and studied at Geneva Medical School (1847–49) in New York, the only school to admit her, and at various schools abroad. She opened her own hospital (1853; known as New York Infirmary from 1857), staffed it with women, and established training for nurses. The Women's Medical College of the New York Infirmary was founded in 1868. She returned to England in 1869 where she founded and taught at the London School of Medicine for Women.

black widow A venomous *spider, also called button or redback spider, that belongs to a genus (*Latrodectus*; about 6 species) found in tropical and subtropical regions. The female of *L. mactans*, the most common North American species, has a shiny black body, 1 in (25 mm) long, with red markings on the abdomen. (The male is about 0.24 in (6 mm) long and usually killed and eaten by the female after mating.) The bite of this spider—although serious—is rarely fatal. Family: *Theridiidae*.

bladder In anatomy, any hollow organ containing fluid, especially the urinary bladder situated in the pelvis, into which urine drains from the *kidneys (via the ureters). Urine is stored in the bladder and released at intervals by relaxation of a circular (sphincter) muscle at its opening into the urethra (which leads to the exterior). Bladder emptying is normally under voluntary control. *See also* enuresis.

bladderwort A plant of the widely distributed genus *Utricularia* (about 200 species, many tropical). Most bladderworts are submerged aquatic plants with finely divided leaves bearing small bladders, which trap tiny aquatic animals by a trapdoor mechanism triggered by sensitive hairs. The two-lipped tubular flowers protrude above the water. Some bladderworts are troublesome weeds of ricefields. Family: *Lentibulariaceae*.

Blaine, James Gillespie (1830–93) US politician and statesman. A Republican, he served in the US House of Representatives (1863–76) and was speaker (1869–75). He became a US senator in 1876 and was appointed secretary of state by President James A. Garfield in 1880. Blaine was the Republican candidate for president in 1884 and again served as secretary of state (1889–92) under President Benjamin Harrison. He was outspoken in advocating the abolition of slavery; later, he was instrumental in securing American interests in the Panama Canal.

WILLIAM BLAKE *An engraving (plate 14) from The Book of Job. These biblical illustrations, of which Blake produced 22, were commissioned in 1821 and engraved 1823-25.*

Blake, William (1757–1827) British visionary poet, painter, and engraver. His books of poems, the texts of which he engraved and illustrated, include *Songs of Innocence* (1789), *Songs of Experience* (1794), various "Prophetic Books," *Milton* (1808), and *Jerusalem* (1820). All were influenced by his unorthodox Christian and political beliefs and by such mystics as *Böhme. As an artist his imaginative watercolors for *The Book of Job* (1826) and Dante's *Divine Comedy* (1827) were inspired by his visions, gothic sculpture, and engravings after Michelangelo. Although largely unrecognized by his generation, he was a precursor of Romanticism.

Blanc, Louis (1811–82) French socialist. A utopian and revolutionary, from 1839 Blanc propagated his doctrines of economic equality in his journal *Revue du progrès*; the axiom "from each according to his ability, to each according to his needs" formed the basis of his thought. Although a member of the provisional government in the *Revolution of 1848, he found little support for his views among his colleagues and fled to England. Returning to Paris in 1870, he remained active in left-wing causes until his death. His books include *Organisation du travail* (1840).

Blanche of Castile (c. 1188–1252) The daughter of Alfonso VIII of Castile, she married (1200) *Louis VIII of France. As regent of France for her husband (1223–26) and her son *Louis IX (1226–36, 1248–52), she ruled firmly, suppressing a revolt of the nobility and effecting peace with England.

Bland-Allison Act (1878) US law that regulated the federal purchase and coinage of silver. Congressman Richard P. Bland (1835–99) campaigned for unlimited coinage of silver, which was unacceptable to Congress. When modified by Senator William B. Allison (1829–1908), the bill, which put limits on but provided for consistent coinage, passed.

blank verse Unrhymed iambic pentameter lines, the distinctive form of English narrative and dramatic verse since its introduction from Italy in the early 16th century by Henry Howard, Earl of *Surrey. It was used in the plays of *Marlowe and *Shakespeare. The form allows considerable variation and has been used by most major English poets to suit their different ends: in *Milton's *Paradise Lost* (1667) it is formal and grand, in *Wordsworth's *Prelude* (1805) it is intimate and casual.

Blanqui, Louis Auguste (1805–81) French revolutionary. Interested in the practice of revolution rather than in abstract ideas, Blanqui introduced the notion, later taken up by Marx, that revolutions must begin with temporary dictatorship of a revolutionary elite devoted to the socialist cause. From 1830 he built up a network of secret societies committed to violent insurrection. In 1871, although in prison, he was elected president of the *Commune of Paris. His followers, the Blanquists, joined with the Marxists in 1881.

Blantyre (*or* Blantyre-Limbe) 15 46S 35 00E The largest city in Malawi, in the Shire Highlands. In 1956 it was linked with the nearby town of Limbe, a major railroad center, and is Malawi's chief commercial and industrial center. Industries include distilling, textiles, and cigarette production. Population (1977): 228,520.

Blarney 51 56N 8 34W A village in the Republic of Ireland, in Co Cork. Blarney Castle contains the famous Blarney Stone, which is kissed in order to receive the gift of "blarney" or smooth talk. Population (1971): 1128.

Blasco Ibáñez, Vicente (1867–1928) Spanish novelist. He wrote many novels set in Valencia but is best known for his World War I novels, especially *The Four Horsemen of the Apocalypse* (1916), three times filmed. He was frequently penalized for his political activities and in 1923 exiled himself to France.

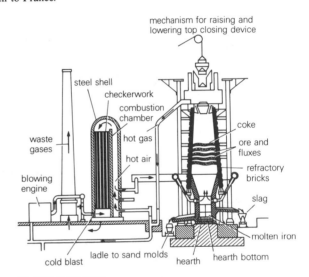

BLAST FURNACE

blast furnace A furnace heated by solid fuel, usually coke, through which a blast of air is blown to aid combustion. Blast furnaces are used in the *smelting of ore. In steel making, iron ore, coke, and limestone are poured in at the top of a vertical furnace and hot air is blown in at the bottom to burn the coke. Molten iron is drawn off at the bottom. A glassy waste, called slag, is also produced.

blastula A hollow sphere of cells (blastomeres) produced by repeated *cleavage of a fertilized egg cell (zygote). It is an early stage in embryonic development, before differentiation into tissues and organs has begun. A blastula consists of an outer layer (the blastoderm) surrounding a cavity (the blastocoel).

Blaue Reiter, Der. *See* Blue Rider, The.

Blavatsky, Helen Petrovna (1831–91) Russian theosophist, who founded the Theosophical Society in New York in 1875. She later established a following in India, but her claims to supernatural powers were discredited by scientific investigations during the 1880s and 1890s. Her best-known book is *Isis Unveiled* (1877). *See also* theosophy.

bleaching The whitening, lightening, or removing of color by chemical treatment, exposure to sunlight, air, or moisture. Most bleaching agents are oxidizing agents, which convert a pigment into an oxidized colorless form. Examples are hydrogen peroxide, *bleaching powder, and hypochlorites. In some processes reducing agents, such as sulfur dioxide, are used. Bleaching is an important part of textile and paper manufacture.

bleaching powder (*or* chloride of lime) A whitish powder containing calcium hypochlorite ($Ca(OCl)_2$), calcium chloride ($CaCl_2$), calcium hydroxide ($Ca(OH)_2$), and water. It reacts with dilute acids to produce chlorine, which acts as a bleaching agent.

bleak A fish, *Alburnus alburnus*, related to the *carp, with a slender silvery-green body, about 8 in (20 cm) long. It lives in schools near the surface of fresh waters in N Europe and feeds on invertebrates. The scales are used in the manufacture of artificial pearls.

bleeding. *See* hemorrhage.

bleeding heart An ornamental plant of the genus *Dicentra*, especially *D. spectabilis* from Siberia and Japan and *D. eximia* from North America. They are perennials with arching stems, up to 35 in (90 cm) long, bearing strings of large rose-red heart-shaped flowers with whitish tips, which glisten when the blooms are fresh. Some species have attractive fernlike foliage. Family: *Fumariaceae*.

Bleeding Kansas (1854–56) Name given to Kansas during conflicts between pro-slavery and abolitionist settlers. Bloody skirmishes among the territory's settlers were common before President Pierce established a fragile peace in 1856.

Blenheim, Battle of (August 13, 1704) The battle won by the Duke of *Marlborough and *Eugene of Savoy against the French army in the War of the *Spanish Succession. It was fought at Blenheim (now Blindheim) on the Danube River. Blenheim Palace was built for Marlborough by a grateful government.

Blenkinsop, John (1783–1831) British engineer, who built the first practical steam locomotive (1812), a twin-cylinder engine driving cogs that engaged with rack rails. It was used for transporting coal from Middleton to Leeds.

blenny A small fish belonging to a family (*Bleniidae*; about 300 species) found among rocks in shallow waters of tropical and temperate seas. Blennies have an elongated scaleless body with a blunt nose, a long dorsal fin, and one- to three-rayed pelvic fins located in front of the larger pectoral fins. Many have small tentacles on their heads. The name is also used for several other fish of the order *Perciformes*.

Blériot, Louis (1872–1936) French aviator. Beginning his career as a motorcar engineer he was the first to fly the English Channel (1909), from Calais to Dover, in a monoplane. He later became a manufacturer of □aircraft.

blesbok A small fast-running South African antelope, *Damaliscus dorcas*. About 44 in (110 cm) high at the shoulder, blesboks are red with a white muzzle, rump, and shanks and have lyre-shaped ridged horns. Bonteboks (*D. dorcas dorcas*) are a subspecies with a larger rump patch and more white on the legs.

blewits An edible *mushroom, *Tricholoma* (or *Lepista*) *saevum*, occurring mainly in open pastures. It has a bluish-gray stalk and a flat clay-colored cap, 2–5 in (6–12 cm) in diameter, producing pale-pink spores. The wood blewits (*T. nudum*) has a lilac or purple cap and is usually found beneath trees. It also is edible. Family: *Tricholomataceae*.

Bligh, William (1754–1817) British admiral. He accompanied *Cook on his second voyage around the world and in 1787 was sent to Tahiti on the *Bounty* to collect specimens of the breadfruit tree. Setting sail for home, his crew mutinied and deserted, leaving Bligh and 18 officers aboard a small boat without maps. He eventually reached safety. He was made governor of New South Wales (1805–08) where another mutiny took place. (*See* Rum Rebellion.)

blight A severe disease of plants caused by pests, fungi, or other agents or by a mineral deficiency. Symptoms commonly include spotting followed by wilting, and the plant eventually withers and dies. The notorious potato blight that devastated Ireland in the mid-19th century was caused by the fungus *Phytophthora infestans*. Control measures against blights vary according to the cause of the disease.

blindness Partial or complete loss of sight (degrees of visual impairment less severe than total loss of sight are classified as blindness for administrative purposes). Sudden blindness may be caused by direct injury to the eye or to the part of the brain that receives the visual signals. Blindness that develops gradually is caused by a wide variety of diseases, including *trachoma, *glaucoma, *cataracts, diabetes mellitus, and tumors (especially of the pituitary gland), that compress the optic nerve. There are various aids available for the visually handicapped, including books in *Braille or on tape or records and specially trained *guide dogs. In many countries the blind are entitled to special education and financial benefits. *See also* color blindness.

blindworm. *See* slowworm.

blister An accumulation of fluid (usually colorless serum) within the skin. Blisters can be caused by continuous friction, sensitivity to chemicals, and *burns. They may also develop in certain diseases, including chickenpox. Blisters usually heal spontaneously, but some (especially severe burns or those on the feet, in contact with shoes) require dressings. They should not be burst intentionally as this provides an entrance for infection.

blister beetle A brightly colored beetle, about 0.4–0.6 in (10–15 mm) long, belonging to a widely distributed family (*Meloidae*; about 2000 species), which also includes the *oil beetles. The larvae are parasitic upon other insects, while the adults generally feed on plants—often causing severe damage. Their secretion of cantharidin, a powerful blistering agent, has led to the medicinal use of various European and Asian species, especially *Spanish fly.

Blitzkrieg (German: lightning war) A military tactic aiming to shock and disorganize enemy forces by swift suprise attacks using tanks and aerial bombardment. It was extensively used by the Germans in *World War II in Poland, Belgium, the Netherlands, France, and Africa. It was also used by the US general Patton, in Europe in 1944. The **Blitz** refers to the intensive German air raids on London during the battle of Britain in *World War II. Between July and December, 1940, 23,000 civilians died.

Blixen, Karen. *See* Dinesen, Isak.

Bloch, Ernest (1880–1959) Swiss-born composer of Jewish descent. He lived in various countries before taking up residence in the US in 1916. His opera *Macbeth* (1903–09), a rhapsody for cello and orchestra entitled *Schelomo* (1916), *Concerto Grosso* (1925), and *Sacred Service* (1930–33) incorporate Jewish musical elements into a cosmopolitan 20th-century style.

Bloch, Felix (1905–83) US physicist, born in Zurich. After working in Germany he left Europe when Hitler came to power and emigrated to the US, becoming a citizen in 1939. He developed the *nuclear magnetic resonance technique for magnetic field measurements in atomic nuclei, for which he shared the Nobel Prize (1952) with the independent discoverer, E. M. *Purcell. Bloch's concept of magnetic neutron polarization (1934) enabled him, in conjunction with L. *Alvarez, to measure the neutron's magnetic moment. During World War II he worked on the development of the atomic bomb.

Block Island 41 11N 71 35W An island in S Rhode Island, in the Atlantic Ocean at the beginning of Long Island Sound and separated from the mainland by Block Island Sound. The island was discovered by Adriaen Block in 1614; it was settled in 1661, joined the colony in 1664, and became the town of New Shoreham in 1672. Tourism and fishing are its main industries. Length: 7 mi (11.5 km); width: 1.5–3.5 mi (2.5–6 km). Population (1980): 620.

Bloemfontein 29 07S 26 14E The judicial capital of South Africa and the capital of the Orange Free State. Founded in 1846, it is an important transportation and agricultural center. Industrial development is being encouraged with the opening of new gold mines nearby. It has the University of the Orange Free State (1855) and the US universities of Harvard and Michigan have observatories here to take advantage of the dry clear atmosphere. Population (1980 est): 230,688.

Blois 47 36N 1 20E A city in France, the capital of the Loir-et-Cher department on the Loire River. It has a famous chateau, begun in the 13th century, and trades in wine, brandy, and grain. Population (1975): 51,950.

Blok, Aleksandr Aleksandrovich (1880–1921) The leading Russian symbolist poet. His early poetry, notably *Verses about the Beautiful Lady* (1901–02), celebrated the spiritual fulfillment of his love for Liubov Mendeleyeva, whom he married in 1903. But his love for Russia was the deeper theme, and in *Scythians* (1918) and *The Twelve* (1918) he expressed a revolutionary optimism that soon turned to deep disillusion.

Blondel, Maurice (1861–1949) French philosopher. He invented a philosophy of action, seeking a compromise between intellectualism and pragmatism. His chief works are *Action* (1893), *The Process of Intelligence* (1922), and *Being and Beings* (1935).

Blondin, Charles (Jean-François Gravelet; 1824–97) French acrobat and tightrope walker. In 1859 he walked across a tightrope suspended over Niagara Falls and later repeated the feat several times with various acrobatic variations.

blood The red fluid contained within the arteries and veins and pumped around the body by the *heart. Blood consists of a watery fluid (*see* plasma) in which are suspended various blood cells—the red cells (*see* erythrocyte), containing the red oxygen-carrying pigment hemoglobin, and several kinds of white cells (*see* leukocyte), concerned with the body's defense mechanisms. The *platelets are small particles involved in blood clotting.

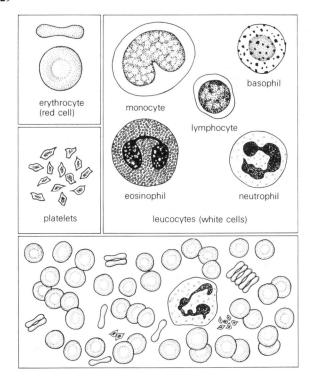

BLOOD *Blood cells and platelets, showing surface and side views of a red cell and five types of white cell (above). Human blood, magnified about 1500 times (below) containing a single white cell, a mass of red cells, and two clusters of platelets.*

Blood acts as a medium for transporting oxygen, carbon dioxide, digested food, hormones, waste materials, salts, and many other substances to and from the tissues. An average adult has about 2.3 fluid oz (70 milliliters) of blood per pound (0.45 kilogram) of body weight (i.e. about 4.5 quarts [5 l] in an average man). Blood is present in all animals with a circulatory system: its functions are similar to that of human blood although its composition varies. *See also* blood clotting; blood groups; circulation of the blood.

Blood, Council of   (*or* Council of Troubles; 1567–74) A court established in the Low Countries during the *Revolt of the Netherlands by the Spanish governor, the Duke of *Alba, to suppress Protestantism and particularism. Thousands were imprisoned or executed without proper trial and, following the arrest of two prominent magnates, *Egmont and *Horn, many others fled abroad. Alba used the threat of the council to impose the tenth penny, an unpopular tax that united Catholics and Calvinists against Spain. After Alba's departure (1573), the council was abolished.

blood clotting   The mechanism by which blood is converted from a liquid to a solid state, which normally occurs after injury to blood vessels and prevents loss of blood. The process involves a number of chemical reactions between certain soluble proteins (clotting factors) in the blood, resulting in the formation of a fibrous protein (fibrin), which forms the basis of the blood clot. *Platelets accumulate at the site of the injury, their presence being essential for the reactions to occur. *See also* thrombosis.

blood fluke   A parasitic flatworm of the genus *Schistosoma* (3 species), which causes the disease *schistosomiasis among human populations in many parts of the world. The flukes are carried by freshwater snails and enter their human hosts to inhabit blood vessels, feeding on blood and causing severe debilitation. *See also* fluke.

blood groups   The different types into which blood can be classified on the basis of the presence or absence of certain proteins (*see* antibody) on the surface of the red cells, which is genetically determined. The major grouping is the ABO system, which was the first human blood system to be discovered—in 1900, by Karl Landsteiner (1868–1943). It consists of four groups: A, B, AB, and O. Group A cells carry the A antigen and the plasma contains *antibodies against B antigen (anti-B antibodies); the converse applies to group B blood. Transfusion of blood between these groups will cause destruction of the donor blood cells (*see* blood transfusion). Group O blood contains neither antigen and can therefore be used in trans-

fusions to people of groups A and B. Group AB blood contains neither anti-A nor anti-B antibody: people of this blood group can accept both A and B blood during transfusion. There are numerous other minor blood-group systems of which the rhesus system is the most important (*see* rhesus factor).

bloodhound   An ancient breed of dog with a keen sense of smell, widely used for tracking purposes. It has a sturdy frame and a large dome-shaped head with long drooping ears and wrinkled skin around the eyes. Bloodhounds are black and tan, liver and tan, or red in color. Height: 25–27 in (63–69 cm) (dogs); 23–26 in (58–64 cm) (bitches).

blood poisoning   (*or* septicemia) The presence of bacteria or bacterial toxins in the blood. The symptoms include fever, rigors, and various aches and pains. The bacteria may come from any infected region (such as an abscess) and they may be carried to other parts of the body, including the brain and kidneys. Treatment consists of the injection of large doses of antibiotics.

blood pressure   The pressure that blood exerts on the walls of the arteries, due to the pumping action of the heart. Blood pressure is at its lowest between heartbeats (i.e. at diastole) and at its highest when the ventricles of the heart are contracting (i.e. systole). It is recorded, using an instrument called a *sphygmomanometer, as the height in millimeters of a column of mercury (mmHg). Blood pressure varies with age and individual variations are common within each age group depending on such external factors as stress, but a healthy adult might have a systolic pressure of about 120 mmHg and a diastolic pressure of 80 mmHg. This is normally expressed as 120/80. Abnormally high blood pressure (*see* hypertension) may be associated with various diseases or it may arise without any obvious cause. Abnormally low blood pressure occurs in *shock.

bloodstone   A mineral of a green color speckled with red. It is a variety of *chalcedony. Birthstone for March.

blood test   An analysis of a blood sample. Such tests may be useful in the diagnosis of disease. A common test is the measurement of the erythrocyte sedimentation rate (ESR)—the rate at which red blood cells settle out of plasma, which increases in rheumatic disease, cancer, and some infections. Other tests include plasma viscosity, red-cell counts (in the diagnosis of anemia), blood-sugar estimation (when diabetes mellitus is suspected), and the determination of alcohol, drugs, or bacteria in the blood or the individual's blood group. The blood is usually taken from a vein using a hypodermic needle.

blood transfusion   The transfer of blood from one individual (the donor) to another (the recipient). As blood of a different *blood group from that of the recipient may cause a serious reaction, the blood groups of both the donor and the recipient must be determined beforehand. Direct person-to-person transfusion is now rarely performed; the donor blood is usually stored, at a temperature of 34°F (4°C), in a **blood bank** and should be used within 3–4 weeks of collection. Blood transfusion is performed when there has been extensive loss of blood; for example, during surgery or following an accident. Some people (e.g. Jehovah's Witnesses) object to transfusions on religious grounds.

bloodworm   The larva of nonbiting *midges of the genus *Chironomus*. It lives in stagnant water and is red owing to the pigment *hemoglobin, which it uses to help increase its supply of oxygen.

Bloody Assizes.   *See* Jeffreys of Wem, George, 1st Baron.

Bloomfield, Leonard   (1887–1949) US linguist, whose book *Language* (1933) outlines a strictly scientific behaviorist framework for the description of language, on which modern American structural *linguistics is based. He also did pioneer descriptive fieldwork in both Malayo-Polynesian and American Indian languages.

Bloomington   39 10N 86 32W A city in SW Indiana, founded in 1815. Indiana University was established here in 1820. Industries include electrical equipment and limestone quarrying. Population (1980): 51,646.

Bloomsbury group   A group of English writers and artists active in the 1910s and 1920s who met in private houses in Bloomsbury, London, for aesthetic and philosophic discussions. The group included the writers Virginia *Woolf (and her sister Vanessa Bell; 1879–1961), E. M. *Forster, and Lytton *Strachey, the art critics Clive Bell (1881–1964) and Roger *Fry, and the economist J. M. *Keynes. Most of them had studied at Cambridge University and were influenced by G. E. *Moore's *Principia Ethica* (1903) in their belief in the overriding importance of personal relationships and aesthetic experience.

blowfly   A large buzzing fly belonging to the family *Calliphoridae*. Some blowflies lay their eggs in human food, but more commonly the larvae develop in dung or decaying organic material. The larvae of certain species (e.g. of the American genus *Cochliomyia*)—known as screwworms—are serious pests of sheep and cattle, eating away the flesh at wounded areas. Chief genera: *Calliphora* (bluebottles), *Lucilia* (greenbottles).

Blücher, Gebhard Leberecht von, Prince of Wahlstatt (1742–1819) Prussian general, known as Marshal Forward. He fought in the campaigns against Revolutionary France and subsequently held command in the War of Liberation against Napoleon, whom he defeated at Leipzig (1813). In 1814 he crossed the Rhine and marched to Paris. His pursuit of Napoleon's forces at Waterloo contributed to the allied victory.

Bluebeard A European folktale character who murders successive wives and locks their bodies in a forbidden room. His new wife discovers the bodies and is herself threatened with death, but is rescued by her brothers. The story may have been based on the crimes of Gilles de *Retz or of an ancient Breton chieftain.

bluebell One of several plants having bell-shaped blue flowers. In England the bluebell is *Endymion non-scriptus*, a perennial herb, up to 20 in (50 cm) high, very common in woods and shady places. It overwinters as a bulb and produces blue (sometimes white or pink) flowers in spring. Family: *Liliaceae*. In Scotland the name is applied to the *harebell.

bluebird A songbird of the New World genus *Sialia* (3 species). The eastern bluebird (*S. sialis*) of E North America is about 6.5 in (17 cm) long and has a blue back and red-brown breast. Family: *Turdidae* (thrushes). *Compare* fairy bluebird.

bluebottle. *See* blowfly.

Bluefields 12 00N 83 49W The chief Caribbean port of Nicaragua, in the SE near the Escondido River. A 17th-century base (as Blewfeldt) of Dutch pirates, it was the capital of the British Mosquito Coast until 1850. Population (1978 est): 18,252.

bluefish A food fish, *Pomatomus saltator* (or *P. saltatrix*), also called tailor or snapper. The only member of the family *Pomatomidae*, it is found in all warm seas. It has a blue-green elongated body, up to 4 ft (1.2 m) long, with a whitish belly, a large mouth, and two dorsal fins. It lives in large schools and preys voraciously on other fish. Order: *Perciformes*.

blue fox. *See* Arctic fox.

bluegrass A perennial grass, *Poa pratensis*, also called meadow grass, native to Europe, Asia, and North America. It has erect stems, 12–35 in (30–90 cm) high, soft smooth leaves (which may be blue-tinged or green), and flower clusters 2–8 in (5–20 cm) long. It is widely cultivated for pastures and lawns.

blue-green algae Microscopic *algae of the division *Cyanophyta* (1500 species), which contain a blue pigment (phycocyanin), in addition to the green chlorophyll. They are single cells or filaments and resemble bacteria in their primitive structure (e.g. the genetic material is not organized into a distinct nucleus). Reproduction is asexual. Blue-green algae are widely distributed on land and in water. They occur on moist surfaces of rocks and trees, and in the soil, where they contribute to *nitrogen fixation. Aquatic blue-green algae are a constituent of plankton, sometimes forming dense concentrations (blooms), which color the water.

blue gum A fast-growing evergreen Australian □tree, *Eucalyptus globulus*, up to 130 ft (40 m) high with patchy gray and fawn bark. It has sickle-shaped blue-green leaves up to 10 in (25 cm) long. The timber is used for construction work and pulp, and eucalyptus oil is distilled from the leaves. Family: *Myrtaceae*. *See also* Eucalyptus.

Blue Mountains A mountain range in Australia, in New South Wales. Part of the *Great Dividing Range, it reaches 3871 ft (1180 m) at Bird Rock and contains the Blue Mountains National Park. It is a popular tourist area.

Blue Rider, The A group of artists formed in Munich in 1911 by *Marc and *Kandinsky when the latter's work was rejected by an exhibition committee. Their manifesto *Der Blaue Reiter Almanac* (1911) and their exhibitions illustrated their diverse influences: primitive naive art, children's pictures, and religious paintings on glass. Their aim was to unite in an expressionist style (*see* expressionism) the symbolic and spiritual elements manifest in the art of all ages. The group, which also included Paul *Klee and August *Macke, disbanded during World War I.

Blue Ridge Mountains A mountain range that extends NE from N Georgia to E West Virginia and W Virginia, part of the Appalachian Mountains. The highest point is Mount Mitchell 6684 ft (2038 m) in North Carolina. Noted for their scenic beauty, the Mountains include Shenandoah National Park (Virginia), Great Smoky Mountains National Park (North Carolina), the Appalachian Trail, and the Blue Ridge Parkway.

blues A type of American folk music that evolved from the Negro spirituals and work songs of the 1860s and became a song form used in jazz, rhythm and blues, and rock. The blues is a slow bitter-sweet song the syncopated melodic line and harmonies of which contain "blue" notes, which are flattened versions of certain notes in the major or minor scale. In origin it always consisted of three sets of four bars, in which the second set is a repetition of the first. The final line is improvised. The first published blues were "Memphis Blues" (1912) by W. C. Handy (1873–1958) and Jelly Roll Morton's "Jelly Roll Blues" (1915). The blues influenced the development of jazz and rock music and influenced classical composers such as George Gershwin, who wrote the orchestral *Rhapsody in Blue* (1924). Famous blues singers include Blind Lemon Jefferson (1897–1930), Bessie Smith (1898?–1937), and Billie Holiday (1915–59).

blue shark A *shark, *Prionace glauca*, that is abundant in warm-temperate and tropical seas. It has a slender dark-blue body, up to 13 ft (4 m) long, with a white belly and long sickle-shaped pectoral fins. It is found usually near the surface and feeds voraciously on shoaling fish, squid, and other sharks. Family: *Carcharhinidae*.

Blue Sky Law A term referring to any law that protects those who buy stocks and bonds from unscrupulous schemes that promise "the blue sky." The first law was passed by Kansas in 1911 and upheld by the US Supreme Court in 1917. Usually, blue sky laws provide for dealer licensing, issue registration, and penalties for fraudulent practice.

Bluestockings A group of intellectual society hostesses in 18th-century England. They included Lady Mary Wortley *Montagu and the novelist Fanny *Burney; their guests were Samuel *Johnson, Horace *Walpole, David *Garrick, and others, some of whom were accustomed to wearing ordinary blue, rather than formal dress, stockings to the meetings. The term is still used to describe intellectual women.

bluetit A European tit, *Parus caeruleus*, formerly a woodland species but now common in towns and gardens. It has a blue crown and wings, a yellow breast, white face and wing bars, and a black collar and eyestripe. Bluetits are acrobatic birds and feed chiefly on insect larvae.

bluets A tufted herb of the genus *Houstonia* (about 25 species), native to North America but often grown in rock gardens. The small white, blue, or purple funnel-shaped flowers are borne singly or in clusters. Some creeping species form mats, providing a close ground cover in shade. Family: *Rubiaceae* (madder family).

blue whale The largest living *whale, *Balaenoptera musculus*, probably the largest animal ever. It grows to over 98 ft (30 m) and weighs over 150 tons. Widely distributed in world oceans, blue whales are approaching extinction due to overhunting. Family: *Balaenopteridae* (*see* rorqual). □mammal.

Blum, Léon (1872–1950) French socialist, statesman, and writer; prime minister (1936–37, 1938, 1946–47). His *popular front government of 1936–37 brought about radical reforms in labor organizations and nationalized the Bank of France. After the fall of France to the Germans in 1940 Blum was arrested by the Vichy government and spent the remainder of the war in prison. From 1946 until his death he led the moderate socialist wing in France. His books include *L'Exercice du pouvoir* (1937) and *À l'échelle humaine* (1945).

blunderbuss A short-range smoothbore gun with a bell-shaped muzzle, firing many balls. In use from the 17th to 19th centuries, its name is derived from the Dutch word *donderbus*, thunder gun. It ranged in size from the pistol to the small artillery piece.

B'na-i B'rith (Sons of the Covenant) An international Jewish organization devoted to the betterment of life in the Jewish community. Founded in 1843 as a fraternal order, it included women by 1897 and now has over 500,000 members in almost 50 countries. It promotes civil rights and fights antisemitism through its Anti-Defamation League (1913), educates its youth through the Hillel Foundation on college campuses, and has many vocational services, hospitals, and philanthropic organizations.

boa A snake belonging to the subfamily *Boinae* (40–60 species) of the *constrictor family and occurring in Old and New World regions. 8 in–15 ft (20–760 cm) long, boas may be terrestrial, semiaquatic, or arboreal and are usually green, brown, or yellowish with a camouflaging pattern of blotches and diamonds. They kill their prey by biting and then constricting. The boa constrictor (*Boa constrictor*), occurring from Mexico to Argentina, is about 12 ft (3.5 m) long, hunts birds and small mammals at night, and bears live young.

Boadicea (Latin name: Boudicca; d. 60 AD) Queen of the *Iceni. Her husband Prasutagus ruled in what is now Norfolk (England). At his death in 60, Roman officials attempted to seize his wealth and maltreated Boadicea and her daughters. She led the Iceni into open rebellion and they sacked Colchester, London, and St Albans. The Roman governor Suetonius Paulinus defeated the rebels at or near Fenny Stratford on Watling Street. Boadicea committed suicide.

boar, wild A Eurasian wild *pig, *Sus scrofa*, once common in forests throughout Europe. Up to 5 ft (1.5 m) long and 40 in (1 m) high at the shoulder, wild boars have a rough bristly coat colored grayish brown. The ancestors of domestic pigs, they are still hunted for sport in some regions. Males have four tusks.

Boas, Franz (1858–1942) German-born US anthropologist. In 1886 Boas left his post of assistant curator of the Berlin Royal Ethnological Museum and embarked upon extensive research among the Indians of the NW American coast. In 1899 he became the first professor of anthropology at Columbia University. His most famous books are *The Mind of Primitive Man* (1911), *Primitive Art* (1927), and *Race, Language and Culture* (1940). Boas was concerned not only with the physical features of ethnic groups, but also with cultural and psychological aspects. He strongly opposed the racial theories propounded by the Nazis.

boatbill A nocturnal heron, *Cochlearius cochlearius*, occurring in tropical American swamps. It is about 20 in (50 cm) tall and has a gray plumage with black markings on the head and neck. It closely resembles the *night heron but has a characteristic broad flattened hook-tipped bill.

Boa Vista 2 51N 60 43W A town in N Brazil, the capital of Roraima territory on the Rio Branco. Important mineral resources include diamonds, gold, bauxite, and cassiterite. Population (1970): 37,062.

bobcat A short-tailed cat *Felis rufa*, resembling a lynx, found in North America from S Canada to Mexico. About 35 in (90 cm) long, it is brown with gray or white markings and has large ears tipped with a tuft of hairs. Bobcats feed at night on a wide variety of small birds, rodents, and deer.

Bobo-Dioulasso 11 11N 1 18W A city in SW Upper Volta. It is the country's main trade, industrial, and communications center. Industries include food processing and handicrafts. Population (1975): 115,063.

bobolink An American *oriole, *Dolichonyx oryzivorus*, that nests in Canada and the northern states of the US and migrates to South America in winter. It is black below and white above and nests on the ground, foraging for insects and seeds.

Bobruisk (or Bobruysk) 53 08N 29 10E A port in the W central Soviet Union, in the Belorussian SSR on the Berezina River. It has an 18th-century fortress and its industries include engineering, timber, and tire manufacturing. Population (1981 est): 203,000.

bobsledding The sport of racing bobsleds (also called bobsleighs or bobs), which was developed by British sportsmen at St Moritz (Switzerland) in the late 19th century. A bobsled is a steel-bodied toboggan with two pairs of runners, the front pair steerable, and a rear brake, holding two or four people. In a race, the bobsleds slide one at a time down a narrow icy chute some 1640 yd (1500 m) long with high walls and banked turns, reaching speeds of over 81 mph (130 km per h).

Boccaccio, Giovanni (1313–75) Italian writer and poet. Son of a merchant of Florence, he was sent to Naples about 1328 to learn business. Literature interested him more, however; between then and 1341, when he returned to Florence, he wrote *Filocolo*, a prose romance, *Filostrato*, which supplied the plot of Chaucer's *Troilus and Criseyde*, and *Teseida*, the source of Chaucer's *Knight's Tale*. Between 1348 and 1353 he composed the *Decameron*, a collection of a hundred stories told by a party of young people escaping from plague-stricken Florence in 1348. He met *Petrarch in 1350 and was much influenced by him. In later life he chiefly wrote scholarly works in Latin and lectured on Dante's *Divine Comedy*. He also founded the first chair of Greek in W Europe, at the University of Florence.

Boccherini, Luigi (1743–1805) Italian violoncellist and composer. He became famous in Rome while still a boy. Boccherini produced his first opera *La confederazione* (1765) in Lucca. His large output includes cello concertos and sonatas, symphonies, choral works, and string quintets and quartets.

Boccioni, Umberto (1882–1916) Italian futurist painter and sculptor. He trained under *Balla before settling in Milan (1907), where, influenced by the poet *Marinetti, he aimed to express the violence and speed of modern life in such paintings as *The City Rises* (1910; New York). His manifesto of futurist sculpture (1912) advocated the use of materials such as glass, cement, lightbulbs, etc.

Bochum 51 28N 7 11E A city in NW West Germany, in North Rhine-Westphalia. It is the site of the Ruhr University (1965). The manufacture of cars, textiles, and chemicals has replaced coalmining and iron and steel production. Population (1980 est): 402,000.

Bodawpaya (d. 1819) King of Burma (1789–1819). His aggressive policies ensured considerable expansion of Burmese territory during his reign. He annexed Arakan (1785), Manipur (1813), and Assam (1816) and almost precipitated an Anglo-Burmese war by demanding the surrender of Chittagong, Dacca, and Murshidabad from the British Indian government. His sudden death averted a confrontation. The *Burmese Domesday Book* (1784), a survey of Burma, was compiled during his reign.

Bodensee. *See* Constance, Lake.

Bode's law (or Titius-Bode law) A relationship between the distances of the planets from the sun. Take the number sequence 0, 3, 6, 12, 24, . . ., add 4 to each number, and divide each sum by 10. The resulting sequence is in good agreement with observed planetary distances (in astronomical units) out to Uranus, provided the belt of *minor planets is considered a single entity. Formulated by Johann Titius (1729–96) and popularized in 1772 by Johann Bode (1747–1826), it is still unexplained by theory.

Bodhidharma (6th century AD) Indian Buddhist patriarch from Conjeevaram, near Madras. He entered China about 520. Teaching a form of meditation called *dhyana* (Chinese *ch'an*, Japanese *zen*), he is credited with founding *Zen Buddhism.

Bodhisattva In Mahayana Buddhism, the title of a person who is to become a Buddha. The term is also used to describe the Buddha (Gautama) before his enlightenment. The Bodhisattva ideal is that of the individual who seeks enlightenment not for himself alone but for all beings. In Indian art the Bodhisattvas are depicted as youthful and represent various aspects of the nature of Buddha.

Bodin, Jean (1530–96) French philosopher and jurist. Although a Protestant, he was a successful lawyer and became parliamentary representative of Vermandois (1576). He visited Britain in 1581 where his belief in witchcraft, propounded in *Démonomanie des sorciers* (1580), later influenced James I. His greatest work, *La République* (1576), is a comprehensive political philosophy.

Bodleian Library The major *library of Oxford University, first established in 1409 and restored and enlarged by Sir Thomas Bodley from 1598 to 1602. Since 1610 it has been entitled to receive a free copy of every book published in Britain; it contains well over 2.5 million volumes.

Bodoni, Giambattista (1740–1813) Italian printer. In 1768 he became the Duke of Parma's printer and, influenced by François-Ambroise Didot (1730–1804), began to design his own typefaces. The best known, designed in 1790 and named for him, is still in use.

Boehm, Theobald (1794–1881) German flautist. He invented the **Boehm System**, a keyed mechanism for the flute that is still in use today and has been applied successfully to the clarinet and the oboe.

Boehme, Jakob. *See* Böhme.

Boeotia A region of central Greece, N and W of *Attica. Its main geographical features are rich central plains, surrounded by hills and mountains, and Lake Copaïs (now drained). The dozen or so city states that shared the territory formed a federal state dominated by *Thebes in 446 BC. The Boeotians had a reputation for good living and stupidity, belied by the military success of Thebes and the poetry of *Hesiod and *Pindar, among others. Boeotians took no part in Greek colonization overseas.

Boer. *See* Afrikaner.

Boer Wars (or South African Wars) The wars fought against the British by the Boers or *Afrikaners of South Africa. In the first (1880–81) the Boers of the Transvaal under *Kruger rebelled against British rule. After inflicting a massive defeat on the British garrison at *Majuba Hill, the Transvaal regained its independence under the *Pretoria Convention. In the second Boer War (1899–1902) the Boer forces of the South African Republic (previously the Transvaal) and Orange Free State were initially successful, besieging Ladysmith, Mafeking (held courageously by *Baden-Powell from October, 1899, until his relief in February, 1900), and Kimberley. They suffered reverses during 1900 but, using guerrilla tactics, were able to hold off the British under *Kitchener and F. S. *Roberts. The British devastated the countryside, rounded up Boer women and children, of whom some 20,000 died in concentration camps, and finally defeated the Boers, who lost their independence in the Peace of Vereeniging (1902).

Boethius, Anicius Manlius Severinus (c. 480–524 AD) Roman statesman and philosopher. A patrician by birth, Boethius was consul in 510 during the Gothic occupation of Rome under *Theoderic, to whom he became chief minister. His championing of Roman traditions and institu-

BOER WAR On Cronjé's Heels *(1900), by the British war artist H. Seppings Wright. The tactics of the Boers and the unfamiliar terrain caused problems for the conventionally trained British troops.*

tions earned Theoderic's displeasure, and Boethius was imprisoned, tortured, and eventually executed. His translations of Aristotle and treatises on music and mathematics were standard texts in medieval Europe but his most famous work is *The Consolation of Philosophy,* written while he was in prison. A dialogue between the author and the personification of philosophy, the *Consolation* seeks to prove that virtue alone remains constant and the knowledge of God is the only true wisdom.

HUMPHREY BOGART *With Rod Steiger (right) in* The Harder They Fall *(1956).*

Bogart, Humphrey (1899–1957) US film actor. He achieved international success in the 1940s with his portrayals of tough heroes whose cynicism masked a romantic idealism. His films include *The Petrified Forest* (1936), *The Maltese Falcon* (1941), *Casablanca* (1942), *To Have and Have Not* (1944), in which Lauren Bacall (1924–), whom he subsequently married, made her screen debut, *The Big Sleep* (1946), *The African Queen* (1951) for which he won an Academy Award, and *The Harder They Fall* (1956).

Boğazköy (*or* Boğazkale). *See* Hattusas.

Bogomils. *See* Cathari.

Bogor (former name: Buitenzorg) 6 34S 106 45E A city in Indonesia, on W Java. It is famed for its botanical garden (1817) and former Dutch governor general's residence (1745). It is an agricultural center with an agricultural university (founded 1963) and an important research institute. Population (1971): 195,882.

Bogotá, Santa Fé de 4 38N 74 15W The capital of Colombia, on a fertile central plateau of the E Andes at an altitude of 8600 ft (2640 m). Founded by the Spanish in the early 16th century on the site of the conquered Indian settlement of Bacatá, it became capital of the viceroyalty of New Grenada and an important cultural center. Today it possesses a university (1867), a number of colleges, and several notable technical schools. Regular airlines have helped to improve its rather isolated position from the rest of the country. Population (1978 est): 3,831,098.

Bohai. *See* Chihli, Gulf of.

Bohemia (Czech name: Čechy; German name: Böhmen) An area and former province (1918–49) of W Czechoslovakia. It consists chiefly of a plateau enclosed by mountains. The most industrialized part of Czechoslovakia, Bohemia possesses important mineral resources, including uranium, coal, and iron ore. Agriculture is well developed. It is renowned for its many mineral springs. *History*: Bohemia derives its name from the Boii (the first known inhabitants), who were displaced by the Czechs (1st-5th centuries AD). Bohemia became part of the greater Moravian empire in the 9th century, during which period Christianity was introduced. St Wenceslas was the first great Bohemian ruler but his brother, Boleslav I (d. 967; reigned 929–67), was forced to acknowledge the rule of Emperor Otto I and for many centuries thereafter Bohemia was linked with the Holy Roman Empire. During the 11th century there was a successful expedition into Moravia, which was linked from then on with Bohemia. It achieved the height of its power following the acquisitions of the Přemyslid Otakar II (1230–78; reigned 1253–78). The Přemyslid dynasty came to an end with the assassination of Wenceslas III (1289–1306; reigned 1305–06) and John of Luxemborg was subsequently elected king (1310). The golden age of Bohemia was established by his son Charles I (Emperor *Charles IV), who founded the university at Prague in 1348. The reigns of his successors were marked by religious upheavals inspired by Jan Hus (*see* Hussites).

The accession (1526) of Archduke Ferdinand began the long Habsburg domination of Bohemia. It was laid waste during the Thirty Years' War and after the Peace of Westphalia (1648) forcible Germanization and oppressive taxation reduced most Czechs to misery. There was a rebirth of Czech nationalism during the 19th century but full independence was only attained at the end of World War I, when Bohemia became part of the Republic of Czechoslovakia.

Bohemond I (*or* Bohemund; c. 1056–1111) Prince of Antioch (1099–1111). He fought (1080–85) with his father Robert Guiscard against Alexius I Comnenus and was a leader of the first Crusade, during which he took Antioch (1098). He was captured by the Turks (1100–03) and after renewed warfare with Alexius became his vassal (1108).

Böhm, Karl (1894–1981) Austrian conductor, who was noted particularly for his performances of operas by Mozart and Richard Strauss. He was conductor of the Dresden State Opera (1934–43) and the Vienna State Opera (1943–45).

Böhme, Jakob (*or* Boehme; 1575–1624) German Lutheran theosophist, who lived most of his life as a shoemaker in Silesia. His first work, the *Aurora* (1612), was condemned by the local authorities. Although forbidden to write, he later published such works as *Der Weg zu Christo* and *Mysterium magnum* (both 1623). He was influenced by *Paracelsus, alchemy, and astrology but also claimed divine inspiration for his writings. His central belief was that God was the source of everything, including evil, since he had two wills, one good and the other evil. He has influenced many thinkers, notably *Hegel and *Schelling.

Bohr, Niels Henrik David (1885–1962) Danish physicist. He made an immense contribution to atomic theory by combining *Rutherford's nuclear model with Planck's quantum theory. The model of the atom he proposed (the *Bohr atom) was modified by *Sommerfeld but is essentially the basis for modern atomic theory. Bohr also invented the concept of complementarity to combine the particle and wave aspects of subatomic particles. He was awarded a Nobel Prize in 1922. During the 1930s his Institute of Theoretical Physics in Copenhagen became a haven for many Jewish and other physicists expelled by Hitler. In 1939 he took news of Meitner's and Hahn's uranium fission work to the US and started the process that culminated in the manufacture of the atomic bomb. Bohr himself later worked at Los Alamos on the bomb, after escaping from German-occupied Denmark. A fervent advocate of atomic energy for peaceful uses, he organized the first Atoms for Peace Conference in 1955. His son **Aage Bohr** (1922–) shared the 1975 Nobel Prize for Physics for his work on atomic theory.

Bohr atom A model of the atom, put forward by Niels *Bohr in 1913. His model assumes that electrons move around a central nucleus in circular orbits. The electrons are confined to fixed orbits at fixed distances from the nucleus, each orbit corresponding to a specific energy level. If the electron gains or loses the right amount of energy, in the form of a photon of electromagnetic radiation, it jumps or falls into another orbit. The jumps are quantized (*see* quantum theory), the energy associated with each jump being equal to hf, where h is the Planck constant and f is the frequency of the radiation. The model gives a good explanation of the spectral emission of the hydrogen atom and was later modified by *Sommerfeld to explain the fine structure of the hydrogen lines, by assuming that the electrons move in precessing elliptical orbits.

Boiardo, Matteo Maria, Conte di Scandiano (1441–94) Italian poet. He served the Dukes of Ferrara as governor of Modena (1480–82) and Reggio (1487–94). His chief work was the unfinished *Orlando innamorato* (1483), a chivalrous epic about Roland (*see* Charlemagne) and the precursor of the more famous *Orlando furioso* by *Ariosto.

boil An inflamed pus-filled swelling on the skin, usually caused by infection of a hair follicle with the bacterium *Staphylococcus aureus*. Boils are more likely to develop when constitutional resistance is low or when the diet is inadequate. The application of a warm poultice will bring the boil to a head and allow the pus to drain. A **carbuncle** is a collection of boils situated close together; it is slightly more difficult to treat and may require the use of antibiotics.

Boileau(-Despréaux), Nicolas (1636–1711) French poet and critic. After the publication of his satires in 1666 he became friendly with *Molière, *Racine, and other leading writers. *L'Art poétique* (1674) was received as a definitive guide to the classical principles in literature and had a powerful contemporary influence in France and England. He also wrote a mock epic, *Le Lutrin* (1674), and translated *Longinus' treatise *On the Sublime*.

boiling point The temperature at which the *vapor pressure of a liquid is equal to the atmospheric pressure. The boiling point of a liquid is usually given at standard atmospheric pressure (101,325 pascals).

Bois de Boulogne A park in W Paris, France, bordering on the Seine River. It was presented to the city in 1852 by Napoleon III and contains the Auteuil and Longchamp racecourses. Area: 2125 acres (860 ha).

Boise 43 38N 116 12W The capital and largest city of Idaho. The center of a gold rush in 1862, it has timber, food-processing, and agricultural industries. Population (1980): 102,451.

Boito, Arrigo (1842–1918) Italian composer and librettist. An accomplished poet, he wrote the librettos for Verdi's last operas, *Otello* (1887) and *Falstaff* (1893). He adapted the libretto of his own opera *Mefistofele* (1868) from *Goethe's *Faust*.

Bokassa I (Jean Bedel B.; 1921–) Emperor of the Central African Empire from 1977 until his overthrow in 1979. He seized power in the Central African Republic in 1966, becoming president and later proclaiming himself emperor.

Bokhara. *See* Bukhara.

Bolesław (I) the Brave (c. 966–1025) The first King of Poland, who extended the territory of the Polish principality, which he inherited in 992, and was crowned king (1000) by Emperor Otto III. He reorganized the Polish church, making it responsible directly to the pope and independent of the German church.

Bolesław (II) the Generous (1039–81) King of Poland (1058–79), recognized by the pope in 1076. Bolesław successfully pursued Polish interests at the expense of German influence until a revolt of the clergy and nobility led to his excommunication and deposition.

Bolesław (III) the Wry-Mouthed (1086–1138) Ruler of Poland (1102–38). Bolesław never took the title of king. Between 1113 and 1135 he reconquered and christianized Pomerania.

Boletus A genus of mushrooms (about 50 species). The undersurface of the cap bears a series of vertical tubes (instead of gills), in which the spores are formed. Most grow near trees and they are generally edible or harmless (*see* cèpe). An exception is Satan's boletus (*B. satanas*), which is poisonous but not deadly. It has a short stalk and a gray or grayish-green cap 4–8 in (10–20 cm) in diameter. Family: *Boletaceae*; class: *Basidiomycetes*.

Boleyn, Anne (c. 1507–36) The second wife (from 1533) of Henry VIII of England and the mother of Elizabeth I. Henry soon tired of Anne, who was accused of adultery and executed.

Bolingbroke, Henry St John, 1st Viscount (1678–1751) English statesman and philosopher. A Tory, he became a member of parliament in 1701 and was secretary of war (1704–08) before becoming secretary of state for the north in 1710. A supporter of the *Jacobites, he fled to France (1715–25) after their failed rebellion. There, he encountered the major thinkers of the *Enlightenment (including Voltaire) and wrote *Reflections upon Exile* and *Reflections Concerning Innate Moral Principles*. He became the bitter opponent of Robert *Walpole and wanted to create a Country Party of Whigs and Tories united by their opposition to Walpole. In 1735 he returned to France. He also wrote *The Idea of a Patriot King* (1749).

Bolívar Simón (1783–1830) South American soldier and statesman, known as the Liberator. The son of a wealthy Venezuelan creole family, his childhood tutor and subsequent travels in Europe instilled in Bolívar a lasting admiration for the ideas of the Enlightenment. He returned to Latin America in 1807 and devoted the rest of his life to its liberation from Spain. In 1813 he seized Caracas but after defeat in 1814 went into exile until 1817. His victory at the battle of *Boyacá (1819) achieved the liberation of New Granada, which was renamed Colombia. Bolívar became its president after liberating Venezuela and Quito (Ecuador) in 1821, and organized a federation of the three newly independent states. Latin America was finally freed of the Spanish by campaigns in Peru, and Upper Peru took the name Bolivia in honor of Bolívar, who became its president. His dream of a united Andean republic was never realized and he died disillusioned by the political bickering that thwarted this goal.

Bolivia, Republic of An inland country in central South America consisting of low plains in the N and E, crossed by the Madre de Dios, Bené, and Mamoré river systems; in the W, ranges of the Andes rise to over 21,000 ft (6400 m) and the Altiplano, a plateau averaging about 13,000 ft (3900 m), contains Lakes Titicaca and Poopó. Bolivia has some of the world's highest inhabited regions, most of the population, which is of mixed Indian and Spanish descent, living at altitudes of over 3000 m (10,000 ft). *Economy*: Bolivia is one of the poorest South American countries. Tin mining has long been of the first importance to Bolivia's economy and remains the principal industry. The main tin producers have been nationalized in recent years. Other minerals include zinc, lead, antimony, and copper. Silver is much less important than previously. Agriculture is being improved in the E part and the main crops are sugar cane, potatoes, maize, rice, and wheat. Livestock, including llamas, is raised and forestry is being developed. Main exports include tin and other minerals, oil (through a pipeline to Arica on the Chilean coast), natural gas (to Argentina), hides and skins, and vicuña wool. Poor transportation is a detriment to growth. *History*: ruins near Tiahuanaco indicate the existence of a pre-Inca civilization (the Aymaras) going back to the 10th century. The area later became part of the Inca Empire and was conquered by the Spanish in the 16th century, when it became known as Alto Peru. The discovery of tin and silver at Potosí soon after the Spanish conquest led to great prosperity. In 1776 it became part of the viceroyalty of Buenos Aires. After a long war it gained its independence with the help of Simón Bolívar in 1825 and became a republic with Antonio José de *Sucre as first president. During the remainder of the century as a result of civil wars and struggles with neighboring countries Bolivia lost much territory, including access to the Pacific coast. Political unrest and violent changes of government have continued into the 20th century and in 1971 a military coup brought General Hugo Banzer Suárez to power. He achieved a measure of political stability, remaining in office until overthrown in a coup in 1978. Since then frequent political upheavals have resumed with a resulting succession of presidents. Disputes with Peru and Chile continue over the question of access to the Pacific coast and these have heightened in recent years. Official languages: Spanish, Quechua, and Aymara. Official currency: peso boliviano of 100 centavos. Area: 424,160 sq mi (1,098,580 sq km). Population (1983 est): 5,883,000. Capital: La Paz (legal capital: Sucre).

Böll, Heinrich (1917–85) German novelist. After infantry service in World War II, he eventually settled down as a full-time writer in 1951. His novels and stories include *The Train Was on Time* (1949), *The Clown* (1963), *The Lost Honor of Katharina Blum* (1975) and *The Safety Net* (1982). His writing frequently depicts ironically the moral degeneration of postwar German society. He won the Nobel Prize in 1972.

Bollandists The *Jesuit scholars who continued the work on the *Acta Sanctorum*, an authoritative edition of the lives of the saints, begun by the founder and first editor of the project, John van Bolland (1596–1665). The first two volumes of the work were published in Antwerp in 1643, and the most recent one appeared in 1940.

boll weevil A stout brownish *weevil, *Anthonomus grandis*, also called cotton boll weevil. Originally a native of the New World tropics, it is now a major insect pest of cotton crops in the W hemisphere. The female lays a single egg within each cotton boll, which thus fails to develop.

Bologna 44 30N 11 20E A city in N Italy, the capital of Emilia-Romagna. The history of the site of Bologna dates from Etruscan times. It became a free city in the middle ages and the Emperor Charles V was crowned here in 1530. It has an ancient university (1088) and a 14th-century gothic church. Its industries include engineering and food processing. Population (1980 est): 466,593.

Bologna, Giovanni da. *See* Giambologna.

Bolsheviks One of the two factions into which the Russian Social Democratic Workers' Party split in 1903 in London (the other was the *Mensheviks). The Bolsheviks, which means those in the majority, were led by *Lenin, who believed that the revolution must be guided by a single centralized party of professional revolutionaries (*see also* Leninism). The Bolsheviks came to power in the *Russian Revolution (1917) and from 1918 until 1952 the Soviet Communist Party was termed Communist Party (Bolsheviks).

Bolshoi Ballet The principal Russian ballet company, based at the Bolshoi Theater in Moscow. It originated from a dancing class established by the Moscow orphanage in the late 18th century and moved into its present premises in 1856 after fire had destroyed the first Bolshoi Theater. Known for its dramatic style and its realistic and elaborate scenery, it first appeared in the West in 1956 in London and has since become one of the world's leading ballet companies.

Bolton 53 35W 2 26W A city in NW England, in Greater Manchester. Traditionally a cotton-spinning town (Samuel Crompton, inventor of the spinning mule, was born here), Bolton also manufactures textile machinery and chemicals and is involved in engineering. Population (1981): 146,722.

Boltzmann, Ludwig Eduard (1844–1906) Austrian physicist, who developed statistical mechanics with J. C. *Maxwell and J. W. *Gibbs, notably the Maxwell-Boltzmann statistics of particle systems obeying classical laws. He also linked thermodynamics with molecular physics by showing that increasing entropy is related to increasing disorder among particles. Working with his teacher Josef Stefan (1835–93), he showed that Stefan's

law could be derived thermodynamically and it is now usually known as the *Stefan-Boltzmann law.

Boltzmann constant (k) A constant, obtained by dividing the *gas constant by *Avogadro's number, equal to 1.3806×10^{-23} joule per kelvin. Named for Ludwig *Boltzmann.

Bolyai, János (1802–60) Hungarian mathematician, who (with *Lobachevski) was the first to study the properties of spaces with *non-Euclidean geometry.

Bolzano 46 30N 11 22E A city in Italy, in Trentino-Alto Adige. It has a 14th-century gothic cathedral. Bolzano is a center for tourism and trades in fruit and wine. There are steel and textile industries. Population (1980 est): 105,854.

Boma 5 50S 13 03E A port in SW Zaïre, on the Zaïre River. It was formerly the capital of the Congo Free State, later the Belgian Congo (1886–1926). Forest products, such as palm oil, are exported. Population (1970): 61,054.

bombardier beetle A blue-gray and orange beetle, about 0.35 in (9 mm) long, belonging to a widely distributed genus (*Brachinus*) of *ground beetles. It has an efficient means of chemical defense, emitting puffs of an irritant secretion from the anal glands. Similar beetles of the genus *Pherosophus* occur in Africa, Asia, and the East Indies.

Bombay 18 56N 72 51E A city in India, the capital of Maharashtra and the country's main seaport on the W coast. The city proper occupies a group of islands that are united by a system of causeways and breakwaters; the site, known as Bombay Island, is linked with Salsette Island in the N. Its natural harbor, 7 mi (11 km) wide, is the focus of most of India's international trade. Bombay is also the financial and commercial center of the country. Industry includes cotton textiles, food processing, and oil refining. The city is also the site of the country's first nuclear reactor. The harbor is dominated by the monumental Gateway of India arch (1911). The University of Bombay (1857) and numerous government buildings are situated in the center of the city and the many temples (dating from the 8th century AD and earlier) reflect the cultural and religious diversity to be found in the city. The population is mainly Hindu but there are large Muslim, Christian, and Jewish minorities. The city's island location has led to problems of overcrowding and a twin city on the mainland is planned. *History*: ceded to the Portuguese in 1534, it passed to Charles II of England in 1661 and to the British East India Company in 1668. The arrival of the railroads, the opening of the Suez Canal, and land reclamation led to considerable expansion in the 19th century. Population (1971): 5,970,575.

Bombay duck A fish, *Harpodon nehereus*, found in the estuaries of N India, where it is widely used for food. It has a gray or brown body, about 16 in (40 cm) long, with small dark speckles and large pectoral and pelvic fins. Order: *Myctophiformes*.

Bon The pre-Buddhist religion of Tibet, characterized by the belief in a supreme sky god and a hierarchy of good and evil spirits, gods, demons, and ghosts. Elaborate ritual, including animal or even human sacrifice, abounded; religious practice was presided over by a class of shamans (*see* shamanism), priest-magicians who could influence the spirits by means of white or black magic, even being able to open the gate between earth and heaven. It was absorbed into Tibetan Buddhism, to which it lent a very individual character.

Bon, Cape 37 05N 11 02E A peninsula in NE Tunisia, extending into the Mediterranean Sea. Its fertile plains produce oranges, olives, and market-garden produce. Length: about 46 mi (75 km). Width: 22 mi (35 km).

Bonaparte (*or* Buonaparte) A Corsican family that included the French emperors, *Napoleon I and *Napoleon III, and the nominal emperor, *Napoleon II. **Carlo Bonaparte** (1746–85), a lawyer, had four sons. **Joseph Bonaparte** (1768–1844) was a diplomat of indifferent qualities who rose to high office by virtue of the position of his brother Napoleon I, from whom he received the thrones of Naples (1806) and Spain (1808). After Napoleon's defeat at Waterloo (1815) Joseph lived in exile. **Lucien Bonaparte** (1775–1840) was president of the Council of Five Hundred under the Directory and became a critic of Napoleon's policies. The brothers were reconciled, however, on the eve of Waterloo and after Napoleon's defeat Lucien lived in exile in Italy. **Louis Bonaparte** (1778–1846) was created King of Holland by Napoleon in 1806 but, exasperated by Louis' inability to enforce the *Continental System, Napoleon obliged him to relinquish the crown in 1810. He too died in exile. His son by Hortense de *Beauharnais became Napoleon III. **Jérôme Bonaparte** (1784–1860) was created King of Westphalia in 1807 and was a commander in Napoleon's Russian invasion and at Waterloo. He survived to become a dignitary in the Second Empire (1852–70), established by his nephew Napoleon III.

The exploits of these and other members of the Bonaparte family formed the iconography of **Bonapartism**, a movement that sought to recreate the Napoleonic empire and to establish the dynasty in France. Louis Napoleon's *Des idées napoléoniennes* (1839) typified the romantic and conservative nature of Bonapartism.

Bonaventure, St (Giovanni di Fidanza; c. 1221–74) Italian Franciscan theologian, known as Doctor Seraphicus. He studied and lectured at Paris, in 1257 receiving the degree of doctor and becoming minister general of the Franciscan Order. He wrote the official biography of St Francis. As a theologian, he supported the traditional teachings of St Augustine, as opposed to the new Aristotelian thought that influenced his contemporary St Thomas *Aquinas. Feast day: July 14. Emblem: a cardinal's hat.

bond A security issued by a government, local authority, or public company as a means of raising capital. Most bonds pay a fixed rate of interest and are redeemable on a stated day. *See also* gilt-edged securities.

bone A rigid tissue that forms most of the skeleton of higher animals and man. The shape of individual bones is governed by their function (*see* skeleton). Most bones have a central cavity filled with *marrow. Bone is composed of a matrix of fibers of the protein collagen, responsible for the strength of bones, and bone salts, chiefly calcium salts (*see* apatite). This tissue is formed by activity of bone cells (osteoblasts), which become enclosed in the matrix when they have ceased to function. Bone formation starts during embryonic life. Most bones (including the long bones) develop from cartilage and the process is complete at birth. Membrane bones (e.g. the skull bones) are formed directly in connective tissue, the process being completed after birth (hence the gap (called a fontanelle) in a newborn baby's skull). The branch of medicine concerned with the diagnosis and treatment of diseases of bones is called **osteology**.

Bône. *See* Annaba.

boneset A plant of the genus *Eupatorium*, also called thoroughwort, found in tropical South America, Mexico, and the West Indies but grown elsewhere as greenhouse or border plants. Boneset is a perennial herb, shrub, or small tree. The flat-topped flower heads consist of disk florets, usually rose or white, with protruding styles. Family: *Compositae*. *See also* comfrey.

bongo An antelope, *Boocerus euryceros*, of dense tropical central African forests. About 48 in (120 cm) high at the shoulder, bongos are red-brown with vertical white body stripes and white markings on the head and legs. The male has spiraled horns up to 40 in (100 cm) long. Bulls are solitary; cows and calves live in small herds. They feed on leaves and shoots. ◻mammals.

Bonhoeffer, Dietrich (1906–45) German pastor and theologian. As a young theological lecturer and pastor, Bonhoeffer identified himself with the German *Confessing Church, which opposed the pro-Nazi part of the Lutheran church, and during the war became involved with anti-Hitler conspirators. He was arrested in 1943, sent to Buchenwald concentration camp, and finally hanged. His posthumous *Letters and Papers from Prison* (1953) and radical theological writings continue to be influential.

Boniface, St (*or* St Wynfrith; c. 680–754 AD) English missionary, known as the Apostle of Germany. He was born in Crediton, Devon, and entered the Benedictine Order. He visited Frisia in 716 and in 718 was granted papal authority to evangelize the Germans. He successfully established Christianity in several German states and instituted church reforms elsewhere, culminating in his appointment as Archbishop of Mainz in 751. He was martyred with 53 companions in Frisia. Feast day: June 5.

Boniface VIII (Benedict Caetani; c. 1234–1303) Pope (1294–1303). He was elected after a long career in papal administration. An expert in canon law, he repeatedly clashed with *Philip IV of France concerning papal supremacy and the royal claim to judge and tax the clergy (which he also disputed with *Edward I of England). The bull *Unam Sanctam* (*One Holy*; 1302) proclaimed papal supremacy over temporal powers. In 1304 he was captured in Italy by Philip's forces and although soon released died shortly afterward.

Bonin Islands A Japanese group of about 30 forested volcanic islands in the central Pacific Ocean, the most important being Chichi-jima. Strategically important during World War II, they were captured by the US in 1945 (returned 1968). Sugar cane, cocoa, and bananas are produced, timber is exported, and there is offshore whaling. Area: 40 sq mi (103 sq km). Population (1970 est): 300. Chief settlement: Omura.

bonito A swift marine food and game fish, belonging to the worldwide genus *Sarda*, which is related to *mackerel and *tuna. About 30 in (75 cm) long, bonitos are greenish blue above, with dark longitudinal stripes, and silvery below. Other related fish called bonito include the leaping bonito

(*Cybiosarda elegans*), plain bonito (*Orcynopsis unicolor*), and *skipjack tuna. ◻oceans.

Bonn 50 43N 7 07E The capital of the Federal Republic of Germany (West Germany), in North Rhine-Westphalia on the Rhine River. The old part of the town contains the cathedral (12th–13th centuries) and Beethoven's birthplace (now a museum). The university was founded in 1786. *History*: originally settled by the Romans, it was destroyed by the Normans in the 9th century AD, and was the seat of the Electors of Cologne from the 13th to the 16th centuries. It passed from France to Prussia in 1815 and was made the federal capital in 1949. Population (1980 est): 287,100.

Bonnard, Pierre (1867–1947) French painter. He took up art in Paris in the 1880s, after studying law, and as a member of the *Nabis, he painted decorative domestic scenes, influenced by Japanese prints. More original works of this period were his lithographs, *Aspects of the Life of Paris* (1895), and illustrations for Verlaine's book *Parallèlement* (1900). After 1900 his paintings of interiors, landscapes, and bathing women were treated increasingly with dazzling color and light.

Bonnet, Charles (1720–93) Swiss naturalist, noted for his speculations about evolution. He demonstrated that aphid eggs could develop without fertilization (*see* parthenogenesis). This led him to propose that every organism contained a sequence of preformed individuals corresponding to successive generations. His catastrophe theory of evolution argued that periodic destruction of most life forms was followed by evolutionary advancement of the survivors.

Bonneville Salt Flats (*or* Bonneville Flats) A barren salt plain in the US, in NW Utah. The flats form part of the Great Salt Lake Desert and are a relict feature of an ancient lake. Several world land speed records have been established here since 1935.

Bonnie Prince Charlie. *See* Charles Edward Stuart, the Young Pretender.

Bonny, Bight of (name until 1975: Bight of Biafra) An inlet of the Atlantic Ocean, bordering on Nigeria and Cameroon. It is the innermost bay of the Gulf of Guinea.

bonsai An ordinary shrub or tree, such as a conifer or flowering cherry, that is developed as a miniature (up to about 24 in [60 cm] high). The technique was first practiced as an art form in China over 700 years ago, probably using weather-beaten trees, which were considered aesthetically pleasing. It was later perfected by the Japanese (who treat good specimens as heirlooms) and has now spread to the W hemisphere. Bonsais grow from seeds or cuttings planted usually in earthenware pots with one or more drainage holes and containing a compost with a limited nutrient and water supply. Both branches and roots are trained and pruned. The trees may take ten years or more to acquire an aged appearance, and some live 300–400 years. Good hardy species may be kept outdoors for most of the year.

bontebok. *See* blesbok.

Bonus Army (1932) Unemployed veterans who marched on Washington, DC to demand payment of adjusted compensation certificates voted them in 1924, but deferred until 1945. After much rioting and violence, the veterans were given travel money and persuaded to leave the city, and by 1936 had received their compensation.

bony fish Any fish belonging to the class *Osteichthyes* (or *Pisces*), which includes the majority of food and game fishes (*see* teleost). They have bony skeletons and their gills are covered by a structure called an operculum. Many species use a swim bladder for buoyancy control and even for breathing air (*see* lungfish). Fertilization of the eggs occurs outside the body. Subclasses: *Actinopterygii*; *Sarcopterygii*.

booby A large tropical seabird belonging to the family *Sulidae* (gannets, etc.; 9 species) characterized by a large head, a long stout tapering bill, large webbed feet, and a wedge-shaped tail. Boobies are 26–33 in (65–85 cm) long and typically have a white plumage with brown markings. Boobies soar high over the sea, diving to catch fish and squids.

boogie-woogie A piano blues in which the left hand establishes a driving repetitive pattern with eight beats to the bar, while the right provides a variety of syncopation. Originating in the SW US, it was popular in the 1930s.

book A set of sheets of paper or similar material, usually bearing printed or handwritten words, folded and bound together between protective covers. The handwritten book (the codex), combining compactness, strength, and ease of use, began to oust its predecessor, the cumbersome papyrus scroll, during the 2nd century AD. Vellum (or parchment), being more durable than papyrus, became the preferred writing surface until the use of *paper spread slowly across Europe from 11th-century Byzantium. Printing at first brought no radical changes in book production, the sheets still being folded and bound by hand. Development of more efficient presses and cheaper paper production in the late 18th and early 19th centuries gradually brought the price of books within reach of the general public. During the 20th century paper binding (paperbacks), brought about a revolution in publishing so that in the US alone over 32,000 new titles are published each year. In response to this deluge libraries have evolved new methods of data storage, using microfiche and microfilm (*see* microcopy).

BOOBY *Blue-footed boobies (Sula nebouxii) of the Galapagos Islands in courtship display. The male (left) can be distinguished from the female by its smaller eye pupil.*

bookbinding The practice of sewing or gluing together the pages of a *book along one edge and securing them between protective covers (boards) joined across the back (spine) by a flexible hinge. Utilitarian in purpose, bookbinding has nonetheless long been practiced as a decorative art. In the middle ages wooden boards were common and elaborate examples were encrusted with precious metals and gems. The advent of printing encouraged diversification in the types of material used for binding, with leather and vellum becoming paramount. Gold tooling, the commonest form of decoration, reached a peak of elaboration in the 17th and 18th centuries. The spread of literacy caused a demand for still cheaper binding materials; cloth bindings (1822), and in the 20th century paper and plastics, have catered to this need.

Nowadays books are bound by machinery, first invented in the late 19th century. The bindings are similar to hand bindings except in paperbacks, which are simply glued together. Hand binding remains a specialist craft employed in the production of luxury books.

Booker McConnell Prize An annual prize of 10,000 for a work of British fiction. It was set up in 1968 by the British engineering and trading company Booker McConnell, in conjunction with the Publishers Association, on the lines of the French Prix Goncourt (*see* Edmond de Goncourt). Since 1971 it has been administered by the National book League. Recent winners include William *Golding (1980), Salman *Rushdie (1981), Thomas Keneally (1982), J. M. Coetzee (1983), and Anita Brookner (1984).

booklouse A soft-bodied wingless insect 0.04–0.28 in (1–7 mm) long, also called dustlouse, belonging to the order *Psocoptera* (about 1600 species). Booklice inhabit buildings, often feeding on old books, papers, and entomological collections. *See also* bookworm.

bookmaking The occupation of accepting bets, chiefly involving horse racing and professional and college sports events, but also other sports, current events, etc. The bookmaker (bookie) lays odds against a particular horse winning a race, which the bettor accepts. Licensed betting shops have been established in some states. *See also* Totalizator.

Book of Changes. *See* I Ching.

Book of the Dead A collection of ancient Egyptian texts dating from the 16th century BC. They consist of charms, formulas, and spells written on papyrus and placed inside mummy cases for use by the dead in the afterlife.

bookworm Any insect that damages books by gnawing the bindings and boring holes in the paper. Bookworms therefore include *silverfish, booklice, moth and beetle larvae, etc.

Boole, George (1815–64) British mathematician, who applied the methods of algebra to logic. Replacing logical operations with symbols, Boole showed that the operations could be manipulated to give logically consistent results. His method, known as Boolean algebra or symbolic logic, led to mathematics being given a logically consistent foundation. The subject was further developed by G. Frege, B. A. W. *Russell, and A. N. *Whitehead.

boom The phase in the *trade cycle in which output reaches a peak. Booms are characterized by full employment, rising prices, high profits, and high investment that goes with business confidence. *Compare* depression; recession.

boomerang A curved hand-thrown wooden missile used by Australian Aborigines to kill game, as a weapon of war, or in play. The angled shape and the spin given to the missile when thrown enables the light types to return to the thrower if they miss their target. Up to 30 in (75 cm) long, they can be effective to a distance of 50 yd (45 m).

boomslang A venomous green snake, *Dispholidus typus*, occurring in African savanna and reaching 6 ft (1.8 m) in length. It feeds on birds and chameleons, lying in wait and often holding its body erect and motionless before striking. Small amounts of its venom can cause fatal hemorrhaging in man. Family: *Colubridae*.

DANIEL BOONE *A renowned frontiersman who explored Kentucky and helped open the area for American settlers.*

Boone, Daniel (1734–1820) American pioneer. Born in Pennsylvania, he left home at an early age and became a hunter in North Carolina and later served in the *French and Indian War. In 1767 he led a group of settlers along the Wilderness Road through the Cumberland Gap into Kentucky. After several years of exploration there, he guided another group of settlers into Kentucky in 1775 to found a colony for the Transylvania Company. The settlement was later named Boonesboro. During the Revolutionary War, Boone was taken prisoner by the Shawnees, but he was adopted by the tribe and set free. After the war, he was appointed to several public offices in Kentucky but lost all his land holdings, due to a failure to register them properly. Late in his life he moved to Missouri, where he received a small land grant from Congress.

Boonesboro (*or* Boonesborough) A former fort in central Kentucky, SE of Lexington, on the Kentucky River. Settled by frontiersman Daniel Boone in 1775, it was the end of a branch of the Wilderness Road.

Boötes (Latin: herdsman) A large constellation in the N sky near Ursa Major. The brightest star is *Arcturus.

Booth, Edwin (1833–93) US actor. Born in Maryland, the son of the prominent actor Junius Brutus Booth (1796–1852) and older brother of John Wilkes *Booth, he first appeared on stage at age 16. He was best known for his performances in Shakespearean tragic roles, especially Hamlet, which he performed for one hundred consecutive nights in 1864. As a result of his great popularity and commercial success, he constructed Booth's Theater in New York in 1869, appearing there frequently until its closure in 1874. Financial difficulties forced him to spend the rest of his life touring the United States and Europe. He was the founder and first president of the Player's Club in 1889.

Booth, John Wilkes (1838–65) US actor and assassin of President Abraham *Lincoln. Born in Maryland, he was the younger brother of Edwin *Booth and achieved considerable success during his brief dramatic career. A partisan of the South during the Civil War, he masterminded a plot to assassinate the leading members of the Lincoln cabinet. On April 14, 1865, he shot and fatally wounded President Lincoln in Ford's Theater in Washington, DC. Booth fled Washington but was cornered and killed by federal troops near Bowling Green, Va two weeks later.

Booth, William (1829–1912) British preacher and founder of the *Salvation Army. An itinerant Methodist preacher, he left the Methodists in order to do evangelistic work among the poor. The reluctance of established churches to accept his slum converts led to the foundation of the Salvation Army, with Booth as General (1877). His eldest son **William Bramwell Booth** (1856–1929) was chief of staff of the Salvation Army from 1880 and later General (1912–29). His daughter **Evangeline Booth** (1865–1950) was also a leading officer and then General (1934–39).

Boothia Peninsula A peninsula of N Canada projecting into the Arctic Ocean, in Franklin district. The northernmost part of the North American mainland, it is sparsely populated, with a police post and trading post. Area: 12,500 sq mi (32,375 sq km).

Bootle 53 28N 3 00W A city in NW England, on the River Mersey adjacent to N Liverpool. Bootle's docks are extensive and modern and its industries include engineering, tanning, tin smelting, and flour milling. Population (1981): 62,463.

bootlegging The illegal distribution or production of highly taxed goods, especially liquor or cigarettes. During *Prohibition (1920–33, when the manufacture, sale, and transportation of alcohol was banned, a well-organized illegal industry developed. Gangsters, such as Al *Capone, controlled both speakeasies (illegal bars) and private distribution systems. Other illegal activities (graft, extortion, protection rackets, prostitution) accompanied bootlegging and became the basis of an organized crime empire still active. Bootlegging, including the use of illegal stills, continues in certain areas of the US, especially "dry" areas (where liquor is not sold).

bootstrap theory The theory in which no elementary particle is regarded as being more fundamental than any other. Each particle exists by virtue of the existence of all the others. Its name derives from the phrase "to pull oneself up by the bootstraps." The theory avoids the problem of a series of classes of particles, each more fundamental than the last. *See also* particle physics.

bop (*or* bebop) A type of *jazz that originated in the US in the 1940s as a reaction against swing. Bop emphasized the art of melodic improvisation neglected during the swing era, but was also characterized by harmonic and rhythmic experimentation. In New York City, Dizzy Gillespie and Charlie "Bird" Parker established small bop bands that required the audience to listen rather than dance.

Bophutha Tswana, Republic of A small country in South Africa, consisting of several separate landlocked areas. The majority of the population is Tswana. *Economy*: chiefly subsistence agriculture, especially livestock; much is being done to improve production by means of irrigation schemes. Large numbers of people still work and live in South₁Africa. Rich mineral resources include chrome, platinum, asbestos, and iron. *History*: in 1972 it became the first *Bantu Homeland to receive self-government under the Bantu Homelands Constitution Act (1971). It was granted independence in 1977, but this is recognized only by South Africa; the granting of independence in effect wrested South African citizenship from its people. Presi-

dent and prime minister: Chief L. M. Mangope. Official currency: South African rand. Area: 14,769 sq mi (38,261 sq km). Population (1983 est): 1,482,000, of whom 65% lived in South Africa. Capital: Montshiwa.

borage A widely grown annual Mediterranean herb, *Borago officinalis*. Borage is a stiff hairy plant, up to 60 cm high, with terminal clusters of small blue flowers with backward-pointing petals. It is used in herbal remedies, pot-pourri, beverages, and salads and the flowers may be candied. Family: *Boraginaceae*.

Borah, William Edgar (1865–1940) US politician and lawyer. After successfully practicing law and chairing the Idaho Republican State Central Committee, he became a US senator (1907–40) and headed the Senate Foreign Relations Committee (1925–33). While in office he was responsible for the creation of the Department of Labor (1913), for the US not joining the League of Nations after World War I, and for the Washington Disarmament Conference (1921–22). Although known as an isolationist, he advocated recognition of the Soviet Union.

boranes Compounds of boron and hydrogen. The simplest is diborane B_2H_6, which is made by reacting sodium borohydride ($NaBH_4$) with *sulfuric acid. The formulas of boranes are not accounted for by classical theories of valence and their molecules contain electron-deficient bonds.

Borås 57 44N 12 55E A city in S Sweden. It is an important center of the textile industry. Population (1978 est): 102,129.

borax (*or* sodium tetraborate; $Na_2B_4O_7$) A natural substance, usually occurring in hydrated crystalline form. It is found in some salt lakes and in alkaline soils and is used in the manufacture of glass and enamel.

Bordeaux (Latin name: Burdigala) 44 50N 0 34W A city in SW France, the capital of the Gironde department on the Garonne River. It is a major seaport and wine center. Industries include shipbuilding, engineering, oil and sugar refining, and chemicals. There are many fine 18th-century buildings and squares, a cathedral (12th-15th centuries), and a university (1441). *History*: an important commercial center under the Romans, it became the capital of Aquitania (*see* Aquitaine) but declined following the collapse of the Roman Empire. It flourished once again under English rule (1154–1453). It became a center of the Fronde in the 17th century and of the Girondins during the French Revolution. It was the seat of the French government for a brief period in 1914 and again in 1940. Population (1975): 226,281.

Borden, Lizzie (Andrew) (1860–1927) US murder suspect. Thought to have axed to death her well-to-do father and stepmother in Fall River, Mass, in 1892, she was acquitted by a jury in 1893. The mystery that still surrounds the case has long been talked, sung, and written about.

Borden, Sir Robert Laird (1854–1937) Canadian statesman; Conservative prime minister (1911–20). An advocate of economic independence, he opposed a reciprocal trade agreement with the US and came to power after defeating the Liberals on this issue. He formed a coalition government to introduce conscription in 1917 and gave women the vote in 1918. Borden supported British policies but claimed more independence for Canada in world affairs, winning separate Canadian representation at the League of Nations.

Border States Slave-holding states (Delaware, Maryland, West Virginia, Kentucky, Missouri) that bordered the South and stayed in the Union during the US Civil War. During the war they continued slavery, having been exempted from the Emancipation Proclamation (1863) by President Abraham *Lincoln, while fighting for the Northern cause.

border terrier A breed of working dog originating in the border region of England and Scotland. It has a deep narrow body, triangular forward-falling ears, and a short strong muzzle. The coat is red, yellowish-brown, gray and tan, or blue and tan. Weight: 13–15 lb (6–7 kg) for dogs; 11–13 lb (5–6 kg) for bitches.

Bordet, Jules Jean Baptiste Vincent (1870–1961) Belgian bacteriologist, who discovered (1895) the two factors (antibody and complement) in blood serum responsible for the rupture of bacterial cells. This fundamental discovery paved the way for diagnostic tests for many bacterial diseases, including syphilis. Bordet founded the Pasteur Institute, Brussels (1901), and was awarded the 1919 Nobel Prize for Medicine.

bore In oceanography, a tidal flood wave with a steep front occurring in certain estuaries and traveling upstream at great speed, sometimes to a distance of several kilometers. It occurs when the spring flood tide brings sea water into an estuary more quickly than it can travel up the river, so that a ridge of water builds up.

Borelli, Giovanni Alfonso (1608–79) Italian physicist and physiologist, who attempted to explain the workings of the body in purely mechanical terms (*De Motu Animalium*, 1680–81). A friend of *Galileo, Borelli made contributions to astronomy, including ideas concerning the attractive forces between planets, their orbits, and the path taken by comets through space.

BJORN BORG   *Playing at Wimbledon, England, in 1979.*

Borg, Bjorn (1956–) Swedish tennis player, the world's leading player in the late 1970s. In 1980 he won the men's singles at Wimbledon for the fifth consecutive year, thus beating the record of three consecutive wins. He retired from the world class competition in 1983.

Borgå. *See* Porvoo.

Borges, Jorge Luis (1899–) Argentinian writer and scholar. Educated in Europe, he joined the Spanish avant-garde Ultraist movement in 1920. In 1921 he returned to Argentina, where he founded three literary journals and published a book of poems in 1923. His best-known works are collections of intricate, fantastic, and paradoxical stories, especially *Fictions* (1944, 1966) and *The Aleph* (1949, 1970). He became director of the National Library in 1955, when already almost totally blind.

Borghese An Italian family that originated in Siena and rose to wealth and fame following its move to Rome in the 16th century and the election in 1605 of **Camillo Borghese** (1552–1621) as Pope Paul V. He advanced his family's fortunes, particularly those of his adopted nephew **Scipione Caffarelli** (1576–1633), an astute church politician and lavish art patron, who sponsored *Bernini and built the Villa Borghese (now an art gallery) in Rome. In 1803 **Camillo Filippo Ludovico Borghese** (1775–1832) married Napoleon's sister, Marie Pauline (1780–1825). The family split into two branches later in the 19th century.

Borgia, Cesare (c. 1475–1507) Duke of the Romagna and captain general of the armies of the Church. The illegitimate son of Pope *Alexander VI, Borgia became Archbishop of Valencia and a cardinal following his father's election to the papacy (1492). He surrendered his cardinalship to marry the sister of the King of Navarre and to become captain general of the Church. He won the Romagna, with French help, in three campaigns (1499–1502), for which Machiavelli regarded him as the savior of Italy. Borgia was forced to relinquish the Romagna after Alexander's death (1502) and was imprisoned. He escaped and died in the employ of the Navarrese king. His sister **Lucrezia Borgia**, unfairly notorious for immorality, was married three times by her father Alexander VI to further his political aims. Her third husband Alfonso (1486–1534) became Duke of Este and she presided over a culturally distinguished court at Ferrara.

Borglum, Gutzon (1867–1941) US sculptor, famous for his gigantic sculptured heads of US presidents, inspired by similar ancient Egyptian monuments. Best known are those carved on rocks of the *Mount Rushmore National Memorial, the head of Lincoln in the US Capitol rotunda, and the 12 apostles in the cathedral of Saint John the Divine in New York City.

Boris (I) of Bulgaria (d. 907 AD) Khan of Bulgaria (852–89). Boris was converted to Orthodox Christianity in 865 and encouraged the spread of Christianity among the Bulgars. His reign gave birth to Slavonic-Bulgarian literature and civilization. In 889 he abdicated and entered a monastery.

Boris III (1894–1943) King of Bulgaria (1918–1943). Boris ruled as a dictator from 1938 and supported the Axis Powers in World War II. He apparently died of a heart attack but may have been assassinated.

Borlaug, Norman (1914–) US plant breeder, who developed new strains of wheat and rice for underdeveloped countries. Working in Mexico since 1944, he received the Nobel Peace Prize (1970) for his role in the "green revolution." His miracle grains have had their greatest impact in Mexico and India.

Bormann, Martin (1900–45) German Nazi leader. Prominent in the Nazi Party from 1925, he became Hitler's personal secretary in 1942. He was sentenced to death in absentia at Nuremberg. In 1973 it was established that he had committed suicide in May, 1945.

Born, Max (1882–1970) British physicist, born in Germany. He shared the 1954 Nobel Prize with W. Bothe for his work in statistical mechanics. Born and *Heisenberg developed matrix mechanics, which *Schrödinger was able to show was equivalent to his own wave mechanics. Born was professor of natural philosophy at Edinburgh University from 1936 to 1953.

Borneo An island SE of Peninsular Malaysia, in the Greater Sunda Islands, the third largest island in the world. During the 19th century Borneo was settled and virtually partitioned by the Dutch and British to protect their East India companies from piracy. It now consists politically of the Indonesian territory of *Kalimantan (about 70%), the Malaysian states of *Sabah and *Sarawak, and the independent nation of *Brunei. It is mountainous with coastal swamps and dense jungle. The chief population groups are the coastal Malays and indigenous Dyaks. It possesses valuable resources of oil, coal, and gold. Area: 290,000 sq mi (750,000 sq km).

Bornholm 55 02N 15 00E A Danish island in the Baltic Sea, SE of Sweden. Dairy farming is practiced and industries include pottery, using locally worked clay, and watchmaking; tourism is important during summer. Area: 227 sq mi (588 sq km). Population (1971): 47,121. Chief town: Rⅰ÷ⅰo/nne.

Bornu A former Muslim Negro kingdom in West Africa. It existed from the 11th century until the late 19th century, when it was divided between Britain, France, and Germany. Most of the area was incorporated into the protectorate of Northern Nigeria in 1900 and the modern Nigerian state of Bornu encompasses part of the former kingdom.

Borobudur A huge Buddhist stupa (shrine) complex in central Java, built about 800 AD and abandoned, unfinished, about 1000. It has five square terraces of diminishing size, one on top of the other, on the vertical surfaces of which is carved a continuous relief depicting the Buddha's life and doctrine. On top, three circular terraces support 72 stupas around a crowning central stupa, all with a Buddha icon.

Borodin, Aleksandr Porfirevich (1833–87) Russian composer, one of the *Five. A professor of chemistry and medicine, he had little formal training and lacked time to compose. Nevertheless, he produced two symphonies (1867 and 1876), the tone poem *In the Steppes of Central Asia* (1880), three string quartets, and the opera *Prince Igor* (completed by *Rimsky-Korsakov and Glazunov in 1890), which contains the famous *Polovtsian Dances.*

boron (B) A nonmetallic element isolated (1808) by Sir Humphry Davy. It has two forms: an impure brownish amorphous powder and pure brown crystals. The main source, kernite ($Na_2B_4O_7.4H_2O$), is mined in California. Boron is used in semiconductors and in hardened steel. Boron fibers are used in lightweight composite materials. The isotope boron-10 absorbs neutrons: boron carbide (B_4C) and boron alloys are used in the control rods and shielding of nuclear reactors. Other compounds include borax ($Na_2B_4O_7.10H_2O$), used in glass manufacture, and boric acid (H_3BO_3), used in ceramics and fireproofing. At no 5; at wt 10.81; mp 2300°C.

Borromeo, St Charles (1538–84) Italian churchman, Cardinal and Archbishop of Milan. He was appointed to his offices in 1560 by his uncle, Pope Pius IV. He played a leading part in the third convocation of the

Council of Trent (1562–63) and actively supported the evangelization of Switzerland. These activities and the capable reforms he carried out in his archdiocese made him an important Counter-Reformation figure. Feast day: Nov 4.

Borromini, Francesco (1599–1667) Italian baroque architect. Born in N Italy, he settled in □Rome, where all his work was executed. With his rival *Bernini, he brought the baroque style in Rome to its peak. His highly individual approach expressed the classical architectural style in forms never before achieved. Although much less successful than Bernini he was in many ways a greater genius as an architect. His main buildings, S Carlo (1641), S Ivo (1660), and the oratorio of S Filippo Neri (1650), showed a virtuosity of decoration and a command of complex spatial effects that Bernini never approached.

Borstal system An English penal system established (1908) for the rehabilitation and training of offenders aged between 15 and 21. They may be detained in an institution called a Borstal for between six months and two years. Following release, the offender remains under supervision for two years and may be recalled to a Borstal if he commits an offense. The name derives from the prison at Borstal, where the system was introduced in 1902.

borzoi A breed of large □dog originating in Russia, also called Russian wolfhound and used originally for hunting wolves and for hare coursing. The borzoi is a lightly built swift runner with a long silky coat, which is usually white with black to light-brown patches. Height: about 28 in (70 cm).

Bosanquet, Bernard (1848–1923) British philosopher. His early neo-Hegelian philosophy saw the individuality of persons, institutions, and works of art as a combination of abstract general concepts (universals). His *Philosophical Theory of the State* (1899) presents a solution to the problem of communal will and individual liberty. *Bradley influenced his later work.

Bosch, Carl (1874–1940) German chemist, who developed the *Haber process for the conversion of atmospheric nitrogen into ammonia, so that it could be used industrially. This Haber-Bosch process has been used to manufacture enormous quantities of nitrates for both explosives and fertilizers. He shared the 1931 Nobel Prize for Chemistry for his work on high-pressure reactions.

Bosch, Hieronymus (Jerome van Aeken; c. 1450–c. 1516) Dutch painter. He was born in 's-Hertogenbosch (hence his name), where from 1486 he belonged to the Roman Catholic Brotherhood of Our Lady. His allegories have been interpreted variously as forerunners of *surrealism or as expressions of heretical beliefs but as his patrons, including Philip II of Spain, were devout Catholics, they were probably intended as sermons on evil and its consequences. The often inexplicable symbolism and fantastic imagery of half-animal half-human creatures and devils was inspired by contemporary proverbs and writings. Among his major works are *The Haywain* (El Escorial) and *Garden of Earthly Delights* (Prado).

Bose, Sir Jagadis Chandra (1858–1937) Indian plant physiologist and physicist. His research into plant behavior, in which he showed how plants responded to external stimuli (such as injury), revealed parallels between plant and animal tissues. He also invented the crescograph (a device for measuring plant growth) and founded the Bose Research Institute, Calcutta.

Bose, Subhas Chandra (c. 1897–c. 1945) Indian nationalist leader. He was a civil servant before joining Gandhi's movement of noncooperation with the British. He became president of the *Indian National Congress in 1938 but resigned in 1939 because of disagreement with Gandhi over policy. Arrested and imprisoned in Calcutta (1940), he left India in 1941. With Japanese help he organized in Singapore the Indian National Army to free India from British rule (1943). He was said to have been killed in an air crash in 1945.

Bose-Einstein statistics One of two statistical approaches to quantum mechanical problems: it assumes that any number of identical particles may occupy the same energy level. The other statistical method is called *Fermi-Dirac statistics. Particles that obey Bose-Einstein statistics are called *bosons. Named for— S. N. Bose (1894–1974) and A. *Einstein.

Bosnia and Hercegovina (Serbo-Croat name: Bosna I Hercegovina) A constituent republic of Yugoslavia. It consists of a chiefly mountainous triangular-shaped area with karst topography in the SW. It is primarily agricultural, producing mainly cereals, vegetables, fruit, and tobacco; sheep are also raised. *History*: part of ancient Illyria, the region was inhabited by Slavs from the 7th century AD onward. Bosnia became a separate political entity in the 10th century but later came under the control of Hungary. It became an independent kingdom in the late 14th century and annexed

Hercegovina but fell to the Turks in 1463, remaining under their control for four centuries. In 1908 it was annexed to Austria-Hungary; Serbian opposition to this led to the assassination of Archduke Francis Ferdinand, precipitating World War I. Area: 19,737 sq mi (51,129 sq km). Population (1978): 4,125,000. Capital: Sarajevo.

boson A class of elementary particles with integral spin. Bosons always obey *Bose-Einstein statistics and include all the *mesons and the *photon. *See particle physics.*

Bosporus (Turkish name: Karadeniz Boğazi) A strait separating Europe and Asia and connecting the Black Sea with the Sea of Marmara. It has Istanbul at its S end and it is spanned by one of the world's longest suspension bridges. Length: about 19 mi (30 km). Width: about 0.4–2.5 mi (0.6–4 km).

boss In architecture, a small projection in a roof vault, covering the crossing of the supporting ribs. Although sometimes plain, medieval bosses were frequently carved into elaborate decorative shapes. *See also* gothic architecture.

Bossuet, Jacques Bénigne (1627–1704) French Roman Catholic bishop and preacher. He became famous for several funeral orations on prominent persons, such as that on *Henrietta Maria delivered in 1669. He became Bishop of Meaux in 1681, having first been tutor to the dauphin, and later attempted to bring about a compromise between Louis XIV and the pope on the issue of *Gallicanism. He wrote a number of devotional and apologetic works.

Boston 42 20N 71 05W The capital of Massachusetts, on Massachusetts Bay. It is an important port and market for fish and a major financial center. Its industries include publishing, food processing, and the manufacture of machinery. An architecturally exceptional city, its most notable buildings are the old State House (1748), Faneuil Hall (1762), and the State Capitol (1798). Boston is a major cultural and educational center. It is the site of Boston University (1869), Northeastern University (1898), and Boston Latin School (established in 1635 and one of the country's first free secondary schools). Harvard Medical School is also situated here. Notable residents have included Nathaniel Hawthorne, Henry Thoreau, Ralph Emerson, and Longfellow. *History*: founded in 1630 by Puritan Englishmen, it prospered as the main colony of the Massachusetts Bay Company. It became a center of opposition to the British prior to the American Revolution (*see* Boston Tea Party). Often dubbed the "Hub of the Universe," Boston flourished as the commercial, industrial, and financial center of the New England states during the early 19th century. It was a leading force in the antislavery movement during the 1830s. Population (1975 est): 562,994.

Boston Massacre (1770) An incident in which 5 Americans, part of a crowd protesting the quartering of British soldiers in their homes, were killed by the British. Crispus *Attucks was the first fatality. The British soldiers were arrested, tried, and acquitted, due to the efforts of American lawyers, who then turned around and used the incident to promote the cause of the patriots. Eventually, the troops were moved from the city to islands in the harbor.

Boston Tea Party (1773) An expression of colonial hostility toward Britain before the *American Revolution. A group of Americans dressed as Indians, objecting to the import of cheap tea, enforced by the Tea Act to rid the East India Company of its surplus stocks, threw a cargo of tea into Boston harbor. Britain retaliated with the *Intolerable Acts. *See also* Stamp Act.

Boston terrier A breed of □dog originating in the US from crosses between bulldogs and terriers. It is compactly built with a short square muzzle and a short tail. The short smooth coat is brown to brownish-yellow with white markings. Height: about 15 in (38 cm).

Boswell, James (1740–95) Scottish writer, the biographer of Samuel *Johnson. Son of an Edinburgh advocate, he came to London in 1760 and first met Johnson in 1763. He traveled widely on the Continent from 1764 to 1766, meeting other famous men, such as Voltaire and Rousseau. Although he practiced law in Edinburgh from 1766 to 1788 he maintained a close relationship with Johnson. The biography, published in 1791, was widely acclaimed but in later years he suffered from severe depression and alcoholism.

Bosworth Field, Battle of (August 22, 1485) The battle fought near Market Bosworth, Leicestershire, in which Henry Tudor defeated Richard III, thereby ending the Wars of the *Roses. Richard was killed in the battle and Henry became the first *Tudor monarch, as Henry VII.

botanic gardens Collections of growing plants designed to display both familiar native plants and more unusual alien species, particularly ornamentals. Often the plants are grouped to demonstrate their evolutionary and geographical relationships or their similar ecological requirements. Some gardens concentrate on certain types of plants: an arboretum is one specializing in trees and shrubs. Botanic gardens originated in ancient China, as collections of fruit, vegetables, and medicinal plants, but it was not until the 16th and 17th centuries that they became popular in Europe, the first being established in Italy, at Pisa (1543) and Padua (1545). Today the larger botanic gardens have extensive herbaria, where dried labeled specimens are kept for reference. Many have their own laboratories and libraries, providing facilities for research scientists, and often hold courses in horticultural techniques for trainee gardeners. Most also concentrate on preserving and propagating rare species, with greenhouses and culture techniques for those with specialized needs. *See also* Kew Gardens.

botany The scientific study of plants. From ancient times plants have figured prominently in human cultures as man is dependent on them for food, shelter, drugs, and many other purposes. Scientific botany dates from the 4th century BC, with the studies of the ancient Greeks—notably *Theophrastus, who is said to have founded the science, and *Dioscorides, who published one of the first herbals. Until the 17th century botany was almost entirely restricted to the description and properties of medicinal plants. The basic principles of modern plant classification were laid down by John *Ray at the end of the 17th century, and by the middle of the 18th century *Linnaeus had published his works on the naming and classification of plants, which established the principles of *taxonomy still used today for both plants and animals. The invention of the microscope in the 16th century enabled detailed studies of plant structure, culminating in *Schleiden's theory of the cellular nature of plants in the 1830s. The 18th century saw important advances in plant physiology with the discovery of *photosynthesis, the food-manufacturing process of green plants. During the 19th century the origin of plant species was elucidated in Charles *Darwin's theory of evolution and Gregor *Mendel—working with plants—established the mechanisms of inheritance.

Botany in the 20th century has been revolutionized by advances in physiology, biochemistry, and breeding techniques, which have greatly increased the economic importance of plants and enabled a scientific approach to the related disciplines of *horticulture, *agriculture, and forestry. *See also* biological sciences.

Botany Bay An inlet of the Tasman Sea, in SE Australia. It was the site of Capt Cook's first landing in Australia (1770). The bay is now surrounded by the suburbs of Sydney. Industries, located chiefly on the N shore, include chemicals, plastics, and fiberglass, with an oil refinery on the SE shore. Area: about 16 sq mi (42 sq km).

bot fly A hairy beelike fly belonging to the families *Gasterophilidae* (horsebot flies), *Calliphoridae* (e.g. the deer bot fly), or *Oestridae* (e.g. the sheep bot fly). The larvae are parasitic in mammals, often living within nasal and sinus cavities or in the digestive tract to cause irritation, weakening, and vertigo. When mature the larvae pass out with the feces. *Compare* warble fly.

Botha, Louis (1862–1919) South African statesman; the first prime minister of the Union of South Africa (1910–19). Botha grew up in the Orange Free State, where his parents had settled after the Great Trek from Natal. In 1897 he became a member of the Transvaal Volksraad (parliament) and commanded the Transvaal's forces during the second *Boer War. He became prime minister of the Transvaal in 1907 and of the newly formed Union in 1910.

Botha, Pieter Willem (1916–) South African statesman; prime minister (1978–84) and state president (1984–). As defense minister (1966–78) under his predecessor, Vorster, he was largely responsible for South Africa's intervention in 1975 in the civil war in Angola. Following a 1983 referendum, Botha's government began a policy of allowing some non-whites limited participation in the political process, although blacks would not be included. In 1984 he signed a joint security pact with Mozambique intended to end conflict between the two countries.

Bothe, Walther Wilhelm Georg Franz (1891–1957) German experimental physicist, who (with H. *Geiger) developed the coincidence method for particle counting. The use of this technique in cosmic radiation research brought him a share (with Max *Born) in the Nobel Prize for 1954. During World War II he built Germany's first cyclotron. He was responsible for discovering the particle later identified by *Chadwick as the neutron.

Bothnia, Gulf of A shallow section of the Baltic Sea, between Sweden and Finland. It remains frozen for about five months of the year because of its low salinity. Its many small islands restrict navigation. Area: about 45,200 sq mi (117,000 sq km).

Bothwell, James Hepburn, 4th Earl of (c. 1535–78) The third husband of Mary, Queen of Scots. He was almost certainly responsible for the murder of her former husband *Darnley in 1567, after which he allegedly abducted Mary and married her; they may already have been lovers. Following their defeat at Carberry Hill, Bothwell escaped to Denmark, where he died, insane, in captivity.

bo tree An Indian tree, *Ficus religiosa*, up to 98 ft (30 m) high, also called the peepul or pipal. It has heart-shaped leaves, the tips of which are drawn out into a long narrow tail, and globular fleshy purple fruits. Related to the fig, the bo tree is sacred to Buddhists, as it was the tree under which Buddha sat when he attained enlightenment. Family: *Moraceae* (mulberry family).

Botswana, Republic of (former name until 1966: Bechuanaland) A country in the center of S Africa, lying between the Zambezi and Molopo Rivers. It is largely an arid plateau, with the Kalahari Desert in the S and W and some hills in the E. The Okavango River in the N, with its marshy basin, is important for irrigation. The majority of the population, consisting mainly of the Bantu-speaking Tswana group, lives along the E border. The original inhabitants, the Bushmen, now comprise only a small minority. *Economy*: chiefly agricultural, with livestock, especially cattle, taking precedence over crops, which are still largely dependent on the rather sparse rainfall. In 1975 land ownership was reformed to permit more modern use of land. Large quantities of minerals, discovered in the 1960s, are now being developed and these include diamonds, nickel, copper, and coal. The main exports are beef and by-products of cattle but minerals are rapidly becoming an important source of export revenue. *History*: the area became the British Protectorate of Bechuanaland in 1885 and was annexed to the Cape Colony in 1895. It later became a British High Commission Territory, gaining internal self-government in 1965 and full independence in 1966 as the Republic of Botswana within the Commonwealth of Nations. Until 1980 it was under the democratic rule of Sir Seretse *Khama, who maintained a delicate balance in his opposition to the policies of neighboring countries, in spite of being dependent on them for communications and trade. Official language: English; the main African language is Tswana. Official currency: pula of 100 thebe. Area: 222,000 sq mi (575,000 sq km). Population (1983 est): 1,003,600. Capital: Gaborone.

Botticelli, Sandro (Alessandro di Mariano Filipepi; c. 1445–1510) Florentine *Renaissance painter, named for his brother's nickname, meaning "little barrel." He trained under Filippo *Lippi. His chief patrons were the Medici, for whom he produced illustrations for Dante's *Divine Comedy* and allegorical paintings, influenced by humanist writers, such as *Primavera*, *Birth of Venus* (both Uffizi), and *Mars and Venus* (National Gallery, London). They are notable for their graceful draftsmanship. In 1481–82 he worked on frescoes for the Sistine Chapel, in the Vatican. Probably under the influence of the religious leader *Savonarola, his later works, e.g. *Mystic Nativity* (1501; National Gallery, London), became more religious and emotional.

bottlebrush An evergreen Australian shrub or tree of the genus *Callistemon* (25 species). Growing to a height of about 20 ft (6 m), it has stiff narrow leaves, 2 in (5 cm) long. The flower heads consist mainly of bunches of fluffy red or yellow stamens, resembling bottle brushes. The fruits are woody. Bottlebrushes may be grown as ornamental hedges and shrubs. Family: *Myrtaceae*.

bottlenose A *dolphin, *Tursiops truncatus*, with a short beak. Gray-blue and growing to 13 ft (4 m), bottlenose dolphins are a shallow-water species and have become popular in dolphinariums. They have been the subject of research into the social behavior and language of whales. □mammal.

Bottrop 51 31N 6 55E A city in NW West Germany, in North Rhine-Westphalia in the *Ruhr. Its main industries are coalmining and the manufacture of by-products. Population (1980 est): 114,600.

botulism A rare and serious form of *food poisoning from foods containing the toxin produced by the bacterium *Clostridium botulinum*. The toxin can affect the cardiac and respiratory centers of the brain and may result in death by heart or lung failure. The bacterium thrives in improperly preserved foods, such as canned raw meats. The toxin is invariably destroyed in cooking.

Botvinnik, Mikhail Moiseivich (1911–) Soviet chess player, who was world champion (1948–57, 1958–60, 1961–63), losing the title to *Petrosian (1963). He was also a successful electrical engineer.

Bouaké 7 42N 5 00W A city in the central Ivory Coast. It is an important trade center, linked by rail and road to Abidjan, with a trade in coffee, cocoa, and rice. Population (1977): 805,356.

Boucher, François (1703–70) French *rococo painter, born in Paris, the son of a lacemaker. He studied in Italy (1727–31) but was chiefly influenced by *Watteau, many of whose drawings he engraved. He worked for Louis XV, and Madame de Pompadour, whom he painted (Wallace Collection, London), and to whom he gave art lessons. He became director of both the Gobelins tapestry factory (1755), for which he produced designs, and of the French Academy (1765). His paintings are mainly mythological and pastoral scenes and nudes.

Boucher de Perthes, Jacques (1788–1868) French antiquary. In the Somme valley he discovered stone implements together with extinct animal remains; these made him challenge contemporary theories about human origins. His *De la création* (1838–41) and *Antiquités celtiques et antédiluviennes* (1847) argue for the human race's great antiquity.

Boudicca. *See* Boadicea.

Boudin, Eugène (1824–98) French painter and forerunner of *impressionism, born in Honfleur. He painted his coastal scenes in the open air instead of the studio and encouraged *Monet in this practice.

Bougainville A volcanic forested island in the SW Pacific Ocean, the largest in the *Solomon Islands archipelago and a province of Papua New Guinea. Copra, cocoa, timber, and tortoise shell are exported. Area: about 4000 sq mi (10,360 sq km). Population (1971): 96,363. Chief town: Kieta.

Bougainville, Louis Antoine de (1729–1811) French navigator. After service in the Seven Years' War in Canada he joined the navy. Between 1766 and 1769 he circumnavigated the world and wrote an account of the journey in *A Voyage round the World* (1771). He was later a successful commander in the American Revolution. Several geographical features, including the island Bougainville, and the plant genus *Bougainvillea* are named for him.

Bougainvillea A genus of tropical South American shrubs (18 species) climbing by means of hooked thorns. The shrubs bear numerous showy "flowers," usually reddish-purple, for most of the year. The colored parts are actually large bracts, which surround the small inconspicuous flowers. *Bougainvillea* is grown as an ornamental throughout the tropics and subtropics. Family: *Nyctaginaceae*.

NADIA BOULANGER *Rehearsing the Boston Symphony Orchestra in 1962.*

Boulanger, Nadia (Juliette) (1887–1979) French composer, teacher, and conductor. Lennox *Berkeley and Aaron *Copland have been among her pupils. Her works include the cantata *La Sirène* (1908; awarded the Prix de Rome), the opera *La Ville morte* (1911), choral works, and instrumental pieces.

Boulder. *See* Kalgoorlie-Boulder.

Boulder 40 01N 105 17W A city in N central Colorado, on the E edge of the Rocky Mountains. The town was settled in 1858, and the University of Colorado was established here in 1876. It is a center of scientific research; mining, agriculture, and tourism are other important activities. Population (1980): 76,685.

boulder clay. *See* till.

boules A French game similar to *bowls, often played on rough ground. The players aim small metal bowls at a target ball (*cochonnet*).

Boulez, Pierre (1925–) French composer and conductor, a pupil of Messiaen. Boulez has been active as a conductor of contemporary music

and his own work reflects the influence of Schoenberg, Webern, and Cage. He has used total *serialism in such works as *Structures I and II* (for two pianos; 1951–52 and 1956–61) and has set poems by René Char in *Le Marteau sans maître* (for contralto and 6 instruments; 1953–55) as well as poems by Mallarmé in *Pli selon pli* (for soprano and orchestra; 1957–60).

Boulle, André Charles (or Buhl; 1642–1732) French cabinetmaker in the service of Louis XIV. He gave his name to the technique of boullework (or buhlwork), a style of marquetry using brass, tortoiseshell, mother of pearl, etc., inlaid on ebony.

Boulogne-sur-Mer 50 43N 1 37E A port and resort in N France, in the Pas-de-Calais department on the English Channel. It was severely damaged in World War II. It is the country's main fishing port and has a ferry service to England. Industries include boatbuilding, textiles, and steel. Population (1975): 49,284.

Boulton, Matthew. *See* Watt, James.

Boumédienne, Houari (Mohammed Boukharouba; 1925–78) Algerian statesman; president (1965–78). In 1960 he became chief of staff of the nationalist forces fighting the French. After independence in 1962 he became minister of defense and then vice president under *Ben Bella. In 1965 he overthrew Ben Bella to become president.

Bounty, HMS. *See* Bligh, William.

Bourbaki, Nicolas A pseudonym for a group of French mathematicians who, since 1939, have been producing a rigorous development of mathematics from a few basic premisses. Their work is often at variance with conventional mathematics.

bourbon (whiskey). *See* whisky.

Bourbons A European ruling dynasty that originated in Bourbonnais (now Allier, central France). It acquired ducal status in 1272, when Agnès Bourbon married the sixth son of Louis IX. The first Bourbon king of France was *Henry IV (reigned 1589–1610) after whom the house continued to rule until the *French Revolution (1792). The Bourbons were briefly restored under *Louis Philippe (1830–48), a member of a cadet branch. The present pretender to the French throne is Henry, Count of Paris (1908–).

The Bourbon Louis XIV's grandson became (1700) *Philip V of Spain, where the Bourbons ruled almost continuously until the abdication of *Alfonso XIII in 1931. His grandson *Juan Carlos was restored to the Spanish throne in 1975. In Naples and Sicily Bourbons ruled between 1734 and 1860.

Bourdelle, Émile (1861–1929) French sculptor. Influenced by his teacher *Rodin, Bourdelle initially relied on vigorous surface carving for expensive effect. After 1910 he became popular and influential with his sculptures inspired by classical Greek art.

Bourgeois, Léon (1851–1925) French statesman; prime minister (1895–96). He was the chief theorist of solidarism, the concept that an individual's rights in society must be balanced by his responsibility to it. Prominent in the League of Nations, he won the Nobel Peace Prize in 1920.

bourgeoisie Originally, the urban merchants who developed trade at the end of the middle ages and who led the struggle against the feudal aristocracy for the rights of citizenship. The meaning was later extended to include the whole middle class. In the 19th century, *Marx used the concept within his theory of class struggle to describe the propertied entrepreneurs who created industrial capitalism and liberal democracy; conflict between the bourgeoisie and the *proletariat would ultimately lead to revolution. *See* Marxism.

Bourges (Latin name: Avaricum) 47 05N 2 23E A city in central France, the capital of the Cher department. An important town of Aquitaine, it became the capital of Berry in the 12th century and the French center of power following the battle of Agincourt (1415). It has a fine gothic cathedral. Industries include textiles and armaments. Population (1975): 80,379.

Bourguiba, Habib (1902–) Tunisian statesman; president (1956–). A leading figure in the struggle for Tunisian independence, he formed the Neo-Destour Party in 1934. He spent ten years between 1934 and 1955 in French prisons. On independence in 1956 he became president, being reelected three times (1959, 1964, 1969), and in 1974 became life president.

Bourmont, Louis Auguste Victor de Ghaisnes, Comte de (1773–1846) French marshal, who lived in exile (1793–99) during the French Revolution but subsequently served Napoleon. He deserted Napoleon for the allies shortly before Waterloo. In 1829 he became minister of war but went into exile after the July Revolution (1830).

Bournemouth 50 43N 1 54W A resort in S England, in Dorset on Poole Bay. It is a large all-year-round resort with many tourist attractions, including 6 mi (10 km) of beach. It has a famous symphony orchestra. Population (1981 est): 144,803.

Bouts, Dierick (c. 1400–75) Netherlandish painter, born in Haarlem, who lived and worked in Louvain. His paintings, strongly influenced by van der *Weyden, are notable for their treatment of landscape. *The Last Supper* (S Pierre, Louvain) and *The Justice of Emperor Otto* (Brussels) are his major works.

Bouvet 54 26S 3 24E An uninhabited Norwegian island in the S Atlantic Ocean. It is rocky with ice cliffs. Area: 19 sq mi (48 sq km).

Bouvines, Battle of (July 27, 1214) The battle in which *Philip II Augustus of France defeated the Holy Roman Emperor *Otto IV. The failure of the planned diversionary attack by King John of England facilitated Philip's victory, which increased the baronial opposition to John in England (*see* Barons' Wars).

Boveri, Theodor Heinrich (1862–1915) German cell biologist, noted for his studies of chromosomes. Boveri showed that the egg nucleus and the sperm nucleus both contribute hereditary material during the formation of a new cell (zygote) and that irregular distribution of chromosomes leads to abnormal development. These findings led *Sutton to propose his chromosome theory of inheritance in 1903.

Bovet, Daniel (1907–) Swiss pharmacologist, who discovered pyrilamine, the first of the allergy-relieving antihistamine drugs (1944). He also made various synthetic substitutes for the muscle-relaxing drug curare (1947). For his discoveries he received the 1957 Nobel Prize for Physiology.

Bovidae A family of hoofed *ruminant mammals (about 128 species), comprising antelopes, cattle, sheep, and goats. Most live in herds and graze on the plains, although some inhabit mountainous regions. Several species have been domesticated by man for meat, milk, hides, and wool. Order: *Artiodactyla.

Bow, Clara (1905–65) US film actress. She personified the vivacious spirit of the 1920s in such films as *Mantrap* (1926) and *It* (1927) after which she became known as the "It" girl. She retired from acting in the 1930s, after being unsuccessful in sound films.

Bowdler, Thomas (1754–1825) British doctor and editor. His *Family Shakespeare* (1818) expurgated all words, expressions (and even plots) "which cannot with propriety be read aloud in a family." He similarly "bowdlerized" Gibbon's *History of the Decline and Fall of the Roman Empire* (1826).

Bowdoin, James (1726–90) US politician, governor of Massachusetts (1785–87). He played an active role in Massachusetts politics before, during, and after the American Revolution; he headed the state constitutional convention (1779). As governor he was responsible for containing *Shays' Rebellion (1786–87). He founded the American Academy of Arts and Sciences (1780); Bowdoin College was named for him posthumously.

BOWERBIRD *The male satin bowerbird (Ptilonorhynchus violaceus), which has a blue-black plumage, builds an avenue of upright sticks to attract the female.*

Bowen, Elizabeth (1899–1973) British novelist. Born in Dublin, daughter of an Anglo-Irish landowner, she was brought to England as a child. Her novels, in which themes of loneliness and personal relationships are delicately explored, include *The Death of the Heart* (1938) and *The Heat of the Day* (1949).

bowerbird A songbird belonging to a family (*Ptilonorhynchidae*; 18 species) found in Australasian forests. About 8–14 in (22-35 cm) long, it is closely related to the bird of paradise but has a duller plumage, often gray or black. Male bowerbirds court females by building typically dome-shaped bowers with twigs, moss, and stones, often decorating them with feathers, flowers, and shells.

bowfin A *bony fish, *Amia calva*, also called grundle or mudfish, found in fresh waters of E North America. It has a mottled green body, up to 24 in (60 cm) long, a long dorsal fin, and feeds on fish and invertebrates. Family: *Amiidae*; order: *Amiiformes*.

Bowie, David (David Jones; 1947–) British pop singer. Both his style of singing and his theatrical public image have undergone several changes during the course of his career in progressive pop music. His albums include *Ziggy Stardust* (1972) and *Stage* (1978). He has also acted in films, notably *The Man Who Fell to Earth* (1976).

Bowie, James (c.1796–1836) US soldier, pioneer, and popularizer of the Bowie knife. After engaging in some land deals in Louisiana, he settled in Texas, married the daughter of the Mexican vice-governor and became active in the movement to free Texas of Mexican rule. A colonel in the Texas army, he was one of the officers in charge at the Alamo where he died. It is thought that he or his brother invented the Bowie knife that was widely used in the West.

bowling (*or* tenpin bowling) A game in which two players or teams compete by attempting to knock down standing pins with rolling balls. The ten pins, 15 in (38.1 cm) high and each weighing about 3.5 lb (1.5 kg), are placed in a triangle 20 yd (18.29 m) distant at the end of a wooden lane. The balls, which have a thumb hole and two finger holes, have a maximum circumference of 27 in (68.5 cm) and a maximum weight of 16 lb (7.26 kg). Each player has two tries to knock the pins down, points being awarded accordingly. The pins are then reset for the next frame. Ten frames comprise a game.

bowls A game in which biased bowls ("woods") are rolled toward a smaller one (the "jack"). **Flat green bowls** is played on a level grass surface 40–44 yd (36.6–40.2 m) square (for championship greens). Matches are usually played between two sides of four, each player using two bowls; a contest consists of three to six simultaneous matches. The jack is rolled onto the green by the first player and is followed by the other bowls in turn, the object being to position them as near the jack as possible. Playing all the bowls constitutes one "end." Scoring is determined by the closeness of the balls to the jack. *See also* boules.

box A small evergreen tree, *Buxus sempervirens*, up to 30 ft (9 m) high, native to S Europe, Africa, and S England. The leaves are small and glossy and the flowers and seedpods inconspicuous. Being slow growing, box is widely grown as hedges for topiary or screening. The hard fine-grained wood is used for decorative inlay work and engravings. Family: *Buxaceae*.

box elder A *maple tree, *Acer negundo*, up to 65 ft (20 m) high, native to North America but widely planted in Europe as a street ornamental. Also called ash-leafed maple, it has compound pale-green leaves with five toothed leaflets.

boxer A breed of working dog originating in Germany. It has a powerful frame with long straight legs and a broad muzzle. The short glossy coat is fawn to yellowish-brown or brindle, sometimes with white markings, and the mask is black. Height: 22–24 in (56–61 cm) (dogs); 21–23 in (53–58 cm) (bitches).

Boxer Rising (1900) A rebellion in China so called because the rebels belonged to a secret society named the Fists of Righteous Harmony. They opposed the western presence in China and engaged in violence against foreign missionaries and Chinese Christians. Wearing yellow sashes and believing themselves invulnerable to foreign weapons, they marched on Peking, killing and pillaging as they went. The rebellion was eventually suppressed by an international force of troops from seven nations and a crippling indemnity was imposed on China.

boxing Fist-fighting between men wearing gloves in a roped-off ring. Organized boxing in modern times began in 18th-century England, where it became an aristocratic pastime. The basis of modern boxing rules are the **Queensberry Rules**, drawn up under the patronage of the Marquess of Queensberry (1844–1900), published in 1867, and first used in 1892. They established the use of gloves as opposed to fighting with bare fists, which was the custom in the prize fights of the time. In professional boxing the ring is 14 × 20 ft (4 × 6 m) square. The weight limits for professional boxers are: flyweight, 112 lb (50.8 kg); bantamweight, 118 lb (53.5 kg); featherweight, 126 lb (57.2 kg); lightweight, 135 lb (61.2 kg); light welterweight, 140 lb (63.5 kg); welterweight, 147 lb (66.7 kg); light middleweight, 154 lb (69.8 kg); middleweight, 160 lb (72.6 kg); light heavyweight, 175 lb (79.4 kg); heavyweight, unlimited. A bout consists of up to 15 3-minute rounds, separated by 1-minute intervals, and is presided over by a referee. A boxer is assisted by cornermen. A fight may be decided on points (scores awarded by the referee or judges after each round), by disqualification, or by knockout. A boxer is deemed to be knocked out if he cannot rise within ten seconds (he is considered down if any part of his body besides his feet is touching the ground) or if the referee decides that he is not in fit condition to continue.

box turtle A terrestrial turtle belonging to the North American genus *Terrapene* (6 species). Up to 7 in (18 cm) long, box turtles have a high-domed rounded carapace patterned with brown and yellow and a hinged plastron, which allows tight closure of the shell, forming a protective box. They feed on worms, insects, and berries. Family: *Emydidae*.

Boyacá, Battle of (August 7, 1819) The victory, after a heroic crossing of the Andes, of Simón *Bolívar's army of 3000 men over a Spanish force. It assured the liberation of Venezuela and Colombia.

Boycott, Charles Cunningham (1832–97) British estate manager in Ireland. Boycott clashed with the *Land League over its request for rent reductions and as a result the local community refused to associate with, or "boycotted," him.

Boyd-Orr of Brechin Mearns, John, 1st Baron (1880–1971) Scottish scientist and expert on nutrition. In the 1930s he identified nutritional problems among the British population and helped formulate adequate nutritional standards. First director general of the United Nations Food and Agriculture Organization (1945–48), he was awarded the Nobel Peace Prize (1949).

Boyer, Charles (1899–1977) French film actor. He went to Hollywood in 1929 and specialized in the roles of romantic lovers in such films as *Mayerling* (1937) and *Love Affair* (1939). □Dietrich, Marlene.

Boyle, Robert (1627–91) British physicist and chemist, born in Ireland. Boyle showed that air possesses weight, that it is necessary for sound propagation, and that its pressure affects the boiling point of water. His chemical work, summarized in *The Skeptical Chymist* (1661), distinguished between elements, compounds, and mixtures and dismissed the Aristotelian concept of the four elements. His work on gases and vacuums, with Robert *Hooke, led to the law that bears his name. Boyle published his law in 1663, but in France the law is known as Marriotte's law, after Edmé Marriotte (1620–84), who did not publish it until 1676.

Boyle's law At constant temperature, the pressure of unit mass of a gas is inversely proportional to its volume. This law is only approximately true for real gases. A gas that obeys Boyle's law exactly is called an *ideal gas. Named for— Robert *Boyle.

Boyne, Battle of the (July 1, 1690) The victory of William III of England over the former King James II in Ireland. The battle was fought at the River Boyne, N of Dublin, where James hoped to halt the Williamites' advance southward. It was not an overwhelming victory, losses being comparatively slight on both sides, but the sensation of two kings fighting in Ireland for an English throne ensured its fame. The battles of the Boyne and of *Aughrim are still celebrated by Ulster Unionists on the latter's anniversary, July 12.

Boyoma Falls (former name: Stanley Falls) A series of seven cataracts in NE central Zaïre, on a 62-mi (100-km) stretch of the River Lualuba, where it becomes the Zaïre River, close to Kisangani.

Boy Scouts. *See* Scouting.

Bo Zhu Yi (*or* Po Chü-i; 772–846) Chinese poet, imperial official, he became a governor in the provinces and eventually president of the imperial board of war (841). His many poems and ballads deal with the social problems of his age. Their lasting popularity rests on their lucid language, which, according to tradition, he achieved by reading his work to a peasant woman and deleting anything she did not understand.

Brabant **1.** A former duchy in the Low Countries, between the Meuse and Scheldt Rivers. On Belgian independence (1830) it was divided, forming the Belgian provinces of Antwerp and Brabant and the Dutch province of *North Brabant. **2.** A province in central Belgium. It is densely populated with large industrial areas, including Brussels. Agriculture is highly developed, with dairy farming and the production of cereals, fruit, and vegetables. Area: 1268 sq mi (3284 sq km). Population (1980 est): 2,221,782. Capital: Brussels.

Brabham, Jack (John Arthur B.; 1926–) Australian motor-racing driver, who won 14 Grand Prix races between 1955 and 1970 and was world champion in 1959, 1960, and 1966. From 1961 he built his own cars.

Brachiopoda A phylum of primitive marine invertebrate animals (about 250 species) called lamp shells because of their resemblance to ancient Roman oil lamps. The body is protected by two shell valves, usually attached to the sea bed by a fleshy stalk (peduncle). Ciliated tentacles filter food particles from the water and propel them into the mouth. Eggs and sperm are discharged into the sea and produce free-swimming ciliated larvae.

bracken (*or* brake) A *fern, *Pteridium aquilinum*, that is abundant almost throughout the world. Its black underground rhizome creeps extensively, producing aerial fronds, up to 16 ft (5 m) high, with stout erect stalks bearing triangular blades made up of branches of paired leaflets. Spore capsules occur in brownish clusters (sori) around the margins on the underside of the leaflets. Bracken is sometimes considered a pest by farmers; the roots have been used in tanning and the fronds in thatching and as fodder. Family: *Dennstaedtiaceae*.

bracket fungus A fungus that forms a fruiting body resembling a shelf or bracket, usually on trees or timber. The spores are produced in fine tubes that open at pores on the surface. A common species is *Coriolus versicolor*, the semicircular brackets of which, 1–2 in (3–5 cm) across, are found on stumps and branches of deciduous trees. The brackets are marked with concentric colored zones of brown, yellow, gray, or green. Family: *Polyporaceae*; class: *Basidiomycetes*.

bract A modified leaf, often small and scalelike, found at the base of a flower or inflorescence (flower cluster). Occasionally bracts are large and brightly colored, resembling petals, as in the poinsettias. Smaller bracts (bracteoles) may be found on the flower stalk.

Bradbury, Ray (1920–) US science-fiction writer. Many of his works of fantasy and science fiction deal essentially with the themes of conventional fiction, and his literary style has been much admired. His novels include *The Illustrated Man* (1951) and *Fahrenheit 451* (1953) and his many collections of stories include *The Golden Apples of the Sun* (1953), *I Sing the Body Electric* (1969), and *The Stories of Ray Bradbury* (1980).

Braddock, Edward (1695–1755) British general in command of British troops in North America (1755) at the beginning of the French and Indian War. While on an expedition to take Fort Duquesne (Pittsburgh, Pa), his army was ambushed by Canadian and Indian forces, whose fighting tactics were unlike any the British had seen. Defeated and in retreat, Braddock was killed near Fort Duquesne.

Bradford 53 48N 1 45W A city in N England, in West Yorkshire near Leeds. It is the foremost wool textile town in the UK and a world center for the raw-wool market. Besides woolens and worsteds, many other fabrics are manufactured and engineering is important. Bradford has a university (1966) and is the birthplace of J. B. Priestley. Population (1981): 280,691.

Bradford, William (1663–1752) British printer, who emigrated to Pennsylvania in 1682. In 1725 he founded the *New York Gazette*, the first New York newspaper.

Bradley, Bill (1943–) US basketball player and politician. He was an All-American basketball player for Princeton University (1963–65) and later played professionally for the New York Knickerbockers (1967–77). A Rhodes scholar (1965–67), he studied at Oxford. Upon retirement from basketball he served in the US Senate (1970–) as a Democrat from New Jersey.

Bradley, Francis Herbert (1846–1924) British philosopher. He lived as a semi-invalid, holding a sinecural fellowship at Oxford. Indebted to *Hegel, his idealist metaphysics are often brilliant in detail and grandiose in conception, but unwieldy in overall effect. In his greatest work, *Appearance and Reality* (1893), he argues against the acceptance of any general categories as absolutely real. Truth is relative and reality is unknowable and transcendent.

Bradley, Omar Nelson (1893–1981) US general. In World War II, he was in command in North Africa and at the invasion of Sicily. He later commanded the First US Army in the invasion of France (1944). In 1948 he became army chief of staff and was then the first chairman of the joint chiefs of staff (1949–53) until his retirement.

Brady, "Diamond Jim" (James Buchanan B.; 1856–1917) US financier. An entrepreneur who earned his fortune through selling of railroad equipment, he was known for the collection of diamonds he amassed and wore.

He was responsible for funding, in great part, Johns Hopkins University Hospital and New York Hospital.

Brady, Mathew B. (1823–96) US photographer. He was one of the first to learn daguerreotype methods from Samuel F.B. *Morse. By 1854 he had two studios in New York City and one in Washington, D.C. where he photographed most of the famous people of his time, including Abraham Lincoln. Throughout the Civil War (1861–65) he and his team of photographers were active on the battlefields, recording war in pictures for the first time.

Braemar 57 01N 2 34W A village in NE Scotland, in Grampian Region on Clunie Water (a tributary of the River Dee). It is a resort and the scene of the annual Highland games.

Braga 41 32N 8 26W A city in N Portugal. It has a cathedral (12th–17th centuries) and is the seat of the primate of Portugal. A nearby holy sanctuary is visited by many pilgrims. Industries include jewelry and cutlery. Population (1970): 101,877.

Bragança (*or* Braganza) The ruling dynasty of Portugal from 1640 to 1910 and of Brazil from 1822 to 1889. The family was descended from Alfonso, illegitimate son of *John I and 1st Duke of Bragança. The first Bragança king was *John IV (1640–56) and the last was Manuel II (1889–1932; reigned 1908–10), after whose deposition Portugal became a republic. When Brazil became independent (1822), it was ruled by two members of the family, *Pedro I (1822–31) and *Pedro II (1831–89), before becoming a republic (1889).

Bragg, Braxton (1817–76) US Confederate general. He graduated from West Point in 1837 and served in the US Army until 1856. At the outbreak of the Civil War in 1861, he was given command of the Confederate Army of Tennessee and fought an indecisive battle at Murfreesboro (1862–63). He was victorious at Chickamauga (1863), but his defeat at Chattanooga (1863) forced the Confederate Army to leave Tennessee. Relieved of his command in late 1863, he became military advisor to Confederate President Jefferson *Davis and then commanded troops in North Carolina until the end of the war.

Bragg, Sir William Henry (1862–1942) British physicist, who worked in Australia from 1886 to 1908. His early research, described in *Studies in Radioactivity* (1912), concerned the passage of alpha and beta particle and gamma rays through matter. He invented the Bragg diffractometer for measurement of X-ray wavelengths (1912) and with his son **Sir (William) Lawrence Bragg** (1890–1971) discovered the law of X-ray diffraction that bears their name. Together they wrote *X-rays and Crystal Structure* (1915) and were jointly awarded the Nobel Prize for 1915.

Bragg's law A law stating that, if two parallel X-rays of wavelength λ are reflected by adjacent planes, distance d apart, in a crystal lattice and the rays then constructively interfere, then $2d\sin\theta = n\lambda$, where n is an integer and θ the angle between the X-rays and the planes. θ is called the Bragg angle. If n is half-integral, then destructive *interference is observed. Named for— Sir William and Sir Lawrence *Bragg.

Brahe, Tycho (1546–1601) Danish astronomer, who made accurate astronomical instruments and used them to make observations enabling him to revise the existing, often inaccurate, astronomical tables. He first attracted attention by observing a nova in 1572. As a result King Frederick II had two observatories built for him on the island of Hveen, where he worked from 1580 to 1597. During this period he made extensive observations, which led him to support *Copernicus' theory that the planets revolve round the sun. However, he believed the earth to be immovable, with the sun and planets revolving round it. After Frederick's death, he quarreled with his successor and moved to Prague: there he met *Kepler, who became his student. After Tycho's death, Kepler used his teacher's observations to test his laws of planetary motion.

Brahma The creator god of later Vedic religion. Arising from the cosmic Golden Egg, he brings into existence the cyclical process of the creation and destruction of the world. His four heads and arms represent the four *Vedas, castes, and yugas (ages of the world). Brahma represents the creative aspect of supreme deity in the *trimurti triad but since the 7th century his worship has been superseded by that of *Siva and *Vishnu, the other members of the triad.

Brahman (Hinduism) In the *Upanishads, the absolute unmanifest changeless source of the phenomenal universe, seen as self-existent, extra-temporal Being, all-pervading and infinite. Brahman is both the basis of existence and the state of one who has achieved release (*see* atman). Brahman originally meant "the sacred Word," and as such was the exclusive domain of the literate priestly caste. In its extended significance it therefore came to be considered the proper spiritual object of that class alone. *See* Brahmanism.

Brahman (cattle). *See* zebu.

Brahmanas Commentaries on the *Vedas, written in Sanskrit between about 1000 and 600 BC. They systematically explore Aryan legends and folklore in order to account for traditional rituals and are major sources of Indian philosophy, theology, and myth.

Brahmanism An early speculative rather than devotional form of *Hinduism, derived from the *Vedas and characterized by the veneration of an elite priestly caste, who, as the privileged keepers of religious knowledge, were seen as actually embodying the sacred word. *See also* Brahman.

Brahmaputra River A river in S Asia. Rising in SW Tibet as the Tsangpo, it flows generally E across the Himalayas before turning S into the Assam Valley of NE India as the Dihang. From here, as the Brahmaputra, it flows WSW across NE India to join the *Ganges River N of Gaolundo Ghat. Together they enter the Bay of Bengal in a large delta. The floodplains are highly cultivated. Length: 1800 mi (2900 km).

brahmin (*or* brahman) The first of the four major Hindu castes, that of the priests. Observing many social taboos and being innately more ritually pure than the warrior, merchant, or peasant classes, brahmins alone are able to perform the most important religious tasks, to study and recite the scriptures. Since in India spiritual and secular knowledge are virtually inseparable, brahmins frequently hold considerable intellectual and political power. After India achieved independence in 1947, opposition to brahminical elitism strengthened, but this has not yet significantly weakened their sacerdotal role.

Brahmo Samaj A Hindu revivalist movement, arising in response to contact with Christianity. Founded by Rammohan Ray (1772–1833), it intended to restore monotheistic Hinduism and the authority of the *Upanishads. Unlike the *Arya Samaj, it set out to be a universal religion. Disagreements between advocates of devotion or asceticism, rather than rational theism, led to schisms and the incorporation of Christian elements and in some cases to wholly new philosophical formulations.

Brahms, Johannes (1833–97) German composer, born in Hamburg. Brahms' precociousness was demonstrated by his youthful piano compositions; as a young man he became a friend of the violinist Joseph Joachim (1831–1907), Liszt, and the Schumanns. Brahms moved to Vienna in 1863 and later became musical director of the Gesellschaft der Musikfreunde (Society of Friends of Music; 1872–75). Musically conservative, Brahms composed in traditional forms and was unsympathetic to the progressive ideas espoused by Wagner and Liszt, although his compositions abound in lyrical melodies and rich harmonies. His main orchestral works comprise four symphonies, two piano concertos, a violin concerto, and a concerto for violin and cello. His choral works include *A German Requiem* (1868) and the *Alto Rhapsody* (1869). He wrote a large quantity of chamber music, including a piano quintet, three piano quartets, and three piano trios; string sextets, quintets, and quartets; a clarinet quintet and trio; and sonatas for violin, cello, and clarinet. He also composed much piano music and many songs.

Brăila 46 82N 27 58E A port in E Romania, situated at the limit for oceangoing ships on the Danube River. Following the Turkish occupation of the city (1544–1828), it was rebuilt with radiating and concentric streets. It is a major grain center. Population (1979 est): 203,983.

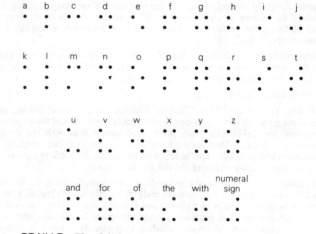

BRAILLE *The alphabet*

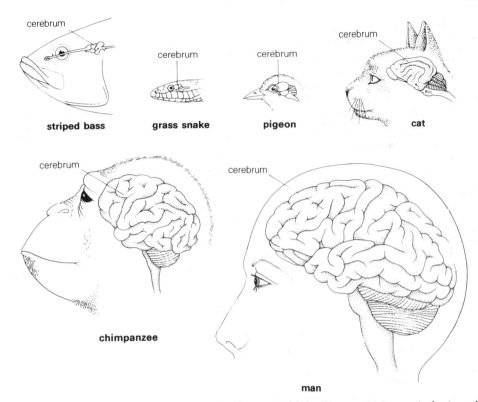

striped bass   grass snake   pigeon   cat

chimpanzee

man

BRAIN   *The brains of these representative vertebrates (drawn to the same scale) show a progressive increase in the size and complexity of the cerebrum. In man this development is such that the cerebrum covers or encloses all the other parts of the brain.*

Braille, Louis   (1809–52) French teacher, who, blinded by an accident at the age of three, published a system of writing that allows the blind to read by touch. He later applied the Braille system to the reading of music. Modern Braille consists of 63 characters, each of which is made up of one to six embossed dots.

brain   The mass of nervous tissue that lies within the skull and is ensheathed by three membranes (meninges). It is the organ of the mind and it controls many bodily activities. The hindmost part of the brain, joining the *spinal cord, is the medulla oblongata: this ascends to the pons, which joins the midbrain. These parts are together called the brainstem, which contains the vital centers controlling breathing and heartbeat and also regulates the level of consciousness and conveys information to and from the cerebrum. The cerebellum is connected to the brainstem and is important in the coordination of movements. The upper end of the brainstem is connected to the largest and most highly developed part of the brain—the cerebrum. This consists of two cerebral hemispheres connected to each other by a tract of nerve fibers. Its surface is intricately folded and is made up of an outer layer of nerve cell bodies (gray matter) and an inner mass of nerve fibers (white matter). The cerebrum is largely responsible for understanding the environment, language, rational thought, and the voluntary control of movements. The hemispheres differ in function: one hemisphere controls the dominant side of the body (normally the left hemisphere in right-handed people) and that hemisphere controls speech. The nondominant hemisphere specializes in analyzing how things are arranged in space. Deep within the cerebrum and brainstem lie cavities (ventricles) filled with *cerebrospinal fluid. The brain of vertebrate animals is similar but less highly developed than the human brain; in lower animals a collection of ganglia (nerve cell bodies) functions as the brain. *See also* electroencephalography; hypothalamus; nervous system; neuron.

Brain Trust   (1932) A group of US academics, advisers to Franklin D. Roosevelt's first campaign for the presidency. Consisting of Columbia University professors Adolph A. *Berle, Jr., Rexford G. Tugwell (1891–1979), and others, the group formulated social and economic policies and were instrumental in developing the president's *New Deal programs.

brake   1. A device used to slow down or stop the rotation of a shaft. An essential component of all vehicles, modern braking systems depend either on the friction between a pair of expanding shoes and the inside of a drum attached to the wheel (**drum brakes**) or between two caliper-operated pads and the two sides of a disk (**disk brakes**). 2. A device that absorbs and measures the power developed by an engine or motor. Brake horsepower is the power so measured. 1 brake HP = 746 watts.

Bramante, Donato   (1444–1514) Italian Renaissance architect. Bramante started his career as a painter and later executed his first building projects in Milan. However, he spent his last 16 years in Rome, where most of the buildings for which he is remembered were erected, showing as they do a much more sophisticated handling of classical forms. His earlier buildings, such as S Maria delle Grazie (1480s) in Milan, although competent, do not show the same assurance that he exhibited in, for example, the Tempietto di S Pietro in Montorio (1502). The Palazzo Caprini (1514) had a lasting influence on secular architects and Bramante's designs for St Peter's can be seen strongly reflected in the later designs of *Michelangelo.

bramble.   *See* blackberry.

brambling   A finch, *Fringilla montifringilla*, 6 in (14.5 cm) long, that breeds in Asia and N Europe and migrates south in winter. It has a brown-speckled plumage with white wing bars and orange underparts but in winter the male has a black head and back.

Bran   A legendary Celtic god-king of Britain, whose story is told in the medieval Welsh collection of tales, the *Mabinogion*. Of giant stature, he once waded across the sea between Britain and Ireland. His severed head lived on for some 80 years, renowned for the good advice and entertainment it gave his followers. In accordance with his wish, Bran's head was finally buried at a spot in London in order to protect Britain from invasion. It gave this protection until it was dug up by King Arthur, who believed that the protection of the country was better served by the valor of individuals.

Branchiopoda   A subclass of small *crustaceans (over 800 species) that, except for the brine shrimp, occur in fresh water. They include the *fairy shrimps, *tadpole shrimps, *water fleas, and clam shrimps, all bearing flat fringed appendages used for locomotion, respiration, and filter feeding. *Parthenogenesis is common.

Brancusi, Constantin   (1876–1957) Romanian sculptor. At first locally trained, he moved to Paris in 1904, where he developed a highly individual style. His stone and metal sculptures show a search for abstract simplicity and surface polish, such as the *Sleeping Muse* series beginning in 1906 and the *Birds* variations (1912–40). In contrast, his wood sculptures, such as the *Prodigal Son* (1915), utilize complex angular forms inspired by *African art and are often mythological or religious in theme.

Brandeis, Louis (Dembitz) (1856–1941) US lawyer, associate justice of the Supreme Court (1916–39). Known as "the people's attorney" during his days as a practicing lawyer (1878–1916), he espoused the causes of the common man. His appointment as the first Jew to sit on the Supreme Court caused much controversy. His court decisions reflected his strong feelings about civil rights, and he defended freedom of expression. He applied sociology to the hard facts of the law and favored experimentation in regard to laws governing ever-changing economic practices and institutions.

Brandenburg 52 24N 12 31E A city in central East Germany, on the Havel River. It was the former capital of the Prussian province of Brandenburg. The city was severely damaged during World War II and has been largely rebuilt. Its industries include steelworks and machinery and textile manufacturing. Population (1973 est): 94,091.

Brandenburg A former state corresponding to the present-day districts of Magdeburg, Potsdam, Neubrandenburg, and Frankfurt of East Germany and to part of W Poland. The region was conquered by the Germans between the 10th and 12th centuries and in 1157 *Albert (I) the Bear became margrave, and then *elector, of Brandenburg. Under *Frederick William, the Great Elector (1640–88), Brandenburg gained suzerainty of Prussia and became a leading German power. In 1701 the Elector of Brandenburg became *Frederick I of Prussia.

Brandenburg Gate A ceremonial gateway now in East □Berlin. The Brandenburg Gate was built (1789) in the neoclassical style by the architect C. G. Langhans (1732–1808). Situated at the W end of Unter den Linden, it became the symbol of the modernized city.

Brandes, Georg Morris Cohen (1842–1927) Danish literary critic. Brandes opposed all that was staid and reactionary in literature, and because of radical and atheistic tendencies he was denied a professorship at Copenhagen University until 1902. *Mainstreams in the Literature of the Nineteenth Century* (1872–75) established his reputation. There followed monographs on *Kierkegaard* (1871), *Ibsen* (1899), and *Anatole France* (1905), and a study of Shakespeare (1897–98).

MARLON BRANDO *In the title role of* The Godfather.

Brando, Marlon (1924–) US film actor. Deeply influenced by his training in the "method" style of acting developed by Lee Strasberg at the New York Actors' Studio in the 1950s from the theories of Konstantin *Stanislavsky, Brando was recognized early in his career as one of the most talented and innovative American actors. His films include *A Streetcar Named Desire* (1951), *On the Waterfront* (1954), *Mutiny on the Bounty* (1962), *Last Tango in Paris* (1971), *The Godfather*, for which he won the Academy Award in 1972, and *Apocalypse Now* (1979).

Brandt, Willy (1913–) West German statesman; chancellor (1969–74). In Norway from 1933, he was a leader of the resistance movement against the Nazis throughout World War II, after which he was Norwegian press attaché in Berlin (1945–48). A member of the Social Democratic Party from 1931, he became its chairman in 1964. As chancellor he negotiated treaties with Russia, Poland, and East Germany and in 1971 was awarded the Nobel Peace Prize. He resigned the chancellorship when it was revealed that one of his aides was an East German spy. He subsequently chaired an international commission on the state of the world economy (the Brandt Commission), which published its report in 1980.

brandy A *spirit distilled from fermented grape juice (wine); the term also denotes drinks distilled from the fermented juices of other fruits. The best types of wine brandy are matured in oak casks and named for— the Cognac and Armagnac districts of France where they are made. Marc (French) or grappa (Italian) brandy is made from the refermented grape pips, skins, and stems left after pressing for wine. VSOP—very superior old pale—brandy is usually 20–25 years old.

Brandywine, Battle of the (Sept. 11, 1777) A battle fought in SE Pennsylvania during the *American Revolution. In an attempt to capture Philadelphia, British Gen William *Howe landed with 15,000 troops at the head of Chesapeake Bay and encircled Gen George *Washington's force, which had taken up a defensive position on the eastern bank of Brandywine Creek. Coordinating his attack with the forward movement of the Hessian troops under Gen William von Knyphausen and of the forces of Gen Charles *Cornwallis, Howe forced the Americans to retreat but was unable to capture the road to Philadelphia.

Brant, Joseph (1742–1807) Mohawk Indian chief. He went to a mission school, where he became an Anglican, and commanded the Mohawks on the British side in the American Revolution. He subsequently settled them in Canada and in 1785 he visited England to claim compensation for war losses. He later resisted the taking of Mohawk lands by speculators.

Brant, Sebastian (?1458–1521) German poet. He studied and taught law at Basle, and was made an imperial councillor by Maximilian I. His most important work was *The Ship of Fools* (1494); a series of satires on contemporary vices (with illustrations ascribed to Dürer). It became popular throughout Europe.

Brantford A city in SE Ontario in SE Canada. Situated on the Grand River, which empties into Lake Erie, it serves as a distribution center, and also produces such items as farming tools, lumber, construction machinery, and paper products. The first long-distance (8 mi; 13 km) telephone call was (1878) made from here by Alexander Graham Bell. Population (1981): 74,315.

Branting, Karl Hjalmar (1860–1925) Swedish statesman; prime minister (1920, 1921–23, 1924–25). His domestic policy pioneered welfare state legislation in Sweden. An enthusiastic supporter of the League of Nations, he was awarded, with the Norwegian pacifist, Christian Lange (1869–1938), the Nobel Peace Prize in 1921.

Brantôme, Pierre, Abbé and Seigneur de Bourdeille (c. 1540–1614) French chronicler. Only nominally a priest, he was a courtier under Marguerite de Valois and Henry II and traveled throughout Europe as a soldier. He began writing when crippled in a riding accident. His *Mémoires* (1665–66) chronicle the lives of illustrious men and women of his time.

Braque, Georges (1882–1963) French painter, who with *Picasso developed *cubism. He was initially influenced by impressionism and later fauvism before painting his earliest cubist landscapes (1908–09) at L'Estaque and Guyon, inspired by *Cézanne. His favorite subjects were still lifes, which during their period of close collaboration, sometimes looked identical to those of Picasso. Notable among Braque's innovations were the use of lettering in compositions, e.g. *The Portuguese* (1911; Basle), mixing paint with sand to produce interesting textures, and papiers collés (paper pasted on canvases). After World War II he painted independently in large flat planes instead of small fragmented cubes. In his later years he produced sculpture and eight paintings of studio interiors (1948–55).

Brasilia 16 0S 48 10W The capital and a federal district of Brazil, situated on the central plateau. The idea of a capital in the interior was first suggested in 1789, but it was not until 1956 that the present site was chosen. It was inaugurated in 1960, the chief designer being Lúcio Costa and the principal architect, Oscar *Niemeyer. Its fine modern buildings include the National Congress Building and the cathedral. The university was founded in 1962. Population (1980): 411,305.

Braşov (German name: Kronstadt) 45 39N 25 35E A city in E central Romania, surrounded by the Transylvanian Alps. It has many historic buildings and the first book printed in Romanian appeared here in the 16th century. Its varied industries include motor vehicles, chemicals, and textiles. Population (1979 est): 299,172.

brass An *alloy of copper and zinc. Brasses containing less than 36% zinc are ductile when cold and can be easily worked into complex shapes. Those with more than 36% zinc are harder and stronger. Brass is easy to machine and stamp into shape and is used for screws, hinges, and a wide variety of articles. It does not rust but exposure to sea water causes dezincification (leaching out of the zinc). This is partially prevented by the addition of tin (1%) in Naval Brass, sometimes with about 0.05% of arsenic. *See also* Muntz metal.

Brassica A genus of mainly annual or biennial herbs (about 40 species, especially in the Mediterranean region), with erect clusters of four-petaled yellow flowers. Many species have basal rosettes of large simple leaves, but in others the leaves are spaced out up the main stem. The genus includes many important vegetables, mostly cultivated varieties of native species; the leaves, buds, stems, or roots may be eaten. *See also* broccoli; Brussels sprout; cabbage; cauliflower; kale; rape; rutabaga; turnip.

BRASILIA *The dramatic interior of the cathedral, which was designed by Oscar Niemeyer.*

brass instruments Wind instruments made of brass. The *French horn, *trumpet, *trombone, and *tuba are commonly used in the symphony orchestra; brass bands use a greater variety, including *bugles and *cornets. Brass instruments have either a cup-shaped or cone-shaped mouthpiece, the shape of which influences the tone quality, as does the type of bore, which may be conical (horn) or cylindrical (trumpet). A brass instrument plays the harmonic series natural to its length; additional series are made available by the use of crooks, slides, or valves.

Bratislava 48 10N 17 10E The third largest city in Czechoslovakia, the capital of the Slovak Republic on the Danube River. It was the capital of Hungary (1526–1784). Notable buildings include the gothic cathedral (13th century), where many of the kings of Hungary were crowned, and its castle. The university was founded in 1919. It is an important industrial center; oil, piped from the Soviet Union via the Friendship Oil Pipeline, is refined here. Population (1980 est): 375,000.

Brattain, Walter Houser (1902–) US physicist, who shared the 1956 Nobel Prize for his part in the invention of the transistor (with W. B. *Shockley and John *Bardeen) while working at the Bell Telephone Laboratories in 1948.

Brauchitsch, Walther von (1881–1948) German general. He became commander in chief of the German army in 1938 but was dismissed (1941) by Hitler after the failure of the Moscow campaign. He died awaiting trial for alleged war crimes.

Braun, Eva (1910–45) The mistress and finally the wife of Adolf Hitler. Their relationship probably began in 1933 and they were married shortly before their suicides on April 30, 1945.

Braun, Wernher von. *See* von Braun, Wernher.

Braunau am Inn 48 16N 13 03E A city in N Austria, in Upper Austria. It has numerous 16th–17th-century houses and several notable gothic churches. Adolf Hitler was born here. It has Austria's largest aluminum plant. Population (1981): 16,185.

Braunschweig. *See* Brunswick.

Brazil, Federal Republic of (Portuguese name: Brasil) A country comprising almost half the area of South America, situated in the NE. The N of the country is dominated by the Amazon basin with its tropical rain forests. The land rises to the Guiana Highlands in the N and the Brazilian Highlands in the S, with large tracts of grassland in between. The Mato Grosso Plateau in the SW is arid savanna. The population is largely of European descent, with some African and Asian minorities and a very small and dwindling Indian minority. Most of the inhabitants live along the coast, especially in the S and SE, although the government has launched ambitious road and regional plans in an attempt to open up and develop the interior. The building of *Brasília was the most impressive single attempt to draw the population away from the overcrowded coastal areas. *Economy*: despite a remarkably high annual growth rate (especially in the period

1960 to 1970) and recent industrialization, Brazil is still mainly an agricultural country, the chief crops being sugar cane, manioc, maize, rice, and beans. Brazil was formerly the world's largest producer of coffee but overproduction has led to a decline in its position. Severe frosts in 1975 caused a 60% loss in the coffee crop. Cocoa, bananas, and oranges are also important. Numbers of livestock have increased and Brazil is now ahead of Argentina as a cattle producer. The fishing industry has been nationalized and in 1971 territorial waters were extended to 200 mi (320 km). Brazil is exceptionally rich in mineral resources, many of them as yet untapped, although more mines are now being opened up as the government attempts to exploit the vast regions of the interior. The iron-ore reserves are estimated to be the largest in the world. There are gold deposits in most parts of the country and the large mine at Minas Gerais was discovered in the late 17th century. Recently large deposits of phosphates have been discovered there, as well as uranium, manganese, and copper. The country's many other minerals include high-grade quartz crystal. Efforts to encourage industrial development since the 1960s have included an increase in steel production, which in turn is designed to encourage shipbuilding. The most important manufacturing industry, however, is textiles, although motor-vehicle production is on the increase. 90% of power comes from hydroelectric sources. There is now an agreement with West Germany, based on Brazil's rich uranium deposits, to build eight nuclear power stations. Oil production only provides a fraction of Brazil's domestic needs although new offshore fields have been found near Campos. Main exports include sugar, coffee, cotton, and minerals, especially iron ore. *History*: claimed by the Portuguese in 1500, it became a Portuguese settlement. During the Napoleonic Wars the Portuguese court was transferred to Brazil and in 1815 it was made a kingdom. In 1822 independence was declared by *Pedro I, son of John VI of Portugal, with a constitution that proclaimed him emperor. In 1889 his son *Pedro II was deposed and Brazil became a republic. From 1930 to 1945 it was ruled under the benevolent dictatorship of Getúlio *Vargas. Less stable governments followed, including a further period under Vargas. In 1964 the left-wing president, João Goulart, was overthrown in a military coup led by General Humberto Castelo Branco. In 1966 Marshal Artur da Costa e Silva was elected president and in 1968 he assumed absolute powers. He resigned in 1969 and the government was taken over by a junta comprising the three heads of the armed forces. The transition from military to democratic rule in the early 1980s was marked by civil disruptions resulting from severe economic measures imposed on the country to satisfy Brazil's foreign creditors. The demand for stringent economic cutbacks by the International Monetary Fund, Brazil's chief lending agent, led to riots and looting. In an attempt to avoid default by Brazil and the chaos it would create in international banking, the IMF softened its demands. Head of state: President Tancredo Neves (1910–). Official language: Portuguese. Official currency: cruzeiro of 100 centavos. Area: 3,286,000 sq mi (8,511,965 sq km). Population (1984 est): 131,200,000. Capital: Brasília. Main port: Rio de Janeiro.

Brazil nut The seed of a tall forest tree, *Bertholletia excelsa*, up to 145 ft (45 m) high, native to tropical South America. The tree produces showy fluffy flowers that develop into hard woody fruits, up to 6 in (15 cm) in diameter, each containing 12–24 seeds (the nuts). Commercial supplies come entirely from wild trees. Family: *Lecythidaceae*.

brazilwood An evergreen tree, *Caesalpinia brasiliensis*, of tropical South America. The leaves are bipinnate—each leaflet is divided into smaller leaflets—and the irregular orange flowers develop into seed pods. The tree yields a very hard wood from which a red dye is extracted; the wood is also used for cabinetwork. Family: *Leguminosae*.

brazing. *See* solder.

Brazos River A river in central Texas that flows E and mainly S past Houston to the Gulf of Mexico at Freeport. Several dams on the river provide power for electricity and irrigation. Length: 850 mi (1369 km).

Brazza, Pierre Paul François Camille Savorgnan de (1852–1905) French explorer of Italian descent. In 1878 he explored, claimed, and colonized French Equatorial Africa, founding Brazzaville. He was the first governor of the French Congo (1886–97).

Brazzaville 4 07W 15 15E The capital of the People's Republic of Congo, situated in the S on the Zaïre River opposite Kinshasa (Zaïre). Founded in the 1880s, it developed as a European center and an important riverport, and became capital of French Equatorial Africa in 1910. During World War II it was the center of the Free French forces in Africa. It became capital of the newly independent Republic of Congo in 1960. The Marien-Ngouabi University was founded in 1972. Population (1980 est): 310,500.

bread A staple food made basically by baking a mixture of *flour and water. Ordinary leavened bread is made by mixing a dough of flour, water, yeast, sugar, salt, and sometimes other ingredients. The dough is kneaded and left to rise twice, a process that can take several hours, before being baked. White loaves, rolls, French sticks, and brown bread are made from different types of wheat flour. Rye bread is another variety, which has a stronger more bitter flavor and can be black, brown, or white.

Bread has been baked since the earliest times, evidence of barley cakes having been found in Neolithic dwellings.

breadfruit The starchy fruit of a tropical tree *Artocarpus communis*. When roasted it forms a staple part of the diet in the Pacific islands, to which it is native, and it is widely cultivated elsewhere. The tree grows to a height of 98 ft (30 m) and has thick shiny divided leaves. The large round fruits, as much as 12 in (30 cm) across, have a thick warty rind and develop from long female catkins. Family: *Moraceae*.

bread mold A fungus that grows on bread, especially one of the genera *Rhizopus* or *Mucor*. Black bread mold (*R. stolonifer*) forms a filamentous branching structure from which arise erect stalks bearing black spore cases resembling pinheads. It also grows on fruit, manure, and other decaying organic matter. Class: *Phycomycetes*.

bream One of several *teleost fishes, especially *Abramis brama*, a food and game fish related to *carp that occurs in European lakes and slow-moving rivers. Its deep body, 12–28 in (30–70 cm) long, is bluish gray or brown above and silvery below. It lives in schools in deep water and feeds on invertebrates or small fish. *See also* sea bream.

Bream, Julian Alexander (1933–) British guitarist and lutenist. Taught by his father, Bream gave his first public performance at the age of 12. His outstanding talent attracted Andrés Segovia's attention. His repertoire includes arrangements of baroque and Renaissance pieces as well as works written for him by Britten and Henze.

breast The milk-producing (mammary) gland of women. Each of the two breasts consists of a mass of fatty tissue in which are embedded milk-secreting lobes, which drain through a series of ducts to the nipple. Breast cancer is the commonest form of cancer in women. Treatment usually involves surgical removal of the breast (*see* mastectomy), sometimes with radiotherapy or *cytotoxic drugs. The activity of the gland is controlled by the hormone prolactin, secreted by the pituitary gland (*see* lactation).

breathalyzer A roadside test used by the police to estimate the amount of alcohol in the breath, which reflects the level of alcohol in the blood.

breathing. *See* respiration.

Brébeuf, St Jean de (1593–1649) French Jesuit missionary and patron saint of Canada. Ordained in 1623, he evangelized the Huron Indians in New France in several expeditions, until he was captured and tortured to death by the Hurons' enemies, the Iroquois. Feast day: Sept 26.

breccia A sedimentary rock consisting of relatively large (over 0.08 in (2 mm) in diameter) angular fragments of pre-existing rocks. These fragments have usually undergone little transport from their source and are poorly sorted. Scree material cemented together forms one kind of breccia.

Brecht, Bertolt (1898–1956) German dramatist and poet. He first studied medicine, serving briefly as a medical orderly in 1918. He abandoned the exuberant expressionism of his early plays after his conversion to Marxism in 1928, producing his best-known work the next year, *Die Dreigroschenoper*, an adaptation of John Gay's *The Beggar's Opera* with music by Kurt Weil. In 1933 he left Germany and lived in Scandinavia and the US (1941–47). During these years he wrote his most powerful plays, notably *Galileo* (1938), *Mother Courage* (1939) and *The Caucasian Chalk Circle* (1949). These exploit his "distancing" technique, in which by emphasizing the unreality of the play he increases its didactic impact. In 1949 he returned to East Berlin and founded his famous Berliner Ensemble Company.

Breckinridge, John Cabell (1821–75) US politician, vice president (1857–61), and Confederate general. Before becoming vice president in President James *Buchanan's administration he was a congressman from Kentucky (1851–57). He worked to fend off secession by the South prior to the outbreak of the Civil War, but favored slavery in the territories. A senator for a short time in 1861, he was expelled when he accepted a commission of general in the Confederate Army. Later in the war he served as the Confederate secretary of war.

Breda 51 35N 4 46E A city in the SW Netherlands, in North Brabant province. Occupied several times, its capture by the Spanish in 1625 is depicted in Velázquez' famous painting, *The Surrender of Breda*. Its industries include textiles and engineering. Population (1981 est): 117,107.

breeder reactor. *See* fast reactor.

breeding The controlled mating of selected animals or plants, usually in order to produce offspring with improved performance, such as a higher

milk yield in dairy cattle, or certain desirable characteristics, such as a particular flower color in garden plants. Based on careful selection of parents (often over many generations) and a knowledge of genetics, modern plant and animal breeding is aimed at improving yield, resistance to disease, hardiness to climate, consumer appeal of the product, etc., and has helped meet increased world demand for food.

Bregenz 47 31N 9 46E A city in W Austria, the capital of Vorarlberg on Lake Constance. A tourist resort, it manufactures textiles and machinery. Population (1981): 24,624.

Brehon Laws A collection of ancient Irish laws, dating back to the 8th century, which constitute one of the most important sources for the history of contemporary Irish society. The Brehon was an official who pronounced upon the law. The Laws describe conditions of tenure and transfer of land and the legal status and responsibilities of clan members, besides fixing penalties and fines for criminal acts.

Breitenfeld, Battles of Two battles fought in Germany during the *Thirty Years' War and won by Sweden. *Gustavus II Adolphus led the Swedish-Saxon army to victory against the Catholic and imperial forces under *Tilly in 1631. The second battle (1642) was a Swedish victory against the imperial army in a campaign to win Saxony.

Bremen 53 05N 8 48E The second largest port in West Germany, capital of the *Land* of Bremen on the Weser River. Its cathedral (founded 1043) was restored following damage during World War II. Its industries include shipbuilding, oil refining, and food processing. Population (1980 est): 555,700.

Bremen The smallest *Land* of West Germany, comprising the cities of *Bremen and *Bremerhaven enclosed by the *Land* of Lower Saxony. Area: 156 sq mi (404 sq km). Population (1976 est): 694,600.

Bremerhaven 53 33N 8 35E A city in N West Germany, in Bremen on the Weser estuary. A major fishing, freight, and passenger port, its industries include fish processing and shipbuilding. Population (1980 est): 138,900.

bremmstrahlung Electromagnetic radiation emitted by a charged particle when it is decelerated on passing close to a nucleus. The effect is most often observed with electrons since they are light and therefore easily decelerated. The radiation from one particle is emitted as a single photon. It is an important method by which *cosmic rays dissipate their energy on entering the earth's atmosphere.

Brendan, St (484–c. 578 AD) Irish abbot. He is traditionally credited with founding the monastery at Clonfert (Cluain Fearta), Co Galway. The Latin *Navigation of St Brendan* (c. 1050) recounts his legendary voyage to "northern and western islands," which may refer to the Orkneys and Hebrides. Feast day: May 16.

Bren gun A gas-operated light machine gun with interchangeable barrels first built at *Br*no, Czechoslovakia (1933), and later manufactured at *En*field, UK (1935). Widely used in World War II, it was accurate, reliable, easily maintained, and used 0.303 caliber ammunition.

Brennan, William J(oseph), Jr. (1906–) US jurist and lawyer; Supreme Court associate justice (1956–). He graduated from Harvard Law School (1931) and entered private practice, specializing in labor law. He was a judge of New Jersey Superior Court (1949–52) and on the New Jersey Supreme Court (1952–56). He was appointed to the US Supreme Court in 1956 by President *Eisenhower and confirmed by the Senate in 1957. A defender of the First Amendment and known as a moderate liberal, he championed civil rights, especially in *NAACP* v. *Button* (1963) and *New York Times Co.* v. *Sullivan* (1964).

Brenner Pass (German name: Brenner Sattel; Italian name: Passo del Brennero) 47 02N 11 32E The lowest of the chief passes in the Alps, on the Austrian-Italian border. Important since Roman times, it links Innsbruck (Austria) with Verona (Italy) by road and rail.

Brentano, Clemens (1778–1842) German writer, a member of the Heidelberg School of Romantic writers. With Achim von Arnim he published the influential folksong collection, *Des Knaben Wunderhorn* (1805–08). Emotionally unstable in early life, he became a Roman Catholic in 1817, and for six years was a monk.

Brentano, Franz (1838–1916) German psychologist and philosopher. He trained as a priest but resigned over the doctrine of papal infallibility. Thinking psychology a necessary foundation for philosophy, he suggested distinguishing marks for psychic phenomena, chief among which was intentionality ("directedness-to-an-object") adopted by *Russell and *Moore. His main works are *Psychology from an Empirical Standpoint* (1874) and *The Origin of Ethical Knowledge* (1889).

brent goose A dark-colored *goose, *Branta bernicla*. 21–23 in (53–58 cm) long, it breeds in the Arctic and winters in temperate N Atlantic coastal regions, feeding chiefly on eelgrass on mudflats. The pale-bellied form occurring in Canada and the eastern US and the dark-bellied form of Arctic Russia and European coasts are both geographic races.

Brescia 45 33N 10 13E A city in Italy, in Lombardy. It has Roman remains, 9th-century and 17th-century cathedrals, and a 12th-century palace. A railroad junction, its manufactures include metal goods, firearms, machinery, and textiles. Population (1980 est): 210,027.

Breslau. See Wroclaw.

Bresson, Robert (1907–) French film director. In most of his austere films concerning moral and religious dilemmas he uses unknown actors. His films include *Le Journal d'un curé de campagne* (1950), *Mouchette* (1967), and *Lancelot du lac* (1974).

Brest (name until 1921: Brest-Litovsk; Polish name: Brześć nad Bugiem) 52 08N 23 40E A port in the W Soviet Union, in the Belorussian SSR on the Bug and Mukhavets Rivers near the Polish border. The Treaties of *Brest-Litovsk were negotiated here in World War I. It is a major industrial, commercial, and transportation center. Population (1981 est): 194,000.

Brest 48 23N 4 30W A port and naval base in NW France, in the Finistère department on the Atlantic Ocean. A German U-boat base in World War II, it was almost entirely destroyed by Allied bombing. It is the site of the University of Brittany. Industries include fishing, chemicals, and clothing. Population (1975): 172,176.

Brest-Litovsk, Treaties of (1918) The peace treaties between the Central Powers and, respectively, the Ukraine and Soviet Russia toward the end of World War I. An independent Ukraine was recognized by the first treaty. By the second, Russia acknowledged Ukrainian independence and also lost its Polish and Baltic possessions. The treaties were annulled following the ultimate defeat of the Central Powers.

Brethren Members of the Protestant Brethren Churches. The largest, called the Church of the Brethren, was founded in Germany in the early 18th century. Persecution forced its members to emigrate to America, where they became known as "Tunkers," "Dunkers," or "German Baptists." They believe in temperance and pacifism and practice adult baptism by triple immersion.

Brétigny, Treaty of (1360) The treaty that concluded the first phase of the *Hundred Years' War. Never fully effective, it promised a ransom of 500,000 for *John II of France (captured at Poitiers in 1356) and granted territories, including Aquitaine, to Edward III of England. In return, Edward was to renounce his claim to the French throne.

Breton A Celtic language with four distinct dialects spoken in Brittany by about one million people. It was originally introduced to this area by immigrants from SW England, who had been displaced by invading Anglo-Saxon tribes. It is related to *Cornish and *Welsh but has been strongly influenced by French. It has a literature that dates from the 15th century. Official encouragement of French has tended to decrease the number of Breton speakers.

Breton, André (1896–1966) French poet. After involvement with *dada, he became the leader of French *surrealism in 1922 and wrote three manifestos (1924, 1930, 1942) defining its aims. His many essays explore surrealist themes, such as the relationship between dreams and reality. His novel *Nadja* (1928) freely blends real and surreal; *Poèmes* (1948) seeks to express the unconscious mind. Briefly a Communist Party member, he lived in the US from 1938 to 1946.

Bretton Woods Conference (1944) A conference held at Bretton Woods, New Hampshire, at which the US, Britain, and Canada established a system of international financial rules, which led to the setting up of the *International Monetary Fund (IMF) and the *International Bank for Reconstruction and Development (World Bank). The chief features of the system were, first, an obligation for each country to maintain the exchange value of its currency within 1% of a value fixed in terms of gold; and, secondly, the provision by the IMF of finance to bridge temporary payments imbalances. In the face of increasing strain, the system eventually collapsed in 1971, following the US government's suspension of convertibility from dollars to gold.

Breuer, Josef (1842–1925) Austrian physiologist and pioneer of psychoanalysis. After successfully treating hysteria in one of his patients, Breuer collaborated with Sigmund *Freud in writing *Studies in Hysteria* (1895). Earlier, working with Ewald Hering (1834–1918), Breuer described the Hering-Breuer reflex involved in the nervous control of breathing movements.

Breuer, Marcel Lajos (1902–81) US architect, furniture designer, and teacher, born in Hungary. In the 1920s he taught at the *Bauhaus, designing the first tubular steel chair (1925). After 1937 he practiced in the US as an architect. One of the best-known buildings on which he worked is the UNESCO headquarters in Paris (1958).

Breuil, Henri (1877–1961) French archaeologist, famous for his work on *Paleolithic art. Although ordained an abbé (1900), Breuil devoted his outstanding talents as a draftsman to copying cave paintings all over Europe (see also Altamira) and in N Africa, China, and S Africa. He was professor at the Collège de France (1929–47) and published over 600 books and articles.

brewing. See beer and brewing.

Brewster, Sir David (1781–1868) Scottish physicist, who studied the polarization of light, double refraction in crystals, and relations between crystalline forms and optical properties (see Brewster's law). He also invented and patented the kaleidoscope. In 1831 he helped to found the British Association for the Advancement of Science.

Brewster, William (1567–1644) US Pilgrim leader. Educated in England, he broke from the Anglican Church in 1606 and formed the Separatists, a group that went to Holland to avoid persecution in 1608 and finally to America in 1620 aboard the *Mayflower. He was a signer of the *Mayflower Compact* (1620) and served as Plymouth Colony's spiritual leader.

Brewster's law Light reflected from a solid surface is plane polarized, with maximum polarization occurring when the tangent of the angle of incidence is equal to the refractive index. Named for Sir David *Brewster.

Brezhnev, Leonid Ilich (1906–82) Soviet statesman; secretary of the Soviet Communist Party (1964–82) and president of the Soviet Union (1977–82). Brezhnev, a metallurgist, was a political leader in the Red Army during World War II. After holding offices in the Ukraine and Moldavia, he became a member of the presidium in 1957 and its chairman in 1960. He and *Kosygin forced Khrushchev to resign in 1964 and Brezhnev became first secretary of the Communist Party. By the late 1960s he had became the most powerful Soviet leader and in 1977 became president.

Brian Boru (926–1014) High King of Ireland (1001–14) after victories over the Danes and the other Irish. He was murdered after his victory at the battle of Clontarf. Brian was the last high king with effective jurisdiction over most of Ireland.

Briand, Aristide (1862–1932) French socialist statesman; prime minister (1909–11, 1913, 1915–17, 1921–22, 1925–26, 1929) and foreign minister (1925–32). The crisis of Verdun in *World War I precipitated the fall of his government in March, 1917, when Clemenceau's attacks upon Briand for his attempt to negotiate peace forced him to retire. From 1919 he was a leading advocate of international cooperation and was instrumental in securing the *Locarno Pact (1925) and *Kellog-Briand Pact (1928). With Gustav *Stresemann, he shared the Noble Peace Prize in 1926.

briar A shrubby rambling *rose with arching prickly stems, found in hedgerows and scrub in many parts of Europe. The principal species are *Rosa rubiginosa, R. micrantha, R. agrestis,* and *R. elliptica.* See also sweet briar.

Briar is also the name of a shrubby white *heath (*Erica arborea*), the roots and knotted stems of which are used for making briar pipes.

bribery and corruption The giving of a gift to a person in a position of trust, particularly a public official, to induce him to act contrary to his duty. If such a gift is secretly given and received it is presumed to be corrupt. The federal statute defines an official to include "any officer or employee or person acting for or on behalf of the United States, or any department or agency or branch of government thereof . . . ."

brick A traditional building material in the form of a rectangular block usually measuring 9 × 4½ × 3 in (225 × 112 × 75 mm). They are normally made from clay and baked or fired in a kiln at about 1650°F (900°C). Water is driven off, organic matter becomes oxidized, and some of the clay minerals fuse and fill the gaps between the clay particles. Iron oxide gives the brick its reddish color. Bricks are laid in various patterns, known as bonds. Refractory bricks made from fireclay are used to line furnaces.

Bride, St See Bridget, St

bridge A card game deriving from *whist. **Straight bridge** was first played about 1880; having overtaken whist in popularity, about 1911 it was displaced by its descendant, **auction bridge**, in which the opposing pairs of partners competed to decide the trump suit. By 1929 the American game of **contract bridge**, popularized by Ely *Culbertson and putting greater emphasis on skill, supplanted other forms of bridge. Two pairs of partners (referred to as North-South and East-West in bridge notation) bid to name the trump suit (or to play without a trump suit, i.e. in "no trumps") and "contract" to win a specified number of tricks (e.g. "four spades") above the six tricks of the "book." A game consists of 100 points, with each spade or heart trick counting 30, each diamond or club 20, and for a bid in no trumps 40 for the first trick and 30 for subsequent tricks. Only the tricks contracted for in the bidding are counted toward game; extra points are awarded separately for "honors" (ace to ten of trumps), overtricks, and for slams (when the partners have bid for and won all the tricks or all but one trick in a hand). Penalty points are awarded to the opponents for undertricks (when the partners who have declared trumps fail to win the number of tricks they contracted for in the bidding). The side winning two games consecutively or two games out of three wins the rubber, which counts as either 500 or 700 extra points. The playing of the hand after the bidding is similar to whist, except that the declarer's partner, called the dummy, puts his entire hand face upward on the table to be played by the declarer.

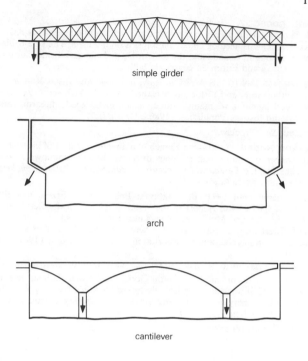

BRIDGES   *The arrows show how forces are exerted onto or away from the foundations in each of the basic structural types.*

structures. **Beam** (*or* girder) **bridges** are supported at their ends by the ground, with the weight thrusting downward. The cantilever is a more complex form of girder. **Arch bridges** thrust outward— as well as downward at their ends and are in compression. **Suspension bridges** use cables under tension to pull inward— against anchorages in the ground. The roadway, or a truss supporting it, hangs from the main cables by a network of vertical cables. In certain bridges, there is insufficient room to allow traffic to pass underneath them. In these cases the bridges are designed with movable parts. Swing bridges can rotate horizontally. Bascule bridges are cantilever-type bridges with a counterweight and hinge to rotate the bridge vertically. Draw bridges and vertical lift bridges have towers that lift the whole of one section of the bridge upward. *See also* Bailey bridge; pontoon bridge.

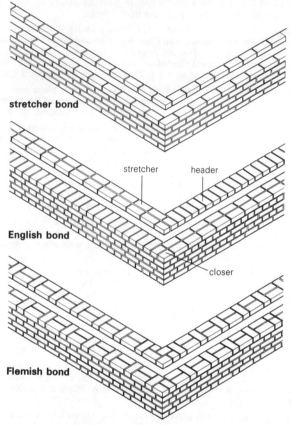

BRICKS   *The factors of cost, strength, and decorative effect influence a bricklayer's choice of bond for a particular task.*

Bridge of Sighs (Italian name: Ponte dei Sospiri)   A covered bridge in Venice (Italy) linking the Doge's Palace with the state prison. Its name derives from the sighs of the prisoners who were conducted over it.

Bridgeport   41 11N 73 11W A city in SW Connecticut, on the Poquonock River at its entrance to Long Island Sound. Connecticut's largest city, Bridgeport was settled in 1639. The University of Bridgeport was established in 1927. Products manufactured include electrical appliances, brass hardware, drugs, clothing, and plastics. Population (1980): 142,546.

Bridger, Jim (James B; 1804–81)   US fur trapper, explorer, and scout. In his travels looking for furs he discovered Great Salt Lake (1824) and what is now Yellowstone Park. He led many expeditions through unexplored territory and established Fort Bridger, a trading post, in Wyoming in 1843. He also acted as a scout for the US Army.

bridges   Structures that provide a means of crossing a river, valley, road, or railroad. There are three basic designs, which differ in the way they bear the weight of the bridge and its load; some bridges consist of composite

Bridges, Robert Seymour   (1844–1930) British poet. Educated at Oxford, he worked as a doctor until 1882. He published several volumes of lyrics and a long philosophical poem, *The Testament of Beauty* (1929), but an even greater contribution to literature was his edition of the poems of his friend Gerard Manley *Hopkins. He was made poet laureate in 1913.

Bridget, St (St Bride *or* St Brigit; died c. 523 AD) Irish abbess and second patron saint of Ireland. The traditions regarding her life are various, but she is believed to have founded the first Irish convent, at Kildare. Feast day: Feb 1.

Bridgetown   14 05N 59 35W The capital of Barbados, a port in the SW on Carlisle Bay, founded in 1628. The main industries are sugar, rum, and tourism. The University of the West Indies was founded in 1963. Population (1980): 7517.

Bridgman, Percy Williams   (1882–1961) US physicist, whose experiments with high pressures led to the invention of a seal the efficiency of which increased with pressure, enabling him to attain pressures of up to 20,000 atmospheres. Bridgman studied the effects of such pressures on solids and, in 1955, his methods were used by the General Electric Company to synthesize diamonds. For this work he was awarded the Nobel Prize in 1946. In *The Logic of Modern Physics* (1927) he made an important contribution to the (operational) concept of scientific meaning.

Brie An area in N France, between the Seine and Marne Rivers. Predominantly agricultural, it produces wheat and sugar beet and is noted for its cheese. Area: 2510 sq mi (6500 sq km).

brig A sailing vessel with two masts, both carrying square sails.

brigantine A sailing vessel with two masts, square-rigged on the foremast, with a fore-and-aft mainsail and square topsails.

Briggs, Henry (1561–1630) English mathematician. On hearing of *Napier's use of *logarithms, which have a base of e, Briggs realized that logarithms to the base ten, known as common or Briggsian logarithms, would make calculations simpler. Common logarithms are now widely used although Napierian logarithms are used for some purposes.

Bright, Richard (1789–1858) British physician, who described many disorders, particularly the group of symptoms, including edema (retention of body fluid), that he showed to be due to kidney disease. This is sometimes called **Bright's disease** (*see* nephritis).

Brighton 50 50N 0 10W A resort in S England, on the East Sussex coast. Originally a fishing village, its growth began with the development of sea bathing in the 1750s. The Prince Regent (later George IV) had the Royal Pavilion redesigned by John Nash in oriental style. Other notable features include the Lanes and the boating marina (completed in 1979). Brighton is also a conference center and site of the University of Sussex (1961). Population (1981): 146,134.

Brigit A Celtic goddess of fire, fertility, learning, culture, and crafts. Elements of her cult were passed into the traditions surrounding St *Bridget, notably the burning of a sacred fire by her shrine.

brill An edible *flatfish, *Scophthalmus rhombus*, related to *turbot, that occurs in European coastal waters, down to depths of 230 ft (70 m). Its smooth body, up to 28 in (70 cm) long, is sandy to gray or dark-brown with light and dark spots above and white with darker blotches below.

Brillat-Savarin, Anthelme (1755–1826) French lawyer and writer. His *Physiologie du goût* (1825) is a collection of gastronomical anecdotes and aphorisms. After the Revolution he became a judge of the French supreme court.

brilliant cut A method of cutting diamonds and other gems to impart maximum brilliance. The upper and lower halves of the stone are cut into 33 and 25 polished facets respectively. These facets meet around the girdle or perimeter of the circular stone.

brimstone A lemon-yellow butterfly, *Gonopteryx rhamni*, found in Europe, N Africa, and parts of Asia. Adults hibernate, flying early in spring. The next generation emerges in June or later, the caterpillars feeding on buckthorn. Family: *Pieridae*.

Brindisi (Latin name: Brundisium) 40 37N 17 57E A seaport in SE Italy, in Apulia. It was an important Roman naval base and a center of the Crusades in the middle ages. It has a 12th-century cathedral and a castle. Virgil died here. Population (1971): 79,784.

brine shrimp A crustacean belonging to a genus (*Artemia*) of *fairy shrimps that lives in salty pools and lakes. The widely distributed species *A. salina*, 0.40 in (10 mm) long, is often cultivated for fish food.

briquette A block of compressed coal dust bound with pitch or a similar substance. Briquetting converts fuel that would otherwise be of little use into one of higher quality that can be sold.

Brisbane 27 30S 153 00E The third largest city in Australia, the capital and chief port of Queensland on the Brisbane River. The chief industries are engineering, shipbuilding, oil refining, food processing, and wool scouring. Exports include wool, meat, mineral sands, and wheat. The University of Queensland was established in 1910 and Griffith University in 1975; other notable buildings include Parliament House (1869), two cathedrals, the Observatory (1829) built by convicts, and the Queen Elizabeth II Stadium built for the 1982 Commonwealth Games. *History*: originally a penal colony, the settlement was opened to colonists in 1842. It became the state capital when Queensland was formed in 1859. Population (1976): 957,710.

brisling. *See* sprat.

Brissot, Jacques-Pierre (1754–93) French journalist and revolutionary. A legal reformer and humanitarian before the French Revolution, he became leader of the Brissotins, later called the *Girondins, in 1789. A proponent of revolutionary war, his policies led to the French declaration of war on Austria in 1792. Internal rivalries and disputes over the conduct of the war produced a power struggle between the *Jacobins and Girondins. After the defeat of the Girondins, Brissot was executed.

bristlecone pine A *pine tree, *Pinus aristata*, native to mountainous regions of Colorado, Arizona, and New Mexico. Up to 49 ft (15 m) tall, it has needles grouped in clusters of five, and cones about 3 in (7.5 cm) long with distinctive bristles on each scale. Bristlecone pines are among the longest-lived trees: it has been estimated that some trees have reached an age of 5000 years and they have been used to date archeological sites (*see* dendrochronology).

bristletail A slender wingless insect, 0.20–0.80 in (5–20 mm) long, that has two or three long tail bristles and belongs to the orders *Thysanura* (three-pronged bristletails) or *Diplura* (two-pronged bristletails). Most bristletails live in damp sheltered places, e.g. under stones and logs, and feed on plant detritus. However, a few species feed on books and papers or anything containing starch (*see* silverfish; firebrat).

bristle worm. *See* annelid worm.

Bristol 51 27N 2 35W A port and industrial city in SW England, the administrative center of Avon on the Avon River, 7 mi (11 km) from the Bristol Channel. An important port in the 17th and 18th centuries, concentrating on trade with the Americas, its docks on the Bristol Channel now handle much of the British import and export trade. Bristol University dates from 1909. Bristol's industries include engineering (particularly aircraft manufacture), chemicals, tobacco, soap, paper manufacture, chocolate, printing, and nonferrous metal refining. Population (1981): 387,977.

Bristol Channel An inlet of the Atlantic Ocean in the UK, between South Wales and SW England. It forms an extension of the Severn Estuary and has the greatest tidal range in England. Length: about 85 mi (137 km).

Britain, Battle of. *See* World War II.

Britannia metal An *alloy of tin (80–90%) with variable amounts of antimony and copper. It resembles silver and was formerly used for tableware instead of *pewter.

British Academy A learned society formed in 1901 and incorporated in 1902. The Academy aims to promote the study of languages and literatures, history, archaeology, philosophy, religion, law, economics, and the visual arts, from which academic fields its Fellows are elected.

British Antarctic Territory A British colony established in 1962 that consists of the South Orkney and South Shetland islands and a part of the Antarctic. It is used as a base for the British Antarctic Survey stations.

British Blue A breed of short-haired cat originating in the UK. They have a powerful body, a short thick tail, and a broad head with slightly rounded ears. The coat is an evenly shaded blue and the eyes are copper, orange, or yellow.

British Broadcasting Corporation (BBC) A radio and television broadcasting network in Britain. The BBC was first set up as a private company in 1922 and was incorporated in 1927; it is responsible to Parliament and is politically neutral and independent. It relies on revenue from television licenses as it is not permitted to carry advertising.

British Columbia The westernmost province of Canada, on the Pacific Ocean. Mostly in the mountainous Cordilleran region, it is bounded by the *Rocky Mountains in the E and the *Coast Range, including islands, in the W. The main rivers (the Fraser, Kootenay, Thompson, and Columbia) and their tributaries are swift flowing and there are many lakes and waterfalls. Forests cover over 55% of the surface and provide the basis for most manufacturing. Fishing, hydroelectricity, and tourism are also economically important. There are rich mineral resources; gold, silver, lead, zinc, copper, coal, and oil are all produced. Although only a small area is farmed, dairy produce, mixed farming, and fruit are valuable. Prosperous and urbanized, British Columbia is Canada's fastest-growing province; half the population lives in the Lower Mainland. *History*: visited by Captain Cook (1778), British Columbia also attracted Russians, Spaniards, and Canadians. A British colony established on Vancouver Island (1849) spread to the mainland when gold was discovered (1858). Entry into Canada (1871) and the transcontinental railroad (1885) provided the basis for economic development. Area: 359,277 sq mi (930,528 sq km). Population (1978 est.): 2,533,200. Capital: Victoria.

British Expeditionary Force (BEF) Army formations that helped France counter German invasions in World Wars I and II. In World War I, its 6 divisions had increased to 65 by 1918 and it suffered almost 3 million casualties, of which 900 000 were fatal. In World War II it consisted of 10 divisions until its evacuation from Dunkirk (1940).

British Guiana. *See* Guyana, Republic of.

British Honduras. *See* Belize.

British Indian Ocean Territory A British colony established in 1965 consisting of Chagos Archipelago, largest island of which is Diego Garcia, claimed by Mauritius. Aldabra, Farquhar, and Desroches were returned to the Seychelles in 1976. Although the islands are at present leased to companies that run copra plantations, they were acquired as a base for military activities. Population (1972 est): 350.

British Isles An archipelago separated from the mainland of NW Europe by the North Sea and the English Channel. It consists of Great Britain, Ireland, the Isle of Man, and the Channel Islands. Area: about 121,577 sq mi (314,950 sq km).

British Museum The national museum containing one of the finest collections of antiquities in the world. Founded in 1753, its Egyptian, Assyrian, Greek, Roman, Chinese, and Cambodian collections are unique and include a number of Egyptian mummies, the Elgin Marbles, and the Rosetta Stone. The natural history exhibits were transferred to a separate building (built 1873–80) known as the Natural History Museum.

British North America Act (1867) An act passed by the British parliament uniting the colonies of Novia Scotia, New Brunswick, Canada West (now Ontario), and Canada East (now Quebec) as the Dominion of Canada.

British thermal unit (btu) A unit of energy equal to the amount of heat required to raise the temperature of 1 lb of water through 1°F. It is equal to 1055.06 joules (251.997 calories).

British Virgin Islands. *See* Virgin Islands.

Britons The indigenous inhabitants of Britain before the Anglo-Saxon settlements. They spoke languages of the Brythonic branch of the *Celtic language family. At the Roman conquest (1st century AD) Britain was divided into a number of tribal kingdoms with a common Celtic culture (*see* La Tène). Religious affairs were conducted by priests known as *Druids. *See also* Belgae.

Brittan, Leon (1939–) British Conservative politician; home secretary (1983–). Trained as a barrister, he entered politics in 1974, becoming minister of state at the Home Office (1979–81) and chief secretary to the Treasury (1981–83).

BENJAMIN BRITTEN *His opera* Gloriana (1953), *on the story of England's Queen Elizabeth I and her courtier, the Earl of Essex, was written for the coronation of Elizabeth II.*

Brittany (Breton name: Breiz; French name: Bretagne) A planning region and former province in NW France. It consists of a peninsula between the Bay of Biscay and English Channel. It was part of ancient Armorica and in 56 BC was conquered by Julius Caesar. During the 5th–6th centuries AD Celts from Britain migrated here to escape the Anglo-Saxon invasion. Finally incorporated into France in 1532, it has retained its own distinctive culture. An important area for tourism, Brittany suffered from oil pollution on many beaches following the *Amoco Cadiz* oil tanker disaster in March,

1978. Area: 10,494 sq mi (27,184 sq km). Population (1981 est): 2,665,200.

Britten, (Edward) Benjamin, Baron (1913–76) British composer and pianist. He spent the years 1939–42 in the US and subsequently founded the English Opera Group (1947) and the Aldeburgh Festival (1948). He wrote many works, as well as leading roles in his operas, for his lifelong friend, the tenor Peter Pears. Among Britten's best-known compositions are the operas *Peter Grimes* (1945), *Billy Budd* (1951), and *Death in Venice* (1973); the orchestral works *Variations on a Theme by Frank Bridge* (1937) and the *Cello Symphony* (1964); choral works, such as the *Spring Symphony* (1949) and *A War Requiem* (1962); and many chamber and instrumental works.

brittle star A marine invertebrate animal, also called sand star or serpent star, belonging to a class (*Ophiuroidea*) of *echinoderms. It has a small disklike body bearing five long fragile arms, used for locomotion. Brittle stars sometimes occur in large numbers on soft muddy sea beds and are active at night, feeding on small crustaceans, mollusks, and bottom debris. □oceans.

Brno (German name: Brünn) 49 12N 16 40E The second largest city in Czechoslovakia, in S Moravia, formerly the capital of the province of Moravia. A fortified town in the middle ages, it contains the Spilberk fortress, an Austrian political prison (1621–1857). Other notable buildings include the 15th-century cathedral; its university was founded in 1919. The botanist Gregor Mendel devised his fundamental principles of heredity here (1865). Brno is now an important industrial center specializing in engineering and textiles; the *Bren gun was originally developed here. Population (1980 est): 373,000.

broad bean A stiff upright annual plant, *Vicia faba*, 24–60 in (60–150 cm) tall, with a ribbed stem and compound gray-green leaves composed of a few large leaflets. The flowers have white petals and dark-purple blotches on the wings. The large pod has a woolly lining surrounding large flat edible beans, for which the plant is cultivated throughout Europe, both as a vegetable and as an animal feed. *See also* bean.

broadbill A brightly colored passerine bird belonging to a family (*Eurylaimidae*; 14 species) of tropical African and Asian forests. It is about 5 in (12 cm) long with a large head, partly joined toes, and a very broad short bill. Most species are insectivorous, feeding in trees or on the wing.

Broadway A major street in New York City along and near which are sited most of the leading commercial theaters. The word is used to refer to commercial theater in the US in general. *See also* Off-Broadway theaters.

broccoli A cultivated variety of wild *cabbage (*Brassica oleracea*) with a stout upright stem and a loose cluster of flower heads at the top. The leaves are narrow and curly; the lower ones are shed as the plant grows, leaving a scarred stem. Sprouting broccoli has purple or white flowers. Calabrese or green sprouting broccoli is an Italian variety, often with fused parallel stems. Both are eaten as vegetables while the flowers are in bud. *See also* Brassica.

Broch, Hermann (1886–1951) Austrian novelist. In 1927 he sold the family textile business to return to the University of Vienna. His trilogy *The Sleepwalkers* (1931–32) is a historical study of Europe in a variety of literary forms. Briefly imprisoned by the Nazis, he emigrated to the US in 1940. There he continued to experiment with innovative literary techniques, most notably in *The Death of Virgil* (1945).

Brocken 51 48N 10 37E A mountain in W East Germany, the highest of the Harz Mountains. According to legend, this bare granite peak is the scene of the witches' sabbath (*see* witchcraft) on Walpurgis Night (May 1). The **Brocken specter** (*or* Brocken bow), first observed here, is a magnified shadow of the observer cast against mist or cloud below the level of the summit and surrounded by colored fringes resulting from the diffraction of light.

Broglie, Louis Victor, 7th Duc de. *See* de Broglie, Louis Victor, 7th Duc de.

Broken Hill 31 57S 141 30E A mining city in Australia, in W central New South Wales. The rich silver, lead, and zinc deposits were discovered in 1883. Population (1975 est): 28,310.

Broken Hill (Zambia). *See* Kabwe.

Bromfield, Louis (1896–1956) US writer. He wrote about rural life in such novels as *The Green Bay Tree* (1924), *Possession* (1925), *Early Autumn* (1926), for which he won a Pulitzer Prize, *The Rains Came* (1937), *Wild is the River* (1941), and *Malabar Farm* (1948).

bromine (Br) A dense reddish-brown liquid element, discovered by A. J. Balard (1802–76) in 1826. It is extracted from sea water and other natural brines by electrolysis or by displacement with chlorine. The liquid element is volatile and its vapor has a pungent smell reminiscent of chlorine with severe irritating effects on the eyes and throat. Compounds include silver bromide (AgBr), used in photography, and ethylene dibromide ($C_2H_4Br_2$), used to scavenge lead in making additives for motor fuel. Other compounds are used as fumigants, dyes, flame-proofing agents, and in medicine. At no 35; at wt 79.904; mp –7.2°C; bp 58.78°C.

bronchial tubes. *See* lung.

bronchitis Inflammation of the bronchi—the tubes conducting air to the lungs. Acute bronchitis is often due to a virus infection, particularly a cold or influenza. Chronic bronchitis is common in middle-aged and elderly men in the UK, being aggravated by cigarette smoking and air pollution. Irritation of the mucus-secreting glands in the bronchi results in a persistent cough, with the production of large amounts of sputum. The patient is breathless and liable to chest infections. Treatment consists of stopping smoking (and reducing exposure to other irritants) and the prompt management of any chest infection.

Bronowski, Jacob (1908–74) British mathematician, science writer, and broadcaster, born in Poland. He became widely known for his highly successful television series *The Ascent of Man* (1973), a history of the development of science and technology. His writings include commentaries on poetry, particularly that of William *Blake, and the importance of the scientific method, especially in *The Commonsense of Science* (1951).

BRONTË SISTERS *A family portrait (c. 1834) of (from left) Anne, Emily, and Charlotte by their brother Branwell.*

Brontë sisters Three British novelists, daughters of the rector of Haworth, an isolated village in Yorkshire. After briefly attending a local boarding school, **Charlotte Brontë** (1816–55) and **Emily Brontë** (1818–48) rejoined their sister **Anne Brontë** (1820–49) at home. Their early writings chronicled the imaginary kingdoms of Angria and Gondal. All the sisters worked for brief periods as governesses and teachers to help pay off the debts of their artist brother, **Patrick Branwell Brontë** (1817–48), an alcoholic and opium addict who died of tuberculosis. In 1846 the sisters published *Poems by Currer, Ellis, and Acton Bell* and in 1847, under the same pseudonyms, the novels *Jane Eyre* (by Charlotte), *Wuthering Heights* (by Emily), and *Agnes Gray* (by Anne). In 1848 Emily died of tuberculosis, as did Anne in 1849. Charlotte published *Shirley* (1849) and *Villette* (1853). She married her father's curate in 1854 and died in pregnancy a year later.

Brontosaurus A huge herbivorous dinosaur, also called *Apatosaurus*, of the late Jurassic period, which ended about 135 million years ago. Up to 68 ft (21 m) long and weighing over 30 tons, it had massive pillar-like legs, a long neck and tail, and spent most of its time in swamps, coming

ashore to lay eggs. With its nostrils placed high on its head, it was able to stand almost fully submerged. Order: *Saurischia. □fossil.

Brontotherium A genus of extinct North American hoofed mammals—*titanotheres—that lived during the Oligocene epoch (between 38 and 26 million years ago). Standing 8 ft (2.5 m) at the shoulder, *Brontotherium* had a large skull with a pair of bony horns.

Bronx, the 40 50N 73 52W One of the five boroughs of New York City, US, situated NE of the Harlem River. It is mainly residential but has an industrialized waterfront. Problems of overcrowding and poor housing conditions have made it the object of local and federal urbanization programs. Area: 41 sq mi (107 sq km). Population (1976 est): 1,255,500.

bronze An *alloy of copper and (4–11%) tin. Because it melts between 900°C and 1000°C, about the temperature of an ordinary wood fire, it was one of the first metals to be used for making weapons and utensils, being known around 2000 BC in Britain. It is harder than pure copper and "copper" coins are usually made of bronze containing 95% copper, 4% tin, 1% zinc, and occasionally other metals. Phosphor bronze contains 0.5% phosphorous. *See also* gun metal.

Bronze Age The cultural phase during which metallurgical technology, based first on copper (in the Chalcolithic period) and then on bronze (copper alloyed with tin), replaced the stone technology (*see* Stone Age) of the *Neolithic period. In Eurasia the development of international trade, literacy, the plow, and the wheel took place during this phase, which began at varying dates according to locality (the earliest being about 6500 BC in Anatolia); it gave way to the *Iron Age in about 1000 BC. In Africa, iron, discovered about 800 BC, replaced stone without an intervening Bronze Age. In the Americas, copper, discovered about 100 AD, was followed rapidly by iron, while in Australasia, the introduction of metallurgy occurred in the colonial period.

Bronzino, Il (Agnolo di Cosimo; 1503–72) Florentine mannerist painter (*see* mannerism). His religious and allegorical works, such as *Venus, Cupid, and Folly* (National Gallery, London), were influenced by *Michelangelo and Bronzino's teacher *Pontormo. As court painter to Cosimo I de' Medici he painted many portraits, including *Eleanor of Toledo and Her Son Giovanni* (Uffizi), a characteristic work having a cold detached dignity and a marble-like finish.

Brook, Peter (1925–) British theater director. His work for the Royal Shakespeare Company, of which he became a director in 1962, included experimental productions of Shakespeare. Since 1970 he has worked with the International Center for Theater Research in Paris, where he has developed acting techniques evolved during a tour of Africa and Asia. He has also directed films, including *Lord of the Flies* (1963) and *King Lear* (1971).

Brooke, Rupert (Chawner) (1887–1915) British poet and critic. His scholarship, charm, and good looks gained him many influential friends in literary and political circles. He received a naval commission in 1914 but died of blood poisoning on a hospital ship in the Aegean, without having seen action. His romantic image and the idealistic patriotism of his wartime poetry, *1914 and Other Poems* (1915), made him a national hero.

Brookeborough, Basil Stanlake Brooke, 1st Viscount (1888–1973) Northern Irish statesman; prime minister of Northern Ireland (1943–63). He became a Unionist MP in 1929 and was minister of agriculture (1933–41) and then minister of commerce (1941–43). He was firmly committed to union with Great Britain.

Brook Farm (1841–47) US utopian community in W Roxbury, Mass. It was established by George *Ripley, a Unitarian minister who had become a transcendentalist. He wanted to experiment with the intellectual and the worker living a simple life together, earning equal pay. Charles A. Dana (1819–97), Nathanial *Hawthorne, Ralph Waldo *Emerson, Theodore Parker (1810–60), Amos Bronson *Alcott, and Margaret Fuller (1810–50), among others participated at Brook Farm in one way or another. Poor farming land, lack of water, natural disasters, and failing finances forced its closing in 1847.

Brooklyn 40 40N 73 58W One of the five boroughs of New York City, situated at the SW end of Long Island. Settled by Dutch farmers in 1636, it has many colonial buildings and is the site of Pratt Institute (1887), Brooklyn Institute of Arts and Sciences (1823; comprising Brooklyn Museum, Brooklyn Children's Museum, and Brooklyn Botanic Garden and Arboretum), and branches of four New York universities. The New York Naval Shipyard, which was established here in 1801, was converted to civilian use in the 1960s. Three bridges, including the famous Brooklyn Bridge (1869–83), span the East River connecting Brooklyn with Manhattan. A major port, it handles a vast amount of shipping and its waterfront is 33 mi

(53 km) long. Area: 81 sq mi (210 sq km). Population (1976 est): 2,313,200.

Brooks Range A mountain range in N Alaska, just below the Alaskan North Slope, crossing the state to the Canadian border and including the De Long, Baird, Endicott, and Davidson mountains. The highest point, Mt Michelson 9239 ft (2816 m).

broom A bushy deciduous shrub, *Sarothamnus scoparius* (or *Cytisus scoparius*), 24–80 in (60–200 cm) high, with shiny green five-angled stems and small pointed compound leaves. The bright-yellow flowers are clustered at the ends of the twigs. Broom is found in heaths and woodland glades in Europe. It is poisonous to livestock but is often grown as an ornamental. The branches are used for brooms and thatching. Family: *Leguminosae*.

broomrape A parasitic plant of the worldwide genus *Orobanche* (about 100 species), lacking chlorophyll but having underground tubers attached to the roots of the host plant. The flowering shoots rise 2–28 in (5–70 cm) above ground on scaly stems topped by spikes of tubular two-lipped flowers, which may be white, yellow, or purple. The fruit is a capsule. Family: *Orobanchaceae*.

brotulid A fish, also called brotula, belonging to the family *Brotulidae* (it is sometimes placed with the cusk eels in the family *Ophidiidae*). Brotulids have an eel-like body, up to about 35 in (90 cm) in length, and most live in deep marine waters. Order: *Perciformes*.

Brough, Louise (1923–) US tennis player, who in 1948 and 1950 won all three titles at Wimbledon (singles, doubles, and mixed doubles). She also won all 22 of her *Wightman Cup rubbers (1946–57).

brougham A compact four-wheeled carriage light enough to be drawn by one horse. The original brougham was designed by Lord Brougham (1778–1868) in 1838.

Brouwer, Adriaen (c. 1605–38) Flemish painter, who worked in Holland, initially as a pupil of *Hals, and later in Antwerp. He excelled in small paintings of brawling and drunken peasants, the somber coloring of which was increasingly influenced by Dutch art.

Brouwer, L(uitzen) E(gbertus) J(an) (1881–1966) Dutch mathematician, who made important contributions to the development of *topology. He is often regarded as the founder of the subject in its modern form. He is also the founder of a school of mathematics known as intuitional mathematics, which holds that mathematics is a mental construction in which laws should be self-evident and derived by intuition.

Brown, Sir Arthur. See Alcock, Sir John.

Brown, Ford Madox (1821–93) British painter, born in France. After studying in Belgium, Paris, and Rome, he returned to England, where he was influenced by the Pre-Raphaelites. He painted chiefly historical themes, although his most famous paintings, *Work* and *The Last of England*, are contemporary subjects.

Brown, Jerry (Edmund Gerald B., Jr.; 1938–) US politician and lawyer. After graduation from Yale Law School (1964) he went into private practice, but, by 1970, was California's secretary of state. Elected Democratic governor of the state in 1974, a position his father "Pat" had also held (1959–67), he served until 1983. He was unsuccessful in seeking the presidential nomination in 1976 and 1980 and in his bid for the US Senate in 1982.

Brown, John (1800–59) US abolitionist. Believing that the slaves of the US should be encouraged to rise up against their masters, Brown established an anti-slavery colony in Kansas and carried out the massacre of 5 local slave owners in 1856. In 1859, supplied with funds by northern abolitionists, Brown and his followers raided the federal arsenal at Harper's Ferry in order to acquire arms for an expected slave rebellion throughout the South. Brown and his men were quickly captured by US Army troops under the command of Lt Col Robert E. *Lee. Brown was later tried and convicted of insurrection, treason, and murder. He was hanged on Dec. 2, 1859, and was considered by many to be a martyr to the abolitionist cause.

Brown, Robert (1773–1858) Scottish botanist, who in 1831 first recognized the *nucleus as a fundamental constituent of cells. Four years earlier, while observing a solution of pollen grains in water under a microscope, he discovered, but was unable to explain, the effect now known as the *Brownian movement.

brown algae *Algae of the division *Pheophyta* (1500 species), which contain a brown fucoxanthin (pigment) in addition to and sometimes masking the green chlorophyll. Brown algae include all the larger *seaweeds, such as wracks and kelps. They are mainly marine and are abundant along coasts in colder regions. Many show an *alternation of generations.

brown bear A large bear, *Ursus arctos*, of the N hemisphere. Brown bears have a thick shaggy coat, humped on the shoulders and varying in color from blackish-brown to gray, and they take a wide variety of food including fish, fruit, and cattle. There are many local races and subspecies, including the North American grizzly and Kodiak bears. The reputedly ferocious grizzly bear (*U. arctos horribilis*), mostly restricted to N Canada and Alaska, reaches a length of 8 ft (2.5 m) and a weight of 1213 lb (550 kg); the Alaskan Kodiac bear—a giant race of grizzly—is the largest living land carnivore, reaching a length of 9 ft (2.8 m) and a weight of 1675 lb (760 kg).

Browne, Hablot Knight (1815–82) British artist, better known as Phiz. He is renowned mainly for his illustrations of books by Charles Dickens, notably *The Pickwick Papers*. He also produced cartoons for *Punch* and watercolors.

Brownian movement The continuous random movement of very small particles (less than about one-thousandth of a millimeter in diameter) when suspended in a fluid. It is caused by collisions between the particles and the atoms or molecules of the fluid. Brownian movement can be observed in smoke suspended in air and in a suspension of pollen grains in a liquid. Named for Robert *Brown.

Browning, Robert (1812–89) British poet. The son of a bank clerk, his early education consisted chiefly of wide reading in his father's library. After the failure of his autobiographical poem *Pauline* (1833) he wrote several verse dramas and dramatic monologues, including the famous "My Last Duchess" (1842). The epic but uneven poem cycle *The Ring and the Book* was his last major work. His wife **Elizabeth Barrett Browning** (1806–61) was also a poet. A spinal injury when she was 15 made her a lifelong semi-invalid. She met Robert Browning in 1845 and in 1846 she defied her domineering father and eloped with Browning to Italy. Here she wrote her most famous work, *Sonnets from the Portuguese* (1850). In later years she became involved in Italian politics, the abolition of slavery, and spiritualism.

Browning Automatic Rifle (BAR) A gas-operated shoulder-fired automatic *rifle designed in 1917 by John Moses Browning (1855–1926). The standard automatic weapon in the US army until the Korean War, it weighed over 19 lbs (8.6 kg), including its 20-round magazine.

Brownshirts The colloquial name for the Nazi Sturmabteilung (SA; stormtroopers). Their name refers to their brown uniforms. They were founded in 1921 and reorganized by Ernst *Röhm in 1930. Squads of thugs, who molested and murdered the Nazis' opponents, they numbered two million by 1933. In 1934 Hitler eliminated Röhm and greatly reduced the power of the Brownshirts. See also SS.

Brownsville 25 54N 97 30W A city and port on the S tip of Texas at the Mexican border, on the Rio Grande, just E of the Gulf of Mexico. Originally a fort, it was important during the Mexican War and to the Confederacy during the Civil War. The oil industry, the processing of foods and chemicals, the production of machinery, and tourism are important. Population (1980): 84,997.

Brown v. Board of Education (of Topeka) (1954) US Supreme Court case that held that segregation in public schools on the basis of race is unlawful. The "separate but equal" doctrine was overturned in a majority opinion written by Chief Justice Earl *Warren who said, "Separate educational facilities are inherently unequal."

Brown v. Board of Education (1955) US Supreme Court ruling that directed implementation of the *Brown v. *Board of Education (of Topeka)* ruling "with all deliberate speed." Local courts were ordered to find solutions to individual problems as they arose.

Brubeck, Dave (1920–) US jazz pianist and composer, who studied composition with Darius Milhaud and Arnold Schoenberg. Brubeck introduced complex rhythms into jazz and formed a quartet in 1951. Among his most famous pieces are "Take Five," and "Blue Rondo à la Turque."

Bruce, James (1730–94) British explorer, who in the course of an arduous expedition that set out from Cairo in 1768 reached Lake Tana, source of the Blue Nile (1770). He described his experiences in *Travels to Discover the Source of the Nile* (1790).

Bruce, Robert. See Robert (I) the Bruce.

brucellosis (*or* undulant fever) An infectious disease of cattle and other farm animals that is caused by the bacterium *Brucella abortus* and can be contracted by man through drinking unpasteurized contaminated milk. Symptoms include fever (which may be intermittent), sweating, weakness, cough, joint pain, and sometimes swelling of the lymph nodes. Tetracycline usually cures the disease. The slaughter of infected animals has reduced the incidence of brucellosis.

Bruce of Melborne, Stanley Melborne, 1st Viscount (1883–1967) Australian statesman; prime minister (1923–29). He fought with the British Army in World War I and entered politics as a member of the National Party in 1918. His coalition government of National and Country Parties implemented social and welfare legislation in the areas of public health and devised a scheme of national insurance against unemployment. He represented Australia in the British war cabinet (1942–45).

Bruch, Max (1838–1920) German composer. He wrote in a romantic but conservative style. He is best known for his first violin concerto (1868) and *Kol Nidrei* (1880) for cello and orchestra, based on a Jewish hymn.

Brücke, Die (German: The Bridge) An organization of German artists founded in 1905 to promote modern art. Its members, notably *Kirchner, were influenced, like their French contemporaries, the fauves (*see* fauvism), by *Van Gogh, *Gauguin, *Munch, and primitive art. However, unlike the fauves, their crudely painted and vibrantly colored figure studies and landscapes expressed an underlying anxiety more typical of such early German artists as *Grünewald. Although the group broke up in 1913, it has had a lasting influence on the graphic arts, particularly the *woodcut. *See also* expressionism.

Bruckner, Anton (1824–96) Austrian composer and organist. He was a professor at the Vienna conservatoire (1871–91). In 1891 he was granted a pension and apartments in the Belvedere palace in Vienna, where he revised his compositions and worked on his ninth symphony (1887–96), which remained unfinished at his death. His symphonies, which exhibit the influence of Wagner and Schubert, had a mixed reception during his lifetime and were frequently performed in shortened versions. Bruckner also composed choral music in a polyphonic style, chamber music, organ music, and a *Te Deum* (1881–84) for orchestra, soloists, and chorus.

Brueghel the Elder, Pieter (*or* Bruegel; 1525–69) Flemish painter, noted for his often satirical scenes of peasant life and his landscapes. Although popularly called Peasant Brueghel, he was a learned man, whose patrons included Cardinal de Granvelle (1517–86). He studied under Pieter Coecke van Aelst (1502–50), whose daughter he later married, but was chiefly influenced by *Bosch in such works as the macabre *Triumph of Death* (Prado). He visited Italy (c. 1551–53) but Italian art influenced his style only in his last years. In 1563 he settled in Brussels, where he executed his best-known works, e.g. *Peasant Wedding* (Kunsthistorisches Museum, Vienna), and a landscape series entitled the *Labors of the Months*. Many of his paintings were copied by his eldest son **Pieter Brueghel the Younger** (?1564–?1638). His younger son Jan son— Brueghel the Elder (1568–1625), popularly called Velvet Brueghel, is noted for his flower and landscape paintings. He was a friend and sometimes assistant of Rubens.

Bruges (Flemish name: Brugge) 51 13N 3 14E A city in NW Belgium. It was the capital of Flanders in the 12th century and during the 13th and 14th centuries it became the center of the Hanseatic League in N Europe. It has many fine gothic buildings, including the 14th-century cathedral, the Church of Notre Dame (containing Michelangelo's marble statue, the Virgin and Child) and the Market Hall (13th–15th centuries) with its famous belfry and 47-bell carillon. It is linked by canal to many European ports. The traditional industry is lace; newer industrial developments include the manufacture of ships and electronic equipment. Population (1981 est): 118,212.

bruise An area of discolored skin caused by the leakage of blood from damaged blood vessels beneath the skin. Bruises are usually caused by a blow to the skin and are always more pronounced where the blood vessels are loosely suspended in the tissue (e.g. around the eye). They change from bluish to greenish yellow, as the blood pigment is chemically broken down and absorbed.

Brummel, George Bryan (1778–1840) British dandy, known as Beau Brummel. He was a prominent member of fashionable society and a close friend of the Prince Regent, later George IV. He fled to France to evade his creditors in 1816 and died in an asylum.

Brunei, State of A small sultanate in NW Borneo, on the South China Sea. It consists of two separate areas, entirely bounded (except for its coast) by the Malaysian state of Sarawak. It is mainly low lying with some hills in the S; the interior is largely dense forest. The people are mainly Malays, while about a quarter of the population are Chinese or other small minorities. *Economy*: dominated by oil (the main export) since the discovery of the Seria oilfield in 1929, production is being maintained by the addition of offshore oilfields. Recent efforts to diversify the economy include the construction of a deepwater port and a natural-gas liquefaction plant. Agriculture is also being encouraged in an attempt to make Brunei more self-sufficient in food production. *History*: a powerful state in the 16th century controlling the whole of Borneo, as well as parts of the Philippines,

it became a British protected state in 1888. In 1962 there was a revolt, mainly in protest against the proposal to join the Federation of Malaysia, and since then the sultan has ruled by decree. In 1967 Hassanal Bolkia Mu'izuddin Waddaulah (1946–) succeeded his father as sultan. In 1971 internal self-government was achieved and full independence was attained in 1984. Offical language: Malay; Chinese and English are also widely spoken. Official religion: Islam. Official currency: Brunei dollar of 100 cents. Area: 2,230 sq mi (5,776 sq km). Population (1983 est): 209,000. Capital and main port: Bandar Seri Begawan.

Brunel, Isambard Kingdom (1806–59) British engineer, who was one of the most original inventors of the 19th century. His most famous works were the Clifton suspension bridge, which spanned the Avon Gorge, near Bristol, England, completed in 1864, and his ships the *Great Western* (1837), the *Great Britain* (1843; □ship), the first large ship to be driven by screw propellers and now preserved in Bristol, and the *Great Eastern* (1858). Much of his work was done for the Great Western Railroad, for which he built over 990 mi (1600 km) of track, using the 7 ft (2 m) broad gauge rather than the 4 ft 8½ in (1.5 m) standard gauge. His father **Sir Marc Isambard Brunel** (1769–1849) was also an engineer. Born in France, he worked in New York after fleeing the French Revolution in 1793. He moved to England in 1799, where he became famous for his work on tunneling. In 1818 he patented the tunneling shield, which allowed tunnels to be dug below water.

Brunelleschi, Filippo (1377–1446) Italian architect. The founder of Renaissance architecture, Brunelleschi began his career as a goldsmith, only taking up architecture in his thirties, after spending some time studying Roman remains. His taste for classical architecture probably arose from a desire to understand Roman building techniques. This is demonstrated by his most famous construction, the dome of Florence cathedral (1430s), which used classical methods of construction. The Ospedale degli Innocenti (1419–26) is often regarded as the first architectural expression of the Renaissance.

Brunhild (*or* Brynhild) A heroine of Norse and Germanic legend. In the *Volsungasaga* she is the daughter of Odin, doomed to sleep on a fire-encircled rock until wakened by a mortal (*see* Siegfried). In the *Nibelungenlied* she is the queen of Issland.

Brüning, Heinrich (1885–1970) German statesman. As chancellor without a majority in the Reichstag, he governed by decree from 1930 to 1932. His deflationary policies brought him unpopularity and he resigned. In 1934 he left Germany, holding academic posts at Harvard (1937–52) and then at Cologne Universities.

Brünn. *See* Brno.

Brunner, Emil (1889–1965) Swiss Protestant theologian. A professor at the University of Zurich from 1924 to 1953, he became a supporter of the theological views of *Barth. However, he differed from Barth in allowing that God's image in mankind survived the Fall, despite man's fundamental sinfulness.

Bruno, Giordano (1548–1600) Italian philosopher. He became a Dominican (1563) but in 1576 his heretical opinions forced him to flee, first to Geneva, then to France, England, and Germany. Returning to Italy (1592) he was tried by the Inquisition, refused to recant, and was burned. His pantheistic philosophy, viewing all creation as one life, animated by God as "world-soul," influenced *Spinoza, *Descartes, and *Leibniz among others.

Bruno of Cologne, St (c. 1032–1101) German founder of the Carthusian order. He was educated at Cologne and Rheims, where he later taught at the cathedral school. He eventually withdrew with six companions to the mountainous region near Grenoble and built a monastery on the site of the present Grande Chartreuse, which became the mother house of the Carthusians. Called to Italy by Pope Urban II, his former pupil, he founded the monastery of La Torre in Calabria, where he died. Feast day: Oct 6.

Brunswick (German name: Braunschweig) 52 15N 10 30E A city in NE West Germany, in Lower Saxony on the Oker River. It was the capital of the former duchy of Brunswick. Notable buildings include the castle and the romanesque cathedral (both 12th-century), the old town hall (14th–15th centuries), and the ducal palace (1768–69). It also has the oldest technical university in Germany (1745). Its industries include metal working and the manufacture of motor vehicles and pianos. Population (1980 est): 261,500.

brush turkey A *megapode bird, *Alectura lathami*, occurring in dense rain forests of New Guinea and E Australia. It is 26–28 in (65–70 cm) long with a black plumage and builds a huge mound of fermenting plant material in which the eggs are incubated.

BRUSSELS *The European Economic Community building.*

Brussels (Flemish name: Brussel; French name: Bruxelles) 50 51N 4 22E The capital of Belgium, situated in the center of the country on the Senne River. As headquarters of the EEC and NATO, it is an important international center. Its varied industries include the manufacture of machinery, chemicals, and lace. Fine buildings include the 15th-century gothic town hall, the 13th-century Maison du Roi, the church of St Gudule, the 18th-century Palais de la Nation (parliament building), and the Royal Palace. The Free University was founded in 1834 and a Flemish-speaking counterpart became independent in 1970. *History*: settled by the French in the 7th century AD, it developed into a center of the wool industry in the 13th century. It became the capital of the Spanish Netherlands in the 15th century and later of the Austrian S Netherlands. In 1830 it was chosen as capital of the new kingdom of Belgium. It was occupied by the Germans in both World Wars. Population (1981 est): 1,000,221.

Brussels sprout A variety of wild cabbage, *Brassica oleracea* var. *gemmifera*, cultivated for its large edible buds. The stout erect shoots, up to 31 in (80 cm) high, have long-stalked curly leaves arranged spirally up the stem; in the angle between the leaf bases and the stem are large buds, like miniature cabbages up to 2 in (5 cm) in diameter. The lower leaves gradually fall, leaving the stem densely covered with buds. *See also* Brassica.

Brutus, Marcus Junius (?85–42 BC) Roman soldier and one of the assassins of Julius Caesar. Brutus, who supported Pompey against Caesar in the civil war, was pardoned by Caesar and made governor of Cisalpine Gaul (46) but subsequently joined the conspiracy to murder Caesar (44). He committed suicide after his defeat by Antony and Octavian at Philippi (42).

Bryan, William Jennings (1860–1925) US politician, orator, and lawyer. A Democrat from Illinois, he served as a congressman (1891–95), ran for president three times (1896, 1900, 1908) but was defeated each time, and served as secretary of state (1913–15) under Pres. Woodrow Wilson. He was a strong proponent of free silver; his "Cross of Gold" speech (1896) led to his endorsement by four political parties in the 1896 presidential election. Called the "Great Commoner," he championed liberal causes; advocated an income tax, prohibition of alcohol, and women's rights; and worked for the creation of a federal department of labor. In 1925, just before his death, he was the prosecutor in the anti-evolution Scopes trial, which was won by defense attorney Clarence *Darrow.

Bryansk 53 15N 34 09E A city in the W Soviet Union, in the RSFSR. It dates from at least the 12th century and is a communications center with varied industries. Population (1981 est): 407,000.

Bryant, William Cullen (1794–1878) US poet, journalist, and literary critic. He wrote his most famous poems, "Thanatopsis," when he was 17. The success of his *Poems* (1821) enabled him to abandon his law practice and move to New York. From 1829 he was editor of the newspaper *Evening Post* which became, over the next fifty years, an advocate of many liberal causes.

Bryce Canyon National Park A national park in SW Utah, just N of Arizona. Established as a national park in 1928, it is noted for its naturally-carved limestone cliffs, horseshoe-shaped amphitheater-like eroded rock structures, and glowing colored rocks. Area: 36,010 acres (14,584 hectares).

bryony Either of two unrelated Eurasian plants. **Black bryony** (*Tamus communis*) is a herbaceous climber with heart-shaped leaves that turn yellow in autumn. The bell-shaped yellow flowers are borne in separate male and female spikes. The fruits are scarlet berries, and the plant overwinters as a tuber. Family: *Dioscoreaceae* (yam family).

White bryony (*Bryonia dioica*) is a perennial herb climbing by means of tendrils. The hairy stem arises from a large rootstock and the leaves are palmately lobed. Greenish male and female flowers occur on separate plants and produce poisonous scarlet berries. Family: *Cucurbitaceae* (gourd family).

bryophyte A small flowerless green plant of the division *Bryophyta* (about 25,000 species), comprising the *liverworts and *mosses. The plant body is either differentiated into stems and leaves or is a flat branching structure (thallus). Bryophytes range in size from microscopic to over 40 in (1 m) long; they lack true vascular (conducting) tissues and roots (the rootlike rhizoids serve mainly for anchorage). Bryophytes show *alternation of generations: the plant itself is the sexual (gametophyte) phase, which bears male and female sex organs (antheridia and archegonia, respectively). Fertilization of an egg cell results in the development of a spore capsule—the asexual (sporophyte) phase—which remains attached to the gametophyte and largely dependent on it. The spores are dispersed by wind, insects, or water and germinate to form new plants.

Bryozoa (or Ectoprocta) A phylum of aquatic colonial invertebrate animals (about 6000 species), called moss animals, found chiefly in seas as matlike encrustations on rocks. A colony consists of individuals, each up to 0.12 in (3 mm) long and with a chitinous or gelatinous case and a ring of ciliated tentacles around the mouth. These are extended, creating a feeding current that brings food particles into the U-shaped digestive tract. Ciliated larvae establish new colonies by budding off more individuals.

Brythonic languages. *See* Celtic languages.

Brześć nad Bugiem. *See* Brest.

Bubastis (modern name: Tall Bastah) A ruined temple city in Lower Egypt. Bubastis was the capital of the 18th nome (province) and attained importance when the pharaohs of the 19th dynasty (1320–1200 BC) moved their capital to the Nile Delta. It became a royal residence when Sheshonk I was pharaoh (952 BC). After the Persian conquest (525 BC) the city declined. Bubastis was sacred to the cat goddess Bast.

bubble chamber An instrument that makes visible the tracks of ionizing particles, used for observing particle decays and interactions. It contains a liquid, usually hydrogen, helium, or deuterium, under pressure and at a temperature slightly above its normal boiling point. The particle induces boiling along its path and the bubbles are photographed to record the particle's track and those of any charged decay or reaction products.

Buber, Martin (1878–1965) Austrian-born Jewish religious philosopher. He wrote on *Hasidism, to which he was deeply sympathetic, and from 1925 produced, with F. *Rosenzweig, a remarkable German translation of the Bible. However, his best-known and most influential work was *I and Thou* (1923), which sets out his philosophy of religious faith in the form of a dialogue between man and God. Buber was a committed Zionist (he settled in Palestine in 1938), and advocated a joint Arab-Jewish state.

bubonic plague. *See* plague.

Bucaramanga 7 08N 73 10W A city in N Colombia. Situated in mountainous country, it is the commercial center for an area producing coffee and tobacco; manufactures include cigarettes and textiles. The Industrial University of Santander was founded here in 1947. Population (1978 est): 387,886.

buccaneers Bands of pirates who lived by plunder in the Caribbean in the second half of the 17th century. Most were English or French and they preyed primarily on Spanish shipping and settlements. They were often hired by the French governors of Tortuga and the English of Jamaica. By 1670 they had become, under the leadership of Henry *Morgan, a major problem for all countries and a number of treaties promised to bring them under control. In 1685 the English navy began to hunt buccaneers and after 1697 no European country employed them.

Bucer, Martin (1491–1551) German Protestant reformer. A Dominican friar, Bucer abandoned his vows and married in 1522, settling in Strasbourg. He advised Henry VIII on his divorce from Catherine of Aragon and tried to mediate between *Luther and *Zwingli in their debate concerning the Eucharist. In 1549 he went to England and became professor of divinity at Cambridge.

Buchanan, James (1791–1868) US statesman; 15th president of the US (1857–61). Trained as a lawyer, Buchanan served as a member of the US House of Representatives (1821–31), US minister to Russia (1832–33), and US senator from Pennsylvania (1835–45). Buchanan resigned from the Senate to become secretary of state in the cabinet of President James *Polk (1845–49) and US minister to Great Britain during the administration of President Franklin *Pierce (1853–56). As the 1856 presidential nominee of the *Democratic Party, Buchanan defeated the Republican John *Fremont and attempted to effect a compromise over the issue of slavery during his single term in the White House. Hoping to prevent the secession of the southern states, he supported the legalization of slavery in Kansas and proposed a Constitutional amendment that would recognize the rights of slave owners. Buchanan's efforts were ultimately unsuccessful; less than a month after leaving office, the southern states seceded from the Union and the *Civil War began.

Bucharest (Romanian name: Bucureşti)   44 25N 26 07E The capital of Romania, in the SE on a tributary of the Danube. As well as being the administrative and cultural center of the country, Bucharest has many industries, including flour milling, textiles, chemicals, and oil refining. *History*: there is evidence of human settlement from prehistoric times. A fortress was built against Turkish invasion in the 15th century and it became capital of Wallachia in 1659. During the 19th century Bucharest played an important role in revolutionary movements, becoming capital of Romania in 1862. The university was founded in 1864. It was badly damaged by German bombing in World War II and since then has developed considerably. Population (1979 est): 1,832,015.

Bucharest, Treaties of   1. (1812) The treaty ending the Russo-Turkish war of 1806–12. It assigned Bessarabia to Russia and Walachia and Moldavia to Turkey; the Serbs were to receive autonomy. 2. (1886) The treaty ending the Serbian-Bulgarian war (1885–86) over Eastern *Rumelia, which was kept by Bulgaria. 3. (1913) The treaty ending the second *Balkan War, which partitioned Macedonia between Serbia, Greece, Romania, and the defeated Bulgaria. 4. (1918) The treaty in which Romania acknowledged its defeat by the Central Powers in World War I. It was annulled after their defeat by the Allies.

Büchner, Georg   (1813–37) German dramatist. A medical student, he fled to Zürich after publishing a revolutionary pamphlet in 1834. He wrote three plays, the tragedies *Danton's Death* (1835) and *Woyzeck* (1836) and the comedy *Leonce und Lena* (1836), and a fragment of a novel, *Lenz* (1836). His innovatory techniques influenced later expressionist writers.

Buck, Pearl S (ydenstricker)   (1892–1973) US novelist. The daughter of Presbyterian missionaries, she grew up in China and later returned there as a teacher. Her novels about China include *The Good Earth* (1931), *A House Divided* (1935), *Dragon Seed* (1942), and *The Three Daughters of Madame Liang* (1969). She won the Nobel Prize in 1938.

Buckingham, George Villiers, 1st Duke of   (1592–1628) A favorite of James I of England. He replaced Robert Carr, Earl of *Somerset, in the king's favor (1615), becoming Earl of Buckingham (1617), Lord High Admiral (1619), and Duke of Buckingham (1623). His attempt to negotiate the marriage of Prince Charles to the daughter of the Spanish king failed (1623), as did the expedition he planned to Cádiz (1625) in the subsequent hostilities. James resisted parliament's attempts to demote Buckingham, who was assassinated after his unsuccessful expedition to relieve the Huguenots at La Rochelle (1627). His son **George Villiers, 2nd Duke of Buckingham** (1628–87) was a member of the powerful political group the *Cabal, under Charles II. After his father's death he was brought up in the royal family, with whom he went into exile after the final royalist defeat in the Civil War (1651). Becoming a privy councillor at the Restoration, he helped oust *Clarendon (1667) but was overshadowed by *Arlington when the Cabal came to power. Also a playwright, he wrote the satirical *The Rehearsal* (1671); he is portrayed by Zimri in Dryden's *Absalom and Achitophel*.

Buckingham Palace   The London residence of the British monarch. It was built about 1705 for the Duke of Buckingham, becoming a royal residence in 1761. It was completely redesigned by Nash for George IV, although its main façade was not added until 1913.

Buckinghamshire   A county in the South Midlands of England, bordering on Greater London. It is known appropriately as Leafy Bucks because of the many trees throughout the county. It is mainly agricultural, the chief crops being barley, wheat, and oats; sheep, cattle, poultry, and pig farming is also significant. Industry includes the manufacture of furniture based on the extensive beech woods. Area: 725 sq mi (1878 sq km). Population (1981): 565,992. Administrative center: Aylesbury.

Buckley, William F (rank) Jr.   (1925–   ) US journalist and writer. A conservative, he founded and edited *National Review* (1955) magazine. He also writes a syndicated newspaper column. His works include *God and Men at Yale* (1951), *The Unmaking of a Mayor* (1966; about his unsuc-

cessful bid to be mayor of New York City), *Saving the Queen* (1976), and *Overdrive* (1983).

buckthorn   A small thorny deciduous tree or shrub of the genus *Rhamnus* (about 13 species), widespread in the N hemisphere. The leaves are oval, with attractive autumn colors. The small green flowers produce blue-black berries. The wood is used for charcoal and slow fuses, and the bark for dyes. The alder buckthorn (*Frangula alnus*) is a similar and related shrub that lacks thorns. Family: *Rhamnaceae*.

buckwheat   A herbaceous plant of the genus *Fagopyrum*, especially *F. esculentum*. Up to 24 in (60 cm) tall, they have arrow-shaped leaves and clusters of densely packed small pink or white flowers. Buckwheats are native to Asia but widely cultivated for their seed, used as a cereal substitute, or as green fodder. Family: *Polygonaceae* (dock family).

Budapest   47 33N 19 03E The capital of Hungary, situated in the N of the country on the Danube River. Most of Hungary's industry is sited here and includes machinery, iron and steel, and chemicals. The university was founded in 1635. *History*: from the 14th century the fortress of Buda, on the W bank of the Danube, was the seat of the Magyar kings. After occupation by the Turks, it came under Habsburg rule in the 17th century. In 1872 it united with Pest, on the E bank of the river, to form the modern city that became the capital of Hungary in 1918. In 1956 it was the scene of a popular rising, suppressed by Soviet troops. Population (1980 est): 2,060,000.

BUDDHA *A sculptured head from Gandhara, NW Pakistan, made in the 4th or 5th century* AD.

Buddha, title of **Gautama Siddhartha**   (c. 563–c. 483 BC) Indian prince, whose teachings formed the basis of Buddhism. The son of Suddhodana and his queen, Maya, in Kapilavastu (Nepal), Gautama was reputed to have been a child of exceptional intelligence and beauty about whom many stories and legends have been told. At the age of 16 he married his cousin Princess Yasodhara, who some 13 years later bore him a son, Rahula. Soon after this event Gautama, renouncing his life of indolence and luxury, abandoned his family and set out to seek solutions to the problems of the transience and suffering of human existence. He was then about 29. After six years of emaciating asceticism he reluctantly concluded that austerity was as unlikely as triviality to provide the solution he sought. Abandoned now by his five companions for his rejection of mortification, he determined to seek enlightenment, alone, within himself. According to tradition, this he achieved while seated beneath a banyan tree, in what is now called Buddh Gaya, in Bihar (his title, *Buddha*, is Sanskrit for the Awakened One). Probably 35 years old at this time, he devoted the rest of his life to teaching the principles (*see* dharma) of this enlightenment, first moving to Benares, where he founded the Buddhist order of monks, and thereafter teaching in various places in N India. He died at Kusinagara in Uttar Pradesh. *See also* Buddhism.

Buddhaghosa (5th century BC) Buddhist scholar. A Brahman convert from Buddh Gaya, he wrote the *Visuddhi-magga* (*Path of Purity*), a collation of Sinhalese Buddhist commentaries that he collected in Ceylon and translated into Pali.

Buddh Gaya (*or* Bodh Gaya) 24 42N 85 00E A village in India, in Bihar. It was here that Gautama Buddha attained enlightenment under the sacred bo (*or* bodhi) tree. Population (1961): 6299.

Buddhism The nontheistic religion and philosophical system founded in NE India in the 6th century BC by Gautama Siddhartha (the *Buddha). His followers seek to emulate his example of perfect morality, wisdom, and compassion, culminating in a transformation of consciousness known as enlightenment. Buddhism teaches that greed, hatred, and delusion separate the individual from the true perception of the nature of things, causing him to remain tied to the *bhavachakra. The apparent substantiality of all objects, including the self, is illusion; everything mundane is impermanent and ultimately unsatisfying. The central beliefs of Buddhism are based on the Buddha's *Four Noble Truths, the last of which is the *Eightfold Path by which enlightenment may be attained and the individual self annihilated in *Nirvana. Buddhism is not dogmatic, but through its long history has developed into many schools (*see* Mahayana; Theravada; Zen Buddhism). With more than 500 million followers in Sri Lanka, Nepal, Japan, and elsewhere in the Far East, Buddhism is currently gaining adherents in the West.

budding In biology, a method of asexual reproduction in lower plants and animals, for example liverworts and coelenterates, in which new individuals develop from outgrowths of cells (buds) on the parent. The process also occurs in single-celled fungi, for example yeasts. In horticulture the term is used for the *grafting of a bud onto a stock.

Buddleia A genus of trees and shrubs (about 100 species), mostly native to tropical or warm temperate regions but widely introduced. The small four-petaled flowers are usually clustered in dense heads; the fruit is a capsule or berry. Many species are grown as ornamentals, especially *D. davidii* (butterfly bush) 13–16 ft (4–5 m) high, the long purple flower heads of which attract many butterflies; and *B. globosa*, which has round orange flower heads. Family: *Buddleiaceae*.

Budé, Guillaume (1467–1540) French Renaissance scholar. Budé wrote many important Greek commentaries and philological works. He founded the Collège de France (1530) and as royal librarian built the library that formed the nucleus of the Bibliothèque Nationale.

Budge, (James) Don(ald) (1916–) US tennis player, the first to win all four major singles titles (Australian, French, US, and Wimbledon) in one year (1938). He was also an outstanding doubles player.

budgerigar A small *parakeet, *Melopsitticus undulatus*, occurring in large flocks in arid regions of Australia. It is 7.6 in (19 cm) long and has a green and yellow plumage with barred upper parts. Since its introduction to Britain in 1840 it has become a popular cagebird; white, violet, yellow, blue, and gray forms have been produced by selective breeding.

budget A prediction of the financial behavior of a firm, government, etc., over a specified period. Careful budgeting enables any deviation from a plan to be noted early and the appropriate action to be taken.

Buenaventura 3 54N 77 02W A port in W Colombia, on the Pacific Ocean. Exports include coffee and sugar from the Cauca Valley and gold and platinum from the Chocó district. Population (1973): 115,770.

Buena Vista, Battle of (1847) Battle during the *Mexican War. US General Zachary *Taylor's forces met the much larger forces of Mexican General Antonio Lopez de *Santa Anna near Monterrey, Mexico. After several days of fighting the Mexicans retreated, leaving NW Mexico in possession of the Americans.

Bueno, Maria (Esther) (1939–) Brazilian tennis player. She won the US singles title four times, the US doubles four times, the Wimbledon singles three times, and the Wimbledon doubles five times.

BUENOS AIRES *Avenida 9 de Julio, one of the world's widest streets.*

Buenos Aires 34 50S 58 37W The capital of Argentina, the largest city in South America and one of the world's largest ports, situated on the Río de la Plata estuary. It is the financial, commercial, and industrial center of the country. Its chief exports are beef and wool. A cultural center, Buenos Aires possesses many universities (including the University of Buenos Aires, 1821), the national library, and a famous opera house (the Teatro Colón). There are several fine avenues, including the Avenida de Mayo and the Avenida de Julio. Notable buildings include the cathedral (completed in 1804). *History*: founded in 1580, after Indian attacks on earlier settlements, it became capital of the newly created viceroyalty of the Río de la Plata in 1776 and of the new Republic of Argentina in 1880. In the late 19th and early 20th centuries its population was greatly swelled by European immigrants, especially Spanish and Italian. Population (1975 est): 2,972,453.

buffalo A large African hoofed mammal, *Syncerus caffer*, also called Cape buffalo. Weighing over 1543 lb (700 kg) and measuring 44–60 in (110–150 cm) at the shoulder, buffaloes have massive curved horns and a smooth black coat. They live in large herds in grassy areas where both tree cover and water are available. Once numerous, their numbers have been reduced by hunting and disease. Family: *Bovidae. Compare* bison; water buffalo.

Buffalo 42 52N 78 55W A city in New York state on Lake Erie and the Niagara River. The state's second largest city, it is linked to New York City by the New York State Barge Canal (formerly Erie Canal). A major port, its industries include the manufacture of iron and steel, motor vehicles, and electrical equipment. Population (1980 est): 357,870.

Buffalo Bill. See Cody, William F(rederick).

buffalo gnat. *See* black fly.

buffer solution A solution the *pH of which is insensitive to dilution or the addition of moderate amounts of acid or base. Generally it consists of a mixture of a weak acid or base and its salt. If, for example, acid is added to an acetic acid-acetate mixture, the hydrogen ions will combine with acetate ions to form acetic acid molecules, thus lowering the acidity. Buffers are present in many living organisms, as fluctuations in pH would destroy the activity of enzymes, etc.

Buffet, Bernard (1928–) French painter. Precociously talented, he established his reputation by 1948. His realistic paintings are notable for their strong black lines, melancholy colors, and elongated forms.

Buffon, Georges Louis Leclerc, Comte de (1707–88) French naturalist, who formulated a crude theory of evolution and was the first to suggest that the earth might be considerably older than suggested by the Bible. He estimated the age of the earth to be 75,000 years, with life emerging some 40,000 years ago.

bug A common name for any insect-like animal. Specifically, the term refers to insects of the order *Hemiptera (the true bugs), especially the *bedbug and insects of the suborder *Heteroptera* (plant bugs, water bugs, etc.).

Bug River 1. (*or* Western Bug) A river in E central Europe, rising in the Soviet Union, in the SW Ukrainian SSR, and flowing NW as part of the border between the Soviet Union and Poland to the Vistula River. Length: 450 mi (724 km). 2. (*or* Southern Bug) A river in the SW Soviet Union, rising in the W Ukraine and flowing SE to the Dnieper estuary on the Black Sea. Length 530 mi (853 km).

Buganda   A former kingdom in East Africa, now comprising an administrative region of Uganda bordering on Lake Victoria. The UK government assumed responsibility for Buganda in 1893. When Uganda became a republic (1963) the kabaka (king) of Buganda became president of Uganda. His arrest (1966) by the former prime minister Dr Milton Obote caused widespread rioting in Buganda.

Bugatti, Ettore (Arco Isidoro)   (1881–1947) Italian □car manufacturer. In 1909 he founded a factory in Molsheim, Alsace, to produce cars to race at Le Mans. His finest car was probably the Type 41—the Golden Bugatti.

bugle   A high-pitched brass (or copper) instrument with a wide conical tube, a cup-shaped mouthpiece, and a small bell. It lacks valves and so can only play a single harmonic series (usually having the fundamental of C). Formerly much used for military signaling, it is also used on ceremonial occasions and in the brass band.

bugloss   A biennial herb of the Eurasian genus *Echium* (about 30 species), e.g. viper's bugloss (*E. vulgare*). Up to 35 in (90 cm) high, the plants are covered with bristly hairs and produce spikes of funnel-shaped flowers, about 0.8 in (2 cm) long, usually bluish with several protruding stamens. Another plant called bugloss is *Lycopsis arvensis*, an annual similar to *Echium* species but with smaller flowers. Family: *Boraginaceae*.

Bujumbura   (former name: Usumbura)   3 30S 29 20E The capital of Burundi, a port on the NE shore of Lake Tanganyika. Founded in the 19th century, it became the capital of Ruanda-Urundi after World War I. The university was founded in 1960. Population (1976 est): 157,100.

Bukavu   (name until 1966: Costermansville)   2 20S 28 52E A port in E Zaïre, on Lake Kivu. A commercial center, it has local agricultural and brewing industries. Population (1976 est): 209,051.

Bukhara   (or Bokhara)   39 47N 64 26E A city in the SW Soviet Union, in the Uzbek SSR. The Bukhara region (*oblast*) of which it is the capital was the center of a powerful kingdom, which was ceded to Russia in 1868. It grew rapidly in the 1950s after the discovery of natural gas. It has textile industries, and the traditional crafts of gold embroidery and metalworking are still practiced. Population (1981 est): 192,000.

Bukhari, al-   (810–70 AD) Muslim scholar and historian. After extensive travels, he collected more than 600,000 traditional records (*see* Hadith) of the words and deeds of the prophet Mohammed. He published a selection of these, arranged by subject, which he considered authentic teachings. The resulting collection is revered by orthodox Muslims as second in authority only to the Koran.

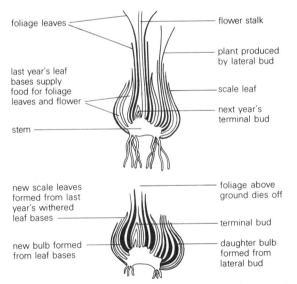

BULB   *A section through a daffodil bulb in spring (above) and summer (below) to show growth cycle.*

Bukharin, Nikolai Ivanovich   (1888–1938) Soviet politician and communist theoretician. In exile after 1911, Bukharin edited the socialist newspaper *Novy Mir*, in New York. He returned to Russia during the Revolution and became editor of the newspaper *Pravda*. He believed that Russia

should achieve socialism slowly and therefore supported Lenin's New Economic Policy (1924). He was chairman of the Comintern until dismissed by Stalin in 1929. He helped draft the 1936 constitution but was expelled from the Communist Party shortly afterward and died in Stalin's purges.

Bukovina   (or Bucovina)   An area in E Europe, in the NE Carpathian Mountains. As part of the principality of Moldavia, it fell to the Turks in 1512 and was ceded to Austria in 1775. Occupied by the Romanians in 1918, the N part was ceded to the Soviet Union (1940), later becoming part of the Ukrainian SSR. S Bukovina remained a Romanian province until it was abolished in 1952.

Bulawayo   20 10S 28 43E The second largest city in Zimbabwe. It was founded on its present site in 1894 by the British, near to its original site of the kraal of Lobengula, the center of the Ndebele tribe. Nearby are the popular tourist attractions of Rhodes Matapos National Park and the Khami Ruins. The city is the country's chief industrial center with metal, tire, and cement industries. Population (1980 est): 373,000.

bulb   A modified underground stem of certain perennial herbaceous plants, for example onions, daffodils, and tulips, that serves as an overwintering organ. Food is stored in overlapping fleshy leaves or leaf bases, borne on a very short stem, and is used to produce one or more plants the following season. When a bulb produces two or more plants it acts as an organ of vegetative reproduction. East Anglia (UK) and the Netherlands are centers for the commercial production of spring-flowering bulbs.

bulbul   A gregarious forest-dwelling songbird belonging to an Old World family (*Pycnonotidae*; 120 species). 5–9 in (12–22 cm) long, bulbuls are yellow, green, or brown, sometimes with bright patches on the head and beneath the tail. They have a slender bill surrounded by stiff bristles and feed largely on fruit and berries.

Bulfinch, Charles   (1763–1844) US architect. Strongly influenced by architecture in England and Italy, he introduced the Federal style in the US. His buildings include the state houses in Boston, Mass (1787–88), Hartford, Conn (1792–96), and Augusta, Maine (1828–31). He was responsible for designing the east portico of the US Capitol building (1817–30).

Bulganin, Nikolai Aleksandrovich   (1895–1975) Soviet statesman; prime minister (1955–58). Bulganin began his career in 1918, when he joined *CHEKA. In World War II he became (1944) a member of Stalin's war cabinet and in 1947, defense minister. As prime minister, Bulganin participated in the attempt to oust Khrushchev in 1957 and was subsequently dismissed.

Bulgaria, People's Republic of   A country in SE Europe, in the E Balkans on the Black Sea. The low-lying Danube basin in the N rises to the Balkan Mountains in the center of the country; further S, beyond the valley of the Maritsa River, the Rhodope Mountains reach heights of almost 10,000 ft (3000 m). The inhabitants are mainly Bulgars, with minorities of Macedonians, Turks, and Gypsies. *Economy*: industrialization has proceeded rapidly since World War II, following the introduction of a centrally planned economy. Particular emphasis has been given to heavy manufacturing industries. The industrial sector has recently been reorganized into several large combines. Coal, iron, and other minerals are mined and hydroelectricity and nuclear energy contribute to power supplies. Oil has been found offshore in the Black Sea and natural gas is also being produced. Agricultural production, the traditional mainstay of the economy prior to 1945, has been mechanized and organized on a cooperative basis, the main crops being wheat, maize, beet, and barley. Tourism has been considerably developed in recent years. Main exports include machinery, chemicals, food products, textiles, tobacco, and nonferrous metals. Bulgaria is a member of *COMECON. *History*: following the invasion of the Bulgars in the 7th century AD and their gradual adoption of the culture and language of the conquered Slavs, Bulgaria became a significant power in SE Europe. Despite coming under Turkish rule in 1396, the Bulgars succeeded in retaining their national identity over the centuries until they once again became independent in 1908 under the Saxe-Coburg ruler *Ferdinand, who took the title of tsar. Bulgaria aligned itself with Germany in both World Wars. In 1944 it was occupied by the Soviet Union and power was seized by the Fatherland Front, a left-wing alliance, which formed a pro-Soviet government that declared war on Germany. In 1946 a People's Republic was proclaimed and since then Bulgaria has remained one of the most loyal of the Soviet Union's satellite states. Under a new constitution in 1971 Todor *Zhivkov became chairman of the Council of State and first secretary of the Communist Party. Official language: Bulgarian. Official currency: lev of 100 stotinki. Area: 42,823 sq mi (110,912 sq km). Population (1980 est): 8,880,000. Capital: Sofia. Main port: Varna.

Bulgarian   A language belonging to the South *Slavonic group spoken by eight million people in Bulgaria, Greece, Romania, and areas of the Soviet

Union. It differs from other Slavonic languages in several respects as it lacks case declensions for nouns and shares grammatical features and vocabulary elements with other non-Slavonic Balkan languages. The literature written in Bulgarian dates from the establishment of Christianity (9th century).

Bulge, Battle of the. *See* World War II.

bulk modulus. *See* elastic modulus.

bull (from Latin: *bulla*, seal) Originally, the seal attached to papal edicts. The term was later used for the documents themselves, but now refers only to the most important missives. Named by their opening word or phrase, for example *Pastor Aeternus* (Eternal Father; 1870), they are issued to assert doctrine.

Bull, John (caricature). *See* John Bull.

bullace A type of *plum, *Prunus insititia*, cultivated for centuries but probably originating in SW Asia. The young branches are very hairy and have few thorns. The blue-black fruit is similar to that of the blackthorn but larger and sweeter.

bulldog A breed of dog originating in England, where it was used in bull-and bear-baiting. It has a compact rounded body with short sturdy legs and a short tail. The relatively large head has an undershot jaw (i.e. the lower jaw projects in front of the upper) and loose folds of skin. The fine short coat can be of any color except black. Weight: 55 lb (25 kg) (dogs); 51 lb (23 kg) (bitches).

bulldozer A powerful caterpillar tractor equipped with a blade or shovel for moving or digging earth and often used for preliminary clearing and leveling of building sites, roads, etc. The blade can be raised or lowered hydraulically or set at an angle for sideways shifting of earth.

bullfighting Subduing and killing bulls. The national spectator sport of Spain, it is also popular in parts of France and Latin America, and mounted bullfighting is practiced in Portugal. The bulls are specially bred. At a normal *corrida de toros* (bullfight) three matadors kill two bulls each. Following the initial ceremonial procession the first bull enters the ring. Preliminary passes are made by the *banderilleros* (assistants) with their capes to attract the bull's attention and allow the matador to assess the bull's reactions. The matador then makes his first series of passes with his cape, controlling the direction and extent of the bull's charge. During the next stage, the matadors make the bull charge at a mounted picador, who uses a form of lance to stab the bull's neck, weakening the muscle so that it lowers its head. This procedure is repeated up to three times, each of the three matadors taking turns to draw the bull away from the horse and continue the capework. During the following stage the neck muscle is further weakened by pairs of barbed sticks (*banderillas*) thrust into it by the *banderilleros*. In the final stage the matador performs a series of passes with his *muleta* (a small red cape folded over a stick) to weaken the bull further until he can reach over its head to thrust his sword in at the right angle to sever its aorta.

bullfinch A plump woodland *finch, *Pyrrhula pyrrhula*, of N Eurasia. It is about 6 in (14 cm) long and has a gray back, a pinkish breast, and black head, wings, and tail. Bullfinches have strong stout bills and strip buds and flowers from trees, for which they are often regarded as pests.

bullfrog A large frog, *Rana catesbiana*, of North America. Dull green with a slightly warty skin, bullfrogs grow to about 8 in (20 cm) and can jump up to 7 ft (2 m). Females are larger than males. They are the only common American frogs large enough to be used as food.

Other large frogs—*Pyxicephalus adspersus* in Africa and *Rana tigrina* in India—are also called bullfrogs.

bullhead One of several predatory bottom-dwelling fish, also called sculpin, belonging to the family *Cottidae*, including the Eurasian miller's thumb (*Cottus gobio*). Bullheads have a tapering conical body, up to 12 in (30 cm) long and often covered with spiny bony plates, a broad spiny head, and two dorsal fins. They are found in fresh water and shallow seas of the N hemisphere. Order: *Perciformes. See also* catfish.

bull market A stock or commodity market in which there is a continuing upward movement in prices. An initial rise in prices, caused by favorable economic factors, is often magnified by consequent buying by investors. *Compare* bear market.

bull mastiff A breed of dog resulting from crosses between bulldogs and mastiffs. It is sturdily built with a short broad muzzle and folds of skin surrounding the face. The short coat is red, fawn, or streaked brown. Height: 25–27 in (63–68 cm) (dogs); 24–26 in (61–66 cm) (bitches).

Bull Run, Battles of (*or* Battles of Manassas) Two battles in the *Civil War fought in NE Virginia. Both were Confederate victories. In the first

(July 21, 1861) Union forces failed to prevent the unification of Confederate forces under General P. G. T. Beauregard (1818–93) and General Joseph E. Johnstone (1807–91) at Manassas Junction near a stream named Bull Run. The untried Union troops were repulsed after an unsuccessful attack. The second battle (August 29–30, 1862) followed an unsuccessful Union attempt to capture Gordonsville, a rail junction near Richmond, the Confederate capital. The 70,000 Union troops had withdrawn to await reinforcements when Stonewall *Jackson attacked and forced their retreat to Washington.

bull terrier A breed of ☐dog originating in the UK from crosses between bulldogs and terriers. It is strongly built with a courageous temperament. The coat is either pure white (with darker head markings) or colored. Height: 19–23 in (48–56 cm). (Miniature bull terriers must not exceed 14 in (36 cm) in height.)

Bülow, Bernhard Heinrich, Fürst von (1849–1929) German statesman and diplomat; chancellor (1900–09). He pursued aggressive foreign policies that contributed to German isolation in Europe. He alienated France over the Moroccan crisis in 1905 and Russia over the Bosnian crisis in 1908. He resigned after losing the confidence of Emperor William II and of the Reichstag and served from 1914 to 1915 as ambassador to Italy.

Bülow, Hans Guido, Freiherr von (1830–94) German pianist and the outstanding conductor of his time. Bülow championed Wagner until his wife Cosima (Liszt's daughter) eloped with Wagner in 1866. From that time he championed the works of Brahms.

bulrush A widely distributed perennial herbaceous plant, *Scirpus lacustris*, growing in ponds, lakes, and rivers. Forty in–10 ft (1–3 m) high, it has cylindrical leafless stems bearing branched clusters of small reddish-brown flowers. Family: *Cyperaceae* (sedges, etc.). The name is also applied to the *reedmace, and the biblical bulrush is the *papyrus.

Bultmann, Rudolf (Karl) (1884–1976) German New Testament scholar. A professor at Marburg University (1921–51), he allied himself with the anti-Nazi *Confessing Church during the Third Reich. In his influential writings he argued that the New Testament message must be "demythologized" (or stripped of its no longer acceptable mythical concepts) if it was to have any relevance to contemporary man.

Bulwer-Lytton, Edward George Earle. *See* Lytton, Edward George Earle Bulwer-Lytton, 1st Baron.

bumblebee A social *bee, also called humblebee, belonging to a genus (*Bombus*) found mainly in temperate regions. Bumblebees, 0.6–1 in (15–25 mm) long, are usually black with yellow or orange bands. They live in colonies, on or below the ground, containing 100–400 workers in the summer. Their life cycle is like that of the *honeybee, although only young fertilized queens survive the winter. Solitary parasitic bumblebees belong to the genus *Psithyrus*. Family: *Apidae*. ☐insect.

Bunche, Ralph (1904–71) US political scientist and UN official. As a government official Bunche specialized in colonial areas during World War II and became the first black American to hold an important position in the State Department. He was a founder of the UN and director of its trusteeship division. Bunche won the Nobel Peace Prize for negotiating the 1949 Arab-Israeli truce and supervised the UN Congo peace force in 1960.

Bundelkhand A region in present-day Madhya Pradesh state, in N central India, taking its name from the Bundela Rajputs, a dynasty that ruled here from the 14th to the 18th centuries. The area is rich in architectural history; in the 10th and 11th centuries the Candella kings built many beautiful temples at Khajuraho and a fine fortress was erected later at Jhansi.

Bunin, Ivan Alekseevich (1879–1953) Russian poet and novelist. He published his first book of poems in 1891, and translated works by *Byron and *Longfellow. His prose works include novels (*The Village*, 1910), short stories (*The Gentleman from San Francisco*, 1916), and autobiographical works (*The Well of Days*, 1910). In 1920 he emigrated to Finland. He won the Nobel Prize in 1933.

bunion A deformity and swelling at the joint at the base of the big toe. It is usually caused by pressure from ill-fitting shoes: the toe becomes bent toward the others and a fibrous fluid-filled sac (bursa) develops over the affected joint. Bunions may require surgical treatment.

Bunker Hill, Battle of (June 17, 1775) A battle of the *American Revolution actually fought on Breed's Hill (next to Bunker Hill) in Charlestown, near Boston. The Americans defended the strategic hill from three British attacks but Sir William *Howe displaced the Americans at the third attempt. The American defense helped raise support for the Revolutionary cause.

Bunsen, Robert Wilhelm (1811–99) German chemist, after whom the Bunsen burner is named. He did not, however, invent the Bunsen burner although he did popularize it. In collaboration with *Kirchhoff, Bunsen developed the technique of *spectroscopy, using a Bunsen burner to heat the substance. In 1860 they used the technique to discover the elements *rubidium and *cesium. He also invented a carbon-zinc electric cell (1841).

Bunsen burner A gas burner for laboratory use, popularized by R. *Bunsen. It consists of a vertical metal tube with a variable air inlet at the bottom. Gas is led into the bottom of the tube and the gas–air mixture burned at the top. Adjustment of the air inlet allows control of combustion intensity, temperature, sooting, and other flame properties.

bunting A sparrow-like bird belonging to a subfamily (*Emberizine*) of the *finches. Buntings are 5–8 in (12–20 cm) long and usually have a brownish or grayish plumage. They live on the ground or in bushes and thickets and scratch for seeds with their characteristically large feet. The subfamily includes the *yellowhammer and the *snow bunting. *See* Plate V.

Buñuel, Luis (1900–83) Spanish film director. He worked mainly in France and Mexico. His films are characterized by surrealist techniques and by their anticlericalism and satire on social hypocrisy. They include *Un Chien andalou* (1928), *Viridiana* (1961), *The Discreet Charm of the Bourgeoisie* (1972), and *That Obscure Object of Desire* (1977).

bunya bunya. *See* Araucaria.

Bunyan, John (1628–88) British writer. Son of a tinker, he fought in the parliamentary army during the Civil War. From 1650 to 1656 he underwent a spiritual crisis, finally resolved by his conversion to religion. He became the leader of a group of Baptists in Bedford and in 1660 he was imprisoned for preaching without a license. During his 12 years in prison he wrote his spiritual autobiography, *Grace Abounding* (1666), and began his major work, *The Pilgrim's Progress* (1678). An imaginative allegory written in plain but majestic prose, it has been widely read and admired for centuries.

Bunyan, Paul US legendary giant of the frontier logging camps; a symbol of bigness and American ingenuity. Paul Bunyan and his companions – Babe the Blue Ox, Johnny Inkslinger, and Shot Gunderson – all larger than life, grew out of the lumber camps of the 1800s and were credited with creating Puget Sound, the Grand Canyon, and the Rocky Mountains. His legend was highly publicized, and he appeared in the works of poets and composers such as Carl *Sandburg, Robert *Frost, W. H. *Auden, and Benjamin *Britten.

Burbage, Richard (c. 1567–1619) English actor. He played leading roles in the first productions of many of Shakespeare's plays. He also acted in plays by Kyd, Webster, and Ben Jonson, and was a shareholder in the Blackfriars and the Globe theaters.

Burbank, Luther (1849–1926) US plant breeder. Largely self-taught and using methods he devised himself, primarily the cross-breeding of different varieties, he developed many new varieties of agricultural importance. His first commercial success, the Burbank potato, enabled him to settle in California, where—by skilful selection and breeding techniques—he originated more than 800 new strains and varieties of fruit, vegetables, and flowers.

Burbank 34 12N 118 18W A city in SW California, just NW of Los Angeles. Established in 1887, it is home to major television and movie studios, among them Walt Disney Productions. Burbank also has a large aerospace industry. Population (1980): 84,625.

burbot A food fish, *Lota lota*, that is similar and related to the *ling. Up to 3.6 ft (1.1 m) long, it lives on the bottom in cold fresh waters of Europe, Asia, and North America and feeds voraciously on other fish.

Burckhardt, Jacob Christoph (1818–97) Swiss art and cultural historian. The son of a Protestant clergyman, he studied at the Universities of Berlin and Bonn. From 1843 he lectured at Basle University, becoming professor of history there in 1858, after three years at Zürich. His most important work, *The Civilization of the Renaissance in Italy* (1860), was a model for later cultural histories, with its thorough and systematic analysis of the period.

burdock A tall stiff biennial plant of the genus *Arctium* (about 5 species), 25–52 in (60–130 cm) high, found in Europe and Asia. They have broad heart-shaped leaves and reddish-purple thistle-like flower heads, surrounded by many large stiff hooked bracts, which are retained by the fruits. Family: *Compositae.

Burgas 42 30N 29 29E A city in E Bulgaria, on the Black Sea. Bulgaria's second largest port (after Varna), its industries include fishing, mining, and oil refining. Population (1979 est): 165,994.

Bürge, Joost (1552–1632) Swiss mathematician, who invented *logarithms independently of, and probably before, John *Napier. He also con-

tributed to the exponential notation (i.e. y^x to indicate y multiplied by itself x times).

Burgenland A federal state in E Austria, bordering on Hungary. It was ceded to Austria by Hungary following World War I. Predominantly agricultural, it produces cereals, root crops, and fruit and vegetables; livestock are also extensively raised. Area: 1531 sq mi (3965 sq km). Population (1981): 272,568. Capital: Eisenstadt.

Bürger, Gottfried (1747–94) German poet. At Göttingen University he studied law and eventually became professor of aesthetics. His ballad *Lenore* (1773) influenced writers of the early Romantic period throughout Europe. He translated traditional English and Scots ballads and wrote many more of his own.

Burger, Warren Earl (1907–) US jurist and lawyer; Supreme Court chief justice (1969–). He practiced law in St Paul, Minn, and taught at St Paul's Mitchell College of Law. In 1953 he was appointed US assistant attorney general and then, in 1955, to the US Court of Appeals for the District of Columbia by President *Eisenhower. Chosen by President *Nixon to replace Earl *Warren as chief justice on the Supreme Court in 1969, Burger presided over a court more conservative than Warren's, while upholding certain rights of criminals and aliens. Burger himself was a strong advocate of reforming the judicial system.

Burgess, Anthony (John Burgess Wilson; 1917–) British novelist and critic. A teacher and lecturer in English literature and phonetics, he became a full-time writer in 1959. His novels include the sinister tragicomedy *A Clockwork Orange* (1962), which was filmed by Stanley *Kubrick, *Inside Mr Enderby* (1963), *Nothing like the Sun* (1964), and *Napoleon Symphony* (1974), *Earthly Powers* (1980), and *Enderby's Dark Lady* (1984).

Burgess, Guy. *See* Maclean, Donald.

Burghley, William Cecil, Lord (1520–98) English statesman; close adviser to Elizabeth I. A moderating influence on Elizabeth, his pragmatism is evident in her religious settlement (*see* Reformation). He helped to bring about the Treaty of Edinburgh (1660) with Scotland, which undermined French influence there. He influenced Elizabeth's pro-Protestant foreign policy, aiding the Revolt of the Netherlands against Spain, and helped to prepare England for the threatened Spanish invasion (*see* Armada, Spanish). He was instrumental in securing the execution of Mary, Queen of Scots, in 1587. He was succeeded as royal adviser by his son **Robert Cecil, 1st Earl of Salisbury** (c. 1563–1612), who negotiated the accession of James VI of Scotland to the English throne as James I (1603). As lord treasurer (1608–12), he was James' chief adviser.

burglary In law, entering a building, ship, or other inhabited vehicle without leave or right to, intending to commit serious crimes, such as theft, rape, grievous bodily harm, or unlawful damage. A person is not guilty of burglary if the premises at the time are open to the public.

Burgos 42 21N 3 41W A city in N Spain, in Old Castile. Its fine cathedral (13th–16th centuries) contains the remains of the legendary hero El Cid. Population (1974 est): 136,409.

Burgoyne, John (1722–92) British general. In the American Revolution he commanded the British force in the N, ordered in conjunction with a column from New York under Sir William *Howe to divide the Americans along the Hudson River. Howe's progress was blocked and Burgoyne was defeated by *Gates at Saratoga (1777).

Burgundian school A group of musicians working at the court of the Dukes of Burgundy in the 15th century. Under Philip the Good, who reigned from 1419 to 1467, there was a great flowering of the arts. Two composers are outstanding: Guillaume *Dufay and Gilles Binchois (c. 1400–60). Their compositions include chansons with French texts, motets, masses, and magnificats. The composers of the Burgundian school were influenced by such English composers as John *Dunstable.

Burgundy A region in France, E of the Rhône and Saône Rivers. The Burgundians were a Scandinavian people who occupied the region in the 4th century AD, establishing a powerful kingdom that was conquered by the Franks in 534. The NW part of the former kingdom became a duchy in the 9th century and passed to the French crown in the mid-14th century. John the Good transferred it to his fourth son, Philip the Bold, and after the death (1477) of his descendant Charles the Bold it was annexed by the crown.

Buridan, Jean (c. 1297–c. 1358) French scholastic philosopher. He became professor of philosophy at Paris and famed as a debater. He is associated with "Buridan's ass," an illustration of a position in arguments about free will; the animal starves through being unable to choose between equally attractive piles of hay.

Burke, Edmund (1729–97) British political philosopher and politician. A member of Parliament from 1765, he attacked George III's exalted view of the monarch's political role. In the pamphlet *Thoughts on the Cause of the Present Discontents* (1770) and in two famous speeches, "On American Taxation" (1774) and "On Moving His Resolutions for Conciliation with the Colonies" (1777), he blamed the unrest in the American colonies on British misgovernment. He also campaigned against the corrupt Indian administration of the *East India Company. An opponent of democracy, he believed that the common good was best secured by responsible aristocratic government. He thus condemned the French Revolution (*Reflections on the Revolution in France*, 1790). He has been regarded as the foremost Conservative philosopher. He also wrote a widely read work on aesthetics, *A Philosophical Enquiry into the Origin of Our Ideas of the Sublime and Beautiful* (1757).

Burkina Faso (former name: Republic of Upper Volta; French: République de Haute-Volta) A landlocked country in West Africa, bordered by Mali (W and N), Niger (NE), Benin (SE), Togo, Ghana and Ivory Coast (S). It consists mainly of a low-lying plateau, crossed by the headwaters of the Volta River: the Black, Red, and White Voltas. The population is almost entirely African, the largest groups being the Mossi and Fulani. *Economy*: chiefly agricultural, the main food crops being millet and sorghum; livestock is important and is the main export. Production of rice, groundnuts, cotton, and sugar is being increased by means of schemes to improve water supplies, although these advances were hampered by the severe droughts affecting the Sahel region in the early 1970s. Some minerals, including manganese, have been found but lack of communications makes their exploitation difficult. *History*: the area was occupied by powerful Mossi states from the 14th century. It became part of the French protectorate of Soudan in 1898 and in 1919 the separate protectorate of Upper Volta was formed. In 1932 it was divided between Niger, Ivory Coast, and Soudan but was reconstituted in 1947. In 1958 Upper Volta became an autonomous republic, gaining full independence outside the French Community in 1960. A military coup in 1966 brought Lieutenant Colonel (later General) Sangoulé Lamizana (1916–) to power. Lamizana was elected president in 1978 but was overthrown in a coup in 1980. Another military coup (1982) brought Major Jean-Baptiste Ouédraogo to power. He was ousted by Captain Thomas Sankara (1983), supported by paratroopers, who then set up a military government. In 1984 the name was changed from Upper Volta to Burkina Faso (Land of the Incorruptible Men) to reflect better the nation's African heritage. Official language: French. Official currency: CFA (Communauté financière africaine) franc of 100 centimes. Area: 105 764 sq mi (274 002 sq km). Population (1983 est): 6,569,000. Capital: Ouagadougou.

Burlington 44 29N 73 13W A city and port in NW Vermont, on the E shore of Lake Champlain. Vermont's largest city, it served as a naval base during the War of 1812 and is the home of the University of Vermont (1790). Wood, maple syrup, and electrical, metal, and cereal products are some of its manufactures. Tourism is an important industry. Population (1980): 37,712.

Burma, Socialist Republic of the Union of A country in SE Asia, on the Bay of Bengal and the Andaman Sea. The principal river system, that of the Irrawaddy and its main tributary, the Chindwin, forms a narrow plain running N-S, rising to the Arakan Mountains and the Chin Hills in the W and the Shan Plateau in the E. The Tenasserim Hills lie along the coast in the SE. The majority of the population, concentrated in the Irrawaddy delta, is Burmese, but there are several minorities, including the Shan, Karen, Chachin, and Chin peoples. *Economy*: priority has been given to the development of agriculture, the main crop being rice, and in 1976 plans were introduced by the government to set up cooperative farming, mainly on virgin land. Almost half the land (all of which is nationalized) is under forest and teak is a valuable export. There is some mining, especially of lead and zinc. Other industries are mainly based on food processing and all industry is now nationalized. Inland waterways provide an important means of communication. All foreign trade is carried out through government trading organizations and the main exports include rice and rice products, rubber, jute, and timber. *History*: by the 13th century the Burmese had developed a civilization based on Hinayana Buddhism. In the centuries following defeat by the Mongols in 1287, the area was under the rule of the Shans and the Mons. The rule of the Burmese Alaungpaya in the 18th century began a period of increased prosperity. After successive wars it came totally under British rule in 1885 as part of British India. In 1937 it attained a certain measure of self-government and was separated from India. In World War II it was occupied by Japanese forces, fighting first with the Japanese and later against them in support of the British. In 1948 it became a republic outside the Commonwealth. In 1962 its parliamentary democracy was overthrown in a military coup by General U *Ne Win.

1974 saw the end of military rule and the formation of a one-party socialist republic. Following U Ne Win's resignation in 1981 Gen San Yu was elected president. Burma has avoided close ties with both East and West, maintaining a policy of strict neutrality. In 1983 a bomb explosion in Rangoon, apparently aimed for visiting South Korean president Chin Doo Hunin, killed 21 people. The bombing was alleged by Burma to have been the work of North Korean terrorists, some of whom were captured. Burma, departing from its neutral stance, broke ties with North Korea. Official language: Burmese. Official currency: kyat of 100 pyas. Area: 261,789 sq mi (678,000 sq km). Population (1983 est.): 37,061,000. Capital and main port: Rangoon.

Burmese A language of the Tibeto-Burman branch of the *Sino-Tibetan language family spoken by 20 million people in Burma, where it is the official language. Written in an alphabet derived from the *Pali script of India, Burmese literature dates from the 11th century AD.

Burmese cat A breed of short-haired cat originating from an Asian hybrid imported into the US in 1933. The Burmese has a long slender body, a small head with large ears and greenish-yellow eyes, and usually a dark-brown coat. Other recognized colors include silvery-gray (the Blue Burmese), lilac, red, and cream.

Burne-Jones, Sir Edward Coley (1833–98) Pre-Raphaelite painter and designer. After meeting *Rossetti (1856) he abandoned his studies for an art career but only established his reputation in an exhibition in 1877. Typical of his dreamy romantic paintings, inspired by Botticelli's style, medieval legends, and classical mythology, is *King Cophetua and the Beggar Maid* (Tate Gallery). More influential for the 20th century were his designs for stained glass and tapestries.

burnet A slender perennial herb of the genera *Sanguisorba* (about 3 species) and *Poterium* (about 25 species), of N temperate regions. 20–40 in (50–100 cm) high, they have pinnate toothed leaves and oval heads of crimson or greenish petal-less flowers borne on long stems. The leaves are used to flavor salads and soups. Family: *Rosaceae*.

Burnet, Sir Frank Macfarlane (1899–) Australian physician, who advanced understanding of virus diseases and immunology. Burnet discovered the phenomenon of acquired immunological tolerance to foreign tissue transplants, for which he shared a Nobel Prize (1960) with Sir Peter *Medawar. He did important work in the identification of bacteria and in the culture of viruses.

Burnet, Gilbert (1643–1715) English bishop and historian, born in Edinburgh. He was a minister in the Church of Scotland and a professor at Glasgow University before settling in England in 1674. While abroad during James II's reign, he became a friend of William of Orange, with whom he sailed to England in 1688 and who appointed him Bishop of Salisbury in 1689. His books include *History of My Own Time* (1723–34).

Burnett, Frances Eliza Hodgson (1849–1924) British novelist. The daughter of a Manchester manufacturer, she moved to the US in 1865. Her best-known works are the children's books *Little Lord Fauntleroy* (1885), *The Little Princess* (1905), and *The Secret Garden* (1909).

Burnley 53 48N 2 14W A city in N England, in Lancashire in the Calder Valley. Traditionally a cotton-weaving town (with some spinning and dyeing), there has been some diversification of industry in recent years (light engineering, chemicals). Population (1973 est): 74,300.

burns Damage to the skin caused by heat, electricity, chemicals, or radiation. In order of increasing severity, burns may cause reddening of the skin, as in sunburn (first-degree burn), blistering (second-degree burn), and finally damage to the tissues beneath the skin (third-degree burn). The extent rather than the thickness of the burn determines its effect. Both second- and third-degree burns cause fluid loss, which may be extensive enough to lead to *shock. Treatment consists of the application of wet dressings and later the administration of intravenous fluids and transfer of the patient to clean surroundings, where the burns are exposed and allowed to heal. The danger of infection can be prevented by the use of antibiotics. Skin grafting may be necessary to replace the skin destroyed by severe burns.

Burns, Robert (1759–96) Scottish poet. Son of a poor farmer in Ayrshire, in 1783 he began writing poems in traditional styles. *Poems, Chiefly in the Scottish Dialect* (1786), published in Kilmarnock, won him immediate fame; from 1786 until 1788 he was lionized by Edinburgh society, which was little to his taste (he was a lifelong radical) or his profit. His return to farming was a failure and from 1789 he worked for the excise service. His poems range from sentimental love lyrics, often patterned on traditional songs, to broad humor, as in "Tam o'Shanter" (1788), and scathing satire, as in "The Twa Dogs" (1786) and "Holy Willie's Prayer"

ROBERT BURNS *A portrait of the 18th century Scottish poet by Alexander Nasmyth.*

(1785). He collected and wrote numerous songs for inclusion in *The Scots Musical Museum* (1787–1803) and *Select Scottish Airs* (1793–1818).

Burnside, Ambrose Everett (1824–81) US military leader and politician. Appointed commander of the Union's Army of the Potomac in 1862, he was defeated at Fredericksburg (1862) and removed from command. He participated in the early stages of the Wilderness Campaign (1864–65) but resigned when his tactics at Petersburg were criticized. He was governor of Rhode Island (1866–69) and was a senator from Rhode Island (1875–81). Sideburns were named for him.

Burr, Aaron (1756–1836) US statesman; chosen by the Senate to be Republican vice president (1801–05) after tying with Jefferson in the election of 1800. In 1804, after killing his political rival Alexander *Hamilton in a duel, Burr fled to Philadelphia and plotted to establish an empire in the West. Arrested for treason but acquitted (1807), after further intrigues, including a scheme for Napoleon to conquer Florida, Burr gave up politics for law.

Burra, Edward (1905–76) British painter. His early watercolors were chiefly scenes of Mediterranean low life. Later, in response to the horrors of the Spanish Civil War and World War II, he began to paint sinister subjects in a realistic style. His works include *Soldiers* (1942).

Burroughs, Edgar Rice (1875–1950) US novelist. After a variety of unsuccessful jobs he gained wealth and international fame from his fantasy fiction. *Tarzan of the Apes* (1914) introduced his most famous character, an English nobleman's child, abandoned in the African jungle and reared by apes. Among the approximately 70 works he published were western, crime, and science fiction adventures.

Burroughs, William (1914–) US novelist. He graduated from Harvard in 1936 and wandered in the US and Europe. In 1944 he became a drug addict. *Junkie* (1953) and *The Naked Lunch* (1959) were influential novels of the *Beat movement. He lived mostly in Paris, London, and Tangiers, continuing his literary experiments in such novels as *Nova Express* (1964).

burrowing owl A long-legged ground-dwelling *owl, *Speotyto cunicularia*, of grasslands from Florida and the western US to Argentina. 9 in (22 cm) long, it nests in colonies, often in disused rodent burrows, and feeds at night on frogs, lizards, mice, and insects.

Bursa 40 12N 29 04E A city in NW Turkey. It was the capital of the Ottoman Turks for most of the 14th century and contains notable mosques and sultans' tombs and a university (1975). Population (1980): 445,113.

Burton, Sir Richard (1821–90) British explorer, diplomat, and translator. After military service in India he traveled in Arabia (entering the sacred city of Mecca in 1853 disguised as a Muslim) and Somaliland. He made two attempts (1855, 1857–58) to discover the source of the Nile and on the second, with *Speke, discovered Lake Tanganyika. The two men later quarrelled over Speke's claim to have discovered the Nile source in Lake Victoria. Apart from his many travel books, he published superb translations of oriental erotica, including *Kama Sutra of Vatsyayana* (1883) and the *Arabian Nights* (16 vols, 1885–88). After his death his wife burned almost all his diaries.

Burton, Richard (Richard Jenkins; 1925–84) British actor, born in Wales. He first achieved success as a stage actor, especially in Shakespearian roles, but since the 1950s acted almost exclusively in films. These include *Look Back in Anger* (1959), *Becket* (1964), and *Who's Afraid of Virginia Woolf?* (1966). His two marriages to Elizabeth Taylor were highly publicized.

Burton, Robert (1577–1640) British scholar. He was educated at Oxford and spent his life there as a don. *The Anatomy of Melancholy* (1621, revised five times) is a vast, witty, and erudite miscellany of Jacobean knowledge on what is now called depression; it includes folklore, superstitions, and the learning of the ancient Greeks and Arabs.

Burundi, Republic of A small inland country in central Africa, bordering on Lake Tanganyika in the SW. It consists chiefly of high plateau along the main Nile-Congo dividing range, descending rapidly to the Great Rift Valley in the W. Most of the population belongs to the Hutu, a Bantu tribe, but the rulers are Tutsi and there are other tribal minorities. *Economy*: mainly subsistence agriculture; coffee is the main export and tea is also being developed. Minerals have been found including gold, cassiterite, and nickel, and there has been considerable development in recent years, although industry still provides only a very small proportion of the revenue. *History*: the area (with present-day Rwanda) became part of German East Africa in 1890 and from 1919, as the S part of Ruanda-Urundi, it was administered by Belgium, first under League of Nations mandate and then as a UN trust territory. It became independent in 1962 and in 1964 a monetary and customs union with Rwanda was dissolved. In 1966 the hereditary Mwami Mwambutsa IV was deposed by his son, who was enthroned as Mwami Ntare V. In the same year, following a military coup, Captain (later Lieutenant General) Michel Micombero (1940–83) set up a republic with himself as president. In 1972 he assumed absolute powers and fighting broke out in which thousands were killed, including the deposed king. Further intertribal killings took place in 1973. In 1976 Micombero was overthrown in a coup and Jean-Baptiste Bagaza became president. Micombrero later died in exile in Somalia. Bagaza proceeded to civilianize the Burundi government. He was confirmed uncontested as president in 1982 by election. Official languages: French and Kirundi; Swahili is also used commercially. Official currency: Burundi franc of 100 centimes. Area: 10,759 sq mi (27,834 sq km). Population (1983 est.): 4,561,000. Capital: Bujumbura.

Bury 53 36N 2 17N A city in NW England, in Greater Manchester on the River Irwell. A textile town concentrating on cotton spinning and weaving, the woolen and felt industries are important. John Kay and Sir Robert Peel were born here. Population (1981): 67,529.

Buryat Autonomous Soviet Socialist Republic (*or* Buryatia) An administrative division in SE central Soviet Union, in the RSFSR. Over half its area is covered by forest. The Buryats, who comprise about 35% of the population, are traditionally nomads and speak a Mongolian language. The region is one of Siberia's most prosperous, having valuable mineral deposits, including coal, molybdenum, and gold. The main industries are mining, timber, and food processing; spring wheat and fodder crops are grown and stock breeding is also important. Area: 135,650 sq mi (350,300 sq km). Population (1977 est): 879,000. Capital: Ulan Ude.

burying beetle A strong beetle, also called a sexton beetle, belonging to a genus (*Necrophorus*) occurring chiefly in N temperate regions. Burying beetles are 0.05–0.41 in (1.5–35 mm) long and feed and lay their eggs on the dead bodies of small animals, which they first bury: the larvae use the same food source. Family: *Silphidae* (carrion beetles).

Bury St Edmunds 52 15N 0 43E A city in E England, in Suffolk. Its ruined abbey, which was built to house the shrine of St Edmund, last King of East Anglia, became a famous place of pilgrimage. Bury St Edmunds is a market town with brewing, sugar-refining and agricultural machinery industries. Population (1981): 28,914.

GEORGE BUSH *Vice president who played an active role in world affairs for President Ronald Reagan.*

BUSHBABY *The enormous eyes and large sensitive ears of the common bushbaby make it well suited to a nocturnal existence.*

Bush, George (Herbert Walker) (1924–) US politician and statesman, vice president (1981–). The son of Prescott Bush, a Connecticut senator, he served in World War II, graduated from Yale University (1948), and went to Texas, where he was successful in the petroleum industry. A Republican, he served Texas in the US House of Representatives (1967–71), was appointed ambassador to the United Nations (1971–72), chaired the Republican National Committee (1972–73), and was director of the Central Intelligence Agency (CIA) 1976–77). His unsuccessful bid for the Republican presidential nomination in 1980 eventually brought him the vice presidency under Ronald *Reagan. As vice president he headed a government reform task force and traveled extensively representing the president. Although he was initially opposed by more conservative Republicans, his loyalty to Reagan won him many supporters in the party.

Bush, Vannevar (1890–1974) US electrical engineer and inventor of the differential analyzer, an electronic analog computer. He was a professor (1919–38) at Massachusetts Institute of Technology, became president (1938–55) of the Carnegie Institution of Washington, and headed the Office of Scientific Research and Development during World War II.

bushbaby A small nocturnal *prosimian primate belonging to the genus *Galago* (4 species), of African forests and bush. They are 11–31 in (27–80 cm) long including the tail (6–16 in [15–40 cm]). Common bushbabies (*G. senegalensis*) have soft dense grayish fur and a long bushy tail. They live in small groups and climb acrobatically among the trees in search of large insects; they also eat fruit and leaves. Family: *Lorisidae*.

bushbuck A small antelope, *Tragelaphus scriptus*, of tropical African bush and forest, also called harnessed antelope. 26–43 in (66–109 cm) high at the shoulder, bushbucks are red with white spots and stripes on the flanks and legs. Males have black-tipped horns with a single spiral turn. They are shy and nocturnal, living in pairs.

bush cricket A *cricket belonging to the family *Tettigoniidae* (over 4000 species), having a green or brown body and short tail appendages (cerci). Bush crickets rarely fly or jump, but crawl among bushes and trees in fields and meadows. The swordlike ovipositor with which the female inserts eggs into plant tissues can cause considerable damage. Many species are carnivorous, usually eating small insects. □insect.

bushel A unit of capacity (dry or liquid) equal to 2150.42 cubic inches in the US and 8 gallons or 2219.36 cubic inches in the UK.

Bushido The military and ethical code of the Japanese *samurai class. It originated in about the 13th century, although the term was not used until the 17th. Obedience to one's lord and fearlessness were its main virtues, along with austerity, honesty, and kindness. In the 13th–14th centuries it was influenced by Zen Buddhism and in the 17th–19th centuries, by Confucianism. In the mid-19th century it became the basis of Japanese emperor worship and nationalism. *See also* martial arts.

Bushire (*or* Bandar-e Bushehr) 28 59N 50 50E A city in SW Iran, on the N shore of the Persian Gulf. The port serves inland Iran but has lost trade to Abadan. Population (1972 est): 45,000.

Bushman. *See* Khoisan.

bushmaster A *pit viper, *Lachesis muta*, occurring in scrub and forests of Central and South America. The longest venomous snake of the New World, it reaches a length of 6 ft (1.8 m) and is brownish pink with dark diamond-shaped blotches. Its venom can prove fatal to man.

Bushnell, David (1742–1824) US inventor, who in 1776 built the first submarine, nicknamed the Turtle. It was intended to be a combat vessel, laying mines on the hulls of enemy ships, but it lacked the necessary maneuverability.

bushrangers Outlaws in the Australian outback in the late-18th and 19th centuries. They robbed farmsteads and stagecoaches, murdered, and plundered, but while some were ruthless and cruel, others shared their gains with the poor. The most famous of the Australian bushrangers is probably Ned *Kelly.

Busoni, Ferruccio (1866–1924) Italian virtuoso pianist and composer. An admirer of Liszt, he exploited the extreme possibilities of the piano in both his playing and in his transcriptions and compositions for the instrument. Among his works are a piano concerto (1903–04), the *Fantasia contrappuntistica* (for piano; 1910), and the opera *Doktor Faust* (1916–24).

Bustamante y Sirvén, Antonio Sánchez de (1865–1951) Cuban lawyer. He is best known for the Bustamante Code, a system of international law regarding the security of people and property. It was ratified by the sixth Pan-American Congress in 1928.

bustard A large omnivorous bird belonging to a family (*Otididae*; 22 species) occurring in grassland regions of the Old World and having long legs adapted for running. Bustards have a long stout neck, broad wings, and a gray or brown mottled plumage, often with ornamental plumes. The great bustard (*Otis tarda*), 48 in (120 cm) long and weighing 31 lb (14 kg), is the largest European land bird. Order: *Gruiformes* (cranes, rails, etc.).

butadiene (H_2C:CHHC:CH_2) A colorless flammable gas made from *butanes and butenes. It is used in making synthetic rubbers.

butane (C_4H_{10}) A colorless flammable gaseous *alkane found in crude oil. It is used in the manufacture of synthetic rubber and, in its pressurized liquefied form, as a fuel.

butcherbird. *See* shrike.

butcher's broom A small evergreen European shrub, *Ruscus aculeatus*, up to 31 in (80 cm) high. The leaves are reduced to small brown scales, but the plant has oval flattened branches that function as leaves. There are separate male and female flowers, which are small and greenish and grow on separate plants. The fruit is a red berry. Family: *Liliaceae.*

Bute, John Stuart, 3rd Earl of (1713–92) British statesman; prime minister (1762–63). A close friend of George III and extremely unpopular, he was forced to resign after securing the passage of a cider tax. He continued unofficially to influence the king until 1765.

Butler, Benjamin Franklin (1838–93) US statesman; Republican congressman (1866–75, 1877–79). A Union general, Butler was hated by southerners for his military governorship of New Orleans during the Civil War. As a Radical Republican congressman, he advocated the impeachment of President Andrew *Jackson and harsh Reconstruction policies. After several attempts he became governor of Massachusetts for one year (1882) and ran unsuccessfully for the presidency on a populist ticket in 1884.

Butler, Reg(inald) Cotterell (1913–81) British sculptor. Butler trained as an architect and practiced as an engineer (1939–50) before devoting himself to sculpture. Influenced by Henry *Moore and Alexander *Calder, he produced iron and stainless steel constructions suggestive of plant and insect forms.

Butler, Samuel (1835–1902) British novelist. Son of a village rector and grandson of a bishop, he rejected his family, religion, and prospects, emigrating to New Zealand from 1859 to 1864, when he returned wealthy. After failing as an artist, he turned to literature and engaged in the Darwinian controversy. *Erewhon* (1872), which made him famous, satirizes Victorian utopian ideals. The autobiographical *The Way of All Flesh* (1903) recounts his painful liberation from his claustrophobic family background.

Butor, Michel (1926–) French experimental novelist and critic. He studied philosophy at the Sorbonne and has taught in Egypt, Thessalonika, Geneva, and Manchester. His novels, employing the techniques of the anti-novel (*see* nouveau roman), include *Passing Time* (1956), *Second Thoughts* (1957), *Degrees* (1960), *Mobile* (1962), and *Third Below* (1977).

butte A small steep-sided mass of rock left upstanding after the erosion of a *mesa. It usually consists of a resistant rock capping that protects the underlying rock from erosion.

buttercup An annual or perennial herbaceous plant of the worldwide genus *Ranunculus* (about 300 species), usually with much divided leaves. The flowers are usually yellow, with spirally arranged petals and stamens. The fruit is a head of small nutlets (achenes). A common Eurasian species, widely introduced, is the perennial meadow buttercup (*R. acris*), up to 28 in (70 cm) high. The genus, which is poisonous to livestock, also includes the *crowfoots. Family: *Ranunculaceae. See* Plate VI.

butterflies and moths Insects belonging to the order *Lepidoptera* (about 100,000 species), distributed worldwide. The adults have two pairs of scale-covered wings, which are often highly colored and patterned. They range in size from the smallest moths, with a wingspan of only 0.16 in (4 mm), to butterflies with wingspans of up to 12 in (300 mm). They all undergo a complete metamorphosis comprising a four-stage life cycle: egg, larva (*see* caterpillar), *pupa (chrysalis), and adult (imago). The caterpillars feed mainly on plants, eating leaves or boring into stems and roots, in some cases becoming serious crop pests (e.g. the cabbage white butterfly and the spruce budworm). Some species pupate by spinning silken cocoons (*see* silkworm moth). The adults are often strong fliers, seeking out a mate and migrating long distances. They feed mainly on nectar and other plant juices using a long tubular proboscis and may aid plant pollination in the process (*see* yucca moth). The forewings and hindwings of moths are locked together by a "bristle-and-catch" device (frenulum). Butterflies generally are active by day and rest with their wings held together vertically; moths, which are mainly nocturnal, generally rest with their wings flat. Another differentiating feature is the antennae, which are smooth and club-shaped in butterflies and plumed or feathery in moths. *See* Plate VII.

butterfly bush. *See* Buddleia.

butterwort A *carnivorous plant of the genus *Pinguicula* (about 30 species), found in the N hemisphere and South America. These perennial herbs, 5–6 in (12–15 cm) high, have a rosette of yellow-green leaves covered with sticky glands on which insects are trapped. The single spurred funnel-shaped violet or pink flower arises on a slender stalk. Family: *Lentibulariaceae.*

button quail A small ground-dwelling bird belonging to a family (*Turnicidae*; 15 species) found in warm Old World grassland regions. Button quails are 5–8 in (13–19 cm) long with a brown streaked plumage, short wings, and a small slender bill. The female courts the male and leaves

him to incubate the eggs and tend the young. Order: *Gruiformes* (cranes, rails, etc.).

buttress A projecting mass of masonry strengthening a wall. The huge vaults of Roman and Byzantine public buildings caused buttresses to be built to counteract the outward thrust of the roof. In *gothic architecture, the graceful but highly functional **flying buttress** developed to support the upper walls of large churches.

butyl rubber A synthetic *rubber made by copolymerization of isobutylene with small amounts of *isoprene. It is less permeable to gas than natural rubbers and is used in tire inner tubes.

Buxtehude, Dietrich (1637–1707) Danish organist and composer. He settled in Germany in 1668 as organist at the Marienkirche, Lübeck. In 1673 he started his famous *Abendmusiken* ("evening concerts"); J. S. Bach walked 200 miles to Lübeck to hear Buxtehude's music. One of the most influential of the North German school of organists, he composed much organ music and sacred music.

buzzard A *hawk belonging to a widespread genus (*Buteo*) characterized by broad wings, a large rounded tail, and a brown plumage. Buzzards hunt in open country for small mammals, reptiles, insects, and carrion and soar gracefully at great heights. The common Eurasian buzzard (*B. buteo*), 22 in (55 cm) long, occurs in a number of races; the migratory rough-legged buzzard (*B. lagopus*) is distinguished by its feathered legs.

buzz bomb. *See* V-1 missile.

Byblos 34 08N 35 38E A *Phoenician city state on the E Mediterranean coast, now Jubeil (Lebanon). Egyptian records from the 14th to the 10th centuries BC attest a thriving trade with Byblos; excavations here have revealed strong cultural links with Egypt. Under Greek and Roman rule Byblos dwindled in relative commercial importance but remained famous as the center of orgiastic worship of Astarte (*see* Aphrodite) and her lover *Adonis. *See also* Sidon; Tyre.

Bydgoszcz (German name: Bromberg) 53 16N 17 33E A city in N Poland. It is an important inland port on a canal linking the Vistula and Oder Rivers. Industries include engineering, printing, and the processing of forest products. Population (1979 est): 344,000.

Bylot, Robert. *See* Baffin, William.

Byng, George, Viscount Torrington (1663–1733) English admiral. A supporter of William III, he gained rapid promotion and in the War of the Spanish Succession captured Gibraltar (1704). He defeated the fleet of *James Stuart, off Scotland (1708) and crowned his career by destroying a Spanish fleet off Messina (1717).

Byng of Vimy, Julian, 1st Viscount (1862–1935) British field marshal. He won distinction in World War I first at *Gallipoli, then as commander of the successful Canadian troops at Vimy Ridge. After the war he was governor general of Canada (1921–26).

Byrd, Harry Flood (1887–1966) US politician. After serving as Virginia's Democratic chairman, he was elected governor (1926–30) before becoming a US senator (1933–65). As chairman of the Senate Finance Committee (1955–65) he was known as a conservative who opposed increased federal power.

Byrd, Richard E(velyn) (1888–1957) US explorer. A naval pilot, he served in World War I and in 1926 began a series of record-breaking flights over the two Poles and the Atlantic Ocean. In 1928 he set out on the first of several expeditions to explore Antarctica from the air. In 1934–35, he spent five months alone in a hut at Bolling Advance Base, describing his experience in *Alone* (1938).

Byrd Land. *See* Marie Byrd Land.

Byron, George Gordon, Lord (1788–1824) British poet. Born with deformed ankles and a clubfoot, he grew up lacking parental affection. His first book, *Hours of Idleness* (1807), was followed in 1809 by a satire aimed at its ungenerous reviewers. After two years traveling in Europe he published *Childe Harolde's Pilgrimage* (1812) to immediate acclaim and was lionized by London society. He was bisexual and among many love affairs had an incestuous relationship with his half-sister Augusta Leigh. He married Annabella Milbanke in 1815 but she left him the following year. Byron then left England forever. He stayed near Geneva with *Shelley and then went to Italy. In 1818 he began writing the witty verse satire *Don Juan*. In 1823 he became involved in the Greek struggle for independence and he died while training troops at Missolonghi.

Bytom (German name: Beuthen) 50 21N 18 51E A town in SW Poland. It is a major heavy-industry center in a coal, zinc, and lead mining area. Population (1979 est): 232,000.

LORD BYRON   *Portrait by Thomas Phillips (1770-1845).*

Byzantine art and architecture   The painting, architecture, and decoration that developed in the ancient city of Constantinople (formerly Byzantium; modern Istanbul) after 330 AD, when it became the new Roman imperial capital, until 1453, when Constantinople fell to the Turks. Primarily religious and often symbolic or didactic, Byzantine art suppressed both realistic portrayal and opportunities for individual artistic expression. Owing to Constantinople's position as a meeting point of Asia and Europe, the bright colors and intricacy of oriental design mingle in Byzantine mosaics and *icons with Christian symbolism. Three main phases of Byzantine art succeeded one another between 330 and 1453 AD. The first phase (330–726) came to an end with the Iconoclastic controversy (726–843), which resulted in the destruction of many works of art (*see* iconoclasm). During the second golden age (843–1204) and the final phase (1204–1453) a complicated iconography of religious pictures was evolved, wherein each divine person, prophet, saint, angel, and apostle was allocated their strict position on the wall, apse, or dome of the church. This was possible because of the design of the Byzantine *basilica with its characteristic dome rising from a square base—an innovation that greatly extended the versatility of the Roman dome, which was restricted to circular buildings. The Church of Holy Wisdom (Hagia Sophia) in Constantinople, built between 532 and 537, is the outstanding example of a Byzantine basilica with a central dome (in this case buttressed by semidomes). The characteristic brickwork, pillars, and internal mosaics of Byzantine buildings also had a profound effect on western architecture from the spectacular St Mark's (11th century) in Venice to the somewhat surprising Westminster Cathedral in London in the 20th century.

Byzantine Empire (*or* Eastern Roman Empire)   The Roman territories E of the Balkans separated from the western *Roman Empire by *Diocletian in 293 AD. An eastern emperor and magistrates coexisted with their western counterparts at Rome. Under *Constantine the Great the Empire became Christian. Constantinople (previously Byzantium; now *Istanbul) was inaugurated as the "New Rome" in 330 AD. The Byzantine Empire survived until the fall of Constantinople to the Ottoman Turks in 1453 – almost a millennium after the western Empire.

Byzantium.   *See* Istanbul.

C

Cabal Five ministers of Charles II of England who dominated politics from 1667 to about 1674. They were Sir Thomas Clifford (1630–73), Lord Ashley (later 1st Earl of *Shaftesbury), the 2nd Duke of *Buckingham, the Earl of *Arlington, and the Earl of *Lauderdale. It was not a united body: the king played one minister off against another to retain control of policy. Clifford and Arlington supported a secret pro-Catholic policy of friendship with France, which, owing to parliamentary opposition, cost them their offices in 1673–74.

Caballé, Montserrat (1933–) Spanish soprano. She sang at La Scala, Milan, and in 1965 made her debut in New York. She became a member of the Metropolitan Opera and specializes in bel canto roles, such as the title role in Bellini's *Norma*.

cabbage A flowering plant, *Brassica oleracea* var. *capitata*, widely cultivated as a vegetable. The short stem bears a round heart, up to 10 in (25 cm) in diameter, of tightly compressed leaves. Many different cultivated varieties have been developed, of various shapes, colors, and densities, used for cooking, salads, and pickling. For example, the Savoy cabbage is a cooking variety with dark-green wrinkled leaves. All cabbages and many other brassicas—including cauliflower, broccoli, kale, and Brussels sprouts—are derived from the wild cabbage (*B. oleracea*), a perennial herb native to coastal regions of W Europe. 12–24 in (30–60 cm) high, its straggling stem bears a spike of yellow flowers. Family: *Cruciferae*.

cabbage palm A West Indian palm tree, *Roystonea oleracea*, that may grow to a height of 98 ft (30 m) but is often cut when young for its head of young leaves, which resembles a cabbage and is eaten as a vegetable. An oil and a type of sago are obtained from the fruit. The name is also given to several other palms, including *Livistona australis*, of E Australia.

cabbage root fly A plant-eating fly, *Erioischia brassicae*, whose larva is a serious economic pest. The larvae feed on the roots of cabbages, radishes, turnips, etc., having developed from eggs laid around the stems. Family: *Muscidae*.

cabbage white butterfly A white butterfly belonging to the genus *Pieris*, whose caterpillars eat cabbages and related vegetables. The species are the large white (*P. brassicae*), the green-veined white (*P. napi*), and the small white (*P. rapae*).

caber tossing An event in Scottish athletics. A competitor carries the caber, a tapering tree trunk 13–17 ft (4–5 m) long, vertically in his cradled hands and then tosses it forward. As the top end hits the ground, the other end should continue over it so that the tossed caber should lie in the direction in which it was thrown; a toss more than 90° off-line is invalid.

Cabimas 10 26N 71 27W A city in NW Venezuela, on the NE shore of Lake Maracaibo. It is an important center within the Ambrosio oilfields. Population (1976 est): 159,000.

Cabinda (*or* Kabinda) A district of Angola, forming an enclave between the Congo and Zaïre on the Atlantic coast. Extensive oil deposits were discovered offshore in 1968 and led to the expansion of the chief town, Cabinda. The area also produces coffee, palm oil, timber, and cocoa. Area: 2806 sq mi (7270 sq km). Population (1960): 58,547.

cabinet A committee of the executive heads of government. In the US, the cabinet comprises the heads of the various departments of the executive branch. They are Secretary of State, Secretary of Defense, Secretary of the Treasury, Secretary of Labor, Secretary of the Interior, Secretary of Transportation, Secretary of Education, Secretary of Health and Human Services, Secretary of Energy, Secretary of Commerce, Secretary of Agriculture, Secretary of Housing and Urban Development, and the Attorney General, who heads the Department of Justice. All cabinet members are appointed by the president and subject to confirmation by the Senate. The extent of the cabinet's influence in the formation of national policy depends on the extent to which the president chooses to consult its members. The American cabinet system was developed from the British cabinet, which originated in the 18th century with the selection of a royal adviser, called the *prime minister, from the majority party in *parliament. Unlike the members of the American cabinet who are responsible only to the president, all British ministers also fulfill legislative functions. British cabinets consist of about 20 leading ministers, from either house of parliament, appointed by the prime minister. They serve until dismissed by the prime minister or

until their party loses its parliamentary majority. This parliamentary system has also been adopted by many other countries.

Cabora Bassa Dam 15 34S 33 00E A dam in Mozambique, on the Zambezi River. It is the largest dam in S Africa.

Cable, George Washington (1844–1925) US author and reformer. Through his novels and short stories he gave a feeling for the Southern life, especially that of his native New Orleans. He was a strong advocate for the rights of the newly-freed blacks and published many essays on the subject. They are collected in *The Silent South* (1885) and *The Negro Question* (1888). His short stories are collected in *Old Creole Days* (1879).

Cabot, John (Italian name: Giovanni Caboto; c. 1450–c. 1499) Italian explorer. He settled in England in about 1484 and under Henry VII's patronage discovered Cape Breton Island (which he thought to be Asia) in 1497. He set out on a second voyage in 1498 and appears to have died at sea. His son **Sebastian Cabot** (c. 1476–1557) was a cartographer to Henry VIII. In Spanish service he explored the coast of South America (1525–28).

Cabral, Pedro Álvares (?1467–1520) Portuguese navigator. In 1500, on his way to India with 13 ships, he landed in Brazil, which he claimed for Portugal. Resuming his voyage E, he landed at Mozambique, of which he later gave an interesting account, and thence reached Calicut, where he established the first commercial treaty between Portugal and India. He returned to Portugal in 1501 with only four ships.

Cabrini, St Frances Xavier (1850–1917) Italian founder of the Missionary Sisters of the Sacred Heart, known as Mother Cabrini. She sailed in 1889 to the US and established 67 houses there and in Buenos Aires, Paris, and Madrid. She worked mainly among poor Italian immigrants in the US and was the first US citizen to be canonized. Feast day: Nov 13.

cacao. *See* cocoa and chocolate.

Caccini, Giulio (c. 1545–c. 1618) Italian singer and composer. He developed the monodic style (a single vocal line supported by a chordal bass), which led to the earliest operas; his opera *Euridice* was performed in 1602.

Cáceres 39 29N 6 23W A market city in W Spain, in Estremadura. It produces textiles and cork. The old part of the town is surrounded by Roman and Moorish walls. Population (1970): 56,064.

cachalot. *See* sperm whale.

cacomistle An arboreal nocturnal mammal of the American genus *Bassariscus* (2 species). Cacomistles are grayish brown with small faces, long ears, and pointed snouts; the long bushy tail, patterned with black and white rings, accounts for about half the total body length 24–40 in (60–100 cm). They feed on small animals and fruit. The North American cacomistle, or ring-tailed cat (*B. astutus*) occurs from the SW US to S Mexico; the South American cacomistle extends from Central America to Peru. Family: *Procyonidae* (raccoons, etc.); order: *Carnivora*.

Cactoblastis. *See* cactus moth.

cactus A flowering plant belonging to the family *Cactaceae* (over 2000 species). These perennial herbs and shrubs grow chiefly in the drier regions of tropical America and the West Indies. Plant size and shape varies widely; the larger species may grow to a height of 33 ft (10 m) or more. Cacti show pronounced modifications to prevent water loss—their leaves or shoots are reduced to spines, they have thick waxy outer layers, and many possess succulent water-storing stems. The flowers, borne singly, are large and brightly colored. Some genera are cultivated for their soft timber or alkaloid content, and the fruits of many species are edible (*see* prickly pear). Cacti are grown as ornamentals in many regions of the world.

cactus moth A South American cactus-boring *pyralid moth, *Cactoblastis cactorum*, that was introduced into Australia in 1925 as a means of biologically controlling the prickly pear cactus, which had ruined large areas.

caddis fly A mothlike insect, also called sedge fly, belonging to the worldwide order *Trichoptera* (about 5000 species). Caddis flies— 0.05–1.6 in (1.5–40 mm) long, with long antennae—are found in cool damp places and feed on nectar. The omnivorous larvae (called caddis worms) live in flowing fresh water, often in portable cases constructed from sand, stones, pieces of leaf, etc.

Caddo A North American Indian language spoken by a confederation of related tribes formerly inhabiting areas in Arkansas, Louisiana, Oklahoma, and Texas. The Caddoan group of languages takes its name from the ancient Caddo, who were a semisedentary agricultural people who established villages of conical huts around a central temple mound. Political and religious affairs were conducted by a hereditary elite. The present Caddoan population, numbering approximately 1000 members of the various member tribes, is now settled primarily in the Wichita Reservation in Oklahoma.

cade A *juniper tree or shrub, *Juniperus oxycedrus*, native to Mediterranean coastal regions and growing to a height of 26 ft (8 m). Also called prickly juniper, it has needles and rounded reddish berry-like fruits, 0.24–0.40 in (6–10 mm) in diameter. Oil of cade is distilled from the wood and used in medicine and veterinary work.

CACTUS *Two ornamental cacti:* Rhipsalidopsis *"Electra" (above) from Brazil and* Opuntia microdasys *(below) from Mexico.*

Cade, Jack (d. 1450) English rebel, who led a rebellion in 1450 against Henry VI. The rebels, who were chiefly opposing high taxes and court corruption, demanded the recall of Richard Plantagenet, Duke of York, from Ireland. In spite of initial successes in Kent and London the rebellion was soon quelled and Cade was killed.

Cádiz 36 32N 6 18W A city and seaport in SW Spain, in Andalusia on the Gulf of Cádiz. Founded by Phoenician merchants (c. 1100 BC), it was taken from the Moors by Alfonso the Wise of Castile in 1262. Following the discovery of America it prospered as a base for the Spanish treasure fleet; the harbor was burned by Sir Francis Drake in 1587, destroying many ships. It has two cathedrals and a notable collection of works by the artist Murillo. An important port and naval base, it has tuna fisheries and shipbuilding industries. Population (1974 est): 142,136.

cadmium (Cd) A soft dense metal, discovered in 1817 by Friedrich Strohmeyer (1776–1835). Cadmium occurs naturally as the mineral greenockite (CdS) and in zinc, copper, and lead sulfide ores. It is chemically similar to lead and is a component of low-melting-point alloys. It is used in the control rods of nuclear reactors, in light meters, television-tube phos-

phors, batteries, solders, and in special low-friction alloys for bearings. Cadmium and its compounds are poisonous and care should be taken in working with solders (e.g. silver solder) that contain cadmium. Compounds include several salts, the yellow sulfide (CdS) and the oxide (CdO). At no 48; at wt 112.40; mp 320.9°C; bp 765°C.

Cadmus A legendary Greek hero. Obeying the oracle of Delphi, he followed a cow into Boeotia and founded the city of Thebes where it lay down. From the teeth of a dragon he had killed a race of fierce warriors is said to have emerged. He married Harmonia, daughter of Ares and Aphrodite, and is reputed to have introduced the alphabet into Greece from Phoenicia.

caecilian A limbless burrowing *amphibian of the order *Apoda*, or *Gymnophiona* (over 150 species), found in tropical and warm temperate regions of the world. Resembling earthworms, caecilians are 4–42 in (11–140 cm) long and feed on termites and earthworms.

Caedmon (died c. 680 AD) English poet, known only from the account given by *Bede in his *Ecclesiastical History*. He was an illiterate herdsman who in his old age was suddenly divinely inspired to compose a hymn on the Creation. The *Hymn* is a typical example of Old English oral verse. Caedmon later entered the monastery of Whitby, where he composed many poems on biblical themes.

Caen 49 11N 0 22W A city and port in NW France, the capital of the Calvados department on the Orne River. Situated at the center of an agricultural and horse-breeding area, Caen has iron, silk, and leather industries. Stone from nearby quarries was used to build several cathedrals and churches in England. A cultural center, its university was established in 1432 (reorganized in 1970). It has many fine churches. *History*: captured by the English in 1346 and again in 1417, it became a Huguenot stronghold in the 17th century. Caen was badly damaged during the Normandy campaign (1944) of World War II. Population (1975): 122,794.

Caernarfon (English name: Caernarvon) 53 08N 4 16W A town in North Wales, a tourist center, market town, and small port. Its castle (built by Edward I in 1284) is the likely birthplace of Edward II, the first Prince of Wales, and was the scene of the investiture of Prince *Charles as Prince of Wales in 1969. Population (1981): 9506.

Caerphilly 51 35N 3 14W A market city in South Wales, in Mid Glamorgan. Situated in a coalmining area, it is best known for Caerphilly cheese (originally made here) and its castle, the largest in Wales. Population (1981): 42,736.

Caesar, (Gaius) Julius (100–44 BC) Roman general and statesman, whose career marked the end of the Roman Republic. Caesar, born of a patrician family, allied himself with the popular party by his marriage in 84 to *Cinna's daughter Cornelia. After her death in 68, he married Pompeia, whom he divorced in 62, and in 59 he married Calpurnia.

During the 60s Caesar ascended the political ladder, joining *Pompey and *Crassus in the first *Triumvirate (60) and becoming consul (59) and then governor of Gaul. Caesar's subjugation of Gaul (58–50), and his brief campaigns in Britain (55, 54), confirmed his military reputation and made him a popular hero. Crassus's death (53) and Pompey's developing association with Caesar's opponents in the Senate brought the Triumvirate to an end (50) and the Senate, with Pompey's support, asked Caesar to resign his armies. He refused and, crossing the Rubicon River into Italy (49), initiated the civil war. Caesar defeated Pompey at *Pharsalus (48) and spent the following winter in Alexandria with *Cleopatra, who became his lover. She is reputed to have had a son, Caesarion, by him. Caesar then campaigned in NE Anatolia, defeating Pharnaces II at Zela (47), the victory provoking his comment "veni, vidi, vici" ("I came, I saw, I conquered"). He went on to defeat the remnants of Pompey's party at *Thapsus (46) and Munda (45), after which he returned to Rome as dictator. There, he introduced many reforms, including the sponsorship of a revised (Julian) *calendar, but on the Ides of March (March 15, 44), Caesar was assassinated in the Senate House by republicans, including *Brutus and *Cassius, who feared his monarchical aspirations.

A distinguished prose stylist, Caesar wrote outstanding accounts of his campaigns in Gaul (*De bello gallico*) and the civil war (*De bello civili*).

Caesarea 32 30N 34 54E An ancient town in Israel, on the Mediterranean coast between Tel Aviv-Yafo and Haifa. Built by Herod the Great, it had a large early Christian community and was for a time the capital of Roman Palestine. Caesarea was twice held by the Crusaders and finally destroyed by Muslims in 1265. The Israelis have excavated many Roman remains and are developing a tourist resort here.

Caesarean section A surgical operation in which a baby is delivered through an incision made in the abdominal wall and the womb, so called because Julius Caesar was said to have been born in this way. Caesarean section is employed when a baby cannot be delivered through the vagina; for instance, because it is abnormally positioned in the womb or is too large to pass through the birth canal.

Caetano, Marcello José das Neves Alves (1906–80) Portuguese statesman; prime minister (1968–74). He succeeded Salazar and initially proved a more liberal head of state. He was overthrown in a military coup.

Caffaggiolo majolica An important category of Italian pottery mainly produced from about 1504 to 1540 under Medici patronage. Its main characteristic is bold bright decoration in orange, yellow, red, and green, on a cobalt-blue background. *See* majolica.

caffeine (*or* theine; $C_8H_{10}O_2N_4$) The substance in coffee and tea that acts as a stimulant. In its pure form it is white and crystalline.

Cage, John (1912–) Avant-garde US composer, who studied with Schoenberg and Varèse. His works include *Sonatas and Interludes* (1946–48) for prepared piano (with pieces of wood, metal, etc., fixed across its strings); *Imaginary Landscape No 4* (1951) for 12 randomly tuned radio sets; *4 minutes 33 seconds* (1954), silence in three movements for any instrument(s); *Reunion* (1968); and *Apartment Building 1776* (1976). His books, including *Silence* (1961), reflect his philosophy of indeterminism.

Cagliari 39 13N 9 08E A seaport in Italy, in Sardinia. It has Roman remains, a 14th-century cathedral, and a university (1606). There are milling, tanning, and fishing industries. Lead, salt, and zinc are exported. Population (1980 est): 240,366.

Cagliostro, Alessandro, Conte di (Giuseppe Balsamo; 1743–95) Italian adventurer. His pretended skills in alchemy and magic gained him fame throughout Europe, especially in Paris. He was arrested for promoting freemasonry and died in prison in Italy.

Cagney, James (1899–) US actor. He began making films in the 1930s, after working as a vaudeville singer and dancer, and became famous for his portrayals of tough gangsters. His films include *Public Enemy* (1931), *The Roaring Twenties* (1939), and *Ragtime* (1981). He won an academy award for *Yankee Doodle Dandy* (1942).

Caicos Islands. *See* Turks and Caicos Islands.

Caillaux, Joseph (1863–1944) French statesman; prime minister (1911–12). He was finance minister three times before World War I and introduced direct income tax into France. In 1914 his wife shot and killed Gaston Calmette (1858–1914), the editor of *Le Figaro*, who had cast aspersions on his financial dealings while in office. An advocate of a negotiated peace during World War I, Caillaux was arrested in 1917 on a charge of dealing with the enemy. His civil rights were restored in 1925.

Cain In the Old Testament, the elder son of Adam and Eve. He became jealous of his younger brother Abel, a shepherd whose burnt offerings were accepted by God in preference to his own. He murdered Abel and was banished, marked as the world's first murderer.

Cain, James M (allahan) (1892–1977) US novelist. He worked in journalism after college but left in 1931 to concentrate on writing racy fast-paced crime novels. His first, *The Postman Always Rings Twice* (1934), became a stage play (1936) and a movie (1946). Other well-known novels that later became films were *Double Indemnity* (1936) and *Mildred Pierce* (1941).

Cainozoic era. *See* Cenozoic era.

cairn. *See* barrow.

Cairns 16 51S 145 43E A port in Australia, in NE Queensland on Trinity Bay. It is the commercial center for an agricultural, mining, and timber region; sugar is exported. Population (1980 est): 37,100.

cairn terrier A breed of small □dog originating in the Scottish Highlands, where it was used to flush game from cover (such as stone cairns). It has a long outer coat and a short soft undercoat; the color varies from red, sandy, or mottled gray to almost black. Height: about 10 in (25 cm).

Cairo (Arabic name: El Qahira) 80 01N 31 14E The capital of Egypt, situated in the N of the country on the E bank of the Nile River. It is the largest city in Africa and the cultural and commercial center of Egypt. Industry has developed dramatically since the 1920s and in particular since the revolution of 1952, with traditional textile manufacturing and food processing retaining importance alongside newer industries, such as metallurgy and plastics. Its many mosques include the Mosque of Omar (643 AD), Cairo's earliest remaining Arabic building, and the Mohammed Ali Mosque, housed in the 12th-century citadel. The Mosque and University of El Azhar was founded in 970 AD; three other universities were established in the 20th century. *History*: the Arabic city of El Fustat was founded in 641 AD, and from the 9th century, as El Qahira, it was successively the

capital of the Fatimid, Ayyubite, and Mameluke dynasties. It was under the Mamelukes that the city enjoyed the period of its greatest prosperity. Following its conquest by the Turks in the 16th century, it declined in power, but in the 19th century its prosperity was restored under Mehemet *Ali and his successors. During World War II it was the seat of the Allied headquarters in the Middle East. Population (1976): 5,084,000. *See also* Giza, El.

CAIRO   *The Mohammed Ali Mosque now dominates Saladin's citadel, built in the 12th century.*

caisson A large cylindrical or box-shaped structure sunk into the ground during excavation work. Caissons aid construction of underwater foundations, for example in the construction of piers for bridges, and may become part of the permanent structure.

caisson disease. *See* decompression sickness.

Caithness A former county of NE Scotland. Under local government reorganization in 1975 its boundaries were adjusted to form a district of the same name, in the Highlands Region.

cakewalk A ballroom dance popular in the early 1900s, originally performed by slaves satirizing the elegance of plantation society. Couples walked around in a square, being judged for the grace and inventiveness of their movements. The winners were awarded a cake, from which the expression "to take the cake" derives.

Calabar (former name: Old Calabar) 4 56N 8 22E A port in SE Nigeria. It was a center of the slave trade in the 18th and 19th centuries; exports now include palm oil, rubber, timber, and cocoa. Population (1975 est): 103,000.

calabash A tree, *Crescentia cujete*, 25–49 ft (7.5–15 m) tall, native to tropical America (particularly Brazil). Funnel-shaped flowers are borne on the old stems and produce gourdlike fruits, up to 20 in (50 cm) long. These fruits have woody outer layers and, after removal of the inner pulp, are used as pots, cooking utensils, etc. Family: *Bignoniaceae*.

Calabria A mountainous region occupying the southern "toe" of Italy. It is basically a poor agricultural region (producing olives, citrus fruits, vines, and cereals) with the lowest per capita income of any Italian region. Crotone is the main industrial center. Area: 5822 sq mi (15,080 sq km). Population (1980 est): 2,087,231. Capital: Catanzaro.

Calais 50 57N 1 52E A port in N France, in the Pas-de-Calais department. Its prosperity lies in being on the shortest sea route to England. It produces lace, tulle, and other textiles. *History*: besieged and captured by the English under Edward III in 1346, Calais remained in English hands until 1558. In World War II it was the target of savage bombardment and was heroically defended in support of the withdrawal from *Dunkirk. Population (1975): 79,369.

calamine An ore of zinc. In English usage it refers to zinc carbonate (smithsonite) and in the US it refers to zinc silicate (hemimorphite). A skin lotion of the same name contains zinc oxide.

Calamites An extinct genus of treelike pteridophyte plants, prominent during the Carboniferous period, 345–280 million years ago. Their fossilized remains form a major constituent of the Carboniferous coal seams (*see also* Lepidodendron). Class: *Sphenopsida* (*see* horsetails).

Calamity Jane (Martha Canary; c. 1852–1903) US frontierswoman, who featured in many stories and legends of the Wild West. She worked in frontier towns and camps, claimed to have been a Pony Express rider and US Army Scout, frequently dressed as a man, and was skilled in riding and shooting. She later appeared in wild west shows.

Calas, Jean (1698–1762) French Huguenot, who was accused of the murder of his son in 1761 in order to prevent his becoming a Roman Catholic. He protested his innocence but was tried and executed. His conviction was reversed after *Voltaire, at the request of his widow, led a campaign for religious toleration and legal reform and succeeded in having the trial reviewed.

Calceolaria A genus of perennial herbs and shrubs (300–400 species) native to temperate South America. The plants grow to a height of 12–28 in (30–70 cm) and bear brightly colored slipper-shaped flowers. Some species and hybrids are grown as ornamentals. Family: *Scrophulariaceae*.

Calchas A legendary Greek prophet who foretold the length of the *Trojan War and advised the Greeks to build the wooden horse by which they gained entry to Troy. He died after being defeated by Mopsus in a trial of prophecy.

calcite A common rock-forming mineral consisting of crystalline calcium carbonate. It is usually colorless or white. It occurs in igneous, metamorphic, and sedimentary rocks. Most *limestones consist largely of calcite, sometimes in the form of fossil shells, and calcite is a common cementing material in coarse-grained sedimentary rocks. Calcite is very soluble in slightly acidic water.

calcitonin A polypeptide hormone, secreted by the thyroid gland in mammals, that reduces the level of calcium in the blood when this rises above normal. A hormone from the *parathyroid gland raises blood calcium levels and therefore acts antagonistically.

calcium (Ca) A reactive metal, first isolated by Sir Humphry Davy in 1808. It occurs in nature as *limestone ($CaCO_3$), *fluorite (CaF_2), and *gypsum ($CaSO_4.2H_2O$) and is an essential constituent of shells, bones, and teeth. The element is extracted by electrolysis of the molten chloride ($CaCl_2$). It forms many compounds. These include quicklime (CaO), which has many industrial uses as a base in addition to its role in *cement, the nitrate ($Ca(NO_3)_2$), chloride ($CaCl_2$), and carbide (CaC_2), from which acetylene is produced by the addition of water. The metal itself is reactive. It is used to clear residual gases from vacuum systems and as a reducing agent in the production of thorium and uranium. At no 20; at wt 40.08; mp 839 ± 61°F (2°C); bp 2731°F (1484°C).

calculator Any device for carrying out mathematical functions ($+,-,\times,\div$). Originally mechanical, they were later electrically operated; purely electronic calculators, based on the digital *computer, have now largely replaced all earlier types. Electronic calculators use a silicon chip *integrated-circuit package, often smaller than a dime, that contains the equivalent of hundreds of *transistors built into complex logic circuits. These logic circuits perform the basic functions of addition and subtraction using binary arithmetic (*see* binary system). Multiplication and division are performed by repeated additions or subtractions. The high speed of a modern calculator enables the solution to a problem to appear on the digital display apparently instantaneously.

Many electronic calculators have more complex functions available (percentages, square roots, trigonometric functions, etc.) by pressing a single key and some provide a memory in which the intermediate results of a chain of calculations can be stored. Advanced types enable the user to program a sequence of functions for the calculator to perform automatically.

calculus The mathematical techniques, developed by *Newton and *Leibniz, that are based on the concept of infinitely small changes in continuously varying quantities. For example, calculus is used to define the velocity of a moving body as the rate of change of its position at any instant. Velocity (v) is said to be the derivative of position (x) with respect to time (t); in calculus it is written $v = dx/dt$. In this notation dt is a vanishingly small time interval and dx is the distance the body travels in this time. If x is a known function of t, values for v at any time can be obtained by calculating the derivative of (differentiating) this function with respect to time. Similarly, the derivative of the velocity (or the second derivative of position) at any instant gives its acceleration (a), i.e. $d^2x/dt^2 = dv/dt = a$. The simpler notation $x'' = v$ and $x''' = a$ is sometimes used.

The **differential calculus** is the system of rules for making such calculations. On a graph, the derivative of a function is the gradient of the curve at any point. A maximum or minimum value of the function can be found, as they occur when the gradient is zero. The **integral calculus** is concerned with the same process in reverse. If velocity is a continuously varying function of time, the change in position over a measurable time interval is calculated by summing the products of v and dt for each of the infinitely small intervals of time (dt) that make up the measurable interval. As with differential calculus, the extraction of integrals follows general rules, each type of mathematical function having a corresponding integral. The integral of v between time t_1 and t_2, written

$$\int_{t_1}^{t_2} v.dt,$$

gives the change in position in this interval. On a graph, the area between the curve of a function and the horizontal axis is the integral of the function over the specified time interval.

Equations that contain derivatives are called **differential equations**. They are solved by guessing at a general form of solution and trying it in the equation, using the rules of differential calcuius. For well-known differential equations, such as those that describe wave motion and the diffusion of gases, there are standard forms of solution.

1 *The derivative dx/dt at P gives the slope of the curve at P. When the function has a stationary (e.g. a maximumum as at A or a minimum as at B) value, $dx/dt = 0$.*

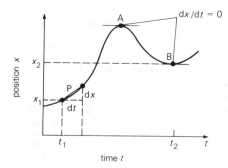

2 *The integral $\int_{t_1}^{t_2} v.dt (= x_2 - x_1)$ is the shaded area, i.e. it is the sum of all the areas $v.dt$ of the infinitely thin slices. The area between A and B is subtracted since v is negative.*

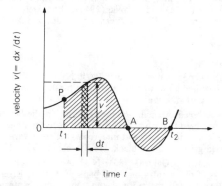

CALCULUS *The two basic techniques are (1) differentiation and (2) integration.*

Calcutta 22 35N 88 21E A city in India, the capital of West Bengal on the Hooghly River. It is a major industrial center and the most important seaport on the E coast of India. Jute manufacturing dominates the industrial sector, while engineering, cotton textiles, and chemicals are also important. A large section of the population is employed in small workshops and handicraft industries. Calcutta is the focal point of rail, road, and air routes and its port is a major outlet for iron, coal, manganese, and mica as well as the large exports of manufactured jute goods. The city itself is part of a conurbation that has a combined population of over seven million people, many of whom live in appalling conditions; less than one third of the conurbation is sewered, water supplies are inadequate, and many thousands of the inhabitants sleep on the streets. By way of contrast, the city center contains many imposing buildings, situated around Fort William (a British building dating from 1758). There are three universities, including Calcutta University (1857). *History*: founded in 1692 as a trading post for the British East India Company, it was the scene of much fighting (1756–57) between the British under Clive and the forces of Siraj-ud-Dawlah, Nawab of Bengal (*see* Black Hole of Calcutta). Population (1981 est): 9,165,650.

Calder, Alexander Stirling (1870–1945) US sculptor. His busts of John James *Audubon and William *Penn are in the Hall of Fame of Great Americans. He also sculpted fountains, sundials, and memorials. His son **Alexander Calder** (1898–1976) was also a sculptor. Trained as an engineer, Calder began his professional career as a commercial artist. During the 1920s he worked in Paris and became known for his unique moving sculptures, which were given the name "mobiles" by one of Calder's colleagues and admirers, the French artist Marcel *Duchamp. Calder's mobiles, consisting of flat metal disks suspended from wires, were influenced by the work of Joan *Miró and Piet *Mondrian. Calder later became famous for monumental free-standing constructions, which were named "stabiles" by another of his colleagues, Jean *Arp.

caldera. *See* volcano.

Calderón de la Barca, Pedro (1600–81) Spanish dramatist. He studied law and theology but rejected a career in the Church; in 1623 he began writing plays at the court of Philip IV. After the death of *Lope de Vega he became the leading Spanish dramatist. His many plays include *The Constant Prince* (1629), *Life Is a Dream* (1635), and *The Mayor of Zalamea* (1640). He was ordained priest in 1651, after which he wrote mainly masques and operas for the royal court and religious dramas.

Caldwell, Erskine (1903–) US novelist. After taking a wide variety of jobs he gained international fame with his novels *Tobacco Road* (1932) and *God's Little Acre* (1933). His social criticism, which in his fiction is blended with comedy and sex, is most forcefully expressed in his journalism, notably in *You Have Seen Their Faces* (1937) and *In Search of Bisco* (1965). His *Stories of Life/North and South* (1983) is a collection of short stories.

Caldwell, Sarah (1928–) US conductor and opera director. She began her career at the New England Opera Theater under Boris Goldovsky and at Tanglewood Music Festival under Serge Koussevitsky. Head of the Opera Workshop department at Boston University, she started to assemble the Opera Company of Boston in 1957. Her ability to search out and put together little-known operas and to bring out all phases of characterization earned her worldwide acclaim.

Caledonia The name given by ancient Roman writers to Scotland. Remote and rugged, Caledonia was scarcely known in antiquity. The Roman governor in Britain, Gneus Julius Agricola, in an exploratory expedition defeated the Caledonians in 83 AD near present-day Inverness, as did the emperor Lucius Septimius Severus in 209, but the clans and their chieftains remained independent until united under Kenneth I MacAlpine in the 9th century.

Caledonian Canal A system of lakes and canals in Scotland, linking the North Sea with the Irish Sea, via the Great Glen. Engineered by Thomas Telford, it was opened to navigation in 1822. Today it is used mainly by small craft. Length: about 60 mi (100 km).

Caledonian orogeny. *See* orogeny.

calendar Any of a variety of systems for the reckoning of time over an extended period. The period is divided into years containing a whole number of days, the days being grouped into months. Calendars are usually based on the earth's orbital period around the sun (a year), although in some systems the moon's orbital period around the earth (a month) is taken as the basis. Since the seasons recur after each tropical *year (which contains 365.2422 days), the length of the calendar year, averaged over many years, should correspond as closely as possible to that of the tropical year. This is achieved by using leap years, which contain one more day than the usual calendar year.

In 46 BC, Julius Caesar established the so-called **Julian calendar** in which a period of three years, each of 365 days, was followed by a leap year of 366 days. The average length of the year was therefore 365.25 days. Since this was over 11 minutes longer than the tropical year, an extra day appeared about every 128 years. This discrepancy was amended by the **Gregorian calendar**, which was introduced in Roman Catholic countries in 1582 by Pope Gregory XIII, was made law in Britain and its colonies in 1752, and is now in almost worldwide use. Leap years are restricted to century years divisible by 400 (e.g. 1600 and 2000) and any other year divisible by four. This reduces the average length of the calendar year to a much more acceptable 365.2425 days. *See also* French Republican calendar.

Calgary 51 05N 114 05W A city in W Canada, in Alberta. It developed with the arrival of the railroad (1884) and local oil discoveries, becoming the center of Canada's petroleum industry. Calgary is the distribution and farming center of S Alberta and is the site of the University of Calgary (1945). The Calgary Stampede, a famous rodeo, is celebrated annually. Population (1976): 469,917.

Calhoun, John C (aldwell) (1782–1850) US statesman; vice president (1825–32), a champion of the southern states and a defender of slavery. A South Carolinian, he was a member of the House (1811–17) and then secretary of war (1817–25) before becoming vice president. Resigning as Andrew Jackson's vice president (1832), he immediately entered the Senate, where he stayed, except while secretary of state (1844–45), until his death. His famous Nullification theory claimed the rights of states to nullify congressional laws that they considered unconstitutional. He encouraged the annexation of Texas to provide another slaveholding state and to strengthen the power of the South.

Cali 3 24N 76 30W The third largest city in Colombia. It is the industrial and commercial center for a rich agricultural area producing coffee, sugar, and cotton. Its university was founded in 1945. Population (1978 est): 1,255,198.

calico A simple woven cotton fabric that originated as a printed fabric from Calicut, India. Strong and serviceable with a wide range of textures, it is used mainly for dresses and domestic purposes. British calico is now usually bleached or plain white; US calico is generally printed.

Calicut. *See* Kozhikode.

California The third largest state in the US, on the W coast. California is bounded by Oregon on the N, Nevada and Arizona (whose border with California is formed by the Colorado River) on the E. Mexico lies to the S and the Pacific Ocean to the W. It consists of a narrow coastal plain rising to the Coast Range, with the fertile central valleys of the Sacramento and San Joaquin Rivers, deserts in the S, and the Sierra Nevada in the E. The Sierra Nevada contain Kings Canyon, Sequoia and Yosemite national parks, and Mt Whitney, the highest point in the state. The giant redwood is native to California. The state's spectacular scenery and favorable climate contribute to its popularity as a tourist attraction. The San Andreas Fault, extending through two thirds of the state, has caused numerous tremors and serious earthquakes throughout the coastal area. It is the most populous state in the US and the predominantly urban population is concentrated along the coast. It is the most prosperous state and has a varied economy. Oil is exploited along with natural gas, cement, sand and gravel, and borate. Aircraft and ship construction are important industries, as well as general construction and food processing; wine production is especially important. Employment is also provided by the many military bases and the film industry. Tourism is important in the many national parks throughout the state. California's agriculture is famous and the state produces grapes, tomatoes, cotton, sugar beet, strawberries, citrus fruits, hay, beef cattle, and turkeys. The state has a large number of cultural and educational institutions, many supported by public finance like the University of California. *History*: first discovered by Spain (1542), it became part of New Spain and was gradually settled by the Spanish and Mexicans from present-day Mexico. The Spanish established many missions, including that founded (1776) by Father Junipero Serras, a Franciscan missionary, on the present site of San Francisco. American settlers began to move westward to California in the 1840s. California remained under Spanish, and then Mexican, rule after Mexico achieved independence from Spain. Two presidents, Andrew Jackson and Alexander Polk, unsuccessfully attempted to purchase California from Mexico. In 1846 a group of Californians under the flag of the Republic of California declared themselves independent. In the meantime, Polk had set out to annex California forcibly. In the resulting conflict, the Mexican War, the US won California (1848). In the same year gold was discovered, leading to a rapid increase in the number of immigrants. The Transcontinental Railroad (completed 1869) linked the state with the East. Industry grew rapidly during World War II, and California has now become the country's center for defense-related industries. A large portion of high-technology computer firms are located in "Silicon Valley." In 1978 Californians, leading what became known as the "tax revolt," brought Proposition 13 to the voters. Its passage resulted in a 57 percent cut in property taxes and a $7 billion loss in revenues for the state. Area: 158,693 sq mi (411,013 sq km). Population (1980): 23,668,562. Capital: Sacramento.

California, Gulf of An inlet of the Pacific Ocean, in Mexico between the state of Sonora and the peninsula of Lower California. Length: 760 mi (1223 km).

California, University of US university, founded in 1868. Nine campuses, each with its own chancellor, are overseen by a president and board of regents. The campuses are at Berkeley (1873), San Francisco (1873), Davis (1905), Riverside (1907), Los Angeles (1919), Santa Barbara (1944), San Diego (1912), Irvine (1965), and Santa Cruz (1965).

californium (Cf) A synthetic transuranic element first isolated in 1950. Californium-252 is an intense neutron emitter. It is used as a neutron source in instruments for determining moisture contents and discovering precious metals. At no 98; at wt (251).

Caligula (Gaius Caesar; 12–41 AD) Roman emperor (37–41), son of Germanicus Caesar and Agrippina the Elder. Succeeding Tiberius, he initially enjoyed great popularity but his subsequent tyrannical and extravagant behavior brought allegations of madness, from both contemporaries and historians, and he was assassinated.

caliph The title borne by the leaders of Islam. The first caliph was *Abu Bakr, who succeeded Mohammed in 632. The *Umayyads ruled from 661 to 750 and were overthrown by the *Abbasids, who ruled in Baghdad until 1258 and then in Egypt, until ousted by the Ottomans in 1517. The title was then borne by the Ottoman sultans until 1922 and was abolished in 1924. Rival Muslim dynasties, such as the Egyptian *Fatimids (909–1171), also claimed the title.

calisaya. *See* Cinchona.

calisthenics. *See* gymnastics.

calla. *See* arum.

Callaghan, (Leonard) James (1912–) British statesman; Labour prime minister (1976–79). Entering parliament in 1945, he was chancellor of the exchequer (1964–67), home secretary (1967–70), and foreign secretary (1974–76). He became prime minister when Harold *Wilson resigned and was defeated in the 1979 election by Margaret *Thatcher, but remained leader of the Labour Party, until 1980.

Callao 12 05S 77 08W A major port in W Peru, on the Pacific Ocean. It was the site of the first railroad in South America (1851) connecting Callao with Lima. Chief exports include minerals, metals, and fishmeal. Population (1972): 296,721.

Callas, Maria (Maria Anna Kalageropoulos; 1923–77) US-born soprano of Greek parentage. She possessed a brilliant coloratura voice and fine acting ability. From 1950 she was prima donna of La Scala, Milan, where she was famous for her interpretations of Bellini, Donizetti, Verdi, and Puccini.

Calles, Plutarco Elías (1877–1945) Mexican soldier in the post-1910 revolutionary movement and statesman. As president (1924–28) his anticlerical policies caused the rebellion of the Church's supporters (the *cristeros*) and his attempts to control oil rights brought conflict with the US. He wielded dictatorial power from 1928 to 1934, when he was succeeded by Lázaro *Cárdenas, who forced Calles into exile in 1936.

Callias (5th century BC) Athenian diplomat. He may have negotiated the so-called peace of Callias with Persia (c. 450), which established Persian and Athenian spheres of influence. He probably also helped negotiate the Thirty Years' Peace with Sparta (c. 446).

Callicrates (5th century BC) Athenian architect, chiefly famous for his collaboration with *Ictinus over the design of the *Parthenon. The temple of Athena Nike (450 BC) on the Athenian Acropolis was also his work.

calligraphy The art of handwriting. The term derives from the Greek words meaning beautiful writing. The aim of the calligrapher is to produce a script of intrinsic beauty appropriate to the subject matter, using the type of paper, ink, and writing instrument most suited to his purpose. In Europe, monks practiced calligraphy from the 6th century, at first using Roman capital letters called majuscules, but scripts using *minuscules were soon developed. From these arose the beautiful *italic and 19th-century copperplate scripts suitable for formal and commercial documents. In China, Japan, and Islamic countries calligraphy has a long history as a pure art form in which the artist combines the medium, the sentiment, and the format into an artistic composition.

Callimachus (c. 305–c. 240 BC) Greek poet and scholar. His many works, of which only fragments remain, include a catalogue of the Library of Alexandria, some fine epigrams, of which 64 survive in the *Greek Anthology*, and the *Aetia*.

Callimachus (late 5th century BC) Greek sculptor, reputedly the inventor of the Corinthian *capital and an innovator in the use of the drill in sculpture. Little is known of his work, but ancient critics accused him of overelaboration.

Calliope In Greek legend, goddess of epic poetry and the chief of the nine *Muses. She was loved by Apollo; her children included Hymen, Ialemus, and *Orpheus the musician.

Callot, Jacques (c. 1592–1635) French graphic artist, born in Nancy. In Italy (c. 1609–21) he worked for the Medici, principally on etchings of pageants. After returning to Nancy he made many etchings of beggars, hunchbacks, etc., which show his gift for caricature, but his best work is the *Miseries of War* series (1632–33) evoked by the Thirty Years' War.

callus A region of thickened hardened skin produced by constant friction or pressure. Skin calluses occur most commonly on the palms of the hands and soles of the feet. A bone callus is the mass of tissue that forms around the broken ends of a fractured bone, enabling normal healing and union. A similar tissue is produced by plants at the site of an injury.

Calmette, Albert Léon Charles (1863–1933) French bacteriologist. A pupil of Louis *Pasteur, he developed the vaccine Bacillus Calmette-Guérin (*see* BCG vaccine) in conjunction with Camille Guérin. He founded the Pasteur Institute at Lille, France (1896).

calomel. *See* laxatives.

calorie A unit of heat now being replaced by the joule. Formerly defined as the amount of heat required to raise the temperature of 1 gram of water through 1°C, the calorie is now defined as 4.1868 joules. The kilocalorie or Calorie (with a capital "C") is equal to 1000 calories and was formerly used to express the energy value of foods.

Caltanissetta 37 29N 14 04E A city in Italy, in Sicily. It has a 17th-century cathedral. It has an important sulfur industry. Population (1971): 60,072.

Calvary A hill beyond the walls of Jerusalem where Christ was crucified. The Hebrew name is Golgotha (a skull). Its precise location is unknown. Traditionally it has been taken as the spot, now within the Church of the Holy Sepulcher, where St Helena discovered a supposed relic of the Cross in 327 AD. Some have suggested that it was outside Jerusalem's Damascus Gate.

Calvin, John (1509–64) French Protestant reformer, founder of *Calvinism. He studied law and theology and in the early 1530s openly sided with Protestantism. Settling in Basle in 1536, he published the first edition of his influential *Institutes*. During a visit to Geneva in 1536 he met the Protestant reformer Guillaume *Farel, who persuaded him to stay. Their efforts to organize the Reformation in the city resulted in their exile (1538). Calvin then preached in Strasbourg, where he met other reformers, notably *Bucer. He was invited back to Geneva in 1541, remaining there as its virtual dictator until his death. He sought to shape Geneva as a model community where every citizen came under the legal discipline of the Church.

Calvin, Melvin (1911–) US biochemist, who determined the series of reactions by which green plants use carbon dioxide to manufacture starch during *photosynthesis. Calvin was awarded a Nobel Prize in 1961.

Calvinism The Christian teaching of John *Calvin, much of it published in his work *The Institutes*. On it are based the doctrines of most of the reformed Churches that are not Lutheran, including the state Churches of Holland and Scotland (*see* Presbyterianism), various Nonconformist Churches, and some Churches in North America and Germany. Calvin's systematic writings stress the transcendent power of God and man's total depravity outside God's redeeming grace. Like Luther, Calvin believed that faith must be based on Scripture alone, that justification (that is, righteousness in God's eyes) could only be achieved through faith, and that men lacked free will. Unlike Luther, he believed that some people, the elect, were predestined for salvation and the rest for damnation and also that the church should control the state.

calx. *See* phlogiston theory.

calypso A type of popular song that originated in Trinidad. The text, often containing nonsense syllables, is sung rapidly and without regard for natural word stress. Accompanied by guitars and percussion, the calypso usually satirizes local events. Calypso melodies have been popularized by steel bands playing on tuned oil drums.

calypso orchid A rare and highly prized perennial orchid, *Calypso bulbosa*, also known as the fairy slipper orchid, native to cold N temperate regions. 3–4 in (8–10 cm) high, it has a solitary pink flower with brown, purple, and yellow markings and a single crinkled dark-green leaf.

Camagüey 21 25N 77 55W A city in E central Cuba. Founded in the 16th century, it has many old buildings, including the cathedral (1617). It is the center of an area important for cattle raising and sugar. Population (1981): 480,620.

Camargue, la   The Rhône delta area in S France, between the river channels of the Grand Rhône and the Petit Rhône. Once chiefly marshy, much land reclamation has occurred and cattle, especially bulls for the bullring, and horses are reared. Rice is also grown here. Area: about 215 sq mi (560 sq km).

Cambacérès, Jean Jacques Régis, Duc de   (1753–1824) French lawyer. During the French Revolution he was a member of the National Convention and then of the Committee of Public Safety. Under Napoleon, he served as arch chancellor of the empire. His chief interest was in the development of principles of revolutionary jurisprudence and he contributed to the *Code Napoléon.*

Camberwell beauty   A *nymphalid butterfly, *Nymphalis antiopa*, occurring in temperate Eurasia and in North America, where it is called mourning cloak because of its somber coloration: purple wings with cream edges. The adults hibernate and the caterpillars feed on various trees.

cambium   A layer of cells in woody plants that is responsible for producing additional *xylem and *phloem tissue, bringing about an increase in girth. The cambium also produces bark and protective callus tissue after injury. *See also* meristem.

Cambodia   (officially: Democratic Kampuchea)   A country in SE Asia, in the Indochina peninsula on the Gulf of Thailand. It consists mainly of an alluvial plain drained by the Mekong River and enclosed by mountains. Most of the inhabitants are Khmers, with small minorities of Vietnamese and Chinese. *Economy:* predominantly agricultural, the staple crop being rice. Production has been severely reduced by the recent political upheavals and there is little industry. Kampuchea is rich in forests, and phosphates, gemstones, and gold are produced: there are also known quantities of unexploited iron ore and manganese. There is an abundance of freshwater fish. Exports include rubber and dried fish. *History:* the kingdom of Funan (1st–6th centuries AD) was conquered by the Buddhist *Khmers. Following the collapse of their empire in the 15th century, Cambodia was prey to attack from the Thais and Vietnamese until 1863, when it became a French protectorate. In 1887 it became part of the Union of *Indochina. In 1949 it achieved self-government as a member of the French Union, gaining full independence in 1953. Under Prince *Sihanouk Cambodia was used as a base by North Vietnamese (communist) forces (*see* Vietnam War) and, following the failure of his attempts to negotiate their withdrawal, he was deposed (1970) by General Lon Nol, who was supported by the US. Shortly afterward US and South Vietnamese troops invaded the renamed Khmer Republic to support Lon Nol against the communist Khmer Rouge guerrillas. In the ensuing civil war the Khmer Rouge was finally victorious in 1974 and, after the formation of a new constitution in 1975, the Khmer Republic became Democratic Kampuchea. The Khmer Rouge government, led by Pol Pot, attempted to reshape the country's economy on cooperative lines by driving the Kampucheans out of the towns, depriving them of their property, and killing some three million of the aged, sick, or dissenting. Although Pol Pot's regime maintained an uneasy relationship with the Chinese, China failed to come to its aid when the Vietnamese invaded the country on December 25, 1978. Pol Pot was overthrown and a People's Revolutionary Council was set up under the pro-Vietnamese Heng Samrin. The retreating Khmer Rouge burned existing rice stocks and devastated the land leaving behind them a trail of famine and disease, which has only partly been mitigated by the efforts of international charities. Samrin was succeeded as leader by Pen Sovran. Border warfare with Vietnamese guerrillas was followed by a Vietnamese invasion in 1979. A rebel communist government backed by Hanoi was set up in opposition to Pol Pot, and Cambodia was named the People's Republic of Kampuchea. Guerrilla attacks by the Khmer Rouge and other Cambodian resistance groups (both communist and anti-communist) sought to unseat the Hanoi government. Soviet military backing sustains the Vietnamese regime in Phnom Penh, the capital, whereas China supports the Cambodian resistance. In 1982 a coalition government-in-exile was formed by Sihanouk (president), Khieu Samphan, and Son Sann, former premier. Official language: Khmer; French is widely spoken. Official currency: riel of 100 sen. Area: 71,000 sq mi (181,000 sq km). Population (1983 est): 5,996,000. Capital and main port: Phnom Penh.

Cambrai   (ancient name: Camaracum)   50 10N 3 14E A city in NE France, in the Nord department. Industries include textiles (cambric was first made here in the 16th century) and sugar refining. The town suffered damage in both World Wars. Population (1975): 41,109.

Cambrian Mountains   A mountain system in Wales, extending N–S and including Snowdonia, Plynlimon, and the Black Mountains.

Cambrian period   The earliest geological period of the *Paleozoic era. It began about 590 million years ago and lasted at least 70 million years, lying between the Precambrian and Ordovician periods. Rocks of this period are the first to contain an abundance of fossils, including primitive representatives of most invertebrates living today. Trilobites were very abundant, as well as brachiopods and gastropods. The Cambrian period is divided into Lower, Middle, and Upper.

Cambridge   52 12N 0 07E A city in E England, the administrative center of Cambridgeshire on the River Cam (*or* Granta). The city is dominated by its university (*see* Cambridge, University of). Cambridge has electronics and printing industries and manufactures scientific instruments. It is also an important market center. Its many historic university buildings and Bridge of Sighs make it a popular tourist center. Population (1981): 90,440.

Cambridge   42 22N 71 06W A city in Massachusetts, on the Charles River opposite Boston. A famous educational center, it is the site of Harvard University (1636) and the Massachusetts Institute of Technology (MIT). The first printing press in America was set up here (1639) and at the start of the American Revolution, George Washington established his headquarters (1775–76) in Craigie House, later the home of Longfellow. Industries include printing and publishing. Population (1980): 95,322.

Cambridge, University of   One of the oldest universities in Europe. It is organized as a federation of colleges, the oldest of which, Peterhouse, dates from 1284. Kings College was founded in 1441 and its chapel is a distinctive landmark. The largest college, Trinity, was founded by Henry VIII in 1546. The first college for women, Girton, opened in 1869 (although it was not initially located at Cambridge).

Cambridge Platonists   A group of 17th-century English philosophers and theologians under the leadership of Benjamin Whichcote (1609–83). Philosophically they took their ideas from *Platonism and *Neoplatonism and opposed the rationalism of *Hobbes. In religion they favored mysticism and religious tolerance and attempted to reconcile Christianity with the new ideas being produced by the rapid scientific advances made in their time. They believed in an absolute standard of morality based on reason that is independent of the divine will of God.

Cambridgeshire   A county of E England. It consists chiefly of low-lying fenland, crossed by the Ouse and Nene Rivers. It is predominantly agricultural, the main products being cereals, fruit, and vegetables. Area: 1316 sq mi (3409 sq km). Population (1981): 575,177. Administrative center: Cambridge.

Cambyzes II   King of Persia (529–522 BC) of the Achemenian dynasty; the son of *Cyrus the Great. He conquered Egypt (525), where, according to the Greek historian Herodotus, his tyrannical disrespect for native religion caused resentment. He campaigned unsuccessfully against Carthage and Ethiopia. Cambyzes died, perhaps a suicide, during a revolt against his rule.

Camden   39 52N 75 07W A city in New Jersey on the Delaware River. The former home of Walt Whitman, it manufactures textiles and radio and television appliances. Population (1980): 84,910.

Camden, Battle of   (August 16, 1780) A battle of the *American Revolution. In an attempt to take the British stronghold at Camden, South Carolina, after the fall of *Charleston, the Americans were surprised and routed by Lord *Cornwallis. The Americans retreated in disorder.

camel   A hoofed ☐mammal belonging to the genus *Camelus* (2 species). Camels are now almost entirely domesticated and are used for riding, as pack animals, and as a source of milk, meat, wool, and hides. The one-humped Arabian camel (*C. dromedarius*) is about 7 ft (2 m) high at the shoulder and generally brown in color. The dromedary is a long-legged breed of Arabian camel, developed for racing and riding. The heavier two-humped Bactrian camel (*C. bactrianus*) is native to central Asian steppes, where wild herds still exist.

Adapted to living in sandy deserts, camels can close their nostrils, have heavy protective eyelashes, hairy ear openings, and horny knee pads for kneeling. Although unable to store water, camels can replace rapidly the water that is lost from the body, drinking up to 54 qts (60 l) of water at a time. Fat is stored in the hump, which shrinks when food is scarce. Family: *Camelidae*; order: *Artiodactyla*.

Camellia   A genus of evergreen shrubs and trees (80–100 species) native to India, China, and Japan. Several species are widely grown as ornamentals. The best known, *C. japonica*, grows to a height of 30 ft (9 m) and has attractive glossy oval leaves. The popular double-flowered varieties have overlapping petals ranging from white to pink and red. The genus also includes the *tea plant. Family: *Theaceae*.

CAMELOT *A 19th-century romantic rendering of Arthur's capital by Gustave Doré in his illustrations of Tennyson's* Idylls.

Camelot The legendary capital of King Arthur's kingdom (*see* Arthurian legend). Cadbury Camp, near Yeovil, and Winchester are among the places identified with it.

Camembert 48 52N 0 10E A village in NW France, in the Orme department. Camembert is famous for the creamy cheese named for it.

cameo A semiprecious stone ornamented with a portrait or figures carved in relief. Cameo makers achieved brilliant skills during the Renaissance, when collectors paid high prices for modern gems, as well as for the earliest Hellenistic and Roman examples.

camera, photographic A device for producing a photographic image. Basically, a camera consists of a light-tight box containing a lens and light-sensitive *film or plate. The light image coming through the lens is brought into focus on the film by adjusting the distance between the film and the lens. A picture is taken by opening the shutter over the lens for a certain period to expose the film. The exposure time is determined by the shutter speed. The diameter of the opening (aperture) in front of the lens is measured by its *f-number. Shutter speed and lens aperture determine the light available to record the image on the film. In the simplest cameras they are fixed, but more sophisticated cameras have variable settings. Sometimes the aperture or the shutter speed can be controlled automatically by an *exposure meter. *See also* cinematography.

camera, television A camera for the instantaneous transmission of moving pictures. The scene to be televised is focused onto a screen in the electronic camera tube. This optical image is scanned in horizontal lines, fast enough to appear as a continuous moving picture to the human eye; in most cameras, the image is scanned 25 to 30 times per second. The intensity of light at each point of the image is converted to an electrical signal, which is amplified before being transmitted together with the sound and synchronization signals. *See also* television.

Cameron, Julia Margaret (1815–79) British photographer, born in Calcutta. In England, she devoted herself chiefly to spiritually penetrating portrait photographs, notably of her friends Tennyson, Longfellow, Charles Darwin, and Ellen Terry. She died in Ceylon.

Cameroon, United Republic of (French name: République Unie du Cameroun) A country in West Africa, on the Gulf of Guinea. Hot swampy coastal plains rise to forested plateaus in the center and to the Adamwa Highlands in the N. The main river is the Sanaga. The population consists of over a hundred different ethnic groups, the most numerous being the Bamileke. *Economy*: chiefly subsistence agriculture with varied crops; the main cash crop is coffee. Hydroelectricity is a valuable source of power and is used for aluminum smelting, which is the chief industry. Oil was discovered in 1973 and is responsible for half of the country's revenue. *History*: the area was largely uninhabited when the coast was explored by the Portuguese and others in the 15th and 16th centuries. In 1884 the German protectorate of Kamerun was established and after World War I it was divided into the French and British Cameroons, which were governed from 1922 under League of Nations mandate and from 1946 as UN trust territories. The French Cameroons attained self-government in 1957 and became independent as the Federal Republic of the Cameroon in 1960 with Ahmadou Ahidjo as its first president (1960–82). After a plebiscite in the British Cameroons in 1961, the S joined Cameroon and the N became part of Nigeria. The country is now governed on a one-party basis by the Cameroon National Union. Political and economic stability for the most part characterized the country into the mid 1980s. President: Paul Biya (1933–). Official languages: French and English. Official currency: CFA (Communauté financière africaine) franc of 100 centimes. Area: 183,530 sq mi (475,442 sq km). Population (1983 est): 9,251,000. Capital: Yaoundé. Main port: Doula.

Camisards Protestants in the Bas-Languedoc and Cévennes regions of S France who in 1702 rebelled against the persecution of Protestants by Louis XIV. They sacked and burned churches and killed or expelled priests. The government responded with executions and the burning of villages. By 1705 the revolt was virtually over, although sporadic fighting continued until 1710.

Camões, Luís de (c. 1524–80) Portuguese poet and soldier of fortune. Few biographical facts about him are certain. After 1553 he spent 17 years wandering in the Portuguese colonies in India and China, suffering shipwreck and returning destitute to Lisbon. In 1572 he published *The Lusiads*, a national epic celebrating the 1497 voyage of Vasco da Gama and the Portuguese empire. His lyrical poetry, largely ignored in his own lifetime and published posthumously in 1595, is now greatly admired.

camomile (*or* chamomile) A perennial scented European herb, *Anthemis nobilis* (or *Chamemelum nobile*). The spreading much-branched stems (4–12 in [10–30 cm] in length) carry long-stalked daisy-like flowers. An infusion of the flowers (camomile tea) is used as a general tonic. Family: *Compositae* (daisy family).

Camorra A criminal secret society, at its height in 19th-century Naples. The Bourbon kings used its members in the police, army, and civil service but after Naples became part of a united Italy (1861) the society was suppressed and eventually many of its members fled to the US, where they were ultimately absorbed by the *Mafia.

Campagna di Roma A plain in W central Italy, surrounding Rome. Well populated and fertile during classical times, it subsequently deteriorated into malarial marshes. Recently drained, it now produces fruit and vegetables for Rome. Area: about 800 sq mi (2000 sq km).

Campanella, Roy (1921–) US baseball catcher. He played for the Brooklyn Dodgers (1948–57) and was voted most valuable player (MVP) in the National League three times (1951, 1953, 1955). An automobile accident (1958) left him paralyzed. He was inducted into the Baseball Hall of Fame in 1969.

Campanella, Tommaso (1568–1639) Italian philosopher and Dominican friar. He opposed *Aristotelianism, believing that the foundations of philosophy should be empirical. From 1599 to 1629 he was imprisoned by the Spaniards ostensibly for political reasons but probably because of his religious heterodoxy. After 1634 he lived under *Richelieu's protection in Paris. His *City of the Sun* (1623) describes a Platonic-Christian utopia (*see* utopianism).

Campania A region in S Italy. It consists of a coastal plain along the Tyrrhenian Sea and mountains in the interior and the Sorrento Peninsula. Although most of the population is urban, centered mainly around Naples, agriculture is important. The region produces fruits, vegetables, vines, olives, walnuts, tobacco, and hemp. An industrial belt stretches from Caserta along the Bay of Naples. There are many modern coastal resorts. Area: 5249 sq mi (13,595 sq km). Population (1980 est): 5,491,658. Capital: Naples.

Campanula A genus of annual and perennial herbaceous plants (about 300 species), often known as bellflowers, native to N temperate zones (particularly the Mediterranean region) and tropical mountains. The plants grow to a height of 6–48 in (15–120 cm) and bear spikes of blue, pink, or white bell-shaped flowers. The fruit is a capsule. Some species (including *Canterbury bell) are grown as ornamentals. Family: *Campanulaceae*.

Campbell, Sir Malcolm (1885–1949) British automobile engineer, who broke the land-speed record nine times between 1924 and 1935 and the water-speed record three times between 1937 and 1939. He was the first man to exceed 300 mph (483 km per hour; 1935). His son **Donald Malcolm Campbell** (1921–67) also set land- and water-speed records, including 403.1 mph (648.7 kph) for a wheel-driven car (1964). He was killed in an attempt to break his own water-speed record.

Campbell, Mrs Patrick (Beatrice Stella Tanner; 1865–1940) British actress. Her stage career included notable successes in plays by Shakespeare and Ibsen. She was famous for her wit as well as her passionate acting and created the role of Eliza Doolittle in *Pygmalion*, written by her friend George Bernard Shaw.

Campbell-Bannerman, Sir Henry (1836–1908) British statesman; Liberal prime minister (1905–08), whose personal popularity held together a cabinet of great talent, including *Lloyd George, *Asquith, *Churchill, and *Haldane. Campbell-Bannerman's government passed the Trades Disputes Act (1906), which gave trades unionists greater freedom to strike.

Camp David The retreat in the Appalachian Mountains, Maryland, of the president of the US. It was here that Anwar Sadat and Menachem Begin agreed in September, 1978, to a framework for establishing peace in the Middle East. This agreement, mediated by President Jimmy Carter, laid the foundations for the peace treaty between Israel and Egypt signed in March, 1979.

Campeche 19 50N 90 30W A port in SE Mexico, on the Gulf of Mexico. Founded in 1540, its importance as a port has declined since Spanish occupation and the shallow waters hinder further development. The chief exports include timber, fish, and sugar cane and it has a university (1954). Population (1978 est): 103,613.

Camperdown A village in the NW Netherlands, in North Holland province, on the North Sea. The British defeated the Dutch in a naval battle off the coast here (1797).

camphor ($C_{10}H_{16}O$) A colorless crystalline *ketone. It is obtained from the wood of the camphor tree and also made synthetically; it is used in the manufacture of celluloid and as an insect repellent.

camphor tree A tree, *Cinnamomum camphora*, native to China, Japan, and Formosa. It is cultivated for the *camphor that can be distilled from its wood and young shoots. Family: *Lauraceae*.

Campi, Giulio (1502–72) Italian Renaissance architect and the founder of the Cremonese school of painting, which was influenced by such painters as Titian and Correggio. His followers included his brothers **Vincenzo Campi** (1539–91) and **Antonio Campi** (1536–c. 1591).

Campina Grande 7 15S 35 53W A city in NE Brazil, in Paraíba state. It is an important commercial and industrial center and has a university (1966). Population (1975 est): 236,443.

Campinas 22 54S 47 06W A city in S Brazil, in São Paulo state. It is a trading center for coffee and serves an extensive agricultural area. Population (1980 est): 566,517.

campion An annual or perennial flowering plant of the genus *Silene*. Campions are native to N temperate (particularly the Mediterranean) and cold regions, grow to a height of 12–40 in (30–100 cm), and bear pink, red, or white flowers. The fruit is a capsule. Species include moss campion (*S. acaulis*) and bladder campion (*S. vulgaris*). Family: *Caryophyllaceae*.

Campion, Edmund (1540–81) English Jesuit martyr. Ordained an Anglican deacon, but uneasy about his commitment, he was received into the Roman Catholic Church (1571), and became a Jesuit. After distributing copies of an anti-Anglican pamphlet in Oxford in 1581, he was convicted of treason and hanged, refusing to deny his faith. He was beatified in 1886. Feast Day: Dec 1.

Campo Formio, Treaty of (1797) The settlement between France and Austria signed at present-day Campoformido, NE Italy, following Austria's defeat by Napoleon during his first Italian campaign. Austria gained Venice, thus ending Venetian independence, and ceded its Belgian provinces to France.

Campo Grande 20 24S 54 35W A city in SW Brazil, the capital of Mato Grosso do Sul state situated on the São Paulo-Corumbá railroad. Its university was founded in 1970. Population (1975 est): 180,361.

Campos 21 40S 41 21W A city in E Brazil, in Rio de Janeiro state. The chief products are cacao, sugar cane, and *aguardiente* (a form of brandy). Population (1975 est): 336,996.

Cam Ranh Bay 11 53N 109 10E An inlet of the South China Sea, on the coast of central S Vietnam. About 12 mi (20 km) wide and almost enclosed by two peninsulas, it makes an excellent harbor: the bay and the northern peninsula were used as a vast US military, naval, and air base during the Vietnam War.

camshaft A rotating shaft equipped with a series of eccentric circular or pear-shaped disks (cams). These enable irregular or intermittent motion to be transferred to "followers" set perpendicularly to the camshaft, which move up and down as the cams rotate. Camshafts thus convert rotary motion into reciprocating motion and are used to control the valves in a four-stroke *internal-combustion engine. An **overhead camshaft** is set in the cylinder head and operates the valves directly, but in many engines the camshaft is at the base of the engine and operates the valves through pushrods.

Camus, Albert (1913–60) French novelist, an exponent of *existentialism. Born in poverty in Algiers, he won a school scholarship and studied philosophy as a university undergraduate. During World War II he edited *Combat*, a journal of the French Resistance. He published several collections of essays and plays, and three novels, notably *The Outsider* (1942), *The Plague* (1947), and *The Rebel* (1953); *The Rebel* provoked a fierce intellectual controversy with Jean-Paul *Sartre. In 1957 he won the Nobel Prize. He was killed in a car accident.

Canaan An area roughly corresponding to modern Israel, W Jordan, and S Syria, known from the Bible as the land promised by God to the Israelites before the Exodus. As early as the 18th century BC Canaan was mentioned in a document from *Mari as a political entity, probably comprising loosely allied city states. Excavations at *Jericho, Hazor, and elsewhere have revealed sophisticated Bronze Age cultures prior to the Hebrew settlement (c. 1200 BC).

Canada, Dominion of A country occupying the entire northern half of the North American continent (except for Alaska). More than half of Canada consists of the Canadian Shield, at the center of which lies the Hudson Bay lowlands. The Western Cordillera, which is partly made up of the Coast Mountains and the Rocky Mountains, runs parallel to the Pacific coast and contains Mount *Logan, Canada's highest peak. Between the Rocky Mountains and the Canadian Shield lie the Interior Lowlands (consisting of prairies, plains, and the Mackenzie Lowlands). The SE region of Canada is dominated by the St Lawrence River and the *Great Lakes and is the most densely populated area in the country. The N end of the Appalachian Mountains lies in the extreme SE. The N Arctic region of lakes and islands is one of the world's least populated areas. The population is mainly of British and French descent but there are several substantial minorities, including Germans, Italians, Ukrainians, and Dutch as well as the original inhabitants, the Indians and Inuit. *Economy*: both agriculture and industry are highly developed and the numerous manufacturing industries (concentrated mainly in Ontario and Quebec) include paper, iron and steel, motor vehicles, and food processing. As well as iron ore, the rich mineral resources include asbestos, nickel, zinc, molybdenum, uranium, silver, and gold. Oil production has increased considerably since the discovery of large oilfields in Alberta and an extensive pipeline system includes the Interprovincial Pipeline from Edmonton (Alberta) to Montreal (Quebec) and the Trans-Mountain pipeline from Edmonton to Vancouver. Natural gas is also produced and the Trans-Canada pipeline from the prairies to Montreal is the longest in the world. Agriculture, most of it highly mechanized, is important, with cereals in the Prairie Provinces and considerable fruit growing in British Columbia and Ontario. There is a valuable fishing industry; salmon, lobster, and cod are the most important catches. Forests cover over a third of the land and forestry has long been important to Canada's economy. The other traditional industry, the fur trade, continues, especially with mink farms and the trapping of beaver in the wild. Tourism is an important source of revenue, the majority of visitors coming from the US, with whom Canada has very close links. Almost two thirds of its trade is with the US. Main exports include motor vehicles, oil, wheat, wood pulp, and paper. *History*: there is evidence of Viking settlement in the NE of Canada around 1000 AD. In 1497 John Cabot reached the coasts of Newfoundland and Nova Scotia, the first of which was claimed for England in 1583. In 1534 Jacques Cartier explored the Gulf of St Lawrence. In 1605 the French established Port Royal in *Acadia and in 1608 Quebec. Known as New France, the latter settlement became a royal province in 1663. In the course of early explorations Champlain supported the *Huron Indians in their alliance with the northern tribes against the *Iroquois and later in the 17th century, when the Iroquois defeated the Huron, the French colony was almost completely destroyed. The fur trade was of extreme importance to all settlers and in 1670 the English set up the Hudson's Bay Company. By 1696 the French and English were in open conflict: in 1713 the Treaty of Utrecht gave Acadia, Newfoundland, and Hudson Bay to Britain and after the Seven Years' War, during which General Wolfe defeated the French under General Montcalm (1759), Canada was ceded to Britain by the Treaty of Paris (1763). In the late 18th century the United Empire Loyalists, fleeing from the American Revolution, settled in Canada. The ensuing ethnic tension led to the division of Quebec into French-speaking Lower Canada and English-speaking Upper Canada (1791), which were reunited again in 1841. By the British North America Act (1867) a confederation of Lower Canada (Quebec), Upper Canada (Ontario), Nova Scotia, and New Brunswick was established. In 1869 Rupert's Land was bought from the Hudson's Bay Company and the province of Manitoba was created from it in the following year. In 1871 British Columbia and in 1873 Prince Edward Island joined the confederation. Alberta and Saskatchewan were created from the NW Territories in 1905. Canada's present position as an independent constitutional monarchy in the Commonwealth of Nations was defined by the Statute of Westminster in 1931. It played an important part in both World Wars. The main political problem in recent years has been French-Canadian separatist agitation, led by the Quebec Liberation Front (Parti québecois). The Liberal Party, which had held office for 36 out of the previous 43 years (the last 11 under the leadership of Pierre *Trudeau), was ousted from power in May, 1979, by the Progressive Conservatives under Joseph Clark. In the elections of February 1980, the Liberal Party under Trudeau was again returned to power. In 1982 a new constitution for Canada was signed by Elizabeth II. In 1984 Trudeau retired and although a successor from his own party led the government briefly, the Liberals lost the ensuing general election. Progressive conservative Prime Minister Brian Mulroney formed a new government. Official languages: English and French. Official currency: Canadian dollar of 100 cents. Area: 3,851,809 sq mi (9,976,169 sq km). Population (1981 est): 24,200,000. Capital: Ottawa. Main port: Montreal.

Canada balsam   A transparent resin obtained from fir trees. It is used as an adhesive in optical instruments because its refractive index is similar to that of glass.

CANADA GOOSE   *These birds pair for life and both male and female may incubate the eggs and care for the young.*

Canada goose   A large *goose, *Branta canadensis*, that breeds in Canada and Alaska, migrating in flocks to the southern US for the winter. It is 24–40 in (60–100 cm) long and has a black head and neck, white throat, dark-brown back, and pale underparts. The Canada goose has been introduced to parts of Europe as a sporting bird.

Canadian railroads   Canada has two great transcontinental systems: the Canadian Pacific Limited (CP Rail) and the Canadian National Railroad

(CN). The CP, running from Halifax on the Atlantic Ocean to Vancouver on the Pacific Ocean was the first to be completed in 1885.

Canadian River   A river in the S central US, flowing generally E from NE New Mexico to the Arkansas River in Oklahoma. Length: 906 mi (1458 km).

Canadian Shield.   *See* shield.

Canaletto   (Antonio Canal; 1697–1768) Venetian painter, famous for his views of Venice. He trained under his father, a theatrical-scenery painter, before visiting Rome (1719–20), where he designed opera sets. His popularity with English collectors led to a stay in England (1746–55), where he painted views of London. His early work, painted in the open air, was considerably freer than his later much more architectural painting, for which he used mechanical drawing instruments.

canals   Man-made open water channels. They are divided into two categories: conveyance canals and navigation canals. The former carry water for irrigation, power, or drainage; the latter, to facilitate transportation, often connect two natural waterways. Canals have been dug from ancient times. The Grand Canal in China, started in 109 BC, was 620 mi (1000 km) long by the 8th century and carried 1.8 million tons of freight per annum. The completion of the Erie Canal (1825), linking the Great Lakes with the Hudson River, had an immense effect on the economy of New York and helped to open the Midwest. Some modern ship canals achieve spectacular reductions in voyage distances, especially the *Suez Canal (completed in 1869) and the *Panama Canal (1914). Others of considerable local importance include the Corinth Canal (1893), the Kiel Canal (1895), and the St Lawrence Seaway (1959) connecting the Great Lakes with the Atlantic Ocean. In canal construction, the availability of water is the primary concern. Conveyance canals are often narrow, have a high water velocity, and are earth lined and consequently are subject to erosion. Barge or ship canals are often completely lined with concrete or have concrete edges to prevent wave erosion. Variations in land or water level are common and *locks must be installed to conserve water and allow for the passage of vessels.

canary   A small songbird, *Serinus canarius*, native to the Canary Islands, Madeira, and the Azores. Wild canaries have an olive-green plumage with yellow to gray underparts streaked with black. Popular as cagebirds since the 15th century, they have been selectively bred both for their musical song and attractive plumage—usually pure yellow but sometimes white or striped and occasionally with ornamental plumes. Subfamily: *Cardueline*; family: *Fringillidae* (finches).

canary grass   An annual grass, *Phalaris canariensis*, 8–24 in (20–60 cm) high, native to the Canary Islands and N Africa and cultivated commercially in Europe for birdseed. The related reed canary grass (*P. arundinaceae*), which is widely distributed, is an important forage grass and grows 24–71 in (61–183 cm) high.

Canary Islands   (Spanish name: Islas Canarias)   A group of Spanish islands in the Atlantic Ocean, close to NW Africa. Since 1927 they have constituted two provinces named for their capitals of Las Palmas (including the islands of Fuerteventura, Gran Canaria, and Lanzarote) and Santa Cruz de Tenerife (including the islands of Ferro, Gomera, La Palma, and *Tenerife). The islands became Spanish possessions in the 15th century; the earliest inhabitants, the Guanches, are now extinct. The islands are of volcanic formation and, with the help of irrigation, fruits such as bananas and tomatoes are grown for export. Tourism is also a major source of revenue. Total area: 2807 sq mi (7270 sq km). Population (1970): 1,138,801.

canasta.   *See* rummy games.

Canaveral, Cape   (name from 1963 until 1973: Cape Kennedy)   A barrier island in E central Florida separated from the mainland by lagoons. It is the site of operations by NASA at the Kennedy Space Center. The first flight to land on the moon was launched here in 1969. In 1973 Skylab, the first orbiting laboratory, was launched from here.

Canberra   35 15S 149 10E   The capital of Australia, in the Australian Capital Territory on the Molonglo River. As a result of a competition in 1911, it was planned by the American architect Walter Burley Griffin, as the new federal capital, being formally inaugurated in 1927. The establishment of the National University in 1946 and the growth of government departments have led to sizable increases in population. Population (1980 est): 245,500.

cancan   A boisterous dance originally performed in Parisian dance halls around 1830 as a solo or by groups of women. Tourists flocked to see its spectacular and indecorous high kicking. Famous cancan music includes the galop from Offenbach's *Orpheus in the Underworld.*

cancer A group of diseases caused by the abnormal and uncontrolled division of cells to form tumors that invade and destroy the tissues in which they arise. Such tumors are described as malignant: their cells spread through the bloodstream or lymphatic system or across body cavities to set up secondary tumors at other sites in the body (this spread is called metastasis). The cause of cancer remains uncertain, although it is known that exposure to certain substances (*see* carcinogen) will produce it. Cancer can arise in almost any tissue: in the western world the breasts, colon, lungs, bronchi, prostate gland, and stomach are common sites. Carcinomas are cancers arising in *epithelium; less common but more malignant are sarcomas—cancers of connective tissue (bone, cartilage, muscle, etc.). *Leukemia is a form of sarcoma affecting the bone marrow and other blood-forming tissues. Treatment, which varies with the type of cancer, includes *cytotoxic drugs, radiotherapy, and surgery.

Cancer (Latin: Crab) An inconspicuous constellation in the N sky, lying on the *zodiac between Leo and Gemini. It contains the star cluster *Praesepe.

candela (cd) The *SI unit of luminous intensity equal to the intensity of 1/600,000 square meter of the surface of a black body maintained at the freezing point of platinum.

Candela, Felix (1910–) Mexican architect and engineer, born in Spain. Employing a naturalistic modern style, his work is characterized by use of thin, prestressed concrete roofs, often spanning large distances, e.g. the Church of the Miraculous Virgin, Mexico City (1953).

Candia. *See* Iráklion.

Candida A genus of yeastlike fungi. They are typically spherical, ovoid, or elongated cells that reproduce by budding and spore formation; they do not undergo sexual reproduction. Several species, especially *C. albicans*, cause *candidiasis. Family: *Cryptococcaceae*; class: *Blastomycetes*.

candidiasis An infection caused by a species of yeast (*Candida albicans*). Popularly known as thrush, it affects the mouth and vagina most frequently; it may develop after treatment with certain antibiotics and with diseases (e.g. leukemia) and drugs (e.g. steroids) that reduce the natural immunity of the body. The infection is cleared readily by such fungicides as nystatin.

Candlemas The Christian feast of the Purification of the Virgin Mary and the Presentation of Christ in the Temple (Luke 2.22–38), which is observed on Feb 2. It is so called because of the distribution of candles, symbolizing Christ's appearance as the "light of the world."

candytuft An annual or perennial flowering plant of the genus *Iberis* (about 30 species), native to S Europe and Asia and growing well in dry chalky soils. The stems (up to 6–20 in [15–50 cm] in height) bear white, pink, red, or blue flowers in flat-topped clusters. The fruits are pods containing winged seeds. Some species are grown as garden plants. Family: *Cruciferae*.

cane The stem of certain large grasses and of some palms. In some species it is hollow and jointed, e.g. *reeds (*Phragmites* species), *bamboo (*Bambusa* species), and *sugar cane; in others it is solid, e.g. *rattan and Malacca (*Calamus* species) used for making furniture, walking sticks, etc.

Canea (Greek name: Khaniá) 35 31N 24 01E The capital of Crete, on the Gulf of Khaniá. Founded by Venetians in 1252, it is surrounded by massive Venetian walls. The island's main port with an important coastal trade, it exports leather, olives, olive oil, and fruit. Population (1981): 47,804.

cane rat An African *rodent belonging to the genus *Thryonomys* (2 species) common in reed beds. About 16 in (40 cm) long, cane rats have bright-orange incisor teeth, feeding on reeds, roots, bulbs, grasses, and sugar cane and can become a pest in plantations. Family: *Thryonomyidae*.

Canidae The dog family: a family of mammals belonging to the order *Carnivora. It includes the dogs, wolves, jackals, coyote, and foxes.

Canis Major (Latin: great dog) A conspicuous constellation in the S sky near Orion. The brightest stars are *Sirius, the giants Adhara and Mirzam, and the supergiant Wezen.

Canis Minor (Latin: little dog) A small constellation in the S sky, lying near Canis Major and Orion. The brightest star is *Procyon.

canker 1. A disease of plants, especially fruit trees, caused by various fungi and bacteria. Cankers can be seen as dead, discolored, irregular, or cracked areas on the stem and branches; mechanical or climatic injury and attack by insect pests often predispose to infection. Treatment is by removal of the diseased parts. 2. A chronic disease of horses' hooves, caused by

continually wet conditions underfoot. The affected hooves become soft and swollen and eventually infected, causing inflammation and discharge. Treatment is by removing affected tissue and dressing with antibiotics. Prevention is by ensuring a dry stable floor. 3. Inflammation of the outer ear affecting dogs, cats, and rabbits and causing irritation and itching. Treatment is by application of an antiseptic lotion or powder.

canna A genus of ornamental herbaceous plants (about 155 species), native to tropical and subtropical America. Up to 10 ft (3 m) high, they have spirally arranged leaves, which may be green, bronze, or purple, and terminal clusters of showy flowers, 6 in (15 cm) across and ranging from pale yellow to scarlet. Cannas are grown widely as bedding plants. Family: *Cannaceae*.

cannabis The resin (hashish) or crushed leaves and flowers (marijuana, "grass," or "pot") obtained from certain species of *hemp. The drug is eaten or inhaled and produces a variety of effects on the mind. These include euphoria, distortion of time sense, and increased awareness of sight, sound, and memory. Occasionally feelings of anxiety and apprehension are experienced. The long-term effects of cannabis use are obscure but may affect memory. Cannabis causes mild dependence but there is also a danger of progression to "hard" drugs, such as heroin. *See also* drug dependence; hallucinogen.

Canne, Battle of (216 BC) The battle, fought at the village of Canne in Apulia (SE Italy), in which *Hannibal and the Carthaginians killed almost 50,000 Romans. It is the worst Roman defeat on record.

Cannes 43 33N 7 00E A resort in S France, in the Alpes-Maritimes department on the French Riviera. Its development as a fashionable resort dates from the early 19th century. It has numerous hotels, sports facilities, boulevards, and casinos. The Île St Honorat contains the oldest monastery in W Europe. There are aircraft and textile industries and fruit and flowers are grown. Population (1975): 71,080.

cannibalism The practice of eating human flesh, either as food or for ritual or magical purposes. Extreme hunger has prompted modern occurrences among concentration-camp prisoners and aircrash survivors. In ritual cannibalism certain parts of a defeated enemy may be eaten in order to absorb his strength and courage or to prevent his spirit taking revenge. In other cases (endocannibalism) it forms part of rituals performed at the death of a kinsman. The word is derived from the *Arawak term for the *Carib Indians among whom it was common. Ritual cannibalism was practiced also by the New Zealand Maoris, the Fijian islanders, in Polynesia, in parts of Africa, in New Guinea, and among some North American Indian peoples.

canning The preservation of meat, fish, or fruit in vacuum-sealed airtight metal containers, which have been sterilized by heating followed by rapid cooling. Fruit keeps safely for at least one year, meat and vegetables for two, although in practice they may stay fresh for much longer, especially if kept cool. Canning was introduced in the 18th century and originally used pure *tin cans. Now cans are made of *tinplate. Canned foods may be reheated but do not need further cooking. *See also* food preservation.

Canning, George (1770–1827) British statesman; foreign secretary (1807–09, 1822–27) and Tory prime minister (1827). A member of parliament from 1793, he became foreign secretary in 1807 but resigned in 1809. He again became foreign secretary and was partly responsible for the liberalization of Tory policies in the 1820s. He supported the revolt of Spain's American Colonies (1823) and the War of *Greek Independence (1825–27), before briefly becoming prime minister.

Canning Basin (former name: Desert Artesian Basin) An arid and largely unexplored sedimentary basin of NW Western Australia. It forms part of the *Great Sandy Desert and is covered chiefly by active longitudinal sand dunes. Area: about 150,000 sq mi (400,000 sq km).

Cannizzaro, Stanislao (1826–1910) Italian chemist, who resurrected *Avogadro's hypothesis, which had been neglected for 50 years, and used it to clarify the problem of representing compounds by formulas. He also discovered a method, called Cannizzaro's reaction, of converting an aldehyde into an acid and an alcohol.

Cannon, Joseph Gurney (1836–1926) US politician, Speaker of the House (1903–11). A lawyer in Illinois, he was elected to the US House of Representatives in 1872 and served 1873–91, 1893–1913, and 1915–23. During his term as speaker, several attempts were made to break his arbitrary handling of appointments and other matters, but it was not until 1910 that fellow House members were able to pass resolutions that provided for more democratic House procedures.

cannon An early form of *artillery firearm used primarily until 1670 as a siege gun. A 14th-century invention (by the German monk, Berthold

Schwarz), early cannon were made of wrought-iron rods welded together, covered with lead, and wrapped with iron bands. Some had a removable breech. Cast guns were made in England after 1500. They fired stones, cast-iron and wrought-iron balls. Modern cannons include *guns, *mortars, and *howitzers.

Cannon, Walter Bradford (1871–1945) US physiologist, who pioneered the use of X-rays in physiological studies. By administering a suspension, or meal, of radio-opaque bismuth, the intestine could be revealed on X-rays. Cannon also investigated the body's reaction to stress, particularly the role of the sympathetic nervous system, and he identified an adrenaline-like chemical transmitter secreted by sympathetic nerve endings, which he termed "sympathin."

Cano, Juan Sebastián del (c. 1460–1526) Spanish navigator. He accompanied Magellan's expedition, taking command after Magellan's death. He successfully completed the voyage—the first around the world—in 1522. He died on a second expedition.

canoe A double-ended vessel designed mainly for propulsion by paddles, although certain kinds are equipped with sails (sailing canoe). The modern canoe is, typically, about 10–20 ft (3–7 m) long, and they are usually single or two seaters although Canadian canoes can accommodate up to four people. It is made of waterproofed canvas stretched over a ribbed frame or of aluminum, wood, or fiberglass. The modern canoe is modeled on native craft that have been in use in the Americas and in the Pacific for thousands of years. Some Pacific native war canoes, equipped with outriggers, could accommodate as many as 40 people. Other large canoes served, until the 20th century, as the chief means of transport among the islands of the Pacific. Depending on their age and location, native canoes were made by hollowing out logs or by stretching animal skins or birchbark over a ribbed frame. Canoes are much favored for recreation on lakes and rivers, being easy to maneuver and readily portable. See also kayak.

canonization In the Christian Church, the conferring of the status of *saint on a dead person. In the Roman Catholic Church this is done by a formal declaration of the pope after a long investigation of the person's suitability. Beatification, by which the Church permits the veneration of a person, with the title "Blessed," within a particular diocese, order, or other limited area, precedes canonization and depends on evidence of the person's exceptional virtue and authentic miracles. The Church then puts the case for the canonization and appoints someone, the *Promotor Fidei* (Latin: promoter of the faith, popularly known as the devil's advocate), to oppose it, and completes the process after proof of further miracles. In the early days of Christianity each area recognized its own saints, who were usually local martyrs. Ulrich of Augsburg (c. 890–973) is the first person known to have been canonized by a pope (in 993 AD). About 1170 Pope Alexander III decreed that only the Roman Catholic Church could add new names to the list of saints.

canon law The laws of Christian Churches, particularly the Roman Catholic, Anglican, and Orthodox Churches. They include regulations governing the clergy, the ecclesiastical courts, matters of worship and doctrine, and so on. The origins of canon law lie in the decrees of the various councils of bishops in the early Church, in authoritative pronouncements of important bishops, and in the Decretals, or letters having the force of law, of the Popes. In the 12th century many laws from these sources were included by Gratian (died c. 1179) in his *Decretum*, a collection of rules that the Roman Catholic Church recognized as authoritative. The *Decretum* in turn formed part of a later collection, the *Corpus Juris Canonici, which in 1917 was revised to form the Codex Juris Canonici, the present Roman Catholic code of law.

Canopic jars Earthenware jars used in ancient Egypt in sets of four as containers for the internal organs removed from mummified bodies. Their lids, originally plain, were later modeled as the human, falcon, dog, and jackal heads of the four sons of the god *Horus.

Canopus A conspicuous luminous white supergiant, apparent magnitude –0.7 and 98 light years distant, that is the brightest star in the constellation Carina and the second brightest star in the sky.

Canossa A 10th-century castle near Reggio nel Emilia, in Italy. It is famous as the place in which Emperor Henry IV received absolution from Gregory VII in 1077 to end the *investiture controversy.

Canova, Antonio (1757–1822) Italian sculptor. One of the finest interpreters of the style of *neoclassicism, Canova worked first in Venice, in Rome after 1781, in Vienna, and in Paris, where he was employed by Napoleon. He achieved a wide reputation with his idealized marbles, usually of classical subjects. His best-known works are *The Tomb of Clement XIII* (1783–87; SS Apostoli, Rome) and *Pauline Borghese as Venus Victrix* (1805–07; Borghese Gallery, Rome).

Cánovas del Castillo, Antonio (1828–97) Spanish statesman and writer. Following the overthrow of the First Republic in 1874 and the restoration of the monarchy he created a system of government by two parties in rotation, which remained in force until 1923. He led the conservative party and was many times prime minister. He was assassinated by an anarchist.

Cantabrian Mountains (Spanish name: Cordillera Cantábrica) A mountain range in N Spain extending E–W along the Atlantic coast and rising to 8868 ft (2648 m).

Cantacuzino A family prominent in Romania from the 17th century. Descended from an imperial Byzantine family, the Cantacuzino settled in Moldavia and Walachia (present-day Romania) in the 16th century. Its members included Şerban Cantacuzino (d. 1688), who ruled Walachia from 1679 to 1688, and his nephew Ştefan Cantacuzino, who ruled from 1714 until ousted and executed in 1716. Şerban's cousin Dumitraşcu Cantacuzino (1648–85) was an unpopular ruler of Moldavia (1673–75, 1684–85). A descendant Constantin Cantacuzino (1793–1877) governed Walachia (1848–49, 1854).

Canterbury 51 17N 1 05E A city in SE England, in Kent on the River Stour. The cathedral (11th–15th centuries), where Thomas *Becket was martyred in 1170, is the seat of the Archbishop and Primate of the Anglican Church. Canterbury is a tourist, market, and educational center; the University of Kent (1960) overlooks the city. Population (1981): 34,404.

Canterbury, Archbishop of The chief bishop of the *Anglican Communion of churches, called Primate of All England. The first of the line was St *Augustine of Canterbury. The current archbishop is Robert Alexander Kennedy Runcie (1921– ; 102nd Archbishop 1980–).

Canterbury bell An annual or biennial flowering plant, *Campanula medium*, native to S Europe and frequently grown as a garden ornamental. The plant grows to a height of 30 in (70 cm) and bears spikes of pink, rose, lavender, blue, or white bell-shaped flowers, each 2 in (5 cm) or more long. Family: *Campanulaceae*.

Canterbury Plains A low-lying area of New Zealand, on E central South Island bordering on the Pacific Ocean. It is the most densely populated area of South Island and is important agriculturally, especially for fat-lamb raising and the production of cereals, fodder crops, and vegetables. Area: about 4000 sq mi (10,000 sq km). Chief town: Christchurch.

cantharidin. See Spanish fly.

Can Tho 10 03N 105 46E A port in S Vietnam, on the Mekong delta. It is the industrial center of an important rice-growing area, with a university (1956). Population (1973 est): 182,424.

Canton (Chinese names: Guangzhou or Kuang-chou) 23 08N 113 20E A port in S China, the capital of Guangdong province on the Zhu Jiang (Pearl River) delta. Densely populated, it is the commercial and industrial center of S China and attracts much of the country's foreign trade through its biannual trade fair. It has a university and various colleges. Its industries include steel, shipbuilding, paper, textiles, and the manufacture of machinery and chemicals. *History*: Chinese since the 3rd century BC, it was the first Chinese city to trade regularly with Europeans (from the 16th century), having long traded with Hindus and Arabs, and was the focus of the first Opium War (1839–42). The birthplace of *Sun Yat-sen, it was the starting point of the revolution against the Qing (1911). His Guomindang (Nationalist) government was based here in the early 1920s. Canton was occupied by Japan (1938–45). Population (1977 est): 5,000,000.

Canton 40 48N 81 23W A city in NE Ohio. An important industrial center, it has a large iron and steel industry. It was the home of President McKinley. Population (1980): 94,632.

Canton and Enderbury Two uninhabited coral atolls in the S Pacific Ocean, in the Phoenix Islands. Claims between the US and the UK were settled in 1939, when they agreed to exercise joint control over the islands for 50 years. Canton was used as an international airport for transpacific flights until the advent of long-range jets.

Cantonese. See Chinese.

Cantor, Eddie (Edward Israel Iskowitz; 1892–1964) US entertainer. He began in vaudeville and then appeared in Ziegfield's *Follies* (1916–19) and the stage shows *Kid Boots* (1923–26), *Whoopee* (1928), and *Banjo Eyes* (1941). A comedian and singer, he had his own radio show in the 1930s, appeared in the films *Roman Scandals* (1933) and *Forty Little Mothers* (1940), and entertained on television's *Colgate Comedy Hour* (1950–53).

Cantor, Georg (1845–1918) Russian mathematician, born in St Petersburg. Cantor's family moved in 1856 to Germany, where he spent the rest of his life. He was the first mathematician to set the concept of infinity on a rigorous mathematical foundation. He defined different types of infinity for the set of integers, the set of real numbers, etc., each type being represented by a number known as a transfinite number. His ideas created great controversy and were viciously attacked, by Leopold Kronecker (1823–91) in particular. Cantor broke down in 1884 under the strain and died in a mental asylum.

Canute II (*or* Cnut; c. 994–1035) Danish King of England after defeating *Edmund Ironside (1016). He became King of Denmark (1019) and of Norway (1028). He defended England from Viking attacks (1017, 1026, 1028) and subjected Malcolm II of Scotland (1028). He went on a pilgrimage to Rome in 1027 to attend the coronation of Emperor *Conrad II. According to legend, he proved to flatterers the limits of his powers by demonstrating his inability to induce the waves to recede.

canyon A deep steep-sided gorge found mainly in arid and semiarid areas, the depth of which considerably exceeds its width. Canyons are often formed by rapidly eroding rivers down-cutting into soft rock in arid areas. The lack of rainfall hinders weathering and maintains the steep slopes; where hard- and soft-rock bands occur, a stepped formation results. The largest and best-known canyon is the *Grand Canyon.

Canyon Lands National Park A national park in SE Utah including the area surrounding the junction of the Green and Colorado rivers. Established in 1964, it is noted for its unusual rock formations and mesas. Area: 527 sq mi (1,365 sq km).

Cao Chan (*or* Zao Zhan; ?1715–63) Chinese novelist, famous for the semiautobiographical *Dream of the Red Chamber*, a novel written in the last years of his life. It combines a tragic love story with a description of the downfall of a great Chinese family. It mirrors the fortunes of Cao Chan's own family, which held the hereditary office of commissioner of imperial textiles in Nanking.

Capablanca y Graupera, José Raúl (1888–1942) Cuban chess player, who was world champion from 1921 to 1927. Extraordinarily gifted, he played a fast-paced game with exceptional insight. He worked as a diplomat and wrote books on chess, including *Chess Fundamentals* (1922).

capacitance The ability of an electrical component to store charge. It is measured in *farads and defined as the ratio of the stored charge in coulombs to the voltage drop across the component. Capacitance is one of the factors that control the frequency response of circuits and components to alternating currents.

capacitor An electrical component (formerly called a condenser), with an appreciable *capacitance. It consists of two conductor or semiconductor plates separated by a *dielectric. The value of the capacitance is a function of the geometry and the electrical properties of the dielectric and often also of the operating voltage and the frequency. Variable capacitors are used for tuning electronic circuits.

Cape Breton Island An island in SE Canada, in Nova Scotia, separated from the mainland by the Strait of Canso. Hilly and forested, it encloses tidal salt lakes. Coal, steel, fishing, and tourism are important. It was ceded to Britain by the French (1763). Area: 3975 sq mi (10,280 sq km). Population (1971): 170,007.

Cape Coast 5 10N 1 13W A city in central Ghana, on the Gulf of Guinea. It was the capital of the British colony of the Gold Coast until 1874. It has a cathedral and a university (1962). Fishing industries are important. Population (1970): 71,594.

Cape Cod A sandy peninsula in Massachusetts, between Cape Cod Bay and the Atlantic Ocean. A popular summer resort area, it also produces cranberries and asparagus. The **Cape Cod National Seashore Recreational Area** is an area on the Atlantic Ocean side of Cape Cod. It was established in 1961 to preserve the natural seashore and wildlife on the outer shores of Cape Cod. Length: 65 mi (105 km).

Cape Fear River A river rising in N central North Carolina and flowing SE to Wilmington where it empties into the Atlantic Ocean at Cape Fear. Length: 202 mi (326 km).

Cape Frontier Wars (1779–1878) The wars fought intermittently in S Africa between the white settlers moving E from the Cape and the *Xhosa people who had settled in the E Cape area. Conflict between the two groups arose mainly over land and cattle. The Xhosa had been driven back along the coast by the colonists beyond the Keiskamma River by 1819 and in 1846 the land between the Fish and the Keiskamma Rivers was annexed as British Kaffraria. The final war was in 1877–78 in which the Xhosa were defeated and their lands absorbed into the Cape Colony.

Cape Horn (Spanish name: Cabo de Hornes) The most southerly point in South America, at the S end of Horn Island, Chile. It is notorious for its stormy weather.

Capella A conspicuous yellow giant, apparent magnitude 0.1 and 45 light years distant, that is the brightest star in the constellation Auriga. It is a triple star.

Cape of Good Hope A headland in South Africa, in the SW extremity of Cape Province to which it gave its official name of Cape of Good Hope Province. It was discovered (1488) by Dias, who named it the Cape of Storms.

Cape Province (official name: Cape of Good Hope Province; Afrikaans name: Kaapprovinsie) The largest province in South Africa, in the extreme S of the African continent. It consists chiefly of plateaus separated by mountain ranges. In the diversified economy agriculture is important. The SW produces most of South Africa's fruit and vegetables for export and has many vineyards; sheep and cattle rearing is extensive and wheat and alfalfa are grown. Diamonds and copper are the chief minerals, others being asbestos, manganese, and iron ore. Industries include food processing and canning, textiles, and motor-vehicle production. *History*: first settled by the Dutch (1652), it was ceded to Britain in 1814, becoming known as the Cape Colony. The discovery of diamonds in Griqualand West led to its annexation to the Cape Colony (1871). In 1910 the colony became a province in the Union of South Africa. Area: 400,762 sq mi (646,332 sq km). Population (1980): 4,007,875. Capital: Cape Town.

caper A bramble-like spiny shrub, *Capparis spinosa*, native to drier regions of S Europe. The pickled flower buds are the capers used in flavoring. The fruit is a berry. Family: *Capparidaceae*.

capercaillie The largest European *grouse, *Tetrao urogallus*, of Eurasian coniferous forests, where it feeds on pine buds and needles. The male, almost 40 in (100 cm) long, is black with a blue-green gloss and red wattles above the eyes. The smaller female is brown with black and white markings.

Capernaum 32 53N 35 34E An ancient town in N Israel, on the N shore of the Sea of Galilee. It is the site of many biblical events, and a synagogue dating from about 200 AD has been excavated.

Capetians The ruling dynasty of France from 987 to 1328. It was founded by *Hugh Capet, who became King of France in 987, replacing the Carolingians. Successive kings, notably *Philip II Augustus and *Louis IX, expanded their own authority and the territory under their control (originally comprising little more than the Île-de-France). The Capetians established a royal bureaucracy, from which the *parlements developed, and were the first kings to summon the *States General.

CAPE TOWN *The city is noted for its scenic beauty set against Table Mountain. 3550 ft (1082 m) high.*

Cape Town (Afrikaans name: Kaapstad) 33 56S 18 28E The legislative capital of South Africa and capital of Cape Province, on the Atlantic Ocean. Founded by Jan van Riebeeck in 1652 as a supply post for the Dutch East India Company, it is the oldest white settlement in South Africa. The famous National Botanical Gardens at Kirstenbosch were part of the home of Cecil Rhodes. Cape Town castle (17th century) is the oldest building in South Africa; the university was established in 1918 and has an observatory. Cape Town is a major port, with modern dockyard facilities, and is an important commercial and industrial city. Its industries include oil refining, chemicals, motor vehicles, and textiles. Population (1980): 213,830.

Cape Verde, Republic of (Portuguese name: Cabo Verde) A country occupying an archipelago in the N Atlantic Ocean, off the coast of West Africa. It consists of ten islands and five islets, most of which are mountainous. The majority of the population is of mixed African and European descent. *Economy*: mainly subsistence agriculture. Ship refueling is important and fishing has considerable potential for development; fish and fish products are the main exports. *History*: the Cape Verde Islands were settled by the Portuguese in the mid 15th century, becoming a Portuguese colony in the 19th century and gaining full independence in 1975. Plans for union with Guinea-Bissau on the African coast still meet with opposition in certain quarters, although there is already a considerable amount of cooperation. A nonaligned nation, Cape Verde has become a center for international conferences of heads of government. President: Aristides Maria Pereira (1924–). Official language: Portuguese. Official currency: Cape Verdean escudo of 100 centavos. Area: 1557 sq mi (4033 sq km). Population (1983): 297,000. Capital: Praia. Main port: Mindelo.

Cape York Peninsula The most northerly part of Australia, in Queensland, situated between the Gulf of Carpentaria and the Coral Sea. It is mainly low-lying grass and scrubland in the W, rising to the Great Dividing Range in the E and contains large areas that are uninhabited although bauxite mining is important.

Cap Haïtien (*or* Le Cap) 19 47N 72 17W A port in N Haiti, on the Atlantic Ocean. The chief exports are coffee and sugar and it is the site of one of the world's largest sisal plantations. Population (1975): 54,691.

capillary In anatomy, a minute thin-walled blood vessel (0.005–0.02 mm diameter), networks of which connect the smallest *arteries with the smallest *veins. Nutrients and oxygen diffuse across the capillary walls to nourish the tissues. Waste products and carbon dioxide return from the tissues to the capillary blood.

capital An element of architecture used to join a column to the part of the building it supports. In classical architecture there are five orders of columns with strictly defined types of capital, of varying degrees of ornateness, for each (*see* orders of architecture). In romanesque and gothic architecture, the rules became less strict and the type of capital used depended mainly on the skill and taste of the masons involved. Thus the capital could vary from the plain (called a cushion capital) to the highly ornate, decorated with carvings of foliage, people, and animals (grotesque and historiated types).

capitalism An economic and political system that developed following the industrial revolution. Essential features of the system are uncontrolled free markets, based on the profit motive, and unrestricted ownership of the means of production (capital). If the system is allowed to develop without restriction it has certain undesirable attributes (*see* laissez-faire). This has led western countries to restrict capitalism by the establishment of mixed economies, characterized by substantial government regulation. Communist countries have followed the doctrines of Karl Marx (*see* Marxism), who maintained that capitalism contains the seeds of its own destruction, and have abolished capitalism and the free-market system, replacing them with central direction of the economy by the government.

capital levy. *See* wealth.

capital punishment The punishment of a convicted criminal by death. Although execution by hanging was a sentence often applied by US courts during the 19th century and execution by the electric chair, the firing squad, and the gas chamber was common in the early 20th century, capital punishment has been infrequently applied since the Supreme Court decision of *Furman* v. *Georgia* (1967). Its questionable effectiveness as a deterrent to serious crimes such as murder, the apparent arbitrariness of its application, and the possibility that an innocent person might be put to death have given rise to serious legal and moral questions. Since 1977, however, with a reversal of the earlier Supreme Court decision, the use of capital punishment has been a matter left up to the individual states. Great Britain, which as late as the 18th century had used beheading or hanging for the punishment of many crimes, such as forgery and petty theft, abolished public execution in 1868. In 1957 the application of the death penalty in Great Britain was severely restricted, and in 1965 it was banned except in cases of treason and piracy. Many countries of Western Europe have enacted similar laws abolishing the use of capital punishment. It is still, however, applied in many countries in other parts of the world.

Capitol Reef National Park A national park in S central Utah, including an area along the Fremont River. Established in 1971, it had been a national monument since 1937. There are rock formations, cliffs, and gorges in many different colors. The reefs along the Fremont River resemble domes and are topped by white rock. Area: 60 sq mi (156 sq km).

capitulary Legal and administrative instruments of the *Carolingian kings, arranged in *capitula* (articles). These documents are concerned with many topics, both secular and ecclesiastical, including law and order, the regulation of trade, and the administration of royal estates. Although originals do not survive, copies amply illustrate the scope and power of early Carolingian administration.

Capone, Al (1899–1947) US gangster, born in Italy. He dominated the Chicago underworld of organized crime in the late 1920s. He was particularly successful in the illegal liquor traffic during Prohibition. In the St Valentine's Day Massacre of 1929, his men killed seven members of a rival gang. He was imprisoned in 1931 for income-tax evasion.

Caporetto. *See* Kobarid.

Capote, Truman (1924–84) US novelist. In his early novels and stories, such as *Other Voices, Other Rooms* (1948), he explored traditional southern literary themes of loneliness and the macabre. Later he turned to journalism, an interest reflected in *In Cold Blood* (1966), a novel about an actual multiple murder. Other works include *The Grass Harp* (1951), *Breakfast at Tiffany's* (1958), and *Music for Chameleons* (1980).

Capp, Al (Alfred Caplin; 1909–79) US cartoonist. He is famous for his comic strip *Li'l Abner* depicting the hillbillies of Dogpatch, Kentucky, which first appeared in the *New York Mirror* in 1934. He continued to produce *Li'l Abner* until 1977.

Cappadocia The eastern region of Asia Minor. After early colonization by Semitic merchants, subjection to the Hittites, and invasions from the east, Cappadocia was conquered by the Persians in 584 BC but became an independent kingdom in the 3rd century BC. Feudal and isolated, Cappadocia resisted the hellenizing efforts of its ruling dynasty, which was largely pro-Roman; as the Roman Empire expanded eastward Cappadocia became strategically important and was a Roman province by 17 AD.

Capra, Frank (1897–) US film director, born in Italy. His best-known films include several popular sentimental comedies, notably *It Happened One Night* (1934), *Arsenic and Old Lace* (1942), *It's a Wonderful Life* (1946), and *A Hole in the Head* (1957). During World War II he directed propaganda films for the US War Department.

Capri, Island of (Latin name: Capreae) An Italian island at the SW entrance to the Bay of Naples. Its mild climate, fine scenery, and beaches have made it a popular resort since Roman times. The Blue Grotto, a cavern accessible only by sea, is a notable feature. Area: about 5 sq mi (13 sq km). Population (1971): 7723.

capriccio. *See* veduta.

Capricorn (astrology). *See* zodiac.

Capricornus (Latin: Goat) A constellation in the S sky, lying on the *zodiac between Aquarius and Sagittarius.

Caprivi Strip A narrow extension of NE Namibia giving the country access to the Zambezi River. Length: about 450 km (280 mi).

Capsicum A genus of annual and perennial flowering plants (about 50 species), native to Central and South America. The fruits (berries) of some species, particularly the various cultivated varieties of *C. annuum* and *C. frutescens*, are the *chilies and peppers used in cookery. Large fruits (up to about 4 in [10 cm] long) are the sweet peppers, which have a mild taste and are used in salads or cooked as a vegetable. They are usually green but may be red (the red varieties—paprika—can be ground to produce a spice). Smaller berries (about 1 in [2 cm] long) are the hot-tasting red peppers (or chilies); when dried and ground these form cayenne pepper. Dwarf varieties are grown for ornament. Family: *Solanaceae*.

capsid A delicate *plant bug belonging to the family *Miridae* (about 8000 species). Capsids are 0.08–0.24 in (2.5–6 mm) long and usually green or brown. They are found among all types of vegetation, feeding on plant juices, and are often serious crop pests. A few species prey on small arthropods.

capsule In botany, a type of dry *fruit that releases its seeds at maturity through pores, teeth, or slits: an example is the poppy capsule. The term also refers to the spore-producing structures of mosses and liverworts and the slimy envelope surrounding some bacterial cells. In zoology, it is the layer of connective tissue surrounding some organs, for example the kidney.

Capua 41 06N 14 12E A market city in S Italy, in Campania on the Volturno River. It has Roman remains and a cathedral dating from the 9th century. Population (1971): 17,582.

capuchin monkey A long-tailed *monkey belonging to the genus *Cebus* (4 species), of South America. Capuchins are 28–35 in (70–90 cm) long including the tail 16–20 in (40–50 cm) and live in large troops in the treetops, feeding chiefly on fruit but also eating insects, birds, and eggs. They became familiar as organ-grinders' monkeys. Family: *Cebidae*.

Capuchins A Roman Catholic order of friars founded in 1525. They are reformed *Franciscans and are named from their adoption of the pointed cowl (capuche) worn in emulation of St Francis. Opposed by the established Franciscans, they were almost suppressed in 1542, but survived to become an important force during the Counter-Reformation, being recognized in 1619 as one of the three independent branches of the Franciscan order. From their foundation they were noted for their works of charity and their asceticism.

CAPYBARA *These rodents are semiaquatic; they can swim underwater for considerable distances using their partly webbed feet.*

capybara The largest living rodent, *Hydrochoerus hydrochaeris*. Resembling giant guinea-pigs, up to 5 ft (1.25 m) long and 20 in (50 cm) high, capybaras graze on river banks in Central and South America, living in groups of up to 20 individuals. They have short coarse yellowish-brown hair and partially webbed feet (they are expert swimmers). The capybara is the only member of its family (*Hydrochoeridae*).

car *See* automobile.

caracal A long-legged short-tailed *cat, *Felis caracal*, of African and Asian deserts, bush, and mountains. Caracals are about 26 in (70 cm) long with a reddish-brown coat, and feed mainly on birds but also catch small mammals.

Caracalla (Marcus Aurelius Antoninus; 188–217 AD) Roman emperor (211–17). Rivalry between Caracalla and his brother and coemperor Geta (189–212) threatened to divide the Empire until Caracalla procured Geta's murder. Caracalla extended Roman citizenship to all free inhabitants of the Empire—probably for financial reasons (212). In 214 he embarked on war against the Parthians, claiming to be following Alexander the Great's ambition to unite East and West, but was assassinated during the campaign.

caracara A long-legged *falcon belonging to the subfamily *Daptriine*, of Central and South America. Caracaras can run swiftly and spend much time on the ground. They are omnivorous and frequently feed on carrion.

Caracas 10 35N 66 56W The capital of Venezuela, situated near the N coast and linked by road to its port, La Guaira. Founded by the Spanish as Santiago de León de Caracas in the 16th century, it suffered damage and destruction from the English and the French in the 16th and 18th centuries and later from severe earthquakes. In the 20th century it has grown considerably, especially since the oil boom of the 1950s. The Central University of Venezuela was founded in 1725, and there are three other universities. It is the birthplace of Simón Bolívar. Population (1976 est): 1,662,627.

carat 1. A unit of weight for precious stones, formerly defined as 4 grains (Troy), but now equal to 0.200 grams. 2. (also karat) A measure of the fineness of gold equal to the number of parts of gold by weight in 24 parts of the alloy. Thus 18-carat gold contains 18/24ths pure gold.

Caratacus (or Caractacus; 1st century AD) King of the Catuvellauni; son of *Cunobelinus (Cymbeline). Caratacus organized resistance to the Roman invasion of 43 AD. Defeated, he fled first to Wales then to the north British queen, Cartimandua, who betrayed him. He was pardoned by Emperor Claudius but died in exile.

Caravaggio (Michelangelo Merisi; 1573–1610) An influential Italian *baroque painter, whose nickname derives from his birthplace. In Rome his chief patron was Cardinal Francesco del Monte, for whom he painted scenes of the life of St Matthew in S Luigi dei Francesi. He executed numerous altarpieces, some of which, e.g. *Death of the Virgin* (Louvre), were condemned for depicting sacred personages as coarse peasants. He is also noted for his dramatic contrasts of light and shade in such paintings as *Supper at Emmaus* (National Gallery, London), which were extremely influential, particularly in N Europe. His violent temper led him to kill a man after a disputed tennis match in 1606. He spent his last years in exile in Naples, Malta, and Sicily.

caravel A sailing vessel used by the Spanish and Portuguese from the middle ages onward. It was usually rigged with a lateen sail on two or more masts.

caraway A perennial flowering plant, *Carum carvi*, native to N temperate regions from Europe to the Himalayas. The much-branched stem grows to a height of 10–24 in (25–60 cm) and terminates in clusters of small white flowers. The fruit is an oblong capsule containing the familiar caraway seeds, used in cookery. Family: *Umbelliferae*.

carbohydrate One of a large group of chemical compounds containing the elements carbon, hydrogen, and oxygen and having the general formula $C_x(H_2O)_x$. Green plants manufacture carbohydrates—such as *sugars and *starch—during *photosynthesis and their cell walls consist largely of carbohydrates—predominantly *cellulose. Hence plant carbohydrates are the primary source of food energy for animals. *Glycogen is a carbohydrate energy reserve found in animals, while chitin is a structural carbohydrate occurring in arthropods (and also in fungi). Chemically, carbohydrates can be classified according to the number of sugar units they contain—one (*see* monosaccharides), several (oligosaccharides), or many (*see* polysaccharides).

carbolic acid. *See* phenol.

carbon (C) A chemical element that is unique in terms of the huge number and variety of its compounds. Carbon is the basis of organic *chemistry and of all living systems. The element occurs naturally in two forms: *graphite, which is a soft grayish-black mineral, and *diamond, the hardest substance known. *Charcoal and *coke are also composed of carbon. Large amounts of carbon are fixed as calcium carbonate ($CaCO_3$) in *limestones. The extensive and varied chemistry of carbon results from its ability to form single, double, and triple bonds with itself and other elements. Simple compounds of carbon may join together to form large polymers; for example polyethylene, $(C_2H_4)_n$, from ethylene. At no 6; at wt 12.011; sublimes at 3367 $\pm$ 32°F (25°C).

carbonaceous chondrite. *See* meteor.

Carbonari Members of a secret society in early 19th-century Italy that advocated constitutional government. The Carbonari emerged as opponents of Joachim *Murat, who ruled Naples for Napoleon. The movement spread to N Italy and was supported by those dissatisfied with the conservative regimes imposed on Italy after the fall of Napoleon. Support for the Carbonari dwindled following the formation of *Young Italy by Mazzini but the society had helped pave the way for the unification of Italy (*see* Risorgimento).

carbon cycle (biology) The process by which carbon (in the form of carbon dioxide) in the atmosphere is taken up by plants during photosynthesis and transferred from one organism to the next in a *food chain, i.e. the plants are eaten by herbivorous animals that are themselves eaten by carnivores. At various stages carbon is returned to the environment with the release of carbon dioxide at *respiration and through decay.

carbon cycle (physics) A cycle of thermonuclear reactions in which a nucleus of carbon-12 acts as a catalyst in converting four hydrogen nuclei into a helium nucleus. The cycle produces energy and is believed to be a major source of energy in some stars. The reactions are:

$$^1_1H + {}^{12}_6C \rightarrow {}^{13}_7N \rightarrow {}^{13}_6C + {}^0_1e$$
$$^1_1H + {}^{13}_6C \rightarrow {}^{14}_7N$$
$$^1_1H + {}^{14}_7N \rightarrow {}^{15}_8O \rightarrow {}^{15}_7N + {}^0_1e$$
$$^1_1H + {}^{15}_7N \rightarrow {}^{12}_6C + {}^4_2He.$$

carbon dioxide (CO_2) A colorless odorless noncombustible gas. It is present (about 0.03% by volume) in air, being produced by combustion of carbon compounds and by respiration. Industrially, CO_2 is made from chalk or limestone and is used as a coolant in nuclear reactors, as a refrigerant, in fire extinguishers, and in "fizzy" drinks.

carbon fibers Black silky threads of pure carbon, made by the heat treatment of organic textile fibers (such as Courtelle) so that the side chains of the molecules are removed. They are some eight times stronger than steel and are used to reinforce resinous, ceramic, or metallic substances (with up to 600,000 fibers per square centimeter) to make components for jet engines, rockets, etc., where strength at high temperature is required.

Carboniferous period A geological period of the *Paleozoic era occurring about 370–280 million years ago between the Devonian and Permian periods. During the period land plants increased prolifically and led to the formation of the world's major coal deposits. Amphibians became more common and by the end of the period some reptiles had evolved. The Carboniferous is divided into Lower and Upper (Mississippian and Pennsylvanian). Limestone deposits were widespread in the Lower Carboniferous; millstone grits and the Coal Measures (alternating beds of coal, sandstone, shale, and clay), in the Upper.

carbon monoxide (CO) A colorless odorless flammable gas. It is produced by the incomplete combustion of carbon compounds (e.g. coke or natural gas) and is used as a fuel (see water gas). CO is highly toxic, combining with red blood cells and preventing them from carrying oxygen. It is present in the exhaust fumes of internal-combustion engines.

carbon tetrachloride (CCl_4) A colorless nonflammable heavy liquid that gives off toxic fumes. It is used as a solvent but its use in fire extinguishers has been discontinued owing to its toxic products of combustion.

carborundum A dark crystalline compound (silicon carbide) manufactured by heating silica (sand) with carbon (coke). It is used as an abrasive and as a refractory material.

carboxylic acids. See fatty acid.

carbuncle. See boil.

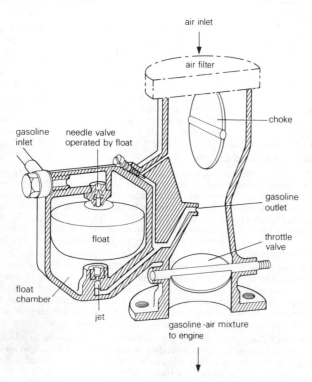

air inlet

air filter

choke

gasoline inlet

needle valve operated by float

gasoline outlet

throttle valve

float

gasoline-air mixture to engine

float chamber

jet

CARBURETOR *The level of gasoline is kept constant in the float chamber. After atomization by passing through the fine jet it is mixed with air and passed to the engine. The engine speed is controlled by the throttle valve. The mixture strength is varied by the choke, a richer mixture being required for starting from cold.*

carburetor The device in a gasoline engine that vaporizes the fuel and mixes it with air in the correct proportions. Vaporization is carried out by sucking the liquid fuel through a fine jet situated in (or near to) the throat of a tube through which the combustion air enters the engine. The carburetor also contains a choke to make the fuel-air mixture richer (i.e. contain more fuel and less air) for cold starting, a throttle valve (which controls the speed of the engine by admitting more or less of the mixture), and an air filter. In some gasoline engines the carburetor is replaced by a *fuel-injection system.

Carcassonne 43 13N 2 21E A city in SW France, the capital of the Aude department. It comprises a medieval fortified town, surrounded by towers and ramparts crowning a hill on the right bank of the Aude River, and a largely modern town, where there is a 13th-century cathedral (restored), on the left bank. A tourist center, Carcassonne is situated in a wine-producing region. Population (1975): 44,623.

Carchemish A *Hittite stronghold on the Upper Euphrates in E Turkey. After the Hittite empire's collapse (12th century BC), Carchemish survived as an independent kingdom until conquered by *Sargon II of Assyria (717 BC). In 605 BC it was the scene of a battle in which the Babylonians defeated an Egyptian army. *Woolley and T. E. *Lawrence excavated fine Hittite reliefs there (1912–14, 1919).

carcinogen An agent that causes cancer. Carcinogens can be chemicals, radiation, and some viruses. Chemical carcinogens include tar (such as that produced by cigarette smoking), aniline, and azo dyes. Large doses of radiation and the polyoma virus are known to cause cancer, particularly leukemia.

carcinoma. See cancer.

cardamon A perennial herb, *Elettaria cardamomum*, native to India. 5–10 ft (1.5–3 m) tall, it has large leaves, green and purple veined flowers, and small capsules filled with hard angular seeds. The spice cardamon consists of whole or ground dried fruit or seeds. It is cultivated in India, Sri Lanka, and Guatemala. Family: *Zingiberaceae* (ginger family).

Cardano, Girolamo (1501–76) Italian mathematician, who contributed to the development of negative and imaginary *numbers and, being an inveterate gambler, constructed a mathematical theory of chance. He also published a method of solving cubic equations known as Cardano's rule, although it was first derived by Niccolò Tartaglia (1500–57). His main works were *De subtilitate rerum* (1551) and *De varietate rerum* (1557).

Cárdenas, Lázaro (1895–1970) Mexican statesman. As president (1934–40) Cárdenas strove to realize many of the promises of the post-1910 revolutionary movement. He redistributed land, promoted mass education, and supported organized labor. His most famous achievement was the nationalization of the oil industry in 1938.

Cardiff (Welsh name: Caerdydd) 51 30N 3 13W The capital of Wales, situated in the SE of the country at the mouth of the River Taff. At the center of the city lies the Norman castle. University College, Cardiff (founded 1883), the University of Wales Registry (1893), the University of Wales Institute of Science and Technology, the Welsh National School of Medicine, and the National Museum of Wales are all located in the city. The cathedral at *Llandaff and the Welsh Folk Museum are situated on the outskirts of the city. *History*: originally a small Roman fort, the site was reoccupied by the Normans. It received its first royal charter in 1581, at which time it was a favorite haunt of pirates. It was not until 1881, however, that Cardiff expanded from a small market town to become the largest city in Wales. Its prosperity was based on coal from the valleys to the N of the city and by 1913 it was the largest coal-exporting port in the world. Trade declined rapidly, however, after World War I. Cardiff was chosen as the capital of Wales in 1955. Population (1981): 273,856.

Cardigan, James Thomas Brudenell, 7th Earl of (1797– 1868) British cavalry officer. In 1824 Cardigan bought himself a command in the Hussars, where his arrogant behavior led to a notorious duel. In 1854, during the Crimean War, he led the fatal charge of the Light Brigade at *Balaclava, made famous by Tennyson. The woolen garment known as a cardigan was named for— him.

Cardin, Pierre (1922–) French fashion designer, who after opening a fashion house in Paris (1949) made his reputation in the 1950s with his oriental styles and slim coats with huge collars. He was the first couturier to show a collection for men (1960).

cardinal A North American *bunting, *Pyrrhuloxia cardinalis*, having a strong stout bill and a crested head. The male, about 20 cm long, has a bright scarlet plumage with a black bib; the female is yellowish brown with a red crest.

cardinals, college of (*or* Sacred College)   The body of the highest dignitaries next to the pope in the *Roman Catholic Church. Originating in the advisory roles played by the parish priests and deacons of the city of Rome, the body was later extended to include six cardinal bishops responsible for the election of the pope. This function was invested in the college as a whole by the Third *Lateran Council (1179). Since then the number of cardinal bishops, priests, and deacons has increased from a total of 70 under Sixtus V (1586) to the present membership of 125 established under John XXIII and Paul VI. Cardinals from all over the world are nominated and elected by the pope, who invests them with the flat broad-brimmed red hat symbolic of their rank. They assist the pope as a privy council, conducting the temporal affairs of the Church, advising on questions of doctrine, etc.; they elect the pope from among their own number.

Cardozo, Benjamin Nathan   (1870–1938) US lawyer, jurist, associate justice of the Supreme Court (1932–38). After a successful career as a courtroom lawyer (1891–1913), he served on the New York State Court of Appeals (1914–32), sitting as the chief judge from 1927. Considered a liberal, his main concern during his career as a judge was simplification of the law to fit the social needs of the case and of the times.

Carducci, Giosuè   (1835–1907) Italian poet and critic. The son of a country doctor, he became professor of Italian literature at Bologna University in 1860 and won the Nobel Prize in 1906. He was elected senator in 1890. He wrote vigorous, patriotic, and anticlerical poetry but *Rime nuove* (1861–87) and *Odi Barbare* (1877–89) also contain more lyrical verse with classical influences.

cargo cults   Religious cults found chiefly in Melanesia since the late 19th century. Their adherents believe that a new paradise will be heralded mainly by the arrival of a supernatural cargo of goods brought by spirits, who are variously viewed as gods, ancestors, or white foreigners. The cults probably evolved from Christian millennial teachings and native jealousy of the colonial European's material wealth.

Caria   A mountainous area in SW Asia Minor under the rule of *Lydia until 546 BC, when it passed to the Persians. The Carians joined the Ionian Greeks' unsuccessful revolt against the Persians (499–493 BC). Under the Hecatomnid dynasty (395–334 BC), Caria was absorbed into the Greek world.

Carib   An American Indian people of the Lesser Antilles and northern South America, after whom the Caribbean was named. The maritime island Caribs were warriors and cannibals, who before the advent of the Spaniards expelled the *Arawak Indians from the Lesser Antilles, enslaving the women and killing and eating the men. As a consequence, in these islands men spoke Carib and women, Arawak. The mainland Caribs were less aggressive and their culture was adapted to the tropical forest region. They cultivated manioc and hunted with the blowpipe.

Caribbean Community (CARICOM)   An association of 12 states in the Caribbean region (Antigua and Barbuda, Barbados, Belize, Dominica, Grenada, Guyana, Jamaica, Montserrat, St Kitts-Nevis, St Lucia, St Vincent and the Grenadines, and Trinidad and Tobago). It was established in 1973 and aims to coordinate the economic policies of member states through the Caribbean Common Market (which replaced the Caribbean Free Trade Area (CARIFTA) formed in 1968); to coordinate foreign policies; and generally to foster cooperation. Its headquarters are in Georgetown (Guyana).

Caribbean Sea   A section of the Atlantic Ocean, between the West Indies, E Central America, and N South America. With the opening of the Panama Canal (1914) it became an important shipping route. Its tropical climate and warm waters have led to the increasing importance of tourism throughout the Caribbean islands. Area: 1,049,500 sq mi (2,718,200 sq km). Maximum depth: 25,216 ft (7686 m).

caribou.   *See* reindeer.

CARICOM.   *See* Caribbean Community.

caries   Cavities in the teeth caused by bacterial erosion of the enamel and dentine. The bacteria feed on sugar from the diet: the sugar and bacteria become attached to the teeth to form a layer called plaque, and acid formed by bacterial breakdown of the sugar causes the damage of caries. Caries is most marked in those of Anglo-Saxon origin and it is particularly common in children and adolescents; a high-sugar diet and poor oral hygiene increase its incidence. Treatment consists of drilling away the damaged part of the tooth and replacing it with filling. Regular and adequate brushing of the teeth is the best preventive measure. The absorption of fluoride by growing teeth strengthens them against bacterial attack; *fluoridation of the public water supply is an aspect of preventive dentistry.

carillon   A set of bells hung in a tower, activated from a manual and pedal console similar to that of an organ. It is a popular instrument in Belgium and Holland. Carillons vary in size from two to four octaves. The wooden keys are depressed with the closed hand. The name is also applied to an organ stop that produces a bell-like sound.

Carina (Latin: Keel)   A constellation in the S sky near Crux. The brightest star is *Canopus.

Carinthia (German name: Kärnten)   A federal state in S Austria. It first came into Austrian possession in 1335; following World War I parts were ceded to neighboring Italy and Yugoslavia. Chiefly mountainous, it has picturesque alpine scenery and many lakes. The main occupations are livestock rearing, forestry, mining, and tourism. Area: 3681 sq mi (9537 sq km). Population (1981): 537,212. Capital: Klagenfurt.

Carl August   (1757–1828) Duke (1758–1815) and Grand Duke (1815–28) of Saxe-Weimar-Eisenach, who was the first German ruler to grant his state a liberal constitution. Carl August— participated in the wars against Napoleon and made territorial gains at the Congress of Vienna (1815). He was a friend and patron of *Goethe and other German writers.

Carl XVI Gustaf   (1946–) King of Sweden (1973–), succeeding his grandfather Gustaf VI (1882–1973). The Swedish monarch became little more than a figurehead under a new constitution effective from Carl's succession. In 1976 he married Silvia Sommerlath (1943–).

Carlisle   54 54N 2 55W A city in NW England, on the River Eden. Once a Roman military center (Luguvallum) and important fortress in the border wars with the Scots, it has a 12th-century cathedral and a castle (11th–13th centuries). Industries include flour milling, textiles, and agricultural engineering. Population (1976 est): 71,503.

Carlisle   40 12N 77 12W A city in SE Pennsylvania, SW of Harrisburg. Originally an army post, it now houses the US Army War College. The Carlisle Indian School (1879–1918) and Dickenson College (1783) are here. Manufactures include radio and electronic crystals. Population (1980): 18,314.

Carlism   A Spanish conservative movement, initiated by those who supported as *Ferdinand VII's successor in 1833 his brother Don *Carlos, rather than Ferdinand's daughter *Isabella II. The Carlists wanted a more severe repression of liberals, the restoration of the Spanish Inquisition, and the maintenance of traditional regional liberties (*fueros*). In the first Carlist War (1833–39), they were supported by the small landowners in the northeast but were eventually defeated. Carlism survived in its strongholds of Navarre and Aragon but in the second Carlist War (1872–76) was again defeated. During the Spanish Civil War Carlist regiments fought with Franco's armies but many Carlists became critical of Franco's government. The present Carlist pretender is Carlos Hugo de Bourbon-Parma (1930–), who married (1964) Princess Irene of the Netherlands.

Carlos, Don   (1788–1855) Spanish pretender. The brother of *Ferdinand VII and an ultra-Catholic reactionary, he contested the succession of his niece *Isabella II in 1833. His followers, who became known as Carlists, opposed Isabella's government in a series of Carlist wars (*see* Carlism).

Carlow (Irish name: Ceatharlach)   A county in the E Republic of Ireland, in Leinster. Chiefly low lying, it rises to mountains in the E. Agriculture is intensive producing barley, wheat, and sugar beet. Area: 346 sq mi (896 sq km). Population (1979): 38,668. County town: Carlow.

Carlsbad   32 25N 104 14W A city in SE New Mexico on the Pecos River. Founded in 1887, the nearby Carlsbad Caverns National Park (containing large limestone caves) makes it a popular tourist center. Potash, discovered in 1931, is extensively mined and it is a shipping point for cotton, alfalfa, oil, and livestock. Population (1970): 21,297.

Carlyle, Thomas   (1795–1881) Scottish historian and essayist. He worked unhappily as a teacher until 1819. In 1826 he married Jane Baillie Welsh and moved to London in 1834. *Sartor Resartus*, a blend of fiction, philosophy, and autobiography, was published in 1836 and was followed by his major work, *The French Revolution*, in 1837. This and later works express his view of history as shaped by the "Hero," or inspired individual. After his wife's death in 1866 he became grief-stricken at his neglect of her and retired from public life.

Carmel, Mount   32 45N 35 02E A mountain in N Israel, extending in a ridge for 16 mi (25 km) SE from the coast at Haifa. The Carmelite religious order was founded here. Height: 1791 ft (546 m).

Carmelites   A Roman Catholic religious order founded around the mid 12th century by St Berthold (died c. 1195), who claimed direct inspiration from Elijah and established a monastery at Mount Carmel. With the collapse of the Crusader kingdoms, the order moved to Europe. The original strict rule was relaxed in some respects. In 1452 an order of Carmelite nuns was instituted. In the 16th century the order was reformed by St *Teresa of Ávila and emphasized the cultivation of the contemplative life, which became a distinctive feature of the order.

Carmina Burana   A miscellany of lyrics, mainly in Latin, preserved together with six religious dramas in a 13th-century manuscript from Benediktbeuern, Bavaria. The work of earlier medieval wandering scholars, they encompass religious, pastoral, and erotic themes and range from satires on the Church to drinking songs. *See also* Orff, Carl.

CARNAC *Nearly 3000 menhirs still stand in the Carnac alignments.*

Carnac   47 35N 3 05W A village in Brittany (NW France). It is famous for the megalithic monuments in its vicinity (*see* megalith). Chief of these, and unique of their kind, are the avenues (alignments) of monoliths, set upright in parallel rows that run continuously for hundreds of meters. The three main groups, called Ménec, Kermario, and Kerlescan, may have had both ritual and astronomical significance.

Carnap, Rudolf   (1891–1970) German-born logical positivist philosopher. A founder of the *Vienna Circle, he was professor of philosophy successively at Vienna, Prague, Chicago, and California Universities. He worked on formal logic and its applications to science and *epistemology, believing that the analysis and clarification of knowledge should be the purpose of philosophy. By developing logical syntax and *semantics, he tried to construct a formal language for the empirical sciences to eliminate confusion, ambiguity, and similar obstacles to knowledge.

Carnarvon Range   A plateau in Australia, in SE Queensland. Part of the Great Dividing Range, it lies within a nature reserve and is being developed as a tourist area.

Carnatic music   The music of S India as opposed to that of N India. Not having been subjected to the influences of invading cultures, the S has kept an unbroken tradition that lays stress on complex rhythmic patterns. The scale is subdivided into 12 sections similar to those of the European chromatic scale. Primarily vocal, it also employs instruments, especially drums.

carnation   A large-flowered cultivated form of the clove pink (*Dianthus caryophyllus*). These perennials grow to heights of 16–24 in (40–60 cm), have tufts of dense grasslike foliage, and double flowers in white, yellow, orange, pink, red, or lavender. Hardy border carnations are suitable for outdoor cultivation, while the perpetual flowering varieties should be grown under glass. Flowers of carnations (and pinks) are noted for their clovelike fragrance. Family: *Caryophyllaceae*. *See also* Dianthus.

carnauba wax   A hard high-quality wax gathered from the leaves of the Brazilian carnauba palm (*Copernica cerifera*) and used for making high-gloss polishes. The tree secretes the wax to prevent excess evaporation from its leaves.

Carnegie, Andrew   (1835–1919) US industrialist, born in Scotland. He founded the Keystone Bridge Company (1865) to manufacture iron and, increasingly, steel. By 1888 he owned auxiliary coal- and iron-fields, railroads, and steamships and in 1901 his companies merged with the US Steel

Corporation. A noted philanthropist, he believed that a rich man should distribute his wealth for the benefit of society and donated over $350 million to causes in the US and Britain. He founded the Carnegie Institute of Technology in Pittsburgh in 1900, the Carnegie Institution in Washington in 1902, and many libraries. He also contributed substantially to the building of Carnegie Hall.

Carnera, Primo   (1906–67) Italian boxer, who was idolized during the 1930s although he was heavyweight champion only briefly (1933–34). 6.5 ft (1.98 m) tall, he was known for his knockout victories. He later took up wrestling and acted in the film *On the Waterfront* (1954).

Carnivora   An order of mammals adapted for hunting and eating flesh. Carnivores have strong jaws, with sharp incisor teeth and pointed canine teeth; some of the cheek (molar) teeth, called carnassials, act as shears to chop up meat. They are the major predators and most species are terrestrial, stalking or pouncing on their prey. The 252 species are divided into seven families: *Canidae (dogs); *Ursidae* (*see* bears); *Procyonidae* (*see* raccoons; pandas); *Mustelidae (weasels, skunks, etc.); *Viverridae (genets, mongooses, etc.); and *Felidae (cats).

carnivorous plant   A plant that obtains at least some of its nutrients by the digestion of insects and other small animals. Carnivorous, or insectivorous, plants show remarkable structural adaptations for their mode of life. *Butterworts and *sundews trap and digest insects by means of the sticky secretions produced by glands in the leaves. The *Venus flytrap traps its prey between bilobed hinged leaves with marginal teeth. Another common method of capture and digestion is by means of liquid-filled "pitchers" into which the insects fall (*see* pitcher plant).

Carnot, (Nicolas Léonard) Sadi   (1796–1832) French scientist and soldier, whose investigations of the efficiency of steam engines led him to the concept of ideal reversible cycles, a fundamental idea in the study of *thermodynamics. He described what are now known as the *Carnot cycle and Carnot's theorem (no engine can be more efficient than a reversible engine working between the same temperatures). His father **Lazare Nicolas Marguerite Carnot** (1753–1823) was a statesman and military engineer, known as the "organizer of victory" in the French Revolutionary Wars. He was a member of the Legislative Assembly (1791), the National Convention (1792), and the Committee of *Public Safety. Carnot was exiled in 1815 and settled in Magdeburg. His *De la défense de places fortes* (1810) became a classic work on fortifications.

Carnot cycle   A reversible thermodynamic cycle of changes of pressure and temperature in the gas in an ideal heat engine. The gas is compressed adiabatically (at constant heat content), thus raising its temperature, say from T_1 to T_2. It is then expanded isothermally (at constant temperature). The gas is then expanded adiabatically, lowering its temperature from T_2 back to T_1, and finally compressed isothermally at T_1, thus completing the cycle. The efficiency of this cycle depends not on the nature of the gas but only on the temperature range, i.e. it is equal to $(T_1-T_2)/T_1$, where T_1 and T_2 are absolute temperatures. Named for Sadi *Carnot.

Caro, Joseph   (1488–1575) Jewish legal scholar and mystic. A refugee from Spain (1492), he settled in Safed (Galilee), an important center of the *kabbalah. His most enduring work is the legal code *Shulhan Arukh* (*The Prepared Table*; 1564–65), which is still regarded as authoritative by orthodox Jews.

carob   The horn-shaped edible fruit pod of the carob tree, *Ceratonia siliqua*, an evergreen native to the Mediterranean region. The pods, sometimes known as algaroba or St John's bread, contain a sugary pulp and are used for fodder. The seeds are believed to have been the original carats of jewelers. Family: *Leguminosae*.

carol   A song of a joyful nature, originally accompanied by dancing. During the middle ages the word was applied to a variety of different types of song. Generally written in a simple verse-plus-refrain form, carols became associated with Christmas or Easter, but often had roots in pre-Christian beliefs. The first printed carol was the *Boar's Head Carol* (1521), one of many associated with the feast of the winter solstice. Others derive from miracle and mystery plays; the few that survive in manuscripts of the 15th century celebrate the events of the first Christmas; carols continued to be written on this theme until the 19th century.

Carol I   (1839–1914) The first King of Romania (1881–1914). Carol was a German prince, who was elected to the Romanian princedom in 1866 and became king when Romania gained independence from the Ottoman Empire. He introduced reforms and exploited Romania's oilfields but his economic program failed to help the peasants, who rebelled in 1907.

Carol II   (1893–1953) King of Romania (1930–40). In 1925 Carol renounced his right of succession to the throne to live in Paris with his mistress Magda Lupescu and his son *Michael succeeded in 1927. Carol returned to Romania in 1930 and was proclaimed king but was forced to abdicate in 1940 by the pro-German *Antonescu. He settled finally in Mexico, where in 1947 he married Mme Lupescu.

Carolina. *See* North Carolina; South Carolina.

Caroline Affair (1837) A US-Canadian incident that strained relations between the two countries. Canadian rebels were using the American steamboat *Caroline* for delivering supplies to Navy Island, their refuge on the Niagara River. Canadians still loyal to the British sank the steamboat in American waters, and the US protested to the British minister to Canada. Although the Canadian commander was tried, he was acquitted.

Caroline Islands An archipelago in the W Pacific Ocean, part of the UN trust territory of the *Pacific Islands, administered by the US. It includes the Truk, Yap, and Palau island groups and the large volcanic islands of Kusaie and Ponape. Copra is the main export. Area: 457 sq mi (1183 sq km). Population (1971): 70,815.

Caroline of Brunswick (1768–1821) The wife of George IV of the United Kingdom. After their separation (1796), he forbade her to see their child Charlotte. When George became king (1820), his attempt to divorce Caroline failed owing to popular support for her but she was excluded from the coronation (1821).

Carolingians The second Frankish ruling dynasty. It was founded by *Pepin the Short, who deposed the last *Merovingian king in 751, and it was named for Pepin's son *Charlemagne, who greatly expanded the Frankish territories. Crowned Emperor of the West in 800 by Pope Leo III, Charlemagne and his son *Louis the Pious were great patrons of learning, fostering the Carolingian renaissance (*see* Alcuin; Einhard). After the death of Louis the Carolingian empire was split into three kingdoms (843). The middle Frankish kingdom was divided into Italy, Lotharingia (Lorraine), and Provence; in the eastern Frankish kingdom (Germany) the dynasty survived until 911; and the western Frankish kingdom (France) was ruled by Carolingians until the failure of the line in 987.

Carossa, Hans (1878–1956) German novelist. A practicing doctor, he was influenced by Goethe's scientific theories as well as his literary works. Among his best-known novels are the autobiographical sequence *Eine Kindheit* (1922), *Rumänisches Tagebuch* (1924), and *Verwandlungen einer Jugend* (1928) and the anti-Nazi *Ungleiche Welten* (1951).

carotenoids A group of yellow, orange, or red pigments manufactured by bacteria, fungi, and plants and essential in the diet of animals. There are two groups—carotenes (including beta-carotene, a precursor of *vitamin A) and xanthophylls. Carotenoid pigments are important for display and camouflage coloring in both plants and animals and also as eye pigments.

carp An omnivorous freshwater fish, *Cyprinus carpio*, native to Asia but widely introduced elsewhere and raised for food. It has an elongated body, usually about 14 in (35 cm) long, with large scales, greenish or brownish above and paler below, four barbels on the upper lip, and a long dorsal fin. During the winter it hibernates in the bottom mud. Related fish include the Crucian carp and golden carp (*see* goldfish). Family: *Cyprinidae* (about 2000 species); order: *Cypriniformes*.

Carpaccio, Vittore (c. 1460–c. 1525) Venetian painter, noted for his paintings of his native city and his narrative cycles. His works, influenced by Gentile and Giovanni *Bellini, include a cycle of *Scenes from the Life of St Ursula* and *The Miracle of the Cross* (Accademia, Venice).

Carpathian Mountains A mountain range in Czechoslovakia, Poland, Hungary, the Soviet Union, and Romania. They form a rough semicircle about 90 mi (1450 km) long, including the Transylvanian Alps, which are also known as the **Southern Carpathians**) between Bratislava and the Iron Gate, both on the Danube River. The highest peak is Mount Gerlachovka, at 8737 ft (2663 m), in NE Czechoslovakia.

carpel The female organ of a flower, consisting of the stigma, style, and ovary (□plant). After fertilization, each carpel may ripen to produce a fruit containing one or more seeds. *See also* pistil.

Carpentaria, Gulf of A shallow inlet of the Arafura Sea, in N Australia situated between Arnhem Land and Cape York Peninsula. It contains many islands, the most important being *Groote Eylandt and Wellesley. There are important bauxite and manganese deposits. Area: about 11,000 sq mi (287,500 sq km).

Carpenter, (Malcolm) Scott (1925–) US astronaut. A Navy test pilot and air intelligence officer, he joined the National Aeronautics and Space Administration (NASA) in 1959 and, in 1962, made a three-orbit flight in Project Mercury's *Aurora 7*, becoming the second American to orbit in space. He retired from the Navy in 1969, after participating in Sealab II (1965) and Sealab III (1967), experimental underwater living stations.

carpenter bee A large black solitary *bee belonging to the European genus *Xylocopa*. *X. violacea* (1 in [25 mm long]) excavates galleries in wood or large plant stems to make its nest. The lesser carpenter bees (genus *Ceratina*) are found mainly in Africa. Family: *Apidae*.

Carpentier, Georges (1894–1975) French boxer, who was world light-heavyweight champion from 1920 to 1922. His unsuccessful fight against Jack *Dempsey (1921) drew the first million-dollar gate. He also fought at several other weights.

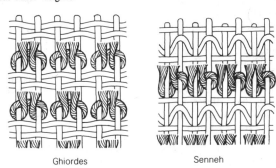

Ghiordes   Senneh

CARPET *The two varieties of knot used in oriental handknotted carpets are the Ghiordes (Turkish) and Senneh (Persian) knots.*

carpet A floor covering of fabric. Although tapestries were sometimes used as floor coverings in the middle ages, knotted carpets originated in Asia and date back to about the 3rd century BC. They are woven with tufts of wool, or sometimes silk, knotted around the warp threads as the carpet is woven or around a jute or hessian backing to form a pile. Oriental carpets traditionally have symbolic designs and colors, which distinguish them as Persian, Turkish, Indian, etc. From the 12th century onward, these designs have been used and adapted by European carpet manufacturers, the Savonnier carpets of 17th-century France being a typical example. Modern machine-made carpets, such as Wilton, have the pile formed by cut loops instead of knots, while Brussels carpet has uncut loops. In the type of carpet now called "tufted" the tufts are held in place by a foam-rubber backing. Synthetic fiber is replacing wool, especially for wall-to-wall carpet, which is made in rolls instead of the traditional squares or rectangles and cut to meet individual requirements.

Carpetbaggers Northern profiteers during the *Reconstruction of the South (1865–77) after the US Civil War, who often carried their possessions in a heavy cloth satchel (carpetbag). By manipulating the uneducated newly enfranchised black voters, the carpetbaggers helped the Republicans gain local and state control. A few carpetbaggers, however, were sincere advocates of equal rights for blacks.

carpet beetle A small oval beetle, up to 0.4 in (10 mm) long, belonging to a genus (*Anthrenus*) of worldwide pests. It is the hairy red-brown or golden-brown larvae that cause the damage, by feeding on virtually all materials of animal origin, especially furs and fabrics. *A. museorum* is a major pest of museum collections. Family: *Dermestidae*.

Carpini, Giovanni da Pian del (c. 1180–c. 1252) Italian traveler in Mongolia. A Franciscan friar, at Pope Innocent IV's behest he led a remarkable mission to the Mongols, whose incursions into Christian lands were causing alarm. He departed from Lyon in 1245, reached Karakoram, where he was presented to the khan, in 1246, and then made the return trip largely in winter (1246–47).

Carracci A family of Bolognese painters, who were instrumental in reviving the Renaissance art of Raphael, Titian, and Correggio after the heyday of *mannerism. They founded an influential teaching academy (1582) and collaborated on decorations for Bolognese palaces. **Ludovico Carracci** (1555–1619) devoted his life to art instruction and painting altarpieces. His cousin **Agostino Carracci** (1557–1602) was a noted engraver and assisted his brother **Annibale Carracci** (1560–1609), the most famous of the three, on decorations in the gallery of the Farnese Palace, Rome.

carrageen (*or* carageen) An edible brownish-red *seaweed, *Chondrus crispus*, also called Irish or sea moss, that grows abundantly on rocky coasts of W Britain and Ireland, N Europe, and North America. A red alga, it has thin, usually flat branching fronds, about 2–12 in (5–30 cm) long, and contains a gelatinous carrageenin (substance) used in jellies, lotions, cosmetics, food products, shoe polishes, etc.

Carrantuohill 52 00N 9 45W The highest mountain in Ireland, in Co Kerry, in Macgillicuddy's Reeks. Height: 3414 ft (1041 m).

Carranza, Venustiano (1859–1920) Mexican statesman and soldier in the post-1910 revolutionary movement. He was the first president (1917–20) under the 1917 constitution and his nationalist policies brought him into conflict with the US. He was deposed and killed in a coup in 1920.

Carrara 44 04N 10 06E A city in central Italy, in Tuscany. It is famous for its white marble, which was used by the sculptor Michelangelo. Population (1971): 67,758.

Carrel, Alexis (1873–1944) French surgeon, who pioneered the technique for sewing (suturing) blood vessels together. He perfected this after moving to the US, where he also worked on techniques for keeping organs alive outside the body. He was awarded a Nobel Prize (1912).

Carrhae, Battle of (53 BC) The battle near Carrhae (now Haran, Turkey) in which the Roman forces under Marcus Licinius *Crassus were defeated by the Parthians.

Carrington, Peter Alexander Rupert Carington, 6th Baron (1919–) British Conservative politician. As foreign secretary (1979–82) he was instrumental in establishing Zimbabwe's independence (1980); he resigned following the Argentinian invasion of the *Falkland Islands (1982). Carrington was appointed secretary general of NATO in 1984.

carrion crow An omnivorous Eurasian crow, *Corvus corone corone*, about 17 in (46 cm) long with a pure-black plumage and a harsh croaking call. It is a notorious egg thief, unpopular with gamekeepers. *See also* hooded crow.

carrion flower A cactus-like succulent plant belonging to the genus *Stapelia* (60 species), native to arid parts of Africa. Several are grown for their showy purplish flowers, although they have a fetid odor. *S. gigantea* has a leafless square stem, 2–12 in (5–30 cm) high, bearing a flower with a diameter of 12 in (30 cm). Family: *Asclepiadaceae*.

The name is also given to a species of *greenbrier, *Smilax herbacea*, which has small green evil-smelling flowers.

Carroll, Lewis (Charles Lutwidge Dodgson; 1832–98) British writer and mathematician. He lectured in mathematics at Oxford University (1855–81) and was ordained in 1861. The children's classic *Alice's Adventures in Wonderland* (1865) was written for a young friend, Alice Liddell. It and the sequel, *Through the Looking-Glass* (1872), are sophisticated books that combine elements of fantasy, logic, and nonsense and have had a lasting appeal to adults as well as children. He also wrote nonsense verse, notably *The Hunting of the Snark* (1876), and was a pioneer of portrait photography.

carrot A biennial flowering plant, *Daucus carota*, found in grassy places in temperate regions from Europe to India. The stem grows to a height of 12–40 in (30–100 cm) and bears a head of small white flowers. *Daucus carota sativus* is the cultivated carrot. This is grown as an annual, and produces an orange thick fleshy edible root. Many varieties of the cultivated carrot have been developed. Family: *Umbelliferae*.

Carson, Edward Henry, Baron (1854–1935) Irish politician and lawyer, solicitor general for Ireland (1892) and England (1900–06). In 1895 Carson gained fame in his successful prosecution for homosexuality of Oscar Wilde. As a member of the English parliament (1892–1921), he led the Ulster opposition to the Irish *Home Rule bill (1912) and raised the Ulster Volunteers to oppose its enactment. In World War I he served in Asquith's and Lloyd George's cabinets.

Carson, Kit (Christopher C.; 1809–68) US frontiersman. A saddler in Missouri, stationed on the Santa Fe trail, he joined a wagon train in 1826 and made Taos, New Mexico, his headquarters for a career as a guide. Well-versed in Indian ways, he was a guide in *Frémont's expeditions to the West in the 1840s and after distinguished service in the Mexican War became US Indian agent at Taos (1853). He subsequently fought for the Union in the Civil War. Illiterate, Carson dictated his memoirs (1856), published as *Dear Old Kit*.

Carson, Rachel Louise (1907–64) US science writer, who worked as a genetic biologist (1936–52) and later as editor for the US Fish and Wildlife Service. Her books, notably *The Sea around Us* (1951) and *Silent Spring* (1962), greatly increased public awareness of the natural environment and warned of the dangers of pollution.

Carson City 39 10N 119 46W The capital city of Nevada. It is named for the famous frontiersman Kit Carson. Although silver and copper are mined, the main industry is gambling. Population (1980): 30,807.

Cartagena 10 24N 75 33W A port in N Colombia, on the Caribbean Sea. It is important industrially, producing textiles, petrochemicals, and pharmaceuticals. It receives oil by pipeline from Berrancabermeja; exports include coffee and oil. The University of Cartagena was founded in 1827. Population (1978 est): 418,953.

Cartagena (*or* Carthagena) 37 36N 0 59W A port in SE Spain, in Murcia on the Mediterranean Sea. Founded by the Carthaginian general Hasdrubal in the 3rd century BC, it was destroyed by Ferdinand II of Castile in 1243. In the 16th century, under Philip II of Spain, it became a great naval port and remains the country's chief Mediterranean naval base. It exports minerals, olive oil, and fruits and has boatbuilding industries. Population (1970): 146,904.

Cartago 9 50N 83 52W A town in central Costa Rica, at the foot of the volcano Irazú. It serves an agricultural area. Population (1981 est): 26,341.

Carte, Richard D'Oyly. *See* D'Oyly Carte, Richard.

cartel An association of producers who join together to secure a higher price for their products by restricting the supply. However, a cartel is inherently unstable; all the members have an interest in producing as much as they can at the new price, in defiance of the cartel agreement. The need to enroll all producers and to maintain strict discipline explains why the highly successful oil cartel OPEC has not been followed by other primary-product cartels.

Carter, Howard (1874–1939) British archeologist. Carter worked in Egypt from 1892 and collaborated with Lord Carnarvon (1866–1923) after 1907. In 1922 they discovered the tomb of *Tutankhamen, work on which occupied Carter for the next ten years.

JIMMY CARTER *The president brings together Sadat of Egypt (left) and Begin of Israel (right) at Camp David.*

Carter, James Earl Jr. ("Jimmy") (1924–) US statesman; 39th President of the US (1977–81). A graduate of the US Naval Academy, Carter spent most of his adult life managing his family's peanut farm and warehouse in Plains, Ga. Carter later embarked on a political career, serving as governor of Georgia (1971–75) and receiving the Democratic presidential nomination in 1976. Carter defeated President Gerald *Ford in the general election and soon after his inauguration attempted to implement an ambitious program of national energy conservation and environmental regulations. His greatest achievements and greatest failures, however, came in the field of foreign policy. In 1978 he sponsored negotiations at *Camp David between Egyptian president Anwar *Sadat and Israeli prime minister Menachem *Begin that led to a peace treaty between the two countries in the following year. In 1978, Carter also supported and signed a treaty relinquishing US control of the *Panama Canal. The most serious crisis of Carter's presidency came in 1979, when the US embassy in Teheran was seized by Iranian students and its staff was held hostage. Unsuccessful US appeals to the United Nations and the World Court and an abortive attempt at a military rescue mission in 1980 failed to gain the hostages' release. Carter's popularity declined dramatically, and he was defeated for re-election by Ronald *Reagan in 1980. A personal memoir of his presidency, *Keeping Faith*, was published in 1982.

Carteret, John. *See* Granville, John Carteret, 1st Earl.

Cartesian coordinates. *See* coordinate systems.

Carthage (Punic name: *Kart-Hadasht*, New City)   An ancient city of N Africa, near modern Tunis. Traditionally founded 814 BC by *Dido and exiles from *Tyre, Carthage rapidly became leader of the *Phoenician trading cities of N Africa, waging intermittent war with the Greeks of Marseilles and Sicily. From 264 BC Carthage fought the three *Punic Wars with *Rome, her former ally, and was totally destroyed (146 BC). Refounded by Julius *Caesar (45 BC), Carthage became, in turn, the commercial, cultural, and administrative capital of Roman Africa, the capital of the *Vandal kingdom (439–533 AD), and a Byzantine outpost, until destroyed by the Muslims in 697 AD.

Carthusians   A contemplative Roman Catholic religious order founded in 1084 by St Bruno and taking its name from the location of the first community, La Grande Chartreuse, near Grenoble. Although originally without a written rule, the Carthusians observed a rigorous life of fasting and solitude and were vowed to silence. The order remained fairly small but disciplined. At the time of the dissolution of the monasteries there were nine Carthusian monasteries, or *Charterhouses, in England. At present the order's English headquarters is the Charterhouse, Parkminster, Sussex. The French monks are noted for the liqueur Chartreuse, which they make.

Cartier, Jacques   (1491–1557) French navigator. In 1534, under the patronage of Francis I, he sailed in search of the *Northwest Passage and explored the coast of N Canada and Newfoundland. The next year he sailed up the St Lawrence as far as what became Montreal but failed to found a colony there (1536). His discoveries were important to French claims in Canada in the 17th century.

Cartier-Bresson, Henri   (1908–) French photographer and pioneer of photojournalism. He studied painting before taking up photography in 1932. Although also providing a record of events on his worldwide travels, his often poignant photographs, collected in such books as *The Decisive Moment* (1952), concentrate on ordinary people and their fleeting expressions and gestures. As a film maker, he collaborated with Jean *Renoir in the late 1930s and returned to this medium in the 1960s.

cartilage   A flexible supportive tissue consisting chiefly of a *polysaccharide—chondroitin sulfate—in which elastic or collagen fibers may be embedded. Cartilage lines the bone ends at joints and also provides the skeleton of the nose, external ear, and parts of the throat (larynx) and airways of the respiratory tract. A tough cartilage forms the intervertebral disks between the bones of the spine. During development a large amount of *bone is formed from pre-existing cartilage.

cartilaginous fish   Any *fish belonging to the class *Chondrichthyes*, comprising the *sharks, *rays, and *chimaeras. They have a cartilaginous skeleton, usually a ventrally situated mouth, and exposed gill slits. The males have pelvic fins modified to form copulatory organs (claspers) and fertilization occurs inside the female's body. Some species deposit their eggs on the sea bed while in others the eggs are retained and develop internally resulting in the birth of live young.

cartography   The science of map and chart making. Belief in the flatness of the world, the centrality of the Mediterranean lands (or Jerusalem in Christian maps), and an all-encircling Ocean dominated classical and medieval cartography. Maps and charts were individually hand drawn at first, but 15th- and 16th-century maps were printed by woodblock and colored by hand. More elaborate maps and charts, richly decorated with lettering and illustrations were introduced by the Italians in the mid-16th century. The difficulty of accurately representing the curved surface of the earth on the plane surface of a map is dealt with by using different □map projections for different purposes. Modern map making is assisted by aerial surveying and satellite photography.

cartoon   1. A full-sized preparatory drawing or painting for a mural, easel painting, tapestry, or mosaic. Among the most famous are Raphael's cartoons for tapestries for the Sistine Chapel in the Vatican. 2. A nonrealistic portrait or figure drawing transferring a person's most readily recognizable features into a comic likeness. Beginning in Italy as a branch of high art with *Leonardo da Vinci's grotesque heads and *Bernini's political drawings, caricatures became a favorite genre in popular art with political satires. This tradition was carried into middle-class journalism in the Victorian period and has now become the widely used cartoon strip of modern newspapers.

Cartwright, Edmund   (1743–1823) British inventor and industrialist, who contributed to the mechanization of weaving and spinning. In 1785 he invented a power loom and then set up a factory for weaving and spinning yarn. Four years later he invented a machine for combing wool.

Caruso, Enrico   (1873–1921) Italian tenor, born in Naples. The greatest lyric tenor of his time, he excelled in Verdi and Puccini and was acclaimed

in Europe and the US, where he sang at the Metropolitan Opera in New York City.

GEORGE WASHINGTON CARVER *Agriculturalist whose research in crop diversification and land rejuvenation aided farmers.*

Carver, George Washington   (1864–1943) US agriculturalist, born into a slave family. Carver demonstrated to southern farmers how fertility could be restored to their land by diversification, especially by planting peanuts and sweet potatoes. He also discovered a wide range of by-products that could be obtained from these crops. At Tuskegee Institute in Alabama, he devoted most of his life to teaching and conducting research.

Cary, (Arthur) Joyce (Lunel)   (1888–1957) British novelist. His early novels, notably *Mister Johnson* (1939), are mostly set in West Africa, where he worked before settling in Oxford in 1920. His best-known book, *The Horse's Mouth* (1944), is part of a trilogy about art; he also wrote a second trilogy, about politics.

caryatid   A carved column in the shape of a draped female figure that first appeared in Greek architecture around 500 BC. The most notable caryatids to have survived are on the Erechtheum on the *Acropolis of Athens. Caryatids were infrequent in Roman architecture but enjoyed a limited revival in 19th-century classicism.

caryopsis   A grain: the small dry *fruit of grasses and cereals. It resembles an achene, being single-seeded and indehiscent, but differs in having the seed completely fused to the fruit wall.

Casablanca   (Arabic name: Dar-el-Beida)   33 39N 7 35W A port in Morocco, on the Atlantic coast. First established by the Portuguese (1515), it was taken by the French in 1907. During World War II it was the scene of the Casablanca Conference (1943), a summit meeting between Franklin D. Roosevelt and Sir Winston Churchill. The largest and most important city in Morocco, its port handles most of the country's trade, the chief export being phosphates. Its major industries include textiles, electronics, chemicals, cement, and food processing. Fishing and tourism are also important. Population (1973 est): 1,371,330.

Casals, Pablo   (Pau C.; 1876–1973) Spanish cellist, conductor, and composer. He performed and conducted in every European country and in the US. Casals revolutionized the style and technique of cello playing and excelled as an interpreter of Bach's six suites for unaccompanied cello and of the cello concertos of Dvořák, Elgar, and Schumann. An opponent of the Franco regime in Spain, Casals settled in Prades in France, near the Spanish border; he established a chamber-music festival there in 1950.

Casanova, Giovanni Giacomo, Chevalier de Seingalt (1725–98) Italian adventurer. He lived in many European cities, working at different times as a violinist, a spy, and a librarian. His adventures, which included a dramatic escape from prison in Venice in 1756 and many romantic liaisons, are recorded in his memoirs, of which the first complete edition was published in 1960.

Cascade Range A volcanic mountain range in North America. It extends N–S, nearly parallel to the Pacific coast, between the Fraser River in British Columbia (Canada) and N California (US), where it becomes continuous with the *Sierra Nevada. It reaches 14,408 ft (4392 m) at Mount Rainier.

case hardening A surface-hardening process in *steel manufacture, in which the metal is heated to over 900°C for several hours in the presence of carbon. The carbon is absorbed on the surface to a depth depending on the temperature and duration of the treatment. The steel is then cooled quickly (quenched) to complete the process. *See also* heat treatment.

casein The major protein present in milk. Casein is easily digested and contains a good balance of essential *amino acids, making it—in dietary terms—a high-quality protein. Cheese consists largely of insoluble para-casein, formed from casein by the action of enzymes. Casein is also used industrially to make thermoplastics (e.g. knife handles), paints, and adhesives.

Casement, Sir Roger (David) (1864–1916) British consular official and Irish nationalist, who was executed by the British for treason. Casement spent his consular career in Africa. He retired to his birthplace, Ireland, in 1912. In World War I he tried unsuccessfully to raise German help for the Irish nationalists. Returning to Ireland in a German submarine, he was arrested, tried, and, in spite of opposition, hanged.

Caserta 41 04N 14 20E A market city in S Italy, in Campania. The center of Garibaldi's campaigns for the unification of Italy in the 19th century, it has a 12th-century cathedral and a palace. Its manufactures include chemicals. Population (1971): 62,928.

cashew A tree, *Anacardium occidentale*, native to tropical America and cultivated widely in the tropics. It grows to a height of about 40 ft (12 m) and has sweet-scented red flowers. The fruit is a kidney-shaped nut that develops at the end of a hanging pear-shaped receptacle. The edible kernel—the cashew nut—is extracted after the fruit is roasted. Family: *Anacardiaceae*.

cashmere A warm soft wool-like fabric made from the undercoat of the *Kashmir goat, produced mainly in China, Mongolia, and Iran. Originally used in shawls from Kashmir, it is an expensive fabric as each goat produces only small quantities of fine soft hair and processing is costly. Imitations are common and any soft woolen textile, natural or synthetic, is frequently called cashmere.

Casimir (III) the Great (1310–70) King of Poland (1333–70). Casimir extended Polish territory, codified laws, and founded Cracow University (1364). He encouraged the development of Polish culture and bettered the lot of the peasants.

Casimir IV (1427–92) Grand Duke of Lithuania (1440–92) and King of Poland (1447–92), whose reign saw a flowering of Polish culture. Casimir greatly enhanced the prestige of the Jagiellon dynasty by his own and his children's political marriages. After a 13-year war with the *Teutonic Knights he won control of W Prussia (1466).

Caspian Sea The largest inland sea in the world, bounded by Iran and the Soviet Union and fed chiefly by the Volga River. Its surface is 93.5 ft (28.5 m) below sea level and is generally becoming lower due to irrigation and increased evaporation from the Volga. The chief ports are Astrakhan and Baku, both in the Soviet Union. Sturgeon and seals are caught here and oil and gas extracted. Area: about 142,827 sq mi (370,000 sq km).

Cass, Lewis (1782–1866) US politician and statesman. A lawyer and state legislator in Ohio, he was then governor of Michigan Territory (1813–31). Appointed secretary of war in 1831 by President Andrew *Jackson, he served through the Black Hawk and Seminole wars before being appointed minister to France (1836–42). He was a senator from Michigan (1845–48; 1849–57), ran for president in 1848, and was secretary of state (1857–60) under President James *Buchanan. During his extensive career he successfully negotiated with the Indians and supported the popular sovereignty doctrine of allowing the territorial settlers to settle the question of slavery among themselves.

Cassander (c. 358–297 BC) King of Macedon (305–297). In the wars of succession that followed the death of Alexander the Great in 323, Cassander fought for control of parts of Alexander's empire and won most of Macedon and Greece. He murdered Alexander's mother, widow, and son to secure his position.

Cassandra A legendary Greek prophetess, daughter of King Priam of Troy. After she had refused to submit to Apollo's advances, he condemned her prophecies to eternal disbelief. When Troy fell she was taken by Agamemnon, with whom she was later murdered.

MARY CASSATT Morning Toilet, *painted in 1886.*

Cassatt, Mary (1844–1926) US painter. She worked chiefly in Paris, where she exhibited with the impressionists (1879–81, 1886) the only American to do so. Although she was influenced by her friend *Degas she developed a distinctly American style. Typical of her work are mother-and-child scenes.

cassava A shrubby flowering plant, *Manihot esculentus* (or *M. utilissimus*), also known as manioc, native to tropical America. Many varieties of this species—divided into two groups, sweet and bitter cassavas—are cultivated in the tropics for their edible starchy tuberous roots. These can be processed into tapioca, ground to produce manioc or cassava meal (Brazilian arrowroot), used as animal fodder, or cooked and eaten as a vegetable. Family: *Euphorbiaceae* (spurge family).

cassette A plastic case containing a length of magnetic recording tape wound onto two spools. Cassettes are easy to use but can hold only relatively short tapes, their length being limited by the minimum thickness of tape that can be used without breakage. Commercial cassettes are two-track, i.e. can be used to record in both directions, and are available with 30, 60, 90, or 120 minutes playing time.

cassia The aromatic bark of a Chinese tree, *Cinnamomum cassia*, used as a substitute for cinnamon. The dried unripe fruits (cassia buds) are also used as a spice. Family: *Lauraceae*.

Cassia A genus of trees, shrubs, and herbs (500–600 species) of tropical and warm regions of Asia, Africa, and America. The laxative drug senna is extracted from the dried leaves and pods (fruits) of many cultivated species. The fruit of *C. fistula* (Cassia pods) is also used as a laxative. Some species are grown as ornamentals. Family: *Leguminosae*.

Cassini's division. *See* Saturn.

Cassino 41 29N 13 50E A city in central Italy, in Lazio. It was a key position during World War II and the town and Benedictine monastery (Monte Cassino) were destroyed in the fighting of 1944. Population (1971): 24,796.

Cassiodorus, Flavius Magnus Aurelius (c. 490–c. 583 AD) Christian writer, born in S Italy, who helped to preserve classical learning. After serving in the government of the Ostrogothic king Theodoric I, Cassiodorus retired to found a monastery at Vivarium in Calabria (550); his most famous work, the *Institutiones*, was a guide to the education of monks.

Cassiopeia A conspicuous constellation in the northern sky, lying partly in the Milky Way. The five brightest stars form a W-shape. It contains the remnants of two recent *supernovae—**Tycho's star** and the intense radio source **Cassiopeia A**.

cassiopeium. *See* lutetium.

Cassirer, Ernst (1874–1945) German philosopher and historian. He taught in Hamburg (1919–34) until Nazism forced him into exile in the US. Interested in people's formation of concepts, he added mythical, historical, and practical categories, based on analysis of language, to *Kant's scientific ones, seeing these as complementary views of one reality. His works include *Substance and Function* (1910) and *Philosophy of Symbolic Forms* (1923).

cassiterite The only commercial ore of tin, consisting of stannic oxide. It is found in association with acid igneous rocks and as alluvial deposits. It is brown or black.

Cassius Longinus, Gaius (d. 42 BC) Roman general. Having shown competence in eastern campaigns, Cassius supported *Pompey until Pompey's defeat by Julius Caesar at *Pharsalus. He was then pardoned by Caesar but joined the conspiracy to assassinate him in 44. Outlawed, Cassius committed suicide after defeat in the battle of *Philippi.

Cassivelaunus King of the Catuvellauni, who organized, with some success, resistance to Caesar's invasion of SE Britain in 54 BC. Only after his stronghold was captured did Cassivelaunus agree to peace terms.

cassowary A large flightless bird belonging to a family (*Casuariidae* ; 3 species) occurring in rain forests of Australia and New Guinea. The largest cassowary (*Casuarius casuarius*) is 60 in (150 cm) tall and has a black plumage, two red throat wattles, and a blue head with a protective bony helmet. Cassowaries have long powerful legs, each having a long sharp claw, and feed on seeds and berries. Order: *Casuariiformes*.

Castagno, Andrea del (Andrea di Bartolo de Simone; c. 1421–57) Italian *Renaissance painter, who was born near Castagno but settled in Florence. His major frescoes depict the *Last Supper* and the *Passion* (Sta Apollonia, Florence). Later works, showing the influence of *Donatello, include the equestrian portrait of *Niccolò da Tolentino* (Duomo, Florence).

castanets A percussion instrument used in Spain and Italy, consisting of two small cup-shaped pieces of wood (usually chestnut) attached to the finger and thumb of each hand. These are clapped together and dancers often accompany themselves with them. In the symphony orchestra the characteristic sound is produced by two wooden cups attached to a handle and shaken. □musical instruments.

Castel Gandolfo (Latin name: Alba Longa) 41 45N 12 39E A village in central Italy, in Lazio on the shore of Lake Albano. The summer residence of the pope is situated here.

Castellammare di Stabia 38 01N 12 52E A seaport and resort in Italy, in Campania on the Bay of Naples. It was the site of the Roman resort of Stabiae, which was destroyed by the eruption of Vesuvius in 79 AD. Industries include marine engineering and textiles. Population (1971): 68,629.

Castellón de la Plana 39 59N 0 03W A city in E Spain. Its industries include textiles and paper and it exports oranges and almonds through its port, El Gráo. Population (1974 est): 108,021.

Castelo Branco, Camilo (1825–95) Portuguese novelist. An illegitimate child with little formal education, he led an adventurous life that is reflected in his many popular novels and stories. His best-known work, *Amor de Perdição* (1862), was written while he was in prison for adultery. Suffering from blindness, he committed suicide.

castes The elements of a system of social stratification in which social boundaries are very definite. A pure caste system consists of a hierarchy of hereditary endogamous occupational groups, in which positions are fixed and mobility from one caste to another is prevented by ritual systems. The classical Hindu caste system (Sanskrit word: varna) of India provides the cardinal example. Traditionally there are four main caste divisions: brahmins (priests), ksatriyas (warriors), vaisyas (merchants), and sundras (serfs). Outside these groups are the "outcastes" or "untouchables." Each stratum is elaborately subdivided; the 1901 census identified 2378 main castes, some of which had several hundred subcastes. Vigorous attempts have been made to abolish the system, especially by Mahatma Gandhi, but despite legislation (1947) abolishing "untouchability" and prohibiting discrimination on the basis of caste, prejudice remains strong.

Castiglione, Baldassare (1478–1529) Italian courtier and writer. A member of an aristocratic family, he was born near Mantua and in 1503 entered the service of the Duke of Urbino, whose court was one of the most distinguished in Renaissance Italy. He performed important diplomatic missions for the Duke; he was later Mantuan ambassador in Rome and after 1524 in the service of Pope Clement VII as papal nuncio in Spain. His literary reputation rests on *Il Cortegiano* (1528), prose dialogues, set in the court of Urbino, which describe the qualities of the ideal courtier. The work was translated into English as *The Courtier* by Sir Thomas Hoby (1530–66) in 1561 and exercised a great influence on such writers as Surrey, Wyatt, and Sidney.

Castile A former kingdom in central Spain. Originally a district at the foot of the Cantabrian Mountains, Castile expanded to the Duero River in the 9th and 10th centuries, becoming a united county. In 1035 it became a kingdom and in 1230 was united with the kingdom of *León, a union dominated by Castile. In 1479 Spain was virtually united following the marriage of *Isabella of Castile to *Ferdinand of Aragon and Castile became the political, administrative, cultural, and linguistic center of Spain. Today, opposition to Castilian dominance persists.

Castilho, Antonio Feliciano de (1800–75) Portuguese poet. Blind from childhood, he achieved literary distinction after publishing several volumes of romantic poetry, notably *A Noite de Castelo* (1836). After 1840 he worked mainly on translations, and his advocacy of neoclassical doctrines provoked fierce controversy.

casting metals The process of shaping molten metals in a mold. In casting individual items a sand mold is often used. A solid pattern of the shape, made of wood, plastic, or metal, is placed in a molding box packed tightly with sand bonded with oil or clay. The pattern is then carefully removed leaving a shaped cavity into which the molten metal is pored and allowed to solidify. If the casting is to be repeated, permanent metal molds called dies are used. **Die casting** is faster and can make more complex shapes than foundry sand casting. **Centrifugal casting**, spinning the molten material at a high speed so that the centrifugal force flings it outward into a surrounding mold, is used for pipes and similar shapes.

cast iron A form of impure iron containing between 2.5% and 4.5% of carbon by weight. The high carbon content makes it relatively hard and brittle and it tends to crack under tension. Cast iron is made by casting *pig iron and adjusting its composition to improve the strength. It is used for complicated shapes.

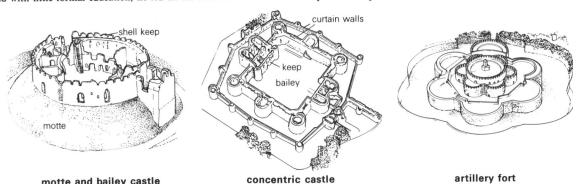

motte and bailey castle   **concentric castle**   **artillery fort**

CASTLE *The early medieval motte and bailey plan gave way to the massive fortifications of the 14th and 15th centuries, which were in turn superseded by the artillery fort with its low walls and sweeping lines of fire.*

castle A fortified defensive building. Its name deriving from Latin *castellum*, a small fortified place, the castle underwent many changes in its history to counteract the development of increasingly powerful weapons. In the early middle ages a castle consisted of a simple building on a mound of earth surrounded by a wooden fence (the motte and bailey castle), a design later copied in stone. The simplest stone castle, such as the White Tower in London, is called a keep or donjon. Later designs became more complicated, involving extensive outworks of battlemented towers and walls (curtain walls), for example Caernarfon Castle in Wales. As they could not be built to withstand cannon fire castles lost their military usefulness; some, such as Windsor Castle, were converted into large houses.

Castle Hill Rising (1804) A rising in New South Wales (Australia) led by Irish convicts against the government. The rebels seized the convict station at Parramatta but were defeated by government troops, who killed 15 convicts. Nine rebels were tried and hanged.

Castlereagh, Robert Stewart, Viscount (1769–1822) British statesman, born in Ireland; foreign secretary (1812–22). A member of the Irish parliament (1780), he became Viscount Castlereagh in 1796. Appointed chief secretary for Ireland in 1798, he resigned in 1801, when George III rejected the Catholic Emancipation bill. He was secretary for war (1807–09), and as foreign secretary he played an important role at the Congress of *Vienna (1814–15).

Castner process The production of sodium cyanide from molten sodium, charcoal, and ammonia. Sodamide and sodium cyanamide are byproducts. The extremely poisonous sodium cyanide finds use in the extraction of gold and silver, in hardening steel, and in dye manufacture. Named for Hamilton Young Castner (1859–99).

Castor A white star, apparent magnitude 1.56 and 46 light years distant, that is the second brightest star in the constellation Gemini. It is a *multiple star. Castor and *Pollux are named for the twins of classical mythology.

Castor and Pollux Twin heroes of classical mythology, also known as the Dioscuri. Pollux was immortal, the son of *Zeus and *Leda; Castor was mortal, the son of Tyndareus and Leda. When Castor died, Pollux successfully petitioned Zeus to allow them to remain unseparated. They were transformed into the Gemini constellation and were the patrons of mariners.

castor oil A pale yellow viscous oil extracted from the seeds of the *castor-oil plant. It is used as a laxative and is also a raw material for the manufacture of resins, plastics, and lubricants.

castor-oil plant A flowering plant, *Ricinus communis*, up to 40 ft (12 m) high, native to tropical Africa and Asia. It is cultivated widely, in the tropics for its seeds, from which castor oil is extracted, and in temperate regions as an ornamental shrub with attractive fanlike leaves (ornamental forms are seldom taller than 7 ft [2 m]). Family: *Euphorbiaceae* (spurge family).

castration Removal of the testes (orchidectomy) or ovaries (oophorectomy). In medicine, castration may be performed in cases of cancer of the testes: it always produces sterility but—unless done before puberty—need not cause impotence. Testicular castration is widely used in livestock management to increase meat production or docility.

castrato A eunuch singer, fashionable in Italian opera and in church choirs during the 17th and 18th centuries. Castration before puberty ensured that the soprano (or sometimes alto) voice quality remained in adulthood. Among the most technically brilliant of the castrati was Giuseppe Farinelli (1705–1782). Composers of Italian opera, such as Handel, frequently wrote the leading male role in the soprano range for a eunuch.

Castres 43 36N 2 14E A city in S France, in the Tarn department. A Huguenot stronghold in the 16th century, it has a major machine-tool industry. Population (1975): 47,527.

Castries 14 01N 60 59W The chief city and main port of St Lucia, in the Windward Islands. Founded by the French in 1650, it has a fine harbor. Population (1970): 45,000.

Castro (Ruz), Fidel (1926–   ) Cuban statesman. The son of a wealthy sugar planter, Castro became an opponent of the dictator Fulgencio *Batista. On July 26, 1953, he led an unsuccessful attack on the Moncada barracks and was imprisoned until 1955. In 1956 he invaded Cuba from Mexico with a small armed band and after a long guerrilla war he defeated government troops. He entered Havana on January 1, 1959. Castro established a socialist government, which the US attempted to subvert. As a result, Cuba became heavily dependent on the Soviet Union. *See also* Bay of Pigs.

Castrop-Rauxel 51 33N 07 18E A city in NW West Germany, in North Rhine-Westphalia in the *Ruhr. Its industries include coalmining and chemicals. Population (1971 est): 83,100.

FIDEL CASTRO *The Cuban leader exhorts the UN General Assembly to give more aid to the developing countries.*

Casuarina A genus of shrubs and trees (about 45 species) native to Australia, tropical SE Asia, Malaysia, Polynesia, the Mascarene Islands, and Pacific islands. The young branches, which are slender, green, and drooping, function as leaves (the true leaves are reduced to scales). The she oak (*C. equisetifolia*) up to 145 ft (45 m) tall, is widely cultivated in warm regions for its very hard reddish-brown wood (beefwood or ironwood) and as an ornamental. Family: *Casuarinaceae*.

cat A carnivorous mammal belonging to the family *Felidae* (36 species). Most cats have sheathed claws and sharp canine teeth to kill their prey, which consists of mammals, birds, and fish. Their acute vision (especially in poor light), sense of smell, and hearing are adaptations for hunting stealthily, often at night. With no natural enemies, the kittens (or cubs) are born blind and toothless and learn hunting techniques through play.

The wide range of different breeds of domestic cat (*Felis catus*), including *Persian, *Siamese, and *Abyssinian, are thought to have been developed from the African wildcat, or cafer cat (*F. lybica*) and possibly the European *wildcat. Wild species range in size from the *tiger to the tiny South African black-footed cat (*F. nigripes*), which is smaller than the average domestic cat.

catabolism. *See* metabolism.

catacombs Subterranean cemeteries, especially those containing early Christian graves. The earliest and biggest catacombs are in Rome, particularly those of St Calixtus and St Sebastian along the *Appian Way. Most catacombs consist of narrow passages into the walls of which the burial niches were cut. With the acceptance of Christianity they fell into disuse, although some remained as centers of pilgrimage.

Catalan A *Romance language spoken by about five million people in Catalonia and the Balearic Islands in Spain, Andorra, and the Roussillon region of France. It is closely related to Spanish and to the Occitan language of France. It was the official language of Aragon in the 12th century and has a literature dating from this period.

Catalaunian Plains, Battle of the (451 AD) The battle on the Catalaunian Plains, probably near modern Châlons-sur-Marne in Champagne (E France), in which the Huns under *Attila were defeated by a combined force of Romans and Visigoths under *Aetius and Theodoric I.

catalepsy A condition associated with certain abnormal mental states, including schizophrenia and hysteria, in which the patient, usually female, remains motionless, often with the limbs in fixed positions, for a variable length of time.

Catalhüyük A Neolithic site SE of Konya (S Turkey), discovered in 1958. It was a settlement of cattle breeders and agriculturalists, dating from the late 7th and early 6th millenniums BC. Houses built to a standard pattern and luxury goods, such as obsidian mirrors, suggest advanced social organization. Notable finds include numerous shrines with frescoes or plasterwork decorations depicting animals.

Catalonia (Spanish name: Cataluña; Catalan name: Catalunya) A mainly mountainous region of NE Spain, on the Mediterranean Sea. Agriculture is important, the main crops being cereals, olives, and grapes. It is the most highly industrialized region in Spain, being well provided with hydroelectric power from the Ebro River (and its tributaries). Tourism is important, especially on the coast. *History*: united with Aragon in 1137 and Castile in 1497, Catalonia has nevertheless maintained a strong separatist tradition. In 1932 an autonomous government was established and this lasted throughout the Civil War (1936–39), in which Catalonia played a prominent role on the Republican side. A center of opposition throughout the Franco regime, the Catalan government was restored provisionally in 1977. Area: 12,329 sq mi (31,932 sq km). Population (1970): 5,122,567. Capital: Barcelona.

Catalpa A genus of trees (11 species) native to E Asia, North America, and the West Indies. They were widely grown as ornamentals for their attractive heart-shaped leaves, 5–12 in (12–30 cm) long, and trumpet-shaped flowers, which are white with yellow and purple markings. The fruit is a long pod. The genus includes the Indian bean tree (*C. bignonioides*), up to 49 ft (15 m) high, which yields a durable timber. Family: *Bignoniaceae*.

catalysis The acceleration of a *chemical reaction by a substance (catalyst) that is not itself consumed in the reaction. Virtually every reaction must overcome an energy barrier as the molecules of the reactants rearrange to form the products. The catalyst allows the reaction to proceed via a different lower-energy pathway. Since the reverse reaction is also accelerated, catalysis does not shift the chemical equilibrium, merely speeds its attainment. Catalysis may be homogeneous (all substances in the same phase), as the catalysis of carbon-monoxide combustion by steam; or heterogeneous (at an interface) as in the *Haber-Bosch process. Catalysis by a reaction product is called autocatalysis. Catalysis is used extensively in industrial chemical processes. In living organisms *enzymes are catalysts for biochemical reactions.

catalytic cracking A chemical process used in *oil refining. Crude oil, which contains large molecules, is decomposed by heat and pressure in the presence of a catalyst, usually a clay-type substance containing alumina and silica. Without a catalyst the same process, known as thermal cracking, needs a pressure of between 20 and 40 atmospheres and a temperature of 332°F (540°C). Catalytic cracking is carried out at between two and three atmospheres at a slightly lower temperature.

catamaran A modern sailing vessel with two identical hulls, rigidly fastened parallel to one another, and, usually, a single mast with a triangular mainsail and jib. Because of their buoyancy, the hulls of a catamaran offer very little resistance to the water, making it extremely fast. The modern catamaran is modeled on a native canoe-like vessel of the SW Pacific, which in some forms was basically a raft with a sail. *See also* trimaran.

Catania 37 31N 15 06E A port in Italy, in E Sicily near Mount Etna. Destroyed by an earthquake in 1693, it was rebuilt in a baroque style. The university was founded in 1434. Its industries include sulfur refining. Population (1980 est): 398,168.

Catanzaro 38 54N 16 36E A market city in S Italy, the capital of Calabria. Citrus fruit is grown in the area. Population (1971): 85,316.

cataract (geography). *See* waterfall.

cataract (ophthalmology) Opacities in the lens of the eye resulting in blurred vision and caused by the deposition of small crystals or changes in the composition of the lens substance. The former condition increases with age; such cataracts are a common cause of blindness in the elderly. Certain diseases, such as poorly controlled diabetes mellitus, can also lead to cataracts. Cataracts are usually treated by surgical removal of the lens and the use of appropriate glasses. In some cases a plastic lens may be implanted to replace the one removed.

catarrh Inflammation of the mucous membranes lining the nose, nasal sinuses, throat, or air passages, causing the production of thick phlegm. Catarrh is commonly due to viral infections, particularly the common cold, and hay fever.

catastrophe theory A theory of dynamic systems using methods of *topology. Originally, catastrophe theory was developed by the French mathematician René Thom (1923–), in 1972, as a theory of biological differentiation, in which gradual growth stimulates and is stimulated by "catastrophic" large-scale changes. It has since been applied to other fields, including optics, engineering, sociology, economics, and linguistics. The theory is based on analogy with topological form. For instance, if a system depends on three factors, a particular state of the system can be represented by a point in three-dimensional space and possible states are represented by a region (or shape). The behavior of the system is investigated by considering the topological classification of these representations, in particular the theory shows how discontinuous catastrophic changes can occur. In engineering, a structure may be stable under a certain range of conditions and collapse if other conditions are applied.

catastrophism A formerly held theory according to which geological changes have occurred as a result of sudden short-lived catastrophes. Such events do occur (e.g. floods), but they have temporary and local effects. *Compare* uniformitarianism.

Catawba American Indian tribe, Siouan-speaking, found in S US in present-day North Carolina and South Carolina. Potters and basketweavers, they allied with the colonials and helped fight off other Indians, especially the *Cherokee and *Iroquois. Today, fewer than 400 Catawba live on a South Carolina reservation.

catchment area The area from which a river is fed with water; it is usually bounded by a *watershed or divide.

catechism A form of instruction in the essentials of Christian doctrine. Catechisms were originally for the instruction of converts preparing for *baptism, frequently taking the form of a set of responses. With the spread of infant baptism, from the 6th century their function became the basic education of children in the faith, often as preparation for *confirmation. After the Reformation, printed forms of catechisms were also used as an expression of particular churches' beliefs.

catechol (pyrocatechol *or* 1,2 dihydroxy-benzene; $C_6H_4(OH)_2$) A colorless crystalline *aromatic compound used as a developer in photography. *See also* catecholamines.

catecholamines Amine derivatives of the chemical compound *catechol. They include the biologically important compounds *adrenaline, *noradrenaline, and dopamine, which act as neurotransmitters and hormones.

catechu A vegetable extract containing *tannin and used in tanning and dying. Black catechu is obtained mainly from the wood of trees. Pale catechu (gambier; terra japonica) is produced from leaves and is used in medicine as an astringent. Extract from betel or areca nuts is also called catechu.

categorical imperative The fundamental moral law in *Kant's ethical theory: an act is moral only if the principle on which it is justified is universally applicable.

catenary The curve obtained by suspending a string between two points. If the middle of the string, the lowest point, is at height a above a reference level, then the height, y, at distance x along the string from the middle is given by: $y = \frac{1}{2}a\,(e^{x/a} + e^{-x/a})$

caterpillar The larva of a butterfly or moth. Soft-bodied and wingless, all caterpillars have a head and 13 body segments with 3 pairs of true thoracic legs and 5 pairs of abdominal prolegs, which aid in locomotion. The mouthparts are variously adapted for chewing leaves or feeding on sap. Some species are serious crop pests. Caterpillars exhibit a wide variety of camouflaging or warning coloration and patterning. Some produce irritating or poisonous secretions. *See also* butterflies and moths.

catfish A *bony fish of the order *Siluriformes* (about 2500 species), with a stout scaleless body, 2–180 in (4–450 cm) long, a broad flat head, and long whisker-like barbels. Freshwater catfish (family *Ictaluridae*), sometimes called bullheads, occur worldwide; marine catfish (family *Ariidae*) inhabit tropical and coastal waters and are generally bottom-dwelling scavengers used as food, game, and aquarium fish. *See also* candiru; wels.

The name is also used for marine fish of the family *Anarhichadidae* (order *Perciformes*).

catgut The tough cord made from the intestines of the sheep or sometimes the ox and the horse (but not the cat). It is used for stringing tennis rackets, violin strings, and for surgical stitching.

Cathari (*or* Cathars) A heretical sect in medieval Europe. It spread from Bulgaria, where its adherents were called Bogomils, to W Europe in the 11th century. From the mid-12th century the Cathari flourished in S France (*see* Albigenses) and in Italy until they were wiped out in the 14th century by the Inquisition. Their doctrine, influenced by *Gnosticism and *Manicheaism, taught that the material world was irredeemably evil but that man's soul was good and could secure his reunion with God. They were skeptical about much biblical doctrine, holding, for instance, that Christ was only an angel. They were divided into two classes, the perfect and the believers. The perfect lived in celibacy, marriage being regarded, with all other fleshly indulgences, as evil. The believers could join the perfect immediately before death by receiving the Cathari's chief rite, a laying on of hands, called the *consolamentum*.

Cathay The medieval European name for China, derived from Khitan, the name of a Mongol people who invaded N China in the 10th century. It was introduced to Europe by such early travelers as Marco Polo. China is still called Khitan by the Russians.

cathedral The principal church of an ecclesiastical area (diocese), governed by a bishop or an archbishop. The name comes from Latin *cathedra*, bishop's seat. Generally larger and more magnificent than other churches, cathedrals, such as *St Peter's Basilica, Rome, *St Paul's Cathedral, London, and *Notre-Dame de Paris, contain some of their country's finest works of art.

Cather, Willa (1873–1947) US author. She wrote about the pioneers and their lives on the Nebraska frontier, where she had lived during her formative years, and the Southwest, which she had visited. As a young woman she worked on *The Home Monthly* and taught school before becoming editor (1908–12) of *McClure's Magazine*. Her works include *O Pioneers!* (1913), *My Antonia* (1918), *One of Ours* (1922), for which she won a Pulitzer Prize, *A Lost Lady* (1923), *The Professor's House* (1927), *Death Comes for the Archbishop* (1927), and *Shadows on the Rock* (1931).

Catherine I (1684–1727) The second wife from 1712 of Peter the Great and Empress of Russia (1725–27). Of Lithuanian peasant origin, Catherine was captured in 1702 in the Great Northern War and became Peter's mistress. After Peter's death in 1725, his adviser Prince A. D. Menshikov (1672–1729), supported by the palace guards, secured the throne for Catherine.

Catherine (II) the Great (1729–96) Empress of Russia (1762–96), who gained the throne in a coup in which her unpopular husband, Emperor Peter III (1728–62; reigned 1762), was murdered. Catherine's reign was noted for the expansion of Russian territory largely as a result of her successful wars against the Turks (1768–72, 1787–92) and the partition of Poland (1772, 1793, 1795). Influenced by the ideas of the Enlightenment, she professed an interest in reform but abandoned her scheme to emancipate the serfs in the face of opposition from their masters, whose privileges she ultimately reinforced. Of the series of lovers for whom Catherine achieved notoriety, only *Potemkin exerted a durable influence on government.

Catherine de' Medici (1519–89) Regent of France (1560–63) during the minority of her second son, Charles IX, and virtual ruler until his death (1574). The daughter of Lorenzo de' Medici, Duke of Urbino, she married Henry II of France in 1533. Intent on upholding royal authority during the *Wars of Religion, she initially advocated tolerance for the *Huguenots but later supported the Catholic party. She was largely responsible for the *St Bartholomew's Day Massacre. Catherine's influence waned during the reign of her third son *Henry III.

Catherine of Aragon (1485–1536) The first wife (1509–33) of *Henry VIII of England and the mother of Mary I. Failing to bear him a son, she was divorced by Henry, who argued that their marriage was invalid because Catherine was the widow of his brother Arthur. The pope's refusal to accept their divorce provoked the English *Reformation.

Catherine of Braganza (1638–1705) The wife (from 1662) of Charles II of England. A Portuguese princess and a devout Roman Catholic, her unpopularity was intensified by her failure to produce an heir to the throne.

Catherine of Genoa, St (1447–1510) Italian mystic. From a noble family, she married at the age of 16 but underwent a religious conversion 10 years later and devoted herself to caring for the sick. She had a number of mystical experiences, which are recounted in *Vita e dottrina* (1551), a book that is perhaps not all her own work in its present form. Feast day: Sept 15.

Catherine of Siena, St (Caterina Benincasa; 1347–80) Italian nun and mystic. Devout from the earliest age, she joined the Dominican Tertiary Order at 16 and devoted herself to caring for the sick and poor and to contemplation. In 1376 she undertook a journey to Avignon to persuade Pope Gregory IX to return to Rome. She was reported to have received the stigmata on her body in 1375. Her letters and a work on mysticism, the *Dialogue*, are extant. Feast day: April 30.

catheter A tube inserted into a hollow organ of the body in order to drain or introduce fluids. A urinary catheter is inserted into the bladder through the urethra to relieve obstruction (commonly caused by enlargement of the prostate gland in elderly men) to the flow of urine. Cardiac catheters are used to measure blood pressure in the heart; similar catheters are used to inject radio-opaque substances into blood vessels for X-ray examination.

cathode The negative electrode of an electrolytic cell, valve, etc. It is the electrode by which the electrons enter the system. *Compare* anode.

cathode-ray oscilloscope (CRO) An instrument that displays electrical quantities on the screen of a *cathode-ray tube. It can be used to show the variation of a signal strength with time or with another electrical quantity. The CRO is used extensively in electronics laboratories and in other scientific work.

cathode rays A stream of electrons emitted by a *cathode, when a voltage is applied between a cathode and an *anode either in an evacuated glass tube or one containing gas at low pressure. The electron beam can be focused onto a fluorescent screen to produce a visual display. This effect is used in the *cathode-ray tube used in television receivers, radar screens, and oscilloscopes.

cathode-ray tube (CRT) A vacuum tube that converts electrical signals into visible form by projecting a beam of electrons onto a fluorescent screen. It is an essential component of the television receiver and the *cathode-ray oscilloscope (CRO). The electron beam is produced by an electron gun, and deflected horizontally and vertically by an arrangement of plates and magnets, which move it back and forth across the screen and focus it by creating an *electromagnetic field, the strength of which varies according to input signals. In a television tube the beam intensity varies to form the light and dark regions of the picture.

Catholic emancipation A campaign in Britain and Ireland to secure full civil and political rights for Roman Catholics. Since the Reformation, Catholics had been subject to a number of restrictions concerning property ownership, inheritance, and government employment and could not sit in parliament. In the late 18th century several relief acts were passed but parliamentary representation was still denied until the Catholic Emancipation Act of 1829 restored most rights.

Catiline (Lucius Sergius Catilina; d. 62 BC) Roman politician, who plotted to seize power in 62. Thwarted by Cicero, Catiline fled to a rebel force in Etruria and his fellow conspirators were executed. He was defeated and killed in battle.

GEORGE CATLIN *A painting by the artist depicting himself (left) in the lodge of a Mandan Indian chief. Catlin made a number of drawings and paintings of this people in 1832.*

Catlin, George (1796–1872) Pennsylvania artist and author. He is famous for his painted and written studies of the American Indians, among whom he lived (1832–40). His best-known book is *Manners, Customs, and Conditions of North American Indians* (1841).

catmint A perennial flowering plant, *Nepeta cataria*, native to chalky regions of temperate Europe. The branching stem grows to a height of 16–40 in (40–100 cm) and bears toothed heart-shaped leaves and small white flowers spotted with purple. The plant has a strong minty scent, attractive to cats. Family: *Labiatae*.

Cato Street Conspiracy (1820) A conspiracy against the British government led by Arthur Thistlewood (1770–1820). A fanatical idealist, Thistlewood and four others planned to murder all the ministers of the cabinet as a prelude to insurrection. Their attempt was foiled and the leaders, arrested in Cato Street, London, were hanged.

Cato the Elder (Marcus Porcius C.; 234–149 BC) Roman statesman, who wrote the first history of Rome. A moral and political conservative, Cato as censor (184) legislated against luxury and sponsored improvements in public works. His embassy to Carthage (153) led him to fear the resurgence of Rome's old enemy; "Carthage must be destroyed" was his repeated cry until the third *Punic War was declared (149). His simple writing style was influential and he is the first important Latin prose author.

Cato the Younger (Marcus Porcius C.; 95–46 BC) Roman politician; the great-grandson of Cato the Elder and an opponent of Julius Caesar. Caesar created the first *Triumvirate (60) to neutralize Cato's opposition to his dictatorial ambitions. Forced to support Pompey in the civil war in an attempt to save the Republic, Cato escaped after Pompey's death to Utica, in Africa. There, on hearing of Caesar's victory at *Thapsus, he committed suicide after ensuring the evacuation of his supporters.

Catskill Mountains A mountain range in the N Appalachian Mountains of New York. Consisting of forested steep-sided mountains, it rises to 4204 ft (1261 m) at Slide Mountain. The area supplies water to New York City and is a popular vacation and recreation area for New Yorkers. The mountains are associated with the fictional character Rip Van Winkle, created by Washington Irving.

cat's-tail. See reedmace.

Catt, Carrie Lane Chapman (1859–1947) US reformer. She was a leader in the woman's suffrage movement and was, in great part, responsible for the ratification of the 19th Amendment in 1920. She headed the National American Woman Suffrage Association (1915–47), reorganizing it into the League of Women Voters after 1920. She was also deeply interested in peace and disarmament movements, Prohibition organizations, and the United Nations, and she helped found the Daughters of the American Revolution (DAR).

cattle *Ruminant mammals belonging to the genus *Bos* (7 species), also called oxen, native to Eurasia and Africa. Modern domestic cattle (*B. taurus*), which are probably descended from such ancestors as the *auroch, vary in body shape, size, and color according to breed but are generally 35–44 in (90–110 cm) high at the shoulder and weigh 882–1984 lb (400–900 kg). *Zebus and *gayals are similarly now found only in the domestic state. Cattle are used for milk and meat production and for draft purposes (see livestock farming). Family: *Bovidae*. See also banteng; gaur; yak.

Cattleya A genus of tropical American epiphytic *orchids (about 65 species), grown commercially for ornament and the florist trade. They have large pseudobulbs, one or two leaves, and clusters of 1–30 large brightly colored flowers. *C. labiata* has been crossed with other orchid genera to produce many showy hybrids.

Catton, (Charles) Bruce (1899–1978) US historian, especially of the Civil War. Editor of *American Heritage* magazine from 1954, he wrote about the Civil War from the participants' point of view. His works earned him a Pulitzer Prize twice, for *A Stillness at Appomattox* (1953) and *The American Heritage Picture History of the Civil War* (1960). Other works include *Mr. Lincoln's Army* (1951), *Glory Road* (1952), *This Hallowed Ground* (1956), *Grant Moves South* (1960), and *The Terrible Swift Sword* (1963).

Catullus, Valerius (c. 84–c. 54 BC) Roman poet. Born in Verona, he became the leading member of a group of young innovatory poets in Rome. 116 poems survive, of which the most famous are the 25 lyrics addressed to a married woman named Lesbia, recording in passionate language the shifting moods of love from ecstasy to despair. The other poems include elegies and vicious satirical attacks on Julius Caesar and other politicians.

Caucasian languages. See Northeast Caucasian; Northwest Caucasian; South Caucasian.

Caucasoid A race or group of races and peoples originally inhabiting Europe, North Africa, and the Near East. In modern times Caucasoids have spread to North and South America, Australia, New Zealand, parts of Africa, and elsewhere. They are characterized by skin pigmentation ranging from very pale to dark brown, straight to curly hair, narrow high-bridged noses, plentiful body hair, and a high frequency of Rh-negative blood type.

Caucasus Mountains (Russian name: Kavkaz) Two mountain ranges in the SW Soviet Union extending NW–SE between the Black Sea and the Caspian Sea and separated by the Kura River: the **Great Caucasus**, some 621 mi (1000 km) long, to the N and the **Little Caucasus**, about half that length, along the Turkish border. Their highest point is Mount *Elbrus. See also Ciscaucasia; Transcaucasia.

Cauchy, Augustin Louis, Baron (1789–1857) French mathematician, who pioneered the study of functions of *complex numbers. He also derived a mathematical basis for the luminiferous ether. An outspoken and extreme conservative, Cauchy went into exile in Italy in 1830 on the accession of King Louis Philippe.

cauliflower A variety of wild *cabbage, *Brassica oleracea* var. *botrytis*, cultivated as a vegetable. The short stem bears a round white heart, up to 25 cm in diameter, of tightly compressed flower buds surrounded by green leaves. See also Brassica.

Cauvery River (or Kaveri R.) A river in S India. Rising in the Western Ghats, it flows mainly ENE to the Bay of Bengal. It has a wide delta, the principal channel being the Coleroon, and it irrigates the area by way of a system of canals. It is sacred to the Hindus. Length: 470 mi (756 km).

Cavafy, Constantine (C. Kavafis; 1863–1933) Greek poet. He lived nearly all his life in Alexandria, where he worked as a civil servant. Many of his poems are ironic treatments of subjects from the ancient Hellenistic world; he also wrote erotic homosexual love poems. He spoke and read English and had a strong influence on E. M. *Forster and Lawrence *Durrell.

Cavalcanti, Guido (c. 1255–1300) Italian poet. A friend of Dante, he wrote about 50 poems on themes of love and emotional suffering. He died of a disease contracted while exiled from Florence for his political activities.

Cavalier poets A group of English poets connected with the court of Charles I (1625–49). They included Richard *Lovelace, Robert *Herrick, Thomas Carew, Edmund Waller, and Sir John *Suckling. Their love lyrics and poems about war and honor were characterized by a sophisticated elegance appropriate to their positions as courtiers and gentlemen.

Cavaliers The royalist party during the English *Civil War. After the *Restoration of the monarchy (1660) the name was kept by the court party and was given to the parliament that sat from 1661 to 1679. The cavaliers were distinguished by their elaborate dress, with lace ruffles, feathers, and velvet, in contrast to the sober attire of the *Roundheads.

Cavalli, Francesco (1602–76) Italian composer of opera and church music. A pupil of Monteverdi in Venice, he wrote over 40 dramatic works based on legends of gods and heroes.

Cavallini, Pietro (c. 1250–c. 1330) Roman fresco painter and mosaicist. He was the first to abandon the stylizations of *Byzantine art and his chief works are the mosaics of the *Life of the Virgin* for Sta Maria in Trastevere and the frescoes in Sta Cecilia.

cavalry A force of mounted soldiers. Employed throughout the ancient world for its speed and mobility, the invention of stirrups (c. 400 AD) increased its usefulness by enabling heavily armored lancers and swordsmen to fight on horseback. The introduction of *small arms in the 15th century shifted the emphasis in warfare to infantry and the use of *machine guns from the late 19th century rendered the role of cavalry in battle suicidal. Modern armored units have adopted the name and role of cavalry.

Cavan (Irish name: Cabhán) A county in the NE Republic of Ireland, in Ulster. It is generally hilly, drained chiefly by the River Erne, with lakes and *drumlins. Although largely infertile, agriculture is the mainstay of the economy producing oats, potatoes, and dairy products. Some small industries exist in the towns. Area: 730 sq mi (1890 sq km). Population (1979): 53,720. County town: Cavan.

cave fish One of several cave-dwelling *teleost fishes, especially members of the family *Amblyopsidae*, found in fresh water in dark limestone caves of North America. They have translucent colorless elongated bodies, about 4 in (10 cm) long, reduced nonfunctional eyes, and numerous sensory papillae covering the body to compensate for blindness.

Cavell, Edith (1865–1915) British nurse. From 1907 she worked at a training institute for nurses in Brussels. She was executed by the Germans in 1915 for helping Allied soldiers to escape from German-occupied Belgium.

Cavendish, Henry (1731–1810) British physicist. He discovered hydrogen and investigated its properties. He also identified the gases in the atmosphere and showed that water is a compound. The first to measure accurately the universal gravitational constant, he used it to calculate the mass of the earth.

caves Underground hollows, usually opening directly onto the ground surface or connected with it by a passage. In limestone regions, where most caves occur, many constitute part of a system of natural underground drainage and are connected by subterranean streams. These caves are excavated by the slow solution of limestone by slightly acidic rain water percolating through its joints. The other main type of cave is that eroded from the base of a cliff by the sea. Such caves are located at some point of weakness in an otherwise resistant rock, such as a fault plane or bed of softer material.

caviar A delicacy, eaten as an hors d'oeuvre, which consists of sturgeon's roe, salted and freed from all fat. It is a Russian specialty. The roe of the beluga is considered the best, although caviar is also obtained from other types of sturgeon. Real caviar is extremely expensive, but a substitute made from lumpfish roe is relatively inexpensive.

Cavite 14 30N 120 54E A city in the N Philippines, in SW Luzon on Manila Bay. Formerly a center of opposition to Spanish and US rule, it is the site of a major US naval base. Population (1970): 75,739.

Cavour, Camillo Benso di, Count (1810–61) Italian statesman; the architect of Italian unification (*see* Risorgimento). Committed to liberal politics from boyhood, he helped to found the organ *Il risorgimento* in 1847. In 1852 he formed his first government under *Victor Emmanuel II of Sardinia-Piedmont. Cavor accepted an alliance with France and Britain during the Crimean War and negotiated a further alliance with France at Plombières in 1859 to oust Austria from Italy. He resigned when France came to terms with Austria but became prime minister again in 1860, negotiating the union of Sardinia-Piedmont with Parma, Modena, Tuscany, and the Romagna, and by 1861 had achieved the establishment of a united Italy.

cavy A small South American *rodent belonging to the genus *Cavia* (6 species); the ancestor of the domestic guinea pig. Cavies are mainly nocturnal and live in groups in scrub and grassland, digging burrows and feeding on vegetation and seeds. The adults generally breed twice a year and the young cavies are independent at three weeks. Family: *Caviidae*.

EVONNE CAWLEY *In action at Wimbledon, England, in 1971, where she beat Virginia Wade to win the women's championship.*

Cawley, Evonne (*born* E. Goolagong; 1951–) Australian tennis player, who twice became Wimbledon singles champion (1971, 1980) and won the doubles in 1974. She was Australian singles champion (1974–76) and Australian doubles champion in 1971, 1974, and 1975.

Cawnpore. *See* Kanpur.

Caxton, William (c. 1422–91) The first English printer. A cloth merchant, Caxton lived in Bruges from 1446 until 1470, when he moved to Cologne. There he learned the technique of printing and in 1474 set up a press that produced the first printed book in English, *Recuyell of the Historyes of Troye* (1475). On returning to England (1476), he set up a press at Westminster, where he printed a long and varied list, including Chaucer's *Canterbury Tales* (1478) and an encyclopedia that was the first illustrated English book, *The Myrrour of the Worlde* (1481).

Cayenne 4 55N 52 18W The capital and main Atlantic port of French Guiana, in the NW of the Île de Cayenne. Founded by the French in 1643, it served as a French penal settlement (1854–1938). Cayenne pepper derives its name from a plant grown in the area. Population (1980): 36,215.

Cayley, Sir George (1773–1857) British engineer and pioneer designer of flying machines. He studied the effects of streamlining, the properties of different shapes of wings, and the basic shape of heavier-than-air aircraft. He tested his theories with models and in 1853 built the first successful manned glider. He also invented the caterpillar tractor.

cayman (*or* caiman) An amphibious reptile occurring in rivers of Central and South America. 4–15 ft (1.2–4.5 m) long, it feeds on fish, birds, and insects. Genera: *Caiman* (2 species), *Melanosuchus* (1 species), *Paleosuchus* (2 species); subfamily: *Alligatorine* (alligators and caimans); order: *Crodilia* (*see* crocodile).

Cayman Islands A British colony in the Caribbean Sea, consisting of three low-lying coral islands (Grand Cayman, Little Cayman, and Cayman Brac) lying about 200 mi (320 km) NW of Jamaica. The population is mainly of mixed African and European descent. *Economy*: depends mainly on tourism, although favorable tax laws have encouraged banking. The main exports are turtle shell, dried turtle meat, and tropical fish. *History*: discovered in 1503 by Columbus, who named them Las Tortugas because of the abundance of turtles. Formerly attached to Jamaica, they gained some self-government in 1959 and became a separate British colony in 1962. Official language: English. Official currency: Jamaican dollar of 100 cents. Area: 100 sq mi (260 sq km). Population (1981 est): 17,035. Capital and main port: Georgetown.

Cayuga North American Iroquoian-speaking Indian tribe, branch of the Five Nations of the *Iroquois League. Found in central New York, they were cultivators, hunters, and warriors. As part of the Iroquois League they supported and fought with the British against the French and against the colonists in the *American Revolution. Today, the remaining Cayuga live on reservations in New York and Oklahoma.

Ceará. *See* Fortaleza.

Ceaucescu, Nicolae (1918–) Romanian statesman, noted for his opposition to Soviet interference in Romanian affairs. Ceaucescu's rise in the Party hierarchy began in 1948. In 1965 he became the Party's general secretary and in 1967 Romania's leader as president of the state council; he became the first president of the Republic in 1974.

Cebu 10 17N 123 56E A port in the central Philippines, in E Cebu. The first Spanish settlement in the Philippines (founded 1565), it has a Roman Catholic cathedral and bishop's palace. Its four universities include the University of San Carlos (1595). An important commercial center, its industries include textiles and food processing. Population (1980): 489,208.

Cebu An island in the central Philippines, in the Visayan Islands. Its populous coastal plains are cultivated chiefly with coconuts, maize, sugar cane, and hemp. Coal and copper are mined. Area: 1964 sq mi (5086 sq km). Population (1970): 1,634,182. Chief town: Cebu.

Cecil, Robert Gascoyne-Cecil, 1st Viscount (1864–1958) British statesman. Cecil was minister of blockade and then deputy foreign secretary in World War I. He took part in the Paris Peace Conference (1919) and helped draft the charter of the League of Nations; he was awarded the Nobel Peace Prize in 1937.

Cecilia, St (2nd or 3rd century AD) Roman Christian martyr. According to legend, she converted her pagan husband Valerian and his brother Tiburtius, who were martyred before her. Although there is doubt concerning her authenticity, she remains the patron saint of sacred music. Feast day: Nov 22. Emblem: an organ.

cecropia moth A large brown and reddish *Saturniid moth, *Platysamia cecropia*. With a wingspan of 6 in (155 mm), it is the largest North American moth. The caterpillars are green and feed on a variety of trees.

cedar A conifer of the genus *Cedrus* (4 species), native to the Mediterranean region and the Himalayas and widely planted for ornament and timber. Cedars usually grow to a height of 130 ft (40 m). Their stiff needle-like leaves grow in tufts of 10–40 on short spurs and their cones are erect and barrel-shaped, 2–6 in (5–14 cm) long. The best-known species are the *deodar; the Atlas cedar (*C. atlantica*), from the Atlas mountains; and the cedar of Lebanon (*C. libani*), of the E Mediterranean. Family: *Pinaceae*.

A number of unrelated trees are also known as cedars (*see* incense cedar; Japanese cedar; pencil cedar), and conifers of the genus *Thuja* (*see* arbor vitae) are sometimes called cedars.

Cedar Rapids 41 59N 91 39W A city in E central Iowa. Its industries include cereals and agricultural machinery. Population (1980): 110,243.

celandine Either of two unrelated perennial herbaceous plants. **Greater celandine** (*Chelidonium majus*) is found in cool temperate and subarctic regions throughout Europe and Asia. The brittle branching stems, 12–35 in (30–90 cm) long, bear deeply lobed leaves and bright-yellow flowers. The fruit is a narrow capsule, 1–2 in (3–5 cm) long. Family: *Papaveraceae*.

Lesser celandine (*Ranunculus ficaria*), sometimes known as pilewort, is native to Europe. The branching stems, 2–10 in (5–25 cm) long, bear long-stalked leaves and bright-yellow flowers, which fade to white. The roots form numerous tubers. Family: *Ranunculaceae*.

Celaya 20 32N 100 48W A city in central Mexico. An agricultural trading center, it contains several churches by the noted Mexican architect Francisco Eduardo de Tresguerras (1763–1833). Population (1978 est): 114,365.

Celebes. *See* Sulawesi.

celeriac A variety of cultivated *celery, Apium graveolens* var. *rapaceum*, also known as turnip-rooted or knob celery, grown for its globular edible root. The root, up to 6 in (15 cm) in diameter, has a celery-like flavor.

celery The cultivated form of wild celery, or smallage (*Apium graveolens*), a biennial herb native to grassy coastal areas from Europe to India and Africa. Many varieties of cultivated celery have been developed for their edible leafstalks (up to 12 in [30 cm] in length), which may be pink, yellow, or green. Traditionally, the green varieties are blanched to tenderize the tissues. The wild plant has an erect grooved stem, 12–24 in (30–60 cm) long, bearing whorls of clusters of small greenish-white flowers. Family: *Umbelliferae*.

celesta A small keyboard instrument the quiet bell-like tone of which is produced by hammers striking steel plates hung over wooden resonators. Invented about 1880, it was used by Tchaikovsky in his ballet *Casse-Noisette*.

celestial mechanics The study of the motions of celestial bodies subject to mutual gravitational interaction through the application of the laws of *gravitation and of *mechanics.

celestial sphere The imaginary sphere, of immense size, at the center of which lies the earth and on the inner surface of which can be projected the stars and other celestial bodies. The directions of these bodies, as seen from earth, are measured in terms of their angular distances from certain points and circles on the celestial sphere. These circles include the *ecliptic, the observer's horizon, and the **celestial equator**, where the earth's equatorial plane meets the celestial sphere. The reference points include the *equinoxes, the *zenith, and the **celestial poles**, where the earth's axis meets the celestial sphere. The earth's daily rotation causes an apparent and opposite rotation of the celestial sphere.

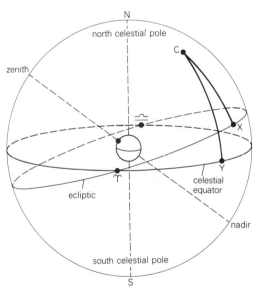

♈	first point of Aries; vernal equinox
♎	first point of Libra; autumnal equinox
C	celestial object
♈Y	right ascension of C (in hours counterclockwise from ♈)
♈X	celestial longitude of C (in degrees counterclockwise from ♈)
YC	declination of C
XC	celestial latitude of C

CELESTIAL SPHERE

celiac disease A disease in which the small intestine is abnormally sensitive to gliadin (a component of the protein *gluten, found in wheat). It results in abnormalities in the cells of the intestine, which cannot digest or absorb food. The symptoms include diarrhea, stunted growth, and general malaise; the condition is treated by a gluten-free diet.

Céline, Louis Ferdinand (L. F. Destouches; 1884–1961) French novelist. The unrelieved cynicism of his controversial first book, *Journey to the End of the Night* (1932), was characteristic of all his novels, including *Death on the Instalment Plan* (1936) and *North* (1960). He suffered imprisonment and exile in Denmark for his outspoken antisemitic opinions.

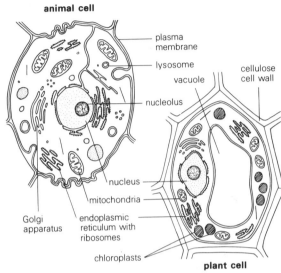

CELL *Plant and animal cells are basically similar but plant cells are supported by cellulose cell walls and contain the green pigment chlorophyll within chloroplasts. Plant cells often also have large fluid-filled vacuoles, which help to control turgidity of the cell.*

cell The basic unit of living matter, which performs the vital processes of producing energy, synthesizing new molecules from raw materials, division, and self-replication. All plants and animals are composed of cells, the average size of which ranges from 0.0004 to 0.004 in (0.01 to 0.1 mm); the simplest organisms (bacteria, protozoa, etc.) consist only of a single cell. The fundamental importance of cells was first recognized by *Schleiden and Schwann in 1838–39. A cell consists essentially of a mass of protoplasm bounded by a membrane. All cells except those of bacteria and blue-green algae and mammalian red blood cells possess a *nucleus, containing the genetic material, and cytoplasm, within which are structures (organelles) specialized for different metabolic functions (*see* Golgi apparatus; lysosome; mitochondria; ribosome). The cells of the body that are not involved in reproduction (called the somatic cells) divide by *mitosis to produce daughter cells identical to themselves. The reproductive cells divide by *meiosis to produce gametes, each containing half the number of chromosomes of the somatic cells. The basic difference between plant and animal cells is the presence in the former of a rigid cellulose cell wall and chlorophyll for use in photosynthesis (*see* chloroplast).

Celle 52 37N 10 05E A town in NE West Germany, in Lower Saxony. Its former ducal palace (1292) is famed for its theater, used since 1674. Wax and dyes are long established manufactures. The concentration camp of Belsen was nearby. Population (1971 est): 57,000.

Cellini, Benvenuto (1500–71) Florentine goldsmith and sculptor, famous for his autobiography (1558–62). First published in 1728, it provides a valuable account of his life and times. Cellini worked chiefly as a medalist and craftsman for the papacy in Rome, the Medici in Florence, and Francis I in France. The famous gold saltcellar (Kunsthistorisches Museum, Vienna) was made for Francis. As a sculptor he was largely unfulfilled, although his *Perseus* (Loggia dei Lanzi, Florence) attests to his skills in this medium.

cello (full name: violoncello) A musical instrument of the *violin family, held between the knees and supported at its lower end by an adjustable pin. It has an extensive range above its lowest note (C two octaves below middle C). Its four strings are tuned C, G, D, A. Used to strengthen the bass line in baroque music, it emerged as a solo instrument in the 18th and 19th centuries. In the 20th century its greatest exponent has been Pablo Casals.

celluloid A highly flammable thermoplastic material made from cellulose nitrate and *camphor. It was the first commercially made plastic, introduced over a hundred years ago. Although superseded for many applications by less flammable plastics, there are many specialist uses for which it is still the most suitable material because of its resistance to water, oils, and dilute acids. These include table-tennis balls, mortar-bomb capsules, and film.

cellulose ($C_6H_{10}O_5)_n$ A *carbohydrate that is an important constituent of the cell walls of plants and consists of linked glucose units. Industrially, it is made from wood pulp and is used to manufacture rayon and cellulose-acetate plastics. Cellulose has an important role in the human diet since it—together with other indigestible plant products—constitutes dietary *fiber.

cellulose nitrate (*or* nitrocellulose) A range of compounds made by treating cellulose with a mixture of nitric acid and sulfuric acid. As it is a nitric acid ester the correct name is cellulose nitrate. It is used as an explosive (gun cotton) and rocket propellant.

Celsius scale The official name of the *centigrade temperature scale. It was devised by the Swedish astronomer Anders Celsius (1701–44), who originally designated zero as the boiling point of water and 100° as the freezing point. The scale was later reversed.

Celsus, Aulus Cornelius (1st century AD) Roman scholar, who wrote an encyclopedic work embracing agriculture, law, philosophy, and medicine, of which only the medical section has survived (*De medicina*). Popular during the Renaissance, this work is today of great historical interest, dealing with hygiene, heart attacks, the surgical removal of gallstones, and many other topics common to contemporary medicine.

Celtiberia A region of NE Spain, S of the Ebro River. From the 3rd century BC the area was inhabited by the warlike Celtiberians, who were descendants of the Celtic invaders of Spain and the Iberian natives. The Celtiberians were defeated by the Romans in 195 BC but their capital, Numantia, was not taken until Scipio Aemilianus forced its capitulation in 133 BC.

CELTIC ART *A Bronze Age hand mirror decorated with characteristic Celtic patterns.*

Celtic art The style of ornamentation developed by ancient tribes in central Europe (*see* Celts). Primitive examples, found in the middle Rhine and Champagne districts, date from around 450 BC: masks and brooches in bronzework with increasingly sophisticated geometric patterns, animal and floral motifs, and, eventually, realistic human-head designs. The most elaborate jewelry, decorated swords, scabbards, and helmets belong to the *La Tène period (c. 350 BC). In Britain, Celtic craftsmanship flourished throughout the Roman occupation, producing work in gold and silver, shields inlaid with enamel, and bronze mirrors. Subsequently, Christian monks adapted traditional designs to adorn religious manuscripts, as in the 9th-century Book of *Kells.

Celtic languages A branch of the Indo-European language family formerly widespread in W Europe. It is divided into two subgroups: Gaulish

and Insular Celtic. The Gaulish languages are now extinct, being superseded in early medieval times by *Romance, *Germanic, and other languages. Insular Celtic can be further divided into a Goidelic branch (including *Manx and *Gaelic) and a Brythonic branch (including *Welsh, *Cornish, and *Breton).

Celts A people who occupied a large part of Iron Age Europe. They were known to the Greeks as Keltoi and to the Romans as Gauls. There were numerous Celtic tribes and chiefdoms sharing a culture that can be traced back to the Bronze Age of central Europe (c. 1200 BC). Distinct stages in its development are represented by the *Urnfield and *Hallstatt cultures and it reached its highest level around the 5th century BC, a period represented by the *La Tène culture. The Celtic warrior aristocracy commanded considerable wealth and power. Burials (e.g. at Vix, France) were often rich and elaborate, containing objects of excellent craftsmanship and aesthetic quality. The Druidic priesthood conducted sacrifices and was responsible for the education of young nobles.

cement A powdered mixture of calcium silicates and aluminates. On mixing with water it undergoes complex hydration processes and sets into a hard solid mass. **Portland cement** and similar materials are made by heating limestone with clay and grinding the product. Portland cement was invented by a British stonemason and named for the stone quarried at Portland, Dorset, which it resembles. It is used extensively in *mortars and in *concrete.

cementation The heating of *wrought iron with charcoal powder to form steel. The process was used to make swords and cutting tools before modern methods were developed. It is similar to *case hardening but the iron was often heated for days before quenching.

cementite Iron carbide (Fe_3C), a constituent of *steel and *cast iron. It is a hard brittle white material that combines with ferrite (pure iron) in different ways depending on the type of steel. *See also* pearlite.

Cennini, Cennino (di Drea) (c. 1370–c. 1440) Florentine painter. His paintings have disappeared but he is famous for his *Il libro dell' arte.* Translated as *The Craftsman's Handbook* (1933), it is a valuable source of information about early artistic techniques, particularly *tempera painting.

Cenozoic era (*or* Cainozoic era) The geological era beginning about 65 million years ago and following the *Mesozoic era. It is usually taken to include both the Tertiary and Quaternary periods. During this era the mammals flourished, after the extinction of most of the reptiles dominant in the Mesozoic; the Cenozoic is sometimes known as the age of mammals. Birds and flowering plants also flourished. The *Alpine orogeny took place in the earlier part of this era.

censors Civil magistrates of ancient Rome responsible for the census, public morality, revision of the senatorial roll, and property investment. Two censors were elected every five years. They generally held office for 18 months. The censorship was instituted in about 443 BC and became the most prestigious magistracy until Sulla curtailed its authority in 81. It lasted until 22 BC.

censorship The examination of printed matter, plays, films, broadcasts, etc., and the suppression of any material considered immoral, obscene, or indecent. Censorship is thus the instrument by which religious, political, and moral freedom can be curtailed. It was practiced throughout the ancient world and in the middle ages, but controlling the dissemination of texts and doctrines considered undesirable by the authorities only really became a problem when *printing enabled material to be widely distributed. Now such actions are frequently challenged as unconstitutionally denying freedom of press and speech in contravention of the First Amendment.

The most notorious instance of religious censorship was the Roman Catholic Church's *Index Librorum Prohibitorum.* Instituted in 1564 in reaction to the spread of Protestantism and scientific inquiry, it only ceased publication in 1966.

census A survey ordered by a government to discover certain characteristics of the population, such as its size, occupations, distribution, and trends in fertility, emigration, and immigration. Censuses were taken in ancient China and ancient Rome but the earliest regular census was initiated in the US in 1790. A census is commonly conducted at five- or ten-year intervals. Information about sex, age, race, housing, education, and language spoken may also be gathered to facilitate government policy making.

Census, Bureau of the US agency that collects, tabulates, and publishes a wide variety of statistical data about the nation's people and economy. It takes a census of population and housing every ten years and five-year censuses of agriculture, trade, manufactures, and transportation; it also compiles current statistics on US foreign trade. It also estimates and projects population and housing. Established in 1902, its headquarters are in Suitland, Md.

centaur In Greek legend, one of a race of wild creatures, half-human and half-horse, living in the mountains of Thessaly and descended from Ixion, King of the Lapiths. They were defeated by the Lapiths in a battle resulting from their characteristically unruly behavior at the wedding of Ixion's son. *See also* Chiron.

Centaurus (Latin: centaur) A large conspicuous constellation in the S sky near Crux. The brightest stars are *Alpha and *Beta Centauri. The constellation contains the huge intense radio source **Centaurus A** and the X-ray binary star **Centaurus X-3**.

centaury An annual or perennial flowering plant belonging to the genus *Centaurium* (or *Erythraea*) (40–50 species), found in most regions except for tropical and S Africa. The common centaury (*C. erythraea*) is widely distributed in temperate regions. Growing to a height of up to 20 in (50 cm), the branching stems bear clusters of small pink flowers. Family: *Gentianaceae*.

Certain plants closely related to *Centaurium* species are also called centaury, e.g. yellow centaury (*Cicendia filiformis*) and Guernsey centaury (*Exaculum pusillum*).

centigrade scale A temperature scale using the freezing point of water as zero and the boiling point of water as 100 degrees. The scale is now officially called the *Celsius scale. Each centigrade (*or* Celsius) degree is equal to one *kelvin.

centipede An *arthropod belonging to the worldwide class *Chilopoda* (about 2800 species). It has long antennae and a slender flattened body of 15–181 segments. The first segment bears a pair of poison claws and nearly all the remaining segments bear a single pair of legs (*compare* millipede). The tropical order *Scolopendrida* contain the largest species, up to 11 in (280 mm) long. Centipedes are found under stones, logs, and leaf litter during the day and at night prey on earthworms, insects, and sometimes small vertebrates. They lay eggs or produce live young.

CENTO. *See* Central Treaty Organization.

Central African Federation. *See* Rhodesia and Nyasaland, Federation of.

Central African Republic (name from 1976 until 1979: Central African Empire) A country in central Africa, consisting mainly of a plateau lying at about 3000 ft (900 m). The dense forests in the S are drained by the Ubangi River, an important channel of communication. Most of the population belongs to the Banda and Baya tribes. *Economy*: chiefly subsistence agriculture, although diamonds have been successfully mined in recent years and there is now a state uranium mine. The main exports are cotton and coffee. *History*: as Ubangi-Shari it was one of the four territories of French Equatorial Africa and from 1958 had internal self-government as a member of the French Community. It became independent in 1960 as the Central African Republic under the presidency of David Dacko (1930–). In a military coup in 1965, Jean Bédel *Bokassa came to power. A new constitution was adopted in 1976 in which the country became a parliamentary monarchy known as the Central African Empire, with Bokassa as Emperor Bokassa I. He was ousted following allegations of massacres and forced to flee the country in 1979. Dacko returned to power but was overthrown in a bloodless coup in 1981; he was succeeded by Gen André Kolingba. Official language: French; Sango is the national language. Official currency: CFA (Communauté financière africaine) franc of 100 centimes. Area: 241,250 sq mi (625,000 sq km). Population (1981 est): 2,420,000. Capital: Bangui.

Central America An isthmus of S North America, extending from the Isthmus of Tehuantepec to the NW border of Colombia and comprising an area of 596,000 sq km (230,000 sq mi). It consists of Belize, Costa Rica, El Salvador, Guatemala, Honduras, Nicaragua, and Panama, together with four Mexican states. It is chiefly mountainous with many volcanoes, including Tajumulco, which rises to 13,846 ft (4210 m), and its fertile volcanic regions yield many crops (especially bananas, coffee, and cocoa). The people are mainly of mixed European and Indian origin. Following the overthrow of Spanish colonial rule Costa Rica, El Salvador, Guatemala, Honduras, and Nicaragua formed (1823–38) the **Central American Federation** (*or* United Provinces of Central America). In 1960 Costa Rica, El Salvador, Guatemala, Nicaragua, and Honduras (which withdrew in 1970) formed the **Central American Common Market** to coordinate their economic policies.

central bank A bank that implements a government's *monetary policy, acting as banker to the government and to the commercial banks. Central banks are responsible for holding a country's gold reserves, conducting monetary relations with other countries, and financing the government debt. These objectives sometimes conflict: for example, the bank may wish to depress interest rates to stimulate investment at home, while wishing to raise interest rates to attract money into the country to aid the balance of payments. Most countries have a central bank; in the US it is the *Federal Reserve Bank.

Central Intelligence Agency (CIA) A US government department established in 1947 to coordinate US intelligence operations. In addition to gathering information on the operations and plans of hostile governments, the CIA has also sponsored covert military operations such as the *Bay of Pigs invasion of Cuba in 1961. By law the CIA is not permitted to operate within the US, but its involvement in the *Watergate affair raised considerable concern. In 1976 the Senate Intelligence Committee held extensive hearings on past CIA actions and established strict guidelines for the agency's future operation.

Central Powers The coalition, including Germany, Austria-Hungary, Turkey, and Bulgaria, that opposed the *Allied Powers during *World War I.

Central Treaty Organization (CENTO) A mutual defense alliance between the UK, Iran, Pakistan, and Turkey. It succeeded the *Baghdad Pact. Its objective is military cooperation and the economic development of its Middle Eastern members. Because the UK and the US, which is an associate member, saw CENTO primarily as an anti-Soviet military alliance and neglected the economic development of the organization's Middle Eastern members, Iran, Turkey, and Pakistan founded the Regional Cooperation for Development in 1964.

center of gravity A fixed point through which the resultant gravitational force on a body always passes no matter what its orientation.

centrifugal force. *See* centripetal force.

centrifuge A device for rotating mixtures of substances at high speed so that the heavier components can be separated from the lighter; the heavier components experience a greater centrifugal force, thus enabling components of different densities (e.g. milk and cream) to separate. The ultracentrifuge is a high-speed device used in the determination of molecular weights and in biochemistry. Large centrifuges are used in physiological research and in training programs to obtain a high *acceleration of free fall (g).

centripetal force A force that acts on a moving body causing it to move in a curved path. An object is constrained to move in a circle by a centripetal force directed toward the center. It has an acceleration toward the center of v^2/r, where v is the objects' velocity and r the radius of the circle. The centripetal force is necessary to overcome the object's tendency to move in a straight line and appears to be balanced by an equal **centrifugal force** directed radially outward.

century The ancient Roman unit of a hundred. In the Roman army centuries were the 60 subdivisions, composed of about a hundred infantrymen, of a legion and were commanded by centurions. Centuries were also political divisions of Roman citizens, each of which had a group vote in the assembly of centuries (*see* comitia).

century plant A perennial herbaceous plant, *Agave americana, native to SW North America. It is stemless but has spiny leaves, 5–6 ft (1.5–1.8 m) long, and after 10–15 years it produces a branched spike of yellow flowers, 25–40 ft (7.5–12 m) tall. After flowering it dies, leaving small plants growing around its base. Century plant is cultivated indoors and outdoors as an ornamental. Family: *Agavaceae*.

ceorl The free peasant (as distinct from the slave) of Anglo-Saxon England. The economic pressures of the Danish invasions and the Norman conquest contributed to the ceorl's declining status and eventual absorption among the unfree *villeins. Thus "churl" has come to mean an uncouth person.

cèpe An edible mushroom, *Boletus edulis. Common in temperate woodlands from August to November, it has a stout whitish or brown stalk and a hemispherical cap, brown to white in color and 6–20 cm in diameter.

Cephalonia (Modern Greek name: Kefallinía) A Greek island in the E Ionian Sea, the largest of the Ionian group. It is mountainous, rising to 5341 ft (1628 m), but produces crops that include olives and grapes. Area: 360 sq mi (935 sq km). Population (1971): 36,742.

cephalopod A *mollusk belonging to the class *Cephalopoda* (about 600 species), which includes *octopuses, *squids, and *cuttlefishes. The most advanced of the mollusks, cephalopods are carnivorous and mostly free swimming, with a ring of tentacles around the mouth, well-developed eyes, and shells that are reduced and often absent. They are found in both shallow and deepwater marine habitats. In cephalopods the sexes are usually separate and fertilization is internal, often preceded by courtship behavior.

cephalosporins A group of *antibiotics with a similar action and chemical structure to penicillin. They may be used to treat penicillin-resistant bacterial infections and infections of the urinary tract.

Cepheid variable A highly luminous supergiant star the brightness of which varies very regularly in a period (1–50 days) that depends on the *luminosity of the star. By measuring the period and the average apparent *magnitude of a Cepheid, its distance can be determined. *See also* variable stars.

Cepheus (Latin: whale) A constellation in the N sky near Cassiopeia. The brightest star is the 2nd-magnitude Alderamin. *See also* Cepheid variable.

Ceram (*or* Serang) An Indonesian island in the Moluccas. Mountainous and forested, its exports include copra, dried fish, and birds of paradise. Area: 6622 sq mi (17,150 sq km). Chief town: Wahai.

ceramics Any nonmetallic inorganic material that is made by heat treatment into useful articles. The main categories are heavy articles made of baked clay, such as bricks and tiles, refractories to withstand high temperatures, such as furnace linings, sintered articles, such as abrasives, and domestic products made from earthenware, stoneware, or *porcelain (*see also* pottery). Earthenware is made from clay, which when strongly heated fuses into a hard porous substance. The defect of porosity is overcome by glazing with a vitreous coating of silicate. Chinese examples date from about 3000 BC. Stoneware is made from a more silicaceous clay and fired at a higher temperature than earthenware. It is vitrified, resonant, and almost impervious. Porcelain, developed by the Chinese from stoneware, is vitrified, impervious, resonant, translucent, and white. It need not be glazed but usually is.

Cerberus In Greek legend, the monstrous dog who guarded the entrance to the underworld, usually portrayed as having three heads and a dragon's neck and tail. The final task of *Heracles was to overpower this monster.

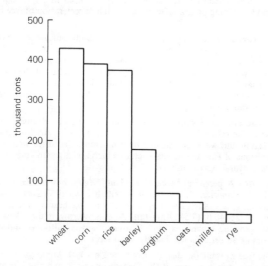

CEREALS *World production of cereals.*

cereals Cultivated *grasses selected for their high yields of grain, which constitutes a major item in the diet of man and livestock. *Wheat, *rice, and *corn are the most important cereals, but *barley, *oats, *rye, and *millet are also widely cultivated. Cereals are usually sown annually and, under certain conditions (especially with rice), two or more harvests may be possible in one year. *See also* arable farming.

cerebellum. *See* brain.

cerebral palsy Damage to the developing brain resulting in uncoordinated movements and muscular weakness and paralysis. The brain damage may be caused by injury during birth, insufficient oxygen before birth, or a viral infection of the brain. In some cases intelligence is affected. Treatment includes appropriate physiotherapy to improve movement and special education; speech therapy may also be needed.

cerebrospinal fluid The fluid that surrounds the *brain and *spinal cord. It is produced by special blood vessels inside the cerebrum and is reabsorbed by special bunches of veins. It acts as a shock absorber and support for the central nervous system. A normal adult has 4 oz (130 ml) of clear fluid; samples of it are taken for diagnostic tests for diseases of the nervous system.

cerebrum. *See* brain.

Ceres (astronomy) The largest *minor planet, 623 mi (1003 km) in diameter, and the first to be discovered (in 1801 by Piazzi). It orbits at between 2.55 and 2.98 astronomical units from the sun, with a period of 4.6 years.

Ceres (mythology). *See* Demeter.

cerium (Ce) The most abundant lanthanide element, discovered in 1803 by Berzelius and others. It occurs naturally in several minerals including monazite, (Ce,La,Th)PO_4, and allanite, a complex aluminosilicate. It is used as a catalyst in self-cleaning ovens, in gas mantles, as a polishing agent, and as an oxidant for volumetric analysis. At no 58; at wt 140.12; mp 475°F (799°C); bp 1916°F (3426°C).

Cernauti. *See* Chernovtsy.

Cervantes, Miguel de (1547–1616) Spanish novelist. Son of an unsuccessful surgeon, he was largely self-educated. In 1569 he went to Italy and fought at the battle of Lepanto in 1571. Returning to Spain in 1575, he was captured by pirates and imprisoned in Algiers for five years. After 1580 he held several minor jobs in the civil service while writing a pastoral novel, *La Galatea* (1585), and several plays. *Don Quixote* (Part I, 1605; Part II, 1615), his revolutionary picaresque novel about a self-deluding knight errant and his simple but cunning squire, Sancho Panza, won him fame throughout Europe but little financial reward.

cervix The lower part (neck) of the womb, leading into the vagina (the term is also used for any necklike part). Childbirth is dependent on the effective dilation of the cervix.

Cesenà 44 09N 12 15E A city in N Italy, in Emilia-Romagna on the Savio River. It is the site of the Malatesta library (15th century), which contains many valuable manuscripts. Pope Pius VI and Pope Pius VII were born here. Pasta, wine, and beet sugar are produced. Population (1971): 86,584.

cesium (Cs) The most reactive and electropositive alkali metal. It was discovered by Bunsen and Kirchhoff in 1860 and occurs naturally in the mica lepidolite and as pollucite, $(Cs,K)AlSi_2O_6 \cdot nH_2O$. Cesium reacts explosively with water to give the hydroxide (CsOH) and is used in *cesium clocks and in photoelectric cells. Chief compounds are the nitrate ($CsNO_3$) and chloride (CsCl). At no 55; at wt 132.905; mp 28.40°C; bp 690°C.

cesium clock An *atomic clock that depends on the energy difference between two states of the cesium nucleus in a magnetic field. A nonuniform magnetic field is used to split a beam of cesium atoms into two components. Nuclei in the lower energy state are irradiated by radio-frequency radiation at the difference frequency between the two states, so that some are excited to the higher state. By reanalyzing the mixture, the radio-frequency oscillator can be locked to the difference frequency of 9 192 631 770 hertz with an accuracy of one part in 10^{13}. This extremely accurate clock is now used in the definition of the *second.

České Budějovice (German name: Budweis) 49 00N 14 30E An industrial city situated in W Czechoslovakia. Founded in 1265, it has an arcaded town square. Manufactures include chemicals, machinery, and pencils. Population (1980 est): 89,000.

Cestoda. *See* tapeworm.

Cetacea An order of carnivorous marine mammals comprising *whales and *dolphins.

cetane number A quality rating for Diesel fuel, similar to the *octane number for petrol. Two reference fuel compounds, cetane and alpha-methylnaphthalene, are given the numbers 100 and 0 respectively. Mixtures of these two have intermediate numbers and other Diesel fuels are compared with them in a standard engine. Most Diesel engines can run on fuel that has a cetane number of 40 or 50.

Cetatea Alba. *See* Belgorod-Dnestrovski.

Cetinje 42 23N 18 55E A city in S central Yugoslavia, in Montenegro. The former capital of the principality of Montenegro, it has a fortified monastery, which was the seat of the Montenegrin prince bishops. Population (1971 est): 11,800.

Cetshwayo (c. 1826–84) King of the Zulus (1873–79), whose kingdom was conquered by the British. Although Cetshwayo inflicted a severe defeat on the British at Isandhlwana (1879) he could not hold out against them and was overwhelmed at Ulundi (1879). Captured, he was allowed to present his case in London and in 1883 was restored to central Zululand.

Ceuta 35 53N 5 19W A Spanish military post and port, forming an enclave in NW Morocco on the Mediterranean coast. It has a fine 15th-century cathedral. Population (1970): 73,182.

Cévennes A mountain range in SE France, constituting the SE edge of the Massif Central and rising to 5755 ft (1754 m).

Ceylon. *See* Sri Lanka, Democratic Socialist Republic of.

Cézanne, Paul (1839–1906) French postimpressionist painter, born in Aix-en-Provence, the son of a banker. After studying law for two years, he was encouraged by his childhood friend Emile *Zola to settle in Paris (1861). His crude and often erotic early paintings failed, however, to find favor. In 1872, while working with *Pissarro in Pontoise, he turned to *impressionism, a period represented by *The Suicide's House* (Louvre) but he soon rejected its flickering effects of light and movement in favor of more stability and solidity. His view that nature should be painted in the forms of the cone, cube, and cylinder and his distortion of perspective strongly influenced the development of *cubism. Living mainly in Provence, he painted portraits, e.g. *The Card Players* (Louvre), still lifes, landscapes, especially of Mont St Victoire and L'Estaque, and a series of *Bathers*.

c.g.s. system A metric system of units based on the centimeter, gram, and second. It includes dynes, ergs, and both electrostatic and electromagnetic units. It has been replaced for scientific purposes by *SI units.

Chablis 47 49N 3 48E A village in central France, in the Yonne department. Chablis is famous for the white wine named for it.

Chabrier, Emmanuel (1841–94) French composer. Prevented by his father from becoming a professional musician, he graduated in law and composed in his spare time. A performance of Wagner's *Tristan and Isolde* in 1880 made him decide to devote his whole life to music. His most famous composition is the colorful orchestral rhapsody *España* (1883).

Chabrol, Claude (1930–) French film director. He was a leading member of the *New Wave group of French directors in the late 1950s. His films, many of which are influenced by Alfred Hitchcock and use tense murder plots to illuminate bourgeois social relationships, include *Les Biches* (1968) and *Le Boucher* (1969).

Chaco. *See* Gran Chaco.

Chaco War (1932–35) The war between Bolivia and Paraguay resulting from a long-standing dispute over the vast Gran Chaco region. The dispute, which had arisen in the 19th century, flared up again in the 1920s when new Paraguayan settlements and word of oil deposits in Chaco upset the uneasy truce. Over 100,000 men died in this bloody war. The League of Nations failed to arbitrate a settlement but mediation by Argentina, Brazil, Chile, Peru, and the US led to an armistice. The treaty, signed in 1938, favored the military victor, Paraguay, which received most of the Chaco.

Chad, Lake A lake in West Africa, between Chad, Niger, Nigeria, and Cameroon. It is shallow and has no outlet; its area varies between about 3860 and 9650 sq mi (10,00–25,000 sq km).

Chad, Republic of (French name: Tchad) A country covering an extensive area in N central Africa, consisting mainly of poor semidesert. The land rises from Lake Chad in the SW to the Tibesti Mountains in the N, reaching heights of about 3400 m (11,000 ft). The majority of the rather sparse population (concentrated in the S) is Sara, a Bantu people; most of the nomadic peoples of the N are Muslims. *Economy*: mainly subsistence agriculture with livestock and fishing. Some oil and other minerals have been found but there is very little industry. The main exports are cotton and meat. *History*: one of the four territories of French Equatorial Africa, it had internal self-government as a member of the French Community from 1958, gaining independence in 1960. Since 1963 there has been considerable rebellion and unrest in the N where the Muslim inhabitants have traditionally opposed the black population of the S. The level of hostilities has increased in recent years, causing deteriorations in Chad's international relations. In 1975 President Nagarta Tombalbaye was assassinated in a military coup and succeeded by Gen Félix Malloum. In 1979, following negotiations held in Nigeria, a transitional government under President Goukouni Oueddei was formed. Conflict between rebel and government forces continued and in 1982 the capital N'djamena was taken by rebel forces led by Hissene Habré. In 1983 the civil war was resumed with the taking of Faya-Largeau by Libyan forces led by Oueddei. Oueddei's support by Libya's Qaddafi was quickly countered. Allying itself with Habré, the US dispatched military and financial aid. Zaire, Nigeria, and eventually France, also lent support. The crucial dispatch of 1000 French troops and other French military reinforcements succeeded in halting Libyan ad-

vances. A cease-fire was reached in 1984, and French and Libyan forces began a mutual withdrawal of troops. Official language: French. Official currency: CFA (Communauté financière africaine) franc of 100 centimes. Area: 495,624 sq mi (1,284,000 sq km). Population (1983 est): 4,990,000. Capital: N'djamena (formerly Fort Lamy).

Chadwick, Sir James (1891–1974) British physicist, who worked at Cambridge with *Rutherford and went on to discover the *neutron in 1932. Physicists had previously suspected the existence of neutrons but had been unable to detect them: by analyzing the radiation emitted by beryllium when bombarded with alpha particles, Chadwick was able to show that it consisted of neutrons. He was awarded the 1935 Nobel Prize.

Chaeronea, Battles of 1. (338 BC) The battle in which *Philip II of Macedon, and his crack army, defeated Athenian and Theban forces at Chaeronea (on the Cephisus River in N Boeotia). It forced the Greek city states to acknowledge Philip's hegemony over Greece and the end of their autonomy. 2. (86 BC) The battle won by the Roman general *Sulla over *Mithridates VI Eupator of Pontus at the same spot.

chafer A herbivorous beetle belonging to the family *Scarabaeidae* (see scarab beetle). Chafers cause much damage to trees and crops by eating the foliage and flowers; the larvae, which live in the soil, attack the roots. Chief genera: *Melolontha* (see cockchafer), *Cetonia* (rose chafers), and *Phyllopertha* (garden chafers).

CHAFFINCH *Although the nest is built by the female, both the male (seen here) and the female care for the young.*

chaffinch A *finch, *Fringilla coelebs*, about 6 in (15 cm) long, that is common in woods and parks in Europe, W Asia, and N Africa. The male chaffinch has a chestnut back, pinkish breast, grayish-blue crown and nape, and two conspicuous white wing bars. The female has a duller plumage with an olive-green back. Chaffinches are often migratory and have a lively song.

Chagall, Marc (1887–1985) Russian-born painter and printmaker of Jewish parentage. After studying in St Petersburg (1907–10) under *Bakst, he visited Paris (1910). There he painted some of his best-known works, recalling Russian village life, such as *Me and the Village* (1911; New York). His childlike figures and objects, distorted in scale and often floating upside down in space, influenced the surrealists. Moving to France (1922), he illustrated Gogol's *Dead Souls* and La Fontaine's *Fables*. During World War II he lived in the US, where he designed ballet sets and costumes and subsequently worked on mosaics and tapestries for the Israeli Knesset building (1966).

Chagas' disease A South American disease caused by infection with a protozoan of the genus *Trypanosoma*. Named for— a Brazilian physician, Carlos Chagas (1879–1934), it is a form of *trypanosomiasis transmitted by bugs. It may result in serious damage to the heart and brain; there is no effective treatment.

Chagos Islands. *See* British Indian Ocean Territory.

chain 1. A measure of length equal to 66 feet (20 m). 2. A measuring device used in surveying. A Gunter's chain is 66 feet (20 m) long (consisting of 100 links), whereas an Engineer's chain is 100 feet (30 m) long (also 100 links).

Chain, Sir Ernst Boris (1906–79) British biochemist, born in Germany, who—with Lord *Florey—isolated and purified penicillin and performed the first clinical trials. Coming to England in 1933, Chain worked first at Cambridge under Sir Frederick *Hopkins and then at Oxford with Florey. For their work, Chain, Florey, and Sir Alexander *Fleming, the discoverer of penicillin, were awarded a Nobel Prize (1945).

chainmail Body armor made by welding or riveting interlaced iron rings. Light and providing adequate protection, it was popular from about 1100 to about 1400, when plate, first worn under and then over chainmail, began to replace it. Chainmail garments include coifs, mittens, and stockings and ultimately covered the entire body. Worn over felt or leather coats, examples from about 1200 weigh between 30 lb (14 kg) and 50 lb (23 kg).

chain reaction A series of reactions in which the product of each reaction sets off further reactions. In a nuclear chain reaction each nuclear fission is induced by a neutron ejected by a previous fission. For example, the fission of a uranium-235 nucleus produces either two or three neutrons each of which can induce the fission of another uranium-235 nucleus. Chain reactions can be used as a source of energy in *nuclear reactors and *nuclear weapons. *See also* critical mass.

chaise A light two- or four-wheeled carriage drawn by one, two, or four horses. A chaise usually had a collapsible hood (calash). "Chaise" could also apply to a *curricle or *phaeton. *Compare* postchaise.

Chaitanya movement A Hindu *Bhakti school, named for— its founder, the Bengali brahmin mystic Chaitanya (1485–1533). Through the ecstatic singing of hymns and mantras, devotees express their blissful surrender to *Krishna and Radha, who epitomize the quasi-erotic mutual love of God and the human soul; Chaitanya himself came to be worshiped as an incarnation of these divine lovers. The Sanskrit scriptures of the movement were subsequently evolved by a group of disciples, known as the six *gosvamins*. Most of the present sect leaders are their descendants and bear the same title.

Chakkri The ruling dynasty of Thailand (formerly Siam). Its first king, Phraya Chakkri (1737–1809), styled himself Rama I after his accession in 1782. A capable military commander, he had put an end to the hostilities of the neighboring Burmese by 1792 and then established the new capital of Bangkok. During the reigns of Rama II (1768–1824; reigned 1809–24) and Rama III (d. 1851; reigned 1824–51) Siam's relations with the West improved. Mongkut (posthumously styled Rama IV; 1804–68; reigned 1851–68) and *Chulalongkon (Rama V; reigned 1868–1910) introduced various social and administrative reforms. A revolt against Prajadhipok (Rama VII; 1893–1941; reigned 1925–35) led to the establishment of a constitutional monarchy in 1932; he abdicated in 1935. The present king, Bhumibol Adulyadej (1927–), ascended the throne in 1946.

Chalcedon (modern name: Kadiköy) A Megarian colony founded in the 7th century BC on the Asian side of the Bosporus. It was known as the city of the blind because it occupied a less strategic site than the opposite side of the Bosporus on which Byzantium (*see* Istanbul) was built. Absorbed first by Pergamum and later forming part of the Roman province of Asia, Chalcedon eventually became a suburb of Byzantium. It was the site in 451 AD of the Council of Chalcedon, the fourth ecumenical council of the Church. It condemned heresies relating to the dual (human and divine) nature of Christ and reaffirmed the doctrines of the Council of *Nicaea and the first Council of *Constantinople.

chalcedony A cryptocrystalline (submicroscopically grained) sometimes fibrous *silica mineral. The numerous varieties include carnelian (red); agate, onyx, and sardonyx (banded); jasper (red or brown); and chert and flint (opaque gray or black). The last two occur in limestones; others occur mainly in veins and amygdales.

Chalcidice (Modern Greek name: Khalkidhikí) A peninsula in NE Greece. It ends in three promontories, the northernmost of which contains

Mount *Athos. There are fertile low-lying areas but it is mostly wooded and mountainous. Area: 1149 sq mi (2945 sq km).

Chalcis (modern name: Khalkís) 38 28N 23 36E The capital of the Greek island of *Eubea, famous as a trading and metalworking center from the 8th to the 1st centuries BC; Aristotle died here in 322 BC. Chalcis established colonies in Italy, Sicily, and the peninsular region named for it, *Chalcidice. It joined Athens against the Persians in 480 BC but the two cities' traditional rivalry was successfully exploited by Philip of Macedon in the 4th century BC. It was partly destroyed in 146 BC by the Romans but was subsequently developed by the Venetians from the 13th century AD and was incorporated in the kingdom of Greece in 1830. Population (1981 est): 44,774.

chalcopyrite The principal ore of copper, sometimes called copper pyrites, of composition $CuFeS_2$. It is brassy yellow with a greenish black streak and contains 34.5% copper. It occurs mainly in veins associated with the upper part of an acid igneous intrusion.

Chaldea (*or* Chaldaea) The region of S Babylonia where the new Babylonian empire was established by Nabopolassar (d. 605 BC) in 625 in the last years of the Assyrian empire. At its height under *Nebuchadnezzar II (reigned 604–562), the Chaldean empire, centered on the rebuilt city of Babylon, dominated the Middle East for about 70 years until overthrown by the Achemenians in 539. The Chaldeans' reputation as astronomers survived undiminished until Roman times.

Chaliapin, Feodor Ivanovich (1873–1938) Russian bass. After a penurious youth, he was discovered as a singer and made his debut at La Scala, Milan, in 1901. He became world famous in the title role of Mussorgsky's *Boris Godunov*.

chalk A sedimentary rock that is a pure-white fine-grained variety of *limestone (calcium carbonate). Coccoliths (the calcareous remains of extinct unicellular organisms) are the main constituents of chalk although other invertebrate remains are included. Chalk is very characteristic of the Upper Cretaceous period in W Europe and the Chalk is sometimes used synonymously with the Upper Cretaceous. Nodules of flint are often found in chalk; these are formed from the remains of siliceous organisms, dissolved and redeposited.

Chalmers, Thomas (1780–1847) Scottish preacher and theologian. Ordained in the Church of Scotland in 1803, Chalmers was an influential minister in Glasgow, where he introduced important changes in parish structures. From 1823 he was a university professor at St Andrew's and then in Edinburgh. He was a leader in the Disruption of 1843, which led to the founding of the Free Church of Scotland.

chalones A group of substances, found in mammalian tissues, that can inhibit cell division. They are thought to be important in aging processes and in cancer.

Châlons-sur-Marne 48 58N 4 22E A city in NE France, the capital of the Marne department. In 451 AD Attila and the Huns were defeated by the Romans on a nearby plain. The 13th-century cathedral suffered damage in World War II. It is the center of the wine trade of Champagne. Population (1975): 55,709.

Chalon-sur-Saône 46 47N 4 51E A city in E central France, in the Saône-et-Loire department on the Saône River. An important commercial center, it has an engineering industry and a wine market. Population (1975): 60,451.

chamberlain An officer appointed by a monarch, nobleman, or corporation to carry out ceremonial duties. The chamberlains of medieval England were financial officers and were figures of great political importance in the 12th century.

Chamberlain, Joseph (1836–1914) British politician. He became a Liberal member of parliament in 1876 and in 1885 presented a program that advocated such radical policies as free education. In 1886 he left the Liberal Party. As leader of the anti-Gladstonian Liberal-Unionists, he supported the Conservatives and became colonial secretary in the Conservative Government (1895–1903). His eldest son **Sir (Joseph) Austen Chamberlain** (1863–1937) became a Liberal-Unionist member of parliament in 1892. He was chancellor of the exchequer (1919–21) and then foreign secretary (1924–29), when he negotiated the *Locarno Pact and was awarded the Nobel Peace Prize (1925). Joseph's son **(Arthur) Neville Chamberlain** (1869–1940) was Conservative prime minister (1937–40), when he advocated a policy of appeasement toward the fascist powers. He recognized Italy's conquest of Ethiopia and kept out of the Spanish Civil War. To avoid a European war he visited Hitler three times in 1938, coming to the *Munich Agreement, which recognized Germany's possession of the Sudetenland. He returned to Britain claiming to have brought "peace for our time" but was forced by Hitler's invasion of Czechoslovakia to abandon appeasement. He declared war after Hitler's attack on Poland but his ineffective direction of the war led to his resignation in May, 1940, when he joined Churchill's war cabinet.

Chamberlain, Owen (1920–   ) US physicist, who shared the 1959 Nobel Prize with Emilio *Segrè for their discovery of the antiproton (*see* antimatter) in 1955. They created the particle by bombarding a copper target with high-energy protons in the Berkeley *bevatron. During World War II he worked on the development of the atom bomb.

Chamberlain, Wilt (Wilton Norman C.; 1936–   ) US basketball player. He played for the Harlem Globetrotters (1957) before joining the Philadelphia (later San Francisco) Warriors (1958–65), the Philadelphia 76ers (1965–68), and the Los Angeles Lakers (1968–73). Nicknamed "Wilt the Stilt," he long held the career record for points and was elected to the Basketball Hall of Fame (1978).

chamber music Music written to be played in the intimacy of a room rather than in a large hall, church, or theater. In the baroque period chamber sonatas were distinguished from church sonatas and in the late 18th century Haydn, Mozart, and Beethoven established the piano trio (violin, cello, and piano), the duo sonata (one instrument and piano), and the string quartet (two violins, viola, and cello) as the main chamber music forms. Chamber music has been written for other combinations of players, including the woodwind quintet (oboe, flute, clarinet, horn, and bassoon), the clarinet quintet (clarinet and string quartet), and the piano quintet (piano and string quartet). Haydn, Mozart, Beethoven, Schubert, Brahms, Dvořák, and Britten all wrote important chamber music compositions.

chamber of commerce An organization that protects and promotes the interests of a town's or city's manufacturers and merchants. Chambers of commerce occur in many countries, sometimes government sponsored and sometimes, as in the US, as voluntary organizations. Many are authorized to issue certificates of origin and to certify commercial documents, and some provide an *arbitration service for their members.

Chambéry 45 34N 5 55E A city in E France, the capital of the Savoie department. It was the capital of Savoy (1232–1562) and has a 16th-century cathedral. Industries include tourism, aluminum, and vermouth production. Population (1975): 56,788.

Chambord A chateau in the Loire Valley (France). Chambord was begun by Francis I in 1519 and was one of his most extravagant building projects. Elaborately decorated and much imitated, Chambord was never completed after work stopped in 1540.

chameleon An arboreal lizard belonging to the Old World family *Chamaeleontidae* (84 species) and characterized by its ability to change its skin color. 7–10 in (17–25 cm) long, chameleons have a narrow body, an extensile tongue for capturing insects, and bulging eyes that can move independently. Some species have a helmet-shaped head or conspicuous horns. They may be green, yellow, cream, or dark brown, often with spots, and change color by concentration or dispersion of pigment in skin cells. Genera: *Brookesia, Chamaeleo.* □reptile.

chamois An agile hoofed *mammal, *Rupicapra rupicapra*, of mountainous regions in Europe and SW Asia. Chamois grow to about 30 in (75 cm) high at the shoulder and have distinctive narrow upright horns with backward-pointing hooked tips. Their tawny coat becomes darker and longer in winter, when they descend from the high slopes to the forests below. Family: *Bovidae*.

chamomile. *See* camomile.

Chamonix 45 55N 6 52E A town in E France, in the Haute-Savoie department near the Swiss and Italian borders. Close to Mont Blanc, it is a mountaineering and winter-sports center. Population (1968): 5907.

Champa An ancient Indochinese kingdom. The Chams were Indonesian in origin but when they established their kingdom on the coastal region of South Vietnam in 192 AD following the collapse of the Chinese Han dynasty their culture became predominantly Indian. Champa's prosperity was greatest between the 6th and 10th centuries, after the demise of Chinese domination and before the Vietnamese kingdom threatened its autonomy. Champa was finally absorbed by Vietnam in the 17th century.

champagne A wine, usually sparkling, produced in the districts around Reims and Épernay, NE France. Champagne is usually made from black (*pinot noir*) and white (*pinot chardonnay*) grapes. After fermentation sugar and yeast are added to the still wine, which, when bottled, undergoes a secondary fermentation, which produces the sparkle. A dosage of sugar syrup determines whether it will be sweet (*sec*) or dry (*brut*) champagne.

Champagne A former province in NE France, now incorporated in the planning region of **Champagne-Ardenne**. Ruled by counts during the mid-

dle ages, it became important for its trade fairs and at the end of the 17th century began to produce the sparkling *champagne for which it is famous.

Champaigne, Philippe de (1602–74) Painter of portraits and historical and religious scenes, born in Brussels. In 1621 he moved to Paris, where he worked for Marie de' Medici and Richelieu. His association with the Jansenists at Port Royal influenced his later portraits, notably *Ex Voto de 1662* (Louvre), which shows his daughter, a nun, after her recovery from paralysis.

champignon One of several edible mushrooms of the family *Agaricaceae* (*see* agaric). The fairy-ring champignon (*Marasmius oreades*), common on meadows and lawns, has a light-brown cap, 0.8–2 in (2–5 cm) in diameter, and a slender stalk. It often occurs as part of a fairy ring—a ring of mushrooms marking the roughly circular perimeter of the underground body of the fungus.

Champlain, Lake A long narrow lake in North America. It extends S from the Richelieu River in Canada, forming the boundary between Vermont and New York state for much of its length. It is named for Samuel de Champlain. Length: 107 mi (172 km).

Champlain, Samuel de (1567–1635) French explorer. In 1603 he followed in *Cartier's footsteps, exploring the St Lawrence and the coast from a base in Acadia. In 1608 he founded a colony at Quebec—New France—of which he became commandant (1612). When Quebec was captured by the English in 1629 he was taken prisoner. Lake Champlain, which he visited in 1609, is named for him.

CHAMOIS *The hide of this increasingly rare animal was formerly used for chamois leather, which is now made from the skins of sheep and goats.*

champlevé (French: raised field) A technique of decorating metal surfaces with polychrome *enamelwork. The enamel is held in depressions incised in the metal. Fine examples of champlevé survive from Celtic England, medieval Europe, and India.

Champollion, Jean-François (1790–1832) French Egyptologist. After studying *Coptic, he tackled the decipherment of Egyptian *hieroglyphics, building on the intuitions of Thomas *Young about royal names on the *Rosetta Stone. His *Lettre à M. Dacier* (1822) correctly identified and assigned phonetic values to about 40 symbols. These results were confirmed and expanded in the *Précis du système hiéroglyphique* (1824).

chancellor In the UK, the name of various state officials. The chancellor, dating from the 10th century, was the head of the Chancery, the secretarial department of the *Curia Regis (King's Court). By the 12th century he was the monarch's chief minister but his political prominence subsequently declined as his judicial activities developed and since the 17th century the **Lord (High) Chancellor**, as he came to be called, has always been a lawyer. He is appointed by the prime minister, is a member of the cabinet, and speaker of the House of Lords as well as being head of the judiciary. The **chancellor of the exchequer** is the minister responsible for the national economy and the presentation of the annual budget.

Chancellorsville, Battle of (1863) Confederate victory in the Civil War, in N central Virginia. Union forces under General Joseph Hooker and Confederate forces under Generals Robert E. Lee and Stonewall Jackson met at Chancellorsville, near the Rappahannock River. The Union Army of the Potomac hoped to advance to and take Richmond, the Confederate capital. Lee sent Jackson to attack Hooker's advancing rear units, thus forcing the retreat of the Union troops. Casualties numbered in the thousands for both sides, and Jackson died of wounds 5 days later.

Chancery, Court of In English law, a court that developed in the 15th century as the personal court of the king's chief law officer, the Lord Chancellor (*see* chancellor), in which he dealt with cases for which the *common law could not provide a remedy. It dealt with such matters as partnerships, the administration of estates, and the execution of *trusts.

Chan Chan The capital city of the pre-Inca *Chimú Kingdom, near Trujillo (Peru). Its adobe (mud brick) ruins of temples, residential buildings, cemeteries, and storerooms are divided into nine compounds, covering 14 sq mi (36 sq km). The multiplicity of reservoirs and aqueducts indicate the importance of irrigation in this arid region.

Chandernagore 22 52N 88 22E A port in India, in West Bengal on the Hooghly River. A former French settlement (1673–1950), its industries include jute and cotton. Population (1971): 75,960.

Chandigarh 30 43N 76 47E A Union Territory and city in NW India, on the Haryana-Punjab border. The joint capital of both states, it is a modern city (1953) planned by *Le Corbusier in 30 rectangular sectors for housing, government, and industry. Punjab University was established here in 1947. Area: 44 sq mi (114 sq km). Population (1971): 257,251.

Chandler, Raymond (1888–1959) US novelist. Educated in England, he returned to the US and worked in business before starting to write detective stories in the 1930s. The detective Philip Marlowe features in all his nine novels, which include *The Big Sleep* (1939), *Farewell My Lovely* (1940), and *The Long Goodbye* (1954).

Chandra Gupta I Emperor of India (320–c. 330 AD), who founded the Gupta dynasty. Crowned at Pataliputra, he married the daughter of the king of the neighboring Lichavi clan and established the beginnings of a large empire.

Chandra Gupta II (c. 375–415 AD) Emperor of India (c. 380–c. 415) of the Gupta dynasty; the grandson of *Chandra Gupta I. He extended the imperial boundaries to the Arabian Sea and was a patron of the arts.

Chandragupta Maurya Emperor of India (c. 321–c. 297 BC), who founded the Maurya dynasty (c. 321–185 BC). He ousted the previous Nanda dynasty. According to tradition, he destroyed the garrison left behind by Alexander the Great. He extended his empire over the whole of India. The Greek ambassador and historian Megasthenes left accounts of the splendor of his reign.

Chanel, Coco (Gabrielle C.; 1883–1971) French fashion designer, who revolutionized women's clothes, introducing a note of simplicity and comfort. She opened a fashion house in Paris in 1924, becoming known particularly for her jersey dresses and suits and for her perfumes, including Chanel No 5. She retired in 1939 but began designing again in 1954.

Chang-chia-k'ou. *See* Zhangjiakou.

Chang-chou. *See* Changzhou.

Changchun 43 50N 125 20E A city in NE China, the capital of Jilin province. Jilin University was established here in 1958. Its chief industry is the manufacture of motor vehicles. Population (1957 est): 975,000.

Chang E In Chinese mythology, the moon goddess. She stole the drug of immortality from her consort and fled to the moon, where she lives in the form of a toad.

Chang Jiang. *See* Yangtze River.

Changsha 28 10N 113 00E A port in S China, the capital of Hunan province on the Xiang (*or* Siang) River. It has long been a commercial and cultural center, Hunan University being established here in 1959. Population (1957 est): 703,000.

Changzhou (*or* Chang-chou) 31 45N 119 57E A city in E China, in Jiangsu province on the *Grand Canal. A long-established commercial center for agricultural produce, it has textile and engineering industries. Population (1953): 296,500.

Channel Islands (French name: Îles Normandes) A group of islands in the English Channel, off the coast of NW France. The chief islands comprise *Jersey (the largest), *Guernsey, *Alderney, and *Sark. Since the Norman conquest (1066) they have been a dependency of the British crown. During World War II they were the only British territory to come under German occupation. Tourism is of major economic importance but

the islands are also noted for their early agricultural and horticultural produce, most of which is exported to the UK. This includes flowers, fruit, potatoes, and tomatoes; the Jersey and Guernsey breeds of cattle are world famous. Area: 75 sq mi (194 sq km). Population (1981): 133,000.

Channel tunnel (*or* Chunnel) A proposed tunnel linking Britain with France. First suggested to Napoleon in 1802, digging was actually started by two private companies in each country in 1882 but the project was abandoned in 1883. In 1964 the two governments revived the project, simultaneously considering plans for a Channel bridge. The tunnel was agreed upon and in the early 1970s work again started, to be abandoned on economic grounds in 1974. Recent developments include possible EEC participation.

Channing, William Ellery (1780–1842) US churchman. The pastor (1803–42) of the Federal Street Congregational Church in Boston, he was a founder of Unitarianism. He wrote and delivered his sermon entitled *Unitarian Christianity* in 1819 and is credited with starting the American Unitarian Association in 1825.

CHA-NO-YU *The Japanese tea ceremony requires humility from its participants, who enter the tearoom on their knees.*

cha-no-yu The Japanese tea ceremony. The ceremony originated in China but was practiced by Zen priests in Japan from the 14th century and later by other members of society. Taking place in a room of simple perfection, it is presided over by a tea master. Its object is to achieve a contemplative calm, in which attention is exclusively fixed on the ritual and utensils used. The kettle, tea bowls, bamboo whisk, and serving ladle are chosen for their artistic merit.

chanson de geste A type of epic poem composed in Old French. Versions survive from the early 12th century but the genre is probably at least a century older. Loyalty and valor are typical themes in the *chanson*, many of which relate the real or imaginary deeds of Charlemagne's knights. The most famous is the *Chanson de Roland* about the heroic last stand of some of these knights at Roncesvalles in the Pyrenees (778).

chant The short melodies to which psalms and canticles are sung in the Anglican Church. They may be single (one tune adapted for each verse) or double (alternating tunes for alternating verses). "Triple" or "quadruple" chants are less common. Many are adaptations from Latin plainsong made by John Marbeck (died c. 1585) in his *Booke of Common Praier Noted* (1550).

chanterelle An edible *mushroom, *Cantharellus cibarius*, occurring in temperate woodlands. It is funnel-shaped and yellow with the gills clearly visible and measures 3–10 cm across the cap. The flesh is regarded as a delicacy if cooked slowly. Family: *Cantharellaceae*; class: *Basidiomycetes*.

Chantilly 49 12N 2 28E A town in France, in the Oise department near the Forest of Chantilly. Once renowned for its lace making, Chantilly is famous for its racecourse and the Grand Château's art collection. Population (1975): 10,684.

Chao K'uang Yin. *See* Song.

Chao Phraya River The chief river in Thailand, rising in the N and flowing S through Bangkok to a delta on the Gulf of Thailand. Length: 750 mi (1200 km).

CHARLIE CHAPLIN *In a scene from* The Gold Rush *(1924).*

Chaos In earliest Greek mythology, the goddess representing the primeval emptiness from which evolved Night, Erebus (darkness), Tartarus (the underworld), and Eros (desire). The concept of a confused and formless mass, out of which the ordered universe was created, dates from the time of Ovid.

chaparral A scrub form of vegetation occurring in S California and NW Mexico. It consists chiefly of sclerophyllous broad-leaved evergreen shrubs and bushes and is closely related to the maquis of lands bordering the Mediterranean. The climate with which this form of vegetation is associated, with mild wet winters and hot dry summers, is sometimes described as the Mediterranean type.

chapbook A small cheap booklet or tract of a few stitched pages in multiples of four. Catering to popular tastes, they related heroic tales, legends, lessons, etc., and were often illustrated with woodcuts. From the 16th century chapmen sold them throughout Europe and subsequently in North America, until they were superseded by magazines in the 19th century.

Chapel Hill 35 55N 79 04W A city in N central North Carolina. Home of the University of North Carolina since 1789, it is mainly a residential town that developed around the university. Population (1980): 32,421.

Chaplin, Charlie (Sir Charles C.; 1889–1975) British film actor. He was recruited by the Keystone Studio while touring the US in 1913. He gained immediate popular and financial success with his portrayals of the tramp, a sensitive but pathetic figure dressed in baggy trousers and a bowler hat, and from 1918 he wrote and directed his own films. These included *The Gold Rush* (1924), *City Lights* (1931), and, following the introduction of sound, *Modern Times* (1936) and *The Great Dictator* (1940). Accused of having communist sympathies, he left the US in 1952 to live in Switzerland. He was awarded an Oscar in 1973 and was knighted in 1976.

Chapman, George (c. 1560–1634) British poet and dramatist, famous for his translations of Homer's *Iliad* (1598–1611) and *Odyssey* (1616). His epic poem *Euthymiae Raptus* (1609) expresses his complex philosophy. His plays include the comedy *Eastward Ho* (1605), for which he and his collaborators John *Marston and Ben *Jonson were imprisoned, and the tragedy *Bussy d'Ambois* (1604).

char A food and game fish belonging to the genus *Salvelinus*, related to *trout, especially *S. alpinus*, found in Arctic coastal waters and fresh wa-

ters of Europe and North America. Its torpedo-shaped body, about 12 in (30 cm) long, is olive-green to moss-green with yellow spots above and silvery or bright red below.

characin A predatory freshwater fish of the family *Characidae* (about 1000 species), found in tropical Africa and America. Characins have toothed jaws and two dorsal fins. Although they range from 1–61 in (2.5 to 152 cm) long, most species are small and make colorful lively aquarium fish. Order: *Cypriniformes*. *See also* piranha; tetra; tigerfish.

charcoal The form of *carbon that is produced as a black porous residue from the partial burning of wood, bones, etc. It is a very clean smokeless fuel useful, for example, in barbecues and saunas. It is also extensively used in gas filters. *See also* activated charcoal.

Charcot, Jean-Martin (1825–93) French physiologist, noted for his studies of the nervous system. He described various diseases, including **Charcot's joint**—degeneration of the joints associated with disease of the nervous system. He was a famous teacher—Sigmund *Freud was one of his students—and interested in hypnosis.

chard 1. The blanched leaves of a sucker growth of the globe *artichoke, used as a vegetable. 2. The edible leaves of a variety of beet, *Beta vulgaris cicla*, also called Swiss chard.

Chardin, Jean-Baptiste-Siméon (1699–1779) French painter of still lifes and domestic interiors in the Dutch tradition of *Vermeer. The writer *Diderot admired the simplicity of his paintings, e.g. *The Housewife* (Louvre) and *The Young Schoolmistress* (National Gallery, London), and his skill at rendering textures. Working in pastel in his later years because of failing eyesight, he produced his celebrated portraits of himself and his wife (both Louvre).

Charente River A river in W central France. Rising in the Haute-Vienne department, it flows mainly W through Angoulême and Cognac to the Bay of Biscay. Length: 225 mi (362 km).

Chari River (*or* Shari R.) A river in N central Africa. Rising in the N Central African Republic, it flows N to Lake Chad, forming part of the Chad–Cameroon border. Length: 1400 mi (2250 km).

chariot 1. A two-wheeled horsedrawn vehicle used for warfare in ancient Asian and European civilizations. Commonly drawn by two horses, a war chariot generally carried two men: the driver and an archer or spearman. 2. A fashionable small traveling carriage of the 18th and early 19th centuries, drawn by two or four horses.

THE PRINCE AND PRINCESS OF WALES *A wedding portrait of the couple. Their marriage on July 29, 1981, in St. Paul's Cathedral, London, was watched on television by an estimated 750 million people throughout the world.*

Charlemagne (c. 742–814) King of the Franks (771–814) and the first postclassical western emperor (800–14). The son of Pepin the Short, he conquered the Saxon tribes (772–81) and became King of Lombardy (773). In 778 he campaigned in NE Spain, where at Roncesvalles his paladin Roland, later to be immortalized as the hero of the *Chanson de Roland*, was killed. In 800, having conquered most of western Christendom, he was crowned emperor of the West by Pope Leo III.

Charlemagne did much to centralize the administration of the empire while maintaining the traditional customs of his conquered territories. His court at Aix-la-Chapelle became a great European center, where Charlemagne, the patron of such scholars as *Alcuin and *Einhard, fostered the cultural revival known as the Carolingian renaissance.

Charleroi 50 25N 4 27E A town in S central Belgium, on the Sambre River. The center of a major coal-producing area, its industries include iron foundries and cutlery. Population (1981 est): 218,944.

Charles (1887–1922) The last emperor of the Dual Monarchy of *Austria-Hungary (1916–18). Charles failed in his attempts to withdraw Austria-Hungary from World War I and following its defeat was exiled. He was formally deposed in 1919.

Charles (Philip Arthur George) (1948–) Prince of Wales and heir-apparent to the throne of the United Kingdom as the eldest son of Elizabeth II. After studying at Trinity College, Cambridge (1967–70), he served in the armed forces before undertaking public duties. In 1981 he married Lady Diana Spencer (1961–). Their first child, Prince William Arthur Philip Louis of Wales was born in 1982; a second son, Henry, was born in 1984.

Charles I (1226–85) The first Angevin King of Naples and Sicily, after defeating Manfred (c. 1232–66; reigned 1258–66) at Benevento (1266) and Conradin (1252–68; reigned 1266–68) at Tagliacozzo (1268). Charles' rule gave rise (1282) to the revolt known as the *Sicilian Vespers and he was driven from his kingdom in 1284.

CHARLES I Charles I in Three Positions *by Van Dyck (c. 1637), the English king's painter.*

Charles I (1600–49) King of England, Scotland, and Ireland (1625–49), succeeding his father James I. Charles' disputes with parliament led ultimately to the *Civil War and his execution. His first three parliaments (1625; 1626; 1628–29) were dominated by Puritan members, who distrusted Charles' Roman Catholic queen and his own High Church loyalties. Parliament attempted to make its award of financial grants to the king dependent on his agreement to its demands. Charles resorted to levying taxes without parliamentary consent and ruled without parliament from 1629 to 1640. His government became increasingly unpopular and his attempt to impose an Anglican prayer book on Presbyterian Scotland led to the *Bishops' Wars (1639–40). The financial demands of the Wars forced Charles to summon parliament again but the so-called Short Parliament (May Parliament 1640) proved so critical that he soon dissolved it. The *Long Parliament, summoned in November following Charles' defeat by the Scots, demanded far-reaching reforms. In 1642 the Civil War broke out. After his defeat at Naseby (1645), Charles' cause was lost and he surrendered in 1646. He was handed to parliament (January, 1647), seized by the

army (June, 1647), and escaped to the Isle of Wight. Charles was tried at Westminster Hall, found guilty of treason, and beheaded (January 30, 1649).

Charles I (King of France). *See* Charles II (Holy Roman Emperor).

Charles (II) the Bald (823–77) Holy Roman Emperor (875–77) and, as Charles I, King of France (843–77). After the death of his father Louis I, civil war broke out between Charles and his three older brothers. By 843 Charles had procured by the Treaty of Verdun the western Frankish territories, which formed the nucleus of what was to become France.

Charles II (1630–85) King of England, Scotland, and Ireland (1660–85). He fought with his father, Charles I, in the Civil War and, after his father's execution (1649), was crowned by the Scots. Defeated by Cromwell (1651), he was forced into exile. After the fall of the Protectorate (1659), Charles became king after promising a general pardon and liberty of conscience. His advisers were a group of ministers known as the *Cabal. In 1670 he negotiated the Treaty of Dover with Louis XIV, promising to aid France against Holland and, in a secret clause, to declare himself a Roman Catholic, in return for annual French subsidies. His Roman Catholic sympathies became clear with his Declaration of Indulgence (1672). Parliament responded with the Test Act (1673) excluding Dissenters and Roman Catholics from office. Fear of Roman Catholicism exacerbated by the lack of an heir to the throne came to head with the *Popish Plot (1678). Charles resisted subsequent parliamentary attempts to exclude his brother James from the succession and from 1681 ruled without parliament. On his deathbed he acknowledged his Roman Catholicism.

Charles II (1661–1700) The last Habsburg King of Spain (1665–1700). Charles became effective ruler in 1675. His reign saw Portugal regain its independence (1668) and the final eclipse of Spanish power in Europe. Charles' childlessness gave rise on his death to the War of the *Spanish Succession.

Charles II (King of France). *See* Charles III (Holy Roman Emperor).

Charles (III) the Fat (839–88) Holy Roman Emperor (881–87) and, as Charles II, King of France (884–87). Charles was the great-grandson of Charlemagne, whose empire he reunited for the last time after becoming King of Swabia (876), of Italy (879), and of the eastern Franks (882) and western Franks (France; 884).

Charles III (1716–88) King of Spain (1759–88). Charles ascended the Spanish throne after ruling (1734–59) Naples and Sicily. An enlightened despot (*see* Enlightenment), he encouraged efforts to modernize Spain, to develop its economy, and restore its international position. He sided with France in the Seven Years' War, losing Florida until 1783, when he regained it after the American Revolution.

Charles (IV) the Fair (1294–1328) King of France (1322–28). Charles was the brother of *Isabella of France, with whom he conspired against her husband Edward II of England.

Charles IV (1316–78) King of Bohemia (1346–78) and Holy Roman Emperor (1355–78). He made Prague his capital, where he founded (1348) Charles University. In 1356 he issued the Golden Bull, an imperial constitution, which confirmed the status of the seven imperial *electors.

Charles IV (1748–1819) King of Spain (1738–1808), who was dominated by his wife María Luisa (1751–1819) and her favorite Manuel de *Godoy. Military defeat and Godoy's unpopularity led to aristocratic and popular opposition, which caused Charles to abdicate.

Charles (V) the Wise (1337–80) King of France (1364–80) during the Hundred Years' War with England. As regent (1356–60) for his father John II, Charles suppressed the peasants' revolt known as the Jacquerie (1358). Between 1369 and 1375 he regained with the help of Bertrand du *Guesclin most of the territory lost to England by the disastrous Treaty of Brétigny (1360).

Charles V (1500–58) Holy Roman Emperor (1519–56). Charles inherited Burgundy and the Netherlands (1506) from his father Philip of Burgundy (1478–1506); he became King of Spain and Naples (1516) on the death of his maternal grandfather Ferdinand II of Aragon and Holy Roman Emperor on the death of his paternal grandfather Maximilian I. Charles' vast possessions provoked intermittent warfare with *Francis I of France: in 1525, having defeated Francis at Pavia, Charles briefly took the French king prisoner and in 1527, in response to an alliance between France, the papacy, Venice, and Milan, Charles' troops sacked Rome. Their contest for European hegemony ended inconclusively with the Treaty of Crépy (1544). Charles also faced the aggression of the Ottoman Turks, who twice besieged Vienna (1529, 1532), but his commitments elsewhere in the Empire prevented a decisive confrontation and the Turks continued to threaten Christendom.

Charles' reign saw the emergence of the *Reformation and in 1521 he presided over the Diet of Worms, which condemned *Luther. His subsequent attempts to conciliate the Protestants failed and in 1546 Charles took up arms against the Protestant Schmalkaldic League, defeating it at Mühlberg (1547). In 1551, however, two German Protestant rulers allied with Henry II of France and Charles was forced to accept Protestant demands (see Augsburg, Peace of). Exhausted by the great and complex problems of his Empire, Charles retired to a Spanish monastery, dividing his possessions between his son, who became *Philip II of Spain, and his brother, Emperor *Ferdinand I.

Charles (VI) the Well-Beloved (1368–1422) King of France (1380–1422). Charles suffered attacks of insanity from 1392 and the ensuing conflict for the regency led to civil war between the Armagnacs and the Burgundians. In 1415 Henry V of England invaded France and defeated the French at *Agincourt. Henry married Charles' daughter Catherine of Valois (1401–37) and was named as Charles' heir.

Charles VI (1685–1740) Holy Roman Emperor (1711–40), who issued the Pragmatic Sanction (1713) to secure the succession of his daughter *Maria Theresa to his Austrian possessions. His claim (1700) to the Spanish throne gave rise to the War of the *Spanish Succession (1701–14), in which he was unsuccessful. In 1716–18 and 1736–39 he fought the Turks; he lost the War of the Polish Succession (1733–38).

Charles VII (1403–61) King of France (1422–61). He suffered losses to the invading English and their Burgundian allies until 1429 when, with *Joan of Arc, he liberated Orleans. By 1453, he had driven the English from all of France, except Calais. He instituted reforms to strengthen the monarchy but his last years were troubled by the intrigues of the dauphin. See also Hundred Years' War.

Charles VII (1697–1745) Holy Roman Emperor (1742–45) during the War of the *Austrian Succession. The Elector of Bavaria (1726–45), Charles joined the alliance against Maria Theresa when she claimed the Austrian inheritance. He was elected emperor in opposition to Maria Theresa's husband Francis (subsequently Emperor Francis I).

Charles VIII (1470–98) King of France (1483–98), who unsuccessfully claimed the throne of Naples. He entered Naples in 1495 but was forced to withdraw in the face of an alliance between Austria, Milan, Venice, and the papacy.

Charles IX (1550–74) King of France (1560–74) during the *Wars of Religion. His mother *Catherine de' Medici dominated his reign and was largely responsible for the *Saint Bartholomew's Day Massacre of Huguenots that Charles ordered in 1572.

Charles IX (1550–1611) King of Sweden (1607–11). During the absence of his nephew King Sigismund (1566–1632; reigned 1592–1604), who was also King of Poland (1587–1632), Charles virtually ruled Sweden, restoring Lutheranism (1593–99). He defeated Sigismund (1598) to become king.

Charles X Gustavus (1622–60) King of Sweden (1654–60), who attempted to establish a united northern state. He invaded Poland in 1655 and declared war on Denmark in 1657, from which he regained lands in S Sweden by the Treaty of Roskilde (1658). He died during a second campaign against Denmark.

Charles X (1757–1836) King of France (1824–30). Charles lived abroad after the French revolution, returning at the Bourbon restoration (1815), when he became leader of the ultraroyalist party. His reactionary rule led to his overthrow (1830) and he fled to England.

Charles XI (1655–97) King of Sweden (1660–97), who reduced the power of the nobles to establish absolute rule. He was defeated (1675) by the Dutch alliance in the Dutch War of 1672–78 but was victorious (1678) against Denmark, marrying (1680) the sister of the Danish king. Thereafter he maintained Swedish neutrality.

Charles XII (1682–1718) King of Sweden (1697–1718) during the Great *Northern War. In the face of an alliance between Denmark, Poland, and Russia, Charles invaded Denmark (1699) and attacked Russia, winning a victory on the Narva (1700). He dethroned the hostile Polish king (1704) and again invaded Russia (1707), where he suffered defeat and fled to Turkey. He died while invading Norway.

Charles XIV John (King of Sweden). See Bernadotte, Jean Baptiste Jules.

Charles, Ray (Ray Charles Robinson; 1932–   ) US singer and pianist. Blind since he was a young boy, he combines gospel, blues, and rock to create a type of soul sound. He rocketed to stardom in the 1950s with his recordings of "I Got a Woman" (1954) and "What'd I Say" (1959).

Charles Albert (1798–1849) King of Sardinia-Piedmont (1831–49) during the Risorgimento (the movement for Italian Unification). Charles Albert introduced many administrative and economic reforms but reluctantly granted representative government to Sardinia in 1848. He joined Milan's revolt against its Austrian government but was defeated at Custoza (1848) and Novara (1849) and abdicated.

Charles Edward Stuart, the Young Pretender (1720–88) The son of the Old Pretender, *James Edward Stuart. Romantically known as Bonnie Prince Charlie, in 1745 he landed in Scotland, rallied his *Jacobite supporters and marched S to claim the English throne. Lack of support forced his withdrawal again to Scotland. Defeated in battle at Culloden (1746), he escaped to exile in Europe.

Charles Martel (c. 689–741) Mayor of the palace of Austrasia (the eastern Frankish empire). After the death (714) of his father Pepin of Herstal, Charles, an illegitimate son, competed for the succession with Pepin's widow, Plectrude, who was regent for her grandsons. Successful by 719, Charles extended his rule over all the Franks. In 732 near Poitiers, he won a great victory over the invading Muslims.

Charles's law For a gas at constant pressure, its volume is directly proportional to its absolute temperature. The law is not strictly obeyed but is closely approximated in gases above their *critical state. An alternative statement of the law is that gases expand by 1/273 of their volume at 32°F (0°C) for every 7.8°F (1°C) rise in temperature. Named for Jacques Charles (1746–1823).

Charles the Bold (1433–77) The last Duke of Burgundy (1467–77), who attempted to create a Burgundian kingdom. In 1465 Charles joined a revolt against Louis XI of France, with whom he was repeatedly in conflict until 1477. He extended his territory to the Rhine, conquering Lorraine in 1475. He then invaded Switzerland (1476) but was defeated near Granson and at Morat and died in battle while laying siege to Nancy.

Charleston 38 23N 81 40W The capital of West Virginia. It was the home (1788–95) of Daniel Boone. Industries include chemicals, glass, and paints. Population (1980): 63,968.

Charleston 32 48N 79 58W A city in South Carolina near the Atlantic coast. Founded in 1670, the first military action of the Civil War took place here with the bombardment of Fort Sumter by Confederate troops in 1861. Despite further damage from an earthquake in 1866, many of Charleston's colonial buildings remain, making it a popular tourist center. Its gardens are famous throughout the world. A major port, its manufactures include fertilizer, paper, and steel. Population (1980): 69,510.

CHARLESTON *A cartoon view of the 1920s dance craze.*

Charleston A ballroom dance of the 1920s named for Charleston, S. C. where it had been a popular black dance in the early 1900s. It became a national craze following the musical *Runnin' Wild* (1923). Its chief characteristics are 4/4 time, syncopated rhythms, and twisting toe-in steps.

Charleston, Battles of Two battles of the *American Revolution fought at Charleston, S. C. In the first (1776) the Americans repulsed the British, whose invasion of the South was thus delayed. In the second the Americans surrendered (May 12, 1780) Charleston after a 45-day siege.

charlock An annual herb, *Sinapis arvensis*, also called wild mustard. 12–31 in (30–80 cm) high, with bright-yellow flowers and hairy toothed leaves, it is found throughout Eurasia and N Africa and has been introduced to the Americas, South Africa, Australia, and New Zealand. It is a serious weed, especially of spring-sown crops. Family: *Cruciferae.

Charlotte 35 03N 80 50W A city in North Carolina. The commercial and industrial center of the Carolina manufacturing belt, its products include textiles, machinery, and chemicals. Population (1980): 314,447.

Charlotte Amalie (name from 1921 until 1936: St Thomas) 18 21N 64 56W The capital of the US Virgin Islands, a port on St Thomas Island. Established by the Danes in 1672, it is now a tourist resort. Population (1980): 11,756.

Charlottenburg 52 31N 13 15E A district of West Berlin, West Germany, on the Spree River. The 1936 Olympic Games were held here. Population (1970 est): 207,732.

Charlottesville 38 02N 78 29W A city in central Virginia. It was the home of Thomas Jefferson, who established the University of Virginia here in 1819. Population (1970): 110,938.

Charlottetown 46 14N 63 09W A city and port in E Canada, the capital of Prince Edward Island. Founded in 1790, it is the province's commercial, industrial, and educational center. Population (1976): 17,063.

charm A property of matter, expressed as a *quantum number, postulated to account for the unusually long lifetime of the psi particle (discovered in 1974). According to this hypothesis a quark (see particle physics) exists having the property called charm. The psi particle itself is a meson having zero charm as it consists of a charmed quark and its antiquark. However, there is evidence that some charmed *hadrons exist. Charm is believed to be conserved in *strong interactions and in electromagnetic interactions.

Charon In Greek legend, the ferryman who carried the souls of the dead over the Styx and Acheron Rivers to the underworld. Only the correctly buried dead were taken. A coin placed in the mouth of the corpse was his payment.

Charpentier, Gustave (1860–1956) French composer and pupil of Massenet. He wrote one successful opera, *Louise* (1900), a naturalistic treatment of the life of a Parisian working girl.

Charron, Pierre (1541–1603) French theologian and philosopher. An intimate of *Montaigne, Charron studied law but entered the Church, becoming a fashionable preacher with a court appointment. *Les Trois Vérités* (1594) is a defense of Roman Catholicism. *De la sagesse* (1601), contrastingly skeptical and rationalistic, foreshadows *deism, and offers a moral philosophy divorced from Christian sanctions.

Chartier, Alain (c. 1385–c. 1440) French poet and prose writer. He served as secretary to Charles VI and as foreign emissary for Charles VII. His works include the *Quadrilogue invectif* (1422), a debate on the state of France and a call for national unity, and the poem *La Belle Dame sans merci* (1424).

Chartism A British working–class movement for political reform, centering on William *Lovett's London Working Men's Association (LWMA). Founded in June, 1836, the LWMA drew up a People's Charter (1838) of six points: universal male suffrage, the secret ballot, equal electoral districts, abolition of the property qualifications for members of Parliament, payment of MPs, and annual general elections. The Chartists quickly gained support throughout the country and presented their Charter with 1.2 million signatures to parliament (1839). It was rejected, as were their two later petitions (1842, 1848). Chartism lost support in the 1840s because of lack of organization, rivalry between its leaders, Lovett and Feargus *O'Connor, and reviving trade and greater prosperity. The movement was spent by the end of the decade.

Chartres 48 27N 1 30E A city in N central France, the capital of the Eure-et-Loire department on the Eure River. The gothic cathedral (begun c. 1194) is famous, especially for its 13th-century stained glass, and there are several other noteworthy churches (particularly St Pierre). Chartres is the principal market town of the Beauce region. Population (1975): 41,251.

Chartreuse, La Grande A *Carthusian monastery in a remote valley in SE France, in the Isère department. The buildings date mainly from the 17th century. The liqueur Chartreuse is made by the monks, the income from it being devoted to maintaining Carthusian monasteries and to several charities.

Charybdis A legendary Greek monster and the whirlpool she formed, traditionally in the Strait of Messina. The dangerous channel between Charybdis and *Scylla was successfully navigated by both Odysseus and the Argonauts.

Chase, Salmon Portland (1808–73) US politician, lawyer, and chief justice of the Supreme Court (1864–73). He spent his early career as a lawyer in Ohio, where he was active in the abolitionist movement. He

served as US senator (1849–55; 1860–61), governor of Ohio (1855–59), and secretary of the Treasury (1861–64). As chief justice he presided over the impeachment trial (1868) of President Andrew Johnson, who was acquitted, and he handled a number of landmark cases, such as *Hepburn* v. *Griswold* (1870), in which he held that legal tender was unconstitutional. He sought his party's nomination for president several times but was unsuccessful.

Chase, Samuel (1741–1811) US jurist and lawyer, associate justice of the Supreme Court (1796–1811). He was an active patriot in his native Maryland, serving in the Continental Congresses (1774–78; 1784–85); he was a signer of the Declaration of Independence (1776). In 1804 impeachment proceedings were initiated against him by the Senate for his actions as a Federalist judge; he was acquitted of all charges in 1805.

chat A songbird belonging to the *thrush family. True chats include *stonechats, *whinchats, *wheatears, and *redstarts although the name is also given to certain Australian wrens (family *Muscicapidae*) and to American wood warblers (family *Parulidae*).

chateau A French castle or large country house. In the middle ages it was the fortified stronghold of the local seigneur. By the 16th century, however, defense needs had decreased and chateaux became the lightly fortified country residences of the nobility. Among the most famous are the chateaux of *Blois (1498–1524), *Chambord (1519–40), and d'Azay-le-Rideau (1520) in the Loire Valley. Under Louis XIV chateau building declined with the aristocracy's increasing dependence on the crown for its income and the resultant need to live in Paris.

Chateaubriand, Vicomte de (1768–1848) French writer and diplomat. Son of a minor nobleman, he sailed to America in 1791 but soon returned to fight in the royalist army. He lived in England from 1793 to 1800. On returning to France, he published *Atala* (1801), an unfinished epic based on his experiences with the American Indians, and *Le Génie du Christianisme* (1802). After the restoration of the monarchy in 1814 he served as ambassador and as minister for foreign affairs. He is best known for his *Mémoires d'outre-tombe* (1849–50).

Chateauroux 46 49N 1 41E A city in central France, the capital of the Indre department on the Indre River. Named for its 10th-century chateau, it has textile, machinery, and tobacco industries. Population (1975): 55,629.

Château-Thierry 49 03N 3 24E A town in N France, in the Aisne department on the Marne River. The site of many battles throughout the centuries, it was the scene of the second battle of the Marne (1918) during *World War I. Population (1968): 10,858.

Chatham 51 23N 0 32E A city in SE England, in Kent on the Medway estuary. It is a naval base dating from Tudor times, with extensive dockyards. Population (1981): 61,909.

Chatham, 1st Earl of. *See* Pitt the Elder, William.

Chatham Islands 44 00S 176 30W A group of islands in the S Pacific Ocean, comprising part of New Zealand. The main occupation is sheep farming. Area: 372 sq mi (963 sq km). Population (1971): 716. Chief settlement: Waitangi.

Chattahoochee River A river that rises in NE Georgia, flows SW and then S, where it forms the border with Alabama from West Point until its entry into NW Florida. Here it meets the Flint River to form the Apalachicola River. Length: 435 mi (701 km).

Chattanooga 35 02N 85 18W A city in SE Tennessee on the Tennessee River. It was settled in 1815 and was the site of a decisive battle in the US Civil War (1863). It grew rapidly following the provision of cheap hydroelectric power by the Tennessee Valley Authority in the 1930s. Its varied industries include the manufacture of textiles, boilers, nuclear reactors, furniture, and chemicals. Population (1980): 169,565.

Chatterjee, Bankim Chandra (1838–94) Indian novelist. A pioneer of the novel in India, he wrote romances, such as *Anandamath* (1882), the heroes of which are usually champions of Hindu nationalism. Many of his books were first published serially in *Banga Darshan*, the journal he founded in 1872.

Chaucer, Geoffrey (c. 1342–1400) English poet, whose works established the Southern English dialect as the literary language of England. Chaucer made various journeys to Europe as a soldier and diplomat, held positions in the customs service, and received pensions from Richard II and Henry IV. He translated part of the French poem *Le Roman de la rose* into English and his own poems *The Book of the Duchess* and *The Parliament of Fowls* derive from the French tradition of the allegorical dream poem. Chaucer was also influenced by Dante, Petrarch, and Boccaccio: he parodied Dante's *Divine Comedy* in *The House of Fame* and used Boccaccio's poem *Il filostrato* as the basis for *Troilus and Criseyde*, a long poem dealing with the transitoriness of earthly love, human free will, and divine foreknowledge. Chaucer's best-known work is *The Canterbury Tales*, a collection of stories told by a group of pilgrims traveling from London to Canterbury. The tales range from the tragedy of *The Knight's Tale* to the bawdiness of *The Miller's Tale*. Colorful portraits of each pilgrim are contained in the famous Prologue.

GEOFFREY CHAUCER *An engraving based on an illumination in a manuscript of Chaucer's works.*

chaulmoogra   Either of two trees, *Hydnocarpus wightiana* of SW Asia or *Taraktogenos kurzii* of Burma, both of which yield a medicinal oil used in treating leprosy. Family: *Flacourtiaceae*.

Chausson, Ernest   (1855–99) French composer. His compositions were influenced by his teacher Franck and by Wagner. His small output includes *Poème de l'amour et de la mer* (for voice and orchestra; 1882–92), *Poème* (for violin and orchestra; 1896), and a symphony (1890). He was killed in a cycling accident.

Chautauqua   A system of adult education started in the US by John H. Vincent and Lewis Miller at Lake Chautauqua, New York, in 1874. Originally a summer training program for Protestant Sunday school teachers in a rural, peaceful setting, it broadened into general education, with guest lecturers and recreation, followed by home reading and correspondence courses. By 1900 there were adult summer school sessions (called chautauquas) throughout the country; although the system weakened after 1924, due to the rise of advanced media techniques, it is still carried on at Chautauqua, N.Y.

Chavez, Cesar Estrada   (1927–   ) US labor leader. He worked for the Community Service Organization (1952–62), serving as its director from 1958. In 1962 he founded the United Farm Workers (UFW), which became the AFL-CIO's United Farm Workers Organization Committee in 1966. He led boycotts of grapes, citrus fruits, and lettuce in the late 1960s and 1970s, but disagreements between management and farm laborers continued.

Cheb   (German name: Eger)   50 04N 12 20E A city in W Czechoslovakia. It was a major border fortress, with a 12th-century castle, guarding the NW approach to Bohemia. Wallenstein was murdered here (1634). Following World War I it was a center of the Sudeten-German movement. Population (1968 est): 26,098.

Chebishev, Pafnuti Lvovich   (1821–94) Russian mathematician, who made many discoveries in the field of *prime numbers, the most important of which was a method of determining the number of primes below a given number. He also contributed to probability theory and mechanics.

Cheboksary   56 08N 47 12E A port in the central Soviet Union, the capital of Chuvash ASSR in the RSFSR on the Volga River. Its manufactures include electrical equipment and it has a large hydroelectric station. Population (1981 est): 340,000.

Checheno-Ingush Autonomous Soviet Socialist Republic   An administrative division in the S Soviet Union, in the RSFSR in the N Caucasus. The population is 50% Chechen and 10% Ingushe (both Muslim) and 35% Russian. Checheno-Ingush has one of the major Soviet oilfields as well as sizable deposits of natural gas and minerals. Its main industries are engineering, chemicals, manufacture of building materials, food canning, and wine and cognac making. The presence of mineral waters has resulted in the development of health resorts. *History*: the Chechens and Ingushes were conquered by Russia in the late 1850s. Each nationality became (1922 and 1924 respectively) a separate autonomous *oblast* (region) before uniting in 1936 to become one autonomous republic. Following collaboration with the Germans in World War II, many Chechens and Ingushes were deported to Central Asia, being returned in 1956. The republic was re-established in 1957. Area: 7350 sq mi (19,300 sq km). Population (1981 est): 1,170,000. Capital: Grozny.

checkers   (UK name: draughts)   A boardgame for two players that was developed in 12th-century Europe from an ancient Egyptian game. Each player has 12 disk-shaped pieces (usually black for one and white or red for the other), which are placed on the 12 black squares at the opposite ends of a chessboard. The pieces move only on the black squares and black always starts. One piece per turn is moved diagonally forward into a vacant adjacent square. If the next square is occupied by one of the opponent's pieces but the square beyond that is vacant, the playing piece must jump onto the vacant square, removing his opponent's piece from the board. He must make a further jump from there if possible (in the same turn). The 16th-century rule of "huffing" enables a player to remove an opponent's piece that could have jumped but did not. If a piece reaches the opposing back line it becomes a "king" (a second piece is placed on top of it) and it may then move forward or backward. The winner is the player who takes or immobilizes all his opponent's pieces.

cheese   A dairy product made from separated milk solids (curd). Curd is made by coagulating milk with rennet or some other enzyme and removing the liquid (whey). It is then salted, pressed into blocks, and left to mature. Cheese is a rich source of protein and calcium. It contains fat but little carbohydrate since most of it is left in the whey. **Hard cheeses**, such as Emmental and Cheddar, are left to mature for some time—years in the case of Italian Parmesan. Cheshire, Port Salut, Edam, and Gouda are **semihard cheeses**. **Soft cheeses** may be eaten relatively fresh, after one day in the case of fresh cream cheese. Brie, Camembert, and Limburg are surface-ripened soft cheeses. Blue cheese, Stilton, Gorgonzola, and Roquefort are ripened by molds inside the cheese.

cheetah   A large *cat, *Acinonyx jubatus*, of Africa and SW Asia, also called hunting leopard. It has a reddish-yellow coat with black spots and grows to about 7 ft (2 m) in length. Cheetahs have nonretractable claws and rough pads and they hunt by running down prey, such as antelope. They are the fastest mammals, sprinting at up to 70 mph (110 kph).

Cheever, John   (1912–82) US author. Although his first collections of short stories, *The Way Some People Live* (1943) and *The Enormous Radio* (1953) dealt with urban life, the bulk of his work told of the suburbs with which he was familiar. His short story collections include *The Housebreaker of Shady Hill* (1958), *The World of Apples* (1973), and *The Stories of John Cheever* (1978; Pulitzer Prize). Among his novels are *The Wapshot Chronicle* (1957), *The Wapshot Scandal* (1964), *Bullet Park* (1969), *Falconer* (1977), and *Oh, What a Paradise It Seems* (1982).

Chefoo.   *See* Yantai.

CHEKA   The first Soviet secret police agency. Founded in 1917, its full name was the Extraordinary Commission to Combat Counterrevolution, Sabotage, and Speculation. It was headed by Feliks Dzerzhinskii (1877–1926) and fought all anti-Bolshevik groups. Owing to its extreme brutality, it came under severe criticism and was reorganized in 1922.

Chekhov, Anton Pavlovich   (1860–1904) Russian dramatist and short-story writer. He began writing comic sketches while studying medicine at Moscow University and developed as a more serious writer after graduating in 1884. Suffering from tuberculosis, he bought a farm at Melikhovo in 1892 and, after a hemorrhage in 1897, lived at Yalta in the Crimea. His first play, *The Seagull* (1896), failed at first but succeeded triumphantly when revived in 1898 by Stanislavsky's Moscow Art Theater. His major plays—*Uncle Vanya* (1897), *The Three Sisters* (1901), and *The Cherry Orchard* (1904)—were written for this company, and in 1901 he married one of the actresses, Olga Knipper.

Chekiang. *See* Zhejiang.

chelate An inorganic chemical complex in which a closed ring of atoms is formed including a metallic ion. For example, two molecules of ethylenediamine form two chelate rings with a cupric ion. Chlorophyll (with a central magnesium ion) and hemoglobin (with a central iron ion) are chelates. Chelating agents are used for sequestering unwanted metal ions. For example, they are added to shampoos in order to soften the water used with them by "locking up" calcium and magnesium ions.

Chelmsford 51 44N 0 28E A city in SE England, the administrative center of Essex. It is a market town and manufactures electronic communications equipment, electronic equipment, and bearings. Population (1981): 58,159.

Chelonia An order of reptiles (600 species) comprising the aquatic *turtles and *terrapins and the terrestrial *tortoises, widely distributed in warm and temperate regions. They have a protective shell consisting of an upper carapace and a lower plastron joined together at the sides with openings for the head, tail, and limbs. The neck is long and mobile and can be withdrawn into the shell.

Chelsea porcelain A pioneer soft-paste *porcelain made in the Chelsea district of London between 1743 and 1785. Products included octagonal table wares from Japanese models, copies of Chinese vases and figures, perfume bottles and toilet articles in *Meissen style, and splendid *rococo vases and figures in the Sèvres style.

Cheltenham 51 54N 2 04W A city in SW England, in Gloucestershire. A fashionable spa town in the 18th century, it is famous for its schools (Cheltenham College, a boys' public school, and Cheltenham Ladies' College) and racecourse. Population (1981): 73,229.

Chelyabinsk 55 12N 61 25E A city in the W Soviet Union, in the RSFSR. It is one of the country's major industrial centers, whose products include steel and chemicals. Population (1981 est): 1,055,000.

Chelyuskin, Cape 77 44N 103 55E A headland in the central N Soviet Union, the most northerly point of any continent.

chemical bond The force that holds the atoms together in a molecule or the ions together in a crystalline solid. In general, atoms combine to form molecules and ions combine to form crystals in order to increase their stability by sharing or transferring outer electrons in such a way that the stable noble-gas configuration results (*see* atomic theory). In **covalent bonds**, atoms are held together by sharing pairs of electrons in their outer shells. In methane (CH_4), for example, each hydrogen atom forms a bond by sharing its only electron with one of the four electrons in the outer shell of the carbon atom. Each hydrogen atom then has a pair of electrons, giving it the stable two-electron outer shell of helium. The carbon atom, with four pairs of electrons in its outer shell, has the stable eight-electron outer shell of argon. In the **electrovalent** (*or* ionic) **bond** an outer electron is transferred from one atom to another so that ions are formed. The electrostatic force between the ions holds the molecule or crystal together. For example, a molecule of sodium chloride (NaCl) is formed when the single electron in the outer shell of the sodium atom is transferred to the chlorine atom. As the chlorine atom has seven electrons, the additional electron gives it the eight-electron argon stability. **Coordinate** (*or* dative) **bonds** are covalent bonds in which both electrons are donated by the same atom. They thus combine the concepts of sharing and transferring. *See also* hydrogen bonds.

chemical energy Energy released in a usable form by a chemical reaction. In molecules, energy is stored as the potential energy of the electrons. During a reaction, rearrangement of the electrons takes place and excess energy is converted to other forms. The energy is usually transformed into heat, as in combustion, acid-base neutralization, etc., but it can be made available as electrical energy in cells. Occasionally, it gives rise to *luminescence.

chemical engineering The design, maintenance, and operation of equipment used in industrial chemical processes. Chemical engineers study both chemistry and engineering subjects.

chemical reaction A process in which one or more chemical substances change to other substances, either spontaneously or as a result of heat, irradiation, etc. Chemical reaction involves partial or complete transfer of one or more electrons between reacting species and a rearrangement of atoms to form different molecules. For a reaction to occur, reactant atoms (or molecules, ions, etc.) must collide. Most reactions are thus bimolecular

(involving collision between two molecules); a few are termolecular (three molecules). Many apparently complicated reactions proceed in a sequence of simple steps. *See also* catalysis.

chemical warfare The use of toxic substances to kill or disable personnel, pollute food or water supplies, or make any other military use of chemicals, for example smoke screens, etc. (explosives are excluded). Toxic substances are generally fired in shells as liquids or solids that form aerosols on explosion. Chlorine, phosgene, and mustard gas were used in World War I but are ineffective against modern protection. They were not used in World War II. Poisons have now been developed to penetrate the skin, circumventing gas masks. Chemical warfare permits great flexibility in the amount and type of injuries inflicted, ranging from the relatively humane *tear gas to the lethal *nerve gases.

chemiluminescence The emission of light without heat in the course of a chemical reaction; often known as cold light. It occurs when the reaction yields product molecules in an excited energy state; light is emitted as the molecules revert to their ground state. Under certain conditions, the oxidation of many organic compounds, including glucose and formaldehyde, results in chemiluminescence. *See also* bioluminescence.

chemin de fer. *See* baccarat.

chemisorption. *See* adsorption.

chemistry The scientific study of matter, especially the changes and interactions it can undergo. Chemistry can be said to have originated with *Aristotle's four-element (earth, air, fire, water) analysis of matter. This totally incorrect view of the substance of the world persisted unchallenged, untested, and unrefuted from the 4th century BC, through some 2000 years of *alchemy, until it was finally demolished by Robert *Boyle in his *Skeptical Chymist* (1661). The modern concept of an element, as a substance incapable of further decomposition, was provided by Boyle, who also correctly distinguished between elements, compounds, and mixtures. The elucidation of the structure of compounds in terms of the elements they contain was developed by such 18th-century chemists as *Cavendish, *Priestley, and *Lavoisier. *Berzelius' law of constant proportions and *Dalton's atomic theory, produced at the beginning of the 19th century, established chemistry on a quantitative basis. However, it was not until the beginning of the 20th century that the work of J. J. Thomson and Rutherford (*see* atomic theory) had established the structure of the atom, enabling the electronic theory of *valence to emerge. This theory made sense of the work of Newlands and *Mendeleyev in ordering the elements into the structure of the *periodic table. **Inorganic chemistry** is concerned with the study of all these elements (except carbon) and their compounds and interactions. **Organic chemistry** is the study of the enormous number of compounds of carbon. It originated with *Wöhler's synthesis of urea in 1828 and developed throughout the 19th century. Organic chemicals fall broadly into two classes: *aliphatic compounds (*see also* alkanes; alkenes; alkynes) and *aromatic compounds. Many industries, including dyeing, explosives, plastics, and pharmaceuticals, depend very largely on organic chemistry. **Physical chemistry** is concerned with the application of physics to a quantitative assessment of the structures and properties of compounds and the laws that control chemical reactions. Electrochemistry and *electrolysis, reaction kinetics, photochemistry, chemical *thermodynamics, and colloid chemistry are some of its main branches.

Chemnitz. *See* Karl-Marx-Stadt.

chemoreception The reception by an organism of chemical stimuli. In man and other air-breathing vertebrates, chemicals ingested in food, etc., are sensed by taste buds on the tongue and walls of the mouth, while airborne chemicals are detected by smell (olfactory) receptors in the lining of the nasal passages (*see also* pheromones). Both smell and taste organs are present in fish but worms and other animals have only a general sensitivity to chemicals over the body surface. Chemoreception is used by animals for locating and identifying other organisms, food sources, and scent marks and trails.

chemotherapy The treatment of disease by means of drugs. The term was originally coined by Paul *Ehrlich, for the synthetic chemicals used to treat infectious diseases (e.g. salvarsan for syphilis), but it was later expanded to include antibiotics. Today chemotherapy commonly refers to the chemical treatment of cancer—by means of *cytotoxic and other drugs, which inhibit the action of cancer cells—as distinct from treatment with X-rays (*see* radiotherapy).

Chenab River A river in NW India and Pakistan, one of the five rivers of the Punjab. Rising in the Himalayas, it flows SW to join the Sutlej River in Pakistan. Length: 675 mi (1087 km).

Chen-chiang. *See* Jinjiang.

Cheng Ch'eng-kung. *See* Zheng Cheng Gong.

Cheng-chou. *See* Zhengzhou.

Chengde (*or* Ch'eng-te; English name: Jehol) 40 48N 118 06E A city in NE China, in Hebei province. During the 18th and 19th centuries the Qing emperors spent the summers here. It was the capital of the former province of Jehol (1928–56). Population (1953): 92,900.

Chengdu (*or* Ch'eng-tu) 30 37N 104 06E A city in central China, the capital of Sichuan province and the site of its university. An ancient cultural, and now also an industrial, center, it produces textiles, chemicals, and machinery. Population (1957): 1,107,000.

Cheng Ho. *See* Zheng He.

Ch'eng-te. *See* Chengde.

Ch'eng-tu. *See* Chengdu.

Chénier, André de (1762–94) French poet, born in Istanbul of Greek-French parentage. He studied in Paris and worked in London before returning to Revolutionary France in 1789. An outspoken political journalist, he was arrested and guillotined. His posthumously published poems, notably the *Iambes* and *Odes*, had a strong influence on later Romantic poets.

Cheops. *See* Khufu.

Chephren. *See* Khafre.

Cher River A river in central France, rising in the Massif Central near Aubusson and flowing NW to join the Loire River near Tours. Length: 220 mi (354 km).

Cherbourg 49 38N 1 37W A seaport in NW France, in Manche department on the Cotentin Peninsula. Cherbourg has civil and military docks and large shipbuilding yards. In the heyday of ocean liners Cherbourg was an important transatlantic port; the cross-channel service to Southampton, England, remains important. Population (1975): 34,637.

Cheremkhovo 53 08N 103 01E A city in the Soviet Union, in the SE RSFSR. A coalmining center, it also refines oil and produces chemicals. Population (1969 est): 104,000.

Cherenkov, Pavel Alekseievich (1904–) Soviet physicist, who discovered **Cherenkov radiation** in 1934. This radiation consists of blue-white light emitted by the atoms of a medium through which a high-energy charged particle is passing at a velocity in excess of the velocity of light in that medium. Three years later the effect was explained by *Franck and Igor Tamm (1895–1971). The three physicists shared the 1958 Nobel Prize for their work.

Cherepovets 59 09N 37 50E A city in the Soviet Union, in the RSFSR on the Volga-Baltic waterway. It is a major transportation center and has a large iron and steel plant. Population (1977 est): 246,000.

Cheribon. *See* Tjirebon.

Cherkassy 49 27N 32 04E A port in the SW Soviet Union, in the Ukrainian SSR on the Dnepr River. Once a *Cossack center, it grew rapidly in the 1960s with the growth of its chemical industry. Population (1981 est): 242,000.

Chernigov 51 30N 31 18E A city in the SW Soviet Union, in the Ukrainian SSR on the Desna River. Chernigov was heavily bombed during World War II and most of its buildings are postwar, although several medieval buildings remain. It is an important railroad junction and its manufactures include tires, pianos, and consumer goods. Population (1981 est): 252,000.

Chernenko, Konstantin Ustinovich (1911–) USSR statesman; president (1984–). Closely allied with Leonid *Brezhnev, he served under him in various positions. Chernenko was chief of staff of the Presidium (1960–82), head of the Central Committee General Department (1965–83), and became a member of the Central Committee in 1971. By 1976 he was the Central Committee's secretary in charge of administration and security. In 1977 he became a non-voting member of the Politburo and was granted full membership the following year. Although he was not selected to be Brezhnev's successor in 1982, he remained in favor and assumed the presidency upon the death of Yuri *Andropov in February, 1984.

Chernovtsy (Romanian name: Cernauti) 48 19N 25 52E A city in the SW Soviet Union, in the Ukrainian SSR on the Prut River. It was held by Romania between 1918 and 1940. It is an important rail junction, industrial, cultural, and scientific center. Population (1981 est): 224,000.

chernozem (*or* black earth) A type of soil that is characteristic of the grasslands of the continental interiors. There is a dark surface layer rich in alkaline humus, underlain by calcium carbonate concretions. Chernozems are agriculturally among the richest soils in the world.

Cherokee A North American Indian people speaking an Iroquoian language and formerly inhabiting extensive areas in Georgia, Tennessee, and North Carolina. The Cherokees supported themselves by agriculture and inhabited towns ruled by chiefs who were responsible for the performance of religious and military ceremonies. During the *American Revolution, the Cherokees fought on the side of the British and in 1829, by order of President Andrew *Jackson, they were forced to leave their homelands and resettle in a reservation in Oklahoma. They called this painful and difficult migration the *Trail of Tears. The present Cherokee population is about 75,000, with the majority living in Oklahoma. In 1984 the Cherokees were permitted to reestablish a tribal center in their former homeland.

cherry A tree or shrub of the genus *Prunus, of N temperate regions, having small rounded juicy fruits surrounding a hard stone containing a seed. Cherry trees produce clusters of white or pinkish flowers in spring, and some varieties are grown only for ornament. Cherries cultivated for their fruits are of two main types—sour and sweet. Sour cherries have been developed from *P. cerasus*, a widespread shrubby tree growing to 23 ft (7 m). Morello—the best variety—has dark-red fruits used in jams and liqueurs. Sweet dessert cherries arose from the gean (*P. avium*), native to Eurasia and N Africa. Found in woods and hedges, it grows to 80 ft (25 m). Fruits of cultivated forms vary from pale yellow to dark red. Hybrids between *P. cerasus* and *P. avium* are used for cooking. *See also* bird cherry.

cherry laurel An evergreen shrub, *Prunus laurocerasus*, 7–20 ft (2–6 m) high, producing spikes of fragrant whitish flowers in spring. A native of SE Europe and SW Asia, it has been introduced and locally naturalized elsewhere in hedges and woodlands. Family: *Rosaceae*.

chert A rock that is a variety of chalcedony, occurring in a stratified form. It consists of minute crystals of silica, of either organic or inorganic origin, found in sedimentary rocks.

cherubim and seraphim Supernatural beings who, according to *Dionysius the Areopagite, are the two highest orders of *angels in the celestial hierarchy. The seraphim are described by Isaiah (Isaiah 6.2–7) as six-winged attendants upon God's throne. The cherubim, who are tradionally depicted as winged heads, appear in the Bible as guardians of the divine presence; for instance, they bar the approaches to the Garden of Eden after the Fall (Genesis 3.24).

Cherubini, Maria Luigi (1760–1842) Italian composer. He spent much of his life in France, becoming director of the Paris Conservatoire in 1822. He was primarily an operatic composer; his *Deux Journées* (1800; English title: *The Watercarrier*) influenced Beethoven. He also wrote two settings of the requiem mass and six string quartets in an original style.

chervil An annual herb, *Anthriscus cerefolium*, 12–20 in (30–50 cm) high, grown for its leaves, used for salads and seasonings. Its white flowers grow in umbrella-like clusters. A native of central, E, and S Europe, it is widely introduced, growing on hedgebanks and waste ground throughout Europe, the Americas, N Africa, and New Zealand. Family: *Umbelliferae*.

Chesapeake Bay The largest inlet on the Atlantic coast, bordering on Virginia and Maryland. Length: approximately 200 mi (320 km).

chess A board game for two players, each of whom controls 16 pieces. The pieces are moved according to strict rules, the object of the game being to force the opponent's king into a position from which it cannot escape. A player attempts to weaken his opponent's position by capturing his pieces. This he does by moving his own pieces onto the squares occupied by his opponent's pieces. Only the kings cannot be captured in this way. After an initial lottery to choose the player who makes the first move, the game becomes one of pure skill with a vast literature devoted to its tactics and strategy. Chess has been variously described as a game, sport, art, science, vocation, and (with advertising) the greatest waste of human ingenuity. To the extent that it simulates war it has been regarded as a psychological sublimation of human aggression, although more lyrical writers have seen it as a source of Indian symbolism and allegory.

Chess pieces dating back to the 2nd century demonstrate the game's antiquity. Well known to 5th-century Hindus, it seems to have reached Europe, via Persia and Arabia, in the 10th century. The rules of the game have hardly changed since the 16th century, although the identities of some of the pieces have.

Since 1922 the rules have been controlled by the Fédération internationale des Échecs (FIDE), which has also organized world championships since 1946. Famous world champions include Emanuel *Lasker (1894–1921), José *Capablanca (1921–27), Alexander *Alekhine, (1927–35; 1937–46), Boris *Spassky (1969–72), Bobby *Fischer (1972–75), and Anatoly *Karpov (1975–).

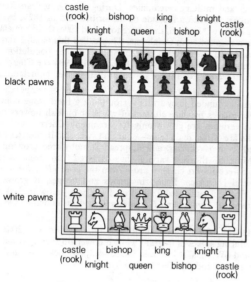

castle (rook)
knight
bishop
queen
king
bishop
knight
castle (rook)

black pawns

white pawns

castle (rook)
knight
bishop
king
queen
bishop
knight
castle (rook)

The chessboard ready for play. A white square is always on the player's right. The queen always starts on a square of her own color.

	a	b	c	d	e	f	g	h	
8	QR1 / QR8	QN1 / QN8	QB1 / QB8	Q1 / Q8	K1 / K8	KB1 / KB8	KN1 / KN8	KR1 / KR8	**8**
7	QR2 / QR7	QN2 / QN7	QB2 / QB7	Q2 / Q7	K2 / K7	KB2 / KB7	KN2 / KN7	KR2 / KR7	**7**
6	QR3 / QR6	QN3 / QN6	QB3 / QB6	Q3 / Q6	K3 / K6	KB3 / KB6	KN3 / KN6	KR3 / KR6	**6**
5	QR4 / QR5	QN4 / QN5	QB4 / QB5	Q4 / Q5	K4 / K5	KB4 / KB5	KN4 / KN5	KR4 / KR5	**5**
4	QR5 / QR4	QN5 / QN4	QB5 / QB4	Q5 / Q4	K5 / K4	KB5 / KB4	KN5 / KN4	KR5 / KR4	**4**
3	QR6 / QR3	QN6 / QN3	QB6 / QB3	Q6 / Q3	K6 / K3	KB6 / KB3	KN6 / KN3	KR6 / KR3	**3**
2	QR7 / QR2	QN7 / QN2	QB7 / QB2	Q7 / Q2	K7 / K2	KB7 / KB2	KN7 / KN2	KR7 / KR2	**2**
1	QR8 / QR1	QN8 / QN1	QB8 / QB1	Q8 / Q1	K8 / K1	KB8 / KB1	KN8 / KN1	KR8 / KR1	**1**
	a	b	c	d	e	f	g	h	

BLACK

WHITE

Chess notations. In the algebraic notation each square is referred to by a file letter a–h and a rank number 1–8. In the descriptive notation the files bear the names of the piece on the first rank. The ranks are counted 1–8 away from the player.

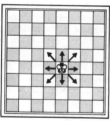

The king, weak and vulnerable, moves only one square at a time (in any direction). The name of the game is a corruption of the Persian word for king–shah.

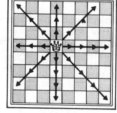

The queen, the most powerful piece, moves any distance in any direction. Originally known as the counsellor, its present name and moves were adopted in the 15th century.

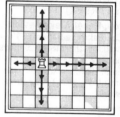

The castle or rook moves any distance vertically or horizontally. Originally represented as a chariot (Arabic: rukh), it is known in many languages as a castle or tower (French: tour).

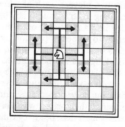

The knight, the only piece to jump over other pieces, moves one square horizontally and two vertically or two horizontally and one vertically. Usually represented by a horse's head, it is sometimes known as the horse (as it was in the Arabic version).

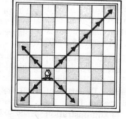

The bishop moves in any direction diagonally. In the Hindu and Arabic games the piece was called an elephant. In the European games the piece has acquired a variety of identities: a bishop in English, a jester (fou) in French, a runner (Laufer) in German, but still an elephant (slon) in Russian.

The pawn moves forward one square (or two on its first move). In Arabic it was called a foot-soldier, the English word deriving from the Latin pes, pedis. In some European languages the piece is called a peasant (e.g. German: Bauer).

chest A large domestic storage box. Chests from ancient Egypt are among the earliest surviving furniture. In Europe they were essential pieces of portable furniture doubling as a bed, table, or seat. The simplest consist of six boards nailed together with one forming a lid, but between the 15th and the 18th centuries they were elaborated into fine decorative furniture. In Europe specimens were paneled and carved but 16th-century Italian chests (cassoni) might be carved and gilded.

Chester 53 12N 2 54W A city in NW England, the administrative center of Cheshire on the River Dee. It was a Roman fortress (Deva) and a medieval walled city and port (the walls remain intact and there are many half-timbered buildings). The Rows are two-tiered arcades of shops with covered balustrades. Its cathedral dates from the 11th century. Chester is a commercial and railroad center, with clothing and metallurgical industries. Population (1981): 58,436.

chesterfield A kind of settee introduced in 19th-century England. It has a low back curving to form upright armrests and is comfortably upholstered with coil springs.

Chesterfield 53 15N 1 25W A city in N central England, in Derbyshire. Its 14th-century parish church has a famous crooked spire. Chesterfield's industries include engineering, iron founding, chemicals, glass, and pottery. Population (1981): 70,546.

Chesterfield, Philip Dormer Stanhope, 4th Earl of (1694–1773) British statesman, diplomat, and writer. He served as ambassador to The Hague (1728–36), lord lieutenant of Ireland (1745–46), and secretary of state (1746–48). A patron of many authors, he is best remembered for his worldly and sophisticated *Letters to His Son* (1774).

Chesterton, G(ilbert) K(eith) (1874–1936) British essayist, novelist, and poet. His best work was done as literary journalism, although the detective stories featuring a Roman Catholic priest and beginning with *The Innocence of Father Brown* (1911) were also highly successful. He met Hilaire *Belloc in 1900. Their names were often linked as romantic opponents of the socialism of G. B. Shaw and H. G. Wells. Chesterton was converted to Roman Catholicism in 1922, and thereafter most of his work was devoted to religious subjects, for example *St Francis of Assisi* (1923). His published work amounts to more than 100 volumes, among which are the critical studies *Dickens* (1906) and *The Victorian Age in Literature* (1913) and the fictional works *The Napoleon of Notting Hill* (1904), *The Club of Queer Trades*, (1905), and *The Man Who Was Thursday* (1908).

chestnut A tree, *Castanea sativa*, also called sweet or Spanish chestnut, bearing large brown edible nuts inside prickly burs. Native to Europe and N Africa and widely introduced, it grows to a height of 98 ft (30 m). The leaves—4–10 in (10–25 cm) long—are toothed and pointed and the flowers grow in yellow catkins, 4–5 in (10–12 cm) long. The North American chestnut (*C. dentata*)—once one of the largest common trees of eastern areas—has been largely destroyed by the chestnut blight fungus. Family: *Fagaceae* (beech family). *Compare* horse chestnut.

Chetniks Members of a Yugoslav resistance movement in World War II. They were organized in groups by General Draža *Mihajlović in March, 1941, against the German invasion but were chiefly in conflict with the communist Partisans under *Tito. In 1944 the Allies transferred their support from the Chetniks to Tito. After the war the Chetniks were proscribed.

Chevalier, Maurice (1888–1972) French singer and actor. Starting as an entertainer in Parisian revues, he went to Hollywood in the 1930s and starred in many successful musical films. These included *Love Me Tonight* (1932), *Love in the Afternoon* (1957), and *Gigi* (1958).

cheviot A woolen fabric manufactured from the soft fine easily spun fleece of Cheviot sheep found in the English-Scottish border country. The cloth is much used as heavy suiting material; *worsted is sometimes added for greater firmness of texture.

Cheviot Hills A range of hills in the UK. They extend along the border between Scotland and England, mainly in Northumberland, reaching 2677 ft (816 m) at The Cheviot.

chevrotain A small hoofed mammal of the family *Tragulidae*. Asiatic chevrotains (genus *Tragulus*; 3–6 species), also called mouse deer, of SE Asia, measure 8–13 in (20–30 cm) at the shoulder and resemble small deer. Their brownish coats have white underparts; some species have white stripes or spots on the body. They are not true deer, lacking antlers and having a three-chambered stomach; males have enlarged upper canine teeth that form tusks. The African water chevrotain (*Hyemoschus aquaticus*) is very similar.

chewing gum A sweetened flavored gum made from *chicle or a synthetic substitute, the milky juice of the sapodilla tree, which is chewed to extract its flavor but not swallowed. It was first patented (1871) in the US.

Cheyenne An Algonkian-speaking North American Indian people of the Great Plains. Originally supporting themselves by agriculture and inhabiting the present state of Minnesota, intertribal wars in the mid 18th century forced abandonment of farming for the nomadic buffalo-hunting culture of the Plains. After a period of wandering, they eventually divided into the Northern Cheyenne and the Southern Cheyenne, who joined the *Arapaho nation in Oklahoma. Both groups shared an elaborate religious ritual, which included the Sun Dance. They were governed by a council of 44 chiefs; an important feature of their social organization was military or warrior societies. With increasing settlement in their territories, they joined other Plains tribes in armed resistance; the Northern Cheyenne joined the *Sioux at the Battle of *Little Big Horn in 1876. The present Northern Cheyenne population, mainly in Montana, is about 2000. The Southern Cheyenne-Arapaho group numbers approximately 3500.

Cheyenne 41 08N 104 50W The capital and largest city of Wyoming. It is an agricultural trading center. Population (1980): 40,207.

Cheyenne River A river that rises in E central Wyoming and flows E into SW South Dakota. Here, at Angostura Dam, it turns NE and meets the Missouri River about Pierre. Length: 527 mi (849 km).

Chiang Ch'ing. *See* Mao Tse-Tung.

Chiang Ching-kuo. *See* Chiang Kai-shek.

CHIANG KAI-SHEK *At the Cairo Conference (1943) with Roosevelt (center) and Churchill (right). The Allies discussed a joint operation in N Burma.*

Chiang Kai-shek (*or* Jiang Jie Shi; 1887–1975) Nationalist Chinese soldier and statesman. He took part in the overthrow of the *Qing dynasty in 1911, joined *Sun Yat-sen's *Guomindang (Nationalist People's Party) in 1918, and became commandant of the Whampoa military academy in 1923. After Sun's death (1925), Chiang became leader of the Guomindang and in 1926, in alliance with the communists (*see* United Fronts), launched the Northern Expedition to regain China from the *warlords. The Communist-Guomindang coalition ended in 1927 and Chiang, with his capital at Nanjing, fought the communists until Japan invaded China in 1931. Chiang's own army (*see* Xi An incident) forced him to join forces with the communists against their common enemy, Japan (*see* Sino-Japanese Wars), but following Japan's defeat in World War II civil war again broke out in China (1946), ending with Guomindang defeat (1949). Chiang was forced to flee to *Taiwan, where he established the Republic of China. His son **Jiang Jing Guo** (*or* Chiang Ching-kuo; 1910–), prime minister (1971–78) and president (1978–) studied in the Soviet Union and married a Russian. On returning to China in 1937, he joined the Guomindang, fleeing with his father to Taiwan in 1949.

Chianti A region of hills in N central Italy, in the Apennines between Florence and Siena. Chianti wine is produced here.

chiaroscuro (Italian: light-dark) The overall pattern of light and shade in a picture. Controlled chiaroscuro was an important element of *Renaissance composition, while strong contrasts of light and shade were a main feature of *baroque painting. Chiaroscuro is displayed to supreme effect in the etchings of *Rembrandt and *Whistler.

Chiba 35 38N 140 07E A city and seaport in Japan, in central Honshu on Tokyo Bay. It is the site of an 8th-century Buddhist temple and a university (1949). Industries include steel, paper, and textiles. Population (1980): 746,000.

Chibcha A South American Indian people of the central highlands of Colombia. At the time of the Spanish conquest they were more advanced socially and politically than any people in the area, except the *Inca. Chiefs, treated with great respect, inherited their position matrilineally. Their accession ceremonies, at which the new chief coated his body with gold dust before immersion in a sacred lake, are the probable origin of the *Eldorado legend.

Chicago 41 50N 87 45N A city and major port in Illinois on Lake Michigan. The second largest city in the country, it is the focal point of air, rail, and road routes and the commercial, financial, and industrial center for a large region. Its manufactures include iron and steel, textiles, and chemicals and there are large grain mills and meat-packing plants, although many of the stockyards are now closing as this industry moves further W. The first of its towering skyscrapers was built in 1887 and the Sears Tower (1974) is the world's tallest building, 1454 ft (443 m) high. It has several universities, including the University of Chicago (1892) and Northwestern University (1851); the Chicago Symphony Orchestra enjoys worldwide fame. *History*: founded in 1803 near the site of Fort Dearborn, it became a city in 1837 and expanded rapidly with the construction of the railroads. In 1871 it was almost completely destroyed by a disastrous fire, in which several hundred people were killed. Chicago was subsequently rebuilt in stone and steel. During the Prohibition years (1919–33), Chicago was notorious for its gangster activities, especially those of Al *Capone. Population (1980): 3,005,072.

Chicago River A short river in NE Illinois. It rises at Lake Superior and flows through Chicago where it forks into two branches. The South Branch flows SW as part of the Illinois Waterway and as the Chicago Sanitary and Ship Canal to meet the Des Plaines River. The river serves as boundaries for Chicago's North, West, and South sides. Length: 24 mi (39 km).

Chichén Itzá A Maya city in N Yucatán (Mexico) that was the political and religious center of a wide area under Toltec influence from the late 10th to the 13th centuries. Remains include El Castillo (a pyramidal temple mound), an astronomical observatory, and a cenote (natural well), from which gold, jade, and other sacrificial objects have been recovered.

Chicherin, Georgi Vasilievich (1872–1936) Soviet statesman. Chicherin began his career in the Tsarist ministry of foreign affairs but in 1904, having become a revolutionary, he left Russia and lived in W Europe. In 1918, after the Revolution, he returned to Russia and was entrusted by Lenin with Soviet diplomacy. Chicherin lost his position in 1928, following Stalin's rise to power.

Chichester, Sir Francis (Charles) (1901–72) British yachtsman. He won the first solo transatlantic race (in 40 days) in *Gipsy Moth III* (1960) and in 1966–67, in *Gipsy Moth IV*, was the first to sail round the world singlehanded: he sailed from Plymouth, England, reaching Sydney, Australia, in 107 days, and then back to Plymouth, in 119 days. He was knighted with Sir Francis Drake's sword.

Chickamauga, Battle of (1863) Confederate victory in NW Georgia during the Civil War. The troops of Union General William S. Rosecrans, defending Chattanooga, Tenn and its valuable railroad facilities, battled the Confederate forces of General Braxton Bragg at Chickamauga for two days. Eventually, Rosecrans's forces were forced to retreat, and the South had gained an important victory. Casualties on both sides were high.

chicken. *See* poultry, domestic.

chickenpox A common very infectious virus disease. It is usually contracted in childhood and one attack normally gives an immunity that lasts for life. At the end of the incubation period (about a fortnight) the patient develops a fever and an irritating rash. Small raised spots appear on the chest and spread—in the next few days—over the body, face, and limbs. The spots become sore reddened blisters, which then dry and flake off, usually in less than a week. The patient is infectious until the last blister has flaked off. *See also* shingles.

chick pea An annual plant, *Cicer arietinum*, up to 16 in (40 cm) high, with whitish flowers and edible pealike seeds. It is the chief pulse crop of India, where the cooked seeds are called dhal. Probably native to W Asia, it has long been cultivated in S Europe and is widely introduced, though of little commercial importance, elsewhere. Family: *Leguminosae*.

chickweed A widely distributed annual or overwintering herb, *Stellaria media*, 2–16 in (5–40 cm) high with small star-shaped white flowers. The plant is a common weed and is readily eaten by birds. It was formerly used as a poultice for ulcers and carbuncles. Family: *Caryophyllaceae*.

Chiclayo 6 47S 79 47W A city in N Peru, in the Lambayeque Valley. It is the commercial center for an area producing sugar cane, cotton, and rice. Population (1972): 187,809.

chicle A gum formed from the coagulated milky substance obtained from the *sapodilla tree found in Central America. Chicle was formerly used in the manufacture of chewing gum, but it has now been replaced by synthetic substances.

chicory A perennial herb, *Cichorium intybus*, 12–48 in (30–120 cm) high, with bright-blue flowers. The dried ground roots yield chicory, a coffee additive, while the blanched leaves are used in salads. A native of Eurasia and N Africa, it is widely cultivated elsewhere. Family: *Compositae*. *See also* endive.

Chicoutimi Canadian city in SE Quebec, on the Saguenay River. Part of the Chicoutimi-Jonquière metropolitan area, it was founded (1676) as a trading station and mission. Industries include lumber and wood products, metals, and agricultural products. Population (1981): 60,064.

Chiemsee (*or* Bayrisches Meer) 47 53N 12 25E A lake in SE West Germany. On one of its islands Louis II of Bavaria built a palace imitating that of Versailles. Area: 33 sq mi (85 sq km).

Chiengmai (*or* Chiang Mai) 18 48N 98 59E A city in NW Thailand, near the Burmese border. The northern commercial and cultural center, it has teak, silver, and silk industries. The university was established in 1964. Population (1979 est): 105,230.

Ch'ien-lung. *See* Qian Long.

chiffchaff A woodland *warbler, *Phylloscopus collybita*, about 4 in (10 cm) long, with a gray-green plumage and whitish underparts. It occurs in Europe and W Asia during the summer and winters in S Europe and Africa. It resembles the willow warbler but can usually be distinguished by its "chiff-chaff" call.

Chifley, Joseph Benedict (1885–1951) Australian statesman; Labor prime minister (1945–49). He introduced welfare reforms and nationalization policies, and encouraged postwar development.

chigger. *See* harvest mite.

chigoe A *flea, *Tunga penetrans*, 0.04 in (1 mm) long, also called jigger or sand flea, that spread to Africa and Asia from South America to become a pest of man. The female burrows beneath the skin, especially on the feet, to form ulcer-like sores that cause intense itching and can become gangrenous. Family: *Pulicidae*.

Chihli, Gulf of (Chinese name: Bohai *or* Po Hai) A large inlet of the Yellow Sea on the coast of NE China.

Chihuahua 28 40N 106 06W A city in N Mexico. Miguel Hidalgo y Costillo, a leader in the Mexican independence movement, was executed here (1811). Its varied industries include smelting, timber, and meat packing and it has a university (1954). Population (1978 est): 369,545.

Chihuahua A breed of □dog originating from an ancient Mexican breed and developed in the US. Perhaps the world's smallest dog, it has an alert saucy expression. The coat is variable in color and either smooth and glossy or long and soft. Height: about 5 in (13 cm).

Chikamatsu Monzemon (Sugimori Nobumori; 1653–1724) Japanese dramatist. His psychological insight and realistic techniques revolutionized the previously unsophisticated tradition of puppet theater. *The Battles of Coxingo* (1715) and *The Love Suicide at Amijima* (1720) are the best-known examples of his two main types of plays, historical romances and domestic tragedies.

chilblain An itchy red swelling, usually on the fingers or toes, that develops in cold weather. A chilblain may lead to scaling and blistering of the affected part. Prevention, by wearing warm clothing, is the best form of treatment, but drugs that dilate the blood vessels may also be used.

Child, Lydia Maria (Francis) (1802–80) US reformer and writer. Best known for her antislavery stands, she wrote *An Appeal in Favor of That Class of Americans Called Africans* (1833) and was editor of *The National Anti-Slavery Standard* (1841–49). She also advocated women's suffrage. Popular works include the novels *Hobomok* (1824), *The Rebels* (1825), and *Philothea* (1836) and the guidebooks *The Frugal Housewife* (1829) and *The Mother's Book* (1831).

child abuse Injuries inflicted on babies or young children by their parents, usually in the first six months of life. It commonly takes the form of facial bruises, cigarette burns, head injuries (often with brain damage), and fractured bones. The parents are often emotionally disturbed or have themselves suffered from physical abuse in infancy or early childhood. Two thirds of these children suffer further injury if discharged from the hospital without the support of a social worker and surveillance of family doctor.

childbirth (*or* labor) The series of events that lead to the birth of a baby. It usually starts spontaneously about 280 days (plus or minus 14 days) after conception but it may be induced by artificial means. The first stage of childbirth may last several hours: it is marked by rupture of the membranes surrounding the fetus and by regular contractions of the womb (uterus). This stage ends when the cervical canal is fully dilated. In the second stage continuing uterine contractions—assisted by conscious pushing by the mother—eases the baby through the cervix and out through the vagina. The *placenta (afterbirth) is delivered in the third stage of labor. The baby is normally born headfirst, although childbirth can occur with the baby in a variety of positions. *See also* Caesarean section; infant mortality.

Children's Crusade (1212) One of the more bizarre episodes of the *Crusades, in which some 50,000 children set out from France and Germany to capture Jerusalem. None reached their destination and few returned home, most being sold into slavery. The enthusiasm aroused by the Children's Crusade encouraged Pope *Innocent III to summon the fifth Crusade.

Chile, Republic of A country in South America, extending in a narrow strip along the W coast of the S half of the continent. There are many islands off the coast, some of which (including *Easter Island) are well out into the Pacific Ocean. Chile also includes half of the island of Tierra del Fuego and has claims to part of Antarctica. The country is dominated by the Andes, which are separated from a lower coastal range by a central valley. The majority of the population is of mixed Spanish and Indian descent. *Economy*: based chiefly on the export of minerals, found principally in the N. Chile is one of the world's largest producers and exporters of copper, while the production of iron ore now exceeds that of nitrates. Coal is also mined in quantity and oil was found in the S in 1945. Production of natural gas is more than enough for domestic needs. The enormous agricultural potential of the country, however, is far from developed, a situation that has been made worse by recent political events. Major land reforms were introduced (1970–73) but much of the land has been returned to its original owners since the fall of the Allende government. The main crops are wheat, sugar beet, potatoes, and maize and there is an expanding wine industry. Fruit and forest production is growing in importance and there are government attempts to promote the dairy industry. *History*: when Magellan, the first European to set eyes on what became Chile, sailed through (1520) the strait named for him, S Chile was occupied by the Araucanian Indians, who continued to control the region until the 19th century. In the N the Atacama Indians had been subjugated in the 15th century by the Incas, who were themselves conquered by the Spaniards in 1532. A Spanish colony was founded at Santiago in 1541 and Chile was attached to the viceroyalty of Peru. It maintained, however, a certain independence and individuality throughout the colonial period, partly because of its inaccessibility. The revolt against Spain began in 1810, when a provisional republic was declared, but victory over the Spaniards was achieved only in 1817 with the military help of the Argentine liberator José de *San Martín. In 1818 the Republic of Chile was established under Bernardo *O'Higgins. Following the ratification of a constitution in 1833 Chile enjoyed political stability and prosperity, becoming the world's leading copper producer. Frontier disputes with Bolivia and Peru culminated in the War of the *Pacific (1879–83), in which Chile, with its superior navy, was victorious, gaining the provinces of Antofagasta from Bolivia and Tarapacá and Arica from Peru. The early 20th century witnessed economic decline, exacerbated by considerable European immigration and resistance from landlords to reform. The enlightened first presidency (1920–25) of Arturo Alessandri Palma (1868–1952) was followed by a military dictatorship and his increasingly right-wing second term (1932–38) led to the election of a socialist Popular Front government. The postwar period saw a return to conservatism and in 1964 Eduardo *Frei, the first Christian Democratic president, was elected. In 1970 Salvador *Allende became the first democratically elected Marxist head of state but was overthrown in 1973 by a military coup led by General *Pinochet. In 1978 Pinochet announced civilian appointments to his cabinet as a step toward the reintroduction of democracy but strong opposition to the regime continues both at home and abroad. The regime's history of repressive measures and human rights violations caused opposition to foment even more fiercely. Chile is a member of the OAS and LAFTA. Official language: Spanish. Official currency: Chilean peso of 100 centavos. Area: 286,397 sq mi (741,767 sq km). Population (1983 est): 11,486,000. Capital: Santiago. Main port: Valparaiso.

chili A tropical American shrubby plant, *Capsicum frutescens*, also called red pepper, bearing elongated hot-tasting red fruits, 0.8–1.2 in (2–3 cm) long. Sun-dried for storage, they are used in cooking and are also an essential ingredient of curry powder and tabasco sauce. Family: *Solanaceae*.

Chillán 36 37S 72 10W A city in central Chile, in the Central Valley. It has suffered much damage from earthquakes. Chillán serves an agricultural region producing chiefly grapes, fruit, cereals, and livestock. Population (1976 est): 108,500.

Chillon A mainly 13th-century fortress at the E end of Lake Geneva (Switzerland). It was the prison (1530–36) of François Bonward (?1494–1570), the Genevan patriot made famous by Byron's poem *The Prisoner of Chillon* (1816).

Chiloé Island An island administered by Chile, off the W coast of South America in the Pacific Ocean. The chief export is timber. Area: 3241 sq mi (8394 sq km). Chief town: Ancud.

Chiltern Hills A chalk escarpment in S central England. It extends NE from the Goring Gap in the Thames Valley, reaching 852 ft (255 m) at Coombe Hill. Many of its hills are covered with beech woods.

Chi-lung. *See* Jilong.

chimaera 1. A *cartilaginous fish, also called ghost shark, ratfish, or rabbit fish, belonging to the order *Chimaeriformes* (about 28 species). It has a dark or silvery body, 24–80 in (60–200 cm) long, a slender whiplike tail, a sharp spine in front of the first dorsal fin, and a variously shaped snout. It lives in cold ocean waters, down to 8200 ft (2500 m), and feeds on fish and invertebrates. Subclass: *Holocephali*. □fish. **2.** (or chimera) An organism that is composed of cells of two genetically different types. Plants with variegated leaves are chimaeras resulting from a mutation in a cell in the growing region (apical meristem). Plant chimaeras can also be produced by *grafting, being known as graft hybrids.

Chimborazo, Mount 1 29S 78 52W An extinct volcano in the Andes, the highest point in Ecuador. Height: 20,681 ft (6267 m).

Chimbote 9 04S 78 34W A port in NW Peru, on the Pacific Ocean. Steel processing and fishmeal production are the chief industries. Population (1972): 159,045.

Chimera A legendary Greek fire-breathing monster with a lion's head, a goat's body, and a serpent's tail. After ravaging Lycia she was killed by Bellerophon. The name now applies to any fantastic imaginary creation.

Chimkent 42 16N 69 05E A city in the Soviet Union, in the S Kazakh SSR. It is an important railroad junction and has chemical and textile industries. Population (1981 est): 334,000.

CHIMPANZEE *Probably the most intelligent of nonhuman primates, chimpanzees have great manual dexterity, considerable curiosity, and are capable of simple reasoning.*

chimpanzee An ape, *Pan troglodytes*, of West African forests. Chimpanzees are 40–67 in (100–170 cm) tall when standing erect and live in small groups, mostly on the ground, feeding chiefly on fruit and leaves but occasionally eating meat. They communicate by facial expressions and a repertoire of calls and possess considerable intelligence, often using tools (such as branches). Bonobos are a race of smaller chimpanzees with black faces.

Chimú A South American Indian people who established a large kingdom in Peru during the 14th century AD. Its capital was at *Chan Chan. They were conquered (c. 1470) by the *Incas, whose civilization was based on Chimú achievements in building, road construction, irrigation, and political organization. The Chimú produced elaborate pottery with molded reliefs, fine textiles, and precious metalwork,

Ch'in. *See* Qin.

China, People's Republic of A country in E Asia, covering vast areas of land ranging from the low-lying and densely populated plains of the NE to the high peaks of the Tibetan Plateau in the W, rising well over 16,500 ft (5000 m). In the far NW much of the land is desert or semidesert. China proper falls into three natural regions, formed around the three main rivers: the Yellow River in the N, the Yangtze in the center, and the Xi Jiang in the S. Over 90% of the inhabitants are Han Chinese. *Economy*: mainly dependent upon agriculture, which is constantly threatened by drought and flood. There are however schemes to safeguard and increase production by means of irrigation, soil conservation, and fertilization. Agriculture is now socialized through a system of communes, although there are still some very small private holdings. The emphasis is on foodcrops, rice in the S, wheat and millet in the N, as well as livestock, especially pigs. Cotton is grown in the N and tea in the S. The once vast forests have been largely cleared over the centuries but considerable reforestation is now taking place. Coal is extensively mined in all parts of the country and is the major source of power. China has been self-sufficient in oil since 1973 and small amounts of natural gas are also produced. The potential for hydroelectric energy is extensive and there are several projects throughout the country. Iron ore is the most important mineral deposit and China is the main world producer of tungsten ore. Other minerals include antimony, lead, bauxite, and manganese. Traditional small industries continue but there has been considerable development of more modern industries, especially textiles, steel, flour mills, and chemicals. Exports include farm produce, textiles, and minerals. *History*: China is one of the world's oldest civilizations, with a history of organized society going back over nearly four millenniums. The first important recorded dynasty was the Shang in the valley of the Yellow River (18th-12th centuries BC). From the 12th to the 3rd centuries BC the *Zhou spread S and E. Under the *Qin, in the 3rd century BC, a unified empire came into being and the first Great Wall was built. The rule of the *Han dynasty, from the 3rd century BC to the early 3rd century AD, saw spectacular advances in technology and manufacturing but its decline was followed by centuries of struggle between different parts of the empire. With the *Tang dynasty (7th–10th centuries) China was once more reunited and reached the high point of its civilization. It was followed by the *Song (10th–13th centuries), the *Mongol (13th–14th centuries), the *Ming (14th–17th centuries), and the *Qing, which lasted until 1912. From the 16th century Europeans came to China and set up trading posts despite opposition from the Qing. British efforts to open up the country to free trade led to the Opium War in 1839 and to the opening of treaty ports (and also to the cession of Hong Kong). Later other trade concessions were made to several European countries and Chinese opposition to these moves included the Taiping Rebellion (1851–64) and the antiforeign Boxer Rebellion (1899–1900). In 1911 a revolution under the leadership of Sun Yat-sen ousted the Qing and a republic was set up. The 1920s saw the rise of the Guomindang (Nationalist People's Party) under Gen Chiang Kai-shek and the foundation of the Chinese Communist Party in 1921. In 1926 relations between them broke down and a struggle began that, in effect, continued until after World War II. In the 1930s threats from Japan culminated in open attack and the occupation of parts of the country, which lasted until the end of World War II. This put a temporary halt to internal party struggles, but in 1949 the Guomindang was defeated by the communists and a People's Republic was set up by *Mao Tse-tung. Chiang Kai-shek retreated to Taiwan, where he set up the Republic of China. During the early years of the communist regime relations with the Soviet Union were close but they later deteriorated, particularly after 1960 when Soviet aid was withdrawn. In 1966 Mao Tse-tung launched the Great Proletarian Cultural Revolution, designed to eradicate "revisionism" and to prevent the rise of a ruling class. From the late 1960s the question of a successor to Mao Tse-tung became an important issue and first *Lin Biao and later *Deng Xiao Ping rose and fell, the latter being dismissed by a "radical" faction of the Politburo, pursuing a policy of constant revolution. Both Mao Tse-tung and the prime minister, Chou En-lai, died in 1976 and were succeeded by the moderate *Hua Guo Feng. Attempts by the "radical" faction (known as the Gang of Four and including Mao's widow Jiang Qing) to gain power were thwarted by the arrest of its members. Deng

Xiao Ping was reinstated in 1977, since when he has been a dominant force in government. Hua was succeeded by Zhao Ziyang as prime minister in 1980 and by Hu Yaobang as chairman of the Chinese Communist Party in 1981. In 1982 the post of chairman was abolished and Hu became secretary general. Since 1971 China has had a seat at the UN. Official language: Mandarin Chinese. Official currency: yuan of 10 chiao and 100 fen. Area: 3,704,400 sq mi (9,597,000 sq km). Population (1982): 1,076,000,000. Capital: Peking. Main port: Shanghai.

china clay A mineral deposit consisting mainly of kaolin, a hydrous aluminum silicate. Kaolin is produced by weathering or by hydrothermal processes acting on the feldspars in granite. It is used for making high-grade ceramic products and in many industrial processes, including paper making.

chinch bug A *ground bug, *Blissus leukopteris*, that has a black body (up to 0.2 in [5 mm] long), red legs, and white wings. Native to tropical America, it has spread to North America to become a serious pest of cereal crops. The female lays eggs on the roots and stems and the larvae suck the sap.

chinchilla A *rodent belonging to the genus *Chinchilla* (2 species), widely bred for its valuable long soft blue-gray fur. Measuring 12–20 in (30–50 cm) long, wild chinchillas are found high in the Andes, living among rocks and feeding at night on vegetation. They faced extermination before the Chilean government banned hunting and established breeding farms. South American captive chinchillas are mostly short-tailed (*C. brevicaudata*) while in North America the long-tailed species (*C. laniger*) is bred. Family: *Chinchillidae*.

Chinchilla cat A breed of long-haired cat. Chinchillas have a compact body with short legs and a broad head with a snub nose and small tufted ears. The white fur is tipped with black on the back, flanks, head, ears, and tail, giving it a silvery luster. The eyes are emerald or blue-green.

Chinchilla rabbit A breed of domesticated rabbit originating in France in the early 20th century. Although its thick bluish coat does not resemble that of the South American *chinchilla, it has been bred for its pelts.

Chindits The 77th Indian Brigade, organized by Orde *Wingate in 1943 in Burma as a "long-range penetration" infantry division. A guerrilla force, the Chindits were so called after the mythological Burmese temple guardian, the *chinthe*, and because they operated beyond the Chindwin River. Initially successful in severing Japanese lines of communication they were later in danger of being encircled and were forced to return to India in small groups.

Chindwin River A river in N Burma, flowing S to join the Irrawaddy River near Myingyan. Length: 650 mi (1046 km). (650 mi).

Chinese A language or group of languages of the Sino-Tibetan family spoken widely in E Asia. The many distinct forms or dialects of Chinese, which include Mandarin, Min, Kan, Hakka, Hsiang, Wu, and Cantonese (or Yüeh), are mutually unintelligible. In China there have been attempts recently to standardize the language, using Mandarin as a basis. Chinese is a tonal language, many words, otherwise identical, having quite distinct meanings according to intonation. Words are usually monosyllabic and do not change their form to indicate part of speech. The language is written in logographic characters or symbols of pictorial origin (*see* ideographic writing systems), which enables them to be understood by speakers of any Chinese dialect. There are as many as 40,000 of these of which 10,000 are in common use. Literacy requires knowledge of about 2000 of them. For transliteration purposes, Pinyin (phonetic spelling) is superseding the older Wade-Giles system, which does not attempt as close a phonetic description of the language. Pinyin is used in this book.

Chinese art Early Chinese art (c. 1550–480 BC) consisted of magical, symbolic, and ritualistic objects of jade and bronze. These combine a few symbols to produce evocative nonrepresentational forms. During the Han dynasty (206 BC–220 AD) these forms were succeeded by sculptural art and painting, both influenced by the rise of Buddhism. Funerary ceramic art flourished and produced animal and human forms and copies of everyday artifacts. The Tang dynasty (618–906 AD) continued to make funerary objects, particularly realistic horsemen, warrriors, and tomb guardians, but sculptures of Buddhist figures are dominant. The realistic outlook of the period was also reflected in landscape and figure painting.

The ensuing Song dynasty (960–1279 AD) was a golden age, when dreamlike landscape, animal, and bird painting flourished alongside *calligraphy, one of the most ancient and important Chinese arts. Monochrome ceramics of very refined form were made as objects of contemplation. This period saw the end of real creativity, the following Yuan dynasty being one of Mongol-inspired taste with a few exceptions, notably the four masters of the Yuan Dynasty. During the following Ming and Qing periods

(14th–20th centuries) ceramic art excelled, the most famous example being the blue and white porcelain. At first it was restorative and of native origin and later innovatory, responding to European influence.

Chinese Exclusion Act (1882) US law limiting immigration of Chinese into the country, the first US law to limit immigration. Large-scale Chinese immigration aroused opposition to them, particularly in the West, and the law banned the immigration of Chinese workers for 10 years. It was subsequently renewed, and eventually immigration quotas were set, a practice that continued into the 1960s.

Chinese lantern plant A hardy ornamental, *Physalis alkekengi*, also called bladder cherry or winter cherry. A native of S and central Europe, it grows to a height of 8–24 in (20–60 cm). The edible fruit is enclosed in a reddish inflated calyx resembling a lantern. Family: *Solanaceae*.

Chinese literature The oldest written records in Chinese date from about 1400 BC. The earliest major literary productions, however, were written mainly between about 200 BC and 200 AD. These were the Confucian classics, nine texts for instruction and discussion by *Confucius and his disciples. They are devoted to poetry, philosophy, history, ceremonies, and codes of protocol and have had a profound effect on Chinese thought and literary style to the present. The earliest is probably the manual of divination, the *I Ching*. The *Shu Jing* (or *Shu Ching*; *Book of Documents*) covers political aspects of Confucian thought; the *Shih Jing* (or *Shih Ching*; *Book of Songs*) contains lyrics some of which are perhaps as early as the 10th century BC. Of the remaining classics, the best known are two books belonging to the historical work *Zuo Zhuan* (or *Tso Chuan*): the *Analects*, a collection of Confucius' sayings and discussions with his disciples, and *The Book of Mencius*. The work of China's first known poet, *Chu Yuan, is a long poem occupying the most prominent place in the *Chuchi* (or *Ch'u Tz'u*), an anthology that, together with the *Book of Songs*, had an enduring effect on verse forms. During the Qin and Han dynasties (221 BC–220 AD), the development of poetry was fostered by the creation in 133 BC of the Yuefu (Music Bureau) for the collection of folksongs. Under Buddhist influences poetry became increasingly individualistic and enjoyed a golden age during the Tang dynasty (618–906 AD). *Li Bo, *Du Fu, and the Buddhist Wang Wei (699–759) were the leading poets, while Han Yu (768–824) pioneered new genres of prose. Musical drama was the major literary genre during the Yuan (Mongol) dynasty (1279–1368), and the novel, originating in printed versions of the tales of professional storytellers, flourished during the Ming dynasty (1368–1644). The two major novels of this period are the *Romance of the Three Kingdoms* and *The Water Margin*, both attributed to Luo Guan-zhong (*or* Luo Kuan-chung; 14th century). These works, dealing with heroic adventures, are skillfully shaped from episodic material and contrast with *The Dream of the Red Chamber* by *Cao Chan (*or* Zao Zhan), which is more realistic and partly autobiographical. The Qing (Manchu) dynasty (1644–1911) was unremarkable for literary work, but western influences were introduced through translations during the 19th century, and in the 20th century there arose a number of writers indebted to western ideas, for example to Romanticism and Symbolism. After the establishment of the republic in 1911, the outstanding poet was Hu Shi (1891–1962) and the leading writer was the satirist Lu Xun. Since the late 1930s literature has been generally subservient to political orthodoxy; although recent official patronage of the arts has encouraged a large number of new writers, no single reputation has become well established outside China.

Chinese water deer A very small *deer, *Hydropotes inermis*, most common along the banks of the Yangtze River in China. Only 20 in (50 cm) high at the shoulder, with a pale-brown coat and short tail, it has no antlers; the male's upper canine teeth are elongated into tusks.

Ch'ing. *See* Qing.

Ch'ing-hai. *See* Qinghai.

Ching-te-chen. *See* Fuliang.

Chinkiang. *See* Jinjiang.

chinoiserie Decorative art and architecture that incorporated Chinese motifs into European fantasy designs and was popular in the late 17th and 18th centuries. The fashion was inspired by importation into Europe of Chinese porcelain, lacquer, etc., in the 17th century. French *rococo artists and architects enthusiastically adopted the style for interiors, furniture, silver, wallpaper, textiles, etc., as did *Meissen designers. Instances of chinoiserie in England include the *willow pattern, combining Chinese elements into a new design.

Chinook A North American Indian people of the NW Pacific coast of the US. The Chinook language is a subdivision of the *Penutian language family. The Chinook supported themselves by salmon fishing and trade, their location along the lower Columbia River being ideally suited for ex-

changing goods with peoples to the N and S and in the interior. Chinook Jargon, a combination of Chinook, *Nootka, and other Indian languages mixed with English and French words, became the trading language of the entire Pacific coast. The Chinook practiced the *potlatch, and their religion emphasized the quest for a personal guiding spirit by undergoing ordeals of various kinds. They were also known as the Flatheads for their cosmetic custom of intentionally deforming the shape of their children's heads during infancy. The present Chinook population is about 400.

CHINOISERIE *A bedstead in the Chinese style, probably made (c. 1750-55) by Thomas Chippendale.*

Chioggia 45 13N 12 17E A fishing port in Italy, on an island in the Venetian lagoon. Population (1973 est): 50,000.

chipmunk A *ground squirrel belonging to the genus *Tamias* (18 species), of North America and Asian forests. Chipmunks are 6–12 in (15–30 cm) long and have a black and white striped back and strong feet and claws for digging. They live in burrows and, in the winter, do not hibernate but feed on a store of nuts and dried fruit carried under ground in their large cheek pouches.

Chippendale, Thomas (1718–79) British cabinetmaker, famous for his elegant furniture designs, especially his chairs. His illustrated collection of rococo furniture designs, *The Gentleman and Cabinet Maker's Director* (1754), was the first comprehensive furniture catalogue and was widely influential in England and America, although his later neoclassical styles are considered the finest.

Chippewa. *See* Ojibwa.

Chirac, Jacques (1932–) French statesman; prime minister (1974–76) under the presidency of Giscard d'Estaing. Differences with Giscard led to Chirac's resignation, after which he reorganized the Gaullist Union des Démocrates pour la République into the Rassemblement pour la République. He became mayor of Paris in 1977.

Chirico, Giorgio de (1888–1978) Italian painter and forerunner of *surrealism, born in Greece. He trained in Munich and was influenced by Nietzsche's philosophy. In Paris (1911–15) he worked on scenes of eerie and deserted Italian squares. At Ferrara (1917) he established with Carlo Carrà (1881–1966) the school of *metaphysical painting, but reverted to a traditional style after 1919.

chiromancy. *See* palmistry.

Chiron In Greek legend, a *centaur, son of Cronos and the sea nymph Philyra. Unlike his fellow centaurs, he was revered for his wisdom and knowledge of medicine. After being accidentally wounded by Heracles he bequeathed his immortality to Prometheus and was transformed into the constellation *Sagittarius.

chiropody The paramedical specialty that deals with the care of feet and the treatment of minor ailments of the feet, such as corns, calluses, and ingrowing toenails.

chiropractic A medical specialty based on the assumption that most diseases originate from disorders of the nervous system, particularly as a result of compression of the nerve roots as they emerge from the spine. A chiropractor attempts to relieve symptoms by manipulating the spine with his hands.

Chiroptera. *See* bat.

chiru An antelope, *Pantholops hodgsoni*, of Tibetan plateaus. About 31 in (80 cm) high at the shoulder, chirus have a dense woolly pinkish-brown coat with white underparts; males have slender black horns up to 28 in (70 cm) long. They live singly or in small groups and excavate shallow depressions for shelter.

Chisholm v. Georgia (1793) A Supreme Court decision that affirmed the right of citizens of one state to sue the government of another state. Alexander Chisholm's heirs, residents of South Carolina, sued the state of Georgia for return of Chisholm's property there, which was confiscated during the American Revolution. The implications of this ruling prompted the passage of the Eleventh Amendment (1798) prohibiting such suits.

Chita 52 03N 113 35E A city in the SE central Soviet Union, in the RSFSR. Founded by the *Cossacks (1653), it is a prosperous city with machine-building, textiles, and food-processing industries. Population (1981 est): 315,000.

chital. *See* axis deer.

chitarrone (Italian: big guitar) A large fretted instrument of the lute family, able to accommodate bass strings of over 5 ft (1.5 m) in length. It was popular for accompanying singing in the early 17th century.

chitin A complex carbohydrate that, in association with proteins, is the principal component of the outer cuticle of insects and other arthropods. Chitin occurs in several other animal groups and is a constituent of the cell walls of fungi.

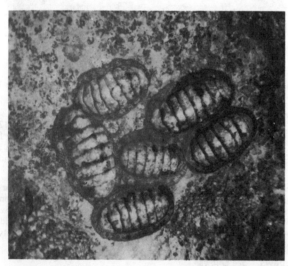

CHITON *Resembling woodlice, these primitive mollusks have a broad muscular foot which enables them to creep over rocky surfaces.*

chiton A primitive *mollusk of the class *Amphineura* (about 600 species), also called sea cradle. Elliptical and measuring up to 12 × 6 in) 30 × 15 cm), chitons live on rocky shores, clinging tightly and grazing on encrusted algae. They have eight shell plates with a fleshy girdle and curl up when detached.

Chittagong 22 20N 91 48E A city and major port in Bangladesh, on the Indian Ocean. The focal point of road, rail, and air routes, it is the second most important industrial center in the country. Its university was established in 1966. Population (1974): 889,760.

chivalry The ideology and code of conduct of the knightly class of medieval Europe. Chivalric behavior depended on the concepts of honor and courtesy and received a notable impetus during the 12th century from the *Crusades and the development of the ideals of *courtly love in such literature as the Arthurian romances. All ties between the chivalric code and military conduct ended with the decline of cavalry and the invention of gunpowder, although elaborate jousts and tournaments kept its memory alive until the 16th century.

chive A small hardy perennial plant, **Allium schoenoprasum*, native to Europe. It has small white elongated bulbs and produces clumps of thin tubular leaves and dense attractive spherical heads of bluish or lilac flowers on long stalks. The leaves are used for seasoning and garnishing foods. Family: *Liliaceae*.

chloral (*or* trichlorethanal; CCl_3CHO) A colorless oily liquid made by treating acetaldehyde with chlorine. It is used in the manufacture of DDT.

chloramphenicol An *antibiotic usually reserved for severe bacterial infections. It is particularly useful in the treatment of typhoid fever and some forms of pneumonia and meningitis. In rare cases chloramphenicol causes serious blood disorders.

chlordiazepoxide. *See* benzodiazepines.

Chlorella A genus of unicellular *green algae found in fresh water or damp soil, some forming symbiotic relationships with fungi to give *lichens. Because they are rich in proteins, carbohydrates, and fats and reproduce rapidly by cell division, their use as a food source for man is now under study.

chlorine (Cl) A greenish poisonous *halogen gas, discovered in 1774 by C. W. Scheele. It is found in nature only in compounds, especially common salt (NaCl), sylvite (KCl), and carnallite ($KMgCl_3.6H_2O$). Chlorine is liberated by the electrolysis of brine. It irritates the respiratory system and was used as a poisonous gas in World War I. Chlorine gas is reactive and combines directly with most elements. Its oxidizing properties make it a useful disinfectant for drinking-water supplies and swimming pools. It is used in the manufacture of *bromine, in bleach (NaOCl), hydrochloric acid (HCl), and carbon tetrachloride (CCl_4). Chlorinated organic chemicals are used in dyes, antiseptics, and insecticides. At no 17; at wt 35.453; mp −149.8°F (−100.98°C); bp −30.3°F (−34.6°C).

chloroform (*or* trichloromethane; $CHCl_3$) A colorless volatile liquid. It is made by reacting *bleaching powder with acetone, acetaldehyde, or ethanol. Its main use is now in the manufacture of *fluorocarbons but it is also used as a solvent and as an anesthetic.

chlorophyll A green pigment present in organisms capable of *photosynthesis. Higher plants possess chlorophylls *a* and *b*, located in *chloroplasts; chlorophyll *c* is found in some primitive marine plants, and bacteriochlorophyll occurs in photosynthetic bacteria. The chlorophylls absorb red and blue light, trapping light energy for photosynthesis.

chloroplast A structure within a plant cell in which the process of *photosynthesis takes place. It is bounded by a membrane and contains the green pigment *chlorophyll. Chloroplasts vary greatly in shape and number within a cell. The greatest concentration occurs in the palisade mesophyll tissue of the leaves—the main photosynthesizing region.

chloroquine A drug used to prevent and treat malaria. It acts by preventing the digestion of hemoglobin (the red pigment of blood) by the malaria parasite. Chloroquine is also used in the treatment of rheumatoid arthritis and related diseases.

chlorpromazine. *See* phenothiazines.

chocolate. *See* cocoa and chocolate.

Choctaw A North American Indian people formerly inhabiting territories in Mississippi and Alabama. The Choctaw language was a subdivision of the Muskoegan language family. They supported themselves by agriculture, raising corn and beans. The Choctaw practiced an elaborate green corn ceremony to ensure the abundance of their crops. They wore their hair long and practiced head flattening through intentional deformation during infancy. After supporting the French against the English in the 18th century, they were forced to move west in the 1830s, settling in Oklahoma. The present Choctaw population there is approximately 40,000.

Chodowiecki, Daniel Nikolaus (1726–1801) German painter and engraver, who specialized in scenes of middle-class life. A noted book illustrator, he engraved editions of Cervantes' *Don Quixote* and Goldsmith's *Vicar of Wakefield*. His best-known painting is *The Parting of Jean Calas from his Family* (1767; Berlin-Dahlem Museum).

choir 1. A group of trained singers. In the Christian Church the use of a choir was derived from Judaism and traditionally consisted of men and boys only. The choir leads the singing of the congregation as well as singing anthems. The most usual division of parts in a choir is into four: soprano, alto, tenor, and bass (SATB). In secular music the choir is often called a chorus. **2.** The part of the chancel of a church where the choir sits.

Choiseul, Étienne François, Duc de (1719–85) French statesman; foreign minister (1758–70). As ambassador to Vienna in 1757 he began negotiations for the marriage of Marie Antoinette to the future Louis XVI. He secured good terms for France in the Treaty of *Paris at the close of the Seven Years' War (1763). The influence of Louis XV's mistress, Mme *Du Barry, undermined his position at court and he was exiled in 1770.

cholera An acute infection of the intestine caused by the bacterium *Vibrio cholerae*, which is transmitted in drinking water contaminated by feces of a patient. Epidemics of cholera occur in regions where sanitation is poor. After an incubation period of 1–5 days, cholera causes severe vomiting and diarrhea, which—untreated—leads to dehydration that can be fatal. Treatment consists of replacement of fluid and salts by intravenous injections. Vaccinations against cholera provide only temporary immunity.

cholesterol A compound derived from steroids and found in many animal tissues. Cholesterol is manufactured by the liver and other tissues and its derivatives form constituents of cell membranes, bile, blood, and gallstones. High levels of cholesterol in the blood have been associated with an increased risk of heart disease, as a result of fatty deposits in the walls of arteries. *See also* atherosclerosis.

Cholon 10 45N 106 39E A port in S Vietnam, a part since 1932 of present-day *Ho Chi Minh City. It is the city's Chinese quarter (founded c. 1778). A trading center for rice and fish, it has rice-milling, timber, and pottery industries. It suffered badly during the Vietnam War.

Cholula (*or* Cholula de Rivadabia) 19 05N 98 20W A city in central Mexico. A major religious center dedicated to the god Quetzalcoatl before the Spanish conquest, it is the site of a pyramid 177 ft (53 m) high, which was begun in the Teotihuacán period and subsequently enlarged. Population (1969 est): 12,820.

Chomsky, Noam (1928–) US linguist, under whose influence the aims and methods of general linguistic theory and especially of *grammar were radically revised. His writings on the subject include *Syntactic Structures* (1957) and *Aspects of the Theory of Syntax* (1965). Chomsky's work draws on and develops that of his teacher Zellig *Harris. Chomsky has also undertaken controversial studies of the theory of speech sounds and of semantic structures.

Ch'öngjin 41 50N 129 55E A city and seaport in North Korea, on the NE coast. Originally a small fishing village, it developed rapidly under Japanese occupation (1910–45). It is an important center for the manufacture of iron and steel; other industries include shipbuilding, chemicals, and textiles. Population (1970 est): 200,000.

Chongqing (Ch'ung ch'ing *or* Chungking) 29 32N 106 45E A port in central China, in Sichuan province at the confluence of the Yangtze and Jialing (*or* Chia-ling) Rivers. A major commercial and industrial center, it is a former capital of China (1937–46). Population (1957 est): 2,121,000.

Chopin, Frédéric (François) (1810–49) Polish composer and pianist of French descent. He studied in Warsaw but later settled in Paris and never returned to Poland. He lived with the novelist George *Sand from 1838 to 1847, but never married her. A fervent nationalist, he was a student of Polish culture and much of his music was influenced by Polish folk music. He developed a highly characteristic style of writing for the piano, for which he composed 2 concertos, 3 sonatas, 24 preludes, and many waltzes, nocturnes, polonaises, and studies. He also wrote a cello sonata, a piano trio, and songs.

Chordata A phylum of animals that comprises the primitive *protochordates and the vertebrates (*see* Vertebrata). They are distinguished from other animals by three features: a hollow dorsal nerve cord; a rodlike *notochord that forms the basis of the internal skeleton; and paired gill slits in the wall of the pharynx behind the head, although in higher chordates these are apparent only in early embryonic stages.

chorea Involuntary jerky movements, particularly of the hips, shoulders, and face, caused by disease of the part of the brain controlling voluntary movement. Sydenham's chorea—formerly known as *St Vitus's dance—is often associated with rheumatic fever in children. It causes no permanent damage and responds to sedatives.

choreography The art of composing *ballet and other theatrical dances. Choreography originally referred only to a dance notation, the lack of which has made precise reconstruction of many ballets difficult. The most comprehensive system for recording dance steps is that devised by the Hungarian dancer Rudolph Laban (1829–1958), known as Labanotation. The

choreographer is usually a professional dancer, who selects, arranges into sequences, and teaches the dancers each step of the dance. Often he works in close collaboration with composers, notable partnerships being between *Tchaikovsky and *Petipa and *Stravinsky and *Fokine. Famous contemporary choreographers include *Robbins, *Béjart, *Ashton, and *Balanchine.

chorus **1.** In Greek drama, a group of actors who described and commented on the dramatic action through dance, song, and chanting. Greek tragedy originated in songs and dances performed by a chorus in honor of Dionysus. The dramas of Aeschylus were performed by a chorus and only two actors, but its dramatic role declined in the plays of Sophocles (who introduced a third actor) and Euripides. The chorus, not directly involved in the actions of the main protagonists, represented the responses and judgments of average humanity. Its role has been revived in certain plays by *Brecht, Eugene *O'Neill, and T. S. *Eliot. **2.** A body of singers or dancers who perform together (in contrast to soloists) as in opera or ballet.

Chorzów 50 19N 18 56E A city in SW Poland. One of Silesia's first coal-mining centers (1790), it remains a major mining and metallurgical town. Population (1979 est): 150,000.

Chota Nagpur. *See* Bihar.

Chou. *See* Zhou.

Chouans Peasants in W France, including dealers in contraband salt, who revolted in 1793 against the government established by the French Revolution. They were provoked by such measures as the abolition of the salt tax (which ruined the contraband trade) and the enforcement of conscription. The revolt, ultimately unsuccessful, is the subject of Balzac's *Les Chouans* (1829).

CHOU EN-LAI *A communist from his student days in France, the Chinese statesman played a prominent part in the establishment (1949) of the People's Republic of China, exerting a moderating influence on policy until his death.*

Chou En-lai (*or* Zhou En Lai; 1898–1976) Chinese communist statesman; prime minister (1949–76) and foreign minister (1949–58). Chou studied in Japan, France, and Germany. In 1924 he became a political instructor at the Whampoa Military Academy and secretary of the Canton provincial Communist Party. He led workers in the 1927 general strike in Shanghai, after which he escaped *Guomindang (Nationalist) assassins and fled to Nanchang, where he helped to organize an uprising. In 1932 he became political commissar to the Red Army and during the *Sino-Japanese War (1937–45) his reputation as a negotiator grew. After the establishment in 1949 of the People's Republic of China, he gained worldwide prominence as a diplomat and at home was largely responsible for establishing communist China's bureaucracy. Regarded as a moderate he exercised a stabilizing influence on his extremist colleagues.

chough A large black songbird, *Pyrrhocorax pyrrhocorax*, about 14 in (37 cm) long, with red legs and a long red down-curved bill. It occurs in the Alps, Spain, and a few sea cliffs around Britain where it can be seen giving displays of aerial acrobatics. The yellow-billed Alpine chough (*P.*

graculus) occurs at high altitudes in European mountains. Family: *Corvidae* (crows).

Chou Shu-jen. *See* Lu Xun.

Chouteau, (René) Auguste (1749–1829) US pioneer and fur trader. Born in New Orleans, he worked for fur trading companies on the Mississippi and Missouri rivers. He helped to build the city of St Louis, Mo and, when Missouri became part of the US, he served the city and federal government in several capacities. With his half-brother (**Jean**) **Pierre Chouteau** (1758–1849) he controlled trade with the Osage Indians. By 1804 Pierre was the agent for all the Indian tribes west of the Mississippi and in 1809 founded the St Louis Missouri Fur Company.

chow chow A breed of □dog originating in China more than 200 years ago. The chow has a compact body and—unusually—a blue-black tongue. The thick coat forms a mane around the neck and shoulders and the tail is held well over the back. Height: 18–20 in (46–51 cm).

Chrétien de Troyes (12th century AD) French poet, author of the earliest romances dealing with the *Arthurian legend. He was a native of Champagne and a member of the court of Marie, countess of Champagne, to whom his romance *Lancelot* was dedicated. Little else is known of his life. His octosyllabic verse introduced a psychological subtlety in the treatment of *courtly love and chivalry that contrasts strongly with the heroic themes of the *chansons de geste*. His romances include *Erec, Cligés, Yvain,* and *Perceval* (or *Conte del Graal*), in which the *Holy Grail appears in a literary work for the first time.

Christchurch 50 44N 1 54W A resort in S England, in Dorset on Christchurch Harbor. It has a famous priory church. Population (1981): 32,789.

Christian I (1426–81) King of Denmark and Norway (1450–81) and Sweden (1457–64), who founded the Oldenburg ruling dynasty of Denmark (1450–1863). His claim to the Swedish crown, which was disputed by Charles VIII of Sweden (d. 1470; reigned 1448–57, 1464–65, 1467–70), was finally ended by Christian's defeat at Brunkeberg (1471). In 1460 he gained Schleswig and Holstein but in 1469 the Norwegian islands of Orkney and Shetland were mortgaged to Scotland as part of his daughter Margaret's dowry on her marriage to the Scottish king James III.

Christian (II) the Cruel (1481–1559) King of Denmark and Norway (1513–23) and of Sweden (1520–23). He acquired his nickname for his massacre of Swedish nobles in his conquest of Sweden. He was subsequently deposed and, following an attempt to regain Norway, imprisoned (1532–59).

Christian III (1503–59) King of Denmark and Norway (1534–59), who established the state Lutheran Church in Denmark (1536) after the *Count's War (1533–36). His administrative reforms laid the foundation for 17th-century Danish absolutism.

Christian IV (1577–1648) King of Denmark and Norway (1588–1648). He entered the *Thirty Years' War in 1624 to defend the Protestant cause and Danish interests in the Baltic but was defeated by the Catholic League and withdrew (1629). At war with Sweden (1643–45), he suffered a crushing defeat (1645) with considerable loss of territory and domestic authority. He founded many new towns, including Christiania (now Oslo).

Christian IX (1818–1906) King of Denmark (1863–1906), who fought unsuccessfully with Germany over *Schleswig-Holstein. He succeeded to the throne through his marriage to the cousin of the childless Frederick VII of Denmark (1808–63; reigned 1848–63). He supported minority conservative governments until 1901, when he was forced to accept a liberal ministry.

Christian X (1870–1947) King of Denmark (1912–47), whose courage and dignity during the German occupation of his country (1940–45) won him international respect; rejecting Nazi antisemitic legislation in 1942, he was imprisoned from 1943 to 1945.

Christian Democrats Political parties having programs based on Christian principles and generally of a conservative nature. In West Germany the **Christlich-Demokratische Union** (Christian Democratic Union; CDU), founded in 1945 held power, in alliance with the Christlich-Soziale Union (Christian Social Union; CSU), from 1948 to 1969 under Konrad *Adenauer. In Italy the **Democrazia Cristiana** (Christian Democratic Party; DC), founded in 1943 as the successor to the Partito Popolare Italiano (Italian Popular Party), has dominated government since 1945. In 1963 Aldo *Moro brought the Italian Socialist Party into a coalition government with the DC, which has depended on the support of the Communist Party. Other Christian Democratic parties are found in Austria, Belgium, France, Norway, and Spain.

Christianity The religious faith based on the teachings of *Jesus Christ, which had its origin in *Judaism. Its believers hold that Jesus is the Messiah prophesied in the Old Testament. It began as a movement within Judaism, and one of the first disputes among the early Christians was the right of the Gentiles to be admitted to the faith. Chiefly through the missionary activities of St Paul, the Apostle of the Gentiles, Christianity spread rapidly through the Roman Empire, despite persecutions under Nero and later emperors. Christian belief was at first taught by the Apostles by word of mouth; however, the need for a written record of Jesus' life and teaching was soon fulfilled by the *Gospels. The definition of Christian belief and the authority of bishops and scriptures was well developed when Constantine became emperor (312). A series of general councils, the first held in 325 at *Nicaea, defined orthodox Christian belief. Constantine's establishment of his new capital, Constantinople, led to a growing polarization between the Eastern *Orthodox Church and the Western *Roman Catholic Church. Despite the collapse of the Western Empire, Western Christianity, under the Bishop of Rome who claimed authority as St Peter's successor, spread vigorously. The Orthodox Church, not so rigorously centralized, became increasingly isolated, and with the development of doctrinal differences the two Churches drifted apart. The date of the formal separation is generally regarded as 1054. The Orthodox Church, under pressure from Islam to the east and often hostile Christians to the west, nevertheless established itself among the Slavs. The Western Church by the end of the first millennium was rapidly gaining power, the papacy reaching the zenith of its influence in the 13th century under Pope *Innocent III. In the later middle ages increasing nationalism and the assertion of power by temporal rulers weakened the united structure of the papacy and *Holy Roman Empire. With the attack on central authority came a greater boldness in dissident criticism of the Church, such as that of John *Wycliffe in England.

By the 16th century the Church no longer had the power to override national interests; in this weakened state it was unable to resist the inevitable fragmentation caused by the *Reformation. Some reformers, such as the followers of Martin *Luther and the English Church, were comparatively conservative, while the *Calvinists, centered in Geneva, were considerably more radical. Coinciding with the exploration of the globe, the Reformation and the Roman Catholic response to it, the *Counter-Reformation, in fact stimulated the spread of Christianity throughout the world, giving rise to the many different Christian denominations and communions of the modern world.

Challenged in the 19th and 20th centuries by materialism, atheism, and agnosticism, the Christian Churches have come under severe pressure in many parts of the world. The ecumenical movement of the 20th century has sought to unite Christendom and after centuries of hostility has had some success in healing its various schisms. The belief of Christianity is based on the New Testament and for most Christians is summarized in the traditional *creeds of the Church. The doctrines of the *Trinity, the *Incarnation of Christ, and the Resurrection are central, as is Christ's role as the redeemer of mankind. The total number of Christians has been estimated at more than 944 million, or approximately 24% of the world population.

Christian Science A religious movement founded by Mary Baker *Eddy in 1866. After being healed of various illnesses by the well-known mesmerist and faith healer Phineas Parkhurst Quimby (1802–66), Eddy formulated a set of principles for curing physical and moral disorders through the use of prayer. This method of universal faith healing, based on the healing powers of Jesus Christ, which Eddy called the "Divine Mind," was expounded fully in her book *Science and Health with Key to the Scriptures* (1875). This work has become one of the central texts of the Christian Science movement, which teaches the denial of the reality of the material world and healing through spiritual control. The form of service is simple, including hymns, Bible readings, and relevant commentary from Mrs Eddy's works. The First Church of Christ, Scientist opened in Boston, Massachusetts in 1879. The movement spread to Europe, and since Mrs Eddy's death in 1910 it has been regulated by a board of five directors. Among the most well-known publications of the Christian Science movement, which operates public reading rooms throughout the world, is the *Christian Science Monitor*, a daily newspaper founded by Mrs Eddy in 1908.

Christian Social Union (German name: Christlich-Soziale Union; CSU) A West German political party, the affiliate of the Christian Democratic Union (*see* Christian Democrats). The two parties held power from 1948 to 1969. In 1976, while in opposition, the CSU, led by Franz Josef Strauss (1915–), staged a walkout on the Christian Democrats. Both parties stood to lose from a split, and after a month the coalition had reformed and is now led by Strauss. Despite its name, the CSU forms the conservative wing in German politics.

Christians of St Thomas   The Christians of the Malabar Coast, in SW India. According to tradition, St Thomas the Apostle brought Christianity to the area. Their Church used a Syriac liturgy and originally held *Nestorian beliefs, but since the 16th century the Roman Catholic Church has played a prominent role in its development.

Christie, Dame Agatha   (1891–1975) British author of detective fiction and playwright. She introduced her most famous character, the Belgian detective Hercule Poirot, in *The Mysterious Affair at Styles* (1920); he met his end in *Curtain* (1975). Later detective novels include *The Murder of Roger Ackroyd* (1926), *Murder on the Orient Express* (1934), and *Death on the Nile* (1937). She wrote over 50 popular detective stories, creating other well-known fictional detectives, including Miss Jane Marple. A number of her stories have been filmed, and her play *The Mousetrap* has had an unparalleled long run in London since its opening in 1952.

Christina   (1626–89) Queen of Sweden (1632–54). After reaching her majority (1644), she clashed repeatedly with her former regent *Oxenstierna. Her secret conversion to Roman Catholicism (then illegal in Sweden) led to her abdication, after which she lived in Rome. There, she became an outstanding patron of the arts, sponsoring the composers Scarlatti and Corelli and the architect and sculptor Bernini.

Christmas   The Feast of the Nativity of Christ. In the West it has been celebrated on Dec 25 since 336 AD, partly in order to replace the pagan sun worship on the same date. In the East, both the Nativity and Epiphany were originally celebrated on Jan 6, but by the end of the 4th century Dec 25 was almost universally accepted, although the Armenian Church still celebrates Christmas on Jan 6. Many of the popular customs associated with Christmas can be traced back to pagan origins.

Christmas Island   An island in the Indian Ocean, SW of Java. It became a territory of the Commonwealth of Australia in 1958. The only commercial activity is phosphate mining. Area: 52 sq mi (135 sq km). Population (1980 est): 3184.

Christmas Island   A large coral atoll in the W central Pacific Ocean, in Kiribati in the Line Islands. British and US nuclear tests were held here between 1957 and 1962. It has coconut plantations. Area: 139 sq mi (359 sq km). Population (1980 est): 1265.

Christmas rose   A perennial herbaceous plant, *Helleborus niger*, about 14 in (35 cm) tall, native to central and S Europe and Asia Minor. Grown in gardens for its attractive white or pink winter-flowering blossoms, it prefers rich moist shady sites. The poisonous rhizomes are irritant to the skin when fresh. Dried, they have been used medicinally. Family: *Ranunculaceae*.

Christoff, Boris   (1919–) Bulgarian singer. His powerful bass voice and skilful characterization have made him a world-famous opera singer. He is particularly well known in the title role of Mussorgsky's opera *Boris Godunov*.

Christophe, Henri   (1767–1820) Haitian ruler. An ex-slave, Christophe served with *Toussaint L'Ouverture against the French and then joined *Dessalines' revolt. After Dessalines' assassination, in which Christophe took part, he ruled N Haiti (1808–20; as king from 1811). His cruelty caused a revolt and he shot himself.

Christopher, St   (3rd century AD) Christian martyr of Syria. According to legend, he carried a child across a river where he was working as a ferryman. The child grew heavier and he learned that it was in fact Christ and he was thus carrying the weight of the world. He is the patron saint of travelers. Feast day: 25 July.

chromaticism   The use in music of notes that are not part of the normal diatonic *scale: the word comes from the Greek *chroma*, color. Under the system of equal *temperament the octave is split into 12 equal parts, containing 7 diatonic and 5 chromatic notes. The practice of "coloring" music by the use of these chromatic notes dates from the 16th century and was widely used by Liszt and Wagner to effect frequent modulations from one key to another. In the early music of Schoenberg chromaticism became so heavy that the concept of key became meaningless and *atonality resulted.

chromatid.   *See* chromosome.

chromatography   A method of chemical analysis in which a mixture to be analyzed constitutes a mobile phase, which moves in contact with an absorbent stationary phase. In **gas chromatography** (*or* gas-liquid chromatography) the mobile phase is a mixture of volatile substances diluted with an inert gas (e.g. argon). The stationary phase consists of a non-volatile liquid supported on an inert material of uniform particles (e.g. diatomaceous earth) in a tall column. The components of the mobile phase are selectively absorbed by the stationary phase. A detector measures the conductivity (or some other property) of the gas leaving the column, the

resulting peaks on a strip chart of the detector output indicating the presence and concentration of the various components of the mixture. When the mobile phase is a liquid it can be introduced into a column of the solid stationary phase. The components of the mixture are selectively absorbed and form colored bands down the length of the column. This method is known as **column chromatography**. In column chromatography, the stationary phase is an absorbent material such as alumina. **Thin-layer chromatography** is a similar technique used for analysis. The stationary phase is a thin layer of alumina on a glass plate, and a spot of sample is separated into spots of the constituents. More commonly, **paper chromatography** is used, in which the stationary phase is a sheet of absorbent paper. The solvent soaks along the paper carrying the constituents with it at different rates. Colorless compounds can be made visible by ultraviolet light or chemical developers. The rate at which a constituent moves relative to movement of the solvent can be used to identify it.

chromatophore   A granular cell containing pigment, found in great numbers in the skin of many animals. The distribution of the chromatophores accounts for the distinctive colors of these animals. Some animals (e.g. chameleons) have the ability to change the concentration and dispersion of pigment within the chromatophore very rapidly, effecting a change of skin color that is of value in camouflage.

chrome dyes   Pigments consisting of chromium salts. **Chrome yellow** and **chrome orange** contain lead chromate ($PbCrO_4$), lead sulfate ($PbSO_4$), and lead monoxide (PbO). They display a range of shades, depending on the composition, and are used in paints. **Chrome green** contains chromic oxide (Cr_2O_3) and, unlike chrome yellow, is resistant to light and heat.

chromium   (Cr)   A hard gray transition metal, discovered in 1798 by Louis Nicolas Vauquelin (1763–1829). It occurs in nature principally as chromite ($FeCr_2O_4$), which is mined in the Soviet Union, Zimbabwe, and elsewhere. The metal is extracted by reducing the oxide (Cr_2O_3) with aluminum. The principal uses of chromium are in electroplating steel and in making alloys with iron. All chromium compounds are colored and the most widely used, other than the oxide, are chromates (for example K_2CrO_4) and dichromates ($K_2Cr_2O_7$), which are used as oxidizing agents and in the dyeing industry. Lead chromate ($PbCrO_4$) is bright yellow and is used as a pigment. At no 24; at wt 51.996; mp $1857 \pm 20°C$; bp $2482°C$.

chromophore   A group of atoms, generally in an organic compound, that absorbs light of characteristic wavelengths, thus imparting color to the compound. Typical examples are the *azo ($-N=N-$) and nitroso ($-N=O$) groups. In dyes, groups called auxochromes (color enhancers) help to modify the color conferred by the chromophore, as well as the solubility and related properties of the dye molecule. A group derived from sulfonic acid ($-SO_3H$) is a typical auxochrome.

chromosome   One of the threadlike structures that carry the genetic information (*see* gene) of living organisms and are found in the nuclei of their cells. Chromosomes consist of a central axis of *DNA with associated *RNA and proteins. Before cell division, the long filamentous threads contract and thicken and each chromosome can be seen as two identical threads (chromatids) joined at the centromere. The chromatids later separate to become the daughter chromosomes (*see* mitosis).

Chromosome number is characteristic of a species. For example, a normal human body cell has 46 chromosomes comprising 22 matched pairs (called autosomes) and two *sex chromosomes. A human sperm or egg cell has half this number of chromosomes (*see* meiosis). Abnormal numbers or parts of chromosomes often lead to abnormalities in the individual concerned. *Down's syndrome (mongolism) in man is caused by the presence of an extra number 21 chromosome.

chromosphere   The layer of the *sun's atmosphere, a few thousand kilometers thick, that lies between the visible surface (the *photosphere) and the *corona. The temperature increases rapidly from about 2252°F (4000°C) near the photosphere to about 277,532°F (500,000°C) at the base of the corona, with the atmosphere becoming increasingly rarified with height. The chromosphere cannot be seen without special equipment, except at a total solar *eclipse.

chronicle plays   Plays that dramatize historical events in order to convey general moral lessons. The successors to the medieval *morality plays, they were popular in England during the Elizabethan era. Examples are Marlowe's *Edward II* (first produced in 1592) and Shakespeare's *King John* (c. 1596). Many of the plots were taken from Holinshed's *Chronicles* (1578).

Chronicles, Books of   Two Old Testament books covering the history of Judah from the Creation to the end of the *Babylonian exile (538 BC). They were probably written in the 4th century BC and originally formed a continuous history with the books of Ezra and Nehemiah. After opening with genealogies from Adam, they describe the reigns of David and Solomon and the succeeding Kings of Judah. Special emphasis is given to the building of the Temple at Jerusalem.

chronometer. *See* clock.

chrysalis The *pupa of most insects of the order Lepidoptera. *See also* butterflies and moths.

Chrysanthemum A genus of herbaceous plants and shrubs (about 200 species) native to Eurasia, Africa, and North America. The wild ancestors of the horticultural chrysanthemums are not known, but probably more than one species—almost certainly of Japanese and Chinese origin—was involved. The showy forms are widely and easily cultivated, having colorful single or double long-lasting flower heads. The different varieties may bloom at any time from early spring to autumn. Family: *Compositae. See also* pyrethrum.

Chrysler, Walter Percy (1875–1940) US businessman. A machinist by trade, he joined the Buick Motor Company in 1912 and became its president in 1916. In 1921 he took over Willys-Overland Company and Maxwell Motor Company, reorganized them and combined them to form the Chrysler Corporation. Dodge, DeSoto, and Plymouth cars joined the Chrysler line in 1928. He was responsible for the construction of the Chrysler building (1929) in New York City.

Chrysoloras, Manuel (c. 1365–1415) Greek scholar and envoy. Chrysoloras was sent on several diplomatic missions by the Byzantine Emperor Manuel Paleologus. In Florence, Chrysoloras taught the humanists Bruni, Poggio, and Guarino. His work on grammar, *Erotemata*, introduced Greek to the West.

chrysoprase An apple-green variety of *chalcedony, used as a gem.

Chrysostom, St John (c. 347–407 AD) Bishop of Constantinople and Doctor of the Church. After a period as a hermit, he was ordained in 386 in Antioch and preached extensively there, soon gaining the epithet Chrysostom (Greek: golden-mouthed). As Patriarch of Constantinople from 398, he was a zealous reformer but alienated the Empress Eudoxia (d. 404) and other powerful persons. In 403 he was unjustifiably condemned on a number of charges, deposed from his see, and banished. He died while journeying to the Black Sea. His *Homilies* are important expositions of various biblical books. The liturgy in general use in the Orthodox Churches is attributed to him, although in its present form it dates from a much later period. Feast day: Jan 27.

Chuang-tzu. *See* Zhuangzi.

chub One of several freshwater fish related to *carp, found in Europe and North America and used as food, game, or bait fish. The European chub (*Leucixus cephalus*) has a plump elongated body, usually 12–16 in (30–40 cm) long, and is dark blue or green above and silvery below. Certain unrelated freshwater fish of the genus *Leucichthys* (order: *Salmoniformes*) are also called chub.

Chu Chiang. *See* Zhu Jiang.

Ch'ü Ch'iu-pai. *See* Qu Qiu Bai.

chuckwalla A North American lizard, *Sauromalus obesus*, occurring in SW arid and rocky regions. 20 in (50 cm) long, it is dark-gray with a red-banded and blotched tail. It feeds on vegetation, storing water in sacs beneath the skin, and shelters in rock crevices; if molested it inflates its lungs to increase its body size making it difficult to dislodge. Family: *Iguanidae*.

Chukchi A people of the Chukchi peninsula in extreme NE Siberia. One branch consists of nomadic reindeer herders; the other is a maritime fishing people whose members also hunt whale, walrus, and seal, and live in fixed villages. Their language is of Paleo-Siberian type.

Chukchi Sea 69 00N 171 00W A part of the Arctic Ocean between NW Alaska and NE Soviet Union, just above the Bering Strait. Icebound for most of the year, it is navigable only from mid-summer until early fall.

Chulalongkorn (1853–1910) King of Siam (now Thailand) from 1868 to 1910. He built roads and railroads, improved education, abolished slavery, and remodeled Siam's administration on western lines. His diplomatic handling of France and Britain ensured Siam's continued independence.

Chungking. *See* Chongqing.

Chur (French name: Coire; Romansh name: Cuera) 46 52N 9 32E A city in E Switzerland. A tourist center, it also trades in Valtelline wines. Population: 31,193.

Churchill, Lord Randolph Henry Spencer (1849–95) British Conservative politician; father of Sir Winston *Churchill. He entered parliament in 1874. After serving as secretary for India (1885–86), he was briefly

chancellor of the exchequer, when his budget was not accepted by the prime minister, Lord *Salisbury, because Churchill wished to reduce funds allocated to the armed forces. He married (1874) Jeanette (Jennie) Jerome (1854–1921), an American.

SIR WINSTON CHURCHILL *Touring the London docks with his wife following an air raid in World War II.*

Churchill, Sir Winston (Leonard Spencer) (1874–1965) British statesman and author. The son of Lord Randolph *Churchill, he was a direct descendant of the 1st Duke of Marlborough. Churchill served in the army and as a war correspondent in the second Boer War before becoming a Conservative member of Parliament in 1900. In 1904 he joined the Liberals and subsequently served as president of the Board of Trade (1908–10), home secretary (1910–11), and first lord of the admiralty (1911–15). In 1915, during World War I, he rejoined the army and served in France. In 1917 he became minister of munitions, supporting the development of the *tank. Churchill lost his parliamentary seat in 1922 but was re-elected as a constitutionalist in 1924, becoming chancellor of the exchequer in Baldwin's government. From 1929 he was out of office until the outbreak of World War II, when he became first lord of the admiralty and then, in 1940, prime minister of a coalition government. During *World War II, his remarkable oratory and outstanding qualities as a leader made him a symbol of British resistance to tyranny throughout the free world. He was largely responsible for Britain's victorious alliance with the Soviet Union and the US (1941) but came to view Soviet communism as a future threat, speaking later of an "iron curtain" drawn across Europe. Churchill's coalition government was defeated in 1945 but he returned as Conservative prime minister in 1951, serving until his resignation in 1955.

His writings include *The Second World War* (1948–54) and *A History of the English-Speaking Peoples* (1956–58); he won the 1953 Nobel Prize for Literature.

Churchill, Winston (1871–1947) US novelist. He served in the New Hampshire legislature (1903–05) and ran for governor in 1912. From these experiences he drew material for *Coniston* (1906) and *The Dwelling Place of Light* (1917). His earlier novels covered the American Revolution (*Richard Carvel*; 1899), the Civil War (*The Crisis*; 1901), and pioneer days (*The Crossing*; 1904).

Churchill Falls A waterfall in E Canada in W Labrador on the Churchill River. In 1967 work began on a huge hydroelectricity project expected to generate 5,222,000 kW. Height: 245 ft (75 m); 1038 ft (316 m) including rapids.

Churchill River (formerly Hamilton River) A river in Canada that rises in Ashuanipi Lake in SW Labrador. It loops N and then SE before turning NE to empty into Lake Melville near Goose Bay. Along its course, just below Lobstick Lake, is Churchill Falls, a drop of over 300 ft (90 m). It is the site of a large hydroelectric power plant. From its headwaters to Churchill Falls, it is known as the Ashuanijai River. Length: 450 mi (725 km).

Church of England The established church in England, which embodies Protestant elements but also claims continuity with the English Church as established by St *Augustine, the first Archbishop of Canterbury. Christianity was probably introduced in Britain during the Roman occupation in the 2nd century AD. Conflicts between the indigenous Celtic Church and' Rome were resolved in favor of Roman usage at the Synod of *Whitby (664), and thereafter the English Church remained under papal authority until the *Reformation. Under *Henry VIII, papal supremacy was rejected and the king was acknowledged Supreme Head of the Church, but there were otherwise no doctrinal changes. The two bases of Anglican doctrine and worship were formulated in the succeeding reigns: the Book of *Common Prayer, introduced in the reign of *Edward VI, and the *Thirty-Nine Articles, published under Elizabeth I, whose excommunication (1570) by the pope completed the break with Rome. The two provinces of the Church are the archbishoprics of Canterbury (see Canterbury, Archbishop of) and York, each of which is further divided into bishoprics. Ecclesiastical affairs are supervised by the General Synod (established 1970 to replace the Church Assembly), composed of bishops, clergy, and laity; its decisions are subject to parliamentary approval.

Church of Scotland The Established Church in Scotland. The Scottish Church's secession from Rome was effected in 1560, largely under the influence of John *Knox. The argument over Church government between Episcopalians and Presbyterians continued until the reign of William of Orange, who established the Presbyterian Church in 1690.

church year The organization of the Christian churches' calendar around the great festivals of Christianity. In the Western Churches, the beginning of Advent (the Sunday nearest to the Feast of St Andrew, Nov 30) marks the opening of the year. The Sundays of Advent are numbered one to four, leading to Christmas Dec (25). Epiphany (Jan 6) follows after one or two intervening Sundays. The other major festivals are linked to the date of Easter, itself associated with the Jewish Passover. There are six Sundays in Lent and eight from Easter to Pentecost. The dates of Ash Wednesday, Good Friday and Ascension Day are dependent on Easter. The Eastern Churches' year begins with Easter and ends with Lent.

Churriguera A Spanish family of architects consisting of three brothers, José (1665–1725), Joaquín (1674–1724), and Alberto (1676–1750). The Churrigueras evolved a distinctive, highly decorative form of the *baroque later dubbed "Churrigueresque." This can be seen in all their work, notably in José's church of S Estéban, Salamanca (1693). It stimulated many imitators all over Spain and Mexico.

Chu Teh. See Zhu De.

Chuvash Autonomous Soviet Socialist Republic An administrative division in the W central Soviet Union, in the RSFSR. The region is a wooded steppe with peat bogs and mineral deposits. The Chuvash, who comprise about 70% of the population, are a Turkic-speaking people. Industries include engineering, oil and natural-gas refining, chemicals, and food processing, but the economy is predominantly agricultural, producing chiefly cereals and fodder crops; livestock is also important. Area: 7064 sq mi (18,300 sq km). Population (1981 est): 1,311,000. Capital: Cheboksary.

Chu Xi (or Chu Hsi; 1130–1200) Chinese philosopher, born in Fujian province, the son of a government official. He was a precocious student and entered the government service, holding various important public posts for most of his life. His major work consists of four commentaries known as the Ssu shu or Four Books. These contain the formulation of *Confucianism that was adopted as the official philosophy of China until the communist revolution in the 20th century.

Chu Yuan (c. 343 BC–c. 289 BC) Chinese poet, the earliest known by name. A nobleman of the state of Ch'u, he was banished to the S after court intrigues and drowned himself in the Mi-lo River. His contribution to the anthology Ch'u tz'u greatly influenced the development of early Chinese poetry.

CIA. See Central Intelligence Agency.

Ciano, Galeazzo (1903–44) Italian fascist leader. *Mussolini's son-in-law, Ciano was foreign minister from 1936 to 1943 and helped to form the military pact with Germany. In 1943 he voted against Mussolini in the Fascist Supreme Council and was shot by Mussolini's supporters in N Italy.

Ciardi, John (1916–) US poet and editor. Poetry editor of Saturday Review, he wrote in contemporary poetic language for both adults and children. His works include I Met a Man (1961), The Man Who Sang the Sillies (1961), and The Wish-Tree (1964) for children; Other Skies (1947), From Time to Time (1951), I Marry You (1958), 39 Poems (1959), You Know Who (1964), and Lives of X (1971), all poetry collections. He also translated Dante's Divine Comedy (Inferno, 1954; Purgatorio, 1961; Paradiso, 1970).

Cibber, Colley (1671–1757) British actor, dramatist, and theater manager. Son of a Danish sculptor, he wrote the sentimental comedy Love's Last Shift (1696) to supplement his earnings as an actor. His adaptation of Shakespeare's Richard III was the preferred acting version until the 19th century. His appointment as poet laureate in 1730 made him the target for satirical attacks by *Pope.

cicada An insect belonging to the mainly tropical family Cicadidae (over 2000 species). Cicadas are 0.8–2.0 in (20–50 mm) long and have large membranous wings. Males produce a variety of loud noises by vibrating two membranes at the base of the abdomen (this is called stridulation). Cicadas usually inhabit trees and the females lay eggs in the wood. The *nymphs (immature cicadas) drop to the ground and burrow underground to feed on plant juices from roots. After 1–17 years they emerge as adults. Order: *Hemiptera.

cicely A perennial herbaceous plant, Myrrhis odorata, also called sweet cicely. 24–40 in (60–100 cm) high, it has umbrella-like clusters of white flowers and a strong aromatic smell. Cicely is native to Europe and also occurs in Chile (where it was probably introduced). Formerly widely used as a vegetable, it is still used for seasoning. Family: *Umbelliferae.

Cicero, Marcus Tullius (106–43 BC) Roman orator and statesman. Established as a prominent lawyer by 70 BC, he was elected consul in 63 BC. His execution of the Catiline conspirators without trial lost him support and he was exiled in 58 BC for 18 months. During the civil war he supported Pompey against Caesar and lived privately in Rome during the latter's dictatorship. After the assassination of Caesar in 44 BC he made a series of attacks on Antony, the Philippics, for which he was later arrested and killed. The greatest of Roman orators, he also wrote treatises on rhetoric and philosophical works influenced by Greek political theory.

cichlid A freshwater fish of the family Cichlidae (over 6000 species), found in tropical regions, especially Africa. Cichlids have a brightly colored deep body, up to 12 in (30 cm) long, and a single long dorsal fin; they feed on plants or animals. Most build nests for their eggs and guard the young but some species carry the eggs in their mouths (see mouthbrooder). Many are popular aquarium fish. Order: Perciformes.

cider An alcoholic drink made from fermented apple juice. In England cider is made from apples grown specifically for cider making. They are crushed to press out the juice, which ferments spontaneously. Fermentation lasts weeks or months, varying according to the apples used. Cider is also made in France, especially in Normandy and Brittany, Spain, and the US, where cider denotes unfermented apple juice and hard cider denotes the English type of cider.

Cienfuegos 22 10N 80 27W A port in S Cuba, on the Caribbean Sea. A picturesque city with many fine buildings, it trades in tobacco, cattle products, and molasses and is the site of a naval base. Population (1981): 235,293.

cigar A cylindrical roll of tobacco leaf, smoked originally by the Indians of the Americas and copied by sailors from Portugal and Spain; by the 19th century they became common in N Europe. The most expensive cigars are still made by hand in Cuba and Jamaica, machine-made cigars being made extensively in the US, Europe, and the Far East. The cigar was replaced to some extent by the cigarette from the end of the 19th century, but small cigars have enjoyed some popularity in recent years.

cigarette A cylindrical roll of fine-cut tobacco, rolled in thin paper. Cigarettes became popular in the late 19th century and is now the form in which most tobacco is smoked. The tobacco most commonly used for cigarettes is Virginia-cut, a type that originated in the US, successfully grown in other countries. Since the 1960s there has been widespread concern over the effects that smoking has on health; it is associated with lung *cancer, lung disease, and *heart disease.

Ciliata A class of microscopic single-celled animals (see Protozoa) having two nuclei and tracts of hairlike cilia over the cell surface, used for feeding and swimming. Most are free-swimming (see Paramecium) but some are attached to the substrate by a stalk (see Stentor; Vorticella). Most ciliates feed on organic detritus, other protozoans, etc., but some are parasitic, especially on fish and other aquatic animals.

Cilicia The SE coastal region of Asia Minor. It was subject consecutively to the Hittites, the Assyrians, the Achemenians, the Macedonians, and the Seleucids. From the 2nd century BC pirates based on Cilicia seriously threatened Mediterranean trade until suppressed by Pompey in 67, after which the region was incorporated into a series of Roman provinces.

Cilician Gates (Turkish name: Külek Boğazi) 37 17N 34 46E A mountain pass in central S Turkey, in the Taurus Mountains. It lies on the route from Ankara to Adana and has been used for centuries.

Cimabue, Giovanni (Cenni de Peppi; c. 1240–c. 1302) Florentine painter, who introduced a degree of naturalism into the stylized *Byzantine art of his period. His only certain work is a mosaic of St John (Duomo, Pisa) but the fresco cycle in the upper Church of St Francis, Assisi, and the Santa Trinità Madonna (Uffizi) are attributed to him. *Giotto was probably his pupil.

Cimarosa, Domenico (1749–1801) Italian composer. He became court musician in St Petersburg and Vienna and was famous for his many operas. His best-known work is the *opera buffa *The Secret Marriage* (1792), which shows his flair for vocal ensemble writing and fine comic talent. He also wrote church music and chamber music.

cimbalom The traditional musical instrument of Hungary; a type of dulcimer. The cimbalom has ten pairs of wire strings stretched over a shallow three-sided soundbox. The strings are struck with a small hammer. The Hungarian composer Kodály used it in the suite *Háry János* (1927).

Cimbri A Germanic tribe from N Jutland. At the end of the 2nd century BC the Cimbri migrated southward, defeating Roman armies in 113 BC (Noricum), 110 BC (Rhône valley), and 105 BC (Arausio, now Orange, France). In 101 BC Marius destroyed them; a remnant survived in Jutland.

Cimon (died c. 450 BC) Athenian general and politician. The son of *Miltiades, Cimon opposed *Themistocles' policy of enmity toward the Spartans, believing Persia was the common Greek enemy, and in about 466 he scored a great victory against the Persians. His opponents, including *Pericles, caused him to be ostracized (461) but after his return to Athens, Cimon negotiated a truce with Sparta (c. 450) and died fighting the Persians in Cyprus.

Cinchona A genus of trees (40 species) of the South American Andes, now cultivated elsewhere in the tropics, especially India. One of the most important species is calisaya (*C. calisaya*). The bark yields powerful medicinal drugs, including cinchonidine and *quinine, used in the treatment and prevention of malaria, and cinchona, useful for coughs and sore throats. Cultivation, which is generally by coppicing, has lost importance since the development of similar synthetic drugs lacking side-effects. Family: *Rubiaceae*.

Cincinnati 39 10N 84 30W A city in SW Ohio, on the Ohio River. Founded in 1788, it developed as a meat-packing center in the 19th century. Today it is an important inland port and major manufacturing center best known as a producer of machine tools. The University of Cincinnati was established here in 1819. Population (1980): 385,457.

Cincinnatus, Lucius Quinctius (5th century BC) Roman statesman. He was made dictator to rescue a Roman legion that was besieged by an Italian tribe. After his victory he returned to his farm, despite pleas that he remain dictator. His rejection of autocratic rule made him a symbol of traditional Roman values.

Cinderella The heroine of a folktale, of which the first recorded version dates from 9th-century China. The story is of a girl treated cruelly by her stepfamily who receives help from a supernatural agent, in most versions an animal or her dead mother, and finally marries a prince.

cinema *See* motion pictures.

cinematography The recording of moving pictures. Essentially a motion film records a rapid sequence of still pictures (each slightly different from the previous one) fast enough to appear continuous to the human eye. The film moves through the camera in a series of jumps. There are usually 18 pictures (frames) per second in silent film and 24 per second in sound film. The sequence of transparencies produced by developing the film is passed through a *projector in the same way. Sound can be carried as a magnetic or optical signal on a narrow strip at the side of the film, to synchronize with the picture. Various widths of film are used: 8 mm for educational and laboratory applications; 16 mm with portable equipment for amateur filming and many other uses; 35 mm for the professional cinema.

cineraria A herbaceous perennial pot plant developed from *Senecio cruentus* of the Canary Islands. There are numerous horticultural varieties, noted for their handsome, sometimes brilliantly colored, daisy-like flowers. Useful for spring and winter flowering, they require a cool moist draft- and frost-free atmosphere. Family: *Compositae*.

Cinna, Lucius Cornelius (d. 84 BC) Roman politician. Expelled from Rome by his opponent Sulla (87), Cinna with *Marius returned and captured Rome. He tried to restrain Marius' brutal revenge on their opponents and as consul (86–84) restored order. He was killed in a mutiny shortly before Sulla's return to Italy.

cinnabar (moth) A moth, *Callimorpha jacobaeae*, of Europe and Asia. Both the adults—scarlet and black—and the caterpillars—striped black and yellow—taste bad: their warning coloration discourages predators. The caterpillars feed on ragwort and have been used to control this weed. Superfamily: *Caradrinoidea* (noctuids, tiger moths, etc.).

cinnabar (ore) A mineral consisting of mercury sulfide, the chief ore of mercury. It is bright red and occurs in veins and impregnations associated with volcanic rocks. Spain, the Soviet Union, Italy, and Mexico are the main producers.

cinnamon An evergreen tree, *Cinnamomum zeylanicum*, 23–35 ft (7–10 m) high, native to Sri Lanka and cultivated widely in the tropics. Before 1776 only wild plants were used, owing to the belief that cultivation would destroy its flavor. It is coppiced, the bark of the twigs being peeled off and rolled up to form the spice. Family: *Lauraceae*.

cinquefoil A shrub or herbaceous plant of the genus *Potentilla*, having leaves with five divisions each. Creeping cinquefoil (*P. reptans*) has been used medicinally, and shrubby cinquefoil (*P. fruticosa*) is often grown in gardens. Family: *Rosaceae*.

Cinque Ports An association of five English ports (Sandwich, Dover, Hythe, New Romney, Hastings) in Kent and Sussex formed during the 11th century to defend the Channel coast. After the Norman conquest they were granted considerable privileges in return for providing the nucleus of the navy. Winchelsea and Rye were added to their number and many other towns in the southeast became associate members. In the later middle ages their power declined both because of competition from other ports and the silting-up of their harbors. The Lord Warden of the Cinque Ports survives as an honorary office.

Ciompi, Revolt of the (1378) A rising of the poorer wage-earners of Florence against the oligarchic rule of the major guilds. The Ciompi (wool workers) seized power together with the minor guilds, but a split in this alliance allowed the major guilds to destroy the revolt and to abolish the Ciompi's newly formed guild.

Circassia An area in the Soviet Union, NW of the Great Caucasus. It is inhabited by the Circassian (*or* Cherkess) people, who, although Christian since the 6th century, adopted Islam under the influence of the Ottoman Empire in the 17th century and subsequently strongly resisted Russian rule until the Ottoman Turks ceded Circassia to Russia in 1829.

Circe Legendary Greek sorceress, who had the power to transform men into beasts. Odysseus, who visited her island of Aeaea on his voyage from Troy, was protected by the herb moly, and forced her to restore his men to human form.

circle A curve defined as the locus of all the points lying in a plane at a certain distance, called the radius, from a fixed point, called the center. Its diameter is any straight line joining two points on the circle and passing through the center. The ratio of the distance around any circle (the circumference) to its diameter is equal to the number π (*see* pi). The area of a circle, radius r, is πr^2.

circuit breaker A mechanism for breaking an electrical power circuit under load. Similar in function to a fuse, it has the advantage of being able to be reset immediately. It is used extensively in power stations and high-voltage distribution lines and now often replaces fuses in low-voltage circuits.

circulation of the blood The passage of blood through the ▢heart and the network of arteries and veins associated with it. By supplying the tissues with blood, the circulatory system effects the transport of oxygen, nutrients, etc., and the removal of waste products. Oxygen-rich blood is pumped out of the *heart into the aorta and then, via the arteries, to all the tissues of the body. Here oxygen is removed, and deoxygenated blood returns, through the veins, to the heart. This blood is then pumped to the lungs, where it is reoxygenated, and returned to the heart to repeat the circuit. The circulation of the blood was first discovered by William *Harvey in 1628.

circumcision The removal of all or part of the foreskin of the penis. In many primitive societies circumcision usually forms part of a ceremony initiating young men into adulthood. Among some Islamic peoples it is performed just before marriage; Jewish babies are circumcised in a religious ceremony when they are eight days old. Its origin is unknown but it has hygienic advantages, especially in hot climates, and cancer of the penis occurs infrequently among circumcised men. It is also carried out for medical reasons in certain circumstances. Female circumcision (the removal of the clitoris) is also practiced among some primitive peoples.

cire perdue (French: lost wax) A technique of metal casting used for small detailed castings, particularly statuary. A wax original model is encased in a mold. When molten metal is poured into the mold the wax melts and is replaced by metal. The process was already known in *Ur (c. 3000 BC) and was perfected in China about 500 BC.

cirque (*or* corrie) A rounded rock basin with steep sides, often containing a lake or cirque glacier. Common in glaciated mountain ranges, cirques form through freeze-thaw action on the headwall and basin floor together with abrasion by slipping ice and debris.

cirrhosis Destruction of the cells of the liver followed by their replacement with fibrous tissue, which eventually produces symptoms of liver failure (e.g. jaundice, swelling of the legs and abdomen, and vomiting of blood). Cirrhosis may be caused by *alcoholism, *hepatitis, obstruction of the bile duct, and heart failure, but in many cases the cause is not known. The treatment of cirrhosis is determined by the underlying condition.

Cirripedia. *See* barnacle.

cirrocumulus cloud (Cc) A high *cloud with a mottled appearance composed of ice crystals; it is sometimes known as "mackerel sky."

cirrostratus cloud (Cs) A high thin veil of *cloud composed of ice crystals, visible as a halo around the sun or moon.

cirrus cloud (Ci) A high detached *cloud occurring in the troposphere above 20,000 ft (6000 m), composed of ice crystals and appearing wispy and fibrous. It is usually associated with fair weather.

Ciscaucasia (*or* North Caucasia) A region in the SE Soviet Union. Mainly steppe, it rises in the S to the Great *Caucasus range. Its main product is oil.

Ciskei. *See* Bantu Homelands.

Cis-Sutlej states Sikh principalities in India, so called by the British because they were on the British side (Latin *cis*, on this side of) of the Sutlej River. They were first united in 1785 under the Maratha, whose rule was broken by the rise of *Ranjit Singh and British power in the subcontinent. The majority of the Cis-Sutlej states came under British government in 1809, the remainder passing to Ranjit Singh. They continued to exist until the attainment of Indian independence in 1947.

Cistercians An order of Roman Catholic monks founded by St Robert of Molesme (c. 1027–1111) as a stricter offshoot of the *Benedictine order. The mother house at Cîteaux, France, from whence the order took its name, was founded in 1098. St *Bernard of Clairvaux contributed considerably to the order's prestige, and communities were established throughout W Europe in the 12th century. In the 17th century the order underwent a reform resulting in two groups: the monks of the Strict Observance, as opposed to the Common Observance, are known as *Trappists.

Citlaltépetl (Spanish name: Volcan Citlaltépetl) 19 00N 97 18W A dormant volcano in S central Mexico, the highest point in the country. Height: 18,697 ft (5699 m).

citric acid An organic compound that occurs in plant and animal tissues and is involved in the series of metabolic reactions called the *Krebs cycle. A commercial preparation of citric acid is used as a flavoring agent in foods.

citron A *citrus tree, *Citrus medica*, 7–10 ft (2–3 m) high. Originally from the Far East, it was introduced into the Mediterranean region in about 300 BC; this remains the main center of commercial cultivation. The rough yellowish sour fruits are used to make candied peel, produced by soaking in brine and preserving in sugar.

citronella A *grass, *Cymbopogon nardus*, cultivated in tropical regions of Africa and Asia and introduced into tropical America. It forms dense tufts and contains geraniol or citronella oil, which is used in cosmetics and insect repellents.

Citrus The largest and most important genus of tropical and subtropical fruits (10 species), originating in SE Asia. All the species are small evergreen trees or shrubs with simple glossy leaves and five-petaled, usually white, flowers. The juicy fruits are rich in vitamin C, citric acid, and pectin (used in jam making). The most important are the *orange, *lemon, *lime, *grapefruit, *citron, and *tangerine, of which commercial varieties as well as various hybrids have been developed. All contain essential oils used in perfumery and soap making (the *bergamot is grown especially for this). Family: *Rutaceae*.

cittern An instrument of the guitar family with a pear-shaped body, a fretted fingerboard, a flat back, and four pairs of wire strings. Being small and easy to play, it was popular between the early 16th and mid 18th centuries.

city states Independent municipalities, each comprising a town and its surrounding countryside, characteristic of ancient Greece. There were several hundreds of city states, of which Athens was the largest. Each enjoyed autonomy, its own laws and constitution (democratic, as at Athens, or oligarchic, as at Sparta), and its own presiding deity. The geography of Greece encouraged life in small communities and the Greeks were so proud of their allegiance to the city state that Greek unity was somewhat precarious.

Ciudad Bolívar 8 06N 63 36W A port in E Venezuela, on the Orinoco River. Accessible to oceangoing vessels, its chief exports include gold, diamonds, and chicle. Population (1976 est): 130,000.

Ciudad Guayana (former name: Santo Tomé de Guayana) 8 22N 62 37W An industrial complex in E Venezuela, on the Orinoco River. Founded in 1961, it amalgamated several existing industrial centers into one; industries include iron and steel processing and gold mining. Population (1976 est): 180,000.

Ciudad Juárez 31 42N 106 29W A city in N Mexico, on the Rio Grande. Its importance is due to its location on the US border and as a marketing center for cotton. Its university was founded in 1973. Population (1978 est): 597,096.

Ciudad Real 38 59N 3 55W A city in S central Spain, in New Castile. It has a 13th-century gothic cathedral. An agricultural center, it produces flour and brandy. Population (1970): 41,708.

CIVET *A 2-month-old African civet cub.*

civet A solitary nocturnal mammal belonging to the family *Viverridae*. The African civet (*Viverra civetta*) is cat-like, about 50 in (1.2 m) long with coarse grayish spotted fur. Mainly carnivorous, civets also eat some fruit and roots. The secretion of their anal glands is used in the manufacture of perfumes as a fixative, making other scents last longer. *See also* palm civet.

Civil Aeronautics Board (CAB) A federal agency that promoted, developed, and regulated commercial air transportation to, from, and within the US. Established in 1940, as an outgrowth of the Civil Aeronautics Authority (1938), it consisted of five members appointed by the president. The agency was abolished at the end of 1984.

civil engineering The branch of *engineering that deals with the design and construction of buildings and public structures, such as roads, railroads, dams, canals, etc. The term was first used in 1750 by John Smeaton (1724–92) to distinguish himself from military engineers, although the practice of civil engineering went back to ancient times. It has diversified into numerous branches calling on specialized mathematical and scientific knowledge and developing such new materials as prestressed concrete.

Civilian Conservation Corps (CCC) (1933–42) US federal work camp program, part of the New Deal, that gave conservation work to unmarried unemployed men. Established during the *Depression, projects included tree planting, dam building, and forest maintenance.

civil law The body of law governing the rights of private individuals and their relationships with each other rather than with the state. It is also called private law, as distinguished from public law and *criminal law. The term is especially used of the European legal systems derived from *Roman law, which are different from *common law in important respects. For example, in civil law court decisions have no legal force in the decision of similar cases. Roman law was revived in Europe from the 11th and 12th centuries and formed the basis of the *Code Napoléon (1804), on which other European, Latin American, and some Asian states modeled their legal systems. English-speaking countries generally use common law, although the law of Scotland is more closely related to civil law.

civil rights The individual's rights to liberty, equality of treatment, education, etc., afforded to him under law and safeguarded by the state. In the US, the basic rights of all citizens are specifically protected by the first ten amendments to the Constitution, known as the *Bill of Rights. These include freedom of speech and religion, the right to bear arms, protection against unreasonable search and seizure by law enforcement authorities, the right to a jury trial, protection against self-incrimination, and protection against cruel and unusual punishment. These rights were developed from the English legal tradition of the *Magna Carta (1215) and of the English Bill of Rights (1689). In the US, the abolition of slavery in 1865 and the *Reconstruction programs after the end of the Civil War initiated a long struggle to ensure the civil rights of black Americans. In the 1950s and 1960s several important US Supreme Court decisions and the growth of the American *civil rights movement were instrumental in the establishment of legal protection for minority rights. On the international level, the United Nations proclaimed a Universal Declaration of Human Rights in 1948.

Civil Rights Acts (1957, 1960, 1964, 1968) US laws that guaranteed equal rights to blacks. The 1957 law established the Civil Rights Commission, while the law of 1960 assured protection of voting rights for blacks. The most important law, the Civil Rights Act of 1964, proscribed discrimination in public places and segregation in the schools and was followed in 1968 by a law that guaranteed fair and nondiscriminatory housing and real estate practices.

Civil Rights Cases (1883) A series of Supreme Court rulings that racial discrimination in private enterprise did not violate the 13th and 14th amendments. The decision voided the Civil Rights Act of 1875, which had outlawed discrimination in public places, and were not overturned until 1964 when the court ruled racial discrimination in the private sector unlawful in *Heart of Atlanta Motel* v. *US*.

civil rights movement In the US, the political and legal campaign for racial equality. Although the rights of black Americans were guaranteed by the 13th, 14th, and 15th Amendments to the US *Constitution, racial segregation in the public schools remained in effect in the South until the ruling of the US Supreme Court in the case of *Brown* v. *Board of Education* (1954). Soon after that decision, Dr Martin Luther *King, Jr, assumed the leadership of a movement to defend the rights of black Americans in every important aspect of public life. The first success of the civil rights movement came in Montgomery, Alabama, in the campaign to desegregate the city's buses (1955–56). During the following decade, the movement gained widespread public support, and its efforts led to the passage of wide-ranging federal laws against racial discrimination. One of the most important of these was the Civil Rights Act of 1964, which prohibited discrimination in housing, transportation, voting rights, and employment. Since that time, many federal programs have been established to provide funds to promote equal opportunity in education and business.

civil service The bureaucracy that implements government policy and provides governmental services. In the US, the civil service comprises government employees on the municipal, county, state, and federal levels who carry out the work of the various departments and agencies. During the 19th century, federal civil servants were customarily recruited by political patronage, but the establishment of the Civil Service Commission in 1883 introduced competitive examinations and a merit system as a means of hiring qualified candidates. In Great Britain, a Civil Service Commission was established in 1855 and was placed under the supervision of a special Civil Service Department in 1968. The secretariats of the various agencies of the UN are regarded as forming an international civil service.

Civil Service Commission (1883) US federal agency that regulates federal employment. Created to administer a merit system form of government employment, it is responsible for giving competitive exams, classifying jobs, and setting salaries, tenure, and benefits.

Civil War, English (1642–51) The war between Charles I and parliament, which led to the execution of the king (1649) and the establishment of Oliver Cromwell's *Protectorate (1653). The Civil War was the outcome of a conflict between king and parliament that had steadily worsened during the reigns of James I (1603–25) and Charles. The struggle for power culminated in the events of the *Long Parliament (summoned in 1640). War was precipitated by Charles' rejection of parliament's Nineteen Propositions in June, 1642. The first battle, at Edgehill, ended indecisively but during 1643 the royalists (*or* *Cavaliers) gained ground. The parliamentarian alliance (*see* Roundheads) with the Scots led to a victory at *Marston Moor (1644). The formation of the *New Model Army brought about the decisive defeat of Charles at *Naseby (1645). In 1646 Charles surrendered to the Scots at Newark and the first Civil War was brought to an end. He was handed over to parliament in January, 1647, but escaped to the Isle of Wight. The second Civil War ensued (1648), with royalist uprisings in Wales and Kent, ending with Cromwell's defeat of the Scots at Preston. In the following year, Charles was tried and executed and the *Commonwealth was established by the Rump Parliament. The Civil War

was concluded by Cromwell's subjection of Ireland (1649–50), his defeat of Charles' heir (later Charles II) at Dunbar (1650), and his victory against the Scots at Worcester in 1651. In 1653 he dismissed the Rump and established the *Protectorate, which governed England until preparations for the *Restoration of the monarchy were initiated in 1659.

Civil War, US (1861–65) The conflict between the US federal government and the 11 southern states that formed the *Confederate States of America. The war arose from an economic and political conflict of interest between the predominately agricultural slave-owning South and the industrialized North. The 1860 election of President Abraham *Lincoln, who was opposed to slavery, precipitated the secession of the southern states in the following year. In February 1861, the Confederate States of America was established, its new constitution was adopted, and Jefferson *Davis was elected its president. War broke out in April when the Confederates opened fire on Fort Sumter, South Carolina, which the federal government had refused to evacuate. The opening skirmishes of the war took place in Virginia and culminated in the unexpected Confederate victory at the first battle of *Bull Run in July. Early in 1862 the Confederate general Thomas "Stonewall" *Jackson conducted a brilliant campaign in Virginia's Shenandoah Valley, but in April, Union general Ulysses S. Grant won an important victory at the Battle of *Shiloh in Tennessee and in May the federal Army of the Potomac under George B. *McClellan captured Yorktown, Virginia, and defeated Robert E. *Lee's force in the Seven Days' Battles near Richmond in July. The Confederates counterattacked in August, pushing northward into Maryland. Although Lee's forces were defeated at *Antietam in September, he gained an important victory at *Fredericksburg at the end of the year. In 1863, following his victory at *Chancellorsville, Virginia, Lee began his second invasion of the North, only to be defeated at *Gettysburg in July. In the West, Grant's forces captured Vicksburg, Mississippi, after a long siege and despite defeat at *Chickamauga, won the battle of Chattanooga in November. In 1864, Grant was appointed commander-in-chief of Union forces and he advanced against Lee in the *Wilderness Campaign and began the siege of Peterburg, Virginia. General William *Sherman, who had succeeded Grant in command of Union forces in the West, captured Atlanta in September before making his historic March to the Sea. After taking Savannah in December, Sherman moved north through the Carolinas. In April 1865, he won a decisive victory at Five Forks, Virginia, the last major battle of the war. Lee surrendered to Grant at Appomattox Court House on April 9. By June, the federal victory was complete and the task of *Reconstruction lay ahead.

civitas Citizenship in ancient Rome acquired either by birth or by grant from the people or emperor. It was a much coveted privilege, entailing voting rights and facilitating an administrative or military career. As Rome expanded *civitas* was gradually extended to its Italian allies (89 BC) and to subjects of some Roman provinces (from 43 BC). In 212 AD all free inhabitants of the Empire were made citizens. An autonomous provincial city was also known as a *civitas*.

Civitavecchia 42 05N 11 47E A seaport in central Italy, in Lazio. It has Etruscan and Roman remains and a citadel designed by Michelangelo. There is a fishing industry. Population (1971): 48,460.

Clair, René (René Chomette; 1898–1981) French film director. Both his early silent comedies and his pioneering sound films, such as *Sous les toits de Paris* (1930), were distinguished by his gifts for humor and fantasy. During World War II he worked in Hollywood, and his later films included *Les Belles de nuit* (1952).

Clairvaux (Latin: *clara vallis*, beautiful valley) The *Cistercian monastery founded (1115) by St *Bernard of Clairvaux in the Aube Valley (NE France), which remained the most influential Cistercian house until its suppression (1790) during the French Revolution.

clairvoyance. *See* extrasensory perception.

clam A *bivalve mollusk with two equal shells and a muscular burrowing foot. Burrowing clams live buried in sand and mud, mainly in shallow coastal waters; they feed by taking in water through a tube (siphon) extended into the water. The largest burrowing clam is the geoduck (*Panopea generosa*), weighing up to 11 lb (5 kg), while the giant clam (*Tridacna gigas*) can exceed 550 lb (250 kg).

clan A group tracing actual or putative descent in either the male or female line from a common ancestor. Clans are frequently important divisions in primitive societies, as in the pre-18th-century Scottish Highlands. They are often exogamous (prohibiting marriage between members). Many have a totemic emblem taking the form of an animal or plant, from which members are believed to descend, and perform collective ceremonies.

The Scottish clans, until their suppression following the *Jacobite rebellions of 1715 and 1745, controlled distinctive territories and were frequently rivals. The members of a clan wore characteristic clothing (*see* Highland dress) and often bore the name of its founder preceded by Mac (son of), e.g. MacDonald. The clan chiefs are still officially recognized, both in Scotland and Ireland.

CLAM *The largest of the bivalve mollusks, the giant clam reaches 4 ft (1.2 m) across. This specimen is from the Great Barrier Reef.*

Clare (Irish name: Chláir) A county in the W Republic of Ireland, in Munster situated between Galway Bay and the Shannon estuary. It consists of a low-lying central plain rising E to mountains and W to the limestone area of the Burren. Agriculture is the chief occupation with cattle rearing and dairy farming. The salmon fisheries are important. Area: 1231 sq mi (3188 sq km). Population (1971): 75,008. County town: Ennis.

Clarendon, Constitutions of (1164) Regulations concerning the relations between church and state issued by Henry II of England. They aimed to limit the power of the church, especially of the ecclesiastical courts, and to bring the church more firmly under royal authority. Thomas *Becket, Archbishop of Canterbury, repudiated his allegiance to the Constitutions, which action eventually led to his murder.

Clarendon, Edward Hyde, 1st Earl of (1609–74) English statesman and historian. In the events that led up to the English *Civil War he tried to influence Charles I toward moderation. He went into exile in 1646, settling eventually with the future Charles II in France. At the Restoration (1660) he became Lord Chancellor. His daughter Anne married the future James II. He was criticized for the sale of Dunkirk to France (1662) and for his handling of the second *Dutch War (1664–67). Forced again into exile, he completed his monumental *History of the Rebellion and Civil Wars in England* (1702–04).

Clarendon Code (1661–65) A series of Acts, passed by Charles II's government, that were directed against *Nonconformists (*or* Dissenters). They included the Corporation Act (1661), which excluded Nonconformists from municipal office, and the Act of Uniformity (1662), which enforced the use of the Church of England's Book of Common Prayer. The Code is named for the king's first minister, the Earl of *Clarendon.

Clare of Assisi, St (1194–1253) Italian nun, founder of the "Poor Clares." Influenced by the teaching of St *Francis of Assisi, she gave up all her possessions and followed him. St Francis established a community of women with Clare as abbess in 1215. They lived in absolute poverty without even communal property. She was canonized in 1255. Feast day: Aug 12.

clarinet A woodwind instrument with a single reed and a cylindrical bore. It is a transposing instrument existing in several sizes and generally has a fundamental of A or B flat; it has a range of three and a half octaves. The clarinet did not become a regular member of the orchestra until the late 18th century. Mozart popularized it, using it in several symphonies and writing a concerto and quintet for the instrument. The **bass clarinet** is pitched an octave lower than the B flat clarinet. □musical instruments.

Clark, Champ (James Beauchamp C.; 1850–1921) US lawyer, politician, speaker of the House (1911–19). After attending schools in his native Kentucky and setting up a law practice in Missouri, he served in the US Congress (1893–95; 1897–1921). Democratic minority leader in 1907, he was elected speaker in 1911 after the Democrats became the majority. He ran unsuccessfully for the Democratic presidential nomination in 1912.

Clark, George Rogers (1752–1818) US pioneer, soldier, and surveyor. After doing survey work in the Ohio Valley, he served in the Virginia militia during the Revolutionary War and, participating in the Northwest Campaign, led successful attacks on key British-held posts in the Illinois country (now Illinois and Indiana).

Clark, Jim (James C.; 1937–68) British automobile race driver, who won a total of 25 Grand Prix races between 1959 and 1968, when he was killed in a crash. He was world champion in 1963 and 1965.

Clark, Joe (Charles Joseph C.; 1939–) Canadian politician; prime minister (1979–80). President of the Progressive Conservative Party Student Federation (1962–65), he served his party in the House of Commons (1972–76) and as leader of the Progressive Conservative Party. Elected prime minister in 1979 to succeed Pierre Trudeau, he held the position for nine months before his government fell to the Liberals.

Clark, Kenneth B(ancroft) (1914–) US psychologist, educator, and reformer; born in the Panama Canal Zone. After completing his education at Howard and Columbia universities, he taught psychology at City College of New York from 1942. His report on racial discrimination in the schools (1950) was used in the 1954 Supreme Court ruling on the unconstitutionality of public school segregation. His works include *Prejudice and Your Child* (1955), *Dark Ghetto* (1965), and *The Pathos of Power* (1974).

Clark, Kenneth (Mackenzie), Baron (1903–83) British art historian. As a young man, Clark worked with *Berenson in Florence. He was director of the National Gallery (1934–45), professor of fine art at Oxford (1946–50, 1961–62), and professor of art history at the Royal Academy, and the author of many works on individual artists and aspects of art. His television series *Civilization* greatly stimulated public appreciation of art.

Clark, Mark Wayne (1896–1984) US Army general. A West Point graduate (1917), he saw action in France during World War I and commanded US ground forces in Europe during World War II. He served under General Dwight D. *Eisenhower and led invasions of North Africa (1942) and Italy (1943). He commanded US troops in Austria (1945–47) and UN troops in Korea (1952–53). After retiring from the Army (1953), he became president of the Citadel (1954–66).

Clark, Ramsey (1927–) US lawyer and public official; son of Tom C. *Clark. During his term as US attorney general (1967–69) he supported civil rights and opposed capital punishment, police violence, wiretapping, and the Vietnam War. He ran unsuccessfully for the Senate (1974) as a Democrat from New York and, defying a travel ban, headed a delegation to Iran (1980) to argue for the release of the American hostages held there. He wrote *Search and Destroy* (1972).

Clark, Tom C(ampbell) (1899–1977) US lawyer, associate justice of the Supreme Court (1949–67). After practicing law in his native Dallas, Tex., he worked in the US Department of Justice (1937–45) until he was appointed US attorney general (1945–49) by President Truman. Appointed by Truman to the Supreme Court in 1949, he is most noted for his opinion that upheld desegregation of public facilities as stated in the Civil Rights Act of 1964. He retired from the court in 1967 when his son, Ramsey *Clark, was appointed US attorney general.

Clark, William (1770–1838) US explorer and politician; younger brother of George Rogers *Clark. He traveled and explored the Northwest Territory with Meriweather *Lewis in 1804–06. He and Lewis left St Louis, crossed the Rocky Mountains, traveled to the mouth of the Columbia River at the Pacific Ocean, and returned to St Louis, mapping and chronicling the entire journey. He served as head of Indian affairs for the Louisiana Territory (1807–13; 1821–38) and as governor of Missouri Territory (1813–21).

Clarkia A genus of herbaceous plants (36 species) found naturally in semiarid environments in California and Chile. Horticultural varieties are grown as summer annuals. About 12 in (30 cm) tall, they are slender, showy, and mostly pink-flowered. Family: *Onagraceae* (willowherb family).

classical art and architecture. *See* Greek art and architecture; Roman art and architecture.

classical literature. *See* Greek literature; Latin literature.

classicism The aesthetic qualities that were embodied in the visual arts and literature of ancient Greece and Rome and served as ideals for various later European and American artistic movements. Qualities associated with this concept include harmony and balance of form, clarity of expression, and emotional restraint.

The Italian *Renaissance of the 15th and 16th centuries was the first and most general attempt to revive these qualities in the arts. Major productions of this period included the sculpture of *Michelangelo, the paintings of *Raphael and *Titian, and the architecture of *Palladio. These achievements provided the artistic standards that other European artists attempted to emulate for the next two centuries. The art of the French 17th century painters *Poussin and *Claude Lorraine was greatly influenced by their study of Renaissance and classical models. Examples of the various neoclassical movements in the 18th century include the paintings of *David and *Ingres in France and the sculpture of *Canova in Italy, while in England the lectures of Sir Joshua *Reynolds at the Royal Academy were based on classical and Renaissance doctrines.

In literature, Renaissance interpretations of Aristotle's *Poetics* influenced writers throughout Europe in the 17th and 18th centuries, notably in the reigns of Louis XIV (1643–1715) in France and Anne (1702–14) in England. The tragic dramas of *Racine and *Corneille represent classicism in literature at its height.

Toward the end of the 18th century there was a general reaction against the rigid neoclassicist doctrines, but in England and the US, the popularity of the Greek Revival school of architecture continued the classical ideal in its use of columns, entablatures, and friezes.

clathrate A compound formed by the physical trapping of the molecules of one substance in the crystal lattice of another. No chemical bonds are formed between the host compound and the trapped molecule. Zeolites form clathrates with many simple compounds by virtue of their cagelike crystal structure. Ice can also form clathrate compounds with some of the *noble gases.

Claude Lorraine (Claude Gellée; 1600–82) French landscape painter. He was born in Lorraine but settled permanently in Rome (1626), where he had earlier received his training. His idealized paintings of the Roman countryside sometimes include small biblical or classical figures and his seascapes and harbor scenes are remarkable for their glowing sunlight. Both were highly esteemed by such patrons as Pope Urban VIII. His *Liber veritatis* (British Museum), dating from 1635, documents his career through drawings and notes and was intended to prevent later forgeries.

Claudian (c. 370–404 AD) Roman poet. Born in Alexandria, he went to Rome in 395. His praise for Stilicho, elected consul in 400, gained him high civil status. His works include panegyrics, satires, epigrams, and the epic poem *The Rape of Proserpine*.

Claudius I (10 BC–54 AD) Roman emperor (41–54). Claudius owed his accession to the chaos that followed the murder of his nephew Emperor *Caligula. His rule was generally efficient: he extended the Empire, taking part in the invasion of Britain (43), but his susceptibility to the influence of freed men and of his third wife Valeria *Messalina alienated the Senate. *Agrippina the Younger, his niece and fourth wife, was suspected of his murder. Claudius had been taught by Livy and he himself wrote histories.

Clausewitz, Karl von (1780–1831) Prussian general and military theorist. In 1812 Clausewitz negotiated the Treaty of Tauroggen, which set in motion the joint Prussian, Russian, and British war effort against Napoleon. In 1818 Clausewitz became director of the German War Academy. Of his many military works the posthumously published *Vom Kriege* is the most famous. Rejecting old ideas of strategy and systems of war in favor of total warfare backed by the will of the people, *Vom Kriege* became a military classic and had a profound influence up to World War I.

Clausius, Rudolf Julius Emanuel (1822–88) German physicist, who in 1854 formulated the concept of *entropy and used it in a statement of the second law of thermodynamics. He also contributed to the development of the *kinetic theory of gases and suggested that electrolysis involved the dissociation of molecules into charged particles.

clavichord A keyboard instrument, popular from the 15th to the 18th centuries and revived in the mid-20th century. Its delicate tone is produced by small brass plates (called tangents) fixed to the end of each key, which strike the strings. Its body consists of a rectangular wooden box, usually without legs, which is portable and able to be placed on a table. It is strung lengthways and has a range of about four octaves. It is said to have been J. S. Bach's favorite instrument.

clavicle The collar bone. There are two clavicles, each running from the upper end of the breastbone to form a joint with the shoulder blade. They brace the shoulders and help to support the arms. Fractures of the clavicle are fairly common, caused by any fall involving the upper arm. *See* Plate IV.

clawed frog A South African aquatic frog, *Xenopus laevis*, also called platanna. Up to 5 in (12 cm) long, with a flattened head and body, it has three short black claws on its hind feet, probably used for stirring up mud to confuse enemies. It is well known as the frog originally used in pregnancy tests.

clay A sedimentary deposit that has plastic properties when wet and hardens and cracks when dry. It consists of fine rock particles (less than 0.0002 in [0.004 mm] in diameter), formed from the decomposition of other rocks. The principal minerals present in clays (the clay minerals) are hydrous silicates, mainly of aluminum and magnesium, which occur as crystals with a layered structure, capable of absorbing and losing water. The main groups of clay minerals are kaolinite, montmorillonite-smectite, illite, and vermiculite.

Clay, Cassius. *See* Ali, Muhammad.

Clay, Henry (1777–1852) US politician; secretary of state (1825–29). A lawyer, he served in the US Senate (1806–07, 1810–11) before moving to the House (1811), where he was elected Speaker (1811–20, 1823–25). In the House he was a leader of the War Hawks, who advocated the expansionist *War of 1812 with Britain. In the election of 1821 he supported John Quincy Adams and then became his secretary of state. Later he returned to the Senate (1831–42; 1849–52). Called "The Great Compromiser," he is best known for his various efforts (e.g. the Missouri Compromise of 1820 and the Great Compromise of 1850) to hold the Union together on the issue of slavery.

clay-pigeon shooting. *See* shooting.

Clayton Anti-Trust Act (1914) US law that strengthened anti-trust regulations and increased the power of unions. Passed to strengthen the *Sherman Antitrust Act (1890), it specifically prohibited such practices as price fixing, stock and directorate interlocking, and competitive contract exclusion. It increased the powers of the unions in regard to picketing, striking, and restricting court injunctions in labor disputes.

Clayton-Bulwer Treaty (1850) A US-British treaty regarding a shipping canal between North and South America. It stated that if either country built a canal in the isthmus separating the two continents certain rules must be observed: the canal would be jointly owned and controlled; Central America would not be colonized or fortified further; the canal would be considered neutral. Forged by Britain's Sir Henry Bulwer and John Middleton Clayton, US secretary of state, the compromise was quite controversial and unpopular.

Cleanthes (c. 310–230 BC) Greek philosopher and follower of *Zeno of Citium. Cleanthes taught that reason is inherent in the nature of living things and virtue is voluntary assent to natural reason. *See also* Stoicism.

Clear and Present Danger A doctrine, indicated in the US Supreme Court case *Schenck* v. *United States* (1919) that stated that freedom of speech could be restricted to preserve national security.

clearing house Any institution that settles debts between members. For example, banks establish clearing houses to exchange, usually each business day, checks drawn against each other. This procedure reduces the payments made to, or received from, other banks to a single payment rather than one for each check processed. Commodity markets often use a clearing house to avoid passing checks between strings of brokers, dealers, etc., all debts being settled by difference accounts through the clearing house on an appointed account day.

Clearwater 27 58N 82 48W A city in W central Florida, N of St Petersburg, on Clearwater Bay. Clearwater Beach Island separates Clearwater Bay from the Gulf of Mexico and is connected to Clearwater by a causeway. Although its main industry is tourism, the processing of citrus fruits and the canning of fish are important activities. Population (1980): 85,528.

clearwing moth A moth of the widely distributed family *Sesiidae* (about 700 species), also called wasp moth. Many have clear wings and dark slender bodies with red or yellow markings, resembling bees and wasps. The larvae bore into roots and stems and are often serious pests.

cleavage The repeated division of a fertilized egg cell (zygote) to produce a ball of cells that forms the *blastula. In egg cells with little yolk, such as those of frogs and mammals, the entire cell divides: this is termed holoblastic cleavage. Meroblastic cleavage occurs in yolky egg cells, such as those of birds, when only the yolk-free region divides.

Cleaver, Eldridge (Leroy Eldridge C.; 1935–) US black activist and author. A convert to the Black Muslim religion, he served time in prison (1954–66) for various crimes; *Soul on Ice* (1968) is about his experiences. He was active in the Black Panther Party. In 1968, to avoid jailing for parole violation, he fled to Algeria and, subsequently, France and Cuba, and did not return to the US until 1975.

cleavers An annual herb, *Galium aparine*, also called goosegrass, native to Eurasia and widely introduced elsewhere. 6–48 in (15–120 cm) high, this pernicious weed is named because of its habit of clinging by means of tiny hooks on its stems and leaves. Its hooked fruits enable efficient seed dispersal via humans and animals. Family: *Rubiaceae* (madder family).

clef (French: key) The symbol placed at the beginning of a musical stave to indicate the pitch of the notes. The treble clef, a decorative G, indicates that the second line up of the stave is the G above middle C; the bass clef, an archaic F, indicates that the fourth line up is the F below middle C. The C clef can be set on any of the lines of the stave to establish it as middle C; the alto clef (used for viola music) has the C on the middle line; the tenor clef (used for cello music) has the C on the fourth line up.

cleft palate An abnormality caused by failure of the left and right halves of the palate to fuse during embryonic development. It leaves the nasal and oral cavities in continuity and it may be associated with a *harelip. The cleft can be repaired surgically at 16 to 18 months of age.

Cleisthenes (d. 508 BC) Athenian politician, regarded as the architect of Athenian democracy. Cleisthenes, a member of the *Alcmeonid family, achieved political power by appealing to the people for support and his democratic reforms (508) broadened the basis of political power in Athens. He is reputed to have introduced *ostracism.

Cleland, John (1709–89) English novelist. He served as consul in Turkey and as an agent for the East India Company, but was later several times imprisoned for debt. His best-known book is the pornographic novel *Fanny Hill* (1748–49).

Clematis A genus of herbaceous or woody plants (about 250 species), mainly climbing perennials, widely distributed in temperate regions. The fruits are often covered with persistent silky hairs, conspicuous and attractive in winter, as in traveler's joy, or old man's beard (*C. vitalba*) of Europe. There are many horticultural varieties, grown for their showy flowers, usually purple, pink, or white. Some species from which popular garden varieties have been developed are *C. alpina, C. montana,* and *C. patens.* Family: *Ranunculaceae. See* Plate VI.

Clemenceau, Georges (1841–1929) French statesman; prime minister (1906–09, 1917–20). A member of the chamber of deputies from 1876 to 1893, when he became known as the Tiger for his attacks on other politicians, he subsequently devoted much of his energies to polemical journalism. During his first premiership he strengthened ties with Britain and broke irrevocably with the socialists at home. During the prewar years he urged military preparation against Germany and then attacked the World War I government for defeatism until again becoming prime minister, when he led France to victory. He condemned the failure of the Treaty of Versailles to provide for French security.

Clement I, St (late 1st century AD) The fourth bishop of Rome. He was the supposed author of several patristic texts, including a letter to the church of Corinth and the *Apostolic Constitutions,* which suggest that he was highly esteemed by the Church as a mediator and legislator. He probably suffered martyrdom. Feast day: Nov 23.

Clement V (Bertrand de Got; 1264–1314) Pope (1305–14), first of the Avignon popes (*see* Avignon papacy). Clement was appointed by the influence of *Philip IV of France. Although he was a patron of learning, his pontificate was marked by venality, nepotism, and high taxation.

Clement VII (Giulio de' Medici; 1478–1534) Pope (1523–34). A cousin of *Leo X, as pope he attempted to follow a middle course between the conflicting policies of Emperor *Charles V and *Francis I of France. This affected his ability to deal effectively with *Henry VIII's divorce from Catherine of Aragon and explains his failure to curb Protestantism. Like other early Renaissance popes, he was a patron of the arts and learning.

Clement IX (Giulio Rospigliosi; 1600–69) Pope (1667–69). His pontificate was marked by disputes with Louis XIV concerning control of the French Church and Louis' harsh policy toward the Jansenists, whose persecution was stopped by the Peace of Clement IX (1669). Clement wrote both sacred and comic opera libretti besides sacred poetry and drama.

Clement XI (Giovanni Albani; 1649–1721) Pope (1700–21). Although austere and pious, he largely failed in the exercise of papal diplomacy, especially in the War of the *Spanish Succession, in the latter stages of which he reluctantly supported the Habsburg candidate. He also met with little success in attempts to defeat *Jansenism.

Clementi, Muzio (1752–1832) Italian pianist and composer. After settling in England in 1766, he became famous as a virtuoso, a composer of piano music, a teacher, a music publisher, and a piano manufacturer.

clementine A small *citrus tree bearing edible fruits, regarded by some as a hybrid between the tangerine and sweet orange; by others as a variety of tangerine. It is grown mainly in N Africa.

Clement of Alexandria (c. 150–c. 215 AD) Greek Christian theologian. He was probably born in Athens and is known to have studied Christianity at the school at Alexandria, of which he became head in 190. He was succeeded by his pupil *Origen after he had been forced to flee from Alex-

andria in 202 because of persecutions. Clement's writings are much influenced by *Gnosticism and his importance lies in bringing Greek philosophical ideas in to supplement Christian belief.

Cleon (c. 422 BC) Athenian politician and demagogue. An artisan by birth, Cleon opposed the moderate imperialism of the aristocrats in the Peloponnesian War. He persuaded the Athenians to execute the rebellious citizens of Mytilene (427) but the decision was eventually reversed. Cleon opposed peace with Sparta (425) and was killed fighting at Amphipolis.

CLEOPATRA *A relief at the temple of Horus at Edfu shows Cleopatra (second from the right) as the goddess of love.*

Cleopatra VII (69–30 BC) Queen of Egypt (51–48, 47–30), famous as the mistress of Julius Caesar and then of Mark Antony. Cleopatra was coruler with her brother Ptolemy XIII (61–48), who ousted her in 48. Restored by Caesar, she accompanied him to Rome and gave birth to (allegedly) his son Caesarion. After Caesar's murder, Cleopatra returned to Egypt and in 41 she met Antony. In 37 he abandoned his wife Octavia and lived with Cleopatra, who bore him three sons. In 31 Antony's brother-in-law Octavian defeated Antony and Cleopatra at *Actium and in 30 they both committed suicide. Shakespeare's reconstruction of their story follows Plutarch's romantic account.

Cleopatra's Needles A pair of ancient Egyptian *obelisks carved in the reign of Thutmose III (c. 1475 BC) at Heliopolis. They were moved by *Augustus Caesar to Alexandria in 12 BC. They were moved again in 1878, one being set up on the Victoria Embankment, London, the other in Central Park, New York.

Clermont-Ferrand 45 47N 3 05E A city in central France, the capital of the Puy-de-Dôme department. Founded by the Romans, it was the ancient capital of Auvergne in the 16th century. It has a fine gothic cathedral and its university was established in 1810. Clermont-Ferrand has France's largest rubber industry and manufactures textiles, chemicals, food products, and metal goods. Population (1975): 161,203.

Cleveland 41 30N 81 41W A city in the US, in Ohio on Lake Erie. It is a major Great Lakes port and the largest city in Ohio. One of the country's leading iron and steel centers, its other industries include oil refining, food processing, and the manufacture of motor vehicles. Population (1980): 573,822.

Cleveland, Stephen Grover (1837–1908) US statesman; 22nd and 24th President of the United States (1885–89, 1893–97). Trained as a lawyer, Cleveland served as mayor of Buffalo, N.Y. (1881–82) and as governor (1882–84) before receiving the Democratic nomination for president in 1884. After defeating Republican James G. *Blaine in the general election, Cleveland embarked on an ambitious program of civil service reform and tariff reduction. These policies provoked considerable opposition, and he was defeated ror re-election in 1888 by the Republican candidate Benjamin *Harrison. Nominated again by the Democratic Party in 1892, Cleveland returned to office and supported the repeal of the Sherman Silver Purchase Act, which had permitted the free coinage of silver and which was believed to be largely responsible for the economic crisis of 1893. In 1894 he authorized the use of federal troops to put an end to the *Pullman Strike. In foreign affairs, Cleveland was opposed to US intervention abroad and opposed the annexation of Hawaii. He also helped to mediate the boundary dispute between Great Britain and Venezuela in 1895. Although he hoped to run for re-election in 1896, Cleveland lost the Democratic nomination to William Jennings *Bryan.

Cleveland Bay A breed of horse developed in the Cleveland region of N Yorkshire, England, and always reddish brown (bay) with black mane, tail, and legs. It has a deep muscular body with relatively short legs and was used as a pack and coach horse. Today Clevelands are used mainly for crossing with Thoroughbreds to produce showjumpers. Height: 15½–16½ hands (1.57–1.68 m).

Clianthus A genus of shrubs (4 species) found in Australia, New Zealand, Indochina, and the Philippines. Several are cultivated for their attractive flowers. The glory pea (*C. formosis*) is an evergreen semiprocumbent shrub, 40 in (100 cm) high, with red and purple flowers. Family: *Leguminosae*.

Cliburn, Van (Harvey Lavan C., Jr.; 1934–   ) US pianist. He won the National Music Festival Award (1948) and from 1951 studied in New York City. In 1958 he became the first American to win the International Tchaikovsky Piano Competition in Moscow. He subsequently toured widely and made numerous recordings.

click beetle A long narrow flat beetle, also called skipjack beetle, belonging to a large and worldwide family (*Elateridae*; 8000 species). If upturned it is able to right itself by springing into the air, making a clicking sound in the process. The larvae, known as wireworms, are serious pests of root crops. Species of the genus *Pyrophorus* are luminous, resembling *firefly beetles.

cliffbrake A *fern of the genus *Pellaea* (about 80 species), found worldwide on rocks, mainly limestone. It has small elongated blue-green branched fronds, which overlap at the leaf margins to protect the spore capsules. Family: *Sinopteridaceae*.

climate The long-term weather conditions prevalent in an area. Climate is determined by three main factors. The first is latitude and the tilt of the earth's axis, which determines the amount of solar radiation received by an area. Second, the distribution of land and sea will affect climate as the land heats and cools far more rapidly than the sea. Ocean currents will also modify a region's climate. The third factor is the altitude and topography of an area; temperature will fall with increased altitude and hills and mountain barriers force clouds to rise and produce rainfall. Over long periods major changes in climate may occur, as in the *Ice Age. The study of the climate is called **climatology**.

climax In ecology, the final stage in the process of ecological *succession, in which a stable community of plants and animals becomes established. A typical climax community would be a deciduous woodland.

climbing perch A *labyrinth fish, *Anabas testudineus*, also called climbing or walking fish, that occurs in ponds and ditches of Asia. Its brownish-gray or greenish-gray body is about 10 in (25 cm) long. It can travel overland for short periods using its tail, pectoral fins, and gill covers and during the dry season it lies dormant in mud.

clingfish A *bony fish, also called sucker, belonging to the family *Gobiesocidae* (about 100 species), found mainly in salt water. Clingfish have an elongated scaleless body, up to 3 in (7.5 cm) long, a wide flattened head, and a suction disc formed from the pelvic fins with which it attaches itself to the bottom. Order: *Gobiesociformes*.

Clinton, De Witt (1769–1828) US statesman; governor of New York (1817–21, 1825–28). He became famous for his scheme to build the Erie Canal—"Clinton's Ditch," which was finished in 1825. It opened up the West by linking the Hudson River with the Great Lakes and made New York City the most important US port.

Clinton, George (1739–1812) US politician, soldier, governor of New York (1777–95; 1800–04) and US vice president (1805–12). He served in the French and Indian War, then studied law in his native New York, and eventually went to the Second Continental Congress, from which he was called back in 1776 to serve in the New York militia. As governor of New York, he opposed ratification of the US Constitution, fearing a loss of states' rights. He served as vice president under Thomas *Jefferson and James *Madison.

Clio In Greek legend, goddess of history and one of the nine *Muses. She loved Pierus, King of Macedonia, and bore him a son, Hyacinthus.

clipper ship A fast sailing vessel developed in the 19th century for international commerce, so called because it clipped short the time required for a given passage. Clipper ships were designed more for speed than for their cargo capacity, which was relatively limited.

clitellum An external glandular beltlike swelling around the bodies of earthworms and leeches. It secretes the cocoon that contains the fertilized eggs.

clitoris. *See* penis.

Clive of Plassey, Robert, Baron (1725–74) British soldier and colonial administrator, who established British supremacy in India. He joined the East India Company in 1743 and went to Madras, India. He captured and held Arcot (1751) against a French-Indian force for 53 days. In 1757 he recaptured Calcutta from the Nawab of Bengal, whom he then defeated at *Plassey. This victory assurred the East India Company control of Bengal, of which Clive was virtual ruler until 1760. He was appointed governor and commander in chief of Bengal (1764–67). He instituted many reforms but was subsequently named in an inquiry into the East India Company's affairs. He was vindicated (1773).

cloaca The posterior chamber of the body in all vertebrate animals except the placental mammals, into which the digestive, urinary, and genital tracts open. Feces, urine, and eggs or sperm are discharged through its vent.

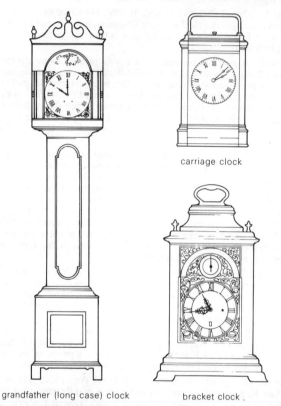

carriage clock

grandfather (long case) clock　　　　bracket clock

CLOCK *Three traditional forms of domestic clock.*

clock A mechanical device for measuring the passage of time. Clockwork has two essential components: an energy store (a raised weight or a coiled spring) and an escapement that regulates the release of energy from the store. The earliest recorded escapement was in a giant Chinese astronomical clock (c. 1090 AD). Early European clocks (caled turret clocks from their usual position in church towers) were crude ironwork with verge escapements, driven by falling weights and recording time by striking on the hour, but the 14th-century Italian family of Dondi introduced dials on their sophisticated astronomical mechanisms. Late medieval clocks, such as the one (1392) in Wells Cathedral, England, were often embellished with ingenious automata. The innovation of mainsprings about 1500 enabled portable clocks (*see also* watch) to be made. Refinements in the 17th century were the anchor escapement (1671) and the application of pendulums to clockwork (*see* Huygens). Both resulted in greatly increased accuracy and during the next 150 years clocks successfully challenged *sundials as the principal domestic timekeepers. Long-case (grandfather) and bracket clocks assumed their modern forms. Carriage clocks were introduced in 1810 by the French firm of Breguet. An important advance in the 18th century was the development of an accurate marine chronometer, used by navigators to determine position. Scientific advances in the 20th century have led to the development of clocks powered by the natural vibrations of atoms (*see* atomic clocks). The *cesium clock, first made in 1955, is so accurate that one specific line in the spectrum of cesium is now the stan-

229

dard by which time is defined (see second), replacing the period of the earth's rotation.

Clodion (Claude Michel; 1738–1814) French *rococo sculptor. Working in Rome (1762–71) and Paris, he enjoyed a wide reputation until the French Revolution, when the rococo style was superseded by *neoclassicism. Although he specialized in small terracotta sculptures of nymphs, satyrs, etc., he also produced more sober works, notably the lifesize marble sculpture of Montesquieu (1783; Versailles).

cloisonné (French: partitioned) A technique of decorating metal surfaces with polychrome *enamelwork. Thin metal strips are soldered edgewise to the surface following the outlines of the design and the resulting compartments filled with colored enamels. The work is then fired, fusion of the colors being prevented by the strips, and the surface ground smooth and polished. Beautiful cloisonné vases, brooches, etc., were produced in medieval Europe, while China and Japan perfected the technique in the 17th, 18th, and 19th centuries.

clone A population of organisms produced from a single parent cell by asexual division—for example by vegetative reproduction in plants or parthenogenesis in animals. The individuals of a clone are genetically identical. Thus cloning, if it could be achieved in humans, would provide the means of producing a whole generation of identical siblings—a concept that still remains in the realms of science fiction. However, some lower animals have been successfully cloned by inserting the nucleus of a somatic (body) cell of the animal to be cloned into an egg cell from which its own nucleus has been removed.

closed-end investment company A company that buys and sells *securities in order to make profits to distribute to its shareholders. The company has a fixed capital and its shares are bought and sold on the *stock exchange. Investors (shareholders) have the advantage of being part owners of a professionally managed portfolio of securities.

closed shop A place of work in which all employees are required to be members of one or more specified labor unions. Closed shops are usually sanctioned by the employer, whose *collective bargaining position may be made simpler if the union (or unions) can speak for the whole workforce. The disadvantage of closed shops is that they exclude from employment those who object to belonging to a labor union.

Clostridium A genus of rod-shaped spore-forming bacteria that occur widely in soil and the gastrointestinal tract of animals and man. Some produce powerful toxins (poisons), particularly *C. tetani*, which causes *tetanus, and *C. botulinum*, which causes *botulism.

clothes moth A small *tineid moth whose larvae feed on clothes, carpets, blankets, etc. There are a number of species of widespread distribution. Adults generally have a wingspan of 0.5–1.0 in (12–25 mm) and are pale gray-brown in color. They prefer dark places. Pesticides, dry cleaning, and man-made fibers have reduced their damaging effects.

Clotho. See Fates.

Clotilda. See Clovis.

cloud A mass of minute water droplets or ice crystals, or a combination of both, produced by the condensation of water vapor in the atmosphere. When conditions are favorable the droplets grow and precipitation may occur. Various classifications of clouds exist but the one internationally agreed upon and most extensively used by meteorologists is based on cloud appearance and height and comprises ten principal forms. The high clouds, normally above 16,000 ft (5000 m) are *cirrus (Ci), *cirrostratus (Cs), and *cirrocumulus (Cc). The medium clouds at 6500–16,000 ft (2000–5000 m) comprise *altocumulus (Ac) and *altostratus (As). Below this level the low clouds are *stratus (St), *stratocumulus (Sc), and *nimbostratus (Ns). Some clouds grow vertically and cannot be classified solely by height; these are chiefly *cumulus (Cu) and cumulonimbus (Cb).

cloud chamber A device, invented by C. T. R. *Wilson, that makes visible the tracks of ionizing particles; it is used for studying their properties. It contains a chamber filled with a saturated vapor. The vapor is expanded adiabatically (usually using a piston) to cool it and so make it supersaturated. When an ionizing particle passes through the chamber drops of liquid condense along its trail, thus making the trail visible.

clouded leopard A large nocturnal forest *cat, *Neofelis nebulosa*, of SE Asia, Borneo, Sumatra, and Java. It is 48–75 in (120–190 cm) long including its tail 24–35 in (60–90 cm) and has a grayish or yellowish coat with black markings. It is an expert climber, using its heavy tail for balance, and feeds on birds and small mammals. □mammal.

Clouet, Jean (c. 1485–1540) Portrait painter, probably of Flemish origin. He worked in France as court painter to Francis I. The influence of Italian *Renaissance portraiture was stronger in the court portraits of his son **François Clouet** (c. 1515–72), who succeeded to his father's post in about 1540. François introduced informal poses, as in his portrait of *Diane de Poitiers (Washington), which shows her in her bath.

clove An evergreen Indonesian tree, *Eugenia caryophyllata*, growing to a height of 40 ft (12 m). The dried flower buds are used as spice. The whole tree is aromatic, clove oil being distilled from the buds, stalks, and leaves for use in medicine and as artificial vanilla. Clove production was once a Dutch Indonesian monopoly but the trees are now grown in many regions, including Madagascar, Brazil, and Tanzania. Family: *Myrtaceae*.

clover An annual or perennial plant of the genus *Trifolium* (about 290 species), which also includes the *trefoils. Clovers, which occur mainly in N temperate regions, have leaves divided into three leaflets and dense heads of flowers. Extensively cultivated as fodder plants, they are also valuable for their nitrogen-fixing ability. *Alsike, red clover (*T. pratense*), and crimson clover (*T. incarnatum*) are three widely grown and naturalized species. Family: *Leguminosae*.

Clovis (c. 466–511) King of the Salian *Franks (481–511), of the Merovingian dynasty, who conquered N Gaul (494), founding a kingdom that dominated western Europe. He married (c. 493) Clotilda, (c. 475–c. 545), a fervent Christian, whose efforts to convert him succeeded after an important victory over the Alamanni (496), when he was baptized with some 3000 warriors. He was regarded as defender of the faith against *Arianism. After defeating the Visigoths near Poitiers (507), he established his capital at Paris. Clovis sponsored the promulgation of the *Salic Law.

Clovis point A fluted stone weapon point found in sites in many parts of North America after about 10,000 BC. They vary in length from 1 in (2.5 cm) to 7½ in (19 cm). *Compare* Folsom point.

clubfoot A deformity in which the foot is abnormally twisted at the ankle joint, so that the sole cannot rest flat on the ground when the person is standing. Its medical name is talipes. When the defect is present at birth it can often be corrected by strapping the foot in the correct position. Surgical correction may be necessary for severe deformities.

clubmoss A perennial mosslike plant, also called ground pine, belonging to a genus (*Lycopodium*; about 200 species) of *pteridophytes, found mainly in tropical and subtropical forests and mountainous regions. It has a creeping stem with wiry branches, densely covered with green, yellowish, or grayish needle-like leaves. The spore capsules occur at the base of special leaves (sporophylls), which are often arranged in conelike clusters (strobili). Family: *Lycopodiaceae*; class: *Lycopsida*. See also Selaginella.

clubroot A disease, caused by the fungus *Plasmodiophora brassicae*, that affects the roots of plants of the family *Cruciferae*, especially brassicas (cabbages, etc.). The infected cells become greatly enlarged, resulting in the deformed nodular roots characteristic of the disease. Control measures include liming, growing in clean soil, and using appropriate fungicides.

Cluj (German name: Klausenburg, Hungarian name: Koloszvár) 46 47N 23 37E A city in NW Romania, on the Someşul River. A former capital of Transylvania, it possesses several educational institutions, including a university (1872). A major industrial center, its manufactures include metal products, chemicals, and textiles. Population (1979 est): 274,095.

Cluny 46 25N 4 39E A town in E France, in the Saône-et-Loire department. Its famous Benedictine abbey (founded 910 AD) became the center of the Cluniac order, a reformed Benedictine order that was widely influential in Europe (c. 950–c. 1130). Population (1968): 3552.

clutch A device enabling two rotating shafts to be coupled and uncoupled. Positive clutches have square or spiral jaws to transmit torque without slipping. They can be used where slow speeds and light loads are involved, but normally both shafts have to be at rest for engagement. Friction clutches provide a period of slipping while the shafts are being engaged, and they do not have to be stopped for engagement. The torque is transmitted by friction between attachments to each shaft: in a plate clutch the attachments are flat disks, which press against each other; in a hydraulic clutch they are radial vanes immersed in a fluid. In a motor vehicle a clutch is used between the engine and the gearbox, usually a plate clutch for manual gearboxes and a hydraulic clutch for automatic transmissions.

Clutha River A river in New Zealand, the longest river in South Island. It flows generally S from Lake Wanaka, in the Southern Alps, to enter the Pacific Ocean near Kaitangata. Length: 210 mi (340 km).

Clyde, River A river in W Scotland. Rising in SE Strathclyde Region, it flows NW through Glasgow and the Clydebank to enter the Atlantic Ocean at the Firth of Clyde. It is important for its large shipbuilding industries. Length: 106 mi (170 km).

Clydebank 55 54N 4 24W A city in W central Scotland, in Strathclyde Region on the River Clyde. Shipbuilding and the manufacture of sewing machines are the main industries. Population (1981): 51,656.

Clydesdale A breed of horse developed in the Clydesdale region of Scotland in the 18th century. Used for draft purposes, it has a deep compact body with strong legs and feet and may be bay, brown, black, or chestnut. Height: about 17 hands (1.75 m).

Clytemnestra In Greek legend, the daughter of Tyndareus, King of Sparta, and Leda, and wife of *Agamemnon. She and her lover Aegisthus killed Agamemnon on his return from the Trojan War and she herself was killed by her son *Orestes.

Cnidos An ancient Greek city at the SW extremity of Asia Minor. Never politically important, Cnidos was known for its wine, *Praxiteles' statue of Aphrodite, and its medical school. The rebuilt city's rectangular street plan (c. 350 BC) is an outstanding example of Greek town planning.

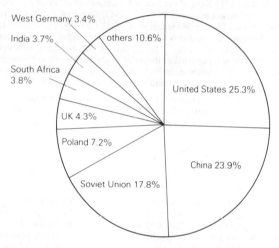

COAL *World production.*

coal A carbonaceous mineral deposit used as a fuel and raw material for the plastics and chemical industries. Coal results from the compaction and heating of partially decomposed fossil vegetable matter. During the coalification process the plant remains are changed progressively from a peatlike material into lignite (brown coal), sub-bituminous and bituminous coal, semianthracite, and anthracite. During this process the percentage of carbon present increases and the moisture and volatile content decreases; anthracite is about 90% carbon. These coals are known as the humic coals. The sapropelic coals (cannel coal and boghead coal) are derived from finely divided vegetable matter (algae, spores, and fungal material). Most coal was formed in the Carboniferous period, although some of the younger coals, for example lignite, date from Mesozoic and Tertiary times.

Coal has been mined since Roman times but on a small scale until the industrial revolution. In about 1800 coal was being carbonized on a commercial scale for the first time, the resulting *coal gas being used for gas lighting and the coke for smelting iron ore. By the middle of the 19th century, interest in the by-products (coal tar, ammonia, and pitch) was awakening. The chemistry of the constituents of coal tar developed into the study of organic chemistry, and the use of aromatic compounds from coal tar led to the development of the dyestuffs and explosives industries. In the 20th century these products also became the foundation of the plastics industry. During the 1920s and 1930s processes were also developed (mainly in Germany) for converting coal into oil—providing Germany with valuable quantities of oil during World War II. Subsequently, *natural gas has largely replaced coal gas and petrochemicals (*see* oil) have to a considerable extent replaced coal tar as sources of organic raw materials. However, the rising price of oil products in the 1970s, reflecting their diminishing reserves, has reawakened a worldwide interest in coal. Recent world consumption is slightly in excess of 3000 million tons per annum and known reserves are capable of supplying this quantity for several centuries.

coal gas A gas consisting mainly of hydrogen (50%) and methane (30%), with some carbon monoxide (8%) and other gases. It is made by destructive distillation of coal, a process that involves heating it to 587°F (1000°C). Coal gas was formerly supplied to homes for heating and cook-ing, but it has now been largely replaced, in the UK, by *natural gas from the North Sea.

Coal Measures. *See* Carboniferous period.

coal tit A Eurasian *tit, *Parus ater.* It is about 11 cm long with a gray back, buff underparts, a black crown and bib, and distinctive white cheeks and nape. It occurs in coniferous woodland, using its slender bill to extract insects from cones and beneath bark.

Coast and Geodetic Survey US agency of the Department of the Interior that measures the land and the earth's curvature and shape. It also conducts coastal area studies.

Coast Guard A naval force established by many nations to prevent maritime evasion of customs duties and to ensure the safety of navigation. The US Coast Guard was established in 1790 as a division of the Department of the Treasury. Originally called the Revenue Cutter Service, it received its current name in 1915. The Coast Guard now provides meteorological information to mariners, maintains navigational aids and lighthouses, and is responsible for customs, immigration, pollution control, and the enforcement of maritime law. In 1967 the Coast Guard was placed under the supervision of the Department of Transportation. In wartime or at the request of the president, however, it functions as a branch of the US Navy.

Coast Mountains A mountain range of W Canada, extending from the US border 1000 mi (1600 km) N into Alaska. Very rugged, it rises steeply from the Pacific coast. It includes Canada's largest mountain mass and a long glacier belt. Mount Waddington at 13,260 ft (3978 m) is the highest point.

Coatbridge 55 52N 4 01W A city in central Scotland, in Strathclyde Region. It has important metallurgical industries. Population (1981): 50,866.

Coates, Joseph Gordon (1878–1943) New Zealand statesman; Reform Party prime minister (1925–28). He is best known for his stringent policies while minister of finance (1931–35, when he devalued the New Zealand pound, lowered interest rates, and encouraged trade within the British Commonwealth.

coati A carnivorous mammal, belonging to the genus *Nasua* (3 species), related to the *raccoons and occurring in Central and South American forests. About 1 m long including a 50-cm tapering tail, coatis have long snouts and grayish, reddish, or brown fur; they are good climbers, foraging in groups in trees or on the forest floor for seeds, eggs, and small mammals.

cobalt (Co) A transition metal similar to iron and noted for its deep-blue color when reacted in ceramics. It was discovered by G. Brandt (1694–1768) in 1735 and occurs naturally as cobaltite (CoAsS) and in copper, nickel, iron, silver, and lead ores. Cobalt is mined chiefly in Zaïre and Canada. It is used as an alloy in the manufacture of cutting steels and magnets. The chloride ($CoCl_2$) and oxides (CoO and Co_3O_4) are used in the glass and ceramics industry. The isotope ^{60}Co is a strong gamma-emitter produced in nuclear reactors and used in radiotherapy (the **cobalt bomb**) and in industry. At no 27; at wt 58.9332; mp 2725°F (1495°C); bp 5203°F (2870°C).

Cobb, Ty (Tyrus Raymond C.; 1886–1961) US baseball player. Nicknamed the "Georgia Peach," he played the outfield for the Detroit Tigers (1905–26) and the Philadelphia Athletics (1927–28). With a lifetime hitting average of .367, a career total of 892 stolen bases, and a record 4191 hits, he set 90 records before retirement. He was a member of the first group elected to the Baseball Hall of Fame (1936).

Cobden, Richard (1804–65) British politician and economist, who was a leading advocate of free trade. A Manchester manufacturer, with John *Bright he formed the *Anti-Corn Law League (1839), which successfully fought for the repeal of the *Corn Laws (1846). A member of Parliament from 1843, he opposed Palmerston's "glory and gunpowder" foreign policy, negotiated an Anglo-French commercial treaty for the reduction of tariffs (1860), and campaigned for the 1867 Reform Act.

Coblenz. *See* Koblenz.

cob nut. *See* hazel.

COBOL (*common business oriented language*) An international computer-programming language, developed in the US and used to express problems in commerce. A high-level language, it can describe business procedures in the form of readable English statements that are sufficiently standardized for presentation to a computer. *See also* program.

cobra A highly venomous snake occurring in warm regions of Africa and Asia and able to expand its neck ribs to form a hood. The king cobra (*Ophiophagus hannah*) of S Asia is over 12 ft (3.6 m) long, making it the largest venomous snake; it preys chiefly on other snakes. The common Indian cobra (*Naja naja*), used by snake charmers, is 6 ft (1.7 m) long and frequently enters houses at night in search of rats. The spitting cobra, or ringhals (*Hemachatus hemachatus*) and the black-necked cobra (*Naja nigricollis*), spit their venom into the eyes of attackers, causing blindness. Family: *Elapidae* (cobras, mambas, coral snakes). □reptile.

coca A Peruvian tree, *Erythroxylon coca*, cultivated in Java, South America, and Sri Lanka for its leaves, which—when dried—yield cocaine. Coca leaves have been chewed for centuries in South America for their effect in relieving fatigue and hunger; prolonged use can cause addiction and serious mental and physical deterioration. Family: *Erythroxylaceae*.

cocaine An alkaloid ($C_{17}H_{21}O_4N$) powder or solution derived from *coca leaves and also made synthetically. Cocaine was the first drug to be used for local anesthesia, but it has now largely been replaced for clinical use by safer, non-addictive drugs such as novocaine. Because cocaine is habit-forming and often causes dangerous side-effects, its non-medical use is strictly prohibited by law in most countries. *See* anesthesia; drug dependence.

coccus Any spherical bacterium. Cocci may occur singly, in clusters, or in chains. Examples are *Neisseria gonorrheae* (the gonococcus, which causes gonorrhea), *Staphylococcus, and *Streptococcus.

coccyx. *See* spine.

Cochabamba 17 26S 66 10W A city in Bolivia, situated in the E Andes. It is an important agricultural trading especially for grain (center). Industries include oil refining and it is the site of a university (1832). Population (1976): 194,156.

Cochin 9 56N 76 15E A major port in India, in Kerala on the Malabar Coast. Founded by the Portuguese in the 16th century, it achieved its greatest prosperity under Dutch rule (1663–1795). It is the Indian Navy's major training center. Population (1971): 439,066.

Cochin China A region in S Vietnam, long ruled from Saigon (now Ho Chi Minh City). It was divided for centuries before being annexed by *Annam in the 18th century. Following the dissolution of the Vietnamese empire it was a French colony (1867–1945) and then an overseas territory before becoming part of independent Vietnam (1949).

cochineal A natural red dye obtained from the dried bodies of certain female scale insects, especially *Dactylopius coccus* of Mexico. It has now been largely replaced by aniline dyes, but continues to be used for coloring foodstuffs and cosmetics.

Cochise (d. 1874) Apache Indian chief, who terrorized the SW US during the 1860s trying to prevent white settlement on his homeland. His band surrendered in 1871. His people were given a reservation on their own land. After his death there, his people were ordered to a more distant area.

cochlea. *See* ear.

Cockaigne An imaginary land of wealth and luxury, celebrated in medieval folklore. There are houses of barley sugar, roast pigs running in the streets with knives and forks in their backs, and a mountain of cheese. It features in some of the fairytales of the brothers Grimm.

cockatiel A small Australian *cockatoo, *Nymphicus hollandicus*, of interior grasslands. It is 13 in (32 cm) long and has a gray plumage with white wing patches, a yellow head and crest, and reddish ear patches.

cockatoo A *parrot belonging to a genus (*Cacatua*; 17 species) ranging throughout Australia, Malaysia, and the Philippines. Cockatoos are usually white, often with a pink or yellow blush, although some species are black; all have a long erectile crest and a large hooked bill used to crack open nuts and extract grubs from wood.

cockchafer A European beetle, *Melolontha melolontha*, also called maybug, that is very destructive to plants (*see* chafer). Up to 1.4 in (35 mm) long, it is black with reddish-brown legs and wing cases and has a loud buzzing flight. The larvae—which cause the most damage, particularly to cereals and grasses—are also called white grubs or rookworms.

Cockcroft, Sir John Douglas (1897–1967) British physicist, who shared the 1951 Nobel Prize with Ernest *Walton for their development of the first particle *accelerator. Their machine, built in 1932, was used for accelerating protons to split an atomic nucleus (of lithium) for the first time. In World War II he worked on the development of the atom bomb.

cocker spaniel A breed of gundog, thought to be of Spanish origin. It is compact with short legs, a short tail, and a square muzzle. The long flat silky coat is usually black, red, or cream, either plain or in mottled combinations. Height: 15–16 in (39–41 cm) (dogs); 15 in (38 cm) (bitches). □dog.

cockfighting A blood sport in which two or more gamecocks fight against each other, often to the death. Although illegal in some countries, it is still practiced in certain parts of the world. The cocks are carefully bred and trained, equipped with steel or bone spurs on their legs and set against each other in a cockpit. Being naturally fearless and very aggressive the cocks peck and gouge each other with intense fury. Heavy betting is a feature of the sport.

cockle A *bivalve mollusk of the widely distributed family *Cardiidae* (about 250 species). The ribbed shell valves, 0.4–9.2 in (1–23 cm) in diameter, are rounded, producing a relatively globular bivalve. Cockles burrow in sand or mud, straining food particles from water drawn in through their protruding siphons. The European cockle (*Cardium* (or *Cerastoderma*) *edule*) is edible.

cocklebur An annual plant, *Xanthium strumarium*, 8–30 in (20–75 cm) high, the fruiting heads of which are densely covered with hooked spines, which catch onto fur and clothing. It has been so widely and unintentionally dispersed by man and animals in warm and temperate regions that its place of origin is uncertain. Family: *Compositae.

cockroach A nocturnal □insect belonging to the mainly tropical family *Blattidae* (3500 species). It has a black or brown flat body, 0.5–2.0 in (12–50 mm) long, with long antenne and leathery forewings. Cockroaches seldom fly; they feed on plant and animal materials and are household pests in dirty places. A widely distributed species is the common cockroach, or black beetle (*Blatta orientalis*). Order: *Dictyoptera*.

cocksfoot A perennial *grass, *Dactylis glomerata*, also known as orchard grass, cultivated throughout North America, Eurasia, and Africa as a pasture grass. It grows in dense tussocks, up to 40 in (1 m) tall.

cocoa and chocolate Foods derived from the seeds of the cacao □tree (*Theobroma cacao*), native to tropical South America and cultivated mainly in West Africa. The tree is pruned to a height of 16–20 ft (5–6 m) and woody pods, 10–12 in (23–30 cm) long, grow directly from its trunk. The pods contain 25–50 seeds (cocoa, or cacao, beans) embedded in a whitish pulp, which are scraped out, fermented, and dried before export. Manufacturing is carried out mainly in the importing countries, where the beans are shelled, roasted, and ground. From them cocoa powder and chocolate are made. Cocoa butter, a fat retained in chocolate but removed from cocoa powder, is a rich source of food energy. Molded chocolate is run into molds, which sometimes contain dried fruit, nuts, etc., to make blocks and bars of chocolate. Couverture (or confectionery) chocolate is used for covering cookies, dried fruit, or fruit fillings, etc. Family: *Sterculiaceae*.

cocodemer A *palm tree, *Lodoicea maldivica*, also known as double coconut, native to the Seychelles Islands. It grows 98 ft (30 m) tall and bears fleshy male and female flower spikes on separate plants. The female flowers produce the largest known fruit, up to 20 lb (9 kg) in weight, which takes ten years to ripen. It consists of a fleshy fibrous envelope surrounding a hard two-lobed nutlike portion, containing edible flesh.

coconut The fruit of the coconut *palm, *Cocos nucifera*; one of the most important tropical crops. The tree has a slender trunk, up to 80 ft (25 m) high, which bears a crown of giant feather-like leaves. The coconuts, 12–18 in (30–45 cm) long and 6–8 in (15–20 cm) in diameter, take a year to ripen and have a thick fibrous husk surrounding a single-seeded nut. The hollow core contains coconut milk; the white kernel is eaten raw or dried to yield copra, from which coconut oil is extracted for use in soaps, synthetic rubbers, and edible oils. The residual coconut cake is used as a livestock feed and the coarse husk fiber (coir) is used for matting, etc.

coconut crab. *See* robber crab.

Cocos Islands (or Keeling Islands) Two Australian coral atolls in the E Indian Ocean. They were visited by Charles Darwin (1836). First settled in 1826, they were controlled by the family of a Scottish settler, John Clunies-Ross, from 1827 to 1972, although under Australian administration after 1955. Copra is produced and there is an important meteorological station. Area: 5 sq mi (13 sq km). Population (1980): 487.

Cocteau, Jean (1889–1963) Immensely versatile French poet and artist. He made his name with the novel *Les Enfants terribles* (1929) and sketches written for *Diaghilev's ballet company, such as *Parade* (1917). In World War I he served as an ambulance driver and became acquainted with *Picasso, *Modigliani, *Apollinaire, and other leading painters and writers. In 1923 he was treated for opium addiction. His creative work includes poetry (*L'Ange Heurtebise*, 1925), plays (*Orphée*, 1926), novels, films (*Le Sang d'un poète*, 1929, and his own *Les Enfants terribles*, 1950), and graphic work in various media.

cod A carnivorous fish, *Gadus morhua*, that lives near the bottom in temperate N Atlantic waters and is commercially fished for food and liver oil (*see* Cod Wars). Its elongated body, up to 6 ft (1.8 m) long, is generally dark gray with spots and has three dorsal fins, two anal fins, and a whisker-like barbel on its lower jaw. *G. macrocephalus* is a similar N Pacific species. Family: *Gadidae* (haddock, ling, pollack, whiting, etc.); order: *Gadiformes*.

JEAN COCTEAU *With Sergei Diaghilev (right), about 1924. Cocteau's memoirs are one of the best sources of information on Diaghilev's circle and the Ballets Russes.*

codeine An *analgesic drug used to relieve mild pain. It is a derivative of morphine but less toxic and less likely to become addictive. The combination of aspirin and codeine is a stronger pain killer than either of the two drugs used separately. Codeine combined with a chalky substance, such as kaolin, is an effective treatment for diarrhea. It depresses the cough center of the brain and is therefore often added to cough mixtures.

Code Napoléon The systematic collection of the *civil law of France. Drafted by a commission set up by *Napoleon I when he was first consul, the code—properly called the *Code Civil*—was brought into force in 1804. Representing the progressive legal thought of the time, it set out to be as clear and easily accessible as possible. It and the other codes subsequently produced under Napoleon's administration remain the basis of present French law and served as a model for civil law codes throughout Europe and the rest of the world.

codling moth A small European moth, *Cydia pomonella* (wingspan about 0.71 in [18 mm]), whose caterpillars eat apples and similar fruit. A serious economic pest, it has spread worldwide wherever apples are cultivated.

cod-liver oil A pale yellow fatty oil obtained from the liver of the cod. It is a rich source of vitamins A and D and is used in medicine to correct the effects of such diseases as rickets.

Cody, William F(rederick) (1846–1917) US showman, known as Buffalo Bill. An army scout and pony express rider, he gained his nickname from his success in supplying the men working on the Union (later Kansas) Pacific Railroad with buffalo—killing 4280 in 1867–68. In 1883 he began touring the US and Europe with his Wild West Show.

Coe, Sebastian (1956–) British middle-distance runner. He was a world record holder in the 800 m, the 1500 m, and the mile.

coeducation The education of both sexes together. Although support for the idea dates back to Plato, it has only recently been practiced to any extent. Coeducation could be found in some US elementary schools in the 17th century but it did not become widespread at all levels until the 20th century. Coeducation is also the norm in Scandinavia and in communist countries, and following World War II all Japanese schools became in

principle coeducational. National attitudes still vary enormously, however, and many Muslim and Roman Catholic countries still favor the separate education of the sexes, especially during adolescence.

coelacanth A *bony fish of the suborder *Coelacanthini*. Once thought to have been extinct for 60 million years, several living representatives have been found since the discovery, in 1938, of *Latimeria chalumne* off the coast of SE Africa. It has a heavy body, up to 5 ft (1.5 m) long, with a short head and limblike fins, and crawls on the bottom, feeding on other fish. Order: *Crossopterygii*.

coelenterate An aquatic invertebrate animal belonging to the phylum *Coelenterata* (or *Cnidaria*; about 9000 species), including *Hydra, *jellyfish, *sea anemones, *corals, etc. There are two different generations of the life cycle (*see* polyp; medusa) and either or both may occur. Coelenterates have a body cavity with a single opening (mouth) and stinging cells (nematocysts) used for defense or catching prey.

coelom The body cavity of many animals. In mammals (including man) the embryonic coelom is divided into three cavities, which become occupied by the lung, heart, and intestines. In the fully developed mammal the coelom is reduced to the virtually nonexistent spaces between the membranes lining the heart (the pericardium), the lungs (the pleura), and the intestines (the peritoneum). Jan

Coen, Pieterszoon (1587–1629) Dutch colonial administrator; governor general of the Dutch East Indies (1618–23, 1627–29). He first visited the East Indies in 1607, in the employ of the Dutch East India Company, which in 1614 appointed him to direct the Company's commerce in Asia. He was responsible for the conquest of the Banda Islands and for the first Dutch settlement in Formosa (now Taiwan).

coenzyme A nonprotein substance that forms a complex with certain enzymes and is essential for the proper functioning of these enzymes. Coenzymes include nucleotide derivatives, such as *ATP and NAD, coenzyme A (important in the *Krebs cycle), and *vitamins of the B complex.

Coeur, Jacques (c. 1395–1456) French merchant, who became *argentier* (court banker) to Charles VII of France around 1440. He helped to finance Charles' recapture of Normandy from the English (1450) but, disliked and envied for his wealth and power, he was arrested (1451) on a false charge. He escaped from prison and fled to Rome.

coffee The seeds (called beans) of certain tropical evergreen trees of the genus *Coffea*, which—when roasted, ground, and brewed in hot water—yield a stimulating drink. *C. arabica* is the most widely grown coffee tree, producing the best quality beans. It is pruned to a height of 10–16 ft (3–5 m) for easy harvesting. *C. canephora* is more disease resistant, longer living, and can be grown at lower altitudes. *C. liberica*, of still lower quality, is grown in Malaysia and Guyana. The coffee beans are usually fermented, then sun dried before export. The main coffee-producing areas are South and Central America, Jamaica, East Africa, and Mysore in India. Family: *Rubiaceae*.

cofferdam A temporary walled structure to hold back water or earth while excavation or construction work is carried out. Thus they may be used to protect workers during the construction of a permanent *dam or *bridge piers across a river. They are made by driving sheets of sectional steel vertically into the ground and bolting or welding the sheets together. Occasionally concrete is used.

Cognac 45 42N 0 19W A city in W France, in the Charente department. Under French law, the name Cognac may only be applied to brandy produced in a certain area around Cognac. Associated manufactures include bottles, corks, and barrels. Population (1975): 22,612.

Cohan, George M(ichael) (1878–1942) US dramatist, songwriter, and entertainer. A native of Rhode Island, he was part of his family's vaudeville act as a child. He wrote the musicals *The Governor's Son* (1901), *Little Johnny Jones* (1904), *Forty Five Minutes from Broadway* (1905), *George Washington, Jr.* (1906), and *The Song and Dance Man* (1923). Popular songs written by him include "Give My Regards to Broadway," "I'm a Yankee Doodle Dandy," "Over There" (for which he received a congressional medal in 1940), "You're a Grand Old Flag," and "Mary's a Grand Old Name." He wrote nonmusical plays, such as *Broadway Jones* (1913) and *The Tavern* (1920) and acted in *The Phantom President* (1932) and *Ah, Wilderness!* (1933).

coherent radiation Electromagnetic radiation in which different waves have a constant *phase difference. Light from most sources is not coherent because it is emitted in random bursts. However, light from a *laser is coherent.

Cohn, Ferdinand Julius (1839–1884) German botanist, considered to be one of the founders of modern bacteriology. Following his early studies of algae and fungi, Cohn became interested in the identification of bacteria and established the basic elements of modern classifications. He also encouraged *Koch to publish his findings on anthrax.

Coimbatore 11 00N 76 57E A city in India, in Tamil Nadu. It is an agricultural processing center for hides, cotton, and oilseeds and has an expanding manufacturing sector. Population (1971): 356,368.

Coimbra 40 12N 8 25W A city in central Portugal. It was formerly the capital of Portugal (1139–1260). It has two cathedrals and Portugal's oldest university, founded in Lisbon (1290) and transferred in 1537. Industries include the production of beer, wine, and pottery. Population (1970): 108,046.

coke A fuel consisting mainly of carbon. It is made by heating coal in the absence of air and is produced as a by-product of *coal gas. Coke is used in *blast furnaces and other industrial processes as well as for domestic heating.

Coke, Sir Edward (1552–1634) English lawyer and politician. Initially a staunch supporter of the crown, Coke became speaker of the House of Commons in 1593 and attorney general in 1594. Under James I he was appointed chief justice (1613) but was dismissed in 1616 because of his defense of the common law against the royal prerogative. Reviving his political career in 1620, he became a leading spokesman for the protection of parliament's liberties and was largely responsible for the Petition of Right.

cola. See kola.

Cola A dynasty that ruled S India from the 10th to the 14th centuries. The empire of the Cola kings centered on Kanci and Tanjore and was marked by cultural and artistic distinction and social stability. In the early 11th century Cola power spread to Ceylon and Indonesia.

Colbert, Claudette (Lily Claudette Chauchoin; 1905–) US film actress, born in France. She is best known for her performances in Hollywood light comedies during the 1930s and 1940s. These include *Three-Cornered Moon* (1933), *It Happened One Night* (1934), and *Midnight* (1939).

Colbert, Jean-Baptiste (1619–83) French statesman; an outstanding financial reformer. Rising to power through the influence of Cardinal Mazarin, Colbert became comptroller general of finance in 1665 and strove to make France under *Louis XIV the dominant power in Europe. An advocate of *mercantilism, he reformed taxation, tariffs, and financial administration, built roads and canals, and largely created a French navy. He was a lavish patron of the arts and sciences but his cold personality won him the nickname *le Nord* ("the North").

Colchester 51 54N 0 54E A market city in SE England, in Essex on the Colne River. Founded by Cymbeline (Cunobelinus) in about 10 AD, Colchester was an important Roman town (Camulodunum); the Roman walls remain in part and there is a Norman castle. Essex University (1961) is nearby. Colchester's industries include engineering and printing. Population (1981 est): 81,945.

colchicine. See autumn crocus.

cold (or common cold) A mild but widespread viral disease affecting the mucous membranes of the nose and throat. Symptoms include a sore throat, running nose, sneezing, headache, a slight fever, and general aches and pains. The disease, which is transmitted by coughing and sneezing, usually lasts about a week: rest and mild *analgesics such as aspirin provide the only treatment required.

cold-bloodedness. See poikilothermy.

Colden, Cadwallader (1688–1776) US scientist, writer, and politician; born in Scotland. He studied medicine there before coming to America in 1710. He wrote *History of the Five Indian Nations of Canada* (1727) and classified American plants according to the Linnaean System. The plant genus *Coldenia* is named for him. He served as lieutenant-governor of New York from 1761 until the Declaration of Independence in 1776 and was unpopular among the colonists for his support of the British-imposed Stamp Act of 1765.

Cold Harbor, Battles of Two battles in the *Civil War fought near Richmond, Va., the Confederate capital. In the first (June 27, 1862) the Confederate general, Robert E. *Lee defeated the Federal forces under George B. *McClellan, both sides suffering heavy losses. In the second (June 3–12, 1864), the Federal advance on Richmond under Ulysses S. *Grant was temporarily halted when he encountered Lee's entrenched forces. Despite his losses (7000 of his 100,000 men), Grant resumed his advance.

Colditz 51 08N 12 49E A town in East Germany, on the Mulde River. It is famous for its castle, built by *Augustus II on a cliff above the town,

which was used as a top-security prisoner-of-war camp during World War II. Many escapes were attempted, some of which were successful.

cold storage A method of storing food or other perishables, such as photographic film, at a low temperature to prevent deterioration. *Refrigeration is used on a domestic scale in *freezing and also on an industrial scale in refrigerated warehouses, trucks, railroad wagons, and ships' holds.

Cold War The hostility between the US and the Soviet Union, and their respective allies, following World War II. The term was first used in 1947 by the US politician Bernard *Baruch. Fear of nuclear war prevented a military confrontation, and the Cold War was fought on economic, political, and ideological fronts. At its most virulent in the 1950s, it had given way by the 1970s to the movement toward detente.

Cole, Thomas (1801–48) US landscape artist, founder of the *Hudson River School of painting; born in England. He emigrated to the US in 1818. He frequently traveled the Hudson River Valley, sketching the landscape that he later incorporated in oil paintings. He traveled to Europe twice (1829–32; 1841–42), staying mainly in Italy; after the first trip he painted "The Course of Empire" (1836) and "The Voyage of Life" (1839–40). In his paintings he showed the overwhelming force of nature in intimate detail.

Coleoptera. See beetle.

Coleridge, Samuel Taylor (1772–1834) British poet and critic. In 1795 he met William *Wordsworth and their joint publication of *Lyrical Ballads* (first edition 1798) marked a decisive break with 18th-century poetry. His finest poems, such as *Kubla Khan* (1797) and *The Rime of the Ancient Mariner* (1797–98), were written at this time, but his personal life was troubled by his unhappy marriage, his poverty, and his increasing opium addiction. His subsequent creative energies were committed to journalism, lectures, and the writing of the critical and metaphysical *Biographia Literaria* (1817).

Colette (Sidonie-Gabrielle C.; 1873–1954) French novelist. After her divorce from her first husband, who had published her early novels (the *Claudine* series) under his own name, she became a music-hall performer in Paris. With *Chéri* (1920) and *La Fin de Chéri* (1926) she became an established writer, celebrated especially for her treatments of childhood and of the natural world, especially animals. Her long writing career was crowned with many official honors and award.

Coleus A genus of herbaceous or shrubby plants (150 species) originating in the Old World tropics. Many cultivated varieties of the species *C. blumei* are grown for their variegated leaves of a diversity of colors, including red, purple, yellow, and green. They can easily be grown from cuttings at almost any time of year if kept at a temperature of 41°F (16°C). Family: *Labiatae*.

Colfax, Schuyler (1823–85) US politician; vice president (1869–73). He served in the US House of Representatives as a Republican from Indiana from 1855 until 1869, six of those years (1863–69) as speaker of the House. During his term as Grant's vice president, he was implicated in the Crédit Mobilier of America scandal (1872) in which several Congressmen had taken bribes.

colic A severe fluctuating abdominal pain, usually due to contraction of the wall of the intestines and caused by such conditions as constipation or obstruction. Colic in babies is quite common and usually due to air in the intestines.

Coligny, Gaspard II de, Seigneur de Châtillon (1519–72) French *Huguenot leader. He became an admiral of France in 1552 and was converted to Protestantism seven years later. He was chief commander of the Huguenots during the second and third *Wars of Religion but Catherine de' Medici, the mother of Charles IX, determined to end his influence over her son, arranged Coligny's murder in the *Saint Bartholomew's Day Massacre.

colitis Inflammation of the large intestine (the colon), causing abdominal pain and diarrhea (sometimes with the passage of blood). Colitis can be caused by bacterial infection (e.g. dysentery) or by *Crohn's disease. In ulcerative colitis the colon becomes ulcerated. The latter condition, which fluctuates in severity, is treated with corticosteroids or sulfasalazine (a sulfonamide drug). Surgery may be required for severe cases.

collage A picture composed of a variety of glued-on scraps of materials, such as newspaper, wallpaper, cloth, string, wood veneer, etc. The first collage was made by *Picasso in 1912 with a piece of oilcloth. It was later followed by the collages of the *dada painters *Arp, *Ernst, and *Schwitters.

collagen A structural protein that is the main component of the white fibers of connective tissue. Inelastic but with great tensile strength, it is found in tendons and ligaments and also in skin, bone, and cartilage.

collar bone. *See* clavicle.

collards *See* kale.

collateral security Property (e.g. shares of stock, real estate, insurance policies, jewelry) pledged by a borrower, in addition to his promise to repay, as a safeguard for the repayment of a loan. On default the lender sells the collateral, deducts his debt and costs from the proceeds, and pays any balance to the borrower.

collective bargaining Bargaining between labor unions and employers on all matters relating to conditions of employment, rates of pay, etc. If agreement cannot be reached by bargaining, the dispute may be referred to *arbitration, or either side may take action against the other (*see* strikes; lockouts).

collective farms Agricultural cooperatives found especially in communist countries. Collectivization was instituted in the Soviet Union, with considerable ruthlessness, by Stalin in the late 1920s; widespread resistance necessitated some modifications in the mid-1930s. The farms and farm equipment belong to the state, which decides what is to be grown and in what quantities, but farmworkers, who live in surrounding villages, pay rent for their homes and are permitted to have their own garden plots and livestock; profits are shared in collective farms while in state farms workers receive wages. Collectivization was introduced into China in 1955. There, communes correspond to the Soviet collective farms, which are also found in Israel (*see* kibbutz).

collective unconscious In Jungian psychology, a body of images and ideas that are inherited and shared by all humans, rather than acquired by the individual. These ideas are called archetypes and *Jung believed them to be detected in the myths, dreams, and mental disturbances of mankind.

collie A breed of □dog originating in Scotland and widely used as a sheepdog. It has a streamlined body and a pointed muzzle. The rough-coated collie has a long dense coat and bushy tail; the smooth-coated variety has a shorter smooth coat and the bearded collie has a long coat with a shaggy beard. Collies are gray, fawn, or sandy, with or without white markings. Height: 22–24 in (56–61 cm) (dogs); 20–22 in (51–56 cm) (bitches).

collimator 1. A device used in conjunction with certain optical instruments for producing a beam of parallel light. A simple collimator consists of a slit placed at the focal point of a convex lens. 2. A device used to produce a beam of radiation of the required dimensions in *radiotherapy.

Collingwood, Robin George (1889–1943) British philosopher, archeologist, and historian, who taught philosophy at Oxford. His *New Leviathan* (1946) defends free institutions. *Essay on Philosophical Method* (1933), *Idea of Nature* (1945), and *Idea of History* (1946) present his own *idealism in relation to that of *Plato, *Hegel, and *Croce. ₆1

Collins, Michael (1890–1922) Irish nationalist; leading member of Sinn Féin. He was imprisoned for his part in the *Easter Rising (1916) and subsequently became finance minister in the republican government (1919). He played a major part in the negotiations that led to the establishment of the Irish Free State (1921) but was shot by republicans who opposed the Anglo-Irish treaty.

Collins, William Wilkie (1824–89) British novelist. He worked in commerce and practiced law before publishing *Memoirs* (1848) of his father, a landscape painter. During the 1850s he enjoyed a mutually beneficial association with Dickens and in 1860 published his pioneering mystery novel, *The Woman in White*. His other novels include *No Name* (1862) and *The Moonstone* (1868).

colloid A solution in which the solute (*or* disperse phase) is present in the solvent (dispersion medium) in the form of particles 10^{-9} to 10^{-6} m in length, rather than as single molecules or ions. If the disperse phase is solid and the dispersion medium is liquid the colloid is known as a **sol** (examples include milk, glue, and some drug preparations). If both are liquid the colloid is known as an **emulsion** (e.g. mayonnaise and most ointments). A colloidal suspension in which the particles of the disperse phase link together, with the dispersion medium circulating through the meshwork, is called a **gel** (e.g. a photographic emulsion). *See also* aerosols.

Colloids consist of charged particles. In lyophilic (solvent-loving) colloids, stability is achieved by attraction between the particles and the molecules of the dispersion medium. Lyophilic colloids are reversible in the sense that when the particles are removed from the solution, they will re-form a solution by simply mixing with the dispersion medium. Lyophobic (solvent-hating) colloids usually consist of large inorganic particles (e.g. clays, metals, etc.). They maintain stability by repulsion between similarly charged aggregates. They often precipitate on the addition of a salt and are irreversible.

Colman, Ronald (1891–1958) British actor. He went to the US in 1920 after military service during World War I and played leading romantic roles in such films as *Lost Horizon* (1937) and *Random Harvest* (1943).

Colmar 48 05N 7 21E A city in E France, the capital of the Haut-Rhin department. It was held by Germany from 1871 to 1919, and from 1940 until 1945. It has many notable buildings, including a Dominican monastery (13th–14th centuries). A trading center for Alsatian wines, Colmar has an important cotton industry. Population (1975): 62,410.

colobus A leaf-eating *Old World monkey belonging to the genus *Colobus* (3 species), of African forests, also called guereza. 20–28 in (50–70 cm) long, colobus monkeys have long hands with small thumbs and their long silky fur is brightly marked. They have been widely hunted for their skins. □mammal.

colocynth The dried fruit of *Citrullus colocynthus*, a prostrate herbaceous perennial found in N Africa, the Middle East, and India and cultivated in Spain and Cyprus. It is a powerful laxative, used medicinally in very small amounts. It can cause poisoning. Family: *Cucurbitaceae*.

Cologne (German name: Köln) 50 56N 06 57E A city in W West Germany on the Rhine River, the largest in North Rhine-Westphalia. A port and major commercial center, it is famed for its toilet water. Other industries include textiles, iron and steel, chemicals, and motor manufacture. It is the site of a university (1388) and the largest gothic cathedral in N Europe (founded 1248). The cathedral and the old gothic town hall were among the buildings reconstructed after World War II during which most of the city center was destroyed. *History*: founded by the Romans, it became the capital of the northern empire in 258 AD and later the seat of Frankish kings. During the middle ages its archbishops were powerful princes and it flourished as a mercantile and cultural center, where Albertus Magnus, Thomas Aquinas, and John Duns Scotus taught. In 1798 it was annexed by France, passing to Prussia in 1815. Population (1980 est): 976,800.

Colombia, Republic of A country in NW South America, on the Pacific Ocean and the Caribbean Sea. It consists chiefly of a hot swampy coastal plain, separated by ranges of the Andes from the pampas and the equatorial forests of the upper Amazon basin. The majority of the population is of mixed Spanish and Indian descent. *Economy*: mainly agricultural, the chief product is coffee, which accounts for over half the total exports. Although industry is largely undeveloped, the manufacturing section has expanded rapidly in recent decades and the export of such products as textiles and chemicals has risen sharply. The country is rich in mineral resources; gold production is the highest in South America and silver, copper, lead, and mercury are also mined. Colombia is one of the world's richest sources of platinum, as well as being the world's largest producer of emeralds. The most valuable natural resource, however, is oil. There are also large reserves of coal and natural gas. *History*: inhabited by Chibchas and other Indians before the Spanish colonization of the 16th century. In 1819 Simón Bolívar, after a 9-year war, secured the independence of Greater Colombia, which included what are now Panama, Venezuela, and Ecuador as well as present-day Colombia. This lasted until 1830 when Venezuela and Ecuador broke away; Panama became independent in 1903. Strife had plagued the country from the 19th century into the 20th, with a civil war of extreme violence erupting in 1899. Political parties, aligned along opposing conservative and liberal lines, had struggled for years with the conservatives emerging victorious after the war in 1902. In 1948 after more than 40 years of political peace, violent war once again tore the country and hundreds of thousands were killed. General Gustavo Rojas Pinilla emerged as dictator. He was overthrown in a military coup in 1957 and a more democratic government was re-established the following year. Since 1975 there has been considerable unrest, including strikes, student rioting, and guerrilla activity. In 1980 the left-wing guerrilla organization M-19 took a number of hostages prisoner in the Dominican Republic's embassy in Bogotá, gradually releasing them in the next two months. In the 1982 presidential elections Belisario Betancur was elected to succeed Dr Julio Cesar Turbay Ayala, who had been in office from 1978. By the mid 1980s the once powerful M-19 had been isolated militarily and their leader killed in a plane crash. Colombia distanced itself further and further from the US in response to US involvement in Central America. Official language: Spanish. Official religion: Roman Catholic. Official currency: Colombian peso of 100 centavos. Area: 456,535 sq mi (1,138,914 sq km). Population (1983 est): 27,663,0000. Capital: Bogotá. Main port: Barranquilla.

Colombo 6 55N 79 52E The capital and main port of Sri Lanka, on the W coast at the mouth of the Kelani River. Founded by the Arabs in the 8th century AD, it was later developed by the Portuguese, the Dutch, and the

British. Colombo has one of the largest artificial harbors in the world, from which tea, spices, and rubber are exported. The University of Sri Lanka was established here in 1972. Population (1981): 585,776.

Colombo, Matteo Realdo (?1516–59) Italian physician, who first described the circulation of blood between the heart and lungs. From his dissections of human cadavers he also described the membrane surrounding the lungs (pleura) and the membrane enclosing the abdominal organs (peritoneum).

Colombo Plan An agreement, signed in Colombo (Ceylon) in 1951, designed to foster economic development in the countries of S and SE Asia. It now has 27 members—21 countries within the region and Australia, Canada, Japan, New Zealand, the UK, and the US. There is an annual meeting of the Consultative Committee, and financial arrangements are made between individual governments rather than from a central fund.

colon. *See* intestine.

Colón (former name: Aspinwall) 9 21N 79 54W A port in central Panama, at the Caribbean end of the Panama Canal. It is a major commercial center; industries include oil refining. Population (1970): 95,300.

colophony. *See* rosin.

color The sensation produced when light of different wavelengths falls on the human eye. Although it is actually continuous, the visible spectrum is usually split into seven major colors: red, orange, yellow, green, blue, indigo, and violet, in order of decreasing wavelength (from about 6.5×10^{-7} m for red light to 4.2×10^{-7} m for violet). A mixture of all these colors in equal proportions gives white light; other colors are produced by varying the proportions or omitting components. Colored pigments, dyes, and filters selectively absorb certain wavelengths, transmitting or reflecting the rest. Thus a red book illuminated by white light absorbs all the components of white light except red, which is reflected. This is a subtractive process, since the final color is that remaining after absorption of the others. Combining colored lights, on the other hand, is an additive process. A mixture of the whole spectrum gives white light, as will a mixture of lights of three *primary colors.

Colorado One of the Mountain States in the W central US. Wyoming lies to the N, Nebraska to the N and E, Kansas to the E, Oklahoma and New Mexico to the S, and Utah to the W. The flat, grass-covered Great Plains of the E are cut by the South Platte and Arkansas rivers flowing eastward from the Rocky Mountains, which run N–S through the center of the state. Colorado's mean elevation is the highest in the US and the majority of the Rockies loftiest peaks are located within the state. The Rockies contain the valley of the Colorado River, and the Continental Divide forms the mountains' crest. The Colorado Plateau in the SE, an area of flat, semiarid land surfaces with stunted, sparse vegetation is cut by numerous majestic canyons. Much of the plateau region constitutes Indian reservations. Most of the population lives and works in a transition zone, the Colorado Piedmont, which divides the eastern and western regions. Manufacturing is the most important sector of Colorado's economy, especially the production of machinery, chemicals, military equipment, and food products. Mining is declining, although Colorado produces molybdenum, coal, oil, and sand and gravel. Tourism, especially winter sports, is of growing importance. The state's farmers are major cattle, pig, and lamb producers. As well as cultural and educational institutions the state has three important observatories. *History*: explored by the Spanish, part of Colorado was acquired by the US in the Louisiana Purchase (1803) and part from Mexico in 1848. Following the discovery of gold (1859), it became a territory in 1861 and a state in 1876. Colorado's cities grew rapidly during and after World War II and the energy crisis of the 1970s brought expansion of its coal and petroleum industries. The state's great natural beauty and outdoor lifestyle attracted many who sought escape from the cities. Colorado fared better than most states during the recession of 1980–82, although federal cutbacks caused a decline in its fuel-producing industries. Area: 104,247 sq mi (269,998 sq km). Population (1983): 3,139,000. Capital: Denver.

Colorado potato beetle A brown and yellow striped *leaf beetle, *Leptinotarsa decemlineata*, about 0.4 in (10 mm) long. Both the adults and larvae eat potato leaves: the larvae also attack the tubers. It is native to W North America but has spread eastward, throughout Europe, to become a serious pest of potato crops everywhere.

Colorado River A river rising in the Rocky Mountains and flowing SW through Colorado, Utah, and Arizona (where it passes through the *Grand Canyon) to the Gulf of California in Mexico. Its extensive use for irrigation and as a source of power (the many canyons providing ideal sites for dams, of which the Hoover Dam is one) is seen by conservationists as a serious threat to the natural landscape. Length: 1440 mi (2320 km).

COLORADO POTATO BEETLE *A specimen on potato leaves. A heavy infestation of this pest can completely strip a plant of its leaves, so that the tubers do not develop.*

Colorado Springs 38 50N 104 50W A health resort in Colorado situated at the foot of the Rocky Mountains. It is the site of the US Air Force Academy and the US Air Defense Command. Population (1980 est): 215,150.

coloratura (Italian: coloring) A style of vocal music characterized by elaborate and florid decorative passages. A **coloratura soprano** is a soprano whose voice is suited to such music. Donizetti and Verdi made effective use of the coloratura style in many of their operas; the Russian composer Reinhold Glière (1876–1956) wrote a concerto for wordless coloratura soprano voice and orchestra.

color blindness The inability to distinguish certain colors. There are various forms of color blindness, the most common of which is red-green color blindness (the inability to distinguish red and green). Color blindness is an inherited condition: because it is a recessive trait carried on the X chromosome it is far more common in men than women (about 8% of males of Caucasian origin are color blind). Very occasionally color blindness may be due to disease of the retina (the light-sensitive layer of the eye). Diagnosis depends on the use of charts in which symbols made of color dots are buried in a background of other dots. Inherited color blindness cannot be cured, and sufferers must avoid activities in which the distinction of color may be of importance.

color photography The recording of *color images on photographic *film that has three layers of light-sensitive emulsion, one for each of three *primary colors. Most color film uses a subtractive reversal process. Colored light entering the camera first falls on an emulsion sensitive only to blue light. On development of this layer, a black image is formed by deposition of silver where blue light has fallen. The unblackened areas are dyed yellow, the complementary color of blue, and the silver deposit is removed. Since silver halide emulsions cannot be made insensitive to blue light, there is a yellow filter (to remove blue light) between the blue emulsion and the next layer, which is green-sensitive. This is developed to form a magenta image of the parts where no green light has fallen. The bottom layer is red-sensitive and gives a cyan (blue-green) negative image. When white light shines through the three superimposed images, the cyan dye subtracts red where it does not occur in the picture; the magenta subtracts green; and the yellow subtracts blue. The light emerging therefore reconstructs the original picture on a screen, in the case of a transparency, or onto printing paper. Positive color paper prints directly from negatives that are not to be used for transparencies. These negatives incorporate dyes to correct for varying sensitivity in the printing-paper emulsion. For printing from transparencies, reversal color paper is used and good color reproduction is more difficult.

color television. *See* television.

color vision The ability of the human eye (and that of some other animals) to detect differences in the wavelength of light. The ability is due to the presence in the retina of the eye of cells known as cones (*see* retina), of which three types are believed to exist; one type being sensitive to red light, one to blue, and one to green. Light stimulates one or more of these types of cones in varying amounts depending on its color. *See also* color blindness.

Colosseum An *amphitheater in Rome. Now one of the most impressive of all Roman remains, the Colosseum was begun (c. 70 AD) by the emperor *Vespasian. It is an elliptical building, four stories high, 617 ft (188 m) long, and 512 ft (156 m) wide. It could seat 47,000 people and

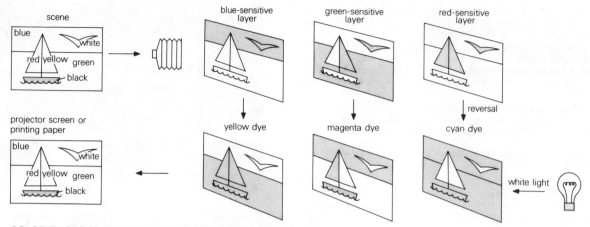

COLOR PHOTOGRAPHY   *In color reproduction with subtractive reversal film, light from the different colored areas of the scene forms negatives for each primary color. These are dyed to form filters that subtract colors from white light to reconstruct the original picture.*

was used mainly for gladiatorial and wild-beast fights, but could be flooded for mock naval battles.

Colossians, Epistle of Paul to the   A New Testament book written by the Apostle Paul about 60 AD to the church in Colossae in W Asia Minor. Its theme is that the Christian faith is sufficient and that speculative philosophy, specifically ideas that appear to be derived from *Gnosticism, diverts attention from this truth.

Colossus of Rhodes   A gigantic statue of the sun god *Helios by the harbor of Rhodes. Cast in bronze by Chares of Lindos about 280 BC and standing about 100 ft (31 m) tall, it was counted among the *Seven Wonders of the World. An earthquake destroyed it 50 years after its completion.

Colt, Samuel   (1814–62) US inventor. A native of Connecticut, his most famous invention was the Colt revolver, a gun with a revolving cylinder that would shoot six times before reloading. The gun became popular during the *Mexican War.

Colt revolver   A *revolver with a multi-shot cylinder rotated and locked in line with the single barrel by cocking the weapon. Invented by the US engineer Samuel Colt (1814–62) in 1835, it became the .45 caliber Frontier Peacemaker (1873) and the standard .45 US army and navy revolver, remaining in service until 1945.

coltsfoot   A perennial early-flowering herb, *Tussilago farfara*, 2–6 in (5–15 cm) high, bearing yellow single flower heads on scaly stems before the leaves appear. Found in Eurasia, N Africa, and North America (introduced), it can be a persistent weed. The dried leaves were previously smoked to cure coughs and asthma. Family: *Compositae.

colugo   An arboreal mammal belonging to the genus *Cyanocephalus* and order *Dermoptera* (2 species), also called flying lemur, found in Asia, Borneo, and the Philippines. About 24 in (60 cm) long, colugos have a membrane of skin, extending from the chin via the fore and hind limbs to the tail, with which they can glide up to 230 ft (70 m). Colugos feed on leaves and fruit.

Colum, Padraic   (Patrick Colm; 1881–1972) Irish poet and folklorist. Associated with *Yeats, *Synge, and other members of the Celtic literary revival, he founded *The Irish Review* in 1911. From 1914 he lived in the US. His works include several volumes of lyrical poetry, plays, folklore anthologies, and a reminiscence of James *Joyce.

Columba, St   (c. 521–597 AD) Irish missionary and abbot. Ordained in 551, he founded churches and monasteries in Ireland before setting up a monastery on Iona. From here, Scotland was evangelized. Feast day: June 9.

Columban, St   (*or* St Columbanus; c. 543–615 AD) Irish missionary and abbot. Establishing himself with 12 companions in Gaul in 590, he founded monasteries in the Vosges. Because of a conflict with the king, his monks went first to Switzerland and then to Italy in 612, where they founded a monastery at Bobbio in N Italy, which became an important center of learning. Feast day: Nov 23. Emblem: a bear.

Columbia   38 57N 92 20W A city in central Missouri. The University of Missouri has been here since 1839 and is the chief industry of the city. Other higher education institutions include Stephens College (1833). Population (1980): 62,061.

Columbia   34 00N 81 00W The capital city of South Carolina. An important commercial center, its industries include textiles, plastics, and machinery. Fort Jackson (a major Army post) is adjacent to the city. The University of Carolina was established here in 1801. Population (1980): 99,296.

Columbia River   A river in North America, flowing SW from British Columbia, through Washington State, to the Pacific Ocean at Oregon. It is an important source of hydroelectric power and forms the only deepwater harbor N of San Francisco. Length: 1200 mi (1930 km).

columbine.   *See* Aquilegia.

columbium.   *See* niobium.

Columbus   39 59N 83 03W The capital of Ohio, on the Scioto River. A major industrial and commercial center of a rich agricultural area, its manufactures include aircraft, machinery, and footwear. It is the site of the Ohio State University (1872). Population (1980): 564,871.

Columbus   32 28N 84 59W A city in W Georgia, on the Chattahoochee River. The state's second largest city, its industries include textiles, food processing, and chemicals. Population (1980): 168,598.

Columbus, Christopher   (1451–1506) Italian navigator, who discovered America. He was born in Genoa, became a pirate, and in 1476 was shipwrecked off the coast of Portugal, where he settled. He conceived the idea of reaching the East by sailing westward but his plan was rejected by the Portuguese king (John the Perfect) and Columbus approached (1486) the Spanish monarchs Ferdinand and Isabella. He eventually won their patronage and on August 3, 1492, set sail in the *Santa Maria*, accompanied by the *Pinta* and the *Niña*. On Oct 12 he landed on Watling Island (now San Salvador Island, in the Bahamas) and in Nov visited Hispaniola. On his return to Spain he was greatly honored: Ferdinand and Isabella stood to receive him at court and offered him a seat. On his second voyage (1493–96) he discovered Guadeloupe, Puerto Rico, and Jamaica and founded the first town in the New World—named Isabella, after his patroness, it is now a ruin in the Dominican Republic. His third voyage (1498–1500) achieved the discovery of Trinidad and the mainland of South America but ended in disaster: in 1499, following a revolt against his command, a Spanish governor was dispatched to relieve Columbus, who was sent back in chains to Spain. On his arrival, however, he was released and compensated and shortly afterward set off on his last voyage (1502–04). From this he returned ill and disheartened, dying not long afterward in Valladolid. In 1542 his remains were taken to Hispaniola.

column.   *See* orders of architecture.

coly   A small gray or brown bird belonging to a family (*Coliidae*; 6 species) of Central and South Africa, also called mousebird because it creeps mouselike along branches. Colies are 12–14 in (30–35 cm) long, including the long stiff tail feathers, and have a short crest, a short curved bill, and red legs with long claws. Order: *Coliiformes*.

coma   In medicine, a state of deep unconsciousness in which the subject is unrousable and does not respond to pain. Coma can be caused by a *stroke, drug overdosage, meningitis, or head injuries. Treatment is that of the underlying condition, with the maintenance of respiration.

Comanche   A North American Indian people formerly inhabiting the southern Plains. Their language, a branch of the Uto-Aztecan linguistic family, is closely related to *Shoshone. During the 18th century, the Comanches migrated from the area of Wyoming, eventually spreading as far south as Texas and Mexico, where they gained a reputation as daring horsemen and raiders. In 1867, after a period of conflict with the US Army, the Comanches agreed to be resettled on reservations in Oklahoma, where the present Comanche population of approximately 3500 still resides.

Comaneci, Nadia (1961–) Romanian gymnast, who in the 1976 Olympic Games won gold medals on the beam, the asymmetrical bars, and also in the individual all-round competition for women.

Combination Acts (1799, 1800) The British laws that made illegal any association (combination) of working men for the purpose of improving their working conditions. They were unsuccessful in preventing the formation of labor unions and were repealed in 1824. An outbreak of strikes followed the repeal and another Act was passed (1825) allowing labor unions to exist but limiting their right to strike.

COMBINE HARVESTER

combine harvester A machine for harvesting grain crops that combines the operations of cutting the crop (reaping) and separating the grain (threshing) from the rest of the plant. Horse-drawn models originated in the US in the 1830s; in the 1940s, the predecessors of the modern self-propelled machines were introduced, replacing the earlier labor-intensive methods.

comb jelly. *See* ctenophore.

combustion A chemical reaction in which a substance combines with oxygen, producing heat and light. For a liquid or a solid to burn, the temperature must initially be high enough to release flammable vapor. To maintain combustion, the heat evolved must maintain this temperature to provide a constant supply of vapor. The oxidation reactions in combustion are generally chain reactions involving free radicals, the principal overall reactions being the oxidation of carbon to carbon dioxide and the oxidation of hydrogen to water ($C + 2H_2 + 2O_2 \geq CO_2 + 2H_2O$).

COMECON. *See* Council for Mutual Economic Assistance.

Comédie-Française The French national theater, founded in 1680 and reconstituted in 1803 by Napoleon. It is organized as a cooperative society, owned by its members. Probationary members are called *pensionnaires* and full members *sociétaires*; a pension is awarded on retirement after 20 years of service. Despite its strong emphasis on tradition, it has produced many of France's most original actors.

comedy A type of dramatic presentation that evokes amusement and laughter. Traditionally, it deals with ordinary characters in everyday situations and ends happily, usually with a marriage or unexpected good fortune. In the comedies of *Shakespeare these elements blend with a more romantic narrative vein.

The earliest surviving comedies are those of the Greek dramatist *Aristophanes and the Romans *Plautus and *Terence (*see* Old Comedy; Middle Comedy; New Comedy; Roman Comedy). During the early 17th century the English dramatist Ben *Jonson pioneered the "comedy of humours" with characters who are gross caricatures of ruling passions. Examples of the satirical comedy of manners, in which more emphasis is placed on sophisticated witty dialogue, are the plays of *Congreve and *Wycherley in the late 17th century. The plays of Oscar *Wilde and Noel *Coward continued the tradition of the comedy of manners in the late 19th and early 20th century.

The development of motion pictures gave rise to a new medium for comedy. Among the most famous of the early silent film comedians were Charlie *Chaplin and Buster *Keaton. In the 1930s, the *Marx Brothers and W. C. *Fields became famous for their satirical, often iconoclastic form of humor. Among the most well-known modern American film comedians are Bob *Hope, Jerry Lewis, and Woody *Allen.

Comenius, John Amos (1592–1671) Czech theologian and educationalist. Comenius wrote widely on education, advocating a broad curriculum incorporating science, handicrafts, economics, and languages. He was commissioned by *Oxenstierna to reform Swedish schools (1641–48). A virulent opponent of the papacy, he was drawn to the mysticism of Jacob *Böhme.

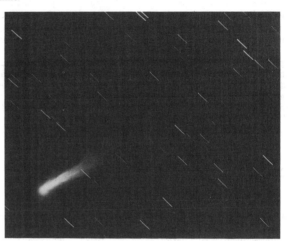

COMET *Comet Morehouse, discovered in 1908. (The short diagonal lines are the images left by stars in the background, as the telescope and camera were moved to follow the comet.)*

comet A small body that moves, usually in a very elongated orbit, around the sun. A typical comet consists of a small nucleus of ice and dust surrounded by an immense tenuous luminous cloud of gas and dust, the coma. Tails of gas and of dust only appear when a comet is near the sun; they point away from the sun and may be millions of kilometers long. **Short-period comets** (such as *Halley's comet) have orbital periods of less than 150 years. The remainder have much longer periods, some exceeding 10,000 years, and move in approximately parabolic orbits. A comet eventually decays to produce a stream of meteoroids around its orbit. *See also* Oort cloud.

comfrey A perennial herbaceous plant, *Symphytum officinale*, also called boneset. Up to 40 in (100 cm) high, it has drooping creamy or purplish flowers. Native to Europe and temperate Asia and formerly used medicinally, it is now grown as a garden flower, as are the related plants *S. grandiflorum* (yellow flowers) and *S. peregrinum* (blue and pink flowers). Family: *Boraginaceae*.

comic opera An opera with a humorous or farcical plot. It is characterized by spoken dialogue and a comic or satirical libretto. Among the most famous comic operas are the Savoy Operas of *Gilbert and *Sullivan. *Compare* opéra comique; opera buffa.

Cominform (Communist Information Bureau) An international communist organization. Founded in 1947, it united the Communist Parties of the Soviet Union, Bulgaria, Czechoslovakia, Hungary, Poland, Romania, Yugoslavia, France, and Italy. In 1948 Yugoslavia was expelled because of its refusal to follow the Soviet line. In 1956, partly in order to improve relations with Yugoslavia, the Soviet Union dissolved the Cominform. *See also* International.

Comintern. *See* International.

comitia Assemblies of the Roman people summoned by magistrates and held at an official meeting place (*comitium*) on an appointed day (*comitialis*). The three *comitia* corresponded to the three divisions of the people into curiae (*see* curia), *centuries, and tribes. The Comitia Curiata was the earliest assembly but its legislative functions became largely formal. The Comitia Centuriata elected the chief magistrates and had some judicial powers. The Comitia Tributa was the assembly of the *plebeians; its enactments had authority after 287 BC.

commedia dell'arte An Italian form of popular theater that flourished throughout Europe from the 16th to the 18th centuries. It was performed by professional actors whose comic and often vulgar improvisations were based on a set of stock situations, usually concerning romantic intrigues and stereotyped characters. These included the clown *Harlequin, the cuckold Pantaloon, and the lover Inamorato. Its influence can be seen in the works of such contemporary dramatists as Molière and in the dramatic forms of *pantomime and *farce. Its characters were popular subjects for 18th-century porcelain figures. *See also* Punch and Judy.

commensalism A relationship between two individuals of different species in which one (the commensal) lives in, on, or with the other (the host), from which it derives food, shelter, support, or transport. The association neither harms nor benefits the host. An example is provided by certain barnacles, which live attached to whales. *See also* symbiosis.

Commerce, Department of US government cabinet-level department that promotes international trade, economic growth, and technological advancement through programs that help increase exports, prevent unfair foreign trade competition, and provide statistics, analysis, and research. Headed by the secretary of commerce, it includes the National Bureau of Standards, Patent and Trademark Office, Bureau of the Census, and the US Travel and Tourism, International Trade, and National Oceanic and Atmospheric administrations. Created as the Department of Commerce and Labor (1903), it became the Department of Commerce in 1913.

commercial banks Institutions that accept demand deposits (checking accounts) and lend money to companies and private individuals. In addition to making loans, these banks offer trust departments, credit cards, safe deposit boxes, and many other services. The commercial banks make a profit by lending at a higher rate of interest than their borrowing rate. Commercial banks are chartered by both the federal and individual state governments.

commesso (*or* Florentine mosaic) A method of making mosaic pictures of flowers, landscapes, religious scenes, etc., with polished semiprecious hard stones, such as lapis lazuli, agate, and jasper. Commesso pictures, which were used chiefly as tabletops and small wall panels, have been made since 1588 at a special Florentine workshop, which is now state supported.

Committees of Correspondence Liaison committees originally appointed by the American colonies for communication with England. As the American Revolution neared, the committees encouraged colonial cooperation against the crown and provided leadership for the coming struggle. These intercolonial committees, first formed in Virginia, organized the first *Continental Congress (1774).

commode A low-level decorative chest of drawers or cupboard. As invented by André-Charles Boulle (1642–1732), the commode was an architectural piece of furniture, sarcophagus-shaped with heavy feet and fitted with drawers. It developed during the 18th century to become an elegantly curved chest of drawers with *marquetry and *ormolu decoration. *Chippendale made important English examples.

commodity trading The buying and selling of products, such as metals, coffee, rubber, grains, sugar, and cocoa, conducted in commodity exchanges or markets by brokers on behalf of clients, who consist of producers, users, and speculators. The majority of dealings are in "futures" (goods for delivery at a stipulated date in the future) although "spots" (goods for immediate delivery) are also traded. Trading in futures rarely involves the exchange of goods, most transactions being closed out by equal sales or purchases on the same market. Commodity exchanges enable producers and users to hedge their transactions in goods and help to stabilize prices by regulating supply and demand.

Commodus, Lucius Aelius Aurelius (161–93 AD) Roman emperor (180–92). The son of Marcus Aurelius, Commodus showed increasing signs of mental imbalance, believing he was the incarnation of the demigod Hercules. He became increasingly unpopular and was finally assassinated.

common law The part of the law that was originally unwritten and based on the common customs of a country. US common law is largely descended from English common law, which developed with the rise of centralized government in England from the 10th to the 13th centuries.

Common Market. *See* European Economic Community.

commons Unenclosed land for the common use of the inhabitants of a particular district. Originally, in every manor there was a tract of uncultivated land over which the inhabitants had **rights of common**, such as the rights to pasture animals, to fish, and to cut wood.

Commons, House of. *See* parliament.

common sense, philosophy of A philosophical movement particularly associated with certain Scottish followers of Thomas *Reid and promoted in the 20th century by G. E. *Moore. It rejected the traditional philosophical *skepticism that had raised doubts about such questions as to whether material objects exist unperceived or whether other people exist. Common-sense philosophers base their case on the universal nonphilosophical consent on such subjects; while particular beliefs may be mistaken, there is none the less a broad base of common-sense views that must be certain.

Commonwealth (1649–53) The period in English history between the execution of Charles I and the establishment of the *Protectorate; the term is sometimes used synonymously with Interregnum to refer to the entire period between the execution of Charles I and the *Restoration in 1660 of his son Charles II.

Commonwealth (British) A loose association of independent nations once subject to the imperial government of the UK (*see* Empire, British). The Commonwealth of Nations was established by the Statute of Westminster (1931), which was based on the principles, enunciated at the 1926 *Imperial Conference, of member states' autonomy, equality, and common allegiance to the English crown; its name was modified to the Commonwealth after World War II. Its member states, the populations of which comprise nearly a quarter of the world's population, are Antigua and Barbuda, Australia, the Bahamas, Bangladesh, Barbados, Belize, Botswana, Canada, Cyprus, Dominica, Fiji, The Gambia, Ghana, Grenada, Guyana, India, Jamaica, Kenya, Kiribati, Lesotho, Malawi, Malaysia, Malta, Mauritius, New Zealand, Nigeria, Papua New Guinea, St Kitts-Nevis, St Lucia, Seychelles, Sierra Leone, Singapore, Solomon Islands, Sri Lanka, Swaziland, Tanzania, Tonga, Trinidad and Tobago, Uganda, the UK, Vanuatu, Western Samoa, Zambia, and Zimbabwe; Nauru, Tuvalu, Maldives, and St Vincent and the Grenadines are special members and are not represented at the meetings of Commonwealth heads of government. Commonwealth heads of government meet every two years but finance ministers meet annually. The Commonwealth Secretariat headquarters are in London.

commune An experimental community based on religious, social, political, or technological ideas, based on the abolition of private property and the sharing of community wealth and resources. In the 19th century, communes based on the philosophies of such men as Robert *Owen, Charles *Fourier, and William *Morris were established in the US, Europe, and South America. The members of these communities sought new physical environments, egalitarian principles of social organization, and a harmonious integration of family, work, and learning. In the US, New Harmony and Brook Farm, of which Nathaniel *Hawthorne was a member, were founded on those principles but survived only a few years.

In the 20th century, there was a revival of interest in experimental communities in various parts of the world. In Israel, the *kibbutz became a successful form of agricultural settlement. In the US, during the 1960s and 1970s, many communes were established by groups dissatisfied with the way of life of modern technological society that turned, at least temporarily, to a way of life based on collective organization.

Commune of Paris (1871) A revolt in Paris against the conservative provisional government established at Versailles following French defeat in the Franco-Prussian War and the collapse of the Second Empire. Fearing a restoration of the monarchy, republican Parisians formed a revolutionary government in March that was reminiscent of the French Revolutionary Commune (1793). Defeated by government troops in May, the Communards lost some 20,000 supporters, 38,000 were arrested, and 7000 deported.

Communications Act (1934) US legislation that set up the Federal Communications Commission (FCC). The act regulated telephone, telegraph, radio, and, later, television transmissions.

communications satellite An unmanned artificial satellite by which long-distance live television broadcasting and telephone communications are achieved. Radio signals, suitably modulated (*see* modulation), are sent from one transmitting station to the satellite, where they are amplified and retransmitted (at a different frequency) to one or more receiving stations. The orbits of communications satellites lie above the earth's atmosphere so that high-frequency radio waves (microwaves), which can penetrate the *ionosphere, must be used. The electronic equipment on board is powered primarily by solar cells (*see* solar power).

The first active satellite was the US Telstar 1, launched in 1962. Telstar and other early satellites were in relatively low elliptical orbits and were only visible for a short portion of their orbit. A communications satellite is now usually placed in a geostationary orbit. This is a circular orbit lying about 36,000 km above the earth's equator. The satellite completes such an orbit in the same time (24 hours) as the earth rotates on its axis and thus to a ground-based radio station appears to remain nearly stationary in the sky. Three or more satellites, suitably placed around the equatorial orbit, can provide worldwide communications links.

Communications Satellite Corporation (COMSAT)   US international satellite communications system, privately owned but controlled by the US government. Established in 1962, COMSAT, with the cooperation of 13 other countries, launched the Intelsat I (Early Bird) satellite in 1965. Other satellites followed.

communism   A movement based on the principle of communal ownership of all property. More specifically, it is associated with *The Communist Manifesto* (1847) of Karl *Marx and Friedrich *Engels according to which the capitalist profit-based system of private ownership is replaced by a communist society in which the means of production are communally owned. This process, initiated by the revolutionary overthrow of the bourgeoisie (*see* Marxism), passes through a transitional period marked by the dictatorship of the proletariat (*see* Leninism) and the preparatory stage of *socialism.

In the late 19th century, Marxist theories motivated several social democratic parties in Europe, although their policies later developed along the lines of reforming *capitalism rather than overthrowing it. The exception was the Russian Social Democratic Workers' Party. One branch of this party, commonly known as the *Bolsheviks and headed by Vladimir *Lenin, succeeded in overthrowing the Czar's regime in the Revolution of November 1917. In 1918 this party changed its name to the Communist Party of the Soviet Union, thus establishing the modern distinction between communism and socialism.

After the success of the Russian Revolution, many socialist parties in other countries became communist parties, owing allegiance of varying degrees to the Soviet Communist Party (*see* International). In 1944–46 communist regimes were set up with the aid of the Soviet army in Poland, East Germany, Czechoslovakia, Hungary, Romania, Yugoslavia, Albania, and Bulgaria. In 1949 the communists in China, led by *Mao Tse-tung, came to power and established the People's Republic of China. Among the other countries in the *Third World that have adopted a communist form of government are Cuba, North Korea, Vietnam, Cambodia, Angola, Ethiopia, South Yemen, and Nicaragua.

Communism never became a popular philosophy in the US, either before or after the establishment of the Communist Party of America in 1919. Federal legislation such as the Smith Act (1940) and the Communist Control Act (1954) greatly restricted the party's activities and controversial hearings conducted by Senator Joseph *McCarthy further reduced its influence.

Since the early 1970s the term **Eurocommunism** has been used to refer to the policies of communist parties in Western Europe, which have sought to break with the tradition of uncritical and unconditional support of the Soviet Union. Such parties are politically active and electorally significant in France and Italy.

Communism Peak   (Russian name: Pik Kommunizma)   38 59N 72 01E The highest mountain in the Soviet Union, in the Pamirs in the S near the Afghan and Chinese borders. Height: 24,589 ft (7495 m).

community   In ecology, an interdependent group of living organisms that occupies a particular habitat. The plants and animals of a community are closely associated with each other in various ecological relationships: for example, they depend on one another for food (*see* food chain). The size and composition of the community depend on the nature of the habitat and its climate; it may show seasonal changes. During ecological *succession, the structure of a community constantly changes until the stable climax community is established. *See also* ecology; ecosystem.

community service   A form of sentence that requires an offender to work for a prescribed number of hours on behalf of the community instead of being imprisoned.

commutative law   The mathematical rule, obeyed by addition and multiplication but not division, that the result of an operation combining two quantities is independent of the order in which they are taken: for addition, $a + b = b + a$, and for multiplication, $ab = ba$.

Commynes, Philippe de   (c. 1445–1511) French statesman and chronicler. He served Charles the Bold, Duke of Burgundy, from 1464 and Louis XI from 1472. On the accession of Charles VIII in 1483 he was imprisoned but later returned to favor. His *Mémoires* (1524) are important historical records of the reign of Louis XI and the Italian expedition of Charles VIII, and embody his advanced political theories.

Como   45 48N 09 05E A city and resort in N Italy, in Lombardy on Lake Como. Known as Comum in Roman times, it is the birthplace of the elder

and younger Pliny. It fell to the Visconti in 1335 and in 1859 was liberated from Austrian occupation by Garibaldi. It has a 15th-century marble cathedral and a gothic town hall. Como is an important tourist center and has several industries, including the famous silk factories. Population (1971): 97,395.

Como, Lake   A lake in central N Italy, lying in a narrow forked valley at the S foot of the Alps. It is about 50 km (31 mi) long, dividing into two arms about halfway along, with a maximum depth of 1345 ft (410 m). There are many fashionable resorts on its shore such as Bellagio, Como, and Lecco. Area: 55 sq mi (145 sq km).

Comodoro Rivadavia   45 50S 67 30W A port in SE Argentina, on the Atlantic Ocean. It is Argentina's main oil-producing center; a natural gas pipeline extends for 1100 mi (1770 km) to Buenos Aires. Population (1970 est): 70,000.

Comorin, Cape   08 04N 77 35E A headland in India, the most southerly point of the subcontinent.

Comoros, Federal and Islamic Republic of the   A country consisting of a group of islands in the Indian Ocean, between the NW coast of Madagascar and the African mainland. The main islands are Grand Comoro, Anjouan, and Mohéli and exclude the island of Mayotte, which has remained French. The population is of mixed African and Arab descent. *Economy*: almost entirely agricultural. The soils are fertile but the relatively undeveloped farming has suffered since French aid was withdrawn in 1975. Sugar cane was formerly the main crop but others, such as vanilla and perfume plants, are now increasing in importance. Exports include vanilla, sisal, and essential oils such as ylang-ylang. *History*: there were successive African, Malay, Malagasy, Arab, and other immigrations to the islands before they became a French colony in the 19th century. At first joined to Madagascar, the Comoros became a separate French overseas territory in 1947. Moves toward— independence in the early 1970s culminated in a referendum in 1974 in which the majority voted in favor of independence, except for the island of Mayotte, which voted to remain French. Mayotte has since been made an overseas department of France. Ahmed Abdallah became the first president in 1975 but later that year he was overthrown in a military coup led by Ali Soilih. The government was taken over by a National Revolutionary Council. In 1976 the independence of the three islands was recognized by France and Soilih was elected president. He was overthrown (and later killed) in a military coup in 1978 and a Political-Military Directorate took over. The exiled Ahmed Abdallah and Mohammed Ahmed were invited to return and appointed copresidents. In October Ahmed Abdallah was elected as the first president of the Federal Islamic Comoro Republic for a six-year term, following the approval of a new federal style constitution, with provision for the inclusion of Mayotte. Official languages: French and Arabic; Swahili is also used commercially. Official currency: CFA franc of 100 centimes. Area: 719 sq mi (1862 sq km). Population (1983 est): 442,000. Capital and main port: Moroni.

compass   A device for determining the direction of magnetic north. The magnetic compass, which has been in use as an aid to navigation probably since the 2nd century BC, consists of a magnetic needle balanced on a point, allowing it to pivot freely. The S end of the magnet indicates magnetic N, as shown on a card (called a compass card) marked with the points of the compass and fixed below it. In some magnetic compasses, the entire card pivots, indicating direction against a mark on the fixed housing. Such compasses are often filled with a fluid (usually alcohol) for damping. A more sophisticated kind of compass, used on larger vessels and in aircraft, is the **gyrocompass**, which employs the effect of the earth's rotation on the orientation of a spinning object's axis of rotation. Magnetic compasses are subject to interference from nearby ferrous metal objects and fittings, and compasses must be adjusted to compensate for distortion. Compensation must also be made, in the reading of a compass, for magnetic N not being in the same direction as geographic N in most longitudes. Up-to-date navigation charts mark on a compass rose the annual correction for position that must be allowed in various longitudes.

compass plant   A perennial herbaceous plant, *Silphium laciniatum*, of the North American prairie. Its oval leaves are orientated N–S to avoid the intense midday radiation. 40 in–7 ft (1–2 m) high, it is sometimes cultivated and is also known as turpentine plant, from the substances that ooze from the stem. Family: *Compositae*.

Compiègne   49 25N 2 50E A city and resort in N France, in the Oise department on the Oise River. Joan of Arc was captured here by the English in 1430. A railroad coach in the forest of Compiègne was the scene of the signing of the Armistice (1918) ending World War I and of the agreement made between the Pétain government and Hitler in 1940. Industries include machinery, printing, and rubber. Population (1975): 40,720.

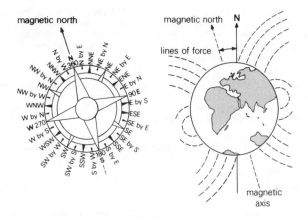

magnetic compass

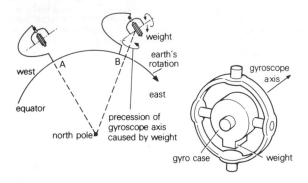

gyro compass

COMPASS *In the magnetic compass, the magnetized needle lines up with the earth's magnetic field. In the gyrocompass a spinning gyroscope is suspended on three mutually perpendicular frames. The axis of spin of a free gyroscope shifts around as the earth rotates: as the axis of the gyrocompass moves from the horizontal at position A to position B, a weight pulls it downwards. As a result of the gyroscopic effect, the axis shifts around at right angles to the gravitational force (precesses) and describes a circle around the N-S direction. When the precession is damped, the gyroscope axis settles down pointing N.*

complementarity principle The principle, proposed by Niels *Bohr, that an elementary particle may be regarded as either corpuscular or wave-like. Thus an experiment designed to detect a corpuscular property cannot, at the same time, detect a wave property, and vice versa. *See also* de Broglie wave.

complex In psychoanalysis, a group of associated ideas that are unacceptable to the conscious mind and have therefore been repressed into the *unconscious. Although the individual is no longer aware of these ideas they continue to influence his (or her) behavior. *See* inferiority complex; Oedipus complex.

complex numbers Quantities that consist of a real number and an imaginary number. They may be written in the form $a + ib$, where a and b are real numbers and $i = \sqrt{-1}$. Two complex numbers can be added and subtracted: for example $(a + ib) + (c + id) = (a + c) + i(b + d)$. They may also be multiplied and divided into each other. A complex number $a + ib$ may be thought of as a pair of ordered numbers (a,b) similar to a pair of *Cartesian coordinates (x,y). Then (a,b) can be regarded as a point on a plane called the complex plane or Argand diagram in which the real axis is taken as horizontal and the imaginary axis as vertical. Complex numbers are widely used in the physical sciences, particularly in electrical engineering in calculations concerning alternating current.

Compositae The largest family of flowering plants (about 900 genera and 14,000 species). They vary from small herbs to trees and are found worldwide. The tiny flowers are grouped into heads that resemble a single large flower. The individual florets may be similar, as in thistles, or of two types (disk and ray flowers), as in daisies. Many composites are cultivated

as ornamentals (e.g. chrysanthemums and dahlias); others are agricultural weeds (daisies, dandelions, etc.) and some are edible (such as lettuce).

Composite order. *See* orders of architecture.

compressor A machine for delivering high-pressure gas. They have a wide variety of uses, from small garage machines for inflating tires to large industrial machines for supplying compressed-air lines. The piston compressor resembles an internal-combustion engine in reverse and is driven by an electric motor or a diesel engine. The centrifugal compressor uses radial vanes to increase the momentum of the gas; they are extensively used in *gas driven by the turbine shaft (turbines) to supply pressurized air to the combustion chambers.

Compromise of 1850 US legislation passed to settle disputes between pro- and anti-slavery forces. Drafted by Henry *Clay, a series of five laws evolved that admitted California to the Union as a free (non-slave) state; admitted the territories of New Mexico and Utah with no mention of slavery; established stricter regulations regarding fugitive slaves; and banned the slave trade in Washington, DC. The issues that had split the political parties were solved, although only temporarily.

Compromise of 1877 US agreement that ended the Reconstruction period. It stated that Federal troops in the South would be withdrawn if Southern Congressmen would give their support to Republican presidential candidate Rutherford B. *Hayes.

Compton, Arthur Holly (1892–1962) US physicist, who discovered the *Compton effect (1923) while analyzing the scattering of X-rays by matter. He could only explain the effect by assuming that the X-rays consisted of photons, then still a novel idea. He shared the 1927 Nobel Prize with C. T. R. *Wilson.

Compton-Burnett, Dame Ivy (1892–1969) British novelist. *Pastors and Masters* (1925) was the first of a series of 17 novels set in a stylized Victorian-Edwardian upper-class world. The series includes *Brothers and Sisters* (1929), *Manservant and Maidservant* (1947), and *Mother and Son* (1955).

Compton effect The increase in the wavelength of electromagnetic radiation when it is scattered by free electrons. The effect can only be explained by regarding the radiation as consisting of particles called photons. Part of the photon's energy is transferred to the electron, the velocity of which is thereby increased. Named for Arthur *Compton.

computer A device for performing calculations at high speed, usually by electronic methods. The principles behind the modern computer were conceived by Charles *Babbage in the 19th century. The first practical machines were built in the US and Britain during World War II. During the immediate postwar years, the developments in *information theory and the invention of the *transistor set the scene for the computer revolution of the next 20 years.

There are two main types of computer: digital and analog. Of these the **digital computer** is the more widely used. It processes information in the form of groups of the binary numbers 1 and 0, which represent the on and off positions of electronic switches. A digital computer requires programming, or *software, to convert the information fed into it into binary form (*see* bit). Computer languages, such as *COBOL, *FORTRAN, and *ALGOL, have been developed to transcribe the *programs from English and mathematical symbols into a notation that a machine can read. The physical equipment, or hardware, of a digital computer system generally has three main components: the central processing unit (CPU), the memory, and the peripheral devices that enable information to be fed into the machine and to be displayed by it after processing. Input is generally by magnetic tape, punched paper tape, or cards. Output is by printout, cathode-ray-tube (CRT) displays, or magnetic tape.

Analog computers deal with continuously varying physical quantities, such as current or voltage. They are used mainly for simulating or monitoring and controlling continuous processes in industry or scientific research.

Hybrid computers use both digital and analog elements. Frequently, an analog input is converted into numbers (the digital form) for processing as digital computation is considerably faster and more efficient.

Advances in solid-state electronics have continually extended the application of computer techniques. Large computers were made possible when vacuum tubes were replaced by solid-state *transistors. Now integrated circuits using silicon chips of decreasing size and increasing complexity have led to the introduction of *microcomputers, which are sufficiently cheap to have wide-ranging applications.

Comte, Auguste (1798–1857) French philosopher. Often said to be the founder of sociology, he coined and defined the term, although work of a sociological nature had been done long before his time. He is best remembered for his positivism (the view that society could be studied scientifically by natural-science methods and was subject to general laws); his Law of the Three Stages of intellectual development (theological, metaphysical, and positive); and his view that the theoretical sciences formed a hierarchy, with sociology at the peak providing a basis for social planning and reorganization. His principal work is *Cours de philosophie positive* (6 vols, 1830–42).

Conakry (*or* Konakry) 9 25N 13 56W The capital of Guinea, a port in the SW on Tombo Island, which is linked to the mainland by a causeway. It was founded by the French in 1884 and became capital of French Guinea in 1893. Population (1972 est): 525,671.

Conant, James Bryant (1893–1978) US educator and statesman. After serving in the US Army (1917–18) during World War I, he taught at Harvard University (1919–33) before becoming its president (1933–53). He was high commissioner to Germany (1953–55) and then ambassador to West Germany (1956–57). After that, funded by Carnegie Corporation, he conducted studies of the US public school system and advised the Ford Foundation on education (1963–65). His many reports on education include *The American High School Today* (1959), *Slums and Suburbs* (1961), and *The Education of American Teachers* (1963).

concentration camps Prisons in which people are held without trial, usually on account of their politics or race. From 1900 to 1902, during the second *Boer War, the British detained civilian Afrikaners in concentration camps, with the loss of some 20,000 lives.

In Germany, camps were first established by the Nazis in 1933 to detain communists and Social Democrats; they were later used to imprison minority groups, such as Gypsies, homosexuals, and, above all, Jews. In 1940 the Nazis established extermination centers, the most notorious being Auschwitz and Treblinka in Poland and Belsen and Buchenwald in Germany. An estimated 20 million people were gassed or died of disease or starvation in Nazi camps, of which some 6 million were Jews—two thirds of European Jewry. Notorious for their torture, medical experiments on living people, and the cruelty of their jailers, the Nazi camps and the *holocaust that took place within them have raised serious doubts as to the moral validity of western civilization.

In the Soviet Union forced labor camps were first established in 1917 and expanded greatly during Stalin's purges in the 1930s. Although many camps were closed following his death in 1953, they continue to be used for the detention of political dissidents.

Concepción 36 50S 73 03W A city in S Chile, on the Bío-Bío River. It suffered damage (1939 and 1960) from earthquakes. It is an important industrial center situated near Chile's chief coalfield; industries include steel processing and oil refining. Its university was founded in 1919. Population (1976 est): 172,510.

concertina A hexagonal musical instrument of the reed-organ family, invented in 1829 by Sir Charles Wheatstone. Similar to the *accordion in construction, the concertina is hand held and notes are produced by pressing buttons on panels at either end of the bellows.

concerto A musical composition for one or more solo instruments and orchestra, usually in three movements (a *sonata form movement, a slow movement, and a rondo finale). In the late 18th century Mozart perfected the form in his piano concertos; 19th-century composers treated it more freely and in the 20th century concertos have been written in a number of different styles and forms. In the baroque period and in the 20th century the word concerto has been applied to a variety of other compositions.

concerto grosso. *See* Corelli, Arcangelo.

conch A heavy-shelled marine *snail of the family *Strombidae* (about 80 species). Conch □shells have a roughly triangular outer whorl with a broad lip and can be 0.8–14 in (2–35 cm) long. Indo-Pacific spider conchs (genus *Lambis*) have long horns around the aperture of their shell.

conciliarism The view of those Roman Catholics who regarded a general council of the Church as a superior authority to the pope. First proposed in the early 13th century, the theory gained support especially in the 15th century. Pius II refuted the doctrine in his bull *Execrabilis* (1460).

Concord 43 13N 71 34W The capital city of New Hampshire. Founded in 1725, it was the home of Mary Baker Eddy (the founder of Christian Science). Industries include printing and publishing. Population (1980): 30,360.

Concord 42 28N 71 17W A city in Massachusetts, on the Concord River. The first battle of the American Revolution occurred here on April 19, 1775. Ralph Emerson, Nathaniel Hawthorne, Louisa May Alcott, and Henry Thoreau all lived in Concord. Population (1970): 16,148.

concordance An index of words used in a single book or all the works of an author, with accompanying citations. Originally used for study of the Bible, concordances are now used as a method of textual analysis of major literary authors.

Concorde. *See* aircraft.

concrete A building material that was used by the Romans but in its modern form came into use after the invention of Portland *cement in 1824. Concrete consists of a mixture of a cement, usually Portland cement, and an aggregate of sand, gravel, and broken stones. The strength of the concrete depends on the proportion of cement to the quantity and type of aggregate. Water is added to this mixture and complex hydration reactions cause the cement to dry out and harden around the aggregate. The material can be reinforced with steel bars (usually up to 2 in [50 mm] in diameter) to increase its tensile strength. **Reinforced concrete** was invented in France in about 1850. In **prestressed concrete** the concrete is maintained in a state of compression by stretching the steel reinforcing wires (usually 0.24 in [6 mm] in diameter) and keeping them in a state of tension after the concrete has set around them. Prestressed concrete is now widely used as a structural material as it has a reduced tendency to bend under load. Concrete parts may be precast in a factory or poured wet on site to harden, usually inside wooden shuttering, into any desired shape.

concussion The sudden and temporary loss of consciousness that may follow a head injury. On recovering consciousness the patient may be disorientated and confused, possibly with some loss of memory. Headache and blurred vision are other possible consequences.

Condé A French princely family, a branch of the *Bourbon royal house. Its first prince **Louis I** (1530–60) was a Huguenot leader during the French *Wars of Religion and was shot after being taken prisoner in battle. He was succeeded as Huguenot leader by his son **Henri I** (1552–88), who fled to Germany following the *St Bartholomew's Day Massacre of Huguenots (1572). Henri's grandson was the general **Condé the Great** (Louis II; 1621–86). During the Thirty Years' War he won victories against Spain at Rocroi (1643) and Lens (1648), subsequently being recalled to suppress the first *Fronde (civil war). In the second Fronde he joined the rebels and fled to Spain. After being defeated by *Turenne at the battle of the Dunes Condé was pardoned and became one of Louis XIV's outstanding generals.

condensation 1. A change of physical state from a gas or vapor to a liquid. Thus as a gas is cooled below a certain temperature it may (depending on the pressure) condense to the liquid. Condensation occurs in buildings when warm moist air comes in contact with cold surfaces, such as windows and uninsulated walls. 2. A type of organic chemical reaction in which two molecules combine to form a larger molecule with elimination of a smaller molecule, such as water or methanol. Condensation reactions are the basis of a type of *polymerization process.

Condillac, Étienne Bonnot de (1715–80) French philosopher and psychologist. His ideas in *L'origine des connaissances humaines* (1746), *Traité des systèmes* (1749), and *Traité des animaux* (1755) resemble *Locke's; all knowledge springs from the senses and association of ideas. After 1800 his high reputation waned, but modern psychology largely vindicates his work.

condition A statement in logic that determines the truth of another statement. A **sufficient condition** always ensures the truth of the second statement. A **necessary condition** must be true if the second statement is true.

conditioned reflex A *reflex response that is evoked by a stimulus other than that which normally produces it. A classic example is provided by *Pavlov's experiments with dogs. The normal stimulus causing salivation (i.e. food) was paired with a different stimulus (a ringing bell) so often that eventually the bell by itself caused the dogs to salivate. A conditioned reflex gradually disappears if the stimulus is presented repeatedly; this process is called extinction. *See also* conditioning.

conditioning The process of modifying behavior by changing the stimuli (and therefore responses) associated with it. Classical conditioning occurs when a response is associated with a stimulus by pairing the stimulus with an event that causes the response by reflex (*see* conditioned reflex). Operant conditioning is brought about by either rewarding or punishing an action by the subject, which thus either encourages or discourages the behavior (*see also* aversion therapy). *Behaviorism uses both forms of conditioning to explain how people learn.

condominium 1. The joint exercise of sovereignty over a territory by two or more sovereign states, usually brought about by treaty to resolve a territorial dispute. The New Hebrides (now the Vanuatu Republic) was the subject of a condominium created by Britain and France in 1906. 2. The multiple ownership of a building by the residents. Condominiums have become increasingly popular as residences as single family homes have become more expensive.

condor A huge South American *vulture, *Vultur gryphus*, found high in the Andes. It is black with a white ruff, bare pink head and neck, and has a wingspan of 10 ft (3 m). It feeds chiefly on carrion but also takes lambs and young deer. The very rare Californian condor (*Gymnogyps californianus*) is smaller with a bare yellow head and red neck.

Condorcet, Marie Jean Antoine de Caritat, Marquis de (1743–94) French philosopher and politician. Distinguished as a mathematician and progressive man of letters in the 1770s and 1780s, after the outbreak of the French Revolution he was elected to the Legislative Assembly (1791). As a moderate *Girondin he was arrested when the *Jacobins became dominant in 1793 and died, perhaps by his own hand, in prison. His most famous work, *Esquisse d'un tableau historique des progrès de l'esprit humain*, was published posthumously (1795).

condottiere A leader of a mercenary army employed by an Italian city or lord between the 14th and 16th centuries. The earliest condottieri (from Italian *condotta*, contract) were foreign, one of the most famous being Sir John Hawkwood (d. 1394), the English adventurer, but by the end of the 14th century the Italians began to raise their own mercenary armies. Condottieri, among them Francesco *Sforza of Milan and Cesare *Borgia, began to conquer territories for themselves. The system disappeared with the foreign invasions and new methods of warfare in the late 15th century.

conductance. *See* resistance.

conduction **1.** (thermal) The transfer of heat from a region of high temperature to one of lower temperature, without the transfer of matter. It occurs as a result of the transfer of kinetic *energy by collisions between atoms and molecules in gases, liquids, and nonmetallic solids. In metals, which are the best thermal and electrical conductors, the energy is transferred by collisions between the free electrons that move through the crystal lattice and the ions of the lattice. **2.** (electrical) The passage of an electric current through a substance. In metals, the best conductors, it results from the passage of free electrons moving in one direction under the influence of an electric field. In a liquid conductor it is due to the passage of positive ions in one direction and negative ions in the other. In gases it is due to positive ions flowing in one direction and electrons in the other. In *semiconductors it results from the passage of electrons in one direction and positive holes in the other.

cone (botany) The structure, also called a strobilus, that bears the reproductive organs (sporophylls) in some pteridophytes (club mosses, horsetails, etc.) and the gymnosperms (conifers and related plants). In conifers both male and female cones are produced: the familiar woody cones of pines, larches, etc., are female strobili, made up of overlapping woody structures called bract scales, which bear the sporophylls in their axils.

coneflower. *See* black-eyed Susan.

cone shell A carnivorous marine *gastropod mollusk of the family *Conidae* (about 400 species), occurring in warm seas. 0.4–12 in (1–30 cm) long and cone-shaped, the highly colored and patterned shells are prized by collectors. The mollusks have a venomous sting and some can be dangerous to man.

Coney Island 40 35N 73 59W A resort in New York City on the S shore of Long Island. With its amusement parks, fine beach, and the New York Aquarium it attracts many tourists.

Confederate States of America (CSA) The 11 southern states of the US that seceded from the Union (1860–61), precipitating the *Civil War. The government of the Confederate States of America was established in February 1861 by South Carolina, Mississippi, Florida, Alabama, Georgia, and Louisiana. Jefferson *Davis of Mississippi was elected president and Alexander *Stephens of Georgia, vice president. The states of Texas, Virginia, Arkansas, North Carolina, and Tennessee joined the Confederacy soon afterward, and Confederate governments were temporarily established in Missouri and Kentucky. The capital of the CSA was originally Montgomery, Alabama, but it was later moved to Richmond, Virginia. The Confederate constitution protected the institution of *slavery and the principle of *states' rights. Its loose organization, however, made efficient conduct of the war with the US difficult. Unable to levy taxes, the government issued unbacked paper currency and caused massive inflation. No foreign government ever recognized the sovereignty of the CSA, and the Confederate government was dissolved soon after the surrender of General Robert E. *Lee in April 1865.

Confederation of the Rhine (1806–13) The union of the German states (except Austria and Prussia) under *Napoleon I. It facilitated the subsequent movement for German unification, which was achieved in 1871.

Confessing Church A movement among German Evangelicals opposed to the rise of Nazism in the 1930s and to the pro-Nazi German Christian Church. Led by Martin *Niemöller, it was openly active until the start of World War II, but lost influence as it was forced underground by the Nazis during the war. It continued as a movement within the Evangelical Church after 1945.

confession The admission of sins made by a penitent seeking forgiveness of them. As a religious practice it originated in Judaism and was taken over by the early Christian Church, in which public confession was customary. The fourth *Lateran Council (1215) made auricular confession (private confession to a priest, who is empowered to grant absolution) incumbent on all Christians once a year. In the Roman Catholic and Orthodox Churches auricular confession is part of the *sacrament of penance. Many Protestant Churches use a form of general confession, made by the whole congregation in public worship, although auricular confession is also practiced in some Anglican and Lutheran Churches.

confirmation A Christian rite generally held to complete the initiation of a member into the Church. Originally associated with *baptism, it became separated with the spread of infant baptism and in the middle ages came to be regarded as one of the seven *sacraments. In the Eastern Orthodox Church, it is administered by a priest immediately after baptism and followed by Holy Communion; in the West, it is conferred by a bishop—in the Roman Catholic Church not before the seventh birthday and customarily at the age of 11 or 12.

Confucianism The traditional philosophy and, until recently, the state religion of China. It was founded in the 5th century BC by *Confucius, whose teaching is contained in five classical works or canonical books (not all of which were actually written by Confucius). While retaining the idea of a divine will (*ming*), Confuciansim emphasizes the moral duty of man to his fellows. Man is born good; the superior man follows his true nature and develops sincerity, fearlessness, compassion, and wisdom. Precise rules of conduct are recorded, regulating social intercourse and establishing the forms of ritual sacrifice to one's ancestors. The canonical books also include works on divination, poetry, and history. Although not sanctioned in China since the Cultural Revolution of 1966–68, Confucianism is still practiced by expatriate Chinese and, as a fundamental ethical attitude, continues to influence Chinese culture.

Confucius (Kong Zi *or* K'ung-fu-tzu; c. 551–479 BC) Chinese philosopher, the founder of *Confucianism. As a minor official in his native Lu, a small state situated in modern Shandong province, he gathered numerous disciples, mainly young gentlemen who wished to enter government service. Promoted to ministerial rank, he became famous for his just and effective policies, but on the ruler's refusing to heed his advice, he left Lu (c. 496) and spent many years wandering from court to court, seeking a prince receptive to his ideas. Most of the works attributed to him are later compilations but the *Analects* (*Lun Yu*) is probably an authentic collection of his sayings and conversations.

conga A modern Cuban dance in march time in which the second beat in alternating measures is accompanied by a 16th note. Originally a parade dance performed by a line of people, it was popularized by the bandleader Xavier Cugat.

conger eel A voracious *eel belonging to a family (*Congridae*; about 100 species) found in all oceans. 40 in–10 ft (1–3 m) long, conger eels have a grayish or blackish body with a paler belly, a large head, and a wide mouth with strong teeth.

conglomerates Sedimentary rocks consisting of rounded fragments of former rocks cemented together, usually in sand. These fragments are over 0.08 in (2 mm) in diameter and generally consist of hard material, such as quartzite or granite. Some conglomerates are used for crushed stone for road making and other purposes.

Congo, People's Republic of (name until 1960: Middle Congo) A country in W central Africa, bordering on the Zaïre River. The narrow coastal plain rises to hills inland and lower valleys in the E provide fertile grasslands. The uplands give way to plains in the NE. The population is composed chiefly of Bantu tribes. *Economy*: largely agricultural, the main cash crops being sugar cane, palm oil, cocoa, and tobacco. Minerals include lead, zinc, and gold, and oil was discovered in 1969. Forests cover about half the country and timber is one of the main exports; others include sugar. The discovery of oil brightened the country's economic outlook considerably, encouraging foreign investment. In the 1980s efforts to decentralize the economy and lessen dependence on oil were aided by loans from the

World Bank and other European and African lending agencies. *History*: in the 15th century the Portuguese established trading relations with the Congo kingdom. In the 19th century the exploration of the Frenchman de *Brazza led to the establishment of the colony of Middle Congo, which in 1910 became one of the four territories of French Equatorial Africa. In 1958 it attained internal self-government as a member of the French Community and in 1960 became independent as the Republic of Congo. In 1968 Major Marien Ngouabi came to power in a military coup and in 1970, under a new Marxist constitution, the country's present name was adopted. Ngouabi was assassinated in 1977 and the government was taken over by a military committee under Colonel Joachim Yhombi Opango until his resignation in 1979. President: Colonel Denis Sassou-Nguesso. Prime minister: Colonel Louis-Sylvain Goma (1941–   ). Official language: French. Official currency: CFA (Communauté financière africaine) franc of 100 centimes. Area: 132,018 sq mi (342,000 sq km). Population (1983 est): 1,694,000. Capital: Brazzaville. Main port: Pointe-Noire.

Congo, Republic of. *See* Zaïre, Republic of.

congo eel A large eel-like North American nocturnal *salamander of the genus *Amphiuma* and family *Amphiumidae* (2 species). The two-toed *A. means* grows to 33 in (85 cm) and the the three-toed *A. tridactylum* up to 46 in (115 cm). Both are light gray-brown, darker above, and feed on snails, crayfish, etc., in their swamp habitats.

Congo River. *See* Zaïre River.

Congregationalism In Christianity, a form of church government that opposes centralized authority and in which each congregation is democratically autonomous. Congregationalist groups first became active at the time of the *Reformation in the 16th century and played an important role in the opposition to King Charles I in England in the 17th century. They were active supporters of Oliver *Cromwell and became one of the most important forces in the early settlement of New England. Congregationalists founded the Plymouth Colony in 1620 and were the dominant political force in the Massachusetts Bay Colony. Now officially called the United Church of Christ, American Congregationalists now number more than 2,000,000. In Great Britain, the unification of the Congregationalists and the Presbyterians in 1972 led to the establishment of the United Reformed Church.

Congress The legislative branch of the US government established by the US *Constitution (1789) and comprising the Senate and the House of Representatives. According to Article I of the Constitution, all legislation must be passed by both the House and the Senate and be signed by the president before being enacted into law. The House of Representatives has the exclusive power to initiate proposals for new taxes, while the Senate has the sole authority to confirm presidential appointments and ratify treaties. There are 435 members of the House of Representatives, allocated among the states according to population. Members must be at least 25 years of age and serve for terms of two years. The House of Representatives is headed by the Speaker of the House and the chairmen of various committees, who are elected by the members of the majority party. The Senate comprises 100 senators, two from each state regardless of population. All senators must be at least 30 years of age and serve for terms of six years. The vice president presides over the Senate and casts the deciding vote in the case of a tie, but a president pro tempore and the Senate committee chairmen are elected by the majority party. In addition to their legislative duties, the two houses of Congress are empowered to remove federal officials from office through the process of impeachment. This proceeding, used only with an official is accused of serious crimes or misconduct, begins with the presentation of formal charges and a vote by the House of Representatives and is decided by a trial in the Senate.

Congress of Industrial Organizations (CIO) A US labor organization. Originally established in 1835 as a part of the *American Federation of Labor to coordinate mass production worker industries, it became a separate organization by 1938. Its first president, John L. *Lewis (1935–40), was successful in unionizing the automobile, steel, textile, rubber, electric, and mining industries. In 1955 it merged with the American Federation of Labor.

Congress Kingdom of Poland (1815–32) A Polish state, formed at the Congress of *Vienna, having administrative autonomy under the Russian crown. Polish nationalists twice attempted to overthrow Russian dominance but were unsuccessful: after the November Insurrection (1830), Congress Poland lost its autonomy and following the January Insurrection (1863–64), it became a Russian province.

Congreve, William (1670–1729) British dramatist. Educated in Ireland, he returned to England in 1688 to study law but under the patronage of *Dryden entered the literary world instead. The comedies *Love for Love*

(1695) and *The Way of the World* (1700) are his best-known plays, although his contemporaries most admired his tragedy *The Mourning Bride* (1697). He wrote little after 1700.

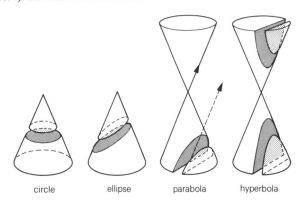

CONIC SECTION *The circle, ellipse, parabola, and hyperbola are produced by slicing through the cone as shown.*

conic section Geometrical figures produced by the intersection of a plane and a cone. If the plane cuts the cone at right angles to its axis the figure is a *circle. If the plane is tilted slightly an *ellipse is formed. If the plane is tilted further, until it lies parallel to the side of the cone, the figure is a *parabola. Tilted more, the figure becomes a *hyperbola. In the case of a hyperbola, the plane also intersects another cone the vertex of which touches the vertex of the first cone, the axes of the two cones being parallel. In this case two conic sections are produced. Therefore a hyperbola has two branches.

conifer A *gymnosperm tree of the widely distributed order *Coniferales* (400–500 species), most abundant in the colder temperate zones, especially in the north; elsewhere they are usually found at high altitudes. Conifers are typically pyramidal in form, with a straight continuously growing stem that can reach great heights (*see* Sequoia). Nearly all conifers are *evergreen (larches are exceptions), with simple needle-like or scalelike leaves. The reproductive organs are typically borne in separate male and female *cones, usually on the same tree, and produce winged seeds that are dispersed by wind (the yew and juniper are exceptions). The wood of conifers—called softwood—is economically important, being used for construction and as a source of paper pulp, etc. (*see* timber).

The principal families are the *Pinaceae* (pines, cedars, spruces, firs, larches, hemlocks, etc.); *Cupressaceae* (cypresses, junipers, arbor vitae, etc.); *Taxodiaceae* (sequoias, swamp cypress, etc.); *Taxaceae* (yews); and *Araucariaceae* (monkey puzzle, etc.).

conjugation The process by which exchange of genetic material occurs in certain lower organisms by means of a connection between the cytoplasm of the two "mating" individuals. In ciliate protozoa and certain algae it is a type of sexual reproduction, the gametes (or gametic nuclei) passing through a cytoplasmic bridge (protozoa) or a conjugation tube (algae). In bacteria the connection between "male" and "female" cells is by means of special hairs (pili) or cell-to-cell bridges.

conjunction An alignment of two celestial bodies in the solar system, usually the sun and a planet, that occurs when the angular distance between them as seen from earth (i.e. the angle planet-earth-sun) becomes zero.

conjunctivitis Inflammation of the conjunctiva—the membrane that covers the surface of the eye and lines the eyelids. Popularly known as pinkeye, it is marked by itching, redness, and watering of the eye. It may be caused by allergy to drugs or pollen; bacterial infection (in which case it usually spreads to the other eye); or mechanical irritation.

Conkling, Roscoe (1829–88) US politician, lawyer, and orator. A lawyer in New York and a leader in the state Republican Party, he served in the US House of Representatives (1859–63; 1865–67) and the Senate (1867–81). He was a strong advocate of *Reconstruction and worked for the passage of the 14th Amendment. He resigned from the Senate when his leadership of the Republican Party was threatened by federal civil service reform.

Conn (2nd century AD) King of Leinster and High King of Ireland. A tireless warrior, known as Conn of the hundred battles, he gained control over the northern half of Ireland and then, shortly before his death, the whole island.

Connacht (or Connaught) A province and ancient kingdom of the NW Republic of Ireland. It consists of the counties of Galway, Leitrim, Mayo, Roscommon, and Sligo. Area: 6611 sq mi (17,122 sq km). Population (1979): 418,500.

Connaught. See Connacht.

Connecticut A state in the NE US, in New England. It is bordered by Massachusetts on the N, Rhode Island on the E, Long Island Sound on the S, and New York State on the W. Uplands in the E and W are separated by the central lowlands, forming the fertile Connecticut River valley. It is one of the most densely populated states in the US with a fairly even demographic distribution; 90% of the inhabitants living in cities. The populous SE forms part of the New York City metropolitan area. Connecticut is highly industrial and manufacturing is an important source of revenue. Traditionally produced goods include clocks, silverware, and brass products, as well as military equipment. Hartford, the capital, is one of the principal US insurance centers. Farming is only a minor activity, producing dairy products, eggs, poultry, and vegetables for local markets with some tobacco for export. The state has a rich tradition and culture dating back to colonial times. Yale University at New Haven is the most famous of its large number of universities and colleges. *History*: one of the original 13 colonies, it was first explored by the Dutch in the early 17th century. The first settlement was by English colonists from the Massachusetts Bay Colony (1633–35). Connecticut joined the other colonies in the American Revolution and was one of the first states to ratify the Constitution. It abolished slavery in 1848. In 1974 Connecticut elected Ella Grasso as governor, the first woman to be elected a governor in her own right. Area: 5009 Sq mi (12,973 sq km). Population (1983 provisional est): 3,138,000. Capital: Hartford.

Connecticut Compromise (1787) A proposal set forth at the US Constitutional Convention by Connecticut delegates that solved the problem of equal representation of states in the federal government. Each state would have representation in the House of Representatives proportionate to its population, while the Senate would have an equal number of representatives from each state.

Connecticut River 41 17M 72 21W A river that rises in the Connecticut Lakes in N New Hampshire and flows S to Long Island Sound at Old Saybrook, Conn. It forms the entire New Hampshire-Vemont border and passes by Springfield, Mass, and Hartford, Conn. Length: 407 mi (656 km).

Connecticut Wits A group of US writers in Hartford, Conn, in the late 1700s and early 1800s. Federalists in favor of strong central government, they grouped together to write satirical verse, such as *The Anarchiad* (1786–87) and *The Political Greenhouse* (1799). *The Echo* (1791–1805) was a series. Members included Theodore Dwight, Joel Barlow, John Trumbull, David Humphreys, and Richard Alsop.

connective tissue The tissue that supports, binds, or separates the specialized tissues and organs of the body. Connective tissue consists of a semifluid ground substance of polysaccharide and protein in which are embedded white collagen fibers, yellow elastic fibers, and various cells (including fibroblasts, which produce the ground substance and the fibers). The amount of collagen determines the toughness of the tissue. Specialized connective tissue includes fatty tissue, blood, bone, and cartilage.

Connelly, Marc (us Cook) (1890–1980) US dramatist. He began writing plays with George S. *Kaufman in the 1920s, while he was a newspaper theater reporter in New York City. In 1930 he wrote *The Green Pastures* for which he received a Pulitzer Prize. Other works include *The Wisdom Tooth* (1926) and, in collaboration with Frank B. Elser, *The Farmer Takes a Wife* (1934).

Connemara An area in the W Republic of Ireland, in Co Galway bordering on the Atlantic Ocean. It contains many lakes, peat bogs, and the Twelve Bens, a group of quartzite mountains.

Connors, Jimmy (1952–   ) US tennis player, who won the US singles title in 1974, 1976, 1978, and 1982 and the doubles title in 1975. He also was Wimbledon singles champion in 1974 and 1982 and doubles champion in 1973.

conquistador (Spanish: conqueror) One of the men who conquered the Indians of Central and South America for Spain in the first half of the 16th century. Few in number, the conquistadores were driven by a fanatical desire to find fame and gold and to serve the Roman Catholic Church. The most famous were Hernán *Cortés and Francisco *Pizarro.

Conrad II (c. 990–1039) German king (1024–39), who founded the Salian dynasty (1024–1125), and Holy Roman Emperor (1027–39). He conquered part of Poland (1028) and Burgundy (1033–34). While attempting to suppress a rebellion in N Italy (1036–38), he lost most of his army in an epidemic.

Conrad III (1093–1152) The first Hohenstaufen German king (1138–52). He was proclaimed antiking (1127) in opposition to Lothair, after whose death (1137) he became king. His election was opposed by the Welf family and although peace was made in 1142 the conflict between the two families was renewed, giving rise to the *Guelf and Ghibelline struggle. In 1147 Conrad joined the second Crusade.

Conrad, Joseph (Teodor Josef Konrad Watęcz Korzeniowski; 1857–1924) Polish-born British novelist, who knew no English before he was 20. Orphaned at the age of 11, he went to Marseilles in 1874, where he became a sailor, serving for 16 years in the British Merchant Navy. He became a naturalized British subject in 1886, and published his first novel, *Almayer's Folly*, in 1895. His seagoing experiences influenced both the themes of his fiction and his own moral outlook. His major novels include *Lord Jim* (1900), *Nostromo* (1904), *The Secret Agent* (1907), and *Under Western Eyes* (1911).

consanguinity Relationship by blood, either real or putative. However, many societies do not consider everyone to whom they are genetically related to be blood kin. For example, some societies do not consider a father to be genetically related to his children and therefore they are not his consanguines. Consanguinity affects laws regarding property inheritance and prohibits marriage between close blood relatives.

Conscience, Hendrik (1812–83) Flemish novelist. The author of over a hundred novels, he began writing sketches in Flemish in the late 1830s, and his historical romance *The Lion of Flanders* (1838) was the first major Flemish novel.

conscientious objection. See pacifism.

conscription The compulsory enlistment of citizens for military service. Conscription was used in the ancient world and during the Middle Ages, when short-term *militia service was enforced for local defense. Universal male conscription was introduced in 1793 in Revolutionary France and was adopted by Prussia in the early 19th century. During the *Civil War, both the Union and the Confederacy used conscription as a means of gaining recruits. There was considerable opposition to this practice, however, especially in the North, where *Draft Riots broke out in 1863. With the entry of the US into World War I in 1917, Congress enacted the first of the *Selective Service Acts, which required the registration of all men between the ages of 18 and 45 for possible military service. Conscription was also used by the US for its participation in *World War II, the *Korean War, and the *Vietnam War. It was officially abolished in 1973, although young men are still required to register with the Selective Service upon reaching the age of 18.

Consejo Real (Spanish: Royal Council) The central organ of government in Spain, created in 1386 in *Castille by Juan I. It was dominated by the clergy and nobility until the reforms of Isabella I in 1480 replaced them with lawyers loyal to the crown. It survived, with diminishing power, until the 19th century.

Consentes Dii The 12 major Roman and Etruscan gods, six male and six female. They are Jupiter and Juno, Neptune and Minerva, Mars and Venus, Apollo and Diana, Vulcan and Vesta, Mercury and Ceres. They were first collectively mentioned in 217 BC.

conservation The rational use of the earth's resources so that life can be sustained indefinitely. Pressure on both mineral and natural resources, resulting from increased agricultural and industrial activity, has required urgent examination of the consequent effects on the world ecosystem. The prudent use of fossil fuels and minerals and the search for alternatives are becoming both political and economic necessities. The destruction of many natural habitats has led to the creation of nature reserves and national parks where wildlife can be protected. Such areas are also often of aesthetic value and serve as recreational areas for urban populations. Legislation can protect some rare species of animals and plants from extinction but international cooperation is needed to protect economically important species (including whales), to conserve fish stocks, and to prevent pollution of the atmosphere and the oceans. In most cases the technological means to solve these problems are available but their high costs, or conflict with sectional interests, prevent their implementation.

conservation of energy supplies The more efficient use of increasingly scarce fuel supplies. In the 1970s several governments began to encourage home-insulation improvements and research into new sources of energy, as well as ways to reduce waste from industrial processes. Similar interest developed in *alternative energy sources. Thus, most new buildings are now designed to minimize heat losses. In electricity-generating stations the warm water produced from condensed steam may be used for local domestic heating in combined heat and power (co-generation) projects. More efficient burners and boilers have been developed for coal-fired power stations. The introduction of transport systems that are less wasteful than the private gasoline-driven car is also likely to become a necessity. *See also* solar power; wave power; wind power.

conservation of mass and energy   The principle that, in any closed system, the total of the mass and energy remains constant. It replaced the older laws in which mass and energy were held to be separately conserved, since the special theory of *relativity demonstrates that mass and energy may, in certain circumstances, be interconvertible. The energy (E) equivalent to a mass (m) is given by Einstein's equation: $E = mc^2$, where c is the speed of light in a vacuum.

Conservative Party   A UK political party that grew out of the *Tory Party in the 1830s under the leadership of Sir Robert *Peel. Under the leadership of *Disraeli the Conservatives acquired a distinct philosophy that combined identification with the monarchy, the British Empire, and the Church of England with social reform. The party was almost continuously in power from 1886 to 1905 and again from 1922 to 1945. It was again in office in 1951–1964, 1970–74, and from 1979 under *Thatcher. The party is now firmly committed to the furtherance of private enterprise and individualism rather than *nationalization.

consols.   *See* gilt-edged securities.

CONSTABLE   *Self-portrait in pencil and watercolor.*

Constable, John   (1776–1837) British landscape painter, He trained in London at the Royal Academy schools. He painted the Suffolk countryside, Hampstead Heath, and Salisbury Cathedral with a particular concern for changing weather conditions, exemplified in *The Leaping Horse* and *Dedham Vale*. Although he exhibited regularly at the Royal Academy, he was only elected a member in 1829. He achieved greater recognition in France, where his *Haywain* won a gold medal and influenced *Delacroix.

Constanta   44 10N 28 40E The chief seaport of Romania, situated on the Black Sea. Founded by the Greeks in the 7th century BC, it was rebuilt by Constantine the Great in the 4th century AD. Oil is pumped here from the Ploieşti fields to be refined and exported. Population (1979 est): 279,308.

Constance   (German name: Konstanz)   47 40N 09 10E A city in SW West Germany, in Baden-Württemberg on Lake Constance. Its 11th-century church was formerly a cathedral. Manufactures include textiles, computers, and chemicals. Population (1971 est): 64,600.

Constance, Council of   (1414–18) The 16th ecumenical council of the Roman Catholic Church, which ended the *Great Schism by electing Pope *Martin V (1417). It decreed that the authority of a general council was superior to that of the pope. The heretics *Wycliffe and *Hus were condemned, and Hus was burned at the stake.

Constance, Lake   (German name: Bodensee)   A lake on the Rhine River in West Germany, Switzerland, and Austria. Area: 205 sq mi (531 sq km).

Constant, Benjamin   (1767–1830) French novelist, born in Switzerland and educated in Germany and Britain. He supported the French Revolution but opposed Napoleon and went into exile. After the restoration of the monarchy he returned to France in 1818 as a leading liberal politician and journalist. His novel *Adolphe* (1816) was based on his passionate affair with Mme de *Staël. Several volumes of his private journals have also been published.

Constanţa   44 10N 28 40E The chief seaport of Romania, situated on the Black Sea. Founded by the Greeks in the 7th century BC, it was rebuilt by Constantine the Great in the 4th century AD. Oil is pumped here from the Ploieşti fields to be refined and exported. Population (1979 est): 279,308.

constantan   An alloy of 55% copper and 45% nickel. It is used in electrical equipment, such as resistors and *thermocouples, because it has a high electrical resistance that does not change with temperature.

Constantine   (ancient name: Cirta)   36 23N 6 29E A city in N Algeria. It was destroyed in 311 AD but rebuilt by Constantine the Great in 313 and renamed for him. The old town is popular with tourists and noted for its handicrafts. Population (1974 est): 350,183.

Constantine I   (1868–1923) King of Greece (1913–17, 1920–22). Constantine led Greece to victory in the *Balkan War (1912–13) but unpopularly maintained neutrality in World War I and was forced to abdicate (1917). Recalled in 1920, he again abdicated following a military revolt against his war with Turkey.

Constantine II   (1940–   ) King of Greece (1964–67). In 1967, following a military coup, Constantine went into exile, eventually moving to Britain. In 1973 he was officially deposed and Greece became a republic. He married (1964) Princess Anne-Marie of Denmark (1946–   ).

Constantine VII Porphyrogenitus   (905–59 AD) Byzantine emperor (913–59). Constantine reigned (919–45) with his father-in-law and coemperor, Romanus I Lecapenus (d. 948), and while Romanus ruled Constantine devoted himself to studying and writing. His works *On Imperial Administration* and *Ceremonies of the Byzantine Court* are invaluable sources for Byzantine social and economic history.

Constantine the Great   (?285–337 AD) Roman emperor in the West (312–24) and sole emperor (324–37). The son of Constantius (c. 250–306), Roman emperor in the West (305–06), Constantine was acclaimed as his father's successor by his troops at York but did not secure his position until he had defeated his rival Maxentius (d. 312). He became sole emperor after defeating the Eastern emperor Licinius (c. 270–325; reigned 311–24). Constantine was the first Roman emperor to adopt Christianity. During his campaign against Maxentius he was reputed to have had a vision of the Christian cross with the words "In this sign, conquer." In 313 Constantine issued the Edict of Milan, which established toleration of Christians, and in 325 summoned the Council of *Nicaea, the first general council of the Church. He was baptized on his deathbed. Constantine introduced administrative and military reforms and founded Constantinople (*see* Istanbul).

Constantinople.   *See* Istanbul.

Constantinople, Councils of   Three general councils of the Christian Church. **1.** (381) The council that was summoned to end the Arian dispute (*see* Arianism) and assert the doctrine of the Council of *Nicaea. **2.** (553) The council that attempted to resolve the conflict between the *Nestorians and *Monophysites. **3.** (680) The council that condemned the *Monothelite heresy and asserted the doctrines of the Council of *Chalcedon concerning the dual nature of Christ's will.

constellations   The 88 areas into which the N and S hemispheres of the sky are now divided, using established boundaries. Each star, galaxy, or other celestial body lies within, or sometimes overlaps, the boundaries of one of the constellations and is often named in terms of this constellation. The constellations all have Latin names. They originally had no fixed limits but were groups of stars forming a distinctive pattern outlining a mythological hero, animal, etc. The constellations that can be observed at night depend on the latitude of the observer and change with the time of night and the time of year.

constipation The condition in which emptying of the bowels occurs infrequently: feces are often hard and dry and there may be pain in passing them. Constipation is often associated with advancing age and a diet deficient in vegetable fiber (probably the commonest cause in the western world). It is also caused by some drugs (e.g. codeine) and by obstruction of the bowel. Long-standing constipation not due to disease of the bowel is treated by increasing the amount of vegetable fiber (e.g. bran) in the diet. *Laxatives may also be used.

constitution The principles according to which a country is governed. Constitutions may comprise the sum of a country's laws and its customs of government, as in the UK, where government is by the monarch in *parliament, or be contained in a single document, as in the US.

Constitution, US (1787) The document that embodies the fundamental laws of the US. It was drawn up in 1787, ratified in 1788, and came into effect in 1789. Framed by James *Madison, it contains 7 articles, which define separation of powers, a system of checks and balances between the legislature (see Congress), the executive (see president), and the judiciary (see Supreme Court). There are 26 amendments, the first 10 of which constitute the *Bill of Rights. Subsequent amendments dealt with prohibiting a citizen of one state from suing another state government (11, 1795), revision of methods for electing the president and vice president (12, 1804), abolition of slavery and full citizenship and voting rights (13, 1861; 14, 1868; 15, 1870), income tax (16, 1913), popular election of senators (17, 1913), prohibition of alcohol (18, 1919), woman suffrage (19, 1920), convening of Congress to eliminate "lame duck" situation (20, 1933), repeal of amendment 19 (21, 1933), number of presidential terms (22, 1951), District of Columbia residents' right to vote for president (23, 1961), prohibition of poll tax (24, 1964), presidential succession (25, 1967), and lowering the voting age to 18 (26, 1971). See Connecticut Compromise; New Jersey Plan; Virginia Plan.

Constitutional Act of 1791 British act that divided Canada into Upper (English-speaking) and Lower (French-speaking) Canada. It was drawn up by Prime Minister William Pitt the Younger (see Pitt the Elder, William, 1st Earl of Chatham) in an effort to keep the colonists under British rule. Under the act the colonists had an elective assembly that worked with a legislative council appointed by the crown.

Constitutional Convention (1787) An assembly of delegates from 12 of the original states (Rhode Island choosing not to participate) that met in Philadelphia to draft a new constitution for the US. Since the original form of federal government for the US, set down in the *Articles of Confederation, had proved to be too weak to permit an effective central authority or a unified foreign policy, an effort was made to create a strong federal government while preserving the rights of the individual states. During the debates at the Constitutional Convention, which lasted from May to September, James *Madison played an instrumental role in shaping the new US *Constitution. The cornerstone of the new system of government was a division of federal power among three separate branches: the executive, the legislative, and the judicial. In order that there be some balance between the influence of the larger states and the smaller states, the legislative branch was to consist of a bicameral *Congress with both proportional and equal representation. After debates in state constitutional ratification conventions, the US Constitution was adopted in 1788.

constrictor A snake belonging to the family *Boidae* (70 species) occurring chiefly in tropical regions. Constrictors are nonvenomous and kill their prey by coiling their thick muscular body around it and squeezing until it suffocates. They often have claws, which are vestigial limbs. The family comprises two subfamilies, *Boine* (see boa) and *Pythonine* (see python).

constructivism A movement in abstract sculpture, architecture, and design, which was launched in Russia by the *Realist Manifesto* (1920) of the brothers Naum *Gabo and Antoine *Pevsner with the aim of freeing contemporary art from political and social overtones. The chief principles of constructivism were functionalism, the articulation of space, and the use of modern materials, such as plastic and steel. Many Russian constructivists left their country for Germany or France in 1922 because of state opposition to the movement. The architect, painter, and designer El *Lissitzky was influential at the *Bauhaus school in Germany, while Gabo spread the style to the UK and the US.

consubstantiation In Christian theology, a doctrine concerning the presence of Christ in the *Eucharist, especially associated with the teaching of Martin *Luther. Traditionally, the consecrated bread and wine were held to become, substantially, the body and blood of Christ (see transubstantiation). According to the doctrine of consubstantiation, the substances of the body and blood of Christ and of the bread and wine were held to coexist together in the consecrated Host.

consuls The two magistrates who held supreme civil and military authority under the *Roman Republic. They were elected annually by the Comitia Centuriata (see comitia) and presided over the Senate. Under the Empire they were nominated by the emperor and held office for only two to four months, the posts becoming honorary.

Consumer Affairs, The Office of US agency within the Department of Commerce that works with the business community on behalf of consumers and assists consumers with market-place problems. It develops cooperative projects with companies, trade and professional associations, consumer organizations, and federal, state, and local agencies to help businesses improve their relations with consumers.

consumerism The idea that consumers should influence the design, quality, service, and prices of goods and services provided by commercial enterprises. Movements based on this idea have developed in the US (see Nader, Ralph) and in Europe as a response to the concentration of economic power in modern corporations and to the increased technical complexity of many contemporary consumer goods.

consumption (economics) Expenditure on goods and services, excluding expenditure on capital goods (see investment). A country's national income is spent either on consumption or on investment. Public consumption consists of government spending on services, such as education, health, defense, etc. Private consumption is money spent by individuals on nondurables, such as food and drink, durables, such as cars and washing machines, and services, such as entertainment. There is some controversy as to whether private consumption is determined by an individual's lifetime prospects or his current income. This controversy has important consequences in economic planning: for example, whether or not tax cuts would reduce unemployment by increasing consumption.

contact lenses A removable form of lens worn directly against the eye to replace spectacles for long or short sight or to protect the eye in some disorders of the outer transparent layer (cornea). Originally made of glass, modern contact lenses are made of plastic and become molded to the shape of the individual's eye. At first the lenses may irritate the eyes, but most people can adapt to them with time.

containerization The use of large cuboid containers built to internationally accepted dimensions (usually $8 \times 8 \times 20$, 30, or 40 ft or $2.4 \times 2.4 \times 6.1$, 9.1 or 12.2 m) for the transport of goods. These containers are transported from the producing factory to the user, distributor, or export dock without being unpacked: thus they cut down on the cost and time involved in handling and reduce the chances of loss through pilferage or damage. Containerization has revolutionized international shipping, as specialized ships are needed to transport the containers efficiently; this has led to the decline of the many docks that are only equipped to handle conventionally packed goods.

conté crayon A stick of soft crayon, named for its inventor, the French scientist Nicholas Jacques Conté (1755–1805). Unlike pastel, its color is durable and nonsmudging, while its size makes it suitable both for line drawing and shading large areas.

contempt of court An act or omission that is designed to obstruct a court in its administration of justice or which is designed to lessen its authority or its dignity. There are two types of contempt: direct and constructive. Direct contempts are committed in court (such as insulting language or acts of violence). Constructive (or indirect) contempts arise from matters occurring out of court, but which tend to obstruct the administration of justice (such as failure or refusal to obey a lawful order, injunction, or decree). Contempt is punishable by fine or imprisonment.

continent One of the major land masses of the earth. The following are usually given as distinct continents: Asia, Africa, North America, South America, Europe, Australia, and Antarctica. (These divisions do not correspond to the rigid plates into which the whole of the earth's crust is divided.) The continents occupy about 30% of the earth's surface area. The crust of which they are formed (mainly granitic) is less dense than the oceanic crust (basaltic). The constituents of the continental crust are called sial and those of the oceanic crust, sima. The continents have not always occupied their present positions; the approximate "fit" of the coastlines of the present continents provided the first evidence for the theory of *continental drift.

Continental Congress (1774–89) The body of representatives of the American colonies, which met in Philadelphia. The first Continental Congress (1774–75) was convened as a response to the passage of the *Intolerable Acts and the *Quebec Act by the British parliament. The members of the First Continental Congress agreed to organize an economic boycott of Great Britain and to reconvene if further action proved to be necessary. Since the British government refused to offer any concessions to the colonists, the Second Continental Congress (1775–76) met to consider the question of American independence and the coordination of a plan for military defense. Its members named George Washington commander of the Continental Army and adopted the *Declaration of Independence on July 4, 1776. With this action, the Continental Congress became the provisional government of the US. It continued to meet yearly until 1789, when it was replaced by the US *Congress established by the Constitution.

continental divide A major *watershed separating the drainage basins of a continent. In North America a continental divide extends generally N–S along the Rocky Mountains dividing the rivers flowing E from those flowing W.

continental drift The theory, first set out in 1912 by Alfred *Wegener and now widely accepted by earth scientists, that the continents are not fixed in position but drift slowly over the earth's surface (*see also* plate tectonics). Wegener's work was based on similarities in rock types, geological structures, flora and fauna, and the coastal outlines of the continents; in recent years geophysical data, particularly from geomagnetic studies, have provided firmer evidence for continental drift. It is believed that about 200 million years ago a supercontinent (termed Pangaea), into which all the continents were joined, began to break up and the fragments drifted apart until the continents reached their present positions. It is probable that continents have been joining together and breaking up throughout the earth's history.

continental shelf The area of sea floor adjacent to the continents, dipping gently from the shoreline to a depth of about 650 ft (200 m). At this depth, the shelf edge, the continental slope begins, dipping more steeply to the ocean bottom. Shelves tend to be wider off low-lying regions than mountainous regions; the average width is about 42 mi (70 km).

Continental System The trade blockade of Britain introduced by Napoleon in 1806 to ruin Britain's commerce and thus force peace on his own terms. Napoleon used his control of the coast from the Baltic to the Adriatic to forbid French allies or neutrals to trade with Britain or its colonies. Britain subjected all countries in alliance with France to counterblockade. The Continental System ultimately failed because of the contraband trade and the new British markets in South America.

contraception The prevention of unwanted pregnancy, also known as birth control and family planning. Of the numerous methods available for preventing conception, the rhythm method and coitus interruptus are the most simple but least reliable. In the former sexual intercourse is avoided around the middle of the menstrual cycle, when ovulation is most likely to occur; in the latter the penis is withdrawn from the vagina before ejaculation. Both the condom (or sheath), which is worn over the penis, and the diaphragm, which is fitted over the cervix of the womb, are more effective since they prevent the sperm from entering the womb. A far more reliable contraceptive is the intra-uterine device (IUD)—a loop or coil, often impregnated with copper, that is inserted by a doctor into the womb. Its method of action is not known. Some women, however, are unable to use an IUD as it causes unacceptable side effects (such as heavy menstrual bleeding or recurrent infection). The most efficient means of preventing pregnancy is by taking hormonal pills (*see* oral contraceptive), but this, too, may produce side effects and is unsuitable for some women. Another hormonal contraceptive method is the injection, at three-monthly intervals, of a synthetic hormone (progestogen). The selection of any contraceptive method depends on its suitability for the individual: there is no universally acceptable method. Permanent contraception is achieved by *sterilization, which includes vasectomy for men and cutting of the Fallopian tubes for women. A contraceptive pill to be taken by men and a morning-after pill for women are actively being sought.

Family planning has had a long history, with early methods ranging from infanticide and abortion to the use of such preventive devices as sheep's bladders as condoms. The need for it, however, was not formally discussed until the beginning of the 19th century, when the writings of *Malthus drew attention to the problems of overpopulation. Moral objections and the absence of an appropriate technology delayed the advent of the first family-planning clinics until 1916. They were pioneered in the US by Margaret Sanger (1883–1966). Until the 1960s and the appearance of the Pill, contraception was almost entirely dependent upon rubber devices (the condom and the diaphragm).

contract In law, an enforceable promise or bargain, usually written but sometimes verbal. A simple promise for which nothing is given in exchange is not a contract and is only enforceable at law as a *deed. Something of value, called "consideration," must be exchanged in return for the promise; the value must be real but need not be equivalent. If a house is sold for a pound of sugar, that sugar represents sufficient consideration. Breach of

contract, meaning failure to fulfil its conditions, may result in the offender being sued for damages by the other party to the contract.

contralto The deepest female singing voice. Range: F below middle C to D an octave and a sixth above.

contrapposto A technique in sculpture for resting a figure's weight on one leg to tilt the body in a realistic pose. Practiced by *Polyclitus of Argos (5th century BC), it was revived during the Renaissance, notably in *Michelangelo's statue of David (Accademia, Florence).

Contreras, Battle of (August 19–20, 1847) A battle of the *Mexican War fought near Mexico City. US forces under Gen Winfield *Scott (1786–1866) put the Mexican forces to flight and gained control of the road to the Mexican capital.

convection The transfer of heat within a fluid by means of motion of the fluid. Convection may be natural or forced. In natural convection, the fluid flows by virtue of the warmer part being less dense than the cooler part. Thus the warmer fluid rises and the colder fluid sinks under the influence of gravity. In forced convection, some external cause, such as a fan or impeller, drives colder fluid into a warmer one, or vice versa.

convergence (*or* convergent evolution) The development in unrelated animals of similarities resulting from adaption to the same way of life. Thus whales (mammals) and fish have evolved similar features independently, associated with their aquatic habitat.

conversos (Spanish: converts) The Spanish Jews who were forced to become Roman Catholics during the persecution of Jews in the late 14th and 15th centuries. The Spanish Inquisition was created to prevent the apostasy of *conversos* and the Muslim *Moriscos.

Convolvulus A widely distributed genus of annual or perennial twining plants (about 250 species). The flowers are funnel or bell-shaped and attractive. The Eurasian *bindweed (*C. arvensis*) is a noxious weed, now widely introduced, with deep persistent roots and rapidly growing stems. Some species, such as *C. altheoides*, are cultivated in gardens. Some have medicinal (purgative) properties. Family: *Convolvulaceae*.

cony. *See* hyrax; pika.

Cook, Captain James (1728–79) British navigator and cartographer. He joined the Royal Navy (1755) and served in the Seven Years' War (1756–63), during which he surveyed the St Lawrence River. His observations on the eclipse of the sun in 1766 were presented to the Royal Society, which gave him command of an expedition to Tahiti to observe the transit of the planet Venus across the sun and to discover Terra Australis, a presumed southern continent. The expedition set sail in the *Endeavour* in 1768 and, Venus observed, Cook went on to discover and chart New Zealand and the E coast of Australia, returning to England in 1771. The voyage was remarkable not least for the absence of scurvy among his crew—the result of a diet, devised by Cook, that was high in vitamin C. His second voyage (1772–75), in the *Resolution*, accompanied by the *Adventure*, achieved the circumnavigation of the Antarctic. He charted Easter Island and discovered New Caledonia, the South Sandwich Islands, and South Georgia Island. Cook's third voyage (1776–79) ended in tragedy: he was killed in a quarrel with Hawaiians.

Cook, Sir Joseph (1860–1947) Australian statesman, born in England; Liberal prime minister (1913–14). He was hampered by a majority of only one in the House of Representatives and a minority in the Senate.

Cook, Mount (Maori name: Aorangi) 43 37S 170 08E The highest mountain in New Zealand, in South Island in the Southern Alps. It is permanently snow capped and flanked by glaciers. Height: 12,349 ft (3764 m).

Cook, Thomas (1808–92) British travel agent, who introduced conducted excursions and founded the travel agents Thomas Cook and Son. He organized his first excursion in 1841, a railroad journey from Leicester to Lowborough for a temperance meeting.

Cooke, Jay (1821–1905) US financier. After working for a banking firm in Philadelphia, he formed his own banking company in 1861. He aided the US Treasury Department during the Civil War by selling war bonds and raising millions of dollars for the war effort. His firm was also instrumental in setting up the new national bank system under the National Bank Act of 1863. The company went bankrupt in 1873, due to railroad speculations, and Cooke turned to other ventures.

Cook Islands A group of scattered islands in the SE Pacific Ocean, a New Zealand dependency. The chief islands are Rarotonga, Atiu, and Aitutaki. Fruit, copra, and mother-of-pearl are exported. Area: 93 sq mi (241 sq km). Population (1976): 18,112. Capital: Avarua.

coolabar A tree, *Eucalyptus microtheca*, growing to 80 ft (25 m), common inland in W Australia. The leaves are mainly persistent and the wood is gray near the outside, deep red within. Called locally by many names, including jinbul, moolar, blackbox, and dwarf box, it is used for building. Family: *Myrtaceae. See also* Eucalyptus.

Coolidge, John Calvin (1872–1933) US statesman; 30th President of the United States (1923–29). After beginning his political career as a Republican member of the Massachusetts legislature, Coolidge was elected governor in 1918 and gained national prominence for his uncompromising and efficient handling of the Boston police strike (1919). Chosen as the vice-presidential running mate of Warren G. *Harding in 1920, Coolidge succeeded to the presidency after Harding's death in 1923. While Harding's administration was marred by scandal and corruption, Coolidge acted decisively to restore the integrity of the federal government and was elected by a large majority to a full term in 1924. In accordance with the belief that "the business of America is business," the Coolidge administration promoted the interests of private industry and, for the most part, avoided active intervention in foreign affairs. While the country achieved unprecedented prosperity, dangerous stock market speculation created the conditions that later resulted in the 1929 financial crash. As a modest, self-effacing individual, popularly known as "Silent Cal," Coolidge chose not to run for re-election in 1928.

cool jazz (*or* progressive jazz) A style of US *jazz developed on the W coast in the early 1950s. Cool jazz was characterized by subtle rhythms as well as by instruments and harmonies borrowed from European classical music. Less frenetic than *bop, cool jazz was also quieter and more economical. Important cool-jazz musicians include Stan Getz (1927–), Miles Davis, and Dave Brubeck.

Cooper, Gary (Frank James C.; 1901–61) US film actor. He is noted for his portrayals of tough but sensitive heroes in Hollywood westerns. His best known films include *The Virginian* (1929), *The Westerner* (1940), *Sergeant York* (1941), and *High Noon* (1952).

Cooper, James Fenimore (1789–1851) US novelist. Expelled from Yale, he served briefly in the navy before his marriage in 1811. Financial need prompted him to start writing, and in *The Pioneers* (1823), his third novel, he portrayed frontier life. Sequels included *The Last of the Mohicans* (1826) and *The Pathfinder* (1840). A parallel series of sea novels, a form that he pioneered, included *The Red Rover* (1827) and *The Sea Lions* (1849). His democratic sympathies were strengthened during his stay in Europe from 1826 to 1833 but his nonfiction writings met with little success.

cooperative societies Organizations set up to manufacture, grow, buy, or sell produce, either without profit or with profits distributed to all members or shareholders as dividends. The cooperative movement was inspired by the ideas of the British philanthropist Robert *Owen in the early 19th century. Owen believed that the pooling of funds and the sharing of expensive equipment by small farmers and tradesmen might eliminate the economic hardships that seemed to be caused by unrestricted competition. Cooperative societies in agriculture, in which heavy farm machinery is shared and produce is marketed jointly by the societies' members, have become common throughout the world. In the US, the *Granger Movement, established in the 1860s, provides the members of local societies, or "Granges," with such agricultural services as low-cost grain storage and cooperative meat packing plants. It also protects the economic interests of small farmers through lobbying activities in Congress. Retail cooperative societies have also been established for consumers in many American cities, providing members with food and other products at reduced prices by bulk purchasing and low merchandising costs.

Cooper Creek (*or* Barcoo River) An intermittent river in E central Australia, in the *Channel Country. Rising in central Queensland it flows generally SW into Lake Eyre. Actual water flow in its lower reaches is irregular, occurring only in times of flood. Length: 880 mi (1420 km).

Cooperstown 42 42N 74 56W A resort town in E central New York where the headwaters of the Susquehanna River flow from Lake Otsego. Here James Fenimore Cooper's *Leather-stocking Tales* took place and Abner Doubleday popularized the game of baseball (1839). It is the home of the National Baseball Museum and Hall of Fame. Population (1980): 2,342.

coordinate systems Geometrical systems that locate points in space by a set of numbers.

In **Cartesian coordinates**, devised by René *Descartes, a point is located by its distance from intersecting lines called axes. In a plane (two dimensions) there are two axes and in space (three dimensions) there are three. Usually the axes are at right angles to each other and are known as rectangular axes, but oblique axes are also used in exceptional circumstances.

Cartesian coordinates

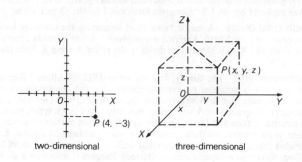

two-dimensional three-dimensional

polar coordinates

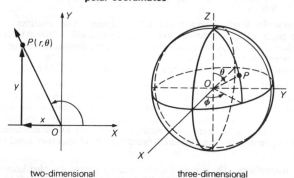

two-dimensional three-dimensional

COORDINATE SYSTEMS *In two-dimensional Cartesian coordinates a point P is located by giving its x- and y-coordinates, in this case 4 and −3 (always given in this order, as shown). In three-dimensional Cartesian coordinates P is located in terms of three axes. In polar coordinates P is located by a radius r and an angle θ. In three dimensions a second angle, ϕ, is required. In the diagrams Cartesian coordinates are superimposed on the polar coordinates.*

Polar coordinates denote position by distance and direction. A fixed point, called the origin, and a fixed line, called the polar axis, are taken as the references. For any point, the polar coordinates are the length, r, of the radius of the circle centered at the origin and passing through the point, and the angle, θ, between this radius and the polar axis. In three dimensions, spherical polar coordinates are used. The radius of a sphere centered at the origin and the two angles it makes with the polar axis define the point.

coot An aquatic *rail of the genus *Fulica* (9 species). Coots have broadly lobed toes, diving deeply to feed on invertebrates and aquatic plants. The European coot (*F. atra*) occurs throughout the Old World and is 14 in (37 cm) long with black plumage and a white bill and frontal shield.

copal Any one of the many resins collected from living or fossilized tropical trees and used in the manufacture of varnishes and inks. Copals can vary from brownish-yellow to colorless.

Copán 14 52N 89 10W A city in Honduras. Extensive ruins with temples, pyramids, astronomical stelae, and a ceremonial stairway remain from its heyday as a *Maya city (c. 300–900 AD). Population (1980 est): 26,100.

Copenhagen (Danish name: Kо́bénhavn) 55 40N 12 35E The capital and chief port of Denmark, on the E coast of Sjælland. It is an industrial as well as a commercial and shipping center, with engineering, food processing, and brewing. Notable buildings include the 17th-century Charlottenborg Palace (now the Royal Academy of Arts) and Christiansborg Palace (now the parliamentary and government buildings). An important center of Scandinavian culture, Copenhagen possesses a university (1479) and several museums. *History*: already a human settlement in the year 900 AD, it became capital of Denmark in 1443. Over the centuries it has been involved in many wars; it was attacked by the Hanseatic League in the middle ages and by Sweden in the 17th century. In 1801 the Danish fleet was destroyed by Nelson at the battle of Copenhagen. In 1728, and again in 1795, it was badly destroyed by fire. Occupied by the Germans in World War II, it became the center of a strong resistance movement. Population (1981 est): 648,720.

Copepoda A subclass of *crustaceans (7500 species), mostly 0.02–0.08 in (0.5–2 mm) long, that have long antennae, a single median eye, and no carapace. There are 11 pairs of appendages on the head and thorax and forked tail filaments (furca). Copepods occur in abundance in fresh and salt water, forming a constituent of plankton. Most feed on microscopic plants or animals but some are parasitic on fish, other crustaceans, etc.

Copernicus, Nicolaus (1473–1543) Polish astronomer, formulator of the modern heliocentric theory of the solar system. After studying mathematics and music at Cracow and Bologna, Copernicus became interested in the problem of calculating planetary positions, since existing tables were out of date. He noticed that by using a system in which the earth revolved round the sun, instead of *Ptolemy's geocentric system, these calculations would be much easier to make. He then realized that such a system could actually describe the solar system, rather than providing a simple working model of it, since it explained the occasional backward motion of the planets. Copernicus, realizing that these ideas were at variance with the Church's view that the earth was at the center of the universe, only circulated them to a few friends. The full text of his book *De revolutionibus orbium coelestium* was not published until 1543: legend has it that Copernicus was presented with the first copy on his deathbed.

Copland, Aaron (1900–) US composer, a pupil of Nadia Boulanger. He has been active as a teacher, pianist, and champion of contemporary music. He is best known for his compositions in a popular style, such as the ballets *Billy the Kid* (1938), *Rodeo* (1942) and *Appalachian Spring* (1944) and the operas *The Second Hurricane* (1937) and *The Tender Lane* (1954). Many of his themes are based on American folklore. His other works employ a variety of styles and include *Piano Concerto* (1927) in a jazz idiom and *Piano Fantasy* (1957) using *serialism.

Copley, John Singleton (1738–1815) US portrait painter. Born in Boston, he worked as an artist from the age of 15 and by his late 20s had become well known for his realistic portraits in America and Europe. In 1774 he brought his family to England and began painting historical subjects. Among these massive works are *The Death of the Earl of Chatham*, *The Death of Major Peirson*, and *The Siege of Gibraltar*. He is best known, however, for his American portraits, such as *Paul Revere* and *John Hancock*.

copper (Cu) A reddish-brown metal, known from prehistoric times and named for the island of Cyprus, which was the principal source in Roman times. It occurs naturally as the native element, the sulfide chalcopyrite (CuFeS$_2$), the carbonate malachite (CuCO$_3$.Cu(OH)$_2$), and other minerals. It is mined in Zambia, Zaïre, Chile, Australia, New Guinea, and elsewhere. Copper is extracted by smelting and electrolysis. It is malleable, ductile, and is important because of its good electrical (second only to silver) and thermal conductivity. Copper is widely used in the electrical industry and in the form of copper pipes in plumbing. It is contained in coins, and in the alloys *brass and *bronze. Common compounds are the oxides (Cu$_2$O, CuO) and copper sulfate (CuSO$_4$). At no 29; at wt 63.546; mp 633°F (1083°C); bp 1472°F (2595°C).

copperhead A North American *pit viper, *Agkistrodon contortrix*, occurring in swampy or wooded regions. Up to 40 in (1 m) long, it is reddish with a coppery head and brown bands on its back. The name is also given to a S Australian snake, *Denisonia superba*, which is about 5 ft (1.5 m) long and usually coppery-brown.

Copperhead A Northerner sympathetic to the South during the *Civil War, especially one who opposed Lincoln's military or civil policies. Mostly midwestern Democrats, the Copperheads were accused of disloyalty to the northern cause and the Democratic Party suffered by association with them. The name derives from a newspaper reference comparing antiwar Democrats to snakes.

Coppermine River A river in N Canada, in Mackenzie district. Rising in Lac de Gras, it flows NW past copper deposits into Coronation Gulf (an arm of the Arctic Ocean). Length: 525 mi (845 km).

copra. *See* coconut.

Coptic A *Hamito-Semitic language spoken in Egypt from the early Christian period until the 8th century AD. It was the last stage of ancient Egyptian and was written in Greek characters with seven additional *demotic letters. There were six dialects of which Sahidic became the standard form in Upper Egypt after the 5th century. Bohairic of Lower Egypt was used for religious purposes by the Coptic Christians and has a literature of scriptural translations from Greek and original writings that reflect Gnostic and Manichaean tendencies within early Christianity.

Coptic Church The largest Christian Church in Egypt. The Copts trace the history of their Church to St *Mark. As a result of its *Monophysite beliefs, which were condemned at the Council of Chalcedon (451), the Coptic Church became somewhat isolated from other Christian bodies. The Muslim conquest of Egypt in 642, together with language and cultural differences, widened the division. The Church suffered some persecution under Arab dominion. In 1741 a number of Copts entered the Roman Catholic communion, becoming the Uniat Coptic Church. Alexandria held an eminent position in the early Church and remains the seat of the Coptic patriarch, who presides over the Church with 12 diocesan bishops. The Copts are in communion with the Armenian and Syrian (Orthodox) Churches.

copyright law The law protecting the exclusive right of authors, composers, artists, publishers, and others who create or publish original literary, dramatic, and artistic works to reproduce them (in whole or in part) and to exploit them. Infringement of copyright is known as piracy. The protection lasts for a certain number of years after the death of the owner of the copyright. Many nations adopted the Universal Copyright Convention in 1952, whereby each signatory undertook to give the same protection to the authors of the other signatories as it gave its own authors.

coracle An ancient boat, usually round, made of wickerwork or laths over which a waterproofed animal skin has been stretched and fitted. Coracles were used in Ireland and in Wales and other parts of W Britain.

coral A sedentary marine animal belonging to a class (*Anthozoa*) of *coelenterates. Individual corals—*polyps—produce a protective skeleton that may be soft and jelly-like, horny, or stony. They usually occur in colonies and are found in all oceans, particularly warm shallow waters, feeding mainly on small animals. Reproduction can be asexual (by budding) or sexual, the eggs being fertilized in the water.

The stony (*or* true) corals (order *Madreporaria*; about 1000 species) secrete a rigid external skeleton made of almost pure calcium carbonate. Coral reefs (*see* reef) are produced by succeeding generations of stony corals, occurring in dense colonies. The principal reef building occurs at depths of less than 165 ft (50 m) and at temperatures above 68°F (20°C). Within this zone symbiotic algae (zooxanthellae) are present in coral tissues and stimulate the secretion of calcium carbonate, accelerating the growth of coral skeletons. The Great Barrier Reef off NE Australia is the best-known example.

Coralli, Jean (J. C. Peracini; 1779–1854) Italian ballet dancer and choreographer. He trained in Paris and was choreographer at the Paris Academy from 1831 to 1845. He choreographed many of the most celebrated Romantic ballets, including *Giselle* (1841) and *La Peri* (1843).

Coral Sea A section of the SW Pacific Ocean between NE Australia, New Guinea, and the New Hebrides. It contains many coral reefs, including the *Great Barrier Reef. During World War II it was the scene of a US victory over the Japanese (1942).

coral snake A New World burrowing venomous snake having a boldly patterned skin. They occur chiefly in the tropics and are generally secretive, preying on other snakes. The main genus, *Micrurus* (40 species), ranges from the S US to Argentina; most species are ringed with red, black, and yellow or white. Old World coral snakes are similar and found in SE Asia (genus *Calliophis*) and Africa (genus *Elaps*). Family: *Elapidae* (cobras, mambas, coral snakes).

The rear-fanged false coral snakes have similar patterning but belong to the family *Colubridae* (grass snakes, etc.).

coral tree A Brazilian tree, *Erythrina crista-galli*, 7–10 ft (2–3 m) high, with clusters of deep-scarlet flowers, for which it is often grown as an ornamental. Family: *Leguminosae.

cor anglais A double-reeded musical instrument, the alto member of the oboe family. It is a transposing instrument, the notes sounding a fifth lower than written. It has a range of two and a half octaves from the E below middle C. Sibelius used its rich tone in the symphonic poem *The Swan of Tuonela*.

Corbusier, Le. *See* Le Corbusier.

Cordaitales An order of extinct *gymnosperm trees that—with *Calamites—formed vast forests during the Carboniferous and Permian periods (370–240 million years ago); coal was formed from their fossilized remains. The trees probably grew up to 98 ft (30 m) high, with a tall columnar trunk and strap-shaped leaves, up to 40 in (1 m) long.

Corday, Charlotte (1768–93) French noblewoman, who assassinated Jean-Paul *Marat in his bath on July 13, 1793. She was guillotined on July 17. She sympathized with the Girondins, the revolutionary party that opposed the more radical Jacobins.

Cordeliers, Club of the A French Revolutionary club founded in Paris in 1790 to defend the rights of man. It was temporarily disbanded following a demonstration against Louis XVI in 1791. After it was restored, it became more radical and was finally disbanded in 1794 following an unsuccessful insurrection.

cordgrass. See Spartina.

Córdoba 31 25S 64 11W A city in central Argentina. Founded in 1573, it has many notable old buildings, including the cathedral (1758) and the university (1613). A commercial and industrial center, its manufactures include automobiles, tractors, and textiles. Population (1975 est): 781,565.

Córdoba 37 53N 4 46W A city in S Spain, in Andalusia on the Guadalquivir River. It became the capital of Moorish Spain in 756 AD and by the 10th century was Europe's largest city and a major cultural center. Its immense Moorish cathedral (8th–10th centuries) was originally a mosque. Industries include silverware and textiles. Population (1974 est): 249,515.

Cordon Bleu Originally, the blue ribbon of the knight's grand cross of the Order of the Holy Spirit, the first order of the Bourbon kings. The term is now used to describe food, or a chef, that achieves an (unspecified) degree of excellence.

Corelli, Arcangelo (1653–1713) Italian violinist and composer. He rationalized contemporary violin technique and wrote sonatas for the instrument. He also established the concerto grosso, in which a small group of soloists (typically two violins and cello) is contrasted with the full orchestra, a form much used by baroque composers. His most famous work is the *Christmas Concerto* for strings and continuo.

Coreopsis A genus of North American, tropical African, and Hawaiian plants (120 species) commonly known as tick-seeds (because of the shape of their seedlike fruits). Annual or perennial herbs, they are often grown in gardens for their daisy-like flowers, which are usually yellow with a darker center. Family: *Compositae*.

Corfu (Latin name: Coreyra; Modern Greek name: Kérkira *or* Kérkyra) A Greek island in the NE Ionian Sea, in the Ionian Islands. It has belonged to many powers, including Venice (1386–1797) and Britain (1815–64). The local produce includes olives, figs, and citrus fruit, and tourism is important. Area: 250 sq mi (641 sq km). Population (1971): 92,933. Chief town: Corfu.

corgi One of two breeds of working □dog originating in SW Wales. Both are low-set: the Cardigan Welsh corgi has a long tail, rounded ears, and a shortish coat, which may be reddish brown, streaked brown, or black and tan; the Pembroke Welsh corgi has a short tail, pointed ears, and a finer coat of red, sable, fawn, or black and tan. Both breeds can have white markings. Height: 12 in (30 cm)) (Cardigan); 10–12 in (25–30 cm (Pembroke).

coriander An annual plant, *Coriander sativum*, 8–28 in (20–70 cm) high, with umbrella-like clusters of small pink or white flowers. Probably native to the Mediterranean, it is widespread in waste places and is also cultivated for its fruits, used in curries, alcoholic beverages, as a condiment, and medicinally for flatulence. Family: *Umbelliferae*.

Corineus A legendary Trojan hero after whom the region of Cornwall, England, is named. According to the medieval chronicler *Geoffrey of Monmouth he was a companion of Brutus, the grandson of Aeneas and legendary founder of Britain, and the killer of the giant Gogmagog (*see* Gog and Magog).

Corinth (Greek name: Kórinthos) 37 56N 22 55E A port in S Greece, in the Peloponnese on the Isthmus of Corinth. The modern port was founded in 1858 near the site of the ancient city; its trade includes wine. *History*: a settlement before 3000 BC, the ancient city of Corinth developed in commercial importance during the 8th century BC. It became the second largest and richest of the Greek city states after Athens, rivalry between the two culminating in the *Peloponnesian War. Corinth resisted Roman pressures but was destroyed by them in 146 BC, later to be revived as a Roman colony (44 BC). The city declined during the middle ages. Extensive excavations have taken place since 1896. Population (1971): 20,733.

Corinth, League of (*or* Hellenic League) An alliance of Greek states formed in 338 BC at Corinth under the leadership of *Philip II of Macedon. The League was formed for a joint Greek and Macedonian campaign against Persia and contributed to the Asian campaign of *Alexander the Great, who succeeded Philip in 336. The League was disbanded after Alexander's death (323), being briefly revived in 303.

Corinthian order. See orders of architecture.

Corinthians, Epistles of Paul to the Two New Testament books written by the apostle Paul to the Christian Church at Corinth in about 57 AD. In the first he deals with problems that had arisen in the Church and answers questions on a number of practical and doctrinal issues, for example marriage and celibacy, the resurrection of the dead, and the Eucharist. In the second he explains the nature of his own apostolic ministry and defends himself against his opponents at Corinth.

Coriolanus, Gnaeus Marcius Roman general, who defeated the Volsci and captured the town of Corioli. Exiled in 491 BC for his contempt for the common people during a famine, he led the Volsci against Rome but was dissuaded from sacking the city by his wife Virgilia and mother Volumnia. The story is the subject of Shakespeare's *Coriolanus* (1607).

Coriolis force A *force required to account for the motion of a body as seen by an observer in a rotating frame of reference. It is often referred to as a fictitious force as it disappears on changing to a nonrotating frame. For example, a shell shot from a gun at the center of a rotating table appears to an outside observer to travel in a straight line. To an observer on the table it appears to have a curved path. The Coriolis force is required to account for this apparent tangential acceleration. The Coriolis force is responsible for the formation and direction of rotation of anticyclones and whirlpools. Named for the French physicist Gaspard de Coriolis (1792–1843).

cork Tissue that forms the outer layer of *bark in woody plants. Cork provides extra insulation and physical protection to the internal cells of the plant. The cork oak (*Quercus suber*), an evergreen oak tree of S Europe and N Africa, is cultivated in Portugal and SW Spain as the source of commercial cork. The cork is stripped from the tree every 8–10 years and is used for shock absorbers, bungs, fishing floats, floor and wall coverings, shoe soles, etc.

Cork (Irish name: Corcaigh) The largest county in the Republic of Ireland, in Munster bordering on the Atlantic Ocean. Mountains in the W extend eastward intersected by valleys, notably that of the Blackwater River. Its many coastal inlets include Bantry Bay and Cork Harbour. Fishing is important; Ballycotton is noted for its game fishing. Agriculture is varied with dairy and arable farming. Its many castles include Blarney Castle, famous for the Blarney Stone. Area: 2880 sq mi (7459 sq km). Population (1979 est): 257,851. County town: Cork.

Cork (Irish name: Corcaigh) 51 54N 8 28W The second largest city in the Republic of Ireland and county town of Co Cork, on Cork Harbour. The settlement grew up around a monastery (founded in about the 6th century AD) and it has remained important as a center of learning with the presence of University College (founded 1845), part of the National University of Ireland. It has many notable buildings, especially its cathedrals and St Ann's Shaldon Church, famous for its bells. It is an important industrial and trading center with a fine harbor. Exports include bacon, dairy produce, and livestock and it has bacon-curing, car assembly, and brewing and distilling industries. Population (1971): 128,235.

corkwood. See balsa.

corm A fleshy underground stem base of certain perennial herbaceous plants, such as the crocus and gladiolus, that acts as an overwintering structure. Growth the following season occurs by one or more buds: if two or more plants are produced the corm is acting as an organ of vegetative reproduction.

cormorant A slender long-necked waterbird belonging to a family (*Phalacrocoracidae*; 30 species) and found on most coasts and some inland waters 20–40 in (50–100 cm) in length, cormorants are typically glossy black with white throat markings and have short legs, webbed feet, a long stiff tail, and a long slender hook-tipped bill; they feed mainly on fish caught underwater. Order: *Pelecaniformes* (gannets, pelicans, etc.).

corn An annual *cereal grass, *Zea mays*, also called Indian corn, sweet corn, or maize, native to the New World and widely cultivated in tropical and subtropical regions, 3–13 ft (1–4.5 m) high, it bears a tassel of male flowers at the top of the stem and spikes of female flowers in the leaf axils; these develop into cobs, each comprising long parallel rows of grains. Corn is used as a vegetable, in breakfast cereals, flour, and livestock feed and for the extraction of corn oil. Cultivated as a grain crop in Central America since at least 2000 BC, corn is a staple food in Latin America and many other countries throughout the world. In terms of world production, it is the third most important cereal crop (after wheat and rice), the US being the chief producing country.

Corn Belt An area in the central US, S and W of the Great Lakes, extending mainly through Indiana, Illinois, Iowa, and Nebraska. It possess

CORMORANT *The common cormorant* (Phalacrocorax carbo) *breeds in colonies, usually on cliffs. The eggs are incubated for a month by both parents.*

es a distinctive agriculture with intensive corn and soybean production used in the raising of fat cattle and pigs.

corn borer A small European *pyralid moth, *Pyrausta nubilalis*, accidentally introduced to North America. It is a serious economic pest, attacking over 200 plant species, including beans, celery, corn, and potatoes. The larvae burrow into plant stems near ground level, sometimes causing them to break off.

corncockle An annual purple-flowered weed of arable land in most temperate regions, *Agrostemma githago*, growing to a height of 40 in (100 cm). Once abundant, it is now rare due to efficient seed clearing. Family: *Caryophyllaceae*.

corncrake A migratory bird, *Crex crex*, also called landrail, that breeds in Eurasian grasslands, wintering in S Africa and Asia. It is 10 in (26 cm) long with a streaked brown plumage and chestnut wing patches and is easily identified by its harsh rasping call. Family: *Rallidae* (rails).

cornea The transparent outer layer at the front of the eyeball, through which light enters the □eye. Corneal grafts have been used successfully to replace diseased areas of cornea; since the cornea has no blood supply the graft cannot be rejected by blood-borne antibodies.

Corneille, Pierre (1606–84) French dramatist. After a Jesuit education he worked in government service in his home town of Rouen from 1628 to 1650. His early comedies, beginning with *Mélite* (1629), were much admired by Cardinal Richelieu. *Le Cid* (1636), the seminal play of French classical tragedy, excited much controversy. Here and in *Horace* (1640), *Cinna* (1641), and *Polyeucte* (1643) he pioneered a dramatic genre the main emphasis of which was on moral conflicts expressed in majestic formal verse, a genre later perfected by his younger contemporary *Racine. In 1647 he moved to Paris and continued to write prolifically until his last play, *Suréna*, in 1674.

Cornelius, Peter von (1783–1867) German painter, born in Düsseldorf. In Rome (1811–19) he was associated with a group of German artists, the Nazarenes, in the revival of fresco painting. He worked subsequently in Munich on frescoes for the museum of classical sculpture and in Berlin.

Corner Brook 48 58N 57 58W A city in E Canada, in Newfoundland. It has one of the world's largest pulp mills. Population (1976): 25,198.

cornet A valved brass instrument, with cup-shaped mouthpiece and conical bore. Pitched in B flat, it is similar to the trumpet but less brilliant. It has a range of two and a half octaves from the E below middle C and plays an important role in the brass band.

cornetfish A tropical marine *bony fish, also called flutemouth, belonging to a family (*Fistulariidae*; about 4 species) related to *pipefish and *seahorses. It has a slender body, up to 6 ft (1.8 m) long, a long threadlike filament extending from the tail fin, and a long siphon-like snout. Order: *Gasterosteiformes*.

cornett A woodwind instrument with a cup-shaped mouthpiece and finger holes. The brilliant tone of the treble cornett was much favored by composers of the 16th and 17th centuries, such as Giovanni Gabrieli.

cornflower An annual, sometimes overwintering, herbaceous plant, *Centaurea cyanus*, growing to about 30 in (75 cm) high. Flower heads are bright blue with a purplish center. Probably native in most of Europe and the Near East, it is widely introduced as a cereal crop weed but is now becoming rare due to improved seed clearing. Horticultural garden varieties are popular. Family: *Compositae*.

Cornforth, Sir John Warcup (1917–) Australian chemist, who shared the 1975 Nobel Prize with Vladimir Prelog (1906–) for their work on stereochemistry. Cornforth showed the importance of stereoisomers in biological systems, using *radioactive tracers to follow the course of their reactions.

Cornish A *Celtic language of the Brythonic group, formerly spoken in Cornwall and Devon, that became extinct in about 1800. It was closely related to Breton, which was introduced to Brittany from this area. A number of miracle and morality plays dating from the 15th century were written in Cornish.

Corn Laws The British laws that regulated (1360–1846) the import and export of wheat and other cereals to guarantee farmers' incomes. These laws were bitterly resented by the working classes, because they kept the price of bread high, and by the manufacturers, who argued that little money was left for the purchase of manufactured goods. Opposition to the Corn Laws was led by the *Anti-Corn Law League and in 1846 Sir Robert *Peel's government repealed them. A nominal duty continued to be levied until 1869.

Cornplanter (c.1746–1836) US Seneca Indian chief. Born of a Dutch or English father and a Seneca mother, he led his people against the white settlers, but gradually sought more peaceful means of resisting the takeover of Indian lands. He signed treaties with the US and tried to prevent other tribes from warring against the Americans. By 1791 he was replaced as chief of the Senecas and was granted land and an annuity by the US government.

corn poppy An annual, or sometimes biennial, poppy, *Papaver rheas*, with scarlet (occasionally pinkish) flowers. Also called field poppy, it grows to a height of 20 in (50 cm). It is a weed of arable and waste places, occurring throughout much of Eurasia and N Africa and introduced to North America, New Zealand, and Australia.

corn salad A slender branching annual plant, *Valerianella locusta*, also called lamb's lettuce. 3–16 in (7–40 cm) high, with small pale-lilac flowers, it grows in dryish places and is sometimes cultivated for salads. It is native to Europe, N Africa, and W Asia and introduced to North America. Family: *Valerianaceae*.

cornucopia A decorative motif from Greek antiquity denoting abundance and wealth. It consists of a goat's horn filled with fruit and flowers and was reputedly presented to the nymph Amalthaea by Zeus or vice versa.

Cornwall (Celtic name: Kernow) The most southwesterly county of England, bordering on the Atlantic Ocean and the English Channel and including the Isles of *Scilly. It consists mainly of rugged hills rising to Bodmin Moor in the E. Dairy farming and market gardening are the main agricultural activities, the equable climate encouraging the growth of early fruit and vegetables. Tourism is a chief source of income and the county is popular for second homes and retirement. Tinmining, important since early times, was revitalized in the 1960s. In 1974 the Cornish nationalist movement led to the revival of the Stannary or Tinners' Parliament and also to attempts to resurrect the Cornish language. Area: 1369 sq mi (3546 sq km). Population (1981 est): 430,506. Administrative center: Truro.

Cornwallis, Charles, 1st Marquess (1738–1805) British general in the *American Revolution. Although he opposed the taxation of the American colonies, he took a command when the revolution broke out and was at first successful, defeating Gates at *Camden (1780). In 1781, however, he was disastrously defeated at Yorktown. He served twice as governor general of India (1786–93, 1805).

Coromandel Coast The SE coast of India between the Krishna Delta and Point Calimere.

Coromandel screens Large 17th-century Chinese screens named for the Coromandel Coast of India, from which they were shipped to Europe. They have up to 12 panels with brown or red lacquer grounds and incised polychromatic decoration.

corona The outer layer of the sun's atmosphere. The **inner corona** lies above the *chromosphere and consists of rapidly moving electrons. Its temperature reaches about 1,110,000°F (2,000,000°C) some 46,500 mi (75,000 km) above the solar surface. The **outer corona** extends for millions of miles and consists of comparatively slow-moving dust particles. The corona cannot be seen without special equipment, except at a total solar *eclipse. It then appears as a pearly usually unsymmetrical halo around the darkened solar disk, the shape depending on the time of the *sunspot cycle. *See also* solar wind.

coronary heart disease The most common form of *heart disease in the western world. It is caused by *atherosclerosis of the coronary arteries, which reduces the blood flow to the heart. This may precipitate the formation of a blood clot in these arteries—**coronary thrombosis**. The patient experiences sudden pain in the chest (*see* angina pectoris) and the result may be a heart attack, when the blood flow to the heart is suddenly stopped (*see* myocardial infarction). Coronary heart disease is associated with smoking, lack of exercise, high-fat diets, hypertension, and middle age; it is commoner in men.

Corot, Jean Baptiste Camille (1796–1875) French landscape painter. After training under two minor landscapists (1822–25), he visited Italy (1825–28), the subject of many of his landscapes. Although he exhibited at the Paris Salon from 1827, he did not achieve critical acclaim until the 1850s, with his poetical misty landscapes populated by nymphs. More popular today are his open-air sketches, small landscapes, and figure studies. He was friendly with the *Barbizon school of painters and influenced the impressionists.

corporate state (*or* corporative state) A society in which the individual is represented in government by the economic group (corporation) to which he belongs rather than according to his geographical location. The ideas were adopted as a system of government by fascist dictators, such as Mussolini, Franco, and Salazar, and the term now has pejorative implications.

Corpus Christi 27 47N 97 26W A city in Texas on Corpus Christi Bay. A popular resort, its port exports cotton, petroleum, and sulfur. Industries include cement and chemicals as well as fishing. Population (1980): 231,999.

Corpus Christi, Feast of (Latin: body of Christ) A Christian feast honoring the institution of the Eucharist, observed in the West on the second Thursday after *Whit Sunday. Originally a local festival in Liège, it was extended to the whole Church by Pope Urban IV in 1264. The chief rite of the feast is the procession of the Blessed Sacrament. It is not generally observed by Protestant Churches.

Corpus Juris Canonici A collection of papal and conciliar decrees comprising the main body of the canon law of the Western Church. It is composed of six collections compiled between the 12th and 15th centuries. Pope Gregory XIII revised it in 1582. It was superseded in 1917 by the Codex Juris Canonici, a revision of the whole of canon law.

Corpus Juris Civilis. *See* Roman law.

corpus luteum. *See* ovary.

Correggio (Antonio Allegri; c. 1494–1534) Italian Renaissance painter, born at Correggio, near Modena. Initially influenced by *Mantegna, he later studied *Leonardo and *Michelangelo. He worked chiefly in Parma, where he decorated the Camera di S Paolo, the domed vaulting of S Giovanni Evangelista, and the cathedral with frescoes that anticipate the *baroque. Using strong contrasts between light and shade, he painted religious subjects, e.g. *Adoration of the Shepherds* or *Night* (Dresden), and sensuous nudes, e.g. *Jupiter and Io* (Kunsthistorisches Museum, Vienna), which later influenced *rococo painters.

Corregidor An island in the N Philippines, in the mouth of Manila Bay. Strategically important, it has been fortified since Spanish times. During World War II US troops on it held Manila harbor against the Japanese for five months although bombed continuously.

Correns, Carl Erich (1864–1933) German botanist and geneticist, whose work on breeding garden peas confirmed the principles of heredity first established by *Mendel. In 1900, simultaneously with *de Vries, he rediscovered Mendel's original paper, which had been ignored since 1865.

Corrientes 27 30S 58 48W A port in NE Argentina, on the Río Paraná. It is an important export center for agricultural products, including cotton, rice, and tobacco. It has a university (1957). Population (1975 est): 136,924.

corrosion. *See* rust.

Corsica (French name: Corse) An island in the Mediterranean Sea, separated from Sardinia by the Strait of Bonifacio. Together with 43 islets it comprises a region of France. It is mountainous with a rugged coastline and much of the island is covered with *maquis*, a dense thorny scrub type of vegetation. Agriculture is relatively undeveloped, producing citrus fruits, olives, vegetables, and tobacco; sheep and goats are extensively reared and

tourism is a major source of income. *History*: under Genoese control from the 14th century, it was sold to France in 1768. During World War II it came under Italian occupation but was liberated by the French in 1943, weakening the German position in Italy. Area: 22,364 sq mi (8722 sq km). Population (1981 est): 230,100. Capital: Ajaccio.

Cortes The Spanish parliament, which first met in the kingdom of Léon in 1188. This was the first time that representatives of the townsmen attended the king's court together with the clergy and nobility. The regional Cortes lost their influence during the 16th century. The first national Cortes met in 1810.

Cortés, Hernán (1485–1547) Spanish conquistador. In Hispaniola and Cuba from 1504, he led a small expedition to Mexico in 1519 and reached Tenochtitlán, the capital of the Aztec Empire. In Cortés' absence, dealing with an attack from a Spanish force from Cuba, the Aztecs launched an attack on Tenochtitlán, forcing the Spaniards' retreat—the *noche triste* (night of sorrows). Cortés eventually rebuilt his forces and destroyed Tenochtitlán (1521) and the Aztec Empire, founding New Spain. After an expedition to Honduras (1524–26) Cortés returned to Spain (1528) but renewed his Pacific explorations in the 1530s. He died in poverty in Spain.

cortex The outer tissues of an animal or plant organ. In plants the cortex is situated between the *epidermis and vascular (conducting) tissues of stems and roots. Its cell walls may contain corky and woody materials or silica, providing strength, and also stored food, usually starch. Other substances that may be present include resins, latex, tannins, and essential oils. In animals the outer tissue of the *adrenal gland, the cerebrum, and the *kidney is called the cortex.

corticosteroids Steroid hormones secreted by the cortex of the adrenal glands (the term also includes synthetic drugs with similar properties). There are two main groups. The glucocorticoids (e.g. cortisone, prednisolone, and dexamethasone) affect carbohydrate metabolism. As anti-inflammatory drugs, they are used to treat allergic conditions (e.g. asthma), inflammatory disorders (e.g. ulcerative colitis and rheumatoid arthritis), and autoimmune diseases. They are also used to treat some cancers. The mineralocorticoids (e.g. aldosterone, fludrocortisone) control the balance of salt and water in the body.

Cortona 43 17N 11 59E A city in Italy, in Tuscany. It is famous for its Etruscan and Roman remains and has a cathedral dating from the 15th century. Population (1971): 21,830.

Cortot, Alfred (1877–1962) French pianist and conductor. He is remembered as an interpreter of Beethoven's piano concertos, as a conductor of Wagner's operas, and as a member of a piano trio with Thibaud and Casals, which achieved international fame.

corundum A mineral consisting mainly of aluminum oxide, the accessory minerals giving rise to a variety of colors. Sapphire is a blue variety containing iron and titanium; ruby contains chromium. It occurs in silica-poor igneous rocks, in metamorphosed shales, and in some metamorphosed limestone veins. The nongem varieties are used as abrasives (corundum is the second hardest mineral to diamond).

Corunna. *See* La Coruña.

corvette A small highly maneuverable lightly armed warship displacing approximately 1600 tons and carrying a complement of a hundred officers and men. They were used mainly for antisubmarine escort duty during World War II. In the days of sail, the corvette, smaller than a *frigate, was a sloop rigged as a ship.

Corvo, Baron. *See* Rolfe, Frederick William.

Corybant One of the Corybantes, the eunuch priests or attendants of the goddess *Cybele, whose worship was accompanied by wild dancing and orgies. They castrated themselves in imitation of the self-mutilation of Cybele's lover, the fertility god Attis.

Corydalis A genus of mainly N temperate herbs (320 species), mostly perennials with underground tubers. The flowers, usually yellow, grow in clusters and resemble those of peas. Garden varieties, 6–24 in (15–60 cm) high, prefer shady cool positions. Family: *Fumariaceae*.

Cos (Modern Greek name: Kos) A Greek island in the SE Aegean Sea, in the Dodecanese. It was a member of the Delian League and the home of the Greek physician Hippocrates. It produces chiefly fruit but also silk and tobacco. Cos lettuce originally came from here. Area: 109 sq mi (282 sq km). Population (1971): 17,939.

Cosenza 39 17N 16 16E A market city in Italy, in Calabria. Its manufactures include furniture and it has a 13th-century cathedral. Population (1980 est): 100,981.

Cosgrave, William Thomas (1880–1965) Irish statesman. A member of *Sinn Féin, he took part in the *Easter Rising (1916) and was elected to the first Irish Assembly (1918). He was first president of the Irish Free State (1922–32) and then led the *Fine Gael opposition until 1944. His son **Liam Cosgrave** (1920–) became leader of Fine Gael in 1965 and was prime minister from 1973 until 1977.

Cosmas and Damian, SS (early 4th century AD) Christian martyrs. Nothing certain is known of their lives, but according to tradition they were twin brothers who practiced as physicians in Asia Minor, refused to accept payment from their patients, and were martyred under Diocletian. They are patron saints of physicians. Feast day: Sept 27 or Oct 27.

cosmetics Beauty aids and preparations intended to improve the appearance of face, hair, or nails or the texture of the skin. Historically, among the most common cosmetics have been kohl, for shading around the eyes, and henna, for dyeing hair, fingertips, and toes; their use dates back at least to ancient Egypt. Rouge and face powders were used by the ancient Greeks and Romans. Although periodically cosmetics have met with public disapproval, as in Puritan and Victorian times, during the 20th century the manufacture of cosmetics has become an important industry, catering increasingly to men as well as women. Although modern western cosmetics no longer contain such dangerous ingredients as the lead compounds found in ancient Greek face powders, some ingredients can nevertheless irritate sensitive skins. Many modern cosmetics, such as eyebrow pencils, are wax-based; lipsticks also contain nondrying oils. Petroleum jelly, liquid paraffin, and coloring are also widely used. Creams and lotions are emulsions of wax or oil in water, which evaporates on application; the oily film left prevents the skin from drying out. Face powder consists principally of zinc oxide, precipitated chalk, talc, and zinc stearate. Nail polish consists of a nitrocellulose base, a plasticizer, and a modifying resin, all in a volatile solvent. Astringent lotions (including aftershave), which close the openings of the hair follicles, are based on alcohol solutions; antiperspirants are usually based on an aluminum salt, which prevents sweat from leaving the sweat ducts.

cosmic rays A continuous stream of very high-energy particles that bombard the earth from space. The primary radiation consists of *protons and light nuclei with smaller numbers of neutral particles, such as *photons and *neutrinos. These particles collide with atomic nuclei in the earth's atmosphere producing large numbers of elementary particles, known as secondary radiation. One primary particle may produce a large number of secondary particles on colliding with a nucleus. This effect is called a shower. Some cosmic rays are believed to originate from the sun, others from outside the solar system.

cosmogony The study of the origin and evolution of the universe and the astronomical objects it contains, or a theory concerning the origin and development of a particular system, especially the solar system.

cosmology The study of the origin, evolution, and structure of the universe. A great variety of cosmological models have been put forward through the ages, based on the observations of astronomers. Ranging from the flat earth draped by a canopy of stars and the earth-centered (geocentric) universe (see Ptolemaic system), these models have changed and evolved as more powerful instruments have been developed to study the heavens (see astronomy). The current model of the universe has emerged from the observation of the *redshift, the advent of *radio astronomy, as well as the discovery of *quasars (1964), the microwave background (1965), and *pulsars (1967). Its origin is seen as a superdense agglomeration of matter that exploded (see big-bang theory), flinging fragments far and wide into space. These fragments passed through various stages to form *stars and galaxies, which are still flying apart from each other like fragments from a bomb (see expanding universe; Hubble constant; steady-state theory).

Cossacks A people of S and SW Russia descended from independent Tatar groups and escaped serfs from Poland, Lithuania, and Muscovy. They established a number of independent self-governing communities, which were given special privileges by Russian or Polish rulers in return for military service. Known for their horsemanship, each Cossack community provided a separate army. The Cossacks slowly lost their autonomy as Russia expanded in the 17th and 18th centuries and there were occasional rebellions. Many fled Russia after the Revolution (1918–21) and collectivization subsumed remaining Cossack communities.

Costa Brava A coastal region in NE Spain, bordering on the Mediterranean Sea. It extends from Barcelona to the French border and is a popular tourist area with many resorts.

cost accounting. See accountancy.

Costa Rica, Republic of A country in the Central American isthmus between Nicaragua and Panama. It includes the island of Cocos, 186 mi (300 km) to the SW. The Caribbean lowlands rise to a central plateau area, with volcanic peaks reaching 12,529 ft (3819 m). The inhabitants are mainly of Spanish and mixed descent, with a dwindling Indian population. *Economy*: chiefly agricultural, the main crops being coffee, bananas, and sugar (the principal export). Livestock is important and crops, such as cocoa, are being introduced as part of a plan to diversify the economy. Almost 75% of the land is forested with valuable woods, such as mahogany, rosewood, and cedar. Mineral resources include gold, hematite ore, and sulfur; many small industries are being encouraged. *History*: discovered by Columbus in 1502, it became a Spanish colony in the 15th century and the native Indian population was practically wiped out. It was part of the captaincy general of Guatemala until gaining independence in 1821. From 1824 until 1838 it formed part of the Central American Federation. In 1948 José Figueres Ferrer, leader of the socialist National Liberation Party, came to power at the head of a junta. A new constitution brought more democratic rule—the army was abolished and banks nationalized. Since then government has been more stable than in most Latin American countries, each election being won by the party in opposition at the time. Costa Rica endeavored to maintain its neutrality in the face of the growing turmoil in Latin America, at the same time seeking to establish closer ties with the US. In 1983 relations with neighboring Nicaragua deteriorated as that country accused Costa Rica of support of anti-Sandinista guerrillas. President: Luis Alberto Monge (1927–). Official language: Spanish. Official religion: Roman Catholic. Official currency: colon of 100 centimos. Area: 19,653 sq mi (50,900 sq km). Population (1983 est): 2,599,000. Capital: San José. Main ports: Limón (on the Caribbean) and Puntarenas (on the Pacific).

cost-benefit analysis An investigation to determine whether a certain investment project is of net benefit to the community or to decide between competing projects. This type of analysis is useful because a purely commercial assessment does not always take account of all the costs and benefits involved; for example, it would not show the benefit of reduced road congestion that might be entailed in building an underground railroad. The weakness of cost-benefit analysis is that it is not always possible to quantify all the consequences, such as the destruction of the breeding grounds of a rare bird.

Costermansville. See Bukavu.

costmary A perennial herb, *Chrysanthemum balsamita*, also called alecost. About 40 in (100 cm) high, it is native to E Mediterranean regions and naturalized in S Europe. The spicy aromatic leaves were formerly used for flavoring ales and salads and to make an antiseptic tea. Family: *Compositae*.

cost of living A measure of the income required to purchase essential goods. Usually the Consumer Price Index based on a standard "basket" of goods, is used as a guide to the cost of living. The cost of living can vary geographically (e.g. depending on whether heating oil is essential) and with time (e.g. as a result of price inflation or revised definitions of what is essential).

Cotman, John Sell (1782–1842) British landscape watercolorist and etcher of the *Norwich school. Although he worked chiefly in Norfolk, he studied and exhibited in London (c. 1798–1806), settling there in 1834. Typical of his sparsely detailed and bold compositions is *Greta Bridge*.

Cotoneaster A genus of shrubs and small trees (about 50 species) of N temperate regions of the Old World. Some species are evergreen. Many are grown in gardens for their attractive foliage and red or black berries. *C. horizontalis* is a popular ground and wall cover; *C. hybrida pendula* is a weeping standard. Family: *Rosaceae*.

Cotonou 6 24N 2 31E The chief city in Benin, on the Gulf of Guinea. A deepwater port, it is the nation's main commercial and financial center and industries include textiles and brewing. Its university was founded in 1970. Population (1979 est): 327,600.

Cotopaxi 0 40S 78 28W The world's highest active volcano, in N central Ecuador, in the Andes. It is noted for the beauty of its symmetrical snow-capped cone. Height: 19,457 ft (5896 m).

co-trimoxazole An *antibiotic widely used in the treatment of urinary-tract infections (such as cystitis). It is a combination of two antibiotics—a *sulfonamide and trimethoprim. Trade names: Bactrim; Septrin.

Cotswold Hills A range of limestone hills in SW central England, mainly in Gloucestershire. It is noted for its picturesque towns and villages, such as Stow-on-the-Wold, built in the local limestone.

Cottbus (*or* Kottbus)   51 45N 14 24E A city in E East Germany, on the Spree River. Cottbus has several medieval churches and is a railroad junction and industrial center. Population (1980 est): 111,502.

cotton   A herbaceous plant of the genus *Gossypium* (20 or 67 species, according to the classification system), native to tropical and subtropical regions. Several species are cultivated for the whitish outer fibers of their seeds. Usually 40 in–7 ft (1–2 m) high, cotton plants bear whitish flowers and produce seed pods (bolls), which burst when filled with the soft masses of fibers. The bolls are harvested mechanically and the fibers separated from the seeds (ginning) and cleaned and aligned (carding), ready for spinning into yarn. The longest and most lustrous fibers are obtained from varieties of Sea Island or Egyptian cotton (*G. bardadense*). Cotton forms a light durable cloth used in a wide range of garments, furnishings, and other products. The seeds are crushed to yield cottonseed oil, used in margarines, cooking oils, soaps, etc., and the residual meal is used as a livestock feed. Family: *Malvaceae*.

cottonmouth.   *See* water moccasin.

cotton stainer   A black and red *plant bug belonging to the genus *Dysdercus*, widely distributed in warm regions. They are serious pests of cotton plants in North America and India, staining the bolls with excrement and rendering them useless. Family: *Pyrrhocoridae*.

cottonwood   A North American poplar the seeds of which resemble cotton seeds, especially *Populus deltoides*, which grows in rich woods and river bottoms and reaches a height of 100 ft (30 m). Its lightweight wood is used commercially.

cotyledon   The seed leaf of seed-bearing plants (gymnosperms and angiosperms): a food store within seeds providing the embryo plant with sufficient energy to germinate. In some plants the cotyledons become the first leaves of the seedling and are often different in form from subsequent leaves. Flowering plants with one cotyledon are classified as *monocotyledons; those with two as *dicotyledons. *See* germination.

couch grass   A *grass, *Agropyron repens*, also known as quack grass or twitch, native to Europe and naturalized in other N temperate regions. 12–48 in (30–120 cm) high, it spreads by underground rhizomes and is a serious weed of arable crops, being difficult to eradicate.

cougar   A red-brown *cat, *Felis concolor*, of North and South America, also called puma, mountain lion, and catamount. It is a slender muscular animal, 5–10 ft (1.5–3 m) long including its tail (20–30 in [50–80 cm]), with long hind legs enabling a powerful leap. It prefers deer, but feeds on a variety of animals.

Coughlin, Charles Edward   (1891–1979) US churchman; born in Canada. He became a Roman Catholic priest in 1916 and came to the US (1926) where, by the 1930s, he was known as the "radio priest" because of his broadcasts expressing his political views. By 1936 he had formed the Union Party to oppose Franklin D. *Roosevelt and by the early 1940s was expressing pro-Nazi and anti-Semitic views. His magazine *Social Justice* and his radio broadcasts were silenced by his superiors in 1942.

coulomb (C)   The *SI unit of electric charge equal to the quantity of electricity transferred by a current of one ampere in one second. Named for Charles de *Coulomb.

Coulomb, Charles Augustin de   (1736–1806) French physicist, who invented the torsion balance and used it to show that the force between charged particles is proportional to the product of their charges and inversely proportional to the square of the distance between them (*see* Coulomb's law). He developed a similar law for magnetic poles. The unit of charge (*see* coulomb) is named for him.

Coulomb's law   The force between two electrically charged bodies is proportional to the product of their charges (q_1 and q_2) and inversely proportional to the square of the distance (d) between them. In free space the law is $F = q_1 q_2/4\pi \epsilon_0 d^2$, where ϵ_0 is the *electric constant. The law is named for its discoverer Charles de *Coulomb. The force is known as the **Coulomb** (or electrostatic) **force**. **Coulomb scattering** is the scattering of a charged particle by a nucleus due to the Coulomb force between them.

council.   *See* local government.

Council for Mutual Economic Assistance (COMECON)   An economic association of communist countries founded in 1949. Its members are the Soviet Union, Bulgaria, Czechoslovakia, East Germany, Hungary, Mongolia, Poland, Romania, and Cuba; Albania ceased to participate in 1961. Its objective, to coordinate the economic policies of its members, has been opposed by Romania and by the more developed East Germany and Hungary, which have argued for greater individualization.

Council of Europe   An association of European states, founded in 1949, that is pledged to uphold the principles of parliamentary democracy and to promote the economic and social progress of its members (Austria, Belgium, Cyprus, Denmark, France, Greece, Iceland, the Republic of Ireland, Italy, Luxembourg, Malta, the Netherlands, Norway, Portugal, Spain, Sweden, Switzerland, Turkey, the UK, and West Germany). Its seat is in Strasbourg.

counterfeiting   The illegal production of false money for gain. Counterfeiting is a form of forgery, distinguished because of the unique position of *money as a general medium of exchange. Most banknotes are produced with exceptionally fine printing on watermarked paper, often with a strip of metal inserted, in an effort to make them difficult to counterfeit. Many countries are signatories to an agreement of 1929 that allows extradition of counterfeiters.

COUNTERPOINT   *An example of counterpoint from J.S. Bach's* Fantasia in C minor.

counterpoint   The art of combining two or more melodic lines simultaneously in music. The word derives from the Latin *punctus contra punctum*, point against point (i.e. note against note). The use of counterpoint continued beyond the end of the polyphonic period (*see* polyphony). Composers continue to make use of it today; contrapuntal techniques have been used by Stravinsky, Hindemith, Tippett, and others.

Counter-Reformation   A movement within the *Roman Catholic Church dedicated to combating the effects of the Protestant *Reformation by reforming abuses within the Church and eradicating heresy by conversion, etc. Extending from the middle of the 16th to about the middle of the 17th century, it witnessed the emergence of the *Jesuits as a leading missionary body throughout the world, the reforms instituted by the Council of *Trent, the extension of the *Inquisition from Spain to other countries, and in general a revival of Catholic spirituality. Although most of N Europe remained Protestant, Poland and S Germany were stabilized as Catholic during this period.

countertenor   A natural high male singing voice, higher than tenor, common in England in the 17th and 18th centuries. It is distinguished from the male *alto voice, which is produced by falsetto, but has the same range. The art of countertenor singing has been revived in the 20th century by Alfred Deller (1917–79) and James Bowman (1941–   ).

country and western   A type of US popular music that evolved from the hillbilly ballads of the Appalachian Mountains and the cowboy songs of the West. Country and western is predominantly vocal music, relating the everyday experiences of the common man in sentimental texts. The singer is accompanied by the guitar and other stringed instruments. Influenced by other styles of popular music, country and western has its own offshoots, such as bluegrass. Famous country hits include "Your Cheatin' Heart" and "Mule Skinner Blues."

country house   In England, a large house on a country estate. The great country houses were mainly built between the reigns of Elizabeth I and Victoria; before about 1550 feudal conditions caused the aristocracy to live in *castles or fortified *manor houses and after 1860 political reform and industrialization shifted the major landowners' power base and attention to the towns. Country houses displayed their owners' wealth and status, enabling them to entertain their political allies in impressive style. Some country houses exhibit the architectural opulence of small palaces (e.g. *Castle Howard and *Chatsworth), contain notable art collections, and are set in magnificent grounds (*see* Blenheim Palace).

Country Party.   *See* National Country Party.

Count's War   (1533–36) The last war of succession in Denmark, constituting a revolt led by Count Christopher of Oldenberg (c. 1504–66) against Christian, heir to the throne. Oldenberg finally surrendered Copenhagen in July, 1536, after which Christian became king as *Christian III.

county   A geographical unit of local government. The US does not have a comprehensive county system and the powers of counties differ widely between states. In Britain counties are long established: the name was applied by the Normans to the Anglo-Saxon *shire. England is divided into 45 counties, Wales into eight, Scotland into nine regions and three island areas. Northern Ireland has 6 counties.

Couperin, François   (1668–1733) French composer, called le Grand, the most famous member of a family that produced five generations of musicians. He was organist to Louis XIV and at St Gervais and is best known for his harpsichord music, a series of *ordres* consisting of pieces in dance forms with descriptive titles. He also wrote organ music, church music, and a book on the art of playing the harpsichord.

Courbet, Gustave (1819–77) French painter, born in Ornans. Self-taught, through copying paintings in the Louvre, he became leader of the school of realism. He painted portraits, including one of his friend Baudelaire, nudes, seascapes, hunting scenes, and everyday life, e.g. *Burial at Ornans* (Louvre) and *Bonjour Monsieur Courbet* (Montpellier). Reacting against academic criticism of his work, in 1855 he organized his first private exhibition. A political radical, he was imprisoned for his participation in the Commune of Paris (1871) and in 1873 he fled to Switzerland, where he died.

Courrèges, André (1923–) French fashion designer, who opened a fashion house in Paris in 1961 after training with *Balenciaga. In 1964 he presented his "space-age" collection, which included close-fitting silver trousers, worn with short-sleeved jackets and calf-length boots. He helped to promote the unisex fashion.

courser A brownish bird belonging to the subfamily *Cursoriine*, having long legs and a pointed curved bill and occurring in arid regions of Africa, India, and Australia. The cream-colored courser (*Cursorius cursor*) of Africa is 10 in (25 m) long with white underparts and eye stripes and feeds chiefly on insects and lizards. Family: *Glareolidae* (pratincoles and coursers).

Court, Margaret (*born* Smith; 1942–) Australian tennis player, the first Australian to win the women's singles at Wimbledon (1963). Wimbledon champion again in 1965 and 1970, she was US singles champion five times, French champion five times, and Australian champion a record 11 times, winning 90 titles in all.

Courtauld Institute of Art An art gallery and college for the study of art history in Portman Square, London. It was originally the home of the manufacturer and art collector Samuel Courtauld (1876–1947), who donated the building and his collection of impressionist paintings to London University.

court cupboard A set of three open shelves supported by corner columns and frequently having a recessed cupboard between the top two. Popular throughout N Europe during the 16th century for displaying plate, they were usually made of oak.

courtly love Essentially a literary convention describing passionate love, arising in 12th-century Provence in the poems of the *troubadors. (The term itself was coined in the 19th century.) It is not certain to what extent courtly love actually existed as a social phenomenon in feudal courts. In the literary convention both lover and beloved are of aristocratic rank. The lover is abjectly devoted as a vassal to his chosen lady, whose virtues are idealized with quasi-religious fervor and who remains unobtainable because she is married to someone else. The lover is bound by rules of gallantry and *chivalry and is ennobled by his attachment to the beloved. On the other hand, his love-sickness may be devastating and he can only be cured if his lady takes pity on him, that is, consents to an adulterous affair. Although the lover's virtue is supposed to be exalted by his love, he suffers enormously from fear of exposure, from the capricious behavior of his lady, etc. The convention, which owes much to the influence of *Ovid, spread from Provence to Italy, influencing the *dolce stil nuovo; to N France, where it formed an important element in the romances of *Chrétien de Troyes and in the 13th-century *Roman de la Rose*; to Germany in the work of the *Minnesingers; and to England, where it was treated in detail by Chaucer, especially in *Troilus and Criseyde*. It continued as an important element in the Elizabethan sonnet through the influence of *Petrarch.

court-martial Legislative criminal courts established in the armed forces. Their jurisdiction is entirely penal and disciplinary. They may be convened by the president, secretaries of military departments and by senior commanders to try and punish offenses committed by members of the armed forces. Appeals are made to the Court of Military Appeals.

Court Packing Bill (1937) A proposal to add six justices to the US Supreme Court. Initiated by President Franklin D. *Roosevelt in an attempt to create a court more sympathetic to his New Deal reforms, the bill was rejected by Congress.

Courtrai (Flemish name: Kortrijk) 50 50N 03 17E A city in Belgium, on the Lys River. It was the site of the battle of the Spurs (1297), in which the French army was defeated by the burghers of Bruges and Ghent. It is an important textile center. Population (1981 est): 76,072.

courts of law Any duly constituted tribunal responsible for administering the law of the state or nation.

court tennis A racket-and-ball indoor court game that originated in France in the 12th–13th centuries as *jeu de paume*. It was originally played with the bare hand; the strung racket was developed in about 1500, when the game became highly popular in France. Many other handball and racket-and-ball court games developed from it. Its world championships are the oldest of any sport, dating back to about 1750, although it is now very much a minority sport. The stone or concrete floor area is approximately 96 × 32 ft (29 × 10 m). The cloth ball is hit over a central net, as in *tennis and *badminton, but it also bounces off the side walls, as in *squash rackets and *fives.

Cousin, Victor (1792–1867) French philosopher. He enjoyed a brilliant career, despite anti-establishment sympathies, and was a superb lecturer and prolific writer. As a minister under *Thiers (1840) he reformed French education. His talents were eclectic rather than analytic and his only truly original work is *Du vrai, du beau, et du bien* (1854).

Cousin the Elder, Jean (1490–1560) French artist and craftsman, who designed tapestries and stained-glass windows. The nude study *Eva Prima Pandora* (Louvre) is attributed to him. His son **Jean Cousin the Younger** (c. 1522–c. 1594) was also a painter, engraver, and stained-glass designer, known particularly for *The Last Judgment* (Louvre).

Cousteau, Jacques Yves (1910–) French naval officer and underwater explorer. He shared in the invention of the aqualung (1943) and invented a way of using television under water. In 1945 he founded the Undersea Research Group of the French navy at Marseilles and in 1950 became commander of the oceanographic research vessel *Calypso*. He became director of the Oceanographic Museum and Institute in Monaco, 1957. He is famous for such films as *The Silent World* (1953) and *The Living Sea* (1963) and for popular television series.

couvade A custom, common in many parts of the world among primitive peoples, in which the father retires to bed during his wife's confinement and simulates the pain of childbirth. Its intention is presumably to establish a role for the father and, by magical association, to lessen the pain of the mother. In the 20th century it has been reported among Basques and in Brazil.

covenant A binding agreement between two parties whereby each promises to do something for the other (*see also* deed). In the Old Testament, the covenant between God and Israel forms the basis of the Jewish religion. In return for obedience to the Law (the *Ten Commandments) as delivered to Moses, the Israelites were promised a privileged relationship with God as the chosen people. The symbol of this agreement was the *Ark of the Covenant containing the tablets of the Law. In the New Testament, this belief is interpreted in Christian terms as including all men, who are regarded as having been redeemed by Christ.

Covenanters Scottish Presbyterians who in the 16th and 17th centuries bonded together (or covenanted) to defend their church. The National Covenant of 1638 was signed by thousands of Scottish Presbyterians after Charles I's attempt to introduce the English Prayer Book. In the English *Civil War the Covenanters joined the parliamentarians in 1643 in return for the promise of church reform. After the Restoration (1660) they were persecuted and suppressed until 1688.

Covent Garden The principal English opera house, officially named the Royal Opera House. The first theater on the site was opened in 1732, and the present building dates from the 1850s; it is currently the home of both the Royal Opera and the Royal Ballet Company. It takes its name from a square (originally a convent garden) onto which it backs, which was laid out in 1631 by Inigo *Jones.

Coventry 52 25N 1 30W A city in central England. Heavily bombed during World War II, the city center was almost entirely rebuilt. Its famous cathedral, designed by Sir Basil Spence, was opened in 1962 and retains the ruins of the old cathedral, which was bombed in 1940. Formerly a weaving town, Coventry is now an important center for the automobile industry and also produces motorcycles, machinery, electrical equipment, and synthetic fabrics. Population (1981): 314,124.

Coverdale, Miles (1488–1568) English Protestant reformer. While an Augustinian friar at Cambridge, he was converted to Protestantism. In exile he published an English translation of the Bible (1535) and was largely responsible for the revisions resulting in the Great Bible of 1539. He was Bishop of Exeter from 1551 until exiled again under Queen Mary. After returning in 1559 he became a Puritan leader.

Covilhã, Pêro da (c. 1460–c. 1526) Portuguese explorer sent by John II to find *Prester John and explore Africa and the East, he left Portugal in 1487 and traveled via Aden to India, visiting Cannanore, Calicut, and Goa. He returned to Ormuz in the Persian Gulf and from Cairo set off for Ethiopia. There he ended his days, honored but forcibly detained.

SIR NOËL COWARD *At Montreux, Switzerland (1967).*

Coward, Sir Noël (1899–1973) British dramatist, composer, and actor. He first established his reputation with *The Vortex* (1924), an intense domestic drama, but his best-known plays are witty and elegant comedies of manners, such as *Hay Fever* (1925) and *Blithe Spirit* (1941). He also contributed as writer, director, composer, and performer to revues, musicals, and films, notably *In Which We Serve* (1942) and *Brief Encounter* (1946). His best-known songs include "Mad Dogs and Englishmen" and "Mad about the Boy."

cowboys Mounted cattle herders and folk heroes of the American West, who from about 1820 worked in the open grassland W of the Mississippi River, from Canada to Mexico. Cowboys used horse, spur, rope, and branding iron to "round-up" the herds and drive them to market. The legendary cowboy of "western" films, drinking and fighting in a saloon, derives from his twice-yearly spree after the round-ups. Rail transport and barbed wire fences rendered the cowboy's jobs of herding and range riding obsolete. *Compare* gaucho.

Cowley, Malcolm (1898–) US literary critic, editor, and author. He was an editor on the *New Republic* (1929–44) and edited collections of writers, such as William *Faulkner, F. Scott *Fitzgerald, and Ernest *Hemingway, and greatly advanced the career of John *Cheever. His works include *Exile's Return* (1934) about his years with the "lost generation" of American writers in Paris in the 1920s, *Dry Season* (1941), *And I Worked at the Writer's Trade* (1978), and *The Dream of the Golden Mountains* (1980).

cow parsley A biennial herb, *Anthriscus sylvestris*, up to 40 in (100 cm) high, with conspicuous umbrella-like clusters of white or pinkish flowers. It is found in hedgerows, wood edges, and waste places throughout much of Eurasia and N Africa and has been introduced to North America. Family: *Umbelliferae*.

cowpea An annual African plant, *Vigna unguiculata*, widely grown in tropical areas and the southern US. Having a high protein content, cowpeas are an important food crop, especially in Africa. There are two forms: a short erect one grown in Africa and America, whose seeds are used dried, and a tall climbing one grown in SE Asia, whose long pods are eaten when young. Family: *Leguminosae*.

Cowpens, Battle of (January 17, 1781) A battle in the American Revolution in which the Americans defeated the British. Led by General Daniel Morgan (1736–1802), the Americans inflicted a surprise defeat on the British force, slowing down *Cornwallis' invasion of North Carolina.

Cowper, William (1731–1800) British poet. With John Newton, he published *Olney Hymns* in 1779. "John Gilpin's Ride" (1783), a comic ballad,

and "The Task" (1785), a long discursive poem on rural themes, were both very successful. He was mentally unstable throughout his life. After the death in 1796 of Mary Unwin, a widow with whom he had lived for many years, he expressed his despair in "The Castaway."

cowpox A contagious virus disease of cattle that can be contracted by man. Resembling a mild form of smallpox, it appears as blisters on the teats and udder. Animals should be isolated and recovery is usually complete. Edward *Jenner used fluid from cowpox blisters to produce the first effective smallpox vaccine.

cowrie A *gastropod mollusk of the family *Cypraeidae* (about 160 species), mostly found in warm seas. 0.4–6 in (1–15 cm) long, cowries have glossy □shells with inrolled lips that are covered by the mantle, which is withdrawn inside the shell when the animal is disturbed. Cowries feed at night on small animals. The shell of the tropical money cowrie (*Cypraea moneta*), about 1.2 in (3 cm) long, is used as a form of currency in Africa and India.

cowslip A perennial spring-flowering Eurasian herb, *Primula veris*, growing to a height of 8 in (20 cm). It has a rosette of crinkled leaves and hanging clusters of bright-yellow five-petaled flowers. It is found from lowland meadows to alpine pastures. Family: *Primulaceae* (primrose family).

Coxey's Army (1894) US unemployed workers, led by Jacob S. Coxey (1854–1951), marched on Washington, DC, to protest against unemployment and to urge the passing of laws to create more jobs and to circulate more paper money. Also known as the Commonwealth of Christ, the group disbanded when Coxey was arrested and accused of treason.

coyote A wild *dog, *Canis latrans*, of Central and North American grassland, also called prairie wolf. Coyotes are about 48 in (120 cm) long, including the bushy tail (12 in [30 cm]), and have yellowish fur. They hunt alone or in packs and take food ranging from insects to small deer.

coypu A South American aquatic *rodent, *Myocaster coypus*. About 24 in (60 cm) long (excluding a long hairless tail), it has thick brown fur and webbed hind feet. The underfur of the belly is known as nutria, and coypus are farmed for fur. In Britain escaped coypus are becoming a pest, especially in East Anglia, eating vegetation and undermining river banks by burrowing. Family: *Capromyidae*.

Cozzens, James Gould (1903–78) US novelist. He was born in Chicago and grew up in New York. *Confusion* (1924) was published while he was in his second year at Harvard University. By 1949 he had won the Pulitzer Prize for *Guard of Honor* (1948). His works include *S. S. San Pedro* (1931), *The Last Adam* (1933), *The Castaway* (1934), *Men and Brethren* (1936), *The Just and the Unjust* (1942), *By Love Possessed* (1957), and *Morning, Noon and Night* (1968).

crab A *crustacean belonging to the tribes *Brachyura* (true crabs; about 4500 species) or *Anomura* (about 1300 species, including the *hermit crab). True crabs have a wide flat body covered by a hard carapace, with the small abdomen tucked underneath. There is a large pair of pincers and four pairs of legs used for walking (typically in a sideways scuttle) or swimming. They are carnivores or scavengers and most species are marine (the *land crab is an exception). The European species *Cancer pagurus* is edible. Order: *Decapoda*.

crab apple A □tree, *Malus sylvestris*, 7–33 ft (2–10 m) high: one of the species from which cultivated *apples have been developed. It has pinkish-white five-petaled flowers that bloom in spring and small sour greenish fruits, used to make jelly. A native of Europe and Asia, it is sometimes grown as an ornamental. Family: *Rosaceae*.

Crabbe, George (1754–1832) British poet. His native Suffolk was the scene of many of his poems. *The Village* (1783) was a brutally realistic portrayal of rural life, in stark contrast to conventional idealized treatments. This theme he took up again in the verse tales of *The Borough* (1810), source of *Britten's opera *Peter Grimes*, and *Tales of the Hall* (1819).

crabeater seal A common Antarctic seal, *Lobodon carcinophagus*, that feeds entirely on krill. About 8.2 ft (2.5 m) long, crabeater seals are dark in winter and almost white in summer; they are slender and can travel fast over ice. □oceans.

Crab nebula A turbulent expanding mass of gas, lying about 6000 light years distant in the constellation Taurus. It is the remnant of a *supernova that was observed in 1054. It emits radiation from all spectral regions and is an especially strong source of radio waves and X-rays. Within the nebula, and supplying energy to it, lies the **Crab pulsar**. This optical pulsar was produced by the supernova and has the fastest period (0.033 seconds) of all known pulsars.

Cracow. *See* Kraków.

Craig, Edward Henry Gordon. *See* Terry, Ellen.

Craiova 44 18N 23 47E A city in S Romania, on the Jiu River. Industries include heavy engineering and food manufacture. Its university was established in 1966. Population (1979 est): 220,893.

crake A small shy bird belonging to the *rail family. Crakes have a short conical bill and are commonly found in marshes and swamps. The Eurasian spotted crake (*Porzana porzana*) is 9 in (23 cm) long and has a streaked olive back, a lightly spotted breast, buff underparts, and a red ring at the base of the bill.

Cram, Ralph Adams (1863–1942) US architect, writer, and reformer. An advocate of a return to the Gothic style in architecture, he designed buildings at Princeton University, the US Military Academy at West Point, Rice University, and other schools. With his partner F. W. Ferguson he redesigned in Gothic style New York City's St John the Divine cathedral. As a reformer he advocated social customs from medieval times. He wrote *The Gothic Quest* (1907), *The Ministry of Art* (1914), *The Nemesis of Mediocrity* (1918), and *The End of Democracy* (1937).

cramp Painful spasmodic contraction of a muscle. Cramp is often caused by overexercise, often of the legs (in swimmers) or hands (writers' cramp). It may also be due to salt deficiency or poor circulation.

Cranach the Elder, Lucas (Lucas Müller; 1472–1553) German artist, born in Kronach (Bavaria). He studied painting under his father before moving to Wittenberg in 1505 to become court painter to Frederick the Wise, Elector of Saxony, and later to his two successors. Because of his portraits of Reformation leaders including his friend Luther, he is sometimes called the Reformation painter. He is also noted for his stylized but sensuous nudes, e.g. *Adam and Eve* (Courtauld Institute, London).

cranberry A low evergreen shrub of the genus *Vaccinium*, bearing red edible berries and growing in acidic boggy areas. *V. oxycoccus* occurs in Europe, N Asia, and North America. *V. macrocarpon* of North America has larger fruits (about 0.6 in [1.5 cm] across). The fruits of both are made into cranberry sauce, eaten with turkey and venison. Family: *Ericaceae* (heath family).

crane (bird) A large long-legged bird belonging to a family (*Gruidae*; 14 species) occurring in Old World regions and North America. Standing up to 56 in (140 cm) tall with a wingspan of over 80 in (200 cm), cranes vary from gray to white with black wingtips; some species are crested. They have heavy bills, feeding in marshes and plains on grain, shoots, and small animals, and are strong fliers; northern species are migratory. Order: *Gruiformes* (rails, etc.). *See also* demoiselle; whooping crane.

crane (machinery) A machine for raising, lowering, or moving heavy objects. It is used in construction work, loading cargoes onto ships, etc. There are many types but most have an engine to wind cables supported by an inclined or horizontal jib or boom, which either has a pulley system at one end or, in the case of a traveling crane, a pulley system that can move along the whole length of the jib. In a gantry crane the jib is fixed on supports at both ends, which themselves travel along rails. Cranes are often mounted on trucks or locomotives.

Crane, Hart (1899–1932) US poet. After an unhappy childhood in Ohio, he settled in New York in 1923 and began writing poems expressive of the personal conflicts caused by his homosexuality and alcoholism. He published *White Buildings* in 1926. *The Bridge* (1930), an epic poem in 15 parts, unites myth, history, and dream in a celebration of contemporary America. He went to Mexico to write another epic and drowned himself on the return voyage.

Crane, Stephen (1871–1900) US novelist. His early work as a journalist in New York provided him with first-hand knowledge of the poverty and destitution portrayed in his novel *Maggie: A Girl of the Streets* (1893). He is best known for the Civil War novel *The Red Badge of Courage* (1895) and his short stories, especially "The Open Boat." He worked as a war correspondent in Cuba and Greece, lived in England, and died in Germany of tuberculosis.

cranefly A harmless fly, also called daddy longlegs, belonging to the family *Tipulidae*. Craneflies are 0.24–3 in (6–75 mm) long with long delicate legs and wings. They are found near water or vegetation and are attracted to light. The larvae generally occur in water or rotting vegetation. However some—the leatherjackets—live in the soil and are plant pests, feeding on the roots of cereals and grasses. □insect.

cranesbill A herbaceous plant of the genus *Geranium* (about 400 species), widely distributed, especially in temperate regions, and usually having pink or purple flowers. They take their name from the long slender beaklike carpels. The meadow cranesbill (*G. pratense*), a perennial up to 24 in (60 cm) high, has violet-blue flowers, 0.6–0.7 in (15–18 mm) long,

and is widespread throughout Eurasia and North America. Family: *Geraniaceae*.

Cranmer, Thomas (1489–1556) Anglican reformer and martyr. He was consecrated Archbishop of Canterbury in 1532. He is especially remembered for his contributions to the Prayer Books of 1549 and 1552. Under Queen Mary he was tried as a heretic and, after initially recanting, burned at the stake.

crannog An artificial island of stone, timber, and peat, constructed as sites for houses in Ireland from the early Neolithic to the medieval eras. A notable example is the Low Gara crannog.

craps A dice game used for gambling, especially in the US. It was developed in the 19th century by black workers from the more complex game of *hazard. Two dice are used. Each player attempts to throw a "natural," a 7 or 11, which wins. 2, 3, or 12 ("craps") are losing combinations. If he throws a 4, 5, 6, 8, 9, or 10 he continues to throw until he wins by throwing the same number again or loses by throwing a 7. Bets are made by the other players against the thrower, among themselves, or (in a casino) against the house.

Crassus, Marcus Licinius (c. 115–53 BC) Roman politician and ally of Caesar, nicknamed *Dives* (wealthy). Crassus suppressed Spartacus' revolt (71), although Pompey took the credit. Failing to manipulate political affairs on his own, Crassus joined Pompey and Caesar in the first Triumvirate (60). He was killed during an invasion of Parthia.

Crater Lake National Park 42 49N 122 08W A national park in SE Oregon, in the Cascade Mountains. Crater Lake, almost 2000 ft (610 m) deep, was formed in the crater of an extinct volcano and is one of the deepest lakes in North America. The lake is surrounded by lava rock cliffs, some as high as 2000 ft (610 m). Other features of the park, which was established in 1902, are Pumice Desert and the Pinnacles. Area: 250 sq mi (648 sq km).

Crawford, Joan (Lucille le Sueur; 1908–77) US film actress. She started her film career in musicals but became famous during the 1930s and 1940s for her dramatic portrayals of ambitious women in such films as *Grand Hotel* (1932), *The Women* (1939), *Mildred Pierce* (1945), *Humoresque* (1946), and *The Best of Everything* (1959).

Crawley 51 7N 0 12W A city in SE England, in West Sussex. Designated a new town in 1947, it has light engineering, electronics, plastics, and furniture industries. Population (1981): 72,756.

crayfish A freshwater *crustacean, also called crawfish and crawdad, belonging to the superfamily *Nephropidea*. It has a small lobster-like body, 1–3 in (25–75 mm) long, and occurs under rocks or debris or in burrows in mud banks during the day. At night it feeds on plant and animal material. Some species are edible. Order: *Decapoda*.

Crazy Horse (c. 1849–77) Leader of the Oglala Sioux, who organized active resistance to the US Army. After their defeat in the First Sioux War (1866–68), the Sioux agreed to be resettled in a permanent reservation in the Dakota Territory. However, the extension of the Northern Pacific Railroad and the arrival of gold miners in the Black Hills was seen by the Sioux as a violation of their treaty with the US government and the Second Sioux War ensued (1875–76). In this war, Crazy Horse joined forces with *Sitting Bull, leader of the Northern Sioux, and they defeated and massacred the troops of General George *Custer at the Battle of Little Bighorn in 1876. Crazy Horse surrendered to the US Army in the following year, but he was killed while resisting imprisonment.

cream of tartar Potassium hydrogen tartrate that occurs in the later stages of the fermentation of grape juice as a deposit on the sides of the cask. After purification and crystallization it is used for culinary (*see* baking powder) and medical purposes.

Crécy, Battle of (August 26, 1346) The first land battle of the *Hundred Years' War, fought in N France, in which the English, led by *Edward III, defeated the French under *Philip VI. It was a triumph for the English longbowmen over heavily armored French knights; about 1500 French soldiers were killed. The victory enabled Edward to move N and besiege Calais.

credit and credit ratings The loan of money to an individual or company by a bank, credit-card organization, retailer, etc. Much consumer purchasing, especially of durables (*see* consumption), in industrial countries is on credit terms. The amount of credit that a person or company can command depends on his credit rating at the bank or on that given by an agency that specializes in listing the creditworthiness of companies. Credit ratings will depend on the applicants' known assets and liabilities, income (profitability for a company), and past record for trustworthiness. Influencing credit is a central part of a government's monetary policy.

credit card A card that enables the holder to obtain goods or services on credit. They are issued by retail stores, banks, and credit-card companies to approved clients. The bank or credit-card company settles the client's bills, invoicing him monthly and usually charging interest on any outstanding debts. The high rate of interest charged, the card-holders' subscriptions, and the fees paid by some organizations that accept cards provide the profit for the credit-card companies and banks.

Cree An Algonkian-speaking North American Indian people closely related to the *Ojibwa and formerly inhabiting large areas of central Canada. Supporting themselves by trapping and hunting in small wandering bands, the Cree nation gradually split into two groups, the Plains Cree and the Woodlands Cree. The Plains Cree migrated southward where they acquired horses and guns and adopted the buffalo-hunting culture of the Great Plains. The Woodlands Cree maintained their traditional way of life, and many became guides for British and French fur-trappers in their territory. The present Cree population, settled mostly in the Canadian province of Manitoba, is approximately 10,000.

Creed, Frederick (1871–1957) Canadian inventor, who moved to Scotland in 1897 and developed the Creed teleprinter (*see* Telex). The first such device was installed in 1912 and was soon in widespread use.

creeds In Christianity, formal summaries of the principal items of belief, often recited as part of the eucharistic service in many Churches. They originated as professions of faith said at baptism and were gradually formalized. The two most widely used are the Apostles' Creed (probably 3rd century AD) and the Nicene Creed, probably a revision by the Council of Constantinople (381) of the creed promulgated at the Council of *Nicaea (325) and accepted by both Western and Eastern churches. The Athanasian Creed, probably dating from the 5th century, is used in the Anglican catechism.

Creek A group of Muskogean-speaking North American Indian peoples, whose main sub-divisions are the Muskogee of Georgia and the Hitchiti of Alabama. Formerly inhabiting extensive territories throughout the SE, the Creek were advanced farmers and villagers who built towns in which rectangular houses were contructed around a central square that often contained a temple mound. Among their characteristic customs was the practice of elaborate body tattooing. In 1813–14 a confederacy of Creek towns began armed resistance to the US Army and were defeated by the forced of Gen Andrew *Jackson in a series of engagements known as the *Creek War. The Creek were later resettled in Oklahoma. The present Creek population numbers approximately 15,000.

Creek War (1813–14) A war between US settlers and the Creek Indians. Aided by the British and carrying Spanish weapons, the Creek Indians in Alabama, Georgia, and Florida attacked and massacred over 500 settlers at Ft Mims, Georgia. US troops under Gen Andrew *Jackson defeated the Creeks at Tallasahatchee, Talladega, and finally Horseshoe Bend, Alabama. The Creeks ceded parts of Alabama and Georgia to the US and ultimately were moved to reservations in Oklahoma.

cremation The disposal of the dead by burning. Practiced by many ancient European peoples, cremation was forbidden by the Christian Church on account of the doctrine of bodily resurrection of the dead. With 19th-century urban overcrowding in the West, cremation was revived and the practice has grown rapidly. The Roman Catholic Church formerly disapproved of cremation but it is now accepted as it is among most Jews. In the East it has remained the most general method of corpse disposal.

Cremona 45 08N 10 01E A city in N Italy, in Lombardy on the Po River. It has a 12th-century cathedral and a 13th-century palace. From the 16th to the 18th centuries it was famous for the manufacture of violins, including those of Stradivari. Population (1971): 81,983.

creodont An extinct primitive carnivorous mammal of the early Tertiary period (55–45 million years ago). They were mostly short-legged and slow-moving, preying on herbivores.

creole **1.** Originally a white person born in Spanish America during the colonial period (16th to 18th centuries). They suffered social and commercial disadvantages in comparison with the Spanish administrative class. **2.** A person of mixed blood living in the Caribbean area or in Latin America, extending to encompass a descendant of slaves in Surinam, a French-speaking descendant of French or Spanish settlers in Louisiana, and various other groups. More loosely, the term refers to people of Caribbean culture. **3.** A patois based on French, English, or Dutch and spoken especially in the West Indies as a mother tongue (*compare* pidgin English).

creosote A substance produced by distilling tar. The creosote used for preserving wood is obtained from *coal tar and is a brownish mixture of aromatic hydrocarbons and *phenols. Creosote made from wood tar is a mixture of phenols and is used in pharmacy.

creosote bush A shrub of the genus *Larrea* (5 species), of arid and semiarid areas of North and South America, where it is the dominant feature of the landscape. Up to 7 ft (2 m) high, these plants contain resinous phenolic substances that deter grazing animals, although some insects are adapted to living and feeding on them. Family: *Zygophyllaceae*.

cresol ($CH_3C_6H_4OH$) A liquid *aromatic compound obtained from *coal tar. It has three *isomers, a mixture of which is used as a disinfectant.

cress A plant of the mustard family (*Cruciferae*) the sharp-tasting leaves of which are used in salads, especially garden cress, or peppergrass (*Lepidium sativum*), believed to be native to W Asia but widely cultivated and naturalized in Europe. The seedlings are eaten, often with those of white mustard (*Sinapis alba*), with which it may be grown in containers. The European winter, or land, cress (*Barbarea verna*) grows to a height of 40 in (100 cm). Its leaves can be picked throughout the winter.

Cressent, Charles (1685–1768) French cabinetmaker. After working with *Boulle he became official cabinetmaker (1715) to the regent, the Duc d'Orléans, and also made furniture for foreign courts. The leading designer of the period, he made popular the use of colored-wood marquetry and *ormolu mountings.

crested tit A dull-brown and gray *tit, *Parus cristatus*, of European coniferous forests. It is about 4 in (11 cm) long and has a pointed black-and-white crest and black C-shaped marking bordering its face. It feeds on insects and seeds, often storing them for winter use.

Cretaceous period A geological period of the Mesozoic era, between about 135 and 65 million years ago, following the Jurassic and preceding the Tertiary (when the Cenozoic era began). It is divided into the Lower and Upper Cretaceous. The period saw a widespread gradual marine transgression, the rocks of the Upper Cretaceous culminating in the thick chalk deposits of N Europe and the midwestern US. The dinosaurs and other giant reptiles, as well as the ammonites and many other invertebrates, became extinct at the end of the Cretaceous.

Crete (Modern Greek name: Kríti) The largest of the Greek islands, in the E Mediterranean Sea approximately 63 mi (100 km) SE of the mainland. It is generally mountainous, rising over 7874 ft (2400 m). The economy is based primarily on agriculture producing olives, wines, and citrus fruits; the raising of sheep and goats is also important. There is a thriving tourist industry, based on Iráklion. *History*: colonized probably in the 6th millennium BC from Asia Minor, Crete achieved extensive maritime power during the Middle Minoan period (c. 2000–c. 1700 BC), from which many artifacts, inscriptions, and buildings have been discovered (*see* Minoan civilization). The most notable are the palace at *Knossos and clay tablets bearing two different scripts known as *Linear A and *Linear B. Politically insignificant in the history of classical Greece, it fell to Rome (67 BC), Byzantium (395 AD), and the Muslims (826). In 1204 it was sold to the Venetians, who gave both the island and Iráklion the name Candia. It fell to Turkey in 1669 and was officially incorporated into Greece in 1913. During World War II it was the scene (1941) of the first ever large-scale airborne invasion, in which the Germans took the island from British and Commonwealth troops, who had been evacuated here from the Greek mainland. Area: 3217 sq mi (8332 sq km). Population (1971): 456,208. Capital: Khaniá.

cretinism The condition resulting from a deficiency of thyroid hormone, which is present from birth. Affected children are mentally retarded dwarfs with coarse skin and facial features. Cretinism is treated with injections of thyroxine, which must be started early and continued throughout life. *See also* hypothyroidism.

Crèvecoeur, Michel-Guillaume-Jean de (*or* J. Hector St John; 1735–1813) French-American writer. After military service in Canada he stayed in America, where he served as French consul between 1784 and 1790. His *Letters from an American Farmer* (1782) and *Sketches of Eighteenth-Century America* (1925) are the thoughtful records of an early immigrant in the New World.

cribbage (*or* crib) A card game attributed to Sir John *Suckling. It is played by 2, 3, or 4 players with a standard pack of 52 cards. The rules vary in detail, but play basically consists of each player alternately playing a card until the total value of the cards played approaches 31. The last player able to play a card without exceeding 31 scores. Points are also scored for having certain combinations of cards in a hand or for playing during certain sequences of cards. The crib (consisting of cards discarded from each hand) scores for the dealer. The score is kept with small pegs on a cribbage board containing rows of holes.

Crick, Francis Harry Compton (1916–) British biophysicist, who (with James D. *Watson) proposed a model for the molecular structure of *DNA (1953). Following this breakthrough, Crick continued to work on

DNA, helping to determine the mechanism of protein synthesis. He shared a Nobel Prize (1962) with Watson and Maurice *Wilkins.

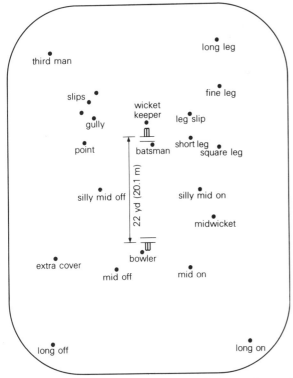

CRICKET   *The pitch, as the field is called, showing the usual fielding positions (for a right-handed batsman).*

cricket (sport)   An 11-a-side bat-and-ball team game, in which the object is to score the most runs. It originated in England among shepherds using their crooks as bats; its rules were laid down in 1744 and the game is played almost exclusively in the UK and its former empire. Presided over by two umpires, it is played on a large field; the pitch is a strip of grass 22 yd (20.12 m) long having at each end a wicket of three stumps surmounted by two bails. The ball is made of cork and twine, encased in leather. The members of one team take turns to bat in pairs, one defending each wicket; the batsmen's objective is to score runs by hitting the ball and exchanging ends before the ball is returned to the pitch. Each player bats until he is bowled, caught, stumped, run out, or judged lbw (leg before wicket). The members of the other team field, some taking turns to bowl the ball. After every over of six balls (eight in Australia) the bowler changes, the new bowler bowling from the other wicket. A match consists of one or two innings and may last for a few hours or up to six days, depending on the type of competition. International cricket, governed by the International Cricket Conference, is played mainly in Test matches between England, Australia, the West Indies, New Zealand, India, and Pakistan.

cricket (zoology)   An insect, resembling a grasshopper but with longer antennae, belonging to one of several families of the order *Orthoptera. The males stridulate (i.e. make a chirping noise) by rubbing the front wings together. True crickets (family *Gryllidae*; 2400 species) have black or brown flattened bodies, 0.12–2 in (3–50 mm) long, with long tail appendages (cerci) and short forewings (they do not fly). The females have long needle-like ovipositors for depositing eggs in soil or crevices. True crickets are omnivorous and live in burrows or among vegetation; some, for example the widely distributed house cricket (*Acheta domesticus*), frequent buildings. *See also* bush cricket; mole cricket.

Crimea (Russian name: *Krym*)   A peninsula and autonomous region (*oblast*) in the Ukrainian SSR, in the SW Soviet Union, almost totally surrounded by the Black Sea and the Sea of Azov and connected to the mainland in the N by the Perekop Isthmus. It is mainly flat but rises to 5069 ft (1545 m) in the S. Iron ore is mined here and wheat, tobacco, and wine are produced. The chief towns are Feodosia, Kerch, Sevastopol, Yalta, Yevpatoria, and the capital of the *oblast*, Simferopol. *History*: colonized by Greeks in the 6th century BC, the Crimea was continually invaded by Goths, Huns, and others and in 1239 was made a khanate by Tatars of the

*Golden Horde. This was overthrown by Turks in 1475, and the area was annexed by Russia in 1783. Many Tatars emigrated then, and the remainder were deported in 1945 for alleged collaboration with the German forces of occupation between 1941 and 1943. Area: about 10,423 sq mi (27,000 sq km). Population (1972): 1,909,000. *See also* Crimean War.

Crimean War (1853–56) The war between Russia, on one side, and Britain, France, the Ottoman (Turkish) Empire, and (from 1855) Sardinia-Piedmont, on the other. Caused by Russia's expansionist ambitions in the Balkans, the war was precipitated by Russia's desire to establish a protectorate over Orthodox Christians in the Ottoman Empire. In July, 1853, Russia occupied Moldavia and Walachia, in October, Turkey declared war, and in March, 1854, following the destruction of a Turkish fleet at Sinope, Britain and France entered the war. The major battles of the year-long siege of Sevastopol, in the Crimea, were of *Balaclava and *Inkerman, and the Russians eventually evacuated the port in September, 1855. Peace was formally concluded at Paris (1856). Over 250,000 men were lost by each side, many from disease in the appalling hospitals of the Crimea. The British Government dispatched Florence *Nightingale to inspect those at Scutari, where her work had a considerable effect in improving conditions.

criminal law   *See* penal law.

criminology   The study of the cause, nature, and prevention of crime. Crime was generally equated with immorality until the 19th century, when the pioneer Italian criminologist Cesare *Lombroso suggested, in *L'uomo delinquente* (1876), that criminals are born and can be recognized by such physical attributes as a receding forehead. Although this view is no longer accepted, at various times evidence has been produced to suggest that such physiological abnormalities as an extra Y chromosome or an endocrine abnormality do predispose to criminality. Poverty, psychological stress, lack of parental affection in childhood, working mothers, and the decline of the extended family have all been suggested as additional or alternative predisposing factors, and some evidence has been produced to support each of them. But none of this evidence can explain why some people succumb to predisposing factors and become criminals while others, exposed to the same factors, do not.

Deep ethical problems are also involved. To what extent, for example, do predisposing factors affect culpability? To what extent should crime be regarded merely as a deviation from social norms? Should punishment fit the crime or the criminal and to what extent should it attempt to be therapeutic? Criminologists have, as yet, no satisfactory answers to most of these questions.

crinoid   A marine invertebrate animal belonging to a class (*Crinoidea*; about 700 species) of *echinoderms, including the sea lilies and feather stars. It has a small cup-shaped body covered with calcareous plates and with five radiating pairs of feathery flexible arms surrounding the mouth at the top. Sea lilies, most of which are now extinct, are fixed to the sea bottom, coral reefs, etc., by a stalk. Feather stars, e.g. *Antedon*, are free-swimming and are usually found on rocky bottoms. Crinoids occur mainly in deep waters and feed on microscopic plankton and detritus caught by the arms and conveyed to the mouth. The larvae are sedentary. □fossil. 60

Cripps, Sir (Richard) Stafford   (1889–1952) British Labor politician. Cripps became solicitor general in 1930, before entering parliament in 1931. In 1939 he was expelled from the Labor Party for campaigning against Neville *Chamberlain's appeasement policy. He was ambassador to Moscow (1940–42), and chancellor of the exchequer (1947–50), when his austere economic policy set Britain on the road to recovery after World War II.

Cristofori, Bartolommeo   (1655–1731) Italian harpsichord maker and inventor of the *piano. He constructed the escapement system in which the hammer falls away from the string immediately after striking it, leaving it free to vibrate. A damper stops the sound when the key is released.

critical mass   The mass of fissile substance that is just capable of sustaining a *chain reaction within it. Below the critical mass, too many of the particles that might have induced a reaction escape and the chain reaction dies away.

critical-path analysis   A planning method based on the use of a schematic representation of the network of activities and events involved in a project. Its aim is to aid coordination by identifying the optimum schedule. A critical path is a sequence of activities in which the key parameters, usually time and cost, cannot be increased without endangering the whole project. In large networks, which often need to be analyzed by computer, there may be more than one critical path. The method is commonly used in large construction projects.

critical state The state of a gas at its critical temperature, pressure, and volume. The critical temperature is the temperature above which a gas cannot be liquefied by increased pressure alone. The vapor pressure of the gas at this temperature is the critical pressure and its volume, the critical volume. In the critical state the density of the vapor is equal to the density of the liquid.

Crivelli, Carlo (c. 1430–95) Venetian painter, who settled in the Marches of Italy in the late 1460s. He is set apart from the Venetian school by his sharp linear style, influenced by *Mantegna, and the decorative detail that appears in such paintings as *The Annunciation* (National Gallery, London).

croaker. *See* drumfish.

Croatia (Serbo-Croat name: Hrvatska) A constituent republic of NW Yugoslavia, bordering on the Adriatic Sea. It is chiefly mountainous, descending to plains in the NE, where it is drained by the Drava River. It is primarily agricultural, producing cereals, potatoes, tobacco, fruit, and livestock. Industries, centered on the larger towns, include metallurgy and the manufacture of textiles. *History*: settled by the Croats in the 7th century AD, the region was successively controlled by Hungary, Turkey, and Austria until the formation of the kingdom of the Serbs, Croats, and Slovenes (later Yugoslavia) in 1918. Following the occupation of Yugoslavia by the Axis Powers in World War II, Croatia was proclaimed an independent state (1941), ruled over by the fascist dictator Ante Pavelić (1889–1959). In 1945 Croatia once more became part of Yugoslavia as a people's republic. Area: 22,050 sq mi (56,538 sq km). Population (1978): 4,601,000. Capital: Zagreb.

Croatian. *See* Serbo-Croat.

Croce, Benedetto (1866–1952) Italian philosopher. Orphaned at 17 by an earthquake, he attended Rome University, studying art, philosophy, and history. His system is expounded in the four-volume *Philosophy of Mind* (1900–10). The only reality is mental and this reality is divided into theoretical and practical. Theoretical reality comprises intuition (art and aesthetics) and conception (philosophy or history—essentially the same, both being accounts of reality). Practical reality comprises individual will (political and economic activity) and universal will (morality). His aesthetic ideas, aired in numerous other works, are the most influential.

Crockett, Davy (1786–1836) US frontiersman. He was a colonel in the Tennessee militia under Andrew Jackson, elected to the state legislature (1821–26), and Tennessee representative to Congress (1827–31, 1833–35). He cultivated the image of a rough frontiersman and became known for his skill as a scout and hunter. He fought for Texas in its struggle for independence from Mexico and was killed at the *Alamo.

crocodile A ◻reptile belonging to either of two genera, *Crocodylus* or *Osteolemus*, and distinguished from alligators and caymans by having a more pointed snout and fewer teeth, the fourth tooth of the lower jaw remaining visible when the mouth is closed. Crocodiles occur chiefly in tropical fresh waters although the estuarine crocodile (*C. porosus*), which reaches a length of 20 ft (6 m), occurs in coastal waters of SE Asia and Australia.

Crocodiles belong to the order *Crocodilia* (about 20 species), along with alligators and caymans. Crocodilians are amphibious mainly nocturnal carnivores living in tropical and subtropical swamps and rivers, where they prey chiefly on fish but also on water birds and land animals. They have long powerful jaws and a covering of thick protective bony plates; the ears and nostrils are placed high on the head and can be closed by valves when under water. The female builds a nest of mud or vegetation in which over a hundred shelled eggs may be laid. She guards the nest until the young, measuring 8–10 in (20–25 cm) in length, begin to hatch. Crocodilians may live for over a hundred years. Their skins are used to make leather goods and this has caused a decline in their numbers.

crocodile bird An African riverbank *courser, *Pluvianus aegyptius*, that feeds on parasites picked from crocodiles. It is 9 in (23 cm) long and is black with white markings on the throat and above the eyes.

Crocus A genus of low-growing plants (75 species), native to Mediterranean regions and widely planted in gardens. They grow from *corms to produce long thin leaves and six-lobed flowers in spring or autumn. Spring-flowering species include *C. vernus*, with white, blue, or purple flowers, and *C. aureus*, with deep-yellow flowers. *C. speciosus* is a purple autumn-flowering species. An Asian species (*C. sativus*) is the source of *saffron. Family: *Iridaceae. Compare* autumn crocus.

Croesus (died c. 546 BC) The last king of *Lydia (c. 560–c. 546 BC), famous for his wealth. He conquered the Greek cities on the coast of Asia Minor but was defeated by the Persian king *Cyrus (II) the Great in 546.

According to legend, Croesus was saved by Apollo from execution by Cyrus, whose counsellor he then became.

crofting A system of subsistence farming that involves the cultivation of a small parcel of land together with access to common grazing land. Crofting was widely practiced in the Scottish Highlands until the introduction of sheep farming together with the eviction of many crofting families in the late 18th century.

Crohn's disease An inflammatory disorder that can affect any part of the intestinal tract, most usually the terminal part of the small intestine (ileum). Crohn's disease, named for the US physician B. B. Crohn (1884–1983), occurs most commonly between the ages of 20 and 40 years; symptoms commonly include abdominal pain and diarrhea. Its cause is not known but it may be a form of *autoimmunity. Patients are treated with drugs, such as prednisolone (a steroid) and sulfasalazine (a sulfonamide); some cases require surgical removal of the affected part of the intestine.

Cro-Magnon A prehistoric race of men believed to be ancestral to modern men. Skeletal remains were found (1868) at Cro-Magnon near Les Eyzies-de-Tayac in the Dordogne (SW France) and similar bones of tall broad-faced individuals have been found at other European sites. They first appeared in Europe about 35,000 years ago and were associated with *Aurignacian and subsequent cultures. They hunted reindeer, bison, and wild horse. They were often cave dwellers but seem also to have constructed huts. They produced the earliest known examples of cave art (*see* Lascaux). *See also* Homo.

cromlech (Welsh: bent stone) A former name for a megalithic table grave or *dolmen and other prehistoric stone monuments. *See also* megalith.

Crompton, Samuel (1753–1827) British inventor of the spinning mule (1779), so called because it was a cross between *Arkwright's water frame and *Hargreaves' spinning jenny. It was able to produce yarn of a higher quality and at a greater speed than had previously been possible. Unable to afford a patent, Crompton sold his idea for very little money but in 1812 he was awarded a parliamentary grant of 5,000.

OLIVER CROMWELL *Dismissing the Rump of the Long Parliament (1653).*

Cromwell, Oliver (1599–1658) English soldier and statesman; Lord Protector of England (1653–58). Cromwell, a country gentleman, was a member of Parliament in the parliament of 1628–29. He emerged as a convinced Puritan and critic of Charles I in the *Long Parliament, summoned in 1640. After the outbreak of the *Civil War he raised a troop of cavalry, and fought at Edgehill (1642). As second in command he decisively defeated Charles at *Naseby (1645). Cromwell acted as mediator between the king, parliament, and the army but his conciliatory attitude hardened after Charles' flight to the Isle of Wight; when the second Civil War ended in Charles' defeat (1648), Cromwell signed the king's death warrant. In the power struggle between parliament and army, he sided with the army and after the establishment of the Commonwealth turned to the final mopping-up campaigns of the Civil War. He ruthlessly subjected Ireland (1649–50) and, after defeating Charles' heir at Dunbar (1650), finally subdued the Scots at Worcester (1651). In 1653 he expelled the Rump of the Long Parliament and following the failure of the Barebones Parliament accepted the Instrument of Government, which established the *Protectorate. As Lord Protector, Cromwell established Puritanism but permitted religious toleration, allowing the Jews to return to England (1656). His foreign policy was dictated by religious and commercial considerations: he ended the first *Dutch War, allied with France against Spain (gaining Dunkirk), and conquered Jamaica (1655). His relations with parliament were strained. He failed to find a workable constitutional basis for his rule, refusing parliament's offer of the crown in 1657. He was succeeded as Lord Protector by his son **Richard Cromwell** (1626–1712), who was forced by the army to abdicate in 1659 and lived in exile in France until 1680.

Cromwell, Thomas, Earl of Essex (c. 1485–1540) English statesman, who drafted the legislation that made the English Church independent of Rome (*see* Reformation). He entered Wolsey's service in 1514, became a member of Parliament in 1529, and by 1532 was Henry VIII's chief adviser; he became chancellor of the exchequer in 1533. He gained Henry's divorce from Catherine of Aragon by a series of acts that made the king, rather than the pope, head of the English Church. Between 1536 and 1540 he organized the dissolution of the monasteries, after which his negotiation of Henry's disastrous marriage to the uncomely Anne of Cleves led to his execution for treason.

Cronin, A(rchibald) J(oseph) (1896–1981) British novelist. He practiced medicine until he published his successful first novel, *Hatter's Castle* (1931). His later novels include *The Citadel* (1937) and *The Judas Tree* (1961).

Cronje, Piet Arnoldus (c. 1840–1911) South African general in the *Boer Wars. He captured Potchefstroom (1881) and the raiders led by *Jameson (1896) and delayed (Magersfontein, 1899) the British advance to relieve Kimberley. He was captured at Paardeburg (1900).

Cronus A Greek deity, the youngest of the Titans. He ruled the universe after castrating his father Uranus. He swallowed all the children he fathered by his sister Rhea except Zeus, for whom a stone was substituted. Zeus was reared secretly in Crete and eventually overthrew Cronus.

Crook, George (1829–90) US general. After graduation from West Point, he served in the Northwest and then saw action as a Union officer in the Civil War from 1862, participating in the battles of Antietam, Chickamauga, Shenandoah, and Petersburg. He was then reassigned to the Western frontier where he successfully fought against Indian uprisings and was victorious against the Apaches and their leader, *Geronimo. He was made brigadier general in charge of the Department of the Platte in 1886 and major general in command of the Division of the Missouri in 1888.

Crookes, Sir William (1832–1919) British physicist, whose work on vacuums led him to investigate the newly discovered phenomenon of *cathode rays. Crookes showed that cathode rays consisted of charged particles rather than electromagnetic radiation, since they were deflected by a magnetic field. He invented the Crookes radiometer and Crookes glass, containing cerium, to protect the eyes of the industrial workers. He also discovered the element thalium.

crop rotation The growing on the same land of different crops in sequence. Crop rotation helps maintain soil fertility, prevents the build-up of crop pests, and enables cultivation of the soil to clear weeds. Nowadays, mechanized farming and the use of artificial fertilizers and pesticides have encouraged monocropping (the repeated growing of the same crop).

croquet A ball-and-mallet game that probably developed from *paillemaille*, a French game played certainly by the 13th century. Croquet was particularly popular in Britain and the US in the mid- to late-19th century. It is played on a grass court or lawn, ideally 35 × 28 yd (32 × 25.6 m), with an arrangement of six hoops and one peg. Two to four players attempt to follow a prescribed course through the hoops, each using a distinctively colored ball, the winner being the first to hit the peg with his ball. If a player's ball hits (roquets) another ball, the player may croquet this ball by placing his own ball next to it and striking his own ball so that the opponent's ball is also moved; the object is to advance his own ball toward the peg and to drive his opponent's ball off course. After passing through a hoop or scoring a roquet a player has another turn.

Crosby, Bing (Harry Lillis C.; 1904–77) US popular singer. He achieved worldwide fame during the 1930s and 1940s as a crooner and is associated with the best-selling recording of all time, Irving Berlin's *White Christmas* (1942). He starred in many films, including *Going My Way* (1944) for which he won an Academy Award, and the "Road" series with Bob *Hope, and also in his own radio and television shows. □Sinatra, Frank.

crossbill A finch of the genus *Loxia* (3 species), 6–7 in (14.5-17 cm) long, whose unique cross-tipped bill is specialized for extracting seeds from unopened cones. The common crossbill (*L. curvirostra*) of Eurasia and North America feeds on spruce seeds. The male is red and the female gray-green; both have dark-brown wings and tail. The parrot crossbill (*L. py-*

tyopsittacus) feeds exclusively on pine seeds, and the Eurasian two-barred crossbill (*L. leukoptera*) feeds on fir seeds. *See* Plate V.

crossbow A short bow mounted on a stock, used in Europe throughout the middle ages. Crossbows were composite, made of wood, horn, tendons, and by the early 15th century of steel (called an arbalest). They were drawn by hand, a belt hook, or a winch. The bolt or *quarrel* was short, iron-tipped, fletched with wood, leather, or brass, and capable of penetrating armor. Slower and less accurate than the *longbow, it could be fired from behind cover. It is now used for sport.

CROSSES *As a Christian symbol the cross was popularized by Constantine the Great and came into wide use in the 4th century.*

crosses Figures formed by a vertical line or bar intersected by a horizontal. As a symbol, the cross is found in the art of several ancient cultures. One of the earliest Egyptian hieroglyphs is the cruciform ankh (*crux ansata*), the symbol of life. The primary association of the cross is with Christianity, in which it represents the instrument used at Christ's *crucifixion. This had several forms, conventionally distinguished by their Latin names: a simple upright stake (*crux simplex*); a stake with a transverse beam toward the top (*crux immissa*), which is known as the Latin cross and is the common form in the Western Church; a stake topped by a transverse beam (*crux commissa*), also known as the tau cross or cross of St Anthony; and an X-shaped structure (*crux decussata*), known as the cross of St Andrew. In European art, the crucifixion is usually depicted with a Latin cross, and the crucifixes (crosses with the image of the crucified Christ) used on altars, rood screens, etc., are given this form. The Greek cross or cross of St George has vertical and horizontal arms of equal length and is the traditional form in use in Orthodox Churches. The cross has influenced innumerable aspects of religious ritual, dress, and art, including the cruciform plan of churches and cathedrals. It is also one of the earliest of monumental designs (*see* Ruthwell Cross). As a charge in *heraldry, it is given various elaborated forms; a familiar example is the Maltese cross, the insignia of the *Hospitallers and, in Britain, of the St John Ambulance Association.

Crossopterygii An order of bony fish—the lobe-finned fishes—most of which are now extinct. Their fins were fleshy and contained elements of the internal skeleton, permitting movement both on land and in water. The suborder *Rhipidistia* were predatory freshwater fishes of the Devonian and Carboniferous periods (about 400–280 million years ago), some of which evolved into the amphibians. The suborder *Coelacanthini* contains *Latimeria*, the only surviving member of the order (*see* coelacanth). Subclass: *Sarcopterygii*.

crossword puzzles A word puzzle with a series of clues, the answers to which are written into a diagram divided into squares, some of which are blacked out. (In most puzzles the pattern of the black squares has to be symmetrical.) The first modern crossword was devised by Arthur Wynne and published in the New York *World* in 1913. They became very popular in the US during the 1920s. They are now a feature of many newspapers, each one having its own style and idiosyncrasies. The more sophisticated puzzles have clues based on literary references, puns, and cryptic sentences as well as anagrams and synonyms.

Croton A genus of tropical trees and shrubs (750 species) many of which are of economic importance. *C. tiglium* of SE Asia produces croton oil, a powerful laxative now considered unsafe. The bark of *C. cascarilla* and *C. eluteria*, trees of the Bahamas, produces cascarilla, used in tonics. *C. laccifer* from India and Sri Lanka provides a lac used in varnishes. Several Brazilian species produce dragon's-blood resin. Family: *Euphorbiaceae* (spurge family).

The evergreen ornamental plants called crotons are members of the genus *Codiaeum*, grown as pot plants for their variegated foliage.

Crotone (ancient name: Croton) 39 05N 17 08E A city in S Italy, in Calabria on the Gulf of Taranto. It was founded in about 700 BC by the Achaeans. There are chemical and zinc industries. Population (1971): 50,970.

crottle A large leafy *lichen belonging to the genus *Parmelia*, which is widely distributed from seashores to mountain tops and resembles crumpled leather. It has a black underside and sometimes reaches 35–48 in (90–120 cm) in diameter. It is used as a dye for fabrics.

croup An acute infection of the respiratory tract, usually caused by viruses, resulting in inflammation and obstruction of the larynx (voice box). Croup occurs most commonly in children under five years of age; symptoms include difficulty in breathing, which is harsh and noisy. Treatment consists of steam inhalations and sedatives; severe cases may require tracheostomy—an operation in which a tube is inserted through a hole in the trachea (windpipe).

crow A large songbird of the widely distributed family *Corvidae* (102 species). 12–26 in (30–65 cm) long, crows typically have a black or brightly colored plumage and a stout bill. They take a variety of food, which often includes carrion, and have a distinctive harsh call. The typical crows are the *carrion, *hooded, and American crows but the family also includes the *rooks, *ravens, *choughs, *jays, and *jackdaws.

Crow A *Siouan-speaking North American Indian people formerly inhabiting the Yellowstone River region. Early in the 18th century, the Crow moved westward, where they adopted the culture of the Great Plains and became traders of guns, horses, and other commodities between the village Indians and the *Shoshoni. In addition to trade, the Crow supported themselves by buffalo hunting. Their religion emphasized a personal quest for a spirit guardian experienced through fasting and other ordeals. They were led by chiefs who had distinguished themselves by acts of personal bravery. The present Crow population, residing mainly in Montana, now numbers approximately 4500.

crowberry A dwarf procumbent shrub, *Empetrum nigrum*, of N temperate and arctic heathlands. 6–18 in (15–45 cm) high, it has oblong leaves, tiny pinkish flowers, and black edible berries. The name derives from the reputation of the fruit for attracting crows. Family: *Ericaceae* (heath family).

crowfoot A widely distributed herbaceous annual or perennial plant of the genus *Ranunculus*, which also contains the buttercups. It has deeply lobed leaves (hence the name) and white or yellow five-petaled flowers. Some species, such as the European water crowfoot (*R. aquatilis*), are aquatic. Family: *Ranunculaceae*.

crown colony A territory that is under the direct legislative control of the UK. Most crown colonies have now been granted independence: the most important one remaining is *Hong Kong; most of the others are small islands, chiefly in the Caribbean and the Pacific.

crown jewels Royal insignia and regalia and the personal jewelry inherited or acquired by a sovereign. They are now frequently museum pieces. The British Crown Jewels, among the most famous, are housed in the Tower of London. Those owned by the czars of Russia are in the Kremlin in Moscow. In Britain they are used for state occasions such as coronations.

crown of thorns 1. A Madagascan shrub, *Euphorbia splendens*, often cultivated for ornament. Up to 40 in (100 cm) high, it has spiny stems at the tips of which are a few leaves and clusters of small flowers, each surrounded by rounded scarlet bracts. See Euphorbia. 2. A spiny vigorous shrub, *Zizyphus spina-christi*, forming thickets or growing singly as a tree. It is widespread in the Mediterranean region and is said to be the source of Christ's crown of thorns. Family: *Rhamnaceae* (buckthorn family).

crown-of-thorns starfish A reddish starfish, *Acanthaster planci*, that has a spiny body, up to 18 in (45 cm) across, with 12–19 arms. With the decimation of its chief predator—the Pacific triton (*Charonia tritonis*)—by shell collectors, it has spread throughout the South Pacific since the mid 20th century and now threatens destruction to the coral reefs and islands on which it feeds.

Cruciferae A family of plants (about 1900 species), mainly annual or perennial herbs, particularly abundant in N temperate regions. The flowers are four-petaled and cross-shaped. Many crucifers are of economic importance as food plants, cattle food, ornamentals, and weeds. Some, such as cabbage and other brassicas, have been grown since ancient times. In some European countries up to 30% of vegetable crop acreage is devoted to crucifers.

crucifixion A form of capital punishment carried out by nailing or binding a person to a *cross by the wrists and feet and leaving him to die from previously inflicted wounds or from exhaustion. It was commonly used in Carthage and adopted in the Roman Empire, where it was regarded as a scandalous form of death and so restricted to slaves and the worst criminals; it could not be inflicted on anyone holding Roman citizenship. Scourging customarily preceded crucifixion and the victim's legs were sometimes broken to hasten death. As a legal punishment it was abolished by the emperor Constantine. The crucifixion of Christ is reported in the four Gospels of the New Testament; the mockery, the crown of thorns, and the piercing of his side with a spear are not typical elements of this form of punishment. According to tradition, St Peter was also crucified, but head downward, and St Andrew was executed on the X-shaped cross that bears his name. In Christian legend, the cross on which Christ was crucified was discovered in 326 AD by St *Helena.

Cruikshank, George (1792–1872) British caricaturist, painter, and illustrator. He achieved early success with his satirical political cartoons. He illustrated such books as Dickens' *Oliver Twist* and Ainsworth's *Tower of London*. His etchings of *The Bottle* and painting of *The Worship of Bacchus* are moralizing sermons on alcoholism.

cruiser A fast heavily armed warship, smaller than a *battleship but larger than a *destroyer and designed for a larger cruising radius. Cruisers with increased firepower, nuclear power that extends their range almost without limit, and greater versatility are replacing the battleships in the world's major navies.

Crusades The military expeditions organized in western Christendom primarily to recover the Holy Places of Palestine from Muslim occupation. The first Crusade (1095–99) was launched under the aegis of the papacy. Jerusalem was captured and the Crusader states of the Kingdom of Jerusalem, the County of Edessa, Antioch, and Tripoli were created. The fall (1144) of Edessa inspired the unsuccessful second Crusade (1147–48) and the capture of Jerusalem by *Saladin in 1187 led to the inconclusive third Crusade (1189–92), led by *Philip II Augustus of France, Emperor *Frederick I Barbarossa, and *Richard (I) the Lionheart of England. The fourth Crusade (1202–04) was diverted from its initial objective, Egypt, and sacked Constantinople (1204). The four Crusades of the 13th century failed to recover lost ground and Acre, the last foothold of the West in Palestine, was lost in 1291. The Crusades failed in their stated objective, but Europe benefited greatly from the resultant growth of East–West trade and the introduction of eastern concepts into medieval culture. *See also* Children's Crusade.

crustacean An *arthropod of the class *Crustacea* (over 35,000 species), which includes the *barnacles, *woodlouse, *shrimps, *lobsters, *crabs, etc. The head bears two pairs of antennae and three pairs of jaws; the head and thorax together are usually covered by a chitinous carapace. There are numerous pairs of forked appendages, which are modified for different functions. Crustaceans are predominantly aquatic, breathing by means of gills. A few, such as the *fish louse, are parasitic on fish, whales, and other aquatic animals. During reproduction the male transfers sperm to the female, which often carries the fertilized eggs until they hatch. The larvae are mainly free-swimming and pass through several stages (*see* metamorphosis) to reach the adult form.

Crux (Latin: cross) A small conspicuous constellation, also called the Southern Cross, in the S sky, lying in the Milky Way. The four brightest stars form a cross, the longer arm of which points approximately toward the S celestial pole.

Cruz, Sor Juana Inéz de la (1651–95) Mexican poet. An infant prodigy, she lived at the Spanish viceroy's court before entering a convent in 1669. She died while nursing nuns during an epidemic. In addition to her metaphysical religious poems she wrote a defense of intellectual freedom and of women's rights to education.

cryogenics The production, effects, and uses of very low temperatures, usually meaning from –150°C down to *absolute zero. The most common method of producing cryogenic temperatures is to use *adiabatic processes. In adiabatic demagnetization, a magnetized paramagnetic substance is thermally isolated and demagnetized, thus cooling it. In adiabatic expansion, a thermally isolated gas is expanded. Cryogenic effects include changes in electrical properties, such as *superconductivity, and changes in mechanical properties, such as superfluidity (*see* superfluid). Cryogenics has been applied to new methods of food preservation, life-support systems in space, and the use of liquid propellants.

cryolite   A rare mineral of composition Na_3AlF_6. It is colorless or white and occurs in pegmatite veins. It is only mined in significant quantities in Greenland, although it is known to occur elsewhere. It is used in aluminum refining. Synthetic cryolite is manufactured from hydrofluoric acid, sodium carbonate, and aluminum.

cryptogam   Any plant that does not produce flowers or seeds but reproduces by means of spores. The nonvascular cryptogams include the mosses and liverworts (bryophytes), lichens, fungi, and algae; the vascular crypto-

gams are the ferns, horsetails, and related plants (pteridophytes). *Compare* phanerogam.

Cryptomeria.   *See* Japanese cedar.

Cryptozoic time   Geological time prior to the *Phanerozoic, i.e. the Precambrian, ending about 590 million years ago. It is the eon of "hidden life"; fossils are rare and obscure.

Crystal Palace   A building designed by Joseph Paxton to house the *Great Exhibition of 1851. The Crystal Palace, which had an area of 772,289 sq ft (69,892 sq m), was built in Hyde Park, London, with the highly advanced use of prefabricated glass and iron. It was later dismantled and reassembled at Sydenham (a suburb in London) but burned down in 1936.

system	edges	angles	minimum symmetry
cubic	$a = b = c$	$\alpha = \beta = \gamma = 90°$	four 3-fold axes (along body diagonals of cube)
tetragonal	$a = b \neq c$	$\alpha = \beta = \gamma = 90°$	one 4-fold axis (along c)
orthorhombic	$a \neq b \neq c$	$\alpha = \beta = \gamma = 90°$	three 2-fold axes (along a, b, and c)
hexagonal	$a = b \neq c$	$\alpha = \beta = 90°$; $\gamma = 120°$	one 6-fold axis (along c)
trigonal	$a = b \neq c$	$\alpha = \beta = \gamma = 90°$	one 3-fold axis (along c)
monoclinic	$a \neq b \neq c$	$\alpha = \gamma \neq \beta = 90°$	one 2-fold axis
triclinic	$a \neq b \neq c$	$\alpha \neq \beta \neq \gamma$	none

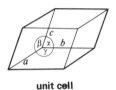
unit cell

CRYSTALS   *The classification of crystals.*

crystals   Solids that have a regular geometrical shape because the constituent atoms, ions, or molecules are arranged in an ordered repeating pattern, known as a crystal lattice. Salt grains, for example, are cubic crystals of sodium chloride with sodium and chlorine ions alternating at the corners of a cubic lattice. There are seven crystal systems, into which all crystals are classified. Crystal structures are studied by a variety of techniques, including *X-ray diffraction and electron microscopy. Specialized mathematical notation and stereographic projections are used to describe lattice structure and symmetry. Many crystalline solids are polycrystalline, i.e. they consist of many small crystals. The physical properties of crystals have found many uses, ranging from *piezoelectric transducers to gemstones. **Crystallography** is concerned with the study of the structure and properties of crystals. Noncrystalline solids, such as glass, are said to be amorphous.

Csokonai Vitéz, Mihaly   (1773–1805) Hungarian poet. His autobiographical play *Tempeföi* (1793) records the struggles and failures of his life as a poet. His work includes a cycle of love poems addressed to "Lilla," a volume of odes, and the highly popular comic epic *Dorottya* (1804).

ctenophore   A marine invertebrate animal, also called comb jelly, sea gooseberry, and sea walnut, belonging to the phylum *Ctenophora* (about 80 species). Its transparent gelatinous body is usually rounded and bears eight rows of ciliated comblike plates, used for locomotion. Ctenophores are mainly free-swimming and often occur in swarms in coastal waters, feeding on other planktonic animals captured by long branched tentacles. Ctenophores were formerly classified as a subphylum of *coelenterates.

Ctesiphon   The capital of *Parthian and *Sasanian kings near Baghdad (Iraq). Taken temporarily by the Roman emperors *Trajan (115 AD) and Carus (283), it fell to the Arabs in 637. The remains of the palace of Khosrow I (reigned 531–79) incorporate the largest known brickwork vault, spanning over 82 ft (25 m).

Cuba, Republic of   A country in the Caribbean Sea, off the S coast of Florida. It consists of two main islands, Cuba (the largest in the Caribbean) and the Isla de Pinos, together with over 1500 small islands and keys. On the island of Cuba fertile plains rise to mountains in the center and SE and there are some lower hills in the NW. The population is mainly of European origin, with large African and mixed minorities. *Economy*: state controlled, it is primarily agricultural and very much dependent upon its sugar crop (its main source of export revenue); production levels have been generally low and attempts to increase efficiency include the part mechanization of the cane-cutting process. Tobacco (especially for cigars) is anoth-

er important export crop and meat production is very important in the domestic economy. Fishing has expanded with government help and in 1977 fishing limits were extended to 200 mi (320 km). Important mineral resources include nickel (the second largest export). Largely dependent upon the Soviet Union for its oil supplies, Cuba has undertaken a program of oil exploration. The fastest growing industries include metallurgy, construction, and textiles. The Cuban economy is heavily subsidized by the Soviet Union but despite this aid it had suffered serious economic declines by the end of 1983. A dramatic drop in the world price of sugar, debts to Western lenders, and high unemployment and inflation forced severe cutbacks and placed the country in a precarious economic position. *History*: discovered by Columbus in 1492, it was a Spanish colony (except in 1762–63, when it was occupied by the British) until 1898, when Spain was forced to withdraw following war with the US. After three years of US occupation Cuba became a republic (1901) but the US, which had invested heavily in the country's economy, continued to intervene in Cuba's internal affairs and to control its foreign policy until 1934. In 1940 *Batista became president, taking Cuba into World War II on the Allied side. His corrupt dictatorship was threatened by Fidel Castro's unsuccessful revolt of July 26, 1953, and in Castro's second attempt (1959) with the aid of Che Guevara, Batista was overthrown. Relations between Castro's socialist government and the US were increasingly strained and Cuba moved closer in international relations to the Soviet Union. In 1961 an invasion by Cuban exiles with US support was defeated at the *Bay of Pigs and in 1962 the Soviet installation of nuclear missile bases in Cuba resulted in a US naval blockade. The Cuban missile crisis aroused worldwide fear of nuclear catastrophe but was resolved when the Soviet Union agreed to remove the bases. In the early 1970s US economic sanctions were lifted and rapprochement between the two countries seemed more possible. In 1976 a socialist constitution was approved by a referendum. As a result of serious unemployment in the late 1970s many Cubans emigrated to countries in E Europe and some sought asylum in South America. In 1980 a flotilla of boats carried Cuban refugees, many of them regarded as "undesirables" by both the US and Cuban governments, to Key West in Florida. In the early 1980s relations between Cuba and the US were further jeopardized by Cuban involvement in Africa (particularly Angola and Ethiopia) and in Central America (mainly Nicaragua and Granada). Increasing drug traffic from Cuba to the US and air piracy worsened US sentiments regarding Cuba. In 1984 Jesse Jackson, a candidate for the Democratic presidential nomination, made an unofficial visit to Cuba and succeeded in negotiating the release of many Cuban political prisoners and Americans held in Cuba primarily on drug charges. Cuba is a member of COMECON. Head of government and first secretary of the Cuban Communist Party: Fidel Castro Ruz. Official language: Spanish. Official currency: Cuban peso of 100 centavos. Area 46,736 sq mi (148,124 sq km). Population (1983): 9,852,000. Capital and main port: Havana.

cubism A style of painting and sculpture, originating in the works of *Picasso and *Braque in about 1907. It started as an intellectual investigation of how a solid form can be represented in two dimensions without resorting to illusionism. Volume was generally suggested by the fusion of multiple viewpoints of an object in one image, which was presented as a complex of geometrical shapes. The subject matter of early cubism was invariably everyday objects of simple form, such as vases, tables, books, pipes, fruit, and musical instruments, many being suggested by the work of a forerunner of cubism, *Cézanne. Figures, which are rare, often resemble primitive sculpture, the observation of which helped Picasso to break with tradition. After 1911 the development of cubism, in which Juan *Gris now also participated, led to the introduction of *collage and also to a more decorative approach, monochrome tones being replaced by rich colors. Cubism was the principal catalystic influence on the evolution of *abstract art.

cubit An ancient unit of length equal to between 18 and 22 inches (46–56 cm); it is based on the distance from the elbow to the tip of the middle finger.

Cuchulain (or Cú Chulainn) A legendary Irish hero, resembling *Achilles in his strength and courageous exploits. He was the son of the god Lug (see Lugus) but was brought up by his mortal uncle, Conchobar, King of Ulster. Cuchulain is the central subject in a series of ancient Gaelic epics and romances known as the Ulster cycle.

cuckoo A bird belonging to a family (Cuculidae; 127 species) occurring worldwide and ranging from 6–28 in (16–70 cm) in length. The European cuckoo (Cuculus canorus), gray with distinctive white barring and a long tail, belongs to a subfamily of parasitic cuckoos (Cuculine; 47 species); these lay their eggs in the nests of other birds, which rear their young. Parasitic cuckoos' eggs resemble those of the host in order to deceive the host bird. On hatching, the young cuckoo removes the other nestlings from the nest, thus obtaining sufficient food from its adopted parents. Order: Cuculiformes (cuckoos and turacos).

cuckoopint A perennial herbaceous European plant, Arum maculatum, also called lords-and-ladies. 12–20 in (30–50 cm) tall, it has large arrow-shaped shiny green leaves and a cylindrical cluster of tiny flowers, which protrudes from a dull-purple funnel-shaped bract (spathe). The flowers give rise to poisonous red berries. Family: Araceae.

cuckoo-shrike A gregarious arboreal songbird of the family Campephagidae (70 species), occurring in tropical regions of the Old World. 5–12 in (13–32 cm) long, they have a mainly gray plumage, long pointed wings, and a notched bill and feed on insects and fruit.

cuckoo-spit insect. See froghopper.

cucumber An annual vine, Cucumis sativus, probably originally from Asia but widely cultivated since ancient times. The long green juicy fruits, up to 24 in (60 cm) long, are eaten raw, cooked, or pickled (see gherkin). In northern regions both glasshouse and outdoor (ridge) varieties are grown. Indoor cucumbers produce fruit without fertilization; if pollinated, the fruits taste bitter. Family: Cucurbitaceae (gourd family).

cucumber tree A slender North American tree, Magnolia acuminata, 53–98 ft (16–30 m) high. Hardiest of all magnolias, it is found in moist rich woodlands, often on mountain slopes. It has tulip-shaped greenish-white flowers and cucumber-like fruit—greenish at first, ripening to dull crimson. The light yellow satiny textured wood is used for furniture, flooring, etc. Family: Magnoliaceae.

Cúcuta (or San José de Cúcuta) 7 55N 72 31W A city in N Colombia, on the Pan-American Highway. It is an important commercial center (especially for coffee). Its university was founded in 1962. Population (1978 est): 358,240

Cudworth, Ralph (1617–88) English scholar, a leading member of the *Cambridge Platonists. His True Intellectual System of the Universe (1678) defends Christianity as the only genuine source of knowledge against the atheism and materialism of *Hobbes.

Cuenca 40 04N 2 07W A city in central Spain, in New Castile. It has a 13th-century cathedral. Industries include tanning, paper milling, and tourism. Population (1974): 104,470.

Cuenca 2 54S 79 00W A city in S central Ecuador. It is the commercial center for S Ecuador with a trade in agricultural products, hides, and marble. The university was founded in 1868. Population 1970: 79,140.

Cuernavaca 18 57N 99 15W A city and resort in S central Mexico. It is the site of Cortés' palace (now government offices), a Franciscan cathedral (1529), and a university (1939). Many writers, artists, and film stars have resided here. Its varied industries include flour milling, textiles, and sugar refining. Population (1978 est): 226,649.

Cuiabá 15 32S 56 05W A city in SW Brazil, the capital of Mato Grosso state on the Rio Cuiabá. It is a collecting center for cattle, rubber, and palm nuts. The Federal University of Mato Grosso was founded here in 1970. Population (1970 est): 99,000.

cuisine minceur A recently developed style of gourmet cookery in which the traditional generous use of butter, cream, and other rich ingredients is minimized. Cuisine minceur was elaborated by the French chef Michel Guérard in the 1970s at his restaurant at Eugénie-les-Bains in SW France. This entirely new approach to elegant cooking recommends using fresh herbs, concentrated stocks, and puréed vegetables to give flavor and texture to sauces and casseroles.

Culbertson, Ely (1891–1955) US bridge authority, born in Romania. He influenced the development of contract bridge. Imprisoned in the Caucasus in his youth for anarchist activity, he emigrated after the Russian Revolution. His life after 1938 was devoted to campaigning for world peace. He founded the magazine The Bridge World (1929) and wrote many books on bridge, as well as an autobiography, The Strange Lives of One Man (1940).

Culdees (Old Irish céle dé: associate of God) Irish and Scottish monks, originally living in solitude but from about the 8th to 12th centuries existing in small groups. They were probably the last surviving remnant of the Celtic Church and were gradually replaced by Roman monastic orders.

Culiacán 24 50N 107 23W A city in W Mexico. It is the commercial center for an irrigated agricultural area. Population (1978 est): 302,229.

Cullen, Countee (1903–46) US poet and writer. He wrote about black society in the Harlem section of New York City and was a leading figure in the Harlem Renaissance. By his senior year at New York University he had published a poetry volume, Color (1925), and had won national poetry contests. His poetry is collected in Copper Sun (1927), The Ballad of the Brown Girl (1927), The Black Christ (1929), and The Meda and Other Poems (1935). He also wrote a novel, One Way to Heaven (1932).

Cullinan diamond An exceptional diamond weighing 3106 metric carats (c. 621 g) when found in the Premier Mine, South Africa, in 1905. It was cut into 9 major and 96 small stones.

Culloden Moor A moor in N Scotland, in the Highland Region near Inverness. In 1746 it was the scene of the last land battle to be fought in Britain, in which the Young Pretender, Charles Edward Stuart, was defeated by the Duke of Cumberland, thus ending the *Jacobite cause in Britain.

Culpeper's Rebellion (1677–79) An American colonial uprising, in which tobacco growers in North Carolina opposed British restrictions on their markets. John Culpeper seized the British deputy governor and governed capably himself until his voluntary surrender for trial in England, at which he was acquitted.

cultivator A farm implement used to till the soil, so destroying weeds and promoting crop growth. Horse-drawn models date from the 19th century but modern tractor-drawn machines consist of a steel frame with curved steel tines to penetrate and disrupt the soil.

Cultural Revolution, Great Proletarian (1966–68) A political rather than cultural movement launched in China by Mao Tse-tung in opposition to bureaucracy and to reinvigorate revolutionary attitudes. Many leading officials were dismissed, the formal educational system was abolished, and reforms to foster correct political views were introduced. Many universities were closed and young people, mobilized as *Red Guards, attacked Party officials and destroyed cultural objects.

culture In microbiology, a colony of micoorganisms grown in a solid or liquid medium for experimental or diagnostic purposes. A widely used medium is agar gel (contained in petri dishes) supplemented with required nutrients, which is inoculated with microorganisms and incubated. Sterile conditions are essential to avoid contamination.

Cumae The first Greek colony in Italy. Founded near Naples about 750 BC by settlers from Chalcis, Cumae expanded rapidly, spreading Greek civilization in S Italy. It repulsed Etruscan influence but was subsequently subject to Rome (from c. 340 BC).

Cumaná 10 29N 64 12W A city in N Venezuela. Exports, through its port of Puerto Sucre on the Caribbean Sea, include sugar, cocoa, and tobacco. Its university was founded in 1958. Population (1976 est): 148,000.

Cumans A nomadic Turkish people, who dominated the W steppes for two centuries until they were driven into Hungary by the Mongol invasions (1237–39). They were absorbed into the Hungarian kingdom in which they had considerable influence.

Cumberland, Richard (1631–1718) English moral philosopher. One of the *Cambridge Platonists, he was renowned for scholarship and virtue. His *De legibus naturae disquisitio philosophica* (1672) opposed *Hobbes' egoism in its principle of universal benevolence and anticipated *utilitarianism.

Cumberland Gap National Historical Park 36 36N 83 40W A national park in the Cumberland Mountains that encompasses an area in SW Virginia, SE Kentucky, and NE Tennessee. A natural pass through the mountains, the Cumberland Gap was part of the 18th century Wilderness Trail, and later played a strategic role during the Civil War. The park includes a paved road through the gap and a tunnel beneath the mountains. Area: 20,177 acres (8166 hectares).

Cumberland River A river that flows from SE Kentucky in the Cumberland Mountains E and S to Nashville, Tenn., and then NW to the Ohio River in southwest Kentucky. Shipping is important along the river as are the Tennessee Valley Authority hydroelectric and flood control projects. Length: 687 mi (1106 m).

cumin An annual herb, *Cuminum cyminum*, up to 12 in (30 cm) high with umbrella-like clusters of small whitish flowers and oblong bristly fruits. Native to the Mediterranean, it has long been cultivated in Europe, India, and China for its fruits, which resemble caraway seeds but are more bitter and are used in curry powders, to flavor liqueurs, etc. Cumin was formerly used medicinally as a stimulant and liniment and in veterinary medicine. Family: *Umbelliferae*.

cummings, e(dward) e(stlin) (1894–1962) US poet. His highly experimental lyric verse is characterized by typographical innovations and eccentric punctuation, which he employed to reinforce the verbal element of his poetry. His works include *Tulips and Chimneys* (1923), *Eimi* (1933), *No Thanks* (1935), and *1 x 1* (1944). He also wrote an experimental novel, *The Enormous Room* (1922), a poetic drama, *Him* (1927), and a ballet, *Tom* (1935).

cumulus cloud (Cu) A low type of *cloud of convective origin having a heaped appearance and developing vertically from a flat base. Fair-weather cumulus clouds are shallow but others are deep and may develop into **cumulonimbus cloud**. This cloud is heavy and dense, extending vertically to about 20,000 ft (6000 m), and is associated with thunderstorms. Its upper part often spreads out to form an anvil shape.

Cunaxa, Battle of (401 BC) The battle fought between *Cyrus the Younger and his elder brother Arsaces, who had seized the Persian throne as *Artaxerxes II in 404 BC. Cyrus gathered an army of Greek mercenaries (including the historian, Xenophon) and met Artaxerxes at Cunaxa, 42 mi (70 km) N of Babylon. Cyrus was defeated by Artaxerxes' superior cavalry forces and died in the battle.

CUNEIFORM *The wedge-shaped strokes of cuneiform writing developed gradually from pictographs.*

cuneiform The oldest *writing system of which records survive, used to represent a number of ancient Near Eastern languages. The name derives from the wedge-shaped marks (Latin *cuneus*, a wedge) made by the imprint of a stylus in soft clay. Originally pictographic, by the 3rd millennium BC cuneiform pictures had become stylized in the form of groups of wedge-shaped imprints, many representing the sounds of syllables. Once hardened the clay tablets were almost indestructible and many are extant today. Probably devised by the Sumerians not later than 3100 BC, cuneiform

spread to other language groups in the area. By 100 BC, however, it had largely been superseded by the North Semitic script that was used to represent the increasingly dominant Aramaic language.

Cunningham, Merce (1919–) US dancer and choreographer. He joined the Martha Graham Company in 1945 and founded his own company in 1952. He has frequently collaborated with the composer John *Cage. His works, which include experimental abstract ballets, include *Suite for Five* (1956), *Aeon* (1961), *Scramble* (1967), *Antic Meet* (1958), *Landrover* (1972), and *Travelogue* (1977).

Cunobelinus (or Cymbeline; died c. 42 AD) British ruler (c. 10–c. 42) of the Catuvellauni tribe. Their lands embraced much of SE England after they overcame the Trinovantes. He founded Colchester (c. 10).

cup fungus A fungus, belonging to the order *Pezizales*, that produces a cup- or saucer-shaped fruiting body. Cup fungi may or may not have a stalk and the spores are released from the upper surface of the cup. The distinctive scarlet elf cup (*Peziza coccinea*), found on dead branches, is a smooth-rimmed cup, 0.8–2.4 in (2–6 cm) in diameter, deep red inside and whitish gray or pink outside. Class: *Ascomycetes*.

Cupid The Roman god of love, identified with the Greek Eros, and lover of Psyche. He is usually portrayed as a winged boy shooting arrows of love.

cuprite A red to black mineral of composition Cu_2O, found where deposits of copper have been subject to weathering.

cupronickel A corrosion-resistant alloy of 75% copper and 25% nickel (by weight). It is often used in coins.

Curaçao A West Indian island, the largest in the Netherlands Antilles. Discovered in 1499, it was settled by the Spanish before being colonized by the Dutch in 1634. The refining of oil from Venezuela is of major importance; other industries include the production of Curaçao liqueur and calcium-phosphate mining. Area: 173 sq mi (444 sq km). Population (1979 est): 256,000. Chief town: Willemstad.

curare A resinous substance obtained from South American trees of the genera *Strychnos* and *Chondodendron*, used as an arrow poison by South American Indians. Curare blocks the action of *acetylcholine, which is released at the junctions of nerve endings and muscles and causes muscular contraction. Curare therefore causes a relaxed paralysis of muscle. Curare-like compounds (e.g. tubocurarine) are injected during general anesthesia to relax muscles and provide the surgeon with better access to the part of the body on which he is operating.

curassow A long-tailed tropical American gamebird belonging to the family *Cracidae*. Curassows have a long neck and long legs and may reach 40 in (100 cm) in length. The black males have a crest of curly feathers and a yellow bill ornament; females are smaller and brownish in color. They are mostly arboreal, feeding on buds, insects, and frogs. Chief genera: *Crax, Pauxi, Mitu*; order: *Galliformes* (pheasants, turkeys, etc.).

curia An ancient division of the Roman people. There were 30 *curiae*, each with a meeting place that was also known as a *curia*. The Senate house of Rome, attributed to Tullus Hostilius, was called the Curia Hostilia and its replacement, built by Julius Caesar, was known as the Curia Julia.

Curia, Roman. See Roman Curia.

Curia Regis The King's Court of early medieval Europe. It fulfilled all the functions of royal government—administrative, legislative, and judicial—and from its specialist departments developed the public government offices, such as, in England, the Chancery and the Exchequer, as well as the courts of law and parliament.

curie (Ci) A unit of radioactivity equal to the amount of an isotope that decays at the rate of 3.7×10^{10} disintegrations per second. Named for Marie *Curie.

Curie, Marie (1867–1934) Polish chemist, renowned for her research into *radioactivity. Born Marya Sklodowska, she emigrated to France in 1891, studied at the Sorbonne, and married (1895) **Pierre Curie** (1859–1906), a French physicist. Interested in *Becquerel's discovery of radioactivity, Marie Curie noticed in 1898 that one particular uranium ore emitted an anomalously large amount of radiation. Realizing that the radiation was caused by a new element, she and her husband spent four years isolating one gram of radium salt from eight tons of the ore. The Curies, together with Becquerel, were awarded the 1903 Nobel Prize for Physics and, for her discovery of radium and polonium, she won the 1911 Nobel Prize for Chemistry. Pierre Curie, before joining his wife's work, had discovered the *piezoelectric effect (1880) and shown that ferromagnetism reverts to paramagnetism (*see* magnetism) above a certain temperature, now known as the Curie point (1895). He was killed in a road accident; she died as a result of the radiation to which she had been exposed. Their daughter **Irène Joliot-Curie** (1896–1956) married the French physicist

Frédéric Joliot (1900–59) in 1926. Working together in the same field as her parents, they were the first to produce radioactivity artificially. For this work they were awarded the Nobel Prize for Chemistry in 1935.

MARIE CURIE *The discoverer of radium working with her husband, Pierre, in their laboratory in 1903, the year they were awarded a Nobel Prize.*

Curie's law The susceptibility of a paramagnetic substance is inversely proportional to its thermodynamic temperature. The **Curie point** (*or* Curie temperature) is the temperature above which a ferromagnetic substance becomes paramagnetic. Named for Pierre Curie.

Curitiba 25 24S 49 16W A city in SE Brazil, the capital of Paraná state. It has two cathedrals and is the site of the Federal University of Paraná (1894). Curitiba is a commercial and industrial center producing chiefly furniture, tobacco, and maté. Population (1980): 843,733.

curium (Cm) An artificial transuranic element discovered by Seaborg and others in 1944 and named for Marie and Pierre Curie. All 13 isotopes are radioactive and some intensely so; ^{242}Cm gives out about three watts of heat per gram. Curium is a silvery reactive metal. Its compounds include the oxides (CmO_2, Cm_2O_3) and halides (CmF_3, $CmCl_3$). At no 96; at wt (247); mp 1340 $\pm$ 40°C.

curlew A streaked brown or gray bird belonging to the genus *Numenius* (8 species). Curlews have a long neck and long curved bill. They breed in inland subarctic regions and migrate south in winter to marshes and mudflats, feeding on worms and crabs. The common Eurasian curlew (*N. arquata*) is almost 24 in (60 cm) long and ranges from Britain to central Asia. Family: *Scolopacidae* (snipe, sandpipers, etc.).

Curley, James Michael (1874–1958) US politician. A Democrat, he served in the US House of Representatives (1911–14) before becoming mayor of Boston in 1914. He served until 1918 and again from 1922 until 1926 and 1930 until 1934, at which time he was elected Massachusetts governor (1935–37). After that he again served in the House (1943–46) and as mayor of Boston (1946–50) for the fourth time. During this last term as mayor he was convicted of mail fraud and spent five months in jail.

curling A game played on ice with stones fitted with handles, played since at least the early 16th century and strongly associated with Scotland, but also played in the US and Canada. Two teams of four players take turns sliding two curling stones, each up to 39 yd (36 m), along the ice toward the "house," a series of concentric circles at the end of the rink. A team scores one point for each stone finishing nearer the center of the house than any of its opponents'. Team-mates are allowed to sweep the ice ahead of a moving stone to remove impediments and influence its course.

currant 1. One of several species of shrubs belonging to the genus *Ribes*. Some are cultivated for their fruit, for example *blackcurrant and *redcurrant, and others, such as the *flowering currant, are grown as ornamentals.

Family: *Grossulariaceae*. **2.** The dried berry of a small seedless *grape, grown in the Mediterranean region and used in cooking.

currawong An Australasian songbird of the genus *Strepera* (6 species). About 20 in (50 cm) long, currawongs are usually black, sometimes with white markings, and have a long hook-tipped bill. They feed on insects, small mammals, and birds and frequently destroy fruit crops. Family: *Cracticidae* (Australian magpies).

currents Flows of water masses moving in a particular direction. The major ocean currents form part of the general circulatory system in the oceans and are permanent, although they may vary with the seasons. They result mainly from the action of the prevailing winds on the sea surface; an example is the North Atlantic Drift. Currents are also induced by the tides, by differences in water density (densities vary with temperature, salinity, and turbidity levels), and by rivers discharging into the sea.

curricle A light two-wheeled carriage usually drawn by two horses harnessed abreast to a pole. Curricles were favored in the 18th and 19th centuries as rapid and stylish conveyances, equivalents to modern sports cars.

Currier & Ives US lithographic company. Founded by Nathaniel Currier (1813–88) in 1834 and joined by James Merritt Ives (1824–95) in 1857, the company published prints of current events and of aspects of everyday American life. Today the lithographs stand as a documentation of life during the second half of the 19th century.

curry A spicy stew of meat, chicken, vegetables, etc., originating in the Indian subcontinent. Long slow cooking over a gentle heat allows the meat to become tender and the different ingredients to intermingle. The essence of curry is the balanced mixture of aromatics: spices (especially yellow turmeric but also cumin, coriander, cardamoms, and ginger), herbs, and seasonings (peppers, chilies, and salt; or sweet seasonings made from sugar or honey; and acid seasonings made from citrus fruit juices). Curries are usually eaten with rice and chutneys. In the West premixed curry powder is often used.

Curtin, John Joseph (1885–1945) Australian statesman; Labor prime minister (1941–45). He implemented many social-welfare policies and developed the military defenses of Australia, introducing wide-ranging conscription measures during World War II. He died in office.

Curtiss, Glenn (Hammond) (1878–1930) US aviator and aeronautical engineer. Curtiss made the first 1-mile flight in the US (1908) and designed and constructed the earliest US seaplanes. He manufactured aircraft for the Allies in World War I.

Curzon, George Nathaniel, 1st Marquess (1859–1925) British politician. As viceroy of India (1898–1905) he made administrative changes but resigned following disagreements with *Kitchener. In World War I he was a member of the War Cabinet (1916–19). As foreign secretary (1919–24) he established a short-lived British protectorate over Persia.

Curzon line A line between Poland and the Soviet Union, which they recognized as the border between them in 1945 after World War II. The boundary, named for Lord *Curzon, had initially been suggested during the Russo-Polish War (1919–20).

cuscus A cat-sized *marsupial mammal belonging to the genus *Phalanger*, found in forests of NE Australia, New Guinea, and nearby islands. Cuscuses have a prehensile tail and climb slowly around trees at night, eating mainly leaves and fruit but sometimes catching lizards or roosting birds. Family: *Phalangeridae* (*see* phalanger).

Cushing, Harvey Williams (1869–1939) US surgeon, noted for his contributions to brain surgery, particularly of the pituitary gland, and his classification of brain tumors. He was the first to describe the hormonal disorder known as *Cushing's disease.

Cushing's disease A disorder resulting from excess *corticosteroid hormones in the body, named for— H. W. *Cushing. The symptoms include obesity, loss of minerals from the bones, and reddening of the face and neck; it may be associated with the symptoms of *diabetes mellitus and high blood pressure. It may be caused by a tumor of the pituitary gland or the adrenal gland or by prolonged therapy with high doses of corticosteroids: the treatment is determined by the cause.

Cushitic languages A subgroup of the *Hamito-Semitic languages. They are spoken in the Sudan, Somalia, Ethiopia, and Eritrea, and include Beja and *Somali. This group is the closest in sound to the common ancestor Proto-Hamito-Semitic.

custard apple A small tree of the genus *Annona* of the American tropics, so called because of the custard-like flavor of its fruits. The common custard apple (*A. reticulata*), 16–26 ft (5–8 m) high and widely grown in the West Indies, produces reddish many-seeded fruits, 3–5 in (8–12 cm) in diameter, with a sweetish pulp. *See also* soursop; sweetsop. Family: *Annonaceae*.

Custer, George A(rmstrong) (1839–76) US cavalry general. A graduate of West Point, he had a distinguished Civil War record, becoming the Union's youngest brigadier general. After the war he became a lieutenant colonel in the Seventh Cavalry during the Western campaigns against the Indians. Sent to round up Sioux and Cheyenne forces under Sitting Bull in South Dakota's Black Hills in 1876, an erroneous reconnaissance report led him to divide his force. He and his force of about 260 were massacred by the main Indian strength at the *Little Bighorn (Custer's Last Stand).

customs and excise duties Indirect taxes (*see* taxation) applied to goods and services. Customs (*or* tariffs) are duties payable on import of foreign goods. They may be either specific duties assessed according to the weight or quantity, or ad valorem duties assessed according to the foreign or domestic price of the imported goods. They raise revenue and restrict imports. An excise tax is a duty chargeable on specific goods produced or consumed within a country, e.g. gasoline, liquor, and tobacco.

customs unions Associations of countries that agree to abolish customs duties and tariffs for each other's products and to institute *free trade between themselves. They usually also agree to common external tariffs for nonmembers. The *European Economic Community is an example of a customs union.

Cuthbert, St (c. 635–87 AD) Celtic churchman and missionary. As a monk and later a prior at Melrose, Ireland, he evangelized, earning a reputation as a miracle worker. With his abbot, St Eata, he moved to Lindisfarne, a coastal island, in 664 and became its bishop in 685. He died on the island of Farne, where he had earlier lived as a hermit. His body was reburied in Durham Cathedral in the 10th century. Feast day: March 20.

cutter 1. A sailing vessel, similar to a *sloop, but with the mast stepped about halfway between the bows and the stern. 2. A fast armed powerboat used by the US Coast Guard for patrolling coastal waters in the enforcement of customs regulations, to rescue vessels in distress, etc.

cuttlefish A *cephalopod mollusk belonging to the family *Sepiidae* (about 100 species), of temperate coastal waters. 1–35 in (2.5–90 cm) long, the body is supported by an internal calcareous leaf-shaped shell—the cuttlebone—which gives buoyancy. When alarmed, the animal emits an inky fluid.

cutworm The larva of a *noctuid moth belonging to the widely distributed genus *Agrotis*. Cutworms destroy crops, such as cabbage, corn, and pasture grasses, by biting through the stems, often at ground level.

Cuvier, Georges, Baron (1769–1832) French zoologist and father of the sciences of comparative anatomy and paleontology. His studies at the Museum of Natural History in Paris showed him how the different parts of an animal skeleton were related to each other and to their functions. By extending this to fossils he was able to reconstruct entire skeletons from the incomplete ones in existence. His classification system, described in *Le Règne animal* (1817), grouped animals (including extinct fossil species) into four phyla. This was an advance on the system of Linneus although it was later superseded.

Cuyp, Aelbert Jacobsz (1620–91) Dutch landscape painter. He was born in Dordrecht, the son and pupil of **Jacob Gerritsz Cuyp** (1594–1651), a portrait and landscape painter. Aelbert's paintings of cattle, river scenes, etc., are distinguished by their glow of golden light, a fine example being *Herdsmen with Cows by a River* (National Gallery, London).

Cuzco 13 32S 71 57W A city in S Peru, in the Andes 11,207 ft (3416 m) above sea level. It was the capital of the Inca Empire prior to the Spanish conquest in 1533; Inca ruins include the Temple of the Sun. It is now a commercial center serving an agricultural region. It has a university (1962). Population (1972): 121,464.

cyanide process The extraction of gold from its ores by chemical treatment with potassium cyanide. The ore is crushed to a fine powder and mixed with a weak solution of cyanide in water. Once the gold is dissolved by the cyanide the resulting compound is precipitated from the solution and the metallic gold separated out by chemically displacing it from the compound with zinc.

cyanocobalamin. *See* vitamin B complex.

cyanogen (C_2N_2) A colorless highly poisonous flammable gas with a smell of bitter almonds. It can be prepared by heating mercury cyanide and has been used as a fumigant, war gas, and rocket fuel.

Cybele An Asiatic earth goddess identified by the Greeks with *Rhea. The center of her worship was Phrygia, whence her cult spread to Athens and later to Rome. She represented the powers of nature and was a protectress of wild animals. Her priests were eunuchs known as Corybantes.

cybernetics The study of communication and control between men, machines, and organizations. The name was derived from the Greek word meaning "steersman" by Norbert *Wiener, who was largely responsible for pioneering the subject. It is an aspect of *bionics, in which the human ability to adapt to changing circumstances and to make decisions is simulated in the design of computer-controlled systems. Ultimately, the application of cybernetics may extend the process of *automation to the point at which almost every operation in a factory is automatic, with very little human supervision.

Cybernetics has also been used as a link between the physical and life sciences, for instance in using *information theory to explain how messages are transmitted in nervous systems and in genetic processes.

cycad A *gymnosperm plant belonging to the order *Cycadales* (about 100 species), native to warm and tropical regions. They resemble small palms or tree ferns, having short stout stems with a crown of frondlike leaves. Reproductive organs are in the form of separate male and female cones borne on different trees, the female cones often being very large (up to 99 lb [45 kg]). The stems of some species yield a type of *sago.

Cyclades (Modern Greek name: Kikládhes) A group of some 220 Greek islands in the S Aegean Sea, including Ándros, Delos, Íos, Míkonos, Melos, Náxos (the largest), Páros, and Syros. Total area: 995 sq mi (2578 sq km). Population (1971): 86,084. Capital: Hermopolis (on Syros).

cyclamate A salt of cyclamic acid ($C_6H_{11}NHSO_3H$). Sodium and calcium cyclamates were formerly extensively used as artificial sweeteners in soft drinks and for diabetics, but their excessive consumption has been shown to have dangerous side effects and their use has been discontinued.

Cyclamen A genus of perennial plants (15 species) native from the European Mediterranean to Iran and widely cultivated as pot and garden plants. The pot varieties are grown from *C. persicum*. The garden cyclamens include attractive dwarf varieties, 2–3 in (5–8 cm) high. All cyclamens produce corms but most can be grown from seed. They have marbled heart-shaped leaves and drooping flowers with red, pink, or white reflexed petals. Family: *Primulaceae*.

cycloid The curve traced out by a point on the circumference of a circle as it rolls along a flat surface.

cyclone An area of relatively low atmospheric pressure with a series of closed isobars around its center. In the N hemisphere wind circulates in an anticlockwise direction around its center, in the S hemisphere it is clockwise. Except in the tropics, cyclones are now usually referred to as *depressions or lows. Tropical cyclones form over the tropical oceans and are accompanied by strong winds; they include *hurricanes and *typhoons.

Cyclops (Greek mythology) Storm gods who made thunderbolts for Zeus. Homer describes them in the *Odyssey* as one-eyed man-eating giants who lived on an island later identified with Sicily. *See also* Polyphemus.

Cyclops (zoology) A genus (44 species) of very small freshwater crustaceans of the subclass *Copepoda*, so named because of their single median eye. In Africa and Asia they transmit the parasitic Guinea worm larvae to man if accidentally swallowed.

cyclostome An eel-like jawless aquatic vertebrate of the class *Cyclostomata*, which includes the *lamprey and *hagfish. Cyclostomes have a long smooth cylindrical body with fins arranged not in pairs but singly (*compare* fish), a cartilaginous skeleton, and a sucking mouth with numerous horny teeth. They occur mainly in temperate fresh waters and salt waters and many are parasitic on fish. Subphylum: *Agnatha*.

cyclotherms Series of beds of sedimentary rocks deposited in a single cycle (in cyclic sedimentation) or repeated group (in rhythmic sedimentation). Carboniferous strata, particularly the Coal Measures, show such sequences, representing the changes in conditions from terrestrial to marine that repeatedly occurred in the period.

cyclotron A type of particle *accelerator in which charged particles are accelerated in an outward spiral path inside two hollow D-shaped conductors (called dees) placed back to back. A magnetic field at right angles to the plane of the dees causes the particles to move in a spiral and, at the same time, they are accelerated by an alternating electric field applied across the gap between the two dees. When the particles reach the edge of the device they are deflected onto the target. The maximum energy of the particles is about 25 MeV. *See also* synchrocyclotron.

Cygnus (Latin: swan) A large conspicuous constellation in the N sky, lying in the Milky Way. The brightest star, *Deneb, and four other bright stars form the **Northern Cross**. The constellation contains many interesting *variable stars, *binary stars, and dark and emission *nebulae—including the old supernova remnant, the **Cygnus Loop**. **Cygnus A** is an intense double radio source while **Cygnus X-1**, thought to be a *black hole, is one of several strong X-ray sources.

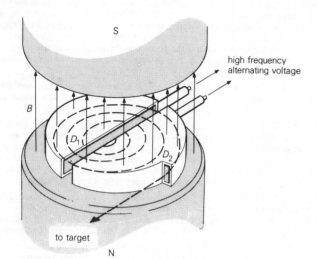

CYCLOTRON   *The charged particles are accelerated in the two D-shaped conductors (D₁ and D₂), which are supported in the magnetic field B.*

cymbals   Circular metal percussion instruments of indefinite pitch. Orchestral cymbals are clashed together, struck with a drumstick, or suspended and rolled with felt-covered timpani sticks. **Choke cymbals** (*or* hi-hat) are a pair of cymbals on a stick, operated by a foot pedal; they are used in dance bands and pop groups. Small tuned cymbals are known as **ancient cymbals**. ☐musical instruments.

Cymbeline.   *See* Cunobelinus.

Cymbidium   A genus of tropical and subtropical *orchids (40–70 species), native to Asia and Australia. Most species have pseudobulbs, straplike leathery leaves, and long-lasting sprays of 6–20 flowers on each flower stalk. Ornamental and very adaptable, cymbidiums are among the most popular orchids in cultivation today. They are popular as ornamentals.

Cynewulf   (early 9th century AD) One of the earliest Anglo-Saxon religious poets (*compare* Caedmon). His work shows him to have been a native of Mercia or Northumbria and from a learned background. Four surviving religious poems, preserved in 10th-century manuscripts, carry his runic signature. They are *Elene, The Fates of the Apostles, The Ascension,* and *Juliana.* All are based on Latin sources and are distinguished by their clear narrative form. Many other Old English poems have been attributed to him.

Cynics   The followers of the Greek moral philosopher *Diogenes of Sinope, who were active from the early 3rd century BC. They are notable less as a coherent school with systematic doctrines than as a succession of flamboyant individuals whose characteristic concern was to discount the pursuit of worldly wealth and success and to demonstrate that basic human needs can be very simply satisfied. They were outspoken critics of accepted social values and often lived notably unconventional lives. Positive freedom could be attained by self-realization, but often it was the negative destructive side of the Cynics' beliefs that was emphasized. Their distinction between natural and artificial values strongly influenced other ancient philosophies, such as *Epicureanism.

cypress   A conifer of the genus *Cupressus* (true cypresses; 20 species), native to S Europe, E Asia, and North America and widely planted for ornament and timber. Cypresses have tiny scalelike leaves, which densely cover the branches and twigs, and rounded cones, 0.4–1.6 in (1–4 cm) in diameter, usually ripening from green to brown. The Italian or funeral cypress (*C. sempervirens*), of the Mediterranean region, is 80–145 ft (25–45 m) high. Cultivated forms, usually narrow and columnar, are planted in gardens and cemeteries. Its strong fragrant long-lasting wood is used for chests, furniture, etc. Family: *Cupressaceae.*

Similar and related trees of the genus *Chamaecyparis* (6 species), of North America and SE Asia, are known as false cypresses. The most important species is Lawson's cypress (*C. lawsoniana*), of W North America, where it grows to a height of 198 ft (60 m). There are many cultivated varieties, up to 38 m high, widely planted for shelter and ornament. *See also* swamp cypress.

Cypress pine   A coniferous tree of the genus *Callitris* (about 16 species), native to Australia and New Caledonia. Their branches are densely covered with small scale leaves and the cones are small and globular. Several species yield a useful timber. Family: *Cupressaceae.*

Cyprian, St   (c. 200–58 AD) African churchman; Bishop of Carthage (from c. 248) and Father of the Church, martyred under the Emperor Valerian. In his treatise, *De unitate ecclesiae,* he argues that the bishop's authority provides the basis for the Church's unity. Feast day: Sept 16.

Cyprus, Republic of   (Greek name: Kypros; Turkish name: Kıbrıs)   An island state in the E Mediterranean Sea, off the S coast of Turkey. A central plain, the Messaoria, rises to the Kyrenia Range in the N, and in the SW the Troödos Massif rises over 6000 ft (1800 m). Most of the population is Greek or Turkish, the former being in the majority. *Economy*: mainly agricultural. Mineral resources include iron pyrites, asbestos, chromite, and copper ores. Though mining is on the decline, other (mainly light) industries are being rapidly developed. Tourism is important, although, like the rest of the economy, it has been badly affected by the unrest of recent years. There is now an intensive development program in the Turkish sector, largely based on agriculture and especially citrus fruit for export, with the aim of creating a self-sufficient economy. Exports include wine, citrus fruits, potatoes, and metals. *History*: there was already a Greek colony on Cyprus almost 4000 years ago. It was conquered by Egypt in the 6th century BC and later formed part of the Persian, Macedonian, Roman, Byzantine, and Arab empires. In 1193 it became a Frankish kingdom and in 1489 a Venetian dependency. In 1571 it was conquered by the Turks and this occupation lasted until 1878 when it came under British administration. It became a crown colony in 1925. In the 1930s Greek Cypriots began advocating Enosis (Union with Greece), and in 1955 a Greek Cypriot organization (*see* EOKA), led by Archbishop *Makarios and General Grivas, began guerrilla warfare against the British. Cyprus became a republic in 1960 and a member of the Commonwealth in 1961. The UK, however, retained sovereignty over several military bases. There were fierce clashes between the Greek and Turkish communities in the 1960s and in 1964 a UN peacekeeping force was sent to the island. Greek and Turkish talks in 1968 aimed unsuccessfully at better relations between the two sides. In 1971 General Grivas began a further terrorist campaign in favor of Enosis; he died in 1974. Following a Greek-supported military coup of the same year, in which Makarios was temporarily overthrown, Turkey invaded the island leading to its virtual partition. In 1975 the Turks set up their own government in the N as the Turkish Federated State of Cyprus, with Rauf Denktash as president. It has not, however, received international recognition. On the death of Makarios in 1977, Spyros Kyprianou was elected president. Cyprus remained divided, with the Turkish-occupied territory in the N constituting about 40% of the country. The rest of the island, occupied by Greek Cypriots, remained under the government of the Republic of Cyprus, internationally recognized as the official government. In 1984 Denktash, president of the Federated States, unilaterally declared the independence of Turkish Cyprus, plunging Cyprus into its worst political crisis since the Turkish invasion. Official languages: Greek and Turkish; English is also widely spoken. Official currency: Cyprus pound of 1000 mils. Area: 3572 sq mi (9251 sq km). Population (1983 est): 653,000. Capital: Nicosia. Main port: Limassol.

Cyrano de Bergerac, Savinien   (1619–55) French writer and dramatist. He became famous in his youth as a soldier and fighter of duels. He wrote a comedy, *Le Pédant joué* (1654), some tragedies on classical subjects, and two fantastic satirical romances describing visits to the moon and sun (published posthumously). He was noted for his comically long nose as well as his chivalrous nature; the conflict between his appearance and his noble character is captured in *Rostand's famous play, *Cyrano de Bergerac.*

Cyrenaica   A region of E Libya, bordering Egypt on the E, largely desert to the S and inhabited mainly by tribesmen of the Senussi, a puritanical Islamic sect. From early pre-Christian times Cyrenaica was colonized or conquered by Greeks, Egyptians, Romans, Vandals, Arabs, Turks, and Italians successively. The scene of many battles in World War II, it was occupied by the British from 1943 until united with Libya in 1951. It was a province of Libya until 1963.

Cyrenaics   A school of Greek philosophers, founded about 400 BC by *Socrates' disciple, Aristippus of Cyrene. The Cyrenaics identified virtue with pleasure and, adopting the *Sophists' view that truth and morality are matters for individual judgment, held that the only purpose of life was immediate gratification of the senses. Among them, Anniceris stressed the pleasures of friendship and family affection, whereas Hegesias, believing that pure pleasure was unattainable, advocated rather the avoidance of pain. Their ethical doctrines foreshadowed those of *Epicureanism.

Cyrene The chief city of ancient Cyrenaica (now in Libya). Founded by colonists from Thera about 630 BC, Cyrene quickly became prosperous, basing its wealth on trade. Its monopoly in silphium, an important Greek medicinal spice, brought the Cyreneans fame as doctors. It fell under the control of the Ptolemies of Egypt in the 4th century BC and was bequeathed by Ptolemy Apion to Rome in 96 BC. Excavations of its extensive remains have provided valuable information about ancient art, architecture, and society.

Cyril, St (c. 827–69 AD) Greek missionary, traditionally the inventor of the *Cyrillic alphabet. With his brother St Methodius (c. 825–84) he was sent to Moravia to evangelize the Slavs by the Patriarch of Constantinople in 863. Although highly successful, the brothers initially incurred much hostility from the German rulers and ecclesiastics for their use of the vernacular in the liturgy. After Cyril's death, Methodius translated the Bible into Slavonic. Feast day: July 7.

Cyrillic alphabet The alphabet used for Russian, Belorussian, Ukrainian, Bulgarian, Serbian, and various other languages of the Soviet Union. It was developed from a Greek alphabet of the 9th century AD in the course of Christian missionary work and is traditionally attributed to the Greek brothers St *Cyril and St Methodius. It originally consisted of 43 letters, but modern versions have reduced this number to about 30.

Cyril of Alexandria, St (c. 375–444 AD) Christian theologian; Patriarch of Alexandria (from 412) and Doctor of the Church. He became a champion of Christian orthodoxy, expelled the Jews from Alexandria, and opposed Nestorius (*see* Nestorians) on the question of Christ's divinity, eventually succeeding in having him banished as a heretic. He produced numerous works, including biblical commentaries and refutations of paganism. Feast day: Feb 9.

Cyrus (II) the Great (d. 529 BC) King of Persia (559–529), who founded the Achemenian Empire. He staged a successful revolt against his overlord Astyages (reigned c. 584–c. 550), gaining control of the empire of the Medes (*see* Media). He then conquered Lydia, Ionia, and Babylonia (539), thereby gaining Syria and Palestine, and territories in Central Asia. He was noted for his humane and tolerant policies toward conquered peoples and permitted the Jews to return to Jerusalem in 537. He was killed fighting in Central Asia: his tomb at *Pasargadae is still to be seen.

Cyrus the Younger (d. 401 BC) The son of Darius II (reigned 423–404) of Persia. Appointed commander of Persian forces in Asia Minor in 407, he helped the Spartan admiral *Lysander defeat Athens in the *Peloponnesian War. When in 404 Cyrus' brother succeeded their father as *Artaxerxes II, Cyrus led a Greek mercenary army, which included the historian *Xenophon, against him. He died leading a cavalry charge at *Cunaxa.

cyst 1. A close fluid-filled sac within the body. Cysts may be caused by blockage of the duct of a gland (e.g. a sebaceous cyst in the skin), dilation of an existing body space (e.g. in the ovary), or by parasitic infection. Some cysts are present from birth. 2. A structure formed during the life cycle of certain lower animals, such as parasitic protozoans and worms. The cysts usually protect the animals when they are most vulnerable.

cystic fibrosis A hereditary disease affecting the mucus-secreting and sweat glands. Symptoms, which appear in early childhood, are due to the production of thick mucus, which obstructs the pancreatic duct, intestinal glands, and bronchi. Patients suffer from malnutrition (because the production of digestive enzymes is blocked) and recurrent chest infections. The sweat contains large quantities of salt, which confirms the diagnosis. Treatment of cystic fibrosis, aimed at relieving its effects, includes antibiotics to combat infections, daily physiotherapy, a low-fat high-protein diet, and the administration of pancreatic enzymes.

cystitis Inflammation of the bladder, usually caused by a bacterial infection. Cystitis is most common in women: symptoms include frequent painful urination and occasionally blood in the urine. It is treated with antibiotics.

cytochromes A group of heme-containing pigments found in the mitochondria of plant and animal cells and involved in cell respiration. Cytochromes b, c_1, c, a, and a_3 form an electron transport chain that captures the energy (in the form of electrons) released by the *Krebs cycle and conserves it for used by the cell through the formation of *ATP molecules. The electrons are transferred ultimately to oxygen with the formation of water.

cytokinins A group of plant growth-stimulating compounds derived from purines. They act in conjunction with *auxins to promote cell division

and retard senescence. Synthetic cytokinins, such as kinetin, are used commercially in the storage of vegetables.

cytology The study of the structure and function of cells. It began with the development of techniques for the sectioning, fixation, and selective staining of materials for study under the light microscope, which enabled the *nucleus and other organelles to be observed. This led to the identification of chromosomes within the nucleus and of their role in heredity. More recent developments have included the use of phase-contrast and electron microscopy, and the biochemistry and physiology of cells has been studied using such techniques as cell separation and analysis, autoradiography, and tissue culture. Cytology has an important function in medicine. The study of diseased cells can reveal the nature of a disease and how it may be controlled, and cytological tests provide the basis for diagnosis of many diseases, including cancer. *See also* biological sciences.

cytoplasm. *See* cell (biology).

cytotoxic drugs Drugs used to kill cancer cells. These drugs, which include nitrogen mustard and vincristine, have led to major improvements in the treatment of some cancers (e.g. leukemia). They act by interfering with the multiplication of the malignant cells, but since they may also affect nonmalignant cells they often cause severe side effects, including damage to bone marrow.

Czech A West Slavonic language related to Slovak and Polish and spoken by nine million people in W Czechoslovakia. It is the official language of this area and is written in the Latin alphabet in a standardized form based on the dialect of Prague. Its development as a literary language dates from the 15th and 16th centuries.

CZECHOSLOVAKIA *The Cathedral of St Vitus (left) and Hradcany Castle (center) in Prague. The statue in the foreground is of the Czech painter Josef Manes (1820-71).*

Czechoslovakia, Socialist Republic of A landlocked country in central Europe. It is mainly wooded and mountainous, the central lowlands surrounding the Morava River rising to the Bohemian plateau in the W and the Slovakian highlands in the E. The population is about two thirds Czech and almost a third Slovak, with small minorities of Hungarians, Germans, Poles, and others. *Economy*: industry, already highly developed before the communist era, is now entirely nationalized and since 1961 the emphasis has shifted from heavy to light industry. An important engineering nation, Czechoslovakia produces a large number of motor vehicles; glass, beer, ceramics, footwear, and textiles are also major products. Mineral resources are sparse and Czechoslovakia is dependent upon the Soviet Union for many raw materials. Agriculture is organized mainly in collectives and state farms and the principal crops include sugar beet, wheat, potatoes, and barley. Forestry is important, with rich natural forests as well as much new afforestation. *History*: Czechoslovakia was created, under the leadership of Tomáš *Masaryk and Edvard *Beneš, in 1918 following the collapse of the Austrian Empire. It comprised the former Austrian possessions of *Bohemia, *Moravia, part of *Silesia, and (from 1920) *Ruthenia. The new state encountered threats from the diverse national minorities that peopled it and was unable to withstand the expansionist ambitions of Hitler's Germany. In 1938 he secured the *Munich Agreement to his annexation of the *Sudetenland and in 1939 took possession of the rest of Czechoslovakia. During World War II a provisional Czechoslovak government existed in London under Beneš' presidency. Following the war the Allies recognized its former territories, except for Ruthenia, which was ceded to the Soviet Union, and some three million Germans were expelled from Czechoslovakia. By 1948 the Communist Party was in power and Czechoslovakia was closely allied with the Soviet Union. In 1968 a liberalization program initiated by Dubček provoked a Soviet invasion and Dubček's overthrow. In 1977 Czech dissidents protested against the violation of human rights in Czechoslovakia in a manifesto entitled Charter 77. President: Dr Gustáv Husák. Official languages: Czech and Slovak. Official currency: koruna of 100 haléřů. Area: 49,365 sq mi (127,877 sq km). Population (1980 est): 15,420,000. Capital: Prague.

Czerny, Karl (1791–1857) Austrian pianist, composer, and teacher. A child prodigy, he had lessons with Beethoven and was influenced by Clementi and Hummel. He was a prolific composer but is best known for his piano studies. He was the teacher of Liszt.

Częstochowa 50 49N 19 07E A city in S Poland, on the Warta River. Formed from two separate communities in 1826, it has a monastery that was defended against the Swedes in the Thirty Years' War and to which Roman Catholics make pilgrimages. Its industries include iron and steel production. Population (1979 est): 233,000.

D

dab One of several *flatfish of the family *Pleuronectidae*, especially the genus *Limanda* found in N Atlantic and N Pacific waters. The European *L. limanda*, up to 12 in (30 cm) long, is light brown, sometimes with dark spots, and is an important food fish.

dabbling duck A *duck that feeds near the surface of water, rarely diving and frequently feeding on land. With relatively small feet and legs set well forward, dabbling ducks walk efficiently on land; they include the *mallard, *pintail, *shoveler, *teal, and *wigeon. Drakes are usually brightly colored and generally have a distinctive patch (speculum) on the wing. *Compare* diving duck.

dabchick A small *grebe, *Tachybaptus ruficollis*, common in quiet inland waters of Europe, S Asia, and Africa. It is 9 in (23 cm) long and has a dark-brown back, pale underparts, and a bright chestnut breast, neck, and cheeks. It feeds on small fish and aquatic invertebrates.

Dacca (Name from 1982: Dhaka) 23 42N 90 22E The capital of Bangladesh, situated in the SE of the country, on the Burhi Ganga River. It is a riverport and commercial and industrial center producing various textiles and jute. The university was founded in 1921. *History*: with a long history of human settlement, it became the capital of the Bengal province of the Mogul Empire in the 17th century. In the 18th century it came under British rule, and upon independence in 1947 was made capital of East Pakistan. Population (1974): 1,730,253.

dace A slender lively fish, also called dart or dare, belonging to the family *Cyprinidae*, which includes chub, roach, minnow, etc. The European dace (*Leuciscus leuciscus*) is up to 12 in (30 cm) long, silvery colored, and lives in fast-flowing streams and rivers, eating plant and animal material.

Dachau 48 15N 11 26E A city in SE West Germany, in Bavaria. It was the site of a notorious Nazi *concentration camp (1933–45). Population (1971 est): 33,200.

dachshund A breed of □dog originating in Germany, where they were developed to pursue badgers to earth. There are two size varieties—standard and miniature—and three coat types—long-haired, smooth-haired, and wire-haired. Dachshunds are usually brownish or black and tan. Height: 7–10 in (18–25 cm) (standard); miniatures are smaller, not exceeding 11 lb (5 kg) in weight.

dacoit An armed robber in a gang in India; the term is also applied to members of guerrilla groups in Burma.

dada A European art and literary movement, beginning in Zürich in 1916 and aimed at deflating the status of the art-object. Dada was originally the name of a Zürich literary periodical published by the poet Tristan Tzara (1896–1963) and *Arp. Since it had no coherent style, much of its ideology was more effectively transmitted in poetry periodicals, such as *L'Intransigeant* in France. Manufactured objects were favored both in graphic art and sculpture. Their violent effect is shown in the collages of Arp, *Ernst, and *Schwitters and the *ready-mades of *Duchamp, who exported dada to the US. For its most fanatical adherents dada was also a way of life, characterized by calculatedly absurd behavior. Although dada petered out in the early 1920s, *surrealism absorbed many of its characteristics.

daddy longlegs. *See* cranefly.

Dadra and Nagar Haveli A Union Territory of W India, on the Gujarat-Maharashtra border. Formerly a Portuguese colony (1789–1954), it is inhabited largely by tribesmen growing cereals and pulses. Area: 190 sq mi (491 sq km). Population (1971): 74,170. Capital: Silvassa.

Daedalus A legendary Greek craftsman and sculptor, said to have built the labyrinth for King *Minos of Crete. Minos imprisoned him but he created wings for himself and his son Icarus and flew away; Icarus was killed when the sun melted his wings but Daedalus reached Sicily safely.

daffodil A perennial European plant, *Narcissus pseudonarcissus*, widely grown as a garden bulb. It has narrow leaves and yellow flowers, each with a trumpet-shaped central crown surrounded by six segments. The bulbs are poisonous and were once used in medicine as an emetic and cathartic. Family: *Amaryllidaceae*.

Dafydd ap Gwilym (c. 1320–c. 1380) Welsh poet. Born into an aristocratic family in S Wales, he traveled widely and was acquainted with the work of the continental troubadours. He was trained in the bardic tradition

but introduced a personal humor and originality into the intricate and obscure conventional forms of his odes.

Dagestan Autonomous Soviet Socialist Republic An administrative division in the S Soviet Union, in the RSFSR on the Caspian Sea. The Caucasus Mountains lie in the S and much of central and N Dagestan is also mountainous. Over 30 different nationalities inhabit the republic, many of whom are Muslim. Its mineral resources remain largely unexploited, although sizable quantities of oil and natural gas have been extracted in coastal areas. There are large engineering, oil, chemical, and food industries and power stations are under construction. Agriculture is varied and crops include wheat and fruit; cattle breeding is also important. *History*: conquered by Arabs, Turks, Mongols, and Persians, Dagestan was annexed by Russia in 1813. It became an autonomous republic in 1921. In 1970, the area suffered a severe earthquake. Area: 19,416 sq mi (50,278 sq km). Population (1981 est): 1,700,000. Capital: Makhachkala.

Dagly, Gerhard (c. 1653–?1714) Belgian artist, a master in baroque lacquer work. At the courts of Electors Frederick William and Frederick III in Berlin (1687–1713) he became known for his cabinet cases, making *chinoiserie popular throughout Europe.

dagoba. *See* pagoda.

Daguerre, Louis-Jacques-Mandé (1789–1851) French inventor of the first practicable photographic process (the daguerreotype). Working initially with Joseph Niepce (1765–1833), who had produced the first permanent photographic image (the heliograph), Daguerre succeeded during the 1830s in producing a photograph by focusing light onto a copper plate that had been coated with a silver salt. Daguerreotypes were widely made in the mid-19th century.

Dahl, Roald (1916–) British author, whose work is pervaded by an ironic and frequently very black humor. Of Norwegian parentage, he served in the RAF during World War II. He has published many collections of short stories, including *Kiss Kiss* (1959) and *Switch Bitch* (1974), and several popular children's books, including *Charlie and the Chocolate Factory* (1976) and *James and the Giant Peach* (1961).

Dahlia A genus of herbaceous perennial tropical American plants (12 species), up to 7 ft (2 m) high, originally cultivated as a food crop for their tubers but now grown mainly for ornament. The brightly colored flowers, 2–20 in (5–50 cm) across, may be single or double and are of two main types. The varieties known as flat heads and pompoms are derived from *D. pinnata*; cactus-type flowers with pointed petals are varieties of *D. juarezii*. Family: *Compositae*.

Dahomey. *See* Benin, People's Republic of.

Daigo II (1287–1339) Emperor of Japan (1318–39), who attempted to restore the power of the throne at the expense of the *shoguns (military overlords). Despite superficial success in 1333, Daigo's plans provoked fierce feudal resistance and led to prolonged civil war and his own exile.

Dáil Éireann The representative assembly of the Republic of Ireland. It is the more important house in the National Parliament, the other house being the Seanad Éireann (the Senate). There are 144 members elected by proportional representation, at least once every 5 years. The president (the nominal head of state) summons and dissolves the Dáil on the advice of the prime minister.

Daimler, Gottlieb (Wilhelm) (1834–1900) German inventor, who contributed to the development of the internal-combustion engine. Daimler started to build his own engines in 1883, which were soon sufficiently light and efficient to power machines; in 1890 he founded a company to manufacture *automobiles. □motorcycles.

daimyo The feudal lords who rose to control one or more provinces of Japan between the 14th and 16th centuries. Their constant warfare was ended by the triumph of *Tokugawa Ieyasu in 1600 but over 250 *daimyo* remained in charge of their own domains until 1871. They were then given pensions and titles and their lands were incorporated into prefectures by a modernizing government.

Dairen. *See* Lüda.

dairy farming The maintenance and management of cattle, goats, and sheep for *milk production. Man has used the milk of his animals as a food for thousands of years and the modern dairy cow is an efficient converter of grass into milk. Herds of 50–200 are milked by machine in milking parlors and the milk passes by pipeline under hygienic conditions to await collection in refrigerated bulk tanks.

Advances in breeding and management of dairy cows have resulted in current annual yields of about 1050 gallons (4000 liters) per cow. *See also* dairy products.

dairy products Foods and other products derived from the processing of milk. Separation of milk by centrifugation yields skimmed milk and cream. Churning the cream disrupts the fat globules, removes water, and produces butter, containing over 80% fat, and buttermilk. Cream is retailed in various stages of concentration, for example light cream and heavy cream; other less concentrated forms include evaporated milk (containing about 65% water) and condensed milk (about 26% water).

Yogurt (*or* yoghurt) is produced by inoculating whole milk with bacteria, principally of the genera *Streptococcus* and *Lactobacillus*. The acid they produce during incubation at about 56°F (43°C) for four to five hours coagulates the milk, to which sweetening and flavoring may be added. Whey is a by-product of *cheese manufacture and, as with skimmed milk, may be dried to a powder form for use in the food industry or fed to farm animals in the fresh liquid state. *See also* dairy farming; milk.

daisy A herbaceous plant of the genus *Bellis* (15 species), native to Eurasia, with flower heads consisting of small central yellow disk florets surrounded by white or purple petal-like ray florets. The entire head is surround by bracts (small leaflike structures). The flower heads are solitary, arising on long stalks from a basal rosette of simple leaves. Many species are garden ornamentals, some with double-flowered varieties. The common wild Eurasian daisy is *B. perennis*, a perennial up to 24 in (60 cm) high, common in grasslands and lawns. Family: *Compositae. See* Plate VI.

Dakar 14 45N 17 08W The capital and main port of Senegal, on Cape Verde peninsula. It was the capital of French West Africa (1904–59). It has a cathedral and a university (1957). The country's main industrial center and one of Africa's most important cities, its industries include sugar refining and groundnut-oil production. Population (1979 est): 978,553.

Dakota. *See* North Dakota; South Dakota.

Dakota *See* Sioux.

Daladier, Édouard (1884–1970) French statesman; prime minister (1933, 1934, 1938–40). He signed the *Munich Agreement in 1938 and resigned in March, 1940, because of the unpopularity aroused by his failure to assist Finland against Russia (*see* Russo-Finnish War). Arrested by the Vichy government (1940) after the fall of France, he was imprisoned by the Germans from 1942 until the end of World War II.

Dalai Lama The title of the spiritual and political ruler of Tibet and head of the Gelukpa Buddhist school. The title, originating in the 14th century, signifies the incarnation of Avalokiteshvara, the *Bodhisattva of compassion. Chosen by oracles after the death of the previous incumbent, the Dalai Lama is regarded as infallible. The 14th Dalai Lama went into exile in India at the beginning of Chinese Communist rule in Tibet in 1959. *See also* Panchen Lama.

Dale, Sir Henry Hallett (1875–1968) British physiologist, who, in 1914, isolated the chemical *acetylcholine from the fungus ergot. His findings of the effects of acetylcholine on living organs corresponded with the discovery by Otto *Loewi, in 1921, that acetylcholine is a chemical transmitter released by the nervous system. Dale shared the 1936 Nobel Prize with Loewi.

d'Alembert, Jean le Rond (1717–83) French mathematician. The illegitimate son of an aristocrat, d'Alembert was raised by a glazier and his wife. His works include the study of vibrating strings, during which he derived the general solution to the wave equation, and a theorem in mechanics known as d'Alembert's principle, which is essentially a form of Newton's second law of motion. He also collaborated with *Diderot in editing the *Encyclopédie* (*see* Encyclopedists).

Daley, Richard J(oseph) (1902–76) US politician; mayor of Chicago (1955–76). A Democrat, he served in the Illinois legislature (1936–46) before becoming mayor of Chicago. As mayor he was known for his reorganization of the police department and urban renewal programs. Known for his complete control of the city's apparatus, during the 1968 Democratic convention held in Chicago he had the police break up anti-Vietnam War demonstrations with a violence that was widely criticized.

Dalhousie, James Ramsay, 1st Marquess of (1812–60) British colonial administrator; governor general of India (1847–56). Elected to Parliament in 1837, he became president of the Board of Trade in 1845 under Peel. The youngest ever governor general, he was criticized for his aggressive annexation of Indian territories. Following the second *Sikh War

(1848–49) he annexed the Punjab and after the second Burmese War (1852) he annexed Rangoon. His annexation of Oudh (1856) caused unrest that contributed to the outbreak of the *Indian Mutiny after his departure.

Dali, Salvador (1904–) Spanish surrealist painter. He joined the Paris surrealists (1929) and, inspired by Freudian theories of the unconscious, painted startling dream images with photographic realism during self-induced hallucinatory states. A similar disturbing imagery occurs in *Un Chien Andalou* (1929), a film he made with *Buñuel. While living in New York (1940–55), he turned to religious subjects and became a Roman Catholic. His taste for self-advertisement is evident in his autobiographical writings, such as *Diary of a Genius* (1966).

Dalian. *See* Lüda.

Dallapiccola, Luigi (1904–1975) Italian composer and pianist. His interest in composition was stimulated by his acquaintance with Alban Berg and he evolved a personal use of *serialism. His compositions include the opera *Ulisse* (1968), as well as many vocal and instrumental works.

Dallas 32 47N 96 48W A city in NE Texas, on the Trinity River. Founded in 1841, it developed as a cotton market during the late 19th century. The discovery of oil in E Texas during the 1930s accelerated the city's growth, which was further enhanced by the introduction of the aircraft and electronics industries during World War II. Today Dallas is the state's second largest city and the financial and commercial center of the SW. A notable cultural center, it is the site of several colleges. President John F. Kennedy was assassinated here on November 22, 1963. Population (1980): 904,078.

Dalmatia A coastal belt in W Yugoslavia, mainly in Croatia bordering on the Adriatic Sea. It is penetrated by a narrow corridor giving Bosnia and Hercegovina access to the sea. Predominantly mountainous with an indented coastline and many offshore islands, its picturesque scenery forms the basis of a thriving tourist industry. Wine production is especially important. The chief towns are Zadar, Split, and Dubrovnik. *History*: Dalmatia formed part of ancient Illyria. Ceded to Yugoslavia in 1920, it was occupied by Italy during World War II before being returned in 1947.

Dalmatian dog A breed named for the Adriatic coastal region of Dalmatia. Dalmatians are strongly built and were formerly used as carriage dogs. The short sleek coat has a pure white background with black or liver (brown) spots. Height: 23–24 in (58–61 cm) (dogs); 22–23 in (56–58 cm) (bitches). □dog.

dalton. *See* atomic mass unit.

Dalton, John (1766–1844) British chemist and originator of the modern *atomic theory of matter. Dalton's earliest researches into gases led to his discovery of *Dalton's law of partial pressures. He believed that gases consist of particles, extending his theory in 1803 to suggest that all matter is particulate, but he did not distinguish between atoms and molecules. His discovery of the law of multiple proportions in the same year strongly supported his atomic theory.

Dalton's law of partial pressures The total pressure exerted by a certain volume of a gaseous mixture is equal to the sum of the pressures (called partial pressures) exerted by each gas, if it alone occupied the same volume. Named for John *Dalton.

dam A barrier across a river. Dams are used for diverting the flow of water; raising the water level for navigation purposes; storing water for irrigation, industrial use, or water control; and providing a high-pressure source of water for *hydroelectric power. Gravity dams depend on the weight of their bulk to provide strength. Usually made of concrete and having a flat vertical face upstream, they are no longer used for the largest dams. Arch dams consist of curved concrete structures presenting their convex faces upstream, so that pressure is transmitted to the sides of the dams. They can thus be much less massive than gravity dams and are therefore cheaper to build. *See also* Aswan High Dam; Grand Coulee Dam; Grande Dixence Dam; Kariba, Lake; Paraná, Rio.

Dam, Carl Peter Henrik (1895–1976) Danish biochemist, who discovered vitamin K. He showed that certain symptoms in chicks, such as a tendency to bleed, were due to deficiency of a vitamin, which he named *Koagulations-Vitamin*, or vitamin K. Later, both he and Edward A. Doisy isolated vitamin K from green leaves. They shared a Nobel Prize (1943).

Daman A region in India, on the Gulf of Cambay. It comprised a district of Portuguese India from 1559 until 1961, after which it became part of the Union Territory of Goa, Daman, and Diu. Area: 176 sq mi (456 sq km). Population (1971): 38,739. Chief town: Daman.

Damanhur 31 03N 30 28E A city in N Egypt, on the Nile Delta. It has an important cotton trade with cotton-ginning and textile industries. Population (1976): 189,000.

Damaraland An area in N Namibia, named for the Damara people, who, however, now live mainly in the S. It is excellent cattle-grazing country.

Damascus (Arabic name: Esh Sham) 33 30N 36 19E The capital of Syria, in the SE of the country close to the Lebanese border. Under Ottoman rule from 1516 until 1918, Damascus was taken by the French (1920) and became capital of independent Syria in 1941. The Great Mosque and the Gate of God are the most notable buildings in the city. The university was founded in 1923. It is now the commercial center of the fertile plain to the E. Population (1977 est): 1,097,205.

damask Originally, a woven silk fabric, reversible and elaborately patterned, manufactured in Damascus. Linen damask was later manufactured in France, Flanders, and Ireland but cotton is now usually used. A firm glossy fabric with interwoven designs, damask is chiefly used as table linen.

damask rose An Asian rose, *Rosa damascena*, about 5 ft (1.5 m) high, with spicy-scented pink and white flowers. It is the main source of attar of roses—the rose oil used as the base of many perfumes. Extraction of rose oil is a major industry in Bulgaria and parts of W Asia.

D'Amboise, Jacques (Jacques Joseph Ahearn; 1934–) US ballet dancer and choreographer. He danced for the New York City Ballet from 1950 and played principal roles in such ballets as *Filling Station*, *Stars and Stripes*, and *Apollo*. He choreographed his own works for the company, including *The Chase* (1963) and *Irish Fantasy* (1964), and worked in movies and television. ABRCHB/28

Damien, Father (Joseph de Veuster; 1840–89) Belgian Roman Catholic missionary. He worked in the leper settlement on the Hawaiian Island of Molokai from 1873 until his death from leprosy.

Damietta (Arabic name: Dumyat) 31 26N 31 48E A port in Egypt, on the Nile River. Its industries include the manufacture of cotton and silk. Population (1975 est): 113,200.

dammar A resin used in making varnish, obtained from various trees of SE Asia, especially species of *Shorea* (family *Dipterocarpaceae*) and conifers of the genus *Agathis* (including the New Zealand *Kauri pine).

Damocles Legendary courtier of Dionysius I of Syracuse in the 4th century BC. Dionysius seated him at a banquet beneath a sword suspended by a single hair, thus illustrating the insecurity of human life, irrespective of wealth or power.

Damodar River A river in NE India. Rising in West Bengal, it flows mainly ESE through Bihar to join the Hooghly River SW of Calcutta. Its valley contains India's most important coalfield, an irrigation works, a hydroelectric project, and important heavy industry. Length: 370 mi (595 km).

Dampier, William (c. 1652–1715) English explorer. As a buccaneer he carried out several raids on Spanish possessions on the W coast of South America and West Africa in the 1680s, reaching Australia in 1686. In 1699 he was sent by the government to explore Australia and New Guinea, returning to England in 1701. The Dampier Archipelago, off the NW coast of Australia, was named for him. During his last voyage (1708–11) he rescued Alexander *Selkirk from the South Seas.

damping-off A disease, usually affecting seedlings, in which the stem base becomes softened and the plant falls over. Fungi of the genus *Pythium* are usually responsible. Soil sterilization may be undertaken as a preventive measure.

damselfish A lively and aggressive deep-bodied fish, also called demoiselle, belonging to the family *Pomacentridae*. Up to 6 in (15 cm) long, damselfish are often brightly colored and live mainly among reefs in the tropical regions of the Atlantic, Indian, and Pacific Oceans. They feed on plant and animal material. Order: *Perciformes*.

damselfly A slender delicate insect belonging to the suborder *Zygoptera*, closely related to the *dragonflies. It has similar habits but is smaller and has weaker powers of flight. The wings are held over the body at rest. □insect.

damson The plumlike stone fruit of *Prunus damascena*, a slender twisted tree found across the N hemisphere. It has small white flowers that develop into purple fruits. Damsons may be eaten cooked, used in jam, or pressed into a cake called damson cheese. Family: *Rosaceae. See also* plum.

Dan, tribe of One of the 12 *tribes of Israel. It claimed descent from Dan, the son of Jacob by his concubine Bilhah. Its territory lay N of the Sea of Galilee and its city of Dan was situated at the northernmost point of

the Hebrew settlement. Some of its people occupied an area NW of Judah, which was gradually absorbed by Judah.

Dana, Richard Henry, Jr. (1815–82) US lawyer and writer. Due to illness he left Harvard University in 1834 and went to sea for two years. After returning and graduating from Harvard in 1837, he wrote *Two Years Before the Mast* (1840), a widely acclaimed novel about life at sea. He practiced law and became active in the movement against slavery, and many of his law cases involved fugitive slaves. He was a founder of the Free-Soil Party (1848).

Danae In Greek legend, the daughter of Acrisius, King of Argos. He imprisoned her because an oracle said he would be killed by her child; Zeus visited her, however, and she gave birth to *Perseus. Acrisius cast mother and son out to sea but Polydectes, King of Seriphos, rescued them.

Da Nang (former name: Tourane) 16 04N 108 14E A port in S central Vietnam, on the South China Sea. It was the site of a major US airbase during the Vietnam War. Textiles are the chief industry. Population (1973 est): 492,194.

dance A social activity or theatrical art in which the body moves rhythmically, usually to music. In ancient times it was primarily used in religious rituals; such dances still exist today among some primitive tribes. During the middle ages the Roman Catholic Church often condemned dancing, particularly when it appeared to be a manifestation of mass hysteria. Dancing as a social activity and as an entertainment largely originated in the European courts. These dances usually developed from peasant dances and among the most popular were the galliard, basse danse, *allemande, and volta. The English country dances, so popular at Elizabeth I's court, eventually spread to the continent and, in the early 18th century and, together with the minuet, dominated ballrooms until the introduction of the *waltz. From the late 19th century the US led the way in social dancing with the *cakewalk, *foxtrot, and *tango; it also introduced the tap dance and contributed to the development of *modern dance. Many 20th-century dances were influenced by jazz, notably the *Charleston (1920s) and the jitterbug (1940s); others, such as the rumba, samba, and conga, were of Latin-American origin. Popular dancing from the 1960s to the 1980s, commencing with the twist, has shown a trend toward freer movement, unregulated by a set sequence of steps and without bodily contact between the partners. *See also* ballet; folk dance; choreography.

dance of death In late medieval art, literature, and drama, an allegorical dance or procession in which the dead lead the living to the grave; also known as the *danse macabre*. It reflected man's preoccupation with death during an age of plague and warfare and was a popular subject for wall paintings in churches and monasteries in France, Germany, and England during the 14th and 15th centuries. The most famous pictorial version is the series of woodcuts designed by *Holbein the Younger between 1523 and 1526.

dandelion A weedy perennial herbaceous plant of the worldwide genus *Taraxacum*, with a basal rosette of jagged toothed leaves and a solitary flower head of bright-yellow florets, up to 2 in (6 cm) across, borne on a stalk up to 20 in (50 cm) high. The seeds have parachutes of fine white hairs and are dispersed by wind. The common dandelion (*T. officinale*) is found throughout the N hemisphere. Its young leaves may be eaten raw in salads or cooked. Family: *Compositae*. □fruit.

Dandie Dinmont terrier A dog breed named for a character in Sir Walter Scott's novel *Guy Mannering* (1812), who owned a pack of them. The Dandie Dinmont has a long body, short legs, and long drooping ears. Its long coat is a mixture of hard and soft hairs and can be either silvery gray to blue-black or fawn to reddish brown. Height: 8–11 in (20–28 cm).

Dandolo, Enrico (c. 1108–1205) Venetian statesman; *doge (1192–1205). He was regarded as the founder of Venice's colonial empire. Dandolo commanded the fleet at the capture of Constantinople during the fourth *Crusade (1204) and secured for Venice a substantial portion of the conquered Greek territories. Defeated near Adrianople in 1205, Dandolo, aged and blind, led the remnants of the Latin army safely back to Constantinople.

dandruff Dry scaling of the scalp, which occurs in everybody to some degree. It is presumed to be due to an infection and may sometimes become more serious, extending to the face. If it is excessive it can be treated with salicylic acid.

Danelaw The area of Anglo-Saxon England E of Watling Street from the Tees River to the Thames River within which Danish laws and customs prevailed from the late 9th to the late 11th centuries.

Daniel (6th century BC) An Old Testament prophet and Jewish exile in Babylon. **The Book of Daniel** is credited to him although some believe it to have been been written in the 2nd century BC. The first six chapters tell of various mainly supernatural episodes involving Daniel and his companions under Kings Nebuchadnezzar and Belshazzar. The remaining six chapters are mostly apocalyptic visions concerning the future of the Jews.

Daniell, John Frederic (1790–1845) British chemist, whose researches into electrochemistry led him to invent the *Daniell cell, the first long-lasting reliable source of electric current. He also invented the hygrometer.

Daniell cell A voltaic cell whose positive pole consists of copper immersed in a solution of copper sulfate and whose negative pole consists of zinc in a solution of sulfuric acid or zinc sulfate. It has an almost constant emf of 1.08 volts. Named for J. F. Daniell.

danio An omnivorous tropical freshwater fish of the genera *Danio* or *Brachydanio*. They have a narrow elongated body, 1.6–2.0 in (4–5 cm) long, often attractively colored, and live in shoals. Family: *Cyprinidae*; order: *Cypriniformes*. *See also* zebra fish.

Danish The official language of Denmark, spoken by about five million people. It belongs to the East Scandinavian branch of the North Germanic languages. Separation from the other Scandinavian languages, to which it is closely related, began in about 1000 AD. It is the most altered form of the common ancestral tongue, having lost the case system and incorporated many words from Low German.

D'Annunzio, Gabriele (1863–1938) Italian poet, novelist, and dramatist. During the 1890s he wrote several novels strongly influenced by *Nietzsche's philosophy, notably *The Triumph of Death* (1894). The erotic novel *The Flame of Life* (1900) described his stormy relationship with the actress Eleanora *Duse, who inspired some of his best poetry and for whom he wrote *The Daughter of Jorio* (1904) and other plays. A militant nationalist, he fought heroically in the air force in World War I and headed the Italian occupation of the Dalmatian port of Fiume in 1919. He joined the fascist party but spent his later years in peaceful retirement.

Dante Alighieri (1265–1321) Italian poet. Born into a noble Guelf family of Florence (*see* Guelfs and Ghibellines), he became actively involved in the political struggle between the Black Guelfs, supported by the Pope, and the White Guelfs, who favored a democratic commune. After the Black Guelfs gained control of Florence in 1301, he lived in exile in various Italian cities, finally settling in Ravenna about 1318. His major works include *La vita nuova* (c. 1292), an autobiographical work concerning his youthful love for the mysterious Beatrice (probably the Florentine aristocrat Beatrice Portinari, who was married and who died at the age of 24), and two influential treatises on the value of vernacular Italian as a literary language. *The Divine Comedy*, begun about 1307, is Dante's spiritual testament, narrating his journey, guided by *Virgil, through Hell and Purgatory and finally, guided by Beatrice, to Paradise.

Danton, Georges Jacques (1759–94) French revolutionary. A leader of the *Cordeliers in 1789 and 1790, he became minister of justice in the new republic in 1792. A member of the first Committee of *Public Safety, he was not included in the second and began to lose power as the *Reign of Terror developed. He and his followers were arrested in March, 1794, charged with a conspiracy to overthrow the government, and Danton was guillotined.

Danu In Celtic mythology, the mother of the gods. She was particularly associated with the *Tuatha Dé Danann, but she was also worshiped in other countries under different names.

Danube River The second longest river in Europe after the Volga River. Rising in the Black Forest in West Germany, it flows mainly ESE across central and SE Europe to enter the Black Sea in Romania. Immensely important commercially, it is linked by the Altmühl River with canals to the Main and Rhine rivers. Major cities along its course include Vienna, Budapest, and Belgrade. Length: 1770 mi (2850 km).

Danzig. *See* Gdańsk.

Daphne (botany) A genus of evergreen and deciduous shrubs (70 species) of the Old World, including many important ornamentals. The leaves, up to 5 in (12 cm) long, are arranged spirally up the stem. The small, often fragrant, flowers occur in clusters near the ends of branches. They have no petals; the calyx (fused sepals) has four spreading lobes. The fruit is a berry. The genus includes the deciduous mezereon (*D. mezereum*), with reddish-purple flowers and red berries, and the evergreen spurge laurel (*D. laureola*), with greenish flowers and black berries. These shrubs are native to Eurasia and grow to a height of 40 in (100 cm); their berries are poisonous. Family: *Thymeleaceae*.

Daphne (Greek mythology) A mountain nymph who rejected Apollo and, to escape him, was transformed by Gaea into a laurel tree. Apollo made the laurel a symbol of honor and victory.

Daphnia. *See* water flea.

Daphnis In Greek legend, a Sicilian shepherd who was punished with blindness for infidelity in love. He consoled himself with songs and was thus revered as the inventor of pastoral poetry and song.

Da Ponte, Lorenzo (1749–1838) Italian author, originally a priest. Banished from Italy in 1779, he settled in Vienna and there wrote the libretti for Mozart's operas *The Marriage of Figaro* (1786), *Don Giovanni* (1787), and *Cosi fan tutte* (1790). In 1805 he went to the US, where he vigorously promoted Italian culture and published four volumes of memoirs (1823–27).

Dardanelles (Turkish name: Çannakale Boğazi; ancient name: Hellespont) A strait separating European and Asian Turkey and connecting the Sea of Marmara with the Aegean Sea. It was the scene of an unsuccessful campaign in *World War I. Length: 37 mi (60 km); width: 1–4 mi (1.5–6.5 km).

Dards A number of peoples of N Pakistan and Kashmir of Aryan origin, who speak Indo-European languages. There are three major subgroups: the Western (*or* Kafir), the Central (*or* Khowar), and the Eastern, including Shina and Kashmiri. The Dards were converted to Islam during the 14th century.

Dar es Salaam 6 48S 39 12E The capital and main port of Tanzania, on the Indian Ocean. Founded in 1862, it was capital of German East Africa (1891–1916) and of Tanganyika (1916–64). The university was established in 1970. It is the terminus of the Tanzam (Tanzania–Zambia) railroad and an important commercial and industrial center. Population (1978): 870,020.

Darién Scheme (1698–99) An attempt by the Company of Scotland to establish a colony in the Darién region, in the E of the Isthmus of Panama. The Scots hoped to control trade between the Atlantic and Pacific Oceans but were forced by the Spanish to abandon their settlement, suffering considerable loss of life.

Darius I (c. 558–486 BC) King of Persia (521–486) of the *Achaemenid dynasty. He obtained the throne after defeating a usurper and on his accession he was forced to deal with revolts throughout the empire. He crushed a revolt of Ionian Greeks (499–94), which precipitated the *Greek-Persian Wars. His invasion of mainland Greece was halted by the Persian defeat at *Marathon (490). Darius was a noted administrator, dividing the empire into provinces known as satrapies. He also encouraged trade and improved communications and may have established *Zoroastrianism as the religion of Persia.

Darjeeling 27 02N 88 20E A city in India, in West Bengal. A popular tourist resort, it has splendid views of the Himalayas, including Mount Kangchenjunga. It is a major tea-growing center. Population (1971): 42,662.

darkling beetle A black or dark brown flightless beetle, also called nocturnal ground beetle, belonging to a widely distributed family (*Tenebrionidae*; 15,000 species), particularly common in warm regions. Darkling beetles vary from .08–1.4 in (2 to 35 mm) in length. Nearly all are scavengers, feeding on decaying vegetation, dung, fungi, or stored grains and cereals. Mealworms (larvae of *Tenebrio molitor*) are common pests of flour mills, etc., and are also reared commercially as food for birds and fish.

Darlan, Jean (Louis Xavier) François (1881–1942) French admiral. He became commander in chief of the navy in 1939 and served in the Vichy government as navy minister and then as vice premier (1941). He lost his post under Laval (1942) and was sent to command French forces in N Africa, where he brought French resistance to the Allies to an end. His assumption of the post of head of state in French Africa aroused considerable hostility. He was assassinated by a French antifascist.

Darling River A river in E Australia, rising in the Great Dividing Range and flowing generally SW across New South Wales before joining the Murray River at Wentworth. Length: 1702 mi (2740 km).

Darlington 54 31N 1 34W A city in NE England, in Durham. The Stockton–Darlington freight railroad (1825) was the world's first railroad. Darlington has engineering and construction industries. Population (1981): 85,396.

Darmstadt 49 52N 08 39E A city in central West Germany, in Hessen. It has a 16th-century palace, which survived the bombing in World War II, and a technical university (1836). Its manufactures include machinery and chemicals. Population (1980 est): 138,300.

darnel A *grass, *Lolium temulentum*, also known as poison grass, native to temperate Eurasia. It is often infected by a fungus of the genus *Claviceps* (see ergot) and is poisonous; it was formerly a serious contaminant of rye bread but modern techniques can separate darnel seeds from rye seeds.

CHARLES DARWIN *In 1860 the Oxford University debate on Darwin's evolutionary theories aroused much controversy and speculation about man's origins, typified by this contemporary cartoon from the English magazine Punch.*

Darnley, Henry Stuart, Lord (1545–67) The second husband of Mary, Queen of Scots, and father of James I of England. He married Mary, his cousin, in 1565 and his unpopularity was intensified by his involvement in the murder of her secretary David *Riccio (1566). Darnley himself was murdered, probably by *Bothwell.

Darrow, Clarence (1857–1938) US lawyer, famous for his defense of union leaders and of people charged with murder. His defense of Eugene Debs in the case arising from the Pullman strike (1894), although unsuccessful, established his reputation. Through his efforts the labor leader William Haywood (1896–1928) was acquitted (1906) from the charge of assassinating the governor of Idaho. He was counsel for the defense in the famous "monkey" trial in Tennessee (1925), in which a science teacher, John Scopes, was tried for teaching Darwin's theory of evolution. He was a passionate opponent of capital punishment.

darter A slender elongated bird belonging to a family (Anhingidae; 4 species) occurring in tropical and subtropical inland waters, also called snakebird because of its snakelike neck. Darters are about 34 in (88 cm) long and black or brown with white markings; males have plumes on the head and neck. They have thin pointed bills for catching fish underwater and are excellent fliers. Order: *Pelecaniformes* (gannets, pelicans, etc.).

Dartmoor A moorland area of England, in SW Devon. A national park since 1951, it consists of a rolling granite upland rising to tors, the highest of which is High Willhays at 2039 ft (621 m). Its many historic remains include stone circles and Bronze Age and Iron Age settlements. Used extensively as a military training area, its dramatic scenery, picturesque wooded valleys, and outdoor recreational facilities have also made it a major tourist attraction. Area: 365 sq mi (945 sq km).

Dartmouth 44 40N 63 35W A city and port in E Canada, in Nova Scotia on Halifax Harbor. It is an industrial and naval center. Population (1976): 65,341.

Dartmouth College v. Woodward (1819) US Supreme Court ruling that the state could not interfere with a corporate charter. Daniel *Webster argued for Dartmouth College trustees that the amending of the college charter by the New Hampshire legislature was unconstitutional because the original wishes of the donors who had given land to the college were altered.

darts An indoor target game, probably deriving from archery, in which players throw weighted metal darts at a round board from a set distance. A standard board is divided into 20 irregularly numbered sectors; outer and inner rings score double and treble respectively and there is a central bull's-eye. Various games are played, but the most common in competitions is 301, in which players score downward from 301 to 0, beginning and ending on a double.

Darwin 12 23S 130 44E A city in Australia, the capital and chief port of the Northern Territory. The harbor, Port Darwin, adjoins Clarence Strait. It was almost completely destroyed by a cyclone in 1974, but was rebuilt on the same site. It is the focus of a pastoral and mining region; exports include uranium ore. Population (1979 est): 50,612.

Darwin, Charles Robert (1809–1882) British naturalist, who originated the concept that living things evolve by means of natural selection. Following attempts to study medicine and theology, Darwin's interest in natural history led him to sail with HMS *Beagle* on an expedition to South America and the Pacific (1831–36). As ship's naturalist, Darwin made exhaustive observations of the geology and natural history of the region, recording these in a journal, which he later published.

Following the voyage, Darwin set about the task of analyzing his observations and forming them into a coherent view of nature. In 1858 he presented his findings to the Linnaean Society and in 1859 published his famous *Origin of Species by Means of Natural Selection* (see Darwinism). His views aroused bitter controversy because they conflicted with the account of the Creation in the Bible. This culminated in the debate at Oxford in 1860 between Darwin's supporters, led by T. H. *Huxley, and Bishop Samuel Wilberforce. Huxley's arguments won the day. In *The Descent of Man* (1871), Darwin applied his theories to mankind, and—slowly—this fundamental principle of biology gained widespread acceptance.

Darwinism The theory of *evolution based on the work of Charles *Darwin. Darwin drew his conclusions from the following observations: (1) in any population the organisms show individual variations; (2) the size of the population remains constant although more offspring are produced than are necessary to maintain it. He concluded that the forces acting on the population—competition, disease, climate, etc.—resulted in the survival of those best fitted to the environment, a process he called **natural selection**. The survivors would breed, thus passing on their inheritable advantageous variations to their offspring. With time—in a gradually changing environment—this process would result in a change in the whole population and ultimately the evolution of new *species.

Darwin's theory has now been reinforced and modified by subsequent discoveries in genetics, which—among other things—have revealed the source of the variation on which it is based (mostly genetic *mutations). The modern version of his theory is known as **neo-Darwinism**.

Darwin's finches A subfamily of *finches (Geospizinae; 13 species) restricted to the Galapagos Islands and also called Galapagos finches. They appear to have evolved from a single species and differ in such features as bill shape, feeding behavior, and habitat preference in order to avoid competition for available resources. The study of these finches by Charles *Darwin provided evidence for his theory of evolution.

dasyure A small carnivorous *marsupial mammal belonging to a family (Dasyuridae; 45 species) occurring in Australia (including Tasmania) and New Guinea, also called marsupial cat or native cat. Dasyures, which vary from 12 in to 67 in (30 cm to 170 cm) in length, are nocturnal and good climbers, hunting prey that ranges from insects to small wallabies. See also Tasmanian devil.

data processing The organization, transmission, and storage of information. **Automatic data processing** usually refers to systems using punchcard machines, paper tape, magnetic tape, etc., as opposed to **electronic data processing**, which is based on electronic computers. In batch processing, data is grouped and coded before processing. The alternative is on-line processing in which each user feeds data into the system continuously. Many systems incorporate both of these forms of processing for different types of work. Most large organizations now use data-processing techniques extensively and have a separate department to provide this service for the rest of the organization.

date A *palm tree, *Phoenix dactylifera*, native to N Africa and SW Asia and cultivated from Morocco to India for its fruits, which are rich in sugar and form a staple food in the producing countries. Male and female flowers grow on separate trees (which reach a height of 80 ft (25 m)); the female flowers develop into clusters of up to 1000 single-seeded berries. The trunk of the tree yields a timber and the leaves are used for basketry, weaving, etc.

dating. See fission-track dating; helium dating; potassium-argon dating; radiocarbon dating; radiometric dating; rubidium-strontium dating; thermoluminescence.

Datura A worldwide genus of shrubs and herbs (about 10 species), with smooth pointed oval leaves and drooping trumpet-shaped flowers, white, pink, orange, or yellow. The commonest species is the *thorn apple. Some species are popular ornamentals: angel's trumpet (*D. suaveolens*), a Mexican shrub up to 16 ft (5 m) high with white musk-scented flowers, is cultivated in greenhouses in temperate regions. Family: *Solanaceae.

Daubenton, Louis Jean Marie (1716–1800) French naturalist, who made detailed anatomical descriptions of many animal species. His other interests included paleontology, plant physiology, and mineralogy. He became the first director of the Museum of Natural History, Paris (1793).

Daubigny, Charles-François (1817–78) French landscape painter. He was associated with the *Barbizon school but painted chiefly by the banks of the Seine and Oise, specializing in twilight and moonlight scenes, e.g. *Evening Landscape* (Metropolitan Museum). He strongly influenced the impressionists.

Daudet, Alphonse (1840–97) French novelist, born at Nîmes. He wrote a number of naturalistic novels on the social and political life of his day but is best remembered for his sketches on Provençal subjects, which were originally written for *Le Figaro* and later collected as *Lettres de mon moulin* (1868). He also wrote plays, notably *L'Arlésienne* (1872), for which Bizet composed incidental music. His son **Léon Daudet** (1867–1942) was a political journalist and novelist. He was violently right-wing in his views and in 1899 helped to found the influential royalist periodical *L'Action française*. His critical essays were published as *Le Stupide XIXe siècle* (1922) and his memoirs, *Souvenirs* (1914–21), cover the years 1890–1905.

Daugavpils (name from 1893 until 1920: Dvinsk) 55 52N 26 31E A city in the W Soviet Union, in the Latvian SSR. It is an important rail junction and a commercial and industrial center. Population (1981 est): 117,000.

Daughters of the American Revolution (DAR) US organization for direct female descendants of participants in the *American Revolution. Founded in 1890 and chartered by the US Congress in 1896, it has a large genealogical library in Washington, DC and promotes history, education, patriotism, and the preservation of historic sites through its almost 3000 chapters and about 190,000 members nationwide.

Daumier, Honoré (1808–79) French caricaturist, painter, and sculptor. As a cartoonist for *La Caricature* in Paris he was imprisoned (1832) for depicting the king as Rabelais' gluttonous giant Gargantua. He produced numerous documentary lithographs, such as *Rue Transnonain*. After 1835 he worked for *Charivari*, satirizing the legal and medical professions and other social and political targets. Although his paintings were largely ignored in his lifetime, *The Washerwoman* (Louvre) and *The Third Class Railroad Carriage* (Ottawa) are admired as forerunners of *impressionism.

dauphin From 1350 until 1830 the title of the heirs to the French crown. It was the personal name, and later became the title, of the rulers of the *Dauphiné, which was purchased by the future Charles V in 1350. After becoming king (1364), he granted the Dauphiné and its accompanying title to his son, thus establishing a precedent that was followed until the abdication of Charles X.

Dauphiné A former province of SE France, corresponding to the present-day departments of Hautes-Alpes, Isère, and Drôme. It formed part of the Holy Roman Empire until 1343, when it was sold to the King of France. From 1350 to 1457, when it was annexed by the crown, it was governed by the French king's eldest son, who thus acquired the title *dauphin.

Davao City 07 05N 125 38E A port in the SE Philippines, in SE Mindanao. The island's commercial center, it grew rapidly in the 1960s and now covers an extensive area. It has timber and fishing industries and exports hemp and coffee. Population (1980): 611,311.

Davenport, Charles Benedict (1866–1944) US zoologist, who introduced the use of statistical techniques into biological research. The need for statistics arose from his studies of population genetics.

Davenport 41 32N 90 41W A city in E central Iowa, on the Mississippi River opposite Rock Island, Ill. It was established as a town in 1838. Aluminum is made here. Machine parts, aircraft parts, and food processing are also important industries. Population (1980): 103,264.

David (d. 962 BC) King of Israel (c. 1000–962). Born in Bethlehem, the son of Jesse, David was anointed by Samuel as the successor of Saul, the first King of Israel. He became a close friend of Saul's son, Jonathan, but his successes against the Philistines, including the slaying of Goliath, aroused Saul's jealousy and he became an outlaw. After the death of Saul and Jonathan, David was proclaimed King of Hebron and then of all Israel. He conquered Jerusalem, making it the nation's political and religious center, finally defeated the Philistines, and united the tribes of Israel. His reign was troubled by the revolt of his son Absalom, who was eventually defeated and killed. David was succeeded by Solomon, his son by Bathsheba. He was the author of some of the psalms. According to the Jewish prophets, the Messiah must be a descendant of David.

David I (1084–1153) King of the Scots (1124–53). The first monarch to recognize Matilda as successor to Henry I of England, he used her cause as an excuse to invade N England (1138) after Stephen had seized the throne. Stephen defeated him in the battle of the Standard (1138), near Northallerton. David founded or refounded over a dozen monasteries.

David II (1324–71) King of the Scots (1329–71), succeeding his father Robert the Bruce. He was forced into exile (1334–41) in France by Edward de *Balliol. He supported France against Edward III of England and was captured and imprisoned (1346–57) by the English.

David, Gerard (c. 1460–1523) Dutch painter, who was born in Oudewater (Holland) but settled in Bruges. Apart from his use of Renaissance detail in *Judgment of Cambyses* (Bruges), he was little influenced by the Italianate style current in Antwerp and continued to paint in the tradition of his predecessors.

David, Jacques Louis (1748–1825) French neoclassical painter, known for his historical paintings and portraits. He trained under Joseph-Marie Vien (1716–1809), before winning the Prix de Rome (1774), which enabled him to study in Italy (1775–80). His mature works depicted heroic scenes from Republican Rome and ancient Greece, e.g. *Oath of the Horatii* (Louvre). During the Revolution he painted some of its martyrs, e.g. *Death of Marat* (Brussels), and actively supported Robespierre; after Robespierre's fall he was imprisoned (1794–95). As court painter to □Napoleon I from 1804, his paintings illustrate imperial successes, e.g. *Napoleon Crowning Josephine* (Louvre). After Napoleon's fall David was exiled and died in Brussels.

David, St (or St Dewi; c. 520–600 AD) The patron saint of Wales and first abbot of Menevia (now St David's). He was also a missionary and the founder of many churches in Wales. Feast day: March 1. Emblem: a dove.

David ap Gruffudd (d. 1283) The brother of *Llywelyn ap Gruffudd, after whose death (1282) David claimed the title Prince of Wales. He was executed by Edward I for leading the Welsh in rebellion against him.

Davies, W(illiam) H(enry) (1871–1940) British poet. He lived for many years as a tramp in England and America before publishing the first of many volumes of simple rural poetry in 1905. G. B. Shaw contributed an introduction to his *Autobiography of a Super-Tramp* (1907).

da Vinci, Leonardo. See Leonardo da Vinci.

Davis, Benjamin Oliver, Sr. (1877–1970) US Army officer; the first black general in the Army. He served in the *Spanish-American War, the Philippines (1901–02), taught at Wilberforce University, Ohio (1905–09), in Liberia (1911–12), and again in the Philippines during World War I. Again teaching military science until 1938, he took over the 369th Harlem Regiment of the New York National Guard and was made a brigadier general in 1940.

Davis, Bette (Ruth Elizabeth D.; 1908–) US film actress. During the 1930s and 1940s she gave intense and dramatic performances in such films as *Of Human Bondage* (1934), *Jezebel* (1938), *Dark Victory* (1939), *The Little Foxes* (1941) and *All About Eve* (1950). In recent years she has appeared in the roles of elderly eccentric or neurotic women.

Davis, David (1815–86) US politician and Supreme Court associate justice. An active layer and judge in Illinois, he was a force behind Abraham *Lincoln's nomination for president in 1860. In turn, he was appointed an associate justice (1862–77) to the US Supreme Court, where he was best known for his decision in *Ex parte Milligan* (1866) that said that military courts are not lawful in nonmilitary areas. He later served in the US Senate as a Democrat from Illinois (1877–83).

Davis, Jefferson (1808–89) US military and political leader; president of the Confederate States of America (1861–65). Born in Todd County, Kentucky, Davis graduated from West Point in 1828 and began his military career with service in the *Black Hawk War in 1832. He later returned to civilian life and was elected to the US House of Representatives from Mississippi in 1845. The following year, Davis resigned from Congress to serve in the *Mexican War. He was later US senator (1847–51) and served as secretary of war in the administration of President Franklin *Pierce. Returning to the US Senate (1857–61), Davis supported slavery and the rights of states against federal interference. With the secession of Mississippi from the Union in 1861, he returned to the South and was elected president of the Confederate government. He held that office until the end of the *Civil War, when he was arrested in Georgia by federal troops. From 1865 to 1867, he was imprisoned and indicted for treason, but all charges against him were eventually dropped. His later years were spent at his home in Mississippi where he wrote *The Rise and Fall of the Confederate Government* (1881).

Davis, John (or J. Davys; c. 1550–1605) English navigator, who went on three voyages in search of the *Northwest Passage (1585, 1586, 1587), passing through the strait named for him to Baffin Bay. In 1592, seeking the Magellan Strait, he discovered the Falkland Islands. On his last voyage to the East Indies, he was killed by Japanese pirates near Singapore.

Davis, Miles (1926–) US jazz trumpeter and composer, one of the originators of *cool jazz. He studied music at the Juilliard School in New York and formed his own band in 1948. He has made a number of influential albums, including *Miles Ahead* and the innovative *Kind of Blue*.

Davis Cup An international tennis competition that was instituted in 1900 for teams of men. The US and Australia have won it most often.

Davis Strait A section of the Atlantic Ocean, between SW Greenland and Baffin Island (Canada). Length: 400 mi (640 km). Width: 200–400 mi (320–640 km). ₃8

Davitt, Michael (1846–1906) Irish nationalist. He joined the *Fenians in 1865 and after seven years' imprisonment founded the *Land League (1879). Davitt urged the reconciliation of extreme and constitutional nationalism.

Davos (Romansh name: Tarau) 46 47N 9 50E A mountain resort in E Switzerland. Comprising two villages at a height of about 5100 ft (1555 m), it is a health resort and winter-sports center, with the renowned Parsenn ski run. Population (1970): 10,238.

Davy, Sir Humphry (1778–1829) British chemist. Davy began his career by discovering the value of nitrous oxide as an anesthetic. For this work he was invited to join the Royal Institution in London, where his most important work was the discovery of many new metallic elements. By passing electricity through molten metallic compounds, he discovered potassium in 1807 and the following year, sodium, calcium, barium, magnesium, and strontium. He also encouraged the young Michael *Faraday, employing him as his assistant.

Dawes, Charles Gates (1865–1951) US financier, political leader, and diplomat. Born in Marietta, Ohio, he served as comptroller of the currency in the administration of President William McKinley and as US budget director for President Warren Harding. He later headed a commission to reconstruct the post-World War I German economy. The report of this commission, known as the Dawes Plan (1924), saved Europe from economic collapse and earned him, jointly with Austen Chamberlain, the Nobel Peace Prize in 1925. From 1925 to 1929, Dawes served as US vice president during the administration of President Calvin Coolidge. President Herbert Hoover named him US ambassador to Great Britain (1929–32).

Dawes Act (1887) US law that prepared for Indian citizenship and terminated the reservation system. Indian reservations were broken up and distributed to individuals for farming. In 1924, when citizenship would be granted to the Indians, these lands could be sold. The act was named for Senator Henry Laurens Dawes (1816–1903), its sponsor.

dawn redwood A deciduous conifer, *Metasequoia glyptostroboides*, thought to be extinct until 1941, when the first specimen of modern times was discovered in SW China. Growing to a height of 113 ft (35 m), dawn redwood has soft needles grouped in two rows and rounded green longstalked cones. It is quite widely grown for ornament. Family: *Taxodiaceae*.

Dawson 64 04N 139 24W A town in NW Canada, in the Yukon on the *Klondike River. During the gold rush it had over 25,000 inhabitants. Population (1981 est): 1252.

Dawson Creek 55 45N 120 15W A city in W Canada, in British Columbia at the beginning of the *Alaska Highway. Population (1976): 10,528.

Day, Clarence Shepard (1874–1935) US writer. After working as a stockbroker and serving in the Navy, he wrote *This Simian World* (1920), *The Crow's Nest* (1921), and *Thoughts Without Words* (1928). He is best known for his works about his family: *God and My Father* (1932), *Life with Father* (1935), and *Life with Mother* (published posthumously; 1937). *Life with Father* was adapted for the stage in 1939.

Dayak (or Dyak) A people of Borneo and Sarawak, speaking languages of the Indonesian section of the Malayo-Polynesian family. There are many groups including the Bahau of central and E Borneo, the Land Dayak of SW Borneo and the Iban (or Sea Dayak) of Sarawak. They are a riverine people, who live in large communal wooden huts (longhouses). They live by rice cultivation, fishing, and hunting with blowpipes. Formerly head hunting was common.

Dayan, Moshe (1915–81) Israeli general. Born in Palestine, during the 1930s he fought with the Haganah (Jewish irregulars) and in World War II in the British Army, losing an eye in battle in 1941. From 1953 until 1958 he was chief of Israel's general staff. He was defense minister in 1967 and from 1973 to 1974, when he resigned after criticism of Israel's unpreparedness in the Arab-Israeli War of 1973–74. In 1977 he became foreign minister but resigned in 1979 as a result of disagreement with Begin's cabinet on policy toward the Arabs.

Day Lewis, C(ecil) (1904–72) British poet and critic. He was a leading left-wing poet of the 1930s but his later verse, as in *The Whispering Roots* (1970), was more purely lyrical. He published translations of Virgil's *Aeneid* (1952) and other works and was appointed poet laureate in 1968. As "Nicholas Blake" he wrote a series of sophisticated detective stories.

Daylight Savings Time A time system in which one hour, usually, is added to local (clock) time, i.e. to Eastern Standard Time, so prolonging useful daylight hours. This system is used in temperate latitudes in spring, summer, and early autumn.

day lily A herbaceous plant of the genus *Hemerocallis*, native to Europe and Asia and cultivated as garden flowers. They have long narrow leaves and long stalks bearing clusters of orange or yellow lily-like flowers, which wither after a short time. *H. lilio-asphodelinus* is grown for its sweet scent, and garden hybrids of *H. flava* bloom for a longer time, producing orange, yellow, pink, and red flowers. Family: *Liliaceae*.

Dayton 39 45N 84 10W A city in Ohio, on the Great Miami River. It was the home of the Wright brothers; the nearby Wright-Patterson Air Force Base is a center for military aviation research. Population (1980): 203,588.

Daytona Beach 29 11N 81 01W A resort in Florida, on the Atlantic coast. Its hard white beach has been used for motor racing since 1902. Population (1970): 45,327.

Dazai Osamu (Tsushima Shuji; 1909–48) Japanese novelist. His fiction exploited the conflict between his wealthy family background and his radical political beliefs. His postwar novels, notably *The Setting Sun* (1947) and *No Longer Human* (1948), expressed the nihilistic mood of a generation bereft of the support of traditional values. He committed suicide in 1948.

D-Day (June 6, 1944) The day on which the Allied invasion of Normandy was launched from Britain during *World War II. It led to the liberation of France from German occupation and the final defeat of Germany.

DDT (dichlorophenyltrichloroethane) An organochlorine compound widely used as a contact *insecticide. It is active against many insects, including mosquitoes, flies, fleas, lice, and bedbugs, specifically affecting the central nervous system. However, many insects have become resistant to DDT, which is a very stable compound and accumulates not only in their tissues but also in the tissues of the animals that prey on them, causing toxic effects. Because the chemical has long-lasting effects, its use is closely regulated.

deadly nightshade (or belladonna) A branching perennial herb, *Atropa belladonna*, up to 5 ft (1.5 m) tall and native to Eurasia. It has dull green leaves, up to 8 in (20 cm) long, and solitary purple or greenish bell-shaped flowers. The shiny black berries taste sweet but contain a deadly poison. The plant is a source of a variety of alkaloids, especially hyoscyamine and atropine. Family: *Solanaceae*. *See also* nightshade.

dead men's fingers A colonial soft *coral, *Alcyonium digitatum*, so called because of its fleshy pink finger-like appearance when out of water. The individual *polyps have an internal skeleton of separate calcareous spicules, which give the tissues a gelatinous consistency. Colonies, which are white, yellow, pink, or orange, are common on rocky coasts of NW Europe.

Dead Sea A lake in E Israel and W Jordan. It is fed by the Jordan River and, having no outlet, is highly saline and supports no life. Area: 401 sq mi (1050 sq km).

Dead Sea Scrolls A group of Hebrew and Aramaic manuscript scrolls, originally stored in jars, found in 11 caves in the area of Khirbat *Qumran, NW of the Dead Sea. The first were accidentally discovered in 1947; the rest were recovered as late as the 1950s. Altogether there are about 500 different documents, dating from 250 BC to 70 AD, which seem to have formed the library of a Jewish, perhaps *Essene, community that existed from about 125 BC to the Jewish revolt in 66–70 AD, when the scrolls were hidden in the caves for safekeeping. They include texts of many Old Testament books, commentaries, prayers, psalms, and material peculiar to the community, including an apocalyptic prophecy. They are valuable as evidence of the accuracy of previously known Old Testament texts, for the information they provide about a Jewish community contemporaneous with early Christianity, and archeologically as examples of the Hebrew and Aramaic scripts of the period.

DEADLY NIGHTSHADE *This notorious plant grows in woodlands, thickets, and scrub. It flowers from June to August and produces its deadly black berries from August to November.*

Deadwood 44 05N 115 40W A town in W Central South Dakota, in the N Black Hills. A frontier mining town named for the dead wood left from a forest fire, it thrived during the gold rush (1875–1876). Calamity Jane and Wild Bill Hickok lived and are buried here. Western frontier days are recreated in tourist attractions. Population (1980): 2035.

deafness A common condition in which hearing is absent or impaired. Deafness is described as either conductive, in which the mechanism for transmitting sound to the inner ear is defective, or sensorineural, when there is damage to the auditory nerve or the part of the brain concerned with hearing. Conductive deafness may be caused by wax in the outer ear, infection in the middle ear, or—as with Beethoven—otosclerosis (a disease of the small bones in the middle ear). Sensorineural deafness occurs commonly in old people but can also be due to infection, head injury, drugs (such as streptomycin), *Ménière's disease, or exposure to continuous loud noise. Some forms of deafness can be treated by removing wax, curing infection, or by microsurgery; untreatable forms can be alleviated with a *hearing aid.

Deák, Ferenc (1803–76) Hungarian statesman. After the *Hungarian Revolution of 1848, Deák became the country's minister of justice and in 1849, after the fall of the revolutionaries, the leader of the opposition to Austrian dominance. Deák believed in the dynastic union of Austria and Hungary but desired separate constitutions and kingdoms and he was largely responsible for the establishment in 1867 of *Austria-Hungary.

Deakin, Alfred (1856–1919) Australian statesman, who was three times prime minister (1903–04, 1905–08, 1909–10). He succeeded Sir Edmund

*Barton, and like him was a member of the Federal Convention that drafted the constitution for the new Commonwealth of Australia. He was a considerable influence on the early development of the Commonwealth and introduced the "White Australia" policy restricting non-white immigration.

Deal 51 14N 1 24E A port and resort in SE England, in Kent. It is one of the Cinque Ports and probable landing place of Julius Caesar (55 BC). Population (1981): 25,989.

Dean, Dizzy (Jay Hanna D.; 1911–74) US baseball pitcher. He played for the St Louis Cardinals (1930, 1932–37) and the Chicago Cubs (1938–41) and achieved 150 career wins before an injury forced his retirement.

Dean, James (James Byron; 1931–55) US film actor. He trained at the Actors' Studio, and became a cult hero for his generation. His films were *East of Eden* (1954), *Rebel Without A Cause* (1955), and *Giant* (1955), released following his death in a car crash.

Deane, Silas (1737–89) US patriot and diplomat. Active in movements leading to American independence, Deane was sent to Paris by the Continental Congress to buy war supplies and negotiate treaties of commerce and alliance with France (1776–78). Accused of embezzlement he went into exile, settling in London.

Dearborn 42 18N 83 14W A city in Michigan, near Detroit. The birthplace of Henry Ford, it is the headquarters of the Ford Motor Company. Population (1980): 90,660.

death The permanent cessation of all bodily functions in an organism. Until recently a person was medically pronounced dead when his heartbeat and breathing movements ceased, but since the advent of mechanical ventilators the heartbeat may be maintained long after "natural" breathing has stopped as a result of irreversible brain damage. Death is therefore now defined on the basis of brain function: when the parts of the brain that control respiration and other vital reflexes have ceased to function the patient is said to be brain dead, i.e. truly dead, although his heart may continue to beat for some time with the aid of mechanical life-support systems. With recent advances in transplant surgery, it is important to establish brain death in those patients who could be suitable donors of kidneys and other organs.

death cap A highly poisonous mushroom, *Amanita phalloides*, fairly common in and near deciduous woodlands. Its cap, 2.8–5.0 in (7–12 cm) in diameter, is usually pale greenish yellow but may be olive green or grayish. The stalk is white or greenish white, with a baglike sheath (volva) at its base. Death cap can be fatal, even in small amounts, and symptoms may not appear for up to 24 hours.

death's-head moth A *hawk moth, *Acherontia atropos*, with a wingspan of 5 in (125 mm), found in Europe, Africa, and Asia, whose thoracic markings resemble a skull and crossbones. These moths emit squeaks when handled and may enter beehives to steal honey.

Death Valley A desert area in SE California. The hottest and driest part of North America, its temperatures exceed 102°F (39°C) during summer. The flora and fauna that survive these harsh conditions are of interest to scientists and many tourists are attracted to the area during winter. In 1933 it was declared a national monument.

deathwatch beetle A widely distributed wood-boring beetle, *Xestobium rufovillosum*, about 28 in (7 mm) long, that can cause immense damage to old buildings and furniture. It lays its eggs in small crevices in the wood and the larvae tunnel in, eventually reducing it to powder. The pupae often make knocking sounds by repeatedly striking their heads against the walls of their burrows. Family: *Anobiidae*.

DeBakey, Michael Ellis (1980–) US physician and surgeon. An innovator in the techniques of heart surgery, he was responsible for the invention of the roller pump for blood transfusions (1932). He pioneered a grafting method for aneurysms, performed the first artery bypass operation (1964), and was the first to successfully implant a heart pump in a human (1966).

de Bary, Heinrich Anton (1831–88) German botanist and founder of mycology (the study of fungi). He determined the life cycles of many fungi, including important disease-causing species. In 1866 he showed that lichens each comprise a fungus and an alga living in a mutually beneficial partnership. For this he coined the word symbiosis.

Debré, Michel (1912–) French statesman; prime minister (1959–62). A Gaullist, Debré became prominent as a member of the Saar Economic Mission in 1947. He became a member of the Rassemblement pour la République upon its formation in 1976 by Jacques *Chirac. Debré is the author of 15 works on politics and economics.

Debrecen 47 30N 21 37E A city in E Hungary. It was a center of Protestantism in E Europe. Lajos Kossuth proclaimed Hungary independent of the Habsburgs in the Great Church of Debrecen in 1849. There are now various industries and a university (1912). Population (1980): 195,000.

Debrett, John (1752–1822) British publisher. He took over a publishing business in 1781; the directory of the peerage, which still bears his name, was first published in 1802.

de Broglie, Louis Victor, 7th Duc (1892–) French physicist, who won the 1929 Nobel Prize for his theory that elementary particles have associated waves, known as *de Broglie waves. The theory was confirmed by the subsequent observation of *electron diffraction and forms the basis of the branch of quantum mechanics known as *wave mechanics.

de Broglie wave A wave associated with any moving elementary particle with nonzero mass, since such particles exhibit wave properties under appropriate conditions. For example, they may be diffracted by a crystal lattice. The de Broglie wavelength of a particle mass m and velocity v is h/mv, where h is the *Planck constant. They were first postulated by Louis *de Broglie in 1923.

Debs, Eugene V(ictor) (1855–1926) US labor organizer and political leader. Born in Terre Haute, Indiana, Debs worked as a railroad employee and became active in the Brotherhood of Locomotive Firemen. In 1880 he was named national secretary and treasurer of the Brotherhood and was elected to the Indiana legislature in 1884. An outspoken advocate of organized labor, he helped to establish the American Railway Union in 1893 and was imprisoned for his role in the *Pullman Strike in the following year. Debs established the Social Democratic Party of America in 1898 and ran for president as a socialist candidate five times. In 1905 he helped to found the *Industrial Workers of the World (IWW). Debs was convicted during World War I of violation of the Espionage Act, and his 1920 campaign for president won almost a million votes. He was released by President Harding in 1921 and wrote *Walls and Bars* (1927), an exposé of prison conditions.

Deburau, Jean-Gaspard (1796–1846) French pantomimist, born in Bohemia. He joined a troupe of acrobats in Paris in 1811 and created the standard pantomime character of Pierrot, the pale and melancholy lover.

Debussy, Claude (Achille) (1862–1918) French composer. He spent most of his life in Paris and is regarded as the originator of musical impressionism. He married twice and wrote his *Children's Corner Suite* (1906–08) for his daughter Chou-chou. Debussy developed an individual style that employed whole-tone, pentatonic, and modal scales as well as unusual harmonies and tone colors. His most famous works include *Prélude à l'après-midi d'un faune* (for orchestra; 1892–94), the opera *Pelléas et Mélisande* (1892–1902), *La Mer* (three symphonic sketches; 1903–05), a string quartet, and a sonata for flute, viola, and harp. He also wrote sonatas for cello and for violin; piano music, including two sets of *Images* (1905, 1907) and 24 preludes (1910–13); and songs.

Debye, Peter Joseph Wilhelm (1884–1966) Dutch physicist and chemist, who was awarded the 1936 Nobel Prize for chemistry for his theoretical work on *dipole moments and the behavior of ions in solution. He also extended the technique of *X-ray crystallography so that it could be applied to powders. Most of his work was done in Germany but in 1940 he left Europe for Cornell University, where he remained until his retirement in 1950.

Decadents A group of late-19th-century French symbolist poets and their contemporaries in England. They aimed to create a literature liberated from all moral and social responsibilities. A journal entitled *Le Décadent* was published in France from 1886 to 1889. Poets linked with the movement included *Rimbaud, *Verlaine, and *Mallarmé in France, and Arthur *Symons, Oscar *Wilde, and Ernest *Dowson in England. *See also* Aesthetic movement.

Decapoda A worldwide order of *crustaceans (over 8500 species), with five pairs of thoracic appendages—anterior pincers and four pairs of walking legs. They include the *shrimps and *prawns (suborder: *Natantia*, "swimming forms") and *lobsters, *crayfish, and *crabs (suborder: *Reptantia*, "walking forms").

decathlon An athletic competition for men, consisting of ten events over two days. On the first are 100 m sprint, long jump, shot put, high jump, and 400 m sprint; on the second are 110 m hurdles, discus throw, pole vault, javelin throw, and 1500 m run. Competitors score for performances in each event, the winner gaining the highest total.

Decatur, Stephen (1779–1820) US naval officer. He established his reputation in the war with the Barbary pirates of Tripoli (1800–05), in which he raided Tripoli harbor and burned the captured US frigate *Phila-*

delphia (1804). In the *War of 1812 he defeated two British frigates (1812, 1815). He was killed in a duel.

Decatur 39 51N 89 32W A city in central Illinois, on the Sagamon River. Abraham Lincoln practiced law and received his first endorsement for president here in 1860. Decatur manufactures heavy brass items, heavy machinery, electronic parts, and food products. Population (1980): 94,081.

Deccan A region of India, considered either as the entire peninsula or as the arid plateau between the Narmada and Krishna Rivers. Sloping gently from the Western to the Eastern Ghats, it is cut by many rivers flowing E.

December Twelfth month of the year. Derived from *decem* (Latin: ten) when it was the tenth month of the Roman 10-month calendar. It has 31 days, and it is on December 25 that Christmas is observed. The zodiac signs for December are Sagittarius and Capricorn; the flowers are holly and narcissus, and the birthstones are the ruby, turquoise, or zircon.

Decembrists (*or* Dekabrists) Members of an anti-Tsarist revolt in December, 1825, following the death of Alexander I. They were members of various clandestine organizations formed after the Napoleonic Wars by former military officers, who, after being exposed to western liberalism, had become discontented on their return to Russia with the country's reactionary government. The revolt failed, largely because of poor organization. Five leaders were executed and their followers imprisoned or exiled to Siberia.

decibel (dB) A unit used to compare two power levels on a logarithmic scale. It is one-tenth of a bel, but this unit is rarely used. Two power levels P and P_0 differ by n decibels when $n = 10 \log_{10} P/P_0$. The unit is often used to express a sound intensity in which case P_0 is usually taken as the intensity of the lowest audible note of the same frequency as P. *See also* phon.

deciduous plants. *See* evergreen plants.

decimal system The number system in common use, having a base 10 and thus using ten separate numerals. It also involves the use of a decimal point to express numbers less than one, instead of the method of fractions: for example $1/4$ is expressed as 0.25. The decimal system was invented by the Hindus and adopted by the Arabs in the 9th century (*see also* mathematics). The use of decimal fractions originated in Italy in the 12th century but was first formalized by the mathematician Simon Stévin (1548–1620) in 1585. The use of the decimal point did not occur until the beginning of the 18th century. Decimalization of currency systems was introduced by France after the Revolution and followed by most other European and American countries, except for Britain, which did not decimalize until 1971. *See also* metric system.

Decius, Gaius Messius Quintus Trajanus (c. 201–51 AD) Roman emperor (249–51). Decius attempted to restore Roman traditions, persecuting Christians in the name of Roman state cults. He was defeated and killed by the Goths at Abrittus.

Declaration of Independence The formal document adopted by the 13 colonies on July 4, 1776. After the decision of the Second Continental Congress early in June 1776 to seek independence from Great Britain, a committee consisting of John *Adams, Benjamin *Franklin, Thomas *Jefferson, Robert *Livingstone, and Roger *Sherman was appointed to draft the formal document. Although Adams and Franklin assisted in its formulation, the text of the Declaration was written by Jefferson. Drawing on the principles of the political philosophy of John *Locke and Charles-Louis *Montesquieu, Jefferson enumerated the specific grievances of the American colonies against the British government and asserted the general principles of human rights that he believed justified independence. The Declaration of Independence quickly became one of the most influential proclamations in the western political tradition.

Declaratory Act. *See* Stamp Act.

declination. *See* magnetic declination; right ascension.

decomposition The breakdown of the complex organic molecules of dead plants and animals and animal wastes into their simple components by bacteria and fungi. These microorganisms (**decomposers**) serve as the ultimate link in *food chains: the simple nitrogenous compounds released into the soil by decomposition can be used by plants (the producers) to manufacture their own food. *See also* nitrogen cycle.

decompression sickness (*or* caisson disease) An occupational hazard of pilots and underwater divers caused by too rapid a return to normal atmospheric pressure. At high pressures large amounts of gas can be carried in the blood. A rapid return to normal pressure causes nitrogen (the main component of inhaled air) to form bubbles out in the blood; this interrupts the blood supply to the tissues, producing joint pain (the bends), general discomfort, and respiratory problems (the chokes). Decompression sickness is prevented by a slow return to atmospheric pressure; it is treated by placing the patient in a hyperbaric chamber.

Decorated The style of □gothic architecture predominant in England between 1300 and 1370. In contrast to the geometric restraint of its predecessor, *Early English, Decorated is characterized by complex flowing patterns, especially in window tracery. Roof vaults were intricately ribbed and the ogee or double curved *arch with elaborate ornamentation became common. The early 14th-century nave of Exeter Cathedral demonstrates the style's profusion of ribs and arches. *Compare* Flamboyant.

decorative arts Arts and crafts the function of which is primarily ornamental. The modern concept of the decorative arts was pioneered by such designers as William *Morris. Despite persistent attempts to demonstrate that mass production need not necessarily compromise design, modern endeavors in the decorative arts tend to center on small workshops producing individually handmade items in such fields as *bookbinding, *enamelwork, *jewelry, *pottery, and wallpaper.

Dedekind, (Julius Wilhelm) Richard (1831–1916) German mathematician, who gave the irrational *numbers the same level of respectability as the rational numbers. He achieved this by means of the Dedekind cut, a method of cutting an infinite line representing the real numbers. He became involved in the controversy between Georg *Cantor and Leopold Kronecker (1823–91), taking Cantor's side against Kronecker's attempt to banish all but the integers from mathematics.

deduction In logic, argument from general principles to particular conclusions. It is thus analytic and certain, in contrast to *induction, the conclusions of which are never more than strong probabilities.

de Duve, Christian (1917–) Belgian biochemist, noted for his contributions to cell biology. De Duve discovered lysosomes, components of living cells that are responsible for breaking down substances within the cell. He shared a Nobel Prize (1974) with Albert Claude (1899–) and George Emil Palade (1912–).

Dee River The name of three rivers in the UK. **1.** A river in NE Scotland, flowing E to the North Sea at Aberdeen. Length: 87 mi (140 km). **2.** A river in North Wales and NW England, rising in Gwynedd and flowing E and N through Llangollen and Chester to the Irish Sea. Length: 70 mi (112 km). **3.** A river in S Scotland, flowing S to the Solway Firth. Length: 50 mi (80 km).

deed In law, a document in writing, signed, sealed and delivered, transferring a right over property (title-deed) or creating an obligation on its maker. To be binding it need not fulfill conditions applicable to a *contract. A deed may be between two parties, to establish mutual obligations, or it may involve one party only (deed poll), as, for example, when a person publishes a change of name.

deer A *ruminant mammal of the family *Cervidae* (41 species), occurring mainly in the N hemisphere, although a few are found in South America and N Africa and they have been introduced to SE Asia and Australasia. Nearly all deer have bony antlers that are shed and replaced every year (the *Chinese water deer and the *musk deer are exceptions). Deer range in size from the *elk (up to 7 ft [2 m] high) to the South American pudu, which is only about 16 in (40 cm) high at the shoulder. Most deer live in herds but some, such as the *muntjac, are solitary.

deerhound A long-established British breed of dog, formerly used for hunting deer. It has a deep-chested long body with long legs and a long tapering head with small ears. The wiry coat is usually blue-gray but may be shades of brown or fawn. Height: 30 in (76 cm) (dogs); 28 in (71 cm) (bitches).

deer mouse A North American rodent belonging to the genus *Peromyscus* (60 species), also called white-footed mouse. 5–15 in (12–37 cm) long including the tail (2–8 in [4–20 cm]), these climbing and burrowing animals have large eyes and ears; they are omnivorous and are often used as laboratory animals. Family: *Cricetidae*.

defamation In law, a false and derogatory statement about another person that causes him to be hated, ridiculed, or held in contempt or that tends to injure him in his profession or trade. It is libel if made in a permanent form (e.g. in writing, newspapers, broadcasts, sound films) and slander if made in a transient form, by spoken words or gestures. The remedy for both types of defamation is by civil proceedings, although libel may also be a crime if its publication is calculated to provoke a breach of the peace. Not only the originator of a libel but everyone who has subsequently repeated or published it may be sued by the person libeled. Action for libel cannot be brought against "privileged" proceedings or statements. Judicial and parliamentary proceedings, for example, are "absolutely privileged" and nothing said in them can be the subject of a libel action. A statement judged to

be a fair comment on a matter of public interest is also not actionable as defamation.

Defense, Department of US cabinet-level agency that provides military forces for deterrence of war and for the protection of the country. The Secretary of Defense directs the department, which includes the *Army, *Navy, *Air Force, and *Marine Corps. Originally established as the war department (1789), it was reorganized (1947; 1949) and renamed (1949).

defense mechanisms In psychoanalysis, the means by which undesirable and antisocial impulses can be unconsciously avoided or controlled by the subject. *Repression, *sublimation, and *projection are important defenses. Others include reaction formation, in which an impulse is turned into its opposite, as when one displays excessive concern for a person whom one secretly hates; and displacement, in which an impulse is transferred onto a more acceptable subject (e.g. kicking the dog instead of the boss). Defense mechanisms are a part of normal life, but if they become excessively strong they can distort the development of personality and even give rise to symptoms of *neurosis.

deficit financing The fiscal policy of stimulating the economy by government spending in excess of revenue by borrowing to finance the resultant deficit. Deficit financing was advocated by the British economist J. M. *Keynes as a method of countering the *Depression of the 1930s; although Keynes' ideas were not assimilated in time to influence that period, deficit financing became normal practice after World War II (*see* multiplier; national debt).

deflation A government action to slow down the economy, with the aim of easing *inflation or cutting down on imports and thus helping the *balance of payments. Both monetary policy (credit "squeeze") and fiscal policy (increasing taxes, cutting government spending) can be used to deflate the economy. *See also* multiplier).

Defoe, Daniel (1660–1731) British novelist, economist, and journalist. His early career as a merchant ended in bankruptcy in 1692. A Nonconformist, he welcomed the arrival of William of Orange in 1688 and wrote *The True-Born Englishman* (1701) in his defense. He subsequently worked as a journalist. His famous novels were written late in his career, *Robinson Crusoe* in 1719 and *Moll Flanders* and *Colonel Jack* in 1722.

defoliant A chemical applied to foliage in order to cause premature shedding of leaves; examples are ammonium thiocyanate and cacodylic acid. Defoliants are used to aid mechanical harvesting of cotton and for other peaceful uses. They are also employed in *chemical warfare.

De Forest, Lee (1873–1961) US electrical engineer, who invented the triode valve (1906), which became the basic *amplifier in all electronic circuits until superseded by the transistor. In the early 1920s he developed a method of converting sound waves into light of varying intensity, which was used as the basis of recording film soundtracks.

Degas, (Hilaire Germain) Edgar (1834–1917) French painter and sculptor, born in Paris. He trained in the École des Beaux-Arts, where he was influenced by the draftsmanship of *Ingres. His early works were portraits, e.g. *The Bellelli Family* (Louvre), recalling the old masters that he had studied in Italy (1856–60), and history paintings, e.g. *Young Spartans Exercising* (National Gallery, London). From the mid-1860s he turned to painting contemporary scenes, particularly of ballet and racecourses. In these works, characterized by informal poses and unusual angles, Degas was indebted both to Japanese prints and to photography. In 1872 he visited his mother's family in New Orleans and painted the *New Orleans Cotton Office* (Pau, France). His pastels of women at their toilet shocked his contemporaries but are now regarded as being among his finest works. He exhibited frequently with the impressionists but was little influenced by their style.

De Gasperi, Alcide (1881–1954) Italian statesman; prime minister (1945–53). After imprisonment (1930–31) as an antifascist, De Gasperi withdrew to the Vatican City, where he worked in the library and organized the moderate Christian Democratic Party during World War II. From 1945 to 1953 he headed coalition cabinets, which included communists until 1947, when De Gasperi expelled them. A Christian Democratic electoral victory in 1948 gave popular sanction to this measure.

de Gaulle, Charles André Joseph Marie (1890–1970) French general and statesman who was an outstanding international figure in the mid-20th century; president (1958–69). An advocate of mechanized warfare during the 1930s, when he wrote his best-known book, *Vers l'armée de métier* (1934), he was promoted early in World War II to general (1940). He entered the cabinet of Paul *Reynaud but opposed the Franco-German armistice, becoming leader of the *Free French in London and a symbol of French patriotism. The Free French contributed heroically to the Allied war effort but de Gaulle resented his dependence on Britain and the US and the antagonism between them was to continue after the war. In 1943 he became head of the newly formed Committee of National Liberation in Algiers and, after the Allied liberation of France (1944), formed a provisional government of which he was president from 1945 until resigning in 1946. In 1947 he formed the unsuccessful Rassemblement du Peuple Français, dissolving it in 1953. In 1958 he was summoned from retirement to deal with the crisis in Algeria, where French settlers, fearing the establishment of Algerian independence, were in revolt. He became president of the new Fifth Republic in 1959 and moved toward the achievement of Algerian independence. Successful by 1962, he subsequently pursued his vision of a Europe of nationally self-conscious states, free of US influence. He thus opposed the postwar multinational organizations, refusing to sign the *Nuclear Test-Ban Treaty (1963) and withdrawing France from the military arm of NATO (1966). He was also passionately opposed to British membership in the European Economic Community. At home his position was greatly weakened by the student and industrial unrest of May, 1968, and in the following year he resigned following defeat in a referendum on constitutional reform. His policies, however, have endured in the right-wing Gaullist movement in contemporary French politics.

CHARLES DE GAULLE

degree 1. A unit of plane angle equal to 1/360th of a complete revolution. It is subdivided into 60 minutes, each of which consists of 60 seconds. 2. An interval on a temperature scale: 1° on the *Celsius (centigrade) scale is equal to one-hundredth of the difference in temperature between freezing and boiling water. It is also equal in magnitude to 1 *kelvin. 1° on the *Fahrenheit scale is 9/5 times the Celsius degree.

De Havilland, Sir Geoffrey (1882–1965) British ☐aircraft designer and manufacturer, who produced some of the first jet-propelled aircraft. During both World Wars he designed several military aircraft, including the well-known Mosquito of World War II.

Dehra Dun 30 19N 78 03E A city in India, in Uttar Pradesh. The Indian Military Academy (1932) is situated here. Population (1971): 166,073.

dehydration A potentially serious condition resulting from excessive loss of water from the body. The water that is continuously lost from the body in urine, sweat, expired air, and feces must be replaced by drinking. Dehydration may result from insufficient intake of water in those shipwrecked or too ill to drink or from excessive loss in fever, vomiting, diarrhea, or from the skin in hot climates. It may lead, if not treated, to shock and death. It can be avoided by ensuring that patients receive fluid in the form of drinks or intravenous infusions. Intravenous fluids can be given slowly to treat those seriously dehydrated.

Deirdre The tragic heroine of the Irish legend known as *The Fate of the Sons of Usnech*, of which the earliest surviving account appears in the 12th-century *Book of Leinster*. To escape marrying King Conchobar of Ulster, Deirdre eloped with Noíse, son of Usnech. When they returned, Noíse and his brothers were killed by the king and Deirdre died of grief. The legend has been dramatized by J. M. Synge and W. B. Yeats.

deism A system of belief in God that, in contrast to *theism, discounts revealed religion, especially Christianity, and takes God as the philosophical *first cause. More specifically, deism was a rationalistic anti-Christian movement in England in the late 17th and early 18th centuries that criticized and rebutted the Scriptures after the manner of *Locke's *empiricism and regarded dogmatic religions as corruptions of man's natural relation with God. Leading deists were Lord *Herbert of Cherbury, Matthew Tindal (1655–1733), and the 3rd Earl of *Shaftesbury. Deism, often tending toward— *atheism, had more influence on German and French thinkers, including *Voltaire, than in England.

Dekabrists. *See* Decembrists.

Dekker, Thomas (c. 1572–1632) British dramatist and pamphleteer. His best-known play, *The Shoemaker's Holiday* (1600), expresses his exuberant affection for London life. He often collaborated with *Webster, *Middleton, and other dramatists. His pamphlets, such as *The Seven Deadly Sins of London* (1606) and *The Gull's Hornbook* (1609), are racy blends of fact, wit, and homily.

de Kooning, Willem (1904–) //US painter of Dutch birth, noted for his figurative subject matter. He also painted abstract compositions, some in black and white, influenced by Arshile *Gorky, *Picasso, and *Miró. His famous but controversial series of *Women* (1950–53), portraying females as grotesque and aggressive creatures, established him as a leading exponent of *action painting.

Delacroix, Eugène (1798–1863) French Romantic painter, born near Paris. He studied with Baron Guérin (1774–1833) but was influenced by *Géricault, *Rubens, and *Constable. His richly colored paintings were often inspired by incidents in Dante, Shakespeare, and Byron, and by contemporary events, e.g. *Massacre at Chios* (1824; Louvre), based on a Turkish atrocity in Greece, and *Liberty Leading the People* (1830; Louvre). The influence of a visit to Morocco (1832) can be seen in some of his exotic later works, e.g. *Women of Algiers* (1834; Louvre). From 1833 he worked on decorations in public buildings, such as the Louvre, Palais-Bourbon, and Saint-Sulpice. He was a friend of *Chopin and George *Sand, both of whom he painted in 1838. His *Journal* contains valuable information on his life and work.

Delagoa Bay (Portuguese name: Baía de Lourenço Marques) An inlet of the Indian Ocean on the coast of S Mozambique. It is about 19 mi (30 km) across and has Maputo at its edge.

De la Mare, Walter (1873–1956) British poet, novelist, and anthologist, whose work is imbued with an atmosphere of mystery and magic. The verse collection *Songs of Childhood* (1902) and the romance *Henry Brocken* (1906) were written while he was working for an oil company, from which he retired to devote himself to full-time writing. Among his best-known works are the poem "The Listeners" (1912), the fantastic novel *Memoirs of a Midget* (1921), and the anthologies *Come Hither* (1923) and *Love* (1943).

De la Roche, Mazo (1885–1961) Canadian novelist. Her romantic saga of the Whiteoak family ran to over 15 books, beginning with *Jalna* (1927), the name of the family estate.

Delaroche, (Hippolyte) Paul (1797–1859) French history and portrait painter. Throughout his life he enjoyed great success with such sentimental history paintings as *The Children of Edward IV in the Tower* (1830; Louvre). He was a professor at the École des Beaux-Arts from 1832, for which he produced the mural of the *Apotheosis of Art* (1837–41).

De La Rue, Warren (1815–89) British astronomer, who pioneered the use of photography in astronomy, discovering solar flares by this process in 1860.

Delaunay, Robert (1885–1941) The earliest French painter of completely abstract compositions. His first major works represented the Eiffel Tower (1910–11) in cubist style but in his series of *Discs* (1912–13) he pioneered *orphism (which he called *simultaneisme*), a style in which color alone was the subject matter.

Delaware The second smallest state in the US. It shares the Delmarva Peninsula with Maryland and Virginia, with Maryland to the W and S and a small portion of Pennsylvania abutting on the N. The Delaware Bay, the mouth of the Delaware River, and the Atlantic Ocean form its seaboard. New Jersey lies across the mouth of the Delaware River to the E. One of the Middle Atlantic states, it occupies part of the low-lying ground of the Atlantic coastal plain, with higher ground in the NW, where most of the state's population and industry are concentrated. It is one of the most industrialized states; Wilmington contains the administrative centers of several large chemical companies and is nicknamed "the chemical capital of the world." Motor vehicles, synthetic rubber, textiles, and food products are also produced. There is limited mining of sand and gravel. The state's farmers produce poultry, soybeans, milk, corn, and vegetables. There is some fishing of coastal and inland waters. *History*: it was discovered by Henry Hudson, who sailed up the Delaware River in 1609. At the time the region was occupied by Delaware Indians. The Dutch established a settlement (1631) but it was the Swedes who founded the first permanent settlement Fort Christiana (now Wilmington) in 1638. Delaware was subsequently captured by the Dutch (1655) and the English (1664). It became part of Pennsylvania in 1682 and shared a governor with that colony until 1776. It was the first of the original 13 states of the US. Eleuthère DuPont's gunpowder mill, founded in 1802, established the state's industrial base. Delaware fought as part of the Union during the Civil War, but many of its rural inhabitants remained loyal to the South. The division between the urban N and the rural S persists today. Area: 2057 sq mi (5328 sq km). Population (1980): 595,225. Capital: Dover.

Delaware River   A river that rises in the Catskill Mountains in SE New York and flows S to Delaware Bay, forming the boundaries between New York and Pennsylvania (from Hale Eddy to Port Jervis), New Jersey and Pennsylvania, and New Jersey and Delaware. During the Revolutionary War, George Washington and his troops crossed the river several times to wage battles in New Jersey. It passes Trenton, NJ, Philadelphia, Pa, and Wilmington, Del, and handles great quantities of their commerce. The scenic Delaware Water Gap, a pass through the Appalachians, is in NW New Jersey and E central Pennsylvania. Length: 280 mi (451 km).

Delaware   American Algonkian-speaking Indian tribe found in what is now New Jersey, Delaware, and Pennsylvania; also known as Lenni-Lenape. Divided into three groups (Munsee, Unalachtigo, and Unami), they were basically an agricultural people who also crafted baskets, pottery, and leather clothing; their most important ceremony was the Corn Dance. With the coming of white settlers they gradually moved westward. Today, most Delaware live on reservations in Oklahoma and Ontario, Canada.

Delbrück, Max   (1906–81) US biologist and Nobel Prize winner (1969); born in Germany. He came to the US in 1937 to study genetics. His discovery that bacterial viruses reproduce or multiply by the hundred thousands in a short period of time proved his theory of genetic recombination. For this and his other work in molecular biology, he shared the Nobel Prize in 1969.

Delcassé, Théophile   (1852–1923) French politician; foreign minister (1898–1905, 1914–15). His conciliatory policy over the *Fashoda incident (1895) and his negotiations leading to the *Entente Cordiale with Britain (1904) paved the way for the *Triple Entente between Britain, France, and Russia. He urged a strong stand against Germany during the 1905–06 Moroccan crisis but, failing to win support, resigned.

Deledda, Grazia   (1871–1936) Italian novelist. Most of her novels, such as *Ashes* (1904) and *The Mother* (1920), are realistic treatments of peasant life in her native Sicily. She won the Nobel Prize in 1926.

Delescluze, Louis Charles   (1809–71) French journalist and radical republican. Active in the revolutions of 1830 and 1848, he was deeply opposed to the Second Empire of Napoleon III. A member of the *Commune of Paris, he was shot at the barricades.

Delft   52 01N 4 21E A city in the W Netherlands, in South Holland province. William the Silent was murdered here in 1584. Since the late 16th century it has been famous for its pottery and porcelain known as delftware. Population (1981 est): 84,129.

Delian League   A confederacy of Greek city states formed in 478 BC during the *Greek-Persian Wars under the leadership of Athens. Members met on the sacred island of Delos, voted on policy, and contributed funds assessed by *Aristides. After the peace between Greece and Persia (c. 450) Athens regarded its allies as subjects. The League treasury was moved to Athens and secession was punished as revolt. The League was disbanded after Athens' defeat (404) in the Peloponnesian War but was revived in defense against Sparta in 378, lasting until the defeat (338) of Athens and Thebes at *Chaeronea.

Delian problem   The problem of constructing a cube that has twice the volume of a given cube. Also known as the duplication of the cube, it was first set by the oracle of Delos in the 5th century BC as a condition for ending a plague. The problem cannot be solved by ruler and compass alone, a fact not recognized until the 19th century.

Delibes, Leo   (1836–91) French composer, a pupil of Adolphe Adam. Early in his career he wrote a number of operas and operettas. In 1863 he became accompanist at the Paris Opéra and, later, second chorus master. His best-known works are the ballets *Coppélia* (1870) and *Sylvia* (1876).

deliquescence   The process in which some crystalline substances, such as calcium chloride ($CaCl_2$), absorb water from the atmosphere to such an extent that they dissolve; this is extreme hygroscopic (water-attracting) behavior. Deliquescent substances are used in several industries to provide dry atmospheres.

delirium   An acute state of mental disturbance in which the patient has hallucinations and delusions and is incoherent, agitated, and restless. It is most commonly associated with a high fever, particularly in children, although it may also be due to a variety of metabolic disorders. It also occurs in association with alcoholic poisoning and with alcohol withdrawal, when it is called **delirium tremens**. It can also be caused by intoxication with other drugs.

Delius, Frederick   (1862–1934) British composer of German descent. After an abortive business career, he went to live in Florida and subsequently made his home at Grez-sur-Loing, near Paris. Largely self-taught, he was influenced by Debussy and Grieg. His works include *Paris, the Song of a Great City* (1899), *Appalachia* (for orchestra and chorus; 1902), *On Hearing the First Cuckoo in Spring* (1912), and *North Country Sketches* (1913–14). He also wrote four operas, four concertos, chamber music, choral works, and songs. Delius became blind in 1925 but continued to compose with the help of his aide, Eric Fenby.

Della Robbia, Luca   (1400–82) Florentine Renaissance sculptor. Working first in marble, Luca produced the *Cantoria* (1431–38), his famous relief depicting singers, musicians, and dancers, for the Duomo, Florence. Subsequently he specialized in enameled terracotta sculptures, the glazing process being his own invention. Their production was carried on by his nephew **Andrea della Robbia** (1435–1525) and Luca's sons **Giovanni della Robbia** (1469–c. 1529) and **Girolamo della Robbia** (1488–1566).

Delorme, Philibert   (?1510–70) French architect of the Renaissance. Influenced by classical architecture, which he studied in Rome in the 1530s, his buildings include the Château d'Anet (c. 1552), designed for Diane de Poitiers, and the palace of the Tuileries (1580). He also wrote two treatises on architecture (1561, 1568).

Delos   (Modern Greek name: Dhílos)   37 23N 25 15E A Greek island in the S Aegean Sea, one of the Cyclades. It was of great importance in antiquity (*see* Delian League), and many ancient temples and other buildings, an altar built of the horns of sacrificed animals, and nine marble lions have been excavated here. Area: 1 sq mi (3 sq km).

Delphi   A village in central Greece. In antiquity, it was the principal sanctuary and oracle of *Apollo. The sacred enclosure, still an imposing sight, is set in spectacular mountain scenery. It contained Apollo's temple, "treasuries" where the Greek states stored their offerings, a theater, and over 3000 statues. A stadium for the *Pythian Games, a gymnasium, and other shrines stood nearby. The oracle's advice about religion, morality, commerce, and colonial projects, interpreted from the trance utterances of a priestess, was eagerly sought by individuals and states. As traditional beliefs declined after the 4th century BC the oracle lost influence. It was closed by the Christian emperor Theodosius (390 AD).

Delphinium   A genus of annual or perennial herbs (250 species), also called larkspur, up to 7 ft (2 m) high with tall spikes of deep-blue flowers and divided leaves. Delphiniums, native to the N hemisphere, are popular garden plants. Cultivated varieties usually range from 12 to 71 in (30 to 180 cm) high and have single or double flowers in shades of blue, pink, purple, or white. Family: *Ranunculaceae*.

delta   A large fan-shaped accumulation of sediment deposited at the mouth of a river, where it discharges into a sea or lake. It forms when the river's flow is slowed down on meeting the comparatively static sea or lake, resulting in a reduction of the river's load-bearing capacity. Clay particles also coagulate on meeting salt water and are deposited. The river is increasingly divided by the deposition into channels. Being fertile, deltas (such as the Nile Delta) are often extensively cultivated but are also prone to flooding.

Delvaux, Paul   (1897–) Belgian painter, who joined the surrealist group in 1935. Influenced by *Magritte and de *Chirico, he specialized in scenes of trancelike nudes and half-clothed women in impressive architectural settings.

demand   The quantity of goods or services that consumers wish to buy. Demand can be elastic (when a small change in price causes a large change in the demand), inelastic (a large change in price results in a small change in demand), or of unitary elasticity (a change in price leads to a proportional demand). The elasticity of demand influences government policy in deciding on which goods to levy a *sales tax.

Demerara River A river in E Guyana, flowing N to enter the Atlantic Ocean at Georgetown. Length: 215 mi (346 km).

Demeter A Greek corn goddess and mother goddess, sister of *Zeus. She was worshipped at Eleusis, whose people, it was said, had aided her in her search for her daughter *Persephone, abducted to the underworld. In gratitude she instructed them in agriculture and religion (*see* Eleusinian Mysteries). She was identified with the Roman goddess Ceres.

de Mille, Cecil B(lount) (1881–1959) US film producer and director. His best-known films were epic productions involving spectacular crowd scenes and special effects. Many of these were based on biblical themes, notably *The Ten Commandments* (1923; remade 1956), *The King of Kings* (1927), and *Samson and Delilah* (1949). His niece **Agnes de Mille** (1909–) is a ballet dancer and choreographer. American themes and traditions were a distinctive feature of her ballets, as in *Rodeo* (1942), choreographed for the Ballets Russes in Monte Carlo. She also choreographed for films and musicals, notably *Oklahoma!* (1943), *Carousel* (1945), and *Paint Your Wagon* (1951). Her autobiographical writings include *Dance to the Piper* (1952) and *Speak to Me, Dance with Me* (1973).

democracy A form of government in which people either rule themselves (direct democracy), as in ancient Athens, or elect representatives to rule in their interests (indirect democracy), as in most modern democracies. Elections, to be democratic, must be held regularly, be secret, and provide a choice of candidates; the elected assembly must also be free to legislate and to criticize government policy. Modern democratic ideas stem from 18th-century *utilitarianism and current debate centers on the elitist theory of democracy—that modern democratic government is by a political elite, which although voted into power invites little participation by the electorate.

Democratic Party One of the two major political parties in the US. Originally founded as the *Democratic Republican Party by Thomas *Jefferson in 1792, it opposed the encroachment of the federal government on the rights of the states and individuals. Under the leadership of Jefferson, James *Madison, and James *Monroe, the party effectively destroyed the power of the *Federalists. During the administration of Andrew *Jackson, it became known as the Democratic Party and began to support the power of the federal government as a means of protecting individual rights and interests. In 1860, just before the *Civil War, the Democrats split over the issue of *slavery into northern and southern factions and the party, dominated by southern Democrats, was eclipsed until regaining northern support in the 1880s. The party gained strength under the administration of Woodrow *Wilson and with the New Deal programs of Franklin *Roosevelt in the 1930s, the Democrats enjoyed the strong support of minorities and organized labor. The policies of Presidents John *Kennedy and Lyndon *Johnson reinforced the party's commitment to civil rights and social legislation.

Democratic Republican Party US political party in the early 1800s. It was the party of Thomas *Jefferson, James *Madison, and James *Monroe and, previously, had been the *Anti-Federalist Party. It opposed a strong federal government and advocated states' rights, strict interpretation of the Constitution, and social reforms at the local level.

Democratic Republicans (Jacksonian) US political party, a faction of the Democratic Republican Party that supported Andrew *Jackson for the presidency. Its members believed in a strong federal government. By Jackson's first term (1829–33) it had become known as the Democratic Party.

Democritus (c. 460–370 BC), Greek philosopher and scientist, born at Abdera (Thrace). He developed the first materialist theory of nature. His *atomism, developed from *Leucippus, considered that all matter consists of minute particles—atoms—the multifarious arrangement of which accounts for different properties of matter apparent to our senses. Democritus wrote also on cosmology, biology, perception, and music. His ethical theory foreshadowed *Epicureanism in valuing spiritual tranquility most highly. Of his works, many fragments, but nothing complete, survives.

demography A branch of the social sciences concerned with the statistical study of the sizes, distribution, and composition of human populations. The subject also includes collecting and analyzing birth, death, and marriage rates for whole populations or groups within them. Demography is primarily a branch of sociology but it also overlaps with such diverse fields as economics, mathematics, geography, and genetics.

demoiselle An elegant *crane, *Anthropoides virgo*, of dry grassy regions of central Europe and Asia. It is smoky gray in color with a black head and neck, long black breast feathers, and long white plumes behind each eye.

De Morgan, Augustus (1806–71) British mathematician and logician. De Morgan was one of the first to recognize that different *algebras may exist other than the one corresponding to the real numbers, which was then

taken to be the only algebra. He also encouraged and collaborated with George *Boole in the development of symbolic logic.

Demosthenes (384–322 BC) Athenian orator and statesman. Demosthenes attacked Philip of Macedon's imperial ambitions in Greece in a series of orations called the *Philippics* (351, 344, 341) and promoted an Athenian alliance with Thebes against Philip. This was defeated by Philip at *Chaeronea (338), whereby Macedonian supremacy in Greece was assured. After the death of Philip's son, Alexander the Great (323), Demosthenes again encouraged a Greek revolt. Condemned to death by Alexander's successors, Demosthenes fled Athens and committed suicide. His simple yet impassioned oratory was much admired in antiquity but his politics were anachronistic; the military power of Macedon could not be denied by even Demosthenes' oratory.

demotic script A form of Egyptian hieroglyphic writing. Pictorial hieroglyphics became less realistic and increasingly cursive from about 2500 BC until in the 7th century BC they developed into the cursive script called demotic. This continued in common use until the 5th century AD. *See also* Rosetta Stone.

JACK DEMPSEY

Dempsey, Jack (William Harrison D.; 1895–1983) US boxer, who was world heavyweight champion from 1919 to 1926. Renowned for his persistence and ferocious punching, he attracted enormous audiences and gate money. He lost his title to Gene Tunney (1897–1978).

dendrite. *See* neuron.

dendrochronology (*or* tree-ring dating) An archeological dating technique based on the *annual rings of trees. Variations in ring widths have been shown to correspond to rainfall and temperature variations and thus very old tree trunks can give a record of past climates. Any construction incorporating timber, for example buildings or ships, can be dated by comparing the timber-ring patterns with a specimen of known age.

dendrology. *See* tree.

Deneb An extremely luminous remote white supergiant star, apparent magnitude 1.25 and about 1600 light years distant, that is the brightest star in the constellation Cygnus.

dengue A tropical disease caused by a virus and characterized by painful joints, fever, and a rash. The virus is transmitted by the bite of a mosquito, and symptoms begin within a week after the bite. Dengue usually lasts for a week and is rarely fatal. There is no specific treatment.

Deng Xiao Ping (*or* Teng Hsiao-p'ing; 1904–) Chinese communist statesman; vice premier (1977–80) and vice chairman of the Central Committee of the Chinese Communist Party (1977–82). He held various prominent Party posts after the establishment of the People's Republic of China in 1949 until being dismissed during the *Cultural Revolution. In 1973 he was rehabilitated but was again dismissed three years later. Following his reinstatement in 1977 he exerted considerable influence on Chinese government and in 1978 made a state visit to the US.

Den Helder 52 58N 4 46E A port in the Netherlands, in North Holland province on the North Sea. It is an important naval and military base. Population (1977 est): 60,828.

denier A unit of weight, used to measure the fineness of woven materials, equal to 1 gram per 9000 meters.

Denikin, Anton Ivanovich (1872–1947) Russian general. After the Russian revolution (1917), he became commander of the *White Russian army, attempting to hold S Russia against the Bolsheviks. He occupied most of the Ukraine but internal divisions and Bolshevik counterattacks led to eventual defeat (1920). Denikin fled to France.

Denis, Maurice (1870–1943) French painter, designer, and art theorist, who was a leading member of the *Nabis. He was responsible for decorating many churches and his religious painting was influential on succeeding generations of religious artists. In 1919 he helped to found the Studios of Sacred Art, which also encouraged the revival of religious art.

Denis, St (3rd century) The patron saint of France. Of Italian birth, he was sent to Gaul as a missionary and there became the first Bishop of Paris. He was martyred under the Emperor Valerian. His shrine is in the Benedictine abbey at St Denis near Paris. Feast Day: Oct 9.

Denison 33 45N 96 33W A city in NE Texas. President Dwight D. Eisenhower was born here. Food processing is a major industry, and the manufacture of electrical equipment and furniture is also important. Population (1980): 23,884.

Denmark, Kingdom of (Danish name: Danmark) A country in N Europe, between the Baltic and the North Seas. It consists of the N section of the Jutland peninsula and about a hundred inhabited islands (chiefly Sjælland (Zealand) Fyn, Lolland, Falster, Langeland, and Bornholm). *Greenland and the *Faeroe Islands are also part of the Danish kingdom. The country is almost entirely flat with some slightly undulating land in the E of the mainland. *Economy*: agriculture, organized on a cooperative basis, is important both for the home and export markets, especially dairy produce and bacon. Since World War II, however, industry has dominated the economy, the main areas being engineering, chemicals, brewing, fishing, and food processing. Furniture, textiles, porcelain, metal goods, and glass are valued for their high-quality design. Its high volume of exports include meat and meat products, dairy produce, cereals, fish, machinery, and metals. *History*: Viking kingdoms occupied the area from the 8th century to the 10th century, when Denmark became a united Christian monarchy under Harald Bluetooth. His grandson, Canute, ruled over Denmark, Norway, and England, forming the Danish Empire, which was dissolved soon after his death. In 1363 Norway again came under the Danish crown by royal marriage. In 1397 Denmark and Norway joined with Sweden to form the Kalmar Union, which lasted until 1523. The Peace of Copenhagen (1660) concluded a long period of conflict between Denmark and Sweden. At this time it became an absolute monarchy, which continued until 1849, when a more liberal government was formed. Having supported Napoleon in the Napoleonic Wars, Denmark was compelled to cede Norway to Sweden by the Treaty of Kiel (1814). In the middle of the 19th century Denmark lost its S provinces of Schleswig, Holstein, and Lauenburg to Prussia, N Schleswig being returned (by plebiscite) in 1920. During World War II Denmark was occupied by Germany but a resistance movement grew in strength and aided the Allied victory. Iceland, which had previously been united with Denmark, became independent in 1944. A new constitution was formed in 1953, with a single-chamber parliament (elected by proportional representation) and executive power in the hands of the monarch through his ministers. In 1973 Denmark joined the EEC. Head of state: Queen Margrethe II (1940–   ). Prime minister: Poul Schluter (1929–   ). Official language: Danish. Official religion: Evangelical Lutheran. Official currency: krone of 100 øre. Area: 16,631 sq mi (43,074 sq km). Population (1983 est): 5,115,000. Capital and main port: Copenhagen.

Dennis v. United States US Supreme Court decision that ruled that the Smith Act (1940), which provided for criminal punishment of anyone teaching, advocating, or encouraging violent overthrow of the government, was constitutional. Members of the US Communist Party appealed their conviction under this law, but the conviction was upheld by the Court, which felt they constituted a "clear and present danger."

density The mass of unit volume of a substance. In *SI units it is measured in kilograms per cubic meter; in these units water has a density of 1000 kg m⁻³. **Relative density** (formerly called "specific gravity") is the density of a substance divided by the density of water at 4°C. This value is numerically one thousandth of the density. In the c.g.s. system, density (in grams per cubic centimeter) is numerically equal to relative density. The density of a gas (vapor density) is often expressed as the mass of unit volume of the gas divided by the mass of the same volume of hydrogen at standard temperature and pressure.

dentistry The branch of medical science concerned with the care of the teeth, gums, and mouth. Scientific dentistry is a relatively recent development—the first dental school was established in Philadelphia in 1840 and the first European school was the Royal Dental Hospital, founded in London in 1858. Modern dentistry includes a number of specialties. Restorative dentistry is concerned with the repair of teeth damaged by *caries and the replacement of teeth lost through injury or extraction. Orthodontics deals with the correction of badly positioned teeth, usually by means of braces or other appliances but sometimes by surgery on the jaw. Periodontics includes the care of the gums and other structures supporting the teeth and the treatment of the diseases affecting them (*see* periodontal disease). Oral surgery deals not only with the extraction of teeth but also with the surgical repair of fractures or abnormalities of the jaws and facial bones. Preventive dentistry is an important branch, concerned with preventing tooth decay and gum disease by such measures as education in oral hygiene and *fluoridation of the public water supply.

Dent du Midi 46 11N 6 55E A massif in SW Switzerland, in the Alps. It rises to 10,692 ft (3259 m) at Haute Cime.

Denver 39 45N 105 00W The capital city of Colorado, on the South Platte River. Founded in 1858 during the Colorado gold rush, Denver is the financial, administrative, and industrial center for a large agricultural area. A US Mint is sited here and it is within easy reach of 12 national parks. Population (1980): 491,396.

deodar A *cedar, *Cedrus deodara*, native to the Himalayas, where it forms vast forests, and widely planted for ornament in temperate regions and for timber in S Europe. Reaching a height of 245 ft (75 m) in the wild, it is distinguished from other cedars by its young branches, which droop down, and by its large barrel-shaped cones, up to 6 in (14 cm) long.

d'Éon, Charles de Beaumont, Chevalier (1728–1810) French secret agent in the service of *Louis XV. His fondness for wearing women's clothes, both as a disguise and in normal life, led to wagers in society about his actual sex. He did nothing to prevent such speculation, which continued until the matter was resolved at the autopsy after his death in London.

deontology A system of *ethics in which duty, rather than rights, virtue, or happiness, is fundamental to morality. It was the title of a book by *Bentham. *Compare* teleology.

deoxyribonucleic acid. *See* DNA.

depreciation The loss in value of capital equipment as a result of wear and tear, obsolescence, etc. For example, a machine that costs $10,000 and is expected to last ten years depreciates at the rate of $1000 a year. To keep its stock of capital equipment, therefore, a firm must set aside a certain sum each year to account for depreciation. The calculation of the depreciation provision is sometimes complicated by the difficulty in judging the life of a machine: changes in taste or technological developments may shorten the useful life of a machine. To encourage firms to maintain their capital equipment, governments usually allow for depreciation when calculating corporation tax.

depression (economics) A period during the *trade cycle in which demand is low compared to industry's capacity to satisfy it. Profits, and therefore confidence and investment, are also correspondingly low (*see* accelerator principle). A depression is also characterized by high unemployment, as occurred in the 1930s (*see* Depression). The influence of the British economist J. M. *Keynes has led governments since World War II to adopt *deficit financing policies to counter depressions, but the advent in the 1970s of the previously unknown combination of depression and *inflation has led to a revival of interest in the rival doctrine of *monetarism. A depression is also called a slump.

depression (meteorology) A *cyclone in the midlatitudes; also called a low or a disturbance. Frequently accompanied by *fronts, depressions move toward the NE in the N hemisphere and toward the SE in the S hemisphere. They are characterized by unsettled weather and are the main source of rainfall in the lowland areas of the midlatitudes.

depression (psychiatry) Severe and persistent misery. It can be a normal reaction to distressing events, such as bereavement (reactive depression). Sometimes, however, it is out of all proportion to the situation or may have no apparent external cause (endogenous depression): it can then be a sign of mental illness. In *manic-depressive psychosis the depression is severe and leads the sufferer to despairing and guilty beliefs and even to delusions of being evil and worthless; sleep, appetite, and concentration can all be disturbed. In depressive neurosis the symptoms are less extreme but may still lead to *suicide. Treatment with *antidepressant drugs is often effective and psychotherapy is helpful. Severe cases may need *electroconvulsive therapy.

Depression, Great The period during the early 1930s when worldwide economic collapse precipitated commercial failure and mass unemployment. Beginning in the US with the stock market crash of October 1929, when share prices fell so disastrously that thousands were made bankrupt and the American banking system was severely shaken, the Depression caused serious economic problems throughout the world. International trade was severely affected, industrial production dropped, and millions were unemployed. In the US, President Herbert *Hoover was criticized for his handling of the economic crisis, and he was defeated by Franklin *Roosevelt in the 1932 election. Roosevelt's *New Deal brought Americans hope of recovery through the use of government funds for public works and social assistance programs. In Europe, however, the Depression caused continuing social unrest and in Germany contributed to the rise of *Hitler's Nazi movement. The Depression was finally ended by the outbreak of World War II and massive military spending by the industrialized nations.

Depretis, Agostino (1813–87) Italian statesman; prime minister (1876–78, 1878–79, 1881–87). At first a supporter of *Mazzini and opponent of *Cavour, Depretis became converted to constitutional monarchism in 1861. He headed several coalitions of moderate Left elements in parliament. His foreign policy contributed to the formation of the 1882 *Triple Alliance of Italy, Austria-Hungary, and Germany.

De Quincey, Thomas (1785–1859) British essayist and critic. In 1802 he ran away from his Manchester business family and then studied at Oxford; there he took opium for toothache and became addicted for life. He lived largely by journalism, writing numerous essays on diverse subjects. Among his friends were *Wordsworth and *Coleridge. His autobiographical *Confessions of an Opium Eater* first appeared in 1822 and was revised in 1856.

Derain, André (1880–1954) French postimpressionist painter. In his bold designs and vibrant colors, particularly in his Thames paintings (1905–06), he was initially a leading exponent of *fauvism, but after 1907 he came under the influence of *Cézanne and painted in a cubist manner. He later reverted to a traditional style after an intensive study of the Old Masters. He produced some notable scenery and costume designs for Diaghilev's *Ballets Russes.

Derby 52 55N 1 30W A city in central England. Its growth as a manufacturing center began in the late 17th century; the first silk mill in England was established here in 1719 and by the 18th century Derby had become a center of porcelain manufacture. Today Derby is an important engineering center (with Rolls-Royce engines). Fine porcelain (see Derby ware), electrical equipment, paints, and textiles are also manufactured. Population (1981): 215,736.

Derby, Edward (George Geoffrey Smith) Stanley, 4th Earl of (1799–1869) British statesman; Conservative prime minister (1852, 1858–59 1866–68). A noted orator, he became leader of the Conservative Party after the defection (1846) of the Peelites over the *Corn Laws. His government's achievements included the Jewish Relief Act (1858) and the *Reform Act (1867).

Derby ware Porcelain first produced by William Duesbury (1725–86) at Derby in the 1750s. Early manufactures resemble *Chelsea porcelain and Duesbury later bought the Chelsea works (1770). Utility products were decorated in bold blue, red, and gilt "Japan" patterns, but important portrait and fictional figures were also made in quantity. Leading artists decorated the fine dessert services with landscapes and specimen flora.

dermatitis Inflammation of the skin (the term eczema is often used synonymously with dermatitis). The patient has an itching red rash that may become scaly. Dermatitis may result from contact with irritant or allergy-provoking substances, infections, drugs, or radiation (particularly sunlight) or it may occur without obvious cause. Treatment is aimed at removing the cause and easing the condition with creams.

dermatology. See skin.

Dermot MacMurrough (?1110–71) King of Leinster. After being defeated by rival kings and banished (1166) from Ireland, he obtained aid from the English and with their support regained his kingdom in 1169–70. He has been unpopular with Irish nationalists ever since, for introducing the English into Ireland.

Derris A genus of tropical woody vines (80 species), especially *D. elliptica* of the East Indies, the roots of which contain rotenone, a useful insecticide. Family: *Leguminosae.

dervishes Members of Sufi religious brotherhoods (see Sufism), which hold various esoteric beliefs and have spread throughout Islam since the 12th century AD. Many of them perform ecstatic rituals, such as hypnotic chanting and whirling dancing, at prayer meetings (called *zikrs*). The dervishes of the Mevlevi order, founded in Anatolia (Turkey) in the 13th century, are famous for their dancing and are commonly called "whirling dervishes."

Desai, (Shri) Morarji (Ranchhodji) (1896–) Indian statesman; prime minister from 1977 until his resignation in 1979. As a young man he was a follower of Mahatma *Gandhi. Later, in the Congress Party, he came to oppose Indira Gandhi and during the state of emergency declared during her first administration he was imprisoned. In the 1977 elections he defeated her to become prime minister as leader of the new Janata Party.

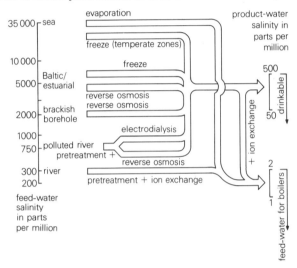

DESALINATION *The initial and final salinities for various desalination techniques and feed-water sources.*

desalination The removal of salt from brine to produce fresh water. Desalination is used to irrigate arid regions in which sea water is available, especially if solar power can be used as an energy source. Several methods are employed, the most common being evaporation of the sea water by heat or by reducing the pressure on it (flash evaporation). The vapor is condensed to form relatively pure water. Freezing is another technique; pure ice forms from brine as it freezes. The method theoretically requires less energy than evaporation but the process is slower and technically more difficult. Reverse *osmosis is another method used. Pure water and salt water are contained on either side of a permeable membrane. The pressure of the salt water is raised above the osmotic pressure, causing water to pass from the brine to the pure side. Because the osmotic pressure required is about 25 atmospheres there are difficulties with large-scale application.

In electrodialysis, the ions are subjected to an electric field instead of increased pressure, the positive and negative ions being filtered off through separate membranes. Another method used for low salinities is ion exchange; in this method the salt ions are chemically removed from the solution.

Descartes, René (1596–1650) French philosopher, one of the most original thinkers of all time. After a Jesuit education he spent nine years in travel and military service before turning to study. After 1628 he settled in Holland, where he lived until 1649, when Queen Christina invited him to Sweden. Here the cold climate and predawn tutorials with the queen caused a fatal attack of pneumonia.

Descartes' *Discourse on Method* (1637) introduced his technique of methodical doubt, which he developed in his greatest work the *Meditations* (1641). Asking "How and what do I know?" he arrived by a process of reduction at his famous statement "Cogito ergo sum" ("I think, therefore I am"). From this core of certainty he proceeded to prove to his own satisfaction God's existence (he was a sincere and lifelong Roman Catholic) and hence the existence of everything else. The importance of this approach lies not in what he proves or discards but in making *epistemology the gateway to knowledge. Equally influential was his dualism: he considered that the world was composed of two different kinds of substance—mind (*res cogitans*), which is the essence of human beings, and matter (*res extensa*). Descartes never satisfactorily answered the problem he thus set of how mind and matter can interact—nor has anyone else.

A distinguished mathematician and scientist, Descartes also contributed to the foundations of geometry (*see* coordinate systems) and optics. He held that mathematics was the supreme science in that the whole phenomenal world could be interpreted in terms of mathematical laws. He avoided confrontation with the Church by separating the realm of mathematics from that of theology and by cautiously suppressing his acceptance of the correctness of the Copernican system (*see* Copernicus).

descent The social recognition of biological relationship to a common ancestor. All societies limit the extent to which such relationships are traced but to differing degrees and in different ways. In many primitive societies the descent system is the basis of group membership, property and other rights, and social status. Unilineal systems count descent in one line only and are termed patrilineal or agnatic when this is through males and matrilineal or uxorial when through females. Double unilineal systems count both lines but for distinct purposes. Cognatic systems, usually found in more advanced societies, count descent in either line.

desensitization In immunology, a method of treating some *allergies, such as hay fever. Small amounts of the substance (allergen) that provokes the symptoms of the allergy are injected at intervals. This stimulates the production of *antibodies in the blood that will combine with the allergen during subsequent exposure and prevent it from reacting with a different set of antibodies, attached to certain cells, to cause the allergic symptoms.

desert A virtually barren area of land where precipitation is minimal and sporadic, limiting vegetation growth. The mean annual rainfall is usually taken as being below 10 in (250 mm) for desert conditions to exist. Deserts may occur in areas of high atmospheric pressure, such as the *Sahara, or near the W coast of continents cooled by cold ocean currents (e.g. the *Atacama and *Kalahari Deserts). They are also found in continental interiors where mountain barriers restrict precipitation, such as the *Gobi Desert. Many deserts are characterized by stony scrublands with occasional resistant rock uplands and some areas of shifting sand dunes. The wind is an important agent of erosion and the rain, falling as violent downpours, is capable of moving large amounts of debris.

Desert cultures A group of Stone Age North American cultures in Nevada, Utah, Arizona, and New Mexico dating from the period 8000–2000 BC. Adapted to arid or semiarid conditions, they were based upon hunting small game and gathering wild plant foods in small nomadic groups. Baskets, milling stones, bone tools, and chipped stone weapon points were made.

desert rat. *See* jerboa.

De Sica, Vittorio (1901–74) Italian film director. He started his career as an actor and began directing in 1940. His postwar films, in which he treated contemporary social themes with compassion and political awareness, included *Shoeshine* (1946), *Bicycle Thieves* (1948), and *Umberto D* (1952). His later films treated less controversial themes and included several romantic comedies.

Desiderio da Settignano (c. 1430–64) Italian Renaissance sculptor. Working chiefly in Florence, he specialized in marble portrait busts. His tomb for the humanist Carlo Marsuppini (Sta Croce, Florence) is renowned.

desman A small aquatic insectivorous mammal belonging to the family *Talpidae* (moles). The Russian desman (*Desmana moschata*) is about 8 in (20 cm) long; the Pyrenean desman (*Galemys pyrenaicus*) is smaller. They have webbed hind feet and partly webbed forefeet, live in burrows in river banks, and feed on invertebrates and fish.

Des Moines 41 35N 93 35W The capital city of Iowa. Founded in 1843, it has developed into an important industrial and commercial center situated in the heart of the Corn Belt. Many insurance companies have their headquarters here. Population (1980): 191,003.

Desmond, Gerald Fitzgerald, 15th Earl of (d. 1583) Anglo-Irish magnate, who opposed the increasing imposition of English authority on Ireland. Periodically imprisoned in the 1560s and 1570s, his 1579 rebellion led to his being outlawed. He was captured and killed.

Desmoulins, Camille (1760–94) French revolutionary and journalist. His fiery oratory contributed to the storming of the *Bastille (July 14, 1789), and in 1792 he became an unremitting critic of the Girondins. Subsequently counseling moderation, he was arrested with the followers of

*Danton in 1794 and guillotined. His best-known work is his *Histoire des Brissotins* (1793).

De Soto, Hernando (c. 1496–1542) Spanish explorer. Setting out from Spain in 1539 to conquer territory for the empire of *Charles V, De Soto landed with 600 men on the W coast of Florida at Tampa Bay and began extensive and destructive explorations in search of gold. Unsuccessful in finding the riches that he sought, in 1541 De Soto led his men up the Mississippi, becoming the first Europeans to explore the river. After progressing as far as the Arkansas River and exploring the region of modern Oklahoma, he died on the return journey.

des Prez, Josquin. *See* Josquin des Prez.

Dessalines, Jean Jacques (c. 1758–1806) Emperor of Haiti (1804–06). He rose to military pre-eminence in the slave revolt led by *Toussaint-L'Ouverture. When Toussaint was captured by the French in 1802 Dessalines assumed the leadership of the Haitians and with British help defeated the French (1803). His habitual cruelty as emperor provoked a palace revolution, during which he was assassinated.

Dessau 51 41N 12 14E A city in W central East Germany, on the Mulde River near its confluence with the Elbe River. Dessau was the former capital of Anhalt state. Many of its historic buildings were destroyed during World War II. Production of armaments, vehicles, and machinery are the main industries. Population (1980 est): 101,969.

destroyer A fast heavily armed naval vessel that is smaller than a *cruiser, has a displacement of about 3000 tons, and is 330–450 ft (110–150 m) long. Destroyers are not armored. Because of their speed, armament, and versatility, they are employed in antisubmarine warfare, in convoy work, and in "hunter-killer" attack groups consisting of one carrier and five or six destroyers.

destroyer escort A smaller lighter somewhat more maneuverable version of the *destroyer, developed during World War II mainly as protection for convoys.

Destutt, Antoine Louis Claude, Comte de Tracy (1754–1836) French philosopher and politician. He narrowly escaped the guillotine during the French Revolution. In prison he planned his *Éléments d'idéologie* (1801–15), in which, inspired by *Locke and *Condillac, he derives all thought from sensory "ideas" and their combinations.

detached retina A condition in which the retina—a layer of specialized light-sensitive cells at the back of the eye—becomes separated from the layer beneath it (the choroid). It happens slowly and painlessly and the patient loses part of his vision. It is caused by injury to the eye or inflammation in the eye and is most common in very near-sighted people. Detached retina is treated surgically, sometimes using a laser beam to weld the retina back into position.

DETECTIVE STORY *Sherlock Holmes, the famous English detective, with his companion Dr. John H. Watson (left).*

detective story A genre of popular fiction in which a mystery, often a murder, is solved by logic and intuition, usually by an individual detective. Ancient Chinese literature had a rich detective tradition, but in the modern West the first true detective story is probably *Poe's "Murders in the Rue

Morgue" (1841). The form was popularized in England by Wilkie *Collins's *The Moonstone* (1868) and the appearance of Sir Arthur Conan *Doyle's detective Sherlock Holmes. The English tradition is typified by Agatha *Christie and Dorothy L. *Sayers, whose first books appeared in the 1920s. In the 1930s the tersely realistic "thrillers" of the US writers Dashiell *Hammett and Raymond *Chandler began a different trend. Among the best writers of the genre are John Dickson Carr, Ellery Queen, Rex Stout, Josephine Tey, Michael Innes, and R. van Gulik. G. K. *Chesterton, "Nicholas Blake" (C. *Day Lewis), Nicholas Freeling, Georges *Simenon, Eric Ambler, Ross McDonald, Ian Fleming, and John Le Carré, among others, have raised it far above a merely popular level.

detergents Chemicals used for cleaning. Although the term includes *soaps it is usually applied in a more restricted sense to synthetic *surfactants. Such detergents have large molecules, typically composed of a hydrocarbon oil-soluble part and a water-soluble part. Alkyl sulfonates are common examples. These compounds are thus able to promote the solution of oil, grease, etc., in water. Household detergents contain other ingredients, including builders, water softeners, bleaches, and fabric brighteners.

determinant. *See* matrix.

determinism The philosophical theory that every event has a cause and that all events are determined by causal physical laws. One view holds that determinism means that every event could be causally explained and could be predicted if the conditions are not too complex for analysis. A stronger view is that a specific event could not have failed to happen, or was predetermined. Applied to human actions, determinism appears to conflict with the concept of *free will. If even desires, intentions, and motives are determined or conditioned (as some psychologists believe) and if actions are, in principle, predictable, this contradicts the idea that actions are freely chosen, and hence the concept of moral responsibility. However, some philosophers believe that determinism and free will are compatible and that a person acts freely if his desires are the cause of his actions. *See also* predestination.

Detmold 51 56N 08 52E A city in NW West Germany, in North Rhine-Westphalia. The capital of the former state of Lippe, it has two palaces. German tribes defeated the Romans here in 9 AD. It has furniture and metallurgical industries. Population (1971 est): 64,400.

detonator A sensitive primary explosive used to ignite a less sensitive high explosive. Detonators may be initiated by percussion, flash, or electrical current. The less sensitive and safer the high explosive is to handle, the stronger the detonator required. Some high explosives require two-stage detonation. A common detonator is mercury fulminate.

Detroit 42 23N 83 05W A city in Michigan, on the Detroit River. Founded in 1701, it was largely rebuilt following a fire in 1805. The fifth largest city in the US, it is dominated by the motor-vehicle industry, with General Motors, Ford, and Chrysler factories comprising 7100 industrial plants. A major port (serving the Great Lakes) and rail center, its other industries include chemicals, steel, and oil refining. It is the home of the University of Detroit (1911) and Wayne State University (1933). Population (1980): 1,203,339.

Deucalion In Greek legend, the son of Prometheus and father of Hellen, the ancestor of the Greek race. Warned of the flood sent by Zeus to destroy mankind, he and his wife Pyrrha survived on a boat and repopulated the earth.

Deus, João de (1830–96) Portuguese poet. His first book, *Flores do campo* (1868), was praised for its simplicity and directness; after the publication of *Campo de flores* (1893) he was acclaimed as the leading poet of his generation. His advanced method of teaching reading was officially adopted in 1888.

deus ex machina (Latin: god from the machinery) A sudden and improbable resolution of an involved situation. The term refers to the convention in ancient Greek drama in which a god was lowered by a crane to conclude a plot.

deuterium (D; *or* heavy hydrogen ^{2}H) An *isotope of *hydrogen having a nucleus consisting of one proton and one neutron. It occurs naturally in hydrogen to an extent of about 0.0156%. It can be separated from the more common isotope by electrolysis of water. It is used as a radioactive tracer. Heavy water (deuterium oxide; D_2O) is used in *nuclear reactors as a moderator. *See also* thermonuclear reactor. At no 1; at wt 2.014.

Deuteronomy The fifth book of the Old Testament, attributed to Moses, although this is widely disputed; it may have been compiled in the 7th century BC. It is a series of addresses by Moses to the Israelites immediately before the occupation of the Promised Land of Canaan (Palestine). After repeating the *Ten Commandments, he exhorts the people to live different-

ly from the surrounding nations, gives a code of religious and civil laws to be observed in Canaan, blesses those who keep the *covenant and curses those who disobey the Law, appoints Joshua as his successor, and gives custody of the book of the Law to the *Levites. The book closes with the song of Moses, his blessing of the people, and an appendix recording his death.

De Valera, Eamon (1882–1975) Irish statesman; prime minister (1932–48, 1951–54, 1957–59) and president (1959–73). A commandant in the 1916 *Easter Rising, he nevertheless escaped execution and in 1917 was elected to the British parliament and became the president of *Sinn Féin. From 1919 to 1922 he was president of the newly declared Irish Republic but rejected the terms of the Anglo-Irish treaty of 1921 (*see* Home Rule). In 1926 he founded *Fianna Fáil.

devaluation A downward change in the value of one country's currency in terms of other currencies. A country that devalues makes its exports cheaper and its imports more expensive; thus devaluation should help correct a *balance-of-payments deficit by increasing the volume of exports and decreasing the volume of imports. The measure is not always effective, however, because the increased import bill may be larger than the increase in receipts from exports: this is likely if the *demand for the country's exports is elastic, while demand for the imports is inelastic. Under the Bretton Woods fixed-rate system (*see* Bretton Woods Conference) devaluations only occurred occasionally but were large and destabilizing. In the floating-rate system that replaced it, the value of a currency in terms of others is determined by supply and demand with a minimum of government interference; as a consequence devaluations are gradual.

Devanagari An alphabetic *writing system used for *Sanskrit, *Hindi, and other languages of India. It has 48 letters and is written from left to right. Vowels are frequently omitted in Devanagari, a short *a* being understood after each consonant unless a different vowel is specified. It was developed from the ancient Brahmi script, which was probably derived from Aramaic in the 7th or 8th century BC. It is therefore historically related to the Hebrew, Arabic, Greek, and Roman alphabets.

developing countries Countries that do not have sophisticated industries and consequently have a low per capita income. They include almost all the countries in Africa, Asia, and South America. The economies of these so-called Third World countries are characterized by abundant cheap unskilled labor and a scarcity of capital for investment. Some observers consider the marked difference in incomes between the industrial and the developing nations (the "north–south split") to be politically as important as the division between *communism and *capitalism (the "east–west split"). Some 70% of the world's population lives in developing countries in largely agricultural economies from which poverty, hunger, disease, and illiteracy have not been eliminated, despite the efforts of various UN agencies. Many of these economies rely shakily on one main crop, which in years of crop failure, poor world demand, or low market prices can cause severe hardship.

Deventer 52 16N 6 10E A city in the E central Netherlands, in Overijssel province on the IJssel River. During the middle ages it was a major educational center; Erasmus and Thomas à Kempis studied here. Population (1981 est): 64,824.

Devil. *See* Lucifer.

devil ray. *See* manta ray.

devil's coach horse A large carnivorous beetle, *Staphylinus olens*, also called a cock-tail. It is about 1 in (25 mm) long and occurs commonly in gardens of W Europe. If threatened it curls its flexible abdomen upward and forward and releases an offensive odor. Family: *Staphylinidae* (*see* rove beetle).

Devil's Island (French name: Île du Diable) 5 16N 52 34W One of the three Îles du Salut, off the coast of French Guiana in the S Caribbean Sea. It contained a convicts' leper colony before becoming a French penal settlement (1895–1938). Area: less than 1 sq mi (2 sq km).

devolution The delegation of political powers from a central government to regional governments. For example, in the UK the establishment of a parliament in Northern Ireland was the first important act of devolution.

Devolution, War of (1667–68) The conflict between France and Spain for possession of the Spanish Netherlands, which *Louis XIV of France claimed had devolved (descended) to him through his wife Maria Theresa, daughter of Philip IV of Spain (1605–65; reigned 1621–65). Louis' troops, under *Turenne and *Vauban, invaded the Netherlands but were withdrawn when an alliance between England, the United Provinces of the

Netherlands, and Sweden threatened to intervene against the French. Peace was made at Aix-la-Chapelle.

Devon A county of SW England, bordering on the Atlantic Ocean in the N and the English Channel in the S. The chief rivers are the Dart, Exe, and Tamar. Agricultural activities include dairy farming and sheep farming. Industry is concentrated around Exeter and Plymouth, a major naval base. There is a thriving tourist industry centered on the coastal resorts. Area: 2591 sq mi (6715 sq km). Population (1981 est): 952,000. Administrative center: Exeter.

Devonian period A geological period of the Upper Paleozoic era, between the Silurian and Carboniferous periods. It lasted from about 415 to 370 million years ago. It is divided into seven stages, based on invertebrate fossil remains, such as corals, brachiopods, ammonoids, and crinoids. The rocks containing these fossils were marine deposits but the Devonian period also shows extensive continental deposits (Old Red Sandstone). Fossils from these rocks include fish, land plants, and freshwater mollusks.

De Voto, Bernard (Augustine) (1897–1955) US writer, teacher, and historian. After teaching at Northwestern University (1922–27) and Harvard University (1929–36), he was an editor for the *Saturday Review of Literature* (1936–38) and wrote (1935–55) for *Harpers* magazine. He edited *Mark Twain in Eruption* (1940) and *The Journals of Lewis and Clark* (1953) and wrote *Mark Twain's America* (1932), *Mark Twain at Work* (1942), *Across the Wide Missouri* (1947; Pulitzer Prize, 1948), and *The Course of Empire* (1952). He was also a novelist; his novels include *The Crooked Mile* (1924), *The Chariot of Fire* (1926), *The House of Sun-Goes-Down* (1928), *We Accept with Pleasure* (1934), and *Mountain Time* (1947). He wrote thrillers under the pseudonym "John August."

de Vries, Hugo Marie (1848–1935) Dutch botanist, who first recognized the importance of *mutation. De Vries observed how, occasionally, a new variety would arise from his plant-breeding experiments. It realized that this sudden variation, which he termed mutation, could play an important part in the evolution of living things. De Vries worked out his own laws of inheritance only to discover, in 1900, *Mendel's original work, which had previously been ignored.

dew The condensation of moisture, which forms on the ground or on objects near the ground, especially at night. It occurs when the cool air near the ground falls to a temperature, called the **dew point**, at which it becomes saturated and the water vapor present condenses into water droplets. The ideal conditions for dew formation are calm weather with a clear sky.

dewberry A straggling Eurasian shrub, *Rubus caesius*, very similar to the *blackberry but with weaker creeping stems and fewer prickles. The fruit has fewer berries per head and a purplish bloom. The name is also applied to many North American *Rubus* species that trail along the ground. Family: *Rosaceae*.

de Wet, Christian Rudolf (1854–1922) Afrikaner politician and soldier. De Wet commanded the Orange Free State forces in the second *Boer War, organizing the guerrilla tactics that were initially so successful. He was later minister of agriculture in the Orange Free State (1907–10). In 1914 he led a revolt against Botha's plan to conquer German South West Africa and was imprisoned for treason.

Dewey, George (1837–1917) US naval officer. He first saw active duty in various naval engagements during the *Civil War. He was promoted to the rank of commodore in 1896. At the time of the outbreak of the *Spanish-American War, Dewey was dispatched to the Philippines in command of the American fleet. His decisive victory over the Spanish fleet in Manila Bay won his national acclaim as one of the heroes of the war. In 1899 he was named Admiral of the Navy, a rank never before attained by an American officer.

Dewey, John (1859–1952) US philosopher and educator. Born in Burlington, Vermont and educated at the University of Vermont and Johns Hopkins University, Dewey became one of the most prominent advocates of philosophical *pragmatism. As chairman of the philosophy department of the University of Chicago and director of its School of Education (1894–1904), he was among the first to experiment with modern teaching methods. He later became a professor at Columbia University (1904–30), where he developed the theory of "instrumentalism," by which he believed that education must equip students to deal with the practical problems they would confront in later life. In works such as *Reconstruction in Philosophy* (1920), *Experience and Nature* (1925), and *Experience and Education* (1938), Dewey held that philosophy must constantly confront changing conditions and produce appreciate new solutions and beliefs.

Dewey, Melvil (1851–1931) US librarian, creator of the Dewey Decimal System for classification of books. He worked as a librarian at Amherst College, his alma mater, from 1874, and it is here that he first introduced

his system of classification. Librarian (1883–88) at Columbia University, he initiated a school for librarians and brought it to Albany, New York, when he became director of the New York State Library (1888–1906). He was a founder of the American Library Association (1876) and helped to establish *Library Journal*.

Dewey, Thomas E(dmund) 1902–71) US lawyer and politician; governor of New York (1943–55). After graduating from Columbia University Law School in 1925, he worked as an assistant US attorney in New York (1931–33) before becoming a US attorney himself. By 1935 he had been appointed a special prosecutor and launched a campaign to destroy the crime syndicate in New York; his successful prosecutions led to his election as New York City's district attorney (1937). He served as the Republican governor or New York (1943–55), working to develop and expand the highway and welfare systems and to eliminate discriminatory practices in employment and housing. He ran unsuccessfully for president in 1944 and 1948.

Dewey Decimal Classification An international system for classifying and arranging the books in a library, originated in 1873 by the US librarian Melvil Dewey (1851–1931) for the Amherst College Library. Books are divided according to subject matter into ten groups, each group having a hundred numbers; principle subdivisions within each group are divided by ten, and with the use of decimal numbers further subdivisions can be generated without limit (e.g. 300: Social Sciences; 370: Education; 372: Elementary Education; 372.3: Elementary Education, Science and Health). The system is being constantly revised and is now in its 18th edition. *See also* Universal Decimal Classification.

dextrose. *See* glucose.

Dhahran 26 18N 50 05E A new town in E Saudi Arabia, on the Persian Gulf coast opposite Bahrain. It ships out oil brought by pipeline from the Abqaiq area just inland.

Dhaka. *See* Dacca.

dharma A Sanskrit term with various religious and philosophical meanings. In Buddhism it signifies the truth, the teaching of the Buddha in whole or in part. It also denotes the law regarding the ultimate nature of things. In Hinduism, it refers to social law or caste duty.

Dharmashastra Traditional Indian lawbooks, still in force. Written in Sanskrit, they comprise some 5000 works, compilations of maxims, treatises, and commentaries. Their composition extended from the 8th century BC to the 19th century AD and is said to be based on the *Vedas. Their emphasis is on outlining the ethical behavior proper to one's caste in any given situation, rather than pronouncing definitive legislation; when properly applied, however, they did act as a valid legal system. British influence hardened and regularized the application of the law and introduced the concept of legal precedent. Since 1955 conventional legislation has been introduced to modify the dharmashastra law as applied by the courts and its importance is diminishing.

Dhaulagiri, Mount 28 39N 83 28E A mountain in NW central Nepal, in the Himalayas. It was first climbed in 1960 by a Swiss team. Height: 26,810 ft (8172 m).

dhole A wild *dog, *Cuon alpinus*, of SE Asia, Sumatra, and Java. Dholes are reddish brown, about 4.5 ft (1.4 m) long including the tail (16 in [40 cm]); they hunt in packs of 5–40 individuals, attacking mainly deer and antelope but occasionally even tigers.

diabase (or dolerite) A dark-colored hypabyssal igneous rock, the medium-grained equivalent of gabbros, occurring mainly as dykes, sills, and plugs. It contains calcic plagioclase feldspar and augite, and sometimes olivine, hypersthene, quartz, or feldspathoids.

diabetes One of several diseases with a common symptom—the production of large quantities of urine. The term usually refers to **diabetes mellitus** (or sugar diabetes), in which the body is unable to utilize sugars to produce energy due to a deficiency of the pancreatic hormone *insulin. Symptoms include thirst, weight loss, and a high level of glucose in the urine and in the blood (hyperglycemia), which—if untreated—leads to coma. Possible long-term complications of diabetes include damage to the arteries, especially in the eyes (which can affect vision). There appears to be a certain tendency to inherit diabetes, which is often triggered by such factors as physical stress. In children the disease appears more suddenly and is usually more severe than in older people. Treatment is based on a carefully controlled diet, often with insulin injections or pills to reduce the amount of sugar in the blood.

Diabetes insipidus is a rare disease due to a deficiency of the pituitary hormone vasopressin, which regulates water balance in the body. The patient produces large quantities of watery urine and is always thirsty. It is treated with doses of the hormone.

Diaghilev, Sergei (Pavlovich) (1872–1929) Russian ballet impresario. He began his career in the imperial theaters in St Petersburg in 1899 and between 1904 and 1908 organized several art exhibitions there and in Paris. His first theatrical production, the opera *Boris Godunov*, staged at the Paris Opéra (1908), was followed by his season of Russian ballet (1909). Its outstanding success resulted in the organization of a permanent company (1911), the *Ballets Russes, which Diaghilev directed until his death. □Cocteau, Jean.

dialect The language of a particular district or group of people. The distinction between language and dialect is not clear cut. As a general rule any two dialects of a language may be expected to be mutually comprehensible. But, for example, the various "dialects" of Chinese are quite separate, being held together only by a common ideographic writing system, while Dutch, Flemish, and Afrikaans are called separate languages for political reasons, although there is a considerable degree of mutual comprehensibility and they might therefore reasonably be regarded as different dialects of the same language. Dialects develop as a result of geographical separation: slightly differing versions of one original language develop in different places within a generation or so of the time of separation. Social factors also affect dialect development. In English, for example, the medieval dialect of London has developed into a socially prestigious class dialect spoken in most parts of Britain (*see* received pronunciation). *See also* idiolect.

dialectical materialism The official philosophy of *Marxism. Materialism, as opposed to *idealism, Marx and Engels derived from contemporary (1850) science; dialectic, or argument from thesis and antithesis to synthesis, they borrowed from Hegel's idealism. Engels even proposed a dialectical theory of evolution. As philosophy, not surprisingly, dialectical materialism is obscure and apparently unrelated to Marxist political theory. However, **historical materialism**, expounded in the *Communist Manifesto*, is a coherent account of history on an economic basis: for every system of production there is an appropriate organization of class and property. While economic forces continually develop production systems, the class and property structure remains unchanged, causing tension between economic forces and social relations, which continues until the ultimate rational socialist society evolves.

dialysis A process, discovered by Thomas Graham (1804–69), for separating mixtures of fluids by diffusion through a semipermeable membrane. Different substances in a solution diffuse at different rates. The passage of large particles, such as *colloids, is almost completely blocked by a semipermeable membrane, whereas salt solutions pass through easily. The technique of dialysis is used in artificial kidney machines, or dialyzers, which take over the function of diseased kidneys by filtering waste material from the blood but leaving behind proteins, blood cells, and other large particles.

diamagnetism A form of magnetism occurring in materials that when placed in a *magnetic field, have an internal field proportional to but less than that outside. Such substances tend to orientate themselves at right angles to the direction of the *flux and tend to move from the stronger part of a field to the weaker part. Diamagnetism is caused by the motion of atomic electrons, which, since they are charged, constitute a current. This current tends to oppose the magnetic field in accordance with *Lenz's law.

diamond The hardest known mineral, comprising a cubic variety of crystalline *carbon, formed under intense heat and pressure. Diamonds are found in ancient volcanic pipes, mainly in S Africa and Siberia, and in deposits off the coast of Namibia. Over 80% of diamonds mined are used industrially, mainly for cutting and grinding tools; the others are used as gems. The largest diamond yet discovered is the *Cullinan diamond (3106 carats), found in 1905 at Pretoria. Many industrial diamonds are produced synthetically from graphite subjected to very high temperatures and pressures (above 1697°F [3000°C] and 100,000 atmospheres). Birthstone for April.

diamondback The largest and most dangerous *rattlesnake. The eastern diamondback (*Crotalus adamanteus*) and the western diamondback (*C. atrox*) may reach lengths of 6 ft (2.5 m).

diamondbird An Australasian *flowerpecker of the genus *Pardalotus* (7–8 species), about 3 in (8 cm) long with a short tail and a white-spotted plumage. Unlike other flowerpeckers, diamondbirds feed on insects and nest in tree holes and rock crevices.

Diamond Head 21 16N 157 49W An extinct volcanic crater on the S tip of the island of Oahu in NW Hawaii. Rising 761 ft (232 m) above the Pacific Ocean, it overlooks Waikiki Beach.

Diana The Roman goddess identified with the Greek Artemis, associated with women and childbirth and with the moon. She is usually represented as a virgin huntress armed with bow and arrows. The position of priest at her shrine of Ariccia (Italy) was customarily held by a runaway slave, who murdered his predecessor.

Diane de Poitiers, Duchesse de Valentinois (1499–1566) The mistress of *Henry II of France, who was 20 years her junior. She dominated court life until his death in 1559, when she was forced by Henry's wife *Catherine de' Medici to retire to Chaumont.

Dianthus A genus of annual and perennial herbs (300 species), mainly from Europe and Asia, having flower stems (often branched) with swollen joints and showy white, pink, or red flowers. Common species include *D. barbatus* (*see* sweet william), *D. caryophyllus* (*see* carnation), and *D. plumarius* (*see* pink). Family: *Caryophyllaceae*.

diaphragm 1. In anatomy, a dome-shaped sheet of muscle that separates the thorax (chest cavity) from the abdomen. The diaphragm is attached to the spine, lower ribs, and breastbone and contains a large opening through which the esophagus (gullet) passes. It plays an important role in producing breathing movements (*see* respiration). 2. *See* contraception.

diarrhea The frequent passing of liquid stools, usually more than three a day. It is a symptom, not a disease; causes include anxiety, allergy, infection or inflammation of the intestines, impaired absorption of food, and side effects of drugs. It can be eased by the use of drugs but proper treatment must aim at eliminating the cause.

Dias, Bartolomeu (c. 1450–c. 1500) Portuguese navigator. In 1486, given command of three ships by John II, he set out to explore the coast of Africa. Blown by a storm around the Cape of Good Hope (which he himself named the Cape of Storms) he reached present-day Algoa Bay on the E coast of Africa but was forced by his unwilling crew to return. He was drowned near the Cape while accompanying *Cabral on the expedition that discovered Brazil.

diaspora (Greek: dispersion) The collective term for Jewish communities outside the land of Israel. Beginning with the *Babylonian exile (6th century BC), Jews spread to most parts of the world, while continuing to regard Israel as their homeland. The resulting tension between Israel and the diaspora has continued to the present day, the dispersion being viewed sometimes negatively, as exile, and sometimes positively. The most important centers of the diaspora were, in antiquity, Babylonia and Egypt; in the middle ages, Spain and France; and in early modern times, E Europe. In the late 19th century there was a massive exodus of Jews from Russia and Poland, and the Nazi *holocaust destroyed many old European communities. The main center is now the US, with some six million Jews.

diastole. *See* blood pressure; heart.

diastrophism The large-scale deformation of the earth's crust resulting in the major structural features of the earth's surface, such as the continents, ocean basins, mountain ranges, fault-lines, etc. It is now widely believed that *sea-floor spreading and the consequent movement of the rigid plates that form the earth's crust (*see* plate tectonics) are responsible for diastrophism.

diathermy The production of heat in the body's tissues by means of a high-frequency electric current passing between two electrodes applied to the patient's skin. It has been used to relieve deep-seated pain in rheumatic conditions. The principle has also been utilized in surgery, one electrode, in the form of a knife, snare, or needle, being used to coagulate blood and therefore seal off blood vessels during incisions or to destroy unwanted tissue.

diatoms Microscopic *yellow-green algae of the class *Bacillariophyceae* (about 16,000 species), occurring abundantly as single cells or colonies in fresh water and oceans (forming an important constituent of *plankton) and also in soil. They have silicon-rich cell walls (called frustules), often beautifully sculptured, composed of two halves that fit together like a pill box. Fossilized frustules form a porous rock called diatomaceous earth (*or* kieselguhr), used in filters, insulators, abrasives, etc.

Díaz, Porfirio (1830–1915) Mexican soldier, who became president (1876–1911) following a coup. He ruled dictatorially, supported by conservative landowners and foreign capitalists. His promotion of economic development benefited only a small elite and no attention was paid to the needs of the Indians. He fled the country in 1911 in the face of a revolution led by Francisco Madero (1873–1913).

diazepam. *See* benzodiazepines.

Dicentra A genus of annual and perennial herbaceous plants (about 300 species) from North America and E Asia, up to 35 in (90 cm) high. They have divided compound leaves and sprays of hanging flowers that are flattened sideways, with the outer petals pouched and the inner ones joined at the tips. Many species are ornamentals (*see* bleeding heart; Dutchman's breeches). Family: *Fumariaceae*.

CHARLES DICKENS *The author with his daughters.*

Dickens, Charles (1812–70) British novelist. Son of a naval clerk, he worked in a factory when his father was imprisoned for debt and later as a solicitor's clerk and court reporter. He began his writing career by contributing to popular magazines, achieving sudden fame with *The Pickwick Papers* (1837), which he followed with *Oliver Twist* (1838) and *Nicholas Nickleby* (1839) and the very successful *Old Curiosity Shop* (1840–41); like all his novels, these first appeared in monthly installments. In the 1840s he traveled abroad, visiting the US in 1842. After 1843, with *The Christmas Carol*, he published many Christmas stories. *David Copperfield* (1849–50) was a strongly autobiographical work, portraying Dickens' father as the feckless Mr Micawber. His later novels, from *Bleak House* (1853) to the incomplete *Edwin Drood* (1870), were increasingly pessimistic in tone; *Great Expectations* (1860–61) and *Our Mutual Friend* (1864–65), in their depiction of the destructive powers of money and ambition, develop most fully Dickens' radical view of society. Although Dickens' marriage was an unhappy one, it produced ten children. In 1856 he and his wife agreed to separate. He formed a relationship with Ellen Ternan, a young actress. In 1858 he began his famous public readings from his work, the strain of which hastened his death.

Dickey, James (1923–   ) US poet and novelist. A pilot during World War II, he wrote of his experiences in his poetry. His poems are collected in *Into the Stone and Other Poems* (1960), *Drowning with Others* (1962), *Helmuts* (1964), *Buckdancer's Choice* (1965; National Book Award, 1966), *The Zodiac* (1976), *The Strength of Fields* (1979), and *Puella* (1982). He also wrote a novel, *Deliverance* (1969), which was made into a movie (1972).

Dickinson, Emily (1830–86) US poet. Daughter of a Calvinist lawyer, she lived a largely secluded life after the age of 30, with her family at Amherst, Mass. She wrote numerous letters and over 1700 poems, mostly brief intense lyrics on themes of love, death, and nature; only seven were published during her lifetime.

dicotyledons The larger of the two main groups of flowering plants, which includes hardwood trees, shrubs, and many herbaceous plants (*compare* monocotyledons). Dicots are characterized by having two seed leaves (cotyledons) in the embryo. Typically the flower parts are arranged in fours or fives (or multiples of these) and the leaves have a netlike pattern of veins. *See also* angiosperms.

dictionaries. *See* lexicography.

Dicynodon A large herbivorous *therapsid (mammal-like) reptile that lived in the late Permian period, which ended 240 million years ago. It occurred worldwide in large numbers and had a long high-domed skull with a horny beaklike jaw and a single upper pair of teeth.

Diderot, Denis (1713–84) French philosopher and writer. With *Voltaire, Diderot helped create the *Enlightenment, mainly through the *Encyclopédie*, which he edited after 1750 (*see* Encyclopedists). Fascinated by science, he developed a form of *pantheism. His writings, notably *Lettre sur les aveugles* (1749), were materialistic and anti-Christian in tenor.

didgeridoo An aboriginal musical instrument, consisting of a wooden tube three to four feet long, sounded by blowing across one of the open ends. The other rests against a hole in the ground to increase resonance. It plays two notes: the fundamental, used to set up a basic rhythm, and a harmonic, used in counterrhythm against it.

Dido In Greek legend, the daughter of a king of Tyre, who fled to Africa when her husband was murdered; there she founded *Carthage. According to legend she burned herself to death on a funeral pyre to avoid marriage to Iarvas of Numidia; in *Virgil's *Aeneid* she killed herself after being abandoned by her lover *Aeneas.

Diefenbaker, John G(eorge) (1895–1979) Canadian statesman; Progressive Conservative prime minister (1957–63). His party's victory in 1957 broke 22 years of Liberal government and in 1958 the Conservatives gained an overwhelming majority (208 out of 256 seats). He lost the 1963 election following opposition to proposals to build nuclear weapons in Canada and resigned the party leadership in 1967.

dielectric A substance that acts as an electrical *insulator and can sustain an electric field. When a voltage is applied across a perfect dielectric there is no energy loss and the electric field strength changes simultaneously with voltage. In the real dielectrics, such as air, ceramics, or wax, which are used in *capacitors, there is always a small energy loss.

dielectric constant. *See* permittivity.

Diels, Otto Paul Hermann (1876–1954) German chemist, who shared the 1950 Nobel Prize with Kurt Alder (1902–58) for their discovery of the **Diels-Alder reaction**, by which linear organic molcules are converted into cyclic molecules. The reaction is now widely used in the synthesis of alkaloids, polymers, etc.

Dieman, Anthony van (1593–1645) Dutch colonial administrator. As governor general of Batavia from 1636, he was responsible for the conquest of Malacca (1641) and parts of Ceylon (1644) important to the spice trade. He also commissioned *Tasman to explore the S Pacific in the interest of trade (1642, 1644), expeditions that discovered Van Dieman's Land (now Tasmania).

Dien Bien Phu, Battle of (March–May, 1954) The decisive battle of the Indochina war, in NE Vietnam, in which Vietnamese forces defeated the French. The collapse of the French fortress coincided with the Geneva Conference, which ended French control of Indochina.

Dieppe 49 55N 1 05E A port and resort in N France, in the Seine-Maritime department on the English Channel. Occupied by the English (1420–35), it became a Huguenot stronghold but declined in importance after the revocation of the Edict of Nantes. It was the scene of heavy fighting during World War II. Population (1975): 26,111.

Diesel engine. *See* internal-combustion engine.

diet, imperial. *See* Reichstag.

dietetics The study of the principles of nutrition and their application to the selection of appropriate diets both to maintain health and as part of the treatment of certain diseases. A balanced diet should contain foods with adequate amounts of all the nutrients—carbohydrates, fats, proteins, minerals, and vitamins—as well as foods with a high content of dietary *fiber. An important aspect of the work of dieticians is to work out the special diets that are required for various diseases. Diabetes mellitus, for instance, requires a diet low in carbohydrate, whereas some liver diseases respond well to a low-protein diet. Obesity can be managed with a low-calorie diet.

Dietrich, Marlene (Maria Magdalene von Losch; 1904–   ) German film actress and singer. Her image of sultry beauty was developed by Josef von *Sternberg in such films as *The Blue Angel* (1930). In 1930 she went to Hollywood, where she made numerous films of varying quality, including *Shanghai Express* (1932), *Blonde Venus* (1932), *Destry Rides Again* (1939), and *Judgment at Nuremburg* (1961). In her later career she gave many cabaret performances.

diffraction The spreading or bending of light waves as they pass the edge of an object or pass through an aperture. The diffracted waves subsequently interfere with each other producing regions of alternately high and low intensity. This phenomenon, first discovered in 1665 by Francesco Grimaldi (1618–63), can be observed in the irregular boundary of a shadow of an object cast on a screen by a small light source. A similar effect occurs with sound waves. *See also* interference.

MARLENE DIETRICH *In* The Garden of Allah *(1936), with Sir C. Aubrey Smith (left) and Charles Boyer (right).*

diffusion 1. The mixing of different fluids, or the distribution of a substance from a region of high concentration to one of lower concentration, by means of the random thermal motion of its constituents. In gases, according to Graham's law (named for Thomas Graham; 1805–69), the rates at which gases diffuse are inversely proportional to their densities. Mixing of fluids is complete after a certain time unless one set of particles is sufficiently heavy for sedimentation to occur. Diffusion also occurs between certain solids; for example gold will slowly diffuse into lead. **2.** The scattering of a beam of radiation on reflection from a rough surface or on transmission through certain media. When diffusion occurs the laws of reflection and refraction are not obeyed.

diffusionism A theory claiming that all civilization and culture were transmitted from certain circumscribed areas of the ancient world and disregarding the possibility of independent invention and discovery. In its most extreme form it held that this original center was Egypt. Other schools believed that certain other centers were also important. Their ideas dominated *ethnology between 1910 and 1925 but are now mainly discredited.

Digby, Sir Kenelm (1603–65) English courtier and scientist. He entered James I's service in 1623 and led a privateering expedition against French ships in the Mediterranean Sea in 1627–28. A Roman Catholic, he was forced to leave England during the Civil War. He finally returned to England in 1654. A founder member of the Royal Society (1663), he discovered that plants need oxygen.

digestion The process by which food is converted into substances that can be absorbed by the *intestine. The process begins in the mouth, where the food is chewed and mixed with saliva, and continues with the action of digestive enzymes secreted by the *stomach, duodenum, and *pancreas. Rhythmic contractions of the muscular layer of the intestinal wall (called peristalsis) ensures a constant mixing of enzymes and food and the propulsion of food along the intestine. The products of digestion include amino acids, various sugars (such as lactose, maltose, and glucose), and fat molecules; these are absorbed by the intestine and conveyed to the bloodstream.

Diggers An English sect that flourished under the *Commonwealth, so called because of their attempts to dig common land. Led by Gerrard *Winstanley, the Diggers believed in the economic and social equality of men. In April, 1649, they established a community where they attempted to put into practice their beliefs in agrarian communism. The support they attracted alarmed the government and they were dispersed in March, 1650. *See also* Levellers.

digger wasp A solitary *wasp of the families *Sphercidae* or *Pompilidae* (*see* spider wasp). Digger wasps are black with yellow or orange markings. They burrow into wood, plant stems, or the ground to build nests, which they stock with insects, such as caterpillars, grasshoppers, and flies; these have been paralyzed to provide food for the developing larvae.

digital computer. *See* computer.

digitalis A crude drug prepared from the dried leaves of foxglove plants. Digitalis is purified to digoxin, digitoxin, and lanatoside C. These drugs are used to improve the action of a failing or inefficient heart and to reduce a dangerously fast heart rate. Side effects of digitalis compounds include nausea, vomiting, and pulse irregularities.

digital recording. *See* recording of sound.

Dijon 47 20N 5 02E A city in France, the capital of the Côte-d'Or department on the Burgundy Canal. The former capital of Burgundy, it is the site of the palace of the Dukes of Burgundy and has a cathedral (13th–14th centuries). An important railroad center, it has varied industries and is famous for its mustard. Population (1975): 156,787.

dik-dik A small African antelope belonging to the genus *Madoqua* (7 species), found in the undergrowth of forested areas. 12–16 in (30–40 cm) high at the shoulder, dik-diks are generally solitary and only the males have horns. When disturbed, they take flight in a series of erratic leaps.

dike A wall-like body of igneous rock that is intruded (usually vertically) into the surrounding rock in such a way that it cuts across the stratification (layering) of this rock. *Compare* sill.

dilatation and curettage (D and C) An operation in which the neck (cervix) of the womb is dilatated (widened) and the lining of the womb is scraped out. D and C may be performed for a variety of reasons, including the removal of any residual membranes after a miscarriage, removal of cysts or tumors, removal of a specimen of tissue for examination in the diagnosis of various gynecological disorders, and for termination of a pregnancy (*see* abortion).

dill A widely cultivated annual or biennial European herb, *Anethum graveolens*, 24 in (60 cm) high. The smooth stem bears feathery leaves and umbrella-like clusters of small yellow flowers, which produce small hard flat fruits. The young leaves and fruits are used to flavor soups, cakes, salads, fish, and pickled cucumbers. Family: *Umbelliferae.

Dillinger, John (1903–34) US criminal and bank robber. After a crime-filled youth, he began robbing banks, was captured and escaped twice, and finally was shot and killed by Federal Bureau of Investigation agents outside a movie theater in Chicago. Because of his daring and notorious escapades he was dubbed "public enemy number one."

Dilthey, Wilhelm (1833–1911) German pioneer of biographical historiography. In contrast to Hegelian reliance on the cosmic spirit and metaphysical enquiry, Dilthey sought to conduct empirical inquiry, using historical facts, biographies, and the surviving records of great personalities. An early sociologist, he studied documents of cultural, religious, and social traditions.

DiMaggio, Joe (Joseph Paul D.; 1914–) US baseball player. An outfielder, he played for the New York Yankees (1936–42; 1946–51). Nicknamed the "Yankee Clipper," he had a career batting average of .325 and hit in 56 consecutive games (1941). He was elected to the Baseball Hall of Fame (1955). He was briefly the second husband (1953–54) of Marilyn Monroe.

dimensional analysis A method of testing or deriving a physical equation in which each term is expressed in the dimensions of mass, length, time, and (if electric or magnetic quantities are present) either charge or current. Each term must have the same dimensional formula if the equation is true. Dimensional analysis is also useful in predicting the behavior of a full-scale system from a model.

diminishing returns, law of The law that as more of a variable factor of production, such as labor, is applied to a fixed quantity of another factor, such as capital (machinery), the returns to each additional unit of the variable factor will eventually decrease. For example, in a small factory, employing one laborer may increase production by freeing machine operators from some tasks, but employing a second laborer will not increase production by as much again.

Dimitrii Donskoi (1350–89) Prince of Moscow (1359–89) and Grand Prince of Vladimir (1362–89). His defeat of Khan Mamai at the battle of Kulikovo on the Don River in 1380 began the liberation of Russia from the *Golden Horde.

Dimitrov, Georgi (1882–1949) Bulgarian statesman. Dimitrov became a member of the executive committee of the *Comintern in 1921. Exiled in 1923, he moved in 1929 to Berlin, where in 1933 he was accused with others of setting fire to the Reichstag. Acquitted, he became a citizen of the

Soviet Union and secretary general of the Comintern. In 1944 he returned to Bulgaria and became prime minister (1946). He died in Moscow.

Dinant 50 16N 04 55E A town in S Belgium, on the Meuse River. It was famous for its artistic metalwork (*dinanderie*) in the middle ages. A popular tourist center, it is overlooked by an 11th-century citadel situated on a cliff above the river. Population (1971 est): 9862.

Dinaric Alps (Serbo-Croat name: Dinara Planina) A mountain range in SW Yugoslavia and N Albania, extending some 435 mi (700 km) NW–SE between the Alps and the Balkan Mountains and rising to 8274 ft (2522 m).

D'Indy, Vincent (1851–1931) French composer, the pupil and biographer of Franck and the cofounder of the Paris Schola Cantorum (1894). He was greatly influenced by Wagner and wrote a number of large-scale orchestral compositions, as well as operas and chamber music. His most famous work is the *Symphony on a French Mountaineer's Song* (for piano and orchestra; 1886).

Dinesen, Isak (Karen Blixen, Baroness Blixen-Finecke; 1885–1962) Danish author, who took up writing after 20 years spent managing a coffee plantation in Kenya. She is best known for two collections of stories in the gothic style: *Seven Gothic Tales* (1934) and *Winter's Tales* (1942).

dingo An Australian wild *dog, Canis familiaris* (formerly *C. dingo*), introduced about 3000 years ago from Asia. It is about 48 in (120 cm) long, including the tail (12 in [30 cm]), and has a smooth tan-colored coat. It is nocturnal and generally solitary.

Dinka A Nilotic people of the Nile basin region of the Sudan. Warlike and independent, the Dinka move with their cattle from dry-season pastures by the rivers to wet-season settlements, where they grow millet. There are many independent tribes of varying size each with numerous levels of segmentation into smaller clans and patrilineal kinship units. Age-set organization is important for men, who attain adulthood by undergoing the ordeals of initiation ceremonial. Ritual life emphasizes sacrificing to ancestral spirits and the god Nhial.

dinoflagellates A group of mostly marine unicellular organisms that form part of the *plankton. Usually measuring 0.0008–0.0039 in (0.02–0.1 mm), many have cellulose cell walls. They move by beating two hairlike structures (flagella). Some species contain the green pigment chlorophyll and can manufacture their own food (by photosynthesis); others can engulf food particles. Since they have characteristics of both plants and animals, dinoflagellates can be classified as algae or protozoans.

dinosaur An extinct reptile that was the dominant terrestrial animal during the Jurassic and Cretaceous periods (200–65 million years ago). Dinosaurs first appeared about 210 million years ago and included many varied forms, ranging in size from about 24 in (60 cm) to such mighty creatures as *Diplodocus*, which reached 87 ft (27 m) in length. There were two orders: the *Saurischia, which were mostly carnivores and included the bipedal *Allosaurus* and *Tyrannosaurus*; and the *Ornithischia, which were all herbivores and included the bipedal *Iguanodon*, the horned *Triceratops*, and *Stegosaurus*. Why both orders died out at the end of the Cretaceous period along with other reptiles, such as *ichthyosaurs, *pterosaurs, and *plesiosaurs, is still not certain. Dinosaurs had large bodies with heavy bones and protective armor and were probably unable to adapt to climatic changes and the effects of a rise in the sea level, which flooded their coastal habitats and led to changes in vegetation.

Dio Cassius (c. 150–235 AD) Roman historian, who was twice elected consul and was appointed governor of Africa and Dalmatia. In 80 books, written in Greek, he recorded the history of Rome from the arrival of Aeneas to his own time.

Dio Chrysostom (2nd century AD) Greek philosopher and orator. A friend of the Emperor Trajan, he admired the Roman state, from his family estates in Bithynia (Asia Minor), and eulogized its compound of monarchy, aristocracy, and democracy.

Diocletian(us), Gaius Aurelius Valerius (245–313 AD) Roman emperor (284–305). He was born in Dalmatia and rose to prominence in the army, to which he owed his accession. In 293 he established the tetrarchy to govern the Empire more effectively in a time of civil strife: the Empire was divided into East and West, with each ruled by an emperor and his associate. Diocletian ruled in the East with *Galerius, who was probably responsible for the persecution of Christians begun in 303. In 305 Diocletian retired to Salona (now Split, Yugoslavia), where his palace can still be seen.

diode. *See* semiconductor diode; thermionic valve.

Diodorus Siculus (1st century BC) Greek historian, born in Sicily. His *Bibliotheca historica* is a history of the Mediterranean countries from their legendary origins up to his own time; of its 40 volumes, only 15 survive.

Diogenes Laertius (3rd century AD) Greek compiler of the opinions and biographical details of classical philosophers, including the *Presocratics. The historical authenticity of his biographical material, for example about the life of *Epicurus, is doubtful.

Diogenes of Sinope (412–322 BC) The founder of the philosophical sect of the *Cynics. Influenced by *Antisthenes, Diogenes claimed, in contrast to almost all Greek thinkers, total freedom and self-sufficiency for the individual. Unlike modern anarchists, he saw no need for violent rebellion to assert his independence, which he thought he already had. His ostentatious disregard for social conventions made him the subject of many stories. He is reported to have lived in a large tub in Athens. According to another story, he went about in daylight with a lamp, saying that he was searching for an honest man.

Diomedes A legendary Greek hero of the Trojan War who commanded 80 ships from Argos. He wounded *Ares and *Aphrodite, took the place of the absent *Achilles in an attack on Troy, and captured the Palladium, the sacred image of *Athena.

Dionysius of Halicarnassus (1st century BC) Greek historian who taught at Rome after 30 BC. He compiled a history of Rome from its origins to the first Punic War in 20 books, of which 10 survive. He also wrote literary criticism and treatises on rhetoric.

Dionysius the Areopagite, St (1st century AD) Greek churchman. He was converted to Christianity by St Paul and was traditionally the first Bishop of Athens. In the middle ages he was thought to be the author of several theological treatises in Greek. These are now attributed to *Pseudo-Dionysius the Areopagite. Feast day: Oct 9.

Dionysius (I) the Elder (c. 430–367 BC) Tyrant of Syracuse (405–367), who fought the Carthaginians in a series of wars, which were ultimately unsuccessful, for control of Sicily and the Greek cities of S Italy. His son **Dionysius (II) the Younger**, who succeeded him as tyrant (367–356, 347–344), was a patron of writers and philosophers and was taught briefly by Plato.

Dionysus (*or* Bacchus) The Greek god of wine, originally a vegetation god. He was the son of *Semele by Zeus, who saved him at her death; he was reared by the nymphs of Nysa. A common theme of many legends concerning him is a people's refusal to accept his divinity and his subsequent retribution: thus Pentheus, King of Thebes, was torn to death by the god's ecstatic female followers, the maenads. Athens held five festivals in Dionysus' honor.

Diophantus of Alexandria (mid-3rd century AD) Greek mathematician; one of the few Greeks to study algebra rather than geometry. He discovered the method of solving problems by means of algebraic equations. His work was preserved by Arabic mathematicians and, in the 16th century, was translated into Latin after which it inspired many advances in algebra. Diophantine equations are named for him.

diopter A unit used to measure the power of a lens equal to the reciprocal of its focal length in meters. The power of a converging lens is taken to be positive and that of a diverging lens as negative.

Dior, Christian (1905–57) French fashion designer, who first became known with his 1947 collection, which introduced the New Look, characterized by fitted bodices and long full skirts. His later designs, which included the H-line and the A-line, aspired to a similar ideal of femininity.

diorite A coarse-grained plutonic igneous rock of intermediate composition. It consists mainly of plagioclase feldspar and ferromagnesian minerals (often hornblende, biotite, or pyroxene). It usually occurs in small intrusive masses or in parts of *batholiths.

Dioscorides Pedanius (c. 40–c. 90 AD) Greek physician, who compiled the first pharmacopoeia. He traveled widely as a surgeon in the Roman army and in his work *De materia medica* (c. 77 AD) he described nearly 600 plants and their medicinal properties.

Dioscuri. *See* Castor and Pollux.

dip circle. *See* magnetic dip.

diphtheria An acute bacterial infection primarily affecting the nose, throat, or larynx. It has been virtually eliminated from most western nations as a result of extensive immunization, although it formerly caused the death of many children. It is still found in Africa and India. Diphtheria produces a membrane across the throat that chokes the child. Alternatively death may be caused by poisons damaging the heart. The disease can be cured using penicillin and antitoxin.

CHRISTIAN DIOR *The French fashion designer at the opening of a 1950 fashion show. His seven mannequins are all modeling New Look evening dresses.*

Diplodocus A huge amphibious dinosaur of the Jurassic period (200–136 million years ago) that was the largest terrestrial vertebrate ever to exist, reaching a length of 87 ft (27 m). It had a narrow body with massive pillar-like legs, a long neck with a tiny head, and a long tail. It fed on soft vegetation found in swamps and shallow lakes and had very few teeth. Order: *Saurischia.

dipole, electric and magnetic A pair of equal and opposite electric charges or *magnetic poles. The dipole moment is defined as the magnitude of one of the charges or poles multiplied by the distance separating them. Some molecules have an electric dipole moment due to the preferential attraction of the bonding electrons for one of the atoms. In the case of hydrogen chloride, for example, the chlorine atom gains a slight negative charge and the hydrogen atom a slight positive charge. Measurement of dipole moments often provides evidence regarding the shapes of molecules.

dipper An aquatic songbird of the family *Cinclidae* (4 species), also called water ouzel, of Eurasia and America. Dippers are found near fast-flowing mountain streams, diving into the water to search for insects and small fish. The Eurasian white-breasted dipper (*Cinclus cinclus*) is about 7 in (17 cm) long and has a dense dark-brown plumage with a white breast.

Diprotodon An extinct Australian giant *wombat that was about the size of a rhinoceros. It lived during the Pleistocene epoch, about a million years ago.

Diptera An order of insects comprising the two-winged, or true, flies. *See* fly.

Dirac, Paul Adrien Maurice (1902–) British physicist, who made two fundamental contributions to the development of the quantum theory. In 1928 he introduced a new notation for handling quantum equations that combined *Schrödinger's use of *differential equations with *Heisenberg's approach using *matrices. Two years later he incorporated *relativity into quantum theory and produced an equation that predicted the existence of antiparticles. For his work he shared the 1933 Nobel Prize with Schrödinger.

direction finder Equipment for locating the source of a radio signal, such as a ship at sea. It consists of one or more directive *aerials (usually in the form of a loop), designed to detect signals from a specific direction, and a receiver. Frequencies normally used are between 0.1 and 2 megahertz. The process can be automatic, often using a rotating aerial with a *cathode-ray tube to display signal strength and direction. Reflections from mountains or tall buildings can cause errors in a land-based direction-finding system. *Radar is a form of direction finding based on picking up reflections of a transmitted signal.

Directory (1795–99) The government of the First Republic of France, comprising five directors who were elected by a Council of Ancients (men over 40 years old) and a Council of Five Hundred. The Directory, which marked a retreat from the extremity of the early years of the *French Revolution, has been criticized for its corruption and administrative incompetence but it achieved successes in the Revolutionary Wars. It was overthrown by a coup d'état on behalf of *Napoleon.

Dire Dawa 9 40N 41 47E A city in central Ethiopia. It is in a hot dry region with little cultivation. Local industries include manufacturing cotton goods and cement. Population (1978 est): 72,202.

Dirichlet's theorem A theorem in *number theory stating that there are an infinite number of *prime numbers contained in the set of all numbers of the form $(a \times n) + b$, where a and b are themselves prime and n is a natural number, i.e. 1, 2, 3, ... The theorem was first suggested by *Gauss and proved by the French mathematician Peter Gustav Lejeune Dirichlet (1805–59).

dirigibles Balloons that obtain their thrust from a propeller. The first airship to fly was a French steam-powered machine, designed in 1852 by H. Giffard; however, the first practical airship was the electrically powered *La France* (1884), built by Renard and Krebs. By 1900 the initiative in airships had passed to Germany, with the machines of Count Ferdinand von Zeppelin (1838–1917) leading the field. Between 1910 and 1914 Zeppelins were in extensive passenger service, carrying some 35,000 passengers, without mishap. In World War I these machines were used by the Germans to bomb England—the first effective use of aerial bombardment. From then onward the history of airships is one of disaster followed by disaster. The British *R101* caught fire at Beauvais in 1930, the US *Shenandoah* and the *Akron* were lost in 1933, and the German *Hindenberg* was destroyed in 1937. These disasters with hydrogen-filled airships cost many lives and gave them a reputation from which they have never recovered. However, the availability of the nonflammable gas helium created a mild revival of interest in the 1970s, especially in the Soviet Union.

disaccharide A carbohydrate comprising two linked *monosaccharide sugar units. *Lactose, maltose, and *sucrose are important disaccharides.

disarmament The reduction of the fighting capability of a nation. Limited disarmament treaties were made under the auspices of the *League of Nations in the 1930s, in an attempt to avoid a repetition of the disastrous loss of life in World War I. But German rearmament under the Nazis and Japanese expansionism in Asia thwarted these attempts. After World War II the main concern was to contain the spread of nuclear weapons. An attempt was made by the UN to limit both conventional arms and nuclear weapons, especially of the defeated countries, but during the Cold War both the Soviet Union and the western powers assisted in the rearmament of their former enemies. In 1963, however, the Soviet Union, the US, and the UK signed a *Nuclear Test-Ban Treaty. In 1967 the same countries signed a treaty banning the use of nuclear weapons in outer space; in the same year 59 countries signed a nuclear nonproliferation treaty. As a result of an initiative by President Johnson, talks between the Soviet Union and US were started in 1969 to limit and reduce strategic nuclear arms; known as SALT (Strategic Arms Limitation Talks) they reached limited agreements in 1974 (SALT I) and again in 1979 (SALT II). *See also* Geneva Conferences; Hague Peace Conferences.

Disciples of Christ (*or* Campbellites) A Christian denomination originating within Presbyterianism in the 19th century but founded as a separate denomination in Philadelphia in 1827 by Alexander Campbell (1788–1866). They preach a simple biblical creed, are congregational in organization, and celebrate weekly communion as the central act of worship.

discriminant A mathematical expression derived from the coefficients of a polynomial that gives information about the roots of the polynomial. An example occurs in the general quadratic equation $ax^2 + bx + c = 0$. This equation has just one solution if its discriminant $b^2 - 4ac$ is zero.

discus throw A field event in athletics. The circular discus is made of wood and metal, the men's weighing 4.4 lb (2 kg) and the women's 2.2 lb (1 kg). It is thrown as far as possible with one hand from within a circle 8.2 ft (2.5 m) in diameter.

disinfectant A substance or process that kills germs or prevents them multiplying. Carbolic acid (phenol) was introduced for this purpose in medicine in the 1870s by Joseph *Lister. It is still used, as are many of its derivatives, in cleaning materials and, in weaker solutions, in skin disinfectants. Chlorine and such compounds as sodium hypochlorite kill bacteria and also some viruses. Chlorinated phenols, such as hexachlorophane, are also widely used in pharmaceutical products. Many other chemicals, including hydrogen peroxide (H_2O_2), iodine (I_2), formaldehyde (HCHO), and other aldehydes, are also used as disinfectants. Dry heating to 110°F (40°C) for about 3 hours will kill all disease-causing germs. Boiling water and ultraviolet light are also effective disinfectants.

dislocation Displacement of a bone at a joint, producing severe pain, difficulty in moving the joint, and usually obvious deformity. Shoulders, elbows, hips, vertebrae, and fingers are all commonly dislocated in injuries.

Often one of the bones in the joint will be broken, and for this reason it is unwise to attempt to put the joint back before an X-ray film has been taken.

Disney, Walt (1901–66) US film producer and animator. His most famous cartoon character, Mickey Mouse, was designed in 1928. His films include full-length cartoon features, such as *Snow White and the Seven Dwarfs* (1938), *Pinocchio* (1939), and *Bambi* (1943), nature documentaries, and adventure films, such as *Treasure Island* (1950) and *Mary Poppins* (1964), all made for family audiences. His *Fantasia* (1940) used colorful visual images and cartoons to accompany several pieces of classical music played by an orchestra under *Stokowski. He opened Disneyland, an amusement park, in California in 1955. Walt Disney World was later opened (1971) near Orlando, Florida.

display In zoology, a specialized means by which animals communicate with each other. Displays can be vocal (such as birdsong), visual (by posture or colorful plumage), chemical (by means of *pheromones), or tactile (for instance bees communicate in a dark hive largely by touch). Displays ensure social integration and cohesion of populations by communicating the whereabouts and identity of individuals. They are used to establish social rank, maintain territory, synchronize breeding, and give warning of danger.

DISRAELI *A contemporary cartoon, entitled, "A Bad Example," shows the prime minister (right) and Gladstone, his political opponent, throwing mud at one another.*

Disraeli, Benjamin, 1st Earl of Beaconsfield (1804–81) British statesman; Conservative prime minister (1868, 1874–80). Of Italian-Jewish descent, Disraeli was baptized a Christian in 1817. He became a member of parliament in 1837. Disraeli was critical of Peel's Conservative Government (1841–46) and opposed the repeal of the *Corn Laws. He was three times chancellor of the exchequer (1852, 1858–59, 1866–68): in 1858 he introduced an unsuccessful parliamentary reform bill but was largely responsible for the 1867 *Reform Act. He became prime minister in February, 1868, but lost office following the autumn election, which was won by the Liberals under Gladstone. His second ministry carried important social legislation. In 1875 he bought Britain a major stake in the Suez Canal and in 1876 secured passage of a bill that conferred the title Empress of India on Queen Victoria. He successfully pursued British interests at the Congress of *Berlin (1878). Under Disraeli's leadership the Conservative Party came to be clearly identified with policies that upheld the monarchy, Empire, and Church of England, while sponsoring social reform. A flamboyant and witty parliamentarian, he earned the respect and friendship of the

queen. Also a writer, Disraeli's novels include *Vivien Grey* (1826), *Coningsby, or the New Generation* (1844), and *Sybil, or the Two Nations* (1845).

dissonance A combination of two or more musical notes that sounds harsh to the ear. This harshness is caused by the *beats that are produced when two notes (or their overtones) of similar pitch are sounded together. For example C and F sharp are dissonant because the second overtone of C is G, which beats with F sharp. A common type of dissonance in diatonic music consists of chords that sound incomplete in themselves and need to resolve onto a consonance. All diatonic music relies on the contrast between dissonances and consonances, without which such music would sound predictable and uninteresting. The use of *chromaticism in the late 19th century increased the amount of dissonance in music; in the 20th century such composers as Bartok and Stravinsky deliberately cultivated the use of unresolved dissonances.

distemper (veterinary science) A highly contagious virus disease affecting dogs, foxes, ferrets, badgers, etc. Canine distemper occurs mainly at 3–12 months; symptoms include fever, loss of appetite, and a discharge from the eyes and nose. Complications may include conjunctivitis, bronchitis, pneumonia, and gastroenteritis. The disease can be prevented by vaccination at about 11 weeks with a booster dose at two years.

distillation A method of purifying or separating the components of a liquid by boiling or evaporating the liquid and condensing the vapor. It is used for separating either liquids from solids or a mixture of liquids whose components have different boiling points. The latter is known as fractional distillation. Distillation is employed in petroleum refineries to separate the various *hydrocarbons, in the production of alcoholic spirits, and in extracting pure water from sea water.

distribution function A mathematical function that gives the probability of finding a system in a particular state or within a range of states. For example, the probability of one of the molecules of a gas having a velocity between v and $v + dv$ in a given direction is Fdv, where F is the distribution function.

distributive law A law concerning the combination of mathematical operations. In arithmetic, for example, multiplication is said to obey the distributive law, or to be distributive, with respect to addition because $a(b + c) = ab + ac$.

District of Columbia A federal district of the E US, coextensive with the federal capital, *Washington. Area: 69 sq mi (178 sq km).

dithyramb An ancient Greek hymn to the god *Dionysus. Originally sung extempore, it developed into a literary form—traditionally originated by the poet Arion—around the 6th and 7th centuries BC. Its best-known authors include *Bacchylides and *Pindar. Aristotle believed that Greek drama developed out of this form.

dittany A perennial European herbaceous plant, *Dictamnus albus*, also known as the gas plant or burning bush. A strong-scented gland-covered plant, it gives off so much aromatic oil that it is said to burst into flames when ignited. Dittany produces a drooping spike of white or pink flowers. Family: *Rutaceae*. The name is also applied to several other plants. Crete dittany (*Origanum dictamnus*) is a herb closely related to marjoram, with thick woolly leaves and pinkish flower clusters. Family: *Labiatae*.

Diu. *See* Goa, Daman, and Diu.

diuretics A large class of drugs that increase the excretion of urine by the kidneys. Diuretics are used in the treatment of diseases in which fluid accumulates in the tissues. These illnesses include heart failure, kidney failure, and some liver diseases (such as cirrhosis). Some diuretics (e.g. frusemide) cause loss of potassium from the body and are prescribed with a potassium supplement. Diuretics may also be used in the treatment of high blood pressure.

diurnal motion The apparent daily motion of astronomical bodies from E to W across the sky, in circles parallel to the celestial equator (see celestial sphere). It is caused by the earth's W-to-E rotation.

diver A large aquatic bird belonging to a family (*Gaviidae*; 3 species) occurring in the N hemisphere, also called loon. Divers breed on lakes and ponds and spend the winter in temperate coastal waters. They have small pointed wings and black and white plumage and they dive deeply, feeding on fish, frogs, and aquatic insects. Order: *Gaviiformes*.

divide. *See* watershed.

dividend A share in the profits of a company paid to stockholders. The rate of dividend is generally declared at the company's annual general meeting and will reflect the preceding year's profit. The dividend **yield** of the share is the income it produces expressed as a percentage of its current value.

divine right of kings A political doctrine claiming that monarchs are responsible only to God and that their subjects owe them unquestioning obedience. The theory originated in the middle ages and was most fully developed in the 16th and 17th centuries, especially in England, where it was associated particularly with the Stuart kings, and in France, where its leading exponent was Louis XIV.

diving beetle An aquatic beetle—a true *water beetle—belonging to a family (*Dytiscidae*; about 4000 species), occurring worldwide but particularly common in Europe and Asia. Diving beetles have dark streamlined bodies and vary in length from 0.08 to 1.5 in (2 to 38 mm): the largest genera are *Cybister* and *Dytiscus*. The adults and larvae (water tigers) are voracious carnivores.

diving duck A *duck that dives to the bottom of lakes or rivers to feed, aided by a dense high-domed skull. Diving ducks, which include the *goldeneye, *pochard, and *scaup, usually have a drab plumage, thick neck, narrow wings, and large feet; the legs are set far back and they walk awkwardly on land. *Compare* dabbling duck.

division of labor The separation of tasks in an industrial process, with the allocation of one worker to each specific task in the manufacture of an object. The term was first introduced by Adam *Smith in his *Wealth of Nations* (1776). The object is to increase output; however, extreme division of labor, as in a car factory, can lead to intense boredom for the worker, who is confined to repeating one operation continuously.

divorce The legal process by which a marriage is ended. Grounds for divorce vary widely among the states, but the trend has been toward easier grounds, such as "irreconcilable differences."

DIWALI *The final day of the five-day festival is dedicated to the tie between brothers and sisters, who exchange special gifts. The bracelet on the boy's wrist, given to him by his sister, symbolizes the bond between them.*

Diwali An important Hindu religious festival. Held over the New Year according to the Vikrama calendar (October–November), it is celebrated especially among the merchant classes and honors *Lakshmi, the goddess of wealth (or in Bengal, Kali). There is feasting, gambling, and lighting of lamps in honor of *Rama. Jains commemorate at this time the death of their saint *Mahavira.

Dix, Dorothea (Lynde) (1802–87) US reformer and crusader for improved conditions in the treatment of the mentally ill. After teaching in Worcester, Mass, she established her own school for girls (1821–35) in Boston. It was while teaching a Sunday school class at the Cambridge jail in 1841 that she was deeply affected by the poor treatment of the mentally ill. After this experience she spent the rest of her life improving conditions for the mentally ill throughout the US and, eventually, in Europe. Legislation, as a result of her efforts, provided for improved conditions in mental institutions.

Dixieland A type of jazz played in imitation of the traditional *New Orleans style, named for the Original Dixieland Jazz Band (founded 1912). It is usually played by small bands. It emerged in the early years of the 20th century but declined during the *swing and bebop eras. Among the most outstanding Dixieland musicians were King Oliver, Jelly Roll Morton, Sidney Bechet, and Louis *Armstrong.

Diyarbakır 37 55N 40 14E A town in SE Turkey, on the Tigris River. It was taken by the Turks in 1515 and has 4th-century walls. Gold and silver filigree work is produced here; wool and grain are traded. It has a university (1966). Population (1980): 235,617.

Djajapura. *See* Jajapura.

Djakarta. *See* Jakarta.

Djambi. *See* Jambi.

Djerba Island 33 45N 11 00E A Tunisian island in the Mediterranean Sea, linked to the mainland by a causeway. Area: 197 sq mi (510 sq km).

Djibouti, Republic of (name until 1977: the French Territory of the Afars and the Issas) A small country in NE Africa, on the Gulf of Aden at its entrance to the Red Sea. It consists chiefly of an arid rocky coastal plain rising to a plateau inland. The main population groups are Somalis (chiefly Issas) and Afars, with Arabic and European minorities. *Economy*: the port of Djibouti (a free port since 1949) is the country's economic focus handling an important transshipment trade but it was adversely affected by the closure of the Suez Canal (1967–75). The port is linked by rail to Ethiopia and handles about half of that country's trade. Exports include hides, skins, sugar, and Ethiopian coffee. Inland the predominantly nomadic population tends goats, sheep, and camels. *History*: French involvement, centered on the port, began in the mid-19th century. It was made a French colony known as French Somaliland in 1896 and proclaimed an overseas territory in 1967. It became independent in 1977 as Djibouti with Hassan Gouled Aptidon as its first president. The country suffered from the war between Ethiopia and Somalia through the disruption of trade. The sustained drought in East Africa in the early 1980s worsened already distressing conditions in Djibouti, where poverty is pervasive. The problem of Ethiopian refugees placed an even greater economic burden on the country's weak economy. Djibouti is entirely dependent on foreign aid for its survival, relying heavily on French support. Official languages: Hamitic languages of Somali. Official currency: Djibouti franc of 100 centimes. Area: 8409 sq mi (21,783 sq km). Population (1983 est): 316,000. Capital and chief port: Djibouti.

Djilas, Milovan (1911–) Yugoslav politician and writer. A member of *Tito's resistance group in World War II, Djilas became a prominent figure in the postwar communist government. His criticism of the regime led to his demotion (1954) and he was twice imprisoned (1956–61, 1962–66) for publishing critical material abroad. His books include *New Class* (1957), *Land Without Justice* (1958), and *Conversations with Stalin* (1962).

Djokjakarta. *See* Jogjakarta.

Djoser (*or* Zoser) King of Egypt (c. 2980–c. 2950 BC) of the 3rd dynasty, famous for his pyramid at *Saqqarah, near Memphis.

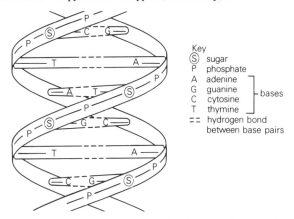

Key
Ⓢ sugar
Ⓟ phosphate
Ⓐ adenine
Ⓖ guanine ⎫
Ⓒ cytosine ⎬ bases
Ⓣ thymine ⎭
== hydrogen bond between base pairs

DNA *The structure of a DNA molecule takes the form of a double helix. The sequence of base pairs constitutes the genetic code, which controls the inheritance of characteristics.*

DNA (*or* deoxyribonucleic acid) A nucleic acid that is the chief constituent of the *chromosomes, carrying genetic information, in the form of *genes, necessary for the organization and functioning of living cells.

The molecular structure of DNA was first proposed by J. D. *Watson and F. H. *Crick in 1953. It consists of a double helix of two strands coiled around each other. Each strand is made up of alternating pentose sugar (deoxyribose) and phosphate groups, with an organic base attached to each pentose group. There are four possible bases: adenine (A), guanine (G), cytosine (C), and thymine (T). The bases on each strand are joined by hydrogen bonds and are always paired in the same way: A always binds with T and G with C. During replication, the strands of the helix separate and each provides a template for the synthesis of a new complementary strand, thus producing two identical copies of the original helix. This special property for accurate self-replication enables DNA to duplicate the genes of an organism during the cell divisions of growth (*see* mitosis) and the production of germ cells for the next generation (*see* meiosis).

Dnepr River (*or* Dnieper R.)   A river in the W Soviet Union. Rising in the Valdai Hills, NE of Smolensk, it flows mainly SE through the RSFSR and the Belorussian and Ukrainian SSRs to enter the Black Sea. It is the third longest river in Europe. Length: 1420 mi (2286 km).

Dneprodzerzhinsk (name until 1936: Kamenskoye)   48 30N 34 37E A port in the SW Soviet Union, in the Ukrainian SSR, on the Dnepr River. A major industrial center, it produces iron and steel, machine tools, and chemicals. Population (1981 est): 257,000.

Dnepropetrovsk (name from 1787 until 1796 and from 1802 until 1826: Ekterinoslav)   48 29N 35 00E A city in the SW Soviet Union, in the Ukrainian SSR on the Dnepr River. It is one of the country's largest industrial cities, producing especially iron and steel, and it is also a transportation center. Population (1981 est): 1,100,000.

Dnestr River (*or* Dniester R.)   A river in the SW Soviet Union. It flows mainly SE from the Carpathian Mountains, through the Ukrainian and Moldavian SSRs, to the Black Sea near Odessa. Length: 877 mi (1411 km).

Dobermann pinscher   A breed of dog developed by Louis Dobermann in Germany in the late 19th century. It has a powerful streamlined body with a very short tail and a long muzzle. The short smooth coat is black, brown, or blue-gray with tan markings. Dobermanns are widely used as police, guard, and guide dogs. Height: 28 in (70 cm) (dogs); 26 in (64 cm) (bitches).

Dobruja (Bulgarian name: Dobrudzha; Romanian name: Dobrogea)   An area in E central Europe, in SE Romania and NE Bulgaria. It consists of a low-lying alluvial plain between the Danube River and the Black Sea.

dobsonfly   A winged insect belonging to the family *Corydalidae*, occurring in all continents except Europe. Male dobsonflies have enormously exaggerated jaws, sometimes over 1 in (25 mm) long. Eggs are laid near fresh water and the larvae (hellgrammites) are aquatic, using their biting jaws to feed on insects and small invertebrates. They migrate to the soil to pupate. Order: *Neuroptera*.

Dobzhansky, Theodosius (1900–75) US geneticist, born in Russia. His studies of wild populations of fruit flies revealed the extent of genetic differences between individuals and how, through natural selection, this enabled the populations to adapt rapidly to changing conditions. Dobzhansky also studied the formation of new species and has written influential articles on evolution and philosophy.

dock   A plant (usually perennial) of the genus *Rumex*, of temperate regions. 4–80 in (10–200 cm) tall, it has a deep stout root and large lance-shaped leaves. The small greenish flowers are borne in small clusters on branched flower stems. They produce small nutlets, often surrounded by the reddish papery remains of the petals. Dock leaves are the traditional antidote to nettle stings. Family: *Polygonaceae*. *See also* sorrel.

docks   Structures designed to enable ships to load and unload cargo or passengers or to undergo repairs. A **wet dock** is situated on a tidal river or on the coast and has gates to maintain the water level irrespective of the tide. Ships can only enter or leave such a dock when the tide brings the water level outside it to the level inside. Where the range of the tide is small (less than 13 ft (4 m)) a **tidal dock** can be used. In this the dock is open to the harbor and ships in dock rise and fall with the tide. In **dry docks** the water enters at one end only and gates enable all the water to be pumped out, so that repairs can be made to a ship's hull. **Floating docks** have the advantage of being movable, but they have a relatively short life. Floating docks also have watertight compartments from which the water can be pumped out and they can be used for repair work. *See also* dredger.

Doctorow, E(dgar) L(awrence) (1931–) US novelist. Known for blending real people with imaginary characters, he wrote *Welcome to Hard Times* (1960), *Big as Life* (1966), *The Book of Daniel* (1971), *Ragtime* (1975), and *Loon Lake* (1980).

documentary film   A film that portrays and interprets factual reality, often for educational purposes. The term was coined by John Grierson, leader of a school of British documentary film directors in the 1930s, to describe one of the most influential early documentaries, Robert *Flaher-

ty's *Nanook of the North* (1920). The propaganda films produced in Nazi Germany, notably Leni Reifenstahl's *Triumph of the Will* (1934), were an exception to the generally left-wing political sympathies of documentary films. Many documentary films have been produced for television.

dodder   A twining parasitic plant of the widely distributed genus *Cuscuta* (150 species), which absorbs food by inserting rootlike organs into the stems of other plants. Dodder has no chlorophyll (green pigment): it consists simply of a yellow or pinkish cordlike stem bearing round clusters of tiny yellow or white bell-shaped flowers. The leaves are reduced to scales and there are no roots. Family: *Cuscutaceae*.

Dodecanese (Modern Greek name: Dhodhekánisos)   A group of Greek islands in the SE Aegean Sea. Although known as the 12 Islands, it in fact consists of some 20 islands and islets, which include Cos, *Rhodes (the largest), and Pátmos. They were taken from Turkey by Italy in 1912 and passed to Greece in 1947. Total area: 1050 sq mi (2719 sq km). Population (1971): 121,017. Capital: Rhodes.

Dodge City   37 45N 100 01W A city in SW Kansas, on the Arkansas River. An important stop for westward travelers on the Santa Fe Trail in the 1880s, it became a major cattle-shipping center with the coming of the Santa Fe Railroad. Meat packing is still carried on, and tourism is important. Population (1980): 18,001.

Dodgson, Charles Lutwidge.   *See* Carroll, Lewis.

dodo   A large clumsy flightless bird, *Raphus cucullatus*, that lived on Mauritius but was extinct by 1681. Weighing about 51 lb (23 kg), it had a gray-blue wispy plumage, stout yellow legs, tiny wings, a tuft of curly white tail feathers, and a large head with a massive hooked bill; it probably fed on fruit or roots. Family: *Raphidae*; order: *Columbiformes* (pigeons, etc.).

Dodoma   6 10S 35 40E A city in E central Tanzania. It has been designated as the future capital to replace Dar es Salaam, and some government operations began to move there in 1983. Population (1978): 45,703.

dog   A carnivorous mammal belonging to the family *Canidae*. Ancestors of the modern domestic dog (*Canis familiaris*), probably derived from wolves or jackals, were first domesticated over 10,000 years ago. Wild dogs generally live and hunt in packs, relying on speed and cooperation to secure their prey. They are specialized hunters with long legs, sharp teeth, strong jaws, and acute hearing and smell.

The intelligence and social nature of dogs have led to their selective breeding by man for a variety of purposes, principally as sporting dogs, working dogs, and ornamental breeds for household pets. There are up to 400 modern breeds and standards for over 100 recognized US breeds have been established.

dogbane   A perennial herb of the genus *Apocynum* (about 7 species), found mostly in the tropics and subtropics, especially the American species *A. androsaemifolium*. Up to 5 ft (1.5 m) high, dogbane has simple leaves and small white or pink bell-shaped flowers clustered at the tips of the shoots. The juice contains alkaloids and has been used in arrow poisons. Family: *Apocynaceae*. *See also* Indian hemp.

doge   The title of the chief magistrate of Venice from about 697 AD to the fall of the Venetian Empire in 1797. The doge was elected for life and wielded considerable power until 1172 when his authority was restricted by the creation of a supreme Great Council of 480 members. Further constitutional checks made the doge little more than a figurehead. The first **Doge's Palace** was built in 814 and destroyed by an uprising in 976. Subsequent structures were destroyed by fire, and the present richly decorated gothic palace originated in the early 14th century, with later additions.

Dogen (1200–53) Japanese Buddhist monk, who introduced the *Soto school of Zen Buddhism to Japan. An orphan of noble birth, he became a monk at 13 and studied the Buddhist scriptures before visiting several Chinese monasteries (1223–27), where he studied Zen. After returning to Japan, he devoted himself to teaching the form of Zen practice that emphasizes quiet meditation. His teaching is embodied in his chief work, *Shobogenzo* (*Knowledge concerning the Dharma*).

dogfish   A small *shark belonging to one of a number of families. *Scyliorhinus stellaris*, up to 40 in (1 m) long, and *S. canicula*, up to 30 in (75 cm) long, are brown-spotted dogfish commonly found in Mediterranean and British coastal waters. They are edible and purchased as "rock salmon." Chief families: *Triakidae* (smooth dogfish or smooth hounds); *Squalidae* (spiny dogfish); *Scyliorhinidae* (spotted dogfish).

DOG

sporting breeds

pointer   cocker spaniel   golden retriever   Irish setter

hounds

dachshund   borzoi   basset   Rhodesian ridgeback

working breeds

corgi   rough-coated collie   Old English sheepdog   German shepherd

terriers

bull terrier   cairn terrier   Airedale   smooth-haired fox terrier   Sealyham

toy breeds

Chihuahua   Pekingese   toy poodle   pug   Yorkshire terrier

non-sporting breeds

Boston   chow chow   shipperke   Dalmatian

Dogger Bank A vast sandbank in the central North Sea, 55–120 ft (17–36 m) below water. Several naval battles have taken place on the bank, notably the battle of Dogger Bank (January 24, 1915) between British and German forces. It is a major fishing ground.

doggerel A crude, naive, form of poetry, often irregular in rhythm and meter. Early examples are John *Skelton's *Colin Clout* (1519) and Samuel *Butler's *Hudibras* (1663–78). It is much used in comic verse, as in the work of the poet Ogden *Nash. The word can be used perjoratively.

dog rose A shrubby *rose, *Rosa canina*, 40 in–16 ft (1–5 m) high. It grows in woods, hedges, and roadsides of Europe, North Africa, and SW Asia. The arching stems have strong curved prickles and bear clusters of scentless white or pink flowers on long stalks.

dog's tooth violet A spring-blooming plant of the genus *Erythronium* (20 species), also known as adder's tongue, native to Eurasia and North America. They have white, yellow, or purple nodding flowers with two leaves at the base; the fruit is a pod. Several species are grown as rock-garden ornamentals. A European species is *E. dens-canis*, with purple flowers. Family: *Liliaceae*.

dogwood A shrub or small tree of the genus *Cornus* (about 45 species), mostly of the N hemisphere. It has oval pointed leaves with prominent curved veins and dense clusters of four-petaled flowers. The fruit is a berry. The common European dogwood (*C. sanguinea*) has white flowers, blood-red shoots and autumn leaves, and black berries; Cornelian cherry (*C. mas*), of central and SE Europe, has small yellow flowers and attractive red berries. The American flowering dogwood (*C. florida*) has showy pinkish blossoms and red berries. Family: *Cornaceae*.

Doha 25 15N 51 36E The capital of Qatar, on the E coast. Its modern development (including an international seaport and airport) has been funded by oil revenues. Population (1981 est): 130,000.

Dohnányi, Ernö (Ernst von D.; 1877–1960) Hungarian composer and pianist. He spent his last years in the US. He was greatly influenced by Brahms, who praised his early works. Unlike his contemporaries, Bartók and Kodály, Dohnányi remained uninfluenced by Hungarian folksong. His best-known composition is the *Variations on a Nursery Theme* (for piano and orchestra; 1913), based on the tune "Baa Baa Black Sheep."

Dolby system An electronic device for reducing the hiss in sound reproduction, particularly in *tape recorders. It was invented by Ray Dolby (1933–), who set up a company to make Dolby noise-reduction units. These are now built into high-quality tape recorders and are increasingly used in film sound tracks and prerecorded cassettes. The Dolby system selectively boosts the higher frequencies in the sound signal before recording it, to drown out the constant hiss produced by the tape, and attenuates them when playing back. Its unique feature is that it operates only when the music is quiet enough for the hiss to be heard. This avoids both distortion that occurs if lower frequencies are boosted to the same level and distortion from boosting already loud higher frequencies.

dolce stil nuovo (Italian: sweet new style) A style of love poetry founded by the Bolognese poet Guido Guinizelli (c. 1240–76) and perfected by the Florentine poets *Cavalcanti and *Dante. It is characterized by a spiritualization of *courtly love, the use of the vernacular, and the sonnet, ballad, and canzone verse forms. Among its best-known examples are Dante's lyrics to Beatrice. The style influenced *Petrarch, *Bembo, Dante Gabriel *Rossetti, and Ezra *Pound.

doldrums The equatorial belt within which the trade-wind zones converge. Winds are light and variable but the strong upward movement of air caused by the meeting of the trade winds produces frequent thunderstorms, heavy rains, and squalls. Navigation by sailing ships was difficult in these areas; ships often became becalmed for several days.

Dole, Sanford (Ballard) (1844–1926) US lawyer and jurist; president (1894–98) and governor (1900–03) of Hawaii. Born of missionary parents in Honolulu, he was educated in the US and returned to Hawaii to practice law. He was an associate justice of the Hawaiian Supreme Court (1887–93) and became president after Queen Liliuokalani was deposed (1893) and Hawaii was proclaimed a republic. Hawaii was annexed by the US in 1898, and he became territorial governor two years later. From 1903–15 he was a district judge.

dolerite See diabase.

Dollfuss, Engelbert (1892–1934) Austrian statesman; chancellor (1932–34). He became prominent as leader of the Lower Austrian Farmers' League. Ruling by decree from 1933, his chancellorship was increasingly strained by his inability to control the Austrian Nazis or to cooperate with the Social Democrats. He suppressed the Social Democratic revolt in February, 1934, and was assassinated in July during an abortive attempt by the Nazis to seize power.

dolmen (Breton: table stone) A prehistoric tomb made of huge stone slabs set upright and supporting a stone roof. Widely distributed in *Neolithic Europe, dolmens were often covered by a *barrow.

dolomite A mineral consisting of calcium magnesium carbonate, $CaMg(CO_3)_2$, colorless, white or gray in color. Rocks containing over 15% magnesium carbonate are called dolomites, those containing less are magnesian limestones, and those containing both dolomite and calcite are dolomitic limestones. Dolomite occurs as a primary sediment, in metalliferous veins and in limestones altered by the process of dolomitization, by which the calcium carbonate is wholly or partly converted to dolomite by magnesium-rich sea water, or by magnesium-rich solutions permeating joints in the rock.

Dolomites (Italian name: Alpi Dolomitiche) A section of the Alps in NE Italy. Composed of dolomitic limestone, they are characterized by their steep-sided rocky peaks, the highest of which is Marmolada at 10,965 ft (3342 m).

dolphin 1. A toothed *whale of the family *Delphinidae* (about 50 species). Agile and streamlined and up to 15 ft (4.5 m) long, dolphins live in large groups, or schools, and feed mainly on fish; they often accompany ships. They are intelligent creatures with well-developed abilities for social communication and *echolocation. The common dolphin (*Delphinus delphus*), which grows to 7 ft (2.1 m), is blue-black with a white belly and striped body. See also bottlenose; porpoise. 2. A fast-moving fish of the family *Coryphaenidae* (2 species). The common dolphin (*Coryphaena hippurus*) has a bluish tapering body, up to 7 ft (2 m) long, with a large blunt head, a forked tail, and a long dorsal fin. It occurs in tropical and temperate seas and feeds on fish and invertebrates. Order: *Perciformes*.

Domagk, Gerhard (1895–1964) German biochemist, who (in 1932) noticed the powerful effects of a dye, Prontosil, in combating bacterial infection. From this dye was isolated the first of the *sulfonamide drugs (sulfanilamide) which paved the way for the treatment of a wide range of bacterial diseases. Domagk received the 1939 Nobel Prize but was prevented from accepting it until 1947, after the fall of Hitler.

dome A roof or ceiling that is hemispherical in section. In classical architecture it was generally supported by a circular drum and topped by a lantern. The Romans developed the technique of building a dome in cast concrete while the Byzantines introduced the use of four pendentives to build a dome over a square section. Another method was invented in the 15th century by *Brunelleschi, using a strong brick cone to bear the weight and a lighter outer shell for visual effect. The Pantheon and St Peter's in Rome, Hagia Sophia, Istanbul, and St Paul's, London, all have famous domes.

Domenichino (Domenico Zampieri; 1581–1641) Italian painter, born in Bologna. He trained under Ludovico *Carracci. In Rome (1602–31) he painted frescoes of the *Life of St Cecilia* (1615–17; S Luigi dei Francesi) and *Last Communion of St Jerome* (Vatican Museum). His landscapes influenced *Poussin and *Claude.

Domenico Veneziano (active c. 1438–1461) Italian painter of the early Renaissance, probably born in Venice. He settled in Florence, where he painted his famous *St Lucy Altarpiece* (central panel; Uffizi).

Dome of the Rock The great mosque in Jerusalem, built in 691 AD by the *Umayyad caliph, 'Abd al-Malik. It is named for the rock (sacred also to the Jews) over which it was built and stands within the enclosure of the destroyed Jewish *Temple of Jerusalem. It is the third most holy place of Islam, after *Mecca and *Medina. The edifice, also erroneously called the mosque of Omar by Europeans, is an impressive example of early Islamic architecture.

Domesday Book (1086) The survey of England ordered by William I to assess the extent of his own possessions and the value for taxation purposes of the estates of his tenants in chief. Royal commissioners collected, shire by shire, details about each *manor, naming its present owner and its owner under Edward the Confessor, changes in its size since Edward's reign, and many other details. Only a few areas of England were omitted, so the book is a key source for the history of early medieval England.

dominance In genetics, the condition in which one of the *alleles of a gene predominates in the function of that gene. Gregor *Mendel, in his famous experiments, crossed pea plants from a line producing yellow seeds with plants from a line producing green seeds. The resulting offspring all produced yellow seeds, i.e. the dominant allele of the gene determining seed color was that carried by the yellow-seeded plants; the allele carried by the green-seeded plants was recessive.

Domingo, Placido (1941–) Spanish tenor, educated in Mexico. He made his debut at the Metropolitan Opera, New York, in 1968. A leading tenor, he sings a wide range of roles but specializes in Verdi and Puccini.

Dominic, St (Domingo de Guzmán; c. 1170–1221) Spanish churchman, who founded the *Dominicans. One of the canons regular attached to the cathedral at Osma, Castile, and later its prior, he became one of the first successful missionaries to the heretical *Albigenses in the south of France. In 1216 with papal encouragement he founded a religious order devoted to preaching. From his headquarters in Rome he sent out his preachers to establish houses in many major cities. Feast Day: Aug 4. Emblems: a star and a dog holding a torch in its mouth.

Dominica, Commonwealth of An island country in the West Indies, the largest of the Windward Islands. It is of volcanic origin and very mountainous. The population is mainly of African descent. *Economy*: chiefly agricultural; exports include bananas, limes, and lime oil. *History*: discovered by Columbus in 1493, it changed hands several times between the French and the British during the 18th century before finally becoming British in 1783. It became internally self-governing in 1967 and an independent republic within the British Commonwealth in November, 1978. Prime Minister Charles, as head of the Organization of Eastern Caribbean States, issued the invitation to the US government to intervene in Grenada in 1983. President: Aurelius Marie. Prime minister: Mary Eugenia Charles. Official language: English. Official currency: East Caribbean dollar of 100 cents. Area: 289 sq mi (728 sq km). Population (1980): 74,089. Capital: Roseau.

Dominican Republic A country in the Caribbean Sea, occupying the E two thirds of the island of Hispaniola (Haiti occupies the W third). It is largely mountainous, rising to over 10,000 ft (3000 m). It is subject to hurricanes. The population is mainly of mixed African and European descent. *Economy*: chiefly agricultural, the principal cash crop is sugar. Other cash crops include coffee, cocoa, and bananas. Mining and light industry are being developed in an attempt to diversify the economy. The principal mineral export is ferro-nickel and gold and silver mining began in 1975. Oil and hydroelectricity are being exploited. There is a growing tourist industry. *History*: the island was discovered in 1492 by Columbus, who named it Hispaniola. The E became a Spanish colony, while the French established themselves in the W, in what became Haiti. The Spanish colony was ceded to the French in 1795 and soon fell to the Haitian *Toussaint L'Ouverture, who proclaimed himself ruler of all Hispaniola. The Spanish were restored in the E in 1809 and in 1821 the colony gained independence. It was held by Haiti from 1822 until 1844, when the Dominican Republic was founded. Political and economic instability led to US occupation (1916–22) and the establishment (1930) of Trujillo's 30-year dictatorship. Following his assassination Juan Bosch (1909–) was elected (1962) president only to be deposed (1963) in a military coup. An attempt by constitutionalists to reinstate Bosch was thwarted by the US in 1965. In 1983 Salvador Jorge Blanco (1927–) was elected president in a landslide victory, promising to create in the Dominican Republic a democratic socialist state based on the Swedish model. A serious economic crisis, the worst in two decades, forced him to impose even more severe economic austerity measures on the populace, dampening their enthusiasm for him and hopes for prosperity in the country. Official language: Spanish. Official currency: Dominican Republic peso of 100 centavos. Area: 18,700 sq mi (48,442 sq km). Population (1983 est): 6,248,000. Capital and main port: Santo Domingo.

Dominicans (Latin *Ordo Praedicatorum*: Order of Preachers) A Roman Catholic order of friars, also known as Black Friars, Friar Preachers, or (in France) Jacobins, founded by St *Dominic and formally organized at Bologna in 1220–21. Their purpose was preaching and teaching, the individual friars leading mendicant lives much of the time. Among their great scholars was St Thomas *Aquinas. They were prominent defenders of orthodoxy in the *Inquisition and leading missionaries to the New World, although the Jesuits superseded them in this role during the Counter-Reformation. There are also two orders of Dominican nuns.

Domino, Fats (Antoine D.; 1928–) US jazz singer, pianist, and songwriter, who became famous in the rock and roll era. His songs, which contain blues elements, include "Blueberry Hill" and "Jambalaya."

dominoes A game played with rectangular pieces marked at each end with a group of dots or a blank space. In a set of 28 pieces, each group adds up to a number from 1 to 6. Dominoes were used in China in ancient times

but not in Europe until the 18th century. There are many games, but in the basic game each player first draws seven pieces. The player with the double six places it face up on the table. The next player places next to it a six on the end of another domino; if this domino has, for instance, a two on the other end the third player must match either the two or the remaining six. Doubles are placed crosswise, the others end to end. A player who cannot make a match misses his turn or in some games takes another domino. The first to get rid of all his pieces wins.

Domitian(us), Titus Flavius (51–96 AD) Roman emperor (81–96). His frustrating inactivity under his father *Vespasian and his brother *Titus made him a harsh ruler. His government became increasingly absolute and from about 84, as censor for life, he controlled the Senate. His suspicion of treachery culminated in a reign of terror, which precipitated his own murder.

Domrémy-la-Pucelle 48 26N 5 40E A village in NE France, in the Vosges, the birthplace of Joan of Arc.

Don River A river in the SE Soviet Union, flowing mainly S to the Sea of Azov. A canal links it to the Volga River. Length: 1224 mi (1981 km).

Donatello (Donato de Nicolo di Betti Bardi; c. 1386–1466) Florentine sculptor. A pioneer of the Renaissance style, Donatello first broke with tradition in his marble sculptures of *St Mark* and *St George* (1415) for the exterior of Orsanmichele. These and his prophets for the campanile of the Duomo are modeled as lifelike rather than idealized figures. Simultaneously he developed a new form of relief sculpture, in which he created perspective by incising the surface of the marble rather than modeling it in depth. Working also in bronze from the early 1420s, he produced *David* (c. 1430–35; Bargello, Florence), the influential equestrian monument in Padua known as the *Gattamelata* (1447–53), and the high altar for S Antonio, Padua (1446–50). His late works include the expressive painted wooden sculpture of *Mary Magdalen* (1454–55; Baptistry, Florence).

Donatists Members of a schismatic North African Christian group of the 4th and 5th centuries AD, named for— Donatus, one of their bishops. They held that the validity of the sacraments depended on the personal holiness of the minister. St *Augustine's repudiation of their views in the early 5th century crystallized Catholic teaching on these matters. He argued that since the true minister is Christ, the personal worthiness of the priest could not affect the validity of the sacraments.

Donatus, Aelius (4th century AD) Roman grammarian and rhetorician. Donatus was the tutor of St Jerome, and his Latin grammar, *Ars Grammatica*, became a universally accepted textbook in the middle ages.

Donbass. *See* Donets Basin.

Doncaster 53 32N 1 07W An industrial city in N England, in South Yorkshire, with railroad workshops and coalmining. Population (1981): 81,610.

Donegal (Irish name: Dún Na Ngall) A county in the N Republic of Ireland, in Ulster bordering on the Atlantic Ocean. Chiefly mountainous, it has a rugged indented coastline. Agricultural products include barley, oats, and potatoes; cattle and sheep are reared. Linen and tweed are manufactured. Area: 1865 sq mi (4830 sq km). Population (1971): 108,000. County town: Lifford.

Donets Basin (or Donbass) An industrial region in the SE Soviet Union, in the Ukrainian SSR. It is the oldest center of coal production in the country and still its major coal-producing and steel-manufacturing area. Area: about 10,000 sq mi (25,900 sq km).

Donetsk (name until 1924: Yuzovka; name from 1924 until 1961: Stalino) 48 22N 40 02E A city in the SW Soviet Union, in the Ukrainian SSR on the Kalmius River. The major city of the *Donets Basin, it has important coalmining and metallurgical industries. Population (1981 est): 1,040,000.

Dong Hai. *See* East China Sea.

Dongola (or Dunqulah) 19 10N 30 27E A small town in the N Sudan, on the Nile River. It was the capital of the Christian kingdom of Nubia (6th–14th centuries). Population (1973): 5937.

Dongting, Lake (or Lake Tung-t'ing) A lake in SE China. Seasonally fed or drained by the Yangtze River, it regulates the river's flooding. Area: (winter) 1500 sq mi (3900 sq km); (summer) about 4000 sq mi (10,000 sq km).

Dönitz, Karl (1891–1980) German admiral. He made his name as a U-boat commander in World War I and in the first three years of World War

II he developed the "pack" system of submarine attack. In 1943 he became grand admiral and then commander in chief of the German navy. He was appointed chancellor after Hitler's death and was imprisoned from 1946 to 1956 for war crimes.

Donizetti, Gaetano   (1797–1848) Italian composer of operas. He became paralyzed and mentally ill toward the end of his life. He wrote with great facility and his 75 stage works rely more on *coloratura display, the popular characteristic of his age, than on intrinsic dramatic effect. Revivals of such operas as *Lucia di Lammermoor* (1835) and *Daughter of the Regiment* (1840) have been successful with such singers as Joan Sutherland or Maria Callas in the title roles.

Don Juan   The great aristocratic libertine of European literature. His probable first appearance was in Tirso de Molina's play *El burlador de Sevilla* (1630), in which he kills the father of his latest victim; he mockingly invites the old man's statue to dinner, and it drags him off to hell. This plot is retained in subsequent versions, most notably *Molière's *Don Juan* (1665) and *Mozart's *Don Giovanni* (1787). In satirical treatments by *Byron (*Don Juan*, 1819–24) and G. B. *Shaw (*Man and Superman*, 1903) Juan is more hunted than hunter.

donkey   A domesticated *ass. Donkeys are more commonly used for pack and draft work than for riding: being stronger in the hindquarters than the forequarters, they must bear the load over the pelvis, which is a less comfortable position for a rider. *See also* hinny; mule.

Donleavy, J(ames) P(atrick)   (1926–) Irish-American novelist. His successful first novel, *The Ginger Man* (1956), was followed by further comic picaresque novels including *The Saddest Summer of Samuel S.* (1967), *The Onion Eaters* (1971), and *The Destinies of Darcy Dancer, Gentleman* (1977).

Donne, John   (1572–1631) English poet, greatest of the Metaphysical school. He received a Roman Catholic education, studied at Oxford and Lincoln's Inn, and took part in naval raids on Spain. In 1601 he secretly married the niece of his patron, Sir Thomas Egerton, and was briefly imprisoned. Failing to gain secular advancement, despite having several influential patrons, he became an Anglican priest in 1615 and was appointed Dean of St Paul's in 1621. His poetry is rich, involved, and often obscure; it combines passionate feeling for God, woman, and humanity with brilliant intellectual wit. Almost all of it, even religious works, such as *La Corona* (1607) and the Holy Sonnets, was written before 1615.

Donner Party   (1846–47) A group of US pioneers en route to California that became trapped by snow in the wilderness. Led by George Donner, a wagon train party of 87 left Illinois, but using a new route around the southern end of the Great Salt Lake, became trapped by mountain snow when they reached a pass through the mountains. Forced to camp for 4 months, the 47 survivors eventually resorted to cannibalism to ward off starvation.

Doolittle, Hilda   (1886–1961) US poet, who wrote under the initials H. D. Born in Pennsylvania, she went to England in 1911 and married Richard *Aldington. A leading exponent of Imagism, her books include *Sea Garden* (1916), *Hymen* (1921), *The Walls Do Not Fall* (1944), and *Helen in Egypt* (1961).

Doppler, Christian Johann   (1803–53) Austrian physicist, who explained and derived, in 1842, an expression for the change in frequency of a wave when the source is moving relative to an observer (*see* Doppler effect). He attempted to apply this principle to the coloration of stars; although the effect is too small to be observed visually, it is now widely used spectroscopically in astronomy.

Doppler effect   The apparent change in the frequency of a wave caused by relative motion between the source and the observer. When the source and the observer are approaching each other, the apparent frequency of the wave increases; when one is traveling away from the other, the apparent frequency decreases. An example of the Doppler effect is the change in pitch of a train whistle as the train passes through a station. The effect can also be observed as a shifting of the wavelength of light from a receding star toward the red end of the spectrum. In this case the effect is known as the *redshift. Named for Christian *Doppler.

dor beetle   A large shiny black convex beetle, with broad digging legs, belonging to a family (*Geotrupidae*; about 300 species) of dung feeders. Dor beetles burrow into the soil beneath dung and lay their eggs on plugs of dung hauled down for use as a food source.

JOHN DONNE   *A miniature portrait (1616) by Isaac Oliver.*

Dorcas gazelle   A small *gazelle, *Gazella dorcas*, of N Africa and S Asia, also called afri. A desert animal, it is light red with a pale flank stripe and distinctive face stripes.

Dorchester   50 43N 2 26W A market town in S England, the administrative center for Dorset on the Frome River. It has several Roman remains and is associated with Thomas Hardy, featuring as Casterbridge in his novels. Population (1981): 14,049.

Dordogne River   A river in SW France. Rising in the Auvergne Mountains, it flows SW and W to enter the Gironde estuary NNE of Bordeaux. It is important for hydroelectric power and has famous vineyards along its lower course. Length: 293 mi (472 km).

Dordrecht (*or* Dort)   51 48N 4 40E A port in the SW Netherlands, in South Holland province. It has a thriving timber trade and metallurgical, shipbuilding, and chemical industries. Population (1981 est): 108,041.

Doré, (Paul) Gustave (Louis Christophe)   (1832–83) French illustrator, painter, and sculptor, born in Strasbourg. He established his wide and lasting popularity in the 1850s with his illustrations of Rabelais' books and Balzac's *Contes drôlatiques*. These were followed by illustrations to Dante, Cervantes, Tennyson, etc., showing his taste for the grotesque and dramatic. His realistic scenes of poverty in *London* influenced Van Gogh. □Camelot.

Dorgon   (1612–50) Prince of Manchuria, who controlled China as regent for a child emperor from 1643 to 1650. Continuing the expansionist policy of his father *Nurhachi, Dorgon helped to lay the foundations of the *Qing dynasty in China, basing its power on centralized government instead of the clan system.

Doria   A family that was prominent in Genoa from the 12th to 18th centuries. The most notable member of the family was **Andrea Doria** (1466–1560). An admiral and condottiere, he served the French against Emperor Charles V, ousted imperial troops from Genoa, and then transferred his allegiance to Charles and expelled the French in return for the emperor's recognition of Genoese liberty (1528). He then became the ruler of Genoa, initiating the period of aristocratic rule (1528–1797) during which the Doria family contributed six doges of Genoa.

Dorians   Iron Age Greek conquerors of the S Aegean region (c. 1100–1000 BC). Moving southward from Epirus and SW Macedonia, they displaced the *Achaeans and brought about the final collapse of the Bronze Age *Mycenaean civilization. They settled in the S and E Peloponnese, near the isthmus of Corinth, in the S Aegean islands, the Dodecanese, and SW Anatolia. There were three major tribes: the Hylleis, Pamphyloi, and Dymanes. The Doric dialects they spoke belonged to the Western Greek group.

Doric order. *See* orders of architecture.

dormancy A period of reduced metabolic activity during which a plant or animal or a reproductive body (e.g. seeds or spores) can survive unfavorable environmental conditions. The onset of dormancy may be triggered by a number of factors, including changes in temperature, daylength (*see* photoperiodism), and availability of water, oxygen, and carbon dioxide. The dormant phase of a life cycle is represented as spores in bacteria and fungi, cysts in protozoans and some invertebrates, and seeds, buds, and bulbs or similar organs in plants. *See also* hibernation.

dormouse A climbing *rodent belonging to the family *Gliridae* (about 10 species) of Eurasia and Africa. The common dormouse (*Muscardinus avellanarius*) is reddish, about 2.4 in (6 cm) long with a 2 in (5-cm) bushy tail. It sleeps in a nest above ground level during the day, feeding at night on nuts, berries, and seeds. During winter it hibernates beneath debris or tree stumps, occasionally waking to feed on stored food.

Dornier, Claudius (1884–1969) German aircraft designer and manufacturer, who constructed the first all-metal aircraft (1911). At his works in Friedrichshafen he manufactured both civil and military planes.

Dorpat. *See* Tartu.

Dorr's Rebellion (1841–42) A US rebellion in Rhode Island, led by Thomas W. Dorr (1805–54), that protested the lack of reforms in the state constitution. Because of restrictions in the constitution regarding landowners' voting rights and representation in the legislature, Dorr, a legislature member, and his followers attacked the state house and proclaimed Dorr governor under their own constitution. Rioting followed, and Dorr was arrested and spent a year in jail. By 1843 a new constitution, incorporating many of the reforms advocated by Dorr, was put into effect.

Dorset A county of SW England, bordering on the English Channel. The chief rivers are the Frome and the Stour. Agriculture is predominant, especially livestock farming. Tourism is important, notably in Bournemouth and Weymouth. Many towns are associated with the writings of Thomas *Hardy, who included Dorset within his fictitious region of Wessex. Area: 1017 sq mi (2634 sq km). Population (1981): 591,990. Administrative center: Dorchester.

Dort. *See* Dordrecht.

Dortmund 51 32N 07 27E A city in NW West Germany, in North Rhine-Westphalia in the *Ruhr. A port on the Dortmund–Ems Canal and a major industrial center, it produces steel, furniture, textiles, coal, and beer. Its university was established in 1966. Population (1980 est): 609,400.

Dortmund–Ems Canal A major canal in West Germany. Opened in 1899, it links the Ruhr industrial area with the North Sea near Emden. Length: about 168 mi (270 km).

dory. *See* John Dory.

Dos Passos, John (1896–1970) US novelist. Born in Chicago, Dos Passos served as an ambulance driver in World War I and returned from that experience to publish his first novel, *Three Soldiers*, in 1921. He later served as foreign correspondent in Spain, Mexico, and the Near East. His greatest work was the trilogy *U.S.A.*, in which he experimented with stream-of-consciousness style and the use of historical personalities as characters to produce a radical interpretation of American history from 1900 until the Depression. It comprises the novels *The Forty-Second Parallel* (1930), *1919* (1932), and *The Big Money* (1936).

Dostoievski, Fedor Mikhailovich (1821–81) Russian novelist. Son of a landowner murdered by his serfs, he graduated as a military engineer in 1843, but resigned his commission and began writing. In 1849 he was sentenced to four years hard labor in Siberia, followed by army service, for printing socialist propaganda. In 1864 his wife and brother died, and he incurred heavy gambling debts. He lived in W Europe from 1867 to 1871 with his new wife, his secretary Anna Snitkina, plagued by his epilepsy and compulsive gambling. He returned to Russia in 1871 and became relatively prosperous, stable, and conservative. His major novels, in which he explored moral and political themes with merciless psychological realism, are *Crime and Punishment* (1866), *The Idiot* (1868–69), *The Possessed* (1869–72), and *The Brothers Karamazov* (1879–80).

dotterel A small Eurasian *plover, *Eudromias morinellus*, that nests in tundra regions and migrates to the Mediterranean and SW Asia for the

winter. It is 8 in (20 cm) long and mottled brown above with a broad white eye stripe and a gray breast separated by a narrow white band from its russet belly.

Dou, Gerrit (1613–75) Dutch painter of domestic interiors and portraits, born in Leyden. He studied under *Rembrandt (1628–31), who influenced his early portrait *Rembrandt's Mother* (c. 1630; Rijksmuseum, Amsterdam). *The Poulterer's Shop* (National Gallery, London), showing his interest in still life, is a more typical work.

Douai 50 22N 3 05E A city in N France, in the Nord department. It became a center for English Roman Catholics following the establishment of a college by William Allen in 1568 and it was here that the *Douai Bible was published. Douai is the coalmining center of N France and has iron and steel industries. Population (1975): 47,570.

Douai Bible The Roman Catholic version of the Bible in English, translated from the *Vulgate by Roman Catholic scholars from Oxford, who had fled to Europe during the reign of Elizabeth I and who were members of the English College at Douai. The New Testament was published at Reims in 1582 and the Old Testament at Douai in 1609–10. Although it retained a number of difficult technical expressions foreign to colloquial English, its language influenced the translators of the *King James Version.

Douala 4 04N 9 43E The largest city in Cameroon, on the Wouri River estuary. A deepwater port and the chief export point of the country, it is also a major West African industrial center with brewing, food-processing, textiles, and timber industries. Population (1976): 458,426.

double bass The lowest-pitched □musical instrument of the violin family. The flat back and sloping shoulders of some double basses are derived from the *viol family. Unlike the violin, viola, and cello, its four strings are tuned in fourths (E, A, D, G). It has a range of over three octaves, from the E an octave below the bass stave. The double bass is a member of the symphony orchestra; it is also played in jazz and dance bands, usually by plucking the strings. Music for the double bass is written an octave higher than it sounds.

Doubleday, Abner (1819–93) US Union general and sportsman. A graduate of West Point, he served in the *Mexican War and, from 1861, in the *Civil War, serving as a general in the battles of Bull Run, South Mountain, Antietam, Fredericksburg, and Gettysburg. He is incorrectly credited with inventing baseball in 1839 in Cooperstown, NY.

double vision The condition in which a person sees two images of a single object. Known medically as diplopia, it is caused by lack of coordination between the muscles that move the eyes. Temporary double vision may occur after taking drugs or alcohol; alternatively it may be due to damage or disease of one of the nerves that supply the eye muscles.

Doubs River A river in E France. Rising in the Jura Mountains and flowing SW to join the Saône River, it forms part of the Swiss–French border. Length: 267 mi (430 km).

Douglas, Stephen Arnold (1813–61) US politician, lawyer, and orator. He practiced law in Illinois and served in the state legislature before serving in the US House of Representatives (1843–47) and as a Democrat senator from Illinois (1847–61). He worked for the passage of the *Compromise of 1850, advocated popular sovereignty in the territories (the right of territorial settlers to decide for themselves the question of slavery), and originated the *Kansas-Nebraska Act of 1854. In 1858 his opponent for the Senate seat was Republican Abraham *Lincoln. From this election campaign evolved the *Lincoln-Douglas Debates, a series of debates on the slavery question. Barely 5 ft (1.5 m) tall, he was often called the "Little Giant."

Douglas, William O(rville) (1898–1980) US jurist, conservationist, and writer; Supreme Court associate justice (1939–75). Born in Minnesota, he practiced law in New York City and Washington and taught at Yale University (1928–36). While a member of the Securities and Exchange Commission (1936–39; its chairman from 1937), he advocated reform of the New York Stock Exchange practices. President Franklin D. *Roosevelt appointed him to the US Supreme Court in 1939. He was known as a liberal who championed civil rights and opposed censorship. Upon retirement in 1975 he had the longest tenure of any judge on the court. An avid conservationist, he wrote *Of Men and Mountains* (1950), *Beyond the High Himalayas* (1952), and *A Wilderness Bill of Rights* (1965).

Douglas fir A conifer, *Pseudotsuga menziesii*, native to W North America and cultivated widely both for ornament and for its high-quality timber, used for construction, poles, masts, etc. 198–295 ft (60–90 m) high, it has flexible blunt-tipped needles and cylindrical cones, about 3 in (8 cm) long, with three-pronged bracts protruding from the scales. Family: *Pinaceae*.

STEPHEN A. DOUGLAS *"The Little Giant," whose doctrine of "popular sovereignty" was the main issue of the Lincoln-Douglas debates.*

Douglas-Home, Sir Alec (Alexander Frederick D.-H., Baron Home of the Hirsel; 1903–) British statesman; Conservative prime minister (1963–64). He was a Member of Parliament (1931–45, 1950–51) before becoming 14th Earl of Home. He was foreign secretary (1960–63) and then, to widespread surprise, succeeded Macmillan as prime minister, renouncing his peerages. Following the Conservative electoral defeat (1964) he resigned the party leadership (1965). He received a life peerage in 1974.

Douglass, Frederick (1817–95) US abolitionist and reformer. An escaped slave (1838), he delivered anti-slavery lectures in New England until forced to flee to England in 1845. He was able to return to the US when his freedom was purchased in 1847, and he started publication of *North Star* (1847–63), an abolitionist newspaper. He worked to aid fugitive slaves, for women's rights, and then, during the Civil War, for the emancipation of blacks. He was later minister to Haiti (1889–91).

Doukhobors (Russian: fighters against the spirit) Russian nonconformist Christian sect founded in the 18th century. Because of their anarchistic doctrines (denial of the state's right to levy tax, etc.) and heterodox religious views (belief in reincarnation, denial of Christ's divinity), they were for a long time persecuted. With the help of *Tolstoy and English Quakers, they emigrated from Georgia to Canada in 1898, where they subsequently came into conflict with the government over such matters as sending their children to state schools. In 1958 some members of the sect were permitted to return to the Soviet Union.

Doulton English pottery works, originally at Lambeth (London), specializing in salt-glazed stoneware. Brown stoneware vessels with relief molded portrait and landscape ornament were typical of the period to 1850. From 1856 Sir Henry Doulton (1820–97) encouraged artist potters to produce unique studio pottery in colored glazes, using wood-fixed kilns. These were exhibited at the 1867 Paris Exhibition.

Douro River (Spanish name: Duero) A river in SW Europe. Flowing W from N central Spain, it forms part of the border between Spain and Portugal before entering the Atlantic Ocean at Oporto. Length: 556 mi (895 km).

douroucouli A nocturnal *monkey, *Aotus trivirgatus*, of Central and South America, also called night monkey or owl monkey. It is 22–30 in (55–75 cm) long including the tail (12–16 in [30–40 cm]) and moves through trees stalking small animals. It also eats fruit and leaves. Family: *Cebidae*.

dove. *See* pigeon.

Dover 51 08N 1 19E A port in SE England, in Kent on the Strait of Dover. An ancient Cinque Port, it is the UK's chief ferry and Hovercraft port for the Continent. Population (1981): 32,843.

Dover 39 10N 75 32W The capital city of Delaware, near Delaware Bay. Founded in 1683, it has many 18th- and 19th-century buildings. Population (1980): 17,488.

Dover, Strait of (French name: Pas de Calais) A channel separating England from NW France comprising the narrowest part of the *English Channel. Minimum width: 21 mi (34 km).

Dow-Jones index A weighted average of the prices on the New York Stock Exchange of 30 industrial shares, computed each working day by Dow Jones and Co. The first index was devised in 1897 using only 12 shares. It is the principal indicator of movements in share prices in the US.

Down A county in E Northern Ireland, bordering on the Irish Sea. It consists of lowlands in the E rising to the Mourne Mountains in the SW. Agriculture is the chief occupation; dairy farming is especially important. Area: 952 sq mi (2466 sq km). Population (1971 est): 311,876. County town: Downpatrick.

Downing Street A street in the Greater London borough of the City of Westminster, adjoining Whitehall. No 10 is the official residence of the prime minister; the chancellor of the exchequer resides at No 11. It was named for the English statesman Sir George Downing (1623–84).

Downpatrick 54 20N 5 43W A market town in Northern Ireland, the county town of Co Down. It is the reputed burial place of St Patrick. Population (1971): 7405.

Downs, North and South Two roughly parallel ranges of chalk hills in SE England, separated by the *Weald. The North Downs extend W–E between Guildford, in Surrey, and Dover, in Kent. The South Downs extend generally SE from Winchester, in Hampshire, to Beachy Head. The Downs have traditionally been sheep-farming areas.

Down's syndrome A genetic disease in which a baby has one extra chromosome; it is named for J. L. H. Down (1828–96), an English physician who studied the disease. Affected children are mentally retarded and their faces resemble those of Orientals, which is why they were formerly called mongols and the disease mongolism. In spite of their handicaps, these children are usually cheerful and with special education can live relatively normal lives in a family. Down's syndrome is more commonly seen in babies of mothers over 40; it can be detected during pregnancy (*see* amniocentesis).

dowsing The use of divining- or dowsing-rods to discover subterranean minerals or water. From the 16th century divining-rods were employed by miners and treasure hunters, a function now largely usurped by metal detectors. Dowsing for water is still of practical value; skilled dowsers can estimate the depth and flow of underground streams. The rod is traditionally a Y-shaped stick which, when its two prongs are grasped, twists in the hands of the dowser as he walks over the relevant place. An alternative means are metal rods, held parallel and a few inches apart, which swing across each other. The nature of the stimuli causing these reactions is still unexplained.

Doyle, Sir Arthur Conan (1859–1930) British author, creator of the archetypal detective Sherlock Holmes. Born in Edinburgh, Conan Doyle graduated from medical school there but soon turned to writing. Holmes, inspired by the diagnostic methods of an Edinburgh lecturer, brought Conan Doyle great success. Holmes first appeared in the novel *A Study in Scarlet* (1887), narrated, as are nearly all the short stories and novels about him, by his dogged but unimaginative friend Dr John H. Watson, almost a self-caricature by the author. Conan Doyle also created the coarsely brilliant Professor Challenger in *The Lost World* (1912) but he valued most highly his historical novels, such as *The White Company* (1890). Knighted in 1902 for his service, and subsequent defense of British involvement, in the second Boer War, Conan Doyle became a champion of *spiritualism after the death of his son in World War I. □detective story.

D'Oyly Carte, Richard (1844–1901) British theater impresario and manager. He produced most of the comic operas of Gilbert and Sullivan. The Savoy Theatre, which he opened in 1881 to house these productions, was the first London theater to have electric lighting.

Drabble, Margaret (1939–) British novelist. Most of her novels concern the moral and emotional problems of women in contemporary society. They include *The Millstone* (1965), *The Needle's Eye* (1972), *The Ice Age* (1977), and *The Middle Ground* (1980). She has also written a study of Arnold Bennett (1974).

Draco (7th century BC) Athenian lawgiver. His legal system is reputedly the first comprehensive code of laws drawn up in Athens. It was so harshly punitive that "draconian" has since been used to describe any rigorous or cruel law. Draco's code prescribed the death penalty by the state for most offenses, taking retribution out of the hands of private citizens. *Solon abolished Draco's code in 590 BC, retaining only his homicide laws.

Dracula, Count The central character of Bram *Stoker's gothic novel *Dracula* (1897) and of many horror films, a Transylvanian *vampire. The name, meaning "demon," was applied to Vlad IV the Impaler, a 15th-century Walachian prince who was the prototype of the fictional character.

Draft Riots (1862–63) Outbreaks of violence in both the North and the South US protesting against conscription methods during the Civil War. The worst riot took place in New York City in 1863. Workers, angry over their inability to buy their way out of the draft, as the wealthy could, rioted in the streets; over 1,000 deaths and $1,500,000 of damage occurred.

dragonet A small spiny-rayed fish, of the family *Callionymidae*, that has a smooth slender body, 4–8 in (10–20 cm) long, flattened anteriorly and often brightly colored. The pelvic fins are located in front of the pectoral fins. Dragonets live on the bottom in temperate and tropical seas and feed on invertebrates. Order: *Perciformes*.

dragonfish A small *bony fish belonging to an order (*Pegasiformes*; about 5 species) found in warm waters of the Indian and Pacific Oceans. They have an elongated body, up to 6 in (16 cm) long, with bony armor, a long snout, and large horizontal winglike pectoral fins.

dragonfly A strong agile brightly colored insect belonging to the widely distributed suborder *Anisoptera* (about 4500 species). It has a long body, large eyes, and transparent veined wings (spanning up to 7 in [180 mm]), which are held horizontally at rest. Both the adults and freshwater nymphs (naiads) are active carnivores and control many insect pests, such as mosquitoes, flies, and gnats. Order: *Odonata*.

dragonroot A perennial North American herbaceous plant, *Arisaema dracontium*, also called green dragon or dragon arum. The flower comprises a central column of sexual organs surmounted by a long tapering cylindrical structure (the spadix) and surrounded by a much shorter pointed green sheath (the spathe). The tuberous roots were formerly used in medicine. Family: *Araceae*.

dragon's blood A red gum that exudes from the fruit of some palms. It was once used in Europe as a medicine because of its astringent and healing properties. It is used as a varnish for violins and in photoengraving.

dragon tree A treelike plant, *Dracaena draco*, native to the Canary Islands. Growing 59 ft (18 m) tall and 20 ft (6 m) wide, it has large sword-shaped leaves at the tips of the branches and clusters of greenish-white flowers followed by orange berries. The dragon tree is sometimes grown as a pot plant for its foliage. The trunk was formerly used as a source of a red gum resin, *dragon's blood. Family: *Agavaceae*.

drag racing 1. A form of *automobile racing that originated in the US. It is held in heats of two cars on a straight strip a quarter of a mile (402 m) long. Using a standing start, races depend heavily on acceleration with the "elapsed time" (from start to finish) and "terminal velocity" of each vehicle measured electronically. Speeds have reached 250 mph (403 kph) in specially constructed light powerful vehicles (slingshots *or* rails), although races are also held for modified production models. 2. A form of motorcycle racing organized in the same way.

Drake, Sir Francis (1540–96) English navigator and admiral. Drake's first important voyages were trading expeditions to Guinea and the West Indies and in 1567 he accompanied Sir John *Hawkins (a relative) to the Gulf of Mexico. In 1572 he embarked on a plundering expedition, destroying towns on the Isthmus of Panama and capturing considerable quantities of booty. In 1578 he became the first Englishman to navigate the Straits of Magellan intending, with Elizabeth I's consent, to raid the Pacific coast. Alone out of five ships, his *Golden Hind* sailed N but unable to find a way back to the Atlantic Ocean crossed the Pacific Ocean, returning home via the Cape of Good Hope. He landed at Plymouth in 1580 and was knighted by Elizabeth on board the *Hind* in 1581. Drake crowned his career by helping to defeat the Spanish *Armada at Gravelines (1588). He died on an expedition to the West Indies.

Drakensberg Mountains (*or* Quathlamba) The chief mountain range in S Africa, extending from Cape Province (South Africa) along the E border of Lesotho to Swaziland, reaching 11,425 ft (3482 m) at Thaba Ntlenyana.

Drammen 59 45N 10 15E A seaport in S Norway, at the mouth of the Drammen River. It exports timber, wood pulp, and paper. Population (1981 est): 49,523.

DRAGON TREE *This plant is unusual in that—like broadleaved trees—it produces true wood. The most famous of these trees was one in Tenerife, which was said to be 6000 years old.*

Drapeau, Jean (1916–) Canadian lawyer and politician; mayor of Montreal (1954–). He formed the Montreal Civic Party (1960) and was reelected as mayor on a platform for city beautification and development. During his terms in office the subway system and Expo '67 were built, and the 1976 Summer Olympics were held in Montreal.

Drava River (*or* R. Drave) A river in E central Europe, flowing E from N Italy through Austria, then SE forming part of the Yugoslav-Hungarian border to join the Danube River. Length: 450 mi (725 km).

Dravidian languages A large language family of up to 20 languages spoken mainly in S India. The major languages of the family are *Tamil, which has a literary tradition dating back 2000 years, *Kanarese (*or* Kannada), Telugu, *Malayalam, and Tulu. These are all spoken in a contiguous area in India, and Tamil is also spoken in Sri Lanka. There is one Dravidian language, Brahui, that is separated from the main bloc by almost a thousand miles and is spoken in Pakistan. The Dravidian languages are all agglutinative (*see* languages, classification of) and this is strong evidence for separating them from the other major language bloc of the subcontinent, the *Indo-European group.

dreams Ideas and images experienced during *sleep. Dreams may take place at any stage of sleep, but they are particularly associated with the paradoxical phase, in which the eyes move rapidly about. Dreams in this stage of sleep are the most vivid in their imagery and the farthest removed from waking thoughts. Everybody has dreams: most people have paradoxical sleep about four or five times a night, for about 20 minutes at a time; whether or not the dream is remembered depends on how quickly after it the sleeper wakes up.

If a person is repeatedly deprived of the chance to dream (by being woken when a dream starts) he becomes irritable, inefficient, and eventually suffers *hallucinations. After such deprivation, he dreams more frequently when he is again allowed to. The new combinations of ideas produced in dreams can be creative and valuable. *Psychoanalysis gives much weight to the content of dreams as an approach to understanding the unconscious mind. Experimental studies indicate that the content of dreams is affected by the dreamer's mood and by stimuli that occur while he sleeps. *See also* nightmares.

Dred Scott v. Sanford (of Sandford; 1857)   A Supreme Court ruling that declared the *Missouri Compromise unconstitutional. Dred Scott, a slave, had been brought from Missouri, a slave state, to Illinois, a free state, and then to Wisconsin, a free territory. Upon his return to Missouri, he filed suit against his owner, John Sanford, maintaining that he was a free man because he had been a resident of a free state and a free territory. Although a step backward in the fight against slavery, the 13th and 14th amendments (1865–1868) rendered this court decision invalid.

dredger   A vessel designed to deepen underwater channels in rivers, docks, canals, etc., by removing material from the bottom. The types used include the suction dredger, which sucks up mud through a rubber pipe from the bottom and either deposits it in barges or in its own tanks; the bucket-ladder dredger, which carries an endless chain of buckets supported on a frame; and the grab dredger, which operates much like a power shovel.

Dreiser, Theodore (1871–1945)   American novelist. Born in Terre Haute, Indiana, son of a poor German immigrant, Dreiser worked as a reporter on various newspapers throughout the Midwest. In 1894 he settled in New York City where he published his first novel, *Sister Carrie*, in 1900. This work, in its disturbing portrayal of the hypocrisy of contemporary sexual mores, was initially attacked by critics and withdrawn by the publisher, but was later recognized as an important work of social realism. Dreiser's most famous novel, *An American Tragedy* (1925), based on an actual murder case, brought him both critical and financial success. Later in his career, Dreiser became increasingly committed to the cause of socialism and published several non-fiction works including *Tragic America* (1932) and *America is Worth Saving* (1941).

Drenthe (*or* Drente)   A low-lying province in the E Netherlands, bordering on West Germany. Parts of its extensive bogs and heaths have been reclaimed for agriculture; produce includes potatoes, rye, and dairy products. Oil is extracted around Shoonebeek. Area: 1037 sq mi (2685 sq km). Population (1981 est): 421,528. Capital: Assen.

Dresden   51 5N 13 41E A city in SE East Germany, on the *Elbe River, the former capital of Saxony. One of the world's most beautiful cities prior to its devastation by bombs in 1945, it has since been rebuilt. Dresden is a center of culture, light industry, and market gardening. The china industry moved to Meissen in 1710. It is the site of a music college and a technical university. Population (1980 est): 516,284.

Dresden, Battle of (August 26–27, 1813)   A battle fought near the capital of Saxony between 120,000 French troops led by Napoleon and an Austrian, Prussian, and Russian force of 170,000. Napoleon inflicted a crushing defeat on the allies, who lost 38,000 men.

Dresden porcelain. *See* Meissen porcelain.

dressage   The training of a riding (*or* carriage) horse to make it calm, supple, and responsive to its rider (*or* driver). It was originally a training for military charges; the present, more humane, methods only developed in the 18th century. The most advanced stage is *haute école* equitation in which a horse is taught to perform intricate leaps and movements. This classical art is practiced by the *Spanish Riding School in Vienna and the Cadre Noir of the French Cavalry School at Saumur. Dressage competitions consist of a sequence of complex prescribed movements. *See also* equestrianism.

Drew, Daniel (1797–1879)   US financier and stockbroker. He entered the brokerage business in 1844 after having run a steamboat company since 1834. He speculated in stock in the Erie Railroad and successfully, although unscrupulously, fought Cornelius Vanderbilt for control of the line (1866–68). He was forced to declare bankruptcy (1876) after the panic of 1873. Drew Theological Seminary (1866) in Madison, N. J., was founded by him.

Dreyer, Carl Theodor (1889–1968)   Danish film director. He began his career in films as a scriptwriter in 1912. His major films concern spiritual and supernatural themes and are distinguished by their atmospheric con-

centration and intensity. They include *La Passion de Jeanne d'Arc* (1928) and *Ordet* (1955).

Dreyer, Johan Ludvig Emil (1852–1926)   Danish astronomer, who compiled the *New General Catalogue of Nebulae and Clusters of Stars* (1888). This work is still a standard reference catalogue for nonstellar objects, which are referred to by their catalogue number, e.g. the galaxy NGC 175.

Dreyfus, Alfred (1859–1935)   French Jewish army officer. Unjustly accused of revealing state secrets to the German military attaché in Paris, in 1894 Dreyfus, the victim of *antisemitism, was deported for life to *Devil's Island. His case was reopened in 1898, largely owing to the championship of Zola and Clemenceau, becoming a cause célèbre and the focus of conflict between royalist, nationalist, and militarist elements on the one hand and socialist, republican, and anticlerical factions on the other. Following a retrial in 1899, Dreyfus was pardoned but not completely cleared until 1906, when he received the Legion of Honor.

Driesch, Hans Adolf Eduard (1867–1941)   German zoologist, whose work gave impetus to modern embryology. His interpretation of studies on developing sea urchin embryos led him to become a lifelong advocate of *vitalism.

drift   1. The debris, including boulders, sand, clay, and gravel, deposited by glaciers or by glacial meltwater. 2. The superficial deposits occurring above the solid underlying rock on the earth's surface. Geological maps are published in both drift and solid editions to distinguish between them.

drill   An *Old World monkey, *Mandrillus leucophaeus*, of central West Africa, smaller than the closely related *mandrill. Drills inhabit inland forests, moving about on the ground in small groups and eating leaves, fruit, and worms.

driver ant   An African *ant of the genus *Dorylus* or related genera, which has a lifestyle similar to the New World *army ant. Subfamily: *Dorylinae*.

Drogheda (Irish name: Droichead Átha)   53 43N 6 21W A port in the Republic of Ireland, in Co Louth on the River Boyne. Its garrison was massacred by Cromwell in 1649. Drogheda exports cattle and has brewing, linen and cotton, and engineering industries. Population (1971): 19,762.

dromedary. *See* camel.

drone. *See* bee.

drongo   A songbird belonging to a family (*Dicruridae*; 20 species) occurring in Old World tropical forests. About 9–14 in (22–35 cm) long, drongos are usually black, often with long tail plumes, and have a harsh song. They have stout sharp-hooked bills and feed on large insects, which are often caught in flight. These birds are noted for fiercely defending their territories against intruders.

dropsy. *See* edema.

dropwort   A perennial herb, *Filipendula vulgaris*, of grasslands and clearings in Eurasia and N Africa. Up to 28 in (70 cm) high, it has compound leaves with 8–20 divided toothed leaflets. The flowers, which occur in flat-topped terminal clusters, have 5–6 red-tinged white petals and long prominent stamens. The tuberous roots may be eaten. Family: *Rosaceae*.

Drosera. *See* sundew.

Drosophila   A genus of small *fruit flies (about 1000 species), also called vinegar flies. Most species feed on fermenting materials, such as rotting or damaged fruit, but a few are predatory or parasitic. Some species, especially *D. melanogaster*, have been used extensively in laboratory studies of heredity and evolution because of the large chromosomes in their salivary glands and their short life cycle. Family: *Drosophilidae*.

drought   An extended period of dry weather with a virtual absence of precipitation, causing a lack of moisture in the soil. Droughts in densely populated areas reliant on agriculture, such as India and China, can have disastrous effects.

drowning   Suffocation due to water in the air passages. Death occurs much more rapidly in fresh water than sea water. This is because fresh water flows through the lungs into the blood, causing the red blood cells to burst and release potassium, which causes the heart to stop. Salt water mechanically prevents the oxygen reaching the lungs. It can take up to ten minutes to drown, and anybody rescued should immediately be given *artificial respiration.

drug dependence   The condition resulting from regular use of a drug such that its withdrawal causes emotional distress (psychological dependence) or physical illness (physical dependence). Drugs causing psychological dependence include cannabis, LSD, and the nicotine in tobacco. Physical dependence is associated with such drugs as morphine, heroin, barbiturates, and alcohol. Withdrawal of these drugs causes unpleasant symptoms (withdrawal symptoms) that disappear on taking further doses. Overdosage of such drugs is common and can be fatal. Physical dependence is invariably associated with severe psychological dependence and requires specialist treatment. *See also* alcoholism.

drugs Compounds that alter the physiological state of living organisms (including man). Medicinal drugs are widely used for the treatment, prevention, and diagnosis of disease. The wide range of drugs available for this purpose includes the anesthetics (*see* anesthesia), *analgesics, *antibiotics, *cytotoxic drugs, *diuretics, hormonal drugs, and *tranquilizers.

Some drugs are taken solely for the pleasurable effects they produce. Many such drugs are addictive (*see* narcotics) and—despite rigorous controls to restrict their use—illegal trade in them continues. The most widely used illicit drugs include *opium and its derivatives and synthetic substitutes, stimulants such as cocaine and amphetamine, hallucinogens such as LSD, marijuana, and some sedatives. *See also* drug dependence.

Druids Ancient Celtic priests who were also revered as teachers and judges. Information about them is largely derived from Julius Caesar's hostile account in his *Gallic Wars*. They worshiped nature gods, believed in the immortality of the soul and *reincarnation, and also taught astronomy. Their central religious rite involved the sacred oak tree, from which they cut mistletoe with a golden knife. They sacrificed humans, usually criminals, on behalf of those near to death. In Gaul and Britain they were wiped out by the Romans, their last stand being in Anglesey (61 AD), but in Ireland they survived until the arrival of Christian missionaries. They had no proven association with *Stonehenge, despite the use of the site by the revived 20th-century Druidic Order.

drumfish A carnivorous fish, also called croaker, belonging to the family *Sciaenidae* (about 160 species), that occurs mainly along warm seashores. They have two dorsal fins and are usually silvery in color. Most species produce sounds by amplifying muscle movements through the swim bladder. Order: *Perciformes*.

drumlin A small streamlined hill, formed through glaciation and composed of glacial till or drift, sometimes with a rock core. Drumlins usually occur in groups or swarms (sometimes called basket-of-eggs topography), their long axes parallel to the direction of ice flow. They are common features in Co Down, Northern Ireland.

drums Musical instruments of ancient origin, in which a pitched or unpitched sound is produced by striking a tight skin stretched over a frame or resonating chamber. Drums are played either with sticks of various kinds or with the hands. The family includes the orchestral *timpani, the bass drum, snare drum, and tambourine. *Compare* percussion instruments; stringed instruments; wind instruments.

drupe A stone fruit, such as a cherry, plum, or peach. The fruit wall (pericarp) develops into three layers: an outer skin (epicarp), succulent flesh (mesocarp), and a stone (endocarp) containing the seed.

Drury Lane Theatre The oldest theater in London, first opened in 1663. The present building dates from 1813. It has housed every form of dramatic production. Its early managers included actor David *Garrick, and playwright R. B. *Sheridan, whose *School for Scandal* had its first performance there.

Druses (*or* Druzes) Adherents of the Druse religion, a sect probably named for one of its founders, al-Darazi, who preached the divinity of the Fatimid caliph al-Hakim (996–1021 AD). After his death they won some support in S Syria and developed extreme heterodox ideas. Druses are not generally accepted as Muslims. Their scriptures are based on the Bible, the Koran, and on Sufi writings. Today they live mainly in Syria, the Lebanon, and Israel.

dryad In Greek mythology, a type of *nymph inhabiting trees, especially oak trees. A dryad was believed to die when the tree died.

dry cleaning Cleaning fabrics using a solvent other than water. Its main advantage over washing is that it rarely affects the shape or color of the article. Commercial dry cleaning plants are mainly automatic and the most common solvent is perchloroethylene. Like washing, the solvent, which may contain a detergent, loosens and flushes away dirt particles. Drying is by spinning and warm air. The solvent is recycled.

Dryden, John (1631–1700) British poet and critic. He welcomed the Restoration of the monarchy with two panegyrics to Charles II and was

appointed poet laureate in 1668. He wrote several successful plays for the recently reopened theaters, for example *Marriage à la Mode* (1673) and *All for Love* (1677). He also wrote brilliant verse satires, notably *Absalom and Achitophel* (1681) and *MacFlecknoe* (1682). He became a Catholic in 1685 and lost the laureateship on the accession of the Protestant William of Orange in 1688. His last major work was a translation of Virgil (1697).

dry farming Crop production in regions receiving less than 20 in (50 cm) of rainfall per annum. This involves special farming techniques, especially planting quick-growing drought-resistant crops to make the best use of limited rainfall. Traditionally, winter wheat is grown in alternation with a fallow year, in which moisture and nutrient levels are allowed to recover. Appropriate husbandry, such as leaving a protective layer of crop residue, contour plowing, and the use of fertilizers, all help to maximize yields under difficult conditions.

Dryopithecus A genus of extinct apes, also called oak apes, with teeth and jaws similar to those of chimpanzees and gorillas. Most *Dryopithecus* remains come from India dating from the late Tertiary period (between 19 and 1 million years ago).

Dryopteris A genus of *ferns (about 150 species), known as buckler ferns, found mainly in N temperate regions. They have firm feathery branched fronds, often growing in crowns, 6–60 in (15–150 cm) high, from short stout scaly rhizomes. Large clusters of spore capsules (sori) occur in two rows on the underside of the leaflets. A common species is the male fern (*D. filix-mas*). Family: *Aspidiaceae*.

drypoint A technique of engraving. The finished print is characterized by a shadowy effect produced by the ridges thrown up by the incision on the copperplate. Early masters of drypoint include *Dürer and *Rembrandt.

dry rot The decay of timber caused by cellulose-digesting fungi, especially *Serpula lacrymans*. Spores are liable to germinate in timber having a moisture content of over 20% and the fungus appears as a whitish mass on the surface. The timber becomes cracked and crumbly and the infection may spread to adjoining dry timbers. Treatment is by removal of infected timbers and application of fungicide to the remaining parts. *Compare* wet rot.

Drysdale, Sir (George) Russell (1912–81) Australian painter, born in England. After training in Melbourne, London, and Paris, he specialized in scenes of the Australian outback.

dualism Any philosophical theory asserting either that the universe is made up of two irreducible and independent substances or that it is based on two fundamental principles (for example, good and evil). It is thus distinguished from monism—the belief in just one substance (or principle)—and pluralism, which holds that there are many. One of the most pervasive dualistic theories in philosophy since *Descartes is the view that the world is constituted of mental substance (mind or consciousness) and physical substance (body or matter).

Dubai. *See* United Arab Emirates.

Du Barry, Marie Jeanne Bécu, Comtesse (?1743–93) The last mistress of *Louis XV of France from 1768 until his death (1774), when she was banished from court. She was guillotined during the French Revolution.

Dubček, Alexander (1921–) Czechoslovak statesman. Dubček participated in the resistance to the Nazi occupation and after World War II rose to become secretary of the Czechoslovak Communist Party in 1968. As leader, he granted Czechoslovakia many liberal reforms, which were opposed by the Soviet Union and led to the Soviet invasion of Czechoslovakia in August, 1968. Dubček was taken to Moscow, where he agreed to cooperate with Soviet demands but in April, 1969, he lost his post and was ousted from the Party in 1970.

Dublin (Irish name: Baile Átha Cliath) 53 20N 6 15W The capital of the Republic of Ireland, on Dublin Bay. An important commercial and cultural center, it is also the largest manufacturing center and the largest port in the Republic. Its industries include whiskey distilling, brewing (it has the largest brewery in the world), clothing, glass, and food processing. It is noted for its wide streets (notably O'Connell Street) and its 18th-century Georgian squares. It has the University of Dublin (founded 1592) and the National University of Ireland (founded 1909); Dublin also contains the famous Abbey Theatre. Literary names associated with the city include W. B. Yeats and J. M. Synge. *History*: during the 18th century Dublin prospered as the second largest city of the British Empire but declined during the 19th century. The Easter Rising of 1916 took place here. Population (1971): 983,683.

DUBLIN *The public viewing the damage in the center of the city following the Easter Rising (1916).*

Dublin (Irish name: Baile Átha Cliath)   A county in the E Republic of Ireland, in Leinster bordering on the Irish Sea. Chiefly low lying, it rises in the S to the Wicklow Mountains and is drained by the River Liffey. The county is dominated by the city of Dublin. Agricultural produce includes barley, wheat, and potatoes, and cattle are reared. Area: 356 sq mi (922 sq km). Population (1971): 862,219. County town: Dublin.

W.E.B. DUBOIS   *A pioneer spokesman in the movement for black equality and an advocate of world socialism.*

DuBois, W(illiam) E(dward) B(urghardt)   (1868–1963) US educator, writer, and reformer. He taught at Atlanta University (1897–1910) after being educated at Fisk, Howard, and Harvard universities. In 1905 he founded the Niagara Movement, which evolved into and merged with the *National Association for the Advancement of Colored People (NAACP) in 1909, and edited *Crisis*, the organization's journal, until 1932. An advocate of African colonial independence, he played leadership roles in the Pan

African conferences (1900, 1919, 1921, 1923, 1927) and chaired the conference in 1945. He joined the American Communist Party in 1961, a result of his interest in socialism, and left the US to live in Ghana. His works include *The Philadelphia Negro* (1899) and *Souls of Black Folk* (1903).

Dubrovnik (Italian name: Ragusa)   42 40N 18 07E A port in S Yugoslavia, in Croatia on the Adriatic coast. It flourished as a city state until the early 19th century, and now, with its picturesque setting and medieval walls, is popular among tourists. The town was damaged by two earthquakes in April, 1979. Population (1972 est): 30,000.

Dubuffet, Jean (Phillipe Arthur)   (1901–85) French painter and sculptor, who achieved notoriety in 1946 with his "junk" pictures. Using plaster, sand, straw, etc., he produced extremely distorted and flattened images, influenced by graffiti on walls and the art of children and the insane. He showed his own collection of works and those of children and psychiatric patients in a Paris exhibition entitled *l'Art brut* (brutal art) in 1949.

Du Cange, Charles du Fresne, Sieur   (1610–88) French historian. An outstandingly prolific writer, Du Cange wrote glossaries of the middle ages that were a significant and original contribution to historical research. He also wrote widely on the Byzantine Empire and edited the works of the medieval chroniclers Villehardouin and Joinville.

Duccio di Buoninsegna   (c. 1255–c. 1318) Italian painter, founder of the Sienese school. His major works are the *Rucellai Madonna* (Uffizi) for Sta Maria Novella, Florence, and the *Maestà* (1308–11), an altarpiece for Siena Cathedral, which contemporaries hailed as a masterpiece and carried in procession through the city. A fusion of *Byzantine and *gothic styles, it illustrates his gift for narrative painting.

Duchamp, Marcel   (1887–1968) French artist. His first success was *Nude Descending a Staircase* (1912; Philadelphia), influenced by *cubism and *futurism. This was followed by his controversial *ready-made objects, for example a urinal, first exhibited in New York. He lived in New York after 1915 and became leader of its *dada art movement. His best-known work is the glass and wire picture of *The Bride Stripped Bare by Her Bachelors, Even* (1915–23; Philadelphia).

duck   A small short-necked waterbird belonging to the family *Anatidae* (ducks, geese, and swans), occurring in salt and fresh waters throughout the world except Antarctica. Ducks are adapted for swimming and diving, having a dense waterproofed outer plumage with a thick underlayer of down. The blunt spatulate bill is covered with a sensitive membrane and has internal horny plates for sifting food from water. The 200 species of duck are mostly gregarious; many are migratory and strong fliers. Ducks feed either at the surface of the water (*see* dabbling duck) or dive to forage in deeper water (*see* diving duck). Order: *Anseriformes* (ducks and geese).

duck-billed platypus   An aquatic *monotreme mammal, *Ornithorhynchus anatinus*, of Australia and Tasmania. Platypuses grow to 22 in (55 cm) long and have webbed feet. They use their broad flat toothless beak for sieving invertebrates from stream bottoms. The female lays two eggs in a grass-lined burrow constructed in a river bank, incubates them for two weeks, then suckles the tiny young (about 0.7 in [17 mm] long). Family: *Ornithorhynchidae*.

duckweed   A small floating aquatic plant of the genus *Lemna* (about 10 species), forming dense carpets on or just below the surface of ponds, streams, etc. The plants have no distinct stems and leaves, consisting of a group of small round leaflike structures (thalli) that continuously reproduce by budding. Minute petalless flowers are enclosed in a sheath on the margin of the thallus. *L. minor, L. gibba,* and *L. polyrhiza* have roots; *L. triscula* is rootless. Duckweeds are the simplest and smallest of flowering plants. Family: *Lemnaceae*.

Dudley   53 30N 2 06W A city in England, in the West Midlands. An important industrial center since the middle ages, clothing and light engineering have now replaced coalmining and iron smelting as the principal industries. Population (1981): 187,228.

Duero River.   *See* Douro River.

Dufay, Guillaume   (c. 1400–74) Burgundian composer and priest (*see* Burgundian school), associated with Cambrai Cathedral for much of his life. He traveled in France and Italy and was a member of the papal choir for several years. One of the outstanding composers of the middle ages, he wrote masses, motets, magnificats, and French and Italian chansons. He was also a famous teacher.

Du Fu (*or* Tu Fu; 712–70 AD) Chinese poet of the Tang dynasty. Du Fu's failure to become a high official forced him to lead a life of poverty and traveling to escape famines and rebellions. The major themes of his poetry are thus the social injustices of his time and the effects of civil strife on Chinese life.

Dufy, Raoul (1877–1953) French painter, born in Le Havre. His early influences were *impressionism and then *fauvism. He later developed an individual style in lively and often witty racecourse and regatta scenes, notable for the way forms are drawn sketchily over areas of thinly applied color. He also designed fabrics, tapestries, and ceramics.

dugong A marine herbivorous mammal, *Dugong dugon*, of the Indo-Pacific region. Up to 10 ft (3 m) long, dugongs—also known as sea cows—have blue-gray rough skin and a bristly snout; the males have short tusks. Their forelimbs are flippers and they lack hind limbs, having a flukelike tail for swimming. Dugongs feed on sea grass on the sea bed and, together with *manatees, are a threatened species. Family: *Dugongidae*; order: *Sirenia*.

Duhamel, Georges (1884–1966) French novelist. Trained as a doctor, he worked as an army surgeon during World War I. His major works are his two novel cycles, *Salavin* (1920–32), exploring the theme of human aspirations in a materialistic age, and *The Pasquier Chronicles* (1933–44).

duiker A small nocturnal African antelope belonging to the subfamily *Cephalophine* (17 species), inhabiting bush or forest. 14–30 in (35–75 cm) high at the shoulder, both sexes usually have smooth backward-pointing horns and often a distinct stripe along the back. They plunge into cover when disturbed, hence their name, which in Afrikaans means "diver."

Duisburg 51 26N 06 45E A city in W West Germany, in North Rhine-Westphalia at the confluence of the Rhine and Ruhr Rivers. Heavily bombed in World War II for its armaments industry, it is the largest European inland port and a steel-producing center. Its university was established in 1972. Population (1980 est): 558,700.

Dukas, Paul (1865–1935) French composer, teacher, and critic. He is best known for his orchestral scherzo *The Sorcerer's Apprentice* (1897). His works also include the opera *Ariane et Barbe-Bleue* (1907) and the ballet *La Péri* (1912). A perfectionist, he destroyed many of his works shortly before his death.

Dukhobors. *See* Doukhobors.

dulcimer A musical instrument consisting of a shallow resonating box with strings stretched over two movable bridges. It is played with two small hammers. Descended from the Persian *santir* and much used in European and Asian folk music, it is particularly popular in Hungarian gypsy music under the name *cimbalom.

Dulles, John Foster (1888–1959) US statesman and diplomat. Educated at Princeton and George Washington University, he began his career as an international attorney. He held various diplomatic positions in the State Department during World War I and served as counsel to the American Peace Commission at the *Versailles Conference. After World War II, Dulles was named delegate to the *San Francisco Conference and was instrumental in the creation of the *United Nations, to which he was US ambassador (1945–49). After an interim appointment to the US Senate, Dulles was named Secretary of State in the Eisenhower administration (1953–59). Throughout the *Cold War, he espoused a policy of active opposition to the expansion of communism throughout the world. He developed a strategy of "brinkmanship" to prevent the People's Republic of China from occupying the islands of Quemoy and Matsu, and during the *Berlin Crisis, he supported a hard line against the Soviet Union. Dulles also helped to formulate the Eisenhower Doctrine, which created a temporary balance of power in the Middle East. His brother, **Allen Welch Dulles** (1893–1969) was also a statesman and diplomat. After serving in several government posts abroad, he was part of the American peace commission in 1918 and the US Department of State's Near Eastern Affairs chief (1922–26). During World War II he served with the Office of Strategic Services (OSS) and then, after working on the establishment of the Central Intelligence Agency CIA (1947), went on to become its deputy director (1951–53) and director (1953–61).

Dulong and Petit's law The product of the mass of 1 mole of a solid element and its specific heat capacity is constant and equal to 25 joules per kelvin. The law is only true for simple substances and at normal temperatures. Named for the French physicists P. Dulong (1785–1838) and A. Petit (1791–1820).

dulse An edible purplish-red *seaweed, *Rhodymenia palmata*, found growing on rocks, shellfish, and other seaweeds on N Atlantic coasts. A red

alga, it has flat leathery lobed fronds, about 5–16 in (12–40 cm) long, which are often eaten as a salty confection of the same name.

Duluth 46 45N 92 10W A city in Minnesota, at the W end of Lake Superior opposite Superior, Wis. It is the commercial and industrial center of N Minnesota and large quantities of iron ore and grain are shipped from its port. Population (1980): 92,789.

Duma The Russian parliament from 1906 to 1917. The Duma, which was established in response to the *Revolution of 1905, transformed Russia into a constitutional monarchy. It was composed of an upper chamber, the state council, and a lower chamber. Half the members of the state council were appointed by the monarch and the remainder of the deputies in both chambers were elected. Owing to their radicalism, the first two Dumas (1906, 1907) were quickly dissolved by Emperor Nicholas II but the third (1907–12) and fourth (1912–17) more conservative Dumas lasted their legal five-year terms. At the beginning of the Russian Revolution the Duma established the provisional government that enforced Nicholas' abdication.

Dumas, Alexandre (1802–70) French novelist and dramatist, often called Dumas *père*. His father was a soldier, the son of a marquis and a black woman, and he became a general in the French Revolutionary armies. Brought up in poverty and largely self-educated, Alexandre began writing melodramatic historical plays in 1829. After 1839 he began writing his famous historical romances, including *The Count of Monte Cristo* (1844–45), *The Three Musketeers* (1844), and *The Black Tulip* (1850). His works were hugely successful but the uninhibited extravagance of his private life kept him continually in debt.

His illegitimate son **Alexandre Dumas** (1824–95), a dramatist, was often called Dumas *fils*. His best-known work is the novel *La Dame aux camélias* (1848), the basis of a play and Verdi's opera *La Traviata*. His other plays, which include *Le Demi-monde* (1855) and *Le Fils naturel* (1858), were mostly moralistic treatments of such themes as adultery and prostitution.

Du Maurier, George (Louis Palmella Busson) (1834–96) British caricaturist and novelist. Born in Paris, he moved to London in 1860 and contributed caricatures to *Punch* and other magazines. His novel *Trilby* (1894), remembered for its sinister hypnotist Svengali, is based on his life as an art student in Paris. The best-known works of his granddaughter **Daphne Du Maurier** (1907–) are romances, usually set in her home county of Cornwall. They include *Rebecca* (1938) and *The Flight of the Falcon* (1965).

Dumbarton Oaks Conference (1944) A conference called by the Allies, in Washington, DC, that led to the formation of the *United Nations. The Soviet Union, the UK, and the US met first and China, the UK, and the US met during the last week of the conference. From these meetings evolved a proposal for an international organization for the promotion of peace and security. The four participants in these meetings were to be permanently represented on the Security Council.

Du Mont, Allen Balcom (1901–65) US engineer, who developed the *cathode-ray tube (CRT). He set up a company to manufacture allied electronic devices in 1931 and invented the oscilloscope (*see* cathode-ray oscilloscope), which incorporated his new durable CRTs. He also utilized them in television receivers, which he began manufacturing in 1937.

Dumont d'Urville, Jules Sébastien César (1790–1842) French navigator. He went on two surveying expeditions to the South Seas (1822–25, 1826–29) and on the second circumnavigated the world in the *Astrolabe*, returning with specimens of plants and rocks. In repeating this exploit (1837–40), he discovered the Adélie (his wife's name) coast of Antarctica.

Dumoriez, Charles François du Périer (1739–1823) French general. During the French Revolution he became commander of a division in Nantes (1791). In 1792 he became minister of foreign affairs but resigned to command the northern army against Austria and Prussia. He won victories at Valmy and Jemappes (1792) but after defeat in early 1793 conspired to overthrow France's revolutionary government. Deserted by his troops he went over to the Austrians, eventually settling in England.

Dunant, (Jean-)Henri (1828–1910) Swiss philanthropist, who inspired the foundation (1864) of the International *Red Cross. In 1859 he organized relief for the wounded at the Battle of Solferino, an experience that led him to propose the establishment of an international relief agency. He won the first Nobel Peace Prize in 1901.

Dunbar, Paul Laurence (1872–1906) US poet and novelist. The son of former slaves, he was known for his poetry and stories written in the black dialect. His poetry is collected in *Lyrics of Love and Laughter* (1903) and *Lyrics of Sunshine and Shadow* (1905). Short story volumes include *The*

Heart of Happy Hollow (1904. One novel, *The Sport of the Gods* (1902), is about blacks, while *The Uncalled* (1898), *The Love of Landry* (1900), and *The Fanatics* (1901) are about the world of whites.

Dunbar 56 00N 2 31W A resort and fishing port in E central Scotland, on the Lothian coast, scene of *Cromwell's victory over the Scots (1650). Population (1973 est): 4609.

Duncan I (d. 1040) King of the Scots (1034–40). His claim to the throne was challenged by Macbeth, by whom he was murdered.

Duncan, Isadora (1878–1927) US dancer. She lived mostly in Europe, where she gained a reputation for both her innovative modern interpretive dancing and her flamboyant lifestyle. Her accidental death was caused by her scarf being caught in the wheel of the car in which she was traveling.

Dundalk (Irish name: Dún Dealgan) 54 01N 6 25W A port in the Republic of Ireland, the county town of Co Louth. Its chief industries are engineering, brewing, printing, and linen manufacturing, and its main exports are beef and cattle. Population (1971): 21,672.

Dundee 56 28N 3 00W A city in E Scotland, the administrative center of Tayside Region on the Firth of Tay. It is a port and university town, known chiefly for the manufacture of jute goods. Dundee also provides supplies and services for the North Sea oil industry and has engineering and shipbuilding industries. Population (1981): 174,746.

Dundee, John Graham of Claverhouse, 1st Viscount (c. 1649–89) Scottish soldier, who led a *Jacobite rebellion (1689) in support of the deposed James VII of Scotland (James II of England). He won an outstanding victory against loyalist forces at Killiecrankie but was mortally wounded.

Dunedin 45 52S 170 30E A port in New Zealand, in SE South Island at the head of Otago Harbor. Founded by Scottish Presbyterians in 1848, it has two cathedrals (Anglican and Roman Catholic) and the University of Otago (the oldest in the country, founded in 1869). Industries include the manufacture of woolen goods, agricultural machinery, and footwear. Population (1974 est): 83,900.

Dunfermline 56 04N 3 29W A city in E Scotland, in Fife Region on the Firth of Forth. Several Scottish kings, including *Robert the Bruce, are buried in the 11th-century abbey. Dunfermline produces silk, synthetic fiber, and rubber products and there are rich coal deposits nearby. It is the birthplace of Andrew *Carnegie. Population (1981): 52,057.

DUNG BEETLE *Using its head and paddle-like antennae, this beetle constructs balls of dung, which it buries and feeds on. The females lay eggs in dung balls, which provide food for the larvae.*

dung beetle A *scarab beetle, also called a tumblebug, that has the habit of rolling dung into balls, which serve as a food source for both the adults and larvae. Dung beetles are usually dark and small, varying between 0.2 and 1.2 in (5 and 30 mm) in length.

Another group of dung-eating beetles belong to the family *Geotrupidae* (*see* dor beetle).

Dunkirk (French name: Dunkerque) 51 02N 2 23E A port in N France, in the Nord department on the Strait of Dover. Sacked by the English (1388), it was ceded to Cromwell in 1658 but was later sold (1662) by Charles II to Louis XIV. During *World War II British and other Allied troops were successfully evacuated from its beaches (1940) following the fall of France. Dunkirk is a rapidly growing industrial center and has an oil refinery and naval shipbuilding yards. Population (1975): 83,759.

dunlin A common *sandpiper, *Calidris alpina*, that breeds in far northern regions, ranging south to N Britain. 8 in (20 cm) long, it has a bill with a curved tip and a black and russet plumage that changes to gray in winter.

Dunlop, John Boyd (1840–1921) Scottish inventor, who is credited with inventing the pneumatic tire (1887). Dunlop began to produce his tires commercially in 1890. Initially for bicycles, they later contributed greatly to the development of motor cars.

dunnock A shy inconspicuous songbird, *Prunella modularis*, also called hedge sparrow (although it is an *accentor and not a sparrow). About 6 in (14 cm) long, the dunnock has a dull-brown plumage with a grayish throat and breast. It has a fine sharp bill and feeds on insects. Cuckoos often lay their eggs in dunnocks' nests.

Dunois, Jean d'Orléans, Comte de (1403–68) French general in the Hundred Years' War. He defeated the English in 1427, then brilliantly held Orléans until relieved by Joan of Arc (1429). Further victories led to his triumphal entry into Paris (1436). After the renewal of war, he drove the English out of N France.

Dunsinane A hill in E Scotland, in the Sidlaw Hills. The ruined fort on its summit is said to be Macbeth's castle and is referred to in Shakespeare's play *Macbeth*. Height: 1012 ft (303 m).

Duns Scotus, John (c. 1260–1308) Scottish-born Franciscan philosopher, who, with Roger *Bacon and *William of Ockham, carried on controversy against *Aquinas. Contradicting Aquinas, Duns Scotus held that what makes one thing distinct from another is its form, or essence, that is its essential properties rather than its accidental properties, as the latter may be removed or change without altering its identity. Although nicknamed the Subtle Doctor by contemporaries, Duns Scotus suffered Renaissance ridicule, so that his name has given rise to the derisive label "dunce."

Dunstan, St (924–88 AD) English churchman and monastic reformer, born near Glastonbury. Of noble birth, he lived as a hermit until appointed Abbot of Glastonbury in 943. He rebuilt its monastery and initiated a revival of English monasticism. The chief minister under Kings Eadred and Edgar, he also became Bishop of Worcester (957), Bishop of London (959), and Archbishop of Canterbury (960). He lost favor under Ethelred II. Feast day: May 19. Emblem: a pair of tongs.

duodecimal system A system of numbers that has a base of 12 as opposed to the base 10 of the normal *decimal system. For example, the number 31 in the decimal system becomes 27 in the duodecimal system since $31 = (2 \times 12) + 7$.

duodenal ulcer. *See* peptic ulcer.

duodenum. *See* intestine.

Duparc, Henri (Marie Eugène Henri Foucques D.; 1848–1933) French composer, a pupil of Franck. His reputation rests on the 14 songs he wrote between 1868 and 1884, some of which have orchestral accompaniments. In 1885 he suffered a breakdown in health and spent the rest of his life in seclusion in Switzerland.

DuPont de Nemours, Eleuthère Irénée (1771–1834) US industrialist; born in France. With his father, Pierre Samuel (1739–1817), he founded E. I. DuPont de Nemours & Company in 1802. He had come from France to the US with his father in 1799 and saw a need for a better quality gun powder in America. By 1802 he had established a gunpowder mill near Wilmington, Del and soon prospered, especially during the War of 1812. The company grew rapidly under his descendants to become one of the giants of US industry.

du Pré, Jacqueline (1945–) British cellist. She studied with Paul Tortelier and Mstislav Rostropovich, making her debut in 1961 in Elgar's cello concerto, a work with which she became particularly associated. In 1967 she married the pianist Daniel *Barenboim, with whom she gave recitals. Multiple sclerosis put an end to her performing career in 1973, but she has since been active as a cello teacher.

Duralumin An aluminum *alloy containing 3.5% copper and 0.5% magnesium. It becomes harder in the few days after heating and quenching and retains this hardness as long as its temperature remains below 115°F (150°C). It is used in aircraft manufacture.

Durance River A river in S France, flowing mainly SSW to the Rhône River near Avignon. It provides Marseilles with water. Length: 189 mi (304 km).

Durand, Asher Brown (1796–1886) US artist and engraver. In the early years of his career he was a partner in several engraving firms. His engraving of artist John Trumbull's (1756–1843) *Signing of the Declaration of Independence* (1820) brought him fame and he later did work for the Federal Bureau of Printing and Engraving. His paintings, done mostly after 1835, concentrated on natural landscapes and were scenes of upper New York and New England. He was a member of the Hudson River School of painting. He served as president of the National Academy of Design (1845–61), which he helped to establish in 1826.

Durango 24 01N 104 40W A city in N Mexico. It lies S of Cerro del Mercado, a hill famous for its iron-ore mines. Industries include iron founding, sugar refining, and textiles. Population (1976 est): 199,822.

Durante, Jimmy (James Francis D.; 1893–1980) US entertainer. Known as "Schnozzola," because of his large nose, he was in vaudeville from the age of 17 and by 1919 was part of a team with Eddie Jackson and Lou Clayton. Several songs became his trademarks, among them "Inka, Dinka, Doo" and "September Song." He appeared in such stage shows as *Show Girl* (1929) and *Jumbo* (1935) and the films, *Ziegfeld Follies* (1946) and *It's a Mad, Mad, Mad, Mad World* (1963), as well as on radio and television.

Durazzo. *See* Durrës.

Durban 29 53S 31 00E The main seaport in South Africa and the largest city in Natal, on the Indian Ocean. Founded in 1835, it has a diversified manufacturing industry, including car assembly and sugar refining, and it is an important tourist center. It contains part of the University of Natal. Population (1980 est): 505,963.

ALBRECHT DÜRER *A self-portrait (detail) painted in 1498, when the artist was 26 years old (Albertina, Vienna).*

Dürer, Albrecht (1471–1528) German *Renaissance painter, engraver, draftsman, and woodcut designer. The son of a goldsmith, he was born in Nuremberg, where he trained under the woodcut designer and altarpiece painter Michael Wohlgemuth (1434–1519). His first Italian visit (1494–95) resulted in a series of watercolors of the Alps. He was influenced by Italian artists, particularly *Mantegna and Antonio *Pollaiuolo, but his woodcuts of the *Apocalypse* (1498) are still *gothic in style. In about 1500, he became preoccupied with the study of human proportions. Paintings of this period include the *Self-Portrait* as Christ (1500; Alte Pinakothek, Munich) and *Adoration of the Magi* (1504; Uffizi). On his second Italian visit (1505–07) he painted *The Feast of the Rose Garlands* (Prague) for the church of the German community in Venice. He worked for Emperor Maximilian I from 1512 to 1519. In this period he executed his most famous engravings, including *Knight, Death, and the Devil* (British Museum, London). His last important work was *The Four Apostles* (Alte Pinakothek, Munich). He was also a friend of Luther and sympathized with the Reformation.

Durham 35 59N 78 54W A city in N central North Carolina, NW of Raleigh. The American Tobacco Company, started in 1881 by the Duke family, was instrumental in the growth of Durham and today is its largest industry. Duke University (1924; 1851 as Trinity College) is here, as is the Duke Medical Center. Other products manufactured include chemicals, machinery, textiles, lumber, and processed foods. Population (1980): 100,538.

Durham, John George Lambton, 1st Earl of (1792–1840) British colonial administrator; governor general of Canada (1838–39). As Lord Privy Seal he helped to draft the 1832 parliamentary *Reform Act and was sent to Canada after serving (1835–37) as ambassador to Russia. In Canada he was criticized for giving amnesty to rebellious French-Canadians and resigned. His *Report on the Affairs of British North America* (1839), greatly influenced subsequent British colonial policy (*see* British Empire).

durian A tree, *Durio zebethinus*, of SE Asia, up to 98 ft (30 m) tall with oblong tapering leaves and large creamy white flowers. The spherical spiny-coated fruit, 6–8 in (15–20 cm) in diameter, is notorious for its noxious smell, but the custard-like pulp is eaten in large amounts by local people and animals. The seeds are roasted. Family: *Bombacaceae*.

Durkheim, Emile (1858–1917) French sociologist and one of the founding fathers of modern *sociology. In opposition to attempts to explain human conduct solely in terms of psychology, he developed an account of stability and change in whole societies in *The Division of Labor in Society* (1893); in *The Rules of Sociological Method* (1895) he set out a methodology for a science of society. His *Suicide* (1897) was a pioneering study in social statistics. Another major work, produced during the latter part of his life, was *The Elementary Forms of Religious Life* (1912), in which he examined the social foundations of religion.

durmast A Eurasian *oak, *Quercus petraea*, up to 130 ft (40 m) tall. It has long-stalked oval leaves with rounded lobes and hairy undersides and unstalked conical acorns (hence its other name—sessile oak). Its durable wood is used for furniture, construction work, and boat building and the bark for tanning.

durra An economically important variety of *sorghum, *S. vulgare* var. *durra*, also called millet, native to the Nile valley. Its grain is used chiefly for livestock feed.

Durrell, Lawrence George (1912–) British novelist and poet. Born in India, he has lived mostly in the Mediterranean countries. His best-known work is *The Alexandria Quartet*, comprising *Justine* (1957), *Balthazar* (1958), *Mountolive* (1958), and *Clea* (1960), an elaborate exploration of the nature of modern love. His work includes poetry (*Collected Poems*, 1968), humorous sketches (*Esprit de Corps*, 1959), and several travel books on the Greek islands. Other novels are *The Black Book* (1938), *Numquam* (1970), and *Monsieur* (1975). His brother **Gerald Malcolm Durrell** (1925–) is a naturalist and popular writer, noted for the autobiographical *My Family and Other Animals* (1956) and *The Stationary Ark* (1976), about his zoo and wildlife conservation trust in Jersey.

Dürrenmatt, Friedrich (1921–) Swiss dramatist and novelist. His plays are often experimental in form and usually satirical in intention, mocking hypocritically conventional values. The best known are *The Old Lady's Visit* (1956) and *The Physicists* (1962). He has also written short stories and detective novels.

Durrës (Italian name: Durazzo) 41 18N 19 28E A port in W central Albania, on the Adriatic Sea. It was founded by Greeks in the 7th century BC and is now Albania's major commercial town and principal port. Products include flour, salt, and bricks. Population (1976 est): 61,000.

durum. *See* wheat.

Duse, Eleonora (1858–1924) Italian actress. She acted in plays by contemporary French dramatists and is especially associated with plays by Gabriele D'Annunzio, her lover, and by Ibsen. Her international reputation as a tragic and romantic actress rivaled that of Sarah Bernhardt.

Dushanbe (name until 1929: Dyushambe; name from 1929 until 1961: Stalinabad) 38 38N 68 51E A city in the SW Soviet Union, the capital of the Tadzhik SSR on the Dushanbinka River. It has food and textile industries and is a cultural and educational center. Population (1981 est): 510,000.

Düsseldorf 51 13N 6 47E A city in NW West Germany, capital of North Rhine-Westphalia on the Rhine River. The birthplace of Heinrich Heine, it is noted for its art academy (1767). A port and major commercial and industrial center of the *Ruhr, its main industry is iron and steel. Population (1976 est): 615,494.

Dust Bowl, the An area extending across W Kansas, Oklahoma, and Texas, and into Colorado and New Mexico. During the 1930s droughts and overfarming resulted in severe erosion of the topsoil. As many as half the residents left. The plight of the farmers was illustrated by the photography of Dorothea Lange (1895–1965) and Steinbeck's novel *The Grapes of Wrath* (1939).

Dutch The national language of the Netherlands, belonging to the West Germanic language group. In Belgium it is one of the two official languages and is known as Flemish (*or* Vlaams). It is derived from Low Franconian, the speech of the Salic Franks, who settled in this area, and has numerous local variants.

Dutch East Indies. *See* Indonesia.

DUTCH ELM DISEASE *The elm bark beetle lays its eggs in burrows beneath the bark of elm trees, where they hatch into larvae (above). The characteristic tunnels seen in affected trees (below) are caused by the burrowing larvae.*

Dutch elm disease A serious disease, first described in the Netherlands in 1919, that reached epidemic proportions in the US and Britain, killing millions of elm trees. The fungus responsible, *Ceratocystus ulmi*, blocks the vessels that carry water to the leaves, which wilt and eventually die. The disease is carried by *bark beetles. Protective measures can be taken but are too expensive for widespread use.

Dutch Guiana. *See* Suriname.

Dutchman's breeches An ornamental perennial herb, *Dicentra cucullaria*, from North American woodlands. Its arching stems bear cream or pale-yellow drooping flowers with saclike spurs. The gray-green fernlike leaves arise from underground tubers. Family: *Fumariaceae* (fumitory family). *See also* Dicentra.

Dutchman's pipe An ornamental climbing vine, *Aristolochia durior* (or *A. sipho*), from the American Midwest. Up to 30 ft (9 m) long, it has large kidney-shaped or heart-shaped leaves. The brown-and-black patterned tubular flowers are attached to swollen greenish-yellow tubes, bent to resemble a pipe, and are pollinated by carrion flies. Family: *Aristolochiaceae*.

Dutch metal A highly ductile gold-colored type of brass that contains between 85% and 88% of copper. It is used for bronzing and imitation gold leaf.

Dutch Republic. *See* United Provinces of the Netherlands.

Dutch Wars 1. (1652–54) The war between England and the Netherlands precipitated by commercial rivalry, which had been aggravated by Oliver Cromwell's *Navigation Act (1651). The English were victorious. 2. (1665–67) The war between England and the Netherlands (supported by France from 1666). Caused by commercial and colonial rivalry, the English defeated the Dutch off Lowestoft (1665) but in 1667 the Dutch entered the Thames and the Medway, bombarding Chatham. The Treaty of Breda concluded the war. 3. (1672–78) The war brought about by the invasion of the Netherlands by Louis XIV of France (supported at sea by England). The English were defeated by the Dutch (1672–73) and concluded the Treaty of Westminister (1674). By late 1673 France had been forced to withdraw from the Netherlands but entered the Spanish Netherlands and defeated the alliance of Spain, Austria, and the Dutch. The war was concluded by the Treaties of *Nijmegen. 4. (1780–84) The war between Britain and the Netherlands caused by Dutch support for the American colonies during the *American Revolution. The Dutch were defeated.

Duvalier, François (1907–71) Haitian politician, known as Papa Doc; president (1957–71). He used his secret police, the Tonton Macoutes, to eliminate all opposition and exploited black nationalism and voodoo practices to maintain popular sympathy. In 1964 he became president for life, a post in which his son **Jean-Claude Duvalier** (1951–) succeeded him.

Dvina River 1. (Northern *or* Severnaya) A river in NW Soviet Union, formed by the confluence of the Sukhona and Yug rivers and flowing generally NW to the White Sea. Length: 466 mi (750 km). 2. (Western *or* Dangava) A river in the W Soviet Union, flowing SW and NW from the Valdai Hills to the Gulf of Riga. Length: 634 mi (1021 km).

Dvinsk. *See* Daugavpils.

Dvořák, Antonín (1841–1904) Czech composer. He was a friend of Brahms and director of the Prague conservatoire (1901–04). From 1892 to 1895 he was director of the National Conservatory in New York, during which time he wrote his famous ninth symphony, entitled "From the New World." Besides the symphonies he wrote concertos for piano, violin, and cello, orchestral tone poems, chamber music, piano music, and songs. His Czech nationalism is particularly evident in his famous *Slavonic Dances* for piano duet (1878–86).

dwarfism Abnormal smallness. The commonest cause is lack of food, and growth can be accelerated if enough food is given. Dwarfism can also occur in children with disease of the pituitary gland, in which insufficient *growth hormone is produced. This can be cured by administration of the growth hormone. Other chronic diseases, such as heart or kidney disease, can cause dwarfism. Children who are emotionally deprived may also fail to grow. The dwarfs seen in circuses are called achondroplastic dwarfs; their small size is due to faulty bone development.

dybbuk (Hebrew: adhesion) In Jewish folklore, an evil spirit, specifically the soul of a sinful person, which, after death, possessed the body of a living person. The dybbuk could be exorcised by invocation of the divine name. Possession by such a spirit is the subject of a famous play, *The Dybbuk*, by the Russian author Solomon Anski (1862–1920).

dyeing The process of permanently changing the color of a material. Natural dyes, such as *madder and *indigo, have been known since 3000 BC. Mauveine, the first synthetic dye, was discovered in 1856 by W. H. *Perkin. Most modern commercial dyes are made from *aromatic hydrocarbons extracted from coal tar or oil. To dye fibers or textiles, the material is immersed in a solution containing the dye, so that the dye molecules adhere to the surface of the fibers. The solvent is usually water but occasionally other solvents are used. An inorganic chemical (such as a salt of chromium), known as a mordant, may be added to make the dye less soluble once it has adhered to the fiber. Dyes used without a mordant are called **direct dyes**. **Vat dyes** are insoluble in water, but are applied in reduced soluble form and then reoxidized. These are used particularly in cellulosic fibers. *See also* pigments.

dyer's broom A stout biennial or perennial plant, *Isatis tinctoria*, also called dyer's greenweed or dyer's furze. 20–48 in (50–120 cm) high, it has arrow-shaped leaves and dense clusters of bright-yellow flowers that produce winged fruits. Native to Eurasia but naturalized elsewhere, its leaves ferment to a distinctive blue dye (*see* woad). Family: *Cruciferae*.

dyer's rocket A biennial herb, *Reseda luteola*, also called weld. It is widespread on waste ground throughout most of the N hemisphere. Up to 28 in (70 cm) high, it has lance-shaped leaves with wavy margins and long slender spikes of pale-yellow flowers, 0.16–0.20 in (4–5 mm) across, formerly used to make a yellow dye. Family: *Resedaceae*.

Dylan, Bob (Robert Allen Zimmerman; 1941–) US singer and songwriter. An outstanding lyricist, he spoke for the protest movement of the 1960s with such folk albums as *The Times They Are A-changin'* (1964). In *Highway 61 Revisited* (1965), he introduced electronic instruments and rock rhythms. *John Wesley Harding* (1968), following a two-year retirement, and *Blood on the Tracks* (1975) confirmed his inventiveness.

dynamics. *See* mechanics; Newtonian mechanics.

dynamite An explosive plastic solid consisting of 75% nitroglycerine and 25% kieselguhr, a porous form of silicon dioxide (SiO_2). It was invented in 1864 by *Nobel. Nitroglycerine alone is very sensitive to shock. The kieselguhr makes it safe to handle. Dynamite is used for blasting, particularly under water.

BOB DYLAN *In concert in 1969.*

dynamo. *See* electric generator.

dyne The unit of force in the *c.g.s. system equal to the force that will impart to a mass of one gram an acceleration of one centimeter per second per second.

dysentery An infection of the large bowel causing painful diarrhea that often contains blood and mucus. It may be caused either by bacteria of the genus *Shigella* or by amebae. It can occur wherever there is poor sanitation, but amebic dysentery is much more common in tropical countries. Treatment for bacillary dysentery is usually by administration of fluids to prevent dehydration, but for amebic dysentery drugs to kill the amebae are also given.

dyslexia Difficulty in learning to write, spell, and read. It is commonly discovered at school when a child cannot read as well as would be expected. Dyslexic children are usually of normal intelligence and with special teaching can improve greatly, although some never manage to deal well with the written word.

dysmenorrhea Painful menstrual periods. In most cases the cause is not known. Treatment is usually with pain killers, but starting a course of oral contraceptive pills will also stop the pain. If the pain starts after years of pain-free periods there may be disease of the reproductive organs.

dyspepsia. *See* indigestion.

dysprosium (Dy) A lanthanide element discovered in 1886. It forms the oxide (Dy_2O_3) and halides (for example DyF_3) and can be separated from the other lanthanides by ion-exchange techniques. At no 66; at wt 162.50; mp 816°F (1412°C); bp 1328°F (2335°C).

Dzerzhinsk (name until 1919: Chernorech; name from 1919 until 1929: Rastyapino) 56 15N 43 30E A port in the central Soviet Union, in the RSFSR on the Oka River. It supports chemical, textiles, and cable industries. Population (1981 est): 263,000.

Dzhambul (name until 1939: Auliye-Ata) 42 50N 71 25E A city in the S central Soviet Union, in the Kazakh SSR on the Talas River. Its industries include phosphates, metal, leather, and food processing. Population (1977 est): 252,000.

Dzungarian Basin. *See* Junggar Pendi.

E

Ea (*or* Enki) The ancient Mesopotamian god of water and the sea, with Anu and Enlil one of the supreme triad. He created the Tigris and Euphrates rivers. A guardian against demons and patron of the arts and sciences, including magic, his main attribute was wisdom.

Eadred (d. 955) King of England (946–55), who reconquered Northumbria by expelling Eric Bloodaxe (954), its Norwegian king. Eadred bequeathed a sum of money to relieve the poor in Northumbria and to aid defense against Viking raids.

Eads, John Buchanan (1820–87) US civil engineer, best known for his design and construction of the steel triple-arched Eads Bridge, which spans the Mississippi River at St Louis, Missouri. Opened in 1874, it is now considered a landmark in the history of civil engineering.

Eadwig (*or* Edwy; d. 959) King of England from 955 to 957, when he lost Mercia and Northumbria. He forced St *Dunstan into exile.

eagle A large broad-winged bird of prey occurring throughout the world, mostly in remote mountainous regions. Eagles have a large hooked bill and strong feet with large curved talons and are typically dull brown but may be a combination of black, gray, white, or chestnut; the head is often crested. With a wingspan of 4.3–7.8 ft (1.3–2.4 m), they can soar for long periods searching for food—generally live prey, such as mammals or reptiles. Family: *Accipitridae* (hawks and eagles). *See also* bald eagle; golden eagle; harpy eagle; Philippine eagle; sea eagle.

eagle owl A large Eurasian *owl of the genus *Bubo*, ranging from cold northern forests to hot southern deserts. It reaches 28 in (70 cm) in length, is tawny with brown mottling, and has orange eyes and large ear tufts.

eaglewood (*or* aloes wood) The resinous heartwood of a tree of the genus *Aquilaria* (especially *A. agallocha*), of SE Asia. Under certain conditions it becomes resinous and fragrant and is used in religious ceremonies and perfumery. Family: *Thymelaeaceae*.

Eakins, Thomas (1844–1916) US painter of portraits and everyday life, particularly sports scenes. He lived mainly in Philadelphia, except for visits to Paris (1866–69) and Spain (1870), where he was influenced by the realism of Velázquez. His teaching methods, particularly his use of live nude models, were controversial, as were some of his paintings, such as *Gross Clinic* (1875), showing a surgeon operating. Other works include *Max Schmitt in a Single Scull* (1871), *The Chess Players* (1876), and *Walt Whitman* (1888).

ealdorman The chief royal official of the Anglo-Saxon shire. Almost always of noble rank, he presided over the shire court, sharing one third of its profits, executed royal orders, and raised the shire military levy. Ealdormen later became the hereditary earls, and the sheriffs succeeded to their duties.

Eames, Charles (1907–78) US designer and architect. He taught at the Cranbrook Academy of Art (1939–41) and there designed, with Eero *Saarinen, an award-winning molded plywood chair for which he became famous. He also designed movie sets, museum and industrial exhibits, and made documentary movies.

ear The organ of hearing and balance in vertebrate animals (including man). The human ear is divided into external, middle, and inner parts. Sound waves are transmitted through the auditory meatus and cause the eardrum (tympanic membrane) to vibrate. These vibrations are transmitted through the three small bones (ossicles) of the middle ear to the fenestra ovalis, which leads to the inner ear. A duct (the Eustachian tube) connects the middle ear to the back of the throat (pharynx), enabling the release of pressure that builds up in the middle ear. The cochlea—a spiral organ of the inner ear—contains special cells that convert the sound vibrations into nerve impulses, which are transmitted to the hearing centers of the brain via the cochlear nerve. The inner ear also contains the organs of balance: three semicircular canals, each of which registers movement in a different plane. The semicircular canals and cochlea are filled with fluid and are known together as the labyrinth of the ear.

AMELIA EARHART *A photograph taken in 1932.*

Earhart, Amelia (1898–1937) US aviatrix, who was the first woman to fly solo across the Atlantic (1932) and from Hawaii to California across the Pacific (1935). Her plane was lost over the Pacific between New Guinea and Howland Island, on an attempted flight around the world with F. J. Noonan.

Early, Jubal (Anderson) (1816–94) US Confederate general. A graduate of the US Military Academy at West Point in 1837, he soon resigned his commission and settled in his native Virginia to practice law. He joined the Confederate Army at the beginning of the Civil War in 1861 and, as a colonel, was instrumental in the Confederate victory at the 1st Battle of *Bull Run. Promoted to general, he served in the major battles in Virginia and was in command of the troops that made an unsuccessful drive toward Washington, DC, in 1864.

Early English The style of □gothic architecture predominant in England in the 13th century. It is characterized by narrow pointed windows and arches, in contrast to the rounded features of the preceding period (*see* Norman architecture). These lancet windows are often grouped in threes or fives (e.g. the Five Sisters window in York Minster). Dog-tooth carving, heavily undercut crockets (stylized foliage) on capitals, and columns with detached shafts in black Purbeck marble are typical decorative elements.

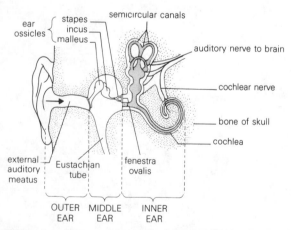

EAR *A vertical section through the human ear shows its internal structure; the middle and inner ears are embedded in the bone of the skull. The arrow indicates the direction of sound waves entering the ear.*

Salisbury Cathedral (begun 1220) and the nave of Lincoln Cathedral (begun 1192) show the style at its best.

earth The third planet from the sun, at an average distance of 93 million mi (149.6 million km) from it. Its diameter at the equator is 7926 mi (12,756 km), slightly less at the Poles; its shape is therefore a flattened sphere (a geoid). It completes an orbit of the sun in 365 days, 6 hours, 8 minutes and makes one rotation on its axis every 23 hours 56 minutes.

The earth is believed to be about 4600 million years old, the oldest rocks so far discovered being 3800 million years old. Geologists divide this time into eras, periods, and epochs (*see* geological time scale). The earth consists of an inner core of solid iron, surrounded by an outer core of molten iron. Surrounding this is the solid mantle, inner and outer, which is separated from the crust by the *Mohorovičić Discontinuity. The crust consists of basaltic oceanic crust surmounted by less dense granitic continental crust, which forms the continents. The crust varies in thickness from 5 km under the oceans to 60 km under mountain ranges. The composition of the crust is approximately 47% oxygen, 28% silicon, 8% aluminum, 4.5% iron, 3.5% calcium, 2.5% each sodium and potassium, and 2.2% magnesium. All other elements are present to an extent of less than 1% each.

70.8% of the earth's surface is ocean. The greatest ocean depth is over 36,000 ft (11,000 m), in the Marianas Trench; the greatest height of land is 29,028 ft (8848 m), at Mount Everest.

earthnut A slender perennial herb, *Conopodium majus*, of European woods and meadows. Up to 40 in (1 m) high, it is also called pignut or hognut, as its tubers are eaten by livestock. It has finely divided leaves and clusters of pinkish white flowers. Family: *Umbelliferae*.

The name is also sometimes applied to the *groundnut.

earthquake A series of shocks felt at the earth's surface, ranging from mild tremblings to violent oscillations, resulting from the fracturing of brittle rocks within the earth's crust and upper mantle. The magnitude of an earthquake depends on the amount of energy liberated when the overstrained rocks fracture. The *Richter scale is used for comparing earthquake magnitudes. The point of origin of the *seismic waves produced is the focus and the point on the earth's surface directly above this is the epicenter. The majority of earthquakes occur in certain well-defined seismic zones, corresponding with the junction of lithospheric plates (*see* plate tectonics); these include the circum-Pacific belt, the Alpine-Himalayan belt, and the midocean ridges.

earthstar A fungus of the genus *Geastrum*, with a starlike inedible fruiting body. Initially globular, the outer layer peels back in segments to form the "rays" of the star, surrounding a thin papery inner globe. Spores are released through a pore in the top. The collared earthstar (*G. triplex*), occurring in woodland, is 2–4 in (6–10 cm) across, pale brown, and has five or more rays. Class: *Basidiomycetes*.

earthworm A terrestrial *annelid worm belonging to a class (*Oligochaeta*) found all over the world. Earthworms feed on rotting vegetation, pulling the dead leaves down into their burrows and improving the fertility of the soil. The body consists of about 100 segments, each with four pairs of bristles for gripping the surface as the worm moves. The largest earthworm is *Megascolides australis*, which reaches a length of about 11 ft (3.3 m).

earwig A nocturnal □insect belonging to an order (*Dermaptera*; about 1100 species) found in Europe and warm regions. It has a dark slender body, 0.2–2.0 in (5–50 mm) long, and a pair of pincers (cerci) at the end of the abdomen. At rest, the membranous semicircular hindwings are covered by short leathery forewings. Most earwigs are herbivorous, sometimes becoming pests in farms and gardens. The females lay eggs in the soil and care for them throughout development.

East Anglia A region in E England, consisting of the counties of Norfolk, Suffolk, and parts of Essex and Cambridgeshire. Originally an Anglo-Saxon kingdom, it became a famous wool center in the middle ages. The University of East Anglia was established at Norwich in 1962.

Eastbourne 51 00N 0 44W A resort in S England, on the East Sussex coast near Beachy Head, where the South Downs reach the sea. One of the larger English resorts, it developed in the 19th century from a group of hamlets. Population (1981): 77,608

East Cape 37 42S 178 35E The easternmost point of New Zealand, on North Island.

East China Sea (Chinese name: Dong Hai) A shallow section of the W Pacific Ocean, between China, South Korea, the Ryukyu Islands, and Taiwan. A monsoon area, it is rich in fish.

EASTER ISLAND *The vast stone statues, of which there are over 600 on the island, occupy stone terraces.*

Easter Island (*or* Rapanui) 27 05S 109 20W A Chilean island of volcanic origin in the S Pacific Ocean. It is famed for its stone sculptures 10–40 ft (3–12 m) high, of unknown origin. The population is of Polynesian stock. Fruit and vegetables are grown and wool is exported. Area: 64 sq mi (166 sq km). Population (1960): 1135. Chief settlement: Hanga-Roa.

Eastern Townships A district of E Canada, consisting of approximately 15 Quebec counties lying S of the St Lawrence River and E of Montreal. A prosperous agricultural area, it also has important asbestos mines. Chief town: Sherbrooke.

Easter Rising (1916) An armed insurrection in □Dublin against the British Government. Patrick Pearse, a leader of the Irish Republican Brotherhood, and James Connolly with his Citizen Army, a total of 2000 men, occupied strategic positions in the city and proclaimed the establishment of the Irish Republic. Serious street fighting ensued with the government employing artillery. Hopes of German arms and munitions were frustrated and the insurgents surrendered unconditionally. The rising was largely confined to Dublin and minor disturbances in Wexford and Galway. Some 15 of the leaders were subsequently executed.

East Germany. *See* Germany.

East India Company 1. (British) A commercial company that was incorporated in 1600 to trade in East Indian spices and came to wield considerable political power in British India. Its dominance in India was established at the expense of the French *East India Company by Robert *Clive's victories in the Seven Years' War (1756–63). For the next decade the Company controlled government, its powers then being restricted by a series of *Government of India Acts. Supreme political power was vested in a Board of Control, responsible to the British parliament, while the Company retained administrative and commercial powers. In the 19th century these were gradually limited and the Company ceased to exist in 1873. 2. (Dutch) A commercial company founded in 1602 to foster Dutch trade in the East Indies. By the late 17th century, it concentrated almost exclusively on the administration of *Java. 3. (French; Compagnie des Indes orientales) A trading company founded by *Colbert in 1664 to administer French commerce and colonialism in India. An unsuccessful rival of the British East India Company, it ceased to exist in 1789.

East Indies A term now usually referring to the *Malay Archipelago but sometimes to Indonesia (formerly called the Dutch East Indies). It may also include SE Asia and India.

East Kilbride 55 46N 4 10W A city in central Scotland, in Strathclyde Region. Designated for development as a new town in 1947, it has engineering and printing industries and manufactures aircraft engines and electrical equipment. Population (1981 est): 71,316.

East London (former name: Port Rex) 33 00S 27 54E A port in South Africa, in SE Cape Province on the Indian Ocean. It is the gateway to the Transkei and Ciskei Bantu Homelands and an important tourist center. Population (1980): 160,582.

Eastman, George (1854–1932) US inventor of the Kodak camera (1888). In 1884 he patented a photographic film consisting of a paper base on which the necessary chemicals were fixed rather than being applied to photographic plates when required. The Kodak camera, containing wind-on film, was improved in 1889, when Eastman replaced the paper-based film with celluloid. He founded (1892) the Eastman Kodak Company. In 1928 he developed a process for color photography. He was also a philanthropist, donating large sums to promote education.

East Pakistan. *See* Bangladesh.

East Riding. *See* Yorkshire.

East River A river in the E US, a tidal strait and navigable waterway flowing through New York City and connecting New York Harbor with Long Island Sound. Length: 16 mi (26 km).

Eaton Affair (1831) A social conflict in Washington, DC, that led to the reorganization of President Andrew *Jackson's cabinet. Secretary of War John Henry Eaton (1790–1856) married for a second time in 1829. His wife, Margaret O'Neill (1796–1879), was not accepted socially by the other cabinet wives, especially Mrs John Calhoun, the vice president's wife. Although she was defended by President Jackson and others, Eaton felt forced to resign from the cabinet.

Ebert, Friedrich (1871–1925) German statesman; first president of the German *Weimar Republic (1919–25). A trade union leader, he later became a deputy in the Reichstag and from 1913 led the Social Democrats. Although a constitutional monarchist, he accepted the republican presidency when the German Empire collapsed in 1918. As president he suppressed extremists of the Right and Left.

Ebla An ancient city (modern Tell Mardikh) S of Aleppo (Syria). It was conquered by *Sargon of Akkad and an archive of over 15,000 Akkadian cuneiform tablets containing trade and other records from this period (c. 2300 BC) was discovered here in 1975.

ebony The valuable heartwood of several tropical evergreen trees of the genus *Diospyros*. Ebony is very hard, heavy, usually deep black, and able to take a high polish. It is used for cabinetwork, inlaying, knife handles, piano keys, and turned articles. The trees have oval leathery leaves, small creamy-white flowers, and round berries. The most important species are *D. ebenum* (up to 49 ft [15 m] high) from India and Sri Lanka and *D. reticulata* from Mauritius. Family: *Ebenaceae*.

Eboracum (*or* Eburacum). *See* York.

Ebro River (Latin name: Iberus) The second longest river in Spain. Rising in the Cantabrian Mountains, it flows generally SE to the Mediterranean Sea. It is an important source of hydroelectricity and irrigation and its delta is canalized. Length: 565 mi (910 km).

Eccles, Sir John Carew (1903–) Australian physiologist, who (in the 1950s) showed how the different nerve endings (synapses) could either allow the transmission of nervous impulses to other nerves (excitatory) or could prevent their passage (inhibitory). He was awarded the 1963 Nobel Prize together with A. L. *Hodgkin and A. F. *Huxley.

Ecclesiastes (Greek: the preacher) An Old Testament book, traditionally ascribed to Solomon (10th century BC) but in fact one of the later books to be accepted as part of the Hebrew Bible. It is pessimistic in tone, consisting of poetic reflections on the futility of human life.

Ecclesiasticus A book of the *Apocrypha, also known as the Wisdom of Jesus the son of Sirach. It was written about 180 BC in Palestine by Joshua (*or* Jesus) ben-Sira. It stresses the need to fear and obey God, gives practical advice for daily living, and underlines the value of having a good name.

Ecevit, Bülent (1925–) Turkish statesman; prime minister (1974, 1977, 1978–79). He represented the Republican People's Party in the Grand National Assembly (1957–60) and was a member of the Constituent Assembly of 1961. From 1961 to 1965 he was minister of labor. In 1974

he ordered the Turkish invasion of Cyprus and in 1978, following violent civil unrest, imposed martial law on Turkey.

Echegaray y Eizaguirre, José (1832–1916) Spanish dramatist. A mathematician and economist, he was appointed minister of finance in 1874. His plays include *Madman or Saint* (1877) and *The Son of Don Juan* (1895), influenced by *Ibsen. He won the Nobel Prize in 1904.

echidna A *monotreme mammal belonging to the family *Tachyglossidae* (5 species), of Australia, Tasmania, and New Guinea. The Australian echidna (*Tachyglossus aculeatus*), or spiny anteater, is about 18 in (45 cm) long, with very long spines among its fur, and digs for ants, picking them up with its long sticky tongue; it has no teeth. Echidnas lay a single egg, which is incubated in a pouch on the female's belly. The young echidna is suckled at a teat in the pouch.

Echidna In Greek legend, a monster, half woman and half serpent. By the monster *Typhon she gave birth to many other legendary monsters, including Chimera, Cerberus, Orthus, Scylla, the Sphinx, and the dragons of the Hesperides and of Colchis.

echinoderm A marine invertebrate animal of the phylum *Echinodermata* (over 6000 species), including *starfish, *sea urchins, *crinoids, *sea cucumbers, *brittle stars, etc. Echinoderms usually have a skin-covered skeleton of calcareous plates, often bearing spines. They use hydrostatic pressure created by a water vascular system to extend numerous small saclike organs (tube feet) used in locomotion, respiration, feeding, etc. Echinoderms generally occur on the sea floor and are found at all depths, usually feeding on other animals or detritus. The sexes are generally separate and sex cells are fertilized in the sea. The larvae are mostly free-swimming.

Echinoidea A class of marine invertebrate animals (900 species) belonging to the phylum *Echinodermata* (*see* echinoderm), in which the body is covered by a rigid skeleton of calcareous plates bearing movable spines. The class includes the *sea urchins, *heart urchins, and *sand dollars.

Echo In Greek legend, a nymph deprived of speech by Hera and able to repeat only the final words of others. Her hopeless love for *Narcissus caused her to fade away until only her voice remained.

echolocation A method by which certain animals can sense and locate surrounding objects by emitting sounds and detecting the echo. Insectivorous bats emit high-frequency sound pulses (12–150 kHz) and, detecting the echo by means of large ears or folds of the nostril, are able to locate their prey when hunting on the wing. Toothed whales and porpoises emit brief intense clicks, enabling them to discriminate objects as small as fine wires. Some shrews and certain cave-dwelling swiftlets also use echolocation as a means of orientation.

echo sounding The use of sound waves to measure the depth of the sea below a vessel or to detect other vessels or obstacles. The device used consists of a source of ultrasonic pulses (about 30 kHz frequency, usually at 1 pulse per second) and an electronic circuit to measure the time taken for the pulse to reach the sea bed or the other vessel and its echo to return to the transducer. This may be displayed on a *cathode-ray tube, paper chart, or neon light. The device was developed originally by the Allied Submarine Detection Investigation Committee (ASDIC) in 1920 and was formerly known by this acronym. The name was changed to sonar (*so*und *na*vigation and *r*anging) in 1963. Echo-sounding depth-measuring devices are now fitted to most ships.

Eck, Johann Maier von (1486–1543) German Roman Catholic theologian. He was a leading defender of Roman Catholicism during the early years of the Reformation. He publicly disputed with *Luther at Leipzig (1519) and with *Melanchthon at Worms (1541).

Eckermann, Johann Peter (1792–1854) German writer. His early work impressed *Goethe, whose unpaid assistant he became in 1823. His *Conversations with Goethe* (1836–48) is a brilliant literary account of the poet's last years.

Eckert, John Presper (1919–) US electronics engineer, who with John W. Mauchly (1907–) built the first electronic computer (1946). Known as ENIAC (*E*lectronic *N*umerical *I*ntegrator *a*nd *C*omputer), it was commissioned by the US Government and used by the army. Eckert and Mauchly also produced Binac (*Bin*ary *A*utomatic *C*omputer) and Univac I (*Univ*ersal *A*utomatic *C*omputer).

Eckhart, Meister (Johannes E.; c. 1260–c. 1327) German Dominican theologian and mystic. Joining the Dominicans in 1275, he studied in Cologne and Paris and became provincial of his order in Saxony in 1303. During his professorship at Cologne University (1320–27) he was charged with heresy and in 1329 his writings were condemned by the pope. They have influenced a number of Protestant theologians and Romantic and existentialist writers.

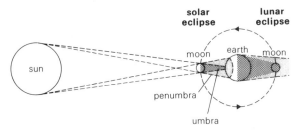

ECLIPSE

eclipse The passage of all or part of an astronomical body into the shadow of another. A **lunar eclipse** occurs when the moon can enter the earth's shadow at full moon. The gradual obscuration of the moon's surface is seen wherever the moon is above the horizon. A **solar eclipse**, which is strictly an *occultation, occurs at new moon, but only when the moon passes directly in front of the sun. The moon's shadow falls on and moves rapidly across the earth. Observers in the outer shadow region (the penumbra) will see a **partial eclipse**, with only part of the sun hidden. Observers in the dark inner (umbral) region of the shadow will see a **total eclipse**, in which the sun's disk is completely but briefly obscured; the *corona can, however, be seen. If the moon is too far away totally to cover the sun, an **annular eclipse** is observed, in which a rim of light is visible around the eclipsed sun.

ecliptic The great circle in which the plane of the earth's orbit around the sun meets the □celestial sphere. As a result of the earth's orbital motion, the ecliptic marks the apparent path of the sun across the celestial sphere, relative to the background stars, over the course of a year.

eclogue A short dramatic poem, originally pastoral in theme and setting. Originated by *Theocritus in the 3rd century BC, the form was used by Virgil and revived during the Renaissance by Dante and other Italian poets. English writers of eclogues include Spenser, Marvell, and Swift. In the 20th century, Louis MacNeice and W. H. Auden have made ironic use of the form.

ecology The scientific study of organisms in their natural environment. Modern ecology, dating from the work of such scientists as Charles *Elton in the 1930s, is concerned with the relationships of different species with each other and with the environment (habitat) in which they live. A *community of organisms and their habitat is called an *ecosystem. Ecologists can calculate the productivity of various ecosystems in terms of energy, with important applications in agriculture. In addition, the effects of man's intervention on natural ecosystems can be predicted, enabling the effective conservation of wildlife and management of game and fish. Ecologists have also introduced biological methods of pest control in certain cases, so avoiding pollution by pesticides.

econometrics The application of statistical techniques to *economics. Econometrics is used in the testing of the validity of economic theories and in forecasting future trends. The usual process is to develop a mathematical model of a specific theory; the model is then tested against observations of the real world and, if the theory is not refuted as a result, the model can then be used to make forecasts.

economic growth An expansion in the output of a nation's economy, measured by an increase in the *gross national product (GNP). Economic growth is generally regarded as desirable because it is the best way of raising the *standard of living; however, it can have drawbacks, such as increased pollution, which do not show up in the GNP. The level of *investment in the economy is an important factor in the rate of growth, but the reasons for faster growth in some countries than in others are not at all certain. It is also necessary to distinguish between growth and growth per capita. In a developing country the rate of growth may be high but the rate of growth per capita may be low because of a large increase in the population.

economics A social science concerned with the production of goods and services, their distribution, exchange, and consumption. **Microeconomics** is concerned with the problems facing individuals and firms, while **macroeconomics** is concerned with the economy of a country and regulation of the economy by governments. The division is useful because what is rational for the individual firm or household is not necessarily rational when considering the whole economy.

Contemporary problems in economics in the western democracies center upon the control of *inflation, *unemployment, and the *balance of pay-

ments, as well as the encouragement of *economic growth. Economics is beset by controversy between the conflicting schools of thought of *monetarism and *Keynesianism as to the extent to which governments can influence economies.

economies of scale An increase in output from a production process that is proportionately larger than the increase in inputs (raw materials, labor, etc.). For instance, a double-decker bus might be able to carry twice as many passengers as a single-decker, using the same number of crew and requiring only 40% more fuel. Such economies of scale are common in the manufacturing industry and are an inducement to use fewer but larger factories.

ecosystem A *community of living organisms together with the nonliving habitat that they occupy. Some ecosystems are clearly defined (for example, a pond or lake); others have no definite boundaries, merging with neighboring ecosystems. An ecosystem receives inputs of solar energy, nutrients, water, and gases and discharges heat, oxygen, carbon dioxide, and organic compounds. The organisms typically comprise producers (plants, manufacturing organic material from inorganic compounds); consumers (animals, feeding on plants and each other); and decomposers (microorganisms bringing about decay). Together they form an interdependent *food chain or food web.

ectopic pregnancy Pregnancy occurring elsewhere than in the womb. The commonest site of an ectopic pregnancy is in a Fallopian tube but it may also occur in the cervix of the womb or very rarely inside the abdomen. It may lead to abortion or, more seriously, to rupture of the tube, with pain, bleeding, and shock. The usual treatment of an ectopic pregnancy is surgical removal of the fetus and tube. Since the patient has a second tube there is usually no reason why she should not subsequently have a normal pregnancy.

Ecuador, Republic of A country in NW South America, lying on the Equator, from which it takes its name. It includes the *Galápagos Islands 600 mi (1000 km) out in the Pacific. It consists chiefly of a coastal plain in the W, separated from the tropical jungles and rivers of the Amazon basin (Oriente) by ranges and plateaus of the Andes (containing several active volcanoes, including *Cotopaxi). There are frequent earthquakes, which are often disastrous. The population is largely of Indian and mixed race, with minorities of European and African descent. *Economy*: mainly agricultural, with livestock, cereals, and vegetables in the upland valleys and tropical farming in the lower coastal areas, where the main cash crops (bananas, coffee, and cocoa) are grown. Much of the country is forested and valuable hardwoods are produced, although a great deal remains to be exploited. Ecuador is the world's leading producer of balsawood. Fishing is important, especially shrimps, and fishing limits have recently been extended to 200 mi (320 km), in spite of opposition from the US. There are some mineral resources; the most important is oil, several new oilfields having been discovered in the Oriente in recent years. In 1972 the construction of the Andean pipeline, which brings oil from the E to the coast, was completed and Ecuador is now South America's second largest oil producer (Venezuela being the first). Industry is being developed, especially the petrochemical, pharmaceutical, cement, and steel industries. Main exports include oil, bananas, cocoa, and coffee. *History*: the Andean kingdom of Quito had already been conquered by the Incas when the Spanish established a colony in 1532. It became part of the viceroyalty of Peru and later of New Granada. It gained independence in 1821 after revolts under Marshal Sucre, and in 1822 joined Gran Colombia under Bolívar. In 1830 it became the independent republic of Ecuador. In 1961 the president, Velasco Ibarra, was overthrown in a left-wing military coup and exiled. After several years of unsettled government he was again elected president. In 1970 he assumed dictatorial powers and in 1972 was deposed by a military regime. This regime was replaced by a three-man junta in 1976 but there are plans for a return to more democratic rule. In the early 1980s the government found itself in a precarious political position, reflected in a number of cabinet reshufflings. Distressing economic and social conditions resulted in ongoing labor strikes, high inflation, and a devalued sucre. Ecuador was forced to borrow heavily from the International Monetary Fund and foreign lenders. In recent years Ecuador has been involved in frontier disputes with Peru. It is a member of OPEC. Head of state: President Osvaldo Hurtado Larrea. Official language: Spanish; the main Indian language is Quechua. Official currency: sucre of 100 centavos. Area: 104,505 sq mi (270,670 sq km). Population (1983 est): 8,811,000. Capital: Quito. Main port: Guayaquil.

ecumenical movement A movement among Christian Churches to reestablish unity. The first major schism within Christianity was caused by the rupture between the Eastern and Western Churches in the 11th century; the second occurred within the Western Church at the *Reformation. It was only with the growth of missionary activity in the 19th century that the need for reunion became pressing. Historical divisions meant nothing to the new converts in countries outside the traditional sphere of Christianity. In 1910 the Edinburgh Missionary Conference opened negotiations among the Churches of the Reformation, a process that ultimately led to the foundation of the *World Council of Churches in 1948. The Orthodox Churches gradually came to take a more active role in this body, and further encouragement to the movement came with Pope *John XXIII's invitation to other Churches to send observers to the second *Vatican Council, the results of which clearly indicated Roman Catholic support for ecumenism. Since then the most obvious progress has occurred on the local level, where interdenominational cooperation is now widespread.

eczema. *See* dermatitis.

Edam 52 30N 5 02E A city in the NW Netherlands, in North Holland province on the IJsselmeer. It is famous for its round red-skinned cheeses. Population (1971 est): 18,495.

Eddas Two Old Norse compilations made in Iceland in the early 13th century. Together they comprise the major store of pagan Scandinavian mythology. The **Poetic** (*or* Elder) **Edda** (c. 1200) contains poems on the gods, heroic legends, and traditional charms and proverbs. The **Prose** (*or* Younger) **Edda** (1223) was the work of Snorri *Sturluson, who planned it as a textbook for writers of *skaldic poetry, prefaced by a section on the Norse cosmogony, pantheon, and myths.

Eddington, Sir Arthur Stanley (1882–1944) British theoretical astronomer, who correctly calculated that the temperature of the sun's interior must be millions of degrees Celsius or it would collapse under gravitational forces. He also showed that the luminosity of a star increases with its mass (the mass-luminosity law). Eddington was a talented popularizer of science: his *Expanding Universe* (1933) contained the novel idea that the galaxies are flying apart.

Eddy, Mary Baker (1821–1910) US religious leader, founder of *Christian Science. Brought up as a Congregationalist and frequently ill as a young woman, Mrs Eddy was much influenced by the faith healer Phineas Parkhurst Quimby (1802–66). She published her beliefs in *Science and Health* (1875) and in 1879 founded the Church of Christ, Scientist, in Boston. The *Christian Science Monitor*, an influential daily newspaper, first appeared in 1908.

eddy current An electric current induced in a conductor that experiences a changing magnetic field. In *electric generators, motors, and transformers, energy is lost by unwanted eddy currents, either producing heat or opposing motion. In these devices eddy currents are reduced by laminating the iron cores to increase their resistance. Eddy currents are useful in some applications, such as eddy-current heating, mechanical damping and eddy-current brakes, and electricity meters.

Ede 52 03N 5 40E A city in the central Netherlands, in Gelderland province. Its museum contains a fine collection of Van Gogh paintings. Population (1981 est): 83,738.

edelweiss A common perennial alpine plant, *Leontopodium alpinum*, from Europe and South America, often grown in rock gardens. About 6 in (15 cm) high, it has woolly leaves arranged like a star and clustered heads of tiny yellow flowers surrounded by whitish felted bracts. Family: *Compositae* (daisy family).

edema The accumulation of fluid in body tissues, leading to swelling, popularly known as dropsy. There are many causes of edema, including heart failure, kidney failure, liver failure, and malnutrition. Fluid in the lungs (pulmonary edema) will cause breathlessness. *Diuretic drugs can usually resolve edema by causing the patient to pass more urine. Swelling of the ankles occurs quite commonly: for example, in hot weather and in women before menstruation. It is usually relieved by resting with the legs raised.

Eden, (Robert) Anthony, 1st Earl of Avon (1897–1977) British statesman; Conservative prime minister (1955–57). Foreign secretary from 1935 to 1938. During World War II he was secretary for war and then (1940–45) foreign secretary. From 1951 to 1955 he was again foreign secretary, playing an important part in the 1954 *Geneva Conference and in the establishment of the *European Defense Community. He succeeded Churchill as prime minister and in 1956, following Nasser's nationalization of the *Suez Canal and an Israeli attack on Egypt, joined France in an offensive against Egypt. Egypt retained control of Suez and, despite Eden's claim that the Anglo-French initiative had ended the war between Egypt and Israel, he was greatly criticized and resigned shortly afterward. He became Earl of Avon in 1961.

Eden, Garden of In the Old Testament, the location of Paradise, in which Adam and Eve were created and lived until expelled because of disobedience (Genesis 2–3). Although the narrative may allude to a place in the fertile part of Mesopotamia, the geographical elements are probably mythological.

Edgar (c. 943–75) The first king of a united England (959–75). He allowed his Danish subjects to retain Danish laws. Edgar promoted a monastic revival and encouraged trade by reforming the currency. He improved defense by organizing coastal naval patrols and a system for manning warships.

Edgar (c. 1075–1107) King of the Scots (1097–1107); a vassal of William Rufus of England. In 1098 he lost the Hebrides to Norway.

Edgar the Aetheling (c. 1050–c. 1130) The grandson of Edmund II Ironside, his title Aetheling means royal prince. His claim to the English throne was rejected in 1066 owing to his minority and ill health. Although he initially submitted to William I, in 1068 and 1069 he led revolts against the king but came to terms with him in 1074.

Edgeworth, Maria (1767–1849) Anglo-Irish writer chiefly famous for her novels of Irish regional life, including *Castle Rackrent* (1800), *Patronage* (1814), and *Ormond* (1817), which influenced Sir Walter *Scott. She also wrote imaginative but moralizing children's stories.

Edinburgh 55 57N 3 13W The capital of Scotland, situated in the E center of the country on the S shore of the Firth of Forth. The financial, legal, and cultural center of Scotland, employment depends largely on service occupations. Food, drink, and printing are the primary manufacturing industries; the city's port is at Leith. Edinburgh is distinguished by its spacious layout and attractive buildings. In the old town, atop cliffs that rise above the city, stands the castle. The Royal Mile extends E from the castle rock to the Palace of Holyrood House (begun c. 1500). The other famous thoroughfare in the city is Princes Street, flanked by the picturesque Princes Street Gardens. The university (1583) is famous for its medical faculty among other notable faculties. The Royal Scottish Academy, the Royal Scottish Museum, and other national institutions are situated in Edinburgh. St Giles Cathedral dates from the 12th century. *History*: strategically important in medieval times in the wars between England and Scotland, Edinburgh emerged as the national capital in the 15th century. After James VI of Scotland (James I of England) moved his court to London in 1605 Edinburgh suffered a decline. It entered a golden age in the mid 18th century as a center of learning. The fame of the city as a cultural center was revived in 1947 with the foundation of the annual Edinburgh International Festival. Population (1981): 419,187.

Edirne (former name: Adrianople) 41 40N 26 34E A city in European Turkey, at the confluence of the Tunca and Maritsa Rivers. Round the main square are three mosques, one of which, the Selimiye Mosque, has 19 domes. Population (1970): 53,806.

Edison, Thomas Alva (1847–1931) US inventor, one of the most prolific of all time, eventually registering more than 1000 patents in his own name. Self-educated, Edison invented an automatic vote recorder at age 22. His improved stock-ticker, invented in 1871, earned him enough money to establish his own manufacturing plant in Newark, NJ. In 1876 he moved his laboratory to Menlo Park, NJ, where he developed some of his most important inventions. The most famous of these, the electric light bulb, took over a year to perfect, but he finally constructed a long-lasting filament bulb in 1879. He also constructed a complete system of electric power distribution for potential customers. Among the other inventions developed at the Menlo Park laboratory were an improved telephone transmitter and the phonograph. He also discovered thermionic emission, called the Edison effect, which later provided the scientific basis for the electron tube. In 1887, Edison moved his laboratory to West Orange, NJ, where he produced, among other inventions, the first motion picture camera, the mimeograph machine, the fluoroscope, and an improved electric battery. His Edison Electric Light Company, established in 1889, later became the General Electric Company.

Edmonton 53 34N 113 25W A city in W Canada, the capital of Alberta on the North Saskatchewan River. A 19th-century trading post, it became an agricultural settlement and grew into a city with the arrival of the railroad (1891). The discovery of oil (1947) stimulated an economy already prosperous from distribution, transportation, manufacturing, and agricultural industries. Edmonton is the site of the University of Alberta (1906) and numerous cultural institutions. Population (1976): 461,361.

Edmund I (921–46) King of England (939–46), who expelled the Norse king Olaf from Northumbria (944). He supported *Dunstan in the reintroduction of the monastic rule of St Benedict. An outlaw stabbed him to death at Pucklechurch.

Edmund II Ironside (c. 981–1016) The son of Ethelred II of England, his struggle with Canute for the vacant throne ended in Edmund's defeat at Ashingdon (1016). However, Canute agreed on the partition of England with Edmund, but after Edmund's sudden death Canute acquired the whole kingdom.

Edmund, St (Edmund Rich; c. 1175–1240) English churchman; Archbishop of Canterbury. After an academic life at Oxford and Paris he was made archbishop in 1234. Supported by the barons he successfully opposed Henry III's policies until his power was diminished by the arrival of the papal legate, Cardinal Otho, in 1237. Feast day: Nov 16.

Edo A people of S Nigeria living to the W of the Niger River. Their language belongs to the *Kwa subgroup of the Niger-Congo family. They live in villages and grow yams, corn, and the cash crops of rubber and cocoa. Their sacred king (or oba) formerly held political, economic, and ritual authority, but most Edo are now Christians or Muslims.

Edom The mountainous and barren land SW of the Dead Sea, which was traversed in antiquity by important caravan routes. The Edomites, according to the Old Testament, were descendants of Esau and may have been subjected by the Israelites under King David. They were converted to Judaism in the late 2nd century BC after being defeated by the *Maccabees. They later migrated to S Judea.

education The process of learning. Highly developed systems of learning emerged early in Asia, especially in China. Institutionalized education could also be found in various forms in ancient Greece and Rome, which later influenced the development of formal education in medieval Europe, although the latter owes a great debt to early Arabic and Hebrew scholarship. Medieval European monastic schools originally established for those intending to enter the monasteries gradually admitted other pupils and extended the curriculum to include grammar, logic, rhetoric, geometry, arithmetic, music, and astronomy. A basic education was also provided in some areas for the children of the poor, usually by the local parish priest. Humanist education based upon the classics emerged during the Renaissance; the Gymnasien, which was established at Strasbourg, provided the model for the academic schools of Protestant Europe, although its influence was slow in reaching England. European schools experienced a decline in standards during the 17th and 18th centuries. Widespread education could be said to stem from the introduction of compulsory attendance at primary schools (see primary education), first established successfully in Prussia in 1763. In the US education patterns originally followed European models. The country developed its own distinctive approaches to education in the 19th century under the impetus of innovators such as Horace Mann and as the college and university network grew. Today, education varies from state to state. Secondary education, however, is nonselective and provides both academic and vocational courses. Approximately 80% of children stay on beyond the compulsory school-attendance age of 16 and about 40% enter higher education. See also adult education; special education.

Education, Department of US cabinet-level executive branch department. It establishes policy for, administers, and coordinates most federal assistance to education. Headed by the secretary of education, the department was created in 1979; previously, it was part of the Department of *Health, Education, and Welfare.

Edward I (1239–1307) King of England (1272–1307), succeeding his father Henry III. He married (1254) *Eleanor of Castile. In the *Barons' War (1264–67) he defeated the barons at Evesham (1265). As king, he is noted for encouraging parliamentary institutions at the expense of feudalism and for subduing Wales, on which he imposed the English system of administration. He later tried to assert his authority over Scotland and died while on his way to fight Robert Bruce (see Robert I).

Edward II (1284–1327) King of England (1307–27), succeeding his father Edward I. He was born in Caernarvon and became the first English Prince of Wales (1301). He married *Isabella of France (1308). His reign was troubled by his extravagance, his military disasters in Scotland, notably at Bannockburn (1314), and the unpopularity of his favorites, Piers Gaveston (d. 1312) and Hugh le Despenser (1262–1326). Isabella and her lover Roger de *Mortimer murdered him.

Edward III (1312–77) King of England (1327–77), succeeding his father Edward II. He married (1328) Philippa of Hainault. Edward assumed effective power in 1330 after imprisoning his mother *Isabella of France and executing her lover Roger de *Mortimer. Thereafter his reign was dominated by military adventures, his victories in Scotland, especially at *Halidon Hill (1333), encouraging him to plan (1363) the union of England and Scotland. Through his mother he claimed the French throne, thus starting (1337) the *Hundred Years' War. His son *John of Gaunt dominated the government during his last years.

Edward IV (1442–83) King of England (1461–70, 1471–83) during the Wars of the *Roses. He married (1464) Elizabeth Woodville. The Yorkist leader, he was crowned after defeating the Lancastrians at Mortimer's Cross and Towton (1461). He was forced from the throne (1470) by the Earl of *Warwick but regained it after defeating the Lancastrians at *Tewkesbury (1471).

Edward V (1470–?1483) King of England (1483), succeeding his father Edward IV. His uncle, the Duke of Gloucester, imprisoned Edward and his brother Richard in the Tower of London, deposed Edward after a reign of only three months, and had himself crowned as Richard III. The two boys, known as the Princes in the Tower, were probably murdered in 1483.

Edward VI (1537–53) King of England (1547–53) and the son of Henry VIII, whom he succeeded, and Jane *Seymour. Effective power was held by the protector, the Duke of *Somerset, until 1550, when the Duke of *Northumberland seized power. Edward became a fervent Protestant and during his reign the *Reformation in England made substantial progress.

Edward VII (1841–1910) King of the United Kingdom (1901–10), succeeding his mother Queen Victoria. He married (1863) *Alexandra of Denmark. As Prince of Wales his indiscretions caused Victoria to exclude him from all affairs of state. A popular king, he ably represented Britain abroad.

Edward VIII (1894–1972) King of the United Kingdom (1936), succeeding his father George V. While both Prince of Wales and king, he expressed sympathy for victims of the Depression. He abdicated on December 11, 1936, because of objections to his liaison with the twice-divorced Mrs Wallis Simpson (1896–   ), whom he married in France in 1937. He became Duke of Windsor and was appointed governor of the Bahamas during World War II. He subsequently lived in France, where he remained until his death.

Edward, Lake (name from 1976 until 1979: Lake Idi Amin Dada) 0 20S 29 35E A lake in Zaïre and Uganda. Its only outlet, the Semliki River, eventually flows into the Nile River. Area: about 820 sq mi (2124 sq km).

Edward, the Black Prince (1330–76) Prince of Wales and the eldest son of Edward III. His nickname is probably posthumous and may refer to the black armor he was said to have worn at Crécy (1346). He won victories against France in the *Hundred Years' War and ruled Aquitaine from 1360 until ousted (1371) by a revolt, during which he was responsible for the massacre of Limoges (1370).

Edwards, Jonathan (1703–58) US theologian and philosopher. As minister of the Congregational Church at Northampton, Mass (1727–50), his strongly Calvinistic preaching led to the revival movement known as the *Great Awakening. Dismissed because of his overzealous orthodoxy, he continued to preach and in the year of his death became president of the College of Princeton, NJ. His best-known theological work, *Freedom of the Will* (1754), is a discussion of determinism.

Edward the Confessor (c. 1003–66) King of England (1042–66), nicknamed for his piety and his foundation of a new Westminster Abbey (consecrated 1065). He lived in Normandy (1016–41) and his early reign was dominated by rivalry between his Norman favorites and his father-in-law Earl *Godwin. After 1053 the Godwins were in the ascendant. Edward's childlessness led ultimately to the Norman conquest. He was canonized in 1161.

Edward the Elder (d. 924) King of England (899–924), succeeding his father Alfred the Great. He defeated the Danes (918), taking East Anglia, and also conquered Mercia (918) and Northumbria (920).

Edward the Martyr (c. 963–78) King of England (975–78), succeeding his father Edgar. He was murdered at Corfe Castle, reputedly by his stepmother Elfthryth. He was canonized in 1001.

Edwin (c. 585–633) King of Northumbria (616–33), who became overlord of all English kingdoms S of the Humber, except for Kent. His marriage to Ethelburh, a Christian, led to his conversion and that of his people to Christianity (627). He was killed in battle against Penda of Mercia.

Edwy. *See* Eadwig.

EEC. *See* European Economic Community.

eel A snakelike *bony fish of the worldwide order *Anguilliformes* (or *Apodes*; over 500 species) having, usually, a scaleless body, no pelvic fins, and long dorsal and anal fins continuous with the tail fin. Most species are marine, occurring mainly in shallow waters and feeding on other fish and invertebrates. The freshwater eels (family *Anguillidae*) migrate to the sea to breed—the *Sargasso Sea in the case of European and American species. The transparent leaflike larvae (leptocephali) develop into young eels (elvers) and return to rivers and streams. □fish. *See also* electric eel.

eelgrass A perennial herbaceous marine plant of the genus *Zostera*, especially *Z. marina*, which grows in muddy intertidal flats and estuaries on the coasts of Europe and North America and is one of the few flowering plants to tolerate sea water. It has creeping underground stems (rhizomes), which help to stabilize mudbanks, and broad dark-green grasslike leaves. Family: *Zosteraceae*.

eelpout A thick-lipped eel-like fish of the family *Zoarcidae* (about 60 species) that lives on the bottom in cold oceanic waters and feeds on small fish and invertebrates. Up to 18 in (45 cm) long, eelpouts have small pelvic fins located near the gills. Many produce live young, for example the European *Zoarces viviparus*. Order: *Perciformes*.

eelworm A very small *nematode worm parasitic on plants, causing damage to agricultural crops. Adult eelworms measure up to 0.05 in (1.5 mm) long. The larvae, on hatching, penetrate plant roots, which may react by forming root galls around them. Chief genera: *Anguina, Ditylenchus, Heterodera*.

Efik A people of Calibar province in Nigeria. Their language, Efik-Ibibio, belongs to the *Kwa subgroup of the Niger-Congo family. Their territory became a major trading center, exporting slaves and, later, palm oil. Most Efik live in forest villages where they farm manioc and yams and there is still a flourishing network of markets. Political and economic power was vested in the Ekpe or Leopard Society, a graded secret society based upon propitiation of forest spirits.

EFTA. *See* European Free Trade Association.

Egbert (d. 839) King of Wessex (802–39), who laid the foundations for the supremacy of Wessex over a united England. He faced the first Danish raiders from 835.

Eger 47 53N 20 22E A town in NE Hungary. It was occupied by the Turks from 1596 to 1687 and has a minaret, 115 ft (35m) high. Wine is produced in the surrounding area. Population (1980): 60,000.

Egeria A Roman goddess associated with fountains; she also presided over childbirth. According to legend she gave advice to Numa Pompilius (the successor of Romulus as king of Rome), who met her nightly at her sacred fountain near Rome.

egg (*or* ovum) The female reproductive cell (*see* gamete), which—when fertilized by a male gamete (sperm)—develops into a new individual of the same species. Animal eggs are surrounded by nutritive material (yolk) and—usually—one or more protective membranes, for example a jelly coat in amphibian eggs, the shell and other layers in birds' eggs. The amount of yolk varies, being greater in the eggs of egg-laying animals since the developing embryo depends on the yolk for nourishment: in mammals the egg is nourished from the maternal circulation and thus has little yolk. *See also* ovary.

eggplant. *See* aubergine.

eglantine. *See* sweet briar.

Egmont, Lamoraal, Graaf van (*or* Egmond; 1522–68) Flemish statesman and soldier, who opposed Philip II of Spain's religious policies in the Netherlands. After distinguished service in the victories against the French he was appointed stadholder (chief magistrate) of Flanders. With William the Silent and other magnates Egmont left the state council in 1565 in protest against the continuing persecution of Protestants by Philip II. He subsequently pledged his loyalty to Philip but was executed as a traitor by the Duke of *Alba in 1568. *See also* Revolt of the Netherlands.

Egmont, Mount 39 18S 174 05E A volcanic mountain in New Zealand, in W North Island. It forms an almost perfect cone and is encircled by a fertile ring plain. Height: 8260 ft (2478 m). *See also* Taranaki.

ego In *psychoanalysis, the part of the mind that is closely in touch with the demands of external reality and operates rationally. It includes some motives (such as hunger and ambition), the individual's learned responses, and his (or her) conscious thought. It has to reconcile the conflicting demands of the *id, the *superego, and the outside world.

egoism A philosophical theory of *ethics claiming that morality should be based on the self-interest of the individual. Egoism also claims that self-interest both explains and provides a motivating force for a general adherence to a set of moral principles. The argument is that a system of morality ensures a stable society and that an individual is better off in a stable society. Egoism is the opposite of altruism, which claims that morality has to be based on concern for the welfare of others. Altruists claim that while egoism may provide the motivation for others to obey moral rules, it does not provide such a motivation for the self. This can only arise from a concern for the welfare of others.

egret A white bird belonging to the *heron subfamily. The great white egret (*Egretta alba*) has long silky ornamental plumes in the breeding season that were formerly used for decorating hats. The smaller cattle egret (*Aroleola ibis*) is 20 in (50 cm) long and follows large grazing animals, feeding on insects disturbed by their hoofs.

Egypt, Arab Republic of (Arabic name: Misr) A country in NE Africa, extending into SW Asia. Most of the country consists of desert—the *Sinai Peninsula, the Eastern Desert (a vast upland area), and the Western Desert (an extensive low plateau), while most of the population is concentrated along the fertile Nile Valley. *Economy*: despite limited resources of water and cultivable land, the introduction of modern irrigation schemes, such as the *Aswan High Dam, has led to an increase in the production of cotton, the chief cash crop, as well as a more diversified agricultural sector (rice, millet, maize, sugar cane, and fruit and vegetables). Nevertheless Egypt is still far from being self-sufficient in food production. Restriction of land ownership under the Agrarian Reform Law (1952) led to increased private investment in industry but the considerable expansion of the industrial sector since the 1950s, especially heavy industries, such as iron and steel, chemicals, and electricity, has been mainly the result of government planning, utilizing aid from communist countries. More recently, however, there has been an increase in private industrial activity. Oil was discovered in 1909 and in recent years production has greatly increased. Natural gas is also being exploited and other minerals include phosphate, iron ore, and salt. Egypt's many historical and archeological remains make tourism an important source of revenue. The chief exports are cotton and cotton goods and oil. *History*: ancient Egyptian history is traditionally divided into 30 dynasties, beginning in about 3100 BC with the union of Upper and Lower Egypt by Menes and ending in 343 BC with the death of the last Egyptian king, or *pharaoh, Nectanebo II. The so-called Old Kingdom (3rd–6th dynasties; c. 2686–c. 2160) reached its peak in the reigns of Khufu and his son Khafre, which saw remarkable building achievements, notably the *pyramids at Giza. The 6th dynasty witnessed a decentralization of government and the consequent rise in power of provincial officials, which resulted in the disunity that characterized the First Intermediate Period (7th–11th dynasties; c. 2160–c. 2040). Egypt was reunited by Mentuhotep II (reigned c. 2060–2010), the founder of the Middle Kingdom (12th dynasty; c. 2040–c. 1786), of which the outstanding kings were Sesostris III and Amenemhet III. In the Second Intermediate Period (13th–17th dynasties; c. 1786–c. 1567) Egypt came largely under the control of the invading Asiatic tribes (the Hyksos), which were finally expelled by Ahmose I, founder of the New Kingdom (18th–20th dynasties; c. 1570–1085). During the New Kingdom Thutmose III extended Egypt's frontiers and acquired new territories in Asia and Amenhotep III sponsored buildings at *Karnak and *Luxor. His own son was the heretic king *Akhenaten, but orthodoxy was restored under *Tutankhamen. The reign of Ramses II was troubled by the *Hittites and that of Ramses III, by the Sea Peoples, and the 20th dynasty also saw the priests' power rise at the kings' expense. The outcome of Egypt's decline under the 21st–25th dynasties (1085–664) was the Assyrian invasion under Esarhaddon (671) and the 26th dynasty (664–525) was brought to an end by the Persian Acheamenians. Acheamenian rule was interrupted by the native 28th, 29th, and 30th dynasties (404–343) and was finally ended by Alexander the Great of Macedon, who obtained Egypt in 332.

On Alexander's death Egypt was acquired by the Macedonian Ptolemy I Soter. The Ptolemies ruled until the suicide of *Cleopatra VII in 30 BC, when Egypt passed under Roman rule. In 395 AD, Egypt became part of the Byzantine (Eastern Roman) Empire. The Arabs conquered Egypt in 642 and it was then governed by representatives of the caliphate of Baghdad, under whom Islam was introduced. After 868 it gained virtual autonomy under a series of ruling dynasties. The last of these, the Fatimids, were overthrown by *Saladin, who restored Egypt to the caliphate in 1171. It was ruled by the Mamelukes from 1250 until 1517, when it was conquered by the Ottoman Turks. The Turks governed Egypt through a viceroy but by the early 18th century power was largely in the hands of the Mameluke elite.

In 1798 Napoleon established a French protectorate over Egypt, which in 1801 was overthrown by the British and Ottomans. A mutiny among Albanian soldiers in the Ottoman army in Egypt brought Mehemet 'Ali to power as viceroy (1805) and in 1840 he was recognized by the Ottomans as hereditary ruler. British and French interests in Egypt intensified in the mid 19th century and in 1869 the opening of the Suez Canal enhanced Egypt's international significance. An Arab nationalist revolt was suppressed in 1882 by the British, who thereafter dominated Egyptian government in spite of nominal Ottoman suzerainty. In 1914, on the outbreak of World War I, Egypt became a British protectorate until independence under King Fu'ad I was granted in 1922. In 1936 his son Farouk signed a treaty of alliance with Britain, which retained rights in the Suez Canal zone, and in World War II Egypt joined the Allies. The immediate postwar period saw the first Arab-Israeli War (1948–49) and a military coup (1952) that overthrew the monarchy (1953) and brought *Nasser to power (1954). Nasser's nationalization of the Suez Canal in 1956 precipitated an invasion by Israeli and Anglo-French forces, which were compelled by the UN to withdraw. In 1958 Egypt, Syria, and subsequently North Yemen formed the *United Arab Republic, a name retained by Egypt, in spite of Syria's withdrawal in 1961, until its present designation was adopted in 1971. Conflict with Israel erupted again in 1967, when in the third Arab-Israeli War (the Six Day War) Egypt lost territories that included the Sinai peninsula, partly regained in the fourth war (1973). In 1970 Nasser was succeeded by Anwar el-Sadat, who in 1972 brought Egypt's close relationship with the Soviet Union to an end by ceasing to employ some 20,000 Soviet personnel. In 1979, under US influence, Egypt and Israel signed a momentous peace treaty. Increasing opposition to Sadat's policies culminated in his assassination by Islamic extremists in 1981. He was succeeded as president by Hasni Mubarak. Under Mubarak, the staged transfer of Sinai territory from Israel to Egypt in accordance with the 1979 peace treaty was completed. But when Israel invaded Lebanon in 1982, Mubarak recalled his ambassador from Israel and relations between the two countries have remained cool though correct. Official language: Arabic. Official religion: Islam. Official currency: Egyptian pound of 100 piastres. Area: 386,198 sq mi (1,000,000 sq km). Population (1983): 45,851,000. Capital: Cairo. Main port: Alexandria.

Ehrenberg, Iliya Grigorievich (1891–1967) Soviet author. From 1908 to 1917 he lived in Paris, where he published some poetry; he returned to Russia in 1920 and immediately went back to Paris as a correspondent. He remained in W Europe until 1940. He was a mildly controversial figure under Stalinism but wrote virulent anti-Western propaganda. His novel *The Thaw* (1954) and his memoirs, *Men, Years, Life* (1960–64), were among the earliest open criticisms of Stalin.

Ehrlich, Paul (1854–1915) German bacteriologist. Ehrlich did much to develop the understanding of acquired immunity to disease in animals and, with *Behring, he prepared a serum against diphtheria. In 1910 he announced the discovery of an arsenical compound (Salvarsan) effective in treating syphilis. Ehrlich shared a Nobel Prize (1908) with *Metchnikov.

Eichendorff, Josef, Freiherr von (1788–1857) German Romantic writer. He studied at Heidelberg and Berlin, where he became involved in the Romantic movement, and rose high in the Prussian civil service. His lyrical nature poems were set by many composers. His best-known novel is *Memoirs of a Good-for-Nothing* (1826).

Eichler, August Wilhelm (1839–87) German botanist, who proposed the system on which modern plant classification is based. Eichler divided the plant kingdom into four divisions: Thallophyta (algae and fungi), Bryophyta (liverworts and mosses), Pteridophyta (ferns), and Spermatophyta (seed plants).

Eichmann, Adolf (1906–62) German Nazi politician, prominent in the extermination of Jews during World War II. After the war he went into hiding in Argentina; traced and captured by the Israelis in 1960, he was then tried and hanged for his war crimes.

eider A large sea *duck, *Somateria mollissima*, of far northern sea coasts. About 22 in (55 cm) long, males are mostly white with a black crown, belly, and tail; females are mottled dark brown. The soft fluffy feathers plucked by the female from her breast to line her nest are the source of eiderdown.

Eiffel Tower A metal tower in □Paris, built for the 1889 Centennial Exposition. The most famous work of the French engineer Alexandre-Gustave Eiffel (1832–1923), the 984 ft (300 m) tower was the highest building in the world until 1930. Although an outstanding engineering achievement, it was originally much disliked, but has become one of the great Parisian landmarks.

Eiger 46 34N 8 01E A mountain in central S Switzerland, in the Bernese Oberland. Its N face, possibly the most difficult climb in the Alps, was not conquered until 1938. Height: 12,697 ft (3970 m).

Eightfold Path (*or* The Noble Eightfold Path) In Buddhism the fourth of the *Four Noble Truths, which summarizes the eight ways that lead the Buddhist to enlightenment. They are: right understanding, right resolve, right speech, right action, right livelihood, right effort, right mindfulness, and right meditation. The Path, which is not a series of successive steps but an integrated spiritual attitude, was described in the Buddha's first discourse at Benares.

Eijkman, Christiaan (1858–1930) Dutch physician, who originated the concept of dietary deficiency disease. As a doctor in the East Indies, Eijk-

man noticed that chickens fed on polished rice developed symptoms resembling beriberi. By including rice hulls in their diet, the disease was cured—an effect he attributed to a dietary factor (later shown to be thiamine, or vitamin B_1). Eijkmann received the 1929 Nobel Prize with Sir Frederick *Hopkins.

Eilat (Elat *or* Elath) 29 33N 34 57E A city in extreme S Israel, on the Gulf of Aqaba. Ancient Eilat declined in the 12th century, and the modern city was founded in 1949 as Israel's only port S of the Suez Canal. There is also an oil-refining industry here. Population (1971 est): 15,900.

Eindhoven 51 26N 5 30E A city in the S Netherlands, in North Brabant province. It is a manufacturing center specializing in electronics and producing light bulbs, radios, and televisions. Population (1981 est): 195,669.

Einhard (*or* Eginhard; c. 770–840) Frankish historian, a courtier of *Charlemagne. His *Vita Caroli magni*, based on intimate knowledge of the emperor's character and government, is one of the major medieval biographies and a probable source of the 12th-century poem *Chanson de Roland*.

EINSTEIN *A photograph taken in 1932.*

Einstein, Albert (1879–1955) German physicist. Born in Ulm, now in West Germany, Einstein was an undistinguished scholar, being interested only in theoretical physics. In 1901 he obtained a post at the Patent Office in Berne, Switzerland, and became a Swiss citizen. While working there, he continued his researches and in 1905 published four highly original papers. One gave a mathematical explanation of the *Brownian movement in molecular terms, the second explained the *photoelectric effect in terms of *photons, the third announced his special theory of *relativity, and the fourth related mass to energy. These papers were so revolutionary that their importance was not immediately recognized and Einstein only secured a university post four years later. In 1915 he extended the theory of relativity to the general case and, when its predictions had been verified in 1917, he became world-famous, receiving the 1921 Nobel Prize for Physics. In 1930, while Einstein was lecturing in California, Hitler came to power; being Jewish, Einstein decided to remain in the US. He spent the rest of his life at the Institute for Advanced Study in Princeton, unsuccessfully seeking a *unified field theory. He became a US citizen in 1940. Originally a pacifist, Einstein was persuaded in 1939 to write to President Roosevelt warning him that an atom bomb could now be made and that Germany might make one first. Although he took no part in its manufacture, he was an active postwar advocate of nuclear disarmament, aware that without his theory of relativity the nuclear age could not have dawned.

einsteinium (Es) An artificial transuranic element discovered by Ghiorso and others in 1952 in fall-out from the first large hydrogen-bomb explosion. It was named for Albert Einstein. Einsteinium behaves chemically as a trivalent actinide. Its 11 isotopes are all radioactive, the longest-lived having a half-life of 276 days. At no 99; at wt (254).

Einthoven, Willem (1860–1927) Dutch physiologist and pioneer of *electrocardiography. In 1903 Einthoven devised a sensitive galvanometer to detect the electrical rhythms of the heart. He developed his recording technique until he was able to correlate abnormalities in electrical activity with various heart disorders. He was awarded the 1924 Nobel Prize.

Éire. *See* Ireland, Republic of.

Eisenach 50 59N 10 21E A city and resort in SW East Germany, on the NW slopes of the Thuringian Forest. Among its many notable buildings is Wartburg Castle, where Martin Luther completed his translation of the

Bible into German. It is the birthplace of J. S. Bach. Its manufactures include motor vehicles and chemicals. Population (1973 est): 50,457.

DWIGHT D. EISENHOWER *US president (1953-61) and Allied Commander in Europe during World War II.*

Eisenhower, Dwight David (1890–1969) US military leader and statesman; 34th President of the United States (1953–61). Born in Denison, Tex, Eisenhower graduated from West Point in 1915 and supervised the training of armored forces during World War I. In 1933, Eisenhower was named special assistant to General Douglas *MacArthur and served as assistant military adviser in the Philippines (1935–39). After the outbreak of World War II, he was assigned to the office of chief of staff, where he headed the War Plans Division. In 1942 he was placed in command of US forces in Europe and led the Allied invasion of North Africa in the same year. Eisenhower became the supreme commander of the Allied Expeditionary Force in western Europe in 1944, and in that capacity he supervised the *D-Day invasion of Normandy. He was promoted to the rank of General of the Army in December, 1944. With the German surrender in 1945, Eisenhower was named commander of the US occupation zone in Germany and he later succeeded General George C. *Marshall as US chief of staff. Eisenhower resigned from the army temporarily to become president of Columbia University (1948–51), but he returned to active duty to accept an appointment by President Truman as supreme commander of the Allied powers in Europe (1951–52).

In 1952, Eisenhower entered politics, gaining the Republican nomination for president and defeating Adlai *Stevenson, the Democratic candidate, in the general election. Eisenhower served two terms in the presidency, defeating Stevenson again in 1956. A popular president, "Ike" initiated important social welfare programs and used federal forces to enforce racial integration in the Little Rock, Ark, public schools. In foreign affairs, the Eisenhower administration, through Secretary of State John Foster *Dulles, pursued a policy of confrontation with the Soviet Union in Europe and direct involvement in the Middle East. During Eisenhower's administration, Alaska and Hawaii were admitted to the Union as the 49th and 50th states, and the American space program was established.

Eisenstein, Sergei (1898–1948) Russian film director. His films are characterized by their use of montage, an editing technique in which isolated images are used to emphasize intellectual points. His experimental theories, developed during his early work in the theater, brought him into frequent conflict with the Soviet authorities. His films include *Battleship Potemkin* (1925), *Alexander Nevsky* (1938), and *Ivan the Terrible* (1942–46).

eisteddfod A Welsh assembly in which bards and minstrels compete for prizes in literature, music, and drama. The main literary prizes are a carved oak chair for the best poem in strict Welsh meter and a silver crown for a poem in free meter. Originating in medieval times, the tradition declined after the 16th century but was revived as the chief national cultural festival during the 19th century.

Ekaterinburg. *See* Sverdlovsk.

Ekaterinodar. *See* Krasnodar.

Ekaterinoslav. *See* Dnepropetrovsk.

El Aaiún 27 00N 13 00W A city in West Africa, the chief city of Western Sahara. Phosphate deposits about 60 mi (100 km) to the SE are exported from here. Population (1974): 20,010.

El Alamein, Battle of. *See* World War II.

Elam An ancient country in SW Iran, roughly corresponding to the present-day province of Khuzistan. The Elamite language, related to no other known tongue, appears in pictographic inscriptions before 3000 BC. Elam's capital was *Susa and it was closely linked culturally and politically with *Sumer and *Babylonia (both of which it temporarily overran in the 2nd millennium BC), before absorption into the Persian *Achaemenian Empire (6th century BC). The Elamites were believed to be descended from Shem, the son of Noah, and were thus related to the Hebrews.

eland An antelope belonging to the genus *Taurotragus* (2 species), of African plains. Up to 71 in (180 cm) high at the shoulder, both sexes have horns. The common eland (*T. oryx*) is light brown with thin vertical white stripes toward the shoulders. The Derby eland (*T. derbianus*) has a black neck with a white band at the base. Both species have a black-tufted tail and dewlap. Elands live in small herds and have been tamed and used as draft animals.

elasticity In physics, the ability of a body to return to its original shape after being deformed. The deforming force is known as a *stress, the resulting deformation is the *strain (*see* elastic modulus). A body is elastic only below a certain stress. Above this point, known as the *elastic limit*, the body is permanently deformed. A substance that is permanently deformed by any stress is said to be plastic. *See also* plasticity.

elastic modulus The ratio of the *stress on a body obeying *Hooke's law to the *strain produced. The strain may be a change in length (Young's Modulus) or a change in volume (bulk modulus).

elastomer A polymer with elastic properties, i.e. one that can be deformed and will revert to its original shape. *Rubber, a natural elastomer, still has many applications, especially for heavy-duty tires. However, synthetic elastomers of styrene-butadiene, polybutadiene, polyisoprene, *silicones, etc., are now far more widely used, not only in car tires, but also in belting for machines, sponge rubber, footwear, and many other products.

Elat (*or* Elath). *See* Eilat.

Elba An Italian island in the Tyrrhenian Sea. It became famous as the place of exile (1814–15) of Napoleon I of France, following his abdication. Area: 86 sq mi (223 sq km). Population (1971): 27,543.

Elbe River (Czech name: Labe) A river in central Europe, flowing mainly NW from N Czechoslovakia, through East and West Germany to the North Sea at Hamburg. It is connected by various canal systems to the Weser and Rhine Rivers as well as to the Oder River. Length: 724 mi (1165 km).

Elberfeld. *See* Wuppertal.

Elbert, Mount A mountain in Colorado. It is the highest peak in the *Rocky Mountains. Height: 14,431 ft (4399 m).

Elblag (German name: Elbing) 54 10N 19 25E A port in N Poland, on the Elblag River. Founded in the 13th century, it became a member of the Hanseatic League and an important port for trade with England. Its chief industries include engineering and shipbuilding. Population (1972 est): 92,600.

Elbrus, Mount (*or* Mt Elbruz) 43 21N 42 29E A mountain in the SW Soviet Union, the highest in the Caucasus Mountains. It is an extinct volcano, with two peaks only 101 ft (38 m) vertically apart, and is a tourist and climbing center. Height: 18,481 ft (5633 m).

Elburz Mountains A mountain range in central N Iran, extending 373 mi (600 km) in an arc parallel with the S shore of the Caspian Sea and rising to 18,386 ft (5604 m) at Mount Demavend.

Elche 38 16N 0 41W A city in SE Spain, in Valencia. Local archeological finds include a 5th-century Iberian statue, known as *La Dama de Elche*. It produces dates, pomegranates, and figs. Population (1970): 122,663.

El Cid (Rodrigo Díaz de Vivar; c. 1040–99) Spanish warrior, also known as el Campeador (the Champion), who was immortalized in the epic poem *Cantar del mio Cid*. A vassal of Alfonso VI of Castile, he was exiled by the king in 1079 and began a long career as a soldier of fortune, fighting for both Spaniard and Moor. Always loyal to his king, he was returned to favor and became protector and then ruler of Valencia.

elder A shrub or tree (up to 65 ft [20 m] tall) of the genus *Sambucus* (40 species), found in temperate and subtropical areas. The compound leaves have toothed leaflets and the tiny cream-colored flowers, grouped into flat-topped clusters, can be used in tea or wine. The red or black berries, rich in vitamin C, are used in wine, jams, and jellies. The common European elder is *S. nigra*. Family: *Caprifoliaceae*.

Eldorado (Spanish: the golden one) An Indian ruler in Colombia who, according to legend, ritually coated himself in gold dust before bathing in a lake. The name was later applied to a region of fabulous wealth the existence of which this legend suggested. The conquest of South America in the 16th century was hastened by expeditions seeking Eldorado, notably those of Francisco *Pizarro (1539) and Jiménez de Quesada (1569–72).

Eleanor of Aquitaine (c. 1122–1204) The wife (1137–52) of Louis VII of France and, after the annulment of their marriage, the wife (1154–89) of Henry II of England. Henry imprisoned her (1174–89) for complicity in their sons' rebellion against him. After Henry's death she helped to secure their peaceful accession as Richard I (1189) and John (1199).

Eleanor of Castile (1246–90) The wife (from 1254) of Edward I of England. A devoted wife, she accompanied Edward on a Crusade (1270–73). He erected the **Eleanor Crosses** wherever her body rested on its way from Nottinghamshire, where she died, to her funeral in London.

Eleatics Greek speculative philosophers, active in the 5th century BC, whose leader was *Parmenides of Elea. Their central doctrine was that reality is timeless, motionless, changeless, and indivisible and that any belief to the contrary was illusion occasioned by the frailty of human senses. The early Pythagoreans (*see* Pythagoreanism) were their major opponents. *See also* Zeno of Elea.

Electoral College The method of election of the president, as provided in the US Constitution (Article II, section I). During a national election citizens vote for a slate of electors in each state that will vote for the president and vice president. The number of each state's electors equals the number of representatives and senators from that state. After a national election, the electors are obliged to vote for that candidate who won the plurality in the state. Discrepancies are settled in the House of Representatives.

electors (1257–1806) The German rulers who elected the Holy Roman Emperor. In 1338 the Archbishops of Mainz, Cologne, and Trier and the dynastic princes of the Palatinate, Saxony, and Brandenburg monopolized the right of election, which was confirmed in 1356. Other electors were the rulers of Bohemia (before 1400 and after 1708), Bavaria (after 1623), and Hanover (after 1708).

Electra In Greek legend, the daughter of Agamemnon and Clytemnestra. She helped her brother Orestes escape after the murder of Agamemnon and later helped him to kill Clytemnestra and her lover Aegisthus. She is the subject of plays by Aeschylus, Sophocles, and Euripides. Electra is also the name of one of the Pleiades, of a daughter of Oceanus, and of the mother of the Harpies.

Electra complex. *See* Oedipus complex.

electrical engineering The branch of engineering concerned with the generation, transmission, distribution, and use of electricity. Its two main branches are power engineering and *electronics (including telecommunications) although the latter is now often regarded as a separate discipline. Electrical engineering emerged in the late 19th century with the mathematical formulation of the basic laws of electricity by James Clerk *Maxwell, followed by the development of such practical applications as the Bell telephone, Edison's incandescent lamp, and the first central generating plants. Electrical power engineers design generators, *power stations, and *electricity supply systems as well as *electric motors and transport and traction systems. Electronics engineers are concerned with all forms of electronic communications and *computers. Electrical engineering is an applied science involving advanced mathematical skills and a profound knowledge of physics, in addition to the basic engineering subjects.

electric-arc furnace A type of furnace used in making high-grade *steels, usually from scrap steel, in which the heat source is an electric arc. Electric furnaces provide clean working conditions and accurate temperature control. They avoid the contamination that occurs when fuel is burned in the furnace. Arc furnaces are gradually replacing the *open-hearth process.

electric automobile An automobile driven by one or more electric motors, which are powered by batteries. Because of diminishing oil reserves and the pollution problems associated with the *internal-combustion engine, the search for an effective electric car has been intensified in recent years. Electric cars are not new; the *Columbia* electric car was in use in the US around 1900, and electric delivery vans have been widely used in the UK for short journeys in towns since the 1930s. The basic problem is that

some seven tons of conventional lead batteries are required to provide an energy store equivalent to five gallons of gasoline. Even allowing that electric motors are several times more efficient than gasoline engines, no electric car has yet been produced to compete with a conventional car. Two lines of research are being pursued: improving batteries and making workable *fuel cells. Several experimental commuter cars using special lead batteries have been produced, with top speeds around 50 mph (80 km per hour) and a range of 30–50 mi (48–80 km). The hybrid electric car carries its own gasoline-engine-driven charging generator for use outside towns.

electric charge A property of certain elementary particles (*see* particle physics) that causes them to undergo *electromagnetic interactions. The magnitude of the charge is always the same and is equal to 1.6021×10^{-19} coulombs (although quarks, if they exist, would have a fractional charge). Charge is of two kinds, arbitrarily called positive and negative. Like charges repel each other and unlike charges attract each other. The force between them can be regarded as being generated by an exchange of virtual photons between the two particles (*see* virtual particles). On a large scale, charge is always due to an excess or deficiency of *electrons compared to the number of protons in the nuclei of a substance.

electric constant (ϵ_0) A constant that appears in *Coulomb's law when expressed in SI units. Its value is 8.854×10^{-12} farad per meter. It is also known as the absolute *permittivity of free space. *Compare* magnetic constant.

electric eel An eel-like freshwater fish, *Electrophorus electricus*, that occurs in NE South America. Up to 10 ft (3 m) long, it swims by undulating its long anal fin and has *electric organs—modified muscle tissue—in the tail, which produce electric shocks capable of killing fish and other prey and of stunning a man. Family: *Electrophoridae*; order: *Cypriniformes*.

electric field The pattern of the lines of force that surround an electric charge. The field strength at any point is inversely proportional to the square of the distance of that point from the charge (*see* Coulomb's law). Any other charge placed in this field experiences a force proportional to the field strength and to the magnitude of the introduced charge. The force is attractive if the charges are opposite and repulsive if they are alike.

electric generator A device for converting mechanical energy into electricity, usually by *electromagnetic induction. A simple electromagnetic generator, or dynamo, consists of a conducting coil rotated in a magnetic field. Current induced in this coil is fed to an external circuit by slip rings in an alternating-current generator or by a commutator, which rectifies the current, in a direct-current generator.

Most of the electricity from *power stations is produced by generators as three-phase alternating current, i.e. there are three windings on each generator, which can have an output of hundreds of megawatts, producing three separate output voltages. For transmission there are three live conductor wires with a common neutral wire. This three-phase system optimizes generator design and minimizes transmission losses, if the three loads are balanced. Generally, all three phases are supplied to large factories but the supply is split to single phase for homes, shops, and offices.

Small generators driven by Diesel engines are used for emergency supplies in factories, hospitals, etc. In the 1970s interest has grown in generators using renewable energy sources, such as hydroelectricity and solar, wave, and wind power (*see* alternative energy).

electricity The phenomena that arise as a result of *electric charge. Electricity has two forms: *static electricity, which depends on stationary charges, and current electricity, which consists of a flow of charges, specifically *electrons.

Static electricity, in the form of an attractive force between rubbed amber and pieces of straw, etc., was known to the ancient Greeks but the word electricity was coined in the 16th century by William *Gilbert (from the Greek *elektron*, amber). The distinction between positive and negative electricity was made at the beginning of the 18th century, but did not acquire a theoretical basis until the discovery of the electron in 1897 by J. J. Thomson.

Current electricity was first demonstrated by *Volta in 1800 and investigated by *Ampère during the next 25 years. *Oersted's discovery (1820) that a magnetic needle was deflected by an electric current inspired *Faraday to a deep investigation of the relationship between electricity and magnetism, which led him to the discovery of *electromagnetic induction, the *electric generator, and the *electric motor. The theory of electromagnetism was elucidated by Clerk *Maxwell in the mid 1850s.

The use of electricity as a source of energy, available in homes and factories for heating, lighting, and motive power, is essentially a characteristic of the

Modern life depends on electricity in so many ways, yet it is not known exactly what it is.

carbon atom

Atoms consist of electrons, protons, and neutrons. The electrons cluster round the central nucleus of protons and neutrons.

−ve   +ve

electron   proton

Electrons have a negative electric charge — protons are positively charged. The charges are equal but opposite.

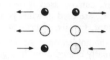

Similar charges repel each other, opposite charges attract each other. These are the forces harnessed to make electricity.

helium atom

An electrical current consists of a flow of electrons in one direction. But in many atoms, such as helium, they are tightly bound to the nucleus. To flow as a current electrons have to be free.

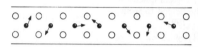

In a metal wire some of the electrons are free to move about between the metal ions (atoms that have lost an electron). Normally they move about at random and no current flows.

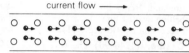

current flow ⟶

When the majority of electrons flow in one direction this is an electric current. 1 ampere is equivalent to a flow of 10^{18} electrons per second.

There are two main methods of making electrons flow to generate a current.

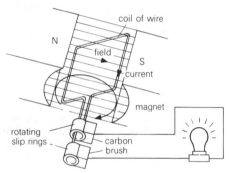

coil of wire

N

field

S

current

magnet

rotating slip rings

carbon brush

One method is to subject them to a changing magnetic field—this is the principle of the dynamo. If a coil of wire is rotated between the poles of a magnet, the electrons are forced round the coil. This is the power-station method; coal or oil is burned to raise steam to drive a turbine, which rotates the coils.

2e

zinc electrode

copper electrode

H_2SO_4 + 2 Zn

2e SO_4^{2-}

2Zn⁻

H_2

2H⁻ +   2e ⟶ 2H

dilute sulfuric acid (H_2SO_4)

The other way is to make use of a chemical reaction in an electric cell to dissociate the electrons from their atoms and molecules. The separated charges then flow in opposite directions as a result of the forces between them. This is how a battery works. The sulfuric acid dissolves the zinc electrode producing 2 electrons, a sulfate ion (SO_4^{2-}), 2 zinc ions (Zn^+), and 2 hydrogen ions (H^-).

ELECTRICITY

20th century. Our dependence upon it is now taken so much for granted that life seems almost unimaginable without it.

electricity supply The system that generates (*see* power station), transmits, and distributes the electric power in an industrialized society. Power stations are interconnected by transmission lines to form a grid. Grid-control centers continuously monitor the load from factories, offices, homes, etc., and match it with the best combination of available generating capacity, maintaining the supply at a constant voltage and frequency. Base-load stations run continuously. These are usually the larger or cheaper-to-run stations. Less economic or smaller stations that are easier to start up and shut down are brought in to supply the peak demand. The grid voltage is reduced at substations for area distribution and further reduced at local substations to the US domestic supply voltage of 110 volts.

electric motor A device that converts electrical energy into mechanical energy usually for driving machinery. Electric motors, which are clean, quiet, and efficient (75–95%), range from tiny models in instrument-control systems using less than a watt to those using several megawatts to drive large pumps.

Electric motors depend on the principle that a current-carrying conductor in a magnetic field experiences a force and that when two electromagnets are placed close together the two magnetic fields force them apart. The simplest type of motor uses this principle to turn a single coil of wire (the armature or rotor) between the poles of a permanent magnet. Practical motors use a stationary winding (stator) in place of a permanent magnet.

Most motors work on an alternating-current (ac) supply. In the induction motor, current is fed to the stator, which induces a current in the rotor; interaction between the magnetic field of the stator and the induced rotor current causes the rotor to rotate. In the synchronous ac motor, current is also fed to the rotor (through slip rings) and the rate of rotation is proportional to the supply frequency. In direct-current (dc) motors, current is also fed to both rotor and stator with the two either in series (series wound) or in parallel (shunt wound). In a dc motor current is fed to the rotor through a commutator. *See also* linear motor.

electric organ In zoology, a group of modified muscle cells in certain fish that are capable of generating electric shocks. These can be used to stun prey, as in the *electric eel and *electric ray. Other species, such as the elephant-snout fishes, generate an electric field for the detection of objects (including prey and predators) and for navigation in dark or cloudy waters.

electric ray A fish, also called torpedo ray, numbfish, or crampfish, belonging to a family (*Torpedinidae*) found mainly in shallow waters of warm and temperate regions. 12–80 in (30–200 cm) long, rays have *electric organs—modified muscle tissue—on each side of the disklike head to produce electric shocks used in defense and food capture. Order: *Batoidea* (*see* ray).

electrocardiography Examination of the electrical activity of the heart. Impulses generated by the contraction of the heart muscle are transmitted through electrodes attached to the skin to a recording apparatus (electrocardiograph). The recording itself, called an electrocardiogram (ECG), indicates the rhythm of the heart and aids in the diagnosis of heart disease, which may produce characteristic changes in heart rhythm.

electroconvulsive therapy (ECT) A treatment for mental disorders in which an electric current is passed through the brain in order to cause a convulsion. The convulsion is greatly reduced by giving an anesthetic and drugs to relax the muscles. ECT is used as a treatment for severe cases of endogenous *depression.

electroencephalography The measurement of the electrical activity of the brain and the recording of the brain waves in the form of a tracing—an electroencephalogram (EEG). Brain waves were first recorded from electrodes on the scalp by Hans Berger (1873–1941) in 1926. Electroencephalography is now used widely to diagnose diseases of the brain and to study brain function. The frequency of the electrical waves and the way they change with stimuli are related to alertness, responsiveness, and expectation.

electroforming A method of manufacturing metallic articles. A metal-coated plastic mold is used as the cathode in *electrolysis and the metal is deposited onto the mold. The method is used for making thin intricately shaped articles.

electroluminescence. *See* luminescence.

electrolysis The chemical decomposition of a substance by passing an electric current through it. If a voltage is applied across two electrodes placed in a liquid (electrolyte) containing ions, the positive ions will drift toward— the negative electrode (cathode) and the negative ions toward the positive electrode (anode). At the electrodes, the ions may give up their charge and form molecules; for example hydrogen gas is released at the cathode when water is electrolyzed. Alternatively, the atoms of the electrode may ionize and pass into solution. Electrolysis is used to electroplate metals and in the manufacture of a number of chemicals, such as sodium and chlorine. It is also a way of separating *isotopes. Deuterium (D *or* ^{2}H), for example, is slower than ordinary hydrogen (^{1}H) to pick up electrons at the cathode, and so electrolyzed water gradually becomes enriched with heavy water (D_2O).

electromagnet. *See* magnets.

electromagnetic field A concept describing electric and magnetic forces that, like gravitational forces, act without physical contact (action at a distance). Although both electricity and magnetism have been observed separately for thousands of years, it was not until the 19th century that their interaction was investigated experimentally by Oersted, Faraday, and others. Faraday explained the electromagnetic interaction in terms of magnetic lines of force, forming a field of force, which is distorted by the presence of a current-carrying conductor or by another magnet. James Clerk *Maxwell developed the mathematical theory that electricity and magnetism are different manifestations of the same phenomenon (the electromagnetic field), magnetism being the result of relative motion of *electric fields.

electromagnetic induction The production of voltage in an electrical conductor when it is in a changing magnetic field or if it moves in relation to a steady magnetic field. The direction of the induced *electromotive force opposes the change or motion causing it. Since a current-carrying conductor itself induces a magnetic field, if the current changes, **self-inductance** occurs, opposing the current change. **Mutual inductance** occurs between two adjacent conductors that carry changing currents.

electromagnetic interaction An interaction that occurs between those elementary particles that possess an electric charge. The interaction can be visualized as the exchange of virtual photons (*see* virtual particles) between the interacting particles. The electromagnetic interaction is 200 times weaker than the *strong interaction but 10^{10} times stronger than the *weak interaction. *See also* particle physics.

electromagnetic radiation Transverse waves consisting of electric and magnetic fields vibrating perpendicularly to each other and to the direction of propagation. In free space the waves are propagated at a velocity of 2.9979×10^8 meters per second, known as the velocity of light (symbol: *c*). Their *wavelength, λ, and *frequency, *f*, are related by the equation $\lambda f = c$. Those with the highest frequencies are known as *gamma radiation; then in descending order of frequency the **electromagnetic spectrum** includes X-rays, *ultraviolet radiation, visible *light, *infrared radiation, *microwaves, and *radio waves. Electromagnetic radiation exhibits typical wave properties, such as *refraction, *diffraction, *interference, and polarization. However, it can also be regarded as a stream of massless elementary

particles called *photons. This dual nature of radiation is analogous to the dual nature of massive elementary particles and *de Broglie waves.

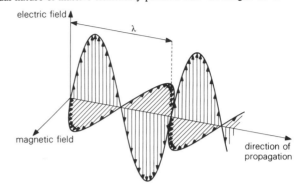

ELECTROMAGNETIC RADIATION

electromagnetic units (emu) A *c.g.s. system of electrical units based on the unit magnet pole, which repels a similar pole one centimeter away with a force of one dyne. Electromagnetic units have the prefix ab- attached to the practical unit (e.g. abvolt).

electromotive force (emf) The electrical potential difference or voltage between two points in an electric circuit. It causes the movement of charge that constitutes an electric current, providing a limited analogy to mechanical force and motion.

electron A stable negatively charged elementary particle with mass $9.109,56 \times 10^{-31}$ kilogram and spin $1/2$. Electrons are responsible for almost all commonly observed electrical and magnetic effects and, since they orbit the nucleus in atoms, are also responsible for most chemical processes. A **free electron** is one that has become detached from an atom. An electric current passing through a metal or low-pressure gas consists of a flow of free electrons; a current of 1 ampere is equivalent to a flow of 6×10^{18} electrons per second.

electron diffraction The *diffraction of a beam of electrons as it passes through spaces, the widths of which are comparable to the wavelength of the electrons. Electrons can be diffracted, for example, by the spacing between particles in a crystal lattice, an effect governed by *Bragg's law. Electron diffraction demonstrates the wave aspect of electrons (*see* de Broglie wave) since diffraction is specifically a wave effect. The effect is used to investigate the structure of surfaces, films, etc.

electronics The study of devices that control and utilize the movement of *electrons and other charged particles. Originating with the invention of thermionic valves and their use in radios and record players, it expanded rapidly during World War II to include radar, missile guidance systems, and the first electronic *computers. The replacement of bulky *thermionic valves by *semiconductor components, such as *transistors, made possible high-speed digital computers and the miniaturized communications and control systems used in spacecraft. The *integrated circuit was a further step toward more compact and reliable equipment. The latest development is the use of computers to produce tiny wafers of silicon functioning as microprocessors.

The social impact of electronics has been immense, with the development of television, communications satellites, the computerization of office and factory systems, and the widespread use of pocket calculators. The emergence of microprocessors is expected to have even greater impact in replacing human labor by automation.

electron microscope A type of microscope in which a beam of electrons is focused by means of magnetic and electrostatic lenses onto a specimen and scattered by it to produce an image. The *de Broglie wavelength of high-energy electrons is very much less than that of light. Therefore both the *resolving power and the magnification of an electron microscope are much greater than can be obtained with an optical microscope. Typically an electron microscope can resolve two points 10^{-9} meter apart and produce magnifications of up to a million. In the **transmission electron microscope** only very thin specimens can be used: the image appears two-dimensional but a high resolution can be obtained. In the **scanning electron microscope** the specimen, which can be of any thickness, is scanned by the beam producing an apparently three-dimensional image but with lower resolution.

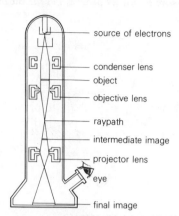

source of electrons

condenser lens

object

objective lens

raypath

intermediate image

projector lens

eye

final image

ELECTRON MICROSCOPE *The beam of electrons in the transmission electron microscope is focused in a similar way to light in an ordinary microscope.*

electron probe microanalysis A method of analyzing a very small quantity (10^{-16} kg) of a substance by bombarding it with a fine electron beam (about 1 micrometer in diameter) and examining the X-ray spectrum produced for characteristic lines of the elements. The method can also be used quantitatively.

electron spin resonance The resonance of an unpaired electron in a paramagnetic substance when placed in a magnetic field and exposed to microwaves. Since the electron is unpaired it acts as a small magnet and may either align itself with the field or oppose it. If the energy of the microwave *photons is equal to the energy difference between the two states then the electron resonates. The effect is used to study chemical bonding and structure. *See also* nuclear magnetic resonance.

electronvolt (eV) A unit of energy, widely used in nuclear physics, equal to the increase in the energy of an electron when it passes through a rise in potential of one volt. $1 \text{ eV} = 1.6 \times 10^{-19}$ joule.

electroplating The process of depositing a layer of one metal on another by making the object to be plated the cathode in an electrolytic bath (*see* electrolysis). Metals used for electroplating include silver (*see* silverplate), gold, chromium, cadmium, copper, zinc, and nickel; they usually form the anode in the bath. The form of the plated layer varies depending on the composition and temperature of the electrolyte, the use of addition agents, and the current density. Some metals do not adhere well to others; for example, chromium does not adhere to steel and it is usual to plate the steel with copper and then nickel before plating with chromium.

electroscope An electrostatic instrument that detects electric charge or radiation. In a gold-leaf electroscope, the deflection of two suspended gold leaves increases with charge. The quartz-fiber electroscope (QFE), which has a quartz fiber instead of gold leaves, is commonly used to detect radiation. The presence of a radioactive source ionizes the air and causes charge to leak away from the initially charged fiber.

electrostatic generators Machines that use mechanical or other energy to separate electric charge, creating an electric potential. They are used to create strong electrostatic fields, particularly in high energy nuclear physics for accelerating charged particles to bombard atomic nuclei. *See also* Van de Graaff generator.

electrostatics. *See* static electricity.

electrostatic separation The use of a strong electric field to separate substances with different electrical properties. The method is used, for example, in separating out iron ores from a mixture of minerals, and to clean air in chimneys by precipitating charged smoke particles.

electrostatic unit (e.s.u.) A *c.g.s. system of electrical units based on the unit of electrical charge, defined as the charge that repels a similar charge one centimeter away with a force of one dyne. Electrostatic units have the prefix stat- attached to the practical unit (e.g. the unit of charged defined above is the statcoulomb).

elementary particles. *See* particle physics.

elements Substances that cannot be broken down into simpler fragments by chemical means. A sample of an element contains atoms that are chemically virtually identical, since they have the same *atomic number and thus the same number of electrons around the nucleus. Samples of a given element may consist of a mixture of *isotopes. Over 100 elements are known, of which about 90 occur naturally, the rest having been synthesized in nuclear reactions. Elements are often classified as *metals, *metalloids, or nonmetals. *See also* periodic table.

African elephant

Indian elephant

ELEPHANT *The African elephant can be distinguished from the smaller Indian species by its larger ears, flatter forehead, smooth skin, and concave back.*

elephant A mammal of the order *Proboscidea*: the African elephant (*Loxodonta africana*) or the Indian elephant (*Elephas maximus*). (The extinct *mammoths also belonged to this order.) Elephants have a tough brownish-gray skin and a muscular prehensile proboscis (trunk)—an extension of the nose and upper lip used to convey food (leaves, branches, and other vegetation) and water to the mouth. The upper incisor teeth are continually growing ivory tusks, for which these animals were formerly extensively hunted. Elephants live in herds; they have a gestation period of 21–22 months and a lifespan of 60–70 years.

The African elephant is the largest land mammal, standing 10–13 ft (3–4 m) high at the shoulder and weighing 5–7.5 tons. The smaller Indian elephant—intelligent and readily trained—is used for transport and heavy work in India, Burma, Thailand, and Malaysia.

elephant birds. *See* Aepyornis.

elephant grass A stout coarse *reedmace, *Typha elephanta*, commonly found in marshes and wet habitats from S Europe to the East Indies. It has long tapering leaves, which have been used to make baskets. The name is sometimes also applied to the tropical napier grass (*Pennisetum purpureum*), which resembles sugar cane.

elephantiasis A condition caused by chronic infection with certain nematode worms, called *filariae. It is therefore a form of filariasis. The worms block the lymphatic channels and cause gross swelling of the legs and scrotum (or vulva). Elephantiasis occurs only in the tropics.

elephant seal   A large seal belonging to the genus *Mirounga* (2 species). The male Antarctic elephant seal (*M. leonina*) grows to over 20 ft (6 m); females are about half that size. The slightly smaller northern elephant seal (*M. angustirostris*) lives off the W coast of North America. Elephant seals feed on fish, crustaceans, octopus, and squid. Family: *Phocidae*.

elephant's ear.   *See* taro.

Eleusinian mysteries   An esoteric religious cult (*see* mysteries) in ancient Greece, with its center at Eleusis. It originated before 600 BC in an agrarian fertility cult, and the main deities worshiped were *Demeter and *Persephone. The myth of Persephone's abduction to the underworld and return was interpreted not only in terms of the dormant seed and the springing corn but also as a symbol of death and resurrection and was probably re-enacted in a darkened room to which only initiates were admitted.

Elgar, Sir Edward   (1857–1934) British composer. He was taught largely by his father, the organist at a Roman Catholic church in Worcester. A professional violinist, Elgar became involved as a conductor with the Three Choirs Festival, where many of his important choral works received their first performance. He also wrote two symphonies and concertos for violin and cello; at the end of his life he wrote three important chamber-music works. His most famous works are the *Dream of Gerontius* (for soloists, chorus, and orchestra; 1900), the *Enigma Variations* (for orchestra; 1899), and the *Pomp and Circumstance* marches (1901–30).

Elgin Marbles   Ancient Greek marble sculptures from the *Parthenon, sold to the British Museum in 1816 by Lord Elgin. He had acquired them from the Turks occupying Athens, who were using the Parthenon for target practice.

Elgon, Mount   1 07N 34 35E An extinct volcano in E Africa, on the Uganda–Kenya border. Its crater is about 5 mi (8 km) in diameter and coffee and bananas are grown on the lower slopes. Height: 14,178 ft (4321 m).

El Greco   (Domenikos Theotokopoulos; 1541–1614) Painter of Greek parentage, born in Crete, who worked mainly in Spain. He trained in Venice under Titian in the 1560s and greatly admired the work of Michelangelo, which he saw during a visit to Rome just before he moved to Spain (1577), where he sought the patronage of Philip II. El Greco submitted his *Martyrdom of St Maurice* (1580–82; El Escorial) to Philip but the king rejected it; El Greco then moved to Toledo, where he spent most of the remainder of his life, becoming friendly with leading churchmen and scholars. His early Spanish works, such as the *Assumption of the Virgin* (1527; Chicago), were Venetian in inspiration, but his later paintings of saints and his masterpiece, *The Burial of Count Orgaz* (1586–88; Santo Tomé), are characterized by strident colors and dramatically elongated figures. He also painted three stormy landscapes and a number of portraits.

Elijah   An Old Testament prophet, who appears to have lived in the 9th century BC. He attacked the cult of Baal among the Israelites (1 Kings 18) and successfully maintained the monotheistic worship of Jehovah. He was considered the greatest of the Hebrew prophets. He was taken into heaven without dying (2 Kings 2.1–18), and it was believed that he would return before the final restoration of Israel to the people.

Eliot, Charles W(illiam)   (1834–1926) US scientist, educator, reformer, and editor. Educated at Harvard University, he taught chemistry at Massachusetts Institute of Technology (MIT) before returning to Harvard to serve as its president in 1869. While there he was instrumental in the rapid growth and raised standards enjoyed by the university. He was also responsible for reshaping US secondary education, believing in adapting schooling to each individual. When he retired in 1909, he started editing the Harvard Classics.

Eliot, George   (Mary Ann Evans; 1819–80) British woman novelist. She was influenced by evangelical Christianity as a girl, but rejected her early religious fervor in 1842. She went to London in 1851, worked on the *Westminster Review*, and lived with the journalist George Henry Lewes, who was married but separated from his wife. After publishing stories based on her childhood she wrote the novels *Adam Bede* (1859), *The Mill on the Floss* (1860), and *Silas Marner* (1861). The pioneering and influential novel *Middlemarch* (1871–72) is a deep and comprehensive depiction of English provincial society. *Daniel Deronda* (1876) contrasts a Jewish family's genuine values with the false ones of society. Lewes died in 1878, and she married a banker, J. W. Cross, six months before her death.

T. S. ELIOT   *A bronze bust by British sculptor Jacob Epstein.*

Eliot, T(homas) S(tearns)   (1888–1965) British-American poet, critic, and playwright. Eliot was educated at Harvard and traveled extensively in Europe, where he became a close acquaintance of Ezra *Pound. Settling in London, he worked briefly as a bank clerk before the publication of his first volume of poetry, *Prufrock and Other Observations*, in 1917. Although *The Waste Land* (1922) is his best-known work, *Four Quartets* (1935–41) is considered to be his most important poetic achievement. In 1927, Eliot became a British subject and converted to Anglo-Catholicism. From 1922 to 1939 he edited *The Criterion* and became recognized as an influential literary critic. His verse dramas include *Murder in the Cathedral* (1935), *The Cocktail Party* (1949), and *The Elder Statesman* (1958). Eliot was awarded the Nobel Prize in literature in 1948.

Elizabeth   40 40N 74 13W A city and port in New Jersey on Newark Bay. Part of the New York conurbation, its industries include sewing machines, aircraft, and chemicals. Population (1980 est): 106,201.

Elizabeth   (1709–62) Empress of Russia (1741–62); the daughter of Peter the Great. Elizabeth came to power in a coup, which ousted the infant Ivan VI (1740–64). She depended on her advisers, such as *Bestuzhev-Riumin, in government and her reign witnessed no reforms and few territorial acquisitions.

Elizabeth I   (1533–1603) Queen of England and Ireland (1558–1603), daughter of Henry VIII and Anne *Boleyn. Her mother's execution and Elizabeth's imprisonment by Mary I made her cautious and suspicious but her devotion to England made her one of its greatest monarchs. Her religious compromise (1559–63) established Protestantism in England (*see* Reformation). Several plots to place her Roman Catholic cousin, *Mary, Queen of Scots, on the throne led to Mary's execution (1587). England won a great naval victory in 1588 by destroying the Spanish *Armada. Elizabeth never married and was called the Virgin Queen, although her relationships with, among others, the Earl of Leicester and the 2nd Earl of Essex caused considerable speculation.

Elizabeth II   (1926–) Queen of the United Kingdom (1952–), noted for her scrupulous fulfillment of the roles of constitutional monarch and head of the Commonwealth. She married Prince *Philip in 1947; their four children are Prince *Charles, Princess *Anne, Prince Andrew Albert Christian Edward (1960–), and Prince Edward Antony Richard Louis (1964–). In 1977 the twenty-fifth anniversary of her accession to the throne was celebrated.

ELIZABETH II *The Queen's Silver Jubilee (1977) not only enhanced the prestige of the Crown, but boosted the morale of the country.*

Elizabeth the Queen Mother (1900–) The wife of George VI of the United Kingdom. Formerly Lady Elizabeth Bowes-Lyon, she married in 1923 and had two children, *Elizabeth II and Princess *Margaret.

Elizabethville. *See* Lubumbashi.

elk The largest deer, *Alces alces*, found in forests of N Eurasia and also in N North America, where it is called a moose. Up to 7 ft (2 m) high at the shoulder, elks have a broad curved muzzle and a short neck with a heavy dewlap. The coat is gray-brown and males grow large palmate antlers spanning up to 71 in (180 cm). They feed on leaves and water plants and form herds in winter. □mammal.

elkhound An ancient breed of working dog originating in Norway and used for tracking and hunting game animals, especially elk. It has a short compact body with the tail curled over the back and a broad head with pricked ears. The thick coat is gray tipped with black. Height: 20.4 in (51 cm) (dogs); 19.3 in (49 cm) (bitches).

Elkins v. United States (1960) US Supreme Court ruling that banned the use of illegally obtained evidence in federal cases.

Ellesmere Island A Canadian Arctic island W of Greenland, the northernmost part of North America. Mostly rugged plateau with large glaciers, it shelters a few weather stations, police posts, and the remnants of Eskimo settlements. Area: 82,119 sq mi (212,688 sq km).

Ellesmere Port 53 17N 2 54W A port in NW England, in Cheshire on the Mersey estuary and Manchester Ship Canal. Its chief industries are the manufacture of petroleum products, cars, chemicals, paper, and engineering. Population (1981 est): 63,134.

Ellice Islands. *See* Tuvalu.

Ellington, Duke (Edward Kennedy E.; 1899–1974) US jazz composer, band leader, and pianist. After leading bands in Washington, DC, Ellington went to New York, where he established a group of musicians that remained the core of his band for 30 years. The worldwide success of "Mood Indigo" in 1930 led to European tours and annual concerts in Carnegie Hall. Ellington concentrated on composing large-scale works for jazz orchestra, writing the suite *Black, Brown, and Beige* in 1943 and the "religious jazz" work *In the Beginning God* in 1966.

ellipse A closed curve having the shape of an elongated *circle. The sum of the distances from any point on the circumference to each of two fixed points, known as the foci, is a constant. In the Cartesian *coordinate system its equation is $(x - h)^2/a^2 + (y - k)^2/b^2 = 1$, where (h,k) is the center of the ellipse and a and b are the largest and shortest radii, which are parallel to the coordinate axes. In the case of a and b being equal, the ellipse becomes a *circle of radius a. The ellipse is one of a family of curves known as *conic sections.

Ellis, (Henry) Havelock (1859–1939) British psychologist and essayist, noted for his studies of human sexual behavior. His major work, *Studies in the Psychology of Sex* (7 vols, 1897–1928), was among the first to deal frankly with sexual problems and met with legal opposition. He was also concerned with women's rights, edited publications in both the arts and sciences, and wrote *Impressions and Comments* (3 vols, 1914–24), a series of essays on art.

Ellis Island 40 42N 74 03W A small island in New York Harbor. It served as an entry center for immigrants to the US (1892–1943).

Ellison, Ralph (Waldo) (1914–) US author. Educated at Tuskegee Institute (1933–36), he wrote of blacks and the opportunities presented in the US and taught at New York University. His *The Invisible Man* (1952) won a National Book Award in 1953. Other works include *Shadow and Act* (1964).

Ellora Caves A cluster of rock-cut Hindu, Buddhist, and Jaina temples in Maharashtra state (W India). They were made mainly between the mid 7th and the early 10th centuries AD. The most sumptuous temple is the Kailashanatha, dedicated to Shiva.

Ellsworth, Lincoln (1880–1951) US explorer. After graduation from Yale and Columbia universities he worked as an engineer in Canada and Alaska and led a geological expedition to Peru. In 1926 he was part of the first successful crossing of the Arctic (with Roald *Amundsen and Umberto *Nobile) from Spitsbergen, Norway, to Teller, Alaska, in the dirigible *Norge*. By 1935 he had become the first to fly across Antarctica. Ellsworth Land is named for him.

Ellsworth, Oliver (1745–1807) US politician, lawyer, and jurist; Chief Justice of the US Supreme Court (1796–1800). A practicing lawyer in Connecticut from 1771, he was a delegate to the Continental Congress in 1777 and co-authored (with Roger Sherman) the *Connecticut Compromise at the Constitutional Convention in 1787. He served in the US Senate (1789–96) and was a principal author of the Bill of Rights (1791). In 1796 he was appointed chief justice of the Supreme Court by President *Washington, a position he held until 1800 when he was forced to resign due to ill health.

Ellsworth Land An area in Antarctica, at the base of the Antarctic Peninsula. It contains the highest peak in Antarctica, *Vinson Massif. UK claims to the area are contested by Argentina and Chile.

elm A □tree of the genus *Ulmus* (about 30 species), widely distributed in N temperate regions. Up to 131 ft (40 m) high, elms have oval pointed toothed leaves, clusters of small reddish flowers, and rounded or heart-shaped winged nuts. Elms are widely planted for shade and ornament and for their strong durable timber. Unfortunately the number of elm trees in Europe and North America has been greatly reduced by *Dutch elm disease. Species include the English elm (*U. procera*), the Eurasian wych elm (*U. glabra*), and the American elm (*U. americana*). Family: *Ulmaceae*. *See also* slippery elm.

elm bark beetle A wood-boring beetle, *Scolytus scolytus*, *S. multistriatus*, or *Hylurgopinus rufipes*, that tunnels under the bark of elm trees and carries the fungus *Ceratostomella ulni*, which causes *Dutch elm disease. Family: *Scolytidae* (*see* bark beetle).

El Obeid 13 15N 30 45E A city in the Sudan. It is a trading center for gum arabic, cereals, and cattle. Population (1973): 89,789.

Elohim One of the Hebrew names of God. It occurs often in the Old Testament and is strictly the plural of *eloah* (which can also be a name of God) but it is used with a singular verb when it denotes God rather than gods.

El Paso 31 45N 106 30W A city in the US, in W Texas on the Rio Grande. Situated on the Mexican border, it is the commercial and industrial center of a mining and cattle-raising area. It is also a major base for the armed forces. Manufactures include refined oil and food products. Population (1980): 425,259.

Elphanta Island 18 58N 72 54E An islet off the W coast of India, in Bombay Harbor. It is famous for its cave temples and a three-headed bust, 20 ft (6 m) high, of the god Shiva.

El Salvador, Republic of A country in Central America, on the Pacific Ocean. Narrow coastal lowlands rise to a fertile plateau, which is enclosed by volcanic mountains. The country is frequently subject to earthquakes. Most of the population is of mixed European and Indian descent. *Economy:* mainly agricultural, the economy has been dominated by coffee since the late 19th century. Cotton is the second main commercial crop. Forests produce not only valuable hardwoods, such as mahogany and walnut, but also dye woods and balsam of which El Salvador is the world's principal source. Most of the cultivated land is controlled by a few families, which has led to considerable movement and even emigration (especially in the 1960s) among the country's farmers, most of whom rent their land. El Salvador has few mineral resources and the main source of power is hydroelectricity. Traditional industries, such as food processing and textiles, remain important, but tourism is also being developed. *History*: the Aztec population was conquered by the Spaniards in 1526 and after the overthrow of Spanish rule the region formed part of the Central American Federation (1823–38). In 1841 it became an independent republic. Tension arising from the emigration of Salvadoreans to Honduras culminated in warfare between the two countries in 1965 and again in 1969, following El Salvador's defeat of Honduras in a World Cup soccer game. In 1978–79 considerable internal unrest occurred in response to the repressive regime of General Carlos Humberto Romero (1924–) with kidnappings of foreigners by left-wing guerrillas, occupations of foreign embassies, and assassinations. Romero was deposed in 1979 and a junta took control but the violence continued, including the assassination in 1980 of the archbishop of San Salvador, Oscar Romero. Following inconclusive elections in 1981 Alvaro Magaña was appointed interim president (1982). Despite substantial US aid, the government has not been able to defeat rebel forces. Right-wing "death squads" have murdered thousands of citizens suspected of liberal sympathies. In 1984 a moderate, José Napoleón Duarte, was elected president with US support, ending the immediate threat of a right-wing takeover. El Salvador is a member of the OAS, the Organization of Central American States, and the Central American Common Market. Official language: Spanish. Official religion: Roman Catholic. Official currency: colón of 100 centavos. Area 8236 sq mi (21,393 sq km). Population (1980): 4,685,000. Capital: San Salvador. Main port: Acajutla.

Elsinore. *See* Helsingør.

Éluard, Paul (Eugène Grindel; 1895–1952) French poet, a friend of André *Breton and Louis *Aragon and with them a leader in the early surrealist movement. Their influence is clear in his early poetry collections, such as *Capitale de la douleur* (1926) and *La Rose publique* (1934). He joined the Communist Party in 1942 and adopted a more realistic style in poems circulated secretly among the Resistance. His postwar poetry was more personal and lyrical.

Élysée, Palais de l' The official residence of the presidents of France since 1873. The palace, which was built in 1718, was formerly the home of Mme de Pompadour.

Elysium (*or* Elysian Fields) In Greek mythology, the fields on the banks of the *Oceanus River where those favored by the gods live in eternal happiness. They are also called (by Hesiod) the Isles of the Blessed. In Roman mythology Elysium is part of the underworld.

Emancipation Act (1861) The edict issued by *Alexander II that freed the serfs of Russia (a third of the country's population). The peasants were to receive land from the landlord and pay for it in labor and crops but inequities in land distribution caused considerable discontent.

Emancipation Proclamation (1863) The edict issued by President Abraham *Lincoln that freed slaves in the rebellious southern states of the US. It was promulgated in part to weaken the Confederate war effort by depriving the South of laborers but Lincoln considered it "the central act" of his administration. The proclamation's limited provisions were extended and confirmed by the 13th Amendment, which abolished *slavery throughout the nation (1865).

Emba River A river in the S central Soviet Union, flowing mainly SW from the Mugodzhar Hills, through the Emba oilfield, to the Caspian Sea. Length: 380 mi (611 km).

embalming The techniques for preserving dead bodies from decay. Embalming was frequent in ancient Egypt (*see* mummy). In medieval Europe it was usually carried out by removing the corpse's internal organs, bathing it in spirits of wine, filling cavities made in the flesh with herbs, and finally wrapping it in waxed or tarred sheets. Since the 18th century arterial injections of preservative solutions, now generally a mixture of formaldehyde, alcohols, and salts, have been used.

embargo A resolution by a country or countries not to supply another country with certain goods, or not to import certain goods from another country, for political reasons. For example, in 1979 the Arab countries imposed an oil embargo on Egypt, after Egypt had signed a peace treaty with Israel.

Embargo Act (1807) A US law that banned trade with Europe for the duration of the Napoleonic Wars. Because both Britain and France had blockaded US trade with Europe, the US decided to end trade with Europe temporarily rather than be brought into the fighting. Passed during the administration of Thomas *Jefferson, it was not successful and was repealed in 1809. *See also* Non-Intercourse Act.

embolism The sudden blocking of an artery by a clot or other material that has come from another part of the body via the bloodstream (the

material is called an embolus). The commonest example is when a clot forms in the leg and pieces break away and lodge in the arteries of the lung—a **pulmonary embolism**. A clot may sometimes come from the heart and lodge in the brain, causing a *stroke. Air and fat can also cause embolism. *See also* thrombosis.

embroidery The decoration of fabrics with needlework, usually in silk but occasionally in gold and silver thread. It was practiced by the ancient Egyptians but the first important western embroidery was the *Bayeux tapestry. From about the 13th century embroidery was chiefly used for state and church vestments. Gros point and petit point are two common kinds of stitch used to form elaborate overall pictures, and from the 17th century such embroidered fabric was much used for curtains, bed hangings, and seat covers.

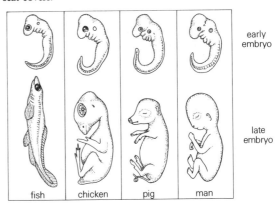

early embryo

late embryo

fish   chicken   pig   man

various vertebrate embryos *The different species are hard to distinguish in the early stages of development; later they develop individual characteristics.*

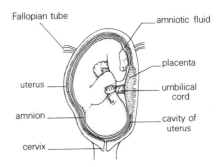

Fallopian tube — amniotic fluid — placenta — umbilical cord — uterus — amnion — cavity of uterus — cervix

human embryo *A few weeks before birth this fetus is practically fully formed.*

EMBRYO

embryo An animal or plant in the earliest stages of its development. In vertebrate animals the embryonic stage lasts from the first division of the fertilized egg until the young animal either hatches from the egg or is expelled from the womb at birth. A human embryo is called a *fetus from the eighth week of pregnancy. In invertebrate animals the embryo is generally called a *larva. In plants, the embryo lies within the *seed and consists of a root (radicle), shoot (plumule), and cotyledons for nourishment. **Embryology** is the study of the development of embryos.

emerald A green variety of *beryl, the color being due to the presence of small amounts of chromium. Used as a gemstone, it occurs mainly in metamorphic rocks, particularly mica schists, the finest specimens coming from Muzo, Colombia. It is less resistant to wear than most gemstones. Birthstone for May.

Emerson, Ralph Waldo (1803–82) American essayist and poet. Born in Boston, Emerson was educated at Harvard and ordained as a Unitarian minister in 1829, but his wife's death in 1831 provoked a radical re-evaluation of his beliefs. After a tour of Europe, during which he met *Wordsworth, *Coleridge, and *Carlyle, he settled in Concord, Mass. where he was one of the founders of the *Transcendentalist movement. His essay *Nature* (1836) was quickly recognized as the most eloquent exposition of the transcendentalist philosophy. A prolific lecturer, poet, and essayist, he expressed his optimistic humanism in his *Poems* (1847), *Representative Men* (1850), and *The Conduct of Life* (1860). The latter work expressed his opposition to slavery and was written during his active participation in the Abolition movement.

emery A granular grayish-black rock composed of *corundum with magnetite, hematite, or spinel. It occurs mainly in metamorphic rocks or sediments, particularly metamorphosed ferruginous bauxite, and altered limestones. It is used as an abrasive, in grinding wheels, emery cloth, and glass polishes, and in the manufacture of certain concrete floors. The principal producers are Turkey and Greece.

emigration. *See* migration, human.

Emilia-Romagna A region in N Italy. It consists of the fertile lowlands of the Po River in the N and E, bounded by the Apennines in the S. It is an important agricultural region producing sugar beet, cereals, vegetables, wine, rice, and fruit. Traditional manufacturing industries associated with agriculture are being replaced by modern chemical and oil-based industries and engineering. Area: 8542 sq mi (22,122 sq km). Population (1980 est): 3,966,649. Capital: Bologna.

Éminence Grise. *See* Joseph, Père.

Emin Paşa, Mehmed (Eduard Schnitzer; 1840–92) German-born physician and naturalist, who became a Muslim and took employment in Egypt. In 1878 *Gordon appointed him chief medical officer in the S Sudan, a post he held until "rescued" (1888) by *Stanley, who thought he was in danger after Gordon's death in Khartoum. He was murdered by Arabs on his way to explore Lake Victoria, but not before making notable contributions to natural history, anthropology, and geography.

Emmen 52 47N 6 55E A city in the NE Netherlands, in Drenthe province. It was formerly a peat-digging center. Industries include metallurgy, timber processing, and chemicals. Population (1981 est): 90,450.

Emmental (*or* Emmenthal) The valley of the upper Emme River, in W central Switzerland. It is famous for its cheese. ₃₃

Emmet, Robert (1778–1803) Irish nationalist, who led a rebellion in Dublin for Irish independence in 1803. It amounted to little more than a riot but Emmet's speech before his execution ensured his immortality.

Empedocles (c. 490–430 BC) Sicilian Greek philosopher. He modified the teachings of *Pythagoras and opposed *Parmenides' view of reality as one and unchanging. Empedocles founded the doctrine that earth, air, fire, and water make up the world, and that love and strife (attraction and antipathy) govern their distribution in a cycle of four stages.

emperor moth A large Eurasian *saturniid moth, *Saturnia pavonia*. Males fly by day, attracted by scent to the stationary females. The caterpillars spin a cocoon with an opening that allows easy exit but prevents entrance by predators.

emperor penguin A large *penguin, *Aptenodytes forsteri*. 3.9 ft (1.2 m) tall and 75 lb (34 kg) in weight, it is the largest seabird and has a blue-gray plumage with a black head and throat, a white belly, and orange patches on the neck.

emphysema A disease of the lungs characterized by destruction of lung tissue and distension of the air spaces. It is most commonly caused by cigarette smoking and is often accompanied by chronic *bronchitis. Patients become very breathless on exertion. It is a progressive condition, but the symptoms may be relieved by giving up smoking, breathing exercises, and administration of oxygen.

Empire, British Britain's overseas possessions from the 16th to early 20th centuries. The Empire's origins lay in the discovery by John *Cabot of Cape Breton Island (1497) but permanent settlements in North America were not established until the early 17th century, when colonists, some escaping religious persecution, were granted royal charters to settle Virginia, Maryland, and New England. The loss of the American colonies in 1783 (*see* American Revolution) was a major blow. In Canada the English came into conflict with the French and only established control in the *Seven Years' War (1756–63) from which they also emerged victorious in India. The East India Company had received its charter in 1600 but its interests in India had remained commercial until the decline of the Mogul Empire provided the chance for territorial expansion. Robert Clive's victory at Plassey (1757) assured British, rather than French, dominance there and the East India Company continued to govern until 1857, when its authority was replaced by the crown's.

The Napoleonic Wars in the early 19th century brought possessions in the West Indies (Trinidad, Tobago, St Lucia) as well as Mauritius, Ceylon, and in South Africa. Britain's first settlement in Africa had been on James Island in the Gambia River (1661) but substantial possessions were not obtained until the late 18th century with the acquisition of what are now Sierra Leone, Ghana, and Nigeria. The 19th-century colonial expansion in Africa was fired by missionary zeal, which motivated such explorers as *Livingstone, as well as by commercial activities. The late 19th century saw the establishment of British dominance in Egypt and the Sudan but in South Africa it was undermined by *Afrikaner hostility.

Colonies in Australia were initially (18th century) penal settlements. New Zealand was controlled by the British from 1840 and the 19th century also achieved the acquisition of Hong Kong (1841) and Burma (1886). In the mid 19th century, following the 1839 *Report on the Affairs of British North America* by Lord *Durham, the self-governing colonies in Canada, Australia, New Zealand, and South Africa received responsible government, whereby governors were advised by local ministers. In 1907 Canada, Australia, and New Zealand (and in 1910 South Africa), by now federated, were termed dominions and regular *Imperial Conferences were instituted. In 1931 the *Commonwealth of Nations was established, giving the dominions autonomy, and in the following decades Britain's other colonies gradually achieved full independence.

Empire style The neoclassical style in the decorative arts developing during the Napoleonic empire (1804–14). It was inspired by classical Greek, Roman, and Egyptian models and reflected contemporary interest in archeology (e.g. *Pompeii). Dark woods, such as rosewood, were favored, sparsely ornamented with *ormolu. Shapes tended to be plain but caryatids were used as supports. The effect was of restrained but opulent elegance. The **Second Empire style** was the official architectural style of the French Government under Emperor Napoleon III (1852–70). Grandiose and ideally suited to public buildings, it became popular throughout Europe and America.

empiricism The philosophical belief that all knowledge is ultimately based on experience, that is, information received through the senses. It is opposed to *rationalism and denies that we have any *a priori knowledge or innate ideas: we owe all our concepts to experience of the world. Concepts only have meaning if they can be associated with some (actual or possible) experience, and statements asserted to be true can only be justified by appealing to experience. (Mathematical and logical knowlege are often exempted from this requirement by being classified as analytically true—true in virtue of syntax and the meaning of symbols alone.) Since the British empiricists, *Locke, *Berkeley, and *Hume, empiricism has been an influential force in much of western philosophy.

Ems telegram (July 13, 1870) A communication from *William I of Prussia to his chancellor *Bismarck, the edited and published version of which precipitated the *Franco-Prussian War. The telegram described a disagreement between William and the French ambassador concerning the succession to the Spanish throne. Bismarck altered the telegram to make it read as if each party had insulted the other.

emu A large flightless long-legged Australian bird, *Dromaius novaehollandiae*, found in open plains and forests. Up to 60 in (150 cm) tall and 100 lb (45 kg) in weight, it has a dark-brown hairlike plumage with a naked blue spot on each side of the neck, and can run at speeds of up to 30 mph (50 km per hr). It is the only member of its family (*Dromaiidae*). *See also* ratite.

emulsion. *See* colloid.

emu wren An Australian *wren of the genus *Stipiturus* (3 species). About 3 in (7.5 cm) long, it has a brownish plumage and a long 3.5 in (9 cm) cocked tail consisting of six wispy gray feathers.

enamel A glaze that is fused onto the surface of metal. Enameled gold jewelry dating back to the 13th century BC has been found, and various methods of enameling have developed since then. Generally, a clear flux made from melted sand, soda potash, and red lead is stained with a metal oxide and left to harden. The resultant enamel cakes are ground and spread on the metal object, which is then placed in a furnace to fuse the enamel with the metal. Painted enamels are applied after the ground enamel has been fired and are not, therefore, true enamels.

enamelwork The art of decorating metal surfaces with colored glass that is fused by heat onto the metal. There are three main kinds: *cloisonné, *champlevé, and painted enamelwork. The technique of painted enamelwork involves painting powdered wet enamel all over the metal before firing. Painted enamel is particularly associated with Limoges, France, (15th and 16th centuries) and with England (18th century).

encaustic painting A method of painting using ground pigments emulsified in hot wax, which are applied thickly with a spatula or brush. Heat is then directed onto the paint to fuse it with the picture surface. Although revived by various artists, it was most successfully employed by ancient Greek and Roman painters.

encephalins (*or* enkephalins)   Short peptide molecules, found in parts of the brain and spinal cord, that are thought to relieve pain. These and similar compounds are called **endorphins**. In the spinal cord encephalins are believed to inhibit painful sensations by reacting with specific receptor sites on the sensory nerve endings. In the brain their function is less certain but may be associated with mood. The pain-relieving effects of acupuncture may be due to the release of the body's encephalins.

encephalitis   Inflammation of the brain. It usually occurs as a result of a virus infection, but can be caused by malaria, fungi, or parasites (rarely by bacteria). The patient is often drowsy and fevered and has a bad headache. There is no specific treatment for viral encephalitis but the patient usually recovers. *See also* sleepy sickness.

Encke's comet   A comet that has a period of only 3.3 years (decreasing by 2.5 hours/revolution) and has been very closely studied during its numerous apparitions. Its period was first established by the German astronomer J. F. Encke (1791–1865).

enclosure   The fencing in of open land to make more efficient use of it. Enclosure has occurred in most parts of Europe but is associated particularly with England, where it reached a peak in the 15th–16th and 18th–19th centuries. The enclosing by landlords, without prior agreement, of land to which tenants had enjoyed traditional grazing rights encountered much opposition and in the 16th century a series of acts against enclosure was passed. The movement again intensified in the 18th century, contributing to the *agricultural revolution. The General Enclosure Acts (1801, 1836, 1845) established procedures to safeguard tenant rights.

encyclical, papal   A decree of the pope addressed to the whole Roman Catholic Church. The term referred originally to a letter to all the churches in a particular area, such as a diocese. The most famous example of an encyclical in recent times is *Humanae Vitae* (1968), which was issued by Paul VI and expressed the teaching of the Church on contraception.

encyclopedia   A reference book summarizing all human knowledge or comprehensively surveying a particular subject. Greek and Roman encyclopedias, such as *Pliny the Elder's *Historia naturalis* (77 AD), were thematically arranged, as were the medieval Latin compilations, such as Vincent of Beauvais' influential *Speculum maius* (c. 1250). After the Renaissance, alphabetical arrangement with articles written in vernacular languages to facilitate use by the layman became accepted. Ephraim Chambers' *Cyclopaedia* (1728) was the earliest to use cross-references. Diderot's 35-volume *Encyclopédie* (1751–65) used specialist contributors and editors (*see* Encyclopedists), but its ideological bias left gaps that the first *Encyclopaedia Britannica* (1768–71) sought to fill. Major encyclopedias that first appeared in the 19th century and are still published in some form include the German *Brockhaus* (1809), the *Encyclopedia Americana* (1833), *Chamber's Encyclopaedia* (1859), and the French *Grand Dictionnaire Universel* (1865–76) of Larousse. In the 20th century the expansion of scientific knowledge has posed particular problems for compilers; in particular the need to keep pace with technology requires frequent updating of reference works. For this reason some modern encyclopedias, including this one, are compiled on computer-based systems and typeset by computer.

Encyclopedists (French name: Encyclopédistes)   The French intellectuals who contributed to *Diderot's monumental *Encyclopédie*, published in 28 volumes between 1751 and 1772. Five more volumes were published in 1776–77. Over 200 scholarly experts, including such leading figures of the *Enlightenment as Voltaire, Rousseau, and d'Alembert, contributed articles that combined scientific facts and radical philosophical thinking. By their appeal to reason rather than faith the Encyclopedists threatened the authority of church and state.

Enderby Land   An area in Antarctica, on the Indian Ocean E of Queen Maud Land. The coast is mountainous and the interior consists of an ice-capped plateau. The site of a Soviet research station, it is claimed by Australia.

Enders, John Franklin (1897–   ) US microbiologist, who shared the 1954 Nobel Prize with Frederick *Robbins and Thomas Weller (1915–   ) for their work on *viruses. In 1948 they discovered a method of growing virus cultures by adding penicillin to prevent the growth of bacteria, a problem that had plagued previous attempts. Their work paved the way for the development of vaccines to prevent virus diseases.

endive   An annual or biennial plant, *Cichorium endivia*, probably native to S Asia and N China and cultivated widely. It has a rosette of shiny leaves, either curled and narrow (var. *crispa*), used for salads, or broad (*latifolia*), used for cooking. The pale-blue daisy-like flowers grow on spikes up to 40 in (100 cm) high. Family: *Compositae. See also* chicory.

Endlicher, Stephan Ladislaus (1804–49) Hungarian botanist, who proposed a system of plant classification based on two groups: thallophytes (algae, fungi, and lichens) and cormophytes (mosses, ferns, and seed plants). Although based on erroneous principles, his system was adopted throughout Europe for a time.

endocrine glands   Ductless glands that produce and secrete *hormones into the bloodstream. Most are regulated by hormones from the *pituitary gland, which is itself controlled by neurohormones secreted by the *hypothalamus. Other endocrine glands include the *thyroid, *adrenal, and *parathyroid glands, parts of the *pancreas (the islets of Langerhans), and the ovaries and testes. The wall of the intestine also contains many endocrine cells that release hormones, such as secretin and gastrin, controlling the secretion of digestive enzymes. The study of the endocrine glands in health and disease is called **endocrinology**.

endorphins.   See encephalins.

endoscopy   Examination of the interior of the body by means of a viewing instrument (endoscope) as an aid to diagnosis. There are many types of endoscope, specialized for viewing different organs. The modern endoscope for examining the stomach and intestine is a flexible *fiberoptic instrument, which is swallowed by the patient. It enables all areas to be observed and photographed and often has attachments for removing tissue specimens for *biopsy. Endoscopy of the gastrointestinal tract is particularly useful for identifying sites of intestinal bleeding and for diagnosing peptic ulcers and tumors.

Endymion   In Greek legend, a beautiful youth, either a shepherd of Caria or a king of Elis, who was put into an everlasting sleep by Selene, goddess of the moon, so that she could enjoy his beauty forever.

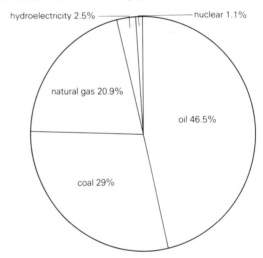

ENERGY   *World primary sources.*

energy   A property of a system that enables it to do work, i.e. to move the point of application of a force. The several forms of energy can be converted into each other under appropriate conditions. *Kinetic energy is energy of motion, whereas *potential energy is stored energy, for example the energy stored in a body by virtue of its position in a gravitational or electric field. Other forms of energy include heat (the kinetic energy of the atoms and molecules in a body), chemical energy (the potential energy stored in the chemical bonds between atoms in a substance), nuclear energy (the potential energy stored in the atomic nucleus), and radiant energy (the energy associated with electromagnetic waves).

As a consequence of the special theory of relativity, mass (m) has also to be regarded as a special form of energy (E), in accordance with the equation $E = mc^2$, where c is the velocity of light. Thus the production of nuclear energy involves a loss of mass in the fuel. However, the sum of the mass and the energy is conserved (*see* conservation of mass and energy). Energy is measured in joules (SI units), calories or ergs (c.g.s. units), kilowatt-hours or British thermal units (Imperial units).

Energy sources: man's first use of energy (other than that of his own body or the body of animals) came with the discovery of fire. For combustion is a process in which chemical energy is converted into heat energy. The first fuel was wood; but fossil fuels (asphalt, coal, oil, natural gas) have been in use for about 8000 years. However, it was the *industrial revolution and the later advent of motorized transport that brought explosive increases in the demand for energy and consequently for fossil fuels. These demands have steadily increased during the 20th century, especially with the spread of technology throughout the world. There is now great concern over the remaining reserves of fossil fuels, which some experts believe will be exhausted in less than a hundred years. Nuclear fission reactors (*see* nuclear energy), a source independent of fossil fuels, now provide some 10% of the world's energy needs and alternative sources, such as solar, tidal, wind, and geothermal power, are being actively explored. However, if it can be successfully harnessed, nuclear fusion (*see* thermonuclear reactor) will be the most abundant energy source in the next century.

Energy, Department of (DOE)   US cabinet-level agency that provides the framework for a comprehensive and balanced national energy plan. Headed by the secretary of energy, it researches and develops energy technology and conservation programs and markets federal power. Established in 1977, it took over certain functions of the departments of Commerce and the Interior.

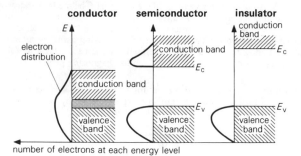

ENERGY BAND   *The distribution of electrons over the various energy levels in a conductor, semiconductor, and insulator. There are no electrons in the "forbidden" band between E_c and E_v in semiconductors and insulators.*

energy band   A concept used to explain the electrical properties of solids, particularly *semiconductors. Electrons need to have a minimum energy, E_v, to free them from the atoms of the solid. Below this energy they are said to be in the valence band. To be able to move through the solid, so that they constitute a current, they need to be above another energy level, E_c, in the so-called conduction band. In an insulator, E_c is significantly greater than E_v and there are effectively no electrons in the conduction band. In a conductor, there are many electrons with energy greater than E_c, and E_c may be less than E_v, i.e. the conduction and valence bands are very close or overlap. A pure semiconductor at *absolute zero behaves like an insulator, but the difference between E_c and E_v is small. With an increase in temperature (a measure of the average energy of the particles in the material), some electrons enter the conduction band. Also, the presence of impurities in a semiconductor crystal brings electrons of an intermediate energy level with it, since E_v and E_c vary from one material to another. Depending on the type of impurity, the number of electrons in either the conduction band or the valence band at a particular temperature, will increase, changing the electrical properties of the solid.

Enesco, Georges   (G. Enescu; 1881–1955) Romanian violinist and composer. He settled in Paris and had a long and brilliant performing career; he composed symphonies, sonatas, and nationalistic Romanian rhapsodies. A distinguished teacher, his pupils included Menuhin.

Engadin   (French name: Engadine)   The Swiss part of the upper Inn Valley, divided into Upper Engadin and Lower Engadin. Tourism is important and it contains several winter-sports centers.

Engels, Friedrich   (1820–95) German socialist and chief collaborator of Karl *Marx. For a time he managed a factory in Manchester, England. In 1844 he met Marx, and was able to introduce him to English economic conditions and the British working-class movement. They wrote the *Communist Manifesto* (1848), in which they predicted the eventual overthrow of capitalism in favor of a classless society. Among Engels' other works are the *Condition of the Working Class in England in 1844* (1845). His *Anti-Dühring* (1878) systematizes *dialectical materialism. After Marx's death, he edited the last volume of *Das Kapital* (1885).

engineering   The systematic application of scientific knowledge to the design, creation, and use of structures and machines. Engineering has its roots in the constructions in classical times by military engineers of harbors, roads, aqueducts, tunnels, canals, and siege machines. *Civil engineering arose from the study and design of such static structures as bridges, dams, buildings, etc., whereas *mechanical engineering is concerned with

dynamical systems, such as machinery and engines. Other important branches of engineering are *electrical engineering, aeronautical engineering, and *chemical engineering.

engineering drawing   A systematic method of producing a drawing to scale of machines, their components, or other technical structures to convey the shape, dimensions, and other information to the constructor. They usually consist of a series of orthogonal projections, side elevations, plans, and other views or details depending on the complexity of the object.

England   The largest political division in the *United Kingdom. With Wales to the W and Scotland to the N, it is separated from the mainland of Europe by the North Sea and the English Channel and from Ireland by the Irish Sea. It consists of two main zones: the lowlands, which extend across the Midlands, the SE, East Anglia, and the Fens, and the highlands of the Pennines and the Lake District in the N and the granite uplands of Dartmoor and Exmoor in the SW. The chief rivers are the Thames and the Severn. The center of government and administration of the UK, England is also the wealthiest and most populous of the UK countries. *Economy*: the development of industry has been a major contributor to England's wealth. Mineral extraction has historically been of importance and the recent exploitation of North Sea oil and gas continues to make an important contribution to the economy. The main English coalfields are situated in the East Midlands, Yorkshire, and Northumberland and Durham. The production of iron ore has declined in recent years and there is an increased reliance on imports. Manufacturing industries are centered on Greater London, Birmingham, Lancashire, Yorkshire, Tyneside, and Teeside, although there has been a dramatic decline in manufacturing employment in London in recent years. The production of motor vehicles faces strong competition from overseas competitors. Other major industries include heavy engineering, petrochemicals, and pharmaceuticals (Manchester), food processing (Liverpool), and steel processing (Sheffield). Despite the expansion of industries based on advanced technology, together with the reorganization and modernization of older industries, the decline of heavy industry (including shipbuilding) has led to high levels of unemployment in these areas. Agriculture has increased in productivity, although the number of people employed in this sector has decreased. The greatest proportion of crop land is in the E and SE, producing chiefly cereals, potatoes, and sugar beet. Fishing and tourism are also important sources of revenue. *History*: there is much archeological evidence of prehistoric settlement in England but historical records begin with the Roman occupation, from 43 AD until the early 5th century. Christianity was introduced in the 4th century, and conquests between the 3rd and 7th centuries by *Angles, *Saxons, and *Jutes led to the establishment of independent kingdoms (*see* Mercia; Northumbria; Wessex), which were united in the 9th century under Wessex. By the late 800s the Danes had established themselves and from 1016 to 1042 the English were ruled successively by the Danish kings *Canute and *Hardecanute. The *Norman conquest (1066) ended the *Anglo-Saxon period of English history and established a new dynasty of Norman kings. In 1455 the rival claims of the Houses of *Lancaster and *York precipitated the Wars of the *Roses, which lasted until Richard III's defeat (1485) by Henry *Tudor. The 16th century saw the establishment of Protestantism in England (*see* Reformation), the formal union of England and Wales (*see* Union, Acts of), and, under Elizabeth I, a significant development in overseas exploration and trade. The consequent rivalry with Spain culminated in the English defeat of the *Armada (1588). The Tudors were succeeded by the *Stuarts in 1603, when James VI of Scotland ascended the English throne as *James I. The unpopularity of James and his son Charles I brought about the *Civil War, which ended with Charles' execution (1649) and the establishment of republican government. The Stuart *Restoration (1660) followed the fall of Oliver Cromwell's *Protectorate but the authoritarian and pro-Catholic policies of James II brought about his deposition in 1688 and the succession of William of Orange and his Stuart wife Mary. The 18th century saw union with Scotland (1707), the development of *cabinet government during the administration of Sir Robert Walpole, and the loss of the American colonies (1783; *see* American Revolution). Following union with Ireland in 1801, England, Wales, Scotland, and Ireland became the United Kingdom of Great Britain and Ireland. With the *industrial revolution the UK evolved from an agricultural to an industrial economy, and political influence shifted from the landowners to the urban middle class. The growing labor movement led to the formation in 1900 of the *Labour Party, which was subsequently to replace the Liberals as one of the two chief political parties. The 19th century also saw the heyday of the British *Empire and the beginning of colonial rivalry with Germany, which was a significant factor in the outbreak of *World War I. The interwar years were dominated by the Depression and the growing threat of fascist governments abroad, which culminated in *World War II. Successive governments have failed to deal effectively with Britain's postwar economic decline and with the prolonged crisis in Northern *Ireland. Area: 50,332 sq mi (130,360 sq km). Population (1981): 46,221,000. Capital: London. *See also* Great Britain.

Engler, Gustav Heinrich Adolf (1844–1930) German botanist, who proposed a system of plant classification that is still widely accepted. Engler adapted *Eichler's system (1883) to encompass the whole plant kingdom. Engler held several important administrative posts in plant science and was an expert on plant geography.

English A West Germanic language spoken originally in Britain but now also in the US, Canada, New Zealand, Australia, and many other parts of the world. It is the world's most widely known and used language. Its history may be divided into three periods. In the Old English period (c. 450–1100 AD), four dialects were spoken: Northumbrian, Mercian, Kentish, and West Saxon. The last became the standard form. Middle English refers to the period from 1100 to 1500, when five dialects were spoken: Northern (developed from Northumbrian), West and East Midlands (diverging from Mercian), South Western (from West Saxon) and South Eastern (from Kentish). Each developed in characteristic ways but in general the influence of French after the Norman conquest brought new vocabulary and sound patterns. Modern English covers the period from 1500 and was much influenced by the speech of London. English slowly became a relatively uninflected language with great flexibility in the way words may function. Its vocabulary is about half Germanic and half Romance with many other borrowings.

English art and architecture The styles of art and architecture found in England. Before the Norman conquest the art of the British Isles was identified with *Celtic art, Roman art and architecture, and Anglo-Saxon art. Illuminated manuscripts constituted the outstanding contribution of Anglo-Saxon artists, and manuscripts of a high quality continued to be produced in the later middle ages. The Normans introduced *romanesque art and architecture (e.g. Durham Cathedral). In the 12th century, *gothic architecture was introduced, which developed into several distinct styles and became the indigenous church architecture of the middle ages. In the early 17th century the architect Inigo *Jones introduced *Palladianism to England and, among painters, the Flemings *Rubens and *Van Dyck towered above their English contemporaries. Architecture in the late 17th century was dominated by *Wren, Vanbrugh, and Hawksmoor, exponents of the *baroque. The 18th and early 19th centuries saw the great era of town architecture; this was followed by the *gothic revival. Notable painters of the 18th century were *Hogarth, *Reynolds, and *Gainsborough. Romanticism found expression in the work of *Turner and *Constable and the 19th century also witnessed the formation of the *Pre-Raphaelite Brotherhood, which, with the work of William *Morris, influenced *Art Nouveau in England. The philosophy of "art for art's sake" was articulated by *Sickert. The 20th century has produced outstanding sculptors, including *Epstein, *Hepworth, and Henry *Moore, and painters, such as Augustus *John, Graham *Sutherland, Stanley *Spencer, L. S. *Lowry, and Francis *Bacon.

English Channel (French name: La Manche) An arm of the Atlantic Ocean in NW Europe, between England and France. It is one of the busiest shipping lanes in the world. Many attempts at swimming the Channel (usually across the Strait of *Dover) have been made; the first successful one was by Capt Webb (1875). *See also* Channel Tunnel.

English literature The earliest works of the Old English period (407–1066 AD) are heroic poems, notably the epic *Beowulf*, which belong to a Germanic oral tradition of alliterative unrhymed verse and were not put into written form until the 7th century. There are also a number of remarkable shorter poems, such as the elegies *The Wanderer* and *The Seafarer*, and many poems on Christian subjects. Major Old English religious writers, such as Bede and Alcuin, wrote in Latin; English prose started with the translations from Latin made by King Alfred and developed in the *Anglo-Saxon Chronicle*, the compilation of which he initiated.

Norman-French displaced Old English as the dominant written language after the Conquest, but the native language, enriched by French, was firmly re-established in the 14th century in the Middle English poetry of Chaucer, whose works were indebted to Italian Renaissance authors, especially Dante, Petrarch, and Boccaccio. The native alliterative tradition continued in such poems as *Piers Plowman*, *Pearl*, and *Gawain and the Green Knight*. Printing was introduced in 1476 by Caxton.

Although Chaucer had introduced Renaissance influences, it was not until the 16th century that the full effects of humanism were felt. The sonnet was introduced, and Spenser produced the Elizabethan allegorical epic *The Faerie Queene* (1590). The blank-verse plays of Kyd and Marlowe prepared the way for the dramas of Shakespeare, Jonson, and their 17th-century successors. Donne and the Metaphysical school are the most important

poets of the early 17th century, while Milton dominates the latter part. Among the most influential prose works were the Authorized Version of the Bible and Bunyan's *The Pilgrim's Progress* (1678).

During the Restoration (from 1660), Dryden developed the heroic couplet in his satires and made an important contribution to modern English prose in his criticism. The classical ideals of the Augustan Age (c. 1690–1740) were embodied in the satirical verse of Pope and the essays of Addison and Steele and were maintained by later writers, such as Johnson, Goldsmith, and Sheridan. Swift was the outstanding prose satirist of the period.

Various economic and social factors during the early 18th century contributed to the emergence of the novel, pioneered by Richardson, Fielding, Defoe, Smollett, Sterne, and various authors of the "gothic" novel of horror. It reached its full development in the works of Jane Austen, Walter Scott, Thackeray, the Brontës, Dickens, George Eliot, Trollope, Meredith, Hardy, Conrad, and the American Henry James.

In the early 19th century the classicism of the previous period was challenged by the Romantic movement. Its precursor was Blake and its leading figures were Wordsworth, Coleridge, Keats, Shelley, and Byron. Their chief successors in the Victorian era were Tennyson, Browning, Matthew Arnold, and Swinburne. Macaulay, John Stuart Mill, Carlyle, Ruskin, and Pater were among the influential prose writers. At the turn of the century the comedies of Wilde and Shaw enlivened the English theater; prior to World War I Kipling, Hardy, Yeats, Belloc, Chesterton, Wells, Housman, and de la Mare produced a distinguished body of verse as well as fiction and criticism. Postwar poetry was dominated by Eliot, Auden, MacNeice, Spender, and the later work of Yeats. Among the leading novelists and prose writers were Forster, Joyce, D. H. Lawrence, Woolf, Aldous Huxley, Orwell, Isherwood, Greene, and Evelyn Waugh. Between World War II and the present appeared the poems of Dylan Thomas and Philip Larkin; the plays of Osborne, Pinter, and Tom Stoppard; and the novels of Kingsley Amis, Muriel Spark, Iris Murdoch, Anthony Powell, and Anthony Burgess.

English-Speaking Union An organization, based in London, that promotes friendship and understanding between English-speaking countries. It was founded by Sir Evelyn Wrench (1882–1966) in 1918 and now has 160 branches in the UK, North America, Australasia, India, and the Caribbean.

engraving A method of producing a reproductive plate by chiseling, carving, or biting the design onto a metal or wood plate. Intaglio engraving denotes such methods as *etching, *mezzotint, and soft- or hard-ground engraving, in which the printed impression pulls ink from inside the carved grooves. By contrast, relief engraving denotes methods, such as *woodcut, in which the carved-away areas are not inked. Intaglio engraving allows for extreme delicacy and detail; relief engraving is often exploited for illustrations, where force and clarity are needed.

Enlightenment (or Age of Reason) An 18th-century philosophical movement that sought to replace orthodox authoritarian beliefs with rational scientific inquiry. During the 17th century, as scientific knowledge increased, such scholars as Newton, Locke, Pascal, and Descartes questioned accepted beliefs, and criticism of established society and assumptions spread throughout Europe. In France the *Philosophes (e.g. Voltaire) attacked established religion (*see* deism) and the Enlightenment beliefs in individual liberty and equality were embodied in the work of Rousseau and other *Encyclopedists. The movement came to an end with the French Revolution.

Enlightened despots were those European monarchs (e.g. Emperor *Joseph II, Frederick the Great of Prussia, and Catherine the Great of Russia) who introduced reforms, based on the ideas of the Enlightenment, by authoritarian means.

Enlil The Sumerian god of the sky and storms. He was the patron deity of *Nippur and with *Anu and *Ea formed the supreme trinity in the Sumerian pantheon.

Ennius, Quintus (238–169 BC) Roman poet. After service in the second Punic War, he was brought to Rome by the elder Cato in 204 and became a Roman citizen in 184. His works include tragic dramas adapted from the Greek, philosophical poems, epigrams, and the *Annals*, a national epic in 18 books narrating the history of Rome from Aeneas to his own time. Only fragments of his works survive.

Enoch An Old Testament patriarch. **The Books of Enoch** are two biblical books ascribed to him; they were in fact written in the 2nd century BC and 1st century AD respectively. The first, a composite work of Jewish origin, is a series of apocalyptic visions. The second is of Hellenistic origin and records revelations supposedly given to Enoch, his journey to heaven, and advice to his children.

enosis. *See* EOKA.

Enragés (French: Madmen)   Members of an extremist French Revolutionary group (1793). Led by Jacques Roux (d. 1794), they demanded direct government action to alleviate food shortages and to help the poor. Actively encouraging food riots, their leaders were arrested by the Committee of *Public Safety and their extremist role was adopted by the Hébertists (*see* Hébert).

Enschede   52 13N 06 55E A city in the E Netherlands, in Overijssel province. It is an important center of the Dutch cotton industry. Population (1981 est): 144,346.

Ensor, James Sydney, Baron   (1860–1949) Belgian painter; his father was English but he was born and spent most of his life in Ostend. He was initially condemned for what was thought his crude technique, but the originality of his grotesque imagery of masks and skeletons, as in the symbolic representation of modern social evils in *Entry of Christ into Brussels* (1888), received popular recognition in the 1920s.

Entebbe   0 05N 39 29E A city in Uganda, in Buganda on the NW shore of Lake Victoria. It was the administrative center of Uganda until 1958 but is now largely residential. It contains Uganda's international airport, where, in 1976, Israeli hostages taken from a hijacked French plane by Palestinian guerrillas were rescued by Israeli troops. Population (1969): 21,000.

entellus. *See* langur.

Entente Cordiale   (1904) An agreement between France and Britain. During the 19th century, colonial expansion, especially in Africa, caused tension between France, Britain, and Germany. France feared a German war and Britain and France, partly through Edward VII's efforts to reconcile their traditional enmity, signed the Entente Cordiale. This was not an alliance but a mutual recognition of each other's colonial interests, especially France's in Morocco and Britain's in Egypt. The agreement brought greater diplomatic cooperation against German pressure.

enthalpy (*H*)   A thermodynamic property of a system equal to its internal energy plus the product of its pressure and volume. The change in enthalpy (ΔH) when a chemical reaction takes place is equal to the heat given out or absorbed. By convention ΔH is negative if heat is evolved by the reaction.

entomology   The study of insects. Entomology probably has its origins in the observations of *Aristotle. Modern entomology dates from the 17th century, when the introduction of microscopy enabled fine details of insect anatomy to be described; for instance, in the work of the Dutch naturalist Jan *Swammerdam. Today attention is focused especially on insect pests, since knowledge of their physiology and ecology is of prime importance in their control or eradication.

entrepreneur   An individual in a capitalist economy who is prepared to commit capital and to initiate a commercial venture. Entrepreneurship is often counted as a fourth factor of production (the others being land, labor, and capital), providing the spark that sets the others off. With the development of large corporations and a large public sector in most economies, the role of the individual entrepreneur has somewhat diminished.

entropy   A measure of the disorder of a system, used in *thermodynamics. Thus a solid has less entropy than a liquid since the constituent particles in a solid are in a more ordered state. Originally defined in connection with the second law of thermodynamics, the change in entropy of a reversible system is equal to the energy absorbed by the system divided by the thermodynamic temperature at which the change takes place. The entropy of a closed system never decreases during a thermodynamic process: if it increases the process is irreversible; if it remains unchanged it is reversible. *See also* heat death of the universe.

Enugu   6 20N 7 29E A city in S Nigeria. It developed following the discovery of nearby coal in 1909 and is an important mining, manufacturing, and trade center. It contains part of the University of Nigeria (1962). Population (1975 est): 187,000.

Enver Pasha   (1881–1922) Turkish soldier and politician, who was a leader of the *Young Turk revolution of 1908. During World War I he was one of the three real rulers of the Ottoman Empire. His aim was to unite the Turks of central Asia with those of Turkey in one state. He was killed in a rising in central Asia against the Bolsheviks.

Environment Protection Agency (EPA)   US executive branch agency that protects and enhances the environment under laws enacted by Congress. It controls and abates pollution in the areas of air, water, solid waste, pesticides, radiation, and toxic substances. Established in 1970, its headquarters are in Washington, DC.

enzymes   An important group of proteins that act as biological catalysts, i.e. they speed up (or slow down) the rate of chemical reactions in living organisms. Enzymes are manufactured by cells according to the *genetic code carried by the chromosomes; because each enzyme catalyzes a specific reaction, it is the enzymes that determine the function of the cell. The structure of enzymes and the nature of their active sites (where they bind to reacting molecules) can be determined by such techniques as X-ray diffraction. Control of *metabolism is largely exerted through regulation of enzyme production and activity, which are inhibited by such poisons as cyanide. Many enzymes require associated nonprotein *coenzymes to function properly.

Eocene epoch. *See* Tertiary period.

eohippus   An extinct ancestor of the *horse, also called *Hyracotherium* or dawn horse, that lived in the Eocene epoch (about 55 million to 40 million years ago). About 11 in (28 cm) tall, it was a browsing forest dweller with a short neck and had four toes on the forefoot and three on the hindfoot. *See also* Hipparion.

Eos. *See* Aurora. 58

Epaminondas   (c. 418–362 BC) Theban general and military strategist, who defeated Sparta at *Leuctra in 371, thereby ending the military supremacy of Sparta in Greece. He was the first to use cavalry to support infantry in a coordinated attack and his military innovations influenced both Philip II and Alexander the Great of Macedon. He died in the battle of Mantinea, in which the Spartans were defeated.

Épernay   49 02N 3 58E A city in NE France, in the Marne department on the Marne River. A center for the wine industry of Champagne, it has famous underground wine cellars. Population (1975): 31,108.

ephedrine   A drug with effects resembling those of *adrenaline. It stimulates the heart, dilates the bronchi (air passages to the lungs), and has marked effects on the nervous system. Ephedrine is used mainly to treat asthma. Side effects include trembling and feelings of anxiety.

ephemeral   A plant that completes its life cycle—from germination to seed production—in under a year, enabling more than one generation to be produced within a single year. Many common weeds, such as groundsel and chickweed, are ephemerals.

ephemeris   (Greek: diary)   A reference manual, usually published annually, that is used in astronomical observation and navigation. It lists the predicted positions of the sun, moon, and planets in the forthcoming year and also gives times of eclipses, stellar positions, and other similar information.

Ephesians, Epistle of Paul to the   A New Testament book that originated as a circular letter from the Apostle Paul to churches in Asia Minor. Written about 60 AD, it deals with a number of religious and moral points and stresses the equality of Jewish and Gentile Christians.

Ephesus   An ancient Greek city and trading center on the Ionian coast of *Asia Minor. *Croesus of *Lydia captured it in 550 BC. It maintained its prosperity under the Persians and Alexander the Great. In Roman times Ephesus was rivaled only by *Alexandria as a commercial center. It was sacked by the *Goths in 262 AD. *See also* Artemis, Temple of.

Ephraim, tribe of   One of the 12 *tribes of Israel. It claimed descent from Ephraim, the son of Joseph and grandson of Jacob and Rachel. It occupied mountainous territory NW of the Dead Sea.

epic   A long narrative poem concerning a heroic theme and written in an appropriately dignified style. The *Iliad* and the *Odyssey* of Homer (8th century BC) are the earliest epics in western literature and are the models of Virgil's *Aeneid* (c. 29–19 BC), in which the hero Aeneas is seen as representing the national spirit of Rome. The *Aeneid* inspired later national epics, such as Camões' *Os Lusíadas* (1572) and Ronsard's *Franciade* (1572). In English literature, examples include the Old English *Beowulf* (8th century AD), Spenser's *Faerie Queene* (1589–96), a mixture of epic and romance, and Milton's *Paradise Lost* (1667).

epicenter. *See* earthquake.

Epictetus   (c. 60–110 AD) Stoic philosopher. A freed slave, Epictetus was banished, with other philosophers, from Rome in 89 AD and settled in Epirus. He taught that loving one's enemies, repudiating pleasure, and understanding that all men are brothers are ways to serenity. Epictetus' teachings were preserved by his pupil *Arrian. *See also* Stoicism.

Epicureanism   A school of philosophy founded by *Epicurus around 300 BC in Athens. He taught that the highest good was pleasure and the avoidance of pain, based on tranquility of mind and conscience. Many seeking a license for the pursuit of pleasure have styled themselves Epicureans, giving the term its common sense of "unashamed sensualist." True

Epicureans, however, seek serenity through detachment from worldly affairs.

Epicurus (341–270 BC) Greek philosopher and founder of the school of *Epicureanism. In 306 BC he began teaching in a garden in Athens. Virtuous and temperate, he was a good friend and citizen but avoided politics, following his maxim "Live unseen and unknown." His surviving works are few and fragmentary but his philosophy, especially his *atomism, was expounded by *Lucretius.

Epidauros A city state of ancient Greece, situated across the Saronic Gulf from *Athens. Its sanctuary of *Asclepius was famous in antiquity. Patients asleep in the temple were visited by the god in their dreams and treated by his priests next morning; grateful inscriptions record numerous cures. The 4th-century BC theater (part of the temple complex) is sufficiently preserved to be still used for plays.

epidemiology The science that investigates the incidence and causative factors of diseases that are associated with a particular environment or way of life. Epidemiologists have enlarged their studies from the classical epidemics of communicable diseases, such as smallpox and cholera, to include noncommunicable diseases associated with modern societies. Thus they have demonstrated the connection between cigarette smoking and lung cancer, diet and coronary heart disease, etc.

epidermis The outermost layer of cells in animals and plants. In lower animals (invertebrates) it often secretes a protective *cuticle. In higher animals (including mammals) it forms the outer layer of the □skin. In plants the epidermis usually consists of a single layer of cells, but aerial organs have extra protection in the form of a noncellular waxy cuticle. Both layers prevent dehydration of internal tissues, lessen damage by bacteria and fungi, and reduce attack by such pests as aphids.

epididymis. *See* testis.

epiglottis A leaf-shaped flap of cartilage at the root of the tongue that prevents food and fluid from entering the windpipe during swallowing. As it is swallowed, the food presses the epiglottis down against the opening of the larynx (at the top of the windpipe). This, combined with the reflex upward movement of the larynx that occurs during swallowing, effectively seals off the entrance to the windpipe.

epilepsy A disease characterized by fits or sudden loss of consciousness. Epilepsy is common—Dostoievski, Van Gogh, Julius Caesar, and Byron all suffered from it. There are several different forms. In grand mal epilepsy the patient suddenly becomes stiff, loses consciousness, and has convulsions. The fit lasts only a few minutes but afterward he is sleepy and confused. Petit mal is a mild form seen only in children, who suddenly lose consciousness but usually do not fall down. Petit mal attacks last only a few seconds. Temporal lobe epilepsy is characterized by peculiar forms of behavior and strange sensations. All forms are treated with anticonvulsant drugs.

Épinal 48 10N 6 28E A city in E France, the capital of the Vosges department on the Moselle River. It is the center for a region manufacturing cotton goods and artificial fibers. Population (1975): 42,810.

epinephrine. *See* adrenaline.

Epiphany (*or* Twelfth Day) A Christian feast celebrated on Jan 6. In Eastern Orthodox Churches it commemorates the baptism of Jesus. Introduced to the West in the 4th century, it developed as a celebration of the coming of the *Magi to Bethlehem, representing the manifestation (Greek: *epiphaneia*) of Christ to the Gentiles. **Twelfth Night** is the night preceding Epiphany and traditionally devoted to festivities and entertainments. In several countries gifts are exchanged on Epiphany rather than at Christmas.

epiphyte A plant that grows on another plant for support. Epiphytes are not parasites: some obtain nourishment from decaying plant remains and many solve the problem of obtaining water by developing such structures as aerial roots. Some orchids are epiphytic.

Epirus (*or* Ípiros) A coastal region of NW Greece and S Albania, bordering on the Ionian Sea. Its tribes were united in the 4th century BC in a kingdom that reached its peak under *Pyrrhus in the early 3rd century BC. Sacked by the Romans in 167, it became part of the province of Macedonia in 148 BC. In the 13th century AD it briefly formed an independent kingdom before falling to the Serbs and Albanians and then (1430) to the Ottoman Turks. It was divided between Greece and Albania in 1913.

episcopacy In Christian Churches, government by bishops. The biblical basis of episcopacy is equivocal, and many Protestant Churches, for example the Congregational and Presbyterian, have adopted different methods. In the Roman Catholic and Orthodox Churches the episcopal hierarchy is seen as a continuation of the original group of apostles chosen by Christ (*see* Apostolic Succession). Among the Reformed Churches episcopal government is retained in whole or in part by Anglicans, Methodists, and Lutherans.

epistemology The philosophical discipline that considers the nature, basis, and limits of knowledge. Ancient Greek philosophers examined the relations between knowledge, truth, and belief, and the question of whether knowledge exists independently of a knower. *Locke and *Kant, however, first treated epistemology as fundamental to all philosophical and scientific enquiry. It is one of the three main branches of modern *philosophy.

Epistles The 21 books of the *New Testament that were written as letters. These are arranged in two groups, those by Paul (13) and those by others (7), divided by the Epistle to the Hebrews, of which the author is unknown. Of Paul's letters nine are to specific churches and four to individuals. The remainder are attributed to James, Peter (2), John (3), and Jude. In the liturgy of many Christian Churches, the Epistle is the name of the first of two passages of Scripture recited or sung at the celebration of the Eucharist, the second being the Gospel. It is usually a passage from the New Testament Epistles but may be a passage from the Old Testament, Acts, or Revelation.

epithelium A tissue that forms the linings of the mouth, nose, pharynx, intestines, respiratory tract, and the skin. There are different types of epithelia specialized for different functions. For example, the cells of the intestinal epithelium are glandular, secreting digestive enzymes, while the skin epithelium produces a tough protective layer of keratin.

epoch. *See* geological time scale.

epoxy resin A type of synthetic *resin made by polymerizing groups containing a three-membered ring that includes the –O– atom (epoxy group). They are themselves viscous liquids but set to hard clear solids on the addition of such curing agents as amines. Epoxy resins are extensively used as adhesives, the resin and the curing agent being mixed immediately before use.

Epstein, Sir Jacob (1880–1959) British sculptor, born in the US. Working in London after 1905, he achieved notoriety with his nude figures for the British Medical Association (1907–08) and his memorial tomb to Oscar Wilde (1912). After 1912 he briefly experimented with avant-garde sculpture, influenced by primitive art, and continued to provoke public criticism with such sculptures as *Rima*, a memorial to the author William Hudson (1925), and *Genesis* (1931). However, his bronze portrait busts of such celebrities as Conrad (1924), Einstein (1933), and T. S. □Eliot were more favorably received.

Equal Rights Amendment (ERA) Proposed amendement to the US Constitution. Reading "equality of rights under the law shall not be denied or abridged by the United States nor by any State on account of sex" and "Congress shall have the power to enforce, by appropriate legislation, the provisions of this article," its purpose is to ban sex discrimination. Passed by Congress in 1971 and 1972, the controversial issue failed to achieve ratification by the necessary 38 states by the extended deadline (June 1982). It was reintroduced in Congress (July 1982), but was defeated in the House of Representatives (1983).

equation A mathematical statement in which two expressions, usually containing at least one variable or unknown quantity, are equated. For example, the simple algebraic expression $2x + 4 = 8$ is an equation that can be simplified, or solved, to give a value of 2 for the unknown quantity x: this is known as the root of the equation. Equations are also used to show the general interdependence of several quantities, without necessarily finding their specific values. The degree of an equation is equal to the highest value of the exponent of the variable. A **linear equation** is of the first degree and has the form $y = mx + c$. A *graph of such an equation is a straight line, which (in the Cartesian *coordinate system) has a *gradient equal to m and cuts the y-axis at c. A *quadratic equation is of the second degree, i.e. contains terms in x^2.

Two or more equations in which all the variables must obey all the equations are called **simultaneous equations**. For a complete solution of simultaneous equations there must be as many equations as there are variables.

equation of time. *See* sundial.

equator The great circle around the earth at latitude $0°$, lying midway between the poles in a plane at right angles to the earth's axis. It is 24,902 mi (40,076 km) long and divides the N from the S hemisphere.

Equatorial Guinea, Republic of A small country in W central Africa, on the Gulf of Guinea. It consists of two provinces: mainland Mbini (formerly Río Muni), which includes several offshore islands; and the island of Bioko (formerly Macías Nguema), which includes the island of Piagalu (formerly Annobón) about 100 miles to the SW. Mbini is mainly tropical forest, with a coastal plain rising gradually to over 3000 ft (1000 m) in the interior; Bioko is dominated by three extinct volcanoes, the highest of which reaches 9865 ft (3007 m). The inhabitants are mainly *Fang, Fernandinos, and the indigenous Bubi (descendants of slaves from West Africa), who inhabit Bioko. *Economy*: chiefly agricultural, the main crops being cocoa on Bioko, and coffee in Mbini, where timber is also produced. There is little industry, apart from fish processing on Bioko; the main exports are coffee and cocoa. *History*: formerly a Spanish colony, the area became two Spanish provinces in 1959. The country attained some internal self-government in 1964 and was one of the last of the African colonial territories to become independent (in 1968). In 1975 Nigerian immigrant workers were expelled after 50 years in the country, and this has had an adverse effect on the economy. In 1979 the life president Francisco Macías Nguema (1924–79) was overthrown and executed in a coup led by Lt Col Teodoro Obiang Nguema Mbasogo. In 1982 voters approved a constitution, hailed as one of the most liberal in Africa, with guarantees of human rights and universal suffrage. In 1983 an abortive coup was mounted against the Obiang government, indicative of unrest in the country. The government subsequently held the country's first elections in 19 years. Official language: Spanish. Official currency: ekuele of 100 céntimos. Area: 10,831 sq mi (28,051 sq km). Population (1983 est): 268,000. Capital and main port: Malabo (formerly Santa Isabel).

equestrianism The art of horsemanship. As a sport, governed by the Fédération équestre internationale (founded 1921), it involves *dressage, *showjumping, and *horse trials.

equinox Either of the two points at which the *ecliptic intersects the celestial equator (*see* celestial sphere). The ecliptic represents the apparent annual path of the sun around the celestial sphere. The sun crosses the celestial equator from S to N at the **vernal** (*or* spring) **equinox**, usually on March 21. It crosses from N to S at the **autumnal equinox**, usually on Sept 23. At the equinoxes the center of the sun is above and below the horizon for equal lengths of time, and night and day are then of almost equal duration.

Equisetum. *See* horsetail.

equity In law, the body of rules applied by the courts to achieve a fair result in cases in which the application of ordinary law would fail to do so. The system developed in England and is followed in the US. The historical distinction between the *common law and equity is due to the failure of the common law to provide a remedy in certain cases, bringing about the custom of applying for redress to the king, who referred the question to the Lord Chancellor's court, the Court of Chancery. Here the rules of equity developed separately from but by the same method (judicial precedent) as the common law. Now all courts administer both law and equity, the rules of equity prevailing if in conflict with the common law.

equivalence The relationship between two mathematical or logical statements linked so that one is true if and only if the other is true. For example "*a* is greater than *b*" is equivalent to "*b* is less than *a*."

era. *See* geological time scale.

Era of Good Feeling (1817–25) A phrase used to describe the mood of the US during James *Monroe's administration. There were no political conflicts, isolationism was predominant, and the US no longer worried as much about European affairs.

Erasistratus of Ceos (3rd century BC) Greek physician, who discovered the difference between sensory and motor nerves and described the heart as part of a system carrying both air and blood to various parts of the body.

Erasmus, Desiderius (1466–1536) Christian humanist and writer, born at Rotterdam. He was perhaps the most influential of Renaissance thinkers and studied and taught all over Europe. His enthusiasm for learning was matched by his zeal for writing, and he produced many original works and compilations, including *Encomium Moriae* (*Praise of Folly*; 1509), written to amuse his host in England, Thomas *More. His translation of the Greek New Testament, the first ever, conclusively exposed the Vulgate as a secondhand document. He opposed dogmatism and priestly power, yet he never rejected Roman Catholic theology and steadfastly remained impartial throughout the Lutheran conflict with the papacy.

Erastianism The subjection of ecclesiastical affairs to secular authority. It is named for Thomas Erastus (1524–83), a Swiss theologian who opposed the strict views of *Calvinists. He argued that the civil authority has complete power in affairs both of church and state. Richard Hooker defended the argument in England in his *Ecclesiastical Polity* (1594). The *Church of England's subjection to the crown is sometimes described as Erastian.

Eratosthenes of Cyrene (c. 276–c. 194 BC) Greek astronomer; a close friend of *Archimedes. His greatest achievement was his calculation of the earth's circumference. His result, obtained by measuring the sun's position at the summer solstice at two different places, was accurate to within 600 miles.

Erbil. *See* Irbil.

erbium (Er) A lanthanide element, which like *yttrium, *ytterbium, and *terbium is named for Ytterby, a village in Sweden near which lanthanide-rich ores are found. It forms an oxide (Eb_2O_3) and halides (e.g. $EbCl_3$). It is added to phosphors, glasses, and alloys. At no 68; at wt 167.26; mp 881°F (1529°C); bp 1425°F (2510°C).

Ercilla, Alonso de (1533–94) Spanish poet. A courtier of *Philip II, he fought the Araucanian Indians in Chile. His epic *La Araucana* (Part I, 1569; Part 2, 1578; Part 3, 1589–90) is noted for its realistic descriptive passages and its sympathetic treatment of the Indians.

Erebus, Mount 77 40S 167 20E An active volcano on Ross Island, in the Antarctic. Discovered in 1841, it was climbed in 1908. Height: 12,520 ft (3794 m).

Eretria An ancient Greek city in *Euboea. An early leader in commerce and colonization, Eretria was defeated by *Chalcis about 700 BC, after which it declined in importance. The Persians sacked Eretria in 490 BC. It was rebuilt and later joined the *Delian League, but it never regained its former significance.

Erevan. *See* Yerevan.

Erfurt 50 59N 11 00E A city in SW East Germany, on the Gera River. One of the oldest German cities, it became a member of the Hanseatic League in the 15th century and was of great commercial importance in the 16th century. Notable buildings include the cathedral (1154–1476) and the 13th-century Church of St Severus. Its university, established in 1392, was closed in 1816. Martin Luther studied there (1501–05). Industries include the manufacture of machinery, electrical equipment, textiles, and footwear. Population (1980 est): 210,687.

erg The unit of energy in the *c.g.s. system equal to the work done when a force of one dyne acts through a distance of one centimeter. 1 erg = 10^{-7} joule.

ergonomics The study of the psychological and physical factors that can be used to improve the design of both machines and systems for human use. In the US the term human-factors engineering is widely used and in other parts of the world ergonomics is known as psychological engineering. The study finds application in many fields, including astronautics, the design of aircraft and cars, and a wide variety of industrial processes. Although it is a young science, having largely grown up since World War II, most university engineering courses now include it.

ergosterol. *See* vitamin D.

ergot A disease caused by the fungus *Claviceps purpurea*, which affects cereals and grasses, especially rye. In affected plants a hard black fungal body develops in place of the grain. Consumption of bread made with diseased grain produces the symptoms of **ergotism**—gangrene of the fingers and toes or convulsions. The gangrenous form of ergotism is accompanied by inflammation and pain in the affected part and in the middle ages it was called St Anthony's fire, since a pilgrimage to St Anthony's tomb was believed to result in a cure. Drugs obtained from ergot include ergometrine, used to induce childbirth, and ergotamine, for relieving migraine.

Erhard, Ludwig (1897–1977) German statesman and economist; Christian Democratic chancellor (1963–66). As minister for economic affairs (1949–63), he was largely responsible for the recovery of German industry after World War II. He succeeded Adenauer as chancellor and subsequently became honorary chairman of the Christian Democratic Party.

Erica. *See* heath.

Ericsson, John (1803–89) US naval engineer, born in Sweden, who in 1836 invented the screw propeller, which replaced paddle wheels in ships. Ericsson also designed the *ironclad *Monitor*, launched in 1862, which was the first warship to have an armored revolving turret. The *Monitor* defeated the Confederate ship *Merrimack* in the first battle between ironclads.

Eric the Red (late 10th century) Norwegian explorer. Exiled as a child with his father he was brought up in Iceland. In 982 he set out from Iceland on an exploration westward and reached Greenland, where he established the first European colony (c. 986). He was the father of *Leif Eriksson.

Eridanus A large constellation in the S sky, named for a river in ancient mythology. The only bright star is *Achernar.

Eridu A city of ancient *Sumer, SW of *Ur (S Iraq), continuously occupied from around 5000 to 600 BC. Excavations (1946–49) revealed a *ziggurat, probably devoted to the worship of Eridu's patron deity *Ea.

Erie North American Iroquoian-speaking Indian tribe found in W New York and N Ohio. Known as the Cat Nation or Panther People, the approximately 15,000 Erie were basically an agricultural people. Spurred on by their neighbors, the Hurons, who had been devastated by the Iroquois, and by threats of Iroquois expansion, the Erie waged an unsuccessful war (1656) against the Iroquois. Severely reduced in numbers, the tribe's remaining members were taken in by the Seneca.

Erie 42 07N 80 05W A city in the US, in Pennsylvania on Lake Erie. Founded in 1753, it is a Great Lakes port and ships coal, timber, iron, and grain. Its manufactures include paper and electrical equipment. Population (1980): 119,123.

Erie, Lake The fourth largest of the Great Lakes in North America, between Canada and the US. Linked with Lake Ontario via the Welland Ship Canal, it forms part of the St Lawrence Seaway system. Its shallow depth causes rapid freezing and it is closed to navigation during winter. Area: 9930 sq mi (25,718 sq km).

Erie Canal A canal that crosses central New York from Albany in E to Buffalo in the W. Built between 1817 and 1825, the canal was 363 mi (585 km) long, 40 ft (13 m) wide and 4 ft (1.3 m) deep, and had 83 locks and 18 aqueducts. It begins on the Hudson River and runs along one of its tributaries, the Mohawk. The early canal revolutionized the freight business, lowering rates 90%. Competition from railroads forced enlargement of the canal, but it was not until after 1909 that the canal was large enough for barges and became the principal part of the New York State Barge Canal System. Today, due to rerouting through Lake Oneida, the canal is 340 mi (548 km) long; it is 150 ft (46 m) wide and 12 ft (3.7 m) deep.

Erigena, John Scotus (c. 800–c. 877 AD) Medieval philosopher, probably born in Ireland. He is said to have traveled widely and after about 846 lived under the protection of Charles the Bald in France, where he was appointed head of the court school at Paris. He defied ecclesiastical orthodoxy in his writings on predestination and cosmology, which show leanings toward *Neoplatonism, *Pelagianism, and *pantheism.

Erik XIV (1533–77) King of Sweden (1560–68), whose ambitions in the Baltic led to an inconclusive war with Denmark (1563–70). He unsuccessfully sought marriage with Elizabeth I of England. After becoming insane, he was deposed and imprisoned.

Erinyes (or Furies) In Greek legend, spirits of vengeance who lived in the underworld and ruthlessly pursued all evildoers. They were three in number and were named (in later writers) Allecto, Tisiphone, and Megaera. In Roman legend they were known as the Furies (Latin *Furiae* or *Dirae*). See also Eumenides.

Eris A Greek goddess personifying strife. She was the sister of *Ares. She threw a golden apple inscribed "To the Fairest" among the gods at the wedding feast of Peleus and Thetis. Aphrodite, Hera, and Athena each claimed the apple. The decision was referred to *Paris, who chose Aphrodite because she offered him in return the most beautiful woman as his wife. This myth, known as the Judgment of Paris, explains the origin of the *Trojan War.

Eritrea A province in Ethiopia, bordering on the Red Sea. It consists of a narrow coastal plain rising inland to the Ethiopian plateau. Locusts and water shortage limit agricultural production, which has also been adversely affected by the recent political upheavals. *History*: made an Italian colony in 1890, it became the base for the Italian invasions of Ethiopia. The area came under British administration in 1941 and was federated as an autonomous unit of Ethiopia in 1952. In 1962 it became an integral part of the Ethiopian empire giving rise to political discontent. During the 1970s this developed into a bloody civil war; many major towns, as well as most of the countryside, fell into the hands of the secessionists but the Ethiopian government, anxious to retain its only two ports (Assab and Massawa), was unwilling to yield to demands for complete independence. In May 1978, a major government offensive backed by Soviet and Cuban aid was carried out, in which most towns were recaptured. The separatists continued to operate from their bases in the countryside. Area: 45,405 sq mi (117,600 sq km).

Erlangen 49 36N 11 02E A city in SE West Germany, in Bavaria on the Regnitz River. The university, shared with Nuremburg, was moved here from Bayreuth in 1743. Its manufactures include electrical equipment and textiles. Population (1980 est): 100,900

Erlanger, Joseph (1874–1965) US physiologist, who, with Herbert *Gasser, developed techniques for recording the electrical impulses in nerve fibers using a cathode-ray oscilloscope. They demonstrated that the conduction rate of impulses depends on the thickness of the fiber and its function and that different fibers transmit different types of impulses, represented by different waveforms. Erlanger and Gasser shared the 1944 Nobel Prize for this work.

ermine A *stoat in its white winter coat. At the onset of winter in northern latitudes, the brown coat is molted, leaving a pure white coat except for the tip of the tail: excellent camouflage on snow-covered ground.

Ermine Street A Roman road built (43–50 AD) along the route now followed by the A1 between London and the River Humber, as part of the military communications system of Roman Britain.

Ernst, Max (1891–1976) German artist, born in Brühl. At first a philosophy and psychiatric student at Bonn University, he achieved artistic prominence in 1919 as a founder of the Cologne *dada movement. He excelled in collage, particularly of cut-out illustrations, and became a leading practitioner of *surrealism in Paris. He invented the technique of frottage, whereby pencil rubbings of leaves, wood graining, cloth, etc., were used to suggest images of the unconscious mind. In 1941 he moved to the US.

Eros (astronomy) An asteroid (about 12 mi [20 km] diameter) that moves in a highly elliptical orbit and in 1975 passed within 14 million mi (23 million km) of earth.

Eros (mythology) The Greek god of love, the son of Aphrodite by Zeus, Hermes, or Ares. He was usually portrayed as a winged youth armed with bow and arrows. He was identified with the Roman Cupid.

Erse. *See* Gaelic.

Erté (Romain de Tirtoff; 1892–) French fashion illustrator and designer, born in Russia. He worked for the US magazine *Harper's Bazaar* (1916–37) and designed extravagant costumes and tableaux for the Folies-Bergère (1919–30) and other theaters. He later produced lithographs and sculpture.

erysipelas A skin infection caused by *Streptococcus* bacteria. It starts suddenly and usually on the face, which is red and hot, and the patient has a high fever. Penicillin quickly cures the infection.

erythrocyte (or red blood cell) A disk-shaped □blood cell, about 0.0003 in (0.007 mm) in diameter, that lacks a nucleus and contains *hemoglobin—a complex iron-bearing pigment responsible for the color of blood. Hemoglobin combines reversibly with oxygen and is the means by which blood transports oxygen from the lungs to the tissues. There are normally about 4.5 million erythrocytes per cubic millimeter of blood. A deficiency of red blood cells or hemoglobin is called *anemia.

Erzgebirge (English name: Ore Mountains; Czech name: Krušné Hory) A range of mountains extending about 81 mi (130 km) along the Czech-East German border between the Fichtelgebirge in the W and the Elbe River in the E. They have been heavily worked for silver, copper, lead, uranium, zinc, iron, and tin ores as well as coal and other minerals. They are also a popular tourist area.

Erzurum 39 57N 41 17E A city in NE Turkey, on the route from Ankara and Trabzon to Iran. Local products include handmade jewelry, and there is a university (1957). Population (1980): 190,241.

Esarhaddon King of Assyria (680–669 BC) in succession to his father *Sennacherib after defeating rivals for the throne. In about 674 he attacked Egypt, conquering it in 671.

Esbjerg 55 28N 8 28E The largest fishing port in Denmark, in the SW on the North Sea coast. Its exports include fish, fish products, meat, and dairy products. Population (1981 est): 79,694.

escalation clause A provision in an industrial contract that allows the contractor to increase his price if his costs exceed a stated limit. Escalation clauses are widely used for long-term projects in a time of inflation.

escalator An automatic moving stairway for transporting passengers from one level to another. Escalators consist of a continuous moving belt of metal stairs, usually driven by an electric motor. The stairs move on tracks between two handrails moving at the same speed. At the top and bottom landings the stairs flatten out and pass through metal combs to dislodge small objects. They are generally about 5 ft (1.6 m) wide and move at 10–12 ft (3–3.5 m) per second.

escape velocity The initial velocity required by a projectile to enable it, without any further source of power, to escape from the gravitational field of the earth or a celestial body. The escape velocity varies with the mass and diameter of the body but not with the mass of the projectile. It is also independent of the angle of launch. For the earth the escape velocity is

36,745 ft (11,200 m) per second and for the moon, 7776 ft (2370 m) per second.

Escaut River. *See* Scheldt River.

eschatology (Greek *eschatos*: last) The part of Christian theology concerned with the last things, often summarized as death, judgment, heaven, and hell. It refers to the ultimate fate of both the individual and of human society. Eschatological writing is common to both Old and New Testaments, where it is linked with the expectation of a coming Messiah. The teaching of Christ has also been explained as based on the assumption that the end of the world was imminent and that consequently a concern with the last things was urgent. Recent theological work has attempted to restore the relevance of these concepts in a less mythologically inclined world.

Esch-Cummins Act (1920) A US act that consolidated the railroads under private operation. The US government had controlled the railroads during World War I. Although the railroads returned to private hands, the Interstate Commerce Commission controlled the rate structure, the sale of stocks in the lines, and profit spending under the terms of the act.

Escobedo v. Illinois (1964) US Supreme Court decision that ruled that an accused person who is refused right of counsel has been denied constitutional rights. Danny Escobedo, accused of murder, was not allowed to consult with his lawyer and was not informed of his right to remain silent. A statement given by him during this period was used in court as major evidence that led to his conviction. The court ruled that the statement could not be used as evidence.

Escoffier, Auguste (1846–1935) French chef. He gained an international reputation while supervising the kitchens at the Savoy and the Carlton hotels in London. He was made a member of the Légion d'Honneur in 1920.

Escorial, El A royal palace, mausoleum, and monastery near Madrid. Built for Philip II beween 1563 and 1584, El Escorial is an austere, square, granite building, measuring 530 ft (162 m) by 670 ft (204 m). Philip himself was probably actively concerned in the design, which was begun by Juan Bautista de Toledo (d. 1567) and completed by Juan de *Herrera. El Escorial houses a magnificent collection of books and paintings.

Esdraelon, Plain of (*or* Valley of Jezreel; Hebrew name: 'Emeq Yizre'el) A lowland area in N Israel, stretching SE from Mount Carmel. In ancient times it was a major commercial route and contains the ancient site of Megiddo. It was swampy until drainage and settlement began in 1921.

Esdras, Books of Two books of the *Apocrypha purporting to be by *Ezra. The first is a compilation of various documents, giving a largely parallel account of events recorded in Chronicles, Ezra, and Nehemiah, but adding a legend explaining how King Darius of Persia was persuaded to permit the rebuilding of the Temple at Jerusalem. The second contains details of several visions consoling the Jews in their suffering and promising them a glorious future.

Esfahan. *See* Isfahan.

esker An elongated ridge consisting chiefly of sands and gravels deposited by glaciers. Once the bed of a stream flowing beneath or in a glacier, eskers are left behind once the ice has melted or retreated. They may extend for hundreds of miles.

Eskilstuna 59 22N 16 31E A city in SE Sweden. A center of the iron and steel industries, its manufactures include machinery, precision instruments, electrical equipment, and cutlery. Population (1978 est): 90,354.

Eskimo A Mongoloid people of the Arctic region of North America and Greenland. Traditionally, the men are hunters of seals, whales, walrus, and caribou, using harpoons, canoes (*or* kayaks), dogs, and sleds. Fishing is also important. Their clothes, made by the women, are of animal skins. Only some of the many different groups build the familiar snow dwellings (igloos). Others construct semisubterranean sod shelters or use snow-covered skin tents. There is no overall sense of identity among them and the main units are small family bands. Their small ivory or stone carvings are highly prized. Modern Eskimo have abandoned much of their traditional ways, adopting the life styles of the Americans and Canadians.

Eskimo-Aleut languages A language group, sometimes included in the classification of American Indian languages. It consists of two distinct languages: Eskimo, spoken in Greenland and in many dialects along the N coast of Canada, and *Aleut, spoken in the Aleutian Islands.

Eskimo dog. *See* husky.

Eskişehir 39 46N 30 30E A city in W Turkey, W of Ankara. Its warm springs are well known, and pipes are made from the local meerschaum deposits. There is a university (1973). Population (1980): 309,431.

esophagus The gullet: a muscular tube, about 10 in (25 cm) long, running from the pharynx at the back of the mouth to the stomach. Contractions of the esophagus propel swallowed food toward the stomach: the food is lubricated with mucus secreted by the walls of the esophagus.

ESP. *See* extrasensory perception.

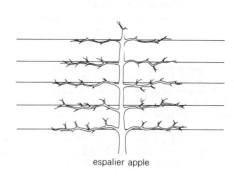

espalier apple

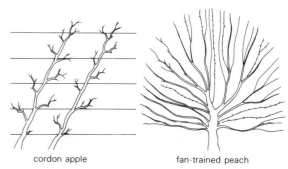

cordon apple   fan-trained peach

ESPALIER *Espalier and cordon apple trees are trained to bring the fruiting stems within arm's reach. Peach trees are particularly suitable for fan training on wires in greenhouses.*

espalier A shrub or tree, especially a fruit tree, that is trained to grow flat against a wall or a framework of wood, iron, or wire to support the fruit-laden branches and facilitate picking the crop. The branches are usually arranged in ladder-like tiers. Other methods result in a fanlike arrangement of branches or a single stem (cordon).

esparto A perennial *grass, *Stipa tenacissima*, also known as alfa or halfa, native to Spain and N Africa, where it is cultivated. It grows in sharp pointed tufts, up to 40 in (1 m) high, and is used to make paper, cord, and rope.

Esperanto An artificial language invented by a Polish philologist, L. L. Zamenhof (1859–1917), in 1887. It was intended to be a universal medium of communication and is indeed the most successful artificial language, being spoken by over 100,000 people. Grammatically it is entirely regular, its pronunciation is consistent with its spelling, and as well as grammatical rules it has the potential for the formation of new words. The rules of the language are laid down in Zamenhof's *Fundamento de Esperanto* (1905).

Espionage Act (1917) An act of Congress to punish any acts intended to interfere with the US effort during World War I. The Department of Justice was given the authority to censor, to survey and confiscate the mails, and to deport those it felt were undesirable.

Espoo (Swedish name: Esbo) 60 10N 24 42E A city in S Finland, just W of Helsinki. It serves mainly as a dormitory town for the capital. Population (1980): 137,409.

ESRO. *See* European Space Research Organization.

essay A short literary prose composition in which a subject is discussed in a personal manner. The word *essai* was coined by *Montaigne, whose *Essais* (1580) are informal and intimate discussions of such subjects as vanity and idleness. In contrast, Francis Bacon's *Essays* (1597) were formal treatments of weighty topics. During the 18th and 19th centuries the literary periodicals provided an outlet for the essays of *Addison, *Steele, *Lamb, and *De Quincey. Among well-known later essayists are Max *Beerbohm, Virginia *Woolf, and Aldous *Huxley.

Essen 51 27N 6 57E A city in W West Germany, in North Rhine-Westphalia near the Ruhr River. The 9th-century cathedral survived the bombing of World War II. Formerly the site of the Krupp steelworks, it is now the administrative center of the *Ruhr. Population (1980 est): 650,200.

Essenes An ancient Jewish sect active between the 2nd century BC and the 2nd century AD in Palestine. Information about them is fragmentary and inconsistent. They seem to have stressed personal purity and asceticism. Many scholars think that the *Dead Sea Scrolls are relics of an Essene community.

essential oils Substances with a characteristic scent produced by the glands of aromatic plants. Essential oils may be extracted by distillation, mechanical pressing, or organic solvents and are used in perfumes, food flavorings, and medicines. Examples include attar of roses, lavender oil, and clove oil.

Essequibo River A river in Guyana, rising on the Brazilian border and flowing generally N to enter the Atlantic Ocean, draining over half of Guyana. Length: 630 mi (1014 km).

Essex, Robert Devereux, 2nd Earl of (?1566–1601) English soldier and courtier to Elizabeth I. He was appointed Master of the Horse (1587) after distinguishing himself against Spain. He commanded an expedition (1591–92) sent to aid Henry IV of France and in 1593 became a privy councillor; he took part in the sack of Cádiz (1596). He was dismissed (1600) after failing to suppress an Irish rebellion and in 1601 raised a riot in London, for which he was executed.

Esslingen 48 45N 9 19E A city in SW West Germany, in Baden-Württemberg on the Neckar River. It is noted for its gothic church (1321–1516) and its wines. Population (1971 est): 87,500.

estate The total property owned by an individual upon his death. Consisting of both real and personal property, it is distributed, often in accordance with the terms of a will, after the owner's death.

Este An Italian princely family of Lombard origin, which under **Obizzo II** (1264–93) gained control of Ferrara, Modena, and Reggio. His successors maintained control of these three regions in spite of papal opposition and were a dominant force in Italian Renaissance politics and culture until Ferrara was incorporated into the papal states in 1598. The Estensi continued to hold Reggio until the French invasion of 1796 and Modena until the unification of Italy in the mid 19th century.

The **Villa d'Este**, at Tivoli, near Rome, was designed (1550) for Cardinal Ippolito II d'Este (1509–72).

Esterházy A family prominent in Hungarian affairs from the 16th to 19th centuries. **Miklós Esterházy** (1582–1645) became imperial governor of Hungary in 1625. His son **Prince Pál Esterházy** (1635–1713) held command against the Turks and became a prince of the Holy Roman Empire (1687). Pál's grandson **Prince Miklós József Esterházy** (1714–90) rebuilt the family castle, Esterháza, and employed Haydn for 30 years. Miklós József's grandson **Prince Miklós Esterházy** (1765–1833) fought against the French in the Napoleonic Wars and accumulated an outstanding art collection. Miklós' son **Prince Pál Antal Esterházy** (1786–1866), a diplomat, was foreign minister in 1848.

esters Organic compounds produced by the reaction of an alcohol with an acid, with the elimination of water. Common organic esters are formed from carboxylic acids and have the general formula R.CO.OR″. The lighter ones often have a pleasant smell and taste and are widely used in perfumes and flavorings. Fats are triesters of long-chain carboxylic acids and glycerol. See saponins; soaps.

Esther An Old Testament woman who became the queen of the Persian King Ahasuerus. **The Book of Esther** recounts an event in Persia during the reign of *Xerxes I (called Ahasuerus in the text), when Esther used her influence to frustrate a plot to massacre the Jews. The deliverance leads to the establishment of the Jewish feast of *Purim.

Estienne (or Étienne; Latin name: Stephanus) A French family of printers and scholars, who published important classical, lexicographical, and theological works. **Henri Estienne** (c. 1465–1520) established the firm in Paris (c. 1502). His son **Robert Estienne** (1503–59) was printer to Francis I but because of political pressure moved the firm to Geneva (1551). Robert's son **Henri Estienne** (1528–98), a renowned scholar, continued the firm in Geneva.

Estonian A language of the Baltic-Finnic branch of the Finno-Ugric division of the Uralic language family. It is spoken by the Estonians, who number about one million people in the Estonian SSR in the Soviet Union.

It is related to Finnish with which it shares the distinctive characteristic of distinguishing three degrees of consonant and vowel length. The written language is based on a northern dialect, Tallinn, and has a literature dating from the 16th century.

Estonian Soviet Socialist Republic (or Estonia) A constituent republic in the NW Soviet Union. Estonia has many lakes and includes numerous islands in the Baltic Sea. Some 70% of the population are Estonians. Fishing is an important occupation, the main catch being herring. Other industries include machine building, radio engineering, and the processing of shale—the most important mineral deposit, from which gas is produced, supplying Leningrad. Pig breeding is the chief agricultural activity and the main crops are barley, oats, and potatoes. *History*: in the 13th century the N was occupied by the Danes and the S by the Livonian Knights (a German order of knighthood). The Danes withdrew in 1346 and the Knights were replaced by the Swedes in the 16th and 17th centuries. Estonia was ceded to Russia in 1721. Rebellions in the 19th century culminated in a declaration of independence (1918), which was recognized by Soviet Russia in 1920. It was assigned to the Soviet Union by the Nazi-Soviet Pact (1939) and became an SSR in 1940. It was occupied by Germany in World War II. Its status is not accepted by the US. Area: 17,410 sq mi (45,100 sq km). Population (1981 est): 1,500,000. Capital: Tallinn.

Estoril 38 42N 9 23W A seaside resort in W Portugal, on the Atlantic Ocean. It has an outstanding avenue of palm trees between its casino and the seafront. Population (1971 est): 15,740.

estrogen A group of steroid hormones that function principally as female sex hormones. The most important estrogens in mammals are estradiol and estrone. Produced by the ovaries under the influence of pituitary *gonadotrophins, they promote the development of the reproductive organs and secondary sexual characteristics (such as enlargement of breasts) at puberty and regulate the changes of the menstrual cycle (see menstruation). Estrogens are also produced by the placenta, adrenal glands, and testes. Synthetic estrogens are used in medicine to treat menstrual and menopausal disorders; they are also constituents of *oral contraceptives.

estrus The period of "heat" in the sexual cycle of female mammals, when the female will attract males and permit copulation. It corresponds to the time of ovulation, so that mating is most likely to result in pregnancy. The estrous cycle is similar to the menstrual cycle of women, except that the lining of the womb is not shed during estrus.

Esztergom 47 46N 18 42E A city in N Hungary, on the Danube River opposite the Czechoslovak town of Stúrovo. Stephen I was born and crowned king here. Population (1970 est): 26,955.

etching A method of making prints from a metal plate covered with an acid-resistant ground, on which a design is drawn with a needle. The plate is then placed in acid, the exposed lines being eaten away. These recessed lines retain ink and the design is transferred to the paper by rolling under pressure. Although the first dated etching was made in 1513, it was *Rembrandt who freed the medium from its technical and formal dependence on *engraving. The process continues to be widely used, with *Picasso among the leading 20th-century exponents.

Eteocles. See Polyneices.

ethane (C_2H_6) A colorless gas, the second member of the *alkane series. It occurs in *natural gas.

ethanol (or ethyl alcohol; C_2H_5OH) A colorless flammable liquid that is the active constituent of alcoholic drinks. It is prepared by fermentation or by the catalytic hydration of *ethylene. It is used as a solvent, a raw material for producing other chemicals, and a fuel. See also alcohol strength.

Ethelbert (c. 552–616 AD) King of Kent, who became overlord of all England south of the Humber. Encouraging the conversion of his people to Christianity, he received Augustine's mission from Rome. He wrote the first extant English code of laws.

Ethelred I (d. 871 AD) King of England (866–71), in whose reign the Vikings launched a full-scale invasion of England. Ethelred died after his victory at Ashdown, leaving his brother *Alfred the Great to fight on.

Ethelred the Unready (968–1016) King of England (978–1016). In the face of Danish raids, he was forced to pay huge tributes (Danegeld) to the enemy. He was driven into exile by *Sweyn in 1013 but returned after Sweyn's death (1014), dying during *Canute's invasion of England (1015–16).

Ethelwulf (d. 858 AD) King of Wessex (839–58). Renowned for his military prowess, he reputedly defeated 350 Viking ships (851). Ethelwulf reduced taxation, endowed the Church, made lay lands heritable, and provided a system of poor relief.

ether Any member of the group of organic compounds with the general formula R–O–R″, which are formed by the condensation of two alcohols. Diethyl ether, $C_2H_5OC_2H_5$, often known simply as ether, is a volatile liquid made by treating *ethanol with concentrated sulfuric acid. It is used as an anesthetic and solvent.

Etherege, Sir George (c. 1635–c. 1692) English dramatist. A diplomat in Turkey from 1668 to 1671, he fled to Paris after the accession of William III. In his comedies of fashionable London life, *The Comical Revenge* (1664), *She Wou'd If She Cou'd* (1668), and *The Man of Mode* (1674), he introduced the comedy of manners to the British theater.

Ethical Culture movement A movement originating in New York in the late 19th century, developed by Felix Adler, to promote the importance of morality in all aspects of life. Adler hoped to encourage ethical behavior independent of religious belief, and thereby promote social reform.

ethics The science of morality, also called moral philosophy. It is one of the three main branches of modern *philosophy and seeks to discover a consistent principle by which human actions and character can be judged. Until about a century ago, ethics was prescriptive, aiming to guide men's conduct. Now it is more descriptive, attempting to discover how moral decisions are actually made. In ancient philosophy, *hedonism, which held that the greatest goal was happiness, and rationalism, which held that it was reason, were the rival schools. Plato and Aristotle combined hedonism and *rationalism. Medieval scholasticism took God's will as the sole ethical standard and grafted this onto Aristotelian ethics. After the Renaissance, pragmatists like *Hobbes, *Bentham, and John Stuart Mill (*see* Mill, James) developed *utilitarianism, in which the good of society rather than of the individual is the criterion. *Kant and other idealists were intuitionists, believing that conscience is to ethics as intelligence is to logic. Today utilitarianism is the implicit basis of commercial, legal, and social ethics, but conscience remains the guide of most individuals.

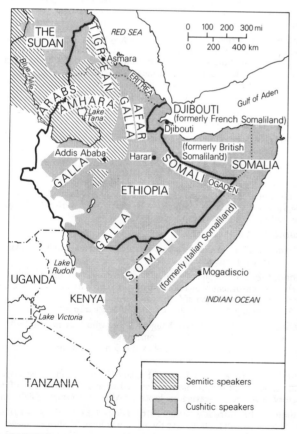

ETHIOPIA *Distribution of main ethnic groups.*

Ethiopia (former name: Abyssinia) A country in NE Africa, on the Red Sea. Ethiopia may be divided into four physiographical regions. The SE consists mostly of desert forming the Ogaden Plateau; further toward the center an elevated plateau region rises to heights of more than 14,000 ft (4250 m) and joins the Great Rift Valley, which constitutes a desert area;

the Ethiopian Plateau extends across the NW, consisting of highlands reaching over 15,000 ft (4570 m). The Blue Nile crosses the Ethiopian Plateau, where the majority of the population lives. The population consists of many ethnic groups, including the Galla and *Amhara. *Economy:* Ethiopia remains one of the poorest countries in the world and agriculture is chiefly at subsistence level. The situation has been worsened in recent years by serious crop failures, causing famines. All land was nationalized in 1975 and much of it is now farmed cooperatively, the main emphasis being on the development of the rural areas. Mineral resources are sparse, though there are small amounts of gold and platinum as well as salt in Eritrea. The disrupted *Ogaden region is thought to be a potential source of mineral wealth. Gas and oil are being explored and exploitation of the country's considerable potential for hydroelectricity has already begun. Some industries, such as textiles, cement, and food processing, are being encouraged. The main export is coffee. *History:* Ethiopia has a longer known history than any other country in Africa apart from Egypt and legend claimed the descent of its rulers from Solomon and the Queen of Sheba. From the 2nd to the 9th century AD the Aksumite Empire enjoyed considerable prosperity and expansion, in the 4th century Ethiopia became the first Christian country in Africa. This period was followed by centuries of struggles (especially with the Muslims) and of internal divisions. It was not until the 19th century that the country was once more reunited under Emperor Tewodros II. In 1896 Italian attempts to conquer it were defeated by *Menelik II. However, in 1935 Italy (under Mussolini) invaded Ethiopia. In spite of Anglo-French attempts (Hoare-Laval Pact) to arrange a settlement and League of Nations sanctions against Italy, in 1936 Addis Ababa fell and the emperor, *Haile Selassie, fled to England. For the next five years Ethiopia formed part of Italian East Africa (with Eritrea and Italian Somaliland). In 1941 the Allies liberated Ethiopia and Haile Selassie returned to the throne. Eritrea again became part of Ethiopia, becoming fully integrated in 1962. Haile Selassie was deposed in 1974 and a provisional military government came to power. After the execution of members of the ruling military council in 1977, the government became known as the Derg (Provisional Military Administrative Council) with Mengistu Haile Mariam as president. During this unsettled period liberation movements in Eritrea and the Somali-speaking Ogaden area seized the opportunity to increase their armed struggle against the government. By the end of 1977 Somali troops had occupied most of the Ogaden region but with the help of Soviet weapons and Cuban troops, Ethiopia regained control of the area. Encouraged by their victories over Somalia, the government launched a successful offensive against Eritrean secessionists (May, 1978), recapturing most of the major towns held by guerrilla forces (*see* Eritrea). In the early 1980s drought led to crop failures, reaching a crisis in 1984, when famine became widespread. An international airlift was organized to bring food to the starving nation. Official language: Amharic; English is widely spoken. Official religion: Ethiopian Orthodox (Coptic). Official currency: birr of 100 cents. Area: 386,000 sq mi (1,000,000 sq km). Population (1983 est): 31,265,000. Capital: Addis Ababa. Main port: Massawa.

ethnology The comparative study and theory of contemporary cultures. In most current usages it is synonymous with cultural *anthropology. However, it has also been used to refer to the historical study of cultures, especially preliterate cultures, and sometimes as a synonym for social anthropology. It may be distinguished from ethnography, which is the descriptive study of culture and is less concerned with the development of theory.

ethology The study of animal behavior. Ethologists are concerned with how animals respond to signals or stimuli (whether from other animals, from their own bodies, or from the environment in which they live), how they sense these signals, and what their response means to other animals and to themselves. They demonstrate the interactions between the inherited (instinctive) aspects of behavior and those determined by experience (learning).

Ethology was founded in Europe in the 1930s by the work of Konrad *Lorenz and Niko *Tinbergen, who studied animals in their natural states. In the US the approach was one of comparative psychology, using laboratory animals under strict experimental conditions. The work of ethologists has provided insights into some aspects of human behavior.

ethyl alcohol. *See* ethanol.

ethylene (*or* ethene; C_2H_4) A colorless flammable gaseous *alkene. It is made by *cracking petroleum and is used to make *polythene (polyethylene). It is also used to ripen fruit artificially.

Etna, Mount 37 45N 15 00E A volcano in E Sicily, having a central crater and over 200 subsidiaries. The first recorded eruption was in 476 BC and significant eruptions this century have occurred in 1928, 1949, and 1971. The coastal town of Catania, 17 mi (28 km) away, has been engulfed twice. Height: 10,705 ft (3263 m).

Eton 51 31N 0 37W A town in SE England, in Berkshire opposite Windsor on the River Thames. Eton College, the famous private school, was founded by Henry VI in 1440. Population (1981): 3523.

Etruria The region of ancient Italy N of Rome, approximating modern Tuscany. Occupied first by *Villanovan peoples, Etruria was inhabited by the *Etruscans from the 8th century BC but by the 3rd century BC had come under Roman control.

Etruscans The ancient inhabitants of Etruria (now Tuscany) in central Italy. From the 8th to the 5th centuries BC their cities, forming a loose political confederacy, dominated their neighbors but after 396 they were rapidly absorbed by the Romans. The Etruscans' origins are mysterious; certain Oriental traits in their artifacts and the frescoes decorating their tombs suggest that they were invaders from Asia Minor, but such traits may have arisen through their extensive trading links. Their language was non-Indo-European and although many inscriptions are known and the alphabet is not dissimilar to ancient Greek, it is still untranslated.

etymology The study of the history of words, in which words are traced back to their earliest recorded forms and, where sufficient evidence exists, even beyond these to hypothetical reconstructed forms. Most English words are derived either from Proto-Germanic (see Germanic languages) or from Latin and French. Many learned English words were taken from Greek or made up from Greek elements, while in the past 200 years English has come to borrow words from languages in every part of the world.

Euboea (Modern Greek name: Évvoia; former English name: Negropont) The second largest Greek island, in the W Aegean Sea. It is separated from the mainland for most of its length by only a narrow channel and rises to 5719 ft (1743 m) at Mount Delphi. Sheep and cattle are raised and grapes, figs, olives, and cereals, grown. Area: 1509 sq mi (3908 sq km). Population (1971): 165,369. Chief town: Chalcis.

Eucalyptus A genus of tropical and subtropical evergreen trees (about 600 species) native to Australia but widely cultivated elsewhere. Eucalypts—also known as gum trees and stringybarks—are among the tallest trees in the world, 300–325 ft (90–100 m) high. The blue-gray bark is smooth and often peeling and the mature leaves are long and narrow (young leaves are rounded or oblong). The flowers are showy, with tiny petals and a fluffy mass of red or white stamens. The fruit is a woody pod. Fast-growing and drought-resistant, eucalypts are important sources of timber. The wood is used as fuel and for buildings and fencing; the bark for paper making and tanning. The best known species are the *blue gum and the red gum (E. ficifolia). Because they take up much water, eucalypts are used to reclaim marshy land. They are also used for street planting. All parts of the trees contain essential oils (oil of eucalyptus comes from blue gum leaves). Some species are shrubby and are known as *mallees. Family: Myrtaceae (myrtle family).

Eucharis A genus of bulb-forming South American plants (10 species), called Amazon lilies. Up to 24 in (60 cm) tall, they have clusters of large fragrant white flowers, up to 5 in (13 cm) across, with protruding slender stamens and six backward curling white sepals. The plants are grown for ornament in greenhouses. Family: Amaryllidaceae.

Eucharist (Greek eucharistia: thanksgiving) The chief *sacrament and central act of worship of the Christian Churches. Also known as Holy Communion, the Lord's Supper, and the Mass, its institution is described in the three Synoptic Gospels. At the last meal of Christ and the apostles, bread and wine were blessed by Christ and shared, representing his death on the cross and the subsequent redemption of mankind. Differing interpretations have been placed on the sense in which Christ is held to be present in the sacrament (see consubstantiation; transubstantiation).

Eucken, Rudolf Christoph (1846–1926) German writer. He upheld idealist metaphysics against 19th-century positivism and materialism and sought to isolate the spiritual content of historical movements. He won the Nobel Prize for literature in 1908.

Euclid (c. 300 BC) Greek mathematician, famous for his book entitled Elements in which he derived all that was known of geometry from a few simple axioms. The geometry that obeys Euclid's axioms is known as *Euclidean geometry, all other kinds being called *non-Euclidean.

Euclidean geometry A system of geometry based on the axioms contained in *Euclid's Elements. In Euclidean geometry, parallel lines never meet and the angles in a triangle always add up to 180°. The geometry of physical space can be assumed for most purposes to be Euclidean. The surface of a sphere, however, is non-Euclidean. Compare non-Euclidean geometry.

Eudoxus of Cnidus (c. 408–c. 355 BC) Greek astronomer and mathematician, who studied under Plato and later founded a school, first on the NW coast of Asia Minor and then in Athens. He studied the motions of the planets and derived many geometric proofs, some of which were later incorporated by *Euclid in his Elements.

Eugene 44 02N 123 05W A city in W central Oregon, on the W bank of the Willamette River. The Universty of Oregon, established in 1872, is here. Lumber and food products are its main produce. Population (1980): 105 624.

Eugène of Savoy, Prince (1663–1736) Austrian general. Born in Paris, he was refused a commission by Louis XIV and entered the service of Emperor Leopold I. He fought outstandingly against the Turks, winning victories at Zenta (1697), which freed Hungary of Turkish domination, Peterwardein (1716), and Belgrade (1717). In the War of *Austrian Succession (1701–14), he won, with Marlborough, the victories of *Blenheim (1704), Oudenaarde (1708), and Malplaquet (1709).

eugenics The science that studies the inheritable factors that determine the physical and mental qualities of the human race, with the aim of improving the quality of life for future generations. The term was first coined by Sir Francis *Galton in 1883. Eugenics is now concerned primarily with the detection and—where possible—elimination of such genetic diseases as Down's syndrome with the aid of *prenatal diagnosis.

Eugénie (1826–1920) The influential wife (1853–73) of *Napoleon III of France. She several times acted as his regent and encouraged French intervention in Mexico. After the fall of the Empire (1870) she retired to England.

Euglena A genus of single-celled microorganisms found chiefly in fresh water. They are spindle-shaped, with a flexible cell wall (pellicle) and a gullet from which protrudes a long whiplike flagellum, used for locomotion. Some species contain chlorophyll or other pigments and can manufacture food by photosynthesis; others feed on small organisms, such as bacteria. Euglenas are regarded by some authorities as algae and by others as protozoans of the class Flagellata. □Protozoa.

Eulenspiegel, Till A German peasant folk hero, a crafty and often savage joker whose exploits inspired numerous folktales and many literary and musical works, notably the epic poem by Gerhard *Hauptmann (1928) and the tone poem by Richard *Strauss.

Euler, Leonhard (1707–83) German mathematician, widely regarded as the greatest mathematician of the 18th century and certainly the most prolific of all time, writing some 800 papers during his lifetime. Many more were published posthumously. He did much work on the number e, the base of natural *logarithms, which is often known as **Euler's number**. He gave that number its symbol, and introduced the symbol i for the square root of −1 and also the notation $f(x)$ for a function of the variable x.

Eumenides (Greek: the kindly ones) In Greek legend, spirits identical with the *Erinyes. After *Orestes was acquitted by the Areopagus of his mother's murder, the pursuing Erinyes became known as the Eumenides.

Euonymus A genus of widely distributed trees, shrubs, and woody climbers (176 species), often grown as ornamentals for their attractive foliage (often with striking autumn colors) and fruits, which are surrounded by a bright-pink or orange fleshy coat (aril). The genus includes the *spindle tree. Family: Celastraceae.

euphonium Brass instrument with a wide conical bore, a cup-shaped mouthpiece, four valves, and a range of about three and a half octaves above the B flat below middle C. Its range is equivalent to that of a tenor *tuba and it is much used in the brass band.

Euphorbia A worldwide genus of herbs and small trees (1600 species), having clusters of small flowers each surrounded by conspicuous petal-like bracts. The genus includes some ornamental shrubs (see crown of thorns; poinsettia; snow-on-the-mountain). The herbaceous euphorbias are known as *spurges. Family: Euphorbiaceae.

Euphrates River A river in SW Asia, rising in E Turkey and flowing SE through Syria into Iraq. 118 mi (190 km) from the Persian Gulf, it joins the Tigris River to form the Shatt al-Arab. It flows past the historic sites of Babylon, Ur, Nippur, and Sippara. Length: 1678 mi (2700 km).

Euphronios (late 6th–early 5th centuries BC) Athenian red-figure potter and vase painter. He signed some 15 surviving vases and is mentioned as a rival by another painter. His drawing shows skill in composition and an interest in characterization.

Eupolis (late 5th century BC) Greek dramatist, a rival of *Aristophanes. His lively and scurrilous comedies satirized contemporary politicians and socialites. Only fragments of his works survive.

Eurasia Europe and Asia considered as one land mass. Geographically, Europe is a peninsula of the Asian continent, with the Ural Mountains generally taken as the dividing line.

EURATOM. *See* European Atomic Energy Community.

eurhythmics A system of teaching music by developing the student's physical response to rhythm. Devised by *Jaques-Dalcroze in about 1905, it has since been used in physical education, *ballet and *modern dance training, and even in mental education because it improves the student's concentration. The student is taught a series of body movements to express different musical rhythms; he is then encouraged to improvise his movements.

Euripides (c. 480–406 BC) Greek dramatist, the third (after *Aeschylus and *Sophocles) of the three major writers of Attic tragedy. According to tradition he was born in Salamis on the day Xerxes' fleet was defeated in the famous battle. In 408 he went to the court of Archelaus in Macedonia, where he remained for the rest of his life. Of approximately 90 plays, 19 survive, including the tragedies *Medea* (431), *Hippolytus* (428), *Electra* (415), *The Trojan Women* (415), *The Bacchae* (405), and *Iphigenia at Aulis* (405). His technical innovations included naturalistic dialogue and a diminution of the role of the chorus. He had a deep interest in feminine psychology and his women, both virtuous and evil, are strongly characterized. His critical attitude toward traditional religion in some of the plays, which offended his contemporaries, is balanced by incidents portraying real heroism and lyrical passages of great beauty.

Eurodollars An international currency based on US dollar balances held by banks outside the US. The Eurodollar market developed from 1957 onward as persistent US *balance-of-payments deficits (largely due to foreign aid and investment programs) led to a large outflow of dollars, which were put to use in Europe often to finance international trade. Oil-producing countries often have large holdings of Eurodollars, which they may move between investment centers in order to take advantage of the highest interest rates. Eurodollars and other expatriate currencies together make up the Eurocurrency market, which deals in large amounts of short-term funds the volatility and freedom from government control of which may at times pose a threat to the stability of international money markets.

Europa In Greek legend, the daughter of King Agenor of Tyre. She was carried to Crete by Zeus in the form of a bull and bore him three sons: Minos, Rhadamanthus, and Sarpedon.

Europe A continent bordering on the Arctic Ocean (N), the Atlantic Ocean (W), and the Mediterranean Sea (S); the Ural Mountains, the Ural River, and the Caspian Sea form its E boundary. Europe is the second (after Australasia) smallest continent but owing perhaps to its latitude and geography has exerted a disproportionate influence on the rest of the world. It comprises a peninsula of the land mass of Eurasia and all geological eras have contributed to its formation. Its long coastline is much indented with several peninsulas (e.g. Scandinavia, Italy) and offshore islands (e.g. the British Isles, Iceland). A central plain, extending from the Ural Mountains to the Atlantic Ocean and divided by uplands and the English Channel, comprises two thirds of the continent. It rises in the S to a series of mountain systems (e.g. the Pyrenees, Alps, Apennines, Carpathian Mountains), and in the N to the mountainous region of Scandinavia and Scotland. The chief rivers flow from the Valdai Hills (e.g Volga, Don, Dnieper) or the Alps (e.g. Danube, Rhine, Rhône, Po). Its four **climatic zones** are characterized by mild winters, cool summers, and rain all the year round (NW); mild winters, hot summers, and chiefly spring and autumn rain (Mediterranean); cold winters, warm summers, and chiefly summer rain (Central Europe); and very cold winters (E Europe). **Vegetation zones** comprise, from N to S: tundra; a coniferous forest belt, predominantly of Scots pine and Norway spruce; a deciduous forest belt, notably of oak and hornbeam in the E and of oak, birch, and holly in the W, with beech in the central lowlands; and the mainly evergreen and scrub vegetation of the Mediterranean. Steppe and semidesert characterize the SE. Forest once covered some 80% of Europe but intense agriculture since the middle ages and industrialization since the 19th century have reduced it to 30% of the land mass. Europe possesses important mineral resources. Coalfields, especially in the UK, Germany, France, Belgium, and the Soviet Union, continue to be an important source of power, and oil and natural-gas reserves are found in the Soviet Union, Romania, Albania, and beneath the North Sea. Iron-ore deposits are found on a large scale only in the Soviet Union, which also has reserves of nickel, tin, and manganese, but nonmetallic minerals, including kaolinite and rock salt, occur widely. Europe's high-density population is concentrated on its industrial regions, which are found chiefly in a central belt extending from England, through N France, the Netherlands, and Germany, to Moscow; N Italy, however, is also densely populated. Most of the unusually large number of national groups in Europe speak an *Indo-European language. The European peoples may be subdivided into racial types (e.g. Nordic, Germanic, Alpine, and Mediterranean) but extensive intermixing has occurred. Christianity, in its various forms, is the dominant religion and has exerted a profound influence on European culture, which also continues to bear the imprint of the civilizations of ancient *Greece and Rome (*see* Roman Republic; Roman Empire). Nevertheless Europe's medieval and modern history is that of its diverse nations, conflicts between which culminated in the 20th century in the two World Wars. The postwar period has witnessed a split between the communist countries of E Europe, dominated by the Soviet Union, and the countries of W Europe, which have sought to resolve their rivalries by means of economic and, increasingly, political union (*see* European Economic Community). Area: about 4,000,000 sq mi (10,400,000 sq km). Population (1969 est): 458,067,000.

European Atomic Energy Community (EURATOM) An international organization founded in 1958 by the Treaty of Rome (1957) to promote and develop the peaceful uses of atomic energy in Europe. In 1967 the merger of EURATOM and the *European Coal and Steel Community with the EEC was begun.

European Broadcasting Union An organization founded in 1950 to improve radio and television communications. Its members include Cyprus, Greece, Iceland, Israel, Lebanon, Morocco, Tunisia, Turkey, and Yugoslavia, as well as all the W European nations.

European Coal and Steel Community (ECSC) A body established in 1952 to coordinate the production of coal and steel in France, Italy, West Germany, and the *Benelux countries. In 1967 the merger of the ECSC and the *European Atomic Energy Community with the EEC was begun.

European Economic Community (EEC *or* Common Market) An organization of W European States created by the Treaty of Rome (1957) to foster economic cooperation and common development with the eventual aim of economic, and a measure of political, unity. Agreements have been reached on the removal of customs tariffs between members, the setting of a Common Customs Tariff for imports from nonmember states, and the abolition of barriers to free movement of labor, services, and capital between member states. The original six signatories were Belgium, France, Italy, Luxembourg, the Netherlands, and West Germany. In 1973 the UK, Denmark, and the Republic of Ireland became members and Greece joined in 1981. In 1967 the merger of the *European Atomic Energy Community and the *European Coal and Steel Community with the EEC was initiated. The EEC implemented a *Common Agricultural Policy (CAP) in 1962 (modified in 1968) and a Common Fisheries Policy in 1983.

The Commission of the European Communities is in Brussels and consists of 14 members; its president is elected for a two-year term. The Commission acts as an advisory body to, and is responsible for implementing policy decided upon by, the Council of Ministers. Also in Brussels, the Council comprises ministers from the governments of the ten member countries. The ten heads of state meet triannually as the European Council. The European Parliament at Strasbourg comments on the Commission's legislative proposals; it must be consulted on the annual budgets and may dismiss the Commission. Members are (since 1979) elected by direct vote in the member countries and sit as political groups (e.g. Christian Democrats, Socialists) in the Parliament. The Court of Justice, at Luxembourg, ensures the observance of law in the interpretation of the treaties establishing the Communities.

European Free Trade Association (EFTA) An association of seven states (Austria, Finland (an associate member), Iceland, Norway, Portugal, Sweden, and Switzerland) founded in 1960 to foster free trade of industrial goods between members. Individual countries may negotiate independent trade agreements with nonmember states.

European Space Agency (ESA) An organization responsible for Europe's space program, formed in 1975 from the merger of the European Space Research Organization and the European Launcher Development Organization. There are 11 full-member nations. All ESA *satellites were launched by NASA before completion of the ESA launcher **Ariane**, the first successful launching of which took place in 1979.

European Space Research Organization (ESRO) An organization founded in 1962 to encourage space research among European states with particular emphasis on its exploitation for peaceful purposes. Activities include the development of scientific, meteorological, and telecommunications programs.

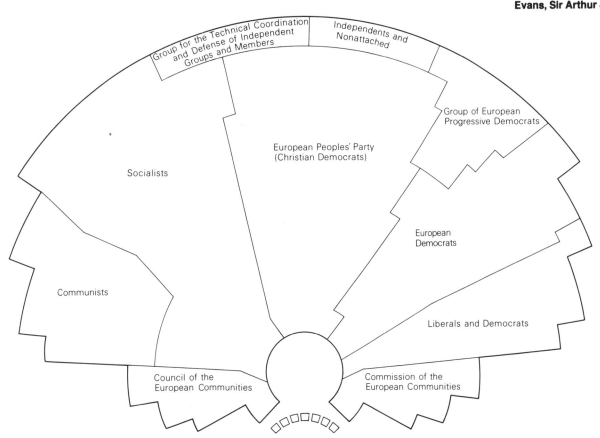

EUROPEAN ECONOMIC COMMUNITY *The plan of the chamber of the European Parliament, showing political groups and their relative strengths.*

europium (Eu)   A *lanthanide element, used in television-tube phosphors. It forms oxides (EuO, Eu_2O_3), and chlorides ($EuCl_2$, $EuCl_3$). At no 63; at wt 151.96; mp 488°F (822°C); 918°F (1597°C).

Europoort.   *See* Rotterdam.

Eurydice   In Greek legend, a *dryad, the wife of *Orpheus. She died of a snake bite. Orpheus descended to the underworld to recover her but lost her forever when he violated the condition of her release and turned to look at her before emerging.

eurypterid   An extinct *arthropod, also called water scorpion, belonging to a subclass (*Eurypterida*) of the Ordovician and Permian periods, i.e. 500–225 million years ago. Its tapering segmented body, up to 10 ft (3 m) long, bore several pairs of oarlike appendages at the head end. Eurypterids, which lived in salt or brackish waters, were predators of worms and small fish or bottom-dwelling scavengers. □fossil.

Eusebius of Caesarea   (4th century AD) Christian churchman and historian. As Bishop of Caesarea from 313, he took a moderate position with regard to *Arianism and sought a compromise between the conflicting views of Arius and Athanasius; he finally accepted the creed proposed by the Council of *Nicaea. He is famous for his *Ecclesiastical History*, an account of the Church from apostolic times to his own day.

Eustace, St   (2nd century AD) Roman martyr and the patron saint of hunters. According to tradition, he was a general who was converted to Christianity through experiencing a miraculous vision of a stag with a crucifix between its antlers. Feast Day: Sept 20.

Eustachio, Bartolommeo   (?1520–74) Italian anatomist and physician, who gave his name to the canal connecting the ear and throat (the Eustachian tube) although this had already been discovered by the Greek physician Alcmaeon of Croton (5th century BC). Eustachio's anatomical studies included the ear, kidney, and nervous system but his *Tabulae anatomicae* was not published until 1714.

eustasy   Worldwide changes in sea level, attributed mainly to the accumulation and release of water in the form of ice during the ice ages. Since the last Ice Age sea level has risen gradually.

Euterpe   In Greek legend, one of the *Muses, the patron of tragedy, flute playing, or lyric poetry.

euthanasia (Greek: easy death)   The taking of life to relieve suffering. Euthanasia is a controversial issue concerned with whether or not those with painful and incurable diseases should be provided with a painless means of dying if they ask for it. This is voluntary euthanasia and includes both active steps for taking life (e.g. administration of drugs) and the withholding of life-supporting treatment (passive euthanasia). Even more unacceptable to some people is the concept of compulsory euthanasia, in which the patient—for example, a severely deformed baby—is unable to express his own wishes and the responsibility for deciding to terminate life rests on society or a person acting on authority. Many societies exist to promote the cause of voluntary euthanasia, but in no country has either voluntary or compulsory euthanasia been legalized.

eutrophication   The overfertilization of lakes, due chiefly to pollution by sewage, runoff from the land, and industrial wastes (inorganic nitrates and phosphates). These compounds act as nutrients, stimulating algal growth to produce huge blooms. Their subsequent decomposition reduces the oxygen content in the water, so killing animals with a high oxygen requirement. Much of the nitrate and phosphate settles to the bottom, to promote further growth at a later stage.

Evangelicalism   A movement within Protestant Churches that advocates adherence to traditional concepts of biblical belief. Evangelicals reject the Catholic and Orthodox view of authority residing in the traditions of the Church and the *Apostolic Succession, while remaining faithful to Trinitarian orthodoxy. They resist the liberalizing trend apparent in nonevangelical Protestant circles, concentrating on the importance of personal salvation and the consequences of accepting the divine inspiration of the Bible.

Evans, Sir Arthur John   (1851–1941) British archeologist. His interest in Cretan sealstones, while Keeper of the Ashmolean Museum, Oxford, led him to his life's work, the excavation of *Knossos (1899–1935). In *The Palace of Minos* (1921–36) he firmly established the chronology and main features of *Minoan civilization.

Evans, Dame Edith (1888–1976) British actress. Her long career included many celebrated performances in Shakespearean roles and in classic comedies such as *The Rivals* and *The Importance of Being Earnest*. She gave some of her most acclaimed stage and film performances during her eighties.

Evans, Oliver (1755–1819) American engineer, who conceived the principle of the continuous production line. In 1784 Evans put his ideas into practice in a flour mill: grain entered one end of an automated production line, was processed, and then discharged as flour at the other end. He also patented a high-pressure steam engine in 1790.

Evans, Walker (1903–75) US photographer. He worked for the Farm Securities Administration and photographed everyday life during the Depression. He also documented New England's architecture of the 19th century in photographs from 1930 on. During the 1940s he photographed the living conditions of Southern sharecroppers and included them in *Let Us Now Praise Famous Men* (1941), with text by James Agee. He was an editor of *Fortune* magazine (1945–65). His works are collected in *American Photographs* (1938), *Message from the Interior* (1966), and *Many Are Called* (1966).

Evanston 42 03N 87 42W A city in NE Illinois, on Lake Michigan, N of Chicago. Northwestern University, around which the community grew opened in 1855. Economic activities include publishing, food processing, and the production of chemicals and communications equipment. Population (1980): 73,706.

Evansville 38 00N 87 33W A city, in SW Indiana, on the Ohio River. Its industries include plastics, meat packing, refrigeration equipment, flour milling, pharmaceuticals, and aluminum. Population (1980): 130,496.

evaporation The conversion of a liquid into a vapor at temperatures below its boiling point. As it is the most energetic atoms and molecules that escape from the surface in evaporation, the average energy of those that remain is reduced and consequently the liquid is cooled.

evening primrose A herbaceous plant of the genus *Oenothera* (100 species), 35–40 in (90–100 cm) tall, native to the Americas but widespread in Europe. The fragrant yellow flowers, 1–2 in (2–5 cm) in diameter, open in the evening. The leaves are spirally arranged and the fruit is a long capsule. Family: *Onagraceae* (willowherb family).

Everest, Mount 27 59N 86 56E The highest mountain in the world, on the Nepal–Tibet border in the Himalayas. It was recognized as the highest in 1852, but the height itself was not established until 1955. Climbing attempts started in 1920 and the 12th expedition was the first to succeed: (Sir) Edmund *Hillary and Sherpa *Tenzing Norgay reached the summit on May 29, 1953. On May 5, 1978, two Austrians became the first to reach the top without the aid of oxygen breathing equipment. Height: 29,028 ft (8848 m).

Everglades A subtropical swampy area in Florida, extending S of Lake Okeechobee. The natural vegetation of sawgrass and rushes is preserved in the Everglades National Park but elsewhere large areas have been drained for agriculture. It was the home of the Seminole Indians until the 1830s.

evergreen plants Plants the foliage of which is retained throughout the year. The leaves of evergreens, which are tough and waxy, are produced and shed at different times all the year round, individual leaves often remaining on the tree for several years. Most conifers and many tropical broad-leaved trees are evergreen. **Deciduous plants** produce softer leaves, which are all shed before winter, leaving only the woody parts and protected buds exposed. Deciduous trees generally occur in temperate regions in which there are seasonal fluctuations in climate.

everlasting flowers Any flowers that can be dried without losing their shape or color and are used in floral arrangements and pictures. They include many members of the *Compositae* (daisy family), such as the true everlastings, or immortelles (*Helichrysum* species), the flower heads of which may be dyed various colors. One of the most popular of these is the strawflower of Australia (*H. bracteatum*). Other plants used include *Anaphalis margaritacea* (the pearly everlasting) and *Gnaphalium* and *Helipterum* species, and striking shapes are supplied by *teasels (*Dipsacus* species). Grasses with showy panicles are often used, especially wild oats and barley.

Everson v. Board of Education (1947) US Supreme Court decision that upheld as constitutional tax-supported school bussing to parochial schools. The court ruled that such a policy did not violate separation of church and state.

Evert, Christine. *See* Lloyd, Christine.

evolution In biology, the gradual and continuous process by which the first and most primitive of living organisms have developed into the diversi-ty of plant and animal life known today. Speculations about the origin of living things go back to the Greek philosophers, notably Aristotle, but until the 18th century it was generally believed that each group of organisms was separately and divinely created. In the 1760s *Linnaeus—in his work on the classification and naming of organisms—recognized the possibility of relationship between similar groups, and his contemporary *Buffon suggested that the differences he observed in fossil organisms were brought about by changes in the environment in which they lived.

The first theory of evolution was published by Lamarck, in 1809 (*see* Lamarckism). His explanation of the process—that changes in form acquired during the lifetime of an animal could be inherited—lacked definite proof, although it has had its supporters. A more satisfactory theory was put forward by Charles *Darwin and A. R. *Wallace in 1858: they proposed that new species arose by a process of natural selection acting on individual inheritable variations in a population (*see* Darwinism). Later work has proved that these heritable changes result from spontaneous genetic mutations, and Darwin's theory—with some modifications—is now generally accepted.

Évora (ancient name: Ebora) 38 34N 7 54W A city in Portugal. It contains many Roman ruins including a Roman temple known as the Temple of Diana. Population (1970): 50,235.

Évreux 49 03N 1 11E A city in NW France, the capital of the Eure department. It has a cathedral (11th–18th centuries) and there are Roman remains nearby. Its manufactures include textiles, rubber, and pharmaceuticals. Population (1975): 50,358.

evzones Members of a Greek infantry regiment, originally from Epirus, who fought with distinction in the Balkan Wars and World War II. Evzones wear a distinctive white-skirted uniform; their name derives from the Greek word meaning "dressed for exercise."

Ewe A people of SE Ghana and S Togo, numbering approximately one million, who originated from *Oyo in Nigeria. Their language belongs to the *Kwa subgroup of the Niger-Congo family. They practice shifting agriculture and, in coastal areas, seafishing. They are divided into independent groups, which form temporary alliances for war.

Excalibur King Arthur's magic sword. In one legend Arthur succeeds, where others had failed, in drawing it from a stone, thereby proving his claim to the English throne. In another he receives it from the Lady of the Lake, to whom it is thrown back at his death. *See also* Arthurian legend.

excavator A self-propeled vehicle equipped with a hydraulically powered movable boom and shovel used for excavating trenches, loading earth, etc. Larger models are used for mining and quarrying and usually consist of a crawler vehicle on which is mounted a boom with one or several digging buckets controlled by cables from a winch.

exchange control Government regulations to control the extent to which a foreign currency can be purchased to prevent a large outflow of foreign exchange, which might precipitate a *balance-of-payments crisis. By controlling foreign exchange a government can restrict imports or limit them to those considered desirable by the government.

exchange rates The value of one country's currency in terms of another's. Foreign trade and tourism make it essential for currencies to be convertible at a stable rate of exchange. Until World War I and again briefly between 1925 and 1931 international currencies were backed by, and convertible into, gold (*see* gold standard). Between 1931 and 1947 various systems were in use.

In 1947 the *International Monetary Fund (IMF) came into operation, as a result of the *Bretton Woods Conference (1944). The IMF fixed par values for members' currencies in terms of gold and these values could not be changed without consulting the IMF. *Special Drawing Rights were introduced in 1970 in an attempt to increase world liquidity, but were unable to maintain the stability of the system: the suspension of convertibility from US dollars to gold in 1971 led to an agreement to allow currencies to float (i.e. to find their own value as a result of market forces). Floating rates avoid the problem of large destabilizing devaluation, which took place under the Bretton Woods fixed-rate system.

excise tax. *See* customs and excise duties.

excitation In physics, the raising of a system from its lowest energy level (the ground state) to a higher energy level (the excited state). The term is usually confined to atoms, molecules, ions, and nuclei and is most frequently caused by the absorption of a *photon. In an atom, ion, or nucleus the photon is absorbed by an electron or *nucleon causing it to move to a higher energy level. Molecules can also be excited into higher states of rotational or vibrational energy.

excommunication The exclusion of a Christian from the community of the Church for misconduct. There are biblical precedents for various forms of excommunication, especially in the Pauline epistles. In the later Church, exclusion from the sacraments was frequently used as a means of censure, and in the middle ages the papacy used it to apply political pressure against sovereigns. It is still used by the Roman Catholic Church as a form of discipline and is theoretically available in some Protestant Churches.

excretion The elimination of the waste products of metabolism by the body. In higher animals and man this includes the excretion of nitrogenous waste in the form of urine by the *kidneys, the egestion of feces—the waste products of digestion—from the bowel, and the exhalation of carbon dioxide from the lungs in breathing. A small amount of urea is also excreted in sweat. Lower animals have various simple organs for the excretion of waste products (see nephridium).

Executive Privilege The right of a US president to withhold information from Congress and the courts if such information would endanger national security. It was first used by President George *Washington in 1796.

Exekias (6th century BC) Athenian potter and vase painter, known from his signatures on several vases. One of the last black-figure painters, Exekias painted dignified symmetrical compositions in painstaking but fluent detail.

Exeter 50 43N 3 31W A city in SW England, on the Exe River. Its 13th-century cathedral, a fine example of gothic architecture, was damaged by bombing in World War II along with many other buildings. Exeter's Guildhall is said to be the oldest municipal building in the country. Industries include tourism, printing, the manufacture of agricultural machinery, and leather goods. Population (1981): 95,621.

existentialism A philosophical movement that rejects metaphysics and concentrates on the individual's existence in the world. The forerunner of existentialism, *Kierkegaard, reacting against German *idealism and the complacency of established Christianity, developed a pragmatic psychologically realistic philosophy of existence. This was adapted by French intellectuals, especially Sartre, after World War II. Sartre's existentialism allows individuals freedom in a nihilistic universe: "All human activities are equivalent, all are destined by principle to defeat." But a man is responsible for his effect on others, though only *his* existence is real to him and he is ultimately his own judge. Sartre expounded existentialism chiefly in *Being and Nothingness* (1943), but his plays and novels (and those of *Camus) present existentialist ideas more accessibly.

exobiology (or astrobiology) The branch of biology that investigates the possibility of life on other planets. Exobiologists monitor the electromagnetic spectrum, including light and radio waves, emitted by the stars for evidence of the organic molecules that are a prerequiste of life on earth. They are also involved in designing life-detecting experiments carried to planets in our own solar system by space probes, such as the Viking series.

Exodus (Greek: going out) The second book of the Bible, traditionally ascribed to Moses. It recounts the events culminating in the departure of the Israelites from Egypt, where they had lived as slaves since the time of Joseph, and their arrival at Mount Sinai, where the *Ten Commandments are given to Moses. The narrative also includes the story of the birth of Moses, the establishment of the *Passover, and the miraculous crossing of the Red Sea. The events themselves perhaps date from the 15th century BC; the book was probably compiled between the 9th and 4th centuries BC.

exorcism The religious practice of driving out evil spirits by means of prayers and other ritual acts. It is a common rite in a number of religions, including ancient Judaism, and was adopted by Christianity on the basis that it was performed by Christ and the apostles in the New Testament. It refers specifically to the prayers, etc., used to expel evil spirits that supposedly possess a person. Although still available in some Churches, the rite may only be performed by a priest with a bishop's permission.

exosphere. *See* atmosphere.

expanding universe The theory that the universe is expanding was first proposed by Edwin *Hubble in 1929 following observations that the light from distant galaxies is subject to a *redshift, which arises from the recession of the galaxies from us (and from each other). The expansion can be explained by the *big-bang theory. *See also* Hubble constant.

expansion The general increase in dimensions of a substance with increasing temperature. In solids it is caused by the greater vibrational energy of the atoms leading to increased interatomic distances. In liquids and gases the expansion is caused by the greater velocities of the atoms or molecules. The thermal expansion of an ideal gas is described by *Charles's law. The

coefficient of linear expansion of a substance is the increase in length per unit length of the substance caused by a rise in temperature of 33°F (1°C).

Ex Parte McCardle (1869) The US Supreme Court decision ruling that Congress regulated the right of the Supreme Court to hear appeals from lower (appellate) courts. Although the Supreme Court is granted the right to hear appeals from lower courts by the Consitution, it is "with such exceptions and under such regulations as Congress shall make." In this case, it was feared that a decision in favor of William McCardle, accused of sedition by the military in the South, would overturn the Reconstruction Acts.

Ex Parte Milligan (1866) The US Supreme Court decision that a civilian could not be tried by a military court outside of a war area. Lambdin P. Milligan, a civilian from Indiana, had been tried for treason by the military and sentenced to death. He appealed to the Supreme Court, contending it unconstitutional for the military to try a civilian when civil courts operated in the same area. This decision overruled President Lincoln's previous Civil War proclamation, issued without approval of Congress, that civilians were subject to military rule.

explosives Substances that can be made to produce a large volume of gas very suddenly. The energy of the expanding gases may be used for a number of industrial or military purposes. There are three main types. **Mechanical explosives** depend on a physical reaction, such as overloading a container of gas until it bursts. They are little used except in specialized mining applications where the release of gas from chemicals is undesirable. In **nuclear explosives**, a nuclear chain reaction (see nuclear energy) takes place in a sudden uncontrolled manner, releasing energy almost instantaneously. This is used for bombs and occasionally for mining. Most explosives used are **chemical explosives**. These include *TNT, *nitroglycerin, and *dynamite. Modern high explosives are often in the form of water gels, which are plastic, water resistant, and easy to handle safely.

exponential function A mathematical function of the general form Ae^{Bx} where A and B are constants and e is the base of natural *logarithms. Bx is called the exponent; if the exponent is a complicated expression, $f(x)$ say, then the function is often written as $\exp[f(x)]$. The function e^x has the important property that its differential is always equal to the function itself. *See also* calculus.

exposure meter A device for measuring the intensity of light falling on a photographic *camera, used to determine the film exposure time and lens *f-number needed to suit the lighting conditions. It often consists of a *photocell that is directed at the subject from the camera, registering light as a reading on an electric current meter. In some cameras this current is used to control the aperture or shutter speed automatically.

expressionism A movement in modern art covering a variety of schools, the common aim of which was to convey the crude force of human emotion. The bright colors and distorted forms of *Van Gogh and *Munch foreshadow expressionism proper. An even earlier forerunner was the German painter *Grünewald. The chief exponents of expressionism were Die *Brücke and Der *Blaue Reiter groups in Germany but independent figures, such as *Rouault, *Soutine, *Schiele, and *Kokoschka also worked in an expressionist style.

extrasensory perception (ESP) Acquisition of information not accessible through normal perceptual processes. Three phenomena are usually classified under this heading: clairvoyance (knowledge of distant events and concealed objects), telepathy (thought transference between people), and precognition (knowledge of future events). Evidence for all three tends to be anecdotal, but some experiments in which subjects have been asked to guess symbols on cards of which they can see only the backs or to reproduce, without having seen it, a simple sketch done by another person show a statistically significant success rate. *See also* Rhine, Joseph.

extroversion (*or* extraversion) The tendency to be interested in the outside world more than in oneself. Extroversion is a quality of personality, first described by Carl *Jung and still used in modern theories of personality. Extroverts are gregarious and outgoing. They prefer frequent changes of activity; their interests tend to be practical and scientific rather than philosophical; and they tend to be resistant to permanent *conditioning. *Compare* introversion.

extrusive rock. *See* igneous rock.

eye The organ of sight. The human eyes lie within two bony sockets in the skull and are attached by six muscles, which produce eye movements. At the front of the eye the white fibrous outer layer (sclera) is replaced by a transparent curved layer (see cornea). A delicate membrane (the conjunctiva) covers the front of the eye and lines the eyelids: it is liable to become inflamed (see conjunctivitis). Light entering the eye is refracted by the cornea and passes through the watery aqueous humor and pupil to the lens. The pigmented *iris controls the amount of light entering the eye. The shape of the lens can be adjusted by means of the ciliary muscles so that an image is focused through the jelly-like vitreous humor onto the *retina. Contraction of the ciliary muscles causes the lens to become flattened for focusing distant objects; relaxation of the muscles increases the curvature of the lens for focusing near objects. Light-sensitive cells in the retina send impulses to the brain via the optic nerve. *See also* blindness; farsightedness; ophthalmology; nearsightedness.

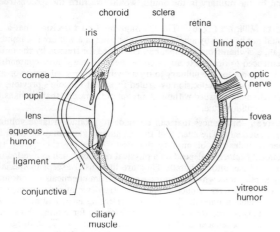

EYE   *The structure of the human eye is revealed in this section. The blind spot, where the optic nerve leaves the eye, contains no visual cells and is therefore insensitive to light. The fovea is the area of acutest vision.*

eyebright   A semiparasitic annual herb of the genus *Euphrasia* (over 130 species), of temperate regions. Eyebrights have small toothed leaves and small unstalked two-lipped flowers, usually white with violet and yellow markings. They grow to a height of 6 in (15 cm). Family: *Scrophulariaceae.*

Eyre, Lake   A shallow salt lake of NE South Australia. It is normally dry except during the rainy season when heavy rains from N Queensland and the Northern Territory are fed into the lake by *Cooper Creek and other streams. The last time it was full was in 1950. Lowest point: about 36 ft (10 m) below sea level. Area: about 3500 sq mi (9100 sq km).

Eyre Peninsula   A peninsula of South Australia, situated between the Great Australian Bight and Spencer Gulf. Iron ore is mined in the Middleback Range in the NE.

Eysenck, Hans Jürgen   (1916–   ) German-born British psychologist. A critic of conventional psychoanalysis, he developed an alternative treatment—*behavior therapy—for neurosis and other mental disorders. Eysenck also developed scientifically based methods of evaluating personality and intelligence, partly based on the distinction between introverts and extroverts. His findings on racial differences in intelligence (*Race, Intelligence and Education*, 1971) caused much controversy.

Ezekiel   An Old Testament prophet, the successor of *Isaiah and *Jeremiah. The **Book of Ezekiel** records his prophecies, probably written during the *Babylonian exile (6th century BC). The prophecies concern the coming destruction of Jerusalem and Israel, denunciations of various foreign states, the renewal of the people, and finally the ideal society and the rebuilding of the Temple at Jerusalem.

Ezra   In the Old Testament, a religious reformer, who was sent by the Persian king, possibly *Artaxerxes II (c. 436–358 BC), to regulate Jewish affairs in Jerusalem.

The Book of Ezra in the Old Testament is a sequel to *Chronicles and was compiled by the author of Chronicles and the Book of *Nehemiah. It records the return of the Jews after the *Babylonian exile in about 537 BC, the rebuilding of the Temple, and legal and religious reforms introduced by Ezra.

F

Fabergé, Peter Carl (1846–1920) Russian goldsmith and jeweler. He designed elegant *objets d'art* and was patronized by European royalty. He was especially famous for the jeweled Easter eggs containing surprise gifts given by the tsars to the tsarinas. He died in exile.

Fabian Society A society, named for *Fabius Maximus, formed in London in 1884 for the purpose of peacefully promoting socialist ideas and establishing a socialist state in Britain. Members included George Bernard *Shaw, Sidney and Beatrice *Webb, and Annie *Besant. The Fabians were active in the establishment of the Labour Party and today continue to press the cause of socialism through public lectures, conferences, and publications.

Fabius Maximus, Quintus (d. 203 BC) Roman general of the second *Punic War. Appointed dictator after *Hannibal's defeat of the Romans at Trasimene in 217, Fabius adopted a policy of attrition, harassing Hannibal but avoiding pitched battles. His derogatory title Cunctator (Delayer) became honorable after Hannibal's victory at *Cannae proved the wisdom of Fabius' tactics. It was *Scipio Africanus' aggressive policies, however, that achieved the final triumph over Hannibal, after Fabius' death.

fable A short narrative in prose or verse, often with animal characters, which illustrates a moral truth. The western literary form had its origins in the collection of fables attributed to *Aesop (6th century BC) and later expanded by the Roman poet *Phaedrus (1st century AD). The medieval genre of *beast epic developed from this form, which reached its highest degree of sophistication in the work of *La Fontaine. Authors of children's literature, notably Rudyard *Kipling, Lewis *Carroll, and Beatrix *Potter, have used this form extensively. Other modern examples are by George *Orwell and James Thurber.

fabliau A medieval French comic and satiric narrative poem, a type that flourished between 1150 and 1400. About 150 examples survive, mostly simple tales the humor of which is usually broad and obscene. Among known authors is Rutebeuf (*see* trouvères). Chaucer's *Miller's Tale* and *Reeve's Tale* (in the *Canterbury Tales*) are the outstanding examples in English.

Fabre, Jean Henri (1823–1915) French entomologist, noted for his studies of bees, wasps, and other insects. From his observations, Fabre realized the importance of inherited instinct in insect behavior. He wrote many popular books about his researches, including *Souvenirs entomologiques* (1879–1907).

Fabricius ab Aquapendente, Hieronymus (1537–1619) Italian physician. Fabricius was a student of *Fallopius and himself became an eminent teacher, one of his pupils being William *Harvey. Among Fabricius' contributions were studies of embryology and fetal development (*De formata foetu*, 1600) and his discovery of one-way valves in veins.

Fabry, Charles (1867–1945) French physicist, who while working at the Sorbonne discovered *ozone in the upper atmosphere (1913). This discovery was made with the Fabry-Pérot interferometer, an instrument that he had designed in collaboration with Alfred Pérot (1863–1925) in 1896.

factoring The commercial practice of buying trade debts and collecting them on behalf of clients. If a manufacturer sells his products to a number of customers, some of whom may be slow payers, he can sell these debts to a factor, who will usually pay 80% of the debt immediately and the balance (less a service charge) when the debt has been collected. This service is often combined (for an extra charge) with credit insurance, enabling the debt to be guaranteed even if the debtor fails.

Fadden, Sir Arthur William (1895–1973) Australian statesman; prime minister (1941) following Menzies' resignation. He was leader of the Country Party (1941–58).

Faenza 44 19N 11 54E A city in N Italy, in Emilia-Romagna. During the 15th and 16th centuries it was famous for the manufacture of majolica earthenware, especially *faience, and a ceramics museum was founded here in 1908. Iron goods and textiles are manufactured. Population (1971): 54,703.

Faeroe Islands (*or* Faroe Islands; Danish name: Faerøerne) A Danish group of self-governing islands in the N Atlantic Ocean, between the Shetland Islands and Iceland. 17 of the 22 islands are inhabited, the chief ones being Strømø, Østerø, and Vaagø. Chiefly hilly, the terrain limits agriculture to sheep raising and the production of hay and potatoes. Fishing and fish processing is important. Area: 540 sq mi (1400 sq km). Population (1980 est): 43,609. Capital: Thorshavn, on Strømø.

Fahd, King (ibn Abdul al-Aziz al-Saud) (1922–) Saudi Arabian king (1982–). The son of *Ibn Saud, founder of Saudi Arabia, and half brother of *Khalid Ibn Abdul Aziz, he served as minister of education (1953–60) and of the interior (1962–75). Named crown prince in 1975, he strengthened Saudi Arabia's petroleum and natural gas industries, planned the construction of two new cities and an airport (1981), and proposed a peace plan for the Middle East. As king, he sought to bolster Saudi Arabia's economy and its role in //the *Organization of Petroleum Exporting Countries (OPEC), to settle Middle-East conflicts, and to maintain close ties with Western countries.

Fahrenheit scale A temperature scale in which the temperature of melting ice is taken as 32 degrees and the temperature of boiling water, as 212 degrees. Named for the German physicist Gabriel Daniel Fahrenheit (1686–1736).

Fa-hsien. See Fa Xian.

faience Several kinds of tin-glazed earthenware made in France. Strictly, *faience* is French shorthand for *porzellana di Faenza*, a species of *majolica made in Italy, and the technique of coating fragile porous earthenware with impervious hard white opaque tin glaze derives from majolica. Italian potters were using the method in France in the 16th century. Centers of production during the 17th and 18th centuries were Lyons, Marseilles, Moustiers, Nevers, and Rouen. Designs drawn from local history (*faience parlante*) and revolutionary events (*faience patriotique*) were popular variations. Richly painted baroque and *rococo styles are common.

Fairbanks, Charles Warren (1852–1918) US politician, US vice president (1905–09). He served as Republican senator from Ohio (1897–1905) until becoming vice president under Theodore Roosevelt. He ran unsuccessfully as the vice presidential candidate with Charles Evans Hughes in 1916.

Fairbanks, Douglas (Julius Ullman; 1883–1939) US film actor. With D. W. Griffith, Charlie Chaplin, and his wife Mary Pickford he founded United Artists Corporation in 1919. His films, in which he played the roles of handsome athletic heroes, include *The Mark of Zorro* (1920) and *The Black Pirate* (1926). His son **Douglas Fairbanks Jr** (1909–) also became a film actor. He played roles similar to those of his father, in films such as *The Prisoner of Zenda* (1937) and *Sinbad the Sailor* (1947).

Fairbanks 64 51N 147 43W A city in E central Alaska, at the confluence of the Tanana and Chena rivers. It was established in 1902 during the gold rush and gold and silver mining are still economically important, as well as coal mining and processing. Lumbering is also carried on. The University of Alaska is in the nearby town of College. Population (1980): 22,645.

Fair Deal The legislative program proposed by President *Truman (1945–1953). First presented in Truman's 1949 inaugural address, the Fair Deal was essentially a continuation of the Roosevelt *New Deal, including expanded social security benefits, federal regulation of working conditions, and ambitious housing programs. Strong opposition by Republicans and Southern Democrats in Congress, however, prevented the implementation of most of the Fair Deal proposals.

Fairfax, Thomas, 3rd Baron (1612–71) English general, who as commander in chief of the *New Model Army defeated Charles I at *Naseby. Fairfax subsequently opposed the king's execution and resigned his command in 1650 in protest against the planned invasion of Scotland. After Cromwell's death he participated in the restoration of Charles II.

fairies Supernatural beings that are half man, half spirit. Folklore depicts them as enigmatic beings skilled in magic and illusion, benevolent or harmful in turn. Some tales tell of their aid to, and even intermarriage with, humans, but others of their abduction of humans, especially children, for whom changelings were substituted. It has been suggested that they represent memories of extinct indigenous peoples, such as the Picts. Modern fairies are usually shown as small, but in folklore they were frequently tall and awesomely beautiful.

Fair Labor Standards Act (1938) A US law that regulated the minimum wage and maximum working hours allowed interstate commerce workers. It provided for overtime pay and banned child labor. Passed during the New Deal, it has long been upheld.

Fair Oaks A battlefield in E central Virginia, E of Richmond. During the Civil War's Peninsular Campaign in 1862 Union General George B. McCellan's forces defeated Confederate General Joseph E. Johnston's troops in 1862. Fair Oaks is also called the Battle of Seven Pines.

fairy bluebird A songbird of the genus *Irena* (2 species), occurring in tropical evergreen forests and feeding chiefly on fruit and nectar. The bluebacked fairy bluebird (*I. puella*) of Indomalaysia has a glossy black plumage with a bright-blue back and tail and red eyes. Family: *Irenidae* (leafbirds).

fairy penguin The smallest of the *penguins, *Eudyptula minor*, also called little penguin. About 12 in (30 cm) tall, it is the only penguin commonly occurring on Australian coasts, breeding in dense colonies and nesting in crevices or disused burrows.

fairy shrimp A *crustacean, belonging to the order *Anostraca*, that occurs in mainly freshwater pools and ponds of arid regions (*compare* brine shrimp). It has an elongated body, up to 1 in (25 mm) long, without a carapace and swims on its back using 11–19 pairs of appendages. Subclass: *Branchiopoda*.

fairy stories Tales for children of a more or less simple kind, involving fantastic or supernatural elements. Most originate in oral tradition, although some are rewritten in sophisticated form, as with *Perrault's *Tales of Mother Goose* (1697); others, like Oscar *Wilde's *The Happy Prince* (1888), are purely literary in origin. The most famous collection of oral tales is *Kinder- und Hausmärchen* (1812–13) by the brothers *Grimm. Probably the most famous writer of original tales is the Dane Hans Christian *Andersen. Fairy tales often transcend national boundaries; similar tales are found throughout the world.

Faisal I (1885–1933) King of Iraq (1921–33). He played an important part in the Arab revolt during World War I. After the war he was briefly King of Syria before the French occupation (1920). In 1921 the British installed him as king in the mandate of Iraq.

Faisal II (1935–58) King of Iraq (1939–58). Until he came of age in 1953, his uncle acted as regent. He was killed in the 1958 revolution led by *Kassem.

Faisal Ibn Abdul Aziz (1905–75) King of Saudi Arabia (1964–75). A son of *Ibn Saud, Faisal represented Saudi Arabia at the UN. In 1958 he became the real ruler of Saudi Arabia, although his brother *Saud was still nominally king until abdicating in 1964. His reign saw economic development and the increased international importance of Saudi Arabia as an oil-producing country. He was assassinated by his nephew.

faith healing (*or* spiritual healing) The curing of illness or disability by supernatural means. The temple of *Asclepius at *Epidauros was a famous faith-healing center in antiquity. Christ is credited with several miraculous cures (Matthew 9.2–7, etc.). Some charismatic healers apparently achieve cures unaccountable to science, particularly at mass rallies where powerful emotional effects operate upon the patients, but the possibilities for deception by callous tricksters are obvious and frauds frequently occur.

Faiyum, El (*or* al-Fayyum) 29 19N 30 50E A city in N Egypt, in the Libyan Desert. Nearby is the ancient site of Crocodilopolis, where the crocodile-god Sobek was worshiped. An agricultural center, it manufactures cotton textiles. Population (1976): 167,000.

Fakhr ad-Din II (c. 1572–1635) Ruler of Lebanon (1593–1633). He took advantage of the weakness of the Ottomans to expand into Syria and Palestine, but in 1635 was captured and executed in Istanbul. He is sometimes seen as a forerunner of Lebanese nationalists.

fakir (Arabic: poor man) A Muslim mendicant who practices ascetic and religious exercises, often a member of a Muslim sect or of a Sufi religious brotherhood (*compare* dervishes). In India the term is applied more generally to any (Muslim or Hindu) ascetic or yogi.

Falabella The smallest breed of pony, developed by the Falabella family in Argentina using Shetland pony stock. It has a fine soft coat of any color and is popular as a mount for small children. Height: 3⅓–7½ hands (38–76 cm).

Falaise 48 54N 0 11W A small town in NW France, in the Calvados department. It is best known as the site of the castle of the Dukes of Normandy, in which William the Conqueror was born. The town was virtually destroyed during the Normandy campaign (*see* World War II).

Falange Española The Spanish Fascist party, created in 1933 by José António *Primo de Rivera. The Falange wanted to regenerate Spain by means of revolution but rejected socialism as atheistic and alien to Spanish

traditions. In 1937 Franco merged the Falange with the various Nationalist parties to create the National Movement, which became Spain's only legal party after the Civil War.

Falashas An Ethiopian tribe, who practice an early form of Judaism. They adhere closely to the Bible but do not have the postbiblical Jewish literature or observances. In recent years many Falashas have been introduced to modern Judaism and some have emigrated to Israel.

falcon A ground-nesting bird of prey belonging to a widely distributed family (*Falconidae*; 58 species). 6–24 in (15–60 cm) long, falcons are characterized by long pointed wings and a notched hooked bill. True falcons belong to the genus *Falco* and are fast, powerful fliers killing small birds in flight with their claws or seizing small mammals from the ground. The small falconets occur in tropical regions and usually feed on insects. Order: *Falconiformes* (falcons, hawks, etc.). *See also* caracara; gyrfalcon; hobby; kestrel; lanner; merlin; peregrine.

falconry (*or* hawking) The sport of hunting small animals or birds with falcons, other hawks, or sometimes eagles. It was practiced in Asia from the 8th century BC and was very popular in Europe from late medieval times to the 17th century. Traditionally the birds are either taken as fledglings (eyasses) or caught as one-year-old birds (passagers) or fully mature birds (haggards), but because many hunting birds are now protected species, they are often bred in captivity. They are then trained to sit hooded on the gloved fist and, by the use of a lure (an imitation bird with meat attached), to hunt and kill (but not retrieve). Large species, such as the peregrine falcon, need very open country, while smaller species are used in wooded country.

Falkirk 56 00N 3 48W A city in Scotland, in Central Region on the Forth-Clyde Canal. Here Bonnie Prince Charlie defeated General Hawley in 1746. Formerly a prominent market town, Falkirk is now important industrially, particularly for iron founding and aluminum rolling. Population (1973 est): 36,901.

FALKLAND ISLANDS *An Argentinian armored personnel carrier patrols the streets of Stanley, the islands' capital, during the Argentinian occupation.*

Falkland Islands (Argentine name: Islas Malvinas) An island group and British crown colony in the S Atlantic Ocean. The main islands of the group of about 100 are East and West Falkland; its dependencies to the SE are *South Georgia and the South Sandwich group. The population is almost entirely of British origin. Sheep farming is the main occupation on the islands' rough moorland, producing wool for export (chiefly to the UK). *History*: the first landing was by Capt John Strong in 1690. In the early 19th century the islands became a British colony. During World War I the naval battle of the Falkland Islands, in which the Germans were decisively defeated by the British, was fought off East Falkland (December, 1914). Argentina has long made claims to the group, and on April 2, 1982, invaded the islands. US and UN attempts to mediate a diplomatic settlement failed and a task force sent by the UK recaptured South Georgia (April 25) and the Falkland Islands themselves on June 14, after considerable loss of life on both sides. Area: 4700 sq mi (12,173 sq km). Population (1980 est): 1813. Capital: Stanley.

Falla, Manuel de (1876–1946) Spanish nationalist composer. He lived in Paris (1907–14), where he met Ravel and Debussy, and spent his last years in Argentina. His music was heavily influenced by Spanish folksong and he is best known for his ballet scores *Love the Magician* (1915) and *The Three-Cornered Hat* (1919), *Nights in the Gardens of Spain* (for piano and orchestra; 1909–15), and a concerto for harpsichord and chamber ensemble.

Fallen Timbers, Battle of (1794) Army victory over the Indians. General Anthony *Wayne attacked Indian tribesmen, who had been aided by the British at Fort Miami, near Toledo, Ohio, in an area of many fallen trees. Victorious, the US signed (1795) with the Indians the Treaty of Greenville, which provided more peaceful opportunities for US exploration of the Northwest Territory.

Fallopian tubes. *See* ovary.

Fallopius, Gabriel (1523–62) Italian anatomist, who discovered the tubes leading from the ovaries to the uterus, which were named for him (Fallopian tubes). A pupil of the great anatomist *Vesalius, Fallopius described the semicircular canals of the ear and many features of the reproductive system in his *Observationes anatomicae* (1561).

fallout Radioactive particles deposited from the atmosphere after a nuclear explosion. If large the particles are deposited within a radius of a few hundred kilometers during the first few hours after the explosion. This is known as local fallout. Tropospheric fallout may occur anywhere along the same line of latitude as the explosion during the first week after the explosion. If the particles are drawn high up into the atmosphere, stratospheric fallout may result, which can last for several years.

fallow deer A *deer, *Dama dama*, native to Mediterranean forests but widely kept in parks and woodlands. About 3 ft (90 cm) high at the shoulder, fallow deer are fawn with white spots in summer, becoming grayish in winter; males have flattened antlers with numerous points. They feed mainly on grass but also browse on leaves.

Falmouth 41 34N 70 38W A resort town in SE Massachusetts, on the S shore of E Cape Cod. The Woods Hole Oceanographic Institution is here. Besides tourism, industries include cranberry growing and processing. Population (1980): 23,640.

False Decretals A collection of mostly forged decrees compiled in 9th-century France, but incorporated into *Isidore of Seville's compilation of decrees of Church councils. They were used to establish the authority of the papacy at the time of its ascendancy up to the 11th century and were accepted as genuine throughout the middle ages, being finally discredited only in 1558.

False Dimitrii. *See* Time of Troubles.

Falster A Danish island in the Baltic Sea, linked by bridge to Sjælland and Lolland. Area: 198 sq mi (513 sq km). Population (1970): 44,467. Chief town: Nykøbing.

Falun 60 37N 15 40E A city in central Sweden. Copper has been mined here since early times, although its importance declined in the 17th century. Other industries include engineering and chemical industries. Population (1978 est): 50,597.

Falwell, Jerry (1933–) US fundamentalist minister; Moral Majority, Inc. leader (1979–). He founded the Thomas Road Baptist Church (1956) in Lynchburg, Va., and that same year started broadcasting his *Old-Time Gospel Hour* program daily on radio; it was televised on Sundays from 1971. By 1980 church membership numbered 17,000 and television listeners 18 million. Moral Majority promotes conservatism and deals with education, lobbying, candidate endorsement, and legal aid.

Famagusta 35 07N 33 57E A port in Cyprus, on the E coast. Founded in the 3rd century BC, it did not develop until the 13th century AD, when Christians fled here from Palestine. It has an old walled town and a gothic cathedral (now a mosque). Its port handles most of the island's freight cargo. Population (1975 est): 39,400.

family planning. *See* contraception.

fandango A Spanish dance with three beats to the bar performed by a man and a woman to the accompaniment of guitar and castanets. The dance begins slowly and becomes gradually faster; the dancers freeze when the music stops.

Faneuil, Peter (1700–43) US businessman. Raised in New Rochelle, N.Y., of French Huguenot parents, he settled in Boston as a young man. He started his own business and eventually inherited his uncle's fortune. In 1740, wishing to give a gift to the city, he built Faneuil Hall, a market place and meeting hall. Although it burned down in 1761 it was rebuilt by 1763 and served as a meeting place during the American Revolution—thus, its name "Cradle of American Liberty." Charles *Bulfinch designed an addition in 1805.

Fang A Bantu people of West Africa comprising a number of tribes in N Gabon, Equatorial Guinea, and S Cameroon. They were originally a warlike hunting people but became ivory traders and craftsmen under colonial rule. Cocoa farming is now important and the Fang have prospered in the postindependence period.

Fangio, Juan Manuel (1911–) Argentinian motor-racing driver, who won 24 Grand Prix races and was world champion a record five times (1951, 1954–57).

Fa Ngum (c. 1316–c. 1373) King of Lan Xang (or Lang Chang), which embraced most of present-day Laos, Thailand, and part of Cambodia (1354–73). He proclaimed himself king after forcing the Lao chiefs of the upper Mekong to accept his sovereignty. He then launched further conquests to the S and W. Wearied by constant warfare, his subjects rebelled in 1373, forcing him to abdicate.

Fanning Island 03 52N 159 22W A coral atoll in the W central Pacific Ocean, in Kiribati in the Line Islands. Copra is exported. Area: 13 sq mi (33 sq km). Population (1973): 340.

fantail A *flycatcher of the genus *Rhipidura* (24 species), of S Asia and Australasia, having a long fan-shaped tail. Fantails are 6–9 in (16–22 cm) long with a gray, black, or reddish-brown plumage, often with patches of white on the breast, tail, and face.

fantasia (*or* fantasy) In the 16th and 17th centuries, a piece of music (typically for viols or a keyboard instrument) having a polyphonic character. In the early 19th century the name was applied by such composers as Mozart and Beethoven to extended compositions that did not follow the *sonata form. It is also a piece of music constructed from themes from an opera or a number of well-known tunes, such as Liszt's fantasia on Mozart's opera *Don Giovanni*.

Fantin-Latour, (Ignace) Henri (Joseph Théodore) (1836–1904) French painter, born in Grenoble. He is best known for his flower paintings and portrait groups, particularly of his impressionist friends in *Studio in the Batignolles Quarter* and *Homage to Delacroix* (both Louvre).

fanworm A marine *annelid worm belonging to the family *Sabellidae*, also called peacock or feather-duster worm. Fanworms build a parchment-like tube, up to 18 in (45 cm) long, from which protrudes a feathery crown of tentacles that trap food particles and absorb oxygen. Class: *Polychaeta*.

FAO. *See* Food and Agriculture Organization.

farad (F) The *SI unit of electrical capacitance equal to the capacitance of a parallel-plate capacitor with a potential difference of one volt across its plates when the capacitor is charged with one coulomb. Named for Michael *Faraday.

Faraday, Michael (1791–1867) British chemist and physicist. Apprenticed to a bookbinder, he found the books to excite his first interest in science. He persuaded Sir Humphry *Davy to take him on as his assistant (1813), eventually succeeding Davy at the Royal Institution as professor of chemistry (1833). His earliest scientific work was on the liquefaction of gases (1823) and his first major contribution to science was the discovery of benzene (1825). However, it is with electricity and electrochemistry that his name is permanently linked. After discovering the process of electrolysis (1832) he went on to work out the laws that control it (*see* Faraday's laws of electrolysis). In electricity, he discovered the connection between electricty and magnetism and, independently of Joseph *Henry, first showed that electromagnetic induction was possible. He used induction to produce the first electrical generator (1831) and also the first transformer.

Faraday constant The quantity of electricity equivalent to 1 mole of electrons, i.e. the product of *Avogadro's number and the electronic charge. It has the value 96,487 coulombs per mole.

Faraday effect The rotation of the plane of polarization of plane-polarized light when it travels through certain substances in a direction parallel to the lines of force of an applied magnetic field. The effect occurs in quartz and water and is named for Michael *Faraday.

Faraday's laws of electrolysis Two laws formulated by M. Faraday in 1813–14. (1) The mass of a substance produced by an electrolytic reaction varies directly with the amount of electricity passed through the cell. (2) The masses of substances produced by a given amount of electricity are proportional to the equivalent masses of the substances.

These empirical laws are now understood to hold simply because electricity is composed of uniform discrete particles (electrons). *See also* electrolysis.

farce (from Latin *farcire*: to stuff) A dramatic genre intended only to amuse its audience, a less sophisticated and less intellectual form than pure comedy. Elements common to most farce include peculiar situations, improbable coincidences, and ridiculous exaggerations of character and physical action. The term originally described comic interludes—"stuffing"—in medieval French religious plays. Some of the best farces were written in the late 19th century, notably those of Feydeau and Labiche in France and Pinero and W. S. Gilbert in England.

Far East The countries and areas of E and SE Asia bordering on the Pacific Ocean. It includes Siberia (Soviet Union), China, North and South Korea, and Japan and sometimes Indonesia, Malaysia, and the Philippines. The term is often generally applied to all the countries of E and SE Asia.

Fareham 50 51N 1 10W A city in S England, in Hampshire on Portsmouth Harbour. Its industries include boatbuilding, engineering, and horticulture (particularly strawberry growing). It is also a market town and sailing center. Population (1981): 88,274.

Farel, Guillaume (1489–1565) French Protestant reformer. Forced to leave France in 1524 because of his beliefs, he settled in Geneva. Although banished from the city, he later returned and succeeded in establishing Protestantism there in 1536. From 1537 he worked with *Calvin, having persuaded him to stay in Geneva.

Farewell, Cape 59 50N 43 40W The S tip of Greenland, on Egger Island. A headland rising to 2000 ft (600 m), it is edged with rocks and is known for its bad weather.

Fargo 46 52N 96 49W A city in North Dakota, on the Red River. Named for the pioneer expressman W. G. Fargo, it is the trading center of an agricultural region. The North Dakota State University was established here in 1890. Population (1980): 61,383.

Fargo, William. See Wells, Henry.

Farnese, Alessandro, Duke of Parma (1545–92) Italian general in the service of *Philip II of Spain (his uncle). In 1571 he fought the Turks at *Lepanto and from 1577 served against the *Revolt of the Netherlands. As governor general of the Netherlands (1578–92), he regained the southern provinces, making peace at *Arras (1579). In 1585 he captured Antwerp following a 13-month siege.

Faro 37 01N 7 56W A port in S Portugal, on the Atlantic Coast. Pillaged by the English in 1596, it was almost destroyed in the earthquakes of 1722 and 1755. It is now a popular tourist town with agricultural industries and sardine fishing. Population (1970): 30,289.

Faroe Islands. See Faeroe Islands.

Farouk I (1920–65) The last king of Egypt (1936–52). His inability to prevent British intervention in Egyptian affairs, and defeat in the first Arab-Israeli War (1948–49), led to his overthrow and exile in Monaco.

Farquhar, George (1678–1707) Irish dramatist. After studying and acting in Dublin he won immediate success in London with his first play, *Love and a Bottle* (1699). His two best-known plays, *The Recruiting Officer* (1706) and *The Beaux' Stratagem* (1707), replaced the highly mannered and cynical conventions of Restoration drama with a more natural sentimental style.

Farragut, David (Glasgow) (1801–70) US admiral. As a young man he became a ship's officer and by 1824 was commander of his own ship. His service during the Civil War involved command of a Union fleet that blockaded parts of the Mississippi River and prevented the Confederates from receiving needed aid. New Orleans (1862) and Vicksburg (1863) fell with his help, and several forts on Mobile Bay, Alabama, were captured (1864) due to his daring run through the mined harbor.

Farrell, James T(homas) (1904–79) US writer. He wrote about his native Chicago and the middle-class Irish-Americans there. His triology, *Young Lonigan* (1932), *The Young Manhood of Studs Lonigan* (1934), and *Judgment Day* (1935), followed one man's life and early death. He also wrote about young Danny O'Neill and would-be writer Bernard Clare (Carr) in a series of novels (1963–68), the novels *Invisible Swords* (1971) and *The Death of Nora Ryan* (1978), and the essay collections *A Note on Literary Criticism* (1936) and *Literature and Morality* (1947).

farsighted(ness) (or hypermetropia) Inability to see close objects clearly, because the lens of the eye focuses light to a point behind the retina (light-sensitive layer). This is less common than nearsightedness among young people, but, owing to changes in the lens with age, many people need glasses for reading by the time they are 50. This type of farsightedness is known as presbyopia.

Fasciola. See liver fluke.

fascism A 20th-century political movement. Taking its name from the *fasces*, the bound bundles of rods that symbolized the authority of ancient Roman magistrates, fascism first became an organized movement in Italy in 1919 under *Mussolini. Social and economic backwardness, fear of communist revolution, and frustrated national ambitions following World War I encouraged its growth, and in 1922 Mussolini's *Blackshirts came to power. Fascism became more doctrinaire, rejecting ideas of individual liberty and equality, emphasizing national or racial superiority, and concentrating authority on a dictatorial cult figure. In Germany Hitler, who came to power in 1933 as leader of the *Nazi Party, added antisemitism to fascist militarism and anticommunism. World War II destroyed Mussolini's and Hitler's dictatorships and fascism won little support in other countries, except in Spain, where Franco's regime survived almost 40 years. The term fascist is now often used pejoratively to describe any advocate of extreme right-wing views.

Fashoda Incident (1898) A confrontation between Britain and France at Fashoda in the Egyptian Sudan over their rival claims to the area. French forces under Jean-Baptiste Marchand (1863–1914) occupied the fort at Fashoda, which quickly brought *Kitchener and his Anglo-Egyptian force to the spot. After several months of diplomatic wrangling, which brought the two countries to the brink of a major war, France was forced to withdraw and Britain's claims were recognized.

Fassbinder, Rainer Werner (1946–82) German film director. Working with a small group of actors in Munich, he produced a rapid succession of bleak realistic films on contemporary social themes. These include *The Bitter Tears of Petra von Kant* (1972) and *Fear Eats the Soul* (1974).

Fast, Howard Melvin (1914–) US writer. A member of the Communist Party (1943–57), he served a prison term (1950) for concealing his membership from the House Committee on Un-American Activities and was awarded the Stalin International Peace Prize (1954). His break with the party is related in *Naked God* (1957). His works include *Two Valleys* (1933), *Citizen Tom Paine* (1943), *Freedom Road* (1944), *Spartacus* (1952), *The Immigrants* (1977), *Second Generation* (1978), *The Establishment* (1979), and *The Legacy* (1981).

fast reactor A nuclear reactor (*see* nuclear energy) in which natural uranium enriched with uranium-235 or plutonium-239 is used without a moderator, the chain reaction being sustained by fast neutrons. In these reactors the core is surrounded by a blanket of natural uranium into which neutrons escape. These neutrons collide with U-238 nuclei to form U-239 nuclei, which decay to the fissionable isotope Pu-239. By suitable design, more Pu-239 can be produced in the blanket than is required to enrich the fuel in the core. These reactors are therefore called **breeder reactors** and they are 50 times more economical in uranium usage than *thermal reactors.

Their main disadvantage is that the temperature is so high that a liquid metal (usually sodium) has to be used as coolant: any leakage of sodium could be disastrous. Also, plutonium is both extremely toxic and can be used to make *nuclear weapons. For these reasons fast breeder reactors, although under development in several countries, are somewhat unpopular.

Fatah, al- (Arabic: the victory) A Palestinian organization, also known as the Palestine National Liberation Movement, established in the late 1950s. Led by Yasser *Arafat, al-Fatah began guerrilla warfare and terrorism against Israel in the mid 1960s.

Fatehpur Sikri 27 06N 77 39E A deserted city in Uttar Pradesh (N India). Founded (1569) by *Akbar, it was the Mogul capital until Akbar's move to *Lahore (1585). Its palaces, mosques, and gateways are masterpieces of *Mogul architecture, notably the Buland Darwaza (Victory Gate).

Fates In Greek mythology, three goddesses who determine human destinies. The daughters of Zeus and Themis, they are: Lachesis, who assigns a person's position at birth; Clotho, who spins out the thread of his existence; and Atropos, who cuts the thread at death.

Fathers of the Church The title given to certain writers of the early Christian Church whose works were regarded as carrying special weight in matters of doctrine and who were noted for their great learning and holiness. The period in which they lived extends from the 1st to the 7th centuries, and they are classified as ante-Nicene or post-Nicene according as to whether they lived before or after the Council of *Nicaea (325). They include Tertullian, Athanasius, Ambrose, Augustine, Jerome, and Gregory the Great.

fathom A unit used to express depths of water. Originally intended to be the distance between a man's fingertips with his arms outstretched, it is equal to six feet. It has now largely been replaced by the meter.

Fátima 39 37N 8 39W A village in central Portugal. It was here that three children allegedly saw a vision of the Virgin Mary (1917); it is now a place of pilgrimage.

Fatimah (d. 632) The daughter of *Mohammed. She married *Ali and was the mother of his sons, Hasan and Husayn, from whom most of the Shiite *imams were descended. She died shortly after her father. The Fatimid caliphs claimed descent from her.

Fatimids A dynasty of *caliphs ruling in N Africa and Egypt (909–1171). The Fatimids claimed descent from *Fatimah, Mohammed's daughter, and formed a subsect of the *Ismaili. They seized power in Tunisia in 909 and conquered Egypt in 969. In the 11th century their power declined and the caliphs became puppets in the hands of their soldiers. In 1171 they were finally overthrown by *Saladin.

fats and oils *Lipid substances formed by the combination of glycerol with *fatty acids. Fats occur widely in animals and plants as an energy store and as insulating material. Vegetable fats and oils are used in making soaps, margarines, cooking oils, paints, and lubricants. Animal fats are used in foods, soaps, and candles. Oils are distinguished from fats by being liquid at 43°F (20°C), whereas fats are solid. Mineral oils are hydrocarbons rather than lipids (see oil).

fatty acid (or carboxylic acid) An organic acid that comprises one or more carboxyl groups (–COOH) attached to an alkyl group. Fatty acids combine with glycerol to form glycerides, the main constituents of *fats and oils. Animal fats tend to be hard because they contain a high proportion of saturated fatty acids; soft fats, such as vegetable and fish oils, contain greater proportions of unsaturated and polyunsaturated fatty acids (containing one or more double bonds). There is evidence to suggest that the risk of heart disease associated with dietary fat is reduced if the fat consumed is rich in polyunsaturated fatty acids. Certain essential fatty acids are normally required in small amounts in the diet.

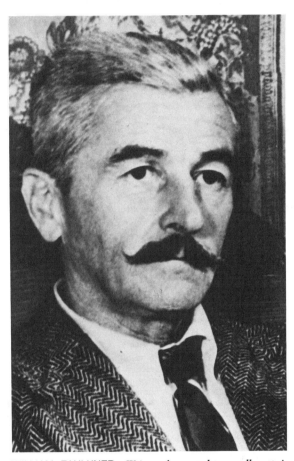

WILLIAM FAULKNER *Writer whose works, usually set in fictional Yoknapatawpha County, Mississippi, portrayed universal man.*

Faulkner, William (1897–1962) US novelist. Born in Mississippi, he abandoned his university education to write. He supported himself with various jobs before publishing his first poetry collection, *The Marble Faun*, in 1924. His first novel, *Soldier's Pay*, appeared in 1926. *Sartoris* (1929), the hero of which is based on Faulkner's great-grandfather, also an author, was the first of his stories set in the fictitious Yoknapatawpha County, based on his native northern Mississippi. Faulkner's characters and their personal tragedies acquire an epic universal grandeur, despite the decaying society within which they occasionally find themselves. His major novels, usually experimental in form and technique, include *The Sound and the*

Fury (1929), *As I Lay Dying* (1930), *Light in August* (1932), *Absalom, Absalom!* (1936), and *The Reivers* (1966). He was awarded the Nobel Prize in 1949.

fault A fracture plane in the rocks of the earth's crust, the rocks on each side being displaced relative to one another, either vertically, horizontally, or obliquely. Faulting occurs as a result of accumulated strain in the rocks, usually at plate margins (see plate tectonics). The extent of vertical displacement of the strata is called the throw; the horizontal displacement is the heave. A horst is an upstanding feature between two parallel faults; conversely a graben or rift valley is downthrown between parallel faults. *See* Plate II.

Fauré, Urbain (Gabriel) (1845–1924) French composer and organist, a pupil of Saint-Saëns. He became organist at the Madeleine (1877) and director or the Paris conservatoire (1905). He was afflicted with deafness in later life. His works include the well-known *Requiem* (1886–87), incidental music for Maeterlincke's play *Pelléas and Mélisande* (1898), the opera *Pénélope* (1913), the orchestral *Pavane* (1887), and much piano music and chamber music. Fauré is probably best known for his songs, such as those in the cycle *La Bonne Chanson* (1891–92).

Faust A legendary medieval German scholar and magician who sold his soul to the Devil in exchange for knowledge and power. Stories of magicians in league with the Devil (often personified by Mephistopheles) combined with the historical Johann Faust (c. 1480–c. 1539), a vagrant scholar and mountebank, to produce a figure who has inspired numerous literary works, notably by *Marlowe (1592), *Lessing (1784), *Goethe (1808, 1832), and Thomas *Mann (1947), as well as musical works, including operas by *Gounod and *Boito. The character of Faust has varied from that of Marlowe's power-seeking magician to that of Goethe's rationalist philosopher.

fauvism A movement in French painting at the turn of the 19th century, characterized by the aggressive use of strong colors. The fauves (French: wild beasts, so called by a critic of their work) included, under the leadership of *Matisse, Raoul *Dufy, Georges *Braque, Georges *Rouault, and Maurice de *Vlaminck. Most of the fauves had become interested in *cubism by 1908.

Fawkes, Guy (1570–1606) English conspirator. A convert to Roman Catholicism, he served in the Spanish army in the Netherlands during the 1590s and on his return to England became involved in the Gunpowder Plot, led by Robert Catesby (1573–1605), to blow up James I and parliament. The conspirators were informed upon and Fawkes was discovered (November 5, 1605) with the gunpowder in a cellar of the Palace of Westminster. Catesby was killed while resisting arrest and Fawkes was — executed. Nov 5 continues to be celebrated with fireworks and the burning on a bonfire of effigies of Fawkes (so-called "guys").

Fa Xian (or Fa-hsien; 5th century AD) Chinese Buddhist monk. He traveled to India and Ceylon in about 402 returning to China in about 413 with a large collection of early Sanskrit Buddhist texts. His translation of these and his account of his journey provide important documentation of the beginning of relations between China and India.

FBI. *See* Federal Bureau of Investigation.

feathers The specialized body covering of birds. Thought to have evolved from the scales of reptilian ancestors, feathers arise from definite tracts over the body surface and are of several types: the down feathers of chicks are short and soft, whereas the quill feathers of adult birds typically have a stiff shaft bearing two vanes with interlocking barbs and are specialized for flight as wing and tail feathers. As well as its role in flight, the plumage has several other functions. Like the hair of mammals, it helps to regulate body temperature and provides protection against the environment. It is also responsible for the bird's distinctive coloration, which is particularly important in courtship or aggressive displays. In order to maintain their function the feathers must be periodically renewed, and most birds undergo at least two molts a year. Molting is controlled partly by hormones and partly by environmental factors.

feather star. *See* crinoid.

February Second month of the year. The name is derived from Februus, the Roman god of purification. It has 28 days with 29 every fourth year, or leap year, to equate the calendar year with the solar year. The zodiac signs for February are Aquarius and Pisces; the flowers are violets and primroses, and the birthstone is the amethyst.

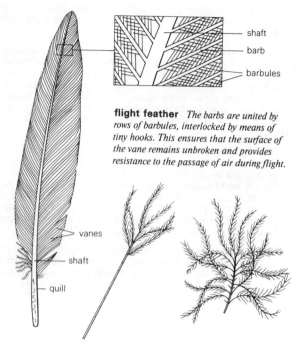

flight feather *The barbs are united by rows of barbules, interlocked by means of tiny hooks. This ensures that the surface of the vane remains unbroken and provides resistance to the passage of air during flight.*

shaft
barb
barbules

vanes
shaft
quill

filoplume *This small hairlike feather, which has very few barbs, is found in large numbers between and beneath the quill feathers.*

down feather *This type of feather forms the insulating body covering of nestlings. Its fluffy appearance is due to the lack of interlocking hooks on the barbules.*

FEATHERS

feces The material that is expelled from the bowels through the anus. It is a solid or semisolid mass consisting of undigested food (chiefly cellulose and other fibers), mucus, bacteria, and material from the liver, including bile pigments (which are responsible for the colour of feces). Any persistent change in the appearance of the feces may be an indication of disease. *See also* constipation; diarrhea.

Fechner, Gustav Theodor (1801–87) German physicist, noted for his work in experimental psychology. Fechner developed techniques for investigating the sensations experienced by human subjects exposed to stimuli of varying strengths. He also proposed a mathematical expression (later shown to be inaccurate) of the theory concerning the just noticeable difference between two stimuli, advanced by E. H. *Weber.

Federal Aviation Administration (FAA) US Department of Transportation agency that oversees aviation. It regulates commercial and civil aviation and coordinates air traffic of both with that of military aircraft. Formerly the Federal Aviation Agency, it took its present name in 1967.

Federal Bureau of Investigation (FBI) The organization within the Department of Justice that carries out investigations into possible breaches of federal law, especially those related to security. Founded as the Bureau of Investigation in 1908, it became the FBI in 1935; under J. Edgar *Hoover (director 1924–72) it developed considerable autonomy. It was prominent in the campaign against organized crime in the 1930s and also in the anticommunist activities of Joseph *McCarthy in the 1950s.

Federal Communications Commission (FCC) An independent US government agency that oversees interstate radio, television, wire, and cable communication services. The Communications Act, passed in 1934, directed the formation of the commission with seven members to be appointed by the president and approved of by the Senate. It consists of four bureaus: the Broadcast Bureau, the Common Carrier Bureau, the Safety and Special Radio Services Bureau, and the Field Engineering Bureau.

Federal Deposit Insurance Corporation (FDIC) A US government agency that insures commercial bank depositors from loss of funds. It was established in 1933 when the Glass-Steagall Act was passed as a future defensive measure against the bank failures of 1929–33. The three-member commission, appointed by the president, insures individual accounts and sets standards for qualifying banks.

Federal Housing Administration (FHA) US government agency, part of the Department of Housing and Urban Development (HUD) since 1965, that insures mortgage lenders that their payments will be met. Created in 1934, it was part of President *Roosevelt's New Deal program to stimulate the housing and construction industry. The standards set for acquiring an FHA insured mortgage have become standards for the housing industry.

federalism The political union of separate states, joined together to serve their common interests while retaining a degree of autonomy. A federation usually provides strong central government in such common matters as defense, a national currency system, etc., leaving to state government affairs that depend on local conditions. In most cases states are not able to withdraw from a federation at will, as the *Civil War demonstrated. In most federations in the 20th century the central government has gained power at the expense of the state government as in the US. An exception is the Soviet Union, where republics have been given a greater control over their budgets and in the management of industry. Canada is a federation that is under severe strain owing to the separatist elements in the province of *Quebec. Other federations include those of Malaysia and Australia.

Federalist Papers (1787–88) A series of essays published in New York newspapers, urging ratification of the US Constitution. The authors of the essays, using the name Publius, were Alexander *Hamilton, James *Madison, and John *Jay. They explained in detail the new federal government and its various departments. The essays were later published (1788) in two volumes, *The Federalist*.

Federalist Party US political party, led by John *Adams and Alexander *Hamilton, that advocated the establishment of a strong central government for the newly independent US. The Federalists emerged in 1787 as those who supported the ratification of the proposed *Constitution, explaining their position in a series of political essays known as the *Federalist Papers. They were opposed by the Republicans led by Thomas *Jefferson, who feared encroachments on individual liberty by a centralized government. With the ratification of the Constitution in 1788 and the election of George *Washington, the Federalist candidate, as the first president, the Federalists emerged as the majority party. During the administration of Washington and his successor, Adams, the Federalists were responsible for establishing a national administration. Their political power declined, however, with the defeat of John Adams and the election of Jefferson as president in 1800. After the *War of 1812, the Federalist Party lost much of its national influence, and many of its members joined the *Whig Party headed by John Quincy *Adams and Henry *Clay.

Federal Reserve System The *central bank of the US, established in 1913, which implements the government's monetary policy. There are 12 Federal Reserve Districts each of which has its own Federal Bank, controlled by the Federal Reserve Board in Washington.

Federal Trade Commission (FTC) A US government agency that regulates competition in interstate commerce. Established in 1914, its five commissioners, appointed by the president, look into unfair competition practices, such as monopolies, restraint of trade practices, and false advertising. Working closely with the Justice Department, the commission enforces antitrust legislation.

feedback In electronics and communications theory, the process of returning to the input of a device a fraction of the output signal. **Negative feedback**, in which the feedback opposes and therefore reduces the input, is often used in *amplifier circuits. It compensates for noise and distortion in the output signal, although it also reduces the overall amplification. **Positive feedback** reinforces the input signal. If it becomes too high, the circuit oscillates and the output becomes independent of the input. This is the cause of the singing noise heard in a public-address system when the microphone picks up feedback from the loudspeakers.

Feininger, Lyonel (Charles Adrian) (1871–1956) US painter and illustrator, born in New York. He studied painting in Germany and Paris and first worked as an illustrator and cartoonist for various German and French periodicals before concentrating on painting in 1907. His works were exhibited with the *Blaue Reiter group and he taught at the *Bauhaus (1919–33), eventually returning to the US in 1937. He developed a personal form of *cubism in his oils and watercolors, his favorite subjects being architectural forms, boats, and the sea.

feldspars The most important group of rock-forming minerals and the major constituents of igneous rocks. There are four components of feldspars: anorthite (calcium plagioclase, $CaAl_2Si_2O_8$); albite (sodium plagioclase, $NaAlSi_3O_8$); orthoclase (potassium feldspar, $KAlSi_3O_8$); and celsian (barium feldspar, $BaAl_2Si_2O_8$, which is rare). Feldspars ranging between albite and anorthite in composition are plagioclase feldspars; those ranging between albite and orthoclase are alkali feldspars. Calcic plagioclase includes anorthite, bytownite, and labradorite; sodic plagioclase includes andesine, oligoclase, and albite. Alkali feldspars include sanidine, anorthoclase, orthoclase, microcline, and adularia.

Felidae The *cat family: a family of mammals of the order *Carnivora. It includes the cats, lion, tiger, leopard, and cheetah.

Felix V (antipope). *See* Amadeus VIII.

Feller, Bob (Robert William Andrew F.; 1918–) US baseball pitcher. He pitched for the Cleveland Indians (1936–41; 1945–56). Nicknamed "Rapid Robert," he had 348 strikeouts in one year (1946) and 266 career wins. During his career he pitched 3 no-hit games. He was elected to the Baseball Hall of Fame (1962).

Fellini, Federico (1920–) Italian film director. He began working in films as an actor and scriptwriter. His films, many of which are characterized by their autobiographical elements and their use of baroque imagery and fantasy, include *La strada* (1954), *8½* (1963), *Roma* (1972), and *Amarcord* (1974).

felony A more serious offense than a misdemeanor involving such crimes as burglary and murder. Conviction for a felony can result in imprisonment for one year or more.

feminism. *See* women's movement.

femur The thigh bone: the longest bone in the human body. It extends from the pelvis, where it forms part of the ball-and-socket hip joint, to the joint of the knee. The head of the femur is commonly fractured in the elderly after falls.

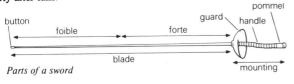

Parts of a sword

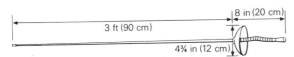

Foil *The foil weighs a maximum of 17.6 oz (500 g). Its blade is quadrangular and very flexible.*

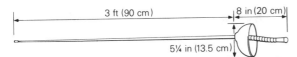

Épée *The épée weighs a maximum of 27.2 oz (770 g). Its blade is triangular and stiffer than that of the foil.*

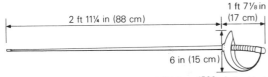

Saber *The saber weighs a maximum of 17.6 oz (500 g). Its blade is is a flattened V-shape.*

FENCING

fencing The art of combat with a sword, of which there are three main forms in sport: foil, épée, and saber. Bouts for all three weapons are fought on a *piste*, or marked-out area 2 × 6.5 × 46 ft (14 m) for foil and épée or 6.5 × 78.5 ft (2 × 24 m) for saber. A hit is scored against a competitor who crosses the rear limit. The winner is the first to score five hits (for men) or four (for women) in a time limit of six minutes (for men) or five (for women), the form of the hit varying between the three weapons. For major competitions the electric foil and épée are used for automatic judging.

Fénelon, François de Salignac de la Mothe (1651–1715) French Roman Catholic prelate and theologian. As director (from 1678) of an institution for recent Roman Catholic converts, he wrote *Traité de l'éducation des filles* (1687), criticizing the coercive conversion of Huguenots. In 1689 he became tutor to Louis XIV's grandson, the Duke of Burgundy, and in 1695 Archbishop of Cambrai. His famous *Aventures de Télémaque* (1699), written for the duke's instruction, alienated the king and his *Explication des maximes des saints* (1697), containing a defense of *Quietism, was condemned by the pope.

Fenian cycle Irish Gaelic tales and ballads of the Fianna, a legendary band of warrior-poets named for their leader, *Finn MacCool, who was said to have flourished in the 3rd century AD. Many of the tales are collected in *The Colloquy of the Ancient Men* (c. 1200) in which Oisin (*see* Ossian) and Caoilte, members of the Fianna, return to Ireland from the Land of Youth and recount their youthful adventures to St Patrick, and in the manuscripts *The Book of the Dun Cow* (c. 1100) and *The Book of Leinster* (c. 1160).

Fenians Members of a secret Irish-American revolutionary society, the Irish Republican Brotherhood (IRB), formed in 1858 by James Stephens (1825–1901). The Fenians staged an unsuccessful rising in Ireland in 1867 but the IRB's influence continued into the 20th century, when it was superseded by the IRA.

fennec A desert *fox, *Fennecus zerda*, of Africa and the Middle East. It is sandy-colored and has large pointed ears. Measuring up to 28 in (70 cm) including the tail 12 in (30 cm), it spends the day in a burrow and hunts at night, finding lizards, birds, and insects by ear. □mammal.

fennel A strong-smelling perennial herb, *Foeniculum vulgare*, native to S Europe and cultivated throughout temperate Eurasia. 20 in–5 ft (0.5–1.5 m) high, it has feathery dark-green leaves and clusters of small yellow flowers. The leaves are used mostly to flavor foods and sauces. The greenish seeds taste of aniseed and are used to flavor liqueurs, candies, pastries, and sweet pickles. The seed oil is used to scent soaps and perfumes. Florence, or sweet, fennel (*F. dulce*) is cultivated for its bulblike leafstalks, which may be eaten cooked as a vegetable or raw in salads. Family: *Umbelliferae*.

fenugreek An annual herb, *Trigonella foenum-graecum*, native to the Mediterranean but widely cultivated. About 24 in (60 cm) high, it has toothed compound leaves and small white flowers that develop into slender curved pods. The brownish seeds are used to flavor curry and chutney. Family: *Leguminosae*.

Ferber, Edna (1887–1968) US novelist. She worked as a reporter in Wisconsin and Chicago, before she started writing short stories and novels in 1911. Emma McChesney, a saleswoman, was one of her most popular early characters and appeared in many short stories. *So Big* (1924) brought her the Pulitzer Prize in 1925 and *Showboat* (1926) was adapted for the musical stage. Other works, most of which were made into motion pictures, include *Cimarron* (1930), *Saratoga Trunk* (1941), *Giant* (1952), and *Ice Palace* (1958). She also wrote plays, including *Dinner at Eight* (1932) and *Stage Door* (1936), with George S. Kaufman.

fer-de-lance A common extremely venomous tropical American *pit viper, *Bothrops atrox*. It is much feared by plantation workers and often visits houses in search of rodents. 4–7 ft (1.2–2 m) long, it has a broad triangular head, is gray or brown with black-edged diamond patterning and a yellowish chin, and generally feeds on small mammals, frogs, and lizards.

Ferdinand (1865–1927) King of Romania (1914–27), who in 1916 joined the Allies in *World War I. In 1918 he annexed Bessarabia from Russia and in 1919 intervened in Hungary to destroy Kun's communist government.

Ferdinand (I) the Great (?1016–65) King of Castile (1037–65). He conquered León (1039) and resumed the offensive against the Moorish border kingdoms, reducing the rulers of Toledo, Saragossa, and Seville to tributaries.

Ferdinand I (1503–64) Holy Roman Emperor (1558–64). His elder brother, Emperor *Charles V, gave him the Habsburg possessions in Germany in 1521 and in 1526 he became King of Bohemia and of Hungary, although his title to the Hungarian crown was challenged by John Zápolya (1487–1540) until 1538. Ferdinand negotiated the religious Peace of *Augsburg (1555).

Ferdinand I (1751–1825) King of Naples and Sicily (Two Sicilies; 1816–25). As Ferdinand IV he was King of Naples (1759–99, 1799–1806), being twice driven into exile in Sicily by the French. He ruled the Two Sicilies despotically.

Ferdinand I (1793–1875) Emperor of Austria (1835–48) and King of Hungary (1830–48). Feeble minded and epileptic, he was dominated by *Metternich. He abdicated during the Revolution of 1848.

Ferdinand I (1861–1948) Prince (1887–1908) and King (1908–18) of Bulgaria. In 1908 Ferdinand declared Bulgaria independent from Turkey but was forced to abdicate in 1918 after supporting the Central Powers.

Ferdinand II (1578–1637) King of Bohemia (1617–37) and Hungary (1618–37) and Holy Roman Emperor (1619–37), who championed the *Counter-Reformation. In 1619 the predominantly Protestant diet (assembly) of Bohemia offered the Bohemian crown to the Protestant *Frederick V of the Palatinate. The ensuing dispute developed into the *Thirty Years' War. Initially successful, Ferdinand suffered reverses with the intervention into the war of France and Sweden, forcing him to accept the compromise Peace of Prague (1635).

Ferdinand III (1608–57) King of Bohemia and of Hungary (1625–57) and Holy Roman Emperor (1637–57). He created a standing army, reformed the imperial council, and helped conclude the *Thirty Years' War by signing the Peace of *Westphalia (1648).

Ferdinand (V and II) the Catholic (1452–1516) King of Castile as Ferdinand V (1474–1504) and of Aragon as Ferdinand II (1479–1516). He ruled Castile jointly with his wife *Isabella I of Castile and after her death was regent for their daughter Joanna the Mad. Ferdinand's accession to the Aragonese throne effected the union of Castile and Aragon, to which Granada, taken from the Moors in 1492, was added. The introduction of the Inquisition (1480) and the expulsion of the Jews (1492) aimed to strengthen both church and monarchy, to which Ferdinand's reforms in Aragon contributed. His ambitions abroad led to wars with France for hegemony in Italy.

Ferdinand VII (1784–1833) King of Spain (1808, 1814–33). In 1808 Ferdinand was forced by Napoleon to abdicate but returned to the throne in 1814. His repressive policies caused a liberal uprising (1820) and the establishment of a liberal government until 1823, when it was ousted with French help. Alfonso repudiated the Salic Law of succession to enable his daughter *Isabella to succeed him, an act that led to the emergence of *Carlism.

Fergana (or Ferghana) 40 23N 71 19E A city in the S Soviet Union, in the Uzbek SSR. It is the industrial and cultural center of the fertile Fergana Valley, one of the country's main cotton- silk-, and fruit-growing districts. Population (1981 est): 180,000.

Feriae The sacred festival days of ancient Rome, which were usually marked by a public holiday, feasts, prayers, and sacrifices to the gods. Feriae were normally held on fixed annual dates.

Ferlinghetti, Lawrence (1919–) US poet. His public readings and his publishing business, the City Lights Bookshop in San Francisco, promoted *Beat movement poetry. His own poetry, published in *Pictures from the Gone World* (1955), *A Coney Island in the Mind* (1958), *Tyrannus Nix?* (1969), and other collections, is largely political satire. A journal, *Back Roads to Far Places*, was published in 1971.

Fermanagh A county in SW Northern Ireland, bordering on the Republic of Ireland. It consists of hilly country contained chiefly in the Erne Basin and is divided by the Upper and Lower Lough Erne. It is predominantly agricultural producing livestock and potatoes. Industries include the production of clothing, cotton thread, and tweeds. Area: 715 sq mi (1851 sq km). Population (1971): 50,255. County town: Enniskillen.

Fermat, Pierre de (1601–65) French mathematician. Professionally a lawyer, Fermat studied mathematics in his spare time. He founded *number theory and, with Blaise *Pascal, *probability theory. He is best known for *Fermat's last theorem and *Fermat's principle.

Fermat's last theorem A theorem, first proposed by Pierre *Fermat, that there are no natural numbers x, y, z, and n such that $x^n + y^n = z^n$ when n is greater than two. The theorem has never been proved for the general case, only for particular examples of n. Fermat himself claimed to have proved it but he never recorded his proof.

Fermat's principle When light travels between two points its path is such that the time taken is a minimum. The principle holds when the light is reflected or refracted between the two points. It is also known as the principle of least time and is named for P. *Fermat.

fermentation The process by which microorganisms and tissues respire in the absence of oxygen (i.e. anaerobically). The fermentation of carbohydrates by yeasts to form alcohol is the basis of making wines and beers (*see* beer and brewing; wine) and the production of industrial alcohol. Other types of fermentation produce lactic acid, as in the souring of milk by bacteria. Fermentation can cause the decomposition of organic materials under anaerobic conditions but the organisms concerned are able to use only a small proportion of the available energy compared to aerobic organisms.

Fermi, Enrico (1901–54) US physicist, born in Italy. His early work in Italy was concerned with the mathematical statistics of nuclear particles; independently of *Dirac he produced the form of statistics known as *Fermi-Dirac statistics. For his work on the bombardment of uranium by thermal neutrons he was awarded the 1938 Nobel Prize. Because of his antifascism and because his wife was Jewish, Fermi and his family sailed direct from the Stockholm Nobel ceremony to the US, where he remained for the rest of his life. He was the first person to achieve a controlled nuclear chain reaction, in a converted squash court at Chicago University (1942). He later played a central role in the development of the atom bomb at Los Alamos. After his return to Chicago (1946) he bitterly opposed *Teller in the development of the hydrogen bomb.

Fermi-Dirac statistics A quantum-statistical method of analyzing a system of indistinguishable particles to determine the probability of the energy distribution. Unlike *Bose-Einstein statistics it assumes that these particles, which are known as fermions, obey the *Pauli exclusion principle. Named for— E. *Fermi and P. A. M. *Dirac.

fermion Any elementary particle that obeys *Fermi-Dirac statistic. These particles, which have half-integral spin, include *leptons and *baryons. *Compare* boson.

fermium (Fm) An artificial transuranic element, named for Fermi. Like *einsteinium it was found in debris from the 1952 hydrogen-bomb explosion. The most stable isotope, ^{257}Fm, has a half-life of 80 days. At no 100; at wt (257).

fern A perennial leafy *pteridophyte plant of the class *Pteropsida* (or *Filicinae* according to some classification schemes; about 9000–15,000 species), most abundant in shady damp tropical regions but also widely distributed elsewhere. The life cycle of a fern shows *alternation of generations. The fern plant itself is the asexual (sporophyte) generation, which has a creeping underground stem (rhizome) bearing roots and aerial fronds, which reach a height of 80 ft (25 m) in the *tree ferns. The fronds are feather-like and usually divided one or more times into leaflets. Asexual spores are produced in spore capsules, which usually occur in clusters (sori) protected by a covering (indusium) on the underside of the leaflets. The spores develop into the inconspicuous sexual (gametophyte) generation—a tiny heart-shaped plant (called a prothallus) producing egg and sperm cells. The fertilized egg cell develops into a new sporophyte plant, which grows up from the prothallus. Many tropical and subtropical ferns are cultivated as house plants for their attractive foliage.

FERNANDEL *In one of his famous roles, as the priest Don Camillo.*

Fernandel (Fernand Joseph Desire Contandin; 1903–71) French comedian. Originally a music-hall singer and comedian, he later acted in numerous films, notably a series in the 1950s in which he played a village priest, Don Camillo, in conflict with the communist mayor.

Fernando Po. *See* Equatorial Guinea.

Ferrara 44 50N 11 38E A city in N Italy, in Emilia-Romagna. Important in Renaissance times as the seat of the Este family, it has a cathedral, castle, citadel, and university (1391). The religious reformer Savonarola was born here. Ferrara has wine, fruit, and grain trades and its manufactures include plastics, sugar, and chemicals. Population (1980 est): 151,643.

Ferrara-Florence, Council of (1438–45) The Church council at which the last concerted attempt was made to resolve the schism between Eastern and Western Churches. The council endeavored to reach agreement on doctrinal differences, such as the *Filioque clause, and to provide assistance for Constantinople against the Turks. Agreement was reached in 1439 but was short lived.

Ferraro, Geraldine Anne (1935–   ) US politician; Democratic candidate for vice president (1984). After graduation from Fordham Law School (1960) she became a Queens, New York, assistant district attorney (1974). The first woman from her district to be elected to the US House of Representatives (1978), she served on the Public Works and Transportation Committee and on the Budget Committee. As the running mate of Democratic presidential candidate Walter *Mondale in the 1984 election, she was the first woman chosen for that role. A frank and engaging speaker, she waged a spirited campaign, despite allegations of financial improprieties lodged against her husband, John A. Zaccaro. After the Democratic defeat, she returned to private life.

ferret A domesticated form of *polecat, *Mustela putorius*, that is slightly smaller than the European polecat and lighter in color (sometimes albino). Ferrets were probably bred from an Asian race (sometimes called *M. eversmanni*) and have been domesticated since at least 400 BC; they are used to drive rats and rabbits from their burrows.

ferrimagnetism A form of magnetism occurring in those *antiferromagnetic materials in which the microscopic *magnetic moments are aligned antiparallel but are not equal. The behavior is weakly *ferromagnetic below the Néel temperature and *paramagnetic above it.

ferrite 1. A compound of iron with the general chemical formula MFe_2O_4, where M is a metal. Most ferrites are *ferromagnetic or *ferrimagnetic ceramic materials and they are used in transformers and computer memories. 2. Iron in its body-centered cubic crystal structure, either pure or as a constituent of *steel.

Ferrol del Caudillo, El 43 29N 8 14W A city in NW Spain, in Galicia on the Atlantic Ocean. A port and naval base, it has ship-building and ship-repairing industries. Gen Franco was born here. Population (1970): 87,736.

ferromagnetism The property of a material that enables it to become a permanent magnet, i.e. ferromagnetic materials when placed in a *magnetic field develop a very strong internal field and retain some of it when the external field is removed. The most common ferromagnetic substances are iron, cobalt, nickel, and alloys of these metals. Ferromagnetism, like *paramagnetism, is caused by the unbalanced spin of atomic electrons, which creates a magnetic dipole moment having the effect of a tiny magnet. In ferromagnetic substances, the application of an external field causes groups of these tiny magnets, called domains, to become aligned; many of them remain aligned when the field is removed. Above a certain temperature, called the Curie point, thermal agitation destroys the domain structure and the substance becomes paramagnetic. The response of a ferromagnetic material to changes in magnetic field is known as the hysteresis effect; the internal field strength remaining after the external field has been reduced to zero is called the remanence.

Fertile Crescent A strip of land in the Middle East roughly comprising the lower Nile Valley, the E Mediterranean coast, Syria, and *Mesopotamia. Formerly enjoying a wetter climate, it was the cradle of civilization, with sites showing evidence of settled communities from at least 9000 BC.

fertility drugs Drugs given to infertile women to stimulate the release of an egg cell from the ovary. The best known are the *gonadotrophins—hormones normally released by the pituitary gland to control activity of the ovary. Another fertility drug is clomiphene. The dosage of these drugs is carefully controlled in order to prevent multiple pregnancies.

fertilization The union of a male and a female *gamete, involving the fusion of hereditary material: it is the essential process of sexual *reproduction. The resulting cell, called a zygote, undergoes division (*see* cleavage), growth, and development to form a new individual, in which half the chromosomes (and therefore the genes) are of paternal origin and half of maternal origin. In **self-fertilization** both gametes are produced by the same individual; in **cross-fertilization** they derive from different individuals (these terms are applied particularly to the processes in flowering plants). In most aquatic animals the gametes are expelled into the water and fertilization is external; in most terrestrial animals the sperms are introduced into the body of the female, where fertilization takes place.

fertilizers Substances added to soils to maintain or improve soil fertility. Natural farmyard manures have long been used as a source of plant nutrients and humus, which maintains the physical structure of the soil. Other traditional fertilizers have included bone meal, dried blood, and other animal products. Modern artificial fertilizers, dating from the 19th century, provided the means for dramatic increases in crop yields. The major plant nutrients required are nitrogen (chiefly provided as ammonium nitrate derived from fixation of atmospheric nitrogen), phosphate (derived from naturally occurring rock phosphate), and potassium (from mined potash deposits). These fertilizers are used either individually as "straights" or in combined or "compound" form to provide ratios of plant nutrients matched to the crop requirements.

Artificial fertilizers have been of immense benefit in helping to feed a rapidly expanding human population. The view that they are inferior to natural fertilizers is largely unfounded. Plants take in nitrogen ions, etc., in solution through their roots whether the source is a sack of fertilizer or farmyard manure. However, excessive application of artificial fertilizers can lead to pollution of streams, rivers, and even drinking water.

Fès (*or* Fez; Arabic name: Fas) 34 05N 5 00W A city in N Morocco. In the 14th century the Islamic city reached its peak as a major center for commerce and learning. It remains important for Arabic and Islamic teaching and has two mosques; the Qarawiyin Mosque is the oldest in Africa and contains a university (859 AD). The city gave its name to the traditional red felt hat worn by Muslims. It is a trade center for hides and leather, fruit, and traditional crafts. Population (1979 est): 744,900.

fescue A *grass of the genus *Festuca* (about 100 species), native to temperate and cold regions of the N hemisphere. It grows in tufts, 19–61 in (46–152 cm) high. Meadow fescue (*F. pratensis*) is sown as a pasture grass and used for livestock fodder; sheep's fescue (*F. ovina*) grows on mountains and in dry and exposed soil and the variety *F. ovina glauca* is used in ornamental borders. Red or creeping fescue (*F. rubra*) is common in grass mixtures for lawns.

fetishism 1. In anthropology, the practice of using charms magically. The term derives from the Portuguese *feitico*, something made. Fetishism is found among W African tribes and, hence, in the West Indies. Auguste *Comte characterized primitive religion as essentially fetishism, by which he meant the attribution of human qualities to nonhuman bodies. Later *Tylor reserved the term for the idea of spirits embodied in or associated with material objects. The term is not very common in modern sociology or anthropology. 2. In psychiatry, the abnormal condition in which sexual satisfaction is obtained by handling or otherwise using nongenital objects (fetishes). The fetish may be an article of clothing (such as shoes or underwear), rubber objects, leather, fur, or hair, and in some cases normal sexual relationships are impossible unless the fetish is present.

fetus (*or* foetus) The developing baby in the womb from the beginning of the ninth week of pregnancy until birth. The fetus is protected by a series of membranes enclosing a fluid (amniotic fluid), which can be extracted and used for diagnostic purposes. The fetus is connected through the *umbilical cord and *placenta to the mother's bloodstream. □embryo. *See also* prenatal diagnosis.

Feuchtwanger, Lion (1884–1958) German novelist and dramatist. Exiled in 1933, he fled to the US in 1940. His best-known novels are historical romances, notably *Jew Süss* (1925) and *The Pretender* (1936). He collaborated with *Brecht on plays and translations.

feudalism The type of land tenure, characteristic of medieval Europe, in which property was held by a vassal of a lord in return for military service and a pledge of homage. Feudalism originated with the collapse of public order in W Europe during the 8th and 9th centuries. Both kings and great lords distributed life grants of lands and offices in return for promises of loyalty and service. This practice developed into the grant of hereditary fiefs or fees (Latin word: *feoda*, from which the word feudalism is derived) in return for military service. The resulting fragmentation of authority was reflected in the rapid growth of feudal armies, often engaged in private wars, the development of the castle as an administrative and military center, and the growth of private justice administered by local lords rather than by a central authority. From the 12th century these implications of feudal tenure were challenged by the growing power of western rulers, especially in England, where it was abolished in 1661. Their governments increasingly depended on a royal bureaucracy and an army of mercenaries rather than the feudal bands. The growth of towns, outside the feudal framework, also contributed to the decline of feudalism.

Feuerbach, Ludwig Andreas (1804–72) German philosopher. Critical of Hegelian *idealism, Feuerbach saw the power of history not as a nebulous succession of spirits of the ages but as the total material conditions in any given period that caused people to behave as they did. This view and also his writings on religion, in which he argued that people lost their essential selves by applying their own attributes to imaginary beings, impressed *Marx and *Engels.

Feuillants, Club of the A moderate French Revolutionary political group that met at the former monastery of the Feuillants in Paris. Founded in 1791, the Feuillants opposed extremism, favoring constitutional monarchy. They disbanded in 1792, when the monarchy was abolished.

fever A body temperature greater than 98.6°F (37°C). This is most commonly due to *infection, but other causes include tumors, drugs, a heart attack, and a blood clot in the leg. Sometimes no cause can be found. The patient usually has a headache, shivers, and feels ill.

feverfew A perennial aromatic Eurasian herb, *Tanacetum* (or *Chrysanthemum*) *parthenium*, about 20 in (50 cm) high, with heads of yellow and white daisy-like flowers. Formerly a popular medicinal herb, it was used to reduce fever. Family: *Compositae.

Feydeau, Georges (1862–1921) French playwright, famous for his many farces, written between 1881 and 1916. They are characterized by fast-moving, intricate, and cheerfully immoral plots, witty dialogue, and complicated stage sets. They include *The Lady from Maxim's* (1889), *Hotel Paradiso* (1894), and *A Flea in Her Ear* (1907).

Feynman, Richard Phillips (1918–) US physicist, who shared the 1965 Nobel Prize with Julian Schwinger (1918–) and Shinitiro Tomonaga (1906–79) for their development of quantum electrodynamics. He is best known for his invention of Feynman diagrams, which illustrate the interactions between charged particles by the exchange of virtual photons.

Fez. *See* Fès.

Fezzan (or Fazzan; Latin name: Phazania) An area in SW Libya, forming part of the Sahara. It was a province until provinces were abolished in 1963.

Fianna Fáil (Irish: Soldiers of Destiny) Irish political party, founded in 1926 by Eamon *De Valera from moderate *Sinn Féin members. The ruling party in the years 1932–48, 1951–54, 1957–73, 1977–81, and 1982–, its leaders have been De Valera (until 1959), Sean Lemass (until 1966), Jack *Lynch (until 1979), and Charles Haughey (1925–).

fiber (or dietary fiber) The constituent of the human diet that is not digested. It consists of the cell walls of plants, i.e. cellulose, lignin, hemicellulose, and pectic substances. Significant amounts are present in whole-wheat cereals and flour, root vegetables, nuts, and fruit: highly refined foods, such as sugar, have a low fiber content. Dietary fiber is considered helpful in preventing constipation, diverticular disease, obesity, diabetes mellitus, and colonic cancer: societies with high-fiber diets rarely suffer from these conditions.

fiberglass (glass fiber *or* spun glass) Material made from glass drawn into fine threads. Glass fiber has excellent heat- and fire-resistant properties and is a good electrical insulator. It is spun and woven into curtain material; made into glass wool for heat, electrical, and sound insulation; woven into coarse mats for filters; and used in reinforcing molded plastics for boats, car bodies, etc.

fiber optics The use of flexible glass fibers for transmitting light. Each fiber, which may be used singly or in bunches, is usually less than a millimeter thick and has a high refractive index. The light inside the fiber is totally internally reflected and travels through the fiber with little loss of intensity. The fibers are highly polished and coated with a substance of lower refractive index to reduce dispersion further. Glass fibers are used for examining otherwise inaccessible places, for example in medical diagnosis and in specialized industrial processes.

fibers Threadlike substances of animal, vegetable, or man-made origin. *Wool and *silk are the most widely used animal fibers. Vegetable fibers include cotton, flax, hemp, jute, and sisal. Man-made fibers fall into two categories: **modified natural fibers**, including *rayon made from wood cellulose, and **synthetic fibers**, most of which are made by the polymerization of petrochemicals. They include *polyesters, nylon, and *acrylics. Some inorganic substances are also used in the form of fibers: examples include glass (*see* fiberglass; fiber optics), *asbestos, and *carbon fibers.

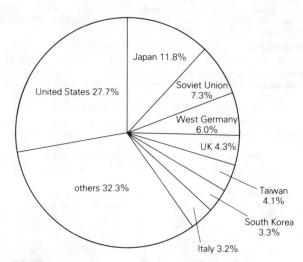

FIBERS *World production of synthetic fibers.*

Fibonacci, Leonardo (c. 1170–c. 1230) Italian mathematician. He traveled widely, especially in North Africa, where he learned the *decimal system of numerals and the use of zero, which al-Khwarizmi had, in turn, learned from the Indians. Fibonacci published the system in Europe, but mathematicians were slow to adopt it. In the **Fibonacci series** (0, 1, 1, 2, 3, 5, 8, . . .) each number is the sum of the preceding two.

fibrositis Inflammation of fibrous tissue, usually of the back muscles and muscle sheaths. This causes sudden pain and stiffness (muscular rheumatism). It is best relieved by rest, but aspirin or similar analgesics may help.

fibula. *See* leg.

Fichte, Johann Gottlieb (1762–1814) German philosopher and follower of *Kant. Fichte, however, debunked Kant's world of numinous "things-in-themselves," holding that practical reason and man's autonomously good will originated all that is worthwhile in the world, as well as creating the highest type of human personality. The outer world, a passive place, is the field of action for this human consciousness; by contrast, the Ego, or self, is the only basic reality. The existence of other Egos was, however, essential for the individual's pursuit of moral perfection. Fichte's philosophical works include *Foundation of the Laws of Nature* (1796) and *System of Moral Philosophy* (1798). His popular works strove to kindle German nationalism against Napoleon.

Fichtelgebirge A mountain range in E West Germany, between Bayreuth and the Czech border. It is mainly wooded (the name means "spruce mountains") and rises to 3448 ft (1051 m) at the Schneeberg. The minerals obtained from it include lead, copper, and marble.

Ficino, Marsilio (1433–99) Italian Platonist scholar. In 1462, under *Medici patronage, he founded the Platonic Academy to disseminate *Platonism and reconcile it with Christianity. His system was a blend of Neo-platonic metaphysics and Augustinian theology expressed in a hierarchical universe, with strata ranging from body to angels and God. Experience consisted of the ascent of man's immortal soul toward God. Ficino's translations of Plato (1484) remained standard for many years.

fiddler crab A small burrowing *crab, 1–1.2 in (25–30 mm) long, belonging to the genus *Uca* (about 65 species). The brightly colored male has an enlarged claw, which it holds somewhat like a violin. Fiddler crabs are found on salt marshes and sandy beaches of tropical and temperate regions, feeding on algae and other organic material. Tribe: *Brachyura.*

Fiedler, Arthur (1894–1979) US conductor; director of the Boston Pops Orchestra (1930–79). After studying in Berlin, Germany, he played for the Boston Symphony Orchestra (1915–30) and, drawing from its members, formed the Boston Pops in 1930. Playing all sorts of music from symphonic to rock, Fiedler and his orchestra became known for free summer concerts on the banks of the Charles River, radio and television appearances, and recordings.

field In physics, a region of space in which a body possessing certain properties can exert a force on similar bodies, when they are not in contact. For example, a body having mass exerts an attractive force on all other massive bodies as a result of its gravitational field. Similarly, an electrically charged body exerts a force (attractive or repulsive, depending on polarity) on other charged bodies and a magnetized body will have a magnetic field around it. A field is often represented by lines of force to indicate the direction in which the force acts at that point. The closeness together of the lines represents the strength of the force, and therefore the field, in that area.

Field, Cyrus West (1819–92) US financier and entrepreneur. Largely self-educated, he amassed a fortune by age 32 through persistence and shrewd investments. Retiring from active involvement in his earlier business interests, he devoted himself to the establishment of a transatlantic telegraph link, first suggested to him by Frederick Gisborne, a Canadian engineer. Field ultimately raised $1,500,000 for the project from a group of New York investors and the first transatlantic cable was laid in 1858 from Valentia, Ireland, to Trinity Bay, Newfoundland. Technical difficulties, however, quickly ended its use. Undeterred by the severe financial losses he had suffered by this failure, Field persisted with the project after the Civil War. He secured the services of the steamboat *Great Eastern* for the laying of an improved cable that went into service in 1866. Although the transatlantic cable project was his most important achievement, Field also invested heavily in railroads and newspapers later in life.

Field, Marshall (1834–1906) US businessman. As a young man he became a partner in a wholesale firm in 1856 in Chicago. After a series of partnerships, Field bought out his partners and established in 1881 Marshall Field and Company, which became the world's largest and most innovative retail store. He revolutionized retailing with one-price marking, liberal credit, a merchandise return system, and a department store restaurant. He supported the University of Chicago and was a founder of the Art Institute of Chicago (1878) and the Columbian Museum (1893), now the Field Museum of Natural History.

field emission The emission of electrons from the surface of certain materials when they are subjected to a very high electric field. Typically fields of about 10^{10} volts per meter are required. The effect is also known as cold emission or autoemission. It is utilized in the **field-emission microscope**, in which a magnified image of a surface is obtained by subjecting it to a high electric field and observing the distribution of emitted electrons on a cathode-ray screen.

fieldfare A *thrush, *Turdus pilaris*, of N Europe and Siberia, migrating to S and W Europe. It is about 10 in (25 cm) long with a speckled brown breast, brown back, white underwings, and blue-gray head.

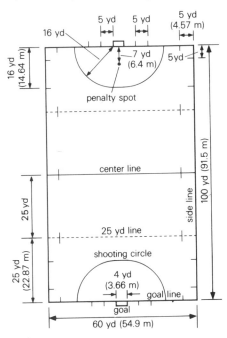

FIELD HOCKEY *The dimensions of the field.*

field hockey An 11-a-side field game for men and women, the object of which is to score goals. It has been played in various forms for at least 4000 years and is an Olympic sport. A team comprises a goalkeeper, two full-backs, three half-backs, and five forwards (left wing, inside left, center,

inside right, and right wing), each of which carries a curved stick for hitting the ball. Play is started at the beginning of the two 35-minute periods (and after each goal) with a face-off in the center of the field. In this brief ritual two opposing players cross their sticks and tap the ground three times. Play proceeds by dribbling the ball with the stick and passing it by hitting it along the ground or through the air. *See also* ice hockey.

Fielding, Henry (1707–54) British novelist and dramatist. He wrote about 25 plays, mostly satirical and topical comedies, between 1728 and 1737, when Walpole's Licensing Act effectively banned his vigorous satire; he then turned to journalism and law studies. *Shamela* (1741), a parody of Samuel Richardson's novel *Pamela* (1740), is almost certainly by Fielding. His major novels include *Joseph Andrews* (1742), the ironical *Jonathan Wild* (1743), and *Tom Jones* (1749).

FIELDMOUSE. *This mouse tends to prefer succulent food (peas, fruit, leaves, etc.) to dry grain and is sometimes found in houses, as well as gardens.*

fieldmouse A small nocturnal long-tailed *mouse, *Apodemus sylvaticus*, of Europe, Asia, and N Africa, also called woodmouse. About 3.3 in (9 cm) long, with an 3.1-in (8-cm) tail, it has a rich brown coat with white underparts. Fieldmice feed on seeds and grain and can become a pest.

Field of the Cloth of Gold (1520) The meeting near Calais of Henry VIII of England and Francis I of France. Francis hoped for English support against Emperor Charles V, with whom, however, Henry subsequently formed an alliance.

Fields, W. C. (William Claude Dukenfield; 1880–1946) US film actor. After working as a vaudeville juggler and comedian he began making films in the 1920s. He frequently portrayed an alcoholic misanthrope. In *It's a Gift* (1934), *You Can't Cheat an Honest Man* (1939), *The Bank Dick* (1940), *My Little Chickadee* (1940), and other films, he exploited his genuine eccentricity and intolerance of sentimentality with comic genius.

Fieschi A leading family of Genoa (Italy) during the 13th, 14th, and 15th centuries. The Fieschi, who were *Guelfs, wielded much influence in Genoese and papal politics as ambassadors, admirals, generals, cardinals, and even popes—*Innocent IV and Adrian V (d. 1276; reigned 1276) were Fieschi.

Fiesole 43 48N 11 17E A city in Italy, in Tuscany situated on a hill near Florence overlooking the Arno River. It has Etruscan and Roman remains and a romanesque cathedral. It is mainly residential. Population (1971): 114,111.

fife A small transverse *flute, pitched in B flat and used in military fife-and-drum bands.

Fife, Duncan. *See* Phyfe, Duncan.

Fifteen Years' War (1591–1606) A struggle between the Austrian Habsburgs and the Ottoman Turks for the possession of Hungary that followed 50 years of intermittent skirmishing. Neither side gained an ascendency but the stalemate was ended when István Bocksay (1557–1606) of Transylvania rebelled against the Habsburgs, made a treaty with the Turks, conquered Habsburg Hungary, and established Transylvania as an effective buffer state between the two belligerents.

fifth column A body of enemy sympathizers working within a country. The term originated in the Spanish Civil War when the Nationalist General Emilio Mola (1887–1937) is supposed to have said "I have four columns operating against Madrid and a fifth inside composed of my sympathizers."

Fifty-Four Forty or Fight (1844) Slogan taken up by those in the US who were in favor of exclusive US rights to the Oregon Territory. The territory between California and Alaska had been occupied jointly by the US and Britain. US expansionists felt the US was entitled to all lands north to latitude 54°40′. A compromise was finally reached in 1846 when the Oregon Treaty set the US boundary at the 49th parallel.

fig A spreading tree or shrub, *Ficus carica*, 40 in–40 ft (1–12 m) high, probably native to W Asia but widely cultivated in warm temperate and subtropical regions. The dark-green leathery leaves are large (up to 12 × 10 in [30 × 25 cm]) and usually deeply lobed. The tiny flowers are borne inside a fleshy pear-shaped structure, up to 3 in (8 cm) long, which develops into the edible fig after fertilization of the flowers. Figs—eaten fresh, dried, or preserved—are rich in sugar and iron and have laxative properties. Family: *Moraceae* (mulberry family).

fighting fish One of several *labyrinth fishes, especially of the genus *Betta*, found in SE Asia and the Malay Archipelago and named for the aggression shown by the males toward each other and to immature females. Some males brood eggs in their mouths. The Siamese fighting fish (*B. splendens*) is about 2.5 in (6.5 cm) long and greenish or brown in color. Long-finned and brightly colored varieties are bred for use in fighting contests.

fig marigold A plant of the genus *Mesembryanthemum* (about 200 species), found in warm regions, especially South Africa, and widely cultivated as ornamentals. Fig marigolds are spreading herbs or shrubs, often succulent, with large brilliantly colored daisy-like flowers and figlike fruits. Family: *Aizoaceae*.

figwort A square-stemmed herbaceous plant of the genus *Scrophularia* (120 species), of N temperate regions. 12–40 in (30–100 cm) tall, they have toothed leaves. The brown, yellow, or green flowers are almost spherical, with five small spreading lobes around the opening, and are borne on a branching flower stalk. A common Eurasian species is *S. nodosa*. Family: *Scrophulariaceae*.

Fiji, State of A country in the S Pacific Ocean. It consists of over 800 islands, only 106 of which are inhabited; the largest are Viti Levu and Vanua Levu. Most of the population are Indians and Fijians with some Europeans, Chinese, and other Pacific islanders. *Economy*: chiefly agricultural, sugar cane being the main cash crop; others include copra and ginger. Some gold is mined on Viti Levu and the chief exports are sugar, copra, coconut oil, and gold. Tourism is being developed and is now the second most important industry. Fiji is an important staging post on the air routes between North America and Australia and New Zealand. *History*: discovered by the Dutch explorer Tasman in 1643, the islands were visited by Capt Cook in 1774. During the 19th century the search for sandalwood brought many ships and tribal warfare was widespread until Fiji was ceded to Britain in 1874. It became independent within the British Commonwealth in 1970. Prime minister: Ratu Sir Kamisese Kapaiwai Tuimacilai Mara. Official language: English. Official currency: Fiji dollar of 100 cents. Area: 7055 sq mi (18,272 sq km). Population (1983 est): 676,000. Capital and main port: Suva.

Filarete (Antonio Averlino; c. 1400–c. 1469) Italian Renaissance architect. Originally a sculptor, he moved in 1451 to Milan where he designed his masterpiece, the Ospedale Maggiore. He wrote a treatise on architecture (1461–64) and, although he built little, was influential in promoting Italian classicism.

filaria A parasitic *nematode worm, mainly of central Africa, Asia, and the SW Pacific. The species *Wuchereria bancrofti* and *Brugia malayi* cause the disease **filariasis**. The tiny larval worm, measuring about 0.06 in (1.4 mm), enters the body in the saliva of a biting mosquito or mite. It then grows up to 3 in (8 cm) long in lymph and blood vessels, causing swelling and pain (*see* elephantiasis).

filbert A Eurasian shrub, *Corylus maxima*, closely related and similar to the *hazel. It is sometimes planted for its nuts, which are larger than hazelnuts and are partly hidden by long bracts.

filefish A *bony fish belonging to a family (*Monacanthidae*) found in warm coastal waters. It has a laterally flattened body, 5–10 in (13–26 cm)

long, covered with small filelike or velvety scales, two dorsal fin spines, and a very small mouth. Order: *Tetraodontiformes*.

Filioque (Latin: and the Son) An article of Christian faith in the Western Church, added to the *Nicene Creed and referring to the *Holy Spirit, "Who proceedeth from the Father *and the Son*" (rather than from the Father alone). It had appeared in Spain as early as 447 but was not adopted at Rome until the 11th century. The Orthodox Church did not accept it and attacked it as an unwarranted addition made to the Creed by Rome. *Photius denounced it in the 9th century and it was one of the central issues—together with disagreement over the nature of the primacy of the *papacy—that culminated in the schism between East and West in 1054.

Fillmore, Millard (1800–74) US political leader; 13th President of the United States (1850–53). Born in Locke, NY, Fillmore began his political career as leader of the Anti-Masonic party in the state legislature. In 1832 he was elected to the US House of Representatives, where he later joined the *Whig Party and became the influential chairman of the Ways and Means Committee. Fillmore returned to New York in 1844 to run for governor, but was defeated. In 1848 he accepted the vice presidential nomination of the Whig Party and was elected to that office as the running-mate of Zachary *Taylor. With Taylor's death in 1850, Fillmore succeeded to the presidency. The most pressing issue faced by the nation during the Fillmore administration was the question of *slavery. In an attempt to resolve the growing bitterness over the issue, Fillmore supported the *Compromise of 1850, but his attempts to enforce the *Fugitive Slave Law aroused considerable opposition within his own party and from the *Abolition movement. He failed to gain renomination by the Whig Party in 1852. Fillmore's last attempt at elective office was his unsuccessful campaign for president as the nominee of the American (*Know-Nothing) party in 1856.

film A thin flexible strip of cellulose acetate, or similar transparent plastic, coated with a light-sensitive emulsion. A black-and-white photographic emulsion usually consists of gelatin containing tiny suspended crystals of silver halide (usually bromide or chloride). After exposure to light in a *camera these crystals are easily reduced to metallic silver when treated with the chemicals in the developer. This produces black deposits of fine particles of metallic silver on the parts of the film upon which the light has fallen, giving a reversed (or negative) image. Fixing of the film consists of bathing it in sodium thiosulfate (hypo) or other fixers to render the unchanged silver halides soluble, enabling them to be washed away with water. The sensitivity (speed) of film is usually quoted as an *ASA rating, which determines the amount of light required to form a given amount of metallic silver. *See also* color photography.

films. *See* motion pictures.

filter A device that allows one substance to pass through it but not others. For example, a filter is used to remove solid particles from a liquid or gas by passing the mixture through a porous substance, such as paper or *fiberglass, the holes in which are fine enough to prevent the passage of the particles. Such filters are used in some air-conditioning units, for water purification, etc. In optics, colored glass filters are used to select light with a certain range of wavelengths. In electronics, filters are circuits used to allow alternating currents of a certain frequency range to pass, while currents with frequencies outside the range are stopped.

finch A songbird belonging to a family (*Fringillidae*; 176 species) occurring in most regions of the world except Australia. Finches have hard conical bills used to crack open seeds, although they also feed on buds and fruit. They range in size from 4–11 in (10–27 cm) and the plumage varies in color with the species. There are two subfamilies: the *Fringillinae*, including the finer-billed *chaffinch and *brambling of the Old World, and the *Carduelinae*, comprising the heavier-billed species found in both the Old World and North America. *Compare* weaverfinch.

Fine Gael (Irish: Tribe of Gaels) Irish political party, formed in 1933. It was the senior member of ruling coalitions in Ireland (1948–51, 1954–57, and 1973–77). It is rather more conservative than the rival *Fianna Fáil.

fineness of gold A measure of the purity of gold equal to the number of parts of pure gold in 1000 parts of the alloy.

finfoot A secretive semiaquatic bird belonging to a family (*Heliornithidae*; 3 species) found in dense vegetation bordering rivers and creeks of tropical and subtropical regions of America, Africa, and Asia. Up to 24 in (60 cm) long, finfoots have olive-brown plumage and large lobed feet, a long neck, and a stiff rounded tail. Order: *Gruiformes* (cranes, rails, etc.).

Fingal's Cave A spectacular cave on the Scottish island of Staffa, in the Inner Hebrides, composed of basaltic columns. Visited by Felix Mendelssohn (1829), it inspired his overture *Fingal's Cave* (1829, revised 1832). Length: 227 ft (68 m). Height: 117 ft (35 m).

Finger Lakes A series of eleven long and narrow lakes in central New York, bounded on the E by Syracuse, the S by Ithaca, and the W by Geneseo. The two largest, Cayuga and Seneca, are approximately 40 mi (65 km) long and 2.5 mi (4 km) wide. The smaller lakes are Otisco, Scaneateles, Owasco, Keuka, Canandaigua, Honeoye, Canadice, Hemlock, and Conesus.

arch   whorl   loop

FINGERPRINT *Loops are the commonest form of pattern (c. 65%), followed by whorls (c. 30%), and then arches (c. 5%).*

fingerprint The impression made by the pattern of ridges on the palmar side of the end joint of the fingers and thumbs. The taking of a person's fingerprints, which are virtually unique, for the purpose of identifying habitual criminals was begun in the early 20th century. The print is taken by rolling the fingers and thumbs, one by one or simultaneously, in ink and then rolling them on paper. Fingerprints left at the scene of a crime may be taken by photography. The FBI has more than 70 million fingerprint records on file. Classification relies on a numerical value given to a print, which identifies the finger and the pattern of ridges (of which there are 1024 primary groups).

Finisterre, Cape 42 52N 9 16W The most westerly point in Spain, on the Atlantic coast.

Finland, Gulf of An arm of the Baltic Sea, extending between Finland and the Soviet Union. The ports of Helsinki and Leningrad lie on the Gulf, which is frozen for 3–5 months of the year. Length: about 249 mi (400 km).

Finland, Republic of (Finnish name: Suomi) A country in N Europe, with S and W coastlines on the Baltic Sea. It includes the *Åland Islands, situated at the mouth of the Gulf of Bothnia. The land is generally low lying apart from some small hills in the NW. Over 10% of the area consists of lakes, which, together with rivers and canals, provide an extensive network of inland waterways. The majority of the population are Finns, with minorities of Swedes, Lapps, and Russians. *Economy*: agriculture is highly mechanized and, together with cereals, dairy produce is of particular importance. Over 70% of the land is under forest, providing ample resources for the timber and pulp and paper industries. Other industries include food processing and textiles. Hydroelectricity provides the main source of power and the principal mineral resources are copper and iron ore. Tourism is an important source of revenue. The main exports are timber, pulp and paper, and machinery. *History*: prehistorically the Finnic peoples migrated into Finland, gradually driving the Lapps northward. Conquered by Sweden in the 12th century AD, Finland continued to enjoy a considerable degree of independence, becoming a grand duchy in the 16th century. The country suffered considerable hardships, however, in the recurring wars between Sweden and Russia. In the 18th century the SE was occupied by Russia and in 1809 the rest of the country was ceded to Russia, becoming an autonomous grand duchy. During this period Finnish nationalism flourished and in 1863 the Finnish language was officially recognized. It became independent in 1917, following the Russian Revolution, and a republic two years later. In 1939 it was invaded by Soviet forces and in 1940, and again in 1944, was forced to cede certain territories to the Soviet Union. A treaty of friendship between the two countries, first signed in 1948, continues in force. Dr Urho Kaleva Kekkonen, who had been president since 1956, resigned in 1981 and was succeeded by Dr Mauno Henrik Koivisto. Official languages: Finnish and Swedish. Official currency: markka of 100 pennia. Area: 117,913 sq mi (305,475 sq km). Population (1983 est): 4,850,000. Capital and main port: Helsinki.

Finlay, Carlos Juan (1833–1915) Cuban physician, who discovered that yellow fever was transmitted by mosquitoes. By 1900, Finlay had persuaded the authorities to control mosquito populations and so eradicate the disease. *See also* Reed, Walter.

Finney, Albert (1936–) British actor. Following his early successful performances in plays by modern dramatists he made several films, notably *Saturday Night and Sunday Morning* (1960). He then returned to the theater to act classic roles, such as Tamburlaine and Hamlet.

Finnic A group of languages of the *Finno-Ugric branch of the Uralic family, which includes Finnish, Estonian, Lapp, Mari, Permic, and a number of other languages, most of which are dwindling in significance. The Finnic peoples, ancestors of the modern Finns and Estonians, migrated in prehistoric times from central Russia to the area of the E Baltic, Finland, and Karelia, bringing grain cultivation with them. Estonia became an important trading area and established a sense of national identity while the Finns inhabited more remote regions and remained fragmented until recent times. The *Lapps in the far north of the region retain their separate identity and language but other groups have mainly lost theirs. All these peoples adopted Christianity during the 11th and 12th centuries.

Finn MacCool A legendary Irish hero, leader of the Fianna (see Fenian cycle). The son of Cumhaill (Cool) and the father of the poet Oisin (see Ossian), he killed Goll MacMorna, his father's murderer, and became leader of the company.

Finno-Ugric languages A large group of languages of the *Uralic family, spoken by more than 20 million people in dispersed communities in Scandinavia, E Europe, and W Asia. Thought to have diverged about five millennia ago, the Finnic and Ugric languages can be further divided into the following major groups: Ugric (*Hungarian and Ob-Ugric) and *Finnic (Finnish, Estonian, Mari, Permic, and a number of other languages mostly spoken in the Baltic and in the region of the Volga). Periodically and to varying degrees, neighboring languages have exercised an influence on the vocabularies of the Finno-Ugric languages. Many Turkic forms, for example, have been absorbed into the Hungarian language. Although phonological processes may be shared by the majority of Finno-Ugric languages no single defining characteristic is common to all members.

fins Organs of locomotion and balance in fish and some other aquatic animals. The fins of fish are supported by bony or cartilaginous fin rays and are either median or paired. The median fins include the tail (or caudal) fin, typically used for propulsion (in conjunction with the muscular body) and the dorsal and anal fins, used for balancing. The paired pectoral fins, just behind the gills, and pelvic fins, further back, are used for steering (although in rays the large pectorals provide motive force).

Finsen, Niels Ryberg (1860–1904) Danish physician, who developed the use of light for treating certain bacterial skin diseases. Although now superseded, his work stimulated research into modern radiation therapy. He founded the Medical Light Institute (now the Finsen Institute), Copenhagen, in 1896 and was awarded a Nobel Prize (1903).

Finsteraarhorn 46 32N 8 08E A mountain in S central Switzerland, the highest in the Bernese Oberland. It was first climbed in either 1812 (disputed) or 1829. Height: 14,022 ft (4274 m).

Fiordland The largest national park of New Zealand, in SW South Island. It is a mountainous region with glacial lakes and fjords, including Lakes Manapouri and Te Anau (famous for its glowworm caves), and Milford Sound. Area: about 4400 sq mi (11,400 sq km).

fir A coniferous □tree of the genus *Abies* (about 50 species). Mostly native to N temperate regions, these trees are also called silver firs, as many species have leaves with a silvery undersurface. Firs have blunt-tipped needles and erect stout woody cones; they are important softwood trees (*see* timber). The European silver fir (*A. alba*), which forms pure forests in the mountains of central Europe, is widely grown for its timber: it reaches a height of 165 ft (50 m) and its cones are up to 6 in (15 cm) long. Another widely planted timber tree is the grand, or giant, fir (*A. grandis*), which grows up to 295 ft (90 m) in its native W North America. Family: *Pinaceae*.

Firdausi (Abul Qasim Mansur; c. 935–c. 1020) The first major Persian poet, famous as the author of the epic poem *Shah-nama* (*The Book of Kings*; 1010), which recounts the history of Iran and its rulers from legendary beginnings to the conquest of the country by Arabs in 641 AD. It includes the tragic legend of Sohrab and Rustum, familiar to English readers in Matthew *Arnold's version. The *Shah-nama* was written in some 60,000 rhyming couplets (*mathnawi*), which are a distinctive feature of Persian poetry.

fire ant An *ant, *Solenopsis saevissima* (or *S. geminata*), that occurs in South America and S North America. Fire ants are serious pests because of their irritant painful sting. Subfamily: *Myrmicinae*.

firearms Any weapon that uses an explosive to discharge a missile. The two main categories are *artillery, with barrels having an internal diameter of more than 20 mm, and *small arms with calibers below 20 mm (this classification is no longer rigidly adopted).

Although gunpowder was invented in China many centuries before its description by Roger Bacon in the 13th century, a practical *cannon was not invented until the 14th century (by a German monk, Berthold Schwarz). *Guns, *mortars, and *howitzers have all evolved from the early cannon. Small-arms development began in the 15th century with the early form of the *musket, called a harquebus. They have evolved into the *pistol, *rifle, and *machine gun. *Guided missiles constitute a separate class of weapons, but can be considered as firearms in some contexts.

firebrat A primitive wingless insect, *Thermobia domestica*: a three-pronged *bristletail that is abundant in buildings all over the world. It prefers warm moist places, such as around stoves, furnaces, and bakery ovens, where it feeds on starchy or sugary materials.

fireclay A soft unbedded clay often occurring beneath coalseams. It is believed that they are fossil soils or earths in which swamp plants grew. Fireclays consist mainly of aluminum oxide and silica, being deficient in iron and alkalis; kaolin is the principal clay mineral. They are used as refractory materials, and poorer quality fireclay is used in the manufacture of sanitary earthenware.

firecrest A tiny European songbird, *Regulus ignicapillus*. It is about 3.5 in (9 cm) long and differs from its close relative, the *goldcrest, only in its black-and-white eyestripe. It uses its fine sharp bill to seek out small insects and larvae.

firefly A nocturnal beetle, also called a lightning beetle, belonging to a family (*Lampyridae*; 2000 species) common in tropical and temperate regions. Fireflies emit a greenish light—often as short rhythmic flashes—from organs on the abdomen (*see* bioluminescence). They are 0.2–1 in (5–25 mm) long and many have conspicuous orange or yellow markings. Most adults never eat (although a few feed on pollen and nectar); the larvae are carnivorous. The wingless females and larvae are called glow-worms. *Lampyris noctiluca* is one of the best-known species.

Some *click beetles are also called fireflies.

Firenze. *See* Florence.

fire prevention Fire prevention and control depend on: elimination of the causes (about 25% of fires are caused by electrical faults; smoking, overheating of machinery, furnace and flue defects, and burner flames are also important causes); fire-safe design using fire-retardant coatings and compartmentalized structures to reduce the spread of fire; the provision of such protective equipment as portable fire extinguishers and automatic sprinklers; and the existence of an efficient fire-fighting service.

Class A fires (paper, wood, furnishings, and other common solid combustibles) are extinguished by cooling with water, carbon dioxide, foam, etc. A common type of extinguisher, the soda-acid device, uses carbon dioxide produced by the reaction of sulfuric acid on sodium hydrogen carbonate to force water out of a container. Class B fires (flammable liquids, such as oil, gasoline, etc.) are extinguished by smothering with chemical foam, dry powder, or carbon dioxide, or by extinguishing with halogenated hydrocarbons (e.g. BCF, bromochlorodifluoromethane). Class C fires involve electrical equipment and require nonconducting extinguishers, such as carbon dioxide, dry chemicals, and halogenated hydrocarbons. Class D fires involve burning metals, such as magnesium, sodium, etc., and require special techniques.

Automatic sprinklers are used in factories, offices, and warehouses and are usually controlled by thermostats, which turn on the sprinklers at a specified temperature. Smoke detectors are used in homes, apartments, and where materials are expected to produce smoke before bursting into flame.

fire salamander A mainly terrestrial *salamander, *Salamandra salamandra*, ranging from S Europe to SW Asia. It is 7 in (18 cm) long and glossy black with yellow or orange stripes and red patches. If molested it secretes a salamandrin (venom), which can be fatal to small mammals, from pores behind its eyes.

Fireside Chats Radio broadcasts, beginning in 1933, made by US President Franklin D. *Roosevelt to update and reassure the nation during the Great Depression and its aftermath.

Firestone, Harvey S(amuel) (1868–1938) US industrialist. After working for a carriage manufacturer and organizing his own rubber company (1896), he formed Firestone Tire and Rubber Company (1900) in Akron, Ohio. He manufactured pneumatic tires for Henry Ford's Model T and was the first to use the balloon tire. Ignoring Britain's plan to increase crude rubber prices, he started his own rubber plantation in Liberia in 1924.

firethorn. *See* Pyracantha.

fireworks Combustible devices, used for signals, flares, and displays. Gunpowder rockets and fire crackers were first used in ancient China for military purposes and celebrations and in Europe from the middle ages. The basic explosive, usually gunpowder, is colored by the addition of metallic salts: sodium salts for yellow, barium for green, strontium for red, and copper for blue. Metal filings are added for sparks and aniline dyes provide colored smokes. Despite safety precautions by firework manufacturers and restrictions on sales to children, fireworks still cause casualties.

firn (*or* névé) A stage in the transformation of fresh snow to glacier ice. Compaction and recrystallization of the snow increases its density and it becomes firm at a relative density of 0.5. Under further compaction firn may be transformed to glacier ice, this occurring at a relative density of 0.89–0.90.

first aid Procedures that can be carried out by a medically unqualified person on someone immediately after injury in order to save life or facilitate specialist treatment given later. The types of injury requiring first aid include bleeding, burns, choking, drowning, electric shock, fracture, and poisoning. The patient should be removed from the cause of injury unless this would worsen his (or her) condition. The patient's breathing should be checked and constricting clothing loosened. In the absence of breathing *artificial respiration should be attempted. Once the patient is breathing he (or she) is put in the recovery position (lying on the stomach with the head to one side and the leg bent at the hip and the knee). In external bleeding the injury is covered and firm pressure applied. Lifting a wounded limb, provided no fractures are suspected, often reduces bleeding. If severe fractures are suspected the patient should not be moved without specialist supervision.

First Amendment First article amending the US Constitution, first part of the Bill of Rights. It guarantees the basic fundamental rights–freedom of religion, freedom of speech, the right to assemble peaceably, and the right to petition the government in the case of grievances.

first cause In the philosophy of Aristotle, and later more generally, the beginning of all the chains of cause and effect that are supposed to explain events in the world on a deterministic basis. The first cause does not itself require a cause. The necessity of a first cause (*or* prime mover) has been used as an argument for God's existence.

fiscal policy Government economic policy in which changes in taxation, social-benefit rates, and government expenditure are used to influence the economy. It has been widely used since World War II, following the widespread acceptance of *Keynesianism. According to *monetarism, however, such "fine tuning" of the economy may actually destabilize it.

Fischer, Bobby (Robert James F.; 1943–) US chess player, who became an International Grandmaster at 15 and world champion in 1972. The championship match, against *Spassky at Reykjavík, was greatly publicized and caused a chess boom around the world. He resigned his title in 1975.

Fischer, Emil Hermann (1852–1919) German chemist, who discovered a method of separating different *sugars from each other. He then determined their structure and showed that their *optical activity depended on the three-dimensional arrangement of the atoms in their molecules, thus founding the subject of stereochemistry. For this work he was awarded the Nobel Prize in 1902. In later life, Fischer showed that proteins consist of amino acids; in 1907 he synthesized the first protein molecule from amino acids.

Fischer-Dieskau, Dietrich (1925–) German baritone. He is renowned for his performances of lieder and of a wide range of operatic roles. He has recorded all the songs of Schubert.

Fischer-Tropsch reaction The formation of a variety of organic compounds, chiefly light liquid *hydrocarbons, upon passing a mixture of hydrogen and carbon monoxide over catalysts at around 143°F (200°C). The reaction is important in the production of synthetic liquid fuels from coal. It was invented by F. Fischer (d. 1948) and H. Tropsch (d. 1935) in 1925 and was extensively used in Germany during World War II.

Fischer von Erlach, Johann Bernhard (1656–1723) Austrian architect, a genius of German baroque. Fischer trained in Rome under *Bernini. Soon after moving to Vienna he became architect to the Habsburg court (1687). The Karlskirche (1716) and Hofbibliotek (1723) in Vienna are probably his finest achievements. He also built numerous palaces and wrote a wide-ranging history of architecture.

Fish, Hamilton (1808–93) US politician; Secretary of State (1869–77). He served his native New York state in various capacities before becoming governor (1849–50) and US senator (1851–57), during which time he transferred his allegiance from the Whigs to the Republican Party. Ap-

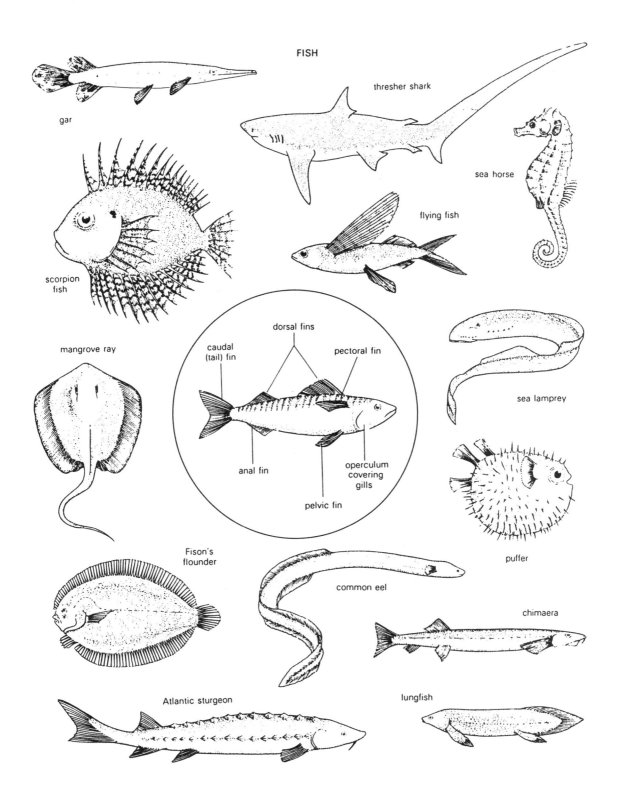

FISH

gar

thresher shark

sea horse

flying fish

scorpion fish

mangrove ray

dorsal fins

caudal (tail) fin

pectoral fin

anal fin

operculum covering gills

pelvic fin

sea lamprey

puffer

Fison's flounder

common eel

chimaera

Atlantic sturgeon

lungfish

FISH *There are numerous variations on the structure of a typical bony fish (mackerel: center). In the flying fish, for instance, the pectoral fins are enlarged as wings; in the lungfish they are fleshy, for moving on land; and in the mangrove ray they are flattened, for swimming. The dorsal and anal fins of the scorpion fish are armed with poisonous spines and the tail of the sea horse is prehensile.*

pointed secretary of state by President *Grant, he was instrumental in negotiating the Treaty of Washington (1871) with Britain, which settled the *Alabama Claims.

fish A cold-blooded aquatic vertebrate belonging to either of the two classes *Chondrichthyes* (*see* cartilaginous fish) or *Osteichthyes* (*see* bony fish), which together comprise over 30,000 species occurring worldwide in seas and fresh waters. Ranging in size from under 0.4 in (10 mm) to over 65 ft (20 m) long, they have streamlined bodies with a covering of bony scales, a fin-bearing tail, an anal fin, one or more dorsal fins, and paired lateral, pectoral (anterior), and pelvic (ventral) fins, which are used in swimming. Oxygen is obtained from water by means of *gills situated in the wall of the mouth cavity, although a few species can also breathe air (*see* lungfish). The majority of fish are carnivorous, feeding mainly on other fish and invertebrates, although some eat plants. Large numbers of small eggs are laid (up to several millions in some cases) and are usually fertilized externally. In some species internal fertilization occurs and live young may be born. Fish are of major importance as a source of food and other products (*see* fishing industry) and for sport (*see* angling). *See also* cyclostomes.

fisher A rare North American mammal, *Martes pennanti* (one of the *martens), also called pekan. Fishers are brown and grow to a length of 40 in (1 m). They feed on porcupines, small animals, and fruit and are named for their habit of fishing out the contents of baited traps.

Fisher, Andrew (1862–1928) Australian statesman, born in Scotland; Labor prime minister (1908–09, 1910–13, 1914–15). He pledged Australian support for Britain in World War I.

Fisher, St John (c. 1469–1535) English prelate and humanist. The chancellor of Cambridge University and Bishop of Rochester from 1504, he opposed Henry VIII's divorce from Catherine of Aragon. He was made a cardinal a month before his execution for refusing to recognize Henry VIII as head of the Church of England. He was canonized in 1935. Feast day: July 9.

fish hawk. *See* osprey.

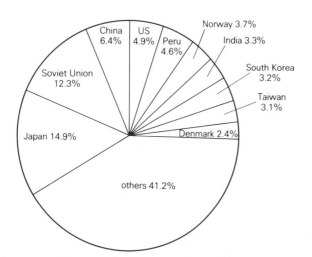

FISHING INDUSTRY *World fish catches.*

fishing industry The recovery and processing of fish, shellfish, etc., for human consumption and other uses. From ancient times man has fished freshwater rivers and lakes and coastal waters using lines and nets. The modern industry uses vessels with refrigerated holds, echo sounding to locate shoals, and efficient nets and recovery gear; the net is often towed behind the vessel (trawling) or left to drift in the ocean. Fish are also dredged up or sucked up, using powerful pumps. The total world catch of about 75 million tons is made up of many species, including cod, haddock, whiting, herring, lobsters, crabs, shrimps, oysters, mussels, octopus, and squid.

Fish are consumed as human food but provide many other by-products, including fish meal, fish oils, glues, pharmaceuticals, shells, pearls, etc. Overfishing of natural populations has led to a decline in many species and smaller catches, sometimes causing friction between fishing nations, such as Iceland and the UK. International agreement is required to regulate fishing and conserve stocks so that yields can be sustained indefinitely. One alter-

native is an increased dependence on **fish farming**, the maintenance and management of fish under controlled conditions to provide food. A long-established practice in China and the Far East, fish farming is now of major importance in many other countries, where trout, catfish, carp, eels, shrimps, and oysters are commonly reared. Hatching of the eggs and rearing take place under optimum conditions in artificial ponds or enclosures situated in lakes or coastal waters. *See also* whaling.

fish louse A tiny parasitic *crustacean of the subclass *Branchiura* (75 species) that uses sucking mouthparts to attach itself to fresh- and salt-water fish. Its flattened body has a large disklike carapace covering the head and thorax.

fish owl An *owl specialized for feeding on fish and frogs. Fish owls have naked legs and rough scaly feet to grip their slippery prey. Genera: *Ketupa* (Asia; 4 species), *Scotopelia* (Africa; 3 species).

Fisk, James (1834–72) US stockbroker. He established a successful stockbrokerage firm in New York City in 1866. He was notorious for his stock manipulation schemes and caused, with Jay *Gould, the "Erie War" (1868) in which they tried to gain control of the Erie Railroad. He and Gould were responsible for Black Friday (1869) when they caused the inflation of gold prices in an attempt to corner the gold market.

fission (biology) A form of asexual *reproduction in which an individual splits into two (binary fission) or more (multiple fission) equal parts, each part becoming a new individual. It occurs in a variety of plants, bacteria, protozoa, and some multicellular animals (e.g. corals).

fission (physics). *See* nuclear energy.

fission-track dating A method of dating based on the spontaneous nuclear fission of uranium-238 in the sample. The fissions are recorded as tracks, which are then compared to the tracks formed by inducing fission in the uranium-235 present. A comparison of the numbers of tracks is used as a measure of the age of the sample.

Fitch, John (1743–98) US inventor; builder of the first steamboat. During 1786–87 he built a side-paddled steamboat that he demonstrated to delegates to the Constitutional Convention. By 1790 he had built a faster and larger stern paddle steamboat that regularly ferried between Philadelphia and a port in New Jersey on the Delaware River. He was never able to make his transportation and freight business a success.

Fittipaldi, Emerson (1946–) Brazilian motor-racing driver, who won his first world championship aged 25 (1972). He won 14 Grand Prix races and was world champion again in 1974.

Fitzgerald, Edward (1809–83) British poet. He lived quietly as a country gentleman with literary tastes. His famous *Rubaiyat of Omar Khayyam* (1859) was a free adaptation of the 12th-century Persian original into his own meter and imagery.

ELLA FITZGERALD

Fitzgerald, Ella (1918–) US jazz singer, known as the "First Lady of Song." Discovered in Harlem by Chick Webb (1902–39), she toured with his band. Later she became famous with the song "A-tisket, A-tasket" (1938), performed with such musicians as Duke Ellington and Oscar Peterson, and made many albums, including *Hello Love, Duke Ellington's Song Book*, and the *Gershwin Song Books*.

Fitzgerald, F(rancis) Scott (Key) (1896–1940) US novelist. The success of his autobiographical first novel, *This Side of Paradise* (1920), enabled him to marry Zelda Sayre (1900–47) and to live out his self-created role as representative of the hedonistic Jazz Age. After 1924 Fitzgerald lived chiefly on the French Riviera, where he wrote his masterpiece *The Great Gatsby* (1925). Zelda suffered increasingly from schizophrenia and after 1930 was confined to an asylum. Fitzgerald, plagued by guilt, declined into alcoholism. His other novels include *The Beautiful and the Damned* (1922) and *Tender is the Night* (1934). *The Last Tycoon*, about Hollywood, where he spent his last years as a screenwriter, was unfinished at his death.

Fitzgerald, George Francis   (1851–1901) Irish physicist, who (independently of *Lorentz) suggested that objects become shorter as their velocity increases, as an explanation of the negative results of the *Michelson-Morley experiment. The phenomenon, now known as the Lorentz-Fitzgerald contraction, was later incorporated by Einstein into his special theory of *relativity, although Fitzgerald did not live to see it.

Fitzsimmons, Bob   (1862–1917) New Zealand boxer, born in England. Of legendary courage and strength, he was world middleweight champion (1891–97), heavyweight champion (1897–99), and light-heavyweight champion (1903–05). He beat many much heavier and bigger men.

Fiume. *See* Rijeka.

Five, the   A group of 19th-century Russian composers dedicated to the formation of a nationalist musical tradition based on folk music. Led by *Balakirev, the other members were *Borodin, César Cui (1835–1918), *Mussorgski, and *Rimsky-Korsakov. The original name of the group was *mogutchaya kutchka* (Russian: the mighty handful).

Five Civilized Tribes   Those US Indian tribes that seemed to be more advanced and more amenable to adopting European ways. All from SE US, the Cherokee, Chickasaw, Choctaw, Creek, and Seminole tribes were later forced to move to reservations in Oklahoma (1832–39). There they also patterned their life style after that of the white settlers.

Five Pecks of Rice Band   A 2nd-century AD religious cult of the later *Han dynasty, so called because its followers paid an annual tribute of five pecks of rice to the sect leader. Together with a sect called the Yellow Turbans, the Five Pecks of Rice Band took part in two mass Taoist rebellions, which lasted over 30 years and played a significant part in overthrowing the Han dynasty (220 AD).

Five Power Constitution   The government constitution drawn up for China by *Sun Yat-sen and put into practice by the *Guomindang (Nationalists) in 1928. The government exercised five powers—executive, legislative, and judicial and those of examination (of candidates for the bureaucracy) and control (of government efficiency). The Constitution is still used by the Guomindang government of the Republic of China (Taiwan).

five-year plans   Economic plans formulated by *developing countries as part of the process of industrialization; they usually include targets for construction, investment, and output to be achieved in the following five years. They were first adopted in the Soviet Union. Capitalist countries (*see* capitalism) committed to economies based on market forces tend to avoid the direction implied in five-year plans, but in a *mixed economy plans based on exhortation rather than direction are sometimes used.

fjord (*or* fiord)   A long narrow sea inlet lying between steep mountain slopes, especially in Norway. Usually U-shaped, fjords are glaciated valleys that have been flooded by the sea. Many are extremely deep, some in excess of 3280 ft (1000 m), but near their mouths they usually have a considerably shallower bar or threshold.

flag   A Eurasian iris, *Iris pseudacorus* (yellow or water flag), growing in marshes and ditches. Up to 50 in (1.2 m) high, it has yellow flowers and long bladelike leaves.

The sweet flag (*Acorus calamus*) is a perennial herbaceous plant native to Asia and North America and naturalized in Britain, growing at the margins of ponds, rivers, etc. About 40 in (1 m) high, it has wavy-edged leaves, which smell of tangerines when crushed, and the small yellow flowers are tightly packed on a tapering spikelike spadix, 3 in (8 cm) long. Family: *Araceae*.

flagella   Long threadlike structures that project from the surface of a cell and produce lashing or undulating movements, used for locomotion or the production of water currents. Flagella occur in protozoa, motile gametes (usually sperms), lower plants, sponges, and also in bacteria (in a simpler form).

Flagellata (*or* Mastigophora)   A class of microscopic single-celled animals (*see* Protozoa) having one or more long whiplike flagella, used for swimming and collecting bacteria, protozoans, and other food particles from water. Some species (subclass *Phytomastigophora*) possess chlorophyll and other pigments and can manufacture food by photosynthesis (*see* Euglena). They may also be classed as algae. Animal-like flagellates (sub-

class *Zoomastigophora*) include the parasites causing *trypanosomiasis and *leishmaniasis as well as free-living forms. mON/39

flageolet   A musical instrument similar to the *recorder but with two thumb holes on the underside and a more complex head fitted with a slender ivory mouthpiece containing a sponge to absorb condensation. The diarist Pepys was a keen player.

Flagg, James Montgomery   (1877–1960) US artist and illustrator. Most famous for his World War I "I Want You" poster of Uncle Sam, he had been a regular supplier of illustrations to magazines since the age of 12. His caricatures of the famous were collected in *The Well-Knowns as Seen by James Montgomery Flagg* (1914).

Flagler, Henry Morrison   (1830–1913) US businessman. After several successful business ventures, he joined John D. Rockefeller, Sr., in the oil business in 1867. By 1870 the business had become the Standard Oil Company. He was instrumental in the development of Florida as a resort state. He organized the Florida East Coast Railway (1886) to Miami and built large luxury tourist hotels. By 1912 he had engineered the connection of the Florida Keys by bridges.

Flagstad, Kirsten Malfrid   (1895–1962) Norwegian soprano, famous for her singing of Wagner roles, such as Brünnhilde in *Der Ring des Nibelungen* and Kundry in *Parsifal*. She also sang the role of Dido in Purcell's *Dido and Aeneas* and championed the songs of Sibelius.

Flagstaff   35 12N 111 39W A city in N central Arizona in the foothills of the San Francisco Peaks. Chiefly a health and recreation resort, tourism is the main industry. Lumbering and livestock raising are carried on, and Northern Arizona University and Lowell Observatory are here. Population (1980): 34,641.

Flaherty, Robert (Joseph)   (1884–1951) US film director. His *Nanook of the North* (1922), filmed during a two-year stay with the Canadian Eskimos, and *Moana* (1926), filmed in the Samoan Islands, were the earliest major documentary films. His later films include *Louisiana Story* (1948).

Flamboyant   In French *gothic architecture, the predominant style during the 15th century. Similar to the earlier English *Decorated style, Flamboyant takes its name from its characteristic slender and elaborate curves that wind into flamelike patterns, especially in window tracery. St Maclou, Rouen (begun 1432), is a fine Flamboyant church.

flamboyant tree   An attractive tree, *Delonix regia*, also called royal poinciana, flame tree, and peacock flower. It grows to a height of 20–40 ft (6–12 m) and has showy flame-colored flowers with long protruding stamens. Native to Madagascar, it is widely planted in the tropics for shade and ornament. Family: *Leguminosae*.

flamenco   A type of Spanish music originating in Andalusia, typically consisting of a song (*cante*) accompanied by dancing, in which the men perform intricate toe and heel tapping steps (*zapateados*) and the women rely on graceful hand and body movements. It was developed by gypsies and shows signs of Moorish influence; the predominant styles are *grande* (anguished) and *chico* (gay and amorous), with a variety of intermediate moods. Flamenco guitar playing has become well known outside Spain; it employs a different technique from that of the "classical" guitar, including a percussive effect obtained by tapping the body of the guitar with the fingers.

flame tree   One of several unrelated trees with flame-colored showy flowers. The name is most commonly applied to *Brachychiton acerifolium* (or *Sterculia acerifolia*), a deciduous Australian tree that bears masses of small scarlet bell-like flowers on leafless branches. Family: *Sterculiaceae*. It may also refer to the *flamboyant tree.

flamingo   A wading bird belonging to a family (*Phoenicopteridae*; 4 species) occurring in large flocks on saltwater lakes in warm regions of the world. 3–5 ft (90–150 cm) tall, flamingos have a long neck, a short tail, a broad wingspan, and white plumage, tinged with pink. They separate algae, diatoms, small mollusks, etc., from mud using their bills, which are lined with sievelike filters. Order: *Ciconiiformes* (herons, storks, etc.).

Flaminian Way   A major Roman road that extended from Rome to Ariminum (now Rimini) on the Adriatic coast. It was named for Gaius *Flaminius, who completed it in 220 BC.

Flamininus, Titus Quinctius   (c. 230–c. 174 BC) Roman general, who defeated Philip V (237–179; reigned 220–179) of Macedon at Cynoscephalae (198). In 196, at the Isthmian Games, Flamininus proclaimed the independence of the Greek states from Macedonian hegemony.

Flaminius, Gaius   (d. 217 BC) Roman popular leader. An advocate of the plebeians' rights, he often challenged or disregarded senatorial authority. In 220, as consul, he built the *Flaminian Way, Rome's road to N Italy.

Popular dissatisfaction with senatorial war policy inspired his election in 217 as leader against *Hannibal, who defeated and killed Flaminius at Trasimene.

Flanders (Flemish name: Vlaanderen; French name: Flandre) A historic region in Europe, in the SW of the Low Countries. It now comprises the provinces of East Flanders and West Flanders in Belgium and parts of N France and the Netherlands. *History*: in the middle ages Flanders formed an autonomous region ruled by the Counts of Flanders and after the 12th century it became a major industrial and commercial center, its cloth being especially important. The scene of many battles during its history, there was heavy fighting here in both World Wars. During World War II the Battle of Flanders (10 May–June 2, 1940) saw the German attack on Holland, Belgium, and France, which resulted in the Allied withdrawal from *Dunkirk.

flash point The lowest temperature at which an inflammable liquid (generally a hydrocarbon or mixture of hydrocarbons) produces enough vapor to ignite on the application of a small flame under specified conditions. Flash points are useful for setting safety standards, especially for the storage of volatile hydrocarbons and for monitoring refinery operations.

flatfish Any carnivorous *bony fish of the order *Pleuronectiformes* (about 600 species), including many important food fishes, such as *halibut, *plaice, *sole, and *turbot. They have a laterally flattened body, 4–80 in (10–200 cm) long, fringed with dorsal and anal fins. Both eyes occur on the same side of the head and they lie on their "blind" side, usually on sandy or muddy bottoms of coastal waters; the upper surface is colored to blend with their surroundings. In the larval stage one eye migrates over the head to lie near the other.

flatfoot Obliteration of the longitudinal arch of the foot, so that the entire sole is in contact with the ground on standing. It is common in young children and they usually grow out of it. Rigid flatfoot is more serious and the result of a congenital abnormality.

Flathead North American Salishan-speaking Indian tribe found in SW Montana. They were called Flatheads by white settlers who had seen deformed heads, probably of slaves, among them, but they never practiced the custom of head flattening. Basically farmers, hunters, and eventually traders, they fought against the Bannock, Shoshoni, and Blackfeet. Missionaries (1841) converted the tribe to Christianity; today, fewer than 3000 live on the Flathead Reservation in Montana.

flathead A bottom-dwelling carnivorous *bony fish of the family *Platycephalidae*, found in tropical Indian, Pacific, and E Atlantic waters. It has a tapering body, up to 55 in (1.3 m) long, and a large flat head covered with ridges and spines. It is an important food fish. Order: *Scorpaeniformes* (or *Scleroparei*).

flat racing A form of horse racing in which the horses are not required to jump obstacles. Flat races are usually run over distances between 0.5 mi (0.8 km) and 1.5 mi (2.4 km). *Thoroughbred horses are used, mainly as two- and three-year-olds. Weight handicaps are allotted in most races. The most prestigious US races are the *Triple Crown.

flatworm A flat-bodied wormlike animal of the invertebrate phylum *Platyhelminthes* (9000 species). Some flatworms are free-living (*see* planarian) but the majority are parasitic (*see* fluke; tapeworm). They have a simple body, with sense organs and a primitive brain at the front end, and range in size from 0.04 in–49 ft (1 mm to 15 m). Many are hermaphrodite, i.e. each individual contains both male and female reproductive organs.

Flaubert, Gustave (1821–80) French novelist. The son of a Rouen surgeon he gave up his law studies in 1843 to dedicate himself wholly to literature. He traveled in the Near East (1849–51) and Tunisia (1857) and was a lover of the poet Louise Colet (1808–76). He worked for five years on his first novel, *Madame Bovary* (1856), a controversially explicit study of an overromantic bourgeois wife. His other major works include the exotic romance *Salammbô* (1862), *L'Éducation sentimentale* (1870), *La Tentation de Saint Antoine* (1874), and the brilliant short stories in *Trois contes* (1877).

flax A herbaceous plant of the genus *Linum* (230 species), mostly of the N hemisphere. Cultivated flax (*L. usitatissimum*) is an annual, up to 40 in (100 cm) high, with narrow leaves and blue five-petaled flowers. Its stem fibers are used to make linen, fine writing paper, and cigarette paper. The seeds contain *linseed oil. Flax is cultivated throughout Europe, the main producing countries being the Soviet Union, Belgium, Holland, and Northern Ireland. Family: *Linaceae*.

flea A small wingless □insect belonging to the widely distributed order *Siphonaptera* (about 1600 species). Fleas are bloodsucking parasites of birds and mammals. A flea's body, which is generally brown, is 0.04–0.40 in (1–10 mm) long and laterally flattened and its legs are modified for jumping. Fleas have irritating bites and change hosts frequently, acting as carriers of some serious diseases. The wormlike larvae use biting mouthparts to feed on dirt, excrement, and dried blood. Two important and widely distributed species are the human flea (*Pulex irritans*) and the oriental rat flea (*Xenopsylla cheopis*), which transmits bubonic plague and typhus to man.

fleabane A perennial herb of the genus *Erigeron* (about 180 species), from America and Europe. 3–16 in (8–40 cm) tall, fleabanes have strap-shaped leaves and small daisy-like flower heads with purple or white ray florets and yellow centers. Herbs of the Old World genus *Pulicaria* are also called fleabane. They have daisy-like yellow flowers, 0.4–1.2 in (1–3 cm) across. Family: *Compositae*.

fleawort One of several herbs of the genus *Senecio*, especially *S. integrifolius*, *S. palustris*, and *S. spathulifolius*, from central and N Europe. The plants are 10–40 in (25–100 cm) high, with yellow daisy-like flowers, 0.8–1.2 in (2–3 cm) across. Family: *Compositae*.

Fleet Street The center of English journalism, a street in London between the Strand and the City in which most of the major newspapers have offices. It is named for the River Fleet (now a covered sewer).

Flémalle, Master of (c. 1378–1444) One of the founders (with the *van Eyck brothers) of the Flemish school of painting (*see* Flemish art). He is usually identified as Robert Campin, an artist active in Tournai from 1406. His name derives from three panels (Frankfurt-am-Main) attributed to him and mistakenly thought to have been commissioned by the abbey of Flémalle near Liège. Other works include the *Mérode Altarpiece* (the Cloisters, New York), the *Annunciation* and *Marriage of the Virgin* (Madrid), and the *Madonna of Humility* (London). His works display the careful realistic rendering of details from everyday life that characterizes the Flemish school as a whole.

Fleming, Sir Alexander (1881–1955) British microbiologist, who discovered the antibiotic *penicillin. In 1928 Fleming noticed that a mold contaminating a bacterial culture had destroyed the bacteria in its vicinity. He identified the mold as *Pencillium notatum* and named the antibacterial substance it produced penicillin. Although he found that penicillin was harmless to human cells, Fleming could not isolate or identify the antibiotic. This was later achieved by Lord *Florey and Sir Ernest *Chain, with whom Fleming shared the 1945 Nobel Prize. Fleming also discovered lysozyme, an antibacterial enzyme found in tears and saliva.

Fleming, Ian (Lancaster) (1908–64) British author and journalist, famous for his creation of the archetypal secret agent, James Bond, in 12 novels and 7 short stories, most of them filmed. Originally a stockbroker, Fleming served as a foreign correspondent in Moscow, and in World War II became a senior naval intelligence officer.

Fleming, Sir John Ambrose (1849–1945) British electrical engineer, who constructed the first rectifying *diode in 1904. His invention greatly stimulated the development of radio and led to the invention of the triode two years later by Lee *De Forest. He also took part in the development of the electric lamp and carried out research into resistance at low temperatures. He was knighted in 1929. *See also* Fleming's rules.

Fleming, Paul (1609–40) German poet. A disciple of Martin *Opitz, his posthumously published love lyrics and religious hymns were distinguished by their sincerity and directness. Many of his poems were inspired by his thwarted love for Elsàbe Niehus, whom he met on a trading journey to Russia and Persia.

Flemings Inhabitants of N and W Belgium who speak Flemish, a dialect of *Dutch known by them as Vlaams. They number approximately 5,500,000. Like the Dutch they are descended from the Salic Franks, a Germanic people, who settled the area during the 3rd and 4th centuries AD. They retain a cultural identity distinct from that of French-speaking Belgians (*see* Walloons).

Fleming's rules A mnemonic, invented by Sir John Ambrose Fleming, for the relationship between the directions of motion, magnetic field, and electric current in *electric motors and generators. The thumb represents motion; the *first* (index) *finger* represents the *field*; and the second finger represents the *current*. If the right hand is held with the thumb and first two fingers straight and mutually at right angles, the directions in a generator are indicated. The left hand indicates the directions in a motor.

Flemish art A tradition of painting that flourished in Flanders, now Belgium, from the 14th to the 18th centuries. The early dominance of manuscript illuminators was replaced in the 15th century by a major school of painters, which included the Master of *Flémalle, the *van Eycks, van der *Weyden, van der *Goes, *Bouts, *Memling, and Gerard *David. In the 16th century Flemish art was Italianized by such painters as *Gossaert and Frans *Floris, although *Bosch and *Brueghel remained largely within the Flemish tradition. Major 17th-century figures were *Rubens, *Van Dyck, *Jordaens, and *Teniers. Flemish art declined in international importance after the 17th century.

Flensburg 54 47N 9 27E A city in N West Germany, in Schleswig-Holstein on the Baltic Sea. Between 1848 and 1867 it was under Danish rule and in 1945 at the end of World War II the German Government capitulated near here. A port and naval base, its industries include shipbuilding and fishing. Population (1971 est): 95,000.

Fletcher, John (1579–1625) English dramatist. He collaborated with Francis *Beaumont on *Philaster* (1610), *The Maid's Tragedy* (1611), and many other plays, and probably with *Shakespeare on *The Two Noble Kinsmen* and *Henry VIII* (1612).

fleur-de-lys A heraldic device, which has three everted petals, resembling the bearded iris. It was the coat of arms of the French monarchy from the middle ages.

Fleury, André Hercule de, Cardinal (1653–1743) French statesman; chief minister (1726–43) of Louis XV. Fleury carried out important reforms, reorganizing finances, building roads, and encouraging commerce. A successful diplomat, he worked to maintain peace in Europe but involved France in the War of the *Polish Succession (1733–38) on the side of Stanisław I Leszczyński.

Flinders Island. *See* Furneaux Islands.

Flinders Range A mountain range in E South Australia. It extends N from Gulf St Vincent between Lake Torrens and Lake Frome, reaching 3904 ft (1190 m) at St Mary Peak.

flint A variety of *chalcedony. It is gray to black, is dense and tough, and breaks with a conchoidal (curved) fracture, leaving sharp edges (hence its use by Stone Age man for tools and weapons). It occurs in nodules in chalk along the bedding planes and as pebbles in river gravels and beach material.

Flint 43 03N 83 40W A city in the US, in Michigan on the Flint River. One of the several cities that surround *Detroit, its main industry is motor vehicles. Population (1981): 159,611.

flint glass A durable, brilliant, and highly refractive glass. It is used in high-quality glassware and also in lenses and prisms since it absorbs very little light. It is also known as lead glass and crystal glass.

FLN. *See* Front de Libération nationale.

Flodden, Battle of (September 9, 1513) The battle in which the English under Thomas Howard, Earl of Surrey (1443–1524), defeated the Scots under *James IV at Flodden Edge, Northumberland. The Scots had invaded England after allying with France against Henry VIII.

flood The overflowing of a river onto the surrounding land (**flood plain**) or the surging of sea water at high tide onto the coastal land. Disastrous floods have occurred throughout history. The flood described in Genesis 6.9 (*see* Noah) is probably apocryphal, although Sir Leonard *Woolley identified at Ur a layer of clay that he believed was deposited during a flood in about 4000 BC. More recent flood disasters include those in Lisbon (1775), Warsaw (1861 and 1964), Paris (1910), Florence (1966), and Bangladesh (1974). However, floods are not always disastrous; the annual floods of the *Nile River have provided a fertile flood plain, the site of one of the earliest civilizations.

The prevention of disasters by flooding involves the accurate prediction of the behavior of rivers and tides and the provision of flood-relief channels and barrages.

Flood, Henry (1732–91) Irish politician. An impressive orator, Flood rapidly became the leader of the patriot party in the Irish parliament. In 1775, however, he accepted a government post and the patriots henceforth branded him as an apostate. In 1781 Flood again espoused the patriot cause but quarreled with its new leader, *Grattan, and declined into political obscurity.

floodgate A movable barrier set up on spillways to control the height of water at *dams. Closure of some of the floodgates at a spillway in times of water shortage may conserve valuable amounts of water, without reducing the full spillway capacity. Vertical-lift gates are raised to permit flow beneath them, while drum gates (solid circular quadrants) rotate downward— to allow water to flow over them.

Flora The Roman goddess of flowers and spring. Her spring festival, the Floralia, instituted in 283 BC, was the occasion for riotous uninhibited behavior.

Florence (Italian name: Firenze) 43 47N 11 15E A city in Italy, the capital of Tuscany on the Arno River. Florence is a major market town as well as an administrative and educational center. The manufacture of luxury goods is important but the principal industry is tourism. Its many famous buildings include the 13th-century cathedral of Sta Maria del Fiore, the campanile of Giotto, the baptistery, and many churches (including Sta Maria Novella and Sta Croce). The Ponte Vecchio (1345) across the Arno River connects the *Uffizi gallery (containing Italy's most important collection of paintings) to the Palazzo Pitti (now an art gallery). Art treasures in Florence include works by Michelangelo, Donatello, Masaccio, Giotto, Fra Angelico, Botticelli, Raphael, Titian, and Rubens. The Italian National Library (Biblioteca Nazionale) is situated here and its university was established in 1321. *History*: an early Roman colony, it had developed into an important center of trade and industry by the 12th century. It was torn by the struggles between the *Guelfs and Ghibellines (13th and 14th centuries) but flourished financially and culturally (14th–16th centuries). The rule of the *Medici family began in 1434 and this continued almost uninterrupted (*see* Savonarola, Girolamo) for three centuries. Following a period of Austrian rule, Florence became part of the new kingdom of Italy in 1861 and was the provisional capital (1865–71). Florence has suffered considerable damage in war (including World War II) and from floods, especially in November, 1966. Population (1980 est): 460,924.

Flores An Indonesian island in the Nusa Tenggara group. Mountainous and volcanic, it is largely unexplored. Agriculture is shifting cultivation producing chiefly maize; sandalwood and copra are exported. Area: 6622 sq mi (17,150 sq km). Chief town: Ende.

Florey, Howard Walter, Baron (1898–1968) Australian pathologist, who, working with Sir Ernst *Chain, isolated and purified the antibiotic *penicillin, first discovered by Sir Alexander *Fleming in 1928. Florey and Chain developed techniques for producing the pure drug in large quantities. In 1941 they conducted the first clinical trials, in which penicillin proved very effective in combating bacterial infections. Florey shared the 1945 Nobel Prize with Chain and Fleming.

Florianópolis (former name: Desterro) 27 35S 48 31W A city and port in Brazil, the capital of Santa Catarina state on Santa Catarina island. It is linked to the mainland by a steel suspension bridge, the longest in Brazil. It exports sugar, tobacco, and fruit and has a university (1960). Population (1975 est): 167,538.

floribunda. *See* rose.

FLORIDA *An aerial view of Miami Beach, the state's most famous resort.*

Florida A state in the extreme SE, forming a 400-mi-long 645-km) peninsula, with the Atlantic Ocean to the E and the Gulf of Mexico to the W; it borders Alabama and Georgia on the N and NE. The Florida Straits, dotted with small chains of islands, including the Florida Keys and the Dry Tortugas, separate the state from Cuba, which has figured prominently in its more recent history. It is predominantly a low-lying peninsula with many lakes and rivers, Lake Okeechobee being the largest lake. In the diversified economy manufacturing is important, especially food processing and the chemical industry. The state's mines produce phosphate, titanium, zircon, and other heavy minerals. Tourism, based on its subtropical climate, is the most important industry, with many popular resorts, such as Miami Beach and Palm Beach. The Everglades, a low-lying subtropical wilderness area of marshlands that extends over a large portion of the S tip of the state, abounds with unique wildlife. Disney World entertainment park near Orlando is the state's most popular tourist attraction. Most recently the state has become a center for space exploration with the John F. Kennedy Space Center at Cape Canaveral. Florida is known for its citrus fruits (producing 75% of the US total), especially oranges, of which it is the nation's leading producer. It also produces large quantities of vegetables. It is also a major region for breeding thoroughbred horses. *History*: following its discovery by Ponce de Leon in his famous search for the Fountain of Youth, Florida was explored by the Spanish, who founded St Augustine, now the oldest permanent white settlement in America. It was ceded to the British in 1763 and remained loyal to it during the American Revolution. Florida was returned to Spain at the end of the war, but the Spanish hold was tenuous and in 1819 it passed to the US. Wars with the Seminoles culminated with the expulsion of most of the Indians from the state. Small Indian populations continue to live in Florida, principally around Lake Okeechobee. It became a state in 1845. It was a supporter of the Confederate cause during the US Civil War. The arrival of the railroads in the 1880s brought access to the agricultural markets of the N and subsequent economic growth. Drainage of the Everglades brought increased settlement as Florida became one of the fastest-growing states. Development accelerated during the 1970s and 1980s, with new residents attracted by the climate and economic prosperity. Area: 58,560 sq mi (151,670 sq km). Population (1980): 9,739,992. Capital: Tallahassee.

Florida Keys A chain of small islands separated from the S coast of Florida by Florida Bay. It includes the islands of Key West and Key Largo and extends for over 100 mi (160 km). The islands are linked by the Overseas Highway, a complex of roads and 42 bridges.

Florio, John (c. 1553–1625) English writer, of Italian descent. While teaching at Oxford he published his important Italian-English dictionary (1598). He later held appointments at James I's court. His main work was an English translation of Montaigne's *Essays* (1603).

Floris Two Flemish artists. **Cornelis Floris** (1514–75) was an architect and sculptor, best known for designing Antwerp town hall (1561–65). His brother **Frans Floris** (c. 1516–70) was a painter. Both studied in Italy and contributed to the spread of the Italian Renaissance style in the Netherlands.

Flotow, Friedrich von (1812–83) German operatic composer. He had much success in his lifetime but his works, with the exception of the opera *Martha* (1847), have not survived.

flotsam, jetsam, and lagan Goods cast into the sea that respectively remain afloat, sink, or would sink but have attached to them a buoy, which keeps them afloat.

flounder A common name for any *flatfish or for certain species. An example is *Platichthys flesus*, which is up to 20 in (50 cm) long and lives in European coastal and fresh waters. It has a greenish or brownish mottled upper surface and is an important food and game □fish.

flour The powdered grain of wheat or other cereals, used in baking. The chief use of flour is in making bread. When the two proteins in wheat, glutenin and gliadin, are mixed with water they form gluten, which permits the dough to expand and retain the carbon dioxide resulting from fermentation of the yeast in bread dough. Different types of flour are made by varying the percentage of flour separated from the wheat. The principal commercial flours are whole wheat (100%), wholemeal and stoneground (92%), wheatmeal (80–90%), and white flours (70–72%). Many nutritionists consider it important to eat food made from whole wheat and wholemeal flour, rather than white flour. The former retain more of the bran (the outer skin of the wheat grain) and have more iron and calcium than white flour. They are also a good daily source of dietary *fiber. Flour with a high gluten content (strong flour) is best when yeast is called for, as in dough for bread. On the other hand a softer flour with a lower gluten content (fine flour) is used for cakes, shortbread, etc. Plain flour is all-purpose, with a moderate gluten content. Self-rising flour is plain flour with the addition of rising agents.

flower The reproductive organ of flowering □plants (angiosperms), which is essential for the production of seeds and fruits. It is made up of the perianth (petals and sepals) and the sexual organs—the *stamens producing pollen (male gametes) and the *carpels containing the female gametes. The petals and sepals serve to protect the sexual organs and—in flowers

pollinated by animals—are brightly colored, scented, and secrete *nectar to attract insects and birds. Wind-pollinated flowers are typically small and inconspicuous and may lack a perianth. See Plate VI.

flowering currant An ornamental garden shrub, *Ribes sanguineum*, native to North America. Up to 8 ft (2.5 m) tall, it has drooping spikes of pink tubular flowers that appear before the maple-shaped leaves. The fruit is a blue-black berry. The shrub has an odor of blackcurrants. Family: *Grossulariaceae* (see currant).

flowering quince. See japonica.

flowering rush A perennial freshwater plant, *Butomus umbellatus*, native to Eurasia but common throughout N temperate regions: it is a popular garden plant. It has tapering leaves, up to 40 in (1 m) long, and an umbrella-shaped cluster of pinkish flowers at the tip of a long stalk. Family: *Butomaceae*.

flowerpecker A songbird belonging to a family (*Dicaeidae*; 55 species) occurring in S Asia and Australasia. Ranging in size from 3–8 in (8–20 cm), they have stumpy tails, short bills, and variable plumage. Flowerpeckers feed on berries and nectar, thereby dispersing seeds and pollinating flowers.

fluidics The use of jets of fluid in a circuit to carry out electronic functions. Fluidic circuits can resist much higher temperatures than electronic circuits and are also unaffected by ionizing radiation and magnetic fields. They therefore have uses in nuclear reactors and spacecraft. They are also used as delay lines since they respond much more slowly than electronic circuits.

fluidization The process of supporting very fine solid particles in a stream of gas so that the combination of solid and fluid behaves like a liquid. The process is used in transporting coal dust and in the cleaning of the catalyst in *catalytic cracking in oil refining.

fluid mechanics The study of the mechanical properties of fluids. *Hydrostatics is concerned with the study of fluids at rest and hydrodynamics (or fluid dynamics) with fluids that are flowing. Hydraulics deals with the practical applications of these sciences. Two important aspects of hydrodynamics are the conservation of energy in fluid flow (see Bernoulli's theorem) and the distinction between streamline and turbulent flow. See also aerodynamics; Reynolds number.

fluke A parasitic *flatworm of the class *Trematoda* (over 6000 species). Typically leaf-shaped, some are elongated to fit the body cavities they inhabit. The monogenetic flukes have a single host and are generally external parasites of fishes; the digenetic flukes have life cycles involving up to four different hosts and are mainly internal parasites of vertebrates, passing early larval stages in various invertebrates.

fluorescence. See luminescence.

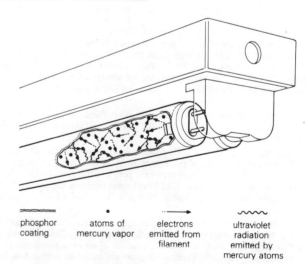

| phosphor coating | atoms of mercury vapor | electrons emitted from filament | ultraviolet radiation emitted by mercury atoms |

FLUORESCENT LAMP *Electrons from the filament collide with atoms of mercury vapor in the tube producing ultraviolet radiation. This is converted to visible light by the fluorescent coating on the tube.*

fluorescent lamp A lamp that uses fluorescence (see luminescence) as its source of light. It consists of a glass tube containing a low pressure gas, such as mercury vapor. As a current passes through the gas, collisions between the electrons and atoms of the gas excite the atoms, which emit *ultraviolet radiation when they return to the ground state. The radiation strikes a phosphor coating on the inner surface of the tube, causing the phosphor to fluoresce emitting visible light.

fluoridation The addition of fluoride (usually sodium fluoride) to drinking water to reduce dental *caries (tooth decay), especially in children. The fluoride combines with apatite—the chief constituent of tooth enamel—to form fluoroapatite, which has a greater resistance to bacterial decay. The recommended level is one part of fluoride per million and if the natural concentration is below this level it is often the policy of local governments to add fluoride to the water. Controversy sometimes arises on the grounds that "medication" is being forced on people who may not wish to accept it. This measure has been shown to be effective, however, and quite safe in low concentrations (many natural water supplies contain up to four or five parts per million).

fluorine (F) A highly reactive pale-yellow halogen gas, the most electronegative element known. It was first isolated by H. Moissan in 1886 and occurs naturally in volcanic gases and as *fluorite (CaF_2) and *cryolite (Na_3AlF_6). It is prepared by electrolysis of potassium hydrogen fluoride (KHF_2) solution in dry hydrofluoric acid (HF). Fluorine became industrially important with the introduction of nuclear power. The gas uranium hexafluoride (UF_6) allows separation of the fissile ^{235}U isotope from ^{238}U by gaseous diffusion. Hydrofluoric acid is used to etch glass and can cause very painful burns to the skin. *Fluorocarbons (for example CF_2Cl_2) are chemically unreactive and have many important uses. Trace amounts of fluoride in drinking water are thought to be important in helping to prevent dental decay (see fluoridation). At no 9; at wt 18.9984; mp $-363°F$ ($-219.62°C$); bp $-306.6°F$ ($-188.14°C$).

fluorite (or fluorspar) A mineral consisting of calcium fluoride, white, green, or yellow in color. It occurs in hydrothermal veins, often as a gangue material in ore deposits, and in some igneous rocks. Most fluorite is used as a flux in iron and steel making; it is also used as a source of fluorine for manufacturing hydrofluoric acid and in the ceramic- and optical-glass industries. Blue John is a deep blue or purple variety used for ornamental purposes.

fluorocarbons Synthetic compounds of carbon and fluorine (sometimes also containing atoms of other halogens). They are extremely resistant to chemical attack, even at very high temperatures, and are nontoxic and nonflammable. They are used as refrigerants, anesthetics, heat-transfer agents, and high-temperature lubricants. The fluoroanalogue of polyethylene, polytetrafluoroethylene (Teflon), is a useful plastic in corrosive environments and has a very low coefficient of friction. Its stability at high temperatures enables it to be used for nonstick coatings in cooking utensils. Fluorocarbons have also been used in enormous quantities as propellants for aerosols, although they have been opposed on environmental grounds as photochemical reactions in the upper atmosphere may lead to depletion of the ozone layer, thereby removing protection against harmful ultraviolet radiation.

fluorspar. See fluorite.

flute A woodwind instrument of ancient origin, existing in many different cultures. The modern side-blown flute (in which a column of air is made to vibrate by blowing across an elliptical mouth hole) and the *recorder are members of the same family. The flute came into prominence in the 16th century, when it was made of wood; today most flutes are metal. The modern orchestral flute (perfected by Theobald *Boehm) is about 2 ft (0.6 m) long and has a range of three octaves above middle C. □musical instruments.

flux (brazing and soldering) A substance applied to pieces to be soldered to aid the formation of the joint. Soft solder, used in electrical joints, commonly contains a core of flux, often tallow or a similar substance. For hard soldering, at higher temperatures, zinc chloride is often used. The flux lowers the melting point of the solder and also reacts with or removes surface oxides from the metals, thus keeping their surfaces clean and allowing the liquid solder to adhere to the surfaces.

flux (physics) The net amount of a directional quantity passing through a surface area at right angles to the surface. The concept of flux is used to describe phenomena that involve forces or the flow of energy, such as electric flux, magnetic flux, and luminous flux.

fly An insect belonging to the order Diptera (over 85,000 species)—the so-called true, or two-winged, flies—of great economic importance in transmitting disease. The adults have only two wings (the front pair), the hind pair being reduced to balancing organs (called halteres). The mouthparts are adapted for piercing or sucking, and most species feed on plant juices or

suck the blood of mammals. The larvae—often called maggots—are typically scavengers on plant and animal refuse or parasites of pest status. Bloodsucking species, such as *mosquitoes and *tsetse flies, may transmit such diseases as malaria, sleeping sickness, and yellow fever. The order also includes the *houseflies, *blowflies, *craneflies, and *horse flies.

The name fly is also used for various flying insects of other orders: the alderfly, caddis fly, damselfly, firefly, and mayfly are examples of nondipterous flies.

fly agaric A poisonous mushroom, *Amanita muscaria, found in woodlands, especially of birch and conifers. Its cap, 2–8 in (6–20 cm) in diameter, is scarlet or orange-red with white scales and the white stalk has a membranous collar beneath the cap. Fly agaric is seldom fatal. It was formerly used as a fly killer, hence its name.

flycatcher A small active songbird belonging to an Old World family (Muscicapidae; 378 species) and feeding on insects, typically caught in flight. They have small bills surrounded by stiff bristles and delicate legs used only for perching. The typical flycatchers are dull colored and include the gray-and-brown European spotted flycatcher (Muscicapa striata) and the black-and-white pied flycatcher (Ficedula hypoleuca). The tropical blue flycatchers and paradise flycatchers are beautifully colored and ornamented. Compare tyrant flycatcher.

Flying Dutchman In sailors' lore, a ghost ship haunting the sea around the Cape of Good Hope. Its captain, driven back from the Cape by a storm, is supposed to have sworn a blasphemous oath to round it or be forever damned. The story became popular in 19th-century literature and inspired Wagner's opera (1843) of the same name.

flying fish A □fish of the family Exocoetidae (about 40 species). Up to 18 in (45 cm) long, flying fish swim just below the surface in warm oceanic waters. If disturbed they launch themselves from the water by rapidly beating the tail and glide through the air using large winglike pectoral fins.

flying fox A fruit *bat belonging to the genus Pteropus (51 species), ranging from Africa to Australia. Flying foxes have foxlike heads and a wingspan of up to 5 ft (1.5 m).

flying lemur. See colugo.

flying lizard A lizard belonging to the genus Draco (15 species) of SE Asia, having large folds of skin between the legs supported by ribs that are spread out when the lizard jumps from a tree. They have greenish bodies and brightly colored "wings." Family: Agamidae (agamas). □reptile.

flying phalanger A squirrel-like *marsupial mammal, also called marsupial glider. Flying phalangers, found in E Australia and Tasmania, range from 6–40 in (14–100 cm) in length. They all have soft fur and long bushy tails and a flap of skin between the fore and hind legs enables them to glide from tree to tree. Genera: Acrobates, Petaurus, Schoinobates; family: Phalangeridae.

flying saucer. See unidentified flying object.

flying snake A slender arboreal snake belonging to the genus Chrysopelea (3 species), occurring in S Asia and the East Indies. They are diurnal, feed on small rodents, bats, birds, and lizards, and can glide short distances by launching themselves in the air and flattening their belly scales. Family: Colubridae.

flying squirrel A nocturnal *squirrel of the subfamily Petauristinae (37 species), occurring in SE Asia, North America, and Eurasia. Flying squirrels have a flap of loose skin from elbow to knee that is stretched tight by extending the legs, enabling them to glide from branch to branch. □mammal.

Flynn, Errol (1909–59) US actor, born in Tasmania. After trying a number of odd jobs, he became an actor in Hollywood, playing the handsome adventurous hero in such films as Captain Blood (1935), Gentleman Jim (1942), and (as John Barrymore) Too Much Too Soon (1958). His private life, which was scarcely less eventful than his film roles, was candidly recounted in two autobiographies, Beam Ends (1934) and My Wicked Wicked Ways (1959).

Fly River A river in New Guinea, rising in W Papua New Guinea and flowing generally S, forming part of the border between Papua New Guinea and West Irian, before entering the Gulf of Papua. Length: 800 mi (1300 km).

flytrap. See Venus' flytrap.

flywheel A large heavy wheel attached to the driving shaft of a motor to act as an energy store and to iron out fluctuations in the speed of the machine. The energy stored depends on the speed of rotation and the weight distribution of the wheel. They are used in *internal-combustion engines, power presses, etc.

f-number The ratio of the focal length of a camera lens to the diameter of the shutter opening (aperture). For example, f-8 means that the focal length is eight times the aperture. The smaller the f-number, the greater the illumination of the film. **Relative aperture** is the reciprocal of f-number.

Foch, Ferdinand (1851–1929) French marshal. At the outbreak of World War I he commanded the Ninth Army and was largely responsible for halting the German advance at the Marne and for the Allied victory at Ypres (1915). After the Somme offensive (1916), he became chief of the general staff (1917). He returned to action in 1918 and as Allied commander in chief forced the Germans back to the Rhine, effecting their defeat.

foetus. *See* fetus.

fog A cloud near the ground surface, within which visibility is reduced to less than 0.6 mi (1 km). Fog is the result of the condensation of water vapor in the lower layers of air, usually through the cooling of air to below its *dew point; it is most likely to occur with light wind conditions and a clear sky at night. It often contains dust and smoke particles and in industrial areas the increased supply of these particles causes a greater incidence of fog; in areas in which smoke occurs *smog can develop.

Foggia 41 28N 15 33E A city in Italy, in Apulia. It has a castle dating from the time of the Holy Roman Emperor Frederick II. Olives, grapes, wheat, and tobacco are grown in the surrounding region and its industries include flour milling, cheese and paper making, and engineering. Population (1980 est): 158,830.

föhn A warm dry wind that descends down the leeward side of mountains. It is a frequent occurrence in the Alps (where the name originated), the Rocky Mountains (where it is known as the **chinook**), and the Andes. In winter it can cause extremely rapid thaws of lying snow, resulting in avalanches.

Fokine, Michel (Mikhail F.; 1880–1942) Russian ballet dancer and choreographer. From 1909 he worked with Diaghilev's Ballets Russes in Paris, for which he choreographed such revolutionary ballets as *The Firebird* (1910) and *Petrushka* (1911). He went to New York in 1923 and became a naturalized US citizen in 1932.

Fokker, Anthony Hermann Gerard (1890–1939) Dutch aircraft manufacturer. Fokker opened an aircraft factory in Germany in 1912. During World War I he supplied Germany with aircraft and invented a method of firing a machine gun through the propeller of an aircraft. He later became a US citizen.

fold A buckling of sedimentary rock strata produced by compressional forces acting on it. Large-scale folding produces mountain ranges; this occurs where two continental plates collide (*see* plate tectonics) and the sediment along their margins is compressed and folded. A simple upfold is called an *anticline and a downfold, a *syncline; however, most folds are much more complex.

folic acid. *See* vitamin B complex.

Folies-Bergère A Parisian variety theater opened in 1869 and celebrated chiefly for its elaborate revues featuring dancing girls and striptease acts. Maurice *Chevalier and many other leading French entertainers have appeared here.

folk dance A form of dance developed by country people, usually for their own amusement. Folk dances derive from ancient ritual dances used in religious worship and to invoke the fertility of the land (the original purpose of the *maypole dance). They have greatly influenced other forms of dances, notably court dancing, 18th- and 19th-century ballroom dances (such as the *waltz and *polka), and *ballet. Many countries have their own traditional dances. The revived interest in folk dancing in the 20th century is reflected in the popularity of professional folk-dance companies and folk-dance societies.

folklore The social, material, and oral culture of primitive societies. The social culture comprises such forms as festivals, dances, and religious rites; the material culture comprises architecture and arts and crafts; the oral culture includes songs, tales, legends, proverbs, and riddles. The study of folklore, spurred by early collections of folk literature, such as Percy's *Reliques of Ancient English Poetry* (1765) and the *Fairy Tales* (1812–14) of the brothers *Grimm, has played an important role in the work of anthropologists, such as Franz *Boas and J. G. *Frazer.

folk music Song or dance music developed from a communal aural tradition and not composed by an individual, e.g. Irish ballads and cowboy songs. The melody and words of folksongs are often changed by a succession of performances. Folk music is characterized by modal melody and simple forms, such as dances, lullabies, work songs, and love ballads. Traditional English folksongs include "Black Is the Colour of My True Love's

Hair" and "Greensleeves." During the revival of folksongs in the US in the 1960s, new music by such composers as Woody Guthrie, Joan Baez, and Bob Dylan was termed folksong or "folk," owing to its similarity to authentic folk music.

follicle-stimulating hormone. *See* gonadotrophin.

FOLSOM POINT   *One of the most developed types of Stone Age weapon heads.*

Folsom point A fluted lanceolate (leaf-shaped) stone spearhead made between 9000 and 8000 BC in the western grasslands of the US. The name derives from Folsom, NM, where one was discovered (1926), with the remains of an extinct form of bison. *Compare* Clovis point.

Fomalhaut A conspicuous star, apparent magnitude 1.15 and 23 light years distant, that is the only bright star in the S constellation Piscis Austrinus.

Fon The predominant people of S Benin (formerly Dahomey), who speak a dialect of *Ewe. They grow maize, manioc, and yams and palm oil as a cash crop. Their villages are headed by the oldest male. A hereditary headman has general authority to arbitrate in disputes. During the 18th and 19th centuries the Fon formed the kingdom of Dahomey. The powerful king and his chiefs conducted war ceremonies, received tribute, and presided over courts. An ancestor cult involved the sacrifice of prisoners of war in return for supernatural aid.

Fonda, Henry (1905–82) US film actor and director, associated particularly with the portrayal of men of solid integrity, notably in *The Grapes of Wrath* (1940). Other films include *War and Peace* (1956), *Twelve Angry Men* (1957), which he directed, and *On Golden Pond* (1981), which earned him his first Oscar and also starred his daughter **Jane Fonda** (1937–), a film actress. Her other films include *Barbarella* (1968), an extravaganza of sexual fantasy, and subsequent more serious roles in such films as *Klute* (1971), *Julia* (1977), and *Coming Home* (1978), for which she won an Oscar. His son **Peter Fonda** (1939–) made his name as an actor and director with *Easy Rider* (1969).

Fontainebleau 48 24N 2 42E A city in N central France, in the Seine-et-Marne department. The surrounding forest inspired the Barbizon school of painters. The Royal Palace, largely built by Francis I, was the scene of Napoleon I's abdication in 1814. Fontainebleau was the headquarters of NATO from 1954 to 1966. Population (1975): 19,595.

Fontainebleau, school of The painters who decorated the Royal Palace of Fontainebleau (France) between about 1530 and 1560. The Italians Giovanni Battista Rosso (1494–1540), Francesco Primaticcio (c. 1504–70), and Niccolò dell' Abbate (c. 1512–71) were chiefly responsible for developing the particularly sensuous and elegant form of *mannerism that characterizes the school.

Fontana, Domenico (1543–1607) Italian architect and engineer. In the employ of the pope in Rome, Fontana designed the Sistine Library (1587–90) and helped complete the dome of St Peter's Basilica. He was also responsible for re-erecting the Egyptian obelisk on its present site in front of St Peter's.

Fontane, Theodor (1819–98) German novelist. He began writing novels at the age of 56 after varied experience as a journalist and war correspondent. *Vor dem Sturm* (1878) is a realistic historical novel dealing with the Prussian nobility. Of several novels dealing with the place of women in society the best known is *Effi Briest* (1898).

Fontanne, Lyn. *See* Lunt, Alfred.

Fontenelle, Bernard le Bovier de (1657–1757) French philosopher and writer, who joined his uncle, Pierre *Corneille, in Paris in 1680, becoming a leading light of the contemporary salons. Renowned for his wit and his learning, he popularized the new scientific theories of Descartes and Newton in such works as *Digressions sur les anciens et les modernes* (1688) and *Éléments de la géométrie de l'infini* (1727). Pouring scorn on ancient myths and beliefs, he was a confirmed "modern," writing his *Théorie des tourbillons cartésiens* when he was 95.

Fontenoy, Battle of (May 11, 1745) The battle in the War of the *Austrian Succession in which France defeated Austria. Fought near Tournai, SE of Brussels, the battle was the French commander de *Saxe's most notable victory, leading to the conquest of Flanders. His artillery and cavalry carried the day against the Austrians, and their Dutch and English allies, who retreated toward Brussels.

Fonteyn, Dame Margot (Margaret Hookham; 1919–) British ballet dancer. She was a member of the Sadler's Wells company and the Royal Ballet from 1934 to 1959 and has also performed with most leading US and European companies, often in partnership with Rudolf *Nureyev. Her most famous performances were in classical ballets such as *Giselle*, *Swan Lake*, and *The Sleeping Beauty*.

Foochow. *See* Fuzhou.

Food and Agriculture Organization (FAO) A specialized agency of the *United Nations constituted in 1945 to coordinate international efforts to raise levels of nutrition and food production and to improve the management of forests. The agency, with headquarters in Rome, conducts research, makes recommendations, organizes educational programs, and encourages the export of agricultural products.

food chain A series of living organisms associated in a feeding relationship: each animal feeds on the one below it in the series. Most commonly, green plants are at the base of a food chain. They are eaten by herbivores, which in turn may be consumed by carnivores. Any animal or plant parasites are also part of the chain, and different food chains are often interconnected to form a **food web**. Other food chains are based on decomposers—organisms that feed on dead organic remains of plants and animals.

food poisoning An acute illness arising from eating contaminated food. Vomiting and diarrhea are the usual symptoms. *Salmonella* is the bacterium that most commonly causes food poisoning (salmonellosis), and symptoms begin 12–24 hours after eating the food. Patients usually recover within a few days. Another kind of food poisoning is due to a toxin (poi-

son) produced by staphylococci: symptoms occur within one to three hours of taking the food. *Clostridium* bacteria may also cause food poisoning, the most severe form of which is *botulism.

food preservation The treatment of food to prevent its deterioration and to maintain its eating quality and nutritional value. Breakdown of food tissues is caused by enzymes, either contained within the food or produced by microorganisms—bacteria, yeasts, and fungi—growing in the food. These organisms also produce unpleasant and sometimes harmful substances. Oxidation and dehydration also contribute to spoilage. The principle of food preservation is therefore to alter the condition of food so that the activities of microorganisms are stopped. One of the oldest methods is drying or dehydration—used for meat, vegetables, cereals, milk products, etc. *Freezing is now widely used for both industrial and domestic food preservation. *Freeze drying involves freezing followed by dehydration. Heating kills microorganisms and is the principle of *pasteurization, *sterilization, etc. Further growth is prevented if food is sealed in airtight containers, such as cans (*see* canning) or bottles. A wide range of chemicals is added to food to inhibit microbial activity. Boiling with sugar (e.g. in jam) and pickling with salt or vinegar (e.g. onions, cucumbers) are traditional methods. Smoking has also been used to preserve meat and fish. Sodium benzoate, propionates, nitrates, nitrites, sulfur dioxide, and sulfites are all used by the modern food industry as well as many other compounds that enhance color, flavor, and texture for the consumer.

Fools, Feast of A festival held in medieval Europe (especially in France) on, or near, Holy Innocents' Day (Dec 28). It was organized by lower clergy. A mock pope or bishop (sometimes a boy) was elected and presided over burlesque church services. There were also processions and carnival plays as well as festive dancing and drinking.

fool's gold. *See* pyrite.

foot The lowermost part of the leg. The human foot contains 14 bones. There are seven tarsal bones, of which one (the talus) forms a hinge joint with the bones of the lower *leg and another (the calcaneus) forms the projection of the heel. The five metatarsal bones form the body of the foot and articulate with the phalanges, the bones of the toes. The first (big) toe is the most important as it provides a springboard for walking and running.

Foot, Michael (Mackintosh) (1913–) British Labour politician and historian. He worked as a journalist until elected to parliament in 1945. He was editor (1948–52, 1955–60) of the left-wing Labour weekly the *Tribune*. He was leader of the House of Commons (1976–79) and leader of the Labour Party (1980–83). His many publications include a biography of Aneurin Bevan (2 vols, 1962–73).

foot-and-mouth disease An infectious virus disease affecting cattle, sheep, goats, pigs, and many wild animals. Symptoms, which appear 1–15

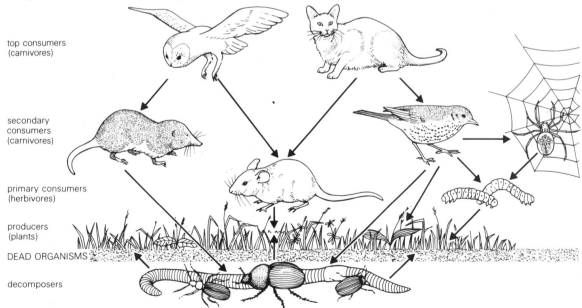

top consumers (carnivores)

secondary consumers (carnivores)

primary consumers (herbivores)

producers (plants)

DEAD ORGANISMS

decomposers

FOOD CHAIN *The feeding relationships between some plants and animals of a meadow habitat are simplified in this food web; in practice many more links and various other organisms are involved.*

days after infection, include fever and the development of blisters in the mouth and on the foot with consequent excessive salivation and lameness. Recovery occurs in 95% of cases but production of offspring and milk yield in females is adversely affected. The disease must be notifed to the authorities in many countries. Infected animals and contacts are usually slaughtered and movement of animals restricted. Vaccination is routine where the disease is endemic.

football A field game played throughout the world, the object of which is to score goals with an inflated ball. Team games using a football were played in China around 200 BC, in ancient Greece and Rome, and from the 12th century in England, where the violence and lawlessness of the game resulted in considerable injury. The modern games evolved during the 19th century as rules were formalized; in this the English public schools played a large role.

American football is similar to rugby football and developed in US colleges in the 1870s; it is played with an oval ball on a field marked out as a gridiron. There are 11 players on the field at any one time, but groups of differently specialized players are used in different phases of the game. The teams toss to decide which is to kick first. The game progresses in downs, or periods when the team in possession of the ball, or offensive team is advancing the ball toward the goal by passing or running with it. A down ends when a play is completed. The offensive team has four downs in which to advance the ball 10 yd (9 m). If this distance is not covered in the first three downs, the offensive team usually kicks the ball to the opponent. The other team then has the chance to substitute offensive for defensive players. If the 10 yd is covered, the offensive team maintains possession of the ball. A touchdown, in which the ball is taken across the opponents' goal line, scores six points; a conversion after a touchdown, in which the ball is taken over the goal line again from scrimmage or is kicked between the goalposts scores respectively two points or one point; a field goal (kicked from anywhere on the field) scores three points; a safety, in which a team scores a touchdown against itself, scores two points for its opponents.

soccer (*or* association football) dates back to the founding in England of the Football Association (1863). It is an 11-a-side game played with a spherical ball weighing 14–16 oz (396–453 g) and having a circumference of 27–28 in (69–71 cm). The traditional positions of the players are: goalkeeper; right and left back; right, center, and left half-back; outside right, inside right, center forward, inside left, and outside left. These positions, established early in the 20th century, have now become very flexible, and a modern line-up consists more generally simply of strikers, midfield players, and defenders. The teams toss for the first kick (the kick-off), following which the teams compete for the ball, trying to kick or head it into the opponents' goal. Only the goalkeeper may use his hands, and then only in his penalty area. Played all over the world, the game is governed internationally by the *Fédération internationale de Football association.

Australian Rules is an 18-a-side game that originated in the Australian goldfields in the 1850s and is extensively played in some states, especially Victoria. It is a fast open game played with an oval ball measuring 22.75 by 29.5 in (57.2 by 73.6 cm), with which players may run as long as they bounce it every 10 yd (9 m). The ball must be punched instead of thrown (as it is in rugby football). There are four goalposts without crossbars at each end. A goal, kicked between the two inner posts, scores six points; a behind, kicked between an inner and an outer post, scores one point.

Canadian football is similar to American football but is played with 12-a-side teams on a larger field and has slightly different scoring and rules.

Rugby football uses an oval ball that is kicked or passed by hand. The game was first played at Rugby School, England, according to tradition in 1823. In 1871 the Rugby Football Union was formed, but its ban on professionalism led in 1893 to the secession of the Rugby League (then called the Northern Union); there are therefore two types of rugby. Rugby Union football (*or* rugger) is a 15-a-side amateur game played throughout the world. The ball is 11–11.25 in (27.9–28.6 cm) long. A try, in which the ball is touched down behind the opponents' goal line, is worth four points; a goal (a try "converted" by kicking the ball over the crossbar of the goalposts), a further two points; a penalty goal, resulting from a kick awarded as a penalty against the opposing team, three points; and a drop goal, from the field, three points. A scrum, in which the forwards of both teams battle for the ball in a tight mass, is used to restart the game after minor infringements. For more serious infringements a penalty kick is given to the opposing side. Rugby League football is a 13-a-side game with slightly different rules and scoring in which professionalism is allowed; it is played mainly in N England.

Foraminifera An order of small single-celled animals (□*Protozoa*) found on the sea bed or as part of the *plankton. They form calcareous often multichambered shells, ranging in size from under 0.02–0.20 in

(0.5 mm to 5 mm), from which they extend fine branching pseudopodia to trap small protozoans and algae. Class: *Sarcodina. See also* Globigerina; Nummulites.

Forbes, George William (1869–1947) New Zealand statesman; prime minister (1930–35). Leader of the United (formerly Liberal) Party, he was forced by economic difficulties into a coalition (1931) with the Reform Party but their combined efforts failed to solve the problems of the Depression.

Forbidden City The central part of *Peking, so called because entry was forbidden to all but the emperor's family and servants. It was surrounded by a wall 2.5 mi (4 km) long and from the 15th century onward it contained the royal palace and residences and offices of the emperor's servants and ministers. It is now a complex of museums.

force The agency that changes either the speed or the direction of motion of a body (symbol: F). It is a *vector quantity defined as the product of the mass of the body and the acceleration produced on it. Force is measured in newtons. *See also* centripetal force; Coriolis force.

Ford, Ford Madox (Ford Hermann Hueffer; 1873–1939) British novelist, grandson of the Pre-Raphaelite artist Ford Madox Brown. Among his 80 or more novels and books of criticism and memoirs are the novels *The Good Soldier* (1915) and *Parade's End* (1924–28), a tetralogy. He founded and edited the *English Review* (1908) and, in Paris, the *Transatlantic Review* (1924), in which he published the early works of *Pound, *Joyce, *Hemingway, and many other writers.

GERALD R. FORD *President (1974-77) who worked to heal the nation in the aftermath of Watergate and Nixon's resignation.*

Ford, Gerald R(udolph) (1913–) US political leader; 38th President of the United States (1974–77). Born in Omaha, Neb and given the name Leslie King, Ford was later renamed for his stepfather. He was educated at the University of Michigan and at Yale Law School and began his political career with election to the US House of Representatives in 1948. Ford gradually distinguished himself as one of the most loyal Republicans in Congress, and in 1964 he was elected House minority leader. With the resignation of Vice President Spiro *Agnew in 1973, Ford was appointed to succeed him by President Richard *Nixon, according to the procedure established by the 25th Amendment to the *Constitution. Following Nixon's resignation as a result of the *Watergate Affair, Ford became the first

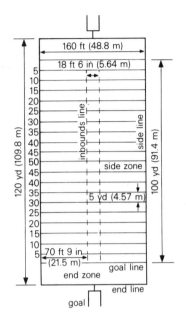

American football

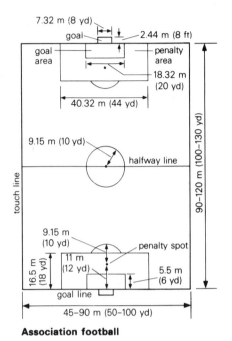

Association football

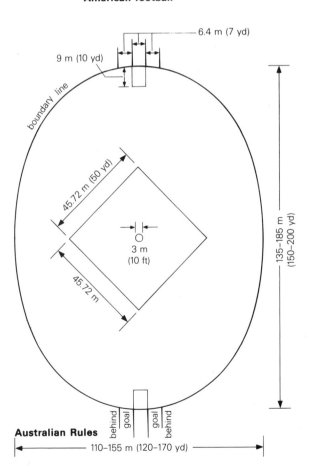

Australian Rules

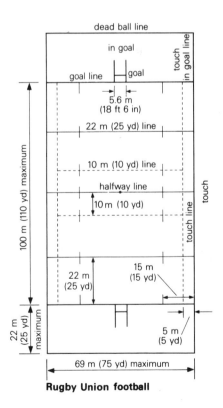

Rugby Union football

FOOTBALL *Dimensions of pitches.*

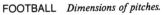

US president to succeed to that office without having been elected. One of Ford's most controversial actions as president was his pardon of Nixon for any crimes he might have committed while in office. For the most part, Ford continued the foreign policy of the Nixon administration, aimed at achieving *détente with the Soviet Union. In 1976, Ford was defeated for re-election by Democratic candidate Jimmy *Carter.

Ford, Henry (1863–1947) US industrialist. He left school at age 15 and worked as a machinist in Detroit for several years. In 1887 he became the chief engineer of the Detroit Edison Illuminating Co., working in his spare time on a new type of gasoline engine, which he perfected in 1892. The prototype proved so successful that Ford began to devote all of his time to automobile production, organizing the Ford Motor Co. in 1903. The most popular of Ford's vehicles, the "Model T" was first manufactured in 1908, and through the introduction of the assembly-line method of production in 1913, millions of Model T Fords were made available to the American public at economical prices. Although Ford was strongly opposed to the unionization of workers at his plants, he voluntarily instituted hour and wage standards. Later in life, he established the Ford Foundation to support his many philanthropic endeavors.

Ford, John (1586–c. 1640) English dramatist, the last major figure of Elizabethan and Jacobean drama. He collaborated with *Dekker and others at first, writing his own major plays between 1627 and 1638. Those most frequently performed are the revenge tragedies *The Broken Heart* (c. 1630) and *'Tis Pity She's a Whore* (c. 1632).

Ford, John (Sean O'Feeney; 1895–1973) US film director. He received much critical acclaim for *The Informer* (1935), *The Grapes of Wrath* (1940), and other films on social themes, but is best known as a director of popular westerns. These include *Stagecoach* (1939), *Rio Grande* (1950), and *How the West Was Won* (1962).

foreign aid Help given to poor countries by richer ones. Foreign aid can take several forms, including gratis payments, low interest loans, gifts in kind, etc. Foreign aid is usually given to the *developing countries to relieve natural disasters, to assist them in their efforts to industrialize, or for political reasons, such as to bolster up a friendly regime. One of the most ambitious programs of foreign aid was the *Marshall Plan in which the US provided funds to assist the recovery of Europe after World War II.

foreign exchange. *See* exchange rates.

Foreign Legion A French military force, the Légion étrangère, formed in 1831 to serve in France's African colonies. Its recruits are international but its officers are usually French. One of its regiments formed the *Organisation de l'Armée secrète (OAS) in Algeria (1961) and was subsequently disbanded. The Legion's headquarters are at Aubagne, near Marseilles, with units in Corsica and Djibouti.

forest An area of land covered largely with trees and undergrowth. Over 20% of world land area is forest, both natural and artificially planted, making forests a vital part of the global ecosystem as major suppliers of oxygen as well as timber. They also provide habitats for wildlife and are widely used for recreation.

The species of trees growing depends mainly on climate. Northern coniferous forests consist largely of pine, spruce, and firs and provide softwood for paper pulp, furniture, construction, etc. In more temperate regions forests consist primarily of mixed deciduous trees, especially oak, ash, elm, beech, sycamore, and other hardwoods, used mainly in furniture. In Mediterranean climates, the trees are adapted to hot dry summers and include the evergreen oaks. Broad-leaved evergreen trees are also found in New Zealand and South America, together with southern conifers. Tropical forests are characterized by a great diversity of species, usually of tall evergreen trees, with many climbing vines and epiphytes. The major tropical rain forests are in the Amazon and Orinoco river basins, with others in Africa and SE Asia. In neighboring regions of lower and more seasonal rainfall, an open savanna forest predominates, consisting of scattered deciduous trees.

Forestry, the cultivation and management of forests, is of major economic importance. Much research and development has been invested in improving varieties of trees for commercial use and in better methods of planting, pest control, thinning, felling, and extraction and of processing the timber into usable products.

Forester, C(ecil) S(cott) (1899–1966) British historical novelist, famous as the creator of Horatio Hornblower, a heroic but self-doubting British naval officer of Napoleonic times whose career he chronicled in a series of novels, beginning with *The Happy Return* (1937). Forester abandoned his medical studies for writing after the success of his first novel, *Payment Deferred* (1926).

forget-me-not An annual or perennial herb of the genus *Myosotis* (50 species), of temperate regions. 2–24 in (5–60 cm) tall, it has oblong hairy leaves and long spikes of small flowers, usually blue with white centers (young flowers are often pink). The fruits are small nutlets. Several species are grown as garden flowers. Family: *Boraginaceae*.

Forlì 44 13N 12 02E A city in Italy, in Emilia-Romagna. It has some ancient buildings, including a 15th-century citadel. Its various manufactures include furniture, textiles, felt, household appliances, and footwear. Population (1980 est): 110,755.

formaldehyde (*or* methanal; HCHO) A colorless toxic gaseous aldehyde. It dissolves in water to produce a solution known as formalin, which is used as a preservative. Formaldehyde is made by the catalytic oxidation of *methanol or petroleum gases and is used to make synthetic resins.

Forman, Miloš (1932–) Czech film director. His films, which include *The Fireman's Ball* (1967), are noted for their blend of humor and social criticism. In 1968 he went to the US, where he made *Taking Off* (1970) and *One Flew over the Cuckoo's Nest* (1976), for which he won an Academy Award.

formic acid (HCOOH) A colorless corrosive liquid *fatty acid with a pungent smell. It is made industrially by treating sodium formate (HCOONa) with sulfuric acid and is used in textile finishing and chemical manufacture. Formic acid occurs naturally in nettles and insects. Its name comes from the Latin *formica*, ant, whose sting is due to the secretion of formic acid.

Formigny, Battle of (April 15, 1450) The battle during the last period of the *Hundred Years' War in which the French forces routed the English army near Caen. The victory led directly to the fall of Caen, and then of Normandy, to the French.

Formosa. *See* Taiwan.

Forrest, Nathan Bedford (1821–77) US Confederate general. He joined the Confederate army as a private in 1861 and quickly rose in the ranks, becoming a general in 1862. With no formal military education, he organized his own cavalry and used them as a base in daring raids and battles at Fort Donelson (1862), Shiloh (1862), Rome, Georgia (1863), Chickamauga (1863), and Nashville (1864). Although he personally was exonerated, his career was marred when black soldiers were massacred at Ft Pillow (1864). He was active in the Ku Klux Klan after the war.

Forrestal, James Vincent (1892–1949) US statesman; Secretary of Defense (1947–49). A banker, who had risen to president of a Wall Street firm by 1938, he was appointed under-secretary of the Navy in 1940 and became secretary in 1944. When the president's cabinet was reorganized to include a secretary of defense he served in that capacity. He was known for his strong stand against the Soviet Union.

Forster, E(dward) M(organ) (1879–1970) British novelist. Educated at King's College, Cambridge, where he returned as a fellow in 1946, his fiction and social criticism stress the importance of human affection and the need to cultivate both the intellect and the imagination. His novels include *Where Angels Fear to Tread* (1905), *The Longest Journey* (1907), *A Room with a View* (1908), *Howard's End* (1910), and *A Passage to India* (1924). *Maurice*, a novel portraying a homosexual relationship, was published posthumously in 1971.

Forsythia A genus of shrubs (about 7 species), sometimes called golden bell, native to E Europe and Asia and widely grown as garden ornamentals. The masses of four-petaled yellow flowers appear before the leaves, which are toothed and oval. The slender stems make the plants suitable for wall shrubs and hedges. The most common garden forsythia is the hybrid *F. × intermedia*. Family: *Oleaceae* (olive family).

Fortaleza (*or* Ceará) 3 45S 38 35W A city and port in E Brazil, the capital of Ceará state on the Atlantic Ocean. Exports include cotton, rice, coffee, and sugar. Its university was established in 1955. Population (1980): 648,815.

Fortas, Abe (1910–82) US lawyer and associate justice of the Supreme Court (1965–69). After holding offices in several government departments, he opened his own law firm in Washington, DC. Appointed a Supreme Court justice by President *Johnson in 1965, he was nominated to fill the chief justice position in 1968. His failure to be approved by the Senate and accusations of bribery and conflict of interest led to his resignation from the court in 1969.

Fort-de-France (former name: Fort Royal) 14 36N 61 05W The capital and main port of Martinique since 1680, on the W coast. It was almost destroyed by an earthquake in 1839 and by fire in 1890. It is an important tourist resort and the site of a French naval base. Exports include sugar, cocoa, and rum. Population (1974): 98,807.

Forth, River A river in SE Scotland, rising on the NE slopes of Ben Lomond and flowing 65 mi (104 km) E through Stirling to Alloa. The river then expands into the **Firth of Forth** (an inlet of the North Sea) extending 51 mi (82 km) in length and 19 mi (31 km) wide at its mouth. It is spanned by the cantilever iron Forth Rail Bridge (designed in the 1880s by Benjamin Baker) and a road bridge (1964). **The Forth and Clyde Canal**, 37 mi (60 km) long, links the Rivers Forth and Clyde.

Fortin barometer A type of mercury *barometer, invented in 1810 by the French instrument maker Nicolas Fortin (1750–1831). The reservoir of mercury is contained in a leather bag attached to an evacuated glass tube marked with a fixed scale. The level of the mercury in the reservoir is set at zero by adjusting the leather bag.

Fort Knox 37 54N 85 59W A military base in N Kentucky. Established in 1917, it is the site of the US Depository, which contains US gold reserves. Population (1970): 37,608.

Fort Lamy. See N'djamena.

Fort Lauderdale 26 08N 80 08W A city and resort in SE Florida, on the Atlantic Ocean. It is the site of one of the largest marinas in the world. Population (1980): 153,256.

Fort Myers 26 37N 81 54W A resort city in SW Florida, on the Caloosahatchee River. Known for its palm-tree-lined streets, it is a popular retirement center. Thomas Alva Edison's winter home (1885) is here. Population (1980): 36,638.

FORTRAN (*fo*rmula *tran*slation) A computer-programming language. It is a high-level language (*see* program) used for representing mathematical formulae in a form that can be processed by a computer. Widely used among scientists and engineers, it has also found applications in the business community.

Fort Stanwix, Treaties of (1768, 1784) Agreements between the British and the Iroquois Indians, in which the British gained present-day W Pennsylvania, West Virginia, New York, and Kentucky for gifts worth $10,000. The fort, located at the site of Rome, New York, was built for defense against the Indians and was renamed Fort Schuyler in 1776.

Fort Sumter. See Charleston.

Fort Ticonderoga A fort in NE New York, in the city of Ticonderoga, between lakes George and Champlain. The French built the fort in 1755 to protect the waterways between New York and Canada. It was captured by the British in 1759 (French and Indian War) and by the Americans under Ethan Allen in 1775 (American Revolution). In 1777 it was briefly recaptured by the British. Originally called Fort Carillon, it was renamed Fort Ticonderoga in 1775 by the Americans and restored as a museum in 1909.

Fortuna The Roman goddess of fortune and good luck. She was usually portrayed standing on a ball or wheel, indicating her mutability, and holding a cornucopia from which she distributes her favors. She is identical to her Greek counterpart, *Tyche.

Fort Wayne 41 05N 85 08W A city in NE Indiana, on the Maumee River. Founded by the French in 1680, the fort was built in 1794. An important communications center, its main manufactures are electrical equipment and motor vehicles. Population (1980): 172,196.

Fort William (Canada). See Thunder Bay.

Fort Worth 32 45N 97 20W A city in NE Texas near Dallas. The center of the N Texas industrial area, its manufactures include aircraft, refined oil, and food products. Population (1980): 385,141.

forty-niners. See Gold Rush.

forum A Roman marketplace, similar to the Greek *agora. The forum was the civic center of the town, containing all the main temples and public buildings. The most famous forum is in Rome; it was laid out in the 1st century BC, but later frequently modified.

fossa A catlike mammal, *Cryptoprocta ferox*, found only in Madagascar. It is about 60 in (150 cm) long including the tail (28 in [70 cm]) and has short legs and short orange-brown fur. It feeds almost entirely on lemurs. Family: *Viverridae; order: Carnivora.

fossil The remains or traces of a plant or animal that lived in the past, usually preserved in sedimentary rock. It may be the whole or part of the organism itself that is preserved, usually chemically altered; alternatively it may have dissolved away leaving an impression (mold), which preserves its exact shape, or a cast, when it has been replaced exactly by mineral matter. Examples of fossils are whole mammoths preserved in ice, insects preserved in amber, and coal (the carbonized remains of extinct swamp plants). Trace fossils include excrement, burrows, or fossil tracks. A derived fossil is found in a more recent sediment than the one in which it was orginally preserved, because of erosion and redeposition. A zone fossil is used in

biostratigraphy to delimit a stratigraphic zone; such fossils must be widely distributed and have a limited vertical range in successive rock strata to be useful for this purpose. The study of fossils is called *paleontology.

fossil fuels The mineral fuels *coal, *oil, and *natural gas that occur in rock formations. They were formed by the deposition millions of years ago of the remains of vegetation (coal) and living organisms (oil and gas), which were buried under subsequent deposition and later subjected to heat and pressure.

Fossil fuels supply a large proportion of our current *energy needs, but the reserves are finite. Gas and oil in particular are rapidly being exhausted. *Alternative energy sources are therefore now being investigated and *nuclear energy is being developed to take their place.

Foster, Stephen Collins (1826–64) US composer of such songs as "Swanee River" (1851) and "Beautiful Dreamer" (1864). Foster was self-taught and turned to black plantation songs for melodic inspiration. Although popular and successful during his lifetime, he died in poverty. Other works include "Oh! Susannah" (1848), "Camptown Races" (1850), "My Old Kentucky Home" (1853), "Jeanie With the Light Brown Hair" (1854), and "Old Black Joe" (1860).

Fotheringhay 52 32N 0 25W A village in England, in Northamptonshire on the River Nene. Fotheringhay Castle (of which little remains) was the scene of Richard III's birth (1452) and the execution of Mary, Queen of Scots (1587).

Foucault, Jean Bernard Léon (1819–68) French physicist, after whom the *Foucault pendulum (1851) is named. He also worked on light, measuring its speed and showing that its speed decreased in water (1850). He also invented the gyroscope (1852).

Foucault pendulum A very long pendulum with a heavy bob, capable of oscillating for a long period. It demonstrates the earth's rotation since, as it swings, its plane of oscillation slowly rotates. At the poles it would rotate through 360° in 24 hours; at a latitude λ, the number of hours for a complete rotation is given by 24/sin λ. It was invented by Jean *Foucault and first demonstrated in 1851 in Paris using a 62-lb (28-kg) lead ball suspended from a wire 220 ft (67 m) long.

Fouché, Joseph, Duc d'Otrante (1759–1820) French politician. A priest and teacher, he became politically active in the French Revolution, being elected a deputy in the National Convention in 1792. He participated in the overthrow of Robespierre (1794) and became minister of police under Napoleon but was forced into exile in 1816 after the restoration of the monarchy.

Fouqué, Friedrich Heinrich Karl, Baron de la Motte (1777–1843) German novelist and dramatist. Of French aristocratic descent, he was a prolific writer of chivalric romances and dramas, many of them adapted from Scandinavian sagas. His best-known work is the romance *Undine* (1811), the story of a watersprite who marries a human.

Fouquet, Jean (c. 1420–81) French painter and manuscript illuminator, born in Tours. After visiting Italy, he worked for Charles VII and later for Louis XI, whose tomb he helped design. For the royal treasurer, Étienne Chevalier, he painted *The Virgin and Child* (Antwerp) and *Chevalier with His Patron St Stephen* (Berlin), which were formerly joined as the *Mehun Diptych*. A manuscript of Josephus' *Jewish Antiquities* (Bibliothèque National, Paris) contains his finest illuminations, noteworthy for their depiction of French towns and countryside.

Fouquet, Nicolas (1615–80) French politician; finance minister (1653–61) under Louis XIV. He amassed a large fortune, partly through fraudulent dealings, which were revealed to the king by *Colbert, and he was arrested and imprisoned for life.

four-eyed fish A freshwater *bony fish of the family *Anablepidae* (2 species), found in Central and South America. Up to 12 in (30 cm) long, they have horizontally divided eyes with separate retinas for cruising just below the water surface, the upper halves being modified for aerial vision. Live young are born. Order: Atheriniformes.

Fourier, (François Marie) Charles (1772–1837) French socialist. Fourier advocated the organization of society on cooperative principles. He sought the abolition of all constrictions, including marriage, and set out his plan of an ideal society in *Le Nouveau Monde industriel* (1829–30).

Fourier, Jean Baptiste Joseph, Baron (1768–1830) French mathematician and physicist. After a career in the army, during which he served in Egypt under Napoleon, Fourier turned to science, his prime interest. While investigating heat, he discovered a method of expanding a periodic function in terms of sine and cosine waves, now known as **Fourier analysis** (*see* harmonic analysis). The discovery attracted widespread interest and Fourier was subsequently made a baron by Napoleon (1808).

FOSSIL

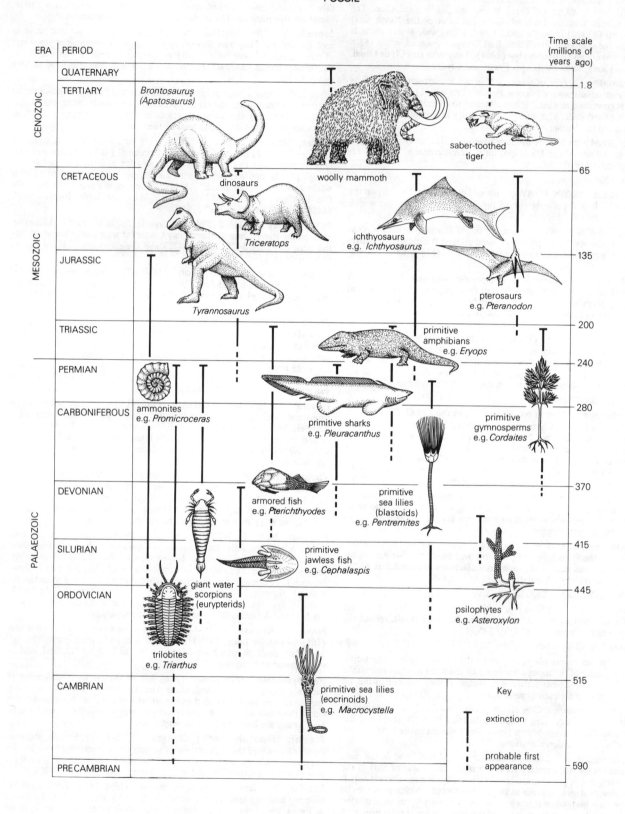

ERA	PERIOD		Time scale (millions of years ago)

- QUATERNARY
- TERTIARY — 1.8
- CRETACEOUS — 65
- JURASSIC — 135
- TRIASSIC — 200
- PERMIAN — 240
- CARBONIFEROUS — 280
- DEVONIAN — 370
- SILURIAN — 415
- ORDOVICIAN — 445
- CAMBRIAN — 515
- PRECAMBRIAN — 590

CENOZOIC
MESOZOIC
PALAEOZOIC

Brontosaurus (Apatosaurus)

woolly mammoth

saber-toothed tiger

dinosaurs

Triceratops

ichthyosaurs e.g. *Ichthyosaurus*

Tyrannosaurus

pterosaurs e.g. *Pteranodon*

primitive amphibians e.g. *Eryops*

ammonites e.g. *Promicroceras*

primitive sharks e.g. *Pleuracanthus*

primitive gymnosperms e.g. *Cordaites*

armored fish e.g. *Pterichthyodes*

primitive sea lilies (blastoids) e.g. *Pentremites*

giant water scorpions (eurypterids)

primitive jawless fish e.g. *Cephalaspis*

psilophytes e.g. *Asteroxylon*

trilobites e.g. *Triarthus*

primitive sea lilies (eocrinoids) e.g. *Macrocystella*

Key

extinction

probable first appearance

FOSSIL *Some extinct animals and plants from past geological ages.*

Fourneyron, Benoît (1802–67) French engineer, who invented the modern water *turbine, producing the first large-scale model in 1832. It was quickly adopted by industry but was not used for generating hydroelectric power until 1895.

Four Noble Truths The fundamental doctrine of Buddhism, set forth by Gautama in the first discourse at Benares. The Truths are: existence is characterized by suffering; the cause of suffering is craving; to end craving is to end suffering; the way to achieve this is the *Eightfold Path.

four o'clock plant A bushy perennial herb, *Mirabilis jalapa*, also called marvel of Peru, native to tropical America but widely grown as an ornamental. 16–30 in (40–75 cm) high, it bears clusters of red, pink, white, yellow, or streaked flowers, which are tubular with a wide flared mouth and open in the late afternoon. Family: *Nyctaginaceae*.

Fourteen Points (1918) Terms for a peace settlement proposed by the US president Woodrow Wilson, in World War I. They called for recognition of national aspirations, free trade, and an international league of nations and inspired the subsequent Treaty of *Versailles.

Fouta Djallon (or Futa Jallon) A mountainous plateau area in NW Guinea. The Niger, Senegal, and Gambia Rivers rise in the range. The area is covered chiefly by savanna and cattle raising is the main activity.

fowl, domestic. *See* poultry, domestic.

Fowler, H(enry) W(atson) (1858–1933) British lexicographer and prescriptive stylist. With his brother **Francis Fowler** (1870–1918) he wrote *The King's English* (1906) and edited the *Concise Oxford Dictionary* (1911). His most famous work, *Modern English Usage* (1926), has been described as "a collection of prejudices erected into a system."

Fowles, John (1926–   ) British novelist, whose works treat philosophical, psychological, and social themes in a rich and often fantastic manner. His novels include *The Collector* (1963), *The Magus* (1966), and *The French Lieutenant's Woman* (1969), which have been filmed, *Daniel Martin* (1977), and *Mantissa* (1982). Other books include the short stories in *The Ebony Tower* (1974).

Fox North American Algonkian-speaking Indian tribe; also known as Mesquakie, or "red earth people." They were found in Wisconsin, where they warred against the French and Sioux, and in the Great Lakes area during the early 18th century. Eventually allied with the Sauk, they were relegated to a Kansas reservation (1842). In 1859 they settled in Tama, Iowa, where the majority reside today.

fox A carnivorous mammal belonging to the *dog family (Canidae). Foxes have pointed ears, short legs with hairy pads on their feet, and large bushy tails. Generally nocturnal, they are solitary stealthy hunters, feeding on small mammals, birds, insects, and some fruit. The most familiar is the *red fox (*Vulpes vulpes*), found in forest and woodland and now venturing into suburban gardens. Some species are specialized for life in difficult habitats, such as the *Arctic fox and the *fennec. The unusual South African bat-eared fox (*Otocyon megalotis*) feeds mainly on termites and has teeth resembling those of an insect-eating mammal. Chief genera: *Vulpes* (9 species), *Dusicyon* (South American foxes; 8 species).

Fox, Charles James (1749–1806) British Whig politician; the first British foreign secretary (1782). He entered parliament (1768) as a supporter of Lord *North but joined the *Rockingham Whigs in opposing North's American policy. Fox resigned and joined North in a coalition that briefly took office in 1783. Fox supported the French Revolution, over which issue many Whigs joined the Tories, and in 1798 he was dismissed from the privy council for opposing war with Revolutionary France. He was foreign secretary again briefly before his death in 1806.

Fox, George (1624–91) English religious leader, founder of the *Quakers. A Puritan by upbringing and originally a shoemaker's apprentice, Fox became dissatisfied with the formalism of established Christianity and the state's control of the church. In 1646 he had a personal revelation and thereafter preached a gospel of love, stressing the immediate guidance of the Holy Spirit. He was frequently imprisoned for his beliefs and he made several missionary journeys abroad, notably to North America in 1671. His best-known work is his *Journal* (1674).

Foxe, John (1516–87) English religious writer. He fled to the Continent during the reign of Mary I and on his return wrote a history of the English Protestant martyrs from the 14th century to his own time. Usually known as *The Book of Martyrs* (1563), it fed the growing Catholic persecution of the time, to which Foxe himself was outspokenly opposed.

foxglove A herbaceous plant of the genus *Digitalis*, especially *D. purpurea*, a biennial herb, 18–60 in (45–150 cm) tall, native to W Europe but naturalized elsewhere. Foxgloves have large gray-green oblong leaves and tall one-sided spikes of drooping bell-shaped flowers, up to 3 in (6.5 cm) long, purple, yellow, or white in color, often with purple spots in the center. The dried leaves contain *digitalis. Family: *Scrophulariaceae*.

foxhound A dog belonging to one of two breeds used for foxhunting. The English foxhound is strongly built with a deep chest and long neck. The American foxhound is descended from the English breed but is of lighter build. In both, the short coat is a combination of black, tan, and white. Height: 23–25 in (56–63 cm).

foxhunting A sport in which huntsmen on horseback pursue a fox with a pack of 20 to 30 *foxhounds, which hunt their quarry by scent. Fully organized in Britain since the 18th century, hunting achieved the status of a national pastime and has influenced many aspects of rural life. Foxhunting is also popular in the E US, and jackalhunting and draghunting (in which hounds follow a prepared trail) are found as substitutes in other parts of the world.

fox terrier A breed of □dog developed in England for hunting foxes and badgers. It is sturdy with a short tail, a broad tapering muzzle, and small ears that are folded forward over the face. There are two coat varieties—smooth-haired and wire-haired—and coloring is mainly white with black and tan markings. Height: 14–16 in (37–39 cm).

foxtrot A ballroom dance in 4/4 time with a syncopated rhythm in which couples combine slow walking steps with quick running steps. It was developed in the US about 1914 from the two-step, a dance in 2/4 time with even rhythms.

Foyle, Lough An inlet of the Atlantic Ocean, in N Ireland. Fed by the Foyle River, it lies between NE Co Donegal in the Republic of Ireland and NW Co Londonderry in Northern Ireland.

fracture The breaking of a bone. This usually occurs as a result of injury but it may happen very easily in bones diseased with cancer or *osteoporosis (pathological fracture). In a simple fracture the ends of the broken bone are not displaced; in a compound fracture the broken bone pierces the skin. A stress fracture is a crack arising in a bone exposed to repeated small injuries, for example in the feet of soldiers marching long distances. The bones of children are relatively soft and flexible; such bones are more likely to be bent than completely broken—this is called a greenstick fracture. Fractures are treated by aligning the ends of the broken bone and immobilizing them. Healing will result quickly. Sometimes, however, it is necessary to pin fractures surgically.

Fragonard, Jean Honoré (1732–1806) French *rococo painter, born in Grasse. He trained with *Chardin and *Boucher in Paris and studied in Italy (1756–61), concentrating on the work of *Tiepolo. He established his reputation with a history painting, *Coresus Sacrificing Himself to Save Callirhoë* (1765; Louvre), but soon turned to more light-hearted and delicately erotic subjects, e.g. *The Swing* (Wallace Collection, London) and *The Progress of Love* (Frick Collection, New York). His interest in Dutch painters, whose influence can be seen in a number of his landscapes and portraits, was strengthened by a visit to Holland in the 1770s. He suffered financial ruin during the Revolution. His subject matter and style of painting no longer found popular favor and he died in obscurity.

France, Anatole (Jacques Anatole François Thibault; 1844–1924) French novelist, son of a Parisian bookseller. His novels are noted for their erudition, skepticism, and elegance. His intervention in the *Dreyfus case (1897) marked the beginning of his commitment to socialism and, during his final years, communism. In such novels as *L'Île des pingouins* (1909) and *Les Dieux ont soif* (1913) his view of mankind is deeply pessimistic. He was awarded the Nobel Prize in 1921.

France, Republic of A country in W Europe, bordering on the English Channel in the N, the Atlantic Ocean in the W, and the Mediterranean Sea in the S. It includes the island of Corsica and several overseas regions (Martinique, Guadeloupe, and French Guiana). Overseas territories include French Polynesia, New Caledonia, and St Pierre and Miquelon. Fertile lowlands cover most of the N and W of France, rising to the Pyrenees in the S, the Massif Central in the SE, and the Vosges, Jura, and Alps in the E. The principal rivers are the Seine, the Loire, and the Rhône. *Economy*: compared with other industrial countries in W Europe, agriculture remains important although the number of people employed in this sector has decreased owing to the reorganization of many of the numerous small peasant holdings into larger units. Animal products make up over half the total output and the production of cereals is important; the wine industry is a major source of revenue. There have been large-scale developments in the industrial sector since World War II, especially in iron and steel, motor vehicles, aircraft, mechanical and electrical engineering, textiles, chemicals, and food processing. Its mineral wealth includes iron ore, potash, bauxite, coal, and sulfur. Natural gas is being developed in the foothills of the Pyrenees, but a considerable proportion of power still comes from hydro-

JEAN HONORÉ FRAGONARD *The Swing (1768-69) was commissioned by the Baron de Saint-Julien, who is seen in the bottom left of the painting eyeing his mistress on the swing. The baron had originally specified that the older man pushing the swing should be a Roman Catholic bishop.*

electric sources. Exports have risen dramatically in the postwar period, especially textiles, iron and steel, motor vehicles, and machinery, and in 1978 France was the world's third largest exporter of arms. Economic growth has slowed down in recent years, however, and the economic strategies of recent prime ministers have failed to deal with the increasing problems of inflation, trade deficits, and soaring unemployment. *History*: present-day France approximates the ancient region of *Gaul, which was conquered by Julius Caesar in the 1st century BC. It became part of the Roman Empire and in the 1st century AD Christianity was introduced to the provinces into which Gaul was divided. From the 3rd to the 5th centuries, it was overrun by German tribes, including the Goths, Vandals, and *Franks (from whom the name France is derived). The Frankish kingdom reached its peak under Charlemagne (reigned 768–814) and his *Carolingian dynasty continued to rule in France until 987, when Hugh Capet became the first *Capetian king. During the 10th century Norsemen (Vikings) established themselves in what became Normandy and in 1066 invaded England. The claims of English kings to French territory were realized on a large scale by the *Angevins and consequent conflict between France and England culminated in the *Hundred Years' War (1337–1453), as a result of which the English were expelled from all of France, except Calais. The Capetians were succeeded by the *Valois dynasty (1328–1589), a period that saw the beginning of France's long rivalry with Spain for hegemony in Europe. During the *Wars of Religion the last Valois king, Henry III, was succeeded (1589) by the first *Bourbon, Henry IV. The first half of the 17th century was dominated by Cardinal de *Richelieu and his successor as chief minister, Cardinal *Mazarin. They were resonsible for France replacing Spain, after the Thirty Years' War, as the supreme European power (1659). During the reign (1643–1715) of *Louis XIV France reached the zenith of its power and brilliance. Decline, however, began before his death and gathered speed in the following decades. The disastrous *Seven Years' War forced France to recognize British supremacy in North America and India and the political reaction and economic incompetence of the later Bourbon kings precipitated the *French Revolution in 1789. The First Republic was proclaimed (1792) and Louis XVI was guillotined (1793) in spite of the military opposition of the major European powers (*see* Revolutionary and Napoleonic Wars). In 1799 *Napoleon Bonaparte overthrew the Directory, becoming first consul and, in 1804, emperor. By 1808 he had brought most of continental Europe under his sway but in 1815 he was finally defeated at Waterloo and exiled. The Bourbons were restored until 1830, when the July Revolution raised Louis Philippe to the throne. Overthrown in the *Revolution of 1848, the monarchy was replaced by the Second Republic of which Louis Napoleon became president; in 1852 he proclaimed himself emperor as *Napoleon III. During the Second Empire France underwent the beginnings of industrialization but its prosperity was not sufficient to achieve victory in the *Franco-Prussian War, in which Napoleon's ignominious leadership led to his overthrow (1870). The subsequent Third Republic lasted until 1940, in spite of scandal (e.g. the *Dreyfus and *Stavisky affairs), *World War I, and political dissension (there were 44 successive governments between 1918 and 1940). After the outbreak of World War II France fell to Germany and a pro-German government was established at Vichy, while *de Gaulle led the Free French resistance in London. In 1944 France was liberated by the Allies and de Gaulle established a provisional government that gave way (1946) to the Fourth Republic. The immediate postwar period was overshadowed by war in Indochina and by the crisis in Algeria that precipitated the fall of the Fourth Republic (1958). De Gaulle was recalled from retirement and, as president of the Fifth Republic, instituted a period of firm government. In May, 1968, however, the Republic was shaken by serious revolts among students and a wave of strikes and in 1969 he resigned. Gaullist principles nevertheless continued to influence government under his successors Pompidou and Giscard d'Estaing. Mitterrand's election (1981) made him the first socialist to hold the office of president in 35 years. Official language: French. Official currency: franc of 100 centimes. Area: 209,912 sq mi (543,814 sq km). Population (1981 est): 53,838,000. Capital: Paris. Main port: Marseilles.

Franche-Comté A planning region and former province in E France, bordering on Switzerland. Part of Burgundy until 843 AD, it was overrun successively by many powers before being finally annexed to France in 1678. The main occupations are farming, especially dairy farming and cattle rearing, and forestry. Area: 6014 sq mi (15,579 sq km). Population (1981 est): 1,090,800.

Francis I (1494–1547) King of France (1515–47). His reign was dominated by rivalry with the Holy Roman Emperor *Charles V. In the course of the conflict, which continued intermittently until 1544, Francis was taken prisoner at *Pavia (1525). At home, he won control over the French church through the Concordat of Bologna (1516), suppressed French Protestantism, and ordered an attack on the *Waldenses in S France (1545).

Francis I (1708–65) Duke of Lorraine (1729–37), Grand duke of Tuscany (1737–65), and Holy Roman Emperor (1745–65). He married (1736) *Maria Theresa, who succeeded to the Austrian dominions in 1740 in the face of much opposition. He was elected emperor during the consequent War of the *Austrian Succession (1740–48).

Francis I (Emperor of Austria). *See* Francis II (Holy Roman Emperor).

Francis II (1544–60) King of France (1559–60); the son of *Henry II and *Catherine de' Medici and husband (1558–60) of *Mary, Queen of Scots. He was dominated by the *Guise family, which used him in its struggle against the Protestant *Condé in the early phase of the *Wars of Religion.

Francis II (1768–1835) The last Holy Roman Emperor (1792–1806) and, as Francis I, the first Emperor of Austria (1804–35). Following three defeats by the French in the Napoleonic Wars, he allied with *Napoleon until 1813. After the Congress of *Vienna (1815), he was guided by his conservative chief minister *Metternich.

Francis Ferdinand (1863–1914) Archduke of Austria and heir apparent to his uncle, Emperor *Francis Joseph. He was known to favor the development of national cultures within the Empire. His assassination (June 28, 1914) by a Serbian nationalist at Sarajevo precipitated *World War I.

Francis Joseph (1830–1916) Emperor of Austria (1848–1916) and King of Hungary (1867–1916). His long reign saw the rise of national tensions in the Empire, which led to the establishment of the Dual Monarchy of *Austria-Hungary, under which Austria and Hungary coexisted as equal partners under the Austrian crown. He was defeated by the Prussians in the Austro-Prussian War of 1866 but in 1879 he allied with the recently formed German Empire and in 1882 with Italy, forming the *Triple Alliance. His ultimatum to Serbia, following the assassination by a Serbian nationalist of his nephew, Archduke *Francis Ferdinand (1914), led to *World War I.

Francis of Assisi, St (Giovanni di Bernardone; c. 1182–1226) Italian friar and founder of the *Franciscans, born in Assisi. The son of a merchant, he renounced his worldly life in 1205 to live in poverty and devote himself to prayer and charitable works. By 1209 he had a band of followers with whom he went to Rome (1210), where he obtained papal approval of his new order. He traveled throughout Spain, the Holy Land, and Egypt, later retiring to Assisi and giving up the leadership of his order. A profoundly humble man, in paintings he is often portrayed in the countryside among animals and birds, which he called his sisters and brothers. His love of nature is also reflected in his famous hymn, *Canticle of the Sun*. He received the *stigmata in 1224, was canonized in 1228. Feast day: Oct 4.

Francis of Sales, St (1567–1622) French Roman Catholic prelate and devotional writer, born in Savoy. He played a leading part in the Counter-Reformation by reconverting the people of Chablais from Calvinism to Roman Catholicism. As Bishop of Geneva from 1602 he cofounded the Order of the Visitation, an order of nuns. Feast day: Jan 29.

Francis Xavier, St (1506–52) Spanish *Jesuit missionary, known as the Apostle of the Indies. While studying in Paris (1523–34) he met St *Ignatius of Loyola and helped him found the Jesuit order. From 1541 he worked in the Indies, India, and Japan, establishing missions and making many converts. Feast day: Dec 3.

Franciscans An order of friars founded in 1209 by St *Francis of Assisi. His rule was devised to impose both personal and corporate poverty on the order's members. The rule was revised in 1221 and again in 1223, when it was confirmed by the pope. Within Francis' lifetime the expanding order found complete poverty practically difficult, and a schism ensued in the early 14th century regarding how strictly the rule should be followed. Despite a resulting decline, the order survived and has remained an important missionary and charitable branch of the Roman Catholic Church.

francium (Fr) The heaviest alkali metal, a very unstable radioactive element discovered in 1939 by Perey. The longest-lived isotope ^{223}Fr has a half-life of 22 minutes; traces of the element exist in nature, as decay products of ^{227}Ac. At no 87; at wt (223).

Franck, César Auguste (1822–90) Belgian composer, organist, and teacher, who settled in Paris in 1834. He became organist of Ste Clotilde in 1858, a post he held until his death. His pupils included D'Indy and Chausson. Franck was influenced by Bach and evolved a highly chromatic form of harmony. He also developed "cyclic form," the use of the same theme in more than one movement of a work. His compositions include *Symphonic Variations* (for piano and orchestra; 1885), a symphony (1886–88), a violin sonata (1886), and a string quartet (1889).

Franck, James (1882–1964) US physicist, born in Germany, whose experiments in collaboration with Gustav Hertz on the excitation of gases when bombarded with electrons won them the Nobel Prize in 1925. Their experiments provided evidence that the energy levels inside atoms were quantized. He also made valuable contributions to photochemistry. During World War II Franck worked on the development of the atom bomb but opposed its use on populated areas.

Franco, Francisco (1892–1975) Spanish general and statesman; dictator from 1939 until his death. He entered the Infantry Academy in 1907, aged 14, was posted to Spanish Morocco in 1912, and became the youngest captain in the Spanish army in 1915. By 1935 he was chief of the General Staff and in the following year, on July 18, staged a military uprising against the Republican Government of *Azaña that precipitated the *Spanish Civil War. In October, 1936, he became head of state in the Nationalist Zone and commander in chief of the rebel forces. By 1939, with help from Hitler and Mussolini, he had defeated the Republican forces and become the absolute leader of all Spain. Franco's fascist government, in which the National Movement (*see* Falange Española) was the only political party, remained sympathetic to Hitler but maintained an officially neutral position throughout World War II. Spain was excluded from the newly formed UN in 1945 but its international isolation was broken during the Cold War, when Franco's anticommunism made him a more attractive ally. In 1953 he signed a military-assistance agreement with the US. Although his government achieved considerable economic advance for Spain, especially in the 1960s, he operated a ruthless dictatorship that tolerated no opposition. However, during his last years he permitted a perceptible liberalization, which foreshadowed the country's move to democracy under his named successor, King *Juan Carlos.

francolin A *partridge belonging to a genus (*Francolinus*; 41 species) occurring in Africa and Asia. 27–46 cm long, francolins are usually a dull brownish color with black, white, or chestnut markings and are popular gamebirds.

Franconia A duchy of early medieval Germany, now in Rhineland-Palatinate, Baden-Württemberg, Hessen, and Bavaria. Its duke, Conrad, was the first elected king of Germany (911–18) but the duchy was subsequently comparatively unimportant and by the 13th century had been fragmented into small principalities.

Franco-Prussian War (1870–71) A war between France and Prussia. Fearing Bismarck's proposals to make a relative of William I of Prussia the king of Spain (*see* Ems telegram), France declared war. Within two months Napoleon III and his army were defeated at the battle of *Sedan but French resistance continued. Napoleon was deposed and the Third Republic was established but the Prussians besieged Paris, which eventually capitulated. The Treaty of Frankfurt imposed a huge indemnity on France, which ceded Alsace and Lorraine to the newly established German Empire; France was left economically weakened and politically divided.

frangipani A tropical American tree, *Plumeria rubra*, cultivated throughout the tropics and known in Asia as pagoda tree or temple flower. Up to 20 ft (6 m) tall, it has tapering long-stalked leaves with parallel veins and round clusters, up to 10 in (25 cm) across, of pink, reddish-purple, white, or yellow flowers, which are very fragrant and used to make perfume. Family: *Apocynaceae*.

Frank, Anne (1929–45) German–Dutch Jewish girl, who died in a German concentration camp. Her diary became a symbol of Jewish resistance and courage following its publication in 1947. She wrote it while hiding from the Nazis in Amsterdam in 1942–43.

Frankfort 38 11N 84 53W The capital city of Kentucky on the Kentucky River. Its major industry is whiskey distilling. Population (1980): 25,973.

Frankfurt am Main 50 06N 8 41E A city in central West Germany, in Hessen on the Main River. A major banking and commercial center, it is famed for its trade fairs, especially the annual book fair. Its gothic cathedral is 13th century and the university was established in 1914. It is the birthplace of Goethe and the original home of the Rothschilds. Its industries include the manufacture of chemicals, pharmaceuticals, and machinery. *History*: it was the seat of the imperial elections (9th to 18th centuries) and coronations (1562–1792) of the Holy Roman emperors. The first German national assembly met here (1848–49). Population (1980 est): 629,200.

Frankfurt an der Oder 52 20N 14 32E A city in E East Germany, on the Oder River. Severely damaged in World War II, the part of the city on the E bank of the river was incorporated into Poland in 1945. A trading center since medieval times, its manufactures include machinery and furniture. Population (1973 est): 65,644.

Frankfurter, Felix (1882–1965) US jurist. Born in Vienna and educated in the US, Frankfurter served as assistant US attorney and as counsel to the War Department before accepting an appointment as professor at Harvard Law School in 1914. After World War I, he was a legal adviser to President Woodrow *Wilson at the *Paris Peace Conference, and in 1920 he helped to found the American Civil Liberties Union. As a strong political supporter of the *New Deal programs, Frankfurter was often consulted on legal matters by President Franklin *Roosevelt. In 1939, Roosevelt nominated him to be an associate justice of the US Supreme Court. Considered a liberal when appointed, he was soon labeled a conservative for his continued belief that judges should practice restraint rather than follow an activist policy. He sat on the court until poor health forced his retirement in 1962.

frankincense (*or* olibanum) An aromatic gum resin obtained chiefly from trees of the genus *Boswellia*, especially *B. carteri*, which grows in the Middle East. It is usually supplied commercially in yellowish blocks covered with white dust, smells of balsam when heated, and burns brightly giving off a fragrant odor. Frankincense has been known since ancient Egyptian times and is still used as an *incense, in fumigants, and in perfumes.

Franklin The northernmost district of Canada, in the *Northwest Territories, consisting of Canada's Arctic archipelago and some northerly peninsulas. Covered by tundra and ice cap, it has large oil reserves. The inhabitants are mostly Eskimo hunters and fishermen. Area: 549,253 sq mi (1,422,565 sq km). Population (1976): 7180.

Franklin, Benjamin (1706–90) US diplomat, scientist, and author. He established a printing business in Philadelphia and became well known for his *Poor Richard's Almanac* (1732–57), which contained many maxims on the virtues of thrift and hard work. His experiments with static electricity, especially the famous episode in which he flew a kite during a thunderstorm (and was lucky not to be killed), established the electrical nature of thunderstorms and led him to invent the lightning conductor. His political prominence began in 1737, when he became deputy postmaster of Philadel-

BENJAMIN FRANKLIN *Statesman, diplomat, and inventor, a leading force in colonial America and the American Revolution.*

phia, where he promoted street lighting and the establishment of a city police force. In the disputes that led to the American Revolution he represented Pennsylvania's case to Britain (1757–62, 1766–75) and as a member of the *Continental Congress helped frame the Declaration of Independence (1775). Famous as a diplomat in Paris (1776–85), he enlisted French help for the colonies and later negotiated peace with Britain (1783). Franklin is also well known as the founder of a club that became (1743) the American Philosophical Society. His *Autobiography* was first published in complete form in 1868.

Franklin, Sir John (1786–1847) British explorer. After service in the Royal Navy, during which he fought at Trafalgar (1805), he was subsequently governor (1836–43) of Van Dieman's Land (now Tasmania). In 1845 he sailed with two ships, never to return, to look for the *Northwest Passage. Successive search expeditions failed to find the men until 1859, when their skeletons and records were found on King William Island. Franklin had virtually discovered the passage but had become ice-bound and he and his companions died of scurvy or starvation.

Franks A Germanic people, who invaded Roman *Gaul from the Rhineland between the 3rd and 5th centuries AD. One of the Frankish tribes, the Salian Franks, gained control of most of Gaul under their ruler *Clovis (d. 511) and were converted to Christianity. The Frankish state was ruled by the *Merovingian dynasty (named for Clovis' grandfather, Merovech) until its replacement by the *Carolingians (named for— *Charlemagne) in 751. The Carolingian empire lasted until its division in 843. The western Frankish kingdom was the nucleus of modern France.

Franz Josef Land (Russian name: Zemlya Frantsa Iosifa) A Soviet archipelago of about 85 islands in the N Barents Sea, the largest being Aleksandra Land, George Land, Graham Bell Island, Salisbury Island, and Wilczek Land. They were discovered in 1873 by Austrians and annexed by the Soviet Union in 1926. They are 90% icebound and have no permanent population. Total area: about 79,905 sq mi (20,700 sq km).

Fraser, (John) Malcolm (1930–) Australian statesman; Liberal prime minister (1975–83). He served in several cabinet posts (1966–72) before becoming Liberal Party Leader. Appointed caretaker prime minister on the dismissal of *Whitlam, he remained in office until the Liberals were defeated in the 1983 elections, when he also resigned as leader of the Liberal Party.

Fraser, Peter (1884–1950) New Zealand statesman; Labour prime minister (1940–49). Born in Britain, he helped form the Democratic Party (1913; the Labour Party from 1916) and entered parliament in 1918. He influenced Allied strategy in the Pacific during World War II and helped to establish the UN (1945).

Fraser, Simon (1776–1862) Canadian explorer and fur trader, born in the US. He started working for the Northwest Company in 1792 and by 1801 had become a partner. He was responsible for the establishment of new trading posts west to the Pacific Ocean and explored the river later named for him. During his leadership (1811–18) of the Red River depart-

ment of the Northwest Company he was accused of attacking and massacring the competition's settlers in that area. Although acquitted, he retired in 1818.

MALCOLM FRASER

Fraser River A river in W Canada, the chief river of British Columbia. Rising near Mount *Robson, it flows rapidly through mountain gorges until it reaches flat farmland in the SW, where it empties into the Strait of Georgia near Vancouver. Length: 850 mi (1370 km).

fraud In law, making a false representation, by words or conduct or by withholding facts where there is a duty to disclose them, in order to obtain a material advantage. To prove fraud it is necessary to show that a false representation was made (1) knowingly, (2) without belief in its truth, or (3) recklessly, without concern whether it was true or not. To obtain damages it must be shown that the defendant intended the injured party to act on the fraudulent representation and that he did so to his detriment. A contract based on fraud may be declared void at the option of the injured party.

Fraunhofer, Joseph von (1787–1826) German physicist, who greatly improved the quality of lenses and prisms and made improvements to the design of optical instruments. His superior equipment enabled him to detect numerous dark lines in the sun's spectrum (1814), now known as **Fraunhofer lines**. The eight most prominent lines are still known by the letters he gave them.

Frazer, Sir James George (1854–1941) British anthropologist, mythologist, and writer. Frazer's major work *The Golden Bough* (first edition 1890) was a description of "the long evolution by which the thoughts and efforts of man have passed through the successive stages of magic, religion, and science." Although his interpretation of his observations was sometimes unsound, the results of his work were far reaching, influencing people outside the anthropological field, including T. S. Eliot.

Frazier, Joe (1944–) US boxer, who was Olympic heavyweight champion (1964), world heavyweight champion (1971–73), and the first man to defeat Muhammad *Ali professionally. He was defeated by George Foreman.

Frederick (I) Barbarossa (c. 1123–90) Holy Roman Emperor (1152–90; crowned 1155), who was engaged in a long struggle with the papacy. He made six expeditions to Italy and was ultimately unsuccessful against the Lombard cities, which regained their independence in 1183. Papal opposition to his ambitions was exacerbated when he set up an antipope to *Alexander III, who excommunicated Frederick in 1160. He finally made peace with the pope in 1177. He failed to subdue his powerful cousin, *Henry the Lion, but he established his authority in Poland, Hungary, Bohemia, and Burgundy. In 1189, he set out on the third *Crusade during which he died.

Frederick I (1657–1713) The first King of Prussia (1701–1713) and, as Frederick III, Elector of Brandenburg (1688–1701). Austria conceded his royal status in return for military aid in the War of the *Spanish Succession (1701–14). He encouraged Prussian industry and agriculture and also fostered the arts and learning; he was a patron of *Leibniz.

Frederick I (King of Sicily). *See* Frederick II (Holy Roman Emperor).

Frederick II (1194–1250) Holy Roman Emperor (1220–50), the last emperor of the *Hohenstaufen dynasty and, as Frederick I, King of Sicily (1198–1250). As leader of the fifth Crusade (1228–29) he captured Jerusalem but remained an opponent of papal policy and was excommunicated three times (1227, 1239, 1245). A man of wide learning, he was a noted patron of the arts and sciences but neglected the government of his possessions, which consequently declined.

Frederick (II) the Great (1712–86) King of Prussia (1740–86), who made Prussia a major European power. He succeeded to the throne after an extraordinarily severe childhood at the hands of his father *Frederick William I. An exponent of enlightened despotism (*see* Enlightenment), he liberalized the Prussian legal code and introduced economic and social reforms that reinvigorated Prussian society and institutions. His conquest of Silesia (1740) gave rise to the War of the *Austrian Succession (1740–48), after which his possession of the region was confirmed. His victory in the *Seven Years' War (1756–63) confirmed the military supremacy of Prussia, both in Germany and in Europe. At his palace of Sans Souci, near Potsdam, a distinguished circle of artists and writers, including *Voltaire, gathered around Frederick, who was himself a writer and composer.

Frederick III (1415–93) The last Holy Roman Emperor to be crowned by the pope in Rome (1452) and, as Frederick IV, German king (1440–93). As Archduke of Austria from 1424, Frederick unified the major Habsburg domains, but failed to win the Bohemian and Hungarian crowns and to resist the Turks. In 1485 *Matthias Corvinus of Hungary conquered Austria, which was recovered in 1490 by Frederick's son *Maximilian I.

Frederick (III) the Wise (1463–1525) Elector of Saxony (1486–1525), whose possession of silvermines made him Germany's richest ruler. A devout Catholic, he nevertheless protected *Luther at the castle of Wartburg after the papal ban of 1521.

Frederick III (Elector of Bradenburg). *See* Frederick I (King of Prussia).

Frederick (V) the Winter King (1596–1632) Elector of the Palatinate (1610–23). Frederick, who was the son-in-law of James I of England, accepted the Bohemian crown in 1619 and led the Protestant revolt against Emperor Ferdinand II (*see* Thirty Years' War). He was defeated at the battle of White Mountain (1620) and died a throneless exile.

Frederick IX (1899–1972) King of Denmark (1947–72), who as regent (1942–47) had encouraged Danish resistance to the Germans in *World War II.

Frederick Henry (1584–1647) Prince of Orange and Count of Nassau. The younger son of *William the Silent, he became stadholder and captain general of the United Provinces in 1625. He successfully waged war against Spanish rule but his autocratic outlook was unpopular. His attempts to make peace were fulfilled at *Westphalia (1648), shortly after his death.

Frederick William (1620–88) Elector of Brandenburg (1640–88), known as the Great Elector. He inherited Germany's weakest electorate. By furthering dynastic claims in Prussia, Pomerania, and the lower Rhineland, he created for his Hohenzollern family the strongest territorial state in N Germany. His fiscal and administrative reforms established the base upon which the great power of *Prussia was created in the 18th century.

Fredericksburg 38 18N 77 29W A city in E Virginia, SW of Alexandria. Here, the Confederates defeated the Union Army in the Battle of *Fredericksburg in 1862. Mary Washington College (1908) is here, as are many historic buildings. Population (1980): 15,322.

Fredericksburg, Battle of (1862) US Civil War battle, a Confederate victory. Union General Ambrose Burnside planned to cross the Rappahannock River in the hope of taking Richmond in the wake of Lee's retreating army. Because of Burnside's hesitancy and delays in constructing pontoon bridges across the river Lee's troops had a chance to regroup and, behind stone walls, constantly repelled Burnside's attacks—14 times in all—leaving behind more than two Union casualties for every Confederate.

Frederick William I (1688–1740) The second King of Prussia (1713–40), who made his country strong and prosperous. He strengthened the army, passed financial reforms, resettled the east, freed the serfs on his own domain (1719), and instituted compulsory primary education (1717);

he also centralized administration and in 1720 acquired most of Swedish Pomerania.

Frederick William II (1744–97) King of Prussia (1786–97), who pursued a policy of territorial aggrandizement. He profited from the second and third partitions of Poland in 1793 and 1795 and from 1792 until 1795 he joined Austria against Revolutionary France. At home his Religious Edict (1788) granted religious toleration, but was limited in effect, and the law code of 1794 included some liberal statutes.

Frederick William III (1770–1840) King of Prussia (1797–1840). His neutral attitude toward Napoleon damaged the prestige of Prussia, which was subjected to France by the Treaty of *Tilsit (1807) following defeat at *Jena and Auerstädt. After Prussia's liberation (1813), Frederick William introduced some reforms but became more repressive in the face of liberal attacks.

Frederick William IV (1795–1861) King of Prussia (1840–61) in a period of social unrest and nationalism. His conservatism triggered off the *Revolution of 1848, which forced him to grant a constitution (1850). This failed to prevent a resumption of reactionary government, which, owing to Frederick William's insanity, was in the hands of his brother, later *William I, from 1858.

Fredericton 45 57N 66 40W A city in E Canada, the capital of New Brunswick. Its industries include the manufacture of wood and plastic products. Tourism, military administration, and distribution are important. The University of New Brunswick was established here in 1785. Population (1976): 45,248.

Freedman's Bureau (1865–74) US government agency established to ensure the welfare of newly freed slaves. Officially the US Bureau of Refugees, Freedmen, and Abandoned Lands, it provided medical aid, food, some jobs, and schools for the former slaves. Its land program for the restoration and redistribution of war-damaged lands in the South failed, as did its programs concerning civil rights.

Freedom of Information Act (1967) US legislation that provided for more public access to government records. It limits the release of information to the public only when that information involves national defense, confidential financial information, or law enforcement and when its release would be harmful to the national interest.

free enterprise. *See* capitalism.

free-form jazz A style of US *jazz developed by Ornett Coleman (1930–), John Coltrane (1926–), and others in the 1960s. Free-form jazz is based on a single theme that is subject to any form of melodic, harmonic, or rhythmic improvisation; it espouses highly complex musical relationships that often result in *atonality.

Free French French forces organized in London by General *de Gaulle in defiance of Marshal Pétain's surrender to Germany in World War II.

freemasonry A secret society for men, which declares itself to be based on brotherly love, faith, and charity. Its origins are uncertain but it probably developed from the medieval stonemasons' guilds. In its modern form freemasonry dates from the establishment (1717) in England of the Grand Lodge, to which over 8000 private lodges are now affiliated. During the 18th century, masonry spread to America and the colonies as well as to continental Europe. Its ceremonies, which are allegorical and illustrated by symbols (many of which are the tools of a working mason), demand a vow of secrecy as well as a belief in God (the great architect of the universe) and are based on Old Testament anecdotes and moralities.

Opposition to masonry orginated with a papal bull (1738) excommunicating masons, since when Roman Catholics have never accepted its principles or its secrecy. In France and some other European countries it assumed a political character and was condemned by governments. Mussolini and Hitler both outlawed masonry and it is banned in E Europe.

free port A port (such as Hong Kong or Singapore) forming a free-trade area, where goods may be landed, handled, processed, and re-exported without incurring *customs duties. Such duties become payable when the goods are moved into adjacent territory. The Hanseatic towns were early examples of free ports.

Freesia A genus of ornamental South African plants (20 species), cultivated commercially, especially as a source of cut flowers. Growing from corms to a height of 30 in (75 cm), they have sword-shaped leaves and funnel-shaped lemon-scented flowers, white, orange, yellow, blue, purple or pink in color, growing in one-sided clusters. Most cultivated varieties are hybrids derived from *F. refracta* (with yellowish flowers) and *F. armstrongii* (rose-purple flowers). Family: *Iridaceae*.

Free Silver A popular campaign of the late 1800s that unlimited silver be coined in the US. Because the coining of silver had been discontinued in

1873 and because the gold supply was dominated by Eastern businessmen, groups made up of less influential persons outside the East and particularly in the West, campaigned for a return to bimetalism. Free silver became a symbol of regeneration of the economy and was an issue of the presidential campaign of 1896 between William McKinley and William Jennings Bryan.

Free Soil Party (1848–54) US political party that advocated barring slavery in territory newly acquired by the Mexican War. Antislavery factions joined together in 1848, after the *Wilmot Proviso had failed to pass in Congress, and chose former President Martin Van Buren as their presidential candidate. Although he failed to win the election his party did manage to elect enough candidates to upset the balance in Congress. By 1854 the party had been absorbed into the Republican Party, which made the Free-Soil antislavery idea part of its platform.

freestyle wrestling. See wrestling.

Freetown 8 20N 13 05W The capital and main port of Sierra Leone, on the Atlantic coast. It was founded in the late 18th century as a refuge for freed slaves and was capital of British West Africa (1808–74), becoming the capital of Sierra Leone in 1961. The University of Sierra Leone was founded here in 1967. It has trade in ginger, diamonds, and gold; industries include fish processing. Population (1974 est): 214,443.

free trade International trade that takes place without tariffs or quotas. World production is maximized by free trade, but the distribution of a particular product may be inequitable and countries may encounter domestic pressures from their own producers to apply *tariffs. Conditions in international trade came closest to free trade in the mid 19th century following the demise of *mercantilism, but since then tariff barriers have been erected again. A group of countries may agree between themselves to lower tariffs and achieve a measure of free trade (see General Agreement on Tariffs and Trade) or they may form a free-trade area (e.g. the *European Economic Community) surrounded by a tariff barrier.

free verse Poetry without regular meter or form and depending on the rhythms and patterns of natural speech. The original French term, *vers libre*, was coined during the 1880s by poets who wished to emphasize rhythm as the essential principle of poetic form. Major exponents of this form include Ezra Pound, D. H. Lawrence, and William Carlos Williams.

free will In philosophy and theology, the ability of man to choose his own destiny, as opposed to the idea that everything that happens to him is inevitable. Philosophers are concerned to discover what the presuppositions and implications of free will are, compared to those of *determinism. They are also concerned to discover to what extent free will and determinism can be compatible. The problem has confronted philosophers since man began to think about abstract matters and is one to which there is no easy solution. In a theistic context, determinism is replaced by *predestination, the view that all events, including human choice, are fixed by the will of God. In the Christian Church, controversy arose in the 5th century between followers of Pelagius, who taught that man is able to choose salvation or damnation, and St *Augustine, who held that man could only be saved by divine grace. The controversy again became a live issue at the Reformation, the Calvinists rejecting free will and claiming that men were consigned from eternity to salvation or damnation, irrespective of merit.

freeze drying A method of drying foods for preservation in which the food is rapidly frozen under very low pressure. Any water present freezes and then sublimes under the low pressure.

freezing The preservation of food by keeping it frozen. The basic principle in all food preservation is to arrest the development of the microorganisms responsible for the decay of the food. Home freezers achieve this by keeping food at a temperature of about –0.4°F (–18°C). On thawing, the deterioration process restarts. Most foods are well preserved by freezing, with little loss in nutritional value, but some with a high water content within the cells of the food, such as strawberries and cucumbers, become soggy after freezing as a result of damage to the cell structure by ice formation. Most vegetables are blanched (boiled for 2–4 minutes) before freezing to arrest the action of enzymes. It is the residual enzymic action that determines the recommended storage time.

Frege, Gottlob (1848–1925) German mathematician and logician, who extended *Boole's work on symbolic logic by using logical symbols not already used in mathematics (symbols for *or, if-then*, etc.). This is now standard practice in logic. Frege published a massive work in which he applied symbolic logic to arithmetic. This, however, was invalidated by a paradox presented by Bertrand *Russell. In Frege's system, some sets, or classes, of things are not members of themselves; for example, the set [all cats] is not itself a cat. Others are; for example, the set [all things that are not animals] is itself not an animal. Russell's paradox is: is the set [all sets that are not members of themselves] a member of itself?

Frei (Montalva), Eduardo (1911–82) Chilean statesman, who defeated Salvador *Allende in 1964 to become the first Christian Democratic president of Chile. His promises of radical reform were not enough to win him re-election and he was defeated by Allende in 1970.

Freiburg. See Fribourg.

Freiburg im Breisgau 48 00N 7 52E A city in SW West Germany, in Baden-Württemberg in the Black Forest. It has a university (1457) and a notable gothic cathedral, built of red sandstone. A major tourist center, its manufactures include precision instruments and pharmaceutical products. Population (1980 est): 173,600.

Fremantle 32 07S 115 44E A major seaport in Western Australia, SW of Perth at the mouth of the Swan River. Kwinana, an important industrial complex with oil and nickel refineries and bulk-grain facilities, is nearby. Population (1976): 29,940.

Frémont, John C(harles) (1813–90) US explorer, cartographer, and political leader. He joined the Topographical Corps of the US Army in 1838. During the 1840s, he explored and mapped large areas of the American Far West. His most important expeditions were along the route of the Oregon Trail in 1842, to the Great Basin west of the Rockies in 1843–44, and through the Sierra Nevada Range in 1846. During this last expedition, which took place at the outbreak of the *Mexican War, Frémont ignored the orders of General Stephen *Kearny and took part in the conquest of California for the US. Frémont was later court-martialed for this action and resigned from the army. After he was granted a pardon by President James *Polk, Frémont began a political career. In 1853–54 he served as US senator from California and in 1856 he waged an unsuccessful campaign for the presidency as the first candidate of the *Republican Party. Frémont returned to the army as a major general during the *Civil War, serving in the Far West and in western Virginia. Later in life he became involved in the construction of western railroads and served as governor of the Territory of Arizona (1873–83).

French, Daniel Chester (1850–1931) US sculptor. As a young man in his native Massachusetts, he sculpted *The Minute Man* (1875) for the town of Concord. It has remained an important symbol of the American spirit. He finished the *Lincoln*, seated in the Lincoln Memorial in Washington, DC, in 1922. Other works include *Europe, Asia, Africa, and America* (1907; in the New York City Custom House) and *Alma Mater* (1915; Columbia University).

French A Romance language spoken by 45 million people in France, and extensively in Canada, Belgium, Switzerland, and elsewhere. It is the official language of 21 countries. Standard French, based upon the Parisian dialect known as Francien, has been France's official administrative language since 1539. It has replaced most northern dialects, known collectively as *langue d'oïl*, and has superseded the Occitan dialects of S France, known as *langue d'oc* (see Provençal). During the 17th century the *Académie Française and the publication of a standard dictionary (1680) quickly stabilized the language. French grammar has been simplified from Latin and the phonology has greatly altered. There are no noun case declensions and the verb is conjugated for three persons. Pronunciation does not, however, distinguish as many grammatical differences as the written form.

French and Indian War (1754–63) The conflict for empire in North America between France on one side and Britain and the American colonists on the other. It constituted the American front of the *Seven Years' War. France and its Indian allies had the initial advantage of superior land forces but British sea blockades eventually defeated the French. The war's climax was reached in the battle for Quebec in which the commanders of each side, *Montcalm and *Wolfe, were mortally wounded. In the concluding Treaty of *Paris (1763) Britain gained Canada and all lands E of the Mississippi.

French art and architecture The styles of art and architecture in France from the early middle ages. Until the *Renaissance, architecture dominated French artistic expression. Many French cathedrals and churches date from the Merovingian or Carolingian periods, which evolved features that anticipated the *romanesque architecture of the 11th and 12th centuries. The *gothic style is celebrated in the cathedrals of Notre-Dame and at Chartres, Rheims, and Amiens. The 13th century also produced some outstanding miniature painting, especially in Paris, a school that reached its height in the 1320s with the work of Jean *Pucelle. The Renaissance in France found expression chiefly in domestic architecture and decoration, notable examples including the chateaux at Amboise and Chambord. The school of *Fontainebleau, founded by Francis I, was profoundly influenced by Italian *mannerism; the 16th century also saw the work of the *Clouet family, who were portraitists, and of the sculptor Jean *Goujon. The great exponents of classicism—*Poussin, *Claude, and *La Tour—dominated French art in the first half of the 17th century, and the influence of *Versailles was felt throughout Europe. The *rococo style of the 18th century was exemplified by the work of *Watteau, *Fragonard, and *Boucher and contrasted the contemporaneous naturalism of *Chardin. The outstanding exponent of late-18th-century *neoclassicism was *David. The latter's followers, *Géricault and *Delacroix, were notable among the Romantics of the 19th century, which also saw the work of *Ingres, *Courbet, and the *Barbizon school. French art in the late 19th century is associated with *impressionism, but the period also witnessed the work of *Gauguin, *Van Gogh, and *Cézanne, an important influence on the development of *modern art (see also cubism). See also Louis XIV; Louis XV; Louis XVI.

French bean An annual herb, *Phaseolus vulgaris*, also called kidney bean, probably native to South America but widely cultivated. It has large heart-shaped leaves and white pealike flowers. Both dwarf and twining varieties are grown for their *beans, usually eaten in the pod. Family: *Leguminosae*. See also haricot bean.

French Canadians French-speaking citizens of Canada descended from immigrants who settled, mainly in Quebec, as farmers during the 17th and 18th centuries. They comprise approximately 30% of the Canadian population, are mainly Roman Catholic, and have a distinct culture. The desire to preserve their identity has promoted a strong separatist movement.

French Community An association of states, comprising France and its former colonies, established by the new Fifth Republic after a constitutional referendum (1958). It succeeded the French Union, which in turn replaced the empire. In addition to France it includes Guadeloupe, Guiana, Martinique, Mayotte, La Réunion, St Pierre and Miquelon, Southern and Antarctic Territories, French Polynesia, New Caledonia, and Wallis and Futuna.

French Equatorial Africa (French name: Afrique Équatoriale Française) A former federation of French territories in W central Africa comprising (1910–59) the present-day independent states of the Central African Republic, Chad, Congo (People's Republic of), and Gabon.

French Guiana A French overseas region on the NE coast of South America. A narrow fertile coastal belt rises to a mountainous interior, which is covered in dense forest rich in valuable timber. *Economy*: timber is the principal export and sugar is the main commercial crop, although the large reserves of minerals, land, timber, and fish have as yet been little developed. *History*: Europeans in search of *Eldorado explored the region from the early 16th century, but it was not settled until the 17th century, when the French, Dutch, Portuguese, and English competed for possession. In 1817 it was finally obtained by the French, who established penal colonies, including the notorious one on Devil's Island, in the territory. The French Guianese have had full French citizenship since 1848 and have been represented in the National Assembly since 1870. Area: about 34,740 sq mi (91,000 sq km). Population (1981 est): 66,400. Capital: Cayenne.

French horn An orchestral brass instrument, which evolved from the hunting horn. It consists of a long narrow coiled tube with a wide bell and a cup-shaped mouthpiece. In its original form the horn could only play its own natural harmonic series of notes; in the 18th century crooks of tubing of different length were inserted to enable it to play in a variety of keys. In the 19th century valves were fitted giving the horn in F a complete range of about three octaves above B below the bass stave. It is a transposing instrument, its music being written a fifth higher than it sounds.

French India A former French overseas territory in India, comprising Chandernagor (an enclave in Bengal) and the coastal settlements of Pondicherry, Karikal, Yanam, and Mahé. It was restored to India (1949–54).

French literature Writings in Old French, the *langue d'oïl*, date from the 10th century AD; major works appeared only in the 12th century. The *chansons de geste* celebrated the military exploits of the French nobility in the Crusades and other wars. From classical and Arthurian romances by Chrétien de Troyes and others developed such allegorical romances as *Le Roman de la rose* (c. 1230) of Guillaume de Lorris. The lyric poetry of courtly love of the southern *troubadours and the northern *trouvères was followed in the 15th century by the more personal poetry of Charles d'Orléans and François Villon.

During the 16th century Pierre de Ronsard and the other members of the *Pléiade rivaled the poets of Renaissance Italy, while the major prose works were the comic masterpieces of Rabelais and the *Essais* of Montaigne. The influence of classicism during the 17th century, the golden age of French literature, is seen in the tragic dramas of Corneille and Racine, the comedies of Molière, and the prose of Descartes and Pascal. During the 18th century the greatest writing was that of Rousseau, Voltaire, and Montesquieu, in the field of social philosophy.

Among the leading figures of the Romantic movement during the early 19th century were Chateaubriand and Victor Hugo. Reacting against Romanticism, such novelists as Stendhal, Balzac, Flaubert, and Zola favored realism and naturalism. Baudelaire, reacting against the Romantic poets de Vigny and de Musset and the Parnassian Gautier, was one of the first Symbolist poets; he was succeeded by Verlaine, Mallarmé, Rimbaud, and, in the 20th century, by Valéry, a contemporary of the surrealist poet Apollinaire.

Major French novelists of the 20th century include Proust, Gide, and Montherlant as well as the existentialists Sartre and Camus. French drama flourished with plays by Anouilh, Jean Cocteau, and the Absurdist writers Ionesco and Beckett. Such novelists as Alain Robbe-Grillet and Nathalie Sarraute pioneered the *nouveau roman*.

French Polynesia (former name: French Settlements in Oceania) A French overseas territory in the S Pacific Ocean consisting of several island groups. The most important of these are the Gambier Islands, the Society Islands, the Tuamotu Archipelago, the Tubuai Islands, and the Marquesas Islands. The islands produce copra and phosphates. Area: about 1500 sq mi (4000 sq km). Population (1980): 155,000. Capital: Papeete.

French Republican calendar The calendar adopted (1793) in France during the French Revolution and retained until 1806, when the Gregorian *calendar was reintroduced. The revolutionaries' purpose was to design a calendar without ecclesiastical associations. The year began on Sept 22 (the date in 1792 when the Republic came into being) and had 365 days divided into 12 months of 30 days each. The remaining 5 days (17–22 Sept) were festivals, an extra one being added in a leap year. Each month was divided into 3 periods of 10 days (a *décade*) and was renamed: Vendémaire (French: vintage; 22 Sept–21 Oct), Brumaire (mist), Frimaire (frost), Nivôse (snow), Pluviôse (rain), Ventôse (wind), Germinal (seedtime), Floréal (blossom), Prairial (meadow), Messidor (harvest), Thermidor (heat), Fructidor (fruits).

French Revolution The overthrow of the French monarchy as a reaction to the corrupt, feudal, and incompetent government of the Bourbon kings. In 1789 Louis XVI was forced to summon the *States General but its Third Estate, opposing aristocratic attempts to dominate proceedings, formed its own National Assembly. Riots followed, the *Bastille was stormed, the king was mobbed at Versailles, and the Assembly (from July the Constituent Assembly) promulgated the Declaration of the *Rights of Man. Feudalism was abolished and in September, 1791, a new constitution was accepted by the king following his thwarted attempt to flee France (the flight to Varennes). However, his continuing uncooperativeness fostered the growing republicanism of what became the Legislative Assembly (October, 1791) and then the National Convention (September, 1792). The Convention proclaimed a republic and in January, 1793, Louis was executed. The moderate *Girondins, discredited by France's war reverses (see Revolutionary and Napoleonic Wars), were now ousted by the *Jacobins and power passed to the Committee of *Public Safety. Under *Robespierre the Committee conducted a *Reign of Terror in which thousands of suspected antirevolutionaries were executed but his extremism brought (1794) his downfall on 9 Thermidor (27 July; see French Republican calendar). The so-called Thermidorean reaction led to the establishment of the *Directory (1795), which struggled for four years with economic crises until Napoleon's coup d'état of 18 Brumaire (1799) brought the Revolution to an end.

French Somalia. See Djibouti, Republic of.

French Southern and Antarctic Territories A French territory (since 1955) comprising *Adélie Land in Antarctica with the islands of Amsterdam and St Paul and the Kerguelen and Crozet archipelagos in the Indian Ocean.

French Sudan. See Mali, Republic of.

French West Africa (French name: Afrique Occidentale Française) The former French territories in West Africa comprising (1895–1958) the present-day independent countries of Benin, Guinea, Ivory Coast, Niger, and Senegal.

Freneau, Philip (1752–1832) US poet. He described his experience as a prisoner during the American Revolution in *The British Prison Ship* (1781). After independence he became a sea captain and later edited the popular *National Gazette* (1791–93). He then went back to sea for a period before retiring to his farm, where he wrote philosophical nature poetry. An impotant early American poet, he wrote "The Wild Honeysuckle," "Eutaw Springs," and "To a Caty-Did."

frequency The number of cycles completed by a vibrating system in unit time, usually one second (symbol: ν or f). The unit of frequency is the *hertz. The angular frequency, ω, is related to the frequency by the equation $\omega = 2\pi\nu$ and is measured in radians per second.

frequency modulation. *See* modulation.

fresco A classical and Renaissance method of wall decoration in which pure pigments dissolved in water were applied to the wet lime-plastered surface of a wall, producing a chemical reaction that made the colors a permanent part of the wall. Up to about 1500 the design was sketched freehand onto the rough plaster surface (the *arricciato*). Separate areas of the sketch were then filled in with fine smooth plaster (the *intonaco*) and detailed color was applied in layers of different pigments. Subsequently the *cartoon, as used by *Michelangelo, *Raphael, *Holbein, and others, allowed for more complicated premeditated design. The composition was drawn on sheets of paper, later applied to the wall, and the design pricked through with a stylus or with charcoal dust forced through the stylus piercings. Fresco painting was revived in the 20th century by the Mexican muralists *Orozco and *Rivera.

Frescobaldi A family of bankers, which dominated the mercantile and political life of Florence until it was divided in the dispute between the *Guelfs and Ghibellines at the end of the 13th century. The Frescobaldi opened a bank in London in the 1270s and financed the wars of Edward I and II. Receiving considerable privileges as reward, they were increasingly unpopular, fleeing the country in 1310 to escape prosecution.

Fresnel, Augustin Jean (1788–1827) French physicist, who (with Thomas *Young) used his work on interference to formulate the wave theory of light. *See also* Fresnel lens.

Fresnel lens A convex optical lens used principally in spotlights. It is thinner and therefore absorbs less light and heat than a normal convex lens with an equally short focal length. This is achieved by making the surface a series of stepped concentric rings, each with the same curvature as the equivalent normal convex surface at that radius. Named for A. *Fresnel.

Fresno 36 45N 119 45W A city in central California, in the San Joaquin River valley. Most of its industries are related to agriculture: grape and wine processing, citrus fruit processing, the manufacturing of containers, and the production of machinery. Population (1980): 218,202.

SIGMUND FREUD *With his grandson Stephan (child of his youngest son Ernst) in Berlin (1922).*

Freud, Sigmund (1856–1939) Austrian psychiatrist and pioneer of psychoanalysis. Freud studied medicine and, in 1882, joined the staff of a psychiatric clinic in Vienna. An interest in hypnosis developed through his collaboration with Josef *Breuer and his meeting, in 1885, with Jean-Martin *Charcot. Following the publication with Breuer of *Studies in Hysteria* (1895), Freud evolved his theory that neuroses were rooted in suppressed sexual desires and sexual experiences of childhood, either real or imagined. In *The Interpretation of Dreams* (1899), he analyzed the content of dreams in terms of unconscious desires and experiences, often dating from childhood. His emphasis on the sexual origin of mental disorders aroused great controversy, particularly his view that the sexual desires of children dated from birth, not puberty. In 1902 Freud established a circle of his colleagues in Vienna, which later (1910) became the International Psycho-Analytical Society. However, many of its members, including Carl *Jung and Alfred *Adler, resigned over disagreements with its founder. Freud left Vienna in 1938, following the Nazi invasion, joining his son in London, where he remained until his death.

Although subsequently modified, Freud's theories shed light on the workings of the unconscious mind and the motives, desires, and conflicts involved in human behavior. His other books include *The Psychopathology of Everyday Life* (1904), *Totem and Taboo* (1913), *Beyond the Pleasure Principle* (1920), and *Moses and Monotheism* (1939). His daughter **Anna Freud** (1895–1982) was a founder of child psychoanalysis. Coming to London with her father in 1938 she established the Hampstead Child Therapy Clinic. Her writings include *Introduction to the Technique of Child Psychoanalysis* (1927) and *Normality and Pathology in Childhood* (1965).

Freyja (or Freya) The Norse goddess of love and fertility, the sister of Frey, the god of sunshine, rain, and fertility. She is the Norse counterpart of Venus and is the leader of the *Valkyries. In some sources she is identified with *Frigga.

friarbird A noisy chattering *honeyeater of the genus *Philemon* (16 species), also called leatherhead. Friarbirds resemble jackdaws but have naked patches on the head and horny outgrowths on the bill.

Fribourg (German name: Freiburg) 46 50N 7 10E A city in W Switzerland. Its many medieval buildings include the Cathedral of St Nicholas (13th–15th centuries) and it has a university (1889). Industries include the production of beer, chocolate, and machinery. Population (1970): 39,695.

Frick, Henry Clay (1849–1919) US industrialist. After forming and running his own coke-oven manufacturing business in Pennsylvania, by the age of 40 he headed Carnegie Brothers and Company (later Carnegie Steel Company). Although often at odds with Andrew Carnegie, Frick ran the company efficiently and was responsible for its expansion and purchase of the Mesabi ore holdings so that the company would no longer be dependent on others for its raw materials.

friction A force exerted at the boundary between two solids or fluids that retards motion between them. In solid friction a distinction is drawn between sliding friction and rolling friction. Sliding friction is further divided into dynamic friction, defined as the minimum force needed to keep a body sliding, and static friction, defined as the minimum force needed to move a stationary body. The latter is slightly greater than the former. In rolling friction the force of resistance is less than in sliding friction as the rolling body moves up the side of a depression made in the stationary body. This accounts for the effectiveness of wheels and ball bearings.

The coefficient of friction is defined as the ratio of the frictional force to the perpendicular reaction between the surfaces. Friction is caused primarily by the two surfaces interlocking at the microscopic level. It is reduced by the use of lubricants, such as grease or graphite (*see* tribology). It is sometimes desirable to increase friction between surfaces, as in brake linings, clutch plates, and shoe soles. For this purpose rough hard-wearing materials are used.

Friedan, Betty (1921–) US feminist; president of the *National Organization for Women (NOW) (1966–70). Her book *The Feminine Mystique* (1963) began the contemporary feminist movement, and by 1966 she had helped to found NOW. Other works include *It Changed My Life* (1976), in which she recounted her life in the feminist movement; and *The Second Stage* (1981), a call for a change of direction in the movement.

Friedland, Battle of (June 14, 1807) A battle in the Napoleonic Wars fought near Friedland, East Prussia (now Pravdinsk, Soviet Union). The French under Napoleon defeated the Russians, under Gen Levin Bennigsen (1745–1826). The victory enabled the French to occupy Königsberg and led to the Treaty of *Tilsit between Napoleon and Alexander I of Russia.

Friedman, Milton (1912–) US economist. A conservative economist, Friedman is known for his theories on monetary supply, which contradict those of *Keynes. His published work, which argues for the free market economy, includes *A Theory of the Consumption Function* (1957) and *Capitalism and Freedom* (1962). He won the 1976 Nobel Prize. He collaborated with his wife Rose on *Free to Choose* (1980), criticizing government involvement in the economy.

Friedrich, Caspar David (1774–1840) German Romantic landscape painter, who studied at the Copenhagen Academy (1794–98). From 1798 he lived in Dresden, where he became friendly with *Goethe and other writers. His first major painting, an altarpiece painted in 1808, initiated a controversy over the use of landscape in religious subjects; successive works, such as *Wreck of the Hope* (1822; Kunsthalle, Hamburg) are notable for their symbolism of despair and man's insignificance in relation to nature.

Friendly Islands. *See* Tonga, Kingdom of.

Friesian cattle A breed of large black-and-white dairy cattle originating from the province of Friesland in the Netherlands. They were exported to North America by early settlers and there developed as Holstein-Friesians. They are very popular high-yielding milk producers and crosses, especially with a Charolais or Hereford bull, are good beef animals.

Friesland A province in the N Netherlands, bordering on the IJsselmeer. Much of the land is below sea level and there are strong dikes and an extensive canal system. Agriculture is important, especially cattle raising and dairy farming; the famous *Friesian breed of cattle came from here. Area: 1468 sq mi (3803 sq km). Population (1981 est): 589,252. Capital: Leeuwarden.

frigate A naval vessel, smaller than a *destroyer, used mainly for carrying guided missiles and displacing about 2400 tons. Earlier sailing frigates included the *Constitution* ("Old Ironsides"), a US vessel that acquired fame in the Revolutionary War.

frigate bird A seabird belonging to the genus *Fregata* and family *Fregatidae* (5 species), occurring in tropical and subtropical oceanic regions, also called man-of-war bird because it often steals food from other birds in midair. 31–45 in (80–115 cm) long, frigate birds have narrow wings spanning up to 7.5 ft (2.3 m), a long hooked bill, and a forked tail. Males are glossy black and develop an inflatable red throat sac in the breeding season; females are brownish black with white underparts. Order: *Pelecaniformes* (gannets, pelicans, etc.).

Frigga (or Frigg) The Norse goddess of married love and the hearth, the wife of *Odin. In some legends she is identified with *Freyja; her name is preserved in *Friday*.

frilled lizard A slender pale-brown arboreal lizard, *Chlamydosaurus kingi*, occurring in dry regions of Australia and feeding chiefly on ants. Up to 40 in (1 m) long, it has a scaly membrane around its neck that forms a large frill, thereby deterring likely enemies. Family: *Agamidae*.

Friml, Rudolph (1879–1972) Czech-born composer and pianist, who settled in the US in 1906. He is remembered for his operettas, such as *Rose Marie* (1916) and *The Vagabond King* (1925). He also wrote a piano concerto and light pieces for the piano.

Frisch, Karl von (1886–1982) Austrian zoologist, best known for his work on animal behavior, especially of bees. He found that bees communicate with each other by means of a circling "dance" or by wagging movements to indicate the location of a source of food from the hive. Von Frisch also worked on the sensory abilities of fish. He shared a Nobel Prize (1973) with *Lorenz and Niko *Tinbergen.

Frisch, Ragnar (1895–1973) Norwegian economist. As professor of economics at Oslo University and editor of *Econometrica*, Frisch was concerned with the application of statistics to economics. He received, with Jan *Tinbergen, the first Nobel Prize for Economics (1969).

Frisches Haff. *See* Vistula Lagoon.

Frisian A West Germanic language formerly spoken along the North Sea coastal region of Holland as far as Schleswig in Germany. It is now principally confined to Friesland province in Holland and certain offshore islands including Heligoland. It is the language most closely related to English. The Frisians were traditionally a seafaring and commercial people. More recently they have become known for dairy and beef farming.

Frisian Islands A chain of islands in the North Sea extending along the coast of, and politically divided between, the Netherlands, West Germany, and SW Denmark. The chain comprises three main groups: the West, North, and East Frisian Islands. The chief occupations are fishing, sheep and cattle raising, and tourism.

fritillary (botany) A bulbous perennial plant of the genus *Fritillaria* (80 species), mostly native to N temperate regions. The leaves are narrow and the bell-shaped flowers droop from slender stalks. The European snake's head (*F. meleagris*), also called leopard lily and toad lily, has reddish-purple chequered flowers. The crown imperial (*F. imperialis*), native to N India, has a cluster of pendant red flowers at the top of a tall (48 in [120 cm]) stem, topped by a tuft of leaves. Both species are popular garden plants. Family: *Liliaceae*.

fritillary (zoology) A *nymphalid butterfly, usually brown or orange marked with black. The caterpillars feed at night—violets are the commonest food plant—but many species hibernate soon after hatching. Chief genera: *Boloria*, *Melitaea*.

Friuli-Venezia Giulia A region in the extreme NE of Italy. It was formed in 1947, incorporating Trieste in 1954, and is semiautonomous. It consists of mountains along the N border with Austria and a coastal plain in the S. The economy is largely based on agriculture, the region's farmers producing cereals and maize in the lowlands, fruit and vines in the foothills, and livestock in the mountains. Manufacturing industries include textiles, food processing, chemicals, and shipbuilding. Area: 3031 sq mi (7850 sq km). Population (1980 est): 1,244,327. Capital: Trieste.

Frobisher, Sir Martin (c. 1535–94) English navigator. He made three attempts (1576, 1577, 1578) to discover the *Northwest Passage, giving his name to a bay on Baffin Island and bringing back "black earth," which was mistakenly thought to contain gold. He later served against the Spanish *Armada and raided Spanish treasure ships.

Froebel, Friedrich Wilhelm August (1782–1852) German pioneer of nursery education. Throughout his life, Froebel was fascinated by the underlying unity of all things. His view of man was one of harmonious growth, and he applied this concept to the development of children in *The Education of Man* (1826). Although influenced by *Pestalozzi, Froebel disagreed with his theory that young children should remain only with their mothers. His view that children should spend time together in creative play led him to found the first kindergarten (1837) at Blankenburg.

frog A tail-less amphibian of the family *Ranidae*, which includes bullfrogs, hairy frogs, and leopard frogs. Many other so-called frogs, such as *tree frogs, are actually toads. The European frog (*Rana temporaria*) grows to 10 cm. Greenish-brown with black markings, it spends most of its life on land, feeding on insects, and only returns to water to breed. Other species, such as the edible frog (*R. esculenta*), may spend most of their lives in water. Order: *Anura*.

frog-bit A Eurasian perennial water plant, *Hydrocharis morsus-ranae*, found in ponds, ditches, etc. It has floating stems arising from submerged roots, rounded leaves, and white flowers, 0.8 in (2 cm) in diameter. Family: *Hydrocharitaceae*.

frogfish A slow-moving carnivorous fish belonging to a family (*Antennariidae*; about 60 species) occurring on the bottom, usually in shallow tropical waters. Frogfish have a robust body, up to 12 in (30 cm) long, with camouflage patterned fleshy flaps and warty skin, limblike pectoral fins, and often a wirelike projection from the snout, which lures prey. Order: *Lophiiformes*.

froghopper A small jumping insect belonging to the family *Cercopidae* (about 2000 species). Froghoppers feed on plant juices, sometimes becoming pests. Eggs are laid on stems or roots and the *nymphs remain stationary until adult. They often protect themselves against predators and desiccation with a cover of white froth ("cuckoo spit"), produced by blowing air mixed with fluid from the anus through a valve in the abdomen. For this reason they are often known as cuckoo-spit insects and spittlebugs. Order: *Hemiptera*.

frogmouth A nocturnal bird belonging to a family (*Podargidae*; 12 species), occurring in forests of SE Asia and Australasia. 10–22 in (25–55 cm) long, frogmouths are well camouflaged with a mottled gray and brown plumage. They have a wide-gaping bill and prey chiefly on beetles, frogs, mice, and small birds. Order: *Caprimulgiformes* (nightjars, etc.).

Froissart, Jean (1337–c. 1400) French chronicler and poet. He traveled widely in Europe and served at the court of Edward III of England. His *Chronicles*, covering the years from 1325 to 1400, are a detailed and colorful record of the Hundred Years' War. He also wrote a verse romance, *Méliador*, and many ballades.

Fromm, Erich (1900–80) US psychologist and philosopher, born in Germany. Fromm left Germany for the US in 1934 and became well known for his controversial analyses of social ills in modern industrial society. In *The Sane Society* (1955), he charged the consumer society with being responsible for isolation, loneliness, and doubt among individuals. His other works include *The Art of Loving* (1956) and *The Revolution of Hope* (1968).

Fronde (French: sling) French uprising between 1648 and 1653 so called because the combatants employed slingshots. The first Fronde, a protest against excessive tax demands and the administration of *Mazarin, was led by the Paris parlement. It was quickly suppressed (1649) by the royal army led by *Condé. In 1650 Condé himself led a second, aristocratic, revolt against Mazarin's authority. Contention among its leaders and an upsurge of support for the monarchy led to its collapse.

front In □meteorology, the interface between two air masses of different thermal characteristics and origins. Where the air masses converge the warm air, being lighter, rises and slopes over the cold air. Distinctive weather phenomena are associated with fronts, particularly the development of depressions, and they are very important in short-term weather forecasting.

Front de Libération nationale (FLN)   An Algerian nationalist group that organized the war of independence against France (1954–62). Formed in 1954, the FLN began a campaign of terrorism and sabotage. In 1956 it organized itself like a government, sending diplomatic missions abroad, and in 1958 set up a provisional government in Tunis under Ferhat *Abbas. In 1962 the French under Gen de Gaulle agreed to Algerian independence and when *Ben Bella became president in 1963 the FLN became Algeria's sole political party.

Frontenac, Louis de Buade, Comte de Palluau et de   (1620–98) French soldier; governor of New France (1672–82, 1689–98), who promoted French expansion in North America. His fur-trading activities, challenged by the Iroquois Indian confederacy, and his policy of expansion, caused dissension that led to his recall. When war broke out with England in 1689 he was reinstated. He attacked New England settlements with the help of Indian allies, defended Quebec, and eventually subdued the Iroquois.

frost   A weather condition that occurs when the temperature falls below 32°F (0°C). It is recognized by the icy deposit that forms but if the air is very dry this will not occur. In weather forecasting grades of severity of frost are distinguished as slight (32 to 26°F [–0.1 to –3.5°C]), moderate (26 to 20°F [–3.6 to –6.4°C]), severe (20 to 11°F [–6.5 to –11.5°C]), and very severe (below 11°F [–11.5°C]). A distinction is made between ground frost, measured at grass level, and air frost, measured at a height of 4 ft (1.4 m).

Frost, Robert Lee   (1874–1963) US poet. In 1885 his family moved to New England, where he spent most of his life and worked as a teacher and farmer. The poetry collections *A Boy's Will* (1913) and *North of Boston* (1914), published during a stay in England, brought him fame. The books

New Hampshire (1923), *Collected Poems* (1930), *A Further Range* (1936), and *A Witness Tree* (1942) were awarded Pulitzer Prizes. His work, often pastoral and lyrical, has a dark undercurrent of fear and suffering relieved only by stoical acceptance.

frostbite   Damage to part of the body, usually a hand or foot, resulting from exposure to extreme cold. The blood vessels to the affected limb constrict so that little blood (and therefore essential oxygen) reaches the skin, nerves, and muscles. This may lead to loss of sensation, ulcers, and eventually gangrene, necessitating amputation. Initial treatment is gently to warm the affected part.

froth flotation   A method of separating mineral ore from waste or one ore from another. The unpurified pulverized ore is agitated with water and a reagent that binds preferentially with the desired ore and alters its surface properties. Air is then passed through the mixture and the ore is carried to the surface by the bubbles to form a froth, which can then be removed.

frottola (Italian: untruth, silly story)   A popular Italian song form of the early 16th century. It was a setting of fashionable verse in four parts, the voice being accompanied by three instrumental parts and the music being repeated for each stanza.

fructose   A simple sugar (monosaccharide) that is sweeter than sucrose and present in green leaves, fruits, and honey. Its phosphate derivatives are important in the carbohydrate metabolism of living organisms.

fruit   The fertilized ovary of a flower, which contains the seed (or seeds) and may incorporate other parts of the flower (e.g. the receptacle in strawberries, the bracts in pineapples). The variation in the structure of fruits reflects the different means they have evolved to ensure dispersal of the seeds, which is essential to prevent overcrowding and enable the plant to spread and colonize new habitats. Fleshy fruits, for example, are usually eaten by animals, the seeds passing out with their feces. Animals can also carry hooked or sticky fruits on their bodies. Seeds dispersed by wind are

FRUITS

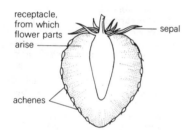

strawberry   *The true fruits, which are formed from the ovary and contain the seeds, are the achenes on the surface of the fleshy receptacle.*

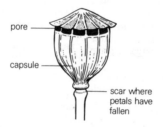

poppy   *The seeds within the capsule are shaken out through the pores.*

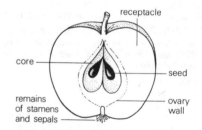

apple   *The flesh of the apple is the receptacle; the core develops from the ovary and contains the seeds.*

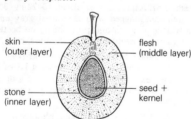

plum   *This fruit, like all drupes (stone fruits), is made up of three layers.*

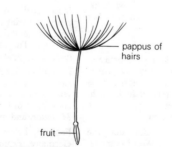

dandelion   *The pappus acts as a parachute.*

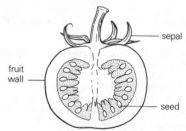

tomato   *The flesh of the tomato (a berry) is formed from the ovary.*

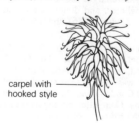

herb bennet   *The hooks cling to the fur of animals, which thus disperse the seeds.*

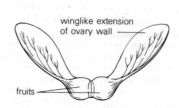

sycamore   *The two winged fruits separate and are carried away by the wind.*

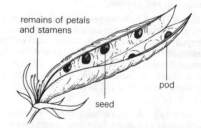

lupin   *When ripe, the pod splits open and curls back, ejecting the seeds.*

usually very light: they are either forcibly ejected from their fruits, for example from the *capsule of poppy and the pods of leguminous plants, or they remain attached to the fruit, which can itself remain airborne for considerable distances, for example the winged fruits of sycamores and ash trees. Some fruits are distributed by water: coconut fruits can be transported several hundred miles by sea. The word fruit is popularly restricted to the fleshy edible fruits, many of which are of economic importance to man: **fruit farming** constitutes an important branch of commercial *horticulture. In terms of world production the most important fruit crops are: apples, pears, and cherries (in cool temperate regions); grapes, peaches, and figs (warm temperate); citrus fruits and dates (subtropical); bananas and pineapples (tropical).

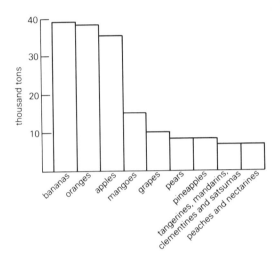

FRUIT   *World production of fruit.*

fruit bat   A vegetarian *bat belonging to the family *Pteropidae* and suborder *Megachiroptera* (150 species). Fruit bats occur in tropical and subtropical regions of the Old World. With a body length of up to 16 in (40 cm), they are typically larger than insect-eating bats and have better vision; only one genus (*Rousettus*, 13 species) uses *echolocation. Most eat fruit although some feed on flowers or nectar. Certain tropical trees are adapted for pollination by fruit bats. *See also* flying fox. □mammal.

fruit fly   A fly belonging to the family *Trypetidae* (1200 species)—the true fruit flies. (Insects of the family *Drosophilidae* are known as small fruit flies: *see* Drosophila.) True fruit flies have spotted or banded wings and the larvae of many species feed on fruit, often causing serious damage. For example, the Mediterranean fruit fly (*Ceratitis capitata*) is a pest of almost all succulent fruits, while the North American apple maggot (*Rhagoletis pomonella*) tunnels into apples.

Frunze   (name until 1925: Pishpek)   42 53N 74 46E   A city in the SW Soviet Union, the capital of Kirghiz SSR on the Chu River. Industries developed rapidly after World War II and include the manufacture of agricultural machinery, textiles, food, and tobacco products. Population (1981 est): 552,000.

Fry, Christopher   (C. Harris; 1907–) British dramatist. The verbal excitement of his earliest verse plays, *A Phoenix Too Frequent* (1946) and *The Lady's Not for Burning* (1948), seemed to presage a revival of poetic drama, but the popularity of his work declined after the early 1950s. His other plays include *Venus Observed* (1950), *The Light Is Dark Enough* (1954), and *Curtmantle* (1962).

Fu'ad I   (1868–1936) King of Egypt (1922–36). He became sultan in 1917 under the British protectorate and king when Britain granted limited independence in 1922. He tried to curb the nationalist Wafd Party and in 1931 suspended the 1923 constitution. Popular pressure forced him to restore it in 1935.

Fuchs, Sir Vivian (Ernest)   (1908–) British explorer. He was director of the Falkland Islands Dependencies Survey Scientific Bureau (1947–50). Later he led the Commonwealth Trans-Antarctic Expedition and with help from Sir Edmund *Hillary he covered and surveyed 2173 mi (3500 km) in 1957–58, during the International Geophysical Year. He was again director of the Falkland Islands Survey (1960–73).

Fuchsia   A genus of shrubs and herbs (100 species) mostly native to tropical America and widely cultivated as ornamentals. The plants range from creeping forms, bushes, and small trees to epiphytes. They have deep-pink, red, or purple drooping flowers all along the branches; each flower has four long flaring colored sepals surrounding the shorter petals, below which the stamens and stigma protrude. Most cultivated forms are varieties of *F. magellanica*, *F. coccinea*, and *F. arborescens* or hybrids between them. Family: *Onagraceae* (willowherb family).

Fucus.   *See* wrack.

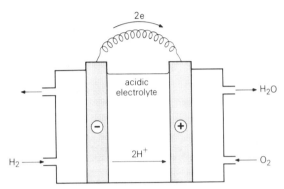

FUEL CELL   *Hydrogen gas (H$_2$) is passed over a negative electrode containing a catalyst, which ionizes the gas into ions (H+) and electrons (e). In an acidic electrolyte the ions migrate to the positive electrode over which oxygen is bubbled. The electrons flow through an external circuit as a current. At the positive electrode water is formed according to the equation* $2H^+ + \frac{1}{2}O_2 + 2e \rightarrow H_2O$.

fuel cell   A device that converts the energy of a chemical reaction directly into an electric current. In the simplest type oxygen and hydrogen are fed through two separate porous nickel plates into an electrolytic solution. The gases combine to form water and thus set up a potential difference between the two plates. Fuel cells are distinguished from *batteries in that the latter need to be recharged and do not consume their chemicals. Fuel cells provide a clean source of power but are rather bulky. Fuel cells are used in space vehicles and experimentally in power stations.

fuel injection   The pumping of fuel in the form of a spray directly into the cylinders of an *internal-combustion engine. This is necessary in the case of continuous-combustion engines, such as rocket motors and *gas turbines. In Diesel engines fuel injection is also used and in some gasoline engines it replaces the normal *carburetor as it gives a more even fuel distribution in the combustion chamber.

fuels.   *See* fossil fuels.

Fugard, Athol   (1932–) South African dramatist, educated at Cape Town University. His plays, which include *Blood Knot* (1969) and *Boesma and Lena* (1969), treat the plight of outcast individuals in an uncaring society with humor and humanity.

Fugger, Hans   (1348–1409) German weaver, who founded a family business that dominated European finance in the 15th and 16th centuries. Through diligence and advantageous marriage the family weaving business expanded under his grandson **Jakob Fugger** (1459–1525) to include mining interests and to handle papal financial business. For a time Fugger financial strength influenced European politics—in 1519 they backed Charles V's election as Holy Roman Emperor—but the family's fortunes subsequently declined and the firm was dissolved after the Thirty Years' War (1618–48).

Fugitives   An influential group of US poets and critics associated with Vanderbilt University in Nashville, Tenn., during the 1920s. They included Allen *Tate, Robert Penn *Warren, John Crowe Ransom (1888–1974), and Cleanth Brooks (1906–). The themes of their writing derived from their concern with the history and traditional culture of the American South. They published the poetry magazine *The Fugitive* (1922–25).

Fugitive Slave Laws   US legislation that protected slave owners and penalized runaway slaves. The two most important were passed in 1793 and 1850. In 1793 Congress sanctioned the rights of slave owners to reclaim their fugitive slaves. Northerners countered with "personal liberty" laws and the Underground Railroad, a system of secretly transporting slaves north to freedom. The 1850 law imposed stronger penalties on those aiding fugitive slaves, precipitating even stronger opposition from the North.

fugue A piece of polyphonic music, generally having three or four parts (*or* voices), in which each part enters in turn with a statement of the main theme (*or* subject). After stating the subject each voice continues with the secondary theme (*or* counter-subject). Fugues are not composed to strict patterns; episodes in different tonalities are often interspersed with subsequent groups of entries of the voices. At the climax the voices are overlapped in close succession (*stretto*).

Fujian (Fu-chien *or* Fukien) A province in SE China, on Taiwan Strait, famous for its beauty. Over a hundred dialects have arisen among its mountain population. Since the 17th century food shortages resulting from insufficient agricultural land have prompted much emigration. It is opposite Taiwan and its military strength has been considerably increased since 1950. Chief products are sugar, rice, tea, timber, and fish. There is some light industry. Area: 47,970 sq mi (123,000 sq km). Population (1972 est): 20,000,000. Capital: Fuzhou.

Fujiwara The most illustrious of Japan's noble families. Fujiwara greatness reached a peak between the 9th and 12th centuries. From 858 the office of regent became a Fujiwara monopoly and government was mainly conducted through the Fujiwara family council. Intermarriage with the imperial family became so common that most emperors were partly of Fujiwara blood. The other base of Fujiwara power was their proprietorship of numerous private estates. From the late 11th century, however, their predominance was challenged by the reinvigorated imperial family and in the 12th century they were forced to yield most of their authority to new provincial warrior leaders.

Fujiwara style A sophisticated and refined sculptural style, also called the Heian style, prevailing in Japan from the 9th to the 12th centuries, when the Fujiwara clan was politically dominant.

Fujiyama (English name: Mount Fuji) 35 23N 138 42E The highest mountain in Japan, it is a dormant volcano in S central Honshu. Long regarded as a symbol of Japan, it has a symmetrical snow-capped (Oct–May) cone and a Shinto shrine. Height: 12,388 ft (3776 m).

Fukien. See Fujian.

Fukuoka 33 39N 130 21E A port in Japan in N Kyushu on Hakata Bay. An ancient commercial center, *Kublai Khan was twice defeated here (1274, 1281). Kyushu University was established in 1910. Industries include textiles and shipbuilding. Population (1976 est): 1,021,623.

Fukushima 37 44N 140 28E A city in Japan, in N Honshu. A major commercial center, its chief industry is silks. Population (1980): 263,000.

Fukuyama 34 29N 133 21E A city in Japan, in SW Honshu. It developed around a 17th-century castle and is now a commercial and industrial center. Population (1976 est): 335,560.

Fulani A Muslim people scattered over a large area of W Africa from Lake Chad to the Atlantic coast. They are a mixed Negroid and, probably, Berber racial type. Their language, known as Fulfulde (*or* Fula), belongs to the Atlantic division of the Niger-Congo family. Their social and cultural patterns are varied, reflecting influences from surrounding peoples. They were originally nomadic herdsmen but many have adopted agriculture and a sedentary way of life. The herdsmen remain egalitarian while the latter are organized more hierarchically. They are generally polygynous and favor cousin marriage, which reflects Islamic influence. In N Nigeria many adopted the *Hausa language and culture and, as a result of religious wars (1804–10), established a Muslim empire in which they were the ruling elite.

Fulbright, J(ames) William (1905–) US political leader. He was president of the University of Arkansas (1939–41) before serving in the US House of Representatives (1943–45) and US Senate (1945–75) as a Democrat. Sponsor of the Fulbright Act (1946), he was responsible for a US government international student exchange program. While chairman of the Senate Committee on Foreign Relations (1959–75), he advocated accommodation with the communists backed by strong deterrents and opposed US involvement in Vietnam.

Fulbright Exchange program An international exchange scholarship program, devised by Senator J. W. Fulbright (1905–) of Arkansas after World War II. The program is ultimately the responsibility of the US Department of State, which, in association with other governments, has made more than 100,000 awards to students and teachers under the scheme.

Fuliang (former name: Ching-te-chen *or* Jingdezhen) 29 17N 117 12E A town in E China, in Jiangxi province on the Chang River. It has been known for its porcelain since the 6th century AD. Population (1953 est): 92,000.

Fuller, Melville Weston (1833–1910) US jurist, lawyer, and Chief Justice of the US Supreme Court (1888–1910). He began to practice law in Chicago in 1856 and, while building up his practice, served in the Illinois state legislature as a Democrat. Appointed chief justice by President Grover Cleveland, he ruled that the US income tax law of 1894 was unconstitutional (*Pollock* v. *Farmers Loan and Trust Co.*, 1895) and that the "separate but equal" segregation laws would be upheld (*Plessy* v. *Ferguson*, 1896). From 1897 to 1899 he arbitrated the Venezuelan-British boundary dispute and from 1900 to 1910 was part of the Hague Court of International Arbitration.

Fuller, Richard Buckminster (1895–1983) US architect and inventor. He briefly attended Harvard and embarked on an unorthodox career in which he sought to maximize energy resources through improved technology. His Dymaxion house (1928) and Dymaxion car (1933) were designed to reduce waste and environmental pollution. In 1948 he experimented with the prototype for the Wichita house, a form of inexpensive, mass-produced housing that could be easily dismantled and rebuilt. His most widely accepted architectural innovation was the *geodesic dome, a lightweight and economical structure built of mutually supporting interlocking rods. In 1958 he supervised the construction of the world's largest geodesic dome in Baton Rouge, La. Among Fuller's published works are *Operating Manual for Spaceship Earth* (1969) and *Earth Inc.* (1973).

fuller's earth A nonplastic *clay rich in montmorillonite, with the property of absorbing and decolorizing oil and grease. It was formerly used for whitening and removing the grease from fleeces (fulling). It is still used in the textile industry and in refining fats and oils. It is believed to have been formed by extremely fine-grained volcanic ash settling in water.

Fullerton 33 52N 117 55W A city in SW California, SE of Los Angeles. Machinery, paper products, and processed foods are made. Population (1980): 102,304.

fulmar A maritime North Atlantic bird, *Fulmarus glacialis*. It is about 18 in (46 cm) long and dark gray above with white underparts. Its range and numbers have increased, as a result of food in the form of offal from trawlers and whalers. Family: *Procellariidae* (petrels).

Fulton, Robert (1765–1815) US engineer and inventor. Trained as a gunsmith and draftsman, he left America in 1786 and lived in Europe for the next twenty years, eventually being recognized as a gifted inventor. Among his most famous inventions in this period were a movable ramp for canal boats, a steam-powered excavator, and an improved process for the construction of cast-iron aqueducts. Fulton also became deeply interested in naval technology, and with the support of the French government he developed (1801) the first submarine, which he called the *Nautilus*. Fulton returned to the US in 1805 and concentrated on the improvement of steam-powered navigation. He designed and constructed the *Clermont*, a side paddlewheeler, which proved its speed and reliability in a trial run from New York City to Albany in 1807. Fulton devoted the rest of his life to the establishment and maintenance of steamboat lines along the Hudson.

fumaric acid. See maleic acid.

fumitory A branching annual herb of the genus *Fumaria* (about 60 species), native to Eurasia and also found in North America. It has much divided compound leaves (feathery in some species) and dense spikes of pink, white, or reddish-purple flattened tubular flowers. The fruit is a nutlet. A common species is *F. officinalis*. Family: *Fumariaceae*.

Funchal 32 40N 15 55W The capital of the Madeira Islands, on the S coast of Madeira. Its mild climate and picturesque setting make it a popular tourist resort and it has a cathedral (1485–1514). The islands' chief commercial center, it exports Madeira wines, embroidery, and wickerwork. Population (1979 est): 265,100.

functionalism (architecture) A doctrine principally associated with the *international style. Its main tenet is that the more fitted to its purpose a building is, the more beautiful it will be. The doctrine was developed under Louis *Sullivan in the 1890s, but found its most vocal advocate in *Le Corbusier, who defined a house as a machine for living in. Functionalism led to a very severe style, lacking in all ornamentation and idiosyncracy. Although still influential, its dominance faded after 1930, and function is no longer accepted as the sole attribute of beauty in architecture.

functionalism (sociology) A perspective, based on an analogy with the workings of a biological organism, which emphasizes the contribution constituent parts of a society (groups and institutions) make it a major influence in sociology of the whole society. Also known as structural-functionalism, the approach was used by *Durkheim and was a major influence in sociology

  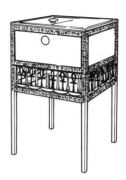

Ancient Egyptian (c. 1330 BC) *Furniture found in the tomb of Tutankhamen is made from imported timber, inlaid with semiprecious stones, ebony, and ivory, and opulently gilded to testify to the wealth and status of its owner.*

 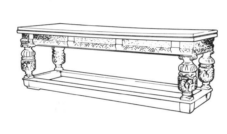 

Elizabethan (16th century AD) *In England and N Europe gothic detail survived on domestic furniture until the 17th century. Solid oak was the most common wood.*

 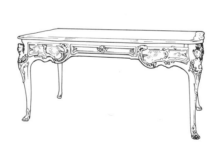 

Louis XV (1723–74) *The reaction in French taste against Louis XIV's monumental baroque led to the graceful curved lines of Louis XV furniture, the epitome of rococo elegance.*

 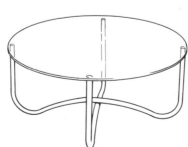 

Modern (20th century) *Although Mies van der Rohe's Barcelona chair (1929) is the product of a skilled craftsman, new materials (plastic, plate glass, etc.) and mass-production have generally predominated in 20th-century furniture making.*

in the US and the UK after World War II as a result of the work of Talcott *Parsons.

fundamental constants Any of several constants that frequently appear in physical equations. The term is often reserved for five constants: the velocity of *light (c), *Planck's constant (h), the charge (e) and mass (m_e) of the *electron, and the fine structure constant (α). The latter is defined as $e^2/2hc\epsilon_0$, where ϵ_0 is the electric constant; its value is approximately $1/137$ and it is a measure of the strength of the *electromagnetic interaction. These constants may be regarded as fundamental in that their values determine the magnitude of many physical effects. Other constants sometimes taken as fundamental include the electric constant, the magnetic constant, Avogadro's number, the Boltzmann constant, and the gravitational constant.

fundamentalism A religious movement among some US Protestants arising after World War I. It insisted on the completely literal truth of the Bible, of the New Testament miracles, and of such traditional teachings as the Virgin Birth and bodily resurrection of Christ. It rejected any scientific knowledge, such as the theory of evolution, which conflicted with a literal reading of the Bible. Interest in fundamentalism increased dramatically in the late 1970s and early 1980s.

Fundy, Bay of An inlet of the Atlantic Ocean in SE Canada, between Nova Scotia and New Brunswick. Long and narrow, it has tides up to 66 ft (20 m) high, from which electricity is generated.

Fünen. See Fyn.

Fünfkirchen. See Pécs.

fungi Unicellular or multicellular organisms belonging to the group *Mycota* (about 50,000 known species), usually regarded as plants and including mushrooms, mildews, molds, yeasts, etc. All fungi lack chlorophyll and therefore (unlike green plants) cannot manufacture their own food by photosynthesis. Some are saprophytes, feeding on dead organic matter by means of digestive enzymes; others are parasites of plants or animals. The body of most fungi consists of a network of branching threadlike structures (hyphae), forming a mycelium. Sexual reproduction results in the formation of spores, which may be produced in a specialized structure called a fruiting body: this is the visible part of mushrooms, puffballs, etc. Other fungi consist of single cells, which can reproduce asexually by simple division into two daughter cells. Fungi are distributed worldwide in terrestrial, freshwater, and marine habitats. Some live in the soil and play a vital role in bringing about *decomposition of dead organic matter. Other fungi (e.g. *Penicillium* and *Streptomyces*) are of great importance as a source of *antibiotics. Many parasitic fungi cause disease in animals and man (see infection) or in plants (e.g. the smuts and rusts), while some saprophytes are destructive to timber (see dry rot). Some fungi form associations with other plants, most notably with algae to form *lichens.

funnel weaver A *spider, also called funnel web spider, belonging to a worldwide family (*Agelenidae*). It builds funnel-shaped webs in grass, among debris, and under rocks and floorboards. The grass spider (*Agelena naevia*), 0.75 in (18–19 mm) long, is a common North American species.

fur The skin of certain mammals including its covering of hair. The hair is usually short and soft next to the skin for insulation with longer guard hairs forming an outer protective layer. The untreated skins (pelts) of such animals as sheep, mink, rabbits, chinchilla, etc., are cleaned and stretched before undergoing tanning to make the skin into *leather. Many wild fur-bearing species are now protected to prevent them from becoming extinct and "furs" made from synthetic fibers have replaced many natural fashion furs.

Furies. See Erinyes.

furlong A unit of length traditionally based on the length of a furrow. It is equal to 220 yards ($\frac{1}{8}$ mile) and is still used in horseracing.

Furneaux Islands 40 0S 148 0E An Australian group of islands, in Bass Strait off the NE coast of Tasmania. The chief islands are Flinders (the largest), Cape Barren, and Clarke. Sheep farming is the principal activity.

furniture Movable domestic artifacts, which are indispensable for civilized life. Examples exist from as early as 3000 BC in Egypt. In Europe medieval furniture was gothic in style and consisted principally of *chests, beds, seats, and tables, but Renaissance designers and craftsmen, working exclusively for the noble and rich, produced work in which function was subordinated to art, such as cabinets, richly ornamented with jewels and precious metals. During the 17th and 18th centuries architects, such as

Robert *Adam, were increasingly concerned with the design of furniture for the interiors of their buildings. Such furniture ranked with paintings and other arts, both socially and economically.

In the 19th century, factory production led to debased design against which a few progressive designers, notably William *Morris, struggled. The 20th century has seen the introduction of simplified design and new materials, such as steel and plastic, reflecting modern functional needs.

Fürstenbund A league of German princes founded in 1785 and led by Frederick the Great of Prussia. Intended as a temporary expedient against Habsburg ambitions in Germany, the league was Prussia's first attempt to unite the other German states under its leadership, finally achieved in 1871.

Fürth 49 28N 11 00E A city in SE West Germany, near Nuremberg in Bavaria on the Regnitz River. The Fürth-Nuremberg railroad line (1835) was the first in Germany. Toys and mirrors are manufactured. Population (1975 est): 101,639.

furze. See gorse.

fuse, electrical A length of wire designed to melt when the electric current passing through it exceeds a specified safe level, thus breaking the circuit. It is used to protect electrical equipment and low-voltage wiring, *circuit breakers being used for higher voltages. Domestic fuses commonly consisted of a length of fuse wire (usually tin or copper alloys) mounted in a glass screw plug.

Fuseli, Henry (Johann Heinrich Füssli; 1741–1825) British painter of Swiss birth. He first worked as a translator of foreign books in London before studying art in Rome (1770–78). On his return his paintings, notably *Nightmare* (1782) and his illustrations of Shakespeare and Milton, showed his taste for horror and drama. He became professor of painting at the Royal Academy in 1799 and Keeper in 1804.

fusel oil A liquid mixture of organic substances including butanol and iso-amyl alcohol. It has an unpleasant smell and taste and is a by-product of the distillation of alcohol produced by fermentation.

Fushun 41 51N 123 53E A city in NE China, in Liaoning province. Its oil, steel, and chemical industries are based on its oil-shale and vast coal deposits. Aluminum production is also important. Population (1957 est): 985,000.

fusion (physics). See nuclear energy.

Fust, Johann (1400–66) German printer, who financed *Gutenberg's development of the printing press. Fust sued Gutenberg for the repayment of his loan and, when Gutenberg was unable to repay it, took possession of his equipment and set up the first successful printing firm.

Futa Jallon. See Fouta Djallon.

Futuna Islands. See Wallis and Futuna.

futurism 1. In Italy, an early 20th-century movement in the arts. It was founded in 1909, when the poet *Marinetti published a literary manifesto demanding the obliteration of past Italian culture and the establishment of a new society, literature, and art glorifying the speed and mechanization of modern life. A second manifesto (1910) was published by artists led by *Boccioni, *Balla, and *Severini. Using a cubist syle and such subjects as cars, trains, moving animals, etc., they aimed to represent multiple phases of motion in one painting. Italian futurism died during World War I but its influence was sustained in subsequent art movements, notably *vorticism. 2. In Russia, a movement that rejected traditional Russian literature. *Mayakovskii and *Khlebnikov were among the writers and artists who signed a manifesto called "A Slap in the Face for Public Taste" (1912) and adopted an experimental and innovatory attitude toward language. The Russian futurists supported the Revolution but were curbed in the 1930s by the Soviet government.

Fuzhou (Fu-chou or Foochow) 26 10N 119 20E A port in SE China, the capital of Fujian province on the Min delta. An ancient capital, it was the center of foreign trade from the 10th to the 19th centuries. It is the site of Fujian Medical University. It has varied industries and its exports include timber and sugar cane. Population (1957 est): 616,000.

Fylingdales The site of an early-warning radar station in NE England, in North Yorkshire, built to give warning of nuclear attack.

Fyn (German name: Fünen) The second largest Danish island, situated between the Little Belt and the Great Belt. Fishing is important and its fertile soil supports cereal growing, dairy farming, and cattle rearing. Area: 1344 sq mi (3481 sq km). Population (1970): 398,255.

G

gabbro A dark-colored coarse-grained basic igneous rock formed by the crystallization at depth of basalt magma. It is the plutonic equivalent of basalt. Calcic plagioclase feldspar (usually labradorite), clinopyroxene (usually augite), and frequently olivine are the main constituents. Gabbro usually occurs in layered complexes or igneous intrusions.

Gaberones. *See* Gaborone.

Gabin, Jean (Jean-Alexis Moncorgé; 1904–76) French film actor. He is best known for his portrayals of brave but vulnerable heroes in films during the 1930s, notably *La Grande Illusion* (1937) and *Le Jour se lève* (1939). His later films include *L'Affaire Dominici* (1973).

Gable, Clark (1901–60) US film actor. He established his popularity as a leading man during the early 1930s, when he played many tough masculine roles. His films include *A Free Soul* (1931), *It Happened One Night* (1934), which earned him an Academy Award, *Gone with the Wind* (1939), and *The Misfits* (1961).

Gabo, Naum (Naum Neemia Pevsner; 1890–1977) Russian sculptor. A pioneer of *constructivism, he and his brother Antoine *Pevsner formulated its main ideals in their *Realist Manifesto* published in Russia in 1920. Working later in Berlin (1923–33), England (1936–45), and the US after 1946, he made numerous constructions of glass, plastic, metals, etc., a favorite device being nylon threads stretched over a plastic framework.

Gabon, Republic of An equatorial country in West Africa, on the Gulf of Guinea. Coastal plains rise to plateaus on either side of the Ogooué basin. The population is mainly Fang. *Economy:* almost three quarters of the land is forested and timber was formerly the most important resource, especially okoumé, a soft wood used for plywood. Now, however, the exploitation of its vast mineral wealth forms the basis of the economy. Oil production is by far the chief revenue producer, giving Gabon the highest per-capita income in sub-Saharan Africa. Production of natural gas is rapidly increasing; other minerals include iron ore, uranium, and manganese, of which Gabon has one of the richest deposits. It is expected, however, that Gabon's oil supply will be depleted by 1990. Mining and forestry are both hindered by transport difficulties but this is now being improved by the construction of the trans-Gabon railroad. Agriculture consists chiefly of subsistence farming. The main exports are oil, timber, manganese, and uranium. *History:* trading posts were set up by the Portuguese in the late 15th century and the area later became a center of the slave trade. Settled by the French in the mid-19th century, it became one of the four territories of French Equatorial Africa in 1910. It gained internal self-government as a member of the French Community in 1958 and became independent in 1960. Gabon instituted a one-party political system in 1967 but in 1980 permitted independent candidates to run in legislative elections. Nonetheless, the ruling party captured all the seats. Student protest movements and opposition from the underground anti-government group known as *morena* characterized Gabon's social and political climate in the 1980s. Anti-French sentiments and pro-*morena* support in some French circles created a strain in relations between the two countries. President: Omar Bongo (Albert Bernard B.; 1935–   ). Official language: French; Bantu languages are widely spoken. Official currency: CFA (Communauté financière africaine) franc of 100 centimes. Area: 103,089 sq mi (267,000 sq km). Population (1983 est): 921,000. Capital and main port: Libreville.

gaboon viper A highly venomous *puff adder, *Bitis gabonica*, occurring in African rain forests. Up to 7 ft (2 m) long, it has a thick body and a broad head with hornlike projections on its snout and is patterned with buff, brown, and purple rectangles and triangles. It feeds on small mammals, gamebirds, lizards, and frogs.

Gabor, Dennis (1900–79) British electrical engineer, born in Hungary. He won the 1971 Nobel Prize for physics for his invention of *holography.

Gaborone (former name: Gaberones) 24 45S 25 55E The capital of Botswana. The seat of government was transferred here from Mafeking in 1965. It contains part of the University of Botswana and Swaziland. Population (1981 est): 59,700.

Gabriel (c. 1776–1800) The leader of the first significant US slave uprising. He planned to attack Richmond, Virginia, with a thousand slaves, seize the arsenal, and establish an independent black state. An informer warned the governor and Gabriel was captured and hanged with other rebels.

Gabrieli, Andrea (c. 1520–86) Italian composer and organist. He became chief organist of St Mark's, Venice, in 1585; he composed madrigals, motets, and instrumental and organ music. His nephew **Giovanni Gabrieli** (c. 1557–1612) became second organist of St Mark's in 1585. He was one of the first composers to incorporate instrumental parts into vocal works and to write antiphonal music for several choirs or orchestras.

Gad, tribe of One of the 12 *tribes of Israel. It claimed descent from Gad, the son of Jacob and his concubine Zilpah. Its territory was in Transjordan, NE of the Dead Sea.

Gaddafi, Moammar al- (or Qaddafi; 1942–   ) Libyan colonel and statesman. In 1969 he led a revolt that overthrew the Libyan monarchy and in 1970 became chairman of the Revolutionary Command Council. His Arab nationalist and Islamic socialist policies have led to a reorganization of Libyan society and an active foreign policy.

Gaddi, Taddeo (c. 1300–?1366) Florentine painter, who was the pupil and assistant of *Giotto. His independent works include the frescoes of the *Life of the Virgin* (Baroncelli Chapel, Sta Croce, Florence). His son **Agnolo Gaddi** (c. 1350–96), also influenced by Giotto, painted frescoes of the *Story of the True Cross* in the choir of Sta Croce and the *Life of the Virgin* (Duomo, Prato).

gad fly A *bot or *warble fly whose parasitic larvae irritate animals, arousing them to bursts of frantic running.

gadolinium (Gd) A *lanthanide element named for the Finnish chemist J. Gadolin (1760–1852). It is used in television-tube phosphors. At no 64; at wt 157.25; mp 1313°C; bp 3233°C.

Gadsden Purchase (1853–54) A treaty between the US and Mexico providing for the transfer of approx. 30,000 sq mi (78,000 sq km) of territory south of the Gila River. Since the Treaty of Guadalupe Hidalgo, which ended the *Mexican War, did not clearly define the boundary between the two countries, President Franklin *Pierce authorized his minister to Mexico, James Gadsden, to negotiate for the purchase of a strip of land that would consolidate American claims in the area. The purchase price eventually agreed upon was $10 million. The territory within the Gadsden Purchase later became part of the states of Arizona and New Mexico.

gadwall A *dabbling duck, *Anas strepera*, that breeds in sheltered inland fresh waters of North America and Eurasia and winters in S Europe, Africa, and the southern United States. It is 19–20 in (48–51 cm) long and has a gray barred plumage, a brown head and rump, and white and reddish wing markings.

Gaea (or Gaia) A Greek goddess personifying the earth. The wife and mother of Uranus (Heaven), by whom she bore the *Titans, the *Cyclops, and the *Gigantes, she incited the revolt of the Titans against him. From the blood of the wounded Uranus were born the *Erinyes.

Gaelic A language of the Goidelic group of *Celtic languages. Irish Gaelic is spoken in Ireland as a first language by approximately 100,000 people and as a second language by around 700,000. It is an official language of the Republic of Ireland. Scottish Gaelic (or Erse), which is spoken in the NW coastal region of Scotland and in the Hebrides, is an offshoot of Irish Gaelic that became a distinct dialect around the 13th century.

Gaeta 41 13N 13 36E A fishing port and resort in S central Italy, in Lazio on the Bay of Gaeta. A popular resort in Roman times, it has several Roman remains. Industries include an oil refinery and glass making. Population (1971): 22,800.

Gafsa (Arabic name: Qafsah) 34 28N 8 43E A city in W central Tunisia, set in an oasis. Its main activities are irrigated fruit growing and the export of phosphates. Population (1975): 236,000.

Gagarin, Yuri Alekseevich (1934–68) Soviet cosmonaut, who on April 12, 1961, became the first person to orbit the earth. He remained in orbit for 89 minutes, reaching a height of about 187 mi (301 km). He died when a plane he was testing crashed.

Gage, Thomas (1721–87) British soldier; commander in chief of British forces in North America (1763–74). His hostility to the grievances of the colonists contributed to the outbreak of the *American Revolution. He helped to draft the *Intolerable Acts in response to the *Boston Tea Party.

He was replaced by William *Howe after military failures at the start of the Revolution.

Gaia. *See* Gaea.

Gaillardia A genus of herbaceous plants (about 20 species), native to North America. Several species are cultivated in gardens, especially the blanket flowers *G. aristata* and *G. grandiflora* (perennials) and *G. pulchella* (an annual). The single or double daisy-like flowers have purple centers and yellow, orange, or white fringed ray florets. Family: *Compositae*.

GAINSBOROUGH The Painter's Daughters with a Cat. *This unfinished picture was painted soon after 1759, when the painter began seeking fashionable clients.*

Gainsborough, Thomas (1727–88) British portrait and landscape painter, born in Sudbury, Suffolk. His London training (1740–46), initially with the French engraver Gravelot, introduced him to *rococo portraiture. In 1759 he moved to Bath, seeking a fashionable clientele. There he studied the art of *Van Dyck, whose elegant style is reflected in Gainsborough's *Countess Howe* (Kenwood House, London) and the *Blue Boy* (San Marino, California). His landscapes were at first influenced by *Ruisdael and *Hobbema and later by *Rubens, particularly in the *Harvest Wagon* (Barber Institute, Birmingham). On his return to London in 1774 he successfully rivaled *Reynolds for commissions and royal favor. In his later years he painted idyllic rustic scenes, the so-called fancy pictures. He was a founder member of the Royal Academy.

Gainesville 29 40N 82 20W A city in N central Florida, SW of Jacksonville. The University of Florida, established in 1853, is here. Important industries are lumber and concrete products and food processing. Population (1980): 81,371.

Gaitskell, Hugh (Todd Naylor) (1906–63) British politician; leader of the Labour Party (1955–63). He was elected to Parliament in 1945 and became chancellor of the exchequer (1950–51). After the defeat of the Labour Party in the 1959 general election, Gaitskell unsuccessfully attempted to change the constitution. After the divisive 1960 party conference, Gaitskell engineered (1961) the reversal of the party's controversial disarmament policy and reunited the party.

galactic cluster. *See* star cluster.

galago. *See* bushbaby.

Galahad In *Arthurian legend, the son of *Lancelot and Elaine. As the most perfect exemplar of knighthood, he was (in many romances) the only knight to succeed in the quest of the *Holy Grail.

galangal A flavoring obtained from the rhizomes of a Chinese perennial herb, *Alpinia officinarum*, that may be used in place of ginger. The plant grows to a height of 20 ft (6 m), with long bladed leathery leaves and pink, yellow, or white fragrant flowers borne in long dense clusters. Family: *Zingiberaceae*.

Galápagos finches. *See* Darwin's finches.

Galápagos giant tortoise A large rare *tortoise, *Testudo elephantopus*, found on the Galápagos Islands, where they were formerly slaughtered for meat. Up to 5 ft (1.5 m) long and weighing up to 331 lb (150 kg), there are numerous subspecies, some now extinct, distinguishable by their different shell shapes. The only other surviving species of giant tortoise is *T. gigantica* of the Seychelles.

Galápagos Islands (Spanish name: Archipiélago de Colón) An archipelago in the Pacific Ocean, W of Ecuador. It consists of 12 main islands and several smaller ones, all of volcanic origin. They became well known following Charles *Darwin's visit in 1835, during which he collected evidence that influenced his theories on natural selection. The islands contain a large number of endemic species, including the giant tortoise; many islands now form nature reserves. Area: 2868 sq mi (7428 sq km). Population (1970 est): 3550.

Galatea 1. In Greek legend, a nymph who loved the shepherd Acis and was loved by Polyphemus. When Acis was killed by his rival she turned him into a river. 2. The name of a statue that came to life in answer to the prayers of *Pygmalion.

Galaţi 45 27N 28 02E A port in E Romania, on the Danube River. Largely rebuilt after World War II, it has a naval base, the country's largest shipyards, and iron, steel, and textile industries. Population (1979 est): 252,884.

Galatians, Epistle of Paul to the A New Testament book written by the Apostle Paul to churches in central Asia Minor in the middle of the 1st century AD. In it he defends his claim to be the apostle to the Gentiles, expounds justification by faith, and warns against those who were encouraging the converts to rely on Jewish ceremonial rites for their acceptance by God.

galaxies Huge assemblies of many millions of stars, gas, and dust, bound together by gravitational interactions. The majority are not independent systems but are members of clusters of galaxies. Almost all the matter in the universe is concentrated in galaxies and clusters of galaxies. **Spiral galaxies** are large flattened systems with spiral arms winding outward from a central nucleus. **Elliptical galaxies** are actually spheroidal, possibly sometimes even spherical, with no clear internal structure. They vary greatly in size and mass, the largest giant ellipticals exceeding 10^{12} solar masses. The third general category, **irregular galaxies**, have no definite shape or structure.

Galaxy (*or* Milky Way system) The spiral *galaxy to which the sun belongs. It contains about a hundred thousand million (10^{11}) stars. Most lie in the flattened galactic disk, comprising two spiral arms that wind out from a bulging central nucleus; the sun is about 33,000 light years from the center. The roughly spherical halo surrounds the nucleus and disk; it is only sparsely populated with stars and globular *star clusters.

Galbraith, John Kenneth (1908–) US economist and diplomat, born in Canada. He became a professor of economics at Harvard University in 1949. As a disciple of the economic philosophy established by John Maynard *Keynes, Galbraith skillfully analyzed the post-World War II US economy in his critically acclaimed works *American Capitalism: The Concept of Countervailing Power* (1952) and *The Affluent Society* (1958). During the administration of President John F. Kennedy, Galbraith served as US ambassador to India (1961–63). Returning to Harvard, Galbraith became increasingly involved in current affairs. Among his later books are *The New Industrial State* (1967), *Economics and the Public Purpose* (1973), and his autobiography, *A Life in Our Times* (1981).

Galen (129–c. 199 AD) Greek physician and scholar, whose ideas dominated medicine until the Renaissance. From his studies of such animals as monkeys and dogs, Galen showed the importance of the spinal cord in muscle activity, the role of the ureter in kidney and bladder function, and that arteries carry blood rather than air. However, he held mistaken views on blood circulation, including the idea that blood seeped through minute pores in the wall of the heart separating the two ventricles. Galen also wrote on philosophy, law, and mathematics and his medical writings were later translated into Arabic and Latin.

galena The principal ore of lead. It is a lead-gray dense but soft metallic mineral, found as cubic crystals of lead sulfide in hydrothermal veins and as replacement deposits in limestones. Galena ore bodies almost always contain silver, and much of the world's silver comes from these ores.

Galerius (Gaius Galerius Valerius Maximianus; c. 250–311 AD) Eastern Roman emperor (305–11) after the abdication of Diocletian. Galerius was probably responsible for continuing the persecution of the Christians begun by Diocletian in 303 but in 311 he proclaimed a limited toleration of Christianity. His authority was challenged by the emperor in the West and the ensuing conflict lasted until 308.

Galicia **1.** A medieval kingdom in NW Spain, now in La Coruña, Pontevedra, Lugo, and Orense. Galicia was colonized by the *Visigoths from the 6th century and became a subkingdom of Castile in the late 11th century. It retained its own flourishing language and culture. **2.** A province in E Europe, which became an independent principality in 1087 until conquered by the Mongols in the 13th century. Subsequently part of Poland (14th century) and Austria (18th century), Galicia was divided between Poland and Austria after World War I and Poland and the Soviet Union after World War II.

Galilee A district of N Israel, bordering on the Jordan River and the Sea of Galilee. It comprised the northernmost region of ancient Palestine and is famous as the scene of Jesus Christ's early ministry. Under the Romans, Galileans were noted for their religious zeal and nationalism and from the fall of Jerusalem (70 AD) to the middle ages Galilee was a center for rabbinic scholarship. From 1892, a number of Zionist settlements were established in Galilee, which was included in its entirety in the state of Israel (1949). *See also* Zealots.

Galilee, Sea of (Sea of Tiberias *or* Lake of Gennesaret; Hebrew name: Yam Kinneret) A lake in NE Israel. It is fed mainly by and drained by the Jordan River; its surface is 686 ft (209 m) below sea level. It was the scene of many episodes in the life of Christ. Area: 64 sq mi (166 sq km).

Galileo Galilei (1564–1642) Italian mathematician, physicist, and astronomer, whose emphasis on mathematical analysis anticipated the experimental method of scientific inquiry. Born in Pisa, legend has it that he demonstrated that the rate of fall of a body is independent of its mass by dropping weights from the Leaning Tower of Pisa. He is also reputed to have worked out that the period of a pendulum is independent of its amplitude by watching a swinging chandelier in Pisa Cathedral. In 1609 Galileo, on learning of the invention of a simple telescope, designed one himself and used it to study the sky. He soon made a number of discoveries, including sunspots and Jupiter's satellites, which convinced him of the superiority of *Copernicus' heliocentric system over the *Ptolemaic system. He wrote a witty and vigorous book, *Dialogue on Two World Systems* (1632), in which he presented these two opposite viewpoints, making Ptolemy's system look foolish. As the Roman Catholic Church had condemned Copernicus' work in 1616, Galileo was forced by the Inquisition to recant his views and placed under house arrest for the rest of his life. In a probably apocryphal story Galileo, following his recantation, is said to have murmured "Eppur si muove" ("Still it moves," referring to the earth, which the Church insisted was stationary at the center of the universe).

gall A swelling or excrescence on plants caused by abnormal proliferation of cells, which can be caused by mechanical injury but is more often the result of attack by insects, mites, fungi, bacteria, or viruses. Some galls are self-limiting, including the oak apples caused by the *gall wasp, while others are tumorous, such as the crown gall induced by the bacterium *Agrobacterium tumefaciens*.

Gall, Franz Joseph (1758–1828) German physician and founder of the practice of *phrenology. He held the view that the shape of the skull reflected the shape of the underlying brain and hence the character of the individual. Although this idea is now discredited, Gall's work did provide a stimulus for research on the brain itself.

Galla A people of Ethiopia numbering about 10 million and making up about 40% of the Ethiopian population. They were originally nomads who spread from the SE region during the 16th century to many other areas, where they largely adopted a sedentary existence and local customs, losing their own distinctiveness. Their language belongs to the *Hamito-Semitic family.

Gallatin, (Abraham Alfonse) Albert (1761–1849) US statesman, born in Switzerland. He settled in Pennsylvania as a young man and was instrumental in helping to settle the Whiskey Rebellion of 1794. He then became a US Congressman (1795–1801), establishing the House Committee on Finance. President Jefferson appointed him secretary of the Treasury (1801–13); during his term he was responsible for reducing the national debt. He went to Europe to negotiate the Treaty of Ghent (1814), which ended the War of 1812, and stayed on as minister to France (1816–23). He also was minister to Britain (1826–27).

gall bladder A saclike organ (2.8–4.0 in [7–10 cm] long), close to the liver, that receives and stores *bile (formerly called gall) formed by the liver. The gall bladder is connected to the liver by the hepatic ducts and to the intestine by the common bile duct. Crystallization of bile components forms *gallstones, which may block the bile duct or cause gall bladder infections (cholecystitis).

Galle (former name: Point de Galle) 6 01N 80 13E A seaport in SW Sri Lanka. The country's chief port under the Portuguese and its capital under the Dutch, it declined with the growth of Colombo. It has a cement factory. Population (1981): 77,183.

Galle, Johann Gottfried (1812–1910) German astronomer, who was the first to observe *Neptune. *Leverrier predicted (1846) the existence of Neptune and asked Galle to search the area in which he expected it to be. Galle discovered it the same day.

galleon A large oceangoing sailing vessel of the 15th–19th centuries, usually having a tall stern and high sides. Galleons were typically square-rigged on the foremast and mainmast and lateen-rigged on one or two after masts. They were widely used by the Spanish in the 16th and 17th centuries as transport between Europe and the New World and were often attacked and captured by pirates. Several sunken galleons, with their treasures still aboard, have been located by divers in the Caribbean Sea.

Gallicanism A movement in France asserting the rights of the French Roman Catholic Church, clergy, and monarchy against papal interference. It was an issue as early as the 13th century but reached its zenith in 1682 with the promulgation by the French bishops, at Louis XIV's instigation, of Four Gallican Articles defending the king's authority in temporal affairs and recognizing the authority of a general council of the Church over that of the pope.

Galli-Curci, Amelita (1882–1963) Italian coloratura soprano. Largely self-taught, she made her debut in Rome in 1909 as Gilda in Verdi's *Rigoletto*. She achieved great success in the same role at her New York debut (1916). She retired, owing to illness, in 1930.

Gallic Wars (58–51 BC) The campaigns in which Julius Caesar annexed Transalpine *Gaul (France). Caesar's intervention in Gallic intertribal warfare was prompted by concern for Italian security; his ambition to conquer Gaul for the Romans developed later. NE Gaul was pacified by 57 BC and the tribes along the Atlantic coast by 56 BC. In 52 Caesar defeated the tribes of central Gaul, led by *Vercingetorix. Caesar's own account of the Gallic Wars has survived.

gallinule A bird belonging to the family *Rallidae* (rails). Gallinules are widely distributed, occurring on semistagnant water, such as ponds, edged by dense vegetation, and commonly have blue, green, or purple plumage for camouflage. They are 12–18 in (30–45 cm) long and have long slender toes enabling them to run over floating vegetation. *See also* moorhen.

Gallipoli (Turkish name: Gelibolu) 40 25N 26 41E A seaport in European Turkey, on the NE coast of the Dardanelles. Taken by Turkey in about 1356, it is strategically important for the defense of Istanbul. The town had to be largely rebuilt after the Gallipoli campaign (*see* World War I). Population (1970): 14,600.

gallium (Ga) A metallic element with a low melting point and high boiling point, discovered in 1875 by Lecoq de Boisbaudran. Gallium is found as a trace element in a number of minerals and is often concentrated in chimney soot. **Gallium arsenide** (GaAs) is a *semiconductor that is widely used in electronic devices, particularly the field-effect *transistor and the Gunn diode (*see* Gunn effect). At no 31; at wt 69.72; mp 86°F (29.78°C); bp 4362°F (2403°C).

Gällivare 67 10N 20 40E A city in N Sweden. The main industry is iron-mining, based on the rich deposits discovered in the 18th century. Population (1970): 25,417.

gall midge A small delicate fly with hairy antennae, also called a gallfly and gall gnat, belonging to the family *Cecidomyiidae*. The majority of species eat plants and lay their eggs in galls. Others are general scavengers or predators and parasites upon other insects. *See also* gall wasp.

gallstones Stones in the *gall bladder formed from *cholesterol, *bile pigments, or most usually a mixture of both. In some people they cause no symptoms; in others they may give rise to pain, indigestion, nausea, and vomiting. The usual treatment is surgical removal of the gall bladder (cholecystectomy).

Gallup, George Horace (1901–84) US public-opinion pollster. The techniques that he devised for gauging public opinion while working in advertising became a standard feature of political life. In 1935 he established the American Institute of Public Opinion and successfully predicted the US presidential election in 1936. Afterwards his polling organization grew rapidly.

gall wasp A small *wasp (0.24–0.31 in [6–8 mm] long), also called gallfly, belonging to the family *Cynipidae*. Gall wasps lay their eggs in plant tissues, particularly oak trees and rose plants, which respond by producing *galls. Thus, *Biorhiza pallida* produces the oak apple gall and *Diplolepis rosae* produces the robin's pincushion gall.

Galois, Évariste (1811–32) French mathematician, who pioneered the branch of modern mathematics known as group theory. His life was dogged by ill luck; three papers that he submitted to the Académie des Sciences were rejected or lost and he was refused admission to the École Polytechnique. He turned to politics, supporting the Republican cause, and was twice arrested. He died following a duel.

Galsworthy, John (1867–1933) British novelist and dramatist. He studied law but embarked on a literary career in 1897 with a volume of short stories, published pseudonymously. *The Man of Property* (1906) began the famous novel series *The Forsyte Saga*, chronicling the decline of a rich English family. His plays, usually rather artificial expositions of moral and social issues, include *The Silver Box* (1906) and *Strife* (1909).

Galton, Sir Francis (1822–1911) British scientist, who studied methods of improving the mental and physical abilities of human populations by selective mating, a science that he called *eugenics. Galton argued that mental as well as physical attributes were inherited, an idea that his cousin Charles *Darwin later endorsed. Galton also made contributions to meteorology and pioneered the use of fingerprinting for personal identification.

Galuppi, Baldassare (1706–85) Venetian opera composer, known as Il Buranello. His comic operas written in collaboration with *Goldoni earned him the appellation "the father of opera buffa." He was also an excellent harpsichordist.

Galvani, Luigi (1737–98) Italian physician, who pioneered research into the electrical properties of living things. He observed how frog muscles twitched when they were touched by metal contacts but he wrongly attributed this to innate "animal electricity" (the current was actually produced by the metal contacts). The *galvanometer was named for him.

galvanized steel Steel coated with zinc to prevent corrosion. The zinc may be deposited by electroplating the steel in molten zinc, spraying with molten zinc, or by coating it with zinc powder and heating it.

galvanometer An instrument for measuring small electric currents. The moving-coil galvanometer consists of a coil of wire suspended in a magnetic field. A current passing through the coil causes it to rotate until balanced by the opposing torsion in the suspending thread. The angle of rotation is used to measure the current. In the moving-magnet instrument the magnet is suspended in the earth's magnetic field and deflection is caused by a current passing through the surrounding coil.

Galveston 29 17N 94 48W A city in Texas, on the Gulf of Mexico. Subject to hurricanes (one of which killed 8000 people in 1900), it has had to undertake large protective schemes. Its port handles sulfur, cotton, and wheat and industries include chemicals and hardware. Population (1980): 61,601.

Galway (Irish name: Gaillimh) 53 16N 9 03W A port in the Republic of Ireland, the county town of Co Galway. It has the University College (founded 1845), part of the National University of Ireland, and a Roman Catholic cathedral (begun 1957). The Galway Theatre produces Irish-language plays. Salmon and eel fishing are important. Population (1979): 167,838.

Galway, James (1939–) Irish flautist of worldwide reputation. He studied in Paris with Jean-Pierre Rampal (1922–). His silver and gold flutes were made to his own specifications. The composer Rodrigo wrote his *Concierto pastorale* (for flute and orchestra; 1978) for him.

Gama, Vasco da (c. 1469–1524) Portuguese navigator. In 1497, under the patronage of *Manuel I, he departed with three ships to continue *Dias' search for the route to India. He rounded the Cape of Good Hope and reached Mozambique and Malindi (now in Kenya). Aided by an Indian pilot he crossed to Calicut (1498). Received with hostility by the Indians, he withdrew. Following the murder of the Portuguese settlers left by Cabral's expedition to Calicut, da Gama was sent out on a punitive expedition (1502) to establish Portugal's influence in the Indian Ocean. He bombarded Calicut and returned to Portugal with considerable amounts of booty. Some 20 years later he went back to India as Portuguese viceroy and died there.

Gambetta, Léon (1838–82) French statesman. A lawyer, Gambetta, who was an opponent of *Napoleon III (1868), was elected to the Legislative Assembly in 1869. Strongly republican, he took advantage of the capture of Napoleon in 1870 in the *Franco-Prussian War to proclaim a provisional government of national defense. His spectacular escape from be-

sieged Paris in a balloon and his courageous organization of the defenses of France from Tours earned him a wide and popular reputation. He was instrumental in founding the *Third Republic but his term as prime minister (1881–82) was unsuccessful because of opposition to his democratic policies and he was forced to resign.

Gambia, Republic of The A country in West Africa, on the Atlantic Ocean, occupying a narrow strip along the Gambia River and surrounded by Senegalese territory. Swamps along the river give way to drier savanna. The majority of the inhabitants are Mandingo. *Economy*: overwhelmingly agricultural, producing groundnuts for export and rice for the home market. Mineral resources are sparse and there is little industry. Attempts to develop the economy include plans for an oil refinery and tourism is being encouraged. *History*: in the 15th century the mouth of the Gambia River was explored by the Portuguese and, in the 16th century, by the English, who established a trading settlement on James Island in 1661. The area was administered from the British colony of Sierra Leone from 1807 until 1843, when it became a crown colony until again coming under Sierra Leone in 1866. Separated again in 1888, it achieved internal self-government in 1963 and independence in 1965 with Sir Dawda Jawara as president, becoming a republic within the British Commonwealth in 1970. An attempted coup in 1981 was subdued with military aid from Senegal; close ties between the two countries were reinforced with the formation of the Senegambia Confederation in 1982. Official language: English. Official currency: dalasi of 100 butut. Area: 4125 sq mi (10,689 sq km). Population (1980 est): 592,000. Capital and main port: Banjul.

Gambia River A river in West Africa. Rising in the Fouta Djallon plateau in Guinea, it flows mainly NW through Senegal and The Gambia to enter the Atlantic Ocean. It is navigable to oceangoing vessels for 200 mi (320 km). Length: 700 mi (1126 km).

Gambier Islands 23 10S 135 00W A group of coral islands in the S Pacific Ocean, in French Polynesia forming an extension of the Tuamotu Archipelago. They have been used for French nuclear tests. Area: 11 sq mi (30 sq km). Population (1971): 1562. Chief settlement: Rikitea.

Gamblers' Anonymous An organization founded in 1957 to bring compulsive gamblers together so that they may help each other to give up their addiction. **Gam-Anon** is an affiliated organization, founded to provide help and comfort for the families of compulsive gamblers.

gamboge (or camboge) A hard brittle gum resin obtained from various SE Asian trees of the genus *Garcinia*. It is orange to brown in color and turns bright yellow when powdered. Artists use gamboge as a pigment and to color varnishes. In medicine and veterinary medicine it is used as a strong purgative.

gamebird A bird that is hunted for sport or for food. Birds that are frequently hunted include pheasants, grouse, partridges, turkeys, guinea fowl, ducks, snipe, and woodcock.

gamelan A type of orchestra common in Indonesia and Thailand, consisting mainly of tuned percussion instruments (particularly gongs and bells). A gamelan was heard at the Great Paris Exhibition of 1889; Debussy was influenced by its sonorities.

gamete A reproductive cell—either male or female—produced in the sex organs of plants or animals and containing half the number of *chromosomes present in a body (somatic) cell. On *fertilization the new individual therefore has a complete set of chromosomes, half from each parent. The female gamete (*see* egg) is large and immotile and contains abundant cytoplasm, while the male gamete (*see* sperm) is motile, with little cytoplasm.

game theory The branch of mathematics that seeks to analyze and solve problems arising in economic, business, or military situations on the assumption that each participant adopts strategies that will maximize gain (payoff) and minimize loss, as in playing a game. Worked out originally by John von *Neumann and Oskar Morganstern, it was successfully used in World War II in an analysis of submarine warfare.

Distinction is made between games for one player (solitaire) in which no conflict arises, games for two players or teams (chess, football) in which conflict is an essential aspect of strategy, and games in which there are more than two participants (poker, roulette) and one persons's gain is not directly reflected by another person's loss. When chance is important, information is incomplete, or participants' goals are obscure, the theory is more complex.

gametophyte. *See* alternation of generations.

Gamliel The name of several important rabbis. **Gamliel the Elder** (Greek name: Gamaliel; early 1st century AD), a grandson of *Hillel, was president of the Jewish council of Jerusalem and a teacher of St *Paul. His grandson

Gamliel II succeeded *Johanan ben Zakkai as head of the school at Jabneh (Yavneh) and is regarded as one of the founders of rabbinic Judaism.

gamma globulin. *See* globulin.

gamma radiation Highly energetic electromagnetic radiation emitted by certain radioactive substances as a result of transitions of nucleons from a higher to a lower energy level and when an elementary particle and its antiparticle annihilate each other. The wavelength of gamma radiation is between 10^{-10} and 10^{-14} meter.

Ganda A Bantu people of the region W and N of Lake Victoria. They are agriculturalists, whose staple crop is bananas. The largest tribe in Uganda, they were formerly ruled by a king (Kabaka) in their own kingdom of *Buganda.

Gander 48 58N 54 34W A town in E Canada, in Newfoundland. A major World War II base, it has one of the world's largest airports, responsible for air-traffic control over the North Atlantic. Population (1976): 9301.

Gandhara An ancient region now in NW Pakistan. It was conquered by the Achaemenians (6th century BC) and by *Alexander the Great (327–325 BC). In the early centuries AD it became a center for a Buddhist art that combined Greco-Roman and oriental characteristics. *See also* Taxila.

Gandhi, Indira (1917–84) Indian stateswoman; prime minister (1966–77; 1980–84). Daughter of Jawaharlal *Nehru, in 1942 she married Feroz Gandhi (d. 1960), who was not a relation of Mahatma Gandhi. She was a cabinet minister under Lal Bahadur *Shastri, whom she succeeded as prime minister. She won substantial victories in the 1971 and 1972 elections. In 1975 she was accused of electoral malpractices and threatened with the loss of her seat. A state of emergency was subsequently declared and strict authoritarian government imposed. She was defeated in the elections of 1977 by Morarji Desai but returned to power in 1980. In the wake of sectarian violence with the Sikh religious sect after she had ordered the army to storm the Golden Temple in Amritsar, Indira Gandhi was assassinated by members of her personal bodyguard who were Sikhs. **Rajiv Gandhi** (1942–), her elder son, succeeded her as prime minister. His efforts to unite the country behind him were successful, and he became prime minister in his own right following elections in December 1984. Her younger son **Sanjay Gandhi** (1946–80) caused controversy over alleged corruption in government office and was later killed in an aircrash.

MOHANDAS (MAHATMA) GANDHI *The architect of non-cooperation in British India leaves a conference in London (1931).*

Gandhi, Mohandas Karamchand (1869–1948) Indian nationalist leader. Mahatma ("Great Soul") Gandhi was born in W India and went to England in 1888 to study law. In 1893 he moved to South Africa and became a champion of the rights of the Indian community, introducing a policy of noncooperation with the civil authorities (*see* satyagraha), which he utilized after his return to India (1914). There he took up the cause of home rule, becoming leader of the *Indian National Congress. His non-cooperation policy was inaugurated in 1919 and was then extended to civil disobedience (e.g. nonpayment of taxes). Following imprisonment (1922–24), Gandhi withdrew from national politics to travel around India.

He campaigned against the degradation of untouchables and encouraged the development of Indian craft industries. Returning to politics in 1927, in 1930 he made his famous walk from Ahmedabad to the sea, where he distilled salt from sea water in protest against the government's salt monopoly, and was again imprisoned. In 1932 he undertook his first "fast unto death," against the government's attitude to untouchables, and in 1933 retired to his ashram at Wardha. Returning to political life in the late 1930s, he became committed to the aim of complete independence for India. In 1942, when the Japanese were threatening India, the British Government offered India complete independence after the war in exchange for cooperation in winning it. Gandhi demanded that the British should withdraw immediately from India. The British responded by jailing Gandhi and the other Congress leaders until 1944, when they were released to discuss independence and partition.

Gandhi, with □Nehru, played a crucial part in the independence talks and although initially opposed to partition he finally accepted the establishment of Pakistan. When violence subsequently broke out in Bengal between Hindus and Muslims, Gandhi undertook a fast in an attempt to halt the conflict. His advocacy of friendship between Hindus and Muslims caused intense resentment among Hindu fanatics, one of whom (Nathuram Godse) assassinated him as he went to a prayer meeting. Gandhi was never a member of the cabinet, but for many years before his death was regarded as the supreme Indian leader.

Gandzha. *See* Kirovabad.

Ganesa One of the principle Hindu deities, portrayed as having an elephant's head on a human body. His father *Shiva beheaded him, but then decided to save him and replaced his human head with that of the first creature he found. A popular god, he is the teacher of the gods and is invoked at the start of any undertaking since he is believed to remove obstacles.

Ganga Two related dynasties in medieval India. The **Western Ganga** ruled over much of Mysore in S India (present-day Karnataka) from the 2nd century until the early 11th century, when they were overthrown by the Cola. The **Eastern Ganga** ruled Kalinga from the 11th to the 15th centuries and were responsible for many glorious monuments, perhaps most notably the Jagannath temple at Puri.

Ganges River (*or* Ganga) The great river of N India. Formed by several headstreams in the Himalayas, one of which emanates from an ice cave, it flows generally E across the broad Ganges plain to join the Brahmaputra River, thereafter continuing as the Padma River, which empties into the Bay of Bengal by way of the largest delta in the world. It is used to irrigate the Ganges plain, which contains several of India's main cities (Delhi, Agra, Varanasi, and Lucknow) and which, after the Yangtze Valley (China), is the world's most populous agricultural area. It is of immense religious importance, being the Hindus' most sacred river. Length: 1557 mi (2507 km).

ganglion (anatomy) A collection of nerve cell bodies, especially one outside the central *nervous system. Sensory ganglia carry out preliminary analysis of the information coming from sense organs. Motor ganglia coordinate the discharges from a number of nerve fibers. *See also* neuron.

ganglion (cyst) A small fluid-filled swelling occurring under the skin and close to a joint, usually the wrist. They are most common in children. Treatment is needed only if the cysts are large or painful, in which case they are surgically removed. A former treatment was to hit them with the family Bible.

Gang of Four. *See* Jiang Qing.

gangrene Death of tissues, most commonly those of a limb. This usually results from narrowing of the blood vessels of the legs by *atherosclerosis or because of diabetes. If the tissues become infected the condition is called wet gangrene. Treatment is aimed at improving the blood flow to the limbs by surgery to the vessels or by rest; in advanced cases amputation may be necessary.

Gangtok 27 20N 88 39E A city in India, the capital of Sikkim. It is an agricultural trading center. Population (1981): 36,768

gannet A seabird belonging to the family *Sulidae*, distributed worldwide. (Tropical members of the family are called *boobies.) The North Atlantic gannet (*Sula bassana*), also called solan goose, reach 35 in (90 cm) in length. It is white with black wingtips and has a long stout bill and a long wedge-shaped tail. Gannets feed on fish and nest in dense colonies on rocky islands and cliffs. Order: *Pelecaniformes* (cormorants, pelicans, etc.).

Gansu (*or* Kansu) A mountainous province in N China, prone in the E to severe earthquakes. Livestock is kept and cereals, cotton, and tobacco are grown in the river valleys. It has oil, coal, hydroelectric power, and a nuclear plant. *History*: it became a part of China in the 3rd century BC, but after the introduction of Islam in the 13th century its Muslim population was continually rebellious and it only came under full Chinese influence in the 19th century. On the route to China from the Middle East, along which traveled Marco Polo, it is strategically important. Area: 137,100 sq mi (355,100 sq km). Population (1976 est): 18,000,000. Capital: Lanzhou.

Ganymede In Greek legend, a Trojan prince of great beauty carried off by Zeus to be his cupbearer in exchange for some immortal horses or a golden vine.

Gao 16 19N 0 09W A city in S central Mali, on the Niger River. It was the center of a powerful Islamic empire (15–16th centuries) and contains the ruined tomb of a Songhai leader. Population (1970): 15,600.

gaon (Hebrew: eminence) A Jewish scholar and communal leader. The geonim were the heads of the Jewish Babylonian academies from the 6th to 11th centuries. Much of their surviving work is in the form of *responsa*, discursive replies to questions concerning the Bible, *Talmud, or *Mishnah. The most celebrated gaon was Sa'adya (892–942), Talmudic scholar, philosopher, poet, grammarian, and the translator of the Bible into Arabic.

Gaoxiong (*or* Kao-hsiung; Japanese name: Takao) 22 36N 120 17E A city in SW Taiwan, the second largest on the island and its leading port. Under Japanese occupation (1895–1945) it became an important naval base. It is a major industrial center, its industries including oil refining, fishing, and food processing. Population (1970 est): 828,191.

gar A freshwater *bony fish, also called garpike, belonging to a family (*Lepisosteidae*; 7 species) found in North and Central America. Gars have a slender body, up to 11 ft (3.5 m) long, covered with enameled scales, and a long alligator-like snout with sharp teeth; they feed mainly on smaller fish. Order: *Semionotiformes*. □fish.

GRETA GARBO *A portrait by Sir Cecil Beaton.*

Garbo, Greta (Greta Gustafson; 1905–) Swedish actress. Her exceptional beauty and aloofness contributed much to her portrayal of tragic heroines in such films as *Grand Hotel* (1932), *Queen Christina* (1934), *Anna Karenina* (1935), and *Camille* (1936). As a comedienne she excelled in *Ninotchka* (1939). She retired in 1941, her private life remaining as enigmatic as it had been during her years of stardom.

García Lorca, Federico (1898–1936) Spanish poet and dramatist. He began writing poems while a student in Granada and Madrid, winning international fame with *Gipsy Ballads* (1928), noted for their boldly original imagery. His visits to the US and Cuba (1929–30) inspired the anguished poems of *Poet in New York* (1940). His masterpiece is the trilogy of folk tragedies *Blood Wedding* (1933), *Yerma* (1934), and *The House of Bernarda Alba* (1936). He was shot by Nationalist partisans at the outset of the Spanish Civil War.

Garda, Lake (Latin name: Lacus Benacus) A lake in central N Italy. Sheltered on the N by the Alps, it has a temperate climate that attracts vacationers and tourists. Area: 143 sq mi (370 sq km).

garden cress. *See* cress.

Garden Grove 33 46N 117 57W A city in SW California, SE of Los Angeles. Industries include ceramics, plastics, aluminum products, and electronic parts. Population (1980): 123,351.

Gardenia A genus of ornamental shrubs and trees (60–100 species) native to tropical and subtropical Africa and Asia. Many are richly scented and used in perfumes and tea. The shiny evergreen leaves are oval and pointed. Single flowers have four or five strap-shaped petals, often creamy white, but many cultivated varieties have showy double flowers. The fruits are large and berry-like. *G. jasminoides* is a popular pot plant. Family: *Rubiaceae* (madder family).

Garden of the Gods An area in Colorado. It consists of remarkable formations of eroded red sandstone rocks, some of which resemble animals, gargoyles, and cathedral spires.

Gardner, John (1933–82) US author. He taught creative writing at the State University of New York at Binghamton. His works, noted for their unusual themes and experimental style, include *Grendel* (1971), *The Sunlight Dialogues* (1972), *Nickel Mountain* (1973), *October Light* (1976), *On Moral Fiction* (1978), *Freddy's Book* (1980), *The Art of Living* (1981), and *Mickelsson's Ghosts* (1982).

Garfield, James A (bram) (1831–81) US statesman; Republican president (1881). A teacher, state legislator, and soldier in the Civil War, he served in the US Congress as a Republican representative from Ohio (1863–80) where he was chairman of the Committee on Appropriations and Republican Chairman. He was elected to the Senate in 1880 but failed to serve because he was nominated to run as president and elected to that position that same year. Four months after his inauguration in 1881, he was shot by a disgruntled voter, Charles J. Guiteau; he lived for 2½ months, thus precipitating the question of succession to the presidency in cases of disablement.

garfish. *See* needlefish.

garganey A small *dabbling duck, *Anas querquedula*, that breeds in shallow fresh waters of N Eurasia and winters along African and Asian coasts. 14–16 in (36–40 cm) long, the male is brown with pale underparts, gray wings, green and white wing bars, and a broad white eye stripe; females are mottled brown.

gargoyle A water spout, in the shape of a grotesque person or animal, that appears chiefly in gothic architecture. Gargoyles project from parapet gutters to carry water draining from the roof clear of the walls.

Garibaldi, Giuseppe (1807–82) Italian soldier, a hero of the movement for Italian unification (*see* Risorgimento). Influenced by Mazzini, he joined an attempted republican revolution in Sardinia-Piedmont (1834) and was forced to flee to South America, where he spent ten years fighting in a series of wars of liberation. He returned to Italy to join the *Revolution of 1848, fighting the Austrians and, after the flight of Pope Pius IX, playing a leading part in the heroic but unsuccessful defense of Rome against the French. Following another period of exile, he gave his support to the unification movement led by Cavour and Victor Emmanuel II of Sardinia-Piedmont. In 1860 he set out from Genoa on the Expedition of a *Thousand, which was·to achieve the conquest of Sicily and Naples and their incorporation in the new kingdom of Italy. He continued to serve Victor Emmanuel in the 1860s and also fought for the French in the Franco-Prussian War (1870–71).

Garland, Judy (Frances Gumm; 1922–69) US singer and film actress. She began her career at the age of five as a singer in vaudeville. Her films included *The Wizard of Oz* (1939), in which she sang "Over the Rainbow" and established herself as a star, *Meet Me in St Louis* (1944), *A Star is Born* (1954), and *Judgment at Nuremberg* (1961). She married five times; although an unhappy private life interfered with her career, she maintained her reputation as an enormously popular singer. Her daughter **Liza Minnelli** (1946–) is also a singer and actress. She is best known for her starring roles in the musical film *Cabaret* (1972) and *Arthur* (1981).

garlic A widely cultivated perennial herb, *Allium sativum*, native to Asia and naturalized in S Europe and North America. Its leafless flower stem grows to a height of 24 in (60 cm). The garlic bulb has a membraneous skin enclosing up to 20 bulblets, called cloves. The bulb has a pungent aroma and taste and is a classic flavoring agent in cooking.

garlic mustard A biennial or perennial Eurasian herb, *Alliaria petiolata* (*A. officinalis*, *Sisymbrium alliaria*), up to 40 in (100 cm) high, also called Jack-by-the-hedge and hedge garlic. The heart-shaped toothed leaves smell of garlic when crushed. Small white four-petaled flowers are borne in a terminal cluster. Family: *Cruciferae*.

Garner, John Nance (1868–1967) US politician and lawyer; vice president (1933–41). After serving in the Texas legislature (1898–1902), he was elected as a Democrat to the US House of Representatives and served 1903–33. He was responsible for the presidential nomination of Franklin D. Roosevelt in 1932 and then was chosen as his running mate. As vice president he expedited New Deal legislation, a program he did not entirely favor. He retired in 1941.

garnet A group of minerals with compositions varying within the series pyralspite (pyrope, $Mg_3Al_2Si_3O_{12}$; almandine, $Fe_3^{2+}Al_2Si_3O_{12}$; and spessartite, $Mn_3Al_2Si_3O_{12}$) or ugrandite (grossular, $Ca_3Al_2Si_3O_{12}$; andradite, $Ca_3(Fe^{3+}, Ti)_2Si_3O_{12}$; and uvarovite, $Ca_3Cr_2Si_3O_{12}$). Garnets occur chiefly in metamorphic rocks. They are used as abrasives, almandine being the most important, and flawless crystals are semiprecious stones. Birthstone for January.

Garonne River A river in SW France. Rising in the central Pyrenees, it flows N through Toulouse and joins the Dordogne River near Bordeaux, entering the Atlantic Ocean by the Gironde estuary. It is linked to the Mediterranean Sea by the Canal du Midi. Length: 360 mi (580 km).

garpike. *See* gar.

Garrick, David (1717–79) English actor. He went to London with Samuel *Johnson in 1737 and began his long theatrical career with a highly acclaimed performance as Richard III in 1741. His natural style of acting contrasted with the prevailing formal conventions. As manager of the Drury Lane Theatre from 1747 to 1776, he introduced innovations in production, lighting, and scenery.

Garrison, William Lloyd (1805–79) US abolitionist and journalist. In the antislavery movement in Boston from the age of 25, he started a newspaper, *The Liberator* (1831–61), and co-founded the American Anti-Slavery Society (1833) serving as its president from 1841. A pacifist, he believed in changing public opinion and exerting moral pressure, unlike those who believed in immediate change, achieved by violence if necessary. When President Abraham Lincoln issued the Emancipation Proclamation (1863) and the 13th Amendment was passed (1865), Garrison turned his attention to women's suffrage, prohibition, and American Indian rights.

Garter, Order of the A British order of knighthood, traditionally founded by Edward III in 1348 and comprising chiefly the sovereign and 25 knights companions. Its motto is *Honi soit qui mal y pense* (The shame be his who thinks badly of it), supposedly the words of Edward III on tying to his leg a garter dropped by a lady at a party. The motto is inscribed on the dark blue garter worn by the knights of the order on the left leg below the knee.

Garvey, Marcus (Mosiah) (1887–1940) US black nationalist leader; born in Jamaica. He promoted black pride and an independent black economy and advocated black separatism and a Back to Africa movement. In 1914, in Jamaica, he established the Universal Negro Improvement Association (UNIA) and by 1916 had started branches in the US. He established a shipping company, Black Star Line, in 1919 and decreed himself the leader of the African Republic, a would-be nation in Africa. By 1923, however, his businesses had gone into bankruptcy and he was on trial for mail fraud. He served 2 years in prison before President Calvin Coolidge commuted his sentence and deported him to Jamaica.

Gary 41 34N 87 20W A city in Indiana, on Lake Michigan. Founded by the US Steel Corporation (1905), it is one of the world's major steel producers. Population (1980): 151,953.

gas constant (R) The constant that occurs in the ideal *gas law: $pV = RT$. Its value is 8.314 joules per kelvin per mole.

Gascony A former duchy of SW France. After Roman rule Gascony was conquered by the Visigoths and then by the Franks. By the end of the 10th century its dukes had achieved autonomy from the French crown but in 1052 it fell to Aquitaine and came under English control in the 12th century. It formed the nucleus of English possessions in France until regained by the French at the end of the Hundred Years' War (1453).

gases Substances that distribute themselves evenly throughout a closed container. The behavior of a gas under variations of temperature, pressure, and volume are fairly accurately described by the *gas laws and the *kinetic theory of gases. When gases are cooled or compressed they become *liquids. However, there is a temperature (the critical temperature) above which a gas cannot be liquefied by pressure alone.

Gaskell, Elizabeth Cleghorn (1810–65) British novelist. In 1832 she settled in Manchester, the industrial setting of her first novel, *Mary Barton* (1848). Her other novels include *Cranford* (1853), and *North and South* (1855). She also wrote the first biography of her friend Charlotte Brontë (1857).

gas laws Relationships between the absolute temperature (T), pressure (p), and volume (V) of a gas. The simplest laws are *Boyle's law ($p \propto 1/V$) and *Charles's law ($V \propto T$), which are combined in the ideal gas equation: $pV = RT$, where R is the *gas constant. However, no real gas obeys this equation exactly. Most later gas laws are modifications of this equation, taking into account the volume occupied by the molecules themselves and the attractive forces between the molecules. The best known of these is *Van der Waals equation.

Gaspé Peninsula A peninsula in SE Quebec province in SE Canada. Bounded on the NW by the St Lawrence River, on the E by the Gulf of St Lawrence, and on the S by Chaleur Bay and New Brunswick province, it is well known for its hunting, fishing, and scenery. The Shickshock Mountains run W to E in N northern Gaspé; the highest point is Mt Jacques Cartier (4,160 ft; 1,268 m) in the NE. First visited by Jacques Cartier in 1534, it was settled by the French Acadians in the 1600s and, during the American Revolution, by refugee British sympathizers from the United States. Farming and fishing in the summer and lumbering in the winter are the chief economic activities. Area: 11,390 sq mi (29,500 sq km).

Gassendi, Pierre (1592–1655) French physicist and philosopher, an ardent believer in the experimental approach to science. He advocated the atomic theory of matter (*see* atomism) and in this influenced the ideas of Robert *Boyle. His astronomical works supported Galileo's ideas. In philosophy he wrote extensively on *Epicureanism and formulated objections to *Descartes' *Meditations*.

Gasser, Herbert Spencer (1888–1963) US physiologist, who shared a Nobel Prize (1944) with Joseph *Erlanger for their work on the function of nerve fibers.

gastric ulcer. *See* peptic ulcer.

gastrin A hormone released by cells of the stomach wall in the presence of food. Gastrin stimulates secretion of gastric juice by the gastric glands.

gastritis Inflammation of the lining of the stomach. Acute gastritis usually results from such irritants as alcohol or aspirin. If the patient stops taking the irritant, the condition usually resolves quickly. Chronic gastritis is common in old people and often symptomless, but it may be associated with pernicious *anemia.

gastroenteritis Infection of the stomach and intestines. Food poisoning is one cause of gastroenteritis, but usually it cannot be related to a meal and no particular bacteria can be incriminated. Gastroenteritis is characterized by diarrhea and vomiting and usually occurs in areas where hygiene is poor. It is particularly dangerous in babies.

gastropod A single-shelled *mollusk belonging to the class *Gastropoda* (about 40,000 species), including *snails and *slugs, *limpets, and *sea hares. Measuring 0.3–8 in (0.1–20 cm) in length, gastropods occupy terrestrial, freshwater, and marine habitats. They move by undulating the muscular foot and have two pairs of retractable sensory head tentacles, one pair bearing simple eyes. They feed by scraping plant or animal matter with a rasping tongue (radula). Most gastropods have internal fertilization: the mating individuals may be of separate sexes or hermaphrodite.

Gastrotricha A phylum of minute wormlike animals (1800 species) found in salt and fresh waters. 0.004–0.06 in (0.1–1.5 mm) long, gastrotrichs have a scaly often spiny cuticle and a ciliated underside; they creep over decaying vegetation, on which they feed. Many are *hermaphrodites and one group exhibits *parthenogenesis, i.e. unfertilized eggs give rise exclusively to females.

gastrula A stage in the embryonic development of an animal in which the cells of the *blastula (the preceding stage) undergo complex movements, resulting in the formation of three distinct germ layers. These layers—the ectoderm, mesoderm, and endoderm—will later differentiate into the tissues and organs of the body. A central cavity (archenteron) is the primitive gut.

gas turbine A form of *internal-combustion engine consisting of a *turbine in which the power to drive the blades is provided by hot gas. The gas turbine is a flexible engine with many applications, the most useful being in aviation (*see* jet engine). It consists of a *compressor, a combustion chamber, and the turbine. Atmospheric air is fed under pressure from the compressor to the combustion chambers, where a fuel, such as natural gas, paraffin, or oil is burned; the hot gases then drive the turbine, which in turn drives the compressor. Power is supplied either in the form of thrust from a jet or rotation of the turbine shaft. ▯heat engine.

Gates, Horatio (?1728–1806) American general. British-born, he saw action in America in the French and Indian War and returned to settle there in 1772. During the American Revolution, his army defeated the British under *Burgoyne at *Saratoga (1777). Defeated by Cornwallis at *Camden (1780), he retired until 1782, when he joined Washington's staff.

Gateshead 54 58N 1 35W A city in NE England, opposite Newcastle across the Tyne River. Gateshead's industries include engineering, clothing, paints, plastics, and glass. Population (1981): 81,367.

GATT. *See* General Agreement on Tariffs and Trade.

Gatun, Lake (Spanish name: Lago Gatún) An artificial lake in the Panama Canal Zone. It was created in 1912 to maintain the water level in the Gaillard Cut. Area: 166 sq mi (430 sq km).

Gatwick 51 08N 0 11W A village in SE England, 27 mi (43 km) S of London. It is the site of one of London's two subsidiary airports. A special railroad service connects the airport to central London.

gaucho A nomadic cattleherder of the Argentine, Uruguayan, and Paraguayan pampas in the 18th and 19th centuries. Often a mestizo (of mixed European and Indian ancestry), gauchos were at first independent herders but, like the US *cowboys, became employees of ranchers. They disappeared following the plowing of the pampas and the introduction of purebreed stock raising. Gauchos were the source of a rich folk tradition.

Gaudí y Cornet, Antonio (1852–1926) Spanish architect with a highly individual approach. Gaudí's work had strong affiliations to *Art Nouveau, but also drew inspiration from gothic and *Mudéjar sources. He also made use of the style of the *gothic revival in the incomplete Sagrada Familia in Barcelona (1880s). He worked exclusively in Barcelona, beginning with the Casa Vicens (1878) and a house for his patron, Count Güell. In the 1890s his style changed radically, and certain later buildings, for example the Casa Battló (1905), tended to resemble natural growths more than architecture.

PAUL GAUGUIN Self-portrait *(1889). Another of the artist's paintings,* The Yellow Christ *(1889), can be seen in the background.*

Gauguin, Paul (1848–1903) French postimpressionist painter, born in Paris. After five years at sea he became a stockbroker (1871), painting only as a hobby. His early works were influenced by the impressionists with whom he exhibited (1881–86). He became a full-time painter in 1883 and moved to Brittany in 1886, where he developed a style called *synthetism in such paintings as *Vision after the Sermon.* He visited Martinique in 1887 and stayed with Van *Gogh in Arles in 1888. Seeking the inspiration of a primitive civilization, he moved to Tahiti (1891), where the symbolism in such paintings as *Nevermore* was influenced by native superstitions. He is noted also for reviving the art of woodcutting.

Gauhati 26 10N 91 45E A city in India, in Assam. The former center of British administration in Assam, Gauhati is an important trading center and has an oil refinery. Its many temple ruins make it a Hindu pilgrimage center. Its university was established in 1948. Population (1971): 123,783.

Gaul An ancient region of Europe. It was divided by the Romans into Transalpine Gaul (the area bound by the Rhine, Alps, and Pyrenees) and Cisalpine Gaul (N Italy). Transalpine Gaul was settled from about 1500 BC by Celtic tribes, who inhabited Cisalpine Gaul after around 500 BC. Subsequent Gallic expansion southward brought conflict with Rome, which the Gauls sacked in 390, and the Roman conquest of Cisalpine Gaul was not completed until the mid-2nd century. In 121 the Romans annexed S Transalpine Gaul, which they called Gallia Narbonensis, and between 58 and 50 Caesar subdued the rest of Gaul, finally crushing the Gallic tribal

leader *Vercingetorix at Alesia. Augustus organized Transalpine Gaul into four provinces—Narbonensis, Belgica, Lugdunensis, and Aquitania. During the 1st century AD Gaul, especially Narbonensis, was extensively romanized and prospered until the barbarian invasions in the 5th century.

Gaullists The supporters of the policies of Gen *de Gaulle, especially his independent foreign policy and drive toward industrial expansion, which were motivated by a wish to re-establish France as a world power. De Gaulle's Rassemblement du Peuple français (1947–53) was succeeded by the Union de Démocrates pour la République, which was reorganized by Jacques *Chirac as the Rassemblement pour la République.

gaur The largest of the wild cattle, *Bos gaurus,* of hilly forests in S Asia. Up to 6 ft (2 m) high at the shoulder, bulls can weigh up to 1 ton. Gaurs are dark brown with white socks and both sexes have horns, the tips pointing upward in bulls and inward in cows.

gauss (G) The unit of magnetic flux density in the *c.g.s. system equal to a flux density of one maxwell per square centimeter. Named for Karl Friedrich *Gauss.

Gauss, Karl Friedrich (1777–1855) German mathematician, regarded (with *Newton and *Archimedes) as one of the greatest mathematicians of all time. He influenced all aspects of mathematics and much of physics. His greatest contributions were in the fields of probability theory, number theory, complex numbers, algebra, and electricity and magnetism.

Gautier, Théophile (1811–72) French Romantic poet and critic. Influenced by Victor *Hugo, his early writings include *Poésies* (1830) and *Les Jeunes-France* (1833). The brief lyrical poems in *Émaux et camées* (1852) embody his belief in the value of art for its own sake. He wrote much influential art, ballet, and dramatic criticism and traveled widely in Europe, the Middle East, and Russia.

gavial (*or* gharial) A long-snouted □reptile, *Gavialis gangeticus,* occurring in N Indian rivers and sacred to Hindus. 13–16 ft (4–5 m) long, it has long slender sharp-toothed jaws, which it sweeps from side to side to catch fish. It is the only member of its family (*Gavialidae*). Order: *Crocodilia* (*see* crocodile).

Gävle 60 41N 17 10E A seaport in E Sweden, on an inlet of the Gulf of Bothnia. Ice free for nine months of the year, it exports timber, wood pulp, and paper. Its industries include shipbuilding. Population (1978 est): 87,378.

Gawain In Arthurian legend, a knight of the Round Table, the nephew of King Arthur and the son of King Lot of Norway and the Orkneys. He was known for his purity and courage.

Gay, John (1685–1732) British poet and dramatist. A friend of Pope and Swift, his *Fables* (1727, 1738) were the most successful of his several satirical poems. His best-known work is the ballad opera *The Beggar's Opera* (1728), a comic blend of social satire and parody of fashionable Italian opera, using traditional tunes.

Gaya 24 48N 85 00E A city in NE India, in Bihar. A center of Hindu pilgrimage, it is situated 6 mi (10 km) S of Buddh Gaya, which is sacred to Buddhists. Population (1971): 179,884.

gayal A species of domestic cattle, *Bos frontalis,* of Burma. Gayals are similar to the wild *gaur, but are smaller, measuring about 60 in (150 cm) at the shoulder, and have a wider spread of horns. Gayals may be a domesticated form of gaur.

Gay Liberation. *See* homosexuality.

Gay-Lussac, Joseph Louis (1778–1850) French chemist and physicist. He discovered the element boron (1808) and the law that gases combine in a simple ratio by volume (**Gay-Lussac's law**). He also discovered *Charles' law independently of Charles and published his results first.

Gaza (Arabic name: Ghazzah) 31 30N 34 28E The largest town in the *Gaza Strip. Gaza has been inhabited continuously for over 3000 years; in biblical times it was a Philistine center, where Samson was killed (Judges 16). Its products now include pottery and textiles. Population (1971 est): 118,300.

Gazankulu. *See* Bantu Homelands.

Gaza Strip A strip of coastal territory, 30 mi (50 km) long, on the SE corner of the Mediterranean Sea. Following the Arab-Israeli War of 1948–49, the only part of Palestine held by Egypt was a strip of land on the coast that became known as the Gaza Strip. Egypt did not integrate the Strip into its own state, but established a military governorship here. Held by the Israelis for a short time in 1956–57, it was taken by them again in 1967, and is now under Israeli military administration. Under the Camp David agreement (1979) between Israel and Egypt, eventual self-government for the area was planned. The Gaza Strip suffers from extreme overpopulation, many Palestine refugees being housed in squalid camps. Agriculture is the chief pursuit, especially the growing of citrus fruit. Population (1967): 390,000, including North Sinai.

gazelle A slender antelope of the genus *Gazella* (about 12 species), of Africa and Asia. 20–35 in (50–90 cm) high at the shoulder, gazelles are distinguished from other antelopes by light and dark horizontal stripes on the face. Brown to gray in color, gazelles may also have a dark band along the sides above the lighter belly. In most species both sexes have horns, which are generally lyre-shaped, ridged, and backward-curving with a forward-pointing tip.

Gaziantep 37 04N 37 21E A city in S Turkey, near the Syrian border. Known for its Hittite remains, Gaziantep is situated near ancient trade routes and has changed hands frequently. It is an important market town. Population (1980): 808,697.

Gdańsk (German name: Danzig) 54 22N 18 41E A port in N Poland, on the Baltic Sea. It is an industrial center with shipbuilding, metallurgy, chemicals, and food processing; exports include coal, grain, and timber. Its university was founded in 1970. *History*: it developed as an important trade center during the Renaissance. It was under Prussian control (1793–1807 and 1814–1919), becoming a free city under the League of Nations in 1919. In 1939 it was annexed by Germany, an act that precipitated World War II; the city was returned to Poland in 1945. Population (1979 est): 448,00.

Gdynia 54 31N 18 30E A port in N Poland, on the Baltic Sea. Originally a fishing village, it was developed (1924–39) to replace Danzig (*see* Gdańsk) as Poland's port, becoming Poland's main shipbuilding center and naval base. Population (1979 est): 231,000.

Ge A group of South American Indian peoples of Brazil and N Paraguay who speak languages of the Macro-Ge group. Its numerous different tribes are very diverse in their range of cultural patterns. They are largely hunters and gatherers but some have adopted cultivation. Their social organization tends to be complex. Besides clan divisions, there is a variety of associations based on age, sex, occupation, etc., each autonomous in its respective sphere.

gean. *See* cherry.

Geber (14th century) Spanish alchemist, whose suggestion that different metals consist of mercury and sulfur in different proportions laid the foundation for the belief in the *philosopher's stone. He was also an experimental chemist, preparing nitric and acetic acids and white lead. He assumed the name Geber, which is the Latin form of Jabir, in honor of the 8th-century Arab alchemist Jabir ibn Hayyan.

gecko A slender long-tailed nocturnal lizard belonging to the widely distributed family *Gekkonidae* (650 species), found in a wide range of habitats including deserts and rain forests. 1.2–14 in (3–35 cm) long, many geckos have fleshy toe pads covered with microscopic hooks enabling them to cling to smooth surfaces, such as ceilings. They feed on insects and have well-developed vocal cords producing a variety of chirps and barks. The tokay (*Gekko gecko*) of E Asia is a large arboreal gecko and lays its eggs in crevices. (□reptile).

Gediminas (c. 1275–1341) Grand Duke of Lithuania (1316–41). One of Lithuania's greatest rulers, he founded the state by unifying the Lithuanian tribes. He extended his dominions, which he defended against the *Teutonic Knights. He was converted to Christianity in 1323. Gediminas made Vilnius the capital of Lithuania.

Geelong 38 10S 144 26E A city and major port in Australia, in S Victoria on Corio Bay. Wool, wheat, and oil are the principal exports. Population (1976): 22,080.

gegenschein (German: counterglow) A very faint glow in the night sky that can sometimes be seen on the *ecliptic in a direction directly opposite the sun's position. It is part of the *zodiacal light.

Gehenna In the Bible, the Valley of Hinnom, outside Jerusalem. At one time it was apparently the site of human sacrifices and was therefore considered an unclean place. In Jewish thought it came to represent a place where sinners are punished and in the New Testament it is a name for hell.

Gehrig, Lou (1903–41) US baseball player. He joined the New York Yankees in 1923 and played for them until illness forced his retirement in 1939. During his career as a first baseman he played in a record 2,130 consecutive games, had a lifetime batting average of .340, hit 493 home runs, held many individual records, and was nicknamed the "Iron Horse." He was voted a member of the Baseball Hall of Fame in 1939.

Geiger, Hans (1882–1945) German physicist, who in 1913 invented the *Geiger counter for detecting ionizing radiation in connection with his work on cosmic rays. During World War II he participated in Germany's unsuccessful attempt to build an atomic bomb.

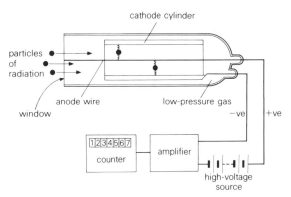

GEIGER COUNTER *The radiation entering the tube causes an electrical discharge through the gas between the anode and cathode, sending an electrical pulse to the counter.*

Geiger counter A device that detects and counts ionizing radiation and particles. Essentially it consists of a metal cylinder containing low-pressure gas and a wire anode running along its central axis. The anode is held at a potential difference just less than that required to produce a discharge in the gas. Ionizing particles passing into the tube through a window at one end induce discharges, which can be counted by a suitable circuit. Named for— Hans *Geiger.

Geisel, Ernesto (1907–79) Brazilian general and president (1974–). After holding a number of military and administrative offices, including the presidency of the state oil company, Geisel was elected president as the nominated candidate of the outgoing president, Emílio Medici.

geisha A Japanese woman whose profession is to entertain men in a restaurant. Geishas, who are not prostitutes, sing and dance or engage their clients in conversation. In modern Japan geishas are employed primarily for the benefit of the tourist trade.

gel. *See* colloid.

Gela 37 04N 14 15E A city in Italy, in Sicily. Founded by Greek colonists in 689 BC, it flourished under the rule of Hippocrates in the 5th century BC. Abandoned in 281 BC, it was refounded in 1233. Its industries include fishing and petrochemicals. Population (1971): 65,736.

gelada A large *Old World monkey, *Theropithecus gelada*, of Ethiopian mountains. 47–59 in (120–150 cm) long including the tufted tail (28–31 in [70–80 cm]), it has a cape of dark-brown hair with two bare patches on the chest and lives in large groups, feeding on roots, leaves, and fruit.

gelatin A protein derived from bones and skins. In solution it forms a reversible gel that becomes fluid as the temperature rises and solidifies on cooling. Because of this property it is widely used in the food industry as a stabilizer in jellies and confectionery, in drug preparations, and in photographic emulsions.

Gelderland A province in the E Netherlands, bordering on West Germany. Predominantly rolling upland, the fertile soils of the Rhine Valley produce vegetables, fruit, and dairy products while the poorer soils in the N produce fodder crops. The NW is also an important tourist area. Manufactured products include cotton and paper. Area: 1981 sq mi (5131 sq km). Population (1981 est): 1,708,860. Capital: Arnhem.

Gell-Mann, Murray (1929–) US physicist, who won the 1969 Nobel Prize for his theoretical work on elementary particles. In 1953 he introduced the concept of *strangeness to account for the absence of certain expected interactions. He also formulated the theory of *unitary symmetry and introduced the concept of quarks (*see also* particle physics).

Gelsenkirchen 51 30N 7 05E A city in NW West Germany, in North Rhine-Westphalia. A *Ruhr coalmining center and port on the Rhine-Herne Canal, it has a moated palace (16th-18th centuries). Its manufactures include steel, chemicals, and glass. Population (1980 est): 305,600.

Gemini (Latin: Twins) A conspicuous constellation in the N sky near Orion, lying on the *zodiac between Cancer and Taurus. The brightest stars are *Pollux and the somewhat fainter *Castor.

Gemistus Pletho. *See* Pletho, Georgius Gemistus.

gemsbok. *See* oryx.

gemstones Minerals or mineral fragments used for decorative purposes, particularly jewelry. Desirability is usually based on the gem's beauty (in terms of color, transparency, and luster), its durability (gemstones must be hard), and rarity. Diamond, ruby, sapphire, and emerald are precious stones, the others (amethyst, agate, jasper, onyx, aquamarine, topaz, garnet, etc.) are semiprecious. Not all are crystalline; for example, opal and jade are amorphous. Gemstones are usually artificially cut (either faceted or rounded) and polished; some, such as onyx, are suitable for engraving, as cameos for instance. Many can be synthetically produced.

gene A unit of the hereditary material of an organism that provides the genetic information necessary to fulfil a single function. The term was first coined by W. L. *Johannsen in 1909.

Genes were initially conceived as a string of beads comprising the *chromosome; they were later defined as lengths of the chromosome that were physically indivisible during the exchange of chromosomal material that occurs during *meiosis. Alternatively, a gene was defined as the shortest length of the chromosome that could undergo *mutation. However, with the discovery of the structure of *DNA and the molecular basis of heredity, a gene is now regarded as being a functional unit (cistron) corresponding to a specific sequence of the *genetic code. Structural genes code for individual polypeptides (see peptides), while regulator genes control the activity of the structural genes.

General Agreement on Tariffs and Trade (GATT) A set of trade agreements, in operation from January, 1948, establishing procedures and tariffs for international trading. Signatories agree to favorable tariffs between members and the reduction of trade restrictions, on condition that home producers do not suffer losses as a result. During the negotiations of 1964–67 the principle of a single tariff for all industrial manufactures was agreed upon, with a resulting reduction in trade costs. There are more than 80 countries, which are responsible for 80% of world trade. The secretariat of GATT, which is a specialized agency of the *United Nations, is in Geneva.

General Services Administration (GSA) US government agency that establishes policy and provides for management of the government's property and records. It is responsible for the construction and operation of buildings; the procurement and distribution of supplies; utilization and disposal of property; transportation, traffic, and communications management; stockpiling of strategic materials; and the management of automatic data processing resources programs. Established in 1949, the GSA headquarters are in Washington, DC.

General Strike (1926) A national stoppage of work by members of Britain's major industries, May 3–12. The General Strike began when the Trades Union Council (TUC) called out its members in support of miners. The strike extended to all forms of transport, the iron and steel industries, and many other trades. However, the government was able to keep essential services going. Nothing was gained and labor unions in general found themselves worse off after the retaliatory Trade Union Act was passed in 1927.

Genesis The first book of the Bible, traditionally ascribed to Moses. It recounts the creation of the universe and of man (Adam), the fall of Adam through disobedience and his exclusion from the Garden of Eden, the events of the Flood and the deliverance of Noah and his family, and the scattering of the nations at *Babel. The remainder of the book gives particular attention to the lives of Abraham, Isaac, Jacob, and Joseph. It also introduces the fundamental Old Testament theme of the *covenant between God and Israel.

Genesee River A river that flows from N central Pennsylvania NW and then NE through New York to Rochester, where it empties into Lake Ontario. Running through the Allegheny Plateau, its valleys yield farm products; hydroelectric projects along the river produce power. Length: 144 mi (232 km).

genet A carnivorous mammal of the genus *Genetta* (9 species) of Africa and Europe. Genets range in size from the 20-in (50-cm) Abyssinian genet (*G. abyssinica*) to the 40-in (100-cm) African giant genet (*G. victoriae*). They have retractile claws, long tails (up to 20 in [50 cm]), foxlike heads, and pale fur with dark spots or stripes. Genets are stealthy nocturnal hunters, preying on roosting birds and small mammals. Family: *Viverridae*.

Genet, Jean (1910–) French novelist and dramatist. His autobiographical *A Thief's Journal* (1948) tells of his life in reformatories and prisons and among the criminals and prostitutes of various European cities. In his novels, which include *Our Lady of the Flowers* (1944) and *Miracle of the Rose* (1946), he describes this underworld with poetic intensity. His plays, in which elements of ritual and fantasy are emphasized, are *Deathwatch* (1947), *The Maids* (1947), *The Balcony* (1956), *The Blacks* (1958), and *The Screens* (1961).

genetic code The means by which information for the organization and function of living cells is carried by *DNA and *RNA molecules. Evidence for the nature of the genetic code was provided in the 1960s by the work of *Crick, M. W. Nirenberg (1927–), *Khorana, and many others. They found that the basic symbol of the code was a sequence of three consecutive bases of the DNA molecule. Therefore, according to the combination of the four possible bases—adenine, guanine, cytosine, and thymine (DNA) or uracil (RNA)—the different triplet sequences (or codons) could specify the 20 or so amino acids commonly used by cells for protein synthesis and give start and stop signals for the process. Investigations in many species have shown that the code seems to apply universally.

genetics The study of heredity and variation in living organisms. The science of genetics is founded on the work of Gregor *Mendel, who, in 1865, established the basic laws of inheritance. In the early 20th century *chromosomes and their *genes were established as the carriers of information determining inheritable characteristics, and with the discovery of the structure of *DNA in 1953, the molecular basis of genetics was revealed.

Genetics is important in plant and animal breeding, in understanding inherited diseases and abnormalities, especially in man, and in obtaining strains of microorganisms beneficial to man, such as yeasts used in brewing and fungi for the production of antibiotics. By means of genetic engineering, genes can now be transferred between species.

Geneva (French name: Genève; German name: Genf) 46 13N 6 09E A city in SW Switzerland, on the SW corner of Lake Geneva. It is a cultural and commercial center with over two-thirds of the population employed in the service sector, banking and international finance being particularly important. Industries include the production of watches, precision instruments, and chemicals. It is the base of many international organizations including the International Red Cross, the World Health Organization, and the International Labor Organisation. The European headquarters of the United Nations is also here, occupying the buildings that formerly housed the League of Nations. It has a cathedral (12th–13th centuries) and a university (1559). *History*: originating as a prehistoric lake dwelling, it was later a Roman city. It became the center of the Calvinist Reformation and a refuge for persecuted Protestants. Population (1980 est): 156,505.

Geneva, Lake (French name: Lac Léman; German name: Genfersee) A lake on the Rhône River lying partly in Switzerland and partly in France. Geneva (at its W end) and Lausanne and Montreux are on the Swiss N shore, while the French resort of Evian lies on its S shore. Its scenic beauty is dominated by the Alps to the S. Area: 223 sq mi (577 sq km).

Geneva Bible An English translation of the Bible published in 1560 by Puritan exiles in Geneva. It is also called the Breeches Bible because of the use of the word in the translation of Genesis 3.7.

Geneva Conferences 1. (1932–34) An international conference on *disarmament. Representatives of 59 states attended the opening meeting, but the major powers were unable to come to an agreement and in 1933 Hitler withdrew Germany from both the conference and the *League of Nations. Continuing deadlock led to the postponement of the conference, which did not reassemble. 2. (1954) A conference convened following the conclusion of the *Korean War. Discussions on the settlement of Korea, attended by representatives of the US, Soviet Union, the UK, France, North Korea, South Korea, and the People's Republic of China ended without agreement. The war in *Indochina was also discussed by representatives of the US, the Soviet Union, the UK, France, China, Vietnam, Cambodia, Laos, and the *Viet Minh; a ceasefire line was settled along the *seventeenth parallel.

Geneva Conventions International agreements covering the care and protection of noncombatants and wounded troops in wartime. Inspired by the establishment of the International *Red Cross, the first conference, attended by representatives from 16 countries, met in Geneva in 1864 to formulate a code of practice for the treatment of wounded soldiers. Later conventions (1906, 1929) ratified further agreements, covering assistance for forces at sea and treatment of *prisoners of war. In 1949 a fourth convention concerning the protection of civilians was incorporated and the others revised. Most states accept the conventions as morally binding. Neutral countries and the International Red Cross have a supervisory role in wartime but enforcement is difficult as violation cannot be punished.

Genghis Khan (c. 1162–1227) The founder of the Mongol empire. Originally called Tamujin, he adopted the title Genghis Khan (Emperor of All) in 1206 after uniting under his command the nomadic Mongol tribes of the Siberian steppes and destroying Tatar power. Organizing his horsemen into highly mobile and disciplined squadrons called *ordus* (hence "hordes"), he attacked China's frontiers. Although his armies breached the Great Wall and captured Peking, they failed to conquer China com-

GENETICS

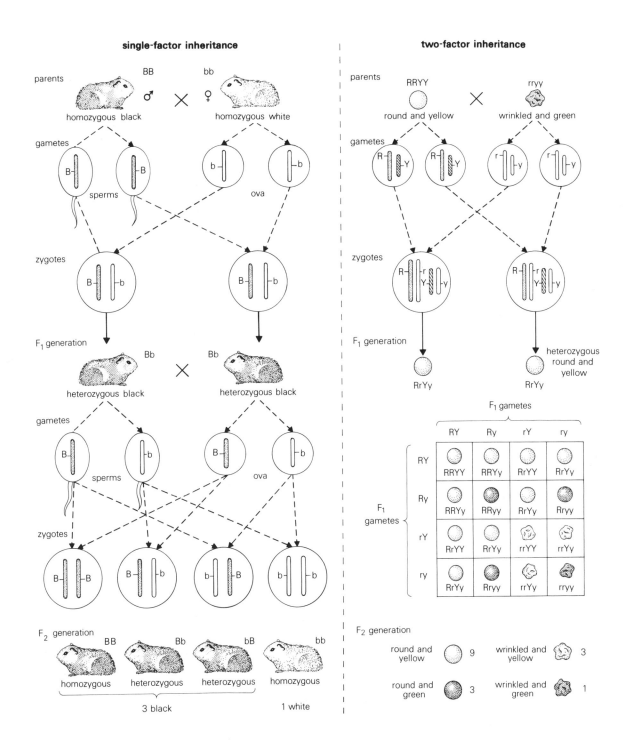

single-factor inheritance

two-factor inheritance

GENETICS *When a purebred (homozygous) black guinea pig (BB) mates with a purebred white one (bb) all the offspring (F₁ generation) will be black (Bb), since the gene for black is dominant. Mating of this heterozygous F₁ generation will produce both black and white guinea pigs (F₂ generation) in the ratio 3:1, since each of the parents carries a white recessive gene. The same principle applies to the inheritance of two factors—seed color and texture—in pea plants. When a plant with round yellow seeds (RRYY—dominant) is crossed with one producing wrinkled green seeds (rryy—recessive) the offspring will all have round yellow seeds (RrYy— heterozygous). Crossing of this generation results in the segregation and reassortment of the genes so that their offspring will show all four possibilities of seed color and texture in the proportions 9:3:3:1. Both these examples of single- and two-factor inheritance obey Mendel's laws.*

pletely. Advancing westward, Genghis, by ruthless massacres and pillage, crushed all resistance in Afghanistan, Persia, and S Russia. After his death his son Ogadai (1185–1241) executed Genghis' plans for the empire's organization.

genipap The fruit of *Genipa americana*, a small West Indian tree. The genipap resembles a brown orange and is used in preserves and beverages. Family: *Rubiaceae* (madder family).

Genk 50 58N 5 30E A city in Belgium. The center of an important coal-mining region, its manufactures include mining machinery. Population (1981 est): 61,399.

Gennesaret, Lake of. *See* Galilee, Sea of.

Genoa (Italian name: Genova) 44 24N 08 56E A port in NW Italy, the capital of Liguria on the Gulf of Genoa. A major maritime city during the middle ages, it possesses many notable buildings dating from then. These include the cathedral of San Lorenzo (1118) and a university (1471). Genoa is Italy's chief port and also a major industrial center with ship-building, heavy engineering, steel processing, and oil refining. Population (1980 est): 774,643.

genotype The genetic constitution of an individual organism, which comprises its *genes and determines the physical characteristics (*see* phenotype) of that individual.

genre painting A type of painting representing some aspect of everyday life. Although earlier examples exist, genre painting first became popular in 17th-century Holland, where the political, economic, and religious structure favored its development under such painters as *Vermeer, *Steen, and de *Hooch. Notable 18th-century examples are the works of *Hogarth and *Chardin. Genre painting became particularly widespread in the 19th century, when the impressionists and Victorian painters enthusiastically adopted it. Although now overshadowed by abstract art it is still practiced.

Genseric (*or* Gaiseric; d. 477 AD) King of the *Vandals (428–77), who played a major role in bringing about the fall of the *Roman Empire. He led the Vandals from Spain to N Africa, which he conquered after seizing Carthage from the Romans in 439. In 455 he sacked Rome.

Gent. *See* Ghent.

gentian A herbaceous plant of the widely distributed genus *Gentiana* (about 400 species), which includes many alpine perennials. The leaves are opposite and unstalked. The flowers have four or five petals, usually blue, arranged to form a bell or funnel with spreading lobes. The fruit of most species is a capsule. Many gentians are cultivated in rock gardens. Family: *Gentianaceae*.

gentian violet A purple dye derived from *aniline. It is used as an antiseptic, a chemical indicator, and as a dye.

Gentile, Giovanni (1875–1944) Italian philosopher. Gentile held to Hegelian theories about the dominance of the will; a thinking person had a spiritual unity that was realized in the *pure act*—hence his doctrine of "actualism." As Mussolini's minister of public education he was instructed to reform the educational system, which for him meant purging it of teachers suspected of democratic or liberal tendencies. Against this process his former collaborator *Croce protested in vain.

Gentile da Fabriano (Niccolò di Giovanni di Massio; c. 1370–1427) Florentine painter of the *international gothic style. His fresco cycles (completed by *Pisanello) for the Doge's Palace, Venice, and the Lateran Basilica, Rome, have perished. The *Adoration of the Magi* (Uffizi) shows his richly decorated style.

geocentric system. *See* Ptolemaic system.

geochemistry The study of the chemical composition of the earth. It involves estimating the absolute and relative abundance of the constituent elements and their isotopes, as well as their distribution and migration in the various geochemical environments (lithosphere, atmosphere, biosphere, hydrosphere) and in the rocks and minerals that make up the earth. In the earth's crust, oxygen (47%), silicon (28%), and aluminum (8%) are the most abundant elements.

geochronology The study of dating geological events, rocks, sediments, and organic remains, either absolutely or relatively. Absolute dating involves radioactive *dating techniques giving an actual date BP (before present). Relative dating establishes the order of geological events in relation to each other, using fossil correlation, pollen analysis, archeological evidence, etc.

geodesy The science of determining the exact shape and size of the earth or portions of it, using precise surveying and exact calculations of gravitational force. Related topics, such as the earth's rotational effects and tides, are also studied. Geodetic surveying is the large-scale surveying of the

earth's surface, taking into account its curvature. This provides the data for fixing exact control points for more detailed surveying (triangulation and leveling).

Geoffrey Martel (1006–60) Count of Anjou (1040–60). Through his marriage (1032) to Agnes the widow of the Duke of Aquitaine he unsuccessfully claimed Aquitaine for his heirs. However, Geoffrey's policy of territorial expansion found fruition in his subsequent acquisition of Touraine and much of Maine.

Geoffrey of Monmouth (c. 1100–54) English chronicler. His major work, *Historia Regum Britanniae*, was the main source for the whole body of medieval European literature concerned with the Arthurian legend and included the stories of King Lear, Cymbeline, and other legendary figures.

Geoffroy Saint-Hilaire, Étienne (1772–1844) French naturalist, who originated the concept that all animals conformed to the same basic structural plan or "unity of composition." Geoffroy saw modern species as unchanging but derived from ancestral species through the appearance of successful "monstrosities." This foreshadowed later concepts of evolution.

geography The study of the features of the earth's surface, together with their spatial distribution and interrelationships, as the environment of man. During the earliest development of geography the Greeks, notably Herodotus, Eratosthenes of Cyrene, and Ptolemy, were concerned with the shape of the earth and the location of land and sea. Through exploration in later centuries more knowledge of the earth was amassed and modern geography was founded as a discipline in the early 19th entury by the German scholars Humboldt and Ritter. During the 20th century geography has moved away from a regional approach, in which different areas were studied and compared, to a more systematic approach. The discipline is now divided between the physical and social sciences. Physical geography includes geomorphology (the study of the landforms of the earth), biogeography (the study of soils and the distribution of animals and plants), and climatology (*see* climate). The main branches of human geography are historical geography (studying spatial change in an area over a period of time or reconstructing past landscapes), economic geography, urban geography, and political geography.

geological time scale A time scale covering the whole of the earth's history from its origin about 4600 million years ago to the present. The largest divisions are eras (Paleozoic, Mesozoic, and Cenozoic); these are subdivided into periods and the Tertiary and Quaternary periods are further subdivided into epochs; epochs consist of several ages, and ages can be divided into chrons. A number of eras together is an eon. This is known as the chronomeric standard scale of chronostratigraphic classification. The stratomeric standard scale refers to the bodies of rocks formed in these time intervals; the corresponding terms are group (era), system (period), series (epoch), stage (age), and chronozone (chron). The divisions are not uniform time intervals but are based mainly on major evolutionary changes. For example, at the beginning of the Cambrian, about 570 million years ago, marine organisms suddenly became abundant and varied. □geology.

geology The study of the earth: its origin, history, structure, composition, and the natural processes acting on it. The branches of geology are historical (including geochronology, stratigraphy, and paleontology); physical (including geomorphology, geophysics, petrology, mineralogy, crystallography, and geochemistry); and economic, involving the distribution and occurrence of the economically important rocks and minerals, such as petroleum.

geomagnetic field The earth's magnetic field, causing a compass needle to align north–south. It is believed to be caused by the liquid-iron core acting as a dynamo resulting from the convection currents moving in it. The magnetic poles do not coincide with the geographic poles, and their positions vary with time. Complete reversals of the earth's magnetic field have occurred in the past; relic magnetism in rocks, which coincides with the magnetic alignment adopted at the time of their formation, provides strong evidence for the theory of sea-floor spreading and continental drift (*see* plate tectonics). The three **magnetic elements** of the earth's field are the *magnetic dip, the *magnetic declination, and the horizontal field strength, which together completely define the earth's field at any point on its surface.

geometrid moth A moth of the family *Geometridae*, occurring in Europe, Asia, and North America. The name is derived from the looping method of locomotion of the caterpillars, which are known as inch worms, loopers, or measuring worms. The adults, known as pugs, umbers, carpet moths, etc., have slender bodies, a weak flight, and camouflaging coloration, often resembling dead leaves.

geometry A branch of mathematics concerned with the properties of space and shapes. In *Euclidean geometry the space corresponds to com-

stages in the evolution of the geological strata of a small area

1 *Desert conditions resulted in the lowest rock layer being sandstone.*

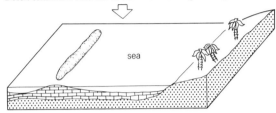

2 *The advance of a warm sea over much of the area saw the deposition of chalk.*

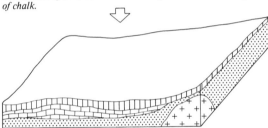

3 *Following the retreat of the sea the area was covered with a fine sediment eventually forming clay and an igneous intrusion of granite was forced up by volcanic activity into the overlying strata.*

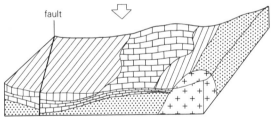

4 *The area was then subjected to folding, faulting, and erosion to form the present day landscape.*

geological map

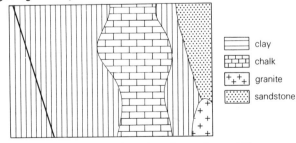

clay
chalk
granite
sandstone

The map of the same area shows the rock types that would be exposed if the overlying soil and vegetation were stripped away.

geological time scale

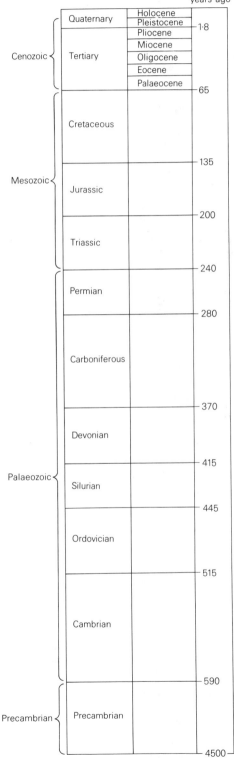

millions of years ago

Cenozoic	Quaternary	Holocene	
		Pleistocene	1·8
	Tertiary	Pliocene	
		Miocene	
		Oligocene	
		Eocene	
		Palaeocene	65
Mesozoic	Cretaceous		
			135
	Jurassic		
			200
	Triassic		
			240
Palaeozoic	Permian		
			280
	Carboniferous		
			370
	Devonian		
			415
	Silurian		
			445
	Ordovician		
			515
	Cambrian		
			590
Precambrian	Precambrian		
			4500

mon notions of physical space and the shapes are idealizations of the common shapes that occur in real life. Other branches of geometry include *non-Euclidean geometry, such as the geometry of the surface of a sphere; *Riemannian geometry, which is used in *relativity theory; and *analytic geometry, in which algebra is used to solve geometrical problems. *See also* topology.

geophysics The study of the physical forces acting on, and particularly within, the earth. Sophisticated equipment is used to study the properties, structure, composition, and evolution of the earth. Important branches of geophysics are seismology, geomagnetism, vulcanology, natural radioactivity, and the earth's rotation and gravitational field. Much geophysical data has been collected in recent years as a result of geophysical prospecting, particularly for petroleum.

geopolitics The study of the influence of geographical factors upon international politics. It suggest that a state's foreign policy is influenced by its desire to obtain, for example, sufficient agricultural land. The term was coined by the Swedish political scientist Rudolf Kjellen (1864–1922) and was used by the Nazis, who justified their expansionist ambitions as the seeking of *Lebensraum* (living space). As a result geopolitics was discredited and has become outdated by technological developments.

George I (1660–1727) The first Hanoverian King of Great Britain and Ireland (1714–27) and Elector of Hanover (1698–1727). He divorced his wife, Sophia Dorothea, for infidelity (1694) and imprisoned her for 32 years. A successful soldier and a shrewd diplomat, he was nonetheless unpopular in Britain because he seemed to subordinate British to Hanoverian interests. He never learned English and left government to his Whig ministers, particularly after they saved George and his mistresses from disgrace in connection with the *South Sea Bubble.

George II (1683–1760) King of Great Britain and Ireland and Elector of Hanover (1727–69), succeeding his father George I. He married *Caroline of Ansbach in 1705. His reliance on his ministers, especially Sir Robert *Walpole, influenced the development of constitutional monarchy. He was an ardent soldier and in the War of Austrian Succession fought at Dettingen (1743), the last British monarch to appear in battle. He was a patron of musicians, notably Handel.

George III (1738–1820) King of Great Britain and Ireland (1760–1820) and Elector (1760–1815) and King (1815–20) of Hanover, succeeding his grandfather George II. He married Charlotte Sophia of Mecklenburg-Strelitz (1744–1818) in 1761. The political instability of the 1760s was blamed by the Whigs unjustly on George's alleged attempts to influence parliament through corrupt "king's friends." He shared with Lord *North the blame for the loss of the American colonies but was more astute in backing William *Pitt the Younger as prime minister (1783–1801). From the 1780s he suffered periods of madness and was permanently insane by 1811.

George IV (1762–1830) King of the United Kingdom and of Hanover (1820–30), succeeding his father George III, for whom he was regent (1811–20). He secretly married a Roman Catholic, Maria Fitzherbert, in 1785 but the marriage was invalid and in 1795 he married *Caroline of Brunswick. They were separated in 1796. Although intelligent and artistic, George's dissipation and extravagance and his heartless treatment of Caroline undermined the prestige of the monarchy.

George V (1865–1936) King of the United Kingdom (1910–36), second son of Edward VII, whose heir he became on the death (1892) of his elder brother Albert Victor. In 1893 George married *Mary of Teck. He gave valuable political advice during the many crises of his reign.

George VI (1895–1952) King of the United Kingdom (1936–52). Second son of George V, he succeeded to the throne when Edward VIII abdicated. He married (1923) Lady Elizabeth Bowes-Lyon (*see* Elizabeth the Queen Mother). His example inspired Britain during World War II.

George, St The patron saint of England and of soldiers. His cult was brought to England by Crusaders returning from Palestine, where he was believed to have been martyred during Emperor Diocletian's rule. In art he is usually portrayed slaying a dragon to rescue a maiden, a legend that probably derives from the *Pegasus myth. Feast day: April 23.

George, Stefan (1868–1933) German poet. He studied in Paris, where he was associated with the Symbolist poets, and in Germany, where he assembled and dominated a group of disciples. In his manifesto *Über Dichtung* (1894) he advocated rigid formal perfection and metrical regularity, goals that he achieved in *Das Jahr der Seele* (1897) and *Der Teppich des Lebens* (1899). His later work glorified a godlike youth, Maximin. The Nazis favored him, but he rejected them, voluntarily exiling himself in 1933.

George, Lake A lake in E New York, N of Albany, that runs NE from the village of Lake George to Ticonderoga near the Vermont border, where it joins an outlet to Lake Champlain. Strategically located, Lake George was important during the French and Indian Wars and the American Revolution. It is a popular resort area. Area: 33 mi (54 km) long; 1–3 mi (1.6–5 km) wide.

Georgetown (*or* Penang) 5 26N 100 16E A city in NW Peninsular Malaysia, the capital of Penang state. The first British Malayan settlement, it is now Malaysia's chief port, exporting tin, rubber, and copra. Population (1980): 250,578.

Georgetown 6 46N 58 10W The capital and main port of Guyana, on the Atlantic Ocean at the mouth of the Demerara River. Founded by the British in 1781, it was later occupied by the French and the Dutch. It has twice in recent years (1945, 1951) been badly damaged by fire. Exports include sugar, rice, and bauxite. Its university was founded in 1963. Population (1970): 63,184.

Georgia A state on the SE coast. It is bordered by Florida on the S, Alabama on the W, Tennessee and North Carolina on the N, and South Carolina on the NE, where the Savannah River forms the boundary between the two states. In the SE Georgia fronts the Atlantic Ocean. The state can be divided into three physiographic regions: the higher elevations of the Appalachian Mountains in the N; a rolling coastal plain with forests and swamps in the S; and the Piedmont Plateau separating the two. Manufacturing is important although largely rurally oriented. Georgia is the nation's major textile producer; other industries include motor vehicles and aircraft assembly, chemicals, and food processing. The state is also a major source of building stone and is noted for its fine marble. Agriculture is important; poultry has replaced cotton as the major item and Georgia is a leading US producer of peanuts. Other products include tobacco, watermelons, and other fruits (especially peaches), with some cattle and pig raising. Forest products are produced throughout the state. Its capital, Atlanta, is the cultural and economic center of the SE and the state has a rich traditional folk culture. *History*: first visited by De Soto in 1540, the state was originally inhabited by Creek and Cherokee Indians. Subsequently, both Spain and England claimed the area. The first British settlers arrived in 1733, led by James Oglethorpe, who intended the colony as a refuge for debtors. Named for George II, it became the 13th of the original colonies. Oglethorpe succeeded in routing Spanish troops in 1743, thus safeguarding the colony's future. A large part of the state fell to the British during the American Revolution. With the development of agriculture after the war, settlement grew. Georgia was the first Southern state to ratify the Constitution (1788). A pro-slavery state with a cotton-based economy, Georgia seceded from the Union and joined the Confederate cause in the Civil War. It suffered considerable damage, most notably the burning of Atlanta (1864) and later in that year General Sherman's March to the Sea. It was the only Southern state to integrate its public schools in the 1950s without incident. In 1976, Jimmy Carter, originally a Georgia peanut farmer and former governor, was the state's first native son to be elected to the US presidency. In 1983 the state passed desegregation legislation governing its institutions of higher learning. Area: 58,876 sq mi (152,488 sq km). Population (1980): 5,464,265. Capital: Atlanta.

Georgian The language spoken by the Georgian peoples of the Georgian SSR, the Azerbaidzhan SSR, NE Turkey, and Isfahan province in Iran. It belongs to the Kartvelian or *South Caucasian group and is written in a script derived from Aramaic with Greek influences and has a literature dating from the 5th century AD. It is the official language of the Georgian SSR.

Georgian Bay A large bay in central Canada, in NE Lake Huron in Ontario. Its many islands and irregular coastline make it a popular recreational area.

Georgian Soviet Socialist Republic (*or* Georgia) A constituent republic in the SW Soviet Union. It is a mountainous region with many holiday resorts on the Black Sea coast. The population is predominantly Georgian. Georgia is rich in minerals, especially manganese and coal, and a gold field was discovered in 1941. The region also has vast hydroelectric resources. The main crop is tea; citrus fruits, grapes, and tobacco are also important to agriculture. *History*: Christianity was introduced in the 4th century AD. An independent kingdom for most of the middle ages, Georgia was divided between Persia and Turkey in 1555, passing to Russia in the 19th century. It became independent in 1918 but subsequently formed part of the Transcaucasian Soviet Federated Republic (*see* Transcaucasia). It became a separate republic in 1936. Area: about 26,900 sq mi (69,700 sq km). Population (1981 est): 5,100,000. Capital: Tbilisi.

Georgian style A style of British architecture prevalent during the reigns of George I to George IV (1714–1830). The period was subject to several different influences but was dominated by *Palladianism and *neoclassicism. Well-proportioned elegance was the keynote of Georgian architecture, characterized by the symmetrical use of twelve-paned sash windows in domestic architecture and the restrained use of classical features in public buildings.

geostationary orbit. *See* communications satellite.

geothermal energy Heat produced in the earth's interior, which may provide a source of usable energy. Volcanoes, geysers, and hot springs are all sources of geothermal energy, although only the latter two provide convenient energy sources. Countries that make use of geothermal energy include Iceland (where it is an important source of power), Italy, New Zealand, and the US. Although geothermal energy is being actively explored as an alternative energy source, it currently supplies only about 0.1% of the world's energy requirements.

Gera 50 53N 12 6E A city in S East Germany, on the Weisse Elster River. Its manufactures include machinery, textiles, and furniture; there are uranium mines nearby. Population (1980 est): 124,146.

geranium A herbaceous plant of the genus *Pelargonium* (250 species), most species of which are native to South Africa and widely cultivated as house and garden plants. They have roundish leaves and rounded clusters of showy flowers, usually red or pink. Most horticultural geraniums are hybrids, of which the most important are the zonal pelargoniums, with a dark ring near the center of each leaf. Family: *Geraniaceae*.

Horticultural geraniums should be distinguished from related plants of the genus *Geranium* (see cranesbill).

Gérard, François (Pascal Simon), Baron (1770–1837) French painter, born in Rome. He was the pupil of *David but later rivaled him at the court of Napoleon with his elegant portraits, e.g. *Josephine Bonaparte* (Louvre), and history paintings. After Napoleon's fall, he became painter to Louis XVIII, who ennobled him in 1819.

gerbil A small *rodent belonging to the subfamily *Gerbillinae* (over 100 species) of Africa and Asia, also called jird and sand rat. Ranging in size from 2–8 in (5–20 cm), gerbils have long hind legs. They inhabit dry open country and spend the day in underground burrows, feeding at night on seeds and roots. Chief genera: *Gerbillus, Tatera*; family: *Cricetidae*.

GERENUK *A male on the lookout for approaching predators, of which the animal has a good view because of its long neck.*

gerenuk A long-necked antelope, *Litocranius walleri*, of E African bush country. About 40 in (100 cm) tall at the shoulder, gerenuks are bright chestnut with white underparts; only males have the curved backward-pointing horns. They feed by rearing up on their hind legs and cropping leaves from thorny shrubs.

geriatrics The medical specialty that deals with the diseases and problems of old age. With improved standards of living and medical care, the number of people surviving to old age has increased and the suitable care of elderly patients is of great importance. In the past little active treatment was given, the patients being virtually bedridden in hospitals, almshouses, etc. Now, however, the aim is to restore as much function and activity as

possible, by encouraging patients to engage in suitable activities with the aid of physiotherapy and occupational therapy.

Géricault, (Jean Louis André) Théodore (1791–1824) French painter, born in Rouen. His famous *Raft of the Medusa* (1819; Louvre), for which he used corpses in the morgue as models, was based on a contemporary shipwreck, which had become a political issue. While visiting England (1820–22), he produced a number of lithographs depicting poor people. He also painted his favorite subject—horses (e.g. *Derby at Epsom*; Louvre). His last works, inspired by a psychiatrist friend, were five portraits of the insane. Despite his early death after a riding accident, he greatly influenced French Romantic painters, especially *Delacroix.

German A language of the West *Germanic language group. It is the official language of Germany and Austria and one of the four official languages of Switzerland. High German, the official and written form, developed from dialects of the highland areas of Germany and Austria. Old High German was spoken before 1100 AD when Middle High German, based on Upper German dialects, became the standard form. Modern High German developed from the 16th-century dialect of Luther, whose biblical translations spread this form. Low German exists only in a spoken form in the lowland areas of N Germany and is derived from Old Saxon and Middle Low German speech. The main difference between Low and High German is the sound system, especially the consonants.

germander A herbaceous plant of the worldwide genus *Teucrium* (300 species), with square stems and simple toothed leaves. The small tubular two-lipped flowers, borne in groups in the axils of leaflike bracts, are usually pinkish-purple. The perennial water germander (*T. scordium*) is a Eurasian species. Family: *Labiatae*.

Germanic languages A subgroup of the *Indo-European language group. Its member languages are spoken in Britain, Scandinavia, Germany, the Netherlands, and Iceland. There are three recognized subgroups: East Germanic, North Germanic, and West Germanic. The first of these is now extinct but it included Gothic, one of the earliest Germanic languages. North Germanic covers the *Scandinavian languages. West Germanic includes modern English and German among its descendants as well as *Dutch (Netherlandic) and *Frisian. These developed from their earlier forms High and Low German, Anglo-Saxon, Middle English, and Old Saxon. Also developed from Germanic origins are *Yiddish and Afrikaans (see Afrikaner). All three branches can be traced back to an unrecorded Proto-Germanic language, which has been reconstructed by philologists by comparing and tracing back similar modern languages using such generalizations as those stated in Grimm's Law (see Grimm).

Germanicus Julius Caesar (15 BC–19 AD) Roman soldier, who was adopted by his uncle, Emperor Tiberius, in 4 AD. In 17 he was appointed to govern Rome's eastern provinces and died mysteriously in Antioch, perhaps as a result of poison. Germanicus married *Agrippina the Elder and was the father of Caligula.

germanium (Ge) A brittle gray-white metalloid, discovered by C. A. Winkler (1838–1904) in 1886. Like *gallium it is present in coal and is concentrated in chimney soot as well as in the flue dusts of zinc smelters, from which it is obtained commercially. The element is a *semiconductor and its most important uses are in the electronics industry. Germanium compounds include the volatile tetrachloride ($GeCl_4$) and the dioxide (GeO_2), which has a high refractive index and is used in lenses. At no 32; at wt 72.59; mp 1721°F (937.4°C); bp 5131°F (2830°C).

German literature Little vernacular German literature earlier than the 12th century survives. The fragmentary *Hildebrandslied* (c. 800) is the only extant example of early heroic verse. The major works of medieval German literature were the epics the *Nibelungenlied* and *Gudrun*, several court epics based on French models, and the love lyrics of the wandering minnesingers, notably those of Walther von der Vogelweide. The Reformation had a great influence, especially through Luther's translation of the Bible (1522; 1534); Lutheran ideals were often expressed in the poetry of the *Meistersingers, the best known of whom was Hans Sachs. The Thirty Years' War, portrayed in Grimmelhausen's novels, resulted in cultural insecurity in the 17th and early 18th centuries and adherence to French models. An upsurge of national feeling in the 18th century resulted in a literary revival; the literature of the Enlightenment, represented most notably by Lessing, was succeeded by the *Sturm und Drang movement and at the end of the century by Romanticism.

Goethe and Schiller outgrew *Sturm und Drang* emotionalism and espoused classicism instead, although Goethe's *Faust* remains balanced by warmth of feeling. The poets Hölderlin and Heine, the novelist and dramatist Kleist, and the dramatist Büchner were not associated with particular literary movements.

The aestheticism of the late 19th and early 20th centuries, found in the poems of George and the plays of Hofmannsthal, was paralleled by the realism of Fontane's novels. The social malaise of Germany at the time of World War I was reflected in Expressionism, elements of which appear in the works of various writers, influencing the mysticism in Rilke's poetry, the nightmare visions in Kafka's novels, and the search for new social and aesthetic values in the novels of Thomas Mann and Hesse and the dramas of Brecht.

The economic and political character of West Germany after World War II has been analyzed in the novels of Böll and Grass. The Swiss playwrights Max Frisch and Friedrich Dürrenmatt have written a number of influential plays. In East Germany postwar literature has suffered from an official insistence on a restrictive form of socialist realism; only recently have poets and novelists emerged who show signs of being able to develop their individual talents.

German measles A common contagious disease of children and young adults caused by a virus. Known medically as rubella, it is a mild infection producing a pink rash and a sore throat. If a woman is infected in early pregnancy she may give birth to a malformed child; for this reason immunization of schoolgirls is encouraged.

German shepherd dog (or Alsatian) A breed of large strongly built □dog originating in Germany. It has a coarse coat that can range in color from white to black but is often black and tan. German shepherds are used as working dogs, especially for police work, as guard dogs, and as guide dogs for the blind. Height: 24–26 in (61–66 cm) (dogs); 22–24 in (56–61 cm) (bitches).

Germany A country in central Europe, now comprising (see below) the German Democratic Republic (East Germany) and the Federal Republic of Germany (West Germany). The region was occupied by German tribes from about 500 BC and came repeatedly into conflict with the Romans from the 2nd century BC. Overrun by the Huns in the 4th and 5th centuries, the area was dominated by the *Franks from the 6th century and was christianized in the late-7th to 8th centuries. After the death of the Carolingian Louis the Pius his empire was divided (843), the E part becoming the eastern Frankish kingdom, the nucleus of Germany. After the failure of the Frankish dynasty the German kings became nominally elective (see electors) but medieval Germany was in practice ruled by a series of hereditary dynasties. The first of these, the Saxons, was founded by Henry the Fowler in 919 and from the election (963) of his son as Holy Roman Emperor (see Otto (I) the Great), the German kings claimed the imperial title by right. The 11th to 13th centuries were dominated by struggle between the emperors and popes over the *investiture controversy, which with the conflict between *Guelfs and Ghibellines gave rise to a sustained period of civil strife. In the 13th century, following the fall of the *Hohenstaufen dynasty, the first *Habsburg emperor was elected and from the 15th century the imperial title remained almost continuously in the family. In the later middle ages the power of the princes was challenged by the *Hanseatic League of northern ports, which wielded political as well as commercial power. The 16th and 17th centuries were dominated by religious strife, following Luther's inception of the *Reformation at Wittenberg in 1520 and the subsequent division of Germany into a predominantly Protestant N and Roman Catholic S. The religious conflict was not resolved until the conclusion (1648) of the *Thirty Years' War. In the 17th century the Hohenzollern Electors of Brandenburg acquired Prussia, which, as a kingdom from 1701, became the dominant German state and, under *Frederick (II) the Great, a major European power. In 1806 the Holy Roman Empire was brought to an end by Napoleon, who formed the *Confederation of the Rhine in its place. The post-Napoleonic German confederation was dominated by Austria and Prussia and in 1834 the latter was the moving influence behind the formation of the *Zollverein (customs union). Prussian power increased further with victory in the *Austro-Prussian War (1866), which permanently destroyed Austrian influence in Germany, and in the *Franco-Prussian War (1870–71). In 1871 Bismarck achieved his cherished ambition of creating a German Empire. The late 19th and early 20th centuries saw rapid industrialization, an aggressive armaments program, and the rise of Germany as a colonial power, especially in Africa; its international aspirations were a major cause of *World War I. Defeated in 1918, the Empire came to an end (1919) and was replaced by the *Weimar Republic, which was plagued by the economic difficulties that facilitated *Hitler's rise to power in the early 1930s. His aggressive foreign policy, aimed at the establishment of a new German empire, led to the annexation of Austria and the Sudetenland (1938) and then of Czechoslovakia (1939). Finally, his invasion of Poland precipitated World War II. Following Germany's defeat the country was divided into British, French, Soviet, and US occupation zones before the subsequent formation of the two separate states, the German Democratic Republic and the Federal Republic of Germany.

German Democratic Republic (GDR; German name: Deutsche Demokratische Republik) The N part of the country, which borders on the Baltic Sea and includes the island of *Rügen, is generally low lying and contains many lakes. The Harz Mountains rise in the W, the Thuringian Forest in the SW, and the Erzgebirge in the SE. The main rivers are the Elbe and the Oder. Economy: highly industrialized and planned in close cooperation with the Soviet Union. Almost all industry is state-owned and great strides forward have been made in the past two decades, particularly in such areas as precision engineering (including optical instruments) and electronics, as well as heavy industries, such as shipbuilding, machinery, and chemicals. However, the growth of light industries, such as textiles and food products, has slowed down recently. The main mineral resource is lignite, which supplies over half of the country's basic energy. It has two nuclear power stations. Oil and coal (all East German coalmines were largely exhausted and closed by the end of 1977) are supplied by the Soviet Union. The agricultural sector, which is organized in collectives and state farms, is gradually declining in importance although forestry remains an important source of revenue. Exports include lignite, potash, textiles, and photographic paper. History: formed from the Soviet-occupied zone of Germany following World War II, it was given a provisional constitution as the German Democratic Republic in 1949, becoming independent in 1954. The leading architect of the new state was Walter Ulbricht, in whose hands real power lay from its establishment, and in 1960, following the death of President Wilhelm Pieck, he became chairman of the newly established Council of State. The early years of economic austerity and curbs on civil liberties led to much discontent and in 1953 serious riots, particularly in East Berlin, were suppressed by Soviet troops, but the flow of refugees to West Germany continued until 1961, when the *Berlin Wall was erected. Since the early 1970s there has been a marked improvement in living standards and relations with West Germany have eased slightly with a treaty calling for closer relations being ratified by both countries in 1973. Disagreement between West and East Germany over the political status of the GDR has continued, and has caused strained relations. West Germany refuses to accept the concept of "two Germanys" whereas East Germany is insistent on its separate status. Chancellor Erich Honecker cancelled a scheduled visit (1984) to West Germany, which would have been the first such state visit in the history of the two Germanys. Afterward, however, West Germany extended a loan to the GDR, and in turn, the GDR eased foreign exchange requirements for West Germany. Trade between the two countries reached an all-time high. East Germany is a member of COMECON and in 1973 was admitted to the UN as a separate state. Chairman of the council of state: Erich Honecker. Official language: German. Official currency: (GDR) Mark of 100 Pfennige. Area: 41,757 sq mi (108,178 sq km). Population (1983 est): 16,724,000. Capital: East Berlin. Chief port: Rostock.

Germany, Federal Republic of (German name: Bundesrepublik Deutschland) For administrative purposes, West Germany is divided into 11 Länder (German Land, state). Extensive plains in the N, which border on the North Sea, rise to a central hilly area with the peaks of the Alps in the extreme S. The chief rivers are the Rhine, Danube, Ems, Weser, and Elbe. Economy: rapid reconstruction, particularly of the industrial sector, followed World War II. There is a large amount of heavy industry, especially in the center and the N, including electrical engineering, iron and steel, motor vehicles, shipbuilding, and chemicals. The manufacture of photographic equipment and optical and other scientific instruments is also important. Considerable mineral resources include coal, iron ore, lead and zinc, and potash. Although the agricultural sector has declined in importance, there is a considerable amount of forestry (now mainly under state control) and an important wine industry, especially in the Rhine and Moselle Valleys. Tourism is an important source of revenue. The main exports include motor vehicles, machinery, chemicals, and electrical-engineering products; in 1978 West Germany superseded the US as the world's principal exporter. History: formed from the British-, French-, and US-occupied zones following World War II, it became fully independent in 1955. The capital was transferred to Bonn although West Berlin remained a part of the Federal Republic. In the postwar years it enjoyed a spectacular economic recovery making it the most prosperous country in W Europe. The import of foreign labor became increasingly essential to the continued industrial expansion, although the total number of Gastarbeiter (guest workers; see migration) has varied according to the fortunes of the economy. Christian Democratic governments under Adenauer and Ehrhard were followed in the early 1970s by the Social Democrats under Willi Brandt, and this contributed to better relations with East Germany and other E European countries. In 1982 the coalition government of Social Democrats and

Free Democrats led by Helmut Schmidt collapsed, after his government received a vote of no confidence in the Bundestag. In a stunning victory, Helmut Kohl, the Bundestag choice, received close to 50% of the German vote and a large majority of the seats in parliament. Mindful of the position of East Germany between Europe's East and West blocs and anxious for good relations with East Germany, West Germany has sought "cordial" relations with the Soviet Union. The two countries remain friendly, despite West Germany's decision to allow Pershing II missiles on its soil as part of NATO's deployment of intermediate-range missiles in Europe. Federal President: Richard von Weizsäcker (1920–). Chancellor: Helmut Kohl. Official language: German. Official currency: Deutsche Mark of 100 Pfennige. Area: 95,989 sq mi (248,620 sq km). Population (1983 est): 61,543,000. Capital: Bonn. Main port: Hamburg.

germination The process by which an embryo plant within a seed is transformed into a recognizable plant with roots, stem, and leaves. Water, warmth, and oxygen stimulate germination, which begins with the emergence of the root (radicle) and is followed by the shoot (plumule). Energy for the process is provided by the *cotyledons (seed leaves), which either remain below ground (hypogeal germination, as in the broad bean) or form the first leaves of the seedling (epigeal germination, as in the marrow squash).

Germiston 26 15S 28 10E A city in South Africa, in the S Transvaal. It contains the world's largest gold refinery and serves the Witwatersrand mines. It is an important railroad junction and has extensive railroad-engineering industries. Population (1980 est): 155,435.

Gerona 41 59N 2 49E A city in NE Spain, in Catalonia. It was besieged several times in the 17th–18th centuries. The fine gothic cathedral (1312–1598) has an exceptionally wide single nave. Industries include textiles, paper, and food processing. Population (1970): 50,338.

GERONIMO *Apache Indian chief who led border raids against both US and Mexican troops before being captured in 1886.*

Geronimo (1829–1909) A leader of the Chiricahua *Apaches. Born in the territory that would later become Arizona, Geronimo led his people in armed resistance to the attempts of the US Army to restrict them to a reservation in the 1870s. Although *Cochise, another Apache leader, agreed to end hostilities in 1872, Geronimo continued his campaign until

his surrender in 1886. The Chiricahuas were subsequently resettled near Fort Sill, Okla, and it was there that he dictated his autobiography, *Geronimo: His Own Story*, shortly before his death.

Gerry, Elbridge (1744–1814) US patriot, politician; US vice president (1813–14). A delegate from Massachusetts to the Continental Congress (1776–81) he was a signer of the Declaration of Independence. He served as a representative in Congress (1789–93) and was part of the group sent to by President John Adams in 1797 to negotiate a treaty with France France (the XYZ Affair). He was Massachusetts governor (1810–12) and then US vice president under President James Madison. The term "gerrymander" was coined from his name and the salamander-shaped result of senatorial redistricting while he was the governor of Massachusetts.

Gershwin, George (Jacob Gershvin; 1898–1937) US composer and songwriter. He wrote many songs for musical shows and films, perhaps the best-remembered being "The Man I Love," "I Got Rhythm," and "Lady Be Good." His jazz-inspired orchestral works include *Rhapsody in Blue* (1924) and *An American in Paris* (1928); the opera *Porgy and Bess* (1935) is still widely performed. His brother **Ira Gershwin** (1896–1983) wrote the lyrics to many of his songs.

Gerson, Jean de (1363–1429) French theologian and chancellor of the University of Paris. He was one of the earliest advocates of restricting papal power (*see* Gallicanism). His efforts to end the *Great Schism of the Western Church by calling a general council were rewarded at the Council of *Constance (1415), of which he was a leading member.

Gesner, Conrad (1516–65) Swiss physician, who was a founder of modern zoology and botany. He compiled a survey of knowledge of animal life, the *Historiae animalium* (5 vols, 1551–87), and described many plant species, often in the form of woodcut illustrations. His other works include a bibliography of authors and their works, a survey of world languages, and a compendium of the recorded knowledge of the world.

Gestalt psychology A school of *psychology that originated in Germany in the early 20th century: Wolfgang *Köhler and Kurt *Koffka were its founders. It regards mental processes as wholes (gestalts) that cannot be analyzed into smaller components. According to this theory, when something is learned the individual's entire perception of the environment has been changed.

Gestapo (German: *Geheime Staatspolizei*, secret state police) The Nazi secret police formed in 1933 under Goering. Administered from 1936 by the *SS, the two organizations were the chief instruments of atrocities carried out by the Nazi Party in Germany and German-occupied Europe.

gestation. *See* pregnancy.

Gesualdo, Carlo, Prince of Venosa (c. 1560–1631) Italian composer. His madrigals employ extraordinary harmonic effects. He was also famous for his lute playing and notorious for the murder of his first (unfaithful) wife.

Getty, J(ean) Paul (1892–1976) US businessman. He made his fortune in oil, becoming a millionaire at the age of 22. He founded the J. Paul Getty Museum at Malibu, California.

Gettysburg 39 50N 77 14W A town in S Pennsylvania, SW of Harrisburg and York. Settled as a town in the late 1700s, it was the scene of Abraham Lincoln's Gettysburg Address and the Battle of Gettysburg in 1863. Population (1980): 7,194.

Gettysburg, Battle of (July 1–3, 1863) One of the most significant battles of the *Civil War, fought in southern Pennsylvania as part of the Confederacy's second invasion of the North. The battle began unexpectedly since both armies were uncertain of the other's position. The first day ended with a slight southern advantage, but a delay in the Confederate attack on the second day shifted the advantage to the Federal troops. On the third day, a large force of Confederates, under the command of General George Pickett, charged the center of the Union line, advancing briefly despite massive artillery fire, but eventually withdrawing with losses of more than 60%. The battle was considered a great victory for Union General George Meade, and it ended the Confederacy's hope of carrying the war to the North. The casualties suffered by both sides were enormous; the Union lost 23,000 men and the Confederates 25,000. Four months after the battle, President Abraham *Lincoln traveled to Gettysburg to dedicate a military cemetery where he delivered the **Gettysburg Address** (Nov. 19, 1863). It later became one of his best known and most quoted speeches.

Geulincx, Arnold (1624–69) Belgian-born philosopher. He was converted to Protestantism and settled in Holland. In response to *Descartes' mind–body relationship problem Geulincx originated the "two clock" theory, whereby body and mind are conceived of as keeping perfect time, side by side, without interaction. For Geulincx, when a mental or physical process takes place, God occasions it, hence the term "occasionalism" applied to this doctrine (*see also* Malebranche).

GEYSERS *The Pohutu geyser, North Island, New Zealand.*

geysers Jets of hot water and steam issuing intermittently from holes in the earth's crust, some reaching heights of up to 230 ft (70 m). Geysers are found in volcanically active or recently active regions, for example, in Iceland. They occur when water from deep within the crust becomes superheated and suddenly boils, gushing up to the surface like a fountain. Cones of sinter (deposits of silica) frequently build up around the vents of geysers.

Gezira, El (*or* al-Jazirah) A triangular plain in the Sudan, between the Blue and White Nile Rivers. The Gezira irrigation scheme using water from the Makwar Dam (completed 1925) makes possible the production of cotton, millet, fodder crops, and groundnuts.

Ghana, Republic of A country in West Africa, on the Gulf of Guinea. Coastal plains rise to undulating country around Accra, and, in the center, the basin of the Volta River rises to plateaus, especially in the N and W. The inhabitants are chiefly of black Sudanese stock but there are a large number of tribal units. *Economy*: chiefly agricultural. Food crops are varied, and increased production is being encouraged through such schemes as "Operation Feed Yourself" in an effort to make the country more self-sufficient. The main cash crop is cocoa, of which Ghana is the world's chief producer. There is also a concentration on such crops as rubber and cotton to provide raw material for industry, in an effort to diversify the economy. Gold and diamonds are mined, as well as manganese, bauxite, and limestone. Hydroelectricity is being developed, particularly through the Volta Dam, and oil was found offshore in 1978. Forestry is important and there are wide reforestation schemes. Fishing limits were extended from 30 mi to 200 mi (48 km to 322 km) in 1977. In spite of government efforts, economic difficulties continue, exacerbated by crop failures and also by such problems as large-scale smuggling. The main export is cocoa; others include timber and gold. *History*: from the middle ages several small kingdoms flourished in what is now Ghana. In 1472 the Portuguese and subsequently other Europeans set up trading posts in the region, which they called the Gold Coast. It became a center of the slave trade and the scene of rivalry between the British and Dutch. The British abolition of slavery led to prolonged wars with the Ashanti slavetraders in the 19th century. The area became the British colony of the Gold Coast in 1874. In 1957, together with the British part of Togo, it became independent, its new name, Ghana, being that of a medieval N African empire. In 1960 it became a republic within the British Commonwealth, with Dr Kwame Nkrumah as its first

president. His government became increasingly dictatorial and in 1966 he was overthrown in a military coup. Military rule continued until 1969, when civilian government was re-established. In 1972, however, a second military coup took place under Colonel Ignatius K. Acheampong. He was forced to resign in 1978 and, with his successor, Lt Gen Fred Akuffo, was executed following a military coup (1979) led by Fl Lt Jerry Rawlings. A new civilian government was formed (1979) with Dr Hilla Limann as president but this was overthrown in another military coup led by Fl Lt Rawlings in December, 1981. To stem smuggling activities all borders were closed in 1982. The expulsion from Nigeria of illegal aliens caused a mass migration of Africans, among them 1 million Ghananians. Ghana was forced to open its borders, and the repatriation of the returning nationals created a national emergency. Four abortive coups against Rawlings' government between 1982 and 1983 were indicative of the growing opposition to his regime. Official language: English. Official currency: cedi of 100 pesawas. Area: 92,010 sq mi (238,305 sq km). Population (1983 est): 13,367,000. Capital: Accra. Main port: Takoradi.

gharial. *See* gavial.

Ghats Two mountain ranges lying along the W and E coasts of India. The **Western Ghats**, which extend about 932 mi (1500 km) from N of Bombay to Cape Comorin, are the higher, rising to 8840 ft (2693 m). With the plentiful rain brought by the W winds, they have dense natural vegetation and are used for tea planting. The **Eastern Ghats** extend, with several breaks, about 880 mi (1400 km) from near Cuttack to the Nilgiri Hills.

Ghaznavids A Turkish dynasty that ruled in E Iran, Afghanistan, and N India (977–1186). The Ghaznavids created the first powerful Muslim state in India and prepared the way for the spread of Islam there. Founded by Sebuktigin (d. 997), a Turkish soldier, the dynasty's territories centered on Ghazna (Afghanistan) and reached its peak with *Mahmud of Ghazna. Following the battle of Dandanqan in 1040, the Ghaznavids lost their lands in Persia to the Seljuqs.

Ghazzah. *See* Gaza.

Ghegs One of the two major ethnic divisions of the Albanian people (*see also* Tosks). The Ghegs live N of the Shkumbi River and differ from the Tosks in dress and other customs.

Ghent (Flemish name: Gent; French name: Gand) 51 02N 3 42E A city in Belgium, at the confluence of the canalized Scheldt and Lys Rivers. One of Belgium's oldest cities, it has a university (1816) and a gothic cathedral. It is a major port and the textile center of the country; other economic activities include metallurgy, chemicals, and banking. Population (1981 est): 239,959.

gherkin A trailing West Indian vine, *Cucumis anguria*, with lobed leaves and small yellow flowers. It is cultivated for its prickly edible fruit, 0.98–3 in (2.5–7.5 cm) long, which is borne on a crooked stalk and used when immature for pickling. The "gherkins" sold in pickle mixtures are immature *cucumbers. Family: *Cucurbitaceae* (gourd family).

ghetto Any slum area occupied by an ethnic minority. Originally a ghetto was that quarter of a city to which Jews were restricted by law. Originating in Italy in the middle ages, ghettos were established during the *Counter-Reformation in many European cities. During the 19th century legal restrictions fell into disuse in W Europe and the communities became bound solely by customs and religion. However, in the 20th century ghettos were revived by the Nazis, for example in *Warsaw. In the US the term is applied to those areas of cities occupied by poor minorities.

Ghibellines. *See* Guelfs and Ghibellines.

Ghiberti, Lorenzo (c. 1378–1455) Florentine Renaissance sculptor. Ghiberti trained as a goldsmith and painter but made his name as a sculptor in 1402, when he won the competition for the bronze relief sculptures for the north doors of the Baptistry of the Florentine Duomo. Finished in 1424, these New Testament scenes, mainly in the *international gothic style, were followed by Old Testament scenes in the Gates of Paradise (1425–52), strongly influenced by antique sculpture. Simultaneously he wrote *I commentarii*, which included histories of ancient and early Renaissance art and an autobiography. His other works include three statues of saints (1416–25) for Orsanmichele.

Ghirlandaio, Domenico (Domenico di Tommaso Bigordi; 1449–94) Florentine painter of the early *Renaissance. From 1481 to 1482 he worked on a fresco in the Sistine Chapel but his major undertaking was the fresco cycle (1486–90) in Sta Maria Novella, Florence. These scenes from the life of the Virgin and St John the Baptist are notable for their portrayal of Florentine personalities in contemporary dress. The tenderly painted *Old Man and Boy* (Louvre) is a fine example of his portraiture.

ghost The disembodied spirit of a dead person, believed in many cultures to be capable of manifesting itself to the living. Ghosts are still venerated in tribal societies in Africa, Asia, and Polynesia (see ancestor worship). Certain feasts in the Roman calendar were devoted to their propitiation. The Roman Catholic doctrine of *purgatory fostered ghost beliefs by sanctioning the notion that the dead could request prayers from the living. Post-Reformation ghosts exhibited more secular interests, demanding revenge or restitution of such wrongs as misappropriated inheritances. Skepticism grew in the 18th century but the *gothic revival initiated a revival in ghost stories, now enjoyed purely for their spine-chilling qualities. In modern times, spirit communication has been the mainstay of *spiritualism and hauntings continue to be reported.

ghost shark. See chimaera.

Giacometti, Alberto (1901–66) Swiss sculptor and painter. Working chiefly in Paris after 1922, he was influenced initially by *cubism and primitive art and later by *surrealism, particularly in his abstract construction of sticks, glass, wire, etc., entitled *The Palace at 4 am* (New York). After breaking with surrealism in 1935, he developed a unique figure style, characterized by spindly elongated forms.

Giambologna (Giovanni da Bologna *or* Jean de Boulogne; 1529–1608) Italian mannerist sculptor of Flemish birth. Working from 1557 in Florence, where he was patronized by the Medici, he produced many fountains and religious sculptures in addition to small bronze statues. His works include *Samson and a Philistine* (1567; Victoria and Albert Museum).

Giant's Causeway 55 14N 6 32W A promontory in N Northern Ireland, in Antrim on the North Channel. It consists of several thousand closely packed basaltic columns, mainly hexagonal in shape, formed by an outpouring of lava into the sea. According to legend it was built as a bridge for the giants to cross between Ireland and Scotland.

giant star A large very luminous star lying above the main sequence on the *Hertzsprung-Russell diagram. See also red giant.

giant tortoise. See Galápagos giant tortoise.

giant water bug A large brown *water bug of the family *Belostomatidae* (up to 200 species), found in tropical and temperate regions. Giant water bugs, sometimes over 0.40 in (10 mm) long, are strong fliers and are often attracted to light. In some species, for example *Belostoma plumineum*, the female forcibly lays her eggs onto the back of the male, attaching them with a glue.

gibberellins A group of organic compounds that stimulate plant growth. First isolated from the fungus *Gibberella fujikuroi*, over 30 gibberellins are now known. When applied to plants they stimulate the growth of leaves, stems, flowers, and fruit and break the dormancy of seeds and tubers; hence their importance in horticulture and agriculture.

GIBBON *These apes are noted for their agility in trees. This individual* (Hylobates lar) *from Borneo manipulates a twig while clinging to a tree branch.*

gibbon A small *ape belonging to the genus *Hylobates* (7 species), of S Asia. 18–26 in (45–65 cm) long, they have long arms with slender hands and hooked fingers used to swing through trees. On the ground they walk upright or run on all fours. They live in family groups, feeding chiefly on fruit and leaves, and have a loud whooping call. Family: *Hylobatidae*. See also siamang.

Gibbon, Edward (1737–94) British historian. Sent to Europe by his father, he traveled in Switzerland and later (1764–65) in Italy. His ironic treatment of Christianity in his monumental *The History of the Decline and Fall of the Roman Empire* (1776–88) aroused contemporary controversy, but the work gained acceptance as successive volumes appeared. Its epic scope and dignity of style have ensured its survival.

Gibbons v. Ogden (1824) US Supreme Court decision that defined commerce as described in the Constitution. It permitted the federal judiciary to void any state law that interfered with interstate commerce. Aaron Ogden, licensed by New York state to operate steamboats in state waters, sought to prevent Thomas Gibbons from using the same waters for the same purpose. The court ruled that Gibbons had a right to use New York state waters and voided the New York commercial monopoly law.

Gibbs, Josiah Willard (1839–1903) US physicist, who was a professor at Yale University (1871–1903). Gibbs founded chemical thermodynamics, which is largely based on the function known as the Gibbs free energy. He is also known for his phase rule, relating the number of parameters that can be varied in a system of more than one phase. His papers were published between 1876 and 1878.

G. I. Bill (Servicemen's Readjustment Act of 1944). Legislation enacted to aid World War II veterans' reentry into civilian life. Job placement, educational expenses, unemployment pay, and home or business financing were made available. In 1945 and during the Korean War the benefits were expanded. The Readjustment Benefits Act of 1966 established benefits for all veterans.

Gibraltar A British crown colony occupying a tiny peninsula at the southern tip of Spain. The sandy isthmus that links it to the Spanish mainland rises sharply to the 1400 ft (427 m) limestock Rock of Gibraltar, which contains numerous caverns and galleries. The population is mainly of Spanish, Genoese, and Portugese descent. *Economy*: its strategic position makes it a naval and air base of great importance; British defense expenditure together with tourist earnings and fees for services to shipping form the basis of its economy. Tourist attractions include the colony's barbary apes, the only monkeys native to Europe. *History*: settled by the Moors in 711 AD, the Rock of Gibraltar was taken by Castile in 1462, becoming part of united Spain. It was captured in 1704 by the British to whom it was formally ceded by the Treaty of Utrecht (1713). The colony became an important British naval base. Claims to Gibraltar have long been made by Spain but a UN proposal to end British occupation was defeated in a referendum in 1967. In 1969 Spain closed its frontier with Gibraltar leading to a manpower shortage (as much of its workforce was domiciled over the border in Spain); the frontier was reopened in 1984. Official languages: English and Spanish. Official currency: Gibraltar pound of 100 pence. Area: 2.5 sq mi (6.5 sq km). Population (1980 est): 29,787.

Gibraltar, Strait of A strait between Europe (Spain and Gibraltar) and Africa (Morocco), joining the Atlantic Ocean and the Mediterranean Sea, of which it is the only outlet. It narrows to 8 mi (13 km) and is of great strategic importance.

Gibran, Khalil (1883–1931) Lebanese mystic and poet. He studied in Beirut and Paris and settled in New York in 1912. His major work in English is *The Prophet* (1923), a romantic blending of religion and philosophy.

Gibson, Althea (1927–) US tennis player. She was the first black to play in major tennis championships (1951) and to win major titles: Wimbledon singles (1957, 1958); United States singles (1957, 1958); and the women's doubles at Wimbledon (1956–58).

Gibson, Charles Dana (1867–1944) US artist and illustrator. Working in pen and ink, he did illustrations for magazines, including *Collier's Weekly*, and was the creator of the "Gibson Girl," the ideal woman of the turn of the century. He also illustrated books, among them *The Prisoner of Zenda*, and painted portraits in oils. His sketches were collected in *The Education of Mr. Pipp* (1899), *The Americans* (1900), *The Social Ladder* (1902), and *The Gibson Book* (1906).

Gibson Desert A desert in central Western Australia. It consists of a vast arid area of active sand dunes and desert grass. Area: 85,000 sq mi (220,000 sq km).

Gide, André (1869–1951) French novelist and critic. Much of his work is semiautobiographical and deals with the conflict between desire and discipline, reflecting his homosexuality and consequent conflict with conventional morality. His visits to North Africa from 1893 to 1896 gave him a sense of freedom, celebrated in *Fruits of the Earth* (1897). In 1895 he married his cousin Madeleine Rondeaux, the inspiration of two short works, *The Immoralist* (1902) and *Strait Is the Gate* (1909). In 1908 he was one of the founders of the important literary journal *La Nouvelle Revue française*. His longer novels are *The Vatican Cellars* (1914) and *The Counterfeiters* (1926). For a short time he was drawn to communism but soon became disillusioned. His *Journal*, which he kept from 1885 until his death, is a major work of literary autobiography. He won the Nobel Prize in 1947.

Gideon v. Wainwright (1963) US Supreme Court decision that guaranteed the right to an attorney for all persons charged with a serious crime. It instructed states to pay attorney's fees for those unable to afford the charges. Clarence Gideon had been tried and convicted by a Florida court without benefit of attorney, despite his request for a state-appointed attorney. The court overruled his conviction; he was retried and acquitted. This case imposed federal regulations on state proceedings.

Gielgud, Sir (Arthur) John (1904–   ) British actor. He is noted for his distinguished speaking voice and for his many fine performances in Shakespearean productions. His *Hamlet*, first performed in 1929, received especial acclaim. During the 1970s he also acted in plays by modern dramatists, such as Harold Pinter and Edward Bond, and in many films.

Gierek, Edward (1913–   ) Polish statesman, who succeeded *Gomulka as first secretary of the Polish United Workers' Party (1970–80). Born in Poland, he lived in France and Belgium from 1923 to 1948. A communist from 1931, he became a member of the politburo in 1956 and came to power following the demonstrations against food prices in 1970.

Giessen 50 35N 08 42E A city in central West Germany, in Hessen on the Lahn River. The university (1607) contains the chemist Liebig's laboratory. Its manufactures include rubber, machine tools, leather, and tobacco. Population (1971 est): 78,100.

Gifu 35 27N 136 46E A city in Japan, in central Honshu. It was *Nobunaga's headquarters in the 16th century. Manufactures include paper lanterns and textiles. Population (1980): 410,000.

Gigantes In Greek mythology, the giant sons of *Uranus (Heaven) and *Gaea (Earth), whose rebellion against the Olympian gods was defeated with the help of Heracles. They were subsequently associated with earthquakes and volcanoes.

Gigli, Beniamino (1890–1957) Italian tenor. He became a world-famous opera singer and was regarded as the successor to Caruso. Toscanini brought him to La Scala, Milan, in 1920, where he made his debut as Faust in Boito's *Mefistofele*. He gave his final concert in 1955.

Gijón 43 32N 5 40W A port in NW Spain, in Asturias on the Bay of Biscay. Its many ancient buildings include Roman baths and medieval palaces. It is an important manufacturing center with metallurgical and chemical industries. Population (1970): 187,612.

Gila monster A rare venomous lizard, *Heloderma suspectum*, occurring in the SW US and N Mexico. 20 in (50 cm) long, it has a stout black body with pink blotches and bands and small beadlike scales and feeds at night on eggs. It has a strong bite and grooved teeth that inject a nerve poison. Family: *Helodermatidae*.

gilbert (Gb) The unit of magnetomotive force in the *c.g.s. system equal to the magnetomotive force produced by a current of 40π amperes passing through a single coil. Named for— William *Gilbert.

Gilbert, Sir Humphrey (c. 1539–83) English navigator. Half-brother of Sir Walter *Raleigh, Gilbert had a notable career as a soldier in Ireland (1567–70, 1579) and the Netherlands (1572). His first attempt to reach North America was a failure (1578) but in 1583 he landed at St John's, Newfoundland, which he claimed for Elizabeth I. He was lost at sea on his return voyage.

Gilbert, William (1544–1603) English physicist and physician to Elizabeth I. One of the early adherents of the experimental method, his *De magnete* (1600) listed many experimental observations concerning magnets, including the discovery of magnetic dip. He suggested that the earth is a spherical magnet, that other magnets point toward its poles, and that the planets are held in their orbits by magnetic attraction. He was the first English scientist to accept the ideas of *Copernicus; he was also responsible for many new terms, including *electricity* and *magnetic pole*.

Gilbert, Sir William Schwenk (1836–1911) British comic dramatist. He wrote comic verses, published as *Bab Ballads* (1869), while studying law. In 1870 he met Arthur *Sullivan, the composer for whom he wrote the libretti for 14 popular operas. His plays written after Sullivan's death in 1900 were less successful.

Gilbert Islands. *See* Kiribati, Republic of.

Gilbert of Sempringham, St (c. 1083–1189) English priest, who founded the Gilbertines, the only indigenous religious order of medieval England, at Sempringham, Lincolnshire. It was composed of nuns, lay sisters and brothers, and canons. It was dissolved by Henry VIII. Feast day: Feb 4.

Gilded Age In the US, an era (1865–1900) marked by ostentatious materialism and governmental corruption. *The Gilded Age* (1873) by Mark *Twain (with Charles Dudley Warner; 1829–1900) described and named the period.

Gilgamesh An ancient Mesopotamian hero whose adventures are related in the collection of fragmentary texts known as the *Epic of Gilgamesh*. These are inscribed on 12 tablets discovered in the library of the Assyrian king Ashurbanipal (reigned 669–626 BC), at Nineveh. They relate how Gilgamesh defeats and then befriends the savage man Enkidu, rejects the love goddess *Ishtar, journeys to consult an immortal wise man, Utnapishtim, about the secret of eternal life, and gains and then loses the plant of immortality.

Gillespie, Dizzy (John Birks G.; 1917–   ) US jazz trumpeter, band leader, and composer, who was one of the originators of *bop. Gillespie played with many different bands in the 1930s and 1940s before forming his own band in 1945. In later years Gillespie incorporated singing and comedy into his performances. His recordings include *Groovin' High* and *Hot vs Cool*; in 1980 he published his autobiographical *To Be or Not to Bop*.

Gillingham 51 24N 0 33E A city in SE England, in Kent on the Medway estuary. The largest of the Medway towns, it has extensive dockyards at Chatham and various light industries. Locally fruit growing is important. Population (1981): 93,741.

gills The respiratory organs of aquatic animals: specialized thin-walled regions of the body surface through which dissolved oxygen is taken into the blood and carbon dioxide released into the water. The gills of fish lie in gill slits on each side of the gullet. Each gill consists of many leaflike gill filaments, which provide a large surface area over which water is pumped. The gills of mollusks (such as the mussel) and fanworms are ciliated and trap food particles in the respiratory currents. The external gills of amphibian larvae (tadpoles) are feathery structures projecting from the body wall.

gillyflower (*or* gilliflower) A name given to various clove-scented flowers, originally applied to plants of the pink family (*Caryophyllaceae*), such as the carnation.

gin A *spirit distilled usually from grain flavored with juniper berries (the name is derived from the Dutch *jenever*, juniper). Gin, with little flavor, is generally drunk with tonic water, *vermouth, fruit juice, etc. Martini cocktails are a mixture of gin and dry vermouth served very cold, sometimes with ice. Dry or London Dry gin is the gin most frequently used for mixed drinks. Sloe gin takes its flavor from the fruit of the blackthorn tree, or sloe berries.

ginger A perennial herbaceous plant, *Zingiber officinale*, native to SE Asia and widely grown in the tropics for its pungent underground stems (rhizomes), used as a spice, food, and flavoring and in medicine. Its leafy stems grow about 40 in (1 m) high; the leaves are 6–12 in (15–30 cm) long and the flowers grow in dense conelike spikes. The plants are sterile, and propagation is by cuttings from the rootstocks. Family: *Zingiberaceae*.

gingivitis Inflammation of the gums. It may be caused by ill-fitting dentures or by infection in debilitated people or those taking antibiotics.

ginkgo A deciduous *gymnosperm tree, *Ginkgo biloba*, also called maidenhair tree, that is the sole living representative of a group of trees that flourished in the Carboniferous period (370–280 million years ago). Growing to a height of 98 ft (30 m), it has lobed fan-shaped leaves, 5 × 4 in (12 × 10 cm), which are pale green and turn yellow in the fall, and fleshy plumlike yellow fruits containing edible kernels. The ginkgo is native to China and widely planted for ornament. Family: *Ginkgoaceae*.

Ginsberg, Allen (1926–   ) US poet. His first book, *Howl* (1956), a rambling attack on contemporary America, was a popular work of the *Beat movement. In the 1960s he traveled in Asia, India, and South America. His later work, in *The Change* (1963), *The Fall of America* (1973), and other books, is fragmentary and rhapsodic.

ginseng An extract of the forked roots of either of two herbs, *Panax quinquefolium* or *P. schinseng*, used as a stimulant drug in the Far East and to make aromatic bitters. It is said to have aphrodisiac and life-prolonging properties. *P. quinquefolium* is grown commercially in North America; *P. schinseng* in Korea and Japan. Family: *Araliaceae* (ivy family).

Giordano, Luca (1632–1705) Neapolitan painter, nicknamed Luca fa presto (Luca works quickly). His enormous output of religious and mythological paintings, at first influenced by *Ribera but later by Venetian art, includes ceiling frescoes in the ballroom of the Palazzo Medici-Riccardi, Florence, and in El Escorial, Spain, where he was court painter (1692–1702).

Giorgione (c. 1477–1510) Italian painter of the Venetian school, born in Castelfranco. He trained under Giovanni *Bellini and worked with *Titian, whom he influenced, on frescoes for the façade of the German Exchange in Venice (1508). Most of his paintings are small-scale secular pictures of a type previously unknown. Their subject matter is often inexplicable, particularly in the *Tempest* (Accademia, Venice), notable for its atmospheric landscape. *The Sleeping Venus* (Gemäldegalerie, Dresden), completed by Titian, and *The Three Philosophers* (Kunsthistorisches Museum, Vienna) show the romantic and dreamlike mood of his paintings. His portraits, e.g. *Laura* (Vienna), influenced many Venetian painters. He probably died of the plague.

Giotto (Giotto di Bondone; c. 1266–1337) Italian painter and architect, who laid the foundation for *Renaissance painting. He was born in Vespignano, near Florence, and was probably the pupil of *Cimabue. The fresco cycle of St Francis, in the upper church of S Francesco, Assisi, is thought to be an early work. Certainly by his hand are the innovative frescoes of scenes from the lives of Joachim and Anne and the Virgin and Christ in the Arena Chapel, Padua. He also painted frescoes in Sta Croce, Florence. In 1334 he became architect of the city and surveyor of Florence Cathedral, for which he designed the campanile.

Gir A breed of *zebu cattle originating from the Gir forest of W India. They have characteristic domed foreheads with backward-curving horns and long ears and are yellowish red to black in color. Traditionally a dairy breed, they are also used for draft purposes.

giraffe A hoofed *mammal, *Giraffa camelopardalis*, of tropical African grasslands. Measuring 10 ft (3 m) at the shoulder, with a neck 8 ft (2.5 m) long, giraffes are marked with a patchwork of reddish-brown blotches on a buff-colored background. They feed on leaves, using their long necks and prehensile lips and tongues. Both sexes have permanent skin-covered horns. Giraffes live in small groups led by a mature male and can go for long periods without drinking. They usually sleep standing up. Family: *Giraffidae*.

Giraudoux, Jean (1882–1944) French dramatist, novelist, and diplomat (from 1910 to 1940). His early literary reputation was established by a series of poetic novels, including *Elpénor* (1919) and *Suzanne et le Pacifique* (1921). His stylized plays, often blending elements of tragedy, comedy, and fantasy, include *Amphitryon 38* (1929), *Tiger at the Gates* (1935), *Ondine* (1939), and *The Madwoman of Chaillot* (1949).

Girl Scouts. See Scouting.

giro A low-cost system for transferring money. It originated in Austria in 1883 and the British National Giro was set up by the Post Office in 1968. All accounts are held at the Giro Center (in Bootle, Lancashire), which transfers money from one account to another on receipt of a completed form. Bank giro operates similarly, but accounts are held at bank branches.

Gironde River A wide estuary in SW France, on the Bay of Biscay. Formed by the confluence of the Garonne and Dordogne Rivers near Bordeaux, it is used by oceangoing vessels. Length: 45 mi (72 km).

Girondins A French Revolutionary political group. Named from the Gironde, where their support was strong, the Girondins were moderate republicans. They became prominent in the newly formed Legislative Assembly (1791), where, suspicious of counter-revolution and seeking to unite the Revolution's supporters, they involved France in war against Austria and Prussia. Military failure undermined their influence and, after the overthrow of the monarchy, they were themselves ousted by the more radical *Jacobins (1793). Many Girondins were subsequently executed.

Girtin, Thomas (1775–1802) British landscape painter, famous for being among the first to perfect watercolor technique. His use of broad transparent washes without the old monochrome underpainting produced heightened atmospheric effects, as in *White House at Chelsea*.

Giscard d'Estaing, Valéry (1926–) French statesman; president (1974–81). He was minister of finance and economic affairs from 1962 until 1966, when he established the Independent Republican Party. He returned to this post (1969) under Pompidou, whom he succeeded as president. In the 1981 presidential elections he was defeated by Mitterand. His attempts at liberal reform were thwarted by his party's dependence on Gaullist support.

VALÉRY GISCARD D'ESTAING *With the German chancellor Schmidt at the meeting of EEC heads of state in Ireland (1979).*

Gish, Lillian (1899–) US actress, who began her career as a child actress on stage with her sister **Dorothy Gish** (1898–1968). Both acted for the director D. W. *Griffith in several early silent films, including *The Birth of a Nation* (1915) and *Intolerance* (1916), and subsequently worked in both films and the theater. The later films of Lillian Gish include *Duel in the Sun* (1946) and *The Night of the Hunter* (1955).

Gislebertus (early 12th century) French *romanesque sculptor. Probably trained in the workshop associated with the Abbey of Cluny, Gislebertus developed an original and powerfully expressive style. His best-known sculptures are those around the west doorway and on the capitals of columns at the Cathedral of St Lazarus, Autun (c. 1125–35).

gittern An early type of guitar with four gut strings, played with a plectrum. It is known to have been a popular instrument for accompanying the voice at various periods between the 13th and 17th centuries but it lost favor after the Restoration.

Giulio Romano (Giulio Pippi; c. 1499–1546) Italian mannerist painter and architect, born in Rome (see mannerism). He was the pupil of *Raphael, whom he assisted in the decoration of the Vatican apartments and the Villa Farnesina. After Raphael's death, Giulio completed some of his works. In 1524 he settled in Mantua, where he designed and decorated the Palazzo del Tè, notable for its Room of the Giants, completely covered with illusionistic frescoes.

Giza, El (*or* al-Jizah) 30 01N 31 12E A city in N Egypt, forming a suburb of Cairo on the Nile River. Nearby are the great pyramids of *Khafre, *Khufu, and Menkaure, one of the Seven Wonders of the World, and the Sphinx. Tourism is important and it has textile and film industries. Population (1976): 1,247,000.

Glace Bay 46 11N 59 58W A city in E Canada, on the coast of *Cape Breton Island. Located over coal seams that have been mined since 1858, it is now chiefly a fishing center. From here Marconi sent his first wireless message (1902). Population (1976): 21,836.

glacier A mass of ice and *firn of limited width lying chiefly, or completely, on land and moving downslope from its source. Different glacier forms exist; **cirque glaciers** are contained in depressions on mountain slopes or valley heads. **Valley glaciers** are contained within pre-existing valleys and are frequently tongue-shaped in plan, originating either from cirque glaciers as an alpine type or from an icesheet as an outlet type. The longest of these is the Lambert Glacier, 250 mi (400 km) long. Where a glacier emerges from a valley onto a lowland area, a lobe-shaped **piedmont glacier** results; an example is the Malaspina Glacier in Alaska (US). **Glaciation** is the action of glacier ice on the land surface. The most recent period of extensive glaciation took place during the Pleistocene epoch, when about 30% of the world's surface area was ice covered. The main landforms resulting from glaciation are either erosional or depositional. Erosional features include the formation of U-shaped valleys and *cirques. Those of depositional origin include glacial *drift and *till. When water is also involved in the formation of glacial landforms the term fluvioglacial is used; fluvioglacial deposits include *eskers and *kames.

Glacier National Park A national park (1911) in the E Rocky Mountains in NE Montana that joins Waterton Lakes National Park in Canada to form Waterton-Glacier International Peace Park (1932). The Continental Divide runs through the park; the highest point is Mt Cleveland (10,448 ft; 3185 m). Area: 1583 sq mi (4100 sq km).

gladiators The slaves, prisoners of war, condemned criminals, or volunteers who fought in amphitheaters for the entertainment of the ancient Roman people. Gladiatorial combats began as a feature of funeral games but their popularity was soon so great that statesmen sponsored shows to enhance their political prestige. Pairs of gladiators would fight to the death unless the audience spared the loser. Several Roman writers condemned gladiatorial shows.

Gladiolus A genus of ornamental perennial herbaceous plants (300 species), native to Europe, Africa, and the Mediterranean regions and widely cultivated. Growing from a corm, the flowering stem reaches a height of 4 ft (1.2 m), with funnel-shaped flowers, usually red, yellow, orange, or white, grouped on one side. The leaves are sword-shaped. Gladioli cultivated for cut flowers have been developed mainly from South and East African species. Principal garden forms are *G. cardinalis, G. primulinus, G. psittacinus, G. purpurea-auratus,* and *G. saundersii.* Family: *Iridaceae.*

W. E. GLADSTONE *The British prime minister summoned all his powers of oratory to convince the House of Commons of the need for Irish Home Rule, but his bill was rejected (1886).*

Gladstone, W(illiam) E(wart) (1809–98) British statesman; Liberal prime minister (1868–74, 1880–85, 1886, 1892–94). Elected to parliament in 1832, he was initially a Tory. He supported the repeal of the *Corn Laws, which split the Tories, with some joining the Whigs (shortly to be termed Liberals). As chancellor of the exchequer (1852–55, 1859–66) Gladstone introduced a series of budgets that reduced tariffs and government expenditure. In 1867 he became leader of the Liberal Party. His first ministry disestablished the Irish Church (1869) and introduced the *Education Act (1870), the first Irish *Land Act (1870), and the Ballot Act (introducing secret ballots). Defeated in the 1874 election, he resigned the Liberal leadership. He again became member of Parliament and prime minister in 1880. His second ministry achieved a second Irish Land Act (1881) and further parliamentary reform (1884) but its failure to save *Gordon from Khartoum led to Gladstone's resignation. His last ministries followed his conversion to Irish *Home Rule.

An impressive speaker, Gladstone with his Conservative opponent Disraeli dominated British politics in the second half of the 19th century.

Glamis 56 37N 3 01W A village in E Scotland. Macbeth was thane of Glamis. Nearby Glamis Castle was the childhood home of Queen Elizabeth the Queen Mother and birthplace of Princess Margaret.

gland An organ or group of cells that is specialized for synthesizing a specific chemical substance (secretion) from constituents of the blood and releasing its secretion for use by the body. Man and higher animals have two kinds of glands. The *endocrine glands lack ducts and release their secretions (which are hormones) directly into the bloodstream. The exocrine glands have ducts through which their products are secreted. Exocrine glands include the salivary glands, the sweat and sebaceous glands in the skin, and the pancreatic cells that secrete digestive enzymes.

Plants also have glands, which secrete a variety of products including latex, resin, nectar, and tannin.

glanders A highly contagious disease of horses, donkeys, and related animals caused by the bacterium *Pfeifferella mallei,* which can also infect other animals and man. Onset of symptoms can occur several months after infection and include the formation of nodules in the lungs, liver, spleen, etc., ulceration of the mucous membranes, enlarged lymph nodes, nasal discharge, and pus-filled blisters. The disease is usually chronic. There is no known cure and slaughter of infected animals is compulsory in most countries.

Glanville, Ranulf de (d. 1190) English jurist; chief minister (1180–89) under Henry II. He assisted Henry with his extensive legal reforms and reputedly wrote the *Tractatus de legibus et consuetudinibus regni Angliae,* the earliest treatise on English common law. He died at the siege of Acre during the third Crusade.

Glaser, Donald Arthur (1926–) US physicist, who was awarded the 1960 Nobel Prize for his invention of the *bubble chamber (1952), an instrument that makes visible the tracks of ionizing particles. His first bubble chamber measured only 6 in (15 cm) across and contained ether.

Glasgow 55 53N 4 15W The largest city in Scotland, the administrative center of Strathclyde Region on the River Clyde. The third largest city in the UK, it is Scotland's chief commercial and industrial center. An important port with a tradition of shipbuilding, Glasgow also has major engineering, textile, chemical, brewing, and whisky-blending industries. *History:* of early religious and educational importance (St Mungo's cathedral dates from the 12th century and the university was founded in 1451), Glasgow's wealth grew rapidly through trade after the union with England (1707), especially in tobacco and sugar from the New World, and through industry in the industrial revolution, having coal and iron ore nearby. Population (1981): 762,288.

glass A translucent and usually transparent noncrystalline substance that behaves as a solid although it has many of the properties of a liquid. Glass itself was known in the 3rd millennium BC and glass objects survive from Egypt's 18th dynasty (1570–1320 BC), but glassblowing was not invented until about 100 BC (in Syria) and windows, which were originally made of blown glass, were not in use until about 100 AD. Ordinary soda glass, used for windows, etc., consists of silica (sand), sodium carbonate, and calcium carbonate (limestone). Flint glass, used for crystal glassware, contains silica, potassium carbonate, potassium nitrate, and lead oxide. Heat-resistant glass also contains borates and alumina; optical glass contains additional elements to control the refractive index and other optical properties, homogeneity being obtained by repeated heating and slow cooling.

Blown glass is melted and blown inside a mold until it fills the mold; bottles and lightbulbs are made in this way by a fully automatic process. Flint glass is also blown to make glassware, but this is usually done by hand. Pressed glass, to make domestic bowls and headlight lenses, is made by pressing the molten glass into a mold. Plate glass, for windows, etc., was formerly made by pouring molten glass onto a flat table and rolling it through heated rollers into sheets, which were then polished. The last stage has now been replaced by floating the rolled sheet of glass on molten tin. This float-glass process was introduced in 1959. *See also* fiberglass; stained glass.

glasses Lenses worn in frames in front of the eyes to correct defective vision. Convex lenses bend parallel light rays inward; they are used by those unable to focus on close objects (*see* farsightedness). Concave lenses have the opposite effect and are used by those unable to focus on distant objects (*see* nearsightedness). *Astigmatism is treated by wearing lenses that produce a compensating distortion of the light rays. Bifocal glasses have convex lenses consisting of upper and lower parts of different curvatures, for focusing on distant and near objects, respectively: they are worn for presbyopia. *See also* contact lenses.

glassfish A fish of the family *Centropomidae* (about 24 species), especially the genus *Chanda,* having a transparent body and a cleft dorsal fin. Glassfish occur along coastlines, in estuaries, and in fresh waters from Africa to the Indian and Pacific regions. Order: *Perciformes.*

glass harmonica. *See* harmonica.

glass snake A legless lizard belonging to the genus *Ophisaurus*, occurring in Europe, S and E Asia, N Africa, and North America. Glass snakes live in loose soil and feed on insects, lizards, mice, and birds' eggs. Unlike true snakes, they have ears, eyelids, and rigid jaws. When attacked, they shed their tail, which breaks into several pieces. Family: *Anguidae*.

glasswort (or marsh samphire) An annual or perennial plant of the genus *Salicornia* (at least 7 species), native to European salt marshes, with jointed green succulent stems that turn red or purple in autumn. The fleshy leaves sheath the stem closely and the flowers are inconspicuous. It was once used in glassmaking as a source of soda. Family: *Chenopodiaceae*.

Glastonbury 51 09N 2 43W A market town in SW England, in Somerset. Here by tradition Joseph of Arimathea founded England's first Christian church; Glastonbury is also the reputed burial place of King Arthur. There are the ruins of an early Benedictine abbey and the site of an excavated iron age lake village. Population (1981): 6773.

glaucoma An eye disease caused by raised pressure inside the eye. Acute glaucoma is often caused by a sudden block to the drainage of the watery fluid (aqueous humor) inside the eye. It leads to pain and disturbed vision, which will result in blindness without urgent treatment. Chronic glaucoma—one of the commonest causes of blindness—comes on slowly and painlessly.

Glazunov, Aleksandr Konstantinovich (1865–1936) Russian composer and pupil of Rimsky-Korsakov. He became director of the St Petersburg conservatory in 1906 but left Russia in 1928 and died in Paris. Glazunov's works, which were influenced by Wagner and Liszt rather than by Russian musical nationalism, included eight symphonies, concertos, ballets, and string quartets.

Gleiwitz. *See* Gliwice.

Glendale 34 10N 118 17W A city N of Los Angeles in SW California. It was part of the first Spanish land grant, Rancho de San Rafael (1798) in California and became a town in 1887. It is largely residential, but there are airplane parts, machines, and home furnishings industries. Population (1980): 139,060.

Glendower, Owen (Welsh name: Owain Glyndwr; c. 1359–c. 1416) Welsh rebel. He led a Welsh rising that became a national war of independence. Allying with Henry IV's opponents, Glendower controlled most of Wales by 1404 but was subsequently defeated and turned to guerrilla warfare. He disappeared in 1416.

Glenn, John (Herschel), Jr (1921–) US astronaut, the first from the US to orbit earth (1962), and senator. A pilot in the Marine Corps (1943–65), he served in World War II and Korea and was later a test pilot. As an astronaut (1959–64) he made three orbits of earth aboard *Friendship 7* on February 20, 1962. He served in the US Senate as a Democrat from Ohio (1975–). He was also an unsuccessful contender for the Democratic presidential nomination (1984).

gliders Light fixed-wing engineless aircraft, sometimes called sailplanes. They are launched into the air by a winch or catapult or by being towed by a car or powered aircraft. Once airborne a glider slowly loses height unless it is lifted by a rising air current created by warm air rising from the ground (a thermal), a ground contour, or a thunderstorm. These air currents enable a skilful pilot to remain airborne for several hours and to travel hundreds of miles.

Pioneered by Otto *Lilienthal in the US, gliders were used by the *Wright brothers in designing their powered aircraft. Gliders towed by aircraft were used in World War II to carry men and equipment. Since the 1920s gliding has been a popular sport and pastime in many countries. *See also* hang-gliding.

Glinka, Mikhail Ivanovich (1804–57) Russian composer. He studied with John Field, made many journeys abroad, and is regarded as the founder of Russian musical nationalism. He composed the first truly Russian opera *Ivan Susanin* (*A Life for the Tsar*; 1836), various works in a Spanish style, piano music, songs, and a second opera *Russlan and Ludmilla* (1842), influenced by oriental music.

Gliwice (German name: Gleiwitz) 50 20N 18 40E A city in S Poland. It is a heavy-industry center within Upper Silesia; industries include coalmining, steel processing, chemicals, and food processing. Population (1976 est): 199,200.

globe artichoke. *See* artichoke.

globefish. *See* puffer.

globeflower A herbaceous plant of the genus *Trollius* (about 15 species), found throughout Europe. It has lobed toothed leaves and solitary many-petaled globe-shaped flowers, yellow or orange, borne on stems 4–26 in (10–70 cm) high. Family: *Ranunculaceae*.

Globe Theatre An Elizabethan theater, in Southwark, England, in which most of Shakespeare's plays were first produced. A cylindrical wooden building open to the sky, it was built in 1598, burned down in 1613, rebuilt in 1614, and finally demolished in 1644.

globe thistle A stout perennial *thistle of the genus *Echinops* (about 15 species), of central and S Europe. 20–79 in (50–200 cm) high, it has lobed leaves, often white and woolly beneath, and large spherical flower heads, usually blue and sometimes woolly. Globe thistles are often planted in gardens.

Globigerina A genus of protozoan animals that are common components of marine plankton. Ranging in size from 0.01–0.08 in (0.3 to 2 mm), their chalky skeletons are a major constituent of the gray mud on some sea beds, forming globigerina ooze. Order: *Foraminifera*.

globular cluster. *See* star cluster.

globulin A type of protein that is generally insoluble in water. Serum (gamma) globulins of the blood include the immunoglobulins (antibodies), which are manufactured by the animal to combat infections. Newborn mammals receive these immunoglobulins in maternal milk. Other globulins occur in eggs, nuts, and seeds.

glockenspiel (German: bell play) A tuned percussion instrument having a keyboard-like arrangement of steel bars played with two small hammers. The notes of its two-and-a-half-octave compass above bottom G of the bass stave sound two octaves higher.

Glomma River (Norwegian name: Glåma) A river in SE Norway and the longest river in Scandinavia. Flowing S from a small lake SE of Trondheim, it enters the Skagerrak at Fredrikstad. It is important for hydroelectric power and for transporting timber. Length: 365 mi (588 km).

Glorious Revolution (1688) The overthrow of James II of England and the establishment of his sister Mary and her husband William of Orange on the throne. The opposition to James' pro-Catholic and absolutist policies invited William and Mary to take the throne and James, offering no resistance, fled to France. As William III and Mary II, the joint monarchs accepted the *Bill of Rights, which established constitutional monarchy in England.

glory pea. *See* Clianthus.

glottis. *See* larynx.

Gloucester 51 53N 2 14W A market city in W England, the administrative center of Gloucestershire on the River Severn. First developed under the Romans (Glevum) in the 1st century AD, its principal building is its cathedral, noted for its inventions in the Perpendicular style. Gloucester has engineering (aircraft components, agricultural machinery) and matchmaking industries. Population (1981): 92,133.

Gloucester 42 41N 70 39W A town in NE Massachusetts, on S Cape Ann, NE of Boston. Settled in 1623 and historically a fishing town, it is a well known resort area and fish processing center. Population (1980): 27,768.

Gloucestershire A county of W England, bordering Wales. It consists of three distinct regions: the Cotswold Hills, the Severn Valley, and the Forest of Dean. It is predominantly agricultural; wheat and barley are the chief arable crops and dairy farming is increasing in importance. Industry includes engineering and timber production. Coal is mined in the Forest of Dean. Area: 1019 sq mi (2638 sq km). Population (1981): 499,351. Administrative center: Gloucester.

glowworm. *See* firefly.

gloxinia An ornamental herb, *Sinningia speciosa*, native to Brazil. Gloxinias have rosettes of large simple velvety leaves and large bell-shaped velvety flowers, usually violet, purple, or pink. New plants can regenerate from the base of the leafstalks. There are many hybrids, which are popular house plants. Family: *Gesneriaceae*.

The genus *Gloxinia* (6 species) of the same family is not cultivated.

Glozel An archeological site SE of Vichy (central France). During the 1920s finds here included engraved pebbles and clay tablets with an alphabetic script. An international commission investigated the site (1927) and cast grave doubts on its authenticity. Scientific dating of Glozel artifacts in the 1970s revived the puzzle, as some objects are undoubtedly ancient.

glucagon A polypeptide hormone, produced by the islets of Langerhans in the *pancreas, that increases the level of glucose in the blood by stimulating the breakdown of *glycogen in body tissues and promoting the utilization of protein and fat as energy sources. At high levels in the blood glucagon stimulates the secretion of *insulin.

Gluck, Christoph Willibald (1714–87) German composer. He reformed *opera seria, making it less artificial. Inspired by Calzabigi's librettos, he composed the operas *Orfeo ed Euridice* (1762) and *Alceste* (1767) in which the music reflected the dramatic situation and merely musical repetition and vocal ornamentation were excluded. He composed over 40 dramatic works as well as other music.

glucose (*or* dextrose) A simple sugar ($C_6H_{12}O_6$) and an essential substance in the carbohydrate metabolism of living organisms. Carbohydrates (such as starch and glycogen) in food or tissue reserves are broken down to glucose, which is easily transported to cells where it undergoes *glycolysis to provide energy for the cell. Organisms can also manufacture glucose from fats and proteins. Glucose levels in blood are regulated by the hormones *insulin and *glucagon and small amounts of glucose are normally present in urine. Fruits and honey are good sources of glucose.

gluten A protein mixture derived from wheat. In bread making, dough rises because the gluten in wheat flour expands, trapping the carbon dioxide bubbles in an elastic network. The properties of gluten vary according to the mixture of the proteins, chiefly gliadin and glutenin. *See also* celiac disease.

glutton. *See* wolverine.

glycerol (*or* glycerine; $CH_2OHCHOHCH_2OH$) A colorless syrupy liquid with a sweet taste. It is made from fats and oils or by fermentation and is used in explosives, cosmetics, and antifreeze solutions.

glycogen A starchlike carbohydrate found in animal tissues as a reserve energy source. Chemically, it consists of branched chains of *glucose molecules: when required to provide energy, glycogen is broken down to glucose under the influence of hormones, chiefly *adrenaline and *glucagon.

glycolysis The sequence of chemical reactions occurring in most living cells by which glucose is partially broken down to provide usable energy for the cell in the form of *ATP. Glycolysis can take place in the presence or absence of oxygen but only a small amount of the available energy is released, the major proportion being released via the *Krebs cycle.

Glyndebourne An estate near Lewes, England, home of an annual international festival of opera. The opera house was built on the estate by its owner, John Christie, who founded the Glyndebourne Festival in 1934 for his wife, the opera singer Audrey Mildmay (1900–53).

Glyptodon An extinct giant *armadillo, whose remains have been found in South America. Glyptodons had a rigid bony shell (unlike the jointed modern armadillo shell) and some had a spiky macelike knob at the end of the tail. They became extinct about 100,000 years ago.

GMT. *See* Greenwich Mean Time.

gnat Any of the smaller delicate species of two-winged flies, the males of which fly in dancing swarms. The term is applied to the less virulent mosquitoes and phantom gnats (family *Culicidae*), winter gnats (family *Trichoceridae*), fungus gnats (family *Mycetophilidae*), craneflies (family *Tipulidae*), and several others.

gnatcatcher A small active songbird belonging to a family (*Polioptilidae*; 11 species) ranging from S Canada to Argentina. 4–5.5 in (10–14 cm) long, gnatcatchers have long wagging tails and fine pointed bills used to pick insects from leaves and crevices. The plumage is typically grayish blue above with lighter underparts and white outer tail feathers.

Gneisenau, August (Wilhelm Anton), Graf Neithardt von (1760–1831) Prussian field marshal, who was instrumental in effecting major reforms in the Prussian army following its defeat by Napoleon (1807). He subsequently played an important part in the wars of liberation (1813–14) and in the defeat of Napoleon at Waterloo (1815).

gneiss A coarse-grained metamorphic rock consisting predominantly of bands of quartz and feldspar alternating with bands of micas and amphiboles. These bands are often irregular or poorly defined. Gneisses are formed during regional metamorphism; those derived from igneous rocks are termed **orthogneiss**, those from sedimentary rocks **paragneiss**.

Gniezno 52 32N 17 32E A city in W central Poland. One of the oldest cities in Poland, it contains many notable historical buildings, including its 10th-century cathedral. It is a commercial center specializing in food processing. Population (1970 est): 50,600.

Gnosticism A religious movement that flourished in the early Christian era. It manifested itself in many ways and contained many elements of pagan thought and magic, but is most fully recorded as a group of heretical Christian sects, attacked by Church Fathers, such as *Tertullian. The Gnostics' defining characteristic was their belief in *gnosis* (Greek: knowl-

edge)—a special revelation from God to initiates, which would ensure their salvation (*compare* mysteries). Their world view was dualistic: God and the spirit were good and matter evil. They interpreted Christ (whose humanity they denied) as being sent to rescue particles of spirit (souls) entrapped in matter. Gnosticism influenced *Manichaeism and several medieval heresies. *See also* Mandaeanism.

GNP. *See* gross national product.

gnu A large ungainly antelope belonging to the genus *Connochaetes* (2 species), also called wildebeest, of African plains. The brindled gnu (*C. taurinus*) grows to 55 in (140 cm) high at the shoulder and is blue-gray with a long black mane, black facial tufts, and a black-tufted tail. The smaller white-tailed gnu (*C. gnou*) has a long white tail and is very rare, surviving only in game reserves.

go (*or* i-go) A board game that originated in China (as *Wei-ch'i*), possibly in the 3rd millennium BC, and is especially popular in Japan. The board is marked with a grid of 19 vertical and 19 horizontal lines, making 361 intersections. There are 361 counters: 181 black "stones" for one player and 180 white for the other. Black begins by placing a stone on any intersection of the empty board. Play alternates, one stone being placed at a time; once played a stone may not be moved except to remove it from the board. The object is to conquer territory by enclosing empty points with one's own stones. Opposing stones that are encircled are captured and removed. The score is calculated by deducting the number of stones a player has lost from the number of intersections he has captured.

Goa A district on the W coast of India, part of Goa, Daman, and Diu Union Territory. A Portuguese overseas territory from 1510 until annexed by India in 1961, it has many fine examples of Portuguese colonial architecture, including the church in which St Francis Xavier is buried. Area: 1363 sq mi (3496 sq km).

Goa, Daman, and Diu A Union Territory of W India. Goa is on the central W coast; Daman lies inland N of Bombay; Diu is an island off the coast of Gujarat. Formerly Portuguese, they depend economically on agriculture, fishing, and tourism. Area: 1472 sq mi (3813 sq km). Population (1981): 1,082,117. Capital: Panaji.

goat A hoofed *ruminant mammal belonging to the genus *Capra* (5 species). Related to sheep, goats are 24–33 in (60–85 cm) tall at the shoulder and have hollow horns, less curled than those of sheep; males have a scent gland beneath the tail and a beard. Wild goats, found in mountainous regions of Eurasia, are grayish in winter, reddish in summer, and live in herds of 5–20 individuals. Goats were first domesticated over 10,000 years ago and are still used to provide milk, meat, and hides in many semiarid regions of the world. Family: *Bovidae*. *See also* ibex; markhor; Rocky Mountain goat; tahr.

goat moth A large moth, *Cossus cossus*, of Europe, Asia, and N Africa. Mottled gray and brown, it has a wingspan of 3 in (70 mm). The reddish caterpillar bores under the bark of trees and emits a characteristic strong odor. It may hibernate for up to four years.

goatsbeard A perennial herb, *Aruncus dioicus* (or *A. sylvestris*), native to N temperate wooded regions, especially Siberia. Often grown as a border plant, goatsbeard is 47–71 in (120–180 cm) tall and has fine compound leaves and branched plumes of small stalkless hay-scented creamy-white flowers. Family: *Rosaceae*.

Gobbi, Tito (1915–84) Italian baritone. He sang in all the world's major opera houses and was a well-known teacher. His most famous parts included the title roles in Mozart's *Don Giovanni* and Verdi's *Falstaff* and Scarpia in Puccini's *Tosca*. He also produced opera.

Gobelins, Manufacture nationale des A French state-controlled tapestry factory, founded in Paris as a dyeworks in the 15th century by Jean and Philibert Gobelin. Manufacturing tapestries from 1529, it was incorporated by Henry IV in 1607. In 1662 Louis XIV purchased it and it was directed from 1663 to 1690 by his First Painter Charles *Le Brun. Since 1826 carpets have also been made here.

Gobi Desert A vast desert of SE Mongolia and N China, one of the largest in the world. On a plateau 2950–4920 ft (900–1500 m) high, it is largely rocky with salt marshes and streams that disappear into the sand. It is rich in prehistoric remains including fossils and stone implements. Area: about 500,000 sq mi (1,295,000 sq km).

Gobind Singh (*or* Govind S.; 1666–1708) The tenth and last Guru of the Sikhs (1675–1708). As a religious reformer he remodeled the Sikh religious belief and practice and renounced social inequality and caste distinctions. He was assassinated by a Muslim.

Gobineau, Joseph Arthur, Comte de (1816–82) French writer and diplomat. He wrote novels, notably *Les Pléiades* (1874), short stories, and scholarly studies, including *La Renaissance* (1877). His influential *Essai sur l'inégalité des races humaines* (1853–55) argued that the continuing strength of the Aryan race depended on its racial purity.

goblin shark A carnivorous *shark, *Scapanorhynchus owstoni*. Up to 14 ft (4.2 m) long, it has long upper teeth that overlap the lower set, a long paddle-shaped nose, and a very long tail fin. It has been found in deep water off Japan, India, and Portugal and is probably the only member of its family, *Scapanorhynchidae*.

goby A fish of the suborder *Gobioidei* (over 800 species), especially the family *Gobiidae* (true gobies). True gobies have smooth elongated bodies, two dorsal fins, and a suction disk formed from fused pelvic fins. Most are 2–4 in (5–10 cm) long, although *Pandaka pygmaea* of the Philippines is the smallest known vertebrate at under 0.51 in (13 mm) long. They are chiefly marine and inhabit sand or mud burrows in tropical coastal regions, sometimes in association with other animals. Order: *Perciformes*.

God The supreme being that is the creator and ruler of the universe. The concept of God perhaps originated in primitive animistic belief, which attributed souls to natural objects and phenomena. It may then have developed into *polytheism, as in India and ancient Greece and Rome. In some religions, principally Judaism, Christianity, and Islam, God is seen as not only the architect of the universe but also as being actively involved with its inhabitants and its destiny (*see* theism). In *deism, God is seen as the creator of the universe who leaves its destiny to natural forces and the will of its inhabitants. In *Hinduism, Brahman, the supreme spirit and ultimate reality, is conceived as operating through the triad Brahma, Vishnu, and Shiva (*see* Trimurti). *Buddhism is, strictly speaking, nontheistic, being concerned more with the attainment of *nirvana than with the nature of a supreme being. The concept of a single supreme deity (*see* monotheism) originated with the ancient Jews (*see* Yahweh). Jews, Christians, and Muslims believe that God reveals himself with supernatural authority in their holy scriptures (*see* Bible; Koran). However, theologians and philosophers have also tried to prove the existence of God by rational means or by means of observed facts about the universe (natural theology). Most of the traditional arguments are associated with St Thomas *Aquinas; these include: the argument from design or the teleological argument (there is an observable design, order, and regularity in the universe and therefore it must have been designed, which argues a designer); the cosmological argument (the mere fact that there is a universe demands further explanation); the degrees of perfection argument (if every thing or quality in the universe can be traced back to a more perfect thing or quality, there must be some ultimate perfect being, i.e. God); the First Cause argument (if everything is caused by something else, at the beginning there must have been an uncaused First Cause). Another important argument is the ontological argument (*see* Anselm of Canterbury, St).

Godard, Jean-Luc (1930–) French film director. During the 1950s he wrote for the magazine *Cahiers du Cinéma* and became a member of the *New Wave. His films, which are characterized by experimental narrative and editing techniques and by his Marxist political convictions, include *À bout de souffle* (1960), *Alphaville* (1965), *Week-End* (1967), and *Tout va bien* (1972).

Godavari River A river in central India. Rising in the Western Ghats, it flows ESE across the Deccan, through the Eastern Ghats, and into the Bay of Bengal. Its delta has an extensive canal irrigation system, which is linked to the Krishna delta. It is sacred to the Hindus. Length: 900 mi (1500 km).

Goddard, Robert Hutchings (1882–1945) US physicist. He was educated at Clark University, where he was appointed professor of physics in 1919. From early in his career, he was interested in the practical application of rocketry and published a scientific article, "A Method of Reaching Extreme Altitudes," that predicted orbital and lunar exploration by means of rockets. During World War I, Goddard took part in the US war effort and developed a prototype *bazooka that was extensively used in World War II. Goddard's greatest achievement came in 1926, when he launched a rocket powered by liquid fuel. By using a mixture of gasoline and liquid oxygen, he was able to improve the speed and reliability of his rockets in the following decade. In 1930 he launched a rocket that rose to a height of 2000 ft (610 m) at a speed of 500 mph (800 km per hr), and five years later, one of his rockets broke the sound barrier. Goddard supervised the jet propulsion program of the US Navy during World War II. He is generally considered to be the father of modern rocketry.

Gödel, Kurt (1906–78) US mathematician, born in Austria, who derived probably the most important proof in modern mathematics. Known as **Gödel's proof**, it states that, in a mathematical system based on a finite number of axioms, there will always exist statements that can be neither proved nor disproved. Gödel's proof, published in 1931, thus ended the search by mathematicians for a complete and self-consistent system.

Godfrey of Bouillon (c. 1060–1100) Crusader and Duke of Lower Lorraine. In 1096 Godfrey joined the first Crusade and played a major role in the siege and capture of Jerusalem. He then became defender of the Holy Sepulcher and effective King of Jerusalem. His exploits were celebrated in the medieval song cycle the *Chansons de Geste*.

Godiva, Lady (d. ?1080) The English woman who, according to the chronicler Roger of Wendover (d. 1236), rode naked through the market place of Coventry in order to persuade her husband Leofric, Earl of Mercia, to reduce the taxes he had imposed on the town. The story was later embellished with a Peeping Tom who, ignoring Godiva's request that the townspeople remain indoors, was struck blind.

Godolphin, Sidney, Earl of (1645–1712) British Whig politician; Lord Treasurer (1685–88, 1700–01, 1702–10). Under Anne (reigned 1702–14) he and *Harley were the most powerful men in politics until the unpopularity of their pursuit of the War of the *Spanish Succession caused their downfall.

Godoy, Manuel de (1767–1851) Spanish statesman; chief minister (1792–97, 1801–08) of Charles IV of Spain. He rose to power through the influence of Charles' wife María Luisa (1751–1819), whose lover Godoy became. He allied Spain with France during the Napoleonic War and, extremely unpopular, was overthrown together with Charles.

Godthåb 64 10N 51 40W The capital of Greenland, a port at the mouth of Godthåb Fjord. Founded in 1721, it is the site of a radio station, hospital, and college. Chief occupations are reindeer and sheep raising, hunting, and fishing. Population (1981): 9423.

Godunov, Boris (Fedorovich) (c. 1551–1605) Russian statesman and tsar (1598–1605). Godunov rose to power in the reign of *Ivan the Terrible and became regent for Fyodor I, whose younger brother and heir, Dimitrii, Godunov may have murdered in 1591. After Fyodor's death (1598), Godunov was elected tsar. His authority was challenged by the first False Dimitrii, a pretender who succeeded Godunov (*see* *Time of Troubles). Godunov was the subject of a play by Pushkin, on which Mussorgsky based his famous opera.

Godwin (*or* Godwine; d. 1053) Earl of Wessex. An Anglo-Danish noble, he rose to power under Canute, after whose death Godwin supported the accession of Edward the Confessor and became a dominant figure in royal government. In 1045 his daughter Edith married Edward. He was overthrown in 1051 but regained his position by force in 1052. He was succeeded by his son Harold (later Harold II).

Godwin, William (1756–1836) British political philosopher and novelist. A utilitarian of the extreme radical kind, Godwin in *Political Justice* (1793) advocated anarchy and communism. As a determinist, he held that the notion of moral desert was irrelevant; Christianity was also a harmful influence, distracting men with bogus promises of immortality. His major novel, *Caleb Williams* (1794), propagates his views on justice. He married Mary *Wollstonecraft (1797).

Godwin Austen, Mount. *See* K2.

godwit A long-legged long-billed migratory bird belonging to a genus (*Limosa*; 4 species) that breeds in N Eurasia and North America. The black-tailed godwit (*L. limosa*) is 16 in (40 cm) long and has a distinctive black-banded white tail, white wing stripe, and, in summer, a chestnut neck and breast. Family: *Scolopacidae* (plovers, sandpipers, etc.).

Goebbels, (Paul) Joseph (1897–1945) German Nazi politician. From 1926, when he became Nazi Party leader in Berlin, he was well known for his skillful propagandist techniques. In 1928 he entered the Reichstag and in 1933 was appointed minister of propaganda by Hitler. He established a vast and complex machine for the control of public information, the arts, cinema, and theater, all of which he manipulated with a cynical disregard for truth to achieve Nazi aims. He committed suicide with his wife after taking the lives of his six children during the collapse of the Third Reich.

Goes, Hugo van der (c. 1440–82) Flemish painter, who worked in Ghent until about 1478. He spent the rest of his life in a monastery near Brussels. His *Portinari Altarpiece* (Uffizi), painted for a Florentine patron, is uncharacteristically large for Flemish paintings. The unharmonious colors and emotional intensity of his last work, *The Death of the Virgin* (Bruges), are perhaps related to mental illness, from which he suffered in the last years of his life.

Goethals, George Washington (1858–1928) US engineer and soldier. After graduating (1880) from West Point, he served in the Army Engineer Corps and in 1907 was made chief engineer of the Panama Canal project (1904–14). He had to deal with the health, housing, and feeding problems of about 30,000 workers, as well as the technical engineering problems of building the canal. He served as governor of the Canal Zone (1914–17) and was made quartermaster general during World War I.

JOHANN WOLFGANG VON GOETHE *After a portrait by Friedrich Bury, drawn when Goethe was about 51 years old.*

Goethe, Johann Wolfgang von (1749–1832) German poet, scholar, and statesman. He studied law at Leipzig and Strasbourg, where his discovery of Shakespeare inspired him to write an epic drama, *Götz von Berlichingen* (1773). The autobiographical novel *The Sorrows of Young Werther* (1774) won him international fame. In 1775 he settled at the court of the Duke of Saxe-Weimar, whom he served as prime minister until 1785 as well as directing the state theater and scientific institutions. At Weimar he fell in love with Charlotte von Stein, who inspired some of his greatest lyric poetry. A visit to Italy (1786–88) made him an enthusiastic advocate of classicism, influencing such plays as *Iphigenia on Tauris* (1787) and *Torquato Tasso* (1790). After the novel *Wilhelm Meister's Apprentice Years* (1795–96) he published the first part of his greatest work *Faust* (1808), a poetic drama of the aspirations of man. Other novels and scientific publications followed, until in 1829 he published *Wilhelm Meister's Journeyman Years*. The second, more philosophical, part of *Faust* he completed shortly before his death. A friend of the dramatist Schiller, Goethe's wide interests included stagecraft, biology, physics, astrology, and philosophy both orthodox and occult; he knew six languages well and translated many works into German.

Gog and Magog In Revelation and other books of the Bible, attendant powers of Satan. In British folklore they appear as the survivors of a race of giants destroyed by Brutus, the legendary founder of Britain. A famous pair of statues depicting them are located in the Guildhall, London.

Gogol, Nikolai Vasilievich (1809–52) Russian novelist and dramatist. Early ambitions to become a poet and an actor and to emigrate to the US all failed, but two volumes of stories based on his Ukrainian childhood won him acclaim from *Pushkin and other leading writers. To escape the controversy aroused by his satirical play *The Government Inspector* (1836) he went to Rome, where he wrote his best-known work, *Dead Souls* (1842), a grotesque lampoon of Russian feudalism. In his last years he became a depressive and a religious maniac.

Goiânia 16 43S 49 18W A city in central Brazil, the capital of Goiás state on the Pan-American Highway. Founded in 1933 to replace the old capital, it serves a cattle-raising and coffee-growing area and has two universities. Population (1980 est): 703,263.

Goidelic languages. *See* Celtic languages.

goiter Swelling in the neck caused by enlargement of the thyroid gland. A goiter is called simple if the thyroid is functioning normally; this occurs in areas where iodine is deficient in the water supply and it may occur sporadically in adolescent girls. A goiter may also be seen when the thyroid is overactive (*see* hyperthyroidism) or underactive (*see* cretinism; myxedema).

Golan Heights A range of hills in SW Syria, under Israeli administration. They are of great strategic importance; Syrian artillery positioned here was able to fire into the upper Jordan and Hula Valleys in Israel. Israeli forces stormed the heights in June, 1967, when most of the local populace fled; Jewish settlements have since been established.

Golconda 17 24N 78 23E A ruined city in S India, in Andhra Pradesh near Hyderabad city. The impressive tombs of the Qutb Shahi dynasty and the fortress, built on a granite ridge, stand as reminders of the city's former status as capital of one of the five Islamic kingdoms of the Deccan (1518–1687).

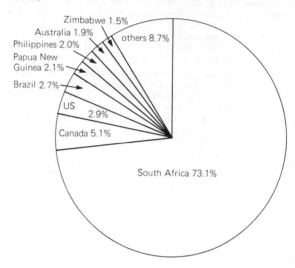

GOLD *World production.*

gold (Au) A soft dense yellow metal known and valued since ancient times. It occurs in nature as the element and in compounds with tellurium, in rock veins and alluvial deposits. The metal is the most malleable and ductile known. It alloys with other metals, is a good conductor of heat and electricity, and is chemically unreactive. The major uses for the element are for jewelry, electrical contacts, and as a currency standard (*see* gold standard). Gold dissolves in aqua regia (a mixture of one-third nitric acid and two-thirds hydrochloric acid) and the most common compound is the chloride ($AuCl_3$). Purity is measured in *karats. At no 79; at wt 196.967; mp 1950°F (1064.43°C); bp 5376°F (2966°C).

Gold, Thomas (1920–) Austrian-born astronomer, who spent 20 years in England before emigrating to the US in 1956 and becoming a professor at Cornell University. With *Bondi and *Hoyle he proposed the *steady-state theory of the universe in 1948. He also described pulsars as being neutron stars that are rapidly rotating.

Goldberg, Arthur J(oseph) (1908–) US statesman, lawyer, and jurist; associate justice of the Supreme Court (1962–65). He practiced law in Chicago, eventually becoming general counsel of the *CIO (1948–55) and the newly-merged *AFL-CIO (1955–61). Named secretary of labor (1961), he served until 1962, when he was appointed to the Supreme Court, a position he resigned in 1965 to become US ambassador to the UN (1965–68). He ran unsuccessfully for governor of New York (1970) and returned to private law practice.

Goldberg, Rube (Reuben Lucius G.; 1883–1970) US cartoonist. In 1907 he joined the *New York Evening Mail*, where he created Professor Lucifer Gorgonzola Butts, who invented elaborate ways to perform simple tasks. Thereafter, any elaborate, complicated system, scheme, or device used to arrive at a simple end was called "a Rube Goldberg." In 1934 he began editorial cartooning, for which he was awarded the 1948 Pulitzer Prize.

Gold Coast The name applied by Europeans to the coastal zone in West Africa between Axim and the Volta River on the Gulf of Guinea. An important source of gold, it came under British control in the 19th century as part of the British colony of Gold Coast (present-day Ghana).

Gold Coast, City of 27 58S 153 20E A resort city of Australia, on the coast of Queensland. It stretches 20 mi (32 km) S of Brisbane, from Southport, the administrative center, to the New South Wales border. Population (1980 est): 112,900.

goldcrest A tiny agile songbird, *Regulus regulus*, occurring chiefly in coniferous woodland of N Europe and Asia and feeding on insects and spiders. It is about 3.5 in (9 cm) long and has a yellow-green plumage with white wing stripes and an orange crest, brighter in the male than the female. Family: *Muscicapidae* (Old World *flycatchers).

Golden Age, Latin The period (70 BC–18 AD) during which some of the highest achievements of Latin literature were produced. The first part of the period (70–43 BC) was dominated by *Cicero. The major writers of the subsequent Augustan age (43 BC–18 AD) include *Virgil, *Horace, *Livy, and *Ovid.

Golden Bull of 1222 A charter of liberties granted by Andrew II of Hungary (1175–1235) that curbed monarchical powers and confirmed the rights of the nobility. The nobles gained important concessions on military service, taxation, and the administration of justice. They had the right to resist if the king violated the Charter's articles.

golden calf An idol made by Aaron for the Israelites to worship when they believed that Moses would not return from Mt Sinai, where he was receiving the tables of the Law (Exodus 32). Moses destroyed the idol upon his return. A similar idol was made by King Jeroboam I (937–915 BC) and set up at Bethel and Dan (I Kings 12.28).

golden cat A small *cat of SE Asia and Sumatra, *Felis temmincki*, also called Temminck's cat. It is about 49 in (125 cm) long, with a plain golden coat and strikingly marked head; it lives among rocks preying on rodents and ground-dwelling birds. The closely related African golden cat (*aurata*) is found on the fringes of forests in West Africa.

golden chain (or golden rain). *See* laburnum.

golden eagle A large dark-brown *eagle, *Aquila chrysaetos*, occurring in mountainous regions of North America and Eurasia. It is 26–33 in (70–85 cm) long and has golden neck feathers, a gray beak, fully feathered legs, large yellow feet, and powerful talons. Golden eagles have a wingspan of up to 90 in (230 cm) and catch small mammals, rabbits, and gamebirds.

goldeneye A *diving duck, *Bucephala clangula*, that breeds in forested areas of N Eurasia and winters in more southerly regions. It is 16–18 in (41–45 cm) long and males are black and white with a greenish head and a circular white patch on the cheek; females are gray with white markings and a brown head.

Golden Fleece The fleece of a sacred winged ram, the recovery of which was the goal of *Jason and the *Argonauts. Athamas, King of Thebes, had two sons, Phrixus and Helle, by his first wife Nephele. His second wife, Ino, hated her stepsons and plotted their death. They escaped across the sea on the golden ram and, having reached Colchis, sacrificed the ram to Zeus and hung the fleece in a grove sacred to Ares, where it was guarded by a dragon.

Golden Fleece, Order of the A chivalric order founded by *Philip the Good, Duke of Burgundy, in 1430, taking as its badge the fleece captured by Jason in Greek mythology. When Burgundy was united to the Habsburg empire (1477) the Order became increasingly aristocratic and was eventually confined to Austria and Spain.

Golden Gate bridge A suspension bridge for road traffic over the Golden Gate strait near San Francisco. Completed in 1937, its total length of 4200 ft (1280 m) made it the longest bridge in the world until the completion of the Verrazano–Narrows bridge (1964) across New York Harbor.

Golden Horde The western part of the Mongol Empire following its fragmentation on the death (1227) of *Genghis Khan. The Horde, which adopted Islam, controlled all of Russia between the Urals and the Danube River until defeated by the Turk *Timur, in the late 14th century.

Golden Horn (Turkish name: Haliç) An inlet of the Bosporus in NW Turkey, on the N side of the peninsula upon which the old quarter of Istanbul stands. It is 4.5 mi (7 km) long and serves as the city's harbor.

golden mole A burrowing insect-eating mammal belonging to the African family *Chryochloridae* (15 species). 2.8–9 in (7–23 cm) long, they are stout-bodied, blind, and almost tailless, with two of the four digits on each forefoot greatly enlarged. Their fur is an iridescent golden-brown. Order *Insectivora*.

golden pheasant A small *pheasant, *Chrysolophus pictus*, native to mountainous regions of E Asia but widespread as an ornamental bird. Its plumage is gold, scarlet, black, and green and the male has a large ruff of broad feathers.

goldenrain tree. *See* lacquer tree.

golden retriever A large strongly built breed of □dog whose ancestors possibly included labradors, setters, and spaniels. The dense water-resistant wavy coat is gold or cream and these dogs are strong swimmers. They are used as gun dogs, guide dogs, and police dogs. Height: 22–24 in (56–61 cm) (dogs); 20–22 in (51–56 cm) (bitches).

goldenrod A perennial herb of the genus *Solidago* (about 120 species), up to 8 ft (2.5 m) tall and mostly native to North America. The stem bears one-sided cylindrical heads of small yellow flowers, forming a branching plumelike inflorescence. Canadian goldenrod (*S. canadensis*) is often grown as a garden ornamental. Family: *Compositae*.

goldfinch, American A North American *finch, *Carduelis tristis*, About 5 in (12 cm) long, the male is bright yellow with a white rump, black forehead, and black tail and wings with white edges. The female is duller. It uses its pointed bill to extract seeds from thistles and dandelions and flocks of goldfinches are commonly seen on farmland.

goldfish A freshwater fish, *Carassius auratus*, also called golden carp, of E Asia origin but introduced elsewhere as an ornamental fish. In its natural state it is greenish brown or gray and up to 12 in (30 cm) long. However, the breeding of abnormal specimens, originally in China and Japan, has produced over 125 varieties, such as the "pop eye," "veiltail," and "lionhead," often with a characteristic red-gold coloration. The goldfish requires cold well-oxygenated water and is omnivorous.

Golding, William (1911–) British novelist. He served in the Royal Navy and subsequently became a schoolteacher. His best-known novel, *Lord of the Flies* (1954), concerns a group of schoolboys who are isolated on a desert island and revert to savagery. His other novels include *Pincher Martin* (1956), *The Spire* (1964), *Darkness Visible* (1979), *Rites of Passage* (1980), *A Moving Target* (1982), and *The Paper Men* (1984). He was awarded the Nobel Prize in 1983.

Goldoni, Carlo (1707–93) Italian comic playwright. A prolific writer of over 250 plays, he revolutionized the rigid conventions of the *commedia dell'arte with his realistic characters and witty dialogue. His plays include *The Liar* (1759), *Mine Hostess* (1753), and *The Fan* (1764). In 1762 he went to Paris, where he wrote his *Mémoires* (1787) and was from 1769 tutor to the daughters of Louis XV.

Gold Rush The transcontinental journey of eastern profiteers after the discovery of gold on John Sutter's land near Sacramento, Calif. (1848). Those (approximately 80,000) who arrived in the first year were called forty-niners. Harsh living conditions and the violent life of the gold fields took many lives and only a few forty-niners made fortunes. There were gold rushes in Australia, South Africa and the Klondike, Canada in the next half century.

Goldschmidt, Richard Benedict (1878–1958) US geneticist. His view of the chromosome as a large-chain molecule led to advances in genetic research. He demonstrated that differences between races were genetically determined and showed how drastic changes in environmental factors could cause changes in the external appearance of fruit flies.

Goldschmidt process The reduction of a metal oxide to the metal by reacting it with aluminum to form aluminum oxide and metal. The process, which produces a great deal of heat, is used to extract chromium from chromium ore. Named for— Hans Goldschmidt (1861–1923).

Goldsmith, Oliver (1730–74) Anglo-Irish poet. Born in Ireland, he was sent to study medicine in Edinburgh and arrived penniless in London in 1756. A friend of Johnson and Boswell, he was inarticulate in conversation and a compulsive gambler. His best-known works are the poem *The Deserted Village* (1770), the novel *The Vicar of Wakefield* (1776), and the play *She Stoops to Conquer* (1773).

gold standard A monetary system in which paper money was convertible on demand into gold. Banknotes were issued fractionally backed by gold (i.e. gold reserves were a fixed proportion of the value of the notes in circulation). Rates of exchange between countries were fixed by their currency values in gold. In classical economics imbalances in international trade were rectified automatically by the gold standard. A country in deficit would have depleted gold reserves and would therefore have to reduce its money supply. The resulting fall in demand would reduce imports and the lowering of prices would boost exports; thus the deficit would be rectified. Most financially important countries were on the gold standard from 1900 until its suspension during World War I because of the problems of transporting gold. It was reintroduced in 1925 but finally abandoned in 1931. *See also* International Monetary Fund.

Goldwater, Barry (Morris) (1909–) US political leader. A Republican senator from Arizona (1953–64; 1969–), he served as a spokesman for right wing, conservative America; he opposed a strong federal government and advocated US escalation in Vietnam. The Republican contender for the presidency (1964), he was defeated by Lyndon B. *Johnson.

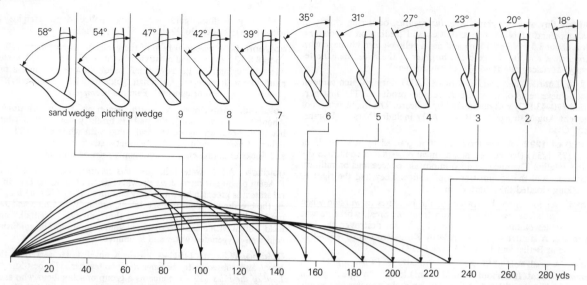

GOLF *Irons are numbered according to the angle of the face; the greater the angle of inclination, the higher the ball is hit into the air. Thus a good player, under normal conditions, knows the range of each iron. The Number One wood (driver) is used from the tee for the maximum distance and the putter is used on the green.*

Goldwyn, Samuel (S. Goldfish; 1882–1974) US film producer, born in Poland. In 1916 he cofounded Goldwyn Pictures, a production company that merged with other concerns to become Metro-Goldwyn-Mayer (MGM) in 1924. His many successful films as an independent producer include *Wuthering Heights* (1939) and *Guys and Dolls* (1955).

golem In medieval Jewish folklore, an image or automaton that can be brought to life by a charm. They were supposed to have been used as servants by rabbis. The word originally referred to anything incomplete or embryonic.

golf A club-and-ball game for two or four players played on a golf course. It was well established in Britain by the 15th century and almost certainly originated in Scotland. A standard course is usually between 4572 m (5000 yd) and 6400 m (7000 yd) and is divided into 18 holes (9 on a small course), each of which is between 90 m (100 yd) and 540 m (600 yd) long. A "hole" comprises the flat starting point, called the "tee," a strip of mown grass about 27–90 m (30–100 yd) wide, called the "fairway," and a smooth putting green. On the green is the actual hole. There are also obstacles around the course, such as trees, ditches, ponds, and sand bunkers. The object of the game is to hit the ball from each tee into each hole with as few strokes as possible ("par" for a hole is the standard number of strokes needed by a first-class player; one stroke less than par is called a "birdie," and an "eagle" is two strokes less). To achieve this a player is allowed a set of 14 clubs of which there are three basic types: woods, irons, and putters.

Golgi, Camillo (1843–1926) Italian cell biologist, whose staining technique using silver nitrate revealed fine details of cells. Golgi distinguished different types of nerve cells in the brain (Golgi cells) and demonstrated a network of tubules and granules within cells (the *Golgi apparatus). He shared the 1906 Nobel Prize with *Ramon y Cajal.

Golgi apparatus (*or* Golgi complex) A structure present in the cytoplasm of nearly all ▢cells, composed of stacks of flattened sacs bounded by membranes and associated with vesicles. Discovered by Camillo *Golgi, it is thought to function in the synthesis and concentration of certain materials, especially secretory products, which are then packaged into the vesicles and transported within the cell.

Golgotha. *See* Calvary.

goliards Wandering scholars (often students or lesser clerics) of medieval Europe who were notorious for their scurrilous verses. Frequently condemned by the Church for their poetry and riotous behavior, by the 14th century the term had lost its earlier connotations, being applied to all minstrels. The largest collection of goliard poetry was published as the *Carmina Burana* in the 19th century.

goliath beetle A large beetle belonging to the group of flower chafers (*see* chafer). The African goliath beetle (*Goliathus giganteus*) has the largest body of all the insects, measuring about 4 in (96 mm) in length. It is white with bold black stripes and brown wing cases. The larvae are found in rotten logs.

goliath frog The largest known living frog, *Rana goliath*, which grows up to 14 in (35 cm) long. This rare shy frog inhabits deep river pools in Africa. Its bones are supposed to have magical properties.

Golovkin, Gavril Ivanovich, Count (1660–1734) Russian statesman. A relative of *Peter the Great, he accompanied the tsar on his early visits to western Europe. In 1706 he became foreign minister and in 1709, state chancellor. In the reign (1725–27) of Catherine I (?1684–1727), he became a member of the supreme privy council. In the 1730 accession crisis, he supported *Anna Ivanovna.

Gomel 52 25N 31 00E A port in the W Soviet Union, in the Belorussian SSR on the Sozh River. It is an important railroad junction and industrial center, producing fertilizers, machinery, timber products, foodstuffs, and textiles. Population (1981 est): 405,000.

Gómez, Juan Vicente (1857–1935) Venezuelan soldier and statesman, who was brought to power in 1908 by a military coup. Elected president in 1910, he governed, either directly or through puppets, until his death. He did much to modernize Venezuela, simultaneously accumulating a vast personal fortune. His power base was in the army and he brutally suppressed all opposition to his regime.

Gomillion v. Lightfoot (1960) US Supreme Court decision that struck down an Alabama law. The law had allowed the redistricting of an area in such a way that most black voters were eliminated from the district.

Gompers, Samuel (1850–1924) US labor leader; born in London. As a young boy in the US he joined the Cigarmakers' Union (1863) and by 1877 had reorganized it. In 1886, when the American Federation of Labor (AFL) was organized, he served as its first president (1886–94; 1896–1924). He held a conservative view toward unions and believed in collective bargaining, a national union, and business-like management of labor affairs.

Gomulka, Władysław (1905–82) Polish statesman. Gomulka was secretary general of the Polish Workers' Party from 1945 until 1948, when his criticism of the Soviet Union led to his demotion and imprisonment (1951–54). Following the *Poznan Riots, which gave Poland more independence from the Soviet Union, Gomulka became first secretary of the Party. In 1970 he resigned after demonstrations over price increases.

gomuti A *palm tree, *Arenga pinnata* (or *A. saccharifera*), also called sugar palm, occurring in SE Asia. The sap yields palm sugar and the fermented juice (palm wine) is distilled to produce arrack. A form of sago is obtained from the pith and the leaf fibers are used to make cord, ropes, etc.

gonad. *See* ovary; testis.

gonadotrophin One of several hormones that control the activity of the testes and ovaries (the gonads) in mammals. The pituitary gland, under the influence of the hypothalamus, produces three gonadotrophins: luteinizing hormone (LH), which stimulates ovulation and *estrogen production by the ovaries and the production of *androgens by the testes; follicle-stimulating hormone (FSH), which promotes ovulation and sperm production;

and *prolactin, which triggers lactation. LH and FSH are glycoproteins and are usually released together. Human chorionic gonadotrophin (HCG) is produced by the placenta, reaching a peak level in the urine in early pregnancy. Measurement of urinary HCG is the basis of pregnancy tests. Gonadotrophins are also used in *fertility drugs.

SAMUEL GOMPERS *Labor movement leader who advocated the use of peaceful, businesslike methods to achieve unionism's goals.*

Gonaïves 12 29N 72 42W A port in W Haiti, on the Gulf of Gonaïves. Exports include coffee, bananas, and mangoes. Population (1975): 36,736.

Goncourt, Edmond de (1822–96) French writer, who collaborated with his brother **Jules de Goncourt** (1830–70) on art criticism, social histories of France, and a series of carefully researched naturalistic novels, most notably *Germinie Lacerteux* (1864) and *Madame Gervaisais* (1869). They are best known for their *Journal*, a lively record of French literary life from 1851 to 1895, and for Edmond's legacy, the Académie Goncourt, which awards France's most prestigious annual literary prize, the Prix Goncourt.

Gondar 12 40N 37 45E A city in central Ethiopia. A former capital of Ethiopia, Gondar was built after the Portuguese Jesuits had been expelled in the 16th century and is now a tourist attraction. Population (1978 est): 68,364.

Gondwanaland The supercontinent in the S hemisphere believed to have existed prior to 200 million years ago, when the drift of the continents to their present positions began. It probably consisted of South America, Africa, Australia, Antarctica, Arabia, and India. *See also* Laurasia.

gong A percussion instrument of indefinite pitch. The orchestral gong (*or* tam-tam) is a disk of metal about 3 ft (1 m) in diameter with a turned-over edge, hanging in a wooden frame.

gong chimes A set of gongs tuned to different pitches, used in many countries of the Far East. The instrument exists in a number of forms, the most elaborate of which, found in Burma and Thailand, consists of 15–20 small gongs set in a circular wooden frame. The player kneels inside the frame and plays the gongs with hammers. □musical instruments.

Góngora y Argote, Luis de (1561–1627) Spanish poet. Son of a judge, he was court chaplain in Madrid from 1617. He wrote many conventional sonnets and satirical verses but is best known for his longer works, *Polifemo* (1612) and *Soledades* (1613), in which he used esoteric allusions and elaborate diction and syntax to create a deliberately obscure and artificial style.

gonorrhea An acute venereal infection caused by a bacterium (the gonococcus). It is now one of the commonest infections in developed socie-

ties. Symptoms in men are discharge from the penis and a burning pain on passing urine. Women may have vaginal discharge and pain on urinating, but half have no symptoms at all, which is one of the reasons the disease is so widespread. It can be treated with penicillin.

Gonzaga An Italian dynasty that ruled Mantua (1328–1707) and Montferrato and Casale (1536–1707). The family was established in Mantua by **Luigi Gonzaga** (c. 1268–1360). His distinguished successors included **Gianfrancesco Gonzaga** (?1394–1444), a soldier and patron of learning under whom *Vittorino da Feltre established a famous school at Mantua, and **Francesco Gonzaga** (1466–1519), who commanded Italian forces against the French invasion in 1494 and was the husband of the distinguished patron of arts Isabella d'Este (*see* Este).

González de Mendoza, Pedro (1428–95) Spanish churchman; cardinal, Archbishop of Toledo, and Primate of Spain (from 1482). He was the most powerful supporter of Isabella in her successful claim to the Spanish throne and in her subsequent attempts to strengthen the monarchy. He took part in the conquest of Granada.

Good Friday The Friday before *Easter, when Christ's crucifixion is commemorated. It is a fast day, and in the Roman Catholic Church the Mass is not celebrated.

Good Hope, Cape of. *See* Cape of Good Hope.

Goodman, Benny (Benjamin David G.; 1909–) US clarinettist, prominent in the development of *swing. A versatile player and band leader, Goodman led big bands and played in small jazz groups from the 1930s to the 1980s. Also active in classical music, Bartok and Aaron Copland wrote works for him.

Good Neighbor Policy The US policy of cooperation and non-intervention in Latin American affairs. After decades of sporadic military involvement in South America, the US government began to change its policy in the late 1920s. This change to a policy of peaceful assistance to Latin American countries was detailed in the 1933 inaugural address of President Franklin *Roosevelt. His Good Neighbor Policy included the withdrawal of American troops, the lifting of trade barriers, and the preparation of a common defense in case of war. In 1948, President *Truman continued this policy, helping to found the *Organization of American States (OAS).

Goodyear, Charles (1800–60) US inventor. He experienced financial difficulties early in his career that resulted in brief imprisonment in a debtors' prison. After his release, he became interested in developing a technique for treating raw India rubber to prevent its melting or stiffening with changing temperatures. In 1837, Goodyear patented his first rubber coating formula and by 1844 he had perfected the *vulcanization process. This method cured the raw rubber by treating it with sulfur at a high temperature, making it strong and elastic. This development led to the use of rubber in many applications. Goodyear's financial difficulties plagued him in later years, and he was forced to sell his rights to his rubber patents.

Goolagong, Evonne. *See* Cawley, Evonne.

goosander A large migratory *duck, *Mergus merganser*, that breeds in North America and N Eurasia, also called sawbill because of its long toothed bill. The male is 30 in (75 cm) long and has a green head, black back, and white body; females are 22 in (57 cm) long and have a chestnut head and gray body. Goosanders feed chiefly on fish.

goose A large long-necked waterbird belonging to the family *Anatidae* (ducks, geese, and swans), occurring in the N hemisphere. Geese have short bills, humped at the base and tapering toward the tip, and short webbed feet. They chiefly feed inland on grass, grain, roots, etc., and are highly migratory, flying in characteristic V-formations and honking loudly in flight. The several breeds of domesticated goose are probably descended from the *graylag goose. Genera: *Anser* (gray geese), *Branta* (black geese); order: *Anseriformes*. *See also* barnacle goose; brent goose; Canada goose; Hawaiian goose; white-fronted goose.

gooseberry A fruit bush of the genus *Ribes*, especially *R. uva-crispa* (or *R. grossularia*), which is widely cultivated in the Old World for its hairy prickly-coated berries used (usually cooked) for preserves, wine, and in desserts. The bush, 40 in–5 ft (1–1.5 m) high, may be upright, spreading, or drooping, with three-lobed toothed leaves and spiny stems. The small drooping greenish flowers arise in the axils of the leaves. Family: *Grossulariaceae*.

goosefish. *See* anglerfish. FDICN/53

goosefoot A herb or small shrub of the genus *Chenopodium* (110 species), of temperate regions, also called pigweed. The stem, 0.5–50 ft (0.5–15m) high, is grooved or angular and the leaves are often fleshy. The whole plant may have a whitish mealy appearance. The small greenish flowers are borne on a branched inflorescence. Family: *Chenopodiaceae*.

goosegrass. *See* cleavers.

gopher. *See* pocket gopher; souslik.

Gorakhpur 26 45N 83 23E A city in N India, in Uttah Pradesh. It served as an army recruitment center for Gurkhas while under British rule. The main industries are sugar refining and fertilizer production and it has a university (1956). Population (1971): 230,911.

goral A small hoofed mammal, *Naemorhedus goral*, of mountainous regions in S Asia. About 26 in (65 cm) high at the shoulder, gorals have short conical horns and a coarse woolly coat, which varies from gray to foxy red. They graze in small herds at dawn and dusk. Family: *Bovidae*. *See also* serow.

Gordian knot A knot binding the yoke and beam of the chariot of Gordius, a legendary king of Phrygia. The knot was extremely complex. According to legend, whoever could unloose the knot would become the ruler of Asia. In 333 BC Alexander the Great is said to have cut the knot with his sword and so laid claim to Asia.

Gordon, Charles George (1833–85) British general. Gordon served in the Crimean War and then in China, where he earned the nickname Chinese Gordon after suppressing the *Taiping Rebellion (1864). In 1874 he was employed by the Khedive of Egypt to open up the country and from 1877 to 1880 was British governor of the Sudan. In 1884 he was sent back to the Sudan to evacuate Europeans and Egyptians, following al *Mahdi's revolt. Gordon was besieged for ten months in Khartoum, which was taken two days before a relief force arrived. Gordon himself was murdered.

Goren, Charles Henry (1901–) US authority on contract bridge. He was US bridge champion more than 30 times and world champion in 1950 and 1957. His many books include *Goren's Bridge Complete* (rev. ed., 1973).

Gorgas, William Crawford (1854–1920) US physician and soldier. After becoming a doctor, he joined the Army Medical Corps (1880) and worked in Havana, Cuba (1898–1902). He was successful in controlling yellow fever and malaria outbreaks in Havana and later (1904–14) during the building of the Panama Canal. He was appointed surgeon general of the Army in 1914.

Gorgon In Greek legend, a monster inhabiting the underworld. Hesiod refers to three Gorgons, the sisters Stheno, Euryale, and *Medusa. They were usually portrayed as winged females with snakes for hair and boars' tusks for teeth.

Gorgonzola 45 32N 9 23E A city in N Italy, in Lombardy. It is famous for Gorgonzola cheese. Population (1971): 12,738.

gorilla The largest living *ape, *Gorilla gorilla*, of tropical African forests. Male gorillas can grow to 6 ft (1.8 m) with a weight of 661 lb (300 kg). They walk on their feet and knuckles, feeding on plant stems and also climbing to reach fruit. Troops are led by a dominant adult male and are generally not aggressive, preferring retreat to attack, although they will fight when cornered. Three races are recognized: the rare shaggy mountain gorilla and two lowland forms—light-colored in the west and black in the east.

Göring, Hermann Wilhelm (1893–1946) German Nazi politician. He served in the air force in World War I and became a Nazi in 1922, taking command of Hitler's Brownshirts. He was elected to the Reichstag in 1928 and became its president in 1932. When Hitler came to power in 1933, Göring was appointed air minister of Germany and prime minister of Prussia. He established the *Gestapo and *concentration camps and probably engineered the Reichstag fire (1933). He directed the development of the Luftwaffe and in 1936 was given charge of mobilizing the economy for war and looted Europe's art treasures. Hitler declared Göring his successor in 1939 but expelled him from the party shortly before the Nazi collapse. Condemned to hang at Nuremburg, he committed suicide before the execution could take place.

Gorizia (German name: Görz; Serbo-Croat name: Gorica) 45 57N 13 37E A city in Italy, in Friuli-Venezia Giulia on the Yugoslav border. It was a noted cultural center under Habsburg rule. Industries include tourism, textiles, and machinery. Population (1971): 42,980.

Gorki, Maksim (Aleksei Maksimovich Peshkov; 1868–1936) Russian novelist. His hard nomadic early life is recounted in his autobiographical trilogy *Childhood* (1913–14), *In the World* (1915–16), and *My Universities* (1923). He established his literary reputation with romantic short stories and followed these with several novels and plays, including *Mother* (1906) and *The Lower Depths* (1906). He lived in exile in Italy from 1906 to 1913 and again from 1921 to 1928. He then returned to Russia, becoming first president of the Soviet Writers Union and an exponent of Stalinism.

Gorkii (Gorki *or* Gorky; name until 1932: Nizhnii Novgorod) 56 20N 44 00E A city in the central Soviet Union, in the RSFSR on the Oka and Volga Rivers. It is one of the country's most important industrial cities, whose manufactures include machinery, chemicals, and textiles. Gorkii's trade fair was the most important in Russia until it was discontinued in 1917. The city was renamed in 1932 in honor of the writer Maksim Gorki. Population (1981 est): 1,367,000.

Gorky, Arshile (Vosdanig Adoian; 1905–48) US painter, born in Armenia, who emigrated to the US in 1920. He worked in most 20th-century styles before adopting, in about 1940, an individual and abstract form of *surrealism. Such works as *The Liver Is the Cock's Comb* (1944; New York) anticipate *action painting in their free application of paint. His promising career was cut short by his suicide.

Görlitz 51 11N 15 0E A city in SE East Germany, on the *Neisse River where it marks the boundary with Poland. Famous since the middle ages for clothmaking, its many industries also include vehicle and machinery manufacture and lignite mining. Population (1973 est): 86,034.

Gorlovka 48 17N 38 05E A city in the SW Soviet Union, in the Ukrainian SSR in the *Donets Basin. It is one of the largest coalmining and industrial centers of the area. Population (1981 est): 338,000.

Gorno-Altai An autonomous region (*oblast*) in the S Soviet Union, in the RSFSR. Formed in 1922 for the Turkic-speaking Altaian peoples, it is now inhabited mostly by Russians. Gold and mercury are mined and livestock breeding is the main agricultural activity. Area: 35,740 sq mi (92,600 sq km). Population (1980 est): 173,000. Capital: Gorno-Altaisk.

Gorno-Badakhshan An autonomous region (*oblast*) in the S Soviet Union, in the Tadzhik SSR. It was formed in 1925 and its population consists mainly of *Tadzhiks. Chiefly agricultural, it produces wheat, fruit, and fodder crops; cattle and sheep are bred. Area: 24,590 sq mi (63,700 sq km). Population (1979 est): 127,000. Capital: Khorog.

gorse (*or* furze) A very spiny densely branched shrub, *Ulex europaeus*, up to 13 ft (4 m) high, with bright-yellow sweet-scented flowers. The leaves, which consist of three leaflets, are reduced to spines or scales on mature plants. The fruit is a black hairy pod that splits open explosively to release the seeds. Gorse is native to grassy areas and heaths throughout Europe and has been introduced elsewhere. Family: *Leguminosae*.

Gorton, Sir John Grey (1911–) Austrálian statesman; Liberal prime minister (1968–71). His administration was responsible for greater federal government intervention in the field of education, and he fostered Australia's involvement in the Vietnam War.

goshawk A large powerful *hawk, *Accipiter gentilis*, ranging throughout forests of the N hemisphere and formerly used in falconry. It is 24 in (60 cm) long with a wingspan of 51 in (130 cm) and a finely barred gray plumage. It feeds chiefly on birds.

Goslar 51 57N 10 28E A city in NE West Germany, in Lower Saxony. An imperial residence in the middle ages, the palace remains. Silver has been mined here since the 10th century. Population (1971 est): 40,300.

Gospels (Old English: good news) The four New Testament accounts of Christ's life, ascribed to *Matthew, *Mark, *Luke, and *John. The word originally referred to the message of Christ's redemptive work rather than to the writings. The first three are known as the Synoptic Gospels, since they report approximately the same synopsis of the events. According to some biblical scholars Mark is the oldest of these and was used as a source by the authors of Matthew and Luke. Material that is not found in Mark but is common to Matthew and Luke is believed to derive from a single lost source, known as Q. The fourth Gospel, John, emphasizes the divinity of Christ and may presuppose a knowledge of the Synoptic Gospels.

Gosport 50 48N 1 08W A port in S England, on Portsmouth Harbour. It is a naval base, linked with Portsmouth by ferry, and has yacht-building and marine-engineering industries. Population (1981): 77,276.

Gossaert, Jan (c. 1478–c. 1532) Flemish painter, whose popular surname, Mabuse, derives from his birthplace Maubeuge. As one of the first Flemish artists to work in the Italian Renaissance style, after visiting Italy (1508) he painted sculptural nudes against Italian architectural backgrounds, e.g. *Neptune and Amphitrite* (Berlin). As a portraitist he was noted for his expressive treatment of hands.

Göta Canal A canal in S Sweden, linking Göteborg on the Kattegat in the W with Stockholm in the E. Opened in 1832, it enters the Baltic Sea near Söderköping. Length: 58 mi (93 km).

Göteborg (English name: Gothenburg) 57 45N 12 00E An important ice-free port in SW Sweden, at the mouth of the Göta River. Sweden's second largest city, it expanded through Napoleon's Continental System and with the opening of the Göta Canal (1832). Notable buildings include

417

the town hall (1750), cathedral (1633), and university (1891). Industries include shipbuilding, oil refining, and the manufacture of cars. Population (1976 est): 442,410.

Gotha 50 56N 10 42E A city in SW East Germany, on the N edge of the Thuringian Forest, former capital of the duchy of Saxe-Coburg-Gotha. It is noted for the *Almanac de Gotha* (an annual record of the royal and noble houses of Europe, published here from 1764 to 1944). Gotha manufactures machinery, vehicles, textiles, and chemicals. Population (1973 est): 57,098.

Gothenburg. *See* Göteborg.

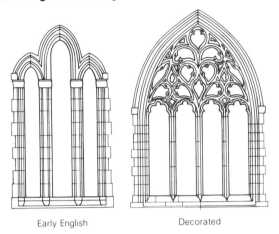

Early English   Decorated

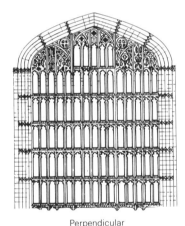

Perpendicular

GOTHIC ART AND ARCHITECTURE *In England the three phases of gothic architecture are characterized by distinctive window designs.*

gothic art and architecture The styles flourishing in Europe from the mid-12th to the end of the 15th centuries. "Gothic" originated as a derisory term used by Renaissance artists, who blamed the destruction of classical art on the Goths who invaded the Roman Empire. The gothic is most closely associated with church architecture, the hallmarks of gothic design being the rib and shaft ceiling, the pointed □arch, the flying buttress, and later great height and the impression of weightlessness. Gothic architecture was initiated in France in the chevet of the Abbey of Saint-Denis, near Paris. It was followed by the cathedrals of *Notre-Dame (begun 1163), Chartres (begun c. 1194), Reims (begun 1211), etc. (*see also* Flamboyant). Although used during the *romanesque period, *stained glass was only fully developed in the gothic period, being characterized by elaborate tracery, brilliant colors, and the reduction of stonework between the windows to very thin stone bars. Gothic sculpture mirrored the development of the architecture it adorned, renouncing its early naturalism for a stylized elegance and an emphasis on line and silhouette. In painting, the early gothic manifested itself chiefly in manuscript illumination. In the 14th century elements of it appear in the art of Simone *Martini, Rogier van der *Weyden, and others, but its full flowering in panel and manuscript painting came with the *international gothic style of the early 15th century. The

gothic was revived in the 19th century by the Victorians, who considered it a perfect embodiment of religious intensity (*see* gothic revival).

gothic novel An English genre, popular in the late 18th and early 19th centuries, characterized by a prevailing atmosphere of mystery and terror and pseudomedieval—"gothic"—settings. Examples include Horace Walpole's *Castle of Otranto* (1765), Ann Radcliffe's *The Mysteries of Udolpho* (1794), and Matthew Gregory Lewis' *The Monk* (1796). The genre wilted under parodies, such as Jane Austen's *Northanger Abbey* (1818), but influenced later writers, among them the Brontë sisters, Poe, and Bram Stoker, in *Dracula* (1897).

gothic revival An architectural style. Initially associated with *Romanticism, the revived popularity for *gothic architecture began in England in the late 18th century, with such buildings as Fonthill Abbey. Common throughout W Europe and the US, it was particularly dominant in Britain after 1818, when parliament voted funds to build new Anglican churches. Over 170 were built in the gothic style. The culmination of the gothic revival was perhaps the new Houses of Parliament (1834–45). One of the last important gothic-revival buildings in London was the Law Courts (1882).

Goths Germanic peoples who originated in Scandinavia (Gotland) and had moved into the Ukraine by the end of the 2nd century AD. Shortly afterward they invaded the Roman Empire N of the Danube and expanded into the Balkans. Converted to Arian Christianity (*see* Arianism) in the mid-4th century, their empire was soon destroyed by the *Huns and their two groups, the *Ostrogoths and *Visigoths, separated.

Gotland (Gothland *or* Gottland) The largest of the Swedish islands, in the Baltic Sea. Long disputed between Denmark and Sweden, it was finally ceded to Sweden in 1645. Its economy is based chiefly on agriculture (cattle and sheep raising) and tourism. Area: 1225 sq mi (3140 sq km). Population (1980 est): 55,346, including associated islands. Capital: Visby.

Gottfried von Strassburg (13th century) German poet. Nothing is known of his life apart from what can be inferred from the erudition and poetic skill of his epic *Tristan und Isolde*, a retelling of the original Celtic legend according to the conventions of courtly love. It inspired Wagner's famous opera.

Göttingen 51 32N 9 57E A city in E West Germany, in Lower Saxony. With its famous university, founded in 1734 by George II of Great Britain, and the Max Planck Association for the furtherance of science, it is a noted educational center. Its manufactures include precision instruments and aluminum goods. Population (1980 est): 128,500.

Gottsched, Johann Christoph (1700–66) German critic, who introduced French classical and rationalist critical principles into German literature. His dramatic academy in Leipzig and his own plays, such as *Der sterbende Cato* (1732), and translations helped to raise the literary standards of German theater.

gouache. *See* watercolor.

Gouda 52 01N 4 43E A city in the W Netherlands, in South Holland province. Its most notable church, the Grote Kerk (1552), has exceptional stained-glass windows (1556–1603). It is famous for its gouda cheese. Population (1981 est): 59,185.

Goujon, Jean (c. 1510–68) French Renaissance sculptor. His best-known works are the marble relief of the *Deposition*, *The Tribune of the Caryatids* supporting a gallery in the Louvre, and reliefs of nymphs for the Fontaine des Innocents. The first two were produced in collaboration with the architect Pierre *Lescot.

Gould, Jay (Jason G.; 1836–92) US businessman. With James *Fisk he caused the "Erie War" (1868) by manipulating illegally the Erie Railroad stock to prevent Cornelius *Vanderbilt from having full control of the line. His attempt to corner the gold market (1869) failed but was the cause of a stock market panic called Black Friday. His later dealings involved holdings in the Union Pacific, Kansas Pacific, Denver Pacific, Wabash, and Missouri Pacific railroads and brought him great profits, but upset the stability of the entire railroad system.

Gounod, Charles François (1818–93) French composer. He began serious composition after studying theology and deciding not to become a priest. His most successful works were the operas *Faust* (1852–59) and *Romeo and Juliet* (1864). Toward the end of his life he composed a large quantity of sacred music, including oratorios and masses.

gourami One of several freshwater tropical *labyrinth fishes, especially *Osphronemus goramy*. It has a brown or gray oval body, up to 24 in (60 cm) long, and a filamentous ray extending from each pelvic fin. Native to the E Indies, it has been introduced elsewhere and cultivated for food.

gourd The fruit of certain plants of the family *Cucurbitaceae*, especially the white-flowered bottle gourd (*Lagenaria siceraria*), a trailing annual herb widely grown in the tropics. Its fruits have woody shells used locally as bottles, pipes, and utensils. Other gourds are grown as ornamentals, having attractive shapes, colors, and surface patterns. The dishcloth gourd (*see* loofah) is used as a bath sponge and the *snake gourd is grown for food.

gout Sudden attacks of arthritis caused by the presence of uric acid crystals in the joints. The big toe is most commonly affected, becoming hot, red, and very painful. Gout is commonest in older men and tends to recur; if not treated (by drugs to reduce the uric acid in the blood) it may lead to destruction of the joint. Gout is associated with an increased incidence of heart disease.

Government Printing Office (GPO) US federal agency that is responsible for all government printing and publishing. Established in 1860 and headed by the Public Printer, it carries out the printing and binding orders of Congress and the federal government departments through the Congressional Joint Committee on Printing. Certain printed materials are available to the public through mail-order catalogues, government bookstores, and selected libraries.

Govind Singh. *See* Gobind Singh.

Gowon, Yakubu (1934–) Nigerian statesman; head of state (1966–76). An army officer, in the 1966 military coup he became chief of staff and then head of state. He was ousted in a bloodless coup in 1976.

Goya (y Lucientes), Francesco (Jose) de (1746–1828) Spanish painter, born near Saragossa. After studying in Italy, he settled in Madrid (1775), where he painted gay scenes of Spanish life for the royal tapestry factory. As court painter from 1789 he produced realistic unflattering portraits of the royal family. He became deaf in 1792, and his works grew pessimistic and sometimes nightmarish, as in his etchings of *Los Caprichos* and *The Disasters of War*, condemning the French invasion of Spain. He settled in France in 1824. Among his best-known paintings are *Maja Clothed*, *The Shootings of May 3 1808*, and the so-called black paintings, such as *Satan Devouring His Children* (all Prado).

Goyen, Jan Josephszoon van (1596–1656) Dutch landscape painter and etcher, who was born in Leiden but after 1630 lived in The Hague. His river and winter scenes were characterized by large expanses of sky and near-monochrome colors.

Gozzi, Carlo (1720–1806) Italian dramatist. He opposed the theatrical reforms of *Goldoni and attempted to revive the techniques of the *commedia dell'arte. His plays, often including elements of fantasy and the grotesque, include *Turandot* (1762), on which Puccini's opera is based, and *L'Augellin Belverde* (1764).

Gozzoli, Benozzo (Benozzo di Lese; 1420–97) Florentine painter. His major works are the frescoes of the *Journey of the Magi* (Palazzo Medici-Riccardi, Florence), which are noted for their detailed landscapes, and portraits of his contemporaries.

Graafian follicle. *See* ovary.

Gracchus, Tiberius Sempronius (163–133 BC) Roman reformer, who as tribune (133) proposed land reforms intended to create a class of small landowners. He was killed in a riot. His brother **Gaius Sempronius Gracchus** (153–121 BC) was tribune in 123 and renewed Tiberius' attempts at land reform. He was killed in riots over his proposal to grant Roman citizenship to Latins. The Gracchi's attempts at reform polarized the aristocracy into hostile factions and thereafter change was difficult to achieve without violence.

grace In Christian theology, God's freely offered forgiveness to his sinful creatures. The nature of divine grace and the conditions on which it is offered and accepted were central to the controversy between *Pelagius and St *Augustine, and between the Calvinists and their opponents at the Reformation. *See also* free will; predestination.

Graces In Greek mythology, the three daughters of Zeus and Hera, representing beauty, grace, and charm. They were named Aglaia, Euphrosyne, and Thalia.

grackle An omnivorous black bird of the North American genus *Quiscalus*. Grackles are about 12 in (30 cm) long and have strong pointed bills used to dig for insect larvae, to kill small vertebrates, and to crack open nuts. They often feed in large flocks, causing damage to crops. Family: *Icteridae* (American orioles).

gradient A measure of the inclination of a slope, often expressed as the rise in height divided by the length of the slope, i.e. the sine of the angle of the slope. Mathematically, however, the gradient is the ratio of the vertical rise to the horizontal distance covered, i.e. the tangent of the angle. For gentle gradients the difference between the sine and the tangent is small. In *calculus the gradient is the slope of the *tangent at any point on a curve in a Cartesian *coordinate system. If the curve is represented by the function $f(x)$, then the gradient is the first derivative of this function.

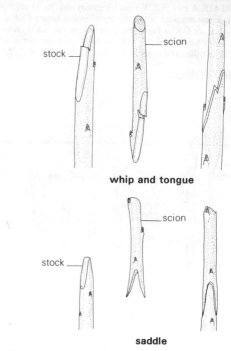

whip and tongue

saddle

GRAFTING *Two commonly used grafting methods. After stock and scion are fitted together they are held securely by tape, string, etc., and protected from desiccation by covering the point of union with wax or moist material.*

grafting 1. (horticulture) The transfer of part of one plant, usually a shoot or a bud, onto another plant. It is often used as a means of vegetative propagation, particularly for fruit trees and roses. The *cambium (a region of actively dividing cells) of the transplanted piece (called the scion) is aligned with that of the recipient plant (called the stock): the wound tissue formed by the two cambia binds the graft together. Grafts will "take" only if the scion and stock are closely related. Genetically identical scions on different stocks may differ considerably, but this is due solely to environmental effects and there is no transfer of genetic material between stock and scion. Occasionally graft hybrids (*see* chimaera) arise from the graft junction, but these are mixtures of the two cell types rather than true hybrids. **2.** (surgery). *See* transplantation.

Graham, Billy (1918–) US evangelist. He began as an evangelist with the Youth for Christ movement before forming the Billy Graham Evangelistic Association (1950) and conducting worldwide crusades. His theatrical and carefully staged meetings, in which the audience are invited to "take a decision for Christ," have attracted very large crowds. His association with prominent personalities brought his movement increased attention.

Graham, Martha (1893–) US dancer and choreographer. She studied with Ruth St Denis and established her own dance academy in New York in 1927. She eventually became one of the most influential teachers of modern dance in America. Her ballets, often concerned with the psychological interpretation of mythological themes, include *Primitive Mysteries* (1931), *Night Journey* (1947), *Circe* (1963), and *Acts of Light* (1981).

Graham, Thomas (1805–69) British physicist, who investigated gaseous diffusion, discovering **Graham's law** (1831), which states that the rates at which gases diffuse are inversely proportional to the square roots of their densities. He continued to study diffusion, investigating the flow of solutions through semipermeable membranes. He coined the terms osmosis, crystalloids, and colloids.

Grahame, Kenneth (1859–1932) British children's writer. His best-known book is the children's classic *The Wind in the Willows* (1908), concerned with Toad, Mole, Rat, and other animal characters that inhabit an ideal riverside world. It was adapted as a play, *Toad of Toad Hall* (1929), by A. A. *Milne.

Graham Land A mountainous peninsula in Antarctica, bordering on the Weddell Sea and comprising part of *British Antarctic Territory. It was formerly a dependency of the Falkland Islands.

Graiae In Greek legend, three goddesses personifying old age, the sisters and protectors of the *Gorgons. They shared one eye and one tooth. *Perseus stole the eye to force them to tell him the whereabouts of the Gorgons.

Grainger, Percy Aldridge (1882–1961) Australian composer and pianist, trained in Germany. He lived in London and in 1914 went to the US, becoming a US citizen. Grainger was a friend of Grieg and Delius and studied and recorded English folksong. Many of his compositions incorporate folk-music intervals and rhythms; they include the orchestral *Shepherds' Hey* (1913), *English Dance* (1925), and *Harvest Hymn* (1933), as well as the "clog dance" *Handel in the Strand* (1913).

gram (g) A unit of mass equal to 1/1000 of a *kilogram. The gram is itself one of the basic units in the *c.g.s. system, but in *SI units the basic unit is the kilogram.

grammar The study of the forms of the words of a language (morphology) and their relationships with one another (syntax). Until 1957 there were two basic types of grammar: **prescriptive grammar**, which expressed value judgments about the correctness of particular expressions, and **descriptive grammar**, which aimed to give an accurate account of the structures observable in recorded texts of a language. The earliest known descriptive grammar is by *Panini (c. 5th century BC) of *Sanskrit. Many grammars of the ancient Greek and Latin languages are still influential today; for example, the traditional parts of speech—noun, verb, adjective, etc.—were invented by Greek grammarians. Descriptive grammarians have been able to show that the judgments of prescriptivists are founded on no more objective basis than the willingness of the community to accept their judgments. Each language has its own patterns; attempts to resolve disputes or difficulties by appealing to authority, history, logic, or the structure of some other language are at best irrelevant, at worst confusing.

Publication in 1957 of *Syntactic Structures* by Noam *Chomsky introduced a new view of the study of grammar—namely that it should be predictive. Chomsky argued that, since the potential number of grammatical sentences in a language is literally infinite, a grammar must predict whether any given utterance is or is not a grammatical sentence of a particular language. Chomsky invented the concept of **generative grammar**, the finite set of linguistic rules that generate an infinite number of grammatical sentences in the language. Every speaker of a language acquires these rules at a very early age in a form to some degree idiosyncratic and different from those of other speakers. The raw material from which sentences are generated (words, phrases, etc.) form in a speaker's memory a store the exact nature of which is disputed. The concept of **transformational** (or transformational-generative) **grammar** seeks to explain the relationships among words in a sentence and among sentences themselves by logical structural analysis. Ambiguities and certain other problems are explained by postulating that behind the "surface structure" of a sentence lies a "deep structure," an abstract underlying form that determines the sentence's meaning. The surface structure is generated from the deep structure by generative rules, some of which are similar to the transformations of theoretical *logic.

Grampians A range of mountains in central Scotland. It extends generally SW-NE, bordered in the S by the Central Lowlands; the Cairngorm Mountains form a northerly extension. Its chief summits include Ben Nevis at 4406 ft (1343 m) and Ben Macdhui at 4296 ft (1309 m).

grampus A small toothed *whale, *Grampus griseus*, of warm and temperate waters, also called Risso's dolphin. About 146 in (3.7 m) long, dark-gray with a pale belly, grampuses live in small herds and migrate toward the Poles in summer and the equator in winter.

Gramsci, Antonio (1891–1937) Italian politician and Marxist theorist. In 1914 he joined the Italian Socialist Party but, dissatisfied with its moderation, broke away in 1921 to form the Italian Communist Party. In 1924 he became its leader in the chamber of deputies. The party was banned by the fascists in 1926 and Gramsci was imprisoned from 1928 until shortly before his death. His voluminous Marxist writings, mostly the work of his prison years, were publishd posthumously as *Prison Notebooks* (1947).

Granada 37 10N 3 35W A city in S Spain, in Andalusia. Formerly the capital of the kingdom of Granada, the last Moorish stronghold in Spain, it was conquered in 1492. Much frequented by tourists, its splendid architecture includes many Moorish buildings (notably the *Alhambra), a cathedral (1523–1703), and the 16th-century Capilla Real, containing the tombs of Ferdinand and Isabella. Population (1974 est): 202,969.

Granada 11 58N 85 59W A city in SW Nicaragua. It is the center of an area producing cotton, sugar, and coffee; manufactures include furniture, soap, and rum. Population (1978 est): 56,232.

granadilla. *See* passionflower.

Gran Chaco A vast plain in S central South America, mainly in N Argentina, E Bolivia, and Paraguay. It consists of a vast alluvial lowland region, drained by the W tributaries of the Paraguay and Paraná Rivers. It was the cause of the *Chaco War between Paraguay and Bolivia (1932–35). Area: 300,000 sq mi (780,000 sq km).

Grand Alliance, War of the (1689–97) The war in which a grand alliance led by England, Austria, Spain, and the Netherlands attempted to curb the expansionist policy of Louis XIV of France. Precipitated by the French invasion of the Palatinate (1688), the war was fought mainly in Flanders. Exhausted by the inconclusive but bloody battles, the participants accepted the Treaty of *Rijswijk in 1697. The conflict was renewed, however, in 1701, with the War of the *Spanish Succession.

Grand Banks A section of the North American continental shelf in the N Atlantic Ocean, extending SE of Newfoundland with a depth of about 130–330 ft (40–100 m). It is an internationally important fishing ground in which cod is especially plentiful. Area: about 494,000 sq mi (1,280,000 sq km).

Grand Canal (Chinese name: Da Yunhe) A canal in E China, the longest in the world, extending about 1000 mi (1600 km) N-S from Peking to *Wuhan. Begun possibly in the 4th century BC, it was built in sections over two millenniums. 100–200 ft (30–61 m) wide and 2–15 ft (0.6–4.6 m) deep, it is still used, chiefly in the S.

Grand Canyon A vast gorge in Arizona, on the Colorado River. It has been eroded through a varied series of virtually horizontal beds of multicolored rock, creating spectacular steps and rock formations. A popular tourist area, it was designated the **Grand Canyon National Park** in 1919. Length: 280 mi (451 km). Width: 4–18 mi (6–29 km). Greatest depth: over 1 mi (1.5 km).

Grand Coulee Dam A large gravity *dam on the Columbia River, in Washington. Completed in 1942, it is 4173 ft (1272 m) long at its crest, 354 ft (108 m) high, and has a reservoir capacity of 11,600 million cubic meters for irrigation, flood control, and hydroelectric power.

Grande Dixence Dam A gravity *dam on the Dixence River (Switzerland). Until 1970 it was the tallest dam in the world (932 ft [284 m] high). It is 2198 ft (670 m) wide at the crest and has a reservoir of 400 million cubic meters.

Grandfather Clause A clause in the constitutions of some Southern US states (prior to 1915) that denied blacks equal voting rights. It stated that anyone who had been able to vote before 1867 was exempt from the high literacy, property, and tax requirements for voting. Since the blacks' right to vote (15th Amendment) had not been granted until 1870, these clauses excluded most blacks and included the poor whites. It was declared unconstitutional by the Supreme Court in 1915 (*Guinn and Beal* v. *US*).

Grand Guignol A type of popular sensational drama, exploiting situations of violence and terror, that flourished in Paris in the late 19th century. The term derives from the name of a theater at which these plays were performed, and from Guignol, a stock character in French puppet shows.

grand mal. *See* epilepsy.

Grand Pré A village in E Canada, in Nova Scotia. It was the center of French-speaking *Acadia until Britain deported its inhabitants for refusing to swear allegiance to the crown (1755), an event romanticized in Longfellow's *Evangeline*.

Grand Rapids 42 57N 86 40W A city in W central Michigan, on the Grand River. Founded in the 1820s, its industries include the manufacture of furniture, motor bodies, paper, and paint. Population (1980): 181,843.

Grand Remonstrance (1641) A list of grievances drawn up by the *Long Parliament on the eve of the English *Civil War. It itemized the past faults of Charles I, the reforms achieved by the Long Parliament, and grievances outstanding.

Grand Teton National Park A national park in NW Montana, on the E edge of the Rocky Mountains, just S of Yellowstone National Park. It encompasses part of the Teton Mountains, a part of Jackson Hole, and many lakes. The highest point is Grand Teton (13,766 ft; 4196 m). The original park was established in 1929, while the Jackson Hole area was added in 1950. Area: 500 sq mi (1295 sq km).

Grange, Red (Harold Edward G.; 1903–   ) US football player. He played running back for the University of Illinois (1923–25), where he was named All-American for three seasons. Nicknamed the "Galloping

Ghost", he played professionally for the American Football League's New York Yankees (1925–28) and for the National Football League's Chicago Bears (1928–35); his success spurred the growth of professional football. He was elected to the Football Hall of Fame (1963).

Granger Movement US rural movement in the 1870s to obtain better business conditions for farmers. The goals of the movement were state regulation of the railroads and grain elevators, reduction of the role of middlemen, and an increase in cooperative buying and selling.

granite A coarse-grained plutonic rock of acid composition resulting from the high silica content. Granites contain quartz, feldspar (usually alkali), and mafic (dark-colored) minerals, usually muscovite and biotite (micas). Most granites crystallize from magma in large igneous intrusions known as batholiths, but some are produced by granitization, which is the transformation of pre-existing rocks into granite by the action of granitic fluids rising from great depths. There are many different types of granite with different modes of formation and mineral content.

Gran Paradiso 45 33N 7 17E The highest mountain entirely in Italy, in the Alps. The surrounding area has been made into a national park. Height: 13,323 ft (4061 m).

Grant, Cary (Archibald Leach; 1904–   ) US film actor, born in England. He went to Hollywood in 1932 and established his reputation as an actor of debonair sophistication in such films as *Holiday* (1938) and *The Philadelphia Story* (1940). He has acted in more than 70 films, including *To Catch a Thief* (1955), and *North By Northwest* (1959), directed by Alfred Hitchcock.

ULYSSES S. GRANT *Commander of the victorious Union forces during the Civil War and then President (1869-77).*

Grant, Ulysses Simpson (1822–85) US military and political leader; 18th President of the United States (1869–77). Born in Point Pleasant, Ohio, Grant graduated from West Point in 1843 and was decorated for gallantry during the *Mexican War. Personal problems forced his resignation from the army in 1854, and for the next six years he remained in private life, settling in Galena, Ill. At the outbreak of the *Civil War, he was commissioned as colonel of the 21st Illinois Volunteers. Grant proved to be an effective commander and won distinction in his capture of Fort Donelson, Tenn. in 1862. Promoted to the rank of major general, Grant won additional victories at *Shiloh, *Vicksburg, and Chattanooga in 1863. The following year, President *Lincoln appointed him commander-in-chief of the Union forces, and after defeating the Confederate forces in the *Wilderness Campaign and at the siege of *Petersburg, he accepted the surrender of General Robert E. *Lee at Appomattox Courthouse, Va on April 9, 1865. Following the war, he was named secretary of war in the administration of President Andrew *Johnson.

In 1868 he was elected president as the candidate of the *Republican Party, and he won re-election in 1872. Among Grant's most important achievements as president were the reform of the civil service system and the ratification of the Treaty of Washington with Great Britain in 1871. The early phases of *Reconstruction were also initiated during his presidency. Charges of corruption and financial mismanagement, however, marred Grant's second term. His autobiography, *Personal Memoirs*, was published in 1885.

Granville, John Carteret, 1st Earl (1690–1763) British statesman; prime minister (1742–44). A bitter opponent of Robert *Walpole, Granville became prime minister after Walpole's fall. His conduct of the War of the *Austrian Succession was criticized for putting George II's Hanoverian interests above Britain's and George was forced to dismiss him.

Granville-Barker, Harley (1877–1946) British theater director, critic, and dramatist. As comanager of the Royal Court Theatre from 1904 to 1907 he produced many plays by G. B. Shaw and by modern European dramatists. His most influential practical criticism is contained in *Prefaces to Shakespeare* (1927–47). His own plays include *The Voysey Inheritance* (1905) and *The Madras House* (1910).

grape The fruit of vines of the genus *Vitis* (about 60 species), especially *V. vinifera*, native to N Asia but cultivated throughout Mediterranean regions and in the US, especially California and New York. The grapevine is up to 30 m long, twining by means of tendrils, with lobed toothed leaves and dense clusters of small greenish flowers. The fruit—a berry—is green, red, or blue-black and used to make *wine, brandy, and liqueurs or eaten fresh or dried (in the form of raisins, sultanas, and currants).

grapefruit A tree, *Citrus paradisi*, 20–39 ft (6–12 m) high, cultivated throughout the tropics and subtropics. It has shiny oval leaves and clusters of white flowers that mature into fleshy yellow-skinned fruits, 4–6 in (10–15 cm) in diameter. Grapefruits are eaten fresh, canned, or crushed to make beverages. *See* Citrus.

grape hyacinth A perennial herbaceous plant of the genus *Muscari* (50 species), mostly native to the Mediterranean region and widely grown as spring-blooming garden bulbs. The leaves are long and narrow and the blue, pink, or white urn-shaped flowers are borne in a dense cluster at the tip of a leafless flower stalk, up to 6 in (15 cm) high. *M. botryoides*, with blue flowers, is a popular species. Family: *Liliaceae*.

graph A method of providing a visual representation of relationships between quantities, usually in the Cartesian *coordinate system. In mathematics graphs are used to solve equations, represent functions, etc. Histograms, in which the height of columns represents the frequency of a result in each of a series of ranges, and pie charts, which show percentages as segments of a circle, are also sometimes referred to as graphs.

graphite An iron-gray to black form of pure carbon, found in many metamorphic rocks, especially metamorphosed coals or other carbonaceous sediments. It occurs in a laminar or massive form. It is very soft, flaky, and greasy to the touch. Graphite is used for making metallurgical crucibles, as a lubricant, in paint, rubber, and pencil leads, in batteries and for other electrical purposes, and as a moderator in nuclear reactors. It has often been called plumbago or black lead, since it was formerly mistaken for lead.

graptolite A small colonial marine animal belonging to the extinct class *Graptolithina*, possibly related to *coelenterates. Their fossils, in the form of carbonaceous impressions, occur in rocks of the Upper Cambrian to Carboniferous periods, about 420–250 million years ago. Graptolites were floating animals, individual polyps living in the cuplike tips of simple or branched hollow tubes.

grass A monocotyledonous annual or perennial herbaceous plant belonging to the family *Poaceae* (or *Gramineae*; 6000–10,000 species), distributed worldwide. The leaves consist of a basal sheath, which encircles the stem, and a long narrow blade. The flowering stems (culms) bear spikelets of inconspicuous flowers; each spikelet has two basal bracts (glumes) and each flower is enclosed by two other bracts—a lower lemma and an upper palea. The hard single-seeded fruit (the grain) is known botanically as a caryopsis, with the ovary wall (pericarp) and seed coat fused. Many species are important in agriculture as a source of food (*see* cereals; sugar cane) and as pasture grasses.

Grass, Günter (1927–   ) German novelist, poet, and political activist. He won international fame with his first novel, *The Tin Drum* (1959), an epic picaresque treatment of modern German history that established him as a moral spokesman for his generation. His other works include the play *The Plebeians Rehearse the Uprising* (1966) and the novels *Dog Years* (1963), *The Flounder* (1978), *The Meeting at Telgte* (1981), and *Headbirths Or the Germans Are Dying Out* (1982).

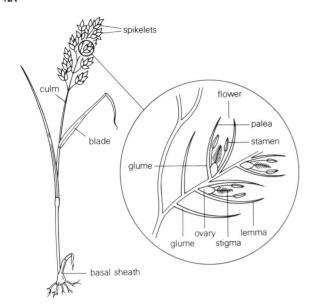

GRASS *The typical structure of a grass is seen in the meadow fescue (Festuca pratensis). The flowers are grouped into spikelets and each consists only of male and female parts; petals and sepals are absent.*

Grasse 43 40N 6 56E A city and resort in SE France, in the Alpes-Maritimes department. It is the center of the French perfume industry. Population (1975): 35,330.

grassfinch A songbird belonging to a subfamily of *weaverfinches, occurring chiefly in arid regions of Australasia. About 4 in (10 cm) long, grassfinches have long tails and stout bills. The group includes a number of colorful popular cagebirds, such as the Gouldian finch (*Poephila gouldiae*) and the *zebra finch.

grasshopper A jumping insect belonging to the family *Acrididae* (about 5000 species). Grasshoppers, 0.94–4 in (24–110 mm) long, are usually green or brown and have short stout antennae and tail appendages. Both sexes produce sound by rubbing the hind legs against the front wings. Some species can fly, sometimes forming dense migratory swarms (*see* locust). Grasshoppers live and feed on grass and low vegetation and the females lay eggs in the soil. Order: *Orthoptera*.

grass monkey A small African *guenon monkey, *Cercopithecus aethiops*, inhabiting thinly wooded regions. The West African green monkey, the East African grivet monkey, and the South African vervet or blue monkey are all local races of grass monkey.

grass of Parnassus A tufted perennial herb of the genus *Parnassia* (about 50 species), especially *P. palustris*, found in wet places throughout Europe and temperate Asia. The basal leaves are stalked and heart-shaped. The solitary white five-petaled flower is borne on an erect stalk with a single unstalked leaf near the base. Family: *Parnassiaceae*.

grass snake A nonvenomous snake, *Natrix natrix*, also called water snake, occurring throughout Europe, usually near ponds, streams, and marshes. 30–37 in (75–95 cm) long, it has a green back with two rows of black spots, vertical black bars along its sides, and a yellow neck patch. It can be distinguished from the *adder, which has a black zigzag line along its back. Its prey includes frogs, tadpoles, fish, lizards, and small mammals. Family: *Colubridae*.

grass tree A woody plant of the genus *Xanthorrhoea* (about 5 species), native to E Australia. They often have palmlike stems, 16 ft (5 m) tall, that end in a tuft of rigid grasslike leaves, from which extend flower spikes resembling those of the *reedmace, about 10 ft (3 m) tall. A red or yellow gumlike resin, used for varnishes, exudes from the bases of old leaves. Family: *Xanthorrhoeaceae*.

Gratian(us), Flavius (359–83 AD) Western Roman emperor (367–83). He was a Christian and abandoned (382) the pagan title *pontifex maximus* (supreme priest). He was deposed by Magnus Maximus (d. 388) and murdered.

Grattan, Henry (1746–1820) Irish politician, who with *Flood was one of the greatest orators in the Irish parliament. From 1775 he led the patriot party and in 1782 obtained Irish free trade and legislative independence from Britain. He opposed, unavailingly, the union of England and Ireland and in 1805 sat in the British parliament. For the remainder of his political career he pressed for *Catholic emancipation.

gravel Unconsolidated rock fragments ranging between 0.08 and 2 in (2 and 60 mm) in particle size, or between coarse sand and cobbles. The term is loosely used for any unconsolidated material coarser than sand, for instance river gravels and glacial gravels.

Gravenhage, 's. *See* Hague, The.

Graves, Robert (Ranke) (1895–) British poet, critic, and novelist. His early autobiography, *Goodbye to All That* (1929), recounts his experiences in World War I. In 1929 he emigrated to Majorca. He has published several editions of *Collected Poems*, historical novels including *I Claudius* (1934) and *Claudius the God* (1934), and studies of mythology, notably *The White Goddess* (1948). A more recent work is *They Hanged My Saintly Billy* (1980).

Gravesend 51 27N 0 24E A port in SE England, in Kent on the River Thames. It is a customs and pilot station for the Port of London and has printing, engineering, and paper-making industries. Population (1981): 52,963.

Gravettian A culture of the Upper *Paleolithic, succeeding the *Aurignacian in W Europe. Named for the cave at La Gravette in the Dordogne (SW France), the Gravettian is characterized by small pointed stone blades with one blunted edge (Gravette points) and dates from between 26,000 and 20,000 BC. The well-known small female figurines called Venuses are of Gravettian origin. The term Eastern Gravettian is applied to similar material from mammoth hunters' camp sites in Russia and E Europe. *Compare* Périgordian.

gravitation An attractive force that occurs between all bodies that possess mass. It was first described by Sir Isaac *Newton in a law stating that the force between two bodies is directly proportional to the product of their masses and inversely proportional to the square of the distance between them. The constant of proportionality is called the universal gravitational constant, G, which has the value 6.673×10^{-11} newton meter squared per kilogram squared. Gravitation is now more accurately described by the general theory of *relativity. In this theory a mass distorts the *space-time continuum around it so that the geometry of the space is locally no longer Euclidean. The force of gravity and the *acceleration of free fall are the result of the attractive force between a body and the earth.

gravitational collapse The sudden collapse of the core of a *star when thermonuclear fusion eventually ceases. The star's internal gas pressure can no longer support the weight of the star and the initial result may be a *supernova explosion. The gravitational pull of all the constituents of the star, or its remains, causes it to contract. The extent of the contraction depends on the mass of the object, producing a *white dwarf, *neutron star, or *black hole.

gravitational interaction One of the four kinds of interaction that occur between elementary particles (*see* particle physics) and by far the weakest (about 10^{40} times weaker than the *electromagnetic interaction). The interaction occurs between all particles with mass and can be explained as the exchange of *virtual particles called gravitons. Such particles have not yet been detected.

gray (Gy) The *SI unit of absorbed dose of ionizing radiation equal to the energy in joules absorbed by one kilogram of irradiated material.

Gray, Asa (1810–88) US botanist, who compiled *Flora of North America* (2 vols, 1838–43), a comprehensive taxonomic guide to the region's plants. He also wrote many popular books on botany, including a *Manual of the Botany of the Northern United States* (1848). Gray was a firm supporter of Darwin's theories of evolution, although he believed that the process of natural selection was controlled by God.

Gray, Elisha (1835–1901) US inventor. Early interested in electricity, he held about 70 patents, the first received in 1867 for an improved telegraph relay. In 1872 he established Gray and Barton Company, the predecessor of Western Electric Company, and in 1876 filed for a patent on his invention, the telephone, just hours after a similar patent application by Alexander Graham *Bell. Years of controversy and litigation followed, but the courts finally ruled in Bell's favor. From 1880 he taught electrical engineering at Oberlin College.

Gray, Thomas (1716–71) British poet. He spent most of his life in scholarly retirement. He published only a few odes apart from his most famous poem, *Elegy Written in a Country Churchyard* (1751), a classical meditation on the graves of the humble villagers of Stoke Poges, Buckinghamshire.

grayling A troutlike fish of the genus *Thymallus*, sometimes placed in a distinct family (*Thymallidae*). Graylings have a silvery-purple scaly body, up to 20 in (50 cm) long, with a sail-like dorsal fin, and live in cold clear fresh waters of Eurasia and N North America, feeding on aquatic insects. They are important food and game fish. Family: *Salmonidae*.

graylag goose A grazing *goose, *Anser anser*, occurring in N and E Europe and central Asia. 30–34 in (75–87 cm) long, it has a heavy orange bill and is dark gray above with pale wings, a finely barred neck, and pink legs.

graywacke (*or* greywacke) A dark-colored sedimentary rock with sand-sized angular rock particles in a finer matrix. Graywackes display a wide range of sedimentary structures and are commonly found in geosynclines.

Graz 47 05N 15 22E The second largest city in Austria, the capital of Styria. Its numerous historical buildings include a cathedral (1438–62) and a notable clock tower (1561). It has a university (1586). An industrial center, it produces iron and steel, textiles, and chemicals. Population (1981): 239,404.

Great Artesian Basin An artesian basin of E Australia. The largest area of artesian water in the world, it extends S from the Gulf of Carpentaria in Queensland into South Australia and New South Wales, underlying the catchments of both the Darling River and Lake Eyre. Area: 676,250 sq mi (1,750,000 sq km).

Great Australian Bight A wide bay of the Indian Ocean, in S Australia situated between Capes Pasley and Carnot. Width: 720 mi (1159 km).

Great Awakening A religious revival in the American colonies in the 18th century. It began in the 1720s among members of the Dutch Reformed Church of New Jersey but flourished in New England in 1740–43, after which it spread to other colonies. It was largely inspired by the preaching of George *Whitefield and Jonathan *Edwards, who, however, disapproved of the excessive enthusiasm or hysteria that was often manifested by those claiming to be converted.

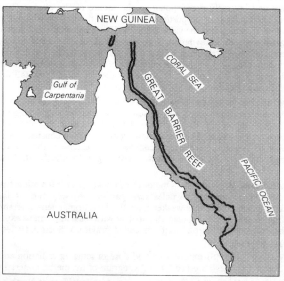

GREAT BARRIER REEF

Great Barrier Reef The largest coral reef in the world, situated in the Coral Sea off the coast of NE Australia. Approximately 15,000 years old, it consists of a complex of coral reefs, shoals, and islets extending for 1250 mi (2000 km) from Breaksea Spit to the Gulf of Papua. Its many fish, crustaceans, birds, exotic plant life, and some 350 species of colorful corals make it popular with tourists.

Great Basin A large semiarid area in the US. Situated between the Sierra Nevada and the Wasatch Mountains, it extends over most of Nevada, Utah, and parts of California and Oregon. It consists of a series of basins, mountain ranges, deserts (including the *Mojave Desert), and salt lakes (including the *Great Salt Lake).

Great Bear. *See* Ursa Major.

Great Bear Lake A lake in N Canada, in Mackenzie district on the Arctic Circle. Frozen eight months of the year, it is the fourth largest lake in North America. It drains into the Mackenzie River via the Great Bear River, 70 mi (112 km) long. Area: 12,275 sq mi (31,792 sq km).

Great Belt (Danish name: Store Bælt) A channel between the Danish islands of Fyn and Sjælland, linking the Kattegat and the Baltic Sea.

Great Britain The largest island in the British Isles and in Europe, separated from the mainland of W Europe by the North Sea and the English Channel. Containing *England, *Scotland, and *Wales, it includes the islands governed with the mainland but excludes the Isle of Man and the Channel Islands. Area: 88,619 sq mi (229,523 sq km). Population (1981 est): 54,128,000.

great circle A circle that is the intersection on the surface of a sphere of a plane passing through the center of that sphere. On the earth, each meridian of longitude is half of a great circle; the equator is the only parallel of lattitude that is a great circle.

great crested grebe A large *grebe, *Podiceps cristatus*, occurring in Eurasia. It is dark brown above with a white face, neck, and underparts, a black two-horned crest and neck frill, and chestnut patches at the sides of the face. Mating pairs perform an elaborate courtship display.

Great Dane A breed of large dog originating in Germany, where they were developed for hunting boar. The Great Dane has a large powerful frame with long legs and a large head with a square muzzle. The short sleek coat can be golden, black, streaked brown, blue-gray, or white with black patches. Height: 30 in (76 cm) minimum (dogs); 28 in (71 cm) minimum (bitches).

Great Dividing Range (Great Divide *or* Eastern Highlands) The E highlands of Australia, comprising a complex of mountains and plateaus. It extends for about 2300 mi (3700 km) from Cape York Peninsula to the Grampians of Victoria and includes the *Blue Mountains and Australian Alps, where it reaches 7316 ft (2230 m) at Mount *Kosciusko.

Greater Antilles The four largest West Indian islands, in the N Caribbean Sea, comprising Cuba, Hispaniola, Jamaica, and Puerto Rico.

Great Exhibition (1851) A display of the products of industrial Britain and Europe, planned by Prince Albert and held in the *Crystal Palace. It contained about 13,000 exhibits and showed the technical progress and industrial supremacy of Britain.

Great Indian Desert. *See* Thar Desert.

Great Lake A shallow freshwater lake in Australia. It lies on the central plateau of Tasmania, at an altitude of 3380 ft (1030 m), and is used as a storage reservoir for hydroelectric power. Area: 44 sq mi (114 sq km).

Great Lakes Five large lakes in E central North America, mostly along the US-Canadian border: Lakes *Superior, *Michigan, *Huron, *Erie, and *Ontario. The world's largest freshwater surface, they drain into the *St Lawrence River and form part of the *St Lawrence Seaway. Canals also link them to the Mississippi River, making them a major transportation route. Their basin is an important economic region, with agriculture, fishing, forestry, mining, hydroelectricity, manufacturing, commerce, and tourism. Recently water pollution has become a major problem, compounded by the many governments with jurisdiction over the lakes.

Great Leap Forward A nationwide campaign in China to promote economic and industrial growth. The movement started in 1958 and aimed to increase industrial production dramatically by using manpower rather than capital in large-scale rural communes and backyard steel furnaces and factories. Ambitious production targets were reached but it proved impossible to coordinate production and control quality, and the movement was revoked in 1960.

Great Ouse River (*or* R. Ouse) A river in E England, rising in Northamptonshire and flowing NE across the Fens to the Wash near King's Lynn. Length: 160 mi (257 km).

Great Plains An extensive area in North America. It consists of a system of rolling plains extending from the Mackenzie River Delta in Canada in the N to the Rio Grande in the S. It is chiefly agricultural with livestock raising and grain production. Length: about 3000 mi (4800 km). Average width: about 400 mi (645 km).

Great Red Spot An immense reddish oval feature in the atmosphere of *Jupiter, lying S of the equator. Observed for over a century, its prominence, color, and size (8694 mi [14,000 km] N–S by up to 24,840 mi [40,000 km] E–W) have been found to fluctuate. Pioneer planetary probes showed it to be a vortex of cold anticlockwise-rotating clouds elevated above the surrounding cloud layer and colored possibly by traces of phosphorus.

Great Rift Valley (*or* East African Rift System) An extensive rift valley in the Middle East and East Africa. It extends from the Jordan Valley in Syria along the Red Sea into Ethiopia and through Kenya, Tanzania, and Malawi into Mozambique. It is marked by a chain of lakes (Lakes Turkana (formerly Rudolf) and Natron) and volcanoes (Mount Kilimanjaro). Length: about 4000 mi (6400 km).

Great Salt Lake A salt lake in NW Utah, in the Great Basin. It is bordered by the Wasatch Mountains and the Great Salt Lake Desert and has no outlet. A salt extraction industry exists along its shores. Its area has fluctuated from less than 1000 sq mi (2500 sq km) to over 2000 sq mi (5000 sq km).

Great Sandy Desert A desert of N Western Australia. It consists of a vast arid region of sand dunes and salt marshes stretching SE from Eighty Mile Beach on the Indian Ocean to the Gibson Desert. Area: 160,000 sq mi (415,000 sq km).

Great Schism (1378–1417) The split in the Roman Catholic Church following the election of two rival popes to succeed Gregory XI. Criticisms of the residency of the papacy in Avignon (*see* Avignon papacy) forced its return to Rome and the election of an Italian, Urban VI. He determined to reform the College of Cardinals, which responded by electing an *antipope at Avignon, Clement VII. The Schism was ended by the Council of *Constance (1414–18) and the election of Martin V in 1417. (For the schism in 1054 between the E and W Christian churches, *see* Filioque.)

Great Slave Lake A very deep lake in N Canada, in Mackenzie district. The fifth largest lake in North America, it drains into the Mackenzie River. Area: 10,980 sq mi (28,438 sq km).

Great Smoky Mountains A mountain range, part of the Appalachians, in E Tennessee and W North Carolina, running NE from the Little Tennessee River to the Pigeon River. Most of the mountains comprise Great Smoky Mountains National Park. Clingmans Dome is the highest point (6643 ft; 2025 m). The mountains are thickly forested with nearly 100 kinds of trees. The hydrocarbons released from some of these trees create the haze that hangs over the mountains and gives them their name.

great tit The largest of the *tits, *Parus major*: a common European bird of woodland, farmland, and gardens feeding on caterpillars, aphids, scale insects, and other pests. It is about 5.5 in (14 cm) long and has a black head with white cheeks, a green back, and a black stripe down its yellow breast.

Great Trek The movement from the mid-1830s to mid-1840s of Dutch settlers (Afrikaners) in South Africa northward across the Orange and Vaal Rivers from the Cape. The so-called Voortrekkers, under such leaders as Andries *Pretorius, moved away from British rule at the Cape in search of more farmland that they could administer themselves. They are considered by Afrikaners to be the founding fathers of South Africa. They established the republics of the Transvaal and the Orange Free State.

Great Victoria Desert A desert of Western and South Australia, between the Gibson Desert and Nullarbor Plain. It consists of a vast arid region of sand hills and salt marshes. Area: 125,000 sq mi (323,750 sq km).

Great Wall of China A medieval defensive fortification in N China. Stretching from the Yellow Sea N of Peking nearly 1500⅜ mi (2400 km) inland, the Great Wall is the world's largest building achievement. Originally begun in 214 ⅝ BC as a defense against nomadic tribes, it was improved and largely rebuilt of stone in the 15th and 16th centuries. It is about 30 ft (9 m) high, with numerous higher watch towers along its length.

GREAT ZIMBABWE *A picture of the ruins of a large round tower, part of the so-called Elliptical Building, published by Britain's Royal Geographical Society in 1892.*

Great Zimbabwe The largest of the ruined Bantu royal centers on the Zambezian plateau in Zimbabwe. The word *zimbabwe* is derived from the Bantu for "revered houses." Great Zimbabwe reached its zenith in the late 14th century but suffered abrupt decline after about 1440. Traces of widespread trade, based on local gold, have been discovered, including Chinese pottery. Parts of the so-called Elliptical Building (a compound enclosing now vanished huts) stand 35 ft (10.5 m) high and consist of regular dry stone courses of dressed granite.

grebe A bird belonging to a primitive family (*Podicipitidae*; 21 species) occurring in rivers and lakes worldwide. Grebes are adapted for swimming and diving by having short wings, a very small tail, and partially webbed feet with lobed toes. They have a long neck and a long pointed bill and feed chiefly on fish and aquatic invertebrates. Grebes are gray, black, or brown, usually with white underparts, and in the breeding season many have brightly colored erectile crests and ear tufts. Order: *Podicipediformes*. *See also* dabchick; great crested grebe.

Greece, Republic of (Greek name: Ellás) A country in SE Europe, occupying the S section of the Balkan Peninsula between the Mediterranean and Aegean Seas. Numerous islands, which comprise about one fifth of the total area of Greece, lie to the S, E, and W, the largest being Crete. Crete as well as the other Greek islands, including Corfu, the Ionian Isles, the Cyclades, and the Dodecanese (especially Rhodes), are popular tourist spots, and tourism constitutes an important source of revenue for the country. About 75% of the terrain is mountainous, the highest point being Mt Olympus (rising to 9570 ft; 2917 m). In the S the Peloponnesus, a mountainous peninsula, is linked to the mainland by the Isthmus of Corinth. The mainland is largely mountainous, with plains in Thrace and Macedonia in the N and Thessaly in the center. *Economy*: since the early 1970s industry has replaced agriculture as the mainstay of the economy. The rapid expansion of the industrial sector (especially metallurgy, chemicals, textiles, rubber, plastics, and electrical machinery) began in the 1960s. Mineral resources, including lignite, bauxite, and iron ore, have been intensively exploited and processed and there has been a dramatic increase in electricity output. The first nuclear power station is expected to be in operation by the 1980s. Recent plans include incentives for the decentralization of industry, which has led to a rapidly changing pattern of growth in N Greece aided by the discovery of natural gas and oil near the island of Thásos. There has been considerable diversification of agriculture and the principal crops include wheat, barley, maize, tobacco, sugar beet, tomatoes, and dried and fresh fruits. *History*: the centuries following the collapse of the *Mycenaean civilization (c. 1200 BC) saw the rise of the Greek city states. From the 8th century, trading activities led to the establishment of colonies around the Mediterranean, in Asia Minor, N Africa, S Italy and Sicily, and in S France. The first half of the 5th century was dominated by the ultimately abortive attempt of the Persians to annex Greece (*see* Greek-Persian Wars) and the late 5th century, by the Peloponnesian War between rival Athens and Sparta. Sparta's subsequent supremacy in Greece lasted until its defeat by Thebes in 371. Greece fell to Philip of Macedon in 338 and was incorporated in the empire of his son Alexander the Great. Following the division of Alexander's possessions at his death (323), the Greek city states remained within the Macedonian orbit but repeatedly attempted to assert their independence until the last Macedonian War (171–168) allowed Rome to dominate Greece. Roman rule lasted until 395 AD, when the Roman Empire was divided between W and E and Greece became part of the Byzantine (Eastern Roman) Empire, centered on Constantinople. In the middle ages Greece was subject to invasions by the Franks, Normans, and the Latin Crusaders. In the early 14th century Byzantium reasserted its control over the area but in 1453 Constantinople fell to the Ottoman Turks; by 1460 they controlled all Greece. Apart from a brief period (1686–1715) of partial Venetian occupation, Greece remained under Ottoman rule until achieving independence in 1829 (*see* Greek Independence, War of). The history of Greece since independence has been characterized by political instability. For over a century, warring republicans and monarchists threw the country into turmoil with monarchs successively toppled and restored in short order. In 1832 the Greek crown was offered to a Bavarian prince, who became Otto I (1815–67), but his despotic rule precipitated his deposition in 1862. In 1863 a Danish prince became king as George I (1845–1913). In the same year Greece acquired the Ionian Islands from Britain and in 1881, in the aftermath of the Congress of Berlin, Thessaly and part of Epirus from Turkey. Greek demands for Crete led to a disastrous war with Turkey in 1897, but in the Balkan Wars (1912–13) Greece gained the island together with territory in Thrace and Macedonia. In 1917 Venizelos took Greece into World War I on the Allied side and the immediate postwar period saw renewed territorial conflict with Turkey, in which Greece lost Smyrna. In 1924 Greece became a republic, which lasted until George II was restored in 1935. In World War II an unsuccessful Italian invasion (1940) was followed by the German occupation (1941–44), after which Greece was plunged into a civil war between monarchists and communists that lasted until 1949. The 1950s were dominated by the question of union with Cyprus, which Greece supported (*see* EOKA), and the 1960s saw a military coup (1967), which deposed Constantine II and established the rule of the colonels under Papadopoulos. He was overthrown in 1973 and succeeded by General Phaedon Ghizikis. The government's involvement in the coup against Makarios in Cyprus led to its collapse (1974). A new constitution (1975) saw the reintroduction of democratic government. Greece became a member of the EEC in 1981 and later in the same year the country's first socialist government was elected. The electoral victory of Andreas Papandreou and his Panhellenic Socialist Movement (Pasko) marked the end of 30 years of Western-style government in Greece. Seeking to assert Greek independence in foreign affairs, Papandreou's election campaign called for withdrawal from the EEC and NATO. Subsequently, however, more pragmatic strategies dominated Greece's relations with the West, resulting in dissatisfaction at home (especially within the Communist Party) because of shelved campaign promises. Head of state: President Constantine Karamanlis. Prime minister: Andreas Papandreou. Official language: Greek. Official religion: Greek Orthodox. Official currency: drachma of 100 lepta. Area: 50,960 sq mi (131,986 sq km). Population (1983): 9,898,000. Capital: Athens. Main port: Piraeus.

GREEK ART   *An Attic black figure cup (c. 550 BC). The names on it are those of Epiketus, the painter, and Hischylos, the maker.*

Greek art and architecture   The arts of ancient Greece from the 8th century BC until Greece's absorption in the Roman Empire after 27 BC, conventionally divided into three main periods: archaic (before c. 550), classical (550–323), and Hellenistic (323–27). Most extant paintings are on pottery. Nonfigurative all-over designs of the earliest period gradually gave way to the more naturalistic black-figure technique in the 7th and 6th centuries BC. The greatest achievements are the Athenian red-figure vases (530–400 BC). As is also the case with sculptors, the work of many Greek painters (e.g. *Zeuxis) is known only through Roman copies, but magnificent Hellenistic wall paintings have recently been uncovered at Vergina. In sculpture, the monumental Egyptian-influenced solidity of the early *kore and *kouros statues yielded to the idealized naturalism of the classical period (480–323 BC). This is exemplified in the *Elgin marbles and in the work of *Phidias and *Praxiteles. In the subsequent Hellenistic period sculpture is characteristically represented by dramatic subject matter and highly complex figure poses and groupings. The small-scale arts of coin engraving, gem carving, jewelry making, and the sculpting of bronze and terracotta figures (*see* Tanagra figurines) also reached a peak of perfection in the Hellenistic era. Greek architecture is perhaps the greatest legacy that the ancient Greeks have left us, for almost all subsequent European architecture is indebted to it. Although the Egyptians invented the colonnade (c. 2500 BC) and the Romans were the first to make use of arches, domes, and vaults as structural features, it was the Greeks who invented the entablature to surmount the colonnade in order to support a hipped roof. They also perfected the design of columns and created the concept of an architect as an artist, engineer, and town planner. Archaic Greek architecture had its roots in Crete (the first palace at Knossos was built about 2000 BC) and in

Mycenae (the famous Lion Gate was erected about 1450 BC). However, classical (*or* Hellenic) Greek architecture did not emerge until about 700 BC, when the Greeks began to build in stone (limestone or marble) instead of wood, rubble, and mud bricks. This development followed slightly different courses on opposite sides of the Aegean Sea. During the 6th century BC the Doric order (*see* orders of architecture; □architecture) emerged as a consistent style in mainland Greece; at about the same time the Ionic order developed on the eastern shores of the Aegean. Both styles reached their zenith in the time of Pericles (490–429 BC); on the Athenian Acropolis the *Parthenon is the prime example of a Doric temple, while the Erechtheum (built by Mnesicles in 405 BC) contains three different Ionic orders. During the Hellenistic period the Doric gave way to the Ionic, and this in turn yielded to the third order of Greek architecture, the Corinthian. This style is exemplified by the Olympieium at Athens, built by Cossutius in 174 BC.

Greek Independence, War of   (1821–32) The war that established a Greek state independent of the Ottoman Empire. The rebels had some initial success until in 1825 the Ottomans were strengthened by Egyptian help. The UK, France, and Russia offered to mediate and when rebuffed by the Ottomans defeated the Ottoman and Egyptian fleet at the battle of *Navarino (1827). The Ottomans fought on briefly but peace negotiations were begun in London in 1829 and independence was proclaimed, being recognized by the Ottoman Empire in 1832, when a Greek monarchy was established. European sympathy for the Greek cause had been encouraged by Lord Byron's championship.

Greek language   An Indo-European language spoken chiefly in Greece and the E Mediterranean islands. Well documented since the 14th century BC (*see* Linear B), ancient Greek was a highly complex inflected language. It had many dialect forms, the main groupings being Ionic (E Greece and Asia Minor), Aeolic (Boeotia and Thessaly), and Doric (the Peloponnese). From Ionic developed the Attic dialect, centered on Athens, which became the chief literary language of classical Greece. When the Greek city states lost their independence (4th century BC), their dialects gave way to a new common dialect (*koine*), which became the language of Hellenistic Greece and the New Testament. During the Byzantine Empire, Greek increasingly diverged from classical forms, with simplified pronunciations and foreign borrowings. Modern Greek has two widely differing forms: the classically based Katharevusa (purified tongue) used in official publications, and Demotic, the living language of speech, poetry, and fiction.

Greek literature   The epics of *Homer date from the 8th century BC, though their echoes of *Mycenaean civilization suggest that they may have existed in oral form for considerably longer. A little later (c. 700) *Hesiod's poems portray the lives and concerns of farmers. *Archilochus of Paros and Alcman (both 7th century) were early masters of lyric verse; they were followed by *Alcaeus, *Sappho, *Solon, and *Anacreon in the 6th century and *Pindar in the early 5th century. Incipient philosophical speculation in 6th-century Ionia stimulated the development of prose, but the earliest prose work to survive entire is the mid-5th-century history of *Herodotus. After the defeat of the Persians (480 BC) Attic writers brought about the flowering of classical Greek literature; major figures were the tragedians *Aeschylus, *Sophocles, and *Euripides, the comedian *Aristophanes (*see* Old Comedy), and the historian *Thucydides. Prose achieved its acme in the 4th century with the works of *Plato, *Xenophon, and the orators *Isocrates and *Demosthenes. During the Hellenistic age Alexandria became the cultural center of the Greek world; it was the home of the poets *Apollonius of Rhodes and *Callimachus, as well as of mathematicians, astronomers, and others who enhanced the status of Greek as a scientific and scholarly medium. Notable among Hellenistic writers elsewhere were the Sicilians *Theocritus and Moschus (c. 150 BC). Under the Roman Empire Greek remained an international literary language, as the works of *Marcus Aurelius, *Plutarch, and the Greek Church Fathers testify. After the 6th century AD, when Byzantium became the center of Greek culture, histories (*see* Procopius), theological works, and scholarly commentaries became the main output. The 10th-century compilation known as the Greek Anthology comprises over 6000 poems ranging in date from the 7th century BC to the 10th century AD. A popular (demotic) tradition also survived, which expressed itself in folksong and epic (e.g. the late 10th-century epic, *Digenìs Akritas*) and led eventually to the birth of modern Greek literature. *See also* Greek language.

Greek Orthodox Church   Strictly, the Orthodox Church in Greece, although the term is often applied to the Orthodox Churches as a whole, to distinguish them from the Latin Church of the West. The Church in Greece dates from the 1st century and St Paul's activities, especially at Corinth. Under the patriarchate of Constantinople Greece was, from the acceptance of Christianity by *Constantine, one of the main Christian centers. With the eventual fall of Constantinople to the Turks, it ceased to be identified with the Byzantine Empire and is now a self-governing Church, the see of Athens holding a primacy of honor after the separation from the patriarchate of Constantinople in 1833.

Greek-Persian Wars An intermittent conflict between the Greeks and Persians. Persian encroachment on Greek territory began in 499 BC, when the Greek cities of *Ionia revolted against their Persian overlords and were crushed by *Darius I. In 490 the Persians were defeated by a small force of Athenians at *Marathon. Darius died in 486 and in 480 *Xerxes I crossed the Hellespont with a large force. The Greeks and Persians fought at *Thermopylae, where the Spartans (under *Leonidas I) heroically held the pass. Xerxes now attacked Attica and Athens was evacuated. At the battle of *Salamis the Persians were defeated by the Greek fleet commanded by *Themistocles and were again defeated at *Plataea (479). Intermittent warfare continued until 449, when the Persians abandoned hope of annexing Greece.

Greek religion The polytheistic religion of ancient Greece. From at least the time of Homer (9th century BC) the myths and deities of the various Greek states were integrated into a more or less coherent system, with a pantheon of 12 anthropomorphic gods who lived on Mount Olympus: *Zeus, *Hera, *Poseidon, *Athena, *Apollo, *Artemis, *Hephaestus, *Aphrodite, *Ares, *Demeter, *Hermes, and *Hestia. All these had appropriate festivals and observances throughout Greece. The orgiastic rites of *Cybele and *Dionysus were slightly later imports from Asia Minor. Deified heroes, such as *Heracles, were also worshiped and there were innumerable local cults for lesser supernatural beings, such as the *nymphs. For those who found the traditional eschatology of *Hades unsatisfactory, the *mysteries held a powerful attraction. During the Hellenistic age king-worship, another oriental import, became important. Religious centers honored throughout Greece included *Delphi, *Delos, Dodona, *Epidaurus, and *Olympia. The forms of the ancient religion were not finally abolished until the Christian emperors closed these shrines (4th century AD), and even today local saints sometimes retain some of the attributes of the pagan gods.

Greeley, Horace (1811–72) US political journalist, who in 1841 founded the *New York Tribune*, championing temperance, liberal reforms, and protectionism. Among his contributors were many well-known people, including, for a time, Karl Marx. In the 1860s he vigorously opposed slavery. After the war he advocated amnesty and suffrage for all males in the South. He made several attempts to enter politics, unsuccessfully running as presidential candidate for the Liberal Republican Party in 1872.

green algae *Algae of the division *Chlorophyta* (about 6000 species), which are bright green, owing to the predominance of the green pigment chlorophyll. Green algae range from simple unicellular plants, for example *Chlamydomonas*, to complex seaweeds, for example *sea lettuce. They are aquatic (mainly freshwater) or terrestrial in moist areas. Reproduction can be sexual or asexual.

Greenaway, Kate (1846–1901) British artist and book illustrator. The daughter of an engraver and draftsman, she is famous for her charming representation of children in such books as *Kate Greenaway's Birthday Album* and *The Language of Flowers*.

Greenback Party (Independent National Party, Greenback Labor Party, National Greenback Party; 1875–84) A US political party in favor of issuing unlimited paper currency to boost the economy. Backed by farmers and workers, it advocated an 8-hour working day, a graduated income tax, the continued circulation of paper money, government controlled interstate commerce, and women's suffrage. It opposed the gold standard and national banks. When the gold standard returned in 1879, the party steadily declined and in 1884 was absorbed by the Anti-Monopoly Party.

Green Bay 44 32N 88 00W A city and port in E Wisconsin, at the head of an inlet of Lake Michigan. Its main industries are paper manufacture and food and dairy processing. Green Bay is the home of the National Railroad Museum and a professional football team, the Green Bay Packers. Population (1980): 87,889.

greenbrier A green-stemmed often evergreen vinelike plant, *Smilax rotundifolia*, that grows in North American woods and thickets, also called catbrier. The leaves are heart-shaped and leathery, and the plant climbs by means of tendrils. The six-part flowers are borne in stalked clusters in the leaf axils and produce blue-black berries. Family: *Liliaceae*.

Greene, (Henry) Graham (1904–) British novelist. After the publication of his first novel, *The Man Within* (1929), he devoted himself to full-time writing. He was converted to Roman Catholicism in 1927, and an intense concern with questions of morality is central in many of his novels, including *Brighton Rock* (1938), *The Power and the Glory* (1940), *The End of the Affair* (1951), *The Human Factor* (1978), *Dr Fischer of Geneva or The Bomb Party* (1980), and *Monsignor Quixote* (1982). He also wrote a number of literary thrillers, which he labeled "entertainments," including *The Ministry of Fear* (1943), *The Third Man* (1950), and *Our Man in Havana* (1958). His other works include plays, film scripts of several of his books, short stories, and essays.

Greene, Nathaniel (1742–86) US military leader. He served in the RI General Assembly (1770–72) and was appointed brigadier general in the Continental Army in 1775. After serving as commander of the army of occupation in Boston, he was promoted to the rank of major general and took part in the battles of *Trenton (1776) and Germantown (1777). In 1778, at *Valley Forge, George Washington named him quartermaster general and Greene successfully organized the supplies to the American troops at the battles of Monmouth and Newport in the same year. Greene was chosen by Washington to succeed General Horatio Gates as Commander of the Army of the South in 1780, and he ultimately forced the British army under Lord *Cornwallis to relinquish its occupation of the Carolinas.

greenfinch A Eurasian *finch, *Carduelis chloris*, about 5.5 in (14 cm) long with an olive-green body and a pale bill. The male has a bright yellow-green breast and both sexes show bright-yellow wing flashes in flight.

greenfly. *See* aphid.

greengage A bush or small tree, *Prunus italica*, related to the *plum, probably native to Asia Minor and widely cultivated. It bears round green fruits, often tinged with red, which are scented and sweet flavored and used in preserves and for canning.

greenheart An evergreen South American timber tree, *Nectandria rodiaei*, native to Guiana, also called sweetwood or bebeeru. Up to 98 ft (30 m) tall, it has branching clusters of inconspicuous flowers and the fruit is surrounded by an acorn-like cup. The wood, which is extremely dense and hard, is used for underwater construction and ships. Family: *Lauraceae* (laurel family).

greenhouse effect An atmospheric effect in which some of the energy of ultraviolet radiation and visible light from the sun is retained by the earth as heat. The radiation is transmitted through the atmosphere to the earth's surface, where it is reradiated as longer wavelength infrared radiation. The atmosphere only partially transmits the infrared back into space and so a heating effect occurs. The phenomenon takes its name from a greenhouse, in which a similar effect occurs.

Greenland (Danish name: Grønland) A large island off NE North America bounded by the N Atlantic Ocean and the Greenland and Norwegian Seas. Lying chiefly within the Arctic Circle, it is largely covered by a vast ice cap through which nunataks protrude around its rim. Many glaciers emerge from this, including the Humboldt Glacier, breaking off to form icebergs along the coast. Eskimos form about 80% of the population, the remainder being chiefly Danish. *Economy*: fishing is the chief occupation, principally for cod and halibut but other catches include shrimps and sea trout. Whaling and seal hunting have declined in recent years. The harsh environment makes agriculture difficult but sheep are reared in the SW. Greenland possesses potentially important mineral resources, notably lead and zinc, which have been exploited since the early 1970s; uranium is also present. *History:* in about 986 AD the Norwegian Eric the Red discovered the island, which he named Greenland to attract settlers. Norse colonies on the island disappeared during the 15th century and until 1721, when a new Danish settlement was established, the Eskimos were the sole inhabitants. A Danish colony from 1721, Greenland became an integral part of Denmark in 1953. In 1979 it gained self-government under Danish sovereignty with its own parliament. Prime minister: Jonathan Motzfeldt. Official language: Greenland Eskimo. Official currency: Danish krone of 100 øre. Area: 840,000 sq mi (2,175,600 sq km). Population (1981): 50,643. Capital: Godthaab.

Greenland Sea An extension of the Arctic Ocean, between Greenland, Svalbard, and Iceland. Covered by drifting ice, it links with the Atlantic Ocean.

Greenland shark A large omnivorous *shark, up to 23 ft (7 m) long, *Somniosus microcephalus*, found usually in shoals in the deeper waters of the N Atlantic and Arctic Oceans. Family: *Squalidae*.

green monkey disease An acute, often fatal, viral infection first described in Marburg, West Germany, and therefore sometimes called Marburg disease. It occurs in vervet monkeys and may be transmitted to laboratory workers by contact with infected animals.

Green Mountain Boys A volunteer militia formed in 1764 to protect the property rights of the settlers of northern New England. In response to attempts by the province of New York to annex portions of Vermont, the Green Mountain Boys, under the command of Ethan *Allen after 1770, successfully defended their land grants. With the outbreak of the *Revolutionary War, they joined forces with the Continental Army, participating in the capture of Fort *Ticonderoga (1775) and in the Battle of Bennington (1777). Their original purpose was attained in 1791 when Vermont was granted statehood.

Green Mountains A mountain range, part of the Appalachians, that extend from N Massachusetts, through central Vermont to S Canada. Mt Mansfield in NW Vermont is the highest point and rises to 4393 ft (1339 m). The mountains yield granite for Vermont's quarrying industry, lumber, and recreation areas, especially for winter sports.

Greenock 55 57N 4 45W A city in W central Scotland, on the Clyde estuary. Shipbuilding is its principal industry; others include engineering, sugar refining, and chemicals. James Watt was born here. Population (1981): 57,324.

Greenough, Horatio (1805–52) US neoclassical sculptor. A pupil of *Thorvaldsen, Greenough worked mainly in Rome. His most important sculpture was of George Washington in a toga commissioned by Congress in 1832.

Green Revolution. *See* agriculture; arable farming.

Greensboro 36 04N 79 47W A city in N central North Carolina, E of Winston-Salem and NW of Durham. The Battle of Guilford Courthouse, a Revolutionary War battle in 1781, was fought near here. Industries include clothing, tobacco, and petroleum-related products, drugs, and building materials. Population (1980): 155,642.

greenshank A bird, *Tringa nebularia*, that breeds in N Eurasian moorland and tundra and winters in South Africa and S Eurasia. It is 12 in (30 cm) long and grayish in color with greenish legs, a white rump, and a long slightly upturned blue-gray bill. Family: *Scolopacidae* (sandpipers).

green turtle A large brown-green marine turtle, *Chelonia mydas*, which has green fat and is used to make turtle soup. Up to 40 in (1 m) long and weighing up to 309 lb (140 kg), they occur in warm Atlantic coastal waters feeding on marine algae and migrate long distances to lay their eggs on Central American beaches. □reptile.

Greenwich A borough of E Greater London, on the S bank of the River Thames. It has important royal and maritime connections. The Greenwich Royal Hospital, designed by *Wren, became the Royal Naval College in 1873. Wren also designed the original *Royal Greenwich Observatory. Population (1981): 211,806.

Greenwich Mean Time (GMT) The local time at Greenwich, London, located on the 0° meridian (*see* longitude), from which the standard times of different areas of the globe are calculated, 15° longitude representing one hour in time.

Greenwich Village A residential section of New York City, in Manhattan. It became a favorite haunt of authors and artists early in the 20th century, acquiring a reputation for bohemianism. It is the site of the main campus of New York University.

Gregorian calendar. *See* calendar.

Gregorian chant The official liturgical plainchant of the Roman Catholic Church as codified during the papacy of Gregory I (590–604 AD). It consists of single unaccompanied melodic lines based on a system of *modes and sung to flexible rhythms. *See* plainchant.

Gregory I, St (c. 540–604 AD) Pope (590–604), known as Gregory the Great. Of senatorial rank, he gave himself to charitable works and was a monk before becoming a papal official. As pope he reorganized and increased papal power in Italy, making peace with the Lombards and limiting imperial authority over the Church. He reformed the papal states and sponsored *Augustine (of Canterbury) in his mission to convert England. Gregory's many pastoral and doctrinal works were of considerable influence, and he introduced the use of *Gregorian chant into the liturgy. He was canonized on his death. Feast day: March 12.

Gregory VII, St (Hildebrand; c. 1021–85) Pope (1073–85). Before his election he worked closely with *Leo IX and Alexander II to reform the Church. As pope, he condemned simony, lay investiture, and clerical marriage. He was ultimately largely successful in asserting the independence of the Church from lay control but during his lifetime he created considerable opposition, especially in France and Germany, where Emperor *Henry IV declared his deposition (1076). He in turn excommunicated Henry and released his subjects from allegiance. Henry was soon forced to accept the pope's reforms and submitted to him at Canossa (1077). The conflict continued, however, when the emperor appointed Wibert, Archbishop of Ravenna, antipope (1080), invaded Italy, and captured Rome (1084). Gregory was rescued by Norman troops whom he had summoned but was nevertheless forced to flee from Rome. He died at Salerno. Feast day: May 25.

Gregory IX (Ugolino of Segni; c. 1148–1241) Pope (1227–41). He was employed as a papal legate by his uncle, *Innocent III, and preached the fifth Crusade (1217). On his election as pope, he immediately excommunicated Emperor *Frederick II for his delay in fulfilling crusading vows. His papacy was marked by conflict with the emperor, and he died while Frederick was besieging Rome. He was a noted canon lawyer and was a friend of St *Francis of Assisi, whom he canonized.

Gregory XIII (Ugo Buoncompagni; 1502–85) Pope (1572–85). His pontificate was marked by support of the *Counter-Reformation and the sponsorship of colleges and reformed orders, especially the *Jesuits and the Oratorians. He founded the English College at Rome (1579) and was responsible for instituting the Gregorian *calendar (1582).

Gregory, Lady Augusta (1852–1932) Irish theater patron and dramatist. With W. B. Yeats, in 1899 she founded the Irish Dramatic Movement, a national theater company that moved into the Abbey Theatre in 1904. She collaborated with Yeats on *The Pot of Broth* (1902) and *Cathleen ni Houlihan* (1902) and wrote many comedies and translations, notably of Molière.

Gregory of Nazianzus, St (c. 330–c. 389 AD) Cappadocian Father of the Church, son of the Bishop of Nazianzus. He was educated in Athens, where he became a friend of St *Basil the Great. With Basil and St *Gregory of Nyssa he became a leading defender of orthodox Christianity against *Arianism. He was Bishop of Caesarea from 370 to 379 and briefly served as Patriarch of Constantinople in 380. Feast Day: May 9.

Gregory of Nyssa, St (c. 335–c. 394 AD) Cappadocian Father of the Church. A leader of the orthodox party, which opposed *Arianism, he was made Bishop of Nyssa in 372 by his brother, St *Basil the Great. He was deposed in 376 but reinstated in 378 on the death of the Arian emperor, Valens. He wrote many theological works. Feast day: March 9.

Gregory of Tours, St (c. 538–594 AD) French churchman and historian; Bishop of Tours (573–94). He is best known for his *Historia Francorum*, which is a history of the world from its creation to the 6th century AD. It is a valuable source of information on early European history. Feast Day: Nov 17.

Grenada, State of An island country in the West Indies, in the Windward Islands in the E Caribbean Sea off the NE coast of Venezuela. It is the smallest nation state in the Western Hemisphere. It also includes some of the Grenadine Islands, the largest of which is Carriacou. The majority of the population is of mixed European and Indian descent. *Economy*: largely agricultural, the chief products are cocoa, bananas, citrus fruits, sugar, and nutmeg (the main export). *History*: discovered by Columbus in 1493, it was colonized by the French and ceded to the British in 1763. In 1967 it became an Associated State under the West Indies Act and in 1974, an independent state within the Commonwealth of Nations. In March, 1979, the government of Sir Eric Gairy (1922–   ) was overthrown in a nearly bloodless coup by the New Jewel Movement (NJM) led by Maurice Bishop (1944–83), who subsequently became prime minister. Following an uprising of armed forces in 1983, during which Bishop was killed, the US invaded the country to take out US nationals. Bishop, a moderate socialist, formed close ties with Cuba and the Soviet Union. In October 1983 Bishop was deposed and executed by rebels under the leadership of Bernard Coard and the military seized control of the government. Later in October President Ronald Reagan ordered an invasion of the island by US forces, supported by troops from several Caribbean nations, that quickly overcame resistance and imposed a stable government. Viewing Grenada as a strategic threat, Reagan cited the presence of Soviet military equipment on the island and Soviet and Cuban assistance in building an airport at Point Salines as evidence that the two countries were using the island as a forward base. Elections were held in 1984 and Herbert Blaize became prime minister. Official language: English. Official currency: East Caribbean dollar of 100 cents. Area: 133 sq mi (344 sq km). Population (1975 est): 107,779. Capital and main port: St George's.

grenadier A carnivorous bottom-dwelling fish, also called rat-tail or torpedo, belonging to a family (*Macrouridae*; about 300 species) found in deep warm and temperate marine waters. It has a stout body, usually 12–24 in (30–60 cm) long, with a long ratlike tail and a large head.

Grenadine Islands A chain of West Indian islets, extending for about 60 mi (100 km) between St Vincent and Grenada and administratively divided between the two.

Grenoble 45 11N 5 43E A city in SE France, the capital of the Isère department. The capital of the Dauphiné until 1341, it has a cathedral (12th–13th centuries) and a university (1339). It is the principal tourist center of the French Alps and has metallurgical, textile, cement, and paper industries. Population (1975): 169,740.

Grenville, William (Wyndham), Baron (1759–1834) British statesman; prime minister (1806–07). As prime minister he led the coalition Ministry of All the Talents, which was notable for its abolition of the slave trade (1807). His government fell owing to royal opposition to the Catholic Relief bill. His father **George Grenville** (1712–70) was prime minister from 1763 to 1765. His government was noted for its *Stamp Act (1765) and prosecution of John *Wilkes.

Gresham, Sir Thomas (c. 1519–79) English financier and philanthropist. He founded Gresham College and the Royal Exchange, both in London, but is best known for the so-called **Gresham's Law**, attributed to him in the 19th century, that "bad money drives out good": if there are two different types of coin in circulation, and one sort of coin is suspected of being debased and is falling in value relative to the other, the more valuable coin will be hoarded and will eventually disappear from circulation.

Greuze, Jean-Baptiste (1725–1805) French painter, born in Tournus. Settling in Paris, he achieved early acclaim with his *Father Reading the Bible to His Children* (1755; Louvre). After an unsuccessful attempt at history painting (1769), he concentrated on sentimental and vaguely erotic portraits of girls, e.g. *The Broken Pitcher* (Louvre).

Grey, Charles, 2nd Earl (1764–1845) British statesman, who as Whig prime minister (1830–34) secured the passage of the parliamentary *Reform Act of 1832 by persuading William IV to create sufficient new peers to carry the bill through the House of Lords. His son **Henry George, 3rd Earl Grey** (1802–94) was Whig colonial secretary (1846–52) and, in advance of his time, advocated colonial self-government. The 2nd earl's nephew **Edward, 1st Viscount Grey of Fallodon** (1862–1933) was Liberal (formerly termed Whig) foreign secretary from 1905 to 1916. He negotiated the *Triple Entente of Britain, France, and Russia (1904–07) and supported France against Germany in the Morocco crises of 1905–06 and 1911. At the outbreak of World War I he remarked: "The lamps are going out all over Europe; we shall not see them lit again in our lifetime."

Grey, Lady Jane (1537–54) Queen of England for nine days (1553) and the great-granddaughter of *Henry VII. The Duke of *Northumberland had her proclaimed queen when Edward VI died but Mary, the rightful heiress, had popular support and Jane abdicated. She was executed for treason with her husband Lord Guildford Dudley, Northumberland's son.

Grey, Zane (1875–1939) US author. Although he graduated from dentistry school, he practiced for only 6 years before turning to writing novels, mostly about the Old West. His works include *Spirit of the Border* (1905), *The Heritage of the Desert* (1910), *Riders of the Purple Sage* (1912), *Desert Gold* (1913), *Wildfire* (1917), *To the Last Man* (1922), *The Call of the Canyon* (1924), and *Western Union* (1939). A noted fisherman, he also wrote sports and outdoor life books for boys.

greyhound An ancient breed of dog used for hare coursing and racing. It has a slender deep-chested streamlined body with long legs and a long muscular neck. The short smooth coat can be of various colors. Greyhounds can reach speeds of up to 45 mph (70 km per hour). Height: 28–30 in (71–76 cm) (dogs); 27–28 in (68–71 cm) (bitches).

greyhound racing (or dog racing) A form of racing popular for betting, in which greyhounds pursue an electrically propelled mechanical hare round a circular or oval track. The sport evolved from *coursing in the US in the early 20th century and is especially popular in Britain and Australia. Races may be on the flat or over hurdles, with distances ranging from 210 m (230 yd) to 1100 m (1200 yd).

gribble A wood-boring marine crustacean of the genus *Limnoria* (about 20 species). It feeds on algae, driftwood, and the submerged sections of docks and piers. *L. lignorum*, common in the N hemisphere, has a gray body up to 0.20 in (5 mm) long. Order: *Isopoda*.

Grieg, Edvard Hagerup (1843–1907) Norwegian composer, who studied in Leipzig and Copenhagen. He spent the latter part of his life in a house near the Troldhaugen fjord and was buried there. The influence of Norwegian folk music is apparent in many of his works, which include the *Lyric Pieces* (for piano; 1867–1901), a very popular piano concerto (1868), incidental music to Ibsen's play *Peer Gynt* (1876), chamber music, and many songs.

griffin A mythological creature with the head and wings of an eagle, the body of a lion, and often a serpent's tail. It is common in many ancient eastern mythologies.

Griffith, Arthur (1872–1922) Irish journalist and nationalist, who organized *Sinn Féin in 1905. He was imprisoned three times (1916, 1918–19, 1920–21) by the British authorities. In 1918 Sinn Féin won the majority of parliamentary seats in Ireland and declared a republic, which Griffith headed from 1919 to 1920. In 1921 he led the Irish delegation to the conference that determined the treaty establishing the Irish Free State. On *De Valera's rejection of the terms, Griffith was elected (1922) president of the Irish assembly (the Dáil Éireann) but died later that year.

Griffith, D(avid) W(ark) (1875–1948) US film director. His intuitive understanding of the artistic potential of the cinema and his innovations in editing and narrative techniques made him the most influential pioneer of the US cinema. His major films include *The Birth of a Nation* (1915), an ambitious epic concerning the Civil War, *Intolerance* (1916), *Broken Blossoms* (1919), and *Isn't Life Wonderful* (1924).

griffon (dog) A breed of toy dog originating in Belgium and of terrier ancestry. It has a square compact body, a docked tail, and a large head covered with long coarse hair. The coat is either rough and wiry or short and tight and may be red, black, or black and tan. Weight: 4–11 lb (2–5 kg).

griffon vulture One of the largest Old World *vultures, *Gyps fulvus*. It is 40 in (100 cm) long and occurs in mountainous regions of S Europe, South Africa, and Asia. It is gray-brown with darker wingtips, a white head and ruff, and whitish downy patches on the neck.

Grignard reagents Organomagnesium compounds, discovered by F. A. V. Grignard (1871–1935) and usually prepared by adding an organic halide to magnesium under ether. They are invaluable in a host of organic syntheses, giving addition products with almost all groups.

Grillparzer, Franz (1791–1872) Austrian dramatist. He worked in government service until his retirement in 1856 and was appointed court dramatist at the Hofburgtheater after the success of his first tragedy, *Die Ahnfrau* (1817). His tragedies ranged from adaptations of Greek myth, such as *The Golden Fleece* (1821), to fantasy plays, such as *A Dream Is Life* (1834).

Grimm Two brothers, German philologists and folklorists. After early work on medieval German texts, **Jakob Grimm** (1785–1863) and **Wilhelm Grimm** (1786–1859) set about collecting German folktales, published in 1812–14 as *Kinder- und Hausmärchen*. The *Deutsche Grammatik* (1819, 1822) is a historical and descriptive German grammar containing observations on the regularity of sound changes in Indo-European languages, known as **Grimm's law**. Their *Deutsches Wörterbuch* is a historical and descriptive German dictionary. A new Grimm brothers tale was found in 1983.

Grimmelshausen, Hans Jacob Christoph von (c. 1625–76) German novelist. Orphaned when a child, he served in the Imperial and Swedish armies during the Thirty Years' War and later worked as a steward, bailiff, and innkeeper. His picaresque *Simplicissimus* novels (1669–72) are a realistic and satirical record of his unsettled times.

Grimsby 53 35N 0 05W A seaport in NE England, near the mouth of the Humber estuary. Although it is the largest fishing port in England, the extension of Iceland's fishing limits (1975–76) combined with overfishing in many of the traditional grounds has led to a considerable reduction in the size of the fishing fleet. Population (1981): 92,147.

Gris, Juan (José Victoriano González; 1887–1927) Spanish-born cubist painter, who worked in Paris from 1906. In contrast to *Picasso and *Braque, his approach to *cubism was mathematical; his starting points were abstract shapes from which he developed real objects in geometrically constructed still lifes, landscapes, and portraits. He also promoted the art of collage and wrote an influential study of painting entitled *Les Possibilités de la peinture* (1924).

grison A mammal belonging to the genus *Grison* (2 species) of Central and South America. Grisons are about 24 in (60 cm) long and grayish black, hunting through forest and grassland for invertebrates and small mammals. Family: *Mustelidae* (weasels, stoats, etc.).

Grissom, Virgil ("Gus"; 1926–67) US astronaut. He was a member of the Mercury space team. His 1961 space flight made him the second person in space. A fire on board a ground-training spaceship took his life.

Griswold v. Connecticut (1965) US Supreme Court decision that upheld right of privacy and struck down a Connecticut law banning the dissemination of information about birth control and sale of birth control devices. Written by Justice William O. *Douglas, aided by Justice Arthur *Goldberg, the decision established the "penumbra theory" – that privacy in marriage was protected in the Bill of Rights (*see* Constitution, US), implied in the 1st, 3rd, 4th, 5th, and 9th amendments.

Grivas, Georgios (1898–1974) Greek general, born in Cyprus. Known as Dighenis, he was the leader of *EOKA, which fought for the union of Cyprus with Greece.

grizzly bear. *See* brown bear.

Grodno 53 40N 23 50E A port in the W central Soviet Union, in the Belorussian SSR on the Neman River. Possessed by Lithuania and then by Poland, it has many historic buildings, including a medieval castle and *Stephen Báthory's 16th-century palace. It is an important railroad center and major industrial city, producing fertilizers, textiles, food products, and tobacco. Population (1981 est): 212,000.

Gromyko, Andrei (1909–) Soviet diplomat; foreign minister (1957–). Gromyko began his diplomatic career in 1939 and served as ambassador to the US (1943–46) and the UK (1952–53). He was Soviet representative at the UN between 1946 and 1949.

Groningen 53 13N 6 35E A city in the N Netherlands, the capital of Groningen province. It has a notable church (the 15th-century Martini-kerk) and a university (1614). An important commercial and market center, its industries include textiles, clothing, and sugar refining. Population (1981 est): 162,952.

Groningen A province in the Netherlands, bordering on the North Sea and West Germany. Low lying and fertile, it is intensively cultivated and agriculture forms the chief occupation. Natural gas is extracted at Slochteren. Area: 900 sq mi (2350 sq km). Population (1981 est): 556,869. Capital: Groningen.

Groote Eylandt 12 20S 135 15E An Australian island, in the Gulf of Carpentaria off the coast of the Northern Territory. It forms part of the Arnhem Land Aboriginal Reserve. Manganese deposits have recently been discovered and exploited. Area: 950 sq mi (2460 sq km). Population (1976): 2059.

Gropius, Walter (1883–1969) German architect, one of the pioneers of the international modern style of architecture. Gropius was influenced by William *Morris and Frank Lloyd *Wright and trained under *Behrens until 1910. His first major building, a factory at Alfeld (1911) is a very early example of the new style. As director of the *Bauhaus (1919–28) he was able greatly to influence all aspects of contemporary design. The rise of Nazi power forced him to leave Germany (1934) In 1937 he moved to America, where he spent 14 influential years teaching at Harvard. He continued to design a few buildings, for example the US Embassy in Athens (1960), and to influence European architecture.

Gros, Antoine Jean, Baron (1771–1835) French painter. A pupil of *David, he later traveled with Napoleon's armies, painting such scenes as *Napoleon Visiting the Plague-Stricken at Jaffa* (1804; Louvre). Although initially successful under the restored Bourbons, he fell into obscurity in the 1820s and finally drowned himself. His style, influenced by *Rubens, anticipates the work of *Delacroix and *Géricault.

grosbeak A finch with a particularly heavy bill used to crack open hard seeds and nuts. The name is given to birds of several genera found in N Eurasia, America, and the tropics. The reddish-brown Eurasian pine grosbeak (*Pinicola enucleator*) uses its bill as a hammer to obtain seeds from pine cones.

gross domestic product. *See* gross national product.

Grossglockner 47 05N 12 44E The highest mountain in Austria, in the Alps. The Grossglockner Road (built 1930–35) crosses it, rising to 7852 ft (2576 m). Height: 12,457 ft (3797 m).

gross national product (GNP) A measure of the total annual output of a country, including net income from abroad; it provides a measure of the economic strength of that country. GNP can be calculated in three ways: based on income, output, or expenditure. If income is used as the basis, all incomes accruing to residents of the country as a result of economic activity (excluding, for instance, pensions) are summed (national income is thus synonymous with GNP calculated in this way). On the basis of output, the value added to a product at each stage of production is summed. If expenditure is used, the value of all consumption products is calculated. All three methods should give the same result. **Gross domestic product** (GDP) is GNP excluding net income from abroad and gives some indication of the strength of industry within a country. **Net national product** differs from GNP in that it makes a provision for *depreciation, i.e. the using up of the country's capital stock.

Gros Ventres Algonkian-speaking North American Indian tribe found in Montana and Saskatchewan, Canada. Originally of the Arapaho, they had broken away and established their own name (meaning "big bellies"), customs, and rituals, which were similar to the Arapaho's. They warred against the Crow and Dakota and, eventually, were defeated by the Blackfoot (1867). The remaining Gros Ventres reside on Fort Belknap reservation in Montana. The Hidatsa, a Siouan-speaking tribe, were also known as Gros Ventres.

Grosz, George (1893–1959) German painter and draftsman, born in Berlin. A member of the *Dada art movement, he is famous for his bitter satirical depictions of war, the bourgeoisie, the church, and German social evils. He was fined and charges of blasphemy were brought against him because of his work. He emigrated to the US in 1932.

Grotefend, Georg Friedrich (1775–1853) German philologist. He did important work on ancient *Italic languages, but after 1800 was increasingly occupied with attempts to decipher Persian *cuneiform inscriptions. He established several facts, including the alphabetic (as opposed to syllabic) nature of the characters, which facilitated their successful decipherment by *Rawlinson.

Grotius, Hugo (or Huig de Groot; 1583–1645) Dutch jurist and diplomat, the founder of international law. Sentenced to life imprisonment in 1619 by Prince Maurice of Nassau for his support of the Arminian faith in the religious controversies of the time, he escaped to France in 1621. There he wrote his famous *De jure belli et pacis* (1625), arguing that natural law should be applied to nations as well as individuals and that war should only be waged for justified causes. He was Swedish ambassador to France from 1635 until his death.

Groton 41 19N 72 12W A city in SE Connecticut, on Long Island Sound at the E mouth of the Thames River. It is a major submarine-building center and is home to a US Navy submarine base. The first nuclear-powered submarine, *Nautilus* (1954), was constructed there. Population (1980): 10,086.

ground beetle A heavily armored long-legged beetle belonging to a family (*Carabidae*; 25,000 species) that is particularly common in temperate regions. Ground beetles are dark in color or have a metallic sheen and are from 0.08–3 in (2–85 mm) long. Most are nocturnal and can be found under stones, logs, and debris during the day. The adults and most larvae are active carnivores, preying on insects, slugs, and snails. *See also* bombardier beetle.

ground bug A *plant bug belonging to the worldwide famiy *Lygaeidae* (about 3000 species). Ground bugs have elongated brown or black bodies, 0.12–0.59 in (3–15 mm) long, often with red markings. They live in moss or rubbish or under stones or low bushes and feed on a variety of plants, in many cases becoming serious pests (*see* chinch bug).

ground elder A perennial herbaceous plant, *Aegopodium podagraria*, also called goutweed, bishop's weed, or herb Gerard, common in Europe on waste ground and as a garden weed. 19–40 in (49–100 cm) tall, it has compound leaves with three leaflets (like those of elder) and umbrella-like clusters of small white flowers. The leaves may be eaten as a salad or vegetable. Family: *Umbelliferae*.

groundhog. *See* marmot.

ground ivy A creeping perennial herb, *Glechoma hederacea* (or *Nepeta glechoma*), found in woods and grasslands across Eurasia. It has long-stalked heart-shaped toothed leaves and its stems, 4–12 in (10–30 cm) high, bear groups of tubular violet two-lipped flowers. Family: *Labiatae*.

groundnut The fruit of *Arachis hypogea*, also called peanut or earthnut, native to tropical South America but widely cultivated in the tropics. The plant is an erect or creeping annual, 12–18 in (30–45 cm) high, with compound leaves and yellow flowers. After fertilization the flower stalk elongates, pushing the developing pod below the soil to ripen under ground. The pod has a thin spongy wall and contains one to three seeds (the nuts), which are highly nutritious. They are used in cooking, canned, and made into peanut butter and peanut oil (used in margarine). Family: *Leguminosae*.

groundsel A weedy herbaceous plant of the genus *Senecio*, especially *S. vulgaris*, 3.1–18 in (8–45 cm) high and common in Eurasia and N Africa. It has lobed toothed leaves and small yellow flower heads, which lack ray florets and are almost enclosed by the sepals. Family: *Compositae*.

ground squirrel A *squirrel that lives in an underground burrow rather than in a tree. Ground squirrels have short strong legs, small ears, and shorter tails than tree squirrels, inhabiting open country in North America, Eurasia, and Africa. Chief genera: *Citellus* (34 species), *Lariscus* (2 species), *Xerus* (4 species). *See also* prairie dog; chipmunk; souslik; marmot.

groundwater The water that has percolated into the ground and become trapped within pores, cracks, and fissures. It is important in *weathering processes through its chemical effects. With depth the *water table is reached, below which all pore spaces are filled.

grouper One of several sedentary food and game fish of the family Serranidae (*see* sea bass), especially the genera *Epinephelus* and *Mycteroperca*, widely distributed in warm seas. Groupers have a dull-green or brown heavy body, up to or exceeding 7 ft (2 m) long, and a large mouth. Some are poisonous when consumed.

group therapy A form of *psychotherapy in which several patients meet together to understand and overcome their problems, usually with the help of a therapist. There are many forms of group therapy: sometimes the aim is to increase patients' insight in psychoanalytic terms, sometimes to teach social skills, sometimes to act out distressing events from the past, and sometimes to support one another in overcoming a common problem (such as alcoholism).

GROUSE   *The male sage grouse* (Centrocercus urophasianus) *in courtship display, during which it fans out its tail and inflates a pouch on its chest to attract females.*

grouse A fowl-like game bird, 12–35 in (30–88 cm) long, belonging to a family (*Tetraonidae*; about 18 species) of the N hemisphere. Grouse are mostly ground-living, with short round wings, a short strong bill, and feathered legs. They are noted for their spectacular courtship displays (called *leks*). The family includes the *black grouse, *red grouse, and *capercaillie of N Europe (including Britain); the *ptarmigans; and the North American ruffed grouse (*Bonasa umbellus*) and *sage grouse. Order: *Galliformes*. *See also* gamebird.

Grove, Sir George (1820–1900) British musicologist, founder and first editor of *Grove's Dictionary of Music and Musicians* (1879–89). His interest in the arts led to extensive musical and biblical research during which he traveled widely. He was founder and first director (1883–94) of the Royal College of Music and was knighted in 1883. *The New Grove Dictionary of Music and Musicians* was published in 1980.

growth hormone (*or* somatotrophin) A protein hormone that promotes the metabolic processes involved in growth of bone and muscle. It is secreted by the pituitary gland and stimulates protein synthesis, mobilizes fat reserves, increases glucose levels in the blood, and affects mineral metabolism. Lack of growth hormone in children causes dwarfism.

Groznyi 43 21N 45 42E A city in the S Soviet Union, the capital of Checheno-Ingush ASSR in the RSFSR. It is one of the country's oldest and richest oil-producing areas. Population (1981 est): 379,000.

Grub Street A street, now renamed Milton St, in London, England, associated in the 18th century with writers of little talent, who earned their livings by whatever literary work they could obtain. *Pope satirized such hacks in *An Epistle to Dr Arbuthnot* (1755) and the name is referred to in the title of George Gissing's novel *New Grub Street* (1891).

Grünewald, Matthias (Mathis Gothardt; d. 1528) German painter, born in Würzburg. His earliest known work is *The Mocking of Christ* (c. 1503; Alte Pinakothek, Munich). For much of his career, he was court painter at Mainz. His favorite subject was the crucifixion, of which perhaps his most tragic treatment is the *Isenheim Altarpiece* (Colmar, France), noted also for its dazzling color. His style, characterized by a distortion of form, influenced 20th-century German expressionists (*see* expressionism).

grunt A small food fish, belonging to the family *Pomadasyidae* (about 75 species), that can produce piglike grunts. It has a colorful elongated body and a large mouth; it occurs in the warm and tropical coastal waters. Order: *Perciformes*.

Gruyère A district in Switzerland, in the middle Saane Valley, famed for its cheese and cattle.

Guadalajara 20 30N 103 20W The second largest city in Mexico, at an altitude of 5413 ft (1650 m). Founded by the Spanish (1530), it has several notable buildings including the cathedral (16th–17th centuries) and the Governor's Palace (begun 1763); there are two universities (1792, 1935). Its key position as a communications center across the Sierra Madre Occidental has led to its rapid expansion in recent years and it now has a large industrial complex. Its handicraft industries (especially glassware and pottery) also remain important. Population (1978 est): 1,813,131.

Guadalcanal 9 30S 160 00E The largest of the Solomon Islands, in the S Pacific Ocean. During World War II the first major US offensive in the Pacific against the Japanese took place here; it was captured after six months of jungle fighting (1942–43). Copra, rubber, and some gold are produced. Area: 2500 sq mi (6475 sq km). Population (1976): 46,619. Chief settlement: Honiara.

Guadalquivir River The main river of S Spain. It flows mainly WSW from the Sierra de Segura to the Gulf of Cádiz and is navigable to Seville by oceangoing vessels. Length: 348 mi (560 km).

Guadalupe Hidalgo (name from 1931 until 1971: Gustavo A. Madero) 19 29N 99 07W A city in central Mexico, a NE suburb of Mexico City. The Basilica of the Virgin of Guadalupe, which was built after an Indian convert reported seeing a vision of the Virgin Mary here in 1531, is a famous place of pilgrimage. The Treaty of *Guadalupe Hidalgo was signed here.

Guadalupe Hidalgo, Treaty of (1848) The treaty that ended the *Mexican War. In exchange for $15 million and the payment of the claims of US citizens, the US received what are now the states of California, Nevada, Utah, parts of Colorado, Wyoming, and Arizona and most of New Mexico.

Guadalupe Mountains National Park A national park in W Texas, E of El Paso that includes part of the Guadalupe Mountain Range, a part of the Rockies. Established in 1966, the park includes the highest point of the range, Guadalupe Peak (8751 ft; 2668 m), a large earth fault and many examples of limestone fossil reef. Area: 82,280 acres (33,299 hectares).

Guadeloupe A French overseas region in the West Indies, in the E Caribbean Sea. It comprises two main islands, Grande Terre and Basse Terre, together with the island dependencies of Marie Galante, La Désirade, Îles des Saintes, St Barthélemy, and the N part of *St Martin. The economy is based on agriculture; sugar cane is the chief crop. Area: 657 sq mi (1702 sq km). Population (1975): 334,900. Capital: Basse-Terre.

guaiacum A small evergreen tree of the genus *Guaiacum*, especially *G. officinale* of tropical America, also called lignum vitae. It has blue flowers, yellow heart-shaped fruits, and very dense hard wood, used to make pulleys, axles, and bowling balls. The greenish resin is distilled for medicinal use. Family: *Zygophyllaceae*.

Guam 13 30N 144 40E An island and US unincorporated territory in the West Pacific Ocean, the largest of the Mariana Islands. Mountainous in the S, it is mantled by jungle. Spanish from 1565 to 1898, it was occupied by the Japanese (1941–44). It is a major naval and air base, especially important during the Vietnam War. Industries include ship repairing. Area: 210 sq mi (450 sq km). Population (1980): 105,821. Capital: Agaña.

guanaco A hoofed mammal, *Lama guanacoe*, closely related to the *llama and found at altitudes of up to 16,404 ft (5000 m) in W South America. Red-brown with a pale face and pale underparts, guanacos grow up to 43 in (110 cm) high at the shoulder and live in small herds on open grassland. Family: *Camelidae*.

Guan Di (*or* Kuan Ti) In Chinese mythology, the god of war. A historical figure and hero of numerous romantic exploits, he was captured and executed in 219 AD. His popularity with both common people and the aristocracy grew until he was pronounced a god in 1594. Various professions and trades, including writers, adopted him as patron and hundreds of temples were built in his honor.

Guangdong (Kuang-tung *or* Kwangtung) A mountainous province in S China, including Hainan and other islands. Heavily populated, it produces rice, sugar cane, tobacco, silk, fish, timber, and minerals. *History*: Chinese from 222 BC, it only came under Chinese cultural influence in the 12th and 13th centuries AD. As China's main trading area, it later had considerable contact with the West and from the mid-19th century overpopulation led to overseas emigration. During the 19th and early 20th centuries it was a center of revolutionary movements. Area: 90,246 sq mi (231,400 sq km). Population (1980 est): 56,810,000. Capital: Canton.

Guangxi Zhuang Autonomous Region (*or* Kwangsi Chuang AR) A mountainous administrative division in S China, on the North Vietnamese border. It has seen great economic growth since 1949, producing sugar cane, rice, timber, manganese, and tin. *History*: its non-Chinese minorities have rebelled periodically and the *Taiping Rebellion started here (1851). It became a center of communist opposition to *Chiang Kai-shek's government and heavy fighting against the Japanese invasion took place here during World War II. Area: 85,956 sq mi (220,400 sq km). Population (1980 est): 34,700,000. Capital: Nanning.

Guang Xu (*or* Kuang-hsü; 1871–1908) The title of Cai Tian (*or* Tsai-t'ien) of the Qing dynasty, who became emperor (1875) at the age of four with his aunt *Zi Xi as regent. When after coming of age he sponsored the *Hundred Days of Reform she imprisoned him for the rest of his life.

Guangzhou. *See* Canton.

guano The accumulated excrement of certain animals, especially seabirds, seals, and bats. It contains 10–18% nitrogen, 8–12% phosphoric acid, and 2–3% potash, according to the age and origin of the deposit. Large amounts have been found on islands off the Peruvian and other coasts and it has been widely used as a fertilizer.

Guantánamo 20 09N 75 14W A city in SE Cuba, N of Guantánamo Bay. It is the center of an agricultural area producing sugar cane and coffee. Industries include coffee roasting, sugar refining, and chocolate manufacture. Population (1981): 246,739.

Guan Yin (*or* Kuan Yin) In Chinese Buddhism, the goddess of compassion. She is the same *bodhisattva who was worshiped in India in male form as Avalokiteshvara and in Japan as the multiheaded or multiarmed Kannon. In Chinese art Guan Yin only took on female form during the 12th and 13th centuries.

guarana A climbing plant, *Paullinia cuparia*, of the Amazon Basin, with large compound leaves and clusters of short-stalked flowers. The fruit is about 0.8 in (2 cm) long and contains one seed. The seeds are roasted to produce a stimulant drink containing more caffeine than coffee or ground to make bread. Guarana is also a source of starch, gum, saponin, oils, and drugs. Family: *Sapindaceae*.

Guarani A group of South American Indian peoples of Paraguay and neighboring areas of Brazil and Argentina who speak languages of the Tupian group. About a million Paraguayans speak Guarani. Few now retain their original culture, typical of the tropical forest, based on hunting and maize cultivation, warfare, and cannibalism.

Guardi, Francesco (1712–93) Venetian painter, who studied under and sometimes collaborated with his elder brother, **Giovanni Antonio Guardi** (1699–1760). His souvenir views of Venice were sometimes copied from *Canaletto but they are distinguished by their romantic style and impressionistic technique.

guardian angels Divine beings that figure in several religions. They derive from the belief that every individual has an angel assigned by God as his guardian. In the Roman Catholic Church they may be invoked as intercessors; feast day: Oct 2.

Guarini, Giovanni Battista (1538–1612) Italian poet. He served at the court of the Duke of Ferrara and in Rome and Florence. His best-known work, *The Faithful Shepherd* (1590), emulating Torquato *Tasso's *Aminta* (1573), helped to establish the genre of pastoral drama.

Guarini, Guarino (1624–83) Italian baroque architect, philosopher, and mathematician. Most of Guarini's work was done in his native Piedmont. Although influenced by *Borromini, his work shows great originality and technical skill. Probably his most successful building is the church of S Lorenzo, Turin (1668–87).

Guarneri An Italian family of violin makers, famous in the 17th and 18th centuries. The first of the line was **Andrea Guarneri** (d. 1698), who was a pupil (with Stradivari) of Amati in Cremona. Andrea's grandson **Giuseppe Guarneri** (1698–1744), known as "del Gesù," was the most famous member of the family; influenced by the makers of the Brescian school, he produced violins with a characteristically powerful tone, signing them "Guarnerius."

Guatemala, Republic of A country in Central America, on the Pacific Ocean, with a small outlet on the Caribbean Sea. The tropical forests of the Petén in the N and a narrower plain on the Pacific rise to a central mountainous region, containing a fertile plateau. The country is subject to hurricanes and earthquakes, which have caused havoc throughout its history. About half the population are *Maya Quiché Indians and most of the rest are of mixed Spanish and Indian descent. *Economy*: mainly agricultural, the land being fertile but subject to erosion. Since the 1950s a new system of land development has been introduced, largely on a cooperative basis. The main crops are coffee, sugar, bananas, and cotton, which are the principal exports. Rubber and essential oils are being developed as well as forest products (chicle and timber). Minerals include zinc and lead concentrates, and nickel mining is being introduced. Oil was discovered in 1974 and production is increasing. Efforts are being made to promote industrial growth in plastics, as well as the more traditional food processing and textile industries. *History*: there is extensive archeological evidence of pre-Spanish civilizations, especially that of the Maya, and, from the 12th century, the Aztecs. From 1524 to 1821 the area was part of the Spanish captaincy general of Guatemala, which included most of Central America. It formed the nucleus of the Central American Federation until 1839, when it became independent. In recent years periods of democratic government have alternated with military dictatorships, accompanied by considerable political unrest. In 1976 a serious earthquake in the center caused further damage to the economy. Guatemala's claims to Belize have intensified in recent years. Following a military coup in 1983, Gen Oscar Humberto Mejìa Victores (1930–   ) succeeded the previous president, Gen Efraín Ríos Montt. Official language: Spanish. Official religion: Roman Catholic. Official currency: quetzal of 100 centavos. Area: 42,042 sq mi (108,889 sq km). Population (1983 est): 7,714,000. Capital: Guatemala City. Main port: Puerto Barrios.

FRANCESCO GUARDI *An architectural caprice, depicting the vaulted arcade of the Doge's Palace in the artist's native city of Venice (c. 1780).*

Guatemala City 14 38N 90 22W The capital of Guatemala, situated in the S of the country in a high valley. Founded in 1776, it was the capital of the captaincy general of Guatemala and later of the Central American Federation. It has four universities; the oldest was founded in 1776. Population (1979 est): 1,500,000.

guava A tropical American tree, *Psidium guajava*, about 33 ft (10 m) tall. Its white four-petaled flowers develop into yellow pear-shaped fruits with white or pink pulp containing many small seeds. Guava fruits, rich in vitamin C, are used to make jam and jelly, stewed for desserts, or canned. Family: *Myrtaceae* (myrtle family).

Guayaquil (*or* Santiago de Guayaquil) 2 13S 79 54W The largest city and chief port of Ecuador, on the Guayas River. It is a major commercial center; industries include food processing, tanning, and textile manufacture. Its university was founded in 1867. Population (1974): 823,219.

gudgeon A freshwater shoaling fish, *Gobio gobio*, related to *carp, found in Europe and N Asia. It has a slender greenish or grayish body, up to about 8 in (20 cm) long, with a row of blackish spots along each side and a pair of barbels at the corners of the mouth. It is used as food and bait.

guelder rose A small tree or shrub, *Viburnum opulus*, 13–16 ft (4–5 m) high, found throughout Eurasia. It has three-lobed leaves and flat-topped clusters of flowers, 2–4 in (5–10 cm) across, in which the outer flowers are large and sterile and the inner ones are small and fertile. The fruits are clusters of red translucent berries. The cultivated form, grown as a garden shrub, is sterile: it has rounded heads of flowers and is called snowball tree. Family: *Caprifoliaceae* (honeysuckle family).

Guelfs and Ghibellines The propapal and proimperial factions respectively in medieval Germany and Italy. Commencing in a German struggle between rival claimants to the Holy Roman Empire, the Guelfs (named for Welf, the family name) and Ghibellines (after Waiblingen, a *Hohenstaufen castle), their conflict acquired an Italian context because of papal opposition to the Hohenstaufen. The Italian city states were led by Florence (Guelf) and Pisa (Ghibelline). Both sides, however, had factions within each city. Defeat of the Hohenstaufen (1268) contributed to Ghibelline decline, while the Guelfs espoused the *Angevin cause in Italy. By the end of the 14th century the factions had only local significance, reflecting urban rivalries.

Guelph 43 34N 80 16W A city in central Canada, in SW Ontario. Founded in 1827, it is an agricultural research and farming center, especially at the University of Guelph (1964). Numerous factories produce electric motors, wire, metal and rubber products, and many other goods. Population (1976): 67,538.

guenon An *Old World monkey belonging to the genus *Cercopithecus* (10 species), of African forests. They are 33–63 in (83–160 cm) long including the tail (20–35 in [50–88 cm]) and move through the trees in troops, feeding on leaves, fruits, insects, and snails. The mona monkey (*C. mona*), dark with creamy-white underparts and rump patches, is a strikingly marked guenon. *See also* grass monkey.

Guercino (Giovanni Francesco Barbieri; 1591–1666) Italian painter, born at Cento, near Bologna. His masterpiece, the ceiling frescos in the Casino Ludovisi, Rome, commissioned by Pope Gregory XV in 1621, were influenced by the *Carracci, under whom he had studied. While in Rome (1621–23) he also painted the *Burial of St Petronilla* (Capitoline Museum, Rome), which his later work never equaled.

Guericke, Otto von (1602–86) German physicist, renowned for his investigation of vacuums. In 1650 he invented the air pump, which he used to perform a series of experiments culminating in a demonstration in which two teams of horses failed to separate a pair of large hemispheres (called the Magdeburg hemispheres after his home town) placed together and evacuated. When air was admitted to the hemispheres they fell apart on their own.

Guernica 43 19N 2 40W A historic Basque town in N Spain, on the Bay of Biscay. During the Spanish Civil War it was bombed and virtually destroyed by German planes supporting the Nationalists on April 27, 1937. This is depicted in a painting by Picasso. Population (1970): 14,678.

Guernsey 49 27N 2 35W The second largest of the Channel Islands, in the English Channel. Roughly triangular in shape, it is low lying in the N and hilly in the S with rugged coastal cliffs. Agriculture and horticulture are important, especially dairy farming (the Guernsey breed of cattle originated here) and the production of tomatoes and flowers for export. Guernsey's mild climate, scenery, and beaches contribute to its popularity as a tourist resort. Area: 24.5 sq mi (63 sq km). Population (1981): 53,303. Capital: St Peter Port.

Guernsey cattle A breed of dairy cattle originating from Guernsey. They have a yellowish coat with a white tail switch and produce high-quality creamy milk.

guerrilla warfare (Spanish: small war) Military action by small irregular armed forces, often supported by a hostile foreign power, intended to erode the war potential and political stability of a country. Relying on hit-and-run techniques and avoiding combat with better equipped regulars, guerrillas usually attempt to gain local support rather than territory. The word was first adopted in reference to the Spanish-Portuguese action against the French conquest in the *Peninsular War. In the 20th century, guerrilla warfare has been employed by many movements, including the Vietnamese in the Vietnam War.

Guesclin, Bertrand du (c. 1320–80) French commander in the *Hundred Years' War. As constable of France from 1370 he was instrumental in recovering the territory previously lost to the English in S and W France.

Guevara, Che (Ernesto G.; 1928–67) Argentine revolutionary and theorist of guerrilla warfare, who became the hero of left–wing youth in the 1960s. A doctor by training, he joined *Castro's invasion of Cuba (1956) and became one of his chief lieutenants in the subsequent guerrilla war. After Castro's victory, Che Guevara influenced Cuba's procommunist foreign relations and directed the land-reform policies. Guevara was an exponent of exporting revolution and in 1967 he was captured and killed by government troops while attempting to instigate a revolt in Bolivia.

Guicciardini, Francesco (1483–1540) Florentine statesman and historian. He was Florentine ambassador to Aragon (1512–14) and then active in Florentine politics before entering the service of the papacy and becoming governor of Modena (1516) and Reggio (1517). After the sack of Rome (1527) by the imperial army, Guicciardini concentrated on his writings, including his famous *Storia d'Italia*, which deals with contemporary events in Italy between 1494 and 1534.

guided missiles Rocket-powered missiles without wings or other lift surfaces that are guided throughout their flight. They comprise a power unit, a guidance system, and a warhead. In most, propulsion is by solid-fuel rocket. Of the many guidance systems the most common methods of controlling the missile depend on a trailing wire or a radio, radar, or laser beam. Some have preset on-board computers, others depend on *inertial guidance, and some home on sources of infrared radiation. Warheads range from relatively small antitank high explosives to nuclear devices in the kiloton range. All missiles are vulnerable to electronic countermeasures (ECM), although cruise missiles, driven by turbofan engines, have a range of over 2000 miles (3000 km) and can change course and direction according to a preset-computer program to confuse defense measures. Missiles may be launched from aircraft (air-to-air or air-to-surface) or from the land or sea (surface-to-air or surface-to-surface). *See also* Polaris missile.

Guido d'Arezzo (c. 990–c. 1050) Italian monk and musical theorist. He developed the hexachord, a six-note scale used to facilitate sight-singing. The notes of the hexachord were named for the first syllables of the first six lines of a Latin hymn: ut, re, mi, fa, sol, and la. The hexachord became the basis of later systems of *solmization. Guido also developed the Guidonian hand, a mnemonic device that gave note names to the tips and joints of the fingers, and popularized the use of colored lines in written music to indicate pitch.

Guildford 51 14N 0 35W A city in SE England, in Surrey on the River Wey. A market and residential town, it is the site of the University of Surrey (1966), and Guildford Cathedral.

guilds (*or* gilds) Associations formed in medieval Europe to further their members' common purposes. Originally religious or social in character, the first such guilds are recorded in the 9th century. Merchant guilds were created in many towns in the 11th century to organize local trade and became a powerful force in local government. Craft guilds, confined to specific crafts or trades, were formed from the 12th century and these too became very powerful, exercising a monopoly over both production and trade and controlling recruitment by the apprenticeship system. In the later middle ages and beyond, their activities were largely superseded by the development of capitalism.

Guilford Courthouse, Battle of (1781) American Revolutionary War battle in N North Carolina. American General Nathanael *Greene's troops made a stand at the Guilford Courthouse against Lord *Cornwallis's British forces. Although the Americans retreated, the British, far more depleted, withdrew to Wilmington in the S of the state and thereafter abandoned the Carolinas.

Guillaume de Lorris (13th century) French poet, author of the first 4000 lines of the verse allegory *Roman de la rose* (c. 1230–40), one of the most influential of medieval poems, translated into English by *Chaucer. Nothing certain is known about Guillaume.

guillemot A bird, *Uria aalge*, occurring in coastal regions of the N hemisphere. It is 16 in (40 cm) long and has a dark-brown plumage with a white belly and wing stripe and a slender bill, feeding on fish, shellfish, and worms. The eggs are shaped so that they do not roll off the cliff ledges where they are laid. Family *Alcidae* (auks).

guillotine A device with which a person may be beheaded. It consists of two vertical posts and a horizontal knife that is dropped onto the victim's neck. Invented by Joseph Ignace Guillotin (1738–1814), it was introduced as a method of capital punishment in France in 1792, during the French Revolution.

Guimarães 41 26N 8 19W A city in NW Portugal. It was Portugal's first capital (12th century) and the birthplace of Alfonso I (1112–85), Portugal's first king. An industrial center, its manufactures include cutlery. Population (1970): 25,113.

Guinea, Gulf of A large inlet of the E Atlantic Ocean, bordering on the *Guinea Coast of West Africa, between Cape Palmas, Liberia, and Cape Lopez, Gabon.

Guinea, People's Republic of A country on the coast of West Africa. A coastal plain, partly swamp, rises steeply to plateaus and mountains. The population is mainly Fulani and Mandingo. *Economy*: chiefly agricultural, now largely collectivized. The chief crops are rice and palm oil and nuts, as well as coffee, peanuts, and fruits. Livestock, especially cattle, is also important. The principal mineral resources are diamonds, iron ore, and bauxite (alumina is the principal export). Most trade and industry are now nationalized. *History*: the N formed part of Ghana from the 5th to the 8th centuries AD and of the Mali empire in the 16th century. From the mid-15th century European traders were active along the coast. In 1849 the French established a protectorate over part of Guinea, which became a colony in 1891. In 1895 it became part of French West Africa. In 1958 French Guinea became an independent republic, with Ahmed Sékou Touré as its first president, rather than joining the French Community. A treaty of cooperation re-established economic relations with France in 1963. Guinea is a single-party state, and in recent years accusations have been made of violations of human rights. Official language: French and the languages of eight ethnic groups. Official currency: syli of 100 cauris. Area: 95,000 sq mi (245,857 sq km). Population (1983 est): 5,430,000. Capital and main port: Conakry.

Guinea-Bissau, Republic of (name until 1974: Portuguese Guinea) A small country on the coast of West Africa, including the archipelago of Bijagós. It consists chiefly of a coastal plain, cut by wide river estuaries and rising to savanna-covered plateau inland. The majority of the population are Fulani, Mandyako, and Mandingo. *Economy*: chiefly agricultural, the principal crops being groundnuts (the main export), rice, and palm oil and nuts. Cattle breeding is important in the interior, and there are plans to diversify crops in order to increase self-sufficiency in food. Land has been nationalized and cooperative farming introduced. Important bauxite deposits have been discovered and there are plans for a major hydroelectric scheme to power an aluminum plant. Other smaller industries are also being developed. *History*: explored by the Portuguese in the mid-15th century, the area became a center of the slave trade. It became a Portuguese colony in 1879 and an overseas province of Portugal in 1951. In 1974 it became an independent republic. Luis de Almeida Cabral (1931–) became the first president; he was replaced by Joao Vieira following a coup in 1980. Official language: Portuguese; Crioulo is widely spoken. Official currency: Guinea-Bissau peso of 100 centavos. Area: 13,948 sq mi (36,125 sq km). Population (1979): 777,214. Capital: Bissau.

Guinea Coast The coastlands of West Africa extending from Gambia to Cape Lopez in Gabon.

guinea fowl A bird belonging to an African family (*Numididae*; 7–10 species). About 20 in (50 cm) long, domesticated guinea fowl are descended from the helmet guinea fowl (*Numida meleagris*), which has a large bony crest, a bare face with red and blue wattles, and a gray white-spotted plumage. Guinea fowl scratch for seeds and insects, especially termites. Order: *Galliformes* (pheasants, turkeys, etc.).

guinea pepper The spicy aromatic fruit of a West African tree, *Xylopia aethiopica*, source of the condiment "Negro pepper." The tree has simple leaves with a metallic sheen arranged in two ranks along the branches and fragrant flowers producing aggregates of berries. Family: *Annonaceae*.

guinea pig A domesticated rodent, *Cavia porcellus*, descended from the *cavy. Guinea pigs were originally bred for food but are now popular as pets. They should be fed on grain, roots, green food, and hay.

guinea worm A parasitic *nematode worm, *Dracunculus medinensis*, that is a serious parasite of man in Africa, India, and the Middle East. The larvae are carried by water fleas (genus *Cyclops*) often present in drinking water. When swallowed by the human host, they burrow into the tissues and grow to maturity: the females reach a length of up to 47 in (120 cm), causing ulcers on the feet and legs.

Guinevere In *Arthurian legend, the wife of King Arthur and lover of *Lancelot. She is featured in various medieval romances. Malory's *Morte d'Arthur* (1485) describes her abduction by Mordred, Arthur's nephew, and her adulterous love for *Lancelot, which triggered the decline of Arthur's chivalric society.

Guinness, Sir Alec (1914–) British actor. He established his reputation as a stage actor in repertory in the late 1930s and played Hamlet in modern dress in 1938. After World War II he achieved success as a character actor in films, including *Oliver Twist* (1948), *Kind Hearts and Coronets* (1949), *The Bridge on the River Kwai* (1957), for which he received an Academy Award, *The Comedians* (1967), *Star Wars* (1977), and *A Passage to India* (1985).

Guiscard, Robert (c. 1015–85) Norman knight, who took part in the invasions of S Italy and extended Norman power into Sicily. He established himself in Calabria and gained papal recognition as Duke of Apulia (1059). He died while campaigning in the Balkans. His brother and nephew later ruled Sicily as Roger I (1031–1101; reigned c. 1071–1101) and *Roger II.

Guise A French noble family prominent during the 16th century. The duchy of Guise was the reward (1528) of **Claude I, Duke of Aumale** (1496–1550) for services to France. His daughter **Mary of Guise** (1515–60) married James V of Scotland and was the mother of Mary, Queen of Scots. Claude's sons **François, 2nd Duke of Guise** (1519–63) and **Charles, Cardinal of Lorraine** (1524–74) became the most powerful men in France and the leaders of the Roman Catholic party in the French *Wars of Religion. François was assassinated by a Huguenot and the Catholic leadership passed to his son **Henri I, 3rd Duke of Guise** (1550–88), who directed the *St Bartholomew Day's Massacre of Huguenots in 1572. Following Henri's assassination the Guise's influence on French politics diminished.

guitar A plucked stringed instrument of Moorish origin, which came to Europe via Spain. The modern Spanish guitar has a flat back, a round sound hole, a fretted fingerboard, and six strings tuned chiefly in fourths. It has a range of over three octaves from the E below the bass stave. Music for it is written an octave higher than it sounds. Guitar technique was developed by Fernando Sor (1778–1839) and in the 20th century by Andrés *Segovia.

guitar fish A *ray fish, belonging to the family *Rhinobatidae*, that has a pointed flattened head with fused pectoral fins and a long muscular shark-like tail. Guitar fish live in shallow waters of tropical and temperate seas and feed on bottom-dwelling animals, especially crustaceans.

Guitry, Sacha (1885–1957) French actor and dramatist. He wrote many light comedies, often concerning the lives of famous men, such as Napoleon and Mozart. He acted in these and occasionally in films, including *Le Comédien* (1949) and *Napoléon* (1955).

Guiyang (or Kuei-yang) 26 35N 106 40E A city in S China, the capital of Guizhou province. Industries, developed since 1949, include steel, machinery, and aluminum. Population (1957 est): 504,000.

Guizhou (Kuei-chou *or* Kweichow) A province in S China, a rather infertile high plateau. There were frequent rebellions among the minority non-Chinese groups, which have rich folk cultures. Rice, maize, tobacco, tea, and timber are grown and silk and minerals produced. Area: 69,278 sq mi (174,000 sq km). Population (1980 est): 27,310,000. Capital: Guiyang.

Guizot, François (Pierre Guillaume) (1787–1874) French statesman and historian. As a professor of history at Paris University (1812–30) he became the chief supporter of constitutional monarchy in France. He was prominent in the revolution that brought Louis Philippe to the throne in 1830 and served as foreign minister (1840–48). The most prominent figure in the government, Guizot was forced by the Revolution of 1848 to resign and devoted the rest of his life to historical writing.

Gujarat A state in W India, on the Arabian Sea SE of Pakistan. Lowlands merge into hills in the S and E and into marshes in the NW. Cotton, tobacco, peanuts, and other crops are raised. An industrial area, Gujarat produces textiles, machinery, and chemicals. *History*: a flourishing area under Muslim princes (13th–17th centuries), Gujarat was conquered by the Maratha in the 18th century before passing to Britain. Area: 75,650 sq mi (195,984 sq km). Population (1981): 33,960,905. Capital: Gandhinagar.

Gujarati An Indo-Aryan language spoken by 20 million people in Gujarat and Maharashtra in India. It is related to Rajasthani, uses a modified Devanagari script, and has a long literary tradition.

Gujranwala 32 06N 74 11E A city in NE Pakistan. The Sikh ruler Ranjit Singh was born here. Manufactures include textiles and leather goods and it has a famous ceramics industry. Population (1972): 366,000.

Gulf States The nations situated on the Persian Gulf. They are Oman, the United Arab Emirates, Qatar, Bahrein, Saudi Arabia, Kuwait, Iraq, and Iran. They comprise the world's major oil-producing area.

Gulf Stream One of the major ocean currents of the world, flowing from the Florida Strait parallel to the North American coast as far as the Newfoundland banks. It bears NE across the Atlantic as the North Atlantic Drift, branching into two main directions, one flowing N toward Spitsbergen and the other flowing S to form the Canary Current. Water from the

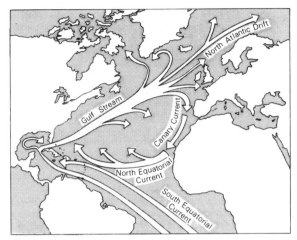

GULF STREAM

North and South Equatorial Currents builds up in the Gulf of Mexico and escapes with force through the Florida Strait as the Florida Current, one of the strongest major ocean currents. The water is warm and although as the Gulf Stream progresses it mixes with cooler waters, the ameliorating effect on the climate of NW Europe is significant.

gulfweed Tropical *brown algae, also called rockweed or sea holly, of the genus *Sargassum*, especially *S. natans*, which forms huge free-floating masses of seaweed in the Sargasso Sea. They have highly branched serrated fronds, with berry-like gas-filled floats or bladders, and most reproduce sexually.

gull A seabird belonging to the subfamily *Larinae* (about 40 species), ranging throughout the world's coastal regions and also found inland. Up to 30 in (75 cm) long, gulls are well built and have long pointed wings and a strong slightly hooked bill. Gulls are typically gray and white, often with dark markings, and some have a dark mask or hood in summer. Some gulls feed on fish but most are scavengers, feeding on invertebrates, eggs, chicks, and refuse. Family: *Laridae* (gulls and terns); order: *Charadriiformes* (gulls, plovers, etc.).

gullet. *See* esophagus.

gum arabic. *See* gums.

gums Adhesive substances exuded by plants. They are odorless tasteless amorphous *carbohydrates that form either clear liquid solutions or gelatinous mixtures with water. **Gum arabic** (*or* gum acacia), the most widely used of the water-soluble gums, is obtained from trees of the genus *Acacia*, although the name is also applied to substitute gums from other plants. It is used for making candies, cosmetics, gummed labels, and textile finishes. **Gum tragacanth** is extracted from shrubs of the genus *Astragalus*: it is not completely water-soluble, but forms a thick mucilage. It is used as an adhesive in pills and as a sauce thickener.

gum tree A tree of the genus *Eucalyptus* (about 600 species), so called because the whole tree is rich in resin and aromatic oils.

gun metal A type of *bronze containing about 90% copper and sometimes a little zinc. Being easy to cast, it was originally used for making cannons. Admiralty gun metal (88% copper, 10% tin, 2% zinc) is used in shipbuilding.

Gunn effect The effect used in solid-state *semiconductor microwave generators (Gunn diodes). When a sufficiently high steady electric field (typically several thousand volts per centimeter) is applied across a sample of n-type gallium arsenide, microwave frequency current oscillations are set up. Named for J. B. Gunn (1928–   ).

gunnel An eel-like fish of the family *Pholididae* (about 8 species), found usually among seaweed or rocks in N Atlantic and N Pacific coastal waters, feeding on invertebrates. The rock gunnel (*Pholis gunnellus*), also called butterfish, is 12 in (30 cm) long and brownish with 9–13 black spots along the dorsal fin. Order: *Perciformes*.

gunpowder An explosive mixture of saltpeter (potassium nitrate), sulfur, and powdered charcoal. Invented by the Chinese many centuries before its description by Roger *Bacon in the 13th century it has had a profound and far-reaching effect on human conflict (*see* firearms). It has now been replaced for most purposes by safer explosives, but is still used in fireworks.

Gunpowder Plot. *See* Fawkes, Guy.

guns *Artillery firearms that discharge high-velocity shells with a relatively flat trajectory. A modern breech-loading gun has a rifled barrel. Its sliding or interrupted screw-thread breech blocks contain linked levers activating the firing pin, which strikes the primer, located either in the round or the block. Buffers absorb the firing shock and recuperators return the barrel to its firing position. Controls elevate and traverse the gun, sometimes electronically. Most ammunition is fused to burst before, on, or after impact. Specialized shells are used in *antitank guns and *anti-aircraft guns. Some shells have nuclear warheads. Guns may be towed or mounted on vehicles or in aircraft or ships. *See also* small arms.

Gunter's chain. *See* chain.

Gunther, John (1901–70) US author. An overseas correspondent (1924–36) for the Chicago *Daily News*, he wrote accounts of his interviews, travels, and experiences in a series of books, including *Inside Europe* (1936), *Inside Asia* (1939), *Inside Latin America* (1941), *Inside U.S.A.* (1947), *Inside Africa* (1955), *Inside Russia Today* (1958), and *Inside South America* (1968). *Death Be Not Proud* (1949) is an account of his son's losing battle with cancer.

Guntur 16 20W 80 27E A city in S India, in Andhra Pradesh. It is an agricultural trading and processing center. Population (1971): 269,991.

Guomindang (*or* Kuomintang) The National People's Party of *Taiwan (Republic of China). Organized in 1912, following the overthrow of the imperial government, from *Sun Yat-sen's Alliance Society, it formed, under Soviet influence, an alliance with the new Chinese Communist Party (CCP) in 1924 (*see* United Fronts). Following Sun's death (1925), the Guomindang was led by *Chiang Kai-shek and with the CCP had gained control of most of China from the *warlords by 1926. A break between the two parties (1927) led to civil war until Japanese conquests in China (*see* Sino-Japanese Wars) necessitated renewed cooperation in 1937. After Japan's defeat (1945), civil war was resumed until a communist victory in 1949 drove Chiang Kai-shek and his Guomindang followers into exile in Taiwan.

guppy A freshwater fish, *Lebistes reticulatus*, native to N South America and the West Indies. Male guppies are up to 1.6 in (4 cm) long and brightly colored, marked with black eyespots and having variably shaped and colored fins. Females, slightly larger and less colorful, are prolific breeders, producing live young (rather than eggs) at monthly intervals. Guppies are popular aquarium fish and—in their native regions—are used to control mosquitoes. Family: *Cyprinodontidae*.

Gupta A powerful Indian dynasty founded in the late 4th century AD. Its founder *Chandra Gupta I was succeeded by *Samudra Gupta and the throne then passed to *Chandra Gupta II. His son Kumara (d. 455; reigned c. 415–55) was followed by Skanda Gupta (reigned 455–67), during whose reign foreign invaders began to conquer parts of the empire. The early Gupta kings fostered Buddhism and presided over a golden age of artistic and cultural achievement. The dynasty was overthrown by the Huns in the 6th century.

Gurdjieff, George Ivanovitch (1873–1943) Russian occultist of Greek parentage, who traveled widely in Europe and Asia before establishing a teaching center near Paris in the 1920s. Believing that man is not usually fully conscious, his students were required to perform a stylized dance to assist them to attain a higher level of perception. Part mystic, part bon viveur, and reputedly part charlatan, this enigmatic man had a considerable following, including P. D. Ouspensky, whose books have outlived Gurdjieff's own *All and Everything, Beelzebub's Tales to his Grandson*.

gurdwara A Sikh place of worship, housing a copy of the *Adi Granth. Although every Sikh home contains one, public gurdwaras are used for meetings, weddings, and services. The most sacred is the Golden Temple or Harimandir at Amritsar.

gurnard A carnivorous bottom-dwelling fish, also called sea robin, belonging to a family (*Triglidae*; about 40 species) found in temperate and tropical seas. It has a tapering body, up to 26 in (70 cm) long, a large armored head, and finger-like pectoral fin rays and produces sound by vibrating its swim bladder. The flying gurnards belong to the family *Dactylopteridae*. Order: *Scorpaeniformes*.

guru In *Hinduism, a venerated spiritual teacher who personally instructs and guides the disciple. In Tibetan Buddhism the guru embodies the Buddha himself and is correspondingly revered. In Sikhism, guru is the title of the first ten patriarchs (*see* Nanak).

Gustavus II Adolphus (1594–1632) King of Sweden (1611–32), who displayed military genius in the *Thirty Years' War. He inherited wars with Denmark, Russia, and Poland, which he successfully terminated in

1613, 1617, and 1629 respectively. He simultaneously, with the help of his chancellor *Oxenstierna, consolidated his internal position and in the 1620s instituted important administrative and educational reforms. In 1630 he entered the Thirty Years' War on the Protestant side, inspired by religious aims as well as a desire for Sweden to dominate the Baltic. He defeated Tilly at *Breitenfeld (1631) and at the Lech (1632) and Wallenstein at *Lutzen, in which Gustavus Adolphus was mortally wounded.

Gustavus I Vasa (1496–1560) King of Sweden (1523–60), who achieved Swedish independence of Denmark and founded the Vasa dynasty. He was taken captive in the 1517–18 war against Denmark but escaped and on returning to Sweden led a successful rebellion against the Danes (1521–23). As king, he dealt effectively with the political and economic consequences of war and established Lutheranism as the state religion (1527–29).

Gutenberg, Johann (c. 1400–c. 1468) German printer, who invented the method of printing with movable metal type (*see* typesetting). Gutenberg worked on his printing process from the 1430s. In 1448 he received the financial backing of *Fust and by 1455 had produced his great 42-line Bible (the Gutenberg Bible). Fust successfully sued Gutenberg in 1455 for the repayment of his loan and the impoverished Gutenberg was forced to relinquish his machinery, with which Fust set up a printing business. He produced a famous psalter (1457), which was largely Gutenberg's work.

Guthrie, (William) Tyrone (1900–71) British theater director. He directed the Old Vic and other British companies and frequently worked abroad, notably at Stratford, Ontario, where he founded the Shakespeare Festival in 1953. He is best known for his inventive productions of Shakespeare, often in modern dress.

Guthrie, Woody (Woodrow Wilson G.; 1912–67) US folksinger and songwriter, many of whose songs reflected the social injustice of the Depression. His most famous song was "This Land Is Your Land." His style and compositions strongly influenced other young musicians. His son, **Arlo** (1947–) is also a singer and songwriter. His best-known song is the satirical "Alice's Restaurant."

gutta percha A brownish leathery material obtained from the *latex of various trees of the family *Sapotaceae*, especially those of the SE Asian genus *Palaquium*. It was once extensively used, for example as an electrical insulator, in golf balls, and in chewing gum, but it has now largely been replaced by synthetics.

Guyana, Cooperative Republic of (name until 1966: British Guiana) A country in the NE of South America, on the Atlantic Ocean. Narrow fertile coastal plains give way to higher undulating areas, rich in minerals and forests. The main rivers, the Demerara, Essequibo, and Berbice give their names to its three counties. Most of the population is of African and East Indian descent. *Economy*: agriculture is important, the main crops being rice and sugar. Fishing, livestock, and cotton growing are being developed as part of a campaign to "feed, house, and clothe" the nation. The most important minerals were formerly gold and diamonds, but these have now been overtaken by bauxite. A local aluminum smelter is planned for the mid 1980s with assistance to come from Jamaica and Trinidad and Tobago. By 1976 nearly all foreign economic interests had been nationalized. Most power comes from hydroelectric sources. *History*: the coast was first explored by the Spanish in 1499 and settlements were founded by the Dutch in the 17th century. The area was occupied by the British (1796–1802, 1803–14) and then formally ceded to Britain, becoming a colony as British Guiana in 1831. In 1961 it gained internal self-government under *Jagan. In 1966, as Guyana, it became independent within the British Commonwealth. It is also a member of CARICOM. Marxist forces in political life led to the formation of a Cooperative Republic in 1970. In 1978 an agricultural commune (Jonestown) 150 mi (240 km) NW of Georgetown was the scene of the mass suicide of some 900 members of the People's Temple sect led by James Warren Jones. President: Linden Forbes Sampson Burnham. Official language: English. Official currency: Guyana dollar of 100 cents. Area: 83,000 sq mi (210,000 sq km). Population (1983 est): 834,000. Capital and main port: Georgetown.

Guyenne A former region of SW France. Ruled by the English kings in the late middle ages, it was regained by France after the Hundred Years' War. The scene of fierce fighting in the 16th-century Wars of Religion and the 17th-century Fronde, Guyenne was later merged with Gascony.

Guzmán Blanco, Antonio (1829–99) Venezuelan statesman. He was president three times (1870–77, 1879–84, 1886–88) but retained despotic power throughout the period 1870–88. He helped Venezuela's economy, encouraging foreign investment and building public works, including the country's first railroad.

Gwalior 26 12N 78 09E A city in India, in Madhya Pradesh. Strategically important, it developed around its impressive fortress, which is believed to date from the 6th century AD. Gwalior is an important commercial and industrial center manufacturing a variety of goods. Jiwaji University was established here in 1964. Population (1971): 384,772.

Gwelo. *See* Gweru.

Gweru (former name: Gwelo) 19 25S 29 50E A city in central Zimbabwe. It is the center of a mining area (with chrome-ore and asbestos deposits) and a cattle-rearing area. Industries include ferrochrome processing. Population (1980 est): 72,000.

Gwyn, Nell (1650–87) English actress. Originally an orange seller in Drury Lane, she achieved fame as an actress and became Charles II's mistress, bearing him two sons. "Let not poor Nellie starve" are said to have been his last words. She helped to establish the Royal Hospital at Chelsea.

gymnastics Exercises designed to perfect balance, strength, and coordination, popular as a sport for individual performers and teams. The modern sport developed in Germany and Sweden in the 19th century from **calisthenics**, rhythmical exercises performed without apparatus or weights. The ancient Persians, Chinese, Indians, Greeks, and Romans also exercised in this way. Competitions consist of prescribed programs of exercises and optional routines, the apparatus being for men the horizontal bar, parallel bars, pommel horse, vaulting horse, and rings and for women the balance beam, asymmetrical bars, and vaulting horse; both men and women do floor exercises. The sport's popularity increased dramatically, especially among girls, after the victories of Olga Korbut (1972) and Nadia Comaneci (1976) in the Olympics. The strong showing of the US men's and women's teams in the 1984 Los Angeles Olympics further spurred the sport's growth in the US. The world governing body is the Fédération internationale de Gymnastique (founded in 1881).

gymnosperms A group of plants, most of which are trees, forming one of the two classes of seed-bearing plants (*compare* angiosperms). The sole consistent characteristic of this variable class is that their seeds are not enclosed within a fruit but are borne naked, in many species on *cone scales. Gymnosperms originated in the late Devonian period (about 380 million years ago) and the principal orders are as follows: *Coniferales* (*see* conifer); *Ginkgoales* (*see* ginkgo); *Cycadales* (*see* cycad); *Gnetales* (e.g. *welwitschia); and several extinct orders, including the *Pteridospermales* (*see* seed fern) and the *Cordaitales*.

gymnure An insectivorous mammal belonging to the family *Erinaceidae* of SE Asia, also called hairy hedgehog. There are four species, including the *moon rat. Short-legged and flat-footed, 6–24 in (15–60 cm) long, they resemble *hedgehogs without spines. They are shy, usually living in thick undergrowth and hunting mainly at night.

gynecology The branch of medicine and surgery concerned with diseases of women and girls, particularly those affecting the reproductive system. The closely related specialty of **obstetrics** deals with the care of women during pregnancy, childbirth, and the period immediately after delivery. Doctors specializing in these fields (gynecologists and obstetricians) work in close association: a gynecologist is usually also an obstetrician.

Györ 47 41N 17 40E A city in NW Hungary, near the confluence of the Rába and Danube Rivers. Györ has many old buildings, including a 12th-century cathedral (rebuilt in the 18th century). It has heavy engineering and lies in an area famous for horse breeding. Population (1980): 125,00.

Gypsies A wandering people found on most continents. The name "Gypsy" is derived from "Egyptian," but they probably originated in India. One group is thought to have migrated through Egypt and North Africa and another through Europe reaching NW Europe during the 15th and 16th centuries and North America in the 19th century. They travel by motorized caravan and live largely by seasonal work, itinerant trade, entertaining, and fortune telling. They have frequently been persecuted, with half a million killed by Nazis in World War II. Their native language is *Romany.

Gypsophila A genus of slender annual or perennial herbs (about 120 species), native to the Mediterranean area. Up to 5 ft (1.5 m) high, they have gray-green strap-shaped leaves and large clusters of white or pink flowers. Some species are grown in rock gardens; others are popular for flower arrangements. Family: *Caryophyllaceae* (pink family).

Gypsum A colorless or white mineral consisting of hydrated calcium sulfate found in clays, shales, and limestones. It occurs mainly as a result of the evaporation of saline water. Rock gypsum is often red-stained, granular, and found in layers. Gypsite is impure and earthy, occurring as surface deposits. *Alabaster is a pure compact fine-grained translucent form. Satin-spar is fibrous and silky. Selenite occurs as transparent crystals in clays and mudstones. Gypsum is used in the manufacture of cement, rubber, paper, plaster of Paris, and blackboard chalk.

gypsy moth A moth, *Lymantria dispar*, distributed throughout the N hemisphere. Males are brownish gray and females white. The grayish larvae, which feed on a variety of trees, were introduced to North America in 1869 and have become a serious pest. *See also* tussock moth.

gyrfalcon The largest *falcon, *Falco rusticolus*, which breeds in N Eurasia, North America, and mountainous regions of Asia. It is 24 in (60 cm) long and its plumage varies from pure white speckled with black to dark gray with dense black barring. It hunts for hares, rodents, and ground-dwelling birds.

gyrocompass. *See* compass.

H

Haakon IV Haakonsson (1204–63) King of Norway (1217–63), who added Iceland and Greenland to Norwegian territories (1262). He subdued rebellions and strengthened the monarchy by improving royal administration and by extensive legislation. In 1247 he was crowned by the pope's legate. He died in an invasion of the Isle of Man and the Hebrides.

Haakon VII (1872–1957) The first King of Norway (1905–57) following the restoration of Norwegian independence. His refusal to abdicate during the German occupation (1940–45), during which he was in England, encouraged Norwegian resistance.

Haarlem 52 23N 4 38E A city in the W Netherlands, the capital of North Holland province. Surrounded by flower fields, it is a major trade center for bulbs. Industries include textiles and printing. It is noted for its Frans Hals museum and its fine cathedral (14–15th centuries). Population (1977 est): 162,774.

Habakkuk An Old Testament prophet of Judah, who lived at the time when a Babylonian invasion was imminent (c. 605 BC). **The Book of Habakkuk** records his perplexity that a just God should make use of an evil nation to inflict punishment on his own people, but the prophet is told to trust in God, who will see to it that all evil will eventually be punished.

habeas corpus (Latin: have the body) A remedy against unlawful confinement, which takes the form of a writ ordering the person having custody of a prisoner to produce him before the court issuing the writ and to submit to whatever the court directs. There are a variety of such writs, the most important being that of *habeas corpus ad subjiciendum* (have the body to submit to whatever the court directs), used to test the legality of imprisonment but not to appeal against a conviction or sentence. The writ is not to determine a prisoner's guilt or innocence; the only issue it presents is whether the liberty of the prisoner is restrained pursuant to the laws of due process.

Haber, Fritz (1868–1934) German chemist and inventor of the Haber process (*see* Haber-Bosch process). The Haber process, developed in 1908, enabled atmospheric nitrogen to be combined with hydrogen to form ammonia, which could then be converted into nitrates. The process was essential to Germany's supply of explosives and fertilizers during World War I. For this work, Haber was awarded the 1918 Nobel Prize. *See also* Bosch, Carl.

Haber-Bosch process A method for the bulk production of ammonia from nitrogen and hydrogen. The pure gases are passed over an iron catalyst at about 933°F (500°C) and a pressure of 500 atmospheres. Ammonia is chiefly used in the manufacture of fertilizers and *explosives. The process was devised by Fritz Haber (1868–1934) and adapted by Carl Bosch (1874–1940), who added a process for making the hydrogen from *water gas and steam.

Habsburgs (*or* Hapsburgs) The most prominent European royal dynasty from the 15th to 20th centuries. The family originated in Switzerland in the 10th century. In 1273 *Rudolf I was elected Holy Roman Emperor and consolidated through marriage and conquest his family's possession of Austria, Carniola, and Styria. After Rudolf's death (1291) the Habsburgs lost the imperial title until 1438 but thereafter kept it until 1740, holding it again from 1745 to 1806. In 1516 *Charles V inherited the Spanish crown, adding Spain with its European and American possessions to the Habsburg domains. When he abdicated in 1556 he left the Spanish crown to his son, *Philip II, and his Austrian possessions to his brother, *Ferdinand I. The Spanish branch ruled until 1700, when it died out and was replaced by the Bourbons. The Austrian Habsburgs continued to rule, becoming emperors of Austria in 1804 and of *Austria-Hungary in 1848, which they ruled until the end of World War I.

Hackney horse An English breed of trotting horse developed from Norfolk trotters. It has a compact body with strong short legs and powerful shoulders, a full tail, and a fine chestnut bay, brown, or black coat. Hackneys were once fashionable carriage horses and are now used mainly for shows. Height: 5–5.2 ft (1.50–1.60 m) ($14\frac{1}{3}$–$15\frac{1}{3}$ hands).

hadal zone. *See* abyssal zone.

haddock A carnivorous food fish, *Melanogrammus aeglefinus*, related to *cod, that usually occurs in shoals near the bottom of N Atlantic coastal waters. It has an elongated body, up to 40 in (1 m) long, gray or brown above and silvery below with a black spot behind each pectoral fin, two anal and three dorsal fins, a small chin barbel, and a dark lateral line. It is eaten both fresh and smoked, Finnan haddock from Scotland being especially well known.

Hades (*or* Pluto) The Greek god of the dead; also the name of the underworld he ruled. He was the brother of Zeus and Poseidon and husband of *Persephone, whom he abducted. The souls of the dead were ferried to Hades across the River Styx by *Charon.

Hadhramaut A region in central South Yemen. It consists of a mountain range parallel to the coast rising to over 6562 ft (2000 m) and the valley, further inland, of an intermittent stream that turns toward the sea E of the mountains. With irrigation, the production of dates, grain, and tobacco is the main industry, and the chief town is Mukalla, on the coast.

Hadith (Arabic: tradition) Traditional records of sayings and deeds attributed to Mohammed that are not contained in the Koran but are accepted as authoritative sources of moral, ritual, and religious law. Extensive compilations of such traditions were made after the Prophet's death. The chief collection is that made by al-*Bukhari.

Hadrian (76–138 AD) Roman emperor (117–38). He was admitted to the imperial household as *Trajan's ward in 85 and a successful military career included special responsibility in Trajan's Parthian campaign. On Trajan's death he became emperor, crushed a conspiracy against him (118), and from 120 to 131 toured the provinces. His foreign policy was generally defensive (he sponsored the building of *Hadrian's Wall in Britain) but he subdued a Jewish revolt (132–35) with considerable severity. From 131 until his death he lived in Rome, instigating building projects, including the *Pantheon and the mausoleum (Castel Sant' Angelo) in which he was buried.

Hadrian IV. *See* Adrian IV.

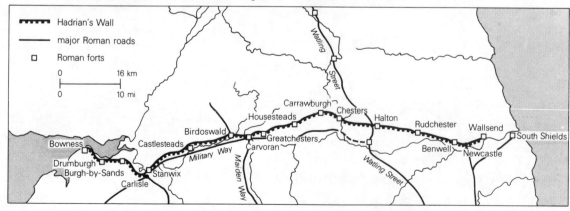

HADRIAN'S WALL *Constructed by the Romans in Britain as a defense against the Scottish tribes.*

Hadrian's Wall A Roman frontier defense work. Begun in 122 AD, it was the N frontier of Roman Britain for 250 years. Designed to control the Scottish tribes, it stretched 85 mi (120 km) from the Tyne River to Solway Firth. Temporarily superseded by the Antonine Wall and several times overrun and rebuilt, it was finally abandoned in 383 AD. Substantial portions still stand.

hadron Any elementary particle that takes part in *strong interactions. The group thus includes all baryons and mesons but not leptons or the photon. *See* particle physics.

Haeckel, Ernst Heinrich (1834–1919) German zoologist, noted for his speculative theories concerning the origin of life and evolution. A firm advocate of *Darwin's theories, Haeckel went even further. He suggested that life originated through spontaneous combination of the elements and he drew genealogical trees to represent the course of evolution. His recapitulation theory (i.e. that stages in the embryological development of an individual reflect stages in the evolution of the species) did much to stimulate embryological research, although the theory is now regarded as unsound.

Ha-er-bin (English name: Harbin) 45 45N 126 41E A port in NE China, the capital of Heilongjiang province on the Songhua River. A trading and industrial center, the site of Heilongjiang University, it was developed by Russia and was a haven for refugees from the Russian Revolution (1917). Population (1957 est): 1,552,000.

Hafiz, Shams al-Din Muhammad (?1326–90) Persian lyric poet, born at Shiraz, where he lived and worked as a religious teacher and copyist of manuscripts. He subsequently became court poet. He is the acknowledged master of the *ghazal*, a short lyric poem on the traditional subjects of love and wine, which are often treated symbolically (the beloved, whether male or female, representing God, and wine symbolizing ecstasy). About 500 *ghazals* are attributed to him. They have been widely translated; Goethe's German versions are perhaps the best known.

hafnium (Hf) A dense ductile metal, first detected in zircon ($ZrSiO_4$) in 1923 and named for the Latin (Hafnia) for Copenhagen, where it was discovered. It is chemically similar to zirconium and the two elements are difficult to separate. The capacity of hafnium to absorb neutrons is used to control nuclear reactors, especially in submarines. Its compounds include the chloride ($HfCl_4$) and other halides, the oxide (HfO_2), the carbide (HfC), and the nitride (Hf_3N_4). At no 72; at wt 178.49; mp 3906°F (2150°C); bp 9762°F (5400°C).

Haganah (Hebrew: defense) The irregular organization of the early Jewish settlers in Palestine established in 1920 to counteract the attacks of the Palestinian Arabs. After the partition of Palestine in 1947, the Haganah became the defense force of the Jewish state, coordinating opposition to the Palestinian and British forces, and in 1948 the national army of the state of Israel.

Hagen 51 22N 7 27E A city in NW West Germany, in North Rhine-Westphalia in the *Ruhr. It has iron and steel, textile, and paper industries. Population (1976 est): 226,301.

Hagen, Walter Charles (1892–1969) US professional golfer, who did much to popularize the game with his exhibition matches and his extrovert personality. Between 1914 and 1929 he won four British and two US Open championships and five US Professional Golfers Association championships.

hagfish A fishlike vertebrate, 16–31 in (40–80 cm) long, sometimes called slime eel, belonging to a family (*Myxinidae*; about 20 species) of *cyclostomes. The eel-like body has 5–16 pairs of gill slits and a sucking mouth surrounded by several thick barbels. They occur on or near the sea bottom in cold regions and feed on dead or dying fish. Hagfishes are initially hermaphrodites but develop either male or female sex organs; fertilization is internal and the eggs hatch to produce young that resemble adults.

haggadah (*or* aggadah) **1.** Nonlegal portions of the Jewish *Midrash, as opposed to *halakhah. **2.** The liturgy recited in the Jewish home over the *Passover meal (*seder*). It contains a narrative of the Exodus from Egypt and various commentaries and hymns.

Haggai An Old Testament prophet. **The Book of Haggai** contains four addresses delivered after the *Babylonian exile (c. 520 BC). Their purpose is to encourage the completion of the Temple; the prophet rebukes the people's failure to complete the rebuilding of it, but prophesies a return of divine favor when it is rebuilt.

Haggard, Sir H(enry) Rider (1856–1925) British adventure novelist. His five years in government service in South Africa provided the background of his first and most popular novel, *King Solomon's Mines* (1885),

notable for a sympathetic treatment of black Africans, reflecting his own liberal views. Of his many later romances, *She* (1887) is the best known.

haggis A traditional Scottish meat dish. Haggis is made from minced sheep's heart, liver, and lungs with onion, oatmeal, suet, seasonings, lemon juice, and stock. The ingredients are stuffed into a bag, made from the sheep's stomach or a substitute, and boiled for several hours.

THE HAGUE *The Peace Palace, home of the International Court of Justice, which was completed in 1913.*

Hague, The (Dutch name: 's Gravenhage *or* Den Haag) 52 05N 4 16E The seat of government of the Netherlands and capital of South Holland province. It developed as a settlement surrounding a 13th-century hunting lodge and became the seat of the States General of the seven United Provinces of the Netherlands in the 16th century. It is the residence of the court and the International Court of Justice is located here. Notable buildings include the 13th-century Binnenhof, in which the government is housed. It is chiefly a commercial and residential center with some light industry. Its port, Scheveningen, is a major herring-fishing center and the most popular Dutch seaside resort. Population (1977 est): 471,137.

Hague Peace Conferences (1899, 1907) Two international congresses on *disarmament, held at The Hague (Netherlands). The first conference, attended by representatives of 26 countries, codified some of the rules of war as recommended by the *Geneva Convention and instituted the permanent Court of Arbitration at The Hague. However, no agreement was reached on disarmament. The second conference, attended by 44 delegates, adopted further conventions on war (*see* neutrality) but again failed to limit armaments.

Hahn, Otto (1879–1968) German chemist and physicist. With Lise *Meitner he discovered protactinium in 1918. He continued to work with Meitner until she was forced to leave Germany in 1938. Together they discovered the process of nuclear fission. Hahn was unwilling to publish the results of this work, but Meitner did so from Sweden in 1939 and *Bohr took the information to the US. Although Hahn remained in Germany for the rest of his life, he did not work on Germany's unsuccessful attempt to make an atom bomb. In 1944 he was awarded the Nobel Prize for chemistry.

Hahnemann, Samuel Christian Friedrich (1755–1843) German physician and founder of *homeopathy. Hahnemann's methods aroused controversy among his contemporaries and he was forced to leave his practice in Leipzig, eventually settling in Paris.

hahnium (Ha; element 105) An artificial transuranic element, synthesized in the US in 1970 by bombarding californium-249 with nitrogen-15 in a particle accelerator and possibly also in the Soviet Union in 1967 by a different method. Named for Otto Hahn. At no 105; at wt (260).

Haifa 32 49N 34 59E A city in NE Israel, on the Mediterranean coast by Mount Carmel. It was the scene of fighting in the 1948–49 Arab-Israeli conflict and has since developed into a manufacturing town based on the deepwater port (opened 1933). Haifa University was founded in 1963. Population (1975 est): 227,200.

Haig, Alexander Meigs, Jr. (1924–) US Army officer and statesman; secretary of state (1981–82). A graduate of West Point (1947), he held positions ranging from aide to General Douglas MacArthur and assistant to Robert McNamara, Henry Kissinger, and Richard Nixon to Army vice chief of staff (1973), chief of the White House staff (1973), and commander of NATO forces in Europe (1974–79); he retired as a full general. Appointed secretary of state by President *Reagan, he resigned over policy difference with the president. He recounted his experiences in *Caveat* (1984).

hail The approximately spherical ice pellets that fall from cumulonimbus clouds. These have been known to weigh almost 2.2 lb (1 kg). They originate as small ice particles around which alternate concentric layers of clear and opaque ice freeze as the ice pellets alternately fall or are uplifted within a cloud. Hailstorms occur most frequently in the continental interiors of temperate latitudes.

Haile Selassie I (1892–1975) Emperor of Ethiopia (1930–36, 1941–74). In 1936 Haile Selassie had to flee to England after the invasion by the Italians, against whom he personally fought, but was restored to the throne by the Allies in 1941. He did much to modernize Ethiopia and became a prominent figure in international affairs. However, his absolute rule provoked opposition and he was deposed by a military coup.

Hainan Island A Chinese island, the largest in the South China Sea, apart from Taiwan, and separated from the mainland by **Hainan Strait**. Sparsely populated, it is one of China's least developed regions. The aboriginal population has moved into the mountainous forested center and S as Chinese farmers have settled the N coastal plain. Rubber and timber are produced and iron ore and other minerals are mined. Area: 13,124 sq mi (33,991 sq km). Population (1956 est): 2,700,000. Capital: Haikou.

Hainaut (Flemish name: Henegouwen; French name: Hainault) A province in SW Belgium, bordering on France. It contains important coalfields and industries include iron and steel processing. Area: 1466 sq mi (3997 sq km). Population (1975 est): 1,321,846. Capital: Mous.

Haiphong 20 50N 106 41E A city in N Vietnam, on the Red River delta. As Hanoi's outport and an industrial center much developed after 1954 with Soviet and Chinese aid, it was severely bombed during the Vietnam War. Textiles, phosphates, and plastics are manufactured and minerals and rice exported. Population (1960): 182,490.

hair The threadlike structures forming the body covering of mammals. Each hair grows from the base of a sheath (hair follicle) embedded in the inner layer (dermis) of the □skin but only a few cells at its root are living. The rest consists of scaly dead cells made largely of *keratin and other proteins. Color is determined by the amount of *melanin pigment in hair. In most mammals hair forms an insulating and protective coat (the pelage), which reduces heat loss from the body and often provides camouflage. In humans hair is important only for personal adornment and display.

Similar structures in lower animals (e.g. insects) often have a sensory function, and plants possess hairs on roots, stems, and leaves.

hairstreak A butterfly belonging to the family *Lycaenidae* and characterized by fine white streaks on the underwings and a small "tail" on each hindwing. Both Old and New World species show a great variety of coloration.

hairy frog A *frog, *Astylosternus robustus*, of the Cameroons. In the breeding season the skin on the sides and thighs of male frogs develops hairlike filaments, containing many blood vessels, that assist in breathing and compensate for its much reduced lungs. The females grow no hairs.

Haiti, Republic of A country in the Caribbean Sea, occupying the W third of the island of Hispaniola (the Dominican Republic occupies the E two thirds). Much of the country is mountainous and forested, with fertile plains lying between the three main mountain ranges. It is subject to hurricanes. The majority of the population is of African descent, with a minority of mulattoes. *Economy*: mainly agricultural, mostly organized in small farms. The main crops are coffee (the principal export), sugar, rice, bananas, and sisal. Mineral resources are largely unexploited although some bauxite and copper are mined. Hydroelectricity is an important source of power. Small industries are being encouraged, particularly manufactures for export. *History*: the island was discovered by Columbus in 1492 and became a Spanish colony. The Spanish virtually wiped out the native Indian population and large numbers of African slaves were imported. The E part was ceded to France in 1697, becoming the most prosperous of the French colonies, and the remainder was temporarily ceded between 1795 and 1809. The slave leader *Toussaint L'Ouverture briefly extended his rule over the whole island and in 1804, under Gen *Dessalines, Haiti gained its independence. A period of unrest was followed by union with the rest of the island (1822–44). For most of the time since it has been a republic; there was a brief period of occupation by the US (1915–34). After

a series of coups Dr François *Duvalier ("Papa Doc") came to power in 1957 and was succeeded in 1971 by his son, Jean-Claude Duvalier ("Baby Doc"). Since then there has been an improvement in the condition of the country (although droughts and soil erosion caused an economic crisis in 1977) and in its relations with other nations. Poor economic conditions caused many Haitians to flee to the US by boat, which led to refugee problems in Florida and strained relations between the countries. Additionally, tourism in Haiti declined sharply in the 1980s because of the link between AIDS (acquired immune deficiency syndrome) and Haitian immigrants in the US. Official language: French; Creole is widely spoken. Offical religion: Roman Catholic. Area: 10,700 sq mi (27,750 sq km). Population (1983): 566,000. Capital and main port: Port-au-Prince.

hajj The pilgrimage to Mecca that every able Muslim is required to make, if means permit, at least once in his lifetime during the first half of the last month of the Islamic year. The pilgrimage includes circumambulations of the *Kaaba and visits to other holy places.

hake A food fish, of the genus *Merluccius*, that is related to *cod and occurs off European, African, and American coasts. Its elongated body, up to about 40 in (1 m) long, is dark gray above and lighter below, with two dorsal fins, the second running to the tail and matching the anal fin.

Hakka A Chinese ethnic minority group found in the provinces of Canton and Fujian and in Taiwan and Chinese settlements in East Asia. The Hakkas (guest people) migrated S from N China in the unrest of the 12th and 13th centuries and for several centuries were social outcasts, having brought with them the different dialect and customs that they still retain.

Hakluyt, Richard (c. 1553–1616) English geographer. As a clergyman he served in various posts, but his chief interest was in exploration, navigation, and the establishment of a colony in Virginia. His major work, *The Principal Navigations, Voyages, Traffics, and Discoveries of the English Nation . . .* (1 vol, 1589; 3 vols, 1598–1600), stimulated English overseas trade and colonization.

Hakodate 41 46N 140 44E A port in Japan, in SW Hokkaido on the Tsugaru Strait. It contains Japan's only western-style fort (1855). Industries include fishing and shipbuilding. Population (1976 est): 310,426.

halakhah Jewish law. The Hebrew word is used in different ways, either for the law as a whole or an individual regulation. The main halakhic sources are the *Torah, *Mishnah and *Talmuds, the gaonic responsa (*see* gaon), and the medieval codes (e.g. those of *Maimonides and Joseph *Caro). The halakhah embraces more than law: it governs every aspect of life and also embodies theological ideas. The authority of halakhah is one of the main points of disagreement between traditional and *Reform Judaism.

Halcyone In Greek legend, daughter of *Aeolus. She threw herself into the sea after her husband, Ceyx of Thrachis, drowned, and they were both transformed into kingfishers.

Hale, Nathan (1755–76) US patriot. A graduate of Yale University and a school teacher, he joined the Continental Army in 1775 and volunteered to spy on British General William *Howe's activities on Long Island. He was captured (1776) and within a day hanged as a spy. The words "I only regret that I have but one life to lose for my country" are attributed to him while on the scaffold.

Haleakala National Park A national park on E Maui Island, E Hawaii. Established in 1961, the park had been a part of the larger Hawaii National Park since 1916. The volcano Haleakala, dormant since 1790, stands 10,023 ft (3055 m) high. Area: 34 sq mi (88 sq km).

Hale Observatories The group of observatories comprising the Palomar Observatory, Mount Wilson Observatory, Big Bear Solar Observatory, all in California, and Las Campanas Observatory, near La Serena, Chile. They are sponsored by the Californian Institute of Technology and the Carnegie Institution, Washington. The principal telescopes are the famous 200 in (5 m) reflector and a 48 in (1.2 m) *Schmidt telescope (Palomar), the oldest 100 in (2.5 m) reflector (Mount Wilson), and a new 2.5 m reflector (Las Campanas). They are named for the US astronomer G. E. Hale (1868–1938), who founded the Mount Wilson Observatory.

Halévy, Jacques François (Fromental Elias Levy; 1799–1862) French composer of Jewish origin. A pupil of Cherubini at the Paris conservatoire, he won the Prix de Rome in 1819. He composed ballets, incidental music, cantatas, and over 30 operas, including *La Juive* (1835).

Haley, Alex Palmer (1921–) US author. He wrote *The Autobiography of Malcolm X* (1965) after retiring from the Coast Guard (1939–59) and then began researching his family lineage, which brought him back to Africa. From this research and from memories recounted by his grandmother in Henning, Tenn., evolved *Roots: The Saga of an American Family* (1976), which was serialized on television (1977).

half-life The time taken for half the atoms in a sample of a radioactive isotope to decay. It is therefore a measure of the activity of an isotope. A very active isotope may have a half-life of only a millionth of a second, whereas some more stable isotopes have half-lives of millions of years.

half-timber work A building technique used since ancient times. It involves constructing a wooden skeleton for a building, which is then filled out with either plasterwork or brick. Frequently the frame is left exposed. A quickly built and strong structure, it is best suited to temperate climates. The technique was frequently used in 15th- and 16th-century England.

Haliç. *See* Golden Horn.

halibut A *flatfish of the genus *Hippoglossus*, especially *H. hippoglossus*—a large food fish, up to about 7 ft (2 m) long, found in N Atlantic coastal waters. The eyed (right) side is brown or dark green with mottling. Family: *Pleuroncetidae*.

Other halibuts include the Greenland halibut and the California halibut, which belong to the family *Bothidae*.

Halicarnassus (modern name: Bodrum) An ancient city of *Caria on the SW coast of Asia Minor. Its rulers included *Artemisia and Mausolus, who made Halicarnassus his capital (c. 370 BC) and is remembered chiefly for his tomb, the *Mausoleum. Herodotus, the Greek historian, was born here.

Halifax 53 44N 1 52W A city in N England, on the River Calder. Halifax has a strong wool textile tradition going back to the 13th century. Carpets, woolens, and worsteds are manufactured as well as machine tools and textile machinery. Population (1973 est): 88,580.

Halifax 44 38N 63 35W A city and major port in E Canada, the capital of Nova Scotia on the Atlantic Ocean. Founded as a British naval base (1749), it dominates the cultural life, commerce, and industry of the *Maritime Provinces. Its industries include shipbuilding, oil refining, steel, and food processing. Population (1976): 117,882.

Halifax, Charles Montagu, 1st Earl of (1661–1715) English statesman. A Whig MP (1689–95), as a lord of the treasury (1692–94) he initiated the national debt and set up the *Bank of England (1694) and as chancellor of the exchequer (1694–95) he introduced a new coinage. In 1697 he became first lord of the treasury but in 1699 was forced by the Tories to resign; he again held the post in 1714–15. He was a patron of writers, including the playwright *Congreve.

halitosis Bad breath. Very foul-smelling breath may be caused by infection in the mouth, teeth, tonsils, or lungs and sometimes by stomach disease. The mild odor that many people have needs no treatment except regular cleaning of the teeth.

Halle 51 30N 11 59E A city in SW East Germany, on the Saale River. The birthplace of Handel, Halle has many fine old buildings. Its diverse industries include sugar refining and coalmining. The university was founded in 1694. Population (1977): 231,480.

Halleck, Fitz-Greene (1790–1867) US poet. A bank employee in New York City, he was part of the Knickerbocker group of poets and coauthored the "Croaker Papers" (1819), satire published in the New York *Evening Post*. He also wrote "On the Death of Joseph Rodman Drake" (1820), "Marco Bozzarius" (1825), and "Young America" (1865).

Hall effect If a conductor carrying an electric current is placed in a magnetic field, so that the field and the current are at right angles to each other, an electric field appears across the material. The electric field is perpendicular to both the current and the magnetic field. The effect is due to the force experienced by all moving charges in a magnetic field: the charges flowing in the material are displaced to one side thus creating a potential difference. Named for Edwin H. Hall (1855–1938).

Haller, Albrecht von (1708–77) Swiss biologist, poet, and one of the founders of modern physiology. Haller showed how the stimulation of a nerve caused contraction of the muscle to which it was attached. He also studied the brain, heart, breathing mechanisms, and embryology; his works include *Elementa physiologiae corporis humani* (8 vols, 1757–66) and four large bibliographies of botany, anatomy, surgery, and medicine. His best-known poem is *Die Alpen*.

Halley, Edmund (1656–1742) British astronomer. He was the first to realize that *comets do not appear randomly but have periodic orbits. In 1705 he identified a particular comet, now known as **Halley's comet**, as having a period of 76 years. The years of its appearance in the 20th century are 1910 and 1986. He also discovered that stars have a proper motion of their own (1718). A friend of Sir Isaac Newton, he had earlier financed the publication of Newton's *Principia*.

hallmarks A set of marks stamped onto gold or silver objects manufactured in the UK, as a guarantee of purity. Each article has up to five marks: the mark of the assay office, an assay mark to indicate quality, a date mark, the sovereign's head (between 1784 and 1890), and the maker's mark. Gold articles also have a mark to indicate their purity in *karats.

Hallowe'en 31 Oct., the eve of All Saints' Day. The name is a contraction of All Hallows (hallowed or holy) Eve. In pre-Christian Britain, Oct 31 was the eve of New Year, when the souls of the dead were thought to revisit their homes. After it became a Christian festival supernatural associations continued and Hallowe'en customs include the shaping of a demon's face from a hollow pumpkin, in which a candle is then placed. Children, wearing disguises, go from door to door on Hallowe'en demanding "treats" on penalty of "tricks."

Hallstatt The phase of the central European Iron Age (700–500 BC) preceding *La Tène. It is named for— the site in the Salzkammergut in Austria, which is famous for its salt mines. Earlier Bronze Age (*see* Urnfield) people in the same area (1200–700 BC) are often included under the term. The wealth of Iron Age Hallstatt depended on extensive trade. Characteristic artifacts were iron swords and elaborate bronze vessels decorated with geometric patterns, solar symbols, or ducks. Wagon burial of chieftains was practiced, e.g. at Vix (France).

hallucination A vivid but false perception of something that is not really there. Any sense can be affected. It may be a result of mental illness, especially *psychosis, when the commonest forms are hearing voices and seeing frightening visions. It can also be caused by drugs, epilepsy, disease of the brain, and sensory deprivation. Transient hallucinations can be experienced by normal people, especially when they are falling asleep (hypnagogic hallucinations) or waking up (hypnopompic hallucinations) or if they have been bereaved (grief hallucinations, of the person who has been lost).

hallucinogens Drugs that produce hallucinations due to their stimulant action on the brain. Such drugs are also described as psychedelic. Hallucinogens, which include *cannabis and *LSD, tend to lead to some form of *drug dependence. The ability of any given hallucinogen to produce a hallucination depends very much on the personality of the individual. Some unlikely drugs (e.g. digitalis) may provoke hallucinations in susceptible individuals.

halogens The elements forming group VII of the *periodic table: fluorine, chlorine, bromine, iodine, and astatine. In chemical reactions they tend to form negative ions or covalent bonds and they have a valence of 1. All are reactive, particularly fluorine and chlorine. They produce salts on contact with metals ("halogen" means salt-yielding) and react with other nonmetals and many organic compounds.

Hals, Frans (c. 1581–1666) Dutch painter of portraits and scenes of everyday life. He was born in Antwerp but worked mainly in Haarlem. Apart from his *Laughing Cavalier* (1624), he is best known for his group portraits, such as those of the companies of archers and musketeers, which are characterized by lively expressions and gestures. Later works, such as *Lady-Governors of the Almshouse at Haarlem* (c. 1664), influenced by *Rembrandt, are more somber and show a greater sympathy for character.

Halsey, William Frederick (1882–1959) US naval officer. He graduated from the Naval Academy in 1904. After service aboard a destroyer in World War I and training as an aviator, he commanded the South Pacific area (1942–44) and the Third Fleet (1944–45) during World War II. His leadership contributed significantly to the American effort in the battles of *Guadalcanal and the Coral Sea (1942), *Leyte Gulf (1944), and Okinawa (1945), which marked the rise of aircraft as decisive weapons in naval warfare.

Hälsingborg (*or* Helsingborg) 56 05N 12 45E A seaport in S Sweden, on the Sound opposite Helsingør, Denmark. It changed hands several times between Denmark and Sweden before finally becoming Swedish in 1710. An industrial center, it has an important shipbuilding industry. Population (1976 est): 101,323.

Hama 35 09N 36 44E A city in W Syria. It dates from Hittite times and still possesses the medieval water-wheels up to 89 ft (27 m) in diameter used for irrigation. It is mainly an agricultural and commercial center. Population (1977 est): 173,459.

Hamadan 34 46N 48 35E A city in W central Iran. Hamadan lies at a high altitude, and visitors are attracted by the cool summers; the winters, however, are severe. A university was founded here in 1973. Population (1976): 155,846.

hamadryas A small *baboon, *Papio hamadryas*, of NE Africa and Saudi Arabia. 40–55 in (100–140 cm) long including the tail (16–24 in

[40–60 cm]), hamadryas baboons have a long silvery-brown mane, pinkish face, and red buttocks and live in groups with a complex social structure. They were sacred animals to the ancient Egyptians.

Hamamatsu   34 42N 137 42E A city in Japan, in S central Honshu. A commercial and industrial center, its manufactures include musical instruments, textiles, and motor cycles. Population (1976 est): 475,552.

Hamburg   53 33N 10 00E A city in N West Germany, on the Elbe and Alster Rivers. A major port and the largest city in West Germany, it is also an important cultural center, with a university (1919), art gallery, and opera house (1678). It is the birthplace of Mendelssohn and Brahms. Its many industries include shipbuilding, engineering, and food processing. *History*: in 834 AD it was made the seat of a missionary archbishop. Its alliance with Lübeck (1241) became the basis of the Hanseatic League. It was a trading center from the middle ages and the first German stock exchange was established here (1558). It was severely bombed during World War II. Population (1976 est): 1,698,615.

Hamburg   One of ten constituent states in West Germany, in the NE, comprising the city of *Hamburg, its surrounding area, and two islands in the Elbe estuary. Area: 289 sq mi (748 sq km). Population (1977 est): 1,680,300.

Hamelin (German name: Hameln)   52 06N 9 21E A city in N West Germany, in Lower Saxony on the Weser River. Its many Renaissance houses include the Ratcatcher's House (1602–03), associated with the legendary Pied Piper. Manufactures include carpets and chemicals. Population (1971 est): 46,800.

Hamersley Range   A mountain range of N Western Australia. It extends W–E between the Fortesque and Ashburton Rivers, reaching 4024 ft (1227 m) at Mount Bruce, and contains large deposits of iron ore.

Hamhŭng (*or* Hamheung)   39 54N 127 35E A city in E central North Korea. Its industry was bombed during the Korean War (1950–53) but has been restored and developed. The principal manufactures are synthetic textiles, chemicals, and machinery. Its seaport, Hungnam, lies to the SE of the city.

Hamilcar Barca   (died c. 229 BC) Carthaginian general and Hannibal's father. Commander in Sicily during the first *Punic War, he negotiated peace in 241. After suppressing rebellious mercenaries in Carthage, he invaded Spain, accompanied by the young Hannibal. He was drowned after the siege of Helice.

Hamilton   43 15N 79 50W A city and port in central Canada, in S Ontario on Lake Ontario. Canada's main center of heavy industry, it is particularly important for iron and steel, motor vehicles, machinery, chemicals, and electrical goods. Hamilton is also a financial, agricultural, transportation, and educational center. McMaster University (1887) was moved here from Toronto in 1930. Population (1976): 312,003.

Hamilton   37 46S 175 18E A city in New Zealand, in N North Island on the Waikato River. It is the most important inland center and serves a pastoral and lumbering region. The University of Waikato was established in 1964. Population (1973 est): 81,600.

Hamilton   55 47N 4 03W A city in W central Scotland, in the Clyde valley. Metal goods, carpets, and electrical equipment are manufactured, local coalmining having declined. Population (1974 est): 45,176.

Hamilton, Alexander   (1755–1804) American political leader. He joined the Continental Army at the outbreak of the *Revolutionary War and was appointed aide-de-camp to General George *Washington in 1777. After the war, he served in the *Continental Congress (1782–83) and practiced law in New York City. Hamilton was an advocate of a strong federal government for the United States, and at the Annapolis Convention of 1786 he was instrumental in persuading the delegates to convene in Philadelphia for a *Constitutional Convention in the following year. He was chosen to be one of the New York delegates to that convention and he worked tirelessly for the ratification of the new *Constitution, collaborating with John *Jay and James *Madison in the publication of the *Federalist Papers.

After the Federalist victory in the elections of 1788, Hamilton was chosen to serve as secretary of the Treasury in Washington's cabinet. In that position, he established the first national bank and structured the repayment program for the national debt. Even after his resignation from public office in 1795, Hamilton remained active in the *Federalist Party. He was a bitter opponent of fellow New Yorker Aaron *Burr and his support for Jefferson in the 1800 elections resulted in Burr's defeat in his campaign for the presidency. In 1804, Hamilton opposed Burr's candidacy for governor of New York and Burr, outraged at Hamilton's continuing political enmity, killed him in a duel.

ALEXANDER HAMILTON   *A Federalist who served as the first secretary of the treasury and established the Bank of the United States.*

Hamilton, Lady Emma   (c. 1761–1815) The mistress of Horatio *Nelson. Wife of Sir William Hamilton (1730–1803), envoy to the court of Naples (1764–1800), she met Nelson in Naples in 1793. They became lovers and in 1801 their daughter Horatia (d. 1881) was born. After Nelson's death (1805), Lady Emma squandered her inheritance and fled to Calais (1814), where she died.

Hamilton, Sir William Rowan   (1805–65) Irish mathematician. A child prodigy, he had mastered 13 languages by the age of 13 and at 22 was appointed professor of astronomy at Trinity College, Dublin. His most important work was the discovery of quaternions, three-dimensional equivalents of *complex numbers. He also made important contributions to the mathematics of light rays and helped to establish the wave theory of light.

Hamito-Semitic languages   A language family spoken in N Africa and S Asia. It is more appropriately known as Afro-Asiatic, especially since the Hamitic section of the name describes no particular characteristics. It has five branches that descend from an ancestor language, Proto-Hamito-Semitic, which was spoken between the 6th and 8th millenniums BC. The five branches are Egyptian, Berber, Cushitic, Semitic, and Chadic. There is some doubt about the membership of the Chadic languages in this group.

Hamlin, Hannibal   (1809–91) US politician; vice president (1861–65). He was a representative from Maine (1843–47) to the US Congress before becoming a senator (1848–57; 1869–81). In 1856 he switched allegiance from the Democratic to the Republican Party and briefly served as governor of Maine in 1857. His one term as vice president under President Abraham Lincoln was not renewed in 1864 because of his association with radical causes.

Hamm   51 40N 7 49E A city in NW West Germany, in North Rhine-Westphalia. The rail center of the *Ruhr, it has the largest marshaling yards in the country. Its chief manufactures are wire, cable, and machinery. Population (1976 est): 171,765.

Hammarskjöld, Dag (Hjalmar Agne Carl)   (1905–61) Swedish international civil servant; the son of Hjalmar Hammarskjöld (1862–1953), who was a prime minister of Sweden (1914–17). As deputy foreign minister (1951–53) he headed the Swedish delegation to the UN and in 1953 succeeded Trygve *Lie as secretary general of the UN. He dealt with the Suez crisis (1956) and the civil war arising from the grant of independence to the Congo (1960). He was killed in a plane crash and awarded the Nobel Peace Prize posthumously in 1961. His diary *Markings* was published in 1964.

Hammerfest 70 40N 23 44E A port in N Norway, on the W coast of the island of Kvaløya (or Kväloy). It is the most northerly town in the world. Its ice-free harbor permits fishing all year. Population (1973 est): 7418.

hammerhead A dark-brown bird, *Scopus umbretta*, that is the only member of its family (*Scopidae*) and occurs in marshes and mangrove swamps of tropical Africa, Madagascar, and the Arabian Peninsula. It has a large bill and a long backward-pointing crest. Hammerheads feed on frogs, fish, and aquatic invertebrates and build a large domed nest of sticks cemented together with mud. Order: *Ciconiiformes* (herons, storks, etc.).

hammerhead shark A *shark of the family *Sphyrnidae*, found in warm and temperate salt waters. Up to 15 ft (4.5 m) long, the head is flattened and extended laterally into two hammer- or spade-shaped lobes, which bear the eyes and nostrils. They feed primarily on fish but may attack other animals, including man.

Hammerstein II, Oscar (1895–1960) US lyricist and librettist, who collaborated with several well-known musical comedy composers, including Jerome Kern, Sigmund Romberg, and Richard Rodgers. His works include *Show Boat* (1927), *Oklahoma!* (1943), *Carousel* (1945), *South Pacific* (1949), *The King and I* (1951), and *The Sound of Music* (1959).

hammer throw A field event for men in athletics. The hammer is an iron or brass sphere weighing 16 lb (7.26 kg) attached to a spring-steel wire handle and grip. It is thrown with both hands from within a circle 7 ft (2.13 m) in diameter. A competitor has six attempts in which to throw the hammer the furthest.

Hammer v. Dagenhart (1918) US Supreme Court decision that declared the Child Labor Act (1916) unconstitutional. The act prohibited interstate shipment of goods produced in factories that employed children under 14 or that imposed unreasonable working hours or conditions on children between 14 and 16. It was the belief of the court that the law violated the extent to which the federal government could regulate states. The decision was overruled by *United States v. Darby* (1941).

Hammett, Dashiell (1894–1961) US novelist. He worked as a private detective for eight years before writing his first detective stories. His novels, the realistic and economical style of which influenced Raymond *Chandler and other detective-story writers, include *The Maltese Falcon* (1930), *The Glass Key* (1931), and *The Thin Man* (1932), all of which were made into successful movies. He was a close friend of Lillian *Hellman.

Hammurabi (d. 1750 BC) King of Babylon (1792–1750). After defeating the kingdoms of Eshunna, Elam, and Ashur, Hammurabi turned against his former allies, the kingdoms of Larsa and Mari. The Code of Hammurabi, a collection of Babylonian laws, has survived in the Akkadian language.

Hampton 37 02N 76 23W A port in SE Virginia, on Hampton Roads Harbor. Founded in 1610, it has large fish-packing and shipping industries. Several military installations are situated nearby. Population (1975 est): 125,013.

Hampton, Lionel (1913–) US black jazz band leader and vibraphone player, who played with Benny Goodman before forming his own orchestra in 1940. Hampton was the first jazz musician to popularize the vibraphone; one of his biggest successes was the record *Flyin' Home* (1942).

Hampton Roads Conference (1865) US peace conference between the Union and the Confederate states at Hampton Roads in SE Virginia. The Union, represented by President Abraham Lincoln and Secretary of State William Seward and Confederate representatives met to discuss peace terms; the conference foundered over the issue of restoration of the pre-war Union versus independence for the Southern states.

hamster A small *rodent of the family *Cricetidae*. The common hamster (*Cricetus cricetus*), native to Europe and W Asia, is solitary and aggressive and has a red-brown coat with white patches on the flanks, neck, and cheek. It feeds on seeds and grains, storing them in underground burrows. The golden hamster (*Mesocricetus auratus*) is a domestic pet and all are thought to have descended from a single family found at Aleppo, Syria, in 1930.

Hamsun, Knut (1859–1952) Norwegian novelist. His early novels, *Hunger* (1890), *Mysteries* (1892), and *Pan* (1894), reflected his interest in nature and the irrational. Much of his subsequent work was influenced by Nietzsche and Strindberg and revealed a distrust of society and civilization; it includes the novels *Vagabonds* (1927) and *Markens grøde* (*The Growth of the Soil*; 1917). He won the Nobel Prize in 1920. He was accused of pro-Nazi tendencies after World War II but was not tried; his own attitude toward the war is commented on in the autobiographical *På gjengrodde stier* (1949).

Han (206 BC–220 AD) A Chinese dynasty founded by the general Liu Bang (or Liu Pang; 256–195 BC), who overthrew the preceding Qin dynasty. The power of the Han was consolidated by the emperor, Wu Di (or Wu Ti; 157–87 BC; reigned 140–87), who completed the conquest of a vast empire. Confucianism was recognized as the state philosophy, Chinese export of silk increased, and a vast canal-building program was started. Paper was invented by the Han Chinese, who also produced early forms of porcelain and kept detailed historical records. The program of expansion led to financial difficulties that enabled *Wang Mang to usurp the throne in 8 AD. However, he was toppled in turn and the Han dynasty was restored for a second period, known as the Later Han (23–220 AD).

Hancock, John (1737–93) US patriot; president of the Continental Congress (1775–77). A prosperous Boston businessman, he led a group of patriots protesting the restrictions imposed by the British. His signature, the first on the Declaration of Independence (1776) has come to mean "signature." He served in the Continental Congress (1775–80; 1785; 1786) and as governor of Massachusetts (1780–85; 1789–93).

Hand, (Billings) Learned (1872–1961) US jurist and writer. He practiced law in New York and served on New York's District Court (1909–24) and on the US Circuit Court of Appeals, 2nd District (1924–51), of which he was chief judge from 1939. Known for his ability to think clearly, write concisely, and speak eloquently, his rulings were, at times, referred to in US Supreme Court cases. His works are collected in *The Spirit of Liberty* (1952) and *The Bill of Rights* (1958).

hand The terminal part of the arm. The human hand contains 27 bones. There are 8 carpal bones, which form the wrist and articulate with the forearm at a hinge joint; 5 metacarpals, in the palm of the hand; and 14 phalanges (the bones of the fingers and thumb). The thumb of man and other primates is unique in being opposable, i.e. it can be rotated to touch each of the other fingers, making possible a wide range of manual skills (including using tools and writing). This—combined with its sensitive skin—has produced a manipulative and exploratory organ that has contributed to the success of man as a species.

handball A court game related to *pelota and fives that probably originated in the Roman baths. It is played in a court against one, three, or four walls with a small rubber ball that is hit with the gloved hand.

Handel, George Frederick (1685–1759) German composer. He became famous as a harpsichordist and as a master of the Italianate style of composition. After visiting England in 1712, he received a court pension from Queen Anne. He became music master to the family of the Prince of Wales and director of the Royal Academy of Music on its foundation in 1720. His Italian operas were successfully produced in London. From 1739 he turned from opera to oratorio, producing such masterpieces as *Saul* (1739), *Israel in Egypt* (1739), and *Messiah* (1742), which maintained his public popularity. In 1751, however, he began to be afflicted with loss of sight and became completely blind, although he continued to compose until his death. His mastery of composition is reflected in the range of his works, which include the *Water Music* (1717), *Music for the Royal Fireworks* (1749), concerti grossi, sonatas, organ concertos, harpsichord suites, and anthems.

Handy, W(illiam) C(hristopher) (1873–1958) US jazz musician, remembered chiefly as "The Father of the Blues." His best known compositions are "Memphis Blues" (1912) and "St Louis Blues" (1914). In later life he became a music publisher, continuing to work until his death, even after becoming blind.

Han fei zi (d. 233 BC) Chinese diplomat and philosopher of law. Although an author of antiquity, he has been studied, along with the Taoists, in the modern period in China. He is best known for his conception of government by law and his advocacy of statecraft.

Hangchow. See Hangzhou.

hang-gliding Unpowered flight in a hang-glider, consisting of a large bat-shaped cloth wing on a light metal framework from which the pilot hangs in a harness, holding a horizontal control bar. In flight, the wing fills to form an aerofoil (see aeronautics). The first hang-glider was built by Otto *Lilienthal, but the prototype for modern design was the sail-wing invented by Frances Rogallo (1912–) as a means of recovering space vehicles. Hang-gliding became popular in the late 1960s, acquiring a reputation as a dangerous sport largely because hang-gliders are relatively easy to attempt to fly without instruction.

hanging. See capital punishment.

Hanging Gardens of Babylon Ancient gardens in the palace of Nebuchadnezzar II (604–562 BC) on the E side of Babylon. One of the Seven Wonders of the World, they were built on top of stone arches 75 ft (23 m) above ground and watered from the Euphrates by a complicated mechanical system.

Hangzhou (Hang-chou *or* Hangchow)   30 18N 120 07E A city in E China, the capital of Zhejiang province on Hangzhou Bay, an inlet of the East China Sea. It was the capital (1132–1276) of the Southern *Song dynasty. A picturesque tourist center, it is the site of three universities. Its varied industries include silk production. Population (1957 est): 784,000.

haniwa   Japanese terracotta sculptures, originally cylindrical in shape, placed on the outside of tomb mounds between about 330 and 552 AD. By the 5th century modeled houses and later horses and human figures were placed on top of the cylinders.

Hankou (*or* Hankow).   *See* Wuhan.

Hanna, Mark   (Marcus Alonso H.; 1837–1904) US politician and businessman. A successful businessman in Cleveland, he engineered the political career of William McKinley through the governorship of Ohio (1891–93) to the presidency (1897–1901) and served as Republican National Chairman (1896). He was a senator from 1897 until his death in 1904.

Hannibal   (247–c. 183 BC) Carthaginian general. Appointed commander in Spain in 221, he deliberately provoked the second *Punic War with Rome. Advancing swiftly, in 218 he crossed the Alps in winter, reaching N Italy after a heroic trek in which he lost about 10,000 of his 35,000 men. For two years he devastated Italy but, after disastrous Roman defeats at Trasimene and *Cannae, Hannibal lost ground in the face of *Fabius' guerrilla tactics. Recalled to defend Carthage after *Scipio Africanus' invasion of Africa, Hannibal was defeated at Zama (202). Domestic politics occupied him until, suspected of rebellion, he was forced to flee Roman retribution. He committed suicide to avoid capture.

Hannibal   39 42N 91 22W A city in NE Missouri, on the Mississippi River. Mark Twain lived here as a boy in the mid-1800s and it is from his life here that many of his stories came. His family's home and memorabilia draw many visitors to the city. Other industries include fertilizers, building materials, machinery, and printing. Population (1980): 18,811.

Hanoi   20 57N 105 55E The capital of Vietnam, situated in the NE of the country on the Red River. The capital of the Vietnamese empire from the 11th until the 17th centuries, it was occupied by the French in 1873 and became the capital of French Indochina. Following the Japanese occupation in World War II, it became the capital of the Democratic Republic of Vietnam. Despite the frequent bombing by the US during the Vietnam War, many ancient buildings in the Vietnamese quarter remain, together with several imposing buildings in the European quarter built by the French. Its university was established in 1956. Population (1976): 1,443,500.

Hanover (German name: Hannover)   52 23N 9 44E A city in N West Germany, the capital of Lower Saxony on the Leine River. It is a transshipment port and a commercial and industrial center, where an important industrial fair is held annually. After the destruction of World War II it was largely rebuilt and some buildings, such as the old town hall (1435–80), were reconstructed. The Leine Palace (founded 1636) is now the *Land* parliament building. Hanover's manufactures include machinery, rubber, textiles, and motor vehicles. *History*: in 1638 Hanover became the capital of an area of Brunswick that was later the electorate and then the kingdom of Hanover. In 1714 Elector George Louis became George I of Great Britain, (*see* Settlement, Act of). The Kings of Great Britain were Electors (later Kings) of Hanover until 1837. Population (1976 est): 547,077.

Hanoverian   A breed of horse developed in Hanover and originally used for hauling. During the 19th and 20th centuries crosses with English Thoroughbreds produced the strong but elegant modern Hanoverian, which is popular for showjumping and hunting. Height: 5–6 ft (1.63–1.73 m) (16–17 hands).

Han River   A river in E central China, rising in S Shenxi province and flowing SE to join the Yangtze River at Wuhan. Length: about 900 mi (1450 km).

Hansberry, Lorraine   (1930–65) US dramatist. She wrote *Raisin in the Sun* (1959), which became the first play by a black to be produced on Broadway. It was also awarded the New York Drama Critics' Circle Award in 1959 and was made into a musical and a movie. She also wrote *The Sign in Sidney Brustein's Window* (1964) and was honored posthumously by a dramatic adaptation of her writings in *To Be Young, Gifted and Black* (1969).

Hanseatic League   An association of N German trading towns (the Hanse) formed in the 13th century to protect their economic interests

overseas. By the mid-14th century, the League, comprising some hundred towns, had become a powerful corporate body and was able to establish trading monopolies in much of NE Europe. It faced considerable opposition from Denmark and England, with which it conducted a number of trade wars. The rise of the non-German Baltic states during the 15th and 16th centuries, as well as changing trade routes, contributed to the League's declining influence. It was finally dissolved in 1669.

hansom cab.   *See* cab.

Hanukka   A Jewish festival, commemorating the revolt of the *Maccabees. It falls in midwinter and is celebrated by lighting of lamps or candles.

Hanuman   In Hindu mythology, a monkey god and one of the principal characters in the *Ramayana*, in which he helps Rama to recover his wife Sita from the demon Ravana. There are numerous temples dedicated to him in both India and Japan.

Hanyang.   *See* Wuhan.

Hapsburgs.   *See* Habsburgs.

hara-kiri   The honorable way of death for Japanese *samurai who wished to avoid shame or demonstrate sincerity. In its strict form it involved ceremoniously cutting one's stomach open with a dagger before one's head was struck off by the single blow of another samurai's sword. In later times, however, there was often only a token gesture of disembowelment before decapitation. It is still sometimes practiced by Japanese suicides, although it is now illegal.

Harappa   The site in the Punjab in Pakistan of a great city of the *Indus Valley civilization. Its cemeteries and brick buildings (excavated 1920s, 1946) equal *Mohenjo-Daro in importance.

Harar (*or* Harer)   9 20N 42 10E A city in E Ethiopia, the capital of Harar province. Situated at 6000 ft (1800 m), it is Ethiopia's only walled city. Its capture by British forces (1941) led to the eventual collapse of Mussolini's African colonial empire. Trade is based on coffee and grain. Population (1974): 53,560.

Harare (formerly, Salisbury)   17 50S 31 02E The capital of Zimbabwe, on a plateau in the NE. Founded in 1890 as Salisbury, is was the capital of the Federation of Rhodesia and Nyasaland (1953–63). The University of Zimbabwe (formerly Rhodesia) was founded here in 1970 and there are Anglican and Roman Catholic cathedrals. The center of a tobacco-growing area, it has an important trade and industry in tobacco. Other industries include textiles and engineering. Population (1980 est): 654,000.

Harbin.   *See* Ha-er-bin.

harbor seal   The common *seal, *Phoca vitulina*, of coastal Pacific and Atlantic waters. Up to 6 ft (1.8 m) long, with a blotchy gray coat, harbor seals inhabit sandbanks and river estuaries, feeding on fish. Family: *Phocidae*. ▢mammal.

Hardanger Fjord   A fjord in SW Norway, S of Bergen, penetrating inland from the North Sea for 68 mi (110 km). It is edged by spectacular mountains and many waterfalls.

Hardecanute   (*or* Harthacanute; c. 1019–42) The last Danish King of England (1040–42), succeeding his illegitimate half-brother Harold I Harefoot, and King of Denmark (1035–42). As the legitimate son of Canute, he ordered Harold's corpse to be disinterred and thrown into the Thames as a revenge for Harold's seizure of the throne after Canute's death. He razed Worcester following a riot there against his tax collectors. He died of a seizure at a marriage feast.

Hardenberg, Karl (August), Fürst von   (1750–1822) Prussian statesman. He was foreign minister under Frederick William III from 1804 to 1806 and prime minister in 1807, when Prussia was subjected to Napoleonic rule. Again prime minister from 1810 until his death, he introduced administrative and economic reforms that strengthened Prussia and enabled it to break away from French control in 1813. However, monarchist opposition to his progressive policies resulted in his declining influence after 1815.

Harding, Warren G(amaliel)   (1865–1923) US statesman; Republican president (1921–23). He built up and ran a successful newspaper, the *Marion Star*, in Ohio before becoming a state senator (1898–1902) and lieutenant governor (1902–04). In 1912 he gave the nomination speech for William Howard Taft at the Republican national convention. He became a US senator (1915–21) and, in 1920, emerged as the dark-horse candidate on the Republican ticket for president. His campaign theme of a "return to normalcy" after World War I helped him win the election as the 29th president of the US. He, urged by others, called the Washington Disarmament Conference (1921–22); he established the Bureau of the Budget. His administration was characterized by complacency and scandal. Under Attorney General Harry M. Daugherty and Secretary of the Interior Albert B. Fall, corruption blossomed, resulting in many scandals, among them the *Teapot Dome incident. He died while on a trip across the country, after receiving news of the scandals and impending congressional investigation.

Hardouin-Mansart, Jules (1646–1708) French *baroque architect, who succeeded Le Vau as court architect to Louis XIV. He built Les Invalides, Paris (1680–91), but is most famous for his huge extensions to *Versailles, begun in 1678. These include the Galérie des Glaces (Gallery of Mirrors) and the orangery. He was also a town planner, his most notable design being the Place Vendôme (1699) in Paris.

Hardwar 29 58N 78 09E A city in N India, in Uttar Pradesh. One of the most sacred Hindu pilgrimage centers, its bathing ghat (or steps) along the Ganges River is believed to contain the footprint of the god Vishnu. Population (1971): 77,940.

Hardy, Thomas (1840–1928) British novelist and poet. The son of a mason, he went to London in 1862 to study architecture. His major novels, which include *The Return of the Native* (1878), *The Mayor of Casterbridge* (1886), and *Tess of the D'Urbervilles* (1891), are tragic tales set in his native Dorset (called "Wessex" in the novels). After the public outrage caused by the alleged immorality of *Jude the Obscure* (1895) he published only verse, beginning with *Wessex Poems* (1898), and an epic drama, *The Dynasts* (1903–08).

hare A mammal belonging to the widely distributed family *Leporidae* (which also includes the *rabbits). Hares are typically larger than rabbits (the European hare (*Lepus europaeus*) weighs up to 9 lb [4 kg]) and have long black-tipped ears. They live and breed in the open (rather than in burrows) and are mainly nocturnal, feeding on grass and bark. The young are born fully furred with open eyes. Chief genus: *Lepus* (about 26 species); order: *Lagomorpha*.

harebell A herbaceous perennial plant, *Campanula rotundifolia*, of N temperate regions, growing to a height of 24 in (60 cm). It has rounded leaves and blue nodding bell-shaped flowers on slender stems. Harebell grows in a variety of open habitats. Family: *Campanulaceae*.

HARE KRISHNA MOVEMENT *The distinctive chant of the saffron-robed members of the society was heard in many cities in the 1970s.*

Hare Krishna movement (Sanskrit: hail Krishna) An international religious community, the International Society for Krishna Consciousness (ISKCON), founded in New York in 1966 on Hindu principles by an Indian, Swami Prabhupada (1895–). Members live according to a strict vegetarian regime that also prohibits gambling, extramarital sex, and the use of drugs. They dress in saffron linen robes and the men have shaved heads. Daily worship includes the chanting of the Hare Krishna mantra and dancing in the streets. The movement is financed by begging, the sale of literature and incense, and donations.

harelip A defect, present at birth, in which there is a cleft in the upper lip. There is often a simultaneous defect in the roof of the mouth (*see* cleft

palate). Both defects interfere with speaking and feeding but they can be repaired surgically.

Hargeisa 9 20N 43 57E A city in N Somalia, near the Ethiopian border. It was the summer capital of former British Somaliland (1941–60). It is a watering and trading place for nomadic herdsmen. Population (1966): 60,000.

haricot bean A variety of *French bean (*Phaseolus vulgaris*) grown in warm climates. The seeds, which are dried for storage and soaked before use, are either brown or light-colored and are used for making baked beans.

Harishchandra (1850–85) Hindi poet, dramatist, and essayist, also known as Bharatendu. He founded two literary Hindi magazines and through his writings and patronage of other writers he contributed to the literary development of Hindi, which eventually became the official language of India. In *Bharat durdasa* (1880) and other plays he attributed the decline of Indian civilization to Muslim and western influences.

Harlan, John Marshall (1833–1911) US jurist. Educated in law at Transylvania University, Harlan served as judge of Franklin County, Ky., in 1858 and later as Kentucky attorney general (1863–67). After two unsuccessful campaigns for governor, he was appointed by President Rutherford B. *Hayes in 1877 to become an associate justice of the US Supreme Court. He remained on the bench until his death and became noted for his dissenting opinions, often in support of minorities. In the case of *Plessy* v. *Ferguson* (1896), he vigorously opposed the Supreme Court's decision upholding the constitutionality of racial segregation in public schools.

Harlem 40 49N 73 57W A residential district of New York City, in Manhattan. It is a political and social focus for blacks. The poets Langston Hughes (1902–67) and Countee Cullen (1903–46) were part of the "Harlem renaissance" of the 1920s.

Harlem Globetrotters A black American professional basketball team formed by Abraham Saperstein (1903–66) in 1926. They traveled in the midwest becoming known for their skill as well as for their clowning and tricky maneuvers. Today they travel all over the world playing in exhibition games. Among their best players have been Reese "Goose" Tatum and George "Meadowlark" Lemon.

Harlem Renaissance A movement in the 1920s, centered in the Harlem section of New York City, that brought black culture into its own—away from the southern dialect and imitation of the white world. Many new works by its black writers and poets, who included James Weldon *Johnson, Claude McKay (1890–1948), Countee *Cullen, and Langston *Hughes, emerged from this movement.

harlequin duck A short-billed *diving duck, *Histrionicus histrionicus*, occurring in coastal waters of Iceland and Greenland. The female is brown with white patches around the eyes; the male is gray-blue with black-edged white markings on the head, neck, breast, and wings and chestnut flanks.

Harley, Robert, 1st Earl of Oxford (1661–1724) English statesman under Queen Anne. An MP from 1688, he was a Tory but allied with the Whigs, becoming speaker of the House of Commons (1701) and then secretary of state (1704). Intriguing against his Whig colleagues *Godolphin and *Marlborough, he was dismissed in 1708 and rejoined the Tories. After the fall of the Whigs, he became Anne's chief minister as chancellor of the exchequer (1710–11) and Lord Treasurer (1711–14). The machinations of his rival *Bolingbroke brought his dismissal and after the accession of George I he was imprisoned (1714–17) for his Tory (and, by implication, *Jacobite) views.

Harlow 51 47N 0 08E A city in SE England, in Essex. It is a new town, developed since 1947 as a satellite town of London with light industries (surgical and scientific instruments, electronics, engineering, furniture, glass). Population (1973 est): 79,160.

Harlow, Jean (Harlean Carpentier; 1911–37) US film actress. Her well-publicized sex appeal and her talent for comedy won great popularity during the 1930s. After such movies as *Platinum Blonde* (1931) and *Bombshell* (1933), she became known as the "blonde bombshell." She died from kidney failure while making *Saratoga* (1937).

harmonica 1. The mouth organ: the smallest member of the reed-organ family; its invention is attributed to Sir Charles *Wheatstone in 1829. Notes and chords are obtained by blowing or sucking rows of parallel reeds. It is used mainly in light music. 2. The glass harmonica: an obsolete instrument consisting of tuned glasses rubbed with a damp finger.

harmonic analysis A procedure, developed in 1822 by Joseph *Fourier, by which complicated periodic functions, such as sound waves, can be written as the sum of a number of simple wave functions known as a Fourier series. One wave function, called the fundamental, has the same frequency as the original function. Those that have frequencies that are integral multiples of the fundamental are called harmonics.

harmonium A keyboard instrument of the reed organ family, patented in 1848 by Alexandre Debain (1809–77) in Paris. It is a free *reed instrument, the air being blown by a bellows activated by foot pedals. It may have several stops (see organ).

harmony In music, the combining of notes into chords, so that they are heard simultaneously. Harmony can be defined as the "vertical" aspect of music in contrast to melody, its "horizontal" aspect; it has greater importance in western music than in any other musical tradition. Before about 1650 composers made use of *polyphony, in which the combination of a number of melodic lines based on *modes was of prime importance. Between about 1650 and about 1900 (the **harmonic period**) a system of harmony evolved based on diatonic chords (see scale). Such chords consist of three notes sounded simultaneously; a note of the scale of the *tonality of the composition and the notes a third and a fifth above it. The constituent notes of any chord can be rearranged to provide variety. A **harmonic progression** consists of a particular sequence of chords, especially one leading (or modulating) into another tonality. When chords are subject to increasing *chromaticism the harmony becomes more complex and the tonality of the music becomes ambiguous. During the last half of the 19th century the music of Wagner, Liszt, and Richard Strauss became increasingly chromatic. In the early years of the 20th century Schoenberg first adopted *atonality and later invented *serialism as a substitute for traditional harmony. Debussy developed novel harmonic practices, such as harmonizing melodies with chords from unrelated tonalities and chords derived from wholetone and pentatonic scales. Composers of the 20th century have made use of a wide range of harmonic styles, some following Schoenberg, some deliberately cultivating dissonance, and others modifying traditional harmonic practice in various ways.

Harnack, Adolf von (1851–1930) German Protestant theologian. A professor at the Universities of Leipzig, Marburg, and Berlin, Harnack was considered the greatest scholar of his day on the early Church Fathers. His influential *History of Dogma* (1886–90), which traced the history of Christian doctrine down to the Reformation, was strongly criticized by conservative theologians.

harness racing A form of horse racing in which each horse pulls a light two-wheeled *sulky with a single driver. The races are of two sorts, according to the pace that the horses are trained to use: trotting (a two-beat gait with legs moving in diagonal pairs) or pacing (a two-beat gait with legs moving in lateral pairs). Races are usually run over 1 mi (1.6 km) on oval dirt tracks. The sport is particularly popular in the US and Australia.

Harold I Harefoot (d. 1040) Danish King of England (1037–40). The illegitimate son of Canute, he became king while Hardecanute, Canute's legitimate son, was preoccupied in Denmark. Before Hardecanute could oust him, Harold died.

Harold II (c. 1022–66) The last Anglo-Saxon King of England (1066), reputedly designated heir by the dying Edward the Confessor. He was the son of Earl *Godwin. After becoming king, he crushed the forces of his brother *Tostig and *Harold III Hardraade of Norway, who claimed the throne, at Stamford Bridge (1066). Harold was killed in the battle of *Hastings by the army of another, successful, claimant to the throne, *William the Conqueror.

Harold III Hardraade (1015–66) King of Norway (1047–66). His nickname means Hard Ruler. Until 1045 he served in the Byzantine army, his exploits in which became the subject of Norse sagas. After his return to Norway he briefly shared the throne with Magnus I (d. 1047); when he became sole ruler, he tried unsuccessfully to conquer Denmark. In 1066 he invaded England in support of *Tostig against Harold II and died at Stamford Bridge.

harp A plucked stringed instrument of ancient origin, consisting of an open frame with strings of varying length and tension. The modern orchestral harp is triangular in shape with about 45 strings stretched between the long soundbox, which rests against the player's body, and the curved neck, which takes the tuning pegs. The pillar, which completes the triangle, contains a mechanism invented in 1810 by Sébastien Érard (1752–1831). This enables the player to raise each string by one or two semitones by means of pedals at the base. It gives the harp a full chromatic range of six and a half octaves from the B below the bass stave. □musical instruments.

Harpers Ferry Raid (1859) The capture of the Federal arsenal at Harpers Ferry, West Va., by John *Brown. An abolitionist (see Abolition Movement), Brown seized the arsenal as a base for a slave insurrection. Robert E. *Lee, in command of federal troops, assaulted and captured Brown's position. Brown was hanged, a martyr to the abolitionist cause.

The town, at the confluence of the Potomac and Shenandoah Rivers, was the site of several engagements during the Civil War.

Harpies In Greek mythology, malicious spirits, originally conceived as winds, who carried off their victims to their deaths. They were later portrayed as rapacious birds with ugly women's faces.

harpsichord A keyboard instrument with strings plucked by quills, rather than hit by hammers (see spinet; virginals; compare clavichord; piano). In the 16th, 17th, and 18th centuries it was an instrument of great importance and it has been successfully revived in the 20th century. It lacks the sustaining power and dynamic variation of the piano; the tone can be changed by the addition of stops, which sound strings an octave below or above the note depressed. A muted effect can be obtained by use of the lute stop.

harpy eagle A tropical South American *eagle, *Harpia harpyja*, that lives in rain forests. It is the largest of the eagles, 40 in (100 cm) long, and has a huge hooked bill and extremely powerful feet for gripping its prey, which includes monkeys, sloths, opossums, and parrots. Mottled gray with a dark-banded tail, it has a large erectile crest.

harquebus (or arquebus). See musket.

harrier (bird) A slender long-legged *hawk belonging to a widely distributed genus (*Circus*). Harriers are about 20 in (50 cm) long and are usually brown (in some species the males are gray), with a small bill and a long tail. They fly low over fields and marshes, searching for frogs, mice, snakes, and insects. See also marsh harrier.

harrier (dog) A breed of hound used for hunting hares. It is similar to the *foxhound but smaller. The short smooth coat is usually black, tan, and white but may be mottled blue-gray. Height: 18–22 in (46–56 cm).

Harriman, Edward Henry (1848–1909) US stockbroker and businessman. As a broker on the New York Stock Exchange he specialized in bankrupt railroads and by 1903 was president of the Union Pacific Railroad, a line he had completely reorganized and rebuilt. He speculated in other railroad stock and his desire to gain control of the Northern Pacific Railroad and ultimately the Chicago, Burlington & Quincy Railroad caused the Panic of 1901.

Harriman, W(illiam) Averell (1891–) US diplomat. Entering government service in 1934, he served as ambassador to the Soviet Union (1943–46), to Great Britain (1946), and as secretary of commerce (1946–48). He was governor of New York (1955–58) and then helped to negotiate the *Nuclear Test-Ban Treaty (1963). He was ambassador to the Paris peace talks on Vietnam (1968–69).

Harrington, James (1611–77) English republican, an admirer of *Hobbes and *Machiavelli. He believed a nation's distribution of land was the factor determining the form of its government, but ignored mercantile and financial influences. His ideal form of government was a "commonwealth," for which he worked out a scheme in his *Oceana* (1656).

Harris. See Lewis with Harris.

Harris, Joel Chandler (1848–1908) US local-color novelist and shortstory writer. His Uncle Remus stories, drawing on his knowledge of Negro folklore gained from his work as a journalist and on plantations, were published in several volumes, beginning with *Uncle Remus, His Songs and His Sayings* (1880).

Harris, Roy (1898–1979) US composer. He studied with Nadia Boulanger in Paris and held various university teaching posts. His compositions, which include 11 symphonies, concertos, chamber music, and choral music, show the influence of Gregorian chant and folk music. Among his best works are *When Johnny Comes Marching Home* (1934), *Third Symphony* (performed 1937), and *Piano Quintet* (1936).

Harris, Townsend (1804–78) US diplomat. While president of New York City's board of education (1846–47) he was instrumental in the founding of the College of the City of New York (1847). After conducting a trading business in the Orient he was appointed consul general to Japan (1855–60), shortly after Japan was opened to Western trade, and negotiated a complete trade and diplomatic representative treaty in 1858.

Harrisburg 40 17N 76 54W The capital city of Pennsylvania, on the Susquehanna River. An important rail center, its manufactures include bricks, steel, and clothing. In March 1979, a failure in the cooling system at the nuclear power plant at nearby Three Mile Island caused widespread concern. Population (1970): 68,061.

Harrison, Benjamin (1833–1901) US statesman; Republican president (1889–93) and grandson of William Henry *Harrison. A lawyer in Indiana, he commanded a regiment during the Civil War. Elected to the US Senate (1881–87), he spoke out in favor of civil rights, reform of the civil service system, and the protection of US industry. Although he was not reelected to the Senate by a Democratic legislature in Indiana, he was nominated to run as the Republican candidate for president in 1888. During his administration the first Pan American Conference (1889) was held, the US participated in the Berlin Conference (1889) that prevented war between Britain and Germany, and international disputes were settled. At home, the *Sherman Anti-Trust Act (1890), the McKinley Tariff Act (1890), and the *Sherman Silver Purchase Act (1890) were passed. Defeated for reelection by Grover *Cleveland, he returned to his law practice, taking time out (1898–99) to negotiate Venezuela's boundary dispute with Great Britain.

Harrison, George (1943–) British rock musician, formerly a member of the *Beatles. When the group disbanded, Harrison embarked on a solo career and made four albums influenced by his interest in eastern mysticism, notably *All Things Must Pass* (1970) and *Extra Texture* (1975).

Harrison, William Henry (1773–1841) US military and political leader; 9th President of the United States (1841). After beginning medical studies at the University of Pennsylvania, Harrison left school to embark on a military career in the *Northwest Territory, gaining distinction in the Battle of *Fallen Timbers (1794). In 1801 he was appointed governor of the newly established Indiana territory by President John Adams. In that post, Harrison led US army forces against the Shawnee Indians of the territory, defeating their leader Tecumseh at the Battle of Tippicanoe (1811). After service in the *War of 1812, Harrison settled in Ohio, where he was elected congressman (1816–19), state senator (1819–21), and US senator (1825–28). He resigned the latter position to become US minister to Colombia. Active in the Whig Party, Harrison unsuccessfully campaigned for the presidency in 1836. In 1840 he was again the Whig nominee and, with vice presidential nominee John *Tyler, ran with the famous campaign slogan "Tippicanoe and Tyler Too". Although Harrison was elected, he died less than a month after taking office.

Harrogate 54 00N 1 33W A residential city and spa in N England, in North Yorkshire. It is a holiday resort, noted for its parks and open spaces. Harrogate has also become an important center for conferences and trade fairs. Population (1973 est): 64,620.

Harsa (*or* Harsha; c. 590–c. 647 AD) King of N India (c. 606–47). He ruled an extensive empire from his capital of Kanauj. In later life he became a devout Buddhist and combined his successful rule with the pursuit of poetry and the arts. His life and reign were well documented by the author *Bana.

Hart, Moss (1904–61) US dramatist. He collaborated with George S. *Kaufman on a great number of successful Broadway comedies, including *You Can't Take It with You* (1936) and *The Man Who Came to Dinner* (1939). He also wrote librettos for musicals by Irving *Berlin and Kurt *Weill, notably *Lady in the Dark* (1941). His autobiography, *Act One*, was published in 1959.

Harte, (Francis) Bret(t) (1836–1902) US local-color writer. He gained international fame with stories about the miners, gamblers, and prostitutes of California, collected in *The Luck of the Roaring Camp and Other Sketches* (1870). He collaborated with Mark Twain on the play *Ah Sin* (1877). After publishing a series of articles in *Atlantic Monthly*, he spent his last years in Europe.

hartebeest A long-faced antelope, *Alcephalus busephalus*, of African plains. About 47 in (120 cm) high at the shoulder, hartebeests are slender fast-running animals. There are several races, ranging in color from dark chestnut to fawn; their horns are united at the base and are generally lyre-shaped. Hartebeests live in small herds, grazing by day.

Hartford 41 45N 72 42W The capital city of Connecticut. Founded in 1633, it has many notable buildings. Trinity College (1823) and the law and insurance schools of the University of Connecticut are situated here. A commercial, industrial, and financial center, Hartford is one of the leading insurance centers in the world. Population (1975 est): 138,152.

Hartford Convention (1814–15) A meeting in Hartford, Conn., of Federalist delegates from Connecticut, Massachusetts, Rhode Island, Vermont, and New Hampshire to protest against President James Madison's policies and conduct of the War of 1812. They proposed a strong states' rights program and came out against the military draft and embargos on trade. The end of the War of 1812 (1815) overshadowed their demands.

Hartlepool 54 41N 1 13W A port in NE England. Originally an old fishing port and medieval walled town, Hartlepool's main industries are engineering, clothing manufacture, and timber working. Population (1977 est): 97,100.

Hartmann, (Karl Robert) Eduard von (1842–1906) German philosopher. He wrote a massive and eclectic work, *Philosophy of the Unconscious* (1869), which sought to reconcile all previous systems and all sciences by means of the hypothesis of the unconscious mind.

Hartmann, Nicolai (1882–1950) Russian-born German philosopher. He was troubled by the problem of cultural relativism pervading all branches of philosophy. Ideas, and even the concepts of logic, were historically conditioned, so that no thinker could begin without preconceptions. Systematic metaphysics, as presented by 19th-century idealists, was impossible, and the task of the philosopher was to draw the boundary between the rational and the irrational.

Harun ar-Rashid (?766–809 AD) The fifth caliph (786–809) of the 'Abbasid dynasty of Islam. He relied greatly on the support of the powerful Barmecide family until it fell from power in 803. His reign was troubled by revolts in subject territories and saw the beginning of Tunisian independence. Harun sent expeditions against the Byzantines and forced them to accept a humiliating treaty in 806. He has become an almost legendary figure because of the references to him in *The Arabian Nights*. Muslim sources, however, say nothing of his alleged close relations with Charlemagne.

Harvard classification system A system, introduced in the 1890s by astronomers at the Harvard College Observatory, by which stars are classified according to features in their spectra. Stellar spectral differences arise mainly from differing surface and atmospheric temperatures, and the stars are grouped accordingly into seven major spectral types: O, B, A, F, G, K, and M, in order of decreasing temperature. These types range in color from blue (O and B) through white, yellow, and orange, to red (M). There are 10 subdivisions for each spectral type, indicated by a digit (0–9) placed after the letter. Stars of one spectral type can be further classified into supergiants, giants, etc., according to their *luminosity. *See also* Hertzsprung-Russell diagram.

Harvard University The oldest university in the US. It was founded in 1636 by a grant from the Massachusetts Bay Colony and located at Cambridge, Mass. It is named for a clergyman, John Harvard (1607–38), who bequeathed his books to the college. Today the library is one of the country's best. The associated women's college, Radcliffe College, dates from 1879.

HARVEST MOUSE *These rodents are small enough to be able to climb cornstalks, with the aid of their prehensile tails, and feed on the grain.*

harvestman An *arachnid, also called harvest spider, belonging to the order *Opiliones* (or *Phalangida*; 2200 species), found in tropical and temperate regions. It has an undivided body, 0.04–0.86 in (1–22 mm) long, and very long delicate legs. It is found in fields, woods, and buildings, feeding on insects and plant materials, and is particularly common in late summer in temperate regions.

harvest mite A *mite, also called chigger and scrub mite, belonging to the genus *Trombicula*. Its larvae are parasitic on vertebrates, including man, feeding on skin to cause intense itching and inflammation. Certain species transmit diseases, including scrub typhus.

harvest mouse A tiny *mouse, *Micromys minutus*, of Europe and Asia. Light red-brown with white underparts, harvest mice are about 1.6 in (4 cm) long with a prehensile tail of the same length. They weave a nest of grass among the stems of plants in cornfields and reedbeds, but are becoming rarer as a result of mechanical farming methods.

Harvey, William (1578–1657) English physician and anatomist, who discovered the circulation of the blood. Harvey studied under the great anatomist *Fabricius ab Aquapendente and later became physician to James I and Charles I. From his numerous dissections and experiments on animals, Harvey concluded that blood flowed from the heart to the lungs, returned to the heart, and was pumped out via the arteries to the limbs and viscera, returning to the heart through the veins. His findings, published in *On the Motion of the Heart and Blood in Animals* (1628), aroused controversy, but by his death the circulation of blood was generally accepted. Harvey also made valuable studies of the development of chick embryos.

Haryana A state in N India, mostly in the fertile Upper Ganges plain. Predominantly rural, it produces wheat, other grains, cotton, sugar cane, and oilseeds. There is some light industry, including textiles, agricultural implements, and sugar refining. *History*: an important center of Hinduism, Haryana lies on the migration route into India. Britain merged it with the Punjab, but it was separated in 1966. Area: 17,070 sq mi (44,222 sq km). Population (1971): 10,036,808. Capital: Chandigarh.

Harz Mountains A mountain range extending about 56 mi (90 km) across the East German-West German border W of Halle. They are the northernmost range of the European mountain system. The highest peak is the *Brocken.

Hasan al-Basri, al- (d. 728) Muslim ascetic and religious thinker. He was active in Basra in Iraq and is important in the development of Muslim theology, although little is known about him. He is said to have supported the idea of human free will against that of divine predetermination.

Hasdrubal (Barca) (d. 207 BC) Carthaginian general; the son of *Hamilcar Barca and the brother of *Hannibal. Hasdrubal commanded the Carthaginian army in Spain following Hannibal's departure to campaign in Italy but was recalled to Africa after being defeated by the Romans in 217. He returned to Spain in 212, campaigning successfully before following Hannibal across the Alps in 207. He was defeated at Metaurus and died in battle.

Hašek, Jaroslav (1883–1923) Czech novelist, who established an early reputation as a satirist and anarchist. During World War I he was captured by the Russians, joined the Czech liberation army, and became a communist. His unfinished novel sequence *The Good Soldier Schweik* (1920–23) is a bawdy and irreverent satire upon bureaucracy and bourgeois values.

Haselrig, Sir Arthur. *See* Hesilrige, Sir Arthur.

Hashemites The Arab descendants of the prophet Mohammed, including the fourth caliph *Ali and the line of hereditary emirs of Mecca. King Hussein of Jordan is a modern representative of the line.

hashish. *See* cannabis.

Hasidism A Jewish religious movement, founded by the *Ba'al Shem Tov. Essentially a blend of *kabbalah and popular pietism, Hasidism spread, against strong opposition, throughout the Jewish communities of E Europe in the 18th and 19th centuries. Led by charismatic teachers (*zaddikim*), the Hasidim stressed simple piety and ecstatic prayer and denounced what they saw as the arid scholasticism of the talmudic academies. A more intellectual approach was adopted by the Habad Hasidim, whose leader is the Lubavitch Rabbi, now based in New York. Most of the Hasidic communities in Europe were wiped out during the *holocaust, but Hasidism still thrives in North America and Israel.

Haskalah (Hebrew: enlightenment) The intellectual movement for spreading modern European culture among the Jews. It began in Germany in the 18th century, largely under the influence of Moses *Mendelssohn, and spread to Russia in the 19th century. Linked to the movement for the political emancipation of the Jews, it attempted to provide them with a modern Hebrew culture of their own and rejected the previous alternatives of the medieval ghetto culture or total assimilation. In its day it exercised an enormous influence, giving birth to modern *Judaism, *Zionism, and

the modern Hebrew language and literature. In the West it succumbed to linguistic and cultural assimilation; in Russia, after enjoying a period of government support, it yielded, in the face of the growing *antisemitism of the 1880s, to attempts to find a political solution to the Jewish problem.

Hassan II (1929–) King of Morocco (1961–). Educated in France, Hassan maintains autocratic rule in Morocco. He introduced some reforms in 1971 following an attempted coup.

Hasselt 50 56N 5 20E A city in NE Belgium. It was the site of a Dutch victory over the Belgians in 1831. Industries include brewing and distilling. Population (1976 est): 40,446.

Hastings 50 51N 0 36E A city on the S coast of England, in East Sussex. Formerly a port (chief of the Cinque Ports), it is now a resort and residential town with a ruined castle built by William the Conqueror, who landed at nearby Pevensey in 1066 (*see* Hastings, Battle of). Population (1973 est): 74,490.

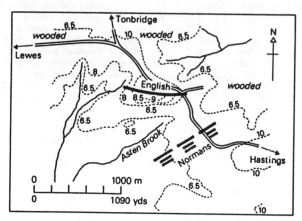

BATTLE OF HASTINGS *The three lines of Norman troops were led by archers, including crossbowmen (making their first recorded appearance in battle), who were able to undermine the advantage of the English position on a ridge above.*

Hastings, Battle of (October 14, 1066) The battle between the Normans and the English at Senlac Hill, near Hastings, in which William, Duke of Normandy, claiming the English throne, defeated Harold II of England. The battle was dominated by the Norman use of archery supported by cavalry to break through the defensive ranks of infantry, which alone made up the English army. Both sides suffered heavy losses but the death of Harold allowed William to conquer England (*see* Norman conquest) and become its king.

Hastings, Warren (1732–1818) British colonial administrator; the first governor general of India (1774–85). He first went to India in 1750 in the employ of the East India Company. After several promotions he became, in 1771, governor of Bengal, and then governor general of India. His outstanding administration consolidated British control of India and introduced administrative, legal, and financial reforms that provided the basis of subsequent British government there. Hastings failed, however, to maintain good relations with his colleagues, especially Sir Philip *Francis, with whom he fought a duel in 1779. On his return to England he was impeached for corruption. The trial before the House of Lords, which lasted until 1795, ended in his acquittal.

hatchetfish A carnivorous hatchet-shaped fish, up to 4 in (10 cm) long, belonging to one of two unrelated groups. Deepsea hatchetfish (family *Sternoptychidae*; 15 species) are related to *salmon and occur in warm and temperate waters down to about 3280 ft (1000 m). The freshwater or flying hatchetfish (family *Gasteropelecidae*; about 9 species) of South America are related to *carp. They swim near the surface and are able to leap out of the water and "fly" short distances by flapping their large pectoral fins. □oceans.

Hathaway, Anne (c. 1556–1623) The wife of William *Shakespeare. She was born at Shottery, near Stratford. She married Shakespeare in 1582 and bore him three children. Her cottage may still be seen in Stratford.

Hathor An Egyptian sky goddess, worshiped as goddess of fertility and of love, happiness, and beauty. She was usually portrayed as a cow or with a cow's horns and is sometimes identified with *Isis.

Hatshepsut Queen of Egypt (c. 1490–1468 BC) of the 18th dynasty. The half-sister and widow of *Thutmose II, she overshadowed the young

*Thutmose III, and assumed the status of pharaoh. During her reign direct communications with Punt (now S Eritrea) were reopened. Illustrated accounts of her expedition there and of the transport of her obelisks from Aswan are carved on her funerary temple at Dayr al-Bahri. After her death Thutmose III attempted to obliterate her memory by defacing her monuments.

Hatteras, Cape 35 14N 75 31W A low sandy promontory in North Carolina, on Hatteras Island. Its shallows are a danger to navigation.

Hattusas The ancient capital of the *Hittite empire (c. 1700–1230 BC) situated at Boğazköy (or Boğazkale) in central Turkey. The massive fortifications still visible date from the reign of *Suppiluliumas (c. 1375–c. 1335 BC). Thousands of tablets, forming part of the royal archives, have been found here and provide invaluable evidence for diplomatic and commercial activity in the period.

Hauptmann, Gerhart (1862–1946) German dramatist. After studying sculpture he turned to writing plays, establishing his reputation with *Before Dawn* (1889). His early work was influenced by *naturalism in its use of dialect and in its social themes, as in *The Weavers* (1892). This element later alternated with a mystical and *Symbolist strain, as in *The Assumption of Hannele* (1893). He also wrote novels (*The Fool in Christ*, 1910), novellas (*Flagman Thiel*, 1888), and poetry (*Der grosse Traum*, 1942). He was awarded a Nobel Prize in 1912.

Hauraki Gulf A large inlet of the South Pacific Ocean, in New Zealand on the E coast of North Island. Waitemata Harbour, on which stands Auckland, is situated in the SW. Area: about 884 sq mi (2290 sq km).

Hausa A people of NW Nigeria and S Niger, numbering about nine million. Their language belongs to the Chadic subgroup of the *Hamito-Semitic family, but has absorbed many Arabic words and influences. It is an official language of Nigeria and a second language in much of West Africa. The Hausa are mainly Muslim. There were once several Hausa states ruled on feudal lines by emirs and titled office holders who held villages as fiefs. This hierarchical system emphasized elaborate etiquette. Slavery was practiced but slaves could attain high office. The economy is based on the cultivation of maize, millet, sorghum, and other crops. Crafts are highly developed and trade is extensive. Cities, such as *Kano, date from precolonial times but most Hausa live in small rural settlements.

Haussmann, Georges-Eugène, Baron (1809–91) French town planner, responsible for extensive rebuilding in Paris under *Napoleon III. Haussmann's long avenues and dramatic vistas, for example the avenues radiating from the *Arc de Triomphe, form much of the city's present-day character. His schemes, while improving sanitation and public utilities, destroyed many remnants of the medieval town.

Havana (Spanish name: La Habana) 23 00N 82 30W The capital of Cuba, a port in the NW. It exports sugar, cotton, and tobacco. The city has been considerably modernized during the Castro regime but much of the Spanish-colonial element remains, including the cathedral. The university was founded in 1728. *History*: the original settlement was on the S coast, but the inhabitants moved to the city's present site in 1519. It became the capital of Cuba in the late 16th century. Because of its excellent natural harbor, Havana has long been of strategic and commercial importance and during the early 19th century it was among the wealthiest commercial centers in the New World. Population (1975 est): 1,008,500.

Havana cat A breed of short-haired cat, formerly known as Chestnut Brown Foreign. The Havana has a lithe slender body with a long tail, a long head, and large ears. The coat is chestnut-brown and the eyes are green and slanting.

Hawaii (former name: Sandwich Islands) 50th US state, one of the 2 states (the other being Alaska) lying outside the coterminous 48 US states, in the central Pacific Ocean 2100 mi (3360 km) SW of San Francisco. Occupying a chain of over 20 volcanic islands, Hawaii consists of 5 major islands and numerous smaller ones. The main islands include Hawaii (the largest), Maui, Oahu, Kauai, and Molokai. Its population, concentrated mainly on Oahu, is more ethnically diverse than that of any other US state, the largest groups being white Americans and Japanese. Its industry relies heavily on imported raw materials; manufactures include oil and chemical products, steel, textiles, and food. Agriculture is important, the main crops being sugar and pineapples. The principal industry, however, is tourism. There is some lumbering and fishing. Hawaii's strategic position for the defense of the US means that there are a large number of military bases. Hawaii's cultural and scientific institutions reflect both Western and Pacific cultures. *History*: the Polynesians who first settled the islands are thought to have occupied Hawaii around the 8th century. In 1788, Captain James Cook became the first European to discover the islands. In 1810 the islands were united under King Kamehameha. Prosperity prevailed until the arrival of European and American traders who introduced infectious diseases previously unknown to the islanders; the population was greatly reduced as a consequence. In the late 1820s, US missionaries and planters established sugar plantations and quickly came to dominate the island's economy. The Japanese attack on Pearl Harbor in 1941 precipitated the US entry into World War II. Hawaii became a state in 1959. Following statehood, the state's economy and population boomed, primarily through tourism and related industries. Area: 6425 sq mi (16,641 sq km). Population (1980): 965,000. Capital: Honolulu.

Hawaiian goose A rare *goose, *Branta sandvicensis*, native to Hawaii and Maui, where it is called néné. It has a gray-brown plumage barred with white and an orange neck. Its numbers are now increasing by breeding programs.

Hawaiian guitar (or steel guitar) A type of guitar held flat on the player's lap. The strings are stopped by a sliding steel bar, which produces a characteristic glissando.

Hawaii Volcanoes National Park A national park on SE Hawaii Island, Hawaii. Within the park are two active volcanoes, Mauna Loa (13,680 ft; 4170 m) and Kilauea (4000 ft; 1220 m). Tourists may drive around the rim of Kilauea's crater and are able to watch its eruptions safely. Area: 344 sq mi (891 sq km).

hawfinch A large *finch, *Coccothraustes cocothraustes*, of Eurasia and N Africa. 7 in (18 cm) long, it has a reddish-brown plumage with paler underparts, a black bib, and black-and-white wings. Its massive bill is used to crack open the stones of cherries, sloes, and damsons to extract the seeds.

Haw-Haw, Lord. *See* Joyce, William.

hawk A bird of prey belonging to a widely distributed family (*Accipitridae*; 205 species) that includes buzzards, eagles, harriers, kites, and vultures. Hawks range in size from small *sparrowhawks to the *harpy eagle and have down-curved pointed bills, powerful gripping feet, and highly developed eyesight. Hawks typically fly fast in pursuit of live prey, using their strong claws for killing, and have broad rounded wings; they usually nest in trees or crags. Order: *Falconiformes*. *Compare* falcon. *See also* falconry.

Hawke, Robert James Lee (1929–) Australian political leader; prime minister (1983–). A Rhodes scholar (1952–55), he joined the Australian Council of Trade Unions (1958) as a researcher and negotiator and eventually served as its president (1970–80). He became president of the Australian Labour Party (ALP) in 1974 and in 1980 was elected to the House of Representatives. In 1983 he defeated Malcolm Fraser by a wide margin to become prime minister. Conservative in nature, he attempted to slow down Australia's economy and to lessen Australia's ambitions internationally.

Hawke Bay An inlet of the SW Pacific Ocean, in New Zealand in E North Island. The surrounding land area of Hawke's Bay is important for sheep rearing. Length: 50 mi (80 km).

Hawkesbury River A river in SE Australia, rising in the Great Dividing Range in New South Wales and flowing generally NE to enter the Tasman Sea at Broken Bay. Length: 293 mi (472 km).

Hawkins, Sir John (1532–95) English navigator. In 1562 he became the first English slave trader, transporting slaves from West Africa to the Spanish West Indies. His third expedition (1567–69), in which Drake participated, met with the Spaniards on its way home and only the ships of Drake and Hawkins escaped. In 1577 he became treasurer of the navy, instituting reforms that greatly contributed to England's victory against the Spanish *Armada (1588), and died at Puerto Rico on a new expedition with Drake.

hawk moth A moth belonging to the widespread family *Sphingidae* (about 1000 species), also called sphinx moth or hummingbird moth. They have large bodies with relatively small wings (spanning 2–8 in [5–20 cm]), which they beat rapidly, hovering over flowers and sipping nectar through their long proboscis. The leaf-eating greenish larvae pupate in soil or litter.

hawk owl An *owl, *Surnia ulula*, that occurs in northern coniferous forests of Eurasia and North America. It is 16 in (40 cm) long and has a long tail, a small head, and short pointed wings, which give a hawklike silhouette in flight. It hunts by day.

Hawks, Howard (1896–1977) US film director. He started as a writer but from 1938 produced and directed numerous movies, the best known of which were comedies like *Bringing Up Baby* (1938), fast-paced action dramas such as *To Have and Have Not* (1944), *The Big Sleep* (1946), a Western, *Red River* (1948), and a musical, *Gentlemen Prefer Blondes* (1953).

HAWK OWL *Unlike many owls, this species is active by day, preying on a wide variety of mammals and birds. Its swooping flight and long tail resemble those of a hawk.*

hawksbill turtle A small sea turtle, *Eretmochelys imbricata*, found in warm waters worldwide. It has hooked jaws, feeds on algae, fish, and invertebrates, and is usually 16–22 in (40–55 cm) long. The polished translucent mottled brown shell is the tortoiseshell used to make ornamental combs, spectacle frames, etc.

hawkweed A perennial herb of the genus *Hieraceum* (about 1000 species), of temperate regions and tropical mountains. It grows to a height of about 24 in (60 cm) and usually has yellow flower heads. The name derives from the old belief that hawks ate these plants to improve their eyesight. Family: *Compositae*.

Hawley-Smoot Tariff (1930) A US law that imposed high taxes on imported goods in an attempt to protect domestic products. Other countries, in retaliation, imposed the same taxes on US goods coming into their countries, and foreign trade as a whole took a sharp drop.

Haworth, Sir Walter Norman (1883–1950) British biochemist, who first synthesized artificial vitamin C (ascorbic acid), thus enabling its cheap production for medical use. He shared a Nobel Prize (1937) with the Swiss chemist Paul Karrer (1889–1971).

hawthorn A thorny shrub or tree of the N temperate genus *Crataegus* (about 200 species). Hawthorns have lobed leaves, usually about 1.6 in (4 cm) long, white spring-blooming flowers, and yellow, black, or red fruits. The common hawthorn, or may (*C. monogyna*), is found in hedgerows and thickets in Europe and the Mediterranean. Up to 33 ft (10 m) high, it has red fruits (haws). There are many horticultural forms, including pink and double-flowered varieties. Family: *Rosaceae*.

Hawthorne, Nathaniel (1804–64) US novelist and short-story writer. His two best-known novels, *The Scarlet Letter* (1850) and *The House of the Seven Gables* (1851), concern the psychological effects of Puritanism in New England. He was a friend of Herman *Melville, who visited him in England after his appointment as consul at Liverpool in 1853. In 1857 he traveled in Italy, the setting of *The Marble Faun* (1860).

Hay, John Milton (1838–1905) US statesman, politician, and writer. He served as a private secretary to President Abraham Lincoln (1861–65) and in various European diplomatic posts, including ambassador to Britain (1897–98). Appointed secretary of state by President William McKinley in 1898, he openly advocated the *Open Door Policy and was instrumental in retaining US influence in the Philippines, China, and Panama. He remained secretary of state until 1905, also serving under President Theodore Roosevelt. He is best known for his 10-volume history of Lincoln (1890).

Haya de la Torre, Victor Raúl (1895–1979) Peruvian politician. In exile following an attempt at revolution in 1923, he founded the radical Alianza Popular Revolucionaria Americana (APRA). He ran for the presidency in 1931 and, successfully, in 1962, only to have the result cancelled by a military coup.

Haydn, Franz Joseph (1732–1809) Austrian composer, born in Rohrau. He became a cathedral chorister in Vienna at the age of eight and subsequently worked as a freelance musician and music teacher, studying the works of C. P. E. Bach to learn the art of composition. He subsequently studied with the Italian composer Nicola Porpora (1686–1768) and in 1760 made an unfortunate marriage. In 1761 he became kapellmeister to the Esterházy family, a post he held for the rest of his life. In 1791 and 1794 he visited London and wrote his last 12 symphonies, which include the *Oxford* and *London* symphonies. Haydn's numerous compositions include piano sonatas, piano trios, string quartets, masses, concertos, 104 symphonies, operas, and the oratorios *The Creation* (1798) and *The Seasons* (1801).

Hayes, Helen (Helen Hayes Brown; 1900–) US actress. At home on the stage from the age of 5, she appeared in *Dear Brutus* (1918), *Caesar and Cleopatra* (1925), *What Every Woman Knows* (1926), *Mary of Scotland* (1933), *Victoria Regina* (1935–39), *Harriet* (1944), *The Glass Menagerie* (1948), *Time Remembered* (1958), and *Harvey* (1970). Her movie credits include *The Sin of Madelon Claudet* (1931) and *Airport* (1969) for which she won Academy Awards in 1932 and 1970. She was married (1928) to playwright Charles MacArthur (1895–1956). Her life and experiences are recounted in *A Gift of Joy* (1965).

Hayes, Rutherford Birchard (1822–93) US statesman; 19th President of the United States (1877–81). A graduate of Kenyon College (1842) and Harvard Law School (1845), Hayes began his political career in Cincinnati, Ohio, where he served as city solicitor (1858–61). During the Civil War, he was active in the *Republican Party and was elected to the US House of Representatives in 1864. Hayes served three terms as governor of Ohio (1868–72, 1876–77) and won the Republican presidential nomination in 1876. Although he received fewer popular votes than his Democratic opponent, Samuel Tilden, he was declared the winner by the *Electoral College. Hayes' administration marked the end of the *Reconstruction period and federal troops were withdrawn from the South. Among Hayes' other achievements was a courageous but unpopular proposal to reform the civil service system. Opposition to this measure within the Republican Party prevented Hayes from gaining renomination in 1880.

hay fever An *allergy to pollen, which leads to sneezing, a streaming nose, and inflamed eyes. If the sufferer is allergic to only one kind of pollen it may be possible to desensitize him (*see* desensitization); otherwise treatment is with *antihistamines or, in severe cases, steroids.

Haymarket Massacre (1886) A riot during a labor union protest rally in Haymarket Square, Chicago, that resulted in the deaths of 7 policemen. Anarchists, who organized the meeting to protest against police brutality at a strike site the day before, bombed police attempting to disperse the crowd. The police retaliated with gunfire; rioting and panic ensued. The anarchist leaders were arrested, charged, and convicted of murder; four were hanged (1887), one took his own life, and three were pardoned (1893).

Hays, Arthur Garfield (1885–1954) US civil liberties lawyer. As a defense attorney with Clarence *Darrow, he participated in the Scopes evolution trial (1925). Other well-known cases in which he was the defense lawyer included the Sacco-Vanzetti case (1927) and the murder trial of the Scottsboro Nine (1931). He also defended Pennsylvania and Kentucky coal miners' attempts to unionize and championed civil rights in Puerto Rico. He wrote *Let Freedom Ring* (1928), *Trial by Prejudice* (1933), and *Democracy Works* (1939).

Haywood, William Dudley (1869–1928) US labor leader. Active in the unionization of miners in the West, he was instrumental in the founding of the Industrial Workers of the World (IWW) in 1905. Also in 1905 he was tried for being involved in the murder of former Idaho governor Frank R. Steunenberg, who opposed unions. Acquitted, Haywood went on to head the IWW and advocated violence to achieve labor's aims. He denounced World War I in 1917, was arrested, convicted of sedition, and given a 20-year prison sentence. He escaped while on bail and fled to the Soviet Union.

hazard A dice game of great antiquity, played in Europe since the middle ages and popular among gamblers since the 17th and 18th centuries. Two dice are used. The person throwing the dice calls a number between 5 and 9; to win he must throw either this number or a 12 if he has called 6 or 8, or an 11 if he has called 7. An ace loses him the throw, as does an 11 if he has called 5, 6, 8, or 9, or a 12 if he has called 5, 7, or 9. He continues to throw until he either wins or loses. *See also* craps.

hazel A hardy shrub or tree of the N temperate genus *Corylus* (15 species), cultivated since ancient times for its edible nuts, also called cob nuts. Flowers appear in early spring, before the leaves (which are rounded and toothed). The male flowers are attractive yellow catkins; each female flower, which consists only of two bright-red stigmas, develops into a nut partly enclosed in a green fringed husk. The best-known species is the European

hazel (*C. avellana*), up to 39 ft (12 m) high. Family: *Betulaceae* (birch family) or, according to some authorities, *Corylaceae*.

Hazlitt, William (1778–1830) British critic and essayist. He studied art and philosophy before becoming a journalist on various dailies and periodicals, including the *Edinburgh Review*. A friend of Wordsworth and Coleridge, Hazlitt held independent opinions in politics and literary matters and expressed them in a style notable for its brilliant invective. His best-known collections of essays and lectures are *Characters of Shakespeare's Plays* (1818–19), *Lectures on the English Poets* (1818) and *The Spirit of the Age* (1825).

Health and Human Services, Department of (HHS) A US cabinet-level executive branch department that deals with human concerns. Headed by the secretary of Health and Human Services, the department includes the Office of Human Development Services; the Public Health Service, which includes Centers for Disease Control; Medicare and Medicaid programs; the Food and Drug Administration; the National Institutes of Health; and the Social Security Administration. Created as the Department of *Health, Education, and Welfare (1953), it assumed its current duties and was renamed in 1979.

Health, Education, and Welfare, Department of US cabinet-level executive branch department (1953–79). It was divided into the Department of *Education and the Department of *Health and Human Services.

health physics The study of the problems that arise from the use of radiation of various kinds, especially those emitted by radioactive substances. Particular areas of study include *radioactive waste disposal, the maximum levels of radiation to which workers may reasonably be exposed, and the causes and effects of *radiation sickness. Health physics is a multidisciplinary subject involving physics, medicine, mathematics, chemistry, biology, and hygiene.

Heard and MacDonald Islands A group of uninhabited subantarctic islands in the S Indian Ocean, under Australian control since 1947. Heard Island is mountainous and chiefly ice covered; its elephant seals and penguins were hunted in the 19th century. The MacDonald Islands consist of a group of rocky islets.

hearing aid A device used by the partially deaf to increase the loudness of sounds. A simple form of hearing aid is the ear trumpet, which by its conical shape increases the sound pressure at the ear. Modern hearing aids are electronic and, since the advent of microcircuitry, can be made sufficiently small to be unobtrusive. An electronic hearing aid consists of a microphone to convert the sound into electrical signals, which are passed into an amplifier. The amplified signal is then fed into an earphone to convert the signal back into a sound wave of increased intensity.

Hearst, William Randolph (1863–1951) US newspaper proprietor. Beginning with the *San Francisco Examiner*, which he took over from his father, and the New York *Morning Journal*, which he bought, he built up a vast newspaper empire whose commercial success was based on popular sensationalism, known as "yellow journalism." His career inspired Orson *Welles' movie *Citizen Kane* (1941).

heart A four-chambered muscular organ that pumps blood around the body. Two chambers—the left and right atria—dilate to receive oxygen-rich blood from the lungs and oxygen-depleted blood from the rest of the body, respectively (this is called diastole). Contraction of the heart (called systole) starts in the atria, forcing blood into the two ventricles. The left ventricle then contracts to force blood into a large artery—the aorta, which leads from the heart and feeds all the other arteries. The right ventricle pumps blood into the pulmonary artery and to the lungs, where it receives oxygen. Valves between the atria and ventricles and at the arterial exits of the heart prevent the backflow of blood. The rhythm of the heartbeat is maintained by the electrical activity of a group of specialized cells within the heart (see pacemaker). The muscle of the heart is supplied with blood by the coronary arteries. *Atherosclerosis of these arteries is the most common form of heart disease in industrial societies: it may lead to a heart attack (see coronary heart disease; myocardial infarction). Other disorders affecting the heart include disease of the valves (which may result from rheumatic fever) and congenital heart disease—defects in the heart present at birth. *See also* circulation of the blood.

heartburn A burning pain felt behind the breastbone. It is usually due to regurgitation of the contents of the stomach into the gullet and may be associated with inflammation of the gullet. It is relieved by antacids (drugs that neutralize stomach acids).

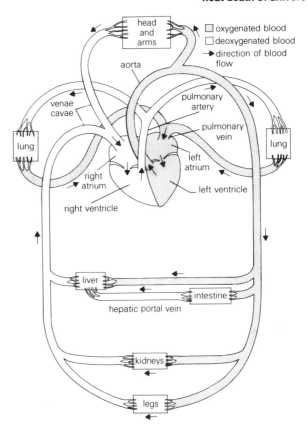

HEART *In man and other mammals the right and left chambers of the heart are completely separate from each other. This ensures that oxygenated and deoxygenated blood do not mix and enables oxygen-depleted blood to receive a fresh supply of oxygen from the lungs before circulating to the rest of the body.*

heart-lung machine An apparatus that temporarily replaces the functions of the heart and the lungs during heart surgery. Blood from two main veins is drained from the body through tubes to an apparatus that bubbles oxygen through it. The oxygenated blood is then returned to a large artery in the body by a mechanical pump.

heartsease. *See* pansy.

heart urchin A marine invertebrate animal belonging to an order (*Spatangoida*) of *echinoderms. It typically has a rigid heart-shaped body, covered with short fine spines used for locomotion and defense. It lives in burrows lined with mucus and uses long tentacles (modified tube feet) to pick up particles of food from the surrounding sand. Class: *Echinoidea*.

heat The form of energy that is transferred from one body or region to another at a lower temperature. The amount of heat gained or lost by a body is equal to the product of its *heat capacity and the temperature through which it rises or falls. Heat is transferred by conduction, convection, or radiation (see heat transfer). The heat contained by a body is equal to the *total* *kinetic energy of its component atoms and molecules; its temperature is the *average* of their kinetic energies. Heat is measured in joules, but older units, such as calories and British thermal units, are still sometimes used.

heat capacity The amount of heat needed to raise the temperature of a body through one degree Celsius (symbol: C). It is measured in joules per kelvin. For a gas, the heat capacity may be measured under conditions of either constant pressure or constant volume. *See also* specific heat capacity.

heat death of universe A hypothetical final state of the universe in which its *entropy is at a maximum and no heat is available to do work. In any closed system the total entropy can never decrease during any process. Thus the entropy of the universe will eventually reach a maximum value and when that happens all matter will be totally disordered and at a uniform temperature. This assumes that the universe can be treated as a closed system.

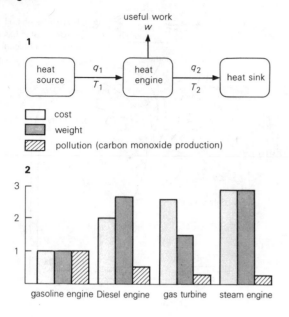

HEAT ENGINE   *The efficiency of a heat engine depends on the temperature* T_1 *at which heat is fed to it and the temperature* T_2 *at which waste heat is discharged* (1). *A comparison of cost, weight, and pollution for various types of heat engine is shown at* (2).

heat engine   A device that converts heat energy into work. Examples are gasoline and Diesel engines, gas turbines, and steam engines. In terms of *thermodynamics, the heat engine converts a quantity of heat q_1 at temperature T_1 into work w; but the conversion can never be complete, some of the heat q_2 will be wasted and can be regarded as being discharged into a heat sink at a temperature T_2. The efficiency of the engine is defined as the work output divided by the heat input (w/q_1). As the work, w, is equal to q_1-q_2 (according to the first law of thermodynamics), the efficiency is $1-q_2/q_1$, or $1-T_2/T_1$. It is therefore important to make T_1 as high as possible and T_2 as low as possible. See also Carnot cycle; internal-combustion engine.

heath   An evergreen shrub or tree of the genus *Erica* (about 500 species) of Europe and Africa (about 470 species are native to South Africa). Heaths have small whorled often needle-like leaves and spikes of bell-shaped or tubular flowers, white, pink, purple, or yellow in color. Dwarf heaths, such as the European species *E. tetralix* (bog heather) and *E. cinerea* (bell heather), are abundant on acid peaty soils, such as moorlands. There are many cultivated varieties, which are popular in rock gardens. Some tree heaths grow to a height of 20 ft (6 m). Family: *Ericaceae.*

Heath, Edward (Richard George)   (1916–) British statesman; Conservative prime minister (1970–74), who took the UK into the EEC (1973). He entered parliament in 1950 and held several cabinet posts. In 1965 he succeeded Douglas-Home as leader of the Conservative Party. His government faced economic difficulties and union strife. Defeated in 1975 he relinquished the party leadership to Margaret Thatcher.

heather   (*or* ling)   An evergreen shrub, *Calluna vulgaris,* up to 24 in (60 cm) high, with scaly leaves and clusters of pale-purple bell-shaped flowers. It grows—often with *heath—on acid soils of heaths, moors, and bogs throughout Europe and in parts of N Africa and North America (where it was probably introduced). Family: *Ericaceae.*

Heathrow   (*or* London Airport)   51 28N 0 27W The chief air terminal for the UK, in the Greater London borough of Hounslow.

heat pump   A device that extracts heat from one substance at a low temperature and supplies it to another substance at a higher temperature. Such a process would violate the second law of *thermodynamics if it occurred spontaneously; therefore the heat pump necessarily consumes energy in the process. Heat pumps are used to extract the low temperature heat from rivers that flow through towns and to convert it to a higher temperature so that use can be made of it, for example in space- and water-heating units. See also refrigeration.

heatstroke   A rise in body temperature associated with *dehydration and exhaustion, caused by overexposure to high temperatures. The emergency treatment is to cool the patient down with water or fans, but medical treatment may be needed in addition.

heat transfer   The transference of energy between two bodies or regions by virtue of the difference in temperatures between them. The three methods of transference are: *convection, *conduction, and *radiation. In convection the heat is transferred by a hotter region flowing into a colder region, either as a result of density differences (natural convection) or by using a fan (forced convection). In conduction, on the other hand, the heat is transferred by direct contact without any apparent relative motion. In radiation the heat is transferred by means of either *infrared radiation or *microwave radiation. Radiation is the only method of transferring heat through a vacuum. The *Dewar (Thermos) flask is designed to minimize heat transfer, whereas the heat exchanger or radiator is designed to maximize it.

heat treatment   The process of heating a metal to a temperature below its melting point and then cooling it in order to change its physical properties. Metals are made up of tiny crystals (grains). Their hardness, strength, and ductility is determined by the concentration and distribution of irregularities (dislocations) in the crystal lattice. In response to stress the dislocations move and change the shape and orientation of the grains. Heating creates and redistributes dislocations, relieving any internal stresses that have built up. This makes the metal softer and more ductile; a process known as annealing. Dislocation movement is restricted by the boundaries between grains and by the presence of impurities, which "pin" the dislocations making the metal harder and less ductile. Because both the impurity distribution and the grain structure are affected by heating and the rate of cooling, so also is the metal's strength. In steel manufacture, rapid cooling (quenching) by immersion in water or oil hardens the steel, leaving it brittle. Slow cooling makes it soft and ductile. The process of heating steel to around 900°C and quenching it, followed by warming to about 300°, is known as hardening and tempering. This results in a tough springy steel. See also case hardening; work hardening.

heaven   In Christian belief, the abode of God and the angels, in which the souls of the virtuous will be rewarded with everlasting life. The iconography of heaven is based upon the account in the Book of Revelation. The peace, light, and harmony of heaven are generally interpreted as metaphors for the bliss enjoyed by beings in the uninterrupted praise and contemplation of God (*compare* hell). Analogous concepts exist in other major religions.

Heaviside, Oliver   (1850–1925) British physicist, who pioneered the mathematical study of electric circuits and helped to develop vector analysis. Independently of *Kennelly, he predicted and then discovered a charged layer of the upper atmosphere that was capable of reflecting radio waves. This region, now known as the E-region of the *ionosphere, was formerly called the Heaviside layer or Heaviside-Kennelly layer.

heavy water   Deuterium oxide (D_2O), the form of water containing the isotope of hydrogen with mass number 2. It is chemically less reactive than normal water and has a relative density of 1.1; its boiling point is 215°F (101.42°C). It is present to an extent of 1 part in 5000 in natural water and it is used as a moderator and coolant in some nuclear reactors.

Hebe   In Greek mythology, the personification of youth. She was the daughter of Zeus and Hera and is described by Homer as cupbearer to the gods and the wife of Heracles.

Hebei   (Ho-pei *or* Hopeh)   A province in NE China, on the Yellow Sea. Its fertile S plain is one of the earliest areas of civilization. Chief products are cereals, cotton, coal, and iron. Area: 79,053 sq mi (202,700 sq km). Population (1968 est): 43,000,000. Capital: Shijiazhuang.

Hébert, Jacques-René   (1757–94) French journalist and revolutionary. With his newspaper *Le Père Duchesne* he attained a wide following among the Parisian working class (*see* sans-culottes), becoming their leading demagogue. In 1792 he helped engineer the overthrow of the monarchy and became the procurator general of the Paris Commune. His unsuccessful attempt to incite a popular uprising against the Committee of *Public Safety resulted in his execution.

Hebrew   A Semitic language. It is written from right to left in an alphabet of 22 letters, all consonants, with vowels indicated by subscript and superscript diacritical marks. The oldest and best-known works of Hebrew literature are those preserved in the *Bible (Old Testament). Mishnaic Hebrew is a somewhat different language, spoken in Palestine until the 2nd century AD. It is the language of the *Mishna and the oldest extant Jewish prayers. Hebrew continued to be a literary language throughout the middle ages, with a particularly rich poetic tradition, besides prose writing. The study of Hebrew grammar was developed by the *Masoretes, and by the *gaon Saadya and later grammarians. In more modern times the *Haskala movement led to a renaissance in Hebrew writing, and from the late 19th century Hebrew was revived as a spoken language, particularly in Russia and Palestine. The *Ashkenazim and *Sephardim differ in their pronunciation of Hebrew. In 1948 it became an official language of Israel.

Hebrew literature A body of literature originating as early as 1200 BC in Old Testament writings and still flourishing in the modern secular idiom of Israel. Not synonymous with Jewish literature (which was frequently composed in other languages, e.g. Arabic or Yiddish), Hebrew literature reflects the vicissitudes of the Hebrew language, being confined after about 200 AD to religious and legal texts and commentaries (see Mishna; Talmud). Medieval Spain produced some original talents, including the poets *Judah ha-Levi and *Ibn Gabirol and the philosopher *Maimonides. The 18th-century Haskala (enlightenment) in E Europe initiated the renaissance of secular literature, and the rise of Zionism encouraged the novelist *Agnon and the poet *Bialik, among others, to mold Hebrew into a modern literary language.

Hebrews, Epistle to the A New Testament book by an unknown author (formerly believed to be Paul), probably written between 62 and 69 AD. The book asserts that Christ is the high priest and greater than any of the *Levites and that his work fulfills and renders obsolete the old *covenant between God and Israel. The book is obviously addressed to readers who had a thorough knowledge of Judaism and is intended to confirm such converts in their new faith.

Hebrides, the A group of about 500 islands off the W coast of Scotland. The islands are subdivided into the Inner and Outer Hebrides, separated by the Minch. The chief islands of the Outer Hebrides include Lewis with Harris and the Uists; those of the Inner Hebrides include Skye, Mull, Islay, and Jura. The main occupations are stock rearing, fishing, and crofting (producing fodder crops, potatoes, and vegetables). Harris tweed is produced, especially in the Uists.

Hebron (Arabic name: Al Khalil) 31 32N 35 06E A city in the S of the *West Bank of the Jordan River. It is one of the oldest continuously inhabited cities in the world and is revered by both Jews and Muslims as the burial place of Abraham. Population (1971 est): 43,000.

Hecate A primitive Greek fertility goddess and a ruler of the underworld. She was associated with witchcraft and magic and was worshiped at crossroads. She witnessed the abduction of *Persephone and accompanied *Demeter in her search for her daughter.

Hecht, Ben (1894–1964) US dramatist and writer. A newspaperman in Chicago from 1910, he co-authored, with fellow newspaperman Charles MacArthur, *The Front Page* (1928). His novels include *Erik Dorn* (1921), *Gargoyles* (1922), *The Florentine Dagger* (1923), *Count Bruga* (1926), and *A Jew in Love* (1930). He wrote and produced screenplays, including *Scarface* (1932), *Design for Living* (1933), *Notorious* (1946), and *The Scoundrel* (1935), which received an Academy Award.

hectare (ha) A unit of area in the *metric system equal to 100 ares or 10,000 square meters. 1 ha = 2.471 acres.

Hector In Greek legend, the eldest son of Priam, King of Troy, and the chief Trojan warrior. He was the husband of Andromache. He fought Ajax in single combat, killed *Patroclus, and was killed in revenge by *Achilles. Priam pleaded for the return of his body, which was buried with great ceremony.

Hecuba In Greek legend, the wife of Priam, King of Troy, and mother of *Hector. She was captured by the Greeks after the fall of Troy, but in revenge for the death of her son Polydorus, she blinded King Polymestor of Thrace and killed his sons.

hedgehog A nocturnal prickly-coated insectivorous mammal belonging to the subfamily *Erinaceinae* (15 species), of Africa, Europe, and Asia. The european hedgehog (*Erinaceus europaeus*) grows up to !2 in (30 cm) long and has brown and cream spines and soft gray-brown underfur. It feeds on worms, beetles, slugs, and snails, hunting mainly by scent and hearing along ditches and hedgerows. Hedgehogs hibernate in colder climates. Family: *Erinaceidae*. □mammal.

hedgehog cactus A cactus of the North American genus *Echinocactus* (10 species), some species of which are cultivated as pot plants. They have round or cylindrical strongly ribbed woolly stems bearing many spines and—at the top—mainly yellow flowers.

hedge sparrow. See dunnock.

hedging A commercial operation enabling a trader or speculator to protect himself against unpredictable changes in price. In *commodity markets, trading in futures (goods for delivery in the future) provides a hedg-

ing facility. For example, a manufacturer may wish to purchase a year's supply of a commodity for regular deliveries throughout the year but may expect the price to fall over the period. In this case he could hedge his purchase by selling short (i.e. selling without buying) on a futures market so that he could cover (buy back) the sales at a lower price if there was a fall in prices.

hedonism The ethical theory holding that pleasure is the greatest good. Varying definitions of pleasure distinguished the classical hedonistic schools but all considered individual rather than communal happiness. *Utilitarianism, the most important modern form of hedonism, uses a social criterion: "The greatest good of the greatest number." *Compare* Epicureanism.

Hefei (*or* Hofei) 31 55N 117 18E A city in E China, capital of Anhui province. The capital of a 10th-century kingdom, it is now a fast-growing industrial center with an industrial university and a scientific university. Population (1957 est): 304,000.

Hegel, Georg Wilhelm Friedrich (1770–1831) German philosopher, one of the greatest and most influential thinkers of the 19th century. He followed *Kant, *Fichte, and *Schelling but exceeded them all in the scale and erudition of his work. He developed his ideas slowly and steadily; his first major work, *The Phenomenology of Mind*, was published in 1807, the *Encyclopedia of the Philosophical Sciences* in 1817, and *The Philosophy of Right* in 1821. Besides these major works, he left voluminous lecture notes on history, religion, and aesthetics. He became an eminent and respected figure, collecting disciples, appointments, and decorations before dying, in Berlin, of cholera. See also Hegelianism.

Hegelianism The idealist school of thought based on the philosophy of *Hegel. His followers built on his idea that philosophy is the highest available form of knowledge and that all other forms (scientific, religious, etc.) must be referred to it. Ambiguity in Hegel's own thought has encouraged considerable diversity in interpreters of Hegelianism. The so-called Old Hegelians thought religion could be brought into harmony with philosophy, while the Young Hegelians saw philosophy as essentially critical of religion. *Marx was influenced by the Young Hegelians, especially *Feuerbach.

Hegira (Arabic *hijrah*: migration) The usual English name for the Muslim era. Based on lunar months, it is reckoned from 622 AD (or 1 AH, from Latin *anno hegirae*), the date of Mohammed's migration from Mecca to Medina. Most Muslim countries now use both the Hegira calendar and the Christian or Common Era calendar.

Heidegger, Martin (1889–1976) German philosopher. His main philosophical work is *Sein und Zeit* (*Being and Time*; 1927). As rector of Freiburg University (1933–34) he supported Hitler and this association, together with logical flaws in his work, has damaged his reputation. Although his preoccupation with *Angst* (dread) as a fundamental part of human consciousness is typical of *existentialism, Heidegger himself denied that he was an existentialist.

Heidelberg 49 25N 08 42E A city in SW West Germany, in Baden-Württemberg on the Neckar River. A tourist center, it has a ruined castle (mainly 16th-17th centuries) and the oldest university in Germany (1386), famed for its student prison. Its varied manufactures include printing presses, cigars, and electrical appliances. *History*: the capital of the Palatinate until 1685, it was devastated during the Thirty Years' War and later by the French. During the 19th century it was the student center of Germany. In 1952 it became the European headquarters of the US army. Population (1976 est): 129,361.

Heifetz, Jascha (1901–) US violinist; born in Russia. A child prodigy, he was performing internationally by 1912. He made his American debut in 1917 at Carnegie Hall, New York City, moved to California, and became an American citizen. He toured extensively, often playing with Gregor Piatigorsky, cellist, and William Primrose, violist.

Heilbronn 49 08N 9 14E A city in SW West Germany, in Baden-Württemberg on the Neckar River. Many historic buildings, including the town hall (1540), were reconstructed after World War II. It is a transshipment point and a center for electrical engineering. Population (1976 est): 112,411.

Heilongjiang (Hei-lung-chiang *or* Heilungkiang) A province in NE China, bordering on the Soviet Union, comprising N Manchuria. The Da Hinggan Ling (mountains) provide valuable timber, while wheat is grown on the S plain. Oil, coal, and gold are produced. Area: 179,000 sq mi (464,000 sq km). Population (1976 est): 32,000,000. Capital: Ha-er-bin.

Heilungkiang. See Heilongjiang.

Heimdall The Norse god of light and dawn, who guarded the Bifrost bridge between *Asgard (the home of the gods) and *Midgard (the earth). He possessed miraculously sharp sight and hearing.

Heine, Heinrich (1797–1856) German-Jewish poet and writer. Before establishing himself as a writer, he worked in banking and studied law. His early works include *Buch der Lieder* (1827), a collection of poetry, and his prose *Reisebilder* (1826–31), in which accounts of his travels are mixed with satirical comment. Sympathetic to revolutionary politics, he moved to Paris in 1831 and remained there until his death. In this period he wrote essays on French and German culture and some satirical poetry, notably *Atta Troll: Ein Sommernachtstraum* (1847).

Heinlein, Robert Anson (1907–) US science fiction writer. A pioneer in science fiction, he wrote *The Green Hills of Earth* (1951), *Double Star* (1956), *Door into Summer* (1957), *Stranger in a Strange Land* (1961), *I Will Fear No Evil* (1970), and *Friday* (1982). His books for children include *Rocket Ship Galileo* (1947) and *The Star Beast* (1954).

Heisenberg, Werner Karl (1901–76) German physicist, who, with *Schrödinger, was the main architect of quantum mechanics. In 1927 Heisenberg created a mathematical system, known as matrix mechanics, to explain the structure of the hydrogen atom. *Dirac soon showed that matrix mechanics and Schrödinger's wave mechanics were equivalent. In the same year he put forward the theory known as the *Heisenberg uncertainty principle, which has had a profound effect on both physics and philosophy. For this discovery he was awarded the Nobel Prize in 1932. Heisenberg was one of the few major physicists to remain in Germany during the Nazi period; during World War II he was in charge of Germany's unsuccessful attempts to make an atom bomb at the Max Planck Institute in Berlin. After the war he became director of the Max Planck Institute for Physics in Göttingen.

Heisenberg uncertainty principle If a simultaneous measurement is made of the position and momentum of a particle then, no matter how accurate the measurements, there is always an uncertainty in the values obtained. The product of the uncertainties is of the same order as *Planck's constant. A similar uncertainty exists with the simultaneous measurement of energy and time. The uncertainty arises because the act of observing the system interferes with it in an unpredictable way. Uncertainty is only important at the atomic and subatomic levels and at this level throws the principle of causality into doubt. Named for Werner *Heisenberg.

Hejaz A province in Saudi Arabia, bordering on the Red Sea. Hilly inland, its coastal plain supports some agriculture; significant income is also derived from light industry and from pilgrims to the holy Muslim cities of Mecca and Medina. The largest town is Jidda. Hejaz, formerly independent, joined *Najd in a dual kingdom in 1926, and both became part of Saudi Arabia in 1932. Area: about 135,107 sq mi (350,000 sq km). Population (1970 est): 2,000,000.

Hel In Norse mythology, the underworld; also called Nifleheim. It was covered with ice and guarded by the dog Garm. It is also the name of the goddess of death and ruler of the underworld, who was the daughter of the giant *Loki.

Helder, Den. *See* Den Helder.

Helen In Greek legend, the daughter of Zeus and *Leda, famed for her supreme beauty. She married Menelaus, King of Sparta, but later fled to Troy with *Paris, thus precipitating the *Trojan War. After the fall of Troy she was reunited with Menelaus.

Helena 46 35N 112 00W The capital city of Montana. It is the commercial center for an agricultural and mining region. Population (1970): 22,730.

Helena, St (c. 248–c. 328 AD) Roman empress, mother of Constantine the Great. A Christian from 313, she made a pilgrimage to the Holy Land (c. 326), where she founded several churches and, according to tradition, rediscovered the cross used at the crucifixion. Feast day: Aug 18. Emblem: the cross.

Helgoland (*or* Heligoland) 54 09N 7 52E A West German island in the North Sea, in the North Frisian group. Ceded to Britain in 1814, it was transferred to Germany in exchange for Zanzibar (1890) and was a major German naval base during both World Wars. With the end of World War II its fortifications were destroyed. Area: about 150 ha (380 acres).

Heliconia A genus of perennial herbaceous plants (about 120 species), native to tropical America and cultivated for ornament in the tropics. They have stout or reedlike stems and the leaves are often coppery with an ivory and pink midrib. The small flowers are contained within brightly colored pointed bracts: *H. psittacorum* has green-yellow black-spotted flowers and red bracts. Family: *Heliconiaceae*.

helicopter An aircraft that obtains both its lift and its thrust from rotors rotating about a vertical axis (*compare* autogiro). The principle was known to Leonardo da Vinci, but the first successful helicopter was made in the US in 1939 by Igor *Sikorsky (his 1909 model, made in Russia, failed to lift a man). A helicopter using a single rotor requires an anti-torque tail propeller and some models also use a vertical propeller for forward thrust. Helicopters can rise and drop vertically, hover, and move backward, forward, and sideways by control of the pitch of the rotors. First used in World War II, helicopters were widely employed for military purposes in the Korean and Vietnam wars. They have since been developed for rescue services, police and traffic observation, and urban passenger services.

heliocentric system Any model of the solar system in which the planets move around the sun. The geocentric *Ptolemaic system was accepted for centuries until the heliocentric system of *Copernicus was published in 1543 and, after much religious and scientific controversy, shown to be true.

Heliopolis An ancient Egyptian city near present-day Cairo dedicated to the cult of the sun god Re. *Cleopatra's Needles came from here.

Helios The Greek sun god, usually represented as a charioteer driving the sun across the sky each day. In later legends he was identified with Hyperion or Apollo. Because he was all-seeing he was called to witness oaths and promises.

heliotrope A herb or shrub of the genus *Heliotropium* (220 species), found in tropical and temperate regions and having heads of blue or white flowers. Many will withstand cold, but none will survive frost. Many horticultural varieties of the cherry-pie plant (*H. peruvianum*) and *H. corymbosa* are used as bedding plants in cooler climates. Family: *Boraginaceae*.

helium (He) The lightest noble gas, first detected in 1868 by Janssen (1838–1904) as an unexpected line in the spectrum of the sun. The term is derived from Greek *helios*, sun. Helium was discovered on earth in 1895 in the uranium mineral, clevite, as a radioactive decay product (*see* radioactivity). Because of its low density and chemical inertness, it is extensively used for filling balloons. It is also used as a gas shield in arc welding, and to replace nitrogen in the breathing mixture used by divers. Helium has the lowest melting point of any element. At no 2; at wt 4.0026; mp −458°F (−272.2°C); bp −452°F (−268.9°C).

helium dating A method of dating materials that utilizes the production of helium in the form of *alpha particles during the radioactive decay of uranium-235, uranium-238, or thorium-232. The amount of helium trapped in the sample may be used to measure its age, after correction to allow for diffusion. The method is used mainly for rocks, minerals, and fossils.

hell In Christian belief, the place in which the fallen *angels under *Lucifer and the souls of the wicked are imprisoned in everlasting torment. The concept of hell as a dark and fiery pit derives from the Book of Revelation and opinions have differed widely regarding its nature. Some Christians insist upon the physical reality of hellfire; others consider it a metaphor for the misery of a soul deprived forever of the vision of God (*compare* heaven). According to the doctrine often condemned as a heresy and known as apocatastasis, hell is not everlasting but will eventually be destroyed and all creatures, even the fallen angels, will be restored to God's grace. *Compare* purgatory.

hellbender The largest North American *salamander, *Cryptobranchus alleganiensis*. Growing to over 24 in (60 cm), it is dark olive-green with a wrinkled shiny skin. Hellbenders inhabit fast-moving oxygen-rich water, emerging from under rocks to feed at night on small animals and carrion. Family: *Cryptobranchidae*.

hellebore A poisonous perennial herb of the genus *Helleborus* (20 species), of Europe and W Asia. The stinking hellebore (*H. foetidus*) grows to a height of 12–20 in (30–50 cm) and bears clusters of cup-shaped purple-edged green flowers. Family: *Ranunculaceae*. *See also* Christmas rose.

helleborine A terrestrial *orchid of either of the genera *Cephalanthera* (about 14 species) or *Epipactis* (about 24 species), native to N temperate regions. They have tall thin stems, crinkled leaves, and clusters of flowers, which are either small, stalked, and drooping (*Epipactis*) or larger, stalkless, and held erect (*Cephalanthera*). The white helleborine (*C. damasonium*) and the marsh helleborine (*E. palustris*) are two Eurasian species.

Hellen In Greek mythology, the grandson of Prometheus and eponymous ancestor of the Greeks, who called themselves the Hellenes and their country Hellas. The four subgroups of the Hellenes, the Aeolians, Dorians, Ionians, and Achaeans, were named for his sons and grandsons.

Hellenistic age The period, between the death of Alexander the Great of Macedon (323 BC) and the accession of the Roman emperor Augustus (27 BC), when Greek culture spread throughout the Mediterranean. Alexander's conquests took Greek ideas to the East and in the political confusion that followed his death city states became cosmopolitan and Greek colonists, following in Alexander's footsteps, implanted Greek ideas in their new environments. In the Hellenistic period Alexandria in Egypt was the major commercial city and center of intellectual life, including scholarly literature and grandiose art, *Epicureanism, *Neoplatonism, Stoic philosophy, *gnosticism, and Christianity. The Koine, common Greek, was the universal language.

Heller, Joseph (1923–) US novelist. He served in the Air Force during World War II and subsequently worked in advertising. His best-known novel, *Catch-22* (1961), is a satirical portrayal of the horrors of modern warfare and bureaucracy. He has also written three other novels, *Something Happened* (1974), *Good as Gold* (1979), and *God Knows* (1984), and a play, *We Bombed in New Haven* (1968).

Hellespont. *See* Dardanelles.

Hellman, Lillian (1905–84) US dramatist. Her plays, often concerning political themes, include *The Children's Hour* (1934), *The Little Foxes* (1939), *Watch on the Rhine* (1941), *The Searching Wind* (1944), and *Another Part of the Forest* (1946). She was a close friend of Dashiell *Hammett and published volumes of memoirs, including *An Unfinished Woman* (1969), *Pentimento* (1973), and *Scoundrel Time* (1976).

Helmand River (Helmund *or* Hilmand) The longest river in Afghanistan. Rising in the E of the country, it flows generally SW then N to enter the marshy lake of Helmand on the Afghan-Iranian border. Length: 870 mi (1400 km).

helmet shell A *gastropod mollusk belonging to the family *Cassidae* (about 60 species), also called bonnet shell. Found in shallow tropical seas and measuring 0.8–10 in (2–25 cm) long, they feed mainly on sea urchins. □shells.

Helmholtz, Hermann Ludwig Ferdinand von (1821–94) German physicist and physiologist, who made contributions to many fields of science. In physiology his main interest was the sense organs, discovering the function of the cochlea in the inner ear and developing T. *Young's theory of color vision (now known as the Young-Helmholtz theory). This work was published in his *Physiological Optics* (1856). His study of muscle action led him to formulate a much more accurate theory concerning the conservation of energy than that earlier proposed by Julius *Mayer and James *Joule. He played a considerable part in the development of thermodynamics, especially in formulating the concept of free energy.

Helmont, Jan Baptist van (1580–1644) Belgian alchemist and physician, who discovered the gas now called *carbon dioxide. Although Helmont was an alchemist he was a skilled and careful experimenter and helped to transform alchemy into chemistry.

Heloise. *See* Abelard, Peter.

helots Indigenous Peloponnesian Greeks who lost their lands and freedom under the repressive state control of Sparta. They formed the farming communities of Messenia and Laconia.

Helsingborg. *See* Hälsingborg.

Helsingfors. *See* Helsinki.

Helsingør (*or* Elsinore) 56 03N 12 38E A seaport in Denmark, in NE Sjælland situated on the *Sound opposite Hälsingborg in Sweden. It contains the fortress of Kronborg (1580), famous as the scene of Shakespeare's play *Hamlet*. Its industries include shipbuilding, brewing, and food processing. Population (1974 est): 55,404.

Helsinki (Swedish name: Helsingfors) 60 13N 24 55E The capital of Finland, a port in the S on the Gulf of Finland. It is the country's commercial and administrative center; industries include metals, textiles, food processing, and paper. Among its fine pale granite buildings are the 18th-century cathedral and the old senate house. The city is well laid out and spacious in appearance and is renowned for its 20th-century architecture. The university was moved here from Turku in 1828. *History*: founded by Gustavus I Vasa of Sweden in 1550 it was largely rebuilt following a fire in 1808. It replaced Turku as capital of Finland (then under Russian rule) in 1812. It was badly bombed in World War II. Population (1975 est): 665,202.

Helvetia. *See* Switzerland, Confederation of.

Helvetii A Celtic tribe that settled about 200 BC in what is now Switzerland. Defeated by Caesar as they migrated southward, they nevertheless retained their former territory, which was a buffer state between Rome and the Germans for over 400 years.

Helvétius, Claude Adrien (1715–71) French philosopher. He followed Hume in holding that self-interest was the only motive of human action. His principle of the artificial identity of interests (i.e. interests manipulated

by government) influenced *Bentham. *De l'esprit* (1758), expounding these views, was furiously denounced and burned by the public hangman.

hematite The principal ore of iron, ferric oxide, varying in color from red to gray to black. It contains over 70% iron. It occurs either in crystalline form (specular iron ore) or in massive form. Most ore deposits are derived from altered iron carbonates and silicates in sedimentary rocks.

hematology The study of blood and its diseases. This medical specialty is concerned particularly with treating *leukemias, *hemophilia, and rare kinds of anemia.

Hemel Hempstead 51 46N 0 28W A city in SE England, in Hertfordshire. Designated a new town in 1946, the principal industries include light engineering (aircraft components, scientific, electronic, and photographic equipment), paper, and pyrotechnics. Population (1977 est): 78,000.

Hemichordata A phylum of marine invertebrate animals (about 100 species), found in coastal sand or mud and on the sea bed. The gill slits and nervous system show similarities with those of chordates—hence their name. The group comprises the *acornworms and the pterobranchs (class *Pterobranchia*). These are up to 0.28 in (7 mm) long and have tentacle-bearing arms. They often form colonies and reproduce both sexually and by budding.

ERNEST HEMINGWAY *Nobel Prize (1954) winning author noted for his short stories and novels emphasizing courage.*

Hemingway, Ernest (1899–1961) US novelist. After serving in the Red Cross during World War I he joined the American expatriate community in Paris. His first successful novel was *The Sun Also Rises* (1926). He was a keen sportsman and adventurer, and in his short stories and his later novels, including *For Whom the Bell Tolls* (1940), about the Spanish Civil War, and *The Old Man and the Sea* (1952), he celebrated the virtues of courage and stoicism in a forceful economical style. His other works include the novels *A Farewell to Arms* (1929), *To Have and Have Not* (1937), *A Moveable Feast* (1964), and *Islands in the Stream* (1970). Among his many memorable short stories were "The Snows of Kilimanjaro" (1936) and "The Short Happy Life of Francis Macomber" (1936). He won the Nobel Prize in 1954. Subject to severe depressions after leaving his home in Cuba in 1960, he committed suicide.

hemiplegia. *See* paralysis.

Hemiptera An order of insects (about 50,000 species)—the true bugs—having piercing mouthparts for sucking the juices from plants or animals. The suborder *Heteroptera* includes plant and animal feeders (*see* plant bug; water bug). The forewings of these insects have both a leathery and a membranous region and are held flat over the body at rest. The suborder *Homoptera*, including the *froghoppers, *aphids, *cicadas, and *scale insects, are all plant feeders and have uniform front wings, held roof-wise over the body at rest.

hemlock **1.** A poisonous biennial plant, *Conium maculatum*, native to Europe, W Asia, and N Africa. It grows in damp places to a height of 7 ft (2 m) and has branching purple-spotted stems that bear much divided leaves and clusters of tiny white flowers. The plant is notorious as the means by which Socrates died. Family: *Umbelliferae*. **2.** A coniferous tree of the genus *Tsuga* (15 species), native to S and E Asia and North America. The narrow bladelike leaves, up to 0.8 in (2 cm) long, are grouped in two rows along the stems and the brown egg-shaped cones are 0.8–1.2 in (2–3 cm) long. The western hemlock (*T. heterophylla*), of W North America, can reach a height of 197 ft (60 m); it is grown both for its strong timber and for ornament. Family: *Pinaceae*.

hemoglobin The substance, contained within the red blood cells (*see* erythrocyte), that is responsible for the color of blood. In humans hemoglobin consists of a protein (globin) combined with an iron-containing pigment (hem). Hem combines with oxygen, which is absorbed into the blood at the lungs, to form oxyhemoglobin, which gives arterial blood its bright-red color and is the means by which oxygen is transported around the body. Oxygen is released at the tissues and the pigment acquires a bluish tinge, responsible for the bluish-red color of venous blood.

hemophilia A hereditary disease in which the blood does not clot properly due to absence of one of the clotting factors. Some of the children of both Queen Victoria and Tsar Nicholas II had this disease, which is almost entirely restricted to boys but is transmitted through the mother. If an affected person (a hemophiliac) cuts himself seriously he may bleed to death without appropriate plasma transfusions. Hemophiliacs also bleed easily into their joints and other parts of the body and must therefore restrict their activities.

hemorrhage Bleeding. Large amounts of blood may be lost in severe injuries, from bleeding peptic ulcers, during operations, in childbirth, or if the patient has a clotting disorder (such as *hemophilia). In these circumstances it may be necessary to give a blood transfusion to avoid *shock and death. If hemorrhage occurs in a confined space, such as the brain or the eye, damage results from destruction of normal tissue.

hemorrhoids (*or* piles) Swollen (varicose) veins in the anal canal, which may enlarge sufficiently to hang down outside the anus. They are very common, usually resulting from chronic constipation, and tend to run in families. Piles may cause bleeding from the anus and itchiness, but rarely severe pain. In severe cases they may need to be surgically removed or injected with a sclerosing agent, which makes them shrivel up. External hemorrhoids are painful swellings at the side of the anus, caused by rupture of an anal vein.

hemp An annual herb, *Cannabis sativa*, native to central Asia and widely cultivated. It grows to a height of 16 ft (5 m) and bears lobed leaves and small yellow flowers. Hemp is cultivated in many temperate regions (e.g. Italy and the Soviet Union) for its fiber, obtained from the inner stem bark and used for ropes, sacking, and sailcloth. The flowers, bark, twigs, and leaves contain a narcotic resin (*see* cannabis)—source of marijuana and related drugs—for which the plant is widely grown, especially in the tropics. Family: *Moraceae*. *See also* Indian hemp.

Henan (*or* Honan) A province in E central China. The Yellow and the Huai Rivers irrigate the E fertile plain. Densely populated, it has been a center of Chinese culture since about 2000 BC. Chief products are cereals, cotton, silk, and coal. Area: 65,000 sq mi (167,000 sq km). Population (1976 est): 60,000,000. Capital: Zhengzhou.

henbane A strong-smelling poisonous annual or biennial herb, *Hyoscyamus niger*, native to Europe and N Africa. Up to 31 in (80 cm) high, it has funnel-shaped yellow flowers, veined with purple, and grows in sandy places. It contains the alkaloid hyoscyamine, used medicinally. Family: *Solanaceae*.

Henderson, Arthur (1863–1935) British Labour politician. He entered Parliament in 1903 and later led the parliamentary Labour Party (1908–1910, 1914–1917). As foreign secretary (1929–31), he ardently supported the League of Nations and the Disarmament Conference, of which he became chairman in 1932. In 1934 he won the Nobel Peace Prize.

Hendricks, Thomas Andrews (1819–85) US politician; vice president (1885). A Democrat, he served in the Indiana state legislature before going to Congress as a representative (1851–55) and senator (1863–69). He was governor of Indiana (1873–77). He attained the vice presidency under President Grover Cleveland, only to die in office 9 months later.

Hendrix, Jimi (James Marshall H.; 1942–70) US rock singer and guitarist. With his group, the Jimi Hendrix Experience, Hendrix recorded such hits as "Purple Haze" and "Foxey Lady" and became famous for his virtuoso electric-guitar playing. He died as a result of a drug overdose.

henequen A perennial herbaceous plant, *Agave fourcroydes*, native to Mexico and cultivated for its leaf fibers called Yucatan, or Cuban, sisal. The plant stems grow to an average height of 35 in (90 cm) in cultivation and the lance-shaped leaves form a dense rosette. Each plant yields 25 leaves annually from 5 to 16 years after planting. The fibers, which have an average length of 4 ft (1.3 m), are made into twines used in agriculture, shipping, and rope. Family: *Agavaceae*.

Hengist and Horsa Legendary leaders of the first Anglo-Saxon settlers in Britain. According to the Anglo-Saxon Chronicle (late 9th century AD) Horsa was killed in 455 AD and his brother Hengist ruled over Kent from 455 to 488.

Hengyang 26 58N 112 31E A city in S China, in Hunan province on the Xiang (*or* Siang) River. A long-established communications, commercial, and cultural center, many historic buildings survive. Chemicals and machinery are manufactured. Population (1953): 235,000.

henna A shrub, *Lawsonia inermis*, occurring in Egypt, India, and the Middle East. Up to 7 ft (2 m) high, it has fragrant white-and-yellow flowers. The leaves are powdered and used for tinting the hair and nails a reddish color. It also has medicinal uses. Family: *Lythraceae*.

henry (H) The *SI unit of inductance equal to the inductance of a closed circuit such that a rate of change of current of one ampere per second produces an induced e.m.f. of one volt. Named for Joseph *Henry.

Henry (I) the Fowler (c. 876–936) Duke of Saxony (912–36) and German king (919–36), founder of the Saxon dynasty (918–1024). In 925 he recovered Lotharingia for Germany, in 933 he defeated the Hungarians, and in 934, after invading Denmark, he won Schleswig for Germany.

Henry I (1069–1135) King of England (1100–35); the youngest son of *William (I) the Conqueror. Henry became king on the death of his brother William Rufus. In England his reign is notable for important legal and administrative reforms, and for the final resolution of the *investiture controversy. Abroad, Henry waged several campaigns in order to consolidate and expand his continental possessions.

Henry (II) the Saint (973–1024) German king and Holy Roman Emperor (1002–24; crowned 1014). After a protracted conflict with Poland he was forced to cede Lusatia but in Italy he successfully defended the papacy against the Greeks and Lombards. He sponsored Church reform, founding monasteries and schools. He was canonized in 1145.

Henry II (1133–89) King of England (1154–89); the son of Matilda and Geoffrey of Anjou and the grandson of Henry I. Henry succeeded Stephen. Married (1152) to *Eleanor of Aquitaine, he ruled an empire that stretched from the River Tweed to the Pyrenees (*see* Angevins). In spite of frequent hostilities with the French king, his own family, and rebellious barons (culminating in the great revolt of 1173–74) and his quarrel with Thomas *Becket, Henry maintained control over his possessions until shortly before his death. His judicial and administrative reforms, which greatly increased royal control and influence at the expense of the barons, were of great constitutional importance.

Henry II (1519–59) King of France (1547–59); the husband from 1533 of *Catherine de' Medici. He concluded war against the Emperor *Charles V at Cateau-Cambrésis (1559), after winning the bishoprics of Metz, Toul, and Verdun. An ardent Roman Catholic, he began the systematic persecution of Huguenots, which ultimately led to the *Wars of Religion. He died of blood poisoning following injury in a tournament.

Henry III (1017–56) German king and Holy Roman Emperor (1039–56; crowned 1046), who greatly enhanced the power of the Empire. He became interested in Church reform under the influence of his second wife, Agnes, and at the synod of Constance (1043) announced his desire to reform the Church. His suppression of heresy, however, was unpopular and toward the end of his reign he faced rebellions in Germany, Hungary, and S Italy.

Henry III (1207–72) King of England (1216–72), succeeding his father John. A minor when he took the throne, Henry did not take the reins of government himself until 1234. Baronial discontent simmered, boiling over in 1258, when Henry, facing financial disaster, attempted to raise large sums from his magnates. Reforms were agreed upon but then renounced by Henry. Simon de *Montfort led a rebellion against the king (*see* Barons' Wars), which was defeated after initial success. Thereafter, the aged Henry ceded much power to his son, the future Edward I.

Henry III (1551–89) King of France (1574–89) during the *Wars of Religion. Elected King of Poland in 1573, he abandoned that country on succeeding to the French throne. In France he was caught between the Huguenot and Roman Catholic parties and after fleeing Paris following an uprising (1588) allied with the Huguenot Henry of Navarre (the future *Henry IV). He was assassinated while besieging Paris.

Henry IV (1056–1106) German king (1056–84) and Holy Roman Emperor (1056–1106; crowned 1084), famous as the opponent of Pope Gregory VII in the *investiture controversy. The conflict over Henry's right to appoint bishops led him in 1076 to depose Gregory, who proceeded to excommunicate Henry. In 1077, however, Henry did penance at Canossa but was then dethroned by the German princes (1078–80). Again excommunicated, in 1084 he entered Rome, deposed Gregory, and nominated the antipope Clement III (d. 1100) by whom he was crowned emperor. He subsequently faced a further rebellion of the German princes and his sons Conrad and the future Emperor Henry V.

Henry IV (1366–1413) King of England (1399–1413); the eldest son of *John of Gaunt. As Henry Bolingbroke, he seized the throne from Richard II. In the early years of his reign Henry faced considerable opposition from Richard's supporters, led by the Earl of Northumberland and his son Hotspur (see Percy, Sir Henry), and from the Welsh under *Glendower. Successful in defeating his enemies, the costs of these wars and resultant taxation led to protracted struggles between king and parliament for control of royal expenditure. Increasingly incapacitated by illness, Henry's last years were marked by bitter factional struggles within his council.

Henry IV (1553–1610) The first Bourbon King of France (1589–1610), who restored peace and prosperity following the *Wars of Religion. A Protestant, he succeeded his mother to the throne of Navarre in 1572. Shortly afterward he married Charles IX's sister *Margaret of Valois and was forced to renounce his religion and confine himself to court. In 1576 he escaped and became a *Huguenot (Protestant) leader in the Wars of Religion. His succession to the throne was only secured in 1594, when he became a Roman Catholic, and civil war continued until he granted the Huguenots freedom of worship by the Edict of *Nantes (1598). Thereafter he sponsored the efforts of his minister *Sully to restore France's shattered economy. Henry died at the hands of an assassin.

Henry V (1081–1125) German king (1089–1125) and Holy Roman Emperor (1106–25; crowned 1111); son of Emperor *Henry IV and first husband of Matilda of England. His reign saw the settlement of the *investiture controversy with the papacy by the Concordat of Worms (1122), which brought him control of the German Church but antagonized his bishops.

Henry V (1387–1422) King of England (1413–22); the eldest son of Henry IV. He vigorously resumed the *Hundred Years' War, partly as a distraction from domestic tensions. His first campaign culminated in the battle of *Agincourt (1415) and by 1420, in alliance with Burgundy, he controlled much of N France. He married Catherine of Valois and gained recognition (1420) as the heir of her father *Charles VI (1420). He was noted by contemporaries as much for his personal piety and love of justice as for military prowess.

Henry VI (1165–97) German king (1169–97) and Holy Roman Emperor (1190–97). Son of *Frederick Barbarossa, he acquired Sicily through his marriage (1189) to Constance of Sicily (1152–98). His reign was dominated by his attempts to secure Sicily and to subdue *Henry the Lion. In 1193 he imprisoned the English king, Richard the Lionheart, and received a large ransom in return for his release.

Henry VI (1421–71) King of England (1422–61, 1470–71), succeeding his father Henry V. He married (1445), and was dominated by, *Margaret of Anjou. His inability to govern led to bitter struggles that culminated in the Wars of the *Roses. Deposed and imprisoned by the Yorkists (1461), he was briefly restored to power (1470–71), only to be again defeated and probably murdered. He was a notable patron of learning and religion: he founded Eton College (1440) and King's College, Cambridge (1447).

Henry VII (c. 1275–1313) Holy Roman Emperor (1309–1313; crowned 1312) and, as Henry VI, Count of Luxembourg (1288–1313). He became King of the Lombards in 1313 but had to contend with *Guelf (anti-imperial) opposition in Italy. He arranged a brilliant match between his son John, the future Count of Luxembourg, and Elizabeth of Bohemia.

Henry VII (1457–1509) King of England (1485–1509). As Henry Tudor, Earl of Richmond, he defeated Richard III at *Bosworth (1485) and his marriage (1486) to Richard's niece Elizabeth of York (1465–1503) united the Houses of *Lancaster and *York, effectively ending the Wars of the *Roses. Until 1499, however, he faced Yorkist plots, such as those of *Simnel and *Warbeck. His domestic rule was noted for its harsh financial exactions, efficient royal administration, and growing prosperity. His foreign policy temporarily put an end to war with France (on favorable terms,

1492), while treaties with Burgundy and the Holy Roman Empire resulted in a new pattern of European alliances.

HENRY VIII *The imposing figure of Henry, in an engraving after a painting derived from a cartoon by Holbein, symbolizes the strength of the Tudor monarchy.*

Henry VIII (1491–1547) King of England (1509–47), who initiated the English *Reformation. In 1512 he joined a European alliance against France, which he defeated at the battle of the *Spurs (1513), gaining Tournai, and in the same year his army thwarted a Scottish invasion at *Flodden. His desire to make England a notable European power was pursued from 1515 by his Lord Chancellor, Cardinal *Wolsey, who arranged the meeting between Henry and *Francis I of France at the *Field of the Cloth of Gold, near Calais (1520). From 1527 Henry was preoccupied by his wish to divorce *Catherine of Aragon, who had been the widow of his elder brother Arthur (d. 1502). He blamed her failure to produce a son (she had given birth to the future Mary I in 1516) on the canonical prohibition against marrying one's brother's widow, a conviction that was enforced by his love affair with Anne *Boleyn. Wolsey's failure to gain a papal annulment of Henry's marriage brought about the cardinal's fall in 1529 but only in 1533, after Thomas *Cromwell had initiated the legislation that made the English Church, under Henry's supreme headship, independent of Rome, could the king marry Anne. In the same year she gave birth to the future Elizabeth I. In 1535 Thomas *More was executed for refusing to acknowledge royal supremacy over the Church and in the following year Anne met the same fate for adultery. Henry then married Jane *Seymour, who died shortly after giving birth to the future Edward VI (1537). His next marriage, arranged by Cromwell, to *Anne of Cleves was short lived, ending in divorce and the execution of Cromwell (1540). Shortly afterward Henry married Catherine *Howard, who was executed in 1542, and finally, in 1543, Catherine *Parr, who outlived him. Henry's last years were dominated by war with France and Scotland, consequent economic problems, and his attempts to hold back the forces of Protestantism, which "the King's great matter" had unleashed.

Henry, Joseph (1797–1878) US physicist, who made important contributions to the investigation of electromagnetism. He built the largest electromagnet then known, which could lift over 660 lbs (300 kg); he also discovered electromagnetic induction independently of *Faraday. Henry invented an early form of the telegraph and the electrical relay. In 1846 he was appointed secretary of the Smithsonian Institution and he was one of the founders of the National Academy of Sciences. The unit of inductance (see henry) is named for— him.

Henry, O. (William Sidney Porter; 1862–1910) US short-story writer. He adopted his pseudonym while serving a prison sentence for embezzlement. He subsequently worked in New York, where he published *Cabbages and Kings* (1904), the first of many volumes of short stories characterized by the use of coincidence and unexpected endings. Other collections include *The Four Million* (1906), *Heart of the West* (1907), and *Strictly Business* (1910).

PATRICK HENRY *Patriot and orator whose "give me liberty or give me death" speech inspired the Virginia militia against Britain.*

Henry, Patrick (1736–99) American Revolutionary orator; first governor of Virginia (1776–79). As a lawyer and member of the Virginia assembly (the House of Burgesses), Henry defended colonial rights against British rule. The mobilization of a Virginia militia on the eve of the American Revolution was ensured by Henry's famous speech ending "give me liberty or give me death." He was again governor of Virginia from 1784 to 1786.

Henry the Lion (?1129–95) Duke of Saxony (1142–81), whose wealth and power brought him into conflict with the Holy Roman Emperors. He gave support to *Frederick Barbarossa in return for regaining Bavaria (1154) but when he broke with Frederick in 1176 most of his lands were confiscated and he was exiled. In 1194, after further conflict, he was reconciled with Frederick's son and successor Emperor *Henry VI.

Henry the Navigator (1394–1460) Portuguese patron of explorers; the fourth son of John I. He won a military reputation at the capture of Ceuta (1415) in N Africa, which kindled his interest in the exploration of the continent. Becoming governor of the Algarve (1419) he set up a school of navigation at Sagres and inspired and sponsored explorers. Under his auspices Madeira, the Azores, and the Cape Verde Islands were colonized, the W coast of Africa was explored, probably as far as Sierra Leone, and many trading stations were established.

Henze, Hans Werner (1926–) German composer, a pupil of Wolfgang Fortner (1907–). His piano concerto won the Schumann Prize in 1951 and he settled in Italy in 1953. He has organized an annual festival at Montepulciano since 1977. Henze has made use of a number of different styles of composition, including serialism and neoromanticism. His Marxist sympathies are evident in such works as the oratorio *The Raft of the Medusa* (1968), for which he wrote both text and music. He has composed symphonies; concertos for piano, violin, viola, and double bass; ballet music; and the operas *Elegy for Young Lovers* (1961) and *The Bassarids* (1966).

heparin An *anticoagulant that occurs naturally in the tissues and is also used in medicine. Heparin is a complex carbohydrate produced and secreted by special cells (mast cells) in connective tissues, especially in the lungs. It inhibits the enzymes responsible for blood clotting.

hepatitis Inflammation of the liver, most commonly caused by viruses. The two main types are infectious hepatitis, usually contracted by ingesting the virus from food or drink, and serum hepatitis, contracted mainly from dirty hypodermic needles or blood products. Some chemicals (e.g. alcohol) can also cause hepatitis. The patient usually has a fever, loses his appetite, and later becomes jaundiced. Hepatitis usually resolves without specific treatment, but sometimes chronic disease develops.

Hepburn, Katharine (1909–) US actress. Her performances in both films and the theater are distinguished by her intelligence and versatility. Among the many movies she made with Spencer *Tracy are *Woman of the Year* (1942), *Adam's Rib* (1949), and *Pat and Mike* (1952). Her other movies include *The Philadelphia Story* (1940), *The African Queen* (1952), and *Summertime* (1955). She won Academy Awards for *Guess Who's Coming to Dinner* (1967), *The Lion in Winter* (1968), and *On Golden Pond* (1981).

Hepburn Act (1906) A US law that increased the powers of the Interstate Commerce Commission over railroads. Regulation of rates, routes, and taxes were strengthened, and the act prohibited railroads from transporting those products in which it had a financial interest.

Hephaestus The Greek god of fire and crafts, the son of Zeus and Hera. According to Hesiod he created *Pandora, the first woman. He is identified with the Roman *Vulcan.

Hepplewhite, George (d. 1786) British furniture designer and cabinetmaker, who established a business in London. His neoclassical furniture is a simplified and more functional version of the designs of Robert *Adam, with whom he sometimes collaborated. Usually in inlaid mahogany or satinwood, it is characterized by straight tapering legs and heart- or oval-shaped chairbacks filled with openwork designs.

heptane (C_7H_{16}) A colorless flammable liquid *alkane. It is obtained from *oil and is used as a solvent and to make other chemicals. Heptane is also a standard in determining the *octane rating of gasoline.

Hepworth, Dame Barbara (1903–75) British sculptor. She studied in Leeds and at the Royal College of Art. A friend of Henry *Moore, she was also influenced by *Brancusi and *Arp. Her abstract carving in wood and stone developed after *Pierced Form* (1931), creating massive shapes broken by holes with wires stretched across their openings.

Hera In Greek mythology, the daughter of Cronus and Rhea and the sister and wife of Zeus. She was jealous of Zeus' many mistresses and cruel to their children but gave loyal support to *Jason and *Achilles. She was worshiped as a goddess of women and marriage. She is identified with the Roman *Juno.

Heracles (*or* Hercules) A Greek legendary hero, famed for his strength and courage. He was the son of Zeus and Alcmene (*see* Amphitryon). After killing his wife and children in a fit of madness inflicted by Hera, he went to the court of King Eurystheus of Tiryns, where he performed the Twelve Labors in expiation: he killed the Nemean lion and the *Hydra of Lerna, captured the Hind of Ceryneia and the Boar of Erymanthus, cleaned the Augean stables, chased away the Stymphalian birds, captured the Cretan bull and the horses of Diomedes, stole the girdle of Hippolyte, captured the oxen of Geryon, stole the apples of the *Hesperides, and finally captured and bound *Cerberus in Hades. The last Labor was taken to represent the conquest of Death itself.

Heraclitus (c. 535–c. 475 BC) Greek philosopher of *Ephesus. His treatise *On Nature* postulates that fire is the universe's basic constituent. Rejecting *Parmenides' doctrine of a unitary static reality, Heraclitus maintained that reality is transitory and every object "a harmony of opposite tensions." Everything was always changing ("you cannot step into the same river twice") and wisdom consisted in seeking to understand this eternal dynamic principle (*see* logos), which unified the diversity of nature.

Heraclius (c. 575–641 AD) Byzantine emperor. Between 613 and 628 he faced the aggression of the Persians, who took Syria, Palestine, and Egypt and besieged Constantinople (626). Finally victorious following a campaign in 626–28, Heraclius restored the Holy Cross to Jerusalem (629), a deed that was immortalized in medieval legend. His success was short-lived for in 634 the Arabs attacked the empire, defeating the Byzantines at Yarmuk (636) and taking Palestine, Syria, and Egypt. He divided Anatolia into military units, from which peasants were enlisted for military service in return for land.

Herakleion. *See* Iráklion.

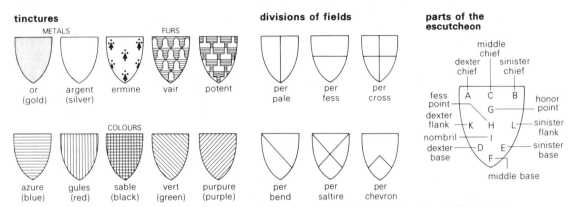

tinctures

METALS

or (gold) argent (silver) ermine vair potent

COLOURS

azure (blue) gules (red) sable (black) vert (green) purpure (purple)

divisions of fields

per pale per fess per cross

per bend per saltire per chevron

parts of the escutcheon

middle chief
dexter chief sinister chief
fess point A C B honor point
dexter flank G sinister flank
K H L
nombril I
dexter base D E sinister base
F
middle base

HERALDRY *The terminology of heraldry, of which a few terms are illustrated, reveals the science's French origins.*

heraldry A system of pictorial devices on shields originally used to identify individuals when wearing armor. Personal devices on shields are of great antiquity but in the early 12th century armorial devices became hereditary in Europe. They were also used as *seals. Coats of arms are also granted to institutions. Coats of arms comprise the shield, a helmet surmounted by a crest, a mantling (stylized drapery behind the shield), a wreath, and a motto. The shield bears the heraldic signs (charges), which have ancient fixed meanings. From these heralds can determine the genealogy and status of the bearer.

Herat (*or* Harat) 34 20N 62 10E A city in W Afghanistan. Near the site of several ancient cities, including one built by Alexander the Great, Herat developed as a scientific and cultural center under the rule of the Turkish conqueror Timur, who seized the city in 1393. An agricultural and commercial center, Herat's industries include flour milling and textiles. Population (1975 est): 157,000.

herbaceous plant A plant that lacks woody stems and the aerial parts of which die each winter. Many herbaceous plants are *annuals but some are *perennials, surviving the winter in the form of underground bulbs, corms, rhizomes, etc.

Herbart, Johann Friedrich (1776–1841) German educational theorist, who pioneered the application of psychology to teaching. Rejecting *Fichte's philosophy with its emphasis on freedom, he preferred *Kant's pluralism, believing that beyond the phenomenal world there existed many real "things-in-themselves," which are inaccessible to the mind. Herbart, like Kant, sought to make psychology a mathematical science and wasted time developing fruitless systems that had no experimental foundation.

herbicide (*or* weedkiller) A chemical used to kill unwanted plants (*see* weed). Selective weedkillers kill the target without harming the plants among which it is growing. Some of these act by interfering with the growth of the weed and are often based on plant hormones. An example is 2,4-D, a synthetic *auxin, which is used to control broadleaved weeds in cereal crops. Herbicides used to clear waste ground are nonselective and kill every plant with which they come into contact. An example is Paraquat.

herb Paris A perennial herbaceous plant, *Paris quadrifolia*, native to woodlands of Europe and Asia. Up to 12 in (30 cm) high, it has a whorl of usually four leaves and a solitary flower with prominent sepals and narrow yellow petals. The fruit is a fleshy capsule. Family: *Trilliaceae*.

herb Robert An annual or biennial herb, *Geranium robertianum*, growing up to 20 in (50 cm) high and found in woods and hedgerows throughout temperate Eurasia and introduced to North and South America. The small flowers are pink or red. Family: *Geraniaceae*.

herbs and spices The fresh or dried parts of aromatic or pungent plants used in food, drink, medicine, and perfumery. Herbs are generally the leaves of plants and are best used fresh. They grow in temperate zones. Common culinary herbs are *basil, *bay leaves, *marjoram, *mint, *parsley, and *thyme. Spices generally grow in hot countries. They were formerly a valuable trade commodity; the Roman Empire's spice trade extended to Indochina and Zanzibar and the quest for spice routes motivated 15th-century European exploration of the East and the Americas. Spices are usually dried and may be obtained from the root (e.g. *ginger), bark (e.g. *cinnamon), flower (e.g. *clove), seed pod (e.g. *chili) or, most commonly, from the seed itself (e.g. *coriander, *cumin, *pepper).

Hercegovina. *See* Bosnia and Hercegovina.

Herculaneum An ancient Italian city near *Naples in Italy. It was destroyed by the same eruption as *Pompeii (79 AD). It was smaller, better planned, and wealthier than Pompeii. Entombment beneath solidified volcanic mud makes excavation there very difficult and much remains buried.

Hercules. *See* Heracles.

hercules beetle A giant green and black beetle, *Dynastes herculeus*, occurring in Central and South America. The male may reach a length of 6 in (15 cm), nearly two-thirds of which is taken up by an enormous pair of horns, extending from the thorax and head. Family: *Scarabeidae* (*see* scarab beetle).

hercules moth A large Australian *saturniid moth, *Coscinoscera hercules*. The adult has broad dark-brown wings, spanning about 11 in (28 cm), with a wing area that is possibly the largest of any insect.

Herder, Johann Gottfried (1744–1803) German philosopher and poet. At first a disciple and later a critic of *Kant, he developed a form of religious humanism based on his readings of Shakespeare, Homer, and the Bible. His works include *A Treatise upon the Origin of Language* (1772) and *Outline of a Philosophy of the History of Man* (1784–91).

Hereford cattle A breed of beef cattle originating from Herefordshire and surrounding areas in W England. They are large and stocky with red coats and white faces. Hardy and maturing quickly, Herefords are often mated with dairy breeds to produce a white-faced beef cross.

Herero A group of Bantu-speaking peoples of SW Africa, Botswana, and Angola. They are traditionally cattle, sheep, and goat herders but some adopted agriculture after European contact. Their social organization is based on the common principle of counting descent in the male line for some purposes and in the female line for others.

hermaphrodite (*or* bisexual) A plant or animal possessing both male and female reproductive organs. Such organisms may show cross- or self-*fertilization: the latter method is particularly common when the opportunity of finding a mate is remote, for example in parasitic invertebrates and deepsea fish. True hermaphroditism rarely occurs in humans. More common is **pseudohermaphroditism**, in which an individual develops secondary characteristics appropriate to the opposite sex (e.g enlarged external genitals in a woman or breasts in a man), due to hormone imbalance.

Hermes In Greek mythology, the messenger and herald of the gods and the guide of travelers. He was regarded as the god of riches and good luck, the protector of merchants and thieves, and the god of dreams. He was usually portrayed as an athletic youth wearing a cap and winged sandals and carrying a golden staff. He was the son of Zeus and Maia. He conducted the souls of the dead to Hades and is credited with the invention of the lyre, which he gave to Apollo. He is identified with the Roman *Mercury.

Hermes Trismegistos (Greek: Hermes the thrice great) The name applied by Greek Neoplatonists to the Egyptian god *Thoth. It is also the name given, after the third century AD, to the author of certain Neoplatonic writings.

Hermeticism An Italian literary movement of the early 20th century. Its leading writers were the poets Ungaretti, Quasimodo, and Montale, whose early poetry was influenced by the theories of the French *Symbolists and characterized by verbal experiment and esoteric symbolism. After World War II all three poets developed more accessible styles.

hermit crab A *crab with a soft unprotected abdomen, belonging to the worldwide families *Paguridae* and *Coenobitidae*. It lives in portable hollow objects, such as snail shells, for protection and changes these for successively larger ones as it grows. Hermit crabs are found in sandy or muddy-bottomed waters and occasionally on land and in trees. Tribe: *Anomura*.

Hermite, Charles (1822–1901) French mathematician, who (in 1873), discovered the first transcendental number: e, the base of natural *logarithms. Such numbers cannot be expressed as a root of a polynomial equation, i.e. an equation of the form $a_0 + a_1x + \ldots + a_nx^n = 0$, where n and the a's are integers. *Liouville had already shown that such numbers exist but could not identify any.

Hermon, Mount 33 24N 35 50E A mountain on the Syrian-Lebanese border, at the S end of the Anti-Lebanon Mountains. It is the highest point near the E coast of the Mediterranean Sea. Height: 9232 ft (2814 m).

Hermosillo 29 15N 110 59W A city in NW Mexico. It is an important commercial center for the surrounding agricultural areas and has a university (1938). Population (1976 est): 264,073.

Herne 51 32N 7 12E A city in NW West Germany, in North Rhine-Westphalia on the Rhine-Herne Canal. It is a coalmining and industrial center. Population (1976 est): 188,357.

hernia The protrusion of an organ or tissue through a weak spot in the wall that normally contains it. The most common types are the inguinal hernia (popularly called a rupture), which is a swelling in the groin caused by the protrusion of the abdominal contents, and the hiatus hernia, in which part of the stomach protrudes into the chest cavity. Other common hernias are femoral (also in the groin) and umbilical (at the navel). Hernias should usually be surgically repaired or they may become painful and cut off from their blood supply (strangulated).

Hero and Leander Legendary lovers whose story was recounted by the Greek poet Musaeus (4th or 5th century AD). Hero was a priestess of Aphrodite at Sestos and Leander swam to her each night across the Hellespont from Abydos. After a stormy night Hero found her lover's drowned body and in despair drowned herself.

Herod (I) the Great (c. 73–4 BC) King of Judaea (37–4); the son of *Antipater. Supported by Mark Antony, he became the Romans' king in Judaea. A Jew of Arab origins, he was regarded as a usurper by nationalists, who resented his encouragement of Greek culture; he retained power by control of the religious establishment and rigorous suppression of opposition. His jealousy and cruelty were exacerbated by feuds among his ten wives and their sons. Shortly before his death he ordered the massacre of the infants of Bethlehem.

Herod Agrippa I (c. 10 BC–44 AD) King of Judaea (41–44); the grandson of *Herod the Great. An impecunious adventurer, he was educated at the Roman imperial court after the execution of his father by Herod the Great. He intrigued in imperial family politics and helped Emperor *Claudius to power, for which he was made King of Judaea. He was a popular ruler but persecuted Christians, executing St James, the son of Zebedee, and imprisoning St Peter.

Herod Agrippa II (died c. 100 AD) King of Chalcis (50–c. 100) in S Lebanon; the son of *Herod Agrippa I. In 60 he heard the case of the arrested St Paul and found him innocent. He attempted to prevent the Jewish rebellion of 66, during which his troops fought on the Roman side, and helped to take Jerusalem in 70.

Herod Antipas (21 BC–39 AD) Tetrarch (governor) of Galilee (4–39 AD) after the partition of the realm of his father *Herod the Great. He divorced his wife to marry his niece Herodias, for which he was censured by John the Baptist. Herodias persuaded her daughter Salome to ask for John's head in return for dancing at Antipas' birthday celebration and John was executed. Jesus Christ, as a Galilean, was brought before Antipas after his arrest, but Antipas returned him to Pontius Pilate of Judaea without passing judgment. After the death of Antipas' friend Emperor *Tiberius, religious riots gave *Caligula an excuse to exile Antipas.

Herodotus (c. 484–c. 425 BC) Greek historian. Born at Halicarnassus, he was exiled for political reasons and moved to Samos. He subsequently moved to Athens and then to the Athenian colony of Thurii in S Italy, where he died. Called "the father of history" by Cicero, he was the first historian to subject his material to critical evaluation and research. His narrative account of the wars between Greece and Persia in nine books contained much incidental anthropological and geographical information gathered on his travels in the Mediterranean countries, Egypt, and Asia, and was written in a lively dramatic style.

heroin (*or* diamorphine) A pain-killing drug with a stronger action and fewer side effects than *morphine, from which it is made. Heroin is used in some countries to alleviate the suffering of terminal illness. Because the regular use of heroin readily leads to physical dependence its use in medicine has been restricted. *See* drug dependence.

heron A wading bird belonging to a subfamily (*Ardeinae*; 60 species) occurring on lakes and rivers worldwide, especially in the tropics. 30–59 in (75–150 cm) long, herons have a slim body, longish legs, long toes, broad wings, a short tail, and a loose plumage colored gray, blue, greenish, white, purple, or reddish. Herons hunt by standing at the water's edge and seizing fish and insects with the long pointed bill. In the breeding season herons may develop ornamental plumes and perform elaborate courtship displays. Family: *Ardeidae* (herons and bitterns). *See also* egret; night heron.

Hero of Alexandria (mid-1st century AD) Greek engineer and mathematician, best known for his invention of the aeolipile, the earliest known steam engine. It consisted of a sphere containing water with two bent tubes extending from it. When heated, steam issued from the tubes, causing the sphere to rotate. However, the device was only used for trivial purposes, such as controlling doors and causing statues to move. He also discovered the well-known formula for calculating the area of a triangle from the lengths of its sides.

Herophilus (c. 335–c. 280 BC) Greek physician, who founded one of the earliest medical schools in Alexandria. Herophilus performed public dissections of human cadavers, distinguished between sensory and motor nerve trunks, and described parts of the brain, duodenum, and several other organs.

herpes A virus that causes *chickenpox, *shingles, and cold sores. Herpes zoster causes chickenpox in children and shingles in adults. Herpes simplex (type 1 or oral type) causes cold sores. The genital type (type 2) is sexually transmitted. The virus is usually dormant, but when active it causes painful sores, during which the disease is highly contagious. No cure is known; however, the drug acyclovir is active against the virus in its active stage.

Herrera, Juan de (1530–97) Spanish architect. After having studied in Italy, Herrera designed a palace in Aranjuez (1569) and the Exchange in Seville (1582) in an Italianate style that had great influence on Spanish architecture. He is best known for his completion of the *Escorial.

Herrera the Younger, Francisco de (1622–85) Spanish baroque painter and architect, born in Seville, the son and pupil of the painter and engraver **Francisco de Herrera the Elder** (1576–1656). After leaving his father's tutelage, he studied in Italy. On his return to Seville, he introduced the dramatic style of Italian baroque in such religious works as *Triumph of St Hermengild* (Prado). He later worked in Madrid, where he designed the high altar of the church of Montserrat.

Herrick, Robert (1591–1674) English poet. A friend of Jonson and other members of London literary society, he was ordained (1623) and served as rector of Dean Prior, Devonshire, from 1630 to 1646 and again after the Restoration. The majority of his secular and religious poems, collected in *Hesperides* (1648), are short lyrics influenced by classical models.

herring An important food fish, *Clupea harengus*, found mainly in cold waters of the N Atlantic and the North Sea. It has a slender silvery blue-green body, up to about 16 in (40 cm) long, with a single short dorsal fin and swims in large shoals, feeding on plankton. A related species (*C. pallasi*) occurs in the N Pacific. Many other small silvery fish of the family *Clupeidae* are called herring. Herrings have long been fished in N Europe, where they are eaten fresh, pickled, and smoked. In the UK, smoked herring are known as kippers, and are produced mainly in Scotland. Overfishing and pollution have greatly reduced catches of herring in European waters in recent years. Order: *Clupeiformes. See also* whitebait.

herring gull A large gray and white *gull, *Larus argentatus*, occurring around coasts in the N hemisphere. It is omnivorous and is commonly seen scavenging at refuse heaps. Adults are 22 in (57 cm) long and have pink legs and a yellow bill with a red spot on the lower mandible.

Herriot, Édouard (1872–1957) French statesman and writer; prime minister of a Radical-Socialist coalition (1924–25, 1926 (for two days), 1932). During World War II, he opposed the Vichy Government and spent the years 1942–45 in prison. From 1947 to 1953 he served as president of the national assembly.

Herschel, Sir William (1738–1822) British astronomer, born in Germany. Working with his sister **Caroline Herschel** (1750–1848), he became expert in grinding lenses and built the largest telescopes then known. In 1781 Herschel discovered the planet *Uranus, the first such discovery since prehistoric times. His other discoveries include binary stars, two new satellites of Saturn, and *infrared rays from the sun (1800).

Hershey, John (Richard) (1914–) US writer; born in China. He was a foreign news correspondent (1937–46) and wrote his first novel, *A Bell for Adano* (1944; Pulitzer Prize; film, 1945), about the Allied campaign in Italy during World War II. His other works include *Men on*

Bataan (1942); *Hiroshima* (1946), about the first atomic bomb; *The Wall* (1950), about revolt in Warsaw ghetto; *The Algiers Motel Incident* (1968); *My Petition for More Space* (1974); *The President* (1975); *The Walnut Door* (1977); and *Aspects of the Presidency* (1980).

Hertogenbosch, 's. *See* 's Hertogenbosch.

hertz (Hz) The *SI unit of frequency equal to one cycle per second. Named for Heinrich *Hertz.

Hertz, Heinrich Rudolf (1857–94) German physicist, who first produced and detected *radio waves (1888). *Maxwell's equations had predicted the existence of *electromagnetic radiation over a wide spectrum of frequencies but, until Hertz's discovery, radio-frequency radiation was unknown. The unit of frequency is named for him.

Hertzog, James Barry Munnik (1866–1942) South African statesman; prime minister of the Union of South Africa (1924–39). In the second *Boer War he led the Orange Free State forces. He formed the Afrikaner Nationalist Party in 1914, becoming prime minister in 1924. In 1933 he formed a coalition government with *Smuts but resigned in 1939, when his motion against entering World War II was defeated. With *Malan he then revived the Nationalist Party but retired from politics in 1940.

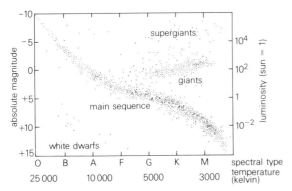

HERTZSPRUNG-RUSSELL DIAGRAM *This graph for bright stars is important in studies of stellar evolution and in determining distance.*

Hertzsprung-Russell diagram A graphic representation of the classification of stars according to spectral type (*see* Harvard classification system) and brightness—usually absolute *magnitude. The stars are not uniformly distributed. Most, including the sun, lie on a diagonal band, the main sequence, the brightest stars of which are spectral types O and B and the faintest are M stars. Main-sequence stars are often called dwarf stars. The somewhat brighter *giant stars, the even brighter *supergiants, and the faint *white dwarfs fall into their own distinct groupings. The diagram was originally produced, independently, in 1911 by E. Hertzsprung (1873–1967) and in 1913 by H. N. Russell (1897–1957).

Herzl, Theodor (1860–1904) Hungarian-born journalist and playwright, who founded the movement to establish a Jewish nation (*see* Zionism). Living mostly in Vienna, he published the pamphlet *The Jewish State* (1896), calling for a world council to discuss the problem of finding a Jewish homeland. At a world congress of Zionists in Basle (1897) the World Zionist Organization was established, Herzl becoming the first president.

Herzog, Chaim (1918–) Israeli soldier and statesman; president (1983–); born in Ireland. Educated in Israel and England, he served in the British Army during World War II. He was in Israeli military intelligence (director, 1948–54) and became military commander of the Jerusalem district (1954–59) and again director of military intelligence (1959–62). He was thrust into the limelight during the Six Days War (1967), when he broadcast war reports, and later was ambassador to the UN (1975–78). As the Labor Party's candidate, he succeeded Yitzhak Navon as president.

Hesiod (8th century BC) Greek poet, the earliest known after Homer. He was a farmer near Mount Helicon in Boeotia in central Greece and was involved in a long dispute with his brother Perses concerning their inheritance. His two major works are the *Theogony*, concerning the gods and their myths, and *Works and Days*, a realistic and personal account of farming life.

Hesperides (Greek: daughters of evening) In Greek mythology, three nymphs who guarded the sacred golden apples of Hera in a garden in the far west. The apples were stolen by *Heracles as one of his Twelve Labors.

Hesperornis A genus of extinct flightless seabirds whose fossils date from the Cretaceous period (125–60 million years ago). It was 7 ft (2 m) long and adapted for swimming and catching fish in shallow seas, having large powerful feet and legs, a long slender neck, a small head, and a long bill (possibly with teeth), but only tiny wing bones and reduced flight muscles.

Hess, Rudolf (1894–) German Nazi politician. Hess joined the Nazi Party in 1920, becoming Hitler's close friend and deputy party leader (1933). However, his declining influence in the late 1930s led to his unsuccessful secret mission to Scotland to negotiate a separate peace with Britain in 1941. There, he was imprisoned until 1946, when he was convicted at the Nuremberg war trials and sent to Spandau prison. In recent years his release from Spandau, where he is now the only prisoner, has been urged.

Hess, Victor Francis (1883–1964) US physicist, born in Austria. Using a balloon to investigate atmospheric background radiation, he discovered that the radiation increased with altitude. This was contrary to expectation, because background radiation was then believed to emanate from rocks. This work led to the discovery of *cosmic rays, for which he shared a Nobel Prize in 1936 with Carl *Anderson.

Hesse (German name: Hessen) A *Land in central West Germany. Formed in 1945, it consists of the former duchies of Hesse-Darmstadt and Nassau. Hilly and forested, it is chiefly agricultural, producing potatoes, sugar beet, and wheat. Industry, concentrated in the S, includes publishing and the manufacture of machinery and chemicals. Iron ore, salt, and coal are mined. Area: 8150 sq mi (21,112 sq km). Population (1977 est): 5,540,600. Capital: Wiesbaden.

Hesse, Hermann (1877–1962) German novelist and poet. He rejected traditional schooling and worked as a bookseller until publication of his first novel, *Peter Camenzind* (1904). His early themes of art and self-knowledge were later extended by his interest in Indian mysticism and Jungian psychology, reflected in *Siddharta* (1922). His other major novels are *Steppenwolf* (1927) and *Narziss und Goldmund* (1930). After publication of his last novel, *The Glass Bead Game* (1943), he was awarded a Nobel Prize (1946). From 1911 until his death he lived in Switzerland.

Hestia The Greek goddess of the hearth, daughter of Cronus and Rhea and the oldest of the Olympian deities. She vowed to remain a virgin, rejecting both Apollo and Poseidon as consorts. She is identified with the Roman *Vesta.

Hevesy, George Charles von (1885–1966) Hungarian-born chemist, who worked in Denmark and Sweden. He discovered the use of *radioactive tracers to follow the course of compounds in a system, for which he received the 1943 Nobel Prize. He also discovered the element *hafnium in 1923, by analyzing zirconium ores.

Heyerdahl, Thor (1914–) Norwegian ethnologist, who led the *Kon-Tiki expedition (1947). The *Kon-Tiki* was a balsawood raft that Heyerdahl built and sailed with five companions from the Pacific coast of South America to Polynesia to show that the pre-Incan inhabitants of Peru might thus have migrated to Polynesia. In 1969–70 he attempted to cross the Atlantic Ocean from Morocco to South America in a papyrus boat—the *Ra*; he reached Barbados, showing the possibility of Egyptian influence on the precolumbian civilization of America. Heyerdahl wrote accounts of both expeditions. In 1978, on his way from Iraq to India, he burned his reed boat, the *Tigris*, in protest against the war in the Horn of Africa.

Heysham. *See* Morecambe.

Heywood, Thomas (c. 1574–1641) English dramatist. An actor as well as a prolific and versatile writer, he wrote numerous comedies, chronicle plays, and scripts for pageants and masques. His best-known work is the domestic tragedy *A Woman Killed with Kindness* (1607).

Hezekiah King of Judah (c. 715–c. 686 BC), noted as a religious reformer. Allied with Egypt, he rebelled against *Sennacherib of Assyria, against Isaiah's advice, and was defeated and forced to pay huge indemnities.

Hialeah 25 49N 80 17W A city in SE Florida, NW of Miami, on the Miami Canal. One of its main attractions is winter horse racing. Industries include the manufacture of metal, chemical, and clothing products. Population (1980): 145,254.

Hiawatha The legendary chief of the Onondaga tribe of American Indians, who was said to have formed the *Iroquois League. His story is the subject of Longfellow's *Song of Hiawatha* (1855).

hibernation A state of *dormancy in winter experienced by many fish, amphibians, reptiles, and mammals of temperate and Arctic regions: it is an adaption to avoid death by heat loss, freezing, or food scarcity. True hibernation is seasonal and not simply a reaction to a drop in temperature. It occurs in a few mammals, including bats and hedgehogs, and some birds. Hibernation involves a period of sleep during which the body temperature drops almost to that of the surroundings, the body processes are slowed, and the hibernator lives on a reserve of body fat until it awakens in the spring.

Hibiscus A genus of tropical and subtropical herbs, shrubs, and trees (about 150 species). Several species are cultivated for their showy five-petaled flowers; two popular shrubs, up to 10 ft (3 m) high, are the Chinese *H. rosa-sinensis* (rose of China), which has red, pink, or yellow flowers with prominent stigmas, and the Syrian *H. syriacus* (rose of Sharon), which has pink, blue, or white hollyhock-like flowers. Both can be grown as pot plants. The genus also includes plants cultivated for their food value (*see* okra; roselle) and for their fiber (*see* kenaf). Family: *Malvaceae*.

hiccup (*or* hiccough) A sudden involuntary intake of breath interrupted by closure of the glottis (in the larynx), producing a characteristic sound. Hiccups are commonly due to indigestion or eating too quickly, but they may be associated with kidney disease or alcoholism.

Hickok, James Butler (1837–76) US lawman, known as Wild Bill Hickok. He was celebrated for his skill and speed as a gunman. After Union army service in the Civil War and against the Indians he was a marshal in several Kansas towns (1866–71) and toured with Buffalo Bill. He was shot dead from behind while playing poker in a saloon.

hickory A tree of the genus *Carya* (20 species), native to E North America and Asia and cultivated for timber, nuts, and ornament. They grow to a height of about 100 ft (30 m) and have compound leaves consisting of paired leaflets. Commercially important species are the shagbark (*C. ovata*), which yields hard durable timber, and the pecan (*C. illinoensis*), which produces thin-shelled nuts resembling walnuts. Both species are North American. Family: *Juglandaceae*.

hide A unit of land measurement in Anglo–Saxon England based on the approximate area of land needed to support a peasant household. Tax assessments were often calculated on the basis of the number of hides comprising an estate. The size of the hide varied, ranging in different areas from 40 to 120 acres.

Hideyoshi (1536–98) Japanese military ruler, who brought feudal Japan under his dominance. Of humble birth, Hideyoshi became by sheer ability a leading commander of *Oda Nobunaga, aiding him to become master of central Japan. Succeeding to Oda's power in 1582, he achieved national hegemony by 1590 but then wasted his energy on an unsuccessful invasion of Korea.

eye   to fly   old age

HIEROGLYPHICS *A picture was used to represent objects, related ideas, and sounds.*

hieroglyphics Originally, an Egyptian system of picture writing in use from about 3000 BC to 300 AD; the term now denotes any *pictographic or *ideographic writing system. The Egyptians used hieroglyphics largely for monumental inscriptions. The characters are careful reproductions of people, animals, and objects and may be interpreted as representing either the objects they portray or the sounds that are featured in the pronunciation of the referent. Hieroglyphic records are coextensive with hieratic, a more cursive stylized form appropriate to brush and ink and the smooth surfaces of papyrus and wood.

hi-fi. *See* high-fidelity sound systems.

high-fidelity sound systems (*or* hi-fi) Systems of recording and reproducing sound in which the quality of the reproduced sound is as close as possible to that of the original source. A typical reproducing system consists of a record player or *cassette player, a stereophonic amplifier, and two loudspeakers. To achieve high fidelity, total distortion in such a system must be less than 2%, the frequency response must be constant between 20 and 20,000 hertz, and the system must be able to reproduce stereophonic or

quadraphonic recordings. While two frontal stereophonic speakers can reproduce the spatial pattern of the sound source, reproduction of the reverberation characteristics of the place at which the recording was made can be reproduced more fully by a quadraphonic system with two additional rear speakers.

The term high fidelity is commonly applied to a wide range of domestic record- and tape-reproducing systems, many of which do not fulfil the requirements of true high fidelity. Stereophonic and quadraphonic radio broadcasts can also be used as sound sources in many hi-fi systems.

high jump A field event in athletics in which jumpers compete to clear a horizontal bar. A competitor is allowed three attempts at a height and is eliminated if he fails to clear it. The height is increased until there is only one jumper left.

Highland Games Scottish athletics meetings, usually professional, held in the Highlands. As amateur competitions they are popular in the US and Canada among those of Scottish descent. Events include standard track and field events as well as such Scottish sports as *caber tossing, and there are also competitions in highland dancing and playing the bagpipes. The modern games date from the early 19th century but they originated far earlier in clan assemblies. The most famous meeting, the Braemar Games, can be traced back to the 8th century AD.

high priest The chief official of the ancient Jerusalem *Temple. The office was hereditary in the family of Aaron. The Hasmonean rulers (*see* Maccabees) claimed the title themselves, and in the last century of the temple the high priests were appointed by political rulers. With the destruction of the temple (70 AD) the office ceased to exist.

Hilary of Poitiers, St (c. 315–c. 367 AD) French churchman; bishop and Doctor of the Church. A leading opponent of *Arianism, he was converted to Christianity from Neoplatonism and became Bishop of Poitiers in about 353. His works include *De trinitate* and *De synodis*. Feast day: Jan 14.

Hilbert, David (1862–1943) German mathematician, who gave geometry a mathematically rigorous foundation. In a book entitled *Foundations of Geometry* (1899), he defined such concepts as the point, the line, and the parallel relationship, which *Euclid in his *Elements* had assumed to be intuitively obvious. Hilbert then developed geometry from a much more rigorous set of axioms than those of Euclid. He also studied the properties of infinite-dimensional space, known as Hilbert space, which is used in the mathematics of quantum theory.

Hildebrand. *See* Gregory VII, St.

Hildesheim 52 09N 9 58E A city in NE West Germany, in Lower Saxony. The romanesque 11th-century cathedral escaped the destruction of World War II. A notable collection of Roman silver was found nearby in 1868. Its manufactures include machinery, textiles, and carpets. Population (1976 est): 104,278.

Hill, Ambrose Powell (1825–65) US Confederate general. A career Army officer who had served in the *Mexican War, he resigned to join the Confederate Army in 1861. By 1862 he was a general and participated in both battles at *Bull Run, at Williamsburg (1862), *Antietam, *Fredericksburg, and *Chancellorsville. He was killed at Petersburg (1865).

Hill, Archibald Vivian (1886–1977) British physiologist, noted for his work on muscle contraction. Hill found that oxygen was needed not for the contraction of a muscle but for its recovery, which provided a clue to the underlying biochemistry involved. Hill shared the 1922 Nobel Prize with Otto *Meyerhoff.

Hill, Graham (1929–75) British automobile racer, who was world champion in 1962 and 1968 and was runner-up from 1963 to 1965. Despite breaking both legs in an accident (1969) he continued to race. He was killed in a flying accident.

Hill, James Jerome (1838–1916) US businessman; born in Canada. He began by acquiring the bankrupt St Paul and Pacific Railroad, reorganizing and extending it, and eventually bringing it and other lines under one parent company, the Great Northern Railway Company (1890). His Northern Securities Company, which oversaw all of his properties, was ruled in violation of antitrust laws in 1904 and ordered dissolved by the US Supreme Court. Other business ventures included banking and mining.

Hillary, Sir Edmund (Percival) (1919–) New Zealand mountaineer and explorer. In 1953 he and *Tenzing Norgay were the first to reach the summit of Mount Everest, for which achievement he was knighted. In 1958–59 he participated in an Antarctic expedition, preparing the way for *Fuchs' crossing of Antarctica.

Hillel (1st century BC) Jewish teacher, lawyer, and biblical scholar. Many of his teachings subsequently became authoritative in rabbinic Judaism. His tolerant character and views are often contrasted with those of his contemporary Shammai.

Hilliard, Nicholas (1547–1619) English portrait miniaturist. He became court painter to Elizabeth I and James I. His high reputation among his contemporaries led many prominent Elizabethans to have their portraits done by him. In his *Treatise on the Art of Limning* (c. 1600), he describes his style and technique of painting miniatures. The elegance and symbolism of his *Unknown Man Against a Background of Flames* is typical of his best work.

hill mynah A glossy black songbird, *Graculus religiosa*, native to India and the East Indies. 10–15 in (25–37 cm) long, it has a yellow bill and yellow wattles on the neck and beneath the eyes. It is a popular cagebird with a remarkable ability to mimic human speech. Family: *Sturnidae* (starlings). *See also* mynah.

Hilo 19 43N 155 05W A city in SE Hawaii on E Hawaii Island. The tourist industry is important; from the city visitors travel to Hawaii Volcanoes National Park to the SW. The city services and ships the fruits and flowers grown on the island. Population (1980): 35,269.

Hilton, James (1900–54) British novelist. His two most popular novels are *Lost Horizon* (1933), set in the Tibetan monastery of Shangri-La, and *Goodbye, Mr Chips* (1934). From 1935 he worked as a scriptwriter in Hollywood, where he died.

Hilversum 52 14N 5 10E A city in the central Netherlands, in North Holland province. It is a summer resort and commuter town for Amsterdam and is the country's main radio and television broadcasting center. Population (1977 est): 93,951.

Himachal Pradesh A state in NW India, in the W Himalayas beside Tibet's border. Long part of the *Punjab, it was formed by the combination of various hill states (1948). Most of the inhabitants are Pahari-speaking Hindus who farm grains, potatoes, maize, and livestock. The forests yield timber and bamboo. Himachal Pradesh has enormous hydroelectric potential, as yet undeveloped. Area: 21,490 sq mi (55,673 sq km). Population (1971): 3,460,434. Capital: Simla.

Himalayas A vast mountain system, the highest in the world, structurally the southern edge of the great plateau of central Asia. They extend about 1550 mi (2400 km) along the N Indian border in a W–E arc, 125–250 mi (200–400 km) wide, reaching 29,028 ft (8848 m) at Mount *Everest.

Himeji 34 50N 134 40E A city in Japan, in SW Honshu. It developed around its famous 16th-century castle, one of the few remaining castles in Japan. Its industries include textiles and steel. Population (1976 est): 439,064.

Himmler, Heinrich (1900–45) German Nazi politician, infamous for his direction of the *SS. He joined the Nazi Party in 1925 and became head of the SS in 1929. From 1936 he also directed the Gestapo and supervised the extermination of Jews in E Europe. After the Nazi collapse he was captured by the Allies and committed suicide.

Hims. *See* Homs.

Hincmar of Reims (c. 806–82) French theologian, archbishop of Reims (845–82). He came into conflict with the emperor Lothair I and successive popes over the extent of his jurisdiction. He also engaged in controversy with the Benedictine monk Gottschalk (d. 868) over the doctrine of predestination.

Hindemith, Paul (1895–1963) German composer and viola player. From the age of 11 he supported himself by playing in dance halls and later studied in Frankfurt am Main, where he led the opera orchestra (1915–23). He also played the viola in the Amar Quartet. In 1927 he began teaching in Berlin. His music was banned by the Nazis in 1933; he moved to Turkey and in 1939 went to the US, becoming an American citizen. His early works were highly dissonant; he later evolved his own system of tonal harmony. Many of his compositions are neoclassical in character (*see* neoclassicism); they include the operas *Cardillac* (1926) and *Mathis der Maler* (1938), the ballet *Nobilissima Visione* (1938), many concertos, instrumental sonatas, and much *Gebrauchsmusik* (German: utility music).

Hindenburg, Paul von Beneckendorff und von (1847–1934) German general, who was recalled from retirement at the outbreak of World War I and with *Ludendorff controlled Germany after the great victory at *Tannenberg (1914). In 1916 Hindenburg became commander in chief and directed the German retreat to the **Hindenburg line** (fortified defense on the Western Front). After Germany's defeat he again retired but became president in 1925. Re-elected in 1932, he was forced to appoint Hitler as chancellor early in 1933.

Hindi The national language of India and the most widely spoken, having approximately 134 million speakers. It is an *Indo-Aryan language, show-

ing strong *Sanskrit influence in its written form but with a much simpler grammar. The standard form, written in Devanagari script, is based on the Khari Boli dialect of Delhi. This belongs to the western dialect division from which *Urdu also developed.

Hinduism The religious beliefs and institutions of about 400 million inhabitants of India and parts of neighboring countries. Hinduism is not a religion with a formal creed, but the complex result of about 5000 years of continuous cultural development. It includes a number of extremely diverse traditional beliefs and practices and over the centuries it has influenced and been influenced by younger religions, including Buddhism, Jainism, Christianity, Islam, and Sikhism. One of its central concepts is that the necessary result of one's actions in life leads to *reincarnation at a higher or lower level of life (*see* karma), a belief that has given rise both to the system of *castes and to a deep respect for all forms of life (*see* ahimsa). The goal of the religion is to find a release from the cycle of rebirth and to return to the ultimate unchanging reality, *Brahman. Release may be sought through good works, devotion to a particular god, such as the popular deity *Krishna, or through various types of meditation and asceticism (*see* samadhi; yoga). The principle gods are Brahma, Vishnu, and Shiva, together known as the *Trimurti; the last two are especially venerated by the two major sects, the Vaishnavas and the Shaivas. These and all the innumerable lesser gods and spirits are seen by many Hindus as manifestations of one reality (Brahman). Popular devotion consists mainly of temple worship and the celebration of numerous festivals. Hinduism originated in early *animism and *totemism (before 2750 BC) and developed a sacrificial worship of a pantheon of nature gods, such as *Indra, during the period of the *Vedas (c. 1500–500 BC). *Brahmanism was the dominant form of Hinduism in the 6th century BC, when Buddhism and Jainism were established in reaction to it. The great Hindu texts, the *Mahabharata and the *Ramayana, were composed at this time. Vishnu and Shiva became the prominent deities in the medieval period (after 800 AD). New schools have continued to emerge in recent times, most of them concerned with universalizing Hindu thought. *See also* Arya samaj; Brahmo samaj; Ramakrishna; Vedanta; Vivekananda.

Hindu Kush A mountain range in central Asia, extending about 500 mi (800 km) W from the Pamirs to the Koh-i-Baba Mountains of central Afghanistan. Its highest peak is Tirich Mir, at 25,236 ft (7692 m).

Hindustani An *Indo-Aryan language that originated in the dialect of the Delhi district. The Moguls and the British promoted its use as a lingua franca throughout India. *Urdu and *Hindi are the literary forms developed from it.

Hines, Earl (Fatha) (1905–83) US jazz pianist and songwriter, who trained as a concert pianist but formed his own jazz band in 1928. He worked with Louis Armstrong from 1948–51 and became well known for his complex and virtuosic piano playing. He wrote the songs "The Earl" and "I Got It Bad."

hinny The sterile offspring of a female ass and a male horse. Smaller than a *mule, hinnies are used as pack animals, especially in hot climates, but are less common than mules.

Hinshelwood, Sir Cyril Norman (1897–1967) British chemist, who became professor at Oxford University in 1937. He pioneered the investigation of reaction kinetics and discovered several chain reaction mechanisms. He shared the Nobel Prize with N. N. Semyonov in 1956. He was knighted in 1948.

hip The part of the body where the legs are joined to the trunk. The skeleton of the hip consists of the *pelvis and the part of the spine (the sacrum) to which it is attached. The hip joint—the articulation between the pelvis and femur (thigh bone)—is a common site for arthritis: in severe cases the whole joint may be replaced by an artificial one or pins or other devices may be inserted into the damaged parts.

Hipparchus (c. 190–c. 120 BC) Greek astronomer, born in Nicaea. He produced the first accurate map of over 1000 stars, indicating their positions by means of latitude and longitude. He also discovered the precession of the equinoxes and accurately measured the distance to the moon by parallax. In mathematics he invented trigonometry by constructing a table of the ratios of the sides of right-angle triangles.

Hipparion An extinct *horse that lived in the Pliocene epoch (about seven million years ago). It was slender and fast-running, about the size of a modern pony, and lived on open plains. Its foot had a distinct hoof, the remaining toes being small and not touching the ground. *See also* eohippus.

Hippeastrum A genus of herbaceous plants (60 species), native to tropical and subtropical America and cultivated as ornamental garden and pot plants. They have large bulbs (about 10 cm in diameter), broad straight-sided leaves, and a stout flower stem terminating in a cluster of white, pink, or red flowers, each 10 cm across. The genus includes the Barbados lily (*H. equestre*), with scarlet flowers. Family: *Amaryllidaceae*.

Hippocrates (c. 460–c. 377 BC) Greek physician and founder of the Hippocratic school of medicine, which greatly influenced medical science until the 18th century. Hippocrates seems to have been a prominent physician, who traveled widely in Greece and Asia Minor. His followers believed that health was governed by the balance of four body fluids, or humors: phlegm, blood, black bile, and yellow bile. The Hippocratic Collection of 60 or so medical works is ascribed to various authors and the Hippocratic Oath, taken by medical students, was probably not written by Hippocrates.

Hippolytus In Greek legend, the bastard son of *Theseus and Hippolyta, Queen of the Amazons. A devotee of *Artemis, his dedication to chastity led him to reject the advances of Theseus's wife *Phaedra, and he was destroyed by a bull from the sea sent by Poseidon.

hippopotamus A large hoofed mammal, *Hippopotamus amphibius*, of tropical Africa. About 59 in (150 cm) high at the shoulder and weighing around 3.5 tons, hippos have virtually naked dark-brown skin and continuously growing tusks up to 24 in (60 cm) long. They spend the day in rivers or waterholes, emerging at night to graze on surrounding pasture. Herds usually number 10–15 individuals. Hippos are highly territorial, marking the boundaries of their grazing ground with piles of dung. Family: *Hippopotamidae*. *See also* pygmy hippopotamus.

Hirabayashi v. United States (1943) US Supreme Court decision that upheld temporary restrictions placed on all persons of Japanese descent living in the US during World War II. The suit, brought by an American of Japanese ancestry, claimed the restrictions and curfews violated the 5th Amendment.

Hirohito (1901–) Emperor of Japan (1926–), having previously been regent for five years after his father Yoshihito (1879–1926) had been declared insane. He married (1924) Princess Nagako Kuai. Ruling as divine emperor until Japan's defeat in World War II, he became no more than a constitutional monarch under the 1946 constitution (introduced under US pressure). The author of several books on marine biology, he is believed to have played a reluctant role in Japan's prewar expansionist aspirations.

Hiroshige (Ando Tokitaro; 1797–1858) Japanese color-print artist of the □Ukiyo-e movement. Trained under another Ukiyo-e master, Toyohiro (1774–1829), Hiroshige first specialized in prints of women. From about 1830 he turned to landscapes, which he often depicted in snow, rain, or moonlight. His best-known print series is *Fifty-Three Stages of the Tokaido Highway* (1833).

Hiroshima 34 23N 132 27E A city in Japan, in SW Honshu on the delta of the Ota River. A former military base and important seaport, it was largely destroyed (August 6, 1945) by the first atomic bomb to be used in warfare; over 130,000 people were killed or injured. Many leading architects helped design the rapid rebuilding of the city and it is now a major industrial center. An international conference is held here annually to oppose nuclear weapons. Its university was established in 1949. Population (1976 est): 842,095.

Hispaniola The second largest West Indian island, in the Greater Antilles. It is politically divided between the *Dominican Republic and the Republic of *Haiti. Area: 29,418 sq mi (18,703 sq km).

histamine An amine, derived from the amino acid histidine, that is released from body tissues after injury or in an allergic reaction, such as asthma or hay fever. It dilates blood vessels, producing inflammation; contracts smooth muscle, which in the lungs leads to breathing difficulties; and stimulates the secretion of gastric juice. Its effects can be counteracted with *antihistamine drugs.

histology The study of *tissues. Originally histology was limited to the study of tissues by light microscopy, but the development of such techniques as electron microscopy, immunofluorescence, and autoradiography has enabled the details of subcellular structure to be revealed. *See also* cytology.

history The story of the past. The student of history discovers, examines, and interprets the records of past human societies. Records of events are found in the inscriptions of the ancient Egyptians but history as a literary activity is generally regarded as beginning with the ancient Greeks, among whom *Herodotus, *Thucydides, and *Xenophon were outstanding. The desire of ancient historians for accuracy was sometimes subordinated to their purely literary ambitions and the Romans (notably *Sallust, *Cicero, *Livy, and *Tacitus) were also concerned to glorify Rome. Early Christian history writing (historiography) was influenced by Jewish historians, such as *Josephus, and Christian preconceptions and subject matter continued

to influence the writing of history throughout the middle ages. Medieval historiography consisted largely of chronicles, such as those of *Bede, Matthew *Paris, and Jean *Froissart. The later middle ages were influenced by Byzantine historians, including *Anna Comnena, and by such Arabs as *Ibn Khaldun and al-*Tabari. The classical interests of early Renaissance scholars (*see* humanism) led to a new concern for textual criticism, which led to the outstanding work of *Machiavelli and *Guicciardini in the early 16th century. Their critical approach to sources was continued by 17th-century historians but the 18th-century Enlightenment enlarged the interests of historians to include a more fundamental study of the pattern of change in human societies. This concern is reflected in the work of the 18th-century British historian Edward Gibbon, who tried to show that the history of mankind is one of continuous progress. In the 19th century, under the influence of the German school of historians, which included von *Ranke and *Mommsen, history was established as an academic discipline in the universities. The scope of historiography has greatly widened in the 20th century under the influence of sociology, anthropology, and psychiatry, and new techniques, such as the use of computers to analyze statistics, have been introduced.

Hitachi 36 35N 140 40E A city in Japan, in E Honshu on the Pacific Ocean. Copper has been mined here since 1591 and the city is Japan's leading producer of electrical equipment. Population (1976 est): 203,626.

ALFRED HITCHCOCK

Hitchcock, Sir Alfred (1899–1980) British movie director. He worked almost exclusively in Hollywood from 1940. He specialized in sophisticated thrillers, using calculated cinematic effects to create an atmosphere of tension and suspense. His technique was appreciated by and influenced directors of the *New Wave. His movies include *The Thirty-Nine Steps* (1935), *Rebecca* (1940), *Notorious* (1946), *Strangers on a Train* (1951), *To Catch a Thief* (1953), *Dial M for Murder* (1954), *Rear Window* (1954), *The Man Who Knew Too Much* (1956), *Psycho* (1960), and *The Birds* (1963).

Hitler, Adolf (1889–1945) German dictator. Born in Austria, the son of a customs officer, he fought in World War I, rising to the rank of lance corporal and winning the Iron Cross. After several years of poverty in Vienna and Munich, often working as a housepainter, he joined (1919) the German Workers' Party, which was renamed the National Socialist (abbreviated to *Nazi) Party in 1920. He became its president in 1921 and two years later staged an abortive coup—the Munich Putsch—against the Bavarian Government. During a brief imprisonment he wrote most of *Mein Kampf* (*My Struggle*), setting out his political philosophy, based on a notion of the innate superiority of the Aryan race, the culpability of the Jews for Germany's defeat in World War I, and a violent anticommunism. In the economic crisis of the late 1920s and early 1930s Hitler's extraordinary powers of oratory and his propaganda machine (headed by *Goebbels) brought the Nazis increasing support, especially from German industrialists, and in 1932 they won a majority of the seats in the Reichstag. In 1933, aided by the machinations of von *Papen, Hitler was offered the chancellorship by *Hindenburg, the German president. The *Reichstag fire enabled him to discredit the opposition and to acquire the far-reaching dictatorial powers he sought; following Hindenburg's death in 1934 he assumed the title of Führer (leader). He proceeded to crush his opponents, institute his fanatical persecution of the Jews by the establishment of *concentration camps, and launch a massive rearmament program in preparation for the wars of conquest that he planned for the Third Reich. He lent his support to Mussolini in Italy and Franco in Spain, precipitating *World War II by invading Austria (1938) and then Czechoslovakia and Poland (1939). Military reverses in 1943 led to Stauffenberg's unsuccessful attempt (1944) to assassinate Hitler, but as the Third Reich collapsed in the face of Allied victory the Führer committed suicide with Eva *Braun (whom he had married shortly before) in the bunker of the chancellory in Berlin. How Hitler was able, unchecked for over a decade, to implement policies of an unparalleled atrociousness is a question that continues to plague mankind.

Hittites An *Indo-European people who appeared in Anatolia around the beginnning of the second millennium BC. By 1340 BC they had emerged as a major power, with their capital at *Hattusas (or Boğazköy) from which they conquered much of Anatolia and also Syria (see Carchemish). In their polytheistic religion, their king was believed to be the representative of god on earth and became a god himself on death. The society was feudal in organization and also upheld the institution of slavery. Their language is extinct, but is known from cuneiform tablets and inscriptions (see Indo-Hittite languages).

hives. See urticaria.

Hoare-Laval Pact. See Laval, Pierre.

hoatzin A primitive bird, Opisthocomus hoazin, that occurs in tropical South American swamps. It is 25.5 in (65 cm) long and has a small head with a wispy crest and a long tail. Its plumage is streaked brown with yellowish underparts and it feeds chiefly on flowers and fruit. It is the only member of its family (Opisthocomidae). Order: Galliformes (pheasants, turkeys, etc.).

Hobart 42 54S 147 18E A city in Australia, the capital and chief port of Tasmania on the Derwent River estuary. It has an excellent natural harbor with small tidal changes. Industries include zinc refining and food processing; the chief exports are apples, wool, timber, and dairy produce. The University of Tasmania was established here in 1890. Population (1976): 131,524.

Hobbema, Meindert (1638–1709) Dutch landscape painter, born in Amsterdam. He often sketched with *Ruisdael but, unlike him, Hobbema specialized in peaceful woodland and rural scenes with watermills. Through his marriage (1668) he gained a minor post in the local excise department but continued with his painting, producing in this period perhaps his best work, The Avenue, Middelharnis (1689; National Gallery, London).

Hobbes, Thomas (1588–1679) English political philosopher. Hobbes was a vigorous proponent of scientific *materialism, particularly with regard to human nature. His interests lay in mathematics, geography, and the classics until the breakdown of English political and social order in the 1640s inspired him to devise his own political theory. Leviathan (1651) argues that because people are inherently selfish they need to be ruled by an absolute sovereign, whose function is to enforce public order. Contemporary theories of natural rights, and the civil rights thought to derive from them, were anathema to him. His theories made him a loyalist both to the English monarchy and, during the Interregnum, to its parliamentary opponents.

hobby A *falcon, Falco subbuteo, occurring in open regions of Eurasia and NW Africa. It is 13 in (33 cm) long and has a dark-gray back, whitish underparts streaked with black, and red "trousers." It feeds on large insects and small birds caught in flight.

Hochhuth, Rolf (1933–) Left-wing Swiss dramatist, who writes in German. His controversial documentary plays include The Representative (1962), criticizing the attitude of Pius XII to the Nazi persecution of the Jews, and The Soldiers (1966), accusing Winston *Churchill of complicity in the death of the Polish general Sikorski. His novel German Love Story (1980) analyzes the extent of the involvement of the German people in Nazi atrocities.

Ho Chi Minh (Nguyen That Thanh; 1890–1969) Vietnamese statesman, who led Vietnam in its struggle for independence from the French. As a young man he lived in England (1915–17) and then in France (1917–23), where in 1920 he joined the French Communist Party. In 1924 he went to communist-controlled Canton, where he formed the Association of Young

Vietnamese Revolutionaries (Thanh Nien), the forerunner of the Indochinese Communist Party (1930). Returning to Vietnam in 1941, following the French defeat by the Germans in World War II, he formed the *Viet Minh, which waged the long and ultimately victorious colonial war against the French (1945–54; see Indochina). According to the Geneva Accords, which Ho Chi Minh attended, Vietnam was divided on either side of the 17th parallel into North Vietnam, of which Ho became president, and South Vietnam. In 1959 he extended support to the *Viet Cong guerrilla movement in the South (see also Vietnam War) with the aim of Vietnamese unification, which was achieved after his death.

Ho Chi Minh City (name until 1976: Saigon) 10 46N 106 43E A city in S Vietnam, on the Saigon River. The University of Saigon (now Ho Chi Minh City) was established in 1917. It is the major commercial and industrial center of the S, with shipbuilding, metalworking, textile, and chemical industries. History: an ancient Khmer town, it was the capital of *Cochinchina and then of French Indochina (1887–1902). During the *Vietnam War, as the capital of South Vietnam, US presence brought an economic boom but left problems of prostitution, crime, and drug addiction. Population (1973 est): 1,825,297.

Hockney, David (1937–) British painter. After studying at the Royal College of Art (1959–62), he traveled widely in the US, where he developed his realistic but witty style, his favorite subjects being figure studies and aquatic themes. He has also designed stage sets and illustrated books.

Hodeida (or Hudaydah) 14 50N 42 58E A city in North Yemen, on the Red Sea coast. It is the country's principal port, exporting cotton and mocha coffee. Population (1970 est): 90,000.

Hodgkin, Alan Lloyd (1914–) British physiologist, who discovered the chemical changes associated with the propagation of a nerve impulse (see action potential) along a nerve fiber. He wrote Conduction of the Nervous Impulse (1964) and shared a Nobel Prize (1963) with A. F. Huxley (his colleague) and Sir John Eccles.

Hodgkin, Dorothy Mary Crowfoot (1910–) British biochemist, who determined the structure of several complex molecules by means of *X-ray diffraction. She helped to determine the structure of penicillin (in the 1940s) and of vitamin B_{12} (in the early 1950s). She was awarded the Nobel Prize in 1964.

Hodgkin, Thomas (1798–1866) British physician, who described the disease of the lymphatic system now known as **Hodgkin's disease** (see lymphoma). Hodgkin made a considerable contribution to the pathology of diseases.

Hofei. See Hefei.

Hoffa, James Riddle (1913–?75) US labor leader. He headed a local Teamsters union in the Midwest during the union movement of the 1930s and by 1952 was vice president of the International Teamsters. He served as president (1957–71) during which time he served almost 5 years in prison (1967–71) for jury and pension fund tampering. He disappeared in 1975, presumed murdered because of his attempts to regain the Teamsters' presidency.

Hoffman, Dustin (1937–) US movie actor. He made his reputation in the movies The Graduate (1967) and Midnight Cowboy (1969). In 1980 he was awarded an Oscar for his performance as a divorced man bringing up his son in Kramer vs Kramer. Other movies include Lenny (1974), in which he played comedian Lenny Bruce, and Tootsie (1982), in which he impersonated a woman.

Hofmann, Joseph Casimir (1876–1957) Polish-born pianist. A performer from the age of six, he was a pupil of Anton Rubinstein. He also composed under the name "Michael Dvorsky." He toured extensively and became a US citizen in 1926.

Hofmannsthal, Hugo von (1874–1929) Austrian poet and dramatist. In 1901, after studying law and philology, he devoted himself to writing. His influential essay "The Letter of Lord Chandos" (1902), expressing his loss of confidence in language, divides the lyrical aestheticism of his short early plays from the social concern of his later ones, such as Der Turm (1925). He was librettist for several Richard *Strauss operas, including Der Rosenkavalier (1911) and Ariadne auf Naxos (1912). He was a co-founder of the Salzburg Festival in 1920.

Hofmeister, Wilhelm Friedrich Benedict (1824–77) German botanist, who pioneered the science of comparative plant morphology. His major work established the relationship between the cryptogams (algae, mosses, ferns, etc.), the gymnosperms (e.g. conifers), and the angiosperms (flowering plants). Hofmeister also discovered that regular alternation between sexual and asexual generations occurs in mosses, ferns, and seed plants.

Hogan, Ben (William Benjamin H.; 1912–) US professional golfer, most of whose major successes, including winning the Masters Tournament in 1951 and 1953, came after a car accident that was expected to cripple him (1949).

WILLIAM HOGARTH   *The British painter and engraver's* Self-Portrait with His Pug.

Hogarth, William (1697–1764) British painter and engraver. He studied under a silverplate engraver before establishing his reputation with the paintings and engravings of *A Harlot's Progress* (1731–32). He excelled in moralizing social satires in such narrative series as *A Rake's Progress, Industry and Idleness, Gin Lane,* and the paintings of *Marriage à la Mode.* As a portraitist the naturalism and vivacity of *Captain Coram* and *Hogarth's Servants* were influential, although unpopular with his contemporaries. His artistic theories are expressed in his treatise *The Analysis of Beauty* (1753).

hogfish A beautifully colored tropical marine fish belonging to a genus (*Bodianus*) of *wrasses. They change color while growing and are very popular in aquaria.

Hoggar Mountains. *See* Ahaggar Mountains.

hogweed A biennial herb, *Heracleum sphondylium*, also called cow parsnip, native to Eurasia and N Africa and introduced to North America. Up to 7 ft (2 m) high, it has hollow ridged stems, divided leaves, and umbrella-like clusters of white or pinkish flowers. The giant hogweed (*H. mantegazzianum*) may reach a height of 11 ft (3.5 m) and is grown as an ornamental. Family: *Umbelliferae*.

Hohenlinden, Battle of (December 3, 1800) The battle in the Napoleonic Wars in which the French under Jean Victor *Moreau defeated the Austrians. It was fought 16 mi (31 km) E of Munich. The French victory brought the collapse of the second coalition against Napoleon. *See* Revolutionary and Napoleonic Wars.

Hohenlohe-Schillingsfürst, Chlodwig Karl Viktor, Fürst zu (1819–1901) German statesman; chancellor (1894–1900). He came to prominence during the 1860s as a vigorous supporter of Bismarck's policy of German unification. He served as ambassador to Paris (1874–78) and as governor of Alsace-Lorraine (1885–94) before becoming chancellor, when he attempted to exercise a moderating influence on William II. He was succeeded by his protégé Bernhard von Bülow.

Hohenstaufen A German dynasty, founded by Frederick, Duke of Swabia (d. 1105), that ruled the Holy Roman Empire from 1138 to 1254. *Conrad III was the first Hohenstaufen emperor and of his successors the most important were *Frederick (I) Barbarossa and *Frederick II. Frequently in conflict with Italian city states and the papacy, the dynasty was destroyed by its defeat at Tagliacozzo by a papal alliance (1268).

Hohenzollern A dynasty, originating in Swabia, that ruled *Brandenburg, then *Prussia, and later Germany. First prominent in the late 12th century, the Hohenzollerns became Electors of Brandenburg in the 15th century. During the next 300 years they acquired other territories, including Prussia, of which *Frederick I became king in 1701. From 1871 they ruled the German Empire until its collapse in 1918.

Hohhot (*or* Huhehot) 40 49N 111 37E A city in NE China, the capital of Inner Mongolia AR. An old frontier trading town, its industry was developed after 1949. The university was established in 1957. Population (1957 est): 314,000.

Hojo Hereditary holders of the regency for the military overlordship (*see* shogun) of Japan between 1204 and 1333. Hojo Tokimasa (1138–1215) became the first regent in 1204 although he had held actual power from the death (1199) of his son-in-law, the first shogun *Minamoto Yoritomo. The Hojo regents were notable for their codification of feudal law, their encouragement of Zen Buddhism, and their repulse of the Mongols (1274, 1281). Their power was destroyed in 1333 by a combination of other feudal lords and the emperor *Daigo II.

Hokan languages An American Indian language group spoken mainly in the NW of the US and in California. Some Hokan languages are found in Mexico, including the most widely spoken, Tlapanccan and Tquistlatecan. The Yuman subdivision found in Colorado and California also has a comparatively large number of speakers. The Mohave language is a member of this subgroup.

Hokkaido (former name: Yezo) The second largest and northernmost of the four main islands of Japan, separated from Honshu by the Tsugaru Strait and from the Soviet island of Sakhalin by La Perouse Strait. Mountainous, volcanic, and forested, with a relatively cool climate, it is popular for winter sports. It has a sizable aboriginal population and the N is largely uninhabited. Main industries are coalmining, agriculture, and fishing. *History*: the Japanese began to settle on the island in the 16th century but did not develop it seriously until after 1868. It became administratively autonomous in 1885. Area: 78,508 sq 30,312 sq mi (km). Population (1970): 5,184,287. Capital: Sapporo.

Hokusai (Katsushika H.; 1760–1849) Japanese painter and book illustrator, the most famous *ukiyo-e designer of color prints. He began as a wood engraver, becoming in 1778 a pupil of the painter and printmaker Shunsho (1726–92). From the 1790s he illustrated historical novels, verse anthologies, etc., and designed greeting and announcement cards. His early prints were chiefly of women and actors but he is best known for his later landscapes, which deeply influenced the impressionists and postimpressionists. His most famous works include his *Views of Mount Fuji* (1835) and his collection of sketchbooks, the *Hokusai Manga*, published from 1814 onward.

Holbein the Younger, Hans (c. 1497–1543) German painter, born in Augsburg. In 1515 he settled in Basle, where he designed woodcuts of the *Dance of Death*. Through his friend Erasmus he obtained the patronage of Sir Thomas More in England (1526–28). Settling in England in 1532, he painted portraits of merchants before becoming court painter and designer to Henry VIII (1536). His portrait of Henry VIII in a wall painting (destroyed) for Whitehall Palace became the prototype for other paintings of the king. He was also commissioned to paint Henry's prospective wives, *Christina, Duchess of Milan* (National Gallery, London) and *Anne of Cleves* (Louvre) and established a thriving portrait-painting business, e.g. *The Ambassadors* (National Gallery, London). Many of the preparatory drawings for his English portraits are in the Royal Collection, Windsor. Holbein died of the plague. His father **Hans Holbein the Elder** (c. 1465–1524) was also a painter, whose major work is the *S Sebastian Altar* (Alte Pinakothek, Munich).

Hölderlin, (Johann Christian) Friedrich (1770–1843) German poet. Trained as a Lutheran minister, he found Christianity incompatible with his enthusiasm for Greek mythology. While working as a private tutor, he fell in love with his employer's wife, who is portrayed in his novel *Hyperion* (1797–99). After her death in 1802 his life was dominated by his schizophrenia, from which he never recovered. His great lyrical talent was unrecognized until the 20th century, when a comprehensive edition of his poetry was published.

hole. *See* semiconductors.

Holguín 20 54N 76 15W A city in E Cuba. It is an important commercial center; the chief exports through its port Gilbara (to the NE) are sugar and tobacco. Population (1975 est): 151,938.

BILLIE HOLIDAY

Holiday, Billie (Eleanor Gough McKay; 1915–59) US jazz singer, known as "Lady Day." She was discovered in Harlem by Benny Goodman and made her first recording in 1933. She subsequently sang with the bands of Count Basie and Artie Shaw. She was best known for singing torch songs, such as "*My Man*," "*Lover Man*," and "*Mean to Me*." Addiction to heroin caused her death.

Holland The low-lying NW region of the Netherlands, now comprising the provinces of *North Holland and *South Holland. A county of the Holy Roman Empire from the 12th century, Holland came under Burgundy in the 15th century and then (1500) under the Habsburgs. Prominent in the 16th-century *Revolt of the Netherlands against Spanish Habsburg rule, Holland became the chief province of the independent United Provinces of the Netherlands. When the kingdom of the *Netherlands was established in 1814, Holland became an administrative province, and its importance diminished. Nevertheless the whole country is still commonly called Holland.

Holland, Sir Sidney (George) (1893–1961) New Zealand statesman; National Party prime minister (1949–57). His government was repressive in industrial disputes and unable to control inflation. His party was defeated shortly after his retirement in 1957.

holly A tree or shrub of the widely distributed genus *Ilex* (300 species). The evergreen English holly (*I. aquifolium*) grows to a height of 50 ft (15 m) and has spiny lustrous dark-green leaves and small white male and female flowers growing on separate trees: the female flowers develop into red berries. It is widely cultivated for hedging and used for Christmas decorations. Family: *Aquifoliaceae*. See also maté.

hollyhock A perennial herb, *Althaea rosea*, native to China but widely cultivated as a garden flower (garden hollyhocks are usually treated as biennials). It grows to a height of 10 ft (3 m) and bears tall spikes of large white, yellow, or red flowers. Family: *Malvaceae*.

holly oak See holm oak.

Hollywood 26 01N 80 09W A NW suburb of Los Angeles, in California. Founded in the 1880s, it has been the center of the US film industry since 1911.

Hollywood 26 00N 80 09W A city in SE Florida, N of Miami, on the Atlantic Ocean. Developed as a winter resort in the 1920s, it has building materials, electronic equipment, and furniture industries. Population (1980): 121,323.

Holmes, Oliver Wendell (1809–94) US essayist and poet. Trained as a physician, Holmes became dean of the Harvard Medical School and wrote several important medical works. In addition to the acclaim he received for his scientific writings, Holmes was recognized for his literary talents. Among his best-known poems are "Old Ironsides" (1830) and "The Chambered Nautilus" (1858). He also published several collections of conversational essays, including *The Autocrat of the Breakfast Table* (1857)

and *Over the Teacups* (1891). His son **Oliver Wendell Holmes Jr.** (1841–1935) was a prominent jurist who became professor of law at Harvard in 1882. In 1902, after service as chief justice of the Massachusetts Supreme Court, the younger Holmes was nominated by President Theodore *Roosevelt to become an associate justice of the US Supreme Court. In that position Holmes distinguished himself as a defender of individual rights, often dissenting from the majority opinions of his colleagues. In particular, he opposed the use of the 14th Amendment to the *Constitution by the federal government to prohibit state wage and hour standards as in the case of *Lochner* v. *NY* (1905). Holmes resigned from the Supreme Court in 1932.

OLIVER WENDELL HOLMES, JR. *Supreme Court justice, "The Great Dissenter," who championed civil rights.*

holmium (Ho) A metallic lanthanide element, discovered in 1879 by P. T. Cleve (1840–1905) and named for his native city, Stockholm. Holmium occurs in rare-earth minerals, such as monazite ($CePO_4$). It forms an oxide (Ho_2O_3) and halides (HoX_3), but has few uses. At no 67; at wt 164.9304; mp 2688°F (1474°C); bp 4888°F (2695°C).

holm oak An evergreen *oak tree, *Quercus ilex*, also called holly oak, native to S Europe and cultivated for ornament and for its durable wood. Growing to a height of 100 ft (30 m), it has a broad dense crown and the leaves of young trees resemble holly leaves.

holocaust The extermination of European *Jews by the Nazis (1939–45). Some six million Jews from many countries, approximately two-thirds of European Jewry, were killed in Auschwitz and other *concentration camps. The holocaust has raised serious theological problems and questions about the nature of European civilization.

Holocene epoch The present, or Recent, epoch in *geological time, including the last 10,000 years from the end of the Pleistocene. Since it follows all the main glacial episodes it is sometimes called the Postglacial, although some authorities consider it to be only an interglacial phase of the Pleistocene. At the beginning of the Holocene the general rise in sea level resulting from the melting of the ice isolated Britain from the rest of the Continent of Europe.

holography A method of producing a stereoscopic image without using a camera. A monochromatic beam of *coherent radiation from a laser is split into two using a semitransparent mirror; one beam falls directly onto a photographic film or plate and the other is reflected by the subject onto the film. The two beams form *interference patterns on the film, which is called a hologram. To reconstruct the image, light of the same wavelength from a

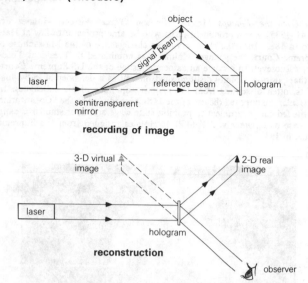

recording of image

reconstruction

HOLOGRAPHY *A three-dimensional image formed by two beams of light is recorded as an interference pattern on a single plate. The two images, giving a 3-D effect, are reconstructed by shining two similar beams through the hologram.*

laser is shone onto the hologram. The interference pattern on the hologram diffracts the beam and splits it into two parts. One part gives a real two-dimensional image and the other a virtual three-dimensional image. The theory of holography was suggested by Denis *Gabor in 1947 but could not be put into practice until the laser was invented 16 years later.

Holst, Gustav (Theodore) (1874–1934) British composer. His interest in oriental philosophy inspired the chamber opera *Savitri* (1908) and other works. Among his most famous compositions are the choral work *The Hymn of Jesus* (1917), the tone poem *Egdon Heath* (1927), and the orchestral suite *The Planets* (1914–16).

Holt, Harold (Edward) (1908–67) Australian statesman; Liberal prime minister from 1966 until his death, apparently by drowning. His administration relaxed immigration and citizenship laws and supported involvement in the Vietnam War.

Holy Grail In medieval legend and romance, a vessel or dish having supernatural power. Originally the grail may have had some significance in pre-Christian Celtic mythology; but by the 12th century, in romances by *Chrétien de Troyes and Robert de Boron's *Joseph d'Arimathie*, it was associated with the chalice used by Christ at the Last Supper and later given to *Joseph of Arimathea, who received the blood of Christ in it at the crucifixion. Chrétien had combined the grail legend with the *Arthurian legend, and the knightly quest for the Holy Grail, undertaken by Percival, Galahad, and other Knights of the Round Table, is a dominant theme in many Arthurian romances. According to a passage in William of Malmesbury, Joseph brought the Holy Grail to Glastonbury, where he also allegedly built the first church in England.

Holy Island (*or* Lindisfarne) 55 41N 1 48W An island, in NE England off the NE coast of Northumberland. Its monastery was founded by St Aidan (635 AD); St Cuthbert was a bishop here (685–87).

Holy Lance The lance said to have pierced Christ's side at the crucifixion. This relic was discovered (1098) after a visionary revelation to a peasant, Peter Bartholomew, at the siege of Antioch during the first *Crusade. Accepted as genuine by most, but not all, of the Crusaders, its discovery raised morale and inspired the capture of Antioch from the Muslims.

Holy League Any of several alliances formed in the 15th, 16th, and 17th centuries usually for the furtherance of papal or Roman Catholic interests. The best known are those formed against the French invasion of Italy (1494) and against the Huguenots in the French *Wars of Religion (1576).

Holyoake, Sir Keith Jacka (1904–83) New Zealand statesman; National Party prime minister (1957, 1960–72). He entered parliament in 1932, became deputy leader of the National Party in 1947, and was deputy prime minister and minister for agriculture from 1949 until Sir Sidney

Holland's resignation in 1957. He was governor general of New Zealand (1977–80).

Holy of Holies The central shrine of the Jewish *tabernacle (Exodus 25–31, 35–40) and later of the *Temple of Jerusalem. Originally it contained the Ark of the Covenant (the receptacle of the two tablets of the law) and other cultic objects. In the second Temple it was apparently empty. The *high priest entered it once a year, on *Yom Kippur, to make atonement for the people.

holy orders In Christian Churches, specifically those accepting *episcopacy, the ranks of bishop, priest, etc., conferred by a bishop. They are traditionally divided into major and minor orders, the former being the ranks of bishop, priest, deacon, and (in the Roman Church) subdeacon. In the Roman Catholic Church, there are four minor orders: porters (or doorkeepers), lectors (or readers), exorcists, and acolytes. Holy orders are considered a *sacrament by the Orthodox and Roman Catholic Churches; they are also held to impose an "indelible character" on the recipient, so that they remain valid after the most serious sin and can be conferred only once.

Holy Roman Empire The successor to the western *Roman Empire of antiquity. The name itself was not employed until the mid-13th century but the institution dates from 800, when *Charlemagne was crowned emperor of the West by Pope Leo III. Its territory came to comprise much of W and central Europe, being centered on Germany and Austria and including areas of E France and N Italy. After the failure of Charlemagne's *Carolingian dynasty the imperial title, which was nominally elective (*see* electors), passed (962) to the German kings, who retained it until the Empire's abolition in 1806; from the 13th century the emperors were almost always *Habsburgs. Between the 11th and 13th centuries the emperors (especially those of the *Hohenstaufen dynasty) vied with the popes for dominance in Europe (*see* investiture controversy; Guelfs and Ghibellines), a conflict from which the Empire emerged much weakened. It was further undermined by the Protestant *Reformation in the 16th century, the *Thirty Years' War in the 17th century, and the rise of Prussia and was finally broken by Napoleon's conquest of imperial territories in the early 19th century.

Holy Spirit (*or* Holy Ghost) In Christian theology, the third person of the Trinity, coequal and of one substance with the Father and the Son. Old Testament references to the spirit of God are given a more specific application in the New Testament Gospels; in St John's Gospel the Holy Spirit is seen as the "Paraclete" or Comforter, sent to inspire Christ's followers after the *Ascension. In Acts, the descent of the Holy Spirit upon the Apostles is described, an event commemorated at the Feast of Pentecost (the 50th day after Easter). In art, the Holy Spirit is usually symbolized by a dove.

homeomorphism In mathematics, a one-to-one correspondence. In *set theory it is a property of two sets in which every member of one set is capable of being paired with one member of the other set and vice versa. In *topology, two shapes are homeomorphic if one can be transformed into the other by a continuous deformation, without being cut; for example, the surfaces of a sphere and a cube are homeomorphic.

homeopathy The system of treating illness developed by Samuel *Hahnemann at the end of the 18th century and based on the principle of "like cures like." To treat a particular disease homeopathists prescribe small doses of a drug that in larger quantities would cause the symptoms of the disease in a healthy person.

homeostasis The self-regulating process by which living organisms tend to maintain their bodies in a constant physiological state regardless of environmental extremes. The extent to which this independence is achieved by a particular group is a measure of its success: protozoans, for instance, are affected by many external factors, whereas man is relatively independent. In man, reflex activity of the nervous system and the action of hormones are important means of achieving homeostatic control. Claude *Bernard was one of the first to recognize the importance of this kind of regulation.

Homer (8th century BC) Greek epic poet, presumed author of the *Iliad* and *Odyssey*. He is believed to have lived in Ionia in Asia Minor and according to legend was blind. Working within a primitive oral tradition, his achievement lay in ordering a wealth of traditional material into a monumental and unified poetic structure. The *Iliad* concerns the Trojan War, and its basic tragic theme is enlivened by the variety and human sympathy of its individual episodes. The *Odyssey* relates the various adventures of *Odysseus during his voyage home from the Trojan War to his kingdom of Ithaca. Both poems were revered by the ancient Greeks for their moral as well as their literary value and have had a profound influence on western culture.

HOMO

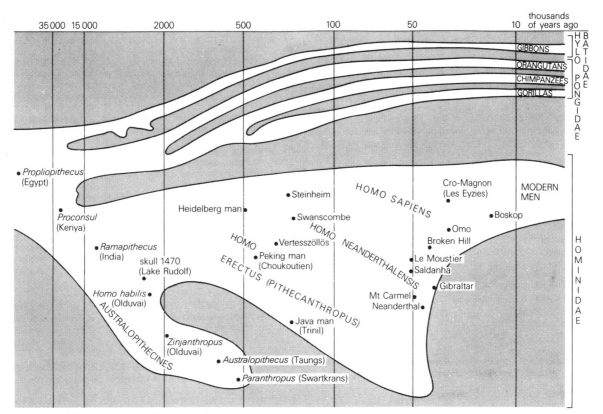

evolution of Homo sapiens *The picture of man's evolution is constantly changing as new fossil evidence comes to light. The fossil* Propliopithecus *represents the apparent divergence of the gibbons (Hylobatidae), great apes (Pongidae), and humans (Hominidae) from the monkeys, but paleontologists are still debating many of the other classifications and relationships shown on this chart. What, for instance, is the connection between* Zinjanthropus *and the older but more highly developed* Homo habilis, *found on the same site?*

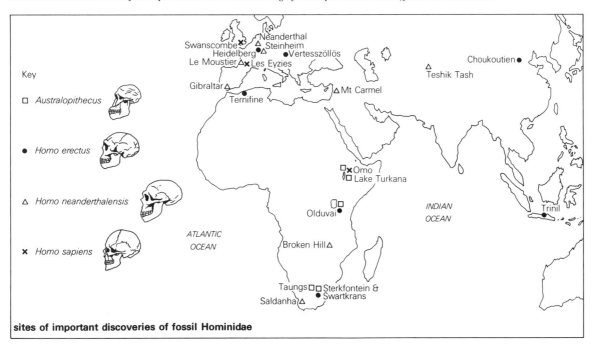

sites of important discoveries of fossil Hominidae

Homer, Winslow (1836–1910) US painter of everyday life, landscapes, and seascapes. In his native Boston he trained under a lithographer. In New York he worked as an illustrator and as an artist-correspondent of the Civil War, achieving prominence with his painting *Prisoners from the Front* (1866). Many of his paintings depict typically American scenes, such as the rural game in *Crack the Whip* (1872). After a visit to England (1881–83), he settled in the Maine fishing village of Prouts Neck, where he painted a number of watercolors of fishermen and the sea, often in dramatic conflict, as in *The Northeaster* (1895) and *The Gulf Stream* (1899).

Home Rule An Irish political movement to repeal the Act of *Union with Britain and give Ireland a legislature responsible for domestic affairs. Founded by Isaac Butt (1813–79) in 1870, the Home Rule movement achieved parliamentary prominence under the leadership of *Parnell from 1880. *Gladstone's conversion to Home Rule produced the Home Rule bills of 1886 and 1893 but both were defeated. In 1914 the third Home Rule bill was passed but suspended for the duration of World War I. A modified act, passed in 1920, was accepted by the north but rejected by the south, which in 1922 gained dominion status as the Irish Free State.

Homestead Act (1862) An act to encourage settlement of the West. Anyone at least 21 years old, and willing to farm for 5 years, was given 160 acres (65 hectares) in the West. After this initial period the land was theirs. The act was instrumental in opening up the West, and about one out of every three farmers was successful.

Homestead Massacre (1892) A clash between strikers and security forces during a steel strike in Homestead, in SW Pennsylvania. The Carnegie Steel Company, in an effort to discourage pickets, hired about 300 Pinkerton detectives to disrupt the pickets. Violence erupted, ten people were killed, and the national guard was posted there for three months. The power of the union remained weak until 1937 when the steel industry was unionized.

homing instinct. *See* migration, animal.

hominid A member of the *Hominidae* family of primates, to which man belongs. Besides man, there are no surviving hominids: the others are known only from fossil remains. The *Hominidae* include the genera *Ramapithecus*, *Australopithecus*, and *Homo*. The hominids appeared between five and one million years ago in Africa and Asia. The first to appear in Europe date from between 600,000 and 800,000 years ago.

Homo A genus of *hominids characterized by a large cranial capacity, erect posture, bipedal gait, a thumb capable of a precision grip, and the ability to make and use tools. The genus includes the species *Homo erectus* (*see* Pithecanthropus), which may have been ancestral to modern man. This species, which first appeared more than one million years ago during the middle *Pleistocene, includes specimens from Java, Peking, Heidelberg, and elsewhere. *Neanderthal man also belongs to the genus *Homo*, as does *Cro-Magnon man, who was probably an early form of the species *Homo sapiens* (modern man). *See also* Australopithecus.

homoiothermy The condition of being warm-blooded, i.e. of maintaining a fairly constant body temperature by physiological mechanisms. Birds and mammals are warm-blooded: in cold climates body heat is conserved and also produced by muscle activity, such as shivering, while in hot weather body heat is lost by sweating and panting. *Compare* poikilothermy.

homosexuality Sexual attraction or relations between persons of the same sex. It is known as lesbianism when the persons involved are females. Homosexuality is an ancient and widespread phenomenon that can involve moral stigma and even punishment, as in the Judeo-Christian tradition, but just as often is regarded as neither abnormal nor immoral, as in ancient Greece. Related phenomena are bisexuality (when an individual is attracted by people of both sexes) and transsexuality (*see* transvestism). Many countries have in recent years liberalized their laws concerning homosexuality. Contemporary movements, such as Gay Liberation, seek to alleviate any residual social problems that may persist for homosexuals in a predominantly heterosexual society.

Homs (Arabic name: Hims) 34 44N 36 43E A city in Syria, on the Orontes River close to the border with N Lebanon. There is a large Crusader fortress here, and Homs is an important trading and industrial town. Population (1977 est): 292,280.

Honan. *See* Henan.

Honduras, Republic of A country in Central America, with a N coastline on the Caribbean Sea and a short S one on the Pacific Ocean. Narrow coastal plains rise to mountainous country, dissected by river valleys. The majority of the population is of mixed Indian and Spanish descent. *Economy*: mainly agricultural, the chief crops are bananas and coffee (the principal exports). Almost half the land is forested, with valuable hardwoods in the NE and pine in the interior. Fishing is important, especially shrimps for export. The considerable mineral resources, some as yet unexploited, include gold, silver, lead, tin and zinc, and mercury. Hydroelectricity is being developed. *History*: the area was a center of Mayan culture from the 4th to the 9th centuries AD and was later occupied by the Lenca Indians. Discovered by Columbus in 1502, it became part of the Spanish captaincy general of Guatemala. It gained independence from Spain in 1821 and then formed part of the Central American Federation (1823–38). Honduras has suffered much internal unrest as well as a long conflict with Guatemala and, more recently, with El Salvador: in 1969 war broke out following El Salvador's defeat of Honduras in a World Cup soccer match. In 1972 a former (1966–71) president, General Oswaldo López, seized power in a bloodless coup but he in turn was overthrown in 1975. Military rule continued under Colonel Juan Melgar Castro, until he was in turn deposed (1978) by a military junta headed by General Paz García. Honduras' growing involvement in the Central American conflict and its escalating struggle against the Sandinista government in Nicaragua created worldwide concern. The US strengthened its ties with Honduras, its closest ally in Central America, by supplying military and economic assistance. Honduras is a member of the OAS and the Organization of Central American States. Official language: Spanish. Official currency: lempira of 100 centavos. Area: 43,227 sq mi (112,088 sq km). Population (1983 est): 4,276,000. Capital: Tegucigalpa. Main ports: Amapala on the Pacific and La Ceiba on the Atlantic.

Honecker, Erich (1912–) East German statesman; first secretary of the Socialist Unity Party (1971–). After his release from Nazi imprisonment, Honecker led a German youth group (1946–1955). From 1958 to 1971 he was responsible for security matters.

Honegger, Arthur (1892–1955) French composer, born in Switzerland. He was a pupil of Widor and d'Indy and one of Les *Six. He developed his own polyphonic and dissonant style. His compositions include five symphonies, the stage works *King David* (1921) and *Joan of Arc at the Stake* (1934–35), an orchestral depiction of a large steam locomotive entitled *Pacific 231* (1923), chamber music, and piano music.

honesty A herbaceous plant of the European genus *Lunaria* (3 species). Up to 40 in (1 m) high, it is often grown in gardens for its decorative disc-shaped papery seed heads. *L. annua* has white to purple flowers while *L. variegata* has crimson flowers and variegated foliage. Family: *Cruciferae*.

honey A sweet thick yellow syrup collected from the honeycomb of bee hives. Bees suck nectar from flowers and empty it into the cells of their hives, where they convert the sugar it contains from sucrose into dextrose and fructose. Honey from heather is golden and that from white clover is greenish-white. It is commercially extracted by heating the honeycomb. Honey consists of about 70% sugars, 18% water, and small amounts of minerals, pollen, and wax. Honey was used for embalming in ancient Egypt and was a favorite food of the ancient Greeks. Mildly antiseptic on account of its acidity, it has also been used medicinally for a variety of purposes.

honey ant An *ant belonging to subfamilies (*Camponotinae* or *Dolichoderine*) occurring in North America, Africa, Australia, and New Guinea. Certain members of the colony, called repletes, gorge themselves with honeydew (mainly from aphids and scale insects) gathered by other workers. They then hang from the ceiling of their underground chamber and regurgitate this food store when stimulated by the other ants.

honey badger. *See* ratel.

honeybee A social *bee, *Apis mellifera*, also called hive bee. Native to SE Asia, it is reared worldwide for its *honey and *beeswax. Honeybees have large colonies with 50,000–80,000 workers during the summer and a well-defined caste system. Workers attend to nest building, food gathering, and brood care; they use dances to communicate the location of food sources to other colony members. The queen lays her eggs in wax chambers (cells). Developing drones and workers are fed on protein-rich "royal jelly" for a few days and then changed to a diet of pollen and honey. Larvae hatching from fertilized eggs and fed on royal jelly throughout their development become queens, rather than workers. New colonies are formed by a swarm of workers led by the old queen (*compare* bumblebee); a young queen continues the established colony. Family: *Apidae*.

honeycreeper A songbird belonging to a family (*Drepanididae*; 22 species) restricted to the Hawaiian Islands, where they appear to have evolved from a single species. Honeycreepers are of two types: nectar feeders with colorful plumage and long slender curved bills and drab-green seed eaters with short bills. Some honeycreepers face extinction due to man's destruction of their specialized habitats.

honeyeater An arboreal songbird belonging to a family (*Meliphagidae*; 160 species) occurring chiefly in SE Asia and Australasia. They are 4–14 in

(10–35 cm) long and have a drab plumage with wattles or naked patches on the face. The slender bill is down-curved and the long extensible tongue has a central trough, through which nectar is drunk, and a brushlike tip for collecting pollen and small insects.

honey fungus A fungus, *Armillaria mellea*, also called bootlace fungus, that forms clusters of toadstools on or near old trees or stumps, to which it is attached by thick black rootlike structures resembling bootlaces. These may be found beneath the bark of an infected tree. The toadstool is 1.2–4 in (3–10 cm) in diameter and may be yellowish, green, brown, gray, or pink. Honey fungus is a serious pest of trees. Family: *Tricholomataceae*; class: *Basidiomycetes*.

honey guide An arboreal bird belonging to a tropical Old World family (*Indicatoridae*; 12 species). Honey guides are 4.5–8 in (11.5–20 cm) long and dull-brown, gray, or greenish in color. They feed mainly on bees and wasps and certain species are known to guide honey badgers or men to bees' nests by chattering and flying in the direction of the nest; the mammal robs the nest and the bird feeds on the remains. Order: *Piciformes* (woodpeckers, etc.).

honey locust A tree of the genus *Gleditschia* (11 species), occurring in warm parts of America, Africa, and Asia. The American species *G. triacanthos* is planted for ornament in Europe. It has stout thorns, compound leaves with paired leaflets, and small green flowers producing long pods. Family: *Leguminosae*.

honey mouse A small marsupial, *Tarsipes spenserae*, of SW Australia, also called honey possum or phalanger. It has a gray-brown body (2.75–3 in [70–85 mm] long) with three dark stripes along the back; a long snout; and a very long prehensile tail 3–4 in (88-100 mm). The honey mouse climbs shrubs to feed on nectar, using its long bristly tongue to reach inside the flowers. Family: *Phalangeridae*.

honeysuckle A shrub or twining plant of the genus *Lonicera* (100 species), of the N hemisphere. The common European honeysuckle (*L. periclymenum*), also called woodbine, is a trailing shrub, up to 20 ft (6 m) long, and bears clusters of elongated tubular yellowish flowers. A number of species are cultivated as ornamentals, including the fragrant climbing honeysuckle (*L. japonica*). Family: *Caprifoliaceae*.

Hong Kong A British crown colony lying off the S coast of China. It consists of the island of Hong Kong, the mainland peninsula of Jiulong, the New Territories, and Stonecutters Island. Much of the land is steep and barren. The majority of the population is Chinese. *Economy*: owing to its strategic position and fine natural harbor, it is an important entrepôt port and banking center. Much of China's foreign trade passes through Hong Kong. The export of manufactured goods has become increasingly important following the rapid industrial expansion since World War II and the textile and clothing industry (developed by immigrants from Shanghai) accounts for over half the total domestic exports. Electronics and plastics are also important and there is some heavy industry, such as ship building and repair and iron and steel manufacture. There is a certain amount of cultivation, although agricultural land is scarce and the reclamation of land from the sea has long been important in the colony's history. Tourism is also a major source of revenue. *History*: the island was ceded to Britain by China at the end of the first Opium War (1842) and Kowloon was added in 1860. In 1898 the New Territories were granted on a 99-year lease from China. Hong Kong was occupied by the Japanese during World War II. Britain's lease on the New Territories (which constitutes most of the colony), scheduled to expire in 1997, caused concern over the future of the colony in the early 1980s. China was firm in its insistence that Hong Kong revert to Chinese control. Pessimism was reflected in a depressed economy, with few new internal investments and a sharp increase in investment outside the colony. In 1984, China and Britain signed an agreement covering the status of Hong Kong after 1997. Under the agreement Hong Kong would be a special administrative region of China, with considerable autonomy with its own legal system and the right to maintain its capitalist system. Official language: English; Cantonese is widely spoken. Official currency: Hong Kong dollar of 100 cents. Area: 398 sq mi (1031 sq km). Population (1983): 5,313,000. Capital and main port: Victoria.

Hong-wu (*or* Hung-wu; 1328–98) The title of Chu Yuan-zhang (*or* Chu Yüan-chang), who became the first emperor (1368–98) of the Ming dynasty. A monk, he became a rebel leader and outstanding military tactician, ousting the Yuan dynasty and declaring himself emperor. He made Nanjing his capital and by 1382 he had united China.

Hong Xiu Quan (*or* Hung Hsiu-ch'uan; 1814–64) Chinese religious leader and revolutionary. After failing to get a place in the civil service, he espoused a strongly political Protestant Christianity, declaring himself God's second son and savior of China. He led the *Taiping Rebellion, but

eventually ceased to take part in politics and committed suicide in Nanjing shortly before it fell.

Honolulu 21 19N 157 50W The capital city of Hawaii, on SE Oahu. Famed for its beauty, it is the economic center of the islands and a transpacific route stop. It is the site of three universities and of Iolani Palace, the former royal residence. *Pearl Harbor is still an important naval base. Population (1980): 365,048.

Honorius II (Lamberto Scannabecchi; d. 1130) Pope (1124–30). An architect of the Concordat of Worms, which ended the *investiture controversy (1122), he re-established relations between the papacy and Empire, supporting the claims of Lothair II against Conrad III. Fearing the growing strength of the Normans under Roger II in Sicily, he led an army against him and was defeated and forced to accept Roger as Duke of Apulia.

Honshu The largest of the four main islands of Japan, situated between the Pacific Ocean and the Sea of Japan. It is mountainous, volcanic, and prone to earthquakes, with a great difference in climate between the subtropical S and the cooler N. The historic center of Japan, it has been the site of its capital since earliest times. Most of Japan's major ports and cities are here, although agriculture is also very important; rice, fruit, cotton, and tea are grown. Mineral wealth includes oil, zinc, and copper. The traditional industry is silk but the many modern industries include shipbuilding, iron and steel, chemicals, and textiles. Area: 88,976 sq"mi (230,448 sq km). Population (1970): 82,559,580. Chief town: Tokyo.

Honthorst, Gerrit von (1590–1656) Dutch painter. Working in Rome (c. 1610–1620), Utrecht, London (1628), and The Hague, he painted biblical, mythological, and everyday scenes, which were influenced by *Caravaggio in their use of candlelight. His portraits include one of Charles I and Henrietta Maria (Hampton Court).

Hooch, Pieter de (1629–c. 1684) Dutch painter, born in Rotterdam. Working in Delft, Leiden, and Amsterdam, he excelled in small paintings, such as *The Pantry* (Rijksmuseum, Amsterdam), depicting household tasks in courtyards or dark interiors that open into sunlit rooms.

Hood, John Bell (1831–79) US Confederate general. After serving in the Indian wars in the West, he resigned (1861) to join the Confederate Army and command the Texas Brigade. He fought at *Bull Run (1862) and, promoted to general, at *Antietam, Gettysburg, and Chickamauga. Although he had lost a leg, he was put in command of the Confederate Army (1864) at Atlanta, where he was defeated. After a crushing defeat at Nashville, he resigned.

hooded crow A crow, *Corvus corone cornix*, identical to the *carrion crow except for its gray back and underparts. It is found in N and E Europe, where the carrion crow does not occur, but in the narrow zone where the two races overlap they hybridize, producing birds of mixed coloration.

hooded seal A *seal, *Cystophora cristata*, of deep Arctic waters, also called bladdernose, or crested seal. About 10 ft (3 m) long, pale gray with dark blotches, hooded seals have a red inflatable bladder on top of the nose. In males the inflated bladder may be used to frighten enemies. Hooded seals are solitary except when breeding. Family: *Phocidae*.

Hooft, Pieter Corneliszoon (1581–1647) Dutch poet and historian, who traveled in France and Italy, where he was influenced by Renaissance art and literature. He gathered a circle of writers, artists, and musicians at the castle at Muiden, of which he was made steward in 1609. Hooft expressed his humanist and pacifist philosophy in the pastoral play *Granida* (1605), while his love poetry echoed that of Petrarch. His history of the Dutch revolt against Spain, *Nederlandsche Historien* (1628–47), remained a model of Dutch prose for over 200 years.

Hooghly River (Hoogli R *or* Hugli R) A river in India, rising in West Bengal. The W stream of the Ganges delta, it flows S through Calcutta to the Bay of Bengal. Length: 145 mi (233 km).

Hooke, Robert (1635–1703) British physicist and instrument maker. In 1660 he discovered *Hooke's law. His work on springs led him into horology and he claimed to have invented the hair spring (also claimed by *Huygens). He was one of the first scientists to examine vegetable matter with a microscope, in 1667 discovering the existence of cells in cork. Many of his microscope studies were published in *Micrographia* (1665).

Hooker, Joseph (1814–79) US Union general. A West Point graduate who had been out of active service since 1853, he joined the Union Army (1861), was made a general, and fought in the major battles of the *Peninsular Campaign. Chosen to lead the Army of the Potomac in 1863, he suffered a crushing defeat at Chancellorsville and was relieved of his command.

Hooker, Thomas (1586–1647) US colonist and minister; born in England. As a Puritan he had gone to Holland in 1630 to escape religious persecution and then emigrated to Massachusetts (1633). Dissatisfied with conditions in Cambridge, the site of his first pastorate, he brought his Congregationalist followers to Connecticut where he was instrumental in the founding of Hartford (1636). He helped to draft the Fundamental Orders of Connecticut (1639) and to found the New England Confederation (1643).

Hooke's law For an elastic body, the *stress is directly proportional to the *strain. For example, if a heavy mass is hung from a wire, the fractional extension is directly proportional to the mass. The law applies only up to the elastic limit (*see* elasticity). Named for its discoverer Sir Robert *Hooke, who stated it in the form *ut tensio, sic vis.*

Hook of Holland (Dutch name: Hoek van Holland) 51 59N 4 07E A port in the SW Netherlands, in South Holland province at the North Sea end of the Nieuwe Waterweg (New Waterway). A ferry service operates from here to Harwich, England.

hookworm A parasitic *nematode worm inhabiting the intestine of animals and man. About 0.4 in (1 cm) long, hookworms attach themselves to the gut lining and feed by sucking blood and body fluids. The two main species infecting man are *Necator americanus*, of the southern US and Africa, and the Eurasian *Ancylostoma duodenale*. Both cause lowered resistance to disease, anemia, and malnutrition. The larvae enter the body through the skin, usually the feet, and migrate to the intestine. Infection can be prevented by wearing shoes and improving sanitation.

hoopoe A bird, *Upupa epops*, of S Eurasia and Africa. 11 in (28 cm) long, it has a pink-brown plumage with black and white barred wings, a long tail, and a long black-tipped crest. It feeds on insects and larvae with its long downcurved bill. It is the only member of its family (*Upupidae*). Order: *Coraciformes* (hornbills, kingfishers, etc.).

HERBERT HOOVER *President (1929–33) whose administration was criticized for its handling of the effects of the Depression, leading to his election defeat in 1932.*

Hoover, Herbert Clark (1874–1964) US statesman; 31st President of the United States (1929–33). Beginning his career as an international mining engineer, Hoover was appointed chairman of American relief commit-

tees in Great Britain and Belgium and US Food Administrator after *World War I. He later served as secretary of commerce in the administrations of Presidents Warren *Harding and Calvin *Coolidge. As the nominee of the *Republican Party, Hoover was elected president in 1928. Soon after taking office, he faced a severe economic crisis with the collapse of the US stock market and the beginning of the *Depression. As a fiscal conservative, however, Hoover was unwilling to initiate massive federal programs to restore the economy and he came under increasing criticism. Defeated for re-election in 1932 by Franklin *Roosevelt, Hoover later headed the Commissions on Organization of the Executive Branch of the Federal Government (known as the Hoover Commissions, 1947–49, 1953–55). His three-volume autobiography, *Memoirs*, was published in 1952.

Hoover, J(ohn) Edgar (1895–1972) US lawyer, director of the Federal Bureau of Investigation (FBI) from 1924 to 1972. He fought the gangsters of the 1930s with his reformed FBI and established the first fingerprint file and crime-detection laboratory. In his later years he was criticized for the power that he had amassed and for his autocratic methods.

HOP *Ripe female flowers ("cones"), which have a bitter flavor and are dried in an oast house before being added to the wort during beer making.*

hop A perennial climbing herb, *Humulus lupus*. Native to Eurasia, where it grows to a length of 10–20 ft (3–6 m) in hedges and thickets, it is widely cultivated for its pale yellow-green female flowers ("cones"), which are used in brewing to flavor beer. The male flowers are smaller. The young shoots have been eaten as a vegetable. Family: *Cannabiaceae*.

Hope, Anthony (Sir Anthony Hope Hawkins; 1863–1933) British novelist. He gave up careers in law and politics after the immediate popular success of *The Prisoner of Zenda* (1894), a tale of adventure set in the imaginary country of Ruritania. He wrote many other successful romances of this kind.

Hope, Bob (Leslie Townes Hope; 1903–) US comedian, born in Britain. He starred in a number of popular movies during the 1940s, including *Road to Zanzibar* (1941) and other "Road" movies with Bing *Crosby and Dorothy Lamour. He gave many performances for US troops in World War II, Korea and Vietnam, as well as in peacetime. He has starred in radio, television, and vaudeville in addition to film.

Hopeh. *See* Hebei.

hop-hornbeam A tree of the N temperate genus *Ostrya* (7 species). Related to hornbeams, they have hard wood, furrowed bark, flowers in catkins, and conelike fruits resembling those of the hop. The European hop-hornbeam (*O. carpinifolia*) may grow to a height of over 65 ft (20 m). Family: *Corylaceae*. *See also* ironwood.

Hopi North American Indians of NE Arizona whose language belongs to the Uto-Aztecan family (*see* Aztec-Tanoan languages). They live in stone and adobe houses forming small towns built on rocky plateaus (mesas). They are peaceful cultivators and sheep farmers, much given to religious practice and ceremonial. There are about 6000 now living but they are rapidly losing their traditional culture. *See also* Pueblo Indians.

Hopkins, Sir Frederick Gowland (1861–1947) British biochemist, who discovered that certain substances—now known as *vitamins—are essential in the diet in trace amounts. He also showed that some amino acids (called essential amino acids) cannot be manufactured by certain animals. He shared a Nobel Prize (1929) with Christian *Eijkman and served as president of the Royal Society (1930–35).

Hopkins, Gerard Manley (1844–89) British poet. He was converted to Roman Catholicism in 1866 and ordained as a Jesuit priest in 1877. In verse of daring originality he rejected conventional meters in favor of a flexible "sprung rhythm." "The Wreck of the Deutschland" and "The Windhover" are among his best-known poems, which were published posthumously in 1918 and were highly influential on poets writing in the 1920s and 1930s.

Hopkins, Harry (Lloyd) (1890–1946) US government administrator. His long-standing interest in social welfare projects culminated in his administration of *New Deal relief programs during the Depression. As aide to President Roosevelt during World War II he negotiated with Churchill and Stalin and headed the US lend-lease program (*see* Lend Lease Act).

Hopper, Edward (1882–1967) US artist. Although initially an illustrator, he studied (1901–06) under Robert Henri and was greatly influenced by the *Ashcan School of painting. His urban scenes are starkly realistic and geometrically exact, depicting loneliness and anonymity. His works include "Model Reading" (1925), "Early Sunday Morning" (1930), "Room in Brooklyn" (1932), "Nighthawks" (1942), "Sunlight in a Cafeteria" (1958), and "Second-Story Sunlight" (1960).

Horace (Quintus Horatius Flaccus; 65–8 BC) Roman poet. He was the son of a freed slave. Although he was reduced to poverty after fighting for Brutus in the Civil War, he became a leading poet under the emperor Augustus and acquired a farm near Rome, celebrated in his poetry. His *Odes* and his more informal *Satires* and verse *Epistles* vividly portray contemporary Roman society and express his own humane and tolerant personality.

Horae Greek goddesses of the seasons. They were originally three in number, the daughters of Zeus and Themis, and associated with the concepts of order, justice, and peace. They later became the four seasons, daughters of Helios and Selene (the sun and moon).

Horatii and Curiatii In Roman legend, two sets of three brothers who fought on opposing sides in the war between Rome and Alba in the reign of Tullus Hostilius, legendary king of Rome. The single survivor, Horatius, killed his grief-stricken sister on finding she had been engaged to one of the Curiatii, but was acquitted after appealing to the people of Rome.

horehound (*or* hoarhound) Either of two Eurasian perennial herbs growing in dry waste places and waysides. White horehound (*Marrubium vulgare*) reaches a height of 10 ft (3 m) and has whorls of white flowers while black horehound (*Balleta nigra*) has whorls of purple flowers and a disagreeable odor. Both have been used medicinally. Family: *Labiatae.*

hormone A substance that is secreted into the blood in small quantities to cause a response in a specific target organ or tissue of the body. Hormones are produced and secreted by *endocrine glands and by specialized nerve cells (*see* neurohormone) under the control of the nervous system or in response to changes in the chemical composition of the blood. Hormones regulate short-term physiological processes, such as digestion, and long-term changes, such as those associated with growth and reproduction; they also help to maintain a constant internal environment in the body (*see* homeostasis). The first demonstration of hormone activity was made in 1905, by *Bayliss and Starling, working with the digestive hormone secretin. The following are some of the more important hormones now known in man: *ACTH, *gonadotrophin, *growth hormone, and *prolactin (secreted by the pituitary); *corticosteroids, *aldosterone, and *adrenaline (from the adrenal glands); *androgens and *estrogens (from the sex glands); thyroid hormone (from the *thyroid gland); *insulin and *glucagon (from the pancreas). Chemically, most hormones are proteins or steroids. The study of hormones—and the diseases caused by their under- or over-production—is called endocrinology. Substances that regulate plant growth, e.g. *auxins, *gibberellins, and *kinins, are sometimes known as plant hormones.

Horn, Filips van Montmorency, Graaf van (*or* Hoorne; ?1524–68) Flemish statesman and admiral, who played a leading part in the resistance to Philip II's religious and domestic policies in the Netherlands. He served his Spanish rulers in military, naval, and administrative capacities, becoming stadholder (chief magistrate) of Gelder and Zutphen in 1555. However, he joined *Egmont and William the Silent in resigning from the state council (1565) and demanding the abolition of the Inquisition. He was executed for treason and heresy by the Duke of *Alba. *See also* Revolt of the Netherlands.

hornbeam A tree of the genus *Carpinus* (26 species), of N temperate regions. The common Eurasian hornbeam (*C. betulus*) grows to a height of 100 ft (30 m) in the wild (cultivated trees are up to 60 ft [19 m] tall); it has smooth gray bark, oval pointed leaves with prominent veins, and small nuts with conspicuous winged bracts. It is planted for ornament and for its hard fine-grained timber. Family: *Corylaceae.*

hornbill A bird belonging to a family (*Bucerotidae*; 45 species) occurring in Old World tropical regions. 15–59 in (38–150 cm) long, hornbills are characterized by a huge bill, often bearing a large bony "helmet," and feed on fruit and berries. Most hornbills nest in treeholes in which the female imprisons herself by plastering the entrance with mud, leaving only a small hole through which the male feeds her, until the young hatch. Order: *Coraciiformes* (kingfishers, etc.).

hornblende A mineral of the *amphibole group, which occurs widely in igneous and metamorphic rocks. It consists mainly of silicates of sodium, calcium, magnesium, and iron. It is black or greenish black and occurs in crystalline or massive form. Hornblende schist is a rock consisting mainly of orientated hornblende crystals.

horned lizard. *See* horned toad.

horned poppy One of two herbs belonging to the *poppy family and having slender hornlike seed pods. The perennial or biennial yellow horned poppy (*Glaucium flavum*) of Eurasia grows to a height of 35 in (90 cm) and is found mainly on seashores. The red horned poppy (*G. corniculatus*) is an annual of the Mediterranean region.

horned toad A desert-dwelling lizard, also called horned lizard, belonging to the genus *Phrynosoma*, occurring in North and Central America and characterized by hornlike spines on its head. 3–5 in (8–13 cm) long, they have a flattened oval body with a fringe of scales along the sides and hide by wriggling sideways until buried in sand. In defense, they may squirt blood from their eyes. Family: *Iguanidae.*

horned viper A mildly venomous desert *viper, *Cerastes cornutus*, that occurs in Africa and the Middle East and has a hornlike scale over each eye. Up to 24 in (60 cm) long, it has a broad head and is pale with dark spots and bars.

hornet A social *wasp, *Vespa crabro*, that is common throughout Europe and has spread to North America and elsewhere. 1 in (35 mm) long, it is tawny-yellow with brown markings and nests in hollow trees. It feeds chiefly on insects, nectar, and fruit juices and its painful sting can be dangerous to man.
Members of the genera *Dolichorespula*, *Paravespula*, and *Vespula* may also be known as hornets.

hornpipe A traditional British dance, originally accompanied by a wooden pipe. It retains its popularity with sailors as it requires no partners and little space. Like the jigs and reels to which it is related, it was often danced in clogs. Handel composed a hornpipe for his *Water Music.*

horntail A *wasp, also called wood wasp, belonging to the family *Siricidae* (about 60 species), having a hornlike projection on its abdomen. Horntails are usually brown, blue, or black with yellow bands and can be up to 1.4 in (37.5 mm) long. The females have strong ovipositors to insert their eggs into hardwood trees, particularly elm, beech, and maple, in which the larvae develop.

hornwort 1. A plant of the widely distributed genus *Ceratophyllum* (3 species), which grows submerged in ponds and streams. *C. demersum* is rootless, with a stem 8–40 in (20–100 cm) long and simple forked leaves, 0.4–8 in (1–2 cm) long. The small flowers produce a three-spined nutlike fruit. Family: *Ceratophyllaceae.* 2. A thallose *liverwort of the order *Anthocerotales*, also called horned liverwort and often classified as a separate class of bryophytes—the *Anthocerotae.* Distributed worldwide, they consist of a flat leaflike gamete-producing plant from which arises a long-lived spikelike spore-producing structure, 0.8–2 in (2–5 cm) long.

horoscope. *See* astrology.

Horowitz, Vladimir (1904–   ) US pianist, born in Russia. He settled in the US in 1940. Horowitz excels in the music of Chopin, Schumann, and Liszt and in his own transcriptions. He has twice made a triumphant return to the concert platform after periods of illness during 1936–39 and 1953–65.

Percheron

Arab horse

Thoroughbred

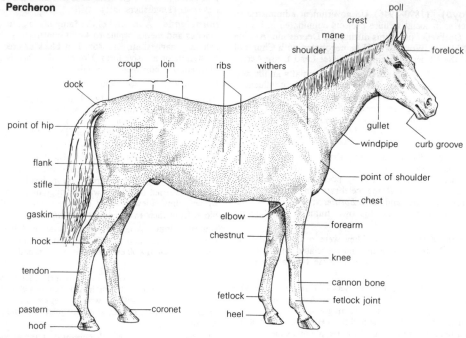

croup loin ribs withers shoulder mane crest poll forelock

dock

point of hip gullet windpipe curb groove

flank point of shoulder

stifle chest

gaskin elbow forearm

hock chestnut knee

tendon cannon bone

fetlock fetlock joint

pastern coronet heel

hoof

points of the horse

Exmoor pony

Lipizzaner

Tennessee Walking Horse

horse A hoofed mammal, *Equus caballus*, domesticated worldwide for pack and draft work, riding, and sport (*see* equestrianism). The earliest horse is believed to have been *eohippus, which is thought to have originated in North America and spread to Asia. Successive larger forms evolved, in which the central toe became enlarged as the hoof and the remaining toes became smaller and fewer (*see* Hipparion). These horses developed from forest browsers to become grazing animals of the plains with well-developed senses to detect predators.

The many breeds of modern horse—thought to have evolved from several different Asian and European forms, including *Przewalski's horse and the *tarpan—are commonly grouped into ponies, light horses, and draft horses. They range in size from the tiny *Falabella to the massive *Shire horse and are measured in hands (1 hand = 4 in = 10.16 cm) to the top of the shoulders (withers). According to breed, horses mature at $3\frac{1}{2}$–5 years of age and the lifespan is usually 20–35 years. Mares have a gestation period of 11 months, producing usually a single foal. Except for breeding stallions, males are usually castrated, being called geldings. Horses belong to the family *Equidae*, which also includes *asses and *zebras.

horse chestnut A broad spreading □tree, *Aesculus hippocastanum*, native to SE Europe and widely planted as an ornamental. It grows to a height of 80 ft (25 m), producing large compound leaves and erect clusters of white flowers; the green spiny fruits ripen to release large brown shiny seeds (conkers). The red horse chestnut (*A.* × *carnea*) is similar but has red flowers. It is a hybrid between the horse chestnut and *A. pavia*. Family: *Hippocastanaceae*.

horse fly A stout-bodied fly of the genus *Tabanus* (the term is also used loosely for the other genera—*Chrysops* (deerflies) and *Haematopota* (cleg flies)—of the family *Tabanidae*; 2500 species). Male horse flies feed on nectar but the females are bloodsuckers and inflict painful bites on man, horses, cattle, etc. A few species may also transmit diseases, such as tularemia and anthrax. The carnivorous larvae live mainly in damp soil and mud.

horsehair worm A long thin hairlike aquatic invertebrate of the phylum *Nematomorpha* (about 80 species), found mostly in fresh water. They range in length from 0.4–40 in (1–100 cm), with a diameter of only 0.01–0.08 in (0.3–2 mm). Their larvae are parasitic in beetles, crickets, and grasshoppers.

horsepower (hp) A unit of power equal to 550 foot-pounds per second. It was devised by James *Watt, who found that a strong horse could raise a weight of 150 pounds 4 feet in 1 second. *See also* watt.

horse racing A form of contest in which horses are ridden or driven. Its three main forms are *flat racing, *steeplechase and hurdling, and *harness racing.

horseradish A perennial herb, *Armoracia rusticana*, probably native to SE Europe and W Asia and widely cultivated. Growing to a height of 50 in (125 cm), it has thick fleshy pungent roots from which horseradish sauce is made and it bears small white flowers. Family: *Cruciferae*.

horseshoe bat An insect-eating *bat belonging to the genus *Rhinolophus* (74 species), found in temperate and tropical regions of the Old World. Horseshoe bats are named for— the fleshy structure surrounding the nostrils, which focuses the ultrasonic signals that the bat emits when navigating. They also have large ears for receiving the echoes. Family: *Rhinolophidae*.

horseshoe crab A large nocturnal marine *arthropod (up to 20 in [50 cm] long), also called king crab, belonging to the subclass *Xiphosura*, most members of which are now extinct. The two living genera, *Limulus* and *Tachypleus*, are found in shallow waters on the E coasts of North America and Asia respectively. They have a hinged body covered by a brown horseshoe-shaped carapace and a long tail spine. They can swim but usually burrow in sand, feeding on worms and thin-shelled mollusks. Class: *Meristomata*.

horsetail A rushlike perennial *pteridophyte plant, also called scouring rush, belonging to the only living genus (*Equisetum*; about 30 species) of the class *Sphenopsida* (which includes many giant extinct forms, such as *Calamites). Horsetails grow in moist rich soils everywhere except Australasia. Their creeping rhizomes give rise to aerial jointed stems of two kinds—green sterile stems, often branched in whorls, and pale fertile stems, bearing cone-shaped clusters of spore capsules. The leaves are reduced to sheaths encircling each stem joint. Tropical horsetails may grow to a height of 20 ft (6 m), but temperate species are much smaller. They are used as abrasives and in folk medicine.

horse trials Contests to test a horse's abilities and the rider's skill in horsemanship. The three-day event is an Olympic sport involving on successive days: *dressage; speed, endurance, and jumping tests on *steeple-chase and cross-country courses; and *showjumping. The one-day event is a reduced version.

horst. *See* fault.

Horta, Victor (1861–1947) Belgian architect, a proponent of *Art Nouveau. His early work, particularly the Hôtel Tassel (1892) and the Maison du Peuple (1896) in Brussels, are fine examples of this style. He later abandoned Art Nouveau for classicism.

Horthy de Nagybánya, Miklós (1868–1957) Hungarian admiral and statesman. After the collapse of *Austria-Hungary (1919), he organized an army against Béla *Kun's communist government. Elected regent of Hungary in 1920, he preserved an independent constititional system, despite alliance with Nazi Germany. When he attempted to negotiate a surrender to Russia (1944) the Germans deposed him.

horticulture The cultivation of vegetables (also known as market gardening) and fruit for food and of trees, shrubs, and other plants for ornament. Traditionally practiced in small gardens and orchards, horticulture is now both a popular domestic pastime and an important commercial activity using large field and glasshouse acreages. The introduction of new higher-yielding and more disease-resistant plant varieties, increased mechanization of planting and harvesting, the use of new cultivation techniques, such as *hydroponics, and the application of fertilizers and pesticides have all contributed to improved productivity and quality. Also, modern refrigeration, storage, and transport mean that many crops are now available throughout the year.

Horus The Egyptian sun-god, usually portrayed as a falcon or with a falcon's head. He was the son of *Osiris and *Isis and avenged his father's death by killing *Set. The pharaohs were conceived as the incarnations of Horus as earthly ruler and added the god's name to their titles.

Hosea (8th century BC) An Old Testament prophet of Israel. In the **Book of Hosea** the unfaithfulness of Israel to God is presented in terms of a spiritual adultery, comparable to the infidelity that the author has experienced in his own life. This familial analogy was later developed in the Christian concepts of the Fatherhood of God and of the Church as the bride of Christ.

hospital An institution providing diagnostic and therapeutic services for the sick on a residential (in-patient) or nonresidential (out-patient) basis. In the ancient world such medical services as existed were provided by religious organizations (e.g. the Temple of Aesculapius at Epidauros in Greece). In Europe in the middle ages many institutions for the care of the sick were founded by monastic orders and later, during the Crusades, by orders of knighthood. St Bartholomew's (1123) and St Thomas's (1207) in London date back to this period. During the 18th and 19th centuries, new voluntary hospitals were founded by philanthropists and staffed by doctors who gave their services free. Municipal hospitals arose alongside the voluntary hospitals; they had paid medical staff. Modern hospitals have a variety of administrative structures and have become increasingly specialized, often concentrating on the treatment of particular diseases (e.g. cancer).

Hospitallers (Order of the Hospital of St John of Jerusalem) A religious order of knighthood that began as a hospital for pilgrims to Jerusalem (c. 1070) and during the *Crusades took on a military function. Immensely wealthy, the Hospitallers were the great rivals of the *Templars. After the fall of Acre (1291) they established themselves in Cyprus, Rhodes, and finally Malta.

Hosta A genus of perennial herbaceous plants (10 species), native to China and Japan and widely planted in gardens. They are grown chiefly for their foliage—the leaves are large (5–10 in [12–25 cm] long), oval, and pointed and come in a variety of colors, often variegated—but they also produce attractive spikes of purplish or white funnel-shaped flowers. Family: *Liliaceae*.

Hot Springs 34 30N 93 03W A health resort city in W central Arkansas, in the Ouachita Mountains. It surrounds Hot Springs National Park, and its economy derives from the therapeutic benefits of the park's hot spring water, which is piped to bath houses in the city and bottled for national distribution. Several medical facilities are housed here. Population (1980): 35,166.

Hot Springs National Park A national park in W central Arkansas, in the Ouachita Mountains. Forty-seven hot springs (143°F; 62°C) are here, as well as mountains for hiking and lakes for swimming. A government-designated health resort since 1832, it was established as a national park in 1921. Area: 5.5 sq mi (15 sq km).

hot spring A spring from which hot water flows continuously from deep within the earth's crust. Like *geysers, hot springs normally occur in areas that are (or have recently been) volcanically active. A distinction is sometimes made between hot springs (at a temperature above that of the human body) and *thermal springs* (above the mean annual temperature of the place where they emerge). The water is charged with minerals and deposits of travertine or sinter usually build up.

Hotspur. *See* Percy, Sir Henry.

Hottentot fig A perennial herb, *Carpobrotus edulis*, native to South Africa but naturalized in many warm temperate regions. It has creeping woody stems, fleshy leaves, showy magenta or yellow flowers, and edible fruits. Family: *Aizoaceae*.

HARRY HOUDINI *Posing with a submersible canister from which he would escape under water.*

Houdini, Harry (Erich Weiss; 1874–1926) US magician. Becoming a professional magician in 1897, he was able to escape from handcuffs, straitjackets, and locked containers, even when under water, which gained him an international reputation. He wrote articles and books on magic and was deeply interested in spiritualism and frequently exposed fraud. His books include *The Unmasking of Robert Houdin* (1908) and *A Magician Among the Spirits* (1924).

Houdon, Jean Antoine (1741–1828) French sculptor. Houdon's highly successful career began in Rome (1764–68) with his *St Bruno* (1767; Sta Maria degli Angeli, Rome). Although he made many religious and mythological sculptures, he was most popular as a portrait sculptor; famous sitters included Voltaire, Benjamin Franklin, Catherine the Great, and Napoleon. He visited the US (1785) to make a statue of George Washington.

Houphouët-Boigny, Félix (1905–   ) Ivory Coast statesman; president (1960–   ). In 1946 he founded the Ivory Coast branch of the Rassemblement démocratique africain and was a member of the French Constituent Assembly (1945–46) and National Assembly (1946–59). In 1959 he became prime minister and, on independence in 1960, president.

housecarl A member of the household bodyguard of the Danish kings of England (1016–51). Originally warriors from the Scandinavian army, the housecarls performed strictly organized military and administrative services for which they were rewarded with gifts of money and land.

House, Edward M (andell) (1858–1938) US diplomat and presidential adviser. Nicknamed Colonel House in his native Texas, he actively campaigned for US President Woodrow Wilson in 1912 and became his confidential adviser. He served on many World War I commissions and represented Wilson at the preliminary peace meetings and at Versailles where he helped to frame Wilson's Fourteen Points (1918) and the Treaty of Versailles (1919).

housefly A dull-gray fly, *Musca domestica*, that is a worldwide household pest. The adult is 0.20–0.28 in (5–7 mm) long, with mouthparts used for sucking up organic liquids of all kinds. Through the contamination of food it spreads many serious diseases, such as typhoid, tuberculosis, and dysentery. The scavenging larvae grow quickly on practically any decaying organic matter, especially dung. Family: *Muscidae*.

houseleek A European perennial herb, *Sempervivum tectorum*, that has a basal rosette of fleshy leaves and bears heads of dull-red flowers on stems up to 24 in (60 cm) long. Growing on walls and roofs, it was formerly believed to guard against fire, sorcery, and death and had many medicinal uses. Family: *Crassulaceae*.

House of Representatives The larger chamber of the US Congress, composed of representatives from each state. The number of representatives (or congressmen) from each state is determined by state population; regardless of population each state is entitled to at least one representative. Each representative represents a congressional district within the state and is elected by those people within the district. Membership is limited to 435, with additional, but nonvoting, members from Puerto Rico, the District of Columbia, the Virgin Islands, and Guam. Each representative serves a 2-year term, must be at least 25 years old, and must be a resident of the state and a US citizen for at least 7 years. Constitutionally-delegated powers of the House are origination of revenue bills, initiation of impeachment proceedings, and authorization to elect the president when a tie or lack of majority exists in the electoral college. The House first met in 1789 with 59 members.

house sparrow A Eurasian *sparrow, *Passer domesticus*, that originated in Africa and spread north with Neolithic man: it is now also found in the New World. The male has a black-streaked brown plumage with gray underparts and a black bib and eye stripe; the female has a paler drabber plumage.

Housing and Urban Development, Department of (HUD) US cabinet-level executive branch department. It is concerned with housing needs, fair housing opportunities, and improving and developing communities. It administers mortgage insurance and rental subsidy programs, anti-discrimination in housing activities, neighborhood rehabilitation, and urban preservation. Directed by the secretary of Housing and Urban Development, it was established in 1965.

Housman, A (lfred) E (dward) (1859–1936) British poet and scholar. Although he failed to earn his degree at Oxford, he continued his classical studies. He was eventually rewarded with professorships. His volumes of lyrics, *A Shropshire Lad* (1896), *Last Poems* (1922), and *More Poems* (1936) are concerned with themes of human vanity and transience and are imbued with an atmosphere of romantic pessimism. He also published editions of the Roman poets Juvenal and Manilius.

Houston, Sam (uel) (1793–1863) US soldier, frontier leader, and statesman. He served in the War of 1812 and then as an Indian agent in Tennessee and Arkansas. From 1819 he had a law practice in Nashville and was elected to Congress (1823–27) and then as governor of Tennessee (1827–29). Following marital problems he resigned the governorship and lived with the Cherokee Indians in Oklahoma. In 1832 he was sent to Texas to negotiate Indian treaties. During the Mexico-Texas border disputes in 1835 the Texas settlers were led into battle by Sam Houston. After he and his troops defeated General *Santa Anna at San Jacinto, Texas became independent and Houston its first president (1836–38; 1841–44). After Texas became a state (1845), he was a US senator (1846–59) and governor (1859–61).

Houston 29 45N 95 25W A city, the main port in Texas. Founded in 1836, it is named for the Texan leader Sam *Houston (1793–1863). It expanded rapidly following the building of a canal (1912–14), linking it to the Gulf of Mexico, and the development of coastal oilfields. Today it is one of the world's major oil and petrochemical centers; other industries include shipbuilding and the manufacture of steel. Among its many educational institutions is the Texas medical center, and the Lyndon B. Johnson Space Center is nearby. Population (1980): 1,594,086.

Hove 50 49N 0 10W A city in S England, on the East Sussex coast. It is a resort and residential town adjoining Brighton. Population (1973 est): 72,000.

Hovercraft (or air-cushion vehicle) A shiplike vehicle equipped with powerful horizontal blowers capable of lifting it off a surface so that it rides on a cushion of air, which is contained within a rubber skirt. It can navigate on almost any kind of surface (water, swamp, or land) and is moved forward at high speed by vertical propellers. Hovercraft are used as ferries between England and France, Hong Kong and Macao, between ports in Scandinavia, and elsewhere.

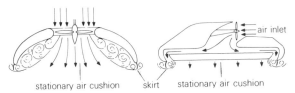

plenum-chamber type   annular-chamber type

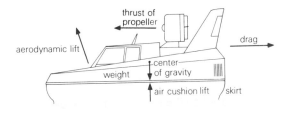

HOVERCRAFT *In the plenum chamber the air cushion is produced by a horizontal fan; the cushion in the center is almost at rest and is surrounded by a fast-moving ring of turbulent air. In the annular chamber the cushion is formed within an annular ring of jets, the nozzles of which are sloped inwards. The lower figure shows the forces acting on a Hovercraft.*

hoverfly A fly, also called a flowerfly or syrphid fly, belonging to the family *Syrphidae* (about 4000 species). Many species are black and yellow, resembling bees and wasps, but they do not sting. The larvae of many hoverflies are scavengers in decaying organic matter or the nests of ants, termites, or bees. Others are predators of aphids and plant lice, while a few are plant pests. *See also* maggot. □insect.

Howard, Catherine (c. 1520–42) The fifth wife (1540–42) of Henry VIII of England. She was beheaded for treason when Henry learned of her premarital love affairs.

Howard, Leslie (Leslie Howard Stainer; 1890–1943) British actor of Hungarian descent. He became famous for his performances as the romantic leading man in both British and US films, including *The Scarlet Pimpernel* (1935), *Pygmalion* (1938), and *Gone with the Wind* (1939).

Howard, Oliver Otis (1830–1909) US Union general. In 1861 he took command of a brigade from Maine in the Civil War, and saw extensive action, losing his right arm at Fair Oaks. In 1864 he was appointed commander of the Army of the Tennessee. After the war he headed the Freedman's Bureau, was a cofounder (1867) and president (1869–73) of Howard University, named for him. Returning to the military in 1874, he fought in various Indian campaigns.

Howard, Trevor (1916–) British actor. After working in the theater in the 1930s he concentrated on films from the 1940s, often appearing in leading romantic roles. His films include *Brief Encounter* (1946), *The Third Man* (1949), *Mutiny on the Bounty* (1962), *Ryan's Daughter* (1970), and *Conduct Unbecoming* (1975).

Howard of Effingham, Charles, 2nd Baron (1536–1624) English Lord High Admiral (1585–1618), who commanded the English victory against the Spanish *Armada (1588). He was a commander of the expedition that sacked Cádiz (1596), for which he was created 1st Earl of Nottingham.

Howe, Elias (1819–67) US inventor, who invented a lockstitch sewing machine, patented in 1846. It was not at first well received but by the 1850s large numbers were being manufactured in infringement of Howe's patent rights. Successful in a series of legal suits, he subsequently earned a fortune from royalties.

Howe, Gordie (1928–) Canadian ice hockey player. He played for the National Hockey League's (NHL) Detroit Red Wings (1946–71) and scored 1850 career points. He came out of retirement to play for the World Hockey League's Houston Aeros and New England Whalers (1973–77) and the NHL's Hartford Whalers (1977–79).

Howe, Julia Ward (1819–1910) US reformer and writer. She and her husband, Samuel Gridley Howe, were active in the abolition movement. She wrote "The Battle Hymn of the Republic" (1862), a poem that, set to music, became associated with the Union cause during the Civil War. Al-ways concerned with women's rights, she was active in many women's suffrage groups.

Howe, Richard, Earl (1726–99) British admiral. In the Seven Years' War (1756–63) he fought with distinction off the N French coast. In 1776 he became commander of the British fleet in the American Revolution. He is best known for the victory in the French Revolutionary Wars of the Glorious First of June— (1793). His brother **William, 5th Viscount Howe** (1729–1814) gained fame in the army. He fought under *Wolfe in North America during the French and Indian War and in the American Revolution commanded at *Bunker Hill (1775), after which he became commander in chief in America. Although he scored successes, notably at *Brandywine (1777), his career ended in anticlimax after the failure at *Valley Forge (1778).

Howel Dda. *See* Hywel the Good.

Howells, William Dean (1837–1920) US editor, critic, and author. He worked for the *Atlantic Monthly* from 1866 and was its editor (1871–81), during which time he was instrumental in publishing Mark *Twain, Bret *Harte, and Henry *James. After 1882 he devoted his time to his own works. His non-fiction criticized the *Haymarket Massacre trial, took issue with various wars, and promoted the cause of blacks. His realistic novels include *Their Wedding Journey* (1872), *The Lady of the Aroostook* (1879), *The Rise of Silas Lapham* (1885), *A Traveler from Altruria* (1894), and *Through the Eye of the Needle* (1907). He also wrote for the "Editor's Study" (1886–92) and "Easy Chair" (1900–20), columns of *Harper's Magazine*.

howitzer A low-velocity *artillery firearm with a shorter barrel and a larger bore than a *gun but a smaller bore and longer barrel than a *mortar. They are often mounted on carriages that enable them to fire either flat gun-type trajectories or arched mortar-type trajectories. They were widely used in World War I but the distinction between a gun and a howitzer in modern practice is now much reduced. The word comes from the Dutch *houwitzer*, catapult.

howler monkey A large monkey belonging to the genus *Alouatta* (6 species), of Central and South American forests. Howlers are 45–71 in (115–180 cm) long including the tail 23–36 in (58–91 cm) and are named for their loud voices. They have beards over their enlarged throats, prehensile tails, and live in groups of up to 40 individuals. Family: *Cebidae*.

Howrah 22 35N 88 20E A city and port in India, in West Bengal situated on the Hooghly River opposite Calcutta. The focal point of rail and road routes, its industries include shipbuilding, jute milling, engineering, and chemicals. Population (1971): 737,877.

Hoxha, Enver (1908–85) Albanian leader (1946–). In World War II Hoxha led Albania's struggle against Italy and founded the country's Communist Party (1941), becoming (1943) its general secretary. He was prime minister (1946–54) and then first secretary (1954–) of the newly named Party of Labor. After the Sino-Soviet disagreement in 1961, Hoxha supported China until 1978.

Hoya. *See* waxplant.

Hoyle, Edmond (1672–1769) British authority on card games. His book *A Short Treatise on the Game of Whist* (1742) was highly successful and his revised rules of 1760 governed whist until 1864. The idiom "according to Hoyle" (meaning according to the rules) is an allusion to this book.

Hoyle, Sir Fred (1915–) British astronomer, who with H. *Bondi and T. *Gold proposed the *steady-state theory of the universe. His other theoretical studies have mainly been concerned with stellar evolution. He is also one of the foremost of today's science writers, his *Galaxies, Nuclei and Quasars* (1965) being a standard work, and a notable science-fiction writer.

Hradec Králové (German name: Königgratz) 50 13N 15 50E A city in NW Czechoslovakia, in E Bohemia on the confluence of the Elbe (Labe) and Orlice Rivers. Industries include the manufacture of musical instruments and photographic equipment. Population (1968 est): 68,160.

Hsia Kuei. *See* Xia Gui.

Hsiang-t'an. *See* Xiangtan.

Hsi Chiang. *See* Xi Jiang.

Hsin dynasty. *See* Wang Mang.

Hsi-ning. *See* Xining.

Hsiung-nu. *See* Xiong Nu.

Hsuan-tsang. *See* Xuan Cang.

Hua Guo Feng (*or* Hua Kuo-feng; 1921–) Chinese communist statesman; chairman of the Chinese Communist Party (1976–81). A communist from boyhood, he became Party secretary in Hunan, which he made one of the most efficiently run provinces in China. He survived a *Red Guard attack during the Cultural Revolution to succeed Chou En-lai as prime minister and then Mao Tse-tung as chairman, the victor of a power struggle with the radicals led by Mao's widow, *Jiang Qing. The pragmatic policies pursued by China under Hua are regarded as being in part the result of the influence of *Deng Xiao Ping.

Huainan 32 41N 117 06E A city in E China, in Anhui province. Situated on a rich coalfield, it has been developed during the 20th century. Industries include iron and steel and chemicals. Population (1953): 286,900.

Huambo (name until 1973: Nova Lisboa) 12 47S 15 44E A city in W Angola. It is a commercial center with a trade in agricultural produce and has important railroad industries. Population (1970): 61,885.

Huancayo 12 05S 75 12W A city in W Peru, the chief commercial center of the central Andes. It has a cathedral and a university (1962). Population (1972): 126,754.

Huang Hai. *See* Yellow Sea.

Huang Ho. *See* Yellow River.

Huari An ancient city in the central Peruvian Andes that was briefly the center of an empire (c. 600–800 AD). Huari itself remained prosperous until abandoned about 1000 and the influence of its pottery styles prevailed over most of its central Peruvian neighbors until the rise of the *Chimú.

Huascar (c. 1495–1532) Ruler of the Incas, who lost his throne and was murdered after being defeated in civil war by his half-brother *Atahuallpa in 1532. Their conflict helped *Pizarro to conquer the Incas.

Huascarán (or Nevado Huascarán) 9 08S 77 36W The highest mountain in Peru, in the Andes. In 1962 an avalanche buried the village of Raurahirca killing about 3500 people. Height: 22,205 ft (6768 m).

Hubble, Edwin Powell (1889–1953) US astronomer, who used the 100-inch telescope at Mount Wilson Observatory to measure the speed of recession of the galaxies. He discovered that the speed of recession of the galaxies is proportional to their distance from the earth, which led to the evaluation of the *Hubble constant.

Hubble constant (H_0) The rate at which the velocity of expansion of the universe changes with distance. It relates the recessional velocity, V, of a distant galaxy to its distance, D. **Hubble's law**, proposed in 1929 by Edwin *Hubble, states that recessional velocity and distance are directly proportional: $V = H_0 D$. A widely accepted value for H_0 is 55 km s^{-1} megaparsec^{-1}, although higher values are and have been used.

Hubei (or Hupei) A province in E central China. Its fertile E plain has many lakes and rivers, including the Yangtze River. It was devastated during the Taiping Rebellion (1851–64) and the 1911 revolution began here. Products include wheat, rice, cotton, fish, and steel. Area: 72,394 sq mi (187,500 sq km). Population (1976 est): 40,000,000. Capital: Wuhan.

Hubli 15 20N 75 14E A city in India, in Karnataka. Together with Dharwar, it forms one of the state's most populous areas. Industries include cotton and newspapers. Population (1971): 379,166.

hubris (or hybris) The ancient Greek concept of human pride or arrogance that results in the transgression of the natural order and subsequent retribution by the gods. The concept is important in Greek tragedies, the protagonists of which, being talented and powerful, were especially prone to this fault.

Huddersfield 58 39N 1 47W A city in N England, at the confluence of the Rivers Colne and Holme. One of the major wool textile towns of West Yorkshire, Huddersfield produces various fabrics and has important engineering (tractors, textile machinery) and metalworking industries. Population (1973 est): 130,060.

Hudson, Henry (d. 1611) English navigator. In 1607, in a small ship with ten sailors, he sailed in search of the *Northeast Passage to China, reaching Spitzbergen. He tried again, unsuccessfully, in 1608. On a third voyage, under the auspices of the Dutch East India Company, he sailed some 150 mi (240 km) down what came to be called the Hudson River, establishing Dutch claims to the area. His fourth voyage (1610–11), in the *Discovery*, took him to what is now Hudson Bay (NE Canada), where his men mutinied and cast him adrift. Nothing more was heard of him.

Hudson Bay A huge shallow oceanic bay in N central Canada, linked to the Atlantic Ocean by Hudson Strait and to the Arctic Ocean by Foxe Channel. Frozen during winter, in summer it carries grain ships from W Canada to Europe.

Hudson River A river in the New York, flowing from the Adirondack Mountains to New York Bay, where it forms part of New York Harbor.

An important commercial waterway, it is linked by canals with the *Great Lakes and the *St Lawrence Seaway. Length: 306 mi (492 km).

Hudson River School (1825–75) Group of US landscape artists, whose paintings depicted the unspoiled beauty of the Catskill Mountains and Hudson River. Its members, the first school of painting to originate in the US, included such artists as Thomas *Cole, Thomas Doughty (1793–1856), Asher Brown *Durand, Martin Johnson Heade (1819–1904), Frederick Edwin Church (1826–1900), and John Frederick Kensett (1818–72). Cole's 4-canvas work, "The Voyage of Life," Doughty's "In Nature's Wonderland," Durand's "Summer Woods," and Kensett's "Lake George" are among the paintings typical of this school.

Hudson's Bay Company A fur-trading company, formed in 1670, that was given settlement and trading rights in Canada; its first governor was Prince *Rupert (*see also* Rupert's Land). The company engaged in bitter rivalry with the *Northwest Company from the 1780s until 1821, when they were united under the name of the Hudson's Bay Company. It maintained a monopoly of the fur trade in Rupert's Land until 1859. In 1870 it sold its territories to Canada but remained a major fur-trading agency with headquarters in London.

Hue 16 28N 107 35E An ancient city in central Vietnam, on the Huong estuary. The University of Hue was established in 1957. A commercial center, Hue has textile, timber, and cement industries. *History*: a Chinese military stronghold from about 200 BC, Hue later fell to Champa and after 1635 was the capital of *Annam and after 1802 of the short-lived Vietnamese empire. It suffered heavily during the Vietnam War, in which it was a part of South Vietnam, and lost many of the historic buildings and treasures of the imperial citadel. Its population was also increased sixfold by refugees. Population (1973 est): 209,043.

Huelva 37 15N 6 56W A port in SW Spain, in Andalusia on the Odiel estuary. It ships copper from the Ríotinto mines and also iron, manganese, and wine. Population (1974 est): 105,625.

Huesca 42 08N 0 25W A city in NE Spain, in Aragon. Quintus Sertorius (c. 123–72 BC) founded his school here in 77 BC. It has a cathedral (13th–16th centuries). Population (1970): 33,185.

Huggins, Sir William (1824–1910) British astronomer, who pioneered the application of spectroscopy to astronomy, using the technique to discover that stars consist of the same elements as those found on the earth. He also discovered the *red shift in the lines of a star's spectrum. He was knighted in 1897.

Hugh Capet (c. 940–96 AD) The first *Capetian King of France (987–96). Son of the Count of Paris, Hugh seized the throne after the failure of the *Carolingian line.

Hughes, Charles Evans (1862–1948) US lawyer and jurist; US Supreme Court chief justice (1930–41). He began practicing law in New York in 1884 and served on state legislature investigating committees. He was governor of New York (1907–10) before being appointed to the Supreme Court by President *Taft in 1910. Known as a liberal associate justice he served until 1916, when he accepted the Republican presidential nomination; he lost to Woodrow Wilson. Hughes was secretary of state (1921–25) under presidents Warren Harding and Calvin Coolidge and organized the Washington Armament Conference (1921–22). Appointed US Supreme Court Chief Justice by President Herbert Hoover in 1930, he was a moderate conservative who presided over a court generally opposed to President Franklin D. Roosevelt's New Deal legislation. When Roosevelt attempted to "pack the court" by increasing the number of justices, Hughes helped to defeat the proposal.

Hughes, Howard (Robard) (1905–76) US aviator, film producer, and entrepreneur. His investments came to include Las Vegas hotels, airlines, and motion picture studios. After founding the Hughes Aircraft Company he broke the air speed record in 1935, reaching a speed of 352 mph (566 km per hr) in a craft of his own design. His films include *Hell's Angels* (1930), *Scarface* (1932), and *The Outlaw* (1944), the last of which he also directed. A billionaire at his death, he left no valid will. From 1950 until his death he lived in seclusion.

Hughes, (James Mercer) Langston (1902–67) US writer and poet; part of the *Harlem Renaissance. His writings portrayed growing up and living as a black in the US. His works include the poem collections *The Weary Blues* (1926), *Fine Clothes to the Jew* (1927), and *Scottsboro Limited* (1932); stage plays and musicals *Simply Heavenly* (1957), *Tambourines to Glory* (1959), *Black Nativity* (1961), and *The Prodigal Son* (1964); and the short story collection *The Ways of White Folks* (1934). His newspaper columns introduced his character Jesse B. ("Simple") Semple, who typified the urban black; the columns were collected in *Simple Speaks His Mind* (1950) and *Simple Stakes a Claim* (1957).

Hughes, Richard (1900–76) British novelist. His best-known novel is *A High Wind in Jamaica* (1929), concerning a family of children captured by pirates. *The Fox in the Attic* (1961) and *The Wooden Shepherdess* (1973) are the first two parts of an unfinished work concerning British and German society during the interwar years.

Hughes, Ted (1930–) British poet. His first volume, *The Hawk in the Rain* (1957), contained many poems concerned with the natural world written in a forceful energetic style. The poems in *Crow* (1970) and subsequent volumes are characterized by increased violence of language and subject matter. He married Sylvia *Plath in 1956.

Hughes, Thomas (1822–96) British writer. *Tom Brown's Schooldays* (1857), his best-known novel, is a celebration of the boarding-school ethos formulated by Thomas *Arnold. He was a Christian Socialist and a Liberal member of parliament from 1865 to 1874.

Hughes, William M(orris) (1864–1952) Australian statesman, born in London; prime minister (1915–23) as leader of the Labor Party (1915–16) and then of the newly founded Nationalist Party. An advocate of Australian federation in the 1890s, he was attorney general (1908–09, 1910–13, 1914–21, 1939–41). As prime minister he attended the Paris Peace Conference (1919) after World War I.

Hugh of Saint-Victor (1096–1141) French theologian. He joined the abbey of St Victor in Paris as a canon regular and, under his direction, its school became a major center of learning. His best-known book is *The Sacraments of the Christian Faith*.

Hugo, Victor (Marie) (1802–85) French poet, dramatist, and novelist. After several early novels and volumes of poetry, his leadership of the Romantic movement was confirmed by the success of his drama *Hernani* (1831). During the 1840s he became increasingly involved in politics as a champion of republican ideals and, after the coup d'état by the future Napoleon III in 1851, he went into exile in the Channel Islands until 1870. His later major works included *Les Contemplations* (1856), a volume of poems, and the novel *Les Misérables* (1862). The greatest French poet of the 19th century, during his last years he was honored as a national literary figure. He died in Paris and was buried in the Panthéon.

Huguenots French Protestants. Their name is derived from the Swiss-German *Eidgenoss*, confederate. The Huguenots, chiefly followers of John Calvin, were soon an influential national minority. The rivalry of their leaders, especially the *Condé, with the prominent Roman Catholic *Guise family gave rise to the *Wars of Religion (1562–94). The Edict of Nantes (1598) guaranteed the Huguenots freedom of worship but in Louis XIV's reign they were increasingly persecuted and after the revocation of the Edict (1685) over 250,000 Huguenots emigrated. Persecution continued until the French Revolution.

Huhehot. *See* Hohhot.

Hui Chinese Muslims of NW China, mainly in the provinces of Hebei, Xinjiang, Gansu, and Qinghai. Numbering about 3.5 million, they are descended from Chinese who were converted as a result of contact and intermarriage with *Turkic peoples during the 14th and 15th centuries. They are also known as Dungan (*or* T'ung-kan).

huia An extinct New Zealand songbird, *Heteralocha acutirostris*, 18 in (45 cm) long, that had a glossy black plumage with a white-tipped tail and orange wattles at the base of the bill. The bill of the male was strong and straight; that of the female was long, slender, and curved. Huias were hunted for the feathers by Maoris but their extinction was caused by the destruction of their habitat and excessive collection of specimens as curios by European settlers. Family: *Callaeidae* (wattlebirds).

Huitzilopochtli The Aztec sun- and war-god. He was portrayed as a hummingbird, or with armor of hummingbird feathers, and dead warriors were believed to be reincarnated as this bird. His temple at Tenochtitlan, founded in 1325 in the Valley of Mexico, was the principal Aztec religious structure. He was identified with the sun as a warrior who defeated the night stars, was reborn each day, and depended for nourishment on the blood of human sacrificial victims.

Huizinga, Johan (1872–1945) Dutch historian. Huizinga was professor of history, first at Groningen and then at Leyden University. His best-known book, *The Waning of the Middle Ages* (1919), was a study of life, thought, and art in late medieval France and the Netherlands. He also wrote *Erasmus* (1924), *In the Shadow of Tomorrow* (1935), an analysis of the malaise of contemporary western society, and *Homo Ludens* (1938).

Hull (official name: Kingston-upon-Hull) 53 45N 0 20W A city and port in NE England, situated on the Humber estuary. An important fishing port, Hull has vast docks and serves as a port for much of the North and Midlands. Its industries include vegetable-oil extraction, saw-milling, flour-milling, paints, chemicals, and engineering, as well as fish-related industries. Its university was established in 1927. Population (1971): 285,472.

Hull 45 26N 75 45W A city in E Canada, in SW Quebec on the Ottawa River opposite Ottawa. One of North America's main pulp-and-paper and timber centers, it has acquired many federal government offices in recent years. Population (1976): 61,039.

Hull, Cordell (1871–1955) US Democratic politician; secretary of state (1933–44) under Franklin D. Roosevelt. He did much to foster good relations with Latin America (*see* Good Neighbor Policy), attending the important Montevideo Conference in 1933, and supported China against Japanese ambitions in East Asia. He was instrumental in the foundation of the UN, for which he won the Nobel Peace Prize in 1945.

humanism 1. The intellectual movement that formed the inspiration and the basis of Renaissance culture. Humanist scholars based their program upon the rediscovery and study of classical Greek and Roman authors, which had been initiated in Italy by such men as *Petrarch and *Boccaccio. They turned away from the exclusively theological bias of their medieval forerunners and concentrated instead upon human achievements in the arts and sciences. *Erasmus was the greatest N European humanist. For him and the other Renaissance thinkers humanism by no means implied rejection of Christianity. 2. A 20th-century philosophical viewpoint that is based on a policy of *atheism, holding religion to be an outmoded superstition unworthy of serious consideration.

human rights Privileges claimed or enjoyed by a human being simply by virtue of being human. The concept developed from Roman ideas of "natural law" entailing "natural rights," via *Locke, *Paine, and the American Declaration of Independence (1776), to 20th-century liberal acceptance of the idea that human beings should have certain equal civil, political, and economic rights. Since the horrors of World War II, moves have been made to ensure international enforcement of human-rights agreements as embodied in the UN Charter. The UN Universal Declaration of Human Rights (1948), itself not a legally binding code, has spawned various subsequent agreements, such as the Covenants on Civil and Political Rights and on Economic, Social, and Cultural Rights (1966), which have been accepted as binding by 35 nations.

Humber An estuary in N England, flowing from the confluence of the Rivers Ouse and Trent to the North Sea past the ports of Hull, Immingham, and Grimsby. It is shortly to be spanned by the world's largest single-span suspension bridge. Length: 40 mi (64 km).

Humboldt, (Karl) Wilhelm von (1767–1835) German scholar and statesman; friend of Schiller and Goethe. As minister of education he founded Berlin University (1809) and was subsequently employed as a diplomat. His writings on language are especially profound: he saw language as a generative process rather than a lifeless structure. He perceived that language and thought are inseparable and identified various kinds of structures by which languages may be differentiated. His brother (**Friedrich Wilhelm Karl Heinrich) Alexander von Humboldt** (1769–1859) was a scientist and explorer. In 1799 he set off with Aimé Bonpland (1773–1858) to explore Central and South America and in the following five years the two men collected a large number of samples and much data relating to earth sciences. He subsequently explored central Asia, again collecting scientific material of great importance. In his great work *Kosmos* (5 vols, 1845–62) he set out his views on the whole universe. The *Humboldt Current and Glacier were named for him.

Humboldt Current (*or* Peru Current) An ocean current constituting part of the South Pacific oceanic circulation system. It flows N off the Peruvian coast of South America. Because of its Antarctic origins and the upwelling of cold water along the W coast of South America, it is a cold current rich in plankton and the fish that feed on them, giving rise to Peru's prosperous fishing industry.

Humboldt Glacier The largest known glacier in the N hemisphere, in NW Greenland. At its end in Kane Basin it is 60 mi (100 km) wide and 300 ft (91 m) high.

Hume, David (1711–76) Scottish philosopher and historian. He spent three years in France (1734–37) but for the rest of his life lived in either London or Edinburgh. In *A Treatise of Human Nature* (1739–40) he developed his influential distinction between impression and ideas, claiming that impressions have more force than ideas. We receive impressions from an unknown source and ideas derive from them through the operations of memory and imagination. For Hume almost nothing about existence was demonstrable; regarding the existence of God, his position throughout his numerous works is an incisive *agnosticism. Although an empiricist like *Locke and *Berkeley, Hume modified problematic aspects of their philosophies in favor of psychological explanations. Another aspect of Hume's thought that is influential among 20th-century philosophers is his analysis of cause and effect as no more than "constant conjunction": we can *observe* that one thing follows another but we can never *know* that it must follow, because of the limitations in the nature and scope of human understanding. Hume's *History of England* (1754–62) was a bestseller for many years.

humerus. *See* arm.

humidity A measure of the amount of water vapor in the atmosphere. Absolute humidity is the mass of water vapor in unit volume of air, measured in kilograms per cubic meter. Relative humidity is the ratio of the absolute humidity at a given temperature to the maximum humidity without precipitation at the same temperature, usually expressed as a percentage.

Hummel, Johann Nepomuk (1778–1837) Hungarian pianist and composer. He numbered Mozart and Haydn among his teachers. He toured Europe as a concert pianist and was famous as an improviser. His compositions include concertos and many piano solos.

HUMMINGBIRD *Gould's long-tailed sylph hummingbird* (Aglaiocercus kingi) *extracting nectar while hovering by a flower. This species is found in the Andes and from Venezuela to Peru and Bolivia.*

hummingbird A brightly colored bird belonging to a New World family (*Trochilidae*; 320 species). Hummingbirds are 2–8 in (5.5–20 cm) long and have a slender often downcurved bill and a brush-tipped tongue for feeding on nectar and small insects. Hummingbirds can hover, fly backward, and produce a humming noise by the rapid vibration of their wings during flight. Order: *Apodiformes* (swifts, etc.).

humpback whale A *rorqual whale, *Megaptera novaeangliae*, found in coastal waters throughout the world. It is 49 ft (15 m) long with long flippers and a large dorsal fin with lobes down to the tail. It is an acrobatic swimmer and lives in communities, feeding on crustaceans and small fish. □oceans.

Humperdinck, Engelbert (1854–1921) German composer. He assisted Wagner with the score of *Parsifal* in 1880–81. Of his many operas only *Hänsel und Gretel* (1893) is still popular: it blends German folklore with Wagnerian operatic techniques.

Humphrey, Hubert Horatio (1911–78) US political leader. As mayor of Minneapolis, Minn. (1945–49), Humphrey gained national prominence as a supporter of civil rights and social legislation. He was elected to the US Senate in 1948 and became active in the leadership of the *Democratic Party. In 1964, Humphrey was chosen by President Lyndon Johnson to become his vice presidential running mate and after Johnson's decision not to run for re-election, Humphrey received the Democratic presidential nomination in 1968. Although he was defeated in that election by Richard Nixon, Humphrey remained active in public life, being elected to two more terms in the US Senate, in 1970 and 1976.

humus · The black organic matter in soil resulting from the *decomposition of dead plants and animals (humification). It is rich in such elements as carbon, nitrogen, phosphorus, and sulfur, which are useful in maintaining soil fertility and hence in promoting plant growth. Humus also improves water absorption and workability of the soil.

Hunan A province in S central China, mountainous and forested in the S and W. The population includes an aboriginal minority. The chief products are rice, cereals, tea, cotton, timber, and such minerals as lead, zinc, tungsten, and gold. *History:* it was devastated during the Taiping Rebellion

(1851–64). Mao Tse-tung was born here. Area: 82,095 sq mi (210,500 sq km). Population (1972 est): 38,000,000. Capital: Changsha.

hundred A subdivision of the shire in England, first mentioned in the 10th century. Of varying size, it may originally have consisted of a hundred *hides. It corresponded to the *wapentake in the areas under Danish law. An administrative and judicial unit, it had its own court sitting every four weeks until the 13th century, when its importance began to decline.

Hundred Days (March 20–June 28, 1815) The period from *Napoleon Bonaparte's return to France, after his escape from Elba, until his final defeat by the allies at *Waterloo.

Hundred Days (March 9–June 16, 1933) The first 100 days of President Franklin D. Roosevelt's New Deal administration. During this time Congress passed many of the bills designed to help recovery from the *Depression. Farmers and homeowners were federally subsidized, banks were nationally regulated, and work was created for the unemployed.

Hundred Days of Reform (1898) A program of reforms announced by the Chinese emperor *Guang Xu, with the help of the reformer *Kang You Wei, to modernize the educational system, administration, and the armed forces and to develop trade, commerce, and industrialization on a western model. Most of the reforms were repealed by Guang Xu's mother *Zi Xi, who with the support of the army imprisoned her son and became regent, thus frustrating a reform movement that might have prevented the overthrow of the *Qing dynasty.

Hundred Flowers A Chinese government campaign to allow greater freedom of speech, particularly among intellectuals. It began in 1956 under the slogan "Let a hundred flowers bloom together, let a hundred schools of thought contend." It led to much open criticism of the government and was harshly suppressed a year later.

Hundred Years' War (1337–1453) A war between England and France. It was precipitated by Edward III's claim to the French throne, although there had long been hostility occasioned by disputes over English territory in France and French support for the Scots. The Treaty of *Brétigny (1360) recognized initial English successes at *Sluys (1340), *Crécy (1346), and Poitiers (1356) but thereafter the war was waged intermittently with frequent truces. Conditions were exacerbated by growing French and Burgundian rivalry, the Burgundians supporting Henry V of England, who achieved recognition as heir to the French throne after his victory at *Agincourt (1415). His early death, the accession of the weak *Henry VI, and more vigorous French prosecution of the war (inspired by *Joan of Arc) reversed his triumph and by 1453 England had been expelled from all French territory except Calais.

Hungarian A language of the *Finno-Ugric branch of the *Uralic family. It is spoken by 14 million people mainly in Hungary, where it is the official language, and in Czechoslovakia, Romania, and Yugoslavia. It uses a modified Latin alphabet and has borrowed many words from surrounding languages. Vowel harmony is characteristic of its sound system and its grammar is based on the use of suffixes. *See also* Magyars.

Hungarian National Council (1918–19) A political coalition formed in October, 1918, by *Károlyi and dedicated to establishing constitutional government in Hungary. In November, after Károlyi had become prime minister, it proclaimed Hungary a republic but the decline of the economy and the opposition of Hungary's minority nationalities forced its resignation (March, 1919) in favor of the communists under *Kun.

Hungarian Revolution (1956) An uprising against Soviet dominance of Hungary. Following the Soviet acceptance of *Gomulka as leader in Poland, a demonstration of students and workers in Budapest demanded the end of the Soviet presence in Hungary and of one-party government. The protestors were joined by army units. Imre *Nagy formed a coalition government, withdrew Hungary from the *Warsaw Pact, and sought UN help. An opposition government was formed by János *Kádár, and Soviet troops attacked Budapest and crushed the rebellion; Nagy and his associates were captured and executed. About 190,000 people left Hungary as a result of the Revolution.

Hungary, People's Republic of (Hungarian name: Magyar Népköztársasag) A country in central Europe. It lies mainly in the basin of the middle Danube, which forms the NW boundary with Czechoslovakia before running N–S across the center of the country. To the E of the Danube lies the Great Hungarian Plain, crossed by the Tisza River; to the W an undulating plain rises to some low hills in the SW and in the NW to the hilly Bakony Forest, S of which lies Lake *Balaton. The people are mainly Magyars, with minorities of Germans, Slovaks, and others. *Economy:* agriculture is now organized collectively, though individuals can still own small plots. The main crops are wheat and maize as well as fruit and vegetables. The wine industry is being encouraged, including the redevelopment of the Takaj region in the NE. The only mineral resource of significance is bauxite. Oil and natural gas have been found but most supplies come by pipeline from the Soviet Union. All industry is nationalized and there has been considerable expansion since World War II, particularly in engineering and chemicals. Since 1968 there has been a new system of economic planning, aiming at a certain amount of decentralization and encouragement of individual initiative, while still maintaining overall state control. The considerable volume of exports (largely to communist countries) includes transport equipment, machinery, fruit and vegetables, and meat. *History*: the Magyars reached the Danube area in the 9th century AD and settled there under the Árpád dynasty. In the 11th century St *Stephen I converted the country to Christianity and became the first Hungarian king. After a long period of dynastic struggles and threats from foreign powers, Hungary was conquered by the Turks in 1526 and in the 17th century it became part of the Habsburg Empire. The 19th century saw the rise of Hungarian nationalism. A revolt under *Kossuth in 1848 was suppressed by the Austrians but in 1867 Hungary gained internal self-government as part of the Dual Monarchy of *Austria-Hungary. Following the collapse of the Dual Monachy in 1918 Hungary became a republic but, after a short period of communist rule, a constitutional monarchy was formed with *Horthy de Nagybanya as regent. Although allied to the Germans in World War II, it was occupied by them in 1944 and liberated by Soviet troops in 1945. After the war it became a republic and in 1949 the communists gained control. In 1956 an anti-Stalinist uprising was crushed by Soviet forces. In 1967 a treaty of friendship with the Soviet Union was renewed and in recent years some reforms and a certain amount of liberalization have taken place. Effective power is in the hands of János *Kádár, first secretary of the Central Committee. Hungary, regarded as the showcase of Eastern European communism, pursues an economic course of "market socialism." In 1983 it had the highest per-capita return on its agricultural production in Europe. Official language: Hungarian (Magyar). Official currency: forint of 100 fillér. Area: 35,911 sq mi (93,035 sq km). Population (1983 est): 10,961,000. Capital: Budapest.

Hung Hsiu-ch'uan. *See* Hong Xiu Quan.

Hungnam. *See* Hamhŭng.

Hung-wu. *See* Hong-wu.

Huns Nomadic peoples, originating in Mongolia, who overran much of SE Europe in the late-4th and 5th centuries, overthrowing the *Ostrogoths and then invading the Roman Empire. Renowned and feared for their military prowess, especially their use of cavalry, the failure of the Empire to continue payment of tribute to them inspired *Attila, under whom the Huns were now united and controlled, to invade Greece, Gaul, and finally Italy (452). The death of Attila (453) fragmented their empire and after defeat by a coalition of tribes at Nedao (455) they ceased to be of importance.

Hunt, (James Henry) Leigh (1784–1859) British poet and journalist. In essays and criticism for many periodicals he supported Keats and other Romantic poets and promoted various political reforms. In 1813 he was imprisoned for his attacks on the Prince Regent. His books include *Imagination and Fancy* (1844) and *Autobiography* (1850).

Hunt, William Holman (1827–1910) British painter, born in London. After studying in the Royal Academy, he helped found the *Pre-Raphaelite Brotherhood, to the principles of which he alone remained faithful. His symbolic but technically realistic paintings, often biblical in subject, include *The Light of the World* (Keble College, Oxford) and *The Scapegoat* (Port Sunlight), inspired by a visit to Syria and Palestine (1854).

Hunter River A river in SE Australia, in New South Wales. It rises in the Eastern Highlands and flows generally S through Glenbawn Reservoir to enter the Pacific Ocean at Newcastle. Length: 290 mi (467 km).

Huntsville 34 44N 86 35W A city in NE Alabama. Founded in 1805, it is a center for rocket and guided-missile research. Industries include textiles and agricultural implements. Population (1975 est): 136,419.

Hunyadi, János (c. 1387–1456) Hungarian military leader and statesman. Following his successful Long Campaign against the Turks (1443–44), he was elected (1446) governor and regent for King Ladislas (1440–57). In 1456, shortly before dying of the plague, he routed the Turkish forces before Belgrade, thus securing a 70-year peace.

Hupa An Athabascan-speaking North American Indian people of the lower Trinity River region of N California. They lived along the river banks in villages consisting of women's houses and men's lodges. They hunted elk and deer, fished for salmon, and gathered acorns. Wealth consisted of dentalium shells and woodpecker scalps of which village headmen possessed the largest amounts. Their religion was characterized by *shamanism and the performance of seasonal ceremonies.

Hupei. *See* Hubei.

hurdling A track event in athletics in which sprinters jump ten hurdles in the course of each race. The standard distances are 110 m and 400 m for men and 100 m for women. For the 110 m the height of the hurdles is 3.5 ft (106.7 cm), for the 400 m it is 3 ft (91.4 cm), and for the 100 m, 2.75 ft (84 cm). Racers are not normally disqualified for knocking hurdles over.

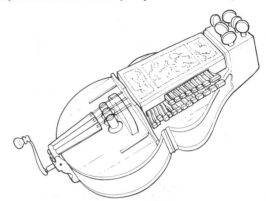

HURDY-GURDY

hurdy-gurdy A stringed instrument sounded by a rosined wheel, turned by the right hand, and stopped by a set of keys played by the left hand; there are also two drone strings. It was very popular in medieval times and survives as a folk instrument in parts of Europe.

hurling (*or* hurley) An Irish 15-a-side stick-and-ball field game similar to field hockey, dating back at least 3000 years. The ball is hit or carried through the air with a broad-bladed curved stick, the hurley (Gaelic word: *caman*), and may be caught in the hand. A standard field measures 137 × 82 m (150 × 90 yd). A goal, hit under the crossbar, scores three points; a hit between the posts but above the bar scores one point.

Huron An Iroquoian-speaking North American Indian people who originally inhabited the St Lawrence River region. Supporting themselves primarily by agriculture, they cultivated maize, beans, squash, and tobacco and occupied villages of bark-covered dwellings. In 1650 they were defeated by the *Iroquois and driven from their lands. Some of the Huron survivors were resettled in Ohio where they were known as the Wyandot Indians. The present Huron population living in small communities in Ohio, Kansas, and Ontario, Canada, is approximately 1250.

Huron, Lake The second largest of the Great Lakes in North America, situated between the US and Canada. It is an important shipping route carrying iron ore, coal, grain, and oil. Area: 23,000 sq mi (59,570 sq km).

Hurrians A people living in E Anatolia and N Mesopotamia during the 2nd millennium BC. The Hurrians probably originated in the Armenian mountains before their expansion. Their language, which is extinct, was neither Indo-European nor Semitic, but may be related to *Georgian and the Caucasian languages. It is largely known from cuneiform tablets from Hattusas, the capital of their neighbors, the *Hittites, whose civilization the Hurrians greatly influenced. There was never a Hurrian empire, but the powerful kingdom of Mitanni (1550–1400 BC) was largely Hurrian in population. *See also* Nuzi.

hurricane 1. A tropical *cyclone with surface-wind speeds in excess of 64 knots (107.3 ft or 32.7 m per second) that occurs around the Caribbean Sea and Gulf of Mexico. Tropical cyclones also occur in the W Pacific Ocean, and Bay of Bengal, but are identified by their own local names (*see* typhoon). The center (eye) of a hurricane is an area of light winds around which strong winds, cloud, and rain bands spiral. 2. Any wind reaching force 12 on the *Beaufort scale (in excess of 64 knots per second) whether or not it is related to a tropical cyclone.

Hurstmonceux. *See* Herstmonceux.

Hus, Jan (c. 1369–1415) Bohemian religious reformer and martyr. Ordained as a priest in 1401, he became a university teacher in Prague and a popular preacher. Under the influence of the writings of *Wycliffe, he criticized the ecclesiastical establishment, chiefly on moral grounds, emphasizing the role of the Scriptures. In 1415, while defending his beliefs at the Council of *Constance, where he had been lured by a promise of safe conduct, he was tried, condemned, and burned at the stake. His followers in Bohemia became known as *Hussites.

Husaynids The ruling dynasty of Tunisia from 1705 to 1957. Their founder, al-Husayn ibn Ali, was recognized as governor of Tunisia by the Ottomans, but he and his successors, who had the title of *bey*, were practically independent. In 1883 their land became a French protectorate. The *beys* lost popularity because it was thought they were too servile to the French and in 1957, when Tunisia became a republic, the dynasty came to an end.

husky One of several breeds of compact sturdy deep-chested dogs used for pulling sledges in Arctic regions. The Siberian husky has small erect ears, a long muzzle, and a brushlike tail curved over the back. The dense double-layered coat may be of various colors and provides insulation against the severe climate. The Eskimo dog, bred in Greenland, closely resembles the Siberian husky, from which it is probably descended. The Alaskan malamute is a similar breed of sled dog. Height: 20–25 in (51–63 cm). *See also* Samoyed.

hussars Light-cavalry regiments originating in Hungary in the 15th century. Most European armies have used hussars for reconnaissance and raids. Their uniform included the characteristic dolman, a cloak worn hanging from the left shoulder.

HUSSEIN *The king has encountered considerable opposition within Jordan and makes frequent tours of his country, piloting his own helicopter.*

Hussein (ibn Talal) (1935–) King of Jordan (1952–). He became king following the deposition because of mental illness of his father Talal. Hussein led Jordan into the 1967 Arab-Israeli War, in which its possessions on the West Bank of the Jordan River were occupied by Israel. The large Palestinian population of the area moved to the East Bank, where al-*Fatah guerrillas established themselves, posing a threat to Hussein's government. In 1970 he ruthlessly crushed the guerrillas in the fighting of "Black September" but in 1974, under pressure from other Arab countries, accepted the claims of the Palestine Liberation Organization to the West Bank.

Husserl, Edmund (1859–1938) German philosopher, influential in the phenomenological tradition (*see* phenomenology). He taught at Halle, Göttingen, and Freiburg Universities. Husserl's philosophy rejected presuppositions about what actually exists (and why it does) and studied instead purely "subjective" data.

Hussites The followers of the Bohemian heretic Jan *Hus (1372–1415). They demanded a reformed national Church with a vernacular liturgy. In spite of papal and imperial crusades led by the Holy Roman Emperor *Sigismund, the Hussites, who were supported by many of the Bohemian aristocracy, remained undefeated until a compromise was reached at the Council of *Basle in 1433. Their more radical wing, the Taborites, rejected this but were quickly defeated. The moderate Utraquists gained many of their demands and, in spite of frequent schisms, survived until the 17th century. *See also* Moravian Brethren.

Huston, John (1906–) US film director. He began his career as a scriptwriter. His first film as director was *The Maltese Falcon* (1941), and subsequent films included *The Treasure of the Sierra Madre* (1948), for which he wrote the script and in which he also acted, *The African Queen* (1951), *The Misfits* (1960), *Fat City* (1972), *The Man Who Would Be King* (1975), and *Annie* (1982).

Hutcheson, Francis (1694–1746) Scottish philosopher. He was a professor at Glasgow University (1729–46) and author of works on ethics and aesthetics. The posthumously published *System of Moral Philosophy* (1755) holds that man has an innate moral sense, so that he is born knowing what is good and right. Hutcheson's phrase, "the greatest happiness of the greatest number," as the criterion of virtuous action, was taken up by the exponents of *utilitarianism.

Hutchinson, Anne (Marbury) (1591–1643) US colonist and religious leader; born in England. She came to Boston in 1634 with her husband and children and began preaching against institutional organized religion. She felt that religion came from within a person, a theory many took to be against Puritanism. Banished from Massachusetts (1637), she and her followers established Portsmouth, RI. In 1643, while living near New York City, she and her family were attacked and killed by Indians.

hutia A large *rodent of the family *Capromyidae* (which also includes the *coypus), found in Cuba and the West Indies. Hutias are 8–24 in (20–60 cm) long excluding the naked tail 1.2–12 in (3–30 cm). They are mainly vegetarian and are either diurnal and arboreal (genus *Capromys*; 4 species) or nocturnal and terrestrial (genus *Geocapromys*; 3 species).

Hutten, Ulrich von (1488–1523) German humanist, who became poet laureate of the Holy Roman Empire in 1517. His reputation was established as a wit and satirist before he devoted himself to the cause of the Reformation and German nationalism. Joining the war against the German princes, he was driven into exile shortly before his death.

Hutton, James (1726–97) Scottish physician, generally regarded as the founder of geology. His investigations led him to believe that the earth was very much older than generally believed at that time. These views were expressed in his book *Theory of the Earth* (1785), which met with strong objections from those who accepted the view of creation contained in Genesis.

Huxley, Thomas Henry (1825–95) British biologist, whose impact spanned both biology and philosophy. A qualified surgeon, he was a staunch supporter and friend of Charles *Darwin and led the debate against opponents of Darwinism at Oxford in 1860. Huxley was instrumental in bringing enlightened change to educational methods. From 1880 onward he challenged orthodox theology and coined the term agnosticism to describe his own position. Three of his grandsons achieved fame in the fields of science and literature. **Sir Julian Huxley** (1887–1975) was a zoologist and scientific administrator, who also made valuable contributions to the philosophy of science. He was appointed first director general of UNESCO (1946–48). His views on evolution appeared in *Evolution: The Modern Synthesis* (1942). His brother **Aldous Huxley** (1894–1964) was a novelist and writer. During the 1920s he lived mostly in Italy and later settled in California. The witty satirical novels *Antic Hay* (1923) and *Point Counter Point* (1928) were followed by *Brave New World* (1932), *Eyeless in Gaza* (1936), and *After Many A Summer Dies the Swan* (1939). His later works, including *The Doors of Perception* (1954) and *Heaven and Hell* (1956), explore such subjects as mysticism and the use of drugs. **Sir Andrew Fielding Huxley** (1917–), half-brother to Sir Julian and Aldous, is a biologist noted for his researches into the mechanisms of nerve-impulse conduction and muscle contraction. For their work on nerve impulses Huxley and his collaborator A. L. *Hodgkin shared a Nobel Prize (1963) with Sir John *Eccles.

Huygens, Christiaan (1629–95) Dutch astronomer and physicist, who discovered Saturn's rings in 1656. He also built the first pendulum clock and designed an arrangement of lenses called a Huygens eyepiece, which is still in use on some telescopes and microscopes. He devised a wave theory of light to explain his observation of double refraction. He claimed to have invented the hairspring (a claim also made by *Hooke).

Huysmans, Joris Karl (1848–1907) French novelist. In his best-known novel, *À rebours* (1884), he epitomized the contemporary taste for decadent aestheticism in the character of Des Esseintes, who devoted his life to the sensual indulgence of his esoteric tastes. He also wrote art criticism and a series of partly autobiographical novels, including *Là-bas* (1891), that charted his spiritual progress and ultimate acceptance of Roman Catholicism.

hyacinth A perennial herbaceous plant of the genus *Hyacinthus* (about 30 species), native to the Mediterranean region and tropical Africa and widely planted as ornamental garden and pot plants. Growing from bulbs, the flower stems, up to 14 in (35 cm) high, bear a dense head of bell-shaped flowers, varying from white and yellow to deep purple. The plants have slender leaves, up to 12 in (30 cm) long. The common garden hyacinths are derived from *H. orientalis*. Family: *Liliaceae*.

Hyades A young open *star cluster in the constellation Taurus, the brightest stars forming a V-shaped group that can be seen with the naked eye. The star *Aldebaran lies in the direction of the cluster but is actually much nearer the sun.

hyaena. *See* hyena.

hybrid The offspring resulting from the mating of two unrelated individuals. The hybrid offspring often shows greater general fitness than either of the two parents, a phenomenon called hybrid vigor (or heterosis). This is commonly used by plant breeders to produce a generation of crop plants giving higher yields and showing improved resistance to disease. Hybrid vigor cannot be maintained in subsequent generations and new hybrids have to be produced for each season.

Hyde, Douglas (1860–1949) Irish scholar, whose translations of Irish literature influenced such writers as Yeats and Synge. He was also the first president of Eire (1938–45). He founded, and was first president (1893–1915) of, the Gaelic League. His books include *The Love Songs of Connacht* (1893), *A Literary History of Ireland* (1899), and *Legends of Saints and Sinners* (1915).

Hyderabad 17 22N 78 26E One of the largest cities in India, the capital of Andhra Pradesh situated on the Musi River. Formerly the capital of the princely state of Hyderabad, it was founded in 1590 by the Muslim Qutb Shahi sultans. The old city was planned around the Charminar (1594), a rectangular building surmounted by four minarets; other notable buildings include the Mecca Masjid, a mosque modeled on the one at Mecca. An educational center, Hyderabad is the site of Osmania University (1918), an agricultural university, and several research institutes. There has been considerable industrial growth in recent years, giving Hyderabad a higher standard of living than many other Indian cities. The chief manufactures include bus and railroad equipment, textiles, and pharmaceutical goods. Population (1971): 1,607,396.

Hyderabad 25 23N 68 24E A city in SW Pakistan, on the Indus River. A focal point of rail and road routes, it has light industries and several institutions of higher education, including the University of Sind (1947). Population (1972): 628,310.

Hyder Ali (1728–82) Muslim Indian ruler of Mysore. A volunteer in the Mysore raja's army from 1749, he became a commander (1759) and in about 1761 deposed the raja. When the British refused to support him against his Indian enemies, he invaded British territory and was narrowly defeated near Madras, coming closer than any other Indian ruler to ousting the British from S India.

Hydra In Greek legend, a monster with many heads who grew two more whenever one was cut off. It was killed by *Heracles, whose own death was later caused by the monster's poisonous blood or gall.

Hydra A widely distributed genus of solitary freshwater invertebrate animals belonging to an order (*Hydroida*) of *coelenterates. They are flexible *polyps, 0.40–1 in (10–30 mm) long, with the mouth at the top surrounded by 6–10 tentacles. Hydras are usually attached to stones, sticks, or aquatic vegetation and feed on small animals. Reproduction is asexual in summer and sexual in winter. Class: *Hydrozoa*.

Hydrangea A genus of shrubs (about 80 species) native to Asia and North and South America, including several popular ornamentals. The showy heads of white, pink, or blue flowers may be sterile and sometimes change color according to the acidity or alkalinity of the soil. *H. macrophylla* is a popular pot plant. Family: *Hydrangeaceae*.

hydraulics The study of the applications of *hydrostatics and *hydrodynamics to design problems. In civil engineering it is used to study the flow of water in pipes, rivers, canals, etc., especially with reference to the construction of dams, reservoirs, and hydroelectric power stations. In mechanical engineering, applications include the design of machinery involving fluids, such as hydraulic presses, *turbines, propellers, etc. Hydraulics is concerned with the bulk properties of fluids, such as density, viscosity, elasticity, and surface tension, rather than their molecular properties.

hydraulis (Greek: water pipe) An early type of *organ in which the air pressure was maintained by water. A clay model found in the ruins of Carthage has three ranks of pipes and suggests an actual height of about 10 ft (3 m). The loud sound it produced made it useful for signaling in battle; it was also played in Roman amphitheaters, the Emperor Nero being an enthusiastic performer.

hydrocarbons Compounds containing carbon and hydrogen. The saturated hydrocarbons are classified as *alkanes. Unsaturated hydrocarbons include the *alkenes and *alkynes. *Aromatic hydrocarbons include *benzene and its many derivatives.

hydrocephalus An excess of fluid in the brain. The brain is normally bathed in cerebrospinal fluid, which is constantly being produced and reabsorbed. A block in the flow or reabsorption of the fluid will result in hydrocephalus. In a baby, the bones of whose skull are not yet joined, the head becomes enlarged. Congenital defects, meningitis, tumors, and injury can all be causes. Hydrocephalus may resolve spontaneously or may require surgical treatment.

hydrochloric acid A solution in water of the colorless pungent gas hydrogen chloride (HCl). It is made by the action of sulfuric acid on salt or by the direct recombination of hydrogen and chlorine from the electrolysis of sea water. It is very soluble in water and forms a strong acid. Concentrated hydrochloric acid contains about 40% HCl by weight and is a clear fuming corrosive liquid. The acid in the human stomach is dilute hydrochloric acid (0.4%).

hydrocyanic acid (*or* prussic acid; HCN) A highly toxic colorless liquid. It is made from ammonia and methane reacted with air in the presence of a catalyst. HCN forms weakly acidic solutions in water and is used in making synthetic fibers and as a fumigant.

hydrodynamics (*or* fluid dynamics) The branch of mechanics concerned with the study of ideal fluids in motion. An ideal fluid is assumed to be incompressible and to be free from frictional forces. Although never achieved, this simplification is often necessary to analyze a complex situation. The velocity, acceleration, and pressure at each point in the flow of an ideal liquid gives an indication of what will happen in a real liquid. *See also* aerodynamics; hydraulics.

hydroelectric power Electricity generation using the energy of falling water. The water turns a *turbine connected to an alternator, generating electricity with an efficiency of over 90% at full load and generally over 60% at quarter-load. Water is led through pipes from high-level natural or artificial reservoirs to the power station. Lower-level reservoirs and dammed rivers are also used in some situations. The higher the reservoir, the less water is needed for the same power output. Hydroelectric power is, therefore, a cheap power source in mountainous areas with high rainfall. Unfortunately these are not usually near the industrial communities that consume the most power. Also, because it depends on rainfall, hydroelectricity has to be backed by other power sources (*see* power station). In pumped storage stations, electricity is stored by using it to drive pumps that raise the water to a high-level reservoir. In times of high demand this water is run back through the turbines. Hydroelectric power stations can have an output of 10,000 megawatts.

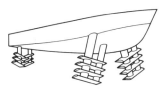

ladder foils

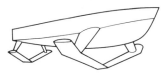

V-shaped foils

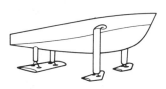

short submerged foils

HYDROFOIL

hydrofoil A type of ship the hull of which is raised out of the water by foils as its speed increases. The foils provide lift in much the same way as an airfoil; once the hull is clear of the water the drag is greatly reduced and the speed can be increased far above that of a normal ship of the same size and weight. The first hydrofoil was built in 1906 by Enrico Fortanini (1848–1930); this had a stack of foils arranged like a ladder. Modern craft use a large V-shaped foil, to provide stability in turns or in rough seas, or small totally submerged foils, which support the hull on streamlined struts. Propulsion is by propeller or by pumped-water jet. Hydrofoils of 150 tons are in use in many parts of the world; some are capable of reaching speeds of up to 70 mph (112 kph).

hydrogen (H) The lightest of all gases, recognized as an element by Cavendish in 1766 and named by Lavoisier after water (Greek *hudro*, water). Hydrogen makes up about three-quarters of the mass of the universe. It is the simplest element, its nuclei consisting of one proton. Heavier elements are formed by nuclear fusion (*see* nuclear energy) from hydrogen in stars. The heavier isotope of hydrogen, *deuterium (D *or* ^{2}H), occurs as about one part in 6000 of ordinary hydrogen. *Tritium (^{3}H) also occurs but is unstable. As well as the gaseous element (H_2) and water (H_2O), hydrogen occurs in organic compounds and in all inorganic *acids and *alkalis. The gas itself is used as a fuel for rockets, in welding, for filling balloons, and in chemical manufacture. It combines (explosively if in the right proportions) with oxygen to form water and can be obtained from water by electrolysis. Liquid hydrogen is used for experiments in low-temperature physics. At no 1; at wt 1.00797; mp –434.45°F (–259.14°C); bp –423.17°F (–252.87°C).

hydrogen bomb. *See* nuclear weapons.

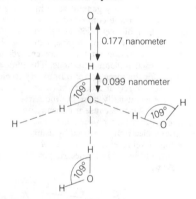

HYDROGEN BOND *The hydrogen bonding between water molecules (H_2O) in ice crystals.*

hydrogen bond A weak attraction (much weaker than a covalent or ionic *chemical bond but much stronger than *Van der Waals forces) between an oxygen, nitrogen, or fluorine atom in one molecule and a hydrogen atom in a neighboring molecule. The hydrogen atom must itself be linked to a similar electronegative atom by a covalent bond. The attraction arises because the atom bonded to the hydrogen atoms exerts a strong pull on the shared electrons and thus confers a partial positive charge on the hydrogen. Consequently electrostatic attraction occurs between this hydrogen atom and the oxygen, fluorine, or nitrogen in the other molecule. Hydrogen bonding is responsible for the anomalous physical properties of many compounds, including water. It is particularly important in biological systems, being responsible for maintaining the structure of proteins and nucleic acids.

hydrography The description, measurement, and charting of the waters of the earth's surface (oceans, seas, lakes, rivers, and streams), particularly for navigational purposes. Tides, currents, and waves are also involved. The term is sometimes used for the shape of the sea floor and the deposits covering it.

hydrology The science that studies the occurrence and movement of water on and over the surface of the earth. The **hydrological cycle** is the cyclic movement of water from the sea to the atmosphere and back, via precipitation, streams, and rivers. The main processes with which hydrology is concerned are precipitation, evaporation and transpiration, stream flow, and groundwater flow. It has many important applications, such as flood control and the supply of water for domestic and industrial purposes, irrigation, and hydroelectric power. □water table.

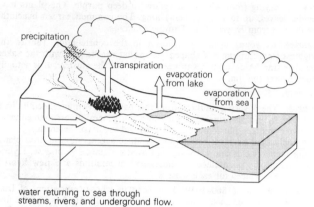

HYDROLOGY *The hydrological cycle.*

hydrolysis The reaction of a chemical compound with water; usually water is the solvent in which the reaction occurs. A common example is the hydrolysis of *esters to form alcohols and carboxylic acids.

hydrometer An instrument for measuring the relative *density of a liquid. It consists of a weighted and sealed glass bulb with a long neck on which a scale is calibrated. The relative density is measured by placing the hydrometer in the liquid and noting the level to which it sinks.

hydrophobia. *See* rabies.

hydrophone A type of *microphone that converts underwater sound waves into electrical signals. It consists essentially of a diaphragm, a *transducer, and an *amplifier. It is used in *sonar equipment, depth sounding, and underwater communications.

hydroponics The cultivation of plants in a liquid nutrient solution instead of soil. A carefully prepared aqueous solution of all the nutrients required for healthy growth is used, usually in conjunction with an inert medium, such as sand or gravel, which provides support for the plant-root system. On a small scale, the solution is simply poured over the substrate and the excess allowed to drain into containers for re-use. On a commercial scale, this is done by an automatic pumping system in which the solution is monitored to maintain nutrient levels and acidity.

Hydroponics enables crops to be produced in arid regions or where the soil is infertile or toxic, but its high cost restricts its use to high-value crops, such as flowers and vegetables.

hydrostatics The branch of mechanics concerned with fluids at rest (*compare* hydrodynamics). It is generally considered to have been instigated by Archimedes. Applications include the design of storage tanks, gates, and valves for hydraulic structures, dams, etc.

Hydrozoa A class of aquatic invertebrate animals (3700 species)—*coelenterates—whose life cycle usually alternates between generations of mainly marine sessile colonial *polyps and free-swimming solitary *medusae. *See also* Hydra; Obelia; Portuguese man-of-war.

hyena (*or* hyaena) A carnivorous □mammal of the family *Hyaenidae*. There are three species: the African spotted hyena (*Crocuta crocuta*); the Asian striped hyena (*Hyaena hyaena*); and the brown hyena (*H. brunnea*) of South Africa, also called strandwolf. Hyenas are doglike in appearance, up to 5 ft (1.5 m) long including the tail, and stand about 35 in (90 cm) high at the shoulder. They hunt in packs, feeding on carrion and killing young or sick animals.

Hyères 43 07N 6 08E A resort and spa in S France, in the Var department on the French Riviera. It has a notable beach and offshore are the Îles d'Hyères, a small group of islands (Porquerolles, Port-Cros, l'Île du Levant, and two islets). Population (1975): 39,593.

Hygiea The Greek goddess of health, worshiped together with *Asclepius, god of medicine, and sometimes identified as his daughter or wife. She was usually portrayed in the act of feeding a serpent from a dish.

hygrometer An instrument that measures the relative *humidity of the atmosphere. In mechanical hygrometers, a material (usually human hair) is used, the length of which varies with the humidity; the variations being transformed into the movement of a pointer along a scale. In the wet-and-dry bulb hygrometer, two thermometers are placed side by side, one having its bulb covered by a moist cloth. The cooling caused by the evaporation from this wet bulb depends on the atmospheric moisture and thus the difference between the two thermometer readings can be related by standard tables to the relative humidity.

Hyksos A nomadic Asiatic tribe, known to the ancient Egyptians as Shepherd Kings or Princes of Foreign Lands. Moving southward about 1750 BC through Palestine and Syria, the Hyksos invaded Egypt and, until driven northward again by the Egyptians about 1570 BC, ruled the Delta area, introducing metallurgy, bronze weapons, the wheel and, traditionally, the use of horse and chariot.

Hymen The Greek god of marriage. He was the son of Apollo or of Dionysus and Aphrodite.

Hymenoptera A large worldwide order of insects (over 100,000 species) including the ants, sawflies, ichneumons, wasps, and bees. Many species show a high degree of social organization. Typically they have two pairs of membranous wings and the first segment of the abdomen is constricted to form a "waist." A tubular egg-laying structure (ovipositor) is generally present and in higher groups is modified for sawing, piercing, or stinging. The larvae (except the sawflies) are legless and have well-developed heads. The males develop from unfertilized eggs. Many species are of benefit to man because they pollinate flowering plants and prey on or parasitize insect pests.

Hymettus, Mount (Modern Greek name: Imittós Óros) 37 57N 23 49E A mountain ridge in SE Greece, running N–S for about 9 mi (15 km) immediately E of Athens. The Kara marble used in ancient times was quarried here. Height: 3366 ft (1026 m).

hymn A song of praise in honor of a deity or saint, often in a metrical verse form. Hymns have been an important part of Christian congregational worship since the end of the 4th century. During the middle ages polyphonic settings became common but after the Reformation Lutheran chorale became the basis of the German and English hymn traditions. Famous hymn writers included Martin Luther, Charles Wesley, and Isaac Watts (1674–1748); many of the hymns sung in the Anglican church today were written in the 19th century.

Hypatia (d. 415 AD) Neoplatonist philosopher and mathematician. She lectured on philosophy at *Alexandria, where her wisdom and learning endeared her to both pagans and Christians. The patriarch Cyril resented her influence, and she was brutally murdered by a Christian mob.

hyperbola The curve, or pair of curves, formed by a *conic section and defined in Cartesian coordinates (see coordinate systems) by the equation $x^2/a^2 - y^2/b^2 = 1$, where a and b are constants. Its two parts have a common axis and are separated by a minimum distance $2a$ along this axis. As it goes out to *infinity, the curve becomes increasingly close to two straight lines, called *asymptotes.

hyperbolic functions A set of mathematical functions written sinh x, cosh x, tanh x, and their inverses csch x, sech x, and coth x respectively. Sinh x is defined as $\frac{1}{2}(e^x - e^{-x})$, where e is the base of natural logarithms; cosh x is $\frac{1}{2}(e^x + e^{-x})$, and tanh x is sinh x/cosh x. Hyperbolic functions are defined by analogy with the trigonometric functions sin x, etc., and are so named because they are related to the *hyperbola in much the same way as the trigonometric functions are related to the circle.

Hyperboreans In Greek mythology, a people who lived in the far north, beyond the north wind (Boreas), in a land of sunshine and luxury. According to *Herodotus, they were devotees of Apollo and sent offerings to him at Delos but did not come themselves.

hyperglycemia A high concentration of sugar in the blood. This occurs in *diabetes mellitus and may, if severe and uncontrolled, lead to coma.

Hyperion In Greek mythology, one of the *Titans, the son of Uranus and Gaea and father of *Eos, *Helios, and *Selene. He was himself a sun god and was often identified with his son Helios.

hypermetropia. See farsightedness.

hypersensitivity. See allergy.

hypertension High *blood pressure. This is a common condition, which can be caused by kidney disease, hormonal disorders, and some congenital diseases; for most cases, however, no cause can be found (this is known as essential hypertension). Usually there are no symptoms, with the consequent danger that untreated hypertension may lead to heart failure, kidney failure, cerebral hemorrhage, and blindness. In some cases surgery can be curative, but usually only drug treatment is necessary and must continue indefinitely.

hyperthyroidism Overactivity of the thyroid gland, which occurs most commonly in women. It may lead to the syndrome of thyrotoxicosis: restlessness, irritability, heat intolerance, weight loss, and palpitations, sometimes with protruding eyes and swelling of the neck (see goiter)—this is

called exophthalmic goiter (or Graves's disease). It can be treated by surgery, radioactive iodine to destroy part of the gland, or drugs that suppress the production of thyroid hormones.

hypnosis The production of a trance state by means of firm suggestion, with the cooperation of the subject. People who have been deeply hypnotized can carry out instructions that would not be possible in a normal waking state; for instance, they can become insensible to pain or regress to childish behavior. First used for therapeutic purposes by *Mesmer in the 18th century, it was developed (and given the name hypnosis) by James Braid (1795–1860) in the 19th century. In France it was used by *Charcot (under whom *Freud studied), and by the turn of the century it was established as a means of treating certain psychiatric disorders (especially those of psychosomatic origin). It has, however, always been regarded as somewhat disreputable, first because of its misuse on the stage as a form of entertainment and second because the mechanism is still not understood. Although it is alleged that a hypnotist cannot force a patient under hypnotism to do anything he would not be willing to do when awake (e.g. commit a crime), the dangers inherent in one person controlling another's actions are obvious.

hypnotics Drugs that cause sleep. Although most drugs that depress the brain's activity have this effect, the ideal hypnotic produces natural sleep without "hangover" effects on awakening. Some drugs of the *benzodiazepine group come closest to this ideal and have now almost entirely replaced *barbiturates as hypnotics.

hypoglycemia A low concentration of sugar in the blood. This may occur in otherwise healthy people who have eaten little and exercised considerably, but is more often seen in diabetics who have taken too much insulin. The patient feels weak, sweaty, and shaky. See diabetes.

hypothalamus A part of the *brain, surrounding the lower part of the third ventricle, that is an important coordinating center for the functions of the autonomic *nervous system. It is particularly involved with the control of body temperature, with regulating how much is eaten and drunk, and with the emotions. It also releases *neurohormones affecting other organs, especially the *pituitary gland.

hypothermia Lowering of the body temperature. This is most commonly seen in old people and young babies—whose body temperature is less well controlled—if they are living in poorly heated rooms. If the body temperature falls very low severe internal changes may occur, but otherwise gentle warming will help the patient to recover. Hypothermia may be deliberately induced for heart surgery.

HYRAX *The rock hyrax, or dassie* (Procavia capensis), *lives in colonies of up to about 40 individuals in caves or other shelters in rocky regions of Africa.*

hyrax An African *mammal belonging to the order *Hyracoidea* (6 species), also called coney. 12–24 in (30–60 cm) long, hyraxes are related to ungulates (hooved mammals), having hooflike toes and a two-chambered stomach for digesting their vegetable diet. They are nimble and live in small colonies in trees or among rocks, being most active at twilight.

hyssop A perennial herbaceous plant, *Hyssopus officinalis*, native to S Europe, Asia, and Morocco. It is grown elsewhere as a garden ornamental and was formerly cultivated as a medicinal herb. Growing to a height of 24 in (60 cm), it has whorls of violet-blue flowers along the stem. Family: *Labiatae*.

hysterectomy　The surgical removal of the womb. A subtotal hysterectomy involves removing the body of the womb but leaving the neck (cervix); in total hysterectomy (or panhysterectomy) the entire womb is removed. It is most commonly performed when the womb contains large fibroids—benign tumors that cause heavy menstrual periods. Other conditions that may require hysterectomy include cancer of the womb or the presence of precancerous cells in the cervix. The operation is usually performed through an incision made in the abdominal wall: it invariably precludes subsequent pregnancy but does not affect sexual activity.

hysteresis　Any of several physical phenomena in which an induced effect lags behind the inducing cause. The term is most often applied to magnetic hysteresis in which the magnetic induction produced in a ferromagnetic material lags behind the magnetic field. Thus a graph of magnetic induction plotted against a magnetizing field is a closed S-shaped loop (hysteresis loop). The area within the loop is equal to the energy dissipation per unit volume during one cycle of magnetization. Other forms of hysteresis include thermal, dielectric, and elastic hysteresis.

hysteria　A neurotic condition of emotional instability and immaturity in which patients are vulnerable to suggestion and develop physical symptoms. Hysterical symptoms are unconsciously adopted by the individual because they bring some gain. The symptoms may be of "conversion hysteria," characterized by physical symptoms, such as paralysis; or of "dissociative hysteria," with changes in thinking, such as multiple personality. Treatment is usually by *psychotherapy.

Hywel the Good　(Howel Dda; d. 950 AD) Welsh prince (c. 909–50 AD). A friend of the English king Athelstan, Hywel eventually united S and N Wales in his remarkably peaceful reign. His famous codification of Welsh law remained effective for over three hundred years.

I

iamb In verse, a metrical foot consisting of an unstressed syllable (or in verse based on quantity, a short syllable) followed by a stressed (or long) syllable. It was developed in quantitative verse by the ancient Greeks, who used it in dramatic dialogue because of its affinity to the natural rhythm of speech, and is the commonest type of metrical foot in English poetry.

Iapetus In Greek mythology, one of the *Titans, the son of Uranus and Gaea and father of Atlas and Prometheus. When the rebellion of the Titans was defeated by Zeus, he was imprisoned in Tartarus.

Iaşi (German name: Jassy) 47 09N 27 38E A city in NE Romania, near the Soviet border. The former capital of Moldavia, it possesses many historic buildings and academic institutions, including a university (1860). It has metal, chemical, and pharmaceutical industries. Population (1979 est): 262,493.

Ibadan 7 23N 3 56E The second largest city in Nigeria. The arrival of the railroad (1901) aided its commercial development and it is now an important industrial, commercial, and administrative center although there are few modern industries. Cocoa, palm products, and cotton are traded. It contains the University of Ibadan (1962). Population (1975 est): 847,000.

Ibagué 4 35N 75 30W A city in central Colombia, on the E slopes of the Central Cordillera. The surrounding area produces cocoa, tobacco, rice, and sugar cane. Tolima University was founded here in 1945. Population (1978 est): 263,669.

Ibarruri, Dolores (1895–) Spanish politician. The foremost Spanish communist in the 1930s, her oratory earned her the name La Pasionaria. She went into exile in 1939 and lived in the Soviet Union until the legalization of the Communist Party allowed her to return to Spain (1977). She subsequently became a member of the Cortes.

Iberian Peninsula A peninsula in SW Europe, occupied by Portugal and Spain. It is separated from the rest of Europe by the Pyrenees and its flora and fauna are similar to those of N Africa. Area: 229,054 sq mi (593,250 sq km).

Iberians A Bronze Age people of S and E Spain in the 1st millennium BC. Their non-Indo-European language, which was displaced by Latin, is known from a variety of inscriptions on stone and other materials. The culture of the tribes of the coastal region of Valencia and in the NE showed considerable Greek influence while that of the SE tribes owed much to the Carthaginians. This is shown, for example, in differences in the alphabets used in each area. The economic basis was agriculture, mining, and metalworking. They lost their identity by cultural assimilation to the *Celts in Roman times.

Ibert, Jacques (1890–1962) French composer. A pupil of Fauré, he won the Prix de Rome in 1919. He directed the Academy of Rome from 1937 to 1955. His compositions include operas, chamber and orchestral music, and songs. His best-known work is the humorous orchestral *Divertissement* (1930).

Iberville, Pierre le Moyne, Sieur d' (1661–1706) French-Canadian explorer. After serving in the French navy he returned to Canada and led raids on the English fur-trading posts on Hudson Bay (1686–97). In 1699 he founded a colony at present-day Biloxi (Mississippi) and in 1700, the first French colony in Louisiana (near present-day New Orleans).

ibex A rare wild *goat, *Capra ibex*, of Eurasian and N African mountains. About 33 in (85 cm) high at the shoulder, ibexes have backward-curving horns up to 26 in (65 cm) long and their coat is brownish-gray with variable markings.

Other species known as ibex include the tur (*C. caucasica*) of Russia and the Spanish ibex (*C. pyrenaica*).

ibis A long-necked wading bird belonging to the subfamily *Threskiornithinae* (20 species), distributed worldwide in warm regions. 22–30 in (55–75 cm) long, ibises have a characteristic slender downcurved bill, and unfeathered face or head and neck, which may be black or brightly colored. They feed on small fish and aquatic invertebrates. Family: *Threskiornithidae* (ibises and spoonbills); order: *Ciconiiformes* (herons, storks, etc.).

Ibiza (Iviza *or* Ivica) A Spanish island in the Mediterranean Sea, in the Balearic Islands. Its climate and fine beaches have made it a popular tourist center. Exports include almonds, dried figs, apricots, and salt. Area: 541 sq km (209 sq mi). Population (1970): 42,456. Chief town: Ibiza.

IBIS *The sacred ibis* (Threskiornis aethiopica) *was revered by the ancient Egyptians as a symbol of the god Thoth: mummified birds have been found in the tombs of the pharaohs. Today the species is restricted to Africa S of the Sahara.*

Iblis The Muslim name for the devil, perhaps derived from Greek *diabolos*. He is also called *al-Shaytan* (Satan). Because of his disobedience and pride, the devil was expelled from Paradise by God, but given power to lead astray those who do not serve God. Muslim tradition gives him a number of names before his fall, such as Azazil. It is disputed whether he was an angel, as in the Koran, or a jinni.

Ibn al-'Arabi, Muhyi-I-din (1165–1240) Muslim mystic and poet born in Murcia (Spain). The leading mystic of his age, he was one of the great geniuses of *sufism. In philosophy, he was a Neoplatonist. Some scholars believe that Islamic sufism, as represented by Ibn al-'Arabi, was an imitation of Christian monastic mysticism.

Ibn Battutah (1304–?1368) Arab traveler. From 1325 to 1354 he traveled extensively in Asia Minor, the Near and Far East, Europe, and Africa. He then settled at Fez and wrote an invaluable and amusing account of his work—the *Rihlah*.

Ibn Ezra, Abraham Ben Meir (1093–1167) Hebrew poet and scholar, born in Toledo, who traveled to England, Italy, France, North Africa, and perhaps to Palestine. His works include a set of famous commentaries on the Hebrew Bible, poems, riddles, and epigrams.

Ibn Gabirol, Solomon (c. 1021–c. 1058) Jewish philosopher and poet, born in Málaga (Spain). He was one of the earliest philosophers of Moorish Spain and a leading Neoplatonist. His outstanding philosophical work, *The Fountain of Life*, influenced generations of western medieval thinkers. *The Kingly Crown* is the summit of his poetic achievement.

Ibn Khaldun (1332–1406) Arab historian and philosopher, who held court posts in Spain and was chief judge in Cairo, where he died. In the *Kitab al-'ibar* (*Book of Examples*) he outlined the history of Islam and a historical theory of cyclical progress and regression in which nation states develop out of, and are subsequently destroyed by, nomadic communities.

Ibn Saud (c. 1880–1953) The first King of Saudi Arabia (1932–53). With the military help of al-*Ikhwan, he extended his territory from the Sultanate of Najd, which he reconquered in 1902, to encompass much of Arabia by 1924, when he took Hejaz. The name Saudi Arabia was adopted in 1932. In 1933 Ibn Saud came to an agreement with a US oil company, which discovered oil in his country in 1936, using the resultant revenues to introduce modernization programs.

Ibo (*or* Igbo) A people of SE Nigeria who speak Igbo, a language of the Kwa subgroup of the *Niger-Congo family. Subsistence cultivators of yams, cassava, and taro, they traditionally lived in scattered small holdings or village clusters of patrilineal kin headed by the eldest male descendant of the founder. Small federations of villages were the largest political units before colonial times. Many have now adopted Christianity. A growing sense of ethnic identity led to the proclamation of the short-lived Ibo secessionist republic of *Biafra (1967–70).

Ibrahim Pasha (1789–1848) Ottoman general; the son (or adopted son) and right-hand man of the viceroy of Egypt, *Mehemet Ali. In Egypt from 1805, he was given various offices by his father, culminating in the command of the Egyptian army after Mehemet Ali had quarreled with the Ottomans (1831). Ibrahim occupied Syria, becoming governor general (1833), until forced to withdraw by the European powers (1840). His modernizing policies were severely imposed and provoked much opposition. In 1848 he succeeded his infirm father as viceroy of Egypt but died after only 40 days in office.

Ibsen, Henrik (1828–1906) Norwegian playwright and poet, the founder of modern prose drama. The son of a rich merchant who became bankrupt when his son was eight, Ibsen was preparing to study medicine when he wrote his first, unsuccessful, play. After working in theaters in Bergen and Kristiania and continuing to write plays, none of which was outstanding, he wrote *Kongsemnerne* (*The Pretenders*; 1864), for which he was granted a scholarship. He traveled to Rome and from 1864 to 1891 lived in Italy and Germany, with occasional visits to Norway. His fame as a dramatist grew with *Brand* (1865) and *Peer Gynt* (1867). In his next several plays he turned to the presentation of social issues: women's emancipation in *A Doll's House* (1879), inherited disease and guilt in *Ghosts* (1881), and public corruption in *An Enemy of the People* (1882), plays which earned him a wide and controversial reputation. Subsequent works, such as *The Wild Duck* (1884) and *Hedda Gabler* (1890), dealt with the problems of individuals. In his last plays, *The Master Builder* (1892), *John Gabriel Borkman* (1896), and *When We Dead Awaken* (1899), he turned to the treatment of autobiographical themes in a symbolic manner.

Icarus (astronomy) A very small (about 0.6 mi [1 km] diameter) *minor planet with the smallest known *perihelion (0.19 astronomical units). It passed only 372,600 mi (600,000 km) from earth in 1968.

Icarus (mythology). *See* Daedalus.

Ice Age A period in the earth's history when ice spread toward the equator with a general lowering of temperatures. The most recent of these was the *Pleistocene epoch ending about 10,000 years ago, during which four major ice advances occurred. Other ice ages occurred in Permo-Carboniferous times about 250 million years ago and in Pre-Cambrian times about 500 million years ago. Between 1550 and 1850 the **Little Ice Age** occurred, with a significant lowering of temperatures in the N hemisphere.

iceberg A large mass of ice in the sea that has originated on land. Many result from the breaking off, or calving, of ice from glaciers. In the N hemisphere icebergs originate chiefly from Greenland, in the S hemisphere most break off from the Antarctic ice. A large part of an iceberg is submerged, causing a hazard to shipping (e.g. the loss of the *Titanic* in 1912).

icefish A name given to several unrelated fish including the family *Chaenichthyidae* (175 species) of the order *Perciformes*, also called white-blooded fish, which occur in Antarctic waters. Others include the semitransparent icicle or glass fish of E Asia (family *Salangidae*) and certain species of *smelt. Order: *Salmoniformes*.

ice hockey A six-a-side team game played with stick and puck on a rink. It derives from field hockey and was first played on the frozen harbor of Kingston, Ontario (c. 1860). Canada is the true home of the game, but it is widely played in the US, the Soviet Union, Sweden, Czechoslovakia, West Germany, and Finland. Each team consists of a goalkeeper, right and left defense, center, and right and left wing and each team is allowed eight reserves. The premier professional league is the National Hockey League (NHL) (instituted 1917). The championship trophy, the Stanley Cup, has been won by the Montreal Canadiens more than any other team. The Canada Cup is a well-known international tournament, and hockey is also played in the Winter Olympics.

Iceland, Republic of (Icelandic name: Ísland) An island country in the N Atlantic Ocean, just S of the Arctic Circle, off the SE coast of Greenland. It consists mainly of a largely uninhabited plateau of volcanoes, lava fields, and glaciers; most of the population live around the deeply indented coast. *Economy*: some crops and livestock are produced, sufficient for local needs, but the basis of the economy is fishing. Hydroelectricity has been used to power an aluminum plant, and geothermal power (from the numerous geysers and thermal springs) is an important source of energy. There is also a thriving tourist industry. The main exports are fish products and aluminum. *History*: the Vikings reached Iceland about 874 AD and by the 10th century it had become an independent state with its own parliament, the Althing, which is considered to be the oldest in the world. In 1264 it came under Norwegian rule and, together with Norway, it passed to the Danish

crown in 1381. In the late 19th century it gained a certain degree of self-government and in 1918 became an independent state under the Danish crown, attaining full independence as a republic in 1944. In recent years, following various extensions of its fishing limits, it has been involved in several *Cod Wars with the UK. President: Vigdis Finnbogadottir. Official language: Icelandic. Official religion: Evangelical Lutheranism. Official currency: króna of 100 aurar. Area: 39,758 sq mi (103,000 sq km). Population (1983 est): 236,000. Capital and main port: Reykjavik.

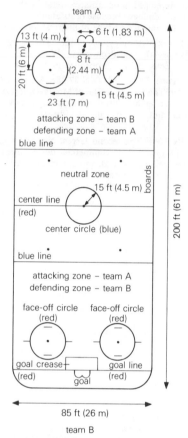

ICE HOCKEY *The dimensions of the rink.*

Icelandic A North Germanic language of the Western Scandinavian subgroup. It is the official language of Iceland. Developed from the *Old Norse spoken by the original settlers of Iceland during the 9th and 10th centuries, Icelandic remains the most conservative of the Scandinavian languages in vocabulary, grammar, and orthography, but there has been much change in pronunciation.

Icelandic literature The greatest period of Icelandic literature was between 1100 and 1350, when the language was a dialect of *Old Norse and the Roman alphabet had only recently replaced the indigenous *runic script. Much of the material then written down drew upon considerably older oral sources. *Skaldic poetry, originating in the pre-Christian (pre-1000) era, remained an important form throughout the middle ages (*see also* Eddas). In prose, stories previously recited were written down for reading aloud (*see* sagas) and the influence of this classical prose has remained a strong conservative force in subsequent Icelandic writing. Despite the small number of Icelandic speakers there was a considerable revival in prose and poetry during the 19th century. In 1955 the Icelandic novelist Halldor *Laxness won the Nobel Prize for literature.

Iceland moss An edible *lichen, *Cetraria islandica*, that grows on moors and alpine areas of the N hemisphere and on lava slopes and plains of Iceland. Up to about 4 in (10 cm) high, it has a dark-brown to gray-white upright body with numerous flattened branches. It contains about 70% digestible starch and a brown dye.

Iceland spar A variety of *calcite consisting of pure colorless transparent crystals having the property of double refraction. It is therefore used for optical purposes and formerly for the nicol prisms in polarizing microscopes. It occurs in large steam cavities in basalt lava in Iceland.

Iceni A British tribe that inhabited the area that is now Norfolk and Suffolk. Their revolt against Roman rule in Britain under the leadership of *Boadicea (60 AD) was brutally suppressed.

ice plant A succulent annual or biennial plant, *Cryophytum crystallinum*, that is covered in glistening papillae and has long prostrate stems reaching 30 in (75 cm). Native to South Africa, it is naturalized in California and the Mediterranean region and widely grown as a garden or pot plant. It is easily propagated from seed. Family: *Aizoaceae*.

ice skating The recreation and sport of sliding over ice on steel-bladed skates. It originated over 2000 years ago and was widely practiced in the middle ages in Scandinavia and on Dutch canals. The main forms of the sport, which is governed by the International Skating Union and is predominantly amateur, are speed skating (long-distance outdoor racing) and two events judged on style—figure skating (compulsory exercises followed by a freestyle performance to music, either singly or in pairs) and ice dancing (a combination of dancing and pairs figure skating). *See also* ice hockey.

I-ch'ang. *See* Yichang.

I CHING   *The* pa kua *are the basis of the 64 hexagrams of the* I Ching, *each of which has a particular significance.*

I Ching A Chinese classic work on divination, also called the Book of Changes, attributed to Wen Wang (12th century BC). It is based on eight named trigrams (*bagua* or *pa kua*) made up of broken and unbroken lines (representing *yin and yang respectively) and arranged in different sequences. Study of the I Ching and its cosmology has exercised many Chinese philosophers.

ichneumon An insect, also called ichneumon fly and ichneumon wasp, belonging to a family (*Ichneumonidae*; about 40,000 species) occurring in Europe, North America, and elsewhere. About 0.47 in (12 mm) long, ichneumons resemble wasps but have longer antennae. They are parasitic upon other insects thereby controlling many insect pests. The female uses a long tubular ovipositor to lay eggs on or in the host. The larvae feed on the host's body fluids and eventually cause its death. Order: *Hymenoptera*.

Ichthyornis A genus of extinct seabirds whose fossils date from the Cretaceous period (125–60 million years ago). It was 8 in (20 cm) long and was probably an active flier, having a large-keeled breastbone and strong wing bones.

ichthyosaur An extinct dolphin-like marine reptile that lived through much of the Mesozoic era but was most abundant in the Jurassic period (200–135 million years ago). 40 in–40 ft (1–12 m) long, it had broad flexible paddles, a large tail fin, and a triangular dorsal fin. Most ichthyosaurs had a long snout and jaws armed with sharp teeth and hunted fish near the surface of the sea but some had few or no teeth and fed on mollusks. □fossil.

icon A painted or mosaic image of Christ or a saint, peculiar to the Byzantine and Orthodox churches. Reverence of icons was castigated as idolatry by the Byzantine iconoclasts (*see* iconoclasm) and they were temporarily banned (730–843 AD). The decree reinstating them proclaimed that an icon must be a recognizable portrait of its subject with his accepted attributes, a formula resulting in a high degree of standardization. Unlike other paintings, therefore, icons have undergone little stylistic development and are characterized by a symbolic rather than realistic approach to color, perspective, etc. *See also* Rublyov.

Iconium. *See* Konya.

iconoclasm The rejection of the veneration of *icons in the Byzantine Church. The movement gained much support, especially in Asia Minor, during the 8th and 9th centuries. Imperial prohibition of icons lasted from 730 to 787 and from 815 to 843, during which times icon worshipers were severely persecuted. Iconoclasm was an expression both of long-standing Christological disputes and of the antagonism toward the portrayal of divinity that was also common to Islam and Judaism in the Near East.

iconography The branch of art history dealing with the interpretation of images and symbols associated with a particular subject in art. Although the term was first used in the 18th century in the study of engravings, it was largely promoted by Aby Warburg (1866–1929) and Erwin Panofsky (1892–1968). *See also* iconology.

iconology The interpretation of the content of a picture in relation to its historical context. The term was adopted by Erwin Panofsky (1892–1968) from the title, *Iconologia*, of a 16th-century book on symbols. Iconology attempts to place *iconography in a broader context and to study visual imagery as a bridge to wider aspects of history and civilization.

Ictinus (5th century BC) Greek architect. With *Callicrates, Ictinus designed the *Parthenon, the most perfect of classical Greek buildings. He also helped rebuild the Telesterion for the temple at Eleusis and possibly designed the temple of Apollo Epicurius at Bassae.

id In *psychoanalysis, the part of the unconscious mind that is governed by irrational instinctive forces, such as *libido and *aggression. These forces seek immediate (actual or symbolic) relief and the id is therefore said to be ruled by the pleasure principle and not by reality or logic. *See also* ego; superego; unconscious.

Ida, Mount (Turkish name: Kaz Daği) A mountain range in NW Asian Turkey, rising to 5797 ft (1767 m). It was important in classical times as it overlooks the plain on which Troy was built.

Idaho A state in the NW, dominated by the N Rocky Mountains. It is bordered by Montana and Wyoming on the E, Utah and Nevada on the S, Oregon and Washington on the W, and British Columbia, Canada, on the N. The valley of the Snake River, famous for its canyons and cataracts, lies in the S of the state. The most spectacular of the river's gorges, Hell's Canyon (7000 ft, 2135 m), is the deepest on the North American continent. Most of the population (70%) lives in the vicinity of the Snake, and the state is sparsely populated. Much of the land is under the control of the federal government in the form of national parks, including Yellowstone National Park. The state is primarily agricultural. On the better soils potatoes (Idaho potatoes are particularly important) are grown while the poorer land supports herds of beef cattle and sheep. Rich in minerals, Idaho is a leading US producer of silver and antimony. Natural gas and oil are increasingly exploited. Idaho is heavily forested, and lumbering is an important activity in the upland regions. *History*: probably first visited by members of the Lewis and Clark expedition in 1805. Fur trappers soon entered the region, establishing trading posts. What is now Idaho belonged to the Oregon Territory, acquired by the US in 1846. The discovery of gold and silver in the 1860s brought a wave of settlers, and labor disputes in the mines dominated the late 19th century. Many of the new settlers also took up ranching and lumbering at the same time. The arrival of the railroads spurred the growth of cities. Idaho became a state in 1890 and has enjoyed prosperity in the 20th century. The state's vast water resources (it has 10 major rivers) have been converted into hydroelectric power with the building of huge dams. In the 1980s environmental issues relating to water pollution and waste disposal and management and conservation of Idaho's natural resources have become important. Area: 83,557 sq mi (216,412 sq km). Population (1980): 943,935. Capital: Boise.

ide. *See* orfe.

ideal gas A hypothetical gas that exactly obeys the ideal gas equation (*see* gas laws). Such a gas has no intermolecular forces and the volume of its molecules is negligible. Also known as a perfect gas, it is closely approximated by real gases at low pressure.

idealism Any doctrine that equates reality with mind, spirit, person, soul, thought, or, as in *Plato, archetypal ideas. *Berkeley was an idealist in holding that all we perceive is sensible ideas. He escaped from *solipsism on the ground that other people were, like himself, spirits—ideas in the mind of God, perceivers of the collections of ideas that were "material objects." In the early 18th century the term came to be used for the belief that the world of common sense was only a projection of our minds. Later it was publicized by *Kant, who called his theory of knowledge "transcendental idealism," the view that the synthetic knowable is confined to the world of phenomena as contrasted with the real world of ideas, or things-in-themselves. *Hegel's absolute idealism conceived the real as being perfect, whole, and complete. *Bradley postulated that there are degrees of truth. It is Hegelian idealism that has led to the organic theory of the state (*see also* Hegelianism).

ideographic writing systems (*or* ideography) Writing systems in which each concept is represented by a symbol. All ideographic systems were probably derived from *pictographic writing systems, stylized representations of abstract concepts being added to the list of symbols. Languages such as Chinese still use ideographic writing systems. However, the huge number of symbols required to represent even a practical selection of the words in a language places a great strain on a person's memory, and hinders the acquisition of literacy skills. Moreover, ideographic systems are inflexible and cannot easily represent new coinages, words borrowed from foreign languages, etc. They have, therefore, been largely replaced by the more efficient phonetic writing systems (*see* alphabets).

Idomeneus In Greek legend, a king of Crete, grandson of *Minos. He was a suitor of *Helen and fought in the *Trojan War. On returning to Crete he killed his son, having sworn to Poseidon to sacrifice the first being he met. Thereafter he lived in exile in Italy.

If A French islet in the Gulf of Lyons. Its 16th-century fortress, Château d'If, was used as a state prison and made famous by Alexandre Dumas in *The Count of Monte Cristo*.

Ife 7 33N 4 34E A town in SW Nigeria. It is the holy city of the Yoruba tribe and is famed for its terracotta and bronze pieces. Today it is primarily an agricultural trade center, the chief products being cocoa and cotton. It contains the University of Ife (1961). Population (1975 est): 176,000.

Ifni An area in Morocco, on the Atlantic coast. First settled by the Spanish (1476), it formed part of Spanish West Africa (1946) and was returned to Morocco in 1969. Chief town : Sidi Ifni.

igloo A temporary dome-shaped dwelling made from blocks of snow by Eskimos. The blocks are cut with a long knife and the joints filled with snow. The igloo is entered by a low and narrow semicylindrical passageway about 10 ft (3 m) long.

Ignatiev, Nikolai Pavlovich, Count (1832–1908) Russian diplomat, who was instrumental in expanding Russian interests into the Far East and the Balkans. After successful diplomatic missions to Bukhara and China (1858–60), Ignatiev served as ambassador to Turkey (1864–77). In 1878 he negotiated the Treaty of *San Stefano, which ended the Russo-Turkish War. He was subsequently minister of the interior (1881–82).

Ignatius of Antioch, St (1st century AD) Christian martyr; Bishop of Antioch. Little is known of his life apart from a series of famous letters to Churches in Rome and Asia Minor, written while he was a prisoner on his way to Rome to be executed. They are a valuable source of information on the beliefs and organization of the early Church. Feast day: Feb 1.

ST IGNATIUS LOYOLA *An engraving after a painting by Rubens. The Latin motto is* Ad Maiorem Dei Gloriam *(To the greater glory of God).*

Ignatius Loyola, St (1491–1556) Spanish founder of the *Jesuits. Of noble birth, his deep interest in religion dated from 1521, after reading the life of Christ while convalescing from a war wound. After visiting the Holy

Land (1523), he studied in Spain and in Paris. There, in 1534 he made vows of poverty, chastity, and obedience, with St *Francis Xavier and other followers. He was ordained in 1537 and then moved to Rome, where he founded the Society of Jesus with the approval of Pope Paul III in 1540. As its first superior general, he sent out missionaries to Japan, India, and Brazil and founded Jesuit schools. His *Spiritual Exercises* (1548) has had lasting influence on the Roman Catholic Church. Feast day: July 31.

igneous rock One of the three major categories of rock (*compare* metamorphic rock; sedimentary rock) consisting mostly of crystalline rocks cooled directly from magma. That cooled at the surface forms extrusive rocks—volcanic lavas with small crystals because they have cooled rapidly (*see also* pyroclastic rock). Some extrusive rocks, such as obsidian, are like glass. Igneous rocks cooled at depth are called intrusive or plutonic. They have larger crystals, granite being a common example. A third category contains the hypabyssal rocks, cooled in dikes or sills at intermediate depth and usually having intermediate crystal sizes, for example dolerite. Silica is the dominant chemical constituent of igneous rocks and the silica content, resulting from the chemical composition of the magma from which the rock cooled, determines whether the rock is acidic (over 66% silica), intermediate (55–66%), basic (45–55%), or ultrabasic (under 45%).

ignis fatuus (*or* will-o'-the-wisp) A phenomenon sometimes observed on marshy ground or graveyards, appearing as a small bluish light. It is believed to be the flame of burning marsh gas (mostly methane), ignited by traces of hydrogen phosphide sometimes found near decaying organic matter.

Iguaçú Falls (*or* Iguassú Falls) 25 35S 54 22W A waterfall in South America, on the border between Brazil and Argentina on the Rio Iguaçú. The spectacular falls are divided by forested rocky islands and are a major tourist attraction. Height: 269 ft (82 m). Width: about 2.5 mi (4 km).

iguana A lizard belonging to the predominantly New World family *Iguanidae* (700 species), comprising desert-dwelling, arboreal, and amphibious species. The green common iguana (*Iguana iguana*) reaches a length of 6 ft [1.8 m] including the long tail (about 4 ft [1.3 m]) and has a short spiny crest along the back; males have a dewlap beneath the throat. They feed on vegetation and are excellent swimmers. The marine iguana (*Amblyrhynchus cristatus*) of the Galapagos is the only lizard that feeds in the sea. *See also* anole; basilisk; chuckwalla.

Iguanodon A large dinosaur that lived in the Jurassic and Cretaceous periods (200–65 million years ago). It stood on powerful hind legs about 16 ft (5 m) tall and measured 36 ft (11 m) from its head to the tip of its heavy balancing tail. Iguanodons were herbivorous, tearing off leaves with their tongues and cutting them with bladelike teeth. Order: *Ornithischia*.

Iguvine tablets Nine inscribed bronze plaques, discovered (1444) at Gubbio (ancient Iguvium) in central Italy. Seven survive, containing ritual records of a priestly brotherhood between 400 and 90 BC. They are important evidence for ancient Italian religion and the extinct Umbrian language.

IJmuiden 52 28N 4 38E A port in the central Netherlands, in North Holland province on the North Sea. It is connected to Amsterdam by canal and has major iron and steel and fishing industries. Population (1974): 66,474.

IJsselmeer (*or* Ysselmeer) A freshwater lake in the NW Netherlands, formed from the S part of the *Zuider Zee by the dam completed in 1932. Out of the original area of 3440 sq km (1328 sq mi) much of the planned 888 sq mi (2300 sq km) has already been drained and cultivated. The last polder to be reclaimed, the Markerwaard, was due to be drained by 1980 but controversy surrounds its final extent.

Ik A small tribe of N Uganda, also known as the Teuso. They are one of the remnants of the original East African hunter-gatherers of Paleolithic times. Their language is unrelated to any other. Recently resettled and forbidden to hunt game they adopted farming but unsuitable conditions and lack of agricultural knowledge have resulted in rapid social and moral disintegration.

ikebana The art of Japanese flower arrangement, first practiced in Japan in the 6th century for Buddhist rituals. Thereafter it evolved into a formal art, being practiced only by men until the 19th century. Famous styles of ikebana include the *shoka*, developed in the 18th century and using three asymmetrically arranged branches.

Ikhnaton. *See* Akhenaton.

Ikhwan, al- (Arabic: the Brethren) Arabian tribesmen united to extend the power of *Ibn Saud in Arabia between 1912 and 1930. Ibn Saud organized the Ikhwan in encampments and with their military help conquered most of Arabia. They then attempted revolt but were defeated by Ibn Saud at the battle of Sabala (1929). He later incorporated the Ikhwan into the National Guard of Saudi Arabia.

Île-de-France A former province in N France, surrounding Paris and enclosed by the Seine, Marne, Beuvronne, Thève, and Oise rivers. It was made a dukedom during the 9th century AD. Following the French Revolution it was divided into departments.

Ilesha 7 38N 4 45E A city in SW Nigeria. Cocoa is exported from here and it is the center of a gold-mining area. Population (1975 est): 224,000.

Ilhéus 14 50S 39 06W A port in E Brazil, in Bahía state on the Atlantic Ocean. Formerly an important export center for cocoa, chief exports now include timber and piassava. Population (1975 est): 119,488.

Ilipa, Battle of (206 BC) A battle in S Spain between *Scipio Africanus and the Carthaginians. Scipio's victory established Roman control of Spain, opening the way for his invasion of Africa.

Illinois A group of Algonkian-speaking North American Indian tribes of Wisconsin, Illinois, Missouri, and Iowa. Their villages were of rush-matcovered dwellings, each housing several families. Separate chiefs were responsible for matters of war and for civil affairs. Men hunted forest game and prairie bison. Women cultivated maize and corn. The Illinois were much reduced in population through wars with other tribes and eventually dispersed from their territory.

Illinois A state in the Midwest. It is bounded by Wisconsin to the N; the S tip of Lake Michigan forms a 60-mi (95-km) border in the NE; Indiana lies directly to the E and Kentucky to the SE and S, where the Ohio River forms the boundary; Missouri and Iowa lie to the W with the Mississippi River forming the boundary. Illinois consists largely of flat prairies drained by over 275 rivers, most notably the Illinois and the Kaskoskia. Approximately half its population is concentrated in the Chicago metroplitan area, the principal grain market of the US interior. Primarily an agricultural state, its farmers are major producers of soy beans, as well as maize, corn, pork, beef, and dairy products. Manufacturing includes machine tools, electrical machinery, printing and publishing, chemicals, iron and steel, motor vehicles, and food processing. It is also an important coalmining state. A deep division exists between upstate Illinois, which contains the Chicago metropolitan area, and the predominantly rural area downstate. *History*: the area was inhabited by Illinois, Fox, and Sac Indians in the 17th century when the French first visited what is now Illinois. Marquette and Jolliet and La Salle subsequently conducted explorations of the region. It formed part of the French province of Louisiana but was ceded to Britain (1763) after the French and Indian Wars. It came under US control (1783) after the American Revolution, becoming a territory in 1809 and a state in 1818. The Black Hawk War (1832) marked the final subjugation of the Indians in Illinois. The Illinois and Michigan Canal (1848) ensured the importance of Illinois as a national transportation center by linking Lake Michigan with the Mississippi River. Abraham Lincoln began his political career in Illinois and in the 1858 senatorial race the now famous debates between Lincoln and Stephen A. Douglas on the slavery issue won national attention. Lincoln went on to become president in 1861 and although Illinois entered the Civil War on the Union side, the populace was divided on the states' rights and slavery questions. Bitter labor disputes characterized the 19th century, but as a consequence Illinois became one of the bellwether states in workers' rights legislation. In 1958 the completion of the St Lawrence Seaway linked Illinois to the Atlantic, making Chicago an important overseas shipping center. Area: 56,400 sq mi (146,075 sq km). Population (1980): 11,418,461. Capital: Springfield.

Illinois River A river in NE Illinois southwest of Joliet. Formed by the function of the Des Plaines and Kankakee rivers, it flows SW to the Mississippi River at Grafton, Ill. It is part of the Illinois Waterway, a barge system that begins in Chicago. Length: 273 mi (440 km).

illiteracy The inability to read or write. The ever-increasing demands of a technological society and the concomitant need for a numerate and literate population has led to a growing awareness of the scale of the problem. Anti-illiteracy campaigns are generally run by voluntary helpers.

illuminated manuscripts Manuscripts of gospels, books of hours, prayers, etc., decorated with designs in opaque or transparent watercolor and frequently gold leaf. The art was first practiced by monastic scribes in the early middle ages, as in the 8th-century Book of Kells. Although it began as the elaboration of capital letters and decoration of margins, by the time printing was invented (mid-15th century) it had become a form of miniature painting, perfected by professional illuminators. The Duke of Berry's book of hours by the de *Limburg brothers is an outstanding example of late medieval illumination. Such illumination laid the basis for medieval panel painting.

ILLUMINATED MANUSCRIPTS *An elaborate capital C from an English writing master's copy sheet (c. 1600).*

Illyria The Adriatic coastal region W of the Balkans. Inhabited from the 10th century BC by warlike but independent tribes, Illyria constantly harassed Macedonia and Epirus, expanding when their power declined. Piratical raids in the Adriatic provoked Roman intervention from 228 BC and Illyria became the Roman province of Illyricum in 167 BC.

ilmenite A black metallic mineral of composition $FeTiO_3$, found in basic igneous rocks, in veins, and as a detrital mineral in sands. It is an ore of titanium.

Iloilo 10 41N 122 33E A port in the central Philippines, in SE Panay. The island's commercial center, famed for its fabrics, it exports sugar and rice. Population (1980): 244,211.

Ilorin 8 32N 4 34E A city in W Nigeria. It is an important trading center for local agricultural and manufactured products, with modern industries producing sugar, matches, and cigarettes. Its university was founded in 1976. Population (1975 est): 282,000.

Ilyushin, Sergei Vladimirovich (1894–1977) Soviet aircraft designer. He first became known for the Il-2 Stormovik, a dive bomber widely used by the Soviet Union during World War II. He later worked on commercial aircraft, designing the jet airliner Il-62.

imaginary number. *See* numbers; complex numbers.

Imagism A literary movement begun in Britain in 1909 that was dedicated to composing poetry characterized by the concise expression of pure visual images. It profoundly influenced British and American poetry for a decade. Its theories derived from criticism of T. E. *Hulme, who rejected the prevailing sentimental romanticism in favor of clarity and hardness. *Des Imagistes* (1914), an anthology edited by Ezra Pound, included poems by Richard Aldington, Hilda Doolittle (H. D.), John Gould Fletcher, and Amy Lowell, who succeeded Pound as leader of the movement.

imago (zoology) The sexually mature adult form of any insect.

imam (Arabic: leader) A Muslim title. **1.** Among Shiite Muslims, the title of the successors of Mohammed, who must be descendants of the fourth caliph *Ali. The imams were regarded as infallible and exercised complete authority. Various Shiite sects recognize different lines of imams and believe that the last of the line (usually considered either the 7th or the 12th after Ali) will return at the end of time. **2.** A title often used by the caliphs and also honorifically given to certain religious leaders, such as *Abu Hanifah. **3.** The title of the leader of prayers in a mosque.

Imbros. *See* Imroz.

Imhotep (c. 2600 BC) Egyptian physician, architect, and adviser to pharaoh *Djoser of the 3rd dynasty. Revered in later times as a healer and magician, Imhotep was eventually deified. He was identified with Asclepius by the Greeks.

Immaculate Conception A dogma of the Roman Catholic Church stating that the Virgin Mary was conceived free from *original sin. It had long been a belief, connected with the feast of the Conception of the Blessed Virgin Mary (Dec 8), which had been celebrated since 1471; but it was the subject of controversy and was opposed by prominent theologians, such as St Bonaventure and St Thomas Aquinas. It was promulgated as dogma in 1854 by Pope Pius IX.

immigration. *See* migration, human.

Immigration and Naturalization Service US Department of Justice division that oversees aliens. It was established in 1891 to enforce the laws that provided for naturalization or deportation of immigrants to the US.

immortelle. *See* everlasting flowers.

immunity In medicine, resistance to infection. Nonspecific immunity is achieved by such agents as polymorphic white blood cells (which engulf invading bacteria) and *interferon, but the term immunity usually refers to that specifically acquired due to the presence of *antibodies. This may be passive, when antibodies derived from another individual are introduced into the body. For example, newborn babies have a temporary passive immunity from antibodies transferred from the mother's blood through the placenta. Active immunity is produced when an individual forms his (or her) own antibodies after exposure to an antigen, such as occurs following an infection. There are two different kinds of immune response produced by antibodies derived from two populations of lymphocytes (white blood cells). Cell-mediated immunity is due to activity of the T-lymphocytes (produced by or dependent on the *thymus). In the presence of antigens these lymphocytes produce cells with antibody bound to their surface. They can attack whole cells and are responsible for such reactions as graft rejection, allergic responses, and delayed hypersensitivity reactions. Humoral immunity is produced by the B-lymphocytes, so called because they are formed in an organ in chickens called the bursa of Fabricius. In man they are probably formed by lymphatic tissue in the gut. B-lymphocytes produce cells that release free antibody into the blood, neutralizing bacterial toxins and coating bacteria to facilitate their ingestion by the polymorphic blood cells.

immunization is the production of immunity by artificial means. This may be achieved by injecting antibodies against specific diseases (e.g. tetanus and diphtheria), providing temporary passive immunity, or by *vaccination to produce active immunity.

immunology The study of the biological processes by which the body reacts to foreign substances. This includes the action of *antibodies both in protecting the body against infection (*see* immunity) and in rejecting foreign tissues (*see* transplantation). Immunologists are also concerned with disorders of the immune system, including *allergy and *autoimmunity.

immunosuppression The condition in which the *immunity of the body is reduced. This can occur in various diseases (e.g. leukemia and severe infections) or it may be deliberately induced by certain drugs (e.g. azathioprine and cyclophosphamide). Immunosuppressive drugs are administered after transplant surgery to enable the body to accept the foreign tissue or organ; they are also used to treat rheumatoid arthritis and other conditions associated with *autoimmunity.

IMPALA *These antelopes usually remain within the cover of dense trees and bushes, like this male. When disturbed they can leap to a height of 10 ft (3m), covering a distance of over 30 ft (9m).*

impala A common antelope, *Aepyceros melampus,* of central and S African savanna. About 40 in (100 cm) high at the shoulder, impalas have a red-brown coat and white underparts; males have lyre-shaped ridged horns. In the rutting season the herds, numbering several hundreds, break up into smaller groups, each led by a mature male. Impalas are known for their agile springing leaps, which are most marked when the animals are alarmed.

impatiens A genus of annual and perennial herbaceous plants (about 700 species), widely distributed in temperate and tropical regions. They have irregular often spurred flowers and (usually) fleshy stems. The genus includes *touch-me-not and various cultivated species, such as the garden *balsam and busy Lizzies—red-, pink-, purple-, and orange-flowered hybrids that are popular pot plants. Family: *Balsaminaceae.*

impeachment A criminal proceeding against a public official. Under the Constitution (Article I), the House of Representatives has the sole power to impeach a federal officeholder, such as the president or vice president, and the Senate has the sole power to try the accused. President Andrew *Johnson was impeached (1868) by the House and acquitted by the Senate.

impedance A measure of the ability of a circuit to resist the flow of an alternating current. It is given by $Z = R + iX$, where Z is the impedance, R is the *resistance, and X is the reactance. The reactance of an inductance L is ωL and that of a capacitance C is $1/\omega C$, where ω is the angular frequency. Impedance and reactance are measured in *ohms.

imperial cities The German cities of the Holy Roman Empire subject directly to the Emperor (by whose officials they were governed). They grew in number during the middle ages, when cities took advantage of political disturbance to assert their freedom. Those that survived flourished, forming themselves into leagues (of which the *Hanseatic League was the most important) and from 1489 were represented in the imperial diet (assembly). In subsequent centuries most cities lost their free status and were incorporated into the provinces; only Hamburg and Bremen maintain their free status today.

Imperial Conferences Meetings between the British government and representatives of the self-governing dominions held between 1907 and 1937 to discuss questions of common interest. Imperial Conferences discussed such matters as migration, naturalization, defense, trade, intraimperial relations, and dominion status. The last Conference discussed the foreign policy of the newly established *Commonwealth of Nations. The Conferences gave way during World War II to the meetings of Commonwealth prime ministers. *See also* Ottawa Agreements.

imperialism The territorial expansion of a nation and its domination over other countries. Powerful nations generally formed their empires by conquest until the 19th century, when imperialism became an economic policy. European powers, especially Britain (*see* Empire, British), ambitious for prestige and anxious for new industrial trading outlets, established their rule over countries in other continents (□Africa). Until World War I ended such imperialism these countries depended on their rulers for government, commerce, and protection. Since World War II imperialism has been used to describe the efforts of world powers to impose, by persuasion or force, their political ideologies on less prosperous nations.

Imperial Valley A former desert area in S California, now an irrigated valley, part of the Colorado Desert, extending from the Salton Sea to just S of the Mexican border. Watered by the All-American Canal, a man-made outlet of the Colorado River, the valley produces alfalfa, milo, cotton, melon, and garden vegetables.

impetigo A highly infectious skin disease, usually caused by staphylococci. Children are most commonly affected and epidemics may occur in crowded schools. Usually occurring on the face, hands, and knees, it starts with a red mark that develops into a blister, which later forms yellow crusts. Antibiotics, applied locally or internally, will cure the condition.

Imphal 24 47N 93 55E A city in India, the capital of Manipur. During World War II, Imphal was the scene of an Anglo-Indian victory over the Japanese. Population (1971): 100,366.

impotence Sexual inadequacy in men, with failure to achieve or maintain an erection or to ejaculate at orgasm. It may be temporary, resulting from tiredness, illness, drunkenness, depression, or taking certain drugs. Long-term impotence is likely to have a deeper cause reflecting the sufferer's fear of women or of castration. It can usually be treated by specialist counseling or by psychotherapy.

impressionism A French art movement that flourished from the late 1860s to the late 1880s. Its name was derived from Monet's painting *Impression: Sunrise* (1872; Musée Marmottan, Paris), shown at the first of the eight impressionist exhibitions (1874, 1876, 1877, 1879, 1880, 1881, 1882,

1886). The leading impressionists were *Monet, *Pissarro, *Sisley, and *Renoir. Among their many forerunners were *Constable, *Turner, *Boudin, *Daubigny, and *Corot. *Manet shared some of their aims and *Degas, although stylistically independent of them, participated in their exhibitions. Painting mainly in the open air, the impressionists aimed to capture fleeting effects of light and weather in paint with dabs of bright color and a minimum of drawing.

imprinting In *ethology, a rapid and irreversible form of learning that takes place in some animals in the first hours of life. Animals attach themselves in this way to whatever creatures they are exposed to at that time—usually, but not necessarily, their mothers. This type of behavior was first described by Konrad *Lorenz working with newly hatched ducks and geese.

inbreeding Mating between closely related individuals. (The term is also used for self-fertilization in plants.) Inbreeding often occurs in small isolated populations of organisms. The effect is to increase the tendency for harmful *recessive genes to express themselves among the population, thus affecting the fitness and survival of individuals. For example, inbreeding in rats reduces fertility and increases mortality. In human societies close inbreeding is prevented by custom and law (*see* incest).

incandescent lamp An electric lamp in which light is produced by passing an electric current through a filament, usually inside a glass bulb containing an inert gas. The filament, of tungsten in the common light bulb, is heated to over 4717°F (2600°C) so that it glows with a white light.

incarnation A central tenet of Christian belief, that the second person of the Trinity took human form and became man. Although in other religions gods temporarily appear in human form (i.e. a theophany), in Christianity the Incarnation is a unique event occurring at a particular time; the union of the divine and human in Christ is permanent and the integrity of both the divine and human natures is maintained. The doctrine is stated in the opening of the Gospel of St John and in St Paul's Epistle to the Colossians and was further defined by the Councils of *Nicaea (325) and *Chalcedon (451).

Incas A Quechua-speaking South American Indian people of the Peruvian Andes. From their capital of *Cuzco, they established, during the 15th century, an empire extending from Ecuador to central Chile. It was destroyed in the 16th century by the Spaniards. The Incas assimilated much of the culture of such people as the *Chimu, whom they conquered. Their hierarchical society, ruled by the King of Inca and a class of aristocratic officials, was highly centralized. Although the wheel and writing were unknown, imperial messengers and an extensive road system enabled the ruler to maintain contact with all parts of his empire. The complex religion was concerned with the propitiation of the sun god Inti, object of the state cult, the creator god Viracocha (*see also* Kon-Tiki), the rain god Apu Ilapu, and others. *See also* Machu Picchu.

incense A mixture of gums and spices (especially gum benzoin) that is burned for its aroma (*see also* frankincense). It was employed in pagan rituals in ancient Egypt, Greece, and Rome as well as in Judaic ritual and was a valued trade commodity. In the Book of Revelation it is a symbol of the prayers of saints and has been used in Christian worship since the 6th century AD. It is used predominantly by the Orthodox and Roman Catholic Churches. The vessel for burning incense is called a censer or thurible.

incense cedar A conifer, *Calocedrus* (or *Libocedrus*) *decurrens*, native to W North America and planted for ornament in Europe, where it is usually narrow and columnar and may reach a height of 148 ft (45 m). It has small scalelike leaves covering the twigs and branches and bright-yellow pointed cones, 0.8 in (2 cm) long, which split open to release the seeds. Family: *Cupressaceae* (cypress family).

incest Proscribed sexual relations between close kin. Such proscriptions are universal, but vary considerably in terms of the categories of kin to which they apply. The most common and universal prohibitions apply to members of the same nuclear family, such as relations between parents and children and between brothers and sisters. These taboos, founded in folklore, have a sound basis in genetics (unfavorable recessive genes can become dominant when consanguineous relatives breed). However, folklore is not always a reliable guide to what constitutes consanguinity, as in the case of taboos forbidding marriage between a man and his mother-in-law.

Inchcape Rock. *See* Bell Rock.

Inchŏn 37 30N 126 38E A city in NW South Korea, Seoul's main seaport on the Yellow Sea. It has a private university (1954). A UN attack here (1950) during the Korean War halted the North Korean invasion. Population (1975): 797,143.

income tax A direct tax on income and a major source of government revenue in many countries. In most countries, including the US, it is a progressive tax (the rate charged increasing with the taxable income) in which a certain amount can be earned without attracting tax. Thus, those with higher incomes pay more tax in proportion to their incomes than the lower paid; therefore the tax, to a certain extent, balances unequal distribution of incomes in the community. However, it acts as a disincentive to increasing income and makes it difficult for the low paid to escape from poverty. Income tax makes no distinction between income that is spent and income that is invested (furthering the productive potential of the economy); higher indirect taxation and lower direct taxation is advocated as a remedy for this disadvantage.

incunabula Books printed during the infancy of modern printing (before 1500) after the invention of movable type by *Gutenberg. N European incunabula have a heavy type design known as black letter; Italian books have a more elegant roman typeface; both were based on current manuscript writing. Paper leaves and a binding of calf leather over wooden boards were usual. Editions were small (200–500), the preferred subjects being religious or scientific.

Independence 39 04N 94 27W A city in Missouri. Situated in an agricultural area, its industries include oil refining and cement. It was the home of President Harry S Truman. Population (1980): 111,806.

Independence Day The national holiday of the US. It marks the anniversary of the adoption of the *Declaration of Independence by the Continental Congress on July 4, 1776.

indeterminacy principle. *See* Heisenberg uncertainty principle.

indexation. *See* price index.

Index Librorum Prohibitorum (Latin: *Index of Prohibited Books*) In the Roman Catholic Church, a list of publications considered dangerous to spiritual wellbeing and not to be read without a bishop's permission. The first formal list of this sort was produced under Pope Paul IV (1555–59); a more comprehensive guide was issued in 1564. The Second *Vatican Council (1962–65) resolved that no new revisions should be undertaken, and the specific limitation on suitable reading is no longer in effect.

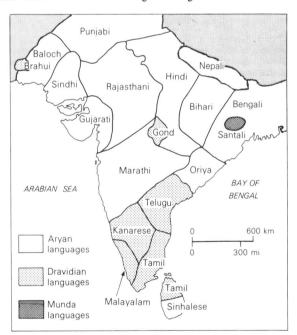

INDIA *The distribution of major language groups in the Indian subcontinent.*

India, Republic of (Hindi name: Bharat) A country in S Asia, the seventh largest in the world and the second most populous. Bordering on Pakistan, China, Nepal, Bhutan, and Burma, it comprises 22 states and 9 Union Territories, reorganized since 1946 according to linguistic groupings. The Himalayas, in which the Ganges River rises, form a natural barrier to the N. Central India consists of a plateau (the Deccan), flanked by the mountains of the Western and Eastern Ghats. N of this lies the Indo-Gangetic plain, with the Thar Desert in the W. The population comprises many ethnic and cultural groups and about 1600 languages and dialects are spoken. The chief religions are Hinduism (83% of the population) and Islam (11%). The *caste system still survives, although untouchability has been abolished. *Economy*: helped by foreign aid, 70% of the workforce is engaged in agriculture, with rice, pulses, and cereals as the main food crops; tea, jute, cotton, and tobacco are also important. Despite land irrigation and reclamation, production is hampered by floods, droughts, insufficient mechanization, and the small size of agricultural units; food supplies are therefore inadequate for the country's needs. Fishing and forestry are also important. India's large mineral resources include iron ore, manganese, bauxite, mica, and ilmenite. Coal is mined, oil is produced from the Arabian Sea, and India also has nuclear power. Industry, much of it state owned, employs only 10% of the workforce, but India is the world's tenth greatest industrial power. Industries include steel, chemicals, electronics, cotton and silk textiles, and handicrafts. The new economic policy of 1977 channeled resources into agriculture and aimed to stimulate rural employment by allowing new capital intensive industries to be established only for goods that could not be produced by cottage or small-scale industries. Chief exports are cotton goods, tea, leather, iron ore, and jute, while chief imports are petroleum, wheat, and machinery. *History*: the *Indus Valley was the site of a civilization for a millennium before the invading Aryans established theirs (c. 1500 BC) between the Indus and the Ganges. From this civilization Hinduism evolved and it has remained India's dominant religion. The Mauryan Empire followed (c. 320 BC–c. 185 BC), which unified most of India. The 4th–6th centuries AD saw a flowering of Hindu culture in the N under the *Gupta dynasty. Muslim raids on the N from the 10th century culminated in the establishment of a Muslim sultanate based on Delhi (1129), under which much of India was again unified. A later Muslim invasion resulted in the magnificent *Mogul Empire (established 1526). At this time Europeans were also arriving. The British *East India Company, grown powerful in the 17th century, fought with French traders in the 18th century for a monopoly as the Mogul Empire declined. With Robert Clive's victory at *Plassey (1757), the British established their supremacy and from 1784 a series of *Government of India Acts shifted power from the East India Company to the British Government. Some of the territory was directly administered by Britain and came to be called British India. The rest of India was administered by Indian princes, with Britain only exercising general supervision; such areas were called princely states. The Indian economy suffered under British trading arrangements, which allowed British goods into India duty free but barred Indian goods from Great Britain by high tariffs, thus provoking social and political unrest. After the *Indian Mutiny (1857–59) reforms were introduced, including the transfer of the East India Company's administrative powers to the India Office, represented by a viceroy and provincial governors. Subsequent reforms allowed greater Indian involvement in government, and in 1919 a parliament was created, the majority of members of which were elected. However, the nationalist movement (*see* Indian National Congress) became increasingly forceful in its demand for home rule and, under the leadership of Mahatma *Gandhi, pursued a policy of civil disobedience. During World War II Gandhi and other Nationalist leaders were imprisoned for refusing to support Britain unless independence was immediately granted. This was finally achieved in 1947 on condition that a Muslim state should be established to satisfy the Muslim faction, active since the late 19th century (*see* Muslim League). The creation of *Pakistan (1947) was followed by violent upheavals in which 500,000 people were killed and by war between the two countries over Kashmir. Trouble between Hindus and Muslims has continued, with riots in 1978, while hostility between India and Pakistan erupted again in 1965 and 1971 (*see also* Bangladesh). India, which became a sovereign state in 1950, has been consolidated by the incorporation of former French and Portuguese territories (1956 and 1961) and the inclusion of Sikkim (1975), although the Kashmir question has not yet been settled. Nevertheless, economic problems and the difficulty of dealing with the large population, coupled with inefficient or corrupt administrations, have aggravated separatist and terrorist reactions, especially during the 1970s. Indira *Gandhi, who served as prime minister from 1966–77 and was returned to power in 1980, sometimes dealt forcefully with the problems confronting her. In 1984 she suppressed a movement of militant Sikhs advocating autonomy for Punjab. Later that year Mrs Gandhi was assassinated by Sikh members of her bodyguard. She was succeeded by her son, Rajiv Gandhi. In the December 1984 elections, voters rallied behind candidates allied with Rajiv Gandhi, who remained prime minister. In foreign affairs India has followed a policy of nonalignment, although it became the world's sixth nuclear power (1974). Zail Singh was elected president of the republic in 1982. Official languages: Hindi and English. Official currency: Indian rupee of 100 paise. Area: 1,269,072 sq mi (3,287,590 sq km), including Jammu and Kashmir. Population (1983 est): 740,009,000. Capital: New Delhi.

Indiana A state in the Midwest, forming part of the Mississippi Basin. It is largely undulating prairie with glacial lakes in the N. Agriculture is important in the fertile central plain, the major crops being soybeans, corn, wheat, and vegetables (especially tomatoes); pigs are the primary livestock. Its manufacturing industry, concentrated in the NW, near Lake Michigan, produces steel, diamond tools, agricultural machinery, motor vehicles, and domestic appliances. Coal and building stone are also exploited. It is an important transport center with the Ohio River linking Indiana with the Mississippi River and Lake Michigan giving access to the Great Lakes and thereby to the St Lawrence Seaway. *History*: explored by the French in the 17th century, the area was ceded to Britain in 1763. During the American Revolution, US troops occupied the region. Increased settlement followed a defeat of the Indians (1794), and Indiana became a territory in 1800. The Indians were subdued by 1811, and Indiana became a state in 1816. The state remained primarily agricultural and rural until the 20th century, when industrialization grew rapidly. Area: 36,291 sq mi (93,993 sq km). Population (1980): 5,490,179. Capital: Indianapolis.

Indian Affairs, Bureau of (BIA) US Department of the Interior division that oversees Indian reservations. It was established in 1832 as part of the War Department to supervise the removal of Indians to reservations and a new lifestyle. Transferred to the Department of the Interior in 1849, it manages the reservations and educates Indians.

Indianapolis 39 45N 86 10W A city in the US, the capital of Indiana. A rail, road, and air center, its varied manufactures include car and aircraft parts and chemicals. It is the scene of annual speedway races, including the **Indianapolis 500**, a 500-mile race for 33 cars first held in 1911. Population (1980): 700,807.

Indian art and architecture The styles evolved in the Indian subcontinent. Evidence for many older art forms is incomplete, as the hostile climate militates against the survival of objects in perishable materials, such as wood. The art of the *Indus Valley civilization is best represented by carved steatite sealstones and miniature sculptures and its architecture by the massive brick ruins at *Harappa and *Mohenjo-Daro. Between about 324 and 185 BC the characteristic Buddhist architectural form of the *stupa appeared, decorated with stone or stucco reliefs depicting scenes from the Buddha's life. Greek and Roman influence is apparent in the art of the N Indian Buddhist kingdom of Gandhara (1st–7th centuries AD). The 10th-century Muslim invasions drove indigenous art to the S. The central spire of Hindu temples became increasingly massive, symbolizing the mythological cosmic mountain; luxuriant carvings, often of erotic scenes, covered every available surface, as in the 13th-century Sun Temple at Konarak (Orissa). The Tamil kingdom of Cola (c. 850–1279) is famous for its exquisite small bronzes. With the spread of Mogul dominance, *Mogul art and architecture became the main tradition until that too declined under British rule.

Indian corn. *See* maize.

Indian hemp A North American perennial herb, *Apocynum cannabinum*, that grows to a height of 5 ft (1.5 m) and bears small greenish-white flowers. The stem fibers were used by Indians to make matting and ropes and the dried roots have medicinal properties. Family: *Apocynaceae*.

True *hemp is also sometimes called Indian hemp.

Indian languages A classification based on the geographically defined area of the Indian subcontinent. Within this area are found languages of widely differing origins. The two major language families to be found are the *Indo-European and the *Dravidian. On the NW borders of India, Baluchi and *Pashto, members of the *Iranian subgroup of the Indo-European family, are spoken. Most of the other Indo-European languages of India are of the *Indo-Aryan subgroup. This includes the lingua franca Hindustani; *Hindi, the official national language; Rajasthani, *Punjabi, *Gujarati, and *Sindhi in the west; *Bengali and *Bihari in the east; and Kashmiri. Most of S India is covered by the Dravidian language family. In addition to these two large families, there are scattered languages of the *Munda group in the NE, and languages of *Sino-Tibetan origins are spoken in the Himalayas.

Indian licorice An Indian plant, *Abrus precatorius*, the roots of which have been used as a substitute for licorice although they contain poisonous resins. The poisonous red and black seeds are used to make necklaces and as weights. Family: *Leguminosae*.

Indian literature Sanskrit literature, the most important division of ancient Indian literature, is divided into three periods: the Vedic period (c. 1500–c. 200 BC), during which the vast and complex sacred literature of Hinduism was accumulated (*see* Vedas; Upanishads); the Epic period (c. 400 BC–c. 400 AD), in which the great Indian epic, the *Mahabharata*, which includes the *Bhagavad-gita*, and the shorter epic, the *Ramayana*, were composed; and the Classical period (from c. 200 AD), characterized by various literary forms including romances, drama, and lyric poetry. *Kalidasa is considered the greatest writer of this period. During the 19th century various regional vernacular literatures of India developed, adopting new western forms and reviving traditional ones. Leading writers of this period include the Bengali poet Rabindranath *Tagore and the Urdu poet Muhammad *Iqbal.

Indian Mutiny (1857–59) A revolt of about 35,000 sepoys (Indian soldiers in the service of the British East India Company), which developed into a bloody Anglo-Indian War. It began with a massacre of Europeans at Meerut in May, 1857, following which the mutineers captured Delhi. The sepoys then rose in many other N Indian towns and were joined by local princes. Extensive British reinforcements were able under Colin *Campbell to regain Delhi in Sept and relieve besieged Lucknow in Nov; by July, 1858, the revolt had largely been contained. The consequent Government of India Act (1858) transferred the administrative powers of the East India Company to the British crown.

Indian National Congress The political party, founded in 1885, that governed India after the declaration of independence in 1947. Though earlier a moderate party, a section of it took up the cause of home rule in 1917. For the next 20 years, chiefly under the guidance of Mahatma *Gandhi, it advocated noncooperation with the British and in World War II refused to support Britain without being promised Indian independence. The party was led by Jawarhalal *Nehru from 1951 to 1964, by Lal Bahadur Shastri (1904–66) until 1966, and then by Mrs Indira *Gandhi until her assassination in 1984, when the leadership passed to her son Rajiv Gandhi.

Indian Ocean The world's third largest ocean, extending between Asia, Africa, Australia, and Antarctica. Lying mainly in the S hemisphere, most is within the tropical and temperate zones. It contains coral and volcanic islands while others, such as the Seychelles, are the peaks of underwater ridges or, like Madagascar, are continental. The ocean floor is extremely rich in minerals.

Indian pipe A fleshy waxy-white to pinkish herb, *Monotropa uniflora*, of North America and Asia, also called corpse plant. Up to 12 in (30 cm) high, it has tiny scalelike leaves, lacks chlorophyll, and obtains nutrients from woodland humus. The stem and single cup-shaped flower resemble a small pipe. Family: *Monotropaceae*.

Indian Removal, Policy of (1830) US program that provided for the removal of Indians in the east to lands west of the Mississippi River. In an effort to prevent hostilities along the expanding US frontier, tribes were moved to Arkansas, Missouri, Iowa, Wisconsin, Minnesota, Kansas, Nebraska, and Oklahoma.

Indian Reorganization Act (Wheeler-Howard Act, 1934) US law designed to encourage Indian self-determination and increase self-sufficiency. It allowed for greater self-government regarding internal affairs and provided funds for credit and education.

Indian Territory The land W of the Mississippi, corresponding to present-day Oklahoma, set aside (1834) for settlement of Indians ejected, sometimes forcibly, from the E. These included the Cherokee, whose journey was known as the Trail of Tears because of the hardships and deaths endured on the way.

indicator A substance used to indicate through changes in color, fluorescence, etc., the presence of another substance or the completion of a chemical reaction. Indicators are usually weak organic acids or bases that yield ions of a different color to the unionized molecule. For example, litmus is red in the presence of acids but blue in the presence of alkalis.

indigestion (*or* dyspepsia) Abdominal discomfort due to disordered digestion. Most people experience indigestion at some time and there is usually no serious cause, but peptic ulcers, a hiatus hernia, and gall bladder disease may all give symptoms that are described as indigestion.

indigo A blue *dye formerly obtained from plants, particularly of the genus *Indigofera*, and present in the woad plant (*Isatis tinctoria*). It is now synthesized from *aniline.

indium (In) A soft silvery metal, named for the bright indigo line in its spectrum. It is used in making transistors, rectifiers, thermistors, and alloys of low melting point. At no 49; at wt 114.82; mp 314°F (156.6°C); bp 2645°F (1450°C).

Indo-Aryan languages A subgroup of the *Indo-Iranian language group, spoken in India, Sri Lanka, and Pakistan. Sometimes called the Indic group, it descends from *Sanskrit, and the earliest Indo-Aryan language dates from about 1100 AD. The most important languages of the group are *Hindi and *Urdu, which are the national languages of India and Pakistan respectively; these are both literary languages with many borrow-

INDIGO *This ornamental shrub* (Indigofera gerardiana) *is closely related to the species formerly used as a source of indigo. It has red flowers and silvery branches.*

ings of Persian and Arabic words dating from the Mogul period. More colloquial *Hindustani is also a member of this group, as are the widely spoken *Sindhi, *Bengali, *Gujarati, *Punjabi, and Sinhalese. The Dardic (see Dards) languages of Pakistan, Afghanistan, and Kashmir, of which the best known is Kashmiri, are often included in the Indo-Aryan group.

Indochina The area of SE Asia comprising present-day *Vietnam, *Kampuchea (formerly Cambodia), and *Laos. It was so called by Europeans because it has been influenced by both Indian and Chinese culture. During the 19th century the French established control over the region, forming (1887) the Union of Indochina from *Cochin China, Cambodia, *Tonkin, and *Annam; Laos was added in 1893. Its capital was Saigon (now Ho Chi Minh City). Except in Cochin China the royal families were retained, although most power lay with the federal government under a French governor general. During World War II the Japanese occupied Tonkin (1940) and then all Indochina (1941). Following Japan's defeat France established the Federation of Indochina, to which Laos and Cambodia submitted while nationalists in Annam, Tonkin, and Cochin China demanded complete independence for a new state of Vietnam (see Ho Chi Minh). In 1946 fighting broke out between nationalists (see Viet Minh) and the French, bitter conflict continuing until 1954, when the *Geneva Conference ended French control of Indochina (see also Dien Bien Phu).

Indo-European languages The largest language family of the world, sometimes called Indo-Germanic. They are spoken throughout Europe as well as in India, Iran, and in parts of the central and E Soviet Union, and the family is generally thought to include the following subgroups: *Germanic; *Italic; *Indo-Iranian; *Celtic; *Baltic; Slavic (see Slavonic); *Albanian; *Greek; *Armenian; *Tocharian; and *Anatolian. Of these, the oldest recorded is Anatolian and the most recent Albanian. Armenian and Greek are single languages rather than subdivided groups like Indo-Iranian or Germanic. Anatolian and Tocharian are now extinct. The only living languages of Europe that do not come from Indo-European origins are *Turkish, *Finnish, *Hungarian, and *Basque. The Indo-European group relates languages as apparently separate as English, a subgroup of Germanic, and *Sanskrit, an ancestor of modern Indian languages. Most of the research needed to support this wide grouping was done by German philologists in the 19th century. See also Indo-Hittite languages.

Indo-Hittite languages A language family proposed by some scholars to include the *Indo-European and *Anatolian languages as subgroups. There has been some confusion about the relation of *Hittite, an Anatolian language, to the Indo-European group. Indo-Hittite has been suggested as an ancestor of both Indo-European and Anatolian. It is more generally accepted that Indo-European is the parent language and Anatolian a subgroup on the same level as the *Celtic or the *Germanic languages.

Indo-Iranian languages A subgroup of the *Indo-European language group, spoken in India, Pakistan, Bangladesh, Nepal, and Sri Lanka. It is subdivided into two branches: *Indo-Aryan and *Iranian. These are among the oldest of the Indo-European group, spoken originally in Turkistan, and there is still much debate about the relation of these languages to the Hittite languages of Anatolia. *Sanskrit was a language of Indo-Iranian origin and the *Romany language spoken by *Gypsies is a member of this group.

Indonesia, Republic of (name from 1798 until 1945: Dutch East Indies) A country in SE Asia, consisting of a series of islands extending E–W for some 3200 mi (5150 km) in the Pacific and Indian Oceans. The main islands are Sumatra, Java and Madura, Bali, Sulawesi, Lombok, the Moluccas, and Timor together with part of Borneo (Kalimantan), and Irian Jaya (the W half of New Guinea). Most of the islands are mountainous and volcanic. Its ethnically diverse population, which belongs mainly to the Malaysian race, may be broadly divided into three main groups: the rice growers of Java and Bali (who make up over half the population), the Islamic coastal peoples, and a group of tribal peoples. The Chinese are the largest nonindigenous group. *Economy*: although rich in natural resources, with large deposits of oil, natural gas, and other minerals as well as some of the richest timber stands in the world, it is a mainly agrarian economy of which the staple crop is rice; cash crops include rubber, palm oil, copra, sugar cane, and coffee. Agricultural output, however, is generally low. The manufacturing sector, which includes shipbuilding, textiles, chemicals, and glass, has been slow to develop. The main exports include oil, timber, and rubber. *History*: in the middle ages kingdoms and empires flourished, including the Hindu Srivijaya empire (7th–13th centuries), based on Palembang, and the Majapahit, which, centered on Java, ruled most of the area in the 15th century. In the 16th century it was occupied successively by the Portuguese, the British, and the Dutch, and from 1602 to 1798 it was ruled by the Dutch East India Company. It became a colony of the Netherlands and, after Japanese occupation during World War II, declared itself a republic in 1945. Dutch colonial interests continued in conflict with the Indonesian nationalists until the country was formally granted independence (1949–50) as a single state. In 1956 ties with the Netherlands were broken off. During the period 1957–65 Dr Sukarno became the central figure pursuing an essentially nationalist policy; Irian Jaya was incorporated in 1963 and there was confrontation with Malaysia (1963–66). A military coup in 1966 under the leadership of Gen Suharto overthrew Sukarno's moderately right-wing authoritarian government replacing it with a harsh military dictatorship; left-wing elements were virtually eliminated. Despite subsequent moves to increase the number of civilian cabinet ministers, the regime remains predominantly military. Changes in foreign policy have led to an influx of capital from the West and Japan and an improvement in relations with Malaysia, but despite the substantial increases in revenue from oil there has been little change in the standard of living for the majority of the population. By the end of 1977 criticism of the Suharto regime increased and there was a series of student riots. Separatist movements have continued in Irian Jaya and East Timor, which was formally incorporated as a province in 1976. President: Gen Suharto. Official language: Bahasa Indonesia. Official currency: rupiah of 100 sen. Area: 735,000 sq mi (1,903,650 sq km). Population (1983): 160,932,000. Capital and main port: Jakarta.

Indore 22 42N 75 54E A city in India, in Madhya Pradesh. Formerly the capital of the princely state of Indore, it is an important trading center with cotton mills and engineering works. Its university was established in 1964. Population (1971): 543,381.

Indra The principal Hindu deity of the Vedic period, god of war and storm, who slew the dragon Vritra, releasing the fertile water and light necessary to create the universe. He is portrayed as wielding a thunderbolt. In later Hinduism, he is supplanted by *Vishnu, *Shiva, and *Krishna and appears as the relatively powerless ruler of the firmament and the east.

indri The largest Madagascan woolly lemur, *Indri indri*. Up to 26 in (70 cm) long, it is gray and black, with long hind legs, a short tail, and a doglike head. It lives in treetops, eating leaves, and has a loud howling cry. Indris are threatened by the destruction of their forest habitats. Family: *Indriidae*.

induction (electromagnetism). *See* electromagnetic induction.

induction (embryology) The process by which an embryonic tissue influences adjacent cells to develop in a certain way, i.e. to differentiate into a particular adult tissue. Absence of the inducer tissue may result in abnormal development or nondevelopment of the induced cells.

induction (logic) The process of making an empirical generalization by observing particular instances of its operation. The conclusion goes beyond the facts, since not all possible instances can be examined. From induction predictions can be made but they are always liable to falsification. *Compare* deduction.

indulgences In the Roman Catholic Church, remissions of the temporal penalties incurred for sins already forgiven by God in the sacrament of penance. Indulgences are based on the belief that a sin, although forgiven, must still have a penalty on earth or in purgatory. The Church may remit these penalties by virtue of the merits of Christ and the saints. The practice of indulgences arose in the early Church when confessors and those about to be martyred were permitted to intercede for penitents and so mitigate the discipline imposed on them. During the later middle ages, indulgences came to command a financial value, which led to widespread abuse and was one of the chief causes of Luther's attack on the Church at the Reformation. Their sale was prohibited in 1567. Today the grant of indulgences, to encourage piety and good works, is largely the prerogative of the pope.

Indus River A river in S central Asia, one of the longest in the world. Rising in SW Tibet in the Himalayas, it flows NW through Kashmir, then SSW across Pakistan to its large delta near Karachi on the Arabian Sea. Its main tributary is the Panjnad, which is formed from the Jhelum, Chenab, Ravi, Beas, and Sutlej rivers. The Indus carries large amounts of sediment and it is also subject to severe flooding but it is an important source of irrigation and hydroelectric power. Waterlogging and salinization have threatened cultivation on the Indus plain and projects have been undertaken to provide an effective drainage system. The Indus contained one of the earliest organized cultures, which lasted from about 2500 until 1700 BC (*see* Indus Valley civilization). Length: 1800 mi (2900 km).

industrial democracy The participation of workers in decisions regarding their work, factory, or company. Various forms of industrial democracy are used in different countries. In the US, the method widely advocated is an extension of *collective bargaining. In West Germany, workers' representatives sit on supervisory boards, which monitor the decisions of the board of directors. In Yugoslavia, there is full worker representation, and at least three-quarters of a management board must consist of production workers. Other methods of encouraging workers' participation include *profit-sharing schemes and *works' councils.

industrial relations Relations between the two sides of industry, employers and employees, usually represented respectively by management and labor unions. In industries with good industrial relations, strikes and lockouts are rare or nonexistent and both sides cooperate to achieve, and to share in, their objectives, whether they be profits, the provision of an efficient service, or simply job satisfaction. Poor industrial relations are easily recognized by frequent and damaging strikes. The key to good industrial relations is probably some measure of *industrial democracy, *profit sharing, and unacrimonious *collective bargaining.

industrial revolution The name given to the process of change that transformed Britain and then other countries from agricultural to industrial economies. The industrial revolution began in Britain about 1750 when the *agricultural revolution was well under way. Inventions were made in the textile industry by such men as James *Hargreaves, Richard *Arkwright, and Samuel *Crompton, which made the production of cloth much faster and the yarn produced of better quality. These new machines could not be used in the home and necessitated the building of factories to house them, at first near rivers for water power and then, when the steam engine was invented, near coalfields. In the factories working conditions were usually intolerable: long hours were worked for low wages and the employment of children was common. Industrial towns sprang up, where living conditions were pitiable, but the current belief in *laissez-faire meant little was done to interfere with the progress of industrial growth. Advances were also made in the production of iron and in communications. The *canals were extended and from about 1830 *railroads were built. By the mid-19th century British industrial methods had spread to continental Europe and the US, laying the foundations for further progress in the 20th century.

Industrial Workers of the World (IWW) US labor organization, established (1905) to organize unskilled workers. Radical in nature, it was founded by Socialist leaders whose ultimate goal was to do away with capitalism. Led by William D. *Haywood, nicknamed the "Wobblies," and drawing its membership particularly from the West, it advocated violence, sabotage, and strikes. It went underground after 1919 and was virtually nonexistent by the mid-1920s.

INDUS VALLEY CIVILIZATION *A seal, probably used for trading purposes, showing a humped bull and pictographic letters. It was found at Mohenjo-Daro (Pakistan).*

Indus Valley civilization A homogeneous culture flourishing between about 2500 and 1700 BC in the area of modern Pakistan. Excavations from the 1920s onward in the great centers of *Mohenjo-Daro and *Harappa have revealed grid-planned streets, municipal drainage, workmen's barracks, granaries and other large public buildings of baked brick, and a standardized system of weights and measures, all testifying to effective centralized administration. Sealstones bearing undeciphered hieroglyphics have also been found. The economy was primarily agricultural but there was some trade with *Sumer and *Akkad. The final downfall of the civilization (c. 1500 BC) was probably because of the *Aryans' incursion.

Ine (died c. 726) King of Wessex (688–726), whose code of law provides valuable information on economic and social life in his time. A patron of the Church, he abdicated (726) to retire to Rome.

inequality A mathematical statement that one quantity is greater or less than another.

$a < (>)b$ means a is less (greater) than b.

$a \leq (\geq)b$ means a is less (greater) than or equal to b.

inert gases. *See* noble gases.

inertia A property of a body that causes it to resist changes in its velocity or, if stationary, to resist motion. When the body resists changes in its linear motion its mass is a measurement of its inertia (*see* mass and weight). When it resists changes in rotation about an axis its inertia is given by its *moment of inertia.

inertial guidance A means of guiding a missile or submarine without communicating with its destination or point of departure. It consists of a set of three gyroscopes, with their axes mounted mutually perpendicular to each other, connected to a computer. The gyroscopes provide a frame of reference, which enables the computer to adjust the controls of the vehicle to steer a preset course.

infallibility A dogma of the Roman Catholic Church promulgated at the first *Vatican Council (1870). It stated that the pope cannot err in defining the Church's teaching in matters of faith and morals when speaking *ex cathedra* (Latin: from the throne), i.e. when intending to make such a pronouncement. The pope is not held thereby to be inspired by God but only to be preserved from error when making such a pronouncement.

infanticide The killing of newborn children. In advanced societies it is generally considered a crime but in many communities, especially in India and China, it has been used to limit population numbers in circumstances of poverty, overpopulation, or famine. Frequently female children and the weak or deformed were at greater risk because they were considered unpro-

ductive. In some societies, for instance among the ancient Phoenicians, a firstborn child would be offered as a sacrifice to the gods.

infant mortality The number of deaths that occur in infants under one year of age. This includes neonatal mortality, occurring in the first four weeks of life, from such causes as asphyxia and other birth injuries, prematurity, and developmental abnormalities. Neonatal deaths account for about two-thirds of infant mortalities in prosperous countries. The quality of a country's obstetric and antenatal care is reflected in its perinatal mortality rate: the number of stillbirths and deaths occurring in the first week of life per 1000 births.

infantry A force of soldiers who fight on foot, even though they may be transported to the battle by air, sea, or mechanized transport. Infantry was predominant in ancient warfare, declined when the emphasis shifted to cavalry (c. 400 AD), and became important again with the development of firearms in the late middle ages. World War I, with its trench warfare, was still essentially an infantry war. The development of fast-moving armor, air power, and the landing craft made World War II a war of combined operations in which infantry played a decisive but not exclusive role. In modern warfare the extensive use of armor and guided missiles has turned the emphasis away from confrontation between massed infantry toward infiltration and *guerrilla warfare.

infection Illness caused by microorganisms, including bacteria, viruses, fungi, and protozoa. Examples of bacterial infections are diphtheria, plague, pneumonia, scarlet fever, tuberculosis, venereal disease, and whooping cough. Viruses cause chickenpox, the common cold, influenza, measles, polio, rabies, and smallpox (among others); malaria and sleeping sickness result from protozoan infection, and fungi cause ringworm. Infectious diseases (also called contagious or communicable diseases) are the commonest cause of sickness and—except in modern industrial societies—have always been the main cause of death. Infections flourish in dirty crowded impoverished conditions, where the inhabitants are malnourished. Methods of transmission include direct contact with an infected person, contact with a human or animal carrier or contaminated objects, and contact with infected droplets produced by coughing and sneezing. The spread of infectious diseases can be prevented by such measures as improving public health, isolation of infected persons, and *vaccination. *Antibiotics are active against a wide range of disease-causing organisms, but as yet there are few effective drugs for viral diseases.

inferiority complex An unconscious belief, first described by Alfred *Adler, that one is severely inadequate in some particular way. This leads to defensive behavior and often to an overcompensation, such as open aggressiveness. *See also* complex.

infinity In mathematics, a quantity larger than any that can be specified. The symbols $+ \infty$ and $- \infty$ are read as "plus infinity" and "minus infinity" respectively. They indicate infinitely large positive and negative values. $x \to + \infty$ means that the value of a variable quantity, x, continues to increase and has no maximum.

inflammation The reaction of the body's tissues in response to injury, infection, chemicals, and poisons, which is characterized by redness, heat, swelling, and pain. Blood flow to the inflamed area increases and white blood cells infiltrate the tissues and begin to engulf the invading bacteria (or other foreign particles). This may result in the accumulation of dead cells and bacteria, which form pus. Inflammation is an essential part of the healing process.

inflation A general sustained increase in prices resulting from excessive demand for goods (demand-pull inflation), increased pricing by sellers in the absence of increased demand (cost-push inflation), or an expansion of the money supply (monetary inflation). **Deflation** is the opposite process and causes a reduction in both output and employment. In the 19th century periods of deflation and inflation alternated regularly. However, the abnormal length and severity of deflation in the 1930s has been followed in the postwar years by a protracted period of inflation, rising in the 1970s to over 10% per annum in many countries. Remedies vary according to the importance ascribed to each contributory factor: control of wages and prices (*see* prices and incomes policy), increased taxation, reduced government spending, and a controlled money supply are among current policies. However, none of them is likely to succeed when the basic cause is an increase in the cost of imported raw materials, such as oil. *Compare* depression.

inflorescence The arrangement of a group of flowers borne on the same main stalk, of which there are two basic types. In a racemose (or indefinite) inflorescence the tip of the main stem continues to grow and flowers arise below it. Examples are the raceme (e.g. foxglove) and the spike, which is similar but the flowers lack stalks (e.g. wheat). Flat-topped racemose inflorescences include the umbel (*see* Umbelliferae), the capitulum

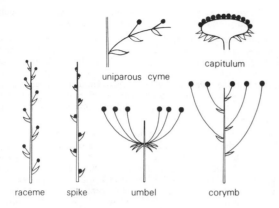

uniparous cyme

capitulum

raceme   spike   umbel   corymb

INFLORESCENCE *All plants except those with solitary flowers show characteristic arrangements of their flowers on the main flowering stalk. All the types shown here, with the exception of the uniparous cyme, are racemose inflorescences.*

(e.g. daisy), and the corymb (e.g. candytuft). A cymose (or definite) inflorescence, or cyme, is one in which a flower is produced at the tip of the main stem, which then ceases to grow. Growth—and further flower production—is continued either by one lateral bud below the tip, to produce a monochasium (e.g. buttercup), or by a pair of buds, giving a dichasium (e.g. stitchwort).

influenza An acute viral infection characterized by chills, fever, headache, and a slight cough. Muscle weakness, aching joints, and loss of appetite may follow. Cases vary from mild to very severe and possibly fatal (particularly if a secondary bacterial infection occurs). Bed rest, aspirin, and fluids provide the only treatment. Usually small outbreaks of influenza occur regularly in winter, but occasionally epidemics sweep across the world. The worst epidemic in the 20th century occurred in 1918–19, when as many as 20 million people died. These epidemics occur because of the development of new strains of influenza viruses, which are not recognized by the body's immune system. Because of this, it is difficult to produce a vaccine, although new ones are constantly produced and are partially effective.

information theory The mathematical theory of communication, involving analysis of the information content of messages and the processes used in their transmission, reception, storage, and retrieval. Statistical concepts, such as probability, are used to assess the extra information (redundancy) necessary to compensate for spurious signals (noise) occurring during communication. The *bit is the basic unit of information and the channel capacity is a measure of the ability of the transmission medium, e.g. a telegraph line, to carry information.

Information theory was developed in the 1940s by Claude E. Shannon (1916–   ). It has been applied widely in such fields as computer science and *cybernetics and has greatly aided the understanding of many processes, ranging from the laws of thermodynamics to the use of language.

infrared radiation Electromagnetic radiation with wavelengths between about 750 nanometers and 1 millimeter. In the electromagnetic spectrum it lies between the red end of visible light and microwaves. It was discovered in 1800 by William *Herschel, who noticed that the solar spectrum contained invisible rays with a heating effect. Infrared radiation is emitted by all bodies at temperatures above absolute zero and is the predominant radiation emitted up to temperatures of about 3000°C.

infrasonics The study of the properties and production of sound waves with a frequency below the threshold of human hearing, i.e. below about 20 hertz. They are produced naturally by earthquakes and tidal waves; in cars traveling at high speeds they have been suspected of having adverse effects on the drivers.

Inge, William (Motter) (1913–73) US dramatist. His plays are set in his native Midwest and deal with the fears, frustrations, and complex feelings of average people, especially in small towns. His works include *Come Back, Little Sheba* (1950), *Picnic* (1953; Pulitzer Prize), *Bus Stop* (1955), *The Dark at the Top of the Stairs* (1957), and the screenplay for *Splendor in the Grass* (1961; Academy Award).

Ingenhousz, Jan (1730–99) Dutch physician and plant physiologist, who discovered the process of *photosynthesis in green plants. Ingenhousz found that plants took in carbon dioxide and gave off oxygen, but only

when exposed to light. This oxygen replenished that used by animals and plants in respiration.

Ingolstadt 48 46N 11 27E A city in SE West Germany, in Bavaria on the Danube River. The Bavarian university was situated here from 1472 to 1800. The cathedral (1425–1500) and castle (1417) survived World War II. An industrial center, it has oil-refining and motor-vehicle industries. Population (1971 est): 71,300.

JEAN-AUGUSTE-DOMINIQUE INGRES   Self-portrait *(1804; Musée Condé, Chantilly).*

Ingres, Jean-Auguste-Dominique (1780–1867) French painter, born in Montauban, the son of an artist. He became a pupil of *David in Paris in 1797. His three paintings of the Rivière family (Louvre) established him as a skilled portraitist. From 1806 to 1820 he lived in Rome, where he produced numerous pencil portraits as well as paintings. Many of his historical and mythological paintings aroused criticism but, on returning to Paris in 1824, his *Vow of Louis XIII* (Cathedral, Montauban) received acclaim and established Ingres as an opponent of the Romantic movement (*see* Romanticism). After holding several posts in the École des Beaux-Arts, he returned to Rome as the director of the French Academy there (1835–41). He is noted for his nudes, e.g. *Valpinçon Bather* (Louvre), and his draftsmanship, which influenced *Degas and *Picasso.

inhibitor A substance that retards a chemical reaction; often called a negative *catalyst. Examples include antioxidants, enzyme inhibitors, and antipolymerization agents.

initiation rites Rituals performed on the transition from childhood to adult status or on joining certain professions, societies, or associations. During the period of transition adolescents among primitive peoples often undergo intensive education in the duties of adulthood. *Circumcision may be practiced at this time. Initiation rites are frequently performed on admission to religious orders, secret societies, and craft guilds. *See also* passage rites.

initiative. *See* referendum and initiative.

injection The introduction of medicinal fluids into the body using a syringe and hollow (hypodermic) needle. The three basic injection routes are under the skin (subcutaneous), for example for insulin; into a muscle (intramuscular), for drugs to be slowly absorbed; and into a vein (intravenous), for drugs to be rapidly absorbed. Drugs are injected when high concentrations are needed or when they are poorly absorbed by the intestines.

injection molding A process, similar to die-casting, for molding thermoplastic materials (plastics that soften on heating and harden on cooling). Injection-molding machines are often fully automatic; the plastic is heated in a cylinder until it has melted and is then forced under pressure into a cooled molding chamber.

Ink A colored fluid for writing or printing. Ordinary permanent blue-black writing ink contains ferrous sulfate, mineral organic acid, and other dyes. Colored inks contain only synthetic dyes, while washable inks use water-soluble synthetic dyes. Marking ink is a mixture of inorganic and organic salts that precipitates aniline black on the surface being marked. India ink, used mainly for drawing, is a black waterproof ink containing carbon black and *shellac. Printing ink consists of pigments suspended in linseed oil, resins, and solvents, the composition depending on the printing process. Ballpoint pen ink is more like printing ink than writing ink since it consists of synthetic dye dissolved in organic liquids with a resinous binder.

Ink cap A *mushroom belonging to the genus *Coprinus*, the gills of which are digested after release of the spores to form an inky fluid that drips from the cap. The common ink cap (*C. atramentarius*) grows in tight clusters, usually at the base of trees and shrubs, and has a pale brownish-gray cap, 1.2–2.8 in (3–7 cm) high, and a whitish stalk.

Inkerman, Battle of (November 5, 1854) A decisive battle of the Crimean War, in which the French and British defeated the Russians at Inkerman, near Sevastopol. In spite of poor direction the Anglo-French force withstood the Russian attack: the Russians lost about 12,000 men, the British, about 2,500, and the French, about 1,000.

Inland Sea A shallow section of the NW Pacific Ocean between the Japanese islands of Honshu, Shikoku, and Kyushu.

Inner Mongolia Autonomous Region (Chinese name: Nei Menggu AR) An administrative division in NE China, bordering on Mongolia and the Gobi Desert in the W. Its steppes are now partly irrigated and cultivated, producing mainly wheat, and the nomadic Mongol herdsmen, now comprising only 7% of the population, are beginning to settle. Some coal is mined. Area: 459,225 sq mi (1,177,500 sq km). Population (1980 est): 18,510,000. Capital: Hohhot.

Inner Temple. *See* Inns of Court.

Innocent III (Lotario de' Conti di Segni; 1160–1216) Pope (1198–1216). He was an outstanding canon lawyer, and as pope his policy was directed to the extension of papal power in all areas of temporal and spiritual government. He successfully intervened in the disputed imperial succession in Germany. In France he condemned the marital behavior of *Philip II Augustus and in England forced the submission of King *John, who recognized the pope as feudal overlord. He also proclaimed the fourth *Crusade (1204). The fourth *Lateran Council (1215) represents the climax of his spiritual rule. In its proclamation of the supremacy of spiritual over temporal power, his pontificate marks the apogee of the medieval papacy.

Innocent IV (d. 1254) Pope (1243–54). Before election to the papacy he was a renowned teacher of canon law at Bologna. Much of his pontificate was taken up with attempts to resolve the conflict between the papacy and Emperor *Frederick II. Innocent was forced to flee Rome (1244) and at the Council of Lyon (1245) condemned and deposed the emperor. Only after Frederick's death, however, did Innocent return to Rome (1253).

Innsbruck 47 17N 11 25E A city in W Austria, the capital of the Tirol on the Inn River. Chartered in 1239, it developed as the junction of several important trade routes, including the *Brenner Pass. It has many fine medieval buildings, and a university (1677). It is a popular tourist and wintersports center and the 1964 Olympic Winter Games were held here. Industries include glass and textiles. Population (1981): 116,025.

Inns of Court Associations in the UK with the exclusive right to confer the rank or degree of barrister-at-law, known as "calling to the Bar." The Inns are Lincoln's Inn (established 1310), Middle Temple (1340), Inner Temple (1340), and Gray's Inn (1357). They are administered by a body of senior barristers and judges known as "benchers," who have absolute discretion as to admission of students to the Bar.

Inoculation. *See* vaccination.

Inönü, Ismet (1884–1973) Turkish statesman; prime minister (1923–37, 1960–65) and president (1938–50). After a successful military career he joined *Atatürk and commanded the fighting against the Greeks in Anatolia (1921). He was prime minister under Atatürk, after whose death (1938) Inönü became president. Following defeat in the elections of 1950 he led the Republican People's Party opposition to the Democratic Party government and after the 1960 coup formed three successive coalition governments (1961–65). He remained in Turkish politics until 1972.

inorganic chemistry. *See* chemistry.

inquilinism An animal relationship in which one species lives in the nest of another species or makes use of its food. For example, some termites live only in the mounds of certain other termite species, although in completely separate compartments.

Inquisition (*or* Holy Office) An institution of the medieval and early modern Church designed to combat heresy and moral offenses. Formally instituted (1231) by Pope *Gregory IX in response to the growing threat of heresy, especially of the *Cathari and *Waldenses, it attempted to place all control of heresy in papal hands. Inquisitors, appointed by the pope, especially from the Dominican and Franciscan orders, and possessing considerable powers, often merited their reputation for cruelty. The use of torture was authorized in 1252 and trials were held in secrecy; fines and various penances were imposed on those who confessed, while those who refused were imprisoned or executed by burning. Almost entirely confined to S Europe, the Inquisition lapsed during the 14th and 15th centuries but was revived in Spain in 1478 against apostate Jews and Muslims. Operating with great severity, especially under the first grand inquisitor, de *Torquemada, the Spanish Inquisition later operated against Protestants in Spain and (with little success) the Netherlands, and achieved some notoriety for its arrest of St *Ignatius Loyola. The growth of Protestantism led to the establishment (1542) of a Roman Inquisition by Pope Paul III. It was given complete independence in matters of doctrine and control of heresy and among its victims was *Galileo. In 1965 the Holy Office became a branch of papal bureaucracy and was renamed the Sacred Congregation for the Doctrine of the Faith; it is now concerned with maintaining Roman Catholic discipline.

In re Gault (1967) US Supreme Court decision that upheld juvenile rights under the 14th Amendment. Gerald Gault, a juvenile, claimed violation of rights, having been denied legal counsel, notification of charges, and appeal of sentence.

In re Neagle (1890) US Supreme Court decision on executive branch powers. The decision upheld the right of the executive branch to carry out its constitutional duties despite previous congressional action, or lack of it.

INRI Abbreviation for *Iesus Nazarenus Rex Iudeorum* (Jesus of Nazareth King of the Jews). According to St John (19.19–20) this inscription, written in Hebrew, Greek, and Latin, was placed by order of Pilate on the cross upon which Jesus was crucified. The initials often appear on the representation of the cross in Christian painting and sculpture.

insanity In law (although not a legal term), defect of reason caused by disease of the mind, making a person not responsible for his acts. A person is presumed sane until the contrary is proved. If a jury finds an accused person committed an act as charged but was insane, it must return a verdict of not guilty by reason of insanity. According to **M'Naghten's Rules** (established following the acquittal in 1843 on the ground of insanity of Daniel M'Naghten, charged with murder) an accused person is insane if he was unaware of the nature or quality of the act or did not know it was wrong. Insanity may affect a person's capacity to make binding contracts or a will or his fitness to plead, i.e. answer to a criminal charge and therefore to stand trial. An insane person contracting with someone aware of his insanity is only bound by contracts for necessaries, such as food, but is liable to pay only a reasonable price irrespective of the contract price. In cases of a person with partial insanity, i.e. with intermittent periods of lucidity, a defense must show that at the relevant time the person was insane.

insect An invertebrate animal, 0.008–14 in (0.2–350 mm) long, belonging to the largest class in the animal kingdom (*Insecta*; about a million known species). Insects occur throughout the world and account for 83% of all animal life. An insect's body, covered by a waterproof cuticle, is divided into three sections: the head, which bears a pair of antennae; the thorax, with three pairs of legs and typically two pairs of wings; and the abdomen. With biting or sucking mouthparts they feed on almost all plant or animal materials. The majority of insects lay eggs, which go through a series of changes (*see* metamorphosis) to reach the adult stage. In the more primitive orders, for example *Orthoptera and *Hemiptera, the young (called nymphs) resemble the adults, but in the higher orders, for example *Hymenoptera, Diptera (flies), and Coleoptera (beetles), the young (called larvae) are unlike the adults, often have a different diet, and go through a resting pupal stage.

Insects play an important role in nature as predators, parasites, scavengers, and as prey. Many are plant or animal pests and disease carriers. Others are useful in pollinating crops or killing insect pests and some produce useful substances, such as honey, beeswax, and silk. Phylum: *Arthropoda*.

insecticides Substances used to kill insects by chemical action. Previously, strong inorganic poisons, such as arsenic compounds and cyanides, were used but these were also toxic to humans and livestock. Synthetic

INSECT

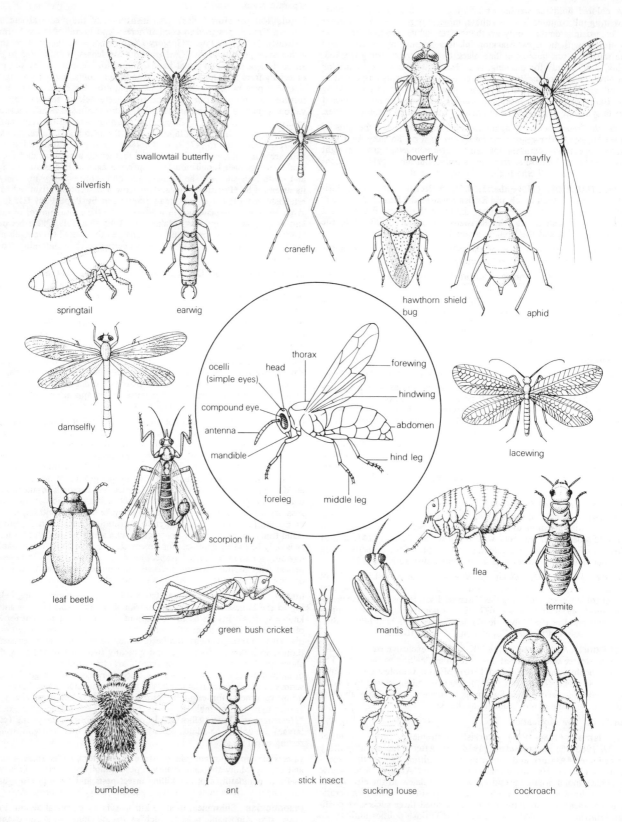

silverfish

swallowtail butterfly

cranefly

hoverfly

mayfly

springtail

earwig

hawthorn shield bug

aphid

damselfly

ocelli (simple eyes)

head

thorax

forewing

compound eye

hindwing

antenna

abdomen

mandible

hind leg

foreleg

middle leg

lacewing

leaf beetle

scorpion fly

flea

termite

green bush cricket

mantis

bumblebee

ant

stick insect

sucking louse

cockroach

INSECT *The structure of a typical insect (center), with representatives from all the principal insect orders.*

organic substances, beginning with DDT in 1945 and including aldrin, endosulfan, and parathion, are now widely used, mainly because of their selectivity, but also because of their cheapness and ease of application. Insecticides are classified according to mode of action or application; for example, **contact insecticides** are applied directly to the insects, while **residual insecticides** are sprayed on surfaces that the insects touch. Problems of insect immunity and environmental pollution have encouraged research into alternative methods involving *biological control.

Insectivora The order of *mammals, comprising about 375 species, that includes *shrews, *tenrecs, *hedgehogs, *moles and *desmans, *golden moles, and *solenodons. Feeding mainly on invertebrates, insectivores are fairly primitive mammals with narrow snouts and sharp simple teeth; their eyes and brains are generally small. Inconspicuous and frequently nocturnal, insectivores are found in nearly all regions; they are absent from the Poles and Australasia and only a few species live in South America.

insectivorous plant. *See* carnivorous plant.

insolvency The inability of a person or company to pay their debts. A creditor may petition a court to declare an insolvent debtor bankrupt (*see* bankruptcy), in which case all his property is sold and the proceeds distributed to his creditors. An insolvent company or partnership is put into liquidation, the court appointing a liquidator, who realizes its assets for distribution to creditors. Although there are state insolvency laws they have generally been superseded by the Federal Bankruptcy Act.

instinct **1.** A complex pattern of behavior, the form of which is determined by heredity and is therefore characteristic of all individuals of the same species. Although the behavior may be released and modified by environmental stimuli, its basic pattern does not depend on the experience of the individual. Birdsong and the complex behavior of social insects (such as bees) are striking examples. It is doubtful whether any human activities are, in this sense, instinctive. **2.** An innate drive, such as hunger or sex, that urges the individual toward a particular goal.

insulator A material that is a poor conductor of electric current and therefore has a high resistivity. Solids, such as glass, rubber, ceramics, and PVC, are used in electric circuits to separate conducting wires and prevent current loss. In overhead power transmission, air acts as the insulator between high-voltage lines. *See also* energy band.

insulin A protein hormone that is secreted by the islets of Langerhans in the *pancreas in response to a high concentration of glucose in the blood, which occurs, for example, after a meal. It stimulates the uptake of glucose and amino acids from the blood by the tissues and the formation of *glycogen. Its effects are counteracted by the hormone *glucagon. Insulin was first isolated in 1921 by *Banting and *Best and its amino acid composition and three-dimensional structure were revealed by Frederick *Sanger and Dorothy *Hodgkin. A deficiency of insulin causes the symptoms of *diabetes mellitus.

insurance A method of providing monetary compensation for a misfortune or loss that may not occur. Events that must occur at some time, such as death, are provided for by life insurance. In many countries insurance against unemployment, sickness, and retirement is provided by the government. Other types of insurance are undertaken by the private sector. Almost any risk can be insured against, the most common being marine and aviation insurance; automobile insurance; fire, burglary, and household insurance; private medical insurance; and weather insurance. The public does not deal directly with the underwriters (insurers) but arranges to cover a risk through an insurance broker, who works for a commission paid by the insurer and advises the client as to the best coverage available, taking into account the cost and reliability of the insurer. Claims are also settled through brokers. The cost to the insured of covering the risk (premium) is calculated by the insurer's *actuary on the basis of the probability of the risk occurring. If the event occurs, the insured's claim is paid by the insurer, as calculated by an insurance assessor or as stipulated in the insurance policy.

intaglio The production of a sunken image, especially in metal or stone, by etching or engraving. It is used in sculpture, gems, and seals, and for making the plates for gravure printing, in which ink is transferred to the paper from only the sunken areas of the plate, the rest having been wiped clean.

integers. *See* numbers.

integrated circuit (IC) A solid-state *semiconductor circuit contained in a single wafer of semiconductor. ICs are made by a process of etching and diffusing a pattern of impurities into the semiconductor surface, forming tiny p-n junctions, which make up individual diodes, *transistors, etc.

Since the 1970s computers have been used to make ICs smaller and more complex, in spite of the fact that further reducing the size makes the doping pattern imprecise. A silicon chip is covered with circuits, and computer-controlled microscopic probes search out the best points for connections for each specific device. The application of this technique has revolutionized many areas of industry and commerce, making cheap *microprocessors available for the automation of production processes.

Intelligence The ability to reason and to profit by experience. An individual's level of intelligence is determined by a complex interaction between his heredity and environment; the Swiss psychologist Jean *Piaget has greatly contributed to present-day understanding of intellectual development. The first **intelligence tests** were devised by Alfred *Binet in 1905 and there are now many tests for assessing intellectual ability. An individual's performance in a test is represented by his **intelligence quotient** (IQ), the product of 100 and the ratio of mental age (obtained from the test results) to actual age. Tests are constructed so that the average IQ is 100 and over 95% of the population come between 70 and 130. However, since it is now widely thought that true intelligence can be expressed only through speech and writing (and is therefore inaccessible to testing) and since each test reflects the constructor's view of the nature of intelligence, the predictive value of the tests as a basis for selection for secondary education is questionable. Tests that measure a wide range of abilities, such as the Weschler Intelligence Scale for Children (WISC), are now regarded as the most useful and relevant for diagnosing educational difficulties.

Intelligence service The government department responsible for obtaining information about the military and economic capabilities and political intentions of another country (intelligence) or for thwarting the attempts of a foreign country to obtain such information for itself (counterintelligence). Sources of intelligence information may be open, such as diplomatic reports, newspapers, and radio broadcasts, or secret, such as aerial reconnaissance, "bugging," and the fieldwork of spies. Intelligence services existed in antiquity and the first known treatise on the subject is Sun Tzu's *The Art of War* (c. 400 BC). Elizabeth I of England had a notable intelligence service, as did Cardinal de Richelieu in 17th-century France and Frederick the Great in 18th-century Prussia. The first specifically military service was established in France under *Fouché (1802) during the Napoleonic Wars, which the British countered (1808) with the Peninsular Corps of Guides in Spain. Intelligence services subsequently grew in complexity and sophistication. The best-known US intelligence services are the *Central Intelligence Agency, the *Federal Bureau of Investigation (counterintelligence), and the National Security Agency (dealing with cryptology).

The development of intelligence services since World War II is linked with technological advances. Modern methods of obtaining secret information about a foreign state, including photoreconnaissance by such aircraft as the U-2 and by satellites, as well as the work of spies, depend on the use of microfilm, recording machines, and computers. The activities of spies have become less significant but remain an enduringly popular theme for books and films and those real-life agents who have been uncovered, such as *Mata Hari, the *Rosenbergs, Burgess and *Maclean, and *Philby, have attracted enormous interest.

Inter-American Development Bank An international bank founded in 1959 to provide assistance for developing countries in Latin America and the Caribbean by making loans at very low *interest rates.

Interest The amount of money charged by a lender to a borrower for the use of a loan. The principal (P) is the amount on which interest is calculated; the term (t), the length of time in years for which the money is lent; and the interest rate (r), the annual rate of return per 100 units of principal. In simple interest, the principal each year is the sum originally lent. The lender is paid $Prt/100$ in interest and repaid P after t years. In compound interest, the interest each year is not paid to the lender but is added to the principal, so that the principal for the next year becomes $P + r/100$. After t years the lender is paid $P(1 + r/100)^t$.

Interference A wave phenomenon in which two waves combine either to reinforce each other or to cancel each other out, depending on their relative phases. The pattern of light and dark strips so produced is called an **interference pattern** (*or* interference fringe). The effect occurs when the two beams have the same frequency and have approximately the same amplitude. Interference was discovered in 1801 by Thomas *Young and provided strong evidence for the wave theory of light.

An **interferometer** is used to produce interference patterns, mainly for the accurate measurement of wavelengths. Several different types are in use, the older instruments being devices for splitting a beam into two parts and then recombining them to form interference patterns after each part has traveled a different distance. In the Michelson interferometer (□Michelson-Morley experiment) the beam is split by a half-silvered mirror in which part of the beam is reflected and the rest transmitted. In the Fabry-Perot interferometer two parallel half-silvered mirrors are placed close to each other. In more modern instruments two lasers are used as separate coherent sources.

Interferon A protein that appears in the plasma during viral infections: it is released from infected cells and inhibits the growth of the viruses. Interferon plays an important role in *immunity because it can enter uninfected cells and render them immune to all viral infections. It was discovered in 1957 by a British virologist, Alick Isaacs (1921–67).

Interior, Department of the US cabinet-level executive branch department that oversees nationally owned public lands and natural resources. It decides on the use of land and water resources; protects fish and wildlife; preserves national parks, forests, and historical places; provides outdoor recreation; assesses and develops mineral resources; and administers Indian reservations and US territories. Directed by the secretary of the Interior, it was established in 1849.

interior design The part of architectural design that deals with the placing and layout of rooms within a building. It chiefly involves the decoration of walls and ceilings and design of normally immovable types of furniture, such as mirrors and fireplaces. It has increasingly concerned movable furniture as well, a field previously left to the skill of the individual craftsman. In the 20th century greater attention has been given to creating a harmonious and functional style for buildings, down to the smallest object of furniture. A notable practitioner of this was Arne Jacobsen, who sometimes specified exact positions for his furniture.

Interlaken 46 42N 7 52E A resort in central Switzerland in the Bernese Oberland between Lakes Brienz and Thun. One of Switzerland's oldest tourist resorts, it is surrounded by spectacular mountain scenery with a fine view of the Jungfrau mountain. Population (1970): 4735.

intermediate vector boson (W) A hypothetical elementary particle thought to be exchanged by particles undergoing a *weak interaction. It would be an unstable *boson, either charged or neutral, and have a mass greater than about 800 MeV. See also particle physics.

internal-combustion engine A *heat engine in which fuel is burned inside the engine, rather than in a separate furnace (see steam engine). This category includes all piston engines, *jet engines, and *rockets. The first practical internal-combustion engine was patented by N. *Otto in 1876. This was a four-stroke engine using gas as a fuel. It was the invention of the □carburetor and the development of the *oil industry that made the liquid-fueled Otto engine a practical source of power for the horseless carriages emerging in the late 19th century (see car). Since then the gasoline engine has powered most road vehicles.

The modern gasoline engine has a compression ratio of 8 or 9 to 1, which requires special fuels (see tetraethyl lead) to avoid *knocking. A simpler but less efficient variety of the gasoline engine is the two-stroke. This does not have the complicated inlet and exhaust valves of the Otto engine, the explosive mixture entering and leaving the cylinder through ports in its walls that are covered and uncovered by the movements of the piston. Two-stroke engines are used where low power is required and in some cars and motorcycles.

The main alternative to the gasoline engine is the oil engine, based on a cycle invented by the German engineer Rudolf Diesel (1858–1913). In the Diesel engine, air is compressed alone inside the engine, causing its temperature to rise to over 1023°F (550°C); oil is then pumped into the combustion chamber as a fine spray and ignites on contact with the hot air. In this case the compression ratio has to be 15 or 16 to 1, making the engine considerably heavier and more expensive than the gasoline engine. The efficiency of both Otto and Diesel engines is limited by their compression ratios and thus their working temperatures (□heat engines). Also, combustion is intermittent and therefore incomplete, causing pollution problems. Moreover, both being reciprocating engines, they have inherent vibrations. This last problem is overcome to some extent in the *Wankel engine. The *gas turbine, however, uses continuous combustion and with a compression ratio of up to 30:1 can reach a working temperature of 2194°F (1200°C). It is therefore more efficient and creates less pollution than piston engines. Jet engines based on the gas turbine are used widely in aircraft and as an easily started and shut down prime mover in some power stations.

Internal Revenue Service (IRS) US Treasury Department arm that enforces tax laws and collects taxes. Established in 1862, the IRS has 8 administrative districts, each with its own director, and has facilities for audit, review, and collection.

Internal Security Act (McCarran Act, 1950) US law passed to curb Communist activity. Sponsored by Senator Patrick A. McCarran, it authorized a commission to require subversive organizations to register as communist, to detain people suspected of sabotage or espionage in times of national emergency, and to bar such individuals from national defense work. The act was amended (1968) to exclude registration requirements.

International An association of national socialist or labor parties formed to promote socialism or communism. The **First International** was an organization of labor and socialist groups founded in London in 1864 as the International Working Men's Association. Karl Marx soon assumed its leadership and its first congress was held in Geneva in 1866. Although the First International was successful in disseminating socialist ideas among workers, it failed to make any political changes, largely because of the conflicting socialist views of its members, especially those of Marx and *Bakunin. Its last meeting was held in 1876 in Philadelphia.

The **Second International** was founded in Paris in 1889; its headquarters were in Brussels. The organization was composed primarily of European, North American, and Japanese social democratic parties, which believed in parliamentary democracy, and of labor unions. Its leaders included Ramsay *Macdonald. At the outbreak of World War I, the organization collapsed because of division between pro- and anti-war groups. A postwar attempt to revive it failed.

The **Labor and Socialist International** was founded in Vienna in 1921; its goal was to create a socialist commonwealth. It has been called the "second and a half International" because it was composed of those out of sympathy with the Second and Third Internationals. It opposed fascism and also communist dictatorship while supporting the Soviet Union. The organization came to an end following Hitler's invasions in W Europe in 1939.

The **Third International** (or Comintern), an organization of world Communist Parties, was founded by Lenin in March, 1919, to encourage worldwide proletarian revolution. Throughout its existence it adjusted its program to political exigencies and to the power struggles within the Soviet party leadership. As a gesture of reconciliation with his western allies, Stalin dissolved the International in 1943 (see also Cominform).

The **Fourth International** was founded by *Trotsky in Mexico City in 1937 in opposition to Stalin and the Third International. It held its first conference in France in 1938 and was composed primarily of those who supported Trotsky's transitional program, which aimed to undermine capitalism in preparation for its revolutionary overthrow.

The **Socialist International** was founded in 1951 as an association of socialist parties that believe in parliamentary democracy and oppose communism. Its headquarters are in London.

International Bank for Reconstruction and Development (IBRD) A specialized agency of the *United Nations, known as the World Bank, with headquarters in Washington, DC. Its function is to finance development in member countries by making loans to governments or under government guarantee. It was set up by the 1944 *Bretton Woods agreements to facilitate reconstruction after World War II. All members must belong to the *International Monetary Fund.

International Brigades A volunteer army recruited during the Spanish Civil War (1936–39) by the Comintern to aid the Republicans against Franco. Comprising at its largest some 20,000 volunteers, of which about 60% were communists, it was organized by nationality into 7 brigades. Ill-armed and badly led, it was disbanded in 1938. Many Americans sympathetic to the Republican cause joined the brigades.

International Civil Aviation Organization (ICAO) A specialized agency of the *United Nations established in 1947 to promote high operating standards and fair competition among international airlines. With headquarters in Montreal, it formulates agreed standards in telecommunications, personnel training, and air-traffic protocols. Its council of representatives of 27 of the member countries implements the decisions of the assembly, its legislative body, and when necessary settles disputes between members.

international commodity agreements Agreements between producers of primary products to regulate their production and sale in order to stabilize prices and conserve supplies; examples include the Tin Agreement (1956), Coffee Agreement (1962), and Rubber Agreement (1976). Natural factors, such as crop failures, and the discovery of new mineral deposits cause fluctuations in the supply and hence the price of commodities. Producers, which are mostly developing countries, have agreed to limit production, fix minimum prices, and establish marketing organizations to build up buffer stocks by buying surpluses, which are sold when prices exceed a specific ceiling.

International Confederation of Free Trade Unions (ICFTU) An international body of national trades-union federations formed in 1949 by federations that had withdrawn from the *World Federation of Trade Un-

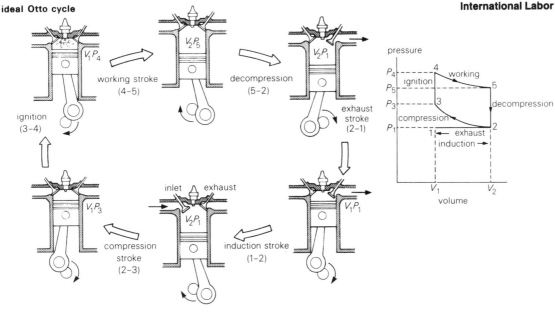

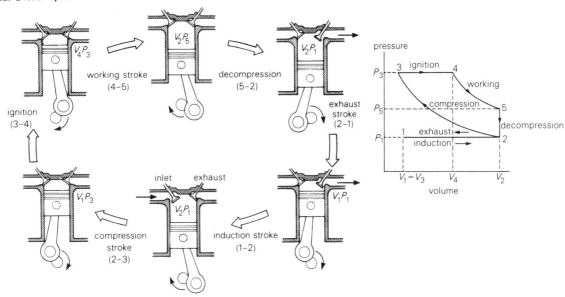

INTERNAL-COMBUSTION ENGINE *In the ideal Otto-cycle (four-stroke) engine, there are four piston strokes (movements up and down) for each explosion. The gasoline-air mixture is drawn into the cylinder by the induction stroke (1-2) and compressed by the compression stroke (2-3). A spark then ignites (3-4) the mixture causing the pressure to rise from P_3 to P_4 before the piston descends (combustion at constant volume). The piston then descends in the working stroke (4-5) and rises again in the exhaust stroke (2-1), when the burned gases are pushed out of the cylinder through the exhaust valve. The graph illustrates the pressure and volume changes during the cycle. In the Diesel cycle, ignition is caused by the high compression achieved by the compression stroke (2-3) and the piston descends, increasing the volume of the burning gas from V_3 to V_4 before the pressure has time to rise (combustion at constant pressure).*

ions (WFTU) following disagreements with the communist members of the WFTU.

International Court of Justice The judicial body set up by the UN to pass judgment on disputes between states. The court, which normally sits at The Hague, comprises 15 judges, each from a different state, elected by the UN General Assembly. The court may only hear disputes between states that have agreed to be brought before it by any other state, either generally or in a specific case. Judgments of the court are enforced by application to the UN Security Council. The court also advises the UN and other specified bodies on questions of *international law.

International Criminal Police Organization. *See* Interpol.

International Date Line A line following the 180° meridian, deviating to avoid some land areas. The date immediately E of the line is one day earlier than to the W since 180°E is 12 hours ahead of *Greenwich Mean Time and 180°W is 12 hours behind.

Internationale The national anthem of the Soviet Union until 1944, composed by P. Degeyter (1848–1932).

international gothic A style of painting and sculpture dominant in W Europe between about 1375 and 1425. Originating in France and Burgundy, it later spread to Italy, Bohemia, and other German states. International gothic retained the figure stylizations of *gothic but introduced naturalism in the depiction of landscape, animals, and costume. Leading exponents were the de *Limburg brothers and Claus *Sluter in Burgundy and *Gentile da Fabriano and *Pisanello in Italy.

International Labor Organization (ILO) A specialized agency of the *United Nations dedicated to the improvement of working conditions and living standards. It was first convened in 1919, when it was affiliated to the *League of Nations, and its headquarters are in Geneva. The organization advocates a world labor code to protect the interests of workers, supports labor research projects, monitors labor legislation, and provides technical assistance to developing nations. In 1977 the US withdrew from the ILO on the grounds that it had come to be dominated by political interests but rejoined in 1980.

international law The rules that determine the legal relationship between independent states (public), or between citizens of such states (private). Public international law, also called the law of nations and administered by the *International Court of Justice, is based on: (1) natural law, being laws recognized by civilized nations; (2) agreements between states, i.e. conventions; (3) customs followed in practice; and, to a lesser extent (4) the writings and opinions of respected jurists. Private international law, also called conflict of laws, determines the laws of which country should apply in given circumstances and which courts should have jurisdiction.

International Monetary Fund (IMF) A specialized agency of the *United Nations, with headquarters in Washington, DC, set up by the 1944 *Bretton Woods agreements to stabilize exchange rates and facilitate international trade. Each member country contributes to the fund in both gold and its own currency. A member with balance-of-payments difficulties can obtain the currency it requires from the fund in exchange for its own, which it must repurchase within five years. The higher a member's contribution the greater its voting rights. *See also* Special Drawing Rights.

International Organization for Standardization (ISO) An organization, situated in Geneva, for establishing and controlling international scientific, industrial, and commercial standards of measurement and design. It was founded in 1946.

International Phonetic Alphabet (IPA) An augmented version of the Roman alphabet, developed by the International Phonetic Association in the late 19th century and kept under continuous revision since. It attempts to symbolize, on phonetic principles, every sound that can be made in human language. It is used internationally in dictionaries to represent the pronunciation of words.

international style The predominant architectural style of the 20th century, so called because it was the first style effectively to breach all national and cultural barriers. Originating in W Europe and the US with such architects as *Gropius, *Wright, *Behrens, and *Le Corbusier, the international style evolved from the new tastes, materials, and advanced technology produced by industrialization. It is chiefly characterized by the use of concrete, often roughcast, a tendency toward monolithic uniformity in the use of undecorated cubic forms, and a functional asymmetry.

International Telecommunication Union (ITU) A specialized agency of the *United Nations founded in 1934 to promote international agreement on standards of use and development of telecommunications systems. It makes recommendations on the regulation and use of radio frequencies, general operating procedures, and the establishment of telecommunications systems in developing countries, including radio, telegraph, telephone, cable, and television. Its headquarters are in Geneva.

International Working Men's Association. *See* International.

Interpol (*Inter*national Criminal *Poli*ce Organization) An association of about 120 national *police forces formed in 1923 to provide a means of international cooperation in the prevention of crime. Its constitution strictly precludes activities of a political, military, religious, or racial nature. Its major concerns are the exchange of police information and the arrest of those who are the subject of an extradition order. Interpol has been most effective in the control of smuggling, particularly of gold and narcotics, and of currency offenses and counterfeiting.

Interregnum. *See* Commonwealth.

interstellar medium The matter, mainly gas and some dust, contained in the region between the stars of the *Galaxy. The gas is mainly hydrogen with some helium. It can exist, for example, as hot ionized clouds, cooler and more tenuous neutral areas, or dense clouds of molecular hydrogen and other molecules. Small dust particles are found throughout the interstellar region. The gas and dust is probably material cast off from old stars, with young stars forming out of the denser clouds.

interstitial An atom that exists in the spaces (interstices) between the atoms or molecules in a crystal lattice. Some interstitial compounds are important *alloys and some are *semiconductors.

intestine The part of the digestive tract, in the abdomen, that extends from the stomach to the anus. It is divided into two parts. The small intestine, which includes the duodenum, jejunum, and ileum, is the principal site of digestion and absorption of food. It secretes digestive enzymes

and mucus and its inner surface is thrown into finger-like processes, which increase the absorptive area. The duodenum is a common site for a *peptic ulcer, since it receives the acid contents from the stomach. The large intestine consists of the colon, cecum, rectum, and anus. It is largely concerned with the absorption of water from digested food and the formation of *feces, which are expelled from the anus. The intestines contain specialized muscle whose rhythmic contractions (called peristalsis) propel food toward the anus.

intimism A branch of postimpressionist painting, specializing in domestic interiors having an atmosphere of intimacy. The chief practitioners were the *Nabis painters Pierre *Bonnard and Édouard *Vuillard.

Intolerable Acts (*or* Coercive Acts; 1774) British parliamentary Acts intended to enforce stricter control over the American colonies following the *Boston Tea Party. The Boston Port Bill (1774) closed the port until reparation for the lost tea had been made. The Massachusetts Government Act repealed the colony's charter and imposed a military government on Massachusetts; the Administration of Justice Act allowed British officials to return home for trial in a criminal case; and the Quebec Act gave the lucrative fur trade between the Ohio and Mississippi rivers to Quebec. The Acts contributed to the outbreak of the *American Revolution.

intoxication Any form of acute poisoning: in popular language it usually refers to alcoholic poisoning. This is characterized by excited, often abusive, behavior, unsteady gait, confused memory, flushed skin, and poor coordination.

intra-uterine device (IUD). *See* contraception.

introversion (*or* intraversion) A quality of personality characterized by interest in oneself rather than in the outside world: it is the opposite of *extroversion. Introverts are reflective and introspective, with a tendency to have a small circle of friends. They are good at persisting for a long time at one task; their interests tend to be philosophical; and they are highly susceptible to permanent *conditioning.

intrusive rock. *See* igneous rock.

intuitionism Any doctrine in which what appears to be self-evident is regarded as the basis of knowledge ("I just *know* that such-and-such is the case"). From the model of mathematics, the Pythagoreans believed that intuition is superior to observation and in modern times the mathematical school of *Brouwer was called intuitionist regarding its views about the nature of mathematics. In contemporary philosophy, intuitionism has been most emphasized in *ethics.

Inuit The *Eskimos of Alaska, Greenland, and Canada. The assertiveness of the Inuit tribes, especially in Canada, brought civil, economic, and social reforms in the late 1970s and early 1980s.

Invar An *alloy of iron with 36% nickel, which expands by only 0.9 mm per km for each centigrade degree temperature rise. This is about one-tenth the expansion of platinum and titanium and less than one-twentieth of that of most other metals. It was discovered in 1896 and since then has been used for accurate measuring tapes and chronometer parts.

Invercargill 46 26S 168 21E A city in New Zealand, in S South Island on the Waihopai River. It is the center of a sheep- and dairy-farming region. Population (1980 est): 53,700.

Inverness 57 27N 4 15W A city in N Scotland, at the head of the Moray Firth. Inverness is a tourist center and has boatbuilding, distilling, ironfounding, and woolen industries. It has a 19th-century cathedral and castle, which occupies the site of an earlier castle destroyed in 1746. Population (1978 est): 44,000.

invertebrate Any animal without a backbone. All animals except vertebrates belong to this category, including the *protochordates—animals that possess a rodlike skeletal notochord. Although widely used, the term is seldom employed in taxonomic systems.

invert sugar A mixture of the sugars glucose and fructose resulting from the action of heat or the enzyme invertase on cane or beet sugar (sucrose). It is sweeter than sucrose and widely used in foods and confectionery.

investiture controversy A dispute between the papacy and the Holy Roman Empire during the late 11th and early 12th centuries concerning the right of secular rulers to appoint bishops and invest them with their office in return for pledges of loyalty. The conflict arose between Pope *Gregory VII and the Holy Roman Emperor *Henry IV and later also involved the Norman kings of England. Compromise was reached with England in 1106 and with the Emperor in 1122. This issue provided a focus for the struggle for supremacy between lay and ecclesiastical powers.

investment 1. The purchase of capital goods (plant and machinery) used in the production of consumer goods and services. Investment and consumption together comprise the national income. A high level of investment is a necessary part of a nation's economic wellbeing and helps to promote *economic growth. In most countries incentives, in the form of tax relief, are available on investment expenditure. What actually motivates investment is a matter of debate: some economists believe the rate of interest is the most important factor, while others assign more importance to the level of demand in the economy. Certainly investment varies a great deal over the *trade cycle. **2.** The use of money to obtain an income or a capital gain in the future. This can be achieved by depositing it with a bank or other financial institution to provide income without capital growth. Investment also includes the purchase of any asset that can be expected to increase in value and can also be linked with insurance policies.

investment bank A financial institution that acts as an intermediary between a company seeking to raise capital on a stock exchange and those wishing to invest. It advises a client on when and how to make a new issue of *securities, advertises it to the public, and often underwrites the issue (i.e., guarantees to buy all the securities that have not been applied for).

investment company. *See* closed-end investment company.

Io In Greek legend, a priestess of Hera, loved by Zeus, who transformed her into a heifer to protect her from discovery. Hera ordered Argus, a herdsman with eyes covering his entire body, to guard her, but she escaped with the help of Hermes and was finally restored to Zeus in Egypt.

Ioánnina (*or* Yannina) 39 40N 20 51E A city in NW Greece, in Epirus on Lake Ioánnina. Conquered by the Turks in 1430, it became the seat (1788–1822) of Ali Pasha. It was captured by the Greeks in 1913. The university was founded in 1970. Population (1971): 40,130.

iodine (I) A purple-black lustrous solid *halogen that evaporates slowly at room temperature to give a purple gas. It was discovered in 1811 by B. Courtois (1777–1838). It is insoluble in water but dissolves readily in organic solvents, such as chloroform ($CHCl_3$) or carbon tetrachloride (CCl_4), to give pink-purple solutions. Iodine is present in sea water and concentrated by seaweeds; it also occurs in saltpeter deposits, such as those in Chile. Potassium iodide (KI) is widely used in photography. The radioactive isotope ^{131}I, with a half-life of 8.1 days, is produced in nuclear reactors; its accidental release into the atmosphere would cause serious problems. It is also used in the diagnosis and treatment of thyroid disorders as it is concentrated in the thyroid gland. Tincture of iodine is used as an antiseptic. At no 53; at wt 126.904; mp 113.5°C; bp 184.35°C.

io moth A large common American *saturniid moth, *Automeris io.* Males are yellow and the larger females reddish brown, with a wingspan of 3 in (70 mm). The greenish spiny larvae feed on trees and are poisonous to touch.

ion An atom or group of atoms that has lost or gained one or more electrons and consequently has an electric charge. Positively and negatively charged ions are called **cations** and **anions** respectively. The sign and magnitude of the charge is indicated by a superscript, as in the potassium ion, K^+, or the doubly charged sulfate ion, SO_4^{2-}. Many compounds (electrovalent compounds) are combinations of positive and negative ions; sodium chloride, for example is formed from sodium ions (Na^+) and chloride ions (Cl^-). *See also* chemical bond; ionization.

Iona 56 19N 6 25W A small sparsely populated island in NW Scotland, in the Inner Hebrides. It has many religious associations; St Columba landed here in 563 AD, establishing a monastery that became the center of the Celtic Church. It later became a burial ground for Scottish, Irish, and Norwegian kings. Area: 2112 acres (854 ha).

Ionesco, Eugène (1912–   ) French dramatist. He was born in Romania of French and Romanian parents and settled permanently in France in 1938. He inaugurated the *Theater of the Absurd with his first play, *The Bald Prima Donna* (1950), which exposed the poverty of language as a means of communication. His later plays, which include *The Lesson* (1951), *The Chairs* (1951), *Rhinoceros* (1960), *Exit the King* (1962), and *Man With Bags* (1977), use a variety of surrealistic techniques to express a nihilistic vision of society.

Ionia In antiquity, the central W coast of Asia Minor and the adjacent islands, settled by Greeks about 1000 BC. Between the 8th and 6th centuries BC *Miletus, *Samos, *Ephesus, and other Ionian cities led Greece in trade, colonization, and culture. The first Greek philosophers, including *Thales, *Pythagoras, and *Anaximander, were Ionian. After 550 BC Ionia passed under the domination of *Lydia and later Persia. The Ionian revolt against Persian rule (499–494 BC) resulted in defeat, economic ruin, subjugation by outsiders, and comparative eclipse.

Ionian Islands A group of Greek islands in the Ionian Sea, extending from Corfu in the N to Zacynthus in the S and including Páxos, Lévkas,

Ithaca, and Cephalonia. They belonged to Britain from the Treaty of Paris (1815) until 1864, when they were ceded to Greece. Several were devastated by earthquakes in 1514, 1893, and 1953. Total area: 891 sq mi (2307 sq km). Population (1971): 184,443.

Ionian Sea The section of the central Mediterranean Sea, bounded by Italy, Sicily, and Greece, that contains the Ionian Islands.

Ionic order. *See* orders of architecture.

ionization The process of producing *ions from neutral atoms or molecules. Solvation (surrounding of an ion by polar solvent molecules), heating (thermal ionization), or bombardment with particles or radiation provide the necessary energy for the process. The minimum energy required to ionize an atom A (i.e. $A \rightarrow A^+ + e^-$) is called its **ionization potential**, which is usually measured in electronvolts.

ionization chamber An instrument used for measuring the intensity of *ionizing radiation. It consists of a gas-filled chamber containing two electrodes with a large potential difference between them. When radiation enters the chamber it ionizes some of the gas atoms or molecules. The ions flow toward the electrodes creating a current, the magnitude of which is a measure of the intensity of the radiation. The *Geiger counter is an example of an ionization chamber.

ionizing radiation Any radiation that ionizes the atoms or molecules of the matter through which it passes. It may consist of particles (such as *electrons) or it may be electromagnetic radiation (*see* ultraviolet radiation; X-rays; gamma radiation). Ionizing radiation occurs naturally in *cosmic rays and is emitted by radioactive substances. It is also produced artificially in X-ray machines, particle accelerators, nuclear reactors, etc. Ionizing radiations are used in medical diagnosis and therapy and in sterilization of food. In biological tissue these radiations create reactive free radicals, especially by ionizing water molecules, which attack proteins, nucleic acids, etc., and can cause damage by changing their structure and function.

ionosphere A region of the upper □atmosphere that reflects short radio waves, enabling transmissions to be made around the curved surface of the earth by sky waves. The gases in the ionosphere are ionized by absorption of radiation from the sun. Its existence was suggested in 1902 by A. E. Kennelly and independently by O. Heaviside. Sir Edward Appleton (1892–1925) provided proof by bouncing radio waves off the different layers of the ionosphere, which vary in behavior with the position of the sun and with the sunspot cycle. The ionization of the D region, at between 30 and 55 miles (50 and 90 km) altitude, disappears during the day. The E region is between 55 and 100 miles (90 and 160 km) high and the F region (sometimes called the Appleton layer) is from 100 miles up to about 250 miles (160 to 400 km). The lower part of the ionosphere (E region) is sometimes called the Kennelly-Heaviside layer. The gas particles in the F region do not lose their charge as quickly as those below because the gas is less dense and therefore ions and electrons are subject to fewer collisions. This enables radio transmissions to continue at night.

Iowa A state in the Midwest. The Mississippi River forms its boundary with Wisconsin and Illinois in the E; Missouri lies to the S; the Missouri River forms its boundary with Nebraska and South Dakota in the W; and Montana lies to the N. The land rises slowly from the Mississippi Valley to form a gentle rolling landscape, with the higher land in the NW. Iowa is predominantly an agricultural state, and its agricultural sector is one of the most important in the country although industry produces more revenue. In the 1930s Iowa moved to diversify its economy, encouraging agriculturally associated industries including the manufacture of agricultural machinery and food processing. It is famed for its livestock, particularly pigs. Major crops are corn, oats, soybeans, and other fodder crops. There is also some mining for portland cement and gypsum. The scattered population and lack of urban areas limit the cultural institutions the state can support. *History*: the Mound Builders were the earliest known inhabitants. When French explorers arrived in the 17th century, they found Sac, Fox, Iowa, and Sioux tribes. *Marquette and Jolliet explored the region in 1673 and La Salle in 1681–82. It formed part of the Louisiana Purchase (1803). The Black Hawk Wars virtually ended the tenure of the Indians in the state, and settlers from the East and from Europe migrated W. With the growth of rural communities, agrarian protest groups, such as the Granger Movement, sprang up. They served as political forums seeking to improve farmers' economic status. Iowa remains essentially agricultural and rural with one of the lowest rates of population growth in the US. Area: 56,290 sq mi (145,790 sq km). Population (1983 provisional est): 2,905,000. Capital: Des Moines.

Ipatieff, Vladimir Nikolaievich (1867–1952) US physicist, born in Russia. While working in Germany he discovered the structure of *isoprene (1897); returning to Russia in 1899 he investigated the catalytic breakdown of *hydrocarbon molecules at high temperatures. In 1930 he emigrated to the US, where he worked on the development of high-octane fuels for internal-combustion engines.

ipecacuanha A South American herbaceous plant, *Uragoga ipecacuanha*, cultivated in the tropics for its root, which yields medicinal alkaloids used as an expectorant and emetic. Large doses cause vomiting and diarrhea. Family: *Rubiaceae*.

Iphigenia In Greek legend, the eldest daughter of *Agamemnon and *Clytemnestra. When the Greek fleet was delayed at Aulis at the beginning of the *Trojan War, Agamemnon was told that Artemis demanded the sacrifice of his daughter before the fleet could sail to Troy. He was about to comply when Artemis took pity on Iphigenia and transported her to Tauris, where she became a priestess of Artemis. The story is the subject of two plays by *Euripides.

I-pin. *See* Yibin.

Ipoh 4 36N 101 02E A city in NW Peninsular Malaysia, the capital of Perak state. The tinmining center of Malaysia, it has noted Chinese rock temples. Population (1980): 300,727.

Ipswich 52 04N 1 10E A city in SE England, at the head of the Orwell estuary. It is a port with engineering, printing, brewing, flour-milling, plastics, fertilizers, tobacco, and textile industries. Cardinal Wolsey was born here. Population (1981): 120,447.

Ipswich 27 38S 152 40E A city in Australia, in SE Queensland. It is the state's second largest coal producer. Population (1975 est): 69,000.

Iqbal, Mohammed (?1875–1938) Indian Muslim poet and philosopher, born in Sialkot (Punjab). He came to England in 1905 (already a noted romantic poet and promoter of Indian nationalism) to study at Cambridge University. From 1908 Iqbal lived in Lahore where he became a leading member of the *Muslim League. He is generally credited with the formulation of the political theory of Pakistan as a separate Muslim state in the Indian subcontinent.

Iquique 20 15S 70 08W A port in N Chile, on the Pacific Ocean. Industries include fishmeal plants and canneries; the chief exports are nitrates, iodine, and fishmeal. Population (1975 est): 63,600.

Iquitos 3 51S 73 13W A port in NE Peru, on the Amazon River 2300 mi (3700 km) from its mouth. The furthest point upstream accessible to oceangoing vessels, it exports rubber, timber, and nuts. Its university was founded in 1962. Population (1972): 110,242.

IRA. *See* Irish Republican Army.

Iráklion (*or* Herakleion; Italian name: Candia) 32 20N 25 08E The chief port of the Greek island of Crete, on the N coast. It is picturesque, possessing many Venetian fortifications, and has become a tourist center. Exports include raisins, grapes, and olive oil. Population (1971): 78,209.

Iran (name until 1935: Persia) A country in the Middle East lying between the Caspian Sea and the Persian Gulf. Its central plateau, containing deserts and marshes, is surrounded by mountains, the *Zagros Mountains in the W, the *Elburz Mountains and the Kopet Mountains in the N, and a barren region of peaks and sand in the E. It suffers great extremes of temperature and severe earthquakes. The most populous areas are the NW and the Caspian coast, which have the greatest rainfall. The population is mainly Persian with groups of Turks, Kurds, Armenians, Arabs, and such tribes as the Bakhtyari. *Economy*: agriculture supports 75% of the population, although lack of rain hampers productivity and much food has to be imported. The development of irrigation has been a high priority. Wheat, rice, tobacco, fruit, sugar beet, and tea are grown; sheep and goats are kept. Iran's chief source of revenue is its oil; it possesses 10% of the world's reserves and has profited greatly from the oil price increases of the 1970s. The main oilfields are in the Zagros Mountains, where oil was first discovered (1908). Other minerals include coal, copper, iron ore, lead, natural gas, and precious stones. The textile industry uses local cotton and silk, and carpet manufacture is an important handicraft. Among Iran's other industries, its steel industry is the largest in the Middle East. Oil revenues have been used to diversify the economy; to this end many capital goods, such as machinery, are imported. *History*: the Caspian coast and the plateau are among the earliest centers of civilization. Early Persian dynasties include the *Achaemenians and the *Sasanians (*see also* Greek-Persian wars). Arab domination, which established Islam in the area, was followed by that of the Turks and Mongols before the Persian Safavid dynasty (1502–1736) came into power. Following a period of great prosperity (1587–1629) Persia again declined, encroached on by Uzbeks, Arabs, Afghans, Turks, and Russians. The next great dynasty, the Kajar dynasty (1794–1925), was marked largely by rivalry for domination between Britain and Russia. Western influence was felt increasingly during the latter half of the 19th century. Repressive rule provoked opposition that became open in about 1900 and was intensified by resentment against the concessions granted to Britain and Russia, made necessary by the Shah's financial difficulties. The Shah was forced to grant a constitution and National Assembly (the Majlis; 1906); his successor disbanded this and was then deposed and replaced (1909). Further disorders resulted in the army coup that established Reza Khan in power (1921), from 1925 as *Reza Shah Pahlavi. Under his virtual dictatorship order returned and the country was industrialized and extensively westernized; he was forced to abdicate in favor of his son *Mohammed Reza Pahlavi (1941). Iran's oil has been a major source of political unrest. In 1945 the Soviet Union supported an Azerbaidzhan and Kurdish revolt to gain oil concessions (later withdrawn). Oil was also a major issue for the militant National Front movement, which nationalized the oil industry (1951); the British responded with a blockade resulting in serious economic difficulties and the Shah was forced to flee the country temporarily. Martial law was ended after 16 years in 1957 but economic and political instability continued; the Shah's reform program, which included in 1963 the enfranchisement of women, the redistribution of land, and compulsory education, was opposed by major religious and political groups. There were riots in the early 1960s and unrest was further provoked by harsh repression, with many dissidents executed or imprisoned; Savak, the secret police, were notorious for their use of torture and imprisonment. By 1978 different opposition groups, including Muslims, politicians, intellectuals, students, communists, and human-rights supporters had united under the exiled Muslim leader Ayatollah Ruholla *Khomeini. Demonstrations and riots in 1977–78 were reinforced by strikes, despite the imposition of martial law in the cities, concessions, and a change of administration; by February, 1979, an estimated 10,000 people had died in political violence, while anti-US and anti-British feeling had forced foreigners to leave the country. The Shah then left the country, later dying in exile (1980), and Ayatollah Khomeini took over the government in the so-called Islamic Revolution. Unrest continued, with Khomeini's strict Muslim administration opposed by progressive groups and Kurdish rebels. In 1979 students occupied the US embassy in Tehran and took 52 of the personnel hostage, only releasing them in January, 1981, after lengthy negotiations. Abolhassan Bani-Sadr, elected Iran's first president in 1980, was dismissed and forced to flee the country in 1981. In the continuing violence his successor, Muhammad Ali Radjai, was killed in a bomb explosion (1981). Hojatleslam Ali Khamenei was later elected president in October, 1981. In September, 1980, Iraq attacked Iran, but the invasion was repelled and a long costly stalemate ensued, the Ayatollah Khomeini refusing to make peace with Iraqi President Sadam Hussein. Official language: Persian (Farsi). Official currency: Iranian rial of 100 dinars. Area: 636,160 sq mi (1,648,000 sq km). Population (1983): 42,480,000. Capital: Tehran.

Iranian languages A subgroup of the *Indo-Iranian language family. Iranian languages are spoken in Iran, Afghanistan, Turkey, and parts of the Caucasus. Like its counterpart the *Indo-Aryan group, the Iranian languages are closely related to *Sanskrit. Modern Iranian languages include Persian, Kurdish, *Pashto, and *Ossetic.

Iraq, Republic of A country in the Middle East, bordering on the Persian Gulf. The SE consists of an alluvial plain around the delta of the Tigris and Euphrates Rivers; this floods in spring. The W is a vast desert while the N is mountainous. The population is about 90% Muslim divided evenly between Shiite and Sunnite sects. The Kurds, who live in the mountainous NE, form about 15–20% of the population. *Economy*: mainly agricultural, the chief crops being wheat, barley, rice, maize, sorghum, sesame, dates, and cotton. Since 1958 cooperative and collective farms have been set up and mechanization and irrigation schemes have increased production. The main industry is oil (first discovered at Kirkuk in 1927) and Iraq is a member of OPEC. Natural gas is also produced, as are textiles, processed foods, cement, and electrical and leather goods. Cereals, meat, machinery, vehicles, chemicals, and consumer goods are imported, chiefly from Japan, Germany, the US, France, and the Soviet Union. *History*: as *Mesopotamia, Iraq was the site of the world's first civilization; it is extremely rich in archeological remains. It was conquered by Arabia and became Muslim in the 7th century AD and was part of the Ottoman Empire from 1534 until World War I, when UK troops expelled the Turks. As a British mandate (1920–32), Iraq became a kingdom (1921). From this period on it has been politically unstable, with ethnic and religious unrest and frequent coups; the monarchy was overthrown in 1958. During the 1960s and 1970s the Kurds have been in intermittent rebellion and there has been opposition to the socialist government (in power since 1968) from Muslims and communists. Although a member of the *Arab League and formerly of the *Baghdad Pact it has been in dispute with Iran and Syria during the 1960s and 1970s, although in 1978 an agreement on military union was signed with Syria. Taking advantage of disorder in Iran, Iraq in September, 1980, attacked its neighbor. Iran repelled the invasion, and the war dragged on at enormous cost to both countries. President: Sadam Hussein (1935–). Official language: Arabic. Official currency: Iraqi dinar of 1000 fils. Area: 169,248 sq mi (438,446 sq km). Capital: Baghdad. Population (1983): 14,509,000.

Irbil (Arbil *or* Erbil)   36 12N 44 01E A city in N Iraq close to the Turkish and Iranian borders. It was important in Assyrian times and is now a trading center for a productive agricultural region. Population (1970 est): 107,400.

Ireland   The second largest island in the British Isles, separated from Great Britain by the North Channel, the Irish Sea, and St George's Channel. It consists of a central lowland area of fertile plains, bogs, and moorland, rising to hills and mountains in the N and S. The River Shannon is the chief river, draining N–S, and Ireland contains many lakes, particularly in the N and W, including Lough Neagh. Since 1920 Ireland has been politically divided, the NE part forming Northern Ireland in the UK and the remainder comprising the Republic of Ireland. *History*: rich in archeological remains, Ireland was invaded in the 4th century BC by the Celts. The country came to be divided into the five tribal kingdoms (the Five Fifths) of Ulster, Meath, Leinster, Munster, and Connaught, which nominally acknowledged the overlordship of the High Kings of Ireland (the rulers of Tara). In the 5th century the country was converted to Christianity—a process in which St Patrick was the outstanding figure—and in the following centuries the Irish Church fostered scholarship, art, and missionary work. The 9th and 10th centuries saw Viking invasions, which were brought to an end by Brian Boru's great victory at Clontarf (1014). In the mid-12th century Ireland was invaded by the Norman conquerors of England and Henry II gained the allegiance of the Irish kings. English law and administration were introduced in the 13th century, and an Irish parliament (composed of the Anglo-Irish and subordinate to the English Crown) began to meet. However, English rule was restricted to the area around Dublin (called the Pale) until the 16th century, when the subjection of the Irish became the aim of the Tudor monarchs of England. Revolts, inspired in part by Roman Catholic opposition to the Reformation, were suppressed and the *Plantation of Ireland by English and later by Scottish settlers was begun. Irish resistance continued, culminating in the rebellion of 1641, which was not suppressed until 1649–50. The subsequent confiscation of the rebels' land and its redistribution among English colonists established the economic and political ascendancy of the Protestant minority in Ireland. It was strengthened by the Restoration settlement and by events after William of Orange's defeat (1690) of the Irish supporters of the deposed Catholic king, James II: the usual land confiscations were accompanied on this occasion by new anti-Catholic penal laws. In the 18th century Ireland's subservience to England came to be opposed by many Irish Protestants and in 1782, under the leadership of Henry Grattan, the Irish parliament obtained legislative independence. However, the abortive Irish rebellion of 1798 led to the complete union of Britain and Ireland (1800; *see* Union, Acts of). Eventually, Catholics received civil rights in 1829 (*see also* O'Connell, Daniel). The appalling social conditions suffered by the majority of Irish renewed Catholic militancy in the 19th century. Nationalist agitation was taken up after the Irish (potato) famine first, abortively, by the *Fenians and then by the *Home Rule movement. While the *Land League pursued agrarian reform with some success, Home Rule was delayed. It was nominally obtained in 1914 but was opposed both by the Republicans, who wanted a greater degree of independence, and the Protestant Ulster Unionists, who feared for their future in a self-governing country with a Catholic majority. Following the proclamation of an Irish republic by Sinn Fein (1919) and virtual civil war Britain proposed partition (1920), with the establishment of separate parliaments in the predominantly Protestant NE and Catholic S and W. The formula was unacceptable to the Republicans and in 1921 the Irish Free State, with dominion status, came into being. The NE (Northern Ireland) immediately withdrew, accepting self-government within the UK.

Northern Ireland The province comprises the counties of Antrim, Armagh, Down, Fermanagh, Londonderry, and Tyrone. *Economy*: there has been a significant change since the 1950s, the traditional industries of shipbuilding and linen manufacture as well as agriculture having declined in importance. Diversification of industry has taken place (chemicals, rubber products, man-made fibers, and engineering) and there has been a large rise in the number of people employed in the service sector. The economy has suffered, however, from the political upheavals of the last decade. *History*: the Government of Ireland Act (1920) established a parliament, which met at Stormont Castle in Belfast and had legislative responsibility for most matters other than foreign affairs. Executive power lay with a prime minister and cabinet. Some 12 representatives were also (and continue to be) returned to the UK parliament. The Protestant majority in Northern Ireland predominantly supports the union with Great Britain, while many of the Roman Catholic minority, dissatisfied with Protestant political dominance, seek union with the Republic of Ireland. Violent conflict broke out between the two groups in 1969, since when the British army has maintained a peacekeeping force in Northern Ireland. Terrorist activities both in Ireland and Great Britain led to the imposition (1972) of direct rule of Northern Ireland by the UK parliament. Bombings and shootings, both by the Irish Republican Army and Protestant paramilitary groups (e.g. the Ulster Volunteer Force) continue to occur. During 1981 violent reprisals followed the deaths of a number of hunger strikers, who had been demanding political status while serving sentences for terrorism at Belfast's Maze Prison. Area: 5452 sq mi (14,121 sq km). Population (1981 est): 1,481,959. Capital: Belfast.

Republic of Ireland (Irish name: Éire) The country is administratively divided into 26 counties. *Economy*: predominantly agricultural, cattle rearing being of major importance, especially in the E lowlands, where cattle are fattened for beef production. Dairy farming is also extensively practiced, particularly in the S. Arable crops produced include barley, wheat, oats, potatoes, and sugar beet. Tourism is the second major source of revenue. Industries have expanded considerably since the 1950s, largely under foreign companies, and are oriented to the export market. They include food processing, brewing, distilling, textiles, and clothing. Peat is extensively cut as a fuel for power stations and as a household fuel. In 1977 Europe's largest lead-zinc mines were opened at Navan. Although the Republic has an extensive coastline its fishing industry is relatively small. *History*: Republican opposition to partition continued immediately after the establishment of the Irish Free State but was quelled by 1923. In 1932 De Valera, leader of Fianna Fáil, became prime minister and, in 1937, introduced a new constitution by which the Irish Free State was renamed Éire. In 1949 a coalition led by Fine Gael took the country, as the Republic of Ireland, out of the British Commonwealth. Since 1969 Irish politics have been dominated by the violent conflict in Northern Ireland and successive Irish governments have declared their desire to see the establishment there of a form of government acceptable to both Roman Catholics and Protestants. In 1973 Ireland became a member of the EEC. Charles J. Haughey (1925–) who, as Jack Lynch's successor, led a Fianna Fáil government (1979–81; 1982), was ousted in November, 1982, and Dr Garret FitzGerald (1927–) became prime minister for a second term, heading a Fine Gael–Labour coalition. In 1983 a "Forum for a New Ireland" that included representatives of the Republic, Northern Ireland, and Britain began to study issues affecting Northern Ireland and the Republic of Ireland. President: Patrick Hillery. Official languages: Irish and English. Chief religion: Roman Catholic. Official currency: Irish pound of 100 pence. Area: 26,599 sq mi (68,893 sq km). Population (1981): 3,443,405. Capital and main port: Dublin.

Ireland, John Nicholson (1879–1962) British composer, a pupil of Stanford and teacher of Britten and E. J. Moeran (1894–1950). His works include orchestral and chamber music, songs, and piano pieces. Many of these, including *The Forgotten Rite* (for orchestra; 1913) and *Sarnia* (for piano; 1941), were inspired by the history of the Channel Islands.

Irene (c. 752–803 AD) Byzantine empress and saint of the Greek Orthodox Church. After the death of her husband Leo IV (reigned 775–80), Irene ruled jointly with their son Constantine VI (771–?797) until 790, when she was banished from court. In 797 she returned, blinded and imprisoned Constantine, and ruled alone. She fought against the iconoclasts (*see* iconoclasm) for the restoration of icons in Christian worship. In 802 she was overthrown and exiled to Lesbos.

Ireton, Henry (1611–51) English soldier, who fought for the parliamentarians in the *Civil War. In 1646 he became Cromwell's son-in-law. Initially favoring negotiations with Charles I, he proposed a constitutional solution to the conflict of power but in 1649 he was a signatory to the king's death warrant. During the Commonwealth, Ireton served in Ireland, where he died of fever at the siege of Limerick.

Irian Jaya. *See* West Irian.

iridium (Ir)   A hard brittle metal, discovered in 1803 by C. Tennant (1768–1838), in the residue left after dissolving platinum in aqua regia. Its salts are highly colored, whence its name (Latin *iris*, rainbow). Its principal use is as a hardening agent for platinum and in electrical contacts. At no 77; at wt 192.22; mp 4374°F (2410°C); bp 7473°F (4130°C).

iris (anatomy)   The muscular tissue in the ☐eye that surrounds the pupil and is situated immediately in front of the lens: it is responsible for eye color. Reflex contraction of the muscles in the iris cause it to become smaller in dim light (which enlarges the pupil and allows more light to enter the eye) and larger in bright light (thus decreasing the size of the pupil).

Iris (botany) A genus of perennial herbaceous plants (about 300 species), native to N temperate regions and widely planted in gardens. Irises grow from bulbs or rhizomes (underground stems) and their flowers, which have three erect inner petals and three drooping outer sepals, can be three or more colors, often with a contrasting "beard" on the lower petals. Many garden varieties are derived from *I. germanica*: up to 40 in (1 m) high, they have purple, white, or yellow flowers and grow from rhizomes. Family: *Iridaceae*. *See also* flag.

Iris (mythology) The Greek goddess of the rainbow and messenger of the gods, especially of *Hera. She is portrayed as carrying a herald's staff and often bearing water that could put perjurers to sleep.

Irish elk A large extinct European *deer belonging to the genus *Megaloceros*, which was abundant during the Pleistocene epoch (2.5 million–10,000 years ago). It stood 71 in (1.8 m) at the shoulder and its massive palmate antlers spanned up to 13 ft (4 m). Several species are known and remains of the largest have been found in Irish bog deposits.

Irish famine (1846–51) The starvation and death of almost a million Irish following a blight that ruined the potato crop (the staple diet of most Irish) in 1846. Another million emigrated.

Irish Literary Renaissance A period of literary activity in Ireland in the late 19th and early 20th centuries inspired by the contemporary resurgence of political nationalism and of interest in traditional Gaelic culture. The strongest individual influence was that of W. B. *Yeats, especially through his *The Wanderings of Oisin* (1889) and *The Celtic Twilight* (1893). Other writers included the poet George Russell (pseudonym AE; 1867–1935), the novelist George Moore (1852–1933), and the dramatist J. M. *Synge.

Irish literature The Gaelic literature of Ireland. The earliest literature, as in other parts of the Celtic world, was the responsibility of an official learned class, the *filid* (or *Druids), who transmitted orally the ancient traditions of the people. The earliest written literature, however, dates from the 7th to 10th centuries. Of most interest in this period are the heroic sagas, written in prose and preserved mainly in three 12th-century manuscript collections, the Book of the Dun Cow, the Book of Leinster, and the Yellow Book of Lecan. These epics, which are shorter than Icelandic sagas, deal with both heroic (warfare, voyages, etc.) and romantic elements. They were grouped in the middle ages into two cycles, the early pagan Ulster cycle and the much later *Fenian cycle. *Deirdre and *Cuchulain are the prominent figures in the Ulster cycle and appear in the two most famous stories, the *Longes Mac Nusnig* (*Exile of the Sons of Usnech*) and the *Táin Bó Cúalnge* (*Cattle-Raid of Cooley*). From the 13th century bardic poets preserved Gaelic culture from the impact of Norman English; their main productions were panegyrics written for aristocratic patrons, but they also responded to influences introduced by the Normans and English, such as, for example, the theme of courtly love. Despite a revival of Gaelic poetry in the 16th century, it declined with the submergence of the Irish aristocracy, particularly after the coming of Cromwell (1649). The work of the poet and historian Geoffrey Keating (c. 1580–c. 1645) is the most important prior to this date; the two outstanding poets of the period were David O'Bruadair (1625–98) and Egan O'Rahilly (1670–1728). Gaelic literature was at its lowest ebb during the 18th century, but was revived in the 19th century, having splintered in the meantime into several dialects. Such 20th-century writers as Liam *O'Flaherty and Brendan *Behan have produced distinguished work in Gaelic, but generally there has been nothing to equal the work of the major modern Irish poets and writers, who have almost without exception written in English. *See also* Irish Literary Renaissance.

Irish moss. *See* carrageen.

Irish Republican Army (IRA) A militant organization established in 1919. It fought a successful war against British forces (1919–21) but the subsequent partition treaty was rejected by many IRA members. The antitreaty faction (keeping the name IRA) was defeated by 1923 and declared illegal but continued to press for an all-Ireland republic. A bombing campaign against England in 1939 and an "offensive" against Northern Ireland (1956–62) both failed. The movement was then quiescent until the present troubles began in 1968. In 1969 both the IRA and *Sinn Féin, to which many IRA members belong, split into the Officials, desiring a socialist 32-county republic, and the Provisionals, concerned only with expelling the British from the North. The Irish National Liberation Army is a breakaway terrorist group.

Irish Republican Brotherhood. *See* Fenians.

Irish Sea A section of the Atlantic Ocean, separating England, Scotland, and Wales from Ireland. Area: about 40,000 sq mi (100,000 sq km). Maximum width: 150 mi (240 km).

Irish terrier A breed of dog originating in Ireland and used for hunting. It has a sturdy streamlined body, a long head, and an alert appearance. The hard wiry coat is red to yellowish-red. Height: 16–18 in (41–46 cm).

Irish wolfhound An ancient breed of large hunting dog originating in Ireland. It has a powerful body and a long narrow head with small ears. The rough wiry coat is long on the brow and under the jaw and can be gray, brindle, red, black, white, or fawn. Height: 31 in (78 cm) minimum (dogs); 28 in (71 cm) minimum (bitches).

Irkutsk 52 18N 104 15E A city in the N Soviet Union, in the RSFSR. It is a major railroad junction and is the industrial, cultural, and educational center of E Siberia. Its industries include ship, aircraft, and vehicle production and repair; machinery, chemicals, textiles, and food are also produced. Population (1981 est): 568,000.

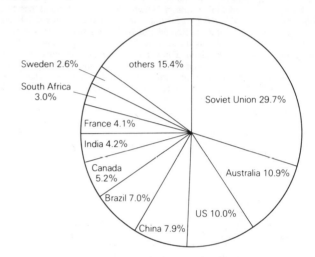

IRON *World production of iron ore.*

iron (Fe) A metallic transition element that has been known and used since prehistoric times. It is the fourth most abundant element in the earth's crust, occurring in the ores hematite (Fe_2O_3), magnetite (Fe_3O_4), and siderite ($FeCO_3$). It is widely used in toolmaking, construction, shipbuilding, car manufacture, and a host of other applications, almost always alloyed with other elements, such as carbon, manganese, chromium, titanium, and vanadium (*see* steel). It is obtained from its ores by smelting in a *blast furnace to give pig iron, which is then converted into cast iron, wrought iron, or steel. Iron has two important valence states forming iron II (ferrous) and iron III (ferric) compounds. Common compounds include the sulfates ($FeSO_4$, $Fe_2(SO_4)_3$), chlorides ($FeCl_2$, $FeCl_3$), and oxides (FeO, Fe_3O_4, Fe_2O_3). Iron is vital to animal life owing to its presence in *hemoglobin. Studies of meteorites and of the magnetic and seismic properties of the earth suggest that the earth has an iron-nickel core, molten on the outside but solid in the interior. At no 26; at wt 55.847; mp 2798°F (1535°C); bp 4987°F (2750°C). *See also* ferromagnetism.

Iron Age The cultural phase during which iron replaced bronze metal technology (*see* Bronze Age). Despite spasmodic earlier use of meteoric iron, it was not until about 1500 BC that iron-working techniques were perfected by the *Hittites. Initially a prestige metal, the superior hardness of which was prized for weapons, iron gradually spread throughout the Middle East after about 1100 BC. It was used in *Hallstatt Europe in the 7th century BC. The Chinese were both forging and casting iron about 500 BC, preceding Europe by about 1700 years in casting. Australia and pre-Columbian America never developed iron metallurgy but African societies moved directly from stone to iron technologies.

ironclad A wooden warship protected by iron armor, the forerunner of the modern battleship. Both the French and the British used ironclad barges against the Russians in the Crimean War (1854–56) but the first ironclad warship, the *Gloire*, was built by France in 1859. The first battle between ironclads occurred off the Virginia coast in 1862 in the Civil War.

Iron Cross The highest German decoration for bravery in battle, instituted by Frederick William III of Prussia in 1813. An iron Maltese cross edged in silver, it was reinstituted by Hitler in 1939.

Iron Curtain The ideological division between the Soviet Union and its satellite countries in E Europe on the one hand, and the democratic countries of W Europe on the other. The term was first used by Winston Churchill in 1946 and came to symbolize the strained relations that persisted well into the 1950s.

Iron Gate (Romanian name: Porţile de Fier; Serbo-Croat name: Gvozdena Vrata) 44 40N 22 30E The deepest gorge in Europe, on the Romanian-Yugoslav border, through which the Danube River flows. A canal, which is used by larger shipping, bypasses the gorge on the Romanian side. A Romanian-Yugoslav hydroelectric plant was opened here (1972). Length: about 2 mi (3 km).

iron lung. *See* respirator.

Ironside, William Edmund, 1st Baron (1880–1959) British field marshal. Disguised as a railroadman he was a secret agent in the second Boer War. In World War I he commanded the Allied forces against Soviet Russia at Archangel (1918). In World War II he was chief of the imperial general staff (1939–40) and commander in chief of the home forces (1940).

ironwood One of several unrelated trees with very hard wood, including *Mesurea ferrea* of India and Malaysia (family *Guttiferae*), used in cabinetwork, and a *hop-hornbeam, *Ostrya virginiana*, of E North America.

Iroquois A coalition of North American Indian peoples living between the Hudson River and Lake Erie, who spoke the Iroquois language belonging to the Iroquois Caddoan family. The Iroquois were farmers and hunters who lived in villages of longhouses, each occupied by several families. The individual clans were grouped into tribes and nations ruled by councils of delegates. In the 16th century, they formed the famous **Iroquois League**, composed of the *Mohawk, Oneida, Onondaga, Cayuga, and Seneca tribes. During the **Iroquois War** (1642–53), these five nations expanded their territory considerably at the expense of neighboring tribes. The Iroquois Confederacy, joined by the Tuscarora tribe in 1722, allied itself with the British in wars against the French and, except for the Oneida and Tuscarora, against the colonists in the *Revolutionary War. The League finally collapsed following the second Treaty of *Fort Stanwix (1784).

irrational numbers. *See* numbers.

Irrawaddy River The chief river in Burma, flowing SSW across the entire country. Joined by the Chindwin River at Mandalay, it enters the Andaman Sea through a swampy delta (one of the great rice bowls of Asia). Length: 1250 mi (2010 km).

Irredentists Italians who sought to bring all Italian-speaking areas into newly unified Italy in the late 19th century, in particular the Austrian-controlled Trentino in the NE. The Irredentists, so called from *Italia irredenta* ("unrecovered Italy"), urged Italy to join the UK and France in World War I. The postwar distribution of territories, giving Italy the Trentino and the Istrian peninsula on the N Adriatic, realized their chief ambitions.

irrigation The artificial watering of land for crop production. Irrigation was practiced in ancient Egypt; traditional systems linked to seasonal changes in river level, using earth banks and channels with water-lifting devices, are still used in many areas. Modern methods involve artificial reservoirs, canals, and pumping systems; the entire field may be flooded, as in rice growing, or the water may run in channels between the rows of the crop. High-pressure sprinklers are also used, especially where the land is undulating. Irrigation may be essential for crop production in arid regions but is also used to supplement rainfall in other regions.

Irtysh River (*or* R. Irtish) A river in central Asia. Rising in the Altai Mountains of China, it flows W and NW to join the Ob River in the Soviet Union. Length: 2760 mi (4444 km).

Irvine 55 37N 4 40W A port in W Scotland, in Strathclyde Region at the mouth of the River Irvine on the Firth of Clyde. Population (1981): 55,278.

Irving, Sir Henry (John Henry Brodribb; 1838–1905) British actor and manager. He established his reputation in London during the early 1870s and remained the leading actor of the London stage for the next 30 years. From 1878 to 1902 he was manager of the Lyceum Theatre, where, with Ellen *Terry as his leading lady, he acted in a notable series of Shakespearean productions. He made several tours in the US, and in 1895 became the first actor to receive a knighthood.

Irving, Washington (1783–1859) US author and historian. Educated as a lawyer, Irving began to publish satirical essays, the most famous of which, *History of New York* (1809), was written under the pen name Diedrich Knickerbocker. From 1815 to 1832 he lived in Europe where he wrote *The Sketch Book* (1819–20), which contains some of his best short stories, including "Rip Van Winkle" and "The Legend of Sleepy Hollow." While in Europe, Irving also served in a diplomatic capacity at the US embassies in Madrid and London. After returning to the US, he was acclaimed as the

SIR HENRY IRVING *As Shylock in* The Merchant of Venice, *one of his most famous roles.*

country's leading man of letters, publishing more short stories, novels, and biographies, among them his five-volume *Life of George Washington* (1855–59).

Isabella (*born* Elizabeth Farnese; 1692–1766) The second wife of Philip V of Spain, whom she dominated throughout their marriage (1714–46). Her ambitions centered on the acquisition of Italian possessions for her sons, the eldest of whom ruled Naples and Sicily before becoming *Charles III of Spain.

Isabella (I) the Catholic (1451–1504) Queen of Castile (1474–1504). Her marriage (1469) to Ferdinand of Aragon brought about the union of the two major Spanish kingdoms, to which Granada was added following its reconquest from the Moors in 1492. The introduction of the Inquisition (1480) and the expulsion of the Jews (1492) were largely due to Isabella's influence. She also supported Columbus' voyages of discovery. *See also* Ferdinand V and II.

Isabella II (1830–1904) Queen of Spain (1833–68). Isabella's reign saw almost continual political turmoil. Her succession was contested by her uncle Don Carlos and only secured in 1839, after the first Carlist War (*see* Carlism). Her governments became increasingly unpopular and she was deposed.

Isabella of France (1292–1358) The wife (1308–27) of Edward II of England; the daughter of *Philip (IV) the Fair. Increasingly isolated by Edward's favorites, she left England in 1325. She became the mistress of Roger *Mortimer and together they returned to overthrow and murder Edward (1327). In 1330 her son Edward III executed Mortimer and confined Isabella to a nunnery.

Isabey, Jean Baptiste (1767–1855) French portrait painter and miniaturist, born in Nancy. He trained under *David and was patronized successively by Marie Antoinette, Napoleon, and the restored Bourbon kings. His son **Eugène Isabey** (1804–86) was also a painter.

Isaiah (8th century BC) Old Testament prophet. He was influential at the court of the rulers of Judah until the Assyrian invasion (701 BC) and, according to tradition, was later martyred.
The Book of Isaiah contains his prophecies, although some scholars attribute chapters 40–66 to others. The prophecies condemn the corruption of both Judah and the surrounding nations, counsel against entering foreign

political alliances, and predict the captivity of the nation in Babylon and its return. Several sections announce the coming of a Messiah. These passages formed the basis of the messianic expectations of the Jews and were interpreted by the Christian writers of the New Testament as referring to Jesus.

ISBN (International Standard Book Number). *See* library.

Ischia, Island of 40 44N 13 57E A volcanic island in Italy, at the entrance to the Bay of Naples. A popular resort, it is noted for its picturesque scenery and mineral springs. Area: 18 sq mi (47 sq km). Population (1971 est): 14,389. Chief town: Ischia.

Ise 34 29N 136 41E A city in Japan, in S Honshu on the Pacific Ocean. It is the site of Japan's most sacred Shinto shrines, some of which possibly date back to the 1st century BC. Population (1976 est): 106,435.

Isfahan (*or* Esfahan) 32 41N 51 41E A city in central Iran. It has some fine examples of Persian architecture, including the 17th-century royal mosque. An industrial quarter was established in the 1930s, and a university was founded in 1950. The city was prominent in the unrest that preceded the Shah's departure from Iran in February, 1979. Population (1976 est): 671,825.

Isherwood, Christopher (1904–) British novelist. His experiences while teaching in Berlin in the 1930s are described in the novel *Mr Norris Changes Trains* (1935) and in the stories *Goodbye to Berlin* (1939), portrayed in the film *Cabaret* (1968). He collaborated with his friend W. H. *Auden on several plays. In 1939 he moved to California, where he cultivated an interest in Hindu philosophy. His other works include *The World in the Evening* (1954), *Down There on a Visit* (1962), and *A Single Man* (1964). In these and several autobiographical works, including *Christopher and His Kind* (1977), homosexuality is a recurrent theme.

Ishtar The supreme Babylonian and Assyrian goddess, the daughter of the sky god Anu or of the moon god Sin. She combined aspects of a beneficent mother goddess and fierce goddess of war and fertility. She descended to the underworld in search of her lover *Tammuz.

Isidore of Seville, St (c. 560–636 AD) Spanish churchman; Doctor of the Church and the last of the western Fathers of the Church. Archbishop of Seville from about 600, he is famous for his encyclopedia of knowledge, the *Etymologiae*, which was much used by medieval scholars. In dealing with such subjects as grammar, mathematics, history, and theology Isidore included etymological explanations of words (hence the title), but these were allegorical rather than scientific. Feast day: April 4.

isinglass A form of gelatin, about 90% pure, made from the swim bladders of fish. It is used in glues and to clarify jellies and alcoholic drinks.

Isis An Egyptian goddess, the sister and wife of *Osiris, whose dismembered body she magically restored to life, and mother of *Horus. She was usually portrayed as holding the child Horus and wearing on her head the solar disk and a cow's horns, the same attributes as *Hathor. She was essentially a goddess of protection, being the perfect mother and having magical powers of healing. Her cult eventually spread throughout the Roman Empire.

Iskenderun (former name: Alexandretta) 36 37N 36 08E A port in central S Turkey. Its main activities are fishing and trading in tobacco, silk, bananas, and cereals. Until 1939 it was in Syria. Population (1980): 124,824.

Islam (Arabic: submission to God) A major world religion, which originated in Arabia in the 7th century AD. The essential creed of Islam, whose adherents are called Muslims, is that there is one God, Allah, and that *Mohammed is his prophet. The revelations received by Mohammed are recorded in the *Koran, which is the basis of Islamic belief and practice and the source of a complex legal and social system (*see also* Islamic law). Islam shares a number of beliefs with Judaism and Christianity and accepts the Books of Moses and the Gospels of Jesus as parts of the same divine scripture that is definitively expressed in the Koran. There is no formally organized church or priesthood. Instead, five fundamental duties are incumbent upon the individual Muslim: expression of belief in the one God, Allah, and in the prophethood of Mohammed; observance at set times of five daily prayers, which are recited facing toward Mecca; fasting during the month of *Ramadan; payment of a special tax for charitable purposes; and performance of the pilgrimage to Mecca (*see* hajj) at least once, if means permit. Given the impetus of the *jihad* or holy war against unbelievers originally prescribed as a duty, the Muslim armies of Arabia extended Islam through the Middle East and N Africa in the 7th and 8th centuries AD. It later spread to sub-Saharan Africa, India, China, SE Asia, parts of Russia, the Balkans, and Spain. It early divided into sects, which originally differed as to who should be the leader of Islam and what should be his powers. The main sects are the *Sunnites (*or* Sunni) and the *Shiites (*or*

Shiah; *see also* Ahmadiya; Wahhabiya). There are an estimated 450 million Muslims.

Islamabad 33 40N 73 08E The capital of Pakistan, situated in the N of the country on the Potwar Plateau. The site was chosen in 1959 and construction began in 1961. The government's first cabinet meeting was held in 1967. The Quaid-i-Azam University was founded in 1965 and the People's Open University in 1974. Population (1972): 77,318.

Islamic art and architecture A distinctive style of art and architecture created and developed by the Muslims in the countries they conquered. Islamic art is generally classified by scholars into five regional groupings: Syrian-Egyptian; Persian; Ottoman-Turkish; Moorish (i.e. North African and Spanish); and Indian. Its most distinctive feature is its elaborate patterning in architecture, painting, ceramics, metalwork, woodwork, glassware, textiles, and carpets. Of all these arts architecture is the most individual, its main characteristics being the dome and the horseshoe □arch. Religious objections to the depiction of human and animal forms inhibited the development of sculpture. Islamic painting is usually associated with Persian, Mogul, and Turkish miniatures, although there were many schools of painting during the middle ages and later. Calligraphy, particularly in decoration, is regarded as an art form in a class of its own. *See also* Mogul art; Persian art.

Islamic law The sacred law of Islam, *shari'ah*, prescibes not only religious duties (*see* Islam) but covers every aspect of the life of a Muslim. Its basic principles were elaborated in the 9th century AD, when the *Koran and the practice of Mohammed (the *sunna*) came to be generally accepted as the main sources of the law. The law covers marriage, divorce, and inheritance; it forbids usury, the depiction of living beings, the drinking of alcohol, the eating of pork, etc., and prescribes penalties and punishments for crimes. When a problem could not be solved by reference to the Koran or *sunna*, other sources were allowed and different legal interpretations developed. Thus among the *Sunnite majority, four equally orthodox schools have arisen, which agree on fundamentals but differ in their interpretation of specific points. In modern times most Muslim states have adopted secular legal systems at least in part and especially with regard to criminal, financial, and property law.

island A piece of land surrounded by water (excluding the continents). The world's largest island is Greenland 840,000 sq mi (2.2 million sq km). Continental islands, such as Britain, lie on the continental shelves, separated usually by a narrow shallow stretch of water from the mainland. Oceanic orogenic islands, such as the Japanese islands, frequently occur in island arcs at the junction of two lithospheric plates (*see* plate tectonics); they are volcanic in origin. Oceanic volcanic islands, such as the Hawaiian islands, occur in the central parts of the deep oceans, particularly the Pacific. They are believed to be formed over "hot spots" in the earth's crust, where molten magma rises to the surface. Many coral islands have a volcanic base. *See also* reef.

Ismaili A *Shiite Muslim sect. In the 8th century AD a group of Shiites recognized Ismail the son of Jafar al-Sadiq as *imam, while the rest of the Shiites supported his brother Musa. In 909 the Fatimid caliphate was established, the rulers of which were Ismaili imams. The Ismaili Fatimids ruled in Egypt and N Africa until 1171, contesting control of the Muslim world with the *Abbasid dynasty of Baghdad. They developed several doctrines that diverge considerably from non-Ismaili Islam and eventually split into many subsects. Today the best-known Ismaili sect is that headed by the *Aga Khan.

Ismailia (Arabic name: al Isma'iliyah) 31 36N 32 15E A city in NE Egypt, midway along the Suez Canal on Lake Timsah. Dependent on the canal trade, much of the population moved elsewhere during the canal's closure (1967–75). It is the center of an irrigated area producing market-garden crops. Population (1976): 146,000.

Isma'il Pasha (1830–95) Viceroy of Egypt for the Ottoman Empire (1863–79). He introduced important reforms but the huge foreign debts that his policies incurred eventually supplied the pretext for British intervention (1882) and led the Ottomans to depose him. Under Isma'il the *Suez Canal was opened in 1869.

ISO. *See* International Organization for Standardization.

Isocrates (436–338 BC) Athenian teacher of rhetoric and political pamphleteer. After developing his highly polished style as a professional speechwriter, Isocrates opened a school, where his method of teaching rhetoric as a preparation for life began the literary tradition of education. His appeals to successive military leaders to unite the feuding Greek states against Persia culminated in the *Philippus* (346 BC), addressed to *Philip of Macedon.

isolationism The policy that opposes participation in world affairs, except in self-defense. The term is most usually used to describe US policies pursued after World War I, when isolationism reached its peak in the Neutrality Acts (1935–37). The Japanese attack on Pearl Harbor in World War II ended isolationism.

structural isomers *Ethanol and dimethyl ether have the same atoms in the molecule but different functional groups.*

cis-trans isomers *A form of stereoisomerism occurring as a result of a double bond.*

optical isomers *Another form of stereoisomerism in which two forms of tartaric acid have different optical properties.*

ISOMERS

isomers Chemical compounds that have the same molecular formulae but different arrangements of atoms in their molecules. In **structural isomerism** the molecules have different molecular formulae. Thus, ethanol (C_2H_5OH) and dimethyl ether (CH_3OCH_3) both have the formula C_2H_6O, although they are quite different compounds. A form of structural isomerism is that in which functional groups occur at different positions in the molecule. For example, there are two alcohols derived from propane: propan-1-ol ($CH_3CH_2CH_2OH$) and propan-2-ol ($CH_3CH_2OHCH_3$), which differ in the position of the OH group on the chain. In **stereoisomerism** the molecules have the same structure and groups but the isomers differ in their spatial arrangements. **Cis-trans isomerism** occurs as a result of the positioning of groups in a planar molecule. A common type occurs in organic molecules with double bonds. Since rotation cannot occur about the bond it is possible to have two isomers: one with groups on both sides of the bond (the cis isomer) and the other with groups on opposite sides of the bond (trans isomer). Similar types of isomer are found in square inorganic complexes depending on opposite (trans) or adjacent (cis) positioning of ligands. Another form of stereoisomerism is **optical isomerism**, in which the two isomeric forms of the molecule are asymmetric and differ in that one molecule is a mirror image of the other. Asymmetric molecules of this type exhibit optical activity, i.e. they rotate *polarized light passed through their solutions. One isomer rotates the light in one sense, the other rotates the light the same amount in the opposite sense. Many naturally occurring organic compounds are optically active. Isomers of all types have different physical properties and, to a greater of lesser extent, different chemical properties. In some cases isomers can exist in equilibrium, a phenomenon known as **tautomerism**.

isomorphism The existence of different chemical compounds with the same crystal structure. Usually it is a reflection of analogous chemical bonding patterns. The *alums, for instance, are all isomorphic compounds.

Isopoda A widely distributed order of *crustaceans (4000 species). The group includes the most successful terrestrial crustacean—the *woodlouse—as well as aquatic forms, such as the *gribble; some marine species are parasites. Isopods have oval flattened bodies, covered by armor-like plates, and—usually—seven pairs of walking legs. The young develop within a brood pouch on the female.

isoprene ($CH_2:C(CH_3)CH:CH_2$) A colorless volatile liquid. It is made from chemicals extracted from oil, coal, or tar and is used to make synthetic rubber. Natural rubber consists mainly of a polymer of isoprene. *See also* polymerization.

isostasy The principle that segments of the earth's outer crust of equal area have the same mass; the higher the feature rises, the deeper the sial of which it is composed extends into the denser sima below. If a change in this equilibrium condition occurs, movements of the crust occur to restore the equilibrium (this is called isostatic compensation). For example, areas of deposition sink, while areas of erosion rise.

isotherm A line on a map joining points of equal temperature. Corrections are usually made to compensate for the effect of altitude on temperature.

isothermal process Any process that occurs without a change in the temperature of a system (*compare* adiabatic process).

isotopes Atoms of the same element that contain equal numbers of *protons but different numbers of *neutrons in their nuclei. They have identical chemical properties but different physical properties. An isotope is indicated by combining its nucleon number and its name or symbol in various ways, for example uranium-235, U-235, ^{235}U. All naturally occurring elements are mixtures of isotopes; hydrogen, for example, consists mainly of ^1H(98.44%) with small amounts of ^2H (deuterium). A third isotope, ^3H (tritium), also exists in nature in minute quantities (1 part in 10^{17}) but can be made artificially. Radioactive isotopes (radioisotopes) are important in nuclear reactors and nuclear weapons. For these purposes sophisticated methods of separation have had to be devised, based on differences in their physical properties. Methods used depend on different rates of gaseous and thermal diffusion, centrifuging, electrolysis, and electric or magnetic effects.

isotopic spin (*or* isospin) A *quantum number used to distinguish between elementary particles (*see* particle physics) having the same properties, except that of electric charge. The concept is not based directly on the idea of rotation but it is analogous in mathematical terms to angular momentum, different charge states of the same particle (e.g. the nucleon) being regarded as having different orientations in a fictitious "isotopic space."

isotropy Any property of a body or medium that is independent of the direction in which it is measured. A body or medium that is not isotropic is said to be anisotropic.

Israel, State of A country in the Middle East, bordering on the Mediterranean Sea. There are mountains in the N, a narrow coastal plain in the W, and the Negev Desert in the S. The Jordan River flowing through the *Great Rift Valley forms part of the E border. The population varies greatly in language and culture, as it consists largely of Jews who have immigrated since 1948. Many Palestinian Arabs left the area when Israel was created but some have since returned. The remaining Arab population lives mainly in the N, with some nomadic Bedouins in the Negev Desert. In 1948 the population consisted of 650,000 Jews and 155,000 Arabs; the population since then has more than quadrupled, with Jews now forming 85% and Arabs 11%; immigration is now decreasing. Some 3% of the population live in *kibbutzim* (*see* kibbutz) and about 5% live in *moshavim*; rural settlements established since 1948 are usually on these lines. *Economy*: both industrial and agricultural output has increased rapidly since 1948, boosted by investments and gifts of capital from abroad. There are resources of copper ore and phosphates; potash and bromine from the Dead Sea are also exploited. One of the chief centers of diamond cutting and polishing, Israel also has food-processing, textile, chemical, and electronics industries and exports finished diamonds and light manufactures. Fishing and tourism are also important. 6% of the work force is employed in agriculture, which depends heavily on artificial irrigation. Between 1949 and 1970 the area of irrigated land increased by six times, with a corresponding increase in production. There has also been extensive reforestation, with a land reclamation scheme in the Negev Desert. Thus, although in 1948 Israel produced only 30% of its food requirements, it now imports only grain in large quantities and exports citrus and other fruit, vegetables, and flowers. Hampered since 1950 by an Arab trade boycott, Israel has had difficulty in building up an export market and still has a large trade deficit. *History*: Israel's history prior to 1948 is that of *Palestine, in which Jewish Zionists had demanded the creation of a Jewish state since the late 19th century. According to a UN recommendation and against Arab opposition, Palestine was to be divided into a Jewish state, an Arab state, and a small internationally administered zone around Jerusalem. As soon as the state of Israel was proclaimed following British withdrawal (1948), however, Arab forces (those of Egypt, Transjordan, Iraq, Syria, and Lebanon) invaded; by early 1949 Israeli forces had not only repulsed them but had gained control of 75% of Palestine, while the rest had been annexed by Jordan (the *West Bank of the Jordan River) and Egypt (the *Gaza Strip). Jerusalem was divided between Jews and Arabs. In 1956, following Nasser's nationalization of the Suez Canal, Israeli forces occupied the Gaza Strip and the *Sinai Peninsula and gained access to the Red Sea, which boosted its international trade. In the Six Day War (1967) Israel defeated Egyptian, Syrian, and Jordanian forces and again occupied the Gaza Strip and the Sinai Peninsula as well as the *Golan Heights, the West Bank, and the Arab sector of Jerusalem. Jerusalem was administered by Israel thereafter as a single unit. Following the Yom Kippur War (1973; so called because the Israelis were taken unawares by Egyptian forces on the Day of Atonement—Yom Kippur) peace talks opened in Geneva. Adjourned in 1974, they were reopened between Israel and Egypt following the visit to Jerusalem of President *Sadat (1977). The Camp David talks, initiated by President Jimmy Carter, resulted in a peace agreement in 1979 following which Israel withdrew from Sinai (1980–82). In 1982, Israel invaded Lebanon, destroyed the Palestine Liberation Organization base there, and occupied the southern part, finally withdrawing from Lebanon in 1985. The unpopularity within Israel of the Lebanon campaign, coupled with raging inflation, led to indecisive results in the 1984 elections. The ruling rightwing Likud Party, led by Yitzhak Shamir, was forced into an uneasy coalition with Shimon Peres' Labour Party, in which Peres leads the government until 1986, when Shamir takes over for two years. Head of State: Chaim Herzog. Official languages: Hebrew and Arabic. Official currency: Israeli shekel of 100 new agorot. Area: 8018 sq mi (20,770 sq km). Population (1983 est): 3,957,000. Capital: Jerusalem. Main port: Haifa.

Issachar, tribe of One of the 12 *tribes of Israel. It claimed descent from Issachar, son of Jacob and Leah. It occupied territory to the S and SE of the Sea of Galilee.

Issas. *See* Somalis.

Issus, Battle of (333 BC) The battle in which Alexander the Great of Macedon defeated an enormous Persian army under Darius III, which was caught in a narrow pass and outmaneuvered. Victory here opened Alexander's way from Asia Minor into Persia proper.

Issyk Kul, Lake A lake in the S Soviet Union, in the Kirgiz SSR in the N Tien Shan. It is 2303 ft (702 m) deep, lying 5279 ft (1609 m) above sea level, and never freezes. Area: about 2401 sq mi (6220 sq km).

Istanbul (or Stamboul) 41 02N 28 57E A city in W Turkey, on both sides of the Bosporus. There are many ancient buildings in the city, including the mainly 6th-century Hagia Sophia (originally a church and now a museum), the Blue Mosque, and the Topkapı Palace (the former sultans' harem). It is a major port and industrial center and has three universities (15th century, 1773, and 1971); tourism is a major source of revenue. *History*: ancient Byzantium was renamed Constantinople in 330, when the emperor Constantine I declared it the capital of the Eastern Roman Empire. It was the capital of the Byzantine Empire until its capture by the Ottoman Turks in 1453, although it had been held by Crusaders from 1204 to 1261. The Ottomans renamed it Istanbul and made it the capital of their empire in 1457. After having been taken by the Allies in World War I, Istanbul became the largest city of the Turkish Republic (established in 1923). Population (1980): 4,741,890.

Isthmian Games In ancient Greece, the biennial festival held near Corinth in Poseidon's honor. Established in 581 BC these games, more lighthearted than the other major Greek festivals, included music and poetry competitions as well as the more usual athletic events and horse racing. The victor's prize was a crown of wild celery.

Istria A peninsula in NW Yugoslavia, in Croatia between the Gulf of Trieste and the Bay of Kvarner. Passing to Italy at the end of World War I, it was ceded to Yugoslavia (1947) except for the Territory of Trieste, which was divided between Italy and Yugoslavia in 1954.

Itaipu Dam. *See* Paraná, Rio.

Italian A language of the *Romance family spoken in Italy. The standard literary and official form is based upon the Tuscan dialect of Florence, the dialect used by *Dante.

Italian art The style of art found in Italy after the collapse of the Roman Empire. Antique motifs continued but were gradually replaced by Christian imagery and the influence, especially in Ravenna and Venice, of *Byzantine art and architecture. The *romanesque style of the 11th and 12th centuries gave way to the *gothic in the 13th century. A truly Italian art developed in the late-13th and 14th centuries, when the foundations of *Renaissance art were laid by *Giotto, *Duccio, and the sculptor Nicola *Pisano. Independent styles arose in the regional centers of Italy, especially in Florence (which dominated the 15th century), Venice (where the Venetian school was founded by the *Bellini family), and Rome. The giants of

the Renaissance, *Leonardo, *Michelangelo, *Raphael, and the Venetians *Giorgione and *Titian dominated the late 15th and early 16th centuries. Their work merged into □mannerism, exemplified by the architect *Giulio Romano, the painter *Parmigianino, and in Venice the painters *Tintoretto and *Veronese. Mannerism gave way around 1600 to the *baroque, the outstanding Italian exponents of which worked in Rome: the architects *Bernini (also a sculptor) and *Borromini and the painter *Caravaggio. After the 17th century Italian art lost its impetus, except in Venice, where it briefly flowered in the 18th century with the work of *Canaletto, *Guardi, and *Tiepolo. A revival occurred in the early 20th century under the influence of *futurism and the outstanding Italian painters of the modern period are *Modigliani and de *Chirico.

Italian East Africa. *See* Somaliland.

Italian literature Latin remained the literary language of Italy until the 13th century, when poets at the Sicilian court of Frederick I (later Emperor Frederick II) began to imitate the poetry of Provence in native Italian. The delicate love poetry of the *dolce stil nuovo school of Florentine poets was followed in the 14th century by the allegorical works of *Dante, the love sonnets of *Petrarch, and the prose tales of *Boccaccio. The gradual development of the Italian language culminated in the Renaissance works of *Ariosto, *Machiavelli, and *Tasso. There followed a long period of decadence until, in the late 18th century, a literary revival was brought about by the dramatists *Alfieri and *Goldoni and the poet *Foscolo. In the 19th century the influence of Romanticism, epitomized in the poetry of *Leopardi, was followed by a reaction represented by the classicism of the poet *Carducci and the realism of the novelist and dramatist Giovanni Verga (1840–1922). Major writers of the early 20th century include the poet *D'Annunzio, the dramatist *Pirandello, and the critic Benedetto *Croce. Literary exploration of social and moral themes was curbed during the fascist regime from 1922 to 1943, but recommenced after World War II, with such writers as Alberto *Moravia, Cesare *Pavese, and Italo Calvino (1923–).

Italic languages A subgroup of the *Indo-European language family spoken in central and NE Italy in the thousand years before the rise of Rome. A parent of modern *Romance languages, this group comprised four related dialects: *Latin, Faliscan, Osco-Umbrian, and Venetic. At the beginning of the 1st millennium BC Osco-Umbrian was the most widely spoken, but with the growth of Roman civilization, Latin quickly came to dominate other dialects, which are now known only through Latin sources.

italic script A style of handwriting adopted in 15th-century Italy by papal scribes and later (c. 1500) adapted for printing. Italic cursive letters eliminate unnecessary lifts of the pen, permitting rapid legible handwriting. *In print its characteristic sloped letters, such as those used in this sentence, are used mainly for display, emphasis, or to indicate that a word is in a foreign language.*

Italy, Republic of A country in S Europe, occupying a peninsula bordered by the Tyrrhenian Sea (W), the Ionian Sea (S), and the Adriatic Sea (E). The principal offshore islands are Sicily and Sardinia. Except for small coastal areas and the Po Valley in the N, the country is generally rugged and mountainous. The main rivers are the Po, Tiber, Arno, and Adige. *Economy*: agriculture is still important, the main crops being wheat, maize, grapes, and olives. Industry, however, has expanded considerably since World War II and is now the most important sector. The principal manufactures are textiles (including silk) and clothing, and machinery, motor vehicles, and chemicals, which together with fruit and vegetables are the principal exports. The wine industry is growing in importance and exports have increased in recent years. Mineral resources are not large and Italy is heavily dependent on imported fossil fuels, although oil is now being extracted, especially in Sicily, and hydroelectricity has been considerably developed. There are also plans to develop nuclear energy. Tourism is an important source of revenue. During the 1970s, however, Italy was faced with severe problems of inflation and economic stagnation and the long-standing problem of integrating the poorer predominantly agricultural S with the industrial N remained unresolved. *History*: pre-Roman Italy was inhabited from the 7th century BC by the *Etruscans in the N, Italics (including the Samnites) and Latins in central Italy, and Greek colonists in the southern mainland and Sicily. By 275 BC most of the peninsula had come under the rule of Rome (*see* Roman Republic). As the western *Roman Empire declined from the 4th century AD, Italy was invaded by a succession of barbarian tribes, including the Visigoths and the Vandals. The last Roman emperor was deposed in 476 by the German king, Odoacer, who in 493 was in turn overthrown by the Ostrogoths. They were expelled in the early 6th century by the Eastern (Byzantine) Roman Empire, the position of which was threatened from the mid-6th century by successive invasions: the Lombards were followed by the Franks in the 8th and 9th centuries, a period that also saw the origins of the pope's temporal power (see papal states); the Muslims invaded the S in the 9th and 10th centuries, Magyars, the N in the 10th century, and Normans, the S in the 11th century. The claim of the German kings to rule Italy was established in 962, when Otto the Great was crowned Holy Roman Emperor in Rome. The conflict from the 11th century between successive popes and emperors over the *investiture controversy embroiled the Italian city states (notably Milan, Pisa, Genoa, Venice, and Florence), which in the 12th century were further divided by the struggle between *Guelfs and Ghibellines. The economic and political development of the city states in the first half of the 14th century was facilitated by the removal of the papacy to Avignon and the preoccupation with German affairs of the Holy Roman Emperors. Many of the Italian cities came to be dominated by single families, such as the *Visconti and then the Sforza in Milan and the *Medici in Florence, who during the Renaissance were often outstanding patrons of culture and learning. Following the French invasion of Italy in 1494 Italy became the scene of conflict between France and Spain and from the 16th to early 18th centuries was largely dominated by the latter. Spain ruled Milan, Naples, Sicily, and Sardinia directly and influenced Savoy, Genoa, and Tuscany; of the major Italian states only the papal states and Venice remained independent. During the 18th century Spanish hegemony was destroyed, passing to Austria until 1796, when Italy was conquered by the French Revolutionary armies under Napoleon. The French occupation gave Italy the experience of unity. After Napoleon's fall and the restoration of Austrian rule this developed into the movement for independence and unification (the *Risorgimento). By 1861, under the leadership of Victor Emmanuel II of Sardinia-Piedmont and his chief minister Cavour, aided by Garibaldi in the S, the Austrians had been expelled and the kingdom of Italy proclaimed with Victor Emmanuel as its first king; unification was virtually complete by 1870. In the late 19th century Italy acquired a colonial empire, notably Somaliland and Eritrea in East Africa, but its attempt to seize Ethiopia was defeated at Adowa in 1896. In 1915 Italy entered World War I on the side of the Allies, obtaining the Trentino and the Istrian peninsula (see Irredentists). The postwar rise of fascism brought Mussolini to power in 1922. In 1936 he conquered Ethiopia and in 1939, Albania. In 1940, loyal to his alliances (1936, 1939) with Hitler, Mussolini took Italy into World War II on Germany's side (1940). The Allied conquest of Sicily (1943) brought Mussolini's fall and in 1946 Umberto II abdicated following a referendum rejecting the monarchy. Since the establishment of the Republic there have been over 40 governments, led by the Christian Democrats. However, their repeated failure to deal effectively with a stagnating economy, widespread corruption, and growing lawlessness exacerbated by such groups as the *Red Brigades and fascists led to an increase in the strength of the Communist Party, which in 1977 achieved a measure of participation in government. In 1983, after an election in which the Christian Democrats received a third of the vote and the Communists slightly less, a Socialist, Bettino Craxi, became premier of a government of center-left parties. The government pursued a policy of fiscal conservatism while successfully suppressing terrorists and intensifying a campaign against the Mafia. President: Alessandro Pertini (1896–   ). Prime minister: Bettino Craxi. Official language: Italian. Official religion: Roman Catholic. Official currency: lira of 100 centesimi. Area: 116,350 sq mi (301,425 sq km). Population (1983 est): 56,345,000. Capital: Rome. Main port: Genoa.

itch mite A parasitic *mite, Sarcoptes scabei, that produces *scabies in man and mange in domestic animals. The female burrows into the skin, where it lays eggs and causes intense itching and irritation. Family: Sarcoptidae.

Ithaca (Modern Greek name: Itháki) A Greek island in the Ionian Sea, one of the Ionian Islands. It is widely believed to have been the home of Homer's Odysseus. Area: 33 sq mi (85 sq km). Population (1971): 4156.

Ithaca 42 27N 76 30W A city in central New York, on the S tip of Cayuga Lake. Cornell University (1865) is here. Settled in 1789, it is a center for the agricultural products of the area and also produces office machinery and clothing. Population (1980): 28,732.

Ito Hirobumi (1841–1909) Japanese statesman, who played a leading part in the abolition of feudalism and the adoption of modern methods and institutions. During the 1880s he assumed responsibility for drafting the Meiji constitution (1889) and between 1885 and 1901 he was prime minister four times. During his second ministry Japan defeated China in the *Sino-Japanese War (1894–95). Ito was assassinated by a Korean nationalist.

Itúrbide, Agustín (1783–1824) Mexican soldier prominent in the independence movement; emperor (1822–23). He used the general unrest in Mexico to further his own advancement in the army. Appointed commander of the combined rebel forces when Mexico declared itself independent of

Spain (1820), he subsequently proclaimed himself emperor. Within months *Santa Anna forced his abdication; Itúrbide returned from exile in 1824 but was executed.

Ivanovo 57 00N 41 00E A city in the central Soviet Union, in the RSFSR on the Uvod River. It played an important part in both the 1905 and 1917 Russian Revolutions. It is one of the country's major textile centers. Population (1981 est): 470,000.

Ivan (III) the Great (1440–1505) Grand Prince of Muscovy (1462–1505). Ivan greatly expanded Muscovite territory and ended Russian subordination to the Tatars. In 1497 he introduced a new legal code. Ivan married (1472) Zoë Palaeologus (d. 1503), the niece of the last Byzantine emperor, and adopted the Byzantine two-headed eagle as his arms.

Ivan (IV) the Terrible (1530–84) Grand Prince of Muscovy (1533–84), who was crowned tsar in 1547. Ivan reformed the legal code and local administration (1555), conquered Kazan and Astrakhan, and established commercial relations with England. After 1560 his reign was marred by his brutality: thousands were executed and in a fit of rage Ivan murdered his son (1581). The effects of his tyranny were aggravated by the financial strains resulting from the abortive *Livonian War (1558–82).

Ives, Charles (Edward) (1874–1954) US composer. An early experimenter with polyrhythms, polytonality, quarter tones, and the superimposition of disparate musical styles, he composed four symphonies, five violin sonatas, songs, and other works. His second piano sonata, subtitled Concord, Mass (1909–15), was inspired by writers associated with the town of Concord. Its movements were subtitled "Emerson," "Hawthorne," "The Alcotts," and "Thoreau." One of his best-known works is Central Park in the Dark (1898–1907). Of the more than 500 works he composed, most remained unpublished. For his Symphony No. 3 (1904) he was awarded a Pulitzer Prize. He was also senior partner of the insurance firm of Ives and Myrick.

ivory The close-grained white tissue forming the tusks of elephants, walruses, and narwhals and the teeth of hippos. So-called fossil ivory is obtained from mammoths. Plastics have now generally replaced ivory for such mundane domestic artifacts as knife handles, but, being easy to carve and polish, ivory is still such a valuable commodity that its main source, the African elephant, is threatened with extinction. Ivory carving is a very ancient art; objects from France date to Paleolithic times and fine examples survive from Egyptian, Minoan, Mycenaean, Assyrian, Greek, and Roman civilizations. In Europe ivory plaques with relief carving became important during the early middle ages for small religious icons, book covers, caskets, etc. India, SE Asia, China, and Japan (see netsuke) have ancient traditions of skilled ivory carving. American Eskimo carvings in walrus ivory are greatly prized by connoisseurs.

ivory-billed woodpecker A rare black-and-white *woodpecker, Campephilus principalis, occurring in North American forests. 18 in (45 cm) long, it has a white bill and the male has a red crest. It feeds on woodboring insects and requires a large feeding territory, hence its decline due to the expansion of the timber industry.

Ivory Coast, Republic of (French name: Côte d'Ivoire) A country in West Africa, on the Gulf of Guinea. Swamps and tropical forests give way to savanna on higher land to the N. The diverse African population includes Baule, Bete, Senufo, and Malinke. Economy: chiefly agricultural, livestock being important as well as crops, including maize, yams, and other tropical plants. The main cash crop is coffee, of which, together with timber (particularly mahogany), Ivory Coast is Africa's leading exporter. Other exports include cocoa, pineapples, and rubber. Mineral resources are on the whole sparse, although some manganese is mined, diamond fields are being exploited, and some oil was found in 1977. Industry is being developed, including tourism. History: explored by the Portuguese in the late 15th century, the area was disputed by several European trading nations over the centuries, becoming a French colony in 1893. It became part of French West Africa in 1904 and an overseas territory in 1946. It possessed internal self-government as a member of the French Community from 1958 and became fully independent in 1960. President: Félix Houphouët-Boigny. Official language: French. Official currency: CFA (Communauté financière africaine) franc of 100 centimes. Area: 124,470 sq mi (322,463 sq km). Population (1983 est): 8,890,000. Capital: Yamoussoukro. Main port: Abidjan.

ivy An evergreen woody climbing plant, Hedera helix, that has glossy three- to five-lobed leaves, aerial roots (with which it clings to supports), clusters of small greenish-yellow flowers, and small round fruits ripening from green to black. Native to Europe and W Asia, it is widely cultivated (ornamental ivies often have variegated foliage). Family: Araliaceae.

Ivy League   A group of seven universities and one college in the NE of high academic and social prestige. They include *Harvard, *Yale, *Princeton, Brown, Dartmouth, Cornell, Columbia, and Pennsylvania and are all members of an athletic conference for intercollegiate sports known as the Ivy League, which dates back to the 1870s.

Iwo   7 38N 4 11E A city in SW Nigeria. Its main activity is the export of agricultural products, especially cocoa. Population (1975 est): 214,000.

Iwo Jima   24 47N 141 19E A Japanese island in the W Pacific Ocean, the largest of the Volcano Islands. Captured by US forces after a severe struggle (1945), it was returned in 1968. Sulfur and sugar are produced. Area: 8 sq mi (20 sq km).

Iwo Jima, Battle of   (1944) World War II battle. US troops invaded the Japanese island stronghold of Iwo Jima and, after more than three weeks of fighting, secured it for a strategic US airplane landing strip. Casualties were heavy, well over 20,000 for each side. The photograph of US Marines raising the flag atop Mt Suribachi has been immortalized in statuary and paintings as a symbol of courage.

Izanagi and Izanami   In Japanese mythology, the male and female creator deities of Japan. They stirred the sea with a spear and drops from its tip formed the Japanese islands, for which they then created other *kami* (spirits) as inhabitants and guardians (*see* Amaterasu).

Izhevsk   56 49N 53 11E A city in the W central Soviet Union, the capital of Udmurt ASSR in the RSFSR. It is a major metallurgical center. Population (1981 est): 574,000.

Izmir   (former name: Smyrna)   38 25N 27 10E A port in W Turkey, on the Aegean Sea. Much was destroyed by fire in 1922, the rebuilt town being a modern commercial center with a university (1953). There is trade in silk, cotton, carpets, figs, raisins, and sponges. Population (1980): 1,976,763.

Izmit   40 47N 29 55E A city in NW Turkey, on the Sea of Marmara. As ancient Nicomedia it was the seat of the kings of Bithynia, and it is now a naval port. Population (1975 est): 164,675.

J

Jabalpur (*or* Jubbulpore) 23 10N 79 59E A city in India, in Madhya Pradesh. An important railroad junction and industrial center, its manufactures include cement, textiles, and military equipment. Its university was established in 1957. Population (1971): 426,224.

Jabir. *See* Geber.

jabiru A large *stork, *Jabiru mycteria*, ranging from Mexico to Argentina. 55 in (140 cm) long, it is white with a dark-blue head and neck with a red patch at the base and has a long slightly upturned heavy bill.

jaborandi A tropical American plant of the genus *Pilocarpus* (22 species), the dried leaves of which yield an alkaloid, pilocarpine, used medicinally in eyedrops to constrict the pupil and to treat glaucoma. Family: *Rutaceae*.

jacamar A bird belonging to a family (*Galbulidae*; 15 species) occurring in tropical American forests. 5–11 in (12–27 cm) long, jacamars have a large head tapering to a long narrow tail and iridescent blue, green, or bronze plumage. They feed on insects caught in flight. Order: *Piciformes* (woodpeckers, etc.).

jacana A waterbird belonging to a family (*Jacanidae*; 7 species) occurring in tropical regions worldwide, also called lily trotter. Jacanas are characterized by long legs with elongated toes and claws, which enable them to run over floating vegetation. 10–13 in (25–32 cm) long, they are commonly reddish to dark-brown in color and can swim and dive well, feeding on aquatic plants and animals. Order: *Charadriiformes* (gulls, plovers, etc.).

Jacaranda A genus of □trees and shrubs (50 species) of South and Central America and the West Indies, often grown as ornamentals. *J. mimosifolia*, up to 49 ft (15 m) tall, has finely divided compound leaves and clusters of blue or violet tubular flowers. In cooler climates it can be cultivated in warm greenhouses. Some species yield commercially valuable timber. Family: *Bignoniaceae*.

jackal A carnivorous mammal of the genus *Canis*, found in Asia and Africa. Jackals are closely related to dogs and have pricked ears and bushy tails. The African black-backed jackal (*C. mesomeles*) is up to 43 in (110 cm) long including the tail (10–13 in [25–33 cm]) and often hunts in packs for carrion, usually at night. The African side-striped jackal (*C. adustus*) is smaller and shyer.

jackdaw An intelligent Eurasian crow, *Corvus monedula*, about 13 in (32 cm) long, having a black plumage with a gray nape, an erectile crest, and pale-blue eyes. Often found in colonies, jackdaws may be seen flying around cliffs, ruins, and large buildings. They feed on insects, grain, and carrion and may rob nests of eggs and chicks.

Jack Russell terrier A breed of dog developed in England from the fox terrier by the Rev John Russell (1795–1883) for flushing foxes from earth. It has a stocky body and a strong muscular head with small drooping ears. The short coat is white, black, and tan. Height: up to 15 in (38 cm).

Jackson 32 20N 90 11W The capital city of Mississippi, on the Pearl River. Founded in 1821, it was virtually destroyed by Gen Sherman in 1863. More recently (1960s) it was the scene of considerable racial tension. Its industries include the production of oil and gas, textiles, and glass. Population (1980): 202,895.

Jackson, Andrew (1767–1845) US military leader and statesman; 7th President of the United States (1829–37). A Tennessee frontiersman, Jackson fought in the *Revolutionary War, served in the US House of Representatives (1796–97) and in the US Senate (1798), and later became a national hero when his defense of New Orleans boosted American morale at the end of the *War of 1812. After the war, he commanded US forces in an invasion of Florida (1818), where he defeated the *Seminoles. Jackson was again elected to the US Senate (1823–25) and ran unsuccessfully for the presidency in 1824. As the leader of an emerging faction of the Jeffersonian Republicans, Jackson is generally credited with the foundation of the modern *Democratic Party. As the victorious presidential nominee of that party in 1828, re-elected in 1832, he relied on support from the middle class and opposed the power of aristocrats and professional politicians. His economic policy strengthened *states' rights and one of the most controversial acts of his presidency was his withdrawal of federal deposits from the *Bank of the United States. After leaving office, he spent his later years at his home, The Hermitage, near Nashville, Tenn.

ANDREW JACKSON *President (1829–37) who, as a general in the War of 1812, had been the hero of the Battle of New Orleans.*

Jackson, Glenda (1936–) British actress. She has acted in many Royal Shakespeare Company stage productions, but first achieved popular success with her portrayal of Elizabeth I in a television series (1971). Her movies include *Women in Love* (1969), *A Touch of Class* (1972), *Hedda* (1976), *The Incredible Sarah* (1976), and *Stevie* (1978).

Jackson, Jesse (1941–) US minister and civil rights leader. He worked closely with Martin Luther *King, Jr. during the 1960s and established and led Operation Breadbasket (1966–77), an antidiscriminatory project of the Southern Christian Leadership Conference, and PUSH (People United to Serve Humanity; 1971–). He campaigned unsuccessfully for the Democratic presidential nomination (1984) and made personal visits to Syria to negotiate the release of an imprisoned US pilot (1983–84) and to Cuba (1984) where he was instrumental in expediting the release of US and Cuban prisoners.

Jackson, Michael (1958–) US singer, dancer, and composer, known for his high tenor voice. A member of the Jackson Five, a group with four of his brothers, he sang and danced from the age of five. Signed by Motown Records in 1969, the group rose to stardom and by 1975 had changed record companies and been renamed The Jacksons. Michael, usually the lead singer in the group, had many solo hits: *Thriller* (1983), an album and a television video, was especially successful. The group's 1983 US tour drew unprecedented crowds.

Jackson, Robert Houghwout (1892–1954) US lawyer and jurist; US Supreme Court justice (1941–54). He worked as a lawyer for the Bureau of Internal Revenue (1934) and the Securities and Exchange Commission (1935) and as assistant attorney general (1936–37), solicitor general (1938), and attorney general (1940) before being appointed to the Supreme Court. He was chief prosecutor at the Nazi war crime trials in Nuremberg, Germany (1946–47). As an associate justice he was known as a moderate in favor of separation of church and state and against the seizure of the steel mills by President Harry S Truman in 1952.

Jackson, Stonewall (Thomas Jonathan J.; 1824–63) US Confederate general. A graduate of West Point (1846), he served in the Mexican War and then left the army (1852). He joined the Confederate cause when the Civil War began. In the first battle of *Bull Run (1861), he and his brigade were described as standing "like a stone wall" in the face of the Federal advance. Jackson was a master of rapid tactical movement, shown particularly in the Shenandoah valley campaign (1862) and he was considered Lee's best lieutenant. His untimely death at Chancellorsville left a gap in the Confederate command that was never filled.

Jackson Hole A valley and wildlife preserve near the Teton Range in NW Wyoming. Part of the valley has been included in Grand Teton National Park since 1950. American elk herds feed here during the winter. Area: 376 sq mi (974 sq km).

Jacksonville 30 20N 81 40W A city and port in NE Florida, on the St Johns River near its mouth on the Atlantic Ocean. Named for President Jackson (formerly the first territorial governor of Florida), it is the state's largest city and main commercial center. A major naval base, its industries include ship repairing, paper, and chemicals. Population (1980): 540,898.

Jack the Ripper An unidentified murderer who killed and mutilated at least seven prostitutes in the East End of London, England, in late 1888. One recent theory suggests that he was Vassily Konovalov, a Russian who committed similar murders in Paris and St Petersburg and who died in a Russian asylum.

Jacobins An extremist group in the *French Revolution. The Jacobin Club was founded in 1789 and (meeting in a Dominican (or Jacobin) monastery) became increasingly radical. Helped by *Danton's rabble-rousing speeches, they proclaimed the republic, had the king executed, and overthrew the *Girondins (1792–93). Through the Committee of *Public Safety, the Jacobins, under the influence of *Robespierre, instituted the *Reign of Terror. They collapsed after Robespierre's execution.

Jacobites Supporters of the exiled *Stuart king, James II, and his descendants. Between 1688, when the Glorious Revolution overthrew James II, and 1745, the Jacobites (mainly Roman Catholics and/or Tories), were the rallying point for opposition to the Hanoverian monarchs. Two Jacobite rebellions, in 1715 and 1745, were suppressed and thereafter the movement lost its political force.

Jacob's ladder A perennial herb, *Polemonium caeruleum*, native of Eurasia and widely cultivated as a garden flower. Growing to a height of 35 in (90 cm), it has bright-blue flowers and leaves consisting of paired ladder-like leaflets. Family: *Polemoniaceae*.

Jacopo della Quercia (c. 1374–1438) Italian Renaissance sculptor, who was the Sienese counterpart to *Donatello. His Sienese works include the Fonte Gaia (1416–19), the now dismantled fountain for the Piazza del Campo, and the Baptistry font, on which he collaborated with *Ghiberti. However, Jacopo's most powerful works are the marble reliefs (1425–35) of scenes from Genesis, which surround the portal of S Petronio, Bologna.

Jacopone da Todi (c. 1236–1306) Italian religious poet. On the death of his wife, he joined the Franciscans as a member of the "Spirituals," the strictest group of the order. In 1298 he was imprisoned by Pope Boniface VIII, whom he had attacked in verse, but was released on the pope's death in 1303. The famous Latin poem *Stabat mater dolorosa* is attributed to him, but most of his poetry was written in the Umbrian dialect of Italian. His *laudi spirituali* (spiritual praises) are vivid devotional poems covering a wide range of mood, from mystical love of God to bitter denunciation of the world.

Jacquard, Joseph-Marie (1752–1834) French inventor of the Jacquard loom, completed in 1801. Its design allowed for the weaving of figured patterns by means of punched cards, which were later employed in the calculator developed by Charles *Babbage and in subsequent computers.

Jacquerie (1358) A peasant revolt in NE France during the Hundred Years' War with England. Its name refers to the aristocrats' contemptuous nickname for a peasant—Jacques Bonhomme. Caused by famine, plague, and war, the rebellion was rapidly suppressed.

jade An extremely hard semiprecious stone, usually green or greenish white, consisting of a tough compact variety of either jadeite (a pyroxene, $NaAlSi_2O_6$) or nephrite (an amphibole). Many highly prized stones come from Upper Burma, where they are found in river terraces or beds.

Jadotville. *See* Likasi.

Jaén 37 46N 3 48W A city in S Spain, in Andalusia. It has a fine Renaissance cathedral. Once famous for silk, it now produces chemicals and has rich leadmines nearby. Population (1970): 78,156.

Jaffa. *See* Tel Aviv-Yafo.

Jagger, Mick (1944–) British rock singer; lead singer of the *Rolling Stones. He became notorious for his aggressive performances on stage and was arrested in 1967 for possessing drugs. He acted in the films *Ned Kelly* (1969) and *Performance* (1970).

Jagiellons The ruling dynasty of Poland and Lithuania (1386–1572), Hungary (1440–1441, 1490–1526), and Bohemia (1471–1526). The dynasty was founded by Jagiełło (1350–1434), Grand Duke of Lithuania, who became King of Poland as Władysław II in 1386, when he married Queen Jadwiga of Poland (1370–99; reigned 1384–99). He was succeeded by his son Władysław III (1424–44), who also became King of Hungary (1440). Władysław III's nephew Władysław (1456–1516) became Vladislav II of Bohemia in 1471 and of Hungary in 1490. The Jagiellons lost Hungary and Bohemia to the Turks at the battle of *Mohács (1526). The last Jagiellon ruler was Sigismund II Augustus (1520–72; ruled Poland 1548–72), under whom a Polish-Lithuanian commonwealth was created by the Union of *Lublin.

jaguar The largest New World *cat, *Panthera onca*, found in the southern US and South America. Up to 8 ft (2.5 m) long including the tail (28–35 in [70–90 cm]), it has dark rosette-shaped spots on its yellow coat. Jaguars inhabit forest and scrub and can swim well and may catch fish. They also hunt peccaries, turtles, and capybaras and may attack domestic livestock.

jaguarundi A weasel-like *cat, *Felis yagouaroundi*, of Central and South America. Up to 43 in (110 cm) long, it stands only 11 in (28 cm) high at the shoulder. It has a red or gray coat, long tail, and small ears. In addition to birds, jaguarundis eat such fruits as grapes, figs, and bananas.

Jahangir (1569–1627) Emperor of India (1605–27); the son of *Akbar the Great, from whom he inherited a powerful empire. After expanding it further he ruled wisely and justly, fostering sport and the arts. He enjoyed good relations with the British *East India Company.

Jainism The religion of between two and three million Indians, followers of *Mahavira. Founded in the 6th century BC in opposition to Vedic religion, Jainism stresses *ahimsa, asceticism, and meditation. Right belief, knowledge, and conduct are the means of release from the perpetual round of rebirth caused by *karma. This release is possible only for monks; the laity aim only for a better rebirth. Jainism is atheistic, although lesser spirits and demons proliferate. The universe, containing heavens and hells revolving eternally in ascending and descending cycles, is seen as the mechanistic interaction of six principles: souls, space, time, matter, right, and wrong. These constitute the opposing categories of life and nonlife.

Jaipur 26 53N 75 50E A city in India, the capital of Rajasthan. Formerly the capital of the princely state of Rajasthan, it has many fine buildings built of pink sandstone, an 18th-century observatory, and a university (1947). Jaipur is famous for its enamel work and jewelry, textile printing, and stone, marble, and ivory carving. Population (1981 est): 1,004,669.

Jajapura (or Djajapura; former name: Sukarnapura) 2 37S 140 39E A port in E Indonesia, the capital of West Irian province on the Pacific Ocean. Liberated from Japanese occupation by US forces in 1944, it became General MacArthur's headquarters. Its university was established in 1962. Population (1971): 45,786.

Jakarta (or Djakarta; name until 1949: Batavia) 6 09S 106 49E The capital of Indonesia, in NW Java linked by canal to its port, Tanjung Priok. The Dutch set up a fort here in the early 17th century and it became a major commercial center as the headquarters of the Dutch East India Company. The University of Indonesia was founded in 1950. Population (1971): 4,576,009.

jalap A climbing plant *Ipomoea purga*, of Mexico and South America, that has crimson flowers. The dried tubers yield a resin that is used medicinally as a laxative. Family: *Convolvulaceae*.

Jamaica, State of An island country in the Caribbean Sea, off the S coast of Cuba. A high plateau is crossed by the Blue Mountains, which reach 7400 ft (2255 m). The population is mainly of African and mixed African and European descent. *Economy*: sugar, bauxite, and tourism form the basis, although the tourist trade was badly affected for several years by domestic unrest. Jamaica is the world's second largest producer of bauxite and alumina and in recent years has increased its control of the industry, which was previously handled by US companies. There is an agreement between Guyana and Jamaica to build two alumina-processing smelters by 1981, and a bauxite and alumina complex is being jointly constructed by Jamaica and Mexico. Other recent industrial developments include the construction of an oil refinery with Mexican aid. *History*: discovered by Columbus in 1494, it was occupied by the Spanish, who exterminated the original Arawak inhabitants. Captured by the British in 1655, it became a colony and a center of the slave trade until the abolition of slavery in 1833. Self-government was introduced in 1944 and extended in 1959, and in 1962 Jamaica became an independent state within the British Commonwealth. There has been considerable political unrest in recent years between the Labour Party (JLP) and the People's National Party (PNP) led by Michael *Manley, an advocate of democratic socialism and republican status for Jamaica. A state of emergency existed in 1976–77 following riots. Enjoying a particularly favorable relationship with the US, Jamaica was the chief beneficiary of the US-sponsored Caribbean Basin Initiative. Jamaica is a member of the OAS and CARICOM. Prime minister: Edward Seaga. Official language: English. Official currency: Jamaican dollar of 100 cents. Area: 4244 sq mi (10,991 sq km). Population (1983 est): 2,535,000. Capital and main port: Kingston.

Jambi (Djambi or Telanaipura)   1 36S 103 39E A port in Indonesia, in SE Sumatra. It is a commercial center producing chiefly rubber and oil. Its university was established in 1963. Population (1971): 158,559.

James (I) the Conqueror   (1208–76) King of Aragon (1213–76). James, who became effective ruler in 1227, was the greatest medieval Aragonese monarch. He reconquered the Balearic Islands and Valencia from the Moors and thus laid the basis for Aragonese expansion in the Mediterranean in the next century. James also contributed to the cultural achievements of his reign, prompting the compilation of the *Chronicle* of his exploits.

James I   (1394–1437) King of the Scots (1406–37), whose actual rule began on his release (1424) from English imprisonment. He strengthened royal authority at the expense of the nobles, whom he treated with some harshness, and extended royal control over the administration of justice and commerce. He was assassinated by a group of disaffected nobles. He is believed to be the author of the poem "The Kingis Quair" ("The King's Book").

James I   (1566–1625) The first Stuart King of England and Ireland (1603–25) and, as James VI, King of the Scots (1567–1625). He succeeded his mother Mary, Queen of Scots, and was brought up by a series of regents. As king he reasserted royal authority against the encroachments of the nobility and the Presbyterians. In England, James encountered opposition from his parliaments, which resented his assertion of the *divine right of kings. James was also unpopular for his choice of favorites and for his attempts to obtain a Spanish marriage for his son. One of the great achievements of his reign was the publication (1611) of the *King James or Authorized version of the Bible. He was the first king to rule both Scotland and England.

James II   (1430–60) King of the Scots (1437–60). He established his authority over rival factions and continued the extension of royal control and justice begun by his father James I. He was killed while besieging the English at Roxburgh Castle.

James II   (1633–1701) King of England, Scotland, and Ireland (1685–88). The second son of Charles I, James (as Duke of York) escaped to Holland (1648) after his father's defeat in the Civil War. In 1659 he married the daughter of the Earl of Clarendon, Anne Hyde (1637–71), by whom he had two daughters (later Queens Mary II and Anne). A few years after the Restoration (1660) of his brother Charles II, James became a Roman Catholic. Successive attempts to exclude him from the succession failed and in 1685 he became king. The Protestant rebellion of the Duke of *Monmouth was suppressed, Roman Catholics were admitted to public office, and religious freedom for all denominations was announced (1687). The threat of a Roman Catholic succession was increased with the birth of a son (see James Edward Stuart, the Old Pretender) to his second wife, Mary of Modena (1658–1718), and precipitated his overthrow in the *Glorious Revolution. James was forced to flee and his subsequent attempt to regain the crown from Ireland failed with his defeat by William III's forces at the *Boyne (1690) and *Aughrim (1691). He died an exile in France.

James III   (1452–88) King of the Scots (1460–88). Until 1469 Scotland was ruled by a regency and his personal rule was marked by baronial revolts. He was killed after defeat by rebel barons near Stirling.

James IV   (1473–1513) King of the Scots (1488–1513). In 1503 he married *Margaret Tudor. He defeated the rebels who had killed his father James III, procuring internal stability and respect for the monarchy. Recurrent hostility with England culminated in the invasion of Northumberland (1513) and his defeat and death, with most of his nobles, at *Flodden.

James V   (1512–42) King of the Scots (1513–42). During his minority (1513–28) Scotland was controlled by rival pro-French and pro-English factions. James favored the French, to whom he was allied by his marriage to Mary of Guise (1515–60). He died shortly after the failure of an invasion of England and was succeeded by his daughter Mary, Queen of Scots.

James VI (King of the Scots).   See James I (King of England).

James, Henry   (1843–1916) US novelist and critic. Much of his childhood was spent in Europe, and in 1875 he moved to Paris, where he met Turgenev, Flaubert, and others who influenced his concern with the technique of fiction. From 1876 he lived mainly in England, becoming a British citizen in 1915. His novel *Roderick Hudson* (1875) introduced the international theme of Americans confronting European culture that he was to develop in many other novels, such as *The Portrait of a Lady* (1881), although he occasionally returned to strictly American settings, as in *Washington Square* (1881) and *The Bostonians* (1886). He wrote more than a hundred shorter works of fiction, of which *The Turn of the Screw* (1898) is perhaps the best known. In his later novels, *The Wings of the Dove* (1902), *The Ambassadors* (1903), and *The Golden Bowl* (1904), action is subordinated to a searching psychological analysis rendered in a highly elaborate style. He was an influential critic; the Prefaces to his novels are important theoretical statements on the novel. He also wrote plays, but they were not successful, although many of his works have been adapted for dramatic performance. His brother **William James** (1842–1910) was a psychologist and philosopher, who developed the theory of *pragmatism in ethics. He held that the truth or falsity of classical philosophical systems made little difference to everyday life and that the function of a theory should be to solve practical difficulties: thus a theory was only true in so far as it successfully helped to solve problems. Religious and moral beliefs were treated in the same nondogmatic way, especially in his influential *Varieties of Religious Experience* (1902) and *The Meaning of Truth* (1909).

James, Jesse (Woodson)   (1847–92) US outlaw. He and his brother Frank fought with southern guerrilla groups during the Civil War before they became outlaws. By 1867 he had formed the James gang and was robbing banks, stagecoaches, and trains in his native Missouri and surrounding states. A $10,000 reward offered by the state of Missouri in 1881 was claimed by a James gang member, Robert Ford, who shot Jesse, living as Thomas Howard in St Joseph. The legends surrounding Jesse James range from those depicting him as a Robin Hood to those portraying a cold-blooded killer.

James, St   In the New Testament, the name of three followers of Christ. **1**. A leader, with St Peter, of the early Christians of Jerusalem. He is described as "the Lord's brother" (Mark 6.3), but the exact relationship is uncertain. He was a devout follower of Jewish practice, being converted to Christianity at the time of the resurrection. He was condemned to death by the Sanhedrin in 62 AD. The **Epistle of James** in the New Testament was traditionally attributed to him and was possibly written early in the 1st century AD. **2**. The Apostle, known as St James the Great, son of Zebedee and brother of *John. He was present with his brother at many events in the life of Christ recounted in the Gospels. He was beheaded by Herod Agrippa I in 44 AD. In the middle ages it was believed that he had preached in Spain and was buried at Santiago de Compostela, the center of international pilgrimages. Feast day: July 25. **3**. The Apostle, known as St James the Less, son of Alphaeus. Nothing further is certainly known about his life. Feast day: May 1.

James Edward Stuart, the Old Pretender   (1688–1766) The son of James II, the deposed Roman Catholic King of England. In exile, he was urged by his supporters, known as *Jacobites, to claim the English throne. After their invasion of Scotland failed in 1715, James abandoned his claim and lived in permanent exile in Rome.

Jameson, Sir Leander Starr   (1853–1917) South African statesman, born in Scotland, who worked closely with Cecil *Rhodes; prime minister of Cape Colony (1904–08). In 1895 he led the **Jameson Raid** into the Transvaal to support British immigrants against the Afrikaners. Imprisoned for three months in England he returned to Cape Colony to become a member of parliament and, on Rhodes' death, leader of the Progressive Party.

James River   A river in the central US, flowing generally ESE through Virginia to *Chesapeake Bay. Jamestown, the first permanent English settlement in America, was established along its lower course in 1607. Length: 340 mi (547 km).

Jamestown   The first permanent English colony in America, established May 14, 1607 on a peninsula in the James River (Virginia) by the London Company. Although many settlers died from disease, lack of food, and Indian attacks in the early years, by 1610, under the leadership of Captain John Smith, the settlement was secure. The marriage of John Rolfe to the daughter of Chief Powhaton, Pocahontas, temporarily improved relations with the Indians. The colonists cultivated tobacco, which became an important crop. The House of Burgesses, the first representative government in the colonies, was established there in 1619. Jamestown was the capital of Virginia until 1699. It is preserved as a colonial historical park.

Jammu and Kashmir A state in N India, forming part of the disputed area of *Kashmir. Area: 38,820 sq mi (100,569 sq km). Population (1981): 5,981,600. Capital: Jammu (winter); Srinagar (summer).

Jamnagar 22 28N 70 06E A city in India, in Gujarat on the Gulf of Kutch. Formerly the capital of the princely state of Nawanagar, it has a fine palace. Industries include textiles and cement. Population (1971): 199,709.

Jamshedpur 22 47N 86 12E A city in India, in Bihar. Founded in 1907 by the industrialist Dorabji Jamsetji Tata, it is the site of India's principal iron and steel works. Population (1971): 356,783.

Janáček, Leoš (1854–1928) Czech composer. He studied at the Leipzig and Vienna conservatoires and became professor of composition at Brno conservatoire in 1919. He was over 60 before he gained wide recognition as a composer. In his vocal works he attempted to reproduce natural speech rhythms; he was also influenced by folk music. His works include the operas *Jenufa* (1894–1903), *The Excursions of Mr Broucek* (1908–17), and *The Makropulos Case* (1923–25), two string quartets, piano music, songs, vocal works, and the *Glagolithic Mass* (1926).

Janissaries The elite troops of the Ottoman sultans. First raised by Sultan Orkhan (1279–1359; reigned 1326–59) about 1330, and organized by his successor Murad I (1319–89; reigned 1359–89) as a professional army, the Janissaries were carefully selected from the Ottoman subject peoples, especially from Christian families. Highly trained, powerful, and close to palace politics, during the 17th and 18th centuries they engineered palace coups, murdering two sultans, and forcing others to abdicate. After their insurrection in 1826 *Mahmud II killed the entire corps.

Jan Mayen 70 10N 9 00W A volcanic island in the Arctic Ocean. It was annexed to Norway in 1929 and has a meteorological station and a NATO radio and navigation station. Area: 144 sq mi (373 sq km).

Jansen, Cornelius Otto (1585–1638) Dutch Roman Catholic theologian and founder of *Jansenism. The director of episcopal colleges in Bayonne (1612–14) and Louvain (1617–30), he became dean of the University of Louvain in 1635 and Bishop of Ypres in 1636. His major work, *The Augustinus* (1640), is the basis of Jansenist doctrine and was condemned as heretical by Pope Innocent X in 1653.

Jansenism A movement in the Roman Catholic Church in the 17th and 18th centuries based on the teaching of Cornelius *Jansen. Stressing the more rigorously predestinarian aspects of St *Augustine's teaching, it brought the Jansenists into conflict with the Jesuits and was condemned by the Church as constituting a threat to traditional sacramentalism. Among other points, Jansenists argued that the efficacy of the sacraments depended on the moral character of the recipient. Jansenism was condemned in 1653 by Pope Innocent X. One of the most famous Jansenists was *Pascal. *See also* Port Royal.

Jansky, Karl Guthe (1905–50) US radio engineer, who discovered a source of radio waves outside the solar system (1932), while investigating static interference. Jansky's discovery led to the new science of *radio astronomy.

Januarius, St (Italian name: San Gennaro; d. ?305) Italian churchman; Bishop and patron saint of Naples. He was probably martyred during the persecution of *Diocletian. The phial of solidified blood in the cathedral in Naples, which is believed to liquefy miraculously several times each year, is revered as one of his relics. Feast day: Sept 19.

January First month of the year. It is named for the Roman god Janus, whose name means "door", and indicates beginning. It has 31 days. New Year's Day (Jan. 1) is a major holiday. The zodiac signs for January are Capricorn and Aquarius, the flowers are the carnation and the snowdrop, and the birthstone is the garnet.

January Insurrection. *See* Congress Kingdom of Poland.

Janus The Roman god of doors, thresholds, and beginnings, after whom the month January is named. He is usually portrayed as having two heads facing forward and backward. His blessing was invoked for the sowing of crops and the beginning of any other major activity.

Japan (Japanese name: Nippon *or* Nihon) A country in E Asia, consisting of a series of islands lying between the Pacific Ocean and the Sea of Japan. The four main islands are *Honshu, *Kyushu, *Hokkaido, and *Shikoku. They have long indented coastlines and much of the land is mountainous, with the highest mountain, *Fujiyama, rising to 12,399 ft (3778 m). The country has long been subject to earthquakes. The population is of mixed Malay, Manchu, and Korean descent; the original inhabitants, the *Ainu, survive in small numbers on Hokkaido. *Economy*: during the past two decades Japan has developed into a highly industrialized country, manufacturing electrical goods, motor vehicles, and petrochemicals; it now produces about half the world's ships. The electronics, paper, and textile industries are also important. Mineral resources, which include limestone, copper, chromite, and coal, are on the whole sparse and Japan relies heavily on imports. There is some oil and natural gas; hydroelectricity is an important source of power. Agriculture is intensive and, although rice is still the main crop, there have been efforts to diversify with such crops as wheat, barley, and soybeans. Vast forests cover over half the land and there is considerable timber production. Although fishing is proportionately less important than before World War II, Japan is still one of the world's leading fishing nations and in 1977 fishing limits were extended to 200 miles. The large volume of exports includes machinery, motor vehicles, metals, textiles, and chemicals. *History*: about 200 BC the country was united under the *Yamato dynasty, already rulers of one of its component kingdoms for about 500 years. Their religion formed the basis of *Shinto, the native religion of Japan, and until 1946 Japanese emperors were regarded as divine descendants of the sun goddess. From 1186 AD real power was in the hands of the military *shoguns until Emperor *Mutsuhito regained power for the House of Yamato in 1867. 1871 saw the end of Hoken Seido (the feudal system) and from the mid-19th century the country was once again opened up to western communications and ideas, from which it had been virtually isolated for 200 years. It expanded colonially, especially in successful wars against China and Russia, and it occupied several Asian countries. It fought against the Allies in World War II and surrendered after the dropping of atomic bombs on Hiroshima and Nagasaki in 1945. Until the peace treaty of 1951 it was under US occupation. In 1956 Japan joined the UN and in 1972 regained the Ryukyu Islands. By a new constitution of 1947 the emperor renounced his former claim to divinity and became a constitutional monarch. The Liberal Democratic Party has been in power since 1955. Relations with the US, Japan's principal trading partner, are clouded by a huge trade surplus in Japan's favor. US exporters claim that the Japanese create obstacles to the entry of American goods into Japan while Japanese goods, often enjoying price advantages made possibly by government policy, have unobstructed access to the US market. The US continues to provide the chief military defense of the Japanese islands. Head of state: Emperor Hirohito. Prime minister: Yashuhiro Nakasone (1917–). Official language: Japanese. Official currency: yen of 100 sen and 1000 rin. Area: 143,777 sq mi (372,483 sq km). Population (1983): 119,205,000. Capital: Tokyo. Main port: Yokohama.

Japan, Sea of A section of the NW Pacific Ocean between Japan and the Asian mainland.

Japanese The language of the Mongoloid people of Japan. Its relationship to other languages is uncertain but it is probably related to *Korean. It is polysyllabic and tonal. There are many very different regional dialects; the standard and official form is based on the speech of Tokyo. Japanese writing systems are extraordinarily complex. The basic kana system has about 1850 characters derived (c. 2nd century AD) from *Chinese script but used to indicate both a syllabic value (the *on*) and a conceptual value (the *kun*). This has two forms, each with 50 characters, developed in the 9th to 10th centuries: the formal hiragana style used for literary works and the katakana or cursive style used for practical purposes and for loanwords.

JAPANESE ART *Mount Fuji (background) from* The Village of Sekiya on the Banks of the Sumida *(1835) by Hokusai, color print from wood blocks.*

Japanese art Neolithic Japanese art consisted of crudely executed terracotta figurines and some ceramic ware. The introduction of Buddhism via Korea in the 6th century and the influence of Chinese culture initiated a great period of temple building, sculpture (chiefly of the Buddha), and the development of the art of flower arrangement (see ikebana). In the Kamakura period (12th–14th centuries) the refined *Fujiwara style was replaced in sculpture by a vigorous naturalism. In painting, a uniquely Japanese style developed in continuous narrative paintings on horizontal scrolls and realistic landscapes. Another entirely Japanese art form was the colored woodblock print of the Tokugawa period (1630–1867). These prints, portraying the transient world of theater, teahouse, etc., and produced by such artists as *Hokusai and *Kitagawa Utamaro, enjoyed a popularity in Europe in the late 19th century, being particularly influential among impressionist painters (see ukiyo-e). Examples of Japanese applied arts are the small wood and ivory carvings (called netsuke) and the gold inlaid sword guards (tsuba). Japanese ceramic art is best illustrated by the *cha-no-yu wares.

Japanese cedar A conifer, Cryptomeria japonica, native to China and Japan, where it is an important timber tree reaching a height of 180 ft (55 m); elsewhere it is grown for ornament and rarely exceeds 115 ft (35 m). Japanese cedar has narrow curved leaves that point toward the tips of the branches and globular spiny cones, 0.8 in (2 cm) across, ripening from green to brown. Family: Taxodiaceae.

Japanese literature Before the mid-8th century AD Chinese was the more prestigious language in Japan and in the 8th century Chinese characters were adapted to render spoken Japanese (see Japanese). Vernacular Japanese folksongs, however, gave rise to a type of lyric poem, the waka, which remained a standard poetic form for over a millennium. This native form appears in the earliest Japanese anthology, the Manyoshu (compiled after 759), which contains about 4500 poems. The emperors of the Heian period (794–1185) encouraged literature, and further anthologies were published, as well as prose tales (monogatari) and fictionalized diaries (nikki). Fiction writing was particularly the province of women; its most famous practitioner was *Murasaki Shikibu, the author of the Genji Monogatari (Tale of Genji; c. 1015). Unsettled conditions in the following 500 years led to a decline in this essentially aristocratic literary output. The last official anthology appeared in 1439. The *no drama, mainly Buddhist in inspiration, however, flowered during the late 14th and early 15th centuries, and the haiku (an epigram comprising 17 syllables) was a product of the early 16th century.

In the Tokugawa period (1603–1867) literature of all kinds enjoyed a renaissance under the patronage of the leisured warrior class and the new mercantile middle class. The haiku reached its peak in the hands of *Matsuo Basho. Fiction encompassed many forms and moods, and nationalistic pride led to official encouragement for writers of philosophy, history, and other learned works. The joruri (puppet theater) at first prospered with playwrights of the caliber of Monzemon writing for it but during the late 18th century it declined in competition with the popular kabuki theater.

After 1868 European influence manifested itself in every branch of literature, mainly with adverse effects as writers strove to imitate western models. In the years after World War II, however, several novelists and poets have established international reputations, including *Kawabata Yasunari and Yukio *Mishima.

Japanese maple A *maple tree, Acer palmatum, up to 43 ft (13 m) tall, the 5–11 lobed leaves of which turn scarlet in autumn. Native to Japan, it is a popular ornamental in many cultivated varieties, including purple-leaved and dwarf types. They require shelter in cooler climates.

japonica A shrub or tree of the genus Chaenomeles (or Cydonia), native to Japan but widely cultivated as an ornamental. Flowering quince (C. japonica) and Japanese quince (C. speciosa) are the most popular species. These have toothed oval glossy leaves and clusters of flame-pink or scarlet five-petaled flowers, 2 in (5 cm) across. The hard greenish-yellow apple-like fruit has a spicy scent and is used in marmalade and jelly. Family: Rosaceae.

Japurá River A river in NW South America, rising as the Río Caquetá in SW Colombia and flowing generally SE to join the Amazon River near Tefé in Brazil. Length: 1750 mi (2800 km).

Jaques-Dalcroze, Émile (1865–1950) Swiss composer and educator. While professor of harmony at the Geneva conservatoire he developed a system of coordinating musical rhythms and bodily movement, which he called *eurhythmics. He founded a number of schools throughout Europe to teach his methods.

jarrah A shrub or tree, *Eucalyptus marginata, of W Australia, that has extremely durable weather-resistant timber, known as West Australian mahogany. It can grow to a height of 52 ft (16 m) and is found in dry areas. Family: Myrtaceae.

Jarry, Alfred (1873–1907) French dramatist. His play, Ubu Roi (1896), is an outrageous satire on bourgeois conventions of respectability. He wrote several sequels and also novels and poems and is regarded as a precursor of *surrealism and the *Theater of the Absurd.

jasmine A shrub of the genus Jasminum (about 300 species), native to tropical and subtropical regions and widely cultivated. Many species are fragrant and yield an essential oil used in perfumery. Two species suitable for temperate gardens are the common jasmine (J. officinalis) from S Asia, which has fragrant white flowers and grows to a height of 20 ft (6 m), and the Chinese winter jasmine (J. nudiflorum), 10–20 ft (3–6 m) tall, the yellow flowers of which open in winter before the leaves. (Winter jasmine can be distinguished from *Forsythia by its green stems.) Family: Oleaceae.

Jason A legendary Greek hero, heir to the throne of Iolcos in Thessaly. Sent by his uncle, the usurper Pelias, to fetch the *Golden Fleece, he and the *Argonauts underwent many adventures before finally recovering the Fleece from Colchis with the help of *Medea. After many years of wandering he died at Corinth.

jasper An impure variety of *chalcedony, usually red or reddish brown. It is slightly translucent and is regarded as a semiprecious stone. It is an abundant mineral, occurring mainly in veins and in cavities in volcanic rocks.

Jasper National Park A national park in Canada, in W Alberta, N of Banff National Park and part of the Rocky Mountains. Established in 1907, it is well known as a recreation center. The park's attractions are numerous: glaciers, mountains, hot springs, lakes, rivers, valleys, canyons, and wildlife. The highest point is Mt Columbia (12,294 ft; 3,748 m). Area: 4,200 sq mi (10,878 sq km).

Jaspers, Karl (Theodor) (1883–1969) German philosopher, a forerunner of *existentialism. Interested in the relation between science and philosophy, he studied medicine and psychology and believed philosophers were better for an acquaintance with the scientific method. His philosophy, expounded in Philosophie (1932), is about the possibilities and quality of human choice. He thought *Kierkegaard and *Nietzsche were exceptional in exhibiting the variety of possibilities open to man.

Jassy. See Iaşi.

Jatakas In the Pali Buddhist canon, a collection of 550 moral tales describing previous existences of the Buddha before his enlightenment. Each story is related to an event in the Buddha's present life. The collection is also a valuable source of folklore.

jaundice Yellowing of the skin and whites of the eyes due to the presence of *bile pigments. Bile pigments are normally produced by the liver from the breakdown of red blood cells and then excreted in bile into the gut. Jaundice may result if there is excessive breakdown of red blood cells, as in hemolytic anemia, or in disease of the liver, such as *hepatitis, or blockage of the bile duct by *gallstones.

Jaurès, Jean (1859–1914) French socialist leader and journalist; a proponent of the international unity of the working class. He was a vehement supporter of Dreyfus and advocated the separation of church and state. In 1905 he was instrumental in founding the French socialist party (the Section française de l'internationale Ouvrière). He helped found L'Humanité in 1904 and was its editor until 1914, when he was assassinated.

Java An Indonesian island, the smallest of the Greater *Sunda Islands. Its chain of volcanic mountains has formed exceptionally fertile soil, and its many rivers feed its intensive wet-rice agriculture. Other food crops, sugar cane, and kapok are grown and forest products include teak. Indonesia's administrative and industrial center, Java has its three largest cities and is heavily overpopulated. The textile industry is of particular importance, especially synthetic textiles, although the village batik industry has declined. Java is subsidized by other islands, which has provoked much unrest. History: Indian colonies in the early centuries AD developed into Hindu and Buddhist kingdoms, with Hindu-Javanese culture reaching its height in the 14th century. Later Islamic control barely influenced the culture. The Dutch East India Company was centered here from 1619. During the anticommunist purges (1965–67) between 500,000 and 1,000,000 people were killed. Area: 51,032 sq mi (132,174 sq km). Population (1971): 76,102,486, with Madura. Capital: Jakarta.

javelin throw A field event in athletics in which a spearlike javelin is thrown as far as possible. The men's javelin is 8.5–8.9 ft (2.6–2.7 m) long and weighs 1.8 lb (800 g). The women's measures 7.2–7.5 ft (2.2–2.3 m) and weighs a minimum of 1.3 lb (600 g). It is thrown with one hand, over the shoulder, after an approach of approximately 120 ft (36 m), and the metal head must hit the ground first. Each competitor has six attempts.

jaw One of the two bones of the face that form a framework for the mouth and provide attachment for the teeth. The lower jaw (*or* mandible) is a horseshoe-shaped bone with a vertical process at each end that forms a joint with the temporal bone of the skull, just in front of each ear. The upper jaw consists of bones (maxillae) that are closely connected to each other and to the other facial bones. Each contains an air *sinus.

Jawara, Sir Dawda (1924–) Gambian statesman; president (1970–). A Muslim, he became minister of education in 1960 and prime minister in 1962, in which post he led his country to independence in 1965. When The Gambia became a republic in 1970 Jawara became president.

Jawlensky, Alexey von (1864–1941) Russian expressionist painter, who spent most of his life in Germany (*see* expressionism). His chief influences were *Kandinsky, with whom he was associated in several artistic groups, notably *Neue Kunstlervereinigung, and *Matisse. Typical of his vibrantly colored and heavily outlined style is his series of heads resembling icons.

jay A crow, *Garrulus glandarius*, of Eurasia and N Africa. It is about 13 in (34 cm) long and brownish pink, with a black tail, white rump, black-barred blue wing patches, and a black-and-white erectile crest. Jays are found mainly in woodland, feeding on insects and larvae in summer and storing acorns and other seeds for winter food. The N American **blue jay** (*Cyanocitta cristata*) lives E of the Rocky Mountains. About 12 in (30 cm) long, it is bright blue above with a white breast, black face markings, and an erectile crest. It also stores acorns and other seeds.

Jay, John (1745–1829) US political leader, diplomat, and jurist. Entering public life as secretary to the N.Y.–N.J. Boundary Commission (1773), Jay emerged as an early advocate of American independence and served in the First and Second *Continental Congresses (1775–76). In 1779, after having helped to draft the N.Y. state constitution, he was sent to Spain as US minister plenipotentiary and later joined Benjamin *Franklin and John *Adams in Paris in the peace negotiations with Great Britain (1782) to end the Revolutionary War. Jay returned to the US and was named secretary of foreign affairs by the Congress (1784), but the restrictions on his policy-making power imposed by the *Articles of Confederation led him to support the formulation of a stronger federal government. Collaborating with Alexander *Hamilton and James *Madison, he published the *Federalist Papers (1787–88), which helped to sway public opinion in favor of the ratification of the US *Constitution. In 1789, President George *Washington appointed Jay to become the first chief justice of the US Supreme Court. While still serving as chief justice, Jay was sent to London to resolve lingering disagreements between the US and Great Britain. The result of his efforts, the **Jay Treaty** (1794), averted war between the two countries, but was seen by many in the US as a surrender to British demands. Jay resigned from the Supreme Court in 1795 to become governor of New York, an office that he held until 1801.

Jaya, Mount (*or* Mount Sukarno) 4 05S 137 09E The highest mountain in Indonesia, in West Irian in the Sudirman range. Height: 16,503 ft (5029 m).

Jayawardene, J(unius) R(ichard) (1906–) Sri Lankan statesman; prime minister (1977–78) and then president (1978–). He became a significant politician in the years before Ceylon (Sri Lanka from 1972) obtained independence in 1948 and as a member of the United National Party, which he led from 1970, held various posts before becoming prime minister.

jazz A form of popular music that originated in New Orleans around 1900, characterized by improvisation and syncopated rhythms. The musical influences responsible for its creation included French and Spanish popular music, ragtime, blues, brass-band music, and African slave songs. It first became popular in the Storyville district of New Orleans and as an accompaniment to funerals, weddings, and country outings. Early jazz bands featured improvised solos on such instruments as the cornet, clarinet, and trombone. Louis Armstrong and Jelly Roll Morton are associated with New Orleans jazz (*see* New Orleans style). In the 1920s jazz spread to larger cities, such as New York and Chicago; the original band was enlarged with saxophones and additional cornets and trumpets. Large dance bands emerged in the era of *swing (the 1930s), in which the bandleaders Paul Whiteman (1891–1967), Benny Goodman, Glenn Miller, and Count Basie were especially important. In the 1940s Dizzy Gillespie and Charlie "Bird" Parker revolted against swing with *bop, using a smaller band and introducing harmonic and rhythmic innovations. *Cool jazz of the late 1940s and 1950s adopted a relaxed behind-the-beat approach as in the playing of Miles Davis and Stan Getz (1927–). In the 1960s and 1970s such musicians as Gunther Schuller (1925–) and John Lewis (1920–) integrated jazz idioms with classical forms and techniques to form *third stream. Ornette Coleman (1930–) and John Coltrane (1926–) ex-

panded the boundaries of jazz to include atonality in a style called *free-form jazz.

Jean de Meun (c. 1240–c. 1305) French poet. His conclusion (18,000 lines) of the verse allegory *Roman de la rose*, contrasting in both style and content with the earlier part written by *Guillaume de Lorris, is valued chiefly for its lengthy and informative digressions on topics of contemporary interest.

Jean Paul (Johann Paul Friedrich Richter; 1763–1825) German Romantic novelist. His novels, such as *Hesperus* (1795) and *Das Leben des Quintus Fixlein* (1796), combine fantasy with humor and psychological realism and later influenced *Keller and *Mörike.

Jeans, Sir James Hopwood (1877–1946) British mathematician and astronomer. His early work was on the kinetic theory of gases and on the quantum theory. Later he concentrated on cosmogony, putting forward a now discredited theory of planetary formation. After 1928 he devoted himself to writing books popularizing science: *The Universe around Us* (1930), *Science and Music* (1937), and *The Growth of Physical Science* (1947) are examples.

Jedda. *See* Jiddah.

Jeffers, Robinson (1887–1962) US poet. From 1916 he lived in isolation near Carmel on the coast of California. *Tamar and Other Poems* (1924) and other volumes of long narrative poems and short lyrics express a bleak view of mankind. He also wrote plays, notably an adaptation of Euripides' *Medea* (1946).

THOMAS JEFFERSON

Jefferson, Thomas (1743–1826) US statesman; 3rd president of the United States (1801–09). Educated as a lawyer, Jefferson began his political career in the Virginia House of Burgesses (1769–75). As one of the most eloquent supporters of the cause of American independence, he wrote an influential pamphlet, *A Summary of the Rights of British America* (1774), which earned him a national reputation and gained him election to the Second *Continental Congress in 1775. In the following year, Jefferson was the principal author of the *Declaration of Independence. During the *Revolutionary War, Jefferson served in the Virginia legislature and as governor (1779–81). He returned to the US Congress in 1783 and was appointed US minister to France in 1784. With the ratification of the US *Constitution and the election of George *Washington, Jefferson became the first US secretary of state (1789–93).

Jefferson, however, opposed the aristocratic policies of the *Federalists and as the leader of the Jeffersonian-Republicans (later to become the *Democratic Party) he resigned from the Washington cabinet in 1793. He later served as vice president under John *Adams (1796–1801) and was elected to the presidency himself in 1800. During Jefferson's two terms in office, he oversaw the war with the *Barbary pirates (1801–05), approved the *Louisiana Purchase (1803), dispatched the *Lewis and Clark Expedition to explore that territory (1804), and encouraged US neutrality in the Napoleonic Wars through the *Embargo Act of 1807. After leaving public office, Jefferson retired to his Virginia estate, Monticello, and was one of the founders of the University of Virginia in 1819.

Jefferson City 38 33N 92 10W The capital city of Missouri, on the Missouri River. Primarily an administrative center, it is the site of Lincoln University (1866). Population (1980): 33,619.

Jeffries, John. *See* Blanchard, Jean Pierre François.

Jehol. *See* Chengde.

Jehovah. *See* Yahweh.

Jehovah's Witnesses A religious movement founded in 1872 by Charles Taze Russell (1852–1916) in Philadelphia. They were first known as the International Bible Students and from 1884 as the Watch Tower Bible and Tract Society. Although based on Scriptural teaching, the movement's beliefs reject Christ's divinity, regarding him as God's prophet. They expect the end of the world in the near future, although the mooted date of 1975 proved incorrect. They originally believed that only the 144,000 elect would be saved but, since the movement increased in numbers, this limitation has been modified. They accept Jehovah as their sole authority and they refuse military service as they will not kill their fellow humans.

Jellicoe, John Rushworth, 1st Earl (1859–1935) British admiral; commander of the grand fleet (1914–16) in World War I. He was criticized for his command at the battle of *Jutland, in which the German fleet escaped relatively unscathed.

jellyfish A free-swimming aquatic invertebrate animal belonging to a class (*Scyphozoa*; about 200 species) of *coelenterates. The translucent gelatinous body, 0.05–79 in (1.5–2000 mm) in diameter, is bell- or umbrella-shaped, with a central tubular projection that hangs down and bears the mouth. Jellyfish occur in all oceans, especially in tropical regions, and usually propel themselves through the water by contracting muscles around the edge of the bell. Stinging tentacles are used to capture and paralyze prey, ranging from plankton to small fish, and can seriously affect man.

The term jellyfish is also used for the free-swimming sexual form of any other coelenterate (*see* medusa).

Jena 51 00N 11 30E A city in S East Germany, on the Saale River. Its university (1558) became famous in the 18th century when Fichte, Hegel, Schelling, Schiller, and August Schlegel taught there. As well as the Zeiss optical works (*see* Jena glass), founded in 1846, Jena has chemical and engineering industries. Population (1980): 103,263.

Jena and Auerstädt, Battles of (October 14, 1806) Simultaneous battles in which Napoleon defeated the Prussians. Following Prussia's challenge to Napoleon after his defeat of Austria at *Austerlitz, Auerstädt and Jena broke Prussia as a military power and left Russia to face Napoleon alone. Prussia remained in the orbit of the French Empire until 1813, when it rejoined the alliance against Napoleon.

Jenkins' Ear, War of (1739–48) A war that arose out of Britain's illicit trade in Spanish America and merged into the War of the *Spanish Succession (1740–48). It followed the accusation of Captain Robert Jenkins that his ear had been cut off by Spanish coastguards in the West Indies.

Jenner, Edward (1749–1823) British physician, who developed the first effective vaccine—against smallpox. Jenner noticed that people who caught the mild disease cowpox never contracted smallpox. In 1796 he inoculated a small boy with cowpox and, two months later, with smallpox. The boy did not get smallpox. Jenner published his findings in 1798 and the process of vaccination—a word that Jenner coined—became a widespread protective measure against smallpox.

Jensen, Johannes (Vilhelm) (1873–1950) Danish novelist and poet, many of whose works were inspired by his travels in the US and the Far East. His most important work was the novel sequence *Den lange Rejse* (*The Long Journey*; 1908–22), a Darwinian account of the origin and early history of mankind.

Jenson, Nicolas (c. 1420–80) French printer, who produced the first distinctive roman typeface, which replaced Gothic (*or* black letter) type. After studying printing under Johann Gutenberg, Jenson opened a printing shop in Venice in 1470.

jerboa A small hopping *rodent belonging to the family *Dipodidae* (25 species) of Asian and N African deserts, also called desert rat. Jerboas are 1.6–6 in (4–15 cm) long and have kangaroo-like hind feet, a long balancing tail, large eyes and ears, and soft sandy-colored fur. They spend the day in tightly closed burrows and emerge at night to feed on seeds and tubers.

Jeremiah (7th century BC) An Old Testament prophet. He is believed to have been born about 650 BC in a village near Jerusalem. The **Book of Jeremiah** contains his prophecies relating to the fall of Judah, its conquest by the Babylonian King Nebuchadnezzar, and the *Babylonian exile of the Jews. A Messiah is prophesied, who will be a descendant of David and who will rule over Jews and Gentiles.

Jerez de la Frontera 36 41N 6 08W A city in SW Spain, in Andalusia. It is renowned for its wine industry and gave its name to sherry. It is also famous for its horses. Population (1970): 149,867.

Jericho 31 52N 35 27E A village in the Jordan Valley (Israel), N of the Dead Sea, now in the Israeli-occupied West Bank area. The nearby site of the old city was excavated by Kathleen *Kenyon, revealing one of the earliest known towns (before 8000 BC), with massive stone fortifications surrounding circular brick-built houses. Later Neolithic burials yielded skulls with features modeled in plaster and shells inset for eyes. Of the biblical Bronze Age city attacked by *Joshua (Joshua 6) nothing remains. The extensive ruins of the magnificent palace, Khirbat al-Mafjar, built (739–44 AD) by the Umayyad caliph Hisham (d. 743) can still be seen.

Jerome, St (c. 342–420 AD) Italian biblical scholar; Doctor of the Church and author of the *Vulgate Bible, the first Latin translation of the Bible from the Hebrew. After a period as a hermit, he was ordained by St *Paulinus of Nola in Antioch. A secretary to Pope Damasus I (reigned 366–94) from 382 until 385, he later settled in Bethlehem, where he established a monastery. He also wrote biblical commentaries and theological works, which are famous for their prose style. Feast day: Sept 30.

Jersey 49 13N 2 07W The largest of the Channel Islands, in the English Channel. Colonized from Normandy in the 11th century, French influence remains strong and French is the official language. It consists chiefly of a plateau incised by deep valleys. Agriculture, particularly dairy farming, is important and the famous Jersey cattle are bred for export. Tourism is also a major source of income. In 1959 the Jersey Zoological Park was founded by Gerald Durrell to protect rare species of wildlife. Area: 45 sq mi (116 sq km). Population (1981): 77,000. Capital: St Helier.

Jersey cattle A breed of dairy cattle originating from the English island of Jersey. Relatively small and fine-boned, Jerseys are golden-brown to black in color, adaptable, and mature rapidly. They produce high-quality creamy milk.

Jersey City 40 44N 74 04W A city in N New Jersey. Founded in 1629, it is connected to nearby New York City by the Hudson River tunnels. Its 12 mi (20 km) of waterfront forms part of the port of New York. A major industrial and commercial center with oil refineries, its products include paper and cigarettes. Population (1980): 223,532.

Jerusalem (Arabic name: El Quds) 31 47N 35 13E The capital of Israel, in the Judea Heights between the Mediterranean and the Dead Seas. Jerusalem is a religious center for three major world religions: Christianity, Judaism, and Islam. Most employment is found in government and the city's main industry, tourism. The Hebrew University of Jerusalem was founded in 1918. The modern city spreads out extensively on the W side of the Old City, which is walled (1537–40) and contains most of the religious shrines, including the Western (Wailing) Wall (Jewish), the Dome of the Rock (begun 661 AD; Islamic), and the Church of the Holy Sepulcher, which was founded in about 335 on the traditional site of Christ's burial and resurrection, although most of the present structure is 19th-century. *History*: Jerusalem was occupied by Alexander the Great (4th century BC) and the Romans (63 BC), under whose fifth procurator, Pontius Pilate, Jesus Christ was put to death in the city. Occupation by the Turks was succeeded by the establishment of the Kingdom of Jerusalem, a feudal state created in 1099 following the conquest of the city by the Crusaders under *Godfrey of Bouillon. It was enlarged in the early 12th century by *Baldwin I and his successors, but their authority was gradually undermined by the religious orders of knighthood, such as the *Hospitallers and the *Templars, and the Kingdom ended when Jerusalem fell to Saladin in 1187. The Turks took the city again in 1517 and held it until 1917, when it was taken by the British, who held it under mandatory rule until 1948. Jerusalem was then divided between the new Zionist state of Israel, of which it became the capital (1950), and Jordan. Israel occupied the whole city in June, 1967, and the status of Jerusalem, of supreme religious and symbolic importance to both Jew and Arab, is the greatest obstacle to settling the *West Bank question. Population (1979 est): 398,200.

JERUSALEM *At the ancient Wailing Wall, men and women each have their own areas of worship.*

Jerusalem artichoke A North American perennial herb, *Helianthus tuberosus*, that grows to a height of 7 ft (2 m), and has edible sweet-tasting knobbly tubers up to 4 in (10 cm) long. They bloom only in hot summers, producing yellow flowers like those of the *sunflower. Family: *Compositae*.

Jerusalem cherry A small shrub, *Solanum pseudocapsicum*, probably of Old World origin, growing to a height of 5 ft (1.3 m) and bearing cherry-sized red or yellow highly poisonous fruits. The false Jerusalem cherry (*S. capsicastrum*) of Brazil is similar. Both are grown as ornamentals. Family: *Solanaceae*.

Jespersen, Otto (1860–1943) Danish linguist. His principal works are *Growth and Structure of the English Language* (1905), *A Modern English Grammar on Historical Principles* (1909–31), *The Philosophy of Grammar* (1924), and *Analytic Syntax* (1937). His approach to language is traditional and historical; his writing is noted for its lucidity.

Jesselton. *See* Kota Kinabalu.

Jesuits Members of the Society of Jesus, an order founded by St *Ignatius Loyola in 1533 to propagate the Roman Catholic faith. The order was organized along military lines; in addition to the traditional vows of chastity, poverty, and obedience, Jesuits were sworn to go wherever the pope might send them. They quickly established themselves as educators and missionaries, becoming one of the dominant forces of the *Counter-Reformation; their argumentative subtlety was proverbial. They also played a prominent role in missions to the New World and the East. Their power and rigorous organization eventually brought them into conflict with civil authorities throughout Europe, and they were expelled from several states. In 1773 Pope Clement XIV suppressed the order, and it was not reinstated until 1814. Today Jesuits are active in most countries and are noted for their schools and universities, including the Gregorian University in Rome; they continue to play a leading role in intellectual life and missions.

Jesus (c. 6 BC–c. 30 AD) The founder of *Christianity; called by his followers the Messiah or Christ (Greek *khristos*, anointed one). Most of the information concerning Jesus comes from the New Testament *Gospels of Matthew, Mark, and Luke. This material was arranged in order to proclaim and interpret his life and teachings to early Christians and therefore does not provide neutral biographical detail, although it is based on historical facts. According to these sources, Jesus was born at Bethlehem in the last years of the reign of *Herod the Great; he was the son of the Virgin *Mary, of Nazareth in Galilee, who belonged to the tribe of Judah and the family of David. Mary's husband, Joseph, was a carpenter, and Jesus was apparently trained as a carpenter in Nazareth. About 27 AD, *John the Baptist, who was related to Jesus, began to preach that the Kingdom of God (a divine last judgment) was approaching and to urge repentance and baptism as a preparation for it. Jesus was baptized by John and shortly (after John had been imprisoned by Herod Antipas) began his public ministry, traveling in Galilee and in the area NW of Lake Gennesaret. He taught in synagogues and in the open, not using sacred texts but adopting a popular style by preaching in parables and proverbial expressions. His teaching, which is summarized in the Sermon on the Mount (Matthew 5–7), emphasized the approaching kingdom of God, the need for repentance, and the importance of such virtues as charity, faith, and humility instead of the ceremonial observance of the Law. Miracles were attributed to him, including healing, driving out demons, and miraculously feeding a multitude of 5000. The beginnings of a movement are evident in Galilee when Jesus summoned the disciples, traditionally 12 in number, instructing them to leave their families and their work in order to preach the imminence of the Kingdom of God. The Gospels devote most attention to the last week of Jesus' life. He went with the disciples to Jerusalem for Passover, apparently aware of the serious opposition that awaited him. There he was acknowledged as the Messiah by many people, but, after betrayal by Judas, was arrested and condemned to death by the chief Jewish tribunal, the Sanhedrin, for the blasphemous claim to Messiahship. The Gospels tend to exonerate Pontius *Pilate in the proceedings against Jesus, but he was executed according to Roman law as a criminal (*see* crucifixion). In the New Testament his death is presented as the fulfillment of a divine purpose that was made clear to the disciples only at the resurrection (on the next day but one after the crucifixion) and by a number of appearances to individuals and groups of disciples. His ascension into heaven is mentioned in the Gospels and in Acts (1.3), where it is said to have occurred 40 days after the resurrection.

jet engine A form of *gas turbine (*see also* internal-combustion engine) in which part of the energy released by burning the fuel is used to drive a turbine, which in turn drives a compressor to increase the pressure of the air required for combustion, and part is used as a high-velocity jet to provide thrust to drive an aircraft. It was first developed in the 1930s. Except for light aircraft, all military and commercial aircraft are now powered by jet engines. Thrust in these engines is equal to the mass of the gas produced multiplied by its acceleration and is due to the forward reaction of the gas jet on the engine itself rather than on the air through which it is flying. It is therefore more efficient at higher altitudes, where the atmosphere is thinner and drag is less.

Early postwar commercial aircraft used a turboprop engine, in which a propeller is driven by the turbine shaft—strictly, therefore, these are not jet engines. For greater speed and economy the turboprop has now been replaced by the turbojet (with reheat) or the turbofan. At over twice the speed of sound (Mach 2), the forward pressure of the air is sufficient for the compressor, and therefore the turbine, to be dispensed with. The resulting engine is called a ramjet. The main drawback of the ramjet is that it needs a rocket-assisted take-off to attain a speed of Mach 2 before it starts to operate. Turboshaft engines, similar to the turboprop, are also in use for driving helicopters, hovercraft, ships, trains, turbogenerators in power stations, and (experimentally) automobiles. In these the turbine shaft is used to provide all the working power. *See also* rockets.

Jewish autonomous region (*or* Birobidzhan) An autonomous region (*oblast*) in the E Soviet Union, in the RSFSR. Formed in 1934 for Soviet Jews, the harsh climate discouraged settlers, and Russians and Ukrainians outnumber Jews, although there is a Yiddish theater, newspaper, and broadcasting service. Industries include metallurgy, timber, and engineering. Area: 13,895 sq mi (36,000 sq km). Population (1980 est): 193,400. Capital: Birobidzhan.

Jews A predominantly Semitic people, claiming descent from the ancient Israelites. The Jews spread or were dispersed in antiquity from the land of Israel, and there are now communities in most countries (*see* Ashkenazim; diaspora; Sephardim). Although they do not share distinctive racial characteristics, they have a strong sense of cultural identity (*see* Bene Israel; Falashas). Their religion is *Judaism (but in recent times some Jews have professed an attachment to the people while rejecting the religion). Under Persian, Greek, and Roman rule the Jews gradually evolved a system of internal self-government and communal administration that enabled them to survive as minority communities through many centuries of Christian and Muslim domination, despite adverse discrimination and frequent persecution (*see* antisemitism). Since the late 18th century they have gradually achieved equal rights as citizens in most countries, although the Nazi slaughter of six million Jews in Europe (*see* holocaust) is one of the ugliest episodes in human history. It did, however, provide the Zionist claim for a national home for the Jews with unanswerable force (*see* Israel; Zionism).

Jew's harp A musical instrument consisting of a metal tongue set in a small frame, held between the teeth. The tongue vibrates when stroked by the finger; the mouth cavity acts as a resonator, different notes being produced by varying its size.

Jezreel, Valley of. *See* Esdraelon, Plain of.

Jhansi 25 27N 78 34E A city in India, in Uttar Pradesh. The heroism of the Rani (female ruler) of Jhansi during the Indian Mutiny has become legendary in modern Indian history. Primarily an agricultural trading center, Jhansi also has a steel-rolling mill. Population (1971): 173,292.

Jhelum 32 58N 73 45E A city in Pakistan, on the Jhelum River. It has a thriving timber industry and there are several oilfields in the surrounding district. Population (1972): 67,900.

Jhelum River A river in India and Pakistan, the most westerly of the five rivers of the Punjab. Rising in Kashmir it flows generally SSW to join the Chenab River. Its lower course is a source of irrigation and hydroelectric power. Length: about 450 mi (720 km).

Jiang Jing Guo *See* Chiang Kai-shek.

Jiang Qing (*or* Chiang Ch'ing; 1912–) Chinese communist politician; the third wife (from 1939) of Mao Tse-tung. A former actress, she attempted with three leftist associates (Zhang Chunjao, Wang Hungwen, and Yao Wenyuan) to seize power on Mao's death. Known as the **Gang of Four**, they were arrested within a month. She remained in prison after a public trial at which she refused to recant.

Jiangsu (Chiang-su *or* Kiangsu) A low-lying province in E China on the Yangtze delta. It is the most densely populated area and one of the richest agricultural regions. It was the center of European trade after 1842 and was badly damaged by Japanese occupation (1937–45). It produces wheat, rice, tea, cotton, salt, fish, and silk. Area: 102,200 sq km (39,860 sq mi). Population (1980 est): 58,930,000. Capital: Nanjing.

Jiangxi (Chiang-hsi *or* Kiangsi) A mountainous province in SE China. It was a center of Confucianism (960–1279), and in the 20th century the Communist-Nationalist conflict originated here (*see* Jiangxi Soviet). One of China's main rice-producing areas, it has mineral resources, including coal and uranium, and is known for its porcelain. Area: 64,300 sq mi (164,800 sq km). Population (1980 est): 32,290,000. Capital: Nanchang.

Jiangxi Soviet (*or* Kiangsi Soviet; 1931–34) A communist republic proclaimed in the Chinese province of Jiangxi. It was a revolutionary base from which Mao Tse-tung and *Zhu De were able to build up their forces in the civil war with the *Guomindang under Chiang Kai-shek. They withstood four encirclement campaigns by the Guomindang but in 1933 Chiang Kai-shek launched a massive fifth campaign in response to which Mao evacuated the base and set off on the *Long March.

Jiddah (*or* Jedda) 21 30N 39 10E A city in Saudi Arabia, on the Red Sea coast. It is a modern industrial city and the chief port for Muslim pilgrims to Mecca. The King Abdulaziz University was opened here in 1967. Population (1974): 561,104.

Jilin (Chi-lin *or* Kirin) A province in NE China, in Manchuria. The E is mountainous, while the W lies on the fertile Manchurian plain. Soybeans, cereals, timber, and minerals are produced. Area: 72,930 sq mi (187,000 sq km). Population (1980 est): 21,850,000. Capital: Changchun.

Jilong (Chi-lung *or* Keelung) 25 10N 121 43E A port and naval base in N Taiwan. It was developed under Japanese occupation (1895–1945). Industries include fishing, chemicals, coal- and gold-mining, and shipbuilding. Population (1970 est): 324,040.

Jim Crow Laws Legislation passed by southern states in the late 19th century to enforce racial segregation; the name derives from that of a black character in a popular song. Under a "separate but equal" doctrine, schools and public facilities were established for each race. Legislation in Oklahoma, for example, provided separate telephone booths for blacks and whites and in Arkansas separate gambling tables were required. Most of the laws were invalidated by the civil-rights legislation of the 1960s.

Jiménez, Juan Ramón (1881–1958) Spanish poet. His early works, such as *Sonetos espirituales* (1915), were influenced by French symbolism but he later developed a pure abstract style in such works as *La estación*

total (1946). He also wrote *Platero y yo* (1914), a portrait of a boy and his donkey.

Jimmu The legendary first ruler of Japan. According to the oldest Japanese writings, Jimmu was descended from the sun-goddess Amaterasu and embarked upon the unification of Japan in 660 BC. This legend was intended to glorify the imperial dynasty and anticipated the dynasty's actual establishment by about seven centuries.

jimsonweed. *See* thorn apple.

Jinan (Chi-nan *or* Tsinan) 36 41N 117 00E A city in E China, the capital of Shandong province. A city since the 8th century BC, it is a cultural center. Industries include textiles, chemicals, and machine building. Population (1957 est): 862,000.

jinja A Shinto shrine dedicated to a deity or nature spirit, situated in a place of exceptional natural beauty. It consists of three parts: the *haiden*, a hall where the laity pray and worship; the *heiden*, where religious ceremonies are performed; and the *honden*, the main inner sanctuary usually accessible only to priests. Before the jinja is a sacred gateway. The architecture is simple and traditional. Larger jinja may incorporate other elements, such as a dance platform, an ablution basin, and animal statues.

Jinja 0 27N 33 14E The second largest city in Uganda, on the N shore of Lake Victoria. Founded by the British (1901), it has developed as an industrial center since the opening of the Owen Falls Dam (1954) with steel rolling, copper smelting, and other industries. Population (1969): 52,509.

Jinjiang (Chen-chiang *or* Chinkiang) 32 15N 119 20E A port in E China, in Jiangsu province at the junction of the Yangtze River and the *Grand Canal. It is a major trading center, its industries including food processing. Population (1953): 201,400.

Jinmen (Chin-men *or* Quemoy) 24 26N 118 20E A Taiwanese island in Taiwan Strait. It is near the Chinese mainland and was bombed from there in 1958, an event that caused an international incident. Area: 50 sq mi (130 sq km). Population (1971): 61,305.

Jinnah, Mohammed Ali (1876–1948) Indian statesman, who was largely responsible for the creation of Pakistan. Born in Karachi, he studied law in England and embarked on an extremely successful legal practice in India before becoming involved in politics. As a member of both the *Muslim League and the *Indian National Congress he championed Hindu-Muslim unity after 1920, when he resigned from the Congress in opposition to Gandhi's policies. He was president of the League in 1916 and 1920 and from 1934, and came to advocate the establishment of a separate state for Indian Muslims. This was achieved with the creation in 1947 of Pakistan, of which he was the first governor general.

Jiulong (*or* Kowloon) 22 20N 114 15E A port in SE China, on the Jiulong peninsula, opposite Hong Kong island and part of the British colony (ceded 1860). Population (1971): 716,272.

Joachim, Joseph (1831–1907) Hungarian violinist and composer. A child prodigy, he studied with Ferdinand David (1810–73) at the Leipzig conservatoire. His interpretations of Bach and Beethoven and his musical perfectionism influenced many composers: Brahms dedicated his violin concerto to him.

Joachim of Fiore (c. 1132–1202 AD) Italian mystic and abbot. He is best known for his philosophy of history, which divided history into three periods: The Age of the Father (Old Testament), The Age of the Son (New Testament and 42 subsequent generations), and The Age of the Spirit, in which all humanity would be converted. Joachim's monastic order, which he founded at San Giovanni in Fiore, was dissolved in 1505.

Joan, Pope A legendary female pope first referred to in the 13th century. She is said to have been elected pope in male disguise about 1100 or earlier, to have ruled for more than two years, and then to have given birth to a child while in a procession, dying immediately thereafter. The legend may be based on a Roman folktale.

Joanna the Mad (1479–1555) Queen of Castile (1504–16). The death of her husband, Philip the Handsome of Castile in 1506, drove her mad. Her father Ferdinand (V and II) of Aragon ruled for her until his death, when he was succeeded by her son, later Emperor *Charles V. He kept Joanna imprisoned in the castle of Tordesillas, where she died.

Joan of Arc, St (French name: Jeanne d'Arc; c. 1412–31) French patriot, known as the Maid of Orléans, whose courageous military and moral leadership against the English invaders led to a reversal of French fortunes in the *Hundred Years' War. Of peasant origin, she claimed to have been told by Saints Michael, Catherine, and Margaret that it was her divine mission to expel the English from France and enable Charles VII to be crowned. She persuaded Charles to allow her to lead an army to relieve the besieged city of Orléans. Her success resulted in Charles' coronation at

Rheims (July, 1429). Other victories followed but she failed to recapture Paris and was subsequently seized by the Burgundians, who sold her to their English allies. They tried her and burned her as a heretic. She was canonized in 1920.

JOAN OF ARC *This portrait of the great French heroine dates to 1584.*

João Pessoa (name until 1930: Paraíba) 7 06S 34 53W A port in E Brazil, the capital of Paraíba state near the mouth of the Rio Paraíba do Norte. The chief exports are cotton, sugar, and coffee. Population (1975 est): 287,607.

Job An Old Testament figure. **The Book of Job**, probably written between the 5th and 2nd centuries BC, develops the theme of the suffering of the innocent. Job experiences the loss of his family, property, and health, but adamantly denies his friends' suggestions that sin is the cause of his misfortunes, for he knows himself to be innocent. No final explanation of the dilemma is reached, but Job is brought to see that man cannot understand the ways of God. Humbled by this knowledge, he prays for his friends and is ultimately granted greater prosperity, etc., than he formerly had.

Jocasta. *See* Oedipus.

Jochho (d. 1057) Leading Japanese sculptor of the Fujiwara period (*see* Fujiwara style). His serene and refined statues of the Buddha for the Fujiwara family temple and his joined-wood technique were influential.

Jodhpur 26 18N 73 08E A city in India, in Rajasthan. Formerly the capital of the princely state of Jodhpur, the city is noted for its handicraft industries, such as ivory carvings and lacquerware. It also gave its name to a style of riding breeches that were introduced into Britain during the 19th century. Jodhpur University was established in 1962. Population (1971): 317,612.

Jodl, Alfred (1890–1946) German general, who was responsible for much of German strategy in World War II. He was executed as a war criminal.

Joel An Old Testament prophet of Judah. **The Book of Judah** records his prediction of a plague of locusts and other disasters as punishment for Judah's sins, followed eventually by a restoration of God's favor and the nation's final triumph over its enemies.

Joffre, Joseph Jacques Césaire (1852–1931) French marshal; commander in chief of the French armies (1915–16) in World War I. As chief of staff he won the victory of the Marne (1914) but the French failure at Verdun (1916) led to his resignation. □Lloyd George, David, 1st Earl.

Jogjakarta (*or* Djokjakarta) 7 48S 110 24E A city in Indonesia, in S Java. It was the capital of the 1945–49 Indonesian Republic. A cultural center, its university was established in 1949. It is rich in Buddhist monuments, notably the temple of Borobudur. Population (1971): 342,267.

Johannesburg 26 10S 28 02E The largest city in South Africa, in the Transvaal on the Witwatersrand. It was founded in 1886 following the discovery of gold in the area and developed rapidly as the center of the gold-mining industry. During the second Boer War it was taken by the British (1900). Today it is a major industrial, commercial, and banking center containing the South African Stock Exchange (1887). Its industries include engineering, chemicals, diamond cutting, and textiles. Linked to the city is the complex of towns known as *Soweto, inhabited by Black Africans. Johannesburg has a number of cultural and educational institutions, notably the University of Witwatersrand (1922) and the Rand Afrikaans University (1966). The fine Johannesburg Art Gallery (1911) was designed by Sir Edwin Lutyens. Population (1980 est): 1,536,457.

Johannsen, Wilhelm Ludvig (1857–1927) Danish geneticist, whose work with plants demonstrated that the physical appearance (phenotype) of individuals was the result of the interaction of their hereditary constitution (genotype) and their environment. He also provided supporting evidence for the mutation theory of *de Vries. Johannsen coined the word *gene* for a unit of heredity as well as the terms phenotype and genotype.

John (1167–1216) King of England (1199–1216), nicknamed John Lackland; the youngest son of Henry II, he succeeded his brother Richard I. His reign saw the renewal of war with *Philip II Augustus of France, to whom he had lost several continental possessions, including Normandy, by 1205. He came into conflict with his barons and was forced to sign the *Magna Carta at Runnymede. His subsequent repudiation of the charter led to the first *Barons' War (1215–17), during which John died.

John I (1357–1433) King of Portugal (1385–1433). The head of the military order of Aviz, John led the nationalist opposition to the succession to the Portuguese throne of John I of Castile (1358–90; reigned 1379–90). After securing the throne, John soundly defeated the Castilians at Aljubarrota. In 1415 he captured Ceuta, the first possession of any European nation in Africa.

John I Tzimisces (925–76 AD) Byzantine emperor (969–76). He increased the power of the Byzantine empire by subjecting the Bulgarians and defeating the Russians (971) and by conquering cities in Syria (974–75).

John (II) the Good (1319–64) King of France (1350–64), who was taken prisoner by the English at the battle of Poitiers (1356) during the *Hundred Years' War. He remained in captivity in London, where he was forced to sign the unfavorable Treaty of *Brétigny, until 1360. Released in 1360, he was unable to raise the ransom demanded by the English and was forced to return to London, where he died.

John (II) the Perfect (1455–95) King of Portugal (1481–95). John encouraged Portugal's overseas expansion, supporting Bartolomeu Dias, and concluded the Treaty of Tordesillas with Spain (1494), which demarcated their respective fields of action in the New World. His home policies reduced the power of the aristocracy.

John II Casimir (1609–72) King of Poland (1648–68), whose reign is known as the Deluge. John faced a revolt of the Ukrainian Cossacks, on whose behalf Russia invaded Poland in 1654, and in 1667 John Casimir was forced to cede the eastern Ukraine. Sweden's invasion of Poland in 1655 resulted in the loss of N Livonia (1660). John Casimir abdicated and died in France.

John III (1502–57) King of Portugal (1521–57). John's reign saw the flourishing of culture in the works of Camoens and others. Spending his country's wealth on his lavish court (rather than economic development), he was responsible for the start of Portugal's decline.

John III Sobieski (1624–96) King of Poland (1674–96), famous as an adversary of the Turks. A brilliant military commander, John Sobieski was elected king after defeating the Turks at Khotin (1663). In 1683 he saved Vienna from the Turks in the great victory at Kahlenberg. His subsequent failure to conquer Moldavia and Wallachia led to a loss of personal prestige, which aggravated the domestic unrest that was a feature of his reign.

John (IV) the Fortunate (1604–56) King of Portugal (1640–56). As Duke of *Bragança, John led a revolt in 1640 against Spanish rule that brought him to the throne. He revived the Cortes and formed foreign alliances against Spain but lost most of Portugal's Asian possessions to the Dutch.

John VI (?1769–1826) King of Portugal (1816–26), having been prince regent from 1799. John lived in Brazil during Napoleon's occupation of Portugal. Returning to Portugal in 1821, he faced a revolt of the reactionaries against constitutional monarchy, which was only defeated with French and British help. In 1825 John recognized the independence of Brazil, which was ruled by his son *Pedro I.

John XXII (Jacques d'Euse; c. 1249–1334) Pope (1316–34) during the *Avignon papacy, a man of great administrative and financial ability. In 1317 he dissolved the austere group of the *Franciscans known as Spirituals, whose cause was taken up by Emperor Louis IV. Aided by the philosophers Marsilius of Padua and William of Ockham, Louis denounced papal supremacy and in 1328 set up an antipope in Rome. John's last years were dominated by theological disputes.

John XXIII (Baldassare Cossa; d. 1419) Antipope (1410–15), one of three claimants to the papacy during the *Great Schism. In 1414 John summoned the Council of *Constance to end the Schism but fled when it demanded his resignation. He was arrested, imprisoned, and deposed.

John XXIII (Angelo Roncalli; 1881–1963) Pope (1958–1963). A papal diplomat and then patriarch of Venice (1953–58) before his election at the age of 77, John was the most popular and innovative pope of modern times. In 1962 he summoned the second *Vatican Council, which marked the climax of John's pursuit of Church reforms and Christian unity. His best-known encyclical, *Pacem in Terris* (*Peace on Earth*; 1963), advocated reconciliation between the western democracies and eastern communist countries. His diary was published as *The Journal of a Soul* (1965).

John, Augustus (Edwin) (1878–1961) British painter. He studied at the Slade School, London (1894–98), displaying a precocious drawing talent, and exhibited at the *New English Art Club from 1903. A flamboyantly unconventional character, he traveled widely, often in Gypsy style. His strongly characterized portraits of contemporaries, such as James Joyce and T. E. Lawrence, are indebted to tradition.

John, Elton (Reginald Kenneth Dwight; 1947–) British rock pianist and singer, who became popular in the US with such songs as "Rocket Man" and "Daniel." He is well known for wearing large and colorful glasses on stage.

John, St In the New Testament, one of the 12 Apostles, son of Zebedee and brother of James. He was present at a number of events in the life of Jesus as recounted in the Gospels and is also thought to be the anonymous disciple "whom Jesus loved" present at the crucifixion. Tradition states that he escaped martyrdom and died at Ephesus. Feast day: Dec 27.

The Gospel according to St John is the fourth book of the New Testament traditionally ascribed to St John and probably written in the late 1st century AD. It is markedly different in a number of details from the other three synoptic Gospels and was specifically written with the intention of inspiring faith in Jesus as the Son of God. It begins with a prologue portraying Jesus as the *Logos* or Word, a theme familiar to current Greek philosophy. Having spoken of his incarnation, it concentrates on his public ministry and especially on claims made in a number of discourses and conversations not recorded in the other Gospels. Over half the book is devoted to the events and teaching occurring during the last week before the crucifixion.

The Epistles of John are three New Testament books traditionally ascribed to St John and written toward the end of the 1st century. The first is addressed to the Churches at large and defines the distinctive marks of a true Christian. The others are brief personal letters. The second warns an unnamed lady against false teachers, while the third commends and encourages a certain Gaius. Tradition also ascribes the Book of *Revelation to John.

John Birch Society A right-wing group founded in 1958 by Robert Welch, Jr. John Birch was a US Army intelligence officer who was killed by the Communist Chinese in August, 1945, and is represented by the Society as the first hero of the *Cold War.

John Bull The personification of England or the English national character. The character first appeared in *The History of John Bull* (1712) by John Arbuthnot, and was popularized in 18th- and 19th-century political cartoons. He is usually portrayed as a stocky countryman noted for his honesty and stubbornness.

John Dory (*or* dory) A fish of the family *Zeidae*, found worldwide in moderately deep marine waters. It has a round narrow body with deep sides, each having a black spot surrounded by a yellow ring, and spiny-rayed fins extended into filaments. *Zeus faber*, up to 35 in (90 cm) long, is a food fish of the Atlantic and Mediterranean. Order: *Zeiformes*.

John Frederick (I) the Magnanimous (1503–54) Elector of Saxony (1532–47), who led the Protestant Schmalkaldic League against Emperor *Charles V. John Frederick was imprisoned (1547–52) after the League's defeat at the battle of Mühlberg and was deprived of his territory and electoral rank.

John of Austria, Don (1545–78) Spanish soldier. The illegitimate son of Emperor *Charles V, his half-brother *Philip II entrusted him with major military commands. He suppressed the revolt of the Moriscos (Moors converted to Christianity) in S Spain in 1569 and in 1571 he commanded the combined fleets of Spain, Venice, and the papacy against the Turks, winning a great victory at *Lepanto. In 1573 he conquered Tunis and in 1576 became governor general of the Netherlands, where he died.

John of Damascus, St (c. 675–c. 749 AD) Greek Orthodox theologian and Doctor of the Church, born in Damascus. While a tax official at the caliph's court at Damascus he wrote several treatises defending the use of images in church worship against *iconoclasm. In about 716 he retired to a monastery near Jerusalem, where he was ordained. There he wrote his most influential work, *The Fount of Wisdom*, which deals with philosophy, heresies, and the Orthodox faith. Feast day: March 27.

John of Gaunt (1340–99) The fourth son of Edward III of England, born at Ghent; Duke of Lancaster from 1362. After a distinguished career in the *Hundred Years' War he assumed an increasingly important role in domestic government during the senility of Edward and the minority of Richard II. From 1386 to 1389 he attempted without success to realize his claim, through his second wife, to Castile. In 1396 he married his mistress Catherine Swynford, and in 1397 their descendants were legitimized but excluded from the royal succession. They included Margaret *Beaufort, the mother of Henry VII.

John of Leiden (Jan Beuckelszoon; 1509–36) Dutch *Anabaptist leader. In 1534 he pronounced himself King of Münster, an Anabaptist stronghold in Germany that had expelled its civil and religious authorities. During his brief rule he legalized polygamy and made property communal. The town was recaptured in 1535 and he was executed.

John of Luxembourg (1296–1346) Count of Luxembourg (1310–46) and, by marriage, King of Bohemia (1311–46); son of Emperor Henry VII. His almost constant warfare and consequent levy of high taxes made him unpopular in Bohemia. He died at Crécy fighting for the French.

John of Nepomuk, St (c. 1340–93) The patron saint of Bohemia. As vicar general of Prague, he opposed Wenceslas IV's plans to create a second bishopric in the city. At the king's instigation he was tortured and drowned. Feast day: May 16.

John of Salisbury (c. 1115–80) English churchman, philosopher, and a leading classical scholar of his age. After studying in Paris under *Abelard he became secretary to Thomas Becket and later Bishop of Chartres (1176). His principal works are the *Polycraticus*, a treatise criticizing contemporary political and courtly life, and the *Metalogicon*, a defense of the study of grammar, logic, and rhetoric.

John of the Cross, St (Juan de Yepes y Alvarez; 1542–91) Spanish mystic, poet, and since 1926 Doctor of the Church. With St *Teresa he founded the Discalced *Carmelites, a reformed branch of the Carmelite order. His poems, which include *Cántico espiritual* and *Noche oscura del alma*, are regarded as the finest examples of Spanish mystical literature. Feast day: Nov 24.

John O'Groats 58 39N 3 02W A village at the NE tip of Scotland, site of the house of John de Groot, a 16th-century Dutch immigrant. John O'Groats is 603 mi (970 km) in a straight line from Land's End, Cornwall.

John Paul II (Karol Wojtyła; 1920–) Pope (1978–). A Pole, he is the first non-Italian pope since 1522. He taught at Lublin and Kraków Universities before becoming Archbishop of Kraków (1964). He has outspokenly defended the Church in communist countries, especially in Poland, and has condemned the politicization of the Church. In 1979 he visited Poland, becoming the first pope to go to a communist state. In 1981 he survived an assassination attempt. His extensive travels have taken him to the US, Britain, South America, and the Far East. He succeeded **John Paul I** (Albino Luciani; 1912–78; reigned August–September, 1978), who took the names of his two predecessors, John XXIII and Paul VI, thus symbolizing his desire to combine the charismatic and intellectual qualities for which they were respectively known.

Johns, Jasper (1930–) US artist, who was a major influence on *pop art. He worked as a commercial artist before establishing his reputation at a one-man show in New York (1958) with paintings of targets and flags. The collages and constructions that followed made a similar use of everyday objects, for example the bronze *Beer Cans* (1960).

Johnson, Andrew (1808–75) US statesman; 17th President of the United States (1865–69). A tailor by trade and with no formal education, Johnson became active in the *Democratic Party, serving as a member of the US House of Representatives (1843–53) and as governor of Tennessee (1853–57). Later elected to the US Senate (1857–62), he was one of the few southern political leaders who maintained his allegiance to the Union at the outbreak of the *Civil War. In 1862, President Abraham *Lincoln appointed Johnson military governor of Tennessee, and Johnson was elected vice president as Lincoln's running mate in 1864. Johnson succeeded to the presidency in the following year, after Lincoln's assassination. During his single term of office, Johnson was a supporter of a conciliatory policy towards the defeated South and came into increasing conflict with the *Radical Republicans who overrode his veto and passed the harsh *Reconstruction Act of 1867. His dismissal of Secretary of War Edwin *Stanton in violation of the Tenure of Office Act led to impeachment proceedings against him by the US Senate, but he was acquitted by a single vote. Johnson did not run for re-election in 1868, but shortly before his death in 1875, he was elected to the US Senate.

JOHN PAUL II *At the Jasna Gora monastery, Czestochowa, during his 1979 visit to Poland. The monastery, a famous place of pilgrimage, contains the image of the Virgin known as* The Black Madonna.

Johnson, Cornelius (Janssen van Ceulen; 1593–1661) English portrait painter, born in London of Dutch parents. Until Van Dyck's arrival (1632), Johnson was the leading portraitist at the courts of James I and Charles I, where he specialized in oval-shaped bust portraits. He settled in Holland in 1643.

Johnson, Jack (John Arthur J.; 1878–1946) US boxer. He began fighting professionally in 1897 and became the first black to hold the heavyweight championship, which he gained in 1908. He held the title until 1915, when he lost to Jess Willard. His self-confidence and showmanship angered many whites, and in 1912 he was charged with taking a white wife-to-be across state lines in violation of the Mann Act. Arrested and convicted, he fled to Canada and Europe. Upon his return to the US in 1920, he served one year in prison.

Johnson, James Weldon (1871–1938) US writer and statesman. After brief careers as a teacher and lawyer, he began writing songs with his brother John. Together they wrote for Broadway musicals from 1901, as well as "Lift Every Voice and Sing," widely popular among blacks. He served as consul to Venezuela (1906–09) and Nicaragua (1909–14), and held several executive positions in the National Association for the Advancement of Colored People (NAACP) (1916–30). His poetry collections include *Fifty Years and Other Poems* (1917) and *God's Trombones* (1927). Other works are *The Autobiography of an Ex-Colored Man* (1912), *Black Manhattan* (1930), and *Along the Way* (1933).

Johnson, Lyndon Baines (1908–73) US statesman; 36th President of the United States (1963–69). Beginning his career as a teacher, Johnson was a strong supporter of the New Deal programs of President Franklin *Roosevelt and was named Texas director of the National Youth Administration in 1935. Johnson later served in the US House of Representatives (1937–49) and Senate (1949–61), becoming majority leader in 1957. An

LYNDON B. JOHNSON *President (1963–69) during the Vietnam War who initiated Great Society domestic programs.*

unsuccessful candidate for the Democratic presidential nomination in 1960, he was chosen as John F. *Kennedy's vice presidential running mate. He succeeded to the presidency after Kennedy's assassination in 1963. As president, Johnson initiated the Great Society program, the most comprehensive plan of social legislation since the New Deal. Among the most important achievements of this program were the establishment of Medicare for senior citizens and the passage of the Civil Rights Act of 1964. Re-elected by a substantial margin in 1964, Johnson became increasingly concerned during his first full term in office with the American involvement in the *Vietnam War. He faced growing domestic criticism for his policies and declined to run for re-election in 1968.

Johnson, Richard Mentor (1780–1850) US lawyer and politician; vice president (1837–41). A hero in the War of 1812, he served in the US House of Representatives (1807–19; 1829–37) and the Senate (1819–29). As running mate to Martin Van Buren in the presidential election of 1836, he did not receive a majority of votes; his election to the vice presidency was decided by the Senate.

Johnson, Samuel (1709–84) British poet, critic, and lexicographer. He left Oxford without taking a degree and went to London in 1737. His early publications include a biography of his friend Richard *Savage (1744) and a long didactic poem, *The Vanity of Human Wishes* (1749). From 1750 to 1752 he produced the weekly *Rambler* almost single handed. His *Dictionary* appeared in 1755 and was well received. His major writings include *Rasselas* (1759), a moral fable, an edition of Shakespeare (1765), and *Lives of the Poets* (1779–81). From the early 1760s he enjoyed the friendship of Reynolds, Goldsmith, Burke, and other men of letters, including his biographer *Boswell, who met him first in 1763 and became a close friend in the 1770s.

Johnson, Virginia Eshelman. *See* Masters, William Howell.

Johnson, Walter Perry (1887–1946) US baseball player. A pitcher (1907–27) for the American League Washington Senators, he was nicknamed "The Big Train" because of his fastball. He won 416 games during his career and struck out 3,508 batters. He later managed and was one of the first players inducted into the Baseball Hall of Fame (1936).

Johnston, Joseph (Eggleston) (1807–91) US Confederate general. After resigning from the US Army at the beginning of the Civil War, he was made a general in the Confederate Army, won the first battle of *Bull Run (1861) and fought at Fair Oaks (1862) where he was critically wounded. In 1863 he lost Vicksburg to *Grant, and in 1864 he led the attempt to hold General *Sherman's march through Georgia. Johnston was then relieved of command, primarily due to a long-standing feud with Confederate President Jefferson. He fought again in the Carolinas (1865) and was forced to surrender to Sherman. After the war, Johnston served in the US House of Representatives (1879–81) and was commissioner of railroads (1885–91).

Johnstown 40 20N 78 55W A city in SW Pennsylvania, on the Conemaugh River, E of Pittsburgh. The Johnstown Flood National Memorial here commemorates 2,100 people who lost their lives in the flood of 1889, when a reservoir dam to the SW burst and flooded the city. Although flood control projects have alleviated the problem, another severe flood occurred in 1977. Industries include coal mining, synthetic fuel and steel making, and clothing and furniture manufacturing. Population (1980): 35,496.

John the Baptist, St In the New Testament, the son of a priest, Zacharias, and Elizabeth, a relative of the Virgin *Mary; known as the "Forerunner of Christ". Born in his mother's old age, he was six months older than Jesus. After living in the desert, he began about 27 AD preaching on the banks of the Jordan River, urging repentance and baptism because of the imminent approach of the Kingdom of God (Matthew 3.2). He baptized Christ, recognizing him as the Messiah. He was beheaded by *Herod Antipas, at the request of *Salome, for denouncing his second marriage to Herodias as illicit. Feast days: June 24 (birth); Aug 29 (beheading).

John the Fearless (1371–1419) Duke of Burgundy (1404–19), a great military leader who earned his nickname on a Crusade in 1396. He competed with the Armagnacs for control over the mad Charles the Well-Beloved of France and arranged the assassination (1407) of their leader (and his cousin) Louis, Duc d'Orléans. His own death, however, was at the hands of an Armagnac assassin.

Johor A swampy forested state in S Peninsular Malaysia. It is economically linked to Singapore, depending on it for trading facilities and supplying it with water. Chief products are rubber, copra, pineapples, palm oil, tin, and bauxite. Area: 7330 sq mi (18,958 sq km). Population (1980): 1,601,504. Capital: Johor Baharu.

Johor Baharu 1 29N 103 44E A city in S Peninsular Malaysia, the capital of Johor state. A trading center with a notable sultan's residence, it is linked to Singapore by a causeway across the Johor Strait. Population (1980): 249,880.

joint The point at which two or more bones are connected to each other. There are three broad categories. Immovable joints allow no movement of the bones; examples are the sutures between the bones of the skull. Slightly movable joints allow a certain degree of movement, as in the joints connecting the individual bones of the spine. Freely movable joints (diarthrodial, or synovial, joints) permit a variety of movements. They include the hinge joints at the knee and elbow, the ball-and-socket joints at the hip and shoulder, and the gliding joints at the wrist and ankle. The bone ends at movable joints are covered by *cartilage and enveloped in a tough capsule thickened in parts to form *ligaments. The inside of the capsule is lined by synovial membrane, which secretes a lubricating fluid.

Joint Chiefs of Staff (JCS) US military advisers who advise the president, National Security Council, and the secretary of defense. Composed of a chairman appointed by Congress and the heads of the *Army, *Navy, and *Air Force, it was established in 1947. The commandant of the *Marines was included from 1978. The JCS coordinates the activities of the armed services as directed by the secretary of defense.

Joinville, Jean de (c. 1224–1317) French chronicler. His record of the seventh Crusade (1248–54), on which he accompanied Louis IX and shared his captivity, constitutes the main part of his *Histoire de Saint Louis*. His work is noted for its vivid descriptions and its honesty and human sympathy.

Joliot, Frédéric, and Irène Joliot-Curie. See Curie, Marie.

Jolliet, Louis. See Marquette, Jacques.

Jolson, Al (Asa Yoelson; 1886–1950) US popular singer and songwriter, born in Russia. He sang in circuses, vaudevilles, and minstrel shows, becoming famous for his blacked-up face and the song "Mammy." In 1927 he appeared in the first full-length sound film *The Jazz Singer* and subsequently made the films *The Singing Fool* (1928) and *Swanee River* (1940).

Jonah (8th century BC) An Old Testament figure. **The Book of Jonah** was probably written after the *Babylonian exile of the Jews. It relates how Jonah was commanded by God to preach to the Gentiles in Nineveh, the Assyrian capital. Attempting to escape this task, he fled by ship, but was thrown overboard, swallowed by a great fish (probably a whale), and after three days was safely cast ashore. He repented of his disobedience and fulfilled God's commandment. The purpose of the story was to emphasize that God was the God of the Gentiles as well as the Jews.

Jones, (Alfred) Ernest (1879–1958) British psychoanalyst. A follower and friend of Sigmund *Freud, Jones helped to establish psychoanalysis in Britain and North America. He wrote many papers, especially on the psychology of literary works, including a famous analysis of *Hamlet* in *Hamlet and Oedipus* (1949). In 1920 he founded the *International Journal of Psychoanalysis* and he also wrote *Sigmund Freud: Life and Work* (3 vols, 1953–56).

Jones, Bobby (Robert Tyre J.; 1902–71) US amateur golfer. Between 1923 and 1930 he won four US and three British Open championships, five

US amateur championships, and one British amateur championship. In 1930 he won all four championships, after which he retired from competition.

Jones, Henry. See Cavendish.

Jones, Inigo (1573–1652) English classical architect. One of the first Englishmen to study architecture in Italy and to understand the rules of classicism, Jones was particularly influenced by *Palladio in his two best-known buildings, the Queen's House, Greenwich (1616–35), and the Banqueting Hall, Whitehall (1619–22). His style was strongly influential in England in the 18th century.

Jones, James (1921–77) US writer. After serving in the Army (1939–44), he wrote the novel *From Here to Eternity* (1951) about military life at Pearl Harbor, which was made into a movie in 1953. He followed with *The Thin Red Line* (1962; film, 1964) and *Whistle* (1978; published posthumously), also about army life. Other works include *Some Came Running* (1957; film, 1958), *Go to the Widow-Maker* (1967), and *A Touch of Danger* (1973).

Jones, John Paul (1747–92) American naval commander, born in Scotland. On the outbreak of the American Revolution he was commissioned into the American navy (1775). Jones captured and sank a number of ships in American and British waters (1776, 1778). In 1779 in the *Bon Homme Richard* Jones defeated the British frigate *Serapis* in a desperate battle lasting almost four hours. He subsequently became a rear admiral in the Russian navy, fighting in the Black Sea against the Turks (1788–89).

Jones, LeRoi (1934–) US dramatist and poet. In *Dutchman* (1964) and other plays and volumes of poetry he deals with social relationships between blacks and whites. As a leading black editor and publisher he has encouraged many other black writers. He changed his name to Imamu Baraka to emphasize his identity with his black heritage and culture.

Jongkind, Johan Barthold (1819–91) Dutch landscape painter and etcher, who settled in Paris in 1846. He was influenced by the Dutch landscape tradition but the atmospheric effects he achieved in his seascapes and watercolors anticipate *impressionism.

Jönköping 57 45N 14 10E A town in S Sweden, at the S end of Lake Vättern. Its manufactures include matches, paper, textiles, footwear, and machinery. Population (1978 est): 107,561.

jonquil. See Narcissus.

Jonson, Ben (1572–1637) English dramatist and poet. In *Every Man in His Humour* (1598) he introduced the "comedy of humors," each character being driven by a particular obsession. Other major satirical plays include *Volpone* (1606), *The Alchemist* (1610), and *Bartholomew Fair* (1614). He also published two collections of poems and translations. Ranked above Shakespeare in the 17th century, Jonson based his finest work on classical principles and influenced a number of younger poets.

Joplin, Scott (1868–1917) US pianist and composer of *ragtime music. One of the first to write down such music, Joplin is remembered for his skillful syncopation in such rags as "Maple Leaf Rag" and "The Entertainer." The revival of the latter, in the film *The Sting* (1973), sparked a renewed interest in Joplin's music. His ragtime operas *A Guest of Honor* (1903), now lost, and *Treemonisha* (1907) were failures and Joplin, having known success, died in poverty.

Jordaens, Jakob (1593–1678) Flemish painter, born in Antwerp. Although he painted numerous religious altarpieces, influenced by *Rubens, he is best known for his allegorical and everyday scenes of merrymaking peasants, such as *The King Drinks* (Brussels). His commissions from the House of Orange included murals for their country house near The Hague.

Jordan, Hashemite Kingdom of A country in the Middle East, its only sea outlet being on the tip of the Gulf of Aqaba. It is mainly desert but more fertile in the W and N, where the population is concentrated. The people are Arab, and most are Sunnite Muslims, with Christian and other minorities. *Economy*: Jordan's major industries are the extraction and some processing of phosphates, which are exported from Aqaba and also used locally in fertilizers. Agriculture is concentrated in the irrigated Jordan Valley. Produce includes cereals, vegetables, wool, and such fruit as melons and olives. Potash from the shore of the Dead Sea is also exploited and some copper is mined. *History*: the area that is now Jordan appears to have flourished in the Bronze Age and was part of the Roman Empire by 64 BC. It was controlled by Arabs from the 7th century, Crusaders in the 11th and 12th centuries, and Turks from the 16th century until 1916, when the part E of the Jordan River was named Transjordan and a League of Nations mandate for its control was given to the UK. It became an independent kingdom in 1946 and was named the Hashemite Kingdom of Jordan in 1949. In the Arab-Israeli War of 1948–49, Jordan overran the *West Bank, but it was occupied by Israel in the Six-Day War of 1967. Palestinians, many of whom were refugees from the West Bank, then began raids on Israel from the East Bank; they were, however, subdued by Jordanian forces in the civil war of 1970–71 to avoid Israeli retaliation against Jordan. This brought Jordan into disfavor with other Arab states, which was only temporarily alleviated by Jordanian participation in the Arab-Israeli War of 1973. Under Arab pressure, Jordan has recognized the *Palestine Liberation Organization as the body entitled to govern the West Bank. The present monarch, King Hussein, succeeded to the throne in 1952. US policymakers hoped that Hussein would represent the interests of the PLO in peace negotiations with Israel after Israel in 1982 had driven PLO fighters out of Lebanon, but the king refused. Prime minister: Mudar Badran (1934–   ). Official language: Arabic. Official currency: Jordanian dinar of 1000 fils. Area: about 37,738 sq mi (97,740 sq km), including the West Bank. Population (1983 est): 3,436,000, including the West Bank. Capital: Amman.

JORDAN   *Camels on the Gulf of Aqaba, the country's only sea outlet.*

Jordan River   A river in the Middle East. It rises in Syria and Lebanon and flows due S through the Sea of Galilee, finally entering the Dead Sea. It forms for some of its course part of the border between Israel and Jordan. Length: 199 mi (320 km).

Jos   9 54N 8 53E A city in central Nigeria. It developed following the discovery of tin (1903); tinmining remains important and it is the world's chief source of the mineral columbite. It has a university (founded 1975). Population (1972 est): 112,912.

Joselito   (José Gómez; 1895–1920) Spanish matador, regarded as one of the greatest. At 17, he was the youngest ever to qualify; together with *Belmonte, he introduced the current style of fighting, working very close to the bull. He died in the ring.

Joseph, Chief   (1832–1904) Nez Percé Indian chief. An advocate of passive resistance, he was forced by more aggressive members of his tribe to go to war (1877) against US troops sent to remove the Indians from their lands in Washington. He spent his time during the fighting caring for women, children, and wounded. The tribe was finally captured during an attempt to retreat to Canada. They were relocated to Oklahoma and then, in 1885, to a reservation in Washington.

Joseph, Père   (François le Clerc du Tremblay; 1577–1638) French Franciscan friar and diplomat, known as the Éminence Grise (Gray Eminence), who as Richelieu's secretary (from 1611) became an active proponent of French participation against Protestant forces in the Thirty Years' War.

Joseph, St   In the New Testament, the husband of the Virgin *Mary. He was a devout Jew belonging to the line of David but worked humbly as a carpenter. He eventually settled in Nazareth. *Jesus grew up there and remained in his house for at least 12 years. He was certainly dead by the time of the crucifixion. Feast day: March 19.

Joseph II   (1741–90) Holy Roman Emperor (1765–90), ruling with his mother *Maria Theresa until 1780. As sole ruler, Joseph, an enlightened despot (*see* Enlightenment), introduced religious freedom and reforms in education, law (issuing a legal code in 1786), and administration, and emancipated the serfs. His sweeping reforms encountered some opposition,

especially in Hungary and the Austrian Netherlands, and his attempt to subject church to state involved the dissolution of over 700 monasteries and much hardship for monks.

Joséphine   (1763–1814) The wife (1796–1809) of Napoleon Bonaparte and Empress of the French from 1804. Her first husband was Alexandre, Vicomte de *Beauharnais, who was guillotined in the French Revolution. She presided over a brilliant court until divorced by Napoleon because of their childlessness.

Joseph of Arimathea, St   In the New Testament, a man described as a councillor. He asked Pontius Pilate for the body of Christ after the crucifixion and arranged for its burial on the same day. According to medieval legend, he came to England after the crucifixion, bringing with him the *Holy Grail, and built the first English church, at Glastonbury. Feast day: March 17.

Josephson, Brian David   (1940–   ) British physicist, who shared the 1973 Nobel Prize for his work on tunneling effects in superconductors and semiconductors. He discovered that when two superconductors are separated by a thin dielectric an oscillating current is set up if a steady potential difference is applied between them (**Josephson effect**).

Josephus, Flavius   (Joseph ben Mattityahu; c. 38–c. 100 AD) Jewish historian and apologist. During the Jewish revolt of 66 AD against the Romans he helped organize the defense of Galilee, but was captured and subsequently accompanied *Vespasian to Rome. Here he wrote his surviving works: a history of the Jewish war, a history of the Jews from the creation up to the war, a defense of Judaism (*Against Apion*), and an autobiography.

Joshua   In the Old Testament, the successor of Moses as leader of the Israelites in the period shortly after the *Exodus. **The Book of Joshua**, which follows Deuteronomy in the Old Testament, relates the history of the Israelites between the death of Moses and the death of Joshua. It describes the invasion and conquest of Canaan (Palestine) and its division among the 12 tribes. Among the well-known episodes in the narrative are the Israelites' miraculous crossing of the Jordan River and the capture of Jericho, the walls of which collapsed at the blast of the Israelites' trumpets.

Joshua tree   A treelike plant, *Yucca brevifolia*, native to desert regions of the SW US. Growing to a height of more than 33 ft (10 m), its branching stem can assume unusual shapes: the name is said to derive from its supposed resemblance to the prophet Joshua extending his arms in blessing. It has stiff sword-shaped leaves and bears waxy white flowers in dense clusters at the tips of the branches.

Josquin des Prez   (c. 1450–1521) Flemish composer. A pupil of Ockeghem, he served at the courts of Milan, Ferrara, and Rome and sang in the papal choir between 1486 and 1494. He was choirmaster at Cambrai Cathedral from 1495 to 1499. His compositions were either elaborately contrapuntal or expressively homophonic; they include masses, motets, and chansons.

Jotunheimen   A mountain range in S central Norway. It rises to 8110 ft (2472 m) at Glittertinden, the highest mountain in the country.

joule (J)   The *SI unit of work or energy equal to the work done when the point of application of a force of one newton moves through a distance of one meter. Named for James *Joule.

Joule, James Prescott   (1818–89) British physicist, who performed a series of experiments during the 1840s to determine the mechanical equivalent of heat. His result, announced in 1847, attracted little attention at first but, supported by Lord *Kelvin, his work greatly contributed toward *Helmholtz's formulation of the law of conservation of energy. He also investigated the heating effect of an electric current (*see* Joule's law) and, with Lord Kelvin, discovered the fall in temperature that occurs when a gas expands adiabatically (*see* Joule-Kelvin effect). The unit of energy is named for— him.

Joule-Kelvin effect (*or* Joule-Thomson effect)   The change in temperature of a gas when it is expanded adiabatically. In most gases it produces a cooling as energy is needed to overcome the attractive forces between molecules when the gas is expanded. The effect is utilized in *refrigeration and in the *liquefaction of gases. It was discovered by James *Joule and William Thomson (later Lord *Kelvin).

Joule's law   A law formulated by James *Joule describing the rate at which a resistance in an electrical circuit converts energy into heat. The heat energy produced per second (in watts) equals the product of the resistance (in ohms) and the square of the current (in amperes).

journalism   The gathering, writing, and publication or broadcasting of news. Journalism developed together with *newspapers and *periodicals and its modern English-language origins lie in the 17th century. Most early

English journalists were essentially propagandists for political parties, although a campaign for freedom from government control was hotly fought throughout the 18th century. The role of journalists became that of objective reporters and investigators only after newspapers became independent of direct political control in the mid-19th century, a period that saw the work of some of the most celebrated journalists. The late 19th century saw the introduction of sensational journalism (the "yellow" press) in the US, particularly by William Randolph Hearst and Joseph Pulitzer, which greatly increased circulation. The first academic courses providing training in journalism were established around the beginning of the 20th century. Awareness of the social responsibilities of journalists and the new specialized demands of radio and television broadcasting increased this trend toward professionalism. *See also* Press Council.

Jouvet, Louis (1887–1951) French actor and theater director. As a director of the Comédie Française from 1936, he directed the first productions of most of the plays of Jean *Giraudoux and gave notable performances in productions of Molière. He published *Réflexions du comédien* in 1939.

Jovian, Flavius (c. 331–64 AD) Roman emperor (363–64). He served with the emperor *Julian the Apostate in Persia. After Julian's death (363), Jovian was named emperor by the army. He made an unpopular peace with the Persians and died before his return to Constantinople.

Joyce, James (1882–1941) Irish novelist and poet. After a distinguished student career at a Jesuit college, Joyce graduated from University College, Dublin, in 1902, having decided to devote himself to writing. Accompanied by Nora Barnacle (whom he did not marry until 1931), he left Ireland in 1904, living first in Trieste (until 1915) and later in Zurich during World War I and Paris (1920–40). *Dubliners* (1914), a volume of short stories, was followed by the semiautobiographical novel *Portrait of the Artist as a Young Man* (1916). In 1922 he published *Ulysses*, a stream-of-consciousness epic portraying a single day in the lives of several Dubliners. He carried linguistic experiment to further extremes in *Finnegans Wake* (1939), a dream recounted in puns and word play.

JP. *See* justice of the peace.

Juan Carlos (1938–) King of Spain (1975–). The grandson of Alfonso XIII, he was designated heir to the throne by Francisco *Franco and became king when he died, presiding over Spain's peaceful transition to democracy. In 1962 he married Sophia (1938–), daughter of King Paul of Greece.

Juan de Fuca Strait A strait between *Vancouver Island (SW Canada) and the Olympic Peninsula (US), linking the Pacific Ocean to Puget Sound and Georgia Strait.

Juan Fernández Islands A Chilean group of three volcanic islands, in the S Pacific Ocean. Alexander Selkirk, who inspired Daniel Defoe's *Robinson Crusoe* (1719), lived on the largest island Más-a-Tierra (1704–09). Area: about 70 sq mi (180 sq km).

Juárez. *See* Ciudad Juárez.

Juárez, Benito (Pablo) (1806–72) Mexican statesman, who was the first Indian president of Mexico (1861–65, 1867–72). He became acting president in 1857 but was forced by conservative opposition to flee from Mexico City. In 1861 he returned and was elected president, winning popularity by nationalizing ecclesiastical property. He led the successful opposition (1864–67) to the French invasion (*see* Maximilian) and was re-elected president in 1867 and 1871, dying in office.

Juba River A river in East Africa. Rising in S central Ethiopia, it flows S across Somalia to enter the Indian Ocean near Kismayu. Length: 1030 mi (1660 km).

Jubbulpore. *See* Jabalpur.

Juchen Nomadic tribes that originated in the area N of Korea and around the Liaodong peninsula. The Juchen became espec ally powerful in *Song times, when they founded their own dynasty (1122–1234) modeled on the Chinese system of government.

Judah ha-Levi (*or* Halevy; c. 1075–1141) Jewish poet and philosopher. He was born and spent most of his life in Spain, living in both Christian (Toledo) and Muslim (Cordoba) centers, where he practiced as a physician. Some 1100 of his poems, on religious and secular subjects, are extant and he is considered one of the greatest of Jewish poets and the most important one to emerge from medieval Arabic culture. His major prose work, *Sefer ha-Kuzari*, is a philosophical dialogue on Judaism and the nature of religious truth. According to tradition, he left Spain in the last year of his life on a pilgrimage to Jerusalem; he was enthusiastically received by the Jews of Alexandria and Cairo but died before reaching the Holy Land.

Judah, tribe of One of the 12 *tribes of Israel. It claimed descent from Judah, the son of Jacob and Leah, and occupied territory W of the Dead Sea, which included Jerusalem and Bethlehem. It became the royal house of David in fulfillment of Jacob's dying prophecy. After the division of Israel (*see* Ten Lost Tribes of Israel), it formed with the tribe of *Benjamin the southern kingdom of Judah.

Judaism The religion of the *Jews. Its fundamental tenet is trust in a single, eternal, invisible God, who created the world and desires its welfare. Man's duty is to serve God with all his being. Judaism's most sacred text is the *Torah, which, according to tradition, contains not only a record of history and revealed law but a complete guide to human life and the mysteries of the universe. Judaism has no official creed and no central authority; it lays stress on right behavior (*see* halakhah) rather than on doctrine.

There is no agreement as to when Judaism began. Tradition attaches importance to the early figures of *Abraham and *Moses, but many of the characteristic ideas and institutions emerged during the *Babylonian exile and the period of the Second *Temple. After the destruction of the temple the *rabbis codified and elaborated the traditional teachings (*see* Midrash; Mishnah; Talmud), and in the middle ages philosophy and the *kabbalah exerted a great influence. The modern enlightenment (*see* Haskalah) undermined traditional values and gave rise to several conflicting movements. Orthodox Judaism asserts the supernatural authority of Torah and halakhah, which is challenged by *Reform Judaism. Conservative Judaism and Reconstructionism, which are strongest in the US, attempt to reach a compromise between these extreme views.

Judas tree A shrub or small tree of the genus *Cercis* (7 species), also called redbud, native to S Europe, Asia, and North America, and cultivated for ornament. The pinkish-red clusters of flowers appear before the heart-shaped leaves have opened. The name is used particularly for *C. siliquastrum*, from which Judas Iscariot is said to have hanged himself. Family: *Leguminosae.

Jude, St In the New Testament, one of the 12 Apostles. He is generally identified with Thaddeus and also known as Judas Thaddeus. Referred to as "Judas of James," he was probably the brother of *James ("the Lord's brother") and therefore a half-brother of Jesus. According to tradition he was martyred in Persia with St *Simon, whose feast is held on the same day. Feast day: Oct 28.

The Epistle of Jude in the New Testament is ascribed to him. Of uncertain date, it is a brief warning against certain immoral teachers who were currently infiltrating the Church.

Judea The southern division of ancient Palestine. The Old Testament kingdom of Judah survived Syrian, Assyrian, and Philistine attacks following Solomon's death but came to an end after conquest by *Nebuchadnezzar II of Babylon, when its capital, Jerusalem, was destroyed (586 BC) and the Jews were exiled. Judea came next under Persian domination, when the Jews were allowed to return and rebuild Jerusalem, but under the Seleucids Antiochus IV Epiphanes' desecration of the temple in 167 BC instigated the *Maccabees' revolt. Judea achieved a shortlived independence until the Roman conquest in 63 BC. After years of unrest the Roman province of Syria absorbed it in 135 AD.

Judges An Old Testament book of unknown authorship, but ascribed by Jewish tradition to Samuel. It covers the history of the Israelites from the death of Joshua to shortly before the commencement of the monarchy under Saul (11th century BC). The book introduces a philosophy of history in which God repeatedly causes nations to oppress Israel, as punishment for its apostasy, and then delivers it through the "judges" or virtuous leaders, such as Gideon and Samson, each time it repents.

Judiciary Acts A series of laws enacted by the US Congress that provided for a structured judicial system. An act of 1789 established the Supreme Court, with a chief justice and five associate justices, 13 district courts, three circuit courts, and the attorney general's office. Subsequent legislation reduced the number of Supreme Court justices (1801) and then added them back (1802), but it was not until 1869 that the number of justices was fixed at nine.

Judith A Jewish widow who deceived and assassinated a general of Nebuchadnezzar's invading army and thus caused the Assyrian army to flee from her home city. The incident is recorded in the **Book of Judith**, a book of the *Apocrypha. Its purpose was probably to inspire Jewish resistance to the policy of *Antiochus IV Epiphanes.

judo An international form of wrestling developed from *jujitsu in Japan by Jigoro Kano (1860–1938). It was included in the Olympic Games for the first time in 1964. Contestants wear kimonos and colored belts to indicate their proficiency. The five *kyu* (pupil) grades wear white, orange, green, blue, or brown belts in order of increasing skill, the 12 *dan* (master)

JUDO *Competitors in the 1976 Judo Championships at Ruislip (England).*

grades all wear black belts. Contests take place on a mat 30 ft (9 m) square and usually last two to ten minutes. The contestants score points by executing prescribed throws, ground holds, and locks. Balance, speed, surprise, and the ability to use an opponent's strength characterize the skillful judoka. *See also* martial arts.

Jugendstil The German equivalent of the *Art Nouveau style. Named for the magazine *Jugend* (*Youth*), which was first published in 1896, Jugendstil originated in about 1894 in the embroideries of curving plant forms by Hermann Obrist (1863–1927). Other leading exponents were the architects Peter *Behrens and Henry *van de Velde.

Juggernaut. *See* Jagannatha.

Jugoslavia. *See* Yugoslavia, Socialist Federal Republic of.

jugular vein A vein that drains blood from the head and neck regions to the larger veins passing to the heart. There are two jugular veins on each side of the neck: a large internal and a smaller external jugular, the latter lying just beneath the skin.

Jugurtha (c. 160–104 BC) King of Numidia (118–105). He was the illegitimate grandson of Masinissa (d. 148) and initially ruled with Masinissa's legitimate grandsons Hiempsal and Adherbal. He assassinated Hiempsal and the Romans divided Numidia, a Roman dependency, between Jugurtha and Adherbal. Jugurtha's attack (112) on Adherbal caused Rome to declare war (the Jurgurthine War), which continued intermittently until 105, when Jugurtha was captured. He was taken to Rome and executed.

Juiz de Fora 21 47S 43 23W An industrial city in SE Brazil, in Minas Gerais state on the Rio Paraibuna. It specializes in the manufacture of textiles, especially of knitted goods, and has a university (1960). Population (1970): 218,832.

jujitsu (Japanese name: *yawara*) The form of self-defense, usually unarmed, used by the Japanese *samurai. The object was to disable, cripple, or kill an opponent by using his own momentum and strength against him. It evolved in about the 16th century and was taught in many forms in different schools. It was misused and fell into disrepute in the late 19th century, when the activities of the samurai were curtailed, but *judo, *aikido, and *karate developed from it.

jujube A small thorny tree of the genus *Zizyphus* that produces sweet edible fruit. *Z. jujuba*, native to China, has been widely introduced to other hot dry regions. It grows up to a height of 30 ft (9 m) and has small yellow flowers; blood-red berries are collected and eaten fresh or made into glacé fruits. Family: *Rhamnaceae*. *See also* crown of thorns.

Juliana (1909–) Queen of the Netherlands (1948–80) following the abdication of her mother Wilhelmina. In 1937 she married Prince Bernhard von Lippe-Biesterfeld. In 1980 Queen Juliana abdicated in favor of her eldest daughter *Beatrix.

Julian calendar. *See* calendar.

Julian the Apostate (Flavius Claudius Julianus; 332–63 AD) Roman emperor (360–63). Julian was the only non-Christian emperor after Constantine. The army proclaimed Julian emperor (360) and he attained power after the death in 361 of Constantius II. In spite of a Christian upbringing, Julian embraced paganism and as emperor restored pagan temples and deprived Christian churches of subsidy. He was killed fighting the Persians.

Julius II (Giuliano della Rovere; 1443–1513) Pope (1503–13). The protégé of his uncle, *Sixtus IV, Julius became a cardinal in 1471 but lived in exile during the pontificate of his rival Alexander VI. Following his election he restored and extended the papal states in Italy. In 1511 he formed a Holy League against the invading Louis XII of France, who, after trying to depose Julius, was forced to withdraw. Julius is best known as a patron of artists, especially Michelangelo and Raphael; he began the building of St Peter's, Rome.

Jullundur 31 18N 75 40E A city in India, in Punjab. An important communications and agricultural center, it manufactures sporting goods. Population (1971): 296,106.

July Seventh month of the year. It is named in honor of Julius Caesar and has 31 days. The zodiac signs for July are Cancer and Leo; the flowers are water lily and larkspur, and the birthstone is the ruby. US Independence Day is celebrated on July 4.

July Revolution Three days of rioting in Paris in July, 1830, which brought *Louis Philippe to the French throne. Rebelling against *Charles X's reactionary ordinances, bourgeoisie and workers alike barricaded the streets. Charles abdicated, and the Chamber of Deputies elected Louis Philippe as king.

Jumna River (Jamuna R *or* Yamuna R) A river in N India. Rising in Uttar Pradesh, it flows S and SE past Delhi to join the Ganges River near Allahabad. This confluence is sacred to the Hindus. Length: 860 mi (1385 km).

jumping bean A Mexican shrub, *Sebastiana pringlei*, the seeds of which may contain the caterpillars of a moth, *Carpocapsa saltitans*. When warmed (for example, when held in the hand) the caterpillars wriggle, causing the seed to jump. The seeds of some species of *Colliguaja* of South America may also contain these caterpillars. Family: *Euphorbiaceae*.

jumping mouse A small long-legged rodent belonging to the subfamily *Zapodinae* (5 species), of North America and Asia 3.1–4 in (8–10 cm) long, jumping mice have long tails (4–6 in [10–15 cm]) and are gray, golden, or yellow-brown in color. Living either in nests on the ground or in very shallow burrows, they feed at night on fruit, seeds, and insects. They hibernate in winter. Family: *Zapodidae*.

Junagadh 21 32N 70 32E A city in India, in Gujarat. An agricultural trading center, it is famous for its Buddhist caves (3rd century BC) and temples. Population (1971): 95,945.

junction transistor. *See* transistor.

June Sixth month of the year. The derivation of the name varies; it is probably named for the Roman goddess Juno, but could come from the Latin *juniores*, which means "youths." It has 30 days. The zodiac signs for June are Gemini and Cancer; the flower is the rose, and the birthstones are the pearl, the moonstone, or the alexandrite.

Juneau 58 20N 134 20W The capital city of Alaska, in the S part of the state, on the Gastineau Channel. A supply center for a fur-trading and mining region, it is also an ice-free port. Industries include salmon fishing and sawmilling. Willow South is planned to replace Juneau as the state capital in the 1980s. Population (1980): 19,528.

June beetle A brown beetle, also called May beetle or June bug, belonging to a genus (*Phyllophaga*) of *chafers. 0.47–1 in (12–25 mm) long, June beetles are commonly seen during early summer evenings, being attracted to lights. They can sometimes be serious pests, destroying crops of corn, potato, and strawberry. The adults feed on the foliage and flowers, while the larvae (white grubs) attack the roots.

Jung, Carl Gustav (1875–1961) Swiss psychiatrist and pioneer psychoanalyst. Jung worked in Zurich and collaborated with Sigmund *Freud until, in 1912, their differences became irreconcilable. Jung originated the concept of introvert and extrovert personalities and made valuable studies of mental disorders, including schizophrenia. In his major work, *Psychology of the Unconscious* (1912), Jung regarded the unconscious part of the mind as containing both the personal experiences of the individual and the common inherited cultural experiences (*see* collective unconscious) of the particular social group to which he belongs. Jung later applied his theories to historical studies of religion and to the way in which the layers of the unconscious become manifest in dreams. He also developed psychiatric methods for the treatment of the elderly.

Jungfrau 46 33N 7 58E A mountain peak in S central Switzerland, in the Bernese Oberland. It forms a massif with the Eiger and the Mönch. A railroad climbs to 11,333 ft (3454 m) at the **Jungfraujoch**, the pass between the Jungfrau and the Mönch. Height: 13,632 ft (4158 m).

Junggar Pendi (Dzungarian Basin) A region in NW China, in Xinjiang Uygur Autonomous Region. A semidesert plateau among mountains, it is inhabited chiefly by nomadic herdsmen. There are some state farms and oil and coal are produced.

jungle fowl An Asian forest bird belonging to the genus *Gallus* (4 species). The males have a large fleshy comb and wattles at the sides of the bill and, in the breeding season, fight fiercely using their sharp leg spurs. The red jungle fowl (*Gallus gallus*) is the ancestor of domestic *poultry. Family: *Phasianidae* (fowl and pheasants).

juniper A coniferous tree or shrub of the genus *Juniperus* (60 species), widely distributed in the N hemisphere. Junipers have two kinds of leaves: needle-like and scalelike. All species have needles when young and some have both needles and scales when mature. Male and female flowers grow on separate trees and the cone is a fleshy "berry." The common juniper (*J. communis*) is native to N Europe, North America, and SW Asia; it rarely exceeds 13 ft (4 m) in height and is often planted for ornament. It has needle-like leaves and blue-black cones, 0.24–0.35 in (6–9 mm) in diameter, used for flavoring gin and foods, as a source of oil, and as a diuretic. Family: *Cupressaceae*. *See also* cade; pencil cedar; savin.

Junius, Letters of A series of letters, written by a still unidentified author, criticizing the government of Britain's King George III. They appeared in the *Public Advertiser* between January 21, 1769, and January 21, 1772. Sir Philip Francis is thought to be the most likely author, although the names of Edmund Burke and Tom Paine, among others, have also been suggested.

Junkers A class of Prussian aristocrats. From small landowners the Junkers rose from the 15th century to control land, industry, and trade. Encouraged by Frederick the Great and Bismarck, they became notorious for arrogance and privilege, enjoying a monopoly of power in the army and civil service that remained unbroken until the 1930s.

Juno (astronomy) A *minor planet (153 mi [247 km] diameter), the orbit of which lies between those of Mars and Jupiter.

Juno (mythology) A principal Roman goddess, the wife of Jupiter. She was concerned with all aspects of women's life, especially marriage and childbirth, and is usually portrayed as a matronly figure. In 390 BC the warning given by her sacred geese on the Capitoline hill saved Rome from an attack by the Gauls. She was identified with the Greek *Hera.

Jupiter (astronomy) The largest and most massive planet, orbiting the sun every 11.86 years at a mean distance of 483 million mi (778.3 million km). Its rapid axial rotation (in less than 10 hours) has produced a nonspherical shape: equatorial diameter 88,675 mi (142,800 km), polar diameter 84,150 mi (135,500 km). In a telescope light and dark bands of clouds are visible, running parallel to the equator, together with spots and streaks.

Jupiter is composed mainly (99%) of hydrogen and helium (in the ratio 88:12). Ammonia, methane, and other compounds are present in the cloud layers. The gaseous atmosphere is 620 mi (1000 km) thick. The planetary interior is liquid hydrogen with possibly a small rocky core. Jupiter radiates, as heat, about twice as much energy as it receives from the sun, suggesting an internal energy reservoir. It is also a source of radio waves. It has a magnetic field and radiation belts of great intensity.

The planet has at least 16 *satellites, 4 of major size, and a satellite ring of rocks, discovered in 1979. *See also* planetary probe.

Jupiter (mythology) The principal Roman god, identified with the Greek *Zeus. Originally a sky god, he controlled the weather and used the thunderbolt as his weapon. His temple on the Capitoline hill was the principal Roman religious structure. He was a protective god and the guardian of honor, being concerned with oaths, treaties, and marriages.

Jura An island in NW Scotland, in the Inner Hebrides, separated from the mainland by the Sound of Jura. It is mountainous and sparsely populated. Area: 147 sq mi (381 sq km). Population (1971): 343, with Colonsay.

Jura Mountains A mountain range in E France and NW Switzerland. It extends along the border in a NE–SW arc between the Rhine and Rhône rivers, rising to 5653 ft (1723 m) at Crêt de la Neige. The area is chiefly agricultural.

Jurassic period A geological period of the Mesozoic era, between about 200 and 135 million years ago, following the Triassic and preceding the Cretaceous periods. The dinosaurs and other reptiles flourished and diversified in this period. Fossils of the earliest birds and mammals have also been found in Jurassic rocks.

Juruá, Rio A river in South America, rising in E central Peru and flowing NE through NW Brazil to join the Amazon River. Length: 1200 mi (1900 km).

jury A body of people, usually 12. They are selected according to law to evaluate the truthfulness of the evidence before them and decide questions of fact arising in a court case.

Jussieu A French family of botanists. **Antoine de Jussieu** (1686–1758) was a physician, who wrote many papers on natural history and made a collection of European plants. He became director of the Jardin des Plantes, Paris. His brother **Bernard de Jussieu** (1699–1777) originated a method of classifying plants that was developed by his nephew **Antoine-Laurent de Jussieu** (1748–1836). The youngest brother of Antoine, **Joseph de Jussieu** (1704–79), spent many years in South America and introduced the garden heliotrope to Europe.

Justice, Department of US cabinet-level executive branch department that represents citizens in enforcing the law in the public interest. It plays a key role in protection against criminals and subversion; in ensuring healthy competition of business; in safeguarding the consumer; and in enforcing drug, immigration, and naturalization laws. Headed by the attorney general, the department conducts all suits concerning the government in the Supreme Court. It was established in 1870.

Justinian I (482–565 AD) Byzantine emperor (527–65). His reign saw chiefly defensive wars on the eastern frontier but in the west his general *Belisarius crushed the Vandals in Africa (533) and the Ostrogoths in Italy (535–53). Justinian, who was greatly influenced by his wife *Theodora, reformed provincial administration and codified *Roman law, which he issued in the *Corpus Juris Civilis* (Body of Civil Law), informally known as the Justinian Code. An orthodox Christian, he attempted to wipe out paganism and built the great church of St Sophia at Constantinople.

Justinian II (c. 669–711 AD) Byzantine emperor (685–95, 705–11), the last of the Heraclian dynasty. He was a notoriously harsh ruler and after a revolt in 695 his nose was cut off (hence his nickname Rhinotmetus) and he was banished to the Crimea. With Bulgar support he returned to Constantinople as emperor, instigating savage reprisals. He was killed in a second revolt.

Justinian Code. *See* Roman law.

Justin Martyr, St (c. 100–c. 165 AD) Christian apologist and martyr, born in Samaria. After his conversion (c. 130) he taught in Ephesus and founded a school of Christian philosophy at Rome, where he was later beheaded. His only certain works are two *Apologies* addressed to the emperor Marcus Aurelius and the Roman Senate and the *Dialogue*, defending Christianity against Judaism. Feast day: April 14.

jute Either of two Indian annual plants, *Corchorus capsularis* or *C. olitorius*, cultivated in India, Pakistan, and Thailand for their fibers. Growing to a height of 10 ft (3 m), they have straight spearlike stems and small yellow flowers. The stems are cut, soaked in water, and beaten to remove the fibers, which are processed into burlap, etc. There are many grades, used for ropes, sacks, carpet backings, hessian, and tarpaulin. Blending jute with man-made fibers has increased its uses. Family: *Tiliaceae*.

Jutes A Germanic people, probably from Jutland, who invaded Britain together with the *Angles and *Saxons in the 5th century AD. Archeological evidence supports *Bede's statement that the Jutes settled in what are now Kent, the Isle of Wight, and Hampshire.

Jutland (Danish name: Jylland) A peninsula in N Europe, between the North Sea, the Skagerrak, the Kattegat, and the Little Belt. It is occupied by the continental part of Denmark and part of the West German *Land* of Schleswig-Holstein.

Juvenal (Decimus Junius Juvenalis; c. 60–c. 130 AD) Roman satirist. The biographical records are unreliable, but it is probable that he was born in Aquinum, SE of Rome, and that he was exiled to Egypt under the emperor Domitian but later became relatively prosperous under the emperor Hadrian. His 16 *Satires*, probably written in the period 98–128 AD, are savage indictments of the corruption and immorality of contemporary Roman society and of the absurd follies of mankind in general.

juvenile delinquency The commission of offenses against the law by a person under a specified age, whatever the age of majority is in a particular state. Most such cases are tried by special Juvenile Courts, to which the press and public are not admitted and in which the terms "sentence" and "conviction" may not be used. The juvenile offender may be bound over to his parents, put under supervision, or committed to a child care officer.

Jylland. *See* Jutland.

K

K2 (*or* Mt Godwin Austen) 35 53N 76 32E The second highest mountain in the world (after Mount Everest), in N Pakistan in the Karakoram Range. As it was the second peak to be measured in the range it was given the symbol K2. The summit was first reached on July 31, 1954, by an Italian team. Height: 28,250 ft (8611 m).

Kaaba The cube-shaped building at the center of the great mosque at Mecca. Muslims believe that it was built by Abraham and Ishmael for the worship of God, was corrupted by Arab paganism, but was then purified and adopted for Islam by Mohammed. In the annual pilgrimage the Muslims circumambulate it and kiss the Black Stone, supposedly brought to Abraham by Gabriel, which is fixed in the interior in the southeast corner.

Kabardino-Balkar Autonomous Soviet Socialist Republic An administrative division in the S Soviet Union, in the RSFSR on the N side of the Caucasus Mountains. A large part of this mountainous region is unsettled and without roads. The population is 45% Kabardinian, 10% Balkar, and 40% Russian. The Kabardinians, most of whom are Muslims, speak a Northwest Caucasian language, while the Balkars are Turkic-speaking. The principal industries of the region are mining, timber, engineering, and food processing. The main crops are cereals, and livestock, poultry, and dairy farming are also important. *History*: the Kabardinians were associated with the Russians from 1557 and, although the Balkars resisted Russian rule, the region was annexed by Russia in 1827. It became an autonomous republic in 1936. In 1943 the Balkars, accused of collaborating with the Germans, were deported; they were returned in 1956. Area: 4825 sq mi (12,500 sq km). Population (1981 est): 688,000. Capital: Nalchik.

kabbalah (Hebrew: tradition) An esoteric Jewish theosophical system. The classical kabbalistic text is the *Zohar* (*Book of Splendor*), written in Aramaic in 13th-century Spain, but kabbalah has much older roots. It has strong connections with *gnosticism and also with magical practices. An important 16th-century kabbalistic school flourished at Safed, in Galilee, around Isaac *Luria, and Christian interpretations of the kabbalah blended with *Neoplatonism in the 16th and 17th centuries. In modern times a thirst for occult teachings has revived considerable amateur interest in the kabbalah.

Kabinda. *See* Cabinda.

Kabuki A form of Japanese popular theater that developed from the aristocratic *No theater during the 17th century. The earliest notable dramatist was Chikamatsu Monzaemon (1653–1724). The plays are performed with musical accompaniment on a wide revolving stage and emphasize visual effects and acting skills. The conventional scenery, costumes, and the actors' make-up are elaborate. Female roles are played by male actors. A traditional program consists of both historical and domestic dramas separated by dance plays.

Kabul 34 30N 69 10E The capital of Afghanistan, situated in the NE of the country at an altitude of 6000 ft (1830 m) on the Kabul River. It is over 3000 years old, with a strategic position commanding high mountain passes. It has been destroyed and rebuilt many times, being in the path of the great invasions of India by Alexander the Great, Genghis Khan, and others. It was capital of the Mogul Empire (1504–1738), becoming capital of Afghanistan in 1773. The university was founded in 1932. Population (1979): 913,164.

Kabwe (former name: Broken Hill) 14 29S 28 25E A city in central Zambia. The first Rhodesian (Zambia was formerly Northern Rhodesia) railroad was built here to serve the mines that now produce some of the world's highest grades of lead, zinc, and vanadium. In 1921 prehistoric hominid fossils were discovered here (*see* Homo). Population (1978 est): 147,000.

Kabyle A *Berber people of NE Algeria. They are Muslims and speak the Sanhajah dialect of the Berber language. The Kabyle are mainly settled cultivators living in autonomous villages (firquahs) occupied by patrilineal clans and governed by assemblies of adult males. There are also several castelike groups of inferior status, such as smiths and butchers.

Kádár, János (1912–) Hungarian leader. Head of the Hungarian secret police (1948–50), in 1956 Kádár led the opposition in the *Hungarian Revolution to Imre *Nagy's government and after the Soviet invasion became first secretary of the Hungarian Socialist Workers' Party. He was also prime minister (1956–58, 1961–65).

KABUKI *The interior of a theater, from a print by Utagawa Toyokuni. The performers enter and leave the stage from the back of the theater along the "flower path," a section of which extends from the stage at the bottom left. Music and sound effects are produced by the group behind the lattice at the right of the stage.*

Kaduna 10 28N 7 25E A city in Nigeria. Formerly a colonial administrative center, it developed as a railroad junction and is a major textile and local trade center. Population (1975 est): 202,000.

Kaesŏng 37 59N 126 30E A city in SW North Korea, a former Korean capital (938–1392). Many historic buildings here were destroyed during the Korean War (1950–53).

Kaffirs The former collective name for the Pondo and Xhosa peoples of the E Cape Province of South Africa, with whom the advancing white settlers fought a series of wars (the *Cape Frontier Wars) in the late 18th and 19th centuries.

Kafirs A people of the Hindu Kush mountains of Afghanistan and Pakistan, who speak a Dardic language (*see* Dards). Their name (Arabic *kafir*: infidel) was acquired from their Muslim neighbors on account of their traditional religion, which is polytheistic and involves sacrifice and divination by shamans.

Kafka, Franz (1883–1924) Czech writer. Born in Prague (then in Bohemia), the son of German Jewish parents, he studied law and worked in an insurance company until tuberculosis forced him to leave. His own inner conflicts are reflected in fantasies and parables that portray the individual isolated in an incomprehensible and uneasy environment. Most of his work was published posthumously, against his instructions, by his friend Max Brod. Among his best-known writings are the stories *Metamorphosis* (1912) and *In the Penal Settlement* (1919) and the novels *The Trial* (1925) and *The Castle* (1926).

Kafuan stone tools Quartz pebbles apparently flaked by human agency, found along the Kafue River (Zambia). They are now considered to be of natural origin.

Kafue River A river in Zambia, rising on the Zaïre frontier and flowing generally S and E to join the Zambezi River. Length: 600 mi (966 km). The **Kafue Dam** (1972) provides about two-thirds of Zambia's hydroelectric power.

Kagoshima 31 37N 130 32E A port in Japan, in S Kyushu on Kagoshima Bay. It was the site of *Francis Xavier's landing in Japan (1549). Its university was established in 1949. It has porcelain and textile industries, a naval yard, and a rocket base. Population (1980): 505,000.

kagu A rare virtually flightless bird, *Rhynochetus jubatus*, occurring on remote forested mountains of New Caledonia. 22 in (55 cm) long, it has a dark-barred gray plumage, an erectile crest, and reddish eyes, legs, and downcurved bill. It lives on the ground, feeding at night on insects and snails. It is the only member of its family (*Rhynochetidae*). Order: *Gruiformes* (cranes, rails, etc.).

Kahn, Louis I(sadore) (1901–) US architect. Kahn's first major building was the Yale University Art Gallery (1951–53) which he designed while he was a professor there. Since then he has developed a striking and individual form of *functionalism, for example at the Medical Research Building, University of Pennsylvania (1957–60). Other designs include the Kimbell Art Museum in Fort Worth, Tex. (1966–72), and the Yale Center for British Art, New Haven, Conn. (1969–74).

Kaieteur Falls 5 09N 59 29W A waterfall in central Guyana, on the Potaro River. It is an important feature of the Kaieteur National Park. Height: 741 ft (226 m). Width: about 350 ft (107 m).

Kaifeng 34 47N 114 20E A city in E China, in Henan province. It was a *Song dynastic capital, and a Jewish colony was established here (12th–19th centuries). It is a commercial and industrial center. Population (1953): 299,100.

Kaikoura Ranges Twin mountain ranges in New Zealand, comprising the Inland and the Seaward Kaikouras. They extend SW–NE in NE South Island, reaching 9465 ft (2885 m) at Tapuaenuku in the Inland Kaikouras, and are separated by the Clarence River.

Kairouan (or Qairouan; Arabic name: al Qayrawan) 35 42N 10 01E A city in N central Tunisia. An ancient town and holy city of Islam, its importance has declined and today it is a local trade center producing carpets and other craft goods. Population (1976 est): 54,000.

kaiser The title (derived from the Latin: Caesar) adopted by the German kings as Holy Roman Emperors (800–1806). It was assumed by William I of Prussia in 1871 and borne by the German emperors until 1917.

Kaiser, Georg (1878–1945) German dramatist. His carefully structured expressionist plays reveal a conflict between his desire for spiritual regeneration and his inherent pessimism. They include *Von Morgens bis Mitternachts* (1916), *Gas I* (1919), and *Gas II* (1920).

Kaiserslautern 49 27N 7 47E A city in SW West Germany, in Rhineland-Palatinate. The site of Barbarossa's ruined castle (1153–58), it shares a university with Trier (1970). Its manufactures include car parts, machinery, and textiles. Population (1976 est): 100,383.

kakapo A rare nocturnal New Zealand *parrot, *Strigops habroptilus*, also called owl parrot. It is the largest and only flightless parrot, having disks of stiff feathers around the eyes resembling an owl. Its green plumage is barred with yellow and brown and it has a heavy bill for grinding plant material.

Kakinomoto Hitomaro (c. 680–710) Japanese poet. He is considered the greatest of the poets whose works appear in the Man'yo-shu, an 8th-century anthology of lyric poetry. He was poet to the court of Empress Jito and Emperor Mommu and many of his poems describe court life.

kala-azar. *See* leishmaniasis.

Kalahari Desert A semiarid area in S Africa, chiefly in Botswana. It is sparsely inhabited by nomadic Bushmen, and although its few rivers are generally dry there is some vegetation. Wildlife is concentrated in the game reserves in the S. Area: about 96,505 sq mi (250,000 sq km).

Kalamazoo 42 17N 85 36W A city in Michigan, on the Kalamazoo River. It produces paper, fishing tackle, and stoves. Population (1980): 79,722.

Kalanchoe A genus of small tropical shrubs (over 100 species) having fleshy leaves and clusters of colorful flowers on tallish stems. They are popular house plants, requiring good draining and water supply and warm temperatures. Most flower in winter, having white, red, yellow, or pink flowers. Family: *Crassulaceae*.

Kalat (or Khelat) A division of SW Pakistan, in S Baluchistan. A former princely state, it was incorporated into Pakistan in 1948. Area: 25,332 sq mi (65,610 sq km). Population (1961): 156,480. Capital: Kalat.

kale A variety of *cabbage, also called borecole, or collards, grown for its large edible leaves, which are used as a winter vegetable and as livestock food. Curly kales, which have curled crimped leaves, are the most popular as vegetables. Some produce tender spring shoots. They are more hardy than most other brassicas.

Kalemie (name until 1966: Albertsville) 5 57S 29 09E A city in Zaïre, on Lake Tanganyika. A port, it handles the Indian Ocean and Zaïre–Tanzania trade. Industries include fishing and textiles. Population (1970): 61,472.

Kalgan. *See* Zhangjiakou.

Kali In Hindu mythology, the goddess of death. The wife of *Shiva in her destructive aspect, she is represented as a hideous four-armed black woman, adorned with skulls, and is propitiated by nocturnal sacrifices of animals.

Kalidasa (5th century AD) Indian poet, considered to be the greatest writer in classical Sanskrit. Almost nothing is known of his life, but he is traditionally associated with the court of Chandra Gupta II. The seven works attributed to him include two epics, two shorter poems, and three dramas, of which the most famous is the *Sakuntala*, concerning the love of King Dusyanta for a semidivine nymph.

Kalimantan The Indonesian part of *Borneo, comprising the SE two-thirds of the island. It is little developed, but its dense forests provide valuable timber. Small-scale agriculture includes the growing of rice, tobacco, sugar cane, coffee, and rubber. It is a long-standing source of gold and also produces oil and coal. Since Indonesian independence in 1949 separatism against the Java-based government has remained strong with active guerrilla activity. Area: 212,388 sq mi (550,203 sq km). Population (1980): 6,723,086. Chief towns: Banjarmasin and Pontianak.

Kalinin (name until 1931: Tver) 56 49N 35 57E A port in the central Soviet Union, in the RSFSR on the Volga River. The city was renamed Kalinin in 1931 in honor of the revolutionary M. I. *Kalinin. It is a major industrial and administrative center, with industries that include engineering and textiles. Population (1981 est): 422,000.

Kalinin, Mikhail Ivanovich (1875–1946) Soviet statesman. A loyal supporter of Stalin, he was formally head of state (1919–46) as chairman of what came to be called the presidium of the Supreme Soviet.

Kaliningrad (name until 1946: Königsberg) 54 40N 20 30E A port in the W Soviet Union, in the RSFSR on the Pregolya River near its mouth at the Baltic Sea. Founded in 1255 as a fortress for the Teutonic Knights, it passed to Prussia in the 16th century and became a major German naval base. It was ceded to the Soviet Union in 1945. Its industries include shipbuilding, timber, paper, textiles, and food processing. Population (1981 est): 366,000.

Kalisz 51 46N 18 02E A city in W central Poland. Originally called Calissia, it is one of the oldest towns in Poland, being mentioned by Ptolemy in the 2nd century AD. Population (1972 est): 83,600.

Kalmar 56 39N 16 20E A port in E Sweden, on Kalmar Sound. The Union of Kalmar (1397) united Sweden, Denmark, and Norway under one ruler. It has a notable 13th-century castle, Kalmar Slott. Shipbuilding is important and nearby are the famous Orrefors glassworks. Population (1978 est): 52,846.

Kalmyk Autonomous Soviet Socialist Republic An administrative division in the S Soviet Union, in the RSFSR on the Caspian Sea. The Kalmyk people, who speak a Mongolian language, are traditionally Buddhists. Industries include fish processing, canning, and manufacture of building materials, but the economy is predominantly agricultural and cattle breeding and fodder crops are particularly important. The Kalmyks were deported to Siberia for collaborating with the Germans in World War II but some were returned in 1957. Area: 29,300 sq mi (75,900 sq km). Population (1981 est): 301,000. Capital: Elista.

Kaluga 54 31N 36 16E A port in the central Soviet Union, in the RSFSR on the Oka River. It produces railroad equipment, electrical equipment, textiles, and consumer goods. Population (1981 est): 276,000.

Kama In Hindu mythology, the god of love. He is the son of *Shiva and his popular epithet of Ananga (bodyless) derives from his having been reduced to ashes by a glance from his father's eye when Kama playfully shot his arrows at him.

Kama River A river in the E Soviet Union, rising in the Ural Mountains and flowing mainly SW to the Volga River. It is a main waterway. Length: 1260 mi (2030 km).

Kamakura 35 19N 139 33E A city in Japan, in SE Honshu on an inlet of the Pacific Ocean. A former Japanese capital (1192–1333), it is now a religious center, noted for its shrines and temples and for its bronze Buddha, 43 ft (13 m) high. Population (1976 est): 168,609.

Kamchatka A peninsula in the extreme E Soviet Union. It is about 746 mi (1200 km) long and separates the Sea of Okhotsk from the Bering Sea. There are many lakes, rivers, and forests, two mountain chains, and about 20 active volcanoes. Area: about 104,225 sq mi (270,000 sq km).

kame A mound consisting chiefly of stratified sands and gravels, deposited by meltwater from a glacier or icesheet. *See also* esker.

Kamehameha I (c. 1758–1819) King of Hawaii (1810–19), who founded the Kamehameha dynasty. Ruler of part of Hawaii from 1782, by 1810 he had united all the Hawaiian islands. He maintained Hawaiian independence despite the arrival of European explorers following James Cook's discovery of Hawaii in 1779. His encouragement of foreign trade established Hawaiian prosperity.

Kamehameha IV (1834–63) King of Hawaii (1854–63). He instituted social reforms, including free medical care, and encouraged greater commercial activity. He successfully opposed annexation by the US in 1853–54 and curbed the political influence of US missionaries by inviting representatives of the Church of England to share their educational work.

Kamenev, Lev Borisovich (1883–1936) Soviet politician. Kamenev failed to win a favorable position in the power struggle after Lenin's death and he was arrested for participating in *Kirov's assassination (1934). He was tried in the first public purge trial and executed.

Kamet, Mount 30 55N 79 36E A mountain in N India, in the Himalayas. It was first climbed in 1931. Height: 25,446 ft (7756 m).

Kamikaze A Japanese aircraft crashed deliberately by its pilot into its target. Such suicide missions were first flown at the battle of Leyte Gulf (1944) in World War II; at Okinawa (1945) some 3000 sorties sunk 21 US ships. Kamikaze means divine wind and refers to the typhoon that scattered Kublai Khan's invasion fleet in 1281.

Kampala 0 20N 32 30E The capital of Uganda, N of Lake Victoria. Founded by the British in the late 19th century, it became the capital in 1962. In 1979 its fall to the combined forces of Tanzanians and exiled Ugandans effected the end of President Idi Amin's regime. It has two cathedrals and Makerere University (1970). It is chiefly an administrative center with some small industries. Population (1969): 330,700.

Kampuchea, Democratic. *See* Cambodia.

Kananga (name until 1966: Luluabourg) 5 53S 22 26E A city in central Zaïre, on the Lulua River. A major commercial center, it serves an agricultural and diamond-producing area. Population (1976 est): 704,211.

Kanarese A *Dravidian language of SW India, also called Kannada. It is the official language of Mysore. Texts written in the Kanarese alphabet date from the 6th century.

Kanazawa 36 35N 136 38E A city in Japan, in central Honshu. It is renowned for its landscape garden. Its university was established in 1949.

Industries include textiles, porcelain, and lacquerware. Population (1980): 418,000.

Kanchenjunga, Mount. *See* Kangchenjunga, Mount.

Kanchipuram (*or* Conjeeveram) 12 50N 79 44E A city in India, in Tamil Nadu. It is one of the oldest cities in S India and is sacred to the Hindus. It is noted for its silk and cotton fabrics. Population (1971): 110,657.

Kandahar (*or* Qandahar) 31 36N 65 47E A city in S Afghanistan. Situated on main routes to central Asia and India, it is built on the site of several ancient cities. It was the first capital (1747) of a unified Afghanistan. Kandahar is a major commercial center. Population (1975 est): 209,000.

Kandinsky, Wassily (1866–1944) Russian expressionist painter and art theorist, born in Moscow, where he graduated in law. In 1896 he moved to Munich to study. Here he painted the first purely abstract pictures in European art (c. 1911). These are characterized by freely applied paint and dazzling colors, from which he drew analogies to music in his book *Concerning the Spiritual in Art* (1911). He was a founder of the *Neue Kunstlervereinigung (1909) and Der *Blaue Reiter (1911); following a stay in Russia (1914–21), he taught at the *Bauhaus school of design, where his style became more geometrical. He settled in France in 1933.

Kandy 7 17N 80 40E A city in central Sri Lanka. Capital of the kingdom of Kandy from 1480 until 1815, when it was occupied by the British, it has a famous Buddhist temple, Dalada Malagawa. Kandy is the commercial center for Sri Lanka's major tea-producing region. Population (1981): 101,281.

Kanem Bornu An African empire that controlled the area around Lake Chad. Kanem, situated on the eastern trade routes, became a center of Muslim civilization in the 11th century. The king was expelled in 1389 and founded a new dynasty in Bornu, which in the 16th century conquered Kanem and expanded the empire. Torn by internal strife, the empire collapsed in about 1800.

kangaroo The largest *marsupial mammal. There are two species, the red kangaroo (*Macropus rufus*) of Australia and the gray kangaroo (*M. kanguru*) of Australia and Tasmania. Red kangaroos can reach a height of 7 ft (2 m) and a weight of 198 lb (90 kg). Kangaroos have short front legs and long hind legs and feet: they travel by a succession of leaps. When moving slowly, they use their long heavy tail as a prop. The red kangaroos graze across the plains while gray kangaroos live in open woodland. Family: *Macropodidae*. *See also* wallaby; wallaroo; tree kangaroo. □mammal.

kangaroo paw A stiff hairy plant of the Australian genus *Anigozanthos* (10 species), also known as Australian sword lilies and sometimes planted in gardens in warm regions. The flowers, borne in short branched terminal clusters, are long, tubular, and hairy, with six pointed flaring lobes, usually yellow, green, or red. Unopened flowers resemble kangaroos' paws. Family: *Hemodoraceae*.

kangaroo rat A North American desert rodent of the genus *Dipodomys* (22 species). Up to 8 in (20 cm) long, kangaroo rats have long back legs and very long hairy tails. They do not need to drink as they obtain water from their food (seeds, tubers, and other vegetation). They spend the day in relatively cool humid burrows, in which they also store food during droughts. □mammal.

Kangchenjunga, Mount (*or* Mt Kanchenjunga) 27 44N 88 11E The third highest mountain in the world (after Mount Everest and K2), on the Sikkim (India)–Nepal border in the Himalayas. It was first climbed in 1955 by a British expedition that stopped just short of the actual summit in deference to the religious wishes of the Sikkimese. Height: 28,208 ft (8598 m).

KaNgwane. *See* Bantu Homelands.

Kang Xi (*or* K'ang-hsi; 1654–1722) Chinese emperor (1661–1722) of the Qing dynasty, who completed the Qing conquest of China started by *Nurhachi. He was a powerful ruler, who led his armies in person against the Mongols and carried out tours of inspection of his vast empire. He built the imperial summer palace at Jehol (now Chengde) and sponsored engineering works to prevent the Yellow River from flooding and to improve communications. His greatest achievement was probably in his sponsorship of the arts.

Kang You Wei (1858–1927) Chinese reformer. A major influence on the *Hundred Days of Reform (1898), he was subsequently forced to flee China and in 1907, in British Columbia, founded the China Reform Association. He returned to China in 1914 and became an opponent of Sun Yat-sen.

Kano 12 00N 8 31E A city in N Nigeria. It was an important trade center for caravans crossing the Sahara. It was captured by the British (1903) and trade developed with the S. It is now an important trade center, particularly for groundnuts and cattle, with some local industries. Population (1975 est): 399,000.

Kanpur (former name: Cawnpore) 26 27N 80 14E A city in India, in Uttar Pradesh on the Ganges River. Ceded to the British East India Company (1801), it became an important British frontier station and during the Indian Mutiny was the scene (1857) of a massacre of British soldiers. Today Kanpur is one of India's largest cities and a major communications and industrial center; the chief manufactures are wool, cotton, jute, leather goods, plastics, and chemicals. Several educational institutions are located here, including a university (1966) and an Institute of Technology (1960). Population (1981 est): 1,685,308.

Kansas A midwestern state in the central US. Missouri lies to the E, Oklahoma to the S, Colorado to the W, and Nebraska to the N. It consists mainly of the Great Plains and is crossed by the Kansas and Arkansas rivers. Famous for its wheat fields, which stretch over the vast, seemingly endless terrain, Kansas is the country's main wheat growing area. Located in the US heartland, it has a continental climate typical of inland regions, with extreme temperatures and dramatic storms, blizzards, and tornadoes. Manufacturing is significant with aircraft production, food and meat processing, and a range of different processing industries. Beef production is especially important, and cattle raising constitutes the leading agricultural revenue producer of the state. Its large mineral resources yield oil, natural gas, coal, sand and gravel, cement, stone, chalk, zinc, and lead. Kansas is also an important agricultural state, being the US's main wheat-growing area; other crops include sorghum grains and hay. Beef production is especially important. *History*: first explored by the Spanish in the 16th century, it was claimed by the French (1682) and formed part of the Louisiana Purchase (1803) by the US. The establishment of Kansas as a territory came late as a result of controversy over the slavery issue. Attempts had been made to organize Kansas and Nebraska as a single territory, but proslavery interests opposed the *Missouri Compromise (which sought to settle the slavery issue in the territories, and would have designated Kansas-Nebraska a nonslavery territory). Thus, attempts to organize the territory were continually defeated. As a concession to the South, Kansas and Nebraska were given free choice, or "squatter sovereignty," on the slavery question. Opposing forces, each seeking to win support for its side, inflamed the sentiments of the settlers to the point of pitched battle. The territory became known as Bleeding Kansas. It was in Kansas that the abolitionist John *Brown formulated a plan to liberate the slaves that culminated in his raid on Harpers Ferry, Va. Kansas fought with the Union in the Civil War. The arrival of the railroad in the late 1860s and 1870s brought many cattlemen. Area: 82,264 sq mi (213,063 sq km). Population (1980): 2,363,208. Capital: Topeka.

Kansas City 39 07N 94 39W A city in NE Kansas, across the Kansas River from Kansas City, Missouri. Settled in 1843 as Wyandot City by the Wyandot Indians, it became Kansas City in 1886. It is known as a meat-packing center, but also has extensive automobile, petroleum, railroad, food processing, paper, metal, and chemical industries. Population (1980): 161,148.

Kansas-Nebraska Act (1854) US law that gave territories the freedom to decide by popular vote (or popular sovereignty) the question of slavery. Sponsored by Senator Stephen A. *Douglas, it was intended to quell the growing acrimony between anti- and pro-slavery factions; instead, it brought the nation closer to war. The act also repealed the *Missouri Compromise, changed existing laws concerning territorial slavery, and created Kansas and Nebraska territories.

Kansu. *See* Gansu.

Kant, Immanuel (1724–1804) German philosopher, who made many original and influential contributions to thought. He spent much of his life (1755–97) teaching at the university in his native Königsberg (now Kaliningrad in the Soviet Union). His early works, notably *Theory of the Heavens* (1755), sought to examine metaphysics in the light of the work of *Newton and *Leibniz. Acquaintance with Hume's *empiricism, however, initiated his so-called "critical period" in which he evolved his doctrine of transcendental idealism. In the famous *Critique of Pure Reason* (1781) he explored the limitations of reason by which mankind interprets experience. The *Critique of Practical Reason* (1788) and the *Critique of Judgment* (1790) deal respectively with *ethics and aesthetic and teleological judgments. Reason makes experience possible by imposing upon the raw data supplied by the senses the forms of understanding. Kant identified 12 of these basic forms (which he called "categories"), such as causality; they were transcendental in as much as they were not derived from experience but were found in pure reason independently of experience. But reason is also practical and as such he identified it with morality. He maintained that there was an absolute moral law, which can never be modified by expediency (it can never be right to tell a lie), and called the obligation to obey this moral law the "categorical imperative," binding upon every rational human being.

Kao-hsiung. *See* Gaoxiong.

kaolin A group of clay minerals consisting of hydrous aluminum silicates. It includes kaolinite (the most important), nacrite, and dickite. Kaolin is the main constituent of *china clay. It has many industrial uses apart from the ceramic industry, particularly as a mineral filler in the manufacture of paper, paint, textiles, rubber, plastics, and cosmetics. It is also used in medicine.

Kapitza, Peter Leonidovich (1894–1984) Soviet physicist, who went to England's Cambridge University in 1921 and worked with *Rutherford on high transient magnetic fields. Returning to the Soviet Union in 1934 he transferred his attention to low-temperature physics, which led him to the discovery of superfluid helium (1941). For this work he was awarded the 1978 Nobel Prize.

KAPOK *The fruit pods of the silk-cotton tree ripen in about two months. They split open to release masses of white kapok, which surrounds the black seeds.*

kapok The fine silky hairs covering the seeds of the silk-cotton tree (*Ceiba pentandra*), which are extracted and used for stuffing mattresses, etc. Impervious to water, kapok can also be used to fill life jackets and oil pressed from the seeds is used in soap making and is edible. The tree is native to tropical America and widely cultivated in the tropics. Growing to 1378 ft (35 m), it has huge horizontal branches, large buttresses at the base of the trunk, and clusters of white or red flowers. Family: *Bombacaceae*.

Kara-Bogaz-Gol A shallow gulf in the SW Soviet Union, on the E Caspian Sea. Its water evaporates fast, drawing more in from the Caspian and creating the richest natural deposits of marine salts in the world. Area: about 5018 sq mi (13,000 sq km).

Karachai-Cherkes An autonomous region (*oblast*) in the W Soviet Union, in the RSFSR. It was formed in 1922 for the Muslim Karachai and Cherkes peoples. Mining, engineering, and chemical industries are important, and the chief agricultural activities are livestock raising and cereal production. Area: 5440 sq mi (14,100 sq km). Population (1980 est): 370,000. Capital: Cherkessk.

Karachi 24 51N 67 02E The largest city and chief seaport in Pakistan, situated on the Arabian Sea just NW of the Indus delta. A modern city, it developed rapidly from the mid-19th century as a port. It became the capital of Pakistan (1947) following partition, which brought a further influx of refugees to an already overcrowded city. The subsequent removal of the capital to Islamabad (1959) and the building of new satellite towns has to some extent eased the housing situation. The University of Karachi was established here in 1957. The city is Pakistan's principal naval base and its port is a major outlet for the agricultural produce of the Sind and Punjab provinces. Industries include jute, silk, wool and cotton textiles, chemicals and plastics, and engineering. Population (1972): 3,498,634.

Karafuto. *See* Sakhalin.

Karaganda 49 53N 73 07E A city in the SW Soviet Union, in the Kazakh SSR. Founded in 1857, Karaganda grew rapidly in the 1920s and

1930s as the Karaganda coal basin was exploited. Today it is one of the largest producers of bituminous coal in the Soviet Union. Although coal-mining and the production of coalmining equipment dominate the city's industries, it also produces building materials and has light industries. Population (1981 est): 583,000.

Karageorge (George Petrović Karadordević; c. 1762–1817) Serbian revolutionary leader. In 1804 he led a successful revolt against Turkey and in 1808 became the "Supreme Serbian hereditary leader." Turkey regained control of Serbia in 1813 and after a five-year exile in Austria Karageorge was murdered, probably by his rivals, the *Obrenović family.

Karajan, Herbert von (1908–) Austrian conductor. Educated at Vienna and the Salzburg Mozarteum, he was musical director of the Vienna State Opera from 1957 to 1964. He founded the Salzburg Easter Festival in 1967 and has conducted the Berlin Philharmonic Orchestra since 1955.

Kara-Kalpak Autonomous Soviet Socialist Republic (*or* Kara-Kalpakia) An administrative division in the S Soviet Union, in the Uzbek SSR on the Aral Sea. The population consists mainly of Kara-Kalpaks, a Turkic-speaking people closely related to the Kazakhs. Kara-Kalpakia's main industries are the manufacture of bricks, leather goods, and furniture and canning and wine making. It is the Soviet Union's chief producer of alfalfa, and other crops grown include cotton, rice, corn, and jute. Cattle and karakul sheep are raised. *History*: the Kara-Kalpaks were under the rule of the *Kazakhs, passing under Russian rule in the late 19th and early 20th centuries. Kara-Kalpakia was within the Kazakh SSR (1925–30) before being incorporated in the RSFSR. It became an autonomous republic in 1932. Area: 63,900 sq mi (165,600 sq km). Population (1981 est): 957,000. Capital: Nukus.

Karakoram Range A mountain range mainly in SW China, NE Pakistan, and NW India. It extends about 280 mi (450 km) between the Pamirs and the Himalayas and includes *K2, the second highest mountain in the world. In 1978 the **Karakoram Highway** was opened connecting China with Pakistan over the Khunjerab Pass, 16,188 ft (4933 m) high.

Karakorum The former Mongol capital founded (c. 1220) by *Genghis Khan in the upper valley of the Orhon Gol River (Outer Mongolia). It replaced the nearby Uighur capital of the same name. After *Kublai Khan moved the capital from Karakorum (1267) the city declined and was eventually destroyed (1388).

karakul A breed of sheep originating in central Asia. The young lambs bear a coat of fine tightly curled black wool, known as Persian lamb.

Kara Kum A desert in the SW Soviet Union, between the Caspian Sea to the W and the Amu Darya River to the E, comprising most of the Turkmen SSR. Area: about 115,806 sq mi (300,000 sq km).

Karamanlis, Constantine (1907–) Greek statesman; prime minister (1955–63, 1974–80), president (1980–). Karamanlis resigned in 1963 and went into exile, returning in 1974, after the fall of the military dictatorship, to form a civilian government.

Kara Sea A section of the Arctic Ocean off the N coast of the Soviet Union, between Novaya Zemlya and Severnaya Zemlya. It is frozen for much of the year but is used to reach the port of Novy Port some 373 mi (600 km) inland on the Gulf of Ob.

KARATE *A championship bout in one of the most popular of the martial arts.*

karate An oriental form of unarmed combat that was systematized in Okinawa, one of the Ryukyu Islands, in the 17th century and spread to Japan in the 1920s, where it absorbed elements of *jujitsu. Breath-control techniques as well as philosophical attitudes, such as the necessity of mental calm, were taken from Zen Buddhism. The aim is to focus the body's total muscular power in one instant. Hands, feet, elbows, etc., are toughened in stylized training sequences against padded or wooden blocks, and karate fighters also perform feats of strength, such as wood breaking. In actual fights, however, which last two or three minutes, blows are stopped short before impact. As in *judo, grades are distinguished by colored belts and points are awarded in combat. *See also* martial arts.

Karatepe A fortified hilltop site near Adana (S Turkey), founded (c. 740 BC) by Asitawandas, King of the Danuna (possibly the same people as the Danaoi, mentioned by Homer). King Sanduarri of Karatepe was beheaded by *Esarhaddon (676 BC). A palace with sculptured reliefs and an important bilingual Phoenician and Hittite hieroglyphic inscription have been found.

Karbala (*or* Kerbela) 32 37N 44 03E A city in central Iraq, S of Baghdad. Muslim pilgrims are attracted to the tomb of Husan (the son of *Ali), who was martyred here. It is a trading center for dates and other agricultural produce. Population (1970 est): 107,500.

Karelian Autonomous Soviet Socialist Republic (*or* Karelia) An administrative division in the NW Soviet Union, in the RSFSR. Comprising largely forest, it also possesses thousands of lakes and rivers. The Karelians speak a Finno-Ugric language, and W Karelia has formed part of Finland for much of its history, but was finally ceded to Russia in 1940. Industries include mining, timber, and chemicals. Some cereals, potatoes, and fodder crops are grown and fishing is very important. Area: 66,560 sq mi (172,400 sq km). Population (1981 est): 746,000. Capital: Petrozavodsk.

Karelian Isthmus A land bridge in the NW Soviet Union, situated between the Gulf of Finland in the W and Lake Ladoga in the E. It connects Finland with the Soviet Union to which it was ceded in 1944. It is 25–70 mi (40–113 km) wide and 90 mi (145 km) long and its principal cities are Leningrad and Vyborg.

Karen A group of peoples of S Burma who speak tonal languages distantly related to those of the Tibeto-Burman branch of the *Sino-Tibetan family. There are many different and distinct groups and languages broadly divided into the White Karens (including Sgaw and Pwo) and the Red Karens (including Bre, Padaung, Yinbaw, and Zayein). Only Sgaw and Pwo have written forms and all are much influenced by surrounding languages. Their religion is animistic.

Kariba, Lake A reservoir in Zambia and Zimbabwe. It is formed by the Zambezi River above the **Kariba Dam** (completed 1959) and is used for generating hydroelectric power. Length: 175 mi (282 km).

Karl-Marx-Stadt (name until 1953: Chemnitz) 50 49N 12 50E A city in S East Germany, on the Chemnitz River. A textile center since the 14th century, it became famous for machine construction in the 19th century, when the first German machine tools and the first German locomotive were made here. Population (1980 est): 316,937.

Karloff, Boris (William Pratt; 1887–1969) British character actor, who worked mostly in US films. Following his great success as the monster in *Frankenstein* (1931), he was typecast in a number of sinister and gruesome roles in horror films.

Karlovy Vary (German name: Karlsbad) 50 14N 12 53E A spa city in W Czechoslovakia, in W Bohemia. It has many hot sodium sulfate springs, including the Vřídlo (Sprudel) at a temperature of 72°C (162°F). Population (1980 est): 61,000.

Karlsbad. *See* Karlovy Vary.

Karlsburg. *See* Alba Iulia.

Karlskrona 56 10N 15 35E A seaport in S Sweden, on the Baltic coast. It has been the main naval station of Sweden since 1680. Its industries include the manufacture of naval equipment, granite quarrying, and sawmilling. Population (1978 est): 60,141.

Karlsruhe 49 00N 8 24E A city in SW West Germany, in Baden-Württemberg. The capital of the former *Land* of Baden, it is the site of the federal court of justice and a university (1825). It has a harbor on the Rhine and varied industries, including oil refining and machinery manufacturing. It is a center for nuclear research and development. Population (1980 est): 270,800.

Karlstad 59 24N 13 32E A port in SW Sweden, on the N shore of Lake Vänern, at the outlet of the Klar River. Its industries are based on timber and heavy machinery and it has a university (1967). Population (1978 est): 74,068.

karma (Sanskrit: action)   The sum of all human actions, which according to Hinduism and Jainism are passed from one individual existence to the next and determine the nature of the individual's rebirth. In *Buddhism, karma is associated with mental and physical elements passed on in the cycle of rebirth until the personal self is annihilated in attaining *nirvana.

Karnak   25 44N 32 39E   A village near *Thebes (Upper Egypt), the site of the huge temple of *Amon, built (c. 1320–1237 BC) mainly by the pharaohs Seti I (reigned 1313–1292) and *Ramses II. *See also* Luxor.

Karnataka (name until 1973: Mysore)   A state in SW India, on the Arabian Sea stretching E over the Western Ghats onto the Deccan plateau. Rice and sugar cane are grown along the coast, coffee and tea on the Ghats, and rice, cotton, and fruit on the Deccan. Hill forests provide teak and most of the world's sandalwood. Iron ore, gold, manganese, and bauxite are mined. Industries include iron and steel, engineering, food products, and silk. Most of the population are Kanarese-speaking Hindus. *History*: long ruled by Hindu dynasties, Karnataka was conquered (1761) by a Muslim, Hyder Ali, whose son Britain dispossessed (1799). Area: 74,024 sq mi (191,773 sq km). Population (1971): 29,299,014. Capital: Bangalore.

Károlyi, Mihály, Count   (1875–1955) Hungarian statesman. Károlyi led the campaign for Hungarian independence during World War I and became (January, 1919) the provisional president of the new Hungarian Democratic Republic. In a confrontation between conservatives and communists, he was forced in March to resign and was succeeded by Béla Kun.

Karpov, Anatoly   (1951–   ) Soviet chess player, who became an International Grandmaster at 19 and subsequently world champion (1975). In 1978 he beat *Korchnoi in a much publicized match at Manila.

karri   A tree, *Eucalyptus diversicolor*, native to SW Australia and cultivated elsewhere. It grows to a height of over 115 ft (35 m) in moist areas and produces excellent timber. The attractive leaves are dark green above and lighter below. Family: *Myrtaceae*.

Karroo   A plateau in S South Africa, divided by the Groot-Swartberge range into the **Great Karroo** and, to the S, the **Little Karroo**. Seasonal rains turn them into rich pasture for sheep.

Kars   40 35N 43 05E   A city in NE Turkey. It was fortified in the 16th century and captured by Russians three times during the 19th century before being restored to Turkey after World War I. Population (1970): 53,338.

karst region   An area of the earth's surface typified by sink holes, uvalas (depressions), and underground drainage, produced by the solution of limestone or dolomite. Such features are notable in the Karst region of Yugoslavia.

karting (*or* go-karting)   A form of *automobile racing that originated in the US in the 1950s. A kart usually has a tubular chassis, no body or suspension system, and a single driving seat. It has a maximum wheelbase of 50 in (1.27 m) and is usually powered by a single-cylinder two-stroke engine. 100 cc, 200 cc, and 270 cc are among the more common engine capacities. Most karts are capable of about 100 mph (160 km per hour). (100 mph).

Kasai River   A river in central Africa. Rising in Angola, it flows N into Zaïre to join the Zaïre River as its main tributary. It forms part of the Angola–Zaïre border and is rich in alluvial diamonds. Length: 1300 mi (2100 km).

Kasavubu, Joseph   (c. 1917–69) Congolese statesman; president (1960–65). A teacher, Kasavubu joined with *Lumumba to lead the Congo (now Zaïre) to independence. In 1961 he deposed Lumumba, until then prime minister, with the help of *Mobutu but was himself deposed in Mobutu's second coup in 1965. He retired to his farm, where he died.

Kashgar.   *See* Kashi.

Kashi (K'a-shih *or* Kashgar)   39 29N 76 02E   A city in NW China, in Xinjiang Uygur AR on a fertile oasis. It is a center of trade with the Soviet Union and the Middle East. Chinese rule has been intermittent here since the 2nd century BC and rebellion among the Muslim population was common in the period 1862–1943. Cloth is manufactured and handicrafts include rug-making. Population (1958 est): 100,000.

Kashmir   The northernmost region of the Indian subcontinent, bordered by China to the NE and Afghanistan to the NW. The S Jammu lowlands rise into the Himalaya and Karakoram Mountains. Except for the Indus Valley and the beautiful Vale of Kashmir, the valleys are small. Rice, other grains, silk, cotton, fruits, and sheep are farmed. Embroidery and other crafts help tourism to thrive. *History*: most Kashmiris became Muslims in the 14th century but in the 19th century Hindu princes won power under British control. Britain's withdrawal (1947) was followed by a Muslim revolt; the Hindu maharajah acceded to India but Pakistan intervened and fighting between the two sides resulted in the partition of the region. Pakistan rules 30,468 sq mi (78,932 sq km) of the W and barren N. China occupies 16,496 sq mi (42,735 sq km) in the E. The remainder forms the Indian state of *Jammu and Kashmir. Area: 85,783 sq mi (222,236 sq km).

Kassala   15 24N 36 30E   A city in the NE Sudan. It has declined as a center for cotton but has an important fruit trade. Population (1973): 106,602.

Kassel   51 18N 9 30E   A city in E West Germany, in Hessen. Notable buildings include the Orangery Palace (1701–11). Bombed for its aircraft and tank industries during World War II, its manufactures now include railroad engines and textiles. Population (1980 est): 195,500.

Kassem, Abdul Karim   (1914–63) Iraqi soldier and statesman; prime minister (1958–63) after leading an army coup that overthrew the monarchy. An opponent of Arab unity, he survived a rebellion (1959) of those who wanted federation with the United Arab Republic but was killed in a revolt led by army officers.

Kassites   A people of mysterious racial origins who moved SW from the Zagros Mountains to overrun *Babylonia in the 16th century BC. Although Indo-European gods were apparently worshiped, the Kassite language is neither Indo-European nor Semitic. The Kassites ruled Babylon for about 400 years until overthrown by *Assyria.

Katanga.   *See* Shaba.

Kathiawar Peninsula   A peninsula in W India, in Gujarat, roughly 118 mi (190 km) square, projecting into the Arabian Sea between the Gulfs of Kutch and Cambay.

Kathmandu (*or* Katmandu)   27 42N 85 19E   The capital of Nepal, near the confluence of the Baghmati and Vishnumati Rivers. Founded in the 8th century AD, it possesses numerous historical buildings and a university (1959) and is the site of several religious festivals. Its development as the country's main commercial center has been assisted by a program of road building. Population (1978 est): 195,260.

Katmai, Mount   An active volcano in S Alaska, in the Aleutian Range. Following its violent eruption in 1912, the *Valley of Ten Thousand Smokes was formed. Height: 7000 ft (2100 m). Depth of crater: 3700 ft (1130 m). Width of crater: about 2.5 mi (4 km).

Katowice (former name (1953–56): Stalinogrod)   50 15N 18 59E   A city in S central Poland. It is an important industrial center within the Upper Silesia coalfield; manufactures include iron and steel. The Silesian University was established here in 1968. Population (1979 est): 353,000.

Katsina   13 00N 7 32E   A city in N Nigeria. From its early foundation (c. 1100), it was an important center for trans-Saharan trade. Active until the 17th and 18th centuries, it has now declined in importance. Population (1972 est): 112,230.

Katsura Taro   (1847–1913) Japanese soldier and statesman, who was instrumental in introducing into the Japanese army a general-staff system on German lines. He was prime minister three times (1901–06, 1908–11, 1912–13) and presided over the victorious *Russo-Japanese War (1904–05) and the annexation of Korea (1910).

Kattegat   A strait between Denmark and Sweden linking the Skagerrak with the Baltic Sea. Length: about 149 mi (240 km).

katydid   A *bush cricket of the subfamily *Pseudophyllinae*, common in the tropics and E North America. It takes its name from the repetitive song—"katy-did, katy-didn't"—of male katydids of the genus *Pterophylla*. Katydids are generally green and have long wings but never fly. They are mainly herbivorous, although some species eat insects.

Katyn Massacre   The execution during World War II of 4250 Polish officers in the Katyn forest, near Smolensk in the Soviet Union. The bodies of the Poles, who had been interned by the Russians following the Soviet occupation of Polish territory in 1939, were discovered by the Germans in 1943. The Russians denied responsibility, countercharging the Germans with the massacre. The Soviet Union forbade the Red Cross investigation requested by the Polish Government in exile, with which it broke diplomatic relations. The weight of evidence points to Soviet accountability.

Kauai Island   An island in NW Hawaii. It was the first Hawaiian island visited by Captain James Cook in 1778. Volcanic mountains rise above fertile valleys where extensive pineapples, sugar cane, and rice are cultivated. The highest point is at Mt Waialeale (5148 ft; 1570 m) deep. The island has the rainiest location in the world – an average of 460 in (1169 mm) of rain falls annually near Mt Waialeale. The seat of island government and largest town is Lihue. Area: 555 sq mi (1438 sq km).

Kaufman, George S(imon) (1889–1961) US dramatist. He worked as a newspaper columnist while collaborating, especially with Moss *Hart, on an enormous number of Broadway comedy hits. With Hart he wrote *You Can't Take it With You* (1936), which won a Pulitzer Prize, and *The Man Who Came to Dinner* (1939). With Marc Connelly he wrote *Beggar on Horseback* (1925), with Edna Ferber *Royal Family* (1927), *Dinner at Eight* (1932), and *Stage Door* (1936), and with Howard Dietz and Arthur Schwartz, *Bandwagon* (1931). With George *Gershwin he wrote *Of Thee I Sing* (1932), and he also wrote the scripts of two *Marx brothers films.

Kaunas (Russian name: Kovno) 54 52N 23 55E A port in the Soviet Union, in the S central Lithuanian SSR at the confluence of the Neman and Viliya rivers. It was held successively by Lithuania, Poland, and Russia before becoming (1918) the capital of independent Lithuania; it was occupied by German forces during World War II. It is a major educational, cultural, and industrial center, with industries that include chemicals, plastics, textiles, and iron and steel production. Population (1981 est): 383,000.

KENNETH KAUNDA *Here he is about to lay the foundation stone of the Chinese-built Tanzam Railway (1975), which connected two countries (Tanzania and Zambia) that were already close political partners.*

Kaunda, Kenneth (David) (1924–) Zambian statesman; president (1964–). He trained as a teacher and joined the African National Congress in 1949. In 1958 he founded the more militant Zambia African National Congress and was imprisoned for subversion. On his release in 1960 he became president of the United National Independence Party, which took Northern Rhodesia to independence as Zambia in 1964.

Kaunitz, Wenzel Anton, Count von (1711–94) Austrian statesman. As chancellor (1753–92) he controlled Habsburg foreign policy under Empress Maria Theresa and her son Emperor Joseph and was also influential in the reform of internal administration. His most striking achievement was to reverse (1756–57) the European alliances of the War of the *Austrian Succession, making France and Russia Austria's allies in the *Seven Years' War against Prussia.

kauri pine A coniferous tree, *Agathis australis*, from New Zealand. Growing to a height of 151 ft (46 m), it has oblong leaves, 2 in (5 cm) long and 0.8 in (2 cm) wide, and spherical cones, 2–3.1 in (5–8 cm) in diameter. It yields a resin (kauri copal or gum) used in making varnishes; the best resin is fossilized, derived from extinct trees and dug out of the ground. Its timber is used for general building purposes. Family: *Araucariaceae*. *See also* dammar.

kava A shrub, *Piper methysticum*, of the Pacific Islands and Australia, the ground and fermented roots of which are made into a narcotic drink. The roots are also chewed, and continued use produces inflammation and ulcers of the mouth. It has been used medicinally and as a local anesthetic. Family: *Piperaceae*.

Kaválla (*or* Kavála; ancient name: Neopolis) 40 56N 24 24E A port in NE Greece, in Macedonia on the Aegean Sea. A Roman naval base, it was visited by St Paul (50–51 AD). It was ceded by Turkey to Greece in 1912. Tobacco is the chief export. Population (1981): 56,260.

Kawabata Yasunari (1899–1972) Japanese novelist. He was one of a group known as the Neo-Impressionists, which opposed the preceding realist movement in Japanese literature. His novels, which include *Snow Country* (1935–47) and *The Sound of the Mountain* (1949–54), are characterized by melancholy and loneliness, probably related to his being orphaned at an early age. In 1968 he was awarded the Nobel Prize.

Kawasaki 35 32N 139 41E A city in Japan, in SE Honshu. Part of the Tokyo-Yokohama industrial complex, it has shipbuilding, iron and steel, and chemical industries. Population (1980): 1,041,000.

Kay, John (1704–c. 1764) British inventor of the flying shuttle (patented in 1733), which contributed to the mechanization of weaving. Kay was defrauded of most of the royalties due to him and died in poverty in France.

kayak A native Eskimo canoe consisting of waterproofed animal skins stretched over a light framework and having one or two openings in the top with flexible watertight closures for one or two occupants.

Kayseri 38 42N 35 28E A city in central Turkey on the site of ancient Caesarea Mazaca. Kayseri has remains of the Seljuq civilization, notably the Great Mosque built in 1136. Population (1980): 281,320.

Kazakh A Turkic people of the Kazakh SSR and Xinjiang Uygur AR in China. With the Kirgiz, *Bashkir, and *Tatars they form the Kipchak division of the Turkic peoples. They were traditionally nomadic herders of horses, sheep, and goats who lived on milk products and mutton. Their movable dome-shaped dwellings (yurts) were constructed of wooden frames across which skins were stretched. Except in Xinjiang Uygur AR they are now settled stock breeders. Clan units, comprising extended-family groups and headed by chiefs, were the main social organization. *See* Turkic languages.

Kazakh Soviet Socialist Republic (*or* Kazakhstan) A constituent republic in the S Soviet Union. The *Kazakhs comprise some 30% of the population, which includes Russians (43%) and Ukrainians (7%). The area is rich in mineral resources, especially coal, oil, copper, and iron ore. The atomic power station on the Mangyshlak peninsula has the world's first industrial fast-breeder reactor. An important agricultural area, it produces cereals, cotton, rice, and fruit. Kazakhstan is also noted for its sheep, from which excellent quality wool is obtained. *History*: conquered by Mongols in the 13th century, the region came under Russian rule in the 18th and 19th centuries. It became a constituent republic in 1936. Area: 1,048,030 sq mi (2,715,100 sq km). Population (1981 est): 15,000,000. Capital: Alma Ata.

Kazan (*or* Kasan) 53 45N 49 10E A city in the E Soviet Union, the capital of the Tatar ASSR in the RSFSR on the Volga River. It is a major historic, cultural, educational, commercial, and industrial center and supports a wide range of industries including oil refining, electrical engineering, chemical production, and food processing. *History*: founded in the 14th century by the *Tatars, it became the capital of an independent khanate and was captured (1552) by Ivan the Terrible. Its trade and industry developed during the 19th century and by 1900 it was one of the chief manufacturing cities in Russia. It became the capital of the Tatar ASSR in 1920. Lenin and Tolstoi studied at Kazan's university (1804). Population (1981 est): 1,011,000.

Kazan, Elia (E. Kazanjoglous; 1909–) US stage and film director and novelist, born in Turkey of Greek parentage. He first achieved success as a stage actor and helped to found the *Actors' Studio in 1947. For the stage he directed *The Skin of Our Teeth* (1942), *A Streetcar Named Desire* (1947), *Death of a Salesman* (1949), and other outstanding plays. His films include *Viva Zapata* (1952), *On the Waterfront* (1954), *East of Eden* (1955), and *The Arrangement* (1969), which is based on his own novel. Other novels include *America, America* (1963) and *The Anatolian* (1982).

Kazantzakis, Nikos (1885–1957) Greek novelist and poet, who also wrote plays, travel books, and essays. His epic poem *I Odysseia* (1938), a continuation of Homer's *Odyssey*, embodies many of his religious and philosophical ideas. He is best known for the novels *Zorba the Greek* (1946) and *Christ Recrucified* (1954).

Kazvin (*or* Qazvin) 36 16N 50 00E A city in NW Iran. It is the trading center for a fertile plain and was the national capital for much of the 16th century. Population (1976 est): 138,527.

Kean, Edmund (c. 1787–1833) British actor, especially famous for his Shakespearean roles. He was particularly successful as Shylock in *The Mer-*

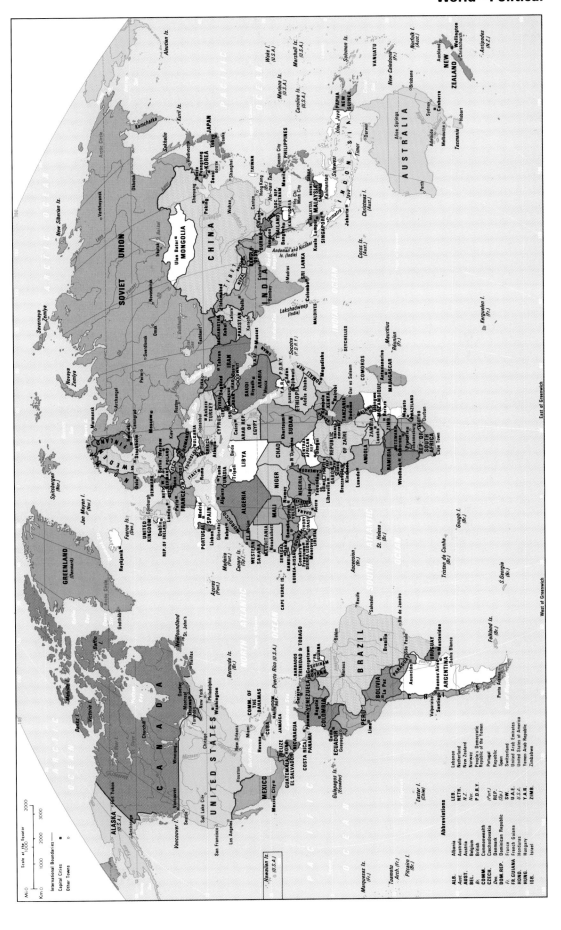

World—Physical

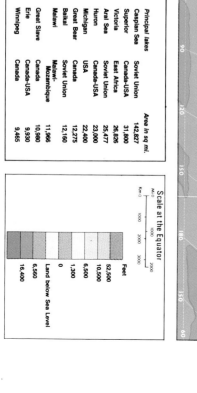

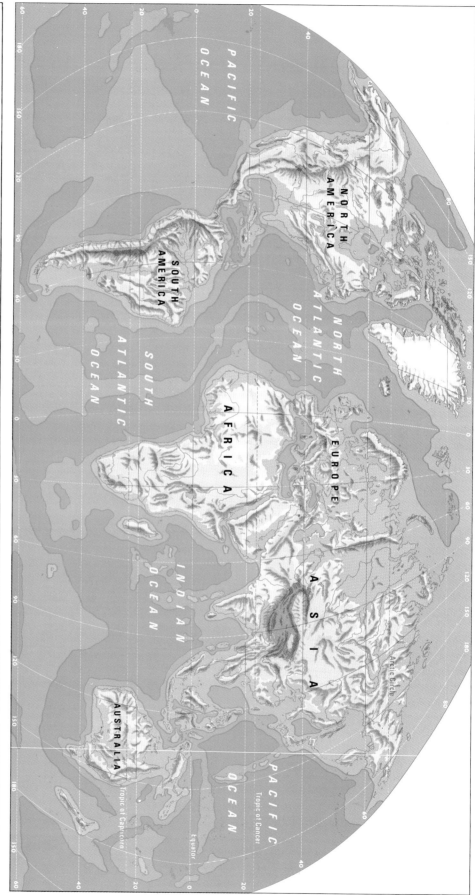

The World-Geographical Facts

Highest peaks

Highest peaks		Height in ft.
Mt Everest	Nepal	29,028
K2	India	28,250
Kangchenjunga	Nepal-India	28,208
Mt Makalu	Nepal-China	27,805
Dhaulagiri	Nepal	26,810
Nanga Parbat	India	26,660
Annapurna	Nepal	26,504
Gasherbrum	India	26,483
Gosainthan	Nepal-China	26,289
Nanda Devi	India	25,645
Rakaposhi	India	25,551
Mt Kamet	India	25,446
Namcha Barwa	China	25,446

Longest rivers

Longest rivers		Length in mi.
Nile	Africa	4,187
Amazon	South America	4,000
Yangtze	China	3,964
Mississippi-Missouri	USA	3,759
Zaire	Africa	3,000
Irtysh	Soviet Union	2,760
Amur	Soviet Union	2,700
Yellow River	China	2,700
Lena	Soviet Union	2,653
Niger	Africa	2,559
Mekong	Asia	2,500
Yenisei	Soviet Union	2,465

Principal seas

Principal seas	Area in sq mi	Greatest depth in ft
Pacific Ocean	63,986,049	36,197
Atlantic Ocean	31,530,024	30,141
Indian Ocean	28,350,021	22,969
Arctic Ocean	5,541,604	17,851
Mediterranean Sea	1,145,000	14,432
Caribbean Sea	1,049,500	25,216
South China Sea	895,000	16,456
Bering Sea	878,000	13,421
Gulf of Mexico	596,000	12,162
Sea of Okhotsk	582,000	12,621
East China Sea	480,000	10,499

Principal lakes

Principal lakes		Area in sq mi
Caspian Sea	Soviet Union	142,827
Superior	Canada-USA	31,800
Victoria	East Africa	26,826
Aral Sea	Soviet Union	25,477
Huron	Canada-USA	23,000
Michigan	USA	22,400
Great Bear	Canada	12,275
Baikal	Soviet Union	12,160
Great Slave	Canada	11,966
Malawi	Malawi-Mozambique	10,980
Erie	Canada-USA	9,930
Winnipeg	Canada	9,465

Scale at the Equator

Km 0   1000   2000   3000
Mi 0   1000   2000

Feet
52,500
10,500
6,560
1,300
0
Land below Sea Level
6,560
16,400

World — Climatic Regions

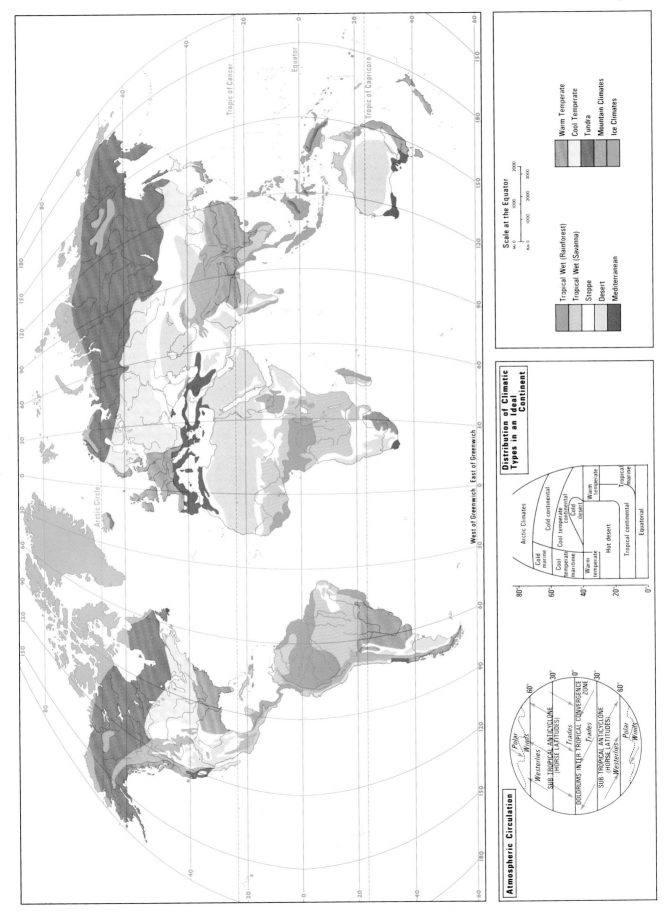

Tropic of Cancer

Equator

Tropic of Capricorn

Arctic Circle

West of Greenwich   East of Greenwich

Legend

Tropical Wet (Rainforest)
Tropical Wet (Savanna)
Steppe
Desert
Mediterranean

Warm Temperate
Cool Temperate
Tundra
Mountain Climates
Ice Climates

Scale at the Equator

Distribution of Climatic Types in an Ideal Continent

Arctic Climates

Cold continental

Cold marine

Cool temperate continental

Cool temperate maritime

Cold desert

Warm temperate

Warm temperate

Hot desert

Tropical marine

Tropical continental

Equatorial

80°
60°
40°
20°
0°

Atmospheric Circulation

Polar Winds
Westerlies
SUB TROPICAL ANTICYCLONE (HORSE LATITUDES)
Trades
DOLDRUMS INTER TROPICAL CONVERGENCE ZONE
Trades
SUB TROPICAL ANTICYCLONE (HORSE LATITUDES)
Westerlies
Polar Winds

60°
30°
0°
30°
60°

World – Vegetation

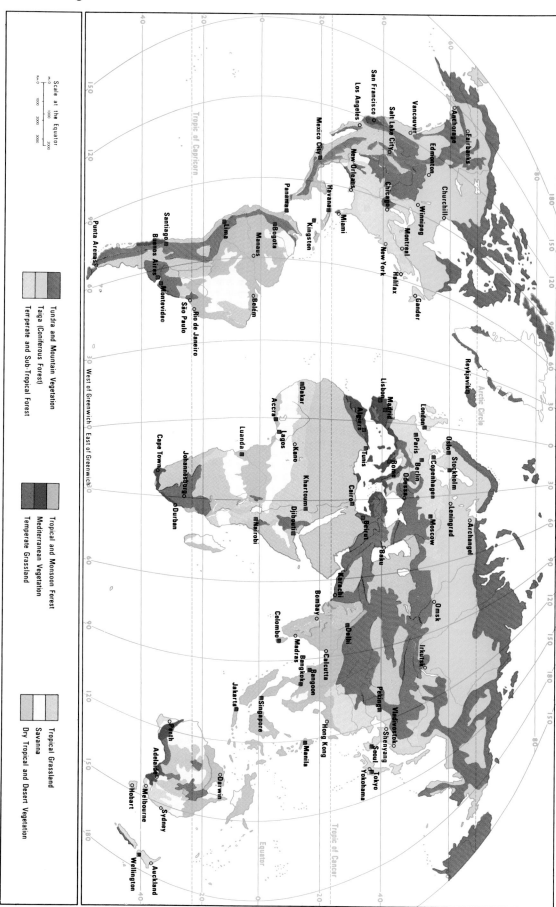

Scale at the Equator

Km.0   M.0
        1000
        2000
3000   2000

Tundra and Mountain Vegetation
Taiga (Coniferous Forest)
Temperate and Sub-Tropical Forest

Tropical and Monsoon Forest
Mediterranean Vegetation
Temperate Grassland

Tropical Grassland
Savanna
Dry Tropical and Desert Vegetation

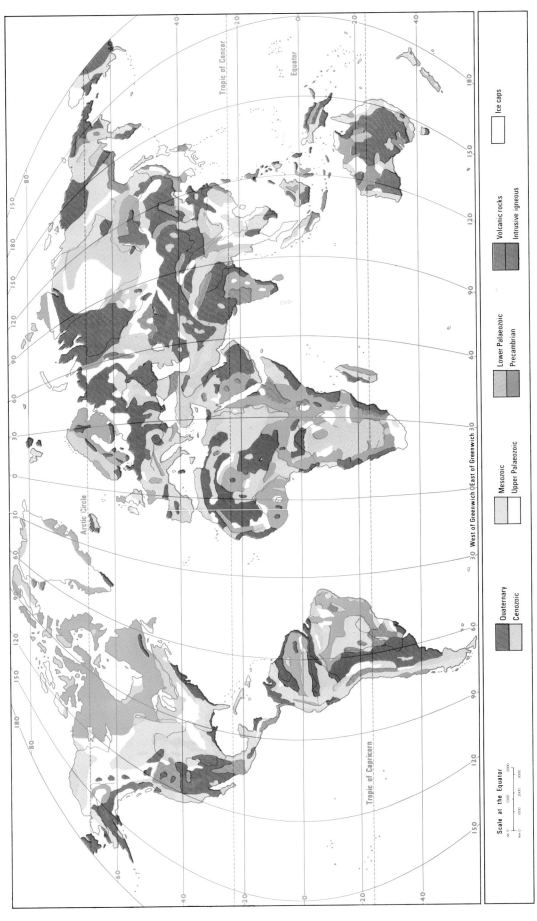

Scale at the Equator

Quaternary

Cenozoic

Mesozoic

Upper Palaeozoic

Lower Palaeozoic

Precambrian

Volcanic rocks

Intrusive igneous

Ice caps

Tropic of Cancer

Equator

Arctic Circle

Tropic of Capricorn

West of Greenwich   East of Greenwich

North America – Physical and Political

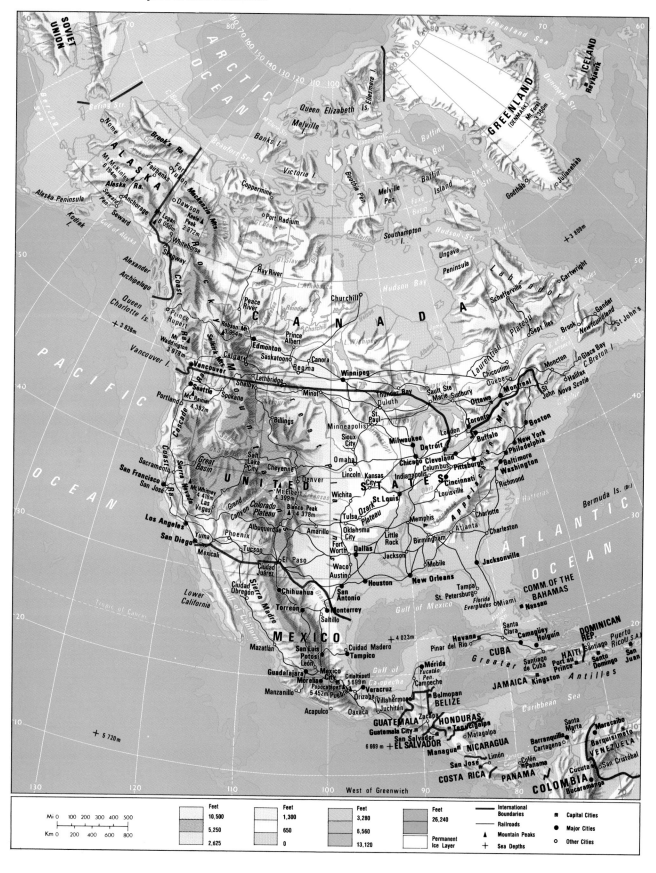

SOVIET UNION

ARCTIC OCEAN

Greenland Sea

ICELAND
Reykjavík

GREENLAND
(DENMARK)
Mt. Forel
3 360m

Queen Elizabeth Is.

Melville

Banks I.

Victoria I.

Ellesmere I.

Baffin Bay

Davis Str.

Godthåb

Julianehåb

Bering Sea

Bering Str.

Nome

Brook's Ra.

ALASKA

Fort Yukon

Fairbanks

Mt. McKinley
6 194m

Alaska Ra.

Anchorage

Mackenzie Mts.

Alaska Peninsula

Seward Pen.

Kodiak I.

Gulf of Alaska

Seward

Mt. Logan
6 050m

Dawson

Keele Pk.
2 972m

Whitehorse

Skagway

Coppermine

Port Radium

Boothia Pen.

Melville Pen.

Baffin Island

Foxe Basin

Southampton I.

Chesterfield

Hudson Str.

Ungava Peninsula

+ 3 809m

Labrador

Cartwright

Schefferville

Sept Îles

Alexander Archipelago

Queen Charlotte Is.

+ 3 828m

Prince Rupert

Coast Mts.

Robson Mt.
3 954m

Mt. Waddington
3 978m

Vancouver I.

Rocky Mountains

Selkirk Mts.

Edmonton

Calgary

Hay River

Peace River

CANADA

Prince Albert

Saskatoon

Canora

Regina

Lethbridge

L. Athabasca

Churchill

Reindeer L.

Gr. Slave L.

Peace

Churchill

Hudson Bay

L. Winnipeg

Plateau

Chicoutimi

Quebec

Laurentian Mts.

Brook

Sander

Glace Bay
C. Breton

Newfoundland

St. John's

Halifax

Moncton

Nova Scotia

St. John

Montreal

Vancouver

Seattle
Mt. Rainier
4 392m

Portland

Spokane

Shelby

Billings

Minot

Winnipeg

Thunder Bay

Sault Ste Marie

Sudbury

Ottawa

Boston

PACIFIC OCEAN

Sacramento

San Francisco

San José

Great Basin

Salt Lake City

Cheyenne

UNITED STATES

Denver

Sierra Nevada

Mt. Whitney
4 418m

Las Vegas

Grand Canyon

Colorado Plateau

Cascade Ra.

Mt. Elbert
4 399m

Blanca Peak
4 378m

Duluth

St. Paul

Minneapolis

Sioux City

Omaha

Lincoln

Milwaukee

Chicago

Detroit

Cleveland

Columbus

Pittsburgh

London

Toronto

Buffalo

New York

Philadelphia

Baltimore

Washington

Richmond

Kansas City

Indianapolis

Cincinnati

Louisville

Ohio

St. Louis

Ozark Plateau

Appalachian Mts.

Charlotte

C. Hatteras

Bermuda Is. (Br.)

Los Angeles

San Diego

Yuma

Phoenix

Tucson

Mexicali

Albuquerque

Amarillo

Wichita

Tulsa

Oklahoma City

Little Rock

Memphis

Birmingham

Atlanta

Charleston

ATLANTIC OCEAN

Lower California

Ciudad Juárez

El Paso

Fort Worth

Dallas

Waco

Austin

San Antonio

Houston

Jackson

Mobile

New Orleans

Jacksonville

Ciudad Obregón

Chihuahua

Rio Grande

Monterrey

Saltillo

Tampa

St. Petersburg

Florida Everglades

Miami

COMM. OF THE BAHAMAS

Nassau

Sierra Madre

Tropic of Cancer

Torreón

Mazatlán

MEXICO

San Luis Potosí

León

Cuidad Madero

Tampico

+ 4 023m

Gulf of Campeche

Mérida

Yucatán Pen.

Campeche

Santa Clara

Havana

Pinar del Río

Camagüey

Holguín

CUBA

Greater

Santiago de Cuba

DOMINICAN REP.

HAITI

Port au Prince

Santiago

Santo Domingo

Puerto Rico (U.S.A.)

San Juan

Guadalajara

Morelia

Mexico City

Popocatépetl
5 452m

Citlaltépetl
5 699m

Puebla

Veracruz

Orizaba

Villahermosa

Juchitán

Manzanillo

Acapulco

Oaxaca

Belmopan

BELIZE

GUATEMALA

Guatemala City

Zacapa

HONDURAS

Tegucigalpa

Matagalpa

6 869 m + EL SALVADOR

San Salvador

Managua

NICARAGUA

JAMAICA

Kingston

Antilles

Caribbean Sea

Santa Marta

Barranquilla

Cartagena

Maracaibo

Barquisimeto

VENEZUELA

+ 5 720m

San José

Limón

COSTA RICA

Colón

Panama

PANAMA

Cúcuta

San Cristóbal

COLOMBIA

Bucaramanga

West of Greenwich

Feet		Feet		Feet		Feet			
10,500		1,300		3,280		26,240		International Boundaries	Capital Cities
5,250		650		6,560				Railroads	Major Cities
2,625		0		13,120		Permanent Ice Layer		Mountain Peaks	Other Cities
								Sea Depths	

Mi 0   100 200 300 400 500

Km 0   200 400 600 800

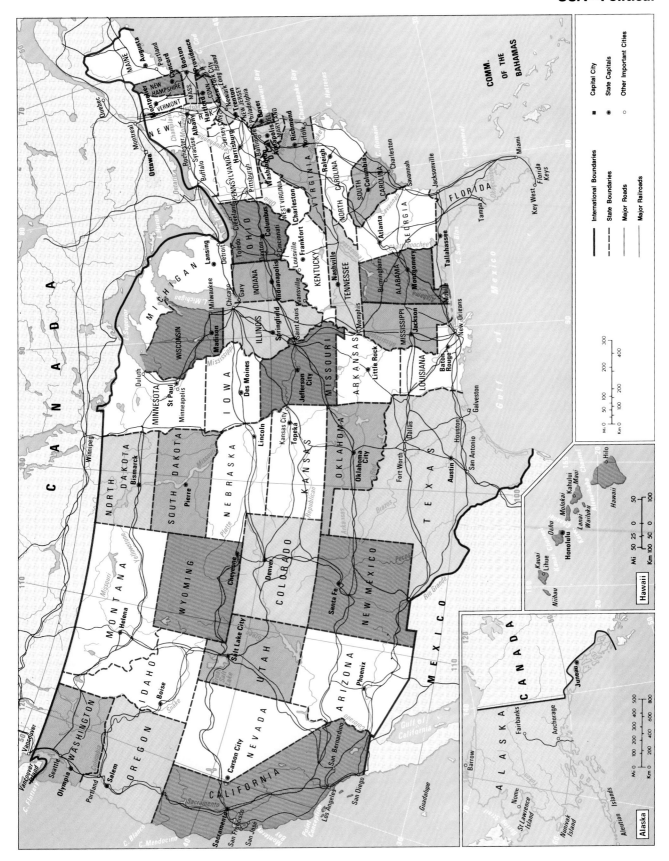

Capital City ■
State Capitals ◉
Other Important Cities ○

International Boundaries
State Boundaries
Major Roads
Major Railroads

COMM.
OF THE
BAHAMAS

Hawaii

Alaska

South America – Physical and Political

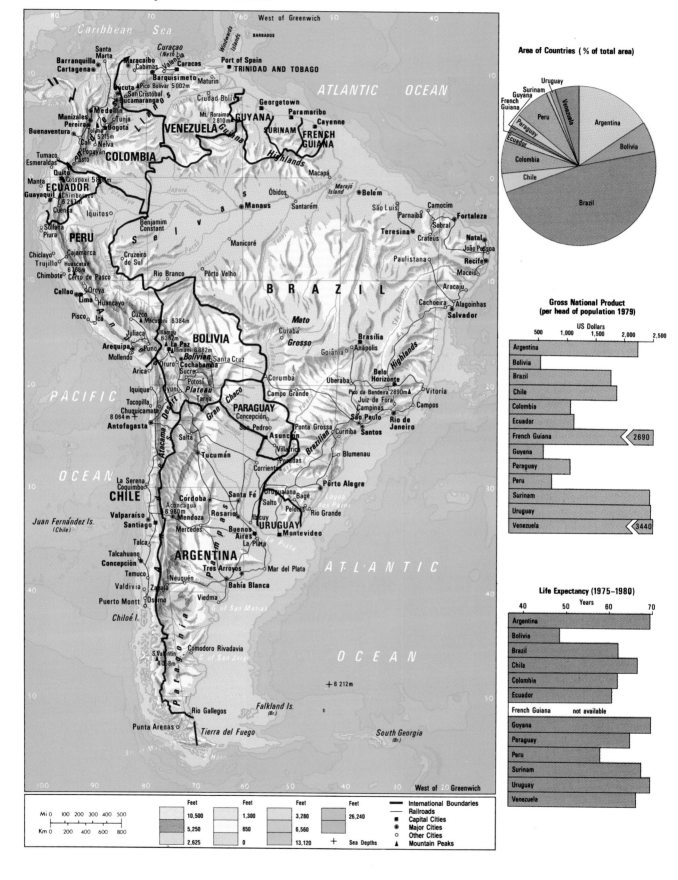

Area of Countries (% of total area)

Uruguay
Surinam
Guyana
French Guiana
Paraguay
Ecuador
Colombia
Chile
Venezuela
Peru
Argentina
Bolivia
Brazil

Gross National Product (per head of population 1979)

US Dollars

	500	1,000	1,500	2,000	2,500
Argentina					
Bolivia					
Brazil					
Chile					
Colombia					
Ecuador					
French Guiana			2690		
Guyana					
Paraguay					
Peru					
Surinam					
Uruguay					
Venezuela			3440		

Life Expectancy (1975–1980)

Years

	40	50	60	70
Argentina				
Bolivia				
Brazil				
Chile				
Colombia				
Ecuador				
French Guiana	not available			
Guyana				
Paraguay				
Peru				
Surinam				
Uruguay				
Venezuela				

Mi 0   100 200 300 400 500
Km 0   200   400   600   800

Feet		Feet		Feet		Feet	
10,500		1,300		3,280		26,240	
5,250		650		6,560			
2,625		0		13,120		+ Sea Depths	

━━━ International Boundaries
─── Railroads
■ Capital Cities
⊛ Major Cities
○ Other Cities
▲ Mountain Peaks

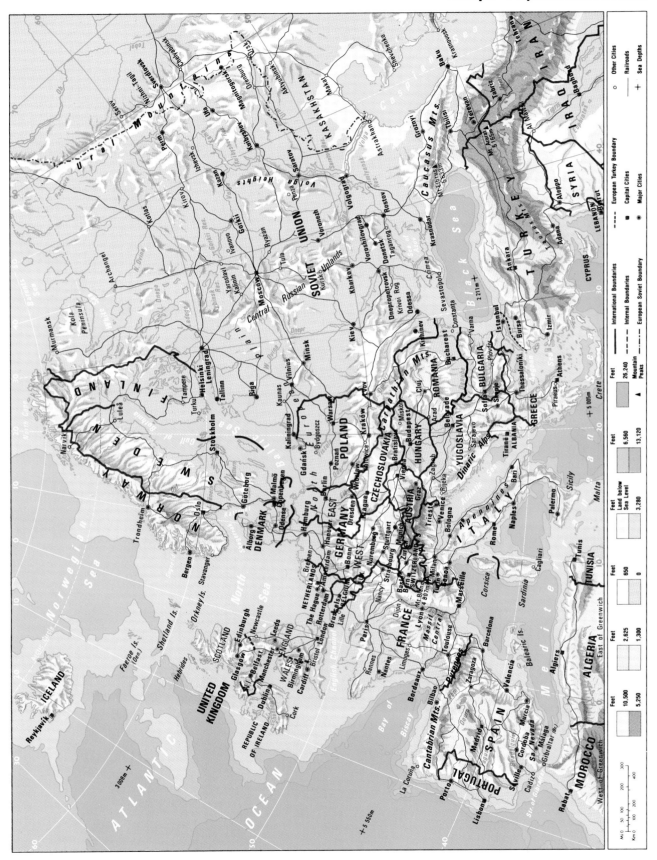

Western Europe – Physical and Political

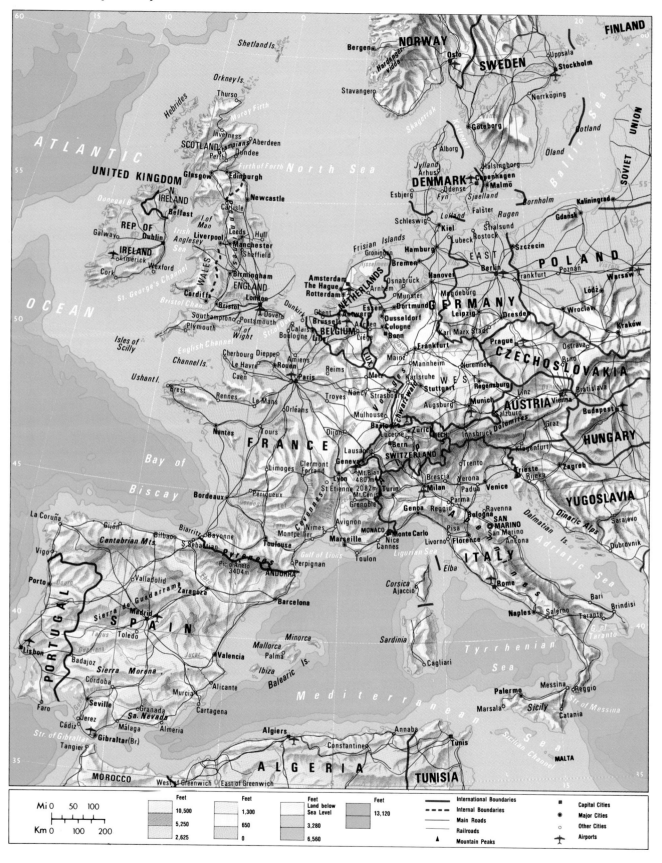

Mi 0   50   100

Km 0   100   200

Feet		Feet		Feet		Feet	
	10,500		1,300	Land below Sea Level			13,120
	5,250		650		3,280		
	2,625		0		6,560		

International Boundaries

Internal Boundaries

Main Roads

Railroads

▲ Mountain Peaks

■ Capital Cities

● Major Cities

○ Other Cities

✈ Airports

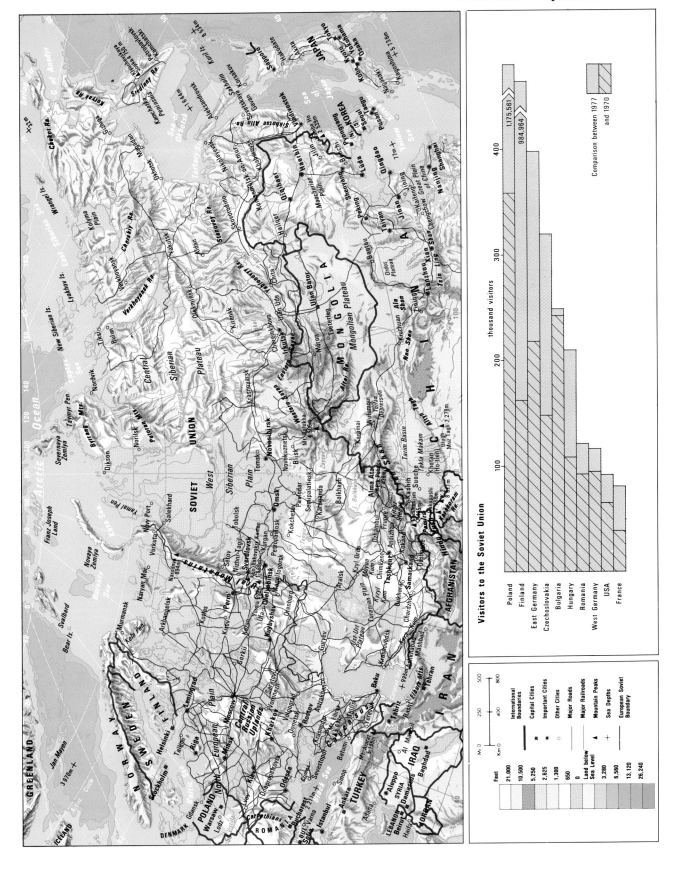

Visitors to the Soviet Union

thousand visitors

Comparison between 1977 and 1970

1,175,561
984,964

100   200   300   400

Poland
Finland
East Germany
Czechoslovakia
Bulgaria
Hungary
Romania
West Germany
USA
France

	Mi. 0	250	500
	Km 0	400	800

Feet		
21,000		International Boundaries
10,500	■	Capital Cities
5,250	■ ●	Important Cities
2,625	○	Other Cities
1,300		Major Roads
650		
0		Major Railroads
Land below Sea Level	▲	Mountain Peaks
3,280	+	Sea Depths
6,560		European Soviet Boundary
13,120		
26,240		

Africa — Physical and Political

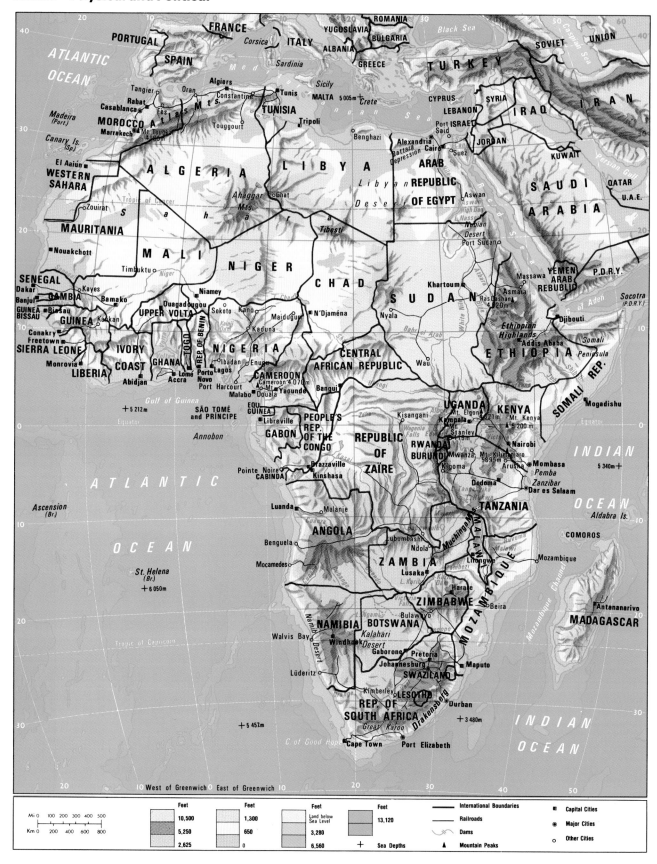

Feet

10,500	
5,250	
2,625	

Feet

1,300	
650	
0	

Feet

Land below Sea Level	
3,280	
6,560	

Feet

13,120	

— International Boundaries
— Railroads
Dams
+ Sea Depths
▲ Mountain Peaks

■ Capital Cities
◉ Major Cities
○ Other Cities

Mi 0 100 200 300 400 500
Km 0 200 400 600 800

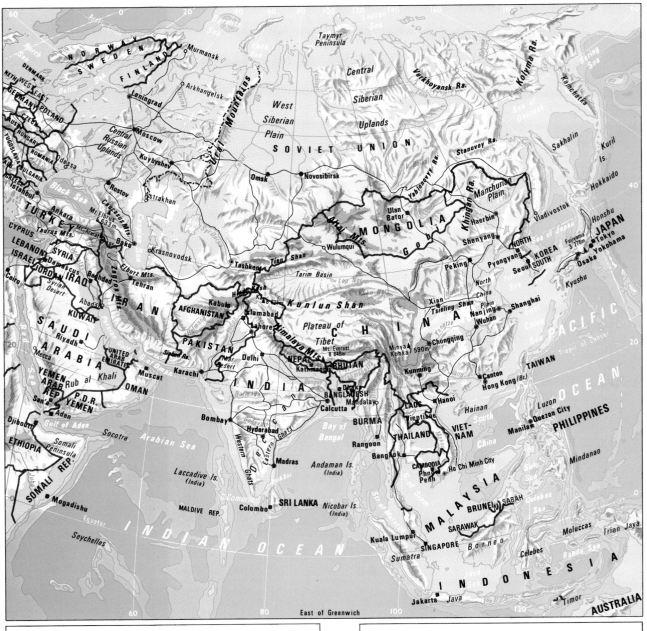

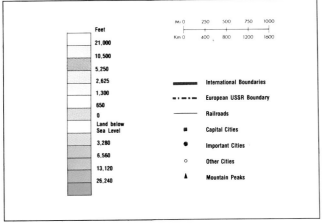

Feet
21,000
10,500
5,250
2,625
1,300
650
0
Land below
Sea Level
3,280
6,560
13,120
26,240

Mi. 0   250   500   750   1000
Km 0   400   800   1200   1600

━━━ International Boundaries
━·━·━ European USSR Boundary
─── Railroads
■ Capital Cities
● Important Cities
○ Other Cities
▲ Mountain Peaks

World	4,124,0	
China	982.6	
India	683.8	
Indonesia	147.4	
Japan	117.1	
Bangladesh	88.7	
Pakistan	82.4	
Vietnam	52.7	
Philippines	48.4	
Thailand	46.5	
S. Korea	37.4	
Burma	35.3	
N. Korea	17.9	
Taiwan	17.5	
Sri Lanka	14.7	
Nepal	14.0	
Malaysia	13.4	

Population (in millions)
of South and East Asia*

1 giant represents 500 million people
1 man represents 10 million people

*latest available figures

Australasia – Physical and Political

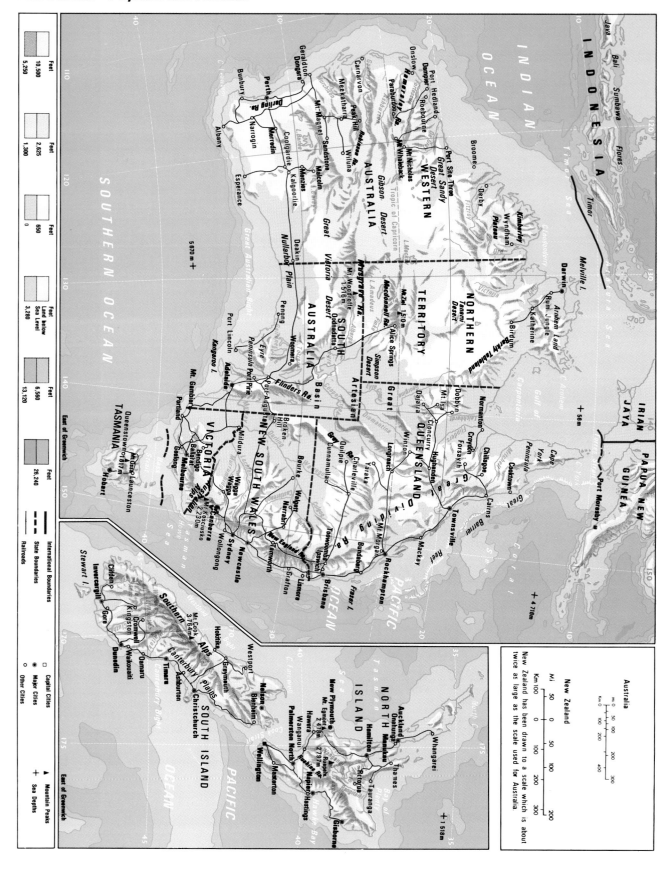

chant of Venice, his first London success in 1814, Richard III, Macbeth, Iago in *Othello*, and Barabas in Marlowe's *The Jew of Malta*, all roles suited to his forceful and passionate style of acting.

Kearny, Stephen Watts (1794–1848) US soldier. He fought in the War of 1812 and then was assigned to frontier duty. By 1846 he commanded, as a general, the Army of the West and during the *Mexican War was responsible for taking New Mexico (1846). He then advanced toward California with a small force, joined those of John C. *Fremont and Robert F. Stockton (1795–1866), and captured San Diego (1846), San Gabriel (1847), and Los Angeles (1847). Kearny finally won the fight over who would administer California. He later served as governor of Veracruz and Mexico City (1848).

Keating-Owen Act (Federal Child Labor Law; 1916) A US law that prohibited products made by child labor from being transported across state lines. It was declared unconstitutional in 1918.

Keaton, Buster (Joseph Francis K.; 1895–1966) US comedian of silent films. He worked with his parents in vaudeville before starting his film career in 1917. He developed his character of the unsmiling and resilient clown in a series of classic silent comedies, including *The Navigator* (1924), *The General* (1926), and *The Cameraman* (1928). He was awarded a special Academy Award for his screen comedies in 1959. His autobiography is *My Wonderful World of Slapstick* (1962).

Keats, John (1795–1821) British poet. Despite the failure of his first volume, *Poems* (1817), which contained the sonnet "On First Looking into Chapman's Homer," and the savage criticism directed at his second, *Endymion* (1818), Keats persisted and between 1819 and 1820 wrote most of his best-known poems. His short life was dogged by tragedies, especially the death of his brother in 1818 and his unrequited love for Fanny Brawne. Such poems as *La Belle Dame Sans Merci*, *The Eve of Saint Agnes*, and the great odes ("To a Nightingale," "On a Grecian Urn," etc.), all published in 1820, eventually established his reputation. He died in Rome of tuberculosis.

Keble, John (1792–1866) British churchman and a leader of the *Oxford Movement. While professor of poetry at Oxford (1831–41) he preached a famous sermon, entitled "National Apostasy," which effectively began the Oxford Movement. Keble College, Oxford, was founded in his memory (1870).

Kebnekaise A mountain range in N Sweden. It rises to 6965 ft (2123 m) at Kebnekaise Sydtopp, the highest mountain in Sweden.

Kecskemét 46 56N 19 43E A city in central Hungary. It lies on a wide fertile plain that is Hungary's most important agricultural area, notably for such fruit as apricots. Population (1980): 93,000.

Kedah A state in NW Peninsular Malaysia, bordering on Thailand. Rice is grown on the W coastal plain; other products include rubber, tin, tungsten, and iron. Area: 3639 sq mi (9425 sq km). Population (1980): 1,102,200. Capital: Alor Star.

Keeling Islands. *See* Cocos Islands.

Keelung. *See* Jilong.

Keeshond A breed of dog traditionally used by the Dutch as barge dogs. It has a compact body with a foxlike face and a long thick gray coat with black-tipped hairs. The tail is carried over the back and a dense ruff surrounds the neck. Height: 17–18 in (43–45 cm).

Keewatin A district of N Canada, in the *Northwest Territories. It consists of the mainland E of 102°W and N of 60°N plus most islands in Hudson Bay. Part of the Canadian Shield, it is mostly tundra. Some fur trapping takes place. Area: 228,160 sq mi (590,934 sq km). Population (1976): 3978. *See also* Barren Grounds.

Kefallinia. *See* Cephalonia.

Kefauver, (Carey) Estes (1903–63) US politician. He practiced law in Tennessee before serving in the US House of Representatives (1939–48) and Senate (1949–63). He achieved national recognition through his televised Senate Crime Investigation Committee hearing in 1951–52. He ran unsuccessfully for vice president in 1956.

Keflavík 64 01N 22 35W A town and fishing port in SW Iceland. It has a NATO air base. Population (1980): 6622.

Keighley 53 52N 1 54W A city in N England, in West Yorkshire on the River Aire. The main products are woolens and worsteds, textile machinery, and machine tools. Population (1981 est): 57,451.

Keitel, Wilhelm (1882–1946) German field marshal, who was Hitler's chief military adviser throughout World War II. In 1945 in Berlin he confirmed the German surrender. He was hanged for war crimes.

Kekulé von Stradonitz, (Friedrich) August (1829–96) German chemist, whose main interest was in valence. He was the first chemist to establish the valence of the elements and to introduce the notion of single, double, and triple bonds. He went on to deduce the structural formulae of many organic molecules, including that of benzene (**Kekulé formula**), which he claimed to have thought of in 1865 while dozing on a bus. *See also* aromatic compound.

Kelantan A state in central Peninsular Malaysia, bordering on Thailand. It was ruled by Siam (now Thailand) from the early 19th century until 1909. Rice is grown on the NE coastal plain, and rubber, copra, and minerals are produced. Area: 5765 sq mi (14,931 sq km). Population (1980): 877,575. Capital: Kota Baharu.

Keller, Gottfried (1819–90) German-Swiss poet and novelist. His early poetry (1846) won him a scholarship to study in Germany. His works include the novel *Der grüne Heinrich* (1854–55) and short stories, including *Die Leute von Seldwyla* (1856–74), describing life in a small town.

Keller, Helen Adams (1880–1968) US social worker and writer. At the age of 19 months she lost her sight and hearing through an illness. Despite these handicaps she learned to speak, read, and write with the dedication of her teacher, Anne Sullivan, and finally graduated from Radcliffe College in 1904. She lectured in many countries and raised money for the education of handicapped people. Her books include *The Story of My Life* (1903), *The World I Live In* (1908), and *The Open Door* (1957). A play about her early life, William Gibson's *The Miracle Worker*, received the 1960 Pulitzer Prize.

Kellogg, Frank Billings (1856–1937) US statesman, diplomat, and politician. A lawyer, he was a special prosecutor in President Theodore Roosevelt's administration and fought monopolies successfully, including the Standard Oil Company (1906) and the Union Pacific Railroad (1907). He served in the US Senate (1917–23) and then was US ambassador to Britain (1924–25). Returning in 1925 to serve as secretary of state under President Calvin *Coolidge, he formulated the *Kellogg-Briand Pact. Awarded the Nobel Peace Prize (1929), he was a member (1930–35) of the International Court of Justice.

Kellogg-Briand Pact (1928) An international agreement that condemned war as a means of settling disputes. The pact of perpetual friendship, negotiated by the US secretary of state, Frank B. Kellogg (1856–1937) and French foreign minister, *Briand, was signed in Paris in 1928 by representatives of 15 nations, and later by 48 others. Some success in South American disputes was achieved by invoking the treaty, but it proved ineffective against the Japanese invasion of Manchuria (1931), the Italian invasion of Ethiopia (1938), and against Hitler's aggression.

Kells (Irish name: Ceanannus Mór) 54 48N 6 14W A market town in the Republic of Ireland, in Co Meath. A monastery was founded here in the 6th century AD by St Columba in which *The Book of Kells*, an 8th-century illuminated manuscript of the Gospels, is reputed to have been written. Population (1971): 2391.

Kelly, Grace (1929–82) US film actress. Her films include *High Noon* (1952), *Dial M for Murder* (1954), *Rear Window* (1954), *The Country Girl* (1955), for which she received an Academy Award, *To Catch a Thief* (1955), and *High Society* (1956). She retired from acting when she married Prince Rainier III of Monaco in 1956. She died following an automobile accident.

NED KELLY *A contemporary engraving of the famous bushranger during his final battle (1880). All members of the gang wore heavy home-made armor.*

Kelly, Ned (1855–80) Australian outlaw. He and his brother Dan formed a gang in 1878 that became notorious for its daring robberies in Victoria and New South Wales. He was captured and hanged in 1880 after a gunfight with the police in which the other gang members were killed.

kelp A large brown *seaweed belonging to the order *Laminariales* (about 30 genera), found in cold seas, usually below the level of low tide, and often covering large areas. The giant kelp *Macrocystis*, of the E Pacific coast, reaches a length of 213 ft (65 m). Its branching fronds are kept afloat by air bladders. The name kelp is also used for the ashes of seaweed, from which potassium and sodium salts and iodine were once obtained. *See also* Laminaria.

kelpie A breed of short-haired dog developed in Australia from the Border Collie and used for herding sheep and cattle. Named for a champion sheepdog of the 1870s, the kelpie has a long muzzle and pricked ears. The coat may be black or red (with or without tan), fawn, chocolate, or smoke-blue. Height: 17–20 in (43–50 cm).

kelvin (K) The *SI unit of *thermodynamic temperature equal to 1/273.16 of the thermodynamic temperature of the triple point of water. Named for Lord *Kelvin.

Kelvin, William Thomson, 1st Baron (1824–1907) Scottish physicist, who was professor at Glasgow University (1846–99). Kelvin was the first physicist to take notice of *Joule's work on heat and to press for its recognition. The two physicists then worked together, discovering the *Joule-Kelvin effect; both also made great contributions to the new science of thermodynamics. In 1848 Kelvin postulated that there is a temperature at which the motions of particles cease and their energies become zero. He called this temperature *absolute zero and suggested a scale of temperature, now known as the Kelvin scale, in which the zero point is absolute zero. In 1852 he suggested that a *heat pump was a feasible device. Kelvin was also active in the study of electricity; during the 1860s he worked on the electrical properties of cables in conjunction with the laying of the first transatlantic cable in 1866. Kelvin was knighted for his contribution to this work in the same year and was created baron in 1896. The unit of temperature (*see* kelvin) is named for him.

Kemal, (Mehmed) Namik (1840–88) Turkish poet, novelist, and dramatist. He was strongly influenced by European Romanticism and became one of the founders of modern Turkish literature. He was a member of a literary group known as the "Young Ottomans" and was imprisoned for the liberal and patriotic ideas he expressed in his most famous play, *Vatan yahnut Silistre* (*Fatherland or Silistria*; 1871).

Kemerovo 55 25N 86 05E A city in the S Soviet Union, in the Tom River. It is the center of the *Kuznetsk Basin coalfield and is one of the country's major chemical-producing cities. Population (1981 est): 486,000.

Kempis, Thomas à. *See* Thomas à Kempis.

Kendall, Edward Calvin (1886–1972) US biochemist, who shared the 1950 Nobel Prize in medicine and physiology with Phillip Hench and Tadeus Reichstein for their work on hormones. In 1916 he isolated the hormone thyroxine produced by the thyroid gland and later isolated several hormones from the adrenal cortex. This work laid the basis for the modern study of endocrinology.

kendo A Japanese *martial art deriving from *samurai sword fighting. Combatants using bamboo staffs or wooden swords try to deliver blows on specified target areas of each other's bodies. Two hits constitute a win.

Kendrew, John Cowdery (1917–) British biochemist, who shared the 1962 Nobel Prize for chemistry with Max *Perutz for his discovery of the structure of the myoglobin molecule. Kendrew, working at Cambridge University, used the technique of *X-ray diffraction, analyzing his results with a computer.

Kenilworth 52 21N 1 34W A city in central England, in Warwickshire. Kenilworth Castle, built in the 12th century, was presented to Robert Dudley, Earl of Leicester, by Elizabeth I in 1563 and described in Sir Walter Scott's novel *Kenilworth*. The city has motor and agricultural engineering and tanning industries. Population (1981): 19,315.

Kenitra (former name: Port Lyautey; Arabic name: Mina Hassan Tani) 34 20N 6 34W A port in NW Morocco, on the Atlantic Ocean. It handles agricultural products, minerals, and timber. Population (1973 est): 135,960.

Kennedy, Cape. *See* Canaveral, Cape.

JOHN F. KENNEDY *President (1961-63) whose assassination in Dallas on November 22, 1963, shocked the world.*

Kennedy, John Fitzgerald (1917–63) US statesman; 35th President of the United States (1961–63). Son of Joseph Patrick *Kennedy, he was educated at Harvard and served as a PT boat commander in the Pacific during World War II. As the grandson of former Boston mayor John F. Fitzgerald, Kennedy became active in the *Democratic Party and began his political career as a member of the US House of Representatives (1947–53). In 1952, Kennedy was elected to the US Senate and quickly rose to national prominence in an attempt to gain the 1956 Democratic vice-presidential nomination. He actively campaigned for the presidency in 1960 and after a bitter primary campaign became the Democratic candidate. Choosing Senator Lyndon *Johnson as his running mate, he defeated Republican Richard *Nixon by a slim plurality. His election marked the first time that a Roman Catholic was elected president and did much to allay opposition to Catholics in public office.

Kennedy's administration was marked by innovation and an ambitious social program that he called the New Frontier. In addition to his active support for the cause of civil rights at home, he worked for cooperation with the nations of Latin America through the *Alliance for Progress and established the *Peace Corps, which sent young Americans to developing nations as educational and technical advisers. In the field of foreign affairs, the Kennedy administration was forced to deal with several serious crises. In 1961 the ill-fated Bay of Pigs invasion of Cuba chilled US-Soviet relations, and the Cuban Missile Crisis of 1962 brought the two superpowers into direct confrontation. A lasting achievement of the Kennedy administration was the ratification of the Nuclear Test Ban Treaty in 1963. While beginning his 1964 re-election campaign, he was assassinated in Dallas, Tex., on November 22, 1963. Riding with him when he was fatally shot was his wife, Jacqueline Bouvier, whom he had married in 1953. She became the wife of Aristotle *Onassis in 1968. As first lady, Jackie, as she was fondly known, had participated actively in arts programs and in redecorating the White House.

Kennedy, Joseph Patrick (1888–1969) US businessman and diplomat. Son of Irish immigrants, Kennedy earned a fortune in the stock market and pursued various business interests. Active in the *Democratic Party, he was appointed chairman of the Securities and Exchange Commission in 1934 by President Franklin Roosevelt. He later served as US Ambassador to Great Britain (1937–40). He had five daughters and four sons, three of whom entered public life. The eldest, **Joseph Patrick Kennedy Jr.** (1915–44), a naval pilot, was killed in World War II. John Fitzgerald *Kennedy

(1917–63), was elected president of the United States. **Robert Francis Kennedy** (1925–68), who served as US attorney general (1961–64) and US senator (1965–68), was assassinated in 1968. The youngest son of the family, **Edward Moore Kennedy** (1932–   ), has served as US senator and one of the leaders of the *Democratic Party since 1962.

Kennelly, Arthur Edwin (1861–1939) US electrical engineer. On learning that *Marconi had succeeded in transmitting radio waves across the Atlantic, despite the earth's curvature, Kennelly guessed that the waves were being reflected by an electrically charged layer in the upper atmosphere. The existence of this layer was confirmed independently by Oliver *Heaviside and was known as the Kennelly-Heaviside layer (now known as the E-layer of the *ionosphere).

Kenneth I MacAlpine (died c. 858) King of the Scots of Dalriada (c. 844–c. 858). He formed the kingdom of Alba, the foundation of modern Scotland.

Kent A county of SE England, bordering on the English Channel and Greater London. It consists chiefly of undulating lowlands, crossed by the North Downs from W to E, and rising to the The Weald in the SW. The chief rivers are the Thames, Medway, and Stour. There are impressive chalk cliffs, notably at Dover. Often called the Garden of England, it is the country's leading fruit and hop-growing area. Other important agricultural activities include market gardening and arable, cattle, and sheep farming. The main industries are paper manufacture, shipbuilding, and oil refining. Area: 1440 sq mi (3730 sq km). Population (1981): 1,463,055. Administrative center: Maidstone.

Kent 41 09N 81 22W A city in NE Ohio, on the Cuyahoga River, NE of Akron. Kent State University (1910), the site of anti-Vietnam War rallies and the shooting of four students by National Guardsmen in 1970, is here. Industries include the manufacture of rubber, plastic, sports and hardware products and of motor vehicles. Population (1980): 26,164.

Kent, William (1685–1748) English architect, landscape gardener, and interior designer. Kent is possibly the most famous exponent of English *Palladianism. His most notable buildings were Holkham Hall, Norfolk (1734), the Horse Guards, London (built after his death), but his greatest contribution to English art was his development of *landscape gardening, later continued by such designers as Capability *Brown.

Kentucky A state in the central US, lying to the E of the Mississippi River. The meandering Ohio River forms the N boundary with Ohio, Indiana, and Illinois. The Mississippi River, which joins the Ohio near Covington, forms the W border with Missouri. (The SW tip of Kentucky is cut off entirely from the rest of the state by a sharp turn in the Mississippi.) The S border with Tennessee forms a straight E–W line across the bottom of the state. In the SE, Kentucky borders Virginia, and in the NE the Big Sandy River forms the boundary with West Virginia. It consists of the Appalachian Mountains in the E, the Bluegrass region in the center, an undulating plain in the W, and the basins of the Tennessee and Ohio Rivers in the SW. Manufacturing in the state includes machinery, iron and steel products, paints, varnishes, textiles, whiskey, and food products. It is an important coalmining state and also produces petroleum and natural gas. Local timber is used in the furniture and wood industries. The principal agricultural products are tobacco, corn, hay, soybeans, cattle, sheep, and pigs. It is also an important region for the breeding of thoroughbred horses. Kentucky is a rural state with a strong rural tradition and folk culture. *History*: Daniel Boone explored the area (1769), blazing the Wilderness Road westward through the Cumberland Gap in Kentucky's Appalachian Mountains and onward to the Ohio River. After rapid settlement Kentucky achieved statehood (1792). As a so-called border state, Kentucky was torn on the slavery issue, but eventually joined the Union side in the Civil War. However, Kentucky soldiers fought on both Union and Confederate sides. In the late 19th century coal mining was begun and has since played a large role in Kentucky's economic life and history. The industry was well established by the 20th century; Kentucky is now the leading US producer of bituminous and lignite coal. As the labor movement gained ground in the 1930s and the United Mine Workers attempted to unionize in Kentucky, violent strife erupted, particularly in Harlan County. Mining subsequently declined but the energy crisis of the 1970s brought new life to the industry. Area: 40,395 sq mi (104,623 sq km). Population (1980): 3,661,433. Capital: Frankfort.

Kentucky and Virginia Resolutions Three resolutions, two (Kentucky) written by Thomas *Jefferson (1798, 1799) and one (Virginia) by James Madison (1798) that recommended repeal of the *Alien and Sedition Acts, which had had strong support from the Federalists. It was felt by the Jeffersonians that states should have the right to decide such matters and that the federal government had far exceeded its powers.

Kenya, Mount 0 10S 37 30E An extinct volcano in Kenya, the second highest mountain in Africa. It has 12 small glaciers radiating from its summit. Height: 17,058 ft (5200 m).

Kenya, Republic of A country in East Africa, on the Indian Ocean. The land rises gradually from the coast to the highlands of the interior reaching heights of over 17,000 ft (5000 m). In the W the Great Rift Valley runs N–S. Most of the inhabitants are Africans, including *Kikuyu, *Luo, *Masai, and Kamba. *Economy*: agricultural production and processing forms the basis of the economy. A variety of subtropical and temperate crops are grown. The chief cash crops are coffee, tea (of which Kenya is Africa's leading producer), sisal, and pineapples; livestock rearing and dairy farming are also important. Forestry is being developed and mineral resources include soda ash, gold, limestone, and salt. Hydroelectricity is a valuable source of power and industries include food processing, with oil refining at Mombasa. Tourism is an important source of income with Kenya's abundant big game; wildlife reserves include the huge Tsavo National Park. *History*: some of the earliest known fossil *hominid remains have been found in the region by the *Leakey family. The coastal area was settled by the Arabs from the 7th century AD and was controlled by the Portuguese during the 16th and 17th centuries. It became a British protectorate (East Africa Protectorate) in 1895 and a colony (Kenya) in 1920. In the 1950s independence movements, especially among the Kikuyu, led to the *Mau Mau revolt. Kenya gained independence in 1963 and in 1964 became a republic within the British Commonwealth, with Jomo *Kenyatta as its first president. Following independence, Kenya gained a reputation for its stable government, democratic policies, and steady economic growth. An abortive coup in 1982, reflecting frustration with a declining economy and with the policies of President Daniel arap Moi, tarnished this image and generated concern among western nations. Moi responded with repressive measures, as the military gained in influence in internal policies. President: Daniel arap Moi. Official languages: Swahili and English. Official currency: Kenya shilling of 100 cents. Area: 224,960 mi (582,600 sq km). Population (1983): 18,580,000. Capital: Nairobi. Main port: Mombasa.

JOMO KENYATTA *Known as Mzee (Grand Old Man), he was invariably seen with a fly whisk, a traditional symbol of power.*

Kenyatta, Jomo (c. 1891–1978) Kenyan statesman; president (1964–78). Son of a poor farmer of the Kikuyu tribe, Kenyatta studied anthropology in London, where his doctoral thesis on the Kikuyu was published in 1938 as *Facing Mount Kenya*. On his return to Kenya he became (1947) president of the Kenya African Union and in 1953 was imprisoned for seven years by the colonial government for his part in the

*Mau Mau rebellion (complicity in which he always denied). While in jail he was elected leader of the Kenya African National Union (1960), which achieved Kenya's independence in 1963. Kenyatta was prime minister before becoming president of a one-party state.

Kenyon, Dame Kathleen (1906–78) British archeologist. Under the influence of Sir Mortimer *Wheeler she promoted sophisticated excavation techniques. Her excavations at *Jericho (1952–58), through which the site's great age was revealed, and at *Jerusalem (1961–67) are renowned.

Kepler, Johannes (1571–1630) German astronomer, who was one of the first supporters of *Copernicus' heliocentric theory of the solar system. In 1597 he went to Prague to study under Tycho *Brahe; on Tycho's death, Kepler inherited his astronomical observations. Kepler used this data to deduce the shape of planetary orbits, discovering that they were elliptical. He published this discovery, the first of *Kepler's laws, together with his second law in *Astronomia Nova* (1609). In 1619 he published his third law relating a planet's year to its distance from the sun. In 1610 he received a telescope built by *Galileo, which he used to observe Jupiter. In 1611 he constructed an improved version, now known as a Keplerian *telescope.

Kepler's laws Three laws of planetary motion proposed by Johannes Kepler in 1609 and (third law) 1619. They state that: (1) each planet moves round the sun in an elliptical orbit with the sun at one focus of the ellipse; (2) the line joining a planet to the sun sweeps out equal areas in equal times, i.e. orbital velocity decreases as distance from the sun increases; (3) the square of the *sidereal period (P) of a planet is directly proportional to the cube of its mean distance (a) from the sun. For P in years and a in *astronomical units, $P^2 = a^3$.

Kerala A state in SW India, extending along the W coastal plain and Western Ghats to India's S tip. Tropical, beautiful, and poor, it is India's most densely populated state, with little industry or mining. Rice, tea, coffee, pepper, rubber, nuts, and fruit are farmed. Fishing is also important. *History*: a civilization separate from Aryan N India, Malayalam-speaking Kerala has traded with the Near and Far East since ancient times, flourishing in the 9th and 10th centuries. Area: 14,998 sq mi (38,855 sq km). Population (1981): 25,403,217. Capital: Trivandrum.

keratin An insoluble fibrous protein that is the major constituent of hair, nails, feathers, beaks, horns, and scales. Keratin is also found in the outer protective layers of the skin.

Kerbela. *See* Karbala.

Kerch 45 22N 36 27E A port in the SW Soviet Union, in the Ukrainian SSR on the Black Sea on the Strait of Kerch. Founded in the 6th century BC by Greek colonists, it was captured from the Tatars by Russia in 1771. Fishing is important, and related activities, together with iron and steel production, form the basis of its industry. Population (1981 est): 159,000.

Kerenski, Aleksandr Feodorovich (1881–1970) Russian revolutionary. A member of the Socialist Revolutionary Party, after the outbreak of the Russian Revolution in February, 1917, Kerenski became minister of justice and then minister of war in *Lvov's provisional government. In July, after Lvov's fall, he became prime minister. His insistence that Russia remain in World War I, and his mismanagement of internal economic affairs, led to the Bolshevik coup d'état in October. Kerenski fled to Paris and in 1940 to the US.

Kerguelen Islands 49 30S 69 30E An archipelago in the S Indian Ocean, in the French Southern and Antarctic Territories. Kerguelen Island, the largest, is mountainous and glacial and the site of several scientific bases. Area: 2786 sq mi (7215 sq km).

Kérkira (*or* Kérkyra). *See* Corfu.

Kerman 30 18N 57 05E A city in E Iran. It is an agricultural trading center and carpet-making town. Kerman University was founded in 1974. Population (1976 est): 140,309.

Kermanshah 34 19N 47 04E A city in W Iran, with a largely Kurdish population. It has a university (1974) and an oil refinery that is connected by pipeline to oilfields near the Iraqi border. Population (1976 est): 290,861.

kermes A scale insect of the genus *Kermes*, especially *K. ilices* of Europe and W Asia, the dried bodies of which were formerly used to produce a red dye. They feed on the small evergreen kermes oak (*Quercus coccifera*), which is native to S Europe, N Africa, and W Asia and grows to a height of 23 ft (7 m).

Kern, Jerome (David) (1885–1945) US composer of musical comedies, the most famous of which was *Show Boat* (1927), written in collaboration with Oscar *Hammerstein II. After 1939 he devoted himself to film music. Two of his best-known songs are "Ol' Man River" and "Smoke Gets in Your Eyes."

kerosene A mixture of hydrocarbons that boil in the range 302–572°F (150–300°C) and have a relative density of 0.78–0.83. It is obtained from crude *oil by distillation and is used as a fuel for domestic heating and for aircraft.

Kerouac, Jack (1922–69) US novelist. He was a leading figure of the *Beat movement, of which his novel *On the Road* (1957) was a seminal work. Other works including *The Dharma Bums* (1958), *Big Sur* (1962), and *Desolation Angels* (1965) were largely autobiographical.

Kerr effects Two effects concerned with optical changes produced by magnetic or electric fields. In the magneto-optical effect, plane-polarized light is slightly elliptically polarized when reflected by the pole of an electromagnet. In the electro-optical effect, the plane of polarization of a beam of light is rotated when passed through certain liquids or solids across which a potential difference is applied. This effect is utilized in the **Kerr cell**, which consists of a transparent cell containing a liquid, such as nitrobenzene; two parallel plates immersed in the liquid enable a field to be applied so that the passage of a beam of polarized light can be interrupted. The cell is used as a high-speed shutter and to modulate *laser beams. Named for the discoverer John Kerr (1824–1907).

Kerry (Irish name: Chiarraighe) A county in the SW Republic of Ireland, in Munster bordering on the Atlantic Ocean. Chiefly mountainous with a deeply indented coastline, it rises in the S to *Macgillycuddy's Reeks and contains the famous Lakes of Killarney, noted for their beauty. The chief occupations are fishing, farming, and tourism. Area: 1815 sq mi (4701 sq km). Population (1979): 120,356. County town: Tralee.

Kertanagara (d. 1292) King of Java (1268–92). Honored as Java's greatest leader, he took advantage of the disunited Malay world in the 13th century to unite Java and became the most powerful ruler in SE Asia. He protected Indonesia from Kublai Khan's efforts to exact tribute and upheld Buddhism and Javanese culture.

Kesey, Ken (1935–) US novelist. His best-known novel, *One Flew Over the Cuckoo's Nest* (1962), a satire based on his own experience in a mental hospital, was made into a successful film by Miloš *Forman. Later works include *Sometimes a Great Notion* (1964) and *Kesey's Garage Sale* (1973).

Kesselring, Albert (1885–1960) German general, who commanded the Luftwaffe in World War II. He held the air command in the invasions of Poland (1939) and France (1940) and in the battle of Britain (1940). In 1943 he became commander of land and air forces in Italy and in 1945 on the Western Front. His death sentence as a war criminal was commuted to life imprisonment and he was released in 1952.

Kesteven, Parts of. *See* Lincolnshire.

kestrel A small *falcon characterized by a long tail and the ability to hover, with the tail fanned out, before diving on its prey. The common kestrel (*Falco tinnunculus*), 13 in (32 cm) long, is widespread in Eurasia and Africa, and hunts small rodents, birds, and insects. The female has a brown streaked plumage; the male is blue-gray with black-streaked pale-brown underparts, a black-tipped tail, and a black eye stripe.

ketch A fore-and-aft-rigged □sailing vessel with two masts, a taller one set approximately one-third of the boat's length from the bows, a shorter one just forward of the rudder post. Ketches are a favored rig for yachts, for the split rig reduces the area of each sail, making handling easier. Ketches do not sail as well toward the wind as *sloops do. *See also* yawl.

ketone A class of organic chemicals having the general formula RCOR', where R and R' are hydrocarbon groups. Ketones are prepared by the oxidation of secondary alcohols. *Acetone (dimethyl ketone) is a common example.

Kettering, Charles Franklin (1876–1958) US engineer, whose inventions, notably the electric starter (1912), greatly improved motor cars. He also pioneered the use of leaded gasoline and antiknock compounds; in 1951 he developed a high-compression car engine.

kettledrums. *See* timpani.

Key, Francis Scott (1779–1843) US lawyer and poet; author of "The *Star-Spangled Banner." He practiced law in Washington, DC and in 1814, during the War of 1812, negotiated the release of a friend who was held prisoner on a British ship in Chesapeake Bay. Because of the British bombardment of Fort McHenry, near Baltimore, Key was forced to spend the night aboard ship. In the morning, relieved to see the American flag still flying over the fort, he was inspired to write a poem; the words, set to the tune of a British drinking song, officially became the US national anthem in 1931.

key. *See* tonality.

Keynes, John Maynard, 1st Baron (1883–1946) British economist, whose ideas continue to exert influence on modern government economic policies (*see* Keynesianism). After attending the Versailles peace conference as a British Treasury representative, Keynes published *The Economic Consequences of the Peace* (1919), which attacked the war reparations imposed on Germany. In his greatest work, *General Theory of Employment, Interest and Money* (1936), written during the Depression years, he argued that unemployment can only be alleviated by increased public spending. During World War II he worked for the British government on war finance and in 1944 was the chief British representative at the Bretton Woods conference, at which the *International Monetary Fund was established.

Keynesianism The economic theories of the British economist J. M. *Keynes, whose *General Theory of Employment, Interest and Money* (1936) has had a pervasive influence. Keynes' central departure from established theory was the premise that what is rational for the individual and the firm is not necessarily rational for the government, and that rather than reinforcing the *trade cycle the government should counter it by public spending with money raised by *deficit financing. This has been developed by later thinkers, not all of whose ideas Keynes himself would have agreed with, into a doctrine of expansive *fiscal policy and government interventionism.

Keystone Kops A zealous but incompetent police force that featured in the silent film comedies produced by Mack *Sennett for the Keystone Film Company between 1912 and 1917. They were the butt of much irreverent slapstick comedy, preserving their imperturbable masks of dignity even during the absurd accelerated chase sequences.

Key West 24 34N 81 48W A city in the US, in Florida, situated at the tip of the Florida Keys. A naval, air, and coastguard base, Key West is a popular tourist center and was the home of Ernest Hemingway. Population (1970): 29,312.

KGB (Committee of State Security) The Soviet secret police concerned with internal security and intelligence. It was founded in 1954, after the fall of *Beria, and replaced the more brutal MGB (Ministry of State Security; 1946–53).

Khabarovsk 48 32N 135 08E A port in the E Soviet Union, in the RSFSR on the Amur River. Situated on the Trans-Siberian Railroad, it is an important transport center. Industries include engineering, machine building, and oil refining. Population (1981 est): 545,000.

Khachaturian, Aram Ilich (1903–78) Soviet composer of Armenian birth. He studied composition at the Moscow conservatoire. His music was deeply influenced by the scales and rhythms of Caucasian folk music. His compositions include concertos for piano (1936) and violin (1940) and the famous ballets *Gayaneh* (1942) and *Spartacus* (1954).

Khafre (Greek name: Chephren) King of Egypt (c. 2550 BC) of the 4th dynasty. He emerged victorious from the dynastic strife that followed the death of his father *Khufu. Khafre built the second pyramid and (probably) the Sphinx at *Giza.

Khakass An autonomous region (*oblast*) in the S Soviet Union, in the RSFSR. It was formed in 1930 for the Turkic-speaking Khakass people, who are Orthodox Christians. Khakass is rich in minerals, including gold, coal, iron ore, and copper, and timber and woodworking industries are also important. Livestock is raised. Area: 23,855 sq mi (61,900 sq km). Population (1980 est): 503,000. Capital: Abakan.

khaki (Hindi-Urdu: dust-colored) A yellowish-brown fabric of cotton, wool, or synthetic fiber used chiefly for military uniforms. Khaki was first worn by British troops in India as a form of camouflage. From about 1900 it became the regular British uniform for battle and has since been adopted by most other nations.

Khalid Ibn Abdul Aziz (1913–82) King of Saudi Arabia (1975–82). Son of *Ibn Saud, the founder of Saudi Arabia, Khalid had a traditional Muslim education. He became king on the death of his brother *Faisal Ibn Abdul Aziz.

Khalifa. *See* Abd Allah.

Khama, Sir Seretse (1921–80) Botswana statesman; president (1966–80). Trained as a lawyer in England, Seretse Khama married an Englishwoman, as a result of which he had to renounce the chieftaincy of the Bamangwato tribe before returning to what was then Bechuanaland in 1956. In 1961 he founded the Bechuanaland Democratic Party, which gained independence for Botswana in 1966.

khamsin A hot dry southerly wind that blows across Egypt from the Sahara Desert. Most common in April and June, it precedes *depressions moving E along the N African coast. According to Arab tradition it blows for 50 days.

Kharga, El (*or* al-Wahat al-Kharijah) A large oasis in Egypt, in the Libyan Desert. It produces dates, figs, olives, and vegetables; efforts have been made to increase irrigation by sinking deep wells. Chief town: El Kharga.

Kharkov 50 00N 36 15E A city in the Soviet Union, in the E Ukrainian SSR. It was almost totally destroyed in World War II, when its importance as a road and railroad junction led to bitter fighting. Today, it is the third (after Moscow and Leningrad) largest railroad junction in the country. The nearby Donets Basin coalfield supports a major engineering industry. Population (1981 est): 1,485,000.

Khartoum (*or* al-Khurtum) 15 40N 32 52E The capital of the Sudan, at the confluence of the Blue and the White Nile Rivers. An Egyptian army camp in the early 19th century, it later became a garrison town. In 1885 *Gordon was besieged and killed here and the town destroyed by the forces of the Mahdi (*see* Mahdi, al-) but was recaptured by Anglo-British forces in 1898 and rebuilt. It has several cathedrals and two mosques; its university was founded in 1956 and it also houses part of Cairo University (1955). An important trading center, it produces textiles and glass. Population (1973): 333,921.

Khazars A Turkic people who inhabited the lower Volga basin from the 7th to 13th centuries. Noted for their laws, tolerance, and cosmopolitanism, the Khazars were the main commercial link between the Baltic and the Muslim empire. In the 8th century the Khazars embraced Judaism. Slavonic and nomadic Turkic invaders brought the downfall of the Khazars in the 11th century. Itil, near modern Astrakhan, was their capital.

khedive The title bestowed in 1867 by the sultan of the Ottoman Empire on the hereditary viceroy of Egypt. It was used until 1914, when Egypt became a British protectorate.

Kherson 46 39N 32 38E A port in the Soviet Union, in the S Ukrainian SSR on the Dnepr River. It is 15 mi (25 km) from the Black Sea and, founded in 1778, was Russia's first naval base on the Sea. Shipbuilding remains the chief industry. Population (1981 est): 329,000.

Khiva 41 25N 60 49E A town in the S Soviet Union, in the Uzbek SSR on the Amu Darya River. It may have existed in the 6th century AD and was the center of the khanate of Khiva from the 16th century until 1873, when it was captured by Russia. Its architectural remains attract many tourists. Cotton spinning is also important.

Khlebnikov, Velimir (Victor K.; 1885–1922) Russian poet, who founded the Russian futurist movement (*see* futurism) with *Mayakovskii. His poetry was characterized by verbal experimentation and technical virtuosity; much of it was written on scraps of paper during his many travels. He died of typhus and starvation while returning from Persia.

Khmer A people of Cambodia (Kampuchea), Thailand, and Vietnam who speak the Khmer language, belonging to the Mon-Khmer Division of the *Austro-Asiatic languages, which includes Vietnamese, *Mon, and Palaung. They are rice cultivators and fishers, living in village communities headed by an elected chief. Their religion is Theravada Buddhism, but magical beliefs and practices survive from pre-Buddhist times. The Khmer empire was founded in 616 AD and between the 9th and 13th centuries Khmer kings presided over the advanced civilization that was responsible for the great stone buildings of *Angkor. The name Khmer was adopted by the anti-French nationalist movement of Cambodia (which was called the Khmer Republic from 1971 to 1975) and the name continues in the communist Khmer Rouge movement (*see* Kampuchea).

Khoisan The racial grouping comprising the Hottentot and Bushmen people of S Africa. The Khoisan languages, of which the Hottentot Nama and the Bushman Kung have been most studied, are noted for their click sounds. Formerly widespread S of the Zambezi River, the Khoisan tribes have been decimated by Bantu and European encroachments since 1700 and their traditional culture and racial integrity almost exterminated. The Hottentots were nomads, herding sheep and cattle. They were divided into clans, each with its own territory and chief, but with no overall political coherence. The Bushmen were traditionally hunters and gatherers, but most are now farm workers. Some groups in the desert regions of W Botswana still roam in small bands, with the women collecting roots and berries and the men hunting with bows and poisoned arrows. Bushman rock paintings survive in many areas of South Africa.

Khomeini, Ayatollah Ruholla (1900–) Iranian Shiite Muslim leader (ayatollah). Following the overthrow of the shah (1979) he returned from 16 years of exile to lead the so-called Islamic Revolution. Subsequently, he ruthlessly suppressed opposition to his rule and instituted a government based on fundamental Islamic principles.

Khorana, Har Gobind (1922–) US biochemist, born in India, who was responsible for deciphering the *genetic code, i.e. the hereditary information carried by DNA molecules. Khorana shared a Nobel Prize (1968) with R. W. Holley (1922–) and M. Nirenberg (1927–). In 1976 Khorana and his team were responsible for constructing the first entirely synthetic yet biologically active gene.

Khosrow I King of Persia (531–79 AD), who came to the throne after prolonged social disturbance and took measures to restore prosperity and to reform the state. He reorganized the army, strengthened his frontiers, and expanded his territory. His only serious rival, the Byzantine empire, was forced to concede tribute and territory but remained hostile. Khosrow's firm yet benevolent rule over an empire stretching from the Oxus River (now Amu Darya) to the Yemen marked the summit of *Sasanian power.

Khosrow II (d. 628 AD) King of Persia (590–628) of the Sasanian dynasty, who accepted Byzantine aid to secure his throne, conceding territory in return. Its subsequent recovery and the conquest of Anatolia, Syria, and Egypt overtaxed Persian resources. The Byzantine counterattack reached his capital, Ctesiphon, and Khosrow was assassinated; the Sasanian empire disintegrated and was soon overrun by the Arabs.

Khrushchev, Nikita S(ergeevich) (1894–1971) Soviet statesman; first secretary of the Soviet Communist Party (1953–64) and prime minister (1958–64). Khrushchev was a close associate of Stalin and emerged victorious from the power struggle that followed his death. In 1956 Khrushchev began a program of destalinization and the degree of liberalization that ensued within the Soviet Union gave rise to revolts in other communist countries, such as the *Poznan Riots in Poland and the *Hungarian Revolution. Owing to the failure of his economic policies and his unsuccessful foreign policy, notably his attempt to install missiles in Cuba (1962) and his antagonism toward China, he was ousted by *Brezhnev and *Kosygin.

Khufu (or Cheops) King of Egypt (c. 2600 BC) of the 4th dynasty; the father of *Khafre. He built the Great Pyramid at *Giza, which was said to have taken 20 years to construct. Khufu's funeral barge has been discovered in good condition.

Khulna 22 49N 89 34E A city in S Bangladesh, on the Ganges delta. An agricultural trading center, its industries include shipbuilding and the manufacture of cotton cloth. Population (1974): 80,917.

Khyber Pass (Khaybar Pass or Khaibar Pass) 34 06N 71 05E A mountain pass in the Safid Kuh range of the Hindu Kush, connecting Kabul in Afghanistan with Peshawar in Pakistan. Rising to 3518 ft (1072 m) in barren country, it is of strategic importance, having been used many times over the centuries by invading armies, the progress of which has often been impeded by hostile Afridi tribesmen.

kiang A wild *ass, *Equus hemionus kiang*, of the Himalayas. It is the tallest wild ass, 5 ft (1.4 m) at the shoulder, and has a chestnut-colored coat. *See also* onager.

Kiangsi. *See* Jiangxi.

Kiangsi Soviet. *See* Jiangxi Soviet.

Kiangsu. *See* Jiangsu.

kibbutz An Israeli collective settlement in which land and property are owned or leased by all its members and work and meals are organized collectively. Adults generally have private quarters but children are housed together. About 3% of the population live in *kibbutzim*. A **moshav** is a smallholders' cooperative in which machinery is shared but land and property is generally privately owned. About 5% of the Israeli population live in *moshavim*.

Kicking Horse Pass A pass through the Canadian Rocky Mountains, NW of Banff. It is the highest point on the Canadian Pacific Railroad. Height: 5339 ft (1627 m).

Kidd, William (c. 1645–1701) Scottish sailor. He spent his youth privateering for the English against the French off the North American coast and in 1695 he was given a royal commission to suppress pirates in the Indian Ocean. He reached Madagascar, a pirates' center, where he seems to have joined them. He was arrested on his return to Boston, sent to England, and executed (possibly unjustly).

Kidderminster 52 23N 2 14W A market city in W central England, in Hereford and Worcester on the River Stour. It is famous for carpet manufacture, begun in 1735. Woolen and worsted yarn, textile machinery, and beet sugar are also produced here. Population (1981): 51,261.

Kidinnu (4th century BC) Babylonian mathematician and astronomer, who discovered the precession of the equinoxes, an effect that causes the position of the sun at equinox to move slowly backward through the zodi-

ac. He also calculated the interval of time between successive new moons to within a second.

kidneys The two organs of excretion in vertebrate animals and man, which also regulate the amount of salt and water in the blood. The human kidneys are bean-shaped, each about 5 in (12 cm) long and weighing about 5 oz (150 g), and situated on either side of the spine below the diaphragm. They contain millions of tubules, the outer parts of which filter water and dissolved substances from blood supplied by the renal artery. Most of the water and some substances are reabsorbed back into the blood further down the tubules: the remaining fluid (*see* urine) contains waste products of protein metabolism and passes on to the pelvis of the kidneys and out through the ureters to the *bladder. The reabsorption of water is controlled by a hormone (vasopressin) from the pituitary gland. The kidneys also secrete a hormone (*see* renin) that assists in controlling blood pressure.

If one kidney ceases to function or is removed the other will enlarge and take over its function. Removal of both kidneys requires the use of an artificial kidney machine (*see* dialysis) unless a suitable donor kidney is available for *transplantation.

Kiel 54 20N 10 08E A city in NE West Germany, the capital of Schleswig-Holstein. A Baltic port, famed for its annual regatta, it was the chief naval port of Germany by the late 19th century. The naval mutiny here in 1918 sparked off revolutions throughout Germany. It has a university (1665) and a 13th-century palace, restored after World War II. Its chief industries are shipbuilding and engineering. Population (1980 est): 250,400.

Kiel Canal (German name: Nord-Ostsee Kanal; former name: Kaiser Wilhelm Canal) A canal in West Germany, in Schleswig-Holstein *Land*, linking Kiel on the Baltic Sea with the Elbe estuary on the North Sea.

Kielce 50 51N 20 39E A city in S central Poland. During World War II it contained four German concentration camps. Notable buildings include its cathedral (12th century). It is a major industrial center. Population (1979 est): 184,000.

Kierkegaard, Søren (1813–55) Danish philosopher. Although critical of *Hegel, particularly in *The Concept of Irony* (1841), he remained under his influence. Kierkegaard was a prolific writer; much of his work is poetic and paradoxical even in its titles, for example *Either-Or* (1843) and *Concluding Unscientific Postscript* (1846). Suspicious of both science and the established Church, he saw man as existing in isolation and relating only to God. Among his specifically religious books is *Works of Love* (1847). His journal reveals him as a deeply religious, if unorthodox, thinker. He greatly influenced 20th-century *existentialism.

Kiev 50 28N 30 29E A city in the SW Soviet Union, the capital of the Ukrainian SSR on the Dnepr River. It is the third (after Moscow and Leningrad) largest city in the country and a major economic and cultural center. Industries include metallurgy, the manufacture of machinery and instruments, chemicals, and textiles. Among its many educational institutions is the Kiev State University (1833), and its opera and ballet companies have a worldwide reputation. Outstanding buildings include the 11th-century St Sophia cathedral, now a museum, and the Golden Gate of Kiev. *History:* Kiev, "the mother of cities," was probably founded in the 6th or 7th century AD and from the 9th to the 13th centuries was the center of a feudal state ruled by the Rurik dynasty—Kiev-Rus, the historical nucleus of the Soviet Union. Recurrent Tatar attacks virtually destroyed the city, which subsequently passed to Lithuania. Russian rule was established in the 17th century. After the Russian Revolution Kiev became the capital of the short-lived Ukrainian republic and in 1934, the capital of the Ukrainian SSR. In World War II the city was occupied after a long siege by the Germans and thousands of its inhabitants were massacred. Its postwar reconstruction has been spectacular, and it remains one of Europe's most beautiful cities. Population (1981 est): 2,248,000.

Kigali 1 58S 30 00E The capital of Rwanda (since 1962). It is the center of the country's mining industry and has a trade in coffee. Population (1978): 117,749.

Kikuyu A Bantu-speaking tribe of Kenya. They cultivate cereals and sweet potatoes and keep considerable numbers of livestock, particularly cattle. Small groups of patrilineal kin occupy scattered homesteads of conical-shaped huts. These kin groups are organized into clans but there is little hierarchical organization or centralization of authority. Age grades are an important basis of social organization, boys being initiated by circumcision. Political authority is held by a council of members of the senior age grade. The largest tribe in Kenya, the Kikuyu were deeply involved in the anticolonial *Mau Mau movement during the 1950s and have had a dominant voice in postindependence government.

Kilauea A volcanic crater in Hawaii, on the E side of Mauna Loa. It is one of the largest active craters in the world. Height: 4090 ft (1247 m). Width: 2 mi (3 km).

Kildare (Irish name: Contae Cill Dara) A county in the E Republic of Ireland, in Leinster. It consists chiefly of a low-lying fertile plain containing part of the Bog of Allen in the N and the Curragh, an area noted for its racehorse breeding and race track. Cattle rearing and arable farming are also important. Area: 654 sq mi (1694 sq km). Population (1979): 97,185. County town: Naas.

Kilimanjaro, Mount 3 02S 37 20E A volcanic mountain in Tanzania on the Kenyan border, the highest mountain in Africa. It has two volcanic peaks: Kibo at 19,340 ft (5895 m), and Mawenzi at 17,300 ft (5273 m).

Kilkenny (Irish name: Contae Cill Choinnigh) A county in the SE Republic of Ireland, in Leinster. Chiefly hilly, it is drained by the Rivers Suir, Barrow, and Nore. Agriculture is the chief occupation with cattle rearing and dairy farming. Area: 796 sq mi (2062 sq km). Population (1979): 69,156. County town: Kilkenny.

Kilkenny (Irish name: Cill Choinnigh) 52 09N 7 15W A city in the Republic of Ireland, the county town of Co Kilkenny. One of Ireland's oldest towns, it has two cathedrals and a 12th-century castle. Population (1971): 9838.

Killarney (Irish name: Cill Airne) 52 03N 9 30W A town in the Republic of Ireland in Co Kerry. A tourist center near the three Lakes of Killarney, it is famous for its lake, mountain, and forest scenery. Population (1971): 7184.

KILLER WHALE *A specimen living in captivity. Killer whales are known for their spectacular jumps, during which they may cover a distance of 40-45 ft. (12-13.5m).*

killer whale A large toothed whale, *Orcinus orca*, common in Pacific and Antarctic waters but found in all other oceans. Up to 30 ft (9 m) long, killer whales are black above and pure white beneath, with an erect dorsal fin as tall as a man. They are notorious for their voracious appetites, hunting in packs and tackling even sharks and other whales. Like other dolphins, they are intelligent and trainable in captivity. Family: *Delphinidae* (dolphins).

killifish One of several small elongated fish, also called egg-laying top minnows, belonging to the family *Cyprinodontidae*, especially the genus *Fundulus*. Killifish occur chiefly in tropical America, Africa, and Asia in fresh, brackish, or salt water and feed at the surface on plant or animal material. Up to 6 in (15 cm) long, many are brightly colored and kept as aquarium fish. Similar related fish are the live-bearing top minnows of the family *Poeciliidae*. Order: *Atheriniformes*.

Kilmarnock 55 37N 4 30W An industrial city in SW Scotland. Industries include engineering, carpets, woolens, lace, whisky, footwear, and earthenware. The Burns museum contains many of his manuscripts. Population (1981): 52,080.

kilogram (kg) The *SI unit of mass equal to the mass of the platinum-iridium prototype kept at the International Bureau of Weights and Measures near Paris.

kiloton A measure of the explosive power of a nuclear weapon. It is equivalent to an explosion of 1000 tons of trinitrotoluene (TNT).

kilowatt-hour (kW-hr) A unit of energy used in charging for electricity. It is equal to the work done by a power of 1000 watts in 1 hour.

kilt. *See* Highland dress.

Kimberley 28 45S 24 46E A city in South Africa, in N Cape Province. It was founded (1871) following the discovery of diamonds and is today the world's largest diamond center. The famous Kimberley Open Mine, 1 mi (1.6 km) in circumference, was closed in 1915. Industries include engineering, clothing, and diamond cutting. Population (1980): 144,923.

Kimberleys. *See* Western Australia.

Kim Il Sung (Kim Song Ju; 1912–) North Korean statesman; prime minister (1948–72) and then president (1972–). He became leader of the Soviet-dominated N in 1945 and with the establishment there of the Democratic People's Republic of Korea in 1948, its first prime minister and chairman of the Korean Workers' Party. In 1950 he ordered the invasion of South Korea in an unsuccessful attempt to reunite Korea (*see* Korean War).

kimono The traditional costume of Japan for men and women from the 7th century AD, now worn mainly by women for formal occasions. It is an ankle-length wide-sleeved robe, often silk, wrapped over at the front and tied with an *obi* (sash) in a large bow at the back of the waist.

Kincardine (*or* Kincardineshire) A former county of NE Scotland. Under local government reorganization in 1975 it became part of Grampian Region.

kindergarten A school for young children, usually aged five to six years, preceding first grade. The term kindergarten, a German word meaning "children's garden," was originated by the German educator Friedrich *Froebel for children aged three to five, but the education of young children is now generally referred to as nursery school.

kinematics. *See* mechanics.

kinetic energy Energy possessed by a body by virtue of its motion. If the body, mass m, is moving in a straight line with velocity v, its kinetic energy is $\frac{1}{2}mv^2$. If it is rotating its rotational kinetic energy is $\frac{1}{2}I\omega^2$, where I is its moment of inertia and ω its angular velocity.

kinetics. *See* mechanics.

kinetic theory A theory developed in the 19th century, largely by *Joule and *Maxwell, in which the behavior of gases is explained by regarding them as consisting of tiny dimensionless particles in constant random motion. Collisions, either between the particles or between the particles and the walls of the container, are assumed to be perfectly elastic. The theory explains the pressure of a gas as being due to collisions between the particles and the walls, its temperature as a measure of the *average* *kinetic energy of the particles, and the heat of the gas as the *total* kinetic energy of the particles. The kinetic theory is based on the concept of an *ideal gas obeying ideal *gas laws; real gases consist of molecules having a finite volume (*see* Van der Waals). The kinetic theory is extended to all matter and regards the heat of a body as the total of the translational, rotational, or vibrational energy of its constituent particles.

King, Billie Jean (*born* Moffitt; 1943–) US tennis player, who was Wimbledon singles champion in 1966, 1967, 1968, 1972, 1973, and 1975. She was champion i n the US Open in 1967 (as an amateur), and again in 1971, 1972, and 1974. She won many other titles and took a record 20th Wimbledon title in 1979.

King, Jr, Martin Luther (1929–68) US civil-rights leader. The son of a minister, he became one himself. He achieved national recognition in 1955–56 by leading a boycott of buses in Montgomery, Ala., in order to end segregation on them. He then helped found the Southern Christian Leadership Conference to work for blacks' civil rights and became its president. An outstanding orator, he followed principles of nonviolent resistance in organizing demonstrations against racial inequality and was one of the leaders of the great March on Washington (1963), joined by over 250,000 people. At the Washington rally he delivered his famous "I Have a Dream" speech. The same year he organized civil rights demonstrations in Birmingham, Ala. His campaigns contributed to the passing of the Civil Rights Act (1964) and the Voting Rights Act (1965) and earned him the Nobel Peace Prize in 1964. He was assassinated in Memphis, Tenn., where he was supporting striking garbage collectors, by James Earl Ray.

MARTIN LUTHER KING *Holding the gold medal of the Nobel Peace Prize (Oslo, 1964).*

King, William Lyon Mackenzie (1874–1950) Canadian statesman; Liberal prime minister (1921–26, 1926–30, 1935–48). His administration enacted moderate welfare legislation and increased Canadian trade with the US and UK. His chief political aim was national unity, achieved by enlisting the support of Progressives and French Canadians.

King Charles spaniel A breed of *spaniel having a compact body, short legs, a short neck, and a large head with a short upturned nose. There are four color varieties: Blenheim, ruby, tricolor, and black and tan, the last being associated with King Charles II. Weight: 7.7–13.2 lb (3.5–6 kg); height: about 10 in (25 cm). The Cavalier King Charles spaniel has a similar coloration but is lighter bodied, with relatively longer legs and a longer muzzle. Weight: 13–18 lb (5–8 kg); height: about 12 in (30 cm).

kingcup. *See* marsh marigold.

kingfisher A bird belonging to a family (*Alcedinidae*; 85 species) divided into two subfamilies: the *Alcedininae* are narrow-billed and live near water, feeding on small fish; the *Dacetoninae* are broad-billed insectivorous birds not closely associated with water. Kingfishers are 5–18 in (12–45 cm) long, mostly compact with a bright plumage of blues, greens, purples, and reds, and are often crested; they have large heads with often brightly colored bills and usually nest in burrows in banks. Order: *Coraciiformes* (hornbills, etc.).

King George's War (1744–48) An indecisive conflict between Britain and France for control of North America. Governor William Shirley of Massachusetts blocked French efforts to take Nova Scotia in 1744, and in 1745 led a colonial force that captured the French fortress of Louisbourg, returned to the French at the end of the war. It was an aspect of the War of the *Austrian Succession.

King James Version The Authorized Version of the English *Bible that appeared in 1611 under the patronage of James I. A scholarly translation from the original languages, it preserved the best from previous versions. It was based on the earlier Bishops' Bible (1568), but the translators also consulted and made use of the *Geneva Bible and the *Douai Bible. It was much indebted to the translations of William *Tyndale. Its rich and vigorous language has had a unique influence on English prose style.

King Philip's War (1675–76) A war of resistance on the part of the Indians, led by King Philip of the Wampanoags, to the westward expansion of English settlers in Massachusetts, Connecticut, and Rhode Island. War broke out after a Wampanoag attack on a settlement in Plymouth colony. The fighting was savage, particularly in the Great Swamp Fight in Rhode Island (1675), in which 300 Indians were killed, lasting until Indian resistance collapsed after the death of King Philip in August, 1676. The war toll was enormous on both sides.

Kings, Books of Two Old Testament books of unknown authorship. They are the major source for the history of the Hebrew kings after David, continuing the narrative from the point where the Books of Samuel end. The first book traces the reign of Solomon (c. 970–933 BC) and his building of the Temple at Jerusalem. After his death, the kingdom was divided into Judah and Israel, the histories of which are continued alternately in the second book. The work of the prophets Elisha and Elijah is treated in detail. After the fall of Israel to Assyria in 722 BC the narrative is devoted to the history of Judah alone up to the *Babylonian exile (586 BC).

Kings Canyon National Park A national park in E central California, in SE Sierra Nevada. Established in 1940, it adjoins Sequoia National Park to the S. The middle and S forks of the Kings River cut through the mountains; the highest peak in the park is North Palisade (14,242 ft [4,341 m]). Scattered throughout the park are groves of giant sequoia trees; in the General Grant Grove stands the General Grant tree, 267 ft (82 m) high and almost 108 ft (33 m) around, which is over 3500 years old. Area: 719 sq mi (1862 sq km).

king's evil. *See* scrofula.

Kingston 17 58N 76 48W The capital and main port of Jamaica, in the SE. Founded in 1692, it became the capital in 1872. In the early 20th century it suffered much damage from hurricanes and an earthquake. The University of the West Indies was founded nearby in 1962. Most industry is associated with agriculture. Population (1970): 111,879.

Kingston 44 14N 76 30W A city and port in central Canada, in SE Ontario at the point where Lake Ontario becomes the St Lawrence River. Founded as a fort (1673), it has Canada's Royal Military College, as well as numerous prisons and Queen's University (1841). Kingston's industry includes ship repairing, aluminum, chemicals, and food processing. Population (1976): 56,032.

Kingston-upon-Hull. *See* Hull.

kinkajou A nocturnal arboreal mammal, *Potos flavus*, of Central and South American forests. Up to 43 in (110 cm) long including the tail (16–22 in [40–55 cm]), it has a soft wooly golden-brown coat, small ears, and a prehensile tail. An agile climber, it feeds mainly on fruit and honey. Family: *Procyonidae* (*see* raccoon).

Kinnock, Neil (Gordon) (1942–) British Labour politician. He became a member of the National Executive Committee of the Labour Party in 1978 and Labour leader (1983–) following Michael Foot's resignation.

kinnor A musical instrument, the ancient Jewish form of the *kithara. A type of *lyre, it is the biblical instrument traditionally reputed to have been played by David.

Kinsey, Alfred (1894–1956) US zoologist and sociologist, who initiated surveys of human sexual behavior. His reports *Sexual Behavior in the Human Male* (1948) and *Sexual Behavior in the Human Female* (1953) aroused great publicity and helped create more open attitudes to sex.

Kinshasa (name until 1966: Léopoldville) 4 18S 15 18E The capital of Zaïre, on the Zaïre River on the S shore of Malebo Pool. It has a long history of human settlement and was occupied by the Humbu when *Stanley discovered it in the late 19th century. A campus of the National University was founded in 1954. One of Africa's largest cities, it is an important industrial and commercial center with food-processing, woodworking, and textile industries. Population (1976 est): 2,443,876.

kinship The social recognition of real or ascribed blood relationship. It is usually distinguished from affinity (relationship by marriage). Kinship implies genetic relationship but this is defined very differently in different societies. Many people deny the genetic contribution of either the father or the mother to the child and count the kin of only one parent as their own. These are known respectively as matrilineal and patrilineal systems. Different societies recognize relationships of very different degrees of distance, some counting as kin those descended from common ancestors many generations back. In primitive societies kinship systems are the fundamental basis of social organization.

Kioga, Lake. *See* Kyoga, Lake.

Kiowa A North American Indian people of Oklahoma. With the *Comanche, they were among the most warlike tribes, raiding settlers in Texas during the 19th century. They also fought against the US Government and were one of the last tribes to be subdued. Their culture was typical of the Plains region. Their language forms part of the *Aztec-Tanoan family.

Kipling, (Joseph) Rudyard (1865–1936) British writer and poet. Born in Bombay, he was educated in England, returning to India in 1882 to work as a journalist. When Kipling returned to London in 1889, he was already famous for his satirical verses and for stories, such as those in *Plain Tales from the Hills* (1888). His popularity was confirmed with *Barrack Room Ballads and Other Verses* (1892), a volume that includes such well-known poems as "The Road to Mandalay," "If," and "Gunga Din." From 1892 to 1896 he lived with his American wife in New England, where he wrote *The Jungle Books* (1894, 1895). *Kim* (1901) is his best novel and the last he wrote with an Indian setting. Among his many other works are *Just So Stories* (1902), for children. He won the Nobel Prize in 1907.

kipper. *See* herring.

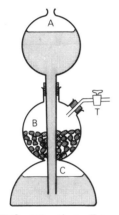

KIPP'S APPARATUS *When the tap* T *is opened the liquid in* C *rises until it reaches the solid in* B, *with which it reacts to produce a gas. When* T *is closed, gas production continues until the liquid has been forced back into* C *against the head produced by the liquid in the reservoir* A.

Kipp's apparatus A laboratory apparatus for producing a gas as a result of a reaction between a liquid and a solid. It is often used to produce hydrogen sulfide by reacting hydrochloric acid with sticks of ferrous sulfide ($2HCl + FeS = FeCl_2 + H_2S$). The device is named for— its Dutch inventor, Petrus Jacobus Kipp (1808–64).

Kirchhoff, Gustav Robert (1824–87) German physicist, who was appointed professor at Heidelberg University in 1854. There, working with Robert *Bunsen, he invented the technique of spectroscopy. Using this technique, Kirchhoff and Bunsen discovered the elements cesium and rubidium in 1861. Kirchhoff, working alone, also discovered several elements in the sun, by investigating the solar spectrum. He is also known for his work on thermal radiation and on networks of electrical wires (*see* Kirchhoff's laws).

Kirchhoff's laws Two laws applying to electrical networks, discovered by G. R. *Kirchhoff. The first states that the net current flowing into and out of any point in the network is zero. The second states that the algebraic sum of the voltages in any closed loop of the network is equal to the algebraic sum of the products of the currents and the resistances through which they flow.

Kirchner, Ernst Ludwig (1880–1938) German expressionist painter and printmaker, who helped found the art movement called Die *Brücke (The Bridge) in 1905 (*see also* expressionism). His diverse influences ranged from *Grünewald to *Munch and African art in paintings notable for their eroticism, vibrant colors, and angular outlines. He painted many satirical street scenes in Berlin (1911–17) before moving to Switzerland, where he concentrated mainly on landscapes. After Nazi condemnation of his work he committed suicide.

Kirgiz Soviet Socialist Republic (*or* Kirgizia) A constituent republic in the S Soviet Union, bordering on China. The Kirgiz, a traditionally nomadic Turkic people, comprise over one-third of the population. Kirgizia, which is mountainous, has important deposits of coal, lead, oil, mercury, and antimony, as well as oil and natural gas. Industries include the manufacture of machinery and building materials and food processing. Wheat, cotton, and tobacco are grown and livestock, especially cattle, sheep, horses, and yaks, are important. *History*: the Kirgiz came under Russian rule in the 19th century and fought the new Soviet Government

after the Russian Revolution. As a result they suffered a famine in 1921–22, in which over 500,000 Kirgiz died. Kirgizia became an SSR in 1936. Area: 76,460 sq mi (198,500 sq km). Population (1981 est): 3,700,000. Capital: Frunze.

Kiribati, Republic of (name until 1979: Gilbert Islands) A country in the S Pacific Ocean comprising the Gilbert Islands, the Phoenix Islands, and some of the Line Islands together with Ocean Island. The majority of the inhabitants are Micronesians. *Economy*: chiefly fishing and subsistence agriculture, including crops such as coconuts, pandanus palm, and breadfruit. Ocean Island is rich in phosphates, which, with copra, are the chief exports. *History*: first sighted by the Spanish in the 16th century, the islands became a center for sperm whale hunting in the 19th century. Part of the British protectorate of the Gilbert and Ellice Islands from 1892, they became a colony in 1915. Links with Ellice Islands (*see* Tuvalu, State of) were severed in 1975 and they became independent in 1979 as the Republic of Kiribati. The Banabans of Ocean Island are seeking independence from Kiribati to become an associate state of Fiji. Chief minister: Ieremia Tabai. Official languages: English and Gilbertese. Official currency: Australian dollar of 100 cents. Area: 332 sq mi (861 sq km). Population (1983): 60,000. Capital and main port: Tarawa.

Kirin. *See* Jilin.

Kirk, Norman (Eric) (1923–74) New Zealand statesman; Labour prime minister (1972–74). He implemented social-welfare and housing measures and recognized the People's Republic of China.

Kirkcaldy 56 07N 3 10W A city in E central Scotland, in Fife Region on the Firth of Forth. It is a port, mainly for coastal trade, and manufactures linoleum and coarse textiles, such as canvas. It is the birthplace of Adam Smith. Population (1973 est): 52,390.

Kirkland, (Joseph) Lane (1922–) US labor leader; head of the *AFL-CIO (1979–). In the merchant marines during World War II, he graduated from Georgetown School of Foreign Service (1948) and worked for George Meany, head of the American Federation of Labor. After being named secretary-treasurer of the merged AFL-CIO in 1969, he succeeded Meany as president in 1979.

Kirkuk 35 28N 44 26E A city in NE Iraq, in a rich oilfield. It is the origin of pipelines to Syria, Lebanon, and, until it was cut in the war of 1948, Haifa (Israel). Population (1970 est): 207,852.

Kirov (name from 1780 until 1934: Vyatka) 58 38N 49 38E A port in the Soviet Union, in the NW RSFSR on the Vyatka River. Founded in 1181, it fell to the Russians in the 15th century and became important as a stopping place on the Moscow–Siberia route. It was renamed in honor of S. M. Kirov. Population (1981 est): 396,000.

Kirov, Sergei Mironovich (1888–1934) Soviet politician. As one of Stalin's closest associates Kirov quickly rose to power and became first secretary of the Leningrad branch of the Communist Party. His assassination, which Stalin claimed to be part of a plot against the entire Soviet leadership and led to the Great Purge trials (1934–38), was probably instigated by Stalin himself.

Kirovabad (name until 1813 and from 1920 until 1935: Gandzha; name from 1813 until 1920: Yelisavetpol) 40 39N 46 20E A city in the Soviet Union, in the NW Azerbaidzhan SSR. A medieval commercial center, it is now an important industrial center, producing especially textiles, building materials, and wine. Population (1981 est): 243,000.

Kirov Ballet A Soviet ballet company based at the Kirov State Theater of Opera and Ballet (formerly the Maryinsky Theater) in Leningrad. The theater was renamed in honor of S. M. *Kirov in 1935. The company's style of dancing owes much to the Imperial Russian Ballet, founded in 1935, of which *Nijinsky was a product. Some of the Kirov's leading dancers, including Rudolf *Nureyev, Natalia Makarova (1940–), and Mikhail *Baryshnikov (1948–), have defected to the West and earned international reputations.

Kirovograd (name until 1924: Yelisavetgrad; name from 1924 until 1936: Zinoviyevsk) 48 31N 32 15E A city in the Soviet Union, in the S central Ukrainian SSR. It is a major agricultural trading center. Population (1981 est): 246,000.

kirsch (*or* kirschwasser) A *spirit distilled from fermented liquor of wild cherries (German *Kirsch*, cherry). It is drunk neat, or used in cooking, especially in cheese fondue or poured over pineapple.

Kiruna 67 53N 20 15E A city in N Sweden, within the Arctic Circle. In area, it is the largest town in the world. It has vast iron-ore deposits. Population (1970): 30,534.

Kisangani (name until 1966: Stanleyville) 0 33S 25 14E A riverport in NE Zaïre, on the Zaïre River. It is an agricultural center and industries include furniture, brewing, and clothing. Zaïre University was founded here in 1963. Population (1976 est): 339,210.

Kish A city of ancient *Sumer, near Babylon. Built on Mesopotamia's fertile alluvial plains, Kish was one of the oldest centers of civilization, retaining its pre-eminence until eclipsed by *Ur (c. 2600 BC). Under the Babylonian empire Kish became obscure but remained inhabited until the 2nd century AD. Excavated between 1923 and 1933, its site has produced valuable evidence of Sumerian civilization, including the earliest known example of writing—pictograms on a limestone tablet dating to soon after 3500 BC.

Kishinev (Romanian name: Chişinău) 47 00N 28 50E A city in the SW Soviet Union, the capital of the Moldavian SSR. Founded in the 15th century, it passed from the Turks to the Russians (1812), becoming the capital of Bessarabia; it was under Romanian rule (1918–40). It is an important food-processing center. Population (1981 est): 539,000.

Kissinger, Henry (Alfred) (1923–) US diplomat and political scientist, born in Germany; secretary of state (1973–76). Appointed adviser to President Nixon on national security (1969), Kissinger and *Le Duc Tho were jointly awarded the Nobel Peace Prize (1973) for helping to negotiate an end to the Vietnam War. Under President Ford he became well known for his flying-shuttle style of diplomacy while negotiating a truce between Syria and Israel (1974). His publications include *Nuclear Weapons and Foreign Policy* (1956), *The White House Years* (1979), and *Years of Upheaval* (1982).

Kisumu 0 03S 34 47E A city in W Kenya, on the NE shore of Lake Victoria. It is an important commercial and industrial center with trade links with Mombasa. Population (1975 est): 149,000.

kit A tiny high-pitched violin used by dancing masters in the 18th century. Its neck, to accommodate the fingers, is disproportionately large.

Kitagawa Utamaro (1753–1806) Japanese artist of the *Ukiyo-e movement, whose color woodblock prints were the first to be popularized in Europe. His book of *Insects* (1788) introduced naturalistic observation into the art of color print. However, he specialized chiefly in scenes of women engaged in everyday tasks or pastimes and half-length portraits of women, such as the series of *Ten Physiognomies of Women* and *Beauties of the Gay Quarters*. In 1804 his prints of the military ruler's wife and mistresses so offended the government that he was handcuffed for 50 days.

Kitakyushu 33 52N 130 49E A city in Japan, in N Kyushu on the Shimonoseki Strait. Formed in 1963 from the cities of Wakamatsu, Yawata, Tobata, Kokura, and Moji, it is one of Japan's leading trade and deepsea fishing ports as well as an important center of heavy industry. Population (1980): 1,065,000.

Kitasato, Shibasaburo (1852–1931) Japanese bacteriologist, who, during an epidemic of bubonic plague in Hong Kong, identified the bacillus responsible. In Berlin Kitasato worked with *Behring on tetanus and diphtheria, demonstrating the value of antitoxin in conferring passive immunity. Kitasato founded a laboratory near Tokyo that was incorporated with the university in 1899. In 1914 he founded the Kitasato Institute.

Kitchener 43 27N 80 30W A city in central Canada, in SW Ontario. Established by German-speaking settlers after 1800, it was called Berlin until 1916. Kitchener is a financial, distribution, and manufacturing center, producing furniture, foods, and leather and rubber goods. Population (1981): 139,734.

Kitchener of Khartoum, Horatio Herbert, 1st Earl (1850–1916) British field marshal. After service with the Royal Engineers, he was appointed to the Egyptian army (1883), becoming commander in chief in 1892. By 1898, with the battle of Omdurman, he had reconquered the Sudan, becoming its governor general (1899). In the second *Boer War he suppressed the guerrillas by a scorched-earth policy and the internment of civilians in concentration camps. In 1914, as war secretary, his recruitment campaign was successful but he lost power in the direction of strategy.

kite A *hawk belonging to the subfamily *Milvinae*, which occurs throughout the world, most commonly in warm regions. Typically reddish brown and 21–23 in (52–57 cm) long, kites have long narrow wings, a long often forked tail, and a narrow bill and feed on insects, small mammals, and reptiles; some are scavengers.

kithara An ancient Greek plucked instrument, traditionally believed to have been invented by Apollo. It was a large wooden-framed *lyre; Greek vases show it held against the player's body. It was used to accompany epic song and declamation.

kittiwake A North Atlantic *gull, *Rissa tridactyla*, that is adapted for nesting on narrow cliff ledges. It is 16 in (40 cm) long and has a white plumage with black-tipped gray wings, short black legs, dark eyes, and a yellow bill. It feeds at sea on fish and offal, going ashore only to breed. Kittiwakes nest in dense colonies, anchoring their seaweed nests with mud.

Kitwe 12 48S 28 14E A city in N central Zambia. It is the chief commercial, industrial, and communications center of the *Copperbelt. Population (1980 est): 341,000.

Kitzbühel 47 27N 12 23E A town in W Austria, in the Tirol in the Kitzbühel Alps. A famous winter-sports center, it is also a health and tourist resort. Population (1971 est): 8000.

Kivi, Alexis (A. Stenvall; 1834–72) Finnish poet, dramatist, and novelist, who was chiefly responsible for establishing the western dialect as the modern literary language of Finland. His greatest work was the novel *Seitsemän veljestä* (*Seven Brothers*; 1870), a naturalistic portrayal of rural life.

Kivu, Lake 1 50S 29 10E A lake between Zaïre and Rwanda. It is 60 mi (96 km) long and drained by the Ruzizi River S into Lake Tanganyika.

kiwi (bird) A secretive flightless bird belonging to a family (*Apterygidae*; 3 species) occurring in forested regions of New Zealand. 10–16 in (25–40 cm) long, kiwis have tiny wings hidden in coarse gray-brown plumage and strong legs with large claws. Kiwis are nocturnal and have weak eyes but well-developed hearing; the long bill is used to probe the soil for worms, insect larvae, etc. The kiwi is the national emblem of New Zealand. Order: *Apterygiformes*.

kiwi (plant) A Chinese climbing shrub, *Actinidia chinensis*, also called Chinese gooseberry. It has hairy leaves, white or yellow flowers, and an edible rough-skinned fruit, up to 2 in (5 cm) long, which has a gooseberry-like flavor. Family: *Actinidiaceae*.

Klagenfurt 46 38N 14 20E A city in S Austria, the capital of Carinthia. It has a cathedral (1578–91) and is a tourist center. Industries include metals, clothing, and shoe production. Population (1981): 86,221.

Klaipeda (German name: Memel) 55 43N 21 07E A port in the W Soviet Union, in the Lithuanian SSR on the Baltic Sea. It has shipyards and other industries include fish canning, textiles, and fertilizers. *History*: dating from the 7th century AD, it was conquered by the Teutonic Knights in 1252, subsequently passing under Prussian rule. In 1919, after World War I, the Allies imposed a French administration over the region, which was seized by Lithuania in 1923. The Memel Statute (1924) recognized Lithuanian possession. It was occupied by the Germans in World War II. Population (1981 est): 181,000.

Klaproth, Martin Heinrich (1743–1817) German chemist, who pioneered the techniques of analytical chemistry. He isolated the oxides of uranium, zirconium, and titanium from minerals and investigated the chemistry of the rare-earth metals.

Klausenburg. See Cluj.

Kléber, Jean Baptiste (1753–1800) French general in the Revolutionary Wars distinguished for his suppression of the uprising in the Vendée (1793). He was recalled from retirement in 1798 and given command in Napoleon's Egyptian campaign. He became governor of Alexandria (1799) but was assassinated after recapturing Cairo.

Klebs, Edwin (1834–1913) Prussian bacteriologist, who, with Friedrich *Loeffler in 1884, isolated the bacillus responsible for diphtheria (the **Klebs-Loeffler bacillus**). He also demonstrated the presence of bacteria in infected wounds and showed that tuberculosis could be transmitted via infected milk, thus establishing the bacterial cause of certain diseases.

Klee, Paul (1879–1940) Swiss painter and etcher, born in Berne. After training in the Munich Academy, he worked initially as an etcher, influenced by *Beardsley and *Goya in the grotesque and symbolic character of his works. Returning to Germany (1906), he became associated with Der *Blaue Reiter and taught at the *Bauhaus school of design (1920–33), but remained an original and independent talent. Inspired by a visit to Tunisia (1914), he turned to painting. Initially he produced small watercolors in brilliant colors; after 1919 he used oils, incorporating signs and hieroglyphs to create a fantasy world influenced by children's art.

Klein, Melanie (1882–1960) Austrian psychiatrist, who moved to England in 1926. She is noted for her psychoanalytical studies of children, which were influenced by Sigmund *Freud and his associates. Using children's play in place of free association, she analyzed the behavior of children in terms of their desires and anxieties, their relationship with their parents, and the significance of their experiences in their emotional and sexual development.

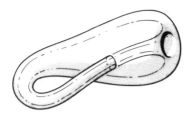

KLEIN BOTTLE *A solid with no edges and only one side.*

Klein bottle In *topology, a surface that has no edges and only one side. It is made by putting the small end of a tapering tube through the side of the tube, stretching it, and joining it to the large end. It was discovered by the German mathematician Christian Felix Klein (1849–1925).

Kleist, Heinrich von (1777–1811) German dramatist. Coming from an old Prussian family, he gave up his early career in the army. His plays vary in mood between the comedy of *Der zerbrochene Krug* (1808), the demonic violence of *Penthesilea* (1808), the romanticism of *Das Käthchen von Heilbronn* (1810), and the spirit of self-discipline of *Prinz Friedrich von Homburg* (1821). A unifying theme, also present is his short stories, is the confusion between illusion and reality. Always unstable, he committed suicide.

Klemperer, Otto (1885–1973) German conductor. He studied in Berlin and became conductor of the German Opera in Prague on the recommendation of Mahler in 1907. He was expelled by the Nazis in 1933 and became first a US and subsequently an Israeli citizen. He was principal conductor of the London Philharmonia Orchestra from 1959 until his death and is particularly remembered for his performances of Beethoven's symphonies.

Klimt, Gustav (1862–1918) Viennese Art Nouveau artist, who founded the Vienna Sezession (1897), an avant-garde exhibiting society. He achieved notoriety with the pessimistic and erotic symbolism of his murals for Vienna University (1900–03). Subsequent paintings and mosaics, allegories or female portraits, are characterized by large patterned areas often predominantly in gold, as in *The Kiss* (Vienna).

Klinger, Friedrich Maximilian von (1752–1831) German dramatist. After touring with a troupe of actors, he made a career in the Russian army. From his tempestuous play *Der Wirrwarr, oder Sturm und Drang* (1776), the *Sturm und Drang* movement took its name.

Klint, Kaare (1888–1954) Danish furniture designer, the originator of the contemporary Scandinavian style of design. Trained as an architect, he founded the Danish Academy of Arts in 1924 and became its first professor of furniture. His pioneering designs in natural unvarnished wood combined craftsmanship with modern functional needs and were influenced by *Chippendale as well as 20th-century styles.

klipspringer A small antelope, *Oreotragus oreotragus*, of rocky regions of S and E Africa. 24 in (60 cm) high at the shoulder, klipspringers have a matted bristly yellowish-brown speckled coat with white underparts; males have short horns, ringed at the base. They are agile and aptly named "cliff-springers."

Klondike The valley of the Klondike River in NW Canada, in the central *Yukon, where gold was discovered in 1896. The subsequent gold rush opened up the Yukon, although the population dwindled when the gold started to run out (1900). The Klondike has passed into Canadian literature and song.

Klopstock, Friedrich Gottlieb (1724–1803) German poet. Inspired by what he felt to be his divine mission as a poet, he achieved success with his early epic *Der Messias* (1745–73) and later with his odes (*Oden,* 1771). In reacting against rationalism by emphasizing emotion and in his enthusiasm for nature, religion, and German history, he anticipated Romanticism. He also wrote plays.

klystron An electronic device used to generate or amplify *microwaves. It consists of a sealed evacuated tube in which a steady beam of electrons from an electron gun is alternately accelerated and retarded by high-frequency radio waves (velocity *modulation) as it passes through a cavity. The resultant radio-frequency pulses are picked up at a second cavity, either as a voltage oscillation or, if connected to a *waveguide, as electromagnetic waves. The second cavity can be tuned to the input frequency or a harmonic of it. *See also* magnetron.

knapweed One of several plants of the genus *Centaurea*, of Eurasia and N Africa, having knoblike purplish flower heads. The lesser knapweed (*C. nigra*), also called hardheads, is a plant of grasslands and open places and has been introduced to New Zealand and North America. Family: *Compositae.

Kneller, Sir Godfrey (1646–1723) Portrait painter of German birth. Beginning a successful career in England (1674), he worked successively for Charles II, William III, Queen Anne, and George I. He founded the first English academy of painting (1711). His best portraits, those of the Whig Kit Cat Club (c. 1702–17) established a standard British portrait type, known as the kit cat (less than half-length but including a hand).

Knight, Dame Laura (1877–1970) British painter, famous for her scenes of circus, gypsy, and ballet life. She exhibited frequently at the Royal Academy, becoming a member in 1936. She was married to the portraitist **Harold Knight** (1874–1961).

knighthood, orders of Societies, found in many countries, to which persons are admitted as a mark of honor. In medieval Europe, companies of knights (e.g. the *Hospitallers) bound by monastic vows fought to defend Christendom (*see* Crusades). Subsequently, secular orders were instituted, usually by rulers who sought the sworn loyalty of their nobles. The most distinguished British orders are those of the Garter, the Thistle, and the Bath.

Knights of Labor US labor union, founded in 1869 in secrecy and designed to protect all who worked for a living. Its requirement of secrecy limited its growth, and it was not until Terence V. Powderly became its head (1879) that secrecy was dropped. The union then grew rapidly; by 1886 membership peaked at 700,000. Public opinion, especially after the *Haymarket Massacre (1886), subsequently turned against the union, which never recovered.

Knights of the White Camellia US secret society that advocated white supremacy. Established in 1867 in Louisiana, it sought to maintain the supremacy of whites in the South following the Civil War. Short-lived, it was dissolved by the early 1870s.

knitting The chain looping of yarn to form a network fabric that is more elastic than woven fabric; it is very suitable for clinging garments, such as sweaters and stockings. Hand knitting, using two or three needles, is an old craft. In addition to shaped flatwork in various relief patterns, tubular shapes can be knitted. Since the 19th century knitting machines have been developed.

knocking A metallic knock heard in gasoline engines as a result of combustion of the explosive charge ahead of the flame front. This is caused by local areas of high pressure in the combustion chamber. It greatly reduces the efficiency of the engine and is controlled by additives, such as *tetraethyl lead, to the fuel. Antiknock compounds that do not contain lead are being sought, owing to pollution of the atmosphere by lead.

Knossos The principal city of Minoan Crete, near present-day Heraklion. It was occupied between about 2500 and 1200 BC. Excavated and reconstructed (1899–1935) by Sir Arthur *Evans, the so-called Palace of Minos was luxurious and sophisticated. It is the probable original of the labyrinth in which, according to legend, *Theseus fought the *Minotaur. Frescoes showing processions, bull sports, and seascapes decorated its walls, there was an elaborate water system, and goods were imported from Egypt. About 1450 BC the palace was burned down and subsequent occupation levels show *Mycenaean influence. *See also* Minoan civilization.

knot (bird) A short-legged bird, *Calidris canutus*, that breeds in Arctic tundra and winters on southern coasts. 10 in (25 cm) long, it has a short black bill and its plumage is mottled gray in winter and reddish in summer. In winter, knots feed in flocks, probing mud and sand for snails, worms, and crabs. Family: *Scolopacidae* (sandpipers, snipe, etc.).

knot (unit) A unit of speed, used for ships and aircraft, equal to 1 nautical mile per hour (i.e. 1.15 miles per hour).

knots Fastenings formed by looping and tying pieces of rope, cord, etc. The mathematical theory of knots, a branch of *topology, was developed mainly in the 20th century, and draws on *matrix theory, algebra, and geometry. A simple closed curve in space may be knotted in various ways, each with specific topological properties. These are classified by knot theory and can be expressed in matrix form.

overhand knot *This is used either to make a knob in a rope or as the basis for another knot.*

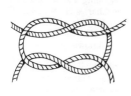

reef knot *A non-slip knot for joining ropes of similar thickness.*

quick release knot *A tug on a will quickly unfasten this knot.*

surgeon's knot *The extra twist in the first part of the knot prevents it from slipping loose while the second part is tied.*

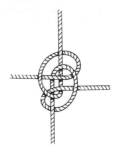

Hunter's bend *A strong, easily tied knot invented in 1978 by Dr Edward Hunter.*

bowline *A knot to form a non-slip loop.*

running bowline *A knot for making a running noose.*

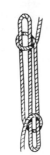

sheepshank *A means of temporarily shortening a rope.*

sheet bend *A knot for securely joining two ropes of different thickness.*

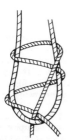

double sheet bend *This follows the same principles as the sheet bend.*

fisherman's knot *Used especially for joining lengths of fishing gut.*

carrick bend *A knot well suited to tying heavy ropes together.*

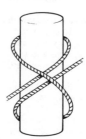

clove hitch *A simple knot for attaching a rope to a ring, rail, etc.*

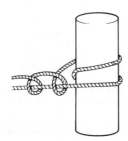

round turn and two half hitches *Used for similar purposes as the clove hitch, this knot does not easily work loose.*

anchor bend *A secure means of attaching a cable to an anchor.*

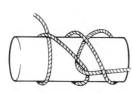

rolling hitch *A quickly made and quickly unfastened knot for attaching a rope to a rail or another, standing rope.*

Know Nothing Party US nativist political party, developed during the 1850s, that opposed the immigrants entering the US, especially Irish Roman Catholics. Also known as the American Party and Native American Party, it was founded in 1845 and acquired its name because members, pledged to secrecy, were to "know nothing" when asked about party policies. The party itself split after the 1856 elections and declined.

Knox, Henry (1750–1806) US soldier; first secretary of war (1785–94). As a colonel during the *American Revolution he brought back from Fort Ticonderoga captured British artillery that enabled the Americans to take Boston in 1776. A general from 1777, he went on to fight in almost every major battle during the Revolution. Named the first secretary of war under the Articles of Confederation, he stayed in that position when George Washington became president in 1789.

Knox, John (c. 1514–72) Scottish Protestant reformer. He was a Catholic priest before adopting the reformed faith in the 1540s. In 1547 he joined the Protestants after Wishart's execution in St Andrew's Castle. The castle was stormed by the French, who imprisoned Knox as a galley slave. After his release (1549) he became a chaplain to Edward VI in England and contributed to the revision of the Second Book of Common Prayer. On Queen Mary's accession he escaped to the Continent, where he met *Calvin in Geneva. Returning to Scotland in 1559, he became its leading reformer. In 1560 the Scottish parliament adopted the *Confession of Faith* that Knox had compiled. His *First Book of Discipline* (1561) outlined a structure for the reformed Church of Scotland, embracing all aspects of life, including education and poor relief.

Knoxville 36 00N 83 57W A city in Tennessee, on the Tennessee River. It is the site of the University of Tennessee (1794) and the headquarters of the Tennessee Valley Authority. An inland port and agricultural trading center, its industries include meat packing and marble processing. Population (1980): 476,517.

koala An arboreal *marsupial, *Phascolarctus cinereus*, of E Australia. About 24 in (60 cm) high, koalas have thick grayish fur, tufted ears, a small tail, and long claws. Groups of koalas move slowly through eucalyptus forests, each adult eating more than 2.2 lb (1 kg) of the leaves every day. The pouch opens toward the female's tail and the young are weaned on half-digested eucalyptus soup from their mother's anus. Family: *Phalangeridae*.

kob An antelope, *Kobus kob*, of African savanna regions, also called Buffon's kob. Males stand about 35 in (90 cm) high at the shoulder; females are smaller. The coat ranges from orange-red to nearly black, with white markings on the face, legs, and belly and a black stripe down the foreleg.

Kobarid (Italian name: Caproetto) 46 16N 13 35E A village in NW Yugoslavia, in Slovenia. Part of Italy until 1947, it was the site of the defeat of the Italians by the Austro-German army in 1917.

Kobayashi Masaki (1916–) Japanese film director. He established his international reputation with *The Human Condition* (1959–61), a trilogy of films concerned with the dignity of the individual in modern society. His other films include *Kwaidan* (1964), an anthology of ghost stories, *Rebellion* (1967), and *Kaseki* (1974).

Kobe 34 40N 135 12E A major port in Japan, in S Honshu on Osaka Bay. It forms the W end of the Osaka-Kobe industrial area and has two of the biggest shipbuilding yards in the country. Other industries include engineering, sugar, chemicals, and rubber. Its university was established in 1949. Population (1980): 1,367,000.

Kφbenhavn. *See* Copenhagen.

Koblenz (Coblenz) 50 21N 7 36E A city in W West Germany, in Rhineland-Palatinate at the confluence of the Rhine and Moselle Rivers. The seat of Frankish kings during the 6th century AD, it was annexed by France in 1798, passing to Prussia in 1815. Notable buildings, many rebuilt after World War II, include the Ehrenbreitstein fortress (c. 1000) and the birthplace of Metternich. It is a wine-trading center and manufactures furniture, pianos, and clothing. Population (1980 est): 113,900.

Koch, Robert (1843–1910) German bacteriologist, who was responsible for major discoveries in the study of disease-causing bacteria. As a young doctor, Koch successfully cultured the bacillus causing anthrax in cattle and determined its life cycle. Devising new and better culture methods, Koch succeeded in 1882 in identifying and isolating the bacillus responsible for tuberculosis. Koch investigated many other diseases including cholera, bubonic plague, and malaria. He was awarded a Nobel Prize (1905).

Köchel, Ludwig von (1800–77) Austrian naturalist and musical bibliographer. He compiled a thematic catalogue of Mozart's works, which was published in 1862; a particular work is referred to by a **Köchel number**, consisting of the letter K followed by the appropriate catalogue number.

Kodály, Zoltán (1882–1967) Hungarian composer. He was educated at Budapest University and conservatoire, where he developed an interest in Magyar folk music. In collaboration with *Bartók he collected and edited Hungarian peasant songs, which influenced his style of composition. He achieved international recognition with his *Psalmus Hungaricus* (1923); other works include the opera *Háry János* (1926), *Dances of Galanta* (1933), masses, chamber music, and orchestral music.

Kodiak 57 20N 153 40W A US island, off the S coast of Alaska in the Gulf of Alaska. First settled by Russians in 1784, it became a base for seal hunting and whaling. In 1964 it suffered an earthquake that lowered it by about 6 ft (1.8 m). Area: 3465 sq mi (8974 sq km). Population (1970): 9409.

Kodiak bear. *See* brown bear.

Kodok (former name: Fashoda) 9 51N 32 07E A small town in the S central Sudan, on the White Nile River. The *Fashoda incident took place here (1898), causing a crisis between Britain and France. Population: about 3000.

Koestler, Arthur (1905–83) British writer, born in Hungary. As a journalist in Berlin, he joined the Communist Party (1931) but left it in 1938. He settled in Britain in 1940, writing in English thereafter. His novel *Darkness at Noon* (1940), depicting the Moscow purge trials, calls on his own experience as a prisoner in the Spanish Civil War. His other novels include *Thieves in the Night* (1946) and *The Call Girls* (1972). His nonfiction was concerned with politics (*The Yogi and the Commissar*, 1945), scientific creativity (*The Sleepwalkers*, 1959; *The Act of Creation*, 1964; *The Ghost in the Machine*, 1967), and parapsychology (*The Roots of Coincidence*, 1972). His autobiographical volumes include *Arrow in the Blue* (1952) and *The Invisible Writing* (1954). His later books include *The Thirteenth Tribe: The Khazer Empire and Its Heritage* (1976) and *Janus: A Summing Up* (1979).

Koffka, Kurt (1886–1941) US psychologist, born in Germany, who was one of the founders of *Gestalt psychology. Among his works was *Growth of the Mind* (1921). He made an influential distinction between the behavioral and the geographical environments—the perceived world of common sense and the world studied by scientists.

Kohl, Helmut (1930–) West German political leader; chancellor (1982–). He served in various state (Rhineland-Palatinate) and national political posts. He was head of Rhineland-Palatinate (1966–69) and a member of the federal legislature. Always active in the Christian Democratic Union (CDU), he became its chairman (1973). He lost the election for chancellor to Helmut Schmidt in 1976, but was elected to that position in 1982.

Köhler, Wolfgang (1887–1967) US psychologist and a founder of *Gestalt psychology. Kohler's experiments on problem solving in apes (*The Mentality of Apes*, 1917) led to his exploration of the physiological basis of perception and the process of learning.

kohlrabi A variety of *cabbage, sometimes called turnip-rooted cabbage. The green or purple stem base, which swells like a turnip, is used as a vegetable and as livestock food.

Kokand 40 33N 70 55E A city in the Soviet Union, in the NE Uzbek SSR in the Fergana Valley. Fertilizers and chemicals are produced. Population (1977 est): 155,000.

Koko Nor. *See* Qinghai, Lake.

Kokoschka, Oskar (1886–1980) Austrian expressionist painter and writer (*see* expressionism). In Vienna and Berlin, he specialized in probing portraits and allegorical poems, plays, and paintings, expressing the struggle of life. After World War I he taught at the Dresden Academy and traveled widely, painting landscapes and city views, particularly of London, where he lived (1938–53). From 1953 he lived and worked in Switzerland.

Kokura. *See* Kitakyushu.

kola (or cola) Either of two trees, *Cola nitida* or *C. acuminata*, native to West Africa and widely grown in the tropics, that produce **kola nuts**. These are rich in caffeine and chewed in Africa and the West Indies for their stimulating effects. Family: *Sterculiaceae*.

Kola Peninsula A promontory in the NW Soviet Union, between the Barents Sea to the N and the White Sea to the S. The area is largely granite but is mined for apatite (for its phosphorus) and nephelinite (for its aluminum). Tundra is extensive with some swampy pine and other forests in the S. The chief town is Murmansk. Area: about 50,182 sq mi (130,000 sq km).

Kolar 13 10N 78 10E A city in India, in Karnataka. To the NW lie the Kolar Gold Fields, which produce almost all India's gold output. Population (1971): 76,112.

Kolarovgrad (*or* Shumen) 43,17 N 26 55E A city in NE Bulgaria. It was an important fort under Turkish rule (15th–19th centuries) and has a notable brewing industry. Population (1972 est): 79,134.

Kolbe, (Adolf Wilhelm) Hermann (1818–84) German chemist, who became professor at Marburg University in 1851. He was one of the first chemists to synthesize organic compounds, his most important discovery being the Kolbe reaction, for synthesizing salicylic acid. This led to the large-scale manufacture of aspirin.

Kolchak, Alexander Vasilievich (1874–1920) Russian admiral. After the Russian Revolution (1917) he became leader of anti-Bolshevik elements at Omsk, clearing Siberia and linking with *Denikin in the south. However, Bolshevik counterattacks, discontent in his territories, and divisions among his followers destroyed Kolchak's forces. He was betrayed by the Allied powers to the Bolsheviks and shot.

Koldewey, Robert (1855–1925) German archeologist. After digging at several classical sites (e.g. *Baalbek), Koldewey excavated *Babylon (1899–1917). Here his training as an architect greatly facilitated recovery of the ancient street plan and reconstruction of the mud-brick buildings.

Kolhapur 16 40N 74 15E A city in India, in Maharashtra. An early center of Buddhism, its industries include sugar processing and textiles and it has a university (1962). Population (1971): 259,050.

Kolmogorov, Andrei Nikolaevich (1903–) Soviet mathematician, who has made notable contributions to many fields of mathematics, particularly topology, probability theory, functional analysis, and geometry. His work in the branch of probability theory known as stochastic processes has found applications in the science of *cybernetics. He is the foremost Soviet mathematician of the 20th century and his influence on younger generations of mathematicians in the Soviet Union has been considerable.

Köln. *See* Cologne.

Koloszvár. *See* Cluj.

Kolyma River A river in the NE Soviet Union. Rising in the Kolyma Range of NE Siberia, it flows mainly NE to the East Siberian Sea. Length: 1615 mi (2600 km).

Komeito A Japanese political party, known in English as the Clean Government Party, formed in 1964 by the Soka-gakkai, a branch of the extreme Nichiren Buddhists. It advocates the establishment of a nonaligned Japan free from extremes of wealth and poverty. Komeito rapidly increased its parliamentary representation to become Japan's third strongest political party. Accused of wishing to impose Nichiru Shoshu as the state religion and of reviving fascism, Komeito severed its links with the Soka-gakkai in 1970.

Komi Autonomous Soviet Socialist Republic An administrative division in the NW Soviet Union, in the RSFSR. It comprises chiefly tundra (in the NE) and coniferous forests. The administrative region was established in 1921 for the Komi people, who speak a Finno-Ugric language, and became an ASSR in 1936. Timbering and mining (notably of coal and oil) are the most important economic activities; livestock raising is the main branch of agriculture. Area: 160,540 sq mi (415,900 sq km). Population (1981 est): 1,147,000. Capital: Syktyvkar.

Kommunizma Pik. *See* Communism Peak.

Komodo dragon A rare *monitor lizard, *Varanus komodoensis*, which, at 10 ft (3 m) long and weighing 298 lb (135 kg), is the largest living lizard. It has a stout neck and body, a long powerful tail, and short strong legs and is powerful enough to attack and kill a man. Komodo dragons feed mainly on carrion but also eat smaller monitors. They occur only on Komodo Island and some of the Lesser Sunda Islands of Indonesia. □reptile.

KOMSOMOL (All-Union Leninist Communist League of Youth) A Soviet youth organization. Organized in 1918, its members fought in the civil war (1918–21). In 1922 it became a social organization to promote communist ideology through social activities. Membership, which is for those aged between 14 and 28, gives good employment opportunities.

Komsomolsk-na-Amur 50 32N 136 59E A city in the Soviet Union, in the W RSFSR on the Amur River. It is named for the *KOMSOMOL, members of which built much of the city (founded 1932). Its industries, including engineering and machine building, are based on the Amurstal steelworks, located here; oil from Sakhalin is refined. Population (1981 est): 274,000.

Konakry. *See* Conakry.

Koniecpolski, Stanisław (1591–1646) Polish soldier and statesman. Koniecpolski fought many victorious battles against the Turks, Tatars, and Swedes. In 1632 he became commander in chief and subsequently influenced the government of Władysław IV (1595–1648; reigned 1632–48). Koniecpolski was extremely wealthy and acquired huge estates in the Ukraine.

Koniev, Ivan Stepanovich (1897–1973) Soviet marshal. A commander in World War II in the Ukraine and the southern front, he ended the war encircling Berlin from the south. He commanded all Warsaw Pact forces in Europe (1955–60).

Königsberg. *See* Kaliningrad.

Konoe Fumimaro, Prince (1891–1945) Japanese noble, who was prime minister three times. His first cabinet (1937–39) escalated the conflict between Japan and China; his second (1940–41) took Japan into alliance in World War II with Germany and Italy; and his third (1941) made the decision to attack the US. After Japan's surrender he avoided trial as a war criminal by committing suicide.

Konstanz. *See* Constance.

Kon-Tiki The name given by Thor *Heyerdahl to the raft built of nine balsawood logs on which, between April 28 and August 7, 1947, he and five companions traveled the 5000 miles (8000 km) between Peru and the Tuamotu islands near Tahiti. The purpose of the voyage was to demonstrate the possibility that ancient peoples of South America could have reached Polynesia. Kon-Tiki was an older name for the Inca creator god, Viracocha, allegedly known in Polynesia as Tiki.

Konya (ancient name: Iconium) 37 51N 32 30E A city in SW central Turkey. It is the center of the Whirling Dervish sect, and the monastery around the tomb of its founder is a religious museum. The town was visited by St Paul and was the capital of the Seljuq kingdom of Rum. Population (1980): 329,139.

kookaburra A large gray-brown Australian *kingfisher, *Dacelo novaeguineae*, also called laughing jackass because of its chuckling call. 17 in (43 cm) long, it is arboreal and pounces on snakes, lizards, insects, and small rodents from a perch.

Köprülü A family, of Albanian origin, of viziers (public servants) of the Ottoman Empire. **Köprülü Mohammed** (c. 1583–1661), grand vizier (1656–61), reformed the Ottoman navy and economy. His son **Köprülü Ahmed** (1635–76), grand vizier (1661–76), conquered Crete. Ahmed's brother **Köprülü Mustafa** (1637–91), grand vizier (1689–91), instituted many financial and military reforms. Their cousin **Köprülü Hussein** (d. 1702), grand vizier (1697–1702), negotiated the Treaty of Karlowitz (1699), in which the Ottoman Empire lost much territory to Austria.

Koran (*or* Quran) The sacred scripture of Islam. According to tradition, the divine revelations given to *Mohammed (d. 632 AD) were preserved by his followers and collected as the Koran under the third caliph, Uthman (d. 656). Written in classical Arabic, they were arranged in 114 suras or chapters according to length, the longer ones first. Admonitions to worship God alone and legal prescriptions predominate. The Koran is one of the main sources of the comprehensive system of *Islamic law. Although the revelations were given to Mohammed piecemeal, Muslims believe that they exist complete in a heavenly book, which contains all that has happened and will happen in the universe.

Korbut, Olga (1955–) Soviet gymnast, who won international acclaim in the 1972 Olympic Games, when she was awarded gold medals for the beam and floor exercises and for the team event. In the 1976 Olympics she did less well, winning a silver on the beam.

Korcë 40 38N 20 44E A city in SE Albania. It is the commercial center of a large wheat-growing area. Population (1978 est): 50,900.

Korchnoi, Victor (1931–) Soviet chess player. An International Grandmaster, he became Soviet champion in 1960, 1962, and 1964. He left the Soviet Union (1976) and later took part in a much publicized match with *Karpov (1978), which he lost.

Korda, Sir Alexander (Sandor Kellner; 1893–1956) British film producer and director, born in Hungary. After settling in London in 1930, he greatly boosted the British film industry during the 1930s and 1940s with a series of extravagant productions, including *The Private Life of Henry VIII* (1932), *The Scarlet Pimpernel* (1934), and *Anna Karenina* (1948).

kore (Greek: maiden) In archaic Greek sculpture, a draped standing female figure, derived originally (c. 650 BC) from Egyptian models. During the next two centuries the drapery, pose, and expression became increasingly naturalistic. *Compare* kouros.

OLGA KORBUT *Her performances did much to make gymnastics a popular spectator sport.*

Korea A country in NE Asia, occupying a peninsula between the Sea of Japan and the Yellow Sea, now divided (*see* below) into the Democratic Republic of Korea (North Korea) and the Republic of Korea (South Korea). Plains in the W rise to mountains in the N and E. Both North and South Koreans are ethnically related to the Mongoloid race. From the 1st century AD three kingdoms flourished in the peninsula: the Koguryo in the N, the Paechke in the SW, and the Silla in the SE. In 668 they were united under Silla and Buddhism subsequently became the state religion. The country long had ties with China but in 1905 became a Japanese protectorate, coming formally under Japanese rule in 1910. In 1945, following Japan's defeat in World War II, the Allies divided Korea at the *thirty-eighth parallel. The communist Democratic People's Republic of Korea under *Kim Il Sung was established in the Soviet-occupied N and the Republic of Korea under Syngman Rhee, in the US-occupied S (1948). Soviet and US troops had withdrawn by 1949 and in 1950 the *Korean War broke out between North and South Korea, ending in 1953 with the country still divided.

Korea, People's Democratic Republic of (Korean name: Chosŏn) The division of Korea left the North with almost all the country's mineral wealth (coal, iron ore, lead, zinc, molybdenum, gold, graphite, and tungsten) and a large proportion of the industries, which had been developed by the Japanese. Although many of the industries were destroyed during the Korean War, reconstruction proceeded rapidly and factory output has expanded considerably in recent times. Textiles, chemicals, machinery, and metals are among the principal manufactures and all industry is nationalized. The rather sparse agricultural land was collectivized in the 1950s and is now almost all farmed in large cooperatives; mechanization has greatly increased production. Exports, mainly to communist countries, include metals and metal products. President: Kim Il Sung. Official language: Korean. Official currency: won of 100 jun. Area: 47,225 sq mi (122,370 sq km). Population (1983 est): 18,802,000. Capital: P'yŏngyang.

Korea, Republic of (Korean name: Han Kook) The repressive government led by the first president of South Korea, Syngman *Rhee, was ended by a military coup in 1961, followed by the rise to power of General *Park Chung Hee, who was assassinated in 1979. The more densely populated South was primarily agricultural when separated from the North but the injection of US aid and other international assistance has led to the predominance of the industrial sector in recent times (especially textiles, chemicals, and food processing). Mineral resources are not large, although it has one of the world's largest deposits of tungsten. The main exports include clothes, plywood, textiles, and electrical goods. President: Chun Doo Hwan. Official language: Korean. Official currency: won of 100 chon.

Area: 38,002 sq mi (98,447 sq km). Population (1983): 41,287,000. Capital: Seoul. Main port: Pusan

Korean The language of the Mongoloid people of Korea. It is probably distantly related to *Japanese and has a somewhat similar grammatical structure. The standard and official form is based on the dialect of Seoul. It is written in a phonetic script called onmun, devised in the mid-15th century to replace the Chinese characters in use before then. Korean literature also dates from about this time, with a royal college of literature being founded in 1420.

Korean War (1950–53) A military conflict between communist and noncommunist forces in Korea. In 1948, after a period of military occupation following World War II, two Korean states were established on either side of the *thirty-eighth parallel. In the north was the communist Democratic People's Republic allied with the Soviet Union and in the south was the Republic of Korea allied with the US. Growing tensions between the two Korean states led to the 1950 invasion of South Korea by northern forces joined by Chinese communist troops. The UN condemned the invasion, and the US and 15 other member nations sent military forces to defend South Korea, under the supreme command of General Douglas *MacArthur of the US. The UN forces staged an amphibious landing at Inchon and eventually captured the North Korean capital of Pyongyang. With massive reinforcements from China, the North Koreans staged a counterattack, pushing back the UN forces and retaking the southern capital of Seoul. A stalemate developed between the contending armies after the fighting progressed slowly northward to the 38th parallel. Because MacArthur was intent on a direct confrontation with China, he was relieved of his command by President Harry *Truman in 1951 and replaced by General Matthew Ridgway. Peace talks were initiated, and an armistice between North and South Korea was signed in 1953.

Korematsu v. United States (1944) US Supreme Court decision that upheld the constitutionality of President Franklin D. Roosevelt's relocation program of Japanese-Americans living on the West coast during World War II. Korematsu, a US citizen of Japanese descent, claimed that his rights under the 5th amendment were violated. The court, declaring the program "an emergency war measure," which would lessen the chances of domestic sabotage, voted in favor of the government's position.

Kórinthos. *See* Corinth.

Kornberg, Arthur (1918–) US biochemist, who discovered how DNA is replicated in bacterial cells. Kornberg and associates were able to reproduce the conditions necessary for DNA replication in a test tube. They found that the "building blocks" (nucleotides) of the new DNA strand were joined together by an enzyme—DNA polymerase I—using existing DNA as a template.

Kornilov, Lavrentia Georgievich (1870–1918) Russian general. After the Russian Revolution (1917) he led the anti-Bolshevik White armies in S Russia. After his death in action, the command was assumed by *Denikin.

Koroliov, Sergei Pavlovich (1906–66) Soviet aeronautical engineer, who designed missiles, rockets, and spacecraft. During the 1930s he headed development of the Soviet Union's first liquid-fuel rocket. After World War II he worked on ballistic missiles and later supervised the Vostok and Soyuz manned spaceflight programs.

Kortrijk. *See* Courtrai.

Koryŏ An ancient Korean kingdom founded and ruled by the Wang dynasty (935–1392). Both Buddhism and Confucianism were influential and Koryŏ was divided by rivalry between pacifist Confucianists and militarist nationalists. The weakened state succumbed to Mongol invasions in the 13th century and virtually became a Mongol dependency in 1231. The last Wang ruler was deposed by the *Yi in 1392.

Kos. *See* Cos.

Kosciusko, Mount 36 28S 148 17E The highest mountain in Australia, in SE New South Wales in the Snowy Mountains. It lies within the Kosciusko National Park, a popular area for winter sports. Height: 7316 ft (2230 m).

Kosciuszko, Tadeusz Andrezei Bonawentura (1746–1817) Polish general and statesman, who served in the American Revolution with George Washington (1776–83). Returning to Poland (1784), he distinguished himself in the war against the Russian invasion, which ended in the partition of Poland. Kosciuszko withdrew to Saxony but returned in 1794 to lead the revolt against the occupation. He was defeated and captured at Maciejourice and imprisoned until 1796.

Košice (German name: Kaschau; Hungarian name: Kassa) 48 44N 21 15E A city in E Czechoslovakia, in E Slovakia. It has a 13th-century cathedral and a university (1959). One of the largest integrated iron and steel complexes in E Europe is situated here. Population (1980 est): 201,000.

Kosinski, Jerzy (Nikodem) (1933–) US writer, born in Poland. Educated in Poland and the USSR, he became a US citizen in 1965. His works include *The Future is Ours* (1960) and *No Third Path* (1962), both written under the pseudonym of Joseph Novak; *The Painted Bird* (1965); *Steps* (1968); *Being There* (1971); *Cockpit* (1975); *Blind Date* (1978); *Passion Play* (1979); and *Pinball* (1982).

Kossuth, Lajos (1802–94) Hungarian statesman, who was one of the leaders of the Hungarian *Revolution of 1848. In March, 1848, when Hungary was granted a separate government by Austria, Kossuth was appointed finance minister. He became governor of an independent Hungarian republic in April, 1849. When Russia destroyed the republic in August, he left Hungary and lived in exile in Turkey, England, and Italy. After his death, his body was returned to Hungary.

Kosygin, Aleksei Nikolaevich (1904–80) Soviet statesman; prime minister (1964–80). Kosygin rose in the Communist Party hierarchy in the 1940s as an expert in economic affairs. He served in the politburo from 1948 to 1952, when he was demoted. In 1960 he was again elected to what was now the presidium and after Khrushchev's fall he became prime minister. He initially shared power with *Brezhnev but in the late 1960s Kosygin's influence declined.

Kota Baharu 6 07N 102 15E A city in NE Peninsular Malaysia, the capital of Kelantan state on the Kelantan delta. It has a major power station. Population (1980): 170,559.

koto A Japanese stringed instrument of the *zither family. The narrow 7-foot (2-meter) sound board has 13 strings, which the player, sitting on his heels, plucks with plectra attached to two fingers and the thumb of the right hand. □musical instruments.

Kotor 42 27N 18 46E A port in S Yugoslavia, on the Gulf of Kotor. The oldest town in Montenegro with a remarkable 12th-century cathedral, it is now protected as a monument. The town was damaged during an earthquake in April, 1979. Population (1971): 4857.

Kottbus. *See* Cottbus.

Kotzebue, August von (1761–1819) German dramatist and novelist. He was a prolific writer of popular sentimental plays, most notably the comedy *Die deutschen Kleinstädter* (1803). He was assassinated as a suspected spy while working for the Russian tsar.

KOUROS *The* Rampin Head *(Louvre, Paris), part of an equestrian statue from the Acropolis, Athens. Its "archaic smile" is typical of Greek sculpture of the second quarter of the 6th century* BC.

kouros (Greek: youth) In archaic Greek sculpture, a nude standing male figure, often more than life-size, derived (c. 650 BC) from Egyptian models. The modeling of the face and body became increasingly naturalistic. *Compare* kore.

Koussevitsky, Sergei (1874–1951) Russian composer. Originally a virtuoso double-bass player, he conducted the State Symphony Orchestra in Petrograd (now Leningrad) but left Russia in 1920. He worked in Paris and subsequently in the US, where he directed the Boston Symphony Orchestra from 1924 to 1949. He was an advocate of contemporary music and founded the Koussevitsky Music Foundation, which continues to commission new musical works.

Kovno. *See* Kaunas.

Kowloon. *See* Jiulong.

Koxinga. *See* Zheng Cheng Gong.

Kozhikode (former name: Calicut) 11 15N 75 45E A seaport on the W coast of India, in Kerala. Formerly famous as a cotton-manufacturing center (Calicut gave its name to calico), it was visited by the Portuguese explorer Vasco da Gama (1498) and in 1664 the British East India Company established a trading post here. Tea, coffee, coconut products, and spices are exported. Population (1971): 333,979.

Kra, Isthmus of The neck of the Malay Peninsula connecting it to the Asian mainland. It is occupied by Burma and Thailand and is 40 mi (64 km) across at its narrowest point.

Krafft-Ebing, Richard von (1840–1902) German psychiatrist, who studied many aspects of mental and nervous disorders. He established the link between syphilis and general paralysis of the insane and made pioneering studies of sexual aberrations in *Psychopathia sexualis* (1886).

kraft process An industrial process for producing cellulose for paper manufacture from pine-wood chips by digestion with alkali. Rosin and fatty-acid soaps are by-products. The pulp produced is especially strong, hence the name (German *kraft*, strong).

Kragujevac 44 01N 20 55E A city in E Yugoslavia, in Serbia. A former center of the Serbian struggle against the Turks, it was the capital of Serbia (1818–39). Its industries include a large car factory. Population (1971): 71,180.

krait A highly venomous snake belonging to the genus *Bungarus* (12 species) occurring in S Asia. Kraits have shiny scales and are usually patterned with blue-and-white or black-and-yellow bands; they prey chiefly on other snakes. The common blue krait (*B. caeruleus*) of India and China is 5 ft (1.5 m) long and its venom can be fatal to humans. Family: *Elapidae* (cobras, mambas, coral snakes).

Krakatoa (Indonesian name: Krakatau) 6 11S 105 26E A small volcanic Indonesian island in the Sunda Strait. During its eruption in 1883, one of the greatest ever recorded, 36,000 people were killed, many by the tidal waves that swept the coasts of Java and Sumatra. Today the island remains uninhabited.

Kraków (or Cracow) 50 03N 19 55E The third largest city in Poland, on the Vistula River. It was the capital of Poland from 1305 to 1609 and remains famous as a cultural center. The Jagiellonian University, one of the oldest in Europe, was founded here in 1364. Other notable buildings include the cathedral (14th century) and many architecturally distinguished churches. Its industry is based at Nowa Huta 6 mi (10 km) to the E. Population (1979 est): 705,000.

Kramatorsk 48 43N 37 33E A city in the Soviet Union, in the E Ukrainian SSR in the Donets Basin. An iron-and-steel center, it manufactures machinery and machine tools. Population (1981 est): 183,000.

Krasnodar (name until 1920: Ekaterinodar) 45 02N 39 00E A city in the Soviet Union, in the SW RSFSR on the Kuban River. It is the center of an agricultural region and food processing is the most important industry. Population (1981 est): 581,000.

Krasnoyarsk 56 05N 92 46E A city in the Soviet Union, in the E central RSFSR on the Yenisei River. It was founded in 1628, developing greatly after the discovery of gold in the region in the 19th century. It produces aluminum, having one of the largest outputs in the country, and has a notable hydroelectric station. Population (1981 est): 820,000.

Krebs, Sir Hans Adolf (1900–81) British biochemist, born in Germany. Working in Germany until 1933, Krebs discovered the cycle of reactions by which waste nitrogenous products are converted to *urea by the body. After his move to Britain came his major achievement—the *Krebs cycle. Krebs was awarded a Nobel Prize (1953) with Fritz Lipmann (1899–).

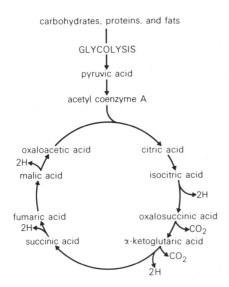

carbohydrates, proteins, and fats

GLYCOLYSIS

pyruvic acid

acetyl coenzyme A

oxaloacetic acid   citric acid
2H
malic acid   isocitric acid

2H

fumaric acid   oxalosuccinic acid
2H   CO₂
succinic acid   α-ketoglutaric acid

CO₂

2H

KREBS CYCLE *For every two atoms of hydrogen transferred, three ATP molecules are generated.*

Krebs cycle (citric acid cycle *or* tricarboxylic acid cycle) The sequence of chemical reactions, taking place in the mitochondria of cells, that is central to the metabolism of virtually all living organisms. Named for its principal discoverer, Sir Hans *Krebs, the cycle involves the conversion of acetyl coenzyme A, derived from the carbohydrates, proteins, and fats of food, into hydrogen atoms or electrons, from which usable energy in the form of *ATP is produced by the *cytochrome electron transport chain. Intermediate products of the Krebs cycle are used for the manufacture of carbohydrates, lipids, and proteins by cells.

Krefeld 51 20N 6 32E A city in NW West Germany, in North Rhine-Westphalia on the Rhine River. It is known especially for its silk and velvet industries. It was the site of a Prussian victory (1758) during the Seven Years' War. Population (1980 est): 223,400.

Kreisky, Bruno (1911–) Austrian statesman; Socialist chancellor (1970–83). After Austria fell to Nazi Germany, he escaped to Sweden (1938), where he lived until 1945. He was foreign minister (1959–66) before becoming chancellor. He retired when the Socialist Party lost its majority.

Kreisler, Fritz (1875–1962) Austrian violinist. A child prodigy, he studied at the Vienna and Paris conservatoires and toured the US in 1889, the beginning of a brilliant career. He frequently played his own compositions, written in the style of older composers and (until 1935) ascribed to them.

Kremenchug 49 03N 33 25E A city in the Soviet Union, in the E central Ukrainian SSR on the Dnepr River. It has a large hydroelectric station and metallurgical and engineering industries. Population (1981 est): 215,000.

Kremlin The citadel of any Russian city, now referring usually to that of Moscow. Built in 1156 but continually extended, it contains the Cathedral of the Assumption (1475–79), the Cathedral of the Annunciation (1484–89), the Great Kremlin Palace (1838–49), etc. Except for the period between 1712 and 1918 it has served continually as the seat of the Russian government and is now also a public museum of Russian architecture.

Kreutzer, Rodolphe (1766–1831) French violinist and composer, renowned for his violin studies. Beethoven's *Kreutzer Sonata* for violin and piano (1803) was dedicated to him.

Krewo, Union of (1385) The union of Poland and Lithuania under Jagiełło, Grand Duke of Lithuania (*see* Jagiellon), whose rule there was threatened by rivals in the ducal family and by the *Teutonic Knights. He agreed to marry the young Polish queen and to accept Christianity while Lithuania was to be annexed to Poland. The union was only made permanent by the Union of *Lublin (1569).

krill Shrimplike marine *crustaceans, 0.3–2.4 in (8–60 mm) long, of the order *Euphausiacea* (82 species). Periodically krill swarms occur in certain regions, for example the Arctic and Antarctic Oceans, to become an important source of food for fishes, birds, and especially baleen whales.

Krishna A popular Hindu deity, the eighth incarnation of *Vishnu and the subject of much devotional worship, art, and literature. In the *Bhagavadgita* he is revealed as the creator, sustainer, and destroyer of the universe (*see* Trimurti). Elsewhere he is worshiped as a fertility god, whose flute playing entrances all and whose erotic love for young maidens expresses God's love for man. He is commonly represented as a beautiful youth with bluish skin wearing a crown of peacock feathers.

Krishna Menon. *See* Menon, Krishna.

Kristiansand 58 8N 08 01E A major seaport in S Norway, on the *Skagerrak. Its numerous industries include shipbuilding, textiles, smelting, and food processing. Population (1981 est): 60,938.

Kristianstad 56 02N 14 10E A city in Sweden, on the Helge River. Originally a Danish fortress (1614), it finally became part of Sweden in 1678. Its industries include textiles and engineering. Population (1978 est): 68,883.

Krivoi Rog 47 55N 33 24E A city in the Soviet Union, in the SE Ukrainian SSR. Founded by the Cossacks in the 17th century, it is now an important ironmining center. Population (1981 est): 663,000.

Krochmal, Nachman (1785–1840) Jewish philosopher and historian, born in Poland. His *Guide to the Perplexed of Our Time* (published posthumously in 1851) offers an original philosophy of Jewish history and marks a significant achievement in the early modern study of Jewish history and literature.

Kronstadt 60 00N 29 40E A port in the NW Soviet Union, in the RSFSR on Kotlin Island in the Gulf of Finland. The *Kronstadt Rebellion (1921) of sailors was instrumental in the Soviet Government's decision to inaugurate the New Economic Policy. Kronstadt is still an important naval base. Population (1969 est): 175,264.

Kronstadt Rebellion (1921) An uprising among Soviet sailors in Kronstadt. The sailors, who had supported the Bolsheviks in the Russian Revolution, demanded economic reforms and an end to Bolshevik political domination. The Red Army crushed the rebels and Lenin's *New Economic Policy (1921) was introduced to relieve the privations that had given rise to the revolt.

Kropotkin, Peter, Prince (1842–1921) Russian anarchist. A noted geographer and geologist, Kropotkin joined the anarchist movement in the 1870s, was arrested, and escaped abroad. He settled in England in 1886 and later wrote his famous autobiography, *Memoirs of a Revolutionist* (1899). In 1917, Kropotkin returned to Russia but, unsympathetic to the authoritarianism of the Bolsheviks, retired from politics.

PAUL KRUGER

Kruger, (Stephanus Johannes) Paul(us) (1825–1904) Afrikaner statesman; president (1883–1902) of the South African Republic (Transvaal). A farmer of Dutch descent, Kruger settled with his parents in the Transvaal after taking part in the *Great Trek. He led the struggle to regain independence for the Transvaal from the British, achieved in 1881, after the first *Boer War. As president he resisted British immigrant demands for political equality with the Afrikaner, a policy that led to the second Boer War (1899–1902). In the course of the war he went to Europe to seek aid for the Afrikaner cause. Unsuccessful, he settled in Holland and then Switzerland, where he died.

Kruger National Park A game and plant reserve in NE South Africa, adjacent to the border with Mozambique. About 202 sw mi (325 km) long and 12–31 mi (20–50 km) wide, it serves to protect most species found in the area, including lions, leopards, zebras, and elephants. Area: about 8106 sq mi (21,000 sq km).

krugerrand A South African coin containing one troy ounce of gold, minted since 1967 for overseas issue and bought for investment purposes. It has never been a true currency coin and was minted to enable investors to escape restrictions on the private ownership of gold.

Krugersdorp 26 06S 27 46E A city in South Africa, in the S Transvaal. Founded in 1887, it is an important mining and industrial center producing gold, uranium, and manganese. Population (1980 est): 102,940.

Krum (d. 814 AD) Khan of the Bulgars (802–14). After defeating a Byzantine army in 811, Krum besieged Constantinople in 813 and 814, dying during the campaign. Krum introduced the basis of a state administrative system to Bulgaria.

Krupp A German family of arms manufacturers. Under **Arndt Krupp** (d. 1624), the family settled in Essen, where in 1811 **Friedrich Krupp** (1787–1826) established a steel factory. His son **Alfred Krupp** (1812–87) diversified the family business into arms manufacture, contributing to Prussian victory in the *Franco-Prussian War (1870–71). Under Alfred's son-in-law **Gustav Krupp von Bohlen und Halbach** (1870–1950), the company developed Big Bertha, the World War I artillery piece named for— Gustav's wife **Bertha Krupp** (1886–1957). Their son **Alfried Krupp** (1907–67) developed Gustav's ties with the Nazis, using concentration-camp internees in his factories. After World War II he was imprisoned for war crimes and his property was confiscated until 1951, when he was granted an amnesty.

krypton (Kr) A noble gas discovered in 1898 by Sir William Ramsay and M. W. Travers (1872–1961), in the residue left after boiling liquid air. Compounds include the fluoride KrF_2 and some *clathrates. It is used for filling some fluorescent light bulbs and the *meter is defined in terms of the wavelength of a specified transition of one of its isotopes. At no 36; at wt 83.80; mp −248.9°F (−156.6°C); bp −241.9°F (−152.2°C).

Kuala Lumpur 3 10N 101 40E The capital of Malaysia, in central Peninsular Malaysia. It became capital of the Federated Malay States in 1895. Formerly also capital of the state of Selangor, it became a federal territory in 1974. The University of Malaya was founded in 1962 and the Technological University of Malaysia in 1972. It is a major commercial center serving an important tinmining and rubber-growing area. Population (1980): 937,875.

Kuang-chou. *See* Canton.

Kuang-hsü. *See* Guang Xu.

Kuan Ti. *See* Guan Di.

Kuan Yin. *See* Guan Yin.

Kuban River A river in the S central Soviet Union. Rising in the Caucasus Mountains, it flows mainly NW into a swampy delta that enters the Sea of Azov. Its main port is Krasnodar. Length: 563 mi (906 km).

Kubelik, Rafael (1914–) Czech conductor. His career in Prague ended in 1948, when he went to live first in Britain and subsequently in the US. He was music director of Britain's Royal Opera (1955–58), and of the New York Metropolitan Opera (1972–74). In 1973 he took Swiss citizenship. His father **Jan Kubelik** (1880–1940) was a famous violinist.

Kublai Khan (1215–94) Emperor of China (1279–94), who founded the Yuan dynasty. Genghis Khan's grandson, Kublai established himself (1259) as chief of the Mongols after years of conflict with his brother Mangu (d. 1259). The conqueror and acknowledged ruler of all China from 1279, he administered from Peking an empire extending from the Danube River to the East China Sea. More humane than his predecessors and much influenced by Chinese culture and civilization, he opened up trade and communications with Europe, largely through Marco *Polo. However, his preoccupation with China and attempts to conquer SE Asia weakened the rest of the empire.

Kubrick, Stanley (1928–) US film writer, director, and producer. His first major film, *Paths of Glory* (1957), which he wrote and directed, concerned an unjust court-martial. His subsequent films, mainly satirical and highly imaginative, include *Lolita* (1962), *Dr Strangelove* (1963), *2001: A Space Odyssey* (1968), *A Clockwork Orange* (1971), *Barry Lyndon* (1975), and *The Shining* (1980).

Kuching 1 32N 110 20E A port in Malaysia, the capital of Sarawak state on the Sarawak River. It exports rubber, sago, and pepper. It has Anglican and Roman Catholic cathedrals. Population (1980): 120,000.

kudu A large antelope, *Tragelaphus strepsiceros*, of African bush regions. About 52 in (130 cm) high at the shoulder, kudus are red-brown with thin white vertical stripes on the flanks. Males have long corkscrew-shaped horns, a fringe on the lower side of the neck, and a mane along the back.

The lesser kudu (*T. imberbis*) is smaller and found only in NE Africa.

kudzu A climbing vine, *Pueraria lobata*, with entire or lobed leaves and fragrant purple flowers. Native to E Asia, it has been introduced to North America for its edible tubers, fiber, and as a quick-growing ornamental along highways, etc. However, its extreme hardiness has made it difficult to contain or control. Family: *Leguminosae*.

Kuei-yang. *See* Guiyang.

Kufah A town 90 mi (145 km) S of Baghdad, in Iraq. Founded as an Arab garrison town in 638 AD, Kufah became one of the most important centers of Islam. From the 10th century it began to decline and it is now an archeological site. Its suburb of Najaf is the burial place of *Ali and a flourishing center of *Shiite Islam.

Kuibyshev (name until 1935: Samara) 53 10N 50 10E A port in the SW central Soviet Union, in the RSFSR on the Volga River. Oil refining is a major industrial activity and market gardening is also important. Population (1981 est): 1,238,000.

Kukai (774–835) Japanese Buddhist monk, famous as a scholar and artist. The founder of the Kongobuji monastery on Mount Koya, Kukai reputedly invented hiragana, the character system of *Japanese writing.

Ku Klux Klan (KKK) A US secret society committed to the racist philosophy of white supremacy. Founded in Tennessee soon after the *Civil War to deter newly-enfranchised blacks from voting, the Klan adopted bizarre membership rituals and was headed by an officer called the Imperial Wizard. During the early *Reconstruction period, Klansmen in white cloaks and hoods, burning fiery crosses, terrorized and killed innocent blacks and destroyed their property. Although the original Klan was disbanded in 1869, it was revived in 1915 as a white supremacist party preaching hatred against immigrants, Catholics, and Jews, as well as blacks. Membership in the KKK dropped during the Depression, but opposition in the South to the *civil rights movement in the 1950s led to another revival. The House Un-American Activities Committee investigated the Klan leadership in 1965, after it had been implicated in the murder of a civil rights demonstrator. The present Klan membership is tiny, but it maintains its fanatical opposition to any form of racial integration.

kulaks Wealthy peasants in late imperial and early Soviet Russia. Before the Russian Revolution (1917) they were prominent in village affairs. After the Revolution, they were favored by the *New Economic Policy (1921) until 1927, when Stalin raised their taxes and then transformed their lands into *collective farms. The dekulakization program led to the exile of many kulaks to remote regions.

Kulturkampf (German: conflict of beliefs) The struggle between *Bismarck and the German Roman Catholic Church during the 1870s and 1880s. Bismarck opposed the church's involvement in politics and subordinated it to the state. However, opposition to the persecution of priests had forced Bismarck to restore the church's rights by 1887.

Kumamoto 32 50N 130 42E A city in Japan, in W Kyushu on the Shira River. One of the strongest centers in feudal Japan, it has a 17th-century castle. Its university was established in 1949. It is an agricultural center, with bamboo, pottery, and textile industries. Population (1980): 526,000.

Kumasi 6 45N 1 35W The second largest city in Ghana. Formerly the capital of Ashanti, it was taken by the British in 1874. It is the commercial and transportation center of Ghana's chief cocoa-growing area. The University of Science and Technology was founded here in 1961. Population (1970): 351,629.

kumquat A shrubby plant of the genus *Fortunella* (6 species), of E and SE Asia, with fruits resembling small oranges. They are acid-tasting and mainly used for pickling and preserves and kumquats can be grown farther N than citrus trees. Family: *Rutaceae*.

Kun, Béla (1886–?1939) Hungarian revolutionary. Kun founded the Hungarian Communist Party in 1918 and led the Soviet Republic that succeeded *Károlyi's government in March, 1919. The populace's reluctance to accept his nationalization program led to a reign of terror, which with his unsuccessful campaigns against Romania forced him to flee in August to Vienna and then to Russia. He reportedly died in Stalin's purges.

KUNG FU *A demonstration of this popular martial art in a city square.*

kung fu An ancient Chinese form of combat, mainly for self-defense. Among the other *martial arts it is most closely related to *karate, which possibly developed from it. In the second half of the 20th century the *wing chun* style (according to tradition devised as a means of self-defense for women) has become particularly well known, partly because of the publicity given it by Bruce *Lee. Like other martial arts, it embodies a philosophy as well as a method of combat.

Kunlun Mountains A mountain system in W China, separating Tibet from the Tarim Basin. It extends 1000 mi (1600 km) E–W, reaching 25,378 ft (7723 m) at Ulugh Muztagh.

Kunming 25 04N 102 41E A city in S China, the capital of Yunnan province. A major commercial and cultural center, it is noted for its Ming bronze temple and is the site of Yunnan University. Industries include iron and steel, engineering, and chemicals. Population (1957 est): 880,000.

Kuomintang. *See* Guomindang.

Kuo Mo-jo (1892–1978) Chinese man of letters, translator of many western classics. Born in Szechwan, he went to Japan in 1913, where in 1921 he founded the Creation Society, dedicated to the reform of Chinese language and literature. He produced a vast amount of work as a poet, novelist, playwright, and critic. He returned to China in 1937 a committed communist and held many major cultural posts under Mao.

Kura River A river in W Asia. Rising in NE Turkey, it flows N into the Soviet Union, through the Georgian and Azerbaidzhan SSRs to enter the Caspian Sea near Baku. It is used for hydroelectric power and irrigation. Length: 941 mi (1515 km).

Kurchatov, Igor Vasilievich (1903–60) Soviet physicist, who headed his country's research into nuclear fission during World War II. His team constructed a nuclear reactor in 1946 and built the Soviet Union's first atomic bomb in 1949 and its first hydrogen bomb in 1952. The element kurchatovium is named for him.

kurchatovium (Ku) An artificial transuranic element and the first transactinide. It was first detected by Soviet scientists in 1964 and named for I. V. *Kurchatov. The claim is disputed by scientists at Berkeley, US, who proposed the name **rutherfordium** (Rf) after Lord *Rutherford, following their independent synthesis. At no 104.

Kurdistan An area in the Middle East inhabited by *Kurds, comprising parts of SE Turkey, N Syria, N Iraq, and NW Iran, including the Iranian province of Kordestan. The Turkish part includes a plateau that supports some agriculture, the remainder being mainly mountainous; the chief towns are Diyarbakir (Turkey), Kirkuk (Iraq), and Kermanshah (Iran). The area was split between different countries on the dissolution of the Ottoman Empire at the end of World War I, and subsequent attempts to form a Kurdish state have been only partially or temporarily successful. Area: 74,600 sq mi (192,000 sq km).

Kurds The major population group in *Kurdistan. Their language, Kurdish, is one of the *Iranian languages and is written in either a modified Arabic or a modified Cyrillic script. The Kurds grow cereals and cotton and are now mostly detribalized but a few nomadic groups still exist. They are Muslims but do not restrict their women to the same extent as other Islamic peoples. Known from Assyrian records (6th century BC), the Kurds have never enjoyed political unity, and nationalistic aspirations issuing in rebellions in the 19th and 20th centuries have led to reprisals, especially in Turkey (1925) and Iraq.

Kure 34 14N 132 32E A port in Japan, in SW Honshu on Hiroshima Bay. An important naval base since 1886, an enormous battleship, the *Yamato*, was built here during World War II. Other industries include engineering and steel. Population (1980): 235,000.

Kurgan 55 30N 65 20E A city in the W central Soviet Union, in the RSFSR on the Tobol River. Machinery is produced and food processed. Population (1981 est): 322,000.

Kuria Muria Islands A group of five islands off the coast of Oman, in the Arabian Sea. Area: 28 sq mi (72 sq km).

Kuril Islands A Soviet chain of 56 islands extending 746 mi (1200 km) NE–SW between Kamchatka (Soviet Union) and Hokkaido (Japan) and separating the Sea of Okhotsk and the main body of the Pacific Ocean. Discovered in 1634 by the Dutch, the islands were Japanese until seized by the Soviet Union in 1945. The largest are Paramushir, Urup, Iturup, and Kunashir. There are hot springs and 38 active volcanoes. Parallel to the chain, about 124 sq mi (200 km) to the E, is the **Kuril Trench**, which has a maximum depth of 34,587 ft (10,542 m). Total area: about 6022 sq mi (15,600 sq km).

Kurosawa Akira (1910–) Japanese film director. His best-known films are action costume dramas such as *Rashomon* (1950) and *Seven Samurai* (1954). Working usually with the actor Toshiro Mifune (1920–), he has also made films on contemporary themes of social injustice and several literary adaptations, notably *Throne of Blood* (1957) from Shakespeare's *Macbeth*.

kuroshio A warm ocean current forming part of the N Pacific circulation. Analogous to the Gulf Stream of the Atlantic, it flows NE along the Pacific coast of Japan, then veers across the N Pacific as the North Pacific Drift.

Kursk 51 45N 36 14E A city in the W central Soviet Union, in the RSFSR. Food processing and metallurgy are important. Population (1981 est): 390,000.

Kusunoki Masashige (1294–1336) Japanese samurai. His steadfast loyalty to Emperor *Daigo II and heroic defense of Chihaya castle became one of the most famous examples of *bushido* (the way of the warriors).

Kut. *See* Al Kut.

Kutaisi 42 15N 42 44E A city in the Soviet Union, in the W Georgian SSR on the Rioni River. It is a historic Transcaucasian city and the 11th-century Bagrati Cathedral survives. It is a major industrial center, producing especially consumer goods. Population (1981 est): 200,000.

Kutch, Rann of An area of salt waste in central W India, near the border with S Pakistan. It consists of the Great Rann in the N and the Little Rann in the SE. It was a navigable lake in the 4th century BC, but is now salt marsh in the wet season and salt desert in the dry. Total area: about 8878 sq mi (23,000 sq km).

Kutenai A North American Indian people of the plateau region between the Rocky and Cascade Mountains of British Columbia. They were a hunting and fishing people, occasionally moving on to the Plains to hunt buffalo. Their language is distantly related to the *Algonkian family.

Kutná Hora (German name: Kuttenberg) 49 58N 15 15E A mining city in Czechoslovakia, in E Bohemia, famous during the 13th century as a silvermining center. It contains the fine gothic Cathedral of St Barbara (13th century), in the form of an imperial crown. Population (1970 est): 18,100.

Kutuzov, Mikhail Ilarionovich, Prince of Smolensk (1745–1813) Russian field marshal. After service in Poland, Austria, and against the Turks, he commanded the forces opposing Napoleon's invasion of Russia. When Napoleon withdrew from Moscow, Kutuzov's army harassed his retreat until barely 100,000 French soldiers remained.

Kuwait 29 20N 48 00E The capital of the sheikdom of Kuwait, on the Persian Gulf. It has a good natural harbor, and its livelihood was based on sea trade, fishing, and boatbuilding until oil became the major industry in the early 1950s and the traditional Islamic town began to develop into a metropolis with modern facilities including a university (1962). Population (1970): 80,405.

Kuwait, State of A country in the Middle East, in Arabia situated at the head of the Persian Gulf. The country is flat, sandy, and barren and has a harsh climate with extremes of temperature. The inhabitants are predominantly Arab, although about half are foreigners, and the Kuwaitis are mainly Sunnite or Shiite Muslim. *Economy*: Kuwait is one of the largest oil producers in the world and has one of the highest per capita incomes; oil revenues account for over half the gross national product and oil-related services for most of the remainder, as the country has almost no other natural resources. Kuwait is a member of OPEC. There are some manufacturing industries, such as plastics and fertilizers, and the traditional fishing (especially for shrimp) and the building of dhows (Arab sailing craft) continue. *History*: Kuwait was originally settled in the early 18th century by nomads from the Arabian interior, who established a sheikdom in 1756. In 1899, to counter German and Ottoman expansionism, Kuwait made an agreement giving Britain control over its foreign affairs and on the outbreak of World War I it became a British protectorate. Its borders were fixed in 1922–23, including those of a neutral zone, the oil revenues from which are shared by Saudi Arabia and Kuwait. Oil was discovered in 1938 but it was not exploited until after World War II, when it transformed the Kuwaiti economy. On gaining independence in 1961, Kuwait almost immediately had to request troops from Britain in order to avert the threatened annexation by Iraq but soon after became accepted as a sovereign state. Kuwait nationalized its oil industry in 1975. War between Iran and Iraq from 1980 raised the fear of Iranian aggression against the Arab states in the Persian Gulf region. In 1984 oil tankers in the Gulf were attacked by both Iranian and Iraqi aircraft. Head of state: Sheik Jabir al-Ahmad al-Jabir as-Sabah (1928–   ). Prime minister: Sheik Saad al-Abdullah as-Salim as-Sabah. Official language: Arabic. Official currency: Kuwait dinar of 1000 fils. Area: 9375 sq mi (24,286 sq km). Population (1983): 1,652,000. Capital: Kuwait.

Kuznets, Simon (1901–   ) US economist, born in Russia. His theory of the *gross national product as a measure of economic output is contained in his major work *National Income and Its Composition (1919–1938)* (1941). Kuznets was awarded the Nobel Prize in 1971.

Kuznetsk Basin An area in the central S Soviet Union comprising the Tom River basin from Novokuznetsk to Tomsk. It has vast coal deposits, which have brought heavy industry to the area, notably iron- and steelworks.

Kwa A major division of the *Niger-Congo language family that includes many languages of West Africa, such as Yoruba, Igbo (*see* Ibo) *Ewe, Twi, and Anyi.

Kwajalein 9 15N 167 30E The largest atoll of the Marshall Islands, in the W Pacific Ocean. It was the first Pacific territory captured by US forces in World War II and is now a US military base.

Kwakiutl A North American Indian people of the coastal region of British Columbia. They speak a *Wakashan language. Their vigorous traditional culture was typical of the NW coast and characterized by extreme competition for status and rank through ostentatious disposal and even destruction of wealth (*see* potlatch). There was an elaborate religious and ceremonial life and a distinctive artistic tradition based upon carving of wooden totem poles, masks, and other objects. Their economy was based on an abundance of salmon and other fish, game, and wild fruits and agriculture was not practiced.

Kwangju 35 07N 126 52E A city in SW South Korea. An ancient commercial and administrative center, it has industries that include motor-vehicle manufacture. Its university was established in 1952. Population (1975): 606,468.

Kwangsi Chuang Autonomous Region. *See* Guangxi Zhuang Autonomous Region.

Kwangtung. *See* Guangdong.

kwashiorkor Severe protein deficiency in children under five years. **Marasmus** is deficiency not only of protein but also of carbohydrate and fat. Kwashiorkor and marasmus often occur together in some combination. Kwashiorkor, which develops in babies soon after they are weaned, occurs in poor countries, especially parts of West Africa, where the diet does not contain sufficient protein (the name derives from a Ghanaian word). The children fail to grow, are apathetic, have swollen stomachs and ankles, sparse hair, diarrhea, and enlarged livers. The slightest infection is usually fatal but the children recover rapidly with a good diet.

KwaZulu. *See* Bantu Homelands.

Kweichow. *See* Guizhou.

Kwinana. *See* Fremantle.

Kyd, Thomas (1558–94) English dramatist. A friend of *Marlowe, Kyd inaugurated the genre of revenge tragedy with *The Spanish Tragedy* (1592). Among his probable works is a play about Hamlet, now lost, which influenced Shakespeare.

Kyoga, Lake (*or* Lake Kioga) A lake in central Uganda. Formed by the Victoria Nile River, it is shallow and reedy and has many arms. Length: about 81 mi (130 km).

Kyoto 35 2N 135 45E A city in Japan, in S Honshu. It has been a leading cultural center since early times, when it was the Japanese capital (794–1192 AD) and the old imperial palace and ancient Buddhist temples still remain. Kyoto university was established in 1897. It is also the center of Japanese Buddhism. Situated within the Osaka-Kobe industrial complex, it is famed for its silk, porcelain, and handicrafts. Population (1980): 1,473,000.

Kyprianou, Spyros (1932–   ) Cypriot statesman; president (1977–   ). When Cyprus became independent in 1960 he was appointed minister of justice and then foreign minister (1960–72). In 1976 he founded the Cyprus Democratic Party.

Kyushu The southernmost of the four main islands of Japan, separated from Korea by the Korea Strait and from Honshu by Shimonoseki Strait. Mountainous and volcanic, it has hot springs and a subtropical climate and is the most densely populated of the Japanese islands. There is a large rice-growing area in the NW, drained by the Chikugo River, while heavy industry is centered on the N coalfield. Other important products are silk, fish, timber, fruit, and vegetables. It is noted for its Satsuma and Hizen porcelain. Area: 13,768 sq mi (35,659 sq km). Population (1970): 12,496,433. Chief cities: Kitakyushu, Fukuoka, and Nagasaki.

Kyzyl Kum A desert in the W central S Soviet Union, lying between the Amu Darya and Syr Darya Rivers in the Kazakh and Uzbek SSRs. Area: about 115,806 sq mi (300,000 sq km).

L

Laaland. *See* Lolland.

Labanotation. *See* illustration at ballet.

labeled compounds. *See* radioactive tracer.

Labiatae A family of herbaceous plants and shrubs (about 3500 species), widely distributed but particularly abundant in the Mediterranean region. They typically have square stems, hairy simple leaves, and clusters of tubular two-lipped flowers. Many of the plants are aromatic and yield useful oils (lavender, rosemary, etc.) and many are used as culinary herbs (marjoram, mint, sage, thyme, etc.).

Labiche, Eugène (1815–88) French dramatist. His numerous popular farcical comedies include *The Italian Straw Hat* (1851) and *The Journey of Mr Perrichon* (1860). They are characterized by intricate plots and the satirical portrayal of contemporary bourgeois conventions.

Labor, Department of US cabinet-level executive branch department that administers laws guaranteeing workers' rights regarding working conditions, wages, discrimination, and compensation insurance. It protects pension rights, provides for job training and employment, strengthens collective bargaining, and measures the nation's economy. Established in 1913, it was originally the Bureau of Labor under the Interior Department.

Labor Party The Australian democratic socialist party. It was formed in New South Wales in 1891 and first held federal office in 1904. World War I provoked a split in the party with the Labor prime minister W. M. *Hughes leading the proconscription majority out of the party to form the National Party (1916). The Labor Party did not regain power until 1929 and in 1931 policies in dealing with the Depression caused another split. In power from 1939 to 1949, the party introduced important social legislation but in opposition in the 1950s another split occurred over attitudes to communism. Labor were again in power from 1972 until 1975 under Gough *Whitlam and from 1983, when Robert *Hawke became prime minister.

Labor Day The day on which the labor movement is celebrated. In 1889, the Second International declared an international labor holiday on *May Day, which has since been thus celebrated in many countries. It is celebrated in the US on the first Monday in September.

labor relations. *See* industrial relations.

labor theory of value The economic theory that the value of a product can be determined by the amount of labor needed to produce it, e.g. a product needing twice as many man hours (of equal skill) to produce it as another is worth twice as much.

labor union An organization of employees joined together to present a collective front in negotiations with an employer and to provide a measure of security for its members. The origins of labor unions lie in the local clubs of skilled craftsmen in 18th-century Britain. The union movement in the US began in the early 19th century but did not gain much support until after the Civil War. Significant gains were made in the early 20th century despite continued opposition by employers and government authorities. Local unions are often affiliated with large national unions, which in turn are part of the *AFL-CIO.

Labour Party The democratic socialist party in Britain. The party was formed in 1900 as the Labour Representation Committee, being renamed the Labour Party in 1906. Its origins lie in the trade-union movement of the 19th century, and the trade unions continue to provide over three-quarters of its funds. The *Fabian Society was also a powerful influence on its formation and political beliefs. In 1922 the Labour Party replaced the divided Liberal Party as one of the two major British parties (*compare* Conservative Party) and in 1924 and 1929–31 Labour formed a minority government under Ramsay *MacDonald. After World War II, under Clement *Attlee, the party won a huge majority in the general election of 1945. In office from 1945 to 1951, the Labour administration undertook widespread *nationalization and set up a comprehensive system of *social security. The party was in office again from 1964 to 1970 and from 1974 to 1979, under Harold *Wilson (1964–76) and then James *Callaghan. The increasing prominence of the extreme left caused splits within the party and in 1981 four members from the right defected to form the *Social Democratic Party. Michael Foot was succeeded as party leader by Neil *Kinnock in 1983.

Labrador A district of NE Canada, on the Atlantic Ocean. Although the coast has belonged to Newfoundland for several centuries, the interior was finally awarded to Newfoundland in 1927 by a judicial decision, which is still not recognized by Quebec. Labrador is mostly a rolling swampy plateau within the Canadian Shield. Generally barren except for forested river valleys, it has vast reserves of high-grade iron ore, which are being mined. Its hydroelectric potential is enormous. Churches and missions are very influential in Labrador, especially in the sphere of education. Area: 99,685 sq mi (258,185 sq km). Population (1976): 33,052. *See also* Churchill Falls.

Labrador Current A major ocean current of the N Atlantic, flowing S from the polar seas down the W coast of Greenland and past Newfoundland, until it meets the Gulf Stream and, being cold and dense, sinks beneath it. The Labrador Current carries icebergs S and is a cause of frequent fogs in the region of Newfoundland.

Labrador retriever A breed of dog originating in Newfoundland, Canada. It is solidly built with a tapering otter-like tail and a short dense water-resistant coat, usually black or yellow-brown. Height: 22.4–22.8 in (56–57 cm) (dogs); 21.6–22.4 in (54–56 cm) (bitches).

La Bruyère, Jean de (1645–96) French satirist. He studied law and then served in the Bourbon household of Louis II, Prince of Condé. His single work, *Caractères de Théophraste, avec les caractères ou les moeurs de ce siècle* (1688), consisted chiefly of satirical portrait sketches (often of real persons under disguised names) and contemporary illustrations of vices; it achieved lasting popularity.

Labuan A Malaysian island in the South China Sea. It became part of the state of Sabah in 1946. Copra, rubber, and rice are produced. Area: 38 sq mi (98 sq km). Population (1970 est): 7200. Chief town: Victoria.

laburnum A tree of the genus *Laburnum*, especially *L. anagyroides*, which is native to mountainous regions of central Europe and widely grown for ornament. Up to 23 ft (7 m) high, it has smooth olive-green or brown bark and its leaves each consist of three dark-green leaflets. The bright-yellow flowers grow in hanging clusters, 4–12 in (10–30 cm) long, and produce slender brown pods. All parts of the plant are poisonous, especially the seeds. Family: *Leguminosae*.

labyrinth fish A small elongated laterally compressed fish of the family *Anabantidae* (about 70 species), found in fresh waters of tropical Asia and Africa. They have an accessory respiratory organ (labyrinth) with which they obtain oxygen from air gulped at the surface—of benefit in poorly oxygenated water. The males often build a floating nest of bubbles to protect the eggs. Some species are popular aquarium fish. Order: *Perciformes*. *See also* climbing perch; fighting fish; gourami.

Laccadive, Minicoy, and Amindivi Islands. *See* Lakshadweep.

LACE *An example of bobbin lace from Brussels made in the first half of the 18th century.*

lace An ornamental network of threads of silk, linen, etc., used mainly for dress collars, cuffs, altar cloths, etc. Needlepoint lace, originating in Italy in the early 16th century, is made with a needle on parchment or fabric. Pillow or bobbin lace, reputedly invented by Barbara Uttmann (b. 1514) in Saxony, is formed by twisting threads around pins stuck in a pillow. The best work was done in Italy, Flanders, France, and England in the 17th and 18th centuries, famous types of lace being Brussels, Valenciennes, Mechlin, and Honiton. Lace making as an art declined in the 19th century after machine manufacture was introduced.

La Ceiba 15 45N 86 45W A port in N Honduras, on the Gulf of Honduras. It is a major port exporting chiefly coconuts, abaca fiber, and oranges. Population (1980 est): 64,000.

lacewing An insect belonging to one of several families of the suborder *Plannipennia*. Lacewings have delicate net-veined wings and are carnivorous, with biting mouthparts. Green lacewings (*Chrysopidae*), also called golden-eyed lacewings, are about 0.4 in (10 mm) long and occur worldwide near vegetation. Eggs are laid individually on hairlike stalks and the larvae feed on aphids, scale insects, etc. The brown lacewings (*Hemerobiidae*) are smaller and often have spotted wings. Order: *Neuroptera*. □insect.

Lachish An ancient city in *Canaan, W of Hebron (Israel), occupied from before 1580 BC. The Israelites held it from about 1220 until its destruction by the Babylonians (588). Inscriptions discovered here are important evidence for the early evolution of the alphabet.

Lachlan River A river in SE Australia, in New South Wales. Rising in the Great Dividing Range it flows generally NW to join the Murrumbidgee River. Length: 922 mi (1483 km).

lac insect An insect of the family *Lacciferidae*, found mainly in tropical and subtropical regions. The legless females have globular bodies covered with a layer of hardened resin. In the Indian species, *Laccifer lacca*, the females become encrusted on twigs to form sticklac, from which *shellac is produced. Suborder: *Homoptera*; order *Hemiptera*.

Laclos, Pierre Choderlos de (1741–1803) French novelist. He was a professional soldier and died while serving as a general under Napoleon in Italy. His novel, *Les Liaisons dangereuses* (1782), written in the form of letters between the main characters, concerned sexual corruption and intrigue in aristocratic society. The seducer Valmont, his accomplice Mme de Merteuil, and their victims are depicted with keen psychological insight.

La Condamine, Charles Marie de (1701–74) French geographer. After service in the army he traveled widely and joined a geographical expedition to Peru (1735–43). He later went down the Amazon River on a raft, studying the region, and brought the drug curare to Europe.

Laconia (modern Greek name: Lakonía) The SE region of the Peloponnese. Once a prosperous Mycenaean kingdom, Laconia was conquered by invading *Dorians about 1000 BC. Settling in *Sparta, the newcomers became rulers of Laconia, using the indigenous inhabitants as serf laborers, called *helots.

La Coruña (*or* Corunna) 43 22N 8 24W A port in NW Spain, in Galicia on the Atlantic Ocean. The Spanish Armada sailed from here on July 26, 1588, and in 1589 the city was sacked by Sir Francis Drake. During the Peninsular War Sir John *Moore was mortally wounded here after ensuring a British victory against the French. An important fishing center, it also manufactures tobacco and linen. Population (1974 est): 193,443.

lacquer Colored and often opaque varnish applied to metal or wood for protection and decoration. In Chinese and Japanese artwork, the sap of the *lacquer tree is used as wood lacquer. Other types of lacquer consist of *shellac dissolved in alcohol, which dries to form a protective film.

lacquer tree A tree, *Rhus vernicifera*, of SE Asia, also called varnish tree. Up to 98 ft (30 m) tall, it has compound leaves each with up to nine pairs of leaflets, which turn red in autumn. Japanese *lacquer is obtained from the milky resin that oozes from cuts in the bark. Family: *Anacardiaceae*.

lacrosse A 10-a-side field game (12 in Canada and for women; 6 in the indoor version) played with a ball and a long-handled stick (the crosse), which has a triangular head with a rawhide strung pocket for catching, throwing, and picking up the ball. Of North American Indian origin, it is played mainly in the US, Canada, and Britain. The object is to score goals by running with the ball and passing it. Each team consists of a goalkeeper, three defensive players, three attackmen, and three midfielders, whose function is both offensive and defensive. Body checking and striking an opponent's stick to dislodge the ball are allowed, and protective clothing is worn. The game developed from the Indian game of bagataway, in which the field was not defined and the teams could number over 1000 players.

lactation The secretion of milk from the breasts or mammary glands. In women lactation is controlled by hormones released from the ovary, placenta, and pituitary gland (*see* prolactin) and starts shortly after childbirth, in response to the sucking action of the baby at the nipple: it will continue for as long as the baby is breastfed. A protein-rich fluid called colostrum is secreted in the first few days of lactation, before the milk has

been produced. It contains antibodies that give the baby temporary immunity to disease.

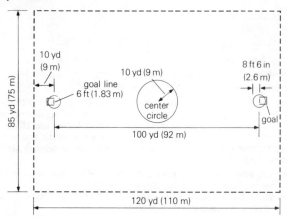

The optimum dimensions of the women's field, although the game is played with no boundaries.

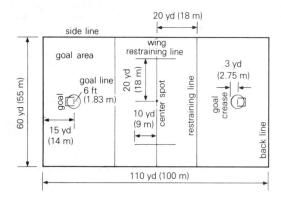

The dimensions of the men's field.

LACROSSE

lactic acid A carboxylic acid ($CH_3CH(OH)COOH$) that is the end product of *glycolysis in animal muscles and of *fermentations (such as the souring of milk) by certain bacteria. A commercial preparation is used as a flavoring and preservative in pickles and salad dressings and in tanning leather.

lactose (*or* milk sugar) A disaccharide carbohydrate ($C_{12}H_{22}O_{11}$) consisting of one molecule of glucose linked to one of galactose. Lactose is found in the milk of all animals and is less sweet than sucrose.

Ladakh Range A mountain range mainly in NW India, extending about 230 mi (370 km) between the Karakoram Range and the Himalayas and rising to over 19,685 ft (6000 m).

Ladin A language spoken in the Dolomite region of Italy that belongs to the Rhaetian branch of the *Romance family. It is related to French and the Occitan dialects, to Romansh, and to Friulian, which is spoken around Udine in N Italy.

Ladino A *Romance language originally spoken by Sephardic Jews in Spain but taken by them after their exile in 1492 to the Balkans, the Near East, N Africa, Greece, and Turkey. It is an old form of Castilian Spanish mixed with Hebrew elements and written in Hebrew characters.

Ladoga, Lake A lake in the NW Soviet Union in the RSFSR, the largest lake in Europe. It discharges via the Neva River into the Gulf of Finland. A canal forming part of the water route from the Gulf of Finland to the Volga River and the White Sea has been built parallel to its S shore to avoid the storms on the lake. *See also* Leningrad. Area: about 6836 sq mi (17,700 sq km).

ladybird beetle A small round beetle, 0.3–0.4 in (8–10 mm) long, that belongs to the widely distributed family *Coccinellidae* (5000 species). Most species are red or yellow with black spots and are of great benefit to man. Both the larvae and adults feed on a variety of plant pests, including aphids, scale insects, mealybugs, and whiteflies. When attacked, ladybirds exude a toxic fluid.

lady fern A delicate *fern, *Athyrium filix-femina*, found in moist shady temperate regions. It has a short stout scaly rhizome that produces a circular cluster of large light-green feathery branched fronds, usually 20–28 in (50–70 cm) long. The clusters of spore capsules (sori) are curved or horseshoe-shaped. Family: *Aspidiaceae*.

lady's slipper A terrestrial orchid, *Cypripedium calceolus*, native to N Europe and Asia. Up to 18 in (45 cm) high, it has broad leaves and the flowers are grouped singly or in twos and threes. Each flower has small twisted red-brown petals and an inflated yellow slipper-like lip. The lady's slipper is nearly extinct in Britain. *See also* slipper orchid.

lady's smock A perennial herb, *Cardamine pratensis*, also called cuckoo flower, found in damp meadows of N temperate regions. 6–12 in (15–60 cm) high, it has compound leaves and a tall spike of pink or violet four-petaled flowers on slender stalks. Family: *Cruciferae*.

Laënnec, René Théophile Hyacinth (1781–1826) French physician and inventor of the stethoscope. Laënnec listened to the chest sounds of his patients using a foot-long wooden cylinder, from which he was able to diagnose diseases of the heart and respiratory system.

Lafayette, Marie Joseph Gilbert Motier, Marquis de (1757–1834) French general and politician, prominent at the beginning of the French Revolution. His early career was distinguished by his military successes (1777–79, 1780–82) against the British in the *American Revolution. In France as a representative in the *States General, he presented the Declaration of the *Rights of Man (1789) and after the storming of the Bastille he became commander of the new National Guard. In 1792 the rising power of the radicals threatened his life and he gave himself up to France's enemy, Austria. Lafayette was also prominent in the July Revolution (1830), which overthrew Charles X.

La Fayette, Mme de (Marie Madeleine, Comtesse de L. F.; 1634–93) French novelist. She was a friend of *La Rochefoucauld and many other prominent writers. Her best-known novel is *La Princesse de Clèves* (1678), a study of the conflict between passion and duty in marriage.

Lafitte, Jean (also Laffite; ?1780–?1825) US privateer; born in France. He led smugglers that looted Spanish ships in the Gulf of Mexico and sold the stolen goods in New Orleans. He aided Andrew *Jackson's defense of New Orleans (1814–15) in the *War of 1812. Pardoned and proclaimed a hero, he returned to pirate life on an island in Galveston Bay until attacked by US ships (1820), after which he moved his activities to Central America.

La Follette, Robert Marion (1855–1925) US politician and lawyer. Born in Wisconsin, he practiced law there before serving as a Republican in the US House of Representatives (1885–91), where he worked on the McKinley Tariff Act (1890). He was elected governor of Wisconsin (1900) on a progressive, anti-Republican platform and by the end of his tenure (1906) had been able to institute many reforms in state government. He was a US senator (1906–25) during which time he founded the National Progressive Republican League (1909), instigated investigation of the Teapot Dome scandal (1921), and ran for president on the Progressive Party ticket (1924).

Lafontaine, Henri-Marie (1854–1943) Belgian jurist and statesman. A senator (1894–1936) and president of the International Peace Bureau (1907–43), he is best known for his contribution to international law. In 1913 he received the Nobel Peace Prize.

La Fontaine, Jean de (1621–95) French poet. He was a friend of many prominent writers and patrons. His major work was the *Fables* (1668–94), sophisticated verse treatments of traditional fables from the collections of *Aesop, *Phaedrus, and later writers. His many other works included the bawdy verse tales, *Contes* (1664), which he is said to have repudiated after his religious conversion in 1692.

Laforgue, Jules (1860–87) French poet, one of the *Symbolists. He was born in Montevideo (Uruguay) and wrote most of his poetry in Berlin while serving as reader to the Empress Augusta (1858–1921). His ironic and slangy poetry in *vers libre* greatly influenced several later French and foreign poets, notably T. S. Eliot.

LAFTA. *See* Latin America.

Lagash A city of ancient *Sumer, N of *Ur, flourishing about 2500 to 2100 BC. *Cuneiform tablets found here bear witness to social, legal, and commercial conditions in Sumer.

Lagerkvist, Pär (Fabian) (1891–1974) Swedish novelist, poet, and dramatist. His early works were pessimistic in tone and influenced by expressionism. In the novels *Bödeln* (*The Hangman*; 1934) and *Dvärgen*

(*The Dwarf*; 1944) he explored the problems of evil and human brutality. His best-known work is the novel *Barabbas* (1950), after which he achieved a worldwide reputation, winning the Nobel Prize in 1951.

Lagerlöf, Selma Ottiliana Lovisa (1858–1940) Swedish novelist, who drew her inspiration from myth, legend, and her early life in Värmland. Her works include *Gösta Berlings Saga* (1891) and the children's storybook *The Wonderful Adventures of Nils* (1907). She was the first woman to be awarded the Nobel Prize (1909).

Lagomorpha An order of mammals (66 species) comprising *pikas, *rabbits, and *hares. Lagomorphs have teeth similar to rodents, with four continuously growing incisors. They are vegetarians and eat their own fecal pellets, thus obtaining the maximum value from their food. Lagomorphs are found all over the world except Antarctica.

Lagos 6 27N 3 28E The capital and main port of Nigeria, on Lagos Island on the Bight of Benin. First settled by Yoruba fishermen in the 17th century, it became the center of the Portuguese slave trade in West Africa and was ceded to Britain in 1861. Its university was founded in 1962. One of Africa's largest cities, it is an important commercial and industrial center. Exports include palm oil and kernels and groundnuts. Population (1975 est): 1,060,848.

Lagrange, Joseph Louis, Comte de (1736–1813) Mathematician and astronomer, born in Italy of French parents. In 1788, he published a book entitled *Mechanique analytique*, in which mechanics is developed algebraically and a wide variety of problems are solved by the application of general equations. In astronomy he solved the problem of predicting how two or more bodies move under each other's gravitational force and worked with *Laplace on planetary perturbations. Lagrange also headed the commission that produced the metric system of units in 1795.

La Guardia, Fiorello Henry (1882–1947) US politician; mayor of New York City (1933–45). As a lawyer and Congressman (1917–21, 1923–33) La Guardia helped initiate such laws as the Norris-La Guardia Act (1932), which allowed organized labor to strike, boycott, and picket. As mayor of New York he fought municipal corruption and supported action for civic improvement.

Lahore 31 34N 74 22E The second largest city in Pakistan, near the Ravi River. Traditionally the chief city of the Punjab, Lahore is situated close to the Indian border and has been the scene of much bloodshed and violence. It is a major railroad, commercial, and political center and the headquarters of the Muslim League. The famous Shalimar gardens lie to the E of the city. An important educational center, it is the site of the University of the Punjab (1882) and Pakistan University of Engineering and Technology (1961). *History:* founded about the 7th century AD, it fell to the Moguls in 1524 and in 1798 it became the seat of Ranjit Singh's Sikh empire. It came under British rule in 1849. Population (1972): 2,165,372.

Lahti 61 00N 25 40E A city in S Finland. A winter-sports resort and growing industrial center, it has sawmilling, furniture, and textile industries and is the site of Finland's main radio and television stations. Population (1980): 94,767.

Laibach. *See* Ljubljana.

Laing, R(onald) D(avid) (1927–) British psychiatrist. He is best known for his explorations of the mind and madness, regarding schizophrenia as a defensive façade and madness as a journey of self-realization (*The Divided Self*, 1960). *The Politics of Experience* (1967) became influential among the radical movements of that period and his views on family life (*The Politics of the Family*, 1969) aroused controversy. His poetry includes *Knots* (1970).

laissez-faire The economic theory that governments should not interfere with market forces based on self-interest and the profit motive. The concept, originally proposed by the 18th-century French economists led by François *Quesnay (*see also* Physiocrats), was advocated by Adam *Smith and widely accepted until the beginning of the 19th century. By then the growth of capitalism had exposed its principal weaknesses: the rise of monopolies, the grossly inequitable distribution of wealth, and the exploitation of labor. In the 20th century, in western economies, laissez-faire policies have been largely abandoned for *mixed economies.

lake (landform) An extensive body of water occupying a hollow in the earth's surface. Rivers generally flow both into and out of lakes although some are landlocked with no outlet. An oxbow lake is crescent shaped and is formed when a river *meander is cut off by the river flow breaching its neck. The larger saline lakes form inland seas, such as the *Caspian Sea. Many lakes are man made, for water supply, hydroelectric-power generation, and irrigation; Lake *Kariba in S Africa is an example.

lake (pigment)   An insoluble pigment formed by the combination of an organic dyestuff with a metallic compound (salt, oxide, or hydroxide). Lakes are used in paints and printing *inks.

Lake District (or Lakeland)   An area in NW England, in Cumbria, a national park since 1951. It consists of a high dome incised by a radial system of glaciated valleys, many of which contain ribbon lakes. High mountains rise between the valleys. Its spectacular scenery, popularized by the Lakeland poets (notably Wordsworth), is now a major tourist attraction, together with facilities for hill walking, rock climbing, and water sports. Traditional occupations include farming, forestry, and quarrying. Area: about 700 sq mi (1813 sq km).

Lake Erie, Battle of   (1813) US-British naval battle during the *War of 1812 that secured Lake Erie and the Northwest for the US. Oliver H. *Perry's fleet successfully engaged in victorious battle the British fleet under Captain Robert H. Barclay that held Lake Erie. To report the victory, Perry wrote his famous message, "We have met the enemy and they are ours . . . "

Lakeland terrier   A breed of dog originating in the English Lake District and used to flush foxes from cover. It has a robust body and a long flat head with small folded triangular ears. The rough dense coat may be black or blue (with or without tan), red, or dark brown. Height: up to 14 in (36 cm).

Lake of the Woods   A lake in S central Canada and N central Minnesota. About one third of the lake is in the US, where the Northwest Angle projects into Canada. In Canada it lies in SE Manitoba and SW Ontario. It is fed by the Rainy River and has almost 14,000 islands. Kenora, Ontario, on the N end of the lake, is the main resort town. Area: 1485 sq mi (3847 sq km).

Lakshadweep (name until 1973: Laccadive, Minicoy, and Amindivi Islands)   A Union Territory of India comprising 27 islands in the Indian Ocean, 186 mi (300 km) W of Kerala. Ruled by Britain from 1792, it was handed over to India in 1956 and depends economically on fish, coconuts, grains, bananas, and vegetables. Area: 12 sq mi (32 sq km). Population (1981): 40,237. Administrative headquarters: Kavaratti Island.

Lakshmi   In Hinduism, the goddess of wealth and happiness, the benign aspect of Shakti, the supreme goddess. As the wife of Vishnu she appears in various forms according to his several incarnations. Many festivals are held in her honor (see Diwali). Lakshmi is also revered by the Jains.

Lalande, Joseph-Jérôme Le Français de   (1732–1807) French astronomer, who published (1801) the most complete catalogue of the stars then known. It listed some 47,000 stars, one of which was found by *Leverrier a hundred years later to be the planet Neptune.

La Línea   36 10N 5 21W A city in SW Spain, in Andalusia on the Strait of Gibraltar. Many of its inhabitants worked in Gibraltar until the closure of the frontier (1969). Industries include textiles and cork. Population (1970): 52,127.

Lalique, René   (1860–1945) French *Art Nouveau jeweler and glassmaker. His jewelry is usually asymmetric with motifs of plants, snakes, etc. He later designed glassware with frosted patterns in relief, establishing a factory at Wingen-sur-Moder (1920).

Lallans   The dialect of the lowlands of Scotland, in which Robert *Burns wrote. A movement to re-establish it as a literary medium occurred after World War I.

Lally, Thomas, Comte de   (1702–66) French general of Irish ancestry. He took part in the *Jacobite rebellion of 1745 and subsequently became commander in chief in the French East Indies (1756), coming into conflict with the British. Forced to surrender in 1761, his action was construed as treason and he was beheaded.

Lalo, (Victor Antoine) Édouard   (1823–92) French composer of Spanish descent. He is best remembered for his Symphonie espagnole (for violin and orchestra; 1873), a cello concerto (1876), and the ballet Namouna (1882).

lamaism.   See Tibetan Buddhism.

Lamar, Lucius Quintus Cincinnatus   (1825–93) US lawyer and politician; Supreme Court associate justice (1888–91). He practiced law in Mississippi before serving in the US House of Representatives (1857–60) where he was in favor of states' rights. At the start of the Civil War he returned home to work with Jefferson *Davis on secession. After the war, he taught at the University of Mississippi and then again became a representative in the House (1873–77), a US senator (1877–85), and secretary of the interior (1885–88), constantly advocating the "new South." His few years on the Supreme Court were devoted to states' rights and restraint in judicial matters.

Lamarck, Jean-Baptiste de Monet, Chevalier de   (1744–1829) French naturalist, noted for his speculations about the evolution of living things, particularly his theory of the inheritance of acquired characteristics (see Lamarckism). Lamarck studied botany under Bernard de *Jussieu and published a flora of France in 1778. In 1793 he became professor of invertebrate zoology at the Museum of Natural History, Paris. Here Lamarck worked on a system of classification for invertebrate animals, published in his Histoire naturelle des animaux sans vertebres (7 vols, 1815–22). In 1809 Lamarck published his theory of evolution (in Philosophie zoologique). Lamarckism has generally been rejected in favor of Charles *Darwin's theory of evolution by natural selection, although some attempts have been made to revive it, most notably by *Lysenko. Lamarck's speculations about the physical and natural world found little favor among his contemporaries and he died blind and poverty stricken.

Lamarckism   The first theory of *evolution as proposed by Jean-Baptiste *Lamarck in 1809, based on his concept of the inheritance of acquired characteristics. He suggested that an organism develops structural changes during its lifetime as an adaptation to its particular environment and that these features are then inherited by successive generations through sexual reproduction. A classic example of these acquired characteristics are the forelegs and neck of a giraffe, which he believed became longer through its habit of browsing on tall trees. There is now little support for Lamarck's theory, although it was revived in a slightly modified form (neo-Lamarckism) by the Soviet geneticist T. D. *Lysenko.

Lamartine, Alphonse de   (1790–1869) French poet, one of the major figures of the Romantic movement. He established his reputation with Méditations poétiques (1820), a volume of lyrical poetry inspired by an unsuccessful love affair. During the 1820s he served as a diplomat in Naples and Florence and in the 1830s he became an active political champion of republican ideals. He was briefly head of the provisional government after the Revolution of 1848. His other major works include the narrative poems Jocelyn (1836) and La Chute d'un ange (1836).

Lamb, Charles   (1775–1834) British essayist and critic. He worked as a clerk for the East India Company, devoting his private life to caring for his sister Mary (1764–1847), who had killed their mother in 1796 during one of her recurrent fits of insanity. He collaborated with Mary on Tales from Shakespeare (1807), a children's book. He is best remembered for his Essays of Elia (1822).

Lambaréné   0 41S 10 13E A town in W Gabon, on an island in the River Ogooué. Its hospital (1913) was founded by the missionary Albert *Schweitzer. Industries include palm products. Population (1970): 10,385.

lambert   A unit of luminance equal to the luminance of a surface that emits one lumen per square centimeter. Named for— J. H. *Lambert.

Lambert, Johann Heinrich   (1728–77) German mathematician and astronomer, who first derived the *hyperbolic functions and proved that π is an irrational *number. As an astronomer he measured the luminosities of stars and planets and introduced the term *albedo; a unit of luminance (see lambert) is named for him.

lamb's lettuce.   See corn salad.

Lamentations of Jeremiah   An Old Testament book, a sequel to the Book of *Jeremiah and traditionally attributed to him, although it is more likely a work of the 5th century BC. It consists of a series of five dirgelike chapters concerned with the capture and destruction of Jerusalem and its Temple by the Babylonians in 586 BC. The event is graphically described, as are the accompanying slavery and famine. Jeremiah sees it as a divine judgment and closes with a prayer for mercy.

Lamerie, Paul de   (1688–1751) English silversmith of French Huguenot parents. Establishing his shop in 1712, he progressed from an unornamented Queen Anne style to *rococo designs, for which he is most famous.

Lamian War   (323–322 BC) The conflict that confirmed Macedon's supremacy in Greece after Alexander the Great's death. *Antipater, the Macedonian regent, was besieged in Lamia by rebellious Greek forces but eventually crushed the city states and reimposed his authority more firmly.

laminar flow   Fluid flow in which the particles move in parallel layers. A fluid moving slowly along a horizontal straight pipe flows in this way. Above a certain velocity, given by the *Reynolds number, the layers no longer remain parallel and the flow becomes turbulent.

Laminaria   A genus of large brown seaweeds (see kelp), also called oarweed, that occurs in abundance along British and Pacific coasts. L. digitata (tangle) is a fan-shaped seaweed that may grow to a length of 165 ft (50 m). Laminaria is a good source of alginic acid and alginates, used in the manufacture of ice cream, tires, etc.

lammergeier A large *vulture, *Gypaetus barbatus*, also called bearded vulture because of the long bristles on its chin. It is over 40 in (1 m) long with a wingspan of 10 ft (3 m) and occurs in mountainous regions of S Europe, central Asia, and E Africa. It is brown with tawny underparts and a black-and-white face. Lammergeiers feed on bones and other carrion.

Lampedusa, Giuseppe Tomasi di (1896–1957) Italian novelist. He lived an adventurous early life as a wealthy Sicilian aristocrat. During his last years he wrote *The Leopard* (1958), a panoramic historical novel concerning Sicily in the late 19th century.

lamprey A fishlike vertebrate belonging to a family (*Petromyzonidae*; about 22 species) of *cyclostomes. 6–40 in (15–100 cm) long, lampreys have an eel-like body with one or two dorsal fins and seven pairs of gill slits. They occur in fresh or salt water and many are parasitic on fish, attaching themselves with a circular sucking mouth and feeding on the blood and flesh. Sexually mature adults move into fresh water to breed and then die after the eggs are laid. The burrowing larvae (ammocoetes) feed on microorganisms and take three to seven years to grow before their metamorphosis into adults and return to the sea. □fish.

lamp shell. *See* Brachiopoda.

Lanai 20 50N 156 55W An island in central Hawaii, S of Molokai and W of Maui. Noted for its pineapple plantations, it has been developed by the Dole Corporation (since 1922), which has been responsible for most construction and settlement. Mt Palawi (3369 ft; 1027 m) is the island's highest point. Area: 141 sq mi (366 sq km).

Lanark 55 41N 3 48W A city in S central Scotland, in Strathclyde Region overlooking the middle Clyde Valley. Nearby New Lanark, founded as a cotton-spinning center in 1784 by David Dale and Richard Arkwright, is well known for the social experiments carried out there by Robert □Owen. Population (1973 est): 8441.

Lancashire A county of NW England, bordering on the Irish Sea. It consists of lowlands in the W rising to the high level plateaus in the E, with the chief river, the Ribble, flowing SW to the Irish Sea. The lowlands are important agricultural regions, especially for dairy farming. Industry is based chiefly on textiles, mining, and engineering. Tourism is important in the coastal towns of Blackpool, Southport, and Morecambe. With industrialization, exploitation of the coalfields accelerated and by the 19th century Lancashire had become the greatest cotton-manufacturing center in the world. Area: 8191 sq mi (3043 sq km). Population (1981): 1,372,118. Administrative center: Preston.

Lancaster 40 08N 76 18W A city in SE Pennsylvania. Settled by German Mennonites in the early 18th century, it developed as an armaments center during the American Revolution. Today it is an agricultural and industrial center, producing tobacco, grain, livestock, and electrical products. Population (1970): 57,690.

Lancaster A ruling dynasty of England descended from Edmund, the second son of Henry III, who was created Earl of Lancaster in 1267. In 1361 the title passed by marriage to the third son of Edward III, *John of Gaunt. His son seized the throne from Richard II and ruled (1399–1413) as Henry IV. He was succeeded by Henry V, whose son Henry VI led the Lancastrians against the Yorkists (*see* York) in the Wars of the □Roses (1455–85), in which their emblem was a red rose. Following Henry VI's death (1471) the royal dynasty came to an end.

lancelet. *See* amphioxus.

Lancelot In *Arthurian legend, a knight of the Round Table, the son of King Ban and Queen Helaine of Benoic. While a child he was kidnapped by the Lady of the Lake, who educated him and later sent him to serve King Arthur. He was a celebrated warrior but failed in the quest of the *Holy Grail because of his adulterous love for *Guinevere.

lancewood Dense strong straight-grained wood obtained from various trees of the family *Annonaceae*, especially *Oxandra lanceolata*, native to the West Indies and South America. It is used in whip handles, fishing rods, etc., for which an elastic wood is essential. Australian lancewood comes from several trees, including *Acacia doratoxylon* (family *Leguminosae*).

Lanchow. *See* Lanzhou.

Land. *See* Germany, Federal Republic of.

Land, Edwin Herbert (1909–) US inventor of *Polaroid, who set up the Polaroid Corporation in 1937 for its manufacture. He also invented the Polaroid Land Camera in 1947, in which pictures are printed inside the camera.

Land Acts, Irish A series of laws passed between 1870 and 1903 to deal with Irish agrarian problems. The three Fs (freedom to sell, fixity of tenure, and fair rents) were obtained in Gladstone's acts of 1870 and 1881.

Later acts (especially those of 1885 and 1903) provided means for the tenant to buy his holding and Ireland thus became a land of owner occupiers.

landau A four-wheeled coach drawn by two or four horses. Landaus, first made in Landau (Germany) in the late 18th century, have fully collapsible tops and are still used in European royal processions.

Landau, Lev Davidovich (1908–68) Soviet physicist, who pioneered the mathematical theory of magnetic domains (*see* ferromagnetism). Working with Peter *Kapitza on *superfluid helium he was able to explain its properties in terms of quantum theory. For this work on superfluidity he was awarded the Nobel Prize in 1962.

land crab A large square-bodied *crab of the tropical family *Gecarcinidae*, specialized for a terrestrial existence. It feeds on plant and animal materials. *Cardiosoma guanhumi*, 4 in (11 cm) across the back, is found in the West Indies and S North America. It lives in fields, swamps, and mangroves, sometimes several miles inland. Tribe: *Brachyura*.

Landes An area of heath and marshland in SW France, bordering on the Bay of Biscay and consisting chiefly of the Landes department. It is bordered by a strip of sand dunes, many over 148 ft (45 m) high, that have been fixed by the planting of pine forests. Area: 5400 sq mi (14,000 sq km).

Land-Grant College US state or territory higher-education institution for agricultural and mechanical arts, funded by the sale of federal lands as provided in the *Morrill Land Grant Act of 1862. Depending upon the circumstances in the state or territory, the school was made a part of an existing college or university or was established separately. By 1890 the second Morrill Act provided for annual funding by Congress to support these institutions.

landing craft Amphibious craft used for military assaults on beaches. Developed mainly by the US Marine Corps in World War II, they were first used on a large scale in the Anglo-American invasion of Sicily (June, 1943), and later were important in the D-Day invasion of Normandy (1944) and in the Pacific campaign from Guadalcanal onward.

Landis, Kenesaw Mountain (1866–1944) US jurist and commissioner of baseball (1920–44). Named for the mountain where his father was wounded during the Civil War, he practiced law in Chicago before being appointed a US district judge (1905–22). He presided over the court that tried Socialist and labor leaders for sedition (1917) during World War I, and ruled in the "Black Sox" case that banned several players for taking bribes during the 1919 World Series. As baseball commissioner he was respected for his fair, honest, and irreversible decisions.

Land League An Irish agrarian organization established by Michael *Davitt in 1879 to press for land reforms. Its most famous tactic was one of organized ostracism (boycotting; *see* Boycott, Charles). After Gladstone's 1881 Land Act, the League's immediate aims were achieved and it was forced to disband.

landlord and tenant relationship The relationship arising from a grant (lease) of absolute possession of an *estate by a landlord to a tenant for a fixed period and, usually, for a regular payment of rent. The relationship is defined by a *contract, express or implied, which is contained in the lease or, for short terms, in a tenancy agreement.

Landon, Alfred Mossman ("Alf"; 1887–) US politician; governor of Kansas (1933–37). By 1912 he owned his own oil company and had become interested in politics. After working behind the scenes for Kansas Republicans, he served as governor for two terms, which led to his nomination as the Republican presidential candidate (1936), an election he lost by a landslide to Franklin D. *Roosevelt. His daughter, **Nancy L. Kassebaum** (1932–) is a US senator (1978–).

Landor, Walter Savage (1775–1864) British poet and prose writer. He lived for many years on the Continent, chiefly in Florence. He wrote poems and dramas based on classical models, and is best known for his *Imaginary Conversations of Literary Men and Statesmen* (1824–28).

Landowska, Wanda (1877–1959) Polish-born harpsichordist and authority on its technique and repertoire. She established a school for advanced performers in Paris and later lived in the US.

Landrace A breed of pig originating in Denmark, where it has been intensively developed as a producer of high-quality lean bacon. It has a relatively small head and neck with light shoulders and long flanks. It can also produce good-quality pork.

Landrum-Griffin Act (also called US Labor-Management Reporting and Disclosure Act; 1959) US law designed to protect labor union members from corruption within a union. Under this legislation union financial records are open, elections are monitored, criminals are prevented from holding office for five years after conviction, and unfair disciplinary practices are discouraged.

landscape gardening The theory and practice of designing and planting a pleasing garden or park. Landscape gardening was carried out in the ancient Middle East, Greece, and Rome. In Europe, geometric formality in rigidly organized enclosed spaces predominated until the mid 18th century, when the possibilities were demonstrated of large-scale remolding of the landscape to achieve a naturalistic impression. Apparently random planting of trees, strategic siting of focal points, and sinuous expanses of water are key components. An excellent example of landscape architecture is Frederick Law Olmsted's design (1856) for Central Park in New York City, which provided an open area in the urban center. With the 20th-century decline of the *country estate, landscape gardening principles (harmony, variety, etc.) have come to be applied on a smaller scale.

Land's End (Cornish name: Pednanlaaz)   50 03N 5 44W The extreme western point of England. A granite headland in Cornwall, it lies at a distance of 603 mi (970 km) from John o'Groats at the N tip of Scotland. The southernmost point of England is the Lizard nearby.

Landshut 48 31N 12 10E A city in SE West Germany, in Bavaria on the Isar River. It is an industrial center and the site of a 13th-century castle. The Bavarian university was sited here (1800–26). Population (1971 est): 52,300.

landslide (*or* landslip) The sudden downward movement of a mass of rock or earth. This may be triggered by an earthquake, or be due to an increase in the weight borne by a steep slope as a result of water soaking into it. Landslides may also occur as a result of undercutting of a slope by water, as in a riverbank or sea cliff.

Landsteiner, Karl (1868–1943) Austrian immunologist, who (in 1900) discovered human *blood groups and devised the ABO system of classification. Landsteiner's discovery enabled safe blood transfusions: by matching the blood groups of donor and recipient the immunological rejection of "foreign" blood by the recipient was avoided. He also discovered, in 1940, the *rhesus (Rh) factor in blood and made valuable contributions to poliomyelitis research. He was awarded the Nobel Prize (1930).

Lanfranc (c. 1010–89) Italian churchman and theologian; Archbishop of Canterbury (1070–89). In about 1043 he founded and became prior of a Benedictine abbey at Bec in Normandy; under the direction of his pupil St Anselm, the abbey became one of the most famous medieval schools. As archbishop under William the Conqueror from 1070, he launched a program of Church reform, which included appointing Normans as abbots of English monasteries and enforcing celibacy among the clergy.

Lang, Fritz (1890–1976) German film director. The best known of a number of distinguished and influential silent films are *Dr Mabuse the Gambler* (1922), *Metropolis* (1926), a nightmare vision of the future, and *M* (1931), a study of a psychopathic murderer. He left Germany in 1933 and went to Hollywood, where he made many commercially successful thrillers and westerns.

Langley, Samuel Pierpont (1834–1906) US astronomer, whose pioneering work on aerodynamics contributed greatly to the design of early aircraft. Langley himself failed to build a working aircraft, in spite of a grant of $50,000 from the US Government.

Langmuir, Irving (1881–1957) US chemist, whose early work on gases and vapors led to the invention of the Langmuir condensation pump. He also developed gas-filled filament lamps. He was awarded the 1932 Nobel Prize for his extensive work on monomolecular layers and surface chemistry.

Langtry, Lillie (Emilie Charlotte le Breton; 1853–1929) British actress, known as the Jersey Lily. After marrying a wealthy husband and becoming well known in London society, she made her stage debut in 1881. She was the first woman in Britain to prove that high social position was not incompatible with an acting career, although her fame was based more on her beauty than her acting talents. She was an intimate friend of the Prince of Wales, later Edward VII.

language The chief means by which human beings communicate with one another. Among the features that distinguish human language from other animals' communication systems are that it is learned, not inborn; the connection between a word or expression and that to which it refers is in principle arbitrary; it can be used to talk about itself, about events, objects, etc., not immediately present, or about any novel or unforeseen situation; and it is organized in recognizable patterns on two levels: *grammar and phonology. The origins of language are unknown, but since it is unique to man and all speech organs have some other more basic physiological function it is probably of quite recent origin in evolutionary terms. It is estimat-

ed that there are some 4000 languages spoken in the world today; countless thousands of others have perished, generally without trace. *See also* dialect; linguistics.

LILLIE LANGTRY *As Rosalind in* As You Like It, *one of her most successful roles.*

languages, classification of The division of languages into groups. There are three methods of classification. The first method is that of geographical or political division, in which languages are grouped together according to the continent or country in which they occur. Examples of the former include *Indian languages and European languages. The latter is represented by the similar but politically distinct languages *Swedish, *Danish, and *Norwegian. Such divisions do not always follow the genetic relationships that exist between languages. This relationship forms the basis for the second method of classification, which maps the historical development from one form of the language to another, as in the relation between Old English and modern *English. Further back both these and other languages can be traced to their common *Indo-European ancestor. However, some languages, such as *Basque, have no discoverable ancestry or relations. The third possible method of classification is on typological evidence, which depends on the grammatical structure of the language. The original three classes were devised by W. von *Humboldt: analytic (or isolating), agglutinative, and inflecting languages. **Analytic languages** (e.g. English, Chinese) show little variation in the forms of words but rely on strict word order to express grammatical relations (compare "The speaker thanked the chairman" with "The chairman thanked the speaker"; the words are the same in both sentences and the subject-object relations are understood purely by the order). In **agglutinative languages** (e.g. Turkish) words have the capacity to be split up into individual components with separate grammatical roles (in Turkish *sev/mek* means "to love"; *sev/dir/il/mek* means "to be made to love"; *sev/ish/mek/* means "to love one another"; and *sev/ish/dir/il/mek* means "to be made to love one another"). In **inflecting languages** (e.g. Latin, Sanskrit) words are characteristically built up of a root plus a component (morpheme) that represents several different grammatical categories (the Latin word *lavo* (I wash) consists of the root *lav-* and a suffix *-o*, the suffix here indicating the distinct grammatical elements of first person, singular number, present tense, indicative mood, and active voice). No language is entirely in one or other of these categories and the system itself has been modified and expanded by 20th-century linguists, but it is possible, on the grounds of predominant characteristics, to make general classifications.

Languedoc A former province in S France, on the Gulf of Lions. Its name derived from *langue d'oc*, the language of its inhabitants (*see* Provençal). In the 10th–12th centuries it flourished as an important cultural center. It is now incorporated chiefly into the planning region of **Languedoc-Roussillon** and is an important wine-producing area. Area: 10,595 sq mi (27,447 sq km). Population (1981 est): 10,117,200.

langur A leaf-eating *Old World monkey of tropical Asia. Langurs have specially adapted stomachs to digest their food. The largest is the hanuman,

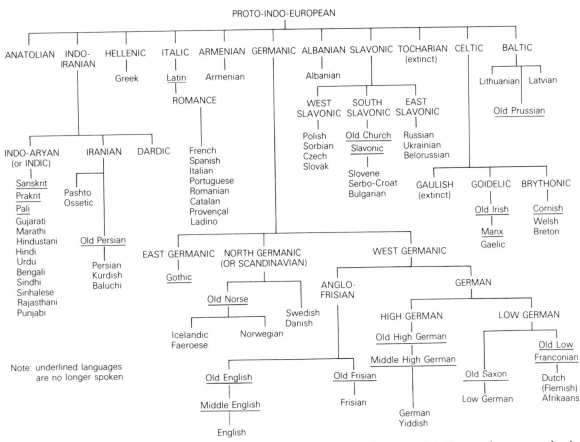

CLASSIFICATION OF LANGUAGES *A simplified family tree shows the relationships of the Indo-European languages, spoken by about half the world's population.*

or entellus langur (*Presbytis entellus*), 30 in (75 cm) long with a 37-in (95-cm) tail. The douc langur (*Pygathrix nemaeus*) of Vietnam is mainly gray with white forearms and is now an endangered species. Chief genera: *Presbytis* (14 species), *Rhinopithecus* (4 species).

Lanier, Sidney (1842–81) US poet. As a Confederate soldier in the Civil War he was imprisoned and contracted tuberculosis, from which he eventually died. His poetry, notably "Corn" (1875), "The Symphony" (1875), and "The Marches of Glyn," was greatly influenced by his musical skills.

lanner falcon A large *falcon, *Falco biarmicus*, occurring in SE Europe and Africa. Up to 18 in (45 cm) long, it has a gray-brown back, white underparts flecked with black on the breast, a tawny head, and a black mustache. Lanner falcons feed chiefly on birds and are used in falconry.

lanolin A purified *wax extracted from wool. It is a mixture of cholesterol and other sterols, aliphatic alcohols, and esters. Because it is easily absorbed by the skin, lanolin is used as a base for creams, soaps, and other skin preparations.

Lansing 42 44N 85 34W The capital city of Michigan, on the Grand River. The site of the Michigan State University (1855), it contains part of the Detroit motor-vehicle industry, manufacturing car components. Population (1980): 130,414.

lantern fish A deepsea *bony fish belonging to the family *Myctophidae* (about 150 species). 1–6 in (2.5–15 cm) long, lantern fish have large mouths and eyes and numerous light-producing organs on the head, underside, and base of the tail. At night, many species migrate toward the surface. Order: *Myctophiformes*.

lanthanides (*or* rare-earth metals) A group of 15 *transition-metal elements, atomic numbers 57–71, which all have remarkably similar physical and chemical properties as a result of their electronic structures. They occur together in monazite and other minerals. They are used as catalysts in the petroleum industry, in iron alloys and permanent magnets, and in glass polishes. The **rare earths** are the oxides of these metals.

lanthanum (La) The first of the series of rare-earth metals (*see* lanthanides), all of which have similar chemical properties. It is used in *misch metal to make lighter flints. Its compounds include an oxide (La_2O_3) and a chloride ($LaCl_3$). At no 57; at wt 138.9055; mp 543°F (921°C); bp 1951°F (357°C).

Lanzhou (Lan-chou *or* Lanchow) 36 01N 103 45E A city in N China, the capital of Gansu province at the confluence of the Yellow and Wei Rivers. It is an ancient trade and communications center and the site of a university. Industries include oil refining, plutonium processing, and the manufacture of chemicals and machinery. Population (1957 est): 699,000.

Laocoon In Greek legend, a Trojan priest of Apollo who warned against accepting the Greek gift of the *Trojan Horse. He and his two sons were killed by sea serpents sent by Apollo, and the Trojans then opened their gates to the wooden horse.

Laodicea 37 46N 29 02E An ancient city of Asia Minor, near present-day Denizli (SW Turkey), founded by *Antiochus II about 250 BC. On an important trade route Laodicea soon prospered; early Christians condemned its worldliness. Under Diocletian it became Phrygia's metropolis (mother city). Its Roman remains include theaters and an aqueduct.

Laoighis (*or* Leix; former name: Queen's County) A county in the E central Republic of Ireland, in Leinster. Predominantly low lying with bogs and drained chiefly by the Rivers Barrow and Nore, it rises to mountains in the NW. Agriculture is the main occupation with dairy farming and cattle rearing. Area: 664 sq mi (1719 sq km). Population (1979): 49,936. County town: Portlaoise.

Laon 49 34N 3 37E A city in N France, the capital of the Aisne department. A former leading town of the kingdom of the Franks, notable buildings include the cathedral (begun in the 12th century) and the bishop's palace. It has metallurgical and sugar-refining industries. Population (1975): 30,168.

Laos, People's Democratic Republic of A landlocked country in SE Asia, in the Indochina peninsula between Vietnam and Thailand. Except for the valley of the Mekong River along its western border, the country is mountainous and forested. Over half the population are Lao (descendants of the Thai) and there are minorities of Vietnamese, Chinese, and others. *Economy*: predominantly agricultural, the difficult terrain combined with recent political upheavals has hindered production and Laos remains the least developed of the nations of the Indochina peninsula. The main crops are rice, corn, coffee, cotton, tea, and tobacco. The valuable mineral resources (tin, iron ore, gold, and copper) have yet to be fully exploited. There is little industry. Hydroelectricity is an important source of power, especially since the opening of the Nan Ngum Dam in 1971. Communications are difficult; there are no railroads and river traffic is hindered by rapids and waterfalls. Meagre exports include timber and tin. *History*: the origins of the area as a nation date from the rule of Fa Ngum in the 14th century. European contacts were initiated in the 17th century and in 1893 Laos became a French protectorate. It was occupied by the Japanese from 1941 to 1945, when the Lao Issara (Free Lao) proclaimed an independent government. This movement collapsed when the French returned in 1946 and a constitutional monarchy was formed in 1947. In 1949 Laos became independent within the French Union. In 1953 civil war, which was to last for 20 years, broke out between the government (supported by the US and by Thai mercenaries) and the communist-led Pathet Lao movement (supported by the North Vietnamese). In 1974 a provisional coalition government was formed but following the collapse of the South Vietnamese the Pathet Lao gained power (December, 1975) and the People's Democratic Republic of Laos was formed with Prince Souphanouvong as president. Relations with Vietnam continue to be close and friction with Thailand has eased somewhat. In 1980 the government announced its decision to adopt more liberal economic policies. Shortages of goods and a subsistence existence for many had led to an exodus of Laotians from their homeland. By the mid 1980s more goods and services were available to the Laotians although ordinary citizens were forced to make purchases with black market or smuggled money. Prime minister: Kaysone Phoumvihan (1920–). Official language: Laotian; French is widely spoken. Official currency: kip of 100 at. Area: 91,000 sq mi (235,700 sq km). Population (1983 est): 3,647,000. Capital: Vientiane.

Laotian A language of SE Asia belonging to the Thai language family. It is a tonal and monosyllabic language and written in an alphabet derived from *Khmer.

Lao Zi (or Lao Tzu; ?6th century BC) The founder of *Taoism. A shadowy, possibly legendary, figure, he was eventually deified. His purpose, propounded mainly in books compiled about 300 years after his likely date of death, was to reach harmony with the *Tao* (way) by dwelling on the beauty of nature, by being self-sufficient, and by desiring nothing.

La Paz 16 30S 68 00W The administrative capital of Bolivia, situated in the W of the country. At an altitude of 11,735 ft (3577 m), it is the world's highest capital. Founded by the Spanish in 1548, it became the seat of government in 1898. The University of San Andrés was founded here in 1830. Population (1976): 654,713. *See also* Sucre.

lapis lazuli A blue semiprecious stone composed mainly of a sulfur-rich variety of the mineral haüyne (a feldspathoid) called lazurite. It is formed by the metamorphism of limestone. It often contains specks or threads of yellow iron pyrites. Lapis lazuli has been mined in Afghanistan for over 6000 years. The pigment ultramarine was formerly made by grinding up lapis lazuli.

Laplace, Pierre Simon, Marquis de (1749–1827) French mathematician and astronomer. Laplace worked with *Lagrange on the effects, known as perturbations, of the small gravitational forces that planets exert on each other. (Newton's work considered only the gravitational force of the sun on the planets.) They deduced that the perturbations only cause small oscillations in the planets' motions and not any permanent movement, thus proving the stability of the solar system. Laplace published their results, without giving Lagrange credit, in a five-volume work, *Mécanique céleste* (1799–1825). At the end of the work, Laplace speculated that the solar system was formed from a condensing rotating cloud of gas.

Lapland (or Lappland) A vast region in N Europe, inhabited by the *Lapps and extending across northern parts of Norway, Sweden, Finland, and into the extreme NW of the Soviet Union. Lying mainly within the Arctic Circle, it consists of tundra in the N, mountains in the W, and forests in the S; there are many lakes and rivers. For many centuries the Lapps were reduced to virtual slavery by their more powerful neighbors. Subsistence farming, fishing, trapping, and hunting are the principal occupations and reindeer are a particularly important source of income. There are rich deposits of iron ore in Swedish Lapland. High unemployment, however, has led to considerable emigration S although there are plans to develop Lapland's fishing potential and to establish fur farms (especially

the silver fox). Recent industrial successes include the new steel works at Tornio on the border between Finland and Sweden.

LA PAZ *Much of the city occupies the slopes of a steep-sided valley, below the high tableland of the Andean Altiplano.*

La Plata (name from 1952 until 1955: Eva Perón) 34 52S 57 55W A city in E Argentina, near the Río de la Plata. Its industries include meat packing and oil refining and it has a university (1884). Population (1975 est): 391,247.

Lapps A people of N Scandinavia and the Kola peninsula of the Soviet Union. They speak a *Finno-Ugric language, which differs from the related Finnish and *Estonian mainly in its sound system. There are three major Lapp dialects, which are very different from one another. The mountain Lapps are nomadic reindeer herders who follow their herds on their seasonal migrations using them as pack animals or to pull sledges. Other Lapps are seminomadic hunters and fishers.

Laptev Sea A section of the Arctic Ocean off the coast of the Soviet Union, between the Taimyr Peninsula and the New Siberian Islands. Half of its supply of fresh water comes from the Lena River and it is frozen for most of the year.

lapwing A Eurasian *plover, *Vanellus vanellus*, also called peewit and green plover. It occurs commonly on farmland, where it feeds on harmful insects, such as wireworms and leatherjackets. 11 in (28 cm) long, it has a greenish-black and white plumage, a long crest, short rounded wings, a short tail, and pink legs. In spring, lapwings perform acrobatic courtship displays.

Laramie 41 20N 105 38W A city in SE Wyoming, on the Laramie River. Founded in 1868 with the arrival of the Union Pacific Railroad, it is a commercial and industrial center for a timber, mining, and livestock region. The University of Wyoming was established here in 1886. Population (1980): 24,339.

larceny. *See* theft.

larch A deciduous conifer of the genus *Larix* (10 species), native to the cooler regions of the N hemisphere. Larches are graceful trees, with needles growing in bunches on short spurs and producing small woody cones. The common European larch (*L. decidua*), from the mountains of central Europe, is widely cultivated both for timber and ornament. It reaches a height of 130 ft (40 m) and its cones, 1–2 in (2–4 cm) long, ripen from pinkish-red to brown. The Japanese larch (*L. kaempferi*) is commonly grown on plantations. Family: *Pinaceae.* □tree.

Lardner, Ring (1885–1933) US short-story writer. He worked as a sports reporter and his early stories included in *You Know Me, Al* (1916) concern the life of a baseball player. His best-known stories are collected in *Gullible's Travels* (1917), *How to Write Short Stories* (1924), *What Of It?* (1925), and *The Love Nest and Other Stories* (1926). *The Story of a Wonder Man* (1927) was autobiographical.

Laredo 27 32N 99 22W A city in Texas, on the Rio Grande. Situated opposite Nuevo Laredo (Mexico), it was founded by the Spanish in 1755 and is a center for US and Mexican trade. It has a thriving tourist industry and is the commercial center for an oil-producing and agricultural region. Population (1980): 91,229.

Lares and Penates Roman household gods. The Lares were originally gods of cultivated land who were worshiped at crossroads and boundaries. The Penates were gods of the storeroom. Together with the *Manes, they were later worshiped in private homes as guardian spirits of the family, household, and state.

Large White A breed of pig originating in Yorkshire, England, also called the Yorkshire. Relatively large-framed, Large Whites are white-skinned with a sparse coat of fine hair. They are extensively used for bacon production. A smaller derivative breed, the Middle White, was formerly popular as a porker.

Lárisa (*or* Larissa) 39 38N 22 25E A city in E Greece, in Thessaly. It is a commercial center; products include silk cloth and tobacco. Population (1971): 72,760.

lark A slender long-winged songbird belonging to a family (*Alaudidae*; 75 species) found mainly in mudflats, marshes, grasslands, and deserts of the Old World and characterized by a beautiful song. Larks commonly have a brown or buff streaked plumage that often matches the local soil color. They have long slender bills and feed on seeds and insects. The only New World lark is the horned lark, or shorelark (*Eremophila alpestris*) of North America. *See also* skylark.

Larkin, Philip (1922–) British poet. His poetry expresses a resigned but honest acceptance of the limitations of daily existence. His volumes include *The Whitsun Weddings* (1964) and *High Windows* (1974). He also edited *The Oxford Book of Twentieth Century English Verse* (1973) and published two novels and a volume of jazz criticism.

larkspur An annual herb of the genus *Consolida*, especially *C. ajacis*, *C. ambigua*, or *C. orientalis*, native to Eurasia but commonly grown for ornament. Larkspurs have feathery leaves and tall stems with branching spikes of white or blue spurred flowers. The name is also applied to species of the genus *Delphinium*. Family: *Ranunculaceae*.

La Rochefoucauld, François, Duc de (1613–80) French moralist. He was born into an ancient aristocratic family and played an active part in intrigues against Richelieu and in the *Fronde revolts against Mazarin (1648–53). Thereafter he lived in retirement, writing his *Mémoires* (1664) and compiling his celebrated *Maximes* (1665), a collection of cynical epigrammatic observations on human conduct.

La Rochelle 46 10N 1 10W A port in W France, the capital of the Charente-Maritime department on the Bay of Biscay. A major seaport (14th–16th centuries), it was a Huguenot stronghold until its capture by Richelieu in 1628. Industries include fishing, shipbuilding, fertilizers, and plastics. Population (1975): 81,884.

Larousse, Pierre (1817–75) French lexicographer, encyclopedist, and publisher. In 1852 he founded the publishing firm of Larousse, which specialized in dictionaries, encyclopedias, and other works of reference. His major work was the *Grand Dictionnaire universel du XIXe siècle* (15 vols, 1866–76). His firm continues as a major French publisher, with such reference works as the *Grand Larousse Encyclopédique* (1960–64).

Lars Porsena (*or* Porsenna; 6th century BC) Etruscan king of Clusium (now Chiusi, near Siena). According to legend, when *Tarquin the Proud, the last Etruscan king of Rome, was deposed, Porsena successfully attacked Rome on his behalf. In another version of the story, Porsena made peace with the Romans from admiration of their bravery.

Lartet, Édouard Armand Isidore Hippolyte (1801–71) French archeologist, who was one of the founders of paleontology. Following his first discoveries of fossil remains in SW France, Lartet excavated many cave sites, finding important evidence for dating the various phases of human culture in the region.

larva The immature form of many animals, which hatches from the egg and often differs in appearance from the adult form. Larvae usually avoid competing for food, etc., with the adults by occupying a different habitat or adopting a different lifestyle. For example, adult barnacles, which are sessile, produce motile larvae, whose role is distribution of the species. Other larvae are responsible for gathering food reserves for the production of a fully formed adult, whose primary function is to breed. Caterpillars and maggots are types of insect larvae with this function. *See also* metamorphosis; tadpole.

laryngitis Inflammation of the larynx. Acute laryngitis is a common complication of colds and similar infections, particularly if the patient talks excessively or is exposed to irritants (such as smoke) in the atmosphere. The main symptoms are hoarseness and pain: sometimes the voice is lost completely. The best treatment is to rest the voice and remain in a warm humid atmosphere; steam inhalations ease the condition.

larynx An organ, situated at the front of the neck above the windpipe (*see* trachea), that contains the **vocal cords**, responsible for the production of vocal sounds. The larynx contains several cartilages (one of which—the thyroid cartilage—forms the Adam's apple) bound together by muscles and ligaments. Within are the two vocal cords: folds of tissue separated by a narrow slit (glottis). The vocal cords modify the flow of exhaled air through the glottis to produce the sounds of speech, song, etc.

La Salle, Robert Cavelier, Sieur de (1643–87) French explorer in North America. La Salle settled in Montreal in 1666 and in 1669 set out on his first expedition, exploring the Ohio region. From 1679 he concentrated on achieving his ambition to descend the Mississippi River to the Gulf of Mexico. In 1682, after two arduous years, he reached the Gulf and named the area watered by the Mississippi and its tributaries Louisiana, after Louis XIV of France. While attempting to found a permanent colony, he was murdered by mutineers.

La Scala (*or* Teatro alla Scala) The principal Italian opera house, opened in Milan in 1776. It is noted for its varied repertoire of new and classical works, and attained its highest reputation under Arturo *Toscanini, director from 1898 to 1907 and from 1921 to 1931.

Las Campanas Observatory. *See* Hale Observatories.

Las Casas, Bartolomé de (1474–1566) Spanish priest, known as the Apostle of the Indies. As a planter on Hispaniola, Las Casas was horrified by the treatment to which the Indians were subjected. He became a priest (1510) and entered the Dominican order, becoming the defender of the Indians at the Spanish court. His agitation included the publication of *The Brief Relation of the Destruction of the Indies* (1552) and bore fruit with the abolition of Indian slavery in 1542.

Las Cases, Emmanuel, Comte de (1776–1842) French writer. He held political office under Napoleon and shared his exile on St Helena. His *Mémorial de St Hélène* (1823) recorded Napoleon's final conversations and opinions on politics and religion and greatly influenced his posthumous reputation.

Lascaux Upper *Paleolithic cave site in the Dordogne (France), discovered in 1940. Lascaux contains rock paintings and engravings of horses, oxen, red deer, and other animals, dating from about 18,000 BC; traps and arrows depicted nearby suggest that the pictures had magical significance in a hunting ritual. Atmospheric changes resulting in deterioration of the paintings caused the cave to be closed again (1963).

laser (*light amplification by stimulated emission of radiation*) A device that produces a beam of high-intensity coherent monochromatic radiation (light, infrared, or ultraviolet). Stimulated emission is the emission of a photon when an atomic electron falls from a higher energy level to a lower level as a result of being stimulated by another photon of the same frequency. In the laser large numbers of electrons are "pumped" into a higher energy level, an effect called population inversion, and then stimulated to produce a high-intensity beam. Laser beams have been produced from solids, liquids, and gases. The simplest type is the ruby laser, consisting of a cylinder of ruby, silvered at one end and partially silvered at the other. A flash lamp is used to excite chromium ions in the ruby to a high energy level. When the ions fall back to their ground state photons (wavelength 694.3 nanometers) are emitted. These photons collide with other excited ions producing radiation of the same wavelength (monochromatic) and the same phase (coherent), which is reflected up and down the ruby crystal and emerges as a narrow beam from the partially silvered end. Lasers are used in civil engineering to aid alignment, in eye surgery, in laser interferometers to measure very small displacements, in *holography, and in scientific research.

Lasker, Emanuel (1868–1941) German chess player, who became world champion in 1894 and remained champion until he conceded the title to *Capablanca in 1921. A Jew, he left Germany in 1933 to settle in the Soviet Union and finally the US.

ruby laser

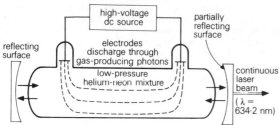

helium-neon gas laser

LASER *In the solid-state ruby laser, chromium ions are excited by an intense flash of light and then stimulated by weak light of one wavelength to emit a pulse of photons. In the helium-neon gas laser, a continuous laser beam is produced from an electrical discharge through low-pressure gas.*

Laski, Harold Joseph (1893–1950) British political theorist. Laski became professor of political science at the London School of Economics in 1926. A socialist, he was influenced by the theories of *Burke and *Mill but became progressively more Marxist in outlook. His writings include *Authority in the Modern State* (1919) and *Faith, Reason, Civilization* (1944).

Las Palmas 28 08N 15 27W The largest city in the Canary Islands, the capital of Las Palmas province in Gran Canaria. It is a popular resort noted for its palms and is a major fueling port between Europe and South America. Population (1970): 287,038.

La Spezia 44 07N 9 48E A port and resort in Italy, in Liguria on the Gulf of Spezia. It is a major naval base, with the largest harbor in Italy. Its industries include shipbuilding, textiles, and the manufacture of porcelain. Population (1980 est): 116,719.

Lassa fever A severe virus disease occurring in West Africa and first described in 1969 in Lassa, a village in Nigeria. It is a rare and often fatal disease that is transmitted to man by certain species of rat.

Lassalle, Ferdinand (1825–64) German socialist politician and theorist. Although deeply influenced by Karl Marx, Lassalle developed a distinctive theory of socialism, stressing the formation of workers' cooperatives as a peaceful way to socialism. He headed working-class opposition to Bismarck and helped to found the General German Workers' Association (1863), the precursor to the Social Democratic party. He was killed in a duel.

Lassen Volcanic National Park A national park in NE California, in the Cascade Ranges. The main feature of the park, established in 1916, is Lassen Peak (10,457 ft; 3188 m), an active volcano that erupted from 1914 through 1921. Lava flows, lava plugs, other volcanoes, and boiling springs and lakes also attract tourists. Area: 167 sq mi (431 sq km).

Lassus, Roland de (Italian name: Orlando di Lasso; c. 1532–94) Flemish composer. He was born in Mons, where he became a chorister. He obtained appointments in Rome (choirmaster at St John Lateran), Antwerp, and with the Bavarian court in Munich. His madrigals, chansons, and motets exhibit great contrapuntal skill. He was afflicted with depression in later life.

Las Vegas 36 10N 115 12W A city in SE Nevada. Founded in 1855, it grew rapidly after construction of the nearby Hoover Dam. It is famous for its nightclubs and the Strip (a row of luxury hotels and gambling casinos). Population (1980): 164,674.

László I, Saint (1040–95) King of Hungary (1077–95). In 1091, László conquered Croatia, to which he introduced Roman Catholicism, founding the bishopric of Zagreb. He also reformed the criminal code, bringing peace and security to Hungary.

Latakia (Arabic name: Al Ladhiqiyah) 35 31N 35 47E A city in NW Syria, on the Mediterranean coast. It dates from Phoenician times and is now Syria's principal port. It is also famous for its tobacco. Population (1977 est): 191,329.

La Tène The second phase of the European Iron Age, succeeding *Hallstatt from the 5th century BC. Named for the site at La Tène (Switzerland), this recognizably Celtic culture spread throughout Europe, coming into contact with the civilizations of Greece and Rome. Aristocratic chariot burials replaced wagon burials and the geometric patterns of Hallstatt metalwork were superseded by the intricate curvilinear designs of *Celtic art. By the 1st century BC Roman expansionism effectively ended coherent La Tène culture. *See also* Celts.

latent heat The amount of heat absorbed or released by a substance when it undergoes a change of state. For example, a liquid absorbs heat (**latent heat of vaporization**) from its surroundings on evaporation, since energy is needed to overcome the forces of attraction between the molecules as the liquid expands into a gas. Similarly a solid absorbs heat (**latent heat of fusion**) when it melts. The heat absorbed or released per unit mass of substance is called the **specific latent heat**; per amount of substance it is the **molar latent heat**.

Lateran Councils Five ecumenical councils of the Roman Catholic Church convened in the Lateran Palace, Rome. **1.** (1123) The council that confirmed the settlement of the *investiture controversy. **2.** and **3.** (1139, 1179) The councils that were principally concerned with the papal-election procedure. **4.** (1215) The council, attended by most major European ecclesiastical and secular powers, that proclaimed the fifth Crusade (1217–21) and was enormously influential in its formulations of doctrine and Church organization and law. **5.** (1512–17) The council that endeavored to counteract hostility to papal power on the eve of the Reformation.

Lateran Treaty (1929) An agreement between the Italian government of Mussolini and the Vatican. The Vatican City state was created and the papacy abandoned its claims to the former *papal states.

laterite A deposit formed from the weathering of rocks in humid tropical conditions. It consists mostly of iron and aluminum oxides. It occurs either under ground, where it is soft, or as a hardened reddish surface capping where the overlying material has been eroded. Most laterites developed in the Tertiary period.

latex A liquid, often milky, emulsion found in certain flowering plants. It has a complex composition and its function in the plant is not fully understood. The latex of the *rubber tree is used in rubber manufacture, while opium and morphine are obtained from the latex of the *opium poppy.

lathe A machine for turning wood, plastic, or metal into cylindrical or conical parts or for cutting holes or screw-threads in them. The piece to be worked is held in a rotating plate or chuck so that a cutting tool can be held against it. The **turret lathe** has a turret containing a set of cutting tools, which can be used independently or simultaneously. Automatic turret lathes perform a sequence of operations on the workpiece without manual interference and are extensively used in mass-production processes.

Latimer, Hugh (c. 1485–1555) Anglican reformer and martyr. While a university preacher, he was converted to Protestantism (1524). He became Bishop of Worcester in 1535, but his opposition to Henry's Six Articles upholding Roman Catholic doctrine resulted in his resignation and imprisonment (1539). A popular preacher under Edward VI, he was arrested at Mary's accession, tried for heresy, and burned at the stake.

Latimeria. *See* coelacanth.

Latin America The countries of Central and South America lying S of the US-Mexican border, including those islands of the West Indies where a Romance language is spoken. Spanish is the most widely used language but Portuguese is spoken in Brazil, the largest country, and French is spoken in Haiti and French Guiana. The population is mainly mestizo (people of mixed Indian and European—usually Spanish—parentage), with minorities of pure Indians and Europeans. The **Latin American Free Trade Association** (LAFTA) was formed in 1961 with the aim of removing all restrictions on trade among its member countries (Argentina, Brazil, Bolivia,

Chile, Colombia, Ecuador, Mexico, Paraguay, Peru, Uruguay, and Venezuela).

Latin American Conferences A series of conferences held in Montevideo, Uruguay (1933); Buenos Aires, Argentina (1936); and Lima, Peru (1938). They discussed US-Latin American relations and inaugurated President Franklin D. Roosevelt's *Good Neighbor Policy. As a result of these meetings, a policy of nonintervention in Latin America affairs was reaffirmed.

Latini, Brunetto (c. 1220–c. 1294) Florentine scholar and politician. A friend of *Dante, Latini contributed to the spread of French learning in Italy and wrote an encyclopedia entitled *Li Livres dou trésor*.

Latin language An Italic Indo-European language, the ancestor of modern Romance languages. First spoken on the plain of Latium near Rome, Latin spread throughout the Mediterranean world as Roman power expanded. An inflected and syntactically complex language, written Latin was gradually molded to express with equal power Cicero's rhetoric and philosophy, Martial's epigrams, and Virgil's subtle poetry. Educated conversational Latin developed contemporaneously with literary Latin, although, with its freer syntax and vocabulary, it remained less static than the formalized written language. Colloquial Vulgar Latin used prepositions and conjunctions freely to replace inflected forms and had a simpler word order; it became the Latin of the provinces, contributing to the early development of the Romance languages. As the western Roman Empire's official language, Latin was used in W Europe for religious, literary, and scholarly works until the middle ages and beyond, and remained the Roman Catholic Church's official language until the mid-20th century.

Latin literature The earliest Latin literature dates from after the conclusion of the first *Punic War (241 BC). Writers such as *Ennius, Naevius, and *Plautus (see Roman comedy) translated Greek epic, tragedy, and comedy and adapted them to Roman themes. Prose, particularly legal and historical writing, developed along more independent lines until the 1st century BC, when *Cicero conclusively established Latin as a mature literary medium. His contemporary *Lucretius perfected the Latin hexameter and, together with the lyric poet *Catullus, they inaugurated the *Golden Age of Latin literature. Their achievements were consolidated in the subsequent Augustan age (43 BC–18 AD), during which the emperor Augustus' adviser *Maecenas was patron to *Virgil, *Horace, and *Propertius. Among their important contemporaries were the poets *Ovid and *Tibullus and the historian *Livy. The spirit of the succeeding *Silver Age is encapsulated in *Seneca's highly rhetorical tragedies. *Juvenal and *Martial were the major poets and *Tacitus, *Suetonius, *Quintilian, and *Petronius contributed notable prose works. Imitations, anthologies, and commentaries later predominated over original work. In the 4th and 5th centuries the Latin Church Fathers set Latin on course for becoming the lingua franca of Christian intellectuals. As the literature of learning, Latin literature's characteristic products were encyclopedias and theological texts. Exceptions to this were the medieval Latin lyrics, which have the spontaneity of their vernacular counterparts. *See also* Latin language.

Latinus A legendary ancestor of the Romans, who gave his name to their language. *Aeneas arrived from Troy in his kingdom of Latium, an area S of Rome, and married his daughter Lavinia.

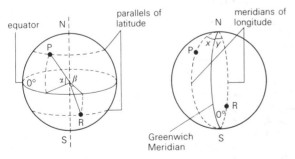

The latitude of P is given by the angle α. In this case it would be α° N. The latitude of R is β° S.

The longitude of P is given by the angle x. In this case it would be x° W. R has a longitude y° E.

LATITUDE AND LONGITUDE

latitude and longitude Imaginary lines on the earth's surface, enabling any point to be defined in terms of two angles. **Parallels of latitude** are circles drawn round the earth parallel to the equator; their diameters diminish as they approach the Poles. These parallels are specified by the angle subtended at the center of the earth by the arc formed between a point on the parallel and the equator. All points on the equator therefore have a latitude of 0°, while the North Pole has a latitude of 90°N and the South Pole of 90°S. Parallels of latitude 1° apart are separated on the earth's surface by about 63 mi (100 km).

Meridians of longitude are half great circles passing through both Poles; they cross parallels of latitude at right angles. In 1884 the meridian through Greenwich, London, England, was selected as the prime meridian and given the designation 0°. Other meridians are defined by the angle between the plane of the meridian and the plane of the prime meridian, specifying whether it is E or W of the prime meridian. At the equator meridians 1° apart are separated by about 70 mi (112 km).

Latium. *See* Lazio.

La Tour, Georges de (1593–1652) French painter, a native of Lorraine. He excelled in candlelit religious scenes, influenced by such Dutch followers of Caravaggio as *Honthorst. His works include *St Joseph the Carpenter* (Louvre) and *The Lamentation over St Sebastian* (Berlin). La Tour's reputation has only been re-established in the 20th century.

La Tour, Maurice-Quentin de (1704–88) French portrait pastelist, born in Saint-Quentin. He settled in Paris, where he enjoyed an immense and lasting popularity. His sitters included Voltaire, Madame de Pompadour, and Louis XV.

Latrobe, Benjamin Henry (1764–1820) US architect and engineer; born in England. Educated as an architect, he came to the US in 1796 and by 1798 had designed the Greek Revival Bank of Pennsylvania building in Philadelphia. He redesigned part of the Capitol building in Washington, DC, in 1803 and rebuilt it (1815–17) after it was burned down. From 1805 until 1818 he worked on the Roman Catholic cathedral in Baltimore, Md.

Latter Day Saints, Reorganized Church of Jesus Christ of A splinter group of the *Mormons that separated from the main group in 1852 and refused to follow the leadership of Brigham Young, successor to Joseph *Smith. Headquarters for its almost 200,000 members is in Independence, Mo.

Latvian A language belonging to the E division of the *Baltic languages division of the Indo-European family, spoken by about two million Latvians. Most live in the Latvian SSR, where Latvian is the official language. Also known as Lettish, it is closely related to *Lithuanian. It is written in a Latin alphabet and written texts date from the 16th century.

Latvian Soviet Socialist Republic (*or* Latvia) A constituent republic in the NW Soviet Union, on the Baltic Sea. It is a fertile lowland with extensive forests. Latvians, who comprise approximately 60% of the population, are mainly Lutheran Christians. Industries include shipbuilding, engineering, chemicals, and textiles. Fishing plays an important part in the economy and Riga, the capital, is an important seaport. *History*: the Latvians were conquered by the Livonian Knights (a German order of knighthood) in the 13th century, passing to Poland in the 16th century, to Sweden in the 17th century, and to Russia in the 18th century. Latvia gained independence in 1918, which was recognized by Soviet Russia in 1920. In 1940 it was incorporated into the Soviet Union as an SSR. It was occupied by Germany in World War II. The US does not recognize Latvia's status as a Soviet republic. Area: 25,590 sq m (63,700 sq km). Population (1981 est): 2,500,000. Capital: Riga.

Laud, William (1573–1645) Anglican churchman and chief adviser to Charles I of Britain immediately before the *Civil War. Successively Bishop of St David's, Bath and Wells, and London, and then Archbishop of Canterbury (1633–45), he supported Charles I's personal rule and his attempt to enforce liturgical uniformity among both Roman Catholics and Puritans. His pressure on the Scots to accept the Book of Common Prayer paved the way for the Civil War and his own downfall. He was impeached for high treason in 1640 and eventually executed.

Lauda, Niki (1949–) Austrian automobile-racing driver, who was world champion in 1975, 1977, and 1984 and won numerous Grand Prix races.

laudanum. *See* opium.

Laue, Max Theodor Felix von (1879–1960) German physicist, who became professor at the University of Berlin in 1919. His early investigations of X-rays led him to discover the technique of *X-ray crystallography, now widely used for determining crystal structures. For this work he won the 1914 Nobel Prize. In 1943 he resigned his chair in protest against the Nazis. After the war he was appointed director of the Max Planck Institute for Physical Chemistry.

laughing jackass. *See* kookaburra.

laughing owl A ground-nesting New Zealand *owl, *Sceloglaux albifacies*, probably now extinct due to the introduction of predatory mammals. It was 15 in (37 cm) long and had a speckled and barred brown plumage with whitish facial feathers.

CHARLES LAUGHTON *As Canon Chasuble with Elsa Lanchester as Miss Prism in Wilde's* The Importance of Being Earnest *(1934).*

Laughton, Charles (1899–1962) British actor. His international reputation was based on his numerous films, which included *The Private Life of Henry VIII* (1933), *Mutiny on the Bounty* (1935), *Rembrandt* (1936), and *Witness for the Prosecution* (1957). He was married to the actress Elsa Lanchester and lived for many years in Hollywood, but made several late appearances in the English theater, notably as King Lear in 1959.

Launceston 41 25S 147 07E A city and port in Australia, in N Tasmania situated at the confluence of the North and South Esk Rivers. It is an important commercial center; industries include aluminum smelting, heavy engineering, textiles, and sawmilling. Population (1976): 63,386.

Laura The subject of Petrarch's love sonnets and other poems. She has been variously identified, traditionally as Laura de Noves (?1308–48), a married woman living in Avignon. The poems suggest that Petrarch's love for her was not returned.

Laurasia The supercontinent of the N hemisphere that is believed to have existed prior to 200 million years ago, when the drift of the continents to their present positions began. It probably consisted of Greenland, Europe, Asia (excluding India), and North America. *See also* Gondwanaland.

laurel One of several unrelated aromatic shrubs or small trees with attractive evergreen leaves. The so-called true laurels (genus *Laurus*) include the *bay tree. Other laurels include the ornamental *cherry laurels, the spotted laurels (genus *Aucuba*; family *Cornaceae*), and the mountain laurel (*Kalmia latifolia*; family *Ericaceae*). The spurge laurel is a species of *Daphne.

Laurel and Hardy US film comedians. **Stan Laurel** (Arthur Stanley Jefferson; 1890–1965), the thin member of the team and originator of the gags, was born in Britain. He joined with **Oliver Hardy** (1892–1957), who played the pompous fat partner, in 1926. They made numerous outstanding two-reel and feature-length comedy films in the 1920s and 1930s, including *The Music Box* (1932), *Our Relations* (1936), and *Way Out West* (1937).

Laurentian Shield. *See* shield.

Laurier, Sir Wilfrid (1841–1919) Canadian statesman; the first French-Canadian prime minister of Canada (1896–1911). His Liberal government was notable for the settlement of the West and the defense of Canadian autonomy within the British Empire.

laurustinus An ornamental evergreen shrub, *Viburnum tinus*, native to the Mediterranean region and up to 10 ft (3 m) tall. It has pointed oval leaves, reddish twigs, and round heads of tiny five-petaled pink-and-white flowers, borne on red stalks and producing blue-black berries. It is often grown as a pot plant. Family: *Caprifoliaceae*.

Lausanne 46 32N 6 39E A city and resort in W Switzerland, on the N shore of Lake Geneva. A cultural and intellectual center, it has a notable cathedral (13th century) and a university (1891) founded as a college in the 16th century. Lausanne is the seat of the Swiss Supreme Court and the headquarters of the International Olympic Committee. Industries include chocolate, precision instruments, and clothing. Population (1980 est): 127,349.

Lausanne, Conferences of 1. (1922–23) A conference between the Allied Powers and Turkey that modified the post-World War I Treaty of Sèvres (1920), which had been unacceptable to Turkey. By the Treaty of Lausanne, Turkey regained territory from Greece and the Allies recognized Turkey's right to control its own affairs. **2.** (1932) A conference between the UK, France, Belgium, and Italy, which ended the payment by Germany of World War I reparations.

lava Magma that has reached the earth's surface through volcanic vents and from which the volatile material has escaped, either molten or cooled and solidified. Basic lavas tend to be liquid and flow over large areas, while acid lavas are viscous.

Laval 45 33N 73 43W A city in E Canada, in Quebec on the island next to *Montreal. Primarily a suburb, it has some industry, including electronics, paper, and metal goods. Population (1980 est): 262,300.

Laval, Pierre (1883–1945) French statesman, whose collaboration with Germany during the German occupation of France in World War II resulted in his execution as a traitor. A socialist, Laval was prime minister in 1930, 1931, 1932, 1935, and 1936 and foreign minister in 1934, 1935, and 1936. In 1935, with Sir Samuel Hoare (1880–1959), the British foreign minister, he proposed an unsuccessful plan (the Hoare-Laval Plan) for the settlement of Mussolini's claims in Ethiopia. After the collapse of France (1940) he joined Marshal *Pétain's Vichy government. Increasingly powerful, he was dismissed and briefly imprisoned by Pétain (December, 1940) but the support of Germany secured Laval the virtual leadership of the Vichy government in 1942. After the liberation of France (1944) he fled to Germany and then to Spain but later gave himself up for trial in France (July, 1945).

La Vallière, Louise de Françoise de la Baume le Blanc, Duchesse de (1644–1710) The mistress of Louis XIV of France from 1661 until 1667, when she was replaced by Mme de Montespan. In 1674 she retired to a convent.

Lavalloisian A Middle *Paleolithic technique of making stone tools by flaking pieces away from a specially shaped lump (prepared core). It is often associated with *Mousterian sites.

lavender A small shrub of the genus *Lavandula* (about 8 species), especially *L. vera* and *L. angustifolia* (or *L. officinalis*). 12–31 in (30–80 cm) high, it has aromatic narrow gray-green leaves and long-stemmed spikes of small mauve or violet flowers. Native to the Mediterranean area, it is widely cultivated for its flowers, which retain their fragrance when dried, and for its oil, which is used in perfumes. Family: *Labiatae*.

laver An edible red *seaweed of the genus *Porphyra*, found growing at the high tide mark in both hemispheres. It has wide irregular membranous fronds, which are dried to provide an important food source in the Orient. In the British Isles it is fried and known as laverbread (*or* sloke).

Laver, Rod (ney George) (1938–) Australian tennis player. In 1962 he took all four major singles titles (Australian, French, US, and Wimbledon) as an amateur and repeated the feat as a professional in 1969.

Laveran, Charles Louis Alphonse (1845–1922) French physician, who (in 1880) first recognized the protozoan parasite responsible for malaria while stationed with the army in Algeria. Laveran investigated other diseases caused by protozoa, including trypanosomiasis and leishmaniasis. He was awarded the 1907 Nobel Prize.

Lavoisier, Antoine Laurent (1743–94) French chemist, regarded as the founder of modern chemistry. Born into an aristocratic family, he became wealthy by investing his money in a private company hired by the government to collect taxes. With his wealth he built a large laboratory where he discovered in 1778 that air consists of a mixture of two gases, which he called oxygen and nitrogen. He then went on to study the role of oxygen in combustion, finally disposing of the *phlogiston theory. Lavoisier also discovered the law of conservation of mass and devised the modern method of naming compounds, which replaced the older nonsystematic method. Lavoisier was arrested during the French Revolution and tried for his involvement with the tax-collecting company. He was found guilty and guillotined.

law That which is laid down, ordained, or established. The body of rules include those that govern and regulate the relationship between one state and another (*see* international law), a state and its citizens (territorial or municipal law), and one person and another when the state is not directly involved (*see* civil law). Rules that must be obeyed and followed by citizens subject to sanctions or legal consequences is a law.

Law, (Andrew) Bonar (1858–1923) British statesman; Conservative prime minister (1922–23). While colonial secretary (1915–16), he fostered the revolt against *Asquith's coalition and in the subsequent coalition led by *Lloyd George became chancellor of the exchequer and leader of the House of Commons. He became prime minister after Lloyd George's resignation.

Lawrence, D(avid) H(erbert) (1885–1930) British novelist, poet, and painter. The son of a Nottinghamshire miner, he was encouraged by his mother to become a teacher; he published his first novel, *The White Peacock*, in 1911. The semiautobiographical *Sons and Lovers* (1913) established his reputation. In 1912 he eloped with Frieda Weekley, the German wife of a professor. Their extensive travels provided material for the novels *Kangaroo* (1923), reflecting a stay in Australia, and *The Plumed Serpent* (1926), set in Mexico. Lawrence explored marital and sexual relations in *The Rainbow* (1915) and *Women in Love* (1921); he treated this subject in more explicit detail in *Lady Chatterley's Lover* (privately printed, 1928). The novel was not published in its unexpurgated form for many years. Lawrence's collected poems were published in 1928. *Fantasia of the Unconscious* (1922) develops ideas that become increasingly prominent in the novels. A number of his critical writings are collected in *Selected Literary Criticism* (1955). He died of tuberculosis.

Lawrence, Ernest Orlando (1901–58) US physicist, who in 1930, at the University of California, designed and built the first *cyclotron, a type of particle *accelerator upon which almost all subsequent models have been based. For his invention he received the Nobel Prize in 1939.

Lawrence, Gertrude (1898–1952) British actress and dancer. She performed in many revues and was especially successful in three productions by Noel *Coward, *Private Lives* (1930), *Tonight at 8:30* (1935–36), and *Lady in the Dark* (1941). She went to the US and made her final appearance in the musical *The King and I* in 1951. She also wrote her autobiography, *A Star Danced* (1945).

Lawrence, St (d. 258) Roman deacon martyred during the reign of Emperor Valerian. According to tradition he distributed ecclesiastical treasure to the poor and was condemned to death by being roasted on a gridiron, which has become his emblem. Feast day: Aug 10.

Lawrence, T(homas) E(dward) (1888–1935) British soldier and writer, known as Lawrence of Arabia. He learned Arabic while excavating Carchemish (1911–14) and after the outbreak of World War I worked for army intelligence in N Africa. In 1916 he joined the Arab revolt against the Turks, leading the Arab guerrillas triumphantly into Damascus in October, 1918. His exploits, which brought him almost legendary fame, were recounted in his book *The Seven Pillars of Wisdom* (1926). Disillusioned by the failure of the Paris Peace Conference to establish Arab independence, in 1922 he joined the ranks of the Royal Air Force (RAF), assuming the name John Hume Ross, and then the Royal Tank Corps (1923), as T. E. Shaw. In 1925 he rejoined the RAF, where he worked as a mechanic. He died in a motorcycle accident.

Lawrence 38 58N 95 14W A city in NE Kansas, on the S banks of the Kansas River, NE of Topeka. The University of Kansas (1863) is here. Founded in 1854, the city was the scene in 1863 of a raid and massacre by William C. Quantrill and his guerrillas. Industries include food processing and the manufacture of greeting cards, chemicals, and paper products. Population (1980): 52,738.

lawrencium (Lr) A synthetic transuranic element discovered in 1961 and named for E. O. *Lawrence. Chemical tests on a few atoms suggest a dominantly trivalent chemistry. At no 103; at wt (257).

laxatives (*or* purgatives) Drugs used to treat constipation. Such laxatives as magnesium sulfate (Epsom salts) mix with the feces and cause them to retain water, which increases their bulk and makes them easier to pass. Irritant laxatives, such as castor oil, senna, and cascara, stimulate the

bowel directly. Another group, which includes bran, both lubricates the feces and increases their bulk.

T. E. LAWRENCE   *Drawing by Augustus John (1919).*

Laxness, Halldór (Kiljan) (1902–) Icelandic novelist and essayist. He spent much of his early life traveling in Europe, where he became a Roman Catholic. The novel *Vefarinn mikli frá Kasmir* (*The Great Weaver from Kashmir*; 1927) marked his abandonment of Catholicism and adoption of socialism, a theme of subsequent works written after his return to Iceland in 1930. These include *Salka Valka* (1934) and *Sjalfstaet folk* (*Independent People*; 1934–35). He was awarded the Nobel prize in 1955.

Layamon (early 13th century) English poet and priest. His alliterative verse chronicle *Brut*, based on the *Roman de Brut* by *Wace, relates the history of England from the arrival of Brutus (a legendary Trojan) to the defeat of the Britons by the Saxons in 689 AD and includes original detail in its treatment of *Arthurian legend.

Layard, Sir Austen Henry (1817–94) British archeologist and diplomat. As excavator of □Nimrud and *Nineveh (1845–51), Layard stimulated popular interest in Mesopotamian archeology by his book *Nineveh and Its Remains* (1848)—actually about Nimrud, as he had at first misidentified the site—and by his feat of transporting colossal statues of winged bulls to Britain.

Lazarists A Roman Catholic order of lay priests known more formally as the Congregation of the Mission. Established by St *Vincent de Paul at St Lazare Priory, Paris, in 1625, the Lazarists now have teaching and missionary communities all over the world.

Lazio (Latin name: Latium) A region in W central Italy. It consists of an extensive coastal plain in the W and mountains in the E, separated by volcanic hills. The majority of the population live in urban centers, such as Rome. Agriculture is important producing cereals, olives, wine, fruits, sheep, and cattle. Rome is an important center for manufacturing industries, such as food processing, chemicals, textiles, and paper; there is also a sizable service industry. Area: 6642 sq mi (17,204 sq km). Population (1980 est): 5,088,641. Capital: Rome.

L-dopa (*or* levodopa) A drug used to treat *parkinsonism, which is caused by a deficiency of dopamine (a chemical secreted at nerve endings when an impulse passes) in the brain. L-dopa is converted to this compound in the brain. It is taken by mouth, combined with carbidopa (Sinemet), which prevents its breakdown in the body.

Lea River (*or* Lee R.) A river in S England, rising in S Bedfordshire and flowing SE and S past Luton to join the River Thames at Blackwall. Its valley is being developed as a recreational park. Length: 46 mi (74 km).

Leacock, Stephen (Butler) (1869–1944) Canadian humorist, born in England. He was educated and taught economics and political science at Canadian universities. *Literary Lapses* (1910) and *Nonsense Novels* (1911) were the first of over 30 popular humorous books.

lead (Pb) A dense soft bluish-gray metal, known from prehistoric times. It occurs in nature chiefly as the sulfide *galena (PbS) but also as cerussite (PbCO₃), anglesite (PbSO₄), and occasionally as the native metal. The metal is very resistant to corrosion and some lead pipes installed by the Romans are still intact. Lead is used in plumbing (although it is now being replaced by plastics). It is also used to shield X-rays, as ammunition, as cable sheathing, in crystal glass (as lead oxide), and as an antiknock (as *tetraethyl lead; $(C_2H_5)_4Pb$). Other common compounds include the sulfate ($PbSO_4$), chromate ($PbCrO_4$), and the oxides red lead (Pb_3O_4) and litharge (PbO). These are colored white, yellow, red, and orange respectively and were formerly extensively used as paint pigments. Most lead salts are insoluble, with the exception of the nitrate, ($Pb(NO_3)_2$), and acetate ($Pb(CH_3COO)_2$). Acute lead poisoning causes diarrhea and vomiting, but poisoning is more often chronic and characterized by abdominal pain, muscle pains, anemia, and nerve and brain damage. Children are particularly vulnerable to excess lead levels from car exhaust fumes. At no 82; at wt 207.19; mp 214°F (327.50°C); bp 998°F (1740°C).

Leadbelly (Huddie Ledbetter; 1888–1949) US folksinger and songwriter, whose blues and work songs foreshadowed the folk revival of the 1960s.

Leadville 39 15N 106 20W A city in central Colorado, in the Rocky Mountains, NE of Aspen. Gold, lead, and silver deposits led to a large, thriving mining community by 1880. The town declined as silver prices fell and today is a large producer of molybdenum and a popular tourist attraction. Population (1980): 3879.

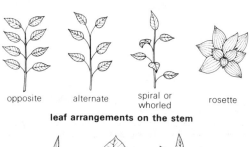

leaf arrangements on the stem

types of simple leaf

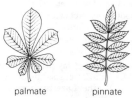

types of compound leaf

LEAF *The type and arrangement of the leaves are characteristic for a particular species of plant. For example, the pear has alternate ovate leaves; the horse chestnut has opposite palmate leaves.*

leaf An outgrowth from the stem of a □plant in which most of the green pigment chlorophyll, used for *photosynthesis, is concentrated. Foliage leaves are typically thin and flat, providing a large surface area for absorbing the maximum amount of light, and they contain pores (stomata) through which exchange of gases and water occurs. They may be simple or compound (composed of a number of leaflets) and with a branching vein system (in *dicotyledons) or parallel veins (in *monocotyledons). Other kinds of leaves include seed leaves (*see* cotyledon) and *bracts. The spines of cacti and the thorns of gorse are modified leaves.

leaf beetle A beetle belonging to a large family (*Chrysomelidae*; 26,000 species) occurring in tropical and temperate regions. Leaf beetles are generally small (less than 0.5 in [12 mm]) and brightly colored. Both the adults and larvae feed on leaves and flowers, although the larvae may also eat roots and stems. Leaf beetles have a wide range of habits: one group is aquatic; in others the larvae carry excrement on their backs (*see* tortoise

beetle); and many are serious pests, including the notorious *Colorado potato beetle. □insect.

leafcutter ant An *ant, also called a parasol ant, belonging to the genus *Atta* and related genera and occurring in tropical and subtropical America. Armies of leafcutter ants damage crops by cutting pieces of leaf and carrying them to their large underground nests. The leaves are used as a medium on which the ants cultivate their diet of fungi. Subfamily: *Myrmicinae*.

leafcutter bee A solitary *bee, about 0.4 in (10 mm) long, belonging to a genus (*Megachile*) of the family *Megachilidae*. It nests in rotten wood and soil, lining the chamber and egg cells with pieces of leaf cut with its strong jaws. Leafcutters are similar to *honeybees in appearance and have pollen-carrying brushes on the underside of their abdomens.

leaf hopper A small slender insect (up to 0.6 in [15 mm] long) belonging to the family *Cicadellidae*. Leaf hoppers are often brightly colored and are powerful jumpers. They feed by sucking plant juices and exude honeydew. Some species are serious pests of plants causing discoloration and weakening or spreading disease. Suborder: *Homoptera*; order: *Hemiptera*.

leaf insect A plant-eating insect, also called a walking leaf, belonging to the family *Phyllidae*. It is excellently camouflaged against foliage, having a broad leaflike body and wings and leaflike flaps on the legs. The female is much larger than the male and lacks hindwings. Order: *Phasmida*.

League of Nations An international organization created (1920) after World War I with the purpose of achieving world peace. The League's Covenant was incorporated into the postwar peace treaties and the failure of the US to ratify the Treaty of *Versailles meant its exclusion from the League. Before 1930 the League, from its Geneva headquarters, organized international conferences, settled minor disputes, and did much useful humanitarian work. However, it failed to deal effectively with the aggression during the 1930s of Japan in China, Italy in Ethiopia (in which the League's use of *sanctions was ineffectual), and Germany, which withdrew from the League in 1933. The UN superseded the League after World War II.

League of Women Voters US organization for women of voting age that keeps the public informed on voting laws and issues. Established in 1920, when women received the right to vote, it is nonpartisan and takes a stand on an issue only when a majority of the membership, after extensive study, indicates the need.

Leakey, Louis Seymour Bazett (1903–72) Kenyan paleontologist. His work at *Olduvai Gorge uncovered crucial evidence for man's early evolution, notably the *Zinjanthropus* skull dating from 1.75 million years ago. In 1974 his wife **Mary Leakey** (1913–   ) unearthed hominid remains at Laetolil (N Tanzania) dating back 3.75 million years. Their son **Richard Leakey** (1944–   ) has made significant fossil finds around Lake Turkana (formerly Lake Rudolf; N Kenya).

Lean, Sir David (1908–   ) British film director. His early films in collaboration with Noël Coward include *In Which we Serve* (1942), *Blithe Spirit* (1945), and *Brief Encounter* (1946). Adaptations of Charles Dickens' *Great Expectations* (1946) and *Oliver Twist* (1947) were followed by the classic *The Bridge on the River Kwai* (1957). Later films include *Lawrence of Arabia* (1962) and *Dr Zhivago* (1965), and *A Passage to India* (1984). He received a knighthood in 1984.

Leander. *See* Hero and Leander.

leap year. *See* calendar.

Lear A legendary British king, probably invented by Geoffrey of Monmouth, who recounts the story of the old king's division of his kingdom among his three daughters. This story is the basis of Shakespeare's *King Lear* (c. 1605) and is referred to in other works of Elizabethan literature.

Lear, Edward (1812–88) British artist and poet. After 1837 he lived mainly abroad, working as a landscape painter and traveling extensively. He died in Italy. He showed great verbal inventiveness in his four books of nonsense verse for children, beginning with *The Book of Nonsense* (1846), and he popularized a form of the limerick.

leasehold. *See* estate.

leasing back An operation to raise liquid cash from a capital asset. The owner of a property, such as a house, sells it on the condition that the buyer leases it back to the seller for a fixed period for a specified rent.

leather Specially treated animal skin. Although any skin can be made into leather, that of domesticated animals, such as cows, sheep, goats, and pigs, is chiefly used. Animals killed exclusively for their skins, such as crocodiles and lizards, produce beautiful but very expensive leather. The skin is first stripped of the fleshy inner and hairy outer layers and then tanned by steeping it in tannin, a preservative. Various finishing processes include rubbing to bring out the grain, as in Morocco leather (goatskin); dyeing; oiling; lacquering for patent leather; and sueding to raise a nap. The uses of leather, which is strong, versatile, flexible, waterproof, and permeable to air, range from industrial parts and saddles to clothing and bookbindings. Synthetic leather has been made since about 1850; modern varieties are usually made from vinyl polymers. *See also* fur; parchment.

leatherback turtle The largest living turtle, *Dermochelys coriacea*, found worldwide. Up to 7 ft (2.1 m) long with a weight of 1200 lb (540 kg), it has no horny external shell and its bones are buried in a ridged leathery brown-black skin. It is a strong swimmer and feeds on marine invertebrates, especially large jellyfish. It is the sole member of its family, *Dermochelyidae*.

Leavis, F(rank) R(aymond) (1895–1978) British literary critic. The moral value of the study of literature was the primary conviction of his teaching at Cambridge University and of his critical journal *Scrutiny* (1932–53). His books include *The Great Tradition* (1948), *The Common Pursuit* (1952), and studies of D. H. *Lawrence (1955) and *Dickens (1970).

Lebanon A country in the Middle East, on the E coast of the Mediterranean Sea. It contains two mountain ranges (the Lebanon and Anti-Lebanon Mountains) extending N–S separated by the Beqaa Valley. The population is mixed, having Arab, Phoenician, Crusader, and Greek origins. Roughly half are Christian and half Muslim; political and official posts are rigorously divided between the two religions. *Economy*: Lebanon was once heavily forested and famous for its cedars, but much has been cleared and converted to arable use, which constitutes a significant part of the country's economy. The fertile Beqaa Valley is the main area of production but has suffered through fighting in the area. The extensive grazing of goats has also seriously depleted the forests and has caused widespread erosion. Industries include traditional crafts and there are two oil refineries, which process oil from Iraq and Saudi Arabia. Until the civil war of 1975–76, international trade, banking, and insurance were the major sources of income. *History*: Lebanon was an early convert to Christianity but in the 7th century broke away from the rest of the Church (*see* Maronite Church) and was invaded by Muslims. Crusaders received support from the Maronites in the 12th and 13th centuries, and Lebanon was held by the Mamelukes during the 14th and 15th centuries and by the Ottoman Turks from the early 16th century to 1918. France, having invaded Lebanon in 1861 to stop the massacres of Christians by Druzes, was given the mandate over Greater Lebanon after World War I. Lebanon became independent in 1941, although France retained control until 1945. In 1958, at the request of President Camille Chamoun (1900–   ), US troops were sent to quell a rebellion against his pro-Western policies. Lebanon did not fight in the 1967 and 1973 Arab-Israeli Wars, but Israel has continually made raids across the border in retaliation for Lebanon's harboring of Palestinian guerrillas. In 1975, a civil war broke out between Christians and Muslims, which lasted 19 months and resulted in virtual religious partition. It was brought to an end by intervention from a Syrian-backed Arab Deterrent Force but unrest continued, especially in the S. In 1982 Israel again invaded S Lebanon, clashing with Syrian forces in the Beqaa Valley and, after besieging Beirut, forced the Palestine Liberation Organization to leave. Bashir Gemayel (1947–82), the president-elect, was killed in a bomb explosion and his brother, Amin Gamayel (1942–   ) succeeded him. Violence continued with US and French troops in the multinational peacekeeping forces suffering heavy casualties in separate terrorist bomb attacks (1983). Leader of the Maronite Christian minority, Gemayel sought to extend his government's authority over bitterly hostile Muslim and Druze factions supported by Syria. Official language: Arabic. Official currency: Lebanese pound of 100 piastres. Area: 3927 sq mi (10,173 sq km). Population (1983 est): 2,598,000. Capital: Beirut.

Lebowa. *See* Bantu Homelands.

Le Brun, Charles (1619–90) French history and portrait painter and designer. During Louis XIV's reign he helped to make Paris the artistic center of Europe. He visited Rome (1642–46) with Poussin and was patronized by the finance minister Colbert and became First Painter to Louis XIV, for whom he decorated rooms in Versailles. He became director of the Gobelins tapestry works (1664) and of the French Academy (1683), which he had helped to found in 1648.

Le Carré, John (David Cornwell; 1931–   ) British novelist. He served in the foreign service in Germany (1961–64). His novels *The Spy Who Came in from the Cold* (1963), *Tinker, Tailor, Soldier, Spy* (1974), *Smiley's People* (1980), and *Little Drummer Girl* (1983), are realistic studies of the world of espionage.

Lecce 40 21N 18 11E A town in SE Italy, in Apulia. It has Roman remains, a 12th-century cathedral, and a university (1956). It has a wine industry. Population (1971): 82,175.

Lech River A river in central Europe. Rising in SW Austria, it flows mainly N through S West Germany and joins the Danube River. Length: 177 mi (285 km).

Le Châtelier, Henri-Louis (1850–1936) French chemist, who discovered (1888) **Le Châtelier's principle**, that a chemical system will react to a disturbance of its equilibrium by tending to compensate for the disturbance. He used this principle to assist in the foundation of chemical thermodynamics. He was also the first to use a thermocouple to measure high temperatures and invented an optical pyrometer.

Leconte de Lisle, Charles Marie René (1818–94) French poet. He was born on Réunion Island in the Indian Ocean and settled in Paris in 1846. His poetry, especially in *Poèmes antiques* (1852) and *Poèmes barbares* (1862), contains powerful descriptions of natural physical beauty. His disciples were known as the *Parnassians.

Lecoq de Boisbaudran, Paul-Émile (1838–1912) French chemist, who used the technique of spectroscopy, newly developed by *Bunsen and *Kirchhoff, to discover the element gallium (1874). He also discovered samarium (1879) and dysprosium (1886).

LE CORBUSIER

Le Corbusier (Charles-Édouard Jeanneret; 1887–1965) French architect, born in Switzerland, one of the most inventive artists of the 20th century. The influence of Le Corbusier's buildings and writings has been enormous. He trained under Auguste Perret (1874–1954) and *Behrens. His career falls into two parts. Until World War II he pioneered a rational, almost cubist, form of design, especially with his villas at Garches (1927) and Poissy (1929). Afterward he became more individual, for example at his extraordinary chapel at Ronchamp (1950; ☐architecture). He was also concerned with town planning (e.g. *Chandigarh, 1950s) and large-scale housing projects (L'Unité, Marseilles, 1945). As a member of the architectural panel, he also contributed much to the UN buildings in New York (1946).

Leda In Greek myth, the wife of Tyndareus, King of Sparta, and mother, either by her husband or by Zeus, of Clytemnestra, Helen, and Castor and Pollux. Helen was born from an egg after Zeus had visited Leda as a swan.

Lederberg, Joshua (1925–   ) US geneticist, who discovered the phenomenon of transduction in bacteria. Lederberg found that fragments of bacterial DNA could be transmitted from one bacterium to another by a virus. For this, together with his earlier work on bacterial sex factors, Lederberg shared a Nobel Prize (1958) with George *Beadle and Edward *Tatum.

Le Duc Tho (1911–) Vietnamese politician. He was a founder member of the Indochinese Communist Party (1930) and the Viet Minh (1945). His negotiations with Henry Kissinger toward the close of the *Vietnam War were instrumental in securing the ceasefire of 1973; the two men were jointly awarded the Nobel Peace Prize (1974) but Le Duc Tho refrained from accepting it.

Lee, Bruce (Lee Yuen Kam; 1940–73) US film actor and *kungfu expert, whose films include *Enter the Dragon*. He became famous for films made in Hong Kong, after only moderate success in Hollywood.

Lee, Francis Lightfoot (1734–97) US statesman; signer of the Declaration of Independence. A political leader in Virginia, he was a delegate to the Second Continental Congress (1775–79) and was instrumental in Virginia's ratification of the Constitution. His brother **Richard Henry Lee** (1732–94) was a statesman and orator. He was a delegate to the first and second Continental Congress; his resolution leading to the Declaration of Independence was adopted in 1776. He served in Congress (1784–87) but was against ratification of the Constitution because it lacked a bill of rights and advocated strong federal government. As a US senator (1789–92), he fought for adoption of the Bill of Rights (1791).

Lee, Gypsy Rose (Rose Louise Hovick; 1914–70) US entertainer, who brought grace and sophistication to the art of striptease. She appeared in the Ziegfeld Follies in 1936 and in several films. A film and a musical were based on her autobiography, *Gypsy* (1957).

ROBERT E. LEE *Confederate general who surrendered for the defeated Confederacy at Appomattox Court House in April 1865.*

Lee, Robert Edward (1807–70) US military leader and commander of Confederate forces during the Civil War. He graduated from West Point in 1829 and joined the Corps of Engineers. After service in the *Mexican War, Lee was appointed superintendent of West Point (1852–53). He was later transferred to Texas to command the frontier cavalry (1855–61). During a leave in Virginia in 1859, he led the federal forces that suppressed the raid of John *Brown on Harper's Ferry. At the outbreak of the *Civil War, Lee was offered the command of the US army by President Abraham Lincoln, but he declined that appointment to accept a commission as the head of Virginia's military forces. Lee saw his role as one of defending his native state, using superior mobility to defeat federal attacks in the Seven Days' battles, the second battle of Bull Run (1862), and Chancellorsville (1863). His subsequent loss at *Gettysburg, however, forced him to adopt a defensive strategy. Appointed general in chief of all Confederate armies in February 1865, he surrendered to US General Ulysses S. *Grant at Appomattox Courthouse on April 9. With the end of the war Lee urged reconciliation between North and South and ended his military career to become president of Washington College, which was later renamed Washington and Lee University as a tribute to him. His father, **Henry Lee** ("Lighthorse

Harry"; 1756–1818), was a US American Revolution soldier. He commanded a cavalry infantry unit during the Revolution (1775–83) and was responsible for the taking of the British fort at Paulus Hook, NJ, in 1779. He later served in the Carolina campaign and was at the surrender at Yorktown (1781). He returned to Virginia politics at the war's end and was governor of Virginia (1792–95) and in the US House of Representatives (1799–1801). His well-known words, "First in war, first in peace, and first in the hearts of his countrymen," eulogized George Washington.

Lee, Tsung-Dao (1926–) US physicist, born in China, who (working with his countryman Chen Ning *Yang) showed that parity is not conserved in *weak interactions. For this discovery the two shared the 1957 Nobel Prize.

leech A carnivorous aquatic *annelid worm of the class *Hirudinea* (about 300 species). Leeches inhabit fresh and salt water throughout the world and also occur in wet soil and rain forest. They have one sucker around the mouth and a second at the rear. Leeches can move by "looping," using their suckers. Most feed on the blood of animals and man, using specialized piercing mouthparts, but some species feed on insect larvae and earthworms.

Leeds 53 50N 1 35W A city in N England, the largest city in West Yorkshire on the River Aire. Canal links with Liverpool and Goole and the local outcropping of coal assisted in promoting Leeds as an important industrial and commercial center. Its main industries are clothing, textiles, printing, engineering, chemicals, and leather goods. The university was founded in 1904. Population (1981): 448,528.

leek A hardy biennial plant, *Allium porrum*, native to SW Asia and E Mediterranean regions and widely grown in Europe as a vegetable. The bulb is hardly differentiated from the stem, which bears long broad leaves. Cultivated leeks are grown from seed and the stems and leaves are eaten in the first year, before flowering. They are set deep in the soil to ensure blanching. The leek is the national emblem of Wales.

Lee Kuan Yew (1923–) Singaporean statesman; prime minister (1959–). As leader of the People's Action Party (PAP) from 1954, he advocated Singaporean self-government within the British Commonwealth and in 1958–59 helped to draft a constitution in preparation for independence. He agreed, in 1963, to lead Singapore into the Federation of Malaysia but constant dissensions led to Singapore's withdrawal in 1965. His government is authoritative and pro-Western.

Leeuwarden 53 12N 5 48E A city in the N Netherlands, the capital of Friesland province. An economic center with trade in cattle and dairy produce, its industries include engineering and glass production. It contains the notable Frisian museum. Population (1981 est): 84,367.

Leeuwenhoek, Antonie van (1632–1723) Dutch scientist, noted for his microscopic studies of living organisms. He was the first to describe protozoa, bacteria, and spermatozoa and he also made observations of yeasts, red blood cells, and blood capillaries. Among his many other achievements, Leeuwenhoek traced the life histories of various animals, including the flea, ant, and weevil; in so doing he refuted many popular misconceptions concerning their origin. Leeuwenhoek ground over 400 of his own lenses during his lifetime, achieving magnifications of up to 300 times with a single lens.

Leeward Islands 1. A West Indian group of islands in the Lesser Antilles, in the Caribbean Sea extending SE from Puerto Rico to the Windward Islands. 2. A former British colony in the West Indies (1871–1956), comprising Antigua, St Kitts-Nevis-Anguilla, Montserrat, and the British Virgin Islands. 3. A group of islands in the Netherlands Antilles, in the Caribbean Sea comprising St Eustatius, Saba, and part of St Martin. 4. A group of islands in French Polynesia, in the Society Islands in the S Pacific Ocean.

leg In human anatomy, the lower limb, which extends from the hip to the foot. The bone of the thigh (*see* femur) is connected by a ball-and-socket joint to the pelvis, permitting a wide range of movements. It forms a hinge joint at the knee with the bones of the lower leg—the shin bone (tibia) and the smaller fibula. This joint is overlain at the front by a bone (the patella, or kneecap) embedded in the tendon of the quadriceps muscle of the thigh.

Le Gallienne, Eva (1899–) US actress, producer, and director, born in England. She translated Henrik *Ibsen's works and played in many of them. Appearing on the New York stage from 1916, she starred in *Liliom* (1921) and in 1926 founded the Civic Repertory Theater, for which she produced many classical revivals, was co-founded by her in 1946. She directed *The Cherry Orchard* (1968) on Broadway. Her well-known roles included leading parts in *Camille* (1931), *Royal Family* (1975), and *To Grandmother's House We Go* (1981).

Legaspi 13 10N 123 45E A port in the E Philippines, in SE Luzon. It was severely damaged by the eruption of Mount *Mayon in 1815. Hemp and copra are exported. Population (1970): 84,090.

Legendre, Adrien Marie (1752–1833) French mathematician, who made important contributions to number theory and mathematical physics. Due to the jealousy of *Laplace, then the foremost mathematician in France, Legendre never in his lifetime received the recognition that he deserved.

Léger, Fernand (1881–1955) French painter, born in Argentan. He settled in Paris (1900) where, associated with *cubism, he produced robotlike figure paintings, followed by an abstract series entitled *Contrasts of Forms* (1913), consisting of brightly colored tubes. His experiences in World War I inspired the machine imagery of such paintings as *The City* (1919; Philadelphia) but later he often returned to the human figure. Broad areas of bright colors are the most characteristic feature of his work. He also painted murals, designed ballet sets, and made the first non-narrative film, *Le Ballet mécanique* (1924).

Leghorn (bird) A breed of domestic fowl originating in Italy and widely used in breeding commercial hybrids for egg laying. It has a full rounded breast, a flat sloping back, a short stout beak, long wattles, and a prominent comb in the male. The plumage can be of various colors, including black, blue, reddish brown, white, and black and white. Weight: 7.5 lb (3.4 kg) (cocks); 5.5 lb (2.5 km) (hens).

Leghorn (port). *See* Livorno.

legionnaires' disease An acute severe pneumonia, caused by the bacterium *Legionella pneumophila*, first described in 1976 after an outbreak among US legionnaires in Philadelphia. There have since been other outbreaks, in the US and other countries. The disease has a mortality rate of less than 5 per cent. The route of transmission is thought to be through air-conditioning systems contaminated by the bacteria.

Legion of Honor (French name: Légion d'Honneur) A French order of knighthood, established by Napoleon in 1802. Its five ranks, to which foreigners are admitted, are knight of the grand cross, grand officer, commander, officer, and chevalier. Its grand master is the president of France.

Legnica (German name: Liegnitz) 51 12N 16 10E An industrial city in SW Poland. Its manufactures include metal products, textiles, and chemicals. Population (1972 est): 77,900.

Leguminosae A worldwide family of herbs, shrubs, and trees (about 7000 species), which includes many important crop plants, such as peas, beans, clovers, and alfalfa. They all have compound leaves and the fruit is a pod containing a single row of seeds. Both pods and seeds are rich in protein. Most species possess root nodules that contain nitrogen-fixing bacteria and leguminous crops replenish nitrogen in the soil (*see* nitrogen cycle).

Lehár, Franz (Ferencz L.; 1870–1948) Hungarian composer. He studied at the Prague conservatoire and after a period as a military band conductor (1894–99) turned to the composition of operettas, of which *The Merry Widow* (1905) was his greatest success. Others include *The Count of Luxembourg* (1911) and *Land of Smiles* (1923).

Le Havre 49 30N 0 06E A port in N France, in the Seine-Maritimes department on the English Channel at the mouth of the Seine River. Severely damaged in World War II, its harbor was subsequently rebuilt and now maintains an important transatlantic cargo service and a car-ferry service to England. Population (1975): 219,583.

Lehmann, Lilli (1848–1929) German operatic soprano. She was taught by her mother. During a long career she sang many roles, including Brünnhilde in *Die Walküre*, Isolde, Donna Anna in *Don Giovanni*, and Leonora in *Fidelio*.

Lehmann, Lotte (1885–1976) German soprano, a US citizen from 1938. She studied in Berlin with Mathilde Mallinger (1847–1920) and became one of the most renowned dramatic sopranos of her time; her most famous role was the Marschallin in Richard Strauss' opera *Der Rosenkavalier*.

Leibniz, Gottfried Wilhelm (1646–1716) German philosopher and mathematician. He put forward a coherent philosophy, which is summarized in his two philosophical books, *New Essays on the Human Understanding* (c. 1705) and *Theodicy* (1710), and numerous essays. Leibniz' best-known doctrine is that the universe consists of an infinite set of independent substances (monads) in each of which a life force is present. In creating the world, God took account of the wishes of monads and this led to a rational harmony in the "best of all possible worlds"—a view satirized in *Voltaire's Candide*. As a rationalist Leibniz founded the distinction

between the logically necessary and the merely contingent truth. His claim to have invented the calculus was disputed by *Newton.

LOTTE LEHMANN

Leicester 52 38N 1 05W A city in central England, the administrative center of Leicestershire. Ancient Ratae Coritanorum on the Fosse Way, Leicester has many Roman remains including the Jewry Wall and sections of the forum and baths. Parts of the Norman castle also remain. The university was established in 1957. The principal industries are hosiery, knitwear, footwear, engineering, printing, plastics, and electronics. Population (1981): 279,791.

Leicester, Robert Dudley, Earl of (c. 1532–88) English courtier. Dudley's good looks attracted the attention of Elizabeth I, who made him Master of the Horse (1558) and then a privy councillor (1659). It was rumored that he might marry the queen after the death of his wife. His incompetent command (1685–87) of an English force against Spain led to his recall but he retained Elizabeth's favor until his death. He was a strong supporter of the Protestant cause.

Leiden (English name: Leyden) 52 10N 4 30E A city in the W Netherlands, in South Holland province. In 1574 it survived a Spanish siege by cutting the dikes and flooding the countryside. Its famous university was founded in 1575 as a reward for this heroic defense. During the 17th and 18th centuries it was an artistic and educational center. The painters Rembrandt and Lucas van Leyden were born here. Industries include textiles and metallurgy. Population (1981 est): 103,246.

Leif Eriksson (11th century) Icelandic explorer; the son of *Eric the Red. He was converted to Christianity by Olaf I Tryggvason of Norway around 1000. According to tradition, Erikson, on his way to promote the faith in Greenland, off course, became the first European to reach America. He landed in a region he called Vinland (Newfoundland or Nova Scotia). His story is told in Icelandic sagas.

Leigh, Vivien (Vivien Hartley; 1913–67) British actress. In the theater, she played many leading Shakespearean roles, frequently appearing with Laurence *Olivier, her husband from 1937 to 1960. Her films include *Gone with the Wind* (1939), in which she played the heroine Scarlett O'Hara, and *A Streetcar Named Desire* (1951).

Leinster A province in the SE Republic of Ireland. It consists of the counties of Carlow, Dublin, Kildare, Kilkenny, Laoighis, Longford, Louth, Meath, Offaly, Westmeath, Wexford, and Wicklow. It incorporates the ancient kingdoms of Meath and Leinster. Area: 7580 sq mi (19,632 sq km). Population (1979): 1,743,861.

Leipzig 51 20N 12 21E A city in S East Germany, near the confluence of the Elster, Pleisse, and Parthe Rivers. Important international trade fairs have been held in Leipzig since the middle ages. It was also the center of the German book and publishing industry until World War II. Notable buildings include the 15th-century Church of St Thomas and Auerbach's

Keller, an inn that provided the setting for Goethe's *Faust*. A famous musical center, the city has associations with J. S. Bach and Mendelssohn. The university was founded in 1409 and renamed Karl Marx University in 1952. Leipzig is the country's second largest city and one of its chief industrial and commercial centers. Its industries include iron and steel, chemicals, printing, and textiles. Population (1980 est): 563,388.

Leipzig, Battle of (or Battle of the Nations; October 16–19, 1813) The battle in which Napoleon was defeated by an alliance including Prussia, Russia, and Austria. The engagement culminated in the allies driving the French into Leipzig and then storming the city. The French army was shattered and its remnants retreated westward across the Rhine, ending Napoleon's empire in Germany and Poland.

leishmaniasis A tropical disease caused by infection with parasitic protozoans of the genus *Leishmania* (*see* Flagellata), which are transmitted to man by the bite of sandflies. The disease may affect the skin, causing open sores or ulcers, or the internal organs, principally the liver and spleen (this form of leishmaniasis is called **kala-azar**). Treatment is by means of drugs that destroy the parasites.

leitmotif (German: leading theme) A short musical phrase characterizing an object, person, state of mind, event, etc. *Wagner developed the technique of constructing large-scale compositions from leitmotifs in his mature operas, such as the cycle *Der Ring des Nibelungen*.

Leitrim (Irish name: Contae Liathdroma) A county in the NW Republic of Ireland, in Connacht bordering on Donegal Bay. Mainly hilly, descending to lowlands in the S, it contains several lakes, notably Lough Allen. Agriculture consists chiefly of cattle and sheep rearing; potatoes and oats are also grown. Area: 589 sq mi (1525 sq km). Population (1979): 27,844. County town: Carrick-on-Shannon.

Leix. *See* Laoighis.

Lely, Sir Peter (Pieter van der Faes; 1618–80) Portrait painter, born in Germany of Dutch parents. He studied and worked in Haarlem before settling in London (1641), where he was patronized by Charles I and later Cromwell. As court painter to Charles II from 1661, he produced his best-known works.

Lemaître, Georges Édouard, Abbé (1894–1966) Belgian priest and astronomer, who originated the *big-bang theory of the universe (1927). Lemaître based his theory on *Hubble's suggestion that the universe is expanding; it went unnoticed until *Eddington drew attention to it.

Léman, Lac. *See* Geneva, Lake.

Le Mans 48 00N 0 12E A city in NW France, the capital of the Sarthe department. Its many historical buildings include the cathedral (11th–15th centuries) in which Queen Berengaria (died c. 1290), the wife of Richard the Lionheart, is buried. The Le Mans Grand Prix, a 24-hour motor race, is held here annually. Le Mans is an agricultural, industrial, and commercial center. Population (1975): 155,245.

Lemberg. *See* Lvov.

lemming A *rodent belonging to the subfamily *Microtini* (which also includes voles), found in northern regions of Asia, America, and Europe. They range from 3 to 6 in (7.5 to 15 cm) in length and have long thick fur. When their food of grass, berries, and roots is abundant, they breed at a great rate but when food is scarce they migrate southward, often in large swarms crossing swamps, rivers, and other obstacles. Although able to swim, they sometimes drown through exhaustion. (Contrary to popular belief, they do not deliberately drown themselves.) Chief genera: *Dicrostonyx* (collared lemmings; 4 species), *Lemmus* (true lemmings; 4 species). Family *Cricetidae*. □mammal.

Lemnos (Modern Greek name: Límnos) A Greek island in the N Aegean Sea. Remains of the most advanced Neolithic communities in the Aegean have been found here. Area: 184 sq mi (477 sq km). Population (1971): 17,789.

lemon A small tree or shrub, *Citrus limon*, 3–6 m high, probably native to the E Mediterranean but widely cultivated in subtropical climates for its fruit. Its fragrant white flowers produce oval fruits with thick yellow skin and acid-tasting pulp rich in vitamin C. The juice is used as a flavoring in cookery and confectionery and as a drink. Family: *Rutaceae*.

lemon sole A *flatfish, *Microstomus kitt*, also called lemon dab, found in the NE Atlantic and North Sea. Up to 18 in (45 cm) long, its upper side is red-brown or yellow-brown with light or dark marbling. It is an important food fish. Family: *Pleuronectidae*.

lemur A small *prosimian primate belonging to the family *Lemuridae* (16 species), found only in Madagascar and neighboring islands. Lemurs are mostly arboreal and nocturnal and often live in groups, feeding mainly

on fruit, shoots, and leaves and also insects. The ring-tailed lemur (*Lemur catta*) is 28–37 in (70–95 cm) long including the tail (16–20 in [40–50 cm]) and is mainly terrestrial, sheltering among rocks and in caves. Dwarf lemurs (subfamily *Cheirogaleinae*) are only 10–20 in (25–50 cm) long including the tail (5–10 in [12–25 cm]).

Lemures In Roman religion, maleficent spirits of the dead. They haunted their former homes and were ritually appeased at the annual festival of the Lemuria, held in May.

Lena River The longest river in the Soviet Union. Rising in S Siberia, W of Lake Baikal, it flows mainly NE to the Laptev Sea. Its large delta, about 11,580 sq mi (30,000 sq km) in area, is frozen for about nine months of the year. Length: 2653 mi (4271 km).

Le Nain A family of French painters, natives of Laon, who established a workshop together in Paris (c. 1680). The individual contributions of **Antoine Le Nain** (c. 1588–1648), **Louis Le Nain** (c. 1593–1648), and **Mathieu Le Nain** (1607–77) are uncertain, since their works were not signed and some were probably joint efforts. Louis probably painted the dignified peasant scenes, such as *The Peasant's Meal* (Louvre); small-scale works on copper, often of family life, are credited to Antoine. All three became members of the newly established French Academy in 1648.

Lenclos, Ninon de (Anne de L.; 1620–1705) French courtesan, whose salon was the meeting place for many prominent literary and political figures of her day. She herself was much interested in Epicurean philosophy. Her lovers included *La Rochefoucauld and *Sévigné.

Lend-Lease Act (1941) Legislation introduced by President Roosevelt enabling Congress to lend or lease information, services, and defense items to any country vital to US defense. Britain and its World War II allies immediately received desperately needed planes, tanks, raw materials, and food.

L'Enfant, Pierre-Charles (1754–1825) French-born US architect and town planner. His principal achievement was his scheme for the design of Washington, DC (1791), which was a layout in a traditional French style, with long parallel avenues and dramatic focal points. The design was inspired by Versailles and a 16th century plan of Rome. Due to the expense involved, the plan was long abandoned. It was not executed until 1901.

Lenglen, Suzanne (1899–1938) French tennis player. She first won the Wimbledon singles in 1919 and subsequently was only once beaten in singles until 1926, when she turned professional. Her accurate play, grace, and daring dress did much to make tennis a spectator sport.

LENIN *Sitting at the center, surrounded by his colleagues in the St Petersburg Union for the Struggle for the Liberation of the Working Class (1895).*

Lenin, Vladimir Ilich (V. I. Ulyanov; 1870–1924) Russian revolutionary and first leader of communist Russia. Lenin became a Marxist after the execution (1887) of his brother Aleksandr for attempting to assassinate the tsar, Alexander III. In 1893 Lenin joined a revolutionary group in St Petersburg (subsequently renamed *Leningrad), where he practiced as a lawyer. In 1895 he was imprisoned and in 1897, exiled to Siberia, where he married (1898) Nadezhda Krupskaya, a fellow Marxist, with whom he worked closely throughout his career. In 1902 he published *What Is to Be Done?*, in which he emphasized the role of the party in effecting revolution. This emphasis led to a split in the Russian Social Democratic Workers' Party between the *Bolsheviks under Lenin and the *Mensheviks. After the failure of the *Revolution of 1905, Lenin again went into exile, settling in

Zurich in 1914, where he wrote *Imperialism, the Highest Stage of Capital-ism* (1917). In April, 1917, after the outbreak of the *Russian Revolution, Lenin returned to Russia. Calling for the transfer of power from the Provi-sional Government to the soviets (workers' councils), he was forced into hiding and then to flee to Finland. Lenin returned in October to lead the Bolshevik revolution, which overthrew the Provisional Government and established the ruling Soviet of People's Commissars under Lenin's chair-manship. He made peace with Germany and then led the revolutionaries to victory against the Whites in the civil war (1918–20). He founded (1919) the Third *International and initiated far-reaching social reforms, includ-ing the redistribution of land to the peasants, but in response to the disas-trous economic effects of the war he introduced the *New Economic Policy (1921), which permitted a modicum of free enterprise.

In 1918 Lenin was injured in an attempt on his life and a series of strokes from 1922 led to his premature death. *See also* Leninism.

Leninabad (name until 1936: Khodzhent) 59 55N 30 25E A city in the S central Soviet Union, in the Tadzhik SSR on the Syr Darya River. Locat-ed on the ancient *Silk Road, it supports a major silk industry. Consumer goods are also produced. Population (1981 est): 130,000.

Leninakan (name from 1840 until 1924: Aleksandropol) 40 47N 43 49E A city in the Soviet Union, in the NW Armenian SSR. Its textile industries are of major importance. Population (1981 est): 213,000.

Leningrad (name from 1703 until 1914: St Petersburg; name from 1914 until 1924: Petrograd) 59 55N 30 25E The second largest city in the Sovi-et Union and the capital of the Leningrad autonomous region (*oblast*), at the head of the Gulf of Finland on the Neva River. It is a major industrial and commercial center and its port, although frozen between January and April, is one of the largest in the world. Industries include heavy engineer-ing (particularly shipbuilding), metallurgy, electronics, chemicals, car manufacture, and light industries; the city is an important railroad junc-tion. Leningrad is rich in baroque and neoclassical buildings and is noted for its broad boulevards and many bridges and canals. The most notable buildings include the Peter-Paul Fortress (Leningrad's oldest building, founded in 1703), the Winter Palace (1754–62, rebuilt 1839), the Gostiny Dvor (1761–85), and Kazan cathedral (1801–11). The city is an important cultural center; it has a university (1918) and many museums, of which the Hermitage Museum, founded by Catherine the Great in 1764, is the most famous with its fine collection of European paintings. *History*: the city was founded (1703) by Peter the Great as a "window on Europe" and was the capital of Russia from 1712 until 1918, replacing Archangel as Russia's main seaport. In the late 19th century it developed as an important indus-trial center and from its labor force emerged several revolutionary parties, later united by Lenin to form the St Petersburg Union for the Struggle for the Liberation of the Working Class. In 1905 a general strike took place and on Bloody Sunday (January 9, 1905) more than a thousand people were killed in a march on the Winter Palace. Leningrad was also prominent in the 1917 revolution (*see* Russian Revolution). During World War II the city withstood a siege by the Germans (September 8, 1941–January 27, 1944), in which nearly a million people perished. In 1941 a road was constructed across frozen Lake Dadoga over which supplies could be brought. Leningrad was awarded the status of "Hero City" in recognition of its ordeal. Population (1981 est): 4,676,000.

Leninism Developments in the theory of scientific socialism (*see* Marx-ism) by V. I. *Lenin. His theory of imperialism is an account of the final stage of capitalism, in which it dominates the entire world, decisive control resting with finance capital (banks) as opposed to industrial capital. Be-cause of the worldwide nature of capitalism, socialist revolution becomes possible even in economically underdeveloped countries, the "weak link" of imperialism. According to his theory of the revolutionary party, the most conscious element of the proletariat provides the leadership for the rest of the working class and the peasantry in organizing the overthrow of the capitalist class.

Lenin Peak (Russian name: Pik Lenina) 39 21N 73 01E The second highest mountain in the Soviet Union, in the Trans-Altai range. Height: 23,406 ft (7134 m).

Leninsk-Kuznetskii (name from 1864 until 1925: Kolchugino) 40 37N 72 15E A city in the central S Soviet Union, in the RSFSR in the Kuznetsk Basin. Coalmining has been the most important industrial activi-ty since its foundation in 1864. Population (1977 est): 131,000.

Lenni-Lenape *See* Delaware.

Lennon, John (1940–80) British rock musician and founding member of the *Beatles. After the Beatles disbanded Lennon recorded solo albums, several of which featured his second wife, **Yoko Ono** (1933–). His most distinctive recording was *Imagine* (1971). He was assassinated in 1980.

Le Nôtre, André (1613–1700) French landscape gardener. Le Nôtre perfected the French version of the formal garden with his use of imposing vistas and was imitated throughout Europe. His first complete garden was at Vaux-le-Vicomte (1656–61) but his largest and most perfect was for Louis XIV at *Versailles, on which he worked for nearly 30 years.

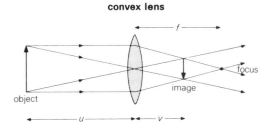

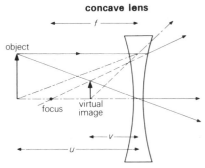

LENS *The lines representing light rays show how a convex lens gives a real inverted image and how a concave lens gives an upright virtual image.*

lens A piece of transparent material, usually glass, quartz, or plastic, used for directing and focusing beams of light. The surfaces of a lens have a constant curvature; if both sides curve outward at the middle the lens is called convex, if they curve inward it is concave. The image formed by a lens may be real, in which case the rays converge to the image point (a converging lens), or virtual, in which the rays diverge from the image point (a diverging lens). The focal length of a lens is the distance from the lens at which a parallel beam of light is brought to a focus. If the focal length of the lens is f, the rays from an object distance u from the lens are focused at a distance v from the lens, where $1/f = 1/u + 1/v$ and u, v, and f all obey certain sign conventions.

Lent The Christian period of fasting and penance preceding Easter. Be-ginning on *Ash Wednesday, the Lenten fast covers 40 days, in emulation of Christ's 40 days in the wilderness (Matthew 4.2). In the middle ages the fast was more or less strictly observed, especially with regard to the prohi-bition on eating meat, but since the Reformation the rules have been gener-ally relaxed in both Roman Catholic and Protestant Churches.

lentil An annual herb, *Lens culinaris*, native to the Near East but widely cultivated. Each pod produces 1–2 flat round green or reddish seeds, which are rich in protein and can be dried and stored for use in soups, stews, etc. Family: *Leguminosae*.

Lenya, Lotte (Caroline Blamauer; 1900–81) Austrian singer and char-acter actress, famous for her interpretations of the songs by her husband, the composer Kurt *Weill.

Lenz's law The direction of an induced current in a conductor is such as to oppose the cause of the induction. For example, a current induced by a conductor cutting the lines of flux of a magnetic field would produce a magnetic field of its own, which would oppose the original magnetic field. Named for Heinrich Lenz (1804–65).

Leo (Latin: Lion) A large conspicuous constellation in the N sky near Ursa Major, lying on the *zodiac between Virgo and Cancer. The brightest stars are the 1st-magnitude Regulus, which lies at the base of the **Sickle of Leo**, and the 2nd-magnitude Denebola and Algeiba.

Leo (I) the Great, St (d. 461 AD) Pope (440–61). One of the greatest medieval popes, Leo was largely successful in his attempts to extend papal control in the West after the fall of the western Roman Empire, but he failed to find support in the East. His treaties with the invading *Huns (452) and *Vandals (455) protected Rome from their onslaughts. His Christology, expressed in the *Epistola Dogmatica* (or *Tome of Leo*; 449), defined the doctrine of the Incarnation and was accepted at the Council of Chalcedon (451). Feast day: April 11.

Leo (III) the Isaurian (c. 675–741 AD) Byzantine emperor (717–41). He repulsed a Muslim attack on Constantinople in 718 and finally secured Asia Minor in 740 after a great victory over the Muslims at Acroïnon. In 730 he issued a decree that established the policy of *iconoclasm (the destruction of Christian images).

Leo III, St (d. 816 AD) Pope (795–816). After his election he was opposed by a Roman faction and was forced to flee to *Charlemagne, who supported his return to Rome. There, in 800, Leo crowned Charlemagne Emperor of the West—an act that marks the start of the Holy Roman Empire. His rule was noted for its munificent church building. He was canonized in 1673. Feast day: June 12.

Leo IX, St (Bruno of Egisheim; 1002–54) Pope (1049–54), the first of the great medieval reforming popes. At successive councils clerical marriage and simony were condemned and, assisted by Hildebrand (later *Gregory VII) and Humbert of Moyenmoutier (c. 1000–61), he attempted to free the papacy from imperial control. Rival claims with the Normans to gain control of S Italy resulted in Leo's defeat at the battle of Civitella (1053). His conflict with the Eastern Church led to the schism between Rome and Constantinople (1054; *see* Filioque). Feast day: April 19.

Leo X (Giovanni de' Medici; 1475–1521) Pope (1513–21), the second son of Lorenzo the Magnificent (*see* Medici), by whose influence Giovanni was made a cardinal in 1489. His pontificate was marked by political vacillation and financial disasters but lavish patronage of the arts. He negotiated the Concordat of Bologna (1516) with Francis I, giving the French crown almost total control over ecclesiastical appointments in France.

Leo XIII (Vincenzo Gioacchino Pecci; 1810–1903) Pope (1878–1903). Elected after a long career as a papal diplomat, Leo fostered relations between the papacy and European powers, the US, and Japan. He also encouraged learning, foreign missions, and lay piety. His encyclical *Rerum novarum* (*Of New Things*; 1891), while condemning socialism, emphasized the duty of the Church in matters of social justice.

LEONARDO DA VINCI *This head of an old man, drawn after 1515, is possibly a self-portrait of the artist.*

León (*or* León de los Aldamas) 21 10N 101 42W A city in central Mexico. It is a commercial and distribution center; industries include the manufacture of footwear and leather goods. Population (1978 est): 589,950.

León 42 35N 5 34W A city in NW Spain, in León. Formerly capital of the kingdom of León, it declined after the 13th century. Medieval in atmosphere, it has a notable gothic cathedral. Population (1974 est): 118,926.

León 12 24N 86 52W A city in W Nicaragua. Moved to its present site after the original city near Lake Managua was destroyed by an earthquake in 1610, it was the capital of Nicaragua until 1855. It is the country's cultural center and has a university (1812). Industries include textiles, distilleries, tanneries, and food processing. Population (1978 est): 81,647.

Leonardo da Vinci (1452–1519) Italian artistic and scientific genius of the *Renaissance, born in Vinci, the illegitimate son of a notary. He trained in Florence under *Verrocchio and painted the *Adoration of the Magi* (Uffizi) for the monks of S Donato a Scopeto (1481). In 1482 he became painter, engineer, and designer to Duke Ludovico Sforza in Milan, where he painted the fresco of the *Last Supper* (Sta Maria delle Grazie) and the first version of the *Virgin of the Rocks* (Louvre). His promised equestrian sculpture glorifying the Duke was never cast but the studies of horses for the project have survived. After the French invasion of Milan (1499), he returned to Florence, becoming military engineer and architect (1502) to Cesare *Borgia. Paintings in this period include the *Battle of Anghiari* for the Palazzo Vecchio, *The Virgin and Child with St John the Baptist and St Anne* (painting, Louvre; cartoon, National Gallery, London) and the *Mona Lisa* (Louvre). Some of his paintings were left unfinished and others, because of his experimental techniques, failed to survive. After working again in Milan (1506–13) and in Rome (1513–15), he was invited by Francis I to France (1516), where he spent his last years in Cloux near Amboise. His notebooks reveal his wide range of interests, including anatomy, botany, geology, hydraulics, and mechanics.

Leoncavallo, Ruggiero (1858–1919) Italian composer of operas. Only *I Pagliacci* (1892) has met with continuing success, although he composed over 15, including a trilogy on Italian historical subjects and, a year after Puccini, his own *La Bohème* (1897).

Leonidas I (d. 480 BC) King of Sparta (?490–480), following the suicide of his half-brother Cleomenes. Leonidas was the hero of the battle of *Thermopylae, in which with indomitable courage he and a small force held the pass for three days before being killed by the Persians.

Leonov, Leonid (1899–) Soviet novelist and playwright. His moral and psychological themes were most powerfully expressed in his early novels, notably *Barsuki* (*The Badgers*; 1924) and *Vor* (*The Thief*; 1927). His later novels are politically and stylistically more orthodox.

Leontief, Wasily (1906–) US economist, born in Russia. He won the Nobel Prize for economics in 1973. After he left the USSR (1925), he worked in Germany and China before coming to the US, where he taught at Harvard University (1931–75). His input-output theory explained the interaction of economic changes and became an international economic forecasting tool. He wrote *The Structure of American Economy* (1919–29) and *Input-Output Economics* (1966).

leopard A large spotted *cat, *Panthera pardus*, found throughout Africa and most of Asia. Leopards are slender, up to 7 ft (2.1 m) long including the 35-in (90-cm) tail, having a yellow coat spotted with black rosettes. Color variations, such as the *panther, sometimes occur. Leopards are solitary and nocturnal, typically lying in wait in a tree for their prey, which includes monkeys, dogs, and antelopes.

Leopardi, Giacomo (1798–1837) Italian poet. His pessimistic philosophy, which is most fully expressed in the long poem *La ginestra* (1836), was largely conditioned by his unhappy home background, his poor health, and his failure in love. He is best known for the intense lyric poetry of *I canti* (1831). He died of cholera in Naples.

leopard lily A perennial herbaceous plant, *Belamcanda chinensis*, also called blackberry lily, native to E Asia and widely planted as a garden ornamental. Growing over 40 in (1 m) tall from an underground stem (rhizome), it has sword-shaped leaves, orange-spotted red flowers, and blackberry-like clusters of seeds. Family: *Iridaceae*.

The name is also given to several other garden flowers, including the snake's head *fritillary and a North American lily (*Lilium pardalinum*).

leopard seal A solitary Antarctic *seal, *Hydrurga leptonyx*, of the pack ice. Leopard seals are fast agile hunters, feeding mainly on penguins. Gray, with dark spots and blotches, females grow to 12 ft (3.7 m) and males to 10 ft (3.2 m). Family: *Phocidae*.

Leopold I (1640–1705) Holy Roman Emperor (1658–1705). Leopold was ultimately successful against the Turks, who had besieged Vienna in

1683, freeing most of Hungary from Turkish dominance by 1699. He also came into conflict with Louis XIV of France, whose claims to the Spanish throne he opposed in the War of the *Spanish Succession. Under Leopold, Vienna became a great European center.

Leopold I (1790–1865) The first King of the Belgians (1831–65). He defended Belgium against William III of the Netherlands (1817–90; reigned 1849–90), who refused to recognize Belgian independence until 1838. A leading diplomat in Europe, at home he encouraged educational and economic reforms. A member of the House of Saxe-Coburg-Saalfield (previously Gotha), he helped to negotiate the marriage of his niece Queen Victoria to Prince Albert.

Leopold II (1797–1870) Grandduke of Tuscany (1824–59). Initially a liberal who granted a constitution in 1848, he became increasingly reactionary after a brief period in exile in 1849 and was forced by radical opposition to abdicate.

Leopold II (1835–1909) King of the Belgians (1865–1909), who sponsored Stanley's exploration of the Congo region of Africa. In 1885 he obtained European recognition of his sovereignty over the Congo Free State, which was annexed as the Belgian Congo in 1908.

Leopold III (1901–83) King of the Belgians (1934–51). He surrendered to the Germans in *World War II, provoking opposition to his return to Belgium in 1945 and forcing his abdication in favor of his son *Baudouin.

Léopoldville. *See* Kinshasa.

Lepanto, Battle of (October 7, 1571) A naval battle off Lepanto, Greece, in which the *Holy League routed the Ottoman navy, which was threatening to dominate the Mediterranean. The Christian force, commanded by *John of Austria, was composed of about 30,000 fighting men, of which over 7000 died. Some 15,000 Turks were killed or captured and 10,000 Christian galley slaves were freed.

Lepidodendron An extinct genus of treelike pteridophytes that—with *Calamites—were dominant forest trees of the Carboniferous period (370–280 million years ago), their fossilized remains forming coal seams. Some species were over 96 ft (30 m) high and 40 in (1 m) wide. Class: *Lycopsida* (clubmosses, etc.).

Lepidoptera. *See* butterflies and moths.

Lepidus, Marcus Aemilius (died c. 13 BC) Roman politician and protégé of Julius Caesar. After Caesar's death, Lepidus joined Antony and Octavian in the second Triumvirate (43 BC), which divided responsibility for the empire, but in 42 they deprived him of his provincial governorships. In 36 Lepidus attempted to secure Sicily and was forced by Octavian to retire.

leprosy A chronic disease, occurring almost entirely in tropical countries, caused by the bacterium *Mycobacterium leprae* (which is related to the tuberculosis bacillus). The incubation period is usually one to three years and—contrary to popular belief—leprosy is contracted only after close personal contact with an infected person. In the lepromatous form of the disease lumps appear on the skin, which—together with the nerves—becomes thickened and progressively destroyed, resulting in disfigurement and deformity. Eyes, bones, and muscles may also be affected. Tuberculoid leprosy usually produces only discolored patches on the skin associated with loss of sensation in the affected areas. There are now potent drugs—sulfones—available to cure the disease.

Leptis Magna An ancient trading center near present-day Homs (Libya). Founded by the Phoenicians (6th century BC) Leptis' importance increased during Roman imperial times; ruins of unusually splendid public buildings attest its former grandeur.

lepton A group of elementary particles, consisting of the *electron, *muon, *tau particle, *neutrinos, and their antiparticles. They take part only in the *weak and *electromagnetic interactions; together with *quarks and photons they are thought to be the only truly elementary particles. *See* particle physics.

Le Puy 45 03N 3 53E A city in S France, the capital of the Haute-Loire department. It has a 12th-century cathedral and is famous for its lace making. Population (1975): 29,024.

Lérida 41 37N 0 38E A city in NE Spain, in Catalonia. It possesses two cathedrals and a massive Moorish castle. An agricultural center, its industries include glass and silk. Population (1974 est): 102,489.

Lermontov, Mikhail (1814–41) Russian poet and novelist. His early Romantic poetry, published while he was a student at Moscow University, was greatly influenced by *Byron. As an army officer and an observer of high society he developed the cynical attitudes expressed in his novel *A*

Hero of Our Time (1840). He was twice exiled to the Caucasus, the first time for a poem attacking the court, and was killed in a duel.

Lerner, Alan Jay (1918–) US lyricist and librettist, who collaborated with the composer Frederick *Loewe in the musicals *Brigadoon* (1947), *My Fair Lady* (1956), and *Camelot* (1960). Lerner also wrote the film scripts for *An American in Paris* (1951) and *Gigi* (1958).

Lesage, Alain-René (1668–1747) French novelist. His best-known work is the picaresque novel *Gil Blas* (1715–35). He also made translations and satirical adaptations of Spanish plays as well as writing over 60 plays and librettos of his own.

lesbianism. *See* homosexuality.

Lesbos (Modern Greek name: Lésvos) A Greek island in the E Aegean Sea, situated close to the mainland of Turkey. Settled by Aeolians about 1000 BC, it is associated with the development of Greek lyric poetry (especially through the work of Alcaeus and Sappho). Lesbos was a member of the Delian League and the chief town, Mytilene, was made a free port in the era of Roman power. Olives, grapes, and cereals are grown here and there is sardine fishing. Area: 629 sq mi (1630 sq km). Population (1971): 114,802.

Leschetizky, Theodor (1830–1915) Polish pianist and piano teacher. His method influenced a generation of pianists, including Paderewski. He was a pupil of Czerny in Vienna and moved to St Petersburg in 1852, becoming head of the piano department at the conservatoire.

LESOTHO *The architecture of this handcraft center at Maseru was inspired by the huts of the Sotho; the decorative top is based on the Mokorotla, the traditional head gear.*

Lesotho, Kingdom of (name until 1966: Basutoland) A small country in SE Africa, enclosed by South Africa. It is largely mountainous, rising to 11,000 ft (3350 m). Most of the inhabitants are *Sotho. *Economy*: chiefly agricultural, the main crops being maize, wheat, and sorghum. Livestock is important but soil erosion due to overgrazing is a serious problem. The main exports, along with diamonds, are cattle, wool, and mohair. Some industry, including tourism, is being developed, but a large proportion of the male population still work in South African mines. *History*: Originally inhabited by San (Bushmen), Lesotho received many refugees of tribal warfare in the 17th and 18th century, and in the 19th century the disparate inhabitants of the country were consolidated into the Basuto tribe by Chief Moshesh. In 1884, following warfare with the Orange Free State, Basutoland came under British protection on the request of Chief Moshesh to protect his people from Boer incursions. When the Union of South Africa was formed in 1910, Basutoland resisted incorporation, but was placed under the authority of the British High Commission in South Africa. In 1966 Lesotho became an independent kingdom within the Commonwealth under King Moshoeshoe II (1939–). A state of emergency existed from 1970 to 1973 and the political climate continues to be unsettled. Prime minister: Chief Leabua Jonathan (1914–). Official languages: Sesotho and English. Official currency: South African rand of 100 cents. Area: 11,716 sq mi (30,340 sq km). Population (1983): 1,438,000. Capital: Maseru.

Lesseps, Ferdinand de (1805–94) French diplomat, who supervised the construction of the Suez Canal, which was completed in 1869. A subsequent project to construct the Panama Canal ended in disaster when Lesseps was prosecuted for embezzling funds.

Lesser Antilles (former name: Caribbees)   A West Indian group of islands, comprising a chain extending from Puerto Rico to the N coast of Venezuela. They include the Leeward and Windward Islands, Barbados, Trinidad and Tobago, and the Netherlands Antilles.

Lessing, Doris   (1919–) British novelist. Born in Iran and brought up in Rhodesia, she came to England in 1949. Political and social themes predominate in her fiction, notably the sequence of five novels entitled *Children of Violence* (1952–69) and *The Golden Notebook* (1962). Later novels include *Memoirs of a Survivor* (1974). She began a series of futuristic science fiction novels with *Marriages Between Zones Three, Four and Five* (1980).

Lessing, Gotthold Ephraim   (1729–81) German dramatist and writer. After studying theology and medicine, he worked as a translator and critic. His *Miss Sara Sampson* (1755) was the first successful German tragedy to reject the classical French model and to use middle-class protagonists, while his comedy *Minna von Barnhelm* (1767) demonstrates the *Enlightenment ideal of reason. In 1765 he was involved in an unsuccessful attempt to create a German national theater; in his influential essays, the *Hamburgische Dramaturgie* (1767–69), he developed his dramatic theories.

Le Tellier, Michel.   *See* Louvois, Michel Le Tellier, Marquis de.

Lethbridge 49 43N 112 48W A city in W Canada, in S Alberta. Founded in 1870 as a coalmining center, it has become an agricultural, distribution, and research center, housing the University of Lethbridge (1967). Most industry is agriculturally based. Population (1976): 46,752.

Lethe   In Greek and Roman mythology, a river in the underworld, the water of which caused those who drank it to forget their former lives.

Leto   In Greek mythology, a daughter of the *Titans loved by Zeus. During her pregnancy she was not welcomed anywhere because of the fear of Hera and was forced to give birth to Apollo and Artemis on the barren island of Delos.

letter of credit   A letter from a bank to a foreign bank authorizing the payment of a specified sum to the person or company named. They are widely used as a means of paying for goods in foreign trade. An **irrevocable letter of credit** cannot be cancelled by the purchaser or the issuing bank. A **confirmed letter of credit** guarantees payment to the beneficiary should the issuing bank fail to honor it. A confirmed irrevocable letter of credit opened at a first-class bank is a safe basis for trading, although it must be negotiated before its expiration date. Unconfirmed or revocable letters of credit do not have great value.

Lettish.   *See* Latvian.

lettres de cachet   (French: letters of the seal) Administrative and judicial orders issued by the Kings of France. They were much misused during the 17th and 18th centuries to authorize arrest and imprisonment without trial or appeal. As symbols of the monarchy's despotism they were abolished (1790) during the French Revolution.

lettuce   An annual herb, *Lactuca sativa*, probably from the Near East and widely cultivated as a salad plant. It has a tight rosette of juicy leaves, rich in vitamin A, and is usually eaten fresh or cooked in soups. Family: *Compositae.

Leucippus   (5th century BC) Greek philosopher. He developed from the teachings of *Parmenides the theory that there are two ultimate realities: (1) an infinite number of tiny irreducible particles (atoms), randomly circulating in (2) empty space. This theory is remarkably close to modern *atomic theory. *See also* Democritus of Abdera.

leucite   A feldspathoid mineral of composition $KAl(SiO_3)_2$, occurring as whitish or grayish crystals in some volcanic rocks deficient in silica. Where sufficiently concentrated it is a source of potash.

Leuckart, Karl Georg Friedrich Rudolph   (1822–98) German zoologist, who founded the science of parasitology. Leuckart described the life cycles of tapeworms and the liver fluke and revealed the importance of wormlike parasites in causing diseases in man.

Leuctra, Battle of   (371 BC) The battle in which the reorganized Theban army under *Epaminondas crushed the Spartan invasion of Boeotia in Sparta's first major defeat on land. Sparta's resultant loss of influence allowed Thebes a short-lived ascendency in Greece.

leukemia   A disease in which the blood contains an abnormally large number of white blood cells (*see* leukocyte). Leukemia is a type of cancer of the blood-forming tissues, which undergo uncontrolled proliferation to produce many immature and abnormal white blood cells that do not func-

tion properly. Leukemias may be acute or chronic, depending on the rate of progression of the disease. They are also classified according to the type of white cell affected. For example acute lymphocytic leukemia (affecting the lymphocytes) occurs most commonly in children and young adults; it can now often be controlled by means of radiotherapy or *cytotoxic drugs. Chronic leukemias occur more often in old people and may not need any treatment.

leukocyte   (*or* white blood cell) A colorless *blood cell, up to 0.008 in (0.02 mm) in diameter, of which there are normally 4000–11,000 per cubic millimeter of blood. There are several kinds, all involved in the body's defense mechanisms. Granulocytes (*or* polymorphs), which have granules in their cytoplasm, and monocytes ingest and feed on bacteria and other microorganisms that cause infection (*see also* phagocyte). The lymphocytes are involved with the production of *antibodies. Cancer of the white blood cells is called *leukemia.

leukotomy   The surgical operation of interrupting the course of white nerve fibers within the brain. It is performed to relieve uncontrollable pain or emotional tension in very severe and intractable psychiatric illnesses, such as severe depression, chronic anxiety, and obsessional neurosis. The original form of the operation—prefrontal leukotomy (*or* lobotomy)—had the serious complication of epilepsy, apathy, and irresponsibility. Modern procedures make small and selective lesions and side effects are uncommon. *See also* psychosurgery.

Leuven.   *See* Louvain.

Levant   A former name for the lands on the E coast of the Mediterranean Sea, now within Turkey, Syria, Lebanon, and Israel. The French mandates (1920–46) of Syria and Lebanon were known as the Levant States.

Le Vau, Louis   (1612–70) French *baroque architect. His first building, the Hôtel Lambert, Paris (1642), was remarkable for its ingenious room planning. As first architect to the crown from 1654, he completed the Louvre, built the Collège des Quatre Nations (begun 1661), and designed the first extension of *Versailles (1669), which was later obliterated by the work of *Hardouin-Mansart. His most famous building is Vaux-le-Vicomte (begun in 1657), a chateau outside Paris built for Nicolas Fouquet.

level **1.** An instrument (also called a spirit level) for indicating whether or not a surface is level. It consists of a sealed glass tube containing spirit (alcohol) and a bubble of gas. The tube is mounted so that the wooden or metal frame supporting it is level when the bubble is in the center of the tube. **2.** An instrument for obtaining a horizontal line of sight. It consists of a telescope with cross hairs on both sights together with a parallel tubular spirit level, mounted on a tripod. Leveling is achieved by means of screw legs on the tripod table.

Levellers   An extremist English Puritan sect, active 1647–49. Led by the pamphleteer John *Lilburne, they campaigned for a written constitution, radical extension of the franchise, and abolition of the monarchy and of other social distinctions. Oliver Cromwell's refusal to execute this program led to mutinies (1647, 1649). After suppression of the last of these, the Levellers lost their identity and influence. *See also* Diggers.

Leverkusen 51 02N 6 59E A city in NW West Germany, in North Rhine-Westphalia on the Rhine River. It is the site of the large Bayer chemical works. Population (1980 est): 161,500.

Leverrier, Urbain Jean Joseph   (1811–77) French astronomer, who predicted the existence of the planet *Neptune (1846) after investigating anomalies in the orbit of Uranus. John *Adams had made similar calculations but the planet was actually first observed by Johann Galle (1812–1910), the German astronomer, in 1846 on information supplied by Leverrier.

Lévesque, René   (1922–) French Canadian politician. An advocate of French separatism, in 1968 he founded the Parti Québecois and in 1976 became Quebec's prime minister. He is the author of *Option Quebec* (1968).

Leviathan   An animal mentioned in several passages (Job, Isaiah, Psalms) of the Old Testament and variously interpreted as referring to the whale or crocodile. Leviathan was mythologically associated with evil and the devil.

Levine, James   (1943–) US pianist and musical conductor and director. A child prodigy, he performed on the piano from six years old and played with the Cincinnati Symphony Orchestra in 1953. He studied conducting at the Juilliard School. He became principal conductor of the Metropolitan Opera (1972) and also its musical director (1976).

Lévi-Strauss, Claude   (1908–) French anthropologist, famous as the founder of structural anthropology. After teaching in America, Lévi-Strauss became professor of ethnology at the University of Paris in 1948 and in 1959 professor of anthropology at the Collège de France. His works include *The Elementary Structures of Kinship* (1949), *Structural Anthropology* (1958), and *From Honey to Ashes* (1967).

Levites   In ancient Israel, the descendants of Levi, the son of Jacob and Leah, who formed one of the 12 *tribes of Israel and became the priestly caste. They were not allocated a specific territory in Palestine but only scattered settlements with grazing rights and they were partly supported by offerings. After the *Babylonian exile, the priesthood was confined to those Levites descended from Aaron.

Leviticus   The third book of the Old Testament, attributed to Moses and concerned with religious and ceremonial law. Its purpose is to give instruction in the laws governing sacrifice and purification, in which the priestly caste of *Levites officiate. It also relates the laws governing diet, hygiene, the five annual national feasts, the use of land, and personal chastity.

Lewes   50 52N 0 01E A market city in SE England, the administrative center of East Sussex, on the River Ouse. At the battle of Lewes (1264) Henry III was defeated by the rebel barons under Simon de Montfort. *Glyndebourne is nearby. Population (1981): 13,770.

Lewis, C. Day.   *See* Day Lewis, C(ecil).

Lewis, C(live) S(taples)   (1898–1963) British scholar and writer. He taught at Oxford University from 1925 to 1954 and at Cambridge University from 1954 to 1963. He wrote science-fiction novels, including *Out of the Silent Planet* (1938), children's books chronicling the land of Narnia, and works on religious and moral themes, notably *The Problem of Pain* (1940), *The Screwtape Letters* (1942) and *Mere Christianity* (1952).

Lewis, John L(lewellyn)   (1880–1969) US labor leader; president of United Mine Workers of America (UMW) (1920–60) and *Congress of Industrial Organizations (CIO) (1935–40). He worked his way up in the ranks of the UMW, an affiliate of the American Federation of Labor (AFL). When he organized what became the Congress of Industrial Organizations for industrial workers in 1935, he and his union were expelled from the AFL. As president of the independent CIO he unionized the steel and automobile industries, often using violent methods. He withdrew the UMW from the CIO in 1942. His union practices were the impetus for the passage of the Smith-Connally Anti-Strike Act (1943) and the Taft-Hartley Act (1947), laws that restricted unions.

Lewis, (Harry) Sinclair   (1885–1951) US novelist. He established his reputation with *Main Street* (1920), a satire on small-town materialism. His other social satires include *Babbitt* (1922), in which he portrayed the archetypal well-meaning but dehumanized businessman; *Arrowsmith* (1925), about an idealistic doctor; and *Elmer Gantry* (1927) a scathing portrait of an evangelical minister. He was the first US writer to win the Nobel Prize (1930). His later novels, such as *Cass Timberlane* (1945) and *Kingsblood Royal* (1947), were less successful.

Lewis, (Percy) Wyndham   (1882–1957) British novelist and painter. After studying art in London and Paris, he helped found *vorticism, the manifestos of which were published in *Blast*, a journal he co-founded with Ezra Pound in 1914. In many polemical works and brilliant satirical novels, which include *The Apes of God* (1930) and the trilogy *The Human Age* (1928–55), he sustained a continual attack on the liberal cultural establishment.

Lewis and Clark expedition   (1804–06) A journey of exploration across the American continent by Meriwether Lewis (1774–1809) and William Clark (1770–1838). Starting in the spring of 1804 they ascended the Missouri, reaching the area of Bismarck, N. Dak., by winter. The next year they crossed the Rockies, greatly aided by the Indian girl Sacajawea. Finally they descended the Columbia River to the Pacific, exploring the Yellowstone River on the return journey to Saint Louis, which they reached in September 1806. Promoted by Thomas Jefferson, the expedition established the US claim to the vast lands of the Louisiana Purchase.

lewisite (*or* chlorovinyl dichloroarsine; $ClCH:CHAsCl_2$)   A colorless volatile liquid that causes blistering of the skin and is used as a war gas. It can be destroyed by oxidizing agents such as *bleaching powder. Named for the US chemist W. L. Lewis (1878–1943).

Lewis with Harris   The largest island of the Outer Hebrides, separated from the coast of NW Scotland by the Minch. Often referred to as separate islands, Lewis in the N is linked with Harris by a narrow isthmus; its most northerly point is the Butt of Lewis. The main occupations are crofting, sheep farming, fishing, and the weaving of the famous Harris tweed. Area: 824 sq mi (2134 sq km). Population (1971): 23,188. Chief town: Stornoway.

lexicography   The compilation of dictionaries. Dictionaries can be monolingual (dealing with only one language) or bi- or multi-lingual (giving equivalents of words in other languages). Both were known in antiquity. Monolingual dictionaries differ in the style and fullness of the definitions, in the audience for which they are intended (e.g. for native speakers or foreign learners), and in the principles on which they are compiled. Some are on historical principles (listing definitions of a word in historical order) while others take the language as it is at the time of compilation (listing definitions in order of current usage). Some dictionaries are prescriptive in that they set out to tell the user how the language should be used; most modern dictionaries tend to be only descriptive, recording without comment the way words are currently used. Almost all dictionaries contain information about spelling and meaning; many also offer guidance on pronunciation, usage, inflected forms of words, *etymology, etc.

The earliest English dictionary was *A Table Alphabeticall of Hard Words* (1604) by Robert Cawdrey; the most famous are Samuel *Johnson's *Dictionary* (1755), the *Oxford English Dictionary on Historical Principles* (1884–1928; chief editor Sir James *Murray), and Noah *Webster's *American Dictionary of the English Language* (1828). Both the Oxford and Webster's have several updated and shortened modern versions.

Lexington   38 02N 84 37W A city in Kentucky. A major horse-breeding center, Lexington is the market and distribution center for E Kentucky's farm produce, oil, and coal. The University of Kentucky was established here in 1865. Population (1980): 204,165.

Lexington   37 47N 79 27W A city in W central Virginia, NE in the Shenandoah Valley. Virginia Military Institute (1839) and Washington and Lee University (1749) are here, as are the graves of Robert E. Lee and Stonewall Jackson. Population (1980): 7292.

Lexington and Concord, Battle of   (April 19, 1775) The first battle in the *American Revolution. British troops led by Lieutenant Colonel Francis Smith intending to destroy American supplies of gunpowder were attacked at Lexington by militiamen under Captain John Parker alerted by Paul *Revere. Going on to Concord they destroyed the stores but were then attacked and forced to retreat to Boston, suffering many casualties.

Leyden.   *See* Leiden.

Leyden jar   An early form of *capacitor, consisting of a glass jar coated with tinfoil on part of its inner and outer surfaces. Named for Leiden (*or* Leyden), the town in the Netherlands in which it was invented.

Leyland   53 42N 2 42W A town in NW England, in Lancashire. Leyland has an important commercial motor vehicle industry and also produces tires, paints, carpets, and cottons. Population (1981): 26,567.

Leyte Gulf, Battle of   (October 23–26, 1944) The battle in World War II in which a US armada of 250,000 men commanded by General MacArthur defeated almost the entire Japanese navy. It initiated the reconquest of the Philippines and US command of the Pacific.

Lhasa   29 41N 91 10E A city in W China, the capital of Tibet, surrounded by mountains. As the traditional center of *Tibetan Buddhism, it is the site of many temples, monasteries, and of the Potala, the former palace of the Dalai Lama, the priest-ruler. Tibet's trading center, it has many traditional handicrafts and some light industry. *History*: the Tibetan capital since 1642, it was closed to foreigners in the 19th century. Before the Chinese occupation (1951) monks comprised half the population. Since then many Tibetans have fled, including the Dalai Lama following the 1959 uprising, while much Chinese immigration has taken place. Population (1960 est): 85,000.

Liaodong Peninsula (*or* Liaotung Peninsula)   A mountainous peninsula in NE China, in Liaoning province. After rivalry with Russia (1895–1905; *see* Sino-Japanese War; Russo-Japanese War) Japan occupied its strategic S harbors (1905–45).

Liaoning   A province in NE China, on the Yellow Sea in S Manchuria. The Japanese controlled it (1905–45) and developed its industry. Rich in coal and iron, it is an important industrial area. Area: 58,500 sq mi (150,000 sq km). Population (1976 est): 33,000,000. Capital: Shenyang.

Libau.   *See* Liepaja.

Libby, Willard Frank   (1908–80) US chemist, who was awarded the Nobel Prize in 1960 for his discovery of *radiocarbon dating. He also perfected a similar technique in which water is dated from its tritium content.

libel.   *See* defamation.

Liberal Party (Australia)   A conservative political party, formed in 1944 from the *United Australia Party, which had performed disastrously in the 1943 election. A Liberal-Country Party (*see* National Country Party) coalition won the election of 1949 and under the leadership successively of Robert *Menzies, Harold *Holt, John *Gorton, and William *McMahon held office until 1972. Under Malcolm *Fraser the Liberals were again in power (1975–83).

Liberal Party (UK) A political party that grew out of the *Whig party. The heyday of the party was from the mid 19th century to World War I, under the prime ministers *Gladstone, *Campbell-Bannerman, *Asquith, and *Lloyd George. Conflict between Asquith and Lloyd George led to a split in the party after World War I, and in 1922 the Labour Party replaced the Liberals as the official opposition. The Liberals enjoyed a small revival in the 1960s and 1970s.

Liberal Republican Party US political party. Founded in 1872 for the purpose of opposing Republican President Ulysses S. Grant's policies, it nominated Horace *Greeley for president. Its platform for reform of the civil service, local and federal government, and tariffs allied the party with the Democrats. When Grant won re-election, the party ceased to exist.

Liberec (German name: Reichenberg) 50 48N 15 05E A city in Czechoslovakia, in Bohemia on the Neisse River. In 1938 it was a center of the Sudeten-German movement. Population (1980 est): 85,000.

Liberia, Republic of A country in West Africa, on the Atlantic Ocean. Coastal plains rise to higher ground inland and to mountains in the N; much of the land is covered with tropical rainforest. Most of the population belongs to indigenous tribes, including the Kpelle, Bassa, and Kru, with a minority who are descended from American slaves. *Economy*: agriculture is extensive, the main food crops being rice and cassava. There have been considerable efforts to increase rice production, including the growing of swamp as well as hill rice and there has been large-scale development in the sugar industry with aid from China. The main cash crop is rubber, some of it grown under concession to US companies. Foreign investment in other areas includes the exploitation of Liberia's rich mineral resources, which form the basis of the country's economy, especially high-grade iron ore and diamonds. These, together with rubber and timber, are the main exports. Ships are easily registered in Liberia and, with many foreign vessels, its merchant fleet is the largest in the world. *History*: it was founded in 1822 by the American Colonization Society as a settlement for freed American slaves. In 1847 it became the Free and Independent Republic of Liberia with a constitution based on that of the US. It has had considerable US aid, and from the 1920s the Firestone Company, developing rubber resources, played an important part in the economy, as have many other foreign companies. Liberia also has close economic ties with Sierra Leone. In 1980 the president, Dr William R. Tolbert, Jr (1913–80), was assassinated in a military coup led by Master Sergeant Samuel Doe. Official language: English. Official currency: Liberian dollar of 100 cents. Area: 43,000 sq mi (111,400 sq km). Population (1983 est): 2,091,000. Capital and main port: Monrovia.

Liberty Party (1840–48) US antislavery political party. It was established by northeastern abolitionists who disagreed with William Lloyd *Garrison over the political approach to abolition. It eventually merged (1848) with the *Free Soil Party.

libido The sexual drive. In *psychoanalysis the libido (like the death instinct) is a fundamental source of energy for all mental life, and changes in the normal course of psychosexual development are responsible for many distortions of the adult personality.

Libra (Latin: Scales) A constellation in the S sky, lying on the *zodiac between Scorpius and Virgo. The brightest star is of 2nd magnitude.

library A collection of books, phonograph records, photographic materials, etc., organized for private or public consultation or borrowing. In ancient Mesopotamia libraries were offshoots of royal archives (*see* Nineveh). Aristotle's teaching library at his *Lyceum inspired the Ptolemaic rulers of Egypt to found a library at Alexandria that became the cultural center of Hellenism. Sizable private libraries were assembled by Roman scholars, such as *Cicero, and Roman and Byzantine emperors founded large public libraries. With the growth of Christian literature it became customary to attach libraries to churches. Monastic libraries grew from the requirement of daily study of religious treatises, especially among the *Benedictines. Late medieval and Renaissance nonecclesiastical collections form the basis of many of today's great libraries, such as the *Bodleian, the Vatican (present building opened in 1571), the *Bibliothèque Nationale, the British Library, and the US *Library of Congress. In response to increasing literacy in the 19th century most European countries developed a municipal library network.

The explosion in the numbers both of items held by libraries and of library users has placed increasing demands on **library science**, a discipline that is concerned chiefly with the acquisition, classification, and cataloguing of items in a library. The acquisition of materials is dictated by a library's selection policy, which is influenced by its budget, storage space, and read-

ers' requirements. The systems of classification of materials into subject fields that are most widely used today are the *Universal Decimal Classification, based on the *Dewey Decimal Classification. and the Library of Congress system. Catalogues, or lists, of holdings generally consist of an alphabetized author catalogue and a subject catalogue. The practice of printing catalogues, with regularly issued supplements, has been complemented since the late 19th century by card catalogues, which facilitate the incorporation of new items. More recent developments include the use of *microcopy systems for recording holdings and of automatic *data processing, which aid the centralization on a regional, national, or international scale of library information. Centralization demands standardization and all publications now bear an International Standard Book Number (ISBN) or an International Standard Serial Number (ISSN), by which an item may be quickly identified.

Formal training for libraries was pioneered by the American Library Association (founded 1876). The International Library Committee was set up in 1927 to try to achieve internationally accepted conventions in such matters as the transliteration of Cyrillic characters into the Roman alphabet, and UNESCO has a division concerned with libraries.

Library of Congress The national library of the US, founded in 1800. First housed in the Capitol, it was moved to its present site in Washington in 1897. It contains over 60 million items, and its system of classification is widely used in academic libraries.

Library of Congress Classification System A numerical system for classifying books by subject, initiated by the US Library of Congress in 1904. Within the system there are 41 subjects, which are, in turn, subdivided.

libretto (Italian: little book) The text of an opera or operetta. The most notable early librettists were the Italians Apostolo Zeno (1668–1750) and Pietro Metastasio (1698–1782), whose elevated style eventually provoked a reaction in favor of greater realism. Dramatists whose plays have been used as libretti include von *Hofmannsthal, *Maeterlinck, and Oscar *Wilde. *Wagner and *Berlioz wrote their own libretti. Notable partnerships between librettists and composers include Calzabigi (1714–95) and Gluck, da Ponte (1749–1838) and Mozart, Boito and Verdi, and Gilbert and Sullivan.

Libreville 0 25N 9 25E The capital of Gabon, a port in the NW on the Gabon Estuary. It was founded by the French in the 19th century, when freed slaves were sent there. The National University was established in 1970. Population (1974 est): 251,400.

Librium. *See* benzodiazepines.

Libya (official name: Popular Socialist Libyan Arab Jamahiriya) A country in N Africa, on the Mediterranean Sea. It consists chiefly of desert, with a narrow coastal plain, rising to the Tibesti Mountains along its southern border and is divided into the three main areas (provinces until 1963) of Cyrenaica, Tripolitania, and Fezzan. The population is mainly of Berber and Arabic origin. *Economy*: between 1955 and 1970 considerable prospecting for oil took place during which time major deposits were discovered, notably at Zelten (1959). Libya is now one of the world's major oil producers and oil constitutes about 95% of exports in value; liquefied natural gas is also exported. Subsistence agriculture is important, livestock farming of sheep, goats, and cattle being the main agricultural occupation, nomadic in the S. The aridity of the land restricts crop production to the narrow coastal areas and scattered oases; barley, wheat, and olives are grown here and esparto grass in semidesert areas. Recently programs have been implemented to improve agriculture, such as in the Fezzan. Manufacturing industry is based largely on traditional crafts. *History*: the area was important within the Roman Empire. During the 16th century it came under Turkish domination and in 1912 was annexed by Italy. It was the scene of heavy fighting in World War II; the French occupied Fezzan and the British occupied Cyrenaica and Tripolitania. In 1951 the United Kingdom of Libya was formed from the federation of these three areas and the Emir of Cyrenaica, Mohammed Idris Al-Senussi (1889–1983), became its first king. He was deposed in a military coup led by Colonel Muammar al-*Gadafi in 1969 and Libya was proclaimed a republic. The Revolutionary Command Council was established to rule the country. In 1973 Gadafi introduced a cultural revolution, an attempt to govern the country according to Islamic principles. Since 1969 Libya has taken an active part in Arab affairs being firmly aligned against Israel. Official language: Arabic; English and Italian are also spoken. Official currency: Libyan dinar of 1000 millemes. Area: 679,216 sq mi (1,759,540 sq km). Population (1979 est): 3,100,000. Capital: Tripoli.

lichee. *See* litchi.

lichens A large group of plants (*Lichenes*; about 15,000 species) consisting of two components, an alga and a fungus, in a mutually beneficial association. Millions of algal cells (the phycobiont) are interwoven with fungal filaments (the mycobiont) to form the lichen body (a thallus), which may be crusty, scaly, leafy, or stalked and shrublike in appearance. Lichens occur in almost all areas of the world, mainly on tree trunks, rocks, and soil, and can survive in extremely harsh conditions. They normally reproduce asexually by fragmentation, *budding, or by producing special structures (soredia), consisting of a few algal cells enmeshed with fungal threads. Lichens are an important source of food for browsing animals of tundra regions (*see* reindeer moss) and they are used by man for food, dyes, medicine, in perfume, and as pollution indicators. *See also* crottle; oak moss; orchil; rock tripe.

Lichtenstein, Roy (1923–) A leading US painter of *pop art. He taught at Ohio and New York Universities and in 1962 had an important one-man show of comic-strip paintings, which pioneered the use of mass-media techniques in the context of noncommercial art. His works include *Whaam* (1963).

licorice A perennial herb, *Glycyrrhiza glabra*, native to S Europe but cultivated throughout warm temperate regions. It bears clusters of blue flowers and long flat pods and its sweet roots, up to 3 ft (1 m) long, are a source of flavoring for confectionery, tobacco, and medicines. The thickened juice of the roots is made into licorice paste (*or* black sugar). Family: *Leguminosae*.

Lidice 50 03N 14 08E A small mining village in W Czechoslovakia. On June 10, 1942, it was destroyed by the Nazis in revenge for the assassination of Reinhard Heydrich, their local administrative head. The 400 or so inhabitants were either shot or deported to concentration camps. The site is now a memorial garden.

Lie, Trygve (Halvdan) (1896–1968) Norwegian Labor politician and international civil servant; the first secretary general of the UN (1946–52). At the UN he dealt with the first Arab-Israeli War and UN armed aid to South Korea in the *Korean War. Soviet opposition to his Korean policies resulted in his resignation.

Liebig, Justus, Baron von (1803–73) German chemist; one of the earliest investigators of organic compounds. His work on fulminates (1920) was followed by the development of a technique for measuring the proportion of carbon and hydrogen in a compound by burning it and determining the amount of carbon dioxide and water released (1831). His later work was concerned with biochemistry and agricultural chemistry. His name is also connected with the Liebig condenser, a much used piece of laboratory equipment.

Liebknecht, Wilhelm (1826–1900) German socialist. He participated in the *Revolution of 1848 and was forced to flee Germany, living in Britain, where he worked with Karl Marx. Returning to Germany in 1862, he was expelled from Prussia in 1865 for his socialist activities but in 1867 became a member of the North German Reichstag. His opposition to the Franco-Prussian War (1870–71) brought imprisonment but he subsequently became a leader of what became (1891) the Social Democratic Party. His son **Karl Liebknecht** (1871–1919) was among the few socialists who refused to support the war effort in 1914. In 1915 he helped to found the revolutionary *Spartacus League, which he led with Rosa *Luxemburg. They were both murdered following the unsuccessful communist revolt of 1919.

Liechtenstein, Principality of A small country in central Europe, between Switzerland and Austria. Mountains rise from the Rhine Valley to heights of over 8000 ft (2500 m). *Economy*: although there is still a considerable amount of farming, the balance of the economy has shifted since World War II to light industry, including textiles, ceramics, tools, instruments, and food processing. Tourism and the sale of postage stamps are also important sources of revenue. *History*: the principality was formed from the union of the counties of Vaduz and Schellenberg in 1719 and was part of the Holy Roman Empire until 1806. It formed a customs union with Switzerland in 1923. Until 1984 women were banned from voting in national elections. Head of state: Prince Franz Joseph II. Head of government: Hans Brunhart. Official language: German. Official religion: Roman Catholic. Official currency: Swiss franc of 100 centimes (*or* Rappen). Area: 62 sq mi (160 sq km). Population (1980): 25,215. Capital: Vaduz.

lie detector An instrument designed to detect whether a person is lying by measuring such factors as blood pressure, respiration rate, skin conductivity, and pulse rate. A sudden change in these factors in a person being questioned is taken to indicate that he is under stress and may be telling a lie. Lie detectors are not usually accepted in a court of law.

Liège (Flemish name: Luik) 50 38N 5 35E A city in E Belgium, on the Meuse River. It has many old churches, including St Martin's (692 AD).

Its university was founded in 1817. The center of a coalmining area, its industries include the manufacture of armaments, iron, textiles, and paper. Population (1981 est): 216,604.

Liegnitz. See Legnica.

Liepaja (German name: Libau) 56 30N 21 00E A port in the Soviet Union, in the W Latvian SSR on the Baltic Sea. It was founded by the Teutonic Knights (1263), passing to Russia in 1795. The independent Latvian Government met here in 1918. A naval base, it has shipbuilding and metallurgy industries. Population (1981 est): 108,000.

Lif and Lifthrasir In Norse mythology, a man and woman destined to sleep during the destruction of the world (*see* Ragnarök), awaking afterward to found a new race.

Lifar, Serge (1905–) Russian ballet dancer and choreographer. He joined Diaghilev's Ballets Russes in 1923 and from 1932 to 1958 was ballet master at the Paris Opéra Ballet, which he revitalized with his experimental choreography. His ballets include *Prométhée* (1929), *Icare* (1935), and *Phèdre* (1950).

life The property that enables a living organism to assimilate nonliving materials from its environment and use them to increase its size and complexity (the process of growth), to repair its existing tissues, and to produce new independent organisms that also possess the properties of life (the process of reproduction). *See also* animal; plant.

Life on earth is thought to have originated between 4500 and 3000 million years ago. The atmosphere then consisted chiefly of methane, hydrogen, ammonia, and water vapor, from which simple organic molecules (such as amino acids, proteins, and fatty acids) were formed as a result of energy supplied by solar radiation, lightning, and volcanic activity. The first "cells" may have arisen spontaneously as simple envelopes of protein and fat molecules. However, the crucial steps toward life would probably have been the inclusion in such a cell of both the enzyme molecules necessary to perform primitive fermentations and the nucleic acid molecules, such as RNA and DNA, capable of directing the metabolic processes of the cell and of self replication, i.e. passing on this information to succeeding generations. These early cells are thought to have arisen in the sea, deriving their energy from the fermentation of simple organic molecules. In the course of time increasingly efficient biochemical pathways evolved, including the process of trapping light energy in cellular pigments, enabling the first simple green plants to develop the process of photosynthesis. This led to the gradual build-up of oxygen in the atmosphere, which started about 2000 million years ago; by about 400 million years ago the *ozone layer in the upper atmosphere was sufficiently dense to shield the land from harmful ultraviolet radiation, enabling plants and animals to survive. With increasing oxygen levels, aerobic respiration—the most efficient method of energy utilization—was adopted by most living organisms.

The factors involved in the origination of life on earth have prompted a search for similar conditions on other planets and in other solar systems, but so far no evidence of life elsewhere in the universe has been discovered. *See* astrobiology.

lifeboat A boat carried aboard a ship, used for accommodating passengers and crew if the ship has to be abandoned.

life cycle The progressive series of stages through which a species of organism passes from its *fertilization or production by asexual means to the same stage in the next generation. The simplest life cycles occur by asexual *reproduction, producing offspring similar to the parent. Life cycles involving sexual reproduction are much more complex and the young do not necessarily resemble the adults: marine crustaceans, for example, pass through several different larval stages before becoming adult. In many plants and animals there is a succession of individuals showing an alternation of sexual and asexual reproduction before completing the cycle (*see* alternation of generations).

Liffey River A river in the E Republic of Ireland, rising in the Wicklow Mountains and flowing mainly W and NE through Dublin to Dublin Bay. Length: 50 mi (80 km).

ligament A strong fibrous tissue that joins one bone to another at a *joint. Ligaments are flexible but inelastic: they increase the stability of the joint and limit its movements to certain directions. Unusual stresses on a joint often damage ("pull") a ligament, as occurs in a "twisted" ankle.

ligature Any material, such as silk, gut, cotton, or wire, used to tie a blood vessel (to stop bleeding) or the base of a tumor (to constrict it). Ligatures are widely used in surgery and are available in various thicknesses.

liger. See tigon.

Ligeti, György (1923–) Hungarian composer. He worked in the West German Radio's studio for electronic music in Cologne (1957–58) and settled in Vienna. His compositions are largely experimental, often involving indeterminacy of pitch and rhythm, and include *Volumina* (1961–62) for organ, a Requiem (1963–65), *Continuum* (1968) for harpsichord, and *Melodien* (1971) for orchestra.

light The form of *electromagnetic radiation to which the eye is sensitive. It forms the part of the electromagnetic spectrum from 740 nanometers (red light) to 400 nanometers (blue light), white light consisting of a mixture of all the colors of the visible spectrum. The nature of light has been in dispute from earliest times, *Newton supporting a corpuscular theory in which a luminous body was believed to emit particles of light. This theory adequately explained reflection and geometric optics but failed to explain *interference and *polarized light. The wave theory, supported in the 19th century by *Fresnel and *Foucault, adequately explains these phenomena and achieved a mathematical basis when *Maxwell showed that light is a form of electromagnetic radiation. The wave theory, however, does not explain the *photoelectric effect and *Einstein reverted to a form of the corpuscular theory in using the *quantum theory to postulate that in some cases light is best regarded as consisting of energy quanta called photons. The present view, expressing *Bohr's concept of complementarity, is that both electromagnetic theory and quantum theory are needed to explain this phenomenon. Light travels at a velocity of $2.997,925 \times 10^8$ m per second in free space, this being, according to the special *relativity, the highest attainable velocity in the universe.

light-emitting diode. *See* semiconductor diode.

lighthouse A tall structure, built on a coastal promontory or cape or on an island at sea, equipped with a powerful beacon, visible at some distance, to mark an obstruction or other hazard. Modern lighthouses are also equipped with radio beacons. Both light and radio signals are emitted in a unique pattern to enable vessels to identify the lighthouse producing them.

lightning An electrical discharge in the atmosphere caused by the buildup of electrical charges in a cloud by such methods as friction between the particles in the cloud. The potential difference causing the discharge may be as high as one thousand million volts. The electricity then discharges itself in a lightning flash, which may be between the cloud and the ground or, much more commonly, between two clouds or parts of a cloud. Thunder is the noise made by the discharge or its reverberations. *See also* ball lightning; thunderstorm.

lightning conductor An earthed conducting rod placed at the top of buildings, etc., to protect them from damage by lightning. It acts by providing a low-resistance path to earth for the lightning current.

lightship A vessel, anchored at sea, used as a lighthouse. In wide use until the mid-20th century, most lightships have now been replaced by fixed structures or, because of advances in sophisticated navigation devices, have been eliminated entirely.

light-year A unit of distance, used in astronomy, equal to the distance traveled by light in one year. One light-year $= 5.88 \times 10^{12}$ miles or 9.46×10^{15} meters.

lignin A complex chemical deposited in plant cell walls to add extra strength and support. It is the main constituent of *wood cells, allowing the trunk to support the heavy crown of leaves and branches.

lignum vitae Wood from trees of the genus *Guaiacum*, especially *G. officinale*, a tropical evergreen of the New World. Lignum vitae is hard, dense, greenish-brown, and rich in fat (making it waterproof). It is used for shafts, pulleys, and bowling balls. Lignum vitae was formerly thought to have medicinal properties: its name (from the Latin) means "wood of life." Family: *Zygophyllaceae*.

Liguria A region in NW Italy. It consists of a narrow strip of land between the Apennines and Maritime Alps in the N and the Gulf of Genoa in the S. It is an important industrial region, concentrating on engineering, shipbuilding, metals, petroleum products, and chemicals. Tourism is a major source of revenue, the region more or less corresponding to the Italian Riviera. Agricultural products include vegetables, olives, and flowers. Area: 2091 sq mi (5415 sq km). Population (1980 est): 1,835,347. Capital: Genoa.

Ligurian Sea A section of the NW Mediterranean Sea, between Italy (N of Elba) and Corsica.

Li Hong Zhang (*or* Li Hung-chang; 1823–1901) Chinese soldier and statesman of the *Qing dynasty. His armies helped suppress the *Taiping Rebellion in 1864 and, as the trusted adviser of the empress *Zi Xi, he encouraged commerce and industry, attempting to introduce modernizing projects, and conducted China's foreign affairs. He amassed a huge personal fortune.

Likasi (name until 1966: Jadotville) 10 58S 26 47E A city in SE Zaïre. Founded in 1917, near the site of old copper workings, it is a major mineral-processing center refining copper and cobalt. Other industries include chemicals and brewing. Population (1970 est): 146,394.

lilac A deciduous bush or small tree of the genus *Syringa* (30 species), especially *S. vulgaris*, native to temperate Eurasia and often grown as a garden ornamental. It has heart-shaped leaves arranged in opposite pairs and dense terminal clusters of white, purple, or pink tubular fragrant flowers with four flaring lobes. The fruit is a leathery capsule. Family: *Oleaceae*.

Lilburne, John (c. 1614–57) English pamphleteer; leader of the radical Puritan sect called the *Levellers. He joined the parliamentarians in the Civil War but resigned from the army in 1645 to organize the Levellers. After 1645 he was frequently in prison and was twice tried and acquitted for treason.

Liliaceae A family of monocotyledonous plants (about 250 species), mostly herbaceous and native to temperate and subtropical regions. They usually grow from bulbs or rhizomes to produce six-lobed flowers and three-chambered capsular fruits. The family includes many popular garden plants, including the lilies, tulip, hyacinth, and lily-of-the-valley. A few are economically important, for example *Asparagus*. Some authorities enlarge this family to include related plants, such as the onion, leek, etc., (*see* Allium), *Agave*, and *Yucca*.

Lilienthal, Otto (1848–96) German aeronautical engineer, who pioneered the construction of gliders. A student of bird flight, Lilienthal demonstrated the superiority of a curved wing over a flat wing. He made some 2000 flights before being killed in a crash.

Lilith In Jewish folklore, a female demon, traditionally the first wife of Adam, who refused to recognize his authority over her. An amulet bearing the names of the three angels who tried to persuade her to return to Adam was worn as protection against her evil powers.

Liliuokalani (1838–1917) The only queen and last sovereign of Hawaii (1891–95). Hawaiian resistance to US attempts to annex the islands led to an insurrection after which she abdicated. She composed the song "Aloha Oe," as a farewell gift to her people.

Lille 50 39N 3 05E A city in N France, the capital of the Nord department on the Deûle River. The center of a large industrial and commercial complex, its industries include textiles, machinery, chemicals, distilling, and brewing. Notable buildings include the citadel (built by Vauban) and the university (1887). *History*: following a prosperous period under the Dukes of Burgundy (14th century), Lille later passed to Austria and then Spain before returning to France in 1668, and was badly damaged in both World Wars. Gen de Gaulle was born here. Population (1975): 177,218.

Lillie, Beatrice (Constance Sylvia Munston, Lady Peel; 1898–) British actress, born in Canada. The sophisticated comedy of her performances in revues and cabaret was successful in both London and New York. She also made several films, notably *Exit Smiling* (1926) and *On Approval* (1943).

Lilongwe 13 58S 33 49E The capital of Malawi. It replaced Zomba as the capital in 1975. Tobacco production is important. Population (1977): 102,924.

lily A perennial herbaceous plant of the genus *Lilium* (80–100 species), native to N temperate regions and widely grown for ornament. Lilies grow from bulbs to produce leafy stems with terminal clusters of showy flowers, usually with backward-curving petals. Some popular species are the tiger lily (*L. tigrinum*), from China and Japan, 24–48 in (60–120 cm) high with purple-spotted golden flowers; the Japanese golden ray lily (*L. auratum*), 35–71 in (90–180 cm) high, whose white flowers are marked with yellow and crimson; the Eurasian Madonna lily (*L. candida*), 24–48 in (60–120 cm) high with pure-white flowers; and the turk's-cap or martagon lily (*L. martagon*), also from Eurasia, 35–60 in (90–150 cm) high, the purplish-pink flowers of which are marked with darker spots. There are numerous varieties and hybrids of these and other species. Family: *Liliaceae*.

The name is also applied to numerous other unrelated plants, such as the *arum lily, *day lily, and *leopard lily.

lily-of-the-valley A fragrant perennial herbaceous plant, *Convallaria majalis*, native to Eurasia and E North America and a popular garden plant. Growing from creeping underground stems (rhizomes), it has a stem, 5–8 in (13–20 cm) long, bearing a cluster of white nodding bell-shaped flowers. Family: *Liliaceae*.

Lima 12 06S 77 03W The capital of Peru, situated in the E of the country near its Pacific port of Callao. Founded by Pizarro in 1535, it became the main base of Spanish power in Peru. Notable buildings include the 16th-century cathedral and the National University of San Marcos (1551). Lima has expanded rapidly in recent years and now has considerable industry; the main manufactures include motor vehicles, textiles, paper, paint, and food products. Approximately one third of the population live in the shanty-town settlements that surround the city. Population (1979): 3,158,417.

Lima bean A herb, *Phaseolus lunatus*, also called butter bean or Madagascar bean, native to South America but widely cultivated in the tropics and subtropics as a source of protein. It is easily stored when dry. Family: *Leguminosae*.

Limassol (modern Greek name: Lemesós; Turkish name: Limasol) 34 40N 33 03E A city in Cyprus, on the S coast. It is the island's second largest city and a major port, exporting notably wine and fruit. Population (1980 est): 105,200.

limbo In medieval Christian theology, the state of existence of souls that merit neither heavenly bliss nor the torments of hell after death. The two categories of soul destined for limbo were unbaptized babies and the patriarchs and prophets of the Old Testament.

Limburg 1. A former duchy in W Europe, divided in 1839 between Belgium and the Netherlands. 2. (French name: Limbourg) A province in NE Belgium, bordering on the Netherlands. In the N, the Kempen heath area has rich coalfields and industries include chemicals and glass. The S is chiefly agricultural (especially dairy farming). Area: 935 sq mi (2422 sq km). Population (1980 est): 716,059. Capital: Hasselt. 3. A province in the SE Netherlands. Its traditional coalmining industry has declined in recent years. Agriculture is varied producing cereals, fruit, vegetables, and sugar beet; cattle, pigs, and poultry are raised. Area: 852 sq mi (2208 sq km). Population (1976 est): 1,073,403. Capital: Maastricht.

Limburg, de (or de Limbourg) A family (active c. 1400–c. 1416) of manuscript illuminators comprising three brothers Pol, Herman, and Jehanequin, born in Nijmegen (Netherlands), the sons of a sculptor. They worked for the Duke of Burgundy (1402–04) and later for the Duke of Berry, for whom they illuminated the *Très Riches Heures* (Chantilly, France), a fine example of the *international gothic style. They influenced the development of Flemish landscape painting.

lime (botany) 1. A large deciduous tree of the genus *Tilia* (about 30 species), also called linden. Growing to a height of 98 ft (30 m), it has toothed heart-shaped leaves and fragrant pale-yellow flowers that hang in small clusters on a long winged stalk. The small round fruits remain attached to the papery wing when shed. Family: *Tiliaceae*. 2. A tree, *Citrus aurantifolia*, growing to a height of about 13 ft (4 m) and cultivated in the tropics for its fruit. Lime fruits are pear-shaped, 2 in (4 cm) in diameter, with a thick greenish-yellow skin and acid-tasting pulp; the juice is used to flavor food and drinks.

lime (chemistry) Calcium oxide (or quicklime; CaO), calcium hydroxide (or slaked lime; Ca(OH)$_2$) or, loosely, calcium salts in general. Ca(OH)$_2$ is prepared by reacting CaO with water and is used in *cement. CaO is used in making paper, as a *flux in *steel manufacture, and in softening water.

limerick A short form of comic and usually bawdy verse having five lines of three or two feet and usually rhyming aabba, as in:

There was a young lady of Lynn

Who was so uncommonly thin

That when she essayed

To drink lemonade,

She slipped through the straw and fell in.

The form, the origin of which is uncertain, was popularized by Edward *Lear in the 19th century and practiced by several notable poets, but the best-known limericks are by anonymous authors. The name is said to have originated in the chorus of an Irish soldiers' song, "Will you come up to Limerick?"

Limerick (Irish name: Luimneach) 52 40N 8 38W A port in the Republic of Ireland, the county town of Co Limerick on the Shannon estuary. It was besieged by William III (1691). Notable buildings include two cathedrals. Its industries include flour milling, tanning, and brewing. Population (1979): 157,407.

Limerick (Irish name: Luimneach) A county in the SW Republic of Ireland, in Munster bordering on the River Shannon estuary. It consists chiefly of lowlands rising to hills in the S. Lying mainly in the fertile Golden Vale, it is important for dairy farming. Area: 1037 sq mi (2686 sq km). Population (1971): 140,459. County town: Limerick.

limestone A common sedimentary rock consisting largely of carbonates, especially calcium carbonate (calcite) or dolomite. Most limestones were deposited in the sea in warm clear water, but some limestones were formed in fresh water. Organic limestones, including *chalk, consist of fossil skeletal material. Precipitated limestones include evaporites and *oolites (spherically grained calcite). Clastic limestones consist of fragments of pre-existing limestones. Marble is metamorphosed limestone. Limestone is used as a building stone, in the manufacture of cement and glass, for agricultural lime, for roadbeds, and as a flux in smelting.

Limoges 45 50N 1 15E A city in W France, the capital of the Haute-Vienne department on the Vienne River. The center of the French porcelain industry, it has Roman remains, a cathedral (13th–16th centuries), and a university (1808). It is the birthplace of Pierre Auguste Renoir. Population (1975): 147,422.

limonite A naturally occurring mixture of hydrated iron oxides and iron hydroxides, both amorphous and cryptocrystalline, derived from the weathering of minerals containing iron. It ranges in color from yellow to brown to black and occurs in bog iron ore, in gossan, and in *laterite.

Limosin, Léonard (or Limousin; c. 1505–c. 1577) French artist, born in Limoges. As court painter to Francis I and later Henry II he was popular chiefly for his enamel portraits, although he also painted plates, vases, etc., and worked in oils.

Limousin A planning region and former province in central France, on the W Massif Central. It was in the possession of the English from 1152 until 1369. Area: 6536 sq mi (16,932 sq km). Population (1981 est): 732,300.

limpet A marine *gastropod mollusk with a flattened shell and powerful muscular foot for clinging to rocks and other surfaces. The true limpets (superfamily *Patellacea*; about 400 species) are oval-shaped and up to 4 in (10 cm) long whereas the keyhole limpets (superfamily *Fissurellacea*; several hundred species) have an opening in the shell for expelling wastes and tend to be smaller.

Limpopo River A river in SE Africa. Rising as the Crocodile River in the Witwatersrand, South Africa, it flows generally NE through Mozambique, to the Indian Ocean, forming part of the border between the Transvaal and Botswana. Length: 1100 mi (1770 km).

Lin Biao (or Lin Piao; 1908–71) Chinese communist soldier and statesman. Lin received military training under *Chiang Kai-shek at the Whampoa Military Academy. He became a Guomindang (Nationalist People's Party) colonel but led his regiment to join the communist uprising in Nanchang. He became commander of the First Red Army Corps and played a major part in the communist victory against the Guomindang (1949). In 1959 he became defense minister and in 1969, vice chairman of the Chinese Communist Party. Lin seemed destined to become Mao Tse-tung's successor but he was the fatal victim of a mysterious aircrash in Outer Mongolia in 1971, when he may have been attempting to flee China after making an unsuccessful bid for power.

Lincoln 53 14N 0 33W A city in E central England, on the River Witham. The British settlement became Lindum Colonia under the Romans. The castle was begun in 1068 and the cathedral in 1075. The principal manufactures are machinery, radios, metal goods, vehicle components, and cattle feed. Population (1981): 76,660.

Lincoln 40 49N 96 41W The capital city of Nebraska. It is the industrial and commercial center of a region producing grain and livestock. The University of Nebraska was established here in 1869. Population (1980): 171,932.

Lincoln, Abraham (1809–65) US statesman; 16th President of the United States (1861–65). A self-educated man who was raised in rural Indiana, Lincoln settled in Illinois, where he became a storekeeper and served in the local militia during the *Black Hawk War (1832). After deciding on a career as a lawyer, he served as the postmaster for New Salem, Ill., (1833–36) while pursuing his legal studies. Admitted to the Illinois bar in 1836, Lincoln moved to Springfield, where he established a successful legal practice. Lincoln was active in Illinois politics and served as a Whig representative in the state legislature (1834–42) and later as a member of the US House of Representatives for a single term (1847–49). Holding long-standing convictions against slavery, he opposed its extension to the new western states as proposed in the *Kansas-Nebraska Act of 1854, sponsored by Illinois Senator Stephen A. *Douglas. In 1856, Lincoln joined the newly formed *Republican Party and ran against Douglas in the senatorial campaign of 1858. Although Douglas won re-election, Lincoln gained a national reputation through his eloquent opposition to slavery in the *Lincoln-Douglas Debates.

ABRAHAM LINCOLN *Civil War President (1861–65) who was known as "The Great Emancipator" and who delivered the Gettysburg Address.*

In 1860, Lincoln received the Republican presidential nomination, and his election to that office precipitated the secession of the southern states from the Union and the outbreak of the *Civil War. Believing that the Union was indivisible, he supervised the military operations intended to force the dissolution of the *Confederate States of America. In 1863, Lincoln issued the *Emancipation Proclamation, liberating the slaves in the southern states, and later in the same year, he gave his famous *Gettysburg Address, reaffirming the principles of equality established by America's founding fathers. Winning re-election in 1864, he appointed General Ulysses S. *Grant commander-in-chief of the Union forces and supported the 13th Amendment to the US Constitution, ratified in 1865, which prohibited slavery in the US. He also advocated a magnanimous *Reconstruction program for the readmission of the Confederate states into the Union after the war, but did not live to see that program carried out. He was assassinated by John Wilkes *Booth in Washington, a few days after the surrender of the South. His wife **Mary Todd Lincoln** (1818–82), whom he married in 1842, bore him four sons, only one of whom, Robert Todd (1843–1926) lived beyond 18 years of age. Her unstableness, due to her husband's assassination and the death of three sons, led to a court declaration of insanity in 1875, a decision that was overturned in 1876.

Lincoln-Douglas Debates (1858) A series of debates on the territorial slavery question during the 1858 Illinois campaign for the US Senate. Abraham *Lincoln and incumbent Senator Stephen A. *Douglas debated at Ottawa, Freeport, Jonesboro, Charleston, Galesburg, Quincy, and Alton, Ill. Lincoln advocated complete abolition of slavery; Douglas furthered his "popular sovereignty" doctrine, that of the right of people to decide whether or not to allow slavery. Lincoln won the popular vote, but lost the election to Douglas due to a Democratic majority in the legislature.

Lincolnshire A county in E England, bordering on the North Sea. It is generally low lying, with the Lincolnshire Edge (a limestone escarpment) in the W and the Lincolnshire Wolds in the E. It is mainly agricultural producing arable crops and livestock; horticulture is also important. Industry is associated with agriculture. Area: 2272 sq mi (5885 sq km). Population (1981): 547,560. Administrative center: Lincoln.

Lincoln's Inn. *See* Inns of Court.

Lind, Jenny (1820–87) Swedish soprano, known as "the Swedish nightingale." Her brilliant career in opera and on the concert platform took her all over Europe. P. T. Barnum arranged her very successful tour of the US (1850–52).

CHARLES LINDBERGH *Aviator, known as "Lucky Lindy," who made the first transatlantic solo flight, from New York to Paris, in 1927.*

Lindbergh, Charles A (ugustus) (1902–74) US aviator who made the first solo nonstop flight across the Atlantic Ocean, from New York to Paris (1927), in the monoplane *Spirit of St Louis.* The success of the flight brought him world-wide fame. After the kidnapping and murder of his two-year-old son in 1932 he and his wife moved to Europe to escape the ensuing publicity. He advocated US neutrality at the start of World War II but subsequently contributed to the Allied cause. His book *The Spirit of St Louis* (1953) won a Pulitzer Prize. His wife **Anne Morrow Lindbergh** (1906–) was an author. Her works include *North to the Orient* (1935), *Listen! The Wind* (1938), *Gift From the Sea* (1955), *The Unicorn and Other Poems* (1956), *Dearly Beloved* (1962), *Hour of Gold, Hour of Lead* (1974), and *War Within and Without* (1980).

linden. *See* lime.

Lindisfarne. *See* Holy Island.

Lindsay, (Nicholas) Vachel (1879–1931) US poet. After an unsuccessful attempt to be a painter he became an itinerant poet, earning his living by reciting his poems. His best-known volumes, *General William Booth Enters into Heaven and Other Poems* (1913) and *The Congo and Other Poems* (1914), owe much to his interest in regional folklore and his mastery of ballad-like verse.

Lindsey, Parts of. *See* Lincolnshire.

Linear A A syllabic script used (c. 1700–1450 BC) to write the lost language of the *Minoan civilization of Crete. It evolved from a pictographic script. Known from fewer than 400 inscriptions, it is still undeciphered, but, like its successor, *Linear B, was mainly used on clay tablets to record inventories.

linear accelerator An *accelerator in which charged elementary particles are repeatedly accelerated along a long straight tube by a radio-frequency electric field. In modern linear accelerators the field is supplied by the electric component of a traveling radio wave in a waveguide. The particles are confined in the tube by a series of magnetic lenses, which focus the beam. The maximum energy attained by a linear accelerator is about 10 GeV for electrons and 2 GeV for protons.

Linear B A syllabic script apparently adapted (c. 1450–1400 BC) from *Linear A by the invading Mycaeneans at *Knossos to write their own language (see Mycaenean civilization). In 1952 Michael *Ventris deciphered this language as an early form of *Greek. Several thousand Linear B clay tablets, mainly containing inventories, survive from Knossos, *Pylos, and elsewhere, dating between about 1400 and 1100 BC.

linear motor A form of electric induction motor in which the stator and the rotor are linear instead of cylindrical and parallel instead of coaxial. The development of linear motors as a method of traction for monorail intercity trains has been proposed by E. R. Laithwaite. In this arrangement one winding would be in the train and the other on the single rail, thus obviating the need for rotating parts.

Line Islands A chain of coral atolls in the W central Pacific Ocean. Of the N islands, Palmyra and Jarvis Islands are US territories while Washington, Fanning, and Christmas Islands, the only permanently inhabited ones, form part of Kiribati. Copra is produced.

linen A fabric manufactured from *flax (*Linum usitatissimum*). Probably the first textile of plant origin, specimens 4500 years old have been found in Egyptian tombs. Flax growing was brought to Britain by the Romans and in the 16th century a flourishing trade grew up, especially in Scotland and Northern Ireland. Greatly reduced by the 18th-century expansion of the cotton trade, and even more so by the advent of man-made fibers, these strong absorbent fibers now constitute less than 2% of world fiber production, being reserved for luxury household fabrics and summer garments.

line of force. *See* field.

ling A deep-sea fish, belonging to a genus (*Molva*; 3 species) related to cod, that is cured and dried for food. The common ling (*M. molva*) has a long slim body, up to about 7 ft (2 m) long, mottled brown or green, a long chin barbel, and two dorsal fins.

lingua franca Any language that is used as a means of communication between speakers with different native languages. It may be a hybrid of other languages, such as *pidgin English, or it may refer to an already existing language, such as French, which was formerly the lingua franca of diplomacy. Lingua franca, meaning Frank language, was originally a pidgin used by Mediterranean traders in the middle ages (Frank being the Arabic word for European).

linguistics The scientific study of *language. The earliest recorded studies of particular languages include the Sanskrit grammar of *Panini (6th/4th century BC) and the Greek grammar of Dionysius Thrax of Alexandria (2nd century BC). In the 19th century the study of language (then called *philology) was mainly concerned with establishing the history and relationships of the *Indo-European languages. The chief influences in broadening the scope of linguistics to its present range were Ferdinand de *Saussure, Leonard *Bloomfield, and Noam *Chomsky. Modern linguistics has three main branches, corresponding to the three main components of language: *semantics, *grammar, and *phonetics. Many linguists at present see it as their task to contribute to the building of a formal model of language, in which the theoretical problems are resolved, the components and processes accurately identified, and the relationships among the components and between linguistic systems and other worlds are plausibly described. Other linguists believe that a coherent one-piece model is simply not possible.

Various specialized interests exist within the field of linguistics. **Comparative linguistics** compares languages either to establish the history of and relationships among related languages (e.g. the Indo-European family) or to test theories about linguistic universals by comparing unrelated languages (see also etymology). The main contribution of **structural linguistics**, which developed in the early 20th century, was to free linguistics from the historical and comparative approach, viewing language as a unique relational structure. **Sociolinguistics** deals with social aspects of language, including such matters as how language affects and reflects the role and status of individuals within the community, attitudes to dialect and "correctness," linguistic taboos and preferences, bilingualism, etc. **Psycholinguistics** is the comparatively recent branch of linguistics that deals with psychological aspects of language, including how children acquire language, how language is stored in and generated by the brain, the relationship between meaning and memory, etc. **Neurolinguistics**, a branch of psycholinguistics, is concerned with the relationship between language and the physiology of the brain, especially with speech disorders that arise from brain damage.

Linköping 58 25N 15 35E A town in SE Sweden. It has a notable romanesque cathedral and its university was established in 1970. Industries include railroad engineering and the manufacture of cars and textiles. Population (1978 est): 112,600.

Linnaeus, Carolus (Carl Linné; 1707–78) Swedish botanist, who established the principles for naming and classifying plants and animals. As a result of his botanical studies, Linnaeus proposed a system for classifying plants based on their flower parts. He published *Systema naturae* in 1735 followed by *Genera plantarum* (1737) and *Species plantarum* (1753). In his system, Linnaeus defined each type of plant by two names: a generic name and a specific name (see binomial nomenclature). Furthermore he grouped related genera into classes and combined related classes into orders. Linnaeus also applied his system to the animal kingdom. His was the first major attempt to bring systematic order to the great array of living things and provided a valuable framework that *Cuvier and others were able to modify and improve. Linnaeus' manuscripts and collections are kept at the Linnaean Society, London, which was founded in his honor in 1788.

LINNET *Nests are built in hedges and thickets and the young are cared for by both parents.*

linnet A small Eurasian *finch, *Acanthis cannabina*, occurring in dry open regions, where it feeds on the seeds of common weed plants. The female has a dull brown-streaked plumage; the male has a crimson crown and breast, a grayish head, and a red-brown back with darker wings and tail. Male linnets have a beautiful flutelike voice and were popular cagebirds in the 19th century.

linotype. *See* typesetting.

linsang A carnivorous mammal belonging to the genus *Prionodon* (2 species) of SE Asia. Linsangs are short-legged, about 30 in (75 cm) long including the tail (12–14 in [30–35 cm]), and have short velvety fur. Nocturnal, with large ears and eyes, they prey on lizards, small mammals, birds, frogs, and insects. Family: *Viverridae.

linseed The flat oval seed of cultivated *flax, which is a source of linseed oil, used in paints, inks, varnishes, oilcloth, and sailcloth. The crushed seed residues form linseed meal, an important protein feed for ruminants and pigs.

Linz 48 19N 14 18E The third largest city in Austria, the capital of Upper Austria on the Danube River. Its many historical buildings include two 13th-century baroque churches and a cathedral (1862–1924). A cultural center, it has art galleries, libraries, and theaters. Its industries include iron and steel processing using local hydroelectric power. Population (1981): 201,421.

Lin Ze Xu (or Lin Tse-hsü; 1785–1850) Chinese statesman and scholar. Lin Ze Xu served as governor of several provinces. While imperial commissioner of Canton (1839–41) he confiscated opium and tried to put an end to its trafficking through British merchants, thus provoking the *Opium War (1839–42). He is also known for his efforts to introduce western defense techniques to China.

lion A large carnivorous □mammal *Panthera leo*, one of the big *cats. Lions are found mainly in Africa (there are a few in India). They are heavily built with sandy-colored coats: the shaggy-maned males grow to 9 ft (2.8 m) while females lack a mane and are more lightly built. Both sexes have a thin tail with a tuft at the end.

Lions inhabit grasslands, living in groups (prides) containing between four and 30 individuals dominated by a supreme male. They hunt mainly at twilight.

Lions, Gulf of (French name: Golfe du Lion)   An inlet of the NW Mediterranean Sea, on the coast of central S France between Marseilles and the Spanish border.

Liouville, Joseph   (1809–82) French mathematician, who proved that there exists a class of numbers, called transcendental numbers, that cannot be expressed as a solution of a polynomial equation (i.e. one of the form $a_0 + a_1x + \ldots + a_nx^n = 0$, where n and the a's are integers). Liouville could not identify any transcendental numbers, a feat first achieved by *Hermite.

Lipari Islands (or Aeolian Is; Italian name: Isole Eolie)   An Italian group of seven volcanic islands in the Tyrrhenian Sea, off the N coast of Sicily. The largest is Lipari and the islands of Stromboli and Vulcano have active volcanoes. Exports include pumice stone, grapes, wine, and figs. Area: 44 sq mi (114 sq km). Population (1971): 16,037. Chief town: Lipari, on Lipari.

lipase   An enzyme that splits the glycerides of fats in food and fatty tissue into their component fatty acids and glycerol. Digestive lipases are secreted by the pancreas and small intestine.

Lipchitz, Jacques   (1891–1973) Lithuanian cubist sculptor, who lived in Paris from 1909 and New York after 1941. Producing his first cubist sculpture in 1914, Lipchitz developed heavy angular forms in such characteristically cubist subjects as bathers and musicians. In 1925 he began experimenting with the use of voids in bronze sculptures, which he entitled "transparents." His later mythological and religious sculptures explored themes of love, evil, and conflict.

Lipetsk   52 37N 39 36E   A city in the central Soviet Union, in the RSFSR on the Voronezh River. Industries include iron and steel and engineering. Its mud spa attracts health devotees. Population (1981 est): 415,000.

lipids   A group of compounds, generally insoluble in water but soluble in organic solvents, that includes *fats, *oils, *waxes, phospholipids, sphingolipids, and *steroids. Fats and oils function as energy reserves in plants and animals and form a major source of dietary energy in animals. Phospholipids are important structural components of cell membranes, and sphingolipids are found predominantly in nerve tissues. Steroids have many important derivatives, including cholesterol, bile salts, and certain hormones. *Prostaglandins, *carotenoids, and *terpenes are also classified as lipids. Lipids often occur in association with proteins as lipoproteins.

Lipizzaner   A breed of ▢horse long associated with the Spanish Riding School in Vienna, where they are trained for spectacular displays. It is named for the stud founded by Archduke Charles at Lipizza, near Trieste, in 1580. The Lipizzaner has a short back, strong hindquarters, a powerful neck, and a small head. Born black, they mature to a gray color. Height: 14½–15 hands (1.47–1.52 m).

Li Po   (Li Bo or Li T'ai Po; 705–62) Chinese poet. Li Po and *Du Fu together are often considered China's greatest poets. Li Po's poetry is mostly light-hearted and romantic and has its stylistic origins in folk ballads and other old traditions. Legend has it that he drowned trying to embrace the reflection of the moon from a boat.

Lipmann, Fritz Albert   (1899–) US biochemist, born in Germany. He won a Nobel Prize in physiology and medicine in 1953. He came to the US (1939) and conducted research at Massachusetts General Hospital (1941–49) where he discovered (1946–47) coenzyme A and its important intermediary role in metabolism and body energy. He taught at Harvard University (1949–57) and worked for Rockefeller Institute from 1957.

Lippe River   A river in NW Germany, rising in the Teutoburger Wald (forest) and flowing generally W to join the Rhine River at Wesel. **The Lippe Canal** (1929), which runs parallel to the river, is the more important waterway. Length: 150 mi (240 km).

Lippershey, Hans   (died c. 1619) Dutch lens grinder, who built the first *telescope. The Dutch Government tried to keep the invention a secret but news of it eventually reached *Galileo, who built his own telescope, which he used for astronomical observations.

Lippi, Fra Filippo   (c. 1406–69) An early Renaissance Florentine painter, who was a Carmelite monk from 1421 to about 1432. During this time he probably trained under *Masaccio. He was frequently patronized by the Medici but his greatest works are his fresco decorations for the choir of Prato Cathedral (1452–64), showing scenes from the lives of St John the Baptist and St Stephen. He is also noted for his idealized Madonnas, e.g. *The Madonna and Child with Two Angels* (Uffizi). He abducted and later married a nun, Lucrezia Buti; their son, **Filippino Lippi** (1457–1504), was

also a painter. Filippino trained under *Botticelli after his father's death and completed Masaccio's fresco cycle in the Brancacci Chapel. His paintings, such as *The Vision of St Bernard* (Badia, Florence), influenced the Florentine mannerists of the 16th century.

Lipscomb, William Nunn   (1919–) US chemist, who won the 1976 Nobel Prize for his elucidation of the structure of *boranes. He discovered the arrangement of atoms inside borane molecules by means of X-ray diffraction and showed how groups of three such atoms are bonded by a single pair of electrons.

liquefaction of gases   Gases are liquefied in several ways. If the temperature of the gas is below its critical temperature (see critical state), it can be liquefied simply by compressing it. If the critical temperature is too low for this, the cascade process can be used. In this a gas with a high critical temperature is first liquefied by compression and then allowed to cool by evaporation under reduced pressure. This gas cools a second gas below its critical temperature, so that it in turn can be liquefied, evaporated, and cooled still further. Thus the temperature is reduced in stages. Other methods include cooling by the *Joule-Kelvin effect, which is used industrially in the Linde process (named for Carl von Linde; 1842–1934), and by adiabatic expansion in which a compressed gas is cooled by performing external work. This is the basis of the Claude process (named for— Georges Claude; 1870–1960).

Liquefied Petroleum Gas (LPG)   Propane, propene, butane, butene, or a mixture of any of these. LPG is a product of *oil refining and is also produced from *natural gas. It is transported by pipeline or in specially built tankers by road, rail, or sea.

Most of the LPG produced is sold in low-pressure cylinders for heating or used as a raw material for chemical manufacture, although it is also used as engine fuel.

liqueurs   Alcoholic *spirits flavored with herbs or other ingredients, usually heavily sweetened. Liqueurs are generally sipped, neat, from small glasses after dinner. Some liqueurs, such as Benedictine, were originated by monks; the yellow or green Chartreuse is still made by the Carthusians. Other liqueurs include Curaçao, Cointreau, and Grand Marnier, which are made with brandy and oranges; Kümmel made with cumin and caraway seeds; Maraschino made with marasca cherries; and Drambuie made with whisky and honey. Aged high-quality brandy and whisky, drunk neat, are sometimes described as liqueurs.

liquid crystal   A substance exhibiting some liquid properties, especially fluidity, and some crystalline properties, in that large clusters of molecules are aligned in parallel formations. As liquid crystals change their reflectivity when an electric potential is applied to them, they are used in the digital display of electronic calculators, etc.

liquidity preference   The proportion of an individual's total assets held in cash. Liquidity preference is determined chiefly by the general price level (if prices are high people need more cash to finance their purchases) and the rate of interest (if interest rates are high people will wish to invest their assets in interest-bearing bonds rather than in money). The concept was originated by J. M. *Keynes to explain the demand for money.

liquids   A state of matter between that of *gases and the *solid state. Liquids assume the shape of a container in the same way as gases but being incompressible do not expand to fill the container. Intermolecular forces are considerably stronger than in gases but weaker than in solids. Molecules are only maintained in an orderly arrangement by intermolecular forces over relatively small groups of molecules. The theory of liquids is much less well established than that of gases and solids.

lira   **1.** Another name for the hurdy-gurdy. **2.** A bowed string instrument of the late middle ages. The **lira da braccio** (Italian: lyre for the arm) resembled the *violin but had a flatter body; it was held against the shoulder. The larger **lira da gamba** (Italian: lyre for the leg) was held like a *cello or viola da gamba. Both instruments had between 7 and 15 strings, some of which were sympathetic strings.

Lisbon (Portuguese name: Lisboa)   38 44N 9 08W   The capital of Portugal, in the SW on the Tagus River. The country's chief seaport, it has one of the finest harbors in Europe; main exports include wine, olive oil, and cork. Lisbon is also a major industrial and commercial center. Historic buildings include the Tower of Belém and the Jerónimos Monastery; its university was founded in 1290. *History*: a settlement from very early times, it was an organized community under the Roman Empire but was later overrun by German tribes. Occupied by the Moors in the 8th century AD, it was captured by the Portuguese in the 12th century and became their capital in 1256. It flourished in the 15th and 16th centuries, the great age of Portuguese exploration and colonization, but later suffered a decline. In 1755 it was almost totally destroyed by an earthquake. It has expanded considerably in the 20th century and in 1966 one of the world's longest suspension bridges was opened across the Tagus River, linking Lisbon with Almada. Population (1974 est): 774,500.

Lisieux 49 09N 0 14E A city in N France, in the Calvados department. The shrine of St Thérèse (1873–1917) attracts large numbers of pilgrims to Lisieux. An agricultural trading center (especially in dairy products), its manufactures include textiles and car components. Population (1975): 26,674.

Lissajous figures Patterns arising from the addition of two *simple harmonic motions at right angles to each other, first studied by Jules Lissajous (1822–80). The shape of the pattern depends on the periods of the two motions and the initial conditions. If one of the two periods is an exact multiple of the other the curve is closed, otherwise the curve is open. Lissajous figures are displayed on a *cathode-ray oscilloscope when two sinusoidal signals control the vertical and horizontal motion of the electron beam.

Lissitzky, El (Eliezer L.; 1890–1941) Russian painter, typographer, designer, and architect, known particularly for his work in advertising and exhibition design. While teaching architecture at Vitebsk (1919–21) he painted his series of abstract geometrical paintings, *Proun*. Between 1922 and 1929 he lived in the West, where he was instrumental in spreading Russian ideas on design (*see* constructivism).

List, Friedrich (1789–1846) German economist, who was exiled in 1825 and emigrated to the US. In *Outlines of American Economy* (1827), he argued the need for tariffs to encourage the growth of industry, especially in a developing country. He also wrote *The National System of Political Economy* (1841).

Lister, Joseph, 1st Baron (1827–1912) British surgeon, who pioneered antiseptic techniques in surgery. In 1865, while surgeon at Glasgow Royal Infirmary, Lister realized the significance of *Pasteur's germ theory of disease in trying to prevent the infection of wounds following surgical operations. Lister devised a means of eliminating contamination and introduced carbolic acid as an antiseptic to dress wounds. Mortality arising from infected wounds declined sharply in Lister's ward and his antiseptic procedures eventually became standard practice in hospitals everywhere.

Liszt, Franz (Ferencz L.; 1811–86) Hungarian pianist and composer. He made his debut at the age of nine. After studying the piano with Czerny and studying composition he began a career as a virtuoso. From 1835 to 1839 he lived with the Comtesse d'Agoult (1805–76); their daughter Cosima married Wagner, of whose works Liszt was an early champion. From 1848 to 1861 Liszt lived with the Princess Sayn-Wittgenstein. In 1865 he took minor orders in the Roman Catholic Church; he spent most of the rest of his life in Weimar, Budapest, and Rome. As a pianist Liszt was considered the greatest performer of his time. As a composer he invented the symphonic poem and made use of advanced harmonies and original forms. His compositions include much piano music (including a sonata in B minor and operatic paraphrases), the *Faust Symphony* (1854–57) and *Dante Symphony* (1855–56), and the symphonic poem *Les Préludes* (1854).

litchi (lychee *or* lichee) A Chinese tree, *Litchi chinensis*, cultivated in the tropics and subtropics for its fruits. The fruit is almost globular, 1 in (2.5 cm) in diameter, with a warty deep-pink rind and is borne in branched clusters. The white translucent watery flesh has a sweet acid flavor and encloses a single large brown seed. The fruit is eaten fresh, canned, or dried as litchi nuts. Family: *Sapindaceae*.

liter A unit of volume in the *metric system formerly defined as the volume of one kilogram of pure water under specified conditions. This definition still applies for most purposes but in *SI units the liter is a special name, not recommended for high-precision measurements, for the cubic decimeter.

litharge. *See* lead.

lithium (Li) The lightest metal (relative density 0.534), discovered by Arfvedson in 1817. It is an alkali metal and gives a crimson-red color to flames. It occurs in nature in lepidolite, spodumene ($LiAlSi_2O_6$), and other minerals; as well as in brine, from which it is extracted commercially by electrolysis of the molten chloride (LiCl). The metal has the highest specific heat capacity of any solid element. It is corrosive, combustible, and reacts with water. Because of its efficiency in reflecting neutrons, lithium has important applications as a blanketing material in both the hydrogen bomb and proposed *thermonuclear reactors. It forms salts, like the other alkali metals, and the hydride LiH. Lithium salts are used in the treatment of some forms of mental depression. At no 3; at wt 6.941; mp 132°F (180.54°C); bp 780°F (1347°C).

lithography. *See* printing.

Lithops A genus of succulent South African desert plants (about 50 species), with no stems and leaves partly buried in the soil. The tips of the leaves are smooth, with a deep cleft across the top, camouflaged to resemble pebbles. The daisy-like flowers are white or yellow. Family: *Aizoaceae*.

Lithuanian A language belonging to the E division of the Baltic languages division of the Indo-European family, spoken mainly by the Lithuanians of the Lithuanian SSR, where it is the official language. The total population of Lithuanian speakers, including those in America, is about 2,750,000. Lithuanian is closely related to *Latvian. It is written in a Latin alphabet and written texts date from the 16th century.

Lithuanian Soviet Socialist Republic (*or* Lithuania) A constituent republic in the NW Soviet Union, on the Baltic Sea. Most of Lithuania comprises a central lowland and is a particularly fertile region, with forests and peat reserves. The Lithuanians comprise about 80% of the population. Lithuania has large fertilizer, textile, and metalworking industries. Agriculture, especially livestock breeding, has been intensified in the postwar period. *History*: one of the largest states in medieval Europe, in the 14th century Lithuania united with Poland under the *Jagiellon dynasty, passing after the partition of Poland in the 18th century to Russia. It became independent in 1918 but was incorporated into the Soviet Union as an SSR in 1940. It was occupied by Germany during World War II, during which the large Jewish minority was virtually exterminated. The US does not recognize Lithuania's status as a Soviet republic. Area: 25,170 sq mi (65,200 sq km). Population (1980 est): 3,400,000. Capital: Vilnius.

litmus A soluble compound obtained from certain lichens. Litmus turns red in an acid solution and blue in an alkaline solution. It is therefore used as an *indicator, often in the form of **litmus paper**, strips of paper impregnated with litmus.

Little America 78 11S 162 10W The main US Antarctic base, near the coast of Ross Dependency. It was established in 1928 as the headquarters for the polar expeditions of Richard *Byrd.

Little Belt (Danish name: Lille Bælt) A strait in SW Denmark, between the mainland and the island of Fyn. It links the Kattegat with the Baltic Sea and narrows to 0.6 mi (1 km).

Little Bighorn, Battle of the (June 25, 1876) The battle fought on the S bank of the Little Bighorn River in the Montana Territory, in which General *Custer and men of the 7th Cavalry were massacred by Sioux Indians led by *Crazy Horse and *Sitting Bull. The battle was also known as Custer's Last Stand. Custer's men were outnumbered nearly 10 to 1. The Indians were resisting incursions by whites into land that had been granted to them by treaty in 1868, but shortly after the battle would be driven from the area. The battlefield is now a national monument.

little owl A small *owl, *Athene noctua*, occurring in Eurasia and North Africa. 8 in (20 cm) long, it has a white-mottled brown plumage with heavily barred underparts, rounded wings, and bright-yellow eyes and hunts over open country at dawn and dusk, feeding on insects, worms, and occasionally mice.

Little Rock 34 42N 92 17W The capital city of Arkansas. In 1957, when black pupils entered the high school for the first time, it was the scene of major race riots protesting against desegregation. Population (1980): 158,461.

Little Turtle (1752–1812) Miami Indian chief. He successfully fought against General Josiah Hormar (1790) and General Arthur St Clair (1791) in their efforts to end Indian raids and to settle the Northwest Territory. In 1793 he was defeated by General Anthony Wayne's forces at Fort Recovery and Fallen Timbers in present-day Ohio. He signed and honored the Treaty of Greenville (1795) and from then on advocated peace.

Litvinov, Maksim Maksimovich (1876–1951) Soviet diplomat; foreign minister (1930–39). Litvinov, who believed in cooperation between the Soviet Union and the West, obtained US recognition of his country in 1934. In the League of Nations he advocated action against the Axis powers and was dismissed shortly before the German–Soviet nonaggression treaty of 1939. After the German invasion of the Soviet Union, Litvinov was ambassador to the US (1941–43).

Liu Shao Qi (*or* Liu Shao-ch'i; 1898–1974) Chinese communist statesman. He joined the Communist Party in Moscow in 1921 and later became a leader of the trade union movement in the *Jiangxi Soviet. In 1959 he succeeded *Mao Tse-tung as chairman of the People's Republic of China but was condemned as a reactionary during the *Cultural Revolution and disappeared from public view.

liver A large glandular organ, weighing 2.6–3.5 lb 1.2–1.6 kg), situated in the upper right region of the abdomen, just below the diaphragm. The liver has many important functions concerned with the utilization of absorbed foods. It converts excess glucose into glycogen, which it stores and reconverts into glucose when required; it breaks down excess amino acids into *urea; and it stores and metabolizes fats. The liver forms and secretes *bile, which contains the breakdown products of worn-out red blood cells, and synthesizes blood-clotting factors, plasma proteins, and—in the fetus—red blood cells. It also breaks down (detoxifies) poisonous substances, including alcohol. *Cirrhosis of the liver is commonly caused by a combination of sensitivity to, and excess of, alcohol.

liver fluke A parasitic *flatworm that inhabits the bile duct of sheep, cattle, and man. The common liver fluke (*Fasciola hepatica*) passes its larval stages in a marshland snail before infecting grazing animals (or, rarely, man). The Chinese liver fluke (*Opisthorchus sinensis*), 0.4–0.8 in (1–2 cm) long, passes two larval stages in a freshwater snail and fish before maturing in a human host.

Liverpool 53 25N 2 55W A major city in NW England, on the estuary of the River Mersey. It is the UK's second most important port and the foremost for Atlantic trade. The most famous landmark is the Royal Liver Building (1910) at the Pier Head. Other notable buildings include St George's Hall (1854). There is a new Roman Catholic cathedral (constructed 1962–67). The Anglican cathedral (begun 1904) is the country's largest ecclesiastical building. Liverpool has one of the largest provincial universities in the UK (1903). Exports include all kinds of manufactured goods, especially textiles and machinery. The main imports are petroleum, grain, ores, nonferrous metals, sugar, wood, fruit, and cotton. These are reflected in some of Liverpool's industries: flour milling, electrical engineering, food processing, chemicals, soap, margarine, tanning, and motor vehicles. *History*: originally trading with Ireland, Liverpool grew rapidly in the 18th and 19th centuries, superseding Bristol as the chief west coast port as a result of trade with the Americas (sugar, tobacco, slaves, cotton). Population (1981): 510,306.

Liverpool, Robert Banks Jenkinson, 2nd Earl of (1770–1828) British statesman; Tory prime minister (1812–27). He became an a member of Parliament in 1790 and held office almost continuously until 1827. He was foreign secretary (1801–04), home secretary (1807–09), and secretary for war and the colonies (1809–12). As prime minister he is remembered for his unenlightened response to the unrest that followed the Napoleonic Wars (1803–15). He also opposed *Catholic emancipation but the last years of his government saw the development of Tory reform.

liverwort A *bryophyte plant of the class *Hepaticae* (10,000 species), found growing on moist soil, rocks, trees, etc. There are two groups: leafy liverworts, in which the plant body is differentiated into stems and leaves; and thallose liverworts, which have a flat lobed liverlike body (thallus). The liverwort plant is the gamete-producing phase (gametophyte) and gives rise to a capsule, the spore-producing phase (sporophyte), which is sometimes borne on a slender erect column (*see* hornwort).

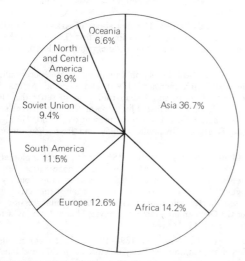

LIVESTOCK FARMING *Distribution of the world's livestock (cattle, sheep, pigs, horses, asses and mules).*

livestock farming The maintenance and management of domesticated animals for the production of milk, meat, eggs, fibers, skins, etc. Farming methods vary widely throughout the world and modern improvements in

livestock breeds and husbandry techniques have enabled dramatic increases to be made in productivity, nutrition and disease control being essential aspects of management.

Cattle produce milk (*see* dairy farming) and beef. The gestation period is about 9 months, followed by about 10 months of lactation and a 2-month dry period before calving again. A cow is known as a heifer until her second lactation. Heifers are reared either for beef or as dairy replacements and bull calves are generally castrated and reared for beef, being known as bullocks or steers. Age at slaughter depends on the breed and level of feeding but is generally about 18 months. Calves for veal are reared on a milk-based diet and are slaughtered at about 14 weeks.

Sheep are farmed worldwide for meat and wool (and in some countries for milk), often grazing on poor mountainous or arid pastures. One or two lambs per ewe are born in early spring. Males are castrated and reared for slaughter at weights of 44–99 lb (20–45 kg). Selected females are reared as replacement ewes. Each sheep yields 4–11 lb (2–5 kg) of wool.

Pigs have traditionally been kept outdoors, foraging for roots, seeds, etc. In modern intensive systems, they are housed under controlled conditions. Young females (gilts) are first mated at 7–8 months. Following the gestation period of 115 days, an average of 7–9 piglets are born per litter. Pork pigs are slaughtered at 88–110 lb (40–50 kg); those reared for bacon are slaughtered at 176–220 lb (80–100 kg).

Poultry are now kept indoors in an artificially controlled environment. Chicks are hatched artificially, the female birds starting to lay after about 20 weeks and producing about 250 eggs per year. Laying flocks are kept in "batteries" of cages with 3–5 birds per cage, feeding, cleaning, and egg collection being automatic. Table birds are fed ad lib and reach a weight of around 4 lb (2 kg) in 8–12 weeks. Turkeys are also reared for meat under intensive conditions.

Apart from producing food, many livestock, especially horses, mules, and donkeys, provide important means of transport and motive power. Goats provide milk in many traditional agricultural systems.

Livia Drusilla (58 BC–29 AD) The wife of Octavian (Emperor *Augustus) from 39 BC and the mother by her first husband of Emperor *Tiberius. As Augustus' consort Livia's image was one of matronly dignity and reports of her machinations on Tiberius' behalf are probably exaggerated. After Augustus' death (14 AD) she received the honorific name Julia Augusta.

living fossil A living organism whose closest relatives are all extinct, being known only as fossils. Such organisms were thought—before their discovery in modern times—to be extinct themselves. Examples of living fossils are the *coelacanth and the *dawn redwood, discovered in 1938 and 1941, respectively.

Livingstone (*or* Maramba) 17 50S 25 53E A city in S Zambia, on the Zambezi River. It was the former capital of Northern Rhodesia (1907–35). It is a tourist center for the nearby Victoria Falls. Population (1980 est): 80,000.

Livingstone, David (1813–73) Scottish missionary and explorer of Africa. A physician and missionary, in 1840 he set out for Bechuanaland (now Botswana). He traced long stretches of the Zambezi, Shire, and Rovuma Rivers, and discovered Lake Ngami (1849), the Victoria Falls (1855), and Lake Nyasa (now Malawi). During an attempt to trace the source of the Nile (1866–73) his famous encounter with Sir Henry Morton *Stanley occurred. He died near Lake Bangweulu.

Livingston, Robert R. (1746–1813) US lawyer and statesman; first secretary for foreign affairs (1781–83). Between service at the Continental Congress (1775–76; 1779–81; 1784–85), he helped to draft the Declaration of Independence (1776), served as chancellor of New York state (1777–1801), and became the first US secretary for foreign affairs, supervising the US delegation to the Paris Peace Conference (1782–83). He was appointed minister to France (1801–04) and, with James *Monroe, negotiated the Louisiana Purchase (1803). He spent the rest of his life promoting steamboating with Robert *Fulton.

Living Theater An experimental theater company founded in New York City in 1947 by Julian Beck (1925–) and Judith Malina (1926–). Their best-known productions include Jack Gelber's *The Connection* (1959), a play about drug addiction, and *Paradise Now* (1968), in which they developed controversial experiments in audience participation.

Livonian Knights (Livonian Brothers of the Sword) A German military and religious order of knighthood founded in 1202 to conquer and christianize the region, notably Livonia, around the Baltic Sea. They merged with the Teutonic Knights in 1237 and were disbanded in 1561.

DAVID LIVINGSTONE   *"Found" by Stanley (on the right) at Ujiji.*

Livonian War (1558–83) A confrontation over Russian expansion toward the Baltic Sea. In 1558 *Ivan the Terrible invaded Livonia and defeated its rulers, the Livonian Knights, who placed Livonia under Lithuanian protection. Russia was eventually defeated by the Polish-Lithuanian commonwealth (*see* Lublin, Union of) and Sweden, losing its Livonian conquests and some border towns on the Gulf of Finland.

Livorno (English name: Leghorn)   43 33N 10 18E A port in central Italy, in Tuscany on the Ligurian Sea. It has a 16th-century cathedral. Its industries include shipbuilding, oil refining, and engineering. Straw (Leghorn) hats are produced. Olive oil, copper products, and marble are exported. Population (1980 est): 176,249.

Livy (Titus Livius; 59 BC–17 AD) Roman historian. He was born in Patavium (Padua) in N Italy and settled in Rome about 29 BC. His monumental history of Rome from its legendary foundation to the death of Drusus in 9 BC, written in an elevated style and emphasizing the moral examples of individual lives, was immediately popular. Only 35 of the original 142 books survive, covering the early history up to the 4th century BC, the second Punic War against Hannibal, and the wars against Macedonia up to 166 BC.

lizard A *reptile belonging to the suborder *Sauria* (3000 species), occurring worldwide but most abundant in tropical regions. They are mainly terrestrial with cylindrical or narrow scaly long-tailed bodies, some with limbs reduced or absent (*see* glass snake; skink), and often with crests, spines, and frills. They range in size from the smallest *geckos to the formidable *Komodo dragon. Lizards lay leathery-shelled eggs although certain species of colder regions and many skinks bear live young. The female builds a simple nest and may guard her eggs until the young hatch and disperse. Some lizards reproduce by parthenogenesis, i.e. unfertilized eggs develop into races of females. Lizards eat chiefly insects and vegetation and have been known to live for 25 years in captivity.

Lizard Point (*or* Lizard Head)   49 56N 5 13W The most southerly point of the British Isles, in SW Cornwall on the Atlantic Ocean. It possesses magnificent coastal scenery with distinctive green- and purple-colored serpentine rock.

Ljubljana (German name: Laibach)   46 04N 14 30E A city in NW Yugoslavia, the capital of Slovenia. Under foreign rule until 1918, it is the center of Slovene culture with a university (1595). It was largely destroyed by an earthquake in 1895. Population (1971): 173,853.

llama A hoofed mammal, *Lama glama*, of S and W South America. Up to 48 in (120 cm) high at the shoulder, llamas are sure-footed, nimble, and hardy, with thick warm coats. They are now only found in the domesticat-

ed state, being used for meat, wool, and as pack animals. Family: *Camelidae* (camels, etc.).

llanos The treeless grasslands of South America that cover about 220,000 sq mi (570,000 sq km) of central Venezuela and N Colombia. Drained by the Orinoco River and its tributaries, the llanos are traditionally a cattle-rearing region but the discovery of oil in the 1930s led to considerable population growth and economic development.

Llewellyn, Richard (R. D. V. L. Lloyd; 1907–83) Welsh novelist. After working in films and journalism, he achieved success with his novel about a Welsh mining village, *How Green Was My Valley* (1939). His other novels include the sequel *Up, Into the Singing Mountains* (1960).

Lloyd, Chris(tine) (*born* Evert; 1954–   ) US tennis player. She won the US singles title 1975–78, 1980, and 1982 and was Wimbledon singles champion in 1974, 1976 and 1981 and doubles champion in 1976.

Lloyd, Harold (1893–1971) US film comedian. He developed the character of the dogged little man in conventional suit and spectacles in numerous early silent comedies, most of them characterized by his use of dangerous stunts. His films include *Just Nuts* (1915), *Safety Last* (1923), and *The Freshman* (1925).

Lloyd George, David, 1st Earl (1863–1945) British statesman; Liberal prime minister (1914–22). He entered parliament in 1890 and gained a reputation for radicalism as a Welsh nationalist. He was president of the Board of Trade (1905–08) and then chancellor of the exchequer (1908–15). In World War I he served as minister of munitions (1915–16) and secretary for war (1916) before succeeding Asquith as prime minister. After the war he continued to lead a coalition government increasingly dominated by the Conservatives. He was criticized for negotiating with Irish militants in the establishment of the Irish Free State (1921) and his government fell when Britain came close to war with the Turkish nationalists. Lloyd George never regained prominence in British politics, although he held his parliamentary seat until 1945.

Lloyd's An association of British insurance underwriters named for the 17th-century London coffee house, owned by Edward Lloyd, where underwriters used to meet. Lloyd's itself does not underwrite insurance business, which is undertaken by private underwriters, who are wholly responsible for losses.

Lloyd Webber, Andrew (1948–   ) British composer. His musicals, with lyrics by Tim Rice (1944–   ), include *Joseph and the Amazing Technicolor Dreamcoat* (1968), *Jesus Christ Superstar* (1970), and *Evita* (1978); later works include *Cats* (1981), *Song and Dance* (1982), *Starlight Express* (1984), and *Requiem* (1985).

DAVID LLOYD GEORGE   *Haig (left) and Joffre (center) argue a point with the British prime minister on the Western Front (1916).*

Llywelyn ap Gruffudd (d. 1282) The only native Prince of Wales (1258–82) to be recognized as such by England. He aided the English barons against Henry III (1263–67) and refused homage to Edward I (1276), who forced Llywelyn into submission but allowed him to remain Prince of Wales by title. Llywelyn was killed in another revolt.

Llywelyn ap Iorwerth (d. 1240) Prince of Gwynedd, N Wales (1194–1238), who achieved supremacy over most other Welsh princes. He supported the barons against his father-in-law King John of England (1215), obtaining recognition for Welsh rights in Magna Carta.

loach A small elongated freshwater *bony fish of the family *Cobitidae* (over 200 species), found mainly in Asia, but also in Europe and N Africa. Loaches feed usually at night on bottom-dwelling invertebrates detected by the three to six pairs of barbels around the mouth. The intestine can serve as an accessory respiratory organ using swallowed air. Order: *Cypriniformes.*

loam A type of soil containing approximately equal proportions of sand, silt, and clay. It is an ideal soil for agriculture since it can retain some moisture and plant nutrients but is well aerated and drained and easily worked.

Lobachevski, Nikolai Ivanovich (1793–1856) Russian mathematician, who (in 1829) produced the first *non-Euclidean geometry. He achieved this by examining what is possible if the fifth axiom in Euclid's *Elements* is neglected. In Lobachevski's geometry the angles of a triangle always add up to less than 180°.

Lobelia A genus of annual and perennial herbs (about 250 species), found in most warm and temperate regions. The leaves are simple and the flowers are tubular, with a two-lobed upper lip and a larger three-lobed lower lip, and are arranged in a terminal spike. Ornamental species, called cardinal flowers, are usually blue or red. Family: *Lobeliaceae.*

Lobengula (c. 1836–94) King (1870–94) of the Matabele (*or* Ndebele) kingdom in S Rhodesia. Son of *Mzilikazi, Lobengula granted land and mineral rights to the British South Africa Company but this was no protection against the conquest of his kingdom in 1893.

Lobito 12 20S 13 34E A port in W Angola, on the Atlantic coast. Its fine natural harbor has made it the country's busiest port. Population (1970): 59,528.

lobotomy. *See* leukotomy.

lobster A large marine *crustacean of the section *Macrura* that has a long abdomen ending in a tailfan. True lobsters (family *Homaridae*) have segmented bodies, a pair of pincers, four pairs of walking legs, and several pairs of swimming legs (swimmerets). They live on the ocean bottom and are mainly nocturnal, feeding on seaweed and animals. Eggs are carried on the swimmerets and hatch into free-swimming larvae that later descend to the bottom. Many species are commercially important as food, for example *Homarus vulgaris* and *H. americanus.* Order: *Decapoda.*

Local Group The small irregularly shaped cluster of *galaxies to which our *Galaxy belongs. Other members include the *Andromeda galaxy, the Triangulum Spiral, and both *Magellanic Clouds. There are 25 or more members.

Locarno (German name: Lugarrus) 46 10N 8 48E A city and health resort in S Switzerland, on Lake Locarno. Its church of Madonna del Sasso (1480) is a place of pilgrimage. The Pact of Locarno was signed here. Population (1970): 14,143.

Locarno Pact (1925) A series of treaties between Germany, France, Belgium, Poland, Czechoslovakia, the UK, and Italy. The most important was an agreement between Germany, France, and Belgium, guaranteed by the UK and Italy, to maintain the borders between Germany and France and Belgium respectively and the demilitarized zone of the Rhineland. The latter was violated by Hitler in 1936.

Lochner, Stefan (c. 1400–51) German painter of the Cologne School, born in Meersburg on Lake Constance. He probably trained in the Netherlands before settling in Cologne. His *Madonna of the Rose Bower* (Wallraf-Richartz Museum, Cologne) combines the delicacy of the *international gothic with the naturalism of Flemish painting.

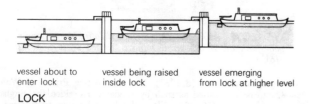

vessel about to   vessel being raised   vessel emerging
enter lock   inside lock   from lock at higher level

LOCK

lock A section of a canal or river, enclosed by gates, that is used to regulate the water level and raise or lower vessels wishing to navigate the waterway. The more common pound lock consists of two sets of mitered gates set a distance apart pointing into the downward force of the water. A vessel wishing to pass from the lower water level to the higher level enters the lock, the lower gates are closed behind it, and water from the upper level is allowed to flow into the lock through gaps in the upper gates. When the two levels are equal the upper gates are opened and the vessel leaves. The reverse procedure enables vessels to travel from the higher to the lower level.

Locke, John (1632–1704) English philosopher. His greatest work, the *Essay concerning Human Understanding* (1690), reveals him as a pioneer of *empiricism. It maintains, contrary to received tradition, that every one of our ideas comes from sense impressions; at birth the human mind is a *tabula rasa* (blank tablet). The *Essay* also attempts to sustain the distinction between primary qualities (found without exception in all bodies) and secondary qualities (originating in the impressions these bodies make on our senses). Locke's two works *Of Government* (1690) were enormously influential in molding modern concepts of liberal democracy. He dismissed any divine right to kingship and advocated liberal government, the function of which was, he thought, to preside over the exchange of "natural" for "civil" rights. He held that, in virtue of the occurrence of some form of *social contract in antiquity, political rulers were obliged to guarantee as civil rights any liberties that their subjects' ancestors might be supposed to have surrendered. However, there were some inalienable rights that could never be given up to a citizen's ruler.

lockjaw. *See* tetanus.

lockout The closure of a workplace by an employer to prevent employees from working, in an attempt to persuade them to accept the employer's terms of employment. In the interests of good industrial relations, the measure is now rarely used.

Lockyer, Sir Joseph Norman (1836–1920) British astronomer, who in 1868 first recognized the existence of an unknown element, which he called helium, in the sun's spectrum. Terrestrial helium was eventually discovered nearly 40 years later by Sir William *Ramsay. Lockyer also founded the scientific journal *Nature.*

locomotive An engine that draws a train on a *railroad. The first locomotives, designed by *Trevithick and *Stephenson were driven by steam engines and steam dominated the railroads until the end of World War II. Even in the mid-1970s, it was estimated that over 25,000 steam locomotives were still in use throughout the world. However, the steam engine has a low efficiency (about 8% in a locomotive, which does not use a condenser), it takes a long time to become operational while steam is raised, it uses an awkward and dirty solid fuel (which it has to pull with it in a tender immediately behind the engine), and it creates pollution. For these reasons steam locomotives have largely been replaced in the industrial countries by electric, Diesel-electric, or Diesel trains, all of which have efficiencies of about 22%.

Where the traffic justifies the cost of installing overhead wires or a conductor rail, electric trains are usually preferred, as it is more efficient to generate electricity centrally than in the locomotive. Various configurations have been tried, but series-wound direct-current motors are the most widely used, with rectification in the locomotive when the supply is alternating current. In some cases a three-phase supply is used, with *thyristor control. For lines in which a permanent installation is not economic, Diesel engines are used as a prime mover. These are either coupled hydraulically to the wheels, using a hydraulic torque converter (or fluid flywheel) and a gearbox, or to an electric generator or alternator, which produces current to power electric motors that drive the wheels. The first Diesel-electric train was used in Sweden in 1912 and the first Diesel-hydraulic in Germany a year later. Because the Diesel provides a very low torque at low speeds, it cannot be used without a hydraulic coupling, but even these units are usually restricted to small trains.

The use of *gas turbines on the railroads began in 1934, when a turbine powered a Swedish experimental train. A gas turbine-electric train was first tried in Switzerland in 1941. Although the gas turbine is lighter than the Diesel, it is only efficient at high power, and most of the long runs that could utilize its smooth full-power output are already electrified. The outlook for gas turbines is therefore not regarded as very promising.

Locri 38 14N 16 15E A city founded by Dorian Greek colonists about 700 BC on the E of the toe of Italy. Well governed by oligarchic rulers, Locri possessed in Zaleucus' legal code (c. 650 BC) Europe's earliest written laws. Its strategic position inevitably brought involvement in Rome's wars with Pyrrhus and Hannibal, and Scipio Africanus conquered it in 205 BC. Locri subsequently declined and was destroyed by Muslims in 915 AD. Excavations in 1889–1900 and the 1950s revealed a temple and many 5th-century terracotta plaques.

Stephenson's "Rocket" *The first locomotive to combine a multi-tubular boiler and a blast pipe, the "Rocket" ran on the earliest public railroad, in NE England, between Stockton and Darlington, in 1829.*

"General" *Typical of the most common type of US locomotive in the 19th century, the "General" was involved in a dramatic sabotage incident in 1862 during the Civil War. One of this class was the first to run at 100 mph (1893).*

C.R. No. 123 *Caledonian Railway's famous locomotive ran the difficult 100.6 miles between Carlisle and Edinburgh, Scotland, in 102.5 minutes in 1888.*

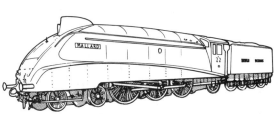

"Mallard" *This locomotive took the world steam traction speed record in July 1938, achieving 126 mph on a brake-test run.*

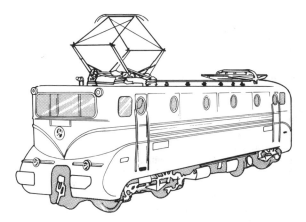

S.N.C.F. BB 9004 *For many years France held the world rail speed record. In 1955, the electric BB 9004 reached a speed of 205.6 mph, hauling three carriages weighing 100 tons.*

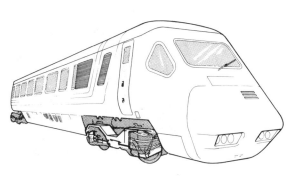

Advanced Passenger Train (APT) *British Rail's prototype gas-turbine APT traveled at 152 mph in 1975. Production APTs are electrically powered.*

locus In mathematics, a set of points that satisfy certain conditions. For example, in two dimensions the set of points a fixed distance from a particular point is a circle.

locust (botany) An evergreen Mediterranean tree, *Ceratonia siliqua*, also called carob tree or St John's bread. 40–49 ft (12–15 m) in height, it has catkins of petalless flowers and produces leathery pods containing a sweet edible pulp and small flat beans. The black locust (*Robinia pseudoacacia*), also called false acacia, is a North American tree widely cultivated for ornament (it is common in streets and parks). Up to 78 ft (24 m) tall, it has deeply ridged dark-brown bark, paired pale-green leaves, hanging clusters of white flowers, and black pods. Family: *Leguminosae*.

locust (zoology) A *grasshopper that undergoes sporadic increases in population size to form huge swarms, which migrate long distances and devour all the crops and other vegetation on which they settle. When the population density is high, due to favorable environmental conditions, the nymphs (immature forms), called hoppers, are brightly colored and crowd together—the gregarious phase, maturing into gregarious swarming adults. Solitary-phase nymphs, whose coloration is that of their surroundings, mature in uncrowded conditions into solitary nonswarming adults. Economically important species include the migratory locust (*Locusta migratoria*), about 2 in (55 mm) long (all locusts are relatively large), found throughout Africa and S Eurasia and eastward to Australia and New Zealand; and the desert locust (*Schistocerca gregaria*), occurring from N Africa to the Punjab.

Lod (or Lydda) 31 57N 34 54E A city in central Israel, between Jerusalem and Tel Aviv-Yafo. Lydda was the scene of many biblical events. Allocated to the Arabs by the UN in 1947, it fell to Israeli forces and is now the site of Israel's international airport. Population (1972): 30,500.

lodestone. See magnetite.

Lodge, Henry Cabot (1850–1924) US Republican politician; a senator from 1893 to 1924. An isolationist, he led the group of Republican senators who rejected the Treaty of *Versailles (1919) and prevented US membership of the League of Nations (1920).

Lodi 45 19N 9 30E A city in Italy, in Lombardy on the Adda River. It has a 12th-century cathedral. Manufactures include iron, majolica, silk, and linen. Situated in a rich dairy-farming district, it has a large trade in cheese, especially Parmesan. Population (1971): 44,422.

Lódź 51 49N 19 28E The second largest city in Poland. It developed rapidly during the 19th century and is now a leading industrial center specializing in textiles. Other manufactures include chemicals and electrical goods. Its university was founded in 1945. Population (1979 est): 832,000.

Loeb, Jacques (1859–1924) US zoologist, born in Germany, who demonstrated that unfertilized eggs of sea urchins and frogs could develop to maturity by means of controlled changes in their environment, which influenced cell division (see parthenogenesis). Loeb also worked on brain physiology, animal *tropisms (involuntary movements), and tissue regeneration.

Loeffler, Friedrich August Johannes (1852–1915) German bacteriologist, who (with Edwin *Klebs in 1884) first isolated the diphtheria bacillus (the Klebs-Loeffler bacillus). Loeffler also showed how some animals were immune to diphtheria, which helped *Behring to develop an antitoxin, and investigated several other animal diseases.

loess A deposit consisting of wind-born dust from desert or vegetation-free areas at the margins of ice sheets. Vast thick deposits occur in NW China; in Europe loess occurs in Germany (the Bördeland), Belgium, and NE France. Deep well-drained soils develop from loess.

Loewe, Frederick (1904–) US composer of musical comedies, born in Austria. He is famous for such musicals as *Brigadoon* (1947), *Paint Your Wagon* (1950), *My Fair Lady* (1956), and *Camelot* (1960), written with the librettist Alan *Lerner. They also wrote the Academy Award-winning film *Gigi* (1958).

Loewi, Otto (1873–1961) US physiologist, who demonstrated that stimulation of nerves causes the release of a chemical transmitter that affects the muscle concerned. He identified this transmitter as *acetylcholine—a substance first isolated by Sir Henry *Dale, with whom Loewi shared the 1936 Nobel Prize.

Lofoten Islands A large group of islands off the NW coast of Norway, within the Arctic Circle. There are rich cod and herring fisheries in the surrounding waters, to which many Norwegian fishermen come during spring. Area: about 1980 sq mi (5130 sq km). Population (1970): 56,066.

log **1.** A book containing a detailed record of the events occurring in and navigation of a vessel. **2.** A device, towed behind or fastened to a vessel, that records the speed of the vessel through the water. Its name comes from chip log, the device formerly used, which consisted of a chip tossed over-

board, at the bow of a vessel; the time required to pass the chip and the distance covered were used to calculate the speed of the vessel.

Logan, Mount 60 31N 140 22W The highest mountain in Canada, in SW Yukon in the St Elias Mountains. Its huge mass towers 13,780 ft (4200 m) above glaciers. Height: 19,850 ft (6050 m).

loganberry A trailing bramble-like shrub that is a cross between a raspberry and a blackberry. It bears heads of juicy wine-red tart-tasting fleshy berries, which are used for preserves, puddings, and wine. It originated in California and is named for James H. Logan (1841–1928), who first grew it in 1881. Family: *Rosaceae*.

logarithms A mathematical function used to facilitate multiplication and division. Based on the law that $a^x \times a^y = a^{x+y}$, two numbers p and q can be multiplied together by writing them in the form $p = a^x$ and $q = a^y$ and then adding together the values of x and y (the exponents). x is called the logarithm of p to the base a, i.e. $x = \log_a p$. Thus $p \times q$ is found by looking up their logarithms in books of tables, adding them together, and looking up the antilogarithm of the result. Division is carried out in a similar way using subtraction, based on the law $a^x \div a^y = a^{x-y}$. The base of common logarithms is 10 (i.e. $a = 10$); Naperian or natural logarithms use the base e. Pocket calculators have obviated the need for logarithms as a method of computation but they remain useful mathematical functions.

logic In the widest sense, the science of reasoned argument. As a mental discipline, it is concerned not so much with the application of argument in specific instances as with the general rules covering the construction of valid inferences. The dialogues of *Plato present *Socrates as pursuing wisdom through rational discourse, but *Aristotle was the first to make a systematic study of the principles governing such discourse (see also syllogism). His six logical treatises, known collectively as the *Organon*, were the sourcebooks for such medieval logicians as *Abelard. After the Renaissance philosophers became increasingly aware of limitations in the Aristotelian approach. *Leibniz, for instance, was worried by the difference between the logical and grammatical structure of sentences; two grammatically identical sentences may be very different logically. (Suppose, for example, that Jemima is a cat and compare the following two sentences: "Jemima is a cat; Jemima is mine; therefore Jemima is my cat." "Jemima is a mother; Jemima is mine; therefore Jemima is my mother.") Rules must therefore be found to formalize ordinary language in such a way as to make plain its underlying logical structure, before further rules for the construction of valid arguments can be drawn up. Since the 19th century formulation of such rules has become mainly the province of mathematicians. *Boole and *Frege were important pioneers in what is now called "mathematical logic" to differentiate it from the wider still current sense. *Russell, whose work had important repercussions for *set theory, called "logic . . . the youth of mathematics, and mathematics . . . the manhood of logic."

logical positivism A philosophical movement that arose from the *Vienna Circle in the 1920s. Influenced by *Mach and *Wittgenstein, it insisted that philosophy should be scientific, regarding it as an analytical (rather than a speculative) activity, the purpose of which was clarification of thought. Any assertion claiming to be factual has meaning only if its truth (or falsity) can be empirically tested. Metaphysical propositions and those of aesthetics and religion are consequently meaningless, since it is impossible to say how they can be verified. A secondary goal of logical positivism was the analysis and unification of scientific terminology. After the Nazi invasion of Austria, members of the Circle emigrated to Britain and the US, where the movement continued to be influential.

logos (Greek: word) A term with several different philosophical interpretations. *Heraclitus used it to mean the pervading rational underpinning of the universe. For the *Sophists logos could simply mean an argument. For the Stoics it was the kind of god from whom stems all the rationality in the universe. Students of St John's Gospel tend to interpret its occurrence there in the Stoic sense. See also Stoicism.

logwood A thorny tropical American tree, *Hematoxylon campechianum*, 30–48 ft (9–15 m) tall, with a short twisted trunk, compound leaves comprising many paired leaflets, and clusters of small yellow flowers. The blood-red heartwood yields the black to purple dye hematoxylin, used in the textile industry and as a biological stain. Family: *Leguminosae*.

Lohengrin In *Arthurian legend, the son of Percival (Parzival). He champions a young noblewoman, Elsa of Brabant, whom he agrees to marry on condition that she does not inquire into his origins. When her curiosity overcomes her, he is taken back by his swan guide to the castle of the *Holy Grail, whence he came. The story was adapted by *Wagner in the opera *Lohengrin* (1850).

Loire River The longest river in France. Rising in the Cévennes Mountains, it flows mainly W to the Bay of Biscay at St Nazaire, passing through

Orléans, Tours, and Nantes. Its tributaries include the Allier, Vienne, and Maine and it drains an area of 40,000 sq mi (119,140 sq km), one fifth of the area of France. The Loire Valley is renowned for its vineyards and chateaux (Amboise, Blois, Chambord, Chaumont, Chenonceaux). It is linked by canal with the Seine River. Length: 634 mi (1020 km).

Loki In Norse mythology, a mischief-making giant with the ability to change his shape and sex, who lived among the gods until imprisoned in a cave for the murder of Balder. His offspring—Hel, the goddess of death, Jörmungandr, the evil serpent surrounding the earth, and Fenris, the wolf—are among the forces of evil, which he leads against the gods at doomsday (□Ragnarök).

Lolland (or Laaland) A Danish island in the Baltic Sea, S of Sjælland. Produce includes cereals, hops, apples, and sugar beet. Area: 480 sq mi (1240 sq km). Population (1970): 78,916. Chief town: Maribo.

Lollards The followers of the English reformer *Wycliffe. Until his retirement from Oxford in 1378, the preaching of his doctrines attacking the Church hierarchy and transubstantiation and advocating the primacy of Scripture was largely confined to the University. Thereafter his teachings were taken up by nonacademics, including merchants, lesser clergy, and a few members of Richard II's court. Henry IV's reign saw considerable repression of the Lollards culminating in the defeat of *Oldcastle's rebellion in 1414. The movement then went underground and became increasingly proletarian. Many of its tenets were adopted by the early Protestants.

Lomax, Alan (1915–) US compiler of folksongs. With his father **John Avery Lomax** (1867–1948), he traveled around the country, recording songs that had never been published. He compiled *American Ballads and Folk Songs* (1934), *Negro Folk Songs As Sung by Lead Belly* (1936), and *Our Singing Country* (1941).

Lombard League A confederacy of Lombard towns formed with papal support in 1167 against attempts by the Holy Roman Empire to weaken their communal liberties. These were confirmed by Frederick (I) Barbarossa at the Peace of Constance (1183). Renewed against the threat of Frederick II the League was disbanded after his death (1250).

Lombardo, Pietro (c. 1438–1515) Italian sculptor and architect. Lombardo worked mainly in Venice, where he was the leading sculptor of his generation. His works include the Pietro Mocenigo monument (c. 1476–81; SS Giovanni e Paolo) and the design and sculptural decoration of Sta Maria dei Miracoli (1481–89). He was frequently assisted by his two sons **Antonio Lombardo** (c. 1458–c. 1516) and **Tullio Lombardo** (c. 1460–1532).

Lombards (Latin name: Langobardi) A Germanic people who, under *Alboin, invaded Italy and established a kingdom centered on Pavia (572 AD). When *Aistulf and then Desiderius (reigned 756–74) threatened Rome, the pope sought Carolingian assistance and in 773–74 the Lombards lost their independence to Charlemagne.

Lombardy (Italian name: Lombardia) A region in N Italy, consisting mainly of mountains in the N and lowlands in the S. Italy's most industrialized region, its economic prosperity has attracted large numbers of immigrants from other parts of the country. The industrial area containing Milan is dominated by textile, chemical, and engineering industries; metal manufacture is also important. Agriculture is highly productive and the most mechanized in Italy, producing a wide range of foods. There are important natural-gas fields and hydroelectric plants. Area: 9191 sq mi (23,834 sq km). Population (1980 est): 8,944,649. Capital: Milan.

Lombok An Indonesian island in the Nusa Tenggara group. The N and S are mountainous, while on the central fertile plain intensive cultivation produces rice, coffee, and tobacco. Under Hindu-Buddhist rule until the 15th century, it resisted later Islamic influence and came under Dutch control in 1894. Area: 1826 sq mi (4730 sq km). Population (1961): 1,300,234. Chief town: Mataram.

Lombroso, Cesare (1835–1909) Italian criminologist. His theories that some criminals are born as such and can be recognized by physical characteristics are no longer considered valid, but his major work, *L'uomo delinquente* (1876), initiated a new emphasis in criminology on the study of the criminal mind.

Lomé 6 10N 1 21E The capital and chief port of Togo, on the Gulf of Guinea. The Lomé Convention was signed here in 1975 between 46 African and Caribbean states providing for trade concessions into the EEC countries. It has a university (1970). Population (1979 est): 247,000.

Lomond, Loch The largest lake in Scotland, in E Strathclyde Region. It is a popular tourist area with picturesque scenery. Length: about 24 mi (38 km). Width: 5 mi (8 km).

Lomonosov, Mikhail Vasilievich (1711–65) Russian poet and scientist. The son of a fisherman, he did innovatory work in the natural sciences and became a professor at the St Petersburg Academy. In 1755 he founded Moscow University. He also wrote classical poetry and works on grammar and rhetoric.

LONDON *Big Ben and the statue of Queen Boadicea, who sacked the city.*

London (Latin name: Londinium) 51 30N 0 10W The capital of the UK, in SE England on the River Thames.

London's financial hub is to be found in its original nucleus, the **City of London**, on the N bank of the Thames, with an area of 1 sq mi (2.6 sq km). London's **East End**, has long provided a home for successive immigrant groups and acquired in the 19th century a reputation for harboring criminals. The **West End** comprises the district around Oxford Street and is the city's shopping and entertainment center.

London's **cultural life** is outstanding. There are remarkable art collections housed in the *National Gallery, the National Portrait Gallery, the *Tate Gallery, and the *Courtauld Institute. Its museums include the *British Museum, the *Victoria and Albert Museum, and the *Imperial War Museum. Most of London's commercial theaters are in the West End.

Many industries have now moved from central London to the suburbs but a wide variety of light industries, including clothing, precision instruments, and printing and publishing, remain. Activities are often localized: for example, the newspaper industry is centered on Fleet Street, and Harley Street is synonymous with doctors.

History: the foundations of London Wall are the chief reminder of the City's origins under the Romans, who built London at the highest point at which the Thames could be forded and at the river's tidal limit. It was sacked by Boadicea in 61 AD and subsequently, on several occasions, by the Vikings. During the reign of William the Conqueror the famous White Tower (*see* Tower of London) was built, and as London prospered in the middle ages both the Church and the *guilds sponsored exceptional building programs. □Westminster Abbey dates from the 11th century. The early Stuart period witnessed the great work of Inigo Jones, notably the Queen's House and the Banqueting Hall (1619–22), its ceiling painted by Rubens. London's population was decimated by the Plague (1665) and much of the city's fabric was destroyed in the calamitous Fire of the following year. The greatest loss—Old St Paul's (□St Paul's Cathedral)—was replaced by Wren, who was responsible for much of the work of reconstruction. Many of London's finest squares were built in the late 17th and early 18th centuries. The 19th century produced the Palace of Westminster, the Law Courts, and the Byzantine-style Westminster Cathedral. London, especially the City and the East End, was seriously damaged by bomb attacks during World War II and subsequent rebuilding has consisted largely of high-rise offices and apartments. Area: 610 sq mi (1580 sq km). Population (1981): 6,696,000.

London 42 58N 81 15W A city in central Canada, in Ontario. Founded in 1826, it has become SW Ontario's center for transportation, manufacturing, finance, and education. London's industries include textiles, printing, food processing, chemicals, electrical and metal goods, motor vehicle parts, and engines. It houses the University of Western Ontario (1878). Population (1981): 254,280.

London, Jack (1876–1916) US novelist. After childhood poverty and imprisonment for vagrancy he embarked on a course of self-education from which he emerged as a committed socialist and best-selling author. *Sea Wolf* (1904) grew out of his life aboard a sealing ship at 17. His best-known novels, *The Call of the Wild* (1903) and *White Fang* (1906), and many short stories were written after his experience of the Klondike gold rush in 1897. His other novels include *The Iron Heel* (1907) and the auto-biographical *Martin Eden* (1909).

London Bridge A bridge spanning the River Thames from the SE region of the City of London to the borough of Southwark. Bridges on this site date back to Roman times but the most famous London Bridge was built in stone between 1176 and 1209. It was replaced by a new bridge in the 1820s. The present bridge was completed in 1973.

Londonderry (or Derry) 55 00N 7 19W A city and port in Northern Ireland, the county town of Co Londonderry on the River Foyle. The City of London Corporation was granted Londonderry and the Irish Society established (1610) to administer it. In a famous siege (1688–89) it held out for 105 days against the forces of James II. Industries include shirt manufacture, light engineering, and food processing. Population (1971): 51,850.

Londonderry (or Derry) A county in N Northern Ireland, bordering on the Atlantic Ocean. It consists of central uplands bordered by lowlands with Low Neagh in the SE. It is drained by the Foyle, Bann, and Roe Rivers. Londonderry is predominantly agricultural producing flax, cereals, and dairy produce. Fishing is also an important source of income. Industries include textiles, chemicals, and light engineering. Area: 814 sq mi (2108 sq km). Population (1971): 130,889. County town: Londonderry.

London Economic Conference (1933) A meeting of the US and League of Nations members in London to discuss financial and economic stability. Also known as the World Monetary and Economic Conference, it aimed at finding ways to equalize the international economy during the Depression, but failed because of disagreement over returning to the gold standard.

London Naval Conference (1930) A meeting of the US, UK, Japan, France, and Italy in London to discuss limitation of warships. The US, UK, and Japan were able to come to agreements regarding the number of submarines and construction of ships, but France and Italy did not agree and did not sign the treaty.

London pride A succulent herb, *Saxifraga umbrosa*, also called St Patrick's cabbage, native to Ireland and Portugal and widely grown as an ornamental. It has a basal rosette of fleshy leaves with wavy edges and small white or pinkish five-petaled flowers in branching clusters on slender stems, 12–20 in (30–50 cm) tall. The garden form is a hybrid, *S.* × *urbium*. Family: *Saxifragaceae*.

Londrina 23 18S 51 13W A city in S Brazil, in Paraná state. Founded in 1930, it is the center of a coffee-growing area and has a university (1971). Population (1975 est): 283,740.

Long, Huey (Pierce) (1893–1935) US politician; nicknamed the "Kingfish." He was elected governor of Louisiana in 1928 and worked to revamp the state public works and welfare programs. He alienated the wealthy by financing his programs with new taxation. As a US senator (1932–35) he continued to run his state by making sure his supporters were in official positions. He proposed a national "Share-the-Wealth" program that would have limited the income of the rich and guaranteed an income and housing for the poor. He was assassinated by the relative of a long-time enemy.

Long Beach 33 47N 118 06W A city and port in California, on San Pedro Bay. It is a major tourist center, with a beach 8.5 mi (13.5 km) long. Other attractions include the former British liner *Queen Mary*, which has been converted into a hotel and conference center. Industries include the manufacture of aircraft and oil refining. Population (1980): 361,334.

longbow A bow of straight-grained yew used from about 1400 to about 1600. Originally Welsh, longbows were up to 6 ft (1.8 m) long and could fire a 37 in (110 cm) arrow capable of piercing chainmail and some plate armor at 200 yd (183 m) every 10 seconds.

Longfellow, Henry Wadsworth (1807–82) US poet. He traveled extensively in Europe and was professor of modern languages at Harvard (1834–54). He achieved enormous popularity with such narrative poems as *Evangeline* (1847), *The Song of Hiawatha* (1855), *The Courtship of Miles Standish* (1858), and *Paul Revere's Ride* (1861). He also produced an undistinguished translation of Dante's *Divine Comedy* (1865–67).

Longford (Irish name: Longphort) A county in the N central Republic of Ireland, in Leinster. Chiefly low lying with areas of bog, it contains part of Low Ree in the SW. Agriculture consists of cattle and sheep rearing and the production of oats and potatoes. Area: 403 sq mi (1043 sq km). Population (1979): 30,785. County town: Longford.

Longhi, Pietro (Pietro Falca; 1702–85) Venetian painter, who specialized in historically interesting scenes of upper-class life. Small in scale, they are distinguished by their doll-like figures and humorous approach, notably in *Exhibition of a Rhinoceros* (National Gallery, London). His son **Alessandro Longhi** (1733–1813) was a portrait painter.

Longinus (1st century AD) Greek rhetorician, supposed author of *On the Sublime*. This treatise, a critical analysis of the quality of excellence in literature with illustrative quotations from numerous Greek writers, greatly influenced many later neoclassical writers, including Dryden, Pope, and Gibbon; it was first translated (1674) into a modern language by the French critic Boileau.

Long Island An island in New York state, separated from the mainland by Long Island Sound. Chiefly residential with many resorts, it contains the New York City boroughs of *Brooklyn and *Queens and the international John F. Kennedy Airport. Aircraft industries have long been a mainstay of the economy. Area: 1723 sq mi (4462 sq km).

longitude. *See* latitude and longitude.

long jump A field event in athletics. Competitors sprint up a runway and leap as far as possible into a sandpit from a take-off board. The competitor who makes the longest jump in three or six tries is the winner.

LONG MARCH *Survivors of the Chinese communist flight from Jiangxi attend a rally in Yan'an.*

Long March (1934–35) The flight of the Chinese communists from the *Jiangxi Soviet, which they were forced by the *Guomindang to abandon, to Yan'an, a distance of 6000 mi (10,000 km). Over 100,000 people, led by Mao Tse-tung, took part in the heroic march but only about 30,000 reached Yan'an. The Long March established Mao as the leader of the Chinese Communist Party.

Long Parliament (1640–60) The parliament that was summoned by Charles I of England following his defeat in the second *Bishops' War. In 1641 it expressed its grievances against Charles in the *Grand Remonstrance, and in 1642 it assumed control of the militia. Charles' rejection of its demands for reform (Nineteen Propositions) precipitated the outbreak of the Civil War. Its power declined as that of the *New Model Army increased, and in 1648 it was purged of its moderate members. The remaining Rump Parliament was dismissed in 1653 by Oliver □Cromwell, who established the *Protectorate. The Rump was reinstated in 1659 and the full membership of the Long Parliament was restored in 1660. Shortly afterward it dissolved itself, being replaced by the Convention Parliament, which effected the *Restoration.

longship A large sailing vessel equipped with a bank of oars on each side for use when there was no wind or when it blew adversely. Longships were used by Scandinavian maritime peoples until the mid 18th century. They had square sails and very high prows and were steered by a long tiller attached to a large rudder. Larger longships could carry about a hundred people and are said to have carried the Vikings from Scandinavia as far as Greenland and to the coast of North America.

Longstreet, James (1821–1904) US Confederate general. After graduating from West Point he served during the *Mexican War. At the outset of the Civil War he resigned from the army to join the Confederates at the first Battle of *Bull Run (1861). By 1862 he had partial command of the Army of Northern Virginia and fought at Bull Run, Antietam, and Fredericksburg. As a lieutenant general he commanded troops at Gettysburg (1863), Chickamauga (1863), Knoxville (1863), and the Battle of the Wilderness (1864) where he was wounded. After the war he became a Republican and served as minister to Turkey (1880–81).

long-tailed tit An acrobatic Eurasian tit, *Aegithalus caudatus*, about 6 in (14 cm) long, with a black, pink, and white plumage and a long (3 in [7 cm]) black-and-white tail. It feeds chiefly on insects and spiders and builds an elaborate domed nest from lichens, animal hair, cobwebs, and feathers.

loofah The fibrous skeleton of the fruit of the tropical dishcloth gourd, or vegetable sponge (genus *Luffa* (6 species), especially *L. cylindrica*). These vines produce cucumber-like straw-colored fruits, about 12 in (30 cm) long. When mature, the pulp and seeds are removed leaving a dense network of fibrous conducting tissue, which is used as a bath sponge, dish washer, and industrial filter. Family: *Cucurbitaceae*.

Lookout Mountain, Battle of (1863) Civil War battle in S Tennessee, part of the Chattanooga Campaign. Lookout Mountain, a ridge near Chattanooga, was held by the Confederate Army. Union troops, under General Joseph *Hooker, advancing on Chattanooga, scaled the ridge under cloud-cover (from which the conflict's nickname of Battle Above the Clouds) and overwhelmed the weakened Confederates.

loom. *See* weaving.

looper. *See* geometrid moth.

Loos, Adolph (1870–1933) Austrian architect. One of the pioneers of modern architecture, Loos was influenced by the styles of Otto *Wagner and Louis *Sullivan. His austere plain style, evident in the Steiner House, Vienna (1910), influenced *Gropius and the development of *functionalism. Later in his career, however, he became less dogmatic, designing buildings with classical motifs.

loosestrife Either of two perennial herbs occurring in marshes, ditches, and along river banks. Purple loosestrife, *Lythrum salicaria* (family *Lythraceae*), native to Eurasia, N Africa, and North America, grows to a height of 24–47 in (60–120 cm) and bears spikes of purple flowers. The Eurasian yellow loosestrife, *Lysimachia vulgaris* (family *Primulaceae*), grows to a height of 40 in (1 m) and forms branching terminal clusters of yellow flowers.

Lope de Vega. *See* Vega (Carpio), Lope Félix de.

López, Carlos Antonio (?1790–1862) Paraguayan statesman. As president (1844–62) he attempted to modernize the country and to end its isolation. He was succeeded by his son **Francisco Solano López** (1826–70), who led Paraguay into the disastrous War of the *Triple Alliance.

Lopez, Nancy (Marie) (1957–) US golfer. She began to play professional golf in 1977 and, in 1978, won nine tournaments, was named Player of the Year, and had total winnings of almost $190,000. She was again named Player of the Year in 1979.

López de Ayala, Pero (c. 1332–c. 1407) Spanish poet and chronicler, who became chancellor of Castile in 1399. His works include translations of Livy, Boethius, and Boccaccio, as well as *Rimado de palacio*, a collection of satirical poetry, and *Crónicas de los reyes de Castilla*.

Lop Nor An area of salt marsh and shallow shifting lakes in NW China, in the *Tarim Basin. Nuclear tests have been carried out here. Formerly a large salt lake, its area now varies widely.

loquat A small evergreen tree *Eriobotrya japonica*, native to China and Japan but widely cultivated in Mediterranean countries. 20–30 ft (6–9 m) high, it bears fragrant white flowers in dense terminal clusters. The yellow or orange fruit is pear-shaped with a woolly skin: it is eaten fresh, in preserves, or in stews. Family: *Rosaceae*.

Lorca, Federico Garcia. *See* Garcia Lorca, Federico.

Lord Dunmore's War (1774) A conflict between Virginia colonials and the Shawnee Indians over lands in Kentucky and W Pennsylvania. John Murray, Earl of Dunmore and royal governor of Virginia, ordered the militia, under Andrew Lewis, to attack the hostile Indians. The battle at Point Pleasant was won by the militia, and by the Treaty of Camp Charlotte that followed the Indians gave up their hunting grounds.

Lords, House of. *See* parliament.

Lorelei A rock in the Rhine River in W Germany noted for its echo and its association with a legend concerning a water nymph whose singing lured sailors to destruction. The legend first appears in the works of Clemens *Brentano.

Loren, Sophia (S. Scicoloni; 1934–) Italian film actress. From working as an extra and then as a supporting actress, she progressed to international stardom in such films as *Two Women* (1961), *The Millionairess* (1961), *Marriage Italian Style* (1964), and *The Cassandra Crossing* (1977). She was married the Italian film producer Carlo Ponti (1913–) in 1957.

Lorentz, Hendrick Antoon (1853–1928) Dutch physicist, who was awarded the 1902 Nobel Prize, with his pupil *Zeeman, for their work on the relationship between magnetism and radiation. Independently of *Fitzgerald, he suggested that bodies become shorter as their velocity increases, in order to explain the negative result of the *Michelson-Morley experiment. This phenomenon, now known as the **Lorentz-Fitzgerald** contraction, was later incorporated into Einstein's theory of *relativity. The mathematical treatment for transforming a set of coordinates from one frame of reference to another was worked out by Lorentz (**Lorentz transformations**) and also formed part of Einstein's theory of relativity.

KONRAD LORENZ *A pioneer of the science of ethology (the behavior of animals in their natural surroundings). Lorenz is pictured here in 1973, the year he received a Nobel Prize.*

Lorenz, Konrad (1903–) Austrian zoologist, who was one of the founders of modern ethology (the study of animal behavior). In the 1930s Lorenz identified the phenomenon of *imprinting in young chicks. He was concerned with determining the elements of behavior, how they were stimulated, their development in an individual, and their evolutionary significance. Lorenz has written several popular books about his work, including *King Solomon's Ring* (1949) and *Man Meets Dog* (1950). He has applied his theories of animal behavior to the human species, with controversial implications (*On Aggression*, 1963). He was awarded a Nobel Prize (1973) with Karl von *Frisch and Niko *Tinbergen.

Lorenzetti Two brothers, both Italian painters of the Sienese school, who were influenced by Giovanni *Pisano and *Giotto. They probably both died in the plague of 1348. **Pietro Lorenzetti** (c. 1280–?1348) was probably the pupil of *Duccio; he introduced a new humanity into his master's style in such works as *The Birth of the Virgin* (Duomo, Siena). His brother **Ambrogio Lorenzetti** (c. 1290–?1348) is renowned for his frescoes of *Good and Bad Government* (1337–39; Palazzo Pubblico, Siena). They are among the first Italian paintings to show scenes of contemporary life and are remarkable for their early mastery of perspective.

Lorenzo Monaco (Piero di Giovanni; c. 1370–1425) Italian painter, born in Siena. He settled in Florence, becoming a monk in 1391. Influenced by both the Sienese school and the Florentine tradition of *Giotto, his *Coronation of the Virgin* (Uffizi) is his major work.

Lorestan. *See* Luristan.

Loreto 43 26N 13 36E A small town in central Italy, in Marche. Pilgrims travel here to see the Santa Casa (Holy House), which is said to have been the home of the Virgin Mary in Nazareth and to have been brought to Loreto by angels in the 13th century.

Lorient 47 45N 3 21W A port in NW France, in the Morbihan department on the Bay of Biscay. Formerly the principal naval shipyard in France, it was badly destroyed in World War II. Today it has an important fishing industry and manufactures car components. Population (1975): 71,923.

loris A nocturnal Asian *prosimian primate belonging to the subfamily *Lorisine* (5 species). Lorises are 8–14 in (20–35 cm) long with almost no tail and very large dark eyes. They are generally slow-moving and arboreal, feeding on insects and fruit. Family: *Lorisidae. See also* angwantibo; potto.

Lorrain, Claude. *See* Claude Lorrain.

Lorraine (German name: Lothringen) A planning region and former province in NE France, bordering on Belgium, Luxembourg, and West Germany. Its valuable iron-ore deposits are the largest in Europe outside Sweden and the Soviet Union. *History*: it was frequently the scene of conflict between France and Germany. In the 9th century AD it formed part of the kingdom of Lotharingia, later becoming a duchy under the Holy Roman Empire. Disputed between France and the Habsburgs, it was finally incorporated into France, as a province, in 1766. Following the Franco-Prussian War (1871) part of Lorraine (now Moselle department) was lost to Germany and united with *Alsace to form the imperial territory of Alsace-Lorraine. Area: 9087 sq mi (23,540 sq km). Population (1981 est): 2,311,500.

Lorraine, Charles, Cardinal de. *See* Guise.

lory A small brightly colored *parrot belonging to the subfamily *Loriinae* (62 species), occurring in Australia, New Guinea, and Polynesia. Lories have a slender bill with a brush-tipped tongue and feed on pollen and nectar, particularly that of gum trees.

Los Alamos 28 54N 103 00W A city in New Mexico. Chosen by the US government (1942) for atomic research, the first atom bombs were made here during World War II. The H-bomb was later developed here by the scientific laboratory of the University of California, which now covers an area of 77 sq mi (199 sq km). Government control of Los Alamos ended in 1962. Population (1970): 11,310.

Los Angeles 34 00N 118 15W A city and seaport in S California on the Pacific coast. Founded in 1781 by Franciscan missionaries, it was made the capital of Mexican California in 1845 but was captured by US forces in the following year. Over the years it has incorporated many neighboring towns so that today it comprises a large industrial and urban complex, with the third largest population in the US. It is the center of the US film industry, which attracts many tourists to the city, and more recently several television studios have been established here. Other major industries include the manufacture of aircraft and oil refining. Industrial pollution, augmented by the high density of cars (Los Angeles is the only major US city without a comprehensive public system of transport), is a serious problem. An educational center, it is the site of several universities. Population (1980): 2,966,763.

Los Angeles, Victoria de (1923–) Spanish soprano. She studied at Barcelona conservatoire, made her London and New York debuts in 1950, and established herself as a popular prima donna, particularly in the title roles of Massenet's *Manon Lescaut* and Puccini's *Madame Butterfly*.

Lost Generation A term applied to the expatriate US writers of the 1920s including Ernest *Hemingway, F. Scott *Fitzgerald, Henry *Miller, John *Dos Passos, and Ezra *Pound, whose works expressed their sense of spiritual alienation. The term derives from a remark attributed to Gertrude Stein and used as an epigraph to Hemingway's novel *The Sun Also Rises* (1926).

Lot River A river in S France, flowing mainly W through the departments of Lozère, Aveyron, Lot, and Lot-et-Garonne to the Garonne River. Length: 300 mi (483 km).

Lothair (c. 835–69 AD) King (855–69) of an area W of the Rhine, inherited from his father Lothair I, that came to be called Lotharingia. His attempts to divorce his childless wife Theutberga developed into a struggle with Pope Nicholas I.

Lothair I (795–855 AD) Coemperor of the West; eldest son of *Louis (I) the Pious, whose coemperor he became in 817. On Louis' death in 840 Lothair's position was challenged by his brothers Louis the German (d. 876) and Charles the Bald and in 843 the Frankish territories were divided between them.

Lothair II (1075–1137) Holy Roman Emperor (1133–37) and, as Lothair III, German king (1125–37). He became Duke of Saxony in 1106 in return for supporting Emperor Henry V against his father in 1104 but subsequently turned against Henry, defeating him at the battle of Welfesholz (1115). The Hohenstaufen family contested his election as king until 1135. As emperor, he tried to expel Roger II of Sicily from Italy.

Loti, Pierre (Julien Viaud; 1850–1923) French novelist. He served as a naval officer and wrote numerous novels of romance and adventure with exotic settings and several travel books. His best-known novels include three studies of Breton sailors, *Mon frère Yves* (1883), *Pêcheur d'Islande* (1886), and *Matelot* (1893).

Lotto, Lorenzo (c. 1480–1556) Venetian painter. He traveled extensively in Italy and his work is consequently marked by a number of influences; he frequently visited Venice but, unable to compete with Titian's success, worked chiefly in Bergamo. He is noted for his altarpieces, e.g. the *Crucifixion* (Monte San Giusto, Bergamo), and the psychological insight of such portraits as *A Young Man* (Kunsthistorisches Museum, Vienna), and *Andrea Odoni* (Hampton Court). He spent his last years in a monastery in Loreto.

lotus Any of several different water plants. The sacred lotus of ancient Egypt was probably *Nymphaea lotus*, a sweet-scented white night-flowering *water lily with broad petals, or *N. caerulea*, a blue-flowered species. The sacred Indian lotus, *Nelumbo nucifera* (family *Nelumbaceae*), has roselike pink flowers and its seeds, called lotus nuts, are eaten raw or in soups. The genus *Lotus* contains about 70 species of herbs, including the birdsfoot *trefoils.

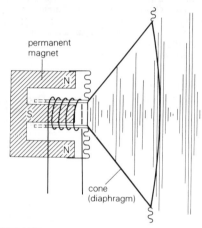

permanent magnet

cone (diaphragm)

LOUDSPEAKER *A moving-coil loudspeaker with a pot-shaped permanent magnet.*

loudspeaker A device for converting electrical signals into sound. It usually consists of a small coil fixed to the center of a movable diaphragm or cone. The coil is in an annular gap between the poles of a strong *magnet. An audio-frequency electrical signal fed to the coil creates a varying magnetic field, which interacts with the steady field in the gap. This causes the coil, and the attached cone, to vibrate and produce sound waves of the same frequencies as the electrical signal. Generally, larger cones give a better response at low frequencies and the smaller cones are best at high frequencies; for the best results two or more different-sized cones are therefore used, either in the same or in separate cabinets. The loudspeaker cabinet is also an important part of the system since it can act as a sound baffle and improve the frequency response.

Louis (I) the Pious (778–840 AD) Emperor of the West (813–40); son of Charlemagne. He fostered Christianity but imperial unity was undermined by his rebellious sons and after his death the Empire was partitioned.

Louis (I) the Great (1326–82) King of Hungary (1342–82) and Poland (1370–82). Louis encouraged commerce and the arts and in 1367 he founded Hungary's first university at Pécs. His campaigns against Venice had brought Hungary most of Dalmatia by 1381.

Louis II (1845–86) King of Bavaria (1864–86) renowned for his extravagant castles, especially Neuschwanstein, and patronage of the composer Richard Wagner. His hopes for Bavaria in the newly founded German empire (1871) were disappointed and he subsequently withdrew from politics. In 1886 he was pronounced mad and shortly afterward drowned himself.

Louis (IV) the Bavarian (?1283–1347) German king and Holy Roman Emperor (1314–47; crowned 1328). In 1324 Pope John XXII excommunicated Louis in support of Frederick III of Austria (c. 1286–1330), who contested the German throne. Louis deposed John in 1327 and in 1328 was crowned emperor by the antipope Nicholas V. From 1294 Louis was Duke of Bavaria, for which he devised a legal code (c. 1335).

Louis (V) le Fainéant (967–87 AD) The last Carolingian King of France (986–87), whose frivolity (his nickname means "feckless") helped to discredit the dynasty, bringing the Capetian *Hugh Capet to power.

Louis (VII) le Jeune (c. 1120–80) King of France (1137–80). He was engaged in a bitter struggle with Henry II of England between 1152, when Henry acquired Aquitaine through his marriage to Louis' former wife *Eleanor of Aquitaine, until 1174.

Louis VIII (1187–1226) King of France (1223–26), known as the Lionheart. He was offered the English throne by King John's baronial opponents but his invasion of England was defeated in 1217. He gained Toulouse and Languedoc for the French crown and in 1226 launched a crusade against the *Albigensians.

Louis IX, St (1214–70) King of France (1226–70), regarded as the model medieval Christian king. After defeating Henry III of England (1242) he set out as leader of the sixth *Crusade (1248), during which he was captured by the Egyptians. On his return to France he introduced administrative reforms and fostered learning and the arts. He died on a Crusade in Tunisia and was canonized in 1297.

Louis XI (1423–83) King of France (1461–83), who united most of France under his rule. In 1447 his father, Charles VII, exiled him to Dauphiné for his part in a conspiracy. After becoming king Louis overcame the aristocratic opposition of the League of the Public Weal (1465) and in 1477 finally defeated Charles the Bold of Burgundy. He extended royal authority over the church and encouraged commerce, gaining the support of the middle classes.

Louis XII (1462–1515) King of France (1498–1515). His reign was dominated by the wars that his father Charles VIII had initiated in Italy, and Louis suffered major defeats (1511–13) on several fronts at the hands of the Holy League.

Louis XIII (1601–43) King of France (1610–43), whose reign was dominated by his chief minister Cardinal de *Richelieu. He was the son of the assassinated Henry IV and of *Marie de' Medici, who was regent during his minority. In 1617 he exiled Marie from court and she raised two revolts against him but mother and son were later reconciled by Richelieu, her adviser, who in 1624 became Louis' chief minister. The king defeated two *Huguenot uprisings (1622, 1628), taking their fortress of La Rochelle in 1628.

LOUIS XIV   *The Sun King portrayed in all his glory.*

Louis XIV (1638–1715) King of France (1643–1715), known as the Sun King because of the splendor of his reign. His minority was dominated by Cardinal *Mazarin, after whose death in 1661 Louis allowed no single minister to dominate. He was ably served by such men as *Colbert, who revived French trade, industry, and agriculture, and *Louvois, who with

his father made France's army the best in Europe, but insisted that *L'état c'est moi* ("I am the state"). He was a firm advocate of the *divine right of kings and subdued the aristocrats, whose rebellion known as the *Fronde had threatened the crown during his minority, by providing diversions at his great palaces—outstandingly *Versailles. His patronage of artists, including the writers Molière and Racine, further enhanced the magnificence of his court. In 1660 he married Maria Theresa (1638–83), the daughter of Philip IV of Spain (1605–65; reigned 1621–65). His mistresses included Mme de *Montespan and then Mme de *Maintenon, whom he secretly married after Maria Theresa's death. Abroad, France became the dominant power in Europe during Louis' reign. His ambitions in the Spanish Netherlands sparked off the War of *Devolution (1667–68) and were renewed by a second invasion in 1672. From this, the third *Dutch War, France emerged (1678) at the pinnacle of its power, a position Louis was unable to retain through the subsequent Wars of the *Grand Alliance (1689–97) and *Spanish Succession (1701–14). France was further weakened by Louis' revocation (1685) of the Edict of Nantes, ending toleration of Protestants and driving many of France's most productive citizens into exile. He left a country weakened by the economic demands of his wars and a monarchy that was to prove unequal to the enormous demands placed on it by his personal rule. His reign was nevertheless one of incomparable brilliance.

The **Louis Quatorze style** of late 17th-century interior design was developed in a deliberate attempt by Louis XIV and his designers to establish a French national idiom. The formal baroque furniture made in the new royal workshops derived from Italian antiquity and was sumptuously gilded or veneered for such regal settings as *Versailles. The most resplendent items were made of cast silver.

Louis XV (1710–74) King of France (1715–74), whose weak rule discredited the crown and contributed to the outbreak of the French Revolution of 1789. His early reign was dominated by *Fleury, after whose death in 1744 Louis' indecisiveness and the influence of his mistresses, especially Mme de *Pompadour and, later, Mme *Du Barry, fostered faction and intrigue. The loss of almost all France's colonies in the *Seven Years' War (1756–63) increased his unpopularity, which hasty judicial and financial reforms at the end of his reign did nothing to alleviate.

The **Louis Quinze style** of French interior decoration and furnishing lasted from about 1723 until Louis' death. A sophisticated and informal style, it was a reaction to the formal baroque pomp of Louis XIV's court. The rococo, with its lighthearted use of eccentric scrolls, replaced symmetrical antique and Renaissance motifs. Chairs, formerly ranged around the walls of large rooms, were designed and arranged for ease of conversation in the new, smaller, and more intimate rooms.

Louis XVI (1754–93) King of France (1774–93), who was guillotined during the *French Revolution. The opposition of Louis' wife *Marie Antoinette and the aristocracy thwarted the attempted reforms of his ministers *Turgot and *Necker. The consequent economic crisis forced the king to summon (1789) the States General, the disaffected Third Estate of which precipitated revolution. The royal family was confined to the Tuileries Palace from which they attempted to flee in 1791, reaching Varennes. Brought back to the Tuileries, Louis was deposed after it had been stormed by the Paris mob. In 1793 he was guillotined and was followed to the scaffold by his wife.

The **Louis Seize style**, a neoclassical French style of furnishing, came into fashion after Louis XVI's accession. It was characterized by rejection of the rococo with straight lines replacing curves and a continuing tendency toward lightness and utility. The predominant idiom was restrained classicism (key patterns, caryatids, garlands, trophies). After the French Revolution (1789–99) this style remained in vogue for some time.

Louis XVII (1785–95) King of France in name (1793–95) following the execution of his father Louis XVI during the French Revolution. He died in prison.

Louis XVIII (1755–1824) King of France, in name from 1795, following the death in prison of his nephew *Louis XVII, and in fact from 1814, following the overthrow of Napoleon. He fled Paris when Napoleon returned from Elba, being restored with diminished prestige after Waterloo "in the baggage train of the allied armies." His attempts to be a moderate constitutional monarch were thwarted by the ultraroyalists.

Louis, Joe (Joseph Louis Barrow; 1914–81) US boxer, called the Brown Bomber, who was world heavyweight champion from 1937 to 1948, when he retired. He defended his title 25 times and has been regarded as the world's greatest boxer.

Louisiana A state on the Gulf of Mexico in the S central US. Mississippi lies to the E, with the Mississippi River forming about half the boundary between the two states. The Gulf of Mexico forms its S shore. Tennessee lies to the W and Alabama to the N. Chiefly low lying, Louisiana is crossed by the Mississippi River, the delta of which dominates the coastal lowlands in the S. The bayous, shallow, swampy rivers, and languid steamy atmosphere of the Mississippi delta lend a distinctive flavor to the region. The main upland area in the state is found in the NW along the Red River Valley. The increasingly urban population (60%) lives mainly in the S. The state produces chemicals and petrochemicals, paper, and food products. Oil is exploited throughout the state and there are major deposits of natural gas, sulfur, and salt. New Orleans and Baton Rouge are important ports and tourism is a growing industry. Its favorable climate and fertile soils make it an important agricultural state; the chief products are beef cattle, rice, soybeans, dairy products, sugar cane, and cotton. It is an important cultural region, famous for its jazz music centered on New Orleans. Distinctive ethnic groups include Creoles (descendants of the original French and Spanish settlers) and Cajuns (descendants of French-speaking Acadians who were expelled from Nova Scotia). *History*: although discovered by the Spanish, it was claimed for France and named for Louis XIV in 1682. It was ceded to Spain (1762) but was restored to France (1800). It was acquired by the US as part of the Louisiana Purchase (1803), becoming a state in 1812. It was a supporter of the Confederate cause in the Civil War. Discoveries of oil and natural gas in the 20th century transformed the economy, and since World War II industrial development has increased substantially. Area: 48,523 sq mi (125,675 sq km). Population (1980): 4,203,972. Capital: Baton Rouge.

Louisiana Purchase (1803) The acquisition by the US government of approximately 828,000 sq mi (2,144,250 sq km) of territory between the Mississippi River and the Rocky Mountains. Concerned by the potential threat to the US posed by extensive French possessions in North America, President Thomas *Jefferson dispatched James *Monroe to Paris in 1801 to negotiate with the French government for the purchase of its American territories. As a result of the negotiations, the US agreed to pay approximately $15 million for the sovereign rights to a huge and largely unexplored tract of land, which doubled the size of the US and established US dominance in North America. Its initial exploration was undertaken by the *Lewis and Clark Expedition in 1804–06.

Louisbourg 45 55N 59 58W A city in NE Nova Scotia, Canada, on E Cape Breton Island. Originally the French fort Fort Louisbourg (1720–45), and now a national historic park, the fort was taken by British forces in 1745, returned to France in 1748, and recaptured by the British under Jeffrey Amherst and James Wolfe in 1758, when it was destroyed. Restoration began in 1961. Population (1981): 1,410.

Louis of Nassau (1538–74) A leader of the *Revolt of the Netherlands against Spain. His opposition to the Spanish led to his exile in 1567 but, after gaining support in Germany and France, he invaded the Netherlands with a Protestant army (1568). The campaign was indecisive and in the second invasion, in 1574, Louis and his younger brother were killed.

Louis Philippe (1773–1850) King of the French (1830–48), the son of the Duke of *Orléans. He supported the *French Revolution until 1793, when he deserted to the Austrians, living abroad until 1814. He joined the liberal opposition to the restored Louis XVIII and came to the throne after the July Revolution had ousted Louis' successor Charles X. Styled King of the French rather than of France and described by Thiers as the Citizen King, Louis Philippe relied on the support of the middle class. His initial moderation turned to repression in the face of the many rebellions against his rule and he abdicated in the Revolution of 1848. He retired to England, dying at Claremont, in Surrey.

Louisville 38 13N 85 48W A city and port in N Kentucky, on the Ohio River. The state's largest city, it has many historical buildings and is the site of the University of Louisville (1798). The American Printing House for the Blind is situated here. Since 1875 the famous Kentucky Derby has been held in Louisville at the Churchill Downs racetrack. Industries include tobacco manufacture, whiskey distilling, milling, and chemicals. Population (1980): 298,451.

Lourdes 43 06N 0 02W A town in SW France, in the Hautes-Pyrénées department situated at the foot of the Pyrenees. It is a major pilgrimage center for Roman Catholics (*see* Bernadette of Lourdes). Population (1975): 18,096.

Lourenço Marques. *See* Maputo.

louse A wingless □insect parasitic on warm-blooded animals. The sucking lice (order *Anoplura*; 225 species) suck the blood of mammals. They have hairy flattened bodies, 0.01–0.24 in (0.5–6 mm) long, and claws for attachment to the host. The eyes are often reduced or absent. One of the most important species is the human louse (*Pediculus humanus*), of which there are two varieties—the head louse (*P. humanus capitis*) and the body

louse (*P. humanus humanus*). Both are transmitted by direct contact and lay their eggs ("nits") on hair or clothing. Body lice are carriers of typhus and related diseases. Biting lice (order *Mallophaga*; 2600 species) resemble sucking lice but have biting mouthparts for feeding on the skin, feathers, etc., of birds—their principal hosts.

Louth (Irish name: Contae Lughbhaidh) The smallest county in the Republic of Ireland, in Leinster bordering on the Irish Sea. It is chiefly low lying. Agriculture is important with cattle rearing and arable farming producing oats and potatoes. Area: 317 sq mi (821 sq km). Population (1979): 86,135. County town: Dundalk.

Louvain (Flemish name: Leuven) 50 53N 04 42E A city in central Belgium. It was a center of the cloth trade in the middle ages and the capital of the duchy of Brabant. It possesses a gothic town hall and a university (1426). Much of the town was destroyed in World War I. Industries include leather and chemicals. Population (1981 est): 85,459.

Louvois, Michel Le Tellier, Marquis de (1641–91) French statesman; minister for war (1666–77). With his father **Michel Le Tellier** (1603–85), war minister (1643–66), he reorganized the French army. Their success was demonstrated by Louis XIV's many military victories. Louvois was the king's chief minister after 1683.

Louvre The national museum of France containing the art collection of the French kings and housed in the former royal palace and Tuileries palace in Paris. It was opened to the public in 1793. Napoleon exhibited his war loot here, of which the celebrated Venus de Milo still remains. Other highlights are Leonardo da Vinci's *Mona Lisa* and a collection of impressionist paintings, housed separately in the Jeu de Paumes in the Tuileries gardens.

lovage A perennial herb, *Ligusticum scoticum*, that grows 6–35 in (15–90 cm) high and has large compound leaves with pairs of divided toothed leaflets and clusters of greenish-white flowers. It is native to Europe and used as a pot herb and salad plant. Family: *Umbelliferae*.

lovebird A small brightly colored *parrot belonging to a genus (*Agapornis*; 9 species) occurring in Africa and Madagascar. 4–6 in (10–16 cm) long, lovebirds typically have a short tail, a red bill, and a prominent eye ring. Lovebirds often feed in large flocks and may damage crops. They are popular cagebirds because they are long-lived, can be taught tricks, and appear to have great affection for each other.

Lovecraft, H(oward) P(hilips) (1890–1937) US novelist and short-story writer. He lived virtually as a recluse and wrote science-fiction stories and tales of macabre fantasy, such as *The Case of Charles Dexter Ward* (1928) and *At the Mountains of Madness* (1931).

love-in-a-mist An annual herb, *Nigella damascena*, also called fennel flower, native to S Europe and grown as an ornamental in temperate regions. It has fernlike leaves and blue or white flowers, 1.6 in (4 cm) across, with many clawed petals surrounded by the leaves. The fruit is a globular head of capsules. Family: *Ranunculaceae*.

Lovelace, Richard (1618–57) English Cavalier poet. During the Civil War, although he was not actively involved, he was committed to and spent nearly all his fortune in the royalist cause, and was twice imprisoned. In prison he wrote one of his best-known poems, "To Althea, from Prison." *Lucasta* (1649) contains most of his best lyrics.

love-lies-bleeding. See Amaranthus.

Lovell, Sir Bernard (1913–) British astronomer. After working on radar during World War II he became interested in *radio astronomy and supervised the construction of a 250-foot radio telescope at *Jodrell Bank Experimental Station, a part of Manchester University. His books include *The Exploration of Outer Space* (1961) and *Out of the Zenith* (1973).

Low Countries The Netherlands, Belgium, and Luxembourg. The Low Countries originally comprised numerous small states, controlled by major powers. In 1568 the N Protestant states revolted against Spanish rule, becoming the independent United Provinces of the Netherlands (*see* Revolt of the Netherlands). Belgium and Luxembourg gained independence in 1830 and 1867 respectively.

Lowell 42 38N 71 19W A city in NE Massachusetts, at the confluence of the Concord and Merrimack Rivers. Its growth began with the establishment of textile mills here in 1822 and it became one of the most famous textile centers in the US. Population (1980): 92,418.

Lowell, Amy (1874–1925) US poet, and critic and biographer. After meeting Ezra *Pound in London in 1913, she became the leading propagandist for *Imagism. The volume *What's O'Clock* (1925) was awarded a Pulitzer Prize. Her *Collected Poetical Works* was published in 1955. She also wrote criticism including *Six French Poets* (1915) and *Tendencies in Modern Poetry* (1917), and a biography of *John Keats* (1925).

Lowell, Francis Cabot (1775–1817) US industrialist; founder of the first complete textile factory. He observed power looms in England (1810–12) and then established the Boston Manufacturing Company (1812) in Waltham, Mass. His factory was the first in the world to process cotton from beginning to end—from just-harvested cotton to finished material. It was long used as a model for other manufacturers. The city of Lowell, Mass, was named in his honor.

Lowell, James Russell (1819–91) US poet, critic, and diplomat. He published literary criticism, political works, and poetry ranging from the satirical *Fable for Critics* (1848) to the dialect *Biglow Papers* (1848, 1867). He edited the *Atlantic Monthly* (1857–61). He served as minister to Spain (1877–80) and Britain (1880–85).

Lowell, Percival (1855–1916) US astronomer, who first predicted the existence of the planet *Pluto, because of certain irregularities in the orbit of Uranus. Lowell never discovered Pluto despite intense searching and it was not found until 14 years after his death. He also made a detailed study of the "canals" on Mars.

Lowell, Robert (1917–77) US poet. In 1943 he was imprisoned as a conscientious objector. *Life Studies* (1959) marked a change from his complex and allusive early poetry, such as *Lord Weary's Castle* (1946), to a looser, more personal style. His left-wing political involvement during the 1960s is reflected in *For the Union Dead* (1964). He also published free translations, collected in *Imitations* (1962), and verse dramas. His last book was *Day by Day* (1977).

Lower California (Spanish name: Baja California) A peninsula in NW Mexico, between the Gulf of California and the Pacific Ocean. It is chiefly mountainous and arid. Within irrigated areas, especially in the N near the US border, cotton, fruit, vegetables, and vines are grown. There are important mineral deposits; these include copper, silver, and lead. Length: 760 mi (1223 km).

Lower Hutt 41 12S 174 54E A city in New Zealand, in S North Island on Port Nicholson (an inlet of Cook Strait). An important industrial center, it has meat freezing, engineering, and textile industries. Population (1973 est): 62,800.

Lower Saxony (German name: Niedersachsen) A *Land* in N West Germany, bordering on the North Sea, the Netherlands, and East Germany. Formed in 1946 from four former states, it lies on the N German plain, with mountains in the S. It is chiefly agricultural but some minerals are extracted, including oil and iron ore. Area: 18,301 sq mi (47,430 sq km). Population (1980 est): 7,246,000. Capital: Hanover.

lowest common denominator The smallest common multiple of the denominators of two or more fractions. For example, the group 2/3, 1/6, 5/8 have the lowest common denominator 24.

Lowestoft 52 29N 1 45E A fishing port in E England, in Suffolk. It suffered considerable damage in both world wars. Besides fishing and associated industries, Lowestoft is concerned mainly with yachting and tourism. Population (1981): 55,231.

Lowry, L(awrence) S(tephen) (1887–1976) British painter, born in Manchester. He worked as a clerk until his retirement at 65, using his spare time for art lessons and painting. He exhibited regularly in Manchester from the 1920s, when he began his most characteristic works, bleak industrial landscapes and towns dotted with matchstick figures. These first attracted serious attention in the 1940s. A large retrospective exhibition was held in 1976.

Lowry, (Clarence) Malcolm (1909–57) British novelist. His first novel, *Ultramarine* (1933), was based on his experience as a deckhand on a voyage to China. After studying at Cambridge he lived in Paris before going to Mexico, the setting of his novel *Under the Volcano* (1947), the semiautobiographical account of the self-destruction of an alcoholic ex-consul. He lived in Canada from 1940 to 1954. Further stories and fragments were published posthumously.

Loyalists. *See* United Empire Loyalists.

Lo-yang. *See* Luoyang.

Lozi A Bantu-speaking people of Zambia, also known as Barotse. They are cereal cultivators on the fertile flood plain of the upper Zambezi, but hunting and animal husbandry are also important. Political authority is vested in a divine king and subordinate queen who rule from separate northern and southern capitals with a council of ministers and regional chiefs drawn from the aristocracy. There is an elaborate system of taxation, centralization, and redistribution of reserves.

LPG. *See* Liquefied Petroleum Gas.

LSD (lysergic acid diethylamide) A drug that—in very small doses—produces hallucinations, altered sensory perception, and a sense of happiness and relaxation or, in some people, fear and anxiety. Long-term use of LSD can cause a schizophrenia-like illness and—if taken by pregnant women—may produce deformities in the developing fetus.

Lualaba River A river in SE Zaïre, the headstream of the Zaïre River. Rising in the Shaba region, it flows N to join the Luvua River and becomes the Zaïre River at the Boyoma Falls. Length: 1100 mi (1800 km).

Luanda 8 58S 13 09E The capital of Angola, a port in the NW on the Atlantic Ocean. Founded by the Portuguese in 1575, it became a center of the slave trade to Brazil. Oil was discovered nearby in 1955 and a refinery was established; main exports include coffee, cotton, diamonds, iron, and salt. The University of Luanda was established in 1963. Population (1970 est): 400,000.

Luang Prabang 19 53N 102 10E A city in N Laos, a port at the head of navigation on the Mekong River. The royal capital of Laos (1946–75), it has many Buddhist pagodas and is the trading center for the surrounding agricultural region. Population (1973): 44,244.

Lubbock 33 35N 101 53W A city in NW Texas. Settled by Quakers in 1879, it is an important market center for cotton, grain, cattle, and poultry. Population (1980): 173,979.

Lübeck 53 52N 10 40E A city in NE West Germany, in Schleswig-Holstein on the Trave estuary. A leading city of the Hanseatic League, it has a cathedral (1173) and city hall (13th–15th centuries), both restored after World War II. Buxtehude lived here (1668–1707) and it is the birthplace of Thomas and Heinrich Mann. West Germany's largest Baltic port, its industries include shipbuilding and metal founding. Population (1980 est): 221,500.

Lubitsch, Ernst (1892–1947) US film director, born in Germany. Following the success of *Madame Dubarry* (1919), a historical romance, he went to Hollywood, where he made a series of sophisticated comedies during the 1920s and 1930s. These include *Forbidden Paradise* (1924), *Bluebeard's Eighth Wife* (1938), and *Ninotchka* (1939).

Lublin 51 18N 22 31E A city in E Poland. The Union of *Lublin, between Poland and Lithuania, was signed here in 1569. Notable buildings include the 16th-century cathedral; its university was founded in 1944. It is an important commercial and industrial center; manufactures include farm machinery, motor vehicles, and beer. Population (1979 est): 298,000.

Lublin, Union of (1569) The act that created a Polish-Lithuanian commonwealth. Poland and Lithuania were to share a common monarch and diet (parliament) but each maintained its own laws, administration, treasury, and army.

Lubumbashi (name until 1966: Elizabethville) 11 30S 27 31E A city in SE Zaïre. Founded in 1910 as a copper-mining settlement, it is the industrial center of an important mining area. It has a cathedral and a campus (1955) of the Université Nationale du Zaïre. Population (1976 est): 451,332.

Lucan (Marcus Annaeus Lucanus; 39–65 AD) Roman poet, nephew of the Stoic philosopher Seneca. He was born in Spain. The *Pharsalia*, his single surviving work, is an epic poem in ten books concerning the civil war between Caesar and Pompey. He committed suicide after the discovery of his involvement in a conspiracy against the emperor Nero.

Lucas, George (1944–) US film director, producer, and writer; creator of *Star Wars* (1977). He produced *American Graffiti* (1973) before the science fiction, fairy-tale trilogy including *Star Wars*, *The Empire Strikes Back* (1980), and *Return of the Jedi* (1983). He also produced *Raiders of the Lost Ark* (1981) and *Indiana Jones and the Temple of Doom* (1984).

Lucas van Leyden (Lucas Hugensz *or* Jacobsz; c. 1494–1533) Northern Renaissance artist. His early paintings include everyday subjects, notably *The Chess Players* (Berlin), but he mainly painted religious works, his masterpiece being the triptych of *The Last Judgment* (Leiden). Best known as an engraver, he was influenced by Dürer, whom he met in Antwerp (1521). He was probably the first to etch on copper rather than iron and to combine *etching with *engraving; his portrait of Emperor Maximilian I (1521) uses these techniques.

Lucca 43 50N 10 30E A city in NW Italy, in Tuscany on the Serchio River. It has Roman remains, an 8th-century church, and a cathedral (11th–15th centuries). Industries include chemicals, engineering, and food processing. It is the birthplace of Puccini. Population (1971): 89,944.

Luce, Henry R(obinson) (1898–1967) US publisher, who was a co-founder of the magazine *Time* (1923), which he edited and published. He founded *Fortune* in 1930, *Life* in 1936, and *Sports Illustrated* in 1954. Over the years he used his position and power to influence US politics. He retired from publishing in 1964. His wife **Clare Booth Luce** (1903–), a playwright, whom he married in 1935, wrote the satire *Kiss the Boys Goodbye* (1938). She sat in the US House of Representatives (1943–47) and was subsequently ambassador to Italy (1953–56) and Brazil (1959).

lucerne. *See* alfalfa.

Lucerne (German name: Luzern) 47 03N 8 17E A city in central Switzerland, on Lake Lucerne. The Lion of Lucerne, a monument to the Swiss guards who fell in Paris (1792), is a notable feature and Lucerne also has a 17th-century cathedral. It is a major tourist center. Population (1980 est): 63,278.

Lucerne, Lake (German name: Vierwaldstättersee) A lake in N central Switzerland. It has four arms formed from deep winding glaciated valleys. Area: 44 sq mi (114 sq km).

Lucian (c. 120–c. 180 AD) Greek rhetorician. He was born in Syria and traveled during his early life as a public lecturer in Asia Minor, Greece, Italy, and Gaul (France). He eventually settled in Athens but also held an administrative post in Alexandria. His many lively satirical works attacking contemporary superstitions and religious fanaticism include *Dialogues of the Dead* and *Dialogues of Courtesans*.

Lucifer In Christian tradition, the leader of the angels expelled from heaven for rebelling against God. Known thereafter as Satan (Hebrew: adversary) or the Devil, he presides over the souls condemned to torment in *hell. He is identified with the serpent that tempted Eve (Genesis 3.1–6) and the great red dragon cast out of heaven by Michael (Revelation 12.3–9). The exact nature of Lucifer's sin was much debated; the commonest view is that his sin was pride.

Lucknow 26 50N 80 54E A city in India, the capital of Uttar Pradesh. Capital of the nawabs of Oudh (1775–1856), it has many notable buildings including the Great Imambara (1784), which is a Muslim meeting place, and the British Residency (1800), which was besieged in 1857 during the Indian Mutiny. The University of Lucknow was established here in 1921. An agricultural trading center, its industries include food processing, railroad engineering, and the manufacture of chemicals, carpets, and copper and brass products. Population (1981 est): 1,006,943.

Lucretia A legendary Roman heroine, wife of Tarquinius Collatinus. After being raped by Sextus, son of Tarquinius Superbus, the Etruscan King of Rome, she committed suicide. Junius Brutus then led a rebellion that expelled the Tarquins and established the Roman Republic.

Lucretius (Titus Lucretius Carus; c. 95–c. 55 BC) Roman philosopher and poet. The biographical records are unreliable, including St Jerome's statements that he became insane but in moments of sanity wrote books that were edited by Cicero and that he committed suicide. His single work, *De rerum natura*, consists of six books that give the most complete exposition of the philosophy of *Epicurus, including his atomic theory of phenomena and the belief that the soul was material (and mortal). His style blends moral intention with poetic sensitivity to the physical world.

Lucullus, Lucius Licinius (died c. 57 BC) Roman general. After service with *Sulla, he successfully conducted the third war against *Mithridates until his troops mutinied and Pompey took command in 67. Lucullus retired to private life and luxury; the splendors of "Lucullan" feasts became proverbial.

Lüda (or Lü-ta) 38 53N 121 37E A port complex in NE China, at the end of the *Liaodong Peninsula. It comprises the two cities **Lüshun** (English name: Port Arthur) and **Dalian** (or Ta-lien; English name: Darien). Industries include shipbuilding, railroad engineering, and fishing. *History*: Lüshun, a major naval base from 1878, was the base of the Russian Pacific fleet during the Russian occupation (1898–1905). The Russians began the construction of the commercial port at Dalian, completed under Japanese occupation (1905–45). Population (1957 est): 1,508,000.

Luddites A group of Nottingham frameworkers, named for their probably mythical leader, Ned Ludd, who destroyed labor-saving machinery in 1811 when the industrial revolution brought unemployment. Luddism, which spread to other parts of industrial England, showed the hostility of the handicraftsmen to the new machines that were taking their livelihood from them. They were severely repressed.

Ludendorff, Erich (1865–1937) German general in World War I. He became chief of staff under *Hindenburg in 1914 and was largely responsible for the German victory at *Tannenberg. After being appointed quartermaster general (1916) Ludendorff exerted considerable political as well as military influence, forcing the resignation of *Bethmann-Hollwegg. He himself resigned after the German defeat and from 1924 to 1928 sat in the Reichstag as a Nazi.

Ludhiana 30 56N 75 52E A city in India, in Punjab. An important grain market, its manufactures include textiles, machinery, and agricultural tools. It is the site of Punjab Agricultural University (1962). Population (1971): 397,850.

Ludwigshafen 49 29N 8 27E A city in SW West Germany, in Rhineland-Palatinate on the Rhine River. It is a transshipment point and center of the chemical industry. Population (1980 est): 160,300.

Luftwaffe The German air force. The Luftwaffe, which fought in World War I, was developed by Göring in the 1930s. In *World War II, countries destined for Nazi invasion were first pounded by aerial bombardment (*see* Blitzkrieg) but the Luftwaffe's failure in the battle of Britain was disastrous to German plans to invade Britain.

Lugano 46 01N 8 57E A city in S Switzerland, on Lake Lugano. Noted for the beauty of its scenery, it is a popular tourist center. It is also a center of international finance. Population (1970): 22,280.

Lugansk. *See* Voroshilovgrad.

Luger pistol A German automatic *pistol developed from a Borchard design by George Luger in 1902. The Parabellum 9-mm model was the standard sidearm of the German navy (1904) and army (1908) until 1938.

Lugus One of the principal Celtic gods. In Ireland he was called Lug and was skilled in many fields, being a warrior, poet, musician, craftsman, magician, etc. His Welsh counterpart was Lleu Llaw Gyffes (skilful hand). Many European placenames, notably, Lyon, Laon, and Leiden, derive from his name.

lugworm A burrowing *annelid worm, *Arenicola marina*, of Atlantic shores, also known as the lobworm. Up to 16 in (40 cm) long, lugworms have about 20 segments, with tufts of red gills on all but the last few. They feed on organic material in the mud, leaving casts of egested mud on the surface. Class: *Polychaeta*.

Lu Hsün (or Chou Shu-jen; 1881–1936) Chinese writer, famous for his short stories criticizing traditional Chinese thought and government. Among the best known are *The True Story of Ah Q* (1921) and those collected in *Call to Arms* (1923) and *Wandering* (1924–25). Although he never joined the Communist Party, the Chinese regard him as a revolutionary hero.

Luik. *See* Liège.

Lukacs, Giorgi (1885–1971) Hungarian Marxist philosopher. Having shown the resemblance between the philosophies of *Hegel and the young *Marx in *History and Class Consciousness* (1923), he disowned the book, which was also condemned by Soviet orthodoxy. For Lukacs, a cultural relativist, the dynamic of all art is the historical movement of its time; in the 20th century this is socialist realism.

Luke, St A New Testament evangelist, traditionally the author of the third Gospel and of the Acts of the Apostles. Although information about him is scarce, he seems to have been a Gentile doctor and to have accompanied *Paul on numerous missions, notably to Greece, Macedonia, and Jerusalem. He is the patron saint of doctors and artists. Feast day: Oct 18.

The Gospel according to St Luke was written in the latter part of the 1st century AD. It was written in idiomatic Greek and with Gentile readers in mind. It contains the most complete account of the life of Jesus. Many historic hymns, such as the *Ave Maria, Magnificat, Benedictus, Gloria in Excelsis*, and *Nunc Dimittis*, are taken from it.

Luleå 65 35N 22 10E A seaport in N Sweden, on the Gulf of Bothnia. Icebound in the winter it exports iron ore from *Gällivare and *Kiruna during the rest of the year. Its university was established in 1971. Population (1978 est): 66,834.

Lull, Ramón (English name: Raymond Lully; c. 1235–c. 1315) Catalan mystic and poet. After an early secular career, he became a Franciscan and devoted himself to missionary work among the Muslims. His mystical writings foreshadow those of St *Teresa and St *John of the Cross. His important theological work, *Ars magna*, was condemned by Pope Gregory XI in 1376 for its attempt to show that the mysteries of faith could be proved by reason. According to tradition, he was stoned to death in N Africa.

Lully, Jean Baptiste (Giovanni Battista Lulli; 1632–87) French composer of Italian birth. The son of a miller, he worked as a scullion in an aristocratic French household but subsequently became composer, violinist, and dancer to Louis XIV. He composed ballets, incidental music to Molière's plays, and operas, being granted a monopoly of operatic production in 1684. He died from gangrene as a result of striking his foot with a pointed stick while conducting.

Luluabourg. *See* Kananga.

lumbago Chronic backache. Almost everybody experiences backache at some time and many biologists regard it as the price man pays for walking upright. More serious backache may be caused by arthritis, a slipped disk, muscle strain, or strained ligaments.

lumbar puncture A procedure in which *cerebrospinal fluid is withdrawn using a hypodermic needle inserted through the spine and into the spinal cord in the region of the lower back. Examination of the fluid assists in the diagnosis of various conditions, for example the presence of blood may indicate a brain hemorrhage.

Lumbini A park and Buddhist shrine in the modern village of Rummindei, in S Nepal. According to legend, the Buddha was born here in about 563 BC.

lumen (lm) The *SI unit of luminous flux equal to the light emitted per second in a cone of one steradian solid angle by a point source of one candela.

Lumière, Auguste (1862–1954) French photographer, who, with his brother **Louis Lumière** (1864–1948), manufactured photographic equipment and made innovations in the techniques of photography, especially in motion pictures. In 1895 they invented the *cinématographe*, which had a camera and projector combined into one. In the same year they used their invention to film and show the first motion picture, *La Sortie des usines lumière*, which was an immediate success. They went on to make a great number of short films, especially comedies. They also greatly improved existing methods of color photography.

luminance The *luminous intensity of a surface in a given direction per unit of orthogonally projected area of that surface. It is measured in candela per square meter.

luminescence The emission of light by a substance for any reason except high temperature. It occurs as a result of the emission of a *photon by an atom of the substance when it decays from an excited state to its ground state. The atom may be excited by absorbing a photon (photoluminescence), colliding with an electron (electroluminescence), etc. If the luminescence stops as soon as the exciting source is removed, it is known as fluorescence; if it persists for longer than 10^{-8} second it is called phosphorescence. The photons emitted may have a different energy (in visible light, a different color) from the absorbed energy. Fluorescent dyes in washing powders make clothes look brighter. Luminous paint is phosphorescent. Other examples of luminescence include triboluminescence, caused by friction, chemiluminescence, caused by chemical reaction. Bioluminescence, which is seen in glow worms, seaweeds, and other organisms, is a form of chemiluminescence. Radioluminescence is caused by radioactive decay.

luminosity The intrinsic brightness of an object, such as a star, equal to the total energy radiated per second from the object. A star's luminosity increases both with surface temperature and with surface area: the hotter and larger a star, the greater its luminosity. Stellar luminosity is related (logarithmically) to absolute *magnitude.

luminous flux The rate of flow of light energy, taking into account the sensitivity of the observer or detector to the different wavelengths. For example, the human eye is most sensitive to the color green. Luminous flux is measured in *lumens.

luminous intensity The amount of light emitted per second by a point source per unit solid angle in a specified direction. It is measured in *candela.

lumpsucker A slow-moving carnivorous *bony fish, also called lumpfish, belonging to the family *Cyclopteridae*, found in cold northern seas. They have a thickset body, sometimes studded with bony tubercles, a cleft dorsal fin, and a ventral sucking disk formed from fused pelvic fins. *Cyclopterus lumpus* is the largest species, reaching 24 in (60 cm) long. The roe is used as a substitute for caviar. Order: *Scorpaeniformes*.

Lumumba, Patrice (Hemery) (1925–61) Congolese statesman; prime minister (1960–61) of the Congo (now Zaïre). Mission-educated, Lumumba was active in labor unionism before entering national politics. He became prime minister of the newly independent Congo under president *Kasavubu in 1960 and opposed the secession of Katanga province under *Tshombe. The following year he was deposed and murdered.

luna moth A large North American saturniid moth, *Actias luna*. It is pale green with a long "tail" on each hindwing, moonlike markings on the forewings, and a wingspan of about 6 in (150 mm). The pale-green larvae feed on trees.

Lund 55 42N 13 10E A town in S Sweden, near Malmö. It has a university (1668) and an 11th-century cathedral. Its varied industries include printing, publishing, and sugar refining. Population (1978 est): 78,487.

Lunda A group of Central Bantu tribes speaking languages of the Benne-Congo division of the *Niger-Congo family. Historically they were united under a paramount chief but their customs and culture vary considerably. Cultivation, hunting and gathering, and trade are all important economic factors.

Lüneburg 53 15N 10 24E A spa in NE West Germany, in Lower Saxony. There are many fine medieval buildings. **Lüneburg Heath** was the site of the surrender of German troops to Britain's *Montgomery in 1945 at the end of World War II. Population (1971 est): 60,200.

lungfish A freshwater *bony fish belonging to the formerly abundant order *Dipnoi*, now reduced to six species including *Lepidosiren paradoxa* of South America, *Protopterus annectens* of Africa, and the Australian *Neoceratodus forsteri*. Up to 7 ft (2 m) long, lungfish have slender bodies, narrow paired fins, and tapering tails. Their swim bladders are modified for breathing air, an adaptation for droughts, when some make burrows in the bottom mud, leaving air vents above the mouth. They re-emerge in the rainy season to feed on bottom-dwelling fish, snails, mussels, etc., and to spawn. Subclass: *Sarcopterygii*. □fish.

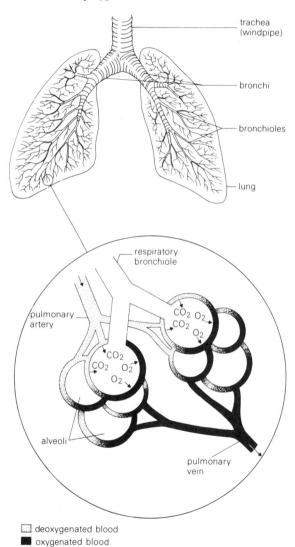

☐ deoxygenated blood
■ oxygenated blood

LUNGS *The air passages in the lungs terminate in millions of tiny air sacs (alveoli), into which blood from the pulmonary artery releases its carbon dioxide. Inhaled oxygen in the alveoli is absorbed by the blood, which is carried back to the heart by the pulmonary vein.*

lungs The respiratory organs of many air-breathing animals and man. The human lungs are situated within the rib cage on either side of the heart. Each lung is enclosed by a smooth moist membrane (the pleura), which permits it to expand without friction, and contains many tiny thin-walled air sacs (alveoli), through which exchange of oxygen and carbon dioxide takes place during breathing (*see* respiration). Air to the lungs passes through the *trachea (windpipe) to the two main airways (bronchi), which subdivide into progressively smaller branches that terminate (as respiratory bronchioles) in the alveoli.

Diseases most commonly affecting the lungs and airways are virus infections and bronchitis; cancer and tuberculosis are less common.

lungworm One of several species of parasitic *nematodes that inhabit the lungs and bronchial passages of cattle, pigs, deer, sheep, and other animals. They damage lung tissue, causing coughing, distress, and debilitation, and may act as reservoirs of such diseases as swine influenza.

lungwort A perennial herb of the genus *Pulmonaria* (about 10 species), especially *P. officinalis*, native to woods of Eurasia. The leaves are heart-shaped or oval, often white-spotted, and the tubular five-lobed flowers, borne in drooping terminal clusters, are pink when young, turning blue later. The plant grows to a height of 12 in (30 cm). Family: *Boraginaceae*.

Lunt, Alfred (1892–1977) US actor, who worked with **Lynne Fontanne** (1887–1983) after their marriage in 1922. They were most successful in sophisticated comedies, such as Noel Coward's *Design for Living* (1933) and Terence Rattigan's *Love in Idleness* (1944), but they also performed in more serious productions, notably Dürrenmatt's *The Visit* (1959).

Luo A Nilotic people of N Uganda and Kenya, who moved into this area from the SE Sudan after about 1500. They speak a Sudanic language. The Luo cultivate cereal crops and herd cattle. For lakeside groups fishing is important. They lack centralized political institutions or chiefs.

Luoyang (*or* Lo-yang) 34 47N 112 26E A city in E central China, in Henan province. A commercial and cultural center, it was the Tang dynastic capital. Manufactures include machinery and ball bearings. Population (1953): 171,200.

Lupercalia An ancient Roman festival of purification and fertility held annually on Feb 15. After performing sacrifices, priests carrying whips of goat hide made a circuit of the Palatine. Women struck by their whips were ensured fertility. The ceremony was suppressed in 494 AD by Pope Gelasius.

lupin An annual or perennial herb of the genus *Lupinus* (about 200 species), native to the N hemisphere and widely cultivated for ornament. They grow 12–47 in (30–120 cm) high and have compound leaves with up to 18 radiating leaflets. Lupins produce dense spikes of blue, purple, white, pink, or yellow flowers. Family: **Leguminosae*.

lupus A skin disease of which there are two forms. Used alone, the term usually refers to **lupus vulgaris**, which is a tuberculous infection of the skin. Without treatment the infection will progress to erode the face (hence the name, which is Latin for wolf, implying a gnawing disease), but it is now readily cured by drugs. **Lupus erythematosus** (LE) is a disease in which inflammation of tissues is brought about by the body's own antibodies. Discoid LE is a chronic condition of scaling and scarring of the skin. Systemic LE affects the connective tissues and so can have serious effects in almost any part of the body, particularly the joints, skin, kidneys, heart, lungs, and brain. LE can be controlled with steroid drugs.

Lurçat, Jean (1892–1966) French tapestry designer. A painter in the cubist style until 1936, he established a tapestry factory at Aubusson in 1939, where he played a major part in the 20th-century revival of tapestry weaving and design.

Luria, Isaac (1534–72) Jewish mystic of Safed (Galilee); the founder of an important school of *kabbalah. He attracted a large band of disciples who, after his early death in an epidemic, collected and developed his teachings, which became extremely influential, especially later in *Hasidism.

Luria, Salvador E (dward) (1912–) US molecular biologist, born in Italy. He won a Nobel Prize in physiology or medicine in 1969. He came to the US (1940) and worked with Max *Delbruck on the study of the structure and reproduction of bacterial viruses.

Luristan (*or* Lorestan) A province in W Iran, comprising part of a larger historical region in which many important archeological finds have been made since 1929.

Lusaka 15 03S 28 30E The capital of Zambia, lying on the Tanzam Railroad. It became the capital of Northern Rhodesia in 1935 and of Zambia on independence in 1964. The University of Zambia was founded here in 1965. The center of an important agricultural region, it has expanded rapidly and industries include food processing, paint, clothing, and plastics. Population (1980 est): 641,000.

Lüshun. See Lüda.

Lusitania A British liner that, although unarmed, was sunk by a German submarine off the Irish coast on May 7, 1915, during World War I. Of the 1195 lives lost, some 128 were Americans and the incident contributed to the anti-German feeling in the US that ultimately brought the country into the war.

Lü-ta. See Lüda.

lute A plucked stringed instrument of Moorish origin; the name derives from the Arabic *al'lud*. The European lute, popular during the 15th, 16th, and 17th centuries, had a body in the shape of a half pear, six or more courses of double strings and a fretted fingerboard. The round sound hole was often intricately carved. Music for the lute was written in tablature, a system of notation using letters or numbers to indicate the position of the fingers. The lute was used chiefly as a solo instrument and to accompany singers; it has been revived in the 20th century.

luteinizing hormone. *See* gonadotrophin.

lutetium (Lu) The heaviest *lanthanide element, separated from ytterbium by G. Urbain (1872–1938) in 1907 and named for Paris (Latin name: *Lutetia*), his native city. It was also discovered independently by C. A. von Welsbach, who called it *cassiopeium*, a name used until the 1950s, especially in Germany. It is present in small amounts in monazite ($CePO_4$) and extracted by reduction of $LuCl_3$ or LuF_3 by alkali metals (e.g. sodium). It is separated from the other lanthanides by ion-exchange techniques. At no 71; at wt 174.97; mp 3028°F (1663°C); bp 6149°F (3395°C).

Luther, Martin (1483–1546) German Protestant reformer, founder of *Lutheranism. An Augustinian monk and from 1507 a priest, he became professor of theology at Wittenberg University in 1511. After experiencing a personal revelation he came to believe that salvation could be attained by faith alone. Several visits to Rome convinced him of the corruption of the papacy, the Dominican monk *Tetzel, who sold *indulgences on behalf of papal funds, being a particular target for his hostility. In 1517 he nailed his 95 theses against this practice to the church door at Wittenberg. He disobeyed the papal summons to Rome (1518) and further attacked the papal system in such writings as *On the Babylonian Captivity of the Church of God* (1520). His public burning of a papal bull condemning his theses and writings resulted in his excommunication in 1521. He appeared before Charles V's imperial diet (legislative assembly) at Worms but refused to recant and was declared an outlaw. While in hiding at Wartburg, under the protection of the Elector of Saxony, he completed a German translation of the New Testament. In 1522 he returned openly to Wittenberg, where he led the reform of its church and in 1525 married the former nun Catherina van Bora (1499–1552). At the same time he lost much popular support because of his opposition to the Peasants' Revolt (1524–25). His contention that human will was incapable of following the good resulted in his rift with *Erasmus and in 1529 he also broke with *Zwingli, maintaining his belief in *consubstantiation. His original intention was reform not schism, but with the *Augsburg Confession (1530) a separate Protestant church emerged. Subsequently the leadership of the German Reformation was gradually taken over by *Melanchthon.

Lutheranism The belief and practice of the Protestant Churches that derive from the teaching of Martin *Luther, especially as formulated in the *Augsburg Confession (1530). There is a wide divergence in matters of belief among Lutherans. Essentially Scripture is taken to be the only rule of faith and conservative Lutherans accept Luther's basic doctrine of justification by faith alone, i.e. that redemption is only through faith in Christ. Lutheranism is the national faith in all Scandinavian countries, where there are some 19 million Lutherans. It is the principal Protestant Church in Germany (about 40 million adherents) and is also strong in North America (over 8 million). The Lutheran World Federation, based in Geneva, claims authority over some 80 million Lutherans world wide, which makes it the largest Protestant body.

Luton 51 53N 0 25W A city in SE England, the largest in Bedfordshire. It has an important motor-vehicle industry and also manufactures household appliances, engineering components, and chemicals. A straw-plaiting industry has survived from the 17th century. Population (1981): 164,049.

Lutoslawski, Witold (1913–) Polish composer. His early works, such as his first symphony, were influenced by Bartók. From the orchestral *Venetian Games* (1961) onward— most of his works contain *aleatoric sections. They include a second symphony (1967), a cello concerto (1970), and *Preludes and Fugue for 13 Solo Strings* (1972).

Lutuli, Albert (John Mvumbi) (1898–1967) South African black leader, whose advocacy of nonviolent opposition to racial discrimination won him the Nobel Peace Prize in 1960. A Zulu chief, in 1952 he became president of the African National Congress, formed in 1912 to further the black cause in South Africa. In 1956 he was arrested for treason and although acquitted in 1957 continued to suffer social and political restrictions.

Lutyens, Sir Edwin Landseer (1869–1944) British architect, known as the last English designer of country houses, a notable example of which is Middlefield, Cambridgeshire (1908). His most spectacular commission was the layout and viceregal palace of New Delhi, India (1912–30).

Lutzen, Battles of 1. (November 16, 1632) The battle in the *Thirty Years' War in which the Swedes under Gustavus II Adolphus clashed with imperial forces in a costly and indecisive battle. Gustavus Adolphus was killed. **2.** (May, 1813) A battle in which Russian and Prussian forces were defeated by Napoleon.

lux (lx) The *SI unit of intensity of illumination equal to the illumination resulting from a flux of one lumen falling on an area of one square meter. Former name: meter candle.

Luxembourg A province in SE Belgium, bordering on the Grand Duchy of Luxembourg and France. The *Ardennes is an important tourist area. Area: 1705 sq mi (4416 sq km). Population (1980 est): 223,396. Capital: Arlon.

Luxembourg, Grand Duchy of A small country in central Europe, between France and Germany. The generally undulating S with its wide valleys rises to the rugged uplands of the Ardennes Plateau in the N. *Economy*: predominantly industrial, the manufacture of iron and steel is especially important although considerable economic diversification has taken place (e.g. chemicals, rubber, and synthetic fibers). Agriculture remains important, especially livestock raising, and wine is produced from the vineyards of the Moselle Valley. The city of Luxembourg is an important international center with the headquarters of the European Parliament and the European Coal and Steel Community, as well as many international companies. *History*: with the Netherlands and Belgium it formed part of the so-called Low Countries. It became a duchy in 1354 and passed to Burgundy in 1443 and to the Habsburgs in 1482. It became a grand duchy in 1815 under the Dutch crown. In 1830 it joined the Belgian revolt against the Netherlands, W Luxembourg joining independent Belgium and the E forming part of the Netherlands until obtaining independence in 1867. It was occupied by the Germans in both World Wars. In 1921 it formed an economic union with Belgium and in 1948 both joined with the Netherlands to form the *Benelux Economic Union. Luxembourg is now a member of the EEC. Head of state: Grand Duke Jean (1921–). Head of Government: Jacques Santer (1937–). Official languages: Luxembourgish, French, and German. Official currency: Luxembourg franc of 100 centimes. Area: 2586 999 sq mi (sq km). Population (1980 est): 365,100. Capital: Luxembourg.

Luxemburg, Rosa (1871–1919) German revolutionary, born in Poland. She was converted to communism in 1890, helped to found the Polish Social Democratic party (later the Communist Party), and from 1898 was a leader of the left wing of the German Social Democratic party. Upon the outbreak of World War I she broke with the majority of German socialists and formed, with Karl *Liebknecht, the *Spartacus League. She spent most of the war in prison and after her release participated in the abortive uprising of 1919, following which she and Liebknecht were murdered.

Luxor (*or* El Aksur) 25 40N 32 38E A city in central Egypt, on the Nile River. It occupies the S part of the ancient city of *Thebes. Its numerous ruins and tombs include the temple built by Amenhotep III to the god Ammon. It is a winter resort. Population (1966 est): 77,578.

Luzern. *See* Lucerne.

Luzon A volcanic island in the N Philippines, the largest and most important. Largely mountainous, its central fertile plain is a major grain growing area with rice terraces to the N. Other products include sugar cane, hemp, timber, and minerals, notably chromite. Most industry is concentrated around Manila. *History*: power struggles for the Philippines have been centered here, including the Japanese invasion during World War II (*see* Corregidor). Area: 41,845 sq mi (108,378 sq km). Population (1970): 18,001,270. Chief town: Quezon City.

Lvov (German name: Lemberg) 49 50N 24 00E A city in the Soviet Union, in the W Ukrainian SSR. A major industrial and cultural center of the W Ukraine, Lvov supports machine building, food processing, and chemical and textile industries, and has a notable university (1661). *History*: founded in the 13th century, it subsequently passed to Poland, Turkey, and then Sweden. Under Austrian rule from 1772, it became the capital of Galicia. It was ceded to Poland after World War I and to the Soviet Union in 1939. It was occupied by the Germans in World War II. Population (1977 est): 642,000.

Lvov, Georgi Yevgenievich, Prince (1861–1925) Russian statesman. Lvov was the first leader of the provisional government in the *Russian Revolution. His unrealistic policies led to the Petrograd uprising in July, 1917, and he resigned. He emigrated to Paris, where he died.

Lyallpur 31 25N 73 09E A city in NE Pakistan. It is the commercial and manufacturing center of an agricultural region specializing in cotton and wheat. Population (1972): 822,263.

Lyautey, Louis Hubert Gonzalve (1854–1934) French marshal and colonial administrator. He served in Indochina and then in Madagascar, where he reformed the colonial government. In 1912 he became resident general of the French protectorate of Morocco, where he again reorganized the administration, maintaining the French position there during World War I. He was briefly war minister (1917–18).

Lyceum The gardens and gymnasium in ancient Athens in which *Aristotle lectured and which gave their name to the school and research foundation that he established there in about 335 BC. The name is now applied particularly to Aristotle's philosophical doctrines.

Lycurgus A legendary Spartan statesman credited with establishing the constitution and military regime of Sparta after a slave rebellion in the 7th century BC. He is mentioned by *Herodotus and his biography was written by *Plutarch. The name refers to several other figures in Greek legend, notably a king of Thrace who opposed the cult of *Dionysus and was subsequently blinded or driven mad.

Lydda. *See* Lod.

Lydgate, John (c. 1370–c. 1450) English poet. He lived at the monastery of Bury St Edmunds. A prolific writer, his major works include the long narrative poems *The Troy Book* (1412–21), written at the request of Henry V, and *The Fall of Princes* (1431–38).

Lydia In antiquity, a region of W Asia Minor with its capital at *Sardis. Its last native king, *Croesus (ruled 560–546 BC), enriched by Lydia's alluvial gold, controlled Anatolia eastward to the Halys River, until his defeat by *Cyrus the Great. The Lydians invented coined money (c. 700 BC).

Lyell, Sir Charles (1797–1875) British geologist, who was mainly responsible for the acceptance of the view that rocks are formed by slow continual processes, such as heat and erosion. Lyell popularized this theory in his *The Principles of Geology* (3 vols, 1830–33). Lyell's work had a great influence on Charles *Darwin and, in turn, Lyell became one of the earliest supporters of Darwin's theory of natural selection.

lymph A clear colorless fluid, consisting of water and dissolved substances, that is contained in a network of vessels called the **lymphatic system**. It is derived from blood and bathes the cells, supplying them with nutrients and absorbing their waste products, before passing into the lymphatic vessels. Here the lymph passes through a series of small swellings called **lymph nodes**, which filter out bacteria and other foreign particles, before draining into the main lymphatic vessels—the thoracic duct and the right lymphatic duct—in the neck. These two vessels are connected to veins in the neck and so drain the lymph back into the bloodstream. The lymph nodes, which also produce lymphocytes (a type of white blood cell), sometimes become enlarged during infections. The lymphatic system is one of the routes by which cancer is spread.

lymphocyte. *See* leukocyte.

lymphoma Cancer of the lymph nodes, which is one of the commonest cancers of young people. There are several different types but the most common is Hodgkin's disease, which can now often be controlled by chemotherapy.

Lynch, Jack (1917–) Irish statesman; prime minister (1966–73, 1977–79). A former hurling star, in 1948 he was first elected as a member of parliament from Cork, enjoying enormous popular support in that city.

Lynd, Robert Staughton (1892–1970) US sociologist. Lynd taught at Columbia University from 1931 to 1961. He collaborated with his wife **Helen Lynd** (1896–1982) on the field study of Muncie, Indiana, their findings being published in *Middletown: A Study in Contemporary American Culture* (1929) and *Middletown in Transition* (1937).

Lynn 42 29N 70 57W A city in Massachusetts. A long-established industrial center, it was the site of the first ironworks (1643) and the first fire engine (1654) in the US. A shoe-manufacturing center since 1636, Lynn also manufactures jet engines and marine turbines. Population (1980): 78,471.

lynx A short-tailed *cat, *Felis lynx*, that inhabits forests of Eurasia and North America. Lynxes are about 40 in (1 m) long with faintly spotted yellow-brown thick fur; their ears are tipped with black tufts. The rare Spanish race has especially bright spots.

Lynxes hunt at night, usually for small mammals (such as lemmings) but sometimes catching moose or reindeer, especially in deep snow. □mammal.

Lyon 45 46N 4 50E The third largest city in France, the capital of the Rhône department at the confluence of the Rhône and Saône Rivers. Notable buildings include the cathedral (12th–15th centuries) and the *hôtel de ville* and Palais des Arts (both 17th century). The university was founded in 1808. A *métro* (underground railroad) was opened here in 1978. The focal point of road and rail routes, Lyon is an important financial center and has been a leading textile center since the 15th century. Manufactures include synthetic fibers, cars, chemicals, and hosiery. Population (1975): 462,841.

Lyons, Joseph Aloysius (1879–1939) Australian statesman; prime minister (1931–39). At first a Labor politician, he resigned over financial policy in 1931 and with the Nationalist Party formed the *United Australia Party. He died in office.

Lyra (Latin: Lyre) A constellation in the N sky near Cygnus. The brightest star is *Vega. The constellation contains the **Ring nebula** (a *planetary nebula) and the *variable stars **RR Lyrae** (a pulsating variable) and **Beta Lyrae** (an eclipsing binary).

lyre An ancient plucked string instrument. It consists of a sound box with two symmetrical arms supporting a cross piece from which strings are stretched to a bridge on the belly. Greek vases often show players holding a lyre in the left hand and a large plectrum in the right.

LYREBIRD *The underside of the tail of the male superb lyrebird forms a silvery shimmering veil during display.*

lyrebird A primitive ground-dwelling passerine bird belonging to a family (*Menuridae*; 2 species) restricted to forests of E Australia. The male superb lyrebird (*Menura superba*), about 51 in (130 cm) long, is brown with gray underparts. Its magnificent tail is spread out into a lyre shape during the courtship display, which is performed on a mound of mud and debris. The smaller Prince Albert's lyrebird (*M. alberti*) does not build display mounds and has a smaller tail. All lyrebirds sing loudly and are excellent mimics.

Lysander (d. 395 BC) Spartan general and politician. He commanded the fleets that defeated the Athenians at Notium (407) and Aegospotami (405) toward the end of the *Peloponnesian War. His plot to make the Spartan throne elective rather than hereditary was thwarted by the government but Lysander escaped punishment. He was subsequently killed in action in Boeotia.

Lysenko, Trofim Denisovich (1898–1976) Soviet biologist, who achieved notoriety for his maverick ideas and damaging influence on Soviet biology. He claimed that changes induced in wheat by his vernalization experiments could be inherited, thus endorsing *Lamarck's discredited theory of evolution through inheritance of acquired characteristics. This led him to attack Mendelian genetics and the chromosome theory of inheritance, which, in the 1930s, were widely accepted elsewhere. With the backing of Stalin, Lysenko's influence grew. In 1939 he attacked the Soviet geneticist *Vavilov, who was later exiled to Siberia, and by 1948, Soviet scientific opposition to his views had been stifled. Lysenko's influence was eclipsed after Stalin's death although he retained his post as director of the Institute of Genetics until 1965, after the fall of Khrushchev.

lysergic acid diethylamide. *See* LSD.

Lysias (c. 459–c. 380 BC) Greek orator. He escaped from Athens during the reign of terror of the Thirty Tyrants (404 BC), but returned to prosecute one of them in his speech "Against Eratosthenes". About 35 of his legal speeches in plain unadorned style survive. He and his family are portrayed in Plato's *Republic*.

Lysippus (4th century BC) The court sculptor of Alexander the Great. Long-lived, original, and prolific, Lysippus worked in bronze and was noted for his portraiture and new system of proportions for human figures. Surviving copies of his works (e.g. the Vatican statue of the athlete scraping oil from his arm) indicate his naturalism.

lysosome A membrane-bounded structure occurring in large numbers in nearly all animal □cells and containing enzymes responsible for the breakdown of materials both within and outside the cell. Functions of lysosomes include the destruction of bacteria in white blood cells, the digestion of food by protozoa, and the breakdown of cellular material after death.

lysozyme An enzyme, present in tears, nasal secretions, and egg white, that destroys bacteria by breaking down their cell walls. It was one of the first enzymes whose molecular structure and mode of action were analyzed by X-ray diffraction techniques.

Lytton, Edward George Earle Bulwer-Lytton, 1st Baron (1803–73) British novelist and politician. His long career in parliament as a Liberal and then a Tory culminated in his peerage in 1866. The best known of his many popular volumes of fiction, verse, and drama are his historical novels, which include *The Last Days of Pompeii* (1834). His son (**Edward**) **Robert Bulwer-Lytton, 1st Earl of Lytton** (1831–91) was viceroy of India (1876–80), initiating the second Afghan War (1878–80).

M

Maas River. *See* Meuse River.

Maastricht 50 51N 5 42E A city in the SE Netherlands, the capital of Limburg province on the Meuse River. It has the Netherlands' oldest church (founded in the 6th century AD) and is a cultural center. Industries include pottery and textiles. Population (1977 est): 110,191.

Maazel, Lorin (1930–) US conductor, formerly a violinist. He directed the German Opera in West Berlin from 1965 to 1971 and was appointed conductor of the Cleveland Orchestra in 1972. In 1980 he became musical director of the Vienna State Opera.

Mabuse. *See* Gossaert, Jan.

McAdam, John Loudon (1756–1836) British inventor of the macadam road surface. It consisted of rocks interspersed with small chips, bound together with slag or gravel and raised to facilitate drainage. In 1823 McAdam's methods were adopted by the British government and in 1827 he became general surveyor of roads.

Macadamia A genus of bushy evergreen trees, 30–49 ft (9–15 m) tall, native to Australia and often grown as ornamentals. *M. ternifolia* has long stiff leaves and slender clusters of small white or lilac flowers. The round hard-shelled fruit contains a single edible seed. These seeds—called macadamia or Queensland nuts—are used as dessert nuts. Family: *Proteaceae*.

Macao (Portuguese name: Macáu; Chinese name: Aomen) 22 13N 113 36E A Portuguese province and free port in S China, across the Zhu estuary from Hong Kong. Although the population is mainly Chinese, there are Portuguese buildings and cultural traditions. Chief industries are textiles and fishing; tourism, gambling, and gold smuggling are also important. *History*: it was a major trading center until the 19th century. Immigration of refugees from Communist China was stopped after procommunist riots (1966–67). Area: 6 sq mi (16 sq km). Population (1975 est): 260,227.

Macapá 9 30S 67 29W A port in N Brazil, the capital of Amapá territory on the N channel of the Amazon delta. Exports include manganese, iron and cassiterite ores, and rubber. Population (1975 est): 108,752.

macaque An *Old World monkey belonging to the genus *Macaca* (12 species), found mainly in the forests of S Asia. 14–31 in (35–78 cm) long (the tail is absent or up to 35 in [90 cm] long), macaques have short legs and areas of hard bare skin on the rump. Intelligent and sociable, they are mainly terrestrial, feeding on plant and animal matter. *See also* Barbary ape; rhesus monkey.

MacArthur, Douglas (1880–1964) US general. A graduate of West Point (1903), he had an outstanding combat record in World War I and then returned to West Point as superintendent (1919–22). Following duty in the Philippines, MacArthur served as US Army chief of staff (1930–35). After reorganizing the Philippine Army (1937–41), he was named Supreme Commander of Allied Forces in the SW Pacific during *World War II (1942–45). As one of the outstanding strategists of the war, he directed the recapture of occupied territories, was named general of the army, and as supreme commander accepted Japan's unconditional surrender in August 1945. MacArthur later headed the military occupation of Japan (1945–51) and was named commander of UN forces in the *Korean War. Despite his initial military success in that conflict, MacArthur developed a serious disagreement with President Truman over the conduct of the war. He was relieved of his command in 1951.

Macassar. *See* Ujung Padang.

Macaulay, Thomas Babington, 1st Baron (1800–59) British essayist and historian. From 1825 he was a leading contributor to the *Edinburgh Review*. He had a long career in parliament (1830–34, 1839–47, 1852–56) and worked in India from 1834 to 1838. His Whig sympathies are clearly evident in his immensely successful *History of England* (5 vols, 1849–61).

macaw A large brightly colored *parrot belonging to one of two genera (*Ara* and *Anodorhynchos*), ranging from Mexico to Paraguay. Up to 40 in (100 cm) long, macaws have a characteristically long loose tail and a huge hooked bill that is used to crack open large nuts.

Macbeth (d. 1058) King of Scots (1040–58), after killing Duncan I in battle at Bothnagowan. He was killed by Duncan's son Malcolm. 50

MacBride, Seán (1904–) Irish diplomat. The son of the nationalist Maud Gonne (1866–1953), he belonged to the IRA before becoming a

member of the Irish assembly (1947). He was chairman of Amnesty International (1961–75) and UN commissioner for Namibia (1973–77). He shared the Nobel Peace Prize in 1974.

DOUGLAS MACARTHUR *General who commanded US troops in the Pacific during World War II and in Korea during the Korean War.*

Maccabees The name applied loosely to the Hasmonean dynasty, founded in Jerusalem by Judas Maccabee (d. 161 BC) after a revolt against Syrian (Seleucid) rule. It continued until the capture of Jerusalem by the Romans in 63 BC. In Christian usage it is applied to seven young brothers martyred during the revolt. In 1895 it was revived in the name of a Jewish athletics organization, Maccabi, the World Union of which was formed in 1921.

The **Books of Maccabees** are four books of the *Apocrypha. I and II Maccabees record the revolt (168 BC) of the Maccabees against the Seleucid king Antiochus Epiphanes and the establishment of an independent Jewish kingdom. They date from the late second century BC. III and IV Maccabees are unrelated works, written probably at the beginning of the Christian era. III Maccabees describes a (probably imaginary) persecution of Jews by Ptolemy IV Philopator of Egypt (late 3rd century BC), while IV Maccabees is a philosophical treatise, with a Stoic flavor, on the superiority of intellect over passions.

McCarran-Walter Act (Immigration and Nationality Act; 1952) US legislation on immigration policies. It retained most of the quotas established in 1924, but lifted the ban on Asiatic and Pacific immigrants, gave priority to higher educated immigrants with necessary skills, and defined admittance and deportation policies regarding aliens considered national security risks.

McCarthy, Eugene Joseph (1916–) US political leader and author. He served in the US House of Representatives (1949–59) and the Senate (1959–71) as a Democrat from Minnesota. An opponent of the Vietnam War, he ran for the Democratic presidential nomination in 1968 and again as an independent in 1976, but was unsuccessful both times. His works include *The Limits of Power* (1967), *The Year of the People* (1969), *The Ultimate Tyranny* (1980), and *Complexities and Contraries* (1982).

McCarthy, Joseph R(aymond) (1908–57) US Republican senator (1947–57) from Wisconsin, who led Senate investigations of supposed communists during the Cold War. His claim in 1950 to have the names of communist infiltrators into the State Department created a sensation but was not proved. In 1954, televised hearings into alleged communism in the army discredited him; he was censured by the Senate, and his anticommunist witchhunt—commonly known as McCarthyism—came to an end.

McCarthy, Mary (1912–) US novelist and critic. Her novels are sensitive to and often satirical of aspects of American society and include *The Groves of Academe* (1952), *The Group* (1963), *Birds of America* (1971), and *Cannibals and Missionaries* (1979). She has published criticism, travel books, the autobiographical *Memories of a Catholic Girlhood* (1957), and journalism, notably *Vietnam* (1967), concerning US involvement in Vietnam.

McCartney, Paul (1942–) British rock musician, formerly a member of the *Beatles. His solo career was launched with the hit "Maybe I'm Amazed" (1970). With his wife Linda McCartney (1942–) he formed (1971) Wings, the band with which he recorded such albums as *Band on the Run* (1973) and toured the world (1975–76).

McClellan, George B(rinton) (1826–85) Union general in the *Civil War. An 1842 graduate of West Point, he served in the Mexican War and later entered civilian life as a railroad executive. He rejoined the regular army in 1861. His 1861 campaign preserved Kentucky and separated W Virginia from the Confederacy. In the *Peninsular Campaign that followed, he fortified Washington, rebuilding the Federal forces there, and in 1862 he was defeated before Richmond. Despite superior strength he did not press *Lee's retreating forces at Antietam and President *Lincoln dismissed him (1862). He ran unsuccessfully as the Democratic candidate against Lincoln in 1864 and later served as governor of New Jersey (1878–81).

McClintock, Barbara (1902–) US geneticist, who was awarded a Nobel Prize in physiology or medicine (1983). She was educated at Cornell University (1919–27) and taught there (1927–31). In 1942 she joined Cold Spring Harbor Laboratory where she conducted experiments on the corn plant and discovered that genes in chromosomes "jump" and cause mutations (1951), opening up new avenues in the fields of antibiotic and cancer research. Her theories were so far ahead of the times that it was not until the 1970s that others understood and took her work seriously.

McClure, Sir Robert John Le Mesurier (1807–73) Irish naval officer and explorer. In 1850, in search of Sir John *Franklin, missing in the Arctic, McClure entered the Beaufort Sea from the Pacific and was marooned in the strait named for him. He was rescued, returning home via the Atlantic (1854), and was thus the first to traverse the *Northwest Passage.

McCormack, John William (1891–1980) US politician; speaker of the House (1962–70). He served in the Massachusetts legislature (1920–26) before representing Massachusetts as a Democrat in the US House of Representatives (1928–70). He was majority leader (1940–47; 1949–51; 1955–61) and minority leader (1947–49; 1953–55). He succeeded Sam Rayburn as the speaker, a post he held until his retirement.

McCormick, Cyrus Hall (1809–84) US inventor and industrialist. He invented (1831), patented (1834), and manufactured and marketed (from 1844) the mechanical reaper. A project started by his inventor father, the reaper did not do well in the hilly East, and it was not until McCormick moved his business to Chicago (1847) to take advantage of the flat Midwest farmlands that he prospered. He founded McCormick Theological Seminary.

McCullers, Carson (1917–67) US novelist and playwright. Her novels, which include *The Heart Is a Lonely Hunter* (1940), *Reflections in a Golden Eye* (1941), and *A Member of the Wedding* (1946), are set in her native South and describe a grotesque and violent world. Other works include *The Ballad of the Sad Cafe* (1951), *The Square Root of Wonderful* (1958), and *Clock Without Hands* (1961).

McCulloch v. Maryland (1819) US Supreme Court decision that upheld the right of the federal government to establish federal banks in states and not be subject to the banking laws of the specific states. The state of Maryland had challenged the power of the Bank of the United States to issue banknotes from its Baltimore branch without affixing state tax stamps.

Macdonald, Sir John (Alexander) (1815–91) Canadian statesman; prime minister (1857–58, 1864, 1867–73, 1878–91). Macdonald helped to establish Canada's dominion status within the British Empire (1867) and served as the first prime minister of the Dominion of Canada. He promoted the expansion of Canada to include Manitoba, British Columbia, and Prince Edward Island.

MacDonald, (James) Ramsay (1866–1937) British statesman; the first Labour prime minister (1924, 1929–31, 1931–35). Elected to Parliament (1906) he became leader of the *Labour Party (1911) but resigned in opposition to World War I (1914) and lost his seat in the 1918 election. Re-elected to parliament in 1922 he again led the Labour Party, becoming prime minister briefly in 1924. His 1929–31 government, failing to deal with current economic problems, was broadened into a coalition (1931–35) that was increasingly dominated by the Conservatives and he was replaced by Baldwin in 1935.

Macdonnell Ranges A system of mountain ranges in Australia. They extend for about 40 mi (65 km) E and 200 mi (320 km) W of Alice Springs, across S Northern Territory reaching 4955 ft (1510 m) at Mount Ziel.

MacDowell, Edward (Alexander) (1861–1908) US composer and pianist. He studied music in New York City, France, and Germany. Returning to the US in 1888, he composed and also developed and headed a music department (1896–1904) at Columbia University. His works include *Second Piano Concerto in D Minor* (1889), *The Saracens* (1891), *Indian Suite* (1892), *Woodland Sketches* (1896), *Sea Pieces* (1898), *Keltic* (1901), and *New England Idylls* (1902).

mace. *See* nutmeg.

Macedonia The central region of the Balkans. Inhabited from Neolithic times, Macedonia was settled by many migrating northern tribes. About 640 BC Perdiccas I became the first ruler of the kingdom of Macedon. *Philip II (359–336 BC) quelled the warlike tribes and founded Macedon's military and economic power, which under his son *Alexander the Great was extended to the East. Alexander's successors were harassed by rebellious uprisings and, after defeat (168 BC) in the *Macedonian Wars, Macedonia became a Roman province (146), losing its independence but remaining a center of Hellenistic culture. The region is now divided between S Yugoslavia (a constituent republic), N Greece, and SW Bulgaria.

Macedonian Wars The three campaigns that secured Roman control of the kingdom of Macedon. The first Macedonian War (214–205 BC) coincided with the intervention of Philip V of Macedon (237–179; reigned 220–179) against Rome in the second *Punic War. The second Macedonian War (200–196) ended with the Roman victory at Cynoscephalae, in Thessaly. Rome instigated the third Macedonian War (171–168) against Philip's son Perseus (reigned 179–168) and finally crushed the Macedonians at the battle of Pydna.

Maceió 9 40S 35 44W A city in NE Brazil, the capital of Alagoas state. It contains many colonial buildings and has sugar-refining, distilling, sawmilling, and textile industries. Population (1975 est): 323,601.

McEnroe, John (Patrick, Jr) (1959–) US tennis player. He won the US singles title in 1979, 1980, 1981. and 1984 and Wimbledon in 1981, 1983, and 1984. An intense competitor noted for his tempestuous court behavior, he is one of the world's finest doubles players, winning many championships with Peter Fleming.

Macgillicuddy's Reeks A mountain range in the Republic of Ireland, in Co Kerry. It extends W of the Lakes of Killarney, reaching 3414 ft (1041 m) at Carrantuohill.

McGovern, George S(tanley) (1922–) US political leader. He served in the House of Representatives (1957–61) and the Senate (1963–81) as a Democrat from South Dakota. Opposed to the Vietnam War, he was the Democratic presidential nominee (1972) and was overwhelmingly defeated by incumbent Richard M. *Nixon.

McGraw, John J(oseph) (1873–1934) US baseball player and manager. He played third base for the Baltimore Orioles (1891–99). As manager of the National League's New York Giants (1902–32), he won 10 pennants and 3 World Series. He was elected to the Baseball Hall of Fame in 1937.

McGuffey, William Holmes (1800–73) US educator; author of *McGuffey's Readers*, the standard elementary school textbooks throughout the Midwest during the 1800s and early 1900s. Self-educated, he began teaching at the age of 13 in frontier Ohio. He graduated (1826) from Washington College and taught (1826–36) at Miami University. In 1836 the first and second McGuffey's school readers were published; they were followed by several other editions. He also served as president of Cincinnati College (1836–39) and Ohio University at Athens (1839–43), and he chaired the moral philosophy department at the University of Virginia (1845–73).

Mach, Ernst (1838–1916) Austrian physicist and philosopher, after whom the *Mach number is named in recognition of his researches into airflow and his observation that as the velocity of sound is reached the airflow changes. Philosophically he was a positivist and as such argued strongly against the concept of atoms, which he regarded as mystical entities since their existence could not be detected but only inferred. *See also* logical positivism.

Machaut, Guillaume de (c. 1300–77) French poet and composer, who held a number of court and ecclesiastical appointments in Bohemia and France before becoming canon of Rheims in 1337. He wrote a number of allegorical poems and developed the *ballade* and *rondeau*. He was one of the leading composers of the *ars nova* style and was the first composer to write a complete musical setting of the mass.

Machel, Samora Moïses (1933–) Mozambique statesman; president (1975–). Machel, who trained as a male nurse, led the FRELIMO (Front for the Liberation of Mozambique) forces in the struggle for independence against Portugal (1966–74) and on independence became Mozambique's first president.

Machiavelli, Niccolò (1469–1527) Italian political theorist. He served the Florentine republic as statesman and diplomat from 1498 to 1512, when the restoration of the Medici family forced him into exile. In *The Prince* (1532), written in 1513, he argued that all means are permissible in the realization of a secure and stable state, and in the *Discorsi* (written 1513–19) he used the example of the ancient Roman Republic to reinforce his arguments. The adjective Machiavellian is used to describe the view, or a supporter of the view, that opportunist or amoral means justify politically desirable ends.

machine gun A *small arm that fires repeatedly without reloading. The first was a rotating cylinder flintlock (1718). By 1862 the Gatling, named for Richard Jordan Gatling (1818–1903), was firing six rounds in a second by means of its several barrels and a hand-rotated breech. Modern weapons are derived from the recoil-operated belt-fed water-cooled weapons designed by Sir Hiram *Maxim toward the end of the 19th century, some of which are still in service. Ammunition from pan, box, belt, or drum is loaded, fired, extracted, and reloaded automatically by recoil or in later models by gas and piston. Classes are: light machine gun (LMG), developed from the rifle; medium machine gun (MMG), normally having a two-man crew and using belt-fed rifle ammunition; and heavy machine gun (HMG), with calibers up to 20 mm (0.8 in). *Submachine guns using pistol ammunition are light derivatives.

machine tools Power-driven mechanical tools used to turn, form, drill, mill, shape, or plane metal or other materials. In *lathes the material to be worked (workpiece) is rotated and the tool is applied to it, whereas in other types of machine tool the workpiece is held stationary and a rotating cutter (milling machine), drill (drilling machine), or reciprocating cutter (shaping machine) is applied to it. In a planing machine the workpiece is reciprocated past the tool. In mass-production techniques a number of operations are carried out on the workpiece without human intervention, often by using a transfer machine to convey it from one machine tool to another. Computer-controlled machine tools are a further step in the automation of production lines.

Mach number The ratio of the velocity of a body in a fluid to the velocity of sound in that fluid. The velocity is said to be supersonic if the Mach number is greater than one. If it exceeds five the velocity is said to be hypersonic. Named for— Ernst *Mach.

Machu Picchu A well-preserved *Inca town in the Urubamba valley (Peru), discovered in 1911. Dramatically sited on a precipitous ridge, Machu Picchu is flanked by extensive agricultural terraces. A typical Inca city, it contains a central plaza, royal palace, and sun temple, all built of polygonal dressed stone blocks.

Macías Nguema. *See* Equatorial Guinea, Republic of.

McKay, Donald (1810–80) US clipper shipbuilder born in Canada. By 1845 he owned his own shipyard in Boston and soon gained fame as the builder of the fastest and the largest clipper ships. The *Flying Cloud* set a speed record from Boston to San Francisco in 1852; the *Great Republic* was the largest clipper ship ever built. The popularity of iron steam-powered ships and a slump in the economy led to the end of the clipper ship business, and the yard closed in 1873.

Macke, August (1887–1914) German painter. During visits to France he was successively influenced by *impressionism, *fauvism, and *cubism. A member of Der *Blaue Reiter group, he became known for his lighthearted subjects, particularly parks and zoos, although his best works were watercolors painted in Tunis (1914), shortly before his death in World War I.

McKenna, Siobhán (1923–) Irish actress. She acted at the Abbey Theater, Dublin, from 1943 to 1946 and made her London debut in 1947. She was particularly successful in the roles of St Joan in G. B. Shaw's play

and of Pegeen in Synge's *The Playboy of the Western World*, a role she also played in the film (1962).

MACHU PICCHU   *The real name of this fortified Inca retreat is unknown, Machu Picchu being the name of the mountain that rises above it.*

Mackenzie A district of N Canada, the westernmost district of the *Northwest Territories. Mountains straddle the W border with the Yukon, the *Mackenzie River valley runs N through the center, and barren plains cover the E. The Territories' most populous district, it produces zinc, lead, gold, and oil. Area: 527,490 sq mi (1,366,199 sq km). Population (1976): 31,457.

Mackenzie, Sir Alexander (?1764–1820) Canadian explorer; born in Scotland. He traveled from Montreal to establish Ft. Chipewyan (1788) on Lake Athabasca in NE Alberta, for the North West Company. Then he traveled along the Mackenzie River NW to its delta at the Beaufort Sea in the Arctic (1789) and, in his next expedition, went S and W across the Rocky Mountains to the Pacific coast of British Columbia (1793). These explorations constituted the first transcontinental crossing N of Mexico. He wrote *Voyage from Montreal on the River St Lawrence, Through the Continent of North America, to the Frozen and Pacific Oceans, in the Years 1789 and 1793* (1801).

Mackenzie, Alexander (1822–92) Canadian statesman and prime minister (1873–78), born in Scotland. A mason and building contractor, he settled in Ontario in 1842; by 1852 he had become editor of a Liberal newspaper, *Lambton Shield*, and in 1861 served in the provincial parliament as a Liberal. After confederation in 1867, he first led the minority Liberals in the House of Commons and then became prime minister in 1873. His five years were spent unsuccessfully trying to change the Conservative policies that had preceded him.

Mackenzie, Sir (Edward Montague) Compton (1883–1972) British novelist. His early novels include the semiautobiographical *Sinister Street* (1913). He served at Gallipoli in World War I and later settled on a Hebridean island. All of his later work is in a lighter vein and includes several volumes of memoirs and many humorous novels, notably *Whisky Galore* (1947).

Mackenzie, William Lyon (1795–1861) Canadian journalist, politician, and reformer; born in Scotland. He used his newspapers (*Colonial Advocate*, 1824; *Constitution*, 1836) to oppose majority Tories in the York (now Ontario) Parliament. Six times elected to the province's parliament, he was ejected each time by the Tories because of his attacks on and his grievances about colonial rule. Attempts to organize a rebellion for independence failed, and he fled to the US (1837), where he was jailed briefly for breaking neutrality laws. Pardoned, he returned to Canada in 1849, was elected to Parliament as a Radical, and continued to fight for independence and agrarian democracy.

Mackenzie Mountains A mountain range in NW Canada that runs N and S straddling the border between Yukon and Northwest Territories, part of the Rocky Mountains. Keele Peak (9750 ft; 2972 m) is the highest point.

Mackenzie River The longest river in Canada, flowing from Great Slave Lake in the North West Territories W and NNW through sparsely settled country to an extensive delta on the Beaufort Sea. Navigable in summer, it carries oil and minerals from the Arctic Ocean to S Canada. Its tributaries generate cheap hydroelectricity. Length: 1065 mi (1705 km).

mackerel An important food and game fish belonging to the genus *Scomber*, related to tuna. Mackerels live in shoals in tropical and temperate oceans, feeding on fish and invertebrates. They have a streamlined body, two dorsal fins, and a series of finlets running in front of the forked tail. The common Atlantic mackerel (*S. scombrus*), about 1 ft (30 cm) long, is marked with black and green bands above and is silvery-white below.

mackerel shark A medium to large carnivorous oceanic *shark of the family *Isuridae*, which includes the *porbeagle and the *white shark. They are heavy bodied and have large keels along both sides of the crescent-shaped tail for stability during fast swimming.

Mackerras, Sir Charles (1925–) US-born Australian conductor. He studied conducting in London and Prague. He was director of the Hamburg State Opera from 1965 to 1969 and director of the English National Opera from 1970 to 1977. He is particularly well known for his performances of Janáček's operas.

McKinley, Mount A mountain in the US, in S central Alaska in the Alaska Range. The highest peak in North America, it was first successfully climbed in 1913 by the US explorer Hudson Stuck (1863–1920). Height: 20,320 ft (6194 m).

McKinley, William (1843–1901) US statesman; 25th president of the US (1897–1901). After serving in the Union army during the Civil War, McKinley became a lawyer and began his political career as a member of the US House of Representatives (1884–91). As an advocate of economic protectionism, he introduced the McKinley Tariff Act of 1890. McKinley later served two terms as governor of Ohio (1892–96) and waged a successful campaign as the Repblican presidential nominee in 1896. As president, McKinley continued to support high tariffs and encouraged the expansion of US economic interests abroad. During his administration, the US became increasingly involved in foreign affairs, gaining territories in the Pacific as a result of the *Spanish–American War (1898) and intervening in China in the suppression of the *Boxer Rising (1900). McKinley was reelected in 1900 but was assassinated in 1901 at the Buffalo Pan-American Exposition by an anarchist, Leon Czolgosz.

Mackintosh, Charles Rennie (1868–1928) Scottish architect and designer. One of the most brilliant exponents of *Art Nouveau, Mackintosh evolved an austere version of the style, which was highly influential throughout Europe, though less so in Britain. All his best work was in Glasgow, in particular the School of Art (1897–1909) and four tearooms (1897–1912), for which he also designed the furniture. In 1923 he moved to London, where his practice collapsed, resulting in his retirement soon afterward.

Macleish, Archibald (1892–1982) US poet. He lived among the expatriate writers in France during the 1920s and later worked in the US government service. Much of the verse in his *Collected Poems* (1952) and *New and Collected Poems 1917–1976* (1976) was influenced by his liberal political principles. He also wrote verse dramas, including *Panio* (1935) and *J. B.* (1958), which was awarded a Pulitzer Prize, and a collection, *Six Plays* (1980).

Macleod, John James Rickard (1876–1935) British physiologist, noted for his work on carbohydrate metabolism. He was professor of physiology at Toronto University (1919–28), where F. G. *Banting and C. H. *Best first isolated the hormone insulin. Macleod was awarded the 1923 Nobel Prize with Banting.

McLeod gauge An instrument that uses *Boyle's law to measure the pressure of a near vacuum. A sample of the vacuum is compressed into a small volume thus raising its pressure, which may then be measured. It is accurate down to about 10^{-6} millimeter of mercury.

Mac Liammóir, Micheál (1899–1978) Irish actor, scenic artist, and dramatist. In 1928 he was a founder of the Gate Theater in Dublin, a home for international drama and a platform for young Irish dramatists. As an

actor, he is best known for his one-man show, *The Importance of Being Oscar* (1960–61), based on the works of Oscar Wilde.

Maclise, Daniel (1806–70) Irish portrait and history painter, born in Cork. He moved to London (1827), where he painted his celebrated *Death of Nelson* and *The Meeting of Wellington and Blücher*.

McLuhan, (Herbert) Marshall (1911–81) Canadian writer and educator. He taught at universities in the US and Canada from 1936 until 1979. An observer of the effects of mass media technology on the human condition, he concentrated on electricity as an extension of the human nervous system. He felt that the media – television, computers, etc. – had the most influence while the impact of print media was fast disappearing. His works include *The Mechanical Bride: Folklore of Industrial Man* (1951), *The Gutenberg Galaxy: The Making of Typographic Man* (1962), *Understanding Media: The Extensions of Man* (1964), and *The City as Classroom* (1977).

MacMahon, Marie Edme Patrice Maurice, Comte de (1808–93) French marshal and statesman; president (1873–79). He came to prominence in the Crimean War (1854–56) and in Italy, where his victory at Magenta (1859) brought him the title Duc de Magenta. He helped to suppress the Commune of Paris (1871) succeeding Thiers as president; he attempted to break the influence of the republican party by appointing a royalist cabinet in defiance of the chamber of deputies. The chamber's successful resistance to this move forced MacMahon to resign.

McMahon, William (1908–) Australian statesman; prime minister (1971–72) of a coalition of Liberal and Country Parties. He became Liberal deputy leader in 1966 and minister for foreign affairs in 1969.

McMillan, Edwin Mattison (1907–) US physicist, who shared the 1951 Nobel Prize with Glenn *Seaborg for their discovery of transuranic elements. The first such element, *neptunium, was discovered by McMillan in 1940 by bombarding uranium with neutrons.

HAROLD MACMILLAN *While prime minister (1957–63) he supported independence for British colonies in Africa but in Europe was frustrated in attempts to join the EEC.*

Macmillan, (Maurice) Harold (1894–) British statesman; Conservative prime minister (1957–63). He was a member of Parliament from 1924 to 1929 and again from 1931. During World War II he held office under Churchill. He became minister of defense (1954), foreign secretary (1955), and chancellor of the exchequer (1955–57). He succeeded Sir Anthony Eden as prime minister. His "wind of change" speech in Africa in 1958 marked his government's support of independence for African states. His second ministry failed to deal effectively with inflation and suffered a major blow when de Gaulle frustrated Britain's attempt to join the EEC (1963). However, he improved relations with the US and helped to achieve the *Nuclear Test-Ban Treaty (1963). He entered the House of Lords in 1984 as Lord Stockton.

MacMillan, Sir Kenneth (1929–) British ballet dancer and choreographer. He choreographed many ballets for companies in Europe and the US, notably *Romeo and Juliet* (1965), *Anastasia* (1967), and *Sleeping Beauty* (1973). He was director of the Royal Ballet from 1970 to 1977.

McNamara, Robert (Strange) (1916–) US executive and public official. An executive of the Ford Motor Company, he served as its president briefly (1960–61) before being appointed secretary of defense (1961–68). He was responsible for revamping the Pentagon and overseeing much of the Vietnam War. Convinced that peace would be achieved through economic stability, not arms, he resigned his position (1967) and took over leadership of the World Bank (1968–81).

MacNeice, Louis (1907–63) Irish-born British poet. A friend of *Auden, *Spender, and *Day Lewis at Oxford in the 1930s, he published his first volume of poetry, *Blind Fireworks*, in 1929. Among his other volumes are *Autumn Journal* (1939), *The Burning Perch* (1963), and a distinguished collection of plays for radio, *The Dark Tower* (1947).

Macon 32 49N 83 37W A city in Georgia, on the Ocmulgee River. It is the industrial center of a large agricultural area. Population (1980): 116,860.

Mâcon 46 18N 4 50E A city in E France, the capital of the Saône-et-Loire department on the Saône River. An important trading center for Burgundy wines, its manufactures include textiles, vats, and agricultural machinery. Population (1975): 40,490.

Maconchy, Elizabeth (1907–) British composer. She studied with Vaughan Williams and in Prague. Her works include ten string quartets and other chamber music, operas, choral music, and ballet music.

McPherson, Aimee Semple (1890–1944) US evangelist; born in Canada. After traveling with her first husband, a Pentacostal evangelist, she started her "Foursquare Gospel" movement and opened Angelus Temple in Los Angeles in 1923, from which she ran a Bible school and radio station. She incorporated the International Church of the Foursquare Gospel in 1927. After a disappearance – supposedly a kidnapping – in 1926, she discontinued public appearances and devoted her time to writing and the business of running her church.

Macquarie Island A subantarctic volcanic island in the S Pacific Ocean, in the Australian Antarctic Territory. The site of a meteorological research station, it is the only known breeding ground of the royal penguin. Area: about 65 sq mi (168 sq km).

McQueen, Steve (1930–80) US film actor. Following his success in *The Magnificent Seven* (1960) he was usually associated with the roles of tough laconic heroes. His later films include *The Cincinnati Kid* (1965) and *Bullitt* (1968), *Papillon* (1973), and *An Enemy of the People* (1976).

Macready, William Charles (1793–1873) British actor and theater manager. One of the most distinguished of 19th-century tragedians, he was particularly successful in the roles of Lear, Hamlet, and Macbeth, and was regarded as the chief rival of Edmund *Kean. He reformed production standards and advocated fidelity to the original texts of Shakespeare.

Madagascar, Democratic Republic of (name until 1975: Malagasy Republic) An island country in the Indian Ocean, off the SE coast of Africa. A narrow coastal plain in the E and a broader one in the W rise to central highlands, reaching heights of over 9000 ft (2800 m). Most of the inhabitants are Merina, Betsimisaraka, and Betsileo, all speaking *Austronesian dialects. *Economy*: chiefly agricultural, now developed on a cooperative basis. Livestock is important and the main crops include manioc as well as coffee, sugar, and spices, which are the main exports. A declining agricultural sector has forced Madagascar to import rice, once a major export. Nonetheless, agricultural products account for 80% of exports. Forests produce not only timber, but also gums, resins, and dyes. Clearing of the forests has, however, seriously depleted the unique indigenous fauna, especially the lemurs. Minerals include graphite, chrome, and ilmenite. Industry, previously based mainly on food processing and tobacco, now includes metals, plastics, paper, and oil refining. *History*: settled by Indonesians from the 1st century AD and by Muslim traders from Africa from the 8th century; the Portuguese visited the island in the 16th century. It remained a native kingdom until the late 19th century, when the French laid claim to Madagascar and, after much bloodshed, established a protectorate (1896). It became a French overseas territory in 1946 and a republic within the French Community in 1958, gaining full independence in 1960. A military government took over in 1972 but was overthrown in 1975. A new socialist constitution was then approved by a referendum and Madagascar became a democratic republic, with Captain Didier Ratsiraka as its first president. Supporting huge foreign indebtedness, Madagascar was forced to impose economic austerity measures on its people, even though in 1984 it was estimated that the cost of living would increase by 50% within the year. Official languages: Malagasy and French. Official currency: Malagasy franc of 100 centimes. Area: 229,233 sq mi (587,041 sq km). Population (1980 est): 9,389,000. Capital: Antananarivo. Main port: Tamatave.

Madariaga y Rojo, Salvador de (1886–1978) Spanish historian and diplomat, who was ambassador to the US (1931) and to France (1932–34). His historical writings include *The Rise and Fall of the Spanish American Empire* (1947) and *Bolívar* (1952).

madder A perennial herb of the genus *Rubia* (about 38 species), especially *R. tinctorum*, native to Eurasia. It has trailing stems with whorls of narrow leaves, clusters of small yellow flowers, and blackish berry-like fruits. A red dye is extracted from the roots. Family: *Rubiaceae*.

Madeira, Rio A river in W Brazil, formed by the union of the Ríos Beni and Mamoré and flowing generally NE to join the Amazon River. Length: 2013 mi (3241 km).

Madeira Islands (*or* Funchal Islands) A Portuguese archipelago in the Atlantic Ocean, about 398 mi (640 km) off the coast of Morocco. It comprises the inhabited islands of Madeira and Porto Santo and two uninhabited island groups. Madeira, the largest and most important island, is densely vegetated and its mild climate attracts many holiday-makers. Its products include basketwork, fruit (such as mangoes), sugar, and the famous Madeira wine. Area: 300 sq mi (777 sq km). Population (1970): 251,135. Capital: Funchal.

Maderna, Carlo (1556–1629) Roman architect. A precursor of the Roman *baroque style of architecture, Maderna's vigorous style first gained full expression in the façade of Sta Susanna (1597–1603). His major work was the completion of St Peter's Basilica, adding the nave and façade to Michelangelo's design.

Madhya Pradesh A state in central India, stretching N over highlands to the S edge of the Ganges plain. The largest state, it is predominantly agricultural, producing grains, cotton, and sugar cane. Its huge hydroelectric potential is harnessed for a few industries, including steel, aluminum, and cement. Coal, iron ore, and other minerals are mined. *History*: under Islamic (11th–18th centuries) and Maratha (18th–19th centuries) rule until Britain established control, Madhya Pradesh became a state in 1956. Area: 170,937 sq mi (442,841 sq km). Population (1981): 52,131,717. Capital: Bhopal.

Madison, Dolley (Payne Todd) (1768–1849) US first lady; wife of James *Madison, fourth president. She married Madison in 1794 after losing her first husband, John Todd, and one of their two sons to yellow fever in 1793. She helped as hostess at the White House during widower Thomas *Jefferson's administration, gaining experience for her husband's two terms (1809–17). During Madison's tenure she was well known for her hospitality.

Madison, James (1751–1836) US statesman; 4th president of the US (1809–17). An influential advocate of a strong federal system for the newly created US, Madison played an important role in the drafting of the US *Constitution in 1787. He later urged its ratification and defended federal powers over *states' rights in the *Federalist Papers, a series of essays he published in collaboration with Alexander *Hamilton and John *Jay. After service in the US House of Representatives (1789–97), Madison was appointed secretary of state in the administration of Thomas *Jefferson (1801–09) and was instrumental in the negotiations leading to the *Louisiana Purchase (1803). In 1809, Madison succeeded Jefferson as president. During Madison's first term in office, US relations with Great Britain deteriorated to the point of open war. The *War of 1812 was initially a military disaster for the Americans, who suffered a blockade of the ports of eastern seaboard. In 1814, British troops occupied Washington, DC, forcing a temporary evacuation by the American government. The war ended in 1815 with the ratification of the Treaty of Ghent. After leaving office, Madison spent his later years at Montpelier, his estate in Virginia.

Madison 43 04N 89 22W The capital city of Wisconsin, situated on an isthmus between Lakes Mendota and Monona. The commercial and industrial center of a rich agricultural region, it is the site of the University of Wisconsin (1848). Population (1980): 170,616.

Madras 13 05N 80 18N A city and major seaport in India, the capital of Tamil Nadu on the Coromandel Coast. Founded (1639) by the British East India Company, the city developed around the small fort, Fort St George, which now contains state government offices and is the site of the first English church built in India (1678–80). The University of Madras was established here in 1857. An important industrial center, Madras manufactures cars, bicycles, and cement and its chief exports are leather, iron ore, and cotton textiles. Population (1981 est): 4,276,635.

Madras. See Tamil Nadu.

Madrid 40 27N 3 42W The capital of Spain, situated on a high plateau in the center of the country on the Manzanares River. Madrid is the focal point of rail, road, and air routes and is the financial center of Spain. Its industries include the manufacture of leather goods, textiles, chemicals, engineering, glassware, and porcelain and the processing of agricultural products. A cultural center, Madrid possesses a university (transferred from Alcalá de Henares in 1836), notable art galleries (especially the *Prado), and the national library (founded in 1712). Fine buildings include the former royal palace, the parliament, many churches, and the 17th-century cathedral. *History*: Madrid was captured from the Moors in 1083 by Alfonso VI. Philip II established it as the capital in 1561. The citizens' uprising against Napoleon's army of occupation in 1808 provided inspiration for the rest of Spain. In the Spanish Civil War Madrid was a Republican stronghold until it fell to the Nationalists in March, 1939, after being besieged for over two years. Population (1974 est): 3,520,320.

madrigal A secular polyphonic composition (*see* polyphony) for voices, often a setting of a love poem. Its first flowering was in 14th-century Florence, where Landini wrote madrigals in two and three parts for voices and instruments. The Italian madrigal of the 16th and 17th centuries developed as an aristocratic art form of great expressiveness in the complex and often chromatic compositions of Marenzio, Monteverdi, and Gesualdo. The English school (Byrd, Morley, Weelkes, etc.) wrote in a simpler but idiomatic style; many sets of madrigals were composed in praise of Elizabeth I.

Madura An Indonesian island in the Java Sea, off NE Java. Largely infertile, its chief industries are cattle rearing and fish farming. It is known for its bull races. The population is Muslim and there is a notable mosque at Bangkalan. Area: 2113 sq mi (5472 sq km). Chief town: Pamekasan.

Madurai 9 55N 78 07E A city in India, in Tamil Nadu. Capital of the Pandya kings (4th–11th centuries AD), it is the site of a large Hindu temple (rebuilt 16th–17th centuries). Its university was established in 1966. Industries include brassware and textiles. Population (1971): 549,114.

Maeander River. *See* Menderes River.

Maecenas, Gaius (d. 8 BC) Roman statesman, who was a close adviser of Emperor *Augustus. Also noted as a literary patron, Maecenas included in his circle the three most important Augustan poets, Virgil, Horace, and Propertius.

Maelstrom A violent whirlpool in a channel in the Norwegian Lofoten Islands, a notorious shipping hazard. The word (uncapitalized) is also used for any whirlpool, particularly one of tidal origin occurring in a narrow irregular channel, as between islands.

Maes, Nicolas (*or* N. Maas; 1634–93) Dutch painter of domestic scenes and portraits, born in Dordrecht. Initially influenced by his teacher *Rembrandt, in such paintings as *Girl at the Window* (c. 1655; Rijksmuseum, Amsterdam), he later adopted the style of Flemish portraiture, after visiting Antwerp in the 1660s.

Maeterlinck, Maurice (1862–1949) Belgian poet and dramatist. Having established his reputation as a poet he became the leading dramatist of the *Symbolist movement with such plays as *Pelléas et Mélisande* (1892), on which Debussy based his opera of the same name, and *L'Oiseau bleu* (1908). He also wrote several philosophical and mystical prose works. From 1890 he lived mostly in France. He won the Nobel Prize in 1911.

Mafeking (*or* Mafikeng) 25 53S 25 39E A city in South Africa, in Bophutha Tswana. It was besieged for 217 days by Boers during the second Boer War (1899–1902) but was held by Colonel *Baden-Powell until relieved. Although outside the territory, it was the capital of the protectorate of Bechuanaland (now Botswana) until 1965. The town was officially surrendered to Bophutha Tswana by South Africa in 1980. It is an important trade center. Population (1970): 6900.

Mafia A criminal organization that originated as a secret society in 13th-century Sicily. The word (meaning "swank") was coined in the 19th century, when the Mafia was employed by the great landowners of Sicily to manage their estates. By extortion, "protection," ransom, and blackmail, the Mafia formed an organization so powerful that it virtually ruled Sicily. Repeated attempts to end its power, including the almost successful efforts of the fascists, have been hampered by the code of absolute silence enforced by reprisals. Italian emigrants took the Mafia to the US in the early 20th century, where as Cosa Nostra (Our Affair), it has flourished despite repeated attempts by federal and local authorities to curtail organized crime.

Magadha An ancient kingdom in NE India, now absorbed by Bihar state. Its early kings included Bimbisara (reigned c. 543–c. 491 BC) and Ajataśatru (reigned c. 491–c. 459). Under *Chandragupta Maurya, *Aśoka, and later the *Gupta kings Magadha, and its capital Pataliputra, became a great cultural and political center.

Magdalena, Río A river in Colombia, rising in the SW of the country and flowing generally N to enter the Caribbean Sea near Barranquilla. Length: 956 mi (1540 km).

Magdalenian A culture of the Upper *Paleolithic, succeeding the *Solutrean in W Europe. Named for La Madeleine cave in the Dordogne (SW France), the Magdalenian is marked by an abundance of bone and antler tools, notably barbed harpoons and spear throwers, both new additions to man's toolkit. Dating from about 15,000 to 10,000 BC, it was the heyday of prehistoric art with magnificent cave paintings (e.g. at *Altamira) and carved and engraved decoration on bone artifacts.

Magdeburg 52 8N 11 35E A city in W East Germany, on the *Elbe River. It achieved fame in the middle ages for its judicial system, the "Magdeburg Law," which was used as a model by many other European cities. It was also a leading member of the Hanseatic League. Bombs destroyed much of the city during World War II, including the town hall (1691), but the cathedral (begun in the 13th century) survived. An important inland port, its industries include iron, oil and sugar refining, chemicals, and textiles. Population (1980 est): 288,725.

Magellan, Ferdinand (c. 1480–1521) Portuguese explorer. He undertook many expeditions to India and Africa for Portugal between 1505 and 1516. In 1519, under Spanish patronage, he set off to seek a passage W to the Moluccas. The expedition of five ships—Magellan's flagship *Trinidad* with *San Antonio, Concepción, Victoria,* and *Santiago*—crossed the Pacific and late in 1520 sailed through the strait that was named for him. In the spring of 1521, after severe privations, they reached the East Indies, where Magellan was killed. Only the *Victoria* returned to Spain, thus completing under del *Cano the first circumnavigation of the world. *See also* Magellanic Clouds.

Magellan, Strait of A channel separating the mainland of South America from Tierra del Fuego. Discovered in 1520 by the Portuguese explorer Magellan, it is an important passage between the S Atlantic and the S Pacific Oceans. Length: 370 mi (600 km). Maximum width: 20 mi (32 km).

Magellanic Clouds Two relatively small irregular *galaxies, the Small and Large Magellanic Clouds are close neighbors of our *Galaxy. They can be seen, by eye, from the S hemisphere and were first recorded by Ferdinand *Magellan in 1519.

Magendie, François (1783–1855) French physiologist, noted for his work on the nervous system. He investigated the finding, first made by the anatomist Sir Charles Bell (1774–1842), that the anterior roots of the spinal cord carry motor nerves and the posterior roots carry sensory nerves. Magendie also experimented on nutritional requirements and studied the effects of drugs on the body.

Magenta 43 28N 8 52E A city in N Italy, in Lombardy. A decisive battle in the struggle for Italian national independence was fought here in 1859, in which the French and Sardinians defeated the Austrians; Magenta dye was named in honor of the event. Population (1971): 23,890.

Maggiore, Lake (Latin name: Lacus Verbanus) A long narrow lake in Italy and Switzerland. Sheltered from the N by the Alps, it enjoys a mild climate: the holiday resorts at its edge include Locarno, in Switzerland. Area: 82 sq mi (212 sq km).

maggot The legless soft-bodied larva of many two-winged flies, such as the *blowfly and *housefly. Rat-tailed maggots are the aquatic larvae of certain *hoverflies, so called because of their long respiratory siphons.

Maghrib (*or* Maghreb; Arabic: west) The area in NW Africa occupied by the states of Morocco, Algeria, Tunisia, and Libya, so called on account of its geographical position in the Arab world. It formerly included Moorish Spain. Its inhabitants are of mixed *Arab and *Berber stock. Although the peoples of the Maghrib have their own distinctive customs and Arabic and Berber dialects they have always formed an integral part of the Arabic cultural tradition. *Compare* Mashriq.

Magi 1. In antiquity, the priests of Zoroaster, renowned for their astronomical knowledge (*see* Zoroastrianism). 2. The sages who came from the East, following a star, to worship the infant Christ at Bethlehem (Matthew 2.1–12). Early Christian tradition embroidered the New Testament account, giving them the title of kings and the names of Caspar, Melchior, and Balthazar. Symbolic significance was ascribed to their gifts: gold (kingship), frankincense (divinity), and myrrh (death). Honored as saints during the middle ages, they became the patron saints of *Cologne, and their adoration of Christ was a favorite theme in Christian art.

magic A system of beliefs and practices by which it is believed that man may control the natural and supernatural forces that affect his life. Generally regarded as "superstition" in industrial societies, magic still lingers in such popular rituals as touching wood to avert ill luck. In many preindustrial societies, magic plays an important social role. Its practitioners may rank next to the chief in prestige and authority, being credited with the ability to communicate with good and evil spirits to ensure success in war and hunting and the fertility of land and livestock. Some primitive rituals, such as pouring water on the ground to bring rain, are purely magical. They differ from religious rituals (praying for rain) because they rely on the naive belief that the poured water can in some way directly affect the mechanics of precipitation.

Maginot line Fortifications built (1929–38) to protect the E frontier of France. They were named for André Maginot (1877–1932), French minister of war (1929–32), who authorized its construction. Outflanked in World War II by the invading Germans (1940), the line was never tested.

Maglemosian A *Mesolithic culture of N Europe, dating from about 8000 to 5000 BC. Named for a site at Mullerup on Sjaelland (Denmark), the Maglemosian extended from E England to NW Russia. Hunters of forest game and fishers in the lakes by which they preferred to live, the Maglemosians used wood, stone, antler, and bone artifacts, including dug-out canoes, but lacked domestic animals (apart from dogs), cultivated crops, and pottery.

magma Molten rock lying beneath the earth's surface, either in the crust or upper mantle. It may rise to the surface through volcanic fissures and be extruded as lava; if it solidifies under ground it forms intrusive *igneous rock. Magma is a hot largely silicate liquid, containing dissolved gases and sometimes suspended crystals.

Magna Carta (1215) The Great Charter that was sealed at Runnymede by King John of England in response to the baronial unrest that resulted from his disastrous foreign policy and arbitrary government. The charter defined the barons' feudal obligations to the monarch, opposed his arbitrary application of justice, and confirmed the liberties of the English Church; its enforcement was to be supervised by 25 men elected by the barons. Although it failed to avert the outbreak of the first *Barons' War and was annulled by the pope, it was reissued, with some changes, in 1216, 1217, and 1225. The charter was subsequently upheld, especially by the parliamentarians in the 17th century, as a statement of fundamental civil rights.

Magnani, Anna (1908–73) Italian film actress, born in Egypt. She began her career as a nightclub singer in Rome. She appeared in Rossellini's *Rome, Open City* (1945), Renoir's *The Golden Coach* (1953), and, after she went to Hollywood, *The Rose Tattoo* (1955).

magnesite A white or colorless mineral consisting of magnesium carbonate. It results from the alteration of magnesium-rich rocks, as in the veins of magnesite in serpentine, and as replacement deposits in limestone and dolomite. It is an important ore of magnesium and is used in the manufacture of refractory material, fertilizers, abrasives, etc.

magnesium (Mg) A light silvery-white reactive metal, first isolated by Sir Humphry Davy in 1808. Magnesium is the eighth most common element in the earth's crust and is a major constituent of the earth's mantle as the minerals olivine (Mg_2SiO_4) and enstatite ($MgSiO_3$). It is extracted by electrolysis of lead chloride ($MgCl_2$), which is obtained from sea water and is responsible for the stickiness of unrefined table salt, since magnesium chloride is deliquescent. Magnesium forms many other ionic salts, such as the sulfate ($MgSO_4$; Epsom salts), the oxide (MgO), the nitrate ($Mg(NO_3)_2$), and the hydroxide ($Mg(OH)_2$; milk of magnesia). It also plays a central role in plant life, occurring in *chlorophyll. It has important commercial uses when alloyed with aluminum to make the strong light alloys used in aircraft construction. It is also used in flares, incendiary bombs, and as magnesium oxide in refractory furnace linings. At no 12; at wt 24.305; mp 1201°F (648.8°C); bp 1996°F (1090°C).

magnet A body that has an appreciable external *magnetic field (*see also* magnetism). Every magnet has two distinct areas around which the field is greatest—these areas are called the north and south poles. If two magnets are brought together, the like poles repel each other and the opposite poles attract each other. Ferromagnetic materials (*see* ferromagnetism) are attracted to magnets because the magnet induces a field in the material in line with its own field. **Permanent magnets** are made of ferromagnetic materials and retain their magnetism unless they are heated above a certain temperature or are demagnetized by a strong opposing field. **Electromagnets** only function when an electric current flows through their coils. The field strength along the axis of the coil is proportional to the number of turns of the coil and the current flowing through it.

magnetic bottle An arrangement of magnetic fields designed to contain a *plasma. Usually the fields are linear with strong magnetic fields called **magnetic mirrors** at both ends so that the plasma is confined within a cylinder. They are used in experimental *thermonuclear reactors.

magnetic constant (μ_0) A constant frequently occurring in magnetic equations in SI units. Also known as the *permeability of free space, its value is $4\pi \times 10^{-7}$ henry per meter. It is related to the *electric constant (ϵ_0) by $\mu_0\epsilon_0 = 1/c^2$, where c is the velocity of light.

magnetic declination The angle between geographical north and the horizontal component of the *geomagnetic field at the same point. It is also known as the magnetic variation.

magnetic dip The angle formed between the horizon and a compass allowed to swing freely in the vertical plane. It thus indicates the direction of the vertical component of the *geomagnetic field. It is measured with a **dip circle**, a vertically mounted magnetic needle surrounded by a circular scale.

magnetic domain. *See* ferromagnetism.

magnetic field The concept, devised by *Faraday, to explain the action-at-a-distance forces produced by a *magnet. The magnet is thought of as being surrounded by a field of force, within which its magnetic properties are effective. The strength and direction of the field is indicated by the lines of force that join the magnet's north and south poles. These lines of force can be seen if a card is laid over a magnet and iron filings sprinkled onto the card; when the card is tapped, the filings congregate along the lines of force. A wire carrying an electric current is also surrounded by a magnetic field, with concentric lines of force. An electromagnet usually consists of a coil of wire, in which the lines of force run through the center of the coil and around its circumference. The strength of the field at the center of the coil is proportional to the current and the number of turns, and inversely proportional to the radius of the coil. *See also* electromagnetic field.

magnetic flux A measure of the current-inducing properties of a magnetic field (*see* flux). It is measured in *webers.

magnetic moment A measure of the strength of a *magnet in terms of the torque or twisting force it experiences in a uniform magnetic field. It is equal to the product of the strength of a magnet's poles and the distance between them.

magnetic monopole A hypothetical particle that would carry a magnetic charge equivalent to either a north pole or a south pole. Such particles would be analogous to charged elementary particles and would provide a complete symmetry between electricity and magnetism. Unlike an electrically charged particle, a stationary magnetic monopole would give rise to a magnetic field and, when moving, an additional electric field. No monopole has ever been discovered.

magnetic tape. *See* cassette; tape recorder.

magnetism A phenomenon in which one body can exert a force on another body with which it is not in contact (action at a distance). The space in which such a force exists is called a *magnetic field. Stationary charged particles are surrounded by an *electric field; when these charged particles move or spin, an associated effect, the magnetic field, is created. Thus, an electric current, consisting of a flow of electrons, produces a magnetic field around the conductor carrying the current. The behavior of materials when placed in such a field depends on how the spinning electrons inside its atoms align themselves to reinforce or oppose the external field. *See also* antiferromagnetism; diamagnetism; ferrimagnetism; ferromagnetism; paramagnetism.

magnetite (*or* lodestone) A black magnetic mineral, a form of iron oxide (Fe_3O_4). It often has distinct north and south magnetic poles and was known around 500 BC for its use as a compass. It is one of the ores from which iron is extracted.

magneto An alternating-current *electric generator that uses a permanent *magnet, rather than an electromagnet, to create the magnetic field. It usually consists of one or more conducting coils rotating between a number of pairs of *magnetic poles. The induced voltage has a frequency equal to the number of magnets times the speed of rotation of the coils. It is used in some small internal-combustion engines to produce the ignition spark, often combined with the flywheel.

magnetohydrodynamics (MHD) A method of generating electricity in which current carriers in a fluid are forced by an external magnetic field to flow between electrodes placed in the fluid. Usually the fluid is a hot ionized gas or plasma in which the current carriers are electrons. The electron concentration is increased by adding substances of low ionization potential (e.g. sodium or potassium salts) to the flame. The method has been used to increase the efficiency of generation of a gas turbine, the exhaust flame of which is used for MHD generation.

magnetomotive force (mmf) A measure of the magnetic effect of an electric current in a coil. It is analogous to *electromotive force and is measured in ampere-turns, being dependent on the number of turns in the coil.

magnetosphere A region surrounding a planet in which charged particles are controlled by the magnetic field of the planet rather than by the interplanetary magnetic field carried by the *solar wind; beyond a magnetosphere, solar-wind particles flow undisturbed. Its shape arises from the interaction between solar wind and planetary magnetic field. The earth's magnetosphere, which includes the *Van Allen radiation belts, extends 37,000 mi (60,000 km) from the sunward side of the planet but is drawn out to a much greater extent on the opposite side.

magnetostriction The mechanical deformation of a ferromagnetic material (*see* ferromagnetism) when it is subjected to a magnetic field. The effect is the result of internal mechanical stress that arises because the energy required to magnetize the crystal domains varies with their orientation in the field. The converse effect, mechanical stress causing a change in magnetization, also occurs. Magnetostriction is used in *echo-sounding oscillators to produce the ultrasonic sound wave.

magnetron An electronic device used to generate and amplify *microwaves. It consists of a sealed evacuated tube containing a central cylindrical cathode (source of electrons) inside a cylindrical anode to which electrons are drawn by an electrostatic field. A steady magnetic field applied along the axis of the tube deflects the electrons from their radial path and, if strong enough, will cause them to rotate around the cathode setting up microwave-frequency oscillations. It is widely used in radar generators.

magnification In optical systems, the ratio of the width of an object to the width of its image, both being measured perpendicular to the axis of the system. For a single lens this reduces to the ratio of the distances of the image and the object from the lens when the image is in focus. For optical instruments the magnification is defined as the ratio of the size of the image on the retina produced by an object with and without the instrument.

Magnitogorsk 53 28N 59 06E A city in the central Soviet Union, in the RSFSR on the Ural River. It is an important metallurgy center and also possesses the largest iron and steel plant in the country. Population (1981 est): 413,000.

magnitude A measure of the brightness of stars and other astronomical objects. An object's **apparent magnitude** is its brightness as observed from earth and depends primarily on its *luminosity and its distance. An object's **absolute magnitude** is its apparent magnitude if it lay at a distance of 10 parsecs (32.616 light years). Both apparent and absolute magnitude are measured at various specific wavebands in the visible, ultraviolet, and infrared regions of the electromagnetic spectrum.

Magnitude values range from about +25 for the faintest objects so far detected through zero to negative values for the brightest objects. One star 5 magnitudes less than another is 100 times brighter; a difference of one magnitude thus denotes a brightness ratio of $\sqrt[5]{100}$, i.e. 2.512.

Magnolia A genus of evergreen or deciduous shrubs and □trees (35 species), native to North America and Asia and widely grown as ornamentals. Up to 148 ft (45 m) high, they have large simple leaves and big showy flowers, with a whorl of white, yellow, greenish, or pink petals and many stamens. These produce papery conelike structures containing winged fruits. A popular ornamental magnolia is the Chinese hybrid *M.* × *soulangeana*, which has pink-tinged flowers. Family: *Magnoliaceae*. *See also* umbrella tree.

magpie A noisy black-and-white crow, *Pica pica*, occurring in Eurasia, NW Africa, and W North America. 17 in (44 cm) long, it has a long wedge-shaped tail and an iridescent blue sheen on the wings. Magpies are omnivorous and notorious predators of eggs and nestlings; they are also attracted to bright objects.

The name is also given to Australian songbirds of the family *Cracticidae*, which includes the *currawongs.

Magritte, René (1898–1967) Belgian surrealist painter. Initially a wallpaper designer and commercial artist, he became associated with the Paris surrealists (*see* surrealism) in the late 1920s. Using a realistic but deadpan technique, he made everyday images appear menacing by the use of unusual juxtapositions.

Magyars The largest ethnic group in Hungary. There are substantial Magyar minorities in neighboring countries. They originated from mixed Ugric and Turkic stock, who migrated from Siberia during the 5th century and eventually reached their present location during the late 9th century. They subjugated the local *Slavs and *Huns and for 50 years raided far into Europe causing widespread disruption and fear. Today they are predominantly peasant farmers. *See also* Hungarian.

Mahabharata (Sanskrit: great epic of the Bharatas) A Hindu epic poem in 18 books. Probably composed about 300 BC, it may record actual events of a thousand years earlier. The main story relates the feud between the Pandava and Kaurava clans and is interwoven with many myths and other episodes, including the *Bhagavadgita in the sixth book. The *Mahabharata* and *Ramayana form the two great classics of Sanskrit literature.

Mahalla el-Kubra 30 59N 31 10E A city in N Egypt, on the Nile Delta. In a region producing rice, cereal, and cotton, it is an important cotton-manufacturing center. Population (1976): 293,000.

Mahan, Alfred Thayer (1840–1914) US sailor and historian. The son of a West Point professor, he went to the Naval Academy (1859). After serving in the Civil War, he devoted his time to writing and lecturing, formulating the role of a strong navy in a nation and profoundly influencing naval planning internationally. He wrote *The Influence of Sea Power upon History, 1660–1783* (1890) and *The Influence of Sea Power upon the French Revolution and Empire, 1793–1812* (2 vols., 1892). He came out of retirement in 1898 to serve on the operations board during the *Spanish–American War.

Maharashtra A state in W central India, on the Arabian Sea. Rising from its coastal plain eastward over the Western *Ghats, it lies mostly on the *Deccan plateau. Cotton, millet, wheat, and rice are farmed. The second most industrialized state, it produces cotton textiles, chemicals, machinery, and oil products. Bauxite, manganese, and iron ore are mined. *History*: conquered by Muslims (1307), the Marathas regained their freedom (16th century) and maintained it until Britain established control (19th century). Maharashtra became a state in 1960. Area: 118,796 sq mi (307,762 sq km). Population (1981): 62,693,898. Capital: Bombay.

Mahavira, title of **Vardhamana** (?599–527 BC) The 24th and final *Tirthankara and founder of *Jainism. Born a member of the warrior caste, at the age of 30 he left his family to become an ascetic, following the teaching of the previous Tirthankara. After 12 years of austere self-mortification, he gained the spiritual knowledge he sought. He devoted the rest of his life to teaching Jaina doctrine.

Mahayana (Sanskrit: Great Vehicle) The school of Buddhism dominant in Tibet, Mongolia, China, Korea, and Japan. More evolved, adaptable, and less conservative and academic than the rival school, the *Theravada, the Mahayana teaching differs from it primarily in promulgating the ideal of the *Bodhisattva—the one who, having gained enlightenment, remains in the world in order to help other beings to their release.

Mahdi, al- (Arabic: the guided one) In Islamic tradition, a messianic leader who will appear shortly before the end of the world and, for a few years, restore justice and religion. According to some *Shiite Muslims, the 12th *imam (9th century AD), who is now hidden, will return as the Mahdi. Of a number of claimants to the title, the best known was the Sudanese leader **Muhammad Ahmad** (1844–85). After a religious experience, he proclaimed himself the Mahdi and led an uprising against the Egyptian Government. In 1884 he attacked Khartoum, which was defended by General *Gordon, and captured it in January, 1885, after a ten-months' siege. He died at Omdurman, near Khartoum, in June, 1885, probably of typhus. His rule was continued by *Abd Allah, the Khalifa.

mahjong An ancient Chinese game. It is usually played by 4 people using 2 dice and 136 tiles of bone, ivory, or plastic. 108 of the tiles are arranged in 3 suits: circles, bamboos, and characters. Each suit comprises tiles numbered one to nine, with four of each type of tile. There are also four each of red, white, and green dragons and four each of east, south, west, and north winds. Many sets have eight additional tiles, the flowers and seasons. The tiles are built into a square of four walls, symbolizing a walled city. Players score by collecting sequences of tiles according to complex rules.

Mahler, Gustav (1860–1911) Austrian composer and conductor. He studied at the Vienna conservatoire and directed the Viennese Court Opera from 1897–1907, where he acquired a brilliant reputation. In 1909 he became conductor of the New York Philharmonic Society, but met resistance to his advocacy of modern music. He died of pneumonia at the age of 50. His nine large-scale symphonies (and uncompleted tenth) were written during brief vacations. The second (*Resurrection Symphony*), third, fourth, and eighth (*Symphony of a Thousand*) employ vocal soloists. He also wrote the song cycles *Kindertotenlieder* (1901–04) and *Das Lied von der Erde* (1907–10).

Mahmud II (1785–1839) Sultan of the Ottoman Empire (1808–39). He continued and increased the modernization and westernization of the Empire that had begun under Selim III (1761–1808; reigned 1789–1807). He destroyed the *Janissaries in 1826 and in 1829 was forced to recognize Greek independence (*see* Greek Independence, War of).

Mahmud of Ghazna (971–1030) The third sultan (997–1030) of the Ghaznavid dynasty, which ruled a kingdom comprising modern Afghanistan. During his reign Mahmud led about 17 expeditions into India, conquering Kashmir and the Punjab, and also expanded his state in Iran. He is regarded as the greatest of his dynasty.

mahogany An evergreen tree of the genus *Swietenia* (7 species), native to tropical America and the West Indies and widely cultivated for timber. Up to about 65 ft (20 m) high, it has large compound leaves with 2–6 pairs of leaflets, greenish-yellow flower clusters, and fruit capsules containing winged seeds. *S. macrophylla* and *S. mahagoni* are the most important species: their hard red-brown wood is highly valued for furniture. Similar wood is obtained from members of other genera (*Khaya, Trichilia,* etc.). Family: *Meliaceae. See also* jarrah.

Mahonia A genus of evergreen shrubs (70 species), native to N temperate regions and South American mountains and often grown as ornamentals. They have leaves with paired, sometimes spiky, leaflets, and bunches of yellow or orange flowers that produce berries; only those of the Oregon grape (*M. aquifolium*) are edible. Family: *Berberidaceae.*

Mahratta. *See* Maratha.

Maiden Castle The 115-acre site on Fordington Hill, near Dorchester, England of a prehistoric fortress that may date back to 2000 BC. Excavations provided evidence that an Iron Age fortified village occupied the site in the 4th century BC. It was captured by the Romans in 43 AD and abandoned in about 70.

maidenhair fern An ornamental *fern of the genus *Adiantum* (about 200 species), especially *A. capillus-veneris*, found worldwide in moist warm places. From a creeping rhizome arise delicate brown or black stalks, about 0.98–12 in (2.5–30 cm) high, bearing fan-shaped green leaflets. Clusters of spore capsules (sori) are situated on the leaf margins, which are folded onto the underside. Family: *Adiantaceae.*

maidenhair tree. *See* ginkgo.

Maidstone 51 17N 0 32E A city in SE England, the administrative center of Kent on the Medway River. It is an ancient city and the center of an important fruit- and hop-growing region. There are brewing, paper, cement, confectionery, and engineering industries. Population (1981): 72,311.

Maiduguri (*or* Yerwa) 11 53N 13 16E A city in NE Nigeria. It comprises the towns of Yerwa and Maiduguri. It mainly exports livestock, hides, crocodile skins, and leather goods. It has a university (1960). Population (1975 est): 189,000.

Maikop 44 37N 40 48E A city in the SW Soviet Union, the capital of the Adygei autonomous region in the RSFSR. It is the center of an oil-producing region and is also important for timber and food processing. Population (1980 est): 128,000.

Mailer, Norman (1923–) US novelist and journalist. He established his reputation with the World War II novel *The Naked and the Dead* (1948). His concern with American society, which provided the themes for novels such as *An American Dream* (1965), is more directly expressed in later works, such as *The Armies of the Night* (1968), concerned with a protest march on the Pentagon, and *Executioner's Song* (1979), about a convicted murderer, in which he attempted to transcend the conventional distinctions between fiction and journalism. Both were awarded Pulitzer Prizes. Other works include *The Deer Park* (1955), *Pieces and Pontifications* (1982), *Ancient Evenings* (1983), and *Tough Guys Don't Dance* (1984).

Maillol, Aristide (1861–1944) French sculptor. Originally a painter and tapestry designer influenced by the *Nabis and *Gauguin, Maillol turned to sculpture in 1896. He made his name in the early 1900s with his monumental female nudes, the best known being *Mediterranean* (c. 1901; New York) and *Night* (1902; Paris). Although influenced by classical Greek models, their extreme simplicity anticipated modern abstract sculpture. Maillol's later works included war memorials and monuments to Cézanne and Debussy.

mail-order business A method of retail trading in which members of the public purchase goods (clothes, household goods, etc.) direct from mail-order houses through the mail, either in response to individual advertisements or from large highly illustrated catalogues. As no retailers' mark-up has to be paid, items can usually be purchased by mail order more cheaply than they can in stores. The customer, however, usually has to pay a delivery or postage charge. This method of trading was pioneered in the US in the 19th century, being especially appropriate to people living in remote areas.

Maimonides, Moses (Mosheh ben Maymun; 1135–1204) Jewish philosopher and physician. He was born in Córdoba (Spain), then under Moorish rule. After the fall of that city to the *Almohads and the subsequent religious persecution of Jews, Maimonides and his family left Spain. They settled in Cairo about 1165, where he later became physician to the Egyptian court. Maimonides' medical theories were advanced for his age. His celebrated philosophical work, *The Guide of the Perplexed*, which attempts to reconcile faith with reason, led to bitter controversy between orthodox Judaism and science.

Main River A river in central West Germany, flowing generally W through Frankfurt to join the Rhine River at Mainz. It is linked by canal with the Danube River. Length: 320 mi (515 km).

Maine A coastal state in the extreme NE. Maine is the largest of the New England states. It is bordered by New Hampshire on the W, the Canadian provinces of Quebec and New Brunswick to the NW and NE, and the Atlantic Ocean to S and SE. It consists of uplands in the W and NW and lowlands along the deeply indented coast in the E. Four fifths of the state is forested although the famous white pine is now almost extinct. It is the most sparsely populated state E of the Mississippi, most of its inhabitants living in the original settlements along the coast and river valleys. Manufacturing is most important and the major products are paper and pulp, leather goods, food, timber, and textiles. An area of considerable mineral wealth, limestone, building stone, and sand and gravel are exploited. The state's major agricultural products are potatoes, poultry, dairying, apples, and beef. *History*: It is thought that the Vikings visited Maine between the 9th and 11th centuries. When white explorers first arrived, the Abnaki Indians inhabited coastal and inland villages. The English also founded an unsuccessful colony in 1607 on the present site of Phippsburg. In 1613 a new French colony and mission was formed on Mt Desert Island but was expelled by English settlers under Sir Samuel Argall. In 1620, Captain John Mason and Fernando Gorges were granted the region, and permanent settlements were soon made. Maine came under the jurisdiction of the Massachusetts Bay Colony in 1653. Succeeding struggles among the British, French, and Indians retarded settlement. In 1691, Massachusetts' control of Maine was settled but Indian rampages threatened expansion; the Queen Anne's War virtually ended Indian raids against the whites in the state. Lumbering, fisheries, and shipbuilding flourished under Massachusetts' administration. Maine entered the Union as part of Massachusetts (1788) and later became a separate state (1820). In the 1970s migration to the S was encouraged by the construction of highways and expanded transportation. In the 1980s a long-standing land claim by Indians in the state was settled with advantageous results for Maine through investments in business and property by the Indians. Area: 33,215 sq mi (86,027 sq km). Population (1980): 1,124,660. Capital: Augusta.

Maine A former province in NW France, approximating to the modern departments of Mayenne and Sarthe. United with Anjou in 1126, Maine became English territory in 1154. It was reconquered by Philip II Augustus in 1204 and was a province from about 1600 until divided into departments in 1789.

Mainland 1. (*or* Pomona) The largest of the Orkney Islands, divided into two main parts by Kirkwall Bay and *Scapa Flow. Area: 190 sq mi (492 sq km). Population (1971): 6502. Chief town: Kirkwall. 2. The largest of the Shetland Islands. Area: about 225 sq mi (583 sq km). Population (1971): 13,150. Chief town: Lerwick.

main sequence. *See* Hertzsprung-Russell diagram.

Maintenon, Mme de (Françoise d'Aubigné, Marquise de M.; c. 1635–1719) The second wife of Louis XIV of France. In 1652 she married the writer Paul *Scarron and after his death became the governess of Louis' illegitimate children (1669) and the king's mistress. She became his wife secretly after the death of Queen Marie Thérèse (1683).

Mainz (French name: Mayence) 50 00N 8 16E A city and port in SW West Germany, the capital of Rhineland-Palatinate at the confluence of the Rhine and Main Rivers. Originally a Celtic settlement, it was the first German archbishopric and in the 15th century Gutenberg set up his printing press here. Its cathedral was founded in 975 AD and its university in 1477 (discontinued 1816–1946). It is a wine-trading center with varied industries. Population (1980 est): 186,700.

Maistre, Joseph de (1753–1821) French monarchist. Settling in Lausanne, he became prominent as an opponent of Revolutionary France with his advocacy of absolutist government, faith in the divine right of kings, and belief, expounded in *Du pape* (1819), that an infallible pope can depose rulers who disregard the laws of God.

maize. *See* corn.

MAJOLICA *An enameled earthenware dish, made in Savona in the 17th century.*

majolica Italian pottery originating in the 15th century. Made from calcareous clay, the soft buff body is coated with white tin glaze and brilliantly painted in luster and rainbow colors. Motifs include narrative pictures, botanical and zoological subjects, grotesques, arabesques, and armorial designs. Items made include tableware, drug jars, and display ornaments. Principal centers of manufacture were Gubbio (famous for lusters by Maestro Giorgio), Deruta (yellow and blue designs on orange backgrounds), Faenza (*see* faience), and *Caffaggiolo. The manufactures of the first quarter of the 16th century, which are sought after and valuable, were often financed by noble patronage. Imitations and forgeries abound.

Majorca (Spanish name: Mallorca) A Spanish island in the Mediterranean Sea, the largest of the Balearic Islands. The chief occupations are agriculture and tourism; cereals, legumes, oranges, olives, and figs are produced and marble is quarried. Area: 1465 sq mi (3639 sq km). Population (1970): 438,656. Capital: Palma.

Majuba Hill A mountain in South Africa, on the border between the Transvaal and Natal in the Drakensberg range. In 1881 it was the scene of a Boer victory over the British. Height: 6500 ft (1981 m).

Makarios III (Mikhail Khristodolou Mouskos; 1913–77) Cypriot churchman and statesman; archbishop of the Orthodox Church of Cyprus (1950–77) and president of Cyprus (1960–74, 1974–77). In 1956 he was deported to the Seychelles by the British because of his support for Greek-Cypriot union (*see* EOKA). He subsequently abandoned this aim, thus facilitating the attainment of Cypriot independence. In 1974 he was deposed in a coup that was backed by the Greek military regime but resumed the presidency before the end of the year.

Makassar. *See* Ujung Padang.

Makeevka(*or* Makeyevka) 48 01N 38 00E A city in the Soviet Union, in the SE Ukrainian SSR in the Donets Basin. Its industry is based on coal-mining and metallurgy. Population (1981 est): 442,000.

Makhachkala (name until 1921: Petrovsk) 42 59N 47 30E A port in the S Soviet Union, the capital of the Dagestan ASSR on the Caspian Sea. It has oil-refining, engineering (especially aircraft), and textile industries. Population (1981 est): 269,000.

Malabar Coast (*or* Malabar) The W coast of India from Goa in the N to Cape Comorin in the S. In 1498 Vasco da Gama landed here, making it the first part of India to be brought into contact with Europe. The shore is fringed by sand dunes and coconut palms, while further inland there are long shallow lagoons and paddy fields.

Malabo (name until 1973: Santa Isabel) 3 45W 8 48E The capital of Equatorial Guinea, a port in the N of the island of Bioko (formerly Macías Nguema), founded by the British in 1827. Population (1960): 37,237.

Malacca 02 14N 102 14E A historic port in W Peninsular Malaysia, the capital of Malacca state. It was colonized successively by the Portuguese,

Dutch, and British after 1511; many Portuguese and Dutch buildings remain. Population (1980): 88,073.

Malacca A state in W Peninsular Malaysia, on the Strait of Malacca. Consisting chiefly of a low-lying coastal plain, it produces rice, rubber, copra, tin, and bauxite. Area: 637 sq mi (1650 sq km). Population (1980): 453,153. Capital: Malacca.

Malacca, Strait of A channel between Sumatra and Peninsular Malaysia, linking the Indian Ocean with the Pacific Ocean. It is one of the world's most important shipping lanes. Length: about 500 mi (800 km).

Malachi An Old Testament prophet who rebuked religious hypocrites and the various social evils of the time, predicted a day of judgment, and urged the people to observe the Law of Moses. **The Book of Malachi** is the last book of the Old Testament.

malachite An ore of copper consisting of hydrated copper carbonate, $Cu_2(OH)_2CO_3$. It is bright green and is found in the oxidized zone of deposits of copper minerals. It occurs in massive form, often with a smooth surface.

malachite green (aniline green *or* China green; $C_{23}H_{25}ClN_2$) A dye that occurs as lustrous green crystals and is soluble in alcohol. It is used medicinally in dilute solution as an antiseptic and in fish breeding to kill fungus and bacteria. It is also used to dye leather and natural fabrics.

Malachy, St (1094–1148) Irish prelate, whose Church reforms initiated a religious revival in Ireland. He became Bishop of Connor in 1124 and Archbishop of Armagh in 1132. On his way to Rome (1139) he visited St *Bernard of Clairvaux, with whose encouragement he founded the first Cistercian abbey in Ireland, at Mellifont (1142). Feast day: Nov 3.

Málaga 36 43N 4 25W A city in S Spain, in Andalusia on the Mediterranean Sea. Founded by the Phoenicians (12th century BC), it passed successively to the Romans, the Visigoths, and the Moors, before falling to Ferdinand and Isabella in 1487. It has a cathedral (begun 16th century) and is the birthplace of the painter Picasso. A major tourist center and port, it exports olives, almonds, and dried fruits. Population (1974 est): 402,978.

Malagasy A language of the *Austronesian family, related to Malay, spoken in Madagascar. The standard form, written in Roman characters, is based on the Merina dialect. It has been influenced by Swahili and Arabic.

Malagasy Republic. *See* Madagascar, Democratic Republic of.

Malamud, Bernard (1914–) US novelist. With witty and ironic short stories and parables and such novels as *The Assistant* (1957) and *A New Life* (1961) he established his reputation as a skilful chronicler of Jewish characters and themes. His other works include the story collections *The Magic Barrel* (1958) and *Pictures of Fidelman* (1969) and the novels *The Fixer* (1966), *The Tenants* (1971), *Dubin's Lives* (1979), and *God's Grace* (1982).

Malan, Daniel F(rançois) (1874–1959) South African politician; prime minister (1948–54). Founder in 1939 with *Hertzog of the Nationalist Party, which won the 1948 elections, Malan instituted *apartheid in South Africa. A minister of the Dutch Reformed Church, he was a right-wing Afrikaner nationalist.

Malang 07 59S 112 45E A city in Indonesia, in E Java. It is the site of ancient ruined royal palaces and Indonesian army and air-force bases. Its university was established in 1961. An agricultural center, it has soap, ceramics, and cigarette industries. Population (1971): 422,428.

Malaparte, Curzio (Kurt Erich Suckert; 1898–1957) Italian political journalist, novelist, and dramatist. He was an active but unorthodox adherent of fascism from the 1920s to the 1940s. His best-known novels are *Kaputt* (1944) and *The Skin* (1949), which drew on his experience as a war correspondent on the Russian front and as a liaison officer with the Allies in Naples during World War II.

malaria An infectious disease caused by protozoa of the genus *Plasmodium. Malaria is transmitted by the female *Anopheles* mosquito, which lives only in the tropics. There are four species of *Plasmodium* that infect man and cause different types of malaria. Malignant tertian malaria (caused by *P. falciparum*) is the most severe; benign tertian malaria (caused by *P. vivax*) is less often fatal but there are repeated attacks. The parasites invade the red blood cells and cause them to burst. There is always fever but, depending on the type of parasite and the number of cells affected, there may also be fits, diarrhea, shock, and jaundice. Chronic infection causes enlargement of the liver and spleen. There are drugs (such as chloroquine) to treat the disease and these can also be taken to prevent it. Attempts by the World Health Organization to limit malaria, which is a major cause of death and ill health in the tropics, by destroying the mosquito have not yet achieved complete success.

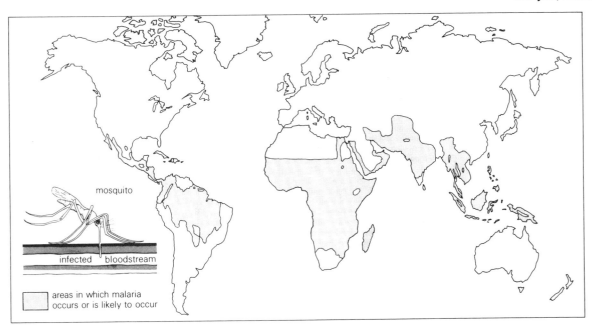

mosquito

infected bloodstream

□ areas in which malaria
occurs or is likely to occur

MALARIA *Despite eradication programs, malaria is still endemic in many parts of the tropics. By sucking the blood of an infected person, the female* Anopheles *mosquito can transmit the malarial parasite to an uninfected person.*

Malatesta A family that ruled Rimini (Italy) from 1295 to 1500. **Malatesta da Verrucchio** (d. 1312) led the local Guelf (papal) faction and came to power in 1295 after ousting the Ghibellines (imperial party; *see* Guelfs and Ghibellines). In the 15th century the family lost papal support and its most famous member, **Sigismondo Pandolfo Malatesta** (1417–68), was expelled from Rimini by Pope Pius II (1461). The family's temporary recovery of Rimini (1469–1500) ended when it was taken by Cesare *Borgia.

Malatya 38 22N 38 18E A city in SE central Turkey dating from 1838. It is in a fertile area producing cotton, tobacco, apricots, and grapes and has a university (1975). Population (1980): 179,074.

Malawi, Lake (former name: Lake Nyasa) A lake in Malawi, Tanzania, and Mozambique. Discovered for Europeans by Livingstone in 1859, it is 370 mi (595 km) long and is drained by the Shiré River S into the Zambezi River. Area: about 11,966 sq mi (31,000 sq km).

Malawi, Republic of (name until 1963: Nyasaland) A country in SE Africa, between Tanzania, Zambia, and Mozambique. Lake Malawi lies at its E border and the land consists mainly of high plateaus reaching heights of over 9800 ft (3000 m). The majority of the population is Bantu. *Economy*: chiefly agricultural. The main subsistence crop is maize, and cash crops include tobacco, tea, sugar, and groundnuts, which are the chief exports. Mineral resources are sparse and most power comes from hydroelectric sources, which are now being intensively developed. *History*: the area was visited by the Portuguese in the 17th century and, after Livingstone's exploration, became a British protectorate in 1891. In 1953, in spite of African opposition, it was joined with Northern and Southern Rhodesia to form the Federation of *Rhodesia and Nyasaland. This was dissolved in 1963 and Nyasaland gained internal self-government, becoming independent in 1964. In 1966 it became a republic within the British Commonwealth with Dr Hastings *Banda as its first president. The Malawi Congress Party is the only political party. Official language: English. Official currency, since 1971: kwacha of 199 tambala. Area: 36,324 sq mi (94,079 sq km). Population (1980 est): 5,900,000. Capital: Lilongwe.

Malay A language of the Indonesian branch of the *Austronesian family spoken in SE Asia and Indonesia. The dialect of the S Malay peninsula is the basis of standard Malay. It can be written in Roman or Arabic script. The Malay people probably migrated to this area from China between 2500 and 1500 BC. They became great seafarers, colonizing as far as Madagascar. Predominantly village dwellers, they live in nuclear families in houses raised on piling. Rice and rubber are the main crops. Distinction between noble and commoner social groups is important. Since the 15th century Islam has been the accepted religion, but vestiges of former Hinduism survive.

Malayalam A *Dravidian language of SW India. It is the official language of Kerala. It is related to Tamil from which its script, Koleluttu, is derived.

Malay Archipelago (former name: East Indies) An island group in SE Asia, the largest in the world. It lies between the Pacific and Indian Oceans and between the Asian and Australian continents. It comprises the Indonesian, Malaysian, and Philippine islands; New Guinea is sometimes included.

Malay Peninsula (*or* Kra Peninsula) A narrow peninsula in SE Asia, between the Andaman Sea and the South China Sea and separated from Sumatra by the Strait of Malacca. Politically it comprises SW Thailand, Peninsular Malaysia, and Singapore. Length: about 200 mi (320 km). *See also* Malaysia, Federation of.

Malaysia, Federation of A country in SE Asia, consisting of the 11 states of Peninsular Malaysia (formerly the Federation of Malaya) and the states of *Sabah and *Sarawak in N Borneo. Peninsular Malaysia consists of coastal plains rising to mountains in the interior, reaching heights of 7000 ft (2100 m). Most of the inhabitants are Malays and Chinese with minorities of Indians, Pakistanis, and others. *Economy*: Malaysia is a major exporter of rubber, tin, and palm oil. Agriculture is the chief occupation; besides the cash crops of rubber and palms, rice (the chief food crop) is extensively produced. Much of the land area is under dense forest producing considerable quantities of timber; fishing is also important. Other than tin, minerals exploited include iron ore, bauxite, ilmenite, and gold. The tourist industry is expanding, an added attraction being Malaysia's ethnic cultures. *History*: from the 9th to the 14th centuries the Srivijaya empire dominated the area. In the 14th century it was overrun by Hindu Javanese from the Majapahit kingdom and in about 1400 Malacca was established as an Islamic center. The spice trade flourished, centered on Malacca, attracting the attention of Europeans. In 1511 the port was taken by the Portuguese and in 1641 by the Dutch. British interest in the Malay states began in the 18th century; the East India Company established stations on Penang, Malacca, and Singapore Island, which became the Straits Settlements (1826). With the opening of the Suez Canal, British trade interests increased and in 1909 British protection was extended over the Federated Malay States (Selangor, Negri Sembilan, Perak, and Pahang) and the remaining five unfederated states. Following occupation by the Japanese during World War II, the Federation of Malaya was established (1948). Malaya became independent in 1957 and in 1963 part of the federal state of Malaysia, together with Sabah, Sarawak, and Singapore (which left the federation in 1965). There has been considerable unrest in recent years caused mainly by Chinese resentment of Malay dominance in the government. A resurgence of communist guerrilla activities has taken place leading to strong measures against communism. In foreign policy Malaysia has moved away from its previous pro-Western stand to a more neutral position. Supreme head of state: Sultan Haji Ahmad Shah Al-Musta'in Billah. Prime minister: Datuk Seri Mahathir Muhammed. Official language: Bahasa Malaysia. Official religion: Islam. Official currency: Malaysian dollar of 100 cents. Area: 127,289 sq mi (329,749 sq km). Population (1983 est): 14,995,000. Capital: Kuala Lumpur. Main port: Georgetown.

Malcolm III (c. 1031–93) King of the Scots (1057–93). He became king after killing *Macbeth, the murderer of his father Duncan I (d. 1040; reigned 1034–40). Malcolm married St *Margaret. He became a vassal of William the Conqueror (1072) and was murdered during the last of frequent raids into N England.

Malcolm X (1925–65) US militant black leader. Formerly a member of the *Black Muslims, he founded the rival militant Organization of Afro-American Unity (1964), which supported violent means of achieving racial equality. He was assassinated while addressing a rally.

Maldives, Republic of (Divehi name: Divehi Raajje; name until 1969: Maldive Islands) A small country in the Indian Ocean, to the SW of Sri Lanka. It consists of a large number of small coral islands, grouped in atolls, of which just over 200 are inhabited. Most of the population is of mixed Indian, Sinhalese, and Arabic descent. *Economy*: the islands are covered with coconut palms, and coconuts, along with fish, are the main export. Other sources of revenue are shipping, tourism, and copra production. *History*: adherents of Islam since the 12th century, the islands were ruled by a sultan. Formerly a dependency of Ceylon, they were officially under British protection from 1887 to 1965. They were ruled by an elected sultan until 1968, when they became a republic. The Republic of Maldives became a special member of the Commonwealth of Nations in 1982. Head of state: President Maumoon Abdul Gayoon. Official language: Divehi. Official religion: Islam. Official currency: Maldivian rupee of 100 larees. Area: 115 sq mi (298 sq km). Population (1983): 168,000. Capital and main port: Malé.

Malebo Pool (former name: Stanley Pool) 4 15S 15 25E A broad section of the Zaïre River in West Africa, on the Congo–Zaïre border. It contains the island of Bamu, which divides the river channel into N and S branches. Area: 174 sq mi (450 sq km).

Malebranche, Nicolas (1638–1715) French philosopher and theologian. Like *Descartes, whose work he publicized, Malebranche was concerned with the mind-body relation. In *De la recherche de la vérité* (1674) he held that the two could not interact causally. God brought about all events, including bodily movements, by direct intervention, a doctrine known as occasionalism.

maleic acid (or *cis*-butenedioic acid; HOOCCH:CHCOOH) A colorless crystalline toxic *fatty acid. It is an *isomer of **fumaric acid** (*trans*-butenedioic acid) and both are used in making dyes and synthetic resins.

Malenkov, Georgi Maksimilianovich (1902–) Soviet statesman; prime minister (1953–55). A close associate of Stalin, Malenkov became first secretary of the Soviet Communist Party and prime minister after Stalin's death. Shortly afterward, he was replaced in the former post by Khrushchev but continued as prime minister until forced, owing to agricultural failures, to resign. He was expelled from the Communist Party in 1961.

Malesherbes, Chrétien Guillaume de Lamoignon de (1721–94) French statesman, a leading figure of the prerevolutionary era of reform in France. In 1750 he became director of censorship and gained a reputation for his liberal attitude, permitting, for example, the *Philosophes to publish their work. Criticism of the monarchy led to his banishment from court in 1771 but he was executed as a royalist during the French Revolution.

Malevich, Kazimir (1878–1935) Russian painter and art theorist, born in Kiev. He worked in most modern styles before exhibiting (1915) his *Black Square on White Ground*, which launched the art movement called *suprematism and made a significant contribution to *abstract art.

Malherbe, François de (1555–1628) French poet and critic. In 1605 he became court poet to Henry IV. In his criticism, mostly contained in letters and commentaries, he anticipated classicism by advocating principles of harmony, regularity, and propriety. His poetry consisted chiefly of conventional verses on political and religious themes.

Mali, Republic of (name until 1959: French Sudan) A large landlocked country in West Africa. It consists largely of desert, extending into the Sahara in the N, and is crossed by the Niger River, the flood plains of which provide most of the fertile land. The majority of the population are Bambara, Fulani, and Senufo. *Economy*: chiefly subsistence agriculture, especially livestock, including cattle, camels, and sheep. The main crops are rice, millet, cassava, cotton, and groundnuts, but all agriculture has been badly affected by droughts (1968–74). River fishing is important and dried

and smoked fish, together with cattle and groundnuts, are the main exports. Industry is based mainly on the processing of food and hides and skins. Mineral reserves of bauxite, uranium, and oil are present but only salt and small quantities of gold are exploited. Tourism is being developed, the main attractions being hunting, fishing, and the ancient city of Timbuktu. *History*: from the 4th century AD the area was occupied by successive empires, including those of Ghana, Mali (the most famous ruler of which was Mansu Musa), and Gao. In the late 19th century it was conquered by the French and, as French Sudan, it became part of French West Africa. It achieved internal self-government as part of the French Community in 1958. It briefly formed with Senegal the Federation of Mali in 1959, becoming a separate and fully independent republic in 1960. It broke away from the French Community but, because of economic problems, rejoined the franc zone in 1967. In 1968 the government was overthrown in a military coup led by Lieutenant Moussa Traoré, who became president in 1969 and was re-elected in 1979. Plans for a union or a confederation of Guinea and Mali were being entertained in the mid 1980s, despite little public support. Official language: French. Official currency: Mali franc of 100 centimes. Area: 464,752 sq mi (1,204,021 sq km). Population (3 est): 7,393,000. Capital: Bamako.

malic acid A dicarboxylic acid ($C_4H_6O_5$) that occurs widely in fruits (including apples, plums, and grapes) as the free acid or its salts. The anion malate is an intermediate compound in the *Krebs cycle.

Malik-Shah (1055–92) The last of the three great Seljuq Sultans of Turkey (1073–92), succeeding his father *Alp Arslan. Malik-Shah, a noted patron of science and the arts, built the famous mosques of Isfahan (his capital) and sponsored the poet *Ömar Khayyam. His government owed its distinction to the work of the vizier *Nizam al-Mulk.

Malines. *See* Mechelen.

Malinke A people of West Africa, also known as Mandingo, who speak a language of the Mande division of the *Niger-Congo family. During the 7th century AD one group founded a state with its capital at Kangaba. This spread to become the empire of Mali, which flourished from about 1250 to 1500. The Malinke are agriculturalists, who live in villages of round huts. Descent follows the patrilineal principle.

Malinowski, Bronisław (1884–1942) Polish anthropologist, regarded as the founder of social anthropology. Between 1914 and 1918 Malinowski lived among the natives of New Guinea and the Trobriand Islands, making a detailed study of their culture. A professor at London University from 1927, he became famous for his functional theory of anthropology, which saw every ritual and belief of a society as fulfilling a particular function. Malinowski's published work includes *The Natives of Mailu* (1915) and *The Father in Primitive Psychology* (1927).

Malipiero, Gian Francesco (1882–1973) Italian composer and teacher. His style owes much to the study of 17th- and 18th-century Venetian composers; his works include operas and orchestral, vocal, and chamber music. He published an edition of the works of Monteverdi.

mallard A *dabbling duck, *Anas platyrhynchos*, common on ponds and lakes in the N hemisphere. About 22 in (55 cm) long, females are mottled brown and males grayish with a green head, white collar, reddish breast, black rump, and a curly tail. Both sexes have a broad yellow bill and a purple wing speculum. The mallard is the ancestor of most domestic breeds of duck.

Mallarmé, Stéphane (1842–98) French poet. He visited England frequently and until 1871 taught English in schools in the French provinces and in Paris. Influenced by Baudelaire and Poe, he became a major figure of the *Symbolist movement, believing that the function of poetry was to evoke the ideal essences that lay behind the world of actual appearances. His best-known works include *Hérodiade* (1864), *L'Après-Midi d'un faun* (1865), and his obscure final poem, *Un Coup de dés jamais n'abolira le hasard* (1897).

mallee Scrubland vegetation of the coastal regions of S Australia, dominated by small trees and shrubs of the genus *Eucalyptus*. Most are 7–10 ft (2–3 m) high, with leathery gray-green leaves and many thick roots that store water.

mallee fowl A white-spotted light-brown bird, *Leipoa ocellata*, occurring in semiarid interior regions of Australia. 25.5 in (65 cm) long, it feeds on seeds and flowers and builds a large nest mound of fermenting plant material and sand, which may reach 15 ft (4.5 m) across. Throughout the incubation period the male maintains the mound at a constant temperature by adding and taking away sand as necessary. Family: *Megapodidae* (megapodes).

Mallorca. *See* Majorca.

mallow A herbaceous plant of the genus *Malva* (30 species), native to N temperate regions. Mallows, which may be creeping or erect, grow up to 35 in (90 cm) tall. They have hairy lobed leaves and five-petaled flowers, which are usually purple, pink, or white and 0.6–2.4 in (1.5–6 cm) across. The name is also given to other plants of the same family. The tree mallow (*Lavatera arborea*) is a shrublike biennial, up to 10 ft (3 m) high, with rose-purple flowers. Family: *Malvaceae*. *See also* marsh mallow.

Malmédy. *See* Eupen-et-Malmédy.

Malmö 55 38N 12 57E A city and port in S Sweden, on the *Sound opposite Copenhagen. It was a prominent trade and shipping center in the middle ages. Malmö's varied industries include shipbuilding, textiles, and food processing. Population (1978 est): 233,803.

malnutrition Ill health resulting from an inadequate diet, usually associated with poverty. The body needs certain amounts of protein, carbohydrate, fat, vitamins, and minerals. Insufficient protein causes *kwashiorkor in children, and a diet deficient in all nutrients causes marasmus. Lack of vitamins causes a wide variety of diseases, including *scurvy, *rickets, *beriberi, and *pellagra. *Obesity can be considered as a form of malnutrition resulting from overeating.

Malory, Sir Thomas (?1400–1471) English writer. He was the author of *Morte d'Arthur* (c. 1469), a narrative in 21 books of the legendary court of King Arthur, drawn mostly from French sources. Malory's identity remains uncertain, but he was probably a Warwickshire knight who had fought in France, became a member of Parliament in 1445, and was several times imprisoned.

Malpighi, Marcello (1628–94) Italian anatomist, whose microscopical studies of living organisms provided new insights into their function. In 1661 he discovered the fine capillaries that connect arteries with veins, substantiating William *Harvey's theory of blood circulation. Malpighi made numerous studies of body organs—the kidney glomeruli (Malpighian corpuscles) and a layer of skin tissue (Malpighian layer) are named for him. He also made valuable early studies of embryology and comparative plant anatomy.

Malplaquet, Battle of (September 11, 1709) A battle in the War of the *Spanish Succession in which the French faced the armies, under Marlborough and Prince Eugene of Savoy, of Britain, the Netherlands, and Austria, fought 10 mi (16 km) S of Mons. By a strategic retreat the French inflicted severe casualties upon the allies, who, although victorious, were checked in their advance upon Paris.

Malraux, André (1901–76) French novelist and essayist. His career included active service with communist revolutionaries in China in the 1920s, with the Republican forces in the Spanish Civil War, and with the French Resistance in World War II. His novels, which are notably objective treatments of the issues involved in these conflicts, include *Man's Estate* (1933) and *Days of Hope* (1938). He was minister for cultural affairs under de Gaulle from 1959 to 1969. He also wrote on art, notably in *Voices of Silence* (1953) and *Museum without Walls* (1967), and a volume of memoirs, *Antimémoires* (1967).

malt Barley or other grain prepared for brewing or distilling. The grain is softened by soaking in water, then either heaped on the malting floor and turned by hand or put in revolving drums to encourage germination. Germ growth is stopped by drying the malt by heat, after which it is ready for brewing. Alternatively, after eight to ten days' germ growth the malt may be used for malt *whisky.

Malta, Republic of A small country in the Mediterranean Sea, to the S of Sicily comprising the two main islands of Malta and Gozo and several islets. *Economy*: previously heavily dependent on foreign military bases, Malta has made efforts to diversify the economy in recent years. The naval dockyards have been converted to commercial use and port facilities are being developed to encourage the use of Malta as a transit center for Mediterranean shipping. Shipbuilding and repair are important and the development of other varied industries is aided by foreign investment (especially from Libya, Algeria, and Saudi Arabia). There is some agriculture, with crops and livestock, and fishing. Tourism is an important source of revenue. Exports include clothing, textiles, machinery, and food. *History*: occupied successively by the Phoenicians, Greeks, Carthaginians, and Romans, the island was conquered by the Arabs in 870 AD. In 1090 it was united with Sicily and in 1530 was granted to the Knights Hospitallers. In 1798 the island was occupied by the French and then by the British, to whom it was formally ceded in 1814. As a crown colony it became an important naval and air base. In World War II Malta's heroic resistance to German attack (1940–42) gained it the George Cross. In 1947 and 1961 it acquired increasing self-government, becoming fully independent in 1964. In 1974 it became a republic within the British Commonwealth. President: Agatha

Barbara (1923–). Prime minister: Carmello Mifsud Bonnici. Official languages: Maltese and English; Italian is widely spoken. Official religion: Roman Catholic. Official currency: Maltese pound of 100 cents and 1000 mils. Area: 122 sq mi (316 sq km). Population (1983 est): 363,000. Capital and main port: Valletta.

Malthus, Thomas Robert (1766–1834) British clergyman and economist, famous for his population theories. In his *Essay on the Principle of Population* (*First Essay*, 1798; *Second Essay*, 1803) Malthus argued that mankind is doomed to remain at near-starvation level as growth in food production, which increases at an arithmetical rate, is negated by the geometrical increase in population. Elaborating ideas from Plato, Aristotle, and Hume, Malthus called for positive efforts to cut the birth rate, preferably by sexual restraint but, failing that, by birth control.

Maluku. *See* Moluccas.

Malvinas, Islas. *See* Falkland Islands.

mamba A large agile highly venomous snake belonging to the African genus *Dendroaspis* (4–5 species). The aggressive black mamba (*D. polylepis*) is 14 ft (4.3 m) long, lives in open rocky regions, and preys on birds and small mammals. The smaller arboreal green mamba (*D. angusticeps*) reaches a length of 9 ft (2.7 m) and is much less aggressive. Mambas are egg-laying snakes. Family: *Elapidae* (cobras, mambas, coral snakes).

Mamelukes (Arabic: *mamluk*, slave) The rulers of Egypt and Syria (1250–1517). The Mamelukes were slave soldiers who seized power and then provided a succession of rulers from their own ranks. They drove back the Mongols and finally expelled the Crusaders from Syria. In 1517 the Ottoman Turks conquered Syria and Egypt but the Mamelukes survived as a class and were frequently the effective rulers of Egypt until destroyed by *Mehemet Ali in 1811.

mammal A warm-blooded animal belonging to the class *Mammalia* (about 4250 species). The evolution of mammals from reptiles involved the development of a temperature-regulation system with an insulating layer of fur and sweat glands in the skin for cooling. This enabled mammals to become highly active, with well-developed sense organs and brains, and to colonize cold climates. The survival of the young was improved by the evolution of milk-secreting *mammary glands, and in placental mammals a specialized nourishing membrane (the *placenta) in the uterus (womb) enabled the young to be born at an advanced stage of development. The stages involved in this evolution can still be seen in such primitive mammals as the egg-laying *monotremes and the *marsupials, which produce young at an early developmental stage.

The majority of modern mammalian species are terrestrial, ranging in size from tiny shrews to the elephant. However, bats are flying mammals and whales have adapted to a wholly marine existence.

mammary gland The gland in female mammals that secretes milk. Believed to have evolved from sweat glands, there are one or more pairs on the ventral (under) side of the body. The number of glands is related to the number of young produced at one birth; for example, rats and mice have five or six pairs; whales and humans have one pair. Each gland consists of branching ducts leading from milk-secreting cells and opening to the exterior through a nipple. In the most primitive mammals (*Monotremata*) there are no nipples and the milk is secreted directly onto the body surface. The secretion of milk (*see* lactation) is under hormonal control. *See also* breast.

mammoth An extinct elephant belonging to the genus *Mammuthus*, whose remains have been found in India, Europe, and North America. Of the four types known, the imperial mammoth (*M. imperator*) was the largest, 15 ft (4.5 m) at the shoulder. The woolly mammoth (*M. primigenius*) had thick body hair and tusks up to 8 ft (2.5 m) long. The well-preserved remains of woolly mammoths, which died out about 10,000 years ago, have been found frozen in the permafrost of Siberia. □fossil.

Mammoth Cave A large cavern in W central Kentucky, in the Mammoth Cave National Park. It consists of a series of limestone caves with spectacular stalactites and stalagmites. The largest cave reaches 125 ft (38 m) in height and a width of 300 ft (91 m).

Mamoré, Río A river in South America, rising in the Andes in central Bolivia and flowing generally N. It forms part of the Bolivia–Brazil border before joining the Río Bení to become the Río Madeira. Length: about 930 sq mi (1500 km).

Ma'mun, al- (786–833 AD) The seventh *caliph (813–833) of the 'Abbasid dynasty. A son of Harun ar-Rashid, al-Ma'mun seized the caliphate from his half-brother al-Amin (c. 785–813). As caliph he was inclined toward Shiite ideas and encouraged philosophical and scientific work.

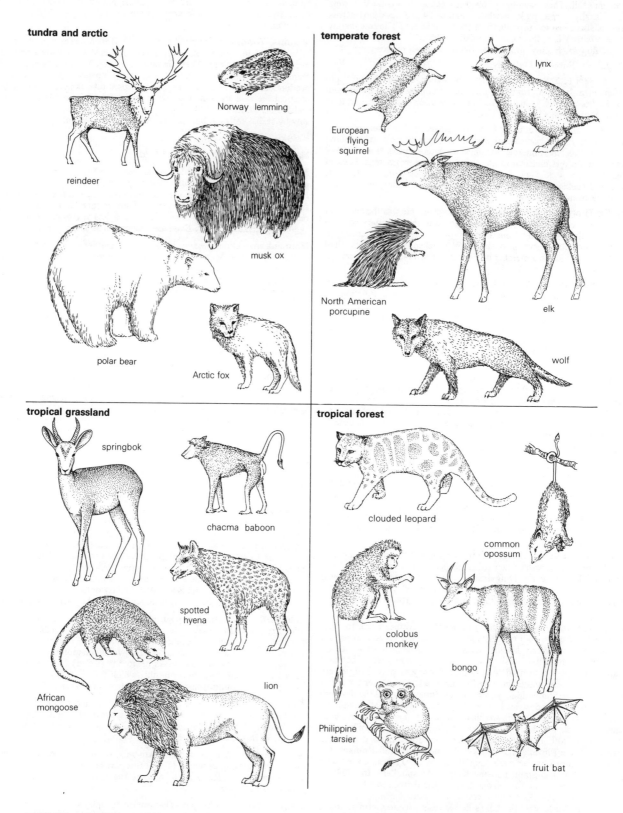

tundra and arctic

reindeer

Norway lemming

musk ox

polar bear

Arctic fox

temperate forest

European flying squirrel

lynx

North American porcupine

elk

wolf

tropical grassland

springbok

chacma baboon

spotted hyena

African mongoose

lion

tropical forest

clouded leopard

common opossum

colobus monkey

bongo

Philippine tarsier

fruit bat

MAMMAL   *This large and diverse group of animals has succeeded in colonizing almost every available habitat on earth, even the most inhospitable. Representative mammals are shown from eight of the world's major habitats (the animals depicted in each habitat are not necessarily from the same geographical region).*

MAMMAL

temperate grassland

American bison

prairie dog

Eurasian hedgehog

saiga antelope

giant anteater

fresh water

beaver

American mink

muskrat

giant otter

desert

Arabian camel

addax

kangaroo rat

fennec fox

red kangaroo

salt water

Florida manatee

blue whale

bottlenose dolphin

walrus

harbor seal

Man, Isle of An island in the Irish Sea, between England and Ireland. It has been a possession of the British crown since 1828, but is virtually self-governing with its own parliament. It consists of central hills rising to 2034 ft (620 m), with lowlands in the N and S. Tourism is the main source of revenue; attractions include its mild climate, scenery, and the annual motorcycle races. The island's low taxation levels encourage a steady influx of retired people. Its agriculture is varied; sheep and cattle are raised and produce includes cereals, turnips, and potatoes. Some manufacturing industry exists including light engineering. *History*: originally inhabited by Celts, the derivative Manx language survived in common usage until the 19th century. The island became a dependency of Norway in the 9th century AD and was ceded to Scotland (1266), coming under English control after 1406. Area: 227 sq mi (588 sq km). Population (1971): 49,743. Capital: Douglas.

Manado. *See* Menado.

Managua 12 06N 86 18W The capital of Nicaragua, on the S shore of Lake Managua. Formerly an Indian settlement, it became capital in 1857. It suffered severe damage from earthquakes in 1931 and 1972 and from the civil war (1979). The Nicaragua campus of the Central American University was founded in 1961. It is the country's principal industrial center. Population (1978 est): 552,900.

manakin A small stocky bird belonging to a family (*Pipridae*; 59 species) occurring in tropical forests of South and Central America. Male manakins are generally dark with bright patches and decorative crests and tail feathers; the females are usually green. Males perform elaborate courtship displays, either on the ground in specially cleared territories or in the trees.

Manama (Arabic name: Al Manamah) 26 12N 50 38E The capital of Bahrain since 1971, situated at the N end of Bahrain Island. An important free port, its economy is based on oil. Population (1980 est): 360,000.

Manassas 38 45N 72 48W A city in N Virginia, SW of Alexandria. Nearby is Manassas National Battlefield Park, which commemorates two Civil War battles fought here in 1861 and 1862. Population (1980): 15,438.

Manasseh, tribe of One of the 12 *tribes of Israel. It claimed descent from Manasseh, King of Judah, son of Joseph and grandson of Jacob. Manasseh's lands lay E and W of Jordan, midway between Galilee and the Dead Sea.

Manasseh ben Israel (Manoel Dias Soeiro; 1604–57) Rabbi of Amsterdam. His *Hope of Israel* (1650) dealt with the supposed discovery of the ten lost tribes in South America. Encouraged by English mystics, he presented a petition to Oliver *Cromwell (1655), asking for the readmission of the Jews to England (they had been expelled in 1290). He died before he could witness the success of his mission.

manatee A herbivorous aquatic □mammal belonging to the genus *Trichechus* (3 species), of warm Atlantic waters and coastal rivers of Africa and America. Up to 15 ft (4.5 m) long, manatees have a rounded body with tail fin and flippers and a squarish snout. The American manatee (*T. manatus*) of Florida feeds mainly at night. Slow and placid, it rests on the bottom during the day, rising regularly to breathe. Family: *Trichechidae*; order: *Sirenia*. *See also* dugong.

Manaus (*or* Manáos) 3 06S 60 00W A city in NW Brazil, the capital of Amazonas state on the Rio Negro. Founded in 1660, it became the center of the rubber boom (1890–1920). It remains the chief inland port of the Amazon basin and is accessible to oceangoing steamers. Exports include rubber, brazil nuts, timber, and other forest products. Notable buildings include the Teatro Amazonas (the opera house, 1896) and the University of Amazonas (1965). Population (1980): 613,098.

Manawatu River A river in New Zealand, in SW North Island flowing generally W and SW to the Tasman Sea NE of Wellington. The surrounding plain is one of New Zealand's most productive farming areas. Length: 113 mi (182 km).

Mancha, La An area and former province in Spain. It consists of an extensive sparsely populated arid plateau. Windmills, used to pump water from under ground, are a distinctive feature. It became famous as the setting of Cervantes' *Don Quixote de la Mancha*.

Manchester 53 30N 2 15W A city in NW England, situated on the Irwell River and forming part of a large conurbation. Linked with the Mersey estuary by the Manchester Ship Canal (opened 1894), it is an important port as well as England's second largest commercial center (banking, insurance). Long the center of Lancashire's traditional cotton industry, its other industries include chemicals, engineering, clothing, printing, publishing, paper, rubber, food products, and electrical goods. *History*: the Roman fort of Mancunium, Manchester developed as a regional wool market place.

From the mid 18th century onward a number of factors, such as new technology, the humid climate, and the availability of labor, combined to make it the world's main cotton-manufacturing town. It became the center of a network of roads, canals, and railroads but its rapid growth led to industrial discontent and political agitation (*see* Peterloo Massacre). Population (1981): 449,168.

Manchester 42 59N 71 28W A city in S New Hampshire, on the W bank of the Merrimack River. It is New Hampshire's largest city and a major distribution center for the surrounding area. Industries include electronics, leather and food processing, wood and paper products, and textiles. Population (1980): 90,936.

Manchu A nomadic people of Manchuria who conquered China during the 16th and 17th centuries and established the *Qing dynasty.

Manchukuo A puppet state set up by the Japanese in Manchuria in 1932 in a bid to occupy all China. It was administered by Chinese with the last Chinese emperor, Henry P'u-i (1906–67), as ruler, and lasted until Japan's defeat in 1945.

Manchuria A region in NE China bordering on the Soviet Union, roughly comprising the provinces of Heilongjiang, Jilin, and Liaoning. It is mountainous in the E and W with a large central fertile plain. The densely populated plain is a major industrial and agricultural area. Products include timber, minerals, such as coal and iron, and fish. *History*: the area was for centuries inhabited and fought over by the Manchu, Mongols, and Chinese. Their power struggles resulted in empires established over China by the Mongols (1279–1368; *see* Yuan) and Manchus (1644–1912; *see* Qing). Although the S had long been colonized by the Chinese, immigration into the whole area increased greatly under the Qing because of land hunger in China. In the late 19th century this fertile area was dominated by Russia (1898–1904) and then by Japan (1905–45), which developed industrial centers in the region. In 1931, following the Mukden Incident (*see* Shenyang), Japanese forces invaded Manchuria and established a puppet state (*see* Manchukuo). After 1945 the area, staunchly communist, received much aid from the Soviet Union until the 1960s, when the break between China and the Soviet Union took place. Since then military forces have been massed along the border. Area: about 502,000 sq mi (1,300,000 sq km).

Manchu-Tungus A group of languages of the *Altaic language family, related to *Mongolian and *Turkic. It comprises only a few languages, of which only the almost extinct Manchu has any literary tradition.

Mandaeanism A Gnostic sect surviving in S Iraq and SW Iran (*see* Gnosticism). It originated in the 1st or 2nd century AD, but its place of origin and its relationship to Christianity, Judaism, and indigenous Iranian religions, on all of which it draws, are disputed. Mandaeans are hostile to Christ but revere John the Baptist. Their most important rite is frequent baptism. The sacred *Ginza* describes their cosmology, which envisages a universe in which hostile spirits (*archons*) endeavor to prevent the soul's ascent to God.

mandala A Buddhist painted or sometimes metal-wrought symbol used in meditation and other religious practices and particularly associated with Tibetan and Japanese Buddhism. It usually consists of a series of concentric circles, representing universal harmony and containing religious figures, the Buddha being represented in the center.

Mandalay 21 57N 96 04E A city in Burma, on the Irrawaddy River. The last capital of the Burmese kingdom, it fell to the British in 1885. It has numerous monasteries, temples, and pagodas and is the site of a university (1964). Mandalay is the principal commercial center of Upper Burma. Population (1973): 418,008.

Mandan North American Siouan-speaking Indian tribe, found in North Dakota, near the Missouri River. The Mandan, whose name means "River people," were basically hunters, weavers, farmers, and traders, who traveled in round bullboats. Smallpox, brought by white traders, devastated the tribe in 1837; today, about 350 descendants of the Mandan live on Fort Berthold Reservation in North Dakota.

mandarin (fruit). *See* tangerine.

mandarin (official) A Chinese bureaucrat, whose appointment to salaried posts in the civil service was from early Han times until the 1911 revolution by examination. Mandarins occupied a privileged position in society, wore special embroidered robes, and spoke the Mandarin dialect of *Chinese, which in its standard, Peking, form is now spoken by 70% of the population.

mandarin duck A brilliantly colored *duck, *Aix galericulata*, native to China—where it was the symbol of marital fidelity—and widespread as an ornamental bird. It is 17 in (43 cm) long. The female is gray-brown with a bluish head, a white eye stripe, and a black bill; the male has a red bill, black-and-white head, purple breast, white underparts, and distinctive chestnut wing fans and whiskers at the sides of the face.

mandate The system whereby former German colonies and Turkish territories were entrusted by the League of Nations to the principal Allied Powers after World War I. The powers were to be responsible for their administration, welfare, and development until the mandatories were ready for self-government. After the establishment of the UN those that remained became *trust territories.

Mandelstam, Osip (1891–?1938) Russian poet. He was a friend of Akhmatova and a leading poet of *Acmeism. His second volume, *Tristia* (1922), contains poems noted for their classical form and spiritual intensity. He was arrested in 1934 and 1938, and is presumed to have died in a labor camp.

Mandeville, Sir John (14th century) The professed author of the immensely popular *Travels* (1356–57), an account that mixes factual and fantastic information about the Middle East, Africa, and Asia. He claimed to be British but was probably fictional and never existed. The book is a translation of a French work itself compiled from other sources.

mandolin A plucked musical instrument, generally having four double courses of wire strings tuned in the same way as the violin. It is played with a plectrum, using a tremolo effect to sustain longer notes. It is used in informal music making and more rarely as a solo or orchestral instrument.

mandrake A herb of the genus *Mandragora*, especially *M. officinarum*, native to Europe. It has large simple leaves, white flowers, and a thick forked root, which resembles the human form and was formerly believed to have healing and aphrodisiac properties. Family: *Solanaceae*.

mandrill A large *Old World monkey, *Mandrillus sphinx*, of West African coastal forests. They are 26–33 in (66–84 cm) long including the tail (2–3 in; 5–7.5 cm), with red and blue muzzle and buttocks and shaggy yellow-brown hair. They live in small family groups and forage for plants and insects, sometimes climbing for berries. *See also* drill.

Manes In Roman religion, the spirits of the dead. The word, a euphemism meaning "the kindly ones," also referred to the underworld and its gods.

Manet, Edouard (1832–83) French painter, born in Paris. After overcoming parental opposition, he trained under the classical painter Thomas Couture (1815–79) between 1850 and 1856. By 1860 he was painting contemporary scenes, but throughout his career he remained indebted to the Old Masters, particularly to Velázquez and Hals. He exhibited mainly at the Paris Salon, where such paintings as *Olympia* and *Déjeuner sur l'herbe* (both Louvre) became targets for considerable scorn and derision. However, his friend Émile *Zola spiritedly defended his work in an article published in 1867. In the 1870s he adopted the technique of the impressionists, although he refused to participate in their exhibitions (*see* impressionism). Such paintings as *The Balcony* (Louvre) and *The Luncheon* (Neue Staatsgaleries, Munich) anticipate 20th-century painting by making brushwork, color, and design more important than the subject matter. His last great work was *A Bar at the Folies-Bergère* (Courtauld Institute, London).

mangabey A large long-tailed *Old World monkey belonging to the genus *Cercocebus* (4 species), of central African forests. Mangabeys are 31–65 in (80–165 cm) long including the tail (17–30 in; 43–75 cm) and have long limbs and muscular bodies. They live in troops, feeding on fruit high in the trees.

Mangalore 12 54N 74 51E A port in India, in Karnataka on the Malabar Coast. Its manufactures include textiles and tiles. Population (1971): 165,174.

manganese (Mn) A hard gray brittle transition element that resembles iron, first isolated in 1774 by J. G. Gahn (1745–1818). It occurs in nature in many minerals, especially pyrolusite (MnO_2) and rhodochrosite ($MnCO_3$), in addition to the extensive deposits of manganese nodules discovered on the deep ocean floors. It is extracted by reduction of the oxide, with magnesium or aluminum, or by electrolysis. The metal is used in many alloys, particularly in steel, in which manganese improves the strength and hardness. Manganese forms compounds in a number of different *valence states: for example MnO, Mn_3O_4, MnO_2. The permanganate ion (MnO_4^-) is a well-known oxidizing agent. At no 25; at wt 54.9380; mp 2273°F (1244°C); bp 3567°F (1962°C).

mange A contagious skin disease, caused by mites, that can affect domestic livestock, pets, and man (*see* scabies). The parasites bite or burrow into the skin causing hair loss, scaly dry skin, pimples, blisters, and intense itching. Treatment is with a suitable insecticide, such as gamma benzene hexachloride.

mangel-wurzel. *See* beet.

mango A large evergreen tropical tree, *Mangifera indica*, native to SE Asia but cultivated throughout the tropics for its fruit. Growing 49–59 ft (15–18 m) high, it has long narrow leaves and large clusters of pinkish flowers. The oblong fruit, up to 5 lb (2.3 kg) in weight, has a green, yellow, or reddish skin and contains a stony seed, surrounded by juicy orange edible flesh that has a spicy flavor. Mangos are eaten fresh and used in preserves or for canning. Family: *Anacardiaceae*.

mangosteen A tropical fruit tree, *Garcinia mangostana*, native to SE Asia and reaching a height of 31 ft (9.5 m). The round or oval fruit, up to 3 in (8 cm) in diameter, has a thick hard purple rind and contains a few seeds surrounded by juicy white edible flesh, which is divided into separate segments and has a slightly sharp taste. Family: *Guttiferae*.

MANGROVES *A young specimen of* Rhizophora stilosa *with conspicuous prop roots, growing in Singapore.*

mangroves Shrubs and trees forming dense thickets and low forests on coastal mudflats, salt marshes, and estuaries throughout the tropics. Many are evergreen, with shiny leathery leaves, aerial supporting (prop) roots, and breathing roots with "knees" that protrude above the water or mud. The main species are the common or red mangrove (*Rhizophora mangle*), the black mangrove (*Avicennia nitida*), and *Sonneratia* species.

mangrove snake A mildly venomous snake belonging to the genus *Boiga* (30 species) occurring in mangrove swamps and lowland forests of Africa, Asia, Australia, and Polynesia. They live on the ground or in trees and prey on frogs, birds, lizards, crabs, fish, etc. The black-and-yellow mangrove snake (*B. dendrophila*) of E Asia can reach a length of 8 ft (2.5 m). Family: *Colubridae*.

Manhattan An island situated at the N end of New York Bay, between the Hudson, East, and Harlem Rivers, comprising one of the five boroughs of New York City. It is a major commercial and financial center focused on Wall Street. Other notable features include the famous Broadway theater district, *Greenwich Village, the United Nations, and its many skyscrapers, including the Empire State Building (1931) and the twin towers of the World Trade Center (1973). Area: 22 sq mi (47 sq km). Population (1980): 1,427,533.

Manhattan Project The code name for a project set up in 1942 to develop an atomic bomb. Research culminated in the construction of the bombs at Los Alamos, New Mexico. In 1945 a uranium bomb and a plutonium bomb were dropped on Hiroshima and Nagasaki respectively (*see* World War II; nuclear weapons).

manic-depressive psychosis A severe mental illness causing repeated episodes of severe *depression, mania (excessive euphoria, overactivity, irritability, and impaired judgment), or both. These episodes can be precipitated by upsetting events but are out of proportion to them. There is a genetically inherited predisposition to this psychosis; long-term treatment with lithium salts can prevent or reduce the frequency and severity of attacks.

Manichaeism A religion influenced by both *Gnosticism and Christianity. It originated in Persia (c. 230 AD), spread throughout Asia and the Roman Empire, and survived in Chinese Turkistan until the 13th century. It influenced several dualistic medieval heresies (see Cathari). Its founder, Mani (c. 216–c. 276), was martyred by the adherents of *Zoroastrianism. Fundamental to his creed was the belief that matter is entirely evil, but within each individual is imprisoned a soul, which is a spark of the divine light. By strict abstinence and prayer man can recover consciousness of the light and be liberated at death from material entanglement. Mani's followers were divided into the elect, teachers who lived in poverty and celibacy, and the hearers, who cared for the elect's material needs and could only achieve salvation after a cycle of reincarnation.

"Manifest Destiny" A phrase applied to US territorial expansion during the 1800s, implying that fate and divine will sanctioned the growth of the country. Coined (1845) by John L. O'Sullivan, editor of *United States Magazine and Democratic Review*, it was meant to justify the US annexation of Texas (1845) and was used afterward regarding annexations in Mexico, Oregon, the Caribbean, Hawaii, Alaska, and Guam.

Manila 14 30N 121 12E The capital and main port of the Philippines, on Manila Bay in Luzon. Founded by the Spanish in 1571, it suffered several foreign occupations over the centuries and the old town was destroyed in World War II. The official capital was transferred to Quezon City on the outskirts (1948–76). An educational center, it has over 20 universities, including the University of Santo Tomas founded in 1611. It has one of the finest harbors in the world and is also an important industrial center; its industries include textiles, pharmaceuticals, and food processing. Manila suffers from severe traffic congestion. Population (1980): 1,626,249.

Manila Bay An inlet of the South China Sea, in the Philippines in SW Luzon. One of the world's finest natural harbors, it was important before the ports of Manila and Cavite were founded. In the battle of Manila Bay in 1898 the US navy defeated the Spanish fleet, and there was again bitter fighting here during World War II. Area: 770 sq mi (1994 sq km).

Manila hemp A strong fiber obtained from a treelike herb, the *abaca, grown in the Philippines. It is largely used to make rope, matting, and strong paper. Finer grades are made into hats and local fabrics.

Manin, Daniele (1804–57) Italian patriot, born in Venice. His opposition to Austrian rule of Venice resulted in his imprisonment in 1847. He was released on the outbreak of the Revolution of 1848, appointed president of the newly restored Venetian Republic, and led a courageous defense of Venice against an Austrian siege. On its surrender (August, 1849) he went into exile in Paris.

manioc. *See* cassava.

Manipur A state in NE India, on the hilly Burmese border. Its largely Mongoloid inhabitants speak many languages. Rice, fruits, sugar cane, and mustard are grown. There is some silk weaving. The jungles yield bamboo and teak. *History*: Burmese threats caused the raja to seek British aid (1824), which became British rule (1891). Manipur became a state in 1972. Area: 8629 sq mi (22,356 sq km). Population (1981 est): 1,433,691. Capital: Imphal.

Manisa (ancient name: Magnesia) 38 36N 27 29E A city in W Turkey. Founded in the 12th century BC, Manisa is a commercial town with trade in such crops as tobacco, olives, and raisins. The Romans defeated Antiochus the Great here in 190 BC. Population (1970): 70,022.

Manitoba A province of W Canada, in the center of North America. Although it is one of the *Prairie Provinces, only the SW is true prairie. Further to the NE lies the *Red River Valley and three large lakes (Winnipeg, Winnipegosis, and Manitoba) with extensive forests in the N and tundra near Hudson Bay. Manitoba's economy is based on large mechanized farms producing grains and livestock. Forests, fisheries, and hydroelectricity are also important. Manitoba produces copper, gold, zinc, silver, nickel, and oil. Manufacturing is based on natural resources and agriculture. The province boasts a rich cultural life centered around Greater *Winnipeg, which contains over half the population. *History*: originally exploited for furs, Manitoba (then known simply as the Red River Settlement) first attracted dispossessed Scots Highlanders as settlers (1812). Acquisition of the area by Canada (1869) provoked the Riel Rebellion (1869–70), an uprising of French-speaking halfbreeds (Métis). Manitoba became a province in 1870. The transcontinental railroad (1882) and steady immigration (especially 1900–14) brought a prosperity that has been interrupted only between the World Wars. Area: 211,774 sq mi (548,495 sq km). Population (1981): 1,026,241. Capital: Winnipeg.

Manitoulin Islands A group of Canadian islands in N Lake *Huron. Timber, farming, and tourism are economically important. The main is-

land, Manitoulin Island, is the largest freshwater lake island in the world. Area (Manitoulin Island): 1068 sq mi (2766 sq km).

Manizales 5 03N 75 32W A city in central Colombia, in the Central Cordillera. It is the commercial center of the country's chief coffee-growing area. Manufactures include textiles, chemicals, and leather products and it has a university (1943). Population (1978 est): 246,036.

Manley, Michael (1924–) Jamaican statesman, who, as leader of the People's National Party, was elected prime minister of Jamaica in 1972 and re-elected in 1976. His socialist policies include nationalizing 51% of the bauxite industry, developing close ties with Cuba, and speaking out for the Third World. He was defeated in the 1980 elections.

Mann, Horace (1796–1859) US educator and politician. Largely self-taught, he studied at college and law school and served in the Massachusetts state legislature. In Massachusetts he was secretary of the nation's first state board of education (1837–48). Here, he formulated his educational philosophy and put it to practical use. Under his guidance the Massachusetts public school system became a model for the rest of the country. He was a US senator (1848–53) and the first president of Antioch College (1853–59).

Mann, Thomas (1875–1955) German novelist. Born into a wealthy merchant family, he chose a similar family as the subject of his first novel, *Buddenbrooks* (1901). Art and the artist are his main themes, however, in the novella *Death in Venice* (1912), *The Magic Mountain* (1924), in which a sanatorium is a microcosm of society, and *Doctor Faustus* (1947), a novel about a modern composer of genius. His other works include *Joseph and His Brothers* (1933–44), a series of four novels based on the biblical story of Joseph, and the picaresque *Felix Krull* (1954). Mann opposed Nazism and was forced to emigrate to the US in the 1930s. He was awarded a Nobel Prize in 1929. His brother Heinrich Mann (1871–1950), also a novelist and opponent of fascism, is best known for his novel *Professor Unrat* (1905; filmed as *The Blue Angel*, 1928).

manna 1. In the Bible, the miraculous food that fell with the dew to sustain the Israelites in the wilderness (Exodus 16.14–15). This phenomenon has been variously identified as an exudation from the tamarisk tree or a form of lichen. 2. A sugary substance obtained from the ash tree and used in medicine.

Mann Act (1910) US law that prohibited the transportation of women across state lines for immoral purposes. Sponsored by US Representative James Robert Mann of Illinois, it was also known as the White Slave Traffic Act.

Mannerheim, Carl Gustaf Emil, Baron von (1867–1951) Finnish general and statesman. He led the antisocialist forces to victory against the Finnish Bolsheviks in 1918 and then retired until 1931. In 1939, at the outbreak of the *Russo-Finnish War, he became commander in chief and, although defeated, was able to obtain good terms for Finland (1941). He re-embarked on war with the Soviet Union (June, 1941) and as president (1944–46) negotiated peace.

mannerism An art movement dominant in Italy from about 1520 to 1600. Mannerism developed out of the *Renaissance style, some of its characteristics being evident in the late work of *Raphael and *Michelangelo. It aimed to surpass the Renaissance style in virtuosity and emotional impact. In architecture this resulted in a clever and playful misuse of the rules of classical architecture, notably in the buildings of *Giulio Romano. In painting it led to a distortion of scale, an elongation of form, and dissonance of color, which frequently resulted in an effect of tension. Leading mannerist painters were *Pontormo, *Parmigianino, *Vasari, and *Bronzino. Features of mannerism also appeared in the work of *Tintoretto and *El Greco. Although largely confined to Italy, it appeared in France in the art of the school of *Fontainebleau and in Bohemia in the paintings of *Arcimboldo and Bartholomeus Spranger (1546–1611).

Mannheim 49 30N 8 28E A city in SW West Germany, in Baden-Württemberg at the confluence of the Rhine and Neckar Rivers. It was the seat of the Electors Palatine (1720–98) and has a notable baroque castle. It is a major port with an oil refinery and its manufactures include motor vehicles and agricultural machinery. Population (1980 est): 303,600.

mannikin A *waxbill of the genus *Lonchura* (30 species) occurring in Africa, S Asia, and Australasia. Mannikins are typically small (about 4 in [11 cm] long) and brown or black with paler underparts. The chestnut mannikin (*L. ferruginosa*) of the Philippines has become so abundant that it is now a pest to rice growers.

Manolete (Manuel Laureano Rodriguez Sánchez; 1917–47) Spanish matador, who became a professional at 17 and achieved a reputation as a bullfighter of great style. He died of injuries received in the ring.

MANNERISM The Madonna with the Long Neck *(1532–40; Palazzo Pitti, Florence) by Parmigianino. The elongated proportions of the Madonna's neck and fingers, the angel's leg, and the child's body are typical of the reaction against naturalism.*

manometer An instrument for measuring pressure differences. The simplest form consists of a U-shaped tube containing a liquid (often mercury), one arm of which is connected to a source of pressure and the other is left open to the atmosphere. The difference between the height of the liquid in the two arms is a measure of the pressure difference.

manor The most common unit of agrarian organization in medieval Europe, introduced into England by the Normans. The manor was essentially the lord's landed estate, usually consisting of the lord's own farm (the demesne), and land let out to peasant tenants, chiefly *villeins, who provided the labor for the demesne and were legally dependent upon their lord.

Manresa 41 43N 1 50E A city in NE Spain, in Catalonia. Below its 17th-century church is the Holy Cave of St Ignatius of Loyola, where he composed his *Spiritual Exercises*. Population (1970): 57,846.

Mansart, François (*or* Mansard; 1596–1666) French classical architect. His first major achievement, the north wing of the chateau at Blois (1635–38) featured the double-angled (Mansard) roof. He built or remodeled several town houses in Paris, notably the Hôtel de la Vrillière (1635) but his most perfect building was Maisons-Laffitte near Paris (1642). He also designed the church of Val-de-Grâce, Paris (1645), but as with many other commissions, his arrogance, reputed dishonesty, and extravagance resulted in his dismissal.

Mansfield 53 09N 1 11W A city in the Midlands of England, in Nottinghamshire. Coalmining is the chief industry; others are cotton textiles, shoe manufacturing, engineering, and chemicals. Population (1981): 58,949.

Mansfield, Katherine (Kathleen Mansfield Beauchamp; 1888–1923) New Zealand short-story writer. She came to Europe in 1908, published her first collection of stories in 1811, and in 1918 married John Middleton

*Murry. *Bliss* (1920) and *The Garden Party* (1922) contain her best-known stories, often compared in stylistic subtlety to those of Chekhov. She died of tuberculosis in France.

Mansfield, Mike (Michael Joseph M.; 1903–) US politician; majority leader of the Senate (1961–77). A Democrat from Montana, he served in the House of Representatives (1943–53) and was elected to the Senate in 1952. He succeeded Lyndon B. *Johnson as Senate majority leader and held the position for a record 16 years. Upon retirement from the Senate, he was appointed US ambassador to Japan (1977) by President Jimmy Carter.

Mansholt, Sicco (1908–) Dutch politician and economist. During World War II he worked secretly to maintain the food supplies of the W Netherlands during the German occupation. After the war he held a number of ministerial posts and was then vice president (1958–72) and president (1972–73) of the EEC Commission. In 1953 he prepared the **Mansholt Plan** for a common agricultural policy among EEC members.

manslaughter The crime of killing a person either (1) accidentally by an unlawful act or by culpable negligence or (2) in the heat of passion, after provocation. The second case is closely related to murder, and a verdict of manslaughter is possible only if there is no evidence of premeditation.

Mansur, Abu Ja'far al- (c. 712–75 AD) The second *caliph (754–75) of the 'Abbasid dynasty. He built Baghdad (begun 762) and made it the 'Abbasid capital. Influenced by Persian ideas, he developed the bureaucracy and is reckoned the real founder of the 'Abbasid caliphate.

Mansura, El (*or* al-Mansurah) 31 03N 31 23E A city in N Egypt, on the Nile Delta. In 1250 it was occupied by Crusaders under Louis IX (St Louis) of France, who was taken and held for ransom by Muslim forces. A market center, it has cotton-ginning and flour-milling industries. Population (1976): 258,000.

manta ray A *ray fish, also called devil ray or devil fish, of the family *Mobulidae*. 24–260 in (60–660 cm) long, they swim near the surface of warm-temperate and tropical waters, feeding on plankton and small animals swept into the mouth by hornlike feeding fins projecting from the front of the head.

Mantegna, Andrea (c. 1431–1506) Italian Renaissance painter and engraver, born near Vicenza. He was trained in Padua by his adopted father Francesco Squarcione, an artist and archeologist. His marriage (1453) to the daughter of Jacopo *Bellini connected him with the Venetian school. As court painter to the Duke of Mantua from 1459, he painted nine panels depicting *The Triumph of Caesar* (Hampton Court, London). His fresco decorations for the bridal chamber of the ducal palace include portraits of members of the Mantuan court and an illusionistic ceiling, which anticipates the *baroque.

mantis An insect belonging to the family *Mantidae* (2000 species), found in tropical and warm temperate regions. Up to 5 in (125 mm) long, mantids blend with the surrounding vegetation and are voracious carnivores, using their forelegs to capture insects and other small animals. The "praying" position held by the forelegs at rest accounts for the name praying mantis, applied in particular to *Mantis religiosa* but also to all other mantids. Eggs are laid in capsules (oothecae) on rocks and plants. Order: *Dictyoptera*. □insect.

mantis shrimp A marine *crustacean of the widely distributed order *Stomatopoda* (over 250 species), especially the genus *Squilla*. 0.04–12 in (1–300 mm) long, it has a short carapace and stalked eyes and the second pair of legs form large pincers for catching prey. Mantis shrimps live in sand burrows or crevices in coastal waters up to depths of 4265 ft (1300 m).

Mantua (Italian name: Mantova) 45 10N 10 47E A city in N Italy, in Lombardy on the Mincio River. Its history dates from Etruscan and Roman times and from 1328 to 1708 it was ruled by the Gonzaga family. It has several notable buildings, including a cathedral (10th–18th centuries), the 15th-century church of S Andrea (designed by Alberti), a 14th-century castle, and a ducal palace. The poet Virgil was born nearby. An important tourist center, Mantua's industries also include tanning, printing, and sugar refining. Population (1971): 65,926.

Manu In Hindu mythology, the ancestor of mankind. Like the biblical *Noah, he survives a flood because supernatural intervention warns him in time to build an ark. He is the reputed author of a Sanskrit code of laws, the *Manusmriti*, probably compiled between 500 and 300 BC.

Manuel I (1469–1521) King of Portugal (1495–1521) during the great period of Portuguese overseas exploration. The crown was greatly enriched by the voyages of Vasco da *Gama and *Cabral, which opened up eastern markets to Portugal. Manuel's reign also saw a revision of the legal code and the expulsion of the Jews (1497–98).

Manukau 37 03S 174 32E A city in New Zealand, in N North Island on Manukau Harbor (an inlet of the Tasman Sea). It serves as the W coast harbor for *Auckland. Population (1977 est): 140,600.

Manutius, Aldus (Aldo Manucci *or* A. Manuzio; 1449–1515) Italian printer and classical scholar, who founded the famous Aldine Press in Venice in about 1490. He specialized in inexpensive compact editions of the Greek and Latin classics, many of them first printed editions. His edition of *Virgil* (1501) was the first book in italic type. After his death the Press was carried on by his brothers-in-law and later by his son **Paulus Manutius** (1512–74) and grandson **Aldus Manutius the Younger** (1547–97).

Manx An extinct language of the Goidelic branch of the *Celtic family. An offshoot of Irish Gaelic, it was spoken on the Isle of Man until the 19th century.

Manx cat A breed of short-haired tailless cat originating from the Isle of Man. The Manx has a short body with deep flanks and a large head. The soft coat has a thick undercoat and may be of any color.

Manzoni, Alessandro (1785–1873) Italian poet and novelist. After living in France from 1805 to 1810 he returned to Italy and established his reputation with the Catholic poems *Inni sacri* (1815), an ode to Napoleon, and two verse dramas. His patriotism and religious convictions are most fully expressed in his masterpiece, *The Betrothed* (1821–27), a historical novel set in 17th-century Milan during the Spanish occupation.

Maoism The theories developed by *Mao Tse-tung. Mao's strategy for revolution in China gave central importance to peasant armies rather than to the action of the industrial working class in urban centers. Similarly, on a world scale, he believed that the socialist revolutions would develop first in the underdeveloped countries rather than in advanced capitalist countries (*compare* Marxism). Mao laid great stress on moral exhortation, indoctrination, and willpower in overcoming objective obstacles and problems in socialist construction. Like Stalin, Mao defended the system of one-party rule and the view that socialism could be constructed in a single country.

Maori A Polynesian people of New Zealand, who make up about 10% of the population. They trace their origins to migrants, probably from the Cook Islands, who came in canoes around 1350. They were an agricultural people who lived mainly in the North Island in large fortified villages of timber dwellings. Descent was counted in both lines, and a person could attach himself to either his mother's or father's descent group (*hapu*) to obtain rights to land and residence. The traditional arts of wood carving and dancing still survive but urbanization and Christianization have largely destroyed the Maoris' way of life.

Maori Wars The wars between the colonial government of New Zealand and the Maoris, fought intermittently between 1845 and 1848 and between 1860 and 1872. They were caused by the enforced sale of Maori lands in infringement of the Treaty of *Waitangi. They resulted in the loss of much Maori land to European settlers.

MAO TSE-TUNG *The cult of Mao finds expression in a portrait on silk measuring 12 ft (3.6 m) by 20 ft (6 m).*

Mao Tse-tung (*or* Mao Ze Dong; 1893–1976) Chinese communist statesman. Born into a peasant family in Hunan province, he was a Marxist by 1920 and helped to form the Chinese Communist Party (CCP) in 1921.

In the late 1920s he became a guerrilla leader against the *Guomindang (Nationalist Party) and in 1931 he became chairman of the *Jiangxi Soviet. Forced to evacuate Jiangxi in 1934, Mao led the communist forces on the *Long March with a price of $250,000 on his head. His arrival in Yan'an in 1935 marked his emergence as a leader of the CCP. Following the defeat of Japan in the *Sino-Japanese War of 1937–45, in which the communists and Guomindang joined forces, civil war was resumed, ending in communist victory. In 1949 Mao, as chairman of the Communist Party, proclaimed the establishment of the People's Republic of China. Mao's political writings formed the theoretical basis of the new government and led to the founding of communes and the *Great Leap Forward. He stepped down as chairman in 1958, purportedly due to ill health, but reappeared with greater standing during the *Cultural Revolution. Following his death, his third wife (from 1939) *Jiang Qing attempted unsuccessfully to seize power and Mao was succeeded by *Hua Guo Feng. *See also* Maoism.

maple A shrub or tree of the genus *Acer* (over 200 species), widespread in N temperate regions and often grown for timber and ornament. Growing 20–115 ft (6–35 m) high, maples usually bear lobed leaves, which turn yellow, orange, or red in autumn, and small yellow or greenish flowers, which give rise to paired winged fruits (samaras). Popular ornamental species are the *sycamore, *Japanese maple, and *box elder. The sugar maple (*A. saccharum*) of E North America is the source of maple sugar (obtained from the sap). Family: *Aceraceae*.

map projection The representation of the curved surface of the earth on a plane surface. The parallels of latitude and meridians of longitude (*see* latitude and longitude) are represented on the plane surface as a network or graticule of intersecting lines. It is not possible to produce a projection of the earth's surface without some distortion of area, shape, or direction and a compromise between these has to be reached. The basic map projections include conical, cylindrical, and azimuthal (*or* zenithal) projections. In the conical form the globe is projected onto a cone with its point above either the North or the South Pole. In the cylindrical projection the globe is projected onto a cylinder touching the equator; the *Mercator projection is of this type. Part of the globe is projected upon a plane from any point of vision in the azimuthal projection; all points have their true compass bearings. Many variations of the basic map projections are in use.

Mapp v. Ohio (1961) US Supreme Court decision that upheld the 4th Amendment. The court ruled that illegally obtained evidence could not be used in state trials.

Maputo (name until 1975: Lourenço Marques) 25 58S 32 35E The capital and chief port of Mozambique, on Delagoe Bay. It became the capital of Portuguese East Africa in 1907. It has a university (1962). A major East African port, its exports include minerals from South Africa, Swaziland, and Zimbabwe. Population (1970): 383,775.

Maquis Groups of provincial guerrillas of the French resistance to the Germans in World War II, as distinct from the urban underground groups. The maquisards took their name from the scrubland (French word: *maquis*) in which they hid. Their operations were usually limited to attacks upon enemy patrols and depots.

marabou A large African *stork, *Leptoptilus crumeniferus*. It is 60 in (150 cm) tall with a wingspan of 8.5 ft (2.6 m) and has a gray-and-white plumage, a bare black-spotted pink head and neck with a pendulous inflatable throat pouch, and a huge straight pointed bill. It feeds chiefly on carrion.

maraca A percussion instrument originating in Latin America, consisting of a dried gourd filled with beads, shot, or dried seeds. Maracas are usually played in pairs, chiefly in jazz bands. □musical instruments.

Maracaibo 10 44N 71 37W The second largest city in Venezuela, a port on the NW shore of Lake Maracaibo. Its economic importance is based on oil production; industries include petrochemicals. The University of Zulia was founded here in 1891. Population (1976 est): 792,000.

Maracaibo, Lake A lake in NW Venezuela. Oil is drilled both in and around the lake, providing about 70% of Venezuela's total oil production. It is connected with the Gulf of Venezuela by a waterway (completed in 1956). Area: about 5000 sq mi (13,000 sq km).

Maracay 10 20N 67 28W A city in N Venezuela, NE of Lake Valencia. It is a military center with two airfields. The chief industry is the manufacture of textiles. Population (1976 est): 301,000.

Marajó Island (Portuguese: Ilka de Marajó) The world's largest fluvial island, in NE Brazil in the Amazon delta. Area: 15,444 sq mi (38,610 sq km).

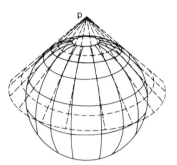 

conical *The globe is projected onto the cone as if it contained a source of light casting a shadow of its features onto the cone, resulting in a flat projection when the cone is unfurled. The cone may touch the globe along one parallel of latitude or intersect along two parallels.*

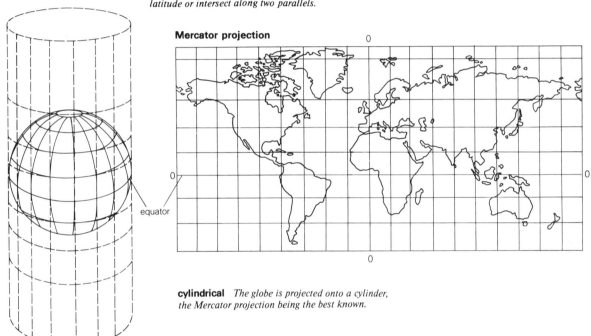

Mercator projection

cylindrical *The globe is projected onto a cylinder, the Mercator projection being the best known.*

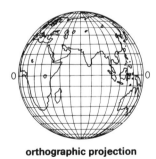 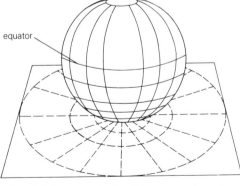 

orthographic projection

Lambert's azimuthal projection

azimuthal *(or zenithal) The globe is pictured as a flattened disc. It may be projected as if it were seen from a point in the center of the earth (gnomonic), from a point on the far side of the earth (stereographic), or from a point in space (orthographic).*

Marañón, Río The headstream of the Amazon River, in South America. Rising in the Peruvian Andes, it flows generally NE forming the Amazon at its confluence with the Río Ucayali. Length: 900 mi (1450 km).

Maraş 37 34N 36 54E A city in central S Turkey. It dates from Hittite times and used to manufacture guns and swords but now exports carpets and embroidery. Population (1980): 178,557.

marasmus. *See* kwashiorkor.

Marat, Jean Paul (1743–93) French politician, journalist, and physician, who devoted himself to radical journalism during the French Revolution. He became editor of *L'Ami du peuple*, supporting the *Jacobin cause of radical reform. Elected to the National Convention in 1792, he was murdered by Charlotte *Corday, a member of the *Girondins, whom Marat had helped to overthrow (1793).

Maratha (*or* Mahratta) A people of India, who live mainly in Maharashtra and speak the *Indo-Aryan Marathi language. More strictly the term applies to the high-ranking castes of this region, who are cultivators, landowners, and warriors of considerable repute. During the 17th century there was a Maratha kingdom in the area and a confederacy of Maratha leaders intermittently resisted the British between 1775 and 1818.

marathon A long-distance running race in athletics over 26 mi 385 yd (42 km 195 m). The marathon derives its name from the story of *Phidippides, who ran from the battlefield of Marathon to Sparta. As different courses vary, there is no official world record. In the Olympic Games there are marathon races for both men and women.

Marathon, Battle of (490 BC) The battle during the *Greek-Persian Wars in which the Athenians under *Miltiades defeated the Persians. *Phidippides was sent to summon Spartan help but the Athenians triumphantly routed the Persians before the Spartans arrived.

marble A rock consisting of metamorphosed limestone, although the term is often used of any rock, particularly limestone, that can be cut and polished for ornamental use. Pure marble is white recrystallized calcite, but impurities, such as dolomite, silica, or clay minerals result in variations of color. Certain quarries in Greece and Italy have been producing large quantities of marble since pre-Christian times. The flawless white marble from Carrara in Tuscany, Italy, is particularly prized by sculptors.

Marblehead 42 30N 70 51W A city in NE Massachusetts, on the NW shore of Massachusetts Bay, NE of Boston. Because of its excellent harbor it was long important in US commerce. Now a resort and boating center, most of its industries concentrate on yachting. Population (1980): 20,126.

Marburg 50 49N 8 36E A city in central West Germany, in Hessen on the Lahn River. It has a gothic castle and an important library and is the site of the country's first Protestant university (1527). Population (1971 est): 47,500.

Marburg disease. *See* green monkey disease.

Marbury v. Madison (1803) US Supreme Court decision that reinforced the supremacy of the Constitution over Congress and established the interpretive role of the Supreme Court. Marbury, appointed a justice of the peace by outgoing President John Adams, was refused his commission by newly-elected President Madison. The court ruled that the Judiciary Act of 1789, under which Marbury was suing, exceeded the judiciary powers outlined in the Constitution and declared it unconstitutional.

Marc, Franz (1880–1916) German expressionist painter, born in Munich. A member of *Neue Künstlervereinigung and a founder of Der *Blaue Reiter art group, Marc is known for his symbolic animal paintings, such as *Blue Horses* (1911; Walker Art Center, Minneapolis). He was killed in World War I.

marcasite A pale bronze mineral form of *pyrite. It occurs as nodules in sedimentary rocks as a replacement mineral, particularly in chalk. Marcasite jewelry is sometimes pyrite but more often polished steel or white metal.

Marceau, Marcel (1923–) French mime. He left conventional acting and began to study mime in 1946, gradually developing the original character Bip, a white-faced clown derived from the traditional pantomime figure of Pierrot. As well as giving solo performances, he formed his own company to produce complete mime plays.

Marcellus, Marcus Claudius (d. 208 BC) Roman general in the second *Punic War. After Roman defeats at Trasimene and Cannae, he was chosen, for his valor, to check Hannibal's advance through Italy. After capturing Syracuse, he harassed the Carthaginian armies in S Italy until his death.

March Third month of the year. Named for the Roman god Mars, it has 31 days. The zodiac signs for March are Pisces and Aries; the flowers are jonquils and daffodils, and the birthstones are aquamarine and bloodstone. St Patrick's Day falls on March 17.

Marchand, Jean Baptiste (1863–1934) French soldier and explorer. After exploring the Niger, W Sudan, and the Ivory Coast, he narrowly avoided causing a war with the British by occupying Fashoda (*see* Fashoda incident).

Marche (*or* the Marches) A region in central Italy, consisting of a narrow undulating coastal plain and a large hilly or mountainous interior. Primarily an agricultural region, it produces wheat, maize, wine, fruit, vegetables, and cattle. Area: 3742 sq mi (9692 sq km). Population (1980 est): 1,420,443. Capital: Ancona.

Marches The border areas of England and Wales, conquered between about 1067 and 1238 by vassals of the English kings. The so-called **marcher lords** enjoyed enormous powers in their lordships until the union of Wales and England in the 1530s.

March on Rome (1922) The display of armed strength by Mussolini's *Blackshirts that established fascist government in Italy. Using threats of violence to support his demands for representation in the government, Mussolini organized the Blackshirts in a march against Rome. They entered unopposed by government or army and Mussolini was asked by Victor Emmanuel III to form a cabinet.

Marciano, Rocky (Rocco Francis Marchegiano; 1923–69) US boxer, world heavyweight champion (1952–56). He became a professional fighter in 1947 and by 1952 had beaten Jersey Joe Walcott for the world title. Known as the Brockton Blockbuster, he defended his title six times before retiring undefeated.

Marconi, Guglielmo (1874–1937) Italian electrical engineer, who invented, independently of *Popov, communication by radio. On reading about the discovery of radio waves, Marconi built a device that would convert them into electrical signals. He then experimented with transmitting and receiving radio waves over increasing distances until, in 1901, he succeeded in transmitting a signal across the Atlantic Ocean. For this work he shared the Nobel Prize for physics in 1909. In 1929 he was made a marchese and an Italian senator; during the 1930s he was a fascist supporter.

Marcos, Ferdinand E (dralin) (1917–) Philippine statesman; president (1965–). His presidency has been threatened by civil unrest and in 1972 he declared martial law and assumed dictatorial powers. Although these controls were ostensibly relaxed in the early 1980s, the murder of opposition leader Benigno Aquino, Jr. probably with government complicity, in 1983 increased opposition to Marcos' rule.

Marcus Aurelius (121–80 AD) Roman emperor (161–80), in association with Lucius Verus (130–69) from 161 and alone from 169. Although he is known as the philosopher emperor on account of his *Meditations* (12 books of aphorisms in the Stoic tradition), his rule was active: from 170 he fought on the Danube frontier, dying during the campaign.

Marcuse, Herbert (1898–1979) German-born US thinker. His radical anti-authoritarian philosophy evolved from the Frankfurt School of social research. Marcuse attacked both western positivism and orthodox Marxism, the former because it led to analysis rather than action, the latter because it lacked relevance to 20th-century conditions. His books include *The Ethics of Revolution* (1966) and *Counter-Revolution and Revolt* (1973).

Mar del Plata 38 00S 57 32W A resort in E Argentina, on the Atlantic Ocean. It possesses extensive beaches, hotels, and a casino. The National University of Mar del Plata was founded in 1961. Population (1975 est): 302,282.

Marduk The supreme god in Babylonian mythology. He created order out of the universe after defeating the sea dragon Tiamat and the forces of chaos. This victory, recounted in the Babylonian and Assyrian creation myth, *Enuma Elish*, was celebrated in a festival at the beginning of each year.

Marengo, Battle of (June 14, 1800) A battle, fought 3 mi (5 km) SE of Alessandria, in Napoleon's Italian campaign (*see* Revolutionary and Napoleonic Wars). Napoleon was surprised by the Austrians with his forces divided and only the timely arrival of reinforcements made French victory possible.

Marenzio, Luca (1553–99) Italian composer, noted for his nine volumes of madrigals containing over 200 works. Some, published in London, influenced English madrigalists. He spent his life in service to various Italian noble families and lived for a time in Warsaw.

mare's tail An aquatic perennial herb, *Hippuris vulgaris*, found in lakes and ponds throughout N temperate regions. It resembles the unrelated *horsetails in having stems, rising up to 12 in (30 cm) above the water surface, bearing whorls of small slender leaves with minute greenish flowers at their bases. Family: *Hippuridaceae*.

Margaret (1353–1412) Queen of Denmark, Norway, and Sweden. Daughter of Valdemar IV Atterdag of Denmark, in 1363 she married Haakon VI of Norway (1339–80; reigned 1355–80). Their son Olaf (1370–87) succeeded Valdemar in Denmark (1375) and Haakon in Norway and following Olaf's death Margaret became queen of both countries, which remained united until 1814. In 1388 she was proclaimed Queen of Sweden by discontented Swedish nobles. The union of the three countries was formalized in 1397, when her heir Erik of Pomerania (1382–1459) was crowned at Kalmar. Margaret remained effective ruler until her death.

Margaret (Rose) (1930–) Princess of the United Kingdom. She is the younger daughter of George VI and sister of Elizabeth II. In 1960 she married Antony Armstrong-Jones (later Lord *Snowdon); they were divorced in 1978.

Margaret, Maid of Norway (?1282–90) Queen of the Scots (1286–90), succeeding her grandfather *Alexander III; she was the daughter of Eric II of Norway (reigned 1280–99). Betrothed to the future Edward II of England, she died while traveling to England and Edward I promptly declared himself overlord of Scotland.

Margaret, St (1045–93) The wife of *Malcolm III of Scotland and the sister of *Edgar the Aetheling. She was noted for her piety and reform of the Scottish Church in accordance with Gregorian principles, for which she was canonized in 1250.

Margaret of Angoulême (1492–1549) An outstanding patron of Renaissance artists and writers; wife of Henry II of Navarre (1503–55). Her own writings include a collection of tales (*Heptaméron*, 1558) and of poetry (*Miroir de l'âme pécheresse*, 1531).

Margaret of Anjou (1430–82) The wife (1445–71) of Henry VI of England; their marriage constituted an attempt to cement peace between England and France during the Wars of the *Roses, in which she was one of the most formidable Lancastrian leaders. She was captured and imprisoned after the Lancastrian defeat in the battle of *Tewkesbury (1471), in which her son Edward was killed. Her husband died, probably murdered, shortly afterward and she returned to France (1476) after Louis XI had paid a ransom for her release.

Margaret of Valois (1553–1615) The wife of Henry IV of France, famous for her *Mémoires* (1628). Daughter of Henry II and Catherine de' Medici, her marriage, which took place in 1572, was dissolved in 1599 to enable Henry to marry Marie de Médicis.

Margaret Tudor (1489–1541) Regent of Scotland (1513–14) for her son James V. The elder daughter of Henry VII of England and the wife of James IV of the Scots (d. 1513), she was ousted from the regency by the English but continued to play an active role in politics until 1534. Her great-grandson, James VI of the Scots, succeeded to the English throne as James I in 1603.

margarine A butter substitute that does not contain dairy-product fat. A type of margarine was first produced in France in 1869 from beef tallow. However, vegetable oils were only able to be used extensively after 1910, when a hydrogenation process was developed to solidify the liquid vegetable oils by adding hydrogen to saturate some of the unsaturated fatty-acid residues in the oils. In modern margarine, pasteurized fat-free milk powder is emulsified with water and such refined vegetable oils as soybean oil, peanut oil, and palm oil. Vitamins A and D are also added. The resulting emulsion is cooled, solidified, and kneaded to remove air. Soft margarines contain only lightly hydrogenated oils, retaining a large part of their unsaturated nature to comply with medical opinion that they are less likely to form damaging *cholesterol in the blood than saturated fats.

Margarita Island A Venezuelan island in the S Caribbean Sea. Pearl and deepsea fishing are of importance. Area: 444 sq mi (1150 sq km). Population (1970 est): 26,000. Capital: La Asunción.

Margate 51 24N 1 24E A resort in SE England, on the N Kent coast, including the resorts of Westgate-on-Sea and Cliftonville. It developed as a resort in the late 18th century, when the bathing machine was invented. Population (1981): 53,280.

margay A spotted *cat, *Felis wiedi* of Central and South America. It is 35 in (90 cm) long including the tail (12 in [30 cm]), found in forests and brush, hunting small mammals and reptiles in trees and on the ground.

Margrethe II (1940–) Queen of Denmark (1972–), who succeeded her father Frederick IX after the Danish constitution had been altered to permit the accession of a woman to the throne.

marguerite A perennial herb, *Chrysanthemum frutescens*, also called Paris daisy, native to the Canary Isles. Each stem bears a single large daisy-like flower. The name is also applied to the similar *oxeye daisy. *See also* Chrysanthemum.

Mari An ancient city on the middle Euphrates River in Syria. Commanding major trade routes, Mari throve during the early Sumerian period (*see* Sumer) and under the rule of *Akkad (c. 2300 BC). Excavated buildings of Mari's final period of prosperity include the palace of the last king, Zimrilim, killed when *Hammurabi destroyed the city (c. 1763). Its archive of 25,000 cuneiform tablets throws light on contemporary diplomacy, administration, and trade.

maria (Latin: seas) Dark expanses of iron-rich basaltic lava that erupted onto the moon's surface (primarily on the nearside) some 3000–3900 million years ago. The lava flooded the immense basins produced by earlier impacts of bodies from space, creating both circular and irregularly shaped maria.

Mariana Islands (*or* Ladrone Islands) A group of mountainous islands in the W Pacific Ocean, comprising the US unincorporated territory of *Guam and the US commonwealth territory of the Northern Marianas. Strategically important, they include the islands of Tinian and *Saipan. Discovered in 1521, the islands were colonized by Spanish Jesuits after 1668. Guam was ceded to the US after the Spanish-American War, while the Northern Marianas were sold to Germany (1899) and occupied by Japan (1914–44) until taken by the US. They voted in 1975 to leave the UN Trust Territory of the *Pacific Islands. Sugar cane, coffee, and coconuts are produced. Area: 370 sq mi (958 sq km). Population (1977 est): 15,000. Administrative center: Garapan, on Saipan.

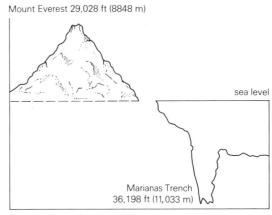

Mount Everest 29,028 ft (8848 m)

sea level

Marianas Trench
36,198 ft (11,033 m)

MARIANAS TRENCH

Marianas Trench A deep trench in the earth's crust in the W Pacific; it is the greatest known ocean depth (36,198 ft; 11,033 m). It marks the site of a plate margin (*see* plate tectonics), where one plate is being submerged beneath another.

Mariánské Lázně (German name: Marienbad) 49 59N 12 40E A city in Czechoslovakia, in W Bohemia. During the 18th and 19th centuries it was a popular spa, patronized by such famous people as Edward VII of the UK and the composer Richard Wagner. Population (1971): 13,402.

Maria Theresa (1717–80) Archduchess of Austria (1740–80). Her father Emperor Charles VI issued the *Pragmatic Sanction (1713) to enable Maria Theresa, as a woman, to succeed to his Austrian territories. Her accession nevertheless precipitated the War of the *Austrian Succession (1740–48), with European powers, especially Prussia, which seized Silesia, hoping to expand their possessions at her expense. In 1745 her husband Francis (whom she married in 1736) became Holy Roman Emperor. Under the influence of *Kaunitz, and determined to regain Silesia, Maria Theresa substituted her English alliance with a French coalition but in the subsequent *Seven Years' War (1756–63) Austria suffered resounding defeat. At home she combined absolutism with a measure of reform, anticipating the Enlightened Despotism (*see* Enlightenment) of her son and successor, Emperor Joseph.

Mari Autonomous Soviet Socialist Republic An administrative division in the W central Soviet Union, in the RSFSR. It is heavily forested. The Mari people, who speak a Finno-Ugric language, are known for their wood and stone carving and embroidery; they came under Russian rule in the 16th century and the region became an autonomous republic in 1936. Industries include machine building, metalworking, timber, paper and food processing; agriculture comprises mainly cereal production. Area: 8955 sq mi (23,200 sq km). Population (1981 est): 711,000. Capital: Yoshkar-Ola.

Maribor (German name: Marburg)   46 35N 15 40E A city in N Yugoslavia, in Slovenia on the Drava River. A former Habsburg trading center, it is now one of Yugoslavia's largest industrial centers. Its university was established in 1975. Population (1971): 97,167.

Marie (1875–1938) The wife of *Ferdinand of Romania. Marie was instrumental in affiliating Romania with the Allies in World War I. A granddaughter of Queen Victoria, Marie wrote several books in English, including an autobiography (1934–35).

Marie Antoinette (1755–93) The wife of Louis XVI of France, whose uncompromising attitude to the *French Revolution contributed to the overthrow of the monarchy. The daughter of Emperor Francis I and Maria Theresa, she married the dauphin Louis in 1770. Her extravagance and alleged immorality contributed to the unpopularity of the crown. After the outbreak of the Revolution she is said to have remarked of the Paris mob: "If they have no bread, let them eat cake." After the overthrow of the monarchy and Louis' execution, she was herself guillotined.

Marie Byrd Land (or Byrd Land)   An area in Antarctica, between the Ross Ice Shelf and Ellsworth Land. The US, although laying no claim to it, has long been active in the area and has established a research station.

Marie de France (12th century AD) French poet. Her identity is uncertain, although it has been suggested that she was a daughter of Geoffrey Plantagenet and half-sister of Henry II of England. Her works include several *lais*, verse narratives based on traditional Celtic stories of love, adventure, and the marvelous.

Marie de Médicis (1573–1642) The wife (1600–10) of Henry IV of France and regent (1610–14) for her son Louis XIII. Banished by Louis from court in 1617 she raised two revolts (1619, 1620) and was readmitted to the king's council in 1622. She persuaded Louis to make her protégé Richelieu chief minister in 1624 but she subsequently tried to oust him and in 1631 fled to Brussels. She built the Luxembourg Palace in Paris, the galleries of which were decorated by Rubens (1622–24).

Marie Louise (1791–1847) The second wife of Napoleon Bonaparte, who married her (1810) following the dissolution of his marriage to Empress Josephine. Their son, his longed-for heir, was entitled King of Rome (see Napoleon II). After her husband's fall she became Duchess of Parma (1816).

Marienbad. See Mariánské Lázně.

Mariette, Auguste Ferdinand François (1821–81) French Egyptologist. Abandoning art teaching, he went to Egypt (1850) to buy Coptic manuscripts for the Louvre, but embarked instead on the excavation of *Saqqarah. He established the Egyptian Antiquities Service (1858) and Cairo Museum (1864) and initiated excavations at *Abydos, *Memphis, *Thebes, and elsewhere.

marigold One of several annual herbaceous plants of the family *Compositae*, popular as garden ornamentals. The pot marigold (*Calendula officinalis*), native to S Europe, bears orange or yellow flowers, which can be eaten in salads. The African and French marigolds (genus *Tagetes*), native to Mexico, have single or double flowers with large outer florets; there are several dwarf varieties. Cape marigolds (genus *Dimorphotheca*) are more daisy-like. See also marsh marigold.

marijuana. See cannabis.

marine biology The study of the organisms that live in the sea and on shore and the features of the environment that influence them. Marine biology is of great economic importance to man in view of his dependence upon the oceans for food, in the form of fish and shellfish, and the effects of pollution upon these organisms. See also fishing industry.

Marine Corps, United States Branch of military service whose members are trained in amphibious warfare, within the Department of the Navy, but separate from the Navy. It is directed by the commandant of the Marine Corps, who is a full member of the joint chiefs of staff, and consists of three active divisions, three active aircraft wings, and three force service support groups. Its primary mission is to provide fleet marine forces for supporting air force and land forces in defense of naval bases and in any land operations essential to a naval campaign. Established in 1775 as part of the Navy, the Marine Corps became a separate service in 1947.

marine insurance *Insurance against the perils of the sea, including storm, collision, theft, stranding, fire, and piracy. Marine insurance falls into three categories: hull, cargo, and freight. Hull insurance provides cover

against losses arising from the perils of the sea as well as accidents caused by the crew, faulty machinery, etc., to the ship itself. Cargo insurance is arranged for each cargo and for each voyage. Freight insurance is the form of marine insurance enabling a buyer or a seller to cover himself against loss for sums paid out in chartering a ship or hiring cargo space.

Mariner probes A series of highly successful US *planetary probes. Mariners 2 and 5 approached Venus in 1962 and 1967, while Mariner 10 flew past Venus in 1974 and then three times past Mercury in 1974–75. Mariners 4 (1964), 6 and 7 (1969), and 9 (1971–72) investigated Mars, with Mariner 9 going into Martian orbit. Mariners 11 and 12 were renamed the *Voyager probes. Mariners 1, 3, and 8 did not achieve their missions.

Marinetti, Filippo Tommaso (1876–1944) Italian poet and novelist. His manifesto published in Paris in 1909 calling for the destruction of traditional literary goals and the creation of new means of expression inaugurated the literary and artistic movement of futurism. His glorification of warfare and technology resulted in his commitment to fascism, which he defended in *Futurism and Fascism* (1924).

Marini, Marino (1901–80) Italian sculptor, born in Pistoia.   Originally a painter, he turned to sculpture in the late 1920s, becoming professor of sculpture at the Brera Academy, Milan, in 1940. Marini, under the influence of ancient Etruscan and Roman sculpture, continued the figural tradition of European art with his bronze horse-and-rider and dancer series.

Marion, Francis (?1732–95) US soldier in the American Revolution. Nicknamed the "Swamp Fox" because of his guerrilla band attacks on the British from the swamps of South Carolina, he was instrumental in US victories throughout South Carolina.

Maritain, Jacques (1882–1973) French Roman Catholic thinker. He was interested in applying St Thomas *Aquinas' methods to contemporary social problems. *Les Degrés du savoir* (1932) treats mystical, metaphysical, and scientific knowledge as complementary. When the metaphysical pretensions of the sciences are abandoned, Maritain thought they would not conflict with Christian faith. He was for a time associated with the reactionary group Action Française.

Maritime Alps (French name: Alpes Maritimes)   A range of mountains in SE France and NW Italy, running about 81 mi (130 km) along the border and constituting the southernmost arm of the Alps. It reaches 10,817 ft (3297 m) at Punta Argentera.

maritime law The branch of law relating to ships and shipping. It evolved from the local customs of certain dominant ports. The Romans, borrowing from the customs of Rhodes, imposed a code in the Mediterranean that was international and uniform in character. This uniformity was preserved until 17th-century nationalism gave rise to various individual codes. The French *Code de Commerce* (1807) treated maritime law as a branch of commercial law and has been widely adopted by other European countries. Outside the Mediterranean the most important early code was the 12th-century Rolls of Oléron (an island off the W coast of France), which codified the customary laws of the Atlantic ports and formed the basis of the maritime law of England, Scotland, France, Flanders, and other countries. The laws of Wisby, the seat until 1361 of the Hanseatic League, were also important and contained the mercantile code of the Baltic. In the US, maritime law is subject to federal regulation and is primarily under the jurisdiction of federal courts.

Maritime Provinces (Maritimes or Atlantic Provinces)   The easternmost provinces of Canada, on the Atlantic coast and the Gulf of St Lawrence. They consist of *New Brunswick, *Nova Scotia, *Prince Edward Island, and usually *Newfoundland and lie in the Appalachian Highlands.

Maritsa River A river in SE Europe. Rising in the Rila Mountains in W Bulgaria, it flows E then S forming part of the Greek-Turkish border, before entering the Aegean Sea. Length: 300 mi (483 km).

Mariupol. See Zhdanov.

Marius, Gaius (c. 157–86 BC) Roman general; an opponent of *Sulla. Military ability outweighing his undistinguished origins and educational deficiencies, he entered Roman politics after campaigns in Numantia, becoming associated with the popular party. After reorganizing the Roman army, he quelled *Jugurtha and crushed Gallic uprisings. In competition with Sulla for the command against *Mithridates, he was forced to flee Italy but in 87 returned with *Cinna and captured Rome, massacring his political opponents. He died shortly afterward.

Marivaux, Pierre Carlet de Chamblain de (1688–1763) French dramatist. His popular comedies, mostly witty and sophisticated treatments of romantic themes, include *La Surprise de l'amour* (1722) and *Le Jeu de l'amour et du hasard* (1730). He also wrote two unfinished novels and much literary journalism.

marjoram One of several aromatic perennial herbs or small shrubs of the Eurasian genera *Origanum* (about 13 species) or *Majorana* (about 4 species). Wild marjoram (*O. vulgaris*), is a hairy plant, 12–31 in (30–80 cm) tall, bearing clusters of small tubular pinkish-purple flowers. Sweet marjoram (*M. hortensis*), is widely cultivated for its aromatic leaves and flowers, which are used as culinary flavoring. Family: *Labiatae*.

Mark, St A New Testament evangelist, traditionally the author of the second Gospel. A cousin of *Barnabas, he went with him and Paul on their first mission. Subsequently he seems to have assisted Paul in Rome, where he also acted as interpreter for Peter. He was believed to have founded the Church in Alexandria and is also associated with Venice, of which he is patron saint. Feast day: April 25.

The Gospel according to St Mark is the earliest of the Gospels and is thought to have been written about 65–70 AD. It is a brief record of the life of Jesus and is believed to have been used by Matthew and Luke in the compiling of their Gospels.

Mark Antony (Marcus Antonius; c. 83–31 BC) Roman general and statesman. Antony fought under Julius *Caesar in Gaul (54–50) and held command in Caesar's civil-war victory at *Pharsalus (48). Following Caesar's assassination, Antony came into conflict with Octavian (*see* Augustus) but they were later reconciled and formed the second *Triumvirate with Lepidus (43). In 42 Antony defeated his opponents Brutus and Cassius at *Philippi. In 41 he met *Cleopatra for the first time; not until 37 did Antony abandon his wife Octavia (Octavian's sister) to live with Cleopatra in Egypt. His strained relations with Octavian were finally severed in about 33. In the following year the Senate declared war on Egypt and Antony was defeated at *Actium. Both he and Cleopatra committed suicide.

market forces. *See* supply and demand.

markhor A large wild *goat, *Capra falconeri*, of the Himalayas. Over 40 in (100 cm) tall at the shoulder, markhors are red-brown in summer and gray in winter and have massive corkscrew-like horns. The species is subdivided into four geographical races, which show variations in the horns.

Markiewicz, Constance, Countess of (?1868–1927) Irish nationalist, who married a Polish count. She fought in the 1916 Easter rising and was imprisoned. She was the first woman to be elected to the British parliament (1918) but did not take her seat.

Markov, Andrei Andreevich (1856–1922) Russian mathematician, who did important work in probability theory, notably on the type of event series known as the Markov chain. In such series the probability of an event occurring depends upon previous events. His work led to the theory of *stochastic processes.

Markova, Dame Alicia (Lilian Alicia Marks; 1910–) British ballet dancer. She joined Diaghilev's Ballets Russes in 1925 and the Vic-Wells Ballet in 1931. Her dancing was noted for its lightness and delicacy, particularly evident in her performances in *Giselle, Swan Lake,* and *Les Sylphides*. She retired in 1962.

marl A calcareous clay that is soft and plastic when wet; consolidated marl is usually called marlstone. Marls are deposited in water, either fresh or marine. The word is also used for any friable clayey soil. Marls and marlstones are used in the manufacture of cement.

Marlborough, John Churchill, 1st Duke of (1650–1722) British general. He suppressed *Monmouth's rebellion against James II (1685) but subsequently supported the *Glorious Revolution (1688) against James. In 1691 he lost favor when suspected of Jacobite sympathies but was reinstated (1701) at the beginning of the War of the *Spanish Succession. As commander in chief under Queen Anne, he won the great victories of *Blenheim (1704), Ramillies (1706), Oudenaarde (1708), and Malplaquet (1709). A *Whig, his political importance owed much to the influence of his wife **Sarah Churchill** (1660–1744), a confidante of Anne. Following Sarah's fall from favor, he was charged with embezzlement and dismissed (1711), living in Holland until 1714.

marlin A large game fish, also called spearfish, belonging to the genus *Tetrapturus* (or *Makaira*). It has an elongated body, up to 8 ft (2.5 m) long, a cylindrical spearlike snout, and a long rigid dorsal fin, which extends forward to form a crest. Marlins are fast swimmers, occurring in all seas and hunting shoals of small fish. Family: *Istiophoridae*; order: *Perciformes*.

Marlowe, Christopher (1564–93) English dramatist and poet. His involvement in secret political activity while a student at Cambridge may have had some bearing on his death in a tavern fight in Deptford. His development of blank verse and dramatic characterization in his plays *Tamburlaine the Great* (written about 1587), *The Jew of Malta* (about 1590), *Faustus* (probably 1592), and *Edward II* (1592), prepared the way for the achievements of Shakespeare. His poetry included lyrics, translations, and the narrative *Hero and Leander* (unfinished; completed by Chapman, 1598).

Marmara, Sea of A sea lying between European and Asian Turkey and between the Bosporus and the Dardanelles. In it lies the island of Marmara, where marble (from which the name Marmara comes) and granite have long been quarried. Area: 4429 sq mi (11,474 sq km).

marmoset A small South American monkey belonging to the genus *Callithrix* (9 species), with claws instead of fingernails. Marmosets are 8–35 in (20–90 cm) long including the tail (4–15 in [10–38 cm]) and have silky fur, often strikingly colored and marked, and long balancing tails. They feed on fruit, insects, eggs, and small birds and have a twittering call. Family: *Callithricidae*.

marmot A large *ground squirrel belonging to the genus *Marmota* (8 species), also called groundhog, of Europe, Asia, and North America. Marmots are 12–24 in (30–60 cm) long and inhabit mountainous or hilly country, feeding on vegetation during the day and living in burrows at night. The woodchuck (*M. monax*) lives in North American woodlands. Marmots live in colonies; at any sign of danger, the whole colony will flee under ground.

Marne River A river in NE France. Rising on the Plateau de Langres, it flows N and W to join the Seine River near Paris. Linked by canal to the Rhine, Rhône, and Aisne Rivers, it was the scene of two unsuccessful German offensives during *World War I (1914, 1918). Length: 326 mi (525 km).

Maronite Church A Lebanese Christian *uniat church named for St Maro (died c. 410). The Maronites apparently originated in a Syrian Orthodox Church group that embraced *Monothelite doctrines in the 7th century and were consequently excommunicated. In the 12th century Crusader influences caused them to enter into full communion with the Roman Catholic Church and in 1584 a Maronite college was established at Rome. Although Catholic in doctrine, the Maronites retain their own Syriac liturgy and Church hierarchy.

Maros River. *See* Mureș River.

Marot, Clément (1496–1544) French poet. He served in the households of Marguerite of Navarre and of her brother Francis II. Suspected of being a Lutheran, he took refuge several times in Italy and died in Turin. He is best known for his metrical translations of the *Psalms* (1539–43), which received the encouragement of John Calvin. He was one of the first French poets to adopt the sonnet. His work marks the transition from the middle ages to the Renaissance and reflects the elegance and style of the new era.

Marquand, J(ohn) P(hillips) (1893–1960) US novelist. His best-known novels are satirical studies of upper-middle-class New England families adrift in an era of social change. These include *The Late George Apley* (1937), *Wickford Point* (1939), and *H. M. Pulham Esq* (1941). He was also the creator of Mr Moto, the Japanese detective who appeared in several novels.

Marquesas Islands A group of 12 volcanic islands in the S Pacific Ocean, in French Polynesia (annexed 1842). Nuku Hiva is the largest and Hiva Oa, where Gauguin is buried, the second largest. Since the 1850s European diseases have reduced the population to a quarter. Mountainous and fertile, the islands export copra, cotton, and vanilla. Area: 497 sq mi (1287 sq km). Population (1977): 5419. Capital: Atuona on Hiva Oa.

marquetry A technique of veneering furniture with different woods, ivory, tortoiseshell, and metals cut into interlocking shapes, which form ornamental or pictorial compositions. It is frequently used on European 17th- and 18th-century fine furniture. *See also* parquetry.

Marquette, Jacques (1637–75) French explorer. A Jesuit, he worked among the Indians in Canada from 1666 and in 1673, with **Louis Jolliet** (1645–1700), he descended the Mississippi River as far as the mouth of the Arkansas River, establishing that it flows into the Gulf of Mexico rather than the Gulf of California.

Marrakech (*or* Marrakesh) 31 49N 8 00W The second largest city in Morocco. Founded in 1062, it was for a time the capital of the Moorish kingdom of Morocco. Its notable buildings include the 12th-century Kotubai Mosque. It is an important commercial center, producing carpets and leather goods, and it is also a tourist center. Population (1973 est): 330,400.

marram grass A coarse perennial *grass of the genus *Ammophila* (2 species), also called beach grass or sand reed, which grows on sandy coasts of temperate Europe, North America, and N Africa. About 40 in (1 m) high, it has spikelike leaves and tough scaly underground stems, which can spread over large areas. It is used to stabilize sand dunes.

marriage The socially, and sometimes legally, acknowledged union between a man or men and a woman or women, such that the resulting children are recognized as legitimate offspring of the parents. Although societies vary greatly in the rules that govern marriage, such legitimacy is always important in determining rights to property, position, rank, group membership, etc. Monogamy, in which each spouse may have only one partner, is general in Christianized societies. Most churches treat marriage as an important rite and in the Roman Catholic and Greek Orthodox Churches it is accounted a *sacrament. Polygyny, in which a man may be married to more than one woman simultaneously, is widespread and sanctioned by Islam. A few societies allow polyandry, in which a group of men, usually brothers, have a wife between them, as in traditional Nayar communities in India. Polygyny and polyandry are collectively known as polygamy. Many societies proscribe certain unions (*see* incest). Others insist on marriage within a particular group (endogamy) or outside it (exogamy). In most countries, social customs and tax laws presuppose some form of marriage as the basis of family life. However, in industrialized societies there has been a marked decline in both the insistence upon strict monogamy and the penalization of unmarried cohabiting couples. Furthermore, changes in the educational and economic status of women, the widespread use of *contraception, and the need for more than one income to support a family have combined to alter the economic structure of marriage. *See also* divorce.

marrow (botany). *See* squash.

marrow (zoology) The soft tissue contained in the central cavities of bones. In early life the marrow of all bones is engaged in the manufacture of blood cells: it is called red marrow. In adult life the marrow of the limb bones becomes filled with fat cells and ceases to function: this is yellow marrow.

Marryat, Captain Frederick (1792–1848) British novelist. His novels based on his long naval career include *Mr Midshipman Easy* (1836) and *Masterman Ready* (1841). He also wrote children's books, notably *The Children of the New Forest* (1847).

Mars (astronomy) The fourth planet from the sun, orbiting the sun every 687 days at a mean distance of 141.5 million mi (227.9 million km). Its diameter is 4129 mi (6794 km) and its period of axial rotation 24 hours 37 minutes 23 seconds. It has two small *satellites. The Martian atmosphere is 95% carbon dioxide and is very thin (surface pressure 7 millibars). The dry reddish dust-covered surface is heavily cratered in the S hemisphere while N regions show signs of earlier volcanic activity: there are several immense volcanoes, the largest being **Olympus Mons** (15 mi [25 km] high), and extensive lava plains. Huge canyons and smaller valleys occur in equatorial regions; the valleys are evidence of running water in the past. *See also* planetary probe.

Mars (mythology) The Roman war god, the son of Juno. He was identified with the Greek *Ares and is usually portrayed as an armed warrior. Originally a god of agriculture, he was later worshiped at Rome as a major deity and protector of the city. The temple of Mars Ultor (Mars the Avenger) was erected by Augustus after the battle of *Philippi and dedicated in 2 BC.

Marsala (ancient name: Lilybaeum) 37 48N 12 27E A port in Italy, in W Sicily. Founded in 397 BC as a Carthaginian stronghold, it has ancient remains and a baroque cathedral. Marsala wine, grain, and salt are exported. Population (1971): 79,920.

Marseillaise, La The French national anthem, written in April, 1792, by *Rouget de l'Isle. It was originally a patriotic song entitled "Le Chant de guerre de l'armée du Rhin". It was taken up by a group of republican soldiers from Marseille, who were prominent in the storming of the Tuileries, and became the revolutionary anthem.

Marseilles (Marseille) 43 18N 5 22E The principal seaport in France, the capital of the Bouches-du-Rhône department. Flanked on three sides by limestone hills, it stands on a bay overlooking the Gulf of Lions. Founded about 600 BC, it was destroyed by the Arabs in the 9th century AD, redeveloped during the Crusades, and came under the French crown in 1481. Most industry is associated with its large world trade and includes oil refining at Fos, which lies to the W and is being developed as an industrial center. The city has few ancient buildings but is noted for Le Corbusier's L'Unité (multiple dwellings). A *métro* (underground railroad) was opened in 1978. Population (1975): 901,421.

Marsh, Ngaio (1899–1981) New Zealand detective-story writer. She came to England in 1928. Her detective novels, which feature Roderick Alleyn of Scotland Yard and often draw on her experience of art and the theater, include *Final Curtain* (1947) and *Last Ditch* (1977).

Marshall, George C(atlett) (1880–1959) US general and statesman. As army chief of staff (1939–45), and President Franklin Roosevelt's strategic adviser, he organized the build-up of US forces, ensuring that recruitment, training, weapons, and strength allocations conformed. He thus contributed greatly to the Allied victory. As secretary of state (1947–49) he devised the **Marshall Plan**, or European Recovery Program, in which the US undertook to provide economic aid to Europe after World War II. For this he won a Nobel Peace Prize (1953).

Marshall, John (1755–1835) US jurist. After serving in the Revolutionary War, Marshall began his political career as a member of the Virginia House of Burgesses (1782–88). He was a strong advocate of the ratification of the US *Constitution and was appointed US minister to France by President John *Adams in 1797. He gained national recognition in the *XYZ Affair for his refusal to authorize American payments to France in return for diplomatic concessions. Returning to the US, Marshall served a single term in the US House of Representatives (1799–1800). He was named secretary of state in the last year of the Adams administration (1800–01) and shortly before the inauguration of Thomas *Jefferson, President Adams appointed him chief justice of the US Supreme Court. Marshall was instrumental in defining the legal relationship between the federal government and the states and in interpreting their constitutional powers. Among his most important opinions were the cases of *Marbury* v. *Madison* (1803), in which he firmly established the right of the Supreme Court to review the constitutionality of federal and state laws; *McCulloch* v. *Maryland* (1819), in which he ruled that Congress may utilize powers implied but not specifically mentioned in the Constitution; and *Gibbons* v. *Ogden* (1824), in which he established the precedent that the federal government has exclusive jurisdiction over interstate trade. Marshall held the office of chief justice until his death.

Marshall, Thurgood (1908–) US jurist and civil rights advocate; associate justice of the US Supreme COurt (1967–). A special counsel for the NAACP (1938–40) and head of legal services (1940–61), he was instrumental in securing and effecting much of modern civil rights legislation. He served on the US Court of Appeals (1961–65) and was US solicitor general (1965–67) before becoming the first black to be appointed to the Supreme Court.

Marshall Islands An archipelago of low-lying atolls in the central Pacific Ocean, in the UN Trust Territory of the *Pacific Islands. It consists of the Ralik (W) and Ratak (E) chains; the chief islands are Kwajalein, Majuro, and Jaluit. Self-government was achieved in 1979 and the islands are negotiating free association with the US. Area: 61 sq mi (158 sq km). Population (1977 est): 27,096.

Marshall Plan US aid program for the recovery of Europe after World War II. Proposed by secretary of state George C. *Marshall in 1947, it was activated by the Economic Cooperation Act (1948) and spent $13.15 billion in aid to 16 countries.

marsh gas. *See* methane.

marsh harrier A temperate Eurasian *hawk, *Circus aeruginosus*, that hunts low over reedbeds and marshes, preying chiefly on water voles, waterbirds, and frogs. It is 21 in (53 cm) long and its plumage is dark brown; the male has a paler streaked breast, bluish wing patches, and a gray tail and the female has a pale head and throat.

marsh mallow A stout perennial herb, *Althaea officinalis*, of marshy coastal areas of Eurasia. Its velvety stems, 24–35 in (60–90 cm) high, bear lobed leaves and clusters of flesh-colored flowers, 2 in (5 cm) in diameter. The fleshy roots yield a mucilage that was formerly used to make marshmallows. Family: *Malvaceae*.

marsh marigold A stout perennial herb, *Caltha palustris*, also called kingcup, growing in marshes and wet woods throughout arctic and temperate Eurasia and North America. It has erect or prostrate stems, up to 31 in (80 cm) long, bearing round leaves and bright golden flowers, 0.8–2 in (2–5 cm) across. Family: *Ranunculaceae*.

Marsilius of Padua (c. 1280–1342) Italian critic of papal imperialism. Marsilius argued in his *Defensor Pacis* (1324) that since the Church is concerned entirely with faith through revelation, and not reason, which belongs to the secular world, it should be regulated by the civil power and should not interfere with government.

Mars-la-Tour and Gravelotte, Battles of (August 16–18, 1870) Successive battles in the *Franco-Prussian War in which the French were defeated. These engagements led to the encirclement of the French in Metz, allowing Prussian forces to march on Paris.

Marston, John (1576–1634) English dramatist. Initially a verse satirist, he was involved in a literary feud with Ben *Jonson until they collaborated (with *Chapman) on the satirical comedy *Eastward Ho!* (1605), for which they were both imprisoned. His best-known play is *The Malcontent* (1604). He was ordained priest in 1609.

Marston Moor, Battle of (July 2, 1644) The battle in the English *Civil War in which the parliamentarians and the Scots decisively defeated the royalists at Marston Moor, W of York. The parliamentary victory, which owed much to Oliver Cromwell's cavalry, destroyed the king's hold on N England.

MARSUPIAL *The newly born young of all marsupials are incapable of independent existence. After a gestation period of only 12½ days, newly born opossums, the size of bees, climb into their mother's pouch, where they remain for nine to ten weeks feeding on milk from the nipples.*

marsupial A primitive *mammal belonging to the order *Marsupialia* (176 species). Most marsupials are found in Australia and New Guinea and include the *kangaroos, *wallabies, *marsupial moles, *dasyures, *bandicoots, and *phalangers. The only New World marsupials are the *opossums.

Marsupials have relatively small brains and they lack a placenta (through which—in other mammals—the embryos are nourished). Young marsupials, which are born in a very immature state, complete their development in a pouch of skin on the mother's belly surrounding the teat, from which they are fed until fully formed. In general, the pouch of herbivorous marsupials opens forward and that of carnivorous ones opens to the rear.

marsupial mole An insectivorous burrowing *marsupial, *Notoryctes typhlops*, of Australia. It is molelike and has short velvety golden fur, powerful forelimbs with digging feet, tiny eyes, a sensitive nose, and a cylindrical body. Family: *Notoryctidae*.

Marsyas In Greek mythology a Phrygian satyr who discovered the flute that Athena had invented and discarded, and challenged Apollo, who played the lyre, to a musical contest. He lost and was bound and flayed alive by Apollo for his presumption.

Martello towers Fortifications containing cannon built in S Britain, Ireland, and Guernsey from 1804 to 1812. The towers were intended to check the potential invasion of Britain by Napoleon—which never materialized. Their construction was proposed after observation of the single tower mounting cannon at Mortella Point, Corsica, whence the term Martello was derived.

marten A carnivorous mammal belonging to the genus *Martes* (8 species), of Eurasian and North American forests. Up to 35 in (90 cm) long including the tail (6–12 in [15–30 cm]), martens are arboreal agile hunters with dark lustrous fur: they prey largely on squirrels but also take sitting birds and their eggs. The two European species are the *pine marten and the smaller stone marten (*M. foina*). The fur of the American marten (*M. americana*) is called American *sable. Family: *Mustelidae*. *See also* fisher.

martensite The hard brittle form of *steel produced after rapid quenching in *heat treatment. When steel is heated to red heat (1396°F [750°C]), the carbon in it forms a solid solution in the iron. On quenching the carbon is frozen into this configuration and the crystal structure of the

steel has internal strains, which cause its hardness. Named for Adolph Martens (1850–1914).

Martha's Vineyard An island off the coast of SE Massachusetts. A former whaling and fishing center, it is now known chiefly as a summer resort. Area: about 100 sq mi (260 sq km).

Martí, José Julián (1853–95) Cuban poet and patriot. He worked for Cuban independence as a journalist in France, Mexico, Venezuela, and the US and died during a military expedition to Cuba. He published many essays on social and literary topics and several volumes of poetry, notably *Versos sencillos* (1891) and *Versos libres* (1913).

Martial (Marcus Valerius Martialis; c. 40–c. 104 AD) Roman poet. Born in Spain, he went to Rome in about 64 AD and gained the patronage of his fellow Spaniards Seneca and Lucan. His best-known works are his 12 books of epigrams, comprising about 1500 short poems describing the contemporary social scene with concise satirical wit and occasional lyricism. Shortly before his death he returned to Spain.

martial arts Styles of armed and unarmed combat developed in the East. The Japanese forms, such as *karate, *judo, *aikido, kendo, and sumo, derive largely from the fighting skills of the *samurai. Since the late 19th century they have become forms of sport, some popular worldwide, as has the Chinese style, *kung fu. They are closely associated with Eastern philosophies, especially Zen Buddhism. *See also* Bushido.

martin A bird belonging to the *swallow family (*Hirundidae*; 78 species). The purple martin (*Progne subis*), about 8 in (20 cm) long, is found from S Canada to the Caribbean and Mexico. It nests in natural holes or martin houses and is valued for the enormous number of insects it eats. The brown sand martin (*Riparia riparia*) is about 5 in (12 cm) long and has white underparts with a brown breast band. It nests in colonies in tunnels excavated in sand or clay banks. The black-and-white Old World house martin (*Delichon urbica*), about 5 in (13 cm) long, commonly nests beneath the eaves of houses.

Martin V (Oddone Colonna; 1368–1431) Pope (1417–31), whose election at the Council of *Constance ended the *Great Schism. He attempted to increase papal power by condemning the view that Church councils have supreme authority and by limiting the power of the national Churches. His attempts to suppress the *Hussites were largely unsuccessful.

Martin, Archer John Porter (1910–) British biochemist, who shared the 1952 Nobel Prize with Richard Synge (1914–) for their development of the technique of paper *chromatography (1944), which they used for separating amino acids. Martin went on to develop gas chromatography in 1953.

Martin, John (1789–1854) British painter. His large and grandiose paintings, often on biblical themes, including *The Fall of Babylon* (1819), *Belchazzar's Feast* (1826), and *The Deluge* (1834), brought him fame throughout Europe.

Martin, Pierre-Émile (1824–1915) French engineer, who invented the Siemens-Martin process of producing steel. In this process Martin employed the open-hearth furnace developed in 1856 by Sir William *Siemens but adopted his own steel-producing process, which utilized pig iron and scrap steel. The Siemens and the Siemens-Martin processes largely replaced the *Bessemer process but the Siemens-Martin eventually became the more widespread.

Martin, St (c. 316–97 AD) A patron saint of France; Bishop of Tours (372–97). A soldier in the imperial army, he later settled at Poitiers and nearby founded the first monastery in Gaul. After becoming Bishop of Tours, he continued to live as a monk at a monastery that he established outside Tours. His military cloak, part of which he reputedly gave to a naked beggar, has become a symbol of charity. Feast day: Nov 11.

Martin du Gard, Roger (1881–1958) French novelist. After active service in World War I he devoted his life entirely to writing. His major work was *Les Thibault* (1922–40), a cycle of novels analyzing contemporary society through family relationships. His other works include the outspoken *Notes sur André Gide* (1951). He won the Nobel Prize in 1937.

Martineau, Harriet (1802–76) British writer. Despite deafness and ill health, she was a leading figure in intellectual life. Her work includes novels, books on religion and economics, and the influential *History of England during the Thirty Years' Peace, 1816–46* (1849).

Martini, Simone (c. 1284–1344) Italian painter, born in Siena and probably the pupil of *Duccio. In 1317 he worked for Robert of Anjou (reigned 1309–43) in Naples, where he was influenced by French gothic art. His *Guidoriccio da Fogliano* (1328), commissioned for the town hall of Siena, is probably the first commemorative equestrian portrait in European art. The *Annunciation* (1333; Uffizi) is the best example of his decorative style and graceful use of line. In about 1340 he moved to Avignon (France), where he worked for the papal court.

Martinique A French overseas region in the West Indies, in the Windward Islands of the Lesser Antilles. It consists of a mountainous island of volcanic origin. Agriculture is of importance, the chief exports being sugar, bananas, and rum. Tourism is being developed. *History*: colonized by the French in 1635, it became a French overseas department in 1946. The volcanic eruption of Mont Pelée (1902) destroyed the town of St-Pierre. Area: 420 sq mi (1090 sq km). Population (1980 est): 308,169. Capital: Fort-de-France.

Martinmas The feast of St *Martin (Nov 11), traditionally the date for slaughtering livestock to be salted as winter food. Fairs, at which servants could be hired, were also held at Martinmas.

Martins, Peter (1946–) US ballet dancer and choreographer; born in Denmark. He danced for the Royal Danish Ballet before joining the New York City Ballet (1969–83) and becoming its ballet master-in-chief (1983). He danced the classical ballets, such as *Swan Lake, Firebird,* and *Serenade,* for the New York City Ballet and choreographed his own works, including *Calcium Light Night* (1978).

Martinů, Bohuslav (1890–1959) Czech composer. He was largely self-taught apart from a period of study with Roussel in Paris from 1923. During World War II he settled in the US. He composed many works, including symphonies, concertos, the ballet *La Revue de cuisine* (1927), the opera *Julietta* (1936–37), and a concerto for double string orchestra and timpani (1938).

Martin v. Hunter's Lessee (1816) US Supreme Court decision that interpreted federal jurisdiction over state courts. Martin, inheritor of Loyalist land confiscated by Virginia and given to Hunter during the American Revolution, sued the state for return of land under the terms of US–British treaties. The state refused, and Martin appealed to the Supreme Court, which ruled that the lands were to be returned to Martin and that the Supreme Court does have jurisdiction over local matters, as determined in the Constitution.

Marvell, Andrew (1621–78) English poet. He was employed as tutor by Cromwell and as secretary by Milton. From 1659 until his death he served as a member of Parliament. He published several satires and pamphlets attacking religious intolerance and government corruption. His poetry, most of which was published posthumously, is noted for its combination of intelligent argument and lyricism. Among his best known poems are "To His Coy Mistress" and "The Garden."

marvel of Peru. *See* four o'clock plant.

KARL MARX *Photographed (c. 1880) towards the end of his life.*

Marx, Karl (Heinrich) (1818–83) German philosopher, economist, and revolutionary. While studying at the University of Berlin, Marx became a member of the Young Hegelians, an antireligious radical group. Unable to obtain a university post because of his radical views, Marx turned to journalism, becoming the editor of a radical paper in 1842. After its suppression Marx left Germany and spent the rest of his life in exile. He stayed first in Paris (until his expulsion in 1845), where he met several leading socialists including Friedrich *Engels, who later collaborated in many of Marx's

writings and provided him with substantial financial support. While in Brussels, Marx's association with a group of German handicraftsmen led to the writing of *The Communist Manifesto* (1848). In 1849 Marx moved to London, where he remained for the rest of his life, publishing *The Class Struggles in France* (1850), *The Eighteenth Brumaire of Louis Bonaparte* (1852), and *A Contribution to the Critique of Political Economy* (1859). Following the establishment of the International Working Men's Association in 1864, Marx devoted many years to the affairs of the First *International, gaining wide recognition among socialists. The first volume of *Das Kapital* was published in 1867 but the rest of his work did not appear until after his death. *See also* Marxism.

Marx brothers A US family of comic film actors: **Chico** (Leonard M.; 1891–1961), **Harpo** (Adolph M.; 1893–1964), **Groucho** (Julius M.; 1895–1977), and, until 1933, **Zeppo** (Herbert M.; 1900–79). Their original vaudeville act also included **Gummo** (Milton M.; 1901–77). Their film comedies, characterized by irreverent comic interplay between the fast-talking Groucho, the incompetent Chico, and the dumb harp-playing Harpo, included *Horse Feathers* (1932), *Duck Soup* (1933), and *A Night at the Opera* (1935). The team disbanded in 1949.

Marxism The theory of scientific socialism introduced by Marx and Engels, which explains the origin, historical development, and demise of the capitalist economic system. It relies heavily on the philosophy of Hegel, in particular Hegel's thesis that change has to be explained in terms of contradiction (*see* dialectical materialism). Class analysis, the central component of Marxism, is not peculiar to Marx but was shared by contemporary political economists, such as Adam Smith and Ricardo. Marxism is distinct in that it developed the theory of proletarian revolution. The transition to a socialist and eventually a classless society would not be a gradual evolution but would involve the violent overthrow of the state power (army, police, bureaucracy, etc.) of the bourgeois class. The working class would have to establish its own state power, which would be more democratic because it would be the rule of the majority of the population, the working class. As classes gradually disappeared, however, state power would also wither away since the state was fundamentally an instrument by which one class ruled over other classes. The classless society of the future would allow the fullest developments of individuals through social cooperation. Since World War I many different versions of Marxism have been expounded (*see also* Leninism; Maoism; communism).

Mary 37 42N 61 54E A city in the S Soviet Union, in the Turkmen SSR. Located in a cotton-growing oasis of the Kara Kum Desert, it has important textile industries. Population (1973): 67,000.

Mary I (1516–58) Queen of England and Ireland (1553–58), succeeding her younger half-brother *Edward VI. The daughter of Henry VIII and Catherine of Aragon, Mary's life after her parents' divorce in 1533 was one of extreme uncertainty until her rehabilitation in the line of succession in 1544. She became queen after the failure of a conspiracy to place Lady Jane *Grey on the throne. Her singleminded aim was to restore Roman Catholicism in England: Edward's Protestant legislation was repealed and in 1554 the heresy laws were reintroduced, resulting in almost 300 deaths at the stake and the queen's nickname, Bloody Mary. Her marriage (1554) to Philip II of Spain, the announcement of which had incited the unsuccessful rebellion (1553) of Sir Thomas *Wyatt, led to England's entanglement in Philip's foreign policy and the loss in 1558 of its last possession on the Continent, Calais. This disaster, coupled with a series of false pregnancies, hastened Mary's death.

Mary II (1662–94) Queen of England, Scotland, and Ireland (1689–94), joint monarch with her husband William III. Daughter of James II, she was brought up as a Protestant and came to the throne after the enforced abdication of her Roman Catholic father during the *Glorious Revolution. She was a popular ruler, governing during William's absences abroad, and died prematurely of smallpox.

Mary, Queen of Scots (1542–87) Scottish queen. The daughter of James V, she succeeded to the throne shortly after her birth. From 1547 Mary, a Roman Catholic, lived at the French court, where in 1558 she married the dauphin (later Francis II). After Francis' death (1561) Mary returned to Scotland and in 1565 married her cousin Lord *Darnley. In 1566 Mary gave birth to the future James VI (James I of England). In 1567 Darnley was murdered by *Bothwell, who then married her. A rebellion of Scottish nobles defeated Mary and Bothwell at Carberry Hill (1567) and Mary was forced to abdicate in favor of her son. She then raised an army that was defeated at Langside (1568). Fleeing to England, where her claim to the English succession had long been an embarrassment to Elizabeth I, she was held prisoner for the rest of her life. She became the focus of a series of plots against Elizabeth and was finally tried for conspiracy and executed.

Mary, the Virgin In the New Testament, the mother of *Jesus Christ. The fullest accounts of Mary are contained in the birth stories in *Luke and *Matthew. *John (19.25) reports that she was present at the crucifixion, and she appears to have been present at the growth of the early Church in Jerusalem (Acts 1.14). Luke records the Annunciation (the announcement by the Angel Gabriel that she was to conceive the Son of God by the Holy Spirit); her betrothal to *Joseph; her meeting with her cousin Elizabeth; and her song of praise (the Magnificat) when Elizabeth had greeted her as the mother of the Lord. The Gospels also state that she was and remained a virgin. Mary's *Immaculate Conception has been recognized as a dogma of the Roman Catholic Church since 1854 and the belief that she was taken up bodily into heaven (the Bodily Assumption) was defined as doctrine in 1950. In the Orthodox and Roman Catholic Churches Mary is venerated as having a secondary mediating role between God and man.

Mary Magdalene, St In the New Testament, the first person to see Jesus after the resurrection. Jesus cured her of possession by evil spirits. She aided his work in Galilee and was present at the crucifixion and burial. Medieval scholars associated her with the repentant sinner who anointed Jesus' feet, mentioned in Luke's Gospel. Feast day: July 22. Emblem: an ointment jar.

Maryborough (Ireland). *See* Portlaoise.

Maryland A state on the E seaboard of the US, one of the mid Atlantic states. Delaware and the Atlantic Ocean lie to the E, Washington, DC, to the S, Virginia and West Virginia to the S and W, and Pennsylvania to the N. It consists of two physical regions: the Atlantic Coastal Plain, which is split by Chesapeake Bay into a low flat plain in the E and uplands in the W; and an area of higher ground, part of the Alleghenies, in the N and W. The Susquehanna and Potomac Rivers empty into Chesapeake Bay. Most of the population (85%) lives in the Baltimore metropolitan area, which is contiguous with the urban area surrounding Washington, DC. Manufacturing is the most important sector of the economy (primary metals, metal products, food processing, transportation and electrical equipment, printing and publishing, and textiles). There is an important service sector and government is the major employer. The state's farmers produce livestock, poultry, and dairy products as well as some corn, tobacco, soybeans, and vegetables. *History*: one of the 13 original colonies, it was first settled by the English. It was granted (1632) to Cecilius Calvert, 2nd Baron Baltimore, by Charles I and named for Charles's wife, Henrietta Maria. Under the Calvert family the colony became a refuge for Roman Catholics persecuted in England. A border state, Maryland was divided on the slavery issue during the Civil War and was placed under military control to ensure loyalty to the Union. The construction of the Chesapeake Bay Bridge and other transportation improvements after World War II helped spur industrialization of the rural E shore. Area: 10,577 sq mi (27,394 sq km). Population (1980): 4,216,446. Capital: Annapolis. Chief port: Baltimore.

Mary Rose A Tudor warship (Henry VIII's flagship), which sank in 1545 in Portsmouth Harbor while sailing into battle. A search for the wreck was begun in 1965 by underwater archeologists and it was positively identified in 1971. The ship's contents, most of which were remarkably preserved, were raised during the following ten years and the hull itself was lifted in 1982 and placed in a dry-dock at Portsmouth. The Mary Rose Trust, of which the Prince of Wales is president, was formed in 1979.

Masaccio (Tommaso di Giovanni di Simone Guidi; 1401–28) Florentine painter of the early Renaissance. He collaborated with *Masolino on the *Madonna and Child with St Anne* (Uffizi) and on the fresco cycle in the Brancacci Chapel in Sta Maria del Carmine. His independent paintings include the *Trinity* (Sta Maria Novella, Florence). Influenced by *Giotto and the innovations of *Brunelleschi and *Donatello, Masaccio initiated the use of linear perspective and a single light source in painting.

Masada 31 19N 35 21E A precipitous rocky hilltop near the W shore of the Dead Sea, in S Israel. The site of one of *Herod the Great's fortified palaces, it was later a center of the *Essene sect and a stronghold of the Jews in their revolt against Rome (66 AD). In the last action of the war (73 AD), after a siege lasting almost two years, the defenders, on the eve of the final assault by the Roman besiegers, committed mass suicide rather than surrender. The site is an Israeli national monument.

Masai A Nilotic people of Kenya and Tanzania who speak a Sudanic language. They are nomads with little centralized political organization. Age sets are the basis of social organization, with three principal stages for every male: boy, warrior, and elder. This system allowed the Masai to form large raiding parties to increase their stock of cattle, which are the basis of their economy. Milk and blood from cattle form an important part of their diet, the blood being drawn from a vein in the animal's neck without killing it. Tall and active, the Masai highly value courage in their warriors.

MASADA *Glass plates found in the Cave of Letters inside the fortress.*

Masaryk, Tomáš (Garrigue) (1850–1937) Czechoslovak statesman, who was one of the founders of Czechoslovakia. In Paris, during World War I, he and Beneš founded the Czechoslovak National Council, which the Allies recognized in 1918. When Austria-Hungary fell in November, 1918, Masaryk was elected Czechoslovakia's first president; he was re-elected in 1920, 1927, and 1934. His administration was marked by a major land reform. He resigned, owing to his age, in 1935. His son **Jan (Garrigue) Masaryk** (1886–1948), a diplomat, was Czechoslovak minister to Britain (1925–38) and foreign minister in Czechoslovakia's provisional government in London (1940–45). Following World War II he returned to Prague but after the communists came to power in 1948 he died in a fall from a window, allegedly a suicide.

Mascagni, Pietro (1863–1945) Italian opera composer. His fame rests chiefly on his one-act opera *Cavalleria Rusticana* (1889), written as an entry for a competition in which it won first prize. He wrote many other operas, including *L'amico Fritz* (1891).

Mascarene Islands (French name: Îles Mascareignes) The heavily populated islands of Mauritius, Réunion, and Rodrigues in the W Indian Ocean. Discovered by the Portuguese in the early 16th century, they were known earlier to the Arabs.

mascons Disk-shaped masses that are located beneath the lunar surface in the younger *maria and are denser than their surroundings. They were discovered when lunar-satellite orbits were found to be slightly perturbed as a result of the higher gravitational attraction over these regions.

Masefield, John (1878–1967) British poet. Having served briefly in the merchant navy, he captured the fascination of the sea in his first volume, *Salt-Water Ballads* (1902). He also wrote narrative poems, such as *Reynard the Fox* (1919), and several adventure novels, including *Sard Harker* (1924) and *Odtaa* (1926). He became poet laureate in 1930.

maser (*m*icrowave *a*mplification by *s*timulated *e*mission of *r*adiation) A device that works on the same principle as the *laser, the radiation produced being in the *microwave region instead of in the visible spectrum. Masers are used as oscillators (e.g. the *ammonia clock) and amplifiers.

Maseru 29 19S 27 29E The capital of Lesotho, near the South African border. It was founded in 1869. The University of Botswana, Lesotho, and Swaziland was established nearby in 1966. Population (1976 est): 45,000.

Mashhad (*or* Meshed) 36 16N 59 34E A city in NE Iran, close to the Afghan and Soviet borders. It is a pilgrimage center for Shiite Muslims; the shrine of the *imam* 'Ali ar-Rida is a magnificent structure. Mashhad is famous for carpets and turquoise; its university was founded in 1956. Population (1976): 670,180.

Mashonaland An area in central and NE Zimbabwe, inhabited by the Shona, a Bantu people. Mashonaland was administered by the British South Africa Company from 1889 to 1923, when it became a part of the new colony of Southern Rhodesia.

Mashriq (Arabic: east) The Arab countries of SW Asia (the Middle East) as compared with the *Maghrib countries of N Africa. Egypt and the Sudan are included in the Mashriq.

Masinissa (c. 240–148 BC) Ruler of Numidia in North Africa. With the support of Rome, whom he had helped against Carthage in the second Punic War (208–201), he established a strong state among the diverse Numidian tribes.

masochism Sexual pleasure obtained from the experience of pain. The condition is named for an Austrian writer, Leopold von Sacher-Masoch (1835–95), whose novels depict it. It is often associated with a pathologically strong need to be humiliated by and submissive to one's sexual partner. Frequently, masochistic and sadistic desires are combined in the same individual.

Masolino (Tommaso di Cristoforo Fini; 1383–?1447) Italian painter, born in Pannicale but active mainly in Florence. He was strongly influenced by *Masaccio, particularly while working with him on the fresco cycle in the Brancacci Chapel, Florence. Later he painted in the *international gothic style. Independent works include *The Miracle of the Snow* (Sta Maria Maggiore, Rome).

Mason, George (1725–92) US politician and patriot. After inheriting a large plantation in Virginia, he became a prominent planter, businessman, and political leader. He was responsible for writing Virginia's constitution and Bill of Rights (1776) upon which Thomas *Jefferson modeled parts of the Declaration of Independence. A delegate to the Continental Congress in 1787, he strongly objected to the slave trade compromise and felt that the proposed constitution leaned too heavily toward central government. He worked actively against its ratification in Virginia, complying only after the Bill of Rights had been added.

mason bee A solitary *bee belonging to the genus *Osmia* and related genera, occurring in Europe, Africa, and elsewhere. It builds nests of soil cemented together with saliva in hollows in wood or stones. Family: *Megachilidae*.

Mason-Dixon line A line drawn in 1767 by two surveyors, Charles Mason and Jeremiah Dixon, to settle the conflict over borders between Pennsylvania and Maryland. Until the Civil War it also represented the division between southern proslavery and northern free states. It has remained a symbolic boundary between the North and South.

masoretes Transmitters of the textual tradition (*masorah*) of the Hebrew Bible. The textual study of the Bible goes back to antiquity (*see* scribes); in the gaonic period (*see* gaon) various schools of masoretes labored to establish a correct text and to mark the pronunciation with the help of accents. The text of Aaron ben Asher (930 AD) was recognized as authoritative by *Maimonides. The masoretic text is the basis of all Hebrew Bibles printed today.

masque A form of dramatic court entertainment popular in England during the late 16th and early 17th centuries. It consisted of a combination of verse, dance, and music, usually with a slight dramatic plot based on a mythological theme. The form was perfected in the collaborations of Ben *Jonson and Inigo *Jones, whose elaborate costumes and scenery were vastly expensive. Other writers of masques include Sir Philip *Sidney and Samuel *Daniel.

mass (physics). *See* mass and weight.

mass (religion). *See* Eucharist.

Massachusetts A state on the NE coast of the US, in New England. It is bordered by New York on the W, Vermont and New Hampshire on the N, the Atlantic Ocean on the E, and Rhode Island and Connecticut on the S. The uplands in the W, which are cut N–S by the Connecticut River, are separated from the lowlands of the Atlantic Coastal Plain and Cape Cod Peninsula by the rolling country of central Massachusetts. The mainly urban population is concentrated along the coast and river valleys. A major manufacturing state, its industries produce electrical and communications equipment, high-quality instruments, chemicals, textiles, and metal and food products. Boston is an important financial and service center. Its farmers produce dairy products, eggs, poultry, cranberries, and horticultural goods. Massachusetts is an important center in US educational and cultural life. *History*: Massachusetts was one of the 13 original colonies. The arrival of the Pilgrim Fathers on the *Mayflower* (1620) heralded major settlement with the formation of the Plymouth Colony. After early hardships, the colony took hold and was followed (1630) by the Massachusetts Bay Colony. The early Puritan government was quasi-theocratic and the perpetuation of Puritan ideas of representative government formed the basis of democracy. By the 1750s Massachusetts was a thriving center for trafficking of molasses, rum, and black slaves (known as the "triangular trade"). It was a center for opposition to British colonial policy, including such demonstrations as the Boston Tea Party. The American Revolution began in Massachusetts with fighting at Lexington and Concord (1775). Massachusetts retained its prominence through the early years of independence, sending several presidents to the White House. With the arrival of the industrial revolution a flourishing textile industry grew up. Boston became a center for many liberal religious and philosophical groups during the 19th century, including transcendentalism, unitarianism, and abolitionism. Labor disputes dominated the early 20th century. After World War II the decline of textile and shoe manufacturing was offset by the growth of computer- and defense-related industries. Area: 8257 sq mi (21,386 sq km). Population (1980): 5,737,037. Capital: Boston.

Massachusetts Bay Company A colony of English Puritans established at Salem, Mass., in 1628. The main body of colonists arrived in 1630 under the leadership of John *Winthrop. The Company's charter was withdrawn in 1684.

Massachusetts Government Act (1774). *See* Intolerable Acts.

Massachusetts Institute of Technology (MIT) A university in Cambridge, Mass. Founded in 1861 at Boston, it moved to its present site in 1916. It is world famous for scientific education and research.

mass action, law of The rate of a chemical reaction for a uniform system at constant temperature varies as the concentration of each reacting substance, raised to the power equal to the number of molecules of the substance appearing in the balanced equation. Thus, for the reaction $2H_2 + O_2 = 2H_2O$ the speed of the forward reaction is proportional to the concentration of O_2 (written $[O_2]$) and to $[H_2]^2$; the reverse reaction depends on $[H_2O]^2$. The law is thus useful for calculation of equilibrium concentrations when reaction speeds are known, and vice versa. It was first proposed in the period 1864–79 by two Norwegian scientists C. M. Guldberg (1836–1902) and P. Waage (1833–1900).

massage Manipulation of the soft tissues of the body for therapeutic purposes. This includes rhythmic stroking (effleurage), kneading (petrissage), and repeated tapping (tapotement); it is used to relieve muscular spasm and pain, improve blood circulation in the skin, and reduces swelling due to accumulation of fluid in the tissues. *See also* physiotherapy.

mass and weight Two physical quantities used to express the extent to which a substance is present; they are sometimes confused. The mass of a body was defined by *Newton as the ratio of a force applied to the body to the acceleration it produces. This is now called the **inertial mass**, as it is a measure of the extent to which a body resists a change in its motion. **Gravitational mass** is defined in terms of the gravitational force between two bodies in accordance with Newton's law of gravitation. Lóránt Eotvos (1848–1919) showed experimentally that inertial mass and gravitational mass are equal, a result used by Einstein in his general theory of relativity.

Mass was also shown by Einstein, in his special theory of relativity, to be a form of energy, according to the relationship $E = mc^2$ (where c is the velocity of light). The total of the mass and the energy of a closed system remains unchanged under all circumstances (the law of the conservation of mass and energy).

Weight is proportional to gravitational mass, being the force by which an object is attracted to the earth. It is therefore equal to the product of the mass and the *acceleration of free fall (i.e. $W = mg$). Thus, the weight of a body may vary according to its position; the mass is a constant. In common usage mass and weight are used synonymously, but in scientific terms they are different, mass being expressed in units of mass (e.g. kilograms) and weight being expressed in units of force (e.g. newtons). *See also* amount of substance.

Massasoit (?1580–1661) American Indian chief; also called Wawmegin ("yellow feather"). Chief of the Wampanoag tribe in Massachusetts and Rhode Island, he made peace with the Pilgrims (1621) in Plymouth Colony and shared the first Thanksgiving with them. He also negotiated a peace treaty (1635) with Rhode Island colonists under Roger *Williams. Although peace reigned under Massasoit, his son Metacomet (King *Philip) warred against the colonists.

Massawa (*or* Mitsiwa) 15 37N 39 28E A port in N Ethiopia, in Eritrea on the Red Sea. It was occupied (1885) by the Italians, who used it as a base for their offensive against Ethiopia in 1935. With good communications to Asmara, 40 mi (64 km) WSW, Massawa is an important outlet for Ethiopia's exports and has a naval base. Population (1971 est): 19,820.

mass defect The difference between the total mass of the constituent protons and neutrons in an atomic nucleus and the mass of the nucleus. This defect is equal to the *binding energy of the nucleus.

Masséna, André (?1756–1817) French marshal. He fought in Napoleon's Italian campaign, winning an important victory at Rivoli (1797). He subsequently defeated the Russians in Switzerland (1799), fought again in Italy, and, outstandingly, against the Austrians (1809–10). In 1810–11 he was defeated by Wellington in the *Peninsular War and lost his command.

mass-energy equation. *See* relativity.

Massenet, Jules (1842–1912) French composer. He studied at the Paris conservatoire and won the Prix de Rome in 1863. Massenet catered to the Parisian musical taste of his day, writing 27 operas, of which *Manon Lescaut* (1884) and *Werther* (1892) are still performed today.

Massey, Raymond (1896–1983) Canadian actor. He first acted on the stage in 1922 and thereafter appeared in a number of films, including *The Scarlet Pimpernel* (1934), *Abe Lincoln in Illinois* (1939), *Arsenic and Old Lace* (1944), and *East of Eden* (1955). He also appeared in the television series *Dr Kildare* (1961–65).

Massey, (Charles) Vincent (1887–1967) Canadian statesman; governor-general of Canada (1952–59); brother of Raymond *Massey. He held various positions in Canada's governor's cabinet before becoming minister to the US (1926–30) and Canada's high commissioner in Great Britain (1935–46). He also headed the University of Toronto (1947–53). He was the first native Canadian to attain the governor-general's post.

Massey, William Ferguson (1856–1925) New Zealand statesman; prime minister (1912–25). He entered parliament in 1894 and became (1903) leader of the Conservative opposition, which in 1909 he named the Reform Party. His administration, in coalition (1915–19) with the Liberals during World War I, is noted for its support of agrarian interests.

Massif Central A plateau area in S central France. Generally considered to be that area over 984 ft (300 m) high, it rises to 6188 ft (1885 m) at Puy de Sancy. The central N area is also known as the Auvergne and the SE rim as the Cévennes. There is dairy and arable farming as well as heavy industry. Area: about 34,742 sq mi (90,000 sq km).

Massine, Léonide (Leonid Miassin; 1896–1979) Russian ballet dancer and choreographer. He joined Diaghilev's company in Paris in 1914 and choreographed his first ballet, *Soleil de nuit*, in 1915. He choreographed for many companies, notably the Ballet Russe de Monte Carlo. His most controversial ballets were the innovatory symphonic ballets *Les Présages* (1933), *Choreartium* (1933), and *Symphonie Fantastique* (1936).

Massinger, Philip (1583–1640) English dramatist. He collaborated with several other writers before succeeding John *Fletcher in 1625 as chief dramatist for the leading theatrical company, the King's Men. His best-known plays are the satirical comedies *A New Way to Pay Old Debts* (1621) and *The City Madam* (1632).

mass number (*or* nucleon number) The total number of protons and neutrons in the *nucleus of an atom.

Massys, Quentin (*or* Matsys, Messys, Metsys; c. 1466–1530) Flemish painter, born in Louvain but active in Antwerp. He was influenced by Italian Renaissance artists, particularly *Leonardo. In portraits, such as *Erasmus* (Galleria Nazionale, Rome), he anticipated *Holbein by depicting his sitter at work. He also painted scenes of daily life, notably *The Banker and His Wife* (Louvre).

mastectomy Surgical removal of a breast, usually for the treatment of breast cancer. There are several varieties of the operation. In a partial mastectomy (or lumpectomy) only the tumor is removed, while in a total mastectomy the entire breast is removed. A radical mastectomy involves removal of the breast together with the lymph nodes in the armpit and the chest muscles associated with it.

Masters, Edgar Lee (1868–1950) US poet. His best-known work is *Spoon River Anthology* (1915), a collection of free-verse epitaphs spoken as monologues by the inhabitants of a small provincial town. A successful stage version was produced in 1963.

Masters, William Howell (1915–) US physician, noted for his studies of human sexual behavior using volunteer subjects under laboratory conditions. Masters and his colleague, the psychologist **Virginia Eshelman Johnson** (1925–), measured physiological changes associated with sex and published their findings in *Human Sexual Responses* (1966). Although criticized, their work established a body of knowledge that is useful in such areas as marriage guidance.

Masterton, Bat (William Barclay M.; 1853–1921) US frontier law enforcer. He was deputy marshal of Dodge City, Kans, while in his early 20s and sheriff of Ford County, Kans, in 1877. In 1880 he was assistant to Wyatt Earp, the federal marshal in Tombstone, Ariz. He became a sportswriter for the *New York Morning Telegraph* in 1902 and eventually became an executive on the paper.

mastic An evergreen shrub, *Pistacia lentiscus*, up to 6 ft (1.8 m) high, native to the Mediterranean region. An aromatic yellowish-green resin is obtained from the bark and used to make varnishes for coating metals and paintings and as an adhesive. Family: *Anacardiaceae*. The name is also applied to other resin-yielding trees, including the related American mastic (*Schinus molle*) and *Sideroxylon mastichodendron* (family: *Sapotaceae*).

mastiff An ancient Eurasian breed of large dog long used as a guard dog and for bull- and bear-baiting. It is powerfully built with a large head and a short deep muzzle. The short smooth coat may be apricot, silver, or fawn; the muzzle, ears, and nose are black. Height: 30 in (76 cm) (dogs); 27 in (69 cm) (bitches). *See also* bull mastiff.

mastodon An extinct elephant that originated in Africa 34 million years ago and spread throughout Europe, Asia, and America. Early mastodons were small and had two pairs of tusks; later forms were larger and more elephant-like. The American mastodons survived until about 8000 years ago and were painted in hunting scenes by early man.

mastoid bone A nipple-shaped process of the temporal bone of the skull, situated behind the ear and containing many air spaces. Infection of the middle ear may spread through these spaces to affect the mastoid bone. Formerly treated surgically, this infection is now readily cured with antibiotics.

Mastroianni, Marcello (1924–) Italian actor. He became one of the best-known international film stars of the 1960s, a representative European leading man. He appeared in Visconti's *White Nights* (1957), Fellini's *La dolce vita* (1960) and *8½* (1963), and Antonioni's *La notte* (1961).

Matabeleland An area in W Zimbabwe, between the Limpopo and Zambezi Rivers. It was named for the Ndebele, a tribe that was driven across the Limpopo by the Voortrekkers in 1837. Consisting chiefly of extensive plains, the area has important gold deposits. Area: 70,118 sq mi (181,605 sq km).

Matadi 5 50S 13 32E The chief port in Zaïre, on the Zaïre River. It was founded in 1879 by *Stanley. It has one of central Africa's largest harbors and is accessible to oceangoing vessels. Population (1976 est): 162,396.

Mata Hari (Margaretha Geertruida Zelle; 1876–1917) Dutch courtesan and secret agent. She lived in Indonesia with her husband, a Dutch colonial officer, from 1897 to 1902. She became a professional dancer in Paris in 1905 and probably worked for both French and German intelligence services. She was executed by the French in 1917.

matamata. *See* snake-necked turtle.

Matamoros 25 50N 97 31W A city in N Mexico, on the Rio Grande on the US border. It is the manufacturing center for a region producing cotton and sugar cane and is an important point of entry for US tourists. Population (1978 est): 186,480.

Matanzas 23 04N 81 35W A port in Cuba, on Mantanzas Bay on the N coast. Its chief export is sugar. It is also a popular tourist center. Population (1981): 421,272.

Matapan, Cape (Modern Greek name: Ákra Taínaron) 36 23N 22 29E The southernmost point of mainland Greece, off which (March, 1941) the British Mediterranean fleet scored a decisive victory over the Italians during World War II.

matches Small lengths of wood, cardboard, etc., tipped with an ignitable substance. The friction match was invented in 1816 (by Dérosne). Modern strike-anywhere matches are usually tipped with phosphorus sesquisulfide, potassium chlorate, and zinc oxide. Safety matches, invented in 1844, have their ignitable substances divided between the tip and a special striking surface. Usually the surface contains red phosphorus and the tip a mixture of antimony sulfide and such oxidizing agents as potassium chlorate and manganese dioxide.

matchlock. *See* musket.

maté The dried leaves of a *holly shrub or tree, *Ilex paraguariensis*, native to Paraguay and Brazil. They are roasted, powdered, and infused with water to make the stimulating greenish tealike beverage, popular in many South American countries.

materialism In classical metaphysics, materialism is the doctrine of *Democritus and *Leucippus that everything in the universe is matter or stuff. All events were explicable in terms of the movements and alterations initiated by this matter. By contrast *Plato sought to establish the existence of some incorporeal objects, called by him Forms. *Aristotle also did not confine himself to a completely materialist explanation of the world, believing that the soul was immaterial. His doctrines nevertheless led to more refined materialistic views than those of the Presocratics, but *Hobbes' uncompromising materialism owed nothing to Aristotle. *Marx's economic materialism, whereby human actions and beliefs are explained solely in terms of economic forces was developed by *Lenin in *dialectical materialism. Some recent materialist philosophers studying the body-mind relationship have reduced thought to (physical) neural processes. In all these senses materialism is a metaphysical doctrine. More popularly, the term has also been used to signify worldly outlooks and behavior.

mathematics The logical study of numerical and spatial relationships. It is usually divided into pure and applied mathematics. In pure mathematics the general theoretical principles are studied, often in abstract. Its branches are *arithmetic, *algebra, *calculus, *geometry, and *trigonometry. Some form of mathematical calculation is an indispensable part of all financial transactions and all measurements. The ancient Egyptians, Sumerians, and Chinese were all using a form of *abacus to carry out these calculations for thousands of years before the Christian era. But it was not until the 9th century AD that *al-Khwarizmi introduced the idea of writing down calculations instead of carrying them out on an abacus. The Venetian mathematicians of the 11th and 12th centuries were largely responsible for the introduction of these methods to the West; indeed it was they who showed that commercial calculations based on algorisms (a word derived from al-Khwarizmi's name) were superior to those performed on an abacus. However, the application of mathematics to the physical sciences (including astronomy) was largely a 16th-century development inspired by *Galileo. It was from this development that applied mathematics grew. It is now largely concerned with *mechanics and *statistics. *See also* new math.

Mather, Increase (1639–1723) US churchman and author. Minister of Second Church in Boston (1664–1723) and president of Harvard University (1685–1701), he traveled to England in 1688 to appeal for a new colonial charter and governor. Partially successful, he returned with a new governor, but the colonists' dissatisfaction caused a decline in Mather's popularity. He was a driving force in ending the mushrooming witchcraft trials in Salem (1692) with the publication of *Cases of Conscience Concerning Evil Spirits* (1692). His son **Cotton Mather** (1663–1728) was also a churchman and author. A Puritan, he served (1685–1728) at Boston's Second Church, where his father was long the minister. He was active in the movement to remove Sir Edmund Andros, royal colonial governor, from office. His *Memorable Providences Relating to Witchcrafts and Possessions* (1689) contributed to the panic that incited the Salem witch trials in 1692. Among his more than 400 works were *The Ecclesiastical History of New England* (1702) and *The Christian Philosopher* (1721). He was a member of the Royal Society of London and a founding father of Yale University.

Mathewson, Christopher ("Christy"; 1880–1925) US baseball player. Also called "Matty" and "Big Six," he was pitcher for the New York Giants (1900–16) and the Cincinnati Reds (1916–18). During his career he pitched 373 victories and in 1936 was one of the first players elected to the Baseball Hall of Fame.

Mathura 27 30N 77 42E A city in India, in Uttar Pradesh on the Jumna River. A pilgrimage center, it is the traditional birthplace of the Hindu god, Krishna. Population (1971): 132,028.

Matilda (or Maud; 1102–67) The daughter of Henry I of England, who designated her his heir. On his death (1135), his nephew Stephen seized the throne and Matilda invaded England (1139) inaugurating a period of inconclusive civil war. She and her second husband Geoffrey, Duke of Anjou (1113–51), captured Normandy and in 1152 the Treaty of Wallingford recognized her son Henry as Stephen's heir. Her first husband was Emperor *Henry V (d. 1125).

Matisse, Henri (1869–1954) French painter and sculptor. Having abandoned his legal studies he became a pupil of the painter Gustave *Moreau in the 1890s. Matisse initiated *fauvism in the early 1900s with his boldly patterned and vibrantly colored still lifes, portraits, and nudes, notably the controversial *Woman with the Hat* (1905). He was the only artist to continue fauvist principles after the development of *cubism. He was also inspired by Islamic art. By 1909 he had achieved worldwide recognition and he remained inventive until his death, a stained glass design for the Dominican chapel at Vence (S France) being among his last works.

Mato Grosso A plateau area in SW central Brazil. It extends across the states of Mato Grosso and Goias, separating the Amazon and Plata River systems. Its height varies between about 328 ft (100 m) and 2953 ft (900 m). It is an important cattle-raising area.

Matopo Hills A range of hills in SW Zimbabwe, S of Bulawayo. Cecil Rhodes is buried here at a point named World's View.

matrix A set of numbers, called elements, arranged in rows and columns to form a rectangular array. It is used to assist in the solution of certain mathematical problems. The *commutative, *associative, and *distributive laws of matrix arithmetic and algebra are different from those of ordinary arithmetic. The **determinant** of a square matrix is a number, or algebraic expression, that is obtained by multiplication and addition of the elements in a specified way. It has properties that are useful for simplifying and solving sets of simultaneous equations. Single column matrices may repre-

$$\begin{pmatrix} a & b \\ c & d \\ e & f \end{pmatrix} + \begin{pmatrix} p & q \\ r & s \\ t & u \end{pmatrix} = \begin{pmatrix} a+p & b+q \\ c+r & d+s \\ e+t & f+u \end{pmatrix} \quad \textbf{addition}$$

$$k \times \begin{pmatrix} a & b \\ c & d \\ e & f \end{pmatrix} = \begin{pmatrix} ka & kb \\ kc & kd \\ ke & kf \end{pmatrix} \quad \textbf{multiplication by a constant}$$

$$\begin{pmatrix} a & b \\ c & d \\ e & f \end{pmatrix} \times \begin{pmatrix} p & q & r \\ s & t & u \end{pmatrix} =$$

matrix multiplication

$$\begin{pmatrix} (ap+bs) & (aq+bt) & (ar+bu) \\ (cp+ds) & (cq+dt) & (cr+du) \\ (ep+fs) & (eq+ft) & (er+fu) \end{pmatrix}$$

the **determinant** of $\begin{pmatrix} a & b \\ c & d \end{pmatrix} = \begin{vmatrix} a & b \\ c & d \end{vmatrix} = ad - bc$

MATRIX *Examples of matrix algebra.*

sent *vectors, enabling them to be handled algebraically and processed by computer.

Ma-tsu. *See* Mazu.

Matsuo Basho (Matsuo Munefusa; 1644–94) Japanese poet. Born near Kyoto, he moved to Edo (Tokyo) in 1667 and in 1680 became a recluse. He transformed the traditional 17-syllable lyric verse form, the haiku, introducing the characteristic concentrated elliptical imagery and the philosophical spirit of *Zen Buddhism. He also wrote travel diaries, of which *The Narrow Road to the Deep North* (1694) is outstanding.

Matsuyama 33 50N 132 47E A port in Japan, in NW Shikoku on the Inland Sea. It is an agricultural and industrial center, with a university (1949). Population (1980): 402,000.

Matteotti, Giacomo (1885–1924) Italian Socialist politician, who was assassinated by fascists after denouncing their party in the Chamber of Deputies. His murder almost brought the fall of Mussolini's government. Three of his assassins were imprisoned following the reopening of the case after World War II.

Matterhorn (French name: Mont Cervin; Italian name: Monte Cervino) 45 59N 7 39E A mountain in Europe, on the Swiss-Italian border in the Alps near Zermatt. First climbed in 1865 by the British mountaineer Edward Whymper, it is conspicuous because of its striking pyramidal shape. Height: 14,692 ft (4478 m).

Matthew, St In the New Testament, one of the 12 *Apostles. He was a tax collector until he became a follower of Jesus. According to tradition, he preached in Judea, Ethiopia, and Persia and suffered martyrdom. Feast day: Sept 21. Emblem: a man with wings. **The Gospel according to St Matthew** is generally believed to have been written sometime after St Mark's Gospel, from which it drew material. It is a narrative of the life and ministry of Jesus that seeks to convince the Jews that he is the Messiah predicted by the Old Testament. It contains the Sermon on the Mount (chapters 5–7).

Matthew Paris (c. 1200–59) English chronicler. He became a monk of the Benedictine abbey of St Albans in 1217 and was a member of the court of Henry III. His careful coverage of the years 1235–59 form the second part of his major work, the *Chronica majora*, a history of the world from the Creation to 1259.

Matthias (1557–1619) Holy Roman Emperor (1612–19). He became King of Hungary (1608) and of Bohemia (1611) following revolts against his brother Rudolph II and was in turn forced to cede these crowns to Ferdinand of Styria (later Ferdinand II) in 1618 and 1617 respectively. Matthias then tried unsuccessfully to moderate Ferdinand's harsh policies against the Bohemian Protestants.

Matthias I Corvinus (?1443–90) King of Hungary (1458–90). The son of János Hunyadi, Matthias brought Hungary to a peak of greatness before its fall in 1526 to the Turks. His reforms embraced administration, law, and the army. He also imposed high taxes, which greatly benefited the treasury but precipitated revolts. His foreign policy was dominated by conflict with Emperor *Frederick III and in 1485 Matthias occupied Vienna. He also added Bosnia, Moravia, and Silesia to his domains but failed in his efforts to take Bohemia. A great patron of Renaissance art and scholarship, Matthias founded the great Corvina library.

Mauchly, John W. *See* Eckert, John Presper.

Maud. *See* Matilda.

Maugham, W(illiam) Somerset (1874–1965) British novelist and dramatist. Born in Paris, he studied and qualified in medicine but abandoned it after the success of his first novel, *Liza of Lambeth* (1896). His later fiction includes *Of Human Bondage* (1915), *The Moon and Sixpence* (1919), *Cakes and Ale* (1930), and *The Razor's Edge* (1944). He wrote popular comedies of manners, such as *The Circle* (1921), and many short stories with Far Eastern or other exotic settings. From 1928 he lived in the South of France. His nephew **Robin Maugham** (1916–81) became famous with a controversial first novel, *The Servant* (1948), which was filmed in 1965. His later novels, often with homosexual themes, include *The Last Encounter* (1972) and *Lovers in Exile* (1977).

Maui 20 45N 156 15W An island in E central Hawaii, NW of Hawaii Island and E of Lanai and Kahoolawe islands. Mountains dominate each end of the island, with a flat isthmus, used for agriculture, joining them. The highest point Haleakala Crater (10,025 ft; 3056 m), in the E, is part of Haleakala National Park. Pineapple and sugar cane crops are the basis of the economy, and tourism is important. Area: 728 sq mi (1886 sq km).

Mau Mau A secret organization among the Kikuyu people of Kenya, which led a revolt (1952–57) against the British colonial government. Secret oaths were administered to participants, who committed appalling atrocities against whites and uncooperating blacks. Jomo *Kenyatta was thought to be a Mau Mau leader and was imprisoned from 1953 to 1961.

Mauna Loa 19 29N 155 36W An active volcano in SE Hawaii, on S central Hawaii Island, part of Hawaii Volcanoes National Park. Standing 13,677 ft (4169 m) high, Mauna Loa's central crater, Mokuaweoweo, and Kilauea, on its S side, have erupted in modern times, including 1950 and 1984.

Maundy Thursday The Thursday before *Good Friday. Its name derives from Latin *mandatum*, commandment, and its traditional foot-washing and almsgiving originated at the Last Supper, when Christ washed the disciples' feet and commanded them to follow his example (John 13). The British sovereign's distribution of special Maundy money in Westminster Abbey is a survival of these rites.

Maupassant, Guy de (1850–93) French short-story writer and novelist. He was introduced into literary circles by Flaubert, his literary mentor, met Zola, and joined his group of naturalist writers (*see* Naturalism). Following the phenomenal success of the first story he published under his own name, "Boule de Suif" (1880), he wrote about 300 short stories and 6 novels, including *Une Vie* (1883) and *Bel-Ami* (1885). He suffered from syphilis, which eventually resulted in mental disorder, and he died in an asylum.

Maupertuis, Pierre Louis Moreau de (1698–1759) French mathematician, best known for his principle of least action, by which the paths of moving bodies, rays of light, etc., are such that the action (momentum multiplied by distance) is a minimum. A quarrelsome and dislikeable man, Maupertuis argued with *Voltaire over his principle and became involved with the controversy between *Newton and *Leibniz over who first discovered the calculus.

Mauretania The coastal area N of the Atlas Mountains in ancient N Africa. Inhabited by Moorish tribes, who retained their independence while permitting settlements of Phoenician traders and later Italian colonists, Mauretania remained rebellious after incorporation in the Roman Empire in 40 AD. It was conquered by the Muslims in the 7th century. *See also* Moors.

Mauriac, François (1885–1970) French novelist. He was born into a middle-class Roman Catholic family near Bordeaux. His novels, which include *Le Désert de l'amour* (1925), *Thérèse Desqueyroux* (1927), and *Le Noeud de vipères* (1933), characteristically portray the conflict between worldly passions and religion in provincial marital and family relationships. He also wrote plays and polemical criticism and journalism. He won the Nobel Prize in 1952.

Maurice of Nassau (1567–1625) Stadholder (chief magistrate) of the United Provinces of the Netherlands (1584–1625), succeeding his father William the Silent. A great military leader and a master of siege warfare, Maurice instituted army reforms that enabled the United Provinces to withstand Spanish attempts to destroy the newly established Protestant republic (*see* Revolt of the Netherlands). He failed to draw the Roman Catholic provinces of the S into the union and was forced to negotiate a 12-year truce with Spain in 1609. His career was marred by the arrest and execution of his colleague *Oldenbarnevelt in 1619.

Mauritania, Islamic Republic of (French name: Mauritanie; Arabic name: Muritaniyah) A country in West Africa, with a coastline on the Atlantic Ocean. The N part is desert while the S is mainly fertile. Most of the inhabitants are Arabs and Berbers with a Negro population, mainly Fulani, in the S. *Economy*: chiefly agricultural. Livestock, especially cattle, are particularly important and the main crops are millet, sorghum, beans, and rice. All agriculture was severely affected by the droughts of the late 1960s and early 1970s. Fishing is important and fish processing is one of the main industries. Iron ore and copper are exploited and, together with dried and salt fish, are now the main exports. *History*: dominated by Muslim Berber tribes from about 100 AD, the coast was visited by the Portuguese in the 15th century and by the Dutch, English, and French in the 17th century. The area became a French protectorate in 1903 and a colony in 1920. It achieved internal self-government within the French Community in 1958 and became fully independent in 1960 with Mokhtar Ould Daddah as its first president. It moved from French to Arab ties in international relations, joining the Arab League and the Arab Common Market. In 1976, with Morocco, it took over Western Sahara, part of the former Spanish Sahara territories, resistance to which led to considerable unrest, including guerrilla attacks from the Polisario, the Western Saharan independence movement. In 1979 Mauritania withdrew from almost all of Western Sahara. In 1978 Daddah was overthrown in a bloodless coup and Lieutenant Colonel Mustapha Ould Mohamed Salek became president until his resignation in 1979. He was succeeded as head of state by Lieutenant Colonel Khouna Ould Kaydala. Mauritania continued to occupy La Guera at the S tip of Western Sahara, fearing for its security if either the Polisario or Morocco gained control. It nonetheless sought to remain neutral in the conflict. Its neutrality was threatened, however, when the military base at La Guera was shelled by what were thought to be Moroccan ships in 1983. President Kaydalla was deposed in a coup in 1984 and was replaced by a military committee headed by former prime minister Moauya Ould Sidi-Ahmad Laya. Official language: French; Arabic, known as Hassaniya, is widely spoken. Official religion: Islam. Official currency: ougiya of 5 khoums. Area: 397, 850 sq mi (1,030,700 sq km). Population (1983 est): 1,591,000. Capital and main port: Nouakchott.

Mauritius, State of An island country in the Indian Ocean, about 500 mi (800 km) to the E of Madagascar. It is mainly hilly and subject to tropical cyclones, which cause severe damage. Dependencies are the Agalega and St Brandon Islands. The majority of the population are of Indian descent, with European, African, and mixed minorities. *Economy*: it is dependent primarily on sugar production; sugar accounting for 90% of its total exports. Fishing is being developed and industry is being encouraged, as well as subsistence agriculture and tourism, in an effort to reduce unemployment. *History*: visited by the Arabs in the 10th century and by the Portuguese in the 16th century, the island was settled by the Dutch in 1598. In 1715 it came under French rule as Île de France and in 1814 it was ceded to Britain. After riots in 1968 it became independent within the British Commonwealth, with Dr Sir Seewoosagur Ramgoolam (1900–   ) as its first prime minister. In the 1970s there was considerable political unrest. Rangoolam was ousted in the 1982 elections and succeeded by Anerood Jugnauth. Official languages: English and French; Creole is widely spoken. Official currency: Mauritius rupee of 100 cents. Area: 720 sq mi (1843 sq km). Population (1980 est): 969,522. Capital and main port: Port Louis.

Maurois, André (Émile Herzog; 1885–1967) French biographer, novelist, and critic. He served in the British army in World War I and had a lifelong affection for English culture. He wrote several novels and short stories but is best known for his biographical studies of Shelley (*Ariel*, 1923), Disraeli (1927), Byron (1930), Voltaire (1935), Chateaubriand (1937), Proust (1949), and Hugo (1954).

Maurras, Charles (1868–1952) French political theorist and essayist. In 1899 he helped found L'Action Française, a political group dedicated to extreme monarchist, antisemitic, and Roman Catholic principles (although condemned and excommunicated by the Church). *Au signe de Flore* (1931) contains his memoirs of his political activities. After World War II, during which he supported the government of Pétain, he was condemned to life imprisonment, but was released because of ill health shortly before his death.

Mauser rifle The first successful metallic-cartridge breech-loading rifle, designed by Paul von Mauser (1838–1914) in 1868. The Model-98 rifle and

Model-98a/b carbine were standard in the German infantry in World War I; the Model-98k (1938) was standard in World War II.

Mausoleum of Halicarnassus An ancient Greek tomb built (363–361 BC) as a monument to Mausolus of Caria by his widow. The building, designed by Pythius, was probably a standard temple form with adorning sculptures, fragments of which are in the British Museum, but raised on a high base and with a stepped pyramid-like roof. It was one of the *Seven Wonders of the World.

Maw, Nicholas (1935–) British composer. He studied with Lennox Berkeley and Nadia Boulanger. His works include *Scenes and Arias* (1962) for voices and orchestra and the opera *The Rising of the Moon* (1970).

Maxim, Sir Hiram Stevens (1840–1916) British inventor, born in the US, who in 1884 invented the first fully automatic *machine gun. The Maxim gun led him to discover cordite, which being smokeless increased the gun's efficiency. He also discovered a method of manufacturing carbon filaments, which were then being used in light bulbs.

Maximilian (1832–67) Emperor of Mexico (1864–67). Maximilian, the brother of Emperor Francis Joseph I, was the Archduke of Austria. He was offered the Mexican crown by France following its invasion of Mexico in 1863. He had no popular support and when in 1867 the French army withdrew under US pressure Maximilian was captured by the forces of Benito *Juarez and executed.

Maximilian I (1459–1519) Holy Roman Emperor (1493–1519). His ambition to rule an empire of all W Europe led him into ultimately unsuccessful wars, especially with France. However, his marriage (1477) to Mary of Burgundy (1457–82), and that of his son Philip the Handsome to Joanna the Mad of Castile, provided his grandson *Charles V with a vast empire.

Maximilian I (1756–1825) King of Bavaria (1806–25); formerly Elector of Bavaria (1799–1806) as Maximilian IV Joseph. In 1799 he joined the second coalition against France (*see* Revolutionary and Napoleonic Wars) but in 1801 negotiated peace. Until abandoning the French alliance in 1813 Maximilian gave military aid to Napoleon, acquiring in return extensive new territories. His government was noted for its liberalism.

maxwell The unit of magnetic flux in the *c.g.s. system equal to the flux through one square centimeter perpendicular to a field of one gauss. Named for James Clerk *Maxwell.

Maxwell, James Clerk (1831–79) Scottish physicist, who was responsible for one of the greatest achievements of the 19th century, the unification of electricity, magnetism, and light into one set of equations (known as **Maxwell's equations**). These equations, first published in their final form in 1873, enabled Faraday's lines of force to be treated mathematically by introducing the concept of the electromagnetic field. Maxwell observed that the field radiated outward from an oscillating electric charge at the speed of light, which led him to identify light as a form of electromagnetic radiation. Maxwell also made important advances in the kinetic theory of gases, by introducing the statistical approach known as Maxwell-Boltzmann statistics (since it was developed independently by *Boltzmann). *See also* Maxwell's demon.

Maxwell's demon A hypothetical creature, postulated by *Maxwell in 1871 as a theoretical construct to disprove the second law of *thermodynamics. The demon was visualized as being able to separate a gas into a hot region and a cold region by opening and closing a shutter to allow only fast-moving molecules to enter the hot region. No violation of the second law on these or any other grounds has ever been observed.

may. *See* hawthorn.

May Fifth month of the year. Named in honor of the Roman goddess Maia, who signified spring, it has 31 days. The zodiac signs for May are Taurus and Gemini; the flowers are lily of the valley and hawthorn, and the birthstone is the emerald. Memorial Day, honoring US military veterans, is celebrated on the last Monday in May.

maya (Sanskrit: illusion) In the Vedas maya is the magic power of a god or spirit. In the *Upanishads, maya is illusion or the mundane world, which is ultimately unreal because of its impermanence. Elsewhere maya is seen as the play of *Brahma, who splits himself into innumerable parts, thereby forgetting himself.

Maya An American Indian people of Yucatán (Mexico), Guatemala, and Belize. There are a number of languages in the Totonac-Mayan language family (*see* Mesoamerican languages). Today the Maya live mainly in farming villages and are nominally Roman Catholic, but between 300 and 900 AD they had established an advanced civilization. They developed hieroglyphic writing and had considerable knowledge of astronomy and mathematics. They devised a precise calendar, which regulated an elaborate ritual and ceremonial life centered on such sites as *Chichén Itzá, *Tikal,

Copan, and Palenque, where large pyramid temples were constructed for the worship of the sun, moon, and rain gods. After 900 the influence of the *Toltecs led to a mixed Toltec-Maya culture in cities such as Mayapan.

MAYA *The Temple of the Sorcerer at Uxmal in Yucatán (Mexico).*

Mayagüez 18 13N 67 09W A port in W Puerto Rico, in the West Indies. It has an important needlework industry; other manufactures include beer, rum, and soap. An experimental station operated here by the US Department of Agriculture has possibly the largest tropical-plant collection in the W hemisphere. Population (1980 est): 95,886.

Mayakovskii, Vladimir (1893–1930) Russian poet. He was a leading member of the futurist movement (*see* futurism) and a prolific propagandist for Bolshevism. Revolutionary politics and his frustrated private life are the main themes of his poetry, which is characterized by aggressive vitality and experimentation. He also wrote two satirical dramas, *The Bedbug* (1929) and *The Bath-House* (1930). He committed suicide.

May Day May 1, traditionally a festival associated with spring fertility rites, celebrated by such customs as dancing around the Maypole. In communist countries May Day is celebrated as International Worker's Day, often the occasion for a display of military technology.

Mayence. *See* Mainz.

Mayer, Julius Robert von (1814–78) German physicist, who (in 1842) was the first to calculate the mechanical equivalent of heat and formulated a form of the law of conservation of energy. However, his work went virtually unrecognized; *Joule received credit for the first achievement and *Helmholtz for the second.

Mayer, Louis B. (1885–1957) US film producer, born in Russia. He helped to create the Hollywood star system. With Samuel *Goldwyn in 1924 he founded the Metro-Goldwyn-Mayer (MGM) production company, whose films were largely determined by his personal taste for lavish but uncontroversial entertainment. He retired in 1951.

Mayfair A fashionable residential district in the Greater London borough of the City of Westminster. It was named for— the annual fair held from the 16th century until 1809.

Mayflower The ship that carried the *Pilgrim Fathers to America. They had intended to settle in Virginia but the *Mayflower* was blown off course and reached Plymouth (Massachusetts) in December, 1620. There, the Pilgrims drew up the **Mayflower Compact**, which based their government on the will of the colonists rather than the English crown.

mayfly A slender ☐insect of the order *Ephemeroptera* (1500 species), found near fresh water. Up to 1.5 in (40 mm) long, mayflies are usually brown or yellow with two unequal pairs of membranous wings. The adults do not feed and only live long enough to mate and lay eggs. The aquatic nymphs feed on plant debris and algae.

May Fourth Movement (1917–21) A Chinese movement for social and intellectual reform that culminated in a student demonstration in Peking on May 4, 1919, against government acceptance of the allocation of Chinese territory to Japan by the Paris Peace Conference following World War I.

The movement aimed to throw off foreign dominance and to build a new modern China.

Mayhew, Henry (1812–87) British journalist. His best-known work is *London Labour and the London Poor* (4 vols, 1851–62), a combination of vivid reportage and amateur social and economic analysis. He was a founder of *Punch* in 1841 and the author of many plays and novels.

Mayo (Irish name: Contae Mhuigheo) A county in the W Republic of Ireland, in Connacht bordering on the Atlantic Ocean. Mountainous in the W it contains several large lakes. Cattle, sheep, and pigs are raised and potatoes and oats are grown. Area: 2084 sq mi (5397 sq km). Population (1979): 114,019. County town: Castlebar.

Mayo A family of US physicians, who pioneered the concept of group practice and established the Mayo Clinic in Rochester, Minnesota, along these lines. The family included **William Worrall Mayo** (1819–1911), his sons **William James Mayo** (1861–1939) and **Charles Horace Mayo** (1865–1939), and Charles' son **Charles William Mayo** (1898–1968). The Mayos also made a number of contributions to medical research.

mayor of the palace An officer of the royal household and later a viceroy appointed by the Merovingian kings of the early middle ages. The most famous were *Pepin of Herstel and his grandson *Pepin the Short, who overthrew the Merovingians and founded the Carolingian dynasty.

Mayotte An island in the W Indian Ocean, in the Comoro Islands group. After the other islands declared independence from France (1975), Mayotte decided by a referendum to remain a French territory. Area: 144 sq mi (374 sq km). Population (1978): 47,246. Chief town: Dzaoudzi.

maypole dance A folk dance of ancient origin, traditionally performed on May 1 as part of the May Day festival. Participants circle around a tall pole, often adorned with ribbons, which they weave into patterns.

Mays, Willie (Howard, Jr.) (1931–) US baseball player. Nicknamed the "Say Hey Kid," he fielded for the New York (later San Francisco) Giants (1950–52; 1954–72) and the New York Mets (1972–73). He hit 660 career home runs and compiled 3283 hits during his career. He was elected to the Baseball Hall of Fame (1979).

Mazarin, Jules, Cardinal (1602–61) French statesman. A papal diplomat, he rose to prominence as a protégé of Cardinal de Richelieu and shortly after Richelieu's death (1642) became chief adviser to the regent Anne of Austria, Louis XIV's mother. The era of Mazarin witnessed a great expansion in the power of the monarchy, achieved largely through his suppression of rebellious aristocrats during the *Fronde. Abroad, he enhanced French supremacy in Europe by the Treaties of *Westphalia (1648) and the *Pyrenees (1659).

Mazatlán 23 11N 106 25W A port and resort in W Mexico, on the Gulf of California. The chief industries are textiles manufacture and sugar refining; exports include tobacco and minerals. Population (1978 est): 177,673.

Mazu (or Ma-tsu) 26 10N 119 59E A Taiwanese island in the East China Sea. It is near the Chinese mainland, from which it was bombed in 1958, causing an international incident. Area: 17 sq mi (44 sq km). Population (1971): 17,061.

Mazurian Lakes Several hundred lakes in NE Poland, around which Germany inflicted two heavy defeats on the Russians in 1914 and 1915.

Mazzini, Giuseppe (1805–72) Italian patriot, who was a leader of the movement for Italian unification (*see* Risorgimento). Forced to live mostly in exile in France, Switzerland, and England, he planned with his *Young Italy movement a rising in Piedmont and an invasion of Savoy in the 1830s but both failed. Mazzini was in Italy during the Revolutions of 1848 in Milan, Piedmont, Tuscany, and Rome, where he became head of a short-lived Roman republic. Although a united kingdom of Italy was finally established in 1861, he never realized his ideal of an Italian republic.

Mbabane 26 30S 31 30E The capital of Swaziland, in the Mdimba Mountains. It was founded in the late 19th century. Tourism is important and nearby is a large iron mine. Population (1976): 22,262.

Mbini. *See* Equatorial Guinea, Republic of.

Mboya, Tom (1930–69) Kenyan politician. Mboya was from the Luo tribe and was an active trade unionist and general secretary of the Kenyan Federation of Labor. He was a founding member and the general secretary (1960–64) of the Kenya African National Union and after the achievement of independence became, under Kenyatta, minister of justice (1963) and later minister of economic planning and development (1964–69). He was assassinated.

Mbuji-Mayi (name until 1966: Bakwanga) 6 10S 23 39E A city in central Zaïre. Diamonds were discovered here in 1909 and the region now produc-

es about 75% of the world's industrial diamonds. Population (1976 est): 382,632.

Mc–. Names beginning Mc are listed under Mac.

mead An alcoholic drink of fermented honey and water. The honey is dissolved in water and boiled with spices. When cool, after brewer's yeast has been added, the mead ferments in a barrel. It should be stored in a bottle for at least six months before serving. It was drunk in Anglo-Saxon England and, called hydromel, by the ancient Romans.

Mead, Margaret (1901–78) US anthropologist. Margaret Mead's anthropological work centers on the study of child rearing and the family. Her field work was done in New Guinea, Polynesia, and other Pacific islands. Her books include *Coming of Age in Samoa* (1929), *Sex and Temperament in Three Primitive Societies* (1935), and *Male and Female* (1949). She also wrote on education, science, and culture. A significant amount of her work was in the field of mental health.

Meade, George Gordon (1815–72) US Union general born in Spain of American parents. He graduated from West Point and participated in the Seminole campaign (1835–36) and the *Mexican War. During the Civil War he led troops in the Peninsular Campaign and at *Bull Run (1862), Antietam, and Fredericksburg. In 1863 he became head of the Army of the Potomac and was victorious at Gettysburg.

meadowsweet A perennial herb, *Filipendula* (or *Spiraea*) *ulmaria*, common in damp places throughout temperate Eurasia. 24–47 in (60–120 cm) high, it has large compound leaves, with 8–20 pairs of toothed leaflets and fluffy terminal clusters of small, creamy-white fragrant flowers, with long stamens. An oil distilled from the flower buds is used in perfumes. Family: *Rosaceae*.

mealworm. *See* darkling beetle.

mealybug An insect of the worldwide family *Pseudococcidae*, closely related to the *scale insects. The female is covered with a white sticky powder, which may be extended into filaments. The species *Pseudococcus citri* is a serious pest of citrus trees in America.

mean. *See* average.

meander A sinuous curve in a river. The velocity of flow in a meandering river is highest on the outside of the meander bends; erosion is concentrated here with deposition occurring on the inside of the bend. The meander will become increasingly looped until the river eventually breaks through its narrow neck creating an oxbow *lake.

mean free path The average distance traveled by a molecule between successive collisions with other molecules. According to the *kinetic theory, the mean free path is directly proportional to the viscosity of the substance and inversely proportional to the average velocity of the molecules.

mean life (or lifetime) The average time for which a radioactive isotope, elementary particle, or other unstable state exists before decaying. *See* radioactivity.

Meany, George (1894–1980) US labor leader. He served as secretary-treasurer of the *American Federation of Labor (AFL) (1939–52) and then as president (1952–55). During this time he was largely responsible for the merger of the AFL and the *Congress of Industrial Organizations (CIO) in 1955, serving as president of the combination (1955–79). He was known for his reforms regarding corrupt union methods and financial practices and was a driving force in the expulsion of the Teamsters Union from the AFL-CIO in 1957.

measles A highly infectious viral disease, which usually affects children. After an incubation period of about two weeks the child becomes irritable and fevered and has a running nose and inflamed eyes. Two or three days later a rash appears on the head and face and spreads over the body. Usually the child recovers after a week, but sometimes pneumonia or encephalitis may develop. There is no specific treatment, but vaccine has reduced the incidence of the disease. *Compare* German measles.

Meath (Irish name: Contae na Midhe) A county in the E Republic of Ireland, in Leinster bordering on the Irish Sea. Consisting chiefly of fertile glacial drifts it is important for agriculture; cattle are fattened and oats and potatoes grown. Area: 903 sq mi (2338 sq km). Population (1979): 90,715. County town: Trim.

Meaux 48 58N 2 54E A city in N France, in the Seine-et-Marne department on the Marne River. The commercial and industrial center of the Brie region, it supplies Paris with agricultural produce. Population (1975): 43,110.

MECCA *The chief problems in the administration of the city (the second largest in Saudi Arabia) arise in providing sufficient water and other services for the pilgrims, who are its main source of revenue.*

Mecca (Arabic name: Makkah) 21 26N 39 49E A city in W Saudi Arabia, in a narrow valley surrounded by barren hills. Mecca and Riyadh are joint capitals of the kingdom, but it is famous as the holiest Muslim city, which every Muslim is expected to visit at least once in his lifetime; nonbelievers are not allowed to enter the city. It has been a holy city since ancient times, but was also the birthplace of Mohammed (c. 570). Inside the court of the al-Haram Mosque in the center of the city are located the chief shrines: the Kabaa (a small windowless building) and the sacred well of Zamzam. In November, 1979, the al-Haram Mosque was seized by armed militants, who held a number of worshipers hostage before being overpowered by the military forces. Population (1974): 366,801.

mechanical advantage The ratio of the force output of a machine to the force input, i.e. the ratio of load to effort. It is useful only as an analysis of simple machines, such as levers, pulleys, jacks, etc., as no account of friction is taken. The **velocity ratio** of the machine is the distance moved by the effort divided by the distance moved by the load; the **mechanical efficiency** of a machine is the ratio of its mechanical advantage to its velocity ratio.

mechanical engineering The branch of *engineering concerned with the application of scientific knowledge to dynamical structures and systems, rather than the static structures of civil engineering. This branch encompasses the design, manufacture, and maintenance of machines of all kinds, engines, vehicles, and many aspects of industrial manufacturing. The subject has numerous specialized subdivisions, including *aeronautics, motor engineering, machine-tool design, etc.

mechanics The study of the motion of bodies and systems and the forces acting on them. The subject is traditionally divided into statics, the study of bodies in equilibrium, and dynamics, the study of forces that affect the motion of bodies. Dynamics is further divided into kinetics, the effects of forces and their moments on motion, and kinematics, the study of velocity, acceleration, etc., without regard to the forces causing them. Aristotelian (*see* Aristotle) mechanics was based on the erroneous concept that a force is required to maintain motion. *Newtonian mechanics recognizes that once a body is moving a force is required to stop it but no force is needed to keep it moving. Newtonian mechanics is the mechanics of classical systems, i.e. large-scale systems moving at relatively low velocities. The more general relativistic mechanics is also applicable to systems moving at speeds comparable to that of light (it reduces to Newtonian mechanics at velocities that are small compared to that of light). *Fluid mechanics is the application of mechanical principles to fluids, both stationary (hydrostatics) and flowing (hydrodynamics).

Mechelen (French name: Malines; English name: Mechlin) 51 02N 4 29E A city in N Belgium, on the Ryle River. Its 12th-century cathedral contains an altarpiece by Van Eyck and there are Rubens masterpieces in two other churches. Once famous for Mechlin lace, industries now include textiles and canned vegetables. Population (1981 est): 77,377.

Mechnikov, Ilya. *See* Metchnikov, Ilya.

Mecklenberg A former German state on the SW Baltic coast, now the Rostock, Schwerin, and Neubrandenburg districts of East Germany. Thinly populated, with many lakes and forests, Mecklenberg was frequently partitioned until its permanent division in 1701 into the Duchies of Mecklenberg-Schwerin and Mecklenberg-Strelitz. After the Congress of Vienna in 1815, both duchies formed part of the German Confederation under Austria's leadership, but in 1866 joined Prussia's North German Confederation; thereafter Mecklenberg's history is linked with Prussia's.

medals Pieces of metal fashioned as coins or crosses to commemorate individuals or special occasions, or awarded in recognition of service to a state or institution. During the Renaissance personal medals, usually bearing a portrait of the owner with an emblem and motto on the reverse, achieved high artistic standards. *Pisanello, *Dürer, and *Cellini were notable medalists. Military medals multiplied in the 18th and 19th centuries. They usually portray a sovereign's head or insignia of the awarding body, bear a commemorative legend, and are worn suspended on a special ribbon. Many are individual rewards for bravery, such as France's Croix de Guerre and Britain's *Victoria Cross but some are general medals to commemorate campaigns and state occasions, such as coronations. In the US, the highest award for gallantry, the Congressional Medal of Honor, was first presented in 1863.

Medan 03 35N 98 39E A city in Indonesia, in N Sumatra. Its state and Islamic universities were established in 1952. An agricultural and trade center that grew around tobacco plantations, it has a seaport (Belawan). Population (1971): 635,562.

Medawar, Sir Peter Brian (1915–) British immunologist, noted for his investigation of the development of the immune system in embryonic and young animals, including the phenomenon of acquired immunological tolerance to foreign tissue grafts. He also showed how genetically determined "markers" (antigens) enable the immune system to discriminate between host cells and foreign cells. Medawar shared the 1960 Nobel Prize with Sir Macfarlane *Burnet.

Medea In Greek legend, a sorceress, the daughter of King Aeetes of Colchis and niece of *Circe. She helped *Jason steal the *Golden Fleece and fled with him to Iolcus. When Jason deserted her for Glauce, daughter of the Corinthian King Creon, she killed Glauce, Creon, and her own two children and fled to Athens.

Medellín 6 15N 75 36W The second largest city in Colombia, in the Central Cordillera. It is the country's leading industrial center; steel processing and the manufacture of textiles are especially important. Its university was founded in 1822. Population (1978 est): 1,442,244.

Media An ancient region SW of the Caspian Sea settled by seminomadic tribes of Medes. Between the 8th and 6th centuries BC they began to unite against Assyria and in 612 under their sovereign Cyaxares (625–585) destroyed Nineveh with the help of Chaldea and overthrew the Assyrian empire. But in 550 the Medes were amalgamated with the Persians in Cyrus the Great's expanding empire.

median 1. The line joining the vertex of a triangle to the midpoint of the opposite side. 2. The middle value of a set of numbers arranged in order of magnitude. For example, the median of $\{2, 3, 3, 4, 5\} \neq \leq 3$.

Medicaid US federal and state health-care assistance-insurance plan for the needy. Established in 1965, it is administered by the states under guidelines established by the federal Welfare Administration. It covers such services as hospital and nursing home care, x-rays, physicians' and dentists' fees, laboratory fees, and medicines.

Medicare US national health insurance program for the aged and severely disabled. It was established in 1966 and is administered by the Social Security Administration of the Department of Health and Human Services. Participants pay nominal premiums and are partially, but almost completely, covered for certain hospital and nursing home care and for physician's services.

Medici A family that dominated Florence from 1434 to 1494, from 1512 to 1527, and from 1530 to 1737 (as grand dukes from 1532). The Medici, who were merchants and bankers, dominated the government of Florence in the 15th century by manipulating elections to the key magistracies. The family's power was established by **Cosimo de' Medici** (1389–1464), entitled Pater Patriae (Father of His Country), who also initiated the Medici tradition of artistic patronage: Brunelleschi, Ghiberti, and Donatello, among others, were employed by Cosimo. His son **Piero de' Medici** (1416–69) succeeded to his position, which then passed to **Lorenzo the Magnificent** (1449–92). Following the *Pazzi conspiracy (1478), in which his brother **Giuliano de' Medici** (1453–78) died, Lorenzo's political prestige was greatly enhanced. An outstanding patron of Renaissance artists (Botticelli, Ghirlandaio, Michelangelo) and scholars (Ficino, Pico della

Mirandola, Politian), Lorenzo tended to neglect the family business, which declined in the late 15th century. He was succeeded by his son **Piero de' Medici** (1472–1503), who was forced to flee Florence in a revolt incited by *Savonarola. Piero's brother **Giovanni de' Medici** (1475–1521) was restored to Florence in 1512, a year before he became Pope *Leo X. The Medici were again ousted, in 1527, but the combined efforts of Emperor Charles V and Pope Clement VII (previously Giulio de' Medici, the illegitimate son of Lorenzo's brother Giuliano) established Clement's illegitimate son **Alessandro de' Medici** (1511–37) as the first Duke of Florence. Subsequent grand dukes included **Cosimo I** (1519–74), **Francesco I** (1541–87), and **Ferdinando I** (1549–1609).

medicine The science and practice of preventing, diagnosing, and treating disease. The term is also used specifically for the management of disease by nonsurgical methods, for example by drugs, diet, etc. (*compare* surgery). Medicine involves study of the anatomy, physiology, and biochemistry of the body in health as well as the changes that occur in disease (pathology). It is closely connected with pharmacology (the study of drugs).
Medicine has its origins in ancient Greece. The medical school at Cnidos, established in the 7th century BC, was concerned purely with the description of symptoms, whereas that founded later by *Hippocrates considered the causes of symptoms in relation to the patient and the environment. In the Alexandrian school the emphasis was on the effects of disease rather than the causes. All existing knowledge of medicine was coordinated and supplemented in the 2nd century AD, by *Galen, whose influence prevailed until the Renaissance. Landmarks in the development of modern medicine were the publication of *Vesalius' major work on anatomy (1543) and of William Harvey's discovery of the circulation of the blood (1628). The nature, treatment, and prevention of infectious diseases were illuminated by the researches of *Pasteur, *Koch, and *Klebs in the 19th century; their work directed *Lister to the discovery of antiseptics, by means of which wound healing and hospital sanitation were greatly improved. Chemotherapy (the treatment of disease by chemical agents) was revolutionized in 1911, when *Ehrlich introduced salvarsan for treating syphilis. The late 1930s saw the development of the sulfonamides—the first powerful general antibacterial drugs—and World War II provided the stimulus for the widespread production and use of antibiotics (the first of which was penicillin). Together these drugs have enabled most infectious diseases to be cured. Viruses, however, do not succumb to antibiotics and the control of viral diseases has relied on immunological methods derived from *Jenner's discovery of vaccination in 1798. With infectious diseases under control, medical research since World War II has concentrated on the organic diseases, especially coronary artery disease, strokes, etc., and cancer. The emphasis has also been on preventive medicine, with the establishment of the *World Health Organization in 1948, campaigns to eradicate epidemic diseases, and the establishment of pre- and ante-natal clinics, medical inspections for schoolchildren, dental clinics, welfare centers, etc., in many parts of the world.

medick An annual or perennial herb of the genus *Medicago* (about 120 species), native to Eurasia and N Africa. The stems are creeping or erect, 2–35 in (5–90 cm) tall, bearing compound leaves with three toothed leaflets, dense yellow or purple flower heads, and curved or spirally twisted pods. Family: *Leguminosae.

Medina (Arabic name: Al Madinah) 24 30N 39 35E A city in W Saudi Arabia, N of Mecca. The tomb of Mohammed is in the mosque at Medina, the second most holy Muslim city after Mecca. Husayn ibn Ali, with the assistance of T. E. *Lawrence, expelled the Turks during World War I by putting the railroad from Damascus out of commission. Date-packing supplements the city's income from pilgrims, and the Islamic University was founded in 1961. Population (1974): 198,186.

Mediterranean Sea An almost landlocked sea extending between Africa and Europe to Asia. It connects with the Atlantic Ocean at Gibraltar, the Black Sea via the Sea of Marmara, and the Red Sea via the Suez Canal. It loses twice as much water through evaporation as it receives from rivers and thus is fed continuously by the Atlantic and to a lesser extent by the Black Sea. Although its waters return to the Atlantic in a ten-year cycle, it is saltier and warmer than the oceans; pollution is a serious problem because of the large quantities of waste discharged into its waters. Tidal variation is insignificant.

medlar A thorny shrub or tree, *Mespilus germanica*, native to SE Europe and central Asia and cultivated for its fruit. Growing to a height of 20 ft (6 m), it bears oblong toothed leaves, 6 in (15 cm) long, and white five-petaled flowers. The globular brownish fruit, 2–2.4 in (5–6 cm) across, has an opening at the top, surrounded by the remains of the sepals, through which the five seed chambers can be seen. Medlars are eaten when partly

decayed and have a pleasant acid taste; they can also be made into jelly. Family: *Rosaceae*.

Médoc An area in SW France, bordering on the left bank of the Gironde estuary. Producing some of France's finest red wines, it contains some famous vineyards including Château Latour.

medulla oblongata. *See* brain.

medusa The free-swimming sexual form that occurs during the life cycle of many animals of the phylum *Coelenterata*. Medusae resemble small *jellyfish and have separate sexes, releasing eggs and sperm into the water. The ciliated larvae settle and develop into the sedentary asexual forms (*see* polyp). *See also* coelenterate.

Medusa In Greek mythology, the only mortal *Gorgon. Athena, angered by her love affair with Poseidon, made her hair into serpents and her face so ugly that all who saw it were turned to stone. She later sent *Perseus to behead her. From her blood sprang *Pegasus and Chrysaor, her children by Poseidon.

Medway River A river in SE England. Rising in Sussex, it flows N and E through Kent to join the Thames River by a long estuary. In 43 AD, near Rochester, the invading Romans defeated the British under Caractacus in the battle of the Medway. Length: 70 mi (113 km).

Meegeren, Hans van (1889–1947) Dutch painter, notorious for his *Vermeer forgeries. He successfully misled the art world, notably with works such as *Christ at Emmaus*, bought by the Boymans Museum, Rotterdam, as an early Vermeer painting. In 1945 he was arrested as a Nazi collaborator, confessed his deceptions, was imprisoned, and died in poverty.

meerkat A small carnivorous mammal, *Suricata suricata*, also called suricate, of South African grasslands. It is about 24 in (60 cm) long including the tail (7–10 in [17–25 cm]), and lives in large colonies of shallow burrows, emerging to sunbathe in the early morning. Meerkats stay close to home, feeding on insects, grubs, reptiles, birds, and small mammals. Family: *Viverridae.

meerschaum A white mineral consisting of hydrated magnesium silicate, $H_4Mg_2Si_3O_{10}$, found in some magnesium-rich rocks, such as serpentine. Turkey has famous deposits of meerschaum; it also occurs in East and S Africa. It is used for making tobacco pipes.

Meerut 29 00N 77 42E A city in India, in Uttar Pradesh. The scene of the first uprising (1857) of the Indian Mutiny, Meerut is an important army headquarters and has diverse industries. Population (1971): 270,993.

megalith (Greek: large stone) A large stone particularly favored for building monuments in the *Neolithic and *Bronze Age (about 3500 BC to 1500 BC). Megaliths could be placed singly or in lines, or in simple or complex circles as at *Stonehenge. Megaliths were also used for tombs and temples in Malta, Egypt, and elsewhere. Stones weighing many tons were set up using simple tackle of timbers and ropes.

Megaloceros. *See* Irish elk.

megapode A bird belonging to a family (*Megapodiidae*; 12 species) ranging from Australia to the Peninsular Malaysia. 19–27 in (48–68 cm) long, megapodes are fowl-like and ground-dwelling with brownish plumage and build a large nest mound in which the eggs are incubated by the heat of fermenting plant material, the sun's rays, or volcanic heat. Order: *Galliformes* (pheasants, turkeys, etc.). *See also* brush turkey; mallee fowl.

Mégara 38 00N 23 20E A city in E central Greece. It was an important city state from the 8th century BC fostering many colonies, including *Chalcedon and Byzantium, before its decline in the 5th century BC. Population (1971): 17,260.

Megatherium A genus of extinct giant ground sloths that lived in North and South America about a million years ago. *Megatherium* was about the size of a modern elephant and probably ate leaves. Giant mammals like this were common in South America before the Panama isthmus closed at the end of the Ice Age, when most of them—including *Megatherium*—became extinct.

megaton A measure of the explosive power of a nuclear weapon. It is equivalent to an explosion of one million tons of trinitrotoluene (TNT).

Meghalaya A state in NE India, NE of Bangladesh on a beautiful plateau falling N to the Brahmaputra Valley. One of the world's wettest areas, it has rich forests but little industry. Rice, potatoes, cotton, and fruits are grown. Meghalaya was separated from Assam in 1972. Area: 8681 sq mi (22,489 sq km). Population (1981 est): 1,327,824. Capital: Shillong.

Megiddo An ancient site in N Israel. Continuously occupied between about 3000 and 350 BC, Megiddo was strategically positioned on the route between Egypt and Syria and was the scene of many battles. Excavations

(1925–39) unearthed hundreds of Phoenician ivories (13th–12th centuries BC) and stabling for about 450 horses, built probably by King Solomon. Megiddo is identified with the biblical Armageddon, where, according to St John the Divine (Revelation 16.16), the last battle will be fought.

Mehemet Ali (1769–1849) Viceroy of Egypt for the Ottoman Empire (1805–48). An Albanian in the Ottoman army, he was recognized as viceroy after he had seized power in Cairo. His important military, agricultural, and educational reforms have led some to see him as the founder of modern Egypt. In 1840 the Ottomans recognized him as hereditary ruler of Egypt and he was succeeded by his son *Ibrahim Pasha. His dynasty survived until 1952.

Meiji. *See* Mutsuhito.

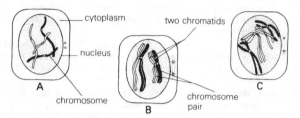

prophase I *The four chromosomes appear as thin threads (A), which form pairs (B). Each chromosome divides into two chromatids and exchange of genetic material occurs between the chromatids of each pair (C).*

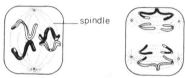

metaphase I *The chromosomes of each pair separate from each other and move to opposite poles of the spindle.*

metaphase II *Two new spindles form and the chromatids of each group separate from each other.*

telophase II *Four new nuclei form, each containing two chromosomes.*

MEIOSIS *The formation of four egg or sperm cells from one parent cell takes place in two divisions, each of which is divided into several phases. Only four phases are shown here.*

meiosis The process by which the nucleus of a germ cell divides prior to the formation of gametes (such as sperm, pollen, or eggs). Meiosis consists of two successive divisions during which one cell with the normal duplicate (diploid) set of chromosomes gives rise to four cells each with only one chromosome of each type (haploid). Meiosis differs from *mitosis in that the chromosomes of each pair become closely associated, enabling the interchange of genetic material between maternal and paternal chromosomes. There is no duplication of chromosomes between the two divisions of meiosis.

Meir, Golda (1898–1978) Israeli stateswoman, born in Russia; prime minister (1969–74). Brought up in the US (1906–21), she emigrated to Palestine in 1921. A founder member of the Israeli Workers' Party (Mapai) she was its secretary general (1966–68). She was minister of labor (1949–56) and minister of foreign affairs (1956–66) before becoming prime minister. She was committed to the establishment of peace in the Middle East and resigned after Israel had been taken unawares in the 1973 *Arab-Israeli War.

Meissen 51 11N 13 23E A city in SE East Germany, on the Elbe River. Meissen is famous for porcelain manufacture, moved here from Dresden in 1710. The process of production of the porcelain (known as Dresden china) was discovered by J. F. Böttger in 1709. Population (1973 est): 43,920.

Meissen porcelain The first hard-paste porcelain made in Europe following discovery (1710) of the technique by the alchemist Böttger (1682–1719) under the patronage of the Elector of Saxony. Initially, the Elector's oriental collection at Dresden was copied. There followed extensive ranges of domestic ware, figures (shepherdesses, monkey bands, Italian comedy, etc.), chinoiseries, small boxes, seals, and ornaments painted with landscapes, flowers, and insects. The styles were extensively copied by all 18th-century factories.

Meissonier, Jean-Louis-Ernest (1815–91) French painter, born in Lyons. He achieved great success at the Paris Salon exhibitions from the 1840s onward with his small, minutely detailed history and military paintings, particularly of Napoleonic battles, for example *Campagne de France, 1814* (1864).

Meistersingers (German: master singers) German singing guilds, which flourished from the 14th to the 17th centuries. As the *Minnesingers declined in Germany, song guilds developed in the artisan class, the first being established in Mainz in 1311. They flourished in most German towns; their contests were regulated by a superabundance of rules, as depicted by Wagner in his opera *The Mastersingers of Nuremberg*.

Meitner, Lise (1878–1968) Austrian physicist. After studying in Vienna under *Boltzmann, she worked with Otto *Hahn in Berlin (1907–38) until expelled by the Nazis. Together they discovered protactinium (1918) and caused the first fission of a uranium atom by neutron bombardment (1934). Hahn did not publish the results of this work and it was first published by Meitner from Stockholm in 1939. In Stockholm she worked with Karl Manne Georg Siegbahn (1886–1978), becoming a Swedish citizen in 1949.

Meknès 33 53N 5 37W A city in N Morocco. It became known as the "Moroccan Versailles" under Mawlay Isma'il (?1645–1727; reigned 1672–1727), when several palaces were built. It is a trade center for agricultural produce and carpets. Population (1973 est): 244,520.

Mekong River A major SE Asian river, rising in Tibet and flowing generally SE through China, Laos, Kampuchea, and Vietnam to the South China Sea. It is navigable for about 340 mi (550 km). The extensive delta is one of the greatest Asian rice-growing areas. Length: about 2500 mi (4025 km).

Melanchthon, Philip (P. Schwarzerd; 1497–1560) German Protestant reformer, who succeeded *Luther as leader of the German Reformation movement. Professor of Greek at the University of Wittenberg, Melanchthon was a convinced humanist, influenced by *Erasmus, and a supporter of Luther in public confrontations, including the debate with *Zwingli over the Eucharist. He was largely responsible for the *Augsburg Confession (1530), the main Lutheran statement of belief.

Melanesia A division of Oceania in the SW Pacific Ocean, consisting of an arc of volcanic and coral islands NE of Australia. It includes the Bismarck Archipelago, the Solomon, Admiralty, and D'Entrecasteaux Islands, Vanuata Republic, New Caledonia, and Fiji. *See also* Micronesia; Polynesia.

Melanesians The people of the Melanesian islands. The term also covers similar peoples of New Guinea, though these are also often known as Papuan. They are of Oceanic Negroid race and speak languages of the *Austronesian family. There are a great many very different languages mostly spoken by only small numbers. The Melanesians cultivate yams, taro, and sweet potatoes and live in small, usually dispersed, homesteads. In coastal areas fishing is important. Pigs play a major role in the economy, being used in the ceremonial exchanges of valuables to establish status that are a common cultural trait. Social organization varies greatly among the different groups.

melanin A pigment, varying from brown-black to yellow, that occurs in hair, skin, feathers, and scales. Derived from the amino acid tyrosine, its presence in the skin helps protect underlying tissues from damage by sunlight. Melanin is also responsible for coloring the iris of the eye.

Melba, Dame Nellie (Helen Porter Armstrong; 1859–1931) Australian soprano, whose professional name was derived from her native city, Melbourne. She studied in Paris, making her debut in 1887 as Gilda in Verdi's opera *Rigoletto*. Her worldwide career culminated in a number of farewell performances in 1926.

Melbourne 37 45S 144 58E The second largest city of Australia, the capital of Victoria on Port Phillip Bay. It is a major commercial center and contains about two thirds of the state's population. Port Melbourne is sited 2.5 mi (4 km) away, on the mouth of the Yarra River; exports include wool, scrap metal, and dairy products. The chief industries are heavy engineering, food processing, and the manufacture of textiles and clothes. A cultural center, Melbourne possesses three universities (including the University of Melbourne founded in 1853), and the new Arts Center of Victoria. Other notable buildings include the State Parliament House and the Anglican and Roman Catholic cathedrals. *History*: founded in 1835, it developed rapidly following the 1851 gold rush. It was the capital of the Commonwealth of Australia from 1901 until 1927. Population (1980 est): 2,759,700.

Melbourne, William Lamb, 2nd Viscount   (1779–1848) British statesman; Whig prime minister (1834, 1835–41), who exerted an early influence on Queen Victoria. He was chief secretary for Ireland (1827–28) and then home secretary (1830–34), when he dealt harshly with the *Tolpuddle Martyrs.

Melchett, Alfred Mond, 1st Baron.   See Mond, Ludwig.

Melchior, Lauritz   (1890–1973) Danish tenor. He studied at the Royal Opera School in Copenhagen and made his debut in 1913. His performances in the roles of Tristan and Siegfried marked him as the leading Wagnerian tenor of the 20th century.

Melchites   Christians of the Orthodox Churches in Syria and Egypt who, during the 5th-century *Monophysite controversy, adhered to the anti-Monophysite doctrine supported by the Byzantine emperor. Their name was therefore derived from a Syriac word meaning "imperial."

Meleager   In Greek legend, the son of Oeneus, King of Calydon. He killed the Calydonian boar, sent by Artemis because Oeneus had neglected to sacrifice to her.

Melilla   35 17N 2 57W A Spanish port forming an enclave on the Mediterranean coast of N Morocco. Iron ore is the principal export. Population (1970): 64,000.

melilot   An herb belonging to the genus *Melilotus* (25 species), also called sweet clover, occurring in temperate and subtropical Eurasia. The leaves consist of three leaflets and the small yellow or white flowers grow in clusters along the stems. The biennial common melilot (*M. officinalis*) has yellow flowers and grows to a height of 51 in (130 cm). Family: *Leguminosae.

Melitopol   46 51N 35 22E A city in the Soviet Union, in the SE Ukrainian SSR. The center of a fruit-growing region, it has food-processing industries. Nearby is the site of ancient Merv, an Islamic center at its height under the Seljuq Turks in the 12th century. Population (1981 est): 165,000.

Mellon, Andrew William   (1855–1937) US financier and philanthropist. As secretary of the treasury (1921–32) he played a major role in the government's postwar tax reforms. He was ambassador to Great Britain (1932–33). An art collector, he donated both his collection and $15 million to the construction of the National Gallery of Art in Washington, DC.

melon   An annual trailing vine, *Cucumis melo*, native to tropical Africa but widely cultivated for its edible fruits. Melon plants have coarse hairy five- to seven-lobed leaves, yellow or orange cup-shaped flowers, and round or oval fruits, up to 9 lb (4 kg) in weight, with tough skins and sweet juicy flesh surrounding a core of seeds. There are several varieties including the muskmelon, with a net-veined skin and pinkish orange flesh; the honeydew melon, with smooth whitish or greenish skin and light-green flesh; the canteloupe, with rough warty skin and orange flesh; and a newer variety produced in Israel with a green skin and sweet green flesh. Melons are usually eaten fresh. Family: *Cucurbitaceae. See also* watermelon.

Melos   (*or* Mílos)   A Greek island in the Aegean Sea, one of the Cyclades. Successive Minoan cities have been excavated here and the famous statue the *Venus de Milo* was discovered here in 1820. Area: 58 sq mi (150 sq km). Population (1971): 4593.

Melpomene   In Greek religion, one of the nine Muses, the patron of tragedy and lyre playing. She was the mother of the *Sirens.

melting point   The temperature at which the solid form of a substance becomes a liquid, usually at atmospheric pressure.

Mélusine   (*or* Melusina)   In French legend, a fairy who was punished for imprisoning her father in a mountain by being changed into a serpent from the waist down every Saturday. When her husband, Count Raymond of Lusignan, broke his promise not to see her on Saturdays, she vanished but her cries were heard at Lusignan castle shortly before the death of each of her descendants.

Melville, Herman   (1819–91) US novelist. In 1841 he joined the crew of a whaler; his experiences in the South Seas form the raw material of *Typee* (1846), *Omoo* (1847), *Mardi* (1849), *Redburn* (1849), and *White Jacket* (1850). His masterpiece, *Moby Dick* (1851), is a narrative about whaling with an underlying philosophical theme on the nature of evil. After the failure of *Pierre* (1852), Melville abandoned professional writing. *Billy Budd*, published in 1924 after his death, formed the basis of a libretto for an opera by Benjamin Britten.

Memel.   *See* Klaipeda.

HANS MEMLING   *Triptych:* The Virgin and Child with Saints and Donors *(c. 1477). The figures on the extreme left and right are St John the Baptist and St John the Evangelist.*

Memling, Hans   (*or* Memlinc; c. 1430–1494) Painter of portraits and religious subjects, born in Seligenstadt (Germany). He settled in the Netherlands, where he probably studied under Rogier van der *Weyden, the strongest influence on his painting. About 1465 he moved to Bruges, where his best-known works, *The Shrine of St Ursula* and *The Mystic Marriage of St Catherine*, were painted for the Hospital of St John.

memory   The recollection of experiences from the past. Three processes are required: registration, in which an experience is received into the mind;

retention, in which a permanent memory trace, or engram, is preserved in the brain, probably in the form of a chemical molecule; and recall, in which a particular memory is brought back into consciousness. Short-term memories are vivid but are forgotten with the passage of time unless they are registered in the long-term memory. Once in the long-term memory, they remain available unless they are interfered with by a similar memory.

Failure of memory (*see* amnesia) is a common consequence of diseases of the brain, especially those caused by *alcoholism and those affecting the part of the *brain called the hippocampus. An abnormally good memory (hypermnesia) can sometimes be produced by hypnosis and is sometimes found in *autism.

memory, computer   The part of a computer that stores information. It usually refers to the computer's internal store, in which the programs and data needed to run the computer are held; this is under the direct control of the central processing unit. In large computers, a high-speed buffer store holds information in active use by the central processing unit, while longer-term storage is provided by the slower main store.

Solid-state electronic memory devices operate at very high speeds and are used for the internal memory. Magnetic tapes and disks form the external memory, which is available to the computer through peripheral devices. The external memory contains information that is not needed frequently.

Memphis   35 10N 90 00W A city and port in Tennessee situated above the Mississippi River. Founded in 1819, it was so called because of the similarity of its riverside position to that of the ancient Egyptian city of Memphis. It is a major cotton, timber, and livestock market and its manufactures include textiles and chemicals. Memphis is associated with W. C. Handy, the composer of the blues. Memphis State University was established here in 1912. Population (1980): 646,356.

Memphis   An ancient city of Lower Egypt, S of modern Cairo. A center for *Ptah worship, Memphis was founded as the capital of all Egypt after its unification by *Menes (c. 3100 BC), remaining the capital until supplanted by *Thebes (c. 1570 BC). The necropolis of *Saqqarah and the *pyramids and sphinx at Giza formed part of its extensive complex of monuments.

Menado (*or* Manado)   01 32N 124 55E A port in Indonesia, in N Sulawesi on the Celebes Sea. A trading center, it exports copra, coffee, and spices. Its university was established in 1961. Population (1971): 169,684.

Menander (c. 341–c. 290 BC) Greek dramatist. The most celebrated dramatist of the *New Comedy, he wrote sophisticated comedies on romantic and domestic themes with strongly individualized characters. His single surviving complete play is the *Dyscolus*, recovered from an Egyptian papyrus in 1958, but many of his other plays are known from their adaptations by the Roman dramatists Plautus and Terence.

Menander (c. 160–c. 20 BC) Greek King of the Punjab and one of the heirs to *Alexander the Great's conquests. His capital was at Sakala (probably present-day Sialkot, Pakistan) and he commanded an extensive empire over NW India. He became a devout Buddhist.

menarche.   *See* puberty.

Mencius (Mengzi *or* Meng-tzu; 371–289 BC) Chinese moral philosopher. He was taught by pupils of *Confucius and produced the *Mencius*, an exposition of Confucian thought read by Chinese schoolchildren until the 20th century. For Mencius, moral thinking was superior to theorizing and he made benevolence (*ren or jen*) the keynote of his political philosophy. He traveled extensively, advocating that rulers should treat their subjects humanely.

Mencken, H(enry) L(ouis) (1880–1956) US journalist and critic. As editor of *The Smart Set* (1914–23) and *American Mercury* (1924–33) he boldly attacked both the political and the literary establishments and championed many young novelists. His miscellaneous essays were collected in *Prejudices* (6 vols, 1919–27). In *The American Language* (1919) he surveyed the development of English in America. *Newspaper Days 1899–1908* (1914) and *Heather Days (1890–1936)* (1943) are autobiographical.

Mendel, Gregor Johann (1822–84) Austrian botanist, who discovered the fundamental principles governing the inheritance of characters in living things (*see* genetics). Mendel was a monk with a scientific education and an interest in botany. In 1856 in the monastery garden at Brünn, Moravia, he began to inbreed lines of pea plants by means of repeated self-pollination. All the dwarf plants produced dwarf offspring only, but of tall plants, only about one third were true-breeding. The majority each produced both tall plants and dwarf plants in the ratio 3:1. Mendel then crossed pure-bred tall and dwarf plants and found that all the resulting hybrids were tall. Crossing these hybrids resulted in a mixture of pure-bred dwarf, hybrid tall, and pure-bred tall plants in the ratio 1:2:1. From these and similar

experiments Mendel concluded that such characteristics were determined by factors of inheritance that were contributed equally by both parents and that sorted themselves among the offspring according to simple statistical rules. He summarized these findings in two principles (now known as *Mendel's laws of inheritance). Mendel reported his findings in 1865 but met with little response. The importance of his achievement was not appreciated until the rediscovery of his work by C. E. *Correns, Hugo *de Vries and E. von Tschermak (1871–1962) in 1900.

mendelevium (Md)   A synthetic element, first produced in 1955 by Ghiorso and others, by bombarding einsteinium with helium ions; it is named for the chemist Mendeleyev. At no 101; at wt (256).

Mendeleyev, Dimitrii Ivanovich (1834–1907) Russian chemist, who was professor at St Petersburg (now Leningrad) from 1866 to 1890. He became interested in the subject of atomic weights after hearing *Cannizzaro lecture on the subject and, in 1869, succeeded in arranging the elements in order of increasing atomic weights so that those with similar properties were grouped together (*see* periodic table). Mendeleyev succeeded where others had failed, by recognizing that the rows of the table were not all of equal length and that there were gaps in the table, representing undiscovered elements.

Mendel's laws   The basic principles governing the inheritance of characters, first proposed by Gregor *Mendel in 1865. His first law, the Law of Independent Segregation, states that the factors of inheritance (now called *alleles of the gene) that determine a particular characteristic segregate into separate sex cells. His second law, the Law of Independent Assortment, states that the segregation of factors for one character occurs independently of that for any other character. (This is true except for alleles of genes located on the same chromosome, which have a tendency to be segregated together.)

Mendelssohn, Felix (Jacob Ludwig Felix Mendelssohn-Bartholdy; 1809–47) German composer; the grandson of Moses Mendelssohn. A child prodigy, his education was strictly supervised by his father. His string octet (1825) and the overture to *A Midsummer Night's Dream* (1826) demonstrated his precocious brilliance. In 1836 he became conductor of the Leipzig Gewandhaus orchestra and subsequently founded the Leipzig conservatoire. His music was popular in Britain and he was entertained by Queen Victoria. His compositions include five symphonies, overtures, the oratorios *St Paul* (1836) and *Elijah* (1846), chamber music, and piano music. He revived Bach's *St Matthew Passion* in 1829.

Mendelssohn, Moses (1729–86) German Jewish philosopher and literary critic. He was admired by *Kant and *Lessing and did much to improve the position of the Jews, for whom he sought civil rights. He also advocated the separation of church and state. Mendelssohn is known for his proofs of the immortality of the soul, in *Phaedon* (1767), and the existence of a personal God, in *Morgenstunden* (1785).

Menderes, Adnan (1899–1961) Turkish statesman; prime minister (1950–60). His repressive policies led to an army coup in 1960 and his execution.

Menderes River (ancient name: R. Maeander; Turkish name: Büyük Menderes)   A river in W Turkey, flowing generally WSW into the Aegean Sea. The ancient name of this winding river gave rise to the term *meander. Length: 249 mi (400 km).

Mendès-France, Pierre (1907–82) French statesman; prime minister (1954–55). A Radical Socialist, Mendès-France was forced to resign because of his unpopular policies, which aimed to restore the failing Fourth Republic; these included strengthening the executive, ending the war with Indochina, and granting independence to Tunisia.

Mendip Hills (*or* Mendips)   A range of limestone hills in SW England, in Somerset. It extends NW–SE between Axbridge and the Frome Valley, reaching 1068 ft (325 m) at Blackdown.

Mendoza   32 48S 68 52W A city in W Argentina. It is the commercial center of an irrigated area specializing in wine production and has a university (1939). Population (1975 est): 118,568.

Mendoza, Antonio de (?1490–1552) Spanish colonial administrator. Mendoza was the first viceroy (1535–50) of New Spain (Mexico), where he fostered economic development and education, bringing the first printing press to the New World. He subsequently became viceroy of Peru (1551–52), where he died.

Menelaus   A legendary Spartan king and husband of *Helen. He served under his brother Agamemnon in the *Trojan War and after the fall of Troy was reunited with Helen.

Menelik II (1844–1913) Emperor of Ethiopia (1889–1913). He greatly expanded Ethiopia and carried out important reforms, limiting the power of the nobility and modernizing the administration. In 1896 he was able to repel an Italian invasion.

Menes The first ruler of a united Egypt (c. 3100 BC); the founder of the 1st dynasty. Perhaps a legendary figure, he was said to have founded *Memphis.

Mengelberg, William (1871–1951) Dutch conductor. He studied at the Cologne conservatoire and was conductor of the Amsterdam Concertgebouw Orchestra from 1895 to 1941. He was famous for his performances of Beethoven.

Mengs, Anton Raphael (1728–79) German painter, born in Aussig, Bohemia. An early exponent of *neoclassicism, he achieved a high reputation particularly in Rome, where he settled (1755), and in Spain, where he worked for Charles III. Apart from numerous portraits, his best-known work is the *Parnassus* fresco (1761; Villa Albani, Rome).

menhir (Breton: long stone) A prehistoric *megalith set upright either by itself or with others in circles (e.g. *Stonehenge) or alignments (e.g. *Carnac).

Ménière's disease A disease of the inner ear causing progressive deafness, tinnitus (ringing in the ear), and vertigo. The disease normally occurs in the middle-aged and elderly and treatment (medical or surgical) is not altogether successful.

Menindee Lakes A series of lakes and reservoirs in Australia. They lie in SW New South Wales, forming part of the Darling River Conservation Scheme, and provide water for irrigation and industrial and domestic purposes.

meningitis Inflammation of the meninges—the membranes that surround the brain. This is usually caused by bacteria or viruses and occurs most commonly in children. Symptoms include headache, vomiting, stiff neck, intolerance to light, tiredness, irritability, and fits. Treatment for bacterial meningitis is with antibiotics and the patient usually recovers rapidly. Viral meningitis is often mild but may have serious effects. Tuberculous meningitis comes on more slowly and—before modern drugs were developed—was always fatal. Complications such as mental handicap, deafness, and weak limbs may occasionally occur.

Menlo Park 37 28N 122 13W An unincorporated community in E central New Jersey, part of the town of Edison. Many of Thomas Alvah Edison's experiments, including the invention of the incandescent light bulb (1879), took place in his laboratory here. A state park houses memorabilia and commemorates the inventor.

Mennonites A Christian sect that originated in Holland and adjacent areas in the 16th century. Their name derives from Menno Simons, who reorganized persecuted *Anabaptist groups after 1536. There are sizable Mennonite communities in Holland and in North America, where the first colony settled in 1683. Common ground between the doctrinally diverse Mennonite groups is their rejection of hierarchical Church organization and of infant baptism. In secular life Mennonites are pacifists and avoid public office.

Menno Simons (c. 1496–1561) Dutch Anabaptist leader. A former Roman Catholic priest, Menno became the traveling shepherd of scattered *Anabaptist groups in N Europe, persecuted by both Roman Catholics and Reformers. His preaching of total pacifism became the mark of the *Mennonites, one section of the Anabaptist movement.

Menon, Krishna (Vengalil Krishnan Krishna Menon; 1896–1974) Indian diplomat. He was secretary of the India League from 1929 and a major figure in the campaign for Indian independence. After this was achieved in 1947 he was high commissioner for India to the UK (1947–52) before becoming a member of the Indian legislature; he was a delegate at the UN (1952–62) and defense minister (1957–62).

menopause The cessation of menstruation. It is the time in a woman's life when the menstrual periods become irregular and finally cease because egg cells are no longer produced by the ovaries. The menopause can occur at any age between the late 30s and late 50s. Some women may experience physical and emotional symptoms, including flushing, palpitations, and irritability, due to reduced secretion of estrogens.

Menorca. *See* Minorca.

Menotti, Gian Carlo (1911–) Italian-born US composer. Living in the US since 1928, he studied and later taught at the Curtis Institute, Philadelphia. Among his compositions are the operas *The Medium* (1946) and *The Saint of Bleeker Street* (1954), both of which received Pulitzer Prizes, *The Consul* (1950) and the television opera *Amahl and the Night Visitors* (1951). In 1958 he founded the Spoleto Festival.

Mensheviks One of the two factions into which the Russian Social Democratic Workers' Party split in 1903 in London. Unlike the rival *Bolsheviks, the Mensheviks (meaning those in the minority) believed in a large and loosely organized party. They supported Russia's participation in World War I and were prominent in the Russian Revolution until the Bolsheviks seized power in October, 1917. They were finally suppressed in 1922.

menstruation The monthly discharge of blood and fragments of womb lining from the vagina. This is part of the **menstrual cycle**—the sequence of events, occurring in women from puberty to the menopause, by which an egg cell is released from the ovary. Menstruation is the stage at which the egg cell (with blood, etc.) is expelled from the womb if conception has not occurred. Ovulation occurs at around the middle of the cycle: it may be associated with abdominal pain. Depression and irritability are common shortly before menstruation (premenstrual tension).

mental retardation A state of arrested or incomplete development of the intellect. Mildly retarded people (with an IQ of approximately 50–70) usually make a good adjustment to life after special help with education; their condition is usually caused by inherited disorders or psychological disturbances. Severely retarded people (with an IQ of less than 50) usually require permanent help from other people and may need care in a special home or a hospital. Severe retardation is nearly always caused by physical diseases affecting the brain, but good education improves the outcome. *See also* intelligence.

menthol ($C_{10}H_{20}O$) A white crystalline solid. It is a constituent of peppermint oil and is responsible for the characteristic smell of the mint plant, but can also be prepared synthetically. Menthol is used as an analgesic in medicine (in skin creams, throat pastilles, and inhalers) as well as in flavoring for sweets and cigarettes.

Menton 43 47N 7 30E A city in SE France, in the Alpes-Maritimes department on the French Riviera near the Italian border. A popular holiday resort, it produces fruit and flowers. Population (1975): 25,314.

Menuhin, Yehudi (1916–) US violinist, living in England. A pupil of Georges Enesco, he became famous in boyhood; Elgar coached him for performances of the composer's violin concerto. From 1959 to 1968 Menuhin was director of the Bath (England) Festival, where he also participated as a conductor. He founded the Yehudi Menuhin School for musically gifted children in 1963. He was frequently partnered in recitals by his sister, the pianist **Hephzibah Menuhin** (1920–81). □Stern, Isaac.

SIR ROBERT MENZIES *The Australian parliament listens to the prime minister speaking on his Communist Party Dissolution Bill (1950). After its enactment it was declared invalid (1951) by the Australian courts.*

Menzies, Sir Robert Gordon (1894–1978) Australian prime minister. Elected to the federal parliament in 1934, he was attorney general (1934–39) before becoming prime minister as leader of the United Australian Party. He resigned in 1941 and formed the Liberal Party in 1944. As Liberal prime minister he increased US influence in Australian affairs and was strongly anticommunist. He encouraged immigration from Europe and developed the Australian universities.

Merca 1 45N 44 47E A city in Somalia, on the Indian Ocean. Merca has a deepwater harbor and exports agricultural produce, especially bananas. Population (1980 est): 60,000.

mercantilism An economic doctrine that flourished in the 17th and 18th centuries. Primarily concerned with international trade, mercantilism attempted to maximize national wealth, which it identified with a nation's bullion reserves. To this end, tariffs were applied to imports in the hope of creating a *balance-of-trade surplus and adding to bullion reserves. Mercantilism was replaced by *free trade, after *Hume and Adam *Smith had shown that mercantilism merely served the self-interest of the merchant classes.

Mercator, Gerardus (Gerhard Kremer; 1512–94) Flemish geographer, best known for his method of mapping the earth's surface, known as the *Mercator projection. He worked at Louvain, but was prosecuted for heresy in 1544 and emigrated to Protestant Germany in 1552, where he was appointed cartographer to the Duke of Cleves. In later life he prepared a book of maps, which, since it had a picture of Atlas supporting the earth on its cover, became known as an atlas.

Mercator projection A cylindrical □map projection, originally used (1569) by Gerardus Mercator. The parallels of latitude are represented as being straight lines of equal length to the equator. The meridians are equally spaced and intersect at right angles. The correct ratio between latitude and longitude is maintained by increasing the distance between the parallels away from the equator causing increased distortion toward the Poles. Compass bearings are accurately shown and the projection is commonly used for navigation charts. The **Transverse Mercator projection** is a development of the Mercator projection but in this case the cylinder is tangential to a meridian rather than to the equator. It is used chiefly for small areas with a N–S orientation and is used in all British *Ordnance Survey maps.

mercerization A finishing process for cotton fabrics and yarns. Named for John Mercer (1791–1866), who investigated the process (1844), mercerization involves treating the cotton by immersion, while under tension, in a caustic soda solution, later neutralized by acid. This process causes the fibers to swell permanently; cotton thus treated dyes better and is stronger and more lustrous.

Merchant Marine Academy, United States Training institution for US Merchant Marine officers. It trains students in nautical and naval science and in ship management. The program offers a bachelor of science degree and a naval reserve commission. It was established in 1943 at Kings Point, NY, on Long Island.

Merchants Adventurers An English trading company, incorporated in 1407, which controlled the export of cloth to continental Europe. Its center was at Bruges until 1446, when it moved to Antwerp; in 1567 it transferred to Hamburg but returned to a series of Dutch marts after 1580. The Adventurers, which rivaled the *Hanseatic League, were criticized for furthering their own interests at the expense of the English economy and lost their charter in 1689.

Merchant Staplers English merchants who controlled the export and sale of wool from the late 13th to late 16th centuries. Exports were sold at one market (the staple), which from 1363 was Calais. At its height in the 15th century, the company declined with the growth of English manufacturing.

Mercia A kingdom of Anglo-Saxon England. The Mercians were *Angles and their territory embraced most of central England south of the Humber between Wales and East Anglia. Mercia became a formidable power under *Penda (c. 634–55) and achieved pre-eminence under *Offa (757–96), who controlled all England S of the Humber. Thereafter it declined and was merged in the 9th century into a united England under Wessex.

Mercouri, Melina (1925–) Greek actress and politician; minister of culture and science (1981–). Her best-known films were made with the US director Jules Dassin (1911–), whom she married, and include *Never on Sunday* (1960) and *Topkapi* (1964). She campaigned in exile against the military junta (1967–74) and returned to Greece when civilian government was restored.

mercury (botany) An annual or perennial herb of the genus *Mercurialis* (8 species), native to Eurasia and N Africa. The perennial dog's mercury (*M. perennis*) of woodland areas has an evil smell and is poisonous to grazing animals. Growing 6–16 in (15–40 cm) high, it has large toothed leaves arranged in pairs and clusters of small green male and female flowers borne on separate plants. The annual mercury (*M. annua*) occurs on wasteland and as a garden weed. Family: *Euphorbiaceae*.

mercury (Hg) The only common metal that is liquid at room temperature (it has a high relative density of 13.546). It occurs chiefly as the sulfide cinnabar (HgS), from which mercury is obtained simply by heating in a current of air. The element was known in ancient Egypt, India, and China and occurs rarely in nature in the metallic state. It is used in thermometers,

barometers, and batteries and as an amalgam in dentistry. Compounds include the oxide (HgO), mercurous and mercuric chlorides (Hg_2Cl_2, $HgCl_2$), and the explosive mercury fulminate ($Hg(ONC)_2$), which is widely used as a detonator. Mercury and its compounds are highly poisonous and are only slowly excreted by the human body. Organo-mercury compounds, such as dimethyl mercury, $(CH_3)_2Hg$, are particularly toxic (*see* Minimata disease). At no 80; at wt 200.59; mp –38.03°F (–38.87°C); bp 674°F (356.58°C).

Mercury (astronomy) The innermost and second smallest (3030 mi [4880 km] diameter) planet, orbiting the sun every 88 days at a mean distance of 36 million mi (57.9 million km). Its long period of axial rotation, 58.6 days, is two thirds of its orbital period. Mercury can only be seen low in the twilight and early morning sky and, like the moon, exhibits *phases. Its surface is heavily cratered, with intervening lava-flooded plains. It has only a very tenuous atmosphere, mainly helium and argon. *See also* planetary probe.

Mercury (mythology) The Roman god of merchants and commerce and patron of astronomy. He is usually portrayed as holding a purse, and also with a cap, winged sandals, and staff, the attributes of the Greek *Hermes, with whom he was identified.

Meredith, George (1828–1909) British poet and novelist. Educated in Germany, he returned to England to study law but embarked on a literary career instead. For many years he was dependent on literary hackwork. His long poem *Modern Love* (1862) was partly based on his unhappy marriage to Mary Ellen Nicholls, daughter of Thomas Love *Peacock. With his novels, including *The Egoist* (1879) and *The Tragic Comedians* (1880), he achieved critical acclaim and financial security.

Meredith, Owen. *See* Lytton, Edward George Earle Bulwer-Lytton, 1st Baron.

merganser A *duck belonging to a genus (*Mergus*) of the N hemisphere, also called sawbill. It occurs on inland lakes in summer and coastal regions in winter. 16–22 in (40–57 cm) long, mergansers have a long serrated bill for feeding on worms, fish, and eels. Males have a dark-green double-crested head, a chestnut breast, and a gray-and-white back; females are brown with a white wing bar. *See also* goosander.

merger The amalgamation of two or more companies to form one new company; usually the shareholders of the old companies exchange their old shares for shares in the new company. **Vertical mergers** involve the amalgamation of companies specializing in different parts of the production process (e.g. a car manufacturer and a steelmaker); **horizontal mergers** involve the amalgamation of related product manufacturers (e.g. car and truck manufacturers); and **conglomerate mergers** are between firms unrelated in production. Mergers usually require government approval, as they can lead to *monopolies.

Mérida (Latin name: Augusta Emerita) 38 55N 06 20W A city in W Spain, in Estremadura on the Guadiana River. Founded by the Romans in 25 BC, it has numerous Roman remains, including an aqueduct, temples, two bridges, and a triumphal arch. Population (1970): 40,059.

Mérida 20 59N 89 39W A city in E Mexico. It is the commercial and industrial center for an agricultural area specializing in henequen (a fiber) production. It has a 16th-century cathedral and is the site of the University of Yucatán (refounded 1922). Population (1978 est): 263,186.

meridian. *See* latitude and longitude.

meridian circle An instrument for determining very accurately the position of a celestial body by measuring the body's altitude and the time as it crosses the observer's meridian (which passes through the observer's zenith and N and S celestial poles). It consists of a telescope pivoted on a horizontal E–W axis so that the telescope's line of sight follows the meridian plane.

Mérimée, Prosper (1803–70) French novelist. His first published works were fake translations of plays and ballads that deceived many leading scholars. His best-known works are his short novels, especially *Columba* (1841) and *Carmen* (1843), the source of Bizet's opera. He was also a distinguished historian and archeologist, and a friend of the empress Eugénie.

Merino A breed of sheep originating from Spain and noted for its long thick high-quality white fleece. Merinos are well adapted to hot arid climates and have been exported to many parts of the world, especially Australia, where the Australian Merino has been developed for its superior fleece.

Merionethshire A former county of NW Wales. Under local government reorganization in 1974 it became part of *Clwyd and *Gwynedd.

meristem An area of actively dividing plant cells responsible for growth in the plant. The main meristematic regions in dicotyledon plants are the shoot tip and root tip (apical meristems) and the *cambium (lateral meristem). A damaged meristem produces distorted growth, but it can be used for plant propagation.

Merleau-Ponty, Maurice (1908–61) French philosopher. He was interested in the nature of human consciousness and its interaction with matter, problems that he examined in *Le Structure du comportement* (1942) and *Phénoménologie de perception* (1945). In his eyes, causal and behavioristic theories misinterpreted consciousness, as did dualism, and he accepted the Marxist view of the dependence of consciousness upon material conditions.

merlin A small *falcon, *Falco columbarius*, occurring in moorland and heathland regions of the N hemisphere. The female is 12.5 in (32 cm) long and is dark brown with heavily streaked underparts; the male is 10 in (26 cm) long and has a gray-blue back and tail. Merlins feed chiefly on small birds, which are caught in flight.

Merlin In *Arthurian legend, the wizard who counsels and assists Arthur and his father, Uther Pendragon. There are various accounts of Merlin's life in *Geoffrey of Monmouth and later writers. He helped Uther to win Igraine, Arthur's mother, made the Round Table, cared for Arthur as a child, and gave him, or arranged for him to be given, the sword Excalibur. In old age Merlin fell in love with Nimue (*or* Vivien), who tricked him into a cave or hollow tree and left him there forever imprisoned by a spell.

mermaid A legendary creature whose form is that of a beautiful woman above the waist and a fish below. A mermaid's male counterpart is called a **merman**. They are generally represented as malicious to man. Such aquatic mammals as dugongs may account for mermaid stories in mythology and folklore.

Merneptah King of Egypt (c. 1236–1223 BC) of the 19th dynasty. His father *Ramses II had neglected frontier defense in his old age and Merneptah faced the aggression of Libya and the Sea Peoples, against whom he scored a victory in 1232.

Meroë The capital of an ancient Nubian kingdom in the area that is now the Sudan. After ruling Egypt (c. 730–670 BC), Nubian kings established Meroë in about 600 BC. Its temples and pyramids show Egyptian influence. Before its abandonment (7th century AD), Meroë may have been the route by which iron technology reached sub-Saharan Africa.

Merovingians The first Frankish ruling dynasty (*see* Franks). It was founded by Merovech, King of the Salian Franks, in the mid-5th century AD. His grandson *Clovis (reigned 481–511) greatly extended Merovingian possessions and the kingdom reached its zenith in the mid-6th century. The last Merovingian king, Childeric III, was deposed in 751 by the *Carolingian Pepin the Short.

Merrill, Robert (1919–) US singer. A baritone, he first sang at the Metropolitan Opera House (1945) in *La Traviata*. With the Met since then, he is known for his roles in such operas as *Carmen*, *Otello*, *A Masked Ball*, and *La Forza del Destino*. He wrote *Once More from the Beginning* (1965) and *Between Acts* (1977).

Merseburg 51 22N 12 0E A city in S East Germany, on the Saale River just S of Halle. Founded in 800 AD, there is a 15th-century castle and a 13th-century cathedral. Industries include tanning, brewing, engineering, lignite mining, and the manufacture of machinery and paper. Population (1973 est): 54,930.

Mersey River A river in NW England. Formed by the confluence of the Goyt and Tame Rivers at Stockport, it flows W to enter the Irish Sea by way of a 16 mi (26 km) long estuary, with the ocean ports of *Liverpool and Birkenhead on its banks. Length: 70 mi (113 km).

Mersin 36 47N 34 37E A port in central S Turkey, the major port on the S coast. It has an oil refinery and exports wool, cotton, and agricultural produce. Population (1980): 216,308.

Merthyr Tydfil (Welsh name: Merthyr Tudful) 51 46N 3 23W A city in South Wales, in Mid Glamorgan on the Taff River. Formerly a world iron and steel center based on the surrounding coalfields, the main industries are now light and electrical engineering. Population (1981): 53,843.

Meru, Mount In Hindu mythology, the cosmic mountain at the center of the universe. It is symbolized in the massive pyramidal towers of Hindu shrines.

Merv. *See* Melitopol.

mesa An isolated flat-topped hill occurring in areas of long-continued erosion of horizontally bedded strata, usually in semiarid climates. The upper slopes are steep, and gentle lower slopes merge into the surrounding plain. The cap rock is of resistant material. Further erosion may reduce the mesa to a *butte.

Mesa Verde A high plateau, in SW Colorado. It contains the remains of numerous cliff dwellings, spanning four archeological periods.

mescaline A hallucinogenic drug obtained from the *peyote cactus of Mexico, where it was once widely used in religious ceremonies. The effect of mescaline varies from individual to individual; it does not cause serious dependence and the hallucinations are mostly visual.

Mesembryanthemum. *See* fig marigold.

Meshed. *See* Mashhad.

Mesmer, Franz Anton (1734–1815) German physician, who claimed to cure diseases by correcting the flow of "animal magnetism" in his patients' bodies during séance-like group sessions. Investigation of "mesmerism" by a commission of his contemporaries concluded that any cures were due to the powers of suggestion. Mesmer's claims stimulated serious study of hypnosis by such men as James *Braid.

Mesoamerican languages A geographical classification of the languages spoken by the American Indian peoples of Mexico, Guatemala, Honduras, Belize, El Salvador, and Nicaragua. It includes around 70 languages belonging to a number of families. The main families are: the Totonac-Mayan (e.g. Mayan); Uto-Aztecan (e.g. *Nahuatl) the Otomangean (e.g. Mixtec); the Hokan-Coahuiltecan; and Tarascan.

Mesolithic The middle division of the *Stone Age, especially in N Europe, where a distinct cultural stage, the *Maglemosian, intervened between the last ice age and the evolution of farming communities. Generally, the Mesolithic is characterized by production of microliths (very minute stone tools), which were hafted into wooden, bone, or other handles. The dog was the only domesticated animal. Outside Europe the Mesolithic distinction is less useful: for example, the Middle Eastern transition between *Paleolithic and *Neolithic was more rapid and less definable and in Japan pottery, a Neolithic characteristic, coexisted with microlith manufacture.

mesons A group of unstable elementary particles (lifetimes between 10^{-8} and 10^{-15} second) that are classified as hadrons; each meson is believed to consist of a quark-antiquark pair (*see* particle physics). The muon was originally called the mu-meson as it was thought to be a meson but is now classified as a lepton.

Mesopotamia The region between the Tigris and Euphrates Rivers, "the land between two rivers." The Sumerians (*see* Sumer) settled in S Mesopotamia about 4000 BC to cultivate the alluvial land left by flooding. They established the world's first civilization and founded city states, such as *Ur, *Kish, and *Uruk. *Babylon became Mesopotamia's capital under *Hammurabi, whose code of laws shows the development of civilized conduct and government. After his death Mesopotamia, overrun successively by Kassites, Assyrians, and Persians, was no longer the most advanced civilization, being overtaken by Egypt.

Mesosaurus A small slender freshwater reptile of the late Carboniferous and early Permian periods (around 280 million years ago). It was 40 in (1 m) long and had a long narrow skull with numerous teeth for straining crustaceans from water.

Mesozoic era The geological era following the Paleozoic and preceding the Cenozoic. It contains the Triassic, Jurassic, and Cretaceous periods, and lasted from about 240 to 65 million years ago. The reptiles were at their greatest development during this era but became extinct before the end of it. The Alpine orogeny began at the end of the Mesozoic.

mesquite A spiny shrub or small tree, of the genus *Prosopis*, with deep penetrating roots, native to the SW US and Mexico. Up to 49 ft (15 m) tall, it has compound leaves, with many narrow leaflets, and creamy flower catkins producing long narrow pods, which are used as cattlefeed. The hard wood is sometimes used in furniture. Family: *Leguminosae.

Messager, André (Charles Prosper) (1853–1929) French composer and conductor. His compositions include the operetta *Véronique* (1898) and the ballet *Les Deux Pigeons* (1886). He directed the first performance of Debussy's *Pelléas et Mélisande* in 1902.

Messalina, Valeria (c. 26–48 AD) The third wife of Emperor Claudius and mother of Britannicus (41–55) and Octavia (the wife of Nero). Messalina was notorious for her promiscuity and, according to Roman scandal, contracted a bigamous and treacherous marriage to the senator Gaius Silius, for which they were both executed.

Messerschmitt, Willy (1898–1978) German □ aircraft designer. He is best known for his World War II military planes, particularly the Me-109 fighter (1935) and the Me-262, the first jet fighter. In 1927 he was appointed chief designer at the Bayerische Flugzeugwerke, which was later renamed Messerschmitt-Aktien-Gesellschaft.

Messiaen, Olivier (1908–) French composer, organist, and teacher. Messiaen was a pupil of Paul Dukas and Marcel Dupré. In 1931 he was appointed organist of La Trinité in Paris. His music has been heavily influenced by Catholic mysticism and the rhythms of eastern music; he has also made use of bird song in his later compositions. His works include *La Nativité du Seigneur* (for organ; 1935), the symphony *Turangalîla* (1948), the *Quatuor pour la fin du temps* (for violin, cello, clarinet, and piano; 1941), and *La Transfiguration* (for chorus and orchestra; 1965–69).

Messier, Charles (1730–1817) French astronomer. In 1760 he began making a list of what he thought were nebulae. The result was the **Messier catalogue**, which listed 109 bright nonstellar celestial objects and was published in 1784–86. The objects were given a number preceded by the letter M, as in M31—the Andromeda galaxy. They are mainly galaxies and star clusters together with some nebulae.

Messina 38 13N 15 33E A port in Italy, in NE Sicily on the Strait of Messina. Originally known as Zancle, after the sickle shape of its harbor, it was successively occupied by Greeks, Carthaginians, Mamertines, Romans, Saracens, Normans, and Spaniards. In 1860 it became the last city in Sicily to be made part of a united Italy. Most of its old buildings were destroyed by severe earthquakes in 1783 and 1903. It has a university (1549) and its manufactures include macaroni, chemicals, and soap. Population (1980): 273,810.

Messina, Strait of A channel in the central Mediterranean Sea, between Italy and Sicily and narrowing to 2 mi (3 km). The rocks on the Italian side and the whirlpool on the Sicilian are possibly the origin of the myth of *Scylla and Charybdis.

Meštrović, Ivan (1883–1962) Yugoslav-born US sculptor. Trained at the Vienna Academy, Meštrović enjoyed an international reputation with his religious and portrait sculptures. His sitters included Herbert Hoover, Pope Pius XI, and Sir Thomas Beecham. Moving to the US (1947), he became a citizen in 1954.

metabolism The sum of the processes and chemical reactions that occur in living organisms in order to maintain life. It can be divided into two components. **Anabolism** involves building up the tissues and organs of the body using simple substances, such as amino acids, simple sugars, etc., to construct the proteins, carbohydrates, and fats of which they are made. These processes require energy, which is provided by the oxidation of nutrients or the body's own food reserves. Oxidation and all other processes involving the chemical breakdown of substances with the production of waste products are known collectively as **catabolism**. Basal metabolism is the energy required to maintain vital functions (e.g. respiration, circulation) with the body at rest. It is measured by estimating the amount of heat produced by the body and is controlled by hormones from the thyroid gland.

metal An element that is usually a hard crystalline solid, opaque, malleable, a good conductor of heat and electricity, and forms a salt and hydrogen when reacted with an acid and a salt and water when reacted with an alkali. Not all metals have all these properties, however: mercury is a liquid at normal temperatures, sodium is soft, and antimony is brittle. Of the 70 odd metals known, the most important are the heavy metals (iron, copper, lead, and zinc) used in engineering and the rarer heavy metals (nickel, chromium, tungsten, etc.) used in *alloys. Other commercially important metals are the *noble metals (gold, silver, platinum, and mercury) and the light metals (aluminum and magnesium). Chemically important metals include the *alkali metals (sodium, potassium, and lithium), the *alkaline-earth metals (calcium, barium, etc.), and the rare-earth metals (*see* lanthanides). Uranium is an important metal in the nuclear power industry (*see* nuclear energy).

Most metals occur in the earth's crust in the combined state and have to be mined (*see* mining and quarrying) before being extracted from their ores (*see* metallurgy). The extracted metal is then usually formed into an alloy (*see also* steel) before being ready for use.

metal fatigue The deterioration of metal caused by repeated stresses. Fatigue, which eventually leads to failure, occurs in vibrating parts of machinery, but only when the stresses are above a critical value, known as the endurance limit. It is an important consideration in the design of aircraft, where high engine speeds and high stresses are unavoidable.

metallography The study of the crystalline structure of metals. It includes various techniques and is used to test the quality of steel after *heat treatment. Usually a small sample is taken from a batch and polished before being examined under a microscope for cracks, impurities, or holes. The polished surface may also be treated chemically to show up the different constituents of an alloy or to highlight cracks. In 1911 Max von *Laue used X-rays to show that the atoms in metals are arranged in a regular geometrical fashion, i.e. they are crystalline. His technique of *X-ray diffraction is still used to examine metallic crystals.

metalloids Elements displaying the physical and chemical properties both of *metals and nonmetals. Examples of metalloids are arsenic and germanium, which both have metallic and nonmetallic allotropes. Chemically, their behavior is intermediate between metals and nonmetals in that they may form positive ions as well as covalently bonded compounds. The metalloid elements are often *semiconductors.

metallurgy The science and technology of producing metals. It includes the extraction of metals from their ores, alloying to form materials with specific properties, and *heat treatment to improve their properties. The art of working metals was known as early as 3500 BC, when copper, lead, tin, gold, and silver were in use in various parts of the world. Modern metallurgy is concerned with all metals, but primarily with those, such as iron, that are abundant and useful (*see* steel). Metallurgy originally developed by finding new *alloys and treatments by trial and error. Techniques, such as *metallography, have reduced the element of chance by identifying the factors in the microscopic structure of metals that contribute to hardness, strength, and ductility.

metamorphic rock One of the three major rock categories (*compare* igneous rock; sedimentary rock) consisting of rocks produced by the alteration (in the solid state) of existing rocks by heat, pressure, and chemically active fluids. Contact (*or* thermal) metamorphism occurs around igneous intrusions and results from heat alone. Regional metamorphism, extending over large areas, results from the heat and pressure created by crustal deformation. Dislocation metamorphism results from localized mechanical deformation, as along fault planes. Metamorphic rocks tend to be resistant to denudation and often form upland masses. Marble is a metamorphic rock formed from recrystallized limestone.

metamorphosis The process in animals by which a *larva changes into an adult. This radical change of internal and external body structures may be gradual or abrupt. Certain insects, such as dragonflies, undergo incomplete metamorphosis, during which successive stages (known as nymphs) become increasingly like the adult through a series of molts. In complete metamorphosis, seen in such insects as butterflies and houseflies, the larva passes into a quiescent pupal stage, during which the adult tissues are developed. Metamorphosis also occurs in amphibians (*see* frog). The process in insects and amphibians is controlled by hormones.

metaphor A figure of speech in which one thing is described in terms of another. The comparison is implicit, lacking such words as *like* or *as* (*see* simile). The metaphor is a common feature of ordinary language, as in such phrases as "time flies" and "to lose one's head," and is a fundamental poetic device. This example is from Shakespeare's *Macbeth* (act 5, scene 3):

Life's but a walking shadow, a poor player

That struts and frets his hour upon the stage.

metaphysical painting A style of painting practiced by Carlo Carrà (1881–1966) and Giorgio de *Chirico in the second decade of the 20th century. Together they established a school in Ferrara in 1917. They illustrated the mystery behind everyday reality by depicting dreamlike illusions, characterized by hallucinatory lighting with stark shadows, incongruous juxtapositions of objects, sharply plunging perspectives of empty streets, and the use of mannequins rather than people. *Surrealism adopted many of their ideas and devices.

metaphysical poets A group of 17th-century English poets whose work was characterized by intellectual wit and ingenuity, especially in their use of elaborate figures of speech. The leading poet was John *Donne, and his successors included George *Herbert, Henry Vaughan, Andrew *Marvell, and Abraham Cowley. They frequently employed colloquial speech rhythms in both their secular and their religious verse. The influential criticism of T. S. Eliot, who praised their union of intellect and emotion, helped to establish their high reputation in the 20th century.

metaphysics The study of existence or being in general. The term derives from the title given to a group of Aristotle's writings by the philosopher Andronicus of Rhodes (1st century BC). The status of metaphysics has been much debated; *Kant thought this kind of investigation impossible because our minds can only cope with the phenomenal world or the world of appearances and *Ayer used the word in *Language, Truth and Logic* (1936) as a pejorative term to indicate the meaninglessness of much traditional philosophy. However, with *ethics and *epistemology, metaphysics is still held to be one of the main divisions of philosophy.

Metastasio, Pietro (Pietro Antonio Domenico Trapassi; 1698–1782) Italian poet and librettist. In 1730 he was appointed court poet in Vienna, where he wrote numerous classical libretti. These include *L'Adriano* (1731) and *La clemenza di Tito* (1732), which has been set to music by many composers.

Metaxas, Ioannis (1871–1941) Greek general; dictator (1936–41). After the monarchy was re-established in 1935, he became premier and then, with George II's support, dictator. He led Greek resistance to the Italian invasion in World War II.

metayage A type of land tenure in which rent is paid in kind. Metayage, a French word (from Latin *medietas*, half), was at one time the dominant form of tenure in S France, involving payment of approximately half the tenant's output to the landowner.

Metazoa A subkingdom of animals whose bodies consist of many cells differentiated and coordinated to perform specialized functions. The Metazoa includes all animals except the single-celled *Protozoa and the Parazoa (*see* sponge).

Metchnikov, Ilya Ilich (*or* I. I. Mechnikov; 1845–1916) Russian zoologist, who discovered that certain cells in animals could surround and engulf foreign particles, such as disease-causing bacteria. He called these cells *phagocytes and was awarded, with Paul *Ehrlich, the 1908 Nobel Prize.

metempsychosis. *See* reincarnation.

meteor A streak of light seen in the night sky when a **meteoroid**—an interplanetary rock or dust particle, usually with a mass from 10^{-7} to 10^{-3} gram but sometimes weighing over 22 lb (10 kg)—enters and burns up in the earth's atmosphere. A decaying *comet gradually produces a **meteor stream** of meteoroids around its orbit. When the earth passes through a meteor stream, an often spectacular **meteor shower** is observed, usually at the same time each year. The August Perseids and December Geminids are examples. A **meteorite** is a large piece of interplanetary debris that falls to the earth's surface, usually breaking up in the process. It produces a brilliant meteor. Meteorite composition is either principally iron or stone, or an intermediate mixture. Meteorites were formed early in the history of the solar system and most are believed to be fragments of minor planets. The rare fragile stony carbonaceous chondrites are possibly cometary fragments.

weather conditions

- rain
- drizzle
- ∇ showers
- ✳ snow
- ▲ hail
- △ ice pellets
- ◠ dew
- ≡ fog
- ⏄ thunderstorm

cloud cover

- ○ clear
- ◔ 1 okta
- ◔ 2
- ◑ 3
- ◑ 4
- ◕ 5
- ◕ 6
- ◕ 7
- ● 8
- ⊗ sky obscured (1 okta = ⅛ of the sky)

wind *The arrow points in the direction from which the wind is blowing.*

knots

- ⊙ calm
- 1–2
- 3–7
- 8–12
- 13–17
- 18–22
- 23–27
- 28–32
- 33–37
- 38–42
- 43–47
- 48–52

weather map *The numbers at the stations show temperature (0°C). Isobars show atmospheric pressure in millibars.*

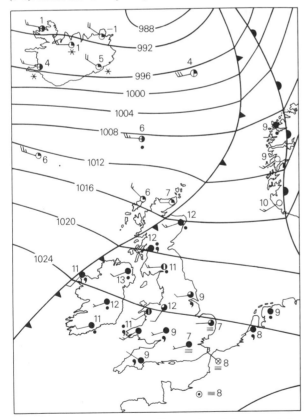

fronts

cold front *boundary between overtaking cold air mass and warm air mass.*

warm front *boundary between overtaking warm air mass and cold air mass.*

stationary *boundary between air masses of similar temperature.*

occluded *line where a cold front overtakes a warm front.*

METEOROLOGY *Internationally agreed symbols are used throughout the world by meteorological stations to represent current weather conditions. These are plotted on weather maps from which forecasts can be made.*

meteorology The study of the physics, chemistry, and movements of the *atmosphere and its interactions with the ground surface. The troposphere and stratosphere, the lower layers of the atmosphere in which most weather phenomena occur, are the chief focuses of meteorology and much attention has been paid to the explanation of surface weather and to weather forecasting. **Weather** is the state of atmospheric conditions (including temperature, sunshine, wind, clouds, and precipitation) at a particular place and time. A **weather forecast** is a prediction of what weather conditions will be over a stated future period; it is made by studying weather maps, especially those obtained from satellites (often feeding the observations into a computer). Short-term forecasts are made usually for a period of 24 hours (less for specialized uses) and long-range forecasts may be made for a month ahead although they are considerably less accurate. Weather forecasts are essential to shipping and aviation and are of use to many other bodies, including power authorities (predicting cold spells) and transport authorities (predicting snow, ice, and fog), as well as to farmers. Attempts have been made to modify weather, including cloud seeding, hurricane steering, and fog clearance, but success has been limited. *See also* climate.

meter (m) The unit of length of the metric system. Originally defined in 1791 as one ten-millionth of the length of the quadrant of the earth's meridian through Paris, it was redefined in 1927 as the distance between two marks on a platinum-iridium bar kept at the International Bureau of Weights and Measures near Paris. It is now defined (General Conference on Weights and Measures, 1983) as the length of the path traveled by light in a vacuum in 1/299,792,458 second, which replaced the 1960 definition based on the wavelength of the emission of a krypton lamp.

meter (poetry) The rhythmic pattern of a line of verse measured in terms of basic metrical units or feet. In accentual verse, as in English, a foot consists of various arrangements of stressed (′) and unstressed (˘) syllables. In classical Greek and Latin verse, the quantity or length rather than the stress of syllables determines the foot. In English the most common feet are the *iamb (˘′), the trochee (′˘), the anapaest (˘˘′), the dactyl (′˘˘), and the spondee (′ ′). A typical line of *blank verse consisting of five iambs is known as an iambic pentameter. Most traditional poetic forms, such as the *sonnet, are written according to strict metrical patterns. Many poets of the late 19th and 20th centuries have written in free verse, which has no regular meter or line length, or syllabic verse, in which each line has a fixed number of syllables but no regular pattern of stress.

methane (CH_4) A colorless odorless flammable gas that is the main constituent of *natural gas. It is the simplest member of the *alkane series and is used as a fuel and a source of other chemicals. Methane is produced in nature by the decay of vegetable matter under water, rising in bubbles from marshes as **marsh gas**. Coal gas also contains methane and is found in coalmines. Recently the generation of methane from sewage has been investigated as an *alternative energy source. It burns with a clear blue flame.

methanol (methyl alcohol *or* wood alcohol; CH_3OH) A colorless poisonous flammable liquid. Originally produced by distillation of wood, it is now usually made from hydrogen and carbon monoxide by high-pressure *catalysis. It is used as a solvent, antifreeze, and a raw material for making other chemicals. *See also* methylated spirits.

Methodism The Christian denomination that developed out of the religious practices advocated by John Wesley and his brother Charles. Although not conceived initially as an institution separate from the Church of England, to which it is very close in doctrinal matters, Methodism evolved its own church organization during the 1790s. The supreme decision-making body is the Conference; local societies (congregations) are highly organized and pastoral and missionary work are major concerns. Methodism in the US dates from the 1780s. It is the second largest US Protestant denomination (after the Baptists).

Methodius, St. *See* Cyril, St.

methyl alcohol. *See* methanol.

methylated spirits A form of *ethanol (ethyl alcohol) that has been made unsuitable for drinking (and is therefore duty free) by the addition of about 9.5% of methanol (methyl alcohol), about 0.5% of pyridine, and a methyl violet dye (as a warning that it is dangerous to drink). In this form it has many household uses, especially as a fuel for spirit burners. It is sometimes drunk by desperate alcoholics, in whom it can cause blindness and other serious medical conditions. Industrial methylated spirits (IMS) consists of ethanol with about 5% of methanol and no pyridine. It is used as a solvent for varnishes, etc.

metric system A system of measurement based on the decimal system. First suggested in 1585 by Simon Stevin (1548–1620), an inspector of dikes in the Low Countries, it was not given formal acceptance until 1795, when a French law provided definitions for the *meter, *are, *stere, *liter, and gram. In 1799 a subsequent law established legal standards, made of platinum, for the meter and the kilogram. However, this form of the metric system was not widely used, even in France, until the third decade of the 19th century; during this period it was also adopted by most European countries. The metric system is not widely used in the US and Great Britain, except by the scientific community.

For scientific purposes, former metric systems (such as the *c.g.s. system and the *m.k.s. system) have been replaced by *SI units, a coherent system of metric units.

metrology The science of measurement. The scientific method is based on making accurate measurements, i.e. of expressing the magnitude of a physical quantity (say, length) in terms of a number and a unit (say, meters). Metrologists study methods of making these accurate measurements and of deciding what units should be used and how they should be defined. Modern metrology is based on *SI units and the methods of defining the system's seven basic units. The decision to adopt this system was taken in 1960 by metrologists from 30 nations meeting at the Conférence Générale des Poids et Mesures.

metronome A small device consisting of a pendulum with a small sliding weight on it, which can be regulated to make the pendulum beat at a desired number of beats per minute. The most common type is the clockwork metronome invented by J. N. Maelzel (1770–1838); electric metronomes also exist. Metronome markings are often given in musical scores to indicate the exact speed of the music.

Metropolitan Museum of Art The largest art museum in the US and one of the most important in the world. Founded in 1870, it was opened in its present premises in New York City's Central Park in 1880. Its enormous collection comprises paintings, drawings, sculptures, ceramics, furniture, etc., from many periods and countries, including China, ancient Egypt, Greece, and Rome as well as an extensive American collection. Since 1938 its collection of medieval art has been housed in the Cloisters, built in Fort Tryon Park, Manhattan, from fragments of medieval monasteries and churches.

Metropolitan Opera Association The principal US opera company, founded in New York City in 1883. *Caruso sang regularly with the company from 1904 to 1921. The general manager from 1950 to 1972 was Sir Rudolph *Bing. The company occupied the Metropolitan Opera House until 1966, when it moved into the Lincoln Center for the Performing Arts, the original building being demolished.

Metsu, Gabriel (1629–67) Dutch painter, who was born in Leyden but lived in Amsterdam from about 1650. His early subjects were often religious but he is better known for his interiors showing middle-class life in such paintings as *The Duet* (National Gallery, London).

Metternich, Klemens Wenzel Nepomuk Lothar, Fürst von (1773–1859) Austrian statesman, the leading figure in European diplomacy from the fall of Napoleon (1815) until the Revolutions of 1848. As foreign minister (1809–48) he sought to maintain the balance of power in Europe, supporting dynastic monarchies and suppressing liberalism. His policies dominated the great Congresses of *Vienna (1814–15), *Aix-la-Chapelle (1818), Troppau (1820), Laibach (1821), and Verona (1822). The Revolution of 1848 forced him to seek refuge in Britain, the constitutional monarchy that he had always condemned.

Metz (Latin name: Divodorum) 49 07N 6 11E A city in NE France, the capital of the Moselle department on the Moselle River. The center of the Lorraine coal and metal industries, it trades in wine and agricultural products and has varied manufacturing industries. It has a fine cathedral (13th–16th centuries) and a university (1971). *History*: part of the Holy Roman Empire until seized by France (1552), it fell to Germany (1871) but returned to France after World War I. Population (1975): 117,199.

Meuse River (Dutch and Flemish name: Maas) A river in W Europe. Rising in NE France and flowing mainly N past Liège in Belgium and Maastricht in the S Netherlands, it enters the North Sea at the Rhine Delta. It was the scene of heavy fighting in World War I (1914) and World War II (1940). Its lower course is an important commercial waterway. Length: 575 mi (926 km).

Mewar. *See* Udaipur.

Mexicali 32 36N 115 30W A city in the extreme NW of Mexico, on the US border. It is the commercial center for a rich irrigated agricultural area. Population (1978 est): 338,423.

Mexican Border Campaign (1916–17) US expedition into Mexico to quell attacks on New Mexico and Texas by Mexican revolutionary Pancho *Villa. Led by General John J. *Pershing, US cavalry chased Villa 300–400 mi (480–640 km) into Mexico, but never captured him.

Mexican War (1846–48) A territorial conflict between Mexico and the US arising from a dispute over the southern border of Texas. Hostilities began when Mexican forces crossed the Rio Grande to attack a detachment of the US Army commanded by General Zachary *Taylor. Taylor repulsed the attackers and pursued them into Mexico, winning a crucial victory at *Buena Vista. At the same time, General Stephen *Kearny was ordered to capture the territories of New Mexico and California. The end of the war came with an invasion of Mexico commanded by General Winfield *Scott, during which American forces captured Mexico City. By the Treaty of

Guadalupe Hidalgo, the Mexicans ceded the disputed territory in Texas as well as New Mexico and California for a payment of $15 million by the US government. The border between the US and Mexico was finalized with the *Gadsden Purchase in 1853.

Mexico, United States of A country in Central America between the Gulf of Mexico and the Pacific Ocean. Narrow coastal plains rise to high mountain ranges in the interior, which include the volcano Popocatépetl. Much of the N is arid with tropical forest in the S, especially in the Yucatán Peninsula in the SE (the only extensive low-lying area). Most of the population is of mixed Indian and Spanish descent. *Economy*: Mexico now ranks among the world's main oil-producing countries following substantial finds in several areas, the most recent being along the E coastline of the states of Tamaulipas and Veracruz. Some 80% of exported oil went to the US in 1978. Mexico also has large reserves of natural gas and there are substantial deposits of uranium, although in 1979 only one nuclear-power plant was under construction. Other minerals extracted include iron ore, zinc, sulfur, silver, and copper, and Mexico is the world's largest producer of fluorite and graphite. Agriculture remains relatively underdeveloped and during the mid 1970s a program to collectivize smallholdings was launched in an effort to increase food production. Corn is the main food crop; cash crops include cotton, sugar, coffee, and fruit and vegetables, as well as sisal in Yucatán. Fishing has been developed considerably in recent years and important catches include sardines, shrimps, and oysters. Tourism is an important source of foreign currency. *History*: Mexico was the site of the Mayan civilization from the 2nd to the 13th centuries AD, and between the 8th and the 12th centuries the *Toltecs flourished. The 14th century saw the rise of the *Aztecs, whose capital was at Tenochtitlán, the site of present-day Mexico City. The Aztecs were conquered by the Spanish under Cortés in 1521 and Mexico became part of the viceroyalty of New Spain. The struggle for independence from Spain began in 1810 and was achieved in 1821. A turbulent period dominated by *Santa Anna was followed by the *Mexican War (1846–48), in which territory was lost to the US. In 1864 *Maximilian, Archduke of Austria, was installed as emperor by the French, but in 1867 he was shot in the successful anti-French revolution led by Benito Juárez. In 1911 the long dictatorship of Porfirio Díaz ended in an uprising under Francisco Madera. The Mexican Revolution culminated in the constitution of 1917, the democratic goals of which have been the declared aims of subsequent governments. Mexico is now a one-party state dominated by the Party of Institutionalized Revolution (PRI), serious demonstrations against which have occurred. Mexico faced perhaps the worst crisis in its history in the 1980s with drastic economic ills brought on by a reduction of exports and a flight of capital from Mexican to US banks. Corruption in previous governments contributed to the dangerous conditions as did the recession of 1980–82. Higher prices of US exports, a reduction of Mexican imports by the US, and increased interest rates on its debts forced further borrowing. By the end of 1982 the inflation rate had soared to over 100%. Mexico responded by devaluing the peso three times in 1982, nationalizing private banks, and imposing severe austerity measures. By the end of 1983 the government held more than 80% of the country's economic resources. The importance of a healthy Mexican economy to global economic stability (Mexico is the third largest trading partner of the US) induced a rescheduling of debts by the International Monetary Fund and further loans by foreign nations. Mexico is a member of the OAS. President: Miguel de la Madrid Hurtado. Official language: Spanish; Indian languages, especially Nahuatl, are widely spoken. Official currency: Mexican peso of 100 centavos. Area: 761,530 sq mi (1,967,183 sq km). Population (1982 est): 75,702,000. Capital: Mexico City. Main port: Veracruz.

Mexico, Gulf of An arm of the Atlantic Ocean that is bounded by the S United States and E Mexico. Its outlets are via the Straits of Florida and the Yucatan Channel-Caribbean Sea to the Atlantic Ocean. Waters warmed in the gulf flow through the Straits of Florida to create the warming Gulf Stream. Large rivers, including the Mississippi in the United States and the Rio Grande that forms the US–Mexican border, flow into the gulf. The average depth is about 4700 ft (1433 m), with a maximum depth of 17,070 ft (5200 m). It yields major quantities of oil, natural gas, and fish and has substantial tourist industries along its coast. Area: 596,000 sq mi (5200 m).

Mexico City (Spanish name: Ciudad de México) 19 25N 99 10W The capital of Mexico, in the S of the high central plateau at a height of 7800 ft (2380 m), surrounded by mountains. The 14th-century Aztec city of Tenochtitlán (built on a lake, since filled in) had a population of almost half a million when it was destroyed by Cortés in 1521. A new Spanish city was built on the site and it rapidly became the most important in the New World. It was captured by the US and then by France in the 19th century and in the 20th century was the center of several revolutions. It has seen rapid growth in recent years and now has considerable industry. A cultural

center, it is the site of the National Autonomous University of Mexico (founded in 1551), the national library, a famous school of mining engineering, the museum (containing the Aztec Calendar Stone), and the Palace of Fine Arts Theater (a notable example of the city's modern architecture). Other famous landmarks include the fine cathedral (16th–19th centuries) and the 17th-century Palacio National. Population (1978 est): 8,988,230.

Meyerbeer, Giacomo (Jacob Liebmann Beer; 1791–1864) German composer and pianist. A child prodigy, he studied the piano with Clementi and composition with Abbé Vogler (1749–1814). His early German operas failed while those in the more superficial Italian style were more successful. It was in Paris that he composed the spectacular works by which he is remembered: *Robert le Diable* (1831), *Les Huguenots* (1836), and *L'Africaine* (performed posthumously; 1865).

Meyerhof, Otto Fritz (1884–1951) US biochemist, born in Germany, who showed that glycogen in muscles is broken down anaerobically into lactic acid when the muscle is working. He shared the 1922 Nobel Prize with Archibald *Hill for this discovery.

Meyerhold, Vsevolod Emilievich (1874–?1943) Russian theater director. He joined the Moscow Art Theater in 1898, but eventually rejected the naturalism of *Stanislavsky and experimented with a symbolic and abstract drama in which the actor's individual role was reduced to a minimum. He supported the Revolution and joined the Bolshevik Party in 1918. In the 1920s he was the first director to specialize in producing Soviet plays, but fell out of favor with the government in the 1930s. He died probably in a Soviet labor camp.

Mezzogiorno (Italian: midday) Southern Italy; the name refers to the heat of the region, which is economically, socially, and politically backward. After the unification of Italy in the 19th century the development of the N received greater attention from the central government than the S, where local government was ineffectual, the *Mafia flourished, and the gulf between landowners and peasants was considerable. Despite special government aid during the 20th century, the problems are still largely unsolved.

mezzo-soprano. *See* soprano.

mezzotint A technique of printing tonal areas (as opposed to lines), invented by a German officer, Ludwig von Sieger (1609–?1680). It was thus particularly suitable for reproducing paintings, being popular in 18th- and 19th-century England for printing Reynolds' portraits, Constable's landscapes, etc. The technique involves roughening and indenting a copper or steel plate with a serrated edged tool (rocker). Some of the roughened parts are then scraped away before the plate's surface is coated with ink. The indentations create the dark tones of the print, while the polished parts produce the lighter accents. Mezzotint is often combined with *etching and line engraving.

Mfecane (1818–28) A period of wars and upheaval among Bantu peoples of southern Africa. The Zulu, under their warrior king *Shaka, turned on neighboring tribes, causing them to abandon their cattle and grain stores and to flee into the territory of other tribes. This movement of peoples radically altered tribal groupings and led to the formation of new groupings, such as the Swazi, Basuto, Kololo, and Ndebele.

Miami 25 45N 80 15W A city and port in □Florida, on Biscayne Bay. A major tourist resort and retirement center, it grew during the Florida land boom of the 1920s and includes Coral Gables (site of the University of Miami, established in 1925) and Miami Beach. It is famous for its citrus fruit and winter vegetables. Industries include aircraft repairing, clothing, and concrete. Population (1980): 346,931.

Miami Beach 25 47N 80 08W A resort city in SE Florida, on islands across Biscayne Bay from Miami. Causeways connect it to the mainland. It was created in the early 1900s from sandy swampy land. It is a major US tourist center in the winter. Population (1980): 96,298.

Miami River, or Great Miami River A river that flows from W central Ohio SW to join the Ohio River at the Indiana border W of Cincinnati. Length: 160 mi (258 km).

Micah (8th century BC) An Old Testament prophet of Judah and contemporary of Isaiah. **The Book of Micah** records his condemnation of a number of specific sins in the corrupt nation and predicts the fall of Jerusalem, the renewal of the people, and the coming of a Messiah.

micas A group of common rock-forming silicate minerals that have a layered structure and complex composition. Muscovite, $K_2Al_4(Si_6Al_2)O_{20}(OH,F)_4$, is a white mica and economically the most important; it occurs in granitic rocks (often pegmatites), gneisses, and schists. The other principal micas are *phlogopite (amber), biotite (dark), paragonite, margarite, zinnwaldite, and lepidolite (a source of lithium). Their perfect cleavage is reflected in the layered structure. In its commercial form it is sold in blocks (sheets), books (flakes resembling the pages of a book), and splittings (loose flakes). Since it is a good insulator and can withstand high temperatures, mica has many electrical uses and is used for furnace windows. Splittings bonded together with shellac or synthetic resins are used to make Micanite.

Michael (1596–1645) Tsar of Russia (1613–45) and founder of the *Romanov dynasty. Michael's election as tsar ended the *Time of Troubles. Michael was a weak ruler, relying upon his father Patriarch Philaret (c. 1553–1633). Serfdom was intensified during his reign.

Michael (1921–) King of Romania (1927–30, 1940–47). Michael succeeded his grandfather in 1927 but lost the crown in 1930, when his father *Carol II returned from exile. After Carol's abdication in 1940, Michael again became king. In 1944 he overthrew the dictatorship of Ion Antonescu and declared war on Germany. He abdicated in 1947.

Michael. *See* archangels.

Michael VIII Palaeologus (1224–82 AD) Byzantine emperor (1259–82), who founded the Palaeologan (the last Byzantine) dynasty (1259–1453). In 1261 Michael captured Constantinople from the Latins and re-established the Byzantine empire there after its 57-year exile. His subsequent policies were determined by the fear of another attack from the West. An alliance with the papacy against Charles I of Naples and Sicily led to the union (1274) of the Greek and Roman Churches, for which he was vilified after his death.

Michaelmas daisy. *See* Aster.

Michelangelo Buonarroti (1475–1564) Italian sculptor, painter, architect, and poet, born at Caprese, in Tuscany. Michelangelo was trained in Florence under the painter *Ghirlandaio and in the school in the Medici gardens, under the patronage of Lorenzo de' Medici. Working in Rome from 1496 until 1501, he produced his first major sculptures, notably the *Pietà* (St Peter's, Rome). This was followed (1501–05) by his work in Florence, including *David* (Accademia, Florence), the painting of the *Holy Family* (Uffizi), and the influential cartoon of the *Battle of Cascina*. The last was commissioned as a fresco for the Palazzo Vecchio but was never finished and was painted over by Vasari. Michelangelo's productive but stormy association with Pope Julius II began in 1505, when the pope commissioned Michelangelo to produce his tomb. Although this proved to be his most checkered and lengthy project, it resulted in such masterpieces as the *Slaves* (Accademia, Florence). The celebrated Sistine Chapel ceiling (1508–12), in the Vatican, established his reputation as the greatest painter of his day. Returning to Florence (1516), Michelangelo became the architect and sculptor of the Medici funerary chapel (1520–34) in S Lorenzo and he also designed the Laurentian Library. These architectural projects and the fresco of the *Last Judgment* (1534–41) for the Sistine Chapel were his first major works in the new mannerist style (*see* mannerism). In his last years he worked mainly as an architect, becoming in 1547 chief architect of St Peter's, Rome, in which capacity he designed its great dome. His last sculptures included the *Rondanini Pietà* (Milan, Castello).

Michelet, Jules (1798–1874) French historian. He established his academic reputation while still young and was appointed Keeper of the National Archives in 1831. His *Histoire de France* (6 vols, 1833–43; 11 vols, 1855–67) and *La Révolution française* (7 vols, 1847–53) were unashamedly nationalist works, written with romantic imagination. During the Second Empire (1852–70) he retired from public life and wrote works on natural science.

Michelin, André (1853–1931) French tire manufacturer, who founded, with his brother **Édouard Michelin** (1859–1940), the Michelin Tire Company (1888). In 1895 they became the first to demonstrate the feasibility of using pneumatic tires on motor cars. The company is now also famous for its maps and guidebooks.

Michelozzo di Bartolommeo (1396–1472) Florentine *Renaissance sculptor and architect. As a sculptor he collaborated first with *Ghiberti and then with *Donatello, but after 1433 he turned to architecture. He designed several buildings for the Medici, including the Palazzo Medici (1444–59), which was the first Renaissance palace.

Michelson, Albert Abraham (1852–1931) US physicist, born in Germany. He designed a highly accurate interferometer known as the Michelson interferometer and used it to measure precisely the speed of light. He also used it in an attempt to measure the velocity of the earth through the ether. This work, carried out in conjunction with Edward *Morley and

known as the *Michelson-Morley experiment, eventually led *Einstein to his theory of relativity. Michelson received the Nobel Prize in 1907.

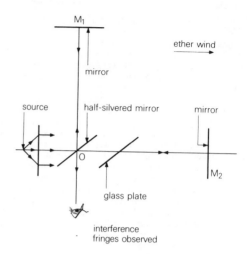

Michelson interferometer

MICHELSON-MORLEY EXPERIMENT *The Michelson interferometer was used in an attempt to detect changes in the velocity of light of the earth's motion through the ether. Distances OM_1 and OM_2 are equal. The glass plate compensates for the thickness of the half-silvered mirror.*

Michelson-Morley experiment An experiment performed by A. A. *Michelson and E. W. *Morley in 1881 in an attempt to demonstrate the existence of the luminiferous ether by measuring the earth's velocity relative to it. They used a Michelson interferometer to obtain interference fringes and then rotated the apparatus through 90° expecting to find a shift in the fringes, since the velocity of light would be different in the two directions. This difference would result from the earth's motion through the ether. However, no shift was detected. This negative result led to the downfall of the ether theory and was explained by Einstein's theory of *relativity in 1905 (*see also* Lorentz, Hendrick Antoon).

Michener, James A (lbert) (1907–) US author. After serving in the Navy, he wrote *Tales of the South Pacific* (Pulitzer Prize; 1947), short stories about his experiences during World War II. *The Bridges at Toko-Ri* (1953) and *Sayonara* (1954) had Oriental themes, while *The Bridge at Andau* (1957) told of the aftermath of the Hungarian Revolution. *Hawaii* (1959) began Michener's epics that covered thousands of years. He followed with *The Source* (1965), *Iberia* (1968), *Centennial* (1974), *Chesapeake* (1978), *The Covenant* (1980), *Space* (1982), and *Poland* (1983).

Michigan A state in the N central US, bordered largely by water (Lakes Superior, Huron, Michigan, Erie, and St Clair). It has land borders with Ohio and Indiana in the S, Wisconsin in the NW, and the Canadian province of Ontario in the E. Michigan is divided by the Straits of Mackinac into the Lower Peninsula (with Lake Michigan on the W and Lakes Huron and Erie on the E) and the Upper Peninsula (with Lake Michigan on the S and Lake Superior on the W). The Lower Peninsula consists of lowlands where most of the state's population and industry are concentrated. The sparsely populated Upper Peninsula, with lowlands in the E and uplands in the W, contains Isle Royale National Park. Michigan is highly industrialized, and its manufacturing sector contributes significantly to US revenues. Especially important is the production of motor vehicles at Detroit; other industries incude machinery, iron and steel, and chemicals. The state exploits its large mineral reserves of gypsum, calcium, and magnesium compounds, natural gas, and oil. Tourism is the state's second largest industry. It is also an important agricultural state, producing corn, beans, other vegetables, fruit, and livestock. *History*: first explored by the French in the 17th century. The region at the time of the arrival of the first whites was inhabited principally by Ojibwa, Ottawa, and Potawatomi Indians. It remained under French control until it was acquired by the British (1763) as part of Canada. Pontiac's Rebellion erupted in the same year, ending with the signing of a peace treaty with the Indians. Michigan came under US control in 1796, although Britain held the area during the War of 1812. The opening of the Erie Canal (1825) between Lake Erie and the Hudson River provided a link from the central states to the Atlantic Ocean, bringing new settlers to the area. The rise of the lumber industry after 1850 resulted in the destruction of huge stands of forest. The state's industrial base was established with the founding of the Ford Motor Company by Henry Ford, who adapted the assembly line to automobile manufacturing. Michigan's economy suffered with the decline in the US automobile industry in the 1970s and early 1980s but prospects for diversifying the economy brightened with the discovery of oil in Grant Traverse Bay in Lake Michigan. Area: 58,216 sq mi (150,779 sq km). Population (1980): 9,258,344. Capital: Lansing.

Michigan, Lake The third largest of the Great Lakes in North America, the only one wholly in the US. It is linked with Lake Huron via the Straits of Mackinac; the city of Chicago is on its S bank. Area: 22,400 sq mi (58,000 sq km).

Mickiewicz, Adam (1798–1855) Polish poet. His early poetry was strongly influenced by the Romantics, especially Byron. In 1823 he was arrested with other students of Vilna University and deported to Russia, where he became a friend of Pushkin. He left Russia in 1829 and settled in Paris in 1832. His works include the Romantic drama *Dziadzy* (1823–32) and the epic poem *Pan Tadeusz* (1832–34).

microbiology The study of microorganisms, or microbes—organisms that are invisible to the naked eye, including bacteria, small fungi (e.g. yeasts and molds), algae, protozoa, and viruses. Microorganisms, which are abundant everywhere, are of immense importance to all living things. They bring about *decomposition and the recycling of nutrients. They are vital to numerous industries, including brewing, baking, dairying, and food processing, and they have revolutionized medical treatment with the discovery of antibiotics. Some microorganisms, however, are parasites that cause disease in plants, animals, and man (*see* infection).

microcomputers Small sophisticated *computers designed for a single user and often for a specific application. The central processing unit, called a *microprocessor, is extremely small. Microcomputers were introduced in the 1970s for a wide range of industrial, commercial, and even domestic applications. They have had a considerable impact in speeding the process of automation.

microcopy A greatly reduced photographic copy of a printed page, drawing, or other image. **Microfilm** is a strip of standard-width film containing microcopies. It was introduced in the 1920s for use in banks and is now widely used for compact storage and ready reference to documents. Special enlarging viewers can rapidly wind the film to the correct page. **Microfiche** is a similar system on cards holding a single film negative, with even greater reduction of the pictures. The viewers often have a printer attached to reproduce paper copies. Microfiche is widely used in data-processing systems as an alternative to paper computer printout, and in libraries to store periodicals, etc.

micrometer An instrument for measuring small lengths with great accuracy. The object to be measured is held between the jaws of a C-shaped metal piece, one jaw of which can be adjusted by a screw. The screw is turned by rotating a drum with a *vernier scale marked on it, from which the required dimension can be read.

micron (μm) An obsolete name for one-millionth of a meter. The correct name is now the **micrometer** (*see* SI units).

Micronesia A division of Oceania in the W Pacific Ocean, consisting of an arc of islands E of the Philippines. It includes the Belau, Kiribati, Mariana, Caroline, and Marshall archipelagos. *See also* Melanesia; Polynesia.

Micronesia, Federated States of An island group within the UN Trust Territory of the *Pacific Islands, comprising Truk, Yap, Ponape, and Yosrae. Self-government was achieved in 1979. Population (1977 est): 69,360.

microphone A device that converts sound into electrical signals. It acts like a *loudspeaker in reverse and some microphones may also be used as loudspeakers. Most consist of a thin diaphragm, the mechanical vibration of which is converted to an electrical signal proportional to the sound pressure. A telephone mouthpiece usually consists of a carbon microphone in which the sound waves exert a varying pressure on carbon granules, so varying their electrical resistance. In capacitor microphones, the most commonly used type in music recording, the diaphragm forms one plate of a capacitor, across which the sound waves produce a fluctuating potential difference. Crystal microphones rely on the *piezoelectric effect. Other types use magnetic induction, and less commonly magnetostriction or other electromagnetic effects. Ribbon microphones have a highly directional response. They consist of a thin strip of aluminum alloy in a strong magnetic field. The ribbon vibrates in the sound waves, inducing in itself an electromotive force proportional to its velocity.

microprocessor The central processing unit of a *microcomputer. Its development was made possible in the 1970s by advances in solid-state electronics, in particular the design of integrated circuits of such complexity that all the main calculating functions can be carried out by a single silicon chip (*see* integrated circuit).

microscope An optical instrument used for producing a magnified image of a small object. There are several distinct types, the most common being the compound microscope, which contains an objective lens system and an eyepiece system. It was invented in 1609 by a Dutch spectacle maker Zacharias Janssen (1580–c. 1638) and his father, but Robert *Hooke gave the first extensive description of its use in biology in his *Micrographia* (1665). In a compound microscope the objective produces a real magnified image, which is further magnified by the eyepiece. At low *magnifications the system is illuminated by a source the light of which is reflected through the specimen by a mirror. At high magnifications special illuminating systems are needed. The magnification, which may be up to a thousand, is limited by the *resolving power of the lenses; the smallest detail capable of resolution by an optical microscope is about 0.2 micrometer. This can be increased by using an *oil-immersion lens (*see also* ultramicroscope). Still higher magnifications are obtained by using shorter wavelength radiations as in the *electron microscope.
A **photomicrograph** is a photograph of the image obtained using a microscope. This enables a permanent record to be kept and also enables ultraviolet radiation to be used for illumination of the specimen.

microwave background radiation. *See* big-bang theory; cosmology.

microwaves Electromagnetic radiation with wavelengths between 1 and 300 millimeters, lying between infrared rays and radio waves in the electromagnetic spectrum. They are used in *radar and **microwave heating**. This method is used in the rapid cooking of food as the radiation penetrates to the interior of the food. The microwave photon is the same order of magnitude as the vibrational energy of atoms and molecules and therefore heats the interior directly, rather than by conduction from the surface. It is also used in sterilization and in drying wood, etc. Microwaves are generated by such devices as *magnetrons and *klystrons.

Midas In Greek legend, a king of Phrygia whose wish that everything he touched be turned to gold was granted by Dionysus in gratitude for his hospitality to the satyr *Silenus. Because he was therefore unable to eat or drink, he was released from this handicap by bathing in the Pactolus River. In another legend, Midas was asked to judge between the music of Pan and Apollo and chose the former. Apollo punished his tactlessness by changing his ears into those of an ass.

Mid-Atlantic Ridge The submarine ridge extending N–S through the Atlantic Ocean. It forms part of the mid-ocean ridge system that crosses all the major oceans. Much of it is over 621 mi (1000 km) wide and rises to between 0.6 and 1.9 mi (1–3 km) above the ocean basin, in places rising above sea level to form islands. Along the crest are rift mountains and a fractured plateau. *See* plate tectonics.

middle ages The period of European history that is generally regarded as commencing in the 5th century with the fall of the western Roman Empire and ending with the Renaissance. This period begins with the creation of the barbarian kingdoms, which developed into the nation states of W Europe. In Church history, the period covers the rise to supremacy of the Roman Catholic Church, centered on Rome, and the development of the papacy as an international religious and political power. Socially and economically the period saw the rising power of the great landed magnates and the creation of a feudal society, while urban growth and the development of trade reached unprecedented heights. The period can be said to end with the fall of Constantinople to the Turks (1453), the discovery of America (1492), and the successful challenge to the papacy of the national reform movements.

Middleback Range A range of hills in S South Australia. It extends N–S for 40 mi (64 km) in the Eyre Peninsula and possesses rich deposits of iron ore; these are worked at Iron Knob, Iron Monarch, and Iron Baron.

Middle Comedy The transitional period of Greek comic drama, lasting from about 400 BC to about 320 BC. Its characteristics are evident in the last two plays of Aristophanes, *Ecclesiazusae* (392) and *Plutus* (388). A more oblique humor replaced the exuberant and scurrilous wit of earlier comedy, perhaps reflecting the Athenians' loss of confidence in themselves after their defeat (404) in the Peloponnesian War. *See also* Old Comedy; New Comedy.

Middle East The area comprising Iran and the countries of the Arabian peninsula and the Mediterranean seaboard. The Middle East, sometimes called the cradle of civilization, is the birthplace of three major world religions, Judaism, Christianity, and Islam, and their attendant cultures. A world crossroads, its troubled history has been dominated at different times by the Jews, Assyrians, Babylonians, Tatars, Macedonians, and Arabs. The present unrest derives from the conflict between superpowers to influence an area that produces 40% of the world's oil, by conflict between Arab countries and Israel (exacerbated by the displaced Palestinians), and by the recent revolution in Iran.

Middlesbrough   54 35N 1 14W A city in NE England, on the Tees estuary. Local iron ore and local coking coal gave Middlesbrough early industrial advantages. Iron and steel, chemicals, constructional engineering, and shipbuilding are the major industries and almost all the traffic through the port is related to the steel and chemical industries. Population (1981): 149,770.

Middletown   41 33N 72 39W A city in central Connecticut, on the W bank of the Connecticut River, SE of Hartford. Wesleyan University (1831) is here. A 19th-century port and shipbuilding center, it now houses banking and insurance firms and produces skis, marine accessories, airplane parts, and electronics. Population (1980): 39,040.

Middle West, the.   *See* Midwest, the.

Midgard   In Norse mythology, the earth, which lies between Hel or Nifleheim, the land of ice, and Muspelheim, the land of fire, and is reached from *Asgard (the home of the gods) by Bifrost, the rainbow bridge. It was formed by the gods from the dead body of the giant Aurgelmir, his flesh being the land, his blood the oceans, etc.

midge   A small fly, also called a nonbiting midge, belonging to the family *Chironomidae* (over 2000 species). It resembles a mosquito but is harmless. Midges are found near fresh water, often in large swarms. The wormlike aquatic larvae are often red (*see* bloodworm) and live in gelatinous or sand tubes, feeding on algae.

The term is also applied loosely to similar but unrelated flies, including the biting or bloodsucking midges (family *Ceratopogonidae*) and the *gall midges.

Midland   32 00N 102 05W A city in W central Texas, S of Lubbock. It is an administrative center for Texas's oil industry. Originally a 19th century cattle-shipping center, it still processes the area's agricultural products; other manufactures include aircraft, chemicals, and tools. Population (1980): 70,525.

Midlands   A collective term for the central counties of England. The area includes the counties of Derbyshire, Leicestershire, Northamptonshire, Nottinghamshire, Staffordshire, Warwickshire, Hereford and Worcester, and the metropolitan county of West Midlands.

midnight sun   The sun when it is seen on or above the horizon at midnight at places within the Arctic or Antarctic circles. At the polar circles it is seen only at the summer *solstice. At the Poles it is seen for the six months between the summer and winter solstices.

Midrash   (Hebrew: inquiry, exposition)   Exposition of the Bible, and more particularly a book consisting of such exposition. There are many Midrashim, mostly dating from the early middle ages, and they are a valuable source for the religious ideas of the Jews of the time. The *Talmuds also contain a great deal of Midrash.

midshipman   A fish, also called singing fish, belonging to a genus (*Porichthys*) of *toadfishes. It is able to produce a whistling sound and has rows of light-producing organs on its underside.

Midway Islands   28 15N 177 25W A small group of US islands in the central Pacific Ocean. A military base, they are unpopulated apart from US military personnel. The sea and air battle that took place here (June 3–6, 1942) resulted in a major Allied victory. Area: 2 sq mi (5 sq km).

Midwest, the (*or* Middle West)   An area in the N central US. Its boundaries are indefinite but it is generally accepted to be N of the Ohio River, W of Lake Erie, and E of the Great Plains. One of the world's most fertile agricultural areas, it produces chiefly corn and wheat.

midwifery   The nursing specialty concerned with the care of women during pregnancy and childbirth. Midwives assist in monitoring the health of the mother and baby during labor and deliver the baby in the absence of complications. Midwives undergo extensive training beyond basic nursing training.

midwife toad   A *toad, *Alytes obstetricans*, found in W Europe up to 7218 ft (2200 m) above sea level. Pale gray and slow-moving, it has an unusual breeding habit. As the eggs are laid, the male winds the two egg strings around his hind legs. He keeps the eggs for about a month, frequently moistening them with dew and finally takes them to hatch in a pool.

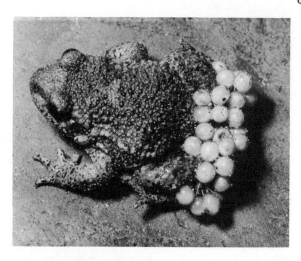

MIDWIFE TOAD   *Mating takes place on land. Soon after fertilization the male twists the eggs around his legs and carries them around, thus protecting them from the predators they would otherwise encounter if laid in water.*

Mies van der Rohe, Ludwig   (1886–1969) German architect. A pioneering architect of the 1920s and 1930s, Mies first achieved fame with his glass skyscrapers (1919–21). However, his most influential building was the glass, steel, and marble German pavilion at the Barcelona international exhibition (1929; □furniture). After a short period running the *Bauhaus, he moved (1937) to the US, where he designed such buildings as the Illinois Institute of Technology (1939) and the Seagram building, New York (1958; □architecture).

mignonette   A bushy annual herb, *Reseda odorata*, native to N Africa and widely grown as an ornamental. Up to 24 in (60 cm) high, it bears dense terminal clusters of tiny yellow or white flowers, which have a musky fragrance and are used in perfumery. The name is also applied to other species of *Reseda*. Family: *Resedaceae*.

migraine   Recurrent headaches, usually affecting one side of the head and thought to be caused by contraction and then dilation of the arteries in the brain. The attacks are often preceded by certain symptoms, usually visual—blurring of vision and flickering lights (called an aura). During the headache itself vomiting commonly occurs. There are some drugs that can reduce the incidence of attacks and others that relieve the severity of an attack.

migration, animal   The periodic movement of animal populations between one region and another, usually associated with seasonal climatic changes or breeding cycles. Migration is best known among birds. Many European species travel to S Africa to avoid the harsh winter weather and the Arctic tern makes a spectacular migration of 11,000 mi (17,600 km) between its breeding grounds in the Arctic and the Antarctic. The phenomenon is seen in many other animals, including fish (notably salmon), which return each year from the sea to spawn in the same river where they themselves were spawned, butterflies, bats, lemmings, and whales.
The mechanism of navigation and homing is not completely understood. In birds it seems to involve sighting of visible landmarks, such as mountains and vegetation, as well as a compass sense, using the sun or the stars as bearings. Other animals are thought to use similar methods. Land mammals may lay scent trails for local direction finding.

migration, human   The movement of groups of people from one country to another in which they intend to settle. Religious persecution has led many (e.g. the *Pilgrim Fathers, the French *Huguenots following the revocation of the Edict of *Nantes, and the Jews) to flee their homelands and settle elsewhere. The 19th century was a period of migration on a large scale, often prompted by severe population pressures, rural unemployment, and the economic opportunities in the country of destination as well as racial persecution. Many of the major countries such as the US, Australia, and South Africa, able to absorb large numbers of immigrants have had historic policies favoring Europeans. Even European immigration in these countries was severely restricted by legislation in the 1920s. Since World War I governments have been more active in controlling migration. War and political upheaval in the late 20th century have prompted many people to flee their native countries in recent years. Such groups include Vietnamese, Cambodians, Cubans, and Haitians.

Mihajlović, Draža (or D. Mihailović; (1893–1946) Yugoslav general. After Germany occupied Yugoslavia in World War II he organized the *Chetniks. In 1943 he was appointed minister of war by Peter II (1923–70; reigned 1934–45) but lost the king's confidence and Allied support, which was given to *Tito. After the liberation he was convicted of treason and shot.

Mikonos (or Mykonos)   A Greek island in the S Aegean Sea, one of the Cyclades. It is popular with tourists and is noted for having a large number of churches. Area: 35 sq mi (90 sq km). Population (1971): 3823.

Milan (Italian name: Milano; Latin name: Mediolanum)   45 28N 9 12E A city in N Italy, the capital of Lombardy on the Olona River. Milan is the focal point of rail and road routes and is the chief commercial and industrial center of Italy. Its manufactures include motor vehicles, machinery, silk and other textiles, and chemicals and it is a major publishing center. Milan has a gothic cathedral (duomo), two universities (both founded in the 1920s), the Brera Palace (containing the city's chief art collection), a library, and the opera house of *La Scala. The convent of Sta Maria delle Grazie contains Leonardo da Vinci's fresco *The Last Supper*. *History*: founded by the Gauls about 600 BC, it was captured by the Romans in 222. Later devastated by the Huns and the Goths, it was involved in much warfare until the 12th century, after which time it enjoyed considerable economic prosperity. It was ruled by the Visconti family from 1310 until 1447, after which it passed to the Sforza family, who ruled almost continuously until the fall of Milan to Spain (1535). It was under Austrian rule (1713–96) and in 1797 Napoleon made it capital of the Cisalpine Republic (1797) and the kingdom of Italy (1805–14). It grew in industrial importance after its unification (1861) with Italy. Population (1980 est): 1,655,599.

mildew   Any fungus that grows as dense filaments forming visible white patches. Many fungal diseases of plants are called mildews: powdery mildews are infestations by fungi of the order *Peronosporales*, while downy mildews are due to infection by fungi of the family *Erysiphaceae*.

mile   A unit of length traditionally used in the US. A statute mile is equal to 1760 yards. The unit is based on the Roman mile of 1000 paces.

Miles Gloriosus (Latin: boastful soldier)   A stock character in comic drama who boasts of brave deeds yet is easily shown to be a fool or coward. The term derives from the title of a play by *Plautus.

Miletus   An ancient Greek city in *Ionia, founded about 1000 BC. Center of the wool trade, early colonizer of the Black Sea area, and commercially active from Italy to Egypt, Miletus exemplified Ionian energy and enterprise. Milesians were prominent among the 6th-century Ionian thinkers, and even after destruction by Persia (494 BC) Miletus recovered, remaining commercially important until its harbors silted up.

milfoil.   *See* yarrow.

Milhaud, Darius   (1892–1974) French composer, a member of Les *Six. He made use of polytonality in many of his compositions, some of which were influenced by jazz. In collaboration with Jean Cocteau he wrote the ballets *Le Boeuf sur le toit* (1919) and *Le Train bleu* (1924); with Paul Claudel he wrote the opera *Christophe Colomb* (1928). His numerous other works include 12 symphonies, 15 string quartets (the last 2 of which can be played simultaneously as an octet), concertos, and Jewish liturgical music.

Military Reconstruction Act   (1867) US law that, after the Civil War, redistricted the South. Because every Southern state except Tennessee refused to ratify the 14th Amendment, Congress divided the South into 5 districts, subject to martial law. The act required the states to call constitutional conventions that would establish governments that would ratify the 14th Amendment before the states could be readmitted to the Union.

militia   A military force composed of reservists enlisted in emergencies to reinforce a standing army. The militia is descended from the Anglo-Saxon *fyrd*, to which all free men were compulsorily recruited for short-term local service.

milk   A fluid secreted by the *mammary glands of mammals to feed their young. Cows' milk consists typically of about 87% water, 3.6% fat, 3.3% protein, 4.7% lactose (milk sugar), small quantities of minerals (mainly calcium and phosphorus), and vitamins (mainly vitamins A and B). (Human milk, in contrast, contains less protein and more lactose.) Although its composition depends on the breed of animal, its diet, and the season, milk forms a well-balanced and highly nutritious food.

Milk River   A river that flows from NW Montana NE through Alberta, Canada, and then SE to NE Montana where it joins the Missouri River.

Used mainly for irrigation, the river is dotted with hydroelectric dams. Length: 625 mi (1007 km).

milk of magnesia   A suspension of magnesium hydroxide ($Mg(OH)_2$) in water. It is a white milky fluid used as an antacid and a mild laxative.

milkweed   A herb of the genus *Asclepias* (120 species), native to North America and often grown in the tropics and subtropics for ornament. Up to 4 ft (1.2 m) high, it bears umbrella-shaped clusters of orange, purple, pink, or red flowers and yields a milky latex. The seeds have long silky hairs ("vegetable silk"), often used in water-safety equipment, in upholstery padding, or as insulation. Family: *Asclepiadaceae*.

milkweed butterfly   A butterfly belonging to the widely distributed mainly tropical family *Danaidae*. The adults are typically large and colorful and may fly long distances (*see* monarch). The caterpillars feed on milkweed and other plants, which makes their taste unpleasant to predators.

milkwort   A perennial herb or small shrub of the genus *Polygala* (500–600 species), native to Europe and North America. The common European milkwort (*P. vulgaris*) has slender branching stems, 2.8–10 in (7–25 cm) long, and spikes of irregular flowers, white, pink, or blue in color. Family: *Polygalaceae*.

Milky Way   The diffuse band of light that is seen, on a clear moonless night, stretching across the sky. It is composed of innumerable stars that are too faint to be seen individually. They lie around the sun in the flattened and densely populated disk of our *Galaxy.

Mill, James   (1773–1836) Scottish writer, historian, and philosophical radical. In the course of a busy journalistic career he met *Bentham (1808), whose enthusiastic disciple he became. Mill's *History of India* (1818) secured him an official post at India House for the remainder of his life. His *Elements of Political Economy* (1821) influenced *Marx and his philosophical stance is reflected by his son **John Stuart Mill** (1806–73), one of the greatest 19th-century thinkers. In economics, J. S. Mill was influenced by the theories of Adam *Smith, *Ricardo, and *Malthus, and his *Principles of Political Economy* (1848) is little more than a restatement of their ideas. He was also the last of the English philosophers in the empirical tradition of Locke. He was a proponent of *utilitarianism, publishing a book under that title (1863). *On Liberty* (1859) shows that he was concerned for the rights of the individual, yet sympathetic to the ideas of contemporary socialists. He believed strongly in the equality of the sexes, publishing his views in *Subjection of Women* (1869).

Millais, Sir John Everett   (1829–96) British painter. He was one of the founders of the *Pre-Raphaelite Brotherhood, the principles of which he applied to his best paintings, notably the controversial *Christ in the House of His Parents* (1850) and *Ophelia* (1852). After abandoning Pre-Raphaelitism in the 1860s, he painted more popular and sentimental works, such as *Bubbles* (1886), a portrait of his grandson.

Millay, Edna St Vincent   (1892–1950) US poet. The rebellious bohemianism of her early lyrical poetry matured into a more profound disillusion, expressed with great technical skill especially in *The Buck in the Snow* (1928) and *Fatal Interview* (1931), a sonnet sequence. *The Harp Weaver and Other Poems* (1923) was awarded the Pulitzer Prize.

millenarianism   A belief, widespread among early Christians and sporadically revived since, that Christ will soon return to reign on earth with his elect for a period of a thousand years preceding the Last Judgment. The idea was fostered by literal interpretations of the Book of Revelation (especially chapter 20) but was rejected by *Origen, whose views on the matter became generally accepted. At the Reformation millenarianism flourished among persecuted minorities, such as the *Anabaptists. Puritan millenarian sects, notably the *Fifth Monarchy Men, proliferated in the mid-17th-century turmoils in England. The political frustrations of colonial rule, combined with fundamentalist biblical teaching, fostered millenarianism among the indigenous peoples of Africa and Polynesia, where it sometimes took the form of *cargo cults. Contemporary millenarian groups include the *Adventists and *Mormons.

Miller, Arthur   (1915–   ) US dramatist. As a Jewish liberal intellectual he has played an active role in political life, and one of the main themes of his plays is social responsibility. His plays include *All My Sons* (1947); *Death of a Salesman* (1947), which won a Pulitzer Prize; *The Crucible* (1953), concerning the Salem witch trials of the 1690s; *A View From the Bridge* (1955); and *After the Fall* (1964), which is in part a portrait of his late wife Marilyn □Monroe.

Miller, Glenn   (1904–44) US jazz trombonist, band leader, and composer of the popular songs "Moonlight Serenade" and "In the Mood." Miller's band, assembled in 1938, recorded many hit swing tunes and entertained the troops during World War II. He died on a routine flight between England and France; the plane and the bodies of the passengers were never recovered.

Miller, Henry (1891–1980) US novelist. During the 1930s he lived in Paris, where he became a close friend of Lawrence *Durrell; he lived in California from 1944. He first gained notoriety with the sexually explicit novels *Tropic of Cancer* (1934) and *Tropic of Capricorn* (1939), which were banned in the US until 1961. His works, which are mostly autobiographical, are anarchic celebrations of life and liberty. Other works include *The Rosy Crucifixion* (1949–60) and *My Life and Times* (1972).

miller's thumb. *See* bullhead.

millet One of various *grasses or their seeds, cultivated in Asia and Africa as a cereal crop and in parts of Europe and North America chiefly as a pasture grass and fodder crop. It grows 12–51 in (30–130 cm) high and the flowers form spikes or branched clusters. Common or broomcorn millet (*Panicum miliaceum*) is used for poultry feed or for flour milling. Pearl millet (*Pennisetum glaucum*) is grown in arid and infertile soils as a food grain; Italian millet (*Setaria italica*) has been cultivated as a grain crop in Asia since ancient times; and Japanese millet (*Echinochloa crus-galli* var. *frumentacea*) is grown mainly for fodder. A variety of sorghum (*see* durra) is also known as millet.

Millet, Jean François (1814–75) French painter of peasant origin, famous for his peasant subjects. He studied in Cherbourg and in Paris under *Delaroche, achieving acclaim in 1844, although later his works were criticized for expressing socialist ideas. After settling in Barbizon (1849), he became associated with the *Barbizon school and painted melancholy and sometimes sentimental agricultural scenes, notably *The Gleaners* (1857) and *The Angelus* (1859; both Louvre).

millibar. *See* bar.

Millikan, Robert Andrews (1868–1953) US physicist, who first measured the charge on the electron. For this and other work, he was awarded the Nobel Prize in 1932. In **Millikan's oil-drop experiment,** he balanced the effects of an upward electromagnetic attraction and the downward pull of gravity on an electrically charged droplet. As changes in the drop's charge (caused by bombardment with X-rays) occur in whole numbers of units of electronic charge, the size of the unit can be calculated from the movement of the drop. Millikan also studied cosmic rays. He was deeply religious and was actively concerned to reconcile religion and science.

millipede A slow-moving *arthropod of the widely distributed class *Diplopoda* (about 8000 species). Its slender cylindrical body, 0.08–11 in (2–280 mm) long, is covered by a calcareous cuticle and consists of 20–100 segments, most of which bear two pairs of legs (*compare* centipede). Millipedes live in dark humid places—under stones, rotting logs, or in soil—as scavengers of dead plant and animal materials. In defense they secrete a toxic fluid containing cyanide and iodine. Eggs are usually sheltered in a nest of excrement.

Mills, Sir John (1908–) British actor. He appeared in the roles of quiet but gallant heroes in *This Happy Breed* (1944) and other war films and later in character roles, as in *Ryan's Daughter* (1971). His daughters **Hayley Mills** (1946–) and **Juliet Mills** (1941–) are both actresses.

Mills, C(harles) Wright (1916–62) US sociologist. He was professor of sociology at Columbia University (1946–62) and concentrated on the theories of German sociologists Karl *Marx and Max *Weber. His works include *From Max Weber* (1946), *White Collar* (1951), *The Power Elite* (1956), *The Sociological Imagination* (1959), *Listen Yankee* (1960), and *The Marxists* (1962).

Milne, A(lan) A(lexander) (1882–1956) British novelist and dramatist. He contributed to *Punch* and wrote several popular comedies, but is best known for his books for and about his son Christopher Robin. These include *When We Were Very Young* (1924), a collection of verse, and two books about toy animals, *Winnie-the-Pooh* (1926) and *The House at Pooh Corner* (1928).

Milo (late 6th century BC) Greek wrestler of legendary strength, who won six Olympic prizes. He is said to have carried a calf on his shoulders once every day from its birth and eventually to have carried the grown cow round the Olympic stadium.

Miloš (1780–1860) Prince of Serbia (1815–39, 1858–60), who led a successful revolt against the Ottoman Empire (1815) and founded the *Obrenović dynasty. Miloš was the alleged assassin of *Karageorge. He was forced to abdicate in 1839 but was recalled in 1858.

Milstein, Nathan (1904–) US violinist, born in Russia, resident in the US since 1929. A pupil of Leopold Auer (1843–1930) and Eugène Ysaÿe (1858–1931), Milstein gave recitals with Vladimir Horowitz in Russia be-

fore establishing a European reputation in 1925. He has published a number of violin transcriptions.

Miltiades (c. 550–489 BC) Athenian general and statesman. Sent to govern the Thracian peninsula in Athenian interests, he ruled as tyrant and fought with *Darius I of Persia in Scythia. Later, after joining the Ionian cities' unsuccessful revolt against the Persians, he had to flee to Athens (493) but escaped punishment. Appointed a general in 490, he devised the strategy by which the Greeks decisively defeated the Persians at the battle of *Marathon.

Milton, John (1608–74) English poet. After leaving Cambridge University he studied privately at his father's house, where he wrote the poems *L'Allegro* and *Il Penseroso* (1632), the masque *Comus* (1633), and the elegy *Lycidas* (1637). In 1638 he traveled in France and Italy. During the 1640s and 1650s he actively supported the Puritan revolution and wrote many polemical pamphlets, notably *Areopagitica* (1644), a defense of free speech. He also wrote a series of pamphlets justifying divorce in cases of incompatibility, a position reflecting his own unhappy marriage (1642) to Mary Powell. In 1649 he was appointed Latin Secretary to the Council of State, but his eyesight began to fail and he had become totally blind by 1652. After the Restoration he retired from public life to write his great epic poem *Paradise Lost* (1667), its sequel *Paradise Regained* (1677), and the dramatic poem *Samson Agonistes* (1671).

Milton Keynes 52 02N 0 42W A city in S England, in Buckinghamshire. Developed since 1967 as a new town, it is the headquarters of the Open University (1969) and has varied light industries. Population (1981): 106,974.

Milwaukee 43 03N 87 56W A city and port in Wisconsin, on Lake Michigan. Originally a fur-trading post, it grew after an influx of German refugees in 1848. The German immigrants established the city's famous brewing industries. The state's largest city and a major shipping center, Milwaukee is a leading producer of heavy machinery, electrical equipment, and diesel and gasoline engines. Population (1980): 636,212.

MIME *Marcel Marceau in the role of Bip, at the Théâtre des Champs-Élysées, Paris.*

mime Acting without words by physical gestures alone. It was practiced in ancient Greek and Roman drama and was an important constituent of the *commedia dell'arte in the 16th century. Modern mime was developed during the early 19th century in France by *Debureau and was revived in the 1920s by Etienne Decroux (1898–), whose pupils included Jean-Louis *Barrault and Marcel *Marceau.

mimesis (Greek: imitation) A philosophical concept introduced by *Aristotle in the *Poetics*. He argues that imitation is the basis of all the arts but they differ as to the means they use and the objects they imitate. Thus, drama is the imitation of an action and the dramatic genres, tragedy and comedy, may be differentiated by their characters, who are either better (in tragedy) or worse (in comedy) than average humanity. Imitation in the arts does not refer to a simple realistic rendering of detail but to the poet's (or artist's) ability to select and present his material so as to express essential truth.

mimicry The phenomenon of two or more organisms (commonly different species) resembling each other closely, which confers an advantage—usually protection—to one or both of them. In **Batesian mimicry**, named for H. W. *Bates, a poisonous or inedible species (the model) has a conspicuous coloration, which acts as a warning to predators. This coloration is adopted by a harmless edible species (the mimic), which derives protection against the same predators. In **Müllerian mimicry**, first described by the German naturalist Fritz Müller (1821–97), two or more species—all inedible—have the same warning coloration. After a predator has associated this pattern with an inedible species it will learn not to select similarly colored species, resulting in a reduction in total mortality.

Mimosa A genus of trees, shrubs, and herbs (450–500 species), mostly native to tropical and subtropical America. They have feathery compound leaves and fluffy round catkins of yellow flowers. The genus includes the sensitive plants, *M. pudica* and *M. sensitiva*, of which the leaflets fold upward and the leafstalks droop at the slightest touch. Florists' mimosas are species of *Acacia* (see wattle). Family: *Leguminosae*.

Mina Hassan Tani. *See* Kenitra.

Minamoto Yoritomo (1147–99) Japanese military leader descended from a 9th-century emperor, who as the first *shogun (military overlord, 1192–99) laid the foundations of feudal government in Japan. After the defeat (1185) of the dominant *Taira clan, Yoritomo built up an extensive vassal network based on Kamakura, near modern Yokohama. In 1192 he obtained the title of shogun from the emperor and his administrative organization gradually moved from coexistence with the imperial government to dominance over it. His half-brother **Minamoto Yoshitsune** (1159–89) was a warrior whose flair and valor contributed greatly to the Minamoto triumph against the Taira but who subsequently incurred the suspicion or jealousy of Minamoto Yoritomo. His adventures before he was finally hunted down and committed suicide have captured the imagination of succeeding generations.

minaret A tall slender tower attached to a mosque from which the muezzin calls Muslims to prayer five times a day.

mind A philosophical term for whatever it is in a person that thinks, feels, wills, etc. Whether it is immaterial or not is controversial. *Materialism denies its existence as an incorporeal entity. For *Aristotle mind was *nous* (intellect), the only part of the soul to survive death. For *Descartes it is his starting point, an incorporeal mental substance by virtue of whose activity (thought) he knew he existed (*cogito ergo sum*—I think therefore I am). Until recently it has been usual to suppose that nonhuman animals do not have minds, the possession of mind being perhaps a defining characteristic of human beings. A more modern view identifies mental attitudes with brain states (see behaviorism).

Mindanao An island in the S Philippines, the second largest. Volcanic and rugged, soil erosion caused by indiscriminate tree felling is a serious problem. Hemp, maize, pineapples, timber, nickel, and gold are the chief products. *History*: the Muslim population has resisted Spanish, US, and now Philippine rule. Separatism, aggravated by rapid economic development in the 1960s, resulted in heavy fighting in 1975. A tribe with a Stone Age culture was discovered here in 1971. Area: 39,351 sq mi (101,919 sq km). Population (1970): 7,484,402. Chief towns: Davao and Zamboanga.

Minden 52 18N 8 54E A city in NW West Germany, in North Rhine-Westphalia on the Weser River. In 1759 the English and Hanoverians defeated the French here. Its cathedral (11th–13th centuries) was rebuilt after World War II. Its varied manufactures include chemicals and glass. Population (1971 est): 50,400.

Mindoro A mountainous island in the central Philippines, S of Luzon. The chief products are timber and coal. Area: 3952 sq mi (10,236 sq km). Population (1970): 472,396. Chief town: Calapan.

Mindszenty, József, Cardinal (J. Pehm; 1892–1975) Hungarian Roman Catholic churchman. He was a vehement opponent of the Nazis and later the Communists, who imprisoned him in 1948. Released by the insurgents in the 1956 Hungarian Revolution, he gained asylum at the US legation in Budapest and eventually settled in Rome in 1971.

minerals Naturally occurring substances of definite chemical composition (although this may vary within limits). Some consist of a single element but most are compounds of at least two. Strictly defined, minerals are solid (except native mercury) and are inorganically formed, although the constituents of organic limestones, for instance, are considered minerals. The term is used loosely for any naturally occurring material that is of economic value, especially if it is obtained by mining, and the fossil fuels (of organic origin) are in this broader sense minerals. Almost all true minerals are crystalline; a few, such as opal, are amorphous. Minerals are identified by the following properties: crystal system (e.g. cubic) and habit or form (e.g. fibrous), hardness (see Mohs' scale), relative density, luster (e.g. metallic), color, streak (color when finely divided), *cleavage, and fracture. *Rocks are composed of mixtures of minerals. If a rock contains an economically extractable quantity of a mineral of commercial value, it constitutes a mineral deposit (see mining and quarrying). **Mineralogy** is the study of minerals (in the strict sense): their identification, classification, and formation.

Minerva A Roman goddess originally of the arts and the crafts of wisdom, later identified with the Greek *Athena. As goddess of war her importance almost equaled that of Mars. Her annual festival was the Quinquatrus, held in March.

minesweeper A powerful fast vessel equipped to cut the cables of floating mines. Partially submerged cables, attached to paravanes that keep them taut and at a desired angle to the boat, are towed through a minefield so that the cable, passing under the mines, cuts their anchor chains, allowing the mines to float so that they can be detonated by gunfire.

Ming (1368–1644) A native Chinese dynasty, which succeeded the Mongol Yüan dynasty. It was founded by *Hong Wu, the first of 17 Ming emperors. The Ming provided an era of stable government personally controlled by the emperor. The examination system to select bureaucrats was restored and overseas expeditions were encouraged. Painting and pottery, especially blue and white porcelain, flourished under the Ming, who built the Forbidden City in Peking in the 15th century.

Mingus, Charlie (1922–79) US black jazz musician, who experimented with atonality and dissonance in jazz. A double-bass player, he played with Louis Armstrong, Lionel Hampton, and others. He also led his own band and appeared in films.

Minho River. *See* Miño River.

miniature painting The art of painting on a very small scale, using watercolor on a vellum, card, or (from the 18th century) ivory base. The medieval Persian and Indian miniatures are the first great examples of the art. In Europe it flourished in the form of oval, circular, and occasionally rectangular portraits from the 16th to mid 19th centuries. There it developed from the medieval art of manuscript illumination (sometimes also called miniature painting) and *Renaissance portrait medals. Although *Holbein the Younger produced some miniatures, Nicholas *Hilliard in England was the first major specialist of the art. His portraits were often worn as jewelry. Other famous miniaturists were the Frenchmen Jean Clovet and Jean Fouquet in the 16th century, and the 17th and 18th century Englishmen Isaac Oliver, Samuel Cooper, and Richard Cosway. The Venetian Rosalba Carriera painted on ivory in the late 17th century. In the US, James Peale was the foremost miniaturist in the late 18th century.

Minicoy Islands. *See* Lakshadweep.

minimal art An abstract style of painting and sculpture developed in New York in the late 1960s. In reaction against the personal character of *action painting, it aims to eliminate artistic self-expression by reducing creativity to a minimum. This has been achieved by using simple hard-edged geometrical shapes and unmodulated vibrant colors. Leading minimalists include the painters Kenneth Noland (1924–) and Frank Stella (1936–) and the sculptor Carl André (1935–).

Minimata disease A form of mercury poisoning that killed 43 people in the Japanese town of Minimata between 1953 and 1956. The disease was contracted by eating fish contaminated with dimethyl mercury, derived from an effluent from a local PVC factory. The symptoms of mercury poisoning include tremors, paralysis, severe anemia, and bone deformities.

mining and quarrying The extraction of useful minerals from the earth's crust. Quarrying is usually regarded as the extraction of stone, sand, gravel, etc., from surface workings. Mining is the extraction by opencast or underground workings of ores producing metals (gold, silver, zinc, copper, lead, tin, iron, and uranium) and other valuable minerals (coal, limestone, asbestos, salt, precious stones, etc.); mining also includes the extraction of oil from wells and the extraction of alluvial deposits. Some 70% of mineral ores come from surface workings, which using modern equipment can reach down to depths of 1640 ft (500 m). After the overburden of rock or sand has been removed, the underlying mineral is blasted by explosives or broken up by machinery and excavated by power shovels, which load it onto conveyors or trucks. To comply with environmental requirements the overburden is often backfilled (deposited behind the current working face). In underground workings many factors have to be taken into account, such as the size, shape, and hardness of the deposit, the nature of the surrounding rock and the surface terrain, and the risk of subsidence. Ores are loosened and excavated by blasting, drilling, and mechanical shoveling. The waste material after the valuable ore has been extracted is often fed back into the mine (sometimes hydraulically, as a slurry) to reduce the risk of subsidence. *See also* coalmining; oil.

minivet An Asian songbird of the genus *Pericrocotus* (10 species), occurring in forests, where it hunts for insects in small flocks. Male minivets, about 7 in (17 cm) long, have a black-and-red plumage; the females are yellowish gray. Family: *Campephagidae* (cuckoo-shrikes and minivets).

MINK *An American mink. This species occurs naturally throughout North America (except in the arid US SW) and is also bred on farms.*

mink A small carnivorous □mammal belonging to the genus *Mustela* (weasels, stoats, etc.), prized for its fur. The American mink (*M. vison*) is the largest species (about 27.5 in [70 cm] long) and has the most valuable fur. It is bred in captivity in many parts of the world, and escaped animals readily adapt to life in the wild. They are nocturnal, semi-aquatic, and efficient hunters both on land and in water, preying on fish, rodents, and waterfowl. Family: *Mustelidae.

Minneapolis 45 00N 93 15W A city in Minnesota, on the Mississippi River. Adjacent to St Paul, the Twin Cities comprise the commercial, industrial, and financial center of a large grain and cattle area; flour milling is the main industry. Minneapolis is noted for its wide streets, many lakes, and parks. The University of Minnesota was established here in 1851. Population (1980): 370,951.

Minnelli, Liza. *See* Garland, Judy.

Minnesingers (German: singers of love) Aristocratic German singing guilds that flourished in the 12th and 13th centuries; the German equivalent of the French *troubadours. Their decline coincided with the rise of the *Meistersingers.

Minnesota A midwestern US state bounded by Lake Superior and the states of Wisconsin on the E, Iowa on the S, South Dakota and North Dakota on the W, and Manitoba and Ontario, Canada, on the N. It consists of rolling prairies rising to the heavily forested, mineral-rich Superior Highlands in the N. Prehistoric glacial activity has left numerous lakes, the largest being the Lake of the Woods. Boulders, also remnants of the glacial age, strew the N hilly regions, giving way to the prairies in the S. Manufacturing industries (especially food processing) now form the most important sector of the economy. The high-grade iron ores, of which it was a major source, are virtually exhausted but mining remains important following new finds of copper and nickel. Agriculture, concentrated chiefly in the S, produces corn and soybeans. Tourism is an important source of revenue. *History*: first explored by the French in the mid 17th century. The Ojibwa and Sioux Indians inhabited the region at the time. Minnesota formed part

of the Louisiana Purchase (1803). Settlers began to arrive in the 1820s; it became a state in 1858. Toward the end of the century many Scandinavian immigrants established homes in Minnesota, becoming a dominant influence in the development of the state. Agrarian reform groups took readily in rural Minnesota, where the Granger Movement was founded. The Populist Party (which held that federal economic policy prejudiced agrarian interests) and the Farmer-Labor Party (uniting farmers and organized labor) received widespread support in Minnesota. In 1944 the Farmer-Labor Party merged with the Democratic Party. Such national political leaders as Hubert Humphrey and Walter Mondale grew out of this political climate. Area: 84,068 sq mi (217,736 sq km). Population (1980): 4,077,148. Capital: St Paul.

Minnesota River A river that flows from Big Stone Lake on the NE South Dakota–W central Minnesota border SE to Mankato, Minnesota, and NE to the St Paul area, where it joins the Mississippi River. It was once an important exploration and trading route. Length: 332 mi (535 km).

minnow One of several fish of the family *Cyprinidae*, especially *Phoxinus phoxinus*, found in clear fresh waters of Europe and N Asia. Its slim body is usually about 3 in (7.5 cm) long, has small scales, and ranges in color from gold to green. Order: *Cypriniformes*.

The name is also applied to various other small fish, including mudminnows (family *Umbridae*; order *Salmoniformes*) and *killifish.

Miño River (Portuguese name: Minho) A river in SW Europe. Rising in NW Spain, it flows mainly SSW, forming part of the border between Spain and Portugal, to the Atlantic Ocean. Length: 210 mi (338 km).

Minoan civilization The civilization of Bronze Age Crete, named by Sir Arthur *Evans after the legendary King *Minos. The most advanced Aegean civilization, the Minoan arose after 2500 BC. It is conventionally divided into three phases: Early (2500–2000), Middle (2000–1700), and Late (1700–1400). During the Middle Minoan period palace building at *Knossos, Mallia, and Phaistos attests Crete's growing wealth. Around 1700 these structures were destroyed and replaced by grander ones, the centers of power in a marine empire covering the S Aegean. A catastrophic eruption on *Thera (c. 1450) ended Minoan prosperity as the sterile volcanic fallout temporarily ruined Crete's agriculture. Subsequent occupation levels show increasing Mycenaean influence (*see* Mycenaean civilization).

Excavated frescoes and artifacts show that Minoan material culture was highly sophisticated; craftsmen included skilled architects, potters, painters, stone cutters, goldsmiths, and jewelers. Three scripts were used: hieroglyphics (c. 1900–1700), *Linear A (c. 1700–1450), and *Linear B (c. 1450–1400). A prominent deity was a snake goddess; religious symbols of bulls' horns suggest ritual significance for the famous bull sports.

Minorca (Spanish name: Menorca) A Spanish island in the Mediterranean Sea, the second largest of the Balearic Islands. It is generally low lying and dry and agriculture is limited, with livestock raising. Shoe manufacture is important and it has an expanding tourist industry. Area: 271 sq mi (702 sq km). Population (1970): 48,817. Chief town: Mahón.

minor planet. See asteroid.

Minos A legendary king of Crete, son of Zeus and Europa. His wife was Pasiphae, by whom he had two daughters, *Ariadne and *Phaedra. Although usually regarded as a good ruler, the Athenians portrayed him as a tyrant, who exacted an annual tribute of seven youths and seven maidens who were fed to the *Minotaur. According to Herodotus, he was killed in Sicily while pursuing *Daedalus after his escape from Crete. He is, with Rhadamanthus and Aeacus, one of the judges of the dead in Hades.

Minotaur In Greek legend, a Cretan monster with a bull's head and a man's body. It was the offspring of Pasiphae, wife of *Minos, and a bull with which Poseidon had caused her to become enamored. It was kept in the labyrinth built by *Daedalus and fed on Athenian youths and maidens sent in tribute to Minos. *Theseus killed it with the help of Ariadne.

Minsk 53 51N 27 30E A city in the W Soviet Union, the capital of the Belorussian SSR. Dating from at least the 11th century, it came under Lithuanian and then Polish rule; it was restored to Russia in 1793. It was virtually destroyed in World War II, and its large Jewish population exterminated during the German occupation. Its varied industries include machine and vehicle manufacturing, textiles, and food processing. It boasts a lively cultural life. Population (1981 est): 1,333,000.

mint An aromatic perennial herb of the genus *Mentha* (about 25 species), native to Eurasia and Australia and widely distributed throughout temperate and subtropical regions. It has creeping roots from which arise square stems, bearing simple toothed leaves and terminal clusters of purple, pink, or white flowers. Many species are grown in gardens for their fragrance or as culinary herbs, especially *peppermint and *spearmint: their leaves are used fresh or dried as flavoring. An oil extracted from mint stems and leaves is used in perfumes and medicines. Family: *Labiatae.

Mint Act (1792) US law that authorized the creation of the first official US mint. It rovided for a mint in Philadelphia for gold and silver coinage and set ratio values on the metal content.

Mintoff, Dom(inic) (1916–) Maltese statesman; Labor prime minister (1955–58, 1971–85). He was an active proponent of Maltese independence from British rule, which was achieved in 1964.

Minton, Sherman (1890–1965) US jurist and politician; associate justice of the US Supreme Court (1949–56). He practiced law in Indiana (1916–25) and Florida (1925–29). He went on to become counselor of the Indiana Public Service Commission (1933–34), a Democratic US senator (1935–41), and US Circuit Court of Appeals judge (1941–49). He was primarily a conservative on the Supreme Court.

Minton ware Porcelain produced at the pottery founded (1796) by Thomas Minton (1765–1836) at Stoke (England). Famous for artistic and technical innovation, the Minton works still make fine porcelain. Remarkable products included imitation *majolica, tiles, and Parian (imitation marble) statuary.

minuet A court dance of the 17th and 18th centuries in triple time. Of rustic origin, it was often included in the instrumental suite and became part of the sonata and symphony in the works of Haydn, Mozart, etc. The first statement of the minuet was followed by a second minuet in a related key (called a trio), after which the first minuet was repeated.

Minya, El 28 06N 30 45E A port in N central Egypt, on the Nile River. It is an important link between the left bank of the Nile and the Bahr Yusuf Canal and trade includes cotton and flour. Population (1976): 146,000.

Miocene epoch. *See* Tertiary period.

Miquelon Island. *See* St Pierre et Miquelon.

Mirabeau, Honoré Gabriel Riquetti, Comte de (1749–91) French statesman. In the years before the *French Revolution he gained notoriety as a libertine and profligate. In 1789 he was elected to the States General, championing the cause of the Third Estate at the outbreak of the Revolution. However, he was out of sympathy with the growing republicanism, advocating the establishment of a constitutional monarchy on the British model. By 1790 he was coming under increasing attack from the *Jacobins but died of natural causes before a crisis was reached.

Mira Ceti A *red giant in the equatorial constellation Cetus that is a *variable star with a mean period of 331 days. Long known to vary considerably in brightness (by 5–6 magnitudes on average), it is the prototype of the **Mira stars**, which are all long-period pulsating variables.

miracle plays Medieval European dramas based on religious themes. In England, they flourished particularly in the 14th and early 15th centuries. A distinction between mystery plays (based on episodes in the Bible) and miracle plays (based on the lives of saints) is often made with regard to French examples of the genre, but in England the plays were almost invariably based on scriptural stories. They were originally performed in churches on religious holidays, especially Corpus Christi and Whitsuntide. They became increasingly secular in form and content and were eventually performed on mobile stages by trade guilds in public marketplaces. Almost complete cycles of plays from York, Coventry, Wakefield, and Chester have survived.

mirage An optical illusion sometimes observed on hot days. It is caused by the air near the ground being considerably hotter than the air above, causing refraction of light rays from the sky, since the refractive index of air depends on its density and therefore on its temperature. Thus rays near the horizon can be bent upward sufficiently to appear to be coming from the ground, creating the illusion of a lake.

Miranda v. Arizona (1966) US Supreme Court decision that upheld the rights of alleged criminals. It ruled that a suspect must be informed of right to counsel and that any statements obtained may be used as evidence for prosecution. It expanded the conditions set forth in *Escobedo* v. *Illinois*.

Miró, Joan (1893–1983) Surrealist painter, born in Barcelona. He moved to Paris (1919), where he participated in the first surrealist exhibition (1925) and began painting in a childlike style under the influence of dreams and poetry. The gaiety of his painting disappeared in the late 1930s with his "savage" paintings, expressing the horrors of the Spanish Civil War; it reappeared, however, in his *Constellations*, painted (during World War II) with his characteristic amebic shapes intertwined with threadlike lines. He is also known for his ballet sets, murals, and sculptures.

mirrors Devices for reflecting light, usually consisting of a sheet of glass with one surface silvered. A plane mirror, in which the sheet is flat, forms a laterally inverted virtual image. Spherical mirrors, concave or convex, magnify or reduce the image. If the distances of the object and image from the mirror surface are u and v, then $1/u + 1/v = 1/f$, where f is the focal length of the mirror, taking all distances as positive in front of the mirror and negative behind it. To avoid spherical aberration, parabolic mirrors are used in reflecting *telescopes.

miscarriage. *See* abortion.

misch metal An *alloy of between 15% and 40% iron with cerium and other rare metals. When rubbed with an abrasive it produces sparks and it is used for flints in cigarette lighters. The name comes from the German *Mischmetall*, mixed metal.

misdemeanor. *See* felony.

Mishima, Yukio (Kimitake Hiraoka; 1925–70) Japanese novelist and playwright of international fame. He also acted in several films. His novels, which include *Confessions of a Mask* (1948) and *Sun and Steel* (1970), dealt with homosexuality, death, suicide, and the importance of traditional Japanese military values. He organized his own military group, the Shield Society, and in 1970 shocked the world by committing harakiri as a protest against the weakness of postwar Japan.

Mishnah (Hebrew: instruction) An early code of Jewish law. Written in Hebrew, it is traditionally thought to have been based on earlier compilations and edited in Palestine by the ethnarch Judah I in the early 3rd century AD. It consists of *halakhah on a wide range of subjects, derived partly from biblical law as interpreted by the early rabbis (called *Tannaim*) and partly from customs that had grown up over a long period of time. *See also* Talmud.

Miskolc 48 07N 20 47E A city in NE Hungary. It has much fine architecture including a 13th-century gothic church and the National Theater. The Technical University of Heavy Industry was established here in 1949. A major industrial center, its manufactures include iron, steel, and chemicals. Population (1980 est): 210,000.

missiles. *See* antiballistic missiles; ballistic missiles; guided missiles; Polaris missile.

Missionary Ridge, Battle of (1863) US Civil War battle in S Tennessee, part of the Chattanooga Campaign. After the Battle of *Lookout Mountain, the Union troops under Generals Joseph *Hooker, William T. *Sherman, and George H. Thomas assaulted Missionary Ridge, broke the Confederate hold, and gained complete control of Chattanooga for the Union.

missions, Christian Enterprises to spread the Christian faith among those who profess other religions or none. The missionary journeys of St *Paul and the Apostles set an example that Christian individuals and organizations have followed ever since. St *Patrick, St *Columba, and St *Augustine of Canterbury were outstanding early missionaries in the British Isles. Isolated medieval missions reached as far as China, but concentrated activity began only with the discovery of the Americas and the sea route around Africa in the late 15th century. Roman Catholic orders, such as the *Dominicans, *Franciscans, and *Jesuits, made substantial conversions, especially in the 17th century, but Protestant denominations, with the exception of the *Moravian Brethren, did not enter the field in force until the 1790s. The 19th century was the peak period of activity with mission stations being established in even the most inaccessible regions. Developing countries frequently recognize the value of this work, which generally includes training in literary, practical, and medical skills, and allow missions to remain in the postcolonial period, although sometimes in conditions of great hardship and danger. Missionary attempts are now felt, ironically, to be necessary against the indifference and materialism of the western world.

Mississippi A state in the S central US, on the Gulf of Mexico. Located in the Deep South, Mississippi is bordered by Alabama to the E, the Gulf of Mexico to the S, Arkansas and Louisiana to the W (with the Mississippi River forming most of the boundary), and Tennessee to the N. Mainly low lying, it consists of the cotton-producing alluvial plain of the Mississippi River (the Mississippi Delta) in the W, an area of extensive swamps in the SW, and a generally infertile region of low hills in the E and NE. The predominantly rural population (only one fourth of the population lives in urban areas) has a large black community (35% of the total population), giving Mississippi the highest proportion of blacks to whites of any state. Still an important agricultural state, its main products are cotton and soybeans, which have superseded cotton in importance. Manufacturing has grown steadily, and in 1965 surpassed agriculture in contribution to revenue. Ship construction and repair is the main industry, with timber and paper products, textiles, chemicals, and food processing also major sources of income. Petroleum is the chief mineral; natural gas, clay, and sand and gravel are also exploited. Mississippi remains, however, one of the country's poorest states. *History*: first visited by De Soto for Spain. Upon his arrival, the indigenous inhabitants were Choctaw, Chickasaw, and Natchez Indians. The French claimed Mississippi and established the first permanent settlement (1690). In 1763, England received Mississippi along with most of the French territory E of the Mississippi River by the Treaty of Paris. Traffic along the Natchez Trace brought settlers to Mississippi. As a cotton state based on slave holdings, Mississippi joined the Southern cause in the Civil War. Jefferson Davis, a native son, became president of the Confederacy. After the Civil War, Mississippi enacted the notorious "Jim Crow" laws, which in effect disenfranchised its black population. The civil rights movement of the 1960s drew world attention to Mississippi, one of the most segregated states in the US. Governor Ross Barnett gained notoriety when he attempted to block the entrance of a black student into the University of Mississippi. By the 1980s the black vote had become significant, and blacks occupied state office in substantial numbers. Area: 47,716 sq mi (123,584 sq km). Population (1980): 2,520,638. Capital: Jackson.

Mississippian period. See Carboniferous period.

Mississippi River A river in the central US, the second longest river in North America. Rising in N Minnesota, it flows generally S into the Gulf of Mexico, through several channels (known as the Passes). Together with its chief tributary, the Missouri River, it forms the third longest river system in the world, at 3759 mi (6050 km) long with the world's third largest drainage basin, covering 1,243,753 sq mi (3,222,000 sq km). Because of the danger of flooding, the lower course has high artificial embankments (levees). Famous for its steamboats, celebrated by Mark Twain, it is now one of the world's busiest commercial waterways, with major ports at St Louis and New Orleans. Length: 3780 km (2348 mi).

Missolonghi (Modern Greek name: Mesolóngion) A city in W Greece, on the Gulf of Patras. It is famous for its defense against the Turks during the War of Greek Independence (1821–29). Lord Byron died here in 1824. Population (1971): 11,614.

Missouri A midwestern state in the central US, lying immediately W of the Mississippi River. It is bounded by Illinois, Kentucky, and Tennessee in the E (where the Mississippi River forms the boundary); Arkansas on the S; Oklahoma, Kansas, and Nebraska on the W; and Iowa on the N. It is divided by the Missouri River (which joins the Mississippi at St Louis) into fertile prairies and rolling hills in the N and W and the hills of the Ozark plateau in the S. Highly urbanized, much of its population lives in the two main cities of St Louis and Kansas City. Manufacturing dominates the economy, with transport and aerospace equipment, food processing, chemicals, and printing and publishing. The leading lead producer in the US, it also exploits barite, iron ore, and zinc deposits. Agriculture is diversified producing livestock and dairy products, soybeans, corn, wheat, cotton, and sorghum grains. *History*: claimed by La Salle for France in 1682; at the time the Osage and Missouri Indians inhabited the region. It was ceded to Spain (1783) before returning to France in 1800. It formed part of the Louisiana Purchase (1803). St Louis, because of its strategic position, became the gateway to the west, experiencing enormous growth with the advent of steamboat traffic on its two great rivers. The question of Missouri's admittance to the US as a state became the focus of the slavery debate in 1820–21. Missouri's entrance as a slave state (most of the inhabitants were Southerners) would have balanced slave and free states. Legislative attempts to emancipate the slaves in Missouri met with sharp opposition, and prolonged controversy over the issue greatly increased sectionalism. The ultimate solution, the *Missouri Compromise, authorized Missouri to adopt a constitution with no restrictions on slavery but prohibited any curtailment of the rights of any US citizens. Missouri was admitted to the Union as a slave state in 1821. The arrival of the railroads and subsequent immigration (most notably thousands of Germans during the 1840s and 1850s) expanded settlement. Missouri fought with the Union during the Civil War. The guerrilla warfare that had characterized fighting in Missouri led to the proliferation of gangs of outlaws after the war, among them the notorious Jesse and Frank James. Industry gradually came to surpass the agrarian sector in importance, particularly with the rise of the automobile industry. (Missouri is the second-largest US manufacturer of automobiles after Michigan.) Area: 69,686 sq mi (180,486 sq km). Population (1980): 4,917,444. Capital: Jefferson City.

Missouri Compromise (1820) US laws that admitted Missouri as a slave state and Maine as a free state to the Union in order to maintain a balance in the Senate. Guided through Congress by Henry *Clay, the compromise also prohibited slavery north of 36°30′ in the Louisiana Purchase territory, with the exception of Missouri.

Missouri River A river in the central US, the longest river in North America and chief tributary of the Mississippi River. Rising in the Rocky Mountains, it flows N and E through Montana, then SE across North and South Dakota before joining the Mississippi at St Louis. A series of dams provides irrigation and has considerably reduced the danger of flooding along its lower course. Length: 2714 mi (4367 km).

Mistinguett (Jeanne-Marie Bourgeois; 1875–1956) French singer and comedienne. She was a leading star of the Moulin Rouge, the Folies-Bergère, and other Paris music halls between the wars. She performed with elaborate costumes and settings, often in company with Maurice *Chevalier.

mistle thrush A heavily built thrush, *Turdus viscivorus*, of Eurasia and NW Africa. It is about 11 in (28 cm) long and has a grayish-brown upper plumage with a thickly speckled yellowish breast and white underwings. It feeds on berries (especially mistletoe—hence its name), snails, and worms.

mistletoe A semiparasitic evergreen shrub of the temperate and tropical family *Loranthaceae* (1300 species), growing on the branches of many trees. The Eurasian mistletoe (*Viscum album*) occurs mainly on apple trees, poplars, willows, and hawthorns. It has rootlike suckers, which penetrate into the host tissues, and woody branching stems, 24–35 in (60–90 cm) long, bearing oval leathery leaves and yellow male and female flowers borne on separate plants. The female flowers give rise to white berries, which are eaten by birds (which thereby disperse the seeds).

Mistletoe was once believed by the Druids to have magic powers and medicinal properties and is a traditional Christmas decoration.

mistral A cold dry northerly wind that is funneled down the Rhône Valley in S France to the Mediterranean Sea. Thick hedges and tree screens orientated E–W protect crops from its force.

Mistral, Frédéric (1830–1914) French poet. In 1854 he helped found the Félibrige, a movement dedicated to the regeneration of Provençal language and culture. His many works in the Provençal vernacular include the epic verse narratives *Mirèio* (1859) and *Lou Pouèmo dóu Rose* (1897). He won the Nobel Prize in 1905.

Mistral, Gabriela (Lucila Godoy Alcayaga; 1889–1957) Chilean poet, who worked as a teacher and cultural ambassador. Her volumes of poetry include *Desolación* (1922), published after the suicide of her fiancé, *Tala* (1938), and *Lagar* (1954). She was awarded the Nobel Prize in 1945.

Mitchell, Margaret (1909–49) US novelist. Her single novel, the international bestseller *Gone with the Wind* (1936), is a historical romance set in Georgia during and after the Civil War. She was awarded a Pulitzer Prize in 1937. The film *Gone With the Wind* (1939) was one of the most popular ever made.

Mitchell, William ("Billy"; 1879–1936) US flier; born in France of American parents. During World War I he commanded US aviation forces and returned a war hero. Always an advocate of air power, he became assistant chief of the air service (1919) and was made a brigadier general (1920). Outspoken in his campaign for increased air power, he was relegated, as a colonel, to San Antonio (1925) where he continued his criticism. When the Navy dirigible *Shenandoah* was lost in a storm (1925), he publicly criticized the inadequacies of the war and navy departments. His accusations resulted in a court-martial, a 5-year suspension, and his resignation (1926). His predictions realized, he was awarded, posthumously, a special congressional medal (1948).

Mitchell, Mount 35 46N 82 16W A mountain in W central North Carolina, in the Black Mountains. It is the highest point (6684 ft; 2038 m) in the United States E of the Mississippi River.

mite A tiny *arachnid (up to 0.24 in [6 mm] long) comprising—with the *ticks—the worldwide order *Acarina* (or *Acari*; over 20,000 species). It has an unsegmented body and eight bristly legs. Mites occur in great abundance in a wide range of habitats, including soil, stored foods, fresh and salt water, plants, and decaying organic material; some are parasitic on animals. They can become serious pests and may also transmit diseases (including *typhus). See also harvest mite; itch mite; spider mite.

Mithra A Persian god of light, truth, and justice. He killed a cosmic bull, whose blood was the source of all animals and plants. The cult of *Mithraism flourished in the Roman Empire from the 2nd century AD, especially in the army, until the official adoption of Christianity in the 4th century.

Mithraism A mystery religion (*see* mysteries) that worshiped Mithra, the Persian god of the sun who represented justice and goodness. It spread through Asia Minor, finally reaching Rome in about 68 BC. Here Mithra was known as Mithras and was worshiped widely among Roman soldiers. He was regarded as the eternal enemy of evil, whose sacrifice of a bull symbolized the regeneration of life. Part of the cult's initiation ceremony was a bath in a sacrificed bull's blood. Mithraism rivaled Christianity until its decline in the 3rd century AD. Remains of a Roman temple to Mithras were discovered (1954) in London; parts of it can still be seen.

Mithridates VI Eupator (120–63 BC) King of Pontus and one of Rome's most persistent enemies. Mithridates extended his kingdom by invading Colchis and Lesser Armenia, antagonizing Rome by proceeding to Paphlagonia, Cappadocia, and Greece. Sulla, Lucullus, and Pompey in turn opposed him in three Mithridatic Wars (88–84, 83–81, 74–64) and he finally committed suicide.

mitochondria Granular rod-shaped structures that occur in the cytoplasm of nearly all □cells. They contain various enzymes that function in cellular *respiration and the metabolism of fat, glycogen, proteins, etc., to produce energy. Therefore in very active cells (i.e. those requiring more energy), such as heart muscle, mitochondria are large and numerous.

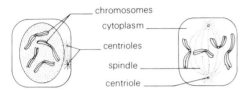

chromosomes
cytoplasm
centrioles
spindle
centriole

prophase *The genetic material becomes visible in the form of chromosomes and the nuclear membrane disappears.*

metaphase *The chromosomes become attached to the equator of a fibrous spindle.*

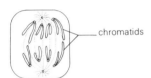

chromatids

anaphase *The two chromatids of each chromosome move to opposite poles of the spindle.*

telophase *Nuclear membranes form around the two groups of chromatids, which become less distinct.*

MITOSIS *Division of the nucleus of an animal cell takes place in four phases, which grade into each other.*

mitosis The process by which the nucleus of a somatic cell (i.e. any cell that is not a germ cell) duplicates itself exactly, producing two daughter nuclei with chromosomes that are identical to those of the parent nucleus. This nuclear division involves the separation of the two chromatids of each chromosome, which move apart to form two groups at opposite ends of the cell. In the final phase each group becomes enclosed in a new nuclear membrane. After this the cytoplasm usually divides to form two new cells. Mitosis occurs in most animals and plants during the normal growth and repair of tissues. *Compare* meiosis.

Mitsiwa. *See* Massawa.

Mittelland Canal (*or* Ems-Weser-Elbe-Kanal) A canal in central Europe. Opened in 1938, it links the Dortmund-Ems Canal in West Germany with the Elbe River in East Germany. Length: 202 mi (325 km).

Mitterrand, François (Maurice) (1916–) French socialist politician; president (1981–). He held ministerial posts from 1947. He was president of a democratic-socialist union (1965–68) and in 1971 assumed leadership of the newly unified Socialist Party. After two unsuccessful runs for the French presidency (1965, 1974) he defeated Giscard d'Estaing in 1981 to become the first socialist president in 35 years.

mixed economy An economy in which there is neither complete capitalist control of resources, nor complete government control. Examples are the democracies of W Europe.

The aim in establishing mixed economies is to temper the "unacceptable face" of capitalism with its incentives and its efficient allocation of resources. Although some critics assert that mixed economies maintain the worst evils of capitalism, their undeniable capacity for economic growth has sub-

stantially improved the lot of the poorer sections of society. In mixed economies, governments seek to control the public services, the basic industries (e.g. coal and steel), and those enterprises that cannot raise adequate capital investment from private sources. This arrangement enables a measure of economic planning to be combined with a measure of free enterprise. In recent years some governments have intervened in the private sector to safeguard jobs in major industries (e.g. shipbuilding, automobile manufacturing, etc.).

Mixtecs An American Indian people originating in W Oaxaca province (S Mexico). After the 10th century they gradually absorbed the neighboring *Zapotecs. The Mixtecs were excellent craftsmen, whose skill in gold working, mosaics, pottery, and painting spread over much of Mesoamerica, influencing both *Maya and *Aztec art styles.

Mizoguchi Kenji (1898–1956) Japanese film director. His films are characterized by a controlled visual style and by a persistent concern with the psychology of women. They include *The Life of O'Haru* (1952), *Ugetsu Monogatari* (1953), and *Street of Shame* (1956).

Mizoram A Union Territory of NE India, in tropical hills between Bangladesh and Burma. Its largely Christian tribes are subsistence farmers of rice, sugar, and potatoes. Mizoram was separated from Assam (1972), following the activities of secessionist factions. Area: 8195 sq mi (21,230 sq km). Population (1981): 487,774. Capital: Aijal.

m.k.s. system A system of *metric units based on the meter, kilogram, and second. It has now been replaced for scientific purposes by *SI units, which are derived from it. The main difference between the two systems is that in SI units, the m.k.s. electrical units are rationalized (i.e. the factor 4π or 2π is introduced when it is demanded by the geometry).

Mnemosyne In Greek mythology, a daughter of the *Titans Uranus and Gaea. She is the personification of memory. After sleeping with Zeus for nine consecutive nights she gave birth to the *Muses.

moa An extinct flightless bird belonging to an order (*Dinornithiformes*; about 25 species) that occurred in New Zealand. Moas were 24–118 in (60–300 cm) tall and had a small head, a long neck, and long stout legs. They were fast runners but were hunted by early Polynesian settlers for food. Members of some smaller species may have survived until the 19th century.

Moabites A highly civilized Semitic tribe living E of the Dead Sea from the late 14th century BC. Closely associated ethnically with their neighbors and rivals the Israelites, they successfully rebelled against Israelite occupation in the 9th century BC. In 582 BC, according to Josephus, they were conquered by the Babylonians. The Moabite Stone, found at Dibon near Amman (Jordan) in 1868 and dating to the 9th century BC, bears an inscription (in the Moabite alphabet) celebrating a Moabite victory against the Israelites.

Mobile 30 12N 88 00W A seaport in Alabama, on Mobile Bay at the mouth of the Mobile River. Founded in 1710, it was occupied by the French, British, and Spanish before being seized for the US in 1813 during the War of 1812. Industries include shipbuilding, oil refining, textiles, and chemicals. Population (1980): 200,452.

MÖBIUS STRIP *A surface with one side and one edge.*

Möbius strip In *topology, a one-sided surface with only one edge, made by taking a strip of paper, twisting it once, and joining the ends. If cut in two lengthwise, it remains in one piece but with no twist. It was discovered by the German astronomer August Ferdinand Möbius (1780–1868).

Mobutu, Lake (former name: Lake Albert) A lake in Uganda and Zaïre. Discovered for Europeans by Baker in 1864, it is some 100 mi (160 km) long and is drained to the N by the Albert Nile River. Area: about 2064 sq mi (5346 sq km).

Mobutu, Sese Seko (Joseph Désiré M.; 1930–) Zaïrese statesman; president (1970–), having come to power in 1965 in a coup. In 1967 he founded the country's only political party—the Popular Movement of the

Revolution—and the stability of his authoritarian government is fostered by his personal cult, Mobutuism.

Moçambique. *See* Mozambique, People's Republic of.

moccasin (snake). *See* water moccasin.

Mocenigo A Venetian family from which came many of the *doges of the Venetian Republic. They included **Tommaso Mocenigo** (1343–1423), doge (1414–23); his nephew **Pietro Mocenigo** (1406–76), who was a distinguished admiral as well as doge (1474–76); Pietro's brother **Giovanni Mocenigo** (1408–85), doge (1478–85); and Giovanni's grandson **Andrea Mocenigo** (1473–1542), a historian.

Mocha (*or* Al Mukha) 13 20N 43 16E A city in SW North Yemen, on the Red Sea coast. It was famous for its export of high-quality coffee but declined following the rise of coffee growing in South America and Java in the early 18th century. Population (1972 est): 5000.

mock epic A form of satiric verse that exposes the absurdity or worthlessness of a trivial subject or theme by treating it in the elevated style appropriate to a genuine *epic. The form originated in classical literature and was practiced by neoclassical writers in the late 17th and early 18th centuries. Examples include *Le Lutrin* (1674–83) by *Boileau and *The Rape of the Lock* (1712–14) and the *Dunciad* (1728–43) by *Pope.

mockingbird A songbird that belongs to an American family (*Mimidae*; 30 species) and is noted for its ability to mimic sounds. Mockingbirds live on or near the ground, feeding on insects and fruit. They were once prized as cagebirds. The common mockingbird (*Mimus polyglottus*), which ranges from S Canada to S Mexico, is about 10 in (25 cm) long with a gray plumage and white wing bars.

mock orange A shrub, also called syringa, belonging to the genus *Philadelphus* (75 species), native to N temperate regions and commonly cultivated for ornament. They have simple leaves and fragrant white flowers resembling orange blossom. *P. coronarius* is the only native European species. Family: *Philadelphaceae*.

Modena (ancient name: Mutina) 44 39N 10 55E A city in N Italy, in Emilia-Romagna. Ruled by the Este family (1288–1860), it has an 11th-century romanesque cathedral, several palaces, and an ancient university (1175). The center of a rich agricultural area, its industries include agricultural engineering, textiles, and motor vehicles. Population (1980 est): 180,526.

modern art The art of the late 19th and 20th centuries, which has largely abandoned traditional subjects, aesthetic standards, and techniques of art. The development of modern art was stimulated by the decline of artistic patronage by church and state, giving the artist more freedom to experiment. These experiments have largely centered on the use of color and form as properties in their own right and not only as a means to mirror the real world (*see* photography). They can be traced back to *Manet and the impressionists. *Cézanne began the dissolution of one of the main foundations of western painting since the Renaissance—the use of linear *perspective. It was completed by *cubism in the early 20th century. Variations of cubism were *futurism in Italy and *vorticism in England but in Russia it developed into a completely nonrepresentational geometric art in the form of *suprematism and *constructivism. Suprematism, constructivism, and neoplasticism (*see* Stijl, de) were highly influential in the 1920s at the German *Bauhaus school of design and geometric abstraction is still a leading artistic trend today in the form of *op art and *minimal art. Color used for its own sake was a major feature of French *fauvism in the early 1900s. Die *Brucke, the German counterpart of fauvism, was also part of another modern movement—*expressionism. However, these two trends were fused in the first abstract painting, which was produced by Kandinsky in about 1910. His heir in the 1940s, when the center of modern art shifted to New York City, was Jackson *Pollock, the inventor of *action painting. Other movements have expanded modern concerns, such as the value of art (*see* dada), the world of dreams and the subconscious (*see* surrealism), and the role of the mass media in society (*see* pop art). *See also* abstract art; sculpture.

Modern Art, Museum of An art gallery in New York City devoted to late 19th- and 20th-century painting. Its extremely comprehensive collection contains major works from all significant movements in Europe and the US of the last century. It was opened in 1929.

modern dance A form of theatrical dance developed in central Europe and the US in the early 20th century in reaction to the technical virtuosity and fairytale subjects of *ballet. The early pioneers were the German dancers Kurt Joos and Mary Wigman and the US dancers Ruth St Denis and her husband, Ted Shawn, Isadora *Duncan, and Martha *Graham.

Modern dance has developed new kinds of movement to express feeling, particularly jerking, thrusting, and contracting movements. It is usually performed in simple clothing against austere scenery. Some of today's leading ballet choreographers, notably *Béjart, *Robbins, Merce Cunningham, Paul Tayler, Alvin Ailey, and Twyla Tharp have been influenced by modern dance.

Modernism A movement among Roman Catholic theologians that arose independently in several countries in the late 19th century. Its adherents sought to bring Roman Catholic thinking into harmony with modern philosophical and scientific trends and in particular with the new critical approach to the Bible. The historical accuracy of the Bible and the problems of dogmatic theology were held to be relatively unimportant. Pope Pius X condemned the movement officially in 1907 and many Modernist clergy were excommunicated.

modes Musical scales derived from ancient Greek music, on which European music was based up to the 16th century. Each mode consists of a different pattern of the five tones and two semitones of the octave; the patterns can be clearly demonstrated using the white notes of the piano keyboard. Some of the most common modes were the Ionian (C-C), the Dorian (D-D), the Lydian (F-F), and the Aeolian (A-A). The Ionian and Aeolian modes became the basis of the major and minor scales of the 17th century and after.

Modesto 37 39N 121 00W A city in central California, SE of Sacramento and E of San Francisco, on the Tuolumne River. Situated at the N end of the San Joaquin Valley, it serves as a processing center for the valley's farm goods and livestock. Wine is also produced. Population (1980): 106,105.

Modigliani, Amedeo (1884–1920) Italian painter and sculptor, born in Livorno of Jewish origin. His mature work, executed in Paris (1906–20), was influenced by *Cézanne and *Brancusi and, in its angular and elongated character, by Negro masks. From 1909 to 1915 he worked chiefly on sculptures; from 1915 until his death from tuberculosis, aggravated by drink and drug addiction, he painted many nudes and portraits.

Modoc North American Shapwailutan-speaking Indian tribe, similar to the Klamath Indians and found by the lakes of NE California and S Oregon. Known for their woven baskets, they fiercely defended their lands in the 1860s but were forced to live, side by side, on an Oregon reservation with their enemy, the Klamath. The Modoc Wars (or Lava Bed Wars; 1872–73), in which renegade Modocs attempted to leave the reservation, resulted in federal imprisonment. About 350 Modoc live on Quapaw Reservation in Oklahoma.

modular construction A method of building construction in which large components of the building are prefabricated for assembly on the site. Where low-cost buildings or many buildings of repeated design are required it has an economical advantage. The modules are usually made of prestressed or precast concrete and may be simply bolted into place, usually around an iron girder frame.

modulation A method of carrying information (the signal) on an electromagnetic wave or an oscillating electric current. In **amplitude modulation** (AM) the amplitude of a carrier wave is changed according to the magnitude of the signal. This is used in medium-wave sound broadcasting in which audio-frequencies (50–20,000 hertz) are carried on radio waves with a frequency of about one megahertz. In **frequency modulation** (FM) the frequency of the carrier wave is changed within a small bandwidth of the reference frequency. FM is used in VHF *radio (about 100 megahertz). Its main advantage over AM is its better signal-to-noise ratio.
In **pulse modulation** the carrier is a series of pulses. It is used in digital equipment, such as computers, and in telegraphy and telemetry. A continuous signal alters the height in pulse-amplitude modulation, the width in pulse-duration modulation, or the time between pulses in pulse-position modulation. Pulse-code modulation uses a coded pattern of pulses to carry the signal, e.g. in *Morse code.

Moers 51 27N 6 36E A city in NW West Germany, in North Rhine-Westphalia in the *Ruhr. It grew rapidly in the 20th century as a coalmining center. Population (1980 est): 100,300.

Mogadishu (*or* Mogadiscio) 2 01N 45 25E The capital and main port of Somalia, on the Indian Ocean. It was founded as an Arab settlement in the 10th century and sold to Italy in 1905 becoming the capital of Italian Somaliland. It has a university (1969). It is the chief commercial center of the republic. Population (1980 est): 400,000.

Mogilev 53 54N 30 20E A city in the Soviet Union, in the E Belorussian SSR on the Dnepr River. Founded in 1267, it passed to Lithuania and then to Poland before being annexed by Russia (1772). It produces metal goods, machinery, and chemicals. Population (1981 est): 308,000.

MOGUL ART AND ARCHITECTURE *An example of late Mogul painting, depicting dancers and musicians performing a nautch, a traditional Indian dance, inside a European palace.*

Mogul art and architecture A style that developed in N India under the patronage of the Mogul emperors. Originally much indebted to *Persian art, Mogul painting developed a more naturalistic style with small-scale scenes of court life and natural history as favored subjects. Book illustration was highly developed. Architecture reached its peak during the reign (1556–1605) of *Akbar, when attempts were made to fuse the opposing traditions of the indigenous Hindu architecture, characterized by solid rocklike masses and use of beams in building, with the Islamic tradition of mathematical clarity in design and use of true arches and internal spaces in construction (*see* Fatehpur Sikri). *See also* Indian art and architecture; Taj Mahal.

Moguls An Indian Muslim dynasty, descended from the Mongol leader *Genghis Khan, that ruled from 1526 until 1858. Its founder was *Babur (reigned 1526–30); he and the first 5 of his 18 successors, Humayun (1508–56; reigned 1530–56), *Akbar (reigned 1556–1605), *Jahangir (1605–27), *Shah Jahan (1627–58), and *Aurangzeb (1658–1707), are known as the Great Moguls, and by the time of Aurangzeb the Empire spread from the far N to the far S of India. During the late 17th and the 18th centuries Mogul power declined in the face of opposition from Hindus to religious intolerance and of European commercial expansion. The last emperor, Bahadur Shah II (1775–1862; reigned 1837–58), was deposed after the *Indian Mutiny and exiled to Burma.

Mohács, Battle of (August 29, 1526) The battle in which the Ottoman Turks under *Suleiman the Magnificent defeated a vastly outnumbered Hungarian and Bohemian army. The battle led to the submission of Hungary to Ottoman overrule.

mohair A wool-like fabric or yarn manufactured from the hair of *Angora goats. Warm, light, and durable and frequently blended with wool, silk, or cotton, mohair is used for lightweight suiting, upholstery, and fluffy fashion knitwear.

Mohammed (*or* Muhammad; c. 570–632 AD) According to Muslims, the last of the prophets and preacher of *Islam to the Arabs. Mohammed is said to have been born in Mecca, a member of the Quraysh clan, which dominated the town. In 610, when he was about 40, he received revelations from God and called upon his pagan fellow townsmen to prepare for the Last Day and to repent. The Meccans rejected him and threatened his life and in 622 he fled to Yathrib (*see* Hegira), where he established the first Muslim community and began to spread Islam. Yathrib now came to be called Medina, "City of the Prophet." By 629 the Muslims in Medina were strong enough to defeat the still pagan Meccans and obtained control of Mecca. By the time of Mohammed's death, Islam had begun to spread throughout Arabia. Mohammed's revelations were collected after his death to form the *Koran. His tomb is venerated in the mosque at Medina.

Mohammed I Askia (d. 1538) Ruler of the West African empire of Songhai (1493–1528), which reached its greatest extent under his rule. He controlled the trade routes to North Africa and was an able administrator. An enthusiastic Muslim, he made the pilgrimage to Mecca in 1495–97.

Mohammed II (1430–81) Sultan of the Ottoman Empire (1451–81). Known as the Conqueror, his fame rests mainly on his conquest in 1453 of Constantinople, which as *Istanbul became the Ottoman capital. He also extended Ottoman territories in the Balkans and Asia Minor.

Mohammed Reza Pahlavi (1918–80) Shah of Iran (1941–79). He became shah when the Allies forced his father *Reza Shah Pahlavi, to abdicate in World War II. In 1979 civil war forced him into exile and an Islamic republic was established in Iran under the leadership of Ayatollah Khomeini.

Mohawk An Iroquoian-speaking American Indian tribe of New York state. They were one of the five tribes that formed the league of the *Iroquois, said to have been founded by the Mohawk chief *Hiawatha. Their culture was typical of that of the neighboring Iroquois tribes.

Mohegan North American Algonkian-speaking Indian tribe, found in E Connecticut, along the Thames River. United with the *Pequot under one chief, Sarcassus, they fought the English settlers in the *Pequot War (1637); under *Uncas, the Mohegan conquered other tribes and occupied most of S New England. A few remaining Mohegan live in Norwich, Conn.

Mohenjo-Daro The site in Sind (Pakistan) of a great city of the □Indus Valley civilization. First excavated in the 1920s, it has extensive brick-built remains. *See also* Harappa.

Mohican An Algonkian-speaking American Indian tribe of New England. Primarily cultivators, they lived in fortified communities of 20 to 30 houses or in enclosed villages, but were displaced by wars with the Mohawks. Each of their five tribal sections was governed by a chief (sachem) together with an elected council.

Mohole An unsuccessful research project embarked upon with US government funds but abandoned in 1966 because of its enormous cost. The aim was to obtain samples of the rocks of the earth's upper mantle by drilling down from the ocean floor through the crust to the *Mohorovičić discontinuity. Drilling was undertaken off W Mexico but the technological difficulties proved enormous.

Moholy-Nagy, László (1895–1946) Hungarian artist. His most influential work was produced while teaching at the *Bauhaus (1923–29), where his experimental abstract paintings and photographs culminated in his *Light-Space Modulators*, plastic mechanical constructions designed to show continuously changing effects of light. His last years were spent teaching in Chicago.

Mohorovičić discontinuity The boundary between the earth's crust and upper mantle, marked by a sudden increase in velocity in seismic waves as the denser mantle is reached. It lies at a depth of 20–22 mi (33–35 km) beneath the continents and 3–6 mi (5–10 km) beneath the oceans. It is named for the Croatian scientist Andrija Mohorovičić (1857–1936), who discovered it in 1909.

Mohs' scale A scale of hardness of minerals named for— the mineralogist Friedrich Mohs (1773–1839). The ten standard minerals in the scale, in ascending order of hardness, are: 1. talc, 2. gypsum, 3. calcite, 4. fluorite, 5. apatite, 6. orthoclase feldspar, 7. quartz, 8. topaz, 9. corundum, and 10. diamond. Each can be scratched by any mineral higher up the scale, and other minerals can be assigned numbers in the scale according to which materials will scratch them.

moiré pattern A wavy cloudy fabric design. Originally applied to mohair (hence its name), this watered effect is obtained by steam pressing the material, usually silk or rayon, between engraved rollers.

Mojave Desert (*or* Mohave Desert) A desert area in S California. It comprises part of the *Great Basin. Area: 15,000 sq mi (38,850 sq km).

Moji. See Kitakyushu.

mold Any fungus that forms a fine woolly mass growing on food, clothing, etc. Examples are the *bread mold and species of *Aspergillus* and *Penicillium*. *See also* slime mold.

Moldavia A former principality in SE Europe. It was occupied by the Mongols in the 13th century, becoming independent in the 14th century and encompassing Bukovina and Bessarabia. It became an Ottoman vassal state in the 16th century, losing Bukovina to Austria in the 18th century and Bessarabia to Russia in the 19th century. In 1859 Moldavia and Walachia formed Romania. Russian Moldavia became the *Moldavian Soviet Socialist Republic in 1940.

Moldavian Soviet Socialist Republic A constituent republic in SW Soviet Union. It was formed in 1940, mainly from areas of *Bessarabia (*see also* Moldavia). Its main industries are wine making, tobacco processing, and food canning, for it is very fertile, producing wheat, maize, fruit, and vegetables, as well as having many vineyards. Area: 13,000 sq mi (33,670 sq km). Population (1981 est): 4,000,000. Capital: Kishinev.

mole (medicine) An area of darkly pigmented skin, known medically as a nevus. Many people have moles and the only reasons for doing anything about them are cosmetic unless they enlarge, bleed, or become painful, any of which may indicate malignant (cancerous) change.

mole (metrology; symbol mol) The *SI unit of amount of substance equal to the amount of substance that contains the same number of entities as there are atoms in 0.012 kg of carbon-12. One mol of any substance contains $6.022,52 \times 10^{23}$ entities (see Avogadro's number). The entities may be atoms, molecules, ions, electrons, etc.

mole (zoology) A burrowing mammal belonging to the family *Talpidae*, of Europe, Asia, and North America. The common Eurasian mole (*Talpa europaea*) is about 5.5 in (14 cm) long including its small bristly tail. It is thickset, with velvety-black fur, and has long-clawed digging forefeet. Moles make an extensive system of underground tunnels, feeding on earthworms and storing surplus worms in a "larder." Practically blind above ground, moles rapidly starve when prevented from digging. Order: *Insectivora. See also* desman.

mole cricket A large *cricket belonging to the family *Gryllotalpidae* (about 50 species). 1.3–2 in (35–50 mm) long, mole crickets are brown and have enlarged and toothed front legs, which are used for digging long shallow tunnels under damp ground. The female lays large numbers of eggs in an underground nest and the young (like the adults) feed on plant roots and insect larvae.

molecular biology The scientific discipline that deals with the molecular basis of living processes. Molecular biology involves both *biochemistry and *biophysics: its growth since the 1930s has been made possible by the development of such techniques as *chromatography, *electron microscopy, and *X-ray diffraction, which have revealed the structures of biologically important molecules, such as DNA, RNA, and enzymes. Heredity, and the development, organization, function, and malfunction of living cells, all depend on the physical and chemical properties of the molecules involved.

molecule The smallest portion of a compound that can exist independently and retain its properties. The atoms that make up a molecule are either bonded together covalently, e.g. CO_2, or electrovalently, e.g. NaCl. However, in crystalline substances the bonds extend throughout the whole crystal structure and the molecule has only a notional existence. In covalent gases and liquids, however, the molecule actually exists as a small group of atoms. **Molecular weight** (*or* relative molecular mass) is the ratio of the average mass per molecule to one-twelfth of the mass of an atom of carbon-12. It is thus the sum of the *atomic weights of the atoms comprising a molecule.

mole rat A burrowing *rodent superficially resembling a mole. Mole rats belong to three families found in Africa and Eurasia: *Bathyergidae* (16 species), *Spalacidae* (3 species), and *Rhizomyidae* (14 species). Mole rats of all three families are similar in appearance with small eyes and ears, a small tail, and powerful digging feet. They feed on roots and tubers.

Molière (Jean-Baptiste Poquelin; 1622–73) French dramatist, the father of modern French comedy. He left home in 1643 to establish a theatrical company and toured the provinces from 1645 to 1658. *Les Précieuses ridicules* (1659) was the first of a series of Paris productions for both court and public audiences that included *Tartuffe* (1664), *Dom Juan* (1665), *Le Misanthrope* (1666), *L'Avare* (1668), *Le Bourgeois Gentilhomme* (1670), and *Le Malade imaginaire* (1673). His ridicule of hypocrisy and his vigorous satire of contemporary manners and types brought him into constant conflict with the religious authorities. He frequently acted in the productions that he both wrote and directed, and he died after collapsing on stage.

Molina, Luis de (1535–1600) Spanish *Jesuit theologian. A professor at Évora in Portugal and later at Madrid, he is best known for his *Concordia liberi arbitrii cum gratiae donis* (1588), which founded the doctrine known as Molinism. This was an attempt to reconcile the concept of divine grace with man's free will. It precipitated a violent dispute between Molina's Jesuit supporters and the *Dominicans, which lasted for several centuries.

Molinos, Miguel de (c. 1640–97) Spanish mystic and priest, who was a leading advocate of *Quietism. From 1669 he lived chiefly in Rome, where he wrote his famous *Spiritual Guide* (1675). He was condemned to life imprisonment by the *Inquisition in 1687.

Molise A mountainous region in S central Italy. Formerly part of Abruzzi e Molise, it was established as a separate state in 1963. It is a poor underdeveloped agricultural region producing wheat, potatoes, maize, sheep, and goats. Area: 1713 sq mi (4438 sq km). Population (1980 est): 334,703. Capital: Campobasso.

mollusk An invertebrate animal belonging to the phylum *Mollusca* (about 100,000 species). Mollusks occupy marine, freshwater, and terres-

trial habitats, being especially common on rocky coasts. They have a soft unsegmented body with a muscular foot, variously modified for crawling, burrowing, or swimming, and a thin dorsal mantle that secretes a shell of one, two, or eight parts. The shell is usually external, as in snails, but it may be internal, as in cuttlefish, or absent, as in slugs. All except bivalves feed using a ribbon-shaped rasping tongue (radula). Most mollusks are herbivorous with some carnivorous and scavenging species. In the more primitive mollusks there are separate male and female sexes and eggs and sperm are released into the water, where fertilization takes place. Some of the more advanced gastropods and bivalves are hermaphrodite and in some gastropods and all cephalopods fertilization is internal. *See also* bivalve; cephalopod; chiton; gastropod.

molly An attractive tropical fish of the genus *Mollienesia*. 2–5 in (5–13 cm) long, several color varieties have been bred for use in aquaria, including the well-known sailfin mollies (*M. latipinna* and *M. velifera*), which have a bluish sheen and, in the male, a large sail-like dorsal fin. Family: *Poeciliidae*; order: *Atheriniformes*.

Molly Maguires (1862–76) US secret terrorist society in the Pennsylvania and West Virginia coalfields. Coal miners, dissatisfied with working and living conditions, banded together, took their name from an Irish anti-landlord organization of the 1840s, and terrorized management and the police. James McParlan, a Pinkerton detective, spied on the group and in 1875–77 gave evidence that resulted in the hanging of 10 men.

Molnár, Ferenc (1878–1952) Hungarian dramatist and writer. He gained international success with his romantic and witty plays, notably *The Devil* (1907) and *The Red Mill* (1923). He also published novels and short stories. He emigrated to the US in 1940.

moloch A grotesque desert-dwelling Australian lizard, *Moloch horridus*, also called thorny devil. Its yellow-and-brown body is covered with thorny spines, which provide good camouflage. Ants are its chief food and a network of microscopic channels on its head collect dew, which drips into its mouth. Family: *Agamidae*.

Moloch A Semitic god whose worship was characterized by the sacrificial burning of children. There are several biblical references to his worship by the Israelites during the period of the Kings (c. 961–c. 562 BC) but his identity remains uncertain.

Molokai A mountainous US island in the N Pacific Ocean, in Hawaii. Father Damien worked in its leper colony. Pineapples and cattle are exported. Area: 261 sq mi (676 sq km). Population (1980): 6076. Chief settlement: Kaunakakai.

Molotov. *See* Perm.

Molotov, Vyacheslav Mikhailovich (V. M. Scriabin; 1890–) Soviet statesman, who assumed the name Molotov in 1906 to escape from the Imperial police. As prime minister (1930–41) and foreign minister (1939–49, 1953–56), Molotov signed the Soviet-German nonaggression treaty in 1939 and, after the German invasion in 1941, he negotiated alliances with the Allies. His subsequent attitude to the West (the frequency with which he said *niet* (no) in the UN was renowned) contributed to the prolongation of the Cold War. Disagreements with Khrushchev led to his demotion in 1956 and he was subsequently expelled from the Communist Party.
The **Molotov cocktail,** named for him, is an incendiary hand-grenade.

Moltke, Helmuth, Graf von (1800–91) Prussian field marshal; chief of the general staff (1858–88). His reorganization of the Prussian army led to the Prussian victories in the wars against Denmark (1864) and Austria (1866) and in the Franco-Prussian War (1870–71). His nephew **Helmuth Johannes Ludwig von Moltke** (1848–1916) was chief of the German general staff (1906–14), directing at the outbreak of World War I the strategy devised by *Schlieffen. Held responsible for the defeat at the Marne, he was relieved of his command.

Moluccas (*or* Maluku) An Indonesian group of islands between Sulawesi and West Irian. It includes the islands of Ambon, Halmahera, and Ceram. Mountainous and volcanic, most are fertile and humid. The indigenous population fishes, hunts, and collects sago, while along the coasts the tropical rain forest is giving way to shifting cultivation; spices, fish, and copra are exported. *History*: before the Portuguese arrival (1512), the islands were ruled by Muslims and already famed for their cloves and nutmeg from which they gained the name of Spice Islands. After great European rivalry, Dutch control was established in the 19th century. With Indonesian independence (1949) the S Moluccas fought to secede but were subjugated by the new government (1950–56). Since 1966 S Moluccans in the Netherlands have drawn attention to their cause with violent protests.

Area: about 28,766 sq mi (74,504 sq km). Population (1980): 1,411,006. Chief town: Ambon.

molybdenum (Mo) A very hard silvery-gray metal of high melting point, it was first prepared in 1782 by P. J. Hjelm (1746–1813). It occurs in nature as molybdenite (MoS_2) and as wulfenite (lead molybdenate; $PbMoO_4$). It is extracted by the reduction of molybdenum trioxide (MoO_3). Molybdenum is used in high-temperature filaments and as an alloying agent in the production of high-strength steels. Trace quantities of molybdenum are important for plant nutrition. At no 42; at wt 95.94; mp 4747°F (2617°C); bp 8342°F (4612°C).

Mombasa 4 04S 39 40E A port in Kenya, on an island in an inlet of the Indian Ocean. It was an important port for Arab traders and was taken in the 16th and 17th centuries by the Portuguese; the Arab influence remains strong. The modern deepwater port at Kinlindini handles most of Kenya's trade; industries include oil refining and a pipeline (opened 1977) supplies Nairobi. Population (1977 est): 371,000.

moment The product of a force and its perpendicular distance from the axis about which it acts. A moment produces a turning effect and is sometimes called a torque. The inertia of a body to a torque is called its **moment of inertia**. This quantity is equal to mr^2 for a single mass (m) rotating about an axis at a distance r from the axis. The moment of inertia of a system of masses is equal to the sum of these products.

momentum The linear momentum of a body is the product of its mass and its linear velocity. The angular momentum of a body is the product of its *moment of inertia and its angular velocity. Momentum is an important quantity in physics as during any process, for example a collision between two bodies, the total momentum of the system always remains constant (the law of conservation of momentum).

Mommsen, Theodor (1817–1903) German historian and politician. In his major historical work, *The History of Rome* (1854–85), Mommsen adopted a modern critical approach, effectively demythologizing Roman history. He also wrote on law and archeology.

Mon A people of lower Burma and central Thailand. They speak an *Austro-Asiatic language, also known as Talaing. It is written in a script derived from *Pali, which the Burmese subsequently adopted. Between about 600 and 1000 AD Mon kingdoms dominated the area. After the fall of rival *Pagan the Mons recovered independence (late 13th to mid-16th centuries) but were subjugated by the Burmese in the 18th century and now survive only as minority groups. They are village-dwelling rice farmers, whose Theravada Buddhism is tinged with earlier pagan beliefs.

Mona. *See* Anglesey.

Monaco, Principality of A small country on the Mediterranean Sea, an enclave within French territory. It consists of three principal localities: the business district around the ports, Monte Carlo with its famous casino, and the capital Monaco. *Economy*: the main sources of revenue are tourism and the sale of postage stamps. *History*: ruled by the house of Grimaldi since 1297, it has been under French protection since 1641 (except for a period, 1815–61, of Sardinian protection). Executive power lies with the hereditary prince and the State Council, and legislative power with the prince and the National Council. Head of state: Prince Rainier III. Official language: French; Monégasque, a mixture of French and Italian, is also spoken. Official currency: French franc of 100 centimes. Area: 467 acres (189 hectares). Population (1980 est): 28,000.

Monadhliath Mountains (or Gray Hills) A mountain range in N Scotland, in the Highland Region. It lies between Loch Ness and the Spey River and reaches 3087 ft (941 m) at Carn Mairg.

Monaghan (Irish name: Contae Mhuineachain) A county in the NE Republic of Ireland, in Ulster bordering on Northern Ireland. It is generally low lying and undulating. Agricultural produce includes oats and potatoes; cattle rearing and dairy farming are also important. Area: 499 sq mi (1551 sq km). Population (1979): 50,376. County town: Monaghan.

mona monkey. *See* guenon.

monarch A widespread American *milkweed butterfly, *Danaus plexippus*. Light brown with black borders and white dots, the adults migrate southward to overwinter in semihibernation. In spring they move north, breeding on the way. Occasionally, individuals may reach Europe. The caterpillars are green with black and yellow bands.

monasticism A system under which men or women devote themselves to a religious life either in solitude or in special communities removed from society. St *Anthony of Egypt probably inaugurated Christian monasticism by organizing ascetic hermits under a rule (c. 305). They were, however, essentially solitaries; communal monastic life was introduced by Anthony's disciple, *Pachomius. Between 358 and 364 St *Basil drew up the rule that

still governs the Orthodox Churches' religious communities. In the 6th century St *Benedict of Nursia introduced a monastic rule in Italy that remained the basic system in the West (*see* Benedictines). It underwent periodic reform, first at *Cluny in the 10th century. The rules of three orders founded in the 11th century—the Camaldolese (1012), *Carthusian (1084), and *Cistercian (1098)—were also stricter variants of the Benedictine rule. The mendicant friars (*see* Augustinians; Carmelites; Dominicans; Franciscans) also took vows and lived according to a rule, but not in seclusion: they continued to perform duties in the world. They had corresponding rules for women, however, who lived enclosed lives as nuns. Two military orders, the *Hospitallers and *Templars, followed monastic discipline. Both monks and nuns were required to take vows of poverty, chastity, and obedience and to devote their lives to prayer and work. Until the Renaissance revived secular learning, the monasteries were the main cultural centers, preserving and transmitting the learning of antiquity. Monasticism was also practiced by the ancient Jews (*see* Essenes), and there is a strong monastic tradition in Buddhism (*see* sangha; tri-ratna).

Monastir. *See* Bitola.

monazite A rare-earth mineral of composition $(Ce,La,Y,Th)PO_4$ and yellow to reddish-brown color, found as an accessory in acid igneous rocks and as placer deposits. Monazite is usually obtained as a by-product of titanium and zircon mining; it is the most common source of the rare earths.

Mönchengladbach (or München Gladbach) 51 12N 6 25E A city in NW West Germany, in North Rhine-Westphalia. The site of a 13th-century cathedral, it is the center of the German textile industry and headquarters of the NATO forces in N central Europe. Population (1980 est): 258,000.

Monck, George, 1st Duke of Albemarle (1608–70) English general. Initially a royalist in the Civil War, he was captured and imprisoned (1644–46). Won over to the parliamentary cause, he defeated the Scots at Dunbar (1650) and pacified Scotland. In the first *Dutch War he became a successful general at sea. In command of Scotland from 1654, he was largely responsible for the Restoration of Charles II.

Moncton 46 04N 64 50W A city and river port in E Canada, in New Brunswick. The railroad and transportation hub of the *Maritime Provinces, it also has light industry and the French-language University of Moncton (1864). Population (1976): 55,934.

Mond, Ludwig (1839–1909) German industrial chemist, who lived in Britain from 1862. He discovered nickel carbonyl and its application to the extraction of platinum from its ores, a method now known as the **Mond process.** He also made improvements to the *Solvay process.

Mondale, Walter F(rederick) ("Fritz"; 1928–) US vice president (1977–81). A lawyer, he worked with the Democratic Farmer-Labor Party and was Minnesota's attorney general (1960–64). He succeeded Hubert *Humphrey in the US Senate (1965–77), where he was known as a liberal. Chosen to be Jimmy Carter's running mate in 1976, he was an active and effective vice president who worked closely with the president and was instrumental in the passage of labor and intelligence-control legislation. He and Carter were defeated (1980) in their bid for re-election. Mondale, chosen as the Democratic presidential nominee in the 1984 elections, named Geraldine *Ferraro as his running mate. Overwhelmingly defeated by incumbent Republican Ronald *Reagan, he returned to private law practice.

Mondrian, Piet (Pieter Cornelis Mondriaan; 1872–1944) Dutch painter, born in Amersfoot. His early still lifes and landscapes became increasingly architectural; however, while in Paris (1912–14) he came under the influence of *cubism. His first abstract compositions (1917) used only horizontal and vertical lines, primary colors, and black and white. During this period he helped to launch the art movement of de *Stijl. After 1919 his style, known as neoplasticism, influenced both the *Bauhaus school and the *international style in architecture. In New York after 1940 his style became more relaxed with such paintings as *Broadway Boogie Woogie*.

Monet, Claude (1840–1926) French impressionist painter, born in Paris (*see* impressionism). He spent his childhood in Le Havre, where his teacher *Boudin encouraged him to paint in the open air. After military service in Algeria (1860–62) he met *Sisley and *Renoir in Gleyre's studio. Initially influenced by the *Barbizon school, in the late 1860s he developed the impressionist technique in views of Paris and in the 1870s in boating scenes at Argenteuil. He excelled in his series of the same scenes painted at different times of day, e.g. *Gare St Lazare, Haystacks, Rouen Cathedral*, and the *Poplars*, the last of which anticipates *abstract art. His last works were his famous murals of water lilies (Orangerie, Paris).

monetarism A revision of old-established economic theories that rivals *Keynesianism. Monetarism's most celebrated proponent is the US economist Milton *Friedman. Monetarists believe that with the exception of *monetary policy government economic policy does not achieve its aims and is harmful. They regard responsible regulation of the money supply as essential to the wellbeing of the economy, advocating a gentle expansion of the money supply at roughly the rate of growth of the economy. Monetarists blame *inflation on overexpansion of the money supply. The essential difference between neo-Keynesians and monetarists is that the former believe in government regulation of the economy, whereas the latter do not.

monetary policy An economic policy in which the money supply is managed by the government, in order to influence the economy. Following the inflation of the 1970s and the impact of monetarist ideas (*see* monetarism), more attention is being paid to monetary policy.

money A medium of exchange. To be an efficient medium of exchange, money should be divisible (for small transactions), have a high value-to-weight ratio (to make it easy to carry about), be readily acceptable, and not easily counterfeited. Money also functions as means of credit and a store of wealth, for which purposes its value must remain stable. The depreciation in the value of money (*see* inflation) is an economic problem, at present besetting the West. Money was reputedly invented by the Lydians in the 7th century BC. It originally took the form of something intrinsically valuable (such as a precious metal) but, so long as it is generally acceptable and retains confidence, this is not necessary. Indeed, most money is now in the form of paper, which is itself almost worthless. Individual countries have their own form of money (currency), which cannot be used in other countries; to be used in another country currencies have to be exchanged (*see* exchange rates). The total stock of money in the economy is known as the **money supply**.

money spider A tiny *spider of the family *Liniphiidae* (over 250 species). It has a reddish or black body and occurs in enormous numbers in fields, etc. Money spiders build sheetlike webs on vegetation to which they cling upside down, waiting to catch insects that drop onto the web. Immature spiders may be seen drifting considerable distances in the air, attached to silken gossamer threads.

moneywort A perennial herb, *Lysimachia nummularia*, also called creeping jenny, native to damp places in Europe. It has a creeping stem, up to 27 in (60 cm) long, shiny heart-shaped leaves, and yellow flowers borne individually on short stalks. Family: *Primulaceae*.

The Cornish moneywort (*Sibthorpia europaea*) is a small trailing perennial with minute pink flowers. Family: *Scrophulariaceae*.

Monge, Gaspard (1746–1818) French mathematician. He was one of the founders of descriptive geometry, the mathematics of projecting solid figures onto a plane, upon which modern engineering drawing is based. He became a close friend of Napoleon and was appointed minister for the navy (1792–93), but was stripped of all honors on the restoration of the Bourbons. He died in poverty.

Mongolian languages A group of languages that, together with *Turkic and *Manchu-Tungus, constitute the Altaic language family. Western Mongolian languages are spoken in parts of the Soviet Union, the Mongolian People's Republic, and Afghanistan; Eastern Mongolian is spoken in China and the Mongolian People's Republic. There are more than three million speakers of these languages, the majority of which remain unwritten.

Mongolian People's Republic A large sparsely populated country in NE central Asia, between the Soviet Union and China. It is mainly high plateau, rising to the Altai and Khangai Mountains in the W and extending into the Gobi Desert in the S. *Economy*: with its nomadic-pastoral tradition, it is still mainly dependent on livestock rearing, now organized in collectives and state farms. In recent years there have been attempts to increase crop growing. Copper mining is being introduced and other minerals include coal, oil, gold, tungsten, lead, and uranium. There is some light industry, mainly based on Ulan Bator. Exports, mainly to communist countries, include cattle and horses, wool, and hair. *History*: in the 13th century Genghis Khan ruled the Mongol empire from Karakoram in the N. As Outer Mongolia, the area was a province of China from 1691 to 1911, when it became an autonomous monarchy under Russian protection. Again under Chinese influence from 1919 to 1921, it then became independent and the Mongolian People's Republic was declared in 1924. Persecution of lama priests (*see* Tibetan Buddhism) precipitated the Lama Rebellion (1932), when several thousand Mongolians with several million head of livestock crossed the border into Inner Mongolia. After World War II its independence was guaranteed by the Soviet Union and China, but relations with the latter have deteriorated since the Sino-Soviet split in the early 1960s.

Head of State: Yumjaagiin Tsedenbal (1916–). Official language: Khalkha Mongolian. Official currency: tugrik of 100 möngö. Area: 604,095 sq mi (1,565,000 sq km). (604,095 sq mi). Population (1981 est): 1,732,000. Capital: Ulan Bator.

mongolism. *See* Down's syndrome.

Mongoloid The racial grouping comprising the populations of E Asia and the Arctic region of North America. They are characterized by medium skin pigmentation, the epicanthic fold of the upper eyelid, straight coarse black hair, a rather flat face with high cheekbones, slight facial and body hair, and a high percentage of B blood type. The American Indian peoples used to be classified as Mongoloid but now only the Eskimo peoples are included.

Mongols An Asiatic people united in the early 13th century by *Genghis Khan, who built up an empire that encompassed much of central Asia. Under his grandson *Kublai Khan the Mongols conquered China and ruled there as the *Yuan dynasty until 1368. They were subsequently confined to the area approximating to the present-day Mongolian People's Republic.

mongoose A carnivorous □mammal belonging to the family *Viverridae* (which also includes civets and genets), found in warm regions of the Mediterranean, Africa, and Asia. There are about 40 species, ranging in size from 20–40 in (50–100 cm) including the long tapering furry tail (10–20 in [25–50 cm]), with short legs, small ears, and long coarse gray-brown fur. Mongooses are renowned for catching snakes and rats and also eat eggs, small mammals, frogs, and birds. Chief genera: *Galidictis*, *Herpestes*, *Helogale*.

monism. *See* dualism.

Monitor and Merrimack Civil War naval battle at Hampton Roads, Virginia, in 1862; the first between ironclad ships. The *Monitor*, the Union ironclad, was engaged by the Confederate *Virginia* (formerly the *Merrimack*), a Northern-built steam frigate converted to an ironclad warship. After much shooting and attempts to ram each other, the *Virginia* returned to home base, each side confident of victory. Although the battle was indecisive, it showed the capabilities of ironclad vessels, raised the morale of both sides, and maintained the Union blockade. In 1978 the wreck of the victorious *Monitor* was identified in 230 ft (75 m) of water outside the harbor.

MONITOR LIZARD *The Australian lace monitor, or goanna* (Varanus varius), *which reaches a length of 6 ft (1.8 m) or more and is mainly black and yellow.*

monitor lizard A lizard belonging to the Old World family *Varanidae* (30 species), occurring in tropical and subtropical regions. 6.5 in–10 ft (0.2–3 m) long, monitors have an elongated body and well-developed legs. They feed on mammals, snakes, lizards, eggs, and carrion. The rare Bornean earless monitor (*Lanthanotus borneensis*) lives in subterranean tunnels and is a good swimmer, feeding on fish and worms. *See also* Komodo dragon.

Moniz, Antonio Egas (1874–1955) Portuguese surgeon, who pioneered the use of brain surgery in the treatment of severe mental illness. In 1935 he performed the first operation of prefrontal lobotomy (*see* leukotomy) and shared the 1949 Nobel Prize with Walter Rudolf Hess (1881–).

Monk, Thelonius (Sphere) (1920–82) US jazz pianist and composer, influential in the development of *bop. He developed a characteristic pianistic style and played alone or in small groups; his compositions include "Off Minor" and "Blue Monk."

monkey A tree-dwelling *primate. Monkeys are 8–43 in (20–110 cm) long and most have a long balancing tail of up to 100 cm used in climbing, although some are tailless. Agile and intelligent, they have fingernails and an opposable thumb enabling manual dexterity. Most monkeys are omnivorous but they prefer fruit, nuts, and other vegetation. *See also* New World monkey; Old World monkey.

monkey flower A fragrant annual or perennial herb or shrub of the mostly North American genus *Mimulus* (100 species), growing near streams and rivers. *M. guttatus* is a naturalized European species. Up to 24 in (60 cm) tall, it has simple toothed leaves and showy yellow tubular flowers with red spots, each with a two-lobed upper lip and a larger three-lobed lower lip. Family: *Scrophulariaceae*. *See also* musk.

monkey puzzle A coniferous tree, *Araucaria araucana*, also called Chile pine, native to Chile and Argentina and widely grown as an ornamental. Up to 100 ft (30 m) high (ornamental trees are much smaller), it has whorled horizontal branches covered with leathery prickly overlapping leaves, 1.2–1.6 in (3–4 cm) long. The globular spiny cones, 4–7 in (10–17 cm) long, ripen from green to brown and break up to release large seeds, which are edible when roasted. Family: *Araucariaceae*.

monkfish A *shark belonging to the family *Squatinidae*. It has a broad flattened head, an elongated tapering body, winglike pectoral fins, two dorsal fins, and no anal fin. Monkfish occur in tropical and temperate seas and feed on bottom-dwelling fish, mollusks, and crustaceans. A species of *anglerfish, *Lophius piscatorius*, is also called monkfish.

monkshood. *See* aconite.

Monmouth, James Scott, Duke of (1649–85) The illegitimate son of Charles II of England who led the Monmouth rebellion against his uncle James II. A Protestant, he became a focus of the opposition to the succession of the Roman Catholic James and was banished (1684). After James' accession (1685), Monmouth landed at Lyme Regis to raise a rebellion and was defeated, captured, and beheaded.

Monnet, Jean (1888–1979) French economist and public official, known for his contribution to European unity. He was deputy secretary general of the League of Nations (1919–23). In 1946 he inaugurated the Monnet Plan for the modernization of French industry and later drafted the *Schuman Plan for the establishment of the European Coal and Steel Community, of which he was president (1952–55). His efforts culminated in the establishment of the EEC.

monocotyledons The smaller of the two main groups of flowering plants, which includes the palms, bananas, orchids, grasses, lilies, and many garden bulbs and corms—daffodils, irises, tulips, crocuses, etc. (*compare* dicotyledons). Monocots are characterized by having a single seed leaf (cotyledon) in the embryo. Typically the flower parts are in threes (or multiples of three) and the leaves have parallel veins. Very few monocots produce true wood. *See also* angiosperms.

Monod, Jacques-Lucien (1910–76) French biochemist, who proposed a mechanism for the regulation of gene activity. Monod and his colleague F. Jacob (1920–) postulated a regulatory gene that controlled the activity of a neighboring gene for protein synthesis. Their theory was later found to be largely true. Monod and Jacob shared the 1965 Nobel Prize with A. Lwoff (1902–).

monomer A simple molecule or group of atoms forming a repeated unit in a dimer (two molecules), trimer (three molecules), or polymer (*see* polymerization).

Monophysites (Greek *monos physis*: one nature) Supporters of the doctrine that the incarnate Christ had only a single divine nature. They opposed the orthodox teaching that he possessed two natures, human as well as divine. The doctrine was provoked by the dogmatic formulations of the Council of Chalcedon (451) and, despite attempts at reconciliation by the Byzantine emperors, the *Coptic and several other Eastern Churches were irrevocably schismatic by the mid-6th century.

monopoly An industry in which the market is supplied by one supplier. The monopolist can obtain a high profit by restricting supply and demanding a high price. Consumers are thus penalized and it is likely that with a secure market there will also be inefficiency in production. In the public sector of a mixed economy monopolies for the supply of public services (electricity, gas, transport, etc.) are commonplace. In the private sector they are usually restricted by legislation such as the *antitrust laws in the US.

monosaccharide (*or* simple sugar) A *carbohydrate consisting of a single sugar unit and possessing either a keto group (C=O) or an aldehyde group (CHO). Monosaccharides are classified according to the number of carbon atoms they possess—the most common being pentoses (with five) and hexoses (with six)—and they can exist as either straight-chain or ring-shaped structures. The most widely occurring monosaccharides are *glucose and *fructose.

monosodium glutamate The sodium salt of the amino acid glutamic acid, used widely in the food industry as a flavoring agent, especially in canned preserved foods.

monotheism Belief in only one God. The great monotheistic religions are Judaism, Christianity, and Islam. Earlier views that monotheism evolved out of *polytheism are now discredited, as Judaism and Islam in particular seem to have grown from conscious opposition to polytheistic systems.

Monothelites (Greek *monos, thelein*: one, (to) will) Supporters of the doctrine that the incarnate Christ possessed only one divine will. Monothelitism was conceived in 624 as a formula for reconciling the *Monophysite churches but failed in its purpose and was formally branded a heresy in 680.

monotreme A primitive *mammal belonging to the order *Monotremata*, found only in Australia (including Tasmania) and New Guinea. The name means "single hole," and monotremes have the reptilian characteristic of a single vent for passing urine, feces, and eggs or sperm. Monotremes lay eggs, suckling their young after these hatch. The only living monotremes are the *echidnas and *duck-billed platypus.

Monroe, James (1758–1831) US statesman; 5th president of the US (1817–25). After service in the Revolutionary War, Monroe studied law under Thomas *Jefferson and was a member of the Continental Congress (1783–86). Although he initially opposed the ratification of the US *Constitution, he served in the US Senate (1790–94) and was named US minister to France (1794–96). After a single term as governor of Virginia (1799–1802), Monroe was sent to France by President Jefferson and was instrumental in the negotiations leading to the *Louisiana Purchase (1803). He later served as a special US minister to Great Britain and Spain (1803–06). In 1811 he was again elected governor of Virginia but resigned that office to become secretary of state in the cabinet of President James *Madison (1811–17) and briefly as secretary of war (1814–15). As the leader of the Jeffersonian Republicans, he was elected president in 1816. His two terms in office were marked by domestic prosperity and stable international relations. Most of the US border with Canada was finalized, and the former Spanish territory of Florida was acquired by the US in 1819. One of the most lasting achievements of the Monroe administration was the proclamation (1823) of the *Monroe Doctrine, which warned against European involvement in the western hemisphere.

MARILYN MONROE *With Arthur Miller.*

Monroe, Marilyn (Norma Jean Baker *or* Mortenson; 1926–62) US film actress. Her childhood was spent in an orphanage and foster homes. Promoted as a sex symbol, in such films as *Niagara* (1952) and *Gentlemen Prefer Blondes* (1953), she later developed a real acting talent and ability as a comedienne. Her third husband was Arthur *Miller, and her last film appearance was in *The Misfits* (1961), which he wrote. She died from an overdose of barbiturates.

Monroe Doctrine. *See* Monroe, James.

Monroe–Pinckney Treaty (1806) Agreement between the US and Britain regarding smuggling, blockading, and the illegal impressment of US sailors into the British Navy. Negotiated by US minister to Great Britain James *Monroe and William Pinckney with the British foreign secretary, it was not ratified by the US Senate.

Monrovia 6 20N 10 46W The capital and main port of Liberia, on the Atlantic Ocean. Founded in 1822 as a settlement for freed North American slaves, it was named for President Monroe of the US. The University of Liberia was founded in 1851. Population (1978): 208,629.

Mons (Flemish name: Bergen) 50 28N 3 58E A city in Belgium, situated between two important coalmining regions. Notable buildings include the town hall (1443–67) and the Church of Ste Waudru (1450–1621). The battle of Mons took place here on August 23, 1914, at the beginning of World War I. Principally a commercial center, its industries include oil, cotton, porcelain, and tobacco. Population (1981 est): 96,336.

Monsarrat, Nicholas (John Turney; 1910–79) British novelist. His best-known novel, *The Cruel Sea* (1951), was based on his naval experiences in World War II. Other novels include *The Tribe That Lost its Head* (1956) and *The Pillow Fight* (1965).

monsoon A seasonal large-scale reversal of winds in the tropics, resulting chiefly from the differential heating of the land and oceans. It is best developed in India, SE Asia, and China; N Australia and East and West Africa have similar wind reversals. The term is derived from the Arabic word *mawsim*, originally applied to the seasonal winds of the Arabian Sea. It is now commonly applied to the rainfall that accompanies the wind reversals, especially the period of heavy rainfall in S Asia extending from April to September, in which the winds are southwesterly.

Monstera A genus of large tropical American herbaceous plants (50 species) that climb by means of aerial roots. *M. deliciosa* is often grown as a house plant for its foliage and in the tropics for its edible green fruits. The leaves, up to 60 cm long, are perforated with slits or holes and the flowers resemble those of the *arum lily. Family: *Araceae*.

Montaigne, Michel de (1533–92) French essayist. Soon after the death of his father, a wealthy merchant, in 1568, he resigned his position as magistrate in Bordeaux and began composing his *Essais*. In 1580 he traveled extensively in Europe and was mayor of Bordeaux from 1581 to 1585. His *Essais*, which inaugurated a new literary genre, expressed his mature humanistic philosophy and constitute a moving self-portrait. They were published in two editions in 1580 and 1588, and a posthumous edition incorporated his final revisions. The *Essais* were translated into English by John Florio in 1603 and influenced the development of the English essay.

Montale, Eugenio (1896–1981) Italian poet. The stoic pessimism and symbolic imagery of his early poetry, especially in *Ossi di seppia* (1925), contrasts with the personal warmth of such later volumes as *Satura* (1971) and *Xenia* (1972). He was an opponent of fascism, and from 1947 literary editor of the newspaper *Corriere della Sera*. He published many translations and literary essays and won the Nobel Prize in 1975.

Montana The fourth largest US state. It is bounded by the Canadian provinces of Saskatchewan, Alberta, and British Columbia to the N; Idaho to the W and SW; Wyoming to the S; and South Dakota and North Dakota to the E. It is mountainous and forested in the W, rising to the Rocky Mountains, with the rolling grasslands of the Great Plains in the E. Its economy is predominantly agricultural, cattle ranching and wheat production being of greatest importance. Other crops include barley and sugar beet. It possesses important mineral resources, notably copper (at Butte) and coal. The extraction of the latter is possible through strip mining but this has caused environmental problems. There are several Indian reservations within the state, notably the Crow reservation. *History*: Once the home of the buffalo and a large number of Indian tribes, including Blackfoot, Sioux, Shoshone, Arapaho, Cheyenne, and Flathead, Montana formed part of the Louisiana Purchase in 1803. The first explorations were probably undertaken by Lewis and Clark, but settlement began with the discovery of gold in the mid 19th century. The capital, Helena, originated as a mining camp called Last Chance Gulch. During the Indian wars the battle of *Little Bighorn (Custer's Last Stand) took place (1876). Range wars between sheep- and cattle-raising ranchers and struggles between copper companies for control of Montana's copper mines dominated the late 19th century. In 1909 open range areas were fenced in to allow farming of the

land. All sectors suffered during the Depression, but World War II brought prosperity. Montana's energy industries flourished during the energy crisis of the 1970s. Area: 145,587 sq mi (377,070 sq km). Population (1980): 786,690. Capital: Helena.

Montanism An early Christian sect founded by a shadowy individual called Montanus in Asia Minor in the mid 2nd century. It spread to N Africa, where *Tertullian became an adherent. It was characterized by *millenarianism, prophesying, and insistence upon strict asceticism.

Montauban 44 01N 1 20E A city in SW France, the capital of the Tarn-et-Garonne department. It has textile and porcelain industries. Population (1975): 50,420.

Mont Blanc (Italian name: Monte Bianco) 45 50N 6 52E The highest mountain in the Alps, on the French–Italian border. It was first climbed in 1786. A road tunnel (1958–62) beneath it, 7.5 mi (12 km) long, connects the two countries. Height: 15,771 ft (4807 m).

montbretia A perennial herb, *Crocosmia crocosmiflora* (a hybrid between *C. pottsii* and *C. aurea*), native to South Africa but naturalized in Europe and often grown as a garden ornamental. Up to 40 in (1 m) high, it has long stiff sword-shaped leaves and clusters of orange-red funnel-shaped flowers, up to 3 in (7.5 cm) across, with spreading petals. The name is also applied to the similar and related flowering herbs of the South African genus *Montbretia* (or *Tritonia*). Family: *Iridaceae*.

Montcalm, Louis Joseph de Montcalm-Grozon, Marquis de (1712–59) French general distinguished for his command (1756–59) against the British in Canada during the Seven Years' War. In 1756 he regained control of Ontario for the French, in 1757 he took Fort William Henry, and in 1758 repulsed the much larger British force from Ticonderoga. He died defending Quebec from assault by Gen James *Wolfe, who, although victorious, was also mortally wounded.

Monte Bello Islands 20 30S 115 30E A group of uninhabited coral islands in the Indian Ocean, off the W coast of Western Australia. They were used for testing British nuclear weapons in 1952 and 1956.

Monte Carlo 43 44N 7 25E A resort in the principality of Monaco, on the Riviera. It is famous for its casino, automobile race, and other cultural and sporting events. Population (1968): 9948.

Monte Cristo An Italian islet in the Tyrrhenian Sea. It is associated with the novel by Dumas, *The Count of Monte Cristo*.

Montefeltro An Italian noble family that ruled the city of Urbino between the 13th and 16th centuries. Originally rulers of the town of Mons Feretri from which they derived their name, the Montefeltri gave military support to the Holy Roman Emperor in his struggle against the pope (*see* Guelfs and Ghibellines). The best-known member of the family is the illegitimate **Federigo Montefeltro, Duke of Urbino** (1422–82), who distinguished himself as a military leader and as an art patron, especially of *Piero della Francesca. Urbino passed into the hands of the Rovere family in the 16th century because there were no Montefeltro heirs.

Montego Bay 18 27N 77 56W A port and tourist resort in NW Jamaica. Its chief exports are bananas and sugar. Population (1971 est): 42,800.

Montélimar 44 33N 4 45E A city in SE France, in the Drôme department. Famous for its nougat, it is an agricultural center and has light industry. Population (1975): 29,149.

Montenegro (Serbo-Croat name: Crna Gora) The smallest constituent republic of Yugoslavia, bordering on the Adriatic Sea. It is predominantly mountainous and forested. Stock raising is important, especially of sheep, goats, and pigs. *History*: it was declared a kingdom in 1910, becoming a province of the kingdom of the Serbs, Croats, and Slovenes (later Yugoslavia) in 1918. Area: 5387 sq mi (13,812 sq km). Population (1978): 583,000. Capital: Titograd.

Monterey 36 39N 121 45W A city in California, on Monterey Bay. One of California's oldest cities, it is a well-known retreat of artists and writers. It forms the background for several of John Steinbeck's novels. Population (1970): 26,302.

Monte Rosa 45 57N 7 53E A massif in S Europe, on the Swiss–Italian border in the Alps. The highest peak, the Dufourspitze, is, at 15,203 ft (4634 m), the highest in Switzerland.

Monterrey 25 40N 100 20W The third largest city in Mexico. Founded in 1579, it has many notable buildings including the 18th-century cathedral. Monterrey is a major industrial center specializing in metallurgy. Population (1978 est): 1,054,029.

Montespan, Françoise Athénaïs de Rochechouart, Marquise de (1641–1707) The mistress of Louis XIV of France from 1667 until replaced by the governess of their seven children—Mme de *Maintenon.

Mme de Montespan remained at court until 1691, when she retired to a convent.

Montesquieu, Charles Louis de Secondat, Baron de (1689–1755) French historical philosopher and writer. Montesquieu's first work, the *Lettres persanes* (1721), was a brilliant satirical portrait of French institutions and society. It was a forerunner of the *Enlightenment. There followed the *Considérations sur les causes de la grandeur et de la décadence des romains* (1734) and the famous *Esprit des lois* (1748). This latter work, a comparative study of ideas on law and government, was perhaps the most important book of 18th-century France. It impressed even *Voltaire, who disliked Montesquieu intensely.

Montessori system A system of education for young children devised by the Italian doctor Maria Montessori (1870–1952). It places emphasis on development of the senses and envisages a limited role for the teacher as the child learns by itself through the use of didactic materials. Her first school opened in Rome in 1907 and her methods continue to be influential in nursery schools today.

Monteux, Pierre (1875–1964) French conductor. He became conductor of Diaghilev's Ballets Russes in 1911 and gave the first performances of Stravinsky's *Petrushka* and *The Rite of Spring*. He subsequently held various posts in Europe and the US and was principal conductor of the London Symphony Orchestra from 1961 to 1964.

Monteverdi, Claudio (1567–1643) Italian composer, a pupil of Marco Ingegneri (1545–92). From about 1590 to 1612 Monteverdi was court musician to the Duke of Mantua. From 1613 until his death he was maestro di cappella at St Mark's Cathedral, Venice. Monteverdi was the first great composer of *opera; enlarging the orchestra, he employed a new range of instrumental effects and made use of an innovatory harmonic style to achieve dramatic effects. He also influenced the development of the madrigal as an expressive form. His works include the operas *Orfeo* (1607) and *The Coronation of Poppea* (1642), a set of *Vespers* (1610), and many madrigals.

Montevideo 34 55S 56 10W The capital and main port of Uruguay, in the S on the Río de la Plata. Founded in 1726 by the Spanish as a defense against Portuguese attacks from Brazil, it suffered several occupations in the early 19th century before becoming capital of the newly independent Uruguay in 1828. In the 20th century it has developed rapidly, as both an industrial and a communications center, and it is now one of South America's largest cities. It is also a popular summer resort. The University of Uruguay was founded here in 1849. Population (1980 est): 1,314,129.

Montez, Lola (Marie Gilbert; 1818–61) Irish dancer and mistress of Louis I of Bavaria (1786–1868; reigned 1825–48). The hostility aroused by her influence led to the abdication of Louis in 1848 and her own expulsion. She later lived for several years in the US.

Montezuma II (1466–c. 1520) The last Aztec Emperor of Mexico (1502–20). During his reign his empire was weakened by tribal warfare, which enabled the Spaniards, led by Hernán *Cortés, to establish themselves in Mexico. The emperor was captured by Cortés and was killed either by the Spaniards or by his own people during the Aztec attack on Cortés' force as it tried to leave Tenochtitlán.

Montfort, Simon de, Earl of Leicester (c. 1208–65) English statesman, born in Normandy; the son and namesake of the leader of the Crusade against the *Albigenses. After serving Henry III of England in Gascony, he joined the antiroyalist faction that demanded greater control of the government, becoming the barons' leader in the subsequent *Barons' War. Initially successful, he became virtual ruler of England, summoning a parliament in 1265. In the same year, however, he was defeated and killed at Evesham.

Montgolfier, Jacques-Étienne (1745–99) French balloonist, who with his brother **Joseph-Michel Montgolfier** (1740–1810) invented the hot-air balloon. The hot-air balloon, so called because it derived its buoyancy from air heated by a fire, was publicly launched in 1782. A much larger balloon, which rose 6562 ft (2000 m), was demonstrated in June 1783 and in October a series of passenger-carrying ascents were made. Jacques-Étienne (who himself never made an ascent) then launched a free-flying balloon and in 1784 Joseph-Michel with five companions ascended in a steerable balloon. Their experiments aroused enormous interest in flying.

Montgomery 32 22N 86 20W The capital city of Alabama, on the Alabama River. Montgomery was the first capital (1861) of the Confederate states during the Civil War. In the mid 1950s it was the scene of a bus boycott by blacks, which played an important part in the growth of the civil-rights movement and brought Martin Luther King to the nation's attention. Montgomery is an industrial city and agricultural trading center. Population (1980): 178,157.

Montgomery of Alamein, Bernard Law, 1st Viscount (1887–1976) British field marshal. In World War II he became commander of the Eighth Army (1942) and after the battle of Alamein drove *Rommel back to Tunis and surrender (1943), an achievement that brought him enormous popularity. Having played a major role in the invasion of Italy (1943), he became chief of land forces in the 1944 Normandy invasion. He helped plan the Arnhem disaster (September, 1944), but restored his reputation by pushing back the subsequent German offensive, receiving Germany's surrender. After the war he was chief of the imperial general staff (1946–48) and deputy commander of NATO forces (1951–58).

month The time taken by the moon to complete one revolution around the earth. The complicated motion of the moon requires the starting and finishing points of the revolution to be specified. The length of the month depends on the choice of reference point. The **sidereal month**, of 27.32 days, is measured with reference to the background stars. The **synodic month**, of 29.53 days, is measured between two identical phases of the moon. The month is one of the basic time periods used in *calendars.

Montherlant, Henry de (1896–1972) French novelist and dramatist. He was born in Paris into an aristocratic family. His works celebrate the virtues of austerity and virility and concentrate on physical pursuits and relationships. His novels include *Les Célibataires* (1934), the tetralogy *Les Jeunes Filles* (1936–39), and *Le Chaos et la nuit* (1963), and his plays include *Malatesta* (1946) and *Port-Royal* (1954).

Montmartre. *See* Paris.

Montparnasse. *See* Paris.

Montpelier 44 16N 72 35W The capital city of Vermont, in N central Vermont, on the Winooski River. Settled in 1789, it became Vermont's capital in 1805. Besides state and federal business carried on in the city, there are also insurance companies headquartered here. Population (1980): 8,241.

Montpellier 43 36N 3 53E A city in S France, the capital of the Hérault department. A Huguenot stronghold, it was besieged and captured by Louis XIII in 1622. Notable buildings include the gothic cathedral, the university (founded 1289), and the Musée Fabre. Montpellier trades in wine and brandy and has numerous manufacturing industries. Population (1975): 195,603.

Montreal 45 30N 73 36W A city and port in E Canada, in Quebec on Montreal Island at the junction of the Ottawa and St Lawrence Rivers. Canada's largest city, it is also the greatest transportation, trade, and manufacturing center. Montreal employs cheap hydroelectricity for many industries, including oil refining, meat packing, brewing and distilling, food processing, textiles, and aircraft. It is the headquarters of banks, insurance companies, airlines, and railroads. Housing two English-speaking and two French-speaking universities, Montreal is a forum for politics, broadcasting, theater, film, and publishing. Two thirds of the population is French speaking, making it the second largest French-speaking city in the world. Among its many beautiful buildings are Notre Dame Church, Christ Church Cathedral, and St James Cathedral. *History*: founded as Ville-Marie (1642), Montreal quickly became a commercial center. Captured by Britain (1760), it acquired an English-speaking merchant community that has dominated Quebec's economy ever since. Recently Montreal was the venue of the world fair Expo '67 and the 1976 Olympics. Population (1976): 1,080,546.

Montreux 46 27N 6 55E A winter resort in W Switzerland, on Lake Geneva. Its 13th-century Château de Chillon is immortalized in Byron's poem the "Prisoner of Chillon". It holds an annual television festival awarding the Golden Rose of Montreux. Tourism is an important source of income. Population (1970): 20,421.

Montrose, James Graham, 1st Marquess of (1612–50) Scottish general. In 1637 he signed the Covenant in support of Presbyterianism but became a rival of the antiroyalist *Argyll. Montrose fought for Charles I in the English Civil War but after a series of victories (1644) his army was defeated (1645) and he fled to Europe. He returned in 1650 but was defeated, captured, and executed by the parliamentarians.

Montserrat A British crown colony comprising one of the Leeward Islands, in the Caribbean Sea to the SE of Puerto Rico. It is largely mountainous with active volcanoes. *Economy*: chiefly agricultural, the main crops are cotton, coconuts, and fruit and vegetables, which with cattle are the main exports. Forestry is being developed. *History*: discovered by Columbus in 1493, it was colonized by the Irish in the 17th century. Formerly administratively joined to the Leeward Islands, it became a separate colony in 1960. It was part of the Federation of the West Indies (1958–62). Official language: English. Official currency: East Caribbean dollar of 100 cents. Area: 40 sq mi (106 sq km). Population (1980): 12,073. Capital and main port: Plymouth.

Montserrat 41 36N 1 48E An isolated mountain in NE Spain, NW of Barcelona. On its E slope is a Benedictine monastery housing a well-known carving, supposedly by St Luke, of the Virgin and Child. Height: 4054 ft (1235 m).

Mont St Michel 48 38N 1 30W A granite islet in NW France, in the Manche department in the Bay of St Michel. The islet is connected to the mainland by a causeway. It is about 256 ft (78 m) high and is crowned by a Benedictine monastery (founded 966 AD), which was used as a prison from the French Revolution until 1863.

Monza 45 35N 9 16E A city in Italy, in Lombardy. An important commercial city in the 13th century, it has a gothic cathedral. Umberto I was assassinated here in 1900. Its manufactures include machinery and textiles. It is noted for its automobile-racing circuit. Population (1981 est): 124,362.

Moody, Dwight Lyman (1837–99) US evangelist. As a successful businessman in Chicago in the 1850s, he was an active lay worker in a Congregational Church. He first achieved fame as a preacher in England (1873–75), and together with his musical colleague Ira David Sankey (1840–1908) compiled a popular collection of hymns, the *Sankey and Moody Hymn Book* (1873). He founded the Moody Bible Institute (1899).

Moog synthesizer. *See* synthesizer.

moon The natural satellite of the earth. The moon orbits the earth every 27.32 days at a mean distance of 238,712 mi (384,400 km), keeping more or less the same face (the nearside) toward the earth. As it revolves, different *phases can be seen from earth, together with up to two or three lunar *eclipses per year. The moon is only 81 times less massive than the earth and has a diameter of 2148 mi (3476 km).
The major surface features are the light-colored highlands on the southern nearside and most of the farside, and the much darker lava plains—the *maria. The maria and more especially the highlands are heavily cratered. These roughly circular walled depressions, ranging greatly in size, were produced by impacting bodies from space. The extremely tenuous atmosphere exposes the surface to considerable temperature extremes (–292°F to 230°F [–180°C to +110°C]).
Much of our information about the moon has been derived from photographs and other measurements taken from orbiting US and Soviet satellites and later from moonrock samples brought back (1969–72) by the Apollo astronauts (and the unmanned Soviet Luna landers) and from experiments set up on the moon by the astronauts. The first landing on the moon was made by Neil Armstrong (1930–) and Edwin Aldrin (1930–) on July 20, 1969. *See* Apollo moon program.

moonfish A deep-bodied fish, also called opah, belonging to the genus *Lampris* and family *Lamprididae*, widely distributed in warm seas. Up to 7 ft (2 m) long, its body is colored blue above, rose-pink below, and is spotted with white; the fins are scarlet. It is uncommon and valued as food. Order: *Lampridiformes*.

moonflower. *See* morning glory.

Moonies. *See* Unification Church.

moon rat The largest living mammal of the order *Insectivora, Echinosorex gymnurus*, of Sumatra, Borneo, and S Asia. It is a *gymnure about 24 in (60 cm) long, black with a white head and long whiskery snout. A secretion of the anal glands gives it a characteristic smell.

moonstone A gem variety of feldspar, usually transparent or translucent orthoclase, albite, or labradorite. It shows a play of colors resembling that of opal.

Moore, Clement Clarke (1779–1863) US poet and teacher; author of *A Visit from St Nicholas* (1823). He taught Oriental and Greek literature at General Theological Seminary (1823–50) in New York City. His famous poem, written as a gift for his children, is better known by its opening words, "'Twas the night before Christmas."

Moore, G(eorge) E(dward) (1873–1958) British philosopher. Moore's work centered on language and the analysis of its meaning. He maintained that the common usage of words is often profoundly different from their analytical meaning. Much of his published work is in the field of ethics and is concerned with the analysis of concepts of goodness. His books include *Principia Ethica* (1903) and *Ethics* (1912). He was professor of mental philosophy and logic at Cambridge (1925–39) and editor of the journal *Mind* (1921–47).

Moore, Henry (1898–) British sculptor. Moore studied at Leeds and the Royal College of Art (1921–24). His fascination with primitive African and Mexican art molded the development of his two characteristic themes: mother and child sculptures and reclining figures. The latter, a lifelong

preoccupation, reached its apogee in the sculpture for UNESCO in Paris (1956–57). After devoting himself to abstract work in the 1930s, Moore reverted to the humanist tradition in the early 1940s with his celebrated drawings of sleeping figures in air-raid shelters. These, his *Madonna and Child* (1943–44), and family groups brought him international fame. His later output continued in this vein, together with more experimental abstract works, such as *Atom Piece* (1964–66).

HENRY MOORE *The sculptor in the indoor studio at his home in England.*

Moore, Marianne (1887–1972) US poet. Her first volume, *Poems* (1921), contained poems contributed to the English Imagist magazine *Egoist*. She edited the literary magazine *Dial* from 1925 to 1929. *Collected Poems* (1951) won the Pulitzer Prize. Her poetry is noted for its qualities of irony and sharply observed detail. She also published a verse translation of *The Fables of La Fontaine* (1954).

moorhen A gray-brown waterbird, *Gallinula chloropus*, also called common gallinule and waterhen, occurring worldwide except for Australia. It is 13 in (32 cm) long and has a red bill and forehead and a white patch beneath the tail. It breeds in thick vegetation near ponds and marshes and feeds on seeds, water plants, and aquatic invertebrates. Family: *Rallidae* (rails, etc.).

Moorish idol A deep-bodied tropical fish, *Zanclus canescens*, found in shallow Indo-Pacific waters. It has a black and yellow vertically striped body, about 7 in (18 cm) long, a beaklike mouth, and a greatly extended dorsal fin. It is the only member of its family (*Zanclidae*). Order: *Perciformes*.

Moors The conventional European name for the *Arab and *Berber inhabitants of NW Africa and, by extension, for the 8th-century Muslim conquerors of the Iberian Peninsula, whose armies consisted of both Arab and Berber troops. The word originates in the Roman name for that region of Africa—Mauretania. The Moors were the dominant power in Spain until the 11th century, after which they fell gradually under Christian rule (*see* Mudéjars). A highly civilized people, the Moors played a major role in transmitting classical science and philosophy to W Europe.

moose. *See* elk.

Moose Jaw 50 23N 105 35W A city in W Canada, in S Saskatchewan. Founded in 1882, it is a railroad and farming center. Food processing, building materials, and oil refining are economically important. Population (1976): 32,581.

moped. *See* motorcycles.

Moradabad 28 50N 78 45E A city in India, in Uttar Pradesh. Founded in 1625, it is an agricultural trading center and has metalworking, cotton-weaving, and printing industries. Population (1971): 258,590.

moraine The clay, stone, boulders, etc. (*see* till), carried along or deposited by glaciers. It may have been deposited by former glaciers as particular landforms or be actively transported on the ice surface, within the ice, or beneath the ice.

morality plays A form of vernacular religious drama popular in England and France from the late 14th to late 16th centuries. Similar in content and purpose to medieval sermons, morality plays were dramatized allegories of good and evil fighting for man's soul. They include *The Pride of Life, The Castle of Perseverance*, and *Everyman*, which is best known.

They influenced Elizabethan drama and at the Reformation in England provided a vehicle for dramatizing the religious issues at stake. *See also* miracle plays.

moral philosophy. *See* ethics.

Moral Rearmament (MRA) An evangelical movement founded by a US evangelist and former Lutheran pastor, Frank Nathan Daniel Buchman (1878–1961), in the 1920s. It initially received most support at England's Oxford University and was called the Oxford Group until 1938. It seeks the regeneration of national and individual spirituality through conversion, God's personal guidance, and living in purity, unselfishness, honesty, and love.

Morandi, Giorgio (1890–1964) Italian still-life painter and etcher, born in Bologna. Although he also painted landscapes and flowerpieces, he is noted for his austere compositions of bottles and jars. He was associated with the school of *metaphysical painting.

Moravia (Czech name: Morava; German name: Mähren) An area and former province (1918–49) of central Czechoslovakia. Lying chiefly in the basin of the Morava River, it rises in the N to the Sudeten Mountains and in the E to the Carpathian Mountains. It contains important mineral deposits, including coal and iron ore. *History*: settled by Slavic tribes in the late 8th century AD, it formed the center of an important medieval kingdom (Great Moravia) until incorporated into the kingdom of *Bohemia in 1029; in 1849 it was made an Austrian crownland. It became part of the Republic of Czechoslovakia in 1918. Chief town: Brno.

Moravia, Alberto (Alberto Pincherle; 1907–) Italian novelist. His early novels, beginning with *The Time of Indifference* (1929), criticized fascism and the corrupt middle-class society that allowed it to flourish. His later works, which include *The Woman of Rome* (1947), *Roman Tales* (1954), *Two Women* (1957), *The Lie* (1966), and *1934* (1983) concern themes of social alienation and the futility of sexual relationships. His literary and political essays are collected in *Man As an End* (1963).

Moravian Brethren A Protestant denomination that continues the ideals of the earlier Bohemian Brethren, a 15th-century group centered in Prague that practiced a simple unworldly form of Christianity. The Moravians date from the establishment of a community in 1722 by Count von *Zinzendorf on his estates in Saxony. In doctrine they are close to *Lutheranism but have a simplified Church hierarchy and liturgy. Hymn singing is important in their services. From the 1730s they were active missionaries; John *Wesley was among those whom they influenced. Many now live in North America.

MORAY EEL *The long jaws of a moray eel are armed with very sharp strong teeth, which are capable of inflicting a severe bite.*

moray eel A thick-bodied *eel of the family *Muraenidae* (over 80 species). Up to 5 ft (1.5 m) long, it is brightly colored and lacks pectoral fins. Moray eels live in rock crevices and reefs of warm and tropical seas and can be dangerous when disturbed. The flesh can be poisonous.

Moray Firth An inlet of the North Sea in NE Scotland, extending SW from a line between Tarbat Ness in the Highland Region and Burghead in Grampian Region. Length: about 35 mi (56 km).

Mordvinian Autonomous Soviet Socialist Republic (*or* Mordovian ASSR) An administrative division in the W central Soviet Union, in the RSFSR. It is heavily forested. The majority of the population is Russian, 35% being Mordvinians, who speak a Finno-Ugric language. The area was annexed by Russia in the 16th century and became an autonomous republic in 1934. The region supports a wide range of industries, including timber, manufacturing of building materials, and textiles, but is predominantly agricultural: the main crops are cereals; sheep and dairy farming are also important. Area: 10,110 sq mi (26,200 sq km). Population (1981 est): 984,000. Capital: Saransk.

More, Henry (1614–87) English philosopher. One of the *Cambridge Platonists, More shared the group's interest in *Neoplatonism. *Descartes, whose work he helped publicize in England, was an early influence, but More later found his philosophy too materialistic. Although he was an opponent of religious fanaticism, More's own writings, such as *The Immortality of the Soul* (1659) and *Divine Dialogues* (1668), are more poetical and mystical than philosophical.

More, Sir Thomas (1477–1535) English lawyer, scholar, and saint, whose martyrdom horrified his contemporaries and has captured the imagination of succeeding generations. He joined Henry VIII's Privy Council in 1518 and succeeded Wolsey as chancellor in 1529. He resigned the chancellorship in 1532 in opposition to Henry's assumption of the supreme headship of the English Church. In 1534 More was imprisoned after refusing to swear to the new Act of Succession because it repudiated papal authority in England, and he was brought to trial for treason in 1535. In spite of a brilliant self-defense, he was convicted on false evidence and beheaded. He was canonized by the Roman Catholic Church in 1935.

His best-known scholarly work is *Utopia* (1516), in which he discussed an ideal social and political system; he also wrote (c. 1513–c. 1518) an unfinished *History of King Richard III*.

Moreau, Gustave (1826–98) French symbolist painter, best known for his detailed and brilliantly colored biblical and mythological fantasies and as the enlightened teacher of *Matisse and *Rouault at the École des Beaux Arts. Most of his works are in the Musée Gustave Moreau, Paris.

Moreau, Jean Victor (1763–1813) French general. He fought in the Revolutionary Wars and, after Napoleon came to power (1799), became commander of the Rhine army, defeating the Austrians at Hohenlinden (1800). In 1804 he was arrested after becoming involved with anti-Bonapartists and was exiled. In 1813 he joined the coalition army formed to oppose Napoleon and died in the battle of *Dresden.

morel A fungus belonging to the genus *Morchella*. Morels are typically club-shaped with the surface of the cap pitted like a honeycomb. The edible common morel (*M. esculenta*) has a yellowish-brown cap, 1.6–3.1 in (4–8 cm) high, and a stout whitish stalk. It is found in clearings and hedgerows. Class: *Ascomycetes.

Morelia (name until 1828: Valladolid) 19 40N 101 11W A city in Mexico, situated on the central plateau. It has a notable cathedral (17th–18th centuries) and is the center of a cattle-raising area. Population (1978 est): 239,377.

Morgagni, Giovanni Battista (1682–1771) Italian anatomist and founder of pathological anatomy. His great work, *On the Seats and Causes of Diseases as Investigated by Anatomy* (1761), was based on over 600 postmortem dissections. Morgagni was professor of anatomy at Padua University for nearly 60 years until his death.

Morgan An American all-purpose breed of horse descended from a stallion with some Thoroughbred and Arabian ancestry, born in about 1790 and named for its owner, Justin Morgan. The Morgan has a compact deep-chested body, powerful hindquarters, and a long crested neck and is usually bay. Height: 4.6–4.9 ft (1.42–1.52 m) (14–15 hands).

Morgan, Charles (1894–1958) British novelist and dramatist. With his novels, which include *The Fountain* (1932) and *The Voyage* (1940), he achieved a considerable reputation in Europe, becoming a member of the French Academy. In England he won greater success with his plays, especially *The River Line* (1949).

Morgan, Sir Henry (c. 1635–88) Welsh buccaneer. Said to have been kidnapped and taken to Barbados, he joined the buccaneers then raiding the Spanish in the Caribbean. In 1671 he led a band over the Isthmus of Panama and sacked the city (1671), thus opening the way to plunder in the S Pacific. He was knighted in 1674 and made lieutenant general of Jamaica.

Morgan, John Pierpont (1837–1913) US financier, who founded J. P. Morgan and Co, one of the most powerful US banking corporations. Son of a successful New York banker, Morgan amassed a fortune through gold speculation during the Civil War. In 1869 he gained control of the Albany & Susquehanna RR and continued to expand his railroad interests throughout the following decades. Morgan later supervised the organization of the United States Steel Corp (1901) and the International Harvester Corp (1902). As a prominent art collector, he was an important patron of the Metropolitan Museum in New York and founded the Pierpont Morgan Library. His son **John Pierpont Morgan, Jr.** (1867–1943) succeeded him as the chairman of J. P. Morgan and Co and helped to organize the credit requirements of the Allies in World War I.

Morgan, Thomas Hunt (1866–1945) US geneticist, who established that *chromosomes carried the units of inheritance proposed by Gregor *Mendel. Morgan was skeptical about Mendelian theory until he began his breeding experiments with the fruit fly *Drosophila*. He discovered that a number of genetic variations were inherited together and demonstrated that this was because their controlling genes occurred on the same chromosome (the phenomenon of linkage). Morgan was awarded a Nobel Prize (1933).

Morgan le Fay In *Arthurian legend, an evil sorceress who plotted the overthrow of her brother King Arthur. According to Malory's *Morte d'Arthur* (1485) she betrayed *Guinevere's adultery to Arthur. However, in the earlier *Vita Merlini* (c. 1150) by *Geoffrey of Monmouth she is a benevolent figure who lives in Avalon, where she once healed the wounded Arthur.

Morgenthau, Henry, Jr. (1891–1967) US statesman; secretary of the treasury (1934–45). An avid conservationist, he held several New York state conservation and agricultural positions (1928–32) during Franklin D. *Roosevelt's term as governor. After Roosevelt became president, Morgenthau was appointed secretary of the treasury, a post he held through the New Deal legislative programs and World War II. After his Morgenthau Plan for the postwar reconstruction of Germany met with President Harry S Truman's disapproval, he resigned and devoted the rest of his life to farming and philanthropic causes.

Mörike, Eduard Friedrich (1804–75) German poet and novelist. A rural clergyman, he found inspiration in country life, which supplied the subjects of his first distinguished collection of lyrics (*Gedichte*, 1838). The best of his prose works is the novella *Mozart auf der Reise nach Prag* (1856).

Moriscos Muslims forced to profess Christianity in Spain. Many Muslims continued to live in Spain after the formerly Muslim areas came under Christian rule and by the 15th century they were forced to become Christians or go into exile. Many chose to remain in Spain while privately remaining Muslims and eventually the government ordered their expulsion. Between 1609 and 1614 about 500,000 Moriscos were forced into exile, settling mainly in Africa.

Morisot, Berthe (1841–95) French painter, granddaughter of the artist *Fragonard. The first female impressionist and an outstanding painter of women and children, she was strongly encouraged by *Corot. *Manet, whose brother Eugène she married (1874), was influenced by her.

Morland, George (1763–1804) British painter, born in London. The son and pupil of the painter Henry Morland (c. 1730–97), he exhibited sketches at the Royal Academy when aged only ten. Popularized through engravings, his work, which included such picturesque rustic scenes as *The Inside of a Stable*, declined after 1794. His dissolute life finally resulted in imprisonment (1799–1802).

Morley, Edward Williams (1838–1923) US chemist, who investigated the relative atomic weights of hydrogen and oxygen. However, he is best known for his collaboration with Albert *Michelson in the *Michelson-Morley experiment.

Morley, Robert (1908–) British stage and film actor. His long career as a character actor dates from 1929, and his films include *Major Barbara* (1940), *Beat the Devil* (1953), and *Oscar Wilde* (1960). Other films are *The Trygon Factor* (1967), *Theater of Blood* (1973), and *The Blue Bird* (1976). Many of his later roles have been those of pompous eccentrics.

Morley, Thomas (1557–1603) English composer, music printer, organist of St Paul's Cathedral, and member of the Chapel Royal. A pupil of Byrd, he wrote madrigals, canzonets, songs, church music, and the textbook *A Plaine and Easie Introduction to Practicall Musicke* (1597).

Mormons Adherents of the Christian sect that is formally called the Church of Jesus Christ of Latter-Day Saints, founded in 1830 by Joseph Smith in New York state. A series of visions culminated in Smith's claim that he had discovered golden tablets that contained the Book of Mormon, a sacred book named for a primitive American prophet who had compiled it. After Smith's murder by a mob, the persecuted Mormons moved W under Brigham Young, establishing their headquarters at Salt Lake, Utah, in 1847. Attempting to revert to the simple sanctity of the early Christians, Mormons have no professional clergy, reject infant baptism, emphasize self-help to avoid want, abstain from alcohol and other stimulants, and run educational and missionary programs. Polygamy (*see* marriage), for which Mormons were once notorious, has been disallowed since 1890.

Mornay, Philippe de, Seigneur du Plessis-Marly (1549–1632) French Huguenot (Protestant) leader during the *Wars of Religion. Escaping the *St Bartholomew's Day Massacre (1572), he rose to a position of considerable influence as one of the chief confidants of Henry of Navarre, later Henry IV of France. When Henry was converted to Roman Catholicism, Mornay retained his Huguenot sympathies and lost the king's favor.

morning glory A trailing or twining plant of the genus *Ipomea*, native to tropical America and Australia and cultivated for its beautiful flowers. The leaves are often heart-shaped and the trumpet-shaped flowers, up to 5 in (12 cm) across, are deep blue, purple, pink, or white. Popular species are *I. purpurea* and *I. alba* (the moonflower). The seeds of certain varieties contain hallucinogens. Family: *Convolvulaceae*.

Moro, Aldo (1916–1978) Italian statesman; Christian Democratic prime minister (1963–68, 1974–76) and foreign minister (1965–66, 1969–72, 1973–74). He included socialists in his first cabinet and in 1976 was instrumental in gaining communist support for the minority Christian Democratic government. In 1978 he was kidnapped and then murdered by the *Red Brigades.

Morocco, Kingdom of A country in NW Africa, bordering on the Atlantic Ocean and Mediterranean Sea. The Atlas Mountains crossing the center of the country rise to 13,665 ft (4165 m) at Mount Toubkal and separate the Atlantic coastal area from the Sahara. The population is mainly of Berber and Arabic origin. *Economy*: the chief occupations are agriculture and mining. Wheat, barley, maize, and citrus fruits are grown, mainly in the coastal areas N of the mountains; livestock, especially sheep and goats, is also important. Morocco is a leading exporter of phosphates, having about 40% of the world's known phosphate reserves. Other mineral resources are iron ore, coal, lead, zinc, cobalt, and manganese. Industries include food processing, textiles, and traditional handicraft industries; a major phosphoric acid plant has been developed. There is a thriving fishing industry, sardines and tuna being the chief catch. Morocco's hot sunny climate and Atlantic and Mediterranean beaches make it a popular tourist center. *History*: part of the Roman province of Mauretania, it fell to the Vandals in the 5th century AD. Conflict between Arabs and Berbers was virtually continuous; in the 15th and 16th centuries Morocco came under attack from Spain and Portugal and until the 19th century was a base for Barbary pirates. Its strategic importance was recognized by the European powers in the 19th century, French and Spanish interests conflicting with those of Germany. The Algeciras Conference was held (1906) to consider the Moroccan question. The French increased their control in the area and the appearance of a German warship at Agadir (1911) was interpreted by the French as a threat of war. Following the Agadir incident Morocco was partitioned into French and Spanish protectorates (1912) and the international zone of Tangier (1923). In 1956 the protectorates were relinquished and Morocco became a sultanate, later a kingdom (1957) under King Mohammed V; his son, Hassan II, acceded to the throne in 1961. In 1975 agreement was reached providing for the partition of Spanish Sahara (*see* Western Sahara) between Morocco and Mauretania; in 1979 Mauretania withdrew from Western Sahara and it came under Moroccan occupation. Prime minister: Mohammed Karim Lamrani. Official religion: Islam. Official language: Arabic. Official currency: dirham of 100 centimes. Area: 144,078 sq mi (458,730 sq km). Population (1979 est): 19,470,000. Capital: Rabat.

Moroni 11 40S 43 16E The capital of the Comoro Islands, a port in the SW of Grande Comore island. Population (1977 est): 16,000.

Moroni, Giovanni Battista (c. 1525–78) Italian painter, born near Bergamo. Although he painted many altarpieces in Bergamo, he is best known for his portraits, notably *The Tailor*.

Morosini A noble Venetian family, prominent from the 10th century, that produced four *doges as well as distinguished generals, admirals, and churchmen. Best known is **Francesco Morosini** (1618–94), who was doge of Venice from 1688 until his death. As commander in chief of the Venetian fleet, he defeated the Turks, Venice's enemies, at sea and in Greece.

Morpheus In Greek mythology, a god of dreams, a son of Somnus, the god of sleep. He sent human forms into the dreams of sleeping men, while his brothers Phobetor and Phantasus sent animal and inanimate forms.

morphine A *narcotic analgesic drug obtained from *opium and used in medicine for the relief of severe pain. Its depressant effect on the brain accounts for the pain-killing properties; in high doses it also inhibits the breathing and cough centers. Other side effects include constipation, nausea, and vomiting. Morphine is an addictive drug and readily leads to severe physical dependence. Nalorphine is a specific antidote to morphine overdosage. *See also* drug dependence.

morphology (biology) The study of the form and structure of plants, animals, and microorganisms. *Anatomy is often used synonymously with morphology but in the former the emphasis is on the gross and microscopic structure of organs and parts.

morphology (language). *See* grammar.

Morphy, Paul Charles (1837–84) US chess player, who between 1858 and 1860 was regarded as the world's best player and whose games still fascinate chess enthusiasts. He traveled to Europe, defeating all opponents, but gave up chess to follow his legal career. This was unsuccessful and he became mentally unstable.

Morrill Land Grant Act (1862) US law that provided for the establishment and financial support of state institutions of higher learning, especially in the fields of agriculture and mechanical arts. Sponsored by US Representative Justin Smith Morrill of Vermont, it promoted education for the "industrial classes." *See also* Land-Grant College.

Morris, Desmond John (1928–) British zoologist, noted for his popularization of biology, especially in his books on human behavior. *The Naked Ape* (1967), *The Human Zoo* (1969), and *Manwatching* (1977) all set out to prove that human beings are still subject to the basic laws of animal behavior.

Morris, Gouverneur (1752–1816) US patriot, statesman, and diplomat. A member of the Continental Congress (1778–79), his financial expertise led to an appointment as assistant superintendent of finance (1781–85), during which time he devised the decimal coinage system, using dollars and cents, a term he invented. A delegate from Pennsylvania to the Constitutional Convention (1787), he played a major role in the final writing of the Constitution, although his idea of a strong central government was not incorporated. He was appointed US minister to France (1792–94), served as US senator (1800–03), and was made chairman of the Erie Canal Commission in 1810.

Morris, Robert (1734–1806) US patriot and businessman; born in England. He came to America in 1747 and by 1754 was a partner in a Philadelphia trading firm. A member of the Continental Congress (1775–78), he signed the Declaration of Independence and distinguished himself as a business and financial expert. He was recalled in 1781 to serve as superintendent of finance and was responsible for raising the funds for the Revolution. He reorganized government finances, established credit, founded the Bank of North America (the first nation's commercial bank, 1781), and established the US currency system. He was a US senator from Pennsylvania (1789–95).

Morris, William (1834–96) British designer, artist, and poet. Associated with the *Pre-Raphaelite Brotherhood, he later started a firm of decorators and designers (1861), who placed great importance on preindustrial crafts. He designed stained glass, carpets, and furniture, and his wallpaper designs are still used. His Kelmscott Press, founded in 1890, influenced book design and printing generally. The 19th-century *Arts and Crafts movement drew much of its inspiration from his work. He was also one of the founders of British socialism.

Morris dance A ritual English folk dance performed by groups of white-clad men wearing bells and often carrying sticks or handkerchiefs. A common theme is fertility through death and rebirth, symbolized by the carrying of green branches. Similar dances are found throughout Europe, India, and the Americas, often featuring animal characters or the black-faced Morisco (Moor), from which the name Morris is thought to derive.

Morris Jesup, Cape 83 40N 34 00W The N tip of Greenland, the world's most northerly land point, 440 mi (708 km) from the North Pole.

Morrison, Toni (Chloe Anthony Wofford; 1931–) US novelist. A graduate of Howard (1955) and Cornell (1957) universities, she worked in publishing from 1967. Her novels, dealing primarily with the lives of blacks, include *The Bluest Eye* (1970), *Sula* (1973), *Song of Solomon* (1977), and *Tar Baby* (1981).

Morristown 40 48N 74 29W A city in N central New Jersey, NW of Newark. Settled about 1709–10, it was the site of General George Washington's winter encampments of 1777 and again in 1779–80. The Morristown National Historical Park commemorates these and other significant Revolutionary War events. The telegraph was invented here by Samuel F. B. Morse and Alfred L. Vail. Industries include stone quarries, clothing, chemicals, and plastics. Population (1980): 16,614.

Morse, Samuel Finley Breese (1791–1872) US painter and inventor. He abandoned his first career as a successful portrait painter because he believed the US market was too limited. From the early 1830s, he worked for several years to perfect the electric telegraph before erecting the first telegraph line, between Washington and Baltimore (1844). Messages were sent by a system of dots and dashes that he had invented for the purpose (*see* Morse code). The first mesage sent, "What hath God wrought!" was particularly appropriate because the telegraph revolutionized communications.

letters			
A	·—	N	—·
B	—···	O	———
C	—·—·	P	·——·
D	—··	Q	——·—
E	·	R	·—·
F	··—·	S	···
G	——·	T	—
H	····	U	··—
I	··	V	···—
J	·———	W	·——
K	—·—	X	—··—
L	·—··	Y	—·——
M	——	Z	——··

numbers		punctuation marks	
1	·————	·	·—·—·—
2	··———	,	——··——
3	···——	:	———···
4	····—	?	··——··
5	·····	'	·————·
6	—····	-	—····—
7	——···	/	—··—·
8	———··	(or)	—··——
9	————·	"	·—··—·
0	—————		

MORSE CODE

Morse code The code invented by Samuel *Morse for transmitting telegraph messages. Each letter of the alphabet and number has a characteristic sequence of dots and dashes (short and long pulses), a dash being three times as long as a dot.

mortar (building material) A mixture of sand, hydrated lime, and Portland cement, used to bind together building bricks, etc. It is applied wet as a paste, which sets to a durable solid.

mortar (weapon) A short-barreled muzzle-loading artillery piece with a low-velocity high-angled trajectory. Although modern designs date from 1915, it originated before 1600. In World War II the largest Allied mortar had a caliber of 4.2 inches (107 mm), the German version being 8.3 inches (210 mm) with six barrels. Used against an enemy behind cover, mortars are principally used to fire high-explosive and smoke bombs.

mortgage Rights in property (usually land, buildings, etc.) given by a borrower (mortgagor) to a lender (mortgagee) as security for a loan. When all the money borrowed and the interest due under the mortgage have been repaid, it is redeemed.

Mortier, Édouard Adolphe Casimir Joseph, Duc de Trévise (1768–1835) French marshal, who fought in the Revolutionary and Napoleonic Wars. In 1803 he occupied Hanover but in 1805 was defeated at Dürnstein by the Russians. He subsequently served in the campaign against Prussia (1806–07) and in the *Peninsular War, winning at Ocaña (1809). He was Louis-Philippe's prime minister (1834–35) and died in an attempt on the king's life.

Mortimer, Roger de, 1st Earl of March (c. 1287–1330) English magnate. He led the baronial opposition to Edward II's favorites (1320–22) and was imprisoned before fleeing to France. There he became the lover of Edward's queen *Isabella with whom he secured Edward's deposition and murder in 1327. He then ruled England in the name of Edward's son, Edward III, until the latter caused him to be executed.

Morton, James Douglas, 4th Earl of (c. 1516–81) Regent of Scotland (1572–78) for James VI (later James I of England). Under Mary, Queen of Scots, he was involved in the murder of Riccio (1566) and then, for which he was eventually executed, of Darnley (1567).

Morton, Jelly Roll (Ferdinand Joseph La Menthe; 1885–1941) US jazz pianist and composer, who began his career playing the piano in New Orleans' Storyville brothels and made recordings in the 1920s with the group Morton's Red Hot Peppers. Claiming that he "invented jazz in 1902," his reputation has been the subject of controversy.

Morton, John (c. 1420–1500) English churchman. A supporter of the Lancastrian cause, under Henry VII he became Archbishop of Canterbury (1486), chancellor (1487), and cardinal (1493). He is remembered for his argument—**Morton's Fork**—that both the rich and those who seemed to be less well off could afford to contribute to royal requests for grants: those who lived in luxury obviously had the money to spare, while those who lived less extravagantly must have saved money by their modest way of life.

mosaic A picture or ornamental design made from small colored cubes of glass, stone, tile, etc. Mosaics were common in ancient Greece, where they were principally used for floors and made from colored pebbles. During the Roman Empire mosaics of opaque glass and glass covered with gold leaf became popular for wall and vault decoration, a development that reached its peak in the early Christian churches in Byzantium and Italy. The 6th-century decorations in S Vitale, in Ravenna, are among the most famous mosaics of the middle ages. During this period mosaics were no longer stylistically dependent on painting but, instead, led artistic trends with their use of two-dimensional forms, rich color, and lavish use of gold. During the Renaissance frescoes became the preferred form of church decoration but mosaics have been revived during the 20th century.

Mosaic law The collective name for the laws contained in the *Torah. They purport to have been revealed by God to Moses on Mount Sinai and in *Judaism they form the basis of *halakhah. In Christianity some of them are accepted, but most are rejected or interpreted allegorically.

mosasaur A member of an extinct family of huge marine lizards that lived during the Cretaceous period (135–65 million years ago). Up to 33 ft (10 m) long, mosasaurs had broad paddle-like limbs and a long flexible tail and were efficient swimmers, feeding on fish, cuttlefish, and squid.

moschatel A perennial herbaceous plant, *Adoxa moschatellina*, also called townhall clock, native to Eurasia and North America. Up to 4 in (10 cm) high, it has compound leaves with round-lobed leaflets and a squarish terminal cluster of greenish flowers. It has a musky smell and is the sole member of its family (*Adoxaceae*).

Moscow (Russian name: Moskva) 55 45N 37 42E The capital of the Soviet Union and of the Moscow autonomous region (*oblast*), in the RSFSR on the Moskva River. It is the economic and political center of the Soviet Union and an important transportation center. Industries include heavy engineering, cars, textiles, electronics, chemicals, publishing, and food processing. Moscow is at the center of the Soviet railroad system and is an important riverport. Its underground railroad (begun 1935) is of note. The city is based on a radial plan; the *Kremlin (citadel) and Red Square are at its heart. The Kremlin, triangular in shape, encloses a number of notable ecclesiastical buildings including the Cathedral of the Assumption (1475–79) and the Cathedral of the Annunciation (1484–89). Red Square is the traditional setting for military parades and demonstrations. Beyond its historical center Moscow is a modern city. It is a major cultural center; its many educational institutions include the University of Moscow (1755), the People's Friendship University (1960) for foreign students, and the Academy of Sciences of the USSR. The Tretyakov Gallery of Russian Art (1856) is the most notable of its many museums. Other famous institutions include the Bolshoi Theater of Opera and Ballet (1780), the *Moscow Art Theater, and the Moscow State Circus. *History*: first documented in 1147, settlement actually dates back to prehistoric times. By the beginning of the 13th century it was the center of the Muscovy principality and became the seat of the Russian Church containing the Kremlin (1326). In 1712–13 the capital was transferred to St Petersburg (Leningrad) but Moscow remained significant. The city was invaded by Napoleon (1812) and the ensuing fire, started either by looting French soldiers or the Moscow people themselves, destroyed much of the city. The workers' movements in Moscow played an important role in the Revolution of 1905. In March, 1918, it was chosen as the capital of the RSFSR and following the arrival of Lenin and other communist leaders (1922) was made the capital of the Soviet Union. Development programs were interrupted by World War II, during which the German invasion of the city was only halted by the severe weather and strong resistance. Since the war, programs of recovery and development have been followed and Moscow has developed an important tourist industry. It was chosen as the site of the 1980 Olympic Games. Population (1981 est.): 8,203,000.

Moscow Art Theater A Russian theater company founded in 1898 by Konstantin *Stanislavsky and Vladimir Nemirovich-Danchenko (1859–1948). Its first major success was a production of *The Seagull* by Chekhov, whose plays were ideally suited to the naturalistic acting style developed by Stanislavsky. Other dramatists whose plays received notable productions include Gorky, Tolstoy, and Maeterlinck. The company

gained international acclaim on its first tour of Europe and the US in 1922 and has continued to maintain high standards of ensemble acting.

Moseley, Henry Gwyn Jeffries (1887–1915) British physicist, who, working under *Rutherford, discovered the connection between the frequency of the X-rays emitted by an atom of an element and its atomic number. This discovery provided a theoretical basis for the periodic classification of the elements. Moseley's career came to a tragic end when he was killed in World War I.

Moselle River (German name: Mosel R.) A river in W Europe, flowing N from NE France to join the Rhine River at Koblenz. It forms part of the border between West Germany and Luxembourg. Its valley is one of the main wine-growing areas of West Germany. Length: 340 mi (547 km).

Moses In the Old Testament, the lawgiver of Israel, who led the people from slavery in Egypt (Exodus) and, after wandering in the desert for 40 years, brought them to an area E of the Jordan River, the border of the Promised Land. He is the central figure in most of the Pentateuch (the first five Old Testament books). As a child in Egypt (according to the Old Testament), Moses was saved from the slaughter of all Hebrew male children ordered by Pharaoh by being hidden in bulrushes on the Nile; he was found and brought up by one of Pharaoh's daughters. On Mt Sinai he was given the Ten Commandments by Jehovah. He died at the age of 120, before the Israelites entered the Promised Land, which he was allowed to see from a distance (Mt Pisgah).

Moses, Grandma (Anna Mary Robertson M.; 1860–1961) US primitive painter, born in Greenwich, New York (*see* primitivism). Entirely self-taught, she only turned seriously to painting at the age of 67 after a life as a farmer's wife. She specialized in naive and nostalgic scenes of farm life, popularized through prints and Christmas cards.

Mosley, Sir Oswald Ernald (1896–1980) British fascist. He was a member of parliament as a Conservative (1918–22), an Independent (1922–24), and then a Labour representative (1924, 1926–31), serving as chancellor of the Duchy of Lancaster (1929–30). In 1932 he established the British Union of Fascists, which incited antisemitic violence, especially in London. In World War II he was interned (1940–43) and in 1948 founded the Union Movement.

mosque A Muslim place of worship. It evolved in various styles from a simple rectangular building, such as the first mosque built by Mohammed at Medina in 622 AD. Larger mosques are usually built around a courtyard, which is surrounded by arcades on all four sides. Prayers are said in a large covered area on the side facing Mecca, the direction being indicated by a niche (*mihrab*) in the wall. Mosques are often domed and have *minarets. Painting and sculpture of living beings are forbidden, but elaborate geometrical designs and Arabic calligraphy frequently adorn both exterior and interior walls. The mosque has traditionally been the center of Muslim life, intellectual and social as well as religious. The three most sacred mosques are those of Mecca, Medina, and Jerusalem.

Mosque of Islam. *See* Black Muslims.

mosquito A small fly belonging to a family (*Culicidae*; about 2500 species) of almost worldwide distribution, being especially abundant in the tropics. It has long legs, elongated mouthparts, and a long slender abdomen. In most species the males feed on plant juices, while the females bite and suck the blood of mammals, often transmitting serious human and animal diseases. The three important genera are *Anopheles, *Aedes, and *Culex* (including the common gnat, *C. pipiens*). The active larvae live in fresh water, feeding on algae, bacteria, and organic debris. Most breathe through a siphon at the rear end.

Mosquito Coast (*or* Miskito Coast) A coastal belt in Central America, bordering on the Caribbean Sea and extending from E Honduras into E Nicaragua. Its name derives from the former inhabitants of the area, the Mosquito (Miskito) Indians. The cultivation of bananas is the chief occupation. Average width: 40 mi (60 km).

moss A *bryophyte plant of the class *Musci* (or *Bryopsida*; about 15,000 species), growing worldwide (except in salt water) on moist soil, trees, rocks, etc. The moss plant is differentiated into stems and leaves and produces sex cells (gametes), which give rise to a spore capsule that grows from the plant on a long stalk. Mosses help control erosion by providing surface cover and retaining water. *Sphagnum, responsible for peat formation, is the only economically important moss.

The name is also applied to several unrelated plants, for example *Spanish moss.

Mossamedes. *See* Moçâmedes.

moss animal. *See* Bryozoa.

Mössbauer effect The emission of a gamma ray (see gamma radiation) by an excited nucleus in a solid. Generally such an emission causes the nucleus to recoil, thus reducing the energy of the gamma ray. In the Mössbauer effect the recoil is distributed throughout the solid. The gamma ray therefore loses no energy and may then raise other nuclei into the same excited state. It was discovered by the German physicist Rudolph Mössbauer (1929–) and enables the structure of nuclei and molecules to be examined.

moss pink. See Phlox.

Mostaganem 36 04N 0 11E A port in NW Algeria, on the Mediterranean Sea. Founded in the 11th century, it has an 11th-century citadel. It trades in wine, fruit, and vegetables, and is at the head of a natural gas pipeline from Hasse R'Mel in the Sahara. Population (1978 est): 766,167.

Mostar 43 20N 17 50E A city in W central Yugoslavia, in Bosnia and Hercegovina on the Neretva River. A center for Serbian culture with a university (1977), it is situated amid mountainous wine-growing country. Population (1971): 47,606.

most-favored-nation clause A clause in a trade agreement between two countries in which each country agrees that any more favorable agreement either may make with a third country shall also apply to the other country. The mechanism is at the heart of the *General Agreement on Tariffs and Trade (GATT), although GATT allows the clause to be waived in treaties with *developing countries and in certain cases involving the formation of a *customs union.

Mosul 36 21N 43 08E A city in N Iraq, close to the Turkish border. From 1534 to 1918 it was an important trading center in the Ottoman Empire, and Turkey continued to claim the town until 1926. Mosul's modern prosperity is derived from nearby oilfields. Its former Faculties of the University of Baghdad became Mosul University in 1967. Population (1970 est): 293,079.

motet A polyphonic composition (see polyphony) for voices, generally unaccompanied. In the medieval motet the fundamental tenor (holding) part was based on a slow-moving plainchant or popular song while the upper triplex (treble) and motetus (worded) parts had a different text and a quicker rhythm. The 16th-century motet with Latin text, used during church services but not a part of the liturgy, is found in its purest form in the works of Palestrina. In England a Latin motet was distinguished from an English *anthem. Since the 17th century the word has been used to describe a serious but not necessarily religious choral work.

mother-of-pearl. See pearl.

Motherwell, Robert (1915–) US abstract painter. Largely self-taught, he turned to painting during World War II, under the influence of the European surrealists. He became a leading exponent of *action painting with his use of dripped and splattered paint, notably in his black and white series entitled *Elegy to the Spanish Republic*. His painting after this period became more structured, showing the influence of *Rothko.

Motherwell and Wishaw 55 48N 4 00W A city in central Scotland, in Strathclyde Region on the Clyde River. Formed by the union of two separate cities in 1920, its industries include iron and steel and engineering. Population (1978 est): 154,000.

moth orchid An epiphytic *orchid of the genus *Phalaenopsis* (about 40 species), native to SE Asia and E Australia. It has a very short stem bearing several broad leathery leaves and larger clusters of flowers. Moth orchids are popular hot-house ornamentals; hybrids produced usually have white or pink long-lasting flowers.

moths. See butterflies and moths.

motion pictures The art form and industry of films. The first motion picture exhibited to a public audience was made in 1895 by the French brothers Louis and Auguste *Lumière, whose equipment was developed from the inventions of Thomas *Edison, and the first commercial success was the American film *The Great Train Robbery* (1903). Influential pioneers of the silent film in the US were D. W. *Griffith, Mack *Sennett, and Charlie *Chaplin. In Europe, technological developments were creatively exploited by such directors as F. W. Murneau (1889–1931) in Germany and *Eisenstein in Russia. The end of the era of silent films was signaled by the success of Al *Jolson's *The Jazz Singer* (1927), which had a synchronized musical score; color film, introduced in the 1930s, added further popular appeal. The French directors René *Clair and Jean *Renoir made notable contributions to the early development of sound pictures. Between 1930 and 1945 the motion picture industry in the US became essentially an entertainment factory, controlled by the giant Hollywood studios, such as MGM and Paramount. The decline in audiences from the late 1940s because of the rival attraction of television caused the break-up of the Hollywood system. After World War II many of the most significant developments in motion pictures were initiated by directors in Europe, including Federico *Fellini and Michelangelo *Antonioni in Italy, Ingmar *Bergman in Sweden, Spain's Luis *Buñuel, and, later, François *Truffaut in France. Asian directors of note included Akira *Kurosawa in Japan and Satyajit Ray in India. British film makers included Carol Reed, David Lean, Tony Richardson, and Ken Russell. Directors such as Alfred *Hitchcock found their work acclaimed throughout the world. Many modern US directors, such as Stanley *Kubrick, Robert Altman, and Francis Ford Coppola, have often concentrated on films with a social message. Others, including George *Lucas and Steven Spielberg, have introduced a new era of futuristic films. Some actors, notably Woody *Allen and Robert Redford, have also achieved success as directors.

motion sickness Nausea and sometimes vomiting caused by traveling in cars, buses, trains, planes, boats (sea sickness), or on any fast-moving machine. It arises when the constant movement disturbs the organs of balance in the inner ear, which causes nausea. Motion sickness is especially common in children and many of them grow out of it. It is treated with drugs to stop the nausea, particularly *antihistamines. As many of these cause sleepiness as well, a person driving should not take them.

motmot A bird of the tropical American family *Motmotidae* (8 species). 6–20 in (16–50 cm) long, motmots have short rounded wings, short legs, and long tails with elongated central feathers. The bill is broad and serrated and the plumage is green, blue, brown, and black. Motmots live in forests and prey on insects, spiders, worms, etc. Order: *Coraciiformes* (kingfishers, etc.).

moto-cross (or scrambling) A form of *motorcycle racing invented in Britain in 1927. It takes place on a circuit marked out across rough country. International events are for 250 cc and 500 cc machines.

motorcycle racing Racing single-seat motorcycles or sidecar combinations, in classes according to engine capacity. In **road racing**, run usually on special circuits, the main classes are 125, 250, 350, and 500 cc. The sport developed in Europe. World championships are awarded according to points won in Grand Prix and other races held in many contries. In the US the sport is regulated by the American Motorcyclist Association (AMA). **Motorcycle trials** are usually events in which a cross-country course has to be completed within a certain time, with points lost in observed sections of the course for stopping, touching the ground, etc. See also drag racing; moto-cross; rally; speedway.

motorcycles Two-wheeled engine-powered vehicles. The evolution of the motorcycle has been closely associated with the development of the *bicycle, *steam engine, and *car. The muscle-powered bicycle was in use by the mid 19th century but the concept of a steam-powered bicycle was first realized by S. H. Roper in the US in the 1860s. Similar machines were being built in Paris at about the same time by Pierre and Ernest Michaux. However, the true forerunner of the modern motorcycle was Gottlieb *Daimler's 1885 bicycle powered by an *Otto four-stroke engine. The first production model was Hildebrand and Wolfmüller's 1894 *Pétrolette*. By 1900 there were some 11,000 motorcycles in France alone. During World War I, motorcycles (often in combination with sidecars) were extensively used. The interwar period—the great era of the motorcycle—saw the development of many classic designs: the Harley-Davidson in the US; the Brough Superior, Triumph Speed Twin, and Ariel Square Four in Britain; and the German DKW two-stroke and BMW four-stroke. All these were in military use in World War II. During and after the war some innovations were made, such as telescopic forks, sprung near wheels, disk brakes, and starter motors, but the basic design remained unchanged. In the 1950s and 1960s interest in motorcycles in Europe and the US declined; their inherent danger and the status symbol of car ownership forced most European manufacturers out of business. The motor scooter, a low-powered Italian-originated version of the motorcycle, and the moped, an engine-assisted bicycle, acquired some popularity. In the 1970s, the Japanese, exploiting the closing of European factories, developed a whole new range of motorcycles, based on European designs. These machines now dominate world markets.

Mott, Lucretia Coffin (1793–1880) US reformer and pioneer in the woman's rights movement. As a Quaker lecturer, she preached against slavery, alcohol, and war. By 1833 she had formed the Philadelphia Anti-Slavery Society. With Elizabeth Cady *Stanton she initiated the 1848 Seneca Falls Convention, from which the woman's rights movement was born. She continued to work for suffrage and equal opportunities for all, especially women and blacks.

Mo-tzu. See Mo-Zi.

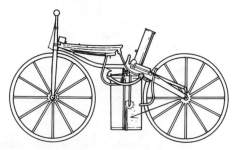

1860s S.H. Roper Velocipede *One of the earliest steam-powered cycles, this machine survives in the Smithsonian Institution, Washington, D.C.*

1885 Daimler *The forerunner of the modern motorcycle, it had a wooden frame, iron tires, and a 264 cc four-stroke engine.*

1894 Hildebrand and Wolfmüller "Pétrolette" *The first production motorcycle, it had direct rearwheel drive, pneumatic tires, and a 1488 cc engine. Production was ten machines a day.*

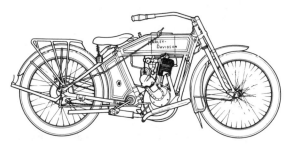

1917 Harley-Davidson *This 989 cc Vee-twin chaindrive machine had the first twist-grip throttle control.*

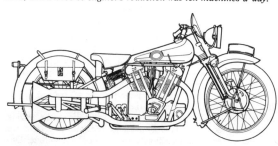

1930 Brough Superior *Built from 1919 to 1940 this Cadillac of motorcycles had a 980 cc Vee-twin JAP engine. Only 3000 were ever made.*

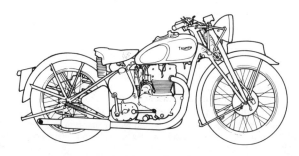

1938 Triumph 500 cc Speed Twin *Capable of over 100 mph, it was widely used by the police.*

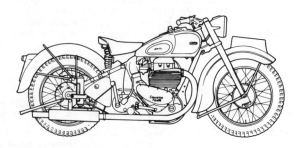

1949 Ariel Square Four *The compact arrangement of the four cylinders gave the machine its name. It had telescopic front forks and a sprung rear wheel.*

1979 Yamaha RD250 *A Japanese twin cylinder two-stroke with capacitor discharge ignition and disc brakes.*

mouflon A wild sheep, *Ovis musimon*, native to Corsica and Sardinia and introduced to other parts of Europe and to North America. Mouflons are about 25.5 in (65 cm) high at the shoulder and males have large curved horns, a distinctive rump patch, and a white saddle on the back.

Moulmein 16 30N 97 39E A port in Burma, on the Salween River. The chief city of British Burma from 1826 until 1852, Moulmein has an important teak trade and exports rice. Population (1973): 171,977.

mountain. *See* orogeny.

mountain ash A tree, *Sorbus aucuparia*, also called rowan, native to temperate Eurasia and commonly cultivated as an ornamental. Up to 49 ft (15 m) high, it has long leaves with numerous paired leaflets and large clusters of small cream flowers, which give rise to bright-scarlet berries with a bitter acid taste, used to make wine and jelly. The similar and related American species is *S. americana*. Family: *Rosaceae*.
The Australian mountain ash (*Eucalyptus regnans*), up to 344 ft (105 m) high, is the world's tallest broad-leaved tree.

mountain beaver. *See* sewellel.

mountaineering A sport that developed in the mid 19th century. Interest in exploring mountains first grew in the 18th century; after Mont Blanc was climbed in 1786 by Michel Paccard and Jacques Balmat interest gradually extended to other areas of the Alps. The English Alpine Club, founded in 1857, was quickly followed by continental clubs. The Matterhorn was climbed in 1865 by Edward *Whymper's expedition, Mount Kilimanjaro in 1889 by Hans Meyer and Ludwig Purtscheller, and Mount Kenya in 1899. No peak over 25,646 ft (7817 m) was climbed until after World War II, when modern equipment and generous funding made high-altitude climbing possible. Annapurna I was climbed in 1950 by Maurice Herzog and Louis Lachenal and Mount Everest in 1953 by Sir Edmund *Hillary and *Tenzing Norgay. Now that the world's highest peaks have been conquered, mountaineering is largely a matter of finding new routes and new methods. Rock climbing and ice climbing, skills always intrinsic to mountaineering, have become independent sports; like mountaineering in general, they make use of such equipment as nylon ropes, down suits, and crampons and are organized through clubs.

mountain lion. *See* cougar.

LORD MOUNTBATTEN *His outstanding contribution to public life was to oversee, as last viceroy of India, the establishment of Indian independence, and here he is greeted by Y. B. Chavan (1913–), India's defense minister (1962–66), at celebrations for Independence Day.*

Mountbatten of Burma, Louis, 1st Earl (1900–79) British admiral and colonial administrator; son of Prince Louis of Battenberg (1854–1921), who took the name Mountbatten and was created Marquess of Milford Haven in 1917, and of Princess Victoria of Hesse-Darmstadt, the granddaughter of Queen Victoria. He entered the Royal Navy in 1913 and in World War II was supreme Allied commander in SE Asia (1943–45), retaking Burma. As viceroy of India (1947) he presided over the transfer of power to India and Pakistan and was then governor general of India (1947–48). He was subsequently commander in chief of the Mediterranean fleet (1952–54) and first sea lord (1955–59), becoming an admiral in 1956. He died in Ireland, the victim of an IRA bomb.

Mounties. *See* Royal Canadian Mounted Police.

Mount McKinley National Park A national park in S central Alaska, in the Alaska Range. Established in 1917, the park surrounds glacier-covered Mount McKinley (20,320 ft; 6194 m), North America's highest peak. Many wildlife species are protected, including dall sheep on the high slopes. Area: 3031 sq mi (7849 sq km).

Mount of Olives The highest point in a small range of four summits situated just E of Jerusalem. It features in the Old and New Testaments. Its W slope was the site of the Garden of *Gethsemane. According to the Acts of the Apostles (1.2–12), Christ ascended to heaven from the Mount of Olives. Many churches and convents of various denominations have been built here since the 4th century AD or earlier.

Mount Rainier National Park A national park in S central Washington, SE of Seattle, in the Cascade Range, Mount Rainier, the focus of the park, which was established in 1899, is an extinct volcano that rises to 14,410 ft (4393 m) and has over twenty glaciers on it. The park is a popular winter sports area. Area: 378 sq mi (979 sq km).

Mount Rushmore National Memorial The gigantic sculpture of the heads of four US presidents—Washington, Jefferson, Lincoln, and Theodore Roosevelt—carved (1927–41) to the design of the sculptor Gutzon Borglum (1871–1941) on the NE cliffs of Mount Rushmore, South Dakota. Each head is about 60 ft (18 m) high.

Mount Saint Helens 46 12N 122 11W A volcano in SW Washington, in the S Cascade Range, NE of Vancouver, Canada. It is 9677 ft (2950 m) high, and, until 1980, had not erupted since 1857. In May 1980, a mamouth eruption blew the top off the mountain and caused widespread destruction in which more than 50 people died. The devastated area of about 172 sq mi (445 sq km) is included in Mount St Helens National Volcanic Monument, established in 1982. Minor eruptions since 1980 have caused minor damage.

Mount Vernon A national shrine in Virginia, S of Washington, DC, on the Potomac River. It was the home (1754–99) of George Washington, whose tomb lies in the grounds of the 18th-century Georgian mansion. The house, outbuildings, and gardens have been carefully restored and preserved.

Mount Wilson Observatory. *See* Hale Observatories.

Mourne Mountains A mountain range in Northern Ireland, in Co Down. It extends SW–NE between Carlingford Lough and Dundrum Bay, reaching 2798 ft (853 m) at Slieve Donard.

mourning dove A common North American *pigeon, *Zenaidura macroura*, that is adapted for survival in hot deserts; it can endure high body temperatures and dehydration and can fly long distances, enabling it to live far from water. 12 in (30 cm) long, it has a long pointed tail and gray-brown plumage with pink and violet patches on the neck.

mouse A *rodent belonging to the suborder *Myomorpha*. The house mouse (*Mus musculus*) is common in buildings worldwide and has long been associated with man. Grayish brown, it is 5.5–6 in (14–16 cm) long including its tail (2.8–31. in [7–8 cm]) and feeds on a variety of foods, from sugar and grain to oil-based paints and putty.
Most mice—together with their larger relatives, the *rats—are grouped into the subfamilies *Murinae* of the Old World and *Cricetinae* of the New World (which also includes hamsters). There are separate subfamilies for African tree mice (*Dendromurinae*; 7 species), jumping mice (*Zapodinae*; 3 species), dormice, and other small groups.

mousebird. *See* coly.

mouse deer. *See* chevrotain.

Mousterian A stone-tool industry of the Middle *Paleolithic, associated with *Neanderthal man. Named for caves at Le Moustier in the Dordogne (SW France), the Mousterian occurs, with variants, throughout Eurasia from France to China and in N Africa. Spanning roughly the period of 70,000 to 35,000 BC, it is characterized by a wide variety of hand axes, scrapers, points, and blades, often made by the *Lavalloisian technique. Mousterian sites have provided the earliest evidence for formal burial of the dead.

mouthbrooder A fish belonging to one of several genera of *cichlid fishes. The eggs are carried in the mouth of the parent, usually the female, until they hatch. Chief genera: *Tilapia; Haplochromis; Pelmatochromis*. Other mouthbrooders include certain *fighting fish, *catfish, and cardinal fish.

mouth organ. *See* harmonica.

Mozambique, People's Republic of (Portuguese name: Moçambique) A country in S East Africa, bordering on the Indian Ocean. Extensive coastal plains, at their widest in the S, rise to plateaus inland with mountains reaching over 6500 ft (2000 m). The chief rivers, notably the Zambezi and Limpopo, flow E and provide both irrigation and hydroelectric power. Most of the population is African, mainly Bantu, with diminishing minorities of Europeans and others. *Economy*: chiefly agricultural, the staple food crops being rice and corn. The main cash crops of cashew nuts (of which Mozambique is the world's largest producer), cotton, and sugar are also the principal exports. Industry is, at present, based largely on food processing and textiles but there are plans to develop heavy industry. Mineral resources, including natural gas and high-grade iron ore, are largely unexploited except for coal and bauxite. The transit trade provides an important source of income and Mozambique was compensated for closing its routes to Rhodesia (now Zimbabwe) in 1976. *History*: the N coast was settled by Arabs from the 10th century and was explored by Vasco da *Gama in 1498, becoming a Portuguese colony in the early 16th century. In 1951 it became an overseas province of Portugal. From 1963 FRELIMO (Frente de Libertaçao de Moçambique) waged a guerrilla campaign that achieved the establishment (1975) of an independent socialist republic. Mozambique provided a base for *Mugabe's arm of the Zimbabwe guerrilla organization, the Patriotic Front, and its borders with Rhodesia (now Zimbabwe) were closed from 1976 until 1980. The South-African-backed Mozambique National Resistance (MNR) applied military pressure in Mozambique with raids on Maputo, the capital. South Africa claimed that the incursions were targeted at a guerrilla movement seeking to overthrow the South African government. In 1984 two US petroleum companies contracted with Mozambique to explore for oil. Official language: Portuguese; the main African language is Makua Lomwe. Official currency: Mozambique escudo of 100 centavos. Area: 303,070 sq mi (784,961 sq km). Population (1983 est): 13,047,000. Capital and main port: Maputo.

Mozarabs Christians living in Spain under Muslim rule. The Mozarabs (meaning "almost Arabs") were so called because in spite of their Christianity they adopted the Arabic culture of their Muslim rulers. They formed autonomous communities within the Muslim state.

MOZART *Lithograph by Jab from a painting by Hamman. Many of Mozart's compositions for the piano were written to display his abilities as an instrumentalist.*

Mozart, Wolfgang Amadeus (1756–91) Austrian composer, born in Salzburg, the son of the violinist and composer Leopold Mozart (1719–87). Mozart exhibited extraordinary musical talent at the age of four; in 1762 his father took him on a tour of Germany and to Paris and London, where he received adulation for his abilities. In 1770 in Rome Mozart was able to write out the entire score of a *Miserere* by Gregorio Allegri (1582–1652) after hearing the work twice; he earned the highest praise for his talents as performer, improviser, and composer. He continued to tour, composing piano sonatas, symphonies, and his early operas but failing to find a permanent position worthy of his exceptional talents. After a period of unhappy service with the Archbishop of Salzburg (1779–81) he settled in Vienna as a freelance musician and teacher, composing such masterpieces as the operas *The Marriage of Figaro* (1786) and *Don Giovanni* (1787). The success of the latter obtained him belated recognition from the emperor but constant traveling, poverty, and frequent overwork contributed to his early death, possibly from typhus. Mozart achieved a fusion of the Germanic and Italianate styles of composition and his immense productivity enriched almost every musical genre. He composed 49 symphonies, over 40 concertos (of which those for piano (25), horn, violin, and clarinet are best known), 7 string quintets, 26 string quartets, numerous divertimenti, piano sonatas, violin sonatas, and much other music. Some of his finest works, such as the operas *Così fan tutte* (1790) and *The Magic Flute* (1791) and the *Jupiter* symphony (1788), were written in the last years of his life. His unfinished *Requiem* was completed after his death by Franz Süssmayr (1766–1803). *See also* Köchel, Ludwig von.

Mo-Zi (*or* Mo-tzu; ?470–?391 BC) Chinese philosopher. Originally a follower of Confucius, Mo-Zi criticized him for stressing ritual rather than virtue. In his chief work, the *Mo-Zi*, he taught universal love, pacifism, and simplicity, principles that formed the basis of a short-lived religious movement, Moism. Although Moism as a religion had ceased to be practiced by the 2nd century BC, as a philosophy it is still highly regarded.

Mtwara 10 17S 40 11E A deepwater port in S Tanzania, on the Indian Ocean. It exports chiefly local produce, mainly cashew nuts. Population (1978): 771,726.

Mu'awiyah I (c. 602–80 AD) The first *caliph (661–80) of the Umayyad dynasty. He participated in the conquest of Syria, where he was made governor in 640. He fought against *Ali, after whose assassination he himself became caliph. Renowned for his tactful control of the Arabs, Mu'awiyah is blamed by Islam for turning the caliphate into a worldly kingship.

Mubarak, (Mohammad) Hosni (Said) (1928–) Egyptian statesman; president (1981–). A general, he commanded the Egyptian air force (1972–75) and was responsibe for reorganization of the air units that fought successfully in the Yom Kippur War with Israel (1973). He became vice president to Anwar *Sadat in 1975 and succeeded him, upon his assassination, to the presidency in 1981. A cautious, conservative president, he held Egypt's inflationary economy in check, kept US-Egypt relations cordial, and attempted, with some success, to end isolation from neighboring Arab countries.

mucous membrane A moist membrane that lines the digestive and respiratory tracts and the nasal sinuses. It is a type of *epithelium containing cells that secrete **mucus**, a slimy substance that protects its surface and—in the digestive tract—also lubricates the passage of food and feces. In the bronchi the mucus traps particles that are inhaled with air.

Mudéjars (Arabic: vassal) The Muslims (*see* Moors) of Spain who had, by the 13th century, become subject to Christian rule during the reconquest of the Iberian peninsula. Many were of mixed *Berber and Spanish descent and continued to preserve their Islamic religion and customs. They were the creators of an architectural style notable for its ornamental brickwork and use of ceramic tiling. Many examples still survive in Castile and Aragon. *Compare* Mozarabs.

mudfish. *See* bowfin.

mudpuppy A salamander, *Necturus maculosis*, of North America. Gray-brown, with four well-developed limbs, mudpuppies retain their dark-red gills throughout their lives, even when mature at about five years old and 8 in (20 cm) long. They are slow moving and generally hunt fish, snails, and other invertebrates at night. The female guards her eggs until they hatch. Family: *Proteidae*. *See also* olm.

mudskipper A fish of the subfamily *Periophthalminae*, especially the genus *Periophthalmus*, found in swamps, estuaries, and mud flats of Africa, Polynesia, and Australia. Mudskippers have an elongated body, up to 12 in (30 cm) long, a blunt head, and dorsally protruding eyes. They are able to climb and walk over land using their limblike pectoral fins. Family: *Gobiidae* (*see* goby).

mufti A Muslim legal expert. They assist judges or private citizens by writing their opinions (*futwas*) on legal matters. These only become precedents in cases of marriage, divorce, and inheritance. In the Ottoman Empire muftis were state officials, the grand mufti being the chief spiritual authority.

Mugabe, Robert (Gabriel) (1925–) Zimbabwe statesman; prime minister (1980–). A teacher, he helped found the Zimbabwe African National Union (ZANU) in 1963 and, after ten years' (1964–74) detention in Rhodesia, formed the *Patriotic Front (PF) with Joshua Nkomo, leader of the Zimbabwe African People's Union (ZAPU). Based in Mozambique and Zambia respectively, they waged guerrilla warfare against the governments of Ian Smith and then Bishop Muzorewa until agreeing through talks (1979–80) to disarm (see Zimbabwe). His party's election victory (1980) brought Mugabe the leadership of newly independent Zimbabwe. Since that time he has consolidated his power and eliminated political opposition.

mugger A broad-snouted *crocodile, *Crocodylus palustris*, found in India, Sri Lanka, and Burma. It was formerly a sacred animal, kept in temples and tended by priests.

mugwort. *See* wormwood.

Mugwumps Group of US Republicans who supported Democrat Grover *Cleveland and would not vote for Republican James G. Blaine in 1884. Coined by New York newspaper editor Charles Dana, it means "big chief" in the Algonkian Indian language and is used to lable any party member that does not support the party's candidate.

Muhammad. *See* Mohammed.

Muhammad Ahmad. *See* Mahdi, al-.

Mühlhausen 51 14N 10 26E A city in SW East Germany, on the Unstrut River. The headquarters of Thomas *Müntzer in the Peasants' War, it has several fine medieval churches. Industries include the manufacture of textiles, machinery, and furniture. Population (1973 est): 44,473.

Muir, Edwin (1887–1959) Scottish poet. He moved to London in 1919, and during the 1930s he and his wife moved to Prague, where they translated the novels of Franz *Kafka and other major German writers. His reputation as a poet was established rather late in life with *The Voyage* (1946) and *The Labyrinth* (1949), in which he made distinctive use of traditional meters and diction. His *Autobiography* (1954) contains much of his best prose.

Muir, John (1838–1914) US naturalist and conservationist; born in Scotland. He settled in Wisconsin in 1849 and, after college (1859–63), traveled the country. He lived in Yosemite Valley for six years from 1868 and during a trip to Alaska (1879) discovered Glacier Bay. Due to his efforts and writings, the National Park bill (1890) established Yosemite and Sequoia national parks and paved the way for 13 national forests by 1897. The Muir Woods National Monument (1908) in California is named for him.

Mujibur Rahman, Sheik (1920–75) Bangladesh statesman; prime minister (1972–75). He was jailed in 1968 by *Ayub Khan's regime in Pakistan for campaigning for the independence of East Pakistan. Following the victory of his party, the Awami League, in the 1970 elections and victory in the subsequent civil war (1971), he became prime minister of the independent state of Bangladesh. Shortly before his assassination he assumed dictatorial powers.

Mukden. *See* Shenyang.

mulberry A tree of the genus *Morus* (12 species), native to N temperate and subtropical regions. The black mulberry (*M. nigra*) is the species most commonly cultivated for its fruit. About 31 ft (12 m) high, it has toothed heart-shaped leaves and round green male and female flower clusters (catkins), borne usually on separate trees. The female flowers give rise to small berries that are grouped together to form a blackberry-like fruit, which has a pleasant slightly acid taste and is used in jellies, desserts, etc. The leaves of the white mulberry (*M. alba*) are the staple food of silkworms. Family: *Moraceae. See also* paper mulberry.

mule The sterile offspring of a female horse and a male ass. Mules are useful pack and draft animals, being hardy, sure-footed, and strong but smaller than a horse and requiring less food. *See also* hinny.

Mülheim an der Ruhr 51 25N 6 50E A city in NW West Germany, in North Rhine-Westphalia on the Ruhr River. There is a 13th-century castle. Its manufactures include power-station generators, pipes and tubes, and machinery. Population (1980 est): 182,100.

Mull An island off the W coast of Scotland, in the Inner Hebrides. It is chiefly mountainous and agriculture is restricted; sheep and cattle are raised. Other occupations include fishing, forestry, and tourism. Area: 351 sq mi (909 sq km). Population (1971): 1560. Chief town: Tobermory.

mullein A biennial or perennial herb of the genus *Verbascum* (about 300 species), native to N temperate Eurasia. The biennial common mullein (*V. thapsus*), also called Aaron's rod, occurs in dry limy regions. It has a single stem, 0.6–2 m tall, bearing large woolly leaves and a dense terminal spike of pale-yellow flowers. Some species, including the European dark mullein (*V. nigrum*), are grown as garden plants. Family: *Scrophulariaceae.*

Muller, Hermann Joseph (1890–1967) US geneticist, who discovered the ability of X-rays to induce changes (mutations) in genetic material. Although useful as an experimental tool, Muller recognized the danger of X-radiation to man. He was awarded a Nobel Prize (1946).

Müller, Paul Hermann (1899–1965) Swiss chemist, who discovered the insecticidal properties of *DDT (1939). Müller found it was relatively harmless to other forms of life and DDT became widely used to combat insect pests. Müller was awarded the 1948 Nobel Prize for Medicine.

mullet A food fish, also called gray mullet, belonging to the genus *Mugil* (about 70 species), found in temperate and tropical coastal waters and estuaries. It has a slender silvery-green or gray large-scaled body, 12–35 in (30–90 cm) long, with two dorsal fins. It feeds in large schools on algae and small invertebrates. Family: *Mugilidae*; order: *Perciformes. See also* red mullet.

Mulliken, Robert Sanderson (1896–) US chemist and physicist, who developed *Schrödinger's theory of wave mechanics to provide a mathematical explanation of chemical bonding in terms of electron probabilities, orbitals, and energy levels. He received the 1966 Nobel Prize for chemistry for this work.

Mulroney, (Martin) Brian (1939–) Canadian statesman and lawyer; prime minister (1984–). He practiced law in Montreal from 1962; in 1977 he was named to head the Iron Ore Company of Canada, where he proved himself adept at settling labor problems. Active in the Progressive Conservative Party from law school days, he became the party's leader in 1983 and in September 1984 was elected prime minister, ousting Liberal Party leader John *Turner. Mulroney pledged to strengthen Canada's economy, extend social services, and improve relations with the US.

Multan 30 10N 71 36E A city in central Pakistan. An ancient settlement on the key route to S India, it has often been besieged and occupied. As well as manufacturing textiles, Multan's cottage industries are noteworthy. Population (1972): 542,195.

multinational corporations Large business enterprises with headquarters (the parent company) in one country and operating divisions (subsidiaries) in one or more other countries. Strategic decision making usually takes place at the head office. Their command of large resources and ability to maneuver around local legislation and taxation have led to demands for international legislation to restrain their activities when these conflict with national interests.

multiple sclerosis A chronic and usually progressive disease of the nervous system in which the fatty sheaths that surround the nerves in the brain or spinal cord are destroyed, which affects the function of the nerves. The disease is also called disseminated sclerosis, as its effects are disseminated in different parts of the body. It usually begins in young adults, and the commonest initial symptoms are sudden severe blurring of the vision or weakness in one limb. The initial symptoms often resolve completely but later the disease returns and progresses slowly, causing permanent handicap.

multiple star A system of three or more stars that move in complex orbits under mutual gravitational attraction.

multiplexer In *telecommunications, a device that combines several signals so that they can be sent along a single transmission path, or channel, and reconstructed at the receiver. One method is to superimpose carrier waves of different frequencies (*see* modulation) on the signals. Multiplexers are used with radio transmissions, telephone lines, etc.

multiplier A number used in economic theory to indicate how many times a specific increase in income, demand, etc., will be multiplied to produce an increase in the overall income, demand, etc., in a nation's economy. For example, if an individual's income is increased by 10 as a result of a cut in direct taxation, half of this increase may be spent in such a way that it becomes income for others, who may in turn also spend half of their increased income. Thus the original 10 could be multiplied to produce a total of 20 of additional income, in which case the multiplier has a value of 2. Opinions differ as to the practical impact of the multiplier, depending on the prevailing view of what motivates consumption.

Mumford, Lewis (1895–) US social philosopher. Mumford's academic posts included research professorships at the Universities of Stanford (1942–44) and Berkeley (1961–62). He wrote widely on architecture and cities, arguing that technological society was repressive. His books include

Sticks and Stones (1924), *Technics and Civilization* (1934), *Values for Survival* (1946), *In the Name of Sanity* (1954), and *The City in History* (1961).

mummers' play An English folk drama based on the legend of St George and the Seven Champions of Christendom; it was a dumb show (*mummer*, from Middle English *mum*, silent), traditionally enacted on Christmas Day by masked performers. Its plot largely consists of a duel between St George and an infidel knight, in which one of them is killed but is later brought back to life by a doctor. The play is still performed in a few villages in England and N Ireland.

mummy A human or animal body prepared and embalmed for burial according to ancient Egyptian religious practice. The internal organs were extracted and sealed in *Canopic jars and the body was desiccated by packing in dry natron, anointed, and encased in linen bandages.

mumps An acute virus infection that usually occurs in children. After an incubation period of 12 to 20 days the child develops headache and fever; later, the parotid salivary glands (situated under the ear) become tender and swollen. The disease is usually mild and resolves rapidly, but sometimes mild *meningitis develops. In adult male patients the infection may spread to the testicles, which may occasionally lead to sterility.

Munch, Charles (1892–1968) French conductor. He made his debut in Paris in 1932 and directed the Boston Symphony Orchestra from 1949 to 1962. In 1967 he founded the Orchestre de Paris but died on its first US tour.

Munch, Edvard (1863–1944) Norwegian painter and printmaker, who was a major influence on 20th-century German *expressionism. Largely self-taught, he developed his mature style in Berlin, following visits to Paris where he was influenced by *Gauguin and *Van Gogh. His symbolic paintings of love, death, and despair, including the famous *Cry* (1893; Nasjonalgalleriet, Oslo), reflect the pessimism caused by family tragedy. After 1910 he lived in Norway, where he painted murals for the festival hall of Oslo University (1913).

München. *See* Munich.

München Gladbach. *See* Mönchengladbach.

Münchhausen, Karl Friedrich, Freiherr von (1720–97) German soldier famous as a raconteur. His hyperbolic accounts of his feats passed into legend and were the subject of a series of adventure tales, *The Adventures of Baron Munchhausen* (1793), written by R. E. Raspe (1737–94).

Muncie 40 11N 85 22W A city in E Indiana, on the White River. It is the "typical American" town of the classic sociological study *Middletown* (1929) by Robert and Helen Lynd. An agricultural trading center, Muncie's varied manufactures include machine tools and glass. Population (1980): 77,216.

Munda Aboriginal tribes living mainly in the hills and forests of central and NE India. Munda languages form a subgroup of the *Austro-Asiatic language family. The northern branch of the Munda languages includes Santali, the most important. The Munda peoples are mainly slash-and-burn cultivators.

mung bean A *bean plant, *Phaseolus aureus*, also known as green gram, native to India and cultivated in tropical and subtropical regions chiefly as a vegetable crop. The slender pods contain up to 15 small edible seeds, which can be dried and stored or germinated in the dark to produce bean sprouts. Family: *Leguminosae*.

Munich (German name: München) 48 08N 11 35E A city in S West Germany, the capital of Bavaria on the Isar River. It has a 15th-century cathedral and many baroque and rococo buildings, including Nymphenburg Palace (1664–1728). Its university was moved here from Landshut in 1826. It is also noted for its technical university, opera, art galleries, and for its annual Oktoberfest (beer festival). A center of commerce, industry, and tourism, its manufactures include precision instruments, electrical goods, chemicals, and beer. *History*: Munich was from 1255 the residence and from 1506 the capital of the Dukes of Bavaria (from 1806 Kings). During the late 19th and early 20th centuries it flourished culturally, attracting such figures as the composer Wagner. The Nazi movement began here in the 1920s. Munich was severely bombed during World War II. Population (1980 est): 1,298,900.

Munich Agreement (1938) The settlement, resulting from the conference between Neville Chamberlain (UK), Daladier (France), Hitler (Germany), and Mussolini (Italy), that recognized Hitler's territorial claims to the *Sudetenland. Described by Chamberlain as achieving "peace in our time," it was followed in March, 1939, by Hitler's invasion of Czechoslovakia and in September by World War II.

Munich Putsch (1923) The attempt by *Hitler to seize power in Germany. Hitler planned to form a national government after first seizing power in Bavaria. This attempt at revolution (German word: *Putsch*) failed and Hitler was imprisoned.

Munn v. Illinois (1877) US Supreme Court decision that upheld right of states to control commerce within the state; one of the Granger cases. Grain elevator owners claimed that only the federal government had the right to regulate interstate trade. The court ruled that states could regulate private businesses that performed a public function, expecially if the business is carried on within the state.

Munro, Hector Hugh. *See* Saki.

Munsell color system A method of classifying *colors based on three parameters: hue (dominant color), luminosity (brightness), and saturation or chroma (strength, i.e. the degree to which it is a pure spectral color). The various colors are set out in a chart known as the colour tree, in which the different gradations of color are exhibited according to the three parameters. The Munsell color system is widely used in the paint industry. Named for Albert H. Munsell (1858–1918).

Münster 51 58N 7 37E A city and port in NW West Germany, in North Rhine-Westphalia on the Dortmund-Ems Canal. It was an important member of the Hanseatic League and the capital of the former province of Westphalia. It has a 13th-century cathedral, restored after the damage of World War II, and a university (1773). Service industries provide employment for most of the workforce. Population (1980 est): 267,600.

Munster A province and ancient kingdom of the SW Republic of Ireland. It consists of the counties of Clare, Cork, Kerry, Limerick, Tipperary, and Waterford. Area: 9315 sq mi (24,125 sq km). Population (1979): 979,819.

Munthe, Axel (1857–1949) Swedish physician and author. Munthe practiced in Paris and Rome before retiring to Capri, where he built the Villa San Michele. *The Story of San Michele* (1929) described his early life and the building of the villa. It has been translated into 44 languages and remains a bestseller.

MUNTJAC *A male Indian muntjac showing the short antlers (about 5 in or 12 cm long), arising from hairy pedicles that extend down the face as bony ridges.*

muntjac A small deer belonging to the subfamily *Muntiacinae* (6 species), occurring in forests of Asia, Sumatra, Java, and Borneo. The Indian muntjac (*Muntiacus muntjak*), also called barking deer or rib-faced deer, is 22 in (55 cm) high at the shoulder, chestnut above and paler beneath with short unbranched antlers and short sharp fangs. Muntjacs are mainly solitary and nocturnal, feeding on grass, leaves, and shoots.

Müntzer, Thomas (c. 1490–1525) German Protestant reformer and *Anabaptist leader. He began preaching reformed doctrines at Zwickau in 1520 but soon diverged from Luther's teachings. Claiming direct inspiration from the Holy Spirit, he called for radical social, political, and religious reform. He was driven out of several towns because of his subversive activities. A leader of the *Peasants' Revolt (1524–25), he was captured at the battle of Frankenhausen (1525) and executed.

Muntz metal A relatively hard strong type of *brass containing 60% copper and 40% zinc. It is not easily worked at room temperature and is usually shaped while hot or by casting. Named for G. F. Muntz (d. 1847).

muon A negatively charged unstable elementary particle (lifetime 2×10^{-6} second; mass 207 times that of the electron) that decays into an electron and two *neutrinos. It has a corresponding antiparticle. It was originally thought to be a meson (and was called the mu-meson) but is now classified as a lepton. *See* particle physics.

mural painting The decoration of walls and ceilings by such varied techniques as *encaustic, *tempera, and *fresco painting. The design of murals is largely dependent on their architectural settings. *Renaissance painters often used perspective and architecture in their murals to create the illusion that the painted walls or ceilings were space extensions of the real architecture. Mural painting was revived during the 20th century, principally by the Mexican painters *Rivera, *Orozco, and *Siqueiros, who used it to reach a wider public with their social and political subject matter.

Murasaki Shikibu (?978–?1026) Japanese writer. She is most famous for her great saga, *The Tale of Genji*, which is probably the world's earliest novel. It deals chiefly with the love life of Prince Genji and is remarkable for its observations of nature and understanding of human emotions. It brought her such fame that she was invited to become lady-in-waiting to Shoshi, the consort of Emperor Ichijo.

Murat, Joachim (1767–1815) French marshal and King of Naples (1808–15). He served as a distinguished cavalry leader in Napoleon's campaigns in Italy (1796–97) and Egypt (1798–99) and fought at *Marengo (1800) and *Austerlitz (1805). In Naples, Murat introduced important administrative reforms. He treated with the Austrians after Napoleon's defeat (1813) but subsequent attempts to regain his throne ended first in defeat at Tolentino and then in his capture and execution.

Murcia 38 59N 1 08W A city in SE Spain, in the province of Murcia. It was formerly the capital of the Moorish kingdom of Murcia and possesses a cathedral and university (founded 1915). Industries include silk and textiles. Population (1974 est): 240,881.

Murdoch, Iris (1919–   ) British novelist. Born in Dublin, she studied and taught philosophy at Oxford. Her first publication was a philosophical study, *Sartre* (1953). Her novels are elaborate and witty explorations of human relationships. They include *Under the Net* (1954), *The Bell* (1958), *A Severed Head* (1961), *The Black Prince* (1974), *The Sea, the Sea* (1978), *Nuns and Soldiers* (1981), and *The Philosopher's Pupil* (1983).

Mureş River (Hungarian name: Maros) A river in E Europe, flowing W from the Carpathian Mountains in Romania across the Transylvanian Basin to join the Tisza River in Hungary. Length: 499 mi (803 km).

murex A *gastropod mollusk belonging to the family *Muricidae* (about 1000 species), mainly of tropical seas. Murex □shells are elaborately ornamented with spines and frills; the snail feeds on other mollusks by drilling holes in their shells and extracting the flesh with its long proboscis. The Mediterranean *Murex trunculus* was the source of the dye Tyrian purple.

Murfreesboro 35 51N 86 23W A city in central Tennessee, SE of Nashville, on the W fork of the Stones River. Once the capital of Tennessee (1818–26), the city was the site of a strategic Civil War battle in December 1862–January 1863 and left the Union forces in control. The site is now part of the Stones River National Battlefield. Industries include textiles, clothing, electrical parts, luggage, furniture, and dairy products. Population (1980): 32,845.

Murillo, Bartolomé Esteban (1617–82) Spanish painter. He spent most of his life in Seville, working for the religious orders and helping to found the Spanish Academy (1660), of which he became first president. After abandoning his early realism, he painted urchins and religious scenes, particularly the Immaculate Conception, in an idealized style influenced by Rubens and the Venetians. Murillo was very popular until the 20th century, when there was a reaction against the sentimentality of such works as *The Two Trinities*.

Murmansk 68 59N 33 08E A port in the NW Soviet Union, in the RSFSR on the Kola inlet of the Barents Sea. Its ice-free harbor was used by the Allied expedition against the Bolsheviks in 1918 and is an important fishing base. Population (1981 est): 394,000.

Murphy, Frank (1890–1949) US lawyer and statesman; associate justice of the US Supreme Court (1940–49). He was mayor of Detroit, Mich (1930–33), governor-general and then US high commissioner of the Philippines (1933–36), and governor of Michigan (1937–39). Appointed US attorney general in 1939, he established a civil liberties division in the Department of Justice. His time on the Supreme Court, except for a brief military stint, fund him defending the rights of Japanese-Americans (by his

dissent in *Korematsu v. United States*; 1944), labor (by his vote in favor of *Thornhill v. Alabama*; 1940), and religion (by his dissent in *Wolf v. Colorado*; 1949).

Murray, Sir James (Augustus Henry) (1837–1915) British lexicographer. Largely self-educated, he became a teacher in 1870. After editing some early English texts, he was in 1878 appointed editor of the *New English Dictionary on Historical Principles* (later called the *Oxford English Dictionary*), to which he devoted the rest of his life, making a practical reality of this project and setting the standards of its scholarship.

Murray cod A carnivorous food and game fish, *Maccullochella macquariensis*, found in fresh waters of Australia. Up to 7 ft (2 m) long, it has a deep broad olive-green body with brown spots and a long dorsal fin.

Murray River The chief river in Australia. Rising near Mount Koscuisko, in New South Wales, it flows generally W and S forming the boundary between Victoria and New South Wales. It enters Encounter Bay on the Indian Ocean through Lake Alexandrina. The main tributaries are the Darling and Murrumbidgee Rivers; it also receives water from the Snowy Mountains hydroelectric scheme. Length: 1609 mi (2590 km).

Murrow, Edward R(oscoe) (1908–65) US radio and television journalist. He joined CBS in 1935 and became head of the European Bureau in 1937. After World War II he became a CBS vice president but continued to broadcast regularly and in the 1950s was a fearless critic of Senator Joseph *McCarthy. He produced and hosted two influential television programs, *See It Now* (formerly *Hear It Now* on radio) and *Person to Person*. In 1961 he became director of the US Information Agency.

Murrumbidgee River A river in SE Australia, rising in the Eastern Highlands in New South Wales and flowing through the Australian Capital Territory before entering the Murray River. The Burrinjuck Dam provides water for irrigation. Length: 1050 mi (1690 km).

Murry, John Middleton (1889–1957) British literary critic. He married Katherine *Mansfield and was a friend of D. H. *Lawrence. He edited the literary magazines *Athenaeum* (1919–21) and *Adelphi* (1923–48). His many books include studies of Keats (1925, 1930, 1949) and Blake (1933) as well as an autobiography, *Between Two Worlds* (1935).

Muscat 23 37N 58 38E The capital of Oman, on the Gulf of Oman. Most port traffic is now handled at Matrah to the NW. There is an oil terminal to the W. Population (1971 est): 7650.

Muscat and Oman. *See* Oman, Sultanate of.

muscle Tissue that is specialized to contract, producing movement or tension in the body. It contains long spindle-shaped cells (muscle fibers) that convert chemical energy (*see* ATP) into mechanical energy. Most of the body's musculature consists of voluntary muscle, which is consciously controlled via the central nervous system. It is also known as skeletal muscle (because it is attached to the bones) and striated (or striped) muscle (because of its banded appearance under the microscope). Individual muscles are made up of bundles of fibers enclosed in a strong fibrous sheath and attached to bones by tendons. Involuntary muscle occurs in the walls of hollow organs, such as blood vessels, intestines, and the bladder. It is responsible for movements not under conscious control and is regulated by the autonomic nervous system. Cardiac muscle is a special type of muscle found only in the heart: its rhythmic contractions produce the heartbeat.

muscovite. *See* micas.

Muscovy Company The first important English joint-stock company. Founded in 1553 to discover a northeast passage to the Orient, it was chartered in 1555 and granted a Russian trade monopoly, which it lost in 1698. It was dissolved in 1917.

Muscovy duck A large tropical American *perching duck, *Cairina moschata*. It has a glossy black plumage with white wing patches. The domesticated form is larger with a gray, white, or speckled plumage and a large scarlet caruncle on the bill.

muscular dystrophy A group of chronic and progressive disorders characterized by wasting and weakening of the muscle fibers. The disease is inherited and the commonest type, Duchenne muscular dystrophy, affects predominantly boys. The muscles affected and the rate of progress of the disease are both very variable. There is no specific treatment but physiotherapy and orthopedic measures can help those who suffer from the disease.

Muses In Greek mythology, the nine patrons of the arts and sciences, daughters of Zeus and *Mnemosyne. Calliope was the muse of epic poetry; Clio, history; Euterpe, flute playing and music; Erato, love poetry and hymns; Terpsichore, dancing; Melpomene, tragedy; Thalia, comedy; Polyhymnia, song and mime; and Urania, astronomy.

MUSICAL INSTRUMENTS

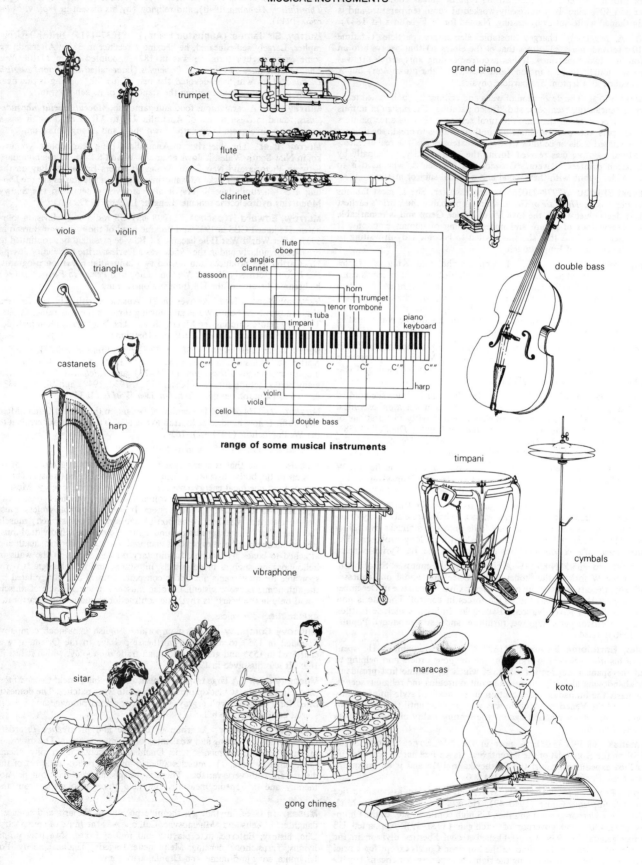

trumpet

flute

clarinet

grand piano

viola

violin

triangle

double bass

castanets

flute
oboe
cor anglais
clarinet
bassoon
horn
trumpet
tenor trombone
tuba
timpani
piano keyboard

C'''' C'' C' C C' C'' C''' C''''

harp

violin
viola

cello

double bass

range of some musical instruments

harp

vibraphone

timpani

cymbals

maracas

sitar

gong chimes

koto

Musgrave Ranges A range of rocky granite hills in NW South Australia. It runs parallel to the Northern Territory border, reaching 4970 ft (1516 m) at Mount Woodruffe.

mushroom The umbrella-shaped spore-forming body produced by many fungi. (Sometimes the word toadstool is used for those species that are inedible or poisonous, mushroom being restricted to the edible species.) It consists of an erect stem (stipe) and a cap, which may be flat, conical, spherical, or cylindrical and has numerous radiating gills on its undersurface in which the spores are produced. The well-known edible mushrooms belong to the genus *Agaricus*; they have a smooth white or scaly brown cap with gills that are white, gray, or pink when immature and become deep brown at maturity. The field mushroom (*A. campestris*) has a white cap 1.6–3.1 in (4–8 cm) in diameter and deep-pink to brown gills.

music The art of organizing sounds, which usually consist of sequences of tones of definite *pitch, to produce melody, harmony, and rhythm. Musical cultures based on *scales evolved in such ancient civilizations as those of China, Persia, India, etc., as well as in Europe. Within each culture both *folk music and classical (*or* "art") music traditions exist. In western music both traditions evolved from the Greek system of *modes established by Pythagoras and codified during the middle ages. In classical music modes became the basis for *plainchant and subsequently for *polyphony, which reached its peak in the 15th and 16th centuries. With the development of the major and minor scales in the early 17th century harmonic composition for instrumental ensembles and in *opera began to evolve. During the 17th and 18th centuries increasing attention was given to the development of musical form in classical music. By the beginning of the 19th century the dominant musical forms were the *sonata, *symphony, *concerto, and string quartet. Opera continued to flourish and *oratorio, invented during the 18th century, remained popular. The influence of Romanticism in music gave rise to the tone poem (*see* symphonic poem) and an increasingly free attitude to traditional forms. *Chromaticism in the music of the late 19th and early 20th centuries led to *atonality and the adoption by some composers of *serialism. In the later 20th century composers have used unpitched sounds, electronic generators, tape recordings, synthesizers, and unconventional instrumental techniques to create music, as well as experimenting widely with musical forms. The 20th century has also seen the development of other important forms of popular music in the western tradition, heavily influenced by African folk music. *See* jazz; rock; pop music.

musica ficta (Latin: false music) A modification of the pitch of certain notes, which, during the 11th to 16th centuries, was made in the course of musical performance. For instance, the harsh tritone F-B, known as *diabolus in musica* (Latin: the devil in music), was avoided by sharpening the F or flattening the B.

musical instruments Devices used to produce music. The chief characteristics of a musical instrument are its *timbre and range (i.e. the highest and lowest notes it can produce). In the *orchestra musical instruments are grouped into families. The *stringed instruments (*or* strings) include the violin, viola, cello, double bass, and harp (*see also* piano). The *wind instruments are divided into the woodwind (flute, clarinet, oboe, and bassoon) and brass (horn, trumpet, trombone, and tuba). The *percussion instruments include a whole range of instruments from the triangle and cymbals to the xylophone and timpani. Many instruments are used chiefly in jazz or pop (e.g. guitar, vibraphone, and maracas) while others, such as the Indian sitar, the Japanese koto, and the Spanish castanets, feature predominantly in the music of particular countries.

musicals Light dramas combined with songs and dances. The genre evolved in the US in the late 19th century and was developed during the 1920s and 1930s by George *Gershwin, Cole *Porter, and Irving *Berlin. In *Oklahoma!* (1943) and other musicals of the 1940s, Richard *Rodgers and Oscar *Hammerstein attempted to integrate the dramatic and musical elements, a trend culminating in Leonard Bernstein's *West Side Story* (1957). Other notable creators of the musical include George M. Cohan, Jerome Kern, Kurt Weill, Lorenz Hart, Alan J. Lerner, Frederick Lowe, and Stephen Sondheim.

music drama. *See* opera.

music hall *See* vaudeville.

Musil, Robert (1880–1942) Austrian novelist. He studied engineering and later philosophy and psychology and served as an officer in World War I. His fame was posthumous and due chiefly to his one major work, *The Man Without Qualities* (1930–43), a long novel describing life during the declining years of the Habsburg empire. Of his other works, only the novel *Young Törless* (1906) is noteworthy.

musique concrète A type of musical composition invented by Pierre Schaeffer (1910–) in 1948. Natural or man-made sounds are recorded on tape and arranged, often in an altered or distorted form, to form a composition made up of "concrete" or already existing sounds, as opposed to "abstract" musical tones.

musk (botany) A perennial plant, *Mimulus moschatus* (a species of *monkey flower), native to North America and grown as an ornamental for its musky fragrance. 8–24 in (20–60 cm) tall, it has oval leaves and tubular yellow flowers. The name is also applied to several other plants with a musky odor including the *moschatel, musk mallow (*Malva moschata*), musk rose (*Rosa moschata*), and musk stork's bill (*Erodium moschatum*).

musk (perfumery) An odorous substance obtained from the male *musk deer. It is included in perfumes because of the strength and persistence of its odor and it has been used as an aphrodisiac and stimulant.

musk deer A small solitary deer, *Moschus moschiferus*, found in mountain forests of central Asia. Musk deer are about 24 in (60 cm) high at the shoulder with long hind legs; males have no antlers but grow long fangs. They have been widely hunted for the secretion of their musk gland, which is used in the manufacture of perfumes.

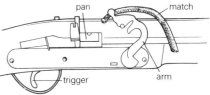

In the matchlock, a slow-burning match was forced into the powder pan by the arm when the trigger was pressed.

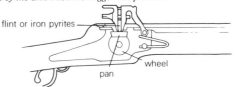

In the wheellock, the flint or iron pyrites was lowered onto a serrated wheel when the trigger was pressed. The sparks produced ignited the charge in the pan. The wheel, wound up by a key, also rotated when the trigger was pressed.

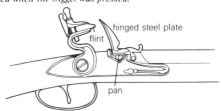

In the flintlock, pressing the trigger caused the flint to strike a hinged steel plate, forcing it back to expose the powder in the pan to the sparks.

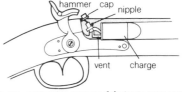

The percussion cap, containing mercury fulminate, was struck by the hammer when the trigger was pressed. The flame produced passed through the hollow nipple into the vent, where it fired the main charge.

MUSKET *The types of lock mechanism used in muzzle-loaders.*

musket A smoothbore firearm fired from the shoulder. The earliest form, known as a harquebus (*or* arquebus from German *Hackenbüsche*, hook gun), evolved in the 15th century as the first hand-held form of the *cannon—a development that depended on the matchlock as a means of igniting the charge. With a range of only 120 yd (110 m), the ball from the harquebus was unable to penetrate armour. In the second half of the 16th century a Spanish general invented a heavy shoulder weapon with a sufficiently large charge to penetrate even the finest armor—this musket still relied on the matchlock, essentially a fair-weather device. It was not until the mid 17th century that wheellocks (working on much the same principle as a flint lighter) and flintlocks were adopted for military use. The next landmark in the development of the musket was the *percussion cap at the beginning of the 19th century, which led to the breech-loading musket with cartridge and percussion-cap ammunition. Muskets were superseded by *rifles in the mid 19th century.

musk ox A large hoofed □mammal, *Ovibos moschatus*, inhabiting the Arctic tundra of North America. About 59 in (150 cm) high at the shoulder, musk oxen have long dark shaggy hair and prominent horns, which curve down the sides of the skull and upward at the tip. They live in herds of 20–30 and feed on grass, etc. Bulls have a strong musky scent in the rutting season. Family: *Bovidae*.

muskrat A large North American water *vole, *Ondatra zibethica*, also called musquash. It grows up to 14 in (35 cm) long, excluding its black hairless tail, and its soft glossy coat is used in the fur trade. Muskrats inhabit marshland, living in earthmounds or burrowing in river banks. They feed on water plants, mussels, and crayfish. Family: *Cricetidae*. □mammal.

Muslim League An organization of Indian Muslims created to safeguard their rights in British India. Formed in 1906 as the All-India Muslim League, it generally supported British rule. In 1940, under the leadership of *Jinnah and with the prospect of Indian independence, the League began to press for a separate state for Indian Muslims. In 1947, after the founding of Pakistan, it became Pakistan's dominant political party. Supported mainly by the westernized middle class, it split into three factions in the 1960s.

muslin A smooth delicately woven cotton fabric. Originally made in Mosul in Mesopotamia (hence its name), it is used for dresses and curtains. In the US coarser cotton fabrics used for shirts and sheeting are also called muslins.

musquash. *See* muskrat.

mussel A *bivalve mollusk belonging either to the family *Mytilidae* (marine mussels) or the superfamily *Unionacea* (freshwater mussels). Marine mussels have wedge-shaped shells measuring 2–6 in (5–15 cm), which are anchored to rocks by strands (byssus threads). Some species burrow into sand or wood. The edible mussel (*Mytilus edulis*) is an important seafood, being farmed commercially. Freshwater mussels inhabit ponds, lakes, and streams, embedded in mud or wedged between rocks.

Musset, Alfred de (1810–57) French poet and dramatist, one of the major figures of the Romantic movement. He published his first volume of poetry, *Contes d'Espagne et d'Italie*, at the age of 20. He lived extravagantly, and his many volumes of poetry and drama include satires on the excesses of the Romantic movement. His autobiographical *La Confession d'un enfant du siècle* (1836) includes an account of his love affair with George *Sand.

MUSSOLINI

Mussolini, Benito (Amilcare Andrea) (1883–1945) Italian fascist dictator. Initially an ardent socialist, his support of Italian participation in

World War I led to his expulsion from the Socialist Party (1915). In 1919 he formed the Fasci di combattimento (*see* Blackshirts) in Milan and came to power following the *March on Rome (1922). He was prime minister until the murder of *Matteotti persuaded him to establish (1924–29) a dictatorship. As *duce* ("leader") his social policies, program of public works, maintenance of law and order, and conciliatory policies toward the Roman Catholic Church (*see* Lateran Treaty) initially impressed the Italian people. However, his expansionist foreign policy, especially his invasion of Ethiopia (1935), and his alliance with Hitler (the Rome-Berlin Axis, 1936) brought him increasing unpopularity. In 1939 he annexed Albania and after the outbreak of World War II he declared war on France and Britain (June, 1940). The Italian war effort was disastrous, leading to defeats in E and N Africa and in Greece. Following the Allied invasion of Sicily, Mussolini was forced by the Fascist Grand Council to resign (July, 1943). Rescued by the Germans to head a new fascist republic in N Italy, he was subsequently captured and shot by Italian partisans. His body was brought to Milan and hung up in a public square before burial.

Mussorgski, Modest Petrovich (1839–81) Russian composer. At first an army officer and later a civil servant, he had little formal training beyond a few lessons with Balakirev. He developed a highly personal style, reproducing Russian speech rhythms in such works as the song cycles *The Nursery* (1868–72) and *Songs and Dances of Death* (1875–77). His masterpieces are the opera *Boris Godunov* (1868–72), the piano work *Pictures at an Exhibition* (1874), and the orchestral tone poem *A Night on the Bare Mountain* (1860–66).

mustang The wild horse of North America. Mustangs are descended from the domesticated European stock of Spanish settlers and have become tough and small in the harsh conditions. Many were caught and tamed by cowboys and Indians, including the Mustang tribe, which was noted for its horse breeding. Wild herds were rapidly declining until protective legislation was passed in 1971.

mustard Any of various annual herbs of the genus *Brassica* and closely related genera, native to Europe and W Asia and cultivated chiefly for their seeds—source of the condiment mustard. They have branched stems, up to 0.6 in (1.5 cm) high, deeply lobed leaves, and terminal clusters of yellow flowers. The leaves may be used as fodder, fertilizer, vegetables, or herbs. The main species are the white or yellow mustard, *Sinapis alba* (or *B. hirta*), black or brown mustard (*B. nigra*), and Indian mustard (*B. juncea*).

Mustelidae A family of mammals of the order *Carnivora. It includes the stoats, weasels, martens, badgers, skunks, and others. Mustelids typically have a long body and tail, short legs, and glands that secrete a musky fluid.

Mutanabbi, Abu At-Tayyib Ahmad Ibn Husayn al- (915–65 AD) Arab poet. From a poor but noble family, he learned his craft from the Bedouins and at Damascus, becoming a court poet in N Syria (948) and later in Egypt. He brought elaborate rhetorical innovations to the traditional odes (*qasidahs*) addressed to his patrons.

Mutare (former name: Umtali) 19 00S 32 40E A city in E Zimbabwe. Situated on the main railroad to Mozambique from Harare, it is an important market center for an area producing fruit and timber. Industries include papermilling, textiles, and food canning. Nearby national parks attract tourists. Population (1980 est): 64,000.

mutation A change in the hereditary material (*see* DNA) of an organism, which results in an altered physical characteristic. A mutation in a germ cell is inherited by subsequent generations of offspring; a change in any other cell (somatic cell) affects only those cells produced by division of the mutated cell. Gene mutations result from a change in the bases of the DNA molecule; chromosome mutations may be due to the addition or subtraction of bases and can usually be seen under a microscope. Both types of mutation affect the *genetic code and hence the corresponding function of the genes.
Very occasionally, mutations occur spontaneously and at random. They can also be induced by certain chemicals, ionizing radiation (such as X-rays), and by ultraviolet light. Most nonlethal mutations are of no benefit to the organism, but they do provide an important source of genetic variation in the population on which natural selection can act, which eventually results in the *evolution of new species.

Mutesa I (c. 1838–84) King of *Buganda in East Africa. An absolute ruler, Mutesa tried to play off the Arab intruders into his kingdom against the Europeans so that neither would become too powerful. He traded with both and encouraged Islam and Christianity.

mute swan An Old World *swan, *Cygnus olor*, found in marshy areas and estuaries and, as a semidomesticated ornamental bird, on rivers and

lakes. It is 63 in (160 cm) long and has a long neck, white plumage, black legs, and an orange bill with a black base. Less vocal than other swans, it is also silent in flight.

Mutsuhito (1852–1912) Emperor of Japan (1867–1912), who presided over Japan's transformation into a modern state. The Meiji (Mutsuhito's title as emperor) restoration (1866–68) ended seven centuries of feudal rule and nominally returned full power to the throne, a change that culminated in the constitution promulgated by Mutsuhito in 1889.

muttonbird A bird whose chicks are collected for meat and oil. The name is used especially for the slender-billed shearwater (*Puffinus tenuirostris*) of Australia and the sooty shearwater (*Procellaria griseus*) of New Zealand. Both belong to the family *Procellariidae* (petrels).

mutualism. *See* symbiosis.

Muybridge, Eadweard (Edward James Muggeridge; 1830–1904) US photographer, born in Britain. He was a pioneer of action photography with his series of animals and humans photographed in consecutive stages of motion. He showed that a trotting horse momentarily raises all four legs simultaneously.

Muzorewa, Bishop Abel (Tendekayi) (1925–) Zimbabwe statesman and bishop of the Methodist Church. One-time president of the African National Congress and the All Africa Conference of Churches, Muzorewa negotiated a new constitution with Ian *Smith's government in 1978 and headed a nominally black government in *Zimbabwe until 1980, when Robert *Mugabe became prime minister.

MYCENAE *The entrance to the citadel of Mycenae is by the Lion Gate, set between massive walls of Cyclopean stonework.*

Mycenae An ancient citadel in the Peloponnese (S Greece). Famed in legend as the home of *Agamemnon, Mycenae attained its zenith between 1600 and 1200 BC. Massive fortifications, including the famous Lion Gate, attest Mycenae's military readiness and exquisite bronze daggers, gold masks, and silver drinking vessels from its royal graves indicate accompanying affluence.

Mycenaean civilization The civilization of Bronze Age Greece. It developed after about 1650 BC in mainland centers, such as *Mycenae and *Pylos, but after the collapse of the Minoan civilization (c. 1450 BC) its influence and political control extended to Crete. The Mycenaeans were a warrior aristocracy, identifiable with Homer's *Achaeans. They spoke a form of Greek, used *Linear B script, and lived in palaces decorated with frescoes and equipped with luxury stone and metal goods. About 1200 BC the palaces were destroyed, either by invaders or in internecine struggles, but recognizably Mycenaean culture survived in debased form until about 1100 BC.

mycology The branch of biology dealing with the study of fungi. Mycology was established as a separate discipline in the early 19th century, when the Swedish botanist Elias Fries (1794–1878) published the first scientifically based classification of the fungi (1821–32).

mycoplasma A minute organism that lacks a cell wall and belongs to the class *Mollicutes*, also called pleuropneumonia-like organisms (PPLOs). Regarded by some authorities as bacteria, mycoplasmas may be rounded, 150–300 nanometers in diameter, or filamentous, up to several micrometers long (*see* SI units). They are the cause of several plant and animal diseases; for example *Mycoplasma mycoides* causes pleuropneumonia in cattle.

myelin A white fatty material that forms a sheath around the large nerve fibers of vertebrates and some invertebrates. Myelin acts as an insulator, thereby increasing the speed of conduction of impulses along the nerve fiber.

Myers, F(rederic) W(illiam) H(enry) (1843–1901) British essayist and poet. As well as poetry and literary criticism, he published several books concerning psychical research, including *Phantasms of the Living* (1886) and *Human Personality and Its Survival of Bodily Death* (1903). He helped to found the Society for Psychical Research in 1882.

Mylae, Battle of (260 BC) A battle in the first *Punic War in which the Romans destroyed the Carthaginian fleet off Sicily. It was Rome's first naval victory.

My Lai A village in S Vietnam, where a massacre of about 347 civilians by US soldiers took place (March 16, 1968) during the Vietnam War. The incident was investigated only after it had been disclosed by an ex-serviceman (1969). The investigation resulted in the court martial of several soldiers. Only one, Lieutenant William Calley, was convicted but his conviction was overturned. The incident provoked much criticism of the role of the US in Vietnam.

Mylodon A genus of extinct South American ground sloths dating from the Pleistocene epoch (one million years ago). About 118 in (300 cm) long, they had a specialized toe on the hind limb that was probably used for gripping branches or digging up tubers. *See also* Megatherium.

mynah A songbird belonging to a genus (*Acridotheres*) native to SE Asia. Mynahs usually have a dark plumage with bright wattles on the face. They feed chiefly on the ground and eat the insects found on cattle. The common mynah (*A. tristis*) lives in close proximity to man and has become a pest in some regions. The Chinese crested mynah (*A. cristatellus*) has been introduced to North America. Family: *Sturnidae* (starlings). *See also* hill mynah.

myocardial infarction Death of part of the heart muscle: the cause of what is popularly described as a heart attack. This is the commonest cause of death in advanced societies and usually results from *atherosclerosis. The patient usually experiences sudden severe central chest pain, which may spread to the neck and arms and is usually accompanied by sweating and nausea. Most people who recover from heart attacks can eventually lead a full and active life: many have survived for as long as 40 years.

myopia. *See* nearsightedness.

Myrdal, Gunnar (1898–) Swedish sociologist and economist. Joint recipient of the 1974 Nobel Prize, Myrdal is best known for his study of the US racial problem, published as *An American Dilemma* (1944). His wife **Alva Myrdal** (1902) won the 1982 Nobel Peace Prize for her work for disarmament.

Myriapoda A group of terrestrial arthropods comprising the *centipedes, *millipedes, *pauropods, and *symphylids. They have elongated bodies and numerous walking legs.

Myrmidons A legendary Greek people from Thessaly. According to one legend, they originated on the island of Aegina when Zeus turned the ants (Greek *myrmex*, ant) into people. They are best known as the loyal warriors commanded by *Achilles in the Trojan War.

Myron (5th century BC) Athenian sculptor. His *Discus-Thrower* and *Marsyas*, described by ancient critics, are known through Roman copies. These free-standing figures show the new stances (made possible by the novel techniques of bronze working) that superseded the stylized poses derived from *kouros and *kore figures.

myrrh An aromatic yellow to red gum resin obtained from small tropical thorny trees of the genus *Commifera*, especially *C. myrrha*, *C. molmol*, and *C. abyssinica*, native to Africa and SW Asia. Myrrh exudes from the bark through slits and hardens on exposure to air. It is used in incense, perfumes, cosmetics, dentistry, and pharmaceuticals. Family: *Commiphoraceae*.

myrtle An evergreen shrub of the genus *Myrtus* (over 100 species). The common myrtle (*M. communis*), native to the Mediterranean area and W Asia, may grow to a height of 16 ft (5 m). It has aromatic dark-green shiny leaves, fragrant five-petaled white flowers, 2–3 cm across, with numerous stamens, and blue-black berries. An oil obtained from the leaves, flowers, and fruit is used in perfumery. Family: *Myrtaceae*. Other plants known as myrtle include the *sweet gale.

Mysore 12 18N 76 37E A city in India, in Karnataka. Industries include textiles, chemicals, and food processing and it has a university (1916). Population (1971): 355,685.

mysteries Secret religious cults in the ancient Mediterranean world that revealed their mystical rites only to initiates and promised them a life after death. Their initiation ceremonies, of which the details are often vague, involved purification, assimilation of occult knowledge, and acting out a sacred drama. The Egyptian cult of *Isis, the Greek *Eleusinian and *Orphic mysteries, and Roman *Mithraism are the most famous.

mystery plays. *See* miracle plays.

mysticism Belief in a type of religious experience in which the individual claims to achieve immediate knowledge of or temporary union with God. Mysticism is an element in most theistic traditions and the validity of the experience is often claimed to be established by the similarity of the accounts by mystics from totally different cultures of their visions, trances, and ecstasies. The usual preliminary is strict *asceticism. Christianity insists that a mystic should demonstrate his spiritual grace by practical works of charity. St *Francis of Assisi, St *Catherine of Siena, St *Teresa of Avila, St *John of the Cross, and *Julian of Norwich are among the many famous Christian mystics. Official Church attitudes have alternated between regarding mysticism as a special spiritual grace and suspecting it of verging on *Gnosticism, *pantheism, *Neoplatonism, or simply dangerous individualism. *See also* Sufism.

mythology Imaginative poetic stories, traditions, etc., concerning religious beliefs, gods, and supernatural and heroic human beings. Mythology often involves a cosmogony—an attempted explanation of the origin of the universe, of mankind, or of a particular race or culture. The term also refers to the formal study of such stories, traditions, etc. Myths have been interpreted in several ways. One ancient theory, first advanced by the Greek Euhemerus (300 BC) and called euhemerism, holds that there is an element of historical truth in myths and that mythical characters are only kings or other heroes given the honor of deification by the populace. *Plato also adopted a critical view of Greek mythology because of its immorality and sought to introduce worthier ideals by inventing more rational myths. Anthropology and psychoanalysis have thrown new light on the function of myths. Among primitive peoples they serve to provide an explanation or justification for social institutions. They also appear to embody universal values or patterns with regard to human psychology, as in Freud's interpretation of the child's relationship to its parents in terms of the *Oedipus myth. The mythologies of particular cultures have provided the material of most of the world's great literature and art, as in Egypt, Greece and Rome, and in Hinduism.

Mytilene (Modern Greek name: Mitilíni) 39 06N 26 34E The chief city of the Greek island of Lesbos, on the Aegean Sea. It is a port trading chiefly in olive oil, citrus fruits, and cereals. Population (1971): 23,426.

myxoedema Underactivity of the *thyroid gland. Patients are slow, tired, dislike the cold, and have a slow pulse and reflexes. The skin may be thick and swollen. Myxoedema can be easily treated with thyroxine, the hormone produced by the thyroid gland.

myxomatosis An infectious disease of rabbits and hares that is caused by a virus. Symptoms include swollen eyes, nose, and muzzle, closed eyelids, and fever. The disease is usually fatal although some strains of rabbits show resistance. A vaccine is available to protect domestic rabbits. The disease was introduced to the UK and Australia during the 1950s as a pest-control measure.

Mzilikazi (c. 1790–1868) Zulu warrior, who in about 1840 founded the Matabele (*or* Ndebele) kingdom in S Rhodesia. A great military leader and an able administrator, Mzilikazi organized his new kingdom on military lines and withstood attacks from neighboring tribes and from the Afrikaners. Not long after his death his kingdom, under his son *Lobengula, was overwhelmed by the whites.

N

Naas (Irish name: Nás na Riogh)   53 13N 6 39W A city in the Republic of Ireland, the county town of Co Kildare. It is a center for horse racing and hunting. Population (1971): 5078.

Nabis (Hebrew: prophets)   A group of French artists formed in Paris in 1888. The leading members—Paul Sérusier (1863–1927), *Denis, *Bonnard, and *Vuillard—were united by their admiration for *Gauguin and Japanese prints. They applied their famous tenet that "a picture is ... essentially a flat surface covered by colors in a certain order" to their activities as painters, poster and stained-glass designers, book illustrators, etc., thus influencing many branches of art. They disbanded in 1899.

Nablus   32 13N 35 16E A city on the *West Bank of the Jordan River. Nablus is the Shechem of the Old Testament: Jacob's Well is nearby. Population (1967 est): 444,233.

Nabokov, Vladimir   (1899–1977) US novelist. Born into an aristocratic Russian family, he was educated at Britain's Cambridge University and lived in France and Germany before emigrating to the US in 1948. He achieved popular success with *Lolita* (1955), whose academic antihero lusts after young girls. His novels, noted for their elegant and witty word play, include *The Defense* (1930), one of several originally written in Russian, *Pale Fire* (1962), and *Ada* (1969). His other works include the autobiographical *Speak, Memory* (1967) and a translation of Pushkin's *Eugene Onegin* (4 vols, 1964).

nacre.   *See* pearl.

Nadar   (Gaspard Felix Tournachon; 1820–1910) French photographer, caricaturist, and writer, born in Paris. Although better known by his contemporaries as a novelist and essayist, his reputation now rests on his photographs of writers and artists, such as Baudelaire and Delacroix, and his pioneering aerial photographs taken from a balloon (1858).

Na-Dené languages   An American Indian language group covering the northern US, NW Canada, and Alaska. It includes the Athabascan, Tlingit, Haida, and Eyak subgroups. Athabascan is the largest group, consisting of more than 20 languages, and is also the most widespread, extending from the Yukon almost to the US border. Another subgroup of Athabascan origin, spoken on the N American Plains, includes *Navajo and several *Apache languages.

Nader, Ralph   (1934–   ) US lawyer and consumer advocate. His book *Unsafe at Any Speed* (1965), which criticized the safety standards of the automobile industry, resulted in the passing of a car safety act in 1966. A champion of consumer rights, he founded the Center for the Study of Responsive Law in 1969. Among the many other consumer issues that he has investigated are fairness in advertising, nuclear power, and meat processing.

Nader Shah   (1688–1747) Shah of Persia (1736–47). Of Turkoman origin, he overthrew the Safavid dynasty to become shah. He had military successes but his internal policies led to many revolts. His attempt at introducing a new rite of Sunni Islam (*see* Sunnites) into Shiite Persia, and forcing his subjects to join it, failed. He was assassinated.

nadir.   *See* zenith.

Naevius, Gnaeus   (c. 270–c. 200 BC) Roman poet. He wrote a number of tragedies and comedies and an epic on the first Punic War, in which he related the mythical origins of Rome (making Romulus a grandson of the Trojan Aeneas). Only fragments of his work are extant.

nevus.   *See* birthmark.

naga   In Hindu mythology, one of a race of minor serpent deities inhabiting an underworld region called Patala, which is filled with gems. They are associated with water and may be regarded as demons and a possible source of evil, but are also worshiped as companions of the gods. □Vishnu is often portrayed sleeping on the naga Sesha, and there is a Buddhist legend of a naga raising the Buddha on its coils above a flood sent to prevent his attaining enlightenment. Nagas are variously depicted as half-snake and half-human, as many-headed cobras, or in human form posed beneath a canopy of cobras.

Nagaland   A state in NE India, on the Burmese border. Mostly in the forested Naga Hills, it produces rice, other grains, pulses, sugar cane, and vegetables. Mahogany and other forest products are important. Local industries include weaving. *History*: after 1947 the Naga tribes resisted Indian

rule as fiercely as they had Britain, winning statehood in 1963. Further talks with the Naga underground movement led to the Shillong Peace Agreement in November, 1975. Area: 6379 sq mi (16,527 sq km). Population (1981): 773 281. Capital: Kohima.

NAGA   *A 10th-century sandstone panel from a temple in central India depicting a naga encircled by a 5-headed cobra.*

Nagarjuna   (c. 150–c. 250 AD) Indian Buddhist monk and philosopher. Probably originally a brahmin from S India, he founded the Madhyamika (Middle Way) school of Mahayana Buddhism, noted for its highly intellectual approach to defining the nature of reality. Works attributed to him survive only in Tibetan and Chinese.

Nagasaki   32 45N 129 52E A port in Japan, in W Kyushu on the East China Sea. The first Japanese port to deal with European traders, it became a center of Christianity following its introduction by the Portuguese in the 16th century. On August 9, 1945, the second of the two atomic bombs used against Japan was dropped on Nagasaki, killing or wounding about 75,000 people, although the damage was not as extensive as at Hiroshima. Rapid rebuilding followed and the city is now an important center of the shipbuilding industry. Its university was established in 1949. Population (1980): 447,000.

Nagorno-Karabakh   An autonomous region (*oblast*) in the W Soviet Union, in the Azerbaidzhan SSR. It was formed in 1923 and its population comprises chiefly Azerbaidzhani and Armenians. It has metal and mineral deposits and supports many light industries but is chiefly agricultural: cotton, grapes, and wheat are grown. Area: 1700 sq mi (4400 sq km). Population (1981 est): 164,000. Capital: Stepanakert.

Nagoya 35 8N 136 53E A port in Japan, in SE Honshu on Ise Bay. The fourth largest city in the country, it was founded in 1610 and by World War II had developed into an important center for the manufacture of aircraft and ammunition. It was largely rebuilt following heavy bombing in 1945 and its industries now include steel and textiles. Its universities were established in 1939 and 1950. Population (1980): 2,088,000.

Nagpur 21 10N 79 12E A city in India, in Maharashtra. Founded in the early 18th century, it fell under British control in 1853. It grew with the arrival of the Peninsula Railroad (1867) and now has cotton, transport equipment, and metallurgical industries. Its university was established in 1923. Population (1981 est): 1,297,977.

Nagy, Imre (1896–1958) Hungarian statesman, who led the revolutionary government of 1956. As prime minister (1953–55) Nagy promised such reforms as an end to the forced development of heavy industry and agricultural collectivization, more consumer goods, occupational mobility, and the closure of labor camps. Opposed by Hungary's Stalinists, he was demoted and in 1956 expelled from the Communist Party. In the subsequent *Hungarian Revolution Nagy again became prime minister but was abducted by Soviet troops and executed.

Naha 26 10N 127 40E A port in Japan, the main city of the *Ryukyu Islands and capital of Okinawa. It is the site of the University of the Ryukyus. Population (1976 est): 304,550.

Nahuatl The most widely used American Indian language of the Uto-Aztecan family, spoken in Mexico. It was the language of the *Aztecs and *Toltecs. A distinctive characteristic is the extensive use of the *tl* sound. The Nahua people are slash-and-burn cultivators, growing maize, beans, tomatoes, and chilis. Crafts, especially weaving, are well developed. The Nahua are nominally Roman Catholic, but pagan beliefs continue to flourish.

Nahum An Old Testament prophet who predicted the imminent destruction of the Assyrian capital of Nineveh by the Medes in 612 BC. **The Book of Nahum** describes this event in detail and interprets it as divine retribution.

naiads In Greek mythology, a class of *nymphs or female spirits of nature associated with rivers, lakes, and springs.

Naipaul, V(idiadhur) S(urajprasad) (1932–) West Indian novelist. He was educated at Oxford and now lives in England. A witty ironic tone characterizes his early comic novels, such as *A House for Mr Biswas* (1961), concerning the life of the poor in his native Trinidad. His later more sombre novels include *In a Free State* (1971), *Guerrillas* (1975), *A Bend in the River* (1979), and *Among the Believers* (1981). He has also published two travel books, a collection of essays (*The Return of Eva Perón*; 1980), and a history of Trinidad (*The Loss of El Dorado*, 1969).

Nairobi 1 17S 36 50E The capital of Kenya, situated on a plateau just S of the equator. Founded as a railroad center in the late 19th century, it is the administrative center of Kenya and trading center of a fertile agricultural region. Its varied manufactures include chemicals, textiles, glass, and furniture. The Nairobi National Park lies on the city's outskirts. The University of Nairobi was established in 1970. Population (1977 est): 776,000.

Naismith, James (1861–1939) US inventor of basketball; born in Canada. He was educated in Canada and then enrolled in the Springfield, Mass., Young Men's Christian Association (YMCA) Training School's physical education course. It was here, as a requirement of the course, that he invented basketball (1891), with two peach baskets and a soccer ball. He later taught physical education at the University of Kansas (1898–1937).

naive art. *See* primitivism.

Najd (*or* Nejd) A province in Saudi Arabia, occupying the center of the country. It is largely desert and much of the population is nomadic. Formerly an independent kingdom, it became part of Saudi Arabia in 1932. Area: about 424,621 sq mi (1,100,000 sq km). Population (1970 est): 4,000,000. Capital: Riyadh.

Nakasone, Yasuhiro (1918–) Japanese prime minister (1982–). After graduation from law school (1941) and service in World War II, he served in the Japanese House of Representatives (1947–). He was transportation minister (1967–68), defense director (1970–71), minister of international trade and industry (1972–74), and administrative management agency director (1980–82). Long a leader in the Liberal-Democratic Party (LDP), he won a majority of the vote in the 1982 election and became prime minister. Elections called in 1983 saw a lessening of the LDP's power, but Nakasone remained in office. He broadened Japan's role internationally, especially in the development of Asia.

Nakhichevan Autonomous Soviet Socialist Republic An administrative division in the S Soviet Union, in the Azerbaidzhan SSR. It is populated mainly by Azerbaidzhani. The economy is predominantly agricultural, producing mainly cereals, cotton, and tobacco. Industries include textiles and food processing. Area: 2120 sq mi (5500 sq km). Population (1977 est): 231,000. Capital: Nakhichevan.

Nakuru 0 16S 36 04E A city in Kenya, on the N shore of Lake Nakuru. It has a large European community and is the trading center of an agricultural area producing wheat, maize, and coffee. Population (1975 est): 66,000.

Namaqualand (*or* Namaland; Afrikaans name: Namakwaland) An arid coastal area in SW Africa, extending S from near Windhoek (Namibia) into Cape Province (South Africa), divided by the Orange River into Little Namaqualand (S) and Great Namaqualand (N). It is occupied chiefly by Namas, consisting of Hottentot tribes, and has important diamond reserves.

Namib Desert A desert chiefly in W Namibia, extending some 994 mi (1600 km) along the Atlantic coast. It is arid and almost devoid of population.

Namibia (name until 1968: South West Africa) A territory in SW Africa, on the Atlantic Ocean. The narrow coastal plains of the Namib Desert rise to the central plateau, with the Kalahari Desert to the N. The Orange River forms its S boundary, and the Kunene and Okavango Rivers form part of its N boundary. The majority of the population is African, the largest group being the Ovambo. *Economy*: chiefly subsistence agriculture with emphasis on livestock, especially stock raising, and some dairy farming. Fishing is important, especially for pilchards. Rich mineral resources include diamonds (the main export), as well as copper, lead, zinc, tin, and vanadium; uranium has been found. Hydroelectricity is a valuable source of power. *History*: a German protectorate from 1884, during World War I it surrendered (1915) to South Africa, which administered South West Africa under a League of Nations mandate. In 1966 South Africa refused to acknowledge the declaration by the League's successor, the UN, that the mandate was at an end and has been condemned by both the UN and the South West Africa People's Organization (SWAPO) as illegally occupying the territory. A constitutional solution put forward by South Africa in 1976 proved unacceptable to SWAPO and efforts to resolve the crisis continue. Official languages: Afrikaans and English. Official currency: South African rand of 100 cents. Area: 318,261 sq mi (824,269 sq km). Population (1983 est): 1,018,000. Capital: Windhoek. Main port: Walvis Bay (an enclave of South Africa).

Namier, Sir Lewis Bernstein (1888–1960) British historian. Born in Poland, he emigrated to England (1906) and was professor of modern history at Manchester University (1931–53). Among his works on 18th-century politics is *The Structure of Politics at the Accession of George III* (1929).

Namur (Flemish name: Namen) 50 28N 04 52E A city in S Belgium, strategically positioned at the confluence of the Sambre and Meuse Rivers. It was besieged and captured many times. Notable buildings include the 18th-century cathedral. Its chief manufactures are glass, paper, and leather and steel goods. Population (1981 est): 100,670.

Nanaimo 49 08N 123 58W A city and port in W Canada, in British Columbia on the E coast of Vancouver Island. With the main ferry links to the mainland, it is Vancouver Island's distribution center and the site of primary industries. Population (1976): 40,336.

Nanak (1469–1539) Indian founder of *Sikhism. Born near Lahore, a member of the mercantile Hindu class he traveled within and perhaps beyond India, visiting both Hindu and Muslim centers in search of spiritual truth. He settled finally in Kartarpur, where he attracted a large community of disciples. His teachings are contained in a number of hymns, many of which are extant.

Nana Sahib (Dandhu Panth; c. 1825–c. 1860) A leader of the *Indian Mutiny (1857). Adopted into a noble family, he led the revolt at Cawnpore, in which the British were massacred. When defeated in 1859 he was driven into the Himalayan foothills, where he probably died.

Nanchang 28 38N 115 56E A city in SE China, the capital of Jiangxi province and the site of its university. China's first commune was briefly established here in 1927. An ancient commercial center, it has varied manufactures. Population (1957 est): 508,000.

Nancy 48 42N 6 12E A city in NE France, the capital of the Meurthe-et-Moselle department on the Meurthe River. The former capital of the Dukes of Lorraine, it passed to France in 1766. It has a fine collection of 18th-century buildings and is the site of a university (1572). Its varied industries include iron, salt, sodium, machinery, and textiles. Population (1975): 111,493.

Nanda Devi, Mount 30 21N 79 50E A mountain in NW India, close to the Tibetan border in the Himalayas. Height: 25,645 ft (7817 m).

Nanga Parbat, Mount 35 15N 74 36E A mountain in NE Pakistan, in the Himalayas. Height: 26,660 ft (8126 m).

Nanhai. *See* South China Sea.

Nanjing (Nan-ching *or* Nanking) 32 05N 118 55E A port in E China, the capital of Jiangsu province on the Yangtze River. An ancient cultural center, it was a Chinese capital (1368–1421, 1928–37) and the center of the Taiping Rebellion (1851–64). The university was established in 1902. It is a center of heavy industry. Population (1977 est): 3,000,000.

Nanking. *See* Nanjing.

Nanning 22 50N 108 19E A city in S China, the capital of Guangxi Zhuang AR. The commercial center of a rich agricultural area, it has many industries, including food processing and the manufacture of paper and agricultural machinery. Population (1957 est): 264,000.

Nansen, Fridtjof (1861–1930) Norwegian explorer, zoologist, and statesman. In 1888 he led an expedition across the Greenland icefield and in 1893, in the *Fram*, specially designed to resist icepacks, set sail across the Arctic. He allowed the vessel to drift attached to an icefloe. In 1895, with F. J. Johansen (1867–1923), he left the ship and reached 18 14N, the nearest point to the North Pole then attained. He subsequently contributed greatly to the League of Nations, becoming its high commissioner for refugees in 1920; he pioneered the **Nansen passport**, an identification card for displaced persons (1922). He won the Nobel Peace Prize (1923).

Nantes 47 14N 1 35W A major port in W France, the capital of the Loire-Atlantique department on the Loire estuary. Its commercial importance dates back to Roman times and it was here that the Edict of Nantes was signed in 1598. It has a 15th-century cathedral and a university (1961). Its port is accessible to oceangoing vessels and its industries include shipbuilding, oil refining, and tanning. Population (1975): 263,689.

Nantes, Edict of (1598) A decree that guaranteed the French Protestants (*see* Huguenots) religious liberty. The edict, proclaimed by Henry IV, established the principle of religious toleration; by permitting the Huguenots freedom of worship and limited civil equality, Henry hoped to prevent further wars of religion in France. The Edict was revoked in 1685 by Louis XIV.

Nantucket An island off the coast of SE Massachusetts. A former whaling center, it is now chiefly a resort. Length: 15 mi (24 km). Width: 3 mi (5 km).

napalm An inexpensive jelly consisting of a mixture of the aluminum salts of *na*pathenic acid and *palm*itic acid used to thicken gasoline so that it can be used in incendiary bombs and flame-throwers. It was used in World War II, the Korean War, and in Vietnam. It ignites easily, burns at temperatures up to 1000°C, and is particularly effective against humans.

Naphtali, tribe of One of the 12 *tribes of Israel. It claimed descent from Naphtali, the son of Jacob by his concubine Bilhah. Its territory was NW of the Sea of Galilee.

naphthalene ($C_{10}H_8$) A white crystalline aromatic hydrocarbon that occurs in coal tar. It is used in the manufacture of dyes, synthetic resins, and mothballs. **Naphthol** ($C_{10}H_7OH$) is the hydroxy derivative. It consists of two isomers; the most important, beta-naphthol, is used in antioxidants for rubbers and dyes and in drugs.

Napier 39 29S 176 58E A port in New Zealand, in E North Island on Hawke Bay. It is the most important center of New Zealand's wool trade. Population (1973): 42,900.

Napier, John (1550–1617) Scottish mathematician, who invented *logarithms. In 1614 he published a table of logarithms to the base e, now known as Napierian logarithms. Logarithms to the base ten (common logarithms) were later adopted, following a suggestion by Henry *Briggs. Napier also produced an elementary calculating machine using a series of rods, known as **Napier's bones**.

Napier of Magdala, Robert Cornelis, 1st Baron (1810–90) British field marshal. He fought in the *Sikh Wars in India (1845–49) and during the Indian Mutiny helped to relieve Lucknow (1857). In 1868 he led the expedition to release British diplomats imprisoned in Ethiopia, capturing Magdala.

Naples (Italian name: Napoli; ancient name: Neapolis) 40 50N 14 15E A city in S Italy, the capital of Campania situated on volcanic slopes overlooking the Bay of Naples. It is an important port and a center of commerce and tourism. As well as traditional industries, such as textiles, food

processing, and oil refining, newer industries (including the manufacture of cars and ball bearings) have grown up in recent years as a result of central government assistance. Its many historic buildings include medieval castles, a gothic cathedral (13th–14th centuries), the 17th-century Royal Palace, and the university (1224). The National Museum houses remains from Pompeii and Herculaneum. *History*: founded by Greek colonists about 600 BC, it fell to Rome in 326 but retained its Greek culture. It was under Byzantine rule (6th–8th centuries AD) and in 1139 it became part of the Norman kingdom of Sicily. It prospered under Charles I, the first Angevin King of Sicily, who made Naples his capital. Following the revolt known as the *Sicilian Vespers (1282), the island of Sicily passed to the House of Aragon and the Italian peninsula S of the Papal States became known as the kingdom of Naples (with Naples as its capital) until it fell to Garibaldi (1860) and was united with the rest of Italy (*see also* Sicily). From this time Naples lagged economically behind the N, resulting in considerable poverty. The city suffered further hardships during World War II, when it was badly damaged. Central government assistance during the postwar period has led to considerable improvements in the life of the city, based on a developed infrastructure (new roads, port installations, modernized transport and communications). Existing industries have been modernized and expanded and new industries have been established. Many thousands of its inhabitants, however, continue to live in slum conditions. Population (1980 est): 1,219,362.

NAPOLEON I *David's portrait (1821; Versailles) of the emperor crossing the Alps splendidly evokes the glory of the Napoleonic legend.*

Napoleon I (1769–1821) Emperor of the French (1804–15). Born Napoleon Bonaparte in Corsica, he became an artillery officer and rose to prominence in 1795, when he turned the guns of the Paris garrison—"a whiff of grapeshot"—on a mob threatening the government of the National Convention. Shortly afterward he married *Josephine de Beauharnais and in January, 1796, was appointed to command the French army in Italy (*see* Revolutionary and Napoleonic Wars). His Italian campaign (1796–97) took the army from the brink of defeat by the Austrians to the conquest of Milan and Mantua. After Sardinia, Naples, and the papacy had sued for peace Napoleon obtained the Directory's support for his plan to break British imperial power by conquering Egypt and India. In Egypt his great victory of the *Pyramids was undermined by Nelson's annihilation of a French fleet at *Aboukir Bay (1798) and in 1799 he returned unobtrusively to France, where he joined a conspiracy against the tottering Directory. In the coup d'état of 18 Brumaire (November 9–10, 1799) he became first consul in a consulate formed on the Roman model; in 1802 he became consul for life and in 1804 had himself proclaimed emperor.

His outstanding domestic achievement was the legal codification, the *Code Napoléon*, that remains the basis of French law, but Napoleon achieved immortality with his exploits abroad. In 1802 he negotiated both the Treaty of Lunéville, which marked his defeat of the Austrians at Marengo, and the Treaty of Amiens with the British; however, his designs upon Italy, Germany, and Switzerland led to a renewal of war in 1805. Despite the disaster at *Trafalgar (1805), which forced him to abandon his plan for the invasion of Britain, his land victories, especially at *Austerlitz (1805), *Jena (1806), and *Friedland (1806), drew almost every continental power within the French orbit.

Napoleon's supremacy was short lived. The *Continental System failed to break the British by blockade and the protracted *Peninsular War (1808–14) drained French resources. In 1812 Napoleon invaded an increasingly recalcitrant Russia with half a million men, of whom nearly 400,000 died in the brutal Russian winter. In 1813 Europe rose against Napoleon, inflicting a massive defeat at Leipzig that forced his abdication and subsequent exile to Elba, of which he was given sovereignty. In 1815, however, he escaped, returned to a rapturous welcome in France, and attempted in the *Hundred Days to regain his former greatness. He suffered a decisive defeat at *Waterloo and spent the remainder of his life confined to the island of St Helena. Napoleon's claim to the French crown was pursued after his death by the son of his second marriage, to Marie Louise of Austria (*see* Napoleon II), and then by his nephew, who became Emperor *Napoleon III. *See also* Bonaparte.

Napoleonic Code. *See* Code Napoléon.

Napoleonic Wars. *See* Revolutionary and Napoleonic Wars.

Napoleon II (1811–32) The title accorded by supporters of the Bonapartist claim to the French throne to the son of Napoleon I and Empress Marie Louise. At birth entitled King of Rome, he was brought up, after his father's fall (1814), in Austria, where he received the title Duke of Reichstadt.

Napoleon III (1808–73) Emperor of the French (1852–70); son of Louis Bonaparte and Hortense de Beauharnais and nephew of Napoleon I. Pretender to the French throne during the reign of Louis Philippe (1830–48), Napoleon used the enormous prestige of his name to win the presidential election after the Revolution of 1848. By a coup d'état at the end of 1851, he dissolved the legislative assembly and, a year later, declared himself emperor. His domestic policies fostered industry and, with the planning work of Baron *Haussmann, transformed the face of Paris. Abroad, his diplomacy embroiled France in the Crimean War (1854–56), in war against the Austrians in Italy (1859), and in a desultory conflict in Mexico (1861–67). Finally, his aggressive stance toward— Bismarck helped to cause the *Franco-Prussian War, in which the Second Empire was destroyed and Napoleon was driven into exile.

Nara 34 41N 135 49E A city in Japan, in S Honshu. Japan's first capital (710–84 AD), it contains many historic monuments, including a bronze Buddha 72 ft (16 m) high. Population (1976 est): 261,813.

Narayanganj 23 36N 90 28E A city in Bangladesh, the chief riverport of Dacca. It is a major trading center and together with Dacca forms the largest industrial region in the country. Population (1974): 186,769.

Narbonne 43 11N 3 00E A market city in SE France, in the Aude department. An important Roman settlement, it was formerly a port (silted up in the 14th century). Population (1975): 40,543.

Narcissus (botany) A genus of perennial herbaceous plants (about 40 species), native to Eurasia and N Africa and widely planted in gardens and parks. Growing from bulbs, they produce strap-shaped or rushlike leaves and erect flower stalks, usually up to 12 in (30 cm) high. The flowers are usually yellow, orange, or white, with a ring of petal-like segments surrounding a central crown. The *daffodils (*N. pseudonarcissus*) have large solitary yellow flowers with trumpet-shaped crowns; the sweet-scented jonquils (*N. jonquilla*) have clusters of smaller pale-yellow flowers with small cuplike crowns; and the poet's narcissus (*N. poeticus*) has solitary flowers with white petals surrounding a short fringed orange-tipped crown. Family: *Amaryllidaceae*.

Narcissus (Greek mythology) A beautiful youth who was punished for rejecting the love of the nymph Echo by being made to fall in love with his own reflection in a pool. He died and was transformed into a flower.

narcotics Drugs that cause stupor or sleep and relieve pain by depressing activity of the brain. The term is used particularly for *opium and its derivatives (opiates), including morphine and codeine. Synthetic narcotics include heroin, methadone, and pethidine. The main medical use of narcotics is for the relief of severe pain, but their use is strictly controlled by law in most countries because they carry the risk of *drug dependence. The term narcotics is also used more loosely for any addictive drug.

Narragansett North American Algonkian-speaking Indian tribe found in S New England. Chiefly in Rhode Island, they had an agricultural society. Partially wiped out from fighting the colonists in *King Philip's War (1675–76), they, along with other tribes in the area, relocated. Descendants, numbering almost 500, live in Rhode Island.

Narragansett Bay A bay in SE Rhode Island. It contains many islands including Rhode Island, Prudence Island, and Conanicut Island.

Narses (c. 480–574 AD) Byzantine general. Originally a slave in Emperor *Justinian I's household, Narses rose to become the emperor's confidant. In 551 he replaced *Belisarius as commander in Italy. He recaptured Rome and eventually subdued the Ostrogoths, governing Italy until 567.

Narva 59 22N 28 17E A port in the W Soviet Union, in the Estonian SSR on the Narva River near the Gulf of Finland. Peter the Great was defeated by the Swedes in a famous battle here in 1700. It is an important textile center and also possesses fish- and food-processing industries. Population (1970): 57,863.

Narvik 68 26N 17 25E An ice-free port in N Norway. Two naval battles between the British and Germans were fought here in 1940 and the port was occupied by the Allies from May 10 until June 9. It exports iron ore from the Kiruna-Gällivare mines in N Sweden. Population (1973 est): 12,839.

narwhal A gregarious Arctic toothed *whale, *Monodon monoceros*, up to 16 ft (5 m) long and feeding on fish and squid. Male narwhals have a long straight spirally twisted tusk that is derived from a tooth and grows to a length of 10 ft (3 m); its function is unknown. Family: *Monodontidae*.

NASA (National Aeronautics and Space Administration) The US civilian agency, formed in 1958, that is responsible for all nonmilitary aspects of the US space program. Its major projects have included the manned *Apollo moon program, *Skylab, and several highly successful *planetary probes. In addition it has launched many artificial *satellites belonging to the US and other nations. The space shuttles *Columbia* and *Challenger*, designed to carry people and materials between earth and permanent space stations, have made numerous flights since the first orbital mission in 1981. *See also* space shuttle.

Naseby, Battle of (June 14, 1645) The battle in the English *Civil War that decided Charles I's defeat. The *New Model Army under Fairfax and Oliver Cromwell routed Prince *Rupert's royalist forces at Naseby, near Market Harborough, Leicestershire, and in the following year Charles surrendered.

Nash, Ogden (1902–71) US humorous writer. He wrote witty comments on social and domestic life expressed in doggerel verse. He contributed to the *New Yorker* magazine, and his books include *Free Wheeling* (1931), *I'm a Stranger Here Myself* (1938), *You Can't Get There from Here* (1957), *Collected Verse* (1961), and *Marriage Lines* (1964). He collaborated with Kurt Weill and S. J. Perelman on the musical *One Touch of Venus* (1943).

Nash, Paul (1889–1946) British painter. After studying at the Slade School, he became known for his symbolic war landscapes during World Wars I and II, the finest example being *Totes Meer* (1940–41; Tate Gallery). Nash was also a leading member of Unit One (1933), a group of artists, including Barbara *Hepworth and Henry *Moore, dedicated to promoting modern art (particularly *abstract art) in the UK. His brother **John Nash** (1893–1977) produced fine watercolor landscapes and botanical illustrations.

Nash, Sir Walter (1882–1968) New Zealand statesman; Labour prime minister (1957–60). Born in Britain, he introduced successful anti-Depression policies while minister of finance (1934–49) and was also a member of the Pacific War Council (1942–44).

Nashe, Thomas (1567–c. 1601) British pamphleteer and dramatist. In *Pierce Penilesse* (1592) and other satiric pamphlets he attacked the Puritans and defended the theaters against them. Among other works are the comic masque *Summer's Last Will and Testament* (1592) and the pioneering picaresque novel *The Unfortunate Traveller* (1594). He collaborated with Ben Jonson and others on the satirical play *The Isle of Dogs* (1597).

Nashville 36 10N 86 50W The capital city of Tennessee, on the Cumberland River. Founded in 1779, it is the site of Vanderbilt University (1873) and is a major center for religious education. A center of the recording industry for country and western music, the Country and Western Music Hall of Fame and Museum are situated here. Since the 1930s, cheap electric power from the Tennessee Valley Authority has made it an important commercial and industrial city. Industries include railroad engineering, glass, printing and publishing, and clothing. Population (1980): 455,651.

Nasik 20 00N 73 52E A city in India, in Maharashtra on the Godavari River. It is a major Hindu pilgrimage center. Industries include printing and distilling. Population (1971): 176,091.

Nassau A former duchy, now in Hesse and Rheinland-Pfalz (West Germany). In 1544 William the Silent, Count of Nassau, inherited the principality of *Orange, thus linking the two states. Nassau joined Napoleon's Confederation of the Rhine in 1806 and in 1866 came under Prussia.

Nassau 25 2N 77 25W The capital of the Bahamas, a port on New Providence Island. Built in 1729, it is an important tourist center. Population (1970): 3233.

Nasser, Gamal Abdel (1918–70) Egyptian statesman; prime minister (1954–56) and president (1956–70). An army officer, he helped to found the nationalist Free Officers group, which overthrew the monarchy in 1952. He became prime minister and then president of the Republic of Egypt (United Arab Republic from 1958). His nationalization of the Suez Canal led to an unsuccessful Israeli and Anglo-French attack on Egypt (1956), after which he was established as a leader of the Arab world. His socialist and Arab nationalist policies brought him into frequent conflict with the West and the more conservative Arab states.

Nasser, Lake. See Aswan High Dam.

Nast, Thomas (1840–1902) US political cartoonist; born in Germany. He began drawing for *Harper's Weekly* in 1859 and then became a staff member (1862–86). His anti-slavery cartoons greatly helped the Union cause during the Civil War. He is best known for his cartoons attacking New York City's Boss Tweed (William Marcy *Tweed) and Tammany Hall, which were instrumental in the breakup of the Tweed Ring and the arrest of Tweed (1876). He created the symbols for the Republican and Democratic parties and popularized the US version of Santa Claus.

nasturtium An annual garden plant of the genus *Tropaeolum* (90 species), also called Indian cress, native to Central and South America. It has round parasol-like leaves with central stalks, and orange, yellow, pink, or red flowers, which are funnel-shaped with a long spur containing nectar. *T. majus* is the most popular ornamental species and its seeds may be used in salads. The canary creeper (*T. peregrinum*) has twining leafstalks. Family: *Tropaeolaceae*.

Natal 5 46S 35 15W A port in NE Brazil, the capital of Rio Grande do Norte state near the mouth of the Rio Potengi. The chief exports are sugar, cotton, and carnauba wax; industries include salt refining and the manufacture of textiles. It has a university (1958). Population (1980): 376,552.

Natal The smallest province in South Africa. The land rises sharply from the Indian Ocean in the E to the Drakensberg Mountains in the W. Economic growth has been rapid. Agriculture and forestry are important. Along the coast sugar cane is the major crop and inland pine, eucalyptus, and wattle plantations supply the timber and paper industries. Other products are tropical fruits, maize, and beef and dairy cattle. Industries include shipping, food processing, chemicals, and sugar and oil refining. Durban is the main industrial center and port. Coal is the chief mineral. *History*: the Boers attempted to establish a republic in Natal (1838) but this was annexed by Britain in 1843 and with additions became a province of the Union of South Africa (1910). Area: 33,578 sq mi (86,967 sq km). Population (1970 est): 4,236,770. Capital: Pietermaritzburg.

Nataraja In Hinduism, *Shiva in his aspect as lord of the cosmic dance, which symbolizes the constant activity of creation and dissolution. During the middle ages, in imitation of this divine dance, dancing became an important part of Hindu temple ritual.

Natchez A Muskogean-speaking North American Indian tribe of the Lower Mississippi. They were cultivators who, like the *Creeks, built mound temples and worshiped the sun. They were ruled by a despotic chief known as the Great Sun and had an elaborate system of social classes. The highest caste, the "suns," were obliged to marry members of the lowest caste, the commoners.

Natchez 31 34N 91 23W A city in SW Mississippi, on the E bank of the Mississippi River. Settled in 1716, it began its growth as a major cotton port in the early 19th century with the opening of the Mississippi River and the advent of the steamboat. It was also the end of the Natchez Trace (1801–08) a road from Nashville, Tennessee, to Natchez. Natchez was the capital of Mississippi from 1817 to 1821. It is still an important shipping center for cotton and other agricultural products. The antebellum architecture and features of Natchez attract tourists. Population (1980): 22,015.

Natchez Trace A road that runs from Nashville, Tennessee, to Natchez, Mississippi. Built over an old Indian trail by the US Army between 1801

and 1808, the road opened up Mississippi and enabled settlers to get to and from Nashville, the nearest major town. It became an important trade and postal route, but declined when the steamboat came into use on the river. Since 1938, it has been part of the Natchez Trace Parkway. Length: 500 mi (800 km).

Nathan, George Jean (1882–1958) US editor and drama critic. He was co-editor, with H. L. *Mencken, of *Smart Set* (1914–23), and with Mencken started *American Mercury* in 1924, in which Nathan enhanced his reputation as a drama critic. He went on to co-found *American Spectator* in 1930 and continued to satirize American culture and to elevate theater standards in numerous magazines and newspapers. He published an annual, *Theatre Book of the Year* (1943–51), and many books of criticism.

Nation, Carrie (Amelia Moore; 1846–1911) US reformer. Her first husband, Dr Charles Gloyd, whom she married in 1867, died from alcoholism. In 1877 she married David Nation, who divorced her in 1901. Living in Kansas, where prohibition was in effect but openly disobeyed, she took it upon herself to destroy, often using a hatchet, the illegal saloons. Through the 1890s and early 1900s, she continued her crusade in Kansas and cities on the east and west coasts, appearing in simulated religious dress, singing hymns, and quoting from the Bible—sometimes with followers. She also opposed short skirts and smoking and favored woman suffrage, but her fanaticism prevented endorsement from organized groups.

National Academy of Sciences (NAS) US organization, founded in 1863, that promotes the use of science for the general welfare. Composed of elected members from the science and engineering community who have distinguished themselves in research and development, the academy advises the government and informs the public through its publications.

National Aeronautics and Space Administration. See NASA.

National American Woman Suffrage Association (NAWSA) US organization, established in 1890, to promote voting rights for women. A result of the merger of the National Woman Suffrage Association (1869) and the National American Woman Suffrage Association (1869), it promoted woman suffrage on the national, state, and local level. Elizabeth Cady *Stanton served as one of its first presidents (1892–1900).

national anthem The official patriotic song of a country, sung or played on ceremonial occasions. The US anthem is "The *Star-Spangled Banner." Other well-known anthems are Britain's "God Save the King" and France's "La Marseillaise."

National Association for the Advancement of Colored People (NAACP) US civil rights organization, founded in 1909, that promotes equality for blacks. Formed by the merging of W. E. B. *DuBois's black militant Niagara Movement and a group of interested whites, it sought to achieve equal rights for blacks through education and legal and legislative means. Its Legal Defense and Education Fund was responsible for bringing about school desegregation in *Brown v. Board of Education of Topeka (1954). It is headquartered in New York City and membership comprises about 500,000 in almost 2000 local units.

National Country Party An Australian political party, formed in 1919 as the Country Party, that represents the interests of farmers. It has held office only in coalition with the *Liberal Party.

national forest US forest land, overseen by the Forest Service, a division of the Department of Agriculture, that is set aside for conservation and recreation. The Forest Service, established in 1905, protects water, forage, wildlife, recreation, and timber to be used in ways that "will best meet the needs of the American people," as reaffirmed in the Multiple Use and Sustained Yield Act (1960). About 200 million acres (81 million hectares) of forest areas in the US and its possessions are administered by the Forest Service.

National Gallery An art museum in London, containing the largest collection of paintings in Britain. Founded in 1824, it originally contained 38 paintings, bought from John Julius Angerstein (1735–1823). William Wilkins (1778–1839) built the present building (1832–38). The National Gallery has aimed to collect paintings of every leading school and period (except the modern) in Europe.

National Gallery of Art US museum, established in 1937, that houses the national art treasures. It is a branch of the Smithsonian Institution and, although privately funded at first, is maintained by the US government. Most gallery acquisitions are privately donated. Started off by Andrew W. *Mellon's collection of American portraits (he also funded the construction of the building), it houses European and American masterpieces.

National Greenback Party. See Greenback Party.

National Industrial Recovery Act (NIRA) US New Deal legislation, passed in 1933, to aid economic recovery during the Depression. It promoted fair competition, improved working conditions and labor standards, and increased consumer buying power. Industrial codes (about 550 in all) covered every facet of business from shortened working hours and child labor to pricing and production numbers and collective bargaining. To oversee implementation of the legislation, President Franklin D. *Roosevelt established the National Recovery Administration (NRA). Although it was agreed that conditions had improved somewhat, the NIRA was ruled unconstitutional by the Supreme Court (*Schechter v. United States*; 1935).

nationalism A doctrine that claims to determine the unit of population entitled to have government of its own. In its revolutionary form it regards existing state boundaries as arbitrary. The doctrine developed in Europe around 1800. The Latin word *Natio* had simply meant a group, regardless of frontiers, as in *Montesquieu's reference to monks as the "pietistic nation." After the French Revolution nationalists, such as *Fichte and *Mazzini, sought to make the boundaries of states coextensive with those of national habitation. Nations were supposed to be recognizable by certain distinguishing characteristics—for Fichte this was the use of a particular language. *Kant's doctrine of the autonomy of the will was used to provide philosophical backing for nationalism. While it was hoped that nationalism would make for peace, nationalistic aspirations in practice have often resulted in xenophobia, rivalry, and war.

National Labor Relations Board (NLRB) US federal agency, established in 1935, that governs labor relations. Its two main objectives are to correct unfair practices in business and labor unions and to insure the employee's freedom of choice, by secret ballot voting, to unionize. It administers the National Labor Relations Act (Wagner Act; 1935), which was amended by the Labor-Management Relations Act of 1947 (Taft-Hartley Act). There are five board members and a general counsel.

National Labor Relations Board v. Jones and Laughlin Steel Corp. (1937) US Supreme Court decision that dealt with the extent of federal regulatory power over interstate trade. The National Labor Relations Board (NLRB) directed Jones and Laughlin to rehire employees who had been fired for union activities. The steel company refused, and a federal court upheld their claim that the federal government could not rule on matters that affected interstate commerce only indirectly. The Supreme Court disagreed, ruled the direction of the NLRB constitutional, and ordered the workers rehired.

National Organization for Women (NOW) US organization, founded in 1966, that supports equal rights for women. Organized by feminist Betty Friedan and others, it advocates, through legislation, full equality for women, especially regarding the right to work and matters of marriage and divorce. It is a major force behind the campaign to ratify the Equal Rights Amendment.

National Park Service US government agency, established in 1916, a division of the Department of the Interior. It oversees the administration of all national historic, natural, cultural, and recreational areas, which include, among others, parks, monuments, rivers, parkways, seashores, reservoirs, and events. The oldest of the national parks is *Yellowstone National Park.

National Portrait Gallery An art museum in London founded in 1856 to house portraits that are authentic likenesses of famous personalities in British history. Its collection includes works by Holbein, Rubens, Reynolds, and Augustus John and an increasing number of photographs.

National Recovery Administration (NRA). *See* National Industrial Recovery Act.

National Republican Party US political party, formed in 1828 by a faction of the Republican Party that opposed Andrew *Jackson's re-election to the presidency in 1832. One of the party's leaders, Henry *Clay, ran against Jackson in the election, but lost. The party platform urged support of the second Bank of the United States. Short-lived, the party became part of the Whig Party by 1836.

National Security Acts (1947, 1949) US legislation that unified the military establishment, strengthened national security, and created the Department of Defense. In the 1947 law the Air Force became separate from the Army and equal to the Army and the Navy; the cabinet post of secretary of defense was created; and the National Security Council, *Central Intelligence Agency (CIA), National Security Resources Board (which no longer exists), and Joint Chiefs of Staff and several other boards were established. By the 1949 act the National Military Establishment was renamed the Department of Defense and raised to executive department level.

National Socialist German Workers' Party. *See* Nazi Party.

Nation of Islam. *See* Black Muslims.

Native American Party. *See* Know Nothing Party.

NATO. *See* North Atlantic Treaty Organization.

Natron, Lake 2 20S 36 05E A lake in N Tanzania, in the *Great Rift Valley. It measures about 30 mi (56 km) by 15 mi (24 km) and contains salt and soda.

natterjack A short-legged European *toad, *Bufo calamita*. About 2.8 in (7 cm) long when fully grown, the natterjack has a yellow stripe down its back. It runs in a series of short spurts and if alarmed raises its inflated body on its hind legs to appear larger to the enemy.

Nat Turner Insurrection (1831). *See* Turner, Nat.

natural gas A naturally occurring mixture of gaseous hydrocarbons consisting mainly of methane with smaller amounts of heavier hydrocarbons. It is obtained from underground reservoirs, often associated with *oil deposits. Like oil it originates in the bacterial decomposition of animal matter. It is a relatively cheap effective fuel, although in short supply (the present known reserves will be exhausted early next century). It also contains nonhydrocarbon impurities, the most important being helium, which is extracted commercially.

Naturalism A literary and artistic movement of the late 19th century characterized by the use of realistic techniques to express the philosophical belief that all phenomena can be explained by natural or material causes. It was influenced by the biological theories of *Darwin, the philosophy of *Comte, and the deterministic theories of the historian *Taine. Its literary manifesto was *Le Roman expérimentale* (1880) by *Zola, whose sequence of 20 novels known as *Le Rougon-Macquart* (1871–93) was intended to demonstrate, by its concentration on the history of a single family, how human life is determined by heredity and environment. Writers influenced by Naturalism include the dramatists *Hauptmann, *Ibsen, *Strindberg, and, in the 20th century, the US novelist Theodore *Dreiser. Its influence is also apparent in the work of such painters as *Courbet and *Van Gogh.

naturalization In law, the process by which an *alien, on taking an oath of allegiance, acquires the rights of a natural-born citizen of a country.

natural selection. *See* Darwinism.

Naukratis (*or* Naucratis) An ancient town on the W side of the Nile delta in Egypt. A community of Greek traders with considerable autonomy flourished here by permssion of the pharaohs from the 7th century BC.

Nauplia (Modern Greek name: Návplion) 37 34N 22 48E A port in S Greece, in the E Peloponnese. It was the capital of Greece from 1829 to 1834. Exports include fruit, vegetables, tobacco, and cotton. Population (1971): 9281.

Nauru, Republic of (*or* Naoero; former name: Pleasant Island) A small country in the central Pacific Ocean, NE of Australia comprising a coral island. The small population consists mainly of Naurians and other Pacific islanders. *Economy*: based entirely on the mining of phosphates, the only export. Deposits are expected to run out in the 1990s, but it is hoped to derive sufficient revenue by developing the island as a transport center and tax haven. *History*: discovered by the British in 1798, it was under British mandate from 1920 to 1947, when it came under the joint trusteeship of Australia, New Zealand, and the UK. In 1968 it became an independent republic and a special member of the British Commonwealth, with Hammer DeRoburt (1922–) as its first president. He faced serious difficulties in 1983, which led to his resignation. Bringing a libel suit against a Guam newspaper for linking DeRoburt and the Nauru government with a loan to Marshall Island separatists, DeRoburt lost the case at great financial cost to the country. In addition, Nauru's proposal to ban the dumping of nuclear wastes in the Pacific was defeated by the superpowers. Four days after his resignation, DeRoburt was re-elected. Official language: English. Official currency: Australian dollar. Area: 8 sq mi (21 sq km). Population (1983): 8000. Capital and main port: Yaren.

Nausicaa In Greek legend, the daughter of Alcinous, King of Phaeacia. She gave help to the shipwrecked *Odysseus, and was offered by her father in marriage, but Odysseus, loyal to his wife, refused.

nautical mile. *See* mile.

nautilus One of several cephalopod mollusks with external shells. The pearly nautiluses (genus *Nautilus*; 3 species) live near the bottom of the Pacific and Indian Oceans. Up to 8 in (20 cm) across, they have 60–90 tentacles surrounding a horny beak and live in the outermost chamber of their flat coiled shells. The others serve as buoyancy chambers from which gases can be absorbed, thus enabling the animals to float at different depths.

The paper nautilus (*Argonauta argo*) is found in the Atlantic and Pacific Oceans. The female, 8 in (20 cm) long, secretes from one of its tentacles a papery boat-shaped shell in which the eggs are laid and fertilized and develop. The male is much smaller (about 0.8 in [2 cm] long).

Navajo A North American Indian Athabascan-speaking people of New Mexico, Arizona, and Utah. Like their relatives, the *Apache, they migrated from the far north, probably during the 17th century. Unlike the Apache, they learned farming and adopted many traits from the *Pueblo Indians. Their social organization is based on the matrilineal principle and they live in small dispersed settlements, traditionally with little centralized political authority. They are farmers and herders and now the most numerous North American Indian tribe.

Navarino, Battle of (October 20, 1827) A naval battle arising from European intervention on behalf of Greece in the War of *Greek Independence from the Ottoman Empire. Ships of the French, Russian, and British navies destroyed the Ottoman-Egyptian fleet in the Bay of Navarinou in the Peloponnese. This was the last fleet action fought wholly under sail.

Navarre A former kingdom in N Spain, corresponding to the present-day Spanish province of Navarre and part of the French department of Basses-Pyrénées. Known as Pampalona until the late 12th century, it was ruled by Muslims until the late 9th century, when a Basque dynasty established control over the kingdom. In 1234 it passed to a French dynasty but in 1512 S Navarre was conquered by Ferdinand the Catholic of Aragon and united with Castile in 1515. French Navarre passed to the French crown in 1589.

navel A depression in the center of the abdomen that represents the site of attachment of the *umbilical cord of the fetus. Its medical name is the umbilicus. Occasionally babies are born with an umbilical hernia, in which the intestines protrude through the navel.

Navigation Acts A series of English acts originally to foster English shipping (1382, 1485, 1540) but subsequently to protect England's colonial trade, especially against its Dutch rivals. During the Commonwealth (1649–53) two ordinances (1650, 1651) respectively banned foreign trading in the colonies and restricted such trade to English or colonial ships, manned by predominantly English crews. These and similar Acts of 1660, 1672, and 1696 were repealed in 1849.

Navratilova, Martina (1956–) US tennis player; born in Czechoslovakia. She defected to the US in 1975 and won her first major title, the Wimbledon singles championship, which she won again in 1979, 1982–84. The dominant women's player of the early 1980s, she took the US title in 1983 and 1984.

navy A nation's warships (see ships), together with their crews and supporting administration. Navies were built by the ancient Greek city states at first to protect their Mediterranean trade routes from pirates and later to undermine the sea power of their rivals and enemies. The first recorded sea battle took place between Corinth and Corcyra (or Corfu) in 664 BC and navies—typically comprising triremes—played an important part in both the Greek-Persian and Peloponnesian Wars. The first permanent naval administration was organized (311 BC) in ancient Rome, which was the supreme Mediterranean power by the early 2nd century BC (see Punic Wars). Rome's naval power passed after the collapse of the western Empire in the 5th century AD to the Byzantine (Eastern Roman) Empire. Meanwhile, the Vikings marauded northern waters, provoking Alfred the Great of England to create (9th century) the origins of the Royal Navy. The later middle ages saw the rise of Italian navies, outstandingly those of Venice and Genoa, and the decline of the Byzantine fleet, under the threat of the Ottoman Turks. By 1571, when, at Lepanto, the Turkish control of the Mediterranean was finally destroyed, Spain had emerged as the supreme naval power. England's defeat of the Spanish *Armada (1588) anticipated its subsequent emergence as a great naval power: by the late 17th century it had overtaken the Netherlands (see Dutch Wars) and by the early 19th century, France (see Revolutionary and Napoleonic Wars). British naval supremacy was threatened in the early 20th century by the German navy, which in spite of defeat in World War I again became a power to be reckoned with in the 1930s. By the end of World War II command of the seas had passed to the US navy. The navies of the US and the Soviet Union now dominate the seas and with their nuclear-powered missile-armed submarines also dominate most of the earth's surface.

Navy, Department of the US government military department within the Department of *Defense. Directed by the secretary of defense and the secretary of the navy, it comprises the US *Navy, the US *Marine Corps, and the US Coast Guard when it is operating as a service in the Navy. Charged with the prosecution of war at sea when necessary and the maintenance of freedom on the seas, the department oversees the activities of its forces. Established in 1798, the department took over activities that had been the responsibility of the secretary of war.

Navy, United States Naval forces of the military. The Navy's mission is to protect the United States by the effective prosecution of war at sea, including the seizure or defense of advanced naval bases (*Marine Corps); to support the forces of all military departments of the US; and to maintain freedom of the seas. Established in 1775, the Navy is headed by the secretary of the navy and the chief of naval operations (CNO), the Navy's highest ranking officer.

Naxalites An extremist communist movement centering on the town of Naxalbari in W Bengal (India). Dedicated to Maoist principles, it attempted a violent seizure of land for the landless in 1967.

Náxos A Greek island in the S Aegean Sea, the largest in the Cyclades. Náxos is traditionally the place where Theseus abandoned Ariadne. It was an ancient center of the worship of Dionysius. Area: 169 sq mi (438 sq km). Population (1971): 14,201. Chief town: Náxos.

Nazareth 32 41N 35 16E A city in N Israel, between Haifa and the Sea of Galilee. The chief attractions of the city are the many churches, which commemorate its associations with the early life of Jesus Christ. Population (1972): 33,000.

NAZI PARTY *Hitler's exploitation of the techniques of mass propaganda, notably at party rallies such as the one pictured here, helps explain his rise to power in prewar Germany.*

Nazi Party (*N*ationalsozialistische Deutsche Arbeiterpartei) The National Socialist German Workers' Party, founded in 1919 as the German Workers' Party and led from 1921 until his suicide in 1945 by Adolf *Hitler. See also fascism.

Nazirites (*or* Nazarites) In the Old Testament, a group of Israelites who consecrated themselves to God by taking special vows, originally perhaps for life but later for a certain period only. The vows were to abstain from wine, not to cut the hair, and to avoid contact with dead bodies. Samson and Samuel were Nazirites from birth.

N'djamena (name until 1973: Fort Lamy) The capital of Chad, a port in the SW on the Chari River. It was founded by the French in 1900. The University of Chad was established in 1971. Population (1976 est): 241,639.

Ndola 13 00S 28 39E A city in N Zambia, near the Zaïre border. It is an important commercial and distribution center for the *Copperbelt and has copper and cobalt refineries. Population (1980 est): 323,000.

Neagh, Lough A lake in Northern Ireland, divided between Co Antrim, Co Armagh, and Co Tyrone. It is the largest lake in the British Isles. Area: 150 sq mi (388 sq km).

Neanderthal man An extinct *hominid race that inhabited Europe and the adjacent areas of Africa and Asia between about 70,000 and 35,000 years ago. Characterized by heavy brow ridges, receding forehead, heavy protruding jaw, and robust bone structure, Neanderthal man nonetheless had a large cranial capacity and upright posture. They were cave-dwelling hunters who made tools and buried their dead in a manner implying some sort of cult and ritual (see Mousterian). Their status as a distinct species (*Homo neanderthalensis*) is now questioned and some paleontologists prefer to see them as a subspecies of *Homo sapiens* (see Homo).

neap tide A □tide of comparatively small range that occurs near the time of the moon's quarters. The range falls below the average range by 10 to 30% (high low tides and low high tides). *Compare* spring tide.

nearsightedness (*or* myopia) Inability to focus on distant objects. This is the commonest kind of visual defect and commonly runs in families: it is not due to excessive reading in bad light but to a slightly misshapen eyeball, in which the light rays are focused in front of the retina (light-sensitive layer). It is corrected by wearing glasses with concave lenses or contact lenses.

Nebraska A state in the midwestern US. It is bordered by Iowa and Missouri on the E with the Missouri River forming the boundary, by Kansas and Colorado on the S, by Wyoming on the W, and by South Dakota on the N. Part of the Central Lowlands cover the eastern third of the state, with the higher Great Plains in the W. Traditionally an agricultural state, it is still a leading producer of cattle, corn, and wheat. Most of the population is situated in the industrial E. Omaha, the largest city, and Lincoln are insurance centers. Food processing (especially meat) is a major industry; machinery, fabricated metal, transport equipment, chemicals, and printing and publishing are also important. *History*: originally inhabited by tribes of Pawnee, Cheyenne, Arapaho, and Sioux who hunted the vast herds of buffalo that roamed Nebraskas's plains, the region was first explored by Francisco Vasquez de Coronado for Spain (1511). The French had developed the fur trade by the time the US acquired the area as part of the Louisiana Purchase in 1803. The Homestead Act (1862) and the arrival of the railroads (1867) encouraged settlement as hordes of pioneers traveled westward to claim the free land. Simultaneously with the arrival of the railroads, Nebraska achieved statehood (1867). The improved transportation spurred the development of cattle ranching. Nebraskan farmers were receptive to the Granger and Populist movements, and William Jennings Bryan, a native Nebraskan, became the national leader of both the Populists and the Democrats. Nebraska's well-being depended on its agricultural productivity, which was severely damaged by a devastating drought that came on the heels of the Depression of the 1930s. After World War II farm mechanization increased and new industries were developed; federal water projects helped the state, particularly with crop irrigation. During the economic recession of the early 1980s the economy remained generally strong with relatively low unemployment although the agricultural industry did suffer. Area: 77,227 sq mi (200,018 sq km). Population (1980): 1,570,006. Capital: Lincoln.

Nebuchadnezzar II (*or* Nebuchadrezzar; c. 630–562 BC) King of *Babylon (605–562). Nebuchadnezzar defeated the Egyptians at Carchemish (605 BC) and extended Babylonian power in Elam, N Syria, and S Asia Minor. He captured Jerusalem in 597 and again in 586, when he destroyed the city and forced the Jews into exile (*see* Babylonian Exile). He restored Babylon to its former glory. Daniel's story of his madness is probably unhistorical.

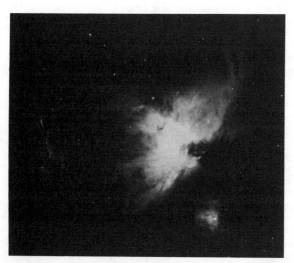

NEBULA *The Orion nebula, one of the brightest emission nebulae.*

nebula A cloud of interstellar gas and dust that becomes visible for one of three reasons. In an **emission nebula** the gas is ionized by ultraviolet radiation, generally from a hot star within the cloud; the ions interact with free electrons in the cloud, and light (predominantly red and green) is emitted. In a **reflection nebula** light from a nearby star is reflected in all directions by dust in the cloud, thus illuminating the cloud. The dust in a **dark nebula** reduces quite considerably the amount of light passing through

it (by absorption and scattering) and a dark region is seen against a brighter background.

Neckar River A river in SW West Germany, flowing mainly N from the Black Forest past Stuttgart and Heidelberg to join the Rhine River at Mannheim. Length: 245 mi (394 km).

Necker, Jacques (1732–1804) French statesman. A successful banker, in 1768 he became a director of the French East India Company. In 1776 he was appointed director of the treasury and in 1777, director general of finance. In retirement from 1781 to 1788, he was recalled to his former post on the eve of the French Revolution in the hope that he would deal with the economic crisis. He persuaded Louis XVI to summon the States General and suggested reforms that aroused the enmity of the aristocrats, who secured his dismissal. Reappointed after the storming of the Bastille, he resigned in 1790. His daughter was Mme de Staël.

nectar A sugary solution produced by glandular structures (nectaries) in animal-pollinated flowers. Nectar attracts insects, birds, or bats to the flower and encourages pollination as the animal collects nectar from different sources.

nectarine. *See* peach.

needlefish A carnivorous fish, also called garfish, belonging to the family *Belonidae* (about 60 species), that occurs in tropical and warm-temperate seas. It has a slender silvery-blue or green body, up to 4 ft (1.2 m) long, with elongated jaws and numerous sharp teeth. Species include the European garfish (*Belone belone*). Order: *Atheriniformes*.

Neer, Aert van der (c. 1603–77) Dutch landscape painter, famous for his moonlight, sunset, and firelight scenes. He also painted ice-bound canals and other winter landscapes.

Nefertiti (died c. 1346 BC) The cousin and chief wife of *Akhenaton of Egypt. She is depicted with her six daughters and the king in many scenes of personal and domestic life, a unique exception to the priestly conventions of Egyptian royal portraiture. Her portrait bust is perhaps the best-known work of Egyptian art.

Negev A desert in S Israel. In recent years large areas have been irrigated by pipeline from the Jordan River and many farming communities established, including over a hundred *kibbutzim*. Area: about 4632 sq mi (12,000 sq km).

Negrín, Juan (1889–1956) Spanish politician. A moderate socialist, Negrín became prime minister of the Republic in 1937 during the *Spanish Civil War. He centralized the military forces of the Republic but Negrín's dependence on the Communist Party brought opposition that forced his resignation.

Negri Sembilan A state in W Peninsular Malaysia, on the Strait of Malacca. It is hilly, producing mainly rubber, rice, coconuts, and tin. Area: 2550 sq mi (6605 sq km). Population (1980): 563,955. Capital: Seremban.

Negro, Río **1.** (Portuguese name: Rio Negro) A river in NE South America. Rising in E Colombia as the Guainía, it flows generally E into Brazil, joining the Amazon River about 10 mi (16 km) below Manaus. Length: about 1400 mi (2250 km). **2.** A river in S Argentina, rising in the Andes and flowing generally SE across Patagonia to the Atlantic Ocean. Length: 630 mi (1014 km).

Negroid The racial grouping comprising populations of sub-Saharan Africa. They are characterized by heavy skin pigmentation, curly to kinky dark hair, broad nose and lips, slight body hair, and high frequency of blood type Ro in the Rh system. Two subtypes exist: the taller darker Congoloid race and the shorter and lighter pygmies, Bushmen, and Hottentots, collectively known as Capoids.

Negros A volcanic island in the central Philippines, in the Visayan Islands. The chief industry is sugar production. Area: 5278 sq mi (13,670 sq km). Population (1970): 2,219,022. Chief town: Bacolod.

Nehemiah In the Old Testament, a Jewish leader of the 5th century BC. He was cupbearer to the Persian king but was granted permission to return to Jerusalem in 444 BC, where, despite opposition, he planned and supervised the restoration of the city walls. In 432 he visited Jerusalem a second time and initiated a number of religious and social reforms. **The Book of Nehemiah**, recording his activities, is by the author of *Chronicles and *Ezra.

JAWAHARLAL NEHRU *Two members of a political dynasty view exhibits at the Summer Palace in Peking. With Nehru is his daughter, Indira Gandhi, who later became prime minister.*

Nehru, Jawaharlal (1889–1964) Indian statesman; the first prime minister of independent India (1947–64). Educated in England, he returned to India in 1912 to practice law but soon left his profession to follow Mahatma *Gandhi; in 1929 he was elected president of the *Indian National Congress in succession to his father Motilal Nehru (1861–1931). Between 1921 and 1945 he served nine prison sentences for participating in the movement of noncooperation against the British. After World War II he was a central figure in the negotiations for the creation of an independent India. Throughout his long premiership he was held in high esteem both in his own country and abroad. He carried through many social reforms and maintained a policy of nonalignment with foreign powers, although he was finally forced to enlist US support against Chinese border attacks in 1962. Vijaya *Pandit was his sister and Indira *Gandhi his daughter.

Neill, A(lexander) S(utherland) (1883–1973) Scottish educationalist, child psychologist, and writer. The best-known British exponent of child-centered education, Neill founded Summerhill (1921), a coeducational boarding school, famous for its informal atmosphere and liberal educational techniques. His books include *Hearts, Not Heads* (1945) and *Talking of Summerhill* (1967).

Neisse River 1. (*or* Glatzer Neisse; Polish name: Nysa) A river in SW Poland, flowing NE to join the Oder River near Brzeg. Length: 159 mi (244 km). 2. (*or* Lusatian Neisse) A river rising in NW Czechoslovakia and flowing mainly N to the Oder River near Gubin in Poland. It forms part of the border between East Germany and Poland. Length: 140 mi (225 km).

Nejd. *See* Najd.

Nekrasov, Nikolai Alekseevich (1821–78) Russian poet. After rejecting the military career proposed by his father, he became a successful editor and manager of various literary periodicals. The main theme of his poetry is the oppression and character of the Russian peasants. He frequently drew on traditional folksongs, especially in his poems for children.

nekton An ecological division of aquatic animals that includes all those swimming actively, i.e. by their own efforts, in the open waters of a sea or lake (*compare* plankton). The nekton includes fishes, squids, turtles, seals, and whales.

Nelson, Horatio, Viscount (1758–1805) British admiral. At the outbreak of the French Revolutionary Wars he was given a command in the Mediterranean. In 1794, at Calvi, he lost the sight in his right eye but went on to play an important part in the victory off Cape St Vincent (1797), for which he was knighted. Shortly afterward he lost his right arm in action but in 1798 he destroyed France's naval power in the Mediterranean by his great victory in the battle of the *Nile. Nelson spent the following year in Naples, where he fell in love with Emma, Lady *Hamilton. Returning to England in 1800, Nelson, now Baron Nelson of the Nile, received a hero's welcome but his affair with Emma Hamilton caused scandal. Given command in the Baltic, he was responsible for the victory at Copenhagen

(1801). In 1803 he became commander in the Mediterranean. He blockaded Toulon but in 1805 the French escaped, with Nelson hot in pursuit, and the ensuing chase culminated in the battle of *Trafalgar (1805). Nelson directed this British triumph from aboard the *Victory* (□ships) but was himself mortally wounded.

HORATIO NELSON *Portrait (1798-1800) by Guy Head.*

Neman River (*or* Nyeman R.) A river in the W Soviet Union. Rising in the Belorussian SSR, it flows mainly NW through the Lithuanian SSR to enter the Baltic Sea. Length: 582 mi (937 km).

nematode A spindle-shaped colorless worm, also called roundworm, belonging to the phylum *Nematoda* (over 10,000 species). Most nematodes are less than 0.12 in (3 mm) long and have a mouth at one end, sometimes containing teeth or stylets, and usually a short muscular pharynx leading to the intestine. The sexes are generally separate. Nematodes live almost everywhere in soil, fresh water, and the sea. Some are parasites of plants or animals; others feed on dead organic matter. Many damage crops or parasitize domestic animals and man. *See also* Ascaris; eelworm; filaria; guinea worm; hookworm; pinworm; vinegar eel.

Nemertina. *See* ribbonworm.

Nemery, Jaafar Mohammed al (1930–) Sudanese statesman; president (1971–). An army officer, Nemery came to power in a coup in 1969 and was chairman of a revolutionary council before becoming president. In 1972 he negotiated an end to the 17-year revolt of the non-Muslims in the S, but N–S tensions remained. In the early 1980s, he was threatened by opposition from Libya.

Nemesia A genus of annual herbs native to South Africa. They are up to 12 in (30 cm) tall, with narrow leaves and showy white, yellow, red, pink, or purple two-lipped flowers, sometimes spurred, with spotted centers. Many species are popular ornamentals, especially *N. strumosa*, *N. floribunda*, and *N. versicolor*. Family: *Scrophulariaceae*.

Nemesis In Greek mythology, a goddess personifying the gods' anger at and punishment of human arrogance or *hubris. According to Hesiod, she is the daughter of night. She is associated with just vengeance and especially the punishment that befalls the impious.

Nemi, Lake 41 43N 12 43E A small crater lake in W central Italy, SE of Rome. Two large pleasure ships from the time of the Roman emperor Caligula were raised from the bottom (1930–31) but burned by the retreating German army in 1944.

Nennius (9th century AD) Welsh antiquary. He is traditionally held to be the author of *Historia Britonum*, a summary of Roman, Saxon, and Celtic legends concerning the early history of Britain. It contains the earliest reference to King *Arthur and mentions the poets *Aneirin and *Taliesin.

neoclassicism **1.** In art and architecture, a style dominant in Europe from the late 18th to mid 19th centuries. Originating in Rome in about 1750, it later spread throughout Europe and to the US. Although essentially a revival of classical art and architecture, it was distinguished from similar revivals by its new scientific approach to the recreation of the past. This was largely stimulated by archeological discoveries at *Pompeii, *Herculaneum, and elsewhere. Key figures in the early development of neoclassicism were the art historian *Winckelmann, who promoted enthusiasm for Greek art, and *Piranesi, who did the same for Roman art. Early neoclassical painters included *Mengs and Benjamin *West but the best known were Jacques Louis *David and *Ingres, who worked in France. Here neoclassicism developed under the stimulus of the *Enlightenment as a reaction to the frivolity of the *rococo style. The neoclassical penchant for themes of self-sacrifice in painting made it popular during the French Revolution. Other leading neoclassicists were the sculptors *Canova and *Thorvalsden and the architects Robert Adam, Soufflot, Claude-Nicholas Ledoux, and Friedrich Gilly. *See also* Empire style.

2. A style of composition originating in the 1920s. It was characterized by the use of counterpoint, small instrumental forces, and the use of such 18th-century forms as the concerto grosso. The leading practitioners of musical neoclassicism were *Stravinsky and *Hindemith.

neodymium (Nd) A *lanthanide element, occurring in the mineral monazite. It is used with lanthanum in *misch metal in lighter flints and, as the oxide (Nd_2O_3), together with praseodymium, to produce special dark glasses used in welding goggles. At no 60; at wt 144.24; mp 1872°F (1021°C); bp 5560°F (3068°C).

neoimpressionism. *See* pointillism.

Neolithic The final division of the *Stone Age. It is characterized by the development of the earliest settled agricultural communities and increasing domestication of animals, apparently occurring first in the Middle East during the 9th millennium BC (*see* Catalhüyük; Jericho). Although man still used only stone tools and weapons, he evolved improved techniques of grinding (as opposed to flaking) stone and the invention of pottery facilitated food storage and preparation.

Neo-Melanesian The form of *pidgin English widely used in Melanesia and New Guinea as a trade and mission language, which has become the native language of some communities. It has a more restricted vocabulary than that of English, on which it is based, a simplified grammar, and a modified sound system.

neon (Ne) A noble gas present in very small amounts in the earth's atmosphere, discovered in 1898 by Ramsay and M. W. Travers (1872–1961) by fractional distillation of liquid air. In an electrical discharge tube, neon glows orange-red and it is commonly used in advertising signs and voltage indicator tubes. Although some ion-pairs have been reported (for example NeH+), no stable compounds similar to those of krypton and xenon are yet known. At no 10; at wt 20.179; mp –415°F (–248.67°C); bp –410.9°F (–246.05°C).

neoplasticism. *See* Stijl, de.

Neoplatonism The philosophy, formulated principally by *Plotinus that emphasizes an eternal world of order, goodness, and beauty, of which material existence is a weak and unsatisfactory copy. The chief influences were Plato's concept of the Good, the analysis of love in the *Symposium*, and the speculations about the soul and immortality in the *Phaedo*; Plotinus had little interest in Plato's political and other systems. Neoplatonism helped to shape both medieval Christian theology and Islamic philosophy. *See also* Platonism.

Neoptolemus In Greek legend, King of Epirus, the son of *Achilles. He took part in the *Trojan War after his father's death and killed *Priam at the altar of Zeus.

Neorealism An Italian literary movement that originated during the early years of the fascist regime in the 1920s and flourished openly after its fall in 1943. Notable writers included the novelists Cesare *Pavese, Alberto *Moravia, and Ignazio *Silone, all of whom suffered political persecution for their accurate portrayal of social conditions. The term Neorealism has also been applied to certain Italian films made after World War II. Often using nonprofessional actors and shot on real locations, Neorealist films include *De Sica's *Bicycle Thieves* (1948).

neoteny The condition in which larval characteristics persist in an animal when it reaches sexual maturity. The *axolotl is a neotenous salamander that rarely assumes the typical adult form under natural conditions, although metamorphosis can be triggered by injection of thyroid hormone. Neotony is also known in certain tunicates (primitive marine chordates).

Nepal, Kingdom of A landlocked country in the Himalayas, between China (Tibet) and India. Most of the country consists of a series of mountain ranges and high fertile valleys, with some of the world's highest peaks, including Mount Everest, along its northern border and a region of plain and swamp in the S. Its predominantly Hindu population is of Mongoloid stock, the Gurkhas having been the dominant group since 1769. *Economy*: chiefly agricultural, the main crops are rice, maize, millet, and wheat. Forestry is also important. Mineral resources are sparse, although some mica is being mined. Hydroelectricity is being developed on a large scale and some industry is being encouraged, including jute and sugar. Tourism is an important source of revenue. Exports, mainly to India, include grains, jute, and timber, as well as medicinal herbs from the mountains. *History*: the independent principalities that comprised the region in the middle ages were conquered by the Gurkhas in the 18th century and Nepal was subsequently ruled by the Shah family and then by the Rana, who continue to reign. In 1959 a new constitution provided for an elected parliament, but in 1960 the king dismissed the new government and in 1962 abolished the constitution. There is now a pyramidal structure of government by local and national councils (*panchayat*) and executive power lies with the king. In international relations Nepal tries to keep a balance between the two neighboring great powers. Head of state: King Birendra Bir Bikram Shah Dev. Prime minister: Lokendra Bahandur Chand. Official language: Nepali. Official currency: Nepalese rupee of 100 paisa. Area: 54,600 sq mi (141,400 sq km). Population (1980 est): 14,300,000. Capital: Kathmandu.

nephritis (*or* Bright's disease) Inflammation of the kidneys. It may result from infection, as in *pyelitis, or from a disorder of the body's system that affects the kidneys (called glomerulonephritis), which causes protein, cells, and blood to appear in the urine and swelling of the body tissues (*see* edema). This sometimes occurs in children after a streptococcal infection of the throat and often resolves, but other types of glomerulonephritis, occurring more often in adults, may become chronic and result eventually in kidney failure or *uremia.

Neptune (astronomy) The most distant giant planet, orbiting the sun every 165 years at a mean distance of 2793 million mi (4497 million km). It is somewhat smaller (30,750 mi [49,500 km] in diameter) and more massive (17.3 earth masses) than *Uranus, exhibits a similar featureless greenish disk in a telescope, and is thought to be almost identical to Uranus in atmospheric and internal structure. It has two *satellites. Neptune's existence was predicted by John Couch Adams and Urbain Leverrier. It was discovered in 1846 by J. G. Galle, using Leverrier's predicted position.

Neptune (mythology) An early Italian god associated with water. When seapower became important to Rome, he became the principal Roman sea god and was identified with the Greek *Poseidon. He is usually portrayed holding a trident and riding a dolphin.

neptunium (Np) The first synthetic transuranic element, produced in 1940 at Berkeley, Calif, by bombarding uranium with neutrons. Trace quantities are produced in natural uranium ores by the same reaction. It is available in small quantities in nuclear reactors and forms halides (for example NpF_3, $NpCl_4$) and oxides (for example NpO_2). At no 93; at wt 237.0482; mp 1185°F (640°C); bp 7063°F (3902°C).

nereids In Greek mythology, a class of *nymphs or female spirits of nature associated with the sea. They were the daughters of the sea god Nereus and Doris, daughter of Oceanus. The best-known Nereids were *Amphitrite, wife of Poseidon, and *Thetis, mother of Achilles.

Nereus A primitive Greek sea god, father of the *Nereids. He had prophetic powers and was capable of changing his form.

Nergal A Mesopotamian god of hunger and devastation and ruler of the underworld. He is also described as a protective god capable of restoring the dead to life and features in the *Epic of Gilgamesh*.

Neri, St Philip (1515–95) Italian mystic, who founded the Congregation of the Oratory (*see* Oratorians). Settling in Rome (c. 1533), he organized a body of laymen dedicated to charitable works. He was ordained in 1551, becoming a priest at the Church of San Girolamo. Over its nave he built an oratory to hold religious meetings and concerts of sacred music, from which both the name of Neri's order and the word *oratorio* derive. He later ordained his followers, finally installing them in Sta Maria at Vallicella in 1575. Feast day: May 26.

Nernst, Walther Hermann (1864–1941) German physical chemist, who first stated the third law of *thermodynamics. He also explained the ionization of certain substances when dissolved in water and showed that hydrogen and chlorine combine, when exposed to light, as a result of a chain reaction involving free radicals. He won the 1920 Nobel Prize for Chemistry.

Nero (Claudius Caesar) (37–68 AD) Roman emperor (54–68), notorious for his cruelty. His early reign was dominated by his mother *Agrippina the Younger, *Seneca, and Sextus Afranius Burrus but by 62 Nero had thrown off these influences: Agrippina was murdered (59), Burrus died, perhaps by poison (62), and Seneca retired (62). Also in 62, he murdered his wife Octavia in order to marry Poppaea, who herself died in 65 after being kicked by her husband. Nero ruled with a vanity and irresponsibility that antagonized most sectors of society. A conspiracy to assassinate him, after which Seneca was forced to kill himself, failed in 65. In 68, however, revolts in Gaul, Spain, and Africa and the mutiny of his palace guard forced him to flee Rome and precipitated his suicide.

Neruda, Pablo (Neftalí Ricardo Reyes; 1904–73) Chilean poet. He served in the diplomatic service from 1927 to 1943, was elected a Communist senator in 1943, and was appointed ambassador to France by Salvador *Allende in 1970. The nihilism of his early poetry, such as *Residencia en la tierra* (1925–31), was later replaced by social commitment in *Canto general* (1950) and other works. He won the Nobel Prize in 1971.

Nerva, Marcus Cocceius (c. 30–98 AD) Roman emperor (96–98), chosen by the Senate to succeed Domitian. Nerva's brief rule was enlightened: land was allotted to poorer citizens, treason charges were abolished, and administration was improved.

Nerval, Gérard de (Gérard Labrunie; 1808–55) French poet. His childhood interest in the occult was furthered by travels in the Near East, described in *Voyage en Orient* (1851). His best-known works, which anticipate the techniques of symbolism (*see* Symbolists) and *surrealism, include the story *Sylvie* (1854), the sonnets *Les Chimères* (1854), and the collection of prose and poetry, *Le Rêve et la vie* (1855). His writing was affected by his thwarted love for an actress and by his mental breakdowns, which recurred from 1841 until his suicide in 1855.

nerve. *See* neuron.

nerve gases War gases that inhibit the action of the enzyme acetylcholinesterase, which is essential for the transmission of impulses from nerve to nerve or muscle. Death results from paralysis of the diaphragm leading to asphyxiation. Most nerve gases are derivatives of phosphoric acid and they are toxic in minute quantities (1 mg can be lethal). *See* chemical warfare.

Nervi, Pier Luigi (1891–1978) Italian engineer and architect, famous for his inventive use of reinforced concrete. His first major building, a stadium in Florence (1930–32), features a concrete cantilevered spiral staircase and curved roof. It was followed between 1935 and 1941 by a series of aircraft hangars (now destroyed) with vaults of lattice-patterned beams. In 1949 he designed the great exhibition hall in Turin and in 1953 was one of the architects of the UNESCO building in Paris. Among his later works were two sports stadiums for the 1960 Rome Olympics and San Francisco Cathedral (1970). He was a professor at Rome University from 1947 to 1961.

nervous system The network of nervous tissue in the body. This comprises the central nervous system (CNS), i.e. the *brain and *spinal cord, and the peripheral nervous system. The latter includes the cranial and spinal nerves with their *ganglia and the autonomic nervous system (ANS). The ANS controls unconscious body functions, such as digestion and heartbeat, and is coordinated by the *hypothalamus. The nervous system is chiefly responsible for communication both within the body and between the body and its surroundings. Incoming information passes along sensory *neurons to the brain, where it is analyzed and compared with *memory; nerve impulses then leave the central nervous system along motor nerves, carrying signals to all parts of the body and enabling it to respond continuously. Man's success as a species is largely due to the complexity of his nervous system.

Ness, Loch A deep lake in N Scotland, in the Highland Region in the Great Glen. The sight of a monster (the **Loch Ness monster**) has frequently been reported. Length: 22 mi (36 km). Depth: 754 ft (229 m).

Nesselrode, Karl Robert, Count (1780–1862) Russian statesman. He represented Russia at the Congress of Vienna (1814–15) and became foreign minister in 1822, dominating the formation of Russian foreign policy until his death. Nesselrode's intransigent policy in the Balkans contributed largely to the outbreak of the *Crimean War in 1853.

Nessus In Greek legend, a centaur who attempted to rape Deianira, the wife of *Heracles, who killed him with an arrow tipped with the *Hydra's poisonous blood. Before he died, Nessus deceitfully told Deianira that she should save some of his own infected blood as a potion to win back Hera-

cles' love. She smeared the centaur's blood on Heracles' shirt and thus caused his death.

nest A structure built or taken over by animals to house their eggs, their young, or themselves. The greatest variety is found among birds, whose nests are typically bowl-shaped and constructed of twigs, leaves, moss, fur, etc., woven or glued together. The nests of certain swifts are made entirely of saliva and form the major ingredient of bird's nest soup. Some birds nest on the ground, without using any nesting material; others use holes, either naturally occurring or excavated in trees. Nest building in birds is a complex behavior, triggered by hormones, in which some components are instinctive and others learned. Nests are also built by ants, termites, bees, and wasps, which construct elaborate tunnel systems, and by fish, amphibians, reptiles, and small mammals.

Nestor In Greek legend, a king of Pylos. His 11 brothers were killed by *Heracles. As a commander in the *Trojan War during his old age, he acted as a wise counselor to the quarrelling Greek leaders.

Nestorians The adherents of the Christological doctrines of the Syrian bishop Nestorius (died c. 451). Appointed Patriarch of Constantinople (428), he maintained, probably in overreaction to *Monophysite theories, that there were two persons, not merely two natures, in the incarnate Christ, and that the Virgin Mary could not therefore properly be called the Mother of God. He was accused of heresy and deposed (431). His supporters in his E Syrian homeland formed their own church, centered on Edessa. Expelled from Edessa (489), they established themselves in Persia until virtually annihilated by the 14th-century Mongol invasions.

Netherlandic A subgroup of the Western *Germanic languages. It first appears in documents in the 12th century. It is now spoken in Holland and Belgium, where it is called Dutch and Flemish respectively, although the two are in fact the same language. It is the parent language of Afrikaans and is also spoken in parts of Indonesia as a result of Dutch colonization.

Netherlands, Kingdom of the A country in NW Europe, on the North Sea. It is almost entirely flat except for some low hills in the SE, and considerable areas of land have been reclaimed from the sea. Rivers, including the Scheldt, Maas, and Rhine, together with the many canals form an efficient system of inland waterways. *Economy:* although popularly considered to be an agricultural nation, industry and commerce are the principal sources of income. Highly developed industries include oil and gas, chemicals, electronics, printing, metals, and food processing. The production of coal, once important, ceased in 1975, when all mines were closed. Agriculture is highly mechanized and market gardening is important. There is also considerable livestock farming, dairy produce being one of the principal exports together with flower bulbs, fuels, chemicals, textiles, and machinery. There is a thriving fishing industry and oysters are a valuable product. Tourism is an important source of revenue as is the Europort at *Rotterdam. *History:* until 1581 the Netherlands formed with present-day Belgium and Luxembourg the region often referred to as the Low Countries. It was under Roman occupation from the 1st century BC to the 4th century AD. It was then overrun by German tribes, of which the Franks had established dominance over the area by the mid-5th century. After the partition of the Frankish empire in 843 the region formed (855) part of Lothair's inheritance and was called Lotharingia. The following centuries saw the rise of powerful principalities, notably the bishopric of Utrecht and the counties of Holland and Guelders, which were fiefs of the German kings before coming under the influence of Burgundy from the 14th century and the Habsburg Emperor Charles V in the early 16th century. Commercial prosperity and the persecution of Protestants fostered a growing movement for independence from the rule of Charles' son Philip II of Spain. In 1581, during the *Revolt of the Netherlands, the seven northern provinces—Holland, Zeeland, Utrecht, Overijssel, Gröningen, Drenthe, and Friesland—proclaimed their independence as the United Provinces of the Netherlands under the leadership of William the Silent. War with Spain continued intermittently until, at the conclusion of the Thirty Years' War, Spain recognized the independence of the Dutch Republic in the Peace of Westphalia (1648). In the 17th century, under the rule of the House of Orange-Nassau, from which the stadholder (chief magistrate) was elected until 1795, the Netherlands reached a peak of prosperity (based on trade and fishing) and international prestige, forming a considerable overseas empire. In the 18th century, however, after the death of William III of Orange, who in 1688 had become King of England, the Netherlands declined. In 1795 it fell to Revolutionary France and in 1806 Napoleon made his brother Louis Bonaparte King of Holland. Following Napoleon's defeat the former Dutch Republic was reunited with the southern provinces (the Spanish Netherlands until 1713 and then the Austrian Netherlands), which had remained loyal to the Habsburgs in the 16th century, to form the Kingdom of the Netherlands (1814). In 1830 the S revolted against the union, forming Belgium (1831), and in 1867 Luxembourg became an independent state. The Netherlands, which flourished economically in the second half of the 19th century, remained neutral in World War I but in World War II was occupied by Germany (1940–45) in spite of fierce Dutch resistance. In 1948 the Netherlands joined with Belgium and Luxembourg to form the *Benelux economic union; it was a founder member of the EEC. The immediate postwar period was dominated by the Dutch colony of Indonesia's fight for independence, achieved in 1950 after bitter and bloody conflict. The peaceful assimilation of non-white immigrants from the former colonies was marred in the 1970s following terrorist activities by the South Moluccans, who were protesting against the Indonesian occupation of their country. In 1980 Queen Juliana abdicated and was succeeded as head of state by her daughter Princess Beatrix. As part of a 1979 NATO agreement the Netherlands agreed to allow the deployment of medium-range missiles on its soil. The final decision on deployment was postponed, however, in response to widespread anti-nuclear sentiments in the country. In the early 1980s the Netherlands was the only European country scheduled to receive missiles that had not decided to go through with the deployment. Official language: Dutch. Official currency: guilder of 100 cents. Area: 15,892 sq mi (41,160 sq km). Population (1983): 14,347,000. Capitals: Amsterdam (legal and administrative); The Hague (seat of government). Main port: Rotterdam.

Netherlands Antilles (Dutch name: Nederlandse Antillen) Two groups of West Indian islands in the Lesser Antilles, in the Caribbean Sea some 497 mi (800 km) apart. The S group lies off the N coast of Venezuela and consists of *Curaçao, *Aruba, and Bonaire; the N group (geographically part of the Leeward Islands) consists of St Eustatius, Saba, and the S part of *St Martin. Under Dutch control since the 17th century, the islands became self-governing in 1954. The economy is based chiefly on oil refining, centered on Curaçao and Aruba. Area: 390 sq mi (996 sq km). Population (1979 est): 256,000. Capital: Willemstad.

net national product. See gross national product.

Neto, Agostinho (1922–79) Angolan statesman; president (1975–79). A physician, he led the MPLA (Popular Movement for the Liberation of Angola) in the struggle against Portuguese rule (1962–74) and on independence became Angola's first president.

nettle An annual or perennial herb of the genus *Urtica* (about 30 species), found in temperate regions worldwide. Up to 5 ft (1.5 m) in height, it has simple leaves with toothed margins and bears clusters of small green unisexual flowers. Stems and leaves may have stinging hairs. Family: *Urticaceae*.

Dead nettles are annual or perennial herbs of the genus *Lamium* (about 40 species), occurring in Europe, temperate Asia, and N Africa. They bear clusters of tubular two-lipped flowers. Family: *Labiatae*.

nettle rash. See urticaria.

Neuchâtel (German name: Neuenburg) 47 00N 6 56E A city in W Switzerland, on Lake Neuchâtel. It possesses a university (1909) and the Swiss Laboratory of Horological Research. Industries include watchmaking and chocolate production; wine trading is important. Population (1970): 169,173.

Neue Kunstlervereinigung (New Artists' Association) An organization of artists founded in Munich in 1909 by *Kandinsky and *Jawlensky, among others. Its aim to provide more favorable exhibiting conditions for modern art in Munich was largely fulfilled in its large exhibition of international contemporary art in 1910. Disagreements among the members resulted in the defection in 1911 of Kandinsky and Marc, who then founded Der *Blaue Reiter.

Neumann, (Johann) Balthasar (1687–1753) German architect, born in Bohemia. One of the greatest rococo architects, Neumann was a military engineer before being appointed court architect to the Bishop of Würzburg (1719), for whom he built his most famous palace. He also designed churches, of which the church of Vierzehnheiligen (1743–72), with its complex plan and lavish ornamentation, was his masterpiece.

Neumann, John von (1903–57) US mathematician, born in Hungary. He invented *game theory, the branch of mathematics that analyzes strategy and is now widely employed for military purposes. He also set quantum theory upon a rigorous mathematical basis.

neuralgia Sharp or burning pain arising from nerves. Causalgia, one form of neuralgia, is pain arising from a single nerve and is usually caused by an injury to that nerve. The commonest form is trigeminal neuralgia, in which paroxysms of pain affect one side of the face, particularly the cheek, along the course of the trigeminal nerve.

neuritis Inflammation of the nerves. This can be caused by leprosy and multiple sclerosis. However, most diseases of peripheral nerves are caused not by inflammation but by degeneration of the nerve, and the word **neuropathy** is used to describe this. Neuropathies can be caused by a variety of conditions, including diabetes, alcoholism, lead poisoning, and vitamin deficiencies, such as beriberi and pellagra.

neurohormone A chemical (see hormone) that is secreted by nerve cells and modifies the function of other organs in the body. The *hypothalamus, for example, releases several hormones that cause the *pituitary gland to secrete its own hormones, the kidney to retain water in the body, and the breast to produce milk.

neurology The study of the structure (neuroanatomy), function (neurophysiology), and diseases (neuropathology) of the *nervous system. A neurologist is a physician who specializes in the diagnosis and treatment of nervous diseases.

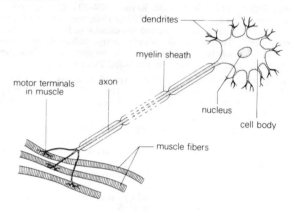

NEURONE *When a nerve impulse transmitted down the axon of a neurone reaches the motor terminals in muscle fibers the muscle is stimulated to contract.*

neurone (*or* nerve cell) The functioning unit of the *nervous system. A neurone consists of a cell body, containing the nucleus; small irregular branching processes called dendrites; and a single long nerve fiber, or axon, which may be ensheathed by layers of fatty material (myelin) and either makes contact with other neurons at *synapses or ends at muscle fibers or gland cells. When a neuron is stimulated from outside or by another neuron, a nerve impulse is transmitted electrochemically down the axon (see action potential). The frequency of these impulses is the basis for the control of behavior. Bundles of nerve fibers are bound together to form **nerves**, which transmit impulses from sense organs to the brain or spinal cord (sensory nerves) or outward from the central nervous system to a muscle or gland (motor nerves).

Neuroptera An order of slender carnivorous insects (4500 species) with long antennae and two similar pairs of net-veined wings. The order includes the *alderflies, *snakeflies, and *dobsonflies (suborder *Megaloptera*) and the *lacewings and *antlions (suborder *Plannipennia*).

neurosis A mental illness in which insight is retained but there is a disordered way of behaving or thinking that causes suffering to the patient (*compare* psychosis). The symptoms of neurosis vary considerably: they include a pathologically severe emotional state, as in *anxiety or *depression; distressing behavior and thoughts, as in *phobias or *obsessions; and physical complaints, as in *hysteria. A neurosis with psychological symptoms is known as a **psychoneurosis**. Neurotic symptoms usually arise through a complex interaction between *stress and a vulnerable personality. Treatment for neurosis can include *tranquilizers, *psychotherapy, and *behavior therapy.

Neusiedl, Lake (German name: Neusiedlersee) A lake in Austria and Hungary. Having no natural outlet, its area varies with the rainfall. Many species of bird are to be found on its reedy shore. Area: about 135 sq mi (350 sq km).

Neuss 51 12N 06 42E A city in NW West Germany, in North Rhine-Westphalia near the Rhine River. Known for its annual rifle-shooting contest, it is a canal port and industrial center. Population (1980 est): 149,300.

Neustria The western Frankish kingdom created by the partition in 511 of the possessions of *Clovis I. Approximating in area to N France, it was the rival to *Austrasia (the eastern kingdom) until 687, when *Pepin of

Herstal, mayor of the palace (viceroy) of Austrasia, defeated the Neustrians at Tertry.

neutrality The legal status of a country that remains impartial in relation to other countries that are at war (belligerents). In *international law the rights and obligations of a neutral state are mainly contained in the Hague Conventions V and XIII (1907; see Hague Peace Conferences) on neutrality in land war and on the sea, respectively. A neutral state must treat belligerents in the same way in matters not relating to war and must not assist either side in furthering its war aims. In particular it must prohibit the use of its territory for the purpose of equipping for war or recruiting men, and it may use force if necessary to prevent any violation of its neutrality. The most important right conferred by neutrality is inviolability of territory: belligerents may not carry on warfare in a neutral state's territory, which includes its water and air space. The term "nonbelligerence" is used when a state that is theoretically neutral is, in fact, sympathetic to one belligerent, for example the relationship between the US and the UK between 1939 and 1941.

neutrinos A group of three elementary particles and their antiparticles. They are classified as leptons, have no charge, and are probably massless. One type of neutrino is associated with the *electron, one with the *muon, and one with the *tau particle.

neutron An elementary particle that is a constituent of all atomic nuclei except hydrogen–1. It has no electric charge and its mass is slightly greater than that of the *proton. Inside the nucleus the neutron is stable but when free it decays by the *weak interaction to a proton, an electron, and an antineutrino (see beta decay). Its mean life is about 12 minutes. The neutron was discovered by *Chadwick in 1932. See also particle physics.

neutron bomb. See nuclear weapons.

neutron star A star that has undergone *gravitational collapse to the extent that most of the protons and electrons making up its constituent atoms have coalesced into neutrons. The density is extremely high (about 10^{17} kg m^{-3}) and the pressure exerted by the densely packed neutrons can support the star against further contraction. Neutron stars are thought to form when the mass of the stellar core remaining after a *supernova exceeds about 1.4 times the sun's mass. See also pulsar.

Neva, Battle of the (July 15, 1240) The battle in which Sweden was defeated by the forces of Prince Aleksandr Yaroslavich of Novgorod (who thus received the name Nevsky; see Alexander Nevsky). His victory ended the expansionist ambitions of Sweden into NW Russia.

Nevada One of the mountain states in the W US. It is bounded by Utah and Arizona on the E, California on the SW and W, and Oregon and Idaho on the N. Lying almost wholly within the Great Basin, most the state consists of a vast plateau with several high mountain ranges rising to well over 5250 ft (1600 m). The only major river is the Colorado, in the SE. The Hoover, or Boulder, Dam, one of the world's major dams, impounds Lake Mead along the Colorado. Nevada is the most arid US state. Many water projects throughout the state supply drinking water and irrigation. Over 85% of Nevada is federally controlled in the form of water projects and military installations. Most of the population and manufacturing industries are located in the two main cities of Las Vegas and Reno. Copper smelting in a major industry; others include stone, clay, and glass products, cement, food processing, and more recently space, electronics, and the atomic industries. A mineral-rich state, it produces metallic ores and other minerals. Tourism (largely because of the state's legalized gambling) is by far the most important industry. Las Vegas, which is also famous for its nightlife, and Lake Tahoe are two of the chief tourist attractions. The land and climate are unfavorable for agriculture but some dairying and livestock raising, especially cattle and sheep, are carried on. *History*: first explored by Americans, the state was ceded to the US by Mexico in 1848 as part of the *Mexican War settlement. The Mormons founded the first permanent settlement in 1858. It became a state in 1864 following the discovery of the Comstock Lode, the richest known US silver deposit (now depleted). During the 1970s Nevadans began suit against the federal government for repossession of its land resources. The movement became known as the Sagebrush Rebellion. The growth of high-technology industries contributed to Nevada's expansion, and in the 1980s it had become one of the fastest growing states. Area: 110,540 sq mi (286,297 sq km). Population (1980): 799,184. Capital: Carson City.

Nevelson, Louise (Louise Berliawsky; 1900–) US sculptor and painter, born in Russia. She used scraps of everyday objects—wood, metals, and plastics—to create her futuristic sculptures. Her "black boxes" of the 1950s, filled with odd pieces of wood and wheels, were wall structures painted black. In the 1960s and 1970s she constructed metal and Plexiglass sculptures, usually painted white or gold. Her works include *Sky Cathedral*

(1958), *Daun's Wedding Feast* (1959), *Homage to the World* (1966), *Transparent Sculpture VI* (1967–68), *Night Presence IV* (1972), and the White Chapel of the Good Shepherd at St. Peter's Lutheran Church in New York City (1977–78).

Nevers 47 00N 3 09N A city in central France, the capital of the Nièvre department on the Loire River. It has a 13th-century cathedral and a palace (15th–16th centuries) and its industries include light engineering and pottery. Population (1975): 47,730.

Nevis. See St Kitts-Nevis.

nevus. See birthmark.

New Amsterdam 6 18N 57 30W A port in NE Guyana, on the Berbice River. It serves an area producing sugar cane, rice, and cattle. Population (1970): 18,000.

Newark 40 44N 74 11W A city in New Jersey, on Newark Bay, part of the Greater New York Metropolitan Area. Founded in 1666, it attracted several inventors, whose developments included patent leather (1818), malleable cast iron (1826), the first photographic film (1888), and electrical measuring instruments (1888). The state's largest city, it is the focus of air, road, and rail routes. Industries include cutlery, jewelry, and chemicals. Population (1980): 329,248.

New Bedford 41 38N 70 56W A city in SE Massachusetts, on Buzzard's Bay at the mouth of the Acushnet River, SE of Fall River. Its history is steeped in the whaling business; during the 18th and 19th centuries it was a major shipping and whaling port, and fishing is still important. Industries include food processing, textiles and clothing, and rubber and metal products. Population (1980): 98,478.

New Britain A volcanic island in the SW Pacific Ocean, in Papua New Guinea, the largest of the Bismarck Archipelago. Copra and some minerals are exported. Area: 14,100 sq mi (36,520 sq km). Population (1970 est): 154,000. Chief town: Rabaul.

New Brunswick A province of E Canada, on the Gulf of St Lawrence. Heavily forested, it consists of rugged uplands with fertile river valleys; the population is concentrated in the *St John River Basin. There is some mixed farming and fishing is important along the Bay of Fundy. Lead, zinc, and some copper are mined at Bathurst. Forestry was a major activity during the last century but overcutting and the loss of protected British markets led to a decline in the industry. Today lumbering and the manufacture of pulp and paper serve mainly local needs. In an attempt to encourage industrial development the federal government has spent considerable sums of money on improving the infrastructure (factories, roads, etc.). *History*: slow settlement by French peasants, beginning in the 17th century, ended shortly after Britain's control of the coastal areas was confirmed in 1713. Colonization from Britain and New England followed, and New Brunswick became a separate colony (1784). It prospered and was a founding member of the Dominion of Canada (627,835 sq mi (72,092 sq km). Population (1981 est): 696,403; approximately 30% are French speaking. Capital: Fredericton.

New Brunswick 40 29N 74 27W A city in NE New Jersey, on the S bank of the Raritan River, W of Perth Amboy. Rutgers University (1766) is here. Settled in 1681, its chief manufactures are drugs and medical supplies. Population (1980): 41,442.

New Caledonia (French name: Nouvelle Calédonie) A French island in the SW Pacific Ocean. Together with its dependencies (the Isle of Pines, the Loyalty Islands, and others) it forms a French overseas territory. The main industries are nickel mining and processing and meat preserving. Nickel, copra, and coffee are exported. Area: 7374 sq mi (19,103 sq km), including dependencies. Population (1976 est): 133,000. Capital: Nouméa.

Newcastle 32 55S 151 46E A city in Australia, in New South Wales on the mouth of the Hunter River. Iron and steel industries are important, using coal from the Newcastle-Cessnock field. Population (1976): 251,132.

Newcastle, Thomas Pelham-Holles, 1st Duke of (1693–1768) British statesman; Whig prime minister (1754–56, 1757–62). He resigned as prime minister in 1756 because of early reverses in the *Seven Years' War but returned in 1757 with foreign affairs in the hands of Pitt the Elder. His brother **Henry Pelham** (1696–1754) was prime minister (1743–54) in the Broad-Bottom administration, which included members of opposing political factions.

Newcastle, William Cavendish, Duke of (1592–1676) British soldier, author, and patron of the arts. He fought for the royalists in the Civil War and after their defeat at *Marston Moor (1644) he went into exile. Returning at the Restoration, he became a patron of writers, including Jonson and Dryden.

Newcastle disease. See fowl pest.

Newcastle-under-Lyme 53 00N 2 14W A city in the Midlands of England, in Staffordshire. There are traces of a 12th-century castle built by John of Gaunt. The principal industries are coalmining, bricks and tiles, clothing, paper, and machinery. Nearby is Keele University (1962). Population (1981): 72,853.

Newcastle upon Tyne 54 59N 1 35W A city in NE England, on the N bank of the Tyne River opposite Gateshead, with which it is linked by tunnel and five bridges. It is the principal port and commercial and cultural center of NE England, with a 14th-century cathedral and a university (1852). The principal industries include shipbuilding, marine and electrical engineering, chemicals, flour milling, soap, and paints. *History*: on the site of a Roman settlement, Newcastle derives its name from the castle (1080) built as a defense against the Scots. Newcastle's well-known trade in coal developed in the 13th century. Population (1981): 192,454.

Newchang. *See* Yingkou.

Newcombe, John (1944–   ) Australian tennis player, who was Wimbledon singles champion in 1967, 1970, and 1971 and US singles champion in 1967 and 1973. Also an outstanding doubles player, he won three successive titles at Wimbledon (1968–70).

New Comedy The final period of Greek comic drama, lasting from c. 320 BC to the mid-3rd century BC and characterized by well-constructed plays on domestic themes. The role of the chorus diminished as the plots became more complicated. The leading writers of this period were *Menander and *Philemon, whose plays influenced the development of comedy in Rome and later in W Europe. *See also* Middle Comedy; Old Comedy.

Newcomen, Thomas (1663–1729) English blacksmith, who in 1712 constructed an early steam engine. It was based on Thomas *Savery's engine and was widely used for pumping water out of mines. It was extremely inefficient, however, and it was not until *Watt invented the separate condenser that steam engines became suitable for use in transportation.

New Deal (1933–41) The sweeping legislative program proposed by President Franklin D. *Roosevelt to help the nation recover from the effects of the *Depression and to initiate social and economic reforms. Promising to offer the American people a "new deal," Roosevelt embarked on an ambitious program of emergency legislation during the first hundred days of his administration in 1933. In order to deal with the country's severe economic crisis, the president ordered a four day bank holiday during which the *Federal Reserve System was completely reorganized; credit, currency, and foreign exchange were regulated; the gold standard was abandoned; and the dollar was devalued. These measures enabled the nation's banks to reopen on a sound basis and averted impending economic catastrophe. The next stage in the New Deal program was the establishment of federal agencies to provide work, relief, and public works programs for the millions of Americans who had lost their jobs. These programs included the *Civilian Conservation Corps, the *Agricultural Adjustment Act, the *National Industrial Recovery Act, and the Tennessee Valley Authority, which was ostensibly set up as a flood control program, but which improved the social and economic status of the undeveloped region by promoting farming and industry. The early New Deal programs achieved notable successes, and they were supplemented in 1935 by the establishment of the *Works Progress Administration (WPA), the *National Labor Relations Board, and the *Social Security Act, which provided retirement and disability payments for all American workers. Although the Roosevelt administration faced opposition from conservative members of Congress and from several adverse rulings of the Supreme Court, the New Deal effectively brought the country out of the Depression and established the social and economic policies carried on by succeeding administrations.

New Economic Policy (NEP) An economic policy adopted by the Soviet Union between 1921 and 1929. Introduced by Lenin, the NEP replaced War Communism, a period during the civil war of forced labor and brutal requisitioning of food supplies. The NEP, by contrast, gave concessions to private enterprise in agriculture, trade, and industry and aimed at the political neutralization of the peasants. Although the NEP met with considerable success, it was followed under Stalin by more radical policies and the *five-year plans.

New England An area in the extreme NE US, bordering on the Atlantic Ocean. It consists of the states of Maine, New Hampshire, Vermont, Massachusetts, Rhode Island, and Connecticut. Explored and named by Captain John Smith (1614), it was first settled by the Puritans (1620). Poor agriculturally, it developed industry early, especially fishing and textiles. Despite the decline of its textile industry the area is now of major economic importance with a flourishing tourist industry. Area: about 63,300 sq mi (164,000 sq km).

New England A district of Australia, in New South Wales. Predominantly agricultural, it occupies the N Tableland between the Moonbi Range and the Queensland border. A separatist movement has existed since the early 20th century but so far has been unsuccessful in making the district a separate state.

New England Confederation A union in 1643 of four colonies—Massachusetts, Plymouth, Connecticut, and New Haven—for purposes of safety, defense, and mutual cooperation. Factors prompting confederation were Indian wars, threat of foreign invasion, desire for a state religion, and the need for mutual cooperation in intercolony matters. Maine and Rhode Island were excluded because of religious differences. It disbanded in 1684.

Newfoundland A province of E Canada, consisting of the sparsely populated Coast of *Labrador on the Atlantic Ocean and the triangular island of Newfoundland, lying between the Ocean and the Gulf of St Lawrence. The island consists of a low forested plateau rolling gently to the NE. Its interior is fairly infertile and most of the population lives along the irregular coast, especially in the SE. Pulp and paper has replaced the declining fisheries as the major industry. Iron, lead, zinc, and copper are mined. *History*: discovered by John Cabot (1497), Newfoundland became an English fishing station where settlement was actively discouraged until the 19th century. The island won representative government (1832) and developed steadily until World War I, when it became a dominion. In 1927 it won possession of Labrador's interior and in 1949 became the newest Canadian province. In the last 50 years Newfoundland has not been very prosperous. The island still has a rich tradition of folksong and story-telling. Area: 143,044 sq mi (370,485 sq km). Population (1981 est): 567,681. Capital: St John's.

Newfoundland dog A breed of working dog originating in Newfoundland. Massively built and strong swimmers, Newfoundlands have been used for life-saving at sea. The heavy dense black, brown, or black-and-white coat enables them to withstand icy water. Height: 28 in (71 cm) (dogs); 26 in (66 cm) (bitches).

New France The French colonies in E Canada. From about 1600 French trading posts extended along the St Lawrence River to the Great Lakes. France lost these colonies to Britain in the *Seven Years' War (1756–63).

New Frontier President John F. *Kennedy's name for the theme of his administration's (1962–63) legislative program. First used in his nomination acceptance speech (1960), he referred to "new frontiers" at home, abroad, and in space that would be challenging, even perilous at times, but would be met and conquered.

New Granada A Spanish colony in South America, which in 1717 became a viceroyalty comprising modern Colombia, Ecuador, Panama, and Venezuela (which was later detached). It was liberated by Simón *Bolívar in 1819. From 1830 to 1858 Colombia and Panama formed the Republic of New Granada.

New Guinea An island in the SW Pacific Ocean, the second largest island in the world separated from Australia by the Torres Strait. It consists of the Indonesian province of *West Irian in the W and *Papua New Guinea in the E. Mountainous and forested, it is largely undeveloped and is famed for its unique species of butterflies and birds. Its linguistically diverse tribal population consists of Melanesian, Negrito, and Papuan ethnic groups. *History*: known to Europeans from 1511, the island was colonized by the Dutch in the 18th century. In 1828 the Dutch controlled the W part; this became part of Indonesia in 1963. The SE was colonized by Britain and the NE by Germany in the late 19th century. Area: 299,310 sq mi (775,213 sq km). Population (1971 est): 1,795,602.

Newham A borough of E Greater London, created in 1965 from the former county boroughs of East Ham and West Ham, and parts of Barking and Woolwich. Population (1981): 209,290.

New Hampshire A NE state in New England. It is generally hilly, with many lakes; a low-lying area adjoins the Atlantic Ocean in the SE. Manufacturing is the principal source of employment, centered mainly in the S. Electrical and other machinery together with paper and wood are the principal products. Tourism is the other major industry. The state's farmers produce livestock, dairy and poultry products, and vegetables. Mining is of minor importance and the large deposits of granite are no longer quarried to any great extent. *History*: one of the 13 original colonies, it was first settled by English colonists about 1627, becoming a royal province in 1679. One of the first states to declare its independence, it became a state in 1788. Area: 9304 sq mi (24,097 sq km). Population (1975 est): 818,000. Capital: Concord.

New Harmony 38 08N 87 56W A town in SE Indiana, on the E bank of the Wabash River at the Illinois border, NW of Evansville. George Rapp named it Harmonie when he settled here in 1815. Rapp's utopian colony disbanded in failure in 1824. Robert Owen's experimental utopian society, New Harmony, (1825–28) also failed, but the name remained. The chief economic activity is agriculture. Population (1980): 945.

New Haven 41 18N 72 55W A city and seaport in Connecticut, on Long Island Sound. It is best known as the site of Yale University (1701). It was here that Charles Goodyear invented vulcanized rubber. Industries include hardware, watches, and firearms. Population (1980): 126,109.

New Haven Colony Colony in S Connecticut and SE New York on the N shore of Long Island, established in 1638 as Quinnipiac by Puritans John Davenport (1597–1670) and Theophilus Eaton (1590–1658) and their followers. A theocracy, rule was based on interpretation of the Bible and voting and office-holding eligibility required church membership. Renamed New Haven in 1640, it became part of the New England Confederation in 1643 and eventually included settlements at Guilford, Milford, Stamford, and Branford, Connecticut and at Southold, Long Island. The smallest of the Puritan colonies, it was absorbed into Connecticut Colony in 1664.

New Hebrides (French name: Nouvelles-Hébrides). *See* Vanuatu.

Ne Win (1911–82) Burmese statesman; prime minister (1958–60, 1962–74); president (1974–   ). From 1943 he fought for Burmese independence and, when this was achieved in 1948, became defense minister. In 1958 he became prime minister after forcing U *Nu's resignation and, after leaving office in 1960, again seized power in 1962. In 1972 the 1947 constitution was abolished and replaced (in 1974) by one introducing a single-party assembly and the presidency of Ne Win.

New Ireland A volcanic island in the SW Pacific Ocean, in Papua New Guinea in the Bismarck Archipelago. Copra is exported. Area: 3340 sq mi (8650 sq km). Population (1973 est): 50,522. Chief town: Kavieng.

New Jersey A state in the NE US, on the mid-Atlantic coast. It is bounded by the Atlantic Ocean on the E, by Delaware (across the Delaware Bay) on the S, by Pennsylvania (across the Delaware River) on the W, and by New York on the N. The Kittatinny Mountains extend across the NW corner of the state, SE of which lies a belt of lowland containing most of New Jersey's major cities. The remaining area to the S consists of coastal plains, which cover more than half the state. One of the most highly urbanized and densely populated states, it is a major industrial center. The most important economic activity is manufacturing, with chemicals, textiles, electrical machinery, and processed foods the major products. Although mining is relatively unimportant, New Jersey is a center for copper smelting and refining as well as a major producer of titanium concentrate. Agriculture is also well developed and a variety of crops are grown, including asparagus, tomatoes, peppers, sweet corn, potatoes, and peaches. Its beaches, forests, and mountain regions form the basis of a thriving tourist industry. *History*: originally inhabited by the Delaware Indians, the region was first explored by Henry Hudson on a voyage for the Dutch East India Company. Other Europeans conducted explorations in the early 17th century. Eventually Dutch trading posts sprang up, but the area was taken over in 1664 by the British, who held it until Delaware declared its independence as one of the 13 original colonies. Many important battles of the American Revolution took place in New Jersey, including those at Trenton, Princeton, and Monmouth. New Jersey became a state in 1787. The 19th century was a period of tremendous economic growth, accompanied by political corruption. The corruption was targeted by Governor Woodrow *Wilson's reform movement (1910–12), which served as a springboard for his nomination for president. The state's highly industrial economy also saw great expansion during and after World War II. In the 1970s casino gambling in Atlantic City was legalized, which served as a boost to the seaside resort and the state's tourist industry. The huge Meadowlands Sports Complex, completed in 1981 in East Rutherford, has also encouraged tourism. Political corruption surfaced once again and New Jersey figured prominently in the Abscam investigations of 1980–81. Area: 7836 sq mi (20,295 sq km). Population (1980): 7,364,158. Capital: Trenton.

New Jersey Plan   (1787) Plan for national government put forth at the Constitutional Convention of 1787 by William *Paterson of New Jersey. The plan aimed at accommodating the smaller states and called for equal representation of states in a federal legislature, as opposed to representation by population as formulated in the *Virginia Plan. Eventually parts of both plans were incorporated in the *Connecticut Compromise, which called for a federal bicameral legislature.

New London 41 21N 72 06W A city and seaport in Connecticut, at the mouth of the Thames River on Long Island Sound. The US Coast Guard Academy and a US naval submarine base (1916) are located here. The

annual Harvard-Yale boat race is held here on the Thames River. Industries include shipbuilding and textiles. Population (1970): 31,630.

Newman, John Henry, Cardinal (1801–90) British churchman and a leader of the *Oxford Movement, until his conversion to Roman Catholicism (1845). He was educated at Oxford, later becoming a fellow and tutor there. While vicar of St Mary's, Oxford (1827–43), he published *Parochial and Plain Sermons* (1834–42) and began the series entitled *Tracts for the Times* in 1833. He wrote many of these, including the most controversial one, *Tract 90*, which argued that the Thirty-Nine Articles were not incompatible with Roman Catholicism. Of his later works the most famous are *Idea of a University* (1852), his poem, *Dream of Gerontius* (1866), and a theological work, *Grammar of Assent* (1870). His spiritual autobiography, *Apologia pro vita sua* (1864), was a reply to Charles Kingsley's criticisms of Roman Catholicism. He was made a cardinal in 1879.

Newman, Paul (1925–   ) US film actor. He has frequently played the roles of cynical and witty heroes, notably in *Hud* (1963), *Butch Cassidy and the Sundance Kid* (1969), and *The Sting* (1973); among his other films are *Buffalo Bill and the Indians* (1976), *Slap Shot* (1977), *Absence of Malice* (1981), and *The Verdict* (1982). From 1968 he also directed and produced films. A political activist, he supports nuclear disarmament. He is married to the US actress Joanne Woodward (1930–   ).

new math The new methods of teaching mathematics and presenting mathematical relationships that incorporate some of the concepts of formal logic. *Set theory and *vectors, for example, formerly considered advanced and abstract, are now taught at an early stage in school mathematics and form part of the logical basis of further learning. New applications of mathematics are being developed to deal with computers, automation, and the accompanying changes in social organization, for example operational research.

New Mexico One of the mountain states in the SW US. It is bordered by Texas on the E, by Texas and Mexico on the S, by Arizona on the W, by Colorado on the N, and by Oklahoma on the NE. There are three main physical regions: a flat tableland in the E, a central mountainous region cut N–S by the Valley of the Rio Grande, and a region of mountains and plains in the W. A generally arid state, its irrigation problems have been mitigated by the presence of two important rivers, the Rio Grande and the Pecos. The relatively sparse population is mainly concentrated in the urban centers, especially in Albuquerque. Its rich mineral wealth forms the basis of the economy. Its oil and natural-gas deposits are especially important, and it is a leading producer of uranium ore, manganese ore, and potash. There are also large commercial forests. Livestock is the main agricultural product, and crops include hay, cotton, wheat, and sorghum grains. There is limited manufacturing. Tourism is an important source of revenue. *History*: inhabited by Indians for some 20,000 years, the region was dominated by the Pueblos when the first Europeans arrived. In the 16th century the Spanish explored the territory. Their efforts to establish missions and form ranching communities were met with tremendous resistance from the Indians. When Mexico achieved independence from Spain (1821), the area became a Mexican province, passing to the US after the Mexican War (1846–48). Settlement continued via the Santa Fe Trail. With the defeat of the Apache chief Geronimo (1886), Indian resistance was finally broken. A boom in ranching, accelerated by the arrival of the railroads (1879), encouraged development, and New Mexico became a state in 1912. In 1943, Los Alamos Laboratories was built by the US government as a center for atomic research. Intense scientific labor at Los Alamos came to fruition in the world's first atomic bomb, exploded near Alamagordo in July 1945. The mushrooming of military installations greatly enhanced the state's economic and population growth. Still a relatively poor state with high unemployment, New Mexico's economic difficulties of the early 1980s increased tensions among the Anglo, Indian, and Spanish communities. Area:121,666 sq mi (315,113 sq km). Population (1980): 1,299,968. Capital: Santa Fe.

New Model Army   The parliamentary army formed in 1645 during the English *Civil War. It was organized by Sir Thomas *Fairfax and united the various local armies. Led by Oliver *Cromwell, it wielded increasing political power, emerging the victor from its power struggle with the *Long Parliament. In 1650 Cromwell became its commander in chief.

New Netherland A Dutch colony in North America. Established in 1613, the colony was centered on New Amsterdam, which after its conquest by the English (1664) was renamed New York.

New Orleans 30 00N 90 03W A city and major port in Louisiana. Known as the Crescent City because of its location on a bend in the Mississippi River, it is one of the leading commercial and industrial centers of the South with food processing, oil, chemical, shipbuilding, and ship-repairing industries. The Vieux Carré (French Quarter) has many historic buildings, including St Louis Cathedral (1794) and the Cabildo (1795). An educational center, New Orleans possesses several universities. The famous Mardi Gras festival is held here annually. *History:* founded in 1718, New Orleans became the capital of the French colonial region of Louisiana before passing to Spain in 1763. It returned briefly to France in 1803 but passed to the US in the same year. Jazz had its origins among the black musicians of New Orleans during the late 19th century. Population (1980): 557,482.

New Orleans, Battle of (1815) US victory and final battle of the *War of 1812. Although it is considered a decisive, morale-boosting battle of the war, it was fought, due to slow communication, two weeks after the peace treaty at Ghent was signed. Aided by the Creoles and the pirate band of Jean *Lafitte, Andrew *Jackson's forces held off the British invasion from ships in the Gulf of Mexico. British casualties were high—almost 300 were killed.

New Orleans style The original style of jazz, which developed in the Storyville district of New Orleans. The New Orleans style began around 1890 with the band of Buddy Bolden (1868–1941) and continued until the 1920s when *swing bands gained popularity. In New Orleans jazz, the melody of a song was treated as a basis for improvisation by the cornet, clarinet, or trombone, supported by double bass, drums, guitar, and piano. Important New Orleans jazz musicians include Louis Armstrong and Jelly Roll Morton. *Compare* Dixieland.

Newport 41 13N 71 18W A city in SE Rhode Island, on S end of Aquidneck Island in Narragansett Bay. Settled in 1639, it grew as a shipbuilding center, port, and cultural center. In the mid 19th century it became popular with the wealthy, who began to build luxurious summer homes. The naval base, established in the late 19th century and expanded after World War I, also helped the economy. Today, tourism is very important. Many of the summer mansions are open to the public and events, such as the America's Cup Yacht races and Tennis Week are traditional. Population (1980): 29,259.

Newport (Welsh name: Casnewydd ar Wysg) 51 35N 3 00W A port in South Wales, the administrative center of Gwent near the mouth of the Usk River. Iron and steel, engineering, chemicals, and fertilizers are important industries. Its parish church became the cathedral for the Monmouth diocese in 1921. Population (1981): 105,374.

Newport News 36 59N 76 26W A city and seaport in SE Virginia, on the James River estuary. A major shipbuilding and ship-repair center, its manufactures include metal products and building materials. Population (1980): 144,903.

New Siberian Islands (Russian name: Novosibirskiye Ostrova) A Soviet archipelago off the N coast, between the Laptev Sea and the East Siberian Sea. Kotelny, Faddeyevskii, and New Siberia are the largest islands and the Lyakhov Islands to the S are sometimes considered part of the group. There is no permanent population. Total area: 13,549 sq mi (35,100 sq km), including the Lyakhov Islands.

New South Wales A state of SE Australia, bordering on the Pacific Ocean. It consists of extensive plains in the W, separated from the narrow coastal belt by the *Great Dividing Range with the *Snowy Mountains and part of the Australian Alps in the SE. The chief rivers are the Murray, Darling, and Murrumbidgee. It is the most populous and economically important state of Australia. Agricultural products include beef cattle, cereals (of which wheat is the most important), fruit and vegetables (especially in the southern *Riverina district), wool, and dairy produce, which includes large quantities of butter and milk products processed at cooperative factories along the coast. Fishing, including oyster farming, and forestry are also important. Minerals extracted include coal, silver, lead, zinc, and copper. Over half the population live in Sydney, where most of the industries are located; these include the manufacture of iron and steel, textiles, electrical goods, and chemicals. Separatist movements, resenting the domination of the state, exist in the districts of *New England and Riverina. Area: 309,433 sq mi (801,428 sq km). Population (1980 est): 5,146,200. Capital: Sydney.

New Spain, Viceroyalty of (1535–1821) A Spanish colony in the New World comprising modern Mexico, the SW US, and parts of Central America. It was established under Antonio de *Mendoza.

newspaper A publication issued at regular intervals and containing information and opinion about current affairs. The earliest newspaper may have been the ancient Roman *Acta Diurna* (59 BC) but newspapers in their modern form originated in Europe in the 17th century. The political influence of newspapers was quickly appreciated by governments, which introduced such legislation as the Stamp Act (1712), imposing a duty of a halfpenny on each half-sheet and a penny on each whole sheet. The most notable victory in the campaign for press freedom was made in the 18th

century in England by John *Wilkes, who obtained the right to publish parliamentary reports, but not until 1855 was the Stamp Act repealed. The rapid expansion of newspapers during the 19th century was influenced by improvements in printing technology, the establishment of international news agencies, and the increase in literacy. Popular *journalism was pioneered in the US by such newspapers as the *San Francisco Examiner* (1880) and the *Morning Journal* (1895), both founded by William Randolph *Hearst. Technological improvements continued in the 20th century, including computer-aided typesetting and satellite transmission of data.

New Sweden (1638–55) Swedish colony in N Delaware on the W bank of the Delaware River; sponsored by the New Sweden Company, a group of Swedish and Dutch under the leadership of Peter Minuit, former governor of the New Netherland (New York) colony. The Swedes remained, settled Fort Christina (now Wilmington) and the surrounding area, and persevered until 1655 when the colony was captured by New Amsterdam's Peter *Stuyvesant.

NEWT *The European palmate newt* (Triturus helveticus), *like other newts, becomes totally aquatic during the breeding season. After an elaborate courtship display the male deposits sperm masses (spermatophores), which are taken into the cloaca of the female and fertilize the eggs internally.*

newt A salamander belonging to a family (*Salamandridae*) occurring in Europe, Asia, and North America. The European smooth newt (*Triturus vulgaris*) is greenish brown with dark-brown spots and has a black-spotted orange belly. It grows to a length of 4 in (10 cm) (including a 2 in [5 cm] tail). Newts live mainly on land, hibernating under stones in winter and returning to water to breed in spring. The European fire salamander (*Salamandra salamandra*) bears live young and produces a poisonous skin secretion when harmed.

New Testament The 27 books that constitute the second major division of the Christian *Bible. The title is intended to convey the belief that the books contain the fulfillment of prophecies made in the *Old Testament. Written in Greek, the New Testament has four divisions: the four Gospels (Matthew, Mark, Luke, and John); the *Acts of the Apostles; the *Epistles, mainly written by St Paul; and the Book of *Revelation. It covers a period from the birth of *Jesus to the spread of Christianity throughout the Roman Empire and was written between about 50 and 100 AD.

newton (N) The *SI unit of force defined as the force required to give a mass of one kilogram an acceleration of one meter per second per second. Named for Sir Isaac *Newton.

Newton, Sir Isaac (1642–1727) British physicist and mathematician, who was a professor at Cambridge University (1669–1701). One of the greatest scientists of all time, Newton did much of his original work in his parents' home immediately after his graduation, while Cambridge was closed (1665–67) during the Great Plague. His first discovery was the law of gravitation, apocryphally inspired by the realization that an apple falling from a tree is attracted by the same force that holds the moon in orbit. Gravitation required a precise definition of force, this Newton also supplied in his laws of motion (*see* Newtonian mechanics). Newton's second major work in this period was the invention of the calculus; *Leibniz and Newton bickered for some years as to who had the idea first. Probably they both invented the method independently. His third contribution was in optics: he recognized that white light is a mixture of colored lights, which can be separated by refraction. His incorrect belief that this effect could not be corrected, when it occurs as the chromatic aberration of a lens, inspired him to invent the reflecting telescope. Newton's principal publications were

Philosophiae naturalis principia mathematica (1686–87) and *Optics* (1704), which held that light is a corpuscular phenomenon.

He was president of the Royal Society from 1703 until his death and was knighted in 1705. A considerable amount of Newton's later life was spent delving into alchemy, astrology, and theological speculation. From biblical chronology he calculated the day of the earth's creation to be about 3500 BC. Einstein said of him: "in one person, he combined the experimenter, the theorist, the mechanic and, not least, the artist in exposition."

Newtonian mechanics The branch of *mechanics concerned with systems in which the results of *quantum theory and the theory of *relativity can be ignored. Also known as classical mechanics, it is based on *Newton's three laws of motion. The first law states that a body remains at rest or moves with constant velocity in a straight line unless acted upon by a *force. This law thus defines the concept of force. The second law, which defines mass, states that the *acceleration (*a*) of a body is proportional to the force (*f*) causing it. The constant of proportionality is the mass (*m*) of the body: $f = ma$. The third law states that the action of a force always produces a reaction in the body. The reaction is of equal magnitude but opposite in direction to the action.

Newton's rings A series of light and dark rings formed in a plano-convex lens if monochromatic light is shone onto the lens when it rests on a plane mirror. First observed by *Newton, they are caused by *interference between light reflected by the mirror and light reflected at the curved surface of the lens.

New Wave (*or* Nouvelle Vague) A group of French film directors in the late 1950s whose films were characterized by their informal and highly original individual styles. The directors, most of whom were associated with the magazine *Cahiers du Cinéma* and the *auteur theory of film criticism, included *Truffaut, *Chabrol, *Resnais, and *Godard.

New Westminster 49 10N 122 58W A city and port in W Canada, in British Columbia on the Fraser River. Bordering on E Vancouver, it manufactures wood products, foods, and oil. Population (1976): 38,393.

New World A name for the American continent, used especially by early emigrants from Europe and in describing the geographical distribution of plants and animals. *Compare* Old World.

New World monkey A *monkey native to the Americas. There are two families: the *Cebidae* (37 species) including *uakaris, *sakis, *titis, *howlers, *capuchins, *squirrel monkeys, *spider monkeys, *woolly monkeys, and the *douroucouli; and the *Callithricidae* (33 species) containing *marmosets and *tamarins. New World monkeys are restricted to Central and South America and are largely arboreal and vegetarian.

New York A state in the NE US. It is bordered by Canada and Lake Ontario on the N, by Vermont, Massachusetts, and Connecticut on the E, by Pennsylvania, New Jersey, and the Atlantic Ocean on the S, and by Pennsylvania, Lake Erie, and Canada on the W. It is basically an upland region, dissected by the valleys of the Mohawk and Hudson Rivers. Traffic flowing from the Great Lakes to the major port of New York City has provided many opportunities for industrial development and today New York is the chief manufacturing state in the US. Its varied products include clothing, electrical machinery, and processed foods and printing and publishing are among the most notable industries. The presence of New York City also makes it the commercial, financial, and cultural center of the nation. The most important agricultural activity is dairying; other leading products include apples, grains, and potatoes. *History*: first explored by Giovanni da Verrazano (1524) and Henry Hudson (1609), the region was the home of Iroquois, Algonquin, Mohegan, and other Indian tribes. The area was originally a Dutch colony (1624) known as New Netherland with New Amsterdam as the capital. In the Second Dutch War (1664–67) Peter Stuyvesant was forced to surrender the colony to the British, who renamed it in honor of the Duke of York and held it until it declared its independence (1776) as one of the 13 original colonies. New York figured prominently in the American Revolution, with close to one third of the war's battles being fought on its soil. The important Battle of Saratoga (1777), a decisive victory for the colonists, took place there. New York became a state in 1788. In the 19th century the growth of commerce was facilitated by the opening of the Erie Canal (1825). Rapid industrial growth followed, particularly in textiles. Formerly a predominantly agricultural region, the growth of industry marked a new direction for New York's economy. During the 1880s the reform movements that flourished throughout the Northeast, including abolitionism and women's suffrage, found a favorable climate in New York. The waves of immigration that had begun in the mid-1800s continued into the early 20th century. Industrial expansion brought New York to the forefront in manufacturing, and it became the leading manufacturing state as well as the state with the largest population. Al-

though the population declined after World War II, it is still the second-largest after California. New York City remains the country's largest metropolis. Many prominent political leaders were native sons, including five presidents (Martin Van Buren, Millard Fillmore, Chester A. Arthur, Theodore Roosevelt, and Franklin Delano Roosevelt) and three distinguished governors (Alfred E. Smith, Thomas E. Dewey, and Nelson A. Rockefeller). Following World War II the demographics of New York began to change significantly, with a shift from the urban areas into the suburbs, a trend also marked by the movement of many urban businesses to outlying areas. Area: 49,576 sq mi (128,402 sq km). Population (1980): 17,557,288. Capital: Albany.

New York 40 45N 74 00W The largest US city, situated in New York state on New York Bay at the mouth of the Hudson River. Divided into five boroughs—*Manhattan, *Brooklyn, the *Bronx, *Queens, and Richmond (coextensive with *Staten Island), it is the nation's leading seaport and one of the most important business, manufacturing, communications, and cultural centers in the country. As one of the world's financial centers (*see* Wall Street), it is the site of many large corporations and the New York and American Stock Exchanges. The principal manufactures include furs, jewelry, chemicals, metal products, and processed foods. New York is also the main center of US television and radio and book publishing. Its most notable features include Central Park, the fashionable shops of Fifth Avenue, the *Statue of Liberty, Times Square, *Greenwich Village, the Brooklyn Bridge (1883), Rockefeller Center, St Patrick's Cathedral (1858–79), and a large number of extremely tall buildings (skyscrapers), such as the Empire State Building (1931), the United Nations Headquarters (1951), and the World Trade Center (1973), which give Manhattan its characteristic skyline. Its cultural life is exceptional. As well as the famous Broadway theater district and the Lincoln Center for the Performing Arts, which houses two opera companies, a symphony orchestra, and a ballet company, there are numerous museums, art galleries, and libraries. The most notable educational institutions include Columbia University (founded as King's College in 1754), the City University of New York (1847), and New York University (1831). *History*: on September 3, 1609, Henry Hudson sailed into New York Bay and his glowing reports attracted its founding Dutch colonists, who arrived in 1620. In 1625 New Amsterdam, situated at the S tip of Manhattan, became the capital of the newly established colony of New Netherland and the following year the whole island of Manhattan was bought from the Indians for the equivalent of $24. In 1664 the city was captured by the English for the Duke of York and promptly renamed. In the 17th century it became a base for prosperous merchants and such pirates as Captain Kidd. From 1789 until 1790 it was the first capital of the US. The opening of the Erie Canal in 1825 ensured its pre-eminence as a commercial city and seaport. Following the Civil War, it began to merge with neighboring towns, such as Brooklyn, and the metropolis began to form. Early in the 20th century the arrival of millions of European immigrants supplied New York with limitless cheap labor. In recent years many of its middle-class inhabitants have moved to the suburbs of the metropolis and the city subsequently lost a considerable amount of tax revenue. During the mid-1970s New York's financial crisis worsened and the city was narrowly saved from bankruptcy by emergency loans. Population (1980): 7,071,030.

New York Times Company v. Sullivan (1964) US Supreme Court decision that upheld the 1st Amendment's freedom of the press clause. The suit was brought against *The New York Times*, which had published an advertisement in which police action in Montgomery, Ala., was criticized, by the Montgomery police commissioner. The Supreme Court reversed a state court libel decision that had been in the commissioner's favor. The court stated that, unless malice could be proven, public officials cannot seek libel damages for criticism of their official functions.

New Zealand, Dominion of A country in the Pacific Ocean, to the SE of Australia. It consists of two main islands, *North Island and *South Island, together with several smaller ones, including *Stewart Island to the S. *Ross Dependency and the *Tokelau Islands are dependencies, and the *Cook and Niue Islands are self-governing. Most of the population is of British descent with a large Maori minority. *Economy*: the main basis of the economy is livestock rearing, especially sheep farming. Farms are highly mechanized and there is considerable research into agricultural science and technology. Meat, wool, and dairy products are the main exports, which were adversely affected when the UK joined the EEC in 1973. However the effects were less than had been feared and New Zealand has opened up markets in other parts of the world. Mineral resources include coal, gold, limestone and silica sand, and oil and natural gas have been found. New Zealand's swift-flowing rivers make hydroelectricity a valuable source of power. Timber production has increased in recent years and there is a growing pulp and paper industry. Other industries, such as food processing and textiles, have also been expanding and tourism is of growing importance. *History*: from about the 14th century the islands were inhabited by the Maoris, a Polynesian people. The first European to discover New Zealand was *Tasman in 1642, who called it Staten Land, later changed to Nieuw Zealand; in 1769 the coast was explored by *Cook. During the early part of the 19th century it was used as a whaling and trading base. By the Treaty of *Waitangi in 1840 the Maori chiefs ceded sovereignty to Britain and a colony was established. British settlement increased rapidly and sheep farming developed on a large scale. After two wars with the Maoris over land rights, peace was reached in 1871. New Zealand was made a dominion in 1907 and became fully independent by the Statute of Westminster in 1931. By the early part of the 20th century its social administration policy was one of the most advanced in the world. Free compulsory primary education was introduced in 1877 and in 1893 New Zealand became the first country in the world to give women the vote. It played an important part in both World Wars. Since World War II New Zealand has played an increasing role in international affairs, especially in the Far East. Its economy has suffered from the recent world recession and efforts to curb inflation have included a prices and wages policy as well as financial measures. Prime Minister: David Lange. Official language: English. Official currency: New Zealand dollar of 100 cents. Area: 103,719 sq mi (268,704 sq km). Population (1983 est): 3,142,000. Capital: Wellington. Main port: Auckland.

Nexø, Martin Andersen (1869–1954) Danish novelist. His upbringing in the slums of Copenhagen led him to become a socialist and subsequently a communist. He achieved worldwide fame with his novels *Pelle erobreren* (*Pelle the Conqueror*; 1906–10) and *Ditte menneskebarn* (*Ditte: Daughter of Man*; 1917–21), depicting the struggles of the working class. In 1949 he left Denmark and settled in East Germany.

Ney, Michel, Prince of Moscow (1769–1815) French marshal, whom Napoleon described as "the bravest of the brave." He served throughout the Revolutionary Wars and, under Napoleon, won the great victory at Elchingen (1805) and fought at *Jena (1806) and *Friedland (1807). His extraordinary courage in the French retreat from Moscow (1812–13) prompted Napoleon's accolade. When Napoleon returned from Elba, Ney rallied to the former emperor's cause and after his defeat at Waterloo was shot as a traitor.

Nez Percé A North American Indian people of the plateau region of Idaho. Their culture, typical of this area, was based on salmon fishing. After acquiring horses in the 18th century, they frequently left their riverside villages to hunt buffalo on the Plains and thus acquired many Plains Indian traits. They became expert horse breeders possessing large herds. Their language belongs to the Sahaptin division of the *Penutian family.

Ngo Dinh Diem (1901–63) Vietnamese statesman; president of South Vietnam (1955–63). Unsympathetic to Ho Chi Minh's *Viet Minh, he went into exile during the war of independence against France. Returning just before the partition of Vietnam, he was appointed prime minister (1954) under US influence and in the following year abolished the monarchy and became president. His government was threatened by the guerrilla activities of the *Viet Cong against whom he sought US aid (*see* Vietnam War). He was assassinated, together with his brother Ngo Dinh Nhu, in a military coup in 1963.

Nguni A division of the *Bantu-speaking peoples of S Africa. It includes the *Swazi, *Xhosa, and *Zulu.

Nha Trang 12 15N 109 10E An ancient port in S Vietnam, at the mouth of the Cai River. Nearby are four shrines dating from the 7th to 12th centuries. The chief industry is fishing. Population (1973 est): 216,227.

Niagara Falls Two waterfalls on the US-Canadian border, on the Niagara River between Lakes Erie and Ontario. The American Falls, 167 ft (51 m) high and 1000 ft (300 m) wide, are straight while the Horseshoe Falls (Canada), 162 ft (49 m) high and 2600 ft (790 m) wide, are curved. Much of their flow is diverted to generate electricity but they remain spectacular tourist attractions. Shipping between the two lakes is diverted past the Falls by way of the Welland Ship Canal.

Niagara Falls 43 06N 79 04W A city in SE Ontario, Canada, on the Niagara River, opposite Niagara Falls, NY, to which it is connected by a bridge. The chief economic activity is tourism, which centers on Horseshoe Falls, the Canadian side of Niagara Falls. Other industries include fertilizer, chemicals, cereals, and silverware. Population (1981): 70,960.

Niagara Falls 43 06N 79 02W A city in W New York, NW of Buffalo on the Niagara River, opposite Niagara Falls, Canada. Tourism is the main economic activity; American Falls, the US side of Niagara Falls and surrounding exhibits of the history of the falls and of the area attract many

visitors. Manufactures here include chemicals, metals, petroleum, wood and paper products, and foodstuffs. Population (1980): 71,384.

Niamey 13 32N 2 05E The capital (since 1926) of Niger, on the Niger River. It has grown rapidly as the country's administrative and commercial center. Its university was founded in 1973. Population (1977 est): 225,314.

Niarchos, Stavros Spyros (1909–) Greek businessman and the owner of one of the largest independent shipping lines in the world. In rivalry with his brother-in-law, Aristotle *Onassis, he pioneered the construction of supertankers during the 1950s.

Nibelungenlied (German: *Song of the Nibelungs*) A Middle High German epic poem composed in the 13th century but drawing on much earlier material. Its main theme is the disastrous rivalries following *Siegfried's killing of the Burgundian princes called Nibelungs and his seizure of their treasure. A variant of the story also occurs in the Old Norse *Volsungasaga* (*see* sagas), in which Siegfried is called Sigurd. *Wagner's operatic cycle, *The Ring of Nibelung*, makes use of elements from both the Germanic and Old Norse versions.

Nicaea, Councils of Two ecumenical councils of the Christian Church held at Nicaea, now Iznik (Turkey). **1.** (325) The council that was summoned by the Byzantine emperor Constantine to establish Church unity and suppress *Arianism. The number of participating bishops was, according to later reports, 318. The *Nicene Creed was the major doctrinal formulation. **2.** (787) The council that was summoned by the Byzantine empress Irene to condemn *iconoclasm. Its initial assembly at Constantinople (786) was disrupted by iconoclasts, but the following year it met at Nicaea and approved a formula for restoring the veneration of icons.

Nicaragua, Republic of A country in Central America between the Caribbean Sea and the Pacific Ocean. Swamp and dense tropical forest on the Caribbean coast, and a broader plain with lakes to the W rise to a central mountain range. Lake Nicaragua in the SW is the largest in Central America. The population is mainly of mixed Indian and Spanish descent, with minorities of African and other descent. *Economy*: chiefly agricultural, the main crops are maize, rice, cotton, coffee, and sugar. Development plans include large irrigation schemes. Production of bananas, formerly the main crop in the E, has been reduced in recent years. There is considerable livestock rearing, and meat packing is an important industry. Minerals include gold, silver, and copper, and large quantities of natural gas were found in 1974. Oil deposits are being explored. Industries, on a small scale, include food processing, textiles, and oil refining. The main exports are cotton, coffee, sugar, beef, and timber. *History*: sighted by Columbus in 1502, it was colonized by Spain from 1522, becoming part of the captaincy general of Guatemala. It broke away from Spain in 1821 and formed part of the Central American Federation until 1838, when Nicaragua became a republic. A treaty with the US in 1916 gave the latter an option on a canal route through Nicaragua as well as naval-base facilities. From 1933 the government was dominated by the Somoza family, opposition to which culminated in a civil war that forced (1979) the resignation and exile of the president, General Anastasio Somoza (1925–80). The victorious Sandinista National Liberation Front (FSLN) established a government that instituted socialist policies. Accusing the Sandinistas of supplying arms to the El Salvador rebels, the US has supported an army of "Contras" that attacks Nicaragua from bases in Honduras and Costa Rica. Head of state: President Daniel Ortega. Official language: Spanish. Official currency: córdoba of 100 centavos. Area: 57,143 sq mi (148,000 sq km). Population (1980 est): 2,568,000. Capital: Managua. Main ports: Corinto (on the Pacific coast) and Bluefields (on the Caribbean).

Nice 43 42N 7 16E A city in SE France, the capital of the Alpes-Maritimes department on the Baie des Anges. Ceded by Sardinia to France in 1860, it is one of the leading resorts of the French Riviera. Notable landmarks include the Promenade des Anglais and it has a university (1965). It is famous for its many carnivals and fêtes and it has a large trade in fruit and flowers. Population (1975): 346,620.

Nicene Creed The statement of Christian belief accepted as orthodox by the first Council of *Nicaea (325). The Nicene Creed used in the *Eucharist service of Orthodox, Roman Catholic, and Protestant Churches is a version of this creed, considerably expanded in the sections on Christ (*see* Filioque) and the Holy Spirit.

Nichiren Buddhism A popular Japanese Buddhist school named for its founder, a 13th-century monk and prophet. He militantly opposed other Buddhist sects and held that *The Lotus Sutra* contained the true teaching and that the historical Buddha was identical with eternal Buddha-nature, in which all men participate. The sincere invocation of the mantra of homage to *The Lotus Sutra* is sufficient to gain enlightenment. Among the numerous subsects of the school, the Nichiren-sho-shu and the related lay group, the Soka-gakkai, are the largest and most influential.

Nicholas I, St (d. 867) Pope (858–67 AD). In the West Nicholas successfully defended and expanded papal authority against both secular rulers, such as *Lothair, and local bishops, notably *Hincmar of Reims. In the East Nicholas strongly opposed the appointment of *Photius to the patriarchate of Constantinople and declared him deposed. Photius, in his turn, declared the deposition of Nicholas (867) but Photius' overthrow prevented further hostilities. Feast day: Nov 13.

Nicholas I (1796–1855) Emperor of Russia (1825–55), notorious as an autocrat. Nicholas' accession was followed by the *Dekabrist revolt, which though unsuccessful hardened his conservatism. His ambitions in the Balkans precipitated the *Crimean War.

Nicholas II (1868–1918) The last Emperor of Russia (1894–1917). Nicholas' ambition in Asia led to the unpopular *Russo-Japanese War, which in turn precipitated the *Revolution of 1905. Forced to accept the establishment of a representative assembly (*see* Duma), Nicholas nevertheless continued attempts to rule autocratically. In 1915 he took supreme command of Russian forces in World War I, leaving Russia to the mismanagement of the Empress *Alexandra and *Rasputin. After the outbreak of the Russian Revolution in 1917, Nicholas was forced to abdicate (March). He and his family were imprisoned by the Bolsheviks and executed at Ekaterinburg (now Sverdlovsk).

Nicholas, St (4th century AD) The patron saint of Russia, sailors, and children. He is thought to have been Bishop of Myra in Asia Minor and his alleged relics are in the Basilica of S Nicola, Bari. Legends telling of his gifts of gold to three poor girls for their dowries gave rise to the practice of exchanging gifts on his feast day, Dec 6. This custom has been transferred to Dec 25 in most countries.

Nicholas of Cusa (1401–64) German prelate and scholar. He was made a cardinal in 1448, appointed bishop of Brixen (present-day Bressanone) in 1450, and became a papal legate. He is known for the breadth of his learning. He wrote important works on mysticism, mathematics, biology, and astronomy.

Nicholson, Ben (1894–1982) British artist. His first one-man exhibition (1922) reflected the influence of *cubism and de *Stijl. Some of his best abstract works were produced in the 1930s, while a member of the British art group Unit One (*see* Nash, Paul). These include white-painted plaster reliefs of rectangles combined with circles. He was the son of **Sir William Nicholson** (1872–1949), an artist renowned for his posters.

Nicholson, Jack (1937–) US film actor. Following his success as a supporting actor in *Easy Rider* (1969), he became one of the most respected stars of the 1970s. His films include *Chinatown* (1974), *The Passenger* (1974), *One Flew Over the Cuckoo's Nest* (1976), and *Terms of Endearment* (1983), for which he won an Academy Award.

Nicholson, William (1753–1815) British chemist, who in 1800 discovered *electrolysis by passing a current from a Voltaic pile through water and noting the bubbles of gas being given off.

Nicias (c. 470–413 BC) Athenian general and politican. An aristocratic opponent of the demagogue *Cleon, Nicias negotiated a temporary peace with Sparta in the Peloponnesian War (peace of Nicias, 421). He opposed Alcibiades' imperialist designs and only reluctantly commanded the ill-fated Athenian campaign to Sicily, during which he and nearly his entire force perished.

nickel (Ni) A hard silvery metal similar to iron, discovered in 1751 by A. F. Cronstedt (1722–65). It occurs in nature chiefly as pentlandite, NiS, and pyrrhotite, (Fe,Ni)S, which are found in Canada and Australia. Iron meteorites typically contain from 5 to 20% nickel. It is chemically similar to cobalt and copper, and forms a green oxide (NiO), the chloride ($NiCl_2$), the sulfate ($NiSO_4$), and other compounds. It is used widely in alloys, such as stainless steel, Invar, Monel, armor plating, and in coinage. Finely divided nickel is also used as a catalyst for hydrogenation reactions in organic chemistry. At no 28; at wt 58.71; mp 2650°F (1453°C); bp 4954°F (2732°C).

Nicklaus, Jack William (1940–) US golfer, who has won more major championships than any other. Between 1959 and 1981 he won two US amateur championships, four US and three British Open championships, five US Professional Golfers Association championships, and five Masters championships.

Nicobar Islands. *See* Andaman and Nicobar Islands.

Nicolai, Otto Ehrenfried (1810–49) German conductor and composer of operas. He held posts in Rome and Vienna and is remembered for *The Merry Wives of Windsor* (1849).

JACK NICKLAUS

Nicolson, Sir Harold (George) (1886–1968) British diplomat and literary critic. Born in Iran and educated at Oxford, he worked in the diplomatic service until 1929 and was later a member of parliament (1935–45). In 1913 he married the novelist Victoria Sackville-West (1892–1962). He published political studies, critical appreciations of Verlaine, Byron, Tennyson, and others, and several volumes of his *Diaries*.

Nicopolis, Battle of (September 25, 1396) The battle in which a coalition of Crusaders under Emperor *Sigismund, at the request of the Byzantine emperor, Manuel II Palaeologus (1350–1425; reigned 1391–1425), were decisively defeated by the Turks under Sultan Bayezid I (1347–1403; reigned 1389–1403). It contributed greatly to further Turkish advances and the ultimate fall of the Eastern Roman (Byzantine) Empire.

Nicosia (Greek name: Leukosía; Turkish name: Lefkosa) The capital of Cyprus, on the Pedieas River. Originally known as Ledra it has been successively under Byzantine, Venetian, Turkish, and British control. It possesses many old buildings, including the Cathedral of St Sophia (completed 1325), now the main mosque in Nicosia. Its industries include textiles, food processing, and cigarettes. Population (1980 est): 161,200.

nicotine ($C_{10}H_{14}N_2$) A toxic colorless oily liquid alkaloid that rapidly turns brown on exposure to air. It is obtained from the dried leaves of the tobacco plant and is present in small quantities in cigarettes.

nicotinic acid. *See* vitamin B complex.

Niebuhr, Barthold Georg (1776–1831) German historian. Niebuhr served as Prussian ambassador in Rome from 1816 to 1823, when he joined the staff of Bonn University. His *History of Rome* (1811–32) was significantly different from previous works on the ancient world, as he adopted a more critical approach and stressed the importance of external factors in the development of Rome. His ideas and methods influenced many scholars, including Theodor *Mommsen.

Niebuhr, Reinhold (1892–1971) US minister, philosopher, and theologian. He was pastor of Detroit's Bethel Evangelical Church (1915–28) where he saw labor injustices in the automobile industry. He taught at Union Theological Seminary (1928–60) and through the 1930s was a pacifist, political activist, and socialist. During the 1940s, however, he favored the war to stop Hitler and totalitarianism and after 1945 cofounded Americans for Democratic Action and was an adviser to the State Department. His early writings—*Moral Man and Immoral Society* (1932) and *Christianity and Power Politics* (1940)—reflected his socialist years. His later works—*A Nation So Conceived* (1963) and *Man's Nature and His Communities* (1965)—dealt with his theory of political realism.

Niedersachsen. *See* Lower Saxony.

Nielsen, Carl (August) (1865–1931) Danish composer and conductor. He began his musical career as a violinist. Nielsen developed the principle of progressive tonality (beginning in one *tonality and ending in another) in his six symphonies, of which the fourth, entitled *The Inextinguishable* (1914–16), and the fifth (1922), are the best known. He also composed concertos for the violin, flute, and clarinet, the operas *Saul and David* (1900–02) and *Maskarade* (1904–06), chamber music, and choral music.

Niemeyer, Oscar (1907–) Brazilian architect. A disciple of Le Corbusier with whom he collaborated on the Ministry of Education (1937–43) in Rio de Janeiro, Niemeyer has made a major contribution to the development of modern architecture in Brazil. His first independent buildings included a casino, club, and church at Pampulha in Bel Horizonte. He has achieved international fame for his designs for □Brasília, notably the president's palace (1959) and the cathedral (1964).

Nietzsche, Friedrich (1844–1900) German philosopher. A friend of Wagner, Nietzsche was influenced by the writings of *Schopenhauer and *Goethe. His first book, *The Birth of Tragedy* (1872), argued that Wagnerian opera was the successor to Greek drama. Nietzsche rejected Christianity and its morality and attempted a "transvaluation of all values." He argued that the "will to power" (the title of his posthumously edited notebooks) was the crucial human characteristic. In *Thus Spake Zarathustra* (1883–92), he eulogizes the man who is free, titanic, and powerful, an ideal adopted by the Nazis for the Aryan superman. His often obscure writings have been variously interpreted by 20th-century psychologists and existentialists. After 1889 he was permanently insane.

Niger, Republic of A large landlocked country in West Africa. Lying mainly in the Sahara, it consists of desert in the N merging to semidesert in the S and rising to the central Aïr mountains. In the extreme SW it is drained by the Niger River, bordered by fertile flood plains. Approximately half the population are Hausa, with large proportions of Zerma, Songhai, and Fulani. *Economy*: agriculture, particularly livestock raising, is important but it suffered badly from the droughts of the late 1960s and early 1970s in the Sahel. Crops include groundnuts, millet, beans, and cassava, with cotton and rice being grown in the wetter river districts. Mineral resources include salt, natron, and tin, and important uranium deposits in the N are being exploited. The main exports are uranium and groundnuts. *History*: occupied by France (1883–99), it became a territory of French West Africa in 1904. It was made an autonomous republic within the French Community in 1958 prior to gaining full independence in 1960 with Hamani Diori as president. Diori was overthrown in a military coup led by Maj Gen Seyni Kountché (1931–), who subsequently became president. Official language: French. Official currency: CFA (Communauté financière africaine) franc of 100 centimes. Area: 458,075 sq mi (1,186,408 sq km). Population (1981 est): 5,619,000. Capital: Niamey.

Niger River The third longest river in Africa. Rising in the S highlands of Guinea, near the Sierra Leone border, it flows NE and then SE through Mali, Niger, and Nigeria to enter the Gulf of Guinea. It has one of the largest hydroelectric-power plants in Africa. Length: 2600 mi (4183 km).

Niger-Congo languages An African language family spoken in central and S Africa. It is subdivided into six groups: the *West Atlantic languages; the Mande languages spoken in Guinea, Mali, and Sierra Leone; the Voltaic languages spoken in Upper Volta, Ghana, and the Ivory Coast; the *Kwa languages of West Africa, such as Yoruba and Igbo; the Benue-Congo group, which includes the *Bantu languages; and the Adamawa-Eastern group spoken in Nigeria. The whole family is sometimes included in the larger Niger-Kordofanian classification, which relates it to the Kordofanian languages of the Sudan.

Nigeria, Federation of A large country in West Africa, on the Gulf of Guinea. Mangrove swamps along the coast give way to tropical rain forest inland rising to open savanna-covered plateaus, with mountains in the E reaching heights of over 5000 ft (2000 m). The N is semidesert and the Niger River flows through the W. The inhabitants are mainly Hausa and Fulani in the N, Yoruba in the W, and Ibo in the E. *Economy*: since the discovery of oil in the 1960s and 1970s there has been a dramatic expansion in the economy and a shift away from agriculture to industry. Oil production accounts for about 90% of exports although production has declined in recent years; Nigeria is a member of OPEC and the world's eighth largest producer. There are also important reserves of natural gas and other minerals, including tin, coal, iron ore, and columbite (of which Nigeria is the world's main supplier). Manufacturing industries to have undergone rapid expansion include brewing, aluminum, motor vehicles, textiles, and cement. Hydroelectricity is a valuable source of power, particularly since the opening of the Kainji Dam on the Niger River (1969). Agriculture is still important and diverse although output has declined in recent years and it suffered severely through the prolonged drought in the Sahel. The main cash crops are groundnuts and cotton in the N and palms, coconut, and rubber in the S. Livestock, fishing, and forestry for timber are also important. *History*: in the middle ages there were highly developed kingdoms in the area, such as those of the Hausa in the N and the Yoruba (e.g. Oyo, Benin) in the SW; the Ibo occupied the SE. The coast was explored in the 15th century by the Portuguese, who developed the slave trade, in which the Dutch and English also participated. In 1861 Lagos was annexed by Britain and in 1886 the Royal Niger Company was incorporated to further British interests. By 1906, the British were in control of Nigeria, which was divided into the protectorate of Northern Nigeria and the colony (of Lagos) and protectorate of Southern Nigeria. These were united in 1914. Nigeria became a federation in 1954, gained independence in 1960, and became a republic within the Commonwealth in 1963. The government was overthrown in a violent military coup in 1966 and, after a further coup, a new government was formed under Lt Col Gowon. In 1967 the Eastern Region, which contained the homeland of the Ibo, withdrew to form the Republic of *Biafra under Lt Col Odumegwn Ojukwu's leadership. Civil war followed, lasting until Biafra's surrender in 1970. Gowon was overthrown in a coup in 1975. In 1979 Alhaji Shehu Shagari became president. He was re-elected in 1983. On the last day of 1983 the Shagari government was overturned, and a military regime under Major General Mohammed Buhari was installed, despite the overwhelming mandate for Shagari in 1982 when the country held its first general election in almost 20 years. Official language: English; the main African languages are Yoruba, Hausa, and Ibo. Official currency: naira of 100 kobo. Area: 356,669 sq mi (923,773 sq km). Population (1983 est): 85,219,000. Capital and main port: Lagos.

nightblindness Inability to see in dim light. This is the earliest sign of vitamin A deficiency and is seen most commonly in young children in poor countries. Vitamin A is found in fruit, vegetables, and fish-liver oil. Preparations of vitamin A and cod-liver oil are used in treatment.

night heron A nocturnal *heron belonging to a subfamily (*Nycticoracini*; 9 species) occurring worldwide. Night herons are comparatively short-legged and squat, with a short neck and a broad bill. Birds of the main genus (*Nycticorax*) are mostly black-headed with long white ornamental head plumes.

nightingale A plump woodland bird, *Luscinia megarhynchos*, that winters in tropical Africa and breeds in S Europe and Asia Minor during the summer. It is about 6 in (16 cm) long with reddish-brown plumage and pale underparts and feeds on ground insects and spiders. Nightingales are noted for their beautiful song and were popular as cagebirds. The thrush nightingale (*L. luscinia*) is a closely related similar species. Family: *Turdidae* (thrushes).

FLORENCE NIGHTINGALE *The legendary Lady with the Lamp tending patients in the hospital at Scutari, during the Crimean War.*

Nightingale, Florence (1820–1910) British hospital reformer and founder of the nursing profession. With strong religious convictions, Nightingale trained as a nurse and was appointed a nursing superintendent in London in 1853. On the outbreak of the Crimean War, in 1854, she volunteered to lead a party of nurses to work in the military hospitals. She set about transforming the appalling conditions, earning herself the title Lady with the Lamp from her patients. After the war she was instrumental in obtaining improved living conditions in the army and, in 1860 she established a school for nurses, the first of its kind.

nightjar A nocturnal bird belonging to a subfamily (*Caprimulginae*; 60–70 species) occurring in most temperate and tropical regions, also called goatsucker. About 12 in (30 cm) long, nightjars have a soft mottled gray, brown, and rufous plumage with spotted and barred underparts and a long tail. Its short bill has a wide gape surrounded by long sensitive bristles enabling it to catch insects in flight. Family: *Caprimulgidae*; order: *Caprimulgiformes* (frogmouths, nightjars, etc.).

nightmares Frightening *dreams, from which the sufferer often wakes with a feeling of suffocation. They are distinguished from **night terrors**, in which a child wakes suddenly in panic but later cannot remember the incident. Nightmares are more common during states of anxiety and depression and in people taking certain sleeping tablets. *See also* sleep.

nightshade One of several plants of the family *Solanaceae. The most notorious is *deadly nightshade (or belladonna). The **woody nightshade**, or bittersweet (*Solanum dulcamara*), is a scrambling shrubby perennial, up to 7 ft (2 m) tall, of Eurasia and N Africa. It has oval leaves, the lower ones much divided, and loose clusters of flowers with five spreading purple lobes and conspicuous yellow stamens. The red berries are poisonous. The **black nightshade** (*S. nigrum*) is an annual, up to 20 in (50 cm) high, widely distributed as a weed. It has oval pointed leaves, small yellowish flowers, and poisonous black berries.

The unrelated **enchanter's nightshade** (*Circaea lutetiana*), of Eurasia, is a herbaceous perennial of shady places. Up to 24 in (60 cm) tall, it has large heart-shaped leaves and a terminal spike of tiny white flowers. Family: *Onagraceae.*

nihilism A view that rejects all traditional values and institutions. *Turgenev invented the label in *Fathers and Sons* (1861) for the philosophy of the character of Basarov, which was based on that of Dmitrii Pisarev (1840–68). The political expression of nihilism is anarchy; its 19th-century Russian proponents held that progress is impossible without the destruction of all existing organizations. Nihilism also undermines accepted standards in *ethics and *aesthetics.

Niigata 37 58N 139 2E A city in Japan, in NW Honshu. The main port for the Sea of Japan, its industries include chemicals and oil refining. Its university was established in 1949. Population (1980): 458,000.

Nijinsky, Vaslav (1890–1950) Russian ballet dancer. In 1909 he joined Diaghilev's company in Paris, and quickly achieved an international reputation for his daring and sensitive dancing. Michel *Fokine created *Petrushka, Scheherazade*, and other ballets for him, and from 1913 he also began to choreograph. He retired in 1919 suffering from schizophrenia and was cared for by his wife until his death.

Nijmegen (German name: Nimwegen) 51 50N 5 52E A city in the E Netherlands, in Gelderland province. The Treaties of *Nijmegen (1678–79) were signed here. Its university was founded in 1923. It is an important industrial center with chemicals and engineering. Population (1981 est): 147,346.

Nijmegen, Treaties of (1678–79) The peace treaties between France and, respectively, the Netherlands (1678), Spain (1678), and the Holy Roman Empire (1679) that ended the third *Dutch War. Terms were least favorable to Spain, Louis XIV securing Franche-Comté and a naturally defensible frontier with the Spanish Netherlands.

Nike The Greek personification of victory, often portrayed as an aspect of *Athena. Among larger representations is the famous statue discovered in Samothrace in 1836 and now in the Louvre, Paris.

Nikisch, Arthur (1855–1922) Hungarian conductor. A brilliant student at the Vienna Conservatoire, he directed the Leipzig Opera (1879–87), the Boston Symphony Orchestra (1889–93), and then the Leipzig Gewandhaus and Berlin Philharmonic Orchestras concurrently (1895–1922).

Nikko 36 45N 139 37E A city in Japan, in central Honshu. Situated within Nikko National Park its beautifully ornamented temples and shrines are a place of pilgrimage and attract a large number of tourists. Population (1970): 28,502.

Nikolaev 46 57N 32 00E A port in the Soviet Union, in the S Ukrainian SSR at the confluence of the Bug and Ingul Rivers about 40 mi (64 km) from the Black Sea. Long a naval base, it has important shipbuilding and flour-milling industries. Population (1977): 447,000.

Nikopol 47 34N 34 25E A city in the SW Soviet Union, in the Ukrainian SSR on the Dnepr River. It is important as the center of a region having the world's largest manganese reserves. Population (1977 est): 146,000.

Nile, Battle of the (August 1, 1798) A naval battle in which the British, under *Nelson, defeated the French during *Napoleon's invasion of Egypt (*see* Revolutionary and Napoleonic Wars). This engagement severed communications between France and Napoleon's army in Egypt and gave Britain control of the Mediterranean.

Nile River A river in N Africa, the longest river in the world. The longest of its three main tributaries, the White Nile, rises in Burundi as the Luvironza River before joining the Kagera River to enter Lake Victoria, the chief reservoir of the Nile. It emerges as the Victoria Nile at Jinja to flow northward— through Lake Mobutu becoming the White Nile at its confluence with the Bahr el Ghazal. At Khartoum it is joined by the Blue Nile (which rises in the Ethiopian highlands) and later by the Atbara River before flowing through a broad delta into the Mediterranean Sea. The Nile's annual floodwaters have supported cultivation on its floodplains

since ancient times. To provide the increasing amounts of water required for irrigation vast dams have been constructed, including the Aswan Dam and *Aswan High Dam. Length: 4187 mi (6741 km).

nilgai A large antelope, *Bosephalus tragocamelus*, inhabiting Indian forests and plains. Up to 55 in (140 cm) high at the shoulder, male nilgais have a slate-gray coat with white underparts and develop short horns and a throat tuft. Females are smaller and tawny brown. They live in small herds, browsing on shrubs and fruit.

Nilo-Saharan languages A family of African languages that covers the smallest geographical area of all the African language groups. It is also the least clearly defined group, there being very great variety within its constituent languages. It includes the Nilotic languages of the Chari-Nile group, such as Dinka and Nuer.

Nilsson, Birgit Marta (1918–) Swedish soprano, who studied at the Stockholm Royal Academy, making her debut in 1946 as Agathe in Weber's opera *Der Freischütz;* she is well known in the roles of Brunnhilde, Salome, Elektra, and Turandot.

nimbostratus A form of *cloud common in temperate latitudes. Dark gray and solid in appearance it has a low base but may show extensive vertical development. Precipitation of snow or rain is often prolonged although not usually heavy.

Nîmes 43 50N 4 21E A city in S France, the capital of the Gard department. An important Roman settlement, it was a Protestant stronghold (16th–17th centuries). It has several notable Roman remains, including an amphitheater and the temple of Diana; the Pont du Gard lies to the NE. A trading center for wine and brandy, its manufactures include textiles, footwear, and agricultural machinery. Population (1975): 133,942.

Nimitz, Chester W (illiam) (1885–1966) US admiral. In World War II, as commander of the Pacific Fleet after Pearl Harbor (1941), he complemented General Douglas *MacArthur's command of the SW Pacific. His victories along the island chains from Japan to New Guinea, which destroyed the Japanese fleet, were made possible by his use of aircraft carriers as support bases.

Nimrod A legendary biblical figure described in Genesis as a mighty hunter. He founded a Mesopotamian kingdom that included the cities of Babel, Erech, and Akkad and is credited with building the cities of Nineveh and Kalhu (modern Nimrud).

Nimrud An Assyrian capital (ancient Kalhu) near Mosul (Iraq). Founded about 1250 BC it was destroyed by the Medes in 612 BC. *Layard's excavations (1845–51) of the 9th-century city yielded gigantic sculptures of winged bulls and a library of *cuneiform tablets. *See also* Nineveh.

Nin, Anaïs (1903–77) US writer; born in France. She spent part of her childhood in the US and most of her young adult years in France. Influenced by the Surrealist writers in Paris and her personal experience with psychoanalysis, she developed her own style of writing, concentrating on themes of women and women's problems. Her works include the novels *The House of Incest* (1937), *Winter of Artifice* (1939), *The Four-Chambered Heart* (1950), *A Spy in the House of Love* (1954), and *The Novel of the Future* (1970); short stories *Under a Glass Bell* (1944) and *Ladders to Fire* (1946); and her diaries, which appeared in 6 volumes.

ninety-five theses. See Luther, Martin.

Nineveh An Assyrian capital (modern Kuyunjik) near Mosul (Iraq). Nineveh was made cocapital with □Nimrud by *Sennacherib (c. 700 BC). The Medes sacked it in 612 BC. Sculptures, reliefs, and inscriptions illuminate Assyrian life at this period, but *Layard's great find was the library of *Ashurbanipal, which preserved masterpieces of *cuneiform literature, including the epic of *Gilgamesh.

Ningbo (or Ning-po) 29 54N 121 33E A river port in E China, in Zhejiang province near the East China Sea. Important for overseas trade (5th–9th centuries), it was also a religious center and has many temples. Its industries include textiles and food processing. Population (1953): 237,500.

Ningxia Hui Autonomous Region (or Ningsia Hui AR) An administrative division in N China. It occupies a plateau and is largely desert, with nomadic herdsmen in the N and some cultivation in the S. Area: 25,896 sq mi (66,400 sq km). Population (1980 est): 3,640,000. Capital: Yinchuan.

Niobe In Greek mythology, the daughter of Tantalus and wife of the King of Thebes. She took great pride in her many children and arrogantly urged the Thebans to worship her instead of Leto, the mother of only two children, Apollo and Artemis. When the Thebans consented to this, Apollo and Artemis avenged their mother's honor and killed Niobe's children. Overcome by grief, Niobe wandered to Mount Sipylus in Lydia, where

NIMRUD *British archeologists directed the excavation and removal of the statue of the winged bull, now in the British Museum, London. It was at first believed to have been the site of Nineveh.*

Zeus changed her into a stone column or statue, the face of which was said continually to shed tears.

niobium (Nb) A soft ductile white metal, discovered in 1801. It was formerly known as columbium in the US. Niobium is used in specialist alloys in spacecraft, and at low temperatures it has superconducting properties. Its compounds include the white oxide (Nb_2O_5), which has interesting structural properties, and the volatile fluoride and chloride (NbF_5, $NbCl_5$). At no 41; at wt 92.9064; mp 4479°F (2468°C); bp 8576°F (4742°C).

nipa A small *palm tree, *Nipa fruticans,* of brackish waters and estuaries of SE Asia. It has a creeping trunk and large feathery foliage, which is used for thatching and basket making. The fruits are sometimes eaten and the flowers are used commercially as a source of sugar.

Nippur A city of ancient *Sumer (modern Niffer in central Iraq). From about 2600 BC it was Sumer's chief religious center with a *ziggurat dedicated to Enlil (built c. 2000 BC) and temples to *Ishtar (Inanna). Quantities of tablets bearing religious, literary, and other texts have been discovered.

Nirenberg, Marshall Warren (1927–) US biochemist, who developed a technique for breaking the genetic code. Nirenberg used synthetic RNA of known base sequence and determined for which amino acid it coded. He shared a Nobel Prize (1968) with *Khorana and Robert W. Holley (1922–) for this work.

nirvana The supreme goal of Buddhism, in which liberation from the limitations of existence and rebirth are attained through the extinction of desire. Whereas the *Theravada school sees nirvana as the negation of the mundane, the *Mahayana regards it as the ultimate achievement of man's essential Buddha-nature. In Hinduism nirvana also means spiritual release in the sense of freedom from reincarnation or of union with God or the Absolute.

Niš 43 20N 21 54E A city in E Yugoslavia, in Serbia on the Nišava River. For five centuries to 1877 it was a center for Serbian resistance to Turkish control. Its products include locomotives and textiles, and it has a university (1965). Population (1971): 127,654.

Nishinomiya 34 44N 135 22E A city in Japan, in S Honshu on Osaka Bay. A heavy industrial center, it is traditionally known for its *sake* (a Japanese rice wine). Population (1980): 410,000.

Niterói 22 54S 43 06W A city in SE Brazil, in Rio de Janeiro state on Guanabara Bay opposite the city of Rio de Janeiro. Although largely residential, it has shipbuilding and textile industries and is a popular resort. Population (1980): 386,185.

nitric acid (HNO_3) A fuming corrosive liquid made by the oxidation of ammonia by air in the presence of a platinum catalyst or the action of sulfuric acid on sodium or potassium nitrate. It is widely used in the manufacture of fertilizers and explosives and in other chemical processes.

nitrocellulose. *See* cellulose nitrate.

nitrogen (N) A colorless odorless gas, discovered by D. Rutherford (1749–1819) in 1772. It makes up 78% of the earth's atmosphere by volume. The element exists as diatomic molecules (N_2) bonded very strongly together. This bond must be broken before nitrogen can react, which accounts for its chemical inertness. It forms a range of chemical compounds including ammonia (NH_3), the oxides (N_2O, NO, N_2O_3, NO_2, N_2O_5), nitric acid (HNO_3), and many nitrates (for example $NaNO_3$). Liquid nitrogen has a wide range of cryogenic applications. Ammonia (NH_3) and nitrates are of great importance as fertilizers. Nitrates are also used in explosives as a source of oxygen, which they liberate when heated. Sodium and potassium nitrates occur naturally in some desert areas. Nitrogen gas is used to provide an inert gas blanket in some welding applications. At no 7; at wt 14.0067; mp –290.86°C; bp –195.8°C.

nitrogen cycle The sequence of processes by which nitrogen and its compounds are utilized in nature. Nitrogen gas in the air is converted (fixed) to ammonia by lightning, cosmic radiation, certain soil bacteria, and fertilizer manufacturers (*see* nitrogen fixation). Nitrifying bacteria in the roots of leguminous plants convert ammonia to nitrites and then to nitrates. Some nitrates are reduced by denitrifying bacteria to nitrogen, but most are used by plants to manufacture amino acids and proteins. When animals eat plants some of this nitrogenous plant material is incorporated into animal tissues. Nitrogenous excretory products and dead organic matter decompose to produce ammonia, so completing the cycle.

nitrogen fixation The conversion of atmospheric nitrogen gas into nitrogen compounds. The process occurs naturally by the action of bacteria in the roots of leguminous plants (*see* nitrogen cycle). Industrial methods of fixing nitrogen are of immense importance in the manufacture of nitrogen fertilizers. One method is the reaction of nitrogen with oxygen to give nitric oxide in an electric arc. The process is only economical in regions in which cheap hydroelectric power is available. The major method of fixing nitrogen is the *Haber-Bosch process for making ammonia.

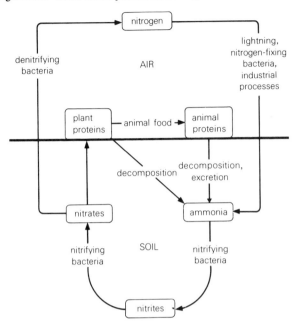

NITROGEN CYCLE

nitroglycerin ($C_3H_5(NO_3)_3$) A yellow oily highly *explosive liquid. It is used as an explosive either alone or as *dynamite or *gelignite.

Niue 19 02S 169 55W A fertile coral island in the S Pacific Ocean, belonging to New Zealand. Copra and bananas are exported. Area: 100 sq mi (260 sq km). Population (1980 est): 3288. Chief town: Alofi.

Niven, David (1909–83) British film actor. His early films include *The Prisoner of Zenda* (1937) and *Wuthering Heights* (1939), and he later appeared in many stylish comedies and action films, including *Separate Tables* (1958), *The Guns of Navarone* (1961), and *Candleshoe* (1977). He published two highly successful volumes of autobiography, *The Moon's a Balloon* (1972) and *Bring on the Empty Horses* (1975).

Nixon, Richard Milhous (1913–) US statesman; Republican president (1969–74). A Californian-born lawyer, he was elected in 1946 to the US House of Representatives, where he was a member of the Un-American Activities Committee. In 1950 he was elected to the Senate as a staunch anti-communist. He achieved early political power partly by discrediting Democratic opponents as communist sympathizers. He was Eisenhower's vice president from 1953 until 1960, when he became the Republican presidential candidate. He was defeated by John F. *Kennedy, and when in 1962 he failed to win the governorship of California his political career seemed over. However, Nixon returned to national politics in the mid-1960s and in 1968 narrowly defeated Hubert Humphrey for the presidency. As president he reduced US troop commitments abroad and in 1973 ended US military involvement in Vietnam. In 1972 he visited the People's Republic of China, a move that was to lead to the establishment of diplomatic relations with China. Participation in illegal efforts to ensure re-election in 1972 and the subsequent cover-up attempt led to the *Watergate scandal. Under threat of impeachment he became the first president to resign office. President *Ford granted him a free pardon after succeeding him as president. In private life he wrote *RN: The Memoirs of Richard Nixon* (1978) and *The Real War* (1980).

Nizam al-Mulk (c. 1018–92) Persian statesman, who was vizier (minister; 1063–92) to the *Seljuq sultans *Alp-Arslan and Malik-Shah. Nizam al-Mulk, who wielded almost absolute power, governed the Seljuq empire at its zenith. He was the author of *The Book of Government*, in which he expressed his political and orthodox religious views. Shortly before Malik-Shah's death, Nizam al-Mulk was assassinated, probably by a rival at court.

Nizhnii Novgorod. *See* Gorkii.

Nizhnii Tagil 58 00N 59 58E A city in the Soviet Union, in the W RSFSR on the Tagil River and on the E slopes of the Ural Mountains. Its metallurgical industries arise from the surrounding ironmining region. Population (1981 est): 404,000.

RICHARD M. NIXON *President (1969-74) who, as a result of the Watergate scandal, became the first to resign the presidency.*

Nkomo, Joshua (1917–) Zimbabwean politician. Secretary general of the Rhodesian African Railway Union in Rhodesia (1945–50), Nkomo became president of the Zimbabwe African People's Union (ZAPU) in 1961. With headquarters in Zambia, it allied with Robert Mugabe's Zimbabwe African National Union (ZANU) in 1976 to form the *Patriotic Front (PF) against the government of Ian Smith in Rhodesia (*see also* Zimbabwe). Nkomo became a minister in Mugabe's government in 1980 but was dismissed (1982) when arms caches were found on his farms.

Nkrumah, Kwame (1909–72) Ghanaian statesman; prime minister (1957–60) and then president (1960–66). A student in the US and the UK, after returning home he formed (1949) the Convention People's Party, which with a policy of noncooperation with the British took the Gold Coast to independence as Ghana in 1957. Nkrumah was deposed by a military coup while visiting China in 1966. He sought exile in Guinea, where Sékou Touré made him cohead of state. An advocate of African unity, he wrote *Toward— Colonial Freedom* (1947) and *Handbook of Revolutionary Warfare* (1968).

No A form of Japanese theater, the early development of which is associated with the work of the actor and dramatist *Zeami Motokiyo (1363–1443). Originating in religious ritual and folk dances and strongly influenced by Zen Buddhism, it is performed with a minimum of scenery and properties and is characterized by the use of dance, mime, and masks. The acting is highly stylized. A traditional No program lasts several hours and consists of five plays separated by three comic interludes known as *Kyogen*. It has remained an aristocratic form, contrasting with the more realistic *Kabuki drama.

Noah An Old Testament figure. After God had determined to destroy the human race because of its wickedness (Genesis 6–8), he made a covenant with Noah as the only man worthy of being saved from the coming flood. Noah was instructed to build an ark for his family and representatives of each animal species, and they would be preserved after the flood subsided. Noah and his sons Ham, Shem, and Japheth and their wives became the ancestors of the present human race. Several other cultures have similar legends about a catastrophic primeval flood.

Nobel, Alfred Bernhard (1833–96) Swedish chemist and businessman. From his invention of dynamite (1867) and a smokeless gunpowder (1889) and his exploitation of the Baku oilfields he amassed a considerable fortune, leaving 1.75 million as a foundation for the **Nobel Prizes**. Five of

	1981	1982	1983	1984
Physics	N. Bloembergen A. Schawlow K. Siegbahn	K. Wilson	S. Chandrasekhar W. Fowler	Carlo Rubbia Simon van der Meer
Chemistry	R. Hoffmann K. Fukui	A. Klug	H. Taube	Robert B. Merrifield
Medicine	D. Hubel R. Sperry T. Wiesel	S. Bergstroem B. Samuelsson J. Vane	B. McClintock	Niels K. Jerne Georges J. F. Koehler Cesar Milstein
Literature	Elias Canetti	Gabriel Garcia Márquez	William Golding	Jaroslav Seifert
Peace	UN High Commission for Refugees (UNHCR)	A. Garcia Robles A. Myrdal	L. Walesa	Desmond Tutu
Economics	J. Tobin	G. Stigler	G. Debreu	Richard Stone

NOBEL *Recent prizewinners.*

the annual awards— (for physics, chemistry, physiology or medicine, literature, and peace) are made by various Swedish academies, except for the Peace Prize, which is awarded by a committee elected by the Norwegian parliament. A sixth prize, for economics, instituted in memory of Alfred Nobel, has been financed by the Swedish National Bank since 1969.

nobelium (No) A synthetic transuranic element discovered in 1957 by bombarding curium with carbon ions in an accelerator. Five isotopes with short half-lives have been discovered. Named for Alfred Nobel. At no 102; at wt (255).

Nobile, Umberto (1885–1978) Italian aeronautical engineer and aviator. He designed the airships *Norge* and *Italia*, piloting the *Norge* in *Amundsen's flight over the North Pole (1926). In 1928 he flew the *Italia* across the Pole but crashed on the return journey, being rescued after 40 days.

Noble, Sir Andrew (1831–1915) British physicist, who founded the science of ballistics. In conjunction with Sir Frederick *Abel he improved the quality of gunpowder and made many innovations in artillery design.

noble gases (*or* inert gases) The elements forming group O of the *periodic table: helium, neon, argon, krypton, xenon, and radon. All are colorless odorless tasteless gases, which are slightly soluble in water. They are virtually inert chemically owing to their filled outer electron shells, although complexes of xenon and krypton have recently been isolated (e.g. XeF_4). Helium is commercially obtained from natural gas, the others (apart from radon) from the distillation of air. Their inertness suits them for such applications as arc welding and filling incandescent lamps.

noble metals Metals, such as gold, silver, and platinum, that do not rust or tarnish in air or water and are not easily attacked by acids.

Nobunaga Oda (1534–82) Japanese general, hero of many legends. As the emperor's chief military commander, Nobunaga was virtual ruler of central Japan from 1568. Thereafter he built up his own regular forces, bringing much of Japan under imperial rule. His work of unification was brought to an end by his assassination.

Noctiluca A genus of minute single-celled animals (□Protozoa) found in coastal waters throughout the world. They are pinkish, about the size of a pinhead, have a single flagellum that wafts food particles toward the mouth, and are luminescent. Class: *Flagellata.*

noctuid moth A moth belonging to the family *Noctuidae* (about 20,000 species), also called owlet moth, widespread in Eurasia and North America. The adults are usually dull brown or gray and fly at night. The caterpillars, which are also known as *army worms and *cutworms, are active at night, eating plant roots and stems.

noctule An insect-eating *bat, *Nyctalus noctula,* of Eurasia. About 5 in (12 cm) long, it has bright-chestnut fur and long narrow wings. Noctules hibernate only from Dec to Jan. Family: *Vespertilionidae.*

noddy. *See* tern.

Noel-Baker, Philip John (1889–1982) British campaigner for disarmament and Labour politician. He worked at the League of Nations (1919–22) and helped to draft the UN Charter; he was an MP (1929–31, 1936–50). The author of *The Arms Race: A Programme for World Disarmament* (1958), in 1959 he was awarded the Nobel Peace Prize.

Noguchi, Hideyo (1876–1928) Japanese bacteriologist, who discovered that paralysis in syphilitic patients was caused by spirochete organisms in the central nervous system. Noguchi also investigated snake venoms, poliomyelitis, and trachoma. He died of yellow fever while investigating the disease in Africa.

SIDNEY NOLAN *Dead Duck Mine.*

Nolan, Sidney (1917–) Australian painter, born in Melbourne. Largely self-taught, he first painted abstract works, influenced by *Klee and *Moholy-Nagy but is internationally known for his paintings of Australian historical figures, and landscapes of the outback.

Nolde, Emil (E. Hansen; 1867–1956) German expressionist painter and printmaker. Although briefly associated (1906–07) with Die *Brucke, he developed an independent style characterized by his distorted forms and clashing colors. Deeply religious, he painted many biblical scenes, bleak landscapes of the Baltic coast, and still lifes of flowers.

Nollekens, Joseph (1737–1823) British neoclassical sculptor (*see* neoclassicism). After executing several portrait busts in Rome (1760–70), he became highly successful with his portrait sculptures in England. His sitters included George III, Benjamin West, William Pitt the Younger, and Charles James Fox. He was also a sculptor of tombs and mythological subjects.

nomads Peoples who live in no fixed place but wander periodically according to the seasonal availability of food, pasture, or trade and employment. Hunters and gatherers (e.g. Australian Aborigines) usually live in small bands that spend anything from a few days to a few weeks in a vicinity, moving within a loosely defined territory. Pastoralists (e.g. many central Asian tribes) often move between summer and winter pastures (*see* transhumance). Traders, tinkers, entertainers, and those who provide certain crafts and services, such as the *gypsies, often travel widely seeking custom.

Nome 64 30N 165 30W A port in W Alaska, on the S shore of the Seward Peninsula. Founded as Anvil City during the gold rush of 1868, it has fishing and handicraft industries. Population (1980): 2301.

nominalism The medieval philosophical theory that general terms (called universals) have no real existence, that is, there is no abstract entity corresponding to a universal. Thus, there exists no such thing as blueness, but only individual blue things (called particulars). Nominalism, therefore, contrasts with *realism. *William of Ockham, *Hobbes, and certain modern analytic philosophers have all made varying statements of nominalist theory.

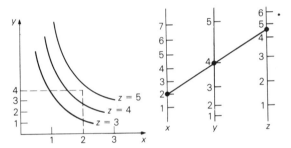

NOMOGRAPH *If x = 2 and y = 4, a value of approximately 4.5 for z is obtained from the two forms of nomograph shown.*

nomograph (*or* nomogram) A *graph showing the relationship between three variable quantities, enabling the value of one variable to be read off if the other two are known. It can take the form of a series of curves on a graph of two quantities, corresponding to constant values of a third. Or it can consist of three straight lines calibrated with the values of the variables. A fourth line is drawn between two known points on two of the straight lines: the point at which this fourth line cuts the third straight line gives the value of the unknown quantity.

Nonconformists In its original early-17th-century sense, the term referred to members of the Church of England who did not conform with its rituals. After the Act of Uniformity (1662), the term's scope widened to include members of dissenting Protestant sects, such as the Quakers and Methodists.

non-Euclidean geometry A form of *geometry in which *Euclid's postulates are not satisfied. In *Euclidean geometry if two lines are both at right angles to a third they never meet (i.e. they remain parallel). In, for example, hyperbolic (or elliptic) geometry they eventually diverge (or converge). Non-Euclidean geometry was developed independently by *Lobachevski (published 1831) and *Bolyai (published 1836). *See also* Riemannian geometry.

Non-Intercourse Act (1809) US law that allowed trade with nations except Britain and France until they stopped the blockade of neutral nations. It superseded the *Embargo Act of 1807.

Nono, Luigi (1924–) Italian composer. A pupil of Francesco Malipiero (1882–1973), he married Schoenberg's daughter Nuria. Nono's compositions frequently employ serialism; many of them consist of settings of texts by Marxist writers. They include *La fabbrica illuminata* (for mezzo-soprano and tape; 1964) and *Non consumiamo Marx* (for voices and tape; 1969).

Nonproliferation of Nuclear Weapons, Treaty on the. *See* disarmament.

nonsense verse A genre of comic verse that is structured according to a kind of surreal logic that defies rational interpretation. It is characterized by strict rhyme schemes and the use of meaningless neologisms. The genre, predominantly English, is usually dated from the publication of *The Book of Nonsense* by Edward *Lear in 1846. Other outstanding writers of nonsense are Lewis *Carroll and Hilaire *Belloc. *See also* limerick.

Nootka A North American Indian people of the NW Pacific coast region who speak a *Wakashan language. They were traditionally hunters, fishers, and expert whale catchers, using large canoes and harpoons. They practiced the *potlatch as did their neighbors, the *Kwakiutl.

noradrenaline (*or* norepinephrine) A hormone that is secreted by the central core (medulla) of the adrenal glands. It is a *catecholamine, structurally similar to *adrenaline but producing different effects in certain target organs, especially the heart, the rate of which it decreases. Noradrenaline is taken up and stored by cells of the sympathetic nervous system and subsequently released by nerve endings to excite adjacent nerves in the transmission of impulses. In the hypothalamus it is thought to inhibit transmission of impulses.

Nordenskjöld, Nils Adolf Erik, Baron (1832–1901) Swedish navigator. After exploration in Spitsbergen he became the first, in the *Vega*, to navigate the *Northeast Passage (1878–79).

Norfolk 36 54N 76 18W A seaport in Virginia, on Hampton Roads. Founded in 1682, it suffered considerable damage in the American Revolution and the US Civil War. It is the headquarters of the US Atlantic Fleet. Norfolk's industries include textiles, cars, and shipbuilding. Population (1980): 266,979.

Norfolk A county of E England, bordering on the North Sea. It is mainly agricultural with arable farming and intensive turkey rearing. Fishing is centered on Great Yarmouth. Tourism is important, especially in Great Yarmouth and on the Norfolk Broads. Area: 1067 sq mi (5355 sq km). Population (1981): 693,490. Administrative center: Norwich.

Norfolk, Thomas Howard, 3rd Duke of (1473–1554) English statesman; the uncle of two of Henry VIII's wives. He became president of the privy council in 1529 and in 1536 suppressed the *Pilgrimage of Grace. He lost power after 1542 and was imprisoned under Edward VI for involvement in treason (1546). Surrey's son **Thomas Howard, 4th Duke of Norfolk** (1538–72) was imprisoned (1559–60) by Elizabeth I for planning to marry Mary, Queen of Scots. He subsequently participated in *Ridolfi's plot against Elizabeth and was executed.

Norfolk Island 29 05S 167 59E A mountainous Australian island in the SW Pacific Ocean. Formerly a British penal colony, some of the descendants of the *Bounty* mutineers were resettled here from *Pitcairn Island (1856). Area: 14 sq mi (36 sq km). Population (1972): 1422. Chief town: Kingston.

Norman 35 13N 97 26W A city in central Oklahoma, on the Canadian River, SW of Oklahoma City. Founded in 1889, it became the home of the University of Oklahoma in 1892. Oil wells and petroleum production are important to the economy. Population (1980): 68,020.

Norman art and architecture The styles that flourished in Normandy and the lands that the Normans had conquered in the 11th and 12th centuries, notably the *romanesque architectural style. First appearing in England before the Norman conquest in Westminster Abbey (consecrated 1065), Norman architecture later developed into a distinctive native style. Characteristic Norman features include massive walls, rounded arches, two-tower church façades and abstract geometrical ornamentation on columns, etc. In S Italy the Norman style was fused with the native Saracen and Byzantine traditions. In the other arts the most notable Norman achievement was the *Bayeux tapestry.

Norman conquest (1066–72) The conquest of England by William, Duke of Normandy (*see* William the Conqueror). After defeating Harold II at the battle of Hastings (1066), William captured London and was crowned. Local uprisings were suppressed by 1070 and with the defeat of the Scots in 1072 the conquest was complete. The Norman influence on Anglo-Saxon England was fundamental. Although structures of government continued virtually unaltered, the English aristocracy was replaced by Normans and other continentals and *feudalism was introduced. Latin became the language of government and Norman French, the literary language; the Norman influence was also felt in church organization and architecture.

Normandy (French name: Normandie) A former province in N France, on the English Channel. It now comprises the planning regions of **Basse-Normandie**, with an area of 6787 sq mi (17,583 sq km) and a population (1975 est) of 1,303,600, and **Haute-Normandie**, with an area of 4732 sq mi

(12,258 sq km) and a population (1975 est) of 1,595,400. A fertile agricultural area with sheep and dairy farming, it also produces flax, hemp, and apples. *History*: during the medieval period Normandy flourished as a major state. William II, Duke of Normandy, conquered England (1066) to become William I of England. Disputed between England and France during the following centuries, it finally reverted to France in 1449. During World War II it suffered severe damage, the Normandy invasion taking place in 1944.

Norman French The dialect spoken in Normandy during the early middle ages and by the Norman invaders of England. Their speech influenced English and introduced new words to the language.

Normans Viking settlers in N France (later Normandy) whose rule, under their leader Rollo, was formally recognized (911) by Charles the Simple (879–929; reigned 898–923). Further expansion in Normandy followed and by the end of the 11th century they had also conquered England (*see* Norman conquest) and much of S Italy and Sicily and had established crusading states in the E, besides gaining a foothold in Wales and Scotland. Noted for their military dynamism and inventiveness (they introduced the castle into England) they adopted and adapted existing administrative practices in countries they conquered with great success, normally possessing a stable government working in close harmony with the Church.

Norns In Norse mythology, the fates, three females who shape the life of man. They are Urth (the past), Verthandi (the present), and Skuld (the future).

Norris, Frank (Benjamin Franklin N.; 1870–1902) US naturalist writer. He was a news correspondent for several newspapers and a magazine from 1895–1902. He wrote *McTeague* (1899) and the first two parts—*The Octopus* (1901) and *The Pit* (1903)—of a trilogy, *Epic of the Wheat*. The third part, *The Wolf*, was never finished.

Norrköping 58 35N 16 10E A port in SE Sweden, on an inlet of the Baltic Sea. Its industries include shipbuilding, engineering, and textiles. Population (1978 est): 119,238.

Norsemen. *See* Vikings.

North, Frederick, Lord (1732–92) British statesman; prime minister (1770–82). He was a Lord of the Treasury (1759–65) and chancellor of the exchequer (1767–70) before becoming prime minister, as which his policies were largely dictated by George III. He was severely criticized for precipitating the *American Revolution (1775–83), and for British defeats in the conflict, and eventually resigned.

North America The third largest continent in the world, in the N of the W hemisphere bordering on the Arctic Ocean, the N Pacific Ocean, the N Atlantic Ocean, the Gulf of Mexico, and the Caribbean Sea. The Isthmus of Panama links it with South America. It is generally accepted as consisting of *Canada, the *United States of America, *Mexico, *Central America, *Greenland, and the *West Indies. The mountains of the Western Cordillera extend down its entire W coast descending E to the Great Plains before rising to the Appalachian Mountains further E, which are separated from the Canadian Shield by the Great Lakes. Area: over 9,500,000 sq mi (24,000,000 sq km). Population (1970 est): 320,000,000.

North American Indian languages A geographical classification of the languages of the indigenous peoples of North America. It is estimated that these languages originally numbered about 300; at least a third of these are dead or dying out, but the number of speakers of a few, such as *Navaho, is increasing. Highly diverse, these languages have been classified in various ways and about 57 families have been identified. *Sapir arranged these into six phyla (1929): *Eskimo–*Aleut; *Algonkian-*Wakashan; *Na-Dené; *Penutian; *Hokan–*Siouan; and *Aztec-Tanoan.

Northampton 52 14N 0 54W A city in central England, the administrative center of Northamptonshire on the Nene River. A manufacturing center, Northampton has undergone considerable expansion since its designation as a new town in 1968. Population (1981): 156,853.

Northampton 39 59N 83 56W A city in W central Massachusetts, on W bank of the Connecticut River, north of Springfield. Smith College (1871) is here. Products manufactured include cutting utensils, wiring, and optical instruments. Population (1980): 29,286.

North Atlantic Drift One of the major ocean currents of the world, flowing NE across the Atlantic from the *Gulf Stream.

North Atlantic Treaty Organization (NATO) An alliance formed in 1949 by Belgium, Canada, Denmark, France, Iceland, Italy, Luxembourg, the Netherlands, Norway, Portugal, the UK, and the US; Greece and Turkey joined in 1952, West Germany in 1955, and Spain in 1982. It was formed during the *Cold War to protect the western world against possible Soviet aggression. All member states are bound to protect any member

against attack. The strategic areas of NATO are divided into three great commands covering the Atlantic, Europe, and the English Channel and North Sea. NATO also seeks to encourage economic and social cooperation among its member states. Its secretariat headquarters is in Brussels and its military headquarters near Mons.

North Borneo. *See* Sabah.

North Brabant (Dutch name: Noord-Brabant) A province in the S Netherlands, bordering on Belgium. Its fertile coastal lowlands were badly flooded in 1953; these produce wheat and sugar beet. Area: 1896 sq mi (4911 sq km). Population (1981 est): 2,071,885. Capital: 's Hertogenbosch.

North Cape (Norwegian name: Nordkapp) 71 11N 25 40E A promontory in Norway, on the island of Magerøy. It is the most northerly point in Europe.

North Carolina A state in SE US. It is bounded on the N by Virginia, on the E by the Atlantic Ocean, on the S by South Carolina and Georgia, and on the W by Tennessee. The extensive coastal plain stretches westward—from the indented coastline to the Piedmont Plateau and the Appalachian Mountains in the E. It is heavily populated and the leading industrial state in the South, producing textiles, furniture, and processed foods. It is the nation's major producer of tobacco and tobacco products. *History*: first visited by Giovanni da Verrazano (1524), the region was inhabited by Tuscarora, Catawaba, and Cherokee Indians. Sir Walter Raleigh tried and failed to establish the first British New World settlement there in the 1580s. With the colonization of the eastern seaboard, small farms gradually grew up, but settlement was hampered by political conflict with North Carolina's colonial proprietors from Virginia. Indian resistance also discouraged settlement. One of the 13 original colonies, it shares its early history with South Carolina. In 1713, North Carolina became a separate colony, and in 1729 it became a royal colony. At the time of the American Revolution it was the first colony to direct its delegates to vote for independence. Following the war, because of strong sentiments against a powerful central government, North Carolina did not ratify the US Constitution or become a state until 1789. The forced removal of the Cherokees (beginning in 1835) spurred expansion into the region. Although antislavery sentiments ran high, it supported the Confederate cause in the Civil War. Reconstruction marked the beginnings of the modern era; industry saw enormous growth and the traditional plantation system was replaced by farm tenancy. Expanded educational opportunities contributed to development, and following World War II industrial diversification and the arrival of hydroelectric power brought prosperity. North Carolina is a bellwether state, a forerunner in the area of social legislation and a major industrial force in the South. Area: 52,586 sq mi (136,197 sq km). Population (1980): 5,874,429. Capital: Raleigh.

North Dakota A state in the N central US. Minnesota lies to the E, South Dakota to the S, Montana to the W, and Canada to the N. It comprises three main physical regions: the Red River Valley along the E border, the Central Lowlands just W of this strip, and the Great Plains in the SW. The population is sparse, particularly in the W. Agriculture and mining are the two principal economic activities; its coal and oil reserves are among the country's largest and it is a major producer of wheat. The small manufacturing sector is growing, especially food processing. *History*: explored by Pierre de la Verendryé (1738) and the Lewis and Clark Expedition (1804–05), the area (except for a portion) formed part of the Louisiana Purchase (1803); the remainder was obtained from the British in 1818. Early attempts to settle were made by Scottish and Irish families at Pembina in 1812, but settlement was slow until the Indians were forcibly subdued in the 1860s. With the arrival of the railroads and the defeat of the Sioux chief Sitting Bull, the area was ripe for settlement. It formed part of the territory of Dakota from 1860 until 1889 when it was made a separate state. Large numbers of Europeans immigrated to the area in the late 1800s. Agrarian dissatisfaction and the emergence of the Populist Party laid the groundwork for numerous reforms. Subsequently drought, dust storms, and the Depression of the 1930s brought severe hardship, but North Dakota experienced recovery with World War II. The construction of air bases and missile sites in the 1960s boosted the local economy. Oil was discovered in 1951 and with the energy shortage of the 1970s, the state undertook efforts to develop further its own energy supplies. Area: 70,665 sq mi (183,022 sq km). Population (1980): 652,695. Capital: Bismarck.

Northeast Caucasian languages A group of about 25 languages of the NE region of the Caucasus, also called the Nakho-Dagestanian family. Chechen, the most important, is part of the Nakh subdivision. The Dagestanian subdivision may be further divided into the Avar-Ando-Dido languages of which Avar is the most important and the only one that is written; the Lakk-Dargwa languages; and the Lezgian languages. Most of these languages fall within the boundaries of the Dagestan ASSR.

North-East Frontier Agency. *See* Arunachal Pradesh.

Northeast Passage (Russian name: Severny Morskoy Put) The sea route along the N Eurasian coast, kept open in summer by Soviet icebreakers. It was first traversed by the Swedish explorer Niels Nordenskjöld (1878–79). *See also* Northwest Passage.

Northern Areas The northernmost districts administered by, although technically not part of, Pakistan, principally Baltistan, Hunza, and Gilgit.

Northern Ireland. *See* Ireland.

Northern Marianas. *See* Mariana Islands.

Northern Rhodesia. *See* Zambia.

NORTHERN TERRITORY *A waterhole on the Finke River at Glen Helen Gorge 100 mi (160 km) W of Alice Springs.*

Northern Territory An administrative division of N central Australia, bordering on the Timor and Arafura Seas. It consists chiefly of a plateau with Arnhem Land in the N (containing Australia's largest Aborigine reservation) and the Macdonnell Ranges in the S. SW of Alice Springs and close to the geographical center of the continent stands *Ayers Rock. The main agricultural activity is the rearing of beef cattle; these are transported in trains of trailers (road trains) along the highways, the chief means of transport. Minerals are important, especially iron ore, manganese, copper, gold, and bauxite. There are also large deposits of uranium, as yet unexploited, but possibly containing a quarter of all the world's known resources of high-grade ore. In 1978 the Northern Territory became an independent state, although the federal government retained control over uranium. Area: 519,770 sq mi (1,346,200 sq km). Population (1980 est): 121,300. Capital: Darwin.

Northern War, Great (1700–21) The war fought between Russia, Denmark, and Poland, on one side, and Sweden, on the other. *Charles XII of Sweden, whose Baltic supremacy was opposed by his neighbors, defeated Denmark, then Russia at Narva (1700), and Poland (1706). He was subsequently overcome by the Russians under Peter the Great (Poltava, 1709) and fled to the Turks, who defeated the Russians at Pruth River (1711). After returning to Sweden Charles suffered a series of setbacks and was forced to initiate peace negotiations. At the same time he continued hostilities in the course of which he died (1718). The war between Denmark, Poland, and Sweden was ended by the Treaties of Stockholm (1719–20). The Treaty of *Nystad (1721) between Russia and Sweden marked Russia's emergence as the major Baltic power.

North German Confederation (1867–71) An alliance of German states under Prussian leadership formed by Bismarck following victory in the Austro-Prussian War (1866). It formed the basis of the German Empire, proclaimed in 1871.

North Holland (Dutch name: Noord-Holland) A province in the W Netherlands, between the North Sea and the IJsselmeer. Much of it lies below sea level. The province contains major urban centers, including Amsterdam, and its industrial activities include shipbuilding, textiles, and motor vehicles. Its farms produce mainly dairy and livestock products. Area:

1124 sq mi (2912 sq km). Population (1981 est): 2,315,676. Capital: Haarlem.

North Island The most northerly of the two principal islands of New Zealand, separated from South Island by Cook Strait. It consists chiefly of a central volcanic plateau with fertile coastal and valley lowlands. Area: 44,281 sq mi (114,729 sq km). Population (1980 est): 2,289,300.

North Ossetian Autonomous Soviet Socialist Republic An administrative division in the S Soviet Union, in the RSFSR. The Ossetians are a Caucasian people, known for their wood and silver carving. The region has metal and oil deposits and industries include textiles and food processing. The main crops are grain, cotton, and grapes. Area: 3088 sq mi (8000 sq km). Population (1981 est): 601,000. Capital: Ordzhonikidze.

North Platte A river that rises in N central Colorado and flows N and then E through Wyoming into Nebraska where it meets the South Platte River at North Platte to become the Platte River. Numerous dam/reservoir systems along the river provide irrigation and flood control for the surrounding valleys. Length: 680 mi (1095 km).

North Rhine-Westphalia (German name: Nordrhein-Westfalen) A *Land* in W West Germany, bordering on the Netherlands and Belgium. It was formed in 1946. Rich in minerals, including coal, it contains the vast Ruhr industrial region and is one of the world's most densely populated areas. Its many industries include steel, textiles, and chemicals. Area: 13,147 sq mi (34,057 sq km). Population (1980 est): 17,040,700. Capital: Düsseldorf.

Northrop, John Howard (1891–) US biochemist, who isolated and purified various digestive enzymes and showed that they were all proteins. He received the 1946 Nobel Prize.

North Sea A section of the Atlantic Ocean in NW Europe, between the British Isles and the continent N of the Strait of Dover. The entire floor is part of the continental shelf, with an average depth of about 914 ft (300 m). It is fished for over 5% of the world's catch, consisting especially of cod, herring, and mackerel; recent exploitation of *North Sea oil and natural-gas finds have further increased its economic importance. Freak high tides have flooded large areas of coastal lowlands, especially in the Netherlands and E England.

North Sea oil The *oil deposits that were discovered under the North Sea in the 1960s. Exploration and development has been carried out by multinational companies from the US and Europe. The area is divided into UK, West German, Norwegian, Danish, and Dutch sectors. The UK has the largest of these. Discovered reserves in the North Sea contain an estimated 2.5 billion tons but exploration is still continuing and new oilfields are being developed.

North Star. *See* Polaris.

North Uist. *See* Uist.

Northumberland The northernmost county of England, bordering on Scotland and the North Sea. The main river, the Tyne, flows SE. There are outstanding Roman remains, notably Hadrian's Wall. The main agricultural activity is sheep farming. Area: 1944 sq mi (5033 sq km). Population (1981): 299,905. Administrative center: Newcastle-upon-Tyne.

Northumberland, John Dudley, Duke of (1502–53) English statesman, who was virtual ruler of England (1549–53) under Edward VI, a minor. In 1553 he married his son Guildford Dudley to Lady Jane *Grey, whom he persuaded the king to name as his heir. On Edward's death Jane was proclaimed queen but lack of support forced a surrender to Mary (I). Northumberland was executed.

Northumbria A kingdom of Anglo-Saxon England north of the Humber, formed in the 7th century by the union of the kingdoms of Deira and Bernicia. Northumbria became politically pre-eminent in England in the 7th century under *Edwin, Saint *Oswald, and *Oswin. Northumbrian scholarship was also unrivaled, boasting such great names as *Bede and *Alcuin. By 829, however, Northumbria had recognized the overlordship of Wessex and in the late 9th century its unity was destroyed by the Danes.

Northwest Caucasian languages A group of languages of the NW region of the Caucasus, also called the Abkhazo-Adyghian family. It includes Abkhaz, Abaza, Adyghian, Kabardian (Circassian), and Ubykh. All but Ubykh are written. A distinctive feature is the small number of vowel sounds and great number of consonants.

Northwest Company A Canadian fur-trading company, founded in 1783, that became a bitter rival of the *Hudson's Bay Company. Conflict between them ended in their forced merger in 1821.

North-West Frontier Province A province in NW Pakistan, SE of Afghanistan in the Himalayas and lower mountains. Its Pathan inhabitants mostly herd livestock or cultivate grains, fruit, sugar cane, and tobacco. There is little industry, but the province controls the strategic Khyber Pass to Afghanistan. Over the centuries each great power in the region has sought to control the province, but it has usually remained semiautonomous because of its rugged terrain and fierce inhabitants. Area: 28,773 sq mi (74,522 sq km). Population (1972): 8,402,000. Capital: Peshawar.

Northwest Ordinance (1787) US congressional ordinance that outlined government for territories carved out of the newly-created Northwest Territory and any future territories. Each territory would have a congressionally-appointed governor, secretary, and three judges. When a population of 5,000 males, eligible to vote, had been reached, the territory could elect a legislature and send one non-voting representative to the US House of Representatives. Statehood could be attained with a population of at least 60,000. A minimum of three and maximum of five states could be carved from the Northwest Territory and all rights, including freedom from slavery, would be accorded citizens of the territory.

Northwest Passage The sea route along the coast of North America, between the Atlantic and Pacific Oceans. It was first traversed by Roald Amundsen (1903–06) and since 1969 has been used for transporting Alaskan oil. *See also* Northeast Passage.

Northwest Territories A territory of N Canada, stretching from 60°N to the North Pole. It consists of the districts of *Franklin, *Keewatin, and *Mackenzie. The territory has never undergone much development, largely because of its harsh climate. One of the most sparsely populated areas in the world, two thirds of the people are Indians and Eskimos, who traditionally live nomadically by hunting, trapping, and fishing. The Eskimos are increasingly settling in larger communities around cooperatives and government institutions. Rich in mineral resources, the economy is dominated by the mining industry; pitchblende, silver zinc, lead, tungsten and gold are all extracted. At present, the territory's vast oil reserves are being explored. Area: 1,253,432 sq mi (3,246,389 sq km). Population (1978 est): 43,500. Capital: Yellowknife.

Northwest Territory Area established by Congress in 1787 and defined as W of Pennsylvania, N of the Ohio River to the Great Lakes, and E of the Mississippi River. The North-west Ordinances (1785; 1787) determined the method of land sale and government. Eventually, the states of Ohio (1803), Indiana (1816), Illinois (1848), Michigan (1837), Wisconsin (1848), and a small part of Minnesota (1858) evolved from the territory.

Norway, Kingdom of (Norwegian name: Norge) A country in N Europe occupying the W part of the Scandinavian Peninsula. It borders on the Arctic Ocean (N), the Norwegian Sea (W), and the Skagerrak (S). It is largely mountainous, reaching heights of almost 8000 ft (2500 m), with a heavily indented coastline. There are numerous glaciers and forests cover approximately one quarter of the country. The archipelago of Svalbard and Jan Meyen Island are also part of Norway together with the dependencies of Bouvet Island, Peter I Island, and Queen Maud Land. Norway is one of the most sparsely populated countries on the continent. *Economy*: abundant hydroelectric power has enabled Norway to develop as an industrial nation. Chemicals, engineering, shipbuilding, and food processing are all important while forestry is a major source of wealth, especially for the pulp and paper industry. Norway is one of the world's great fishing nations and fish is one of the principal exports. It also has one of the world's largest merchant fleets. Revenues from tourism are important. Minerals include iron ore, limestone, coal, copper, zinc, and lead. Heavy borrowing to finance the development of offshore oil and gas deposits (discovered 1968), which have proved to be considerably less than was first thought, has led to a balance-of-payments deficit. *History*: its early history was dominated by the Vikings. The many local chieftains were not subjected to a single ruler until the reign of Harold I Haarfager (died c. 930). Christianity was introduced in the 10th century and became established under Olaf II Haraldsson (reigned 1015–28). During the reign (1204–63) of Haakon IV Haakonsson Norway acquired Iceland and Greenland and in the 14th century, under Margaret, was united with Sweden and Denmark. Sweden broke free in 1523 but Norway remained under Danish domination until 1814, when it was united with Sweden under the Swedish crown, while maintaining internal self-government. Only in 1907 was full independence achieved. Norway declared its neutrality in both World Wars but from 1940 to 1944 was occupied by the Germans, who established a government under Quisling. Abandoning isolationism after World War II, Norway joined the UN (of which the Norwegian Trygve Lie was first secretary general) and NATO. In 1972 Norwegians rejected membership of the EEC in a referendum. In common with other Scandinavian countries Norway has a highly developed social-welfare system. Head of state: Olav V. Prime minister: Kaare Isaachsen Willoch. Official language: Norwegian. Official religion: Evangelical

Lutheran. Official currency: Krone of 100 oere. Area: 125,053 sq mi (323,886 sq km). Population (1983): 4,131,000. Capital and main port: Oslo.

Norwegian A North Germanic language of the West Scandinavian division, spoken in Norway. There are two distinct forms known as Dano-Norwegian (Bokmål or Riksmål) and New Norwegian (Nynorsk or Landsmål). Bokmål derives from written Danish, the language used during the union with Denmark (1397–1814). Nynorsk was created by the scholar Ivar Aasen (1813–96) to revive the tradition of Old Norwegian, which was closely related to *Old Norse speech. Bokmål is more widely used.

Norwegian Antarctic Territory The area in Antarctica claimed by Norway, lying S of latitude 60°S and between longitudes 20°W and 45°E. It consists of the end of Coats Land, Queen Maud Land, and islands. There have been many European, South African, and Soviet research stations along the mountainous coast.

Norwich 52 38N 1 18E A city in E England, on the Wensum River. In the late 16th century it became a major textile center. It has a Norman cathedral (1096) and keep, many medieval churches, and is the site of the University of East Anglia (1963). Industries include shoe manufacturing, electrical and other machinery, food and drink, chemicals, printing, and bookbinding. Population (1981): 122,270.

Norwich school A school of regional landscape painters active in Norwich, England, in the first half of the 19th century. Founded as the Norwich Society in 1803, it held regular exhibitions until 1834. Its leading members included *Cotman.

nose The organ of smell, which is also an entrance to the respiratory tract. The external nose, which projects from the face, has a framework of bone and cartilage and is divided into two nostrils by the nasal septum. It leads to the nasal cavity, which is lined by *mucous membrane, extends back to the pharynx and windpipe, and is connected to the air *sinuses of the skull. Hairs in the nostrils filter particles from inhaled air, which is further cleaned, warmed, and moistened in the nasal cavity. The membrane at the top of the nasal cavity contains olfactory cells, which are sensitive to different smells and are connected to the brain via the olfactory nerve.

Nostradamus (Michel de Notredame; 1503–66) French physician and astrologer, who became famous with his publication of *Centuries* (1555–58), in which he made a number of prophesies in the form of rhyming quatrains. Some of his prophecies, which are obscure and open to various interpretations, appeared to come true and Charles IX appointed him his physician on his accession (1560).

nothosaur A primitive marine reptile of the Jurassic period (200–135 million years ago). 0.98 in–20 ft (0.3–6 m) long, nothosaurs had a long neck and tail and long limbs partly modified into paddles. They fed on fish, which were gripped tightly with long sharp teeth.

notochord A flexible skeletal rod that runs along the length of the body in the embryos of all animals of the phylum Chordata (including vertebrates). In primitive chordates, such as the lancelets and lampreys, the notochord persists throughout life as the main axial support, but in vertebrates it is incorporated into the backbone as the embryo develops.

Notoungulata An extinct order of mammals whose remains have been found mainly in South America. Notoungulates ranged from small rabbit-like forms to the massive *Toxodon*, which stood over 7 ft (2 m) high at the shoulder. They had three-toed feet, with either claws or hooves, and lived from the Paleocene epoch to the Pleistocene epoch (about 70 million to 2.5 million years ago).

Notre-Dame de Paris The gothic cathedral built (1163–1345) on the Île de la Cité, Paris, to replace two earlier churches. The nave, choir, and west front were completed by 1204; the innovatory flying buttresses and the great rose windows, which still retain their 13th-century stained glass, are notable features. Damaged during the French Revolution, Notre-Dame was saved from demolition and redecorated for Napoleon's coronation (1804) and was subsequently fully restored (1845–64) by *Viollet-le-Duc.

Nottingham 52 58N 1 10W A city in N central England, the administrative center of Nottinghamshire on the River Trent. Charles I raised his standard here in 1642 at the outbreak of the Civil War. Notable buildings include the castle (built by William the Conqueror and restored in 1878). Nottingham's chief industries are hosiery, bicycles, cigarettes, pharmaceuticals, engineering, brewing, and printing. The university dates from 1948. Population (1981): 271,080.

Nottinghamshire A county in the East Midlands of England. It consists mainly of lowlands, crossed by the Trent River, with the Pennine uplands in the W and the remnants of Sherwood Forest (famous for its associations with the Robin Hood legend) in the SW. Agriculture is important with arable and dairy farming, orchards, and market gardening. It contains important coalfields. Gypsum, limestone, and gravel are also extracted. The main industrial town is Nottingham. Area: 2164 sq km (835 sq mi). Population (1981): 982,631. Administrative center: Nottingham.

Nouakchott 18 09N 15 58W The capital of Mauritania, in the W near the Atlantic coast. A small village until the 1950s, it was developed as the capital after independence in 1960. Its modern port was situated 4 mi (6.4 km) from the city. Population (1977 est): 70,000.

Nouméa 22 16S 166 26E The capital of New Caledonia. A port, it exports nickel, chrome, manganese, and iron. Population (1976): 74,335.

nouveau roman An experimental type of the novel pioneered by French writers in the 1950s. The leading exponents include Nathalie *Sarraute, Alain *Robbe-Grillet, and Michel *Butor. Reacting against traditional realistic concepts of character and narrative, their works are characterized by a distrust of psychological motives, detailed descriptions of external reality, and the avoidance of any kind of value judgment.

Nouvelle Vague. *See* New Wave.

nova A star that suddenly increases in brightness by perhaps 10,000 times or more and then fades over months or years, usually to its original brightness. Novae all appear to occur in binary systems in which there is (usually) a *white dwarf with a large close companion star. Gaseous material flowing from the large star is thought to accumulate on the white dwarf and trigger the immense nova eruption. Novae are considered *variable stars.

Novalis (Friedrich Leopold, Freiherr von Hardenberg; 1772–1801) German Romantic poet and writer. After studying law, he became an auditor. The death of his fiancée (1797) inspired his celebration of death and love in the *Hymnen an die Nacht* (1800); he himself died prematurely of tuberculosis. His unfinished novel *Heinrich von Ofterdingen* (1802) typifies the Romantic belief in the transforming power of art.

Nova Lisboa. *See* Huambo.

Novara 45 27N 08 37E A city in NW Italy, in Piedmont. It has several notable buildings, including a 13th-century town hall. As well as a rice-milling industry, there are textile and chemical plants. Population (1980 est): 102,039.

Nova Scotia A province of E Canada. It consists of a peninsula protruding into the Atlantic Ocean and *Cape Breton Island. Mostly rolling hills and valleys, Nova Scotia was originally covered by mixed forest but has been largely replanted with conifers. Economic growth is restricted by limited resources and the distance from important markets. Coal output is down significantly, but Nova Scotia also mines gypsum, salt, and copper. Agriculture includes dairying, mixed farming, livestock, and fruit. Iron and steel, pulp and paper, fishing, and tourism are also economically important. *History*: from the first colonization (1605), Britain and France contested the area, Britain eventually gaining possession (confirmed by the Treaty of Paris in 1763). Largely settled by Scots, Nova Scotia prospered in the 19th-century age of sail. But since joining Canada (1867), its economy has lagged. Area: 20,402 sq mi (52,841 sq km). Population (1981 est): 847,442. Capital: Halifax.

Novaya Zemlya A Soviet archipelago off the N coast, between the Barents and the Kara Seas. It is a continuation of the Ural Mountains and consists almost entirely of two islands separated by a narrow strait. There is no permanent population, and the N island is always icebound. Total area: about 32,040 sq mi (83,000 sq km).

novel An extended work of prose fiction dealing with the interaction of characters in a real or imagined setting. The term derives from Italian *novella*, meaning a short tale or anecdote. Latin forerunners of the novel are the picaresque *Satyricon* of Petronius (1st century AD) and *The Golden Ass* by Apuleius (2nd century AD). Cervantes' *Don Quixote* (1605) is considered the most important early novel. In England, a particular combination of social, economic, and literary conditions led to the development of the novel in the 18th century. The first notable English novelists included *Richardson, *Fielding, and *Defoe. The novels of the great 19th-century writers, notably *Melville and *Twain in the US, *Dickens in England, *Tolstoy and *Dostoievsky in Russia, and *Balzac and *Flaubert in France, together constitute one of the great achievements of world literature. In the 20th century the novel has been strongly influenced by developments in psychology and philosophy, and the various proliferating categories of novel—such as *science fiction, the *detective story, and the *nouveau roman—appeal to all levels of readership. *See also* picaresque novel.

Novello, Ivor (David Ivor Davies; 1893–1951) British composer, dramatist, and actor. He composed the World War I song "Keep the Home

Fires Burning," and is best known for his series of romantic musicals including *Careless Rapture* (1936) and *The Dancing Years* (1939).

November Eleventh month of the year. Derived from *novem*, which means nine in Latin, it was the ninth month in the ancient Roman calendar. It has 30 days. The zodiac signs for November are Scorpio and Sagittarius; the flower is the chrysanthemum, and the birthstone is the topaz. In the US, Veterans Day is November 11, and Thanksgiving is celebrated on the fourth Thursday of the month.

November Insurrection. *See* Congress Kingdom of Poland.

Novgorod 58 30N 31 20E A city in the Soviet Union, in the NW RSFSR on the Volkhov River. It has varied manufacturing industries and is a famous tourist center, although many of its magnificent buildings, including the St Sofia Cathedral (1045–50), were badly damaged during World War II. *History*: it is one of Russia's oldest towns, dating at least to the 9th century, and was a notable trading center in the middle ages. Self-governing from 1019, it was forced to acknowledge Tatar overrule in the 13th century and that of Moscow in the 15th century. It was held by the Swedes from 1611 to 1619 and subsequently declined. Population (1981 est): 198,000.

Novi Sad 45 15N 19 15E A port in N central Yugoslavia, in Serbia on the Danube River. It is an important center of Serbian culture with a university (1960). Population (1971): 141,375.

Novokuznetsk 53 45N 87 12E A city in the Soviet Union, in the W central RSFSR. Kuznetsk, a village on the right bank of the Tom River, was founded in 1617 and the industrial town of Stalinsk was developed on the opposite bank in the 1930s. The conurbation was named Novokuznetsk in 1961. It has two large iron plants and is the center of a coalmining region. Population (1981 est): 551,000.

Novorossiisk 44 44N 37 46E A port in the Soviet Union, in the SW RSFSR on the Black Sea. It is a naval base with a shipbuilding industry and produces large quantities of cement. Population (1981 est): 165,000.

Novosibirsk 55 04N 83 05E A city in the Soviet Union, in the W central RSFSR on the Ob River and the Trans-Siberian Railroad. The most important economic center in Siberia, it has machine-building, textile, chemical, and metallurgical industries. Nearby is the Academic Community (Akademgorodk), a complex of science research institutes. Population (1981 est): 1,343,000.

Novotný, Antonín (1904–75) Czechoslovak statesman. One of the founding members of the Czechoslovak Communist Party (1921), he was first secretary of the Party (1953–68) and president of Czechoslovakia (1957–68). He was forced to resign in the face of the reform movement led by *Dubček, after whose fall Novotný was reinstated as a Party member.

Noyes, Alfred (1880–1958) British poet. He wrote patriotic verse about the sea and several epic narrative poems including *Drake* (1906–08) and *The Torchbearers* (1922–30). His traditional views on literature and politics were expressed in his literary criticism and his autobiography, *Two Worlds for Memory* (1953).

Nu, U (*or* Thakin Nu; 1907–) Burmese statesman; prime minister (1948–56, 1957–58, 1960–62). A leading nationalist from the 1930s, he became prime minister on the achievement of independence. He sought to establish parliamentary democracy but when his Anti-Fascist People's Freedom League split in 1958 he was forced by *Ne Win to resign. He was restored, together with parliamentary government, in 1960 but was again deposed in 1962 and in 1966 withdrew into exile. He returned to Burma in 1980.

Nubia A region of NE Africa, in the Nile valley, approximately between Aswan (Egypt) and Khartoum (Sudan). Much of Nubia is now drowned by Lake Nasser. From about 2000 BC the Egyptians gradually occupied Nubia, which they called Cush. Trade, especially in gold, flourished. By the 15th century BC Nubia had an Egyptian viceroy. As Egyptian power waned, Nubian kings, based at Napata and *Meroë, became influential, even dominating Egypt itself (c. 730–670). Their independent nation, culture, and language lasted until the 4th century AD.

Nubian Desert A desert in the NE Sudan, between the Nile River and the Red Sea. It consists of a sandstone plateau with peaks of up to 7411 ft (2259 m) near the coast. Area: about 154,408 sq mi (400,000 sq km).

NUCLEAR ENERGY

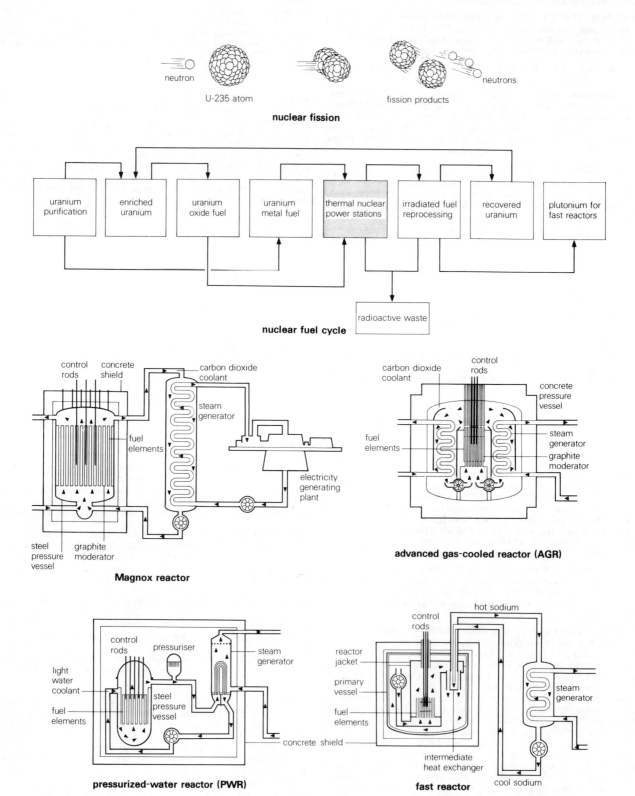

nuclear fission

nuclear fuel cycle

Magnox reactor

advanced gas-cooled reactor (AGR)

pressurized-water reactor (PWR)

fast reactor

NUCLEAR ENERGY   *Natural uranium metal fuel clad in Magnox (magnesium alloy) is used in Magnox thermal reactors. Enriched uranium dioxide pellets clad in steel are used in AGR and PWR fuel elements. Plutonium for fast reactors and recycled enriched uranium is obtained by reprocessing spent fuel from thermal reactors. The electricity generating plant is similar with all reactor types.*

nuclear energy The energy evolved by nuclear fission or nuclear fusion. The energy is liberated in fission when a heavy atomic nucleus, such as uranium, splits into two or more parts, the total mass of the parts being less than the mass of the original nucleus. This difference in mass is equivalent to the *binding energy of the nucleus and most of it is converted into kinetic energy (i.e. the increased velocity with which the parts move) according to Einstein's law, $E = mc^2$. In a fusion reaction, two light nuclei, such as hydrogen or deuterium, combine to form a stable nucleus, such as helium; as the nucleus formed is lighter than the sum of the component nuclei, again energy is released in accordance with Einstein's law.

In the case of fission, when a nucleus of uranium-235 atom is struck by a neutron, a U-236 nucleus is formed, which immediately splits into two roughly equal parts, two or three neutrons being liberated at the same time. As these neutrons can then cause further fissions, a chain reaction builds up and a lump of U-235 will disintegrate almost instantaneously with enormous explosive power, provided that it is in excess of the critical mass (see nuclear weapons).

In nuclear power stations the fission reaction is harnessed to produce heat at a controlled rate (to raise steam to drive a turbine) in one of two ways. Both use natural uranium, which contains only 0.7% of the fissionable U-235 isotope, nearly all of the rest being the isotope U-238. The U-238 isotope absorbs the fast-moving neutrons emitted by the fission of U-235 and prevents a chain reaction from occurring in natural uranium. There are, however, two ways of producing a chain reaction. One is to use a moderator to slow down the fast neutrons so that they are not absorbed by U-238 nuclei (see thermal reactor). The other is to enrich the natural uranium with extra quantities of U-235 (or plutonium-239) so that there are sufficient neutrons to sustain the chain reaction in spite of absorption by U-238 (see fast reactor). All present commercial reactors are thermal, although the fast reactor is under development.

The fusion process is the basis of the hydrogen bomb (see nuclear weapons) and the □thermonuclear reactor, which is unlikely to be a source of energy until the 21st century.

The importance of nuclear energy is that it will almost certainly be increasingly needed to supply world energy requirements as reserves of fossil fuels diminish. It is also important as a source of energy to power submarines, a very small quantity of nuclear fuel providing a very large amount of energy—about 7×10^{13} joules per kilogram, compared to about 4×10^7 J/kg for coal.□p. 886.

nuclear fission. See fast reactor; nuclear energy; nuclear weapons; thermal reactor.

nuclear fusion. See nuclear energy; nuclear weapons; thermonuclear reactor.

nuclear magnetic resonance (NMR) An effect observed when an atomic nucleus is exposed to radio waves in the presence of a magnetic field. A strong magnetic field causes the magnetic moment of the nucleus to precess around the direction of the field, only certain orientations being allowed by quantum theory. A transition from one orientation to another involves the absorption or emission of a photon, the frequency of which is equal to the precessional frequency. With magnetic field strengths customarily used the radiation is in the radio-frequency band. If radio-frequency radiation is supplied to the sample from one coil and is detected by another coil, while the magnetic field strength is slowly changed, radiation is absorbed at certain field values, which correspond to the frequency difference between orientations. An NMR spectrum consists of a graph of field strength against detector response. This provides information about the structure of molecules and the positions of electrons within them, as the orbital electrons shield the nucleus and cause them to resonate at different field strengths.

nuclear reactor A device for producing *nuclear energy in a usable form. See fast reactor; thermal reactor; thermonuclear reactor.

Nuclear Regulatory Commission (NCR) US agency that licenses and regulates the uses of nuclear energy to protect public health and safety and the environment. It regulates the building and operating of nuclear reactors and the ownership and use of nuclear materials. Inspections after licensing are routinely carried out by the commission to ensure adherence to safety rules. Esablished in 1974, it took over functions formerly assigned to the Atomic Energy Commission.

Nuclear Test-Ban Treaty (1963) A treaty banning nuclear testing by its signatories on the ground, in the atmosphere, in space, and under water. The signatories were the US, the Soviet Union, and the UK; many other countries agreed to adhere to the treaty. It made no attempt to limit nuclear stockpiling and therefore was rejected as ineffectual by France and China. See also disarmament.

nuclear weapons Missiles, bombs, shells, or land mines that use fission or fusion of nuclear material (see nuclear energy) yielding enormous quantities of heat, light, blast, and radiation. The first **atomic bomb** (or fission bomb), manufactured by the US in World War II, was dropped on Hiroshima in 1945. It consisted of two small masses of uranium-235 forced together by a chemical explosion to form a supercritical mass, in which an uncontrolled chain reaction occurred. Below the critical mass (estimated at between 35–44 lb [16 and 20 kg]) a chain reaction does not occur, as too many neutrons escape from the surface. The bomb had an explosive power equivalent to 20,000 tons of TNT. Later models used plutonium-239 to even greater effect.

The **hydrogen bomb** (fusion bomb or thermonuclear bomb) consists of an atom bomb surrounded by a layer of hydrogenous material, such as lithium deuteride. The atom bomb creates the necessary temperature (about 180,000,000°F [100,000,000°C]) needed to ignite the fusion reaction (see thermonuclear reactor). Hydrogen bombs have an explosive power measured in tens of megatons (millions of tons) of TNT. The first hydrogen bomb was exploded by US scientists on Eniwetok Atoll in 1952 and although it has never been used in war, hydrogen bombs have been tested by the Soviet Union, Britain, France, and China. Further testing was prohibited by the *Nuclear Test-Ban Treaty of 1963.

The **neutron bomb** (or enhanced radiation bomb) is a nuclear weapon designed to maximize neutron radiation. It is lethal to all forms of life but, having reduced blast, leaves buildings, etc., relatively undamaged.

nucleic acids Organic compounds, found in the cells of all living organisms, that consist of a mixure of nitrogenous bases (purines and pyrimidines), phosphoric acid, and a pentose sugar. The sugar is ribose in the ribonucleic acids (see RNA) and deoxyribose in the deoxyribonucleic acids (see DNA). Nucleic acids store genetic information in living organisms and interpret that information in protein synthesis. See also nucleoprotein.

nucleolus A small dense body, one or more of which can be seen within the *nucleus of a nondividing cell. It contains RNA and protein and is involved in the synthesis of *ribosomes.

nucleon A collective name for a proton or neutron. See also mass number.

nucleoprotein A compound consisting of a *nucleic acid associated with one or more proteins. The nucleoprotein of cell nuclei—the chromosomes—consists of DNA and proteins, mainly histones; cytoplasmic nucleoproteins—the *ribosomes—are ribonucleoproteins comprising some 60% protein and 40% RNA. *Viruses also consist of nucleoprotein.

nucleus (biology) A large granular component of nearly all □cells. It is usually spherical or ovoid in shape and is surrounded by a nuclear membrane, which is perforated with pores to allow exchange of materials between the nucleus and cytoplasm. The nucleus contains the *chromosomes, made up of the hereditary material (DNA), and is therefore essential for the control and regulation of cellular activities, such as growth and metabolism. During cell division the chromosomes are involved in the transfer of hereditary information (see meiosis; mitosis).

nucleus (physics) The central core of the atom (see atomic theory) discovered by Rutherford in 1911. All nuclei consist of protons and neutrons (jointly called nucleons), except for hydrogen, which consists of a single proton. The constituent nucleons are held together by the *strong interaction, which at the minute distances within the nucleus (of the order 10^{-15} m) is some one hundred times stronger than the electromagnetic interaction between protons. The number of protons in the nucleus determines its charge and atomic number; the number of neutrons (in addition to the number of protons) determines the mass number and the isotope. **Nuclear physics** is the study of the structure and reactions of the nucleus. See also particle physics.

Nuevo Laredo 27 30N 99 30W A city in N Mexico, on the Rio Grande. It is an important point of entry from Mexico into the US. Population (1978 est): 214,161.

Nu Jiang. See Salween River.

Nuku'alofa 21 09S 175 14W The capital of Tonga in the S Pacific, in N Tongatabu. It is the site of the Royal Palace (1865–67) and Royal Tombs. Copra and bananas are exported. Population (1976): 18,396.

Nukus 42 28N 59 07E A city in the S Soviet Union, the capital of the Kara-Kalpak ASSR in the Uzbeck SSR on the Amu Darya River. Its industries include food processing. Population (1981 est): 113,400.

Nullarbor Plain A plain of SW South Australia and SE Western Australia, bordering on the Great Australian Bight. It consists of a treeless arid plateau with extensive limestone areas and is crossed by the Trans-Australian Railway. Area: 100,000 sq mi (260,000 sq km).

NUMBAT *This marsupial is well adapted for feeding on ants and termites, having a long sticky tongue, many small teeth, and powerful claws for digging up nests.*

numbat A rat-sized *marsupial, *Myrmecobius fasciatus*, of open eucalyptus woods in SW Australia, also called marsupial (*or* banded) anteater. It is slender and rust-colored, with white stripes across the back and a long tail, and it feeds on ants and termites with its long sticky tongue. Numbats have no pouch. Family: *Dasyuridae*.

numbers Mathematical symbols used to denote quantity. The natural numbers, 1, 2, 3, 4, 5 . . . , etc., were developed first by the Hindus and Arabs for simple counting. Subtraction led to negative numbers and to zero, which together with natural numbers make up the set of integers . . . –3, –2, –1, 0, 1, ... Division of whole numbers results in fractions or rational numbers. Some numbers, such as $\sqrt{2}$, cannot be expressed as the ratio of two integers. These are called irrational numbers and they occur as the solutions to simple algebraic equations. They can be calculated to any required accuracy but cannot be written as exact values. Other numbers, called transcendental numbers, do not come from algebraic relationships. Some of these occur as basic properties of space, for example π, the ratio of a circumference of a circle to its diameter. Real numbers include all rational and irrational numbers. The equation $x^2 = -1$ can have no real solution for x, since the square of any number is positive. The imaginary number, $i = \sqrt{-1}$, was introduced to overcome this problem. *See* complex numbers; number theory.

Numbers The fourth book of the Old Testament, attributed to Moses. It derives its name from the two records of a census that it mentions. The narrative covers the Israelites' journey from Mt Sinai to the borders of Canaan and gives the reasons for their failure to enter Canaan. It recounts the subsequent 40 years wandering in the wilderness and includes miscellaneous laws relevant to the eventual occupation of the Promised Land.

number theory The study of the properties of *numbers. It includes various theorems about *prime numbers, many of which are unproved but apparently true, and the study of Diophantine equations (named for *Diophantus of Alexandria), i.e. equations that have only integer solutions. *Fermat's last theorem deals with the solution of one of these equations and is a famous unproved theorem. Although number theory has existed for thousands of years, its development has been continuous and it now includes analytic number theory, originated by *Euler in 1742; geometric number theory, which uses such geometrical methods of analysis as Cartesian coordinates (*see* coordinate systems), *vectors, and *matrices; and probabilistic number theory, based on *probability theory.

Numidia An ancient kingdom of N Africa, W of *Carthage. Its *Berber population was nomadic until Masinissa (c. 240–149 BC), Rome's ally during the second and third *Punic Wars, promoted agriculture and urbaniza-

tion. After supporting Pompey against Julius Caesar (46 BC), Numidia lost its monarchy and became part of the Roman province of Africa.

numismatics (*or* coin collecting) Collecting and studying coins, medals, or banknotes as a hobby or as a form of historical research. Collecting Greek and Roman coins became popular among aristocrats in Renaissance Italy, although collections then often included copies. During the 19th century numismatics became popular among a wider public; catalogues were produced and societies formed. Museums are now the greatest collectors, while private collectors usually specialize in one field. Coins in good condition are a form of investment, the best being "proof" coins, struck especially for sale to collectors.

Nummulites A genus of protozoan animals, sometimes called money fossils, that was abundant during the Eocene epoch (about 54–38 million years ago) although only one species has survived. Some limestones are almost entirely composed of their shells, which were disk-shaped and biconvex. Order: *Foraminifera*.

nunatak A rock peak protruding above the surface of an ice sheet. Nunataks occur in Greenland, the word originating from the Eskimo language.

Nuneaton 52 32N 1 28W A city in central England, in Warwickshire. Besides its coalmining industry, Nuneaton manufactures textiles, cardboard boxes, and bricks. Its name refers to the 12th-century Benedictine nunnery, now in ruins. Population (1981): 71,530.

Nuremberg (German name: Nürnberg) 49 27N 11 05E A city in SE West Germany, in Bavaria on the Pegnitz River. It was severely bombed during World War II because of its engine industry and is now a major center of the metalworking and electrical industries. It shares a university with Erlangen. *History*: a medieval trading center, it became the center of the German Renaissance, when the mastersingers' contests were held here. It was the site of the Nazi Party congresses (1933–38) and the war-crime trials following World War II. It is the birthplace of Albrecht Dürer and Hans Sachs. Population (1980 est): 483,900.

Nuremberg Trials (1945–46) The trials of *Nazi criminals after World War II. An international military court was set up by the Allied Powers in Nuremberg to try Nazi individuals or groups who had violated the rules of war or committed crimes against humanity, such as the mass murders of Jews in *concentration camps. 12 men were sentenced to hang (including Göring, who committed suicide before the sentence could be carried out, Ribbentrop, Frank, Streicher, and Jodl) and six others were imprisoned for various terms (including Hess, who still remains in Spandau). The trials of the war criminals created precedents, chiefly that war crimes are the responsibility not merely of the state but also of the individual.

Nureyev, Rudolf (1938–) Russian ballet dancer. He danced with the Leningrad Kirov Ballet from 1958 until 1961, when he defected from Russia. In 1962 he joined the Royal Ballet, where he frequently partnered Margot *Fonteyn in such ballets as *Giselle* and *Swan Lake*. In 1977 he starred in the film *Valentino*. He became an Austrian citizen in 1982.

Nurhachi (1559–1626) Manchu chieftain, who founded the Qing dynasty of China. He unified the Juchen tribes of Manchuria to found the Manchu state. He organized all his subjects under the *Banner System, creating a powerful base from which his successors conquered all China.

Nurmi, Paavo Johannes (1897–1973) Finnish middle-distance and long-distance runner. He broke over 20 world records and won 12 Olympic medals, 9 gold and 3 silver. He was Olympic 10,000 meters champion in 1920 and 1928 and in 1924 won both the 1500 meters and the 5000 meters. He was in the habit of running carrying a stopwatch.

nursery rhymes Traditional verses said or sung to small children. They are usually for amusement only, although some, such as counting rhymes, are also instructional. They vary greatly in age and origin: some probably originate in ancient folklore, while others were first composed as popular ballads in the 19th century. The earliest known collection, *Tommy Thumb's Song Book* (1744), includes such perennial favorites as "Sing a Song of Sixpence" and "Who Killed Cock Robin?".

nurse shark A *shark, *Ginglymostoma cirratum*, that occurs in warm shallow waters of the Atlantic Ocean. Yellow-brown or gray-brown and up to 14 ft (4.2 m) long, it is considered dangerous to man only when provoked. Live young are born. Family: *Orectolobidae*.

nursing The medical specialty concerned with the care of the sick. Nursing originated in the religious orders, becoming increasingly secularized in Protestant countries after the Reformation; the standards of professional nursing were established by Florence *Nightingale after her work in the Crimea. Nurses are responsible for the day-to-day welfare of patients and for carrying out routine medical and surgical procedures under the supervision of a doctor. Apart from nursing in hospitals, the profession includes the work of nurse-midwives, home and school nurses, public health nurses, nurse practitioners, and physicians' assistants.

Nusa Tenggara (former name: Lesser *Sunda Islands) A volcanic Indonesian island group E of Java, the chief islands being Bali, Lombok, Sumbawa, Sumba, Flores, and Timor. Area: 28,241 sq mi (73,144 sq km). Population (1971): 7,706,561.

nut Loosely, any edible nonsucculent fruit, including the peanut and brazil nut. Botanically, a nut is a large dry fruit containing a single seed that is not released from the fruit at maturity. An example is the chestnut.

nutcracker A songbird of the genus *Nucifraga* found in coniferous forests of E Europe and Asia. The nutcracker (*caryocatactes*) is dark brown speckled with white, about 13 in (32 cm) long, and cracks open pine cones with its sharp bill to extract the seeds. Clark's nutcracker (*N. columbianus*) is gray with a black tail and wings patched with white. Family: *Corvidae* (crows, jays, magpies).

nuthatch A small stocky bird belonging to a family (*Sittidae*: 30 species) occurring everywhere except South America and New Zealand. Nuthatches have long straight bills, for hammering open nuts, and long-clawed toes, for running up and down tree trunks in search of insects. The European nuthatch (*Sitta europaea*), about 5.5 in (14 cm) long, has a blue-gray upper plumage with paler underparts and a black eyestripe.

nutmeg A fragrant tropical evergreen tree, *Myristica fragrans*, native to Indonesia but widely cultivated in SE Asia and the West Indies. Growing to 65 ft (20 m) high, it has oval pointed leaves and tiny male and female flowers borne on separate trees. The yellow fleshy fruit, about 1.2 in (3 cm) across, splits when ripe to expose the seed, which has a red fleshy covering (aril). The dried aril (mace) and whole or ground seeds (nutmeg) are used as spices. Family: *Myristicaceae*.

nutria. *See* coypu.

nux vomica A poisonous evergreen tree, *Strychnos nux-vomica*, also called the koochla tree, native to lowlands of Burma and India. It has simple leaves and clusters of tubular flowers, each with five spreading lobes. The seeds of the orange-like fruits contain the highly poisonous substances strychnine and curare. Family: *Strychnaceae*.

Nuzi An ancient *Hurrian city SW of Kirkuk (N Iraq). Nuzi flourished in the 15th century BC before being absorbed into the Assyrian Empire. Excavations here in the 1920s revealed a prosperous trading center with archives detailing legal, commercial, and military activities.

nyala An antelope, *Tragelaphus angasi*, of SW Africa. About 40 in (100 cm) high at the shoulder, nyalas are shy and nocturnal, inhabiting dense undergrowth, and have spiral-shaped horns and a grayish-brown coat with vertical white stripes on the flanks. The mountain nyala (*T. buxtoni*) lives in mountainous regions of S Ethiopia.

Nyasa, Lake. *See* Malawi, Lake.

Nyasaland. *See* Malawi, Republic of.

Nyeman River. *See* Neman River.

Nyerere, Julius (Kambarage) (1922–) Tanzanian statesman; president (1962–). Educated at Makerere College (Uganda) and Edinburgh University, in 1954 Nyerere formed the Tanganyika African National Union, which led the fight for independence (achieved in 1960). He became chief minister (1960), prime minister (1961), and then president of Tanganyika, which was renamed Tanzania in 1964 after union with Zanzibar.

Nyerere, who defends the one-party state as being more appropriate for a developing country, is a prominent advocate of African unity. Under his leadership Tanzania was instrumental in the overthrow of Amin in Uganda in 1979.

Nyköping 58 45N 17 03E A seaport in E Sweden, on the Baltic coast. A center of commerce and industry, its manufactures include machinery and textiles. Population (1978 est): 64,099.

nylon A synthetic material with a translucent creamy white appearance, widely used both in fiber form and in solid blocks because of its lightness, toughness, and elasticity. It is made by *polymerization of diamine with *fatty acid or by polymerizing a single monomer, in both cases to form a polyamide. Nylon is used to make small engineering components, such as bearings and gears, because it is hard wearing and easy to machine. It is also spun and woven into fabrics for clothing, etc., and can be colored with pigments. Introduced commercially in 1938, nylon was the first truly synthetic fiber.

nymph A stage in the life cycle of insects that show incomplete *metamorphosis, including dragonflies, grasshoppers, and bugs. The egg hatches into a nymph, which undergoes a series of molts to form a line of nymphs that show increasing similarity to the adult.

nymphalid butterfly A butterfly belonging to the widely distributed family *Nymphalidae*, also called brush-footed butterfly. Nymphalids are characterized by small hairy forelegs, useless for walking. Many, including the migratory *red admiral and *painted lady, are strong fast fliers. The adults are generally orange or brown with black markings and the caterpillars are commonly brown or black and covered with branched spines.

Nymphenburg porcelain Porcelain produced at a factory established (1753) near Munich. It is famed for rococo figures designed by F. A. Bustelli (1723–64). They include Italian comedy, chinoiserie, and mythological models. After Bustelli died table wares, particularly tea services, were made, often based on Meissen. The factory still copies its early models.

nymphs In Greek mythology, female spirits of nature, often portrayed as youthful and amorous dancers or musicians. They were long lived, though not immortal, and usually benevolent. The several classes of nymphs associated with particular natural phenomena include the *dryads, the *naiads, and the *nereids.

Nyoro A Bantu-speaking people of the western lakes region of Uganda. They were traditionally divided into three distinct groups: the Bito clan from whom the hereditary paramount chief (Mukama) always came, the aristocratic Huma pastoralists, and the subordinate Iru cultivators. The Bito and Huma are thought to have originally come from the north as conquering invaders. They are a patrilineal people who live in small scattered settlements.

Nysa River. *See* Neisse River.

Nystad, Treaty of (1721) The peace treaty between Russia and Sweden that concluded the Great *Northern War. Sweden was obliged to cede large tracts of territory, including Livonia, and Russia gained its long-coveted access to the Baltic Sea, thus becoming a European power.

Nyx (Latin name: Nox) A Greek goddess, the personification of night. She was the daughter of Chaos and her offspring included Thanatos (Death), Hypnos (Sleep), the *Fates, and *Nemesis. She lived in Tartarus, from which she emerged as Hemera, the goddess of day.

O

Oahu An island in Hawaii, the most populous and the administrative center. The Japanese attack on *Pearl Harbor (1941) was decisive in bringing the US into World War II. Area: 608 sq mi (1584 sq km). Population (1970): 761,964. Chief town: Honolulu.

oak A deciduous or evergreen □tree or shrub of the genus *Quercus* (over 800 species), found in N temperate and subtropical regions. The simple leaves usually have lobed or toothed margins and the yellow male catkins and tiny green female flowers are borne on the same tree. The fruit—an acorn—is a hard oval nut partly enclosed by a round cup. Often 98–131 ft (30–40 m) high, many species are important timber trees, especially the common or pedunculate oak (*Q. robur*) and the *durmast oak (both Eurasian) and the North American white oak (*Q. alba*) and live oaks. Several are planted for ornament, including the Eurasian Turkey oak (*Q. cerris*), the North American red oak (*Q. rubra*), which has a red autumn foliage, and the Mediterranean *holm oak. The cork oak (*Q. suber*) is the main commercial source of *cork. Family: *Fagaceae*.

Oakland 37 50N 122 15W A port in California, on San Francisco Bay and connected with San Francisco by the San Francisco–Oakland Bay Bridge (1936). Oakland's industries include chemicals and shipbuilding. Population (1980): 339,288.

Oakley, Annie (Phoebe Anne Oakley Mozee; 1860–1926) US sharpshooter. From 1885 she and her husband, Frank Butler, performed daring acts of marksmanship in Buffalo Bill's Wild West Show. A musical, *Annie Get Your Gun* (1948) with music by Irving Berlin, was based on her life.

oak moss An edible *lichen, *Evernia prunastri*, found in mountainous regions of the N hemisphere. It has a pale greenish-gray body, 1.2–3.1 in (3–8 cm) long, with numerous pointed branches. Its heavy fragrance makes it of value in perfumery and it is used in the preparation of drugs for treating wounds and infections.

Oak Ridge 36 02N 84 12W A city in Tennessee. It contains the Oak Ridge National Laboratory (1943) for nuclear research. Population (1980): 27,662.

Oakville 43 27N 79 41W A city in central Canada, in S Ontario. A dormitory suburb of Toronto, it houses a major motor-vehicle factory and produces plastics, paints, and electrical appliances. Population (1976): 68,950.

oarfish A *ribbonfish of the genus *Regalecus*, especially *R. glesne*, found in all seas. It has a long silvery ribbon-like body, up to 30 ft (9 m) long, a long red dorsal fin that extends forward to form a crest, long red oarlike pelvic fins situated near the pectoral fins, and no anal or tail fins. □oceans.

OAS. *See* Organisation de l'Armée secrète; Organization of American States.

oasis An area within a desert where water is available for vegetation and human use. It may consist of a single small spring around which palms grow or be an extensive area where the water table is at or near the ground surface.

Oates, Joyce Carol (1938–) US writer. She writes about violence and of mental and economic poverty. Her collections of short stories include *By the North Gate* (1963), *Wheel of Love* (1970), and *Last Days* (1984). Among her novels are *Expensive People* (1968), *Them* (1969), *Wonderland* (1971), *The Assassins* (1975), *Childworld* (1976), *Bellefleur* (1980), *A Bloodsmoor Romance* (1982), and *The Profane Art* (1983).

Oates, Lawrence Edward Grace (1880–1912) British explorer. He participated in R. F. *Scott's expedition to the Antarctic (1910–12). They reached the Pole but on the return journey Oates, fearing that his lameness (resulting from frostbite) might hinder the expedition, walked out into the blizzard to die. His gallant act failed to save his companions.

Oates, Titus. *See* Popish Plot.

oat grass A perennial *grass of either of the genera *Arrhenatherum* (about 6 species), native to temperate Eurasia, and *Danthonia* (over 100 species), native to S temperate regions. Tall oat grass (*A. elatius*) has been introduced as a pasture grass to many countries; *Danthonia* species are important forage grasses.

oats Annual *grasses belonging to the genus *Avena* (10 species), native to temperate regions. The common oat (*A. sativa*) was first cultivated in Europe and is grown widely in cool temperate regions. Up to 40 in (1 m)

high, it has a branching cluster of stalked flowers; the grain is used as a livestock feed, especially for horses, and for oatmeal, breakfast cereals, etc. The straw is used for livestock fodder and bedding. Wild oats, especially *A. fatua*, can be a serious weed in cereal crops.

OAU. *See* Organization of African Unity.

Oaxaca (*or* Oaxaca de Juárez) 17 05N 96 41W A city in S Mexico, in the Atoyac Valley. Founded in 1486 by the Aztecs, it has flour-milling, cotton, textile, and handicraft industries. Its university was established in 1827. Population (1978 est): 131,193.

Ob River A river in the N central Soviet Union, flowing N from the Altai Mountains to the **Gulf of Ob** on the Kara Sea. One of the world's largest rivers, its drainage basin covers an area of about 1,131,000 sq mi (2,930,000 sq km). Length: 2287 mi (3682 km).

Obadiah An Old Testament prophet who predicted the downfall of Edom, the traditional enemy of Israel. **The Book of Obadiah** records his prophecy and is the shortest book of the Old Testament.

Obelia A genus of marine invertebrate animals belonging to a suborder (*Leptomedusae*) of *coelenterates. Their life cycle alternates between a sedentary asexual phase (*see* polyp) and a free-swimming sexual phase (*see* medusa). The polyps occur in small whitish or brownish colonies attached to the sea bottom, rocks, shells, etc., of shallow coastal waters. Order: *Hydroida*; class: *Hydrozoa*.

obelisk A stone monument generally shaped as a tall tapering rectangular column of stone, ending in a pyramid-like form. First used by the Egyptians, they have also been employed in the modern age. They were normally made of a single piece of stone and erected for religious or commemorative purposes. Perhaps the most famous are those known as *Cleopatra's Needles.

Oberammergau 47 35N 11 07E A town in S West Germany, in the Bavarian Alps. It is noted for its passion play, performed every ten years following a vow made by the villagers (1633) when they were saved from the plague. Population (1970 est): 4700.

Oberhausen 51 27N 6 50E A city in NW West Germany, in North Rhine-Westphalia on the Rhine-Herne Canal in the *Ruhr. It is a port and industrial center. Population (1980 est): 229,300.

oboe A woodwind instrument with a double reed, made in three jointed sections and having a conical bore and small belled end. It derives from the ancient shawm. It has a range of about three octaves above the B flat below middle C and because of its constant pitch usually gives the A to which other orchestral instruments tune.

Obote, (Apollo) Milton (1925–) Ugandan statesman; prime minister (1962–66) and president (1966–71, 1980–). He formed (1958) the Uganda People's Congress, which opposed the existence of the kingdom of *Buganda within Uganda. On independence he became prime minister and in 1966 deposed Mutesa II of Buganda (1924–69). He was overthrown by *Amin in 1971 but was re-elected in 1980.

Obrenović A Serbian ruling dynasty that came to power in 1815, when *Karageorge was assassinated, probably by *Miloš Obrenović. This led to a feud between the Karadordević and Obrenović families, which lasted until *Alexander, the last Obrenović monarch, was assassinated in 1903.

O'Brien, Edna (1936–) Irish author. Her novels include *The Country Girls* (1960), *The Lonely Girls* (1962; filmed as *The Girl With Green Eyes*, 1965), *Casualties of Peace* (1966), *Night* (1972), and *The Dazzle* (1981). She has also written plays, film scripts, and short stories.

O'Brien, Flann (Brian O'Nolan; 1911–66) Irish novelist and journalist. His best-known novel is *At Swim-Two-Birds* (1939), an exuberant comic mixture of folklore, farce, and lyricism that was praised by James Joyce and Dylan Thomas. Other novels include *The Dalkey Archive* (1964) and *The Third Policeman* (1967). He wrote a satirical column for the *Irish Times* under the name Myles na Gopaleen.

O'Brien, William (1852–1928) Irish nationalist politician and journalist. He made a great impression as a fiery member of parliament (from 1883) in the *Home Rule party. He later became more moderate, forming (1910) a short-lived political party that attempted to reconcile different opinions in Ireland.

720

O'Brien, William Smith (1803–64) Irish politician. A member of parliament (1828–48), he was at first a moderate constitutionalist but in the 1840s became a prominent member of the *Young Ireland group and led the abortive 1848 rebellion. O'Brien was transported to Australia but subsequently pardoned.

obscenity. *See* censorship.

obsidian A black glassy volcanic rock with a conchoidal fracture. It is of rhyolitic composition (*see* rhyolite) and contains less water and less crystalline material than pitchstone, a similar volcanic glass. Obsidian is formed by the rapid cooling of acid lava.

obstetrics. *See* gynecology.

O'Casey, Sean (1880–1964) Irish dramatist. Born into a poor Protestant family in Dublin, he was largely self-educated and became involved in the Irish nationalist movement. His early realistic tragicomedies, such as *The Shadow of a Gunman* (1923) and *Juno and the Paycock* (1924), were produced at the Abbey Theatre and dealt with Ireland in the time of the "Troubles." In 1926 he went to live in England. His later work includes the antiwar play *The Silver Tassie* (1929), *Red Roses for Me* (1943), *The Bishop's Bonfire* (1955), and *The Drums of Father Ned* (1958). He published six volumes of autobiography (1939–54).

Occitan. *See* Provençal.

occultation The temporary disappearance of one astronomical body behind another, as when the moon passes in front of and obscures a star. *See also* eclipse.

occultism Theories and practices based on a belief in hidden supernatural forces that are presumed to account for phenomena for which no rational or scientific explanation can be provided. Occultists set great store by ancient texts, secret rituals, esoteric traditions, and the powers of the human mind as keys to the understanding of the universe. *Theosophy, *satanism, *alchemy, *astrology, the *Kabbalah, *gnosticism, and various methods of divination, such as the *I Ching, are all manifestations of occultism.

occupational therapy The ancillary medical specialty concerned with restoring the physical and mental health of the sick and disabled. The occupational therapist plays an important role in keeping long-stay hospital patients interested and usefully occupied, in helping them gain confidence to return to work, and—if necessary—in training disabled persons for new employment. Occupational therapy is of great importance in *geriatrics.

oceanarium A large display tank in which species of marine animals and plants are maintained in the conditions of their natural environment. The first public oceanarium was founded in 1938 at Marineland, Fla.

Oceania The islands of the Pacific Ocean, usually taken to exclude Japan, Indonesia, Taiwan, the Philippines, and the Aleutian Islands, but often including Australasia.

Ocean Island (*or* Banaba) 00 52S 169 35E An island in the SW Pacific Ocean, in Kiribati. Rich in phosphate, it was mined by the UK from 1900 to 1979, when supplies were exhausted. After a long legal battle the Banabans accepted 5 million compensation for the loss of their island. Resettled on Rabi Island in Fiji during World War II, they are demanding independence from the government of Kiribati. Area: about 2 sq mi (5 sq km). Population (1980 est): 300,000.

oceanography The study of the oceans, particularly their origin, structure, and form, the relief and sediments of the sea floor, and the flora and fauna they contain. The physical and chemical properties of sea water, waves, currents, and tides are also involved. The structural geology of the oceans is a major element in the theory of *plate tectonics.

oceans The large areas of water (excluding lakes and seas) covering about 70% of the earth's surface. The whole water mass is known as the hydrosphere. The oceans are the Pacific (covering about one third of the world), Atlantic, Indian, and Arctic; the Southern Ocean (waters south of 40°S) is sometimes distinguished. Major structural features of the oceans are the continental margins (continental shelf and slope), mid-ocean ridges, ocean basins, and trenches (the deepest parts of the oceans). Since 1968 the research vessel *Glomar Challenger*, drilling into the ocean floor at many locations, has provided much data that assists in the understanding of geology.

Oceanus In Greek mythology, a river issuing from the underworld and encircling the earth. It was personified as a *Titan, a son of Uranus and Gaea and father of the gods and nymphs of the seas and rivers.

ocelot A *cat, *Felis (Panthera) pardalis*, also called painted leopard, of Central and South American forests. 40–59 in (100–150 cm) long including the tail 12–20 in (30–50 cm), it has a black-spotted buff coat with stripes on the legs—an attractive target for hunters. It frequently hunts by night to avoid capture, searching for small mammals and reptiles.

ocher A natural pigment, either red or yellow, consisting of hydrated ferric oxide with various impurities. It is therefore a type of *limonite deposit. It has been used as a pigment since prehistoric times and was important in medieval fresco painting.

Ochoa, Severo (1905–) US biochemist, who won a Nobel Prize in physiology or medicine (1959). Born in Spain, he studied medicine at Madrid University. He was one of the first to demonstrate the role of adenosine triphosphate (ATP) in the storage of the body's energy. This led to the discovery of the enzyme polynucleotide phosphorylase, which was later used to synthesize ribonucleic acid (RNA).

Ockham's Razor The metaphysical principle, associated with the English medieval philosopher *William of Ockham, that "Entities should not be multiplied unnecessarily." In analyzing a problem one should always choose the hypothesis that makes the least number of assumptions; only indispensible concepts are real.

O'Connell, Daniel (1775–1847) Irish politician, who aroused popular support in the 1820s for the right of Roman Catholics to sit in the British parliament. Himself a Catholic, his election to parliament in 1828 forced the government to concede *Catholic emancipation. Thereafter, O'Connell was dubbed the Liberator. He subsequently worked for the repeal of union with Britain.

O'Connor, Feargus (1794–1855) Irish politician. From 1832 to 1835 he was a radical member of parliament. He then became a leading Chartist (*see* Chartism), editing the radical newspaper *Northern Star*. He was elected again to parliament in 1847 and presented the 1848 Chartist petition. In 1852 he was pronounced insane.

O'Connor, Frank (Michael O'Donovan; 1903–66) Irish short-story writer. During the 1930s he was director of the Abbey Theatre and a friend of W. B. *Yeats. He published many collections of stories, from *Guests of the Nation* (1931) to *My Oedipus Complex* (1964), and several translations from Gaelic.

O'Connor, Sandra Day (1930–) US jurist; the first woman appointed to the Supreme Court (1981–). She practiced law in Arizona and became that state's assistant attorney general (1965–68), was Republican majority leader of the state senate (1972–74), and sat on Arizona's Court of Appeals (1979–81). A conservative, she was appointed to the Supreme Court by President Ronald Reagan.

octane number A measure of the extent to which a fuel causes *knocking in a gasoline engine. It is the percentage by volume of *iso*-octane (C_8H_{18}) in a mixture of *iso*-octane and *n*-heptane (C_7H_{16}), which has the same knocking characteristics as the fuel under specified conditions.

Octavia (d. 11 BC) The sister of Emperor Augustus, who married her to Mark Antony (40) to seal their reconciliation. Antony divorced her in 32, when he returned to Egypt and Cleopatra.

Octavian. *See* Augustus.

October Tenth month of the year. Derived from *octo*, which means eight in Latin, it was the eighth month in the ancient Roman calendar. It has 31 days. The zodiac signs for October are Libra and Scorpio; the flowers are cosmos and calendula, and the birthstones are opal, tourmaline, and beryl. In the US, Columbus Day falls on October 12, and Halloween is observed on the 31st.

octopus An eight-armed *cephalopod mollusk belonging to the genus *Octopus*, found in most oceans. Octopuses are 2–213 in (5–540 cm) long and a large species may have an armspan of 354 in (900 cm). The common octopus (*O. vulgaris*), weighing up to 4.4 lb (2 kg), has a pair of well-developed eyes, a ring of tentacles around its horny beak, and a saclike body. Octopuses feed mainly on crabs and lobsters and may eject a cloud of ink when alarmed. Family: *Octopodidae*; order: *Octopoda*.

Oda Nobunaga (1534–82) Japanese feudal lord, who began the reunification of feudal Japan. By careful administration, skillful diplomacy, the selection of able generals, and the adoption of novel military tactics based on formations of infantry armed with the newly introduced arquebus, Nobunaga achieved domination between 1560 and 1582 over Kyoto and central Japan. He was treacherously assassinated.

Odense 55 24N 10 25E A seaport in S Denmark, on the island of Fyn. Its gothic cathedral was founded by *Canute II and contains his tomb and shrine. Odense University was established in 1964. It is the birthplace of Hans Christian Andersen. Its varied industries include shipbuilding, sugar refining, textiles, and iron founding. Dairy produce is the main export. Population (1981 est): 169,183.

OCEANS

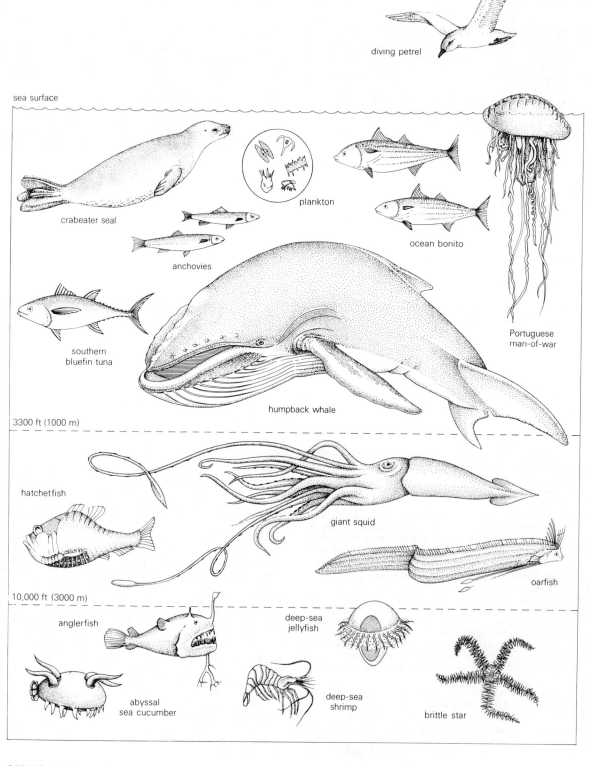

sea surface

diving petrel

crabeater seal

plankton

anchovies

ocean bonito

southern
bluefin tuna

humpback whale

Portuguese
man-of-war

3300 ft (1000 m)

hatchetfish

giant squid

oarfish

10,000 ft (3000 m)

anglerfish

deep-sea
jellyfish

abyssal
sea cucumber

deep-sea
shrimp

brittle star

OCEANS *A selection of animals and plants found at different depths of the ocean.*

Oder River (Polish and Czech name: Odra) A river in E Europe. Rising in the Oder Mountains of Czechoslovakia, it flows N and W through Poland and enters the Baltic Sea at Szczecin. Linked by canals to both E and W Europe, it is of great commercial importance. Length: 551 mi (886 km).

Oder-Neisse Line The boundary between Germany and Poland confirmed by the Allies at the *Potsdam Conference (1945) at the end of World War II. The line ran S from Swinoujście on the Baltic Sea to the Czechoslovak border, following the Oder and Neisse Rivers. It was recognized by East Germany and Poland in 1950 but not by West Germany until 1970.

Odessa 46 30N 30 46E A port in the Soviet Union, in the S Ukrainian SSR on the Black Sea. Fishing and whaling as well as ship repairing are important activities and industries include engineering, chemicals, and oil refining. *History*: founded in the 14th century as a Tatar fortress, it passed to Russia in 1791 and became a naval base. It was the scene in the Revolution of 1905 of the mutiny on the *Potemkin*, the subject of a remarkable film by Eisenstein. Population (1981 est): 1,072,000.

Odets, Clifford (1906-63) US dramatist. He joined the Communist Party in 1934 and was a founding member of the Group Theater, which produced his first successful play, *Waiting for Lefty* (1935). He later became a Hollywood scriptwriter. His other plays include *Awake and Sing* (1935), *Golden Boy* (1937), *The Big Knife* (1949), and *The Country Girl* (1950).

Odin The principal god of the Teutonic peoples, the husband of *Frigga and, according to some legends, the father of *Thor. Also known as Woden and Wotan, he was the god of war, learning, and poetry and possessed great magical powers. He was the protector of slain heroes, who were brought to *Valhalla by his servants the *Valkyries. His desire for learning was so great that he gave up his right eye to drink from Mimir's well of knowledge. The Old English form of his name, *Woden*, is preserved in *Wednesday*. □Ragnarök.

Odoacer (c. 433-93 AD) King of Italy (476-93). A German chieftain, he served with various Roman commanders before rebelling and deposing the last western Roman emperor, *Romulus Augustulus. After acknowledging the overlordship of the Eastern Roman emperor, Zeno (reigned 474-91), he ruled Italy competently until overthrown and treacherously killed by the Ostrogothic king, *Theodoric the Great.

Odontoglossum A genus of epiphytic *orchids (about 250 species) native to mountainous areas of tropical America. Each large swollen stem base bears one or more leaves, and the flowers, which are borne on a spike, vary greatly in color and size. Many *Odontoglossum* species have been crossed both within the genus and with other orchid genera to produce hundreds of beautiful hybrids, prized by orchid growers.

Odo of Bayeux (c. 1036-97) Bishop of Bayeux (1049-97). The half-brother of William the Conqueror, he took part in the Norman conquest of England and helped rule the country during William's absences but subsequently rebelled against William II. He died on the first Crusade.

Odysseus (*or* Ulysses) A legendary Greek king of Ithaca and hero of Homer's *Odyssey*, notable for his cunning. His many adventures during his voyage home from the *Trojan War included encounters with the Cyclops *Polyphemus, the cannibalistic Laestrygones, the enchantress *Circe, and the goddess Calypso, with whom he lived for eight years. Having reached Ithaca, he was reunited with his faithful wife *Penelope after killing her suitors with the help of his son Telemachus.

OECD. *See* Organization for Economic Cooperation and Development.

Oedipus In Greek legend, a king of Thebes who unwittingly fulfilled the prophecy of the oracle at Delphi that he would kill his father and marry his mother. He was brought up by Polybus, King of Corinth. He killed his true father, Laius, in a roadside quarrel, and after winning the throne of Thebes by solving the riddle of the *sphinx he married his mother, the widowed Jocasta. When they discovered the truth, Jocasta committed suicide and Oedipus blinded himself and went into exile. The story is the subject of Sophocles' best-known tragedy.

Oedipus complex The unconscious sexual feelings of a boy for his mother, which are accompanied by aggressive feelings for his father. According to psychoanalysis this is a normal desire, made unconscious by *repression. The female equivalent (in which a girl desires her father) is called the **Electra complex**.

Oehlenschläger, Adam (Gottlob) (1779-1850) Danish poet and playwright. Greatly influenced by Goethe, Fichte, Schelling, and the Schlegels, Oehlenschläger was the founder of Danish Romanticism and Denmark's greatest poet. His works include the blank-verse tragedies *Hakon Jarl* and *Baldur hin Gode* (*Balder the Good*), based on Norse legend and published in *Nordiske Digte* (1807). He also wrote lyric poetry and a ballad cycle based on the poetic Edda, *Nordens Guder* (*The Gods of the North*; 1819).

Oersted, Hans Christian (1777-1851) Danish physicist; professor at Copenhagen University. He discovered the magnetic effect of an electric current and thus established the relationship between electricity and magnetism. He did not, however, take an active part in the elucidation of this discovery. The c.g.s. unit of magnetic field strength is named for— him.

Offa (d. 796) King of Mercia (757-96) and overlord of all England S of the Humber. He engaged in trade with Charlemagne, although Charlemagne had refused to marry his daughter to Offa's son. He accepted greater papal control of the Church, introduced a new currency, and devised a code of laws. **Offa's Dyke**, an earthwork dividing England from Wales, built c. 784-c. 796, marks the frontier established by his wars with the Welsh.

Offaly (Irish name: Uabh Failghe) A county in the central Republic of Ireland, in Leinster bordered in the W by the River Shannon. It is chiefly low lying containing part of the Bog of Allen in the N. Agricultural produce includes oats, barley, and wheat; cattle are reared. Area: 770 sq mi (2000 sq km). Population (1979): 57,342. County town: Tullamore.

Off-Broadway theaters Small-scale professional theaters in New York City that specialize in noncommercial and experimental productions. They were responsible for the most lively drama in the US in the 1950s and 1960s.

Offenbach (am Main) 50 06N 8 46E A city in S central West Germany, in Hessen on the Main River. It is noted for its leather industry. Population (1980 est): 111,200.

Offenbach, Jacques (J. Eberst; 1819-80) German composer of French adoption and Jewish descent. He adopted the name of the town in which his father lived. A professional cellist, at the age of 30 he began writing a series of popular operettas, including *Orpheus in the Underworld* (1858), *La Belle Hélène* (1864), and *La Vie Parisienne* (1866). He also composed one grand opera, *The Tales of Hoffman* (produced posthumously; 1881).

Office of Strategic Services (OSS) (1942-45) US World War II information-gathering agency. Created to gain access to enemy war information, to demoralize the enemy, and to act as liaison with the underground resistance forces within enemy countries, it was administered by Major General William Donovan (1883-1959). The *Central Intelligence Agency later assumed many of its activities.

O'Flaherty, Liam (1897-1984) Irish novelist. Born in the Aran Islands, he worked his way around the world before starting his literary career in London in 1922. His novels, chiefly concerned with themes of violence and terrorism, include *The Informer* (1925) and *The Assassin* (1928). *The Pedlar's Revenge and Other Stories* was published in 1976. After 1935 he lived mostly in the US.

Ogaden, the A semidesert area in E Ethiopia, enclosed by Somalia except to the W. The nomadic inhabitants are chiefly Muslim Somalis and in the 1960s a claim to the area by Somalia provoked border clashes. Somalia invaded the Ogaden in 1977 but withdrew (1978) in the face of counteroffensives launched by Ethiopia with Cuban and Soviet aid. Guerrilla fighting has continued.

Ogam (*or* Ogham) A script found in about 400 Celtic inscriptions in Ireland and W Britain, dating from the 5th to the 7th centuries AD. It is alphabetic and consists of 20 letters, each made from a number of oblique or straight strokes on either side of a central dividing line.

Ogbomosho 8 05N 4 11E The third largest city in Nigeria, on the Yorubaland plateau. Agricultural trade is important and there are local craft industries, including textiles and wood working. There are also shoe and tobacco factories. Population (1975 est): 432,000.

Ogden, C(harles) K(ay) (1889-1957) British writer and scholar. With I. A. *Richards he wrote *The Meaning of Meaning* (1923). From 1925 he developed *Basic English, with a restricted vocabulary of 850 words, intended as a practical medium of international communication.

Oglethorpe, James Edward (1696-1785) English general and colonizer. While serving in parliament, he promoted the establishment of a colony in North America for indigent debtors and persecuted Protestants. In 1733 he led the first group of settlers to the colony that was to become Georgia. He repulsed a Spanish attack against it (1742).

Ogooué River (*or* Ogowe R.) A river in W central Africa. Rising in the SW Congo, it flows mainly NW and W through Gabon to enter the Atlantic Ocean. Length: 683 mi (970 km).

O'Hara, John (Henry) (1905–70) US novelist. After working as a journalist he began publishing ironic stories about middle-class life in the 1930s. His best-known novels are *Appointment in Samarra* (1934), *Butterfield 8* (1935), *Pal Joey* (1940), *Ten North Frederick* (1955), and *From the Terrace* (1958).

O'Higgins, Bernardo (?1778–1842) Chilean national hero. The son of an Irish-born soldier who became Spanish colonial governor, he fought with José de *San Martín against Spain and liberated Chile. He was made dictator of the country in 1817 but his wide-ranging reforms created much resentment and he was deposed after a revolt in the provinces.

Ohio A midwestern state in the US. It is bounded on the E by Pennsylvania and West Virginia, on the S by West Virginia and Kentucky, on the W by Indiana, and on the N by Michigan and Lake Erie. The flat or rolling land of W Ohio gives way in the E to the hill and valley region of the Appalachian Plateau. A major industrial state, it lies at the center of the most industrialized area of the US and is strategically located near many rich markets. The leading industrial products are transportation equipment, raw and fabricated metals, non-electrical machinery, and rubber. It also exploits its abundant natural resources, including clay and stone, lime, coal, natural gas, and oil. Agriculture is important, especially livestock. *History*: Miami, Shawnee, Erie, and Ottawa Indians were the indigenous inhabitants when European explorers arrived. Robert Cavalier, sieur de La Salle (1669) claimed the area for France in 1669. Subsequent Anglo-French rivalry over control of the territory culminated in the French and Indian War, in which England won the region (1763). After the American Revolution the area became part of the Northwest Territory (1787). Ohio became a separate territory in 1799 and a state in 1802. Rapid industrial development, facilitated by the earlier building of railroads and canals, took place after the Civil War. Cleveland became the site of a growing petroleum industry. Flooding, a long-standing problem in Ohio, took a devastating toll in 1913 and prompted the establishment of many state and national water-control projects. The Depression caused severe hardship for factory workers and farmers, but World War II brought economic prosperity. The national energy crisis of the late 1970s resulted in a boom for Ohio's coal industry, and prosperity continued until the 1980s when the entire nation experienced a slowdown. Area: 41,222 sq mi (106,764 sq km). Population (1980): 10,797,419. Capital: Columbus.

Ohio River A river flowing mainly SW from Pittsburgh in W Pennsylvania to join the Mississippi (in Illinois) as its main E tributary. Length: 980 mi (1577 km).

ohm (Ω) The *SI unit of electrical resistance equal to the resistance between two points on a conductor when a potential difference of one volt between the points produces a current of one ampere. This definition replaced the former definition, which was based on the resistance of a specified column of mercury. Named for— Georg *Ohm.

Ohm, Georg Simon (1787–1854) German physicist, who discovered in 1827 that the current flowing through a wire is proportional to the potential difference between its ends (*see* Ohm's law). Ohm also found that the electrical resistance of a wire is proportional to its length and inversely proportional to its cross-sectional area. The unit of electrical resistance is named for him.

Ohm's law The basic law of electric current, named for its discoverer, Georg *Ohm. The current, I, flowing through an element in a circuit is directly proportional to the voltage drop, V, across it. It is written as $V = IR$, where R is the resistance of the circuit element.

oil There are three types of oil: lipids (*see* fats and oils), *essential oils, and mineral oil.

Petroleum (*or* rock oil) is the thick greenish mineral oil that occurs in permeable underground rock and consists mainly of *hydrocarbons, with some other elements (sulfur, oxygen, nitrogen, etc.). It is believed to have derived from the remains of living organisms deposited many millions of years ago with rock-forming sediments. Under the effects of heat and pressure this organic material passed through a number of chemical and physical changes ending up as droplets of petroleum, which migrated through porous rocks and fissures to become trapped in large underground reservoirs, often floating on a layer of water and held under pressure beneath a layer of natural gas (mostly methane).

Mineral oil was used in the 4th millennium BC by the Sumerians to reinforce bricks, and the Burmese were burning it in oil lamps in the 13th century AD. However, the modern oil industry began when oil was discovered in Pennsylvania in 1859 and has grown with the development of the internal-combustion engine, which is entirely dependent on it as a fuel.

The presence of oil in underground reservoirs is detected by geologists, who seek evidence of the type of structures in which oil is known to occur and

measure the gravitational force in likely areas to identify variations of rock density; depth is determined by such measures as the behavior of sound waves produced by small surface explosions. Exploratory narrow-bore drillings are then made to determine the extent of a reservoir. The actual oil well is made by drilling through the rock with a rotating bit supported in a wider shaft; a specially prepared mud is pumped through the hollow bit to collect the debris, which is forced back up the shaft around the drilling bit. When the oil is reached, the pressure of the mud is used to control the pressure of the oil so that none is wasted by "gushers"; when the mud has been removed from the shaft the flow is controlled by valves. This method of sinking wells enables oil over 3 mi (5 km) below the surface to be mined. Drilling for oil below the sea is achieved in a similar manner, except that the drilling rig has to be supported on a base, which has legs sunk into the sea bed.

Petroleum has no uses in its crude form and has to be refined by fractional distillation (i.e. separating the components according to their boiling points) before it is of commercial value. Natural gas is widely used as a substitute for coal gas and as a source of power in the refinery. Products made by blending the distillation fractions include aviation spirit, gasoline, kerosene, diesel oil, lubricating oil, paraffin wax, and petroleum jelly. In addition to fractional distillation, other processes, such as catalytic cracking, are used to split the larger molecules into smaller ones to increase the yield of gasoline and to reduce the viscosity of heavier oils. Catalytic reforming is used to make a number of valuable chemicals (petrochemicals), which are required to manufacture detergents, plastics, fibers, fertilizers, drugs, etc.

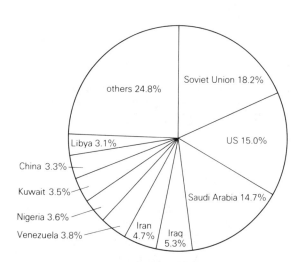

OIL   *World crude petroleum production.*

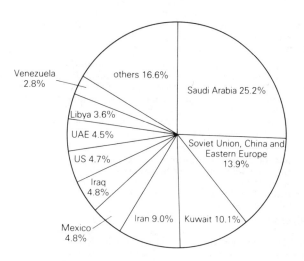

OIL   *World crude petroleum reserves.*

As one of the world's primary energy sources, the price, conservation, and political significance of oil are extremely controversial issues. In 1961 the *Organization of Petroleum Exporting Countries (OPEC) was set up to protect producing countries from exploitation. Its advent ended the era of cheap energy and prices for petroleum products rose sharply during the ensuing decade. In 1974 the International Energy Agency (IEA) was established to protect consumers. Since then various factors, including the flow of North Sea oil, have helped to stabilize prices, although the Iranian revolution of 1979 has led to world shortages and further price increases. World oil reserves are as difficult to estimate as future world consumption. Reserves depend on the estimates for undiscovered sources, while consumption depends on the projected growth of usage, the price of oil in relation to its competitors, and the extent to which nuclear energy will be utilized.

oil beetle   A heavy-bodied flightless beetle belonging to the family *Meloidae* (about 2000 species). If disturbed, it discharges evil-smelling oily blood—an example of reflex bleeding—as a defense mechanism. It has a similar lifestyle to the *blister beetle.

oilbird   A South American cave-dwelling bird, *Steatornis caripensis*, also called guacharo. It is 12 in (30 cm) long and has a fan-shaped tail, a white-spotted black-barred brown plumage, and a hook-tipped bill surrounded by long bristles. It lives in colonies, uses echolocation inside caves, and feeds on fruit. It is the only member of its family (*Steatornithidae*); order: *Caprimulgiformes* (frogmouths, nightjars, etc.).

oil-immersion lens   A lens system used in some *microscopes in which the gap between the objective lens and the specimen is filled with oil (usually cedar-wood oil). It increases the amount of light entering the system.

oil palm   A *palm tree, *Elaeis guineensis*, native to tropical West Africa and cultivated in Africa, Indonesia, Malaysia, and tropical America as the source of palm oil. Growing to a height of 49 ft (15 m), the palms produce fleshy fruits, 1.2 in (3 cm) long, containing a white kernel within a hard black shell. Palm oil is extracted from the pulp and kernel and used in making soaps, margarine, lubricants, etc. The residual meal from the kernels is a valuable livestock feed.

oilseeds   Oil-bearing seeds of plants from which the edible oil is extracted for making margarine, soaps, etc. Examples include rapeseed, cottonseed, groundnuts, and soybeans. The oil is obtained from the seeds by expelling it under pressure or by extracting it using a solvent (with a solvent recovery cycle); the **oilcake** remaining after most of the oil has been removed is called expellers or extractions, respectively. Both forms of oilcake are widely used as animal feeds.

Oise River   A river in N France, flowing mainly SW from the Belgian Ardennes to join the Seine River at Conflans. Length: 188 mi (302 km).

Oistrakh, David   (1908–75) Russian violinist. He made his debut in Moscow in 1933 and won the International Violin Competition in Brussels in 1937. He played frequently in the West, and was well known for his performances of the Brahms, Tchaikovsky, and Prokofiev violin concertos. His son and pupil, the violinist **Igor Oistrakh** (1931–), often gave joint recitals with him and has also conducted.

Oita   33 15N 131 36E A port in Japan, on the NE coast of Kyushu. An important town in the 16th century, it is now an expanding industrial center with an oil refinery and iron and steel industries. Population (1980): 360,000.

Ojibwa   A North American Indian people of the Great Lakes region, who speak a language of the Algonkian family. They are also known as Chippewa; those who now live near Lake Winnipeg in Canada are called Saulteaux. They were traditionally hunters, fishers, and gatherers, who wandered in small bands and sheltered in simply made dome-shaped wigwams. Shamans exercised considerable influence.

Ojos del Salado   27 05S 68 05W A mountain peak on the border between Argentina and Chile, the second highest peak in the Andes. Height: 22,550 ft (6873 m).

okapi   A hoofed mammal, *Okapia johnstoni*, of central African rain forests. Okapis are about 60 in (150 cm) high at the shoulder and have a dark-brown coat with horizontal black and white stripes on the legs and rump, which provide camouflage. The smaller male has short bony backward-pointing horns. They were unknown to science until 1901. Family: *Giraffidae* (giraffes).

Okavango Swamp   A marshy area in NE Botswana, into which the Okavango River drains. It supports a rich and varied wildlife.

Okayama   34 40N 133 54E A city in Japan, in SW Honshu. A commercial and industrial center, it has a 16th-century castle and a traditional

Japanese garden (1786). Its university was established in 1949. Population (1980): 546,000.

OKAPI   *The closest living relative of the giraffe, this nocturnal animal becomes very docile and breeds readily in captivity.*

Okeechobee, Lake   A large freshwater lake in S Florida. It drains into the Atlantic Ocean through the *Everglades. Area: 700 sq mi (1813 sq km).

Okefenokee Swamp   A swamp area extending through SE Georgia and NE Florida. In 1937 a large proportion of it was designated the Okefenokee National Wildlife Refuge; the wildlife includes alligators, snakes, and birds.

O'Keeffe, Georgia   (1887–) US painter. Her first one-person show was presented in 1917 by the photographer Alfred *Stieglitz, whom she married in 1924. She has since specialized in semiabstract paintings of flowers, bones, architecture, and landscapes inspired by the countryside of New Mexico.

Okeghem, Jean d'   (c. 1425–c. 1495) Flemish composer, noted for his innovatory counterpoint. He was composer to Charles VII, Louis XI, and Charles VIII of France and his pupils included Josquin des Prez. He wrote much church music, including 16 masses and 9 motets.

Okhotsk, Sea of   A section of the N Pacific Ocean off the E coast of the Soviet Union, separated from the main ocean by Kamchatka and the Kuril Islands.

Okinawa   A mountainous Japanese island, the main one of the *Ryukyu group. During World War II it was captured by US forces in a major amphibious operation and was only returned to Japan in 1972, the US retaining military bases there. Chief products are fish, rice, sugar cane, and sweet potatoes. Area: 454 sq mi (1176 sq km). Population (1971): 934,176. Capital: *Naha.

Oklahoma   A state in the S central US. It is bounded on the E by Missouri and Arkansas, on the S by Texas, on the W by Texas and New Mexico, and on the N by Colorado and Kansas. It has a diverse landscape, with uplands in the W, the lowlands of the Arkansas River Valley and coastal plain in the center and S, and wooded hills in the E. An oil-rich state, agriculture (especially cattle) remains a major source of revenue. Most industry is located around Oklahoma City and Tulsa (one of the world's leading oil centers). The most important manufacturing industries are food processing, non-electrical machinery, fabricated metal products, and electrical and transport equipment. *History*: occupied by Plains Indians including Apache, Comanche, Kiowa, and Osage, Oklahoma was acquired by the US as part of the Louisiana Purchase (1803). In 1834 the land was designated Indian Territory by the federal government, a repository for Indians evicted from their homelands. The opening of the cattle routes, such as the Chisholm Trail (1860s), which traversed the territory, brought pressure on the government to allow settlement. Homesteading runs and "land lotteries" subsequently brought settlers when a strip of land was released for settlement. In 1906 white settlers were allowed access to the remainder of the Indian Territory. In the 1890s and early 1900s Oklahoma became a major oil producer. It became a state in 1907. Oklahoma was severely affected by the great drought of the 1930s (during the Depression), and thousands saw their farms turn to dust, forcing them to become migrant laborers. During World War II the economy expanded and diversified, allowing for gradual but solid growth after the war. During the postwar period and into the present, energy-related industries have contributed to Oklahoma's position as a rapidly growing state. Area: 69,919 sq mi (181,089 sq km). Population (1980): 3,025,266. Capital: Oklahoma City.

Oklahoma City 35 28N 97 33W The capital city of Oklahoma, on the North Canadian River. Founded in 1889, it expanded rapidly following the discovery of oil (1920s). Today it is a commercial, industrial, and distribution center for an oil-producing and agricultural area. Oklahoma City University was established in 1904. Population (1980): 403,213.

okra An annual African herb, *Hibiscus esculentus*, also called lady's fingers or gumbo, widely cultivated in the tropics and subtropics. It grows 40–80 in (1–2 m) high and has heart-shaped leaves and five-petaled yellow flowers with a crimson center. The pods are picked before they are ripe and eaten fresh, canned, dried, or pickled. They may be used to thicken stews and soups. The seeds are a coffee substitute. Family: *Malvaceae*.

Olaf I Tryggvason (c. 964–c. 1000) King of Norway (995–c. 1000). He took part in the Viking attacks on England (991–94) but the English king, Ethelred the Unready, became his godfather when Olaf was confirmed as a Christian at Andover (994). Olaf subsequently imposed Christianity on Norway. A hero of Scandinavian literature, he died at the hands of the Danes in the battle of Svolder.

Olaf II Haraldsson, Saint (c. 995–1030) King (1015–28) and patron saint of Norway. Baptized in 1013, he attempted to complete the conversion of Norway to Christianity. He was overthrown by Canute II of England and Denmark and died, attempting to regain his kingdom, at the battle of Stikelstad.

Olaf V (1903–) King of Norway (1957–). A talented sportsman, he took part as a yachtsman in the 1928 Olympic Games. In 1929 he married Princess Märtha of Sweden (1901–54) and his heir is his son Prince Harald (1937–).

Öland A long narrow island in Sweden, in the Baltic Sea separated from the mainland by the Kalmar Sound. Area: 520 sq mi (1347 sq km). Population (1970): 20,361. Chief town: Borgholm.

Olbers, Heinrich Wilhelm Matthäus (1758–1840) German astronomer, who was the first to point out the paradoxical nature of the night sky (*see* Olbers' paradox). He was also one of the first astronomers to detect and study the asteroids, discovering Pallas in 1802 and Vesta in 1804.

Olbers' paradox Why is the sky dark at night? Heinrich *Olbers argued, in 1826, that if the universe were infinite, uniform, and unchanging, with innumerable stars, then the night sky would be covered in stars and appear as bright as the average star, i.e. the sun. The paradox is resolved by the facts that the universe does not extend infinitely in space and time and is expanding rather than remaining static and unchanging: as the galaxies recede, their radiation suffers a *redshift (i.e. is diminished in energy), which increases with distance.

Old Believers A schismatic sect of the Russian Orthodox Church that rejected the liturgical reforms of the Patriarch of Moscow (1667). Its members were mainly peasants, who suffered much persecution. The majority, who evolved their own Church hierarchy, was eventually recognized by the state (1881), but the remainder split up into small and often eccentric sects.

Oldcastle, Sir John (c. 1378–1417) English soldier and leader of the *Lollards. An ardent supporter of *Wycliffe, whose works he distributed, he was arrested for heresy and imprisoned in the Tower of London (1413). He escaped but was recaptured four years later and hanged. Shakespeare's character Falstaff is partly based on him.

Old Catholics Christian Churches from several European countries that separated from the Roman Catholic Church at various times and in 1932 entered into communion with the Church of England. They comprise the Church of Utrecht, which supported *Jansenism against Roman Catholic orthodoxy (1724), the Old Catholic Churches of Germany, Switzerland, and Austria, which rejected papal infallibility (1870), the National Polish Church (established 1897), and the Yugoslav Old Catholic Church (1924).

Old Comedy The first period of Greek comic drama, lasting up to the end of the 5th century BC. The episodic choral plays of this period contained elements of song, dance, topical satire, and political criticism and ranged in style from bawdy slapstick to lyrical grace. All the surviving examples are by *Aristophanes. *See also* Middle Comedy; New Comedy.

Oldenbarneveldt, Johan van (1547–1619) Dutch statesman. He supported William the Silent in the *Revolt of the Netherlands against Spain and, with *Maurice of Nassau, became (from 1586) the leading statesman of the newly formed United Provinces of the Netherlands. He presided over a vast expansion of Dutch trade and the formation of the Dutch East India Company. His moderate Protestantism brought him into conflict with Maurice, whose imprisonment and execution of Oldenbarneveldt was a shameful blot on the early history of the United Provinces.

Oldenburg 53 08N 8 13E A city in NW West Germany, in Lower Saxony on the Hunte River. The capital of the former duchy of Oldenburg, it has a 17th-century palace. It is an agricultural and industrial center. Population (1980 est): 136,400.

Oldenburg, Claes (Thure) (1929–) US sculptor, born in Sweden. He became a leading exponent of *pop art in the 1960s, first with his re-creation of ordinary environments, notably *The Store* (1960–61), and later with his "soft sculptures," in which vinyl and stuffed canvas are shaped into everyday objects, such as bathtubs, typewriters, etc.

Old English sheepdog A breed of working □dog originating in England. It has a compact body, a characteristic ambling gait, and a long dense shaggy coat that may be gray or blue-gray with white markings. These dogs are also known as bobtails because their tails are docked at birth. Height: 22–26 in (55–66 cm).

Oldham 53 33N 2 07W A city in N England, in Greater Manchester. Traditionally a cotton-spinning town, Oldham now also has electronics, textile machinery, plastics, and clothing industries. The town hall is a copy of Ceres' Temple in Athens. Population (1981): 95,467.

old man cactus A succulent desert *cactus of the genus *Cephalocereus* (50 species), especially *C. senilis*, native to tropical and subtropical America. Its sturdy stems are coated with long strands of white hair at maturity and may reach a height of 39 ft (12 m).

old man's beard. *See* Clematis.

Old Norse A North Germanic language formerly spoken in Iceland and Norway (c. 1150–c. 1350). It is the language of the Norse *sagas and was closely related to the contemporary speech of Denmark and Sweden. From this group the modern Scandinavian languages are derived.

Old Testament The collection of 39 books constituting the sacred scriptures of *Judaism. Together with the *New Testament they also form the first of the two major divisions of the Christian *Bible. The title derives from the Latin word for *covenant and refers to the pact between God and Israel, a concept that underlies the authors' view of history and is the major theme throughout. The books claim to cover the period from the creation of the universe and man (Adam) to about 400 BC. They are traditionally divided into three parts: the Law or *Torah, the first five books, traditionally ascribed to Moses and often called the Pentateuch by scholars; the Prophets, which are most of the books bearing the names of individual prophets and containing much historical information; and the Writings or Hagiographa (Hebrew: *Kethubim*), the latest books admitted to the canon of the Hebrew Old Testament (c. 100 AD), i.e. Psalms, Proverbs, Job, Ruth, Lamentations, the Song of Solomon, Ecclesiastes, Esther, Daniel, Chronicles, Ezra, and Nehemiah.

Olduvai Gorge A site in N Tanzania yielding an important sequence of Lower *Paleolithic fossils and tools. Here L. S. B. *Leakey found remains of the *Australopithecus he called *Zinjanthropus* (c. 1,750,000 years old) and the *hominid *Homo habilis* (c. 2,000,000 years old), one or both of which manufactured crude pebble choppers.

Old World A name for Europe, Africa, and Asia, used especially by early emigrants from Europe. *Compare* New World.

Old World monkey A *monkey belonging to the family *Cercopithecidae* (58 species), native to Africa or Asia. There are both terrestrial and arboreal species, active mainly by day and either omnivorous or vegetarian. They inhabit forest, savannah, swamps, and rocks. *See also* baboon; colobus; guenon; langur; macaque.

oleander A poisonous evergreen shrub, *Nerium oleander*, also called rosebay, native to the Mediterranean region and widely cultivated in warm regions for its attractive flowers. Up to 23 ft (7 m) high, it has long narrow leaves, clusters of white, pink, or purplish five-petaled flowers (up to 3 in [7.5 cm] across), and dangling pods. Family: *Apocynaceae*.

oleaster A shrub or tree, *Elaeagnus angustifolia*, also called Russian olive, found throughout S Europe and sometimes cultivated for its ornamental silvery foliage. It grows 6.5–40 ft (2–12 m) high and bears small fragrant yellowish flowers. The olive-shaped yellowish fruits have a silvery scaly coat and are dried and used in cakes as Trebizond dates. Family: *Elaeagnaceae*.

olefines. *See* alkenes.

Oligocene epoch. *See* Tertiary period.

oligopoly An economic market structure in which there is imperfect competition between a few suppliers. Oligopoly is common in western economies today. Economic theory is not as successful at predicting the market trends in an oligopoly as it is under the extremes of *monopoly and *perfect competition, because the action of each firm in an oligopoly affects the policies of the others.

olingo A mammal belonging to the genus *Bassaricyon* (3 species), found in tropical forests of South America. Olingos are 30–37 in (75–95 cm) long including the tail 16–19 in (40–48 cm), with buff-colored or golden fur. They apparently nest in hollow trees and feed chiefly on fruit. Family: *Procyonidae* (raccoons, kinkajous, etc.); order: *Carnivora*.

Oliphant, Sir Mark Laurence Elwin (1901–) Australian physicist, who in 1934 discovered *tritium while bombarding deuterium with deuterons. His work contributed to the development of the hydrogen bomb. He also designed the first proton synchrotron accelerator.

Olivares, Gaspar de Guzmán, Conde-Duque de (1587–1645) Spanish statesman. The chief minister of Philip IV (1621–43), he combined reform, especially economic, with a grand imperial vision and attempted to make all the Spanish kingdoms provide him with men and money. Dissatisfaction exploded under the strain of Spain's participation in the *Thirty Years' War into revolt in Portugal and Catalonia and led to his downfall. Olivares supported the painters Rubens and Velázquez and the writer Lope de Vega.

olive An evergreen tree, *Olea europaea*, native to W Asia but cultivated throughout Mediterranean and subtropical regions for its fruits. Up to 40 ft (12 m) high, it has a gnarled gray trunk and lance-shaped leathery gray-green leaves. Small greenish-white flowers produce fleshy oval berries containing a hard stone. Unripe green olives and ripe black olives are usually pickled for use in hors d'oeuvres and other dishes. **Olive oil**, pressed from the fruit, is one of the finest edible oils and can be consumed without refining or processing. It is also used in making soaps, cosmetics, and textiles. Olive wood resists decay and is used for furniture and ornaments. Family: *Oleaceae*.

Oliver, Isaac (?1556–1617) Portrait miniaturist, born in Rouen (France). In about 1568 he moved to London with his Huguenot parents to escape religious persecution. Although he studied under *Hilliard, his naturalistic style was influenced by Italian and Flemish art. He successfully rivaled his master at James I's court, where he painted many portraits of the queen and Henry Frederick, Prince of Wales (1594–1612). □Donne, John.

Olives, Mount of (*or* Olivet) 31 47N 35 15E A hill to the E of the old city of Jerusalem. Near its foot is the Garden of Gethsemane, the scene of the betrayal of Christ (Mark 14.26–50) and it is the traditional site of Christ's Ascension (Acts 1.2–12). Height: 2686 ft (817 m).

olive shell A *gastropod mollusk of the family *Olividae* (300 species) of warm shallow seas. The shiny □shell, 0.4–5 in (1–12 cm) long, is roughly cylindrical with a short spire and is covered by the mantle. The animals prey on smaller mollusks on sandy seabeds.

Olivier, Laurence (Kerr), Baron (1907–) British actor. He played many Shakespearean roles while with the Old Vic Theatre Company from 1937 to 1949 and a number of outstanding modern roles. His films include the Shakespeare adaptations *Henry V* (1944), *Hamlet* (1948), and *Richard III* (1956). He was director of Britain's National Theatre Company from 1961 to 1973, during which time he played many leading roles, including Shakespeare's Othello (filmed 1965) and in plays by Chekhov, O'Neill, and Ionesco. He was knighted in 1947 and created a life peer in 1970.

olivine A group of rock-forming silicate minerals, varying in composition between the end-members forsterite (Mg_2SiO_4) and fayalite (Fe_2SiO_4). Olivines are green, brownish green, or yellowish green, with a conchoidal fracture. Those rich in magnesium occur in basic and ultrabasic igneous rocks, while fayalite occurs in acid igneous rocks. Peridot is a pale green gem variety. Olivine is believed to be a major constituent of the earth's upper mantle.

LAURENCE OLIVIER *Preparing for a scene in his third Shakespearean film*, Richard III.

olm A cave-dwelling salamander, *Proteus anguineus*, found in the Carpathian Mountains. Growing to about 12 in (30 cm), it is white and has bright-red gills throughout its life. The eyes are covered with skin but are clearly visible in young larvae. Although sightless, olms prey on small worms and can survive for long periods without feeding. Family: *Proteidae*. *See also* mudpuppy.

Olmecs An ancient American Indian people of the Gulf Coast of Mexico. Between about 1200 and 400 BC they evolved the first important Mesoamerican culture, with great ceremonial centers at La Venta and San Lorenzo. They invented a hieroglyphic script and a calendar. Outstanding stone carvers, they produced both monumental basalt heads and small jade figures.

Olomouc (German name: Olmütz) 49 48N 17 15E An industrial city in central Czechoslovakia, in N Moravia. Its notable historic buildings include the gothic cathedral and the town hall with its 15th-century astronomical clock. The university was founded in 1576. Population (1980 est): 103,000.

Olsztyn (German name: Allenstein) 53 48N 20 29E A market city in NE Poland. It was founded in 1334 by the Teutonic Knights. Industries include the manufacture of leather. Population (1976 est): 118,000.

Olympia A sanctuary of *Zeus, established about 1000 BC in the NW *Peloponnese, in W Greece. From 776 BC until at least 261 AD it was the venue of the *Olympic Games. Extensive excavations from 1881 have revealed no important buildings before the 6th century BC, when the temple of Hera and the stadium were built. In 457 BC the temple of Zeus in the Altis (sacred grove), which later held *Phidias' famous statue, was completed. Public buildings and monuments, a gymnasium, wrestling area, baths, and guest houses for officials and competitors were built later. The sanctuary was finally closed by the Christian Emperor Theodosius (390 AD).

Olympia 47 03N 122 53W A seaport and the capital of Washington, on Puget Sound. Founded in 1850, it possesses a fine capitol building (1893). Industries include timber, fishing, and mining. Population (1980): 311,681.

Olympic Games A quadrennial international amateur sports contest. The modern games derive from the ancient Greek athletic festival held at *Olympia, first recorded reliably in 776 BC; however, the games probably date back to the 14th century BC and originated in a religious ceremony. Corrupted in Roman times, they were banned by *Theodosius the Great (393 AD). They were revived at Athens in 1896, largely through the efforts of Baron Pierre de Coubertin (1863–1937), a French educator, who wished to improve national and international understanding through sport. The Winter Olympics were first held in 1924. The Games are governed by the International Olympic Committee, a self-elected international body. Although officially a contest between individuals, hosted by a particular city, the Games are often seen as a competition between countries.

Olympic National Park A national park in NW Washington, mainly in the Olympic Mountains but including a narrow strip along the Pacific Ocean. Established in 1938, the park preserves the glaciered Olympic Mountains, as well as rain forests along the coast. Mount Olympus, the highest point, rises to 7954 ft (2425 m). Area: 1401 sq mi (3629 sq km).

Olympus, Mount (Modern Greek name: Óros Ólimbos) 40 05N 22 21E A small group of mountains in NE central Greece, held in ancient times to be the home of the gods. Highest point: 9570 ft (2917 m).

Om In Indian religions, the greatest of the mantras or mystical sounds embodying and representing spiritual power. In Sanskrit *Om* comprises three sounds *A, U, M* (the vowels being equivalent to *O*), which represent the three Vedic scriptures, the three worlds (earth, atmosphere, heaven), the *Trimurti or some other triple, and ultimately the essence of the universe.

Omaha 41 15N 96 00W A city in Nebraska, on the Missouri River. The state's main commercial center, industries include meat processing and agricultural machinery. Omaha is a center for medical research. Population (1980): 311,681.

Oman, Sultanate of (name until 1970: Muscat and Oman) A country in the Middle East, in E *Arabia. It is mainly flat but rises to 10,194 ft (3107 m) near the coast in the N. The majority of the population is Arab, Ibadhi Muslim by religion, nomadic, and illiterate. *Economy*: oil, which has been extracted since 1967, accounts for about 90% of the country's revenue. There is also beef production, fishing for sardines, tuna, and sharks, and the growing of such produce as cereals, tobacco, and dates; dates, limes, and pomegranates are the chief export crops. *History*: Oman was settled by the Portuguese, Dutch, and English in the 16th century. Since the 19th century Britain has been influential in Oman. It supported the present sultan's overthrow of his father in 1970 and has helped fight the guerrillas in *Dhofar. Head of State: Sultan Qaboos ibn Sa'id. Official language: Arabic. Official currency: Rial Omani of 1000 baiza. Area: 120,000 sq mi (300,000 sq km). Population (1980 est): 890,000. Capital: Muscat.

Omar (*or* Umar) (d. 644 AD) The second *caliph (634–44), who is regarded by Islam as the founder of the Muslim state. Omar continued the Muslim conquests and in 638 visited Jerusalem after its capture. He was murdered in Medina by a discontented slave.

'Omar Khayyam (?1048–?1122) Persian poet, who was famous as a mathematician and made astronomical observations for the reform of the calendar. His poems, characterized by an agnostic and hedonistic philosophy, were written in the form of *ruba'is* (quatrains). The free translation of 75 of them by Edward *Fitzgerald in 1859 became widely popular; more recent translations have been made by the British poets Robert Graves and John Heath Stubbs (1918–).

Omayyads. *See* Umayyads.

ombres chinoises (French: Chinese shadows) A form of shadow puppet drama introduced into 18th-century Europe by travelers returning from the Far East. It was popularized in France by the opening of a shadow theater at Versailles in 1774. The technique involved the representation of brief amusing episodes by black silhouettes cast from solid puppets.

ombudsman A person appointed to investigate grievances against central-government administration. The post originated in Sweden in 1809 and exists in most Scandinavian countries.

Omdurman 15 37N 32 29E A city in the Sudan, on the Nile River. The Mahdi made it his capital in 1885 but his successor, the Khalifa, was defeated by Anglo-Egyptian forces under Lord Kitchener in the battle of Omdurman (1898). The Islamic University of Omdurman was founded in 1961. It has trade in hides, textiles, agricultural produce, and handicrafts. Population (1973): 299,401.

Omsk 55 00N 73 22E A port in the Soviet Union, in the W central RSFSR at the confluence of the Irtysh and Om rivers. Also on the Trans-Siberian Railway, it is a significant transportation center and has important engineering industries and oil refineries. Population (1981 est): 1,044,000.

onager A small wild *ass, *Equus hemionus onager*, of Iran. Onagers have a yellow-brown summer coat, which becomes darker in winter, and roam dry grassland in small herds.

Onassis, Aristotle Socrates (1906–75) Greek businessman, who owned one of the largest independent shipping lines in the world. He started his business in 1932 and during the 1950s became one of the first to construct supertankers. In 1968 he married Jacqueline *Kennedy, his second wife, after a long relationship with Maria *Callas.

OMDURMAN *A painting of the Battle of Omdurman (1898) showing the first charge of the Dervishes.*

Oñate, Juan de (d. 1630) Spanish conquistador. In about 1595 he settled the territory NW of Central America, New Mexico, and in 1601 sought the mythical kingdom of Quivira. Later, seeking a strait to the Pacific, he reached the Colorado River and Gulf of California.

Ondes Martenot (English: Martenot waves) An electronic musical instrument invented in 1928 by Maurice Martenot. It consists of oscillators that produce signals, which are then mixed, amplified, and emitted through a loudspeaker. The frequency of the notes is determined by a keyboard and a special metal ribbon, by means of which glissandi can be produced. The keys can also be moved laterally to produce microtonal variations in pitch. The instrument plays an important part in Messiaen's symphony *Turangalila* (1948).

Onega, Lake A lake in the NW Soviet Union, the second largest in Europe. It forms part of the water route from the Gulf of Finland to the White Sea. Area: 3817 sq mi (9887 sq km).

Oneida 43 04N 75 40W A city in New York state. A religious society, the Oneida Community, was established nearby in 1848. Its members, who made silverware and steel traps, held all property in common, but social experiments ceased when it became a joint stock company in 1881. Population (1970): 11,677.

Oneida North American Iroquoian-speaking Indian tribe, part of the *Iroquois League, found in central New York. Descendants of the Oneida now live in New York, Wisconsin, and Canada.

EUGENE O'NEILL *Playwright whose dramas earned him the Nobel Prize for literature and four Pulitzer Prizes.*

O'Neill, Eugene (1888–1953) US dramatist. The son of actors, he was brought up in the theater and worked for six years as a sailor. He began writing one-act plays while recovering from tuberculosis in a sanatorium. He won critical recognition with *Beyond the Horizon* (1920), *Emperor Jones* (1920), *Anna Christie* (1921), and *Desire Under the Elms* (1924). *Mourning Becomes Electra* (1931) transplants Aeschylus' trilogy to Civil War New England. His finest plays, including *The Iceman Cometh* (1946) and *Long Day's Journey into Night* (1956; written 1940–41), were written while he was suffering from Parkinson's disease and alcoholism. He won the Nobel Prize in 1936.

O'Neill, Thomas P(hilip), Jr. ("Tip"; 1912–) US politician; speaker of the House of Representatives (1977–). A Democrat from Massachusetts, he served in the House of Representatives (1952–). As speaker he

effectively worked behind the scenes to bring opposing factions together in compromise.

onion A hardy herbaceous perennial plant, *Allium cepa*, probably native to central or W Asia but now cultivated worldwide, mainly in temperate regions, for its edible bulb. The mature plant has a leafless stalk, about 40 in (1 m) high, which bears a round head of small white flowers, and six long slender leaves growing directly from the bulb. Onions are grown either from seed or from tiny bulbs called sets, produced in the flower head. Immature bulbs, together with their leaves, are eaten raw in salads, etc.: these are spring, or green, onions (*see* scallion). Family: *Liliaceae*.

Onitsha 6 10N 6 47E A port in S Nigeria, on the Niger River. It suffered damage during the civil war (1967–71). It is an important trading center. Agricultural products are the main exports and manufacturing is being developed, including textiles, printing, and tire retreading. Population (1975 est): 220,000.

Onsager, Lars (1903–76) US chemist, born in Norway. His study of the thermodynamics of irreversible processes helped to solve the problems of separating uranium-235 from uranium-238 by gaseous diffusion, which was essential to the production of nuclear fuel. For this work Onsager was awarded the Nobel Prize in 1968.

Ontario The second largest province of Canada, stretching from the Great Lakes N to Hudson Bay. It lies mainly on the mineral-rich Canadian Shield, a rocky forested plateau with many lakes and rivers. Most of the population live in the gentle fertile lowlands near the S Great Lakes, dominated by the highly industrialized belt stretching from Toronto to Windsor. Manufacturing is very important, especially the production of motor vehicles, steel, pulp and paper, textiles, machinery, petrochemicals, and food products. Ontario is Canada's leading mining province, producing half the world's nickel as well as copper, iron, zinc, gold, and uranium. The province's farmers produce tobacco, fruit, vegetables, and dairy products. Ontario is the wealthiest and most populous Canadian province, the country's political and economic heartland, and the cultural and educational center of English-speaking Canada. *History*: penetrated by French explorers and fur traders in the 17th century, Ontario became British (1763) and was settled by *Loyalists after the American Revolution. The province benefited greatly from the formation of Canada (1867), which provided it with a vast hinterland and a larger domestic market. Area: 344,090 sq mi (891,194 sq km). Population (1978 est): 8,449,700. Capital: Toronto.

Ontario, Lake A lake in E North America, the smallest and easternmost of the Great Lakes. It is fed by the Niagara River and empties into the St Lawrence River. Area: 7313 sq mi (18,941 sq km).

ontogeny. *See* phylogeny.

ontology The branch of philosophy that deals with the theory of being and considers questions about what is and what is not. Ontological theories may assert that only minds exist (extreme *idealism), or that only physical objects do (*see* materialism). The term was introduced by *Wolff to cover one of the chief concerns of *metaphysics.

o'nyong-nyong An acute viral infection occurring in East Africa. The disease, transmitted by mosquitoes, is characterized by a rash, aching joints, headache, and fever. Patients usually recover with rest and drugs to relieve the pain and fever.

onyx A semiprecious stone consisting of a variety of *chalcedony characterized by straight parallel bands, often distinctly colored. Onyx occurs in the lower part of steam cavities in igneous rocks. **Sardonyx** (birthstone for August) is a variety with reddish bands.

oolite A variety of *limestone consisting mainly of beds of ooliths, approximately spherical concretions of calcite accumulated in concentric layers around a nucleus (for example a grain of sand or fragment of a shell). Ooliths of greater diameter than 0.08 in (2 mm) are called pisoliths and the resultant rocks pisolites. Although most oolites are calcareous, oolitic ironstones also occur.

Oort cloud A cloud of ten million or more comets, thought to move around the sun in near-circular orbits that lie in a zone far beyond Pluto's orbit. A comet can be perturbed out of the cloud by, say, a passing star and sent toward the sun, taking many thousands of years to complete its orbit. The cloud is named for the Dutch astronomer Jan Hendrik Oort (1900–).

opah. *See* moonfish.

opal A semiprecious stone consisting of a hydrous amorphous variety of silica. Common opal is a dull-white or milky-blue color, with yellow, brown, or red tinges due to impurities. The precious variety, used as a gem, shows a characteristic internal play of colors (opalescence) resulting from internal reflection and refraction of light passing through adjacent thin layers of different water content. It occurs in cavities in many rocks, deposited by percolating silica-bearing water; geyserite is a variety deposited from hot springs. The variety diatomite, made up of diatom skeletons, is used industrially as an insulator, abrasive, and filtering agent. The main sources of opal gems are Australia and Mexico. Birthstone for October.

Op art A form of abstract art, developed in the 1950s and 1960s, that exploits optical techniques to produce dramatic effects, such as the illusion of movement. Violent color contrasts and subtly distorted patterns are commonly used. Notable exponents include Victor *Vasarely in the US and Bridget *Riley in the UK.

OPEC. *See* Organization of Petroleum Exporting Countries.

Open Door A policy promulgated by the US in 1899 to ensure equal trading rights in China for all countries. Its own trade with China threatened by the growing influence there of the other major powers, the US sought and received the guarantee by Britain, France, Germany, Italy, and Japan of the maintenance of Chinese integrity.

open-hearth process A technique for making *steel from *pig iron, scrap steel, and iron ore. It was developed in the 1850s and is still used, although *electric-arc furnaces are being used increasingly, especially for high-grade steel. The process uses gaseous fuel, which is preheated by the exhaust gases from the furnace. The molten metal lies in a shallow pool at the bottom or hearth of the furnace.

opera A staged dramatic work in which all or most of the text is set to music. Opera originated in Florence in the early 17th century as the result of attempts to revive Greek tragedy and to reproduce its musical elements. These became the aria, recitative, and chorus of operatic convention. Opera began in the court but quickly became a popular public entertainment. The earliest opera still in the modern repertory is Monteverdi's *Orfeo* (1607). In *opera seria, the Italian style of opera developed by such composers as Scarlatti, Lully, and Handel, vocal ability became the dominant feature until Gluck reaffirmed the importance of the dramatic element in the mid-18th century. *Opera buffa developed in the early 18th century and was originally performed between the acts of opera seria. At the end of the 18th century Mozart perfected opera buffa, giving it greater depth and expression. In the early 19th century the influence of Romanticism gave rise to the works of Weber and Meyerbeer, while the Italian *bel canto tradition was maintained by Bellini, Rossini, and Donizetti. In the mid-19th century Wagner evolved the theory of music drama, in which the musical and dramatic elements of opera were integrated. He applied it to his opera cycle *Der Ring des Nibelungen* (1869–1876) and his subsequent operas, which embodied his theory of the *gesamtkunstwerk* (German: complete work of art). Verdi extended the emotional and dramatic range of Italian opera and in his late works assimilated the Wagnerian technique of continuous music in each act in place of the traditional division into separate numbers. The realism of Bizet's *Carmen* (1875) influenced Leoncavallo, Mascagni, and Puccini. In the 20th century a wide variety of operatic styles have flourished, including the dramatic realism of Janáček and the neoclassicism of Stravinsky. Richard Strauss's operas were greatly influenced by Wagner, as was Debussy's opera *Pelléas et Mélisande* (1902). Schoenberg and Berg applied atonal and serial techniques to opera. Other important operatic composers of the 20th century include Prokofiev, Britten, Henze, and Tippett. *See also* opéra comique; comic opera; operetta.

opera buffa A form of comic *opera containing some spoken dialogue. It evolved in Italy in the 18th century, an early example being *Pergolesi's *La serva padrona* (1733). The French genre, *opéra bouffe*, evolved from it in the 19th century and is typified by *Offenbach's operettas.

opéra comique 1. A type of French comic opera of the 18th century with spoken dialogue. 2. In the 19th century, any French opera with spoken dialogue, a category including Bizet's *Carmen* and Gounod's *Faust*.

opera seria A type of *opera common in the 18th century, characterized by a mythological or heroic plot, an Italian libretto, and a formal musical scheme of recitatives and arias.

operetta A light or comic *opera, usually with spoken dialogue. Lehar's *The Merry Widow* (1905) is a typical example.

Ophites (Greek *ophis*: serpent) A Gnostic sect that worshiped the serpent who brought about man's fall (Genesis 3) as the source of wisdom. *See* Gnosticism.

ophthalmia The old name for inflammation of the eye (*see* conjunctivitis). **Ophthalmia neonatorum** is conjunctivitis in newborn babies due to gonorrhea that they have caught from their mothers during birth. The babies are treated with antibiotics and silver nitrate eyedrops.

ophthalmology The medical specialty concerned with the study, diagnosis, and treatment of diseases of the eye. Ophthalmologists are doctors

specializing in this. **Optometry** is the assessment and correction of visual defects, and opticians are not doctors: ophthalmic opticians both test eyesight and prescribe suitable lenses; dispensing opticians make and fit glasses.

Ophüls, Max (M. Oppenheimer; 1902–57) German film director. He worked mostly in France, Italy, and the US. His stylish and elaborate romantic films include *La Ronde* (1950), *Madame De* (1953), and *Lola Montes* (1955).

Opitz (von Boberfeld), Martin (1597–1639) German poet and man of letters. Educated at Heidelberg, he served in the courts of various German nobles until he was appointed historiographer to Ladislaus IV of Poland. His own verse, for example *Teutsche Poemata* (1624), lacks originality but was, with his translations and critical works, especially *Buch von der teutschen Poeterey* (1624), extremely influential in providing a model for German verse and in introducing the work of the *Pléiade, Sidney's *Arcadia*, and other foreign writers.

opium The dried juice obtained from the seed capsule of the *opium poppy. A narcotic drug, opium has been used for centuries in medicine for the relief of pain. Although still sometimes given in the form of laudanum (tincture of opium), its main legitimate uses today include the extraction of its active ingredients—*morphine (first isolated in 1803), codeine, papaverine, etc.—and preparation of their derivatives (e.g. heroin). Because opium causes *drug dependence and overdosage can be fatal, its preparation and use are strictly controlled (in spite of this, illegal trading in opium continues). India and Turkey are the main opium-producing countries.

opium poppy An annual *poppy, *Papaver somniferum*, cultivated since ancient times in N temperate and subtropical regions as the source of *opium. 12–24 in (30–60 cm) tall, it has large white to purple flowers with dark centers and the fruit is a round capsule. Opium is extracted from the latex of the plant, which exudes from notches made in the half-ripened capsule and hardens on exposure to air.

Opium Wars 1. (1839–42) The war between Britain and China precipitated by the confiscation by the Chinese Government of British opium stores in Canton and the murder of a Chinese by British sailors. The British victory was confirmed by the Treaty of Nanking in which five *treaty ports were opened to British trade and residence. 2. (1856–60) The war between Britain and France, on one side, and China. Its immediate cause was the boarding of a British ship by Chinese officials. The allied victory opened further ports to western trade (Treaty of Tientsin, 1858, to which the Chinese agreed in the Peking Convention, 1860) and led to the legalization of opium.

Opole (German name: Oppeln) 50 40N 17 56E A city in SW Poland, on the Oder River. It was the capital (1919–45) of the German province of Upper Silesia. Industries include the manufacture of machinery, chemicals, cement, and textiles. Population (1976 est): 107,500.

Oporto (Portuguese name: Pôrto) 41 09N 8 37W The second largest city in Portugal, on the Douro River near the Atlantic coast. Built on terraces, it has many tall granite houses and a modernized 13th-century cathedral; its university was founded in 1911. It is famous for the export (chiefly to Britain) of its port wine; other exports include fruit, olive oil, and cork. Population (1974 est): 311,800.

OPOSSUM *Young common opossums cling to their mother's fur after emerging from the pouch and remain close to her for about three months before leading an independent existence.*

opossum A New World *marsupial belonging to the family *Didelphidae* (65 species). Opossums are the only marsupials outside Australasia. The common, or Virginian, opossum (*Didelphys marsupialis*) is cat-sized, with a large pouch containing up to 16 teats; it produces at least two litters of young every year. After about three months the young ride on their mother's back, leaving the pouch free for another litter. Opossums live in crevices and abandoned burrows, feeding on both animal and vegetable matter. □mammal.

Oppeln. *See* Opole.

Oppenheimer, J. Robert (1904–67) US physicist, who contributed to quantum mechanics and particle physics. In 1943 he was put in charge of the development of the atom bomb at Los Alamos, N.M. After the war he was appointed chairman of the advisory committee to the Atomic Energy Commission but as a result of his opposition to the development of the hydrogen bomb, he lost his post in 1953 and was labeled a security risk by Senator Joseph *McCarthy's committee. He also served as director (1947–66) of Princeton's Institute for Advanced Study.

opposition An alignment of two celestial bodies in the solar system, usually the sun and a planet, that occurs when they lie directly opposite each other in the sky. The angle planet-earth-sun is then 180°. Venus and Mercury cannot come to opposition with the sun. For the other planets, opposition is the most favorable time for observation.

Ops A Roman fertility goddess, wife of Saturn, identified with the Greek *Rhea. She was usually worshiped together with a primitive rustic god, Consus.

optical activity The rotation of the plane of polarization of plane *polarized light as it passes through certain solutions and crystals. The angle through which the plane is rotated is directly proportional to the path length of the light in the substance and, in the case of a solution, to its concentration. If the plane is rotated clockwise (looking at the oncoming light) the substance is said to be dextrorotatory and is indicated by the prefix *d*–. Levorotatory substances, indicated by *l*–, rotate the plane counterclockwise.

optics The branch of physics concerned with *light and vision. Optics is divided into two major branches: geometrical optics and physical optics. Geometrical optics studies the geometry of light rays as they pass through an optical system. Physical optics is the study of the properties of light including *diffraction, *interference, and polarization (*see* polarized light) and the interaction between light and matter as in *refraction, *scattering, and absorption.

option The right to buy or sell something at an agreed price by a specified date. Usually the option costs a sum of money (the option money), which is not returned if the option is not taken up. Options are sought for such diverse assets as the right to buy a house, the film rights of a book, or a line of stocks or shares. On stock and commodity exchanges options to buy shares or commodities (a call option) or to sell them (a put option) are regular features of trading.

Opuntia. *See* prickly pear.

Opus Dei (Latin: God's work) **1.** In Benedictine monasticism, the monk's primary duty of prayer. It specifically refers to the recitation of prescribed prayers (the Divine Office) at set times known as the canonical hours, namely matins, lauds, prime, terce, sext (noon), nones, vespers, and compline. **2.** An international Roman Catholic organization originating in Spain (1928). It was founded to spread Christian ideals, particularly in university and government circles, and its members include priests and laymen.

orache An annual branching herb or small shrub of the genus *Atriplex* (about 100 species), occurring worldwide on sea shores and waste land and growing 40 in–5 ft (1–1.5 m) high. The leaves are narrow or triangular and, in some species, may be used as a vegetable. Tiny green flowers are borne in a branching cluster and the fruit is surrounded by a winglike membrane. Family: *Chenopodiaceae*.

oracle A response given by a deity, usually through the medium of a priest or priestess, to an individual's inquiry; also, the sacred place at which such responses were sought. Although occurring in Egyptian and other ancient civilizations, the best-known oracles were those of classical Greece. The oldest was that of Zeus at Dodona, where the oracle was interpreted from the rustling of the leaves of oak trees. At the oracle of Apollo at Delphi, which attained great political influence during the 6th and 7th centuries BC, the oracular pronouncements made by the Pythian priestess in a state of frenzy were interpreted in verse by the priests.

Oracle. *See* teletext.

Oradea 47 03N 21 55E A city in NW Romania, on the Crişul Repede River. It is situated in a wine-producing area where many Neolithic, Roman, and other artifacts have been found. Its varied industries include the manufacture of machine tools, chemicals, and food products. Population (1979 est): 178,407.

oral contraceptive A hormonal drug—usually a mixture of an *estrogen and a synthetic *progesterone—taken in the form of tablets ("the Pill") by women to prevent conception. Oral contraceptives act by preventing the monthly release of an egg cell from the ovary. They are taken every day from the 5th to the 26th day of the menstrual cycle (menstruation occurs during the week in which they are not taken). The Pill may cause fluid retention (therefore swelling of the ankles), depression, high blood pressure, weight gain, and in rare cases thrombosis.

Oran (Arabic name: Wahran; French name: Ouahran)   35 45N 0 38W A port in Algeria, on the Mediterranean Sea. Under intermittent Spanish occupation from the 16th to the 18th centuries, it was occupied by France from 1831 until Algerian independence (1962). It has a university (1965). Exports include cereals, wine, wool, and esparto grass. Population (1974 est): 485,139.

orange One of several small evergreen □trees or shrubs of the genus *Citrus*, native to SE Asia but cultivated throughout the tropics and subtropics. The thick oval shiny leaves have winged stalks and the fragrant white five-petaled flowers are borne in clusters. The globular fruit has a dimpled orange or yellow rind and a juicy pulp, rich in sugars, acids, and vitamin C. Fruit of the sweet orange (*C. sinensis*) is eaten fresh while that of the Seville orange (*C. aurantium*) is used to make marmalade. Oranges are also used in soft drinks and confectionery. Family: *Rutaceae*. *See also* tangerine.

Orange The ruling dynasty of the Netherlands since 1815. In the 16th century the Princes of Orange, in S France, married into the House of *Nassau, a member of which, *William the Silent, became Prince of Orange-Nassau (1544) and led the Revolt of the Netherlands against Spain. He and his descendants (one of whom became William III of England) were *stadholders (chief magistrates) of the United Provinces of the Netherlands until its collapse in 1795. In 1815 the family were restored as monarchs of the newly established kingdom of the Netherlands. The principality of Orange was seized by Louis XIV in 1660.

Orange 44 08N 4 48E A city in SE France, in the Vaucluse department. It was the capital of the principality of Orange in the middle ages, the descendants of which formed the House of Orange. There are several notable Roman remains. Population (1975): 26,468.

Orange Free State (Afrikaans name: Oranje Urystaat) An inland province in South Africa. Much of the province consists of the undulating plain of the Highveld. It is predominantly rural, with agriculture as the leading economic activity. Wheat, maize, and stock rearing are important. Mining has developed recently; diamonds, gold, uranium, and coal are produced. Chemicals, fertilizers, and oil from coal are manufactured. The province has a strong Afrikaner culture. *History*: first settled by Voortrekkers in the early 19th century, it was under British rule as the Orange River Sovereignty from 1848 until an independent Orange Free State was recognized in 1854. It joined the Union of South Africa in 1910. Area: 49,886 sq mi (129,152 sq km). Population (1970): 1,716,350. Capital: Bloemfontein.

Orange Order An Irish sectarian society, named for— William III of England (previously William of Orange), pledged to maintain the Protestant succession. Formed in 1795, following William's defeat of the Roman Catholic former king James II, it provided the backbone of Ulster resistance to the *Home Rule movement. The embodiment of Protestant Unionism, its parades have contributed to the political unrest of Northern Irish politics.

Orange River A river in SW Africa. Rising in NE Lesotho, it flows mainly W across the South African plateau to the Atlantic Ocean. The largest river in South Africa, it forms part of the border between South Africa and Namibia. In 1963 the **Orange River Project** was begun to provide, through a series of dams, irrigation and hydroelectric power. Length: 1300 mi (2093 km).

orang-utan A long-armed great *ape, *Pongo pygmaeus*, of Borneo and Sumatra. Orang-utans grow up to 47 in (120 cm) tall, with arms spanning more than 79 in (200 cm), and have long coarse reddish-brown hair. Mainly vegetarian, they are especially fond of durian fruit. They are the only great apes outside Africa and there are fewer than 5000 individuals in the wild.

Oratorians Communities of Roman Catholic priests who live together without taking vows and who devote themselves to teaching, preaching, prayer, and administration of the sacraments. There are two orders: the Italian Oratory of St Philip Neri (founded 1564) and the French Oratoire de Jésus-Christ (1611). The former has oratories in England founded by Cardinal Newman. The latter runs seminaries for the training of priests.

oratorio A musical composition, usually on a religious subject, for soloists, chorus, and orchestra. The name derives from the Oratory of St Philip Neri in 16th-century Rome (see Oratorians), where semidramatized versions of biblical stories were performed with musical accompaniment. Among notable oratorios are the *St Matthew* and *St John Passions* of J. S. Bach, Handel's *Messiah*, Haydn's *The Creation*, Mendelssohn's *Elijah*, Berlioz's *Childhood of Christ*, Elgar's *Dream of Gerontius*, and Tippett's *A Child of Our Time*.

orbital An atomic orbital is the region around the nucleus in which there is an appreciable probability that an electron will be found. In *wave mechanics an electron does not have a fixed orbit as it does in the *Bohr atom; it has instead an orbital in which there is a probability distribution, given by a wave function, that it will be found in a particular region. Each orbital has a fixed energy and a shape determined by three *quantum numbers, one (n) indicating the most probable distance of the electron from the nucleus, one (l) giving its angular momentum, and one (m) giving the orientation of the orbital if it is not spherical. In the formation of a covalent bond between two atoms, a molecular orbital containing two electrons is formed.

orb weaver A *spider belonging to a widely distributed family (*Argiopidae*; over 2500 species), noted for its geometrically designed web. For example, the web of the orange garden spider (*Miranda aurantia*), common in grass and bushes, has a zigzag band and reaches 24 in (60 cm) across.

Orcagna, Andrea (Andrea di Cione; c. 1308–c. 1368) Florentine artist. His only certain surviving painting is the altarpiece in the Strozzi Chapel of Sta Maria Novella, Florence; as a sculptor he is known for his marble tabernacle in Orsanmichele. He became architect to Orsanmichele (1355) and to the Duomo in Florence (1357 and 1364–67) and in Orvieto (1358).

orchestra A body of instrumentalists playing music written or arranged for a specific combination of instruments. The modern **symphony orchestra** evolved from the small and variously constituted orchestras of the 18th century; its original instrumentation (first and second violins, violas, cellos, double basses, bassoons, oboes, flutes, horns, and timpani) being that of the typical symphony. Such orchestras were directed from a continuo keyboard instrument or by the leader of the first violin section. In the 19th century the orchestra was enlarged and the range of instruments widened by the addition of clarinets, trumpets, trombones, and percussion instruments; later the harp, cor anglais, piccolo, bass clarinet, contra bassoon, and tuba were added. In the late 19th century the number of woodwind and brass was increased, and such instruments as the saxophone, saxhorn, Wagner tuba, glockenspiel, and xylophone were occasionally used. The role of the conductor became increasingly important from the early 19th century onward. In the 20th century the piano, guitar, mandolin, marimba, vibraphone, as well as various electric and electronic instruments have all had orchestral parts written for them. The modern symphony orchestra comprises at least a hundred players. The **chamber orchestra** corresponds in size to the smaller orchestras of the 18th century.

orchid A herbaceous perennial plant of the family *Orchidaceae* (about 20,000 species), found worldwide, especially in damp tropical regions. Most temperate orchids grow normally in the soil (i.e. they are terrestrial), while tropical orchids tend to grow nonparasitically on trees (i.e. as epiphytes) and form pseudobulbs (storage organs) at the base of the stem. Orchid flowers vary greatly in shape, color, and size and occur usually in clusters. Each flower consists of three petal-like sepals and three petals—the lowest (labellum) being very distinctive. The one or two stamens and stigma are fused to form a central column that bears pollen grains grouped into masses (pollinia), which are transferred to other flowers by insects. The flowers of many species are adapted to receive only a particular species of insects in order to restrict natural hybridization; examples are the bee, fly, and spider orchids (genus *Ophrys*). The fruit is a capsule containing enormous numbers of tiny seeds, which are dispersed by wind. Many orchids are cultivated for ornament, both commercially for the florist trade and by amateur growers (see Cattleya; Cymbidium; Odontoglossum; slipper orchid); one genus—*Vanilla*—is of commercial importance as the source of vanilla flavoring.

orchil (or archil) One of several *lichens (*Umbilicaria, Roccella, Evernia, Lecanova*, and *Ochrolechia*) from which a violet dye can be extracted by fermentation. The name is also applied to the dye itself.

Orczy, Baroness Emmusca (1865–1947) British novelist. Born in Hungary, she went to London to study art. Her best-known novel is The

Scarlet Pimpernel (1905), concerning the adventures of an English nobleman who smuggles aristocrats out of Revolutionary France.

Order of the British Empire, The Most Excellent A British order of knighthood, instituted in 1917 and having five classes: Knights or Dames Grand Cross (GBE); Knights or Dames Commanders (KBE or DBE); Commanders (CBE); Officers (OBE); and Members (MBE). Its motto is *For God and Empire*.

orders of architecture The fundamental elements of classical □architecture, comprising five main types of supportive column—Doric, Tuscan, Ionic, Corinthian, and Composite. The column was first employed by the Egyptians but it was developed by the Greeks and Romans to such an extent that the proportions between the column's constituent parts determined the proportions of the entire building.
Each order usually consists of four main parts, the base, shaft, *capital, and entablature, these having individual shapes and types of decoration. The first order to be developed, the Doric, takes two forms: the Greek Doric, which has no base, and the Roman Doric, more slender in proportion and with a base. Roman Doric's unadorned and unfluted counterpart is the Tuscan order. The Ionic first appeared in Asia Minor in about the 6th century BC and was adopted by the Greeks in the 5th century BC. It has slender proportions and a capital adorned with four spiral scrolls (volutes), two at the front and two at the back. The most decorative order, the Corinthian, was developed by the Romans, although it was occasionally used in ancient Greece. The Romans also combined the Corinthian capital of *acanthus leaves with the volutes of the Ionic capital to form the Composite order.

A **pilaster** is a rectangular column attached to the wall. It conforms to the system of orders but, unlike the cylindrical column, is usually only decorative in function.

Ordovician period A geological period of the Lower Paleozoic era, between the Cambrian and Silurian periods. It lasted from about 515 to 445 million years ago. It is divided into the Upper and Lower Ordovician, based on the graptolite fossils that are abundant in the deepwater deposits.

Ordzhonikidze (name until 1944: Vladikavkas; name from 1944 until 1954: Dzaudzhikau) 43 02N 44 43E A city in the S Soviet Union, the capital of the North Ossetian ASSR in the RSFSR. An important road and rail junction, it has a variety of industries, including metallurgy and food processing. Population (1981 est): 287,000.

ore A rock body or mineral deposit from which one or more useful materials, usually metals, can be economically extracted. The metal content of the various ores differs; iron ore contains about 20–30% iron, whereas copper ores may contain only 0.5% copper. The gangue is the waste material left when the desired mineral has been extracted.

Örebro 59 17N 15 13E A city in S Sweden. An ancient city, it was largely rebuilt following a fire in 1854. It has a university (1967) and its manufactures include footwear, machinery, and chemicals. Population (1978 est): 116,969.

oregano An aromatic perennial herb, *Origanum vulgare*, native to the Mediterranean and W Asia. The dried leaves and flowers are used as a culinary flavoring and the plant is a source of essential oils. Family: *Labiatae*.

Oregon A state on the NW Pacific coast; bordered by California and Nevada to the S, the Pacific Ocean to the W, Washington to the N, and Idaho to the E. Its topography is diverse; the Cascade Range extends N–S dividing the state between the valleys of the W and the dry plateau areas of the E. The Willamette Valley contains the major settlements. The economy is based predominantly on agriculture and forestry. Oregon is the nation's leading timber state and approximately half its area is forested; the Douglas fir is especially important. Much of the timber is used to produce plywood, pulp, and paper. Agriculture includes cattle ranching in the drier areas, dairy farming in the valleys, and wheat growing in the NE; specialized crops, such as cherries, are also grown. Hydroelectric-power resources have led to the development of metal-processing industries. *History*: originally occupied by several Indian tribes, the first extensive US exploration was by the *Lewis and Clark Expedition (1805). Fur traders became active shortly thereafter. There was considerable migration of settlers from the Midwest along the famous *Oregon Trail during the mid-19th century. It became a territory in 1848 and a state in 1859, after being separated from Washington (1853). Industrial development and the state's relatively unspoiled environment spurred growth in the 20th century. Area: 96,981 sq mi (251,180 sq km). Population (1980): 2,632,663. Capital: Salem.

Oregon Trail An overland route from the Missouri to the Columbia River, first followed by explorers and fur traders, and later by settlers. Traversing more than 2000 mi (3200 km) of frontier territory, the Oregon Trail began at Independence, Mo., crossed the Rockies at the South Pass, then followed the course of the Colorado and Snake rivers, and ended at Astoria, a fur trading center at the outlet of the Columbia River. During the Great Migration of 1842–43, thousands of settlers from the American midwest followed the route of the Oregon Trail in wagon trains to establish new homes and towns in the Oregon territory.

Oregon Treaty (1846) US-British agreement that settled the N boundary line of the US west of the Rocky Mountains. A compromise, the treaty set the boundary at the 49th parallel except for the island of Vancouver. The British, through the *Hudson's Bay Company, retained free navigation rights on the *Columbia River.

Orel (or Oryol) 52 58N 36 04E A city in the Soviet Union, in the W RSFSR. Founded in 1564, it was severely damaged in World War II. Industries include engineering. The writer Turgenev was born here, and his house is now a museum. Population (1981 est): 315,000.

Orenburg (name from 1938 until 1957: Chkalov) 51 50N 55 00E A city in the Soviet Union, in the W RSFSR on the Ural River. It was founded in 1735 by the Cossacks on the site of present-day Orsk, subsequently being moved downstream. Industries include engineering and consumer-goods manufacture. Population (1981 est): 482,000.

Orense 42 20N 7 52W A city in NW Spain, in Galicia on the Miño River. It possesses a cathedral and a remarkable bridge built in 1230. Industries include iron founding and flour milling. Population (1970): 73,379.

Oresme, Nicole d' (c. 1320–82) French philosopher and churchman. He became master of the College of Navarre at Paris in 1355 and later Bishop of Lisieux (1377). His writings deal with politics, natural science, geometry, and economics. He was also an early advocate of the theory that the earth revolves around other bodies.

Orestes In Greek legend, the son of *Agamemnon, King of Mycenae, and *Clytemnestra. Encouraged by his sister *Electra, he avenged his father's murder by killing his mother and her lover Aegisthus. In the dramatic trilogy of *Aeschylus he is pursued by the *Erinyes until he is acquitted at the Areopagus in Athens by the deciding vote of Athena.

Øresund (or Öresund). See Sound, the.

orfe A carnivorous food and game fish, *Idus idus*, also called ide, found in rivers and lakes of Europe and NW Asia. Its stout elongated body, 12–20 in (30–50 cm) long, is blue-gray or blackish with a silvery belly. The golden orfe is a reddish-gold variety. Family: *Cyprinidae*; order: *Cypriniformes*.

Orff, Carl (1895–1982) German composer, teacher, conductor, and editor. He developed a monodic style of composition characterized by lively rhythms; his best-known work is the scenic oratorio *Carmina Burana* (1935–36), based on 13th-century Latin and German poems found in a Benedictine monastery in Bavaria. Orff also developed educational percussion instruments, such as the stone chimes.

organ A musical wind instrument of early origin, which developed from the reed pipes and the *hydraulis. The modern organ consists of a large number of graduated pipes, some of which contain reeds, fitted over a wind chest and blown by manual or electric bellows. The pipes are made to sound by depressing keys or pedals. Each pipe sounds one note, but groups of duplicate pipes, called stops, can be made to sound together or successively. Different stops have different tone colors, many of which resemble orchestral instruments. An organ console may have as many as five or more keyboards, known as the great, swell, choir, solo, and echo, as well as pedals. Each keyboard has a separate range of stops and different characteristics; the swell, for example, has shutters over the pipe holes that allow crescendos and decrescendos.

Coupler mechanisms allow one keyboard to become automatically linked to another. These allow, for example the pedals, which normally play the deepest notes, to play notes many octaves higher.

The action linking keys and pipes consists of a series of rods called a tracker action or wires conveying electrical impulses. The modern **electronic organ** consists of a series of electronic oscillators to produce notes, which are then amplified.

organic chemistry. See chemistry.

Organisation de l'Armée secrète (OAS) An organization of French settlers in Algeria opposed to Algerian independence from France. The OAS was established in 1961 and led by General Raoul Salan (1899–). Its campaign of terrorism in Algeria and France included the attempted assassination in September, 1961, of the French president, de Gaulle, who by March, 1962, had reached agreement with the Algerian nationalists (see Front de Libération nationale). Salan was captured in April (and imprisoned 1962–68) and the OAS collapsed.

Organization for Economic Cooperation and Development (OECD) An international organization founded in 1961 to further economic growth among its members, expand world trade, and coordinate aid to developing countries. It succeeded the Organization for European Economic Cooperation, which had been set up in 1948 to coordinate the *Marshall Plan for European economic recovery after World War II. The headquarters of the OECD are in Paris.

Organization of African Unity (OAU) An intergovernmental organization of independent African countries. It was founded in 1963 to provide a forum for discussion of political and economic problems affecting African states and to formulate policies toward such problems. The OAU meets annually but maintains a standing committee in Addis Ababa (Ethiopia).

Organization of American States (OAS) A body founded in 1948 to foster mutual understanding and cooperation between American republics and collective security. It is based on the principle of the *Monroe Doctrine. In 1962 Cuba was expelled from the OAS because of its acceptance of nuclear missiles from the Soviet Union.

Organization of Central American States An international organization founded in 1951. Its members include Costa Rica, El Salvador, Guatemala, Honduras, and Nicaragua, and its headquarters are in Guatemala City. Its aim is to promote social, cultural, and economic development through joint action.

Organization of Petroleum Exporting Countries (OPEC) An organization founded in 1960 to represent the interests of the 11 chief oil-exporting nations (Abu Dhabi, Algeria, Indonesia, Iran, Iraq, Kuwait, Libya, Nigeria, Qatar, Saudi Arabia, and Venezuela) in dealings with the major oil companies. OPEC is the only really successful primary-product *cartel, deciding in 1973 to double its share in the receipts from oil exported; it has continued to control the price of oil.

organ-pipe cactus A branching columnar *cactus, of the genus *Lemacrocereus* or *Cereus*, especially *L. thurberi*, which resembles a candelabrum and is found in deserts of the S US and Mexico. Up to 33 ft (10 m) high, it is grown in hedgerows and used for fuel and construction. The fruit is edible.

organ-pipe coral A *coral, *Tubipora musica*, occurring in shallow waters of the Indian and Pacific Oceans. It is composed of a colony of long upright stalked *polyps supported by bright-red skeletal tubes of fused spicules. Order: *Stolonifera*.

organum (Latin: organ, instrument) A type of medieval polyphonic vocal composition in which a plainchant melody was accompanied by voices at the fixed intervals of the octave and fourth or fifth. See also ars antiqua.

oribi A rare antelope, *Ourebia ourebi*, of African grasslands. About 35 in (90 cm) high at the shoulder, oribis have slender legs, large ears, a fawn coat, and a short bristly tail; males have short straight horns. Hiding among long grass during the day, they graze in small herds at dawn and dusk.

orienteering A navigational sport, held over rugged country, that originated in Sweden in 1918 and is designed to test both intellectual and athletic ability. Using a map and compass, competitors run around a series of control points that must be visited in the prescribed sequence. Distances range from 2 to 8 mi (3–13 km).

origami The oriental art of paper folding, which developed into a traditional Japanese craft. It is used in the formal ceremonial wrapping of gifts and to construct models of birds, animals, sailing boats, etc., which can often be made to move, e.g. birds that flap their wings. It now enjoys a wide popularity outside Japan.

Origen (c. 185–c. 254 AD) Egyptian theologian and Father of the Church, born at Alexandria, son of a Christian martyr. As head of Alexandria's catechetical school he gained fame as a teacher. He was ordained in Palestine (c. 230), but the Bishop of Alexandria immediately unfrocked him, maintaining that he was unfit for priesthood because he had castrated himself. He then settled in Caesarea, where he founded a school. During the persecution of Emperor Decius (c. 250) he was imprisoned and tortured at Tyre. The most famous of his many influential works are his critical edition of the Bible, the *Hexapla*, and his theological treatise, *De principiis*.

original sin In Christian doctrine, the inherent wickedness of mankind occasioned by Adam's fall (Genesis 3). After much debate by the Church Fathers, St *Augustine of Hippo's diagnosis, that it is inescapably transmitted to us by our parents and that only the divine initiative of *grace can redeem us, was accepted as orthodox (*see also* Pelagius). St Thomas *Aquinas accorded greater scope to the human will, and after the Reformation the concept of original sin became unfashionable among many theologians. Many modern thinkers reject it or interpret it symbolically.

Orinoco River (Spanish name: Río Orinoco) The third largest river system in South America. Rising in S Venezuela, it flows in an arc forming part of the Venezuela–Colombia border before entering the Atlantic Ocean via an extensive delta region. It provides an important communications system; oceangoing vessels can penetrate upstream for about 226 mi (364 km). Drainage basin area: 365,000 sq mi (940,000 sq km). Length: about 2575 km (1600 mi).

oriole A songbird belonging to an Old World family (*Oriolidae*; 28 species) occurring mainly in tropical forests. Orioles generally have a black-and-yellow plumage, measure 7–12 in (18–30 cm), and feed on fruit and insects. The golden oriole (*Oriolus oriolus*) is the only species reaching Europe, visiting Britain in the summer.

American orioles belong to the family *Icteridae* (87 species). 6–21 in (16–54 cm) long, they usually have a black plumage with red, yellow, or brown markings.

Orion A very conspicuous constellation that lies on the celestial equator and can therefore be seen from most parts of the world. The brightest stars, *Rigel and the slightly fainter *Betelgeuse, lie at opposite corners of a quadrilateral of stars with Bellatrix and Saiph, both 2nd magnitude, at the other corners. Inside the quadrilateral three 2nd-magnitude stars form **Orion's Belt**, S of which lies the **Orion nebula**, one of the brightest emission □nebulae.

Orissa A state in E India, on the Bay of Bengal. Its coastal plain extends through the Eastern *Ghats via broad valleys into interior highlands. Orissa is grossly overcrowded and its inhabitants farm rice, turmeric, and sugar cane. Fishing, forestry, and the mining of iron ore, manganese, chromite, and coal are economically important. There is also some heavy industry. *History*: known from ancient times, Orissa ruled a maritime empire during the 1st millennium AD. Partitioned by Muslim conquerors (17th century), it gradually fell under British domination (18th–19th centuries). Area: 60,132 sq mi (155,782 sq km). Population (1981): 26,272,054. Capital: Bhubaneswar.

Orizaba 18 51N 97 08W A city and resort in E central Mexico. It is the chief center of the textile industry. Population (1976 est): 111,510.

Orkney Islands (*or* Orkneys) A group of about 70 islands off the N coast of Scotland, separated from the mainland by the Pentland Firth. About 20 of the islands are inhabited; the chief ones are Mainland (Pomona), South Ronaldsay, Westray, Sanday, and Hoy. The population is of Scandinavian descent, reflecting the Islands' long connections with Norway and Denmark. Agriculture is of major importance within the Islands' economy, producing chiefly beef cattle and poultry. It serves as a base for the exploitation of North Sea oil. Area: 376 sq mi (974 sq km). Population (1981): 18,906. Administrative center: Kirkwall.

Orlando 28 33N 81 21W A city in central Florida. A tourist resort, it is the commercial center for citrus growing. Walt Disney World is situated nearby. Population (1980): 128,394.

Orlando, Vittorio Emanuele (1860–1952) Italian statesman; prime minister (1917–19). Representing Italy at the Paris Peace Conference (1919) after World War I, his failure to secure sufficiently favorable terms for Italy led to his resignation. He supported Mussolini and *Matteotti's murder in 1924, retiring from politics until after World War II. He was elected to the Senate in 1948.

Orléans 47 54N 1 54E A city in N France, the capital of the Loiret department on the Loire River. In 1429, during the Hundred Years' War, the city was delivered from the English by Joan of Arc. Its cathedral, which was destroyed by the Huguenots in 1568, was rebuilt in the 17th century. The focal point of road and rail routes, Orléans has an extensive trade in wine, brandy, and agricultural produce. Its manufactures include machinery, electrical goods, and textiles. Population (1975): 105,956.

Orléans, Charles, Duc d' (1394–1465) French poet. He was captured by the English at the battle of Agincourt (1415) and spent the next 25 years in prison in England, where he wrote a collection of poems in English. His son became Louis XII of France.

Orléans, Louis Philippe Joseph, Duc d' (1747–93) French revolutionary. A cousin of Louis XVI of France, he nevertheless supported the dissident Third Estate at the beginning of the *French Revolution. He joined the radical Jacobins in 1791 and voted for the execution of the king. He was himself executed after his son (later King Louis Philippe) had joined the Austrian coalition against France.

Orléans, Siege of (October, 1428–May, 1429) English siege of the strategically important city of Orléans during the *Hundred Years' War, undertaken with little success on either side until the arrival of *Joan of Arc to relieve the city. Her achievement of this aim was a notable factor in French military resurgence and signaled the beginning of the end of English occupation.

Orlov, Grigori Grigorievich, Count (1734–83) Russian soldier, who was the lover of *Catherine the Great. Orlov and his brother **Aleksei Grigorievich Orlov** (1737–1807) led the coup d'état that placed Catherine on the throne in 1862. Grigori Orlov had a favorable position at court but exerted little influence over Catherine.

Ormandy, Eugene (E. Blau; 1899–1985) Hungarian-born US conductor. His early career was as a violinist, but he turned to conducting soon after settling in the US in 1921. He was conductor of the Philadelphia Orchestra, in succession to Stokowski, from 1938 to 1980.

ormolu (French: *d'or moulu*, powdered gold) Ornamental gilded bronze usually used as embellishment on furniture. The 17th- and early 18th-century technique applied the gold coating by means of a mercuric process, which released poisonous fumes. This was abandoned in favor of applying gold dust in a varnish. Ormolu mounts were frequent on French 18th- and 19th-century furniture.

Ormonde, James Butler, 1st Duke of (1610–88) Anglo-Irish general, who in the *Civil War commanded the royalist army in Ireland (1641–50). After the Restoration of the monarchy, he was Lord Lieutenant of Ireland (1661–69, 1677–84).

Ornithischia An order of herbivorous *dinosaurs that lived in the Jurassic and Cretaceous periods (200–65 million years ago). They had hip bones arranged like those of birds (the name means "bird hips") and a horny beak at the front of the jaw (teeth were present only at the rear). Some were bipedal while others evolved to become quadrupedal and heavily armored. There were both amphibious and terrestrial forms. *See* Iguanodon; Stegosaurus; Triceratops.

Ornitholestes A dinosaur that lived in North America during the Jurassic and Cretaceous periods (200–65 million years ago). About 7 ft (2 m) long, it was lightly built and moved on its long slender hind limbs balanced by a long stiff tail. Its fore limbs were short with long slender clawed fingers and it probably lived in forest undergrowth, catching birds, lizards, and mammals.

ornithology The study of *birds. Ornithology is a popular pastime as well as a branch of zoology; the records of bird spottings made by amateur ornithologists can be valuable to professional scientists in helping to determine the ecology and behavior of bird populations. Recovery of rings used in bird-ringing experiments provides information regarding the dispersion and migration of birds. Many species are protected by legislation, and such bodies as the Audubon Society exist to promote the establishment of bird sanctuaries and general interest in birds.

orogeny A period of mountain building. Several major orogenies have occurred in the earth's geological history, the main ones since the Precambrian being the Caledonian (in the Lower Paleozoic), Variscan (including the Armorican and Hercynian phases, in the Upper Paleozoic), and the Alpine (in the Tertiary). **Orogenesis** is the process of mountain building, including folding, faulting, and thrusting, resulting from the collision of two continents, which compresses the sediment between them into mountain chains (*see* plate tectonics).

Orontes River A river in SW Asia. Rising in Lebanon, it flows mainly N through Syria and then SW past Antioch (Turkey) to enter the Mediterranean Sea. Length: 230 mi (370 km).

Orozco, José (1883–1949) Mexican mural painter. His early watercolors of prostitutes were so bitterly attacked that he sought refuge in the US (1917–20). In 1922, however, the Mexican Government commissioned him, *Rivera, *Siqueiros, and others to paint murals in the National Preparatory School, Mexico City. Renewed criticism of his social and political subject matter led to his second visit to the US (1927–34), where he made his name with murals for several educational institutions.

Orpheus A legendary Greek poet and musician, the son of the muse Calliope by either Apollo or Oeagrus, King of Thrace. After sailing with the *Argonauts he married *Eurydice. After her death, he descended to Hades to recover her. *Persephone, charmed by his playing on the lyre, released Eurydice but Orpheus lost her when he disobeyed the gods' command not to look back at her. He met his death at the hands of the Maenads, followers of *Dionysus, who dismembered him. He was believed to be the founder of the *Orphic mysteries, a cult dating from the 7th century BC, which was concerned with the liberation of the soul from the body.

Orphic mysteries An esoteric religious cult (*see* mysteries) in ancient Greece and S Italy. It was based on poems, probably datable to the 7th century BC, which its adherents believed were written by *Orpheus. According to these, the material world was made from the ashes of the Titans, whom Zeus destroyed for devouring his son Dionysus. Vegetarianism, participation in the mystical rites, and high ethical standards were demanded of initiates.

orphism An abstract form of *cubism, which developed in France about 1912. Albert Gleizes (1881–1953), Jean Metzinger (1883–1956), and Gino *Severini all contributed to this brightly colored flat patterned style but the chief exponent, *Delaunay, preferred to call his version *simultaneisme*. His work became purely abstract by 1914, greatly influencing *Klee and *Kandinsky.

Orr, Bobby (Robert Gordon O.; 1948–   ) Canadian hockey player. He played for the Boston Bruins (1967–76). The holder of many scoring records for defensemen, he was named the National Hockey League's top defenseman 8 times (1968–75).

orrisroot The fragrant rhizome (underground stem) of several European plants of the genus *Iris*, chiefly *I. florentina*, *I. pallida* and *I. germanica*. It is dried and ground for use in perfumes and medicines.

Orsini A Roman family, originating in the 10th century, that led the propapal (Guelf) faction in Rome during the 13th century. Several members became high-ranking clerics including two popes, Celestine III (reigned 1191–98) and Nicholas III (reigned 1277–80). They remained a dominant force in the politics of Rome and the papacy during the early modern period, attaining princely status in 1629.

Orsk 51 13N 58 35E A city in the Soviet Union, in the W RSFSR at the confluence of the Ural and Or rivers. It has an oil refinery and also manufactures heavy machinery. Population (1981 est): 254,000.

Ortega y Gasset, José (1883–1955) Spanish philosopher and writer. He became professor of metaphysics at Madrid University in 1910. His philosophy was chiefly concerned with what he called "the metaphysics of vital reason." In his best-known book, *La rebelión de las masas* (1930), he attacked mass rule, which, he argued, would lead to chaos.

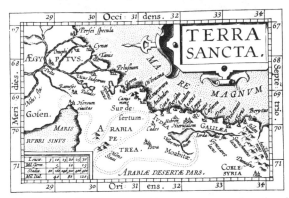

ORTELIUS *The Theatrum orbis terrarum was enlarged and reissued until 1612 and this miniature map of Palestine was first published in 1601. It shows the route taken by Moses and the Israelites on the flight from Egypt.*

Ortelius, Abraham (1527–98) Flemish cartographer. Ortelius traveled widely, buying and selling antiquities and maps. His *Theatrum orbis terrarum* (1570), a collection of maps charting the whole world, became the definitive contemporary cartographical system. Ortelius became geographer to Philip II of Spain in 1575.

orthicon A television camera tube in which a low-energy electron beam scans a target screen, consisting of a thin dielectric plate with a mosaic of photosensitive squares on one side and a thin metallic coating on the other. Each square and its metallic electrode form a tiny capacitor; when light falls on a photosensitive element the capacitor becomes charged. The scanning beam discharges these capacitors and thus becomes modulated by the pattern of light falling on the screen.

orthoclase An alkali potassium *feldspar, $KAlSi_3O_8$. It is formed at intermediate to low temperatures and crystallizes in the monoclinic crystal system, often with twinned crystals. Orthoclase is found in acid igneous rocks and in many metamorphic rocks. It is white, pink, or greenish gray, and is softer than quartz, with a duller luster. Commercially orthoclase is frequently obtained from pegmatites; it is used in the manufacture of glass, ceramic glazes, and enamels.

orthodontics. *See* dentistry.

Orthodox Church The federation of self-governing Churches historically associated with the eastern part of the Roman Empire and separated from the Latin Church since 1054 (*see* Filioque); also called the Eastern Orthodox Church. The four ancient *patriarchs of Orthodoxy are of Constantinople (which has primacy of honor), Alexandria, Antioch, and Jerusalem; in addition there are patriarchs of Moscow, Georgia, Serbia, Bulgaria, and Romania. Independent or autocephalous Orthodox Churches exist in Greece, Cyprus, Albania, Czechoslovakia, and Poland. There are numerous congregations in other countries, many established by Russian immigrants after the Revolution. Government is by bishops, who must be unmarried, priests, who may marry but only before ordination, and deacons, who play an important liturgical role. The Orthodox Church claims the authority of *Apostolic Succession and regards itself as the one true Church, accepting as doctrine only the *Nicene Creed. Its worship is sacramental and centered on the Eucharist and the ancient liturgies of St John Chrysostom and St Basil, which are always solemnly celebrated and sung without accompaniment. Communion is given in both kinds. The veneration of *icons is a distinctive feature of Orthodox worship; statues and other three-dimensional images are forbidden. Easter is the main feast of the Church year, which follows the Julian calendar and therefore varies considerably from Western custom in dating major Christian festivals. *See also* Greek Orthodox Church; Russian Orthodox Church.

orthopedics The medical specialty concerned with treating deformities caused by disease of and injury to the bones and joints. This includes the use of surgery, manipulation, traction, etc., in correcting deformities and fractures, together with rehabilitation to enable patients to lead an independent life. The availability of artificial hip joints has greatly extended the scope of orthopedics in the treatment of severe arthritis of the hip.

Orthoptera A mainly tropical order of generally large stout-bodied insects (15,000 species), including the *grasshoppers and *crickets. The hind legs are enlarged and specialized for jumping and the large blunt head has biting jaws for feeding on vegetation. Typically there are two pairs of wings—the front pair thicker—but few species are good fliers. Many species produce sounds by rubbing one part of the body against another (stridulation).

ortolan A Eurasian *bunting, *Emberiza hortulana*, about 6 in (16 cm) long, having a brown-streaked plumage with a yellow throat and pinkish belly. Prior to its autumn migration to N Africa and the Middle East it stores large amounts of fat and for this reason it is trapped in large numbers as a table delicacy.

Oruro 17 59S 67 08W A city in central Bolivia, 12,160 ft (3705 m) above sea level. It is the center of an important tinmining area; other minerals worked include silver, copper, and wolfram. It has a technical university (1892). Population (1976): 124,091.

Orvieto 42 43N 12 06E A city in central Italy, in Umbria. It is reputed to be the site of the Etruscan city Volsinii, which was destroyed by the Romans in 280 BC. Notable buildings include the gothic cathedral and several palaces. A popular tourist center, it is also famous for its white wine. Population (1971): 23,220.

Orwell, George (Eric Blair; 1903–50) British novelist. Born in India, he was educated at Eton and served in the Burmese Imperial Police from 1922 to 1927. In *Down and Out in Paris and London* (1933) and *The Road to Wigan Pier* (1937) he described his experience of poverty. He criticized official communist policies and practices in *Homage to Catalonia* (1936), an autobiographical account of the Spanish Civil War, and expressed his anti-Stalinist convictions in the political allegory *Animal Farm* (1945). *Nineteen Eighty Four* (1949) is a deeply pessimistic view of a totalitarian future.

Oryol. *See* Orel.

oryx A desert antelope, *Oryx gazella*, which comprises two races, beisa and gemsbok, of S and E Africa. Up to 47 in (120 cm) high at the shoulder, oryxes have long slender straight horns and are grayish brown with black markings on the face and legs. The herds feed at night on desert plants. The white Arabian oryx (*O. leukoryx*) and the grayish-white N African scimitar-horned oryx (*O. tao*) are both endangered species.

Osaka 34 40N 135 30E A port in Japan, in SW Honshu on the Yodo delta. The third largest city in Japan, it was a leading commercial center by the 17th century. Imperial palaces were built here from the 4th century AD and an ancient Buddhist temple (593 AD) still remains. It is overlooked by the 16th-century castle (reconstructed). A cultural center, it possesses several universities and has a famous puppet theater. Together with Kobe, Kyoto, and several small cities it now forms the **Osaka-Kobe** industrial area, second in importance only to the Tokyo-Yokohama area, and in common with Tokyo suffers from serious atmospheric pollution as well as traffic congestion. Major industries are textiles, steel, electrical equipment, and chemicals. Population (1980): 2,648,000.

Osborne, John (1929–) British dramatist. One of the original *Angry Young Men, he gave expression to the rage and frustration of a whole generation in the character of Jimmy Porter, the disillusioned antihero of *Look Back in Anger* (1956). His criticism of contemporary Britain continued in such plays as *The Entertainer* (1957) and *West of Suez* (1971).

Oscar. *See* Academy of Motion Picture Arts and Sciences.

Oscar II (1829–1907) King of Sweden (1872–1907) and of Norway from 1872 until its final separation from Sweden in 1905. He was also a writer, especially of poetry.

Osceola (?1800–38) Seminole Indian leader. Rebelling at attempts to relocate his people from Georgia to west of the Mississippi River, he settled in Florida with a band of followers. In 1835 he was responsible for killing a US Indian agent, precipitating the Second Seminole War (1835–42). Entrenched in the Everglades, he fought guerrilla style until he was captured (1837) while under a flag of truce. He died while in prison.

oscilloscope. *See* cathode-ray oscilloscope.

Oshawa 43 53N 78 51W A city and port in central Canada, in S Ontario on Lake Ontario. A prosperous agricultural center, it houses a major motor-vehicle factory. Other industries include metal goods, furniture, glass, and plastics. Population (1976): 107,023.

Oshogbo 7 50N 4 35E A city in SW Nigeria. It developed as a commercial center after the arrival of the railroad (1906). Its main exports are cocoa and palm oil; there are also local tobacco-processing, cotton-weaving, and dyeing industries. Population (1975 est): 282,000.

osier A small *willow tree, *Salix viminalis*, 10–33 ft (3–10 m) high, with flexible hairy branches used in basket making. The long narrow dark-green leaves are smooth above and white and silky beneath, with inrolled margins. Osiers are found in marshy areas throughout central and S Eurasia and often cultivated.

Osijek 45 33N 18 42E A city in N central Yugoslavia, in Croatia on the Drava River. An agricultural trading center, it manufactures agricultural machinery and footwear. Population (1971): 95,000.

Osipenko. *See* Berdyansk.

Osiris The Egyptian god of the dead, the brother and husband of *Isis; as the father of *Horus (the sun), he was also the god of renewal and rebirth. He was killed by his evil brother *Set. After Isis had magically reconstructed his body, he became ruler of the underworld. The pharaohs, and later all men who passed the judgment of good and evil, became identified with Osiris after death. He is usually portrayed holding the royal flail and crook. He was identified by the Greeks with *Dionysus.

Osler, Sir William (1849–1919) Canadian physician, who pioneered modern clinical teaching methods. In 1872 Osler identified the particles in blood known as *platelets. He was appointed professor of medicine at the new Johns Hopkins University, Baltimore, in 1888. Osler introduced new attitudes and ideas to teaching medicine, encouraging examination of patients in the wards— and the use of laboratories by students. In 1905 he became Regius Professor of Medicine at Oxford University. A classics scholar, he bequeathed his library to McGill University, Montreal.

Oslo (former name (1877–1925): Kristiania) 59 56N 10 54E The capital and main port of Norway, situated in the SE at the head of Oslo Fjord. It is the financial and industrial center of Norway. The principal industries include the manufacture of consumer goods and shipbuilding. A cultural center, Oslo is the site of a university (1811), the National Theater, and several notable museums. Fine buildings include the 17th-century cathedral and the 19th-century royal palace. *History*: founded in the 11th century as a defensive post against the Danes, it became capital in 1299. It developed into an important trading post under the influence of the Hanseatic League and was rebuilt after a fire in the 17th century. It was occupied by the Germans in World War II. Population (1981 est): 452,023.

Osman I (c. 1258–c. 1326) Emir of the small Turkish state in Asia Minor that later developed into the *Ottoman Empire. He was the eponymous ancestor of the Ottoman sultans. Under Osman the state expanded mainly at the expense of the Byzantines and shortly before he died Bursa was captured.

OSIRIS *The third innermost coffin of Tutankhamen, made of gold, portrays the pharaoh as Osiris.*

osmiridium A naturally occurring alloy of osmium and iridium, with minor quantities of platinum, rhodium, and ruthenium. It is used for fountain pen nibs because it is hard and resistant.

osmium (Os) An extremely hard bluish-silver metal of the platinum group. It is one of the densest elements known (relative density 22.6). Its major use is in the production of hard alloys with other noble metals, for pen nibs and electrical contacts. The tetroxide (OsO_4) is volatile (bp 130°C) and very toxic. At no 76; at wt 190.2; mp 3045 ± 20°C; bp 5027 ± 100°C.

osmosis The passage of a solvent from a less concentrated into a more concentrated solution through a semipermeable membrane (one allowing the passage of solvent, but not solute, molecules). Osmosis stops if the pressure of the more concentrated solution exceeds that of the less concentrated solution by an amount known as the **osmotic pressure** between them. In living organisms the solvent is water and osmosis plays an important role in effecting the distribution of water in plants and animals: the passage of water into and out of cells is determined by the osmotic pressures of the extracellular and intracellular solutions. Osmosis can be used in the *desalination of water.

Osmunda A genus of stout leathery *ferns (about 12 species), found in wet tropical and temperate regions. Their short thick branching rhizomes give rise to branching fronds, 20–71 in (50–180 cm) high, made up of light-green tapering leaflets with expanded bases. The upper leaflets of the larger central fertile fronds are reduced to veins covered with clusters of brown pear-shaped spore capsules, which resemble flower clusters in the royal fern (*O. regalis*). The root and rhizome fibers are used as a culture medium for orchids. Family: *Osmundaceae*.

Osnabrück 52 17N 8 03E A city in NW West Germany, in Lower Saxony on the Hase River. The 13th-century romanesque cathedral and episcopal palace (1667–90) survived the bombing of World War II. It has iron, steel, and car industries. Population (1980 est): 157,800.

osprey A large *hawk, *Pandion haliaetus*, also called fish hawk, occurring worldwide (except in South America) around coasts and inland waters. It is 25.5 in (65 cm) long and its plumage is brown above and white below It feeds mostly on pike and trout, caught in its talons, which are covered with rough spikes to help grasp prey. The recent decline in numbers has been due mainly to pesticide poisoning.

Ossa, Mount 41 52S 146 04E A mountain in Australia, the highest peak of Tasmania in the Duana Range. Height: 5305 ft (1617 m).

Ossetia. *See* North Ossetian Autonomous Soviet Socialist Republic; South Ossetian autonomous region.

Ossetic A language belonging to the *Iranian family and spoken in the N Caucasus by the Ossetes. The Ossetes are descended from the ancient Alani, a Scythian tribe. The language is written in the Cyrillic alphabet and has absorbed many influences from Russian and the other Caucasian languages.

Ossian (3rd century AD) A legendary poet and warrior who, as Oisin, features in the *Fenian cycle. The Scots poet James Macpherson (1736–96) claimed to have discovered remains of Ossian's poetry in the Highlands and published his "translations" from the Gaelic between 1760 and 1763. These included the epic poem *Fingal* (1762). Macpherson's work was in fact his own, largely based on a few well-known Gaelic fragments. Although denounced as forgeries by Dr Johnson, the poems were enthusiastically received throughout Europe and had a great influence on European Romanticism.

Ossietsky, Carl von (1888–1938) German pacifist and journalist. He founded a pacifist organization in 1920 and became editor of a liberal newspaper in 1927. Following his arrest in 1933 he spent the rest of his life in a concentration camp and in hospitals. He won the Nobel Peace Prize in 1935.

Ossining 41 10N 73 52W A city in New York state. Known as Sing Sing until 1901, it is the site of the Sing Sing state prison, once notorious for its severe discipline. Population (1970): 21,659.

Ostade, Adrian van (1610–85) Dutch painter and etcher, born in Haarlem. Influenced by *Brouwer, he specialized in scenes of peasant life.

Ostend (Flemish name: Oostende; French name: Ostende) 51 13N 2 55E A seaport in NW Belgium, on the North Sea. Ostend is a pleasure resort, with a casino, a promenade, and a royal chalet. It is the headquarters of the country's fishing fleet and maintains a cross-Channel ferry service to Dover, England. Industries include shipbuilding and fish processing. Population (1981 est): 69,678.

Ostend Manifesto (1854) US communication that stated the intention of the US to seize Cuba if Spain would not sell it to the US. When Spain refused US minister Pierre Soulé's offer to buy Cuba, he, under direction from the US secretary of state, met with James Y. Mason and James Buchanan, US ministers to France and Britain respectively, at Ostend, Belgium, where they signed the manifesto. Condemned in the US, the manifesto was never issued.

osteoarthritis A disease of the joints in which their internal surfaces are rubbed away and they become swollen and painful. This becomes increasingly common as people age: almost all very old people have some osteoarthritis, but it may affect younger people as well. The joints that bear most weight are most commonly affected: back, hips, and knees. Drugs can reduce the pain of the joints but cannot reverse the disease. Artificial hips and knees can be surgically installed to relieve the pain and allow greater movement. *See also* arthritis.

osteology. *See* bone.

osteomalacia Softening of the bones due to shortage of vitamin D: adult *rickets. It is seen most commonly in pregnant women and in old people whose diet is deficient in vitamin D or who do not have access to much sunshine (which activates vitamin D). Fractures occur very easily in osteomalacia. Treatment is with vitamin D preparations.

osteomyelitis Infection of bone. This occurs most commonly in poor communities. Children, particularly boys, are more often affected; symptoms are a high fever and acute pain in the bone affected, which is classically around the knee. Before antibiotics were available death or physical handicap often resulted, but these are now rare and the infection is readily cured with antibiotics.

osteopathy A system of healing by manipulation and massage, based on the theory that nearly all diseases are due to the displacement of bones, especially the bones of the spine. Osteopathy is undoubtedly of use in treating dislocations, fractures, and disorders of the joint, but the theory behind it is unacceptable to the medical profession and osteopathy is not legally recognized as a branch of orthodox medicine. Many doctors of medicine are vehemently opposed to osteopathy.

osteoporosis Weakening of the bone. This occurs most commonly in old people, particularly women, but it also affects bones that are immobilized for long periods. The immobilized bone of a young person will usually regain its strength after mobilization, but an elderly patient's osteoporotic bones are more difficult to treat.

Ostia A town of ancient Rome, at the mouth of the Tiber River. It was probably founded about 350 BC, although it is dated by tradition to the 7th century BC. A major naval base under the Republic, its prosperity was greatest in the 2nd century AD, when it was an important commercial center. It was abandoned in the 9th century. Impressive Roman ruins have been excavated.

ostracism The method in 5th-century BC Athens of banishing unpopular citizens. Each citizen inscribed on a potsherd (*ostrakon*) the name of his candidate for banishment. The man receiving most votes was exiled for ten years. Instituted to curb tyranny, ostracism was in practice uncommon. Prominent ostracized Athenians included Aristides and Themistocles.

Ostracoda A subclass of small *crustaceans (2000 species), 0.04–0.16 in (1–4 mm) long, also called mussel or seed shrimps, found in fresh and salt water. Ostracods have a bean-shaped two-sided carapace, from which protrude two pairs of large hairy antennae and two pairs of legs for swimming or walking. Most ostracods live on or near the bottom and eat anything, but particularly decaying vegetation or small animals. The females lay eggs on stems and leaves of water plants.

Ostrava 49 50N 18 15E An industrial city in Czechoslovakia, in N Moravia on both sides of the Ostravice River. It is a major coalmining center; other industries include iron and steel processing, engineering, and chemicals. Population (1980 est): 325,000.

ostrich A flightless African bird, *Struthio camelus*, occurring in open grassland and semidesert regions. Males may reach 8 ft (2.5 m) tall and are black with white wing and tail plumes; females are smaller and mainly brown. Ostriches have a long almost naked neck, a small head, and a ducklike bill used to feed on plant material. They can reach speeds of up to 40 mph (65 km per hour). Domesticated birds are farmed commercially for leather and ornamental feathers. It is the largest living bird and the only member of its family (Struthionidae). Order: Struthioniformes.

Ostrogoths A branch of the *Goths, originally based in the Ukraine, but forced W of the Dniester River by the *Huns (375 AD). In the 6th century they frequently invaded N Italy and captured much of the Balkans. Between 493 and 526 *Theodoric, their leader, ruled Italy. On his death the Roman Empire, after a long struggle, destroyed the Ostrogoths (562).

Ostrovskii, Aleksandr Nikolaevich (1823–86) Russian dramatist. He established his reputation with realistic comedies about the merchant class, making use of the knowledge of corruption that he had gained as a civil servant. His best-known plays include *Easy Money* (1856) and the tragedy *The Storm* (1859), which became the basis of *Janacek's opera *Katya Kabanova*.

Ostwald, (Friedrich) Wilhelm (1853–1932) German chemist, born in Riga, who was a pioneer in the field of physical chemistry. His greatest work was in developing the theory of catalysis for which he was awarded the Nobel Prize in 1909. He also contributed to the philosophy of science and was an ardent positivist.

Oswald, Lee Harvey (1939–63) The presumed assassin of President John F. *Kennedy. Renouncing his citizenship in 1959 to live in the USSR, he returned in 1962. He shot Kennedy in Dallas, Tex., on November 22, 1963. Two days later he was killed by Jack Ruby, a nightclub owner, in the Dallas police headquarters. Following an investigation into the assassination, the Warren Commission ruled in 1964 that Oswald had acted alone.

Oswald, Saint (c. 605–41) King of Northumbria (634–41) after defeating and killing the Welsh king, Cadwallader. Converted to Christianity while in exile on Iona, he restored Christianity in Northumbria with the help of St *Aidan. Oswald was killed in battle by Penda. Feast day: Aug 5.

Oswald of York, St (d. 992 AD) English churchman. Bishop of Worcester and later Archbishop of York, he founded many new monasteries and was a leading initiator of Anglo-Saxon monastic reform. Feast day: Feb 28.

Oświęcim (German name: Auschwitz) 50 02N 19 11E A town in S Poland. It was the site of a notorious Nazi concentration camp during World War II. Population (1972 est): 41,000.

Oswiu (*or* Oswy; d. 670) King of Northumbria (655–70) and overlord (655–57) of all England S of the Humber, after his forces had killed Penda of Mercia in battle. He summoned the Synod of *Whitby (664) to resolve the differences between the Roman and Celtic Churches.

Otis, Elisha Graves (1811–61) US inventor, who in 1852 designed the first safety elevator, that is one that would not fall to the ground if the cable broke. In 1854 Otis publicly demonstrated the elevator's safety by arranging for the cable of an elevator in which he was riding to be cut.

Otranto 40 08N 18 30E A small port in SE Italy, in Apulia on the Strait of Otranto. Dating from Greek times, it became an important Roman port, later destroyed by Turks (1480). Its ruined castle provided the setting for Horace Walpole's gothic novel *The Castle of Otranto*. Population (1971): 4151.

OTTAWA *The center block of the neogothic Parliament buildings (1859-65) on Parliament Hill. The Peace Tower at the center separates the Commons wing (on the left) from the Senate wing (on the right).*

Ottawa 45 25N 75 43W The capital of Canada, in SE Ontario on the Ottawa River. It is two-thirds English speaking and one-third French speaking. Ottawa University was founded in 1848 and the Carleton University in 1942. *History*: founded (as Bytown) in the early 19th century as a lumbering center, it became capital of the United Provinces of Canada in 1858, and national capital in 1867. Population (1976): 304,462.

Ottawa North American Algonkian-speaking Indian tribe, found in Ontario, Canada; Michigan, and Wisconsin. Traders, they allied with the French during the *French and Indian War and, under Chief *Pontiac, fought British expansion. Today, the Ottawa live in Oklahoma, Michigan, Wisconsin, and Manitoulin Island, Ontario.

Ottawa Agreements (1932) Preferential tariff rates negotiated between the UK and its dominions at the Imperial Economic Conference held at Ottawa (Canada).

Ottawa River A river in central Canada, rising in W Quebec and flowing W, then SE down the Ontario-Quebec border to join the St Lawrence River, as its chief tributary, at Montreal. The numerous rapids along its lower and middle courses are used to generate electricity. It is linked with Lake Ontario by the Rideau Canal. Length: 696 mi (1120 km).

otter A semi-aquatic carnivorous ▢mammal belonging to the subfamily *Lutrinae* (18 species), distributed worldwide except in Polar regions, Australasia, and Madagascar. Otters have a cylindrical body with waterproof fur, short legs, partially webbed feet, and a thick tapering tail.

The Eurasian otter (*Lutra lutra*), grows to a length of about 4 ft (1.2 m) and a weight of about 22 lb (10 kg). Otters inhabit waterways, lakes, and coasts, feeding on frogs, fish, and invertebrates. Chief genera: *Lutra, Paraonyx*; family: *Mustelidae. See also* sea otter.

otterhound A breed of dog of uncertain ancestry, used to hunt otters. It is a strongly built powerful swimmer with large webbed feet and a large head with long drooping ears. Otterhounds have a dense water-resistant undercoat and a long shaggy outer coat, which can be any color. Height: 24–27 in (61–69 cm).

otter shrew A semiaquatic carnivorous mammal belonging to the family *Potamogalidae* (3 species), of West and central Africa. Up to 24 in (60 cm) long, they have long slender brown and white bodies with a shrewlike snout and a flattened tail for swimming. They forage for aquatic invertebrate prey. Order: *Insectivora.

Otto (I) the Great (912–73 AD) Holy Roman Emperor (936–73; crowned 962). He subdued his rebellious vassals, defeated a Hungarian invasion at the great victory of Lechfeld (955), and extended his influence into Italy. He deposed Pope John XII, replacing him with Leo VIII, and established bishoprics as a means of controlling his domains.

Otto IV (c. 1175–1218) Holy Roman Emperor (1198–1215; crowned 1209). He was elected emperor in opposition to the candidate of the Hohenstaufen family but was crowned by Pope Innocent III in return for promising to keep out of Italian territorial disputes. In 1210, however, he invaded S Italy and, after being decisively defeated by France, a Hohenstaufen ally, at *Bouvines (1214), was formally deposed.

Otto, Nikolaus August (1832–91) German engineer, who in 1876 devised the four-stroke cycle, known as the Otto cycle, for the *internal-combustion engine. His engine made the development of the automobile possible.

Ottoman Empire A Turkish Muslim empire ruling large parts of the Middle East as well as territories in Europe from the 14th to the 20th centuries. Its capital was *Istanbul (formerly Constantinople) and its rulers descendants of its founder *Osman I. Originating around 1300 as a small Turkish state in Asia Minor, in 1453 the Ottomans captured Constantinople and destroyed the Eastern Roman (Byzantine) Empire. Ottoman power culminated in the 16th century with the conquest of Egypt and Syria (1517) and, under *Suleiman the Magnificent, Hungary (1529) and territories in the Middle East and N Africa. From the 17th century the Empire declined. Attempts at modernization were only partly successful and in the 1908 *Young Turks revolution a group of army officers seized power. In World War I the Ottomans supported Germany and defeat brought the loss of territories outside Asia Minor. This humiliation led to the nationalist revolution of Kemal *Atatürk, which replaced the Ottoman Empire with the state of Turkey (1922).

Otway, Thomas (1652–85) British dramatist. His best-known plays are the sentimental tragedies *The Orphan* (1680) and *Venice Preserved* (1682), written for the actress Elizabeth Barry (1658–1713), whom he loved. He also wrote Restoration comedies and adapted plays by Racine and Molière.

Ouagadougou 12 25N 1 30W The capital of Upper Volta. Founded in the 11th century as the center of a Mossi empire, it was captured by the French in 1896. Its university was founded in 1974. It is an important communications center. Population (1981 est): 172,661.

Oudenaarde, Battle of (July 11, 1708) A battle in the War of the *Spanish Succession in which the British, Dutch, and Austrians defeated the French. The allied commanders, Marlborough and Prince Eugene of Savoy, unexpectedly joined armies and forced the French to fight a surprise battle.

Oudry, Jean-Baptiste (1686–1755) French *rococo painter and tapestry designer. A pupil of the portraitist Nicholas de Largillière (1656–1746), he was a portrait and still-life painter before specializing (from about 1720) in animal and hunting scenes. As head of the *Beauvais (1734) and *Gobelin (1736) tapestry works, and as favorite painter of Louis XV, he achieved a wide reputation. His illustrations to La Fontaine's *Fables* are particularly well known.

Ouessant. *See* Ushant.

Oujda 34 41N 1 45W A city in E Morocco, near the Algerian border. It is a meeting point of the Moroccan and Algerian railroads. Population (1973 est): 155,800.

Oulu (Swedish name: Uleåborg) 65 00N 25 26E A seaport in NW Finland, on the Gulf of Bothnia. It has a university (1959) and its industries include shipbuilding and saw milling. Population (1980): 93,806.

ounce. *See* snow leopard.

Ouse River The name of several rivers in England, including: **1.** A river in NE England, flowing mainly NE through Yorkshire to join the Trent River forming the Humber estuary. Length: 57 mi (92 km). **2.** A river in S England, flowing E and S across the South Downs to the English Channel at Newhaven. Length: 30 mi (48 km). *See also* Great Ouse River.

Ouspensky, Peter (1878–1947) Russian-born occultist. He trained as a scientist but as *Gurdjieff's close associate (1915–24) he became interested in methods of developing man's consciousness. He taught in London (1924–40) and New York (1940–47) and his writings include *Tertium Organum* (1912) and *A New Model of the Universe* (1914).

Outer Mongolia. *See* Mongolian People's Republic.

ouzel. *See* ring ouzel.

ouzo A Greek liquor flavored with aniseed, similar to *absinthe. It is drunk cold with water, in which it becomes cloudy.

ovary **1.** The organ of female animals in which the *egg cells (ova) are produced. In mammals (including women) there are two ovaries close to the openings of the Fallopian tubes, which lead to the uterus (womb). They produce both eggs and steroid hormones (*see* estrogen; progesterone) in a regular cycle (*see* menstruation). The ovaries contain numerous follicles, some of which—the Graafian follicles—mature to release egg cells at ovulation, after which they form yellowish hormone-producing bodies (*see* corpus luteum). **2.** The part of a flower that contains the *ovules. It is situated at the base of the carpel(s) and becomes the fruit wall after fertilization.

ovenbird A small brown passerine bird belonging to a diverse family (*Furnariidae*; 221 species) occurring in tropical America and ranging in size from 5–11 in (12–28 cm). Ovenbirds usually build elaborate nests in tunnels and crevices but the family name is derived from the nests of the genus *Furnarius*, which build large oven-like globes from wet clay.

Overijssel A province in the NE Netherlands bordering on West Germany. Reclamation in the W has made it an inland province. Dairy farming and the production of fodder crops are especially important. Recently developed industries produce textiles, machinery, and salt. Area: 1516 sq mi (3927 sq km). Population (1981 est): 1,027,836. Capital: Zwolle.

overture An orchestral composition serving to introduce an opera, oratorio, or play or a one-movement work with a programmatic title played in the concert hall (**concert overture**). In the 18th century the two principal forms of opera overture were the **Italian overture**, consisting of a slow movement between two quick ones, from which the symphony evolved, and the **French overture**, consisting of a slow introduction, a quick fugal section, and often a slow final section or separate dance movement.

Ovid (Publius Ovidius Naso; 43 BC–17 AD) Roman poet. After his education he traveled extensively in Greek territories. His poems include the *Amores* and the *Ars amatoria*, both demonstrating his clear and polished style and his characteristic theme of love; the *Heroides*, love letters addressed by legendary heroines to their lovers; and the *Fasti*, a poetic treatment of festivals and rites in the Roman calendar, which he never completed. His greatest work, the *Metamorphoses*, is a poem in 15 books including mythological and historical tales linked by the theme of transformation. In 8 AD he was exiled by the emperor Augustus to Tomi, a remote township on the Black Sea, possibly because of some association with Augustus' licentious daughter, Julia. Despite appeals for mercy in his poems *Tristia* and *Epistulae ex Ponto*, he remained there until his death.

Oviedo 43 21N 5 50W A city in N Spain, in Asturias. It possesses a 14th-century cathedral and a university (founded 1608). Industries include mining and food processing. Population (1974 est): 164,332.

ovule The structure within the *ovary of a flower that contains an egg cell and nutritive tissue. After fertilization it develops into the *seed containing the embryo.

ovum. *See* egg.

ROBERT OWEN *This contemporary engraving shows his model community at New Lanark: the school and kitchens (left), the cotton factories (right), and the village band (lower right-hand corner).*

Owen, Robert (1771–1858) British philanthropist and manufacturer. Born in Wales, in 1800 he became manager of the mills at New Lanark, Scotland, where he established a model community. He introduced better working conditions and housing and established the first infant school in Britain (1816). His advocacy from 1817 of "villages of unity and cooperation" for the unemployed anticipated *cooperative societies and he established such communities at New Harmony, Indiana (1825), Orbiston, Scotland (1826), Ralahine, Ireland (1831), and Queenswood, England (1839). Owen was also active in the trade-union movement. Trades Union in 1834.

Owen, Wilfred (1893–1918) British poet. His poetry written during World War I was motivated by horror at the brutality of war, pity for its victims, and anger at civilian complacency. His most famous poems include "Strange Meeting" and "Anthem for Doomed Youth." While in a hospital near Edinburgh in 1917 he met Siegfried *Sassoon, who edited his *Poems* (1920). He was killed in action.

Owen Falls 0 29N 33 11E A cataract in Uganda, on the Victoria Nile River just below Lake Victoria. The **Owen Falls Dam** (completed 1954) provides hydroelectric power for much of Uganda and Kenya and is used to control the flood waters.

Owens, Jesse (John Cleveland O.; 1913–80) US sprinter, long jumper, and hurdler. In 1935 he set six world records in 45 minutes (in the long jump, 100 yards, 220 yards, 220 meters, 220 yards hurdles, and 220 meters hurdles). At the Berlin Olympics (1936) he won four gold medals; this success of a black athlete was inconsistent with the racist theories of Hitler, who refused to congratulate him. He was awarded the Presidential Medal of Freedom in 1976.

owl A nocturnal bird of prey belonging to an order (*Strigiformes*) of worldwide distribution. There are two families: *Strigidae* (typical owls) and *Tytonidae* (barn and bay owls). Owls have a large head with large forward facing eyes surrounded by a facial disk of radiating feathers, soft plumage, usually brown and patterned, and a short sharp hooked bill. With acute vision and hearing and silent flight, owls hunt mammals, birds, and insects, disgorging the remains in hard pellets. They range in size from the *pygmy owls to the large *eagle owls; most are arboreal but some live in swamps, cactus deserts, or on the ground. *See* barn owl; burrowing owl; fish owl; little owl; snowy owl; tawny owl.

owlet frogmouth A solitary arboreal bird belonging to a family (*Aegothelidae*; 7 or 8 species) occurring in Australian forests. They have a gaping mouth surrounded by long sensitive bristles and feed at night on insects. The little owlet frogmouth (*Aegotheles cristatus*) is 9 in (22 cm) long and has a gray-brown plumage with brown underparts. Order: *Caprimulgiformes* (nightjars and nighthawks).

owlet moth. *See* noctuid moth.

ox. *See* cattle.

oxalic acid (*or* ethanedioic acid; $(COOH)_2$) A colorless poisonous soluble crystalline solid. Potassium and sodium salts are found in plants. Industrially it is prepared from sawdust treated with sodium and potassium hydroxides. Oxalic acid is used as a metal cleaner and for bleaching textiles and leather.

oxbow lake. *See* lake.

Oxenstierna, Axel, Count (1583–1654) Swedish statesman; chancellor (1612–54). He gained great power during the reign of Gustavus II Adolphus, being the effective controller of national finance and commerce. After Gustavus' death in 1632, he directed Sweden in the Thirty Years' War and gained favorable terms at the Peace of *Westphalia. During the minority (1632–44) of Queen *Christina he dominated the regency council, and continued to influence government until his death.

oxeye daisy A perennial herb, *Chrysanthemum leucanthemum*, also called moon daisy or marguerite, found in grassland and wasteland throughout Europe. 8–27.5 in (20–70 cm) high, it has large solitary flower heads, 0.98–2 in (2.5–5 cm) in diameter, with long white rays surrounding a yellow central disk. Family: *Compositae*.

Oxford 51 46N 1 15W A city in S central England, on the Rivers Thames and Cherwell. Important from Saxon times and heavily fortified, Oxford's fame as a center of learning dates from the 13th century, when the first university colleges were founded (*see* Oxford, University of). In the Civil War Oxford was the royalist headquarters. The college buildings dominate the center of the city but there is considerable industrial development. It has one of the world's greatest libraries (the *Bodleian Library, 1602). Population (1981): 98,521.

Oxford, Provisions of (1258) The scheme of constitutional reform imposed upon Henry III by his barons at Oxford following their opposition to excessive taxation. Royal authority was to be contained by an advisory council of 15 barons, which was to reform government. The pope absolved Henry from his promise to observe the Provisions (1261), which led to the *Barons' War.

Oxford, 1st Earl of. *See* Harley, Robert, 1st Earl of Oxford.

Oxford, University of One of the oldest universities in Europe, dating from the 12th century. It is organized as a federation of colleges, which are governed by their own teaching staff ("Fellows"), admit students, maintain their own property (which includes residential accommodation, libraries, playing fields, etc.), and provide members of the University's administrative and legislative bodies, its many faculties, departments, and committees. The University is responsible for organizing a lecture program, maintaining the large libraries (such as the *Bodleian Library), providing all laboratories, and conducting examinations. The University includes University College, (founded in 1249), All Souls (1438), Christ Church (1546), and Lady Margaret Hall (1878), which was the first women's college, and Green College (1979).

Oxford Group. *See* Moral Rearmament.

Oxford Movement A movement within the Church of England in the 19th century aimed at emphasizing the Catholic principles on which it rested. Led by *Newman, *Keble, *Pusey, and *Froude of Oxford University, it was initiated in 1833 by Keble's sermon "On the National Apostasy." Aided by their *Tracts for the Times*, the Tractarians, as they came to be called, unleashed a spiritual force that did much to invigorate Anglicanism.

oxidation and reduction Oxidation is the chemical combination of a substance with oxygen. An example is the combustion of carbon to carbon dioxide: $C + O_2 \rightarrow CO_2$. The converse process, removal of oxygen, is known as reduction; an example is the reduction of iron oxide to iron: $Fe_2O_3 + 3C \rightarrow 2Fe + 3CO$. The terms oxidation and reduction have been extended in chemistry. Thus, reduction also refers to reaction with hydrogen and oxidation to removal of hydrogen. More generally, an oxidation reaction is one involving loss of electrons and a reduction reaction is one in which electrons are gained. Thus, the conversion of ferrous ions to ferric ions is an oxidation: $Fe^{2+} - e \rightarrow Fe^{3+}$. A compound that supplies oxygen or removes electrons is an **oxidizing agent**, whereas one that removes oxygen or supplies electrons is a **reducing agent**. Usually oxidation and reduction reactions occur together. Thus, in the reaction of ferric ions (Fe^{3+}) with stannous ions (Sn^{2+}), the ferric ions are reduced to ferrous ions (Fe^{2+}) and the stannous ions oxidized to stannic ions (Sn^{4+}): $2Fe^{3+} + Sn^{2+} \rightarrow 2Fe^{2+} + Sn^{4+}$. Reactions of this type are called **redox reactions**.

oxidation number (*or* oxidation state) The number of electrons that would have to be added to an atom to neutralize it. Thus $Na+$, $Cl-$, and He have oxidation numbers of 1, –1, and 0, respectively. Rules have been developed for assigning oxidation numbers to covalently bound atoms depending on the electric charge that the atom would have if the molecule ionized.

oxlip A perennial herb, *Primula elatior*, found throughout Europe and W Asia. It is similar to the *cowslip but has larger more flattened pale-yellow flowers with a darker yellow throat. The name is also given to hybrids between the primrose and cowslip. Family: *Primulaceae*.

Oxnard 34 12N 119 11W A city in SW California, W of Los Angeles, near the E end of the Santa Barbara Channel. Sugar beet refining and citrus fruit processing are the principal industries. Population (1980): 108,195.

oxpecker An African songbird of the genus *Buphagus*, also called tickbird, that feeds on ticks and maggots pecked from the hides of cattle and game animals. The yellow-billed oxpecker (*B. africanus*) is about 8 in

(20 cm) long with sharp claws for clinging to the backs of its hosts and a stiff tail used for support in climbing over them. Oxpeckers remove parasites from their hosts but also feed on the blood from the sores. Family: *Sturnidae* (starlings).

Oxus River. *See* Amu Darya River.

oxygen (O) A colorless odorless gas discovered by J. *Priestley. The element exists in two forms—the diatomic molecule (O_2), which constitutes 21% of the earth's atmosphere, and trace amounts of the highly reactive triatomic allotrope, ozone (O_3), which is formed in the upper atmosphere by the interaction of ultraviolet radiation with oxygen and by lightning discharges. The ozone layer is important in absorbing harmful ultraviolet rays from the sun. Oxygen is very reactive and forms oxides with most elements (for example Na_2O, MgO, Fe_2O_3, Cl_2O_7, XeO_3). In addition to its vital importance for plants and animals, its major use is in the production of steel in blast furnaces. It is obtained by the distillation of liquid air. At no 8; at wt 15.9994; mp –218.4°C; bp –182.96°C.

oxygen cycle The process by which oxygen—present in the atmosphere or dissolved in water—is taken in by plants and animals for use in *respiration (intercellular combustion of food materials to provide energy) and released into the environment as a waste product, mostly in the form of free oxygen (by plants in *photosynthesis). Oxygen is often combined in organic and inorganic compounds, which may also be considered as part of the cycle. *See also* carbon cycle; nitrogen cycle.

Oyo Empire A kingdom in SW Nigeria and the most powerful state in West Africa from the mid-17th until the mid-18th centuries. Oyo then began to decline relative to Dahomey and during the next century was broken up by *Fulani invasions, European intrusions, and civil war. Oyo is now a province in Western State, SW Nigeria.

oyster A sedentary *bivalve mollusk belonging to the family *Ostreidae* (true oysters), of temperate and warm seas. The lower plate (valve) of the shell is larger and flatter than the upper valve; they are held together by an elastic ligament and powerful muscles. Edible oysters are cultivated for their white flesh; pearl oysters (family *Aviculidae*) are cultivated for their pearls, which they make by coating a grain of sand lodged inside their shell with calcareous material.

oystercatcher A black or black-and-white wading bird belonging to a family (*Haematopodidae*; 4 species) occurring in temperate and tropical coastal regions. 16–20 in (40–50 cm) long, oystercatchers have long pointed wings, a long wedge-shaped tail, pink legs, and a long or flattened orange-red bill specialized for opening bivalve mollusks and probing in mud for worms and crustaceans. Order: *Charadriiformes*.

Ozark Plateau (*or* Ozark Mountains) An eroded plateau in S Missouri and N Arkansas, reaching over 2000 ft (600 m) in the Boston Mountains. Forestry and mining are important; minerals include lead and zinc.

ozone (O_3) A pale blue gaseous form of *oxygen, formed by passing an electrical discharge through oxygen (O_2). Ozone is a poisonous unstable gas. It is used as an oxidizing agent, for example in water purification. It is present in small amounts in the atmosphere, mostly in the *ozone layer.

ozone layer (*or* ozonosphere) The zone in the upper atmosphere in which the gas ozone (triatomic oxygen; O_3) forms in its greatest concentrations. This is generally between about 6 and 30 mi (10–50 km) above the earth's surface. Ozone forms as a result of the dissociation by solar ultraviolet radiation of molecular oxygen into single atoms, some of which then combine with undissociated oxygen molecules. It absorbs in the 230–320 nm waveband, protecting the earth from dangerous excessive ultraviolet radiation.

P

Pabst, G(eorge) W(ilhelm) (1885–1967) Austrian film director. His films are distinguished by their innovative realistic techniques and their social criticism of decadence and nationalism in Germany. They include *Pandora's Box* (1929), the antiwar *Westfront 1918* (1930), *Die Dreigroschenoper* (1931), and *Kameradschaft* (1931).

paca A large nocturnal *rodent, *Cuniculus paca*, of Central and South America. Up to 34 in (60 cm) long, with a tiny tail and spotted coat, it is found in damp places near rivers and swamps, feeding on leaves and fruit and living in burrows. Part of the skull is specialized as a resonating chamber. It is hunted by all kinds of predators, including man. Family: *Dasyproctidae*.

Pacaraima Mountains A mountain range in NE South America. Comprising part of the Guiana Highlands, it extends W–E along part of the Brazil–Venezuela and Brazil–Guyana borders reaching 9219 ft (2810 m) at Mount Roraima.

pacemaker A small section of specialized heart muscle that initiates heartbeat. It is situated in the right atrium and contracts spontaneously: the impulse to contract is transmitted from the pacemaker to both atria and then to the ventricles. If the pacemaker ceases to function (heart block) it may be replaced by an artificial battery-operated device that stimulates the heart to contract. If required permanently it is surgically implanted under the skin.

Pachomius, St (c. 290–346 AD) Egyptian hermit, who founded the first monastery in 318 at Tabenna, on the Nile River, and the first Christian rule involving a uniform communal existence. Until then *monasticism had been practiced only by solitaries in the desert. Feast day: May 14.

pachyderm A thick-skinned *mammal, such as the elephant, rhinoceros, or hippopotamus. Early naturalists classified these animals, together with pigs and walruses, in a group called *Pachydermata*. The classification is now abandoned but the term is still used.

Pachymeres, Georgius (1242–c. 1310) Byzantine historian and writer. Pachymere's most important work was a history of the period 1261 to 1308, under the emperors *Michael VIII Palaeologus and Andronicus II Palaeologus (1260–1332; reigned 1282–1328). Other works include an outline of Aristotelian philosophy and a treatise on the Holy Spirit. The latter work is significant in that it accepts the controversial Roman *Filioque clause of the formula of St *John of Damascus.

Pacific, War of the (1879–84) The war between Chile and the allies Bolivia and Peru. Also called the Nitrate War, it was provoked by a dispute over Chile's exploitation of nitrate deposits in Bolivia. Within two years Bolivia was defeated, and Peru's capital of Lima captured. According to the peace terms, finally agreed in 1884, Peru and Bolivia ceded territories to Chile, Bolivia losing all access to the sea.

Pacific Islands, Trust Territory of the A UN trust territory administered by the US. It comprises the *Marshall Islands, the Federated States of *Micronesia, and Belau; the Mariana Islands were included until 1978. Taken by Japan from Germany (1914), the islands were captured by the US in World War II (1944) and the trusteeship established in 1947.

Pacific Ocean The world's largest and deepest ocean, covering a third of its surface. It extends between Asia, Australia, Antarctica, and America. It contains a multitude of volcanic and coral islands in the tropical SW and reaches its maximum depth in the *Marianas Trench. The S and E are marked by a uniform climate with steady winds, but the W is known for its typhoons, which often cause coastal flooding. The Pacific has some diurnal and mixed tides, while Tahitian tides follow the sun and not the moon. Its vast mineral resources are unexploited.

pacifism The group of doctrines, religious, moral, or political, that urge nonparticipation either in any war whatsoever or in particular wars that are held to be unjustified. In ancient societies it was assumed that membership of the society involved fighting for it when necessary. This view was not held by early Christians, although not all Christians have been unanimously pacifist; in fact Christian pacifism was relatively unimportant from Constantine's period to the Reformation, when first *Anabaptists, and then *Quakers, adopted total pacifism. In modern times conscientious objectors have been recognized in both World Wars and have often served with distinction in noncombatant (medical) units. Moreover, nonviolent methods of attaining political ends were shown to be effective by *Gandhi in the

1920s, although his achievement was to some extent diminished by the slaughter between Hindus and Muslims that followed his years of pacifism. Martin Luther *King, Jr., adapted Gandhi's methods to the US civil-rights movement.

pack rat A North American *rodent belonging to the genus *Neotoma* (20 species), also called wood rat. With body length of 6–9 in (15–23 cm), it has a hairy tail and inhabits rocky and wooded country, nesting in a pile of twigs and feeding on seeds and vegetation. Family: *Cricetidae*.

Padang 1 00S 100 21E A port in Indonesia, in W Sumatra. An early Dutch settlement, it flourished when railroads were built in the 19th century. It exports coal, cement, coffee, copra, and rubber. Its university was established in 1956. Population (1971): 196,339.

paddlefish One of two species of freshwater *bony fish, *Polyodon spathula* of North America or *Psephurus gladius* of China, also called duckbill cat. Paddlefishes have a smooth body, with an enormous paddle-shaped snout, and feed by straining planktonic organisms from the water. Family: *Polyodontidae*; order: *Acipenseriformes*.

Paderborn 51 43N 8 44E A city in N central West Germany, in North Rhine-Westphalia. Notable buildings include a cathedral (11th–13th centuries) and a Renaissance town hall (1613–20). Its university was established in 1972. An important agricultural market, it manufactures agricultural machinery, computers, textiles, and furniture. Population (1980 est): 109,600.

Paderewski, Ignacy (Jan) (1860–1941) Polish pianist, composer, and statesman. Having studied at Warsaw, Berlin, and Vienna, he achieved an international reputation as a performer and composed a piano concerto and many solo pieces. He was the first prime minister (1919) of newly independent Poland but resigned after ten months to return to his musical career.

Padua (Italian name: Padova) 45 24N 11 53E A city in NE Italy, near Venice. An important city in Roman and Renaissance times, it has several notable buildings, including a 13th-century cathedral and the Basilica of St Anthony, in front of which stands one of Donatello's most famous works, the equestrian statue of Gattamelata. Galileo taught at its university (founded in 1222). Machinery and textiles are produced. Population (1980 est): 241,400.

Paestum The Roman name for Posidonia, a colony of *Sybaris founded about 600 BC on the SW coast of Italy. Paestum is famed for the three great Doric temples the remains of which still stand there. Named for the Greek sea god *Poseidon, it was conquered by Rome in 273 BC and became celebrated in Latin poetry for its twice-flowering roses.

Páez, José Antonio (1790–1873) Venezuelan revolutionary. The leader of a band of cowboys (*llaneros*), he allied himself with *Bolívar against Spain. After the liberation he took Venezuela out of the confederation of Gran Colombia and became its first president (1831).

Pagalu. *See* Equatorial Guinea, Republic of.

Pagan The former capital of Burma on the Irrawaddy River SE of Mandalay. Founded in about 849 AD, Pagan was refounded after the decree adopting Buddhism as the state religion (1056). Hundreds of brick-built temples, monasteries, and pagodas survived Pagan's sack by the Mongols (1287) and some, such as the Ananda temple (1090) and Shwezigon pagoda (12th century), are still in use.

Paganini, Niccolò (1782–1840) Italian virtuoso violinist. After an adventurous youth he toured Europe, astonishing audiences with his techniques, such as left-hand pizzicato, multiple stopping, and artificial harmonics. His skill inspired Liszt and Schumann to compose piano music of transcendent difficulty. He composed six violin concertos, various showpieces for violin, including a set of variations on the G string, and 24 caprices, one of which became the basis for compositions by Rachmaninov, Brahms, and others.

pagoda A Buddhist shrine in the form of a tower for housing relics of the Buddha. Pagodas originated in India, where their standardized form of a basic unit repeated vertically in diminishing sizes was evolved. From India the pagoda spread to Sri Lanka (where it is called a dagoba), SE Asia, China, and Japan. Japanese pagodas are usually five-storied wooden structures built round a central timber post to provide stability against earthquakes. *See also* stupa.

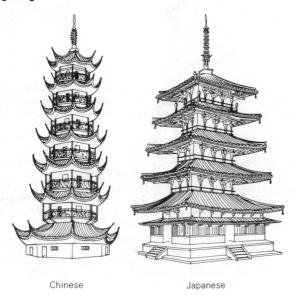

Chinese   Japanese

PAGODA *The exuberantly curving roofs of the typical multi-storied Chinese pagoda contrast with the more restrained Japanese form.*

Pago Pago 14 16S 170 43W The capital of American Samoa, in SE Tutuila on the S Pacific Ocean. A US naval base (1872–1951), it is a port exporting canned tuna. Population (1970): 2451.

Pahang A large state in SE Peninsular Malaysia, on the South China Sea. Lying mainly in the Pahang River basin it rises to the Cameron Mountains in the W. Rubber, rice, coconuts, gold, and tin are produced. Area: 13,873 sq mi (35,931 sq km). Population (1980): 770,644. Capital: Kuantan.

Pahang River The longest river in Peninsular Malaysia, rising in the NW and flowing generally S then E through the state of Penang to enter the South China Sea. Length: 200 mi (322 km).

Paige, Satchel (Leroy Robert P.; 1906–82) US baseball player. Long a pitcher in black baseball leagues, he became a member of the Cleveland Indians in 1948 when blacks began to be allowed in the major leagues. He also pitched for the St Louis Browns (1951–53) and other teams and was elected to the Baseball Hall of Fame in 1971.

Paine, Thomas (1737–1809) British writer and political theorist. His pamphlet *Common Sense* (1776) initiated the American movement toward independence. In 1791–92 his *Rights of Man* was published, in support of the French Revolution and in opposition to *Burke's *Reflections*. Indicted for treason, Paine fled to France, where he was elected to the French Convention. While imprisoned by Robespierre, he wrote the second part of his *Age of Reason* (1796), a deist manifesto that held that "all religions are in their nature mild and benign."

paint A finely powdered insoluble pigment suspended in a binding medium; on application to a surface the volatile components of the binding medium evaporate, the drying oils oxidize, and the resins polymerize, leaving a decorative or protective skin. The pigments impart color and opacity to the skin and extenders (such as barium sulfate, calcium carbonate, or asbestos) are mixed with the pigments to strengthen the skin and reduce raw-material costs. The binding medium consists of a drying oil (e.g. linseed oil or tung oil), a resin (rosin or a synthetic alkyd), a thinner (turpentine, benzene, etc.), and a drier (e.g. lead linoleate) to accelerate film formation. Water-based emulsion paints consist of emulsions of a synthetic resin (e.g. polyvinyl acetate, polystyrene, acrylic resins) in water.

Painted Desert An area in N central Arizona, bounded by the Little Colorado River on the E and S and on the N by the Colorado River. It is about 15–20 mi (24–32 km) wide. At an average altitude of 5000 ft (1525 m), it was named by Joseph C. Ives and John Strong Newberry in 1858 because of the wide range of colors in aged rocks exposed by erosion. Area: 7500 sq mi (19,425 sq km).

painted lady An orange, black, and white butterfly, *Vanessa cardui*, of worldwide distribution. It cannot survive cold winters but migrates from warmer regions each year. The caterpillars feed mainly on thistles and nettles. The American painted lady (*V. virginiensis*) is similar but less widespread.

painting In art, the creation of an aesthetic entity by the skilled covering of a surface with paint. Suitable painting surfaces include paper, canvas, walls, and ivory, and among the many techniques of painting are oil, *watercolor, *tempera, *encaustic, *fresco, and, the most modern method, *acrylic painting. The main subjects of painting were religious until the Renaissance period, when portraits, landscapes, *genre, and *still life began to assume an independent existence. The principal painting styles in the history of art have been classical (ancient Greek and Roman), Byzantine, romanesque, gothic, Renaissance, mannerist, baroque, rococo, neoclassical, impressionist, and abstract.

Paisley 55 50N 4 26W A city in W central Scotland, in Strathclyde Region near Glasgow. Famous for shawls in the 19th century, Paisley's textile industry is still important. The richly colored abstract design used for the shawls, which imitated shawls from India, is still known as **paisley pattern**; any fabric printed with such a design is known as paisley. Population (1981): 84,789. 47

Paisley, Ian (1926–) Northern Irish politician; an uncompromising defender of Protestant unionism. A minister of the Free Presbyterian Church of Ulster from 1946, he was a Protestant Unionist member of parliament in the Northern Irish parliament (1970–72) before becoming (1974) a Democratic Unionist member of Britain's House of Commons.

Paiute North American Shoshonean-speaking Indian tribe, found in Utah, Arizona, Nevada, and California (Southern Paiute) and in parts of Oregon, California, Nevada, and Idaho (Northern Paiute). Basically farmers, weavers, and hunters, they were relocated after 1850 to reservations within the boundaries of their original lands.

Pakistan, Islamic Republic of A country in S Asia, bordering on Iran, Afghanistan, China, and India. The W is mountainous and the E has areas of desert, while the Indus River rises in the Himalayas in the N and flows S across plateau and the Indus Plain to the Arabian Sea. The country is arid with great extremes of temperature but the plain is very fertile, except in areas that have become saline or waterlogged. The population, which is increasing rapidly, is a mixture of many Asian and Middle Eastern racial groups. Of the languages spoken Punjabi is the most commonly used, although Urdu is the language of the educated. 97% of the population is Muslim. *Economy*: mainly agricultural, producing chiefly rice, wheat, sugar cane, and cotton. Productivity has improved during the 1960s and 1970s with increased mechanization, the use of chemical fertilizers, improved strains of crops, and the reclamation of saline land. Irrigation, on which agriculture is dependent, has also been extensively developed since the Indus Waters Treaty was concluded with India (1960). Industry has developed successfully since 1947, at which time the area had very little. Although industry employs only 14% of the workforce and is still largely dependent on imported machinery, petroleum, chemicals, and metals, Pakistan has become a major exporter of cotton and cotton yarn and cloth. Chemical fertilizers, cement, sugar, and handicrafts are also produced, and a steel industry is being developed. Fishing is increasingly important. Resources include coal (mainly low-grade), iron ore, copper, limestone, oil, and large quantities of natural gas. Hydroelectric power is also produced. *History*: the history of Pakistan is that of *India until 1947, when it was created to satisfy the *Muslim League's demand for a separate state for the Muslim minority. It consisted then of two separate areas; West Pakistan comprised Baluchistan, the Northwest Frontier, West Punjab (now Punjab province), and Sind, while East Pakistan was formed from East Bengal. The question of control over Kashmir is still unsettled. The most serious problem has been the unification of Pakistan's diverse population groups, divided by geography, race, and extremes of wealth and poverty. The unifying force of the common religion has not been able to contain demands for regional autonomy and increased democracy. Thus each of Pakistan's three constitutions (1956, 1962, 1973) has been replaced by martial law. Regional unrest was especially serious in East Pakistan, which had a larger population but less political and military power than West Pakistan. The electoral victory in East Pakistan of the Awami League (1970), which demanded regional autonomy, led to its secession as *Bangladesh (1971). This was effected after a two-week civil war in which Indian forces intervened and defeated the Pakistani army, which consisted of troops from West Pakistan. Regionalism later led to guerrilla fighting in Baluchistan and the Northwest Frontier province (1973 onward). On January 30, 1972, Pakistan withdrew from the Commonwealth of Nations. Allegations of ballot rigging following the 1977 elections triggered off more violent unrest, which led finally to a military coup led by Gen Zia ul-Haq. Demonstrations and riots followed when members of the previous government were arrested on charges ranging from corruption to murder and when the former prime minister, Zulfikar Ali Bhutto, was executed for conspiracy to murder (1979). The former president, Fazal Elahi Chaudhry (1904–82), retired from office in 1978 and was succeeded by Gen Zia. Official language: Urdu. Official currency: Pakistan rupee of 100 paise. Area (excluding Jammu and Kashmir): 310,322 sq mi (803,943 sq km). Population (1981): 83,780,000. Capital: Islamabad.

Palace of Westminster The British parliamentary buildings in Westminster, London, containing the *House of Commons and the House of Lords (see parliament). It is also known as the Houses of Parliament. A royal palace until the 16th century, it was rebuilt in the *gothic revival style following a fire in 1834.

Palaeologus The ruling dynasty of the Eastern Roman Empire from 1261 to 1453. Originating in the 11th century, the first Palaeologus emperor was *Michael VIII Palaeologus and they continued to rule until the fall of Constantinople to the Turks in 1453. During this period Byzantine culture underwent a major revival.

palanquin An enclosed litter formerly used in the Far East by high-ranking officials and by women and usually carried by four or six men.

palate The roof of the mouth, which is divided into two parts. The soft palate at the back of the mouth is composed of mucous membrane and prevents food passing into the nose during swallowing. From its center hangs down a flap of tissue, the uvula. The hard palate, further forward, is composed of two fused halves made up of the palatine bone and part of the maxillary (upper jaw) bones. During development the two halves of the palate may fail to fuse, leading to a *cleft palate.

Palatinate Two regions of West Germany: the Lower (or Rhenish) Palatinate is now in Rheinland-Pfalz, Baden-Württemberg, and Hessen and the Upper Palatinate is now in Bavaria. In 1156 the title of count palatine (originally a judicial officer) was bestowed by Emperor Frederick I on his half-brother Conrad, whose territories included what later became the Rhenish Palatinate. When, in 1214, it passed to the *Wittelsbach family, their lands in Bavaria became the Upper Palatinate. From 1356 the counts palatine were *electors of Holy Roman Emperors. During the Reformation the Palatinate became a center of Protestantism and the claim by the Protestant, Elector Frederick, the Winter King, to the Bohemian throne precipitated the *Thirty Years' War. The two Palatinates were separated from 1648 until 1777 but in the early 19th century the Lower Palatinate was divided between France and various German states and the Upper Palatinate passed to Bavaria.

Palau. See Belau.

Palawan A mountainous island in the W Philippines, between the South China and Sulu Seas. Sparsely populated, its chief products are timber, mercury, and chromite; fishing is important. Area: 4550 sq mi (11,785 sq km). Population (1970): 236,635. Chief town: Puerto Princesa.

Palembang 2 59S 104 45E A port in Indonesia, in S Sumatra on the Musi River. It was the capital of a Hindu Sumatran kingdom (8th century AD) and Dutch trade began here in 1617. Its university was established in 1960. The export center of local oilfields, it has Indonesia's largest refinery and many oil-based industries. Population (1971): 582,961.

Palencia 41 01N 4 32W A city in N central Spain, in León. It possessed Spain's first university, founded in 1208 and moved to Salamanca in 1239. The gothic cathedral contains paintings by El Greco, including *St Sebastian*. Manufactures include iron and porcelain. Population (1970): 58,370.

Paleocene epoch. See Tertiary period.

paleography The study of ancient handwriting. Paleography originated as an adjunct to textual criticism of Greek and Latin manuscripts but is now applied to all kinds of scripts. Paleographers assess the cultural and historical implications of the development of writing styles and the output of individual scriptoria (scribal centers) and scribes. Recent technical aids include computerized surveys of large numbers of manuscripts and ultraviolet photography to render faint writing legible.

Paleolithic The earliest division of the *Stone Age. It extends roughly from the emergence of man, or at least of some hominid capable of making simple pebble tools, to the end of the last ice age. The Paleolithic is conventionally divided into three phases: Lower, beginning as much as 3,500,000 years ago and characterized by pebble-tool and hand-axe manufacture; Middle, beginning about 70,000 years ago and associated with *Neanderthal man and *Mousterian industries; and Upper, beginning about 40,000 years ago and associated in Europe with *Cro-Magnon man and cave art.

paleomagnetism The history of the earth's magnetic field (see geomagnetic field) as determined from the remanent magnetism of rocks. The study assumes that the principal component of igneous and sedimentary rocks' magnetism was determined at or near to the time at which the rocks

were formed. Paleomagnetism provides evidence for continental drift (see plate tectonics) and the movement of the magnetic poles.

paleontology The study of ancient organisms from their *fossil remains in the rocks. Their taxonomy, anatomy, ecology, and evolution are studied. Fossils are used to correlate bodies of rock and establish their stratigraphic relationships with each other; this field is called biostratigraphy. Modern methods of *dating rocks by radiometric means give their absolute dates rather than their order in the stratigraphic column. The study of ancient microscopic organisms is called **micropaleontology** and the fossils are known as microfossils.

Paleo-Siberian languages A diverse group of languages of Siberia comprising four unrelated groups: Yeniseian; Luorawetlan, which includes Chuckchi, Koryak, and Aliutor; Yukaghir, which includes Yukaghir and also Omok and Chuvan, both now extinct; and Gilyak, the only one of its group.

Paleozoic era The era of geological time between the Precambrian and the Mesozoic, lasting from about 590 to 240 million years ago. It is divided into the Upper Paleozoic, which contains the Cambrian, Ordovician, and Silurian periods, and the Lower Paleozoic, containing the Devonian, Carboniferous, and Permian. It is the first era of *Phanerozoic time. The Caledonian and Variscan orogenies both occurred in this era.

Palermo 38 08N 13 23E A port in Italy, the capital of Sicily. Founded by the Phoenicians in the 8th century BC, it first established itself as chief town of the island under the Arabs (9th–11th centuries). Its many notable buildings include the gothic cathedral and the Norman palace (now the regional parliament). It has shipbuilding and textile industries. Population (1980 est): 698,254.

Palestine (or Holy Land) A historic area in the Middle East, consisting of the area between the Mediterranean Sea and the Jordan River. It now comprises *Israel and territories belonging to Jordan and Egypt. Sacred to Jews, Christians, and Muslims alike, and caught as it has been between a succession of surrounding empires, the area has been much fought over. It has been inhabited since prehistoric times. Toward the end of the 2nd millennium BC it was settled by the Hebrew people, who in the Old Testament were led out of Egypt by Moses, and in about 1000 BC a Hebrew kingdom was founded by Saul. Following the reign of Solomon it was split into Israel, later conquered by the Assyrians, and Judah (see Judea), later conquered by the Babylonians (see Babylonian exile), who destroyed the *Temple of Jerusalem (rebuilt in 516 BC under the Persians). The Romans conquered the Jewish state that existed briefly in 142–63 BC and also destroyed the Temple (70 AD) while violently suppressing a Jewish revolt. From the late 4th century AD many Jews left Palestine, which became a center first for Christian and later for Muslim pilgrimage (following Arab conquest in 636 AD). Christianity was reinstated in the area by the conquest of the Crusaders (1099 until the 13th century). After a period of Egyptian rule it fell to the Ottoman Turks (1516), who ruled it until World War I. During the 1830s Palestine, inhabited chiefly by Arab peasants, was opened up to European influence and from the mid 19th century Jews returned from the *Diaspora to settle in Palestine. The late 19th century saw the beginning of *Zionism and in 1909 Tel Aviv, the first new Jewish city, was founded. By 1914 there were 100,000 Jews in Palestine, although their numbers were reduced by almost half during World War I, in which they were sympathetic to the Allies. In 1918 Palestine was captured by the British; British administration, effective from 1920, was confirmed by a League of Nations mandate (1922). By the *Balfour Declaration (1917) the British supported the Jewish demand for a Jewish nation in Palestine. This provoked unrest and terrorism among the Arab population, who felt increasingly threatened by Jewish immigration. In 1947 the problem was referred to the UN, which decided to divide Palestine into two separate states, Jewish and Arab. As this was accepted by the Jews but not the Arabs, Britain renounced its mandate in 1948. The state of Israel was then proclaimed and immediately attacked by the surrounding Arab countries. They were repulsed but the rest of Palestine was divided between Jordan and Egypt. See also West Bank.

Palestine Liberation Organization (PLO) An organization of various Palestinian groups opposed to the existence of the State of Israel. Formed in 1964 and led by Yasser Arafat since 1968, the PLO has not been able to maintain unity among all the Palestinian groups; in particular, the Popular Front for the Liberation of Palestine (PFLP), led by Dr George Habash, has remained independent. The PLO has nonetheless managed to gain support from the *Arab League, which recognized it as the sole legitimate representative of the Palestinian people in 1974. Terrorism has been the PLO's chief means of confrontation with Israel. Among its most widely publicized actions was the murder of 11 Israeli athletes in the 1972 Munich Olympics.

Palestrina, Giovanni Pierluigi da (?1525–94) Italian composer. He spent most of his life in Rome, as chorister, choirmaster, or maestro at churches including St Peter's. One of the greatest masters of *polyphony, he composed 93 masses, 179 motets, and many other pieces, mainly for church use. He was twice offered posts elsewhere (Venice and Mantua) but each time he asked too high a salary.

Palgrave, Francis Turner (1824–97) British poet and anthologist. A friend of Tennyson, he published several volumes of verse and became professor of poetry at Oxford. He is best remembered for his influential anthology of English verse, *The Golden Treasury* (1861).

Pali An *Indo-Aryan language originating in N India. It is the language of the Theravada Buddhist canon and is used throughout the Theravada countries of SE Asia but disappeared from India itself during the 14th century.

Palio A horse race run in July and August in the main piazza of Siena. It is named for the painted silk banner that the winner receives. The Palio first took place in 1482 and is accompanied by considerable pageantry.

Palissy, Bernard (1510–89) French potter, famous for his rustic ware, a richly colored lead-glazed earthenware. His dishes are ornamental in relief with mythological subjects or reptiles, plants, etc. He enjoyed court patronage in the 1560s but was persecuted as a Huguenot and died in prison. He is also known for his writings on religion, science, and philosophy.

PALLADIANISM *Chiswick House (begun 1725), which was designed by England's Lord Burlington for his own use.*

Palladianism An architectural style developed in 16th-century Venetia by *Palladio. It was based on classical Roman public architecture and the theories of *Vitruvius and it placed great importance on symmetrical room planning and a harmonious system of proportions. Largely disseminated by Palladio's books, *I quattro libri dell' architettura* (1570), it was first introduced into England in the early 17th century by Inigo *Jones and it was revived early in the 18th century. The style was widely used in England for public buildings and country houses, and imitated in Europe, Russia and North America, where it influenced Southern Plantation homes. It was eventually replaced by *neoclassicism in the mid 18th century.

Palladio, Andrea (1508–80) Italian architect, born in Padua. One of the most sophisticated and widely imitated of classical architects, Palladio is famous for developing the architectural style now known as *Palladianism. Trained as a stonemason, Palladio designed most of his buildings in and around Vicenza. His first job was the remodeling of the basilica in Vicenza (begun 1549) and from that emerged a hugely successful career. He produced villas, for example the Villa Rotonda (near Vicenza) and Villa Barbaro (Maser); palaces, for example the Palazzo Chericati (1550s); churches, the most famous being S Giorgio Maggiore in Venice (begun 1566).

palladium (Pd) A silvery-white noble metal of the platinum group, discovered by W. H. Wollaston (1766–1828) in 1803, and named for the asteroid Pallas, which was discovered at about the same time. Palladium readily absorbs hydrogen and is used as a catalyst for hydrogenation reactions; it is alloyed with gold to form white gold. At no 46; at wt 106.4; mp 2828°F (1552°C); bp 5689°F (3140°C).

Palladium In Greek and Roman religion, an ancient image of Athena, originally the wooden image kept in the citadel of Troy and believed to have been sent from heaven by Zeus. The safety of the city depended on it. It was stolen by Odysseus and Diomedes, who thus made possible the capture of Troy. It was believed to have been taken to Athens or Sparta, or to Rome (by *Aeneas).

Pallas The second largest (377 m [608 km] in diameter) *minor planet, the orbit of which lies between those of Mars and Jupiter.

Pallas Athena. *See* Athena.

Pallas's cat A small wild *cat, *Felis* (or *Otocolobus*) *manul*, of Tibet, Mongolia, and Siberia. About 20 in (50 cm) long, with a very thick tail and long yellow-gray fur, it has a small face with low-set ears—an adaptation for stalking small mammals from the cover of rocks and boulders.

palm A monocotyledonous plant of the family *Palmae* (or *Arecaceae*; about 2500 species), occurring in tropical and subtropical regions. Ranging from 40–196 ft (1 to 60 m) in height, palms typically have an unbranched trunk crowned with a cluster of leaves, which are pleated and fan-shaped or feather-like and often very large (up to 49 ft [15 m] long). The flowers are usually grouped into large clusters and give rise to berries or drupes (stone fruits). Palms are commercially important as a source of food (*see* coconut; date; sago), oil (*see* oil palm), wax (*see* carnauba), and various fibers and building materials.

Palma (or Palma de Mallorca) 39 35N 2 39E The capital of the Spanish Balearic Islands, in Majorca on the Mediterranean Sea. Its historic buildings include the gothic cathedral (1230–1601) and the 14th-century Bellver Castle. Noted as a tourist resort, it is also a port and commercial center; industries include textiles, footwear, and such crafts as pottery. Population (1974 est): 267,081.

Palma Vecchio, Jacopo (J. Negretti; c. 1480–1528) Italian painter of the Venetian school. He is noted for his *St Barbara Altarpiece* (Sta Maria Formosa, Venice) and his portraits of Venetian women.

Palm Beach 26 41N 80 02W A town and fashionable winter resort in SE Florida, on Lake Worth (a lagoon). It is an extension of the much larger West Palm Beach. Population (1970): 9086.

palm civet A mammal of the family *Viverridae* that is smaller than the true civets and more omnivorous than the *genets. Most palm civets are Asian (the two-spotted palm civet (*Nandinia binotata*) is the only African species). The masked palm civet (*Paguma larvata*) of SE Asia is up to 55 in (140 cm) long including the tail 20–25.5 in (50–65 cm) and is mainly arboreal, feeding on fruit, insects, and some vertebrates.

Palmer, Arnold (1929–) US professional golfer, who did much to make golf a spectator sport. US amateur champion in 1954, he won the US Open championship (1960), Masters championship (1958, 1960, 1962, 1964), British Open championship (1961, 1962), and many other events.

Palmer, Samuel (1805–81) British landscape painter and etcher, born in London. He first exhibited at the Royal Academy at the age of 14 but his best landscapes, often moonlit and either in sepia or watercolor, were painted during his association (1826–35) with a group of painters in Shoreham, who shared Palmer's admiration for William *Blake. His imaginative and mystical approach to art declined into conventionality in the late 1830s.

Palmerston, Henry John Temple, 3rd Viscount (1784–65) British statesman; Liberal prime minister (1855–58, 1859–65). He entered parliament in 1807 as a Tory, but by 1830 he had joined the Whigs (later Liberals). His markedly nationalistic foreign policy sought to defend constitutional states and prevent a Franco-Russian combination. As prime minister Palmerston supported the Confederacy in the Civil War but was dissuaded by his colleagues from actively involving Britain.

Palmerston North 40 21S 175 37E A city in New Zealand, in S North Island. It is a center for the agricultural area of the Manawatu Plain and is the site of Massey University (a branch of Victoria University, Wellington). Population (1971): 51,893.

palmistry The study of the lines and ridges on the palm of the hand in order to interpret character and divine the owner's future. Although without scientific basis, palmistry (or chiromancy as it is also called) provides common-sense evidence of a person's way of life and habits and from these something may be deduced of his character and interests.

Palm Springs 33 49N 116 34W A city in California. Long known for its hot springs, it is a popular resort with golf courses and an aerial tramway. Population (1970): 20,936.

Palm Sunday The Sunday before Easter, commemorating Christ's last triumphal ride into Jerusalem (Mark 11). In many Churches crosses or branches of palm leaves are distributed on this day.

palmyra A *palm tree, *Borassus flabellier*, cultivated in India and Sri Lanka. The timber is used for construction and the leaves are used for thatch and made into a type of paper. The sugary sap from the flower heads is fermented to give palm wine and the kernels of the fruits are eaten.

Palmyra (or Tadmor) 34 36N 38 15E An ancient Syrian desert city on the route of the E–W caravan trade in the 2nd and 3rd centuries AD.

Palmyra came under Roman control in the 1st century AD but under *Zenobia regained its independence from 270 until 272, when it was reconquered and then destroyed; subsequently rebuilt, it was taken by the Muslims in 634. The ruins of the ancient city include the remains of the Temple of Bel (Palmyra's chief deity). Inscriptions in the Palmyric alphabet (developed from the *Aramaic) provide important information on Palmyra's trade. The modern town has a population (1970 est) of 12,722.

Palo Alto 37 27N 122 09W A city in W central California, SE of San Francisco, at the S tip of San Francisco Bay. Stanford University (1885) is here. Population (1980): 55,225.

Palo Alto, Battle of (1846) First US-Mexican clash of the *Mexican War. US General Zachary *Taylor, returning to Fort Texas on the Rio Grande near Brownsville, Tex, was blocked by the Mexicans under General Mariano Arista. The American force, although smaller, was victorious, forcing the Mexicans back across the border.

palolo worm (or paolo worm) A large marine *annelid worm, *Eunice viridis*, of the S Pacific. Palolo worms hunt for small prey among coral reefs and their reproduction is synchronized by the phases of the moon. The rear portion of the worm, containing eggs or sperm, separates and swims to the surface, discharging its gametes in the sea. Swarming worms are a local delicacy. Class: *Polychaeta*.

Palomar, Mount A mountain in California. It is the site of the Mount Palomar Observatory operated by the Carnegie Institute of Washington and the California Institute of Technology. Its 200 in (508 cm) reflecting telescope is among the largest in the world. Height: 6140 ft (1870 m). *See also* Hale Observatories.

Palomino A horse that has a yellow or golden coat and a white or silver mane and tail. Palominos are often Arabs or American Quarter horses but may be of any light saddle-horse breed. They are recognized as a color breed in the US but do not breed true.

palynology (or pollen analysis) The study of pollen grains and their distribution in sedimentary rocks in order to provide information about life and environmental conditions of past geological ages. Pollen is extremely resistant to decay and therefore well preserved in rocks. The different genera and species are also very distinctive; therefore the presence of a certain type of pollen indicates the dominant flora—and therefore the climate and other conditions—of the period studied.

Pamirs (or Pamir) A mountainous area of central Asia, situated mainly in the Tadzhik SSR of the Soviet Union and extending into China and Afghanistan. It consists of a complex of high ranges rising over 20,000 ft (6000 m), with the Tian Shan in the N, the Kunlun and Karakoram in the E, and the Hindu Kush in the W. Its highest point is Mount Communism, at 24,590 ft (7495 m).

Pampas The flat treeless plains of Argentina. These extend W from the Atlantic Ocean to the Andes and are bordered by the Gran Chaco in the N and Patagonia in the S. They are of major agricultural importance in the E, producing wheat, corn, and beef in particular.

pampas cat A small wild *cat, *Felis colocolo*, of South America. About the size of a domestic cat, with a long tail and grayish coat, it once hunted in grassland and swamps but is now very rare.

pampas grass A perennial *grass of the genus *Cortaderia*, native to South America and widely cultivated as an ornamental. *C. argentea* grows in dense clumps, with leaves up to 7 ft (2 m) long and flowering stems exceeding 10 ft (3 m) in length. The flowers usually form silvery-white plumes, although various color varieties are possible.

Pamplona 42 49N 1 39W A city in NE Spain, in the Basque Provinces. It has a cathedral and holds a renowned fiesta (during which bulls are driven through the streets to the bullring) described by the novelist Ernest Hemingway, in *The Sun Also Rises* (1926). It is an agricultural center and its industries include traditional crafts and chemicals. Population (1974 est): 169,173.

Pan The Greek god of shepherds and their flocks, the son of Hermes. He is usually portrayed with the legs, ears, and horns of a goat. He lived in the mountains and was associated especially with Arcadia, where he sported with the nymphs and played his pipes, known as the syrinx (see panpipes). He was believed to be the source of a sudden inexplicable fear, or panic, which sometimes overcame travelers in wild and remote places.

Panama, Isthmus of A narrow strip of land linking North and South America, between the Caribbean Sea and the Pacific Ocean. Length: 420 mi (676 km). Minimum width: 31 mi (50 km).

Panama, Republic of A country in Central America occupying the Isthmus of Panama, which connects Central and South America. The *Panama Canal crosses the isthmus, bisecting the country and providing passage between the Atlantic (via the Caribbean Sea) and Pacific Oceans. Narrow coastal plains rise to volcanic mountains. The population is largely of mixed Indian, European, and African descent. *Economy*: considerable revenue comes from receipts from the Panama Canal and from international capital. The main agricultural products are bananas, rice, sugar, and corn and fishing (especially for shrimps) is growing in importance. Industries include oil refining, cement production, and paper and food processing. Tourism is an increasing source of revenue. The main exports include refined oil, bananas, shrimps, and sugar. *History*: discovered by Columbus in 1502 and soon colonized by the Spanish; in 1513 Balboa made his famous journey across the isthmus. Panama later became part of the viceroyalty of Peru and then of New Granada. In 1821 it became part of newly independent Colombia, from which it broke free in 1903 after a revolution supported by the US. Its political history has been turbulent. A military coup in 1968 brought General Omar Torrijos to power and in 1972 a new constitution gave him full executive powers for six years, while also initiating a presidency. In 1978 Torrijos accordingly retired as head of state but retained his command of the National Guard and effectively remained in control until his death in 1981. Panama helped to form the so-called Contadora group, an alliance of Latin American countries that sought a nonaligned political solution to the region's problems. President: Ricardo de la Espriella. Official language: Spanish. Official currency: balboa of 100 centésimos. Area: 29,201 sq mi (75,650 sq km). Population (1983): 2,059,000. Capital and main port: Panama City.

Panama Canal A canal across the Isthmus of Panama connecting the Atlantic and Pacific Oceans. Some 51 mi (82 km) long, it was begun by the French Panama Canal Company under Ferdinand de *Lesseps but construction was halted in 1889 by bankruptcy. In 1903 the US acquired the construction rights from newly independent Panama and the canal was opened in 1914. By the 1903 treaty the US acquired sovereignty in perpetuity over the **Panama Canal Zone**, a region extending 3 mi (5 km) on either side of the canal. In return Panama received $10 million and an annuity. In 1978 two treaties provided for Panamanian sovereignty over the canal and the Zone by 2000 and for their neutrality and in 1979 Panama assumed territorial jurisdiction over the former Canal Zone. Area: 647 sq mi (1676 sq km). Population: 41,800 (37,400 are US citizens).

Panama City 5 58N 79 31W The capital of Panama, situated in the center of the country near the Pacific end of the Panama Canal. Founded by the Spanish in 1519 on the site of an Indian fishing village, it was destroyed by Henry Morgan and his pirates in 1671 and rebuilt two years later 5 mi (8 km) to the SW. It became capital of the newly independent Panama in 1904 and has expanded considerably since the opening of the Canal in 1914. The University of Panama was founded in 1935 and that of Santa Maria de la Antigua in 1965. Population (1980 est): 467,000.

Pan-American Highway A system of highways connecting North and South America. When completed it will consist of about 16,150 mi (26,000 km) of roadway. First proposed as a single route, it is now a whole network of roads. Between Texas and Panama it is called the Inter-American Highway. The sections through the Central American states were built with US aid, while Mexico financed and built its own section. It will eventually connect with roads leading to Santiago, Buenos Aires, Montevideo, and Rio de Janeiro.

Panathenaea In Greek religion, an annual Athenian summer festival consisting of rites, sacrifices, games, and contests in honor of *Athena. Its central feature, a procession up to the Parthenon with the goddess' new robe, is portrayed on the temple frieze.

Panay An island in the central Philippines, in the Visayan Islands. Mountainous in the W, its central fertile plain produces rice, maize, and sugar. It also has timber, fishing, and copper and coalmining industries. Area: 4744 sq mi (12,287 sq km). Population (1970): 2,144,544. Chief town: Iloilo.

Panchen Lama In *Tibetan Buddhism, the title of the chief abbot of Tashilhunpo monastery at Zhikatse, ranking second to the *Dalai Lama. He is said to be a reincarnation of Amitabha, the Buddha of Infinite Light. The present Panchen Lama was enthroned in 1952 at Tashilhunpo, where he apparently still resides despite the Communist Chinese occupation of Tibet and the exile of the Dalai Lama.

pancreas A gland, about 6 in (15 cm) long, situated in the abdomen behind the stomach. When food passes into the intestine the pancreas secretes several digestive enzymes that drain into the intestine through the pancreatic duct. In addition, small clusters of cells (called islets of Langerhans) scattered throughout the pancreas secrete the hormones *insulin and *glucagon, which control blood-sugar levels.

PANDA *The elongated wrist bone of the giant panda acts like a thumb, enabling it to manipulate the bamboo shoots on which it feeds.*

panda A bearlike mammal belonging to the family *Procyonidae* (raccoons, kinkajous, etc.). The giant panda (*Ailuropoda melanoleuca*) is very rare; it lives in the cold bamboo forests of central China, feeding on young bamboo shoots. Giant pandas are up to 5 ft (1.6 m) long, weigh 165–220 lb (75–100 kg), and have bold black and white markings.

The red panda (*Ailurus fulgens*), also called the lesser panda, lives in the forests of the Himalayas and W China. 31–43 in (80–110 cm) long including the bushy tail 12–20 in (30–50 cm), it is red-brown with black markings on its white face. Red pandas live in trees and feed on the ground at twilight on roots, nuts, lichens, and bamboo shoots.

Pandanus. *See* screw pine.

Pandarus In Greek legend, a Trojan archer who wounded the Greek commander Menelaus and was killed by Diomedes. In the medieval story concerning Troilus and Cressida he is the lovers' go-between.

Pandit, Vijaya Lakshmi (1900–) Indian diplomat; sister of Jawaharlal *Nehru. As a member of *Gandhi's movement of noncooperation with the British she was imprisoned. Following independence she was ambassador to the Soviet Union (1947–49) and to the US (1949–51); she then became president of the UN General Assembly (1953–54) and high commissioner to the UK (1955–61).

Pandora In Greek mythology, the first woman, fashioned by *Hephaestus and invented by Zeus as his revenge on *Prometheus, who had stolen fire from heaven. She married Epimethus, brother of Prometheus. Her dowry was a box, which, when opened, released all the varieties of evil and retained only hope.

pangolin An armored mammal belonging to the genus *Manis* and order *Pholidota* (7 species), of Africa and S Asia, also called scaly anteater. 12–31 in (30–80 cm) long with long prehensile tails, pangolins are covered on their backs with overlapping horny scales. Toothless, with a long sticky tongue and strong claws, they sleep in deep burrows, emerging at night to feed on ants and termites. They can walk on their hind legs, climb trees, and curl up into a tight ball if attacked.

Pan Gu (*or* P'an Ku) In Chinese Taoist mythology, the first man. His knowledge of *yin and yang enabled him to shape the world.

Pan Gu (*or* P'an Ku; 32–92 AD) Chinese historian. He expanded the work of *Si-ma Qian to cover the history of the Han dynasty until his own time. His great work *The History of the Former Han* started the Chinese tradition of compiling dynastic histories.

panic grass An annual or perennial *grass of the genus *Panicum* (500 species), mostly of the tropics and subtropics. The flowering stems, up to 31 in (80 cm) high, have many branches, each bearing several slender-stalked spikelets (flower clusters). Some species are cultivated for their grain (*see* millet).

Panini (6th or 5th century BC) Indian grammarian. Panini's analysis of Sanskrit, the *Ashtadhyayi*, is one of the earliest studies of a language and the most comprehensive grammatical work to appear before the 19th century. Although intended to regulate the use of Sanskrit rather than to teach it, the *Ashtadhyayi* is still used in some Brahman schools.

Pankhurst, Emmeline (1858–1928) British suffragette, who founded the Women's Social and Political Union (1903). She was imprisoned several times for destroying property, undergoing hunger strikes and forcible feeding. During World War I, she abandoned her militancy and encouraged the industrial recruitment of women. *See* women's movement.

P'an Ku. *See* Pan Gu.

panorama A narrative scene or landscape painted on a large canvas, which was either hung up around the walls of a circular room or slowly unrolled before an audience. The first panorama was produced by the Scottish painter Robert Barker (1739–1806) in 1788. An antecedent of films, panoramas provided a popular form of entertainment as well as fulfilling an educational function in the 19th century.

panpipes (*or* syrinx) An ancient musical instrument consisting of a row of small graduated pipes bound together. It is played by blowing across the holes. According to Greek legend it was invented by the deity Pan, who pursued the nymph Syrinx. When she was changed into a reed by Apollo, Pan made the instrument from the reed stem.

pansy A popular annual or perennial garden plant that is a hybrid of the wild pansy (*Viola tricolor*), developed in the early 19th century. There are now many varieties, up to 8 in (20 cm) high, with leafy stems and (usually) yellow, orange, purple, brown, or white flowers, up to 2 in (5 cm) across. The wild pansy, or heartsease, found throughout Eurasia, has small flowers colored purple, yellow, and white. Family: *Violaceae. See also* violet.

Pantelleria Island (ancient name: Cossyra) A volcanic island in Italy, in the Mediterranean Sea. Produce includes wine and raisins. Area: 32 sq mi (83 sq km). Population (1971): 8327. Chief town: Pantelleria.

pantheism Any belief or doctrine presenting the natural world, including man, as part of the divine. Pantheism is a predominant tendency in Hinduism but is frowned on by orthodox Christianity. *Spinoza's phrase equating God and Nature (*Deus sive natura*) was an influential formulation of the idea, which enjoyed some currency among 19th-century philosophers. The Romantic poets, particularly *Wordsworth, were also attracted to pantheism.

Pantheon 1. A temple dedicated to the worship of many gods. The most famous is that in Rome begun in 27 BC but rebuilt about 118 AD under Emperor Hadrian. It is a daring circular design built in concrete and topped by a huge concrete dome 142 ft (43 m) wide. In 609 AD it became the Church of Sta Maria Rotonda. 2. A building honoring the famous. The best known is that in Paris designed by *Soufflot in 1759.

panther A color variety of leopard that has a great deal of black pigmentation, which sometimes extends to the tongue and gums. Panthers can occur among a litter of normally spotted leopards.

panzer A mechanized division of the German army. The term panzer, meaning a coat of armor, has become widely used to denote armored forces, tanks, self-propelled artillery, and armored troop carriers.

papacy The office of the pope as temporal head of the Roman Catholic Church. Popes claim to be elected in direct line from St *Peter, to whom Christ deputed his authority on earth (Matthew 16.18–19) and who became the first bishop of Rome. The keys symbolizing this authority are still a papal emblem. The bishop of Rome, however, was not immediately recognized as pre-eminent and the title Pope was only formally reserved for him in 1073. In W Europe the papacy's political influence spread rapidly after 600 and Pope Leo III's coronation of *Charlemagne (800) marked the beginning of a relationship between the papacy and Holy Roman Empire that dominated Europe until the Reformation. In the East the papacy's attempt to assert its authority by excommunicating the Patriarch of Constantinople brought about the schism between the Roman Catholic and Orthodox Churches (1054; *see also* Filioque). Lesser and temporary schisms were caused by the election of antipopes, notably during the 14th century, when, after the popes had been in exile in Avignon (1309–77; *see* Avignon papacy), there was a period called the *Great Schism (1378–1417) during which there were rival popes in France and Rome. The Reformation seriously weakened the papacy's spiritual and temporal power, although papal territories in Italy remained under the pope's sovereignty. During the unification of Italy, these *papal states were appropriated (1870) and the pope's authority over the Vatican City was only formally acknowledged by the Italian state in the Lateran Treaty (1929). In 1870 the promulgation of the doctrine of papal infallibility caused further schism (*see* Old Catholics). In the 20th century the papacy has resolutely opposed communism and has participated tentatively in the ecumenical movement to heal earlier schisms.

Papadopoulos, George (1919–) Greek colonel, who led the military regime that seized power in Greece in 1967. He ruled by decree with the official title of prime minister, and then president, until overthrown by a military revolt in 1973.

papain A protein-digesting enzyme found in the fruit of the *papaw tree (*Carica papaya*). It is used in biochemical research and as a meat tenderizer.

papal states The central Italian states under papal sovereignty between 756, when *Pepin the Short presented Ravenna to Pope Stephen II (reigned 752–57), and 1870. They included parts of Emilia-Romagna, Marche, Umbria, and Lazio. They were a major obstacle to the 19th-century movement for Italian unification (*see* Risorgimento) but, despite papal opposition, were finally annexed in 1870. The popes refused to recognize their loss of temporal power until the *Lateran Treaty (1929) established the Vatican City as an independent papal state.

papaw (*or* papaya) A small tropical American tree, *Carica papaya*, cultivated throughout the tropics. About 25 ft (7.5 m) tall, it has lobed toothed leaves crowded at the tips of the branches and fragrant creamy-white flowers. The yellowish fruit resembles an elongated melon: its succulent pinkish or orange flesh encloses a mass of seeds. The fruits are eaten fresh, boiled, and in preserves or pickles and are a commercial source of the enzyme papain. Family: *Caricaceae*.

Papeete 17 32S 149 34W The capital of French Polynesia, in NW Tahiti. A tourist center, it is a stop on many Pacific routes. Population (1971): 25,342.

Papen, Franz von (1879–1969) German statesman and diplomat; chancellor (1932). A Catholic Center Party politician with extreme right-wing views, he resigned the chancellorship after six months because of lack of cabinet support for his policies and then persuaded Hindenburg to appoint Hitler as chancellor (1933). Papen was ambassador to Austria (1934–38) and then to Turkey (1939–44). He was found not guilty at the Nuremberg war trials and only served three years of an eight-year prison sentence imposed by a German court.

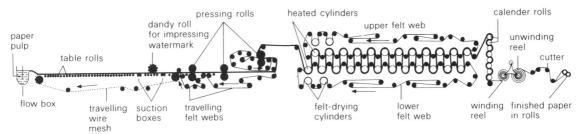

PAPER   *The Fourdrinier paper-making machine is one of the longest machines in use.*

paper A substance in sheet form made from the pulped cellulose fibers of wood, grass, cotton, etc., and used for writing and printing on, wrapping, cleaning, etc. The Chinese invented paper (c. 2nd century BC) and the Arabs learned the secret in 768 AD from Chinese prisoners of war at Samarkand. From Arab manufacture in the Middle East and Spain, paper spread to Byzantium (mid-11th century) and thence all over Europe. Foreign competition meant a slow start to British paper making, the first successful mill being set up about 1589.

All early paper was handmade: shallow wooden frames (molds) with wire mesh bases (*see also* watermark) were dipped into vats of pulp and shaken until the pulp fibers felted together. The resulting sheets were dried, pressed, and, if necessary, sized (dipped in a gelatinous solution to render the surface less permeable). A machine for making paper in a continuous roll (or web) was not invented until 1798, in France. Brought to England in 1803 by Henry Fourdrinier (1766–1854), this machine, of which variants are still in use, picked up the pulp (about 99% water) on a traveling wire mesh and shook it until the fibers were interlaced and the water drained off, before passing it through pressing and drying rollers.

The **pulp** for papermaking is obtained chiefly from wood, but also from esparto grass, rags, and increasingly from recycled wastepaper. Wood pulp may be produced by direct grinding of whole logs, as in making newsprint. For whiter higher quality paper, the wood undergoes a more complex chemical treatment. Esparto grass and rags are used for strong durable high-quality paper, such as bank notes and legal documents. Recycled wastepaper often requires careful sorting and de-inking and is usually mixed with fresh wood pulp.

paper mulberry A shrub or small tree, *Broussonetia papyrifera*, native to E Asia and Polynesia but planted elsewhere as an ornamental, especially in the US. Up to 49 ft (15 m) tall, it has oval pointed leaves, flowers in catkins, and round rough fruits, 1 in (2.5 cm) across. Its bark is used in paper making and to produce tapa cloth in Polynesia. The bast fibers form the basis of coarse fabrics. Family: *Moraceae*.

papilionid butterfly A butterfly belonging to the widely distributed mainly tropical family *Papilionidae* (about 800 species). Papilionids comprise the *swallowtail butterflies, with tail-like projections on the hindwings, and the parnassians, which are mainly alpine.

papilloma A harmless tumor that grows from the surface of the skin or from the lining of a hollow organ, for example the bladder, womb, or lungs. *Warts and *polyps are types of papilloma. If they bleed or undergo any other change they are best treated by removal.

papillon A breed of toy dog, possibly of Spanish origin, associated with such illustrious owners as Mme de Pompadour and Marie Antoinette. Its name is derived from its large forward-facing ears, which resemble the wings of a butterfly (French word: *papillon*). The tail is held over the back and the long fine coat is white with colored patches. Height: 8–11 in (20–28 cm).

Papineau, Louis Joseph (1786–1871) French-Canadian politician. He served in Lower Canada's legislature from 1808 and was speaker (1815–37). He was against British rule in Canada and fought for French-Canadian rights. Opposed to the joining of Upper and Lower Canada, he put forth the "92 Resolutions" (1834), a list of French-Canadian grievances and demands. Although the resolutions were passed in the assembly, they were not enforced and he fled to the US (1837) and eventually to Paris (1839–44). He came back to a united Canada and served in the legislature (1848–54).

Pappus of Alexandria (3rd century BC) Greek mathematician, who wrote an encyclopedia consisting of eight volumes, much of which survives. It summarized Greek mathematics, of which virtually all our knowledge is due to Pappus.

paprika. See Capsicum.

Papua New Guinea, State of A country in the Pacific Ocean, E of Indonesia. It consists of the E part of *New Guinea and several islands, including the Bismarck Archipelago (including New Britain and New Ireland), the N part of the Solomon Islands (including Bougainville), and the Admiralty Islands. Most of the population are Melanesians. *Economy*: subsistence agriculture and the growing of cash crops, such as coconuts, cocoa, coffee, and rubber, are the chief occupations. Livestock rearing is being developed and the country's dense rain forest provides timber. The chief mineral resource and export is copper, the main source being on the island of Bougainville. Other exports include gold, coffee, cocoa, timber, and copra. *History*: the SE part of the island of New Guinea was annexed by Queensland in 1883, becoming a British colony in 1888, known as the Territory of Papua. The NE part was formerly a German territory and came under Australian rule in 1914 as the Trust Territory of New Guinea. In 1921 the two territories including their islands were merged, later becoming a UN Trusteeship under Australia. It was renamed Papua New Guinea in 1971, achieved self-government in 1973, and became fully independent in 1975. Prime minister: Michael T. Somare. Official language: English; Pidgin is widely spoken. Official currency: kina of 100 toca. Area: 178,656 sq mi (462,840 sq km). Population (1980 est): 3,006,799. Capital and main port: Port Moresby.

papyrus An aquatic reedlike plant, *Cyperus papyrus*, up to 10 ft (3 m) tall, originally cultivated in the Nile delta of Egypt and now growing wild in parts of Africa and in Syria. It was used by the ancient Egyptians to make paper: the thick triangular stems were split into thin strips, which were pressed together while still wet. It was also used for rope, mats, sails, and shoes, and the pith was a common food. Family: *Cyperaceae.*

parabola The curve formed by a *conic section, in which the distance from a fixed point (focus) and a fixed line (directrix) are equal. In *Cartesian coordinates a standard form of its equation is $y^2 = 4ax$, for a parabola that is symmetrical about the x-axis and cuts it at the origin (vertex).

Paracel Islands An archipelago of coral islands and reefs in the South China Sea, SE of Hainan Island. They lie above oil deposits and were seized by China from Vietnam in 1974.

Paracelsus (Theophrastus Bombastus von Hohenheim; 1493–1541) Swiss physician, whose radical ideas influenced the development of medicine during the Renaissance. Paracelsus established a reputation for arrogance and aroused controversy by publicly burning the works of *Avicenna and *Galen, denouncing quack remedies, and clashing with the medical establishment. He stressed the importance of chemical compounds in treating disease, refuted the notion that mental illness was caused by demons, and linked goiter with minerals in drinking water.

parachuting The use of a parachute (a fabric canopy) to float down to the ground, usually from an aircraft, either if the aircraft is about to crash, as a way of landing troops in an area, or as a form of sport. Parachutes were used for entertainment long before they were used for safety; the first successful jump was made in 1797 and the first contest held in 1926. In accuracy competitions a contestant uses vents in his parachute to steer himself onto a target area, a red or orange cross with arms 16 ft (5 m) long and 3 ft (1 m) wide. In the middle is a red disk 4 in (10 cm) in diameter. The best parachutists land exactly on the disk. *See also* skydiving.

paraffin wax A wax obtained during the refining of crude *oil. Fully refined, it is a white tasteless solid (mp 50–60°C) consisting of higher *alkanes; it is extensively used in the manufacture of waxed papers, candles, and polishes (especially microcrystalline wax polishes).

Paraguay, Republic of A landlocked country in the center of South America. It is divided by the Paraguay River into two zones: an area of fertile plains and hills to the E and the semidesert of the Gran Chaco to the W. The great majority of the population is of mixed Spanish and Guaraní Indian descent. *Economy*: chiefly agricultural, livestock rearing is of particular importance. Meat packing is one of the main industries, and meat was one of the principal exports, especially to Europe, although this has been reduced since the EEC ban on meat imports. Others include cotton, oilseed, and timber. The main crops are cotton, soybeans, cassava, and sugar cane and there are extensive forests, some of them unexploited. Mineral resources are on the whole sparse, but some limestone, salt, and kaolin is produced. Hydroelectricity is being developed, especially for the export of power to neighboring countries. *History*: explored by the Spanish in the early 16th century, it became a Spanish colony, forming part of the viceroyalty of Peru and later (1776) of the new viceroyalty of Río de la Plata. It became independent of Spain in 1811, and in 1814 José Gaspar Rodríguez de Francia (1766–1840) was elected dictator, becoming dictator for life in 1817. From 1844 to 1870 Paraguay was ruled by the López family. The population suffered great losses in the War of the *Triple Alliance (1865–70) against Brazil, Argentina, and Uruguay and again in the *Chaco War (1932–35) with Bolivia. A period of political unrest was ended in 1954, when General Alfredo Stroessner (1912–) seized power and became president. Paraguay is a member of the OAS and LAFTA. Official language: Spanish; the majority speak Guaraní. Official currency: guaraní of 100 céntimos. Area: 157,042 sq mi (406,752 sq km). Population (1983 est): 3,526,000. Capital and main (river) port: Asunción.

Paraguay River (Portuguese name: Rio Paraguai) A river in South America. Rising in Brazil in Mato Grosso state, it flows generally S to join the Paraná River in SW Paraguay. It is an important means of transport and communications, especially in Paraguay. Length: about 1500 mi (2400 km).

Paraguayan War. *See* Triple Alliance, War of the.

parakeet A small seed-eating *parrot characterized by a long tapering tail and a predominantly green plumage and found especially in SE Asia and Australia. Large flocks may damage crops; brightly colored species are popular as cage birds. *See also* budgerigar; rosella.

paralysis Failure of a muscle or a group of muscles to work. This is most commonly caused by damage to the nerve (and its connections) supplying the muscle, as resulting from injury or infection (*see* poliomyelitis), but it may also be due to failure of the nerve impulse to be transmitted to the muscle (as in myasthenia gravis) or by wasting of the muscle (as in *muscular dystrophy). Paralysis is seen most commonly in western countries following a *stroke: this causes damage to the part of the brain that controls movement and commonly results in **hemiplegia**, i.e. one half of the

body and face becomes paralyzed. *Multiple sclerosis also causes paralysis. **Paraplegia** (paralyzed legs) results from injury to the spinal cord. **Quadriplegia** (paralyzed legs and arms) results when the spinal cord is damaged close to the brain.

paramagnetism A form of *magnetism occurring in materials that when placed in a *magnetic field have an internal field stronger than that outside. This is caused by the presence in atoms or molecules of electrons with unpaired spins. The atom or molecule therefore acts like a tiny magnet (*see* ferromagnetism). In the presence of an external magnetic field these microscopic magnets tend to align with the field, reinforcing it. The effect is destroyed by random thermal motion and, except at low temperatures and high field strengths, the *permeability (a measure of the extent of alignment) is inversely proportional to the temperature.

Paramaribo 5 52N 55 14W The capital and main port of Suriname, near the N coast on the Suriname River. Founded by the French in 1540, it was later under English and then Dutch rule. It has developed considerably since World War II. The University of Suriname was founded in 1968. Population (1971): 151,500.

Paramecium A genus of microscopic single-celled animals (□Protozoa), called slipper animalcules, found in fresh water. They are slipper-shaped, 0.004–0.011 in (0.1–0.3 mm) long, and covered with cilia, which are used for swimming and to waft bacteria and small protozoans into the gullet. They reproduce asexually by binary *fission and sexually by *conjugation. Class: *Ciliata.*

Paraná 31 45S 60 30W A city in E Argentina, on the Paraná River. It is an outlet for agricultural produce (especially cattle, sheep, and grain). Notable buildings include the Cathedral of Paraná (1883). Population (1975 est): 127,635.

Paraná River (Spanish name: Río Paraná) A river in South America. Formed by the confluence of the Rio Grande and Rio Paranaíba in SE central Brazil, it flows generally S for 1800 mi (2900 km) to join the Uruguay River and form the Río de la Plata. The Itaipu Dam, the world's largest dam, which is sited at Foz do Iguaçu near the Paraguayan border, was opened in 1982; the hydroelectric power station is expected to be in full operation by 1989, with a capacity of 12.6 million kW. The cost is being shared by Brazil and Paraguay.

paranoia A mental disorder in which the patient is governed by a rigid system of irrational beliefs (delusions). The sufferer may believe that he is being persecuted by others, or betrayed, or that he is overwhelmingly important. The condition, which can result from *schizophrenia, *alcoholism, or *manic-depressive psychosis, is treated according to the cause. *See also* personality disorder.

paraplegia. *See* paralysis.

parapsychology Scientific investigation into paranormal phenomena. Proper subjects for research include *ghost and *poltergeist hauntings, *extrasensory perception, and *spiritualism. The London Society for Psychical Research (founded in 1882) was the first of numerous kindred organizations throughout the world, but mainstream science is still skeptical about their methodology and conclusions.

Paraquat ($C_9H_{20}N_2(SO_4)_2$) The trade name for a yellow water-soluble solid that is used as a weedkiller. It is highly toxic and some deaths have resulted from swallowing quantities in excess of one gram. It concentrates in the lungs and also causes kidney damage. Treatment for Paraquat poisoning, by *activated charcoal or some other absorbing material, is only effective if carried out immediately.

parasite An organism living in or on another organism of a different species (called the host), from which it obtains food and protection: the relationship may or may not be harmful to the host. A facultative parasite is one that becomes parasitic only under certain conditions, while an obligate parasite must always live parasitically. Many parasites have complex life cycles, with one or more intermediate hosts (of different species) supporting the parasite in the immature stages of its development. The study of parasites—**parasitology**—is of great importance in medicine since many parasites either cause or transmit disease. Disease-causing parasites include bacteria and other microorganisms (*see* infection) and tapeworms; mites, ticks, and fleas are examples of external parasites that transmit disease. Many plants are either partly or completely parasitic, usually on other plants. Mistletoe is a partial parasite.

parasol mushroom An edible mushroom, *Lepiota procera,* found in clearings and around the edges of deciduous woods. Its cap, 4–8 in (10–20 cm) in diameter, is grayish brown with darker scales. The scales form rings on the stem, which has a double collar just below the cap.

parathyroid glands Two pairs of small endocrine glands lying immediately behind the thyroid gland. These glands secrete **parathyroid hormone** in response to a reduction in the level of calcium in the blood. This hormone causes the release of calcium from the bones and its transfer to the blood. Deficiency of parathyroid hormone (and therefore lack of calcium in the blood) results in muscle spasms and cramps (tetany).

paratyphoid fever Infection of the digestive tract caused by the bacterium *Salmonella paratyphi*. It is a mild form of *typhoid fever and can be treated by antibiotic drugs.

parchment Animal skin, usually of the goat, sheep, or calf, treated for writing on but untanned. It derives its name from Pergamum, where in the 2nd century BC the development of improved methods of cleaning, stretching, and scraping skins enabled them to have writing on both sides. It was used for manuscripts and early bound books. More delicate skin from young animals is called vellum. Parchment now often describes high-grade paper manufactured from wood pulp and rag, treated with a special finish. *See also* leather.

parchment worm An *annelid worm, belonging to the genus *Chaetopterus*, that lives in a U-shaped tube made of parchment-like material on muddy shores of the Atlantic and Pacific Oceans. Up to 10 in (25 cm) long, the worm draws in a current of water by beating its paddle-shaped appendages, trapping food particles in a bag of mucus. Parchment worms are strongly luminescent. Class: *Polychaeta*.

Pardubice (German name: Pardubitz) 50 03N 15 45E A city in Czechoslovakia, in E Bohemia on the Elbe River. It has an architecturally distinguished square containing a 16th-century gothic castle and the Green Gate (1507). Population (1980 est): 93,000.

Paré, Ambroise (1510–90) French surgeon and one of the fathers of modern surgery. As barber-surgeon to the army, Paré discarded the practice of treating wounds with boiling oil and hot irons in favor of cleansing, the use of ointments, and surgery to tie off major arteries.

parenchyma The general packing tissue of plants, consisting of simple undifferentiated cells. In young stems, parenchyma encloses the vascular (conducting) tissue and provides support for the plant.

Pareto, Vilfredo (1848–1932) Italian economist and sociologist. Pareto's early work in economics culminated in Pareto's Law, which held that the distribution of incomes could be defined by a mathematical formula. His later sociological work *The Mind and Society* (1916) attacked political liberalism while supporting the free market economy. He is also known for his theory on the rise and fall of governing elites.

Paris 48 52N 2 18E The capital of France and a department of the Paris Region, situated in the N of the country on the Seine River. One of Europe's greatest cities, Paris dominates France as the administrative, commercial, and cultural center. It is also an important industrial base, and many international organizations, including UNESCO, have their headquarters here. The city is in turn dominated by its river, which contributes to the division of Paris into several distinct districts, each with its own characteristics. At the heart of the city, the Île de la Cité contains the cathedral of *Notre-Dame, the Palais de Justice, and the 13th-century Sainte Chapelle. On the Left Bank lie Montparnasse and the Latin Quarter, which is known for its associations with writers and artists and still contains some faculties of the university of the Sorbonne (founded in the 12th century) although much of it has now been moved to other sites. On the Right Bank stands the Palais du Louvre, one of the world's most important museums. Further W is a series of radiating boulevards meeting at the Place Charles de Gaulle (formerly Place de l'Étoile), which were laid out by Baron *Haussmann in the 19th century. The Champs Élysées runs from the *Arc de Triomphe at the center of the Place Charles de Gaulle to the Place de la Concorde. Further N lies Montmartre (the artists' colony of Paris until the migration to Montparnasse in the 1920s), dominated by the Basilica of the Sacré Coeur (1919). The tunnels beneath Montmartre, created by quarrying, are now a major problem, causing subsidence and structural damage to buildings. To the S of the Seine, the *Eiffel Tower, built for an exhibition in 1898, is another reminder of the 19th century. *History*: the earliest known settlement was on the Île de la Cité in Roman times. According to legend, St Denis became the first bishop in the 3rd century AD and Ste Geneviève saved the city from sacking by German tribes in the 5th century. In the 6th century Clovis made it the capital of his Frankish kingdom but it later suffered attacks from Vikings. It regained importance as the capital under the *Capetians and from the 13th century its independence as a city increased. Since the storming of the Bastille (1789), heralding the beginning of the French Revolution, it has been the scene of many revolts, such as the *July Revolution and the *Revolution of 1848; the most recent disturbance was in May, 1968. Occupied by the Germans in World War II, it was liberated by the Allies in 1944. Population (1975): 2,290,000.

PARIS *The Eiffel Tower, probably the city's most famous landmark, seen behind the Alexander III Bridge over the River Seine.*

Paris In Greek legend, a son of *Priam and Hecuba. He was brought up as a shepherd on Mount Ida. His abduction of *Helen with the help of Aphrodite caused the *Trojan War, during which he killed Achilles and was himself killed by Philoctetes. *See also* Eris.

Paris, Matthew. *See* Matthew Paris.

Paris, Treaties of 1. (1763) The treaty that ended the *Seven Years' War. France ceded its North American territories E of the Mississippi River to Britain and Louisiana to Spain, from which Britain acquired Florida. Britain also gained Minorca, Senegal, Grenada, St Vincent, Dominica, and Tobago. 2. (1783) The treaty that ended the *American Revolution. US independence was recognized and Britain ceded Florida to Spain. 3. (1814) The peace between France and the victorious allies (Prussia, Russia, Austria, Britain, Sweden, and Portugal) that confirmed Napoleon's abdication and limited France to its 1792 boundaries. 4. (1815) The peace following Napoleon's final defeat at Waterloo that reduced France to its 1789 boundaries. 5. (1856) The peace that ended the *Crimean War. Russia guaranteed the neutrality of the Black Sea and ceded S Bessarabia to Moldavia.

Paris Peace Conference (1919–20) A conference of representatives of the Allied and Associated Powers held after World War I. Proceedings were dominated by the US (Woodrow Wilson), France (Clemenceau), the UK (Lloyd George), and Italy (Orlando). Five treaties arose from the conference: *Versailles with Germany (1919); Saint-Germain with Austria (1920); Neuilly with Bulgaria (1919); Trianon with Hungary (1920); and Sèvres with Turkey (1920). In addition the conference ratified the Covenant of the *League of Nations.

parity The concept of left- and right-handedness. According to the law of conservation of parity, no fundamental distinction exists between left and right and the laws of physics apply equally to left- and right-handed systems. In 1957 this principle was shown to be violated in *weak interactions between certain elementary particles (*see* particle physics). For example, when a neutron decays the electron produced is always left-polarized (i.e. spins in a direction opposite to that of its motion), whereas if parity was conserved there would be equal numbers of left- and right-polarized electrons. This lack of parity provides a fundamental distinction between left and right. The parity of elementary particles is expressed as a *quantum number.

Park, Mungo (1771–c. 1806) Scottish explorer. A surgeon, he made two explorations of the Niger River. In 1795–96 he ascended the Niger from the mouth of the Gambia River, crossed the Sénégal Basin, and was imprisoned by Arabs. Escaping, he eventually returned to The Gambia. His *Travels in the Interior Districts of Africa* (1797) related his adventures. In 1805, under government patronage and with 40 companions, he resumed his exploration. The expedition was attacked by natives and Park died.

Park Chung Hee (1917–79) South Korean statesman and general; president from 1963 until his murder in 1979. He served in the Japanese army in World War II and then in the South Korean army. He led the coup that established a military regime in 1961, becoming president two years later. In 1972 he declared martial law and assumed quasi-dictatorial powers.

Parker, Charlie (Christopher) (1920–55) US jazz saxophonist and composer, known as "Bird" or "Yardbird." With Dizzy *Gillespie he originated the *bop style of jazz and appeared with a number of bands. In the 1950s he made recordings with a band containing strings and wind and was regarded as one of the greatest jazz musicians.

Parker, Dorothy Rothschild (1893–1967) US humorous writer. Famous as a wit, she established her reputation while working as drama critic for *Vanity Fair* and the *New Yorker* (1927–33). She is best known for her short stories and sketches, collected in *Here Lies* (1939), but she also wrote poems, collected in *Not So Deep As a Well* (1936), plays, and filmscripts.

Parkes, Sir Henry (1815–96) Australian statesman; prime minister of New South Wales (1872–75, 1877, 1878–83, 1887–89, 1889–91). Born in England, he emigrated to Australia in 1839. He campaigned (1849–52) against the British transportation of convicts to Australia and as prime minister worked for the federation of the Australian states and for compulsory free education.

Parkinson, (Cyril) Northcote (1909–) British author, historian, and journalist. He wrote the well-known *Parkinson's Law* (1958), a study of business administration containing the aphorisms that work expands to fill the time allotted to it and that subordinates multiply at a fixed rate regardless of the amount of work produced. His other books include *Britain in the Far East* (1955), *The Law and the Profits* (1960), and *Big Business* (1974).

parkinsonism (or Parkinson's disease) A chronic disease affecting the part of the brain controlling voluntary movement, first described in 1817 by a British physician, James Parkinson (1755–1824). Sometimes the disease may result from infection, side effects of drugs, or injury, but usually no cause is apparent. The symptoms are tremor of the hands and mouth, stiffness, and difficulty in initiating movements. It occurs most commonly in older people and can often be treated effectively with drugs, including *L-dopa, or surgery.

Parkman, Francis (1823–93) US historian. *The Oregon Trail* (1849) is an account of an adventurous expedition undertaken to gain knowledge of the American Indians. Thenceforth he suffered from illness and blindness but completed a monumental colonial history of *France and England in North America* (9 vols, 1851–92). Other works, which often dealt with events in Canadian history include *History of the Conspiracy of Pontiac* (1851) and *The Old Regime in Canada* (1874).

Parks, Gordon, Sr (1912–) US photographer and motion picture director. He worked for *Life* magazine (1948–68) during which time he often photographed black ghetto life. He wrote *The Learning Tree* (1963) and directed the movies *Shaft* (1971) and *Leadbelly* (1976).

parlement The supreme court of France until the French Revolution. The parlement of Paris developed in the 12th century out of the king's court. Membership was at first elective but by the 14th century seats could be bought and in 1614 became hereditable with the introduction of the *paulette* (annual right), which secured a seat by payment of an annual fee. From its duty, and right of refusal, to register royal edicts the parlement derived considerable political power and by the 17th century had become a bastion of reaction. It impeded government attempts to put its own house in order and in 1792, in the wake of the French Revolution, the parlement of Paris, together with its less influential provincial counterparts, was abolished.

parliament The legislative assembly of the UK; it consists of the sovereign, the House of Lords, and the House of Commons; its seat is the *Palace of Westminster. Parliament developed in the 13th century from the *Curia Regis (King's Court), in which the monarch consulted with his barons. In 1213, 1254, and 1258 representatives of the shires were also summoned to attend parliament and in 1265 the parliament summoned by Simon de *Montfort included borough representatives—the origins of the House of Commons. By the reign of Edward III (1327–77) Lords and Commons, meeting separately, were recognized constituents of government. Increasingly assertive under Elizabeth I (1559–1603), its conflict with James I and Charles I over the extent to which the crown was answerable to parliament led to the Civil War (1642–51) and the establishment of republican government under Oliver Cromwell. Following the Restoration of the monarchy in 1660, the attempts of James II to rule arbitrarily led to the Glorious Revolution (1688), which achieved the beginning of parliamentary ascendancy over the crown. The 18th century saw the emergence of party politics (see Whigs; Tories) and of a *prime minister and the development of *cabinet government. In the 19th century the *Reform Acts greatly reduced the influence of the House of Lords, which lost its veto power by the Parliament Act (1911).

Parma 44 48N 10 19E A city in N Italy, in Emilia-Romagna. Dating from Roman times, it became an important cultural center in the middle ages. Its university was established in 1222 and it has a romanesque cathedral and a 16th-century palace, damaged in 1944 during World War II. The center of an agricultural district, Parma's industries include the manufacture of Parmesan cheese, perfume, fertilizers, and glass. Population (1980 est): 175,932.

Parmenides (c. 510–c. 450 BC) Greek philosopher, born at Elea (S Italy). According to Parmenides, things either are or are not. Only "being" is real; "not-being" is illusory. For change to occur "being" must become "not-being," which is absurd. Therefore change does not occur. But our senses indicate that change does occur: therefore our senses are misleading, and "being," as apprehended by reason, is the only reality. Parmenides described "being" as finite, spherical, timeless, undifferentiated, and indivisible. His doctrines strongly influenced *Plato. See also Heraclitus; Zeno of Elea.

Parmigianino (Girolamo Francesco Maria Mazzola; 1503–40) Italian mannerist painter and etcher, whose nickname derives from his birthplace, Parma. After painting frescoes in S Giovanni Evangelista, Parma, he moved to Rome (1524) but was forced to flee to Bologna during the sack of Rome (1527). Characteristic of his elongated figure style is the *Madonna with the Long Neck* (Palazzo Pitti, Florence). His portraits include *Self-Portrait in a Convex Mirror* (Kunsthistorisches Museum, Vienna). □mannerism.

Parnassians A group of French poets in the mid 19th century who reacted against the subjectivism of the Romantics and whose poetry was characterized by objective restraint and verbal and technical precision. They were led by *Leconte de Lisle, whose disciples included Theodore de *Banville, *Sully-Prudhomme, and J.-M. de Hérédia (1842–1905).

Parnassus, Mount (Modern Greek name: Parnassós) 38 32N 22 41E A mountain in S central Greece, held in ancient times as sacred to the god Apollo and the Muses. Height: 8061 ft (2457 m).

Parnell, Charles Stewart (1846–91) Irish politician, who in 1880 became the leader of the *Home Rule party in the British House of Commons. Parnell, a member of parliament from 1875, reconciled constitutional and radical forces and enjoyed widespread popular support in Ireland. He allied his party with the Liberals in 1886, when Gladstone introduced the Home Rule bill. Parnell remained a dominant political figure until 1890, when he was named in a divorce suit brought against Katherine O'Shea, whom he then married.

Páros A Greek island in the S Aegean Sea, in the Cyclades. Marble has been quarried here for sculpture since ancient times. Area: 75 sq mi (195 sq km). Population (1971): 7314.

parquetry The inlaying of geometrically shaped pieces of wood into the plane surfaces of furniture, floors, staircases, etc. The word is often now used to describe geometric *marquetry, particularly as used on 17th- and 18th-century furniture.

Parr, Catherine (1512–48) The sixth wife (1543–47) of Henry VIII of England. She was noted for her kindness to her three stepchildren. After Henry's death, she married (1547) Thomas, Baron Seymour of Sudeley (d. 1549).

Parrish, Maxfield (Frederick) (1870–1966) US illustrator and artist. He illustrated books and magazine covers and painted posters and murals, the most well-known of which is on a wall in the St Regis Hotel in New York City. A painter of intricate, decorative designs, he illustrated Washington *Irving's *Knickerbocker's History of New York* (written in 1809), and Kenneth *Grahame's *The Golden Age* (1895) and *Dream Days* (1898).

parrot A bird belonging to the family (*Psittacidae*; 300 species) occurring worldwide in warm regions. 4–40 in (10–100 cm) long, parrots have a compact body, a short neck, and strong rounded wings suited for fast flight over short distances. The plumage is typically brightly colored and the short stout hooked bill is used to open nuts and to feed on fruits and seeds. Most are arboreal and excellent climbers, having clawed feet with rough scaly toes. They are gregarious and have a harsh screaming voice. Order: *Psittaciformes. See also* cockatoo; kakapo; kea; lory; lovebird; macaw; parakeet.

parrot fish A fish, also called parrot wrasse, belonging to the family *Scaridae* found among tropical reefs. Up to 48 in (1.2 m) long, it has a deep often brilliantly colored body and the teeth are fused to form a hard beak, which is used to feed on coral, mollusks, and seaweed. Order: *Perciformes.*

parsec A unit of distance, used in astronomy, corresponding to a parallax of one second of arc. 1 parsec = 3.26 light-years or 3.084×10^{16} meters.

Parseeism The religion of the descendants of Persians who fled their country in the 8th century AD to avoid persecution following the Arab conquest. Mostly located in Bombay, Madras, Calcutta, and Karachi, they continue to practice *Zoroastrianism in two sectarian forms.

parsley A fragrant biennial herb, *Petroselinum crispum*, native to the Mediterranean region but widely cultivated. The compound leaves are curled or frilled and have an aromatic flavor. They are used fresh or dried in fish and meat dishes, soups, garnishes, and bouquets garnis. The flowering stems, up to 40 in (1 m) high, bear clusters of small yellowish flowers. Family: *Umbelliferae.*

parsnip A hairy strong-smelling biennial plant, *Pastinaca sativa*, native to grassland and wasteland of temperate Eurasia and widely cultivated throughout temperate regions for its large starchy white taproot, which is eaten as a vegetable or used as cattle feed. The leaves consist of paired lobed toothed leaflets on a long furrowed stalk and the clusters of tiny yellow flowers are borne on stems up to 5 ft (150 cm) high. Family: *Umbelliferae.*

Parsons, Talcott (1902–78) US sociologist. His early theories, first expounded in *The Structure of Social Action* (1937), underwent extensive change in *The Social System* (1951), becoming a functionalist (*see* functionalism) systems approach and later incorporating evolutionism and cybernetics. The consequences for adopting such an approach are represented in his analysis of social stratification, in which he emphasized its integrative supportive role. His work has been criticized for obscurity and failure to deal with conflict, power, and deviance.

parthenogenesis A method of reproduction in which the egg develops without *fertilization to produce an individual usually identical to the parent. It occurs commonly among lower plants and animals, particularly aphids, ants, bees, and wasps, principally to accelerate the production of individuals at certain times of the year. In many species, for example aphids, sexual reproduction does take place from time to time to provide genetic variation.

Parthenon A temple on the hill of the Acropolis in □Athens dedicated to the goddess Athena. Built between 447 and 432 BC by *Ictinus and *Callicrates at the instigation of *Pericles, it represents the summit of classical Greek architecture. Its rectangular colonnaded exterior of Doric columns originally contained a walled chamber with *Phidias' gold and ivory statue of Athena. In the 5th century AD it became a Christian church and in the 15th century a mosque. It was blown up by the Turks in 1687. Much that remained of its adorning sculpture was removed by Lord Elgin in the 19th century (*see* Elgin Marbles).

Parthia The region S of the Caspian Sea approximating to present-day Khorasan (NE Iran). Inhabited by seminomadic tribes, Parthia, once a feudal confederacy of vassal kingdoms under the Achaemenians and then the Seleucids, controlled a great empire from about 250 BC to 224 AD with its capital at *Ctesiphon. Parthia's famous cavalry and mounted archers harassed Rome's eastern frontiers, overwhelming Crassus' army in a humiliating defeat at *Carrhae in 53 BC. In 224 AD the Parthian empire was conquered by the *Sasanians of Persia.

particle physics The study of elementary particles and their interactions. Until the discovery of the *electron (J. J. Thomson; 1898), the atom had been thought of as a minute indivisible "billiard ball." The existence of the electron and the discovery of the *proton (Rutherford; 1914) made it clear that the atom had an internal structure. When the *neutron was discovered (Chadwick; 1932), it appeared that the whole universe was constructed of just these three particles. The outstanding problem was the nature of the force that held neutrons and protons together in the atomic

nucleus. The only two fundamental forces known at that time were the gravitational force and the electromagnetic (em) force: the gravitational force was too weak to account for the great stability of the nucleus and the em force had no effect on the electrically uncharged neutron.
In 1935 *Yukawa suggested that there might be in nature a short-lived particle (later called the meson) that jumped between protons and neutrons and held them together in much the same way as two tennis players are held together by the ball passing between them. This concept of exchange forces and the subsequent discovery of short-lived particles led to intensive research into particle physics throughout the world (*see* accelerators). By the 1960s some 200 "elementary" particles had been identified and it became clear that there were four basic types of force; in addition to gravitational and em forces there were *strong interactions (100 times more powerful than em forces) and *weak interactions (10^{10} weaker than em forces). It also became evident that some elementary particles were more elementary than others. In general, there are now believed to be two classes: leptons (the electron, muon, tau particle, and *neutrinos), which interact by the em or the weak forces and have no apparent internal structure; and hadrons (including the proton, neutron, pion, etc.), which interact by the strong interaction and do appear to have an internal structure. During the past 20 years the main preoccupation of particle physicists has been the elucidation of hadron structure. The current model is based on Murray Gell-Mann's concept of the quark, introduced in 1963. In this model, hadrons themselves are divided into two classes: baryons, which decay into protons; and mesons, which decay into leptons and *photons or into proton pairs. Baryons consist of three quarks and mesons consist of a quark-antiquark pair. Thus all the matter in the universe is now seen as being made of leptons and quarks.
Although the quark concept was introduced as a theoretical construct and a single quark has never been identified experimentally, there is now a considerable amount of evidence that they actually exist. Quark theory is fairly elaborate; quarks have fractional electronic charges ($+2/3$ or $-1/3$ of the electronic charge) and come in five "flavors" called up (u; $+2/3$), down (d; $-1/3$), charmed (c; $+2/3$), strange (s; $-1/3$), and bottom (b; $-1/3$). For each flavor there is an equivalent antiquark (ū, đ, etc.). The proton consists of uud ($2/3 + 2/3 - 1/3 = 1$) and the neutron consists of udd ($2/3 - 1/3 - 1/3 = 0$).
In this limited form quark theory conflicted with the *Pauli exclusion principle and it therefore became necessary to introduce the concept of "color." Thus each flavor of quark can have one of the three colors red, yellow, or blue, with antiquarks having the corresponding anticolors. "Color" in this sense has no connection with visual color but the analogy is useful. All hadrons are regarded as white and baryons must consist of a red, a blue, and a yellow (since these visual colors produce white); mesons consist of a quark of any color and its corresponding anticolor. See also antimatter; charm; quantum number; strangeness.

partridge A small gamebird native to the Old World but widely introduced elsewhere. Partridges are 10–16 in (25–40 cm) long and have rounded bodies with short rounded wings and a low gliding flight. The European partridge (*Perdix perdix*) is a common farmland bird and has a grayish plumage with a red face and tail and a dark U-shaped marking on its belly. Family: *Phasianidae* (pheasants, quail, partridges). *See also* francolin.

Partridge, Eric Honeywood (1894–1979) British lexicographer, born in New Zealand. After World War I he settled in England, where he produced many witty, idiosyncratic, and learned works, including *A Dictionary of Slang and Unconventional English* and an etymological dictionary called *Origins*, both of which have had numerous editions.

Pasadena 34 10N 118 09W A city in California. It is a winter health resort and well-known residence for Los Angeles film stars. The annual Tournament of Roses and the Rose Bowl football game are held here. The California Institute of Technology was established here in 1891. Population (1980): 119,374.

Pasadena 29 42N 95 13W A city in SE Texas, just SE of Houston. Sam Houston defeated Mexico's General Santa Anna here in 1836, and Texas independence was established. Oil is refined and petroleum, metal, plastic, paper, and rubber products are manufactured. Population (1980): 112,560.

Pasargadae An ancient Persian city in Fars province, Iran. It was founded as the capital between 546 and 530 BC by *Cyrus the Great, whose tomb still stands there. His successors abandoned it unfinished for *Persepolis in the late 6th or early 5th century BC.

pascal (Pa) The *SI unit of pressure equal to one newton per square meter. Named for Blaise *Pascal.

Pascal, Blaise (1623–62) French mathematician, physicist, and theologian. He made a study of conic sections when still in his teens; later he studied the mathematics of *probability, in collaboration with Pierre de

Fermat, and invented Pascal's triangle for calculating the coefficients of a binomial expansion. He also made discoveries in *fluid mechanics, notably that the pressure in a fluid is everywhere equal (**Pascal's principle**). In 1641 he invented the first calculating machine. At the age of 31 he had a mystical experience and from then on devoted his life to religion. In the same year he became a Jansenist and his *Lettres provinciales* (1656–57) defended *Jansenism against the *Jesuits. His greatest work was *Pensées sur la religion* (1669), a poetical and metaphysical treatise on human nature.

pasha An honorary title applied in the Ottoman Empire to military, naval, and civil commanders. It was abolished in Turkey in 1934 but lasted until 1952 in Egypt.

Pashto The language of the Pathan people of N Pakistan and Afghanistan, which belongs to the *Iranian family. Pashto is the official language of Afghanistan. There are two main dialects, Pashto in Afghanistan and Pakhto in Pakistan. Both are written in a modified Arabic script.

Pashtuns. *See* Pathans.

Pašić, Nicola (1845–1926) Serbian statesman. Pašić was prime minister of Serbia (1891–92, 1904–05, 1906–08, 1909–11, 1912–18). After World War II he was a representative of the newly formed Yugoslavia at the Paris Peace Conference. In 1921 he became prime minister of Yugoslavia, serving until 1924 and again from 1924 to 1926. He believed in a centralized Yugoslavia and Serbian supremacy within it.

Pasionaria, La. *See* Ibarruri, Dolores.

Pasolini, Pier Paolo (1922–75) Italian film director. His films include original treatments of Greek legends, such as *Oedipus Rex* (1967) and *Medea* (1969), a highly acclaimed biblical film, *The Gospel according to St Matthew* (1964), Marxist allegories, such as *Theorem* (1968) and *Pigsty* (1969), and anthologies of bawdy entertainment, such as *The Decameron* (1970).

passage rites Rituals and ceremonies performed on a person's transition from one social status to another. The most common are those at birth, puberty, marriage, death, and succession to office. Practices vary greatly but a pattern consisting of three stages is common to many such rites. First, there is a rite of separation, removing the subject from his previous status; next, a transitional stage in which the person is suspended between statuses; and finally, a rite of aggregation, in which the new status is conferred. In many primitive societies such rites are thought to be essential to ensure success in the new role. *See also* initiation rites.

Passchendaele. *See* World War I.

passenger pigeon A slender long-winged *pigeon, *Ectopistes migratorius*, once common in deciduous woodlands of North America but extinct by the end of the 19th century. It was 12.5 in (32 cm) long and had a pointed tail and a slate-gray plumage with a deep pink breast. It fed on beech nuts, acorns, and fruits and was highly migratory, able to fly long distances for food, and formed flocks numbering millions of birds. Harvesting of eggs, chicks, and adults and rapid deforestation led to its extinction.

passerine bird A bird belonging to the order *Passeriformes*, which includes over half (about 5100) of all bird species. Passerines—the perching birds—are characterized by their feet, which are specialized for gripping branches and stems. They are the most highly evolved birds and occur in large numbers in almost every habitat, although few live or feed in water. Most species are between 5 and 8 in (12 and 20 cm) in length, although some are as small as 3 in (7.5 cm), with others reaching 46 in (117 cm). There are both migratory and sedentary species. Passerines are often of economic importance—as a source of food, for their ornamental plumage, or as cagebirds. Some species, such as the *quelea and *Java sparrow are serious crop pests.
The order is divided into four major groups (suborders): *Eurylaimi* (broadbills); *Tyranni* (includes manakins, ovenbirds, pittas, and tyrant flycatchers); *Menurae* (lyrebirds and scrubbirds); and—the largest and most advanced group—*Oscines* (*see* songbird).

passionflower A climbing plant of the genus *Passiflora* (500 species), native chiefly to tropical and subtropical America and cultivated for ornament. The leaves may be simple or deeply lobed; some are modified as tendrils. The distinctive flowers each consist of a cup-shaped base with five colored sepals and petals at its upper edge surmounted by a colored fringe. From the center of this protrudes a stalk bearing the stamens and ovary. The fruit is a berry or capsule, which in some species (e.g. *P. quadrangularis*) is edible (passionfruits *or* granadillas). Family: *Passifloraceae*.

Passion plays Religious dramas concerning the crucifixion and resurrection of Christ and often including other related religious episodes. They were performed on Good Friday throughout medieval Europe and survived after the Reformation in Switzerland, Austria, and Germany. The Passion play at *Oberammergau in West Germany, the best-known modern example, has been performed every ten years since 1634 in fulfillment of a vow made by the villagers during an epidemic of the plague.

Passover (Hebrew word: *Pesah*) One of the three biblical pilgrimage festivals (the others are Weeks and Tabernacles). It commemorates the Exodus from Egypt and also incorporates a spring harvest festival. In Judaism, it is celebrated for seven or eight days, beginning on the eve of the first day with a formal meal (*see* haggadah). Unleavened bread (*matzah*) is eaten, all leaven being removed from the house. In Christianity it has been replaced by *Easter.

Passy, Frédéric (1822–1912) French economist and politician, whose efforts for peace were rewarded with the first Nobel Peace Prize (1901), which he won jointly with *Dunant. He established a peace arbitration society (Ligue international de la Paix, 1867) and helped found the International Parliamentary Union (1889), as well as arbitrating in international disputes.

pasta An originally Italian dough made from semolina obtained from durum wheat and water, sometimes with the addition of eggs. Among the many varieties of pasta are spaghetti (long thin rods), macaroni (short hollow thicker tubes), lasagne (flat rectangular pieces), ravioli (little squares of pasta stuffed with meat), and tagliatelle (long flat ribbons). Pasta is usually served with well-flavored sauces.

Pasternak, Boris (1890–1960) Russian poet and novelist. He was born into a cultured Jewish family and studied music and philosophy. He published several volumes of Symbolist poetry between 1917 and 1923 and many translations during the 1930s. His epic novel *Dr Zhivago* was banned in Russia but became internationally successful after its publication in Italy in 1957. Under severe political pressure, he declined the Nobel Prize in 1958.

Pasteur, Louis (1822–95) French chemist and microbiologist, who made great advances in the prevention and treatment of diseases caused by microorganisms. A tanner's son, Pasteur became a science master and pursued his interest in chemistry: in 1848 he discovered two different optically active forms of tartaric acid that had differing biological properties. In 1854 Pasteur was appointed dean of the faculty of sciences at Lille University. He found that fermentation was caused by microorganisms and that by excluding these, souring or decay could be prevented (*see* pasteurization). Although partially paralyzed in 1868, Pasteur's interest in germs and disease directed his attention to anthrax (the life cycle of the causative bacillus in cattle had been studied by *Koch). By 1881 Pasteur had devised a means of safely inducing immunity to the disease by injecting a vaccine of heat-treated (attenuated) live anthrax bacilli. Pasteur also produced a vaccine for chicken cholera and—in 1885, his most spectacular achievement—an effective rabies vaccine. The Pasteur Institute was founded in 1888 to treat rabies and has since developed into a world center for biological research.

pasteurization Heat treatment used to destroy the microorganisms in milk. The method involves heating milk for 30 minutes at 140°F (60°C), which kills the tuberculosis bacteria without damaging the milk protein. This process is named for Louis *Pasteur, who demonstrated that heat could prevent the spoilage of wine and beer caused by fermentation of yeasts and other microorganisms.

Pasto 1 12N 77 17W A city in SW Colombia, on a slope of the Pasto volcano. It is the commercial center of an agricultural and cattle-rearing area. The University of Nariño was founded here in 1827. Population (1978 est): 140,700.

Patagonia A geographic area of S South America in Argentina and Chile, extending S of the River Colorado to the Strait of Magellan. It consists chiefly of an arid plateau rising to the Andes. Sheep raising is the principal economic activity. It contains the major oilfield of Comodoro Rivadavia, Argentina's chief source of oil, and the Río Turbio coalfield. Area: about 300,000 sq mi (777,000 sq km).

patas monkey An *Old World monkey, *Erythrocebus patas*, of African grasslands. Patas monkeys are 43–46 in (110–160 cm) long including the tail (20–30 in [50–75 cm]) and are mainly terrestrial and omnivorous. They live in well-ordered troops (hence, their alternative name—military monkeys). A white-nosed eastern race is called the nisnas monkey.

patchouli An aromatic herb, *Pogostemon patchouli*, native to Malaysia. It contains a fragrant essential oil used in perfumery in SE Asia. The dried leaves are used as an insect repellent. Family: *Labiatae*.

PATAS MONKEY *These monkeys have long tails and are well adapted for climbing trees and rocks, although they usually remain on the ground.*

Pater, Walter (Horatio) (1839–94) British critic and essayist. He established his reputation with *Studies in the History of the Renaissance* (1873). His historical fiction *Marius the Epicurean* (1885) advanced his philosophical and aesthetic theories, which greatly influenced the *Aesthetic movement. His many critical essays on art and poetry are noted for their highly polished prose style.

Paterson, William (1745–1806) US jurist and politician; born in Ireland. He held various state positions in New Jersey and went to the Continental Congress (1780–81) and Constitutional Convention (1787), where he proposed the *New Jersey Plan, parts of which were adopted. He served as US senator (1789–90), governor of New Jersey (1791–93), and associate justice of the Supreme Court (1793–1806).

Paterson 40 55N 74 10W A city in New Jersey, part of the Greater New York Metropolitan Area. Founded in 1791, it became known as the Silk City in the 19th century, because of its large silk industry. Its varied manufactures today include cotton, paper, and chemicals. Population (1980): 137,970.

Pathans A large group of tribes of N Pakistan and SE Afghanistan who speak the *Pashto language. They are also known as Pashtuns. Each tribe is subdivided into a number of patrilineal clans, said to be descended from a common ancestor. Genealogical lines of many generations are remembered and determine land rights, succession, and inheritance. Devout Muslims, the Pathans are farmers and warriors, many entering into military service.

pathology The branch of medicine concerned with the study of disease and disease processes in order to understand their causes and nature. The specialty originated in the mid-19th century, when *Virchow demonstrated that changes in the structure of cells and tissues were related to specific diseases. Cellular pathology advanced further with the work of Pasteur and Koch on the bacterial cause of disease, but it was not until the beginning of the 20th century that the knowledge gained in the laboratory was applied to the treatment and prevention of disease in patients. Examples of early work in the science of clinical pathology include Schick's test for diphtheria and Wasserman's test for syphilis. Chemical pathology developed from the observation of changes in the composition and structure of blood in disease, notably with the work of Banting and Best on the importance of insulin in diabetes and contributions from such hematologists as Landsteiner in the discovery of the blood groups. Today pathology includes studies of the chemistry of blood, urine, feces, and diseased tissue, obtained by biopsy or at autopsy, together with the use of X-rays and many other investigative techniques.

Patinir, Joachim (*or* Patenier; c. 1485–1524) Flemish painter, noted for his panoramic landscape views, which dwarf the religious themes that were his ostensible subjects. His paintings include *St Christopher* and *St Jerome* (both Prado).

Pátmos A Greek island in the E Aegean Sea, in the Dodecanese. St John the Divine is believed to have written the Book of Revelation here. Area: 13 sq mi (34 sq km). Population (1971): 2486.

Patna 25 37N 85 12E A city in India, the capital of Bihar on the Ganges River. It was founded in 1541 on the former site of Pataliputra, ancient capital of the Maurya and Gupta empires. Population (1971): 473,001.

pato A four-a-side equestrian sport related to *polo and *basketball, played in Argentina. The mounted players try to throw a ball, to which are attached six leather handles, into a goal (a net attached to a post).

Paton, Alan (1903–) South African novelist. His best-known novel, *Cry, the Beloved Country* (1948), is a passionate indictment of injustice in South African society. His other works include *Too Late the Phalarope* (1953), also dealing with South African social problems, *The Land and the People of South Africa* (1955), *Ah, But Your Land Is Beautiful* (1982), and a collection of short stories, *Debbie Go Home* (1961). He was national president of the Liberal Party from 1953 to 1960.

Patras (*or* Pátrai) 38 14N 21 44E A port in W Greece, in the N Peloponnese on the Gulf of Patras. The War of Greek Independence began here in 1821. Exports include currants, raisins, tobacco, and olive oil. Its university was established in 1966. Population (1971): 111,607.

patriarch 1. In the Old Testament, *Adam and the other ancestors of the human race before the Flood, as well as the later forebears of the Hebrew nation: Abraham, Isaac, Jacob, and Jacob's 12 sons who gave their names to the 12 tribes of Israel. 2. In the Orthodox Church, the title of a bishop with jurisdiction over other bishops. At the Council of Chalcedon (451) five such sees were recognized: Alexandria, Antioch, Constantinople, Jerusalem, and Rome. The patriarch of Constantinople took the title Ecumenical Patriarch, despite Rome's objections (*see* papacy).

patricians The hereditary aristocracy of ancient Rome. Originally the sole holders of political and religious offices, the patricians were gradually forced during Republican times to admit *plebeians to political offices and their privileged position was eroded.

Patrick, St (c. 390–c. 460 AD) The patron saint of Ireland. Legend tells of his abduction from Britain by Irish marauders at the age of 16. A local chief's slave in Antrim, he later escaped to Gaul, finally returning to Ireland as a missionary. He established an archiepiscopal see at Armagh and by the time of his death had firmly established Christianity in Ireland. His only certain works are a spiritual autobiography, the *Confession*, and the *Epistle to Coroticus*. Feast day: March 17. Emblems: snakes and shamrock.

Patriotic Front (PF) A black nationalist organization, founded in 1976, to oppose the government of Ian Smith in Rhodesia (now *Zimbabwe). Using guerrilla techniques, its two wings—the Zimbabwe African National Union (ZANU), led by Robert *Mugabe, and the Zimbabwe African People's Union (ZAPU), led by Joshua *Nkomo—were based in Mozambique and Zambia respectively. In the elections (1980) that followed the Lancaster House agreements, Mugabe became prime minister of Zimbabwe.

Patroclus In Homer's *Iliad*, the companion of Achilles. During the Trojan War he was killed by Hector while wearing the armor of Achilles.

Patti, Adelina (Adela Juana Maria; 1843–1919) Italian-born US operatic soprano. She specialized in the Italian coloratura repertoire, singing both in the US and Europe.

Patton, George S(mith) (1885–1945) US general. Gaining experience in the strategy of armored warfare during his service in World War I, Patton was successively placed in command of the US tank corps in North Africa (1941), the Seventh Army in Sicily (1943), and the Third Army in France (1944) during World War II. Following the *D-Day invasion of Normandy, he led a spectacular advance to the Moselle. In the Ardennes he cleared the W bank of the Rhine and encircled the Ruhr, an operation that was decisive in the final military defeat of Nazi Germany. Patton distinguished himself as an uncompromising commander who demanded total discipline and dedication from his subordinate officers and troops.

Pau 43 18N 0 22W A city in SW France, the capital of the Pyrénées-Atlantique department. It was the former capital of Béarn and residence of the French Kings of Navarre. Pau is a tourist resort and trades in horses, wine, and leather. Population (1975): 85,860.

Paul I (1754–1801) Tsar of Russia (1796–1801). Paul reversed many of the enlightened policies of his mother, Catherine the Great, and pursued an inconsistent foreign policy that isolated Russia. His incompetence and despotism led to his assassination.

Paul I (1901–64) King of the Hellenes (1947–64). The third son of Constantine I, he lived mostly in exile from 1917 to 1935, and again during World War II, succeeding his brother George II (1890–1947; reigned 1922–23, 1935–47). In 1938 Paul married Frederika (1917–) of Brunswick.

Paul III (Alessandro Farnese; 1468–1549) Pope (1534–49). First of the *Counter-Reformation popes, Paul restored the *Inquisition, summoned the Council of *Trent, and actively supported the new orders, especially the *Jesuits. However, he was also noted for his nepotism and worldliness. He was a considerable patron of learning and the arts.

Paul VI (Giovanni Battista Montini; 1897–1978) Pope (1963–78). Succeeding *John XXIII, Paul continued his predecessor's policies of reform, reconvening the second *Vatican Council after his election. While working for ecumenicism and administrative reform he maintained papal authority and traditional doctrines, notably in the encyclical *Humanae Vitae* (*Of Human Life*; 1968), which reiterated the Church's position on birth control.

Paul, St (c. 3–c. 64 AD) Christian Apostle, born Saul of Tarsus, who spread Christianity among the Gentiles; the 13 Epistles attributed to him form a major part of the New Testament. The son of a Pharisee and a Roman citizen, he was educated at Jerusalem and was initially anti-Christian, having participated in the martyrdom of St *Stephen. While traveling to Damascus, he had a vision that led to his conversion to Christianity. He began his activity as an Apostle in Damascus, later joining the other Apostles in Jerusalem. His important missionary work consisted of three journeys in which he traveled to Cyprus, Asia Minor, Macedonia, Greece, Ephesus, and elsewhere, establishing churches or bringing support to previously established Christian communities. After his third journey, he returned to Jerusalem and was arrested by Roman soldiers in order to protect him from the hostility of the mob, who attacked him for teaching transgression of the Mosaic Law. He eventually appealed to Caesar and, as a Roman citizen, was taken to Rome for trial. He was imprisoned for two years; here the New Testament account (in Acts) ends. It appears that he may have been released, before being arrested a final time and beheaded under Nero. Paul's influence was decisive in extending Christianity beyond the Jewish context of the Church at Jerusalem, and the Pauline Epistles formed the basis of all subsequent Christian theology. Feast day: June 29.

Pauli, Wolfgang (1900–58) US physicist, born in Austria, who in 1925 formulated the *Pauli exclusion principle for which he received the 1945 Nobel Prize. In 1931 he postulated that some of the energy of a *beta decay was carried away by massless particles, which *Fermi named neutrinos.

Pauli exclusion principle The principle that no two *fermions may exist in the same state. It is most commonly applied to atomic electrons, which cannot have the same set of *quantum numbers. Named for Wolfgang *Pauli.

Pauling, Linus Carl (1901–   ) US chemist, who originated and developed important concepts concerning the structure of molecules. Successfully using new analytical techniques, Pauling elucidated the nature of chemical bonding in both simple and complex molecules, publishing his highly influential book, *The Nature of the Chemical Bond*, in 1939. He received the Nobel Prize for chemistry (1954) for his research and the Nobel Peace Prize (1962) for his pacifist stance against the use of nuclear weapons.

Paulinus of Nola, St (c. 353–431 AD) Christian Latin poet, born at Bordeaux. After a political career as a senator, consul, and governor of Campania, he became a Christian and was ordained in 394. Bishop of Nola from 409 until his death, he is famous for his poetic epistles. Feast day: June 22.

Paulus, Friedrich (1890–1957) German field marshal in World War II. In command of the Sixth Army on the Eastern Front, he captured Stalingrad (1943) but his army was forced to surrender, thus ending the German offensive in the Soviet Union. *See* Stalingrad, Battle of.

Pausanias (2nd century AD) Greek traveler, whose *Description of Greece* is an invaluable source for places and buildings now destroyed. His accuracy and judgment are attested by his description of those that survive.

Pau-t'ou. *See* Baotou.

Pavarotti, Luciano (1935–   ) Italian operatic tenor. He made his debut at La Scala, Milan, in 1966 and at the Metropolitan Opera in New York in 1968. He has become known for his performances of the works of Bellini, Verdi, and Puccini.

Pavese, Cesare (1908–50) Italian novelist and poet. He was imprisoned for his antifascist journalism in 1935 and later joined the resistance movement. His best-known novels, which concern human isolation, include *Il compagno* (1947) and *La luna e i falò* (1950). He also published poetry and numerous translations of works by US and English writers. Lonely throughout his life, he committed suicide at a time when he was receiving most public recognition. His diaries were published posthumously as *Il mestiere di vivere* (1952).

Pavia (ancient name: Ticinum) 45 12N 9 09E A city in Italy, in Lombardy on the Ticino River. Dating from Roman times, it has a 12th-century church, in which St Augustine is buried, a 15th-century cathedral, a mon-

astery, several palaces, and a university (1361). Pavia is the center of an agricultural region and produces sewing machines, metal goods, textiles and furniture. Population (1971): 90,125.

Pavia, Battle of (February 24, 1525) A major engagement in the Italian wars between *Francis I of France and the Habsburg emperor *Charles V. It marked the beginning of Habsburg ascendancy in Italy. Some 23,000 Habsburg troops relieved the besieged city of Pavia, captured Francis, and virtually destroyed the French army of 28,000.

Pavlodar 52 21N 76 59E A port in the Soviet Union, in the NE Kazakh SSR on the Irtysh River. It was founded in 1720 but remained small until the mid 20th century, since when it has become an important industrial center: food processing is the principal activity. Population (1981 est): 288,000.

Pavlov, Ivan Petrovich (1849–1936) Russian physiologist noted for his studies of digestion and his demonstration of the *conditioned reflex. Pavlov showed how heartbeat is regulated by the vagus nerve and how eating stimulates secretion of digestive juices by the stomach. Pavlov extended his theories of reflex behavior to cover aspects of human behavior, such as learning.

Pavlov was a persistent critic of the communist regime although it continued to provide him with facilities for research. He was awarded the 1907 Nobel Prize.

Pavlova, Anna (1885–1931) Russian ballet dancer. She joined Diaghilev's company in Paris in 1909, and from 1914 she devoted her career to international tours with her own company. She created the chief role in *Les Sylphides* and was especially associated with *Le Cygne*, choreographed for her by *Fokine in 1907.

pawnbroking The lending of money on the security of an item of personal property. An article pawned is pledged to the pawnbroker but can be redeemed within a specified time by the repayment of the loan plus *interest.

Pawnee A confederation of Caddoan-speaking North American Indian tribes of the Platte River area, Nebraska. They were typical of the Eastern Plains Indian semiagricultural and buffalo-hunting culture. Their villages consisted of large circular earth-covered lodges. Shamans were important. The Pawnees worshiped the sun, had a star cult, and observed the morning-star ceremony in which a captured maiden was sacrificed by cutting out her heart.

Pawtucket 41 53N 71 23W A city in NE Rhode Island, on the Blackstone River. The site of the first US cotton mill (1790), its industries include textiles, silks, machinery, and paper. Population (1980): 71,204.

Paxinou, Katina (1900–72) Greek actress. As well as acting in classical Greek tragedies she translated and produced British and US plays for the Greek National Theater. Her films include *For Whom the Bell Tolls* (1943) and *Mourning Becomes Electra* (1947).

Paxton, Sir Joseph (1801–65) British architect. Initially a gardener, Paxton experimented with new techniques of construction employing iron and glass in building greenhouses. This experience culminated in the design of the revolutionary *Crystal Palace in London for the Great Exhibition of 1851. He also designed country houses and practiced landscape gardening.

Payne-Aldrich Tariff Act (1909) US law that attempted reform of tariffs. Originally two separate proposals—by Sereno E. Payne in the House and Nelson Wilmarth Aldrich in the Senate—the merged compromise bill did not greatly change tariff rates and did not include an originally proposed inheritance tax.

Paysandú 32 21S 58 05W A port in W Uruguay, on the Uruguay River. Accessible to oceangoing vessels, its chief exports are cereals, flax, and livestock. It is a meat-processing center and has tanning and sugar-refining industries. Population (1975 est): 80,000.

Paz, Octavio (1914–   ) Mexican poet, critic, and diplomat, whose early poetry was influenced by Marxism and surrealism. His mature poetry is philosophical and deals with the problem of solitude; the collection *La estación violenta* (1958) contains his best-known poem, "Piedra del sol."

Pazzi conspiracy (1478) A plot to assassinate Lorenzo and Giuliano de' *Medici in Florence Cathedral. It was led by their political and business rivals, the Pazzi, and was supported by the papacy. Giuliano died but the Medici maintained control of the government and many of the conspirators were captured and killed. A war with the papacy followed but Lorenzo's dominance over Florence had been demonstrated.

pea An annual herb of the genus *Pisum* (about 6 species), native to the Mediterranean area and W Asia, especially the widely cultivated *P. sativum*. The leaves consist of paired oval leaflets and have curling tendrils used for climbing. The white flowers have a large rear petal and two smaller wing petals enclosing a cuplike keel petal. The edible round seeds are contained in an elongated pod and are an important source of protein for man and livestock. Family: *Leguminosae.

Peace Corps A US government agency and volunteer program established in 1961 by President John F. *Kennedy to provide the underdeveloped countries of the world with skilled technical advisers, teachers, and agricultural experts. Since the inception of the program, thousands of Peace Corps volunteers, all of whom must be US citizens and over 18 years of age, have served in various capacities throughout the Third World, contributing their expertise to the improvement of economic and social conditions and promoting friendship between their host countries and the US.

Peace River A river in W Canada, whose headstreams (Finlay and Parsnip Rivers) rise in the British Columbia Rockies. Flowing generally NE across the N Alberta plains, it empties into the Slave River. It is mostly navigable and is also tapped for hydroelectricity. Its valley is fertile farmland, with important oil and timber reserves. Length: 1195 mi (1923 km), including Finlay River.

peach A small tree, *Prunus persica, probably native to China but widely cultivated in Mediterranean and warm temperate regions. Up to 20 ft (6 m) high, it has toothed glossy green leaves and pink flowers, borne singly or in groups in the leaf axils. The round fleshy fruit (a *drupe) has a distinct cleft and thin velvety skin, yellowish with a crimson tinge. The sweet white or yellow flesh encloses a wrinkled stone. Peaches are eaten fresh, canned, or in preserves. Nectarines (*P. persica* var. *nectarina*) are varieties with smooth-skinned fruits. Family: *Rosaceae.

peacock. *See* peafowl.

Peacock, Thomas Love (1785–1866) British satirical novelist. He worked for the East India Company from 1819 to 1856 and was a close friend of Shelley. His seven novels, which include *Nightmare Abbey* (1818) and *Gryll Grange* (1860), satirize contemporary fashions and ideas.

peacock butterfly A common Eurasian *nymphalid butterfly, *Inachis io*. The adults are brownish purple with a bright eyespot on each wing. They fly from early spring well into summer. The black spiny caterpillars are gregarious and feed on stinging nettles.

pea crab A small pea-shaped *crab belonging to the genus *Pinnotheres*. The female lives within the shell of certain bivalve *mollusks, such as oysters and mussels, obtaining food and shelter but not harming its host (*see* commensalism). The larvae and usually the males are free-swimming. Tribe: *Brachyura*.

peafowl An Old World gamebird belonging to a genus (*Pavo*; 2 species) native to lowland forests of India and SE Asia. Peafowl are 30 in (75 cm) long and the female (peahen) has a green-brown plumage; males (peacocks) have elaborate lacy tails, 60 in (150 cm) long, the feathers of which are tipped by blue-and-bronze markings and raised over the body during display. The blue (Indian) peacock (*P. cristatus*) is a metallic blue color and has been domesticated as an ornamental bird. Family: *Phasianidae* (pheasants, partridges, etc.); order: *Galliformes* (pheasants, turkeys, etc.).

Peale, Charles Wilson (1741–1827) US artist, who painted portraits of the famous, including George *Washington. His son **Rembrandt** (1778–1860) carried on the tradition of portrait painting and was also known for his historical paintings, including *The Court of Death* (1820). Other members of the family, including sons **Raphaelle** (1774–1825), **Rubens** (1784–1865), **Titian** (1799–1885), and **Franklin** (1795–1870), and brother **James** (1749–1831) and his children, worked on miniature, still life, animal, natural history, and portrait paintings.

peanut The fruit of *Arachis hypogea*, also called groundnut or earthnut, native to tropical South America but widely cultivated in the tropics. The plant is an erect or creeping annual, 11–18 in (30–45 cm) high, with compound leaves and yellow flowers. After fertilization the flower stalk elongates, pushing the developing pod below the soil to ripen under ground. The pod has a thin spongy wall and contains one to three seeds (the nuts), which are highly nutritious. They are used in cookery, canned, and made into peanut butter and peanut oil (used in margarine). Family: *Leguminosae.

pear A tree of the genus *Pyrus* (about 20 species), native to temperate Eurasia. The numerous cultivated varieties of orchard and garden pears are derived from *P. communis*. Up to 43 ft (13 m) high, it has oval leaves and bears clusters of five-petaled white flowers. The fruit, which narrows toward the stalk, has freckled brownish-yellow or russet skin surrounding sweet gritty flesh and a core of pips; it is eaten fresh or canned and used to make an alcoholic drink, perry. The wood is used for furniture making. Family: *Rosaceae.

pearl A natural calcareous concretion formed in certain bivalve mollusks popularly known as pearl oysters or pearl mussels. Used for jewelry since earliest times, pearls are usually white or bluish gray and of globular, oval, pear-shaped, or irregular form. A pearl is formed around a foreign body, such as a worm larva, either against the inner side of the shell (a blister pearl) or within the mollusk sealed off as a cyst. It consists of concentric films of nacre, consisting of aragonite, which also forms the smooth lustrous lining (mother-of-pearl) in the shells of pearl-bearing mollusks. Cultured pearls are beads of mother-of-pearl artificially inserted into the mollusk, where they are left for three to five years. Artificial pearls are usually glass beads with a coating prepared from fish scales. Birthstone for June.

pearlfish An eel-like parasitic fish, also called fierasfer or cucumber fish, belonging to the family *Carapidae* (about 27 species), found in shallow tropical marine waters. About 6 in (15 cm) long, it lives in the bodies of echinoderms and mollusks (including pearl oysters), feeding on their reproductive and respiratory organs. The larvae are components of *plankton. Order: *Perciformes*.

Pearl Harbor An inlet of the Pacific Ocean, in Hawaii on Oahu Island. Following the US annexation of Hawaii in 1900, it became a US naval base. On December 7, 1941, the Japanese launched an air attack on US military installations in Hawaii. Four battleships were lost in Pearl Harbor and 3300 service personnel killed. This action precipitated US involvement in World War II. It is now a naval shipyard, supply center, and submarine base.

pearlite A constituent of *steel. It has a regular structure of alternate layers of ferrite (pure iron) and amentite. The name comes from its iridescent appearance under a microscope.

Pearl River. *See* Zhu Jiang.

pearlwort A small tufted or matted annual or perennial herb of the genus *Sagina* (about 20 species), native chiefly to N temperate regions. It has small narrow stalkless leaves and tiny four-petaled white flowers. The evergreen *S. subulata* is cultivated as a rock-garden or border plant. Family: *Caryophyllaceae*.

Pears, Sir Peter (1910–) British tenor. He is well known for his performances of Bach and Schubert and has been closely associated with the music of his friend *Britten, who wrote many works and operatic roles for him, such as the role of Aschenbach in the opera *Death in Venice* (1973). 69

Pearse, Patrick Henry (1879–1916) Irish nationalist, Gaelic enthusiast, and teacher. Pearse became a leader of the Irish Republican Brotherhood (*see* Fenians) and in the *Easter Rising of 1916 proclaimed an independent Irish republic with himself as president. The insurgents were defeated and Pearse and 14 others were executed. Pearse realized the military futility of the rising but believed a blood sacrifice was required for Irish nationalism.

Pearson, Lester B(owles) (1897–1972) Canadian statesman and diplomat; Liberal prime minister (1963–68). Ambassador to the US (1945–46), chairman of NATO (1951), and delegate to the UN, Pearson played a key role in settling the Suez crisis (1956), which earned him the Nobel Peace Prize in 1957.

Peary, Robert Edwin (1856–1920) US explorer in the Arctic. A draftsman and surveyor, he explored areas of Greenland (1886–92). In 1893 he began his efforts to reach the North Pole. In 1909, in the last of six expeditions, he became the first to reach the North Pole. Although his claim was disputed by Frederick Cook, Peary's feat was recognized by Congress in 1911. He achieved the rank of rear admiral.

Peary Land An area in N Greenland, between Victoria Fjord and the Greenland Sea. It is the most northerly land area in the world and was named for the Arctic explorer Robert E. Peary, who first explored it in 1892.

Peasants' Revolt (1381) The only major popular revolt in England during the middle ages. It was occasioned by heavy *poll taxes and reflected a general discontent with government policies. The rising was led by Wat *Tyler and John *Ball. The peasants marched on London, where they were joined by disaffected craftsmen, artisans, and lesser clergy. They achieved initial success, taking the Tower of London, but the revolt soon collapsed and its supporters were ruthlessly suppressed.

Peasants' War (1524–25) A peasant uprising in S Germany, precipitated by economic hardship. The revolt was condemned by Luther and crushed by the Swabian League. Some 100,000 peasants died.

peat Partially decomposed dark-brown or black plant debris laid down in waterlogged conditions in temperate or cold climates. The remains of *Sphagnum (peat or bog moss) are important constituents. Peat is the starting point for the formation of coal and is itself used as a fuel. The more alkaline fen peat is used for horticultural purposes.

pecan. *See* hickory.

peccary A small gregarious hoofed mammal belonging to the genus *Tayassu* (2 species) of South and Central American forests. Resembling a pig, the collared peccary (*T. tajacu*) is dark gray with a light stripe from chest to shoulder and grows to a length of 35 in (90 cm). It has two pairs of short tusks. The white-lipped peccary (*T. albirostris*) is darker and larger and has a white patch on the snout. Both are omnivorous. Family: *Tayassuidae*.

Pechora River A river in the NW Soviet Union. Rising in the Ural Mountains, it flows generally N to enter the Barents Sea and is navigable for much of its length. Length: 1127 mi (1814 km).

Peckinpah, Sam (1926–) US film director. His westerns, which include *Guns in the Afternoon* (1962) and *The Wild Bunch* (1969), show the western myth in conflict with historical progress and include powerful scenes of violence. His other films include *Straw Dogs* (1971) and *The Getaway* (1973).

pecking order (*or* dominance hierarchy) A pattern of social structure found in certain animal groups that denotes the order of precedence of individuals, particularly in relation to feeding. It was first described—and is particularly well developed—in birds, in which the aggressive behavior shown by members of the hierarchy to all those inferior to them takes the form of pecking. It can occur between different species competing for the same food or among a single-species population, especially under captive conditions.

Pecos River A river rising in N New Mexico and flowing SSE through Texas, to join the Rio Grande. It is an important source of irrigation. Length: 1180 km (735 mi).

Pécs (German name: Fünfkirchen) 46 04N 18 15E An industrial city in SW Hungary. An old trading center, it became an important humanist center (14th–15th centuries) and has the earliest established university in the country (1367; reopened 1922). Its rapid growth in the 19th and 20th centuries was based on nearby coalfields. Population (1980): 170,000.

pectin A carbohydrate found combined with cellulose in the cell walls of plants. Ripening fruits change any other pectic compounds present into jelly-like pectin—an essential ingredient for the jelling of jam.

pediatrics The medical specialty concerned with the problems and illnesses of infants and children from birth (or premature birth) to adolescence. Pediatricians must have a detailed knowledge of obstetrics, genetics (to deal with inherited diseases), and psychology. Their work includes the management of handicaps at home and in school as well as the treatment and prevention of childhood diseases.

Pedro I (1798–1834) Emperor of Brazil (1822–31). The son of John VI of Portugal, Pedro became regent in Brazil in 1821 and declared its independence in 1822. On John's death (1826) he refused the Portuguese crown, which was granted to Pedro's daughter. Forced to abdicate in 1831, Pedro returned to Portugal.

Pedro II (1825–91) Emperor of Brazil (1831–89), following the abdication of his father Pedro I. His reign saw an era of prosperity, in spite of wars against Argentina and Paraguay. His gradual abolition of slavery alienated the landowners, who joined the army in deposing him and declaring a republic in 1889.

Pedro the Cruel (1334–69) King of Castile and León (1350–69). He ruled with great cruelty and his brother, Henry of Trastamara (1333–79; reigned, as Henry II, 1369–79), attempted, with French help, to depose him in 1367. England was drawn into the conflict on Pedro's side and Spain thus became a battlefield of the *Hundred Years' War between France and England. Pedro was killed by Henry after defeat at the battle of Montiel.

Peel, Sir Robert (1788–1850) British statesman; Conservative prime minister (1834–35, 1841–46). Elected to parliament in 1809, he was twice home secretary (1822–27, 1828–30). In the Tamworth manifesto (1834), a speech to his constituents, he stated a program of reform that clearly identified the *Conservative Party. His second ministry re-introduced the income tax (1841) and reduced duties on food and raw materials. He is best remembered for the repeal of the *Corn Laws (1846), which caused his followers, the Peelites, to defect from the Conservative Party; they subsequently joined the Liberals.

Peele, George (1556–96) English dramatist. In 1581 he moved from Oxford to the active literary society of London. A prolific writer, his works include the pastoral *The Arraignment of Paris* (1584), the chronicle play *Edward I* (1593), and the satirical play *The Old Wives' Tale* (1595), as well as poems and pamphlets.

Peenemünde 54 09N 13 46E A fishing village in East Germany, on the Baltic coast. The Rocket Test Center was opened in Peenemünde in 1937 and it was here that German rockets (V2) and flying bombs (V1) were developed under Wernher von *Braun during World War II.

peepul. *See* bo tree.

peerage In the UK and Ireland, the temporal hereditary nobility, a body originating in the council of the Norman kings of England, and the life peers, appointed primarily in recognition of public service. The five ranks of the hereditary peerage are, in descending order, duke, marquess, earl, viscount, and baron. A life peer has the rank of baron. All peers are permitted to sit in the House of Lords.

peewit. *See* lapwing.

Pegasus (astronomy) A large constellation in the N sky that contains the **Square of Pegasus**, formed from three of the brightest 2nd- and 3rd-magnitude stars in the constellation together with the 2nd-magnitude star Alpheratz in Andromeda.

Pegasus (Greek mythology) A winged horse that sprang from the blood of *Medusa when she was beheaded by Perseus. It carried the legendary hero Bellerophon in his battles but unseated him when he attempted to ride to heaven. It became a constellation and the bearer of thunderbolts for Zeus.

pegmatite A very coarse-grained igneous rock, usually occurring in veins or dikes within or around bodies of granite. Crystals over 35 ft (10 m) across have been found in pegmatites. Most consist largely of alkali feldspar and quartz but many also contain accessory minerals that are otherwise rare, and these may be of economic importance.

Pegu 17 18N 96 31E A city in S Burma. The former capital of the Mon kingdoms, which dominated Burma at intervals from the 6th century AD until the 17th century, it has an enormous reclining statue of Buddha, 181 ft (55 m) long. Population (1973 est): 254,761.

Péguy, Charles (1873–1914) French poet and essayist. From his socialist bookshop he published the journal *Cahiers de la quinzaine* (1900–14), which expressed the literary ideals of his generation. He was killed in action in World War I.

Pei, I(eoh) M(ing) (1917–) US architect, born in China. He started his own architecture firm in 1955 and was responsible for designing Mile High Stadium in Denver (1956). Through the 1960s he designed many urban complexes as well as the East-West Center at the University of Hawaii and the Everson Museum of Art in Syracuse, NY (1968). He planned the John Hancock Building (1973) and a wing of the Museum of Fine Arts (1981) in Boston, the East Building of the National Gallery of Art (1978), and the US embassy in Peking (1979).

Peipus, Lake (Russian name: Ozero Chudskoye) A lake in the NW Soviet Union, in the Estonian SSR and the RSFSR. It is drained by the Narva River N into the Gulf of Finland. Area: 1356 sq mi (3512 sq km).

PEKING *Commuters stopping on their way to work in order to read the latest wall posters. Worldwide attention was attracted in 1979 by the appearance on "Democracy Wall" of posters critical of the Chinese regime.*

Peirce, Charles Sanders (1839–1914) US philosopher and logician. He spent much of his career in government service, rather than academic life, and his influential *Collected Papers* were only published posthumously (1931–58). Peirce believed that an idea could best be defined by examination of the consequences to which it led. This concept became known as *pragmatism, a name that he later changed to pragmaticism. His work on formal logic was immensely significant.

Peking (Chinese name: Beijing *or* Peiching)   39 55N 116 25E The capital of the People's Republic of China, an administratively autonomous city situated in the NE of the country in Hobei province. The city has expanded considerably since 1949 and there has been rapid development of industries, including iron and steel, machinery, and textiles. A symmetrically laid-out city, its architecture preserves many reminders of its past. It consists basically of two walled cities, the N inner city and the S outer city; the old Imperial City lies within the inner city and at its center the moated "Forbidden City" contains the Imperial Palaces (now museums). There are three universities, the oldest being Peking University (1898). *History*: the site has a long history of human habitation. As Ta-tu, it first became the capital (of N China) under the Yuan dynasty in 1272. Later, when the capital was moved to Nanjing, it became known as Pei-p'ing (*or* Beibing), a name still used by the Republic of China. As Peking (1420), it once more became the capital under the third Ming emperor. In 1928 the Nationalist (Guomindang) government moved the capital to Nanjing and from 1937 until 1945 Peking was occupied by the Japanese. It became the capital of the People's Republic of China in 1949. Population (1980 est): 8,700,000.

Pekingese An ancient breed of toy □dog originating in China and brought to the West by British forces who sacked the Imperial Palace, Peking, in 1860. The Pekingese has a long straight coat forming a luxuriant mane on the shoulders and it may be of any color. The short-muzzled face is always black. Height: 6–9 in (15–23 cm).

Peking man A type of fossil *hominid belonging to the species *Homo erectus* and represented by skeletal remains found at Chou-K'ou-Tien (*or* Zhou kou tian) cave near Peking. Formerly known as *Sinanthropus*, Peking man lived during the middle Pleistocene period (c. 500,000 years ago), used flint and bone tools, hunted, and could make fire.

Pelagius (c. 360–c. 420 AD) The originator of the heretical Christian doctrine known as Pelagianism. Born in Britain, he settled in Rome (c. 380) and later preached in Africa and Palestine. He rejected the doctrines of original sin and predestination, believing in man's free will and inherent capacity for good. These beliefs were hotly disputed by St *Augustine and a series of synods. Pope Innocent I finally condemned them in 417 and excommunicated Pelagius.

Pelargonium. *See* geranium.

Pelasgians (*or* Pelasgi) The inhabitants of Greece before the 12th century BC. They spoke a non-Greek language and lived mainly in the N Aegean. They were scattered during Bronze Age infiltrations of Greek-speaking peoples from the N.

PELÉ *In Brazil he is often nicknamed* La Perola Negra, *the Black Pearl.*

Pelé (Edson Arantes do Nascimento; 1940–) Brazilian soccer player, who played for Santos (1955–74), the New York Cosmos (1975–77), and Brazil. The greatest inside forward of his time, he became a world star at 17 when Brazil first won the World Cup (1958). He scored over 1300 goals.

Pelée, Mount (French name: Montagne Pelée)   14 18N 61 10W An active volcano on the West Indian island of Martinique. In 1902 an eruption engulfed the town of St Pierre. Height: 4800 ft (1463 m).

Peleus In Greek legend, a king of Phthia in Thessaly. He was married to *Thetis and was the father of Achilles.

Pelham, Henry. *See* Newcastle, Thomas Pelham-Holles, 1st Duke of.

pelican A large waterbird belonging to a family (*Pelecanidae*; 7 species) occurring on lakes, rivers, and coasts of temperate and tropical regions. 49–71 in (125–180 cm) long, pelicans are typically white with dark wingtips and have short legs, strong feet, a short tail and very large wings. Their long straight pointed bills have a distensible pouch underneath, in which fish are held before being swallowed. Order: *Pelecaniformes* (gannets, pelicans, etc.).

Pella The capital, about 24 mi (39 km) NW of Thessaloníki (N Greece), of Macedon (*see* Macedonia) from about 400 to 167 BC. Archelaus I (reigned 413–399) established his court here and it is the birthplace of Alexander the Great.

pellagra A disease caused by deficiency of nicotinic acid (*see* vitamin B complex). It occurs mainly in poor countries in people whose diet consists predominantly of maize. The disease causes dermatitis, diarrhea, and delirium or depression. Health can be rapidly restored by giving nicotinic acid, nicotinamide or a diet rich in milk, yeast, beans, or peas.

Pelletier, Pierre Joseph (1788–1842) French chemist, who in 1817 isolated *chlorophyll. He also isolated a number of naturally occurring *alkaloids, including *quinine and *strychnine, which were later introduced into medical preparations by François *Magendie.

Peloponnesus (Modern Greek name: Pelopónnesos) The S peninsula of Greece, joined to central Greece by the Isthmus of Corinth. It includes the towns of Corinth, Patrás (the chief port), and *Sparta. Area: 8354 sq mi (21,637 sq km). Population (1971): 986,912.

Peloponnesian War (431–404 BC) The conflict between Athens and Sparta and their allies, in which Sparta was finally victorious. According to the Athenian historian Thucydides, the war was caused by Spartan fear of Athenian imperialism. Sparta's superior infantry invaded Athens in 431 while Athens, under Pericles, relying for security on walls connecting it to its seaport, attacked at sea. Lacking conclusive victories, both sides agreed to the peace of *Nicias (421). In 415, however, Athens led by *Alcibiades set out to conquer Sicily, which retaliated with Spartan help and destroyed the Athenian fleet (413). The war continued until Sparta under *Lysander captured the partially rebuilt Athenian fleet (405) and beseiged Athens, which then surrendered (404).

Pelops The legendary Greek founder of the Pelopid dynasty of Mycenae, a son of *Tantalus. He won his bride Hippodamia by winning a chariot race with the help of his driver Myrtilus. When Myrtilus demanded his reward, Pelops refused and instead drowned him. The curse pronounced by the dying Myrtilus was passed on to his son *Atreus and all his descendants until it was exorcized by the purification of *Orestes.

pelota A generic name for a variety of court games played with a ball using the hand or a racket or bat. They derive from *real tennis and are widely played in the Basque provinces.

Pelotas 31 45S 52 20W A seaport in S Brazil, in Rio Grande do Sul state on the São Gonçalo Canal. The chief exports are meat, wool, and hides. Population (1975 est): 231,900.

Peltier effect. *See* thermoelectric effects.

pelvis A basin-like structure composed of the hip bones and lower part of the spine. It protects the soft organs of the lower abdomen and provides attachment for the bones and muscles of the legs. The pelvis is larger in women since it must allow the passage of a baby during childbirth.

Pemba 5 10S 39 45E An island in Tanzania, off the NE coast of the mainland. Its major industry is the growing of cloves, of which it is the world's largest producer. Area: 380 sq mi (984 sq km). Population (1978): 205,850.

PEN The acronym of the International Association of Poets, Playwrights, Editors, Essayists, and Novelists, an organization founded in 1921 to promote international fellowship between professional writers. Its presidents have included H. G. *Wells and Heinrich *Böll.

penal law State and federal statutes that determine the acts and circumstances that amount to a crime (a wrong against society prohibited by law) and the punishment for crimes. Most crimes entail both an act (*actus reus*) and a mental element (*mens rea*). However, there is a growing number of crimes in which no mental element is necessary, such as most driving offenses; insanity, infancy (children under the age of ten), or duress (an act committed under threat of death or serious personal injury) may excuse a crime, but ignorance of the law does not if, in cases involving a mental element, the offender intends the result of his acts.

Penang A state in NW Peninsular Malaysia, on the Strait of Malacca, consisting of Penang island and Province Wellesley on the mainland. Ceded to the East India Company in 1786, the island was the first British settlement in Malaya and rapidly became a commercial center. The main products are rice, rubber, and tin. Area: 1031 sq km (398 sq mi). Population (1980): 911,586. Capital: Georgetown.

Penates. *See* Lares and Penates.

pencil cedar A *juniper tree, *Juniperus virginiana*, native to E and central North America and quite widely cultivated for ornament. It has scale-like leaves and blue berry-like fruits, up to 0.24 in (6 mm) long. Its aromatic wood has been used to line clothing chests and cupboards (it repels moths) and for making lead pencils. The tree usually grows to a height of 49 ft (15 m).

Penda (d. 655) King of Mercia (c. 634–55), who made Mercia one of the most powerful English kingdoms. He remained heathen but permitted the conversion of his people to Christianity. He was killed in battle by Oswiu, King of Northumbria.

Penderecki, Krzystof (1933–) Polish composer. He studied in Kraków. His music, for which he has devised a special system of notation, is characterized by note clusters, special tone colors, and unusual sound effects. His compositions include *Threnody for the Victims of Hiroshima* (for strings; 1961), *De Natura Sonoris I* (for orchestra; 1966), the choral work *Utrenja* (1969–71), and a symphony (1973).

Pendleton Act (1883) US law that reformed the civil-service system. Sponsored by Senator George H. Pendleton (1825–89), the bill established the Civil Service Commission to set rules and oversee the granting of government jobs based on competitive examination rather than the spoils system.

pendulum A device in which a mass (the bob) swings freely about a fixed point with a constant period. In the ideal simple pendulum the bob is connected to the fixed point by a length (*l*) of weightless string, wire, etc. Its period is $2\pi (l/g)^{\frac{1}{2}}$, where *g* is the *acceleration of free fall, and is independent of the mass of the bob. A compound pendulum consists of a bob attached to the fixed point via two rigid rods. Pendulums are used to regulate a clock mechanism and in instruments that determine the value of *g*.

Penelope In Homer's *Odyssey*, the wife of *Odysseus. During her husband's absence she put off her many suitors by saying that she must first make a shroud for her father-in-law Laertes. Each night she unraveled what she had woven by day. After 20 years Odysseus returned and killed the suitors.

Penghu Islands (English name: Pescadores) A Taiwanese archipelago of about 64 small islands in Taiwan Strait. Area: 49 sq mi (127 sq km). Population (1972 est): 118,355. Main island: Penghu.

penguin A flightless black-and-white seabird belonging to a family (*Spheniscidae*; 14–18 species) occurring on cold coasts of the S hemisphere. Penguins are adapted for aquatic life, having wings reduced to narrow flippers giving fast propulsion when chasing fish and squid and escaping predators. 16–47 in (40–120 cm) long, they have dense plumage enabling them to tolerate extreme cold. Penguins are highly gregarious and often migrate long distances inland to nest in "rookeries." Order: *Sphenisciformes*. *See also* emperor penguin; fairy penguin.

penicillins A group of *antibiotics. The first penicillin was isolated from the mold *Penicillium notatum*, in 1929, by Sir Alexander *Fleming but was not used to treat infections in man until 1941. Some penicillins must be injected (e.g. benzylpenicillin); others can be taken by mouth (e.g. phenoxymethylpenicillin). Semisynthetic penicillins (e.g. flucloxacillin, methicillin) are effective against infections resistant to naturally occurring penicillins. Ampicillin is a broad-spectrum penicillin, i.e. it kills many species of bacteria. Penicillins can cause severe allergic reactions in susceptible patients.

Penicillium A genus of fungi (about 250 species) that are common molds in soil and on organic matter. The observation of the antibacterial action of *P. notatum* by Sir Alexander *Fleming led to the discovery of penicillin and other antibiotics. *P. camemberti* and *P. roqueforti* are important in cheese making. Family: *Eurotiaceae*; class: *Ascomycetes*.

Peninsular Campaign (1862) US Civil War offensive by the Union Army to take Richmond, Va. Conceived by Union General George B. *McClellan, the Union strategy was to leave Washington protected by 40,000–50,000 troops to proceed, with the rest of the Union Army, from the peninsula between the York and James Rivers to Richmond. McClellan's troops forced Confederate retreats at Yorktown and Norfolk, thus opening up both rivers for the Union fleet, but the Army was stopped near Richmond by Confederate forces under General Joseph *Johnston and later General Robert E. *Lee. The stalemated Battle of Seven Pines and the Seven Days' battles assured the safety of the Confederate capital. Casualties throughout the campaign were high on both sides.

Peninsular War (1808–14) That part of the Napoleonic Wars fought in Spain and Portugal. The French took Portugal in 1807 and in 1808 Napoleon's brother, Joseph *Bonaparte, replaced Ferdinand VII as King of Spain. Popular revolts broke out and turned into a vicious *guerrilla war. The Spanish rebels managed an initial victory at Bailén but against crack French troops could do no more than resist the sieges of Gerona and Zaragoza. British troops under the command of the Duke of *Wellington eventually liberated the Peninsula. After their victory at Vitoria (1813) they invaded France, helping to force Napoleon's abdication (1814).

penis The male copulatory organ of mammals, some reptiles, and a few birds. In man (and other mammals) it contains a tube (urethra) through which both semen and urine can be discharged. The urethra is surrounded by specialized erectile tissue (making up the bulk of the penis): this becomes engorged with blood during sexual excitement, enabling the penis to be inserted into the vagina. The corresponding part in women is the **clitoris**, a small erectile mass of tissue situated in front of the urinary opening.

Pen-ki. *See* Benxi.

Penn, William (1644–1718) English Quaker and founder of Pennsylvania, son of Admiral Sir William Penn (1621–70). Expelled from Oxford (1661) because of his refusal to conform to the restored Anglican Church. He joined the Quakers in 1664. In 1668 he was imprisoned in the Tower for his writings. Here he wrote *No Cross, No Crown* (1669), a classic of Quaker practice. From 1682 he was involved in the establishment of Quaker settlements in America, including Pennsylvania, for which he drew up a constitution, The Frame of Government, allowing freedom of worship. He accomplished peaceful relations with the Indians and designed the city of Philadelphia during his two visits to the colonies (1682–84; 1699–1701). His Charter of Privileges (1701) established a legislature. He was imprisoned for treason and later for debts.

Pennines (*or* Pennine Chain) An upland range in N England. It extends from the Cheviot Hills in the N to the valley of the Trent River in the S. Sometimes known as the "backbone of England" it is the watershed of the chief rivers in N England. It rises to 2930 ft (893 m) at Cross Fell. The **Pennine Way**, a 250 mi (400 km) long footpath, extends between Edale in Derbyshire and Kirk Yetholm in the Borders Region of Scotland.

Pennsylvania A middle Atlantic state. It is bordered on the E by New York and New Jersey, on the S by Delaware, Maryland, and West Virginia, on the W by West Virginia and Ohio, and on the N by Lake Erie and New York. The state is dominated by the uplands of the Appalachian Plateau. Much of the land is under forest or farmed, although it is generally considered to be an urbanized industrial state, dominated by Philadelphia in the E and Pittsburgh in the W. It is a leading iron and steel producer and provides nearly all the country's hard coal. Oil has long been important and the world's first oil well was drilled near Titusville in 1859. Dairy farming predominates in the NE, while the fertile lands of the SE yield cereals, fruit, and vegetables. This latter area is associated with the Pennsylvania Dutch, whose highly decorated barns can be seen throughout the area. *History*: originally the home of the Delaware, Susquehanna, Shawnee, and other Indian tribes, Pennsylvania was first settled by Swedes in 1643. Control passed to the Dutch and then to the British, who granted the region to Quaker William Penn in 1681. Under Penn the colony became a refuge for persecuted religious groups (the Pennsylvania Dutch still live there in large numbers) and a peaceful and successful community, enjoying good relations with the Indians, grew up. The French and Indian Wars (1754–63) interrupted this peace as did the American Revolution two decades later. Benjamin Franklin and other Pennsylvanians became strong voices in the colonial independence movement, and it was at Philadelphia that the signing of the Declaration of Independence took place. Pennsylvania, the nation's capital from 1790 to 1800, achieved statehood in 1787. The late 1700s saw the beginning of iron smelting, and the building of canals (1820s) and railroads facilitated continuing economic expansion. Pennsylvania fought with the Union in the Civil War and was the site of the great Gettysburg campaign (1863). From the close of the Civil War until the end of World War II, Pennsylvania experienced rapid economic and industrial growth with coal mining, oil drilling, and steel production dominating. The state's economy suffered after World War II, but its strong and diversified economic foundation sustained its position as a wealthy and powerful state. Heavy industry was hard hit by the recession of the early 1980s but increasing US energy needs resulted in growing markets for Pennsylvania's coal. Area: 45,333 sq mi (117,412 sq km). Population (1980): 11,866,728. Capital: Harrisburg.

Pennsylvanian period. *See* Carboniferous period.

pennyroyal A perennial herb, *Mentha pulegium*, native to wet places throughout Eurasia and naturalized in North America. 4–20 in (10–50 cm) tall, it has small strongly scented hairy oval leaves and widely spaced whorls of tubular pink or lilac flowers. It is used as a flavoring and to scent soap. Family: *Labiatae.*

Penobscot North American Algonkian-speaking Indian tribe, found in SE Maine in the Penobscot Bay area. Farmers and fishermen, they were members of the Abnaki Confederacy until 1749, when they made their own peace with the British. Today, descendants of the Penobscot live in Old Town, Me, and have limited representation in the state legislature.

Pensacola 30 25N 87 13W A resort city in W Florida, on the W coast of Pensacola Bay, SE of Mobile, Alabama. Settled by the Spanish in 1698, it came under US administration in 1821 as part of Florida Territory. A major US naval flight training base is here. Besides tourism, fish processing and shipping are the major industries. Population (1980): 57,619.

Pentagon The headquarters of the Defense Department, a massive five-sided building in Virginia built (1941–43) during World War II. It houses all three services, the Army, Navy, and Air Force, and extends over 34 acres (14 hectares).

Pentagon Papers (1967–69) Confidential US government papers on the US military situation in Indochina, especially Vietnam. In 1971 several newspapers, including *The New York Times*, started referring to and publishing parts of the study, which revealed that information about Vietnam had been withheld from the US public. The Justice Department, basing its argument on violation of national security, ordered *The Times* to stop publication and prosecuted Daniel Ellsberg, accused of stealing the papers he helped to write, for espionage; both charges were dismissed.

Pentateuch (Greek: five books) The title used by biblical scholars for the first five books of the *Old Testament, traditionally ascribed to Moses. *See also* Torah.

pentathlon An athletic competition comprising five events, the winner being the competitor with the highest total. It originated in an Olympic contest of sprinting, long jumping, javelin throwing, discus throwing, and wrestling (instituted in 708 BC). The current women's version, an Olympic event since 1964, consists of the 100 m hurdles, shot put, high jump, long jump, and 800 m run. The men's pentathlon has been replaced in major competitions by the *decathlon. It has not been an Olympic event since 1924. It comprises the long jump, javelin throw, 200 m sprint, discus throw, and 1500 m run. The **modern pentathlon** is a sporting competition comprising five events: a 5000 m cross-country ride (on horseback), fencing, pistol shooting, a 3000 m swim, and a 4000 m cross-country run. It was first included in the Olympic Games in 1912.

Pentecost. *See* Whit Sunday.

Pentecostal Churches A Christian movement originating in revivalist meetings in the US in 1906. In Pentecostal assemblies people seek spiritual renewal through baptism by the Holy Spirit, as took place on the first Pentecost (Acts 2.1–4). Glossolalia (speaking in tongues, or making utterances in an unknown language under the influence of intense religious experience) is an accompanying phenomenon in many cases as is the ability to perform faith healing. Certain charismatic preachers, generally laymen, evoked an enormous response, especially in the US, where the largest number of Pentecostal Churches are found.

Pentland Firth A channel separating the N Orkney Islands from the mainland of N Scotland. It is notorious for its rough seas and dangerous currents. Length: 20 mi (32 km). Width: 8 mi (13 km).

pentlandite The principal ore mineral of nickel, (Ni,Fe)S, founded in association with pyrrhotite and chalcopyrite in basic and ultrabasic igneous rocks. It is mined in Canada, Australia, and the Soviet Union.

Penutian languages A major family of North American Indian languages spoken along the NW Pacific coast, on the Columbia River plateau, and in California. There are four main divisions: *Chinook and Tsimshian; Coos, Takelma, and Kalapooia; the Sahaptin group, which includes *Nez Percé; and the Californian group.

Penza 53 11N 45 00E A city in the Soviet Union, in the W RSFSR. Founded in 1666, it suffered repeated Tatar attacks. Long an agricultural center, food processing remains important. Other industries include machine manufacturing and paper making. Population (1981 est): 500,000.

peony A large perennial herb or shrub of the genus *Paeonia* (33 species) of N temperate regions, often cultivated for its showy flowers. The large glossy deeply cut leaves arise from underground stems or woody aerial shoots and the solitary white, pink, crimson, or yellow flowers are about 4 in (10 cm) across, with incurving petals and a fleshy central disk supporting the stigma and numerous stamens. The fruit is a large leathery pod containing black seeds. Family: *Paeoniaceae.*

People's Liberation Army (PLA) The military forces of the People's Republic of China. The name was adopted by Chinese communist troops during the civil war of the 1930s and 1940s. Their aim was to liberate the people from the control of the *Guomindang. Since Liberation (1949) the PLA has exercised considerable power in Chinese communist politics.

Peoria 40 43N 89 38W A city in Illinois, on the Illinois River. The state's second largest city, it is the grain and livestock center for an extensive agricultural area. Population (1980): 124,160.

Pepin (II) of Herstal (d. 714 AD) Ruler of the Franks (687–714). He became mayor of the palace (viceroy) of *Austrasia in 679 and virtual ruler of all the Franks after defeating *Neustria at Tertry (687). The Merovingian kings remained nominal rulers until the overthrow of the dynasty by his grandson *Pepin the Short.

Pepin the Short (d. 768 AD) King of the Franks (751–68) after overthrowing the *Merovingians. The son of *Charles Martel, Pepin founded the *Carolingian dynasty and was crowned king by St Boniface. He checked Lombard expansion and in 756 presented Pope Stephen II with the territories around Ravenna—the nucleus of the *papal states. His son *Charlemagne inherited the Frankish kingdom in 771.

pepper A condiment derived from a perennial climbing vine, *Piper nigrum*, native to India. Up to 33 ft (10 m) high, it bears chains of up to 50 inconspicuous flowers that form berry-like fruits (or peppercorns), about 0.20 in (5 mm) in diameter. Whole peppercorns yield black pepper while white pepper is obtained from peppercorns with the outer part of the fruit wall removed. Family: *Piperaceae.*

The fleshy red and green peppers are the fruits of *Capsicum species.

pepperbox A 19th-century firearm, usually a pistol, with a cluster of barrels, each fired separately. Most bizarre was the *Mariette* design (1837) with 18 barrels, firing in groups of three.

peppered moth A European *geometrid moth, *Biston betularia*, the typical form of which has a similar coloration to the lichen-encrusted tree bark on which it rests. During the past century a dark form, var. *carbonaria*, has become common in sooty industrial areas, where it is better camouflaged—and thus better protected from predators—than the typical form.

peppermint A perennial herb, *Mentha × piperata*: a hybrid between water mint (*M. aquatica*) and *spearmint. It has smooth dark-green leaves and oblong clusters of reddish-lilac flowers and is the source of oil of peppermint, used as a flavoring.

pepsin A protein-digesting enzyme found in gastric juice. The inactive form, pepsinogen, is secreted by glands in the stomach wall and converted to pepsin by the hydrochloric acid in the stomach. Pepsin is a powerful coagulant of milk.

peptic ulcer An inflamed eroded area in the wall of the stomach (**gastric ulcer**) or, more commonly, the duodenum (**duodenal ulcer**). Ulcers are very common but it is not known exactly why they occur; they are more common in people who secrete excessive amounts of stomach acid. They may cause abdominal pain, nausea, and vomiting. Serious complications occur when the ulcer bleeds or perforates (bursts). In some patients ulcers disappear as quickly as they come; others require drugs, a special diet, or even surgery (especially if an ulcer perforates).

peptide A chemical compound comprising a chain of two or more *amino acids linked by peptide bonds (–NH–CO–) formed between the carboxyl and amino groups of adjacent amino acids. Polypeptides, containing between three and several hundred amino acids, are the constituents of *proteins. Some peptides are important as hormones (e.g. *ACTH) and as antibiotics (e.g. bacitracin, gramicidin).

Pepys, Samuel (1633–1703) English diarist. His long career in naval administration culminated in his appointment as secretary to the Admiralty (1669–88). He was also a member of parliament and president of the Royal Society. His *Diary*, which extends from 1660 to 1669 and includes descriptions of the Restoration, the Plague, and the Fire of London, is the intimate record of a man for whom every detail of life held interest. It was written in code and deciphered in the early 19th century.

Pequot North American Algonkian-speaking Indian tribe, related to the *Mohegan, found in Connecticut, Rhode Island, and E Long Island, New York. The *Pequot War (1637) forced the few surviving Pequot to seek refuge with neighboring tribes; they were eventually placed by the English in villages near New London, Conn, sold into slavery, or sent to the West Indies.

Pequot War (1637) US colonial war with the *Pequot Indians in Connecticut. Colonists, in retaliation for the murders of colonial traders, attacked the Pequots at Mystic and burned their fort and village. Those that escaped were pursued to swamps near present-day Westport in S Connecticut where the rest of the tribe, with the exception of some women and children, was annihilated.

Perak A populous state in NW Peninsular Malaysia, on the Strait of Malacca. In the Kinta Valley are important tin mines, and rubber, coconuts, and rice are produced. Area: 7980 sq mi (20,668 sq km). Population (1980): 1,762,288. Capital: Ipoh.

Perceval A hero of *Arthurian legend, who played a leading part in the quest of the *Holy Grail. In *Chrétien de Troyes' romance, *Conte du Graal*, and in *Wolfram von Eschenbach's *Parzival*, he succeeds in the quest, but in later romances *Galahad is the only Arthurian knight to succeed in the quest.

Perceval, Spencer (1762–1812) British politician; prime minister (1809–12) remembered for his assassination by a mad and bankrupt broker, John Bellingham.

perch One of two species of freshwater food and game fish belonging to the genus *Perca*. The common perch (*P. fluviatilis*) of Eurasia has a deep elongated body, usually about 10 in (25 cm) long, and is greenish in color, with dark vertical bars on its sides, reddish or orange lower fins, and a spiny first dorsal fin. The yellow perch (*P. flavescens*) is North American. Perch usually live in shoals, feeding on fish and invertebrates. Family: *Percidae*; order: *Perciformes*. *See also* climbing perch; sea bass.

Percheron A breed of heavy draft □horse originating in the Perche district of France. It has a deep muscular body, powerful neck and shoulders, and a characteristically small refined head. Percherons are commonly black or gray. Height: 5–6 ft (1.63–1.73 m) (16–17 hands).

perching duck A *duck belonging to a tribe (*Cairinini*) found chiefly in tropical woodlands. Perching ducks nest in treeholes and have long-clawed toes for gripping branches. Drakes are larger and have brighter colors than females. *See* mandarin duck; Muscovy duck.

percussion cap A device, which came into use in the early 19th century, for igniting the charge in firearms, enabling breech-loading *muskets and *rifles to be developed. Percussion muskets with cartridge ammunition were soon widely adopted in place of flintlocks.

percussion instruments Musical instruments that are struck by the hand or by a stick to produce sounds. The family includes the triangle, gong, rattle, block, cymbals and whip, as well as the pitched xylophone, glockenspiel, bells, celesta, and vibraphone. *Compare* drums; stringed instruments; wind instruments.

Percy, Sir Henry (1364–1403) English rebel, called Hotspur. Together with his father, Henry, 1st Earl of Northumberland (1342–1408), he led the most serious revolt against Henry IV, whom they had helped to the throne in 1399. Headstrong and fearless (hence his nickname) Percy was defeated and killed at Shrewsbury. He appears in Shakespeare's *Henry IV, Part I*.

Père David's deer A rare Chinese deer, *Elaphurus davidianus*, now found only in parks and zoos. About 48 in (120 cm) high at the shoulder, it has a long tail, splayed hooves, and a reddish-gray coat with a white ring round the eye. The male has long branching antlers. A French missionary, Père Armand David (1826–1900), described specimens in the Chinese emperor's hunting park in 1865.

peregrine falcon A large powerful *falcon, *Falco peregrinus*, occurring in rocky coastal regions worldwide. It is 13–19 in (33–48 cm) long and has long pointed wings and a long tail. The male is blue-gray with black-barred white underparts; females are browner. It feeds mainly on ducks, shorebirds, and mammals, soaring high and diving at great speed.

Pereira 4 47N 75 46W A city in W Colombia. Notable buildings include the cathedral (1890) and the university (1961). An agricultural trading center, it has coffee-processing, brewing, and clothing industries. Population (1978 est): 251,861.

Perelman, S(idney) J(oseph) (1904–79) US humorous writer. After publishing his first book in 1929, he worked for a time as a Hollywood scriptwriter, notably on some Marx Brothers films. In the 1930s he began contributing to the *New Yorker*, in which he published most of his short stories and sketches. One of the leading American humorists, he published numerous collections of his pieces, including *Strictly From Hunger* (1937), *Crazy Like a Fox* (1944), *The Most of S. J. Perelman* (1958), *Baby, It's Cold Inside* (1970), and *Eastward, Hi!* (1977).

perennials Plants that can live for many years. In herbaceous perennials, such as the iris and daffodil, aerial parts die down each winter and the plants survive in the form of underground organs (rhizomes, bulbs, corms, etc.). Woody perennials—trees and shrubs—have woody stems, which overwinter above ground. Woody perennials may or may not shed their leaves in winter.

PÈRE DAVID'S DEER *This species would probably now be extinct if a breeding herd had not been established in England at about 1900. All specimens living today are believed to be descended from this herd.*

Pérez de Cuéllar, Javier (1920–) Peruvian diplomat; UN secretary-general (1982–). He served as Peruvian ambassador to Switzerland (1964–66), USSR (1969–71), the UN (1971–75), and Venezuela (1978). From 1975 until 1979 he was under-secretary of the UN in Cyprus. He succeeded Kurt *Waldheim as secretary-general in 1982. He urged negotiations during the Lebanon crises and the *Falkland Islands War.

Pérez Galdós, Benito (1843–1920) Spanish novelist. He wrote a series of 46 historical novels about 19th-century Spain, *Episodios nacionales* (1873–1912), and a second series of novels about contemporary society, of which the best known are *Fortunata y Jacinta* (1886–87) and the *Torquemada* sequence (1889–95). He also wrote several successful plays, including *Realidad* (1892) and the anticlerical *Electra* (1901).

perfect competition A theoretical market structure in economic theory in which no producer supplies a sufficiently large portion of the market to be able to influence prices or to make an exorbitant profit. Perfect competition ensures that resources in the economy are allocated in the most efficient way but is rarely found in practice. *Compare* monopoly; monopsony; oligopoly.

perfect number An integer that is equal to the sum of all its factors (except itself); for example $28 = 1 + 2 + 4 + 7 + 14$. If the sum of all the factors of n is greater or less than n, then n is called excessive or defective respectively. *See also* numbers.

Perga (modern name: Ihsaniye) 36 59N 30 46E An ancient city in SW Turkey, near Antalya. It was the starting point of St Paul's first missionary journey (Acts 13.13) and remains include a theater, an agora, and basilicas.

Pergamum An ancient city of W Asia Minor. After about 230 BC it became capital of a powerful Hellenistic kingdom, allied with Egypt and

Rome against the *Seleucids. Pergamum became rich largely from *parchment and luxury textiles mass-produced by slave labor. Pergamene sculptors led artistic fashion, its library rivaled that of *Alexandria, and the architecture of the upper city was magnificent. The last king bequeathed his realm to Rome (133 BC).

Pergolesi, Giovanni (Battista) (1710–36) Italian composer. He spent most of his short life in or near Naples. His comic intermezzo *La serva padrona* (1733) was influential in the development of *opera buffa. His last work was a *Stabat Mater* (for soprano, alto, and orchestra; 1736).

Perkins, Frances (1882–1965) US stateswoman and reformer. She headed the Consumers' League of New York (1910–12) and served on various New York state industrial commissions. An advocate of better working conditions and unemployment insurance, she was secretary of labor during President Franklin D. *Roosevelt's administrations (1933–45), the first woman appointed to a cabinet position. She was responsible for overseeing and implementing *New Deal legislation. She later served on the Civil Service Commission (1946–53).

Pericles (c. 495–429 BC) Athenian statesman, who presided over Athens' golden age. According to *Plutarch, Pericles became leader of the democratic party in 461 and secured power shortly afterward, following the ostracism of his rival *Cimon. He dominated Athens until 430 by virtue of his outstanding oratory and leadership and his reputation for honesty. Under Pericles, Athens asserted its leadership of the *Delian League and revolts among its members were suppressed: following the Thirty Years' Peace with Sparta, Pericles was able to reduce Euboea (445) and then Samos (439). By 431, rivalry between Athens and Sparta had led to the outbreak of the *Peloponnesian War. The effectiveness of Pericles' strategy, which emphasized Athenian naval power, was undermined by the plague of 430 and Pericles briefly lost office. He died shortly after his reinstatement. In 447 Pericles initiated the great program of public works on the *Acropolis. He also fostered the work of many eminent men, including the playwright Sophocles, the philosopher Anaxagoras, and the sculptor Phidias.

peridotite An ultrabasic igneous rock consisting mainly of olivine; some varieties contain other ferromagnesian minerals, but none contain feldspar. The earth's mantle, believed to be mainly olivine, is sometimes called the peridotite shell. Peridotites are coarse-grained and occur beneath many mountain chains and island arcs.

perigee The point in the orbit of the moon or of an artificial satellite around the earth at which the body is nearest the earth. *Compare* apogee.

Perigordian A culture of the Upper *Paleolithic. Perigordian is the preferred French designation for the pre-*Solutrean industries in W Europe, excluding the typologically different *Aurignacian. Upper Perigordian is approximately equatable with *Gravettian.

Périgueux 45 12N 0 44E A city in SW France, the capital of the Dordogne department. It has Roman remains and a 12th-century cathedral and is renowned for its *pâté de foie gras*, truffles, and wine. Manufactures include hardware and chemicals. Population (1975): 37,670.

perihelion The point in the orbit of a body around the sun at which the body is nearest the sun. The earth is at perihelion on about Jan 3. *Compare* aphelion.

Perilla A genus of herbs (4–6 species), native to India and SE Asia, with simple purplish-green leaves and spikes of tubular lilac flowers. They are cultivated as a source of a fast-drying oil, derived from the seeds and used in printing inks, paints, and varnishes. The leaves are used as a condiment. Family: *Labiatae*.

Perim Island 12 40N 43 24E A South Yemeni island in the Bab (strait) el-Mandeb, off the SW tip of the Arabian Peninsula. It belonged to Aden from 1857 to 1967. Area: 5 sq mi (13 sq km).

period (geology). *See* geological time scale.

period (physics) The interval of time between successive identical configurations of a vibrating system. It is the reciprocal of the frequency of the system.

periodic motion Any motion that repeats itself at constant intervals. The interval of time between successive identical positions is known as the *period of the motion and the maximum displacement of the system from its stationary position is called the amplitude. Examples of periodic motion include a swinging *pendulum, a bouncing ball, and a vibrating string. An important class of periodic motion is *simple harmonic motion.

periodic table A tabular arrangement of the chemical *elements in order of increasing atomic number, such that physical and chemical similarities are displayed. The earliest version of the periodic table was devised in 1871 by D. *Mendeleyev, who successfully predicted the existence of several elements from gaps in the table. The rows across the table are known as periods and the columns as groups. The elements in a group all have a similar configuration of outer electrons in their atoms and therefore show similar chemical behavior. The *halogens, for example, form a group in

PERIODIC TABLE

1A	2A	3B	4B	5B	6B	7B	8			1B	2B	3A	4A	5A	6A	7A	0
1 H																	2 He
3 Li	4 Be											5 B	6 C	7 N	8 O	9 F	10 Ne
11 Na	12 Mg			←		TRANSITION ELEMENTS			→			13 Al	14 Si	15 P	16 S	17 Cl	18 Ar
19 K	20 Ca	21 Sc	22 Ti	23 V	24 Cr	25 Mn	26 Fe	27 Co	28 Ni	29 Cu	30 Zn	31 Ga	32 Ge	33 As	34 Se	35 Br	36 Kr
37 Rb	38 Sr	39 Y	40 Zr	41 Nb	42 Mo	43 Tc	44 Ru	45 Rh	46 Pd	47 Ag	48 Cd	49 In	50 Sn	51 Sb	52 Te	53 I	54 Xe
55 Cs	56 Ba	57† La	72 Hf	73 Ta	74 W	75 Re	76 Os	77 Ir	78 Pt	79 Au	80 Hg	81 Tl	82 Pb	83 Bi	84 Po	85 At	86 Rn
87 Fr	88 Ra	89‡ Ac															

† Lanthanides	57 La	58 Ce	59 Pr	60 Nd	61 Pm	62 Sm	63 Eu	64 Gd	65 Tb	66 Dy	67 Ho	68 Er	69 Tm	70 Yb	71 Lu
‡ Actinides	89 Ac	90 Th	91 Pa	92 U	93 Np	94 Pu	95 Am	96 Cm	97 Bk	98 Cf	99 Es	100 Fm	101 Md	102 No	103 Lr

column 7A. Across each period, atoms are electropositive (form positive ions) to the left and electronegative to the right. For example, in the first period fluorine (F) is the most electronegative element and lithium (Li) the most electropositive. *Atomic theory explains this behavior using the concept of electron shells, corresponding to different energy levels of the atomic electrons. Atoms combine in order to form complete outer shells. The shells are built up by filling the lower energy states (inner shells) first. The first shell takes two electrons, the second, eight, and so on. In larger atoms, the inner electrons screen the outer electrons from the nucleus, resulting in a more complex shell-filling sequence. This explains the partly filled shells of the *transition elements, which form the middle block of the table, in what are known as the long periods. The short periods are from lithium (Li) to neon (Ne) and from sodium (Na) to argon (Ar). The *noble gases in column 0 have complete outer shells and are generally chemically inactive.

periodontal disease   Disease of the gums and other structures surrounding the teeth, formerly known as pyorrhea. Caused by the action of bacteria on food debris that forms a hard deposit (tartar) in the spaces between the gums and teeth, it results in swelling and bleeding of the gums: eventually—if untreated—the teeth become loose and fall out. Periodontal disease is the major cause of tooth loss in adults: it may be prevented (and the early stages treated) by regular brushing, scaling, and polishing, to remove the tartar. Advanced cases require surgery.

Peripatus   A common genus of wormlike *arthropods belonging to the mainly tropical subphylum *Onychophora* (about 90 species). The soft unsegmented body, about 2 in (50 mm) long, bears 14–44 short stumpy legs. The animals live in moist dark places, in rock crevices, or under stones or rotting logs and feed on insects. The young develop within the body of the mother and at birth resemble the adults.

periscope   An optical device consisting, typically, of a tube in which mirrors or prisms are arranged so that light passing through an aperture at right angles to the tube is reflected through the length of the tube to emerge at an aperture at the other end also at right angles to the tube. Periscopes in their simplest form, with cardboard or plastic tubes, are used to see over the heads of a crowd; in their more sophisticated form, they are designed to be extendible and are used by submerged submarines to see above the surface of the water. In this form they may contain aiming devices for weapons, infrared screens, etc.

Perissodactyla   An order of hoofed mammals (16 species) that includes *horses, *tapirs, and *rhinoceroses. The name—meaning odd-toed—reflects the fact that the weight of the body is carried mainly by the central (third) digit of the foot. They are herbivorous, grazing or browsing on leaves, but have evolved separately from other hoofed mammals and have only a single stomach, which is less efficient than the digestive system of *ruminants. *Compare* Artiodactyla.

peritonitis   Inflammation of the peritoneum—the membrane that lines the abdominal cavity. This is a serious condition that results from the bursting of an abdominal organ (such as the appendix, gall bladder, or spleen) or of a peptic ulcer. Alternatively it may result from bacterial infection. The patient will be very ill, possibly in shock, with a painful and rigid belly. An operation is essential to repair the perforated organ and cleanse the abdomen; antibiotics are also given.

periwinkle (botany)   An evergreen creeping shrub or perennial herb of the genus *Vinca* (5 species), native to Europe and W Asia. The attractive solitary blue or white flowers are tubular with five lobes and the fruit is usually a long capsule. They thrive in shade and are cultivated as ornamentals: *V. major* is an important species. Family: *Apocynaceae*.

periwinkle (zoology)   A *gastropod mollusk belonging to the family *Littorinidae*, also called winkle. The common edible winkle (*Littorina littorea*) of European seashores is about 0.8 in (2 cm) high and has a dark-green rounded shell with a pointed spire and grazes on algae. The flat-sided periwinkle (*L. littoralis*) lacks the spire and occurs in many colors.

Perkin, Sir William Henry   (1838–1907) British chemist, who in 1856 synthesized the first artificial dye, aniline purple. Perkin's discovery, when he was only 18, was made by accident.

Perlis   The most northerly state in Peninsular Malaysia, bordering on Thailand. Consisting of a well-watered plain, it produces chiefly rice, with some rubber and coconuts; tin is mined. Area: 310 sq mi (803 sq km). Population (1980): 147,726. Capital: Kangar.

Perm (name from 1940 until 1957: Molotov)   58 01N 56 10E A port in the Soviet Union, in the W RSFSR on the Kama River. Its varied industries include engineering, chemical manufacturing, and oil refining. The *Permian period was first identified here. Population (1981 est): 1,018,000.

permafrost   The permanent freezing of the ground, sometimes to great depths, in areas bordering on ice sheets. During the summer season the top layer of soil may thaw and become marshy, while the frozen ground below remains an impermeable barrier. Problems arise with the construction of roads and buildings in permafrost areas due to the freeze-thaw processes. Permafrost posed problems in the building of the Alaskan pipeline, completed in 1977.

Permalloy   An *alloy of one part iron to four parts nickel, often with other metals added. It has a high magnetic permeability, which makes it useful for parts of electrical machinery that are subjected to alternating magnetic fields.

permeability, magnetic   A measure of the response of a material to a *magnetic field. Magnetic permeability, μ, is the ratio of the magnetic *flux induced in the material to the applied magnetic field strength. The relative permeability, μ_r, is the ratio of μ in the medium to that in a vacuum, μ_o (*see* magnetic constant). Paramagnetic materials have a μ_r greater than unity because they reinforce the magnetic field. Ferromagnetic materials can have a μ_r as high as 100,000. Diamagnetic materials have a μ_r of less than one.

Permian period   The last geological period of the Paleozoic era, between the Carboniferous and Triassic periods, lasting from about 280 to 240 million years ago. Widespread continental conditions prevailed, which continued into the Triassic, and the two periods are often linked together as the Permo-Triassic, during which the New Red Sandstone was laid down.

permittivity   The absolute permittivity of a medium is the ratio of the electric displacement to the electric field at the same point. The absolute permittivity of free space is called the *electric constant. The relative permittivity (*or* dielectric constant) of a capacitor is the ratio of its capacitance with a specified dielectric between the plates to its capacitance with free space between the plates.

Pernambuco.   *See* Recife.

Pernik   42 36N 23 03E A city in W Bulgaria, situated on the Struma River near Sofia. It has engineering and iron and steel industries with coalmining nearby. Population (1976 est): 87,432.

JUAN PERÓN   *He is seen here with his beautiful and popular second wife Evita, a former actress, who was responsible for many reforms (including female suffrage) during his first presidency.*

Perón, Juan (Domingo)   (1895–1974) Argentine statesman; president (1946–55, 1973–74). Elected in 1946 after winning popular support as head of the labor secretariat, his position was strengthened by the popularity of his second wife, **Evita Perón** (Maria Eva Duarte de P.; 1919–52), who was idolized by the poor for her charitable work. After her death, support for Perón waned and he was deposed. He went into exile but remained an influential political force in Argentina, returning in 1973, when he was re-elected president. He died in office and was succeeded by his third wife **Isabel Perón** (María Estella P.; 1930–   ), who was deposed by the army in 1976.

Pérotin   (Latin name: Perotinus Magnus; c. 1155–c. 1202) French composer, active in Paris. A leading exponent of *organum, he composed complex music in the *ars antiqua style.

Perpendicular The style of □gothic architecture predominant in England between about 1370 and the mid 16th century. The name derives from the panel-like effect of the window design, with its pronounced vertical mullions broken regularly by horizontal divisions. Gloucester Cathedral choir (c. 1357) is an early example. The Henry VII chapel, Westminster Abbey (1503–19), is a masterpiece of the Perpendicular style.

perpetual-motion machine A hypothetical machine that produces continuous and unending motion without drawing energy from an outside source. Although such a machine would contravene the laws of *thermodynamics and therefore cannot be made, there have always been, and indeed still are, hopeful inventors who believe that it is possible to find loopholes in the laws of nature. A perpetual-motion machine would need to be frictionless (in contravention of the second law of thermodynamics) or would need to be able to create energy to overcome the friction (in contravention of the first law). Using the heat of the ocean to drive a ship (perpetual motion of the second kind) is also impossible, because it would contravene the second law.

Perpignan 42 42N 2 54E A city in S France, the capital of the Pyrénées-Orientales department situated near the Spanish border. The capital of the former province of Roussillon in the 17th century, it has a gothic cathedral and a 13th-century castle (the former residence of the Kings of Majorca). Perpignan is a tourist and commercial center, trading in wine, fruit, and vegetables. Population (1975): 107,971.

Perrault, Charles (1628–1703) French poet and fairytale writer. As a member of the Académie Française he opposed *Boileau by championing the modern writers against the ancients. He is best known for his collection of fairytales, *Contes de ma mère l'Oye* (1697), translated into English in 1729 and best known by the English title, *Tales of Mother Goose*.

Perrin, Jean-Baptiste (1870–1942) French physicist, who discovered that cathode rays carry a negative charge and therefore consist of particles and not waves, as many physicists then thought. He also used Einstein's equations for the Brownian movement to determine the approximate size of molecules.

Perry, Oliver Hazard (1785–1819) US naval officer, who fought in the war in Tripoli (1801–05) and in the *War of 1812, in which he commanded the US fleet on Lake Erie and was victorious over the British fleet. After the war he served with the Navy in the Mediterranean and in South America. *See also* Lake Erie, Battle of. His brother **Matthew Calbraigh Perry** (1794–1858) was also a naval officer. After service in the *War of 1812, Perry established an educational program for US naval officers (1833) and was later given command of the USS *Fulton*, the first steam-powered vessel in the US Navy (1837). Placed in command of the navy's African Squadron (1843) he helped to suppress the slave trade, and during the *Mexican War, he participated in the naval operations at Vera Cruz. In 1852 he was selected by President Millard *Fillmore to undertake a naval expedition to Japan in order to secure US trading rights there. Anchoring at Yedo Bay at the head of the impressive American Eastern Squadron, he persuaded the Japanese to open diplomatic and economic relations with the US, thus ending Japan's traditional isolation.

Perse, Saint-John (Alexis Saint-Léger; 1887–1975) French poet. He was born in the West Indies, served as a diplomat in the Far East, and became secretary general of the Foreign Ministry in 1933. From 1940 to 1958 he lived in the US. His volumes of poetry, written in long free-verse lines, give prominence to landscapes and the sea and include the long poem *Anabase* (1922), translated by T. S. Eliot in 1930, and *Chronique* (1960). He won the Nobel Prize in 1960.

Persephone (Roman name: Proserpine) Greek goddess of the underworld, daughter of Zeus and *Demeter. She was abducted by *Hades, who made her queen of the underworld. Zeus, moved by Demeter's sorrow for her daughter, allowed her to spend part of each year on earth. Her return to the earth symbolized the regeneration of natural life in the spring.

Persepolis An ancient Persian city in Fars province, Iran. *Darius I (reigned 522–486 BC) planned Persepolis as the ceremonial capital of his empire and its wealth and splendor were legendary. Among the buildings on the vast central terrace were the apadana (royal audience hall), which was approached by monumental stairways flanked by reliefs of tribute bearers, and *Xerxes' throne hall. The Achaemenian royal tombs are nearby. *Alexander the Great destroyed Persepolis in 330 BC.

Perseus (astronomy) A constellation in the N sky near Cassiopeia, lying in the Milky Way. The brightest stars are the 2nd-magnitude Mirfak and the eclipsing binary *Algol.

Perseus (Greek mythology) The son of Zeus and Danae. One of the greatest Greek heroes, he beheaded the *Medusa with the help of Athena, who gave him a mirror so that he could avoid looking at the Gorgon and so

escape being turned to stone. He rescued Andromeda, daughter of the Ethiopian king, and married her. She had been chained to a rock as a sacrifice to a sea monster, which Perseus turned to stone by showing it the Medusa's head.

Pershing, John J(oseph) (1860–1948) US general. A graduate of West Point, Pershing served in the Indian Wars in the Southwest and in the *Spanish-American War. After leading the army in an unsuccessful pursuit of the Mexican revolutionary and outlaw Pancho *Villa (1916), he was appointed commander of the *American Expeditionary Force (AEF) to France during World War I. A sound administrator as well as a strong military leader, he strengthened the AEF, insisting on its independence from the other Allied forces. After the war, he served as army chief of staff from 1921 until his retirement from active duty in 1924.

Persia. *See* Iran.

Persian A language belonging to the *Iranian language family. It is the official language of Iran and is written in a modified Arabic script.

Persian art and architecture The styles associated with the three principal phases of the Persian empire: *Achaemenian (550–331 BC), *Sasanian (224–651 AD), and Islamic. The splendors of Achaemenian and Sasanian architecture are represented respectively by *Persepolis and *Ctesiphon. Sasanian kings commissioned monumental relief sculptures to commemorate victories and coronations. The Persian tradition of fine craftsmanship in metalwork, glassware, and ceramics dates from this period. After 651, Persian styles became an aspect of international trends in *Islamic art. Calligraphy and book illustration became important, the latter evolving into the renowned 15th-, 16th-, and 17th-century Persian miniature painting. The love of subtly brilliant colors is epitomized in the famous Persian carpets and in the architectural use of turquoise colored tiles.

Persian cat A domesticated cat, also called a Longhair, having a long flowing coat with a ruff or frill around the neck. The 20 or so recognized breeds are characterized by their short bodies, deep flanks, short legs, and short bushy tails. The head has a snub nose, large round eyes, and small wide-set ears and the coat may be of any color, although the Blue Persian is most popular.

Persian Empire. *See* Achaemenians.

Persian Gulf An arm of the Arabian Sea, extending some 590 mi (950 km) NW beyond the Gulf of Oman. The large offshore oil deposits are exploited by the surrounding *Gulf States. Area: 89,942 sq mi (233,000 sq km).

Persian Wars. *See* Greek–Persian Wars.

persimmon A tree of the genus *Diospyros* that produces edible fruits. These are the Japanese persimmon (*D. kaki*), the American persimmon (*D. virginiana*), and the Asian date plum (*D. lotus*). Up to 100 ft (30 m) high, they have dark-green oval leaves and produce round orange, yellow, or red fruits, 2–3.1 in (5–8 cm) across. Persimmons are eaten fresh, cooked, or candied. Family: *Ebenaceae*.

perspective Any means of rendering objects or space in a picture to give an illusion of their depth. Perspective in a single object is known as foreshortening and can be seen in even primitive works as a result of accurate observation. The laws of true perspective of an entire scene, known as linear perspective, were formulated by *Brunelleschi in the 15th century and became one of the *Renaissance artists' most important scientific investigations. The earliest known scientific perspective (1436) was constructed by *Alberti in his treatise on painting. Guide lines converge on one, two, or three points on the horizon line, known as vanishing points, according to whether the orientation of a scene is central, angular, or oblique.

perspiration. *See* sweat.

Perth 31 58S 115 49E The capital of Western Australia, on the Swan River. Founded in 1829, it expanded following the discovery of gold (1893) at Kalgoolie. It is the commercial and cultural center of the state; the University of Western Australia was founded in 1913 and there are two cathedrals. Its port, *Fremantle, and Kwinana, both to the S, are growing industrial centers. Population (1980 est): 902,000.

Perth 56 24N 3 28W A city in E Scotland, in Tayside Region on the Tay River. An early capital of Scotland, it was the scene of the assassination of James I (1437). There are dyeing, textiles, whisky distilling, and carpet industries and it is a popular tourist center. Population (1974 est): 41,196.

perturbations Small departures of a celestial body from the orbital path it would follow if subject only to the influence of a single central force. Short-term periodic disturbances arise from gravitational interactions with other bodies. Progressive disturbances or those of very long period can also occur.

Peru, Republic of A country in the NE of South America, on the Pacific Ocean. Narrow coastal plains rise to the high peaks of the Andes, reaching heights of over 21,000 ft (6500 m). The land descends again through an area of forested plateaus to the tropical forests of the Amazon basin. Most of the population is of Indian or mixed Indian and European descent. *Economy*: Peru is one of the world's leading fishing countries, the main product being fishmeal. Agriculture is important, now organized largely in cooperatives, and the main crops include corn, rice, sugar cane, cotton, and coffee. Large-scale irrigation projects are being undertaken. Livestock is particularly important to the economy, especially the production of wool. Rich mineral resources include copper, silver, lead, zinc, and iron; oil has been discovered in considerable quantities, both in the jungles and offshore. In recent years there have been considerable developments in industry and in industrial relations, including moves toward nationalization and worker participation, although such moves have been slowed down by changes of government. With its relics of ancient civilizations, Peru has a valuable tourist trade. The main exports include minerals and metals and fishmeal. *History*: Peru's precolonial history encompasses the civilization of the *Chimú and that of the *Incas, who were conquered by the Spanish under Pizarro in 1533. The viceroyalty of Peru, centered on Lima, enjoyed considerable prosperity in which the Indian population had little share. A revolt in 1780 led by Tupac Amarú was suppressed. Peru was the last of Spain's American colonies to declare its independence (1821) and the Spanish were finally defeated in 1824. Political stability was achieved by General Ramón Castilla; (president 1845–51, 1855–62), who developed Peru's economy, based on guano deposits. However, the country's prosperity was undermined by the War of the *Pacific (1879–83) in which Peru lost the nitrate-rich province of Tarapacà to Chile. Since World War II, in which Peru declared war on Germany in 1945, the country has depended on US aid and has witnessed a series of coups and countercoups, most recently in 1975, when General Francisco Morales Bermúdez became president. In 1980, in Peru's first general elections to be held in 17 years, Fernando Beláunde Terry was elected president. Peru is a member of the OAS and LAFTA. Official languages: Spanish and Quechua; Aymará is also widely spoken. Official currency: sol of 100 centavos. Area: 496,093 sq mi (1,285,215 sq km). Population (1983 est.): 3,526,000. Capital: Lima. Main port: Callao.

Peru Current. *See* Humboldt Current.

Perugia 43 07N 12 23E A city in Italy, the capital of Umbria. Originally an Etruscan city, it has 13th-century city walls, a 14th-century cathedral, an ancient fountain (the Maggiore Fountain), and a university (1200). Perugia is an agricultural trading center and its manufactures include furniture and textiles. Population (1980 est): 140,742.

Perugino (Pietro di Cristoforo Vannucci; c. 1450–1523) Italian Renaissance painter, born near Perugia. He worked on frescoes in the Sistine Chapel, including the *Giving of the Keys to St Peter* (1481–82). His spacious ordered compositions and graceful figure style influenced his pupil *Raphael.

Perutz, Max Ferdinand (1914–) British chemist, born in Austria, who developed the technique of *X-ray diffraction to determine the molecular structure of the blood pigment, hemoglobin. For this work he shared a Nobel Prize (1962) with J. C. *Kendrew.

Pesaro 43 54N 12 54E A city and resort in Italy, in Marche on the Adriatic coast. It is the birthplace of Rossini, who established a school of music here. Population (1971): 84,373.

Pescadores. *See* Penghu Islands.

Pescara 42 27N 14 13E A seaport in Italy, in Abruzzi on the Adriatic coast. Its chief industries are tourism, shipbuilding, and fishing. Population (1980 est): 136,366.

Peshawar 34 01N 71 40E A city in N Pakistan, situated at the E end of the Khyber Pass. One of the oldest cities in Pakistan, it has for centuries been a center of trade between the Indian subcontinent, Afghanistan, and central Asia. Industries include textiles, shoes, and pottery and it has a university (1950). Population (1972): 268,366.

Pestalozzi, Johann Heinrich (1746–1827) Swiss educationalist. A pioneer of mass education, Pestalozzi made several unsuccessful attempts to establish schools for poor children. His book *Wie Gertrud ihre Kinder lehrt* (1801) reflected his ideas on the intuitive method of education. Despite his apparent failures, his theories were of great importance to subsequent educational developments. Pestalozzi's work is commemorated in the **Pestalozzi International Children's Villages**, the first of which was established in 1946 for war orphans at Trogen (Switzerland). A second international village was established in 1958 at Sedlescombe (UK) for the care and education of selected children from developing countries.

pesticides. *See* herbicides; insecticides.

Pétain, (Henri) Philippe (1856–1951) French general and statesman. In World War I he distinguished himself at the defense of Verdun (1916), becoming marshal of France (1918). In World War II, when France was on the verge of defeat (1940), Pétain became prime minister. In June, 1940, he signed an armistice with Hitler that allowed for a third of France to remain unoccupied by Germany. His government of unoccupied France at Vichy was authoritarian and from 1942 was dominated by *Laval and the Germans. Pétain was sentenced to death in August, 1945, for collaboration but was then reprieved and imprisoned for life.

Peter (I) the Great (1672–1725) Tsar (1682–1721) and then Emperor (1721–25) of Russia, who established Russia as a major European power. Peter ruled with his half-brother Ivan V (1666–96) until Ivan's death and under the regency of his half-sister *Sophia until 1689, when he became effective ruler. Peter traveled in W Europe in the 1690s, acquiring knowledge of western technology and returning to Russia with western technicians, who were to implement the modernization programs that marked his reign. He instituted many reforms in government and administration, trade and industry, and in the army. In the *Great Northern War (1700–21), he acquired Livonia, Estonia, and also Ingria, where in 1703 he founded St Petersburg (now *Leningrad). He campaigned less successfully against the Turks (1710–13) but gained territory in the Caspian region from war with Persia (1722–23). Peter's eldest son *Alexis died in prison, having been condemned to death for treason; Peter was succeeded by his wife, who became *Catherine I.

Peter I (1844–1921) King of Serbia (1903–18) and then of Yugoslavia (1918–21). Brought up in exile, Peter was elected king after the assassination of the last Obrenović monarch. His rule was marked by its constitutionalism.

Peter, St In the New Testament, one of the 12 Apostles. He was a fisherman on the Sea of Galilee until called by Jesus along with his brother *Andrew. He became the leader and spokesman for the disciples. Although his faith often wavered, notably at the crucifixion, when he denied Christ three times, Peter was named as the rock upon which the Church was to be built. He was also entrusted with the "keys of the Kingdom of Heaven" (Matthew 16.19)—hence his symbol of two crossed keys. After Christ's death, he dominated the Christian community for 15 years, undertaking missionary work despite imprisonment. Whereas Paul had responsibility for the Gentiles, Peter's was to the Jews. He is believed to have been martyred and buried in Rome. Feast day: June 29.

Peterborough 52 35N 0 15W A city in E central England, on the Nene River. The cathedral (begun in the 12th century) contains the tomb of Catherine of Aragon. Its industries include sugar-beet refining, foodstuffs, engineering, and brick making and it is an important marketing center for the surrounding agricultural area. Population (1981): 114,108.

Peterborough 44 19N 78 20W A city in SE Canada, in Ontario. It is an important manufacturing center and the main commercial center for central Ontario. The largest deposit of nepheline in the world (used in the manufacture of glass) is nearby. Population (1971): 58,111.

Peter Damian, St (1007–72) Italian churchman; cardinal and Doctor of the Church. He is famous as a religious reformer who campaigned for clerical celibacy and attacked simony. Feast day: Feb 23.

Peter Lombard (c. 1100–60) Italian theologian. He studied in Rheims and in Paris, where, between 1136 and 1150, he taught theology at the school of Notre Dame. He became Bishop of Paris in 1159. His most famous work, the *Books of Sentences* (1148–51), was an objective summary of the beliefs of earlier theologians. It was a standard text in the universities until the 16th century and many medieval scholars wrote commentaries on it, including Thomas *Aquinas.

Peterloo Massacre (1819) The name given, by analogy with the battle of Waterloo, to the violent dispersal of a political meeting held in St Peter's Fields, Manchester, England. A peaceful crowd, numbering about 60,000, had gathered to hear a speech on parliamentary reform. The local officials, anxious about the size of the crowd, called in troops. The cavalry were ordered to charge and in the ensuing panic 11 people were killed.

Petersburg 37 13N 77 24W A city in SE Virginia, on the Appomattox River, SE of Richmond. A key Confederate supply base in the Civil War. Petersburg was besieged by General Ulysses S. Grant from June 1864 until it fell in April 1865. Tobacco and peanut processing are important industries, and clothing, furniture, luggage, and paints are manufactured. Population (1980); 41,055.

Peterson, Oscar Emmanuel (1925–) Canadian black jazz pianist, who has played with many leading jazz musicians as well as with his own trio. His many recordings include *The Gershwin Song Book* and *Peterson Plays Basie*.

Peter the Hermit (c. 1050–1115) French monk. A fervent supporter of the first *Crusade under Pope Urban II, he rallied over 20,000 peasants to follow him to the Holy Land, where many were massacred by the Turks. He later founded the monastery of Neufmoutier at Liège.

Petipa, Marius (1819–1910) French dancer and choreographer. He exercised an important influence on the Russian imperial ballet in St Petersburg, where he worked from 1847 until 1903. He became its chief choreographer in 1862. His many ballets include *Don Quixote* (1869) and *The Sleeping Beauty* (1890), on which he collaborated with its composer, Tchaikovsky.

Petit, Roland (1924–) French ballet dancer and choreographer. His innovatory ballets, characterized by elements of fantasy and contemporary realism, include *Carmen* (1949) and *Kraanerg* (1969). He toured with his company in Europe and the US and also choreographed for Hollywood films.

petition of right The procedure by which a person formerly petitioned against the English crown for restoration of property rights. The petition might be for property that the crown had taken possession of or for money due by contract. Although still legal, this method of claiming against the crown, dating back to the reign of Edward I, has been replaced by ordinary court actions. A parliamentary declaration accepted by Charles I (1628) it made illegal imprisonment without trial, taxation without parliamentary approval, and the billeting of soldiers on private individuals.

petit mal. *See* epilepsy.

Petöfi, Sándor (1823–49) Hungarian poet. He came from a peasant background and elements of traditional folksong occur in his early poetry, notably in the narrative poem *Janós the Hero* (1845). His later poetry was chiefly concerned with the cause of nationalism. He disappeared during the battle of Segesvar (1849), in which the Hungarian revolutionary army was defeated by the Austrians and Russians.

Petra An ancient town in S Jordan. It was the capital of the Nabataeans, nomadic Arabs who settled along the caravan routes from Arabia to the Mediterranean. Petra was a great trading center from the 3rd century BC. It was incorporated in the Roman Empire in 106 AD and was superseded by *Palmyra in the 2nd century. Accessible only through a narrow gorge, Petra is renowned for its rock-cut temples and dwellings.

Petrarch (Francesco Petrarca; 1304–74) Italian poet. He was born in Florence, but his family was banished and he lived mostly in Provence from 1312 to 1353, when he returned to Italy. He traveled widely in Europe and in 1341 was crowned as poet laureate in Rome. His humanist works of scholarship anticipated the Renaissance in their combination of classical learning and Christian faith. His other works include *Secretum meum*, his spiritual self-analysis, and *Africa*, a Latin verse epic on Scipio Africanus, but he is remembered chiefly for the *Canzoniere*, a series of love poems addressed to Laura. His work greatly influenced writers throughout Europe, including *Chaucer.

Petrea A genus of tropical climbing plants (about 30 species), native to tropical America and the West Indies. Up to 30 ft (9 m) high, they have oblong leaves and sprays of bluish-purple flowers, each with five widely spaced strap-shaped petals and colored sepals. Popular ornamental species include *P. volubilis* and *P. kohautiana*. Family: *Verbenaceae*.

petrel A marine bird belonging to a widely distributed family (*Procellariidae*; 55 species) characterized by a musky smell, thick plumage, webbed feet, and a hooked bill with long tubular nostrils. 11–35 in (27–90 cm) long, petrels are well adapted for oceanic life, feeding on fish and mollusks and only coming ashore to breed. Diving petrels belong to a family (*Pelecanoididae*; 5 species) occurring in the S hemisphere; they are 6–10 in (16–25 cm) long, have short wings, and feed mostly on crustaceans. Order: *Procellariiformes*. *See also* fulmar; prion; shearwater; storm petrel. □oceans.

Petrie, Sir (William Matthew) Flinders (1853–1942) British archeologist. After surveying British prehistoric sites, Petrie went to Egypt (1880), where his painstaking excavations and meticulous study of artifacts revolutionized and set new standards for archeology. He excavated numerous sites, including *Naukratis, *Tell el-Amarna, and *Abydos, finally leaving Egypt for Palestine in 1926.

Petrified Forest National Park A national park in E central Arizona, E of Flagstaff. The Puerto River runs through the park. Established as a national monument in 1906 and a national park in 1962, it contains petrified multicolored wood, ruins of ancient Indian life, including petroglyphs

(prehistoric rock drawings or carvings), and part of the Painted Desert. Area: 147 sq mi (381 sq km).

petrochemicals. *See* oil.

Petrograd. *See* Leningrad.

petroleum. *See* oil.

petrology The study of rocks, including their formation, structure, texture, and mineral and chemical composition. **Petrogenesis** is the origin or mode of formation of rocks; **petrography** is the description and classification of rocks from hand specimens or thin sections.

Petronius Arbiter (1st century AD) Roman satirist. He was appointed "Arbiter of Taste" at the court of Nero. The *Satyricon*, his picaresque novel of which only fragments survive, relates the scandalous adventures of the youths Encolpius and Ascyltos and includes the famous satirical portrait of a coarse and vulgar millionaire, Trimalchio. Petronius committed suicide after being falsely accused of conspiring against Nero.

Petropavlovsk 54 53N 69 13E A city in the Soviet Union, in the N Kazakh SSR on the Ishim River. It is an important junction on the Trans-Siberian Railway and has varied industries. Population (1981 est): 212,000.

Petropavlovsk-Kamchatskii 53 03N 158 43E A port in the Soviet Union, in the E RSFSR on the Kamchatka Peninsula. Long a major naval base, it was attacked by the French and British during the Crimean War. Fishing, fish processing, and ship repairing are the principal activities. Population (1981 est): 223,000.

Petrópolis 22 30S 43 06W A city and mountain resort in SE Brazil, in Rio de Janeiro state. Notable buildings include the Museum of the Empire (formerly the royal palace) and the gothic-style cathedral. Population (1975 est): 216,582.

Petrosian, Tigran Vartanovich (1929–) Soviet chess player, who was world champion from 1963 to 1969, when he lost the title to *Spassky. Despite his exhaustive preparations, as world champion his matches were often disappointing because his style of play tended to lead to draws.

Petrozavodsk 61 46N 34 19E A city in the Soviet Union, the capital of the Karelian ASSR in the NW RSFSR on Lake Onega. It was founded (1703) by Peter the Great; engineering and lumbering are important activities and there are many educational institutions. Population (1981 est): 241,000.

Petsamo. *See* Pechenga.

Petunia A genus of tropical American herbs (about 40 species), cultivated for their showy funnel-shaped flowers, which are sometimes frilled at the edges. Ornamental species include *P. integrifolia*, with pink, blue, or purple flowers, the white-flowered *P. axillaris*, which has a pleasant night fragrance, and hybrids between them. Family: *Solanaceae*.

Pevsner, Antoine (1886–1962) Russian sculptor and painter, who worked in Paris from 1923. His early career was spent in W Europe but it was in Russia that he and his brother Naum *Gabo pioneered *constructivism in their *Realist Manifesto* (1920). His most characteristic abstract constructions consist of curving and thrusting shapes in striated metal.

pewter An *alloy of tin with lead or copper, antimony, and bismuth. It was formerly used for plates, spoons, and other utensils but now only beer mugs are made from it.

peyote A blue-green *cactus, *Lophophora williamsii*, also called mescal, native to Mexico and the SW US. About 3 in (8 cm) across and 2 in (5 cm) high, it bears white to pink flowering heads, which, when dried, are known as "mescal buttons." They contain the alkaloid *mescaline, which produces hallucinations when chewed.

Pforzheim 48 53N 08 41E A city in SW West Germany, in Baden-Württemberg. It was an important medieval trading center and is the center of the West German watch and jewelry industry. Population (1980 est): 106,700.

pH A measure of the acidity or alkalinity of a solution, equal to the logarithm to the base 10 of the reciprocal of the number of moles per liter of hydrogen ions it contains. Thus a solution containing 10^{-6} mole of hydrogen ions per liter has a pH of $\log_{10}(1/10^{-6}) = 6$. In pure water there is a small reversible dissociation into equal amounts of hydrogen and hydroxide ions: $H_2O \rightarrow H^+ + OH^-$ The product of the concentrations of these ions (moles/liter) is about 10^{-14}: $[H^+][OH^-] = 10^{-14}$. In neutral solutions, therefore, the hydrogen ion concentration is 10^{-7} and the pH is consequently 7. In acid solutions the pH is less than 7; the lower the pH, the more acidic the solution. Conversely, alkaline solutions have pH values greater than 7. The pH scale is logarithmic; for example, a solution with a pH of 2 is ten times more acidic than one with a pH of 1. *See also* acids and bases.

Phaedra In Greek mythology, the daughter of *Minos and Pasiphaë and the wife of Theseus. She fell in love with her stepson *Hippolytus. When he rejected her, she hanged herself, having first written a letter to Theseus accusing Hippolytus of having seduced her.

Phaedrus (1st century AD) Roman writer. Born a slave in Macedonia, he gained his freedom in the household of the emperor Augustus. He wrote poetic versions of the Greek prose fables ascribed to *Aesop. His work was popular in medieval Europe.

Phaethon In Greek mythology, the son of the sun god Helios, who granted him his wish to drive the chariot of the sun for one day. Unable to control the horses, he was about to burn the earth when Zeus struck him down with a thunderbolt.

phaeton A four-wheeled open carriage usually drawn by two horses. Various modifications of the phaeton (pony phaeton, Victoria phaeton, Stanhope phaeton, etc.) were fashionable in the 19th century for pleasure driving.

phagocyte A cell that engulfs and then digests particles from its surroundings: this process is called phagocytosis. Many protozoans are phagocytic, but the word specifically refers to certain white blood cells that protect the body by engulfing bacteria and other foreign particles.

phalanger A small herbivorous *marsupial of the family *Phalangeridae* (48 species), occurring in woodlands of Australia, (including Tasmania), and New Guinea. They range in length from 5–48 in (12 to 120 cm) and are adapted for climbing trees, having strong claws and prehensile tails. The family includes the *cuscuses, *flying phalangers, *honey mouse, *koalas, and *possums.

Phalaris (c. 570–c. 554 BC) Tyrant of Agrigento in Sicily, who established its prominence by subjugating the indigenous Sicels and defying the Phoenicians. Phalaris was noted for his cruelty and was overthrown.

phalarope A lightly built migratory shorebird belonging to a family (*Phalaropodidae*; 3 species) in which the female fights for a territory and courts the male, which rears the young. 8–10 in (20–25 cm) long, phalaropes have a slim neck, lobed toes, and a gray and red-brown plumage. Two species breed in the Arctic and one inland in North America.

phanerogam Any plant that reproduces by means of flowers and seeds. Phanerogams comprise the angiosperms (flowering plants) and the gymnosperms (conifers, etc.). *Compare* cryptogam.

Phanerozoic time Geological time from the end of the Precambrian to the present day, about 590 million years. It refers to the eon of "evident life," when abundant and clearly recognizable fossils were laid down. *Compare* Cryptozoic time.

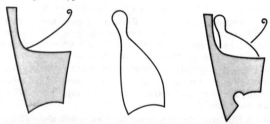

PHARAOH *The pharaoh's double crown, combining the red crown of Lower Egypt with the white crown of Upper Egypt, symbolized the unification of the two lands (c. 3100 BC).*

pharaoh The title of ancient Egyptian rulers. The word derives via Hebrew from the Egyptian for great house. There were various symbols of kingship: the crook and flail and the white, red, or blue crown. The royal cobra, the sun god Ra's symbol, bound around the brow, signified divinity; pharaoh represented Ra reigning on earth. The first dynasty, or line of pharaohs, was founded about 3200 BC.

Pharaoh hound A breed of hunting dog whose ancestors are depicted in sculpture and friezes found in the tombs of the Egyptian pharaohs. The Pharaoh is a slender long-legged hound with a long muzzle and large ears. The short glossy coat is tan, with or without white markings. Height: 22–25 in (56–63 cm) (dogs); 21–24 in (53–61 cm) (bitches).

Pharisees An ancient Jewish religious and political party. They stressed ritual purity and acknowledged a body of traditional laws not contained in the written *Torah. The party originated in the 2nd century BC and vied for political influence with the *Sadducees. In the *Gospels they are frequently criticized by Jesus, although his own teachings are very close to theirs.

After the destruction of the *Temple of Jerusalem they ceased to exist, but many of their teachings were taken over into rabbinic Judaism.

pharmacology The study of the action of drugs on living organisms. Pharmacologists examine the uptake of drugs after administration, the routes by which they reach their site of action, their subsequent effects, how drugs are destroyed by the body, their unwanted side effects, and the interaction between different drugs. Clinical pharmacology (*or* therapeutics) studies the effects of drugs in treating disease. **Pharmacy** is the science concerned with the preparation, manufacture, packaging, quality, and supply of medicinal drugs. The practice of pharmacy should conform to the standards laid down in the official **pharmacopoeia** of the country. This is a government-approved list giving details of the manufacture, dosage, uses, and characteristics of drugs. It is compiled by experts in pharmacy and pharmacology. The World Health Organization has issued the *Pharmacopoeia Internationalis* in an attempt to standardize drug preparations throughout the world.

Pharos of Alexandria An ancient lighthouse, one of the *Seven Wonders of the World. Built in about 280 BC by Sostratus of Cnidos for Ptolemy II of Egypt, it was over 440 ft (135 m) high. It was demolished in the 13th century AD.

Pharsalus, Battle of (48 BC) The decisive encounter near present-day Fársala (Greece) in the Roman civil war, in which Julius Caesar defeated Pompey. Pompey's defeat opened the way to Caesar's dictatorship.

pharynx The muscular tract, lined with mucous membrane, between the back of the mouth and esophagus (gullet) and larynx. It acts as a passageway for food between the mouth and gullet and it also conducts air from the nasal cavity (which opens into it) to the larynx and windpipe. The Eustachian tubes from the middle *ear also open into the pharynx. Inflammation of the pharynx (pharyngitis) is a common cause of a sore throat.

phase (astronomy) The appearance of the illuminated face of the moon or a planet at a particular time in its orbit. Lunar phases vary from new moon (unilluminated) through a waxing crescent, first quarter (half illuminated), a waxing gibbous moon, to full moon (fully illuminated) followed by a waning gibbous moon, last quarter, a waning crescent, and the next new moon.

phase (physics) **1.** The fraction of its whole cycle that a periodically varying system has completed. For example, two *alternating currents of the same frequency are **in phase** if they reach their maximum values at the same instant. If they are out of phase the angle between the *vectors representing the quantities is called the **phase angle**. In an electricity-supply system there are usually three phases, i.e. three separate alternating voltages having the same frequency but being displaced in phase relative to each other by one third of a cycle. **2.** Any portion of a system that is physically distinct, is homogeneous throughout, and can be mechanically separated from other phases. For example, a salt solution is a one-phase system, whereas a mixture of ice and water is a two-phase system. *See also* phase rule.

phase rule A rule stating the conditions of equilibrium for a heterogeneous system. It relates the number of degrees of freedom of a system f, the number of *phases p, and the number of components c, by the rule $f = c - p + 2$. It was proposed by J. W. *Gibbs in 1877 and is important in the study of metallurgy, mineralogy, and ceramics.

Phasmida An order of generally flightless insects (2000 species), occurring mostly in tropical and oriental regions. They comprise the *leaf insects and *stick insects, both of which show a striking resemblance to the vegetation on which they live and feed.

pheasant A long-tailed game bird belonging to an Old World subfamily (*Phasianinae*; 50 species) occurring in open or woodland regions. 20–80 in (50–200 cm) long, pheasants are heavily built and have short rounded wings, a short bill, and strong claws for scratching up grain, roots, and grubs. Males are larger than females and brightly colored, with bright fleshy wattles, large leg spurs, and long tail feathers. They have been introduced to many regions for sport or ornament. Family: *Phasianidae* (pheasants, quail, partridges); order: *Galliformes* (pheasants, turkeys, etc.). *See also* golden pheasant; tragopan.

phenobarbital. *See* barbiturates.

phenols A class of organic compounds with the general formula ROH, in which the –OH group is linked directly to a carbon atom in an *aromatic ring. Although formally similar to alcohols, the phenols have widely different properties; in particular, the aromatic ring confers acidic behavior on the –OH group. The simplest example, phenol itself (or **carbolic acid**), C_6H_5OH, is a white deliquescent solid used as a disinfectant and in the production of drugs, weedkillers, and synthetic resins.

phenomenology A philosophical inquiry into intellectual processes, which is characterized by the vigorous exclusion of any preconceptions about existence or causes. It is thus distinct from *psychology, the aim of which is causal explanations rather than pure description. *Husserl was the first to elevate this method into an independent philosophy.

phenothiazines A group of powerful tranquilizing drugs, including chlorpromazine and fluphenazine. Used in the treatment of *schizophrenia and *manic-depressive psychosis, they are thought to act by inhibiting the action of a chemical (dopamine) in the brain. *See also* tranquilizers.

phenotype The characteristics of an individual, representing the sum total of the effects of the interaction of its inherited characteristics with its environment. A striking example of this occurs in the Himalayan rabbit, which grows either black or white fur according to the temperature. *Compare* genotype.

phenylketonuria A genetic disease that leads to mental deficiency if untreated. Patients are unable to metabolize the amino acid phenylalanine, which is a normal constituent of diet; the amino acid and its derivatives accumulate in the body and prevent proper mental development. Phenylketonuria can now be easily detected at birth by a routine test. Babies with the disease need a special diet that contains little phenylalanine, which should be maintained until adolescence.

pheromone A chemical substance produced by animals to communicate with others of the same species. The best-known pheromones are the sex attractants secreted by moths to attract mates. Pheromones are also used by ants to lay trails and by mammals to mark out territories.

Phidias (c. 490–c. 417 BC) Athenian sculptor, one of the most influential artists of his time. Phidias designed and supervised the sculptures of the *Parthenon (*see* Elgin Marbles). His works included a bronze statue of *Athena on the Athenian *Acropolis and two famous chryzelephantine statues: Athena in the Parthenon and *Zeus at Olympia (where his workshop has been found).

Phidippides (5th century BC) Greek runner who ran 150 mi (241 km) from Athens to Sparta in two days to ask for help against the Persians before the battle of Marathon in 490 BC. The modern *marathon race derives from this feat.

Philadelphia 40 00N 75 10W A city in Pennsylvania, situated on the Delaware River at the junction of the Schuylkill River. Founded in 1681 by the Quaker William Penn, its religious tolerance attracted a large number of immigrants. It has many historic buildings, including Independence Hall (1732–59), where the Declaration of Independence was adopted and the Liberty Bell is kept. Benjamin Franklin is buried here. A cultural center, it is the site of the University of Pennsylvania (1779) and the Franklin Institute (1824) and has a famous symphony orchestra. It is the fourth-largest US city and has the world's largest freshwater port. Its output of manufactured goods is exceeded only by four other US cities. Industries include oil refining, textiles, and shipbuilding. Population (1975 est): 1,815,808.

Philadelphus. *See* mock orange.

PHILAE *The rising waters of Lake Nasser partially submerging the Kiosk of Trajan.*

Philae 24 02N 32 59E A submerged islet in the Nile River, in SE Egypt just above Aswan. Flooding caused by the first Aswan Dam from 1902 onward damaged the many ancient temples on the island. These were moved to a higher island before Philae was totally submerged by Lake Nasser after the construction of the *Aswan High Dam.

philately (*or* stamp collecting) Collecting and studying postage stamps as a hobby, which began immediately following their introduction in En-

gland (1840). Catalogues were first issued in the early 1860s as collecting became increasingly concerned with such details as watermarks, perforations, and numberings. Collectors usually specialize in a particular theme, country, or type of issue. Rare stamps in good condition, which fetch extremely high auction prices, are a form of investment, while the market among collectors for commemorative stamps or first-day covers is an important source of revenue for post offices.

Philby, H(arry) St John (Bridge) (1885–1960) British explorer and Arabist. He joined the Indian civil service in 1907 and in World War I undertook a political mission to central Arabia. He became a Muslim in 1930 and friend and adviser of Ibn Saud of Saudi Arabia. His son **Harold Adrian Russell Philby** (1912–) was an intelligence officer and Soviet secret agent, known as Kim Philby. He became a Soviet agent in 1933 and entered the British intelligence service in 1940. He defected to Russia in 1963.

Philemon (c. 368–c. 264 BC) Greek dramatist. Born in Sicily, he became a citizen of Athens and also worked in Alexandria. His plays, of which only fragments survive, were frequently acclaimed by his contemporaries as superior to those of his rival, *Menander.

Philemon, Epistle of Paul to A New Testament book written in about 60 AD that is the only strictly private letter of Paul to be preserved. In it he requests Philemon, a Christian friend in Colossae, to welcome and forgive Onesimus, his runaway slave, who had become a Christian after meeting Paul. Onesimus delivered the letter.

Philemon and Baucis In Greek mythology, an old peasant couple who offered hospitality to Zeus and Hermes, who were disguised as mortals. They were subsequently spared from a flood that destroyed the land and their cottage was transformed into a temple. They were granted their wishes to serve as priest and priestess in the temple and finally to die together.

Philidor, André Danican (d. 1730) French musician. As assistant librarian of the Royal Music Library at Versailles he made a large collection of instrumental court music. His youngest son **François André Danican Philidor** (1726–95) wrote several operas and was also a considerable chess player.

Philip (I) the Handsome (1478–1506) King of Castile (1506). Son of Emperor Maximilian I and Mary of Burgundy he succeeded to his mother's possessions in 1482. In 1496 he married Joanna the Mad, who inherited the Castilian throne in 1504. Her insanity led Philip to assume sole control in 1506. Their son became Emperor *Charles V.

Philip (II) of Macedon (382–336 BC) King of Macedon (359–336), who founded the Macedonian empire. Philip unified Macedonia, expanded the economy, and trained a professional army with which he gradually bore down on the Greek city states. Despite the resolute opposition of *Demosthenes at Athens, the Greeks were defeated at the battle of *Chaeronea (338). Philip planned to lead a combined force against Persia but he was assassinated and the plan was carried out by his son *Alexander (III) the Great.

Philip II Augustus (1165–1223) King of France (1179–1223), who destroyed the *Angevin empire of the English kings. He waged war with Henry II (1187–89), Richard Lionheart (1194–99), and John; he took Normandy in 1204, followed by Maine, Touraine, and Anjou (1204–05), and in 1214 defeated an English-imperial alliance at *Bouvines. He participated in the third Crusade.

Philip II (1527–98) King of Spain (1556–98). He inherited a vast empire from his father *Charles V, including Naples and Sicily, the Netherlands, and Spanish possessions in America; in 1580 he annexed Portugal. He married Mary I of England in 1554. Philip faced the *Revolt of the Netherlands and the Turkish threat in the Mediterranean, suppressed the *Moriscos, launched the *Spanish Armada against Protestant England (1588), and intervened in the French *Wars of Religion against the Huguenots. On his death Spain was bankrupt and its economy destroyed, largely as a result of the cost of these wars.

Philip (IV) the Fair (1268–1314) King of France (1285–1314). Hostilities with England (1294–1303) were ended by the betrothal of Philip's daughter Isabella of France to Edward II. Conflict with Pope Boniface VIII over the right of lay rulers to tax clergy ended only with Boniface's death (1303) but his successor Clement V was more easily handled and in 1309 moved the papacy to Avignon. In 1306 Philip expelled the Jews from France and his reign also witnessed the suppression of the *Templars (1307–13).

Philip V (1683–1746) The first Bourbon King of Spain (1700–24, 1724–46). The grandson of Louis XIV of France, his accession instigated the War of the *Spanish Succession. He abolished the self-governing privileges of Aragon and centralized the administration. He abdicated in 1724 in favor of his son Luis (1707–24) but returned to the throne when Luis died.

Philip VI (1293–1350) The first Valois King of France (1328–50), succeeding his cousin Charles IV. The failure of the rival claim of Edward III of England to the French throne contributed to the outbreak in 1337 of the *Hundred Years' War, in which Philip suffered severe defeats at Sluis (1340) and Crécy (1346).

Philip, Prince, Duke of Edinburgh (1921–) The husband (from 1947) of Elizabeth II of the United Kingdom. A descendant of Queen Victoria and the son of Prince Andrew of Greece, he assumed the name Mountbatten in 1947, when he took British citizenship. He served in the Royal Navy during World War II.

Philip, St In the New Testament, one of the 12 Apostles. He was a native of Bethsaida and was responsible for bringing Nathanael (probably Bartholomew) to Jesus. In medieval art he is symbolized by loaves because of his participation in the miracle of the loaves and fishes. He may have been martyred. Feast day: May 11.

Philippeville. *See* Skikda.

Philippi, Battle of (42 BC) The battle in which Mark Antony and Octavian (later Emperor *Augustus) defeated *Brutus and *Cassius Longinus in the Roman civil war.

Philippians, Epistle of Paul to the A New Testament book written by Paul in about 60 AD to the church at Philippi in Macedonia, the first church that he founded in Europe. He thanks the Philippians for the gifts they have sent to him in prison in Rome and tells how he has continued to spread Christianity while imprisoned. The epistle contains an important doctrinal passage on the nature of Christ and the Incarnation.

Philippine eagle A rare *eagle, *Pithecophaga jefferyi*, occurring in tropical forests of the Philippines, formerly called monkey-eating eagle because it feeds mainly on macaque monkeys. It is 33–40 in (85–100 cm) long and has a brown plumage with pale underparts, a shaggy crest, a huge bill, and very powerful talons.

Philippines, Republic of the A country in SE Asia, consisting of an archipelago of over 7000 islands, of which some 880 are inhabited, between the Pacific Ocean and the South China Sea. Except for the central plain of Luzon (where most of the population is concentrated) there are few extensive lowlands, most of the larger islands, including Mindanao, being mountainous and volcanic and reaching heights of almost 10,000 ft (3000 m). Most of the inhabitants are Filipinos with small minorities of Chinese and others. *Economy*: based principally on agriculture, forestry, and fishing. The production of the staple crops of rice and maize and the main cash crops (sugar, coconuts, bananas, and pineapples) is concentrated around the central plain of Luzon although attempts are being made to develop economic activities elsewhere. The fastest-growing productive sector in recent years has been mining, based on the country's wide range of metallic minerals, which include copper, gold, iron ore, manganese, molybdenum, zinc, lead, and silver. Forests cover over half the land, providing gums and resins, bamboo, and dyes in addition to good-quality hardwoods. The main industries are food processing, textiles, wood processing, and oil refining. Tourism is an expanding industry. *History*: colonized by Spain in 1565, the islands were ceded to the US in 1898 following the Spanish-American War. Occupied (1942–45) by the Japanese during World War II, they became an independent republic in 1946. During the initial years of independence, a succession of presidents, US economic interests, and the Filipino landowning class did little to improve the standard of living of the peasant majority, but following the election of President Marcos in 1965 rapid economic development and a greatly improved infrastructure brought increased prosperity to the Philippines. During the early 1970s growing communist guerrilla activity in the N and a Muslim separatist movement in the S led to the declaration of martial law. A new constitution was adopted in 1973 under which Marcos became president and prime minister in 1978 and a National Assembly was elected. Martial rule was lifted in 1981, and Marcos was reelected for a six-year term to a presidency strengthened by several constitutional amendments. Exiled opposition leader Benigno S. Aquino, Jr, returning to contest Marcos' political leadership, was assassinated in Manila in 1983. Official languages: Pilipino (a language based on Tagalog) and English. Official currency: Philippine peso of 100 centavos. Area: 115,830 sq mi (300,000 sq km). Population (1980): 47,914,017. Capital: Manila. Main port: Manila.

Philippine Sea A section of the W Pacific Ocean, N and E of the Philippines. It contains deep trenches, volcanic submarine mounts, and coral reefs and is particularly prone to hurricanes. Its warm currents provide important fishing grounds. Maximum depth: 34,580 ft (10,540 m).

Philippopoli. *See* Plovdiv.

Philip the Bold (1342–1404) Duke of Burgundy (1363–1404), so called because of his military courage, particularly at the battle of Poitiers (1356) in the Hundred Years' War. The youngest son of John the Good of France, during the minority of his nephew Charles the Well-Beloved he was one of the regents of France and later, when Charles became insane, virtual ruler. He was also a noted art patron.

Philip the Good (1396–1467) Duke of Burgundy (1419–67). He recognized Henry V of England as heir to the French throne in 1420 but acknowledged Charles VII as King of France in 1435. In 1430 he founded the Order of the *Golden Fleece. He was a notable patron of artists.

Philip the Magnanimous (1504–67) Landgrave of Hesse, an ally of *Luther. Converted to Protestantism in 1524, Philip led the suppression of the *Peasants' War in 1525. He attempted to reconcile Luther and *Zwingli, who became theologically divided over the Eucharist. In 1531 he helped establish the Schmalkaldic League of Protestant princes. However, in 1540 his bigamous marriage, approved by Luther, was used by Emperor Charles V to split the Protestants and in 1547 the League was defeated by Charles at the battle of Mühlberg.

Philistines A non-Semitic people, who were driven from Egypt about 1200 BC and settled in Canaan, resisting Israelite attacks so vigorously that the region took the name Palestine from its new settlers. Tradition holds they were originally one of the *Sea Peoples who left Crete as the Mycenaean world collapsed. A warlike seafaring people, without cultural pretensions (hence the derogatory word philistine), they were largely absorbed into the kingdom of Israel under King David about 1000 BC.

Phillips' curve A relationship between the rate of wage increase and unemployment, plotted by the British economist A. W. Phillips in 1958. The Phillips' curve suggested that there was an option between unemployment and inflation, i.e. a little less of one could be achieved if a little more of the other could be accepted. The monetarists (*see* monetarism) hold that the relationship is theoretically unsound and it has indeed broken down in practice.

Philoctetes A legendary Greek hero, who had inherited from his father the bow and arrows of Heracles. On the way to Troy with the Greek expedition he was bitten by a snake. His cries and the stench of his wound forced the Greeks to leave him on Lesbos. Odysseus and Diomedes later returned to fetch him, needing the help of his bow and arrows. He then killed Paris and helped to bring about the fall of Troy.

Philodendron A genus of woody, usually climbing, plants (275 species), native to tropical America. They have oval, oblong, arrow-shaped, or heart-shaped leaves, either deeply cut or colored along the veins, and they cling to trees or other supports by means of aerial roots growing from their stems. Cultivated as ornamental house plants for their foliage, *P. andreanum* and *P. erubescens* are among the most popular species. Family: *Araceae*.

Philo Judaeus (c. 30 BC–45 AD) Jewish philosopher from the *Diaspora community in Alexandria, then the Greek capital of Roman Egypt. Philo's voluminous treatises, written in Greek, reinterpret Jewish religion in terms of Greek philosophy. Some were designed for sophisticated Jews; others defend Judaism against Greek scorn of Jewish culture. In old age Philo represented the Jews on a deputation to the Roman emperor following antisemitism in Alexandria. Most of his works have survived owing to their popularity with later Christian writers.

philology The study of language in general, before the growth of modern *linguistics. It originally applied to the study of classical languages and literatures but came to be applied to what is now called comparative linguistics. Comparative studies were undertaken in the 19th century by many philologists, including Jacob *Grimm, who helped to identify and trace the relationships of the *Indo-European languages.

Philomela and Procne In Greek legend, the daughters of an Athenian king. Procne married Tereus, King of Thrace. He fell in love with Philomela, raped her, and cut out her tongue to prevent her telling his secret. By means of an embroidery Philomela told Procne of the outrage and in revenge Procne killed her own son, Itys, and fed his flesh to Tereus. He then attempted to kill the sisters but was turned into a hoopoe and the sisters into a swallow and a nightingale.

philosopher's stone A hypothetical substance sought by alchemists for its ability to turn less valuable minerals into gold. In alchemical literature it is also called the elixir, the tincture, and hundreds of other fanciful names. It was sometimes credited with the power of curing all diseases and of making its possessors immortal. *See* alchemy.

Philosophes A group of French philosophers and writers of the 18th century whose faith in the ultimate authority of reason was expressed in their active concern with social and political reform. They included *Montesquieu, *Voltaire, J.-J. *Rousseau, and *Diderot, the chief editor of their literary monument, the *Encyclopédie* (1751–72; *see* Encyclopedists).

philosophy (Greek: love of wisdom) The field generally concerned with the study of ultimate reality and the first principles of thinking, knowledge, and truth. The main theoretical branches of modern western philosophy are *epistemology, *ethics, and *metaphysics; *logic (now closely associated with mathematics) and *aesthetics are also traditionally included. Historically, philosophical as opposed to religious or magical speculation arose in Greece in the 6th century BC in the attempts of the school of Miletus (*see* Thales; Anaximander; Anaximenes) to discover the single element underlying all things. This line of enquiry was pursued further by later Presocratics, including Heraclitus, Pythagoras, Parmenides, and Democritus. The most important phase of ancient philosophy occurred with the teaching of Socrates, who developed the dialectical method and applied it to political and other problems. The works of his successors, Plato and Aristotle, not only shaped the future of European philosophy in most fundamental respects, but also deeply influenced Christian theology. Among later schools of classical philosophy were *Epicureanism, *Stoicism (which strongly appealed to Roman philosophers), and *Neoplatonism. Aristotelianism was preserved in the works of medieval Islamic philosophers, such as Avicenna and Averroes, and re-entered Christian Europe in the *scholasticism of Anselm, Abelard, and Aquinas. Although influenced by scholasticism, the work of Descartes, with its systematic doubt and emphasis on reason, signaled the end of the medieval synthesis and the beginning of the modern period and the dominance of science. Spinoza and Leibniz attempted to deal with problems raised by Descartes; their rationalist systems are usually contrasted with the empiricism of the English philosophers, especially Locke, Berkeley, and Hume. Kant, whose aim was to reconcile these approaches and relate the sensible and the intelligible, was one of the most significant thinkers of the 18th century and stimulated the development of German idealism in the works of Fichte, Schelling, and Hegel. Idealism was also stimulated by the writings of Rousseau, whose ideas were the major source of 19th-century Romanticism and influenced the work of Schopenhauer and Nietzsche. In England utilitarianism was developed by Bentham and J. S. Mill, dialectical materialism by Marx and Engels, and Hegelian idealism by F. H. Bradley. Pragmatism is particularly associated with the Americans William James and, later, John Dewey. Philosophy in the 20th century has been characterized by a marked difference in interests and emphases between most European philosophers and those working in English-speaking countries. The writings of Bergson and Croce had an influence on a number of writers early in the century. The phenomenology of Husserl (and the works of Kierkegaard) led to the existentialism of Heidegger and Sartre. In contrast to their speculative approach to many of the large issues of traditional philosophy, the principal concern of English-speaking thinkers has been a critical approach that concentrates on logical analysis and the role of language—a development that may be traced in the works of Bertrand Russell, A. N. Whitehead, G. E. Moore, Wittgenstein, the logical positivists (the *Vienna circle), and in the current school of "ordinary language" philosophy centered at Oxford University.
Indian and other eastern types of philosophical thought are closely bound to the religious or cultural framework in which they developed (e.g. *Taoism, *Vedanta, Zen Buddhism).

Phiz. *See* Browne, Hablot.

phlebitis Inflammation of a vein, which is always accompanied by some *thrombosis in the vein. The inflammation may be caused by injury or infection or it may occur for no apparent reason: thrombosis of the vein then follows. Alternatively inflammation may develop after thrombosis. Treatment of superficial phlebitis is by rest and support.

phloem Plant tissue specialized to transport synthesized foods, mainly sugars, around the plant. It consists principally of tubelike cells that lack nuclei, the end of one cell being linked to the next by means of a porous wall (sieve plate). The cells are controlled by small neighboring cells, known as companion cells.

phlogiston theory An 18th-century theory of combustion based on the belief that all combustible substances contain phlogiston, which is liberated when the substance is heated, leaving calx or ash. The more combustible the substance, the more phlogiston it contains. The theory was finally overthrown in the late 18th century by A. *Lavoisier, who correctly explained combustion in terms of oxidation.

phlogopite A *mica mineral, $K_2(Mg,Fe^{2+})_6(Si_6Al_2O_{20})(OH,F)_4$. It is brown or bronze colored and occurs in some peridotites and metamorphosed limestones. It is used principally for making commutators.

Phlox A genus of ornamental herbs (about 65 species), mostly native to North America. Growing to about 40 in (1 m) high, they have terminal clusters of tubular flowers with five white, pink, red, or purple spreading petals. The creeping phlox, or moss pink (*P. subulata*), forms carpets of flowers in rock gardens. *P. drummondii* is the source of most garden varieties. Family: *Polemoniaceae*.

Phnom Penh (*or* Pnom Penh; Cambodian name: Phnum Pénh) 11 35N 104 55E The capital of Kampuchea, a port at the head of the Mekong delta. The capital since about 1432, it is now the site of the royal palace and of many museums and pagodas. A cultural center, it has several universities, including a Buddhist university (1954) and the University of Phnom Penh (1960). The country's commercial center, its industries include textiles and food processing. Population (1981 est): 400,000.

phobia A pathologically strong fear of a particular situation or thing. The main kinds are agoraphobia, which is fear of public places and open spaces; claustrophobia (fear of enclosed places); specific phobias of individual things, such as sharp knives; social phobias of encountering people; and animal phobias, as of spiders, rats, or snakes. Phobias are sometimes learned after a frightening incident, sometimes acquired in childhood from other people, and sometimes result from *depression. They are treated with *behavior therapy; *psychotherapy and drug treatment may also be used.

Phocis A region of ancient central Greece, N of the Gulf of Corinth. The Phocians were intermittently engaged in a struggle to retain control of Apollo's shrine at *Delphi (in Phocis). In the first so-called Sacred War (c. 590 BC) the Phocians lost Delphi. The second, precipitated by their seizure of the city, confirmed their possession. Early in the 4th century they again lost it, retaking it in 356. In the ensuing third Sacred War (355–346) the Phocians were defeated by Philip of Macedon, who proceeded to conquer all of Greece.

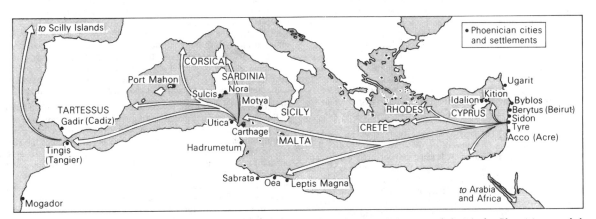

PHOENICIA *From their homeland along the E Mediterranean shore (modern Lebanon and Syria) the Phoenicians traded throughout the Mediterranean and beyond and established many settlements.*

Phoenicia

Phoenicia A group of city states on the coastal plain of Syria N of ancient *Canaan. Semitic peoples settled here sometime before 1800 BC and after about 1000 BC they became outstanding navigators and merchants, establishing trading posts all over the E Mediterranean and beyond. Their major cities—*Tyre, *Sidon, and *Byblos—were ports. The Phoenician alphabet, the ancestor of all western alphabets and perhaps the original one, was the chief Phoenician contribution to cultural progress. Phoenicia fell successively under Egyptian, Babylonian, and Persian influence. It was attacked by *Alexander the Great (332 BC), becoming part of the Hellenistic and later the Roman Empires. Phoenicia's major colony in N Africa was *Carthage.

phoenix A fabulous bird associated with sun worship, especially in Egypt, and representing resurrection and immortality. According to Herodotus, it was like an eagle in size and shape, had red and golden plumage, and lived for 500 years. Only one bird existed at a time. The dying phoenix was consumed by fire in a nest of aromatic materials and from its ashes a new bird arose.

Phoenix 33 30N 112 03W The capital city of Arizona, on the Salt River. The state's largest city, the commercial center for a cotton and farming region, its industries include the manufacture of aircraft and textiles. Its warm dry climate makes it a popular health resort. Population (1980): 789,704.

Phoenix Islands An uninhabited group of coral atolls in the S Pacific Ocean. They comprise *Canton and Enderbury under joint US-British control and the Birnie, McKean, Phoenix, Hull, Sydney, and Gardner islands in Kiribati. Area: about 11 sq mi (28 sq km).

Phoenix Park Murders (1882) The assassination in Phoenix Park, Dublin, Ireland of the new chief secretary for Ireland, Lord Frederick Cavendish, and the permanent undersecretary, Thomas Burke, by extreme Irish nationalists calling themselves the Invincibles.

phon A unit for measuring the loudness of sound equal to the intensity in *decibels of a sound of frequency 1000 hertz, which appears to the ear to be as loud as the sound to be measured.

phonetics The study of the production and perception of sounds in languages. Sounds are classified in terms of the way in which they are produced by the speech organs. There is a wide range of possible speech sounds but each language uses only a selection of them. The study of the system of sounds within any given language is called **phonology** and the selected individual sounds are called phonemes. Phonetics also includes the study of stress and intonation.

phosphorescence. *See* luminescence.

phosphorus (P) A nonmetallic solid element discovered by H. Brand (died c. 1692) in 1669. It exists in at least four forms: white (α and β), red, and black. White phosphorus is a waxy solid, which ignites spontaneously in air to form the pentoxide (P_2O_5). Red phosphorus, a more stable allotrope, is formed when white phosphorus is heated to 753°F (400°C); it is used in matches. Black phosphorus is also stable and forms when white phosphorus is heated to 392–572°F (200–300°C). Phosphorus exists in nature chiefly as the mineral *apatite ($Ca_3(PO_4)_2$), from which the element is obtained, either by reduction with carbon or reaction with silica at high temperatures. Phosphates are used extensively as fertilizers (mainly as "superphosphate"—calcium hydrogen phosphate) but find other uses in detergents, water softeners, and specialist glasses. A wide range of compounds is formed including the hydride (phosphine; PH_3), numerous phosphates (for example Na_3PO_4), and phosphides (for example Na_3P). Phosphorus occurs in DNA and RNA molecules and is therefore essential to life; bones also contain phosphates (*see* apatite) but some organo-phosphorus compounds are extremely toxic and are used as nerve gases. At no 15; at wt 30.9738; mp (white) 111°F (44.1°C); bp (white) 536°F (280°C).

Photius (c. 810–c. 895 AD) Patriarch of Constantinople, whose condemnation of certain practices and doctrines of the Western Church contributed to the rift with the Eastern Church. A leading statesman at the Byzantine court, he was elected patriarch in 858 amid much controversy and before he had been ordained. In 867 he convened a council at Constantinople at which he excommunicated Pope *Nicholas I, who had earlier deposed him, and denounced the *Filioque clause in the creed. Several depositions and reinstatements followed until he was finally exiled to Armenia in 886. He is also famous for his scholarship and is a saint in the Orthodox Church.

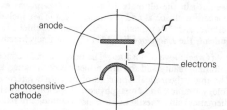

photoemissive cell *Illumination releases electrons from the cathode.*

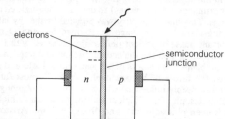

photovoltaic cell *Illumination creates a potential difference at a p–n semiconductor junction.*

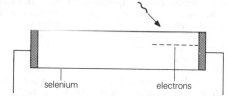

photoconductivity cell *Illumination increases the conductivity of a semiconductor, such as selenium.*

PHOTOCELL

photocell (*or* photoelectric cell) A device that makes use of a *photoelectric effect to measure or detect light or other electromagnetic radiation. In the photoemissive cell, a photosensitive cathode emits electrons when it is illuminated; these photoelectrons constitute a current when they flow to the positive anode of the cell. In solid-state devices the light changes the behavior of a p–n junction (as in the photodiode), creating a potential difference by the *photovoltaic effect. In the conductivity cell, the resistance of a substance, such as selenium, changes when light falls on it as a result of *photoconductivity. Photocells are widely used in light-operated controls, such as automatic doors, fire alarms, and burglar alarms; they are also used in solar cells (*see* solar power) and photographic light meters. *See also* selenium cell.

photoconductivity The increase in the conductivity of certain semiconductors, such as selenium, when exposed to light. It occurs when photons excite electrons in the material from the valence band into the conduction band. *See* energy bands; photocell.

photocopying machine A device that prints black-and-white copies of documents, drawings, etc., from an optical image. The most common technique is a dry electrostatic process known as xerography. A pattern of electric charge is induced by light falling on a layer of *semiconductor material on a conducting surface. Toner powder is sprayed or rolled onto this material, so that it sticks to the highly charged areas. The image so formed is printed onto charged paper, where it is fixed by heating to produce the final copy. Xerography is also used for high-speed printing of computer output, with printing heads instead of a light image.

photoelectric effects A number of effects in which electromagnetic radiation interacts with matter, frequently with the emission of electrons. These effects include *photoconductivity, the *photovoltaic effect, and the *Compton effect and the *Auger effect. The frequency of the radiation (f) has to be such that the energy of the photon (hf, where h is Planck's constant) is sufficient to liberate the electron. For solids, the minimum energy required is called the work function; for free atoms or molecules it is equal to the first *ionization potential, the effect then being known as *photoionization. For most substances, an ultraviolet frequency is needed to eject an electron, but for some metals, such as cesium, visible light is sufficient. *See* photocell.

Photofit. *See* Identikit and Photofit.

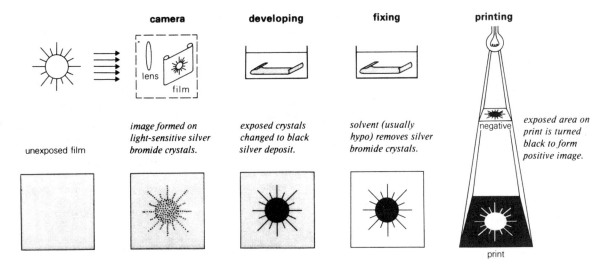

	camera	developing	fixing	printing

image formed on light-sensitive silver bromide crystals.

exposed crystals changed to black silver deposit.

solvent (usually hypo) removes silver bromide crystals.

exposed area on print is turned black to form positive image.

unexposed film

negative

print

PHOTOGRAPHY *The stages in making a black and white photographic print.*

photography The recording of images on sensitized material, by means of visible light, X-rays, or other radiation, and the subsequent chemical processing. The first photograph was taken in 1826 by Joseph Nicéphore Niépce (d. 1833) using the action of light on asphalt solution. In 1839, *Daguerre introduced the daguerrotype, a positive image of milky white on a silver background, produced directly from silver iodide emulsion on plates exposed inside a simple *camera. Modern photography involves a negative made by the development of *film coated with silver salts. The positive picture is obtained by shining light through the negative onto light-sensitive paper with a coating similar to that on the original film. Lenses can be used to enlarge or reduce the size of the final image on the print. Transparencies, for use with a slide *projector, may also be made. Film is usually developed and printed in a darkroom by dipping it in baths of chemicals. Polaroid photography, however, produces positive pictures directly from the camera in one stage. This system was invented by Edwin Land in 1947 and is used for instant pictures for security passes, laboratory records, etc.

Photography as an art dates back almost to the origins of the technique. Portraiture was already established in the 1850s. The Crimean War in the 1850s and more importantly the Civil War in the 1860s provided the first opportunities for the true miseries of war to be realistically portrayed. However, during the last half of the 19th century photographic interest centered on the landscape, especially as horizons broadened with the growth of travel.

In the 1920s the collages of the cubist painters encouraged such photographers as László *Moholy-Nagy to experiment with photomontages. But by the 1930s the Frenchman Henri *Cartier-Bresson had led fashion back to a more realistic technique: using the camera as an extension of the eye, he composed transient scenes in great detail. Picture magazines, such as *Life*, were also a feature of this period. Postwar photography has developed many of these themes, using the new precision cameras and techniques, and many galleries now have permanent exhibitions of photography.

Photography has also had a profound effect on painting. Some art historians believe that the 20th-century trend toward— abstract painting has been primarily a reaction to the camera's ability to do superbly what representationalist painters have often only been able to do indifferently. *See also* color photography; cinematography.

photoionization The *ionization of an atom when it is bombarded with electromagnetic radiation. The frequency of the radiation has to be such that the energy of its *photons exceeds the first *ionization potential of the atom.

photoluminescence. *See* luminescence.

photolysis The breaking of a chemical bond by absorbed electromagnetic radiation. The photon energy of the radiation must exceed the bond energy, and photolytic reactions can be produced by light, ultraviolet radiation, and X-rays. Examples occur in *photosynthesis, suntan, and photography. **Flash photolysis** is a technique for identifying and studying unstable reaction intermediates. The intermediates are produced in a gas by an intense brief flash of light, and their reactions are followed by spectroscopy.

photometry The branch of physics concerned with measuring quantities related to the intensity of light. These quantities are measured in two ways. If the intensity is measured in terms of the energy of the light, they are known as radiant quantities. They may also be measured in terms of their visual effect, since the sensitivity of the eye varies with the wavelength of the light. They are then known as luminous quantities.

photomicrograph. *See* microscope.

photomultiplier An instrument that produces an amplified current when exposed to electromagnetic radiation. Photons striking a photocathode cause the emission of electrons by the *photoelectric effect. These electrons then strike another surface causing a greater number of electrons to be emitted, the process being repeated several times to produce a greatly amplified current. Photomultipliers are used in certain *scintillation counters.

photon The quantum of *electromagnetic radiation, having an energy hf, where h is the *Planck constant and f is the frequency of the radiation. It may also be regarded as an elementary particle with *spin 1 and zero mass that travels at the speed of *light.

photoperiodism The response of an organism to the relative lengths of day and night, based either on a daily, seasonal, or yearly cycle. Flowering in plants, breeding in animals, and bird migration are examples of photoperiodic responses, which may be modified by such factors as temperature and availability of food. In general the response is a reaction to day length, but the flowering of plants actually depends on the length of the dark period. Thus, short-day plants (e.g. chrysanthemums) flower in response to a long night and long-day plants (e.g. certain cereals) flower when nights are short.

photosphere The visible surface of the *sun, acting as a boundary of several hundred kilometers between the opaque outer (convective) zone of the sun's interior and its transparent atmosphere. Almost all the energy emitted by the sun is radiated from the photosphere. Its temperature falls from about 10,850°F (6000°C) at the convective zone to about 7240°F (4000°C) where the photosphere merges with the *chromosphere. *See also* sunspots.

photosynthesis The means by which plants and certain bacteria produce carbohydrates from carbon dioxide and a hydrogen source. The energy for the process is provided by light absorbed by the green pigment chlorophyll, which is contained in the *chloroplasts. Plants use water (H_2O) as the hydrogen source and release its oxygen as a by-product. Thus the atmospheric oxygen that is continually used in respiration by all living organisms is replenished by photosynthesizing plants. Photosynthesis occurs in the chloroplasts and comprises two sets of reactions. One set, which requires light, produces energy-storing and reducing compounds; the other reactions, which may proceed in the light or dark, use these compounds to add hydrogen atoms to carbon dioxide and make carbohydrates. The overall reactions, which are very complex in detail, can be summarized by the equation $6CO_2 + 6H_2O \rightarrow C_6H_{12}O_6 + 6O_2$.

photovoltaic effect The production of a voltage when light falls on certain materials coated with another substance. The effect can be detected by connecting the two materials through an external circuit to generate a current. It occurs in copper (I) oxide on copper and in selenium on iron. *See also* photocell.

phrenology An obsolete approach to the study of the nervous system, first proposed by a Viennese doctor, F. J. Gall (1758–1828). The degree of mental development was supposed to be indicated by the shape of the skull, reflecting the development of the underlying parts of the brain in which the various mental processes were assumed to take place. Although discredited, it was important in developing ideas about the localization of brain function.

Phrygia The central and W areas of Asia Minor inhabited after the Hittite empire collapsed (12th century BC) by Thracian migrants. The short-lived Phrygian kingdom, centered on its capital Gordium, reached its peak in the late 8th century. The legendary *Midas was King of Phrygia. In about 700 BC Phrygia was conquered by Lydia. Phrygia was a center for the cult of *Cybele, which it passed on to Greece; it also influenced early Greek music. The Phrygians are reputed to have invented embroidery.

Phryne (4th century BC) Greek courtesan. She was the lover of *Praxiteles and probably the model for his most famous statue, the Aphrodite of Cnidos, as well as for the painting of Aphrodite Anadyomene by Apelles.

Phyfe, Duncan (or Fife; 1768–1854) US cabinetmaker and furniture designer, born in Scotland. His highly successful firm in New York City produced furniture in the Sheraton, Regency, and French Empire styles.

phyle A tribal subdivision or clan in ancient Greek city states, its members being tied by descent from a common ancestor. The phyle upheld clan traditions, cults and loyalties and encouraged aristocratic rule. By the 5th century BC Athens and Sparta had replaced the phylae with artificial district divisions for administrative and military purposes, engendering allegiance to the city rather than the clan.

Phyllanthus A mostly tropical genus of trees, shrubs, herbs, and aquatic plants (600 species), including a few ornamental greenhouse plants. Many have flattened green stems resembling leaves, with yellow, red, or white flowers along their margins. *P. acidus* (Indian gooseberry) has round fleshy ribbed fruits used in pickles and preserves. Family: *Euphorbiaceae*.

phylloxera A plant-eating insect belonging to the family *Phylloxeridae*, closely related to the *aphids. The grape, or vine, phylloxera (*Phylloxera vitifoliae* or *Viteus vitifolii*) is a notorious pest of grapevines. During a complex life cycle, the insect forms galls on the leaves and roots, which damage the plant. The grape phylloxera spread to Europe from North America in the 19th century and almost destroyed the wine industry in France.

phylogeny The history of the *evolution of a species or other group of organisms. By studying the fossil record, comparative anatomy, embryology, biochemistry, and geographical distribution of the groups involved, one can establish the probable lines of descent and degrees of relationship between broad groups of plants or animals to produce a phylogenetic tree. For example, it is believed that whales and carnivorous land mammals developed from insectivorous mammals living more than 65 million years ago. Phylogeny forms the basis for the classification of organisms (*see* taxonomy). It should be distinguished from **ontogeny**, which is the succession of developmental stages through which an individual organism passes during its lifetime. *See also* biogenetic law.

phylum A major unit of classification for animals (*see* taxonomy). Organisms belonging to the same phylum share basic features but are divided into classes, orders, genera, and species according to their supposed degrees of relationship. For example, the phylum *Arthropoda* is a very diverse group including the insects, spiders, scorpions, crustaceans, etc., which all share the features of a tough segmented external skeleton and jointed limbs. In most plant-classification systems the equivalent term is division.

physical medicine The medical specialty concerned with the treatment of physical disabilities. Originally this was restricted to the diagnosis and management of rheumatic diseases, but it has now been extended to the treatment and rehabilitation of patients disabled by back injuries, polio, asthma, and many other disorders.

physics The study of the interrelationship between matter and energy, without reference to chemical change. Traditionally the subject was divided into the study of mechanics, electricity and magnetism, heat and thermodynamics, optics, and acoustics. More modern aspects of the subject include quantum mechanics, relativity, nuclear physics, particle physics, solid-state physics, and astrophysics.

Physiocrats A group of French 18th-century economists, led by François *Quesnay. The Physiocrats believed that the only real productive sector in the economy was agriculture: industry and merchants were seen as mere processors. As mercantile (*see* mercantilism) interests were no longer identified with the wealth of the nation, *laissez-faire and *free trade were advocated.

physiology The study of the functioning of living organisms and their constituent parts. Physiology is closely linked with both *anatomy (the study of structure) and *biochemistry (the chemical reactions that play a vital role in many physiological processes).

physiotherapy The treatment of injuries or disabilities using physical methods, such as massage, manipulation, exercise, and heat. Physiotherapists play an important role in restoring mobility to patients confined for a long period to bed or a wheelchair; they also enable the rehabilitation of those handicapped by strokes, cerebral palsy, polio, etc., or immobilized by fractures. Physiotherapy is also useful in reducing the pain and stiffness of arthritis.

phytochrome A pigment of green plants that exists in two interchangeable forms, one absorbing red light and the other, far-red light. Day-length responses (*see* photoperiodism), greening of young leaves, and the breaking of dormancy in some seeds are among the processes controlled by phytochrome.

phytosaur An extinct amphibious reptile, resembling a modern crocodile, having long pointed jaws with sharp teeth and protective bony plates beneath the skin. Phytosaurs lived during the late Triassic and Jurassic periods (210–135 million years ago) and probably fed on fish. The nostrils were set on a mound near the eyes and not at the end of the snout (as in crocodiles).

pi In mathematics, the ratio of the circumference of a circle to its diameter, denoted by the Greek letter π. It was proved to be an irrational number by J. H. *Lambert and transcendental by F. Lindemann (1852–1939). Its value is 3.14159 . . . . *See also* numbers.

Piacenza 45 03N 09 41E A city in N Italy, in Emilia-Romagna on the Po River. Dating from Roman times, it has several notable buildings, including a 12th-century cathedral and a 13th-century town hall. Piacenza is primarily an agricultural trading center. Population (1980 est): 108,893.

EDITH PIAF

Piaf, Edith (Edith Giovanna Gassion; 1915–63) French cabaret and music-hall singer. Originally a street singer, her small size earned her the nickname "piaf" (French slang: sparrow). Many of her songs, which include "Je m'en fou pas mal," "Je ne regrette rien," and "La Vie en rose," reflected the defiance and despair of her own tragic life, which was ended prematurely by her addiction to alcohol and drugs.

Piaget, Jean (1896–1980) Swiss psychologist, noted for his studies of thought processes, especially in children. He described the development of perception, judgment, reasoning, and logic during childhood, which had important consequences for children's education. Among his many books are *The Origin of Intelligence in Children* (1954) and *The Early Growth of Logic in the Child* (1964).

piano A □musical instrument consisting of a number of wire strings stretched over a metal frame, which are hit by felt-covered wooden hammers operated by a keyboard. The piano was invented by *Cristofori in the early 18th century; the name derives from the Italian *pianoforte*, soft-loud, referring to the variation in volume obtainable on the piano in contrast to the earlier *clavichord and *harpsichord. In the modern instrument the frame is either horizontal, as in the **grand piano**, or vertical, as in the **upright piano**. Groups of two or three strings are tuned to each note. When a key is struck the escapement mechanism allows the hammer to fall away from the strings after they have been struck; when the key is released a felt damper stops the vibration of the strings. Two pedals allow a wide variation in volume. The right-hand pedal prevents the dampers from cutting off the sound; the left-hand pedal moves the hammers so that they are either closer to the strings (in the upright piano) or only able to strike one or two strings of each group (in the grand piano). The piano has a compass of seven and a quarter octaves; it has the largest repertory of any single instrument. Famous makers of pianos include J. B. Broadwood (1732–1812) and the firms of Bechstein, *Steinway, and Bösendorfer.

pianola. *See* player piano.

Piave River A river in NE Italy. It flows generally S from the Carnic Alps to the Adriatic Sea 20 mi (32 km) NE of Venice. It formed the main Italian line of defense in World War I, following the Austro-German offensive in 1917. Length: 137 mi (220 km).

Picabia, Francis (1879–1953) French painter and writer. Working chiefly in Paris but also in New York (1913–17), Barcelona, and Zürich, he was associated successively with *cubism, *dada, and *surrealism. He is known mainly for his periodical *391* (1917–24), containing his poems, essays, and satirical drawings of machinery.

Picardy (French name: Picardie) A planning region and former province in N France. It was incorporated into France in 1477 by Louis XI of France. During World War I it was the scene of heavy fighting. Area: 7493 sq mi (19,411 sq km). Population (1981 est): 1,723,000.

picaresque novel A type of narrative that recounts the adventures of a single protagonist in a loose episodic form. The term derives from the Spanish *pícaro*, a rogue. Early examples of the form include the Spanish *Lazarillo de Tormes* (1554) and the French *Gil Blas* (1715–35) by *Lesage. English examples include *Moll Flanders* (1722) by *Defoe, *Jonathan Wild* (1743) by *Fielding, and *Peregrine Pickle* (1751) by *Smollett. The form is usually characterized by comedy and social satire rather than by the development of ideas or characters; it was continued in the 19th century by *Thackeray in *Barry Lyndon* (1844) and in the 20th century by Thomas *Mann in *The Confessions of Felix Krull, Confidence Man* (1954).

Picasso, Pablo (1881–1973) Spanish artist, born in Malaga. The most inventive and versatile of 20th-century painters and a precocious draftsman, Picasso trained in Barcelona but worked chiefly in Paris after 1900. Although his most popular paintings are those of the beggars, acrobats, and harlequins of his blue (1901–04) and rose (1905–08) periods, his most original work began with *Les Demoiselles d'Avignon* (1907), influenced by Cézanne and African sculpture, and resulted in his development of *cubism with *Braque. In 1912 he made the first collage. He later began a series of classical paintings of colossal figures, followed by nightmarish distorted figure studies in the 1920s and 1930s, when he was loosely associated with *surrealism. One of his major works, *Guernica* (1937), is a horrific depiction of the destruction of the Basque capital during the Spanish Civil War. He was also a sculptor, lithographer, ceramicist, and stage designer.

Piccard A family of Swiss scientists and explorers. **Auguste Piccard** (1884–1962) and his twin **Jean-Félix Piccard** (1884–1963) pioneered the scientific study of the stratosphere in balloons, reaching a height of 16,940 meters in 1932. In 1948 Auguste designed a bathyscaphe, using it to explore the sea depths, descending to over 3000 meters in 1953. His son **Jacques Piccard** (1927–   ) collaborated with his father in designing bathyscaphes and reached a depth of 10,917 meters in the vessel *Trieste* in 1960.

piccolo A woodwind instrument, the smallest and shrillest member of the *flute family. It is pitched an octave higher than the flute and its music is written an octave lower than it sounds. It is used in the orchestra and in the military band.

Pickering, Timothy (1745–1829) US soldier and statesman. During the American Revolution he served on the Board of War and Ordnance (1777–80) and was George Washington's quarter master general (1780–83). He was Indian Commissioner (1790–95). He held cabinet posts under presidents George Washington and John Adams: postmaster general (1791–95), secretary of war (1795–96), and secretary of state (1795–80). He was a US senator (1803–11) and US representative (1813–17).

picketing The act of guarding the entrance to a workplace by strikers to dissuade nonstrikers from working or to obstruct deliveries.

PICASSO *A photograph of the artist, aged 84, when he lived in southern France.*

Pickett, George Edward (1825–75) US Confederate general. A graduate of the US Military Academy, he distinguished himself in the *Mexican War and then served on the frontier (1849–61). He joined the Confederate Army at the start of the Civil War, fighting in his native Virginia. He was part of the Battle of *Gettysburg where his troops attacked at Cemetery Ridge; thereafter, "Pickett's Charge" was synonomous with bravery.

Pickford, Mary (Gladys Mary Smith; 1893–1979) Canadian-born US film actress. She played the roles of innocent young heroines in early silent films, such as *The Little American* (1917) and *Pollyanna* (1919). In 1919 she cofounded United Artists with Charlie *Chaplin, D. W. *Griffith, and Douglas *Fairbanks, whom she married.

pick-up A device that converts information stored in a phonograph record into an electrical signal. In a record player, the pick-up cartridge, usually a removable assembly, consists of a stylus and a *transducer. The stylus is forced to vibrate by the undulations in the record groove. The transducer responds electrically to these vibrations. The most common types of transducer use the *piezoelectric effect or *electromagnetic induction, but *capacitor, variable-resistance, and variable-reluctance pick-ups are also used. A stereo pick-up has one stylus that picks up vibrations from both sides of the V-shaped groove. The components of the resulting two-dimensional vibration contributed by each side are at right angles and are separated by two suitably oriented transducers.

Pico della Mirandola, Giovanni, Conte (1463–94) Italian Renaissance philosopher. He was converted by *Ficino to *Neoplatonism and became interested in the Hermetic and Zoroastrian writings. Although Pico was concerned to prove the truth of Christianity through these literatures, he was inevitably regarded with suspicion by the Church, which banned a proposed discussion (1486) by him of philosophical and theological topics. He wrote an important study of the *Kaballah.

pictographic writing systems (*or* pictography) Writing systems in which each symbol represents a concept or word in the form of a sketch or diagram of the object it represents (the referent). Prehistoric pictographic records have been found throughout the world. It is a characteristic of primitive (nontechnological) societies that a careful distinction is not maintained between an object, a word denoting the object, and a pictorial representation of it. Pictography is therefore often associated with magic or ritual rather than the straightforward recording of information. Disadvantages of pictography include the difficulty of representing any word except nouns having concrete referents. Pictographic systems that did not die out therefore generally developed into *ideographic writing systems.

Picts (painted people)   The Roman name (referring to their tattoos) for all Scottish tribes living N of the *Antonine Wall. Perpetually hostile to the Romans, the Picts had forced them to withdraw behind *Hadrian's Wall by 200 AD, and remained independent until Kenneth I MacAlpine unified S Scotland in the 9th century.

piddock   A burrowing *bivalve mollusk belonging to the family *Pholadidae*, of cold and temperate seas. Piddocks are adapted for boring into rock, having shells with serrated cutting edges, the largest being 4 in (10 cm) long. They can damage concrete breakwaters, sea walls, and wharves.

pidgin English   A form of English, used to facilitate communication between Chinese and Europeans, having a greatly reduced vocabulary, simplified grammar, and modified sound system. The term may also be applied to *Neo-Melanesian and the Beach-la-Mer of the South Seas. *Compare* creole.

Pieck, Wilhelm   (1876–1960) German communist politician. He opposed both the Weimar Republic and Nazism and advocated their overthrow by violent revolution with the aid of Soviet troops. In 1946 he was elected joint chairman, with Otto Grotewohl, of the Socialist Unity Party in the postwar Soviet zone of Germany and was the first president of the German Democratic Republic (1949–60).

Piedmont (Italian name: Piemonte)   A region in NW Italy. Associated with the House of Savoy since the early 11th century, it became the nucleus of Italian unification in the mid 19th century. It consists of the upper Po Valley, bordered by the Alps in the N and W and the Apennines in the S. Manufacturing is important, with engineering and steel centered on Turin; other industries include textiles, chemicals, rubber, and food products. Agriculture is also important, producing rice, cereals, wine, and dairy products. Area: 9807 sq mi (25,400 sq km). Population (1980 est): 4,517,665. Capital: Turin.

Pierce, Franklin   (1804–69) US statesman; 14th president of the US (1853–57). A Democrat, he served in New Hampshire's legislature before becoming a US representative (1833–37) and US senator (1837–42). After a time as US attorney for New Hampshire and a brief stint as an officer in the *Mexican War, he became the Democrats' compromise presidential candidate in 1852 and won the election. As president he worked hard at patching up differences, the largest being the question of slavery, among the various sections of the country. During his administration the *Gadsden Purchase was completed, the *Kansas-Nebraska Act was passed, and the *Ostend Manifesto proved an embarrassment. He failed to win renomination in 1856.

Piero della Francesca   (c. 1420–92) Italian Renaissance painter, born in Sansepolcro. He probably trained in Florence, where he worked on frescoes in Sant' Egidio in 1439. *The Baptism of Christ* (National Gallery, London) shows his monumental figure style and the influence of Florentine artists, particularly *Masaccio. He frequently worked at the court of Urbino, where he painted the double portrait of the duke and his wife in profile (Uffizi). His lifelong interest in perspective is reflected in his fresco cycle *The Legend of the True Cross*, painted for the church of S Francesco, Arezzo, and in his treatise *On Perspective in Painting*. After his death his work was neglected until it was reappraised in the 20th century.

Piero di Cosimo   (P. di Lorenzo; 1462–1521) Florentine Renaissance painter. He trained under the painter Cosimo Rosselli (1439–1507) but was chiefly influenced by *Leonardo da Vinci and *Signorelli. His mythological paintings and fantasies on the primitive life of mankind are highly original, one of the best examples being *The Death of Procris*.

Pierre   44 23N 100 20W The capital city of South Dakota, on the Missouri River. Founded in 1880, it is a trade center for a grain and dairy-farming region. Population (1980): 11,973.

Pietermaritzburg   29 36S 30 24E A city in South Africa, the capital of Natal. It was founded by Boers (1838) and named for their leaders, Piet Retief and Gert Maritz, massacred by the Zulus. The Church of the Vow (1839), built to commemorate the subsequent Boer victory over the Zulus, now houses the Voortrekker Museum. Part of the University of Natal (1910) stands here. It is the center of a rich farming area. Population (1980 est): 178,972.

Pietism   A movement for spiritual regeneration among Lutherans in 17th-century Germany. It was started by P. J. Spener (1635–1705), whose *Pia Desideria* (1675) proposed instilling new life into official Lutheranism by concentrating upon devotional worship instead of dogmatic theology. Pietism survived in different guises for over 200 years and influenced many subsequent Christian organizations.

piezoelectric effect   The production of electric charges on the opposite faces of certain assymmetric crystals when they are compressed or expanded. The charges are of equal magnitude but opposite in sign on the two faces, the sign on each face depending on whether the crystal is expanded or compressed. Such crystals, known as piezoelectric crystals, include quartz and Rochelle salt. The converse effect also occurs: when a voltage is applied across a piezoelectric crystal, it expands or contracts. The effect is used in the piezoelectric oscillator, the crystal microphone, and the piezoelectric loudspeaker.

pig   A hoofed mammal belonging to the Old World family *Suidae* (8 species). Also called hogs or swine, pigs have a stocky body with short legs, a short neck, and a large head with a long cylindrical snout used for digging up roots, seeds, small animals, etc., from soil. Wild *boars were originally domesticated about 5000 years ago, probably in Asia, and used for meat and clearing vegetation. Modern breeds include the *Landrace and *Large White and are reared for pork and bacon (*see* livestock farming). Other members of the pig family include the *babirusa and *wart hog. *See also* peccary.

pigeon   A bird belonging to a family (*Columbidae*; 300 species) occurring worldwide except in the coldest regions; the smaller long-tailed forms are called doves. 7–30 in (17–75 cm) long, pigeons have soft plumage, a plump body, a small head, short bill and legs, and a characteristic cooing call. Pigeons feed mainly on seeds and other plant material and feed the young on "pigeons' milk"—the sloughed-off lining of the crop. They are often fast fliers and some are highly migratory, domesticated breeds being used as messengers and for racing. Order: *Columbiformes* (pigeons and sandgrouse). *See also* mourning dove; passenger pigeon; wood pigeon.

pigeon racing   The sport of racing homing pigeons back to their home lofts (which they must enter). Pigeons were first, and still are, used for carrying messages; Genghis Khan had a system of pigeon post. The first race of over a hundred miles was held in Belgium (1818), where the sport is still very popular. Birds are banded for racing; their times of departure and arrival are then recorded. Pigeons can cover several thousand miles at speeds of more than 90 mph (145 km per hour).

pigeon wheat.   *See* Polytrichum.

pig iron   The type of iron produced by *blast furnaces, and used as the first stage in *steel making. It has a high carbon content (about 4% by weight) and contains impurities, including some slag, which make it brittle. *See also* cast iron.

pigments   Insoluble substances, in the form of fine particles, that give color and opacity to *paints, *plastics, and *rubber. They can be broadly divided into naturally occurring pigments (such as red iron oxide), inorganic pigments manufactured from minerals, organic pigments, and *lakes.

pigmies.   *See* Pygmies.

pigweed   1. A stout leafy annual herb of the genus *Amaranthus* (about 50 species), found in tropical and temperate regions, often as a weed. Pigweeds have furrowed stems, up to 40 in (1 m) high, with simple pale-green hairy leaves and long branching greenish-white flower spikes. Family: *Amaranthaceae*. 2. *See* goosefoot.

pika   A small mammal belonging to the genus *Ochotona* (14 species), of Asia and North America, also called mouse hare, cony, and rock rabbit. 5–12 in (12.5–30 cm) long and resembling large short-tailed mice, pikas live in cold rocky areas above the tree line. They build stacks of sun-dried vegetation under sheltering ledges to feed on during the winter. Family: *Ochotonidae*; order: *Lagomorpha.

Pike, Zebulon Montgomery   (1779–1813) US soldier and explorer. An army officer on the frontier, he was sent (1805) to find the sources of the Mississippi River. Unsuccessful, he explored most of the southwest (New Mexico and Colorado), discovered *Pikes Peak (1806), and gathered information about the Spanish. He was killed in battle in Canada during the War of 1812. His *Account of the Expeditions to the Sources of the Mississippi and Through the Western Parts of Louisiana* (1810) greatly aided US expansion.

pike (fish)   A freshwater fish of the genus *Esox* found in temperate regions of Eurasia and America. It has an elongated body, up to about 4.5 ft (1.4 m) long, a broad flat snout, and a large mouth with strong teeth. It feeds voraciously on fish and other animals. The common pike (*E. lucius*) is olive-gray above with silvery underparts and pale spots. Family: *Esocidae*; order: *Salmoniformes*.

pike (weapon)   A pre-1800 infantry weapon with a wooden shaft 12–21 ft (4–6 m) long, a steel head on an iron sleeve, and an iron butt. It was useless in the face of missile weapons (arrows, musketry) and was replaced by the *bayonet.

pikeperch   One of several food and game fish related to perch, especially members of the genera *Lucioperca* and *Stizostedion*, found in Europe and North America. The American pikeperches include the species *S. vitreum*,

35 in (90 cm) long, and *S. canadense*, 12 in (30 cm) long. Slender, elongated, and darkly mottled, they are carnivorous, feeding mainly on other fish.

Pikes Peak A mountain in central Colorado, in the Rocky Mountains. It is a popular tourist attraction noted for its spectacular views from the summit, which is ascended by a cog railroad and a road. Height: 14,109 ft (4300 m).

pilaster. *See* orders of architecture.

Pilate, Pontius (1st century AD) Roman governor. As procurator of Judea and Samaria (26–36) he condemned Christ to death but, according to the New Testament Gospels, did so reluctantly, fearing the outcome of any other course. He came into frequent conflict with the Jews and was finally dismissed for his cruel suppression of a Samaritan rebellion. In one tradition he committed suicide, but in the Ethiopian Church he is regarded as a saint and martyr.

pilchard An important food fish, *Sardina pilchardus*, related to the herring and sprat, that occurs in abundance in the Mediterranean, E Atlantic, and English Channel. Its slender body, 10–19 in (25–35 cm) long, is bluish green above and whitish below and it swims in large shoals feeding on crustaceans and fish eggs. Pilchards up to one year old are called *sardines and are fished extensively off the coast of Spain and Portugal. Pilchards are eaten fresh and canned.

Pilcomayo River A river in S central South America, rising in the Bolivian Andes and flowing generally SE, forming part of the Argentina–Paraguay border before joining the Paraguay River. Length: about 1000 mi (1600 km).

piles. *See* hemorrhoids.

Pilgrimage of Grace (1536) A revolt in N England against the government of Henry VIII. The rebels were united by their opposition to the recent *Reformation legislation and the dissolution of the monasteries as well as by economic grievances. Under Robert Ashe (c. 1500–37) they seized York but were persuaded by promises of pardon and a full hearing of their complaints to surrender. However, some 230 men, including Ashe, were executed.

Pilgrim Fathers The 101 English colonists who established the first permanent European settlement in New England in 1620. Among these settlers was a group of 35 English Puritans led by William Bradford and William *Brewster that had lived in Holland for the previous decade in their attempt to escape religious persecution. Granted the right to settle within the American territory of the Virginia Company, the Puritans and other potential colonists set sail in the *Mayflower*, arriving off Cape Cod after a voyage of almost two months. Even though this was beyond the limits of the Virginia Company's possessions, the Pilgrims chose to remain in the area, establishing their first settlement, which they named Plymouth, after their port of departure in England. Although disease and the unexpectedly harsh conditions of the first winter drastically reduced the number of colonists, a sufficient number survived to sow the crops needed to maintain the Plymouth Colony and to reap their first harvest in November 1621 (*see* Thanksgiving Day).

Pill, the. *See* oral contraceptive.

Pillars of Hercules Two promontories at the entrance to the Mediterranean Sea, known in ancient times as Calpe (modern Gibraltar) and Abyla (modern Jebel Musa, at Ceuta, Morocco). According to one legend, the promontories were joined until Heracles tore them apart.

pilot fish A fish, *Naucrates ductor*, that has a pale-blue elongated body, up to 24 in (60 cm) long, marked with five to seven dark vertical bands. It is found in warm and tropical seas, accompanying ships and large fish, especially sharks, to feed on parasites and scraps of food. Family: *Carangidae*; order: *Perciformes*.

pilot whale A gregarious toothed *whale, *Globicephala melaena*. Growing up to 20 ft (6 m), pilot whales are black with a blunt head, narrow tapering flippers, and a broad dorsal fin. They were named by fishermen who found groups of them near herring shoals. Family: *Globicephalidae*.

Pilsen. *See* Plzeň.

Piłsudski, Józef Klemens (1867–1935) Polish statesman, who fought for Polish independence. Piłsudski formed three Polish legions, which fought against Russia in World War I. When Germany refused to guarantee Polish sovereignty, Piłsudski withdrew his support and was imprisoned. After Germany's defeat he declared Poland independent and served as head of state (1919–27). In 1926 he established a military dictatorship, remaining in power until his death.

Piltdown man Skeletal remains once thought to be those of a fossil *hominid, found on Piltdown Common, near Lewes (England), in 1912. In 1953–54 the "find" was shown to be a hoax or fraud. Analysis showed the skull to be made up of a human cranium and an ape's jaw, stained to simulate age. Extinct animal bones and tools had also been placed in the site.

pimento. *See* allspice.

pimpernel A slender annual or perennial herb of the genus *Anagallis* (about 20 species), found in Eurasia, Africa, and America, especially the annual scarlet pimpernel (*A. arvensis*). Growing 2–12 in (5–30 cm) tall, pimpernels have simple leaves and small red, pink, blue, or white bell-shaped flowers with five petals, borne individually on slender stalks. The fruit is a capsule, which opens by a round lid. The yellow pimpernel (*Lysimachia nemorum*) belongs to a closely related genus. Family: *Primulaceae*.

Pinchot, Gifford (1865–1946) US conservationist and politician. He was responsible for the first systematic approach to forest management in the US and became US Forest Service head in 1898. During his tenure (1898–1910) he estblished national forests and guidelines for privately owned forests. After unsuccessful bids for the Republican presidential nomination (1912) and the US Senate (1914), he served as commissioner of forestry in Pennsylvania (1920–22) and as governor of Pennsylvania (1923–27; 1931–35); he also taught forestry at Yale University (1903–36).

Pinckney, Charles (1757–1824) US statesman. He represented South Carolina in the *Constitutional Convention (1787) and his proposals for the new US government—the Pinckney plan—were included in the constitution. He served as governor of South Carolina (1789–92, 1796–98, 1806–08) and as a US senator (1798–1801) and a representative (1819–21). His cousins were **Charles Cotesworth Pinckney** (1746–1825), who was minister to France (1796), and **Thomas Pinckney** (1750–1828), who negotiated **Pinckney's Treaty** (the Treaty of San Lorenzo) with Spain in 1795, determining the boundary between US and Spanish possessions in America at 31°N latitude.

Pindar (518–438 BC) Greek poet. Born into an aristocratic family in Boeotia in central Greece, he was educated in Athens and lived in Sicily for two years from 476 BC. Of his 17 books of choral lyrics only four survive. These contain Epinician Odes written in honor of victors of athletic games and noted for their exalted style and deep religious feeling. He was acclaimed by the ancient Greeks as their greatest poet.

Pindus Mountains (Modern Greek name: Píndhos Óros) A range of mountains extending some 311 mi (500 km) NW–SE across W Greece and S Albania and rising to 8652 ft (2637 m) at Mount Smólikas.

pine A coniferous tree of the genus *Pinus* (about 80 species), widely distributed in the N hemisphere. Pines have long slender needles, usually in clusters of two, three, or five, and hanging cones, of variable shape, made up of overlapping woody scales. Pines are important softwoods: the timber is easily worked and yields turpentine, tar, pitch, and other resinous products. Commercially important and widely planted species include the Scots pine (*P. sylvestris*), of N and W Europe and Asia, up to 131 ft (40 m) high (□tree); the Monterey pine (*P. radiata*), from Monterey, California, up to 115 ft (35 m) high; the shore pine (*P. contorta*), of W North America, up to 80 ft (25 m) high; the Corsican pine (*P. nigra* var *maritima*), up to 148 ft (45 m) high; and the maritime pine (*P. pinaster*), of W Mediterranean regions and N Africa, up to 115 ft (35 m) high. These and other species are also planted for shelter and ornament and some species have edible seeds (*see* stone pine). Family: *Pinaceae*. *See also* bristlecone pine.

A number of other unrelated conifers are called pines, including species of *Araucaria*, the *cypress pine, and the *kauri pine.

pineal gland A small gland within the brain. In the 18th century it was supposed to be the site of the soul. In some lower animals, for example certain lizards, it is receptive to light and is visible externally as a third eye (pineal eye); in man its function is unknown, although it may help to regulate the onset of puberty.

pineapple A perennial herbaceous plant, *Ananas comosus*, native to tropical and subtropical America and cultivated in many warm and tropical regions for its fruit. It reaches a height of 40 in (1 m) and bears a rosette of 30–40 stiff succulent toothed leaves on a thick fleshy stem. Purplish flowers occur at the center of the rosette and—with their bracts—fuse to form the composite fruit, which ripens 5–6 months after flowering begins and can weigh up to 22 lb (10 kg). It takes nearly two years for a plant to bear its first marketable fruit. The major producing countries are the Hawaiian Islands, Brazil, Mexico, Cuba, and the Philippines. Family: *Bromeliaceae*.

pine marten A European carnivorous mammal, *Martes martes*. About 27.5 in (70 cm) long, it inhabits dense evergreen forests, preying on squirrels, birds, insects, and eggs. As with other *martens, the female has a litter

(2–5 cubs) only every second year, a disadvantage for a species widely hunted for fur.

Pinero, Sir Arthur Wing (1855–1934) British dramatist. He abandoned his law studies to become an actor. His early plays, which included *The Magistrate* (1885) and *Dandy Dick* (1887), were hugely successful farces that exploited his professional knowledge of stagecraft. His later plays, notably *The Second Mrs Tanqueray* (1893), were more serious treatments of contemporary social problems.

pink One of several usually perennial herbaceous plants derived from *Dianthus plumarius* and often grown as fragrant garden ornamentals. They have long slender leaves and showy white, pink, or red flowers, often with fringed petals. Family: *Caryophyllaceae*.

Pinkerton, Allan (1819–84) US detective, born in Scotland. He emigrated to the US in 1842. He founded the Pinkerton National Detective Agency in 1850 and organized an intelligence service for the Union during the Civil War.

pinkeye. *See* conjunctivitis.

pink salmon A *salmon, *Oncorhynchus gorbuscha*, also called humpback salmon, found in the North Pacific. It is 16–20 in (40–50 cm) long and marked with large irregular spots. It undertakes the shortest migration of all the salmon and the male develops a hump on its back during the breeding season.

Pinochet, Augusto (1915–) Chilean general and head of state (1973–). He led a military coup that overthrew the government of Salvador *Allende and became the head of a repressive military junta.

Pinsk 52 08N 26 01E A port in the W Soviet Union, in the Belorussian SSR at the confluence of the Pina and Pripet Rivers. A medieval Russian principality, it came under Lithuania (13th century), Poland (16th century), Russia again (1793), and Poland again (1920–39); ceded then to the Soviet Union, it was occupied by the Germans in World War II. Timber, shipbuilding, and metalworking are the principal activities. Population (1970): 61,752.

pintail A *duck, *Anas acuta*, occurring in the N hemisphere, that breeds on inland areas and winters in coastal areas. The male is 28 in (70 cm) long and has a dark-brown head and neck with a white band down the neck, gray flanks, and long black central tail feathers. Females have mottled brown plumage and both sexes have a blue-gray bill.

Pinter, Harold (1930–) British dramatist. His first full-length play, *The Birthday Party* (1958), failed until he had established his reputation with his second, *The Caretaker* (1960), a study of suspicion between a tramp and two brothers. Later plays include *The Homecoming* (1965), *Old Times* (1971), and *Betrayed* (1978). He uses elliptical dialogue to evoke an atmosphere of tension and ambiguity that is rarely explicitly resolved. He has also written film scripts and directed plays.

pinto A horse whose coat consists of sharply defined patches of white and a darker color—either black (piebald pattern) or brown, bay, dun, or roan (skewbald pattern). A pinto may be predominantly white (tobiano pattern) or mainly dark with white splashes (overo pattern). Pintos were commonly used by American Indians. Height: 5 ft (1.42 m) minimum (14 hands).

Pinturicchio (Bernardino di Betto; c. 1454–1513) Italian Renaissance painter, born in Perugia. He was influenced chiefly by *Perugino, whom he probably assisted on frescoes for the Sistine Chapel in the Vatican, where he later decorated the Borgia apartments (1492–94). His other major fresco cycle (1503–08) is in the cathedral library, Siena.

pinworm A slender parasitic *nematode worm, *Enterobius vermicularius*, also called seatworm or threadworm. Up to 0.4 in (1 cm) long, pinworms are white and inhabit the human intestine; they are common in Europe and America. Female worms migrate to the anus to lay thousands of eggs, causing itching, especially at night. The eggs are resistant to drying and to many disinfectants.

pinyin. *See* Chinese.

pion A group of three elementary particles (*see* particle physics) classified as *mesons (symbol: π). The charged pions (π+ and π-) have a mass of 139.6 MeV, the neutral pion (π°) a mass of 136 MeV. The *strong interaction can be represented by the exchange of virtual pions between particles (*see* virtual particle).

Pioneer probes A series of US solar-system space probes, first launched in 1958. Pioneers 4 to 9 went into solar orbit, monitoring solar activity in the 1960s and early 1970s. Pioneers 10 and 11 flew past and studied Jupiter in 1973 and 1974. Pioneer 11 approached Saturn in 1979. Two **Pioneer Venus** probes reached Venus in 1978.

p'i-p'a An ancient Chinese *lute. It is short, with a shallow pear-shaped body and has four silk strings. It is held upright in the lap and played with a plectrum. Poets of the Tang dynasty (618–906 AD) played it to accompany their poems; it is still a popular instrument.

pipal. *See* bo tree.

pipefish One of several slender long-bodied fish belonging to the family *Syngnathidae* (*see also* sea horse). 1–20 in (2.5–50 cm) long, it has a long tubular snout with a small mouth and lives among aquatic plants mainly in warm marine waters, feeding on small organisms. The males carry the young until they hatch. Order: *Gasterosteiformes*.

Piper, John (1903–) British painter and writer. Although he painted abstract works in the 1930s, he is best known for his watercolors and aquatints of architecture, such as Windsor Castle (1941–42). He has also designed stained glass, notably for Coventry Cathedral, and stage sets.

pipistrelle A small insect-eating *bat belonging to the genus *Pipistrellus* (50 species) with a worldwide distribution. The Eurasian pipistrelle (*P. pipistrellus*) is about 1.3 in (3.5 cm) long with a 8-in (20-cm) wingspan. It often flies near houses where insects are attracted to light. Pipistrelles have a prehensile tail, used when crawling into crevices to roost. Family: *Vespertilionidae*.

pipit A small insectivorous songbird of the genus *Anthus* (30 species), 5.5–6 in (14–16 cm) long with a brown-streaked plumage and paler speckled underparts. The meadow pipit (*A. pratensis*) occurs on moors and downs in Britain and is the chief prey of the *merlin. The water pipit (*A. spinoletta*) inhabits the high mountains of Eurasia and North America; it is also found in coastal regions, when it is known as the rock pipit. The Antarctic pipit (*A. antarcticus*) is the only passerine land bird in Antarctica. Family: *Motacillidae* (wagtails and pipits).

Piraeus (Modern Greek name: Piraiévs) 37 57N 23 42E The chief port of Greece, SW of Athens on the Saronic Gulf. It was founded during the 5th century BC as the port of Athens. Following the bombings of World War II extensive industrial renewal has taken place; industries include shipbuilding, oil refining, and chemicals. Its exports include wine and olive oil. Population (1971): 187,362.

Pirandello, Luigi (1867–1936) Italian dramatist and novelist. He was born in Sicily and studied philology in Germany. In 1903 his wife became insane, and his writing was greatly influenced by his life with her. He gained international success with his plays exploring the nature of reality and illusion, notably *Six Characters in Search of an Author* (1921) and *Henry IV* (1922). His other works include the novel *The Late Mattia Pascal* (1904) and the critical study *Humour* (1908). He won the Nobel Prize in 1934.

Piranesi, Giambattista (1720–78) Italian etcher, born in Venice. Initially trained as an architect and stage designer, he achieved a wide reputation with his prints of Rome and its ruins. As an archeologist and champion of the superiority of Roman architecture over Greek (*compare* Winckelmann, Johann Joachim), he was an important figure in early *neoclassicism, although his imaginative and dramatic style, particularly in the *Carceri d'invenzione* (*Imaginary Prisons*), anticipates *Romanticism.

piranha A freshwater fish, also called caribe and piraya, belonging to a genus (*Serrasalmus*) found in South America. It has a deep body, up to 24 in (60 cm) long, ranging from silver to black in color, strong jaws, and razor-sharp teeth. Piranhas swim in groups and feed voraciously on other fish; they will also attack larger animals, including man. Family: *Characidae* (*see* characin).

Pirani gauge A pressure gauge used for measuring low gas pressures. It consists of an electrically heated wire placed in the gas. The rate at which the gas conducts heat away from the wire depends on its pressure; the pressure is measured by observing the resistance of the wire at a fixed voltage or observing the voltage at a fixed resistance.

Pisa 43 43N 10 24E A city in Italy, in Tuscany on the Arno River. Dating from Etruscan times, it developed into a thriving maritime republic (11th–12th centuries) but declined in importance after it fell to the Florentines in 1509. It is the birthplace of Galileo, who taught at the university (founded in 1343). The most famous of its buildings is the Leaning Tower of Pisa, which is 180 ft (55 m) high and about 17 ft (5 m) out of perpendicular. Other notable buildings include the cathedral (11th–12th centuries) and the baptistry (12th–13th centuries). Its many historic monuments make it a popular tourist center. Machinery, textiles, bicycles, and glass are manufactured. Population (1980 est): 103,252.

Pisanello (Antonio Pisano; c. 1395–c. 1455) Italian *international gothic painter, draftsman, and medalist. He worked on frescoes, begun by *Gentile da Fabriano, in Venice and Rome. His portrait medals, influenced by Roman and Greek coins, were popular in court circles, particularly in Ferrara. In such paintings as the *Vision of St Eustace* (National Gallery, London) he recreated the world of chivalry.

Pisano, Andrea   (Andrea de Pontedera; c. 1290–1348) Italian sculptor. Unrelated to Nicola and Giovanni *Pisano, Andrea worked chiefly in Florence, where he succeeded Giotto as architect of the cathedral (1336). His most important works are the bronze reliefs of the life of St John for the south doors of the Baptistry.

Pisano, Nicola   (c. 1220–c. 1278) Italian sculptor. He initiated the revival of antique Roman forms that led eventually to Renaissance sculpture, beginning with his pulpit in the Baptistry, Pisa. Such later works as the pulpit in Siena Cathedral and the fountain in the main square of Perugia reveal the cooperation of his son **Giovanni Pisano** (c. 1250–1314). Giovanni introduced French gothic elements into his sculptures for the façade of Siena Cathedral and his pulpit for S Andrea, Pistoia. He returned to a more classical style in his pulpit for Pisa Cathedral.

Pisces   (Latin: Fish)   A large inconspicuous constellation that lies on the *zodiac between Aries and Aquarius, mainly in the N sky. It contains the vernal *equinox.

Pisistratus   (c. 600–c. 528 BC) Athenian tyrant. After several ultimately abortive attempts to seize power in Athens, Pisistratus succeeded in 546 with a mercenary army. As tyrant, he diminished the power of landed aristocrats by instituting circuit judges to adjudicate local cases. Pisistratus encouraged Athenian agriculture and commerce and his benevolent tyranny promoted the national unity necessary for the later development of democracy.

Pissarro, Camille   (1830–1903) French impressionist painter, born in the West Indies. After running away to Venezuela to become an artist, he was sent by his parents to Paris (1855). He trained in the École des Beaux-Arts, and the Académie Suisse, where he met *Monet. Chiefly influenced by *Corot, he was more interested in landscape structure than the other impressionists. He participated in all eight of the impressionist exhibitions (1874–86) and is noted for his encouragement of younger painters, especially *Cézanne and *Gauguin. In the 1880s he experimented with *pointillism. His son **Lucien Pissarro** (1863–1944) was also a painter.

pistachio   A small aromatic tree, *Pistacia vera*, native to central Eurasia and widely cultivated in Mediterranean regions for its edible green kernels ("nuts"). Growing 23–33 ft (7–10 m) high, it has compound leaves with 1–5 pairs of leathery leaflets and drooping spikes of small male and female flowers, borne usually on separate trees. The oval white fruits, 0.6–0.8 in (1.5–2 cm) long, often split to expose the kernels, which are used as dessert nuts and for decorating and flavoring confectionery, cakes, etc. Family: *Anacardiaceae*.

pistil   The part of a flower consisting of the female reproductive organs. It consists of one or more *carpels, which may be united into a single structure. Some plants, such as the cucumber, have separate male and female flowers: the latter are described as pistillate.

Pistoia   43 56N 10 55E   A city in N central Italy, in Tuscany. *Catiline was killed in battle near here (62 BC). The 12th-century cathedral contains a famous silver altar. Population (1971 est): 94,000.

pistol   A short-range *small arm that can be used with one hand. It evolved from a small cavalry matchlock in the 15th century, later improvements following those of the □musket. The need to make a weapon that would fire more than once without reloading led to the division of pistols into two classes: the *revolver and the automatic. The first revolver (c. 1540) had multiple barrels, which were rotated by hand past the lock. However, the first successful revolver was the *Colt of 1835, in which a magazine chamber revolves behind a single barrel. The first automatics (1893) combined a box magazine in the butt with a recoil loading action. The *Luger 9 mm automatic went into service with the German navy in 1904 and remained the standard weapon until 1938.
Both revolvers and automatics are still in military and police use throughout the world.

Pitcairn Islands   A small island group in the central S Pacific Ocean, a British dependent territory, consisting of Pitcairn Island and three uninhabited islands. Subsistence agriculture is the chief occupation; fruit, vegetables, and souvenirs are sold to passing ships. *History*: Pitcairn Island was occupied in 1790 by mutineers from the *Bounty* and women from Tahiti. By 1856 the island was overpopulated and the inhabitants were moved to Norfolk Island; some later returned. Area: 1.75 sq mi (4.6 sq km). Population (1981): 63. Chief town: Adamstown.

17th-century English wheellock pistol.

18th-century Scottish flintlock with ram's-horn butt.

Colt 45 revolver first produced in 1873 and still in use.

Colt 45 automatic.

PISTOL

pitch (chemistry)   A black or dark-brown residue resulting from the partial evaporation or fractional distillation of coal tars or tar products. The term is sometimes used for the residue obtained from petroleum distillation (bitumen) or for the naturally occurring petroleum residue (asphalt). Bitumen is a mixture of heavy hydrocarbons with a high proportion of free carbon. It is used as a binding agent (it is the main constituent of road tars), as a protective coating in bituminous paints, in roofing felts, and as a fuel.

pitch (music)   The highness or lowness of a note, depending on the frequency of the vibrations producing it. Standard pitch has varied through the centuries: Handel's still extant *tuning fork gives A as 422.5 Hz. Modern **concert pitch** was standardized by international agreement in 1939, and the frequency of the note A was fixed at 440 Hz. **Perfect pitch** is the ability to recognize and name notes by ear alone; since notes have no absolute pitch value, even this depends on relative frequencies. *See also* temperament.

pitchblende   The chief ore of uranium, a massive form of uraninite, UO_2, a black radioactive mineral found in hydrothermal veins and as an accessory mineral in acid igneous rocks. It occurs in North America, Africa, Australia, and central Europe.

Pitcher, Molly   (Mary Ludwig Hays McCauley; 1754–1832) American Revolution heroine. Married to John Casper Hays, an artilleryman, she carried water to him and other troops during the Battle of Monmouth (1778) and took over her husband's cannon when he was wounded. After his death in 1789, she married George McCauley. It was not until 1822 that she was officially recognized as a heroine of the Revolution.

pitcher plant   Any *carnivorous plant with pitcher-shaped leaves, belonging mainly to the families *Nepenthaceae* and *Sarraceniaceae*. The pitcher is often brightly colored and secretes nectar to attract insects, which often fall inside and drown in the digestive juices at the bottom of the pitcher. The *Nepenthaceae* comprises herbs and shrubs of the Old World, many of which are climbers. Their leaf tendrils are swollen to form the pitcher, 2–12 in (5–30 cm) long. The *Sarraceniaceae* are perennial herbs of the New World with rosettes of pitchers arising from a swollen underground stem.

Pithecanthropus   A group of extinct Pleistocene *hominids, now generally called *Homo erectus* (see Homo). The name *Pithecanthropus* (literally apeman) was coined by *Haeckel before any supporting fossil evidence was found for the evolutionary link.

Pitman, Sir Isaac.   *See* shorthand.

pitot tube   A type of *anemometer for measuring the velocity of a fluid, invented by Henri Pitot (1695–1771). It consists of an L-shaped tube placed in the moving fluid; the vertical limb of the tube has an opening facing into the flow. The difference in pressure between the interior of the tube and the surroundings enables the velocity of the fluid to be calculated. The device is used to measure the velocity of liquids, aircraft airspeeds, etc.

Pittosporum A genus of small evergreen trees (about 150 species), called parchment-bark or Australian laurels, native to Australia and New Zealand and often grown as ornamentals. They have long pale leathery leaves and blue, white, yellow, or red flowers. *P. tenuifolium* is popular in flower arrangements. Family: *Pittosporaceae*.

Pitt-Rivers, Augustus Henry Lane Fox (1827–1900) British anthropologist and archeologist. Pitt-Rivers formed a major anthropological collection in his pioneering work on establishing typological sequences for artifacts from different cultures and eras. After 1880 he excavated prehistoric and Romano-British remains in S England.

Pittsburgh 40 26N 80 00W A city in Pennsylvania, at the confluence of the Allegheny and Monongahela Rivers, which here form the Ohio River. Settled in 1758, it was the site of Fort Pitt completed by the British in 1761. The city was founded in 1764. It is the site of several colleges and universities, including the University of Pittsburgh (1787) and the famous Carnegie Institute, which contains a two-million-volume library, several museums, and the Carnegie Music Hall. Pittsburgh has grown as a major center of the steel industry and is the country's largest inland port. Other manufactures include machinery, petroleum, coal, glass, and chemicals. Population (1980): 423,938.

Pittsfield 42 27N 73 15W A city in W central Massachusetts, on the Housatonic River, in the Taconic Mountains. Settled in 1753, it is a popular resort and tourist attraction. The Shaker Village at Hancock is nearby. Population (1980): 51,974.

Pitt the Elder, William, 1st Earl of Chatham (1708–78) British statesman, known as the Great Commoner. Entering parliament in 1735, he established a reputation as an outstanding orator. As paymaster general (1746–55) he was notable for his incorruptibility. In 1756 he became secretary of state and leader of the House of Commons but was dismissed in 1757 and then recalled to form a government with *Newcastle. In charge of foreign affairs, he was largely responsible for British victory in the *Seven Years' War. Forced to resign in 1761, he returned to form a new government in 1766. Plagued by ill health, he resigned in 1768.
His second son **William Pitt the Younger** (1759–1806) was twice prime minister (1783–1801, 1804–06), the youngest in British history. He entered parliament in 1781 and became chancellor of the exchequer in 1782. As prime minister he inherited an enormous public debt, which he reduced by a fiscal policy influenced by Adam *Smith. He introduced new taxes, overhauled customs duties, and introduced a new sinking fund. He also reformed the Indian administration (*see* Government of India Acts). Pitt negotiated the first (1793) and second (1798) coalitions against France (*see* Revolutionary and Napoleonic Wars) and resolved the crisis caused by the Irish rebellion in 1798 by union of Britain and Ireland in 1800. He resigned following George III's refusal to accept Catholic emancipation. His second ministry was marked by an alliance with Russia, Sweden, and Austria against Napoleon, which collapsed shortly before his death in office.

pituitary gland A small *endocrine gland, about 0.5 in by 0.3 in (12 mm by 8 mm), lying within the skull close to the center of the head. The anterior (front) lobe produces *growth hormone, *prolactin, and hormones that regulate the function of other glands, notably the *thyroid and *adrenal glands and the ovary and testis. The posterior (back) lobe is a downgrowth from the *hypothalamus and stores various neurohormones that are synthesized in this part of the brain. The pituitary is therefore the master endocrine gland, from which neural control of the entire endocrine system is effected.

pit viper A New World viper, belonging to the subfamily *Crotalinae*, that has a sensory pit between the eye and nostril used to detect the tiny changes in temperature caused by warm-blooded prey nearby. Pit vipers occur in habitats ranging from deserts to rain forests and are chiefly ground-dwellers. *See also* bushmaster; copperhead; fer-de-lance; rattlesnake; sidewinder; water moccasin.

Pius II (Enea Silvio (*or* Aeneas Silvius) de' Piccolomini; 1405–64) Pope (1458–64), who was also a notable humanist. He served Emperor Frederick III as both imperial poet and secretary before becoming a priest (1446). On his election he attempted to restore papal authority by condemning the view that general councils had supreme authority in the Church. His proclamation of a crusade against the Turks after the fall of Constantinople (1453) was ignored by the secular powers and he died shortly after resolving to lead it in person.

Pius IV (Giovanni Angelo de' Medici; 1499–1565) Pope (1559–65). He continued papal support of the *Counter-Reformation, presiding over the last session of the Council of *Trent and reforming the Sacred College of cardinals.

Pius V, St (Michele Ghislieri; 1504–72) Pope (1566–72). A Dominican friar and noted for his asceticism, he was the greatest of the 16th-century reformer popes. Pius re-edited a number of liturgical texts, including the breviary and missal, enforced the decrees of the Council of *Trent, and expanded the activities of the *Inquisition. He excommunicated the Protestant Elizabeth I of England in 1570. He was canonized in 1712. Feast day: May 6.

Pius VI (Giovanni Angelico Braschi; 1717–99) Pope (1775–99). His pontificate was marked by attempts to combat growing opposition to papal control from both national churches and states, especially in France, where he condemned the state church established during the French Revolution. Pius was captured in the Revolutionary Wars, during which the French attacked the papal states, and died a prisoner.

Pius VII (Gregorio Barnaba Chiaramonti; 1740–1823) Pope (1800–23), who made several unsuccessful attempts to preserve papal privileges in the face of Napoleon's demands. In 1804, under duress, he consecrated Napoleon emperor and in 1809, after the French conquest of Rome, was taken prisoner and forced to make extensive concessions in the Concordat of Fontainebleau (1813). After Napoleon's fall in 1815 Pius gained the restoration of the papal states and negotiated concordats with many of the victorious powers.

Pius IX (Giovanni Maria Mastai-Ferretti; 1792–1878) Pope (1846–78). At first sympathetic to liberal and nationalist movements, he abandoned radicalism for reaction after the Revolution of 1848, in which he fled Rome. He refused to acknowledge the newly established kingdom of Italy, into which Rome was incorporated in 1870. He defined the Immaculate Conception (1854) and papal infallibility (1869–70) and his encyclical *Quanta Cura* (1864), with its *Syllabus of Errors*, condemned modernism in theology and philosophy.

Pius X, St (Giuseppe Sarto; 1835–1914) Pope (1903–14). His pontificate was marked by his defense of the Church's independence against encroachment by the state, support of social reforms (especially in the Catholic Action movement), reform of the liturgy, and a new codification of canon law. He condemned theological modernism and revolutionary political movements. He was canonized in 1954. Feast day: Sept 3.

Pius XI (Achille Ratti; 1857–1939) Pope (1922–39). He attempted to extend the educational and social work of the Church, supporting the role of the laity in the Catholic Action movement. He signed the *Lateran Treaty (1929), establishing the Vatican City as a sovereign state.

Pius XII (Eugenio Pacelli; 1876–1958) Pope (1939–58). Pius' failure to condemn fascism during World War II caused controversy, although he attempted to prevent the outbreak of war, to curb atrocities, and to relieve suffering. He was a staunch conservative both in politics and doctrine, condemning communism and modernist theology.

Pizarro, Francisco (c. 1475–1541) Spanish conquistador. He accompanied Balboa on the expedition that discovered the Pacific (1513) and in the 1520s explored the NW coast of South America. In 1531 having gained Emperor Charles V's assent to the conquest of Peru and an assurance of the major part of the spoils, he crossed the Andes to Cajamarca. There he treacherously murdered the Inca king, Atahuallpa. Over the next nine years he consolidated the Spanish conquest of the Inca empire, founding Lima in 1535. He came into conflict with a fellow conquistador, Diego de Almagro (c. 1475–1538), who was defeated and put to death; his followers, however, subsequently murdered Pizzaro.

PK. *See* telekinesis.

placenta 1. An organ formed within the womb of mammals and other viviparous animals during pregnancy, composed of fetal and maternal tissues. Within the placenta the blood vessels of the fetus and mother come into close contact, enabling exchange of substances in the blood. Thus the fetus receives nutrients, oxygen, and antibodies from the mother's blood and its waste products are absorbed into the mother's circulation. The fetus is attached to the placenta by the umbilical cord. The placenta also secretes hormones that contribute to the control of pregnancy. The placenta is expelled (as the afterbirth) shortly after the baby is delivered. 2. A tissue in plants that connects the ovules (later the seeds) to the ovary (later the fruit wall).

Placodermi An extinct class of fish that lived from the Devonian to the Permian periods (415–240 million years ago). Their bodies, usually 4–16 in (10–40 cm) long, were covered with bony scales, particularly over the head and front half, and had a bony skeleton, primitive jaws, gill covers (opercula), and median and paired fins. Many species were bottom-dwelling carnivores.

plagioclase A group of *feldspar minerals with compositions varying between the two end-members albite ($NaAlSi_3O_8$) and anorthite ($CaAl_2Si_2O_8$). They are milky white or colorless, and occur both as phenocrysts and in the groundmass of most basic and intermediate igneous rocks and in many metamorphic rocks.

plague An infectious disease caused by the bacterium *Pasteurella pestis*, which is transmitted to man by rat fleas. There are three forms of the disease, the most common of which is bubonic plague, in which fever, vomiting, and headache are accompanied by swollen inflamed lymph nodes (buboes). The more severe pneumonic and septicemic plagues develop when the bacteria enter the lungs and bloodstream respectively. Plague is treated with antibiotics. Epidemics of plague afflicted Europe throughout the middle ages, the *Black Death of 1348 being the most devastating.

plaice A commercially important *flatfish, *Pleuronectes platessa*, that occurs in the N North Atlantic and British coastal waters. It is usually 10–16 in (25–40 cm) long, occasionally up to 35 in (90 cm), and is colored brown with bright-red or orange spots above and white beneath. There are four to seven bony warts running backward from the eyes.

plainchant (*or* plainsong) The ritual music of the early Christian Church, as distinct from later polyphonic music. It consists of unaccompanied melodic lines deriving from natural intonation, with flexible rhythms to fit the Latin prose of the daily services. Probably initially influenced by Jewish liturgical chant, its melodic basis derived from the Greek system of *modes. At the end of the 6th century, during the papacy of Gregory I, it was codified as *Gregorian chant and flourished with few changes until the advent of harmonized melody in about 1000.

plains-wanderer An Australian bird, *Pedionomus torquatus*, of dry grassland regions. 4–5 in (10–13 cm) long, it has short rounded wings, a short tail, and a mottled red-brown plumage with a white throat and a collar of black spots. Largely ground-dwelling, it feeds on plant material and insects and is the only member of its family (*Pedionomidae*). Order: *Gruiformes* (cranes, rails, etc.).

planarian A free-living *flatworm of the order *Tricladida*, occurring in marine and freshwater habitats of temperate regions. Flattened and symmetrical, with simple eyespots and olfactory organs, planarians range from 0.08 in (2 mm) to 4 in (10 cm) in length. They glide smoothly by means of beating cilia (hairs) and use a long retractable feeding tube (pharynx) to consume small invertebrates. Class: *Turbellaria*.

Planck, Max Karl Ernst Ludwig (1858–1947) German physicist; the originator of *quantum theory, who was professor at Kiel University (1880–89) and then at the University of Berlin (1889–1926). Planck solved the problem of black-body radiation by assuming that the radiation was emitted in discrete amounts called quanta, the magnitude of a quanta being the product of the frequency of the radiation and a constant, now known as *Planck's constant. For this work he received the Nobel Prize in 1918. He remained in Germany during the Nazi period and attempted to intercede with Hitler on behalf of Jewish scientists. For this he was deprived of the presidency of the research institute that bears his name.

Planck's constant (*h*) A fundamental constant that relates the quantum of energy (*E*) of a photon to the frequency (*f*) of the corresponding electromagnetic radiation by the equation $E = hf$. Its value is $6.626,196 \times 10^{-34}$ joule second. Named for Max *Planck.

Planck's radiation law Electromagnetic radiation is emitted from and absorbed by matter in discrete amounts (quanta) known as *photons. The energy (*E*) of a photon is related to the frequency (*f*) of the radiation by the equation $E = hf$, where *h* is known as *Planck's constant. Max *Planck discovered the law (1900) while investigating the distribution of wavelengths of the radiation emitted by a *black body. It forms the basis of the *quantum theory.

planet A celestial body that moves around a star and shines by light reflected from its surface. The only known planets (*see* Barnard's star) are those orbiting the sun (□solar system): there are nine major planets and numerous *asteroids. The major planets in order from the sun are *Mercury, *Venus, *earth, and *Mars (the **terrestrial planets**), *Jupiter, *Saturn, *Uranus, and *Neptune (the **giant planets**) and, usually outermost, *Pluto.

planetarium 1. A complex instrument that projects an artificial but accurate picture of the night sky, showing planets, stars, and other celestial bodies, on the interior of a hemispherical dome. The dome forms the upper part of an auditorium. The images of the celestial bodies are produced by a considerable number of small optical projectors in the instrument. By moving the individual projectors at the correct speed, the bodies are made to follow their natural paths through the sky. 2. A building housing such an instrument. There are some 60 planetariums in the US.

planetary nebula A luminous cloud of gas cast off and expanding away from a dying star. It is a type of emission *nebula, being ionized by radiation from the hot central star.

planetary probe An unmanned spacecraft that studies conditions on and near one or more planets and their satellites and in the interplanetary medium along the flight path. The information gathered is then transmitted to earth. The transmitters, TV cameras, and other instruments are powered by solar cells or, for deep-space probes, by thermoelectric generators, etc. Midflight course corrections and attitude adjustments can be made by rocket motors. *See* Mariner; Pioneer; Venera; Viking; Voyager probes.

plane tree A large tree of the genus *Platanus* (10 species), native to the N hemisphere and often grown for shade and ornament. Up to 165 ft (50 m) tall, the trees have patchy peeling bark, large lobed leaves, and separate round clusters (catkins) of male and female flowers: the female flowers give rise to bristly round fruits. The London plane (*P.* × *acerifolia*) is a hybrid between the Oriental plane (*P. orientalis*) and North American buttonwood (*P. occidentalis*). The timber is a valuable hardwood used in carpentry. Family: *Platanaceae*.

planimeter A device for measuring small irregular plane areas. A moving arm is traced around a closed curve. The enclosed area is calculated from the revolution of a small wheel attached to the arm.

plankton Minute or microscopic animals (zooplankton) and plants (phytoplankton) that float and drift in the open waters of a sea or lake. The phytoplankton (diatoms and other algae) carry out *photosynthesis in the surface waters and so provide the basic food source for all aquatic animals. The zooplankton include protozoa, small crustaceans, and larvae (e.g. barnacle and fish larvae). Plankton are of great ecological and economic importance as a food source for fish and whales and thus—indirectly—to man, whose fishing industry depends upon them. □oceans.

plant A living organism belonging to the kingdom *Plantae*, of which there are some 400,000 or so species. Plants are typically immobile and most manufacture their own food from simple inorganic nutrients by *photosynthesis, trapping the energy required for the process in the green pigment chlorophyll. (Plants that lack chlorophyll, notably fungi, feed on organic materials.) Plant cells have rigid cell walls, providing support, and growth occurs from specialized zones of tissue (*see* meristem), continuously or periodically throughout life. Plants lack specialized sense organs and a nervous system; response to external stimuli is usually slow and often permanent. Unlike animals, there is considerable variation in form between individuals of the same species. Green plants are the primary source of food and oxygen for all animals.

Plantagenet The surname of the Angevin, Lancastrian, and Yorkist Kings of England (1154–1485). They were descended from Queen Matilda and Geoffrey Martel, Count of Anjou (d. 1151), who was nicknamed Plantagenet because he wore a sprig of broom (*plante genêt*) in his cap. The name was not formally adopted until the 15th century, when it was used by Richard Plantagenet, Duke of *York, to further his claim to the throne in the Wars of the Roses.

Plantagenet, Richard, Duke of York. *See* York, Richard Plantagenet, 3rd Duke of.

plantain 1. An annual or perennial herb of the genus *Plantago* (about 50 species), occurring in temperate regions and on mountains in the tropics, often as a troublesome weed. Plantains have a basal rosette of simple leaves from which arise a stalk, 1.2–27.5 in (3–70 cm) high, bearing a dense terminal head of inconspicuous green, white, yellow, or brown flowers with protruding stamens. The leaves of the greater plantain (*P. major*) of Eurasia are used to treat insect stings. Family: *Plantaginaceae*. 2. *See* banana.

Plantation of Ireland (1556–1660) The government-sponsored settlement of British families in Ireland in the 16th and 17th centuries. Conceived as a method of subjugating the rebellious Irish, the first plantations were not noticeably successful but the Ulster plantation (1608–11), composed of English and Scots, survived and prospered.

plant bug A plant-eating insect belonging to the families *Myridae* (*see* capsid) and *Lygaeidae* (*see* ground bug). The term may also refer to any other herbivorous insect of the suborder *Heteroptera* (*see* Hemiptera).

PLANT

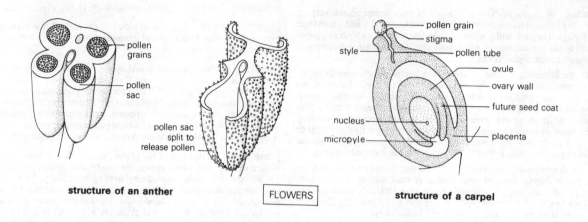

structure of an anther

pollen grains

pollen sac

pollen sac split to release pollen

FLOWERS

structure of a carpel

pollen grain
stigma
style
pollen tube
ovule
ovary wall
future seed coat
nucleus
placenta
micropyle

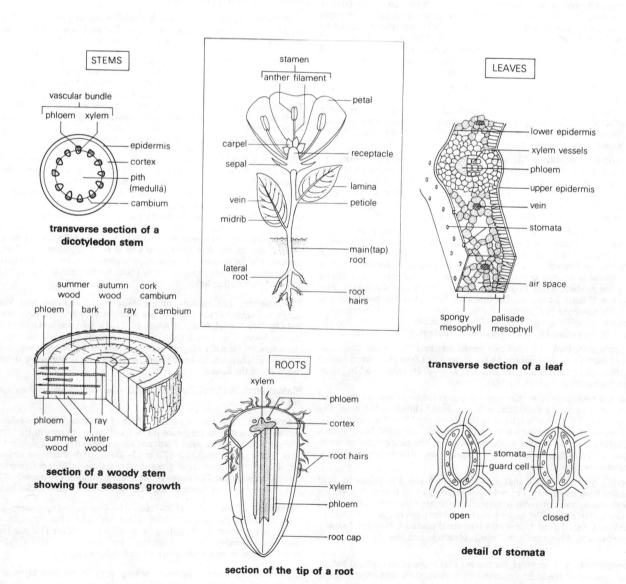

STEMS

transverse section of a dicotyledon stem

vascular bundle
phloem — xylem
epidermis
cortex
pith (medullá)
cambium

section of a woody stem showing four seasons' growth

summer wood — autumn wood — cork cambium
phloem — bark — ray — cambium
phloem — ray
summer wood — winter wood

stamen
anther filament
petal
carpel
receptacle
sepal
lamina
vein
petiole
midrib
main(tap) root
lateral root
root hairs

ROOTS

xylem
phloem
cortex
root hairs
xylem
phloem
root cap

section of the tip of a root

LEAVES

transverse section of a leaf

lower epidermis
xylem vessels
phloem
upper epidermis
vein
stomata
air space
spongy mesophyll — palisade mesophyll

detail of stomata

stomata
guard cell
open   closed

broad category	major groups (usually divisions)	important classes	representative members
ALGAE	Chlorophyta		green algae (*Spirogyra*, sea lettuce, etc.)
	Chrysophyta		yellow-green algae, diatoms
	Phaeophyta		brown algae (wracks, kelps, etc.)
	Rhodophyta		red algae
FUNGI	Myxomycophyta		slime fungi (clubroot, etc.)
	Eumycophyta	Phycomycetes	pin mold
		Ascomycetes	*Penicillium, Aspergillus*
		Basidiomycetes	mushrooms, puffballs, bracket fungi
MOSSES and LIVERWORTS	Bryophyta	Hepaticae	liverworts (e.g. *Pellia*)
		Musci	mosses (e.g. *Sphagnum*)
VASCULAR PLANTS (TRACHEOPHYTES)	Pteridophyta	Lycopsida	clubmosses
		Sphenopsida	horsetails
		Pteropsida	ferns
	Spermatophyta (seed plants)	Gymnospermae	cycads, *Ginkgo*, conifers (pines. larches, spruces, etc.)
		Angiospermae	monocotyledons (grasses, palms, orchids, lilies, etc.), dicotyledons (most trees and flowering plants)

PLANT *A simplified classification of the plant kingdom.*

plant hopper A plant-eating insect belonging to a family (*Fulgoridae*; over 5000 species) found mainly in tropical and subtropical regions. Plant hoppers are 0.40–2 in (10–50 mm) long and often brightly colored, with large unusually shaped heads. Some species are covered with a secretion of white waxy threads or powder. Suborder: *Homoptera*; order *Hemiptera. See also* lantern fly.

plasma (anatomy) The fluid constituent of *blood, in which the blood cells are suspended. Plasma consists of a solution of various salts, sugars, etc., and contains numerous proteins, including those involved in *blood clotting and the immunological response to infection (i.e. antibodies). It is obtained by centrifuging unclotted blood. *Compare* serum.

plasma (physics) A gas the atoms of which have been completely ionized. Sometimes called the fourth state of matter, plasmas occur at enormously high temperatures, such as those in the sun. Plasmas are also created in *thermonuclear reactors.

plasmapheresis A laboratory technique used in blood transfusions in which the fluid constituent (plasma) is separated from the donor's blood and the blood cells are returned to the donor. This technique allows the donor to provide plasma more frequently than would be possible if whole blood were removed, since it is only the red cells that the body requires time to replace. Plasma transfusions are particularly useful for hemophiliacs, who require frequent transfusions, since it contains the blood-clotting factors that they lack.

Plasmodium A genus of parasitic single-celled animals (*see* Protozoa) that cause *malaria in man. *Plasmodium* undergoes the sexual phase of its development in bloodsucking mosquitoes of the genus *Anopheles*, through which it is transmitted to man. Asexual division of the parasite occurs in human liver and red blood cells. Four species cause different forms of malaria: *P. falciparum* (causing the most severe kind), *P. vivax, P. malariae*, and *P. ovale.* Class: *Sporozoa.*

Plassey, Battle of (June 23, 1757) The battle in West Bengal (India) in which Robert *Clive defeated the Nawab of Bengal, Siraj-ud-Dawlah (c. 1728–57). Aided by the mutiny of the nawab's generals, Clive's victory made possible Britain's acquisition of Bengal.

plaster A paste used to give a smooth hard coating to ceilings, walls, etc. A number of formulations are in use, the traditional one being a mixture of lime, sand, and water, which hardens in air owing to drying and reaction with atmospheric carbon dioxide.

plaster of Paris A hydrated form of calcium sulfate ($CaSO_4 \cdot \frac{1}{2}H_2O$) made by partial dehydration of *gypsum by heating. When mixed with water it sets into a hard mass by formation of the dihydrate ($CaSO_4 \cdot 2H_2O$). It is used for casts for broken limbs and for modeling.

plasticity The permanent deformation of a substance after being subjected to a sufficiently large stress. Below a certain stress, called the elastic limit, most substances will recover their original shape when the stress is removed. Such substances are said to be elastic (*see* elasticity). However, single crystals of certain metals are plastic no matter how small the stress.

plastics Synthetic materials that consist of polymers (*see* polymerization) and are molded during manufacture. Plastics are made from synthetic *resins. **Thermosetting plastics** harden on heating to give a rigid product that cannot then be softened. *Polyurethanes, *polyesters, *silicones, and *epoxy resins all form thermosetting plastics. **Thermoplastic materials** soften when heated and harden again when cooled. These include derivatives of *cellulose and polymers, such as *polyethylene, polystyrene, polyvinyl chloride, and polymethylmethacrylate, which contain a reactive double bond.

Natural polymers, such as *shellac and *rubber, have been known for many centuries. The first synthetic material was Celluloid, made in 1870 from cotton and camphor. This highly inflammable substance was replaced during World War I by cellulose acetate and casein products. These materials were all based on naturally occurring large molecules. The first polymers to be made by joining together smaller molecules were the phenol-formaldehyde resins (trade name Bakelite) invented in 1908 by Leo Baekeland (1863–1944). Since then a vast number of different resins have been synthesized.

plastic surgery The branch of surgery concerned with the correction of deformities, disfigurements, or other forms of damage to any part of the body. This includes the reconstruction of developmental defects, such as cleft palate, harelip, and club foot, and the repair of injuries (particularly those of the face) caused by fire, traffic accidents, or wounds. Great advances were made in this aspect of plastic surgery by Sir Archibald *McIndoe, during and after World War II. Cosmetic plastic surgery is performed simply to improve the appearance: an example is facelifting to remove wrinkles.

Plata, Río de la (English name: Plate River) The estuary of the Paraná River and the Uruguay River, on the Atlantic coast of SE South America between Uruguay and Argentina. Its shores are densely populated; Montevideo, the capital of Uruguay, lies on the N shore and Buenos Aires, the capital of Argentina, is situated on the S shore. A naval battle was fought off its mouth in December, 1939 (*see* World War II). Length: 171 mi (275 km). Width (at mouth): 140 mi (225 km).

Plataea An ancient city of Boeotia. Grateful for protection against Thebes, Plataea became Athens' permanent ally; Plataeans alone joined the Athenians at Marathon and they played a crucial role in the battle of Plataea (479 BC), where the allied Greek forces decisively defeated the Persians (*see* Greek-Persian Wars). During the Peloponnesian War Plataea suffered severely for its pro-Athenian policy, being besieged (429–427) and sacked by Sparta. Although rebuilt, it was again destroyed (by Thebes in 373) and then once more restored (by Philip of Macedon in the late 4th century BC).

Plate River. *See* Plata, Río de la.

plateau An extensive area of comparatively level elevated land, sometimes known as a tableland where it is bounded by steep slopes or scarps. It may be crossed by rivers and mountains. One of the world's highest is the Tibetan plateau.

platelet A small particle, 0.00004–0.00008 in (0.001–0.002 mm) in diameter, produced by the bone marrow and found in the □blood. Platelets are essential for *blood clotting, accumulating in large numbers at the site of an injured blood vessel. There are normally 150,000 to 400,000 platelets per cubic millimeter of blood. Absence of platelets causes severe bleeding and may occur in a variety of illnesses (e.g. liver disease).

platemaking The production of *printing plates. Original plates are made by hand engraving (for letterpress), drawing with wax crayons (for lithography), etc., or photographically. In one type of photographic process, metal with a photosensitive coating is exposed to light, usually through a film negative of the type, drawing, or photograph to be printed. The unexposed coating is then washed off and the bare metal underneath turned into nonprinting areas: with a letterpress plate it is etched away; with a typical lithographic plate it is wetted and made grease-repellent, while the exposed areas are inked to make them grease-receptive. A collotype plate has a photosensitive gelatin coating that is hardened, by exposure through a negative, in proportion to the amount of light falling on each area. Collotype can thus reproduce continuous tone, as in a photograph: the more any area is hardened, the less water it will absorb and the more ink it will accept and transfer to the paper. With gravure plates, the printing areas are etched away through an exposed gelatin layer. Continuous tone is simulated in letterpress and lithography by converting the image into a grid of dots of varying size called a half-tone and in gravure by varying the depth of the etched cells and thus the amount of ink that each transfers to the paper. Duplicate (letterpress) plates are made from original plates by one of two methods. In **stereotyping**, a mold (*or* matrix) is made, in which the duplicate is cast in metal or molded from rubber or plastic. In **electrotyping**, a thin layer of copper is deposited electrolytically in a matrix similar to that used in stereotyping and then itself filled with molten metal to make it rigid when the metal cools.

plate tectonics The theory, developed mainly in the 1960s, that the earth's crust is divided into rigid plates (oceanic, continental, or a combination of both), which move about the earth's surface at rates of 0.4–3.5 in (1–9 cm) per annum. The edges of the plates are called plate margins. At constructive plate margins new oceanic crust is created where two plates are moving apart and magma rises to fill the gap; this occurs at midocean ridges (*see* sea-floor spreading). At destructive plate margins two plates collide and one dips beneath the other, producing deep-sea trenches and the associated volcanic island arcs. Where two continental plates collide, mountain chains are formed. All the major structural features of the earth's surface and almost all seismic and volcanic activity can be ascribed to plate movements.

Plath, Sylvia (1932–63) US poet and writer. After college, she married poet Ted *Hughes and moved with their family of two children to England in 1959. She committed suicide in 1963. Her writings, partly autobiographical, tell of rebellion and psychological conflict. Her poetry is collected in *The Colossus and Other Poems* (1960) and *Ariel* (posthumously; 1968); her novels include *The Bell Jar* (1962). Letters to her mother (*Letters Home*; 1975) and her journals (Pulitzer Prize; 1982) were published posthumously.

platinum (Pt) A precious silver-white noble metal, known to the South American Indians. It is malleable, ductile, and has a high melting point. Platinum is found in nature in nickel ore, as about one part in two million of ore. It can absorb large quantities of hydrogen and is used as a *catalyst, particularly in contact process for making sulfuric acid. It is also used in thermocouple wires and in jewelry. It dissolves in *aqua regia to form chloroplatinic acid (H_2PtCl_6). Although unreactive, platinum also forms other compounds, including the hexafluoride (PtF_6), one of the most powerful oxidizing agents known. At no 78; at wt 195.09; mp 3225°F (1772°C); bp 6895 ± 180°F (3827± 100°C).

platinum-iridium An alloy of platinum and iridium that is highly resistant to heat and is used in instruments for measuring high temperatures.

Plato (429–347 BC) Greek philosopher. An Athenian nobleman, he was early disillusioned by both democrats and aristocrats. Seeing no hope for man unless rulers became philosophers or philosophers rulers, he became a devoted follower of *Socrates. After Socrates' death he traveled widely, apparently becoming acquainted with many distinguished thinkers. In 387 he returned to Athens and founded his *Academy. To this he devoted the rest of his life, except that in 367 and again soon afterward, he visited Sicily

to assist his friend, Dion, in his futile attempts to turn *Dionysius II, the young and unstable tyrant of Syracuse, into a philosopher, and Syracuse into a Platonic state. Some of Plato's poetry and all his prose works survive. Apart from 13 possibly spurious letters and the *Apology*, which purports to be Socrates' defense of himself before his judges, they are dramatic dialogues of outstanding literary merit. The early ones illustrate Socrates' character and philosophical methods, focusing especially on the question of whether virtue can be taught. The *Phaedo*, *Symposium*, and *Republic* of Plato's middle period develop Plato's mature views on such topics as metaphysics, love, and government, notably his theory of ideas (Forms), the perfect spiritual entities or prototypes of which the physical world is a feeble and imperfect copy. *See also* Platonism.

Platonism The philosophical tradition originating (c. 385 BC) in the Greek *Academy under *Plato. In the period of Middle Platonism (1st century BC–2nd century AD) interest centered on Plato's thought on God and the supersensible world. Subsequently the philosophers of Alexandria (*see* Plotinus) creatively systematized these and other aspects of their forerunners' work in *Neoplatonism. Works of Platonic character produced by such writers as St *Augustine of Hippo, *Boethius, and Macrobius transmitted Platonism to the medieval West. The impact of *Aristotelianism in the 13th century brought a temporary eclipse, but at the Renaissance Platonism, promoted by such scholars as *Ficino and *Nicolas of Cusa, reasserted itself and exercised enormous influence on artists and writers, such as *Botticelli and *Spenser, as well as on philosophers and theologians (*see also* Cambridge Platonists). Despite modern science's final debunking of Platonic cosmology, elements of Platonism still permeate western thought in areas as diverse as realist logic (*see* realism) and Christian *ethics.

Platt Amendment (1901) Legislation, part of the Army Appropriation Bill, that spelled out Cuban-American relations. Named for Connecticut Republican Senator Orville H. Platt (1827–1905), it provided for a US naval base in Cuba, insured US intervention in Cuban affairs when deemed necessary, and prohibited Cuba from negotiating treaties with any country other than the US. It was made a part of the Cuban-American Treaty in 1903 and repealed in 1934, when a new treaty, granting full independence for Cuba, was negotiated.

Platte River A river in the central US. Formed by the confluence of the North Platte and South Platte Rivers at North Platte, Neb, it flows generally E to join the Missouri River. It is unnavigable but is a source of irrigation and hydroelectric power. Length: 310 mi (499 km).

Platyhelminthes. *See* flatworm.

platypus. *See* duck-billed platypus.

Plauen 50 30N 12 07E A city in S East Germany, on the Weisse Elster River. Several old buildings remain despite damage done during World War II. Famous for lace making since the 15th century, Plauen is a center for textile manufacture and has a textile craft school. Population (1973 est): 81,024.

Plautus, Titus Maccius (c. 254–184 BC) Roman dramatist. He is traditionally believed to have worked as a craftsman in the theater before beginning, in middle age, his career as dramatist. His 21 surviving plays are all adapted from Greek *New Comedy writers, especially Menander and Philemon, and are noted for their robust humor and lively colloquial dialogue. His plays influenced the early development of comic drama by Shakespeare, Molière, and others.

player piano (*or* pianola) A mechanical piano in which the hammers are operated by an airflow produced by pedals or an electrically operated bellows and controlled by perforations on a rotating roll of paper. Rolls are either cut by a special machine attached to a piano and thus record an actual performance or they are produced mechanically. The player can control the volume and the speed by means of special levers.

playing cards Cards with pictures and symbols on one side, used in a wide variety of games, of which *bridge, *whist, *poker, *rummy, and *cribbage are the most popular. Modern cards derive from the *tarot pack; the 52-card French pack with suits of hearts, spades, diamonds, and clubs is now standard, the suits deriving from the tarot suits of cups, swords, money, and clubs respectively. Traditional German, Spanish, and Italian packs with variations in the number of cards and designs of the suits also derive from tarot cards. A connection has been suggested between the suits and the cup, sword, ring, and baton traditionally held by Hindu statues. Playing cards have long been used in divination and conjuring.

plebeians Romans other than the privileged *patricians. At first without civil rights, excluded from state and religious offices, and forbidden to marry patricians, in 493–92 the plebeians forced the Senate to appoint their own tribunes and an assembly. During the subsequent two centuries of conflict, the plebeians gradually gained admission to all Roman offices and the wealthy and ambitious among them merged with the patricians. Thus, from later Republican times, the term plebeian implied low social class.

plebiscite   A vote by the whole electorate on a particular issue. The term is usually used to refer to those *referendums held to decide to which state an area should belong. A plebiscite was first held by France in 1790–91 concerning the papal territory of Avignon.

Pléiade, La   A group of seven French writers in the 16th century who sought to liberate French poetry from medieval tradition. Their principles, deriving from the study of Greek, Latin, and Italian literature, were expounded in *Défense et illustration de la langue française* (1549) by Joachim du *Bellay, and their innovations included the introduction of the sonnet, the ode, and the alexandrine. Led by Pierre de *Ronsard, the group included du Bellay, J.-A. de Baïf (1532–89), Étienne Jodelle (c. 1532–73), Rémy Belleau (c. 1528–77), Pontus de Tyard (c. 1522–1605), and Jacques Peletier (1517–82; for whom the name of Jean Dorat (1508–88) was occasionally substituted by contemporaries).

Pleiades   A young open *star cluster in the constellation Taurus that contains several hundred stars, of which six are clearly visible to the naked eye. The brighter stars are surrounded by reflection *nebula. They were named for the seven daughters of *Atlas, who were changed by the gods into stars while being pursued by Orion.

Pleistocene epoch   The epoch of geological time between the Pliocene and the Holocene, at the beginning of the Quaternary period. It lasted from about 1.8 million to 10,000 years ago. It is often called the *Ice Age because during this time the earth experienced great fluctuations in temperature: cold glacial periods, when the ice margins advanced toward the equator, separated by warmer interglacials, when temperatures at times were higher than today. Four main ice advances are recognized in the Pleistocene. Fossils from the Pleistocene include horses, pigs, and elephants.

Plekhanov, Georgi Valentinovich   (1857–1918) Russian revolutionary and Marxist philosopher. Known as the "father of Russian Marxism," Plekhanov was instrumental in the creation (1898) of the Russian Social Democratic Workers' Party. He believed that Russia must pass through industrialization and capitalism before reaching socialism and came to side with the *Mensheviks against Lenin. After the Bolshevik victory, he lived in Finland.

pleochroism   The ability of certain crystals to transmit light vibrations in one plane only while absorbing those vibrations in other planes. Pleochroic crystals thus produce plane-*polarized light. If the effect occurs along only one axis of the crystal, the crystal is said to be dichroic. *Polaroid, for example, contains dichroic crystals. In trichroic crystals, the effect occurs along two axes perpendicular to each other.

plesiosaur   A widely distributed marine reptile of the Jurassic and Cretaceous periods (200–65 million years ago). Up to about 39 ft (12 m) long, plesiosaurs had broad turtle-like bodies with paddle-like limbs, a long flexible neck, and jaws armed with sharp teeth used to catch fish.

Plessy v. Ferguson   (1896) US Supreme Court case that upheld the "separate but equal" doctrine regarding segregation and that further defined the 14th Amendment. Plessy, of mixed race, was arrested because he refused to leave a "whites only" railroad car in Louisiana; his appeal against his conviction reached the Supreme Court, which ruled that as long as facilities were equal, segregation of races was constitutional. It also ruled that the 14th Amendment did not apply in this type of social situation and that states had the right to determine the race of a citizen.

pleurisy   Inflammation of the pleura—the membrane that covers the lungs and lines the chest cavity. The commonest cause of pleurisy is bacterial or viral infection: pleurisy will often complicate *pneumonia. The patient will often have a fever, a pain in the chest that is worse on coughing or taking a deep breath, and a cough. Bacterial pleurisy is treated with antibiotics.

Pleurococcus   A genus of common unicellular *green algae forming thin green powdery incrustations on the windward side of walls and tree trunks, particularly in tropical regions. The spherical cells are either solitary or form small flat aggregations; reproduction is by cell division.

Pleven   43 25N 24 40E A city in central N Bulgaria. The Russians and the Turks fought here in 1877. It has various industries and serves a mixed agricultural area. Population (1979 est): 122,916.

Plexiglas   (polymethyl methacrylate)   A colorless transparent thermoplastic material made by *polymerization of methyl methacrylate. It can be extruded and molded and colored, for use in light fittings, including colored signals, aircraft parts, and car parts. It is resistant to ultraviolet radiation from fluorescent lights and is widely used as an unbreakable substitute for glass.

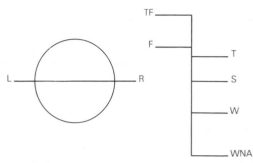

PLIMSOLL LINE   *The lines and letters mark the waterline under various conditions. TF=fresh water in the tropics; F=fresh water; T=salt in the tropics; S=salt water in the summer; W=salt water in the winter; WNA=winter in the N Atlantic. LR represents Lloyd's Register.*

Plimsoll line   A series of lines painted on the outside of a cargo ship's hull showing the various safe levels to which the ship can be loaded. Typically, the loading levels are marked for ships loaded and unloaded, in sea and fresh water, winter and summer, and tropical or northern waters.

Pliny the Elder   (Gaius Plinius Secundus; 23–70 AD) Roman scholar, whose universal encyclopedia, *Natural History*, was a major source of scientific knowledge until the 17th century. During his military career, Pliny assembled material from numerous sources on a wide range of disciplines, including astrology, geography, agriculture, medicine, precious stones, and—most notably—zoology and botany. Pliny did not discriminate fact from fiction and included much folklore and superstition. He finally completed this work of 37 volumes in 77 AD.

Pliny the Younger   (Gaius Plinius Caecilius Secundus; c. 61–c. 113 AD) Roman writer, nephew and adopted son of the encyclopedist Pliny the Elder. He held various administrative posts including that of consul in 100 AD and was a prominent legal orator. His ten volumes of private letters constitute an intimate unofficial history of his time.

Pliocene epoch.   *See* Tertiary period.

pliosaur   An extinct marine reptile that evolved from the *plesiosaurs but had a shorter neck and a longer head with stronger jaws, giving it a more streamlined appearance. It was a powerful swimmer and fed on cuttlefish, squid, etc.

PLO.   *See* Palestine Liberation Organization.

Plock   52 32N 19 40E A city in central Poland, on the Vistula River. Its 12th-century cathedral contains the tombs of Polish kings. Industries include oil refining; it is served by pipeline from the Soviet Union. Population (1974 est): 84,660.

Ploiești   44 57N 26 01E A city in SE Romania, at the foot of the Transylvanian Alps. It is the center for the country's oil production. Population (1979 est): 207,009.

Plotinus   (205–70 AD) Greek philosopher and founder of *Neoplatonism. Born in Egypt, he studied at Alexandria, visited Persia (242–43), and finally settled in Rome, becoming the focus of an intellectual circle. Developing *Plato's mysticism, he taught that the immaterial impersonal indescribable "One" is the ground of all existence and value. From it emanate successively mind, soul, and nature. Mind contemplates and organizes within itself the Platonic Forms; soul thinks less coherently, thus creating time and space; nature "dreams" the chaotic material world, the source of all evil. Man partakes of all these; by rejecting material nature and cultivating the intellect he may briefly become mystically united with the One.

Plovdiv   (former name: Philippopoli)   42 08N 24 45E A city in S central Bulgaria, on the Maritsa River. It is Bulgaria's second largest city and has the remains of the Roman walls. Its industries include food processing and carpet manufacture. Population (1979 est): 342,000.

plover   A bird belonging to a widely distributed family (*Charadriidae*; 56 species) occurring in open regions and along shores. 6–12 in (15–30 cm) long, plovers have brown or gray plumage, often mottled, with white underparts, which become black in summer for some species. They feed on insects and other small invertebrates and nest on the ground. Order: *Charadriiformes* (gulls, plovers, etc.). *See also* lapwing.

Plowright, Joan   (1929–) British actress. Her reputation is based on her performances in both classical and modern plays, the latter including the first productions of Osborne's *The Entertainer* (1957) and Wesker's *Roots* (1959). She married Laurence *Olivier in 1963.

plum A small tree, **Prunus domestica*—a natural hybrid between the *blackthorn and the cherry plum (*P. cerasifera*), native to SW Asia and cultivated in most Mediterranean and N temperate regions for its ▢fruit. 20–33 ft (6–10 m) tall, it has oval toothed leaves and clusters of attractive white flowers. The fruit is round or oval and has a dark-red to blue-black skin (when ripe), enclosing a sweet greenish-yellow pulp and a central oval stony seed. Plums are eaten fresh, cooked in desserts, canned, or dried as prunes. Family: *Rosaceae. See also* bullace; damson.

plumbago. *See* graphite.

Plumbago A genus of herbaceous plants, shrubs, and climbers (12 species), native to warm regions and including a number of ornamentals. They have simple leaves and terminal clusters of white, blue, violet, pink, or red flowers, with five petals arranged to form a narrow tube with spreading lobes. *P. auriculata*, with pale-blue flowers, and *P. rosea*, with red flowers, are popular greenhouse plants. Some species are used for medicinal purposes and some yield a juice that causes blistering. Family: *Plumbaginaceae*.

pluralism. *See* dualism.

Plutarch (c. 46–c. 120 AD) Greek biographer and essayist. He was a citizen of both Athens and Rome, a priest of Delphi, and director of a school in his native town of Chaeronea in Boeotia in central Greece. His *Parallel Lives* consists of biographies of 23 pairs of Greek and Roman statesmen and soldiers. The *Moralia* contain 83 essays on ethical, scientific, and literary topics. His works had a great influence in Europe in the 16th and 17th centuries. The English translation by Sir Thomas North of the *Lives* (1579) was the source of Shakespeare's Roman plays. The *Moralia* served as models for the essays of both Montaigne and Francis Bacon.

Pluto (astronomy) The smallest and usually outermost planet, orbiting the sun every 248 years at a mean distance of 3660 million miles (5893 million km). Its eccentric orbit has brought it inside Neptune's orbit for the period 1979–99. Pluto was discovered in 1930 but little was known about it until its satellite was discovered in 1978. It is apparently a low-density body (relative density 1.3), about 1550 mi (2500 km) in diameter. It is possible that Pluto was once a satellite of Neptune.

Pluto (mythology). *See* Hades.

plutonic rock. *See* igneous rock.

plutonium (Pu) An important synthetic transuranic element discovered in 1940. Trace quantities exist in natural uranium ores. It is produced in large quantities in nuclear reactors by beta-decay from uranium-239. Plutonium is fissile and was used in the atomic bomb dropped on Nagasaki in 1945 (*see* nuclear weapons). It is absorbed into bone marrow and is one of the most toxic substances known. It forms oxides (PuO, PuO_2), halides (for example PuF_3), and other compounds. It is used in *fast reactors and small power units for spacecraft. At no 94; at wt (244); mp 1187°F (641°C); bp 5861°F (3235°C).

Plymouth 50 23N 4 10W A port in SW England, in Devon on Plymouth Sound. The *Mayflower* embarked from here for America in 1620. Severely damaged by bombing during World War II, much of the city center has been rebuilt. Plymouth is an important naval base with associated marine industries. More recent industries include the manufacture of clothing, radio equipment, and processed foods. Population (1981): 243,895.

Plymouth 41 58N 70 40W A town in Massachusetts, on Plymouth Bay. The first European settlement in New England, it was founded by the Pilgrims from the *Mayflower* (1620). Industries include fisheries, boatyards, and tourism. Population (1980): 35,913.

Plymouth Brethren An austere Protestant sect founded at Plymouth in 1830 by a former Anglican priest, J. N. Darby (1800–82). The Brethren have strict standards of behavior and shun many secular trades and professions. They insist on the spiritual priesthood of believers and celebrate communion weekly. Small groups exist throughout the world, often as active missionaries.

Plymouth Colony A settlement of English colonists seeking religious freedom in Plymouth, Mass. Pilgrims from the *Mayflower*, destined for Virginia, landed on New England's shores in 1620 and established Plymouth Colony, also known as New Plymouth. Governed by the Mayflower Compact, the colony expanded but was merged in 1691 with Massachusetts Bay Colony and Maine.

Plymouth Patent Land title (patent) granted to the Pilgrims in *Plymouth Colony from the Council of New England in 1621. A second patent (1630) defined the colony's boundaries from SE Massachusetts to E Rhode Island.

Plymouth Rock A breed of domestic fowl developed and widely used for meat production. It has a deep compact body with large thighs. The plumage can be of various colors, including white with black bars and pure white. Weight: 9 lb (4.3 kg) (cocks); 7 lb (3.4 kg) (hens).

Plzeň (German name: Pilsen) 49 45N 13 25E A city in Czechoslovakia, in W Bohemia. It has been famous for its beer (Pilsener lager) since the middle ages. Local coal and iron ore resources have led to the development of heavy industry, including engineering and chemicals. Population (1980 est): 169,000.

pneumococcus A spherical bacterium, *Streptococcus pneumoniae*, that is commonly found in the throat and causes pneumonia if it infects the lungs. Pneumococci typically exist in pairs and often form capsules, the composition of which is used to identify different strains (pneumococcal typing).

pneumoconiosis Chronic lung disease caused by inhaling dust, most commonly coal dust (causing coalworkers' pneumoconiosis) and silica (causing *silicosis). Considerable coal dust may be taken into the lungs without causing much damage, but later progressive massive fibrosis may develop and the coalworker is disabled by breathlessness. Lung cancer may also complicate pneumoconiosis. There is no effective treatment and prevention is all important. *See also* asbestosis.

pneumonia Inflammation of the lungs, most commonly caused by infection. Pneumonia may arise in only one lobe of the lung (lobar pneumonia) or in patches in both lungs (bronchopneumonia). The infective organisms may be streptococci, viruses (causing a mild disease), tubercle bacilli, or other organisms, such as mycoplasmas. The patient has a fever, cough, and pain in the chest and may be breathless. Treatment is with antibiotics and physiotherapy.

pneumothorax The presence of air in the pleural cavity, which causes the lung to collapse. This may happen for no apparent reason or it may develop in *emphysema or after a penetrating injury of the chest. The patient has pain in the chest and may be breathless. The lung will slowly expand itself or a tube may be inserted into the pleural cavity to allow the trapped air to escape.

Po River (Latin name: Padus) The longest river in Italy rising in the Cottian Alps and flowing mainly ENE through Turin to enter the Adriatic Sea by way of a large delta in the E. The Po Valley is the most fertile and economically important region in Italy. Length: 405 mi (652 km).

Pocahontas (c. 1595–1617) American Indian woman. Daughter of the Indian chief Powhatan, Pocahontas is said to have saved the life of Captain John *Smith from her father's warriors. She married the English colonist John Rolfe (1585–1622) and was entertained as a princess at the English court; she died of smallpox on her return to America.

pochard A large-headed *duck, *Aythya ferina*, occurring in temperate inland waters of Eurasia. It is 18 in (45 cm) long and has gray legs and a gray-blue bill; males have a reddish head, black breast, and gray body; females are brown. It feeds on water plants and small aquatic invertebrates.

Po Chü-i. *See* Bo Zhu Yi.

pocket gopher A *rodent belonging to the subfamily *Geomyinae* (39 species), of North and Central America. Pocket gophers are 4–10 in (10–25 cm) in length and brownish in color. They inhabit open dry country, where they dig extensive burrows, and feed on roots, seeds, insects, and mice. Their large cheek pouches have an outside opening like a pocket.

Pocono Mountains A low mountain range in NE Pennsylvania, part of the Catskills, which are part of the Appalachian Mountains. The highest points are about 2000 ft (600 m). A popular year-round vacation area because of its forests, lakes, and recreation facilities, the Poconos are easily accessible from eastern cities.

Podgorica. *See* Titograd.

Podgorny, N(ikolai) V(iktorovich) (1903–) Soviet statesman. Podgorny was president of the Soviet Union from 1965 to 1977, when he resigned under pressure and was replaced by Brezhnev.

Podocarpus. *See* yellowwood.

Podolsk 55 23N 37 32E A city in the Soviet Union, in the RSFSR 26 mi (42 km) S of Moscow. Lenin and his Bolshevik colleagues often met here before the Russian Revolution. Industries include oil refining, machinery manufacturing, and railroad engineering. Population (1981 est): 205,000.

podzol A type of *soil typical of many cool temperate humid zones especially with coniferous vegetation, as in the taiga of the Soviet Union and North America. It is characterized by an ashen-colored upper layer (A horizon) and an underlying layer (B horizon) of redeposition humus and iron, which may develop into an impermeable pan.

EDGAR ALLAN POE *Writer whose poems, especially "The Raven," and short stories are internationally acclaimed.*

Poe, Edgar Allan (1809–49) US poet, short-story writer, and critic. He was brought up by foster parents after the death of his mother in 1811. He briefly attended Virginia University and West Point. After publishing two volumes of poetry (1827, 1829), he began to contribute to and work for literary magazines. Among his many prose tales and horror stories are "The Fall of the House of Usher" (1839), "The Purloined Letter" (1842), "The Black Cat" (1843), "The Cask of Amontillado" (1846), and the first detective story ever written, "The Murders in the Rue Morgue" (1841). His best-known poems are "The Raven" (1845), and "The Bells" (1849) and his most influential critical work is "The Philosophy of Composition" (1846).

poet laureate A title bestowed by the British monarch on a contemporary poet, whose traditional duties include the writing of commemorative odes on important public occasions. The first official poet laureate was John Dryden, who served from 1668 to 1688.

poetry A form of literature distinguished from prose by the deliberate employment of *meter, rhythm, *rhyme, sound, and figurative language. Poetry probably originated as a form of language distinct from ordinary speech in religious ritual and is an earlier development than prose. The earliest poetic landmarks in western literature are Homer's *Odyssey* and *Iliad*, which developed out of a primitive oral tradition and became models for the epic poems of Virgil and numerous later poets. Poetry was associated with drama from its appearance in the dramatic choruses of ancient Greece until the 19th century; verse drama was revived by T. S. Eliot in the 20th century. The early forms of lyric poetry derived from the dithyrambic poetry of religious ritual; they are characterized by the repetition of song-like elements arranged in stanzas. The sonnet, one of the most popular of all poetic forms, evolved in Renaissance Italy. Narrative poetry, like the epic, derived from oral tradition; the ballad combines lyrical and narrative qualities. A tradition of didactic verse, stretching from Hesiod to Cowper, employed rhyme or meter as an aid to the expression of ideas. Poetry has been used as a medium for satire (Pope), religious and philosophical statement (Lucretius and Wordsworth), and even for scientific classification (Erasmus Darwin). While the poetry of ancient Greece and Rome depended on the variation of fixed metrical patterns, the early poetry of N Europe was characterized by alliteration. Blank verse was evolved by the Earl of Surrey and became the main medium for drama in the works of Shakespeare and his contemporaries and much subsequent serious poetry. In the 19th and 20th centuries some poets adopted free verse, to avoid the constraints of regularity in meter or rhyme.

Poggio Bracciolini, Giovanni Francesco (1380–1459) Italian humanist. A pupil of Manuel *Chrysoloras, Poggio recovered the manuscripts of Lucretius, Quintilian, Silius, and other classical writers. His books include a *History of Florence* and the *Liber Facetiarum*, a collection of humorous tales.

Pogonophora. *See* beardworm.

pogrom (Russian: devastation) An attack on Jews and Jewish property, especially in the Russian Empire. Russian pogroms, which were condoned by the government, were particularly common in the years immediately after the assassination of Alexander II in 1881 and again from 1903 to 1906, though mob persecution of Jews continued until the Russian Revolution (1917).

Po Hai. *See* Chihli, Gulf of.

poikilothermy The condition of being cold-blooded. Invertebrate animals, fishes, amphibians, and reptiles have no physiological mechanism for the control of their body temperature, which therefore fluctuates with that of the environment. They are therefore restricted to environments with a suitable temperature range. *Compare* homoiothermy.

Poincaré, Jules Henri (1854–1912) French mathematician; cousin of Raymond *Poincaré. He is regarded by some as the last universal mathematician because he made important contributions to all fields of mathematics as well as to physics and astronomy. A gifted writer, Poincaré in later life wrote important treatises on the nature of mathematical creativity, emphasizing its intuitional aspects.

Poincaré, Raymond (1860–1934) French statesman; president (1913–20) and prime minister (1912–13, 1922–24, 1926–29). His foreign policy aimed to prevent French isolation in the face of possible German aggression and when, after World War I, Germany delayed in the payment of reparations he ordered French troops to occupy the Ruhr. His postwar economic policy brought a period of stability to France.

poinciana A tropical shrub or small tree of the genera *Caesalpinia* or *Delonix* (both formerly called *Poinciana*), often grown for ornament. Up to 50 ft (15 m) tall, they have large feathery compound leaves and clusters of showy orange or scarlet flowers. Popular species include the Barbados pride (*C. pulcherrima*) and the *flamboyant tree (*or* royal poinciana). Family: *Leguminosae.

poinsettia An ornamental shrub, *Euphorbia pulcherrima, native to Mexico and tropical America and a popular pot plant at Christmas in Europe and North America. Growing 2–10 ft (0.6–3 m) tall, it has simple dark-green leaves and clusters of tiny greenish-yellow flowers surrounded by large scarlet bracts, up to 5.5 in (14 cm) long, which resemble petals. Family: *Euphorbiaceae*.

point 1. A unit of weight for precious stones, especially diamonds, equal to two milligrams. 2. A unit of type size.

Pointe-à-Pitre 16 14N 61 32W The chief town and port of Guadeloupe. It possesses a good harbor and is the chief commercial center for the island. Population (1974): 23,889.

Pointe-Noire 4 46S 11 53E A port in the People's Republic of Congo, on the Atlantic coast. Its port was completed in 1939 and has a considerable entrepôt trade. Population (1975 est): 141,700.

pointer A breed of sporting □dog originating in England and named for its habit of pointing its nose toward game. It is lithely built with a long tapering tail, a long slightly concave muzzle, and drooping ears. The short smooth coat is white combined with yellow, orange, liver, or black. Height: 25–27 in (63–68 cm) (dogs); 24–26 in (61–66 cm) (bitches).

Point Four Program (1950) US program of foreign aid. Named for the fourth point in President Harry S. Truman's inaugural address (1949), the program helped developing nations by sending experts, equipment, and funds to modernize industry and agriculture. By 1953 it became a part of the general US foreign aid program.

pointillism A style of painting using dots of pure color. The pointillists applied primary colors to the canvas in dots and allowed the colors to be mixed by the eye, thus achieving an intense luminosity. Also called divisionism and neoimpressionism, it was developed by *Seurat in France in the 1880s and carried into the 20th century by his disciple *Signac.

poise A unit of viscosity in the *c.g.s. system equal to the tangential force per unit area, in dynes per square centimeter, required to maintain unit difference in velocity, in centimeters per second, between two parallel planes in a fluid one centimeter apart.

poison ivy An extremely poisonous woody vine or shrub, *Rhus toxicodendron* (or *Toxicodendron radicans*), native to North America. It has compound leaves with three broad leaflets and clusters of small round whitish-green flowers, which give rise to whitish berries. All parts contain a poison that causes severe skin inflammation on contact. Family: *Anacardiaceae*.

poisons Substances that injure health or cause death when introduced into the body. The term is often restricted to those substances that are fatal in small doses (e.g. strychnine, cyanide) but can also be applied to those that are harmful when small doses are taken over long periods (cumulative poisons, e.g. lead) and to otherwise safe drugs taken in large doses. Poisons may be classified in various ways, one of which is according to use: i.e. agricultural (pesticides, herbicides, etc.); industrial (poisonous elements and gases, etc.); medicinal (dangerous drugs, e.g. opiates); and natural (bacterial toxins, poisonous plants, animal venoms, etc.). Another way is to group them according to activity: corrosives (acids, alkalis, etc.); blood poisons (e.g. carbon monoxide, warfarin); nerve poisons (e.g. strychnine, cocaine); poisons that interfere with cell function (e.g. cytotoxic drugs, nitrogen mustard, methotrexate); etc.
Toxicology is the study of poisons, which deals with their chemical nature and origin, the pathological changes they induce, their recognition in a poisoned patient, and the determination of specific antidotes.

Poisson, Siméon Dénis (1781–1840) French mathematician, who became professor at the École Polytechnique in 1806. He made important contributions to the mathematical theory of electricity, magnetism, and mechanics. His work on electricity led him in 1837 to discover Poisson's equation, which describes the electric field created by an arbitrary charge density. Poisson's distribution is widely used in probability calculations and **Poisson's ratio** (the ratio of the lateral strain to the longitudinal strain in a stretched wire) is used by engineers in studying the elongation of structural members.

Poitiers (Latin name: Limonum) 46 35N 0 20E A town in W central France, the capital of the Vienne department. The former capital of Poitou, it dates back to Roman times and was the site of a battle (1356) in which the English under the Black Prince defeated the French under John the Good. Notable buildings include the 4th-century baptistry of St John, the cathedral (11th–12th centuries), and the university (1432). Metallurgy, textiles, and brewing are the chief industries. Population (1975): 85,466.

poker A card game, usually for five to seven players, using a single deck of cards. There are many variants but in the standard game of draw poker each player receives five cards, with an option to discard up to three of them and receive replacements. The objective is to make the best hand or to bluff one's opponents into believing one has the best hand. The best hand is (in ascending order) the one containing the highest card; highest pair of cards of the same denomination (irrespective of suit); two pairs; three cards of the same denomination; a straight (a sequence of denominations irrespective of suit); a flush (all of the same suit, irrespective of denomination); a full house (a pair and three of the same denomination); four cards of the same denomination; or a straight flush. Each player makes bets on his hand before and after discarding and the betting continues until the limit (if there is one) is reached or until no one wishes to bet further. Although poker is a game of chance there is an element of skill in the opportunity it provides for bluffing one's opponents into thinking one has the best hand.

Pola. *See* Pula.

Poland, People's Republic of A country in N Europe, on the Baltic Sea. Extensive plains in the N rise to the Carpathian Mountains in the S, which reach heights of over 8000 ft (2500 m). Following the reorganization of the population after World War II, when Poles were transferred from the area ceded to the Soviet Union to that gained from Germany, forcing out the Germans, the majority of the inhabitants are now Polish. Approximately 70% are Roman Catholic. *Economy*: since World War II there has been a significant shift in the balance of the economy from agriculture to industry, but Poland remains one of the world's leading agricultural nations. Although much of the land is organized into collectives and state farms about half is still privately owned. The chief crops are rye, wheat, oats, sugar beet, and potatoes. Its mineral wealth includes rich deposits of copper and sulfur and natural gas has been found as well as some oil. An important shipbuilding nation, Poland is among the world's leading exporters of ships. Other important industries include textiles, engineering, steel, cement, chemicals, and food products. Tourism is an important source of revenue. *History*: Poland first appeared as a separate state in the 10th century, which also saw the introduction of Christianity. From the 14th to 16th centuries its power was extended under the *Jagiellon dynasty, which was succeeded by elected kings. Poland declined in the 17th century, although it was able, under John III Sobieski, to defeat the Turks in 1683. Foreign intervention in the 18th century culminated in partition by Russia, Austria, and Prussia (in 1772, 1793, and 1795), and at the Congress of

Vienna in 1815 the *Congress Kingdom of Poland was created under the Russian crown. After the defeat of the Central Powers in World War I independence was declared under Józef Piłsudski. In 1939 Poland was invaded by Germany, the *casus belli* of World War II, and then by the Soviet Union, being partitioned between them. Some six million Poles, including three million Jews, died during the occupation. Polish resistance to Germany, both within Poland and abroad, directed by Sikorski's government in exile, contributed to the Allied victory, and in 1945 Poland was liberated by the Russians. The *Oder-Neisse line became its W frontier. The first postwar elections, in 1948, brought a communist-controlled government to power under *Gomułka. He was demoted in 1948 for asserting independence from the Soviet Union but returned to power after the *Poznań Riots. Further unrest in 1970 led to his enforced resignation and he was succeeded by Edward *Gierek. Gierek was dismissed in 1980 and succeeded by Stanisław Kania. The political and economic situation in Poland worsened and Kania resigned (1981) to be replaced by General Wojciech Jaruzelski. In December, 1981, the independent labor union Solidarity, led by Lech Walesa, was accused of attempting to overthrow the government, its leaders were detained, and a state of martial law was declared under a military council led by Jaruzelski. Martial law was lifted in 1983, and political prisoners were released, but unrest continued, sometimes expressed through the church's resistance to Communist control of religious and educational matters. Official language: Polish. Official currency: złoty of 100 groszy. Area: 120,624 sq mi (312,677 sq km). Population (1983 est): 36,556,000. Capital: Warsaw. Main port: Gdańsk.

Polanski, Roman (1933–) Polish film director, born in Paris. After his first full-length film, *Knife in the Water* (1961), he worked in Britain and the US. His later films include *Repulsion* (1965), *Cul de Sac* (1966), *Rosemary's Baby* (1968), and *The Tenant* (1976), in all of which he skillfully created an atmosphere of tension and menace.

polar bear A white bear, *Thalarctos maritimus*, living on the shores of the Arctic Ocean. Up to 8 ft (2.5 m) long and weighing 1100–1550 lb (500–700 kg) (depending on the season), polar bears prey mainly on seals, also taking some fish and birds. Males move southward in winter but females sleep in dens prior to the birth of their young in early Dec. □mammal.

Polaris (*or* North Star) A remote cream supergiant, apparent magnitude 2.0 and about 650 light years distant, that is the brightest star in the constellation Ursa Minor. It is the present *pole star, lying about 1° from the N celestial pole; its position is found using the Pointers in the Plow. It is a *Cepheid variable and is the primary component of a *multiple star.

Polaris missile A US navy two-stage solid-fueled nuclear strategic missile launched from a submarine and having a range of 2800 miles (4500 km). Traveling at speeds of over mach 10, some versions (Poseidon) are capable of delivering 10 separately guided 15-*kiloton warheads. When fired from below the surface, the missile is ejected from the vessel by compressed gas, its rocket firing at the surface. Its inertial guidance system is programmed to the launching vessel's exact position. Firing is by two-key control, linked directly to Washington.

polarized light Light in which the direction of vibration is restricted. In ordinary light (and other types of *electromagnetic radiation) the transverse vibrations of the electric and magnetic fields are at right angles to each other in all possible planes. In **plane-polarized light** the vibrations of the electric field are confined to one plane and the magnetic field to one at right angles to it. Plane-polarized light can be produced by reflection at a certain angle (*see* Brewster's law) or by passing light through such doubly refracting substances as *Polaroid. **Circularly** and **elliptically polarized light** occur when the electric vector describes a circle or an ellipse around the direction of the light beam.

Polaroid A trade name for a plastic sheet impregnated with many tiny crystals of a dichroic substance (*see* pleochroism) orientated parallel to each other. The crystals only transmit light vibrating in one plane and absorb all other light. Polaroid is used for reducing glare in headlights, sunglasses, camera filters, etc., by removing stray beams of plane-polarized light.

polder An area of low-lying land reclaimed from the sea or other water, often for agricultural purposes. Polders are usually formed by constructing dikes around the area, which is then drained. Land lying below low-tide mark must be pumped clear of water, while that above may be drained by means of tide gates, which close as the tide rises. The most notable polders are those of Holland, next to the IJsselmeer.

Pole, Reginald, Cardinal (1500–58) English Roman Catholic churchman; Archbishop of Canterbury. He opposed Henry VIII's divorce and in 1532 went to Italy. There he wrote *Pro ecclesiasticae unitatis defensione*

(1536), an attack on Henry's claims of supremacy over the English Church. He was a leading advocate of reform within the Roman Catholic Church and presided at the Council of *Trent. Returning to England on Mary's accession, he became Archbishop of Canterbury in 1556.

polecat A carnivorous mammal, *Mustela putorius*, found in woods and grassland throughout Europe, Asia, and N Africa. About 20 in (50 cm) long, it has a dark-brown coat with yellowish patches on the face and ears. Polecats are nocturnal, foraging for rodents and insects. They eject a pungent fluid when alarmed and were once called "foul martens." Family: *Mustelidae* (weasels, etc.). *See also* ferret; skunk.

Poles, North and South The most northerly and southerly points of the earth's surface and the ends of the earth's axis, about which it rotates. The magnetic north and south poles are the points to which a magnetic compass needle points and where the lines of force of the earth's magnetic field are vertical. They do not coincide with the geographical poles and their positions slowly change. *See also* Arctic Circle; Antarctica.

pole star Either of two bright stars that are nearest the N or S celestial pole. The poles are not fixed in position but, owing to *precession of the earth's axis, trace out two circles in the sky over a period of 25,800 years. There is thus a sequence of stars that slowly, in turn, become the N or S pole star. *See also* Polaris.

pole vault A field event for men in athletics, in which competitors use a fiberglass pole to lever themselves over a horizontal bar. A competitor is allowed three tries at each height and is eliminated if he fails to clear it. The height is increased until only one competitor is left.

Polignac, Auguste Jules Armand Marie, Prince de (1780–1847) French statesman. As chief minister to Charles X (1829–30) he supported the absolute authority assumed by the king, thus helping to bring about the *July Revolution. Arrested and imprisoned until 1836, he was then exiled until 1845.

poliomyelitis A viral infection of the central nervous system that may result in muscle paralysis. It was formerly known as infantile paralysis, because children were most commonly affected. In most cases the infection is mild, with only a nonspecific fever, but sometimes a more severe illness develops three to seven days later, which may lead to severe pain in the limbs followed by permanent paralysis. There is no specific treatment, but an Australian nurse, Elizabeth Kenny (1886–1952), developed the practice of actively exercising affected limbs rather than immobilizing them. Polio is now uncommon in developed countries and a vaccine is available that gives complete protection (*see* Sabin vaccine; Salk vaccine).

Polish (*or* Lekhitic) A West Slavonic language spoken in Poland and closely related to *Czech, *Slovak, and Sorbian. It is written in a Latin alphabet and the standard form is based on the dialect of Poznań.

Polish Corridor A belt of land that separated E Prussia from the rest of Germany and was granted to Poland in the Treaty of Versailles (1919). It allowed Poland access to the sea at Danzig (now Gdańsk). It was annexed by Germany in 1939 and returned to Poland in 1945, after World War II.

Polish Succession, War of the (1733–35) A European war precipitated by the election of rival claimants to the Polish throne in succession to Augustus the Strong: *Stanisław I Leszczyński, supported by France, Spain, and subsequently Sardinia, and Augustus' son, Frederick Augustus III (1696–1763), supported by Russia and Austria. After the fall of Danzig to the Russians (1734) Stanisław fled and the subsequent Treaty of Vienna (1735) recognized Frederick Augustus as king.

Poliziano (*or* Politian; 1454–94) Italian poet and scholar, born Angelo Ambrogini. He gained the patronage of Lorenzo de' *Medici and later of Cardinal Francesco Gonzago in Mantua. His major work is *Stanze per la giostra* (1475–78), an unfinished poem expressing humanist ideals in classical style. His other works include *Orfeo* (1480), a dramatic court entertainment, as well as many translations and Latin poems.

Polk, James Knox (1795–1849) US statesman; 11th President of the United States (1845–49). Beginning his political career as a member of the Tennessee legislature, Polk was later elected to the US House of Representatives, where he became one of the national leaders of the Democratic Party and speaker of the House (1835–39). After serving a single term as governor of Tennessee (1839–41), he received the Democratic presidential nomination in 1844. Polk defeated Henry *Clay in the general election and began his term of office with four distinct aims, all of which he achieved. He established an independent federal treasury; lowered tariffs; resolved the Oregon boundary dispute with Great Britain, placing its border at the 49th parallel; and significantly expanded American territorial possessions in the Far West. As a result of the US victory in the *Mexican War, Texas, New

Mexico, and California became part of the US. Because of poor health, Polk chose not to seek re-election in 1848.

Polk, Leonidas Lafayette (1806–64) US churchman and Confederate general. A bishop in the Episcopal Church, he served in the SW and in Louisiana and was responsible for the establishment of the University of the South (1860) at Sewanee, Tenn. He had graduated from West Point (1827) and resigned his commission shortly after graduation. He accepted a commission in the Confederate Army during the Civil War, defeated General Ulysses S. Grant at Belmont, Mo, and saw action at *Shiloh, Murfreesboro, and *Chickamauga before dying of wounds at Pine Mountain (1864).

polka A Bohemian folk dance in 2/4 time, which became a ballroom dance in 19th-century Europe and rivaled the *waltz in popularity. It is characterized by three steps and a hop.

pollack A popular game fish, *Pollachius* (or *Gadus*) *pollachius*, related to cod, with a protruding lower jaw and no chin barbel. Its elongated body, usually up to 40 in (1 m) long, is brown or olive, sometimes with yellow or orange markings above, and paler below. It occurs in European coastal waters down to 650 ft (200 m).

Pollaiuolo, Antonio (c. 1432–98) Florentine Renaissance artist. He and his brother **Piero Pollaiuolo** (c. 1441–96) trained as goldsmiths and often collaborated on paintings and sculptures. Antonio is famous for his bronze sculptures, the painting of the *Martyrdom of St Sebastian* (National Gallery, London), and the influential engraving *Battle of the Nudes* (Uffizi), which is remarkable for its depiction of movement. He was reputedly the first artist to make anatomical dissections. Piero painted a series of *Virtues* (Uffizi) and *The Coronation of the Virgin* (Duomo, Florence).

pollen The male gametes of seed plants, which are produced in the *stamens of flowering plants and in the male *cones of conifers and other gymnosperms. To ensure fertilization, the pollen must be transferred to the stigma (in flowering plants) or the female cone (in conifers)—the process of **pollination**. Many flowers are cross-pollinated, i.e. the pollen from one plant is deposited on the stigma of another of the same species by means of animal carriers (usually insects), wind, or water. Some flowers are self-pollinated, the pollen being transferred from the anthers to the stigma of the same plant: the stamens are usually bent over the stigma to assist the process. After pollination, a pollen tube grows down from the pollen grain into the pistil of the pollinated flower until it reaches the ovule. Two pollen nuclei travel down this tube: one fertilizes the egg cell, which develops into the embryo plant in the seed; the other fuses with a nucleus in the ovule to become a food source for the seed.

pollen analysis. *See* palynology.

Pollock, Jackson (1912–56) US painter. He trained in New York under Thomas Hart *Benton but early in his career he was influenced by *Orozco and *surrealism. By 1947 he had developed an abstract style (*see* action painting) by which he attempted to express feelings and unconscious thoughts through the act of painting itself. He poured and dripped commercial and metallic paints onto very large canvases to form patterns of interweaving lines. Shortly before his early death in a car crash, he abandoned the use of color, painting only in black and white.

poll tax A levy on every individual (*poll*, head), regardless of means. First levied regularly in England in 1377, it was a direct cause of the *Peasants' Revolt in 1381 and was abolished in 1698. Originally preferred in the US to property-based taxes, the poll tax as a voting qualification was abused as a means of disenfranchising blacks and was constitutionally banned.

pollution The addition to the environment of substances that cannot be rendered harmless by normal biological processes. Modern industrial and agricultural activities have led to the pollution of land, rivers, seas, and the atmosphere by either man-made toxic substances (such as pesticides and fertilizers) or by the overproduction of naturally occurring substances (such as carbon dioxide gas). Pesticides, such as *DDT, can build up in the environment and in the bodies of living organisms until they reach toxic levels. Other forms of pollution may have long-term effects on the health of living things, including man. Current problems include the disposal of radioactive wastes; increasing amounts of heavy metals (such as lead) in the atmosphere; atmospheric pollution by carbon dioxide, carbon monoxide, etc.; the disposal of human refuse and sewage; and unacceptable noise levels. In many cases a technical solution to these problems is available but cannot be implemented because the cost is too high or because of conflict with minority interests. *See also* conservation.

Pollux An orange giant, apparent magnitude 1.15 and 35 light years distant, that is the brightest star in the constellation Gemini.

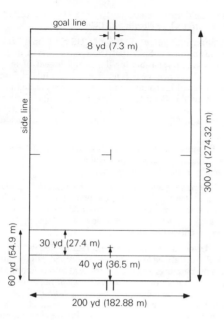

goal line

8 yd (7.3 m)

side line

300 yd (274.32 m)

30 yd (27.4 m)

40 yd (36.5 m)

60 yd (54.9 m)

200 yd (182.88 m)

POLO *The dimensions of the field. If the side lines are boarded, the width is 160 yd (146.4 m) and there is a safety area extending 10 yd (9 m) beyond each side line and 30 yd (27 m) beyond each goal line.*

polo A four-a-side stick-and-ball game in which the players are mounted on ponies (*see* polo pony). It was played in Persia by 600 BC and spread E but had almost died out when it was rediscovered by British officers in India in the 19th century. The riders use long sticks with mallet heads to hit a solid wooden ball, with the object of scoring goals. Several balls are worn out in a game. A game consists of up to eight seven-minute periods, or "chukkas," after each of which mounts are changed. After every goal the teams change ends. It is presided over by two mounted umpires and a referee. Since World War II Argentina has become the leading polo-playing nation but the game has long had an enthusiastic following in the US.

Polo, Marco (c. 1254–1324) Venetian traveler. His father Niccolò Polo and uncle Maffeo Polo undertook a trading expedition to Peking (1260–69) and in 1271 they returned at the request of the Mongol emperor, Kublai Khan, taking Marco with them. Having learned Mongolian, he entered Kublai's service, conducting missions as far as S India, until leaving China in 1292. He subsequently fought for the Venetians against the Genoese and was captured. In prison (1296–98) he dictated an account of his travels, which remained almost the only source of information about the Far East until the 19th century.

polonaise A Polish dance in triple time, with characteristic rhythmic stresses and cadences. Originally a processional folk dance, it evolved into a courtly dance in 18th century Europe; it also became a purely instrumental form, as in Chopin's polonaises for the piano.

polonium (Po) A highly radioactive element discovered in 1898 by Marie Curie in minute amounts in pitchblende. It is 5000 times as radioactive as *radium and liberates considerable amounts of heat. Polonium has 27 isotopes, more than any other element. It is used in compact radiation and thermoelectric power sources. At no 84; at wt (209); mp 490°F (254°C); bp 1765°F (962°C).

polo pony A pony bred and selected as a mount for polo. Polo demands speed, agility, stamina, and courage and the ponies ideally have a strong back, broad deep chest, powerful shoulders and hindquarters, a long flexible neck, and hard legs and feet. Some of the best polo ponies come from Argentina, where they have been specially developed since about 1900. Height: 4.8–5.3 ft (1.47–1.63 m) (14½–16 hands).

Poltava 49 35N 34 35E A city in the Soviet Union, in the E Ukrainian SSR. The center of a fertile agricultural region, it has food-processing industries as well as factories producing machinery, building materials, and consumer goods. *History*: it is one of the oldest Ukrainian towns (dating to the 8th century) and was a Cossack center in the 17th century. Peter the Great defeated Charles XII of Sweden here (1709) during the Great *Northern War. Population (1981 est): 284,000.

poltergeist A noisy, mischievous, and frequently destructive invisible agent that persecutes the occupants of a house, most commonly by throwing or moving objects.

polyanthus A hardy perennial, *Primula × polyanthus*, derived from a cross between the common primrose and the cowslip. There are many varieties, with yellow, brown, blue, or red flowers, grown as garden ornamentals. *See also* Primula.

Polybius (c. 200–c. 120 BC) Greek historian. While he was a political hostage in Rome from 168 to 150 BC he became a friend of the general and literary patron Scipio Aemilianus. His major work was a history of Rome from 220 to 145 BC in 40 books, of which only the first 5 survive intact.

Polycarp, St (c. 69–c. 155) Greek martyr and Bishop of Smyrna. He was reputedly converted to Christianity and made a bishop by St John the Apostle. His fame rests on his *Epistle to the Philippians*, explaining St Paul's teachings and defending Christianity against the leading heresies of his age. The *Martyrdom of Polycarp* is an anonymous letter describing his death and is the earliest of its kind. Feast day: Jan 26.

Polyclitus (5th century BC) Greek sculptor, born at *Argos. A very popular and much copied artist, he was primarily a sculptor of athletes in relaxed poses, combining naturalism with beauty of proportion. His works, as known from later copies, seem less majestic and more individual than those of his contemporary *Phidias.

Polycrates (died c. 522) Tyrant of Samos, whose naval campaigns made Samos an important power in the eastern Mediterranean. Deceived into believing he was joining a revolt against the Persians, Polycrates was captured and crucified by the Persian governor of Lydia, Oroetes.

polycythemia An excessive accumulation of red cells in the blood. This may occur in response to a chronic shortage of oxygen (e.g. in people living at high altitudes) or for no obvious reason (polycythemia vera). The blood becomes much thicker and both *thrombosis and hemorrhage are more common in affected people. Treatment is often with radioactive phosphorus.

polyesters Synthetic resins or *plastics that are polymers of *esters. Saturated polyesters (those with no double bonds), made by a condensation reaction, are widely used in such synthetic fibers as Dacron. Unsaturated polyesters are used as resins to make thermosetting plastics.

polyethylene (polythene) A white translucent thermoplastic material made by *polymerization of *ethylene. **Low-density polyethylene** is made at high pressure and is a soft material used for flexible pipes, sheets, and bags. **High-density polyethylene** is made at lower pressures, is more rigid, and softens at a higher temperature. It is used for molded articles.

polygamy. *See* marriage.

polygon A plane straight-sided geometrical figure with three or more sides; for example a pentagon, which has five sides. A regular polygon has all sides equal and all interior angles equal.

Polygonum A genus of annual or perennial herbs (about 75 species), found worldwide, especially in temperate regions. Ranging usually from 4 to 80 in (10 to 200 cm) in height, they bear simple leaves and small five-lobed white or pink flowers, clustered into dense terminal heads or loose branching clusters. Species include the *knotgrass, *bistort, and persicaria (*P. persicaria*)—a creeping weed. Several others are grown in rock gardens and borders. Family: *Polygonaceae*.

polyhedron A solid bounded by plane *polygons called the faces. Two faces intersect at an edge and three or more at a vertex. In a regular polyhedron all the faces are equal regular polygons. The five regular polyhedrons, called the Platonic solids, are the regular tetrahedron, hexahedron, octahedron, dodecahedron, and icosahedron with 4, 6, 8, 12, and 20 sides respectively.

polymerization The chemical combination of simpler molecules (monomers) to form long chain molecules (**polymers**) of repeating units. In **addition polymerization**, the monomers simply add together and no other compound is formed. Polyethylene is made from ethylene in this way. In **condensation polymerization**, water, alcohol, or some other small molecule is formed in the reaction, as in the production of *nylon.

polymorphism In biology, the functional or structural variation between two or more members of a species, determined by differences in either genetic constitution, environmental conditions, or both. It is a widespread phenomenon in animals and plants. In **transient polymorphism** two different forms exist together temporarily, while one form is replacing the other. This occurs in industrial melanism in moths: with industrial pollution the black variety has an advantage over the normal pale form and eventually replaces it. In **balanced polymorphism** the different forms continue to coexist, as in the *castes in social insects.

Polyneices In Greek legend, a son of Oedipus. Having succeeded to the Theban throne, Polyneices and his brother Eteocles agreed to rule the city in alternate years. At the end of his term Eteocles refused to yield to Polyneices, who then laid siege to the city (see Seven Against Thebes). Eteocles and Polyneices killed each other in the war, fulfilling Oedipus' curse on his sons. See also Antigone.

Polynesia A division of Oceania in the S and central Pacific Ocean. The volcanic and coral islands include those of French Polynesia, Hawaii, Samoa, Tonga, Tuvalu, Kiribati, and the Line and Cook Islands. See also Melanesia; Micronesia.

Polynesian The people of the Pacific islands contained within the roughly triangular area between and including Hawaii, New Zealand, and Easter Island. They are seafarers, with considerable skill in navigation. Fishing and cultivating are also important. There is considerable uniformity in culture throughout this huge area but social organization varies greatly. Kinship is important everywhere. The degree of political centralization and hierarchy varies between the smaller and larger islands. The Polynesian languages belong to the Oceanic branch of the *Austronesian family and include Samoan, *Maori, Tongan, Tahitian, and Hawaiian.

polyp (biology) A sedentary form that occurs during the life cycle of many animals of the phylum *Coelenterata*. It has a cylindrical stalklike body attached at the base, with the mouth at the free end surrounded by tentacles bearing stinging cells (nematocysts). Polyps occur singly or in colonies; colonial polyps are modified for different functions, such as feeding, reproduction, and protection. Polyps reproduce asexually to form new polyps or *medusae or sexually to form polyps.

polyp (medicine) A growth that has a narrow base or stalk. Polyps may occur in the bowel, the nose, the womb, the larynx, and other sites. They often cause obstruction or infection and some forms may become cancerous: for this reason they are best removed by surgery or cauterization.

polypeptide. See peptide.

Polyphemus In Greek mythology, a one-eyed giant, one of the *Cyclops. He lived in Sicily and was an unrequited lover of the nymph *Galatea. Odysseus and his companions escaped from imprisonment in his cave by making him drunk and then blinding him.

polyphony (Greek: many voices) Music that consists of a horizontal combination of melodic strands rather than a series of vertical chords. In its earliest form (9th to 11th centuries) it consisted of voices moving in parallel fourths, fifths, and octaves, called *organum, a development of *plainchant. The true polyphonic period began when the voices became independent, moving in contrary motion and having different note values. The high point of the polyphonic style was reached in the 16th century with *Palestrina's church music, the Italian *madrigal, the compositions of the English madrigalists, and the church music of Tallis and Byrd. The music of later polyphonic composers completed the transition from modal polyphony to the system of major and minor keys and stands at the threshold of the harmonic period. See counterpoint; harmony; modes.

polyploidy A condition in which the number of sets of chromosomes in a cell is greater than normal. Most organisms have two representatives of each chromosome in their body cells—the diploid state. With three of each the cell is triploid, with four—tetraploid, five—pentaploid, and so on. Polyploidy may arise naturally, for example when a sterile hybrid doubles its chromosome number. This results in a fertile organism and is thought to be the means by which many species of plants arose, including wheat. Polyploid plants often show improved size and vigor, and the condition has been induced in crop plants by treating them with chemicals.

polypody A *fern of the genus *Polypodium*, especially *P. vulgare*, which grows on walls, rocks, and trees in temperate regions. It has a creeping slender scaly rhizome with numerous roots, and the tapering branched fronds, 2–30 in (5–75 cm) long, are made up of paired leaflets. The spore capsules are grouped in rounded yellow or orange clusters (sori) and usually occur in two rows on the undersides of the upper leaflets. Family: *Polypodiaceae*.

polypropylene A thermoplastic material made by *polymerization of propylene (CH_2:$CHCH_3$). It is similar to high-density *polyethylene but stronger, lighter, and more rigid. Polypropylene products, such as beer crates, luggage, and hinges, are injection molded. Fibers, which are used to make sacks and carpet backings, are made by extrusion.

polysaccharide A carbohydrate comprising chains of between three and several thousand linked *monosaccharide units. Polysaccharides, such as *starch, *glycogen, and *cellulose, are important as energy reserves and structural components of plants and animals.

polytechnics Institutes of higher education concentrating on courses with vocational relevance while maintaining high academic standards. The first polytechnic was established in Paris in 1794 to provide technical training for artillery and engineering officers. Polytechnics were established in Germany during the first half of the 19th century, while the development of the polytechnic movement in the UK began in 1880.

polytetrafluoroethylene (PTFE) A synthetic material produced by the *polymerization of tetrafluoroethylene (F_2C:CF_2). It can withstand temperatures of up to 750°F (400°C) and has a very slippery surface. PTFE is used to coat nonstick cooking utensils and in gaskets, bearings, and electrical insulation. It is sold under the tradenames Teflon and Fluon.

polytheism Belief in more than one god (compare monotheism). Polytheism characterized the religions of the ancient Indo-European peoples (see Greek religion; Roman religion) and survives today in *Hinduism.

Polytrichum A genus of *mosses (over 100 species), known as pigeon wheat and hair-cap mosses, that form large mats in peat bogs, old fields, and acid soils. *P. commune* is the most widely distributed species and grows up to 6 in (15 cm) high. *Polytrichum* has been used in brooms, baskets, and in stuffing mattresses. Family: *Polytrichaceae*.

polyurethane A synthetic polymer the molecules of which contain the –NH.CO.O– group. Some polyurethanes form thermosetting resins and others, thermoplastic resins. They have a wide range of properties and are used in paints, adhesives, molded articles, rubbers, lacquers, and foams. Polyurethane foam is manufactured from *urethane and can be made flexible or rigid.

polyvinyl acetate (PVA) A vinyl *resin produced by *polymerization of vinyl acetate (CH_2:$CHOOCCH_3$). It is a soft material, used in paints and adhesives.

polyvinyl chloride (PVC) A vinyl *resin or plastic produced by *polymerization of vinyl chloride (chloroethene; CH_2:$CHCl$), a toxic gas. Rigid PVC products are made by molding. The addition of a plasticizer produces flexible PVC. PVC is tough, nonflammable, resistant to moisture, and a good electrical insulator. It is widely used in sheets, pipes, electrical insulators, and clothing.

Pombal, Sebastião José de Carvalho e Mello, Marquês de (1699–1782) Portuguese statesman, who was the virtual ruler of Portugal from 1750 to 1777 as the chief minister of José I (1715–77; reigned 1750–77). A proponent of enlightened despotism (see Enlightenment), he reformed government administration, encouraged manufacturing, and modernized education. He also directed the rebuilding of Lisbon following the earthquake of 1755. His reforms did not achieve lasting success and his unpopular methods caused his downfall after José's death.

pomegranate A shrub or small tree, *Punica granatum*, native to W Asia and widely cultivated in the tropics and subtropics for its fruit. 16–23 ft (5–7 m) tall, it has narrow pointed leaves, about 3 in (7.5 cm) long, and orange-red flowers growing in the leaf axils. The large round fruit has a thick leathery yellowish-reddish skin and contains several chambers, each containing many seeds coated with a pinkish acid-sweet juicy pulp. Pomegranates are eaten fresh or used in beverages or wines. The seeds are used in preserves and syrups. Family: *Punicaceae*.

Pomerania A region of NE Europe on the Baltic Sea between the Oder and Vistula Rivers. Pomerania was Polish territory until the 17th century, when the western and central regions were acquired by Brandenburg (later Prussia). Sweden gained W Pomerania in 1648 but by 1815 it had been reacquired by Prussia, which in 1772 had annexed E Pomerania. Territorial redistribution after World Wars I and II restored Pomerania E of the Oder River to Poland; W Pomerania became part of East Germany.

Pomeranian A breed of toy dog, developed in Pomerania, whose ancestors are thought to have been Scandinavian sled dogs. The Pomeranian has a compact body and foxlike head with small erect ears. The short undercoat is covered by a long straight outercoat and the fluffy tail is held over the back. The coat may be any recognized color, including white, black, brown, or reddish. Height: 5.5–7 in (14–18 cm).

Pomona (mythology) A Roman goddess of fruit to whom a sacred precinct outside Rome was dedicated. She was married to Vertumnus, a god who controlled the change of seasons.

Pomona (Orkneys). See Mainland.

Pompadour, Mme de (Jeanne Antoinette Poisson, Marquise de P.; 1721–64) The mistress of Louis XV, who exerted considerable political influence from 1745 until her death. She influenced the negotiation of an Austrian alliance against Prussia and was blamed for French defeats in the subsequent *Seven Years' War. She was a notable patron of artists and scholars.

MME DE POMPADOUR *Portrait by François Boucher of the mistress of Louis XV.*

pompano A valuable food fish of the genus *Trachinotus*. It has a deep body, usually up to 20 in (50 cm) long, colored silvery blue or gray. Pompanos are carnivorous and live in fast-swimming groups, usually around rocks in warm coastal waters. Family: *Carangidae*; order: *Perciformes*.

Pompeii An ancient city near Naples, in Italy. It was buried 12–18 ft (4–6 m) deep under volcanic ash by the eruption of Mount *Vesuvius (79 AD). Its rediscovery (1748) stimulated general interest in classical archeology. Pompeii, now about three-quarters excavated, provides unparalleled evidence for daily life in Roman times: buildings, often standing to the second floor and with extensive wall paintings and graffiti; normally perishable objects including food, wooden furniture, and paintings, preserved by the ash; and personal possessions abandoned by the fleeing inhabitants.

Pompey (Gnaeus Pompeius; 106–48 BC) Roman general and statesman, called Pompeius Magnus (Pompey the Great). Granted extraordinary powers (67–66) to destroy marauding pirates and then to wage war in Asia, Pompey returned a popular hero. In 60 he joined Julius Caesar and Crassus in the first *Triumvirate, marrying Caesar's daughter Julia (d. 54) in 59, but in 50 he supported the Senate's demand for Caesar to resign his armies. In the civil war that followed Pompey was defeated by Caesar at Pharsalus (48) and fled to Egypt, where he was murdered.

Pompidou, Georges (Jean Raymond) (1911–74) French statesman; prime minister (1962, 1962–66, 1966–67, 1967–68) and president (1969–74). He served under de Gaulle during World War II and was his personal assistant in 1958–59, when he helped draft the constitution of the Fifth Republic. He negotiated a settlement with the Algerians (1961) and with the students in the revolt of May, 1968. He succeeded de Gaulle as president.

Ponce 18 01N 66 36W A major city and port in S Puerto Rico, on the Caribbean Sea. Industries include iron processing, sugar refining, and canning. Population (1980): 188,219.

Ponce de Leon, Juan (1460–1521) Spanish explorer. He accompanied Columbus on his second voyage to Central America (1493–96) and in 1508–09 founded the first settlement in Puerto Rico, of which he became governor (1510). In 1512, searching for the legendary fountain of eternal youth, he discovered Florida. He died while attempting to colonize it, from a wound received from an Indian's poisoned arrow. The port of Ponce is named for him.

Pondicherry A Union Territory in SE India, on the Coromandel Coast. Founded by the French in 1674, it was their chief settlement in India until transferred to Indian administration in 1954. Rice and millet are the chief products. Area: 185 sq mi (479 sq km). Population (1981 est): 604,136. Capital: Pondicherry.

pond skater A *water bug belonging to the family *Gerridae* (about 350 species). Pond skaters, or water striders, have a dark slender body and long legs. They are found mainly in fresh water, running or skating across the surface and feeding on small insects.

pond turtle Either of two species of turtle found in ponds and other still waters. The Pacific pond turtle (*Clemmys marmorata*), of the W coast of North America, is 6–7 in (15–18 cm) long and brown with yellow spots; it

is widely sold for food. The European pond turtle (*Emys orbicularis*) of Europe, N Africa, and W Asia, is 4.7–5.1 in (12–13 cm) long and brown with yellow speckles. Family: *Emydidae*.

pondweed A usually perennial aquatic herb of the genus *Potamogeton* (100 species), found worldwide in fresh water. It has submerged or floating oblong or pointed leaves, 0.8–8 in (2–20 cm) long, and stalked heads of tiny four-lobed greenish flowers. Family: *Potamogetonaceae*.

The Canadian pondweed (*Elodea canadensis*) has submerged stems, up to 10 ft (3 m) long, with whorls of narrow backward-curving dark-green leaves. Native to North America, it is naturalized in Europe. Family: *Hydrocharitaceae*.

Poniatowski, Józef (1763–1813) Marshal of France, born in Austria, who served consecutively in the Austrian and Polish armies before becoming commander of the Duchy of Warsaw, established by Napoleon in 1807. He fought in Napoleon's Russian campaign (1812–13) and died at *Leipzig.

Ponta Delgada 37 29N 25 40W A city in the Azores, the capital of São Miguel Island. Important since 1540, it is a tourist resort and the main commercial center of the Azores. Population (1979 est): 146,600.

Pontchartrain, Lake A coastal lake in SE Louisiana, just NW of New Orleans. It is connected to the Mississippi River and the Gulf of Mexico by lakes and canals and receives excess water from the Mississippi River by way of spillways. The largest lake in Louisiana, it is a popular resort area. Area: 625 sq mi (1620 sq km).

Ponte Vecchio A bridge over the Arno River in Florence. Topped by buildings, it was designed by Taddeo *Gaddi and finished in 1345. It was a highly advanced structure for its period.

Pontevedra 42 25N 8 39W A port in NW Spain, in Galicia. It has a 16th-century cathedral and an episcopal palace. Its manufactures include cloth, leather, and pottery. Population (1970): 52,452.

Pontiac (c. 1720–c. 1769) American Indian chief, who organized local tribes to resist White migration to the NW. In **Pontiac's Conspiracy** (1763–66) the Indians took all but three of the British fortified posts. Fighting continued until 1765, when the posts were all recaptured, and peace was signed at Oswego in 1766.

Pontianak 0 05S 109 16E A port in Indonesia, in W Kalimantan on the Kapuas delta. Formerly Borneo's main gold town, its chief industries are shipbuilding and rubber, palm oil, sugar, and timber processing. Its university was established in 1963. Population (1971): 217,555.

Pontine Marshes (Italian name: Agro Pontino) A reclaimed marshland area in S central Italy, bordering on the Tyrrhenian Sea. An extensive program to drain the marshes was begun in 1928; several towns including Littoria (now Latina) were established and it has become one of the most productive agricultural areas in Italy.

pontoon bridge A type of temporary bridge in which the deck (or roadway) rests on floating flat-bottomed vessels (pontoons). Pontoons were often used in the earliest military campaigns as they could be preassembled, floated into position, and did not need to last forever. Modern pontoon bridges often have a movable section to allow boats to pass; they are useful where the earth is unsuitable for heavy pier foundations or the traffic is too light to justify a piered bridge.

Pontormo, Jacopo da (J. Carrucci; 1494–1557) Italian mannerist painter, born in Pontormo (*see* mannerism). He settled in Florence, where he trained under *Andrea del Sarto. He painted mythological scenes in the Medici villa at Poggio a Caiano (1521) and scenes of the Passion (1522–25) at the Certosa, near Florence, but his major work is the *Deposition* (Sta Felicità, Florence).

Pontus The coastal region S of the Black Sea in NE Asia Minor. Pontus was a kingdom from the 4th century BC, becoming prominent in the 1st century BC under *Mithridates VI Eupator. Pompey conquered Pontus in 64, after which the region was administered by Rome.

pony A *horse that does not exceed 5 ft (1.47 m) (14½ hands) in height at maturity, measured from the top of the shoulders (withers). The many modern breeds of pony are thought to have developed from one or two original types, which may have resembled *Przewalski's horse. Ponies have traditionally been used by man as pack animals and for riding. Today, they are especially popular as children's mounts.

poodle A breed of ☐dog of uncertain origins but long associated with France and Germany. The poodle is an active intelligent dog with a long straight muzzle, drooping ears, and a docked tail. The dense coat, which was originally clipped to enable them to swim and retrieve in water, may be any recognized color, including gray, white, black, brown, or cream. The miniature poodle and toy poodle are derivative breeds of the standard poodle. Height: 15 in (38 cm) minimum (standard); 11–15 in (28–38 cm) (miniature); under 11 in (28 cm) (toy).

pool A form of *billiards played on a table usually 4.5 × 9 ft (1.4 × 2.7 m) with six pockets. The object is to use a white cue ball to sink the 15 colored balls into the pockets.

Poole 50 43N 1 59W A resort in SW England, in Dorset on Poole Harbour. It is a minor port, with boatbuilding, engineering, pottery (using local clays), and chemical industries. Population (1981): 118,922.

Poona (*or* Pune) 18 34N 73 58E A city in India, in Maharashtra. Capital of the Marathas in the late 18th century, it was taken by the British in 1817. It is the site of a university (1949) and a renowned oriental research institute (1919). A commercial, manufacturing, and military center, it has cotton textiles, rubber, paper, and munitions industries. Population (1981 est): 1,685,266.

Poor Laws The laws that governed assistance to the poor in Britain. From the 16th century parishes were responsible for providing for their poor and from 1572 levied a tax for poor relief. The Poor Law Amendment Act of 1834 abolished outdoor relief and those seeking assistance had to enter a workhouse. The Poor Law system was not abolished until 1947.

pop art A modern art movement dominant in the US and Britain in the 1960s. Pop art is strongly influenced by the mass media—television, comics, advertising, etc.—in its subject matter and techniques. Also characteristic is the use of silkscreen *printing, *collage, and the *ready-made. Pioneered in the 1950s by Jasper *Johns and Robert *Rauschenberg, it was influenced by the early 20th-century *dada movement and developed as a reaction to *action painting. Leading pop artists are Andy *Warhol, Roy *Lichtenstein, Claes *Oldenburg, Richard *Hamilton, George Segal, and Peter *Blake.

pope. *See* papacy.

Pope, Alexander (1688–1744) British poet. A severe childhood illness left him a cripple for life. He established his reputation as a poet of biting wit and skill, especially in his masterly use of the heroic couplet, with *An Essay on Criticism* (1711) and the mock epic *The Rape of the Lock* (1712–14). The financial gains from his translations of Homer's *Iliad* (1715–20) and *Odyssey* (1725–26) enabled him to move in 1719 to his comfortable house in Twickenham. Here he wrote the mock epic *The Dunciad* (1728; revised 1742–43), the philosophical poem *An Essay on Man* (1733–34), and poems modeled on the satires of Horace.

Pope, John (1822–92) US Union general. A graduate of West Point, he served in the *Mexican War and during the Civil War. As head of the Army of Virginia (1862) he was defeated at the second battle of *Bull Run. Later, he was in command of the Department of Missouri (1870–83).

Popish Plot (1678) A conspiracy in England, invented by Titus Oates (1649–1705) and Israel Tonge. They alleged the existence of a plot to assassinate Charles II and place his Roman Catholic brother, James, on the throne. The anti-Catholic passions Oates and Tonge thus aroused led to the execution of 35 suspects and the exclusion of Catholics from parliament (*see* Test Acts).

poplar A shrub or tree of the genus *Populus* (about 30 species), native to N temperate regions and grown for wood pulp, shade, and ornament. Up to 130 ft (40 m) tall, the trees may have a broad spreading crown, as in the European black poplar (*P. nigra*), or a tall slender one, as in the Lombardy poplar (*P. nigra* var. *italica*). The oval, triangular, or heart-shaped leaves may have striking autumn colors and the drooping male and female catkins are usually borne on separate trees. The seeds have tufts of silky white hairs. Family: *Salicaceae*. See also aspen.

pop music Any music that is general in its appeal, especially among young people; it includes folk, country and western, and, predominantly, *rock music. It is distinguished from classical music and pure jazz by its lack of sophistication. Pop emerged as a distinctive genre in the 1950s with the emergence of small groups using electronically amplified instruments, simple harmonies, and heavy rhythms. Pop songs are generally about basic human emotions, such as love, happiness, and grief. The emergence of youth movements in the early 1960s lent pop a rebelliousness that expressed itself in the life styles of pop musicians, the lyrics of pop songs, and unconventional styles of dress and performance. The multiplicity of styles in the 1960s, 1970s, and 1980s reflected the development of rock, the predominance of individual performers and groups, and the emergence of disco music. The term **popular music** is generally applied to light music of a romantic or sentimental kind.

Popocatépetl, Mount 19 02N 93 38W A dormant volcano in central Mexico, near Mexico City. Its crater contains sulfur deposits. Height: 17,887 ft (5452 m).

Popov, Aleksandr Stepanovich (1859–1905) Russian physicist, who studied the transmission of radio waves. Popov's work preceded that of *Marconi and in 1897 he succeeded in transmitting over a distance of three miles (five kilometers). However, he failed to pursue the use of radio waves for communication, using them instead to study thunderstorms.

Popper, Sir Karl Raimund (1902–) Austrian-born philosopher. Forced by the Nazi threat to emigrate, Popper was a professor at the London School of Economics (1949–69). His interests were mainly scientific and political. In *The Logic of Scientific Discovery* (1935) he cast doubt upon time-honored methods of establishing scientific laws by observation and experiment: "all crows are black" is an unrestricted generalization that can never be verified (we can never hope to observe *all* crows), but it could be falsified by the observation of one white crow. *The Open Society and its Enemies* (1945) and *The Poverty of Historicism* (1957) promote "methodological individualism," the restoration of the historical importance of the individual against collective doctrinaire systems such as Marxism.

poppy An annual, biennial, or perennial plant of the genus *Papaver* (about 120 species), native mainly to the N hemisphere and often grown for ornament. 6–40 in (15–100 cm) high, it yields a milky sap (latex) and bears large lobed or divided leaves and showy white, pink, or red flowers, sometimes with a dark center, with 4–6 petals surrounding a dense whorl of stamens. The □fruit is a capsule with pores through which the seeds are dispersed. Species include the *corn poppy and *opium poppy. Family: *Papaveraceae*. *See also* horned poppy; prickly poppy; Welsh poppy.

popular front A coalition of left-wing and moderate political groups. Increasingly concerned by the rise of fascism in the mid-1930s, many Communist Parties, with Soviet encouragement, sought political alliances with socialist and liberal groups. In 1936 a popular-front government was elected in France; but generally the different parties were too divided to oppose fascism effectively. *See also* United Fronts.

Populism US farm movement, active in the 1890s. The Populist Party, organized in 1892, evolved from individual farmers' alliances, action groups formed in the West and South in the 1880s to protest poor economic conditions for farmers. Their platform demanded *free silver coinage, government-controlled railroads, and a graduated income tax, among other things—all meant to equalize farmer power with that of business and industry. Although the party made inroads in the elections of 1892 and 1894, it was absorbed into the Democratic Party by 1896.

porbeagle A *mackerel shark, *Lamna nasus*, commonly called the Atlantic mackerel shark, that lives mainly in N temperate shallow waters. It has a dark-blue robust body, 5–10 ft (1.5–3 m) long, with a white belly and may occur in small groups, feeding principally on shoals of fish, especially mackerel.

porcelain White vitrified ceramic evolved by Chinese potters about 900 AD. It was not invented but developed out of stoneware pottery. There are three kinds of porcelain: hard-paste or true porcelain, soft-paste or artificial, and English bone china. Hard-paste porcelain consists of china clay (kaolin) and fusible feldspathic rock (petuntse) finely mixed and fired to about 2550°F (1400°C). This forms a translucent white resonant vitreous body, which is usually glazed with pure petuntse during the firing. Hard-paste porcelain was made in Japan about 1500 AD but the secret of its manufacture defied discovery elsewhere until the early 18th century when the alchemist Böttger (1682–1719) succeeded, after exhaustive secret experiments, in making it at *Meissen. Soft-paste porcelain differs from hard-paste in that the clay or kaolin is mixed with an artificial flux. This might be sand with lime, or flint, soda, etc., depending on the factory. The mixture is fired at about 2015°F (1100°C) and the glaze, usually of glass, is applied in a second firing at about 1835°F (1000°C). Bone porcelain is an 18th-century English invention using bone ash as a flux.

porcupine A large herbivorous spiny *rodent belonging to either of the families *Erethizontidae* (New World porcupines; 11 species) or *Hystricidae* (Old World porcupines; 15 species). American porcupines tend to be arboreal and have prehensile tails. The North American porcupine (*Erethizion dorsatum*) is about 30 in (75 cm) long and grows a soft winter coat that almost conceals its covering of quills. Old World porcupines are mainly ground-dwelling. The Indian crested porcupine (*Hystrix indica*) grows to 40 in (1 m) in length and may have spines 14 in (35 cm) long. Porcupines respond to a threat by turning their backs and raising their spines or even running backward at an attacker. □mammal.

porcupine fish A fish, also called sea porcupine, belonging to a family (*Diodontidae*) related to *puffers, especially *Diodon hystrix*, found in tropical seas. It has a short broad body, up to about 35 in (90 cm) long, which it inflates when provoked, erecting numerous spines in the skin.

porgy. *See* sea bream.

Pori (Swedish name: Björneborg) 61 28N 21 45E A seaport in S Finland, on the Gulf of Bothnia. Its industries include copper refining, textiles, wood processing, steel, and chemicals. Population (1980): 79,405.

porphyria A group of genetic disorders in which there is an accumulation in the body of one or more porphyrins—precursors of the red blood pigment—due to an enzyme defect. The disease affects the digestive tract, causing abdominal pain, vomiting, and diarrhea; the nervous system, causing psychotic disorder, epilepsy, and weakness; the circulatory system, causing high blood pressure; and the skin, causing photosensitivity. There is no specific treatment. The madness of George III is now known to have been due to porphyria.

porphyry An igneous rock, usually hypabyssal, containing numerous large crystals called phenocrysts set in a finer-grained, or sometimes glassy, groundmass. The term porphyry is often given with the name of the porphyritic mineral, for example quartz porphyry.

Porphyry (232–305 AD) Syrian-born philosopher and devoted disciple, editor, and biographer of *Plotinus. Among nearly 80 titles attributed to him are religious and philosophical works, including a *Treatise against Christians*, banned in 448 AD but still partly extant, and commentaries on philosophical authors. He also wrote on literary, grammatical, and scientific topics.

porpoise A small toothed *whale belonging to the family *Phocoenidae* (7 species), of coastal waters. Porpoises are 5–7 ft (1.5–2 m) long and have no beak. The common, or harbor, porpoise (*Phocoena phocoena*) of the N Atlantic and Pacific, has a rounded body, tapering toward the tail, bluegray above and pale gray beneath. It lives in large groups called schools, feeding on fish, squid, and crustaceans.

port A fortified usually dessert *wine from Oporto (N Portugal). The grapes grown on the Douro hillsides are trodden in stone presses. Fermentation is halted by adding brandy. Subsequently the wine is taken to the lodges near Oporto, where it matures in wood. Port-type wines are made in other countries, such as South Africa.

Port Arthur 29 55N 93 56W A city in S Texas. Situated in an oil region known as the Golden Triangle, Port Arthur is a major shipping outlet for oil and has large petrochemical industries. Population (1980): 61,106.

Port Arthur. *See* Lüda; Thunder Bay.

Port-au-Prince 18 40N 72 20W The capital of Haiti, a port in the SW on the Gulf of Gonaïves. Its main exports are coffee and sugar. The University of Haiti was founded here in 1944. Population (1977 est): 703,100.

Port Elizabeth 33 58S 25 36E A city in South Africa, in S Cape Province on Algoa Bay. It was founded in 1820 by British settlers. The university was founded in 1964. Nearby is the Addo Elephant National Park. It is a major port, ore being the chief export, and industries include automobile assembly, fruit canning, and flour milling. Population (1980 est): 492,140.

Porter, Cole (Albert) (1893–1964) US composer of musical comedies and popular songs. He wrote a series of musicals, including *The Gay Divorcée* (1932), *Anything Goes* (1934), *Kiss Me Kate* (1948), and *Can Can* (1953). His songs included "Night and Day" and "Begin the Beguine."

Porter, Katherine Anne (1890–1980) US short-story writer and novelist. As a journalist she traveled in Mexico and Spain. *Flowering Judas*, her first collection of stories, was published in 1930. Her stories, especially those in *Pale Horse, Pale Rider* (1939), are mostly delicate explorations of autobiographical material. Her only novel was the allegorical *Ship of Fools* (1962), which won a Pulitzer Prize.

Port Harcourt 4 43N 7 05E A port in S Nigeria. Founded in 1912, it developed as a port following the arrival of the railroad (1916) from the Enugu coalfields. It now exports coal, tin, and palm oil. It is the major industrial center of the Niger delta oilfields. It has a university (1975). Population (1975 est): 242,000.

Portile de Fier. *See* Iron Gate.

Port Klang (name until 1971: Port Swettenham) 3 01N 101 25E A port in W Peninsular Malaysia, on the Strait of Malacca. Exporting chiefly rubber, it serves the Klang Valley, Malaysia's chief industrial area. Population (1970): 113,611.

Portland 45 32N 122 40W A city in Oregon, on the Willamette River. It was founded in 1829 and its growth was stimulated by several gold rushes along the Oregon Trail. The state's largest city, it is a deepwater port, with shipbuilding, timber, and metallurgical industries. It is the site of the University of Portland (1901). Population (1980): 366,383.

Portland 43 41N 70 18W A city in SW Maine, on Casco Bay. Destroyed by Indians, French, and British, it was the state capital (1820–32). It is a major petroleum port and commercial center. Industries include timber, textiles, and chemicals. Population (1980): 61,572.

Portland, William Henry Cavendish Bentinck, 3rd Duke of (1738–1809) British statesman; prime minister (1783, 1807–09). He was nominal head of the coalition between Lord North and Charles James Fox (1783) and was subsequently home secretary (1794–1801).

Portland vase A Roman vase (c. 1st century AD) of dark blue glass with a white glass relief of figures, discovered in Italy in 1644. It once belonged to the Duke of Portland but is now in the British Museum.

Port Louis 20 10S 57 30E The capital of Mauritius, in the NW of the island. Founded in about 1736, it is the site of two cathedrals. Sugar is exported. Population (1980 est): 147,386.

Port Lyautey. *See* Kenitra.

Port Moresby 9 30S 147 07E The capital and main port of Papua New Guinea, on the Gulf of Papua. It was an important Allied base in World War II and since then the port has been considerably modernized. The University of Papua New Guinea was founded in 1965. Population (1980 est): 122,761.

Pôrto. *See* Oporto.

Pôrto Alegre 30 03S 51 10W A city in S Brazil, the capital of Rio Grande do Sul state on the Lagôa (Lagoon) dos Patos. It is a major commercial and industrial center; industries are chiefly related to agriculture and include meat processing, tanning, and the manufacture of textiles. It is the seat of two universities. Population (1980): 1,108,883.

Port-of-Spain 10 38N 61 31W The capital and main port of Trinidad and Tobago since 1783, on the W coast of Trinidad. It was the capital of the short-lived Federation of the West Indies from 1958 until 1962. Notable buildings include the Anglican and Roman Catholic cathedrals. Petroleum products, sugar, and rum are among the main exports. Population (1970): 11,032.

Porto Novo 6 30N 2 47E The capital of Benin, on the Gulf of Guinea. A former center of the slave trade with the Portuguese, it came under French rule in the late 19th century. Trade includes palm oil and cotton. Population (1979 est): 132,000.

Port Royal A former Cistercian nunnery originally situated a short distance SW of Paris; also called Port Royal des Champs. In the 17th century it became a center of *Jansenism under Abbess Angélique Arnauld (1591–1661), sister of Antoine *Arnauld. After persecution the nuns were dispersed (1709).

Port Said (*or* Bur Said) 31 17N 32 18E A major port in Egypt, situated at the Mediterranean entrance to the Suez Canal. Founded in 1859, it became an important fueling point but suffered from the closure of the Suez Canal (1967–75) and Israeli occupation of the E bank. Population (1976): 263,000.

Portsmouth 50 48N 1 05W A port in S England, at the entrance to Portsmouth Harbour. Notable landmarks include Admiral Nelson's flagship HMS *Victory* and Charles Dickens' birthplace (now a museum). The chief naval base in the UK, Portsmouth is also a commercial port with shipbuilding, ship-maintenance, electronics, and aircraft-engineering industries. Population (1981): 179,419.

Portsmouth 36 50N 76 20W A city and port in Virginia, on Hampton Roads. Founded in 1752, it is the site of the Norfolk Naval Yard, abandoned by Federal troops (1861) during the US Civil War and used by the Confederates to transform the scuttled USS *Merrimack* into the *ironclad *Virginia*. The main industry is shipbuilding and ship repairing. Population (1980): 104,577.

Portsmouth 43 03N 70 47W A city in New Hampshire, on the Atlantic coast. It has several notable buildings, including the John Paul Jones House (1758). The state's only seaport, it is the site of the Portsmouth Naval Yard (established in 1800); it is an important submarine base. Population (1980): 26,214.

Portsmouth Peace Conference (1905) US-sponsored meeting in Portsmouth, NH, to work out peace terms to end the *Russo-Japanese War.

Port Sudan 19 38N 37 07E A port in the Sudan, on the Red Sea. It handles much of the country's trade; exports include cotton, gum arabic, and sesame seeds. It also has an important salt-panning industry. Population (1973): 132,631.

Port Sunlight. *See* Bebington.

Port Swettenham. *See* Port Klang.

Portugal, Republic of A country in SW Europe, occupying the W section of the Iberian Peninsula and bordering on the Atlantic Ocean. The *Madeira Islands are an integral part of Portugal. Coastal plains rise to mountains, reaching 6352 ft (1935 m) in the N. The main rivers are the Douro, Miño, and Tagus. *Economy*: traditionally agricultural, Portugal's principal exports are textiles, clothing, cork, wood products, sardines, and fortified wines. However, recent political upheavals, an inefficient farming system, and drought, combined with loss of cheap raw materials following the independence of former colonies, have led to many economic difficulties. Tourism, an important source of foreign currency, virtually ceased for a while but was being revived by the late 1970s. Rich mineral resources include coal, copper pyrites, kaolin, and hematite, and hydroelectricity is a valuable source of power. *History*: the early history of the region is that of the rest of the Iberian Peninsula (*see* Spain, Kingdom of). Portugal as a distinct Christian territory dates from 868. It became a kingdom in 1139 under Alfonso I and its position was consolidated in the 13th century by the conquest of Muslim territory. Portugal's long alliance with England began in the 14th century. From the 15th century Portuguese explorers opened up new trade routes, allowing for the establishment of an extensive overseas empire that included Angola, Mozambique, and Brazil. In 1580 Portugal came under Spanish domination, which lasted until 1640, after which the Portuguese monarchy became increasingly reactionary, a trend that *Pombal's reforms attempted to reverse. In 1807 Portugal was invaded by the French, who were defeated in the subsequent *Peninsular War. A revolution in 1910 overthrew the monarchy and established a republic. A long period of political instability culminated in a military coup in 1926. A prominent role in the new government was played by *Salazar, who became prime minister in 1932 and established the corporatist New State. His long dictatorship also witnessed bitter colonial wars in Africa. In April, 1974, the government of Salazar's successor, Marcello Caetano, was overthrown in a military coup led by General Antonio de Spinola. Spinola granted independence to Portugal's remaining African colonies before falling from power later the same year, since when there has been a succession of governments as conflict between Left and Right has continued. President: General Ramalho Eanes. Prime minister: Mario Soares. Official language: Portuguese. Official religion: Roman Catholic. Official currency: escudo of 100 centavos. Area: 34,861 sq mi (91,631 sq km). Population (1983 est): 10,008,000. Capital and main port: Lisbon.

Portuguese A *Romance language spoken in Portugal, Galicia (Spain), Brazil, Madeira, and the Azores. It emerged as a distinct language during the early medieval period. The standard form is based on the dialect of Lisbon. Brazilian Portuguese differs slightly in grammar and sound system. A notable characteristic of Portuguese is the use of nasal vowel sounds.

Portuguese East Africa. *See* Mozambique, People's Republic of.

Portuguese Guinea. *See* Guinea-Bissau, Republic of.

Portuguese literature Literature in the Portuguese language commences with the lyrics of a school of poets who flourished under the kings Alfonso III (1248–79) and Dinis (1279–1325) are preserved in three collections of *cancioneiros*. In a later collection, the *Cancioneiro Geral* (1516), the influence of Provençal poetry was replaced by that of Spanish and Italian models. During the 16th century, the golden age of Portuguese literature, Gil Vicente wrote pioneering works of drama, Sá de Miranda (c. 1481–1558) introduced many new poetic forms from Italy, and Luís de Camões composed the national epic poem, *Os Lusíadas* (1572). The subsequent period of decline lasted until the influence of Romanticism in the early 19th century inspired the works of João Baptista da Silva Leitão Almeida-Garrett (1799–1854) and Alexandre Herculano (1810–77). Further stimulation was provided by a reaction against the pseudoclassicism of Feliciano de Castilho led by Antero de Quental (1842–91) and by the influence of French Symbolism. Outstanding individual writers of the 20th century include the poet Fernando Pessoa (1888–1935) and the novelist Manual Ribeiro (1879–1941).

Portuguese man-of-war A colonial marine invertebrate animal belonging to a genus (*Physalia*) of *coelenterates found mainly in warm seas. It has a translucent bladder-like float (pneumatophore), pink, blue, or violet in color, which acts like a sail in the wind. Attached underneath are clusters of *polyps bearing stinging tentacles, up to 165 ft (50 m) long, used to paralyze fish and other prey. The sting can also have a serious effect on humans. Order: *Siphonophora*; class: *Hydrozoa*. □oceans.

Portuguese West Africa. *See* Angola, People's Republic of.

Poseidon The Greek god of the sea and earthquakes, son of Cronus and Rhea and brother of Zeus and Hades. He used his ability to change his

form mainly to further his amorous desires, and his many offspring included Theseus, Polyphemus, and the winged horse Pegasus. He was usually portrayed with a trident and dolphin. He was identified with the Roman *Neptune.

Posen. *See* Poznań.

Po-shan. *See* Zibo.

positivism The philosophical doctrine of *Comte and his successors. It asserts that knowledge of reality can be achieved *only* through the particular sciences and ordinary observation. Positivism rejects all metaphysical propositions, but it has been pointed out (with regard to later *logical positivism) that this rejection itself constitutes a metaphysical proposition. *Hobbes was an earlier positivist with regard to the status of the law. The only law is positive law, the law that is actually enforced; there is no "higher" law such as natural law. *Existentialism, especially in France, has been a reaction against positivism.

positron The antiparticle of the *electron, having the same mass and *spin as the electron but opposite electric charge. A positron and an electron annihilate each other on collision, producing two gamma-ray photons.

possum The most common Australian *marsupial, *Trichosurus vulpecula*, also called brush-tailed phalanger. Nocturnal and arboreal, it is cat-sized and has a soft grayish coat and tail. It feeds mainly on buds, leaves, and fruit, and occasionally fledgling birds. The name possum is often used for other members of the family *Phalangeridae*.

Postal Service, United States Independent agency that provides mail processing and delivery services to individuals and businesses within the US. It protects the mails from loss or theft and apprehends those who violate postal laws. It is headed by the postmaster general, who is appointed by a board of nine governors appointed by the president.

poster art The design of public notices for advertising and propaganda purposes. Poster design originated in the mid-19th century, the first major poster artist being the Frenchman Jules Chéret (1836–1933). Its development was facilitated by the use of lithography (*see* printing), an inexpensive and easy printing process. Leading painters of the period who designed posters included *Toulouse-Lautrec and Aubrey *Beardsley.

POSTIMPRESSIONISM Bathers, Asnières *(1883-84) by Georges Seurat in his pointillism style.*

postimpressionism The art of the late 19th-century French painters *Cézanne, *Seurat, *Van Gogh, *Gauguin, *Toulouse-Lautrec, and their followers whose work developed out of and, to some extent, in reaction to *impressionism. The term was coined by the British art critic, Roger *Fry. Many of them painted impressionist works early in their careers but later rejected the objectivity and fleeting light effects of impressionism. Cézanne was the forerunner of *cubism and Van Gogh of *expressionism, while Gauguin developed a style known as *synthetism, and Seurat introduced *pointillism. The postimpressionists were not an organized group with a coherent style or fixed program.

postmortem. *See* autopsy.

potassium (K) A reactive alkali metal discovered by Sir Humphry Davy in 1807. It is a common constituent of the earth's crust; forming *feldspars ($KAlSi_3O_8$), clays, and evaporite minerals (for example sylvite; KCl). The metal is prepared by electrolysis of the molten hydroxide. It is soft, easily cut with a knife, and reacts readily with water, catching fire and liberating hydrogen. It oxidizes rapidly in air and must therefore be stored under oil. The element is highly electropositive and its chemistry is dominated by its ability to form ionic salts (for example KCl, KNO₃, K₂CO₃, KBr, K₂SO₄, and KCN). Its largest use is in fertilizers, potassium being essential for plant growth. Alloys of potassium and sodium have been proposed as heat transfer media in nuclear reactors, since the lowest melting alloy melts at $9.9°F$ ($-12.3°C$). One of the three isotopes (^{40}K) is radioactive with a half-life of 1.3×10^9 years and is used in *potassium-argon dating. The metal and its salts impart a lilac color to flames. At no 19; at wt 39.102; mp $147°F$ ($63.65°C$); bp $1427°F$ ($774°C$).

potassium-argon dating A method of *radiometric dating of geological specimens based on the decay of the radioactive isotope potassium-40, which is present to a small extent in all naturally occurring potassium. Its half-life is 1.3×10^9 years and it decays to argon-40; thus an estimate of the ratio of the two isotopes in a specimen of rock gives an indication of its age.

potato A perennial herbaceous plant, *Solanum tuberosum*, native to the Andes but cultivated throughout the world, especially in temperate regions, as an important vegetable crop. Potatoes were introduced to England in the late 16th century by Sir Walter Raleigh; they reached Spain and Portugal earlier. The plants grow to a height of 20–40 in (50–100 cm), with compound leaves and clusters of white and purple flowers. The tubers (swollen tips of underground stems) have a thin brownish-white, white, yellow, or pinkish skin and are rich in starch; there are several varieties, up to 3.3 lb (1.5 kg) in weight, and they are eaten cooked or ground into flour. Commercial potatoes are grown from small tubers termed "seed" potatoes. Potatoes are vulnerable to a number of diseases, the most notorious being the potato *blight that ravished Ireland in 1845–47 (*see also* Irish famine). Family: *Solanaceae. *See also* sweet potato.

Potawatomi North American Algonkian-speaking Indian tribe, related to the *Ojibwa and the *Ottawa and found in S Michigan. Basically hunters and farmers, they were driven S by the *Sioux Indians and then W by white settlers and the US Army. Known as the Fire Nation (Potawatomi means "People of the Place of Fire"), they warred successfully against the *Pawnee over land in Kansas. Today, about 2000 Potawatomi live on a Kansas reservation.

Potchefstroom 26 42S 27 06E A city in South Africa, in the S Transvaal. Founded by Voortrekkers (1838), it is the oldest town in the Transvaal. Gold mining and agriculture are important. Population (1970): 60,000.

Potemkin, Grigori Aleksandrovich (1739–91) Russian field marshal and favorite of *Catherine the Great. Potemkin distinguished himself in Catherine's first Turkish War (1768–74) and became her lover for two years as well as her chief adviser. Potemkin retained his political influence, especially in foreign affairs, until his death.

potential, electric A measure of electrical work. The potential at a point in an *electric field is one volt when one joule of energy is needed to bring a positive charge of one coulomb to that point from infinity. Usually the potential difference between two points, rather than the absolute potential, is used. *See also* electromotive force.

potential energy *Energy stored in a body by virtue of its position or configuration. Thus a body, mass m, at a height h above the ground has a potential energy equal to mgh, where g is the *acceleration of free fall, relative to the ground. A compressed spring and an electrically charged body also stores potential energy.

Potentilla A genus of mostly perennial herbs (500 species), found mainly in N temperate and arctic regions. It includes several species and hybrids grown as ornamentals. They have erect or creeping stems, 2–27.5 in (5–70 cm) long, bearing compound leaves and yellow, white, or red four- or five-petaled flowers with many stamens. The fruit is a group of seedlike achenes. Family: *Rosaceae. *See also* cinquefoil; tormentil.

potentiometer A variable electrical *resistance in which a sliding contact can be adjusted to any position along its length so that a variable proportion of the resistance can be included in a circuit. Potentiometers are used for measuring unknown voltages and as a potential divider, producing a voltage output corresponding to calibrated positions of the sliding contact.

potlatch The ceremonial distribution of gifts, practiced by the American Indians of the NW Pacific coast region, in order to affirm claims to rank and status at lavish feasts, to which rivals were invited. Gifts had to be returned with interest at subsequent potlatches to avoid humiliation and loss of status; competition to exceed others in generosity was intense. Among the *Kwakiutl, potlatching developed to an exaggerated extent often involving the ostentatious destruction of property to demonstrate power and rank.

pot marigold A herb, *Calendula officinalis*, native to S Europe and cultivated in temperate regions as an ornamental. About 12–14 in (30–35 cm) tall, it bears simple oblong leaves and yellow or orange daisy-like flowers, often double in cultivated varieties. The fresh petals may be eaten in salads or puddings or are dried and used in medicines. Family: *Compositae.

Potomac River A river in the E central US, rising in the Appalachian Mountains of W Virginia and flowing generally NE through Washington, DC, to Chesapeake Bay. Length: 287 mi (462 km).

Potosi 19 34S 65 45W A city in S Bolivia, at an altitude of 13,340 ft (4066 m). It is the chief industrial center of Bolivia. Mining is important; minerals extracted include tin, copper, and zinc. Its university was founded in 1892. Population (1976): 77,233.

Potsdam 52 19N 13 15E A city in central East Germany, on the Havel River adjoining Berlin. It was the residence of Prussian kings and German emperors. The city was severely damaged by air raids during World War II but extensive restoration has been carried out. Notable buildings include the Brandenburg Gate (1770) and the Sanssouci Palace (1745–47) built by Frederick II. An industrial city, Potsdam has many scientific institutes and is the main center of the East German film industry. Population (1980 est): 129,648.

Potsdam Conference (1945) The conference attended by Truman (US), Stalin (Soviet Union), and Churchill (later Attlee; UK) after the conclusion of World War II in Europe. Its objectives were to confirm the conclusions of the *Yalta Conference, to establish a political and economic program for Allied-occupied Germany, and to decide upon action toward Japan. The Conference was marked by the conflict of interests between the communist and noncommunist powers that developed into the *Cold War.

Potter, Beatrix (1866–1943) British children's writer and illustrator. During a solitary childhood she became a skilled artist and observer of nature. *The Tale of Peter Rabbit* (1900) was the first of a series of famous children's books concerning the domestic lives of such animals as Jemima Puddle-Duck and Mrs Tittlemouse.

Potter, Paul (1625–54) Dutch animal painter and etcher, born in Enkhuizen, the son and pupil of a landscape artist. Working successively in Delft, The Hague, and Amsterdam, he was painting as early as 1640. His best works, such as *The Bull*, were executed in 1647.

Potter, Stephen (1900–70) British humorist and critic. He wrote critical studies of D. H. Lawrence (1930) and Coleridge (1935) but is best remembered for his series of humorous books on the art of establishing personal superiority. These include *Gamesmanship* (1947), *Lifemanship* (1950), and *One-Upmanship* (1952).

potter wasp A solitary *wasp belonging to the genus *Eumerus*, common in North America and Europe. It constructs juglike nests of mud or clay, cemented by saliva and attached to plant stems. A single egg is laid in each nest and paralyzed caterpillars are provided as food for the developing larva.

pottery Generally, all *ceramics other than porcelain, but especially clay that has been shaped into containers (*compare* terracotta) and baked at varying temperatures over $753°F$ ($400°C$). Usually thrown on a potter's wheel, pottery can also be coiled and molded. Being opaque and porous, it is often glazed with an impervious glassy layer. Pottery making is worldwide and of great antiquity. It was being made about 10,000 BC in Japan; from about 3500 BC the fast wheel was used in Mesopotamia. Pottery styles and decorative techniques are important aids to archeologists in identifying and dating cultures. The ancient Greeks (*see* Greek art) and Renaissance Italians (*see* majolica) were among those who raised pottery making to high aesthetic levels, but since the 18th-century advent of porcelain in Europe it has been mainly utilitarian.

potto A *loris, *Perodictus potto*, of African forests. It is about 16 in (40 cm) long with a short tail, a catlike face, stout legs, and strong grasping hands. Pottos have a row of spines on the neck and shoulders, used for butting in self-defense.

pouched rat An African rodent characterized by cheek pouches used for carrying food. They range in size from the African giant pouched rat (*Cricetomys gambianus*), 9.4–18 in (24–45 cm) long excluding the tail (14–18 in [36–46 cm]), to the Cape pouched mouse (*Saccostomus campestris*), 5–6 in (12–15 cm) long, excluding the tail (1.2–2.4 in [3–6 cm]). All are vegetarians.

Poughkeepsie 41 42N 73 56W A city in SE New York, on the E bank of the Hudson River, S of Albany. Vassar College was founded here in 1861. Industries include computers and business machines, dairy farming equipment, chemicals, and ball bearings. Population (1980): 29,757.

Poulenc, Francis (1899–1963) French composer, a member of Les *Six. He was influenced by Ravel and Satie and produced a wide variety of compositions, including the song cycle *Le Bestiaire* (1919), a concerto for piano (1950) and one for two pianos (1932), the operas *Les Mamelles de Tirésias* (1944) and *Les Dialogues des Carmélites* (1953–56), and the ballet *Les Biches* (1923). As a pianist he frequently accompanied the French tenor Pierre Bernac (1899–).

poultry, domestic **1.** Domesticated birds, especially chickens, turkeys, ducks, and geese, that are bred and reared chiefly for eggs and meat but in some cases also for feathers and down. *See* livestock farming. **2.** A domesticated form of the red *jungle fowl, *Gallus gallus*, native to Asian forests. It was first domesticated about 4000 years ago as a religious and sacrificial animal and was used by the Romans for food. Since the 19th century, a large number of breeds and varieties have been selected for size, resistance to disease, egg production, shell color, fertility, and food conversion efficiency. Immature males are castrated and reared for meat as capons. In many countries, males (cockerels) are still used for cockfighting.

Pound, Ezra (1885–1972) US poet and critic. After studying Romance languages, he went to Europe in 1908 and became a dynamic propagandist for modernist literary and artistic movements in London (*see* Imagism; Vorticism). His early poetry included *A Lume Spento* (1908), his first volume, the long poems *Homage to Sextus Propertius* (1917) and *Hugh Selwyn Mauberly* (1920). *The Spirit of Romance* (1910) was a collection of literary criticism. He moved to Paris and, in 1924, to Italy, where he worked on the *Cantos* (1925–69). His support for Mussolini and his broadcasts of fascist propaganda during World War II led to his confinement in a mental hospital in the US (1946–58), after which he returned to Italy.

Pound, Roscoe (1870–1964) US jurist, teacher, and botanist. He directed a botanical survey for Nebraska (1892–1903), during which time a rare moss, *Roscopoundia*, was named for him. He attended Harvard Law School (1889–90), passed the Nebraska bar exam (1890), and began teaching at Harvard in 1910. He served as dean of its law school (1916–36). He was best known for his legal theory of sociological jurisprudence—adapting laws to social conditions—and for his theories on reform of court administration. His works include *The Spirit of the Common Law* (1921), *Law and Morals* (1924), and *Jurisprudence* (5 vols; 1959).

Poussin, Nicolas (1594–1665) French painter, regarded as one of the greatest exponents of *classicism. Poussin lived in Rome from 1624 until his death, apart from two years (1640–42) as painter to the French king Louis XIII. His representation of religious themes, such as *The Martyrdom of St Erasmus* (1628), gave way in the 1630s to an interest in mythology and the Old Testament, for example *The Worship of the Golden Calf* (c. 1635). The pure classicism of his second Roman period is exemplified in such landscapes as *Landscape with Diogenes* (1648).

Powderly, Terence Vincent (1849–1924) US labor leader. A machinist, he rose in the ranks of the Knights of Labor to become its head (1879–93). He believed in arbitration and cooperation and worked against strikes and violence. He also served as mayor of Scranton, Penn (1878–84), US commissioner general of immigration (1897–1902), and head of the information department of the Bureau of Immigration (1907–21).

powder metallurgy The shaping of metals by pressing powdered metal into blocks, heating (*see* sintering), and then shaping it by stamping. Often pressing and sintering are done together in a mold to produce the finished article in one operation. The method is used for working metals, such as platinum and tungsten (used in light-bulb filaments) that are difficult to shape by other means. It has the advantages of leaving no scrap and being suitable for intricate shapes. Nonmetal additives can be easily included, such as the graphite lubricant in self-lubricating bearings.

Powell, Anthony (1905–) British novelist. His novel sequence *A Dance to the Music of Time* comprises 12 social satires beginning with *A Question of Upbringing* (1951) and ending with *Hearing Secret Harmonies* (1975). He has also written a biography of John Aubrey (1948) and two volumes of memoirs.

Powell, Cecil Frank (1903–69) British physicist, who became professor at Bristol University. Powell pioneered the technique of observing particles by the tracks that they leave on specially prepared photographic plates. In 1947 he exposed his plates to *cosmic rays high up in the Andes and discovered the *pion. He was awarded the 1950 Nobel Prize for this work.

Powell, Lewis Franklin, Jr. (1907–) US jurist; associate justice of the Supreme Court (1971–). He was instrumental in achieving desegregation of the Richmond, Va, school system during the 1950s. He served as president of the American Bar Association (1964–65) and the American Bar Foundation (1969–71) and was appointed to the Supreme Court in 1971

by President Richard M. *Nixon. Although generally a conservative he sometimes holds liberal opinions on social and racial issues.

Powell v. Alabama (1972) US Supreme Court decision that established right to counsel in state criminal cases, as provided in due process of law. Seven blacks, accused of raping two white women on a train in Alabama, were tried, convicted, and sentenced to die. The Supreme Court upheld the prisoners' appeal that they had been denied right to counsel, a fair trial, and an unbiased jury (blacks were excluded), fundamental rights accorded in the 14th Amendment.

power The rate at which a body or system does work. It is measured in watts or horsepower.

power station An electricity generating plant that forms part of the *electricity supply system. In **thermal power stations**, heat from the burning of fossil fuels (oil, coal, and gas) or from *thermal nuclear reactors is used to generate steam. The steam drives *turbines connected to alternating-current generators (turbo-alternators), thus converting heat via mechanical energy into electricity. Gas turbines are also used, missing out the steam-generation stage. They are easy to build and flexible to run, but have an efficiency of only about 25%. Sometimes the exhaust gas is used to help generate steam for a steam turbine, in order to increase the station's overall efficiency. Usually in a steam-turbine thermal station about 30 to 40% of the heat is converted to electricity, most of the rest being lost when steam is condensed to water before it is returned to the boilers. *Hydroelectric **power stations** are more efficient (up to 90%) and provide a significant proportion of UK electricity supplies. *See also* energy.

Powhatan A confederation of Algonkian-speaking North American Indian tribes of Virginia. It was founded by the chief known to the European settlers as Powhatan (?1550–1618), the father of *Pocahontas. Although he resented the colonists, violence was avoided when Pocahontas married colonist John Rolfe. The Powhatans were corn cultivators and hunters living in palisaded villages.

Powys, John Cowper (1872–1963) British novelist. He lectured for many years in the US. He wrote poetry, philosophy, and criticism, but his best-known books are his long novels. These include *Wolf Solent* (1929) and *A Glastonbury Romance* (1932), the historical novels *Owen Glendower* (1940), and *Porius* (1951).

Poyang, Lake An area of marsh and lakes in SE China, drained by the Yangtze River. In summer the whole area is flooded. Area (summer): about 1073 sq mi (2780 sq km).

Poynings' Law (1495) A measure introduced by Sir Edward Poynings (1459–1521), Lord Deputy of Ireland, which ensured that the Irish parliament could legislate only in accordance with proposals previously approved by the English crown. A further act applied all English laws to Ireland.

Poznań (German name: Posen) 52 55N 16 53E A city in W Poland, on the Warta River. One of the oldest cities in Poland, it became the first Polish bishopric in 968 AD. It possesses an 18th-century cathedral, rebuilt following extensive damage in World War II; its university was founded in 1919. An important industrial and commercial center, its manufactures include railroad rolling stock, chemicals, and glass. Population (1979 est): 544,000.

Poznań Riots (1956) Labor disturbances in Poland. They began when workers at a steel plant in Poznań staged a strike to protest against the country's political restrictions and economic problems. The ensuing riots were ruthlessly suppressed, with the death of 53 people, but they forced the appointment of a reformist leader, Władysław Gomułka.

Pozzuoli (Greek name: Puteoli) 40 49N 14 07E A port in S Italy, in Campania on the Gulf of Pozzuoli. It is in an area of intense volcanic activity and the local volcanic ash is used to produce cement. Population (1971): 59,813.

Prado An art gallery in the Prado Avenue, Madrid. Designed originally as a natural-history museum by the neoclassical architect Juan de Villanueva (1739–1811), the art gallery was founded in 1818 by Ferdinand VII. Most of its collection consists of paintings collected by the Spanish monarchs from the 16th century onward. Its works by *Velázquez, *Goya, *El Greco, *Titian, and *Bosch are among the finest in the world.

Praesepe An open *star cluster in the constellation Cancer, just visible to the naked eye.

praetor In ancient Rome, originally a consul as leader of an army and subsequently a magistrate responsible for the administration of justice. From about 242 BC a second praetor assisted with lawsuits involving foreigners. Later more praetors were appointed to administer the increasing number of provinces and numbered 18 under Emperor Nerva (96–98 AD).

Praetorian Guard   The official bodyguard of the Roman emperors created by Augustus in 27 BC. Composed of up to 16 long-serving cohorts (infantry divisions) each of 500–1000 men, and stationed as a single unit in Rome, the Guard and its commanders developed great political influence; as senatorial power diminished emperors came to rely upon Praetorian support for election and in later imperial times the emperor's position and even his life depended on the Guard's favor.

Praetorius, Michael   (M. Schultheiss; 1571–1621) German composer. He studied the organ, worked in the service of Julius Heinrich, Duke of Brunswick (1564–1613), and was kapellmeister in Wolfsbüttel (1612–21). He composed a large number of motets, hymns, madrigals, and dance pieces, as well as writing *Syntagma musicum* (1615–20), a valuable account of the musical theory and instruments of the time.

pragmatic sanction   A royal edict establishing a fundamental principle of government. Historically the term is usually applied to the edict of Emperor Charles VI (1713) settling the succession to his Austrian territories in his daughter Maria Theresa. Disregard of this edict by European powers provoked the War of the *Austrian Succession (1740–48). The Edict of Bourges, issued by Charles VII of France in 1438 and limiting papal authority over the French Church, was also a pragmatic sanction.

pragmatism   A philosophical movement initiated by William James (*see* James, Henry) and C. S. *Peirce in the US. It asserts that the truth of a theory can be judged only by its practical consequences, so the question is: what difference would it make if it were true? The comprehensive metaphysical schemes of European philosophers were thus found to have no meaning, since their truth or falsity did not affect human experience. In science, a theory was true if it "worked"—if its expected consequences occurred. In ethics and theology a principle or belief was true if it satisfied its holders. *See also* Dewey, John.

Prague   (Czech name: Praha)   50 8N 14 25E The capital of Czechoslovakia, in the center of the country on the Vltava River. The industrial and commercial center of Czechoslovakia, its various manufactures include machinery, cars, aircraft, processed foods, clothing, and chemicals. A leading cultural center, Prague possesses Charles University (1348) and a technical university (1707). Notable buildings include Hradčany Castle and the mainly gothic Cathedral of St Vitus. *History*: in the middle ages it was the seat of the Přemyslid kings of Bohemia. Following rivalry between the Czechs and Germans, it became the center of the religious reform movement of Jan *Hus. Under Habsburg rule from the 16th century, it was made the capital of newly independent Czechoslovakia in 1918. In 1968 the city was occupied by Soviet troops following Soviet opposition to the liberal Dubček government. Population (1980 est): 1,193,000.

Prague School   A group of language scholars based in Prague during the 1920s and 1930s, including N. S. Trubetskoy and Roman Jakobson. Their work was chiefly in the field of Saussurean structural *linguistics. They originated aspects of modern phonological theory, drew sociolinguistic distinctions between various aspects of language use (for example, between everyday and poetic language), and devised the concept of analyzing both speech sounds and word meanings into ultimate components transcending individual languages.

prairie dog   A large *ground squirrel, *Cynomys ludovicanis*, of North America, also called black-tailed prairie marmot. Heavily built animals, about 12 in (30 cm) long, prairie dogs live in large colonies called "towns." They feed on grass and have been treated as pests by cattle ranchers. Prairie dogs raise a firm rim of soil round their burrows so that the surface water will not enter. □mammal.

Prairie Provinces   The Canadian provinces of *Alberta, *Manitoba, and *Saskatchewan. They lie chiefly in the Great Plains and are major producers of wheat and oil.

prairies   The extensive grasslands of the interior of North America. They occupy a broad N–S belt extending from Alberta and Saskatchewan through the Midwest into Texas, reaching as far W as the Rocky Mountains. Little of the original true prairie now remains, having been extensively plowed for wheat production. *See also* steppes.

prairie wolf.   *See* coyote.

Prakrit   Ancient *Indo-Aryan languages of N India, which were considerably simpler than the standard written form of *Sanskrit. From these spoken forms are derived a number of literary styles and the modern languages of N India. *Pali, the language of the Jain scriptures, is included among the Prakrits.

Prandtl, Ludwig   (1875–1953) German physicist, whose discovery of the boundary layer adjoining the surface of a solid over which a fluid flows led to the foundation of aerodynamics. His major studies were on the effects of streamlining and the properties of aircraft wings. He also made important improvements to such constructions as wind tunnels and his name is remembered in the **Prandtl number**, a dimensionless group used in the study of convection.

Prasad, Rajendra   (1884–1963) Indian statesman; the first president of India (1950–1962). He gave up his legal practice to join *Gandhi's movement of noncooperation with the British and was several times president of the *Indian National Congress (1934, 1939, 1947–48). He helped draft the new Indian constitution.

praseodymium   (Pr)   A *lanthanide element, which was separated from its mixture with neodymium by von Welsbach in 1885. It forms trihalides (for example $PrCl_3$) and an oxide (Pr_2O_3), which is used to give a strong yellow color to glass. At no 59; at wt 140.9077; mp 1709°F (931°C); bp 6360°F (3512°C).

pratincole   A bird belonging to an Old World subfamily (*Glareolinae*; 6 species). 7–9 in (17–22 cm) long, pratincoles have a forked tail, long pointed wings, and a small bill with a wide gape for catching insects. The common pratincole (*Glareola pratincola*) has red-brown underwings and a yellow throat outlined by a black band. Family: *Glareolidae* (pratincoles and coursers); order: *Charadriiformes* (gulls, plovers, etc.).

Prato   (*or* Prato in Toscana)   43 53N 11 06E A city in central Italy, in Tuscany on the Bisenzio River. It has a cathedral (dating from the 12th century) and is an important center of the woolen industry. Population (1980 est): 159,099.

prawn   A large shrimplike *crustacean (up to 8 in [20 cm] long), belonging to the suborder *Natantia*. The antennae are longer than the body and a forward projection of the carapace forms a spike (rostrum) between the eyes, bearing six or more teeth. The second pair of appendages are enlarged to form pincers (*compare* shrimp). The common edible prawn (*Leander serratus*) occurs in temperate coastal waters and is 2–3 in (5–8 cm) long. Large shrimps are often mistakenly called prawns.

Praxiteles   (mid 4th century BC) Athenian sculptor, renowned for his handling of marble. His statue of Hermes, discovered at *Olympia in 1877, exemplifies the sensuous grace and repose for which his work was noted. Most of his statues have perished, but some, such as the famous Aphrodite of Cnidos, are known from Roman copies.

Precambrian   Geological time from the formation of the earth's crust, about 4500 million years ago, to about 590 million years ago when the Paleozoic era began. Precambrian rocks lie below the Cambrian system and fossils are rare and often obscure. The rocks have been subjected to much alteration because of their great age. Most are metamorphosed and have undergone one or more Precambrian mountain-building periods as well as later ones. The largest areas of exposed Precambrian rocks are the *shield areas. Correlation of successive strata is done where possible by radioactive *dating. *See also* Cryptozoic time.

precession   The rotation about an axis of a line that is itself the axis of a rotating body. The effect may be observed in a spinning top, of which the axis of rotation is initially vertical but, as the top slows down, begins to precess about its original position. *See also* precession of the equinoxes.

precession of the equinoxes   The gradual westward motion of the *equinoxes around the *ecliptic in a period of about 25,800 years. It is caused by the *precession of the earth's axis of rotation, which results mainly from the gravitational pull of the sun and moon on the equatorial bulge of the nonspherical earth. As the axis precesses, slowly tracing out a circle in the sky, the celestial equator (lying in a plane perpendicular to the axis) moves relative to the ecliptic. The points of intersection, i.e. the equinoxes, thus continuously change.

predestination   In Christian doctrine, God's foreordaining of salvation for certain people. The idea is explicitly propagated by St *Paul in the Epistles. It raises enormous problems about the nature of divine justice and the role of the human will and endeavors, problems that Christian philosophers have never satisfactorily solved. St *Augustine of Hippo, *Origen, and St Thomas *Aquinas were among those who produced influential approaches to the difficulties. An extreme form of predestination was integral to *Calvinism, with salvation for the elect and eternal damnation for everyone else, whatever their virtues or faults. Modern thinking on the subject tends to stress the universality of God's will to save mankind.

prefect   A high-ranking French government official. Created in 1800 by Napoleon's reorganization of provincial government, prefects are responsible for general administration, public law and order, and the enforcement of central government policies in their own departments. Although dependence on the government in power and a centralized bureaucracy weakens their position, prefects still have considerable civil authority.

pregnancy The period during which a fetus develops within the womb, usually lasting for about 280 days from conception to delivery of the baby. Pregnancy is signaled by cessation of the menstrual periods, tenderness and discomfort in the breasts, and—sometimes—an increase in appetite, nausea, and vomiting. These changes are brought about by the activity of hormones secreted by the *corpus luteum (in the ovary) and *placenta. In the early weeks pregnancy can be definitely diagnosed only by means of pregnancy tests. A commonly used test is based on the detection of the hormone chorionic *gonadotrophin in the urine. *See also* childbirth; prenatal diagnosis.

Pregnancy in animals is usually called gestation, and the period varies between species. In elephants, for instance, it is 18 months and in rats 3 weeks.

Preminger, Otto (Ludwig) (1906–) US film director, born in Austria. He went to the US in 1935 and became a naturalized citizen in 1943. His films range from literary adaptations to large-scale epics and include *Laura* (1944), *Anatomy of a Murder* (1959) and *Exodus* (1960).

premise One of the statements in an argument or chain of reasoning from which the conclusion follows or is said to follow. For example from the premises "only dogs bark" and "Fido barks," the conclusion is that "Fido is a dog."

Premonstratensians A Roman Catholic order of monks, also called Norbertines after St Norbert (c. 1080–1134), who founded them in 1120 at Prémontré (N France). They originally followed an austere rule, which included total abstinence from meat. The order spread all over Europe but was nearly annihilated during the French Revolution. Belgium is now its main base.

prenatal diagnosis Tests made on pregnant women in order to diagnose genetic or developmental abnormalities in the developing fetus. If the tests reveal severe malformation or gross malfunctioning in the fetus the possibility of an *abortion is considered. The investigations include X-rays, scanning using ultrasonic rays, *amniocentesis (involving analysis of a sample of the amniotic fluid surrounding the fetus), and fetoscopy, in which a sample of fetal blood is withdrawn from the placenta and examined for abnormal cells (indicating blood disorders, such as *thalassemia). Some of the techniques may involve risks to the health of the mother or fetus and are not undertaken without good cause.

Preparedness Movement (1915–16) Campaign to bolster the US armed forces in anticipation of involvement in *World War I. Advocated by Theodore *Roosevelt and other national figures when it became obvious that the neutrality of the US was being violated, the movement sponsored legislation to increase national defense.

Pre-Raphaelite Brotherhood The 19th-century British painters Dante Gabriel *Rossetti, John Everett *Millais, and William Holman *Hunt, who joined together in 1848 in reaction to the banality of contemporary British painting and its enthusiasm for *Raphael. Signing all their works PRB, they sought to emulate Italian painters earlier than Raphael and to paint subjects of a moral or religious character, many of their subjects being drawn from medieval literature. Although initially attacked for their lack of idealism, particularly in religious subjects, by 1851 the PRB had won the support of the art critic John *Ruskin. Although the group disbanded soon afterward— (Hunt being the only member to remain faithful to PRB ideas), the PRB had a strong influence on such artists as William *Morris and Edward *Burne-Jones, as well as subsequent painting styles.

Presbyterianism A form of Protestant Church organization based on government by elders (*compare* episcopacy). These elders comprise the ministers and certain laymen from each congregation and all have equal rank; they enforce a strict code of ethics and make decisions on Church policy through a hierarchical system of presbyteries, synods, and general assemblies. Presbyterianism originated with the 16th-century followers of *Calvin who believed that they were returning to a system of the primitive Church. In Scotland the tenets of Presbyterianism were formulated (1560) by *Knox and it became the established Church in 1696. A pan-Presbyterian alliance (founded 1875) embraces the Presbyterian Churches in the US and elsewhere.

Prescott, William Hickling (1796–1859) US historian. Prescott established his reputation with a major work, *The History of the Reign of Ferdinand and Isabella* (1837). There followed *The Conquest of Mexico* (1843), *The Conquest of Peru* (1847), and *The History of Philip II* (1855–58). Although his critical insight was not outstanding, Prescott combined factual accuracy with a vivid narrative style. His discursive memory compensated for his partial blindness.

president In most republics, the executive head of state. In the US the president is the head of the executive branch of government, which was established together with the legislature (*see* Congress) and the judiciary (*see* Supreme Court) by the US constitution (1789). In modern times the president is a member of the *Democratic Party or the *Republican Party and is elected every four years; no one may hold the office for more than eight years. The president is head of the *cabinet. In some other countries (e.g. Germany and Italy) the president fulfills the nonexecutive function of a monarch.

Presidential Powers Those powers invested in the head of a country that enable the country's laws to be carried out. Included in the powers of the US president are command of the armed forces; appointment of cabinet members, agency heads, ambassadors, and Supreme Court justices; and declaring war with the consent of Congress.

Presidential Succession US procedure for transferral of the presidency in cases of emergency, such as death, inability to function, or resignation. Provided for in the US Constitution and amended by the Presidential Succession Act of 1947 and the 25th Amendment (1967), the line of succession is the vice president, the speaker of the House of Representatives, the president pro tempore of the Senate, and the secretary of State.

President of the United States *See* president.

President Pro Tempore of the Senate The presiding officer of the US Senate when the vice president is not available. The position is filled by a senator who is elected by fellow senators.

ELVIS PRESLEY *In a scene from* Girl Happy *(1965).*

Presley, Elvis (Aaron) (1935–77) US popular singer, whose first big hit, "Heartbreak Hotel" (1956), was followed by "Hound Dog" and "Don't Be Cruel." His suggestive performances earned him the nickname "Elvis the Pelvis." Presley also appeared in numerous films and television programs and was long one of the most popular entertainers in the US and the world. His death, probably a result of drug dependence, resulted in his becoming a cult figure.

Presocratics Greek philosophers who lived in Ionia and S Italy (Magna Graecia) during the 6th and early 5th centuries BC, before the time of *Socrates. They were responsible for the earliest philosophical—as opposed to magical and religious—speculation about the universe. The Ionians were *Thales, *Anaximander, and *Anaximenes, all of Miletus, *Xenophanes of Colophon, and *Heraclitus of Ephesus. Notable figures in Italy were *Parmenides and *Zeno, both of Elea (*see* Eleatics), and *Pythagoras.

Pressburg, Treaties of 1. (1491) The treaty in which Maximilian, Habsburg heir to the Holy Roman Empire, recognized Vladislav II of Bohemia (1456–1516) as King of Hungary, renouncing his own claim in return for the restoration of Austria, Styria, and Carinthia, which had been annexed by Matthias I Corvinus in 1486. 2. (1805) The treaty between Austria and France following Napoleon's defeat of Austria at Austerlitz. Austria surrendered territory and paid a large indemnity.

press gang A band of men employed to force paupers, tramps, or criminals into the army or navy. This system of impressment (recruits were paid imprest money), common throughout the world in the 18th century, ceased when improved pay and conditions in the army and navy increased voluntary recruitment.

pressure Force per unit area. For a liquid, density d, the pressure at a depth h is hdg, where g is the *acceleration of free fall. Pressure is usually measured in pascals, millimeters of mercury, or millibars.

pressure gauge An instrument for measuring the pressure of a fluid. Atmospheric pressure is measured with a mercury *barometer or an aneroid barometer. Pressures above atmospheric pressure are usually measured with a Bourdon gauge, which consists of a flattened curved tube that tends to straighten under pressure. As it straightens it moves a pointer around a scale. Low pressures are measured with such vacuum gauges as the *McLeod gauge or *Pirani gauge.

Prestel. See viewdata.

Prester John A legendary Christian priest king. First mentioned in 12th-century chronicles, he became famous as the hero destined to help the Crusaders against Islam. He was sometimes identified as a Chinese prince but more commonly as the King of Ethiopia.

Preston 53 46N 2 42W A city and port in NW England, on the Ribble River. It was the site of a major battle in the English *Civil War. It has plastics, chemical, motor-vehicle and aircraft construction, and electronics industries as well as the traditional cotton and engineering works. Population (1981): 143,734.

Pretender, Old. See James Edward Stuart, the Old Pretender.

Pretender, Young. See Charles Edward Stuart, the Young Pretender.

Pretoria 25 36S 28 12E The administrative capital of South Africa and the capital of the Transvaal. Founded in 1855, it became the capital of the Union of South Africa in 1910. The University of South Africa was founded here in 1873; other important institutions are the University of Pretoria (1930) and the Onderstepoort Veterinary Research Institute. Pretoria is noted for its jacaranda-lined avenues and Voortrekker monument. Its industries include iron and steel processing, engineering, and food processing. Population (1980 est): 528,407.

Pretoria Convention (1881) The peace treaty between Britain and the Transvaal that ended the first *Boer War. The Transvaal acquired self-government under the British crown, which, however, retained control of foreign relations and the power to veto legislation regarding Africans.

Pretorius, Andries (Wilhelmus Jacobus) (1799–1853) Afrikaner leader in the *Great Trek to Natal and then in the Transvaal. He defeated (1840) the Zulu King Dingane and fought the British in Natal (1842) and then in the Transvaal (1848), establishing Transvaal's independence as the South African Republic (1852). The city of Pretoria is named for him. His son **Marthinus Wessel Pretorius** (1819–1901) was president of the South African Republic (formerly and subsequently the Transvaal) from 1857 to 1871 and of the Orange Free State from 1859 to 1863. He returned to politics after Britain's annexation of the Transvaal, finally retiring after Afrikaner victory in the first *Boer War (1880–81).

Prévert, Jacques (1900–77) French poet. He was associated with the surrealist movement in the 1920s. His best-known poems about the street life of Paris, written with anarchic humor, are collected in *Paroles* (1946); later volumes include *Spectacle* (1951) and *Hebromadaires* (1972). He also wrote film scripts, notably for *Les Enfants du paradis* (1944).

Previn, André (Andreas Ludwig Priwin; 1929–) German-born US conductor, pianist, and composer. Active in Hollywood in his youth as a film composer and jazz pianist, he was subsequently conductor of the London Symphony Orchestra (1969–79) and became conductor of the Pittsburgh Symphony Orchestra in 1976. He has done much to popularize classical music through television performances.

Prévost d'Exiles, Antoine François, Abbé (1697–1763) French novelist. His unsettled career included periods of military service, of religious retreat as a Benedictine monk, and of exile in England and Holland. Of his many novels and translations, mostly written to pay off debts, the best known is *Manon Lescaut* (1731), the story of a young nobleman ruined by his love for a courtesan, which was used by both Massenet and Puccini as the basis for operas.

Priam In Greek legend, the last king of Troy, husband of Hecuba. As an old man he witnessed the deaths of many of his 50 sons in the *Trojan War and he pleaded with Achilles for the body of Hector. He was killed at the altar of Zeus by Neoptelemus.

Priapus A Greek fertility god associated with gardens, son of Dionysus and Aphrodite. He was usually portrayed as a comic ugly figure with an enormous phallus. The donkey, symbol of lust, was sacrificed to him.

Pribilof Islands Four US islands in the Bering Sea. They are the breeding ground of the northern fur seal. Since 1911 the seals have been protected by agreements between the US, the Soviet Union, Japan, and Canada. Area: about 65 sq mi (8 sq km).

Price, (Mary) Leontine (1927–) US soprano. After studying at New York City's Juilliard School of Music, she toured internationally as Bess in *Porgy and Bess* (1952–54). She made her debut with the Metropolitan Opera in 1961, singing the role of Leonora in *Il Trovatore*.

price index A single figure used to measure the average percentage change in the price of a set of goods over a period of time, taking a base figure of 100 for a specified year. Thus if a particular price index, in January, 1985, stands at 156 (January, 1975 = 100), there has been a 56% increase in the average prices over the ten-year period. The best-known indexes are the Wholesale Price Index and the Retail Price Index, the latter providing a reliable guide to the *cost of living. Some wages, salaries, and costs are **index-linked** (i.e. increase in proportion to a specified price index) to cover the devaluation of money as a result of *inflation. **Indexation** is commonly used in agreements that extend over a long period during which inflation is expected to be a significant factor.

prickly heat A disorder that occurs most commonly in the tropics due to obstruction of the ducts of the sweat glands. It causes itching and a red rash and often leads to secondary infection.

prickly pear A *cactus of the genus *Opuntia*, native to North and South America and sometimes cultivated for food or ornament. Introduced to Australia and South Africa, it has become a troublesome weed. It has flat jointed spiny stems bearing large orange or yellow flowers, which give rise to edible pear-shaped fruits. The seeds are used to produce an oil and the shoots are eaten as vegetables or used as animal feed.

prickly poppy A plant of the genus *Argemone*, especially *A. mexicana*, also called devil's fig, native to North America and the West Indies and cultivated as a garden ornamental. Growing 12–35 in (30–90 cm) tall, its blue-green bristly stems bear spiny lobed leaves and orange or pale-yellow flowers, with five pointed petals and numerous long stamens. Family: *Papaveraceae*.

Pride, Thomas (d. 1658) English parliamentary soldier during the Civil War, famous for effecting "Pride's Purge" of parliament in 1648. He excluded over a hundred Presbyterian representatives suspected of wanting to negotiate with Charles I, leaving the Rump of the *Long Parliament. He was a signatory of Charles' death warrant.

Priestley, J(ohn) B(oynton) (1894–1984) British novelist and dramatist. He first won popular success with his picaresque novel *The Good Companions* (1929). His plays include social comedies, such as *Dangerous Corner* (1932) and *Laburnum Grove* (1933), and several mildly experimental expressionist dramas, including *The Glass Cage* (1957). A traditionalist by temperament and conviction, he has published many volumes of criticism and memoirs and was a popular broadcaster during World War II.

Priestley, Joseph (1733–1804) British chemist and one of the discoverers of oxygen (together with Carl *Scheele). Priestley, being a firm believer in the *phlogiston theory, named his gas dephlogisticated air and first prepared it in 1774 by heating mercuric oxide. In 1778–79 *Lavoisier demolished the phlogiston theory and named the gas oxygen. Priestley also produced and studied several other gases, including ammonia, sulfur dioxide, and hydrogen chloride. He invented the method of collecting them over mercury, since some of these gases dissolved in water.

primary colors The minimum number of *colors that, when mixed in the correct proportions, are capable of giving all the other colors in the visible spectrum. When light of three **primary additive colors** (usually red, green, and blue) is mixed in equal intensities, white light results. This principle is used in color television and *color photography. Any particular color can also be obtained by subtracting from white light a mixture of three **primary subtractive colors**, usually cyan (blue-green), magenta (purplish red), and yellow, which are complementary to red, green, and blue. Adding pigments of these in equal proportions gives black pigment.

primate A mammal belonging to the order *Primates* (about 195 species), which includes *prosimians, *monkeys, *apes, and man. Primates probably evolved from insectivorous climbing creatures like *tree shrews and have many adaptations for climbing, including five fingers and five toes with opposable first digits (except in the hind feet of man). They have well-developed sight and hearing and—most importantly—enlarged cerebral hemispheres of the brain, most marked in higher primates. Most forms are arboreal but the great apes and man are largely terrestrial.

prime minister A head of government. The best-known example is in the UK, where the post developed in the 18th century with the growth of the *cabinet. Sir Robert *Walpole is generally regarded as the first prime minister (1721–42) but the post was not formally recognized until 1905. The prime minister is customarily a member of the House of Commons and is head of government by virtue of being the leader of the dominant political party in the Commons. The monarch makes all governmental appointments on the advice of the prime minister.

prime number An integer greater than one that has no integral factors except itself and one; for example 2, 3, 5, 7, 11, 13, 17. Every natural number can be expressed uniquely as a product of prime numbers; for example $1260 = 2^2 \times 3^2 \times 5 \times 7$. Prime numbers are of major interest in number theory.

primitivism In art, the style of untrained artists who ignore or are ignorant of both traditional aesthetic standards and avant-garde trends. Its chief characteristics are meticulous detail, brilliant colors, childlike representation, and faulty perspective. Among the first primitives were 17th- and 18th-century American painters who developed in cultural isolation from European artistic trends, but the best known is the French painter Henri *Rousseau. Recent primitives include the Yugoslav peasants Ivan Generalič (1914–) and Mijo Kovačič (1935–) and the American Grandma *Moses. The term is also sometimes applied to African and Polynesian indigenous art.

Primo de Rivera, Miguel (1870–1930) Spanish general, who led a successful coup on September 13, 1923, and was dictator of Spain until 1930. He brought the Moroccan War to a victorious end (1927) but dissatisfaction with his absolute rule, exacerbated by the Depression, caused his downfall. *Alfonso XIII's support of Primo de Rivera discredited the monarchy, which was overthrown a year later. His son **José Antonio Primo de Rivera** (1903–36) founded the Falange, the Spanish fascist party. Executed by the Republic shortly after the start of the Spanish Civil War, his memory was honored by Franco's National Movement.

primrose A perennial herbaceous plant, *Primula vulgaris*, growing in woodlands and hedge banks in Europe and N Africa. It has a basal rosette of puckered spoon-shaped leaves, with solitary pale-yellow flowers on slender stalks, up to 4 in (10 cm) high. Bird's-eye primrose (*P. farinosa*) has pale-purple flowers with yellow centers. Family: *Primulaceae*. See also evening primrose.

Primula A genus of perennial plants (about 500 species), native mainly to N temperate regions and often grown as ornamentals. They have a basal rosette of oval to spoon-shaped leaves and erect flower stalks bearing erect or nodding five-petaled flowers, red, pink, purple, blue, white, or yellow in color and usually with a different colored center. The fruit is a capsule. The genus also includes the *cowslip and *primrose. Family: *Primulaceae*. See also auricula.

Prince Albert National Park A national park in S Canada, in central Saskatchewan. Established in 1927, the park offers a wide variety of plants, animals, and birds. At an average elevation of 1800 ft (550 m), black and white spruce, as well as aspens and grasslands, are found. The many lakes in the park have made it popular for summer vacations. Area: 1496 sq mi (3875 sq km).

Prince Edward Island An island province of E Canada, in the S Gulf of St Lawrence. Its gentle rolling hills and mild climate support small farms producing potatoes, grains, dairy cattle, and other livestock. Tourism and fishing are also important. *History*: discovered (1534) and colonized (1720) by France, the island was captured (1758) and resettled by Britain. In 1873 it joined Canada. Area: 5657 sq km (2184 sq mi). Population (1981): 122,506. Capital: Charlottetown.

Prince of Wales A title customarily conferred on the eldest son of the British sovereign. It was a native Welsh title until 1301, when Edward I, following his annexation of Wales, bestowed it on his son, the future Edward II. The present holder of the title is Prince *Charles.

Princeton 40 21N 74 40W A city in New Jersey. George Washington defeated the British here on January 3, 1777. It is the site of Princeton University (1746) and the Rockefeller Institute for Scientific Research. Population (1980): 12,035.

Princeton University One of the oldest universities in the US, it was founded in 1746 by Presbyterians. A private institution, it has been situated at Princeton, New Jersey, since 1756. Women were first admitted to the university in 1969.

princewood A dark wood with lighter veins, obtained from two tropical trees found in the West Indies, *Hamelia ventricosa*, also called Spanish elm (family *Rubiaceae*), and *Cordia gerascanthoides* (family *Ehretiaceae*). It is used for furniture, doors, boats, etc.

Príncipe Island. See São Tomé and Príncipe.

printed circuit An electronic circuit in which the connections between components are formed by a pattern of conducting film on a board, instead of by wires. The method greatly facilitates mass-production. An insulating board is coated with a conducting material, such as copper, and a protective pattern is deposited on it using photographic techniques. The unprotected metal is then etched away and components are soldered in place. In television receivers, the replacement of thermionic valves by plug-in printed-circuit boards has made maintenance easier. A faulty circuit board can be quickly replaced without tracing the individual failed component.

printing The production of multiple copies of text or pictures, usually on paper. The oldest method, in use in China and Japan before 800 AD, is **letterpress**, in which the raised surfaces of etched, engraved, or cast material are inked and pressed onto the paper. This method was revolutionized by the invention of movable type (see typesetting) in the 15th century, but printing itself remained fundamentally unchanged for four centuries until other methods of mechanization were introduced. Early printing presses were of the hand-operated platen variety in which the type stands on a horizontal surface and the paper is pressed onto it from above. Faster production became possible on the power-driven presses of the 19th century: first the cylinder press, in which the paper is rolled by a cylinder over a flat printing surface, and later the rotary press, in which the printing surface is also a cylinder. Different types of rotary press print either on separate sheets or on a web (see paper), which makes for still faster printing—up to 35,000 impressions per hour.

In **lithography**, a method invented by Aloys *Senefelder in 1798, the printing surface is plane (originally a polished stone but now usually an aluminum sheet), the printing and nonprinting areas being made grease-receptive and grease-repellent respectively (see platemaking). Greasy ink is rolled over the entire area but is taken only by the grease-receptive areas; the ink is then transferred by rolling onto the paper. **Offset printing**, most commonly lithography, involves an intermediate rubber-covered cylinder that transfers the ink from plate to paper. In **gravure printing**, the small square etched holes (cells) in the copper printing plate are filled with a free-flowing ink, the rest of the plate is wiped clean, and the plate is rolled against the paper, which absorbs the ink out of the cells. Nearly all gravure and offset lithography is done on rotary presses.

Letterpress and offset lithography are used for almost all types of printing job; because of the expensive copper plates gravure is limited to long runs, such as cheap illustrated magazines, postage stamps, and packaging. Direct lithography has been used almost exclusively by artists—*Goya and *Manet, for example—and was the principal medium for *poster art in the 19th century. **Flexography** is a widespread form of (usually rotary) letterpress printing using fluid volatile ink and a rubber printing surface. It is used for paperback books, packaging materials, and for printing on nonabsorbent surfaces, such as plastic foil. In **silk-screen printing** (screen-process printing *or* serigraphy), a piece of taut open-weave silk, metal, or synthetic fabric carries the negative of the desired image in an impervious substance, such as glue; ink is forced through the clear (printing) areas by a squeegee onto the paper, glass, fabric, or other material, behind. It is used for printing posters, electronic circuit boards, labeling on bottles, and anything that requires a thick layer of ink or other material. For example pop artists, such as Andy *Warhol, use it to make painted photographic transfers. **Collotype** is a method of printing short runs of high-quality illustrations from gelatin plates; it is not widely used but it is the only method by which continuous tone can be reproduced (see platemaking).

Full-color reproduction is achieved by **color-process printing**, in which all colors can be produced from combinations of three primary colors—yellow, cyan (blue), and magenta. Four separate printing plates are made, one for each primary and one for black; each is printed in succession in exactly the same place. In letterpress and lithography, half-tones are used instead of printing plates (see platemaking). At the normal viewing distance for any piece of color-process printing, the dots are imperceptible, and the effect is of varying shades.

prion A *petrel belonging to a genus (*Pachyptila*; 4 species) found in Antarctica and nearby islands. 8–11 in (20–27 cm) long, prions have a blue-gray plumage with white underparts. The flattened bill has a fringe of strainers with the floor of the mouth forming a small pouch; it feeds by skimming over the sea and straining out small invertebrates.

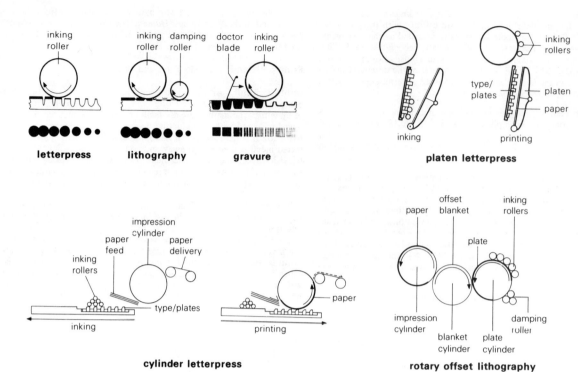

letterpress

lithography

gravure

platen letterpress

cylinder letterpress

rotary offset lithography

PRINTING *Principles of three major printing processes and the three major designs of printing press.*

Prior, Matthew (1664–1721) British poet. He became a member of parliament in 1700 and served as a diplomat in France and Holland. He wrote several long philosophical poems but is best known for *Poems on Several Occasions* (1709).

Pripet River (Russian name: Pripyat) A river in the W Soviet Union. Rising in NW Ukraine, it flows mainly ENE through the Belorussian SSR and joins the Dnepr River near Kiev. The **Pripet Marshes** that lie along its course were the scene of extensive fighting in World War II. Length: 500 mi (800 km).

Priscian (6th century AD) Latin grammarian, born at Caesarea (now Cherchell, Algeria). He taught at Constantinople and was the last considerable Latin scholar in antiquity. His *Institutiones Grammaticae*, in 18 books, which sum up the researches of all previous grammarians, remained a standard work throughout the middle ages.

prism A piece of glass or other transparent material having parallel polygonal ends, with a number of rectangular surfaces meeting them at right angles. They are used in optical instruments, such as cameras and binoculars, for changing the direction of light, either by refraction or by reflection from its walls. They are also used for splitting light into its component colors as a result of double refraction, once on entering the prism and again on leaving it.

prisoner of war A soldier captured by a belligerent in war. Guerrillas are so categorized provided that they have a commander, wear distinctive clothing, carry arms openly, and obey the laws and customs of war. The rights of a prisoner of war, which are defined in the *Geneva Conventions of 1929 and 1949 and are supervised by the International *Red Cross, include: withholding all information except name, rank, and number; receiving adequate amounts of food, drink, and medical care; engaging in correspondence and receiving parcels; and attempting to escape without being punished for so doing. In addition, prison camps must be open for inspection by the representatives of neutral powers.

prisons Institutions for confining convicted criminals (*see* criminal law). In primitive societies, and throughout much of history, offenders were either banished, executed, or physically punished; such prisons as existed were primarily places in which people were held until these punishments could be carried out. It was not until the 18th century that the main purpose of prisons became custodial. The appalling prison conditions at this time led to both reform movements and large-scale prison-building programs in the US in the late 19th century. Reforms since the 19th century have changed the emphasis in penal institutions from retribution to correction and rehabilitation. These have included halfway houses and other measures that prepare prisoners for re-entry into society. Overcrowding, however, has remained a feature of US prisons and became particularly severe in the 1980s.

Pritchett, V(ictor) S(awden) (1900–) British short-story writer and critic. He traveled widely in Europe during the 1920s and has written frequently about Spain. He has written critical works, several volumes of stories including *Collected Stories* (1956) and *Selected Stories of V. S. Pritchett*, (1978), and two much acclaimed autobiographical books, *A Cab at the Door* (1968) and *Midnight Oil* (1971).

private enterprise. *See* capitalism.

privateering The practice of permitting, under government license, private individuals to equip ships to attack and capture enemy merchantmen. Such action constituted piracy without the privateers' official authorization—"letters of marque." Although a useful complement to regular navies and common during the 17th and 18th centuries, privateering frequently degenerated into piracy because these formalities were disregarded; all European countries, except Spain, renounced privateering in 1856. The US abandoned it after the Civil War. *See also* buccaneers.

privet An evergreen or deciduous shrub or small tree of the genus *Ligustrum* (40–50 species), native to Eurasia and Australia and widely used for ornamental hedges, especially the European common privet (*L. vulgare*). Growing up to about 16 ft (5 m) high, it has simple oval leaves and terminal clusters of small creamy four-lobed flowers, which give rise to black berries. Family: *Oleaceae*.

Privy Council A body advising the British monarch, now having chiefly formal functions. It grew out of the Curia Regis (King's Court), forming a distinct group of royal advisers in the 14th century. The emergence of the *cabinet system of government in the 18th century led to a lessening of its power. By convention, it consists of all cabinet ministers, the Archbishops of Canterbury and York, the speaker of the House of Commons, and a number of senior British and Commonwealth statesmen.

probability The mathematical concept concerned with the effects of chance on an event, experiment, or observation. It originated in 1654, when the mathematicians *Pascal and *Fermat worked on problems sent to them by a gambler.

If an event can occur in n ways and r is the number of ways it can occur in a specified way, then the **mathematical probability** of it occurring in the specified way is r/n. For example, the probability of the number 5 coming up on a six-faced dice in one throw is 1/6. The probability of a 5 coming up x times in x throws is obtained by multiplication, i.e. it is $(1/6)^x$. Probabilities are expressed as numbers between 1 (a certainty) and 0 (an impossibility).

If in a number of experiments an event has occurred *n* times and failed *m* times, the **empirical probability** of success in the next trial is *n*/(*n* + *m*). Actuarial tables of life expectancy are based on empirical probabilities.

proboscis monkey A large leaf-eating *Old World monkey, *Nasalis larvatus*, of Borneo. Up to 5 ft (1.5 m) tall, proboscis monkeys have a protruding nose and live in groups in forests, feeding on young palm leaves. They can swim as well as climb.

processionary caterpillar The caterpillar of a moth of Old World genus *Thaumetopoea*. The caterpillars move in columns, guided by a leader, keeping head and tail contact with each other. Resting in nests by day, they feed at night and can be very destructive.

Proclus (410–85 AD) Neoplatonist philosopher, head of *Plato's Academy at Athens. Indefatigable in commenting on, and explaining, earlier philosophers, Proclus integrated pagan religion, philosophy, and mathematics into a single system. His works, translated into Latin and Arabic, transmitted *Neoplatonism to the medieval world.

Procne. See Philomela and Procne.

Proconsul A genus of extinct apes whose remains have been found in E Africa. They lived 20 million years ago and were probably ground-dwellers but could not stand erect. *Proconsul* apes were ancestors of modern apes.

Procopius (6th century AD) Byzantine historian. He accompanied the military commander Belisarius on several campaigns and worked in Constantinople from about 540 AD. His works include histories of the wars and of the public works undertaken during the reign of the Emperor Justinian I.

Procrustes A legendary Greek robber. He tortured his victims by stretching them or cutting off their limbs so that they fitted the exact length of his bed. He was killed by Theseus.

Procyon A conspicuous star, apparent magnitude 0.35 and 11.4 light years distant, that is the brightest star in the constellation Canis Minor and one of the nearest stars to the sun. It is part of a *multiple star, forming a visual *binary star with a *white dwarf.

producer gas A fuel gas containing nitrogen and carbon monoxide, as well as small amounts of hydrogen and hydrocarbons. It is produced by passing air (mixed with a little steam) over incandescent coke. The calorific value is low but heat is also obtained from the heat of reaction. *See also* water gas.

productivity The output of goods and services in a factory, country, etc., in relation to inputs (workers, machines, land) used to produce them. It is difficult to produce a single measure of productivity, but output per man-hour can be used as a rough approximation. Increases in productivity are largely responsible for the large increases in output in western economies since World War II; these increases are probably largely due to increased *investment in new machines and the higher levels of education and skill in the workforce. Two causes of low productivity may be distinguished: overmanning, the use of too many workers to produce a given level of output, and underproduction, a given number of workers producing less output than they should. **Productivity bargaining** is a form of *collective bargaining in which wage increases are agreed subject to a corresponding increase in productivity.

profit sharing Any program for sharing the profits of a firm between employees as well as shareholders. The aim is to give employees an interest in the profitability of a firm both as an incentive to productivity and to promote good *industrial relations. Profits may be shared in the form of bonuses or by making employees shareholders.

progesterone A steroid hormone secreted mainly by the *corpus luteum of the mammalian ovary following ovulation. It prepares the womb for implantation of the embryo and maintains this state during pregnancy. Progestogens—synthetic steroids with progesterone-like actions—are constituents of *oral contraceptives; they are also used to treat menstrual disorders. Progesterone preparations have been used in cattle breeding to suspend the estrous cycle and to enable the mating of the whole herd to be synchronized.

program, computer A series of instructions, written in a special programming language, enabling a *computer to perform a particular function. In a large computer there are several levels of programming. Low-level programming languages are those that resemble more closely the logic of the machine itself. High-level languages, such as *FORTRAN, *ALGOL and *COBOL, are used for the first stage of passing instructions from the human operator to the machine. *See also* software.

program music Music that is based on a literary, descriptive, or emotional subject, in contrast to **absolute music**, which has no overt associa-

tions outside the music itself. Programmatic elements are found in music of almost all periods; one of the first major works of program music was Vivaldi's set of violin concertos entitled *The Four Seasons* (1725), based on four sonnets by the composer. The development of the *symphonic poem and the concert *overture in the 19th century resulted in such well-known programmatic compositions as Mussorgsky's *Night on a Bare Mountain* (a depiction of a witches' sabbath), Liszt's *Les Préludes* (based on Lamartine's *Méditations poétiques*), and Richard Strauss's *Alpine Symphony* (a description of the ascent and descent of a mountain).

Progressive Party (1912–16) US political party; also called the Bull Moose Party. A progressive faction of the Republican Party tried to nominate Theodore *Roosevelt as its presidential candidate in 1912. Defeated at the Republican convention, the faction split from the Republican Party, and Roosevelt became the candidate of the new Progressive Party. Espousing restrictions on business, aid to farmers, and reform in labor and industry, Roosevelt attracted enough votes to cause a loss for Republican presidential candidate William Howard *Taft in 1912. By 1916 it had rejoined the Republican Party to unite behind Charles Evans *Hughes for president.

progressive taxation. See taxation.

Prohibition (1919–33) The period during which the manufacture, sale, and transportation of alcoholic drinks were prohibited in the US by the 18th Amendment to the constitution. The *temperance movement, which attributed crime and poverty to alcohol, combined with the wartime need to divert grain from distilleries to food manufacture, led to national prohibition. It proved impossible to enforce, not least because prohibition agents were outnumbered by gangsters and others profiting from illicit alcohol, and in 1933 prohibition was repealed by the 21st Amendment. See bootlegging.

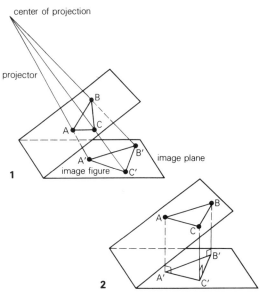

PROJECTION *The mapping of a triangle by* (1) *central and* (2) *orthogonal projections.*

projection (geometry) A mapping of a figure in one plane onto its image in another, called the image plane or plane of projection. A map of the earth's surface is an example of a projection (*see* map projection). The image of each point in the figure is the intersection of a straight line (the projector) and the image plane. In central projection a projector is the straight line drawn through the point and a fixed point (the center of projection). In orthogonal projection a projector is the perpendicular from the point to the image plane. The set of image points makes up the image figure.

projection (psychology) The process of attributing one's own qualities to other people or things. In *psychoanalysis this is a *defense mechanism; people who cannot tolerate their own emotions may cope by believing that other people have them. In projective tests, such as the *Rorschach test, a person's character is assessed from his descriptions of ambiguous objects.

projector, film A device for viewing photographic transparencies by shining a light through them to produce an enlarged image on a screen. Its principal use is in *cinematography although still pictures are also often viewed on slide projectors, particularly for viewing by a number of people together. Motion picture projectors and some home-movie projectors also contain equipment for reproducing sound from the track on the edge of the film.

Prokofiev, Sergei (1891–1953) Soviet composer and pianist. He studied at the St Petersburg conservatoire under Rimsky-Korsakov. He won the Anton Rubinstein Prize in 1914, playing his first piano concerto. He lived abroad from 1918 to 1933 and in 1948 was officially condemned for "undemocratic tendencies" in his music. His work includes seven symphonies (the first of which is the *Classical Symphony*; 1916–17), five piano concertos, two violin concertos, the operas *Love for Three Oranges* (1919) and *War and Peace* (1941; revised 1952), the ballet *Romeo and Juliet* (1935–36), music for the films *Lieutenant Kijé* (1934) and *Alexander Nevsky* (1938), and *Peter and the Wolf* (1936) for speaker and orchestra.

Prokop (*or* Procop; c. 1380–1434) Bohemian priest and leader of the *Hussites. In the 1420s Prokop successfully led the Hussites against the imperial armies detached to destroy them but, after joining the radical (Taborite) Hussites against the moderates (1434), he was killed in the ensuing battle of Lipany.

Prokopyevsk 53 55N 86 45E A city in the S Soviet Union, in the RSFSR. Located in the Kuznetsk Basin, it is an important coalmining center. Population (1981 est): 267,000.

prolactin A protein hormone, produced by the pituitary gland, that initiates and maintains lactation in mammals. In other animals, it has a variety of functions, being involved in growth and the balance of water and salts, as well as reproduction. *See also* gonadotrophin.

proletariat Originally, the lower class of Rome and other ancient states, the term was later used to refer to the lower class of any community. *Marx defined the proletariat as the wage laborers of capitalist economies, who depended on the sale of their labor to live and who owned no property; the struggle between this class and the *bourgeoisie would eventually lead to revolution. *See* Marxism.

Prometheus (Greek: forethought) In Greek mythology, the son of a Titan and Themis who created man and endowed him with reason. He also stole fire from heaven to give to man. Zeus chained him to a rock in the Caucasus and sent an eagle each day to devour his liver, which grew again by night. After thousands of years he was rescued by Heracles.

promethium (Pm) A radioactive element, not known on earth but identified by its spectrum in the light from stars, in which it is continuously being formed by nuclear reactions. The most stable isotope has a half-life of 17.7 years. Promethium salts exhibit bluish-green *luminescence and can be used in photoelectric cells. It is obtained from nuclear reactors. At no 61; at wt (145); mp about 1975°F (1080°C).

pronghorn A hoofed mammal, *Antilocapra americana*, resembling an antelope and found in rocky deserts of the W US. Up to 40 in (100 cm) high at the shoulder, pronghorns are not true antelopes, shedding the horny sheath of their branched horns every year; the bony core is permanent. Brown above and white beneath with white chevrons under the neck, they have brilliant-white rump hairs used for signaling. They are the only surviving members of the family *Antilocapridae*.

proof alcohol. *See* alcohol strength.

propellant **1.** A solid or liquid substance used to provide thrust in a rocket engine or gun. Propellants utilize very fast exothermic chemical reactions to produce large quantities of expanding gas quickly. Generally, they are explosive substances or mixtures. A single unstable substance (such as nitrocellulose) or mixture of combustible material and oxidant (such as alcohol and hydrogen peroxide) is termed a **monopropellant**. If the combustible material and oxidant are mixed in a combustion chamber the mixture forms a **bipropellant**. Generally, bipropellants are hypergolic systems, i.e. systems that ignite spontaneously when mixed. **2.** The pressurized inert liquids used to drive an *aerosol from its container.

propeller A device for converting the rotation of a shaft into thrust in the direction of its axis. A **marine propeller** is attached to a shaft connected to the ship's engine and has between two and six blades, shaped as part of a helical surface. It acts as a screw, accelerating a column of water rearward. An **air propeller** (*or* airscrew), moving in a thinner medium, has longer thinner blades (usually two or four) and a higher rotational speed. It, too, accelerates a mass of air rearward thrusting the aircraft forward by reaction.

proper motion The rate at which a star is observed to move on the *celestial sphere, i.e. perpendicular to the line of sight. Values are very small, often negligible.

Propertius, Sextus (c. 50–c. 16 BC) Roman poet. Born in Assisi in Umbria, he went to Rome as a young man and established himself in literary circles. *Cynthia*, the first of his four surviving books, contains highly personal love poems addressed to his mistress Hostia. His later books contain more generalized poems on various topics, including the psychology of love, written in a style noted for its bold originality.

prophets Ancient Israelite religious leaders and visionaries. The books of the prophets make up the second of the three divisions of the Hebrew *Bible and are grouped into the "Former Prophets" (Joshua, Judges, Samuel, and Kings) and the "Latter Prophets" (Isaiah, Jeremiah, Ezekiel, and the 12 Minor Prophets). Moses is regarded by Jews as the first and greatest of the prophets, and the gift of prophecy is thought to have ceased in the 5th century BC. In Islam, however, Jesus and Mohammed are also regarded as prophets.

proportional representation (PR) A voting system that aims accurately to reflect the wishes of the electorate and to ensure that votes for candidates of minority parties are not wasted. In the system of PR known as the **single transferable vote**, electors indicate their preferences among the candidates by numbering them on their ballot paper (1, 2, 3, etc.). Those candidates who are named as a first choice and who obtain the required quota are elected. First-choice votes for an unsuccessful candidate are then redistributed to second-choice votes for that candidate, and so on until the requisite number of candidates has been elected (the system requires multimember constituencies). In the **party-list system** (widely used in Europe) electors vote for a party, which is then allocated seats in proportion to its total vote.

propositional calculus A system of formal logic that assigns truth or falsehood to compound propositions or statements on the basis of the rules governing the connective words between them. Examples of such connective words are "and," "or," or "if . . . then . . . ." For example, the rule for "and" is that a statement containing it is true only if both the simple statements it connects are true; for "or" it is sufficient that only one of the statements be true. Thus "pigs fly and birds sing" is false, while "either pigs fly or birds sing" is true.

propylaea Ancient Greek monumental gateways, generally the ceremonial entrances to the *acropolis of a town. The best-preserved example is that on the Acropolis of Athens.

proscenium The arch at the front of a □theater stage through which the audience views the play. It became a standard feature of theater architecture following its first use in Italy in the 17th century but has been dispensed with in many theaters built during the 20th century.

Proserpine. *See* Persephone.

prosimian A *primate of the suborder *Prosimii* (53 species), including the *lemurs, *indris, *sifakas, *lorises, *bushbabies, *tarsiers, *tree shrews, and the *aye-aye. Prosimians are the most primitive of the primates and are mainly arboreal. Tree shrews have claws instead of fingernails and only partly opposable thumbs.

prostaglandins Compounds derived from long-chain (essential) fatty acids and found in mammalian body tissues. Their effects include stimulation of contraction in the womb, dilation of blood vessels, and modification of hormonal activity. They are released at sites of inflammation following tissue damage and the pain-relieving properties of such drugs as aspirin are due to their inhibition of prostaglandin synthesis. Synthetic prostaglandins are used to induce labor and abortion in women.

prostate gland A gland in men, situated just beneath the bladder. It secretes an alkaline fluid during ejaculation that forms part of the semen. Enlargement of the prostate commonly occurs in elderly men, obstructing the bladder and preventing urination. It is usually treated by surgically removing the gland in the operation of prostatectomy.

prostitution The practice of offering sexual gratification in return for money or other return. It has always been common, especially in societies in which legitimate sexual relations are closely regulated. Attitudes to prostitution differ greatly in different societies. Sometimes a bride earns her dowry in this way with general approval. It was practiced in ancient Mesopotamia by priestesses for religious reasons. In modern societies it is generally controlled by legislation, usually with the object of preventing the spread of venereal diseases and of making it more difficult for pimps (men who live off the earnings of prostitutes) to introduce young girls into the profession. Male prostitution is less common than female and largely confined to homosexual relations.

protactinium (Pa) A radioactive *actinide element, first identified by K. Fajans (1887–) and O. H. Göhring in 1913. It is present in pitchblende as a member of the uranium decay series. The oxide (Pa_2O_5) and iodide (PaI$_5$) have been produced. The latter decomposes on heating to give the metal. At no 91; at wt (231); mp $< 2900°F < 1600°C$.

Protagoras (c. 485–415 BC) Greek *Sophist. He claimed to teach virtue (more accurately interpreted as "success") and was himself successful and respected for more than 40 years. His saying, "Man is the measure of all things," shows his skeptical and subjectivist attitude to knowledge. His skepticism extended to religion, but not, apparently, to morality.

Protea A genus of evergreen shrubs and trees (over 100 species), native to S and central Africa. They have broad simple leaves and small white, pink, yellow, or orange flowers that are grouped into showy cup-shaped clusters, up to 12 in (30 cm) across, and surrounded by whorls of colored bracts. The flowers are a national emblem of South Africa. Family: *Proteaceae*.

Protectorate (1653–59) The period during which England was governed by Oliver *Cromwell. The Instrument of Government (1653) vested executive authority in the Lord Protector (Cromwell) and a state council and legislative authority in the Protector and a triennial parliament. As modified in 1657, the Instrument gave more power to parliament and less to the state council. Cromwell's relations with parliament subsequently deteriorated and he dismissed it in 1658. Following his death, his son Richard *Cromwell was Protector until his abdication in 1659.

protein A complex organic compound that consists of one or more chains of *amino acids linked by *peptide bonds (–NH–CO–). These chains are variously coiled, wound, and cross-linked to form a three-dimensional molecular structure, revealed by such techniques as *X-ray diffraction, that determines the biological properties of the protein. This structure is irreversibly damaged at temperatures above 140°F (60°C). Proteins are manufactured by cells according to the genetic information carried in the chromosomes and the specific function of the cell (see DNA; RNA). Proteins fulfill many important biological roles: some, including *collagen and *keratin, are important structural materials of body tissues, while the proteins of *muscle—actin and myosin—are responsible for its contractile properties. Proteins vital to the functioning of the body include enzymes—the biological catalysts of metabolic reactions; *antibodies—important in the body's defense mechanisms; and many *hormones—the chemical messengers of the body.

Protestant Episcopal Church Church of England, or Anglican Communion, Christian denomination in the US. Formed and named in 1789, it established seminaries, missionaries, and parish Sunday schools in the early 1800s. Administered by diocesan bishops, local parishes are led by priests who are assisted by curates and the laity. A national General Convention at which a presiding bishop, the national executive officer, is elected, is held every three years. The doctrine of scriptural faith in the Apostles' and Nicene creeds is followed. In 1976 the ordination of women priests was formally accepted.

Protestantism The movement for Catholic Church reform that arose in the Western Church in the 16th century and led to the establishment of the Reformed Churches. The word derives from the *protestatio* of the dissident reforming minority at the Diet of *Speyer (1529). The early leaders of the *Reformation—*Luther, *Calvin, and *Zwingli—each promoted his own brand of Protestantism.
There are many doctrinal divisions among Protestants, but all reject a varying number of tenets and practices retained in Catholicism. In general Protestants rely less upon ecclesiastical tradition, believing the Bible to be the sole source of truth. They deny papal authority and admit a variety of forms of Church government (see episcopacy; Presbyterianism); in some sects the spiritual priesthood of all the faithful is emphasized. *Transubstantiation, *purgatory, special veneration of the Virgin Mary, and invocation of saints are all repudiated. The importance of the sacraments is minimized, with only baptism and the *Eucharist being accorded widespread acceptance, and some groups, such as the *Quakers, reject even these. The preaching and studying of God's word in the Bible is conversely important. Church furnishings, vestments, and music are more austere than their Roman Catholic equivalents. The 20th-century ecumenical movement has gone some way toward reconciling the Roman Catholic and Protestant Churches, but there are still serious doctrinal and other differences, while fresh issues, such as the ordination of women, introduce new elements of divisiveness.

Proteus (bacteria) A genus of motile rod-shaped bacteria found mainly in soil and sewage, where they decompose organic matter, but also in the wounds of animals and man. Some species cause enteritis and urinary-tract infections.

Proteus (mythology) A Greek sea god who served Poseidon as a shepherd of seals. He is usually portrayed as an old man. He had prophetic powers but used his ability to change his form to avoid communicating his knowledge.

Protista A taxonomic group or kingdom that comprises all microscopic organisms, i.e. the algae, some fungi, protozoa, and bacteria.

Protoceratops A dinosaur that lived during the late Cretaceous period (about 100–65 million years ago). It was a short-legged squat quadruped, 7 ft (2 m) long and weighing 1.5 tons, and had long sharp teeth and huge jaw muscles attached to a bony neck frill. Its diet probably consisted of palm fronds. Order: *Ornithischia*.

protochordate Any animal of the subphylum *Chordata* that does not possess a backbone. Protochordates, which include the *tunicates and *amphioxus, may represent the ancestors of the first vertebrates.

Protocols of Zion A document published in 1903 purporting to contain Jewish plans to overthrow Christian civilization. Although conclusively proved a forgery in 1921, Hitler, like earlier antisemitic agitators, used it to justify his persecution of the Jews.

proton A positively charged elementary particle classified as a baryon (see particle physics). It forms part of all atomic nuclei, a single proton being the nucleus of the hydrogen atom. It is a stable particle, 1836 times heavier than the electron.

protostar An embryonic star that has formed out of a contracting cloud of interstellar gas and dust. It continues to contract, the density and temperature at its center rising slowly at first and then increasingly rapidly until they are sufficiently high to cause energy-releasing thermonuclear reactions to begin in the central core. The collapse is then halted, and the object becomes a luminous star.

Protozoa A phylum of typically microscopic single-celled organisms (about 30,000 species), usually classified as simple animals and widely distributed in moist and watery places, including mud, soil, fresh waters, and oceans. Protozoans range in size from 0.0039 in (0.1 mm) to several centimeters. They may have one or several nuclei and a variety of specialized structures, including a contractile vacuole for regulating the water content of the cell and cilia flagella for movement and feeding. The cell may be fairly rigid, with a stiff cell wall (pellicle) or skeletal elements, or flexible and variable. Some protozoans contain pigment and obtain food by photosynthesis in the same way as plants. However, most forms take in dissolved nutrients or solid food particles (detritus, bacteria, etc.). Asexual reproduction is by means of simple division of the parent cell (binary fission) or by budding to form new cells; various forms of sexual reproduction occur, including *conjugation. Protozoans can survive dry or adverse conditions by forming resistant cysts or spores. Some are important parasites of man and animals, including species of *Plasmodium*, which cause malaria, and trypanosomes, which cause sleeping sickness. The phylum includes the classes *Sarcodina*, *Ciliata*, *Flagellata*, and *Sporozoa*.

Protura A worldwide order of primitive wingless insects (150 species) that live in humus and soil, feeding on decaying organic materials. They have a pale cylindrical body (0.02–0.08 in [0.5–2 mm] long), which tapers to a simple tail (telson) and lacks eyes and antennae.

Proudhon, Pierre Joseph (1809–65) French socialist and political theorist. Proudhon was largely self-educated. In his treatises *Qu'est-ce que la propriété?* (1840) and the *Système des contradictions économiques ou philosophie de la misère* (1846), he argued that all property was theft and that in a just society orderly anarchy would replace oppressive government.

Proust, Joseph-Louis (1754–1826) French chemist, who demonstrated by accurate analysis that compounds always contain fixed proportions of elements. This is now known as the law of definite proportion or sometimes as Proust's law. This work contributed to *Dalton's atomic theory.

Proust, Marcel (1871–1922) French novelist. The son of rich bourgeois parents, he suffered from asthma from childhood and was devotedly cared for by his mother. He studied at the Lycée Condorcet and the Sorbonne and in the 1890s became a socialite in the most fashionable aristocratic circles in Paris. After the deaths of his parents (1903, 1905), he dedicated his life to writing and, because of asthma, lived as an invalid recluse in a cork-lined room in an apartment on the Boulevard Haussmann. In 1912 he financed the publication of the first volume (*Swann's Way*) of what was to become his masterpiece, *Remembrance of Things Past*. He then set to work expanding his original conception, realizing that his time was limited because of his ill health. The second volume, *Within a Budding Grove* (1919), won the Prix Goncourt; it was followed by *The Guermantes Way* (1920–21) and *Cities of the Plain* (1921–22). Proust managed to complete but not revise the final volumes, *The Captive* (1923), *The Sweet Cheat Gone*

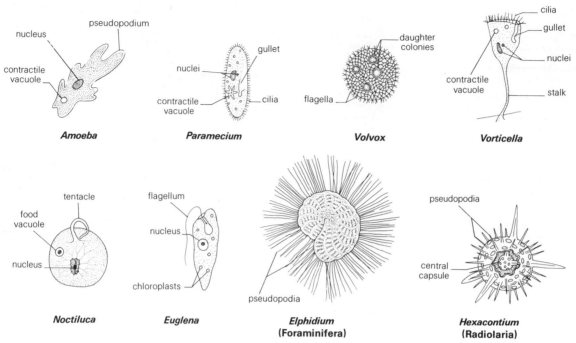

PROTOZOA *Although consisting only of single cells, these primitive animals show a surprising complexity of structure. Many have organs of locomotion (pseudopodia, flagella, or cilia) and some have gullets, through which food is channelled.*

(1925), and *Time Regained* (1927), before his death. Written in an elaborate style and influenced by the philosophy of *Bergson, *Remembrance of Things Past* is a detailed portrait of the society that Proust had abandoned, recreated through the involuntary workings of memory. There is a strong autobiographical element in the narration and in the theme of homosexuality that plays a large part in several sections.

Prout, William (1785–1850) British chemist and physiologist, who in 1824 discovered the presence of hydrochloric acid in the stomach. He was also the first to classify foods in terms of what are now called proteins, fats, and carbohydrates. He also formulated the idea that atomic weights are all multiples of the atomic weight of hydrogen (Prout's hypothesis).

Provençal A *Romance language, strictly the dialect of *Provence, but also used to refer to the dialects of various regions of S France and in this broad sense often called Occitan. These dialects are also collectively described as the *langue d'oc*, in contrast to the *langue d'oïl* spoken in northern and central areas of France (*oc* and *oïl* being the medieval forms for *yes* in these two dialect areas). The primary literary use of Provençal was by the *troubadours; it fell into disuse as a literary language during the later middle ages. About nine million people still speak it.

Provence A former province in SE France, bordering on Italy and the Mediterranean Sea. A kingdom during the 9th century AD, it became part of France in 1481 and now forms the modern planning region of **Provence-Côte-d'Azur**. Chiefly mountainous, its fertile river valleys produce grapes, olives, and mulberries. The perfume industry, centered on Grasse, is important. It contains the French *Riviera, a popular tourist area, along the S coast. Area: 12,134 sq mi (31,435 sq km). Population (1981 est): 3,909,700.

Proverbs An Old Testament book that is a collection of moral and religious maxims, traditionally ascribed to Solomon. Its chief theme is the nature and value of wisdom, which is the result of "fear of the Lord." Also prominent are maxims relating to justice, self-control, purity, industry, friends and family, and life and death.

Providence 41 50N 71 25W A seaport and the capital city of Rhode Island, on Narragansett Bay. Founded in 1636, it is the site of many historical buildings, including the First Baptist Church (1775), the First Unitarian Church, two cathedrals, and Brown University (founded in Warren in 1764 and moved to Providence in 1770). A major outlet for much of New England's oil, its manufactures include jewelry, machinery, and rubber goods. Population (1980): 156,804.

province A territorial subdivision of the empire of ancient Rome administered by a Roman governor. Provincial governors, who in Republican times (510–27 BC) were appointed by the Senate, commanded the garri-

sons, levied taxes, administered justice, and in wartime recruited troops. Under the Empire (after 27 BC), the Senate continued to provide governors for the ten more peaceful provinces while the emperors through their legates controlled those provinces still requiring military occupation. *See also* Roman Republic; Roman Empire.

Provo 40 14 N111 39W A city in N central Utah, on the Provo River, SW of Salt Lake City, east of Utah Lake, and west of the Wasatch Range. The Mormons founded the city in 1849 and established Brigham Young Academy (now Brigham Young University) in 1875. Economic activities include a major steel industry, as well as mining and the production of foodstuffs, electronics, machinery, and clothing. Population (1980): 74,108.

Proxima Centauri. *See* Alpha Centauri.

Prudhoe Bay A small inlet of the Arctic Ocean on the coast of N Alaska. Since the discovery of vast oil deposits in the area (1968) it has been a center of drilling activity. A pipeline transfers oil from Prudhoe Bay to the S.

Prud'hon, Pierre Paul (1758–1823) French painter and draftsman, born at Cluny. He trained in the Dijon Academy and in Rome (1784–7), where he was influenced by the works of *Correggio and *Leonardo. The style of his court portraits, for example *Empress Josephine* (Louvre), and his famous *Crime Pursued by Vengeance and Justice* (Saint-Omer, N France) display a romantic feeling distinctly different from the current neoclassical vogue (*see* neoclassicism).

Prunus A genus of deciduous or evergreen shrubs and trees (over 200 species), mostly native to N temperate regions. It includes the *plums, *almonds, *apricots, *peaches, and *cherries as well as many ornamental species. They have oval toothed leaves, often rolled in the bud, and white or pink flowers, about 0.4 in (1 cm) across, with five petals and many stamens. They produce stone fruits (*see* drupe), often with edible flesh or kernels. Family: *Rosaceae*.

Prussia A former state in N Germany on the NE Baltic coast. Established in the 13th century by the Teutonic Knights, Prussia became a duchy in 1525 under *Hohenzollern rule. United with Brandenburg in 1618, under *Frederick William, the Great Elector, it became the most powerful N German state. In 1701 his son took the title King of Prussia. In the 18th century, under *Frederick the Great, Prussia annexed Silesia and parts of Poland and became a major European power. Following Napoleon's defeat, it made important territorial gains at the Congress of Vienna (1815). Under *Bismarck's ambitious leadership, Prussia defeated Austria and Austria's German allies (1866), acquiring *Schleswig-Holstein and forming the *North German Confederation. Following victory in the

*Franco-Prussian War (1870–71) the German Empire was proclaimed under Prussian leadership. In 1918 Prussia became a republic and was abolished by the Allies after World War II.

prussic acid. *See* hydrocyanic acid.

Przemyśl 49 48N 22 48E A city in SE Poland. During World War I it withstood a five-month siege by Russian armies before surrendering. Its industries are varied and include flour milling, tanning, and the manufacture of machinery. Population (1972 est): 54,800.

Przewalski's horse The single surviving species of wild horse, *Equus przewalskii*, discovered in Mongolia in about 1880 by the Russian explorer Nicolai Mikhailovich Przewalski (1839–88). It is sturdily built with a relatively large head and has a short erect dark-brown mane and a dark dorsal stripe. The coat is reddish brown, becoming paler in winter. Height: 4–5 ft (1.22–1.42 m; 12–14 hands).

Psalms An Old Testament book, also known as the Psalter, containing 150 spiritual songs. They were formerly all attributed to David but are now generally believed to be by a number of different authors; some of them may date from the early period of the Jewish monarchy. They were intended to be sung with musical accompaniment and used in the liturgy of the Temple at Jerusalem; they continue to be used in both public and private worship by Jews and Christians. The majority are expressions of praise and worship of God and his works. A large number deal with aspects of a believer's experience, such as penitence, trust, doubt, fear, and suffering.

psaltery A medieval musical instrument, a type of *zither. It was plucked by the fingers of both hands or by two plectra.

Psamtik I King of Egypt (664–610 BC); the founder of the 26th dynasty. Appointed viceroy of Egypt by *Ashurbanipal of Assyria in 663, he took advantage of Assyria's weakness to repudiate its suzerainty, while remaining its ally. Psamtik encouraged trade with Greece and employed Greek mercenaries (the "brazen men"). During his reign Egyptian national sentiment revived the art and institutions of the pyramid age.

Pseudo-Dionysius the Areopagite (early 6th century AD) Mystical theologian, probably born in Syria, whose real name is unknown. His fame rests on several Greek treatises and letters, which greatly influenced leading medieval scholars. They attempt to combine Christianity with *Neoplatonism and include *The Celestial Hierarchy, The Ecclesiastical Hierarchy, The Divine Names,* and *The Mystical Theology.* They were formerly attributed to St *Dionysius the Areopagite.

pseudopodium A temporary extension of the cytoplasm found in some *Protozoa and used for locomotion and for engulfing food particles. In *Amoeba,* the pseudopodia are blunt lobular processes but in other protozoa they may be slender, filamentous, or branching.

Psilocybe A genus of mushrooms growing in soil and dung. The Mexican species *P. mexicana* contains the hallucinogenic compounds psilocin and psilocybin, which have effects similar to those of *LSD. It was regarded as a sacred mushroom in Mexico and eaten during religious ceremonies. Mushrooms of the liberty cap fungus (*P. semilanceolata*) are common in pastures and lawns, having grayish-brown or olive-green conical caps, 0.4–0.8 in (1–2 cm) in diameter.

psi particle An elementary particle discovered in 1974 and classified as a meson. Its unusually long lifetime led to the extension of the quark model (*see* particle physics) to include a quark (and its antiquark) having a new property called *charm. The psi particle itself is not charmed as it consists of a charmed quark and its antiquark.

psittacosis (*or* parrot disease) An infectious illness caused by a microorganism of the *Chlamydia* group, which is caught from birds, particularly parrots. The severity of the disease varies, but usually it causes pneumonia. Tetracycline antibiotics are used to treat the disease.

Pskov 57 48N 28 26E A city in the NW Soviet Union, in the RSFSR on the Velikaya River, SE of Lake Pskov. Nicholas II abdicated at the railroad station here in 1917. Industries include food processing and tourism, Pskov having many historic buildings. Population (1981 est): 179,000.

Pskov school A school of Russian *icon and mural painting that flourished in the city of Pskov between the late 12th and early 16th centuries. It developed in isolation from other cultural centers since most other parts of Russia were occupied by the Mongols during this period. Characteristics of the school's style were the influence of *Byzantine art, monumental forms, brilliant colors, emotional intensity, and the persistence of archaic methods of representation.

psoriasis A chronic recurring skin disease marked by excessive scaling of the skin. The disease is very common, begins with small red patches covered with scales, and may spread extensively. The knees, elbows, lower back, scalp, and nails are most commonly affected. There is no known cure, but steroid creams and ultraviolet light are used to alleviate the condition.

Psyche In Greek mythology, a personification of the soul, portrayed as a beautiful mortal girl. *Apuleius tells the allegorical story of how she lost her divine lover, Cupid, and of her subsequent quest and suffering before she was finally reunited with him in marriage in heaven.

psychedelic drugs. *See* hallucinogens.

psychiatry The study and treatment of mental disorders. A psychiatrist is a medically qualified physician specializing in mental illness. Modern psychiatry also involves those of other professional disciplines, including nurses, social workers, and psychologists. The range of mental disorders includes *psychosis, *neurosis, *psychosomatic disorders, *drug dependence, and *mental retardation. Within psychiatry there are several specialities, notably child psychiatry, *psychotherapy, forensic psychiatry (which deals with those who have broken the law), and geriatric psychiatry (psychogeriatrics), which cares for the mentally disordered elderly.

psychoanalysis A school of *psychology and a method of treating mental disorders based upon the teachings of Sigmund *Freud (*see also* Adler, Alfred; Jung, Carl). Psychoanalysis stresses the dynamic interplay of unconscious mental forces and the way in which the adult personality is determined by the course of sexual development in childhood. The chief techniques of psychoanalysis are free *association and the recall of *dreams in the course of intensive psychotherapy, which usually requires several 50-minute sessions each week for up to three years. In the course of this treatment transference takes place, in which aspects of the patient's past experiences and relationships are transferred to the analyst, the object being to bring repressed conflicts into consciousness so that they can be resolved. Although analysis was originally intended as a treatment for neurosis, it has been extended to some psychotic conditions by W. R. Bion, Herbert Rosenfeld, and others. Among those who have made significant contributions to the field are Carl Jung, Alfred Adler, Karen Horney, Carl Rogers, Harry Stock Sullivan, Otto Rank, Wilhelm Reich and Eric Fromm. The work of Melanie *Klein was devoted to exploring early infantile experiences on a Freudian basis, while some of Freud's underlying concepts were challenged by other analysts. *See also* defense mechanism; ego; id; Oedipus complex; repression; superego; unconscious.

psychokinesis. *See* telekinesis.

psychology The scientific study of the behavior of man and animals. Different schools of psychology use differing methods and theories. These include *behaviorism; experimental psychology, in which laboratory experiments are used to investigate factors influencing behavior (particularly *memory, perception, and learning); *Gestalt psychology; associationist psychology (*see* association); and *psychoanalysis. Clinical psychology applies these approaches to the understanding and treatment of mental illness (*see also* psychiatry). Educational psychology studies the ways in which children learn, in order to intervene as problems arise. Occupational psychology studies people in their working environment. *See also* ethology.

psychopath A person who behaves violently or antisocially and shows neither guilt nor any feeling for others. Psychopathy can be caused by a constitutional abnormality or an emotionally deprived upbringing.

psychosis A severe mental illness in which the sufferer loses contact with reality. Organic psychoses are caused by diseases affecting the brain, such as epilepsy, alcoholism, and dementia; functional psychoses have no known physical cause. The major functional psychoses are *schizophrenia and *manic-depressive psychosis. All psychoses can cause *hallucinations, delusions, and altered thought processes. They are common and disabling illnesses that account for the occupation of more hospital beds than any other illness.

psychosomatic disorder An illness in which physical symptoms are caused or exacerbated by mental factors. Certain physical illnesses, including asthma, eczema, and peptic ulcer, are thought to be partly a response to psychological and social *stress.

psychosurgery Surgical operations performed on the brain in order to relieve psychological symptoms. The commonest operation is *leukotomy. In lobectomy a whole lobe of the *brain is removed, often because of epilepsy. In amygdalectomy a lesion is made in a small part of the limbic system of the brain to reduce pathological aggression. These are all irreversible treatments and are reserved for the most severe forms of mental illness that are resistant to other therapies.

psychotherapy Psychological methods of treatment for mental disorders. There are many different approaches to psychotherapy, including *psychoanalysis and *group therapy. In client-centered therapy the therapist refrains from giving any direct advice. Family therapy involves several members of a family meeting together with a therapist to improve their relationships. All these approaches share the goal of helping self-understanding and personal development through the relationship between the client and the therapist. *See also* behavior therapy; hypnosis.

Ptah In ancient Egyptian mythology, the creator god. A local deity of *Memphis, he was proclaimed the supreme god when Egypt was first unified (c. 3100 BC), but was later identified with *Osiris and became the patron of craftsmen. He is always shown in the form of a *mummy.

ptarmigan A grouse, *Lagopus lagopus*, found in Arctic tundra and mountain regions. 17 in (35 cm) long, it has white wings and a mottled blackish-brown body that changes to white in winter. Its feet are covered with feathers and it feeds on shoots and fruits in summer and on lichens and leaves dug from the snow in winter.

Pteranodon An extinct flying reptile of the Cretaceous period (135–65 million years ago). 10 ft (3 m) long with a wingspan of 25 ft (7.5 m), it had an enormous bony crest that balanced its large head. It lived around sea cliffs, clinging to them with its long hind claws and gliding over the sea to catch fish in its long toothless beak.

Pteraspis An extinct genus of jawless fishlike vertebrates, belonging to the class *Ostracodermi*, that lived from the Ordovician to the Devonian periods (about 500–370 million years ago). The head and anterior part of the body were covered by a heavy bony shield, the remainder by small scales, and there was an upturned beaklike extension of the head (rostrum). Fins were placed singly, not in pairs. Subphylum: *Agnatha*.

pteridophyte A flowerless perennial vascular plant of the division *Pteridophyta*, which shows a distinct *alternation of generations with the asexual spore-bearing (sporophyte) generation predominating. The sporophyte plant consists typically of leaves, stems, and roots and bears spores in special capsules (sporangia), which are often arranged in clusters (sori) on the leaves. Pteridophytes are subdivided into *Lycopsida* (e.g. *clubmosses), *Sphenopsida* (e.g. *horsetails), *Psilopsida*, or *Psilotopsida* (mostly extinct), and *Pteropsida* (*see* fern).

pterodactyl. *See* pterosaur.

pterosaur An extinct flying reptile, also called pterodactyl, that lived during the Jurassic and Cretaceous periods (200–65 million years ago). A thin wing membrane stretched from the elongated fourth finger of the fore limb along the body to the knee; a second membrane stretched to the neck. It had a compact body and long slender hind limbs, probably used to cling, batlike, to rocks and trees. Its light bones, toothless beaked jaw, large eyes, and large brain resembled those of modern birds. □fossil.

Ptolemaic system A theory concerning the motions of the sun, moon, and planets that was originally advanced in Greece in the 3rd century BC and was completed by Claudius *Ptolemy in the 2nd century AD. It was a geocentric system in which the moon, Mercury, Venus, Sun, Mars, Jupiter, and Saturn were thought to move around the earth. Prediction agreed reasonably well with observation. To achieve this Ptolemy had to propose that each orbiting body moved in a small circle (an epicycle) the center of which moved in a larger circle (a deferent) around the earth. A sphere of stars lay beyond the seven deferents. The Ptolemaic system was finally abandoned when the *heliocentric system of *Copernicus was accepted.

Ptolemies A Macedonian dynasty that ruled Egypt from 323 BC, when *Ptolemy I Soter became governor of Egypt, until 30 BC, when Ptolemy XV Caesar (47–30 BC; reigned 44–30 BC), nicknamed Caesarion, the son of Cleopatra and, perhaps, Caesar, was executed by Octavian (later *Augustus).

Ptolemy (*or* Claudius Ptolemaeus; 2nd century AD) Egyptian mathematician, astronomer, and geographer. Little is known of his life except that he lived and worked in Alexandria, probably publishing his major works between 127 and 145. The foremost of these outlines the *Ptolemaic system of astronomy and was originally known as *He mathematike syntaxis* (*The Mathematical Collection*) but was known to Arab astronomers by the Greek superlative *Megiste*, which took the Arab form *Almagest*, the name by which it is still known. His other works include *Analemma* and *Planisphaerium* on geometry, *Harmonica* on music, and *Geographike hyphegesis*, an extensive guide to geography.

Ptolemy I Soter (?367–?283 BC) The first Macedonian King of Egypt and founder of the Ptolemaic dynasty (*see* Ptolemies). He was a general of Alexander the Great, after whose death he became governor of Egypt as his share of the Macedonian empire. He conquered Palestine, Cyprus, and much of Asia Minor, taking the title of king in 304. He founded the Library of *Alexandria, which he made his capital, and wrote a history of Alexander's campaigns.

Ptolemy II Philadelphus (308–246 BC) King of Egypt (285–246); the son and successor of Ptolemy I. He and his second wife and sister *Arsinoe II were engaged unsuccessfully in war with Syria. He completed the public buildings of *Alexandria, restored the Nile–Red Sea canal, and introduced camels into Egypt.

Ptolemy XIII Theos Philopator (63–47 BC) King of Egypt (51–47), ruling jointly with his sister and wife *Cleopatra VII until he and his advisers expelled her (48). He murdered *Pompey after his defeat by *Caesar, hoping for Caesar's favor, but when Caesar reinstated Cleopatra, Ptolemy opposed him and was killed.

ptomaines Compounds formed during the bacterial decomposition of proteins in animal and plant tissues. Most are amines, such as diethylamine, putrescine, and cadaverine, and they may be poisonous, although the symptoms ascribed to "ptomaine poisoning" are usually due to bacterial toxins in contaminated food (*see* food poisoning).

puberty The onset of sexual maturity. The age at which this occurs is very variable but is usually between 12 and 17 in boys and between 10 and 16 in girls. The sexual organs develop to their adult form and pubic hair starts to grow; in girls the menstrual periods begin (menarche). The secondary sexual characteristics develop: in girls the breasts enlarge and in boys the muscles enlarge, the voice deepens, and facial hair grows. Psychological changes include an increase in the sexual drive and often in anxiety and insecurity.

Public Health Service (PHS) US agency, part of the Department of *Health and Human Services, that is charged with promoting the protection and advancement of the country's physical and mental health. Its functions include implementation of a national health policy, coordination of research programs, and enforcement of safety and drug laws. The National Center for Health Statistics; the Alcohol, Drug Abuse, and Mental Health Administration; and the Food and Drug Administration are among its divisions. It was established in 1798 to oversee marine hospitals.

public relations Efforts by firms, organizations, individuals, etc., to present a good public image. Good public relations are achieved by prompt servicing of complaints and questions from the public, involvement in local affairs, sponsorship of charities, etc. A public relations firm may be hired by a company or an individual to ensure that these tasks are carried out and to promote his employer by such means as obtaining free mention of him or his products in the media.

Public Safety, Committee of A governing body during the French Revolution. When a coalition of European powers attacked France following the king's execution in 1793, the Committee of Public Safety was established to meet the emergency. Coming under the influence of Robespierre, it conducted the *Reign of Terror. After Robespierre's fall in July, 1794, its powers were curtailed.

public sector Those parts of the productive and nonproductive sectors of the economy that are financed out of taxation, are under state control, or both. It embraces all the employees and activities of central and local government, public institutions and utilities, and nationalized industries.

Public Works Administration (PWA) US federal agency established by the National Industrial Recovery Act of 1933 to stimulate the economy and provide jobs for the unemployed. Part of the *New Deal, roads were laid; housing, schools, and hospitals were built; and electrical power and sewage systems were constructed. Secretary of the Interior Harold L. Ickes managed the agency until it was absorbed into the Federal Works Agency in 1939.

publishing The commissioning, production, and distribution of books, *periodicals, and *newspapers. Before the invention of printing, reading matter was produced by hand in the form of papyrus rolls in ancient Egypt, Greece, and Rome, and later in the form of manuscripts copied by hand. With the invention of printing by *Gutenberg, early printed books (*see* incunabula) were sold by the printer, who also functioned as publisher and bookseller. During the 15th and 16th centuries these functions began to separate; the Netherlands was one of the earliest centers of book publishing and the house founded by Louis Elzevir (1540–1617) is still active in Haarlem. After the introduction of the Copyright Act (1709), book publishing, which had previously been financed largely by rich patrons, expanded in the UK and the US as an independent industry.
The growth of libraries, the spread of literacy, and technical innovations in printing and papermaking during the 19th century enabled the independent publisher to flourish. During the 20th century the main innovation in publishing has been the growth of inexpensive paperbacks. The introduction of book clubs has also expanded the market for books.

Puccini, Giacomo (1858–1924) Italian opera composer. He was a church organist before studying at the Milan conservatoire with Amilcare Ponchielli (1834–86). His first major success was *Manon Lescaut* (1893). The operas that followed established Puccini as the master of the Italian stage and of the *verismo* (Italian: realism) style: *La Bohème* (1896), *Tosca* (1900), and *Madame Butterfly* (1904). An opera on an American subject, *La fanciulla del West* (1910) and the three one-act operas of *Il Trittico* (1918) were less successful; his final masterpiece, *Turandot*, was produced posthumously in 1926, having been completed by Franco Alfano (1876–1954).

Pucelle, Jean (?1300–?1355) French miniature painter and manuscript illuminator. His best-known works are the *Belleville Breviary* and *The Hours of Jeanne d'Évreux* (Metropolitan Museum, New York), the latter being a prayer book commissioned by the French queen.

puck In English folklore, a household spirit, malicious fairy, or demon. The famous Puck of Shakespeare's *A Midsummer Night's Dream* is identified with the mischievous fairy Robin Goodfellow.

puddling process A method of making pure iron from *pig iron. The pig iron is melted in a furnace and powdered iron oxide is stirred in to drive off the slag. As the iron becomes purer, its melting point increases and eventually it forms a pasty mass, which is removed and hammered or rolled into shape. Puddling superseded *wrought-iron working by hand and its introduction was an important contribution to the industrial revolution, although it is now little used.

Pudovkin, Vsevolod (1893–1953) Russian film director. He is best known for his early silent films, especially *Mother* (1926), *The End of St Petersburg* (1927), and *Storm Over Asia* (1928). He published influential lectures concerning the technique of montage.

Puebla (*or* Puebla de Zaragoza) 19 03N 98 10W A city in S Mexico. Strategically situated on the route between Mexico City and Veracruz, it was an important fortress city for several centuries. Notable buildings include an ornate cathedral (1649) and the Teatro Principal (1790). A major agricultural and industrial center, Puebla is famous for its onyx products. Population (1978 est): 677,959.

Pueblo 38 17N 104 38W A city in Colorado, on the Arkansas River. Established in 1842, it has important steel industries, which use local coal. Other industrial activities include oil refining and meat packing. Population (1980): 101,686.

Pueblo Indians North American Indian tribes of the SW region including the Tewa, Keres, *Hopi, and Zuni. Their collective name derives from the Spanish term for their villages—*pueblos*. They began to abandon their hunting existence and adopt their present farming economy about 1600 years ago. They were always extremely peaceful peoples, much given to ritual and ceremonial pursuits. Their villages are often constructed around a central courtyard; the buildings, made from mudbrick blocks, have several stories, each set back from the one below. Communities were traditionally governed by a council of the heads of the various secret religious societies, which met in underground rooms called kivas. The diversity of Pueblo languages indicates different origins.

puerperal fever Persistent fever occurring in a woman soon after childbirth, most commonly caused by infection of the genital tract, particularly of the lining of the womb. The infection may be serious and progress to blood poisoning. Formerly many women died of puerperal fever, but with improved hygiene and antibiotics the disease is now rare and can be cured by prompt treatment with antibiotics.

Puerto Rico, Commonwealth of (name from 1898 until 1932: Porto Rico) An island and self-governing commonwealth in association with the US. It is in the West Indies, the smallest and most easterly island in the Greater Antilles. It is largely mountainous, rising over 3937 ft (1200 m) and supports one of the densest populations in the world. *Economy*: rapid industrialization has taken place since the 1940s transforming the economy from a basically agricultural one to a mixed one. Manufacture (chemicals, textiles, plastics, food processing) is the main source of income, while in the agricultural sector income from dairy and livestock farming has overtaken that of sugar, the principal crop. Tourism is an increasingly important source of revenue. *History*: discovered by Columbus in 1508, it was under Spanish rule for nearly 400 years until ceded to the US in 1898. Full US citizenship was granted in 1917 and it attained its present status in 1952, which was ratified by a plebiscite (1967). During the 1940s and 1950s emigration to the US was high, a trend that later moderated. In 1976 the New Progressive Party regained governorship and legislative control, led by Carlos Romero Barceló, who is an advocate of the incorporation of Puerto Rico as a US state. Since 1974, however, there has been growing militant pressure for the independence of Puerto Rico and in August, 1978,

the UN special committee on decolonization reaffirmed the "inalienable right of the people of Puerto Rico" to self-determination. Official language: Spanish; English is also widely spoken. Official currency: US dollar of 100 cents. Area: 3349 sq mi (8674 sq km). Population (1983 est): 3,295,000. Capital: San Juan.

Pufendorf, Samuel von (1632–94) German jurist, philosopher, and historian, known for his contribution to natural and international law. A professor at Heidelberg and later at Lund, he became historiographer to the Swedish court in 1677 and to the Elector of Brandenburg in 1688. In his best-known work, *De Jure naturae et gentium* (1672), influenced by *Grotius and *Hobbes, he argued that all men are entitled to be free and equal and that international law is not restricted to Christendom but is common to all nationalities. His *De habitu religionis christianae ad vitam civilem* (1687) advocated state superiority over the church in civil affairs.

puff adder A large stout-bodied highly venomous *adder belonging to the genus *Bitis* (8 species), occurring in semiarid areas of Africa and characterized by its habit of hissing loudly and inflating its body in a threatening posture. 1–7 ft (0.3–2 m) long, puff adders are brown or gray with yellow chevron patterning.

puffball The globular or pear-shaped fruiting body of certain fungi. As it matures, the outer layer cracks and sloughs off; the spongy interior produces powdery spores, which are released either through a pore (genus *Lycoperdon*) or from the upper surface (genus *Calvatia*). The grayish-white giant puffball (*C. giganteum*) occurs in pastures, woodlands, and roadsides and may reach over 40 in (1 m) across. It is attached to the ground by a short cord. Class: *Basidiomycetes*.

puffer A □fish, also called globe fish, belonging to the family *Tetraodontidae*, that inflates its body with air or water when disturbed. The tough spiny skin contains a highly toxic chemical (tetraodontoxin), which can be fatal. Up to 20 in (50 cm) long, puffers live mainly in tropical and subtropical seas, feeding on corals, mollusks, and crustaceans using their beaklike snouts. They are edible if expertly prepared. Order: *Tetraodontiformes*.

PUFFIN *The bill of this bird, which breeds in large colonies, is armed with serrations that enable it to carry 30-40 fish at a time. Puffins will continue to bring food to the nest even after the young have left.*

puffin A N Atlantic seabird, *Fratercula arctica*. 11.5 in (29 cm) long, it is black with a white face and underparts, red legs, and a blue ring around the eye. Its large triangular bill is striped red, yellow, and blue in the breeding season. It feeds at sea on fish and mollusks and breeds in disused rabbit burrows. Family: *Alcidae* (auks).

pug A breed of toy □dog originating in China and introduced to Holland and the West by Dutch traders in the 17th century. It is stockily built, with the tail curled over the back, and has a wrinkled skin and a large head with a short square muzzle. The short smooth coat can be silver, black, or apricot-fawn with a black mask on the face and a black line along the back. Height: 10–11 in (25–28 cm).

Pugachov, Yemelyan Ivanovich (1726–75) The leader of a Cossack rebellion in Russia, the Pugachov Rebellion (1773–74). Claiming to be the assassinated Tsar Peter III (1728–62; reigned 1762), Pugachov raised a revolt against the government of *Catherine the Great. The revolt collapsed and Pugachov was beheaded.

Puglia. *See* Apulia.

Pugwash Conferences International conferences on science and world affairs, convened at the suggestion of, among others, Albert Einstein and Bertrand Russell, that discuss the problems of *disarmament and the social responsibility of scientists. The first conference was held in the village of Pugwash, Nova Scotia (Canada), in 1957.

Pulci, Luigi (1432–84) Italian poet. He lived mostly at the court of Lorenzo de' *Medici and wrote all his works in Italian. His major work is the epic poem *Morgante* (1483), a colloquial and irreverently comic treatment of French chivalric material concerning Roland (*see* Charlemagne).

puli A Hungarian breed of sheepdog whose unique coat hangs to the ground in long tight cords. The puli is agile and lively; its tail is held over the back and its coat is usually black but may be bronze-black, gray, or white. Height: 16–18 in (41–46 cm) (dogs); 14–16 in (36–41 cm) (bitches).

Pulitzer Prizes Annual awards endowed by editor and publisher Joseph Pulitzer (1847–1911) and first awarded in 1917. Pulitzer stipulated that $500,000 left to Columbia University be used to recognize achievements in journalism and literature. The $1,000 prizes for journalism include local, national, and international reporting, public service and investigative reporting, editorial writing, editorial cartooning, news photography, feature photography, commentary, criticism, and feature writing. The five $500 prizes for literature are fiction, poetry, history, drama, biography, and nonfiction. A prize for musical composition has also been awarded.

Pullman, George Mortimer (1831–97) US businessman and inventor. In 1865, Pullman produced a prototype of a luxurious railroad sleeping car, which he called "The Pioneer" and which proved to be enormously successful. He later founded the Pullman Palace Car Co for the manufacture of similar sleeping cars and experimented with new types of factory organization, including a planned residential town for his employees. His relations with his employees were not always peaceful, however. In 1894 the *Pullman Strike led to a national boycott of all railroads that used his cars and sporadic violence that was ended only by the intervention of federal troops.

Pullman Strike (1894) US railroad labor strike. A strike over wage cuts by workers in the Pullman car factory near Chicago initiated a union boycott against all Pullman cars. When management fired some union leaders, the American Railway Union, under Eugene V. *Debs, struck the railroads nationwide. The government received an injunction against interference, and federal troops were necessary to quell outbreaks of violence. The railroads were kept running with non-union help and military guard. Debs was arrested for violating the injunction.

pulsar A celestial object that emits extremely regular pulses of radiation and is almost certainly a rotating *neutron star. Pulsars were originally discovered, in 1967, at radio wavelengths. The Crab and Vela pulsars also emit pulses at optical and gamma-ray wavelengths. The pulses arise when a beam of radio waves emitted by the rotating star sweeps past the earth, similar to the way in which lighthouse flashes are produced. The radiation (synchrotron radiation) is generated by electrons moving in the star's strong magnetic field; the emission site is still uncertain. The pulsation periods, ranging from 0.033 seconds to 4 seconds, are all very gradually increasing. Pulsars are thought to originate in *supernovae. X-ray pulsars also exist but apparently involve a neutron star as a component of a close binary star.

pulsating stars. *See* variable stars.

pulse The rhythmic contraction and expansion of the elastic walls of the arteries caused by the pressure of blood pumped from the heart. The pulse therefore reflects the heart rate and can be readily felt in arteries just beneath the skin: it is usually measured at the radial artery in the wrist. The average pulse rate of a resting adult is 60–80 per minute; it increases with exercise and emotion. The pulse also changes in disease, becoming faster during a fever and irregular in heart-rhythm disorders. A reduction in blood pressure (e.g. after hemorrhage) will cause a fast feeble pulse.

puma. *See* cougar.

pumice A volcanic rock derived from acidic lava. It resembles sponge in having many cavities produced by bubbles of gas trapped on rapid solidification, often during submarine eruptions. Pumice is light in color and weight and often floats on water.

pumpkin The fruit of certain varieties of *Cucurbita pepo* and *C. maxima*, small bushes or trailing vines cultivated in North America and Europe. The fruit is large and round, up to 66 lb (30 kg) in weight with a lightly furrowed yellow rind surrounding an edible fleshy pulp and numerous seeds. It is cooked and eaten as a vegetable, in pies, puddings, and soups or used as animal feed. Family: *Cucurbitaceae*.

pumps Machines designed to transfer mechanical energy to a fluid. This energy may be required to move the fluid from one place to another, raise its level, increase its pressure, or provide circulation. Pumps are of three kinds: reciprocating, centrifugal, and rotary displacement. The reciprocating pump consists essentially of a piston moving to and fro; liquid is drawn in through one valve on the down stroke, and expelled through an exhaust valve on the upstroke. The centrifugal pump draws liquid into the center of a rotating impeller, which thrusts it out of the exit. Rotating pumps consist of shaped gears or rotors, which move the liquid around a close-fitting chamber.

Punch and Judy A puppet show performed with glove puppets and featuring the violent quarrels of the heartless Punch and his wife Judy. The character of Punch, who wears a striped costume and has a hooked nose and a humped back, derives from the Italian *commedia dell'arte.

Punic Wars Three wars between Rome and Carthage, which gave Rome control of the Mediterranean. The first Punic (from the Latin *Punicus*, Carthaginian) War (264–241 BC) was provoked by Roman intervention in Sicily and was marked by the emergence of Roman naval power: its newly built fleet was victorious off Mylae (260) and again off the Aegates Insulae (241), which brought the war to an end with Carthage's evacuation of Sicily. The second Punic War (218–201) was instigated by *Hannibal's capture (219) of Saguntum, a Roman ally in Spain. His advance into Italy was eventually checked, after disastrous Roman losses at Trebia (218), Trasimene (217), and *Cannae (216), by *Fabius Maximus. Ultimate victory, however, was achieved by *Scipio Africanus, who defeated Hannibal at *Zama (202). Carthage gave up its Spanish conquests and became a dependent ally of Rome. Roman fears of a resurgence of Carthaginian power caused the third Punic War (149–146), in which Carthage was destroyed and its territory became the Roman province of Africa.

Punjab A region of the NW Indian subcontinent, in India and Pakistan below the Himalayan foothills on the flat alluvial plain of five Indus tributaries. Hot and dry, it produces grain surpluses with irrigation. Pulses, cotton, sugar cane, oilseeds, fruit, and vegetables are also grown. Industries include textiles, bicycles, electrical and metal goods, machinery, and food products. The region is comparatively urbanized. Its population is 60% Sikh in India's Punjab state, and almost entirely Muslim in Pakistan's Punjab province. *History*: on the invasion route into India, the Punjab passed successively under different rulers. It was conquered by Muslims (11th century) but eventually became a Sikh stronghold until Britain established control (19th century). On the partition of India and Pakistan (1947), the Punjab was divided on a religious basis. This led to a massacre of minorities and mass migration. The W section became the Pakistan province of West Punjab (renamed Punjab in 1949), with an area of 79,284 sq mi (205,346 sq km) and its capital at Lahore; its population in 1972 was 37,374,000. The Indian section was reorganized in 1956 and again in 1966 on a linguistic basis when the Punjabi-speaking state of Punjab was created, 19,445 sq mi (50,376 sq km), with its capital at Chandigarh; its population in 1981 was 16,669,755.

Punjabi An *Indo-Aryan language of the Punjab (NW India, SE Pakistan). It is similar to *Hindi and written in the Devanagari script or in the Gumurki script of the Sikh scriptures.

Punt, land of A country with which the ancient Egyptians traded from 2750 BC for gold, ivory, incense, and spices. It was probably situated on the Somali coast of NE Africa.

Punta Arenas 53 10S 70 56W A port in S Chile, on the Strait of Magellan. It serves a large sheep-rearing area. Exports include hides, wool, mutton, lumber, and oil. Population (1975 est): 64,450.

pupa A stage in the life cycle of certain insects, including flies, butterflies (in which it is the chrysalis), ants, bees, and beetles, during which complete *metamorphosis from larva to adult takes place. The adult emerges by cutting or digesting the pupal case after a period of a few days to several months.

pupil. *See* eye; iris.

puppetry The art of manipulating puppets or marionettes in a dramatic performance. Puppets were used in religious ritual and folk drama in many early civilizations. In Japan, the form of puppet theater known as *Joruri* and developed by Chikamatsu Monzaemon (1653–1724) is still actively maintained. Introduced into the rest of Europe from Italy in the late 17th century, puppet theater flourished throughout Europe during the 18th century and enjoyed an artistic revival in the late 19th and early 20th centuries.

Purbeck, Isle of A peninsula in S England, in Dorset between the English Channel and Poole Harbour. Purbeck marble, a limestone used in building, is quarried here.

Purcell, Edward Mills (1912–) US physicist, who shared the 1952 Nobel Prize with Felix *Bloch for their independent measurements of the magnetic moments of nuclei in solids and liquids. He also worked in astronomy, discovering an important emission by interstellar hydrogen in the microwave region.

Purcell, Henry (1659–95) English composer and organist. He became organist of Westminster Abbey in 1679. In 1677 he was appointed composer to the orchestra of the Chapel Royal and, in 1682, organist there. He wrote keyboard pieces, sonatas, anthems, songs, cantatas, and much music for the stage, including incidental music for *King Arthur* (1691) and *The Fairy Queen* (1692) and one opera, *Dido and Aeneas* (1689).

Pure Food and Drug Act (1906) US law that banned interstate transport of adulterated packaged food and drugs. It also required accurate labeling of contents. The law is enforced by the Department of Agriculture. It was amended in 1912, 1913, and 1923 to cover false cure claims regarding medicines, accurate weight markings, and milk requirements.

Pure Land Buddhism A popular E Asian devotional form of Mahayana Buddhism, originating in China in the 4th century AD. Its adherents, following the Sukhavativyuha sutras, believe that by reciting the name of Amitabha, the Buddha of Infinite Light, they will be reborn in the Pure Land in the West (Sukhavati), which he has created.

purgatives. *See* laxatives.

purgatory In Roman Catholic doctrine, the state in which souls are purified after death to make them fit for heaven. Masses or prayers for the dead are believed to shorten a soul's purgatorial sufferings. The doctrine of purgatory was officially adopted by the Church in the late 6th century, but at the Reformation the Protestants rejected the concept, holding that souls either go directly to heaven or hell or sleep until the Last Judgment.

Puri 19 49N 85 54E A port in India, in Orissa on the Bay of Bengal. A major religious center, it holds many festivals and has an exceptional 12th-century temple. Population (1971): 72,712.

Purim A Jewish festival, commemorating the frustration of an attempt to exterminate the Jews of the Persian Empire (473 BC), as narrated in the book of Esther. It is celebrated on the 14th Adar (Feb–March), with light-hearted festivities and charitable gifts. The scroll (*megillah*) of Esther is read in synagogues.

purine An organic nitrogenous base ($C_5H_4N_4$) consisting of a two-ringed molecule of carbon and nitrogen atoms. The derivatives adenine and guanine are constituents of the nucleic acids *DNA and *RNA. *Uric acid and *caffeine are also purines.

purism An art movement launched in 1918 by the manifesto, *Après le Cubisme*, of the painter Amédée Ozenfant (1886–1966) and the architect and painter *Le Corbusier. Their aim was to purify *cubism by stripping it of its decorative features and basing their austere geometrical shapes on machine forms.

Puritanism A movement among Protestants in 16th- and 17th-century England. The term originally denoted members of the Church of England in Elizabeth I's reign who wished to eliminate elements in the Church's liturgy and hierarchy that were reminiscent of Roman Catholicism. In the 17th century Puritan criticism of the Anglican episcopacy was intensified and the Puritans, many of them now forming extremist sects became associated with the parliamentarian party in the Civil War. Many Puritans emigrated to the American colonies, several of which were governed according to Puritan principles.

Purple Heart Oldest US military decoration, established as the Badge of Military Merit by George Washington in 1782 and awarded during the American Revolution. Reinstituted in 1932, it is awarded to those wounded in battle. It is a purple heart of cloth, bordered by bronze.

purpura Localized limited bleeding into the skin, causing a rash of purple spots. This is a common and harmless condition of the elderly (senile purpura). Purpura may also result from reactions to drugs and infections, scurvy, and an allergic disease of childhood called Henoch-Schönlein purpura. A deficiency of blood platelets (important in clotting) also leads to purpura.

purslane An annual herbaceous plant, *Portulaca oleracea*, with prostrate reddish stems bearing fleshy oval leaves and dense terminal clusters of tiny pink flowers. It is widespread as a weed and has been used as a culinary herb. Family: *Portulacaceae*.

Sea purslane (*Halimione portulacoides*) is a shrubby perennial of temperate salt marshes, with grayish oval leaves and knobbly heads of tiny golden flowers. Family: *Chenopodiaceae*. *Honkenya peploides*, also called sea purslane, is a creeping perennial plant of N temperate sandy beaches. It has

pointed fleshy leaves and small five-petaled white flowers on short stalks, surrounded by fleshy sepals. Family: *Caryophyllaceae*.

Purus River (Spanish name: Río Purús) A river in NW South America, rising in SE Peru and flowing generally NE through Brazil to the Amazon River. Length: about 2000 mi (3200 km).

pus Thick yellow fluid that arises in infected areas and contains dead bacteria, dead white blood cells, serum, and damaged tissue. It is formed as a result of the body's defensive action against invading bacteria and other particles. Pus is present in boils and similar skin conditions but can be formed anywhere in the body (*see* abscess). *See also* inflammation.

Pusan 35 05N 129 02E A port in SE South Korea, on the Korea Strait, capital of South Kyongsang province and South Korea's second largest city. It is the site of a state and a private university. Refugees gathered here during the Korean War (1950–53). Its varied industries include shipbuilding. Population (1980): 3,160,000.

Pusey, Edward Bouverie (1800–82) British leader of the *Oxford Movement. A Fellow of Oriel College, Oxford, in 1833 he joined the movement at Oriel to revive the Catholic tradition in the Anglican Church. He became its leader in 1841, when John *Newman was converted to Roman Catholicism.

Pushkin (name from 1708 until 1937: Tsarskoye Selo) 59 43N 30 22E A town in the Soviet Union, in the RSFSR 14 mi (24 km) S of Leningrad, with which it was joined by Russia's first railroad (1837). Founded in 1708 by Peter the Great, it was the site of the imperial summer residence, and Catherine the Great's palace (1748–62) is still to be seen. In 1937 it was renamed for the Russian poet, who studied here. It has varied manufacturing industries and a botanical institute. Population (1970): 79,000.

Pushkin, Aleksandr (1799–1837) Russian poet, novelist, and dramatist. In 1820 he was exiled to the southern provinces for his political verse, which was considered revolutionary by the government. In exile he wrote two long Romantic poems strongly influenced by Byron and began the epic verse novel *Eugene Onegin* (1833), on which Tchaikovsky based his opera (1877–78). In 1824 he was transferred to NW Russia, where he wrote the historical drama *Boris Godunov* (1831), which became the basis of Mussorgsky's opera (1874). After his return to Moscow in 1826 he was still hindered by censorship, but during his last years he wrote the epic poem *The Bronze Horseman* (1837) as well as lyrical poetry and several prose works. He was killed in a duel. Pushkin was the most versatile and influential of Russian writers; he broke with a number of artificial conventions of the 18th and 19th centuries, established new literary genres and themes, and made the Russian language a highly adaptable literary medium.

Pushtu. *See* Pashto.

puss moth A moth, *Cerura vinula*, of Europe, Asia, and N Africa. The adult has a fat white hairy body with black spots. The caterpillar is green with black markings and when alarmed it presents a grotesque appearance with the head and tail appendages raised up. It feeds on sallow, willow, and poplar.

putrefaction The decomposition of organic matter, particularly of proteins by bacteria under anaerobic conditions (i.e. in the absence of oxygen). Putrefaction is associated with a characteristic bad smell, produced by the amines, ammonia, hydrogen sulfide, and other compounds that are formed.

putty A mixture of boiled linseed oil and powdered calcium carbonate (whiting) used as a cement. Of doughlike consistency, it is used for cementing sheets of glass into windows.

Putumayo, Río A river in South America. Rising in the Colombian Andes, it flows generally SE forming most of the border between Colombia and Peru. On entering Brazil it is known as the Rio Içá before joining the Amazon River. Length: 980 mi (1578 km).

Puvis de Chavannes, Pierre (Cécile) (1824–98) French painter, born in Lyons. He was an independent artistic figure but also an important influence on such painters as *Seurat and *Gauguin. He is famous for his murals for public buildings, notably *The Life of S Genevieve* (Panthéon, Paris) and his painting *The Poor Fisherman* (Louvre). Imitating in oil the pale colors and simplified forms of frescoes, he chiefly painted allegorical subjects.

Pu Yi, Henry (or H. P'u-i; 1906–67) The last emperor of China (1908–12) as Xuan-tong (or Hsuan-t'ung). He became emperor at the age of two and abdicated two years later after the republican revolution of 1911. He was allowed to live in the summer palace on a government pension until the Japanese made him ruler, as Kang-de (or K'ang-te), of *Manchukuo (1934–45).

PVC. *See* polyvinyl chloride.

Pycnogonida. *See* sea spider.

pyelitis Infection of the central part of the kidney, where the urine collects before passing to the ureter. Infection may spread through the blood or up to the kidney from the bladder. The patient usually has a fever and loin pain and produces urine containing protein, white blood cells, and sometimes red blood cells. In some cases the infection spreads to the rest of the kidney (**pyelonephritis**). The infection will normally settle with antibiotics, but repeated low-grade infections may lead to kidney failure and *uremia.

Pygmalion In Greek mythology, a legendary king of Cyprus who made an ivory statue (known as Galatea in modern versions of the story) and fell in love with it. When he prayed for a wife who would be as beautiful as the statue, Aphrodite gave the statue life and Pygmalion married her.

Pygmies Peoples of the tropical forest region of Africa, who are much smaller in stature than their Bantu neighbors. The males are less than 4 ft 11 in (150 cm) in height. They are nomadic hunters and gatherers, wandering in small and basically patrilineal exogamous bands of around 30 members. They use either the bow and arrow or, more usually, nets and spears. There are no chiefs, decisions being made by general consensus. They speak various Bantu languages.

pygmy hippopotamus A small *hippopotamus, *Choeropsis liberiensis*, of West African forests. Up to 40 in (100 cm) high at the shoulder and weighing about 441 lb (200 kg), pygmy hippos are less aquatic and more solitary than their larger relatives. They frequent river banks, sleeping during the day and feeding in the forest at night.

pygmy owl A very small *owl belonging to a widely distributed genus (*Glaucidium*; 12 species). About 6 in (16 cm) long, pygmy owls hunt small mammals, birds, and insects, which may be larger than themselves.

Pylos (Greek name: Pílos) 36 55N 21 42E A seaport (also called Navarino) in W Greece, on the Peloponnesian coast. It lies at the S end of Órmos Navarínou (Bay of Navarino), scene of two important battles: the Athenian victory over the Spartans during the Peloponnesian War (425 BC) and the decisive battle of *Navarino (1827) in the War of Greek Independence. The Mycenaean town associated with the legendary King *Nestor lies N of the modern town. Here excavations revealed a well-preserved palace and archive of *Linear B tablets.

Pynchon, Thomas (1937–   ) US novelist. He was acclaimed as one of the most original and ambitious writers to emerge in the 1960s. A common theme of his three novels, *V* (1963), *The Crying of Lot 49* (1967), and *Gravity's Rainbow* (1973), is the protagonists' wandering quest through a bizarre and unpredictable landscape.

pyorrhea. *See* periodontal disease.

Pyracantha A genus of thorny evergreen shrubs (about 10 species), known as firethorns, native to SE Eurasia and widely cultivated as garden shrubs in hedges or against walls. A commonly grown species is *P. coccinea*. It has finely toothed leaves and flat-topped clusters of white or pinkish-yellow flowers. The round scarlet berries may last all winter. Family: *Rosaceae*.

pyralid moth A moth of the widespread family *Pyralidae*. The adults have generally narrow forewings and broader hindwings. Both pairs are fringed. The larvae feed on a variety of substances, including dried stored products. They can be serious economic pests, especially the *corn borer, *wax moth, and meal moth (*Pyralis farinalis*). Many larvae spin silken tunnels in which they live.

pyramids Royal funerary monuments in ancient Egypt. The greatest are the pyramids of *Khufu, *Khafre, and Menkaura (Greek name: Mycerinus) at Giza (built c. 2600–2500 BC), the only survivors of the *Seven Wonders of the World. Their tombs were all robbed in antiquity but they nevertheless remain extraordinary feats of engineering. For over four millenniums the pyramid of Khufu, now 453 ft (138 m) high was the highest building in the world. Pyramids were also built in ancient Mexico.

Pyramids, Battle of the (July 21, 1798) The battle in which Napoleon with some 25,000 troops defeated about 40,000 Egyptians near Imbaba on the W bank of the Nile. The battle was followed by Napoleon's defeat of the Ottoman Turks at *Aboukir Bay.

Pyramus and Thisbe Legendary lovers in a Babylonian story retold by *Ovid. The couple were forbidden to marry by their parents but exchanged vows through a chink in the wall between their houses. They arranged a secret meeting. Thisbe arrived first at the meeting place, which was near a mulberry tree; but she was frightened by a lion and fled, dropping her veil. Pyramus, finding her veil and thinking her dead, stabbed himself, and when Thisbe returned she killed herself also. The mulberry tree has borne blood-red fruit ever since. The rustics' farce in Shakespeare's *A Midsummer Night's Dream* is based on this story.

Pyrenean mountain dog (*or* Great Pyrenees) A breed of large dog, possibly of Asian origin, used in Europe for over 3000 years to guard shepherds and their flocks. They are massively built with drooping ears and an ambling gait. The long thick slightly wavy coat is white, with or without gray or brown patches. Height: 28 in (71 cm) (dogs); 26 in (66 cm) (bitches).

Pyrenees (French name: Pyrénées; Spanish name: Pirineos) A mountain range in SW Europe. It extends between the Bay of Biscay in the W and the Mediterranean Sea in the E, forming a barrier between France and Spain. The entire republic of Andorra lies within the range, which rises to 11,168 ft (3404 m) at Pico de Aneto, close to the source of the Garonne River in the center.

Pyrenees, Treaty of the (1659) The treaty that ended the war of 1648–59 between France and Spain and marked the rise of French predominance in Europe. Spain lost Artois and the Catalan counties of Rousillon and Cerdana. Maria-Theresa, the daughter of Philip IV of Spain, was married to Louis XIV of France.

pyrethrum A perennial plant, *Chrysanthemum coccineum* (or *Pyrethrum roseum*), with finely divided leaves and showy red, pink, lilac, or white flowers. It is native to Persia and the Caucasus and widely cultivated for ornament in temperate regions. The name is also given to an insecticide prepared from the dried flower heads of this and related species. Family: *Compositae*.

Pyrex The trade name for a heat-resistant glass containing borosilicate. It is also resistant to many chemicals and is an electrical insulator. Pyrex is used in laboratory glassware, ovenware, and large telescopes.

pyridine (C_6H_5N) A hygroscopic colorless liquid, with a strong odor, which boils at 239°F (115°C). It is a basic aromatic compound with a six-membered heterocyclic molecule, made by passing tetrahydrofurfuryl alcohol and ammonia over a catalyst at 933°F (500°C). It is used as an industrial solvent and in the manufacture of various drugs and pesticides.

pyridoxine. *See* vitamin B complex.

pyrimidine An organic base ($C_4H_4N_2$) consisting of a six-membered ring of carbon and nitrogen atoms. Its derivatives cytosine, thymine, and uracil are constituents of the nucleic acids *RNA and *DNA.

pyrite (*or* iron pyrites) A pale brassy yellow mineral, FeS_2, the most common sulfide mineral. It occurs as an accessory mineral in igneous rocks, in hydrothermal veins, in contact metamorphic rocks, and in sediments laid down in anaerobic conditions. It is usually mined for its sulfur, used for the manufacture of sulfuric acid, or for the gold and copper found in association with it. Because of its color it has been called fool's gold. The term is sometimes used for other sulfides, for example copper pyrites, but if used alone it refers to iron pyrites.

pyroclastic rock Rock formed from fragments thrown out by volcanic explosions, in either the solid or molten state. Fragments less than 0.08 in (2 mm) in diameter are known as ash or, when consolidated, tuff. Lapilli are larger fragments and bombs are even larger, often spindle-shaped. Blocks are large angular fragments ejected in the solid state.

pyroelectricity The development of opposite electric charges on opposite faces of asymmetric crystals when they are heated. The charges occur on those faces that are responsible for the crystal's asymmetry. Quartz and tourmaline have pyroelectric properties. *See also* piezoelectric effect.

pyrogallol (*or* pyrogallic acid; $C_6H_3(OH)_3$) A white soluble crystalline solid. It is a powerful reducing agent, used in developing photographs and to absorb oxygen in gas analysis.

pyrolysis A chemical reaction produced by high temperatures. Common examples include the charring of wood and firing of pottery. Pyrolysis has many industrial applications, a recent one being the recovery of hydrocarbon fuels from waste organic materials.

pyrometer An instrument used for measuring high temperatures. The two most important types are the optical pyrometer and the radiation pyrometer. In the optical pyrometer a filament, heated to a known temperature, is viewed with the hot body in the background. The temperature of the filament is adjusted until it appears to vanish, at which point its temperature is the same as the temperature to be measured. In the radiation pyrometer, radiant heat from the hot body is focused into a *thermopile, which develops a potential difference proportional to the temperature.

P'yŏngyang 39 00N 125 47E The capital of the Democratic People's Republic of (North) Korea, in the NW on the Taedong River. Reputedly the oldest city in Korea, it suffered severely from successive Japanese and

Chinese attacks over the centuries and was almost destroyed by US bombing in the Korean War (1950–53). It is a major industrial as well as administrative and commercial center. Its three universities include the Kim Il Sung University, founded in 1946. Population (1976 est): 1,500,000.

pyrope. *See* garnet.

pyroxenes A group of ferromagnesian rock-forming silicate minerals. They usually occur in basic and ultrabasic igneous rocks but also in some metamorphosed rocks. Those of orthorhombic crystal structure are orthopyroxenes and those of monoclinic structure are clinopyroxenes. Orthopyroxenes vary in composition between the end-members enstatite ($MgSiO_3$) and orthoferrosilite ($FeSiO_3$). Clinopyroxenes, the larger group, include diopside, hedenbergite, augite, pigeonite, aegirine, jadeite, and spodumene (a source of lithium).

Pyrrhon (c. 360–c. 270 BC) Greek philosopher, born at Elis, who was the founder of *skepticism. Pyrrhon believed that objective knowledge was impossible, the limitations of knowledge being explored by later skeptics. He sought a way of achieving mental tranquility by suspension of judgment.

Pyrrhus (319–272 BC) King of Epirus (307–303, 297–272). Having secured his throne (297), Pyrrhus pursued an adventurous policy of expansion but his empire was short-lived: in support of Tarentum against Rome he won victories that cost much in loss of life ("Pyrrhic" victories), especially at Asculum (279), and he was forced to withdraw.

pyruvic acid An organic acid ($CH_3COCOOH$). Its anion, pyruvate (CH_3–CO–COO$^-$), is an important intermediate compound in the carbohydrate metabolism of living organisms.

Pythagoras (6th century BC) Greek philosopher and religious leader. Born at *Samos, he migrated in about 530 BC to Crotone (S Italy), where he founded a religious society that governed Crotone for many years until its suppression (460–440 BC). Its members followed an ascetic regime of dietary taboos, self-examination, and study aimed at purifying the soul and releasing it from "entombment" in successive bodies. Pythagoras probably discovered the geometrical theorem named for him and certainly discovered the arithmetical ratios governing musical intervals, which led him to interpret the universe in terms of mathematics alone. Pythagoreans were pioneers in several branches of science. *See also* Alcmaeon; Archytas; Pythagoreanism.

Pythagoreanism The philosophy of the followers of *Pythagoras, who developed the two main strands in their master's thought: mysticism and mathematics. The former was fostered by an ascetic religious order founded by Pythagoras at Crotone, Italy, the rules of which included silence and vegetarianism. Other disciples extended Pythagoras' interpretation of the physical world through numbers and made substantial advances in geometry. In astronomy they evolved a model of the universe that anticipated the heliocentric system of *Copernicus. An eclectic form of Pythagoreanism, known as Neopythagoreanism, developed in Alexandria during the 1st century BC.

Pytheas (4th century BC) Greek navigator. From Marseilles he made a voyage along the coasts of Spain, France, and E Britain and seems to have reached as far N as Iceland. His narrative is lost but was later used by the Greek geographer *Strabo.

Pythian Games The ancient Greek festival at Delphi in honor of Apollo. Second only to the Olympic Games in importance, the festival originally consisted of musical competitions but from 582 BC also included athletic and equestrian events, taking place every four years.

python A large *constrictor snake belonging to the Old World subfamily *Pythoninae* (20–25 species), occurring in tropical and temperate regions. Pythons usually live near water and tend to be sluggish, catching prey—which may include goats, pigs, and deer—by ambush. The reticulated python (*Python reticulatus*) is the largest of all constrictors, reaching 33 ft (10 m) in length. Many pythons are killed for their meat and skin. Family: *Boidae.* □reptile.

Q

Qaboos ibn Sa'id (1940–) Sultan of Oman (1970–). He became sultan after deposing, with British support, his reactionary father Sa'id ibn Taymur. With Omani oil revenues Qaboos has initiated modernization programs. His rule has been threatened by Chinese-backed guerrillas.

Qaddafi, Moammar al-. *See* Gaddafi, Moammar al-.

Qajars. *See* Agha Mohammad Khan.

Qatar, State of A country in the Middle East, in *Arabia occupying a peninsula on the W coast of the Persian Gulf. It is the smallest Arabian state. The native population is mainly Arab and Wahhabi Sunnite Muslim, but over 80% of workers are immigrants from other countries, including Iran and Pakistan. *Economy:* oil extraction accounts for over 90% of the national income and has led to the development of other industries, such as fertilizer production and water desalination. During the 1980s Qatar experienced sharp declines in oil revenues. Qatar is a member of OPEC. There is also some fishing. *History:* Qatar relied on Britain for most of the 19th and 20th centuries, becoming a protectorate in 1916; it became independent when Britain withdrew in 1971. Head of state: Emir Sheik Khalifa bin Hamad Al-Thani. Official language: Arabic. Official currency: Qatar riyal of 100 dirhams. Area: 4246 sq mi (11,000 sq km). Population (1983 est): 267,000. Capital: Doha.

Qattara Depression An area in NE Egypt descending to 436 ft (133 m) below sea level. Its steep N side proved a defense for the S flank of the British army in the battle of El Alamein. Area: about 7000 sq mi (18,000 sq km).

Qazvin. *See* Kazvin.

Q fever An infection with the microorganism *Coxiella burnetti*, first described in Queensland, Australia (hence *Q* fever) in 1937. The disease affects cattle and sheep but can be transmitted to man through contaminated milk. The incubation period is two–four weeks and the disease usually takes the form of a viral *pneumonia. Treatment is with tetracycline antibiotics.

Qian Long (*or* Ch'ien-lung; 1711–99) The title of Hong-li (*or* Hung-li), Chinese emperor (1736–96) of the Qing dynasty. During his reign the Chinese empire saw its greatest period of expansion through continuing wars of conquest, which, however, undermined China's economy. His government was further weakened by the corruption of his minister He-shen (*or* Ho-shen). Qian Long was a distinguished patron of the arts. He abdicated in favor of his son.

Qin (*or* Ch'in; 221–206 BC) The dynasty under which China became a unified empire. The first Qin emperor, Shi Huangdi (*or* Shih Huang Ti; c. 259–210 BC), consolidated his vast conquest by unifying weights, measures, and coinage and by creating one system of writing for the whole empire. He ordered the burning of all books in China, except for practical handbooks and the history of his own dynasty. Believing in the absolute power of the ruler, his government was so harsh that the dynasty outlasted him by only four years. It was during the Qin reign that much of the *Great Wall of China was built. Excavations in the vicinity of his tomb in the late 1970s revealed several thousand life-size terracotta men and horses.

Qing (*or* Ch'ing; 1644–1911) A Manchu dynasty, founded by *Nurhachi, that ruled China from the fall of the Ming dynasty until the revolution of 1911. The Manchus, living on the borders of Chinese civilization, gradually conquered Chinese territory as the Ming government weakened. The Qing (pure) dynasty was declared in 1636 but Peking was not captured until 1644. At its height in the 18th century under *Qian Long, the Qing ruled a vast empire that included Outer Mongolia, Tibet, and Turkistan. Trade and commerce flourished, as did cultural life and learning. In over two and a half centuries, however, there was little change in the social order with dangerous results. Bureaucratic conservatism resisted modernization, corruption became rife, and China suffered a series of defeats by foreign powers (e.g. *Opium Wars) as well as internal rebellions (e.g. the *Taiping Rebellion) that culminated in the overthrow of the Qing in 1911.

Qingdao (Ch'ing-tao *or* Tsingtao) 36 04N 120 22E A port in E China, in Shandong province on the Yellow Sea. From 1898 to 1922 it was under German and then Japanese control. It is a center of heavy industry. Population (1957 est): 1,121,000.

Qinghai (Ch'ing-hai *or* Tsinghai) A mountainous province in NW China. Tibetan and Mongol nomadic herdsmen keep yaks, sheep, and cattle,

and it is famed for its horses. The monastery near Xining is an important center of Tibetan Buddhism. Salt, oil, coal, and iron are produced. Area: 278,400 sq mi (721,000 sq km). Population (1980 est): 3,720,000. Capital: Xining.

Qinghai, Lake (*or* Koko Nor) A shallow salt lake of N central China, in the mountains of Qinghai province, the largest lake in China. Area: about 1600 sq mi (4100 sq km).

Qom 34 39N 50 57E A city in central Iran, S of Tehran. It is the burial place of many Islamic saints and a pilgrimage center of Shiite Muslims. Population (1973 est): 170,000.

quadratic equation An algebraic *equation in which the greatest power of the *variable is two. It is usually written in the form $ax^2 + bx + c = 0$, in which the two *roots, or possible solutions, are given by $x = [-b \pm \sqrt{(b^2 - 4ac)}]/2a$. Both roots are real *numbers when the quantity under the square-root sign is greater than or equal to zero. They are equal when that quantity is zero. If it is less than zero the roots are complex numbers. The sum of the roots is $-b/a$ and their product is c/a.

quadrature The position of a celestial body in the solar system when its angular distance from the sun, as measured from earth (i.e. the angle body–earth–sun), is 90°.

quadriplegia. *See* paralysis.

Quadruple Alliances 1. (1718) The alliance formed by Britain, France, the Holy Roman Emperor, and the Netherlands to maintain the Treaties of *Utrecht (1713–14), which had been repudiated by Spain. 2. (1814) The alliance formed by Britain, Austria, Prussia, and Russia against Napoleon. It was confirmed at the Congress of *Vienna after Napoleon's fall. 3. (1834) The alliance between Britain, France, Spain, and Portugal that sought to maintain constitutional monarchy in Spain and Portugal.

quaestors Ancient Roman financial officers. Originally two were elected annually; more were appointed as Rome expanded. Two stayed in Rome in charge of the state treasury and records; others supervised Rome's corn supply and the financial administration of the provinces and military campaigns.

quagga An extinct wild horse, *Equus quagga*, that lived on the plains of South Africa. Up to 6 ft (180 cm) high at the shoulder, quaggas had a neck and head striped like a zebra with sandy-colored hindquarters and white legs and tail. The last quagga died in Amsterdam Zoo in 1883.

Quai d'Orsay A street in Paris, on the Left Bank of the Seine River, on which the French Ministry of Foreign Affairs is situated.

quail A round-bodied short-tailed gamebird of open grassland and farmland. Old World quail (subfamily *Perdicinae*; 95 species) are 5–8 in (13–20 cm) long and characterized by a smooth-edged bill and leg spurs; they are stocky and usually sandy in color. New World quail (subfamily *Odontophorinae*; 36 species) are up to 12 in (30 cm) long and have a strong serrated bill, no leg spurs, and are brightly colored and patterned, often with crests; males and females differ markedly. Quail feed on seeds, berries, and leaves. Family: *Phasianidae* (pheasants, partridges, and quail).

Quakers The Christian sect, formally known as the Society of Friends, founded in England by George *Fox in the late 1640s. They suffered violent persecution for many years and in 1682 William *Penn led a colony of Friends to *Pennsylvania. In the US they were leaders in the fight against *slavery, emancipating their own slaves. The early Quakers adopted an unostentatious dress and way of life. They were (and remain) pacifists, refused to take oaths, and rejected the use of titles. In speech they used the old singular form "thou" in preference to the plural form "you" for one person, as more suited to the truth. They rejected the ministry and sacraments of the established church. They worship in meetings, which start with a period of silence until one member is moved by the "inner light," which they believe to be their guide, to address the congregation or to pray.

quaking grass An annual or perennial *grass of the genus *Briza* (about 20 species), mostly native to South America. Their long slender flower stalks bear spikelets of open flower clusters, which quiver in the wind. *B. media* is native to temperate Eurasia and grows 8–20 in (20–50 cm) high. It is sometimes planted for ornament.

quandong A small shrubby Australian tree, *Fusanus acuminatus*, with simple leaves and heads of small inconspicuous flowers. The fruit is fleshy and edible, with a hard stony pitted edible seed. Family: *Santalaceae*.

Quant, Mary (1934–) British fashion designer, one of the first to become known for ready-to-wear rather than *haute couture* clothes. Her miniskirts, created especially for the young, made London a leading fashion center in the 1960s.

quantity theory of money A theory that seeks to explain how the money supply (*see* money) affects the economy. Originally put forward in the 17th century, it has been restated in its modern form by the US economist Milton *Friedman. It states that if there is a change in the money supply, either the price level will change or the supply of goods in the economy will alter. The monetarists (*see* monetarism) assert, on the basis of the quantity theory, that if there is full employment it is the price level that will be affected by altering the money supply.

Quantrill, William Clarke (1837–65) US Confederate guerrilla fighter. After leading a guerrilla band in Kansas and Missouri, he was made a captain in the Confederate Army. He continued his raids, the best-known of which was the sacking of Lawrence, Kan (1863), in which nearly 200 inhabitants were killed and the town was burned down. He was captured by Union forces and died in prison.

quantum number An integral or half-integral number (0, ½, 1, 1½, 2, . . .) that gives the possible values of a property of a system according to the *quantum theory. For example, in Bohr's atomic theory the angular momentum of an electron moving in orbit round an atomic nucleus can only have the values $nh/2\pi$, where n is a quantum number specifying these values and h is Planck's constant. Bohr's theory has now been replaced by the more versatile *wave mechanics, but the concept of quantum numbers is useful in some contexts. It is also used to quantify the properties of elementary particles (*see* particle physics). For example spin is characterized by the quantum numbers $+\frac{1}{2}$ or $-\frac{1}{2}$ for an electron, depending on whether it is parallel or antiparallel to a specified direction. *Parity, *electric charge, *strangeness, *charm, *isotopic spin, etc., are other properties of elementary particles expressed by quantum numbers.

quantum theory The theory first developed by Max *Planck in 1900 to explain the distribution of wavelengths of electromagnetic radiation emitted by a *black body. The experimental observations could only be explained when Planck assumed that the radiation was emitted and absorbed in discrete amounts, which he called quanta. The energy of each quantum has the value hf, where h is a universal constant (now known as the Planck constant) and f is the frequency of the radiation. Planck's quantum theory was used by *Einstein to explain the *photoelectric effect and in 1913 by Niels *Bohr to explain the spectrum of hydrogen. Quantum theory has since become an essential part of modern physics. **Quantum mechanics** is the application of quantum theory to the mechanics of atomic systems; **quantum electrodynamics** is the theory of *electromagnetic interactions between elementary particles; **quantum statistics** is the application of statistical methods to many-particle quantum systems. *See also* wave mechanics.

quarantine The period during which a person or animal suspected of carrying an infectious disease is kept in isolation. The term was originally applied to the 40-day period (French: *quarantaine*) during which ships suspected of carrying infected people were prevented from communicating with the shore. The quarantine period is now slightly longer than the incubation period of the disease; if no symptoms appear during quarantine the individual is considered free of the infection.

quarks. *See* particle physics.

quarrying. *See* mining and quarrying.

Quarter horse A breed of horse developed in colonial America from both local and English stock for racing over short distances, popularly a quarter of a mile. It has a deep compact muscular body and, with its speed and agility, is widely used for ranch work. Quarter horses may be any color. Height: 1.45–1.57 m (14¼–15½ hands).

quartz The commonest of all minerals, consisting of crystalline *silica. It is stable over a wide range of conditions and consequently occurs in many rocks, particularly acid igneous rocks (such as granite), many metamorphic rocks (such as gneisses), and in sands and gravels, which form sandstones on consolidation. It is commonly milky white in color. Pure quartz is colorless and is known as rock crystal; it is used in glassmaking, in jewelry, and (because of its piezoelectric properties) in making electrical oscillators. Some colored varieties, such as amethyst (violet), rose quartz (pink), and citrine (yellow), are used as gemstones. In the form of sand it is used as an abrasive and in cement.

quartzite A resistant pale-colored rock consisting almost wholly of quartz. It is formed by the metamorphism of a pure sandstone, the original quartz grains being recrystallized and interlocking.

quasar (*quasi*-stel*lar* object; *or* QSO) A class of celestial objects discovered in 1964–65, lying far beyond our Galaxy. They appear as starlike points of light but are each emitting more energy than a hundred giant galaxies. Quasar *redshifts are extremely large and indicate that quasars are the most distant and hence the youngest extragalactic objects known. They must therefore be extremely luminous to be visible at such distances. The energy-producing region is compact, and it is thought that the prodigious energy could result from matter spiraling into a supermassive *black hole (maybe 10^9 solar masses) lying at the center of a galaxy.

Quasimodo, Salvatore (1901–68) Italian poet. His early work, such as *And Suddenly It's Night* (1942), was evocative and private, but after World War II his poetry, as in *Il falso e vero verde* (1956), expressed his active concern for social issues. He published several volumes of translations and criticism. He won the Nobel Prize in 1959.

Quassia A genus of tropical Asian trees and shrubs (40 species). Bitterwood (*Q. amara*) is an attractive shrub or small tree with trifoliate leaves and clusters of tubular red flowers. The heartwood is a source of quassiin, a bitter substance used in medicine. Family: *Simaroubaceae*.

Quaternary period The most recent period of geological time, from the end of the *Tertiary (about 1.8 million years ago) to the present day. It includes the *Pleistocene (Ice Age) and *Holocene epochs. It is the period in which man became the dominant terrestrial species. Some authorities consider the Quaternary to be a division of the Tertiary.

Quathlamba. *See* Drakensberg Mountains.

Quebec The largest province of Canada, stretching from the *St Lawrence River N to Hudson Bay and Strait. The rocky forested Canadian Shield covers the N nine-tenths. Most of the population lives in the St Lawrence valley, which has dominated the history and economy of the province. The SE strip of Quebec enters the fertile Appalachian Highlands. The province's highly industrialized economy is based on its abundant natural resources, especially forests, minerals, and water power. Quebec is a major source of the world's paper. Asbestos, the rich iron-ore deposits at Ungava, copper, zinc, gold, and other minerals are mined. Cheap hydroelectricity aids smelting, refining, food processing, and the manufacture of metal and electrical products, textiles, machinery, and chemicals. Fishing, farming, and tourism are also economically important. *History*: claimed by France (1534), Quebec or New France was a French colony (1608–1763) until ceded to Britain. French-Canadian culture was preserved and nationalism increased steadily after the formation of Canada (1867). The Quiet Revolution (1960s) awoke an exciting cultural life and led to the victory of the secessionist Parti Québecois in the 1977 provincial election. A referendum on secession, presented by the Parti Québecois, was defeated in 1980. Area: 523,858 sq mi (1,356,791 sq km). Population (1981): 6,438,403; over 80% are French speaking. Capital: Quebec. *See also* Montreal.

Quebec 46 50N 71 15W A city and port in E Canada, the capital of Quebec. First settled in 1608, it is it is strategically located above a sudden narrowing of the St Lawrence River. Quebec was the key to New France until captured by Britain (1759). It remains a cultural center of French-speaking Canada, housing Laval University. Most of the workforce is employed by government and service industries but textiles, leather goods, printing, publishing, and pulp and paper are also important. Quebec is a major tourist attraction, with its citadel and the steep narrow streets and stone houses of the lower town. The Plains of *Abraham lie to the SW of the city. Population (1981): 166,474.

Quebec Act (1774). *See* Intolerable Acts.

quebracho A tropical or subtropical tree of the genus *Schinopsis*, especially *S. lorentzii* and *S. balansae*. Their reddish-brown wood is an important commercial source of tannin, while *S. quebracho-colorado* is an important timber tree. Family: *Anacardiaceae*.

Quechua The language of the *Incas and of the present-day American Indian peoples of the central Andean highlands. These peoples, having now mainly lost their lands to Spanish settlers, form an impoverished peasantry. Crops are potatoes, corn, and quinoa. Llamas and alpacas are herded. The people are nominally Roman Catholic but many pagan beliefs and rituals survive.

Queen Anne style An English architectural and decorative style with some baroque elements, dating from about 1700 to 1715. It was characterized by increasing restraint in the decorative elements. Beautiful walnut veneered furniture was made; it was curvilinear in outline, exhibiting well-chosen figured woods, and enhanced by the restrained use of herringbone inlays. Gilt and lacquer continued in vogue but in a less flamboyant manner. Chairs became lighter, more comfortable, and invariably had cabriole legs. Plateglass wall mirrors in gilt frames decorated paneled rooms.

Queen Anne's War   (1702–13) US colonial war between England and France; it is the counterpart of Europe's War of the *Spanish Succession. The British captured Spanish-held St Augustine, Florida (1702); Indians, allied with the French, attacked New England from Canada, destroying Deerfield, Mass (1704); and the British took French-held Port Royal in Nova Scotia. By 1712 an armistice was declared, and terms were spelled out in the Treaty of *Utrecht (1713). England gained Nova Scotia, Newfoundland, and Hudson Bay.

Queen Charlotte Islands   An archipelago of W Canada, in British Columbia 100 mi (160 km) off the Pacific coast. Mountainous with lush vegetation (especially forests), the islands are mostly inhabited by Haida Indians engaged in fishing and forestry. Area: 3705 sq mi (9596 sq km). Population (1971 est): 3000.

Queen Maud Land.   *See* Norwegian Antarctic Territory.

Queens   40 45N 73 50W One of the five boroughs of New York city, on Long Island. It is both residential and industrial and is the site of La Guardia and John F. Kennedy airports. Area: 118 sq mi (307 sq km). Population (1976 est): 1,962,700.

Queensland   The second largest state of Australia, situated in the NE. The *Great Dividing Range separates the hilly coastlands from the vast inland plain and the *Great Barrier Reef runs parallel to the Pacific coast. The area is rich in natural resources, with coal the most important mineral. Other important minerals extracted include copper, bauxite, lead, silver, zinc, oil, and natural gas. Manufactures include metals, machinery, chemicals, motor vehicles, textiles, and food. Agricultural activities are also important; large quantities of sugar cane are produced in the E, while elsewhere bananas, pineapples, cotton, and tobacco are grown. Beef and wool are major industries. Another growing industry is tourism. Area: 667,000 sq mi (1,728,000 sq km). Population (1980 est): 2,247,800. Capital: Brisbane.

Queenstown.   *See* Cóbh.

quelea   A small brown African weaverbird, *Quelea quelea*, about 6 in (13 cm) long, also called the red-billed dioch and labeled the most destructive bird in the world. Queleas live in vast colonies: they destroy grain crops, frequently causing famine, and also damage the trees in which they roost by their combined weight. Attempts to control them by poisoning, introducing disease, and by dynamiting their colonies have had little success.

Quemoy.   *See* Jinmen.

Queneau, Raymond   (1903–79) French novelist and poet. He was involved in the surrealist movement in the 1920s and subsequently wrote a series of parodies and other literary exercises the surface humor of which is founded on profound erudition. Notable among these is *Exercices du style* (1947), in which the same episode is rendered in many different styles. His novels include *Le Chien-dent* (1933), *Rude hiver* (1939), *Pierrot mon ami* (1942), and *Zazie dans le métro* (1959).

Quercia, Jacopo della.   *See* Jacopo della Quercia.

Querétaro   30 38N 100 23W A city in central Mexico. The movement for Mexican independence was begun here (1810). There are many Spanish colonial buildings, notably the cathedral and federal palace. Industries include cotton textiles and potteries. Population (1978 est): 176,200.

Quesnay, François   (1694–1774) French economist. Originally the physician of Louis XV, Quesnay devoted himself to the study of economics after 1756. He was founder and leader of the *Physiocrats, a school of economic theorists. He contributed articles to Diderot's *Encyclopédie* and published such books as *Tableau économique* (1758).

Quesnel, Pasquier   (1634–1719) French Jansenist theologian (*see* Jansenism). He was a priest of the French Oratory (*see* Oratorians) until expelled from the society in 1684 for his views. He settled in Brussels but was imprisoned there in 1703 and finally escaped to Holland. His *Nouveau Testament en français avec des réflexions morales* (1692) was condemned by the pope in 1713.

Quetta   30 15N 67 00E A city in W central Pakistan, at an altitude of 5500 ft (1650 m). The chief town of Baluchistan, it was badly damaged by an earthquake in 1935. Quetta is a trading center and summer resort. The University of Baluchistan was established here in 1970. Population (1972): 156,000.

quetzal   A Central American bird, *Pharomachus mocinno*, that lives in cloud forests and feeds on fruit, insects, tree frogs, and lizards. The male

QUETZAL   *These magnificent birds construct nest holes in tree trunks, both parents taking part in nest building, egg incubation, and feeding the young.*

reaches 4.3 ft (1.3 m) in length, including its curved ornamental tail feathers; its plumage is iridescent green, red, and white and the long outer wing feathers curl over the flight feathers. Family: *Trogonidae* (trogons).

Quetzalcoatl   A Mexican wind and fertility god, usually portrayed as a feathered snake. During the Aztec period (14th–16th centuries) he was identified with the planet Venus, symbol of death and resurrection. He was also a creator god, having made humans by sprinkling blood on bones he brought from the underworld.

Quezon City   14 39N 121 01E A city in the N Philippines, in S Luzon near to Manila. It was the nation's former capital (1948–76). The University of the Philippines was established here in 1908. Mainly residential, its chief industry is textiles. Population (1980): 1,165,990.

Quiberon   47 29N 3 07W A peninsula in NW France, on the S coast of Brittany. In 1759, during the Seven Years' War, a naval battle in which the French were defeated by the English was fought off its coast, in Quiberon Bay.

quicksand   A mass of soft unconsolidated sand that, when saturated with water, becomes semiliquid and unable to support any appreciable weight. Quicksands occur where conditions permit large amounts of water to remain in the sand.

Quietism   A form of mystical passivity that discounts all human effort of will or activity and sees perfection in total dependence upon God. Quietism is associated with certain 17th-century theologians, notably the Spanish priest Miguel de *Molinos. It was condemned by the pope (1687) on account of its practical and philosophical implications.

Quiller-Couch, Sir Arthur Thomas   (1863–1944) British critic and novelist who published under the pseudonym "Q." He wrote several adventure novels, many of them set in his native Cornwall, but is best known as compiler of the influential *Oxford Book of English Verse* (1900).

quillwort   A small perennial *pteridophyte plant of the genus *Isoetes* (about 60 species), which grows in water or on land, mainly in swampy cooler regions of N North America and Eurasia. Tufts of stiff spiky quill-like leaves, about 2–7 in (5–18 cm) long, grow from a short stout rhizome that bears numerous roots. The spore capsules are embedded in the expanded bases of the leaves. The common Eurasian quillwort (*I. lacustris*) is aquatic. Class: *Lycopsida* (clubmosses, etc.).

Quimper   48 00N 4 06W A city in NW France, the capital of the Finistère department. A tourist center, it has a gothic cathedral and is famous for its Breton pottery. Industries include textiles and furniture. Population (1975): 60,510.

quince A small tree or shrub, *Cydonia vulgaris*, probably native to W Asia but cultivated in temperate regions for its fruit. 15–20 ft (4.5–6 m) high, it has oval leaves (which are woolly beneath) and white or pink flowers, 2 in (5 cm) across. The pear-shaped fruit is 3–4 in (7.5–10 cm) long with a golden-yellow skin and many pips. When cooked, its flesh turns pink, giving a distinctive color and flavor to preserves and jellies. Family: *Rosaceae*.

Quincy, Josiah (1772–1864) US politician, reformer, and educator. A Federalist from Massachusetts, he served in the US House of Representatives (1805–13), where he was strongly opposed to the Embargo Act (1807), acceptance of Louisiana as a state, and the War of 1812. While mayor of Boston (1823–28), he instituted many reforms in government and housing. His term as president of Harvard University (1829–45) brought about growth, especially in building, faculty, and the curriculum.

Quincy 42 15N 71 00W A city in Massachusetts, on Boston Harbor. It is the birthplace of two US presidents, John Adams and his son John Quincy Adams. Industries include shipbuilding and the manufacture of machinery. Population (1980): 84,743.

Quine, Willard van Orman (1908–) US philosopher. He became professor of philosophy at Harvard in 1955. His philosophy was largely concerned with language and logic. He argued that linguistic adjustments could make any statement valid. His works include *Word and Object* (1960), *Set Theory and Its Logic* (1963), *Philosophy of Logic* (1970), and *The Roots of Reference* (1973).

Qui Nhon 13 47N 109 11E A port in S Vietnam, on the South China Sea. The site of ancient ruins, it was a naval base during the Vietnam War. Its main industry is fishing. Population (1973 est): 213,757.

quinine The first drug used to treat malaria. Quinine, which is obtained from the bark of *Cinchona trees, has now been largely replaced by other drugs (e.g. *chloroquine), which have fewer side effects and are less toxic. Quinine-like compounds (e.g. quinidine) are used to treat abnormal heart rhythms. Quinine may produce allergic reactions in susceptible patients.

quinone ($O:C_6H_4:O$) An *aromatic compound with two hydrogen atoms in the benzene ring replaced by two oxygen atoms. Quinones are used in photography and dye manufacture. They are also found in plants.

quinsy An abscess in the tissue surrounding a tonsil. This arises from infection of the tonsils and may be a complication of tonsillitis. The patient has a sore throat and difficulty in swallowing. Quinsy is sometimes treated by surgical draining of the abscess.

Quintero brothers. *See* Alvárez Quintero brothers.

Quintilian (Marcus Fabius Quintilianus; c. 35–c. 100 AD) Roman rhetorician. He was born in Spain and educated in Rome, where he worked as an advocate and teacher of rhetoric. The emperor Domitian appointed him tutor to his heirs. His *Institutio oratoria*, a practical treatise on rhetoric, includes a comparative survey of Greek and Latin literature and many original observations on the education of children.

Quisling, Vidkun (Abraham Lauritz Jonsson) (1887–1945) Norwegian army officer and Nazi collaborator, whose name is a synonym for "traitor." After serving with the army in Russia, Quisling formed (1933) the fascist National Union Party in Norway. He encouraged the Nazi occupation of Norway (1940), and as "minister president" in the occupation government, sent a thousand Jews to concentration camps. Arrested in 1945, he was found guilty of war crimes and executed.

Quito 0 20S 78 45W The capital of Ecuador, on the slopes of the volcano Pichincha at an altitude of 9350 ft (2850 m). Originally settled by Quito Indians, it became the capital of the Inca kingdom of Quito until 1534, when it was captured by the Spanish. It contains many Spanish-colonial churches with fine wooden sculptures and paintings; its two universities were founded in 1769 and 1946. Population (1974): 599,828.

Qumran, Khirbat The site on the NW shore of the Dead Sea in Jordan, where a Jewish sect called the *Essenes lived from about 125 BC to 68 AD. The community produced the written documents known as the *Dead Sea Scrolls, which were concealed in nearby caves. Excavations from 1951 revealed a complex of buildings.

quotas, import Limits set by a government to the quantity of specified goods that can be imported from abroad (or sometimes from a specified country) in a given period. Quotas are usually operated by a licensing system, importers being granted licenses authorizing them to import a certain quantity of a product and to purchase the requisite amount of foreign exchange. Quotas are used to remedy a weak *balance of payments or to protect domestic manufacturers but they must be used with discretion to avoid provoking retaliation from other countries. *See also* free trade; tariffs.

Qu Qiu Bai (*or* Ch'ü Ch'iu-pai; 1889–1935) Chinese communist leader. He was a leading literary figure in the communist movement and became general secretary of the Chinese Communist Party in 1927. He was captured and executed by *Guomindang (Nationalist) forces in Shanghai.

Quran. *See* Koran.

Qwaqwa. *See* Bantu Homelands.

R

Ra (*or* Re) The Egyptian sun god and lord of creation, usually portrayed with a falcon's head bearing a solar disk. He sailed across the sky by day in his sun boat and through the underworld by night. His center of worship was at Heliopolis. During the 18th dynasty (1567–1320 BC) he became identified with the Theban god *Amon as Amon-Ra.

Rabat (Arabic name: Ribat) 34 00N 6 42W The capital of Morocco, near the Atlantic coast. Founded as a military post in the 12th century, it became the capital under the French protectorate in the early 20th century. It has a university (1957) and its notable buildings include the 12th-century Hassan Tower. It has an important textile industry. Population (1973): 435,510.

Rabaul 4 13S 152 11E A city in Papua New Guinea, the chief town on the island of New Britain. The capital until 1941 of the Territory of New Guinea, it was evacuated in 1937 because of a volcanic eruption and heavily bombed during World War II. Copra is exported. Population (1980 est): 14,973.

rabbi A Jewish scholar and religious authority. The term came into use in the 1st century AD, and the Judaism of the following centuries is often called "rabbinic Judaism." For a long time the rabbinate was not a salaried office; the title indicated scholarly achievement and legal competence. In modern Jewish communities rabbis are communal leaders, preachers, and pastoral workers.

rabbit A burrowing *mammal belonging to the family *Leporidae* (which also includes the *hares). The rabbit from which domestic breeds derive, (*Oryctolagus cuniculus*), grows to about 18 in (45 cm); it has long ears, a short tail, and soft gray-brown fur. The North American cottontail rabbit (*Sylvilagus floridanus*) has a fluffy white tail, gray-brown fur, and white undersides. It grows to about 15 in (38 cm). Rabbits are gregarious, living in large warrens and feeding on grasses and vegetation. They mature at three months and females can produce a litter of up to ten young (kittens) every month. Rabbits can become a serious agricultural pest although populations have been depleted by myxomatosis. Order: *Lagomorpha.

Rabelais, François (1483–1553) French humanist and satirist. He became a Franciscan and then a Benedictine monk, left the monastery to study and practice medicine, and visited Italy with his patron, Cardinal Jean du Bellay (1492–1560). His humanist philosophy is expressed in his works of richly inventive and often frankly coarse comic satire, *Pantagruel* (1532), *Gargantua* (1534), *Tiers Livre* (1546), and *Quart Livre* (1552). The authenticity of the posthumous *Cinquiesme Livre* (1564) has been debated. His attacks on superstition and scholasticism were condemned by theologians but gained him wide popularity. The classic English translation of his works is by Sir Thomas Urquhart (1653).

Rabi, Isidor Isaac (1898–) US physicist, born in Austria, who invented a highly accurate technique for measuring the nuclear magnetic moments of atoms. For this work he was awarded the Nobel Prize in 1944. During World War II Rabi worked on the development of the atom bomb.

rabies An acute viral infection of the brain that can affect all warm-blooded animals and may be transmitted to man through the bite of an infected animal (usually a dog). Symptoms, which appear after an incubation period of from ten days to two years, include painful spasms of the throat on swallowing. Later, the very sight of water induces convulsions and paralysis (hence the alternative name of the disease—hydrophobia, literally "fear of water") and the patient eventually dies in a coma. There is no treatment for the established disease, but antirabies vaccine and rabies antiserum given to patients immediately after they have been bitten may prevent the infection from developing.

raccoon An omnivorous mammal belonging to the genus *Procyon* (7 species), of the Americas. About 40 in (1 m) long, raccoons are stockily built, with long hind legs and short forelegs. A masklike black patch across the eyes and a striped tail contrast with the thick gray coat. Raccoons forage at night for nuts, roots, snails, mammals, and birds and take aquatic prey, such as crustaceans, mollusks, and fish. Family: *Procyonidae*; order: *Carnivora*.

raccoon dog A short-legged wild *dog, *Nyctereutes procyonides*, of Asia. It is golden-brown, about 24 in (60 cm) long, with black eye patches (like a raccoon). It lives near water and feeds on frogs. Its fur is known as Japanese fox.

Rachel (Élisa Félix; 1820–58) French actress. She made her debut at the Comédie-Française in 1838 and gained an international reputation as a leading tragic actress. She was particularly effective in productions of Racine and Corneille. She died of tuberculosis.

SERGEI RACHMANINOV *In London, 1924.*

Rachmaninov, Sergei (1873–1943) Russian composer, pianist, and conductor. He studied in St Petersburg and Moscow, where he became famous as a pianist, particularly in his own compositions. He left Russia in 1917 and spent most of the rest of his life in the US. His works include four operas, three symphonies, four piano concertos (which he also recorded), the *Rhapsody on a Theme of Paganini* (for piano and orchestra; 1934), and *The Bells* (for soloists, chorus, and orchestra; 1910). One of his most popular pieces for piano is the prelude in C sharp minor (1892).

racial discrimination The practice of making unfavorable distinctions between the members of different races. In the US relations were established as slavery grew during the 17th and 18th centuries, with different laws for slaves (blacks). Although conditions improved through the efforts of the *Abolition Movement and emancipation (during the *Civil War), discrimination is still a part of American life despite legislation (*see* Civil Rights Acts and Constitution) and the *civil rights movement. A similar tradition characterizes South Africa (*see* apartheid), where race relations are governed by an inflexible tradition, which has led to the legal and economic separation of peoples on the basis of their ethnic backgrounds. The circumstances that lead to prejudice are many and diverse and much has been written attributing inferiority to particular races (*see* social Darwinism); however, no scientifically accepted work exists to support these contentions.

Racine, Jean (1639–99) French dramatist. He received a Jansenist education at the convent of Port-Royal but was attracted by the Parisian world of theater and began writing plays in 1664. His major classical verse tragedies, influenced initially by those of *Corneille but eventually surpassing them, include *Andromaque* (1667), *Britannicus* (1669), *Bérénice* (1670), and *Phèdre* (1677). In 1677 he retired from the theater, married a young pious girl, and accepted a post at the court of Louis XIV. His final works were two religious dramas based on Old Testament subjects, *Esther* (1689) and *Athalie* (1691). Racine was the outstanding tragedian of the French classical period.

rad The unit of absorbed dose of ionizing radiation in the *c.g.s. system equal to an energy absorption of 100 ergs per gram of irradiated material.

radar (*radio detection and ranging*) A method of locating distant objects used in military surveillance, air traffic control, and marine and air navigation; it was first developed during the years before World War II by a British team led by Sir Robert *Watson-Watt. High-frequency (300 to 30,000 megahertz) radio waves are sent out in pulses from a powerful rotating transmitter and are reflected back by any object they encounter. The reflected signal is picked up by a receiver antenna and is used to deflect the electron beam in a *cathode-ray tube. The beam scans the screen of the tube by rotating at the same speed as the antenna, so that its angular

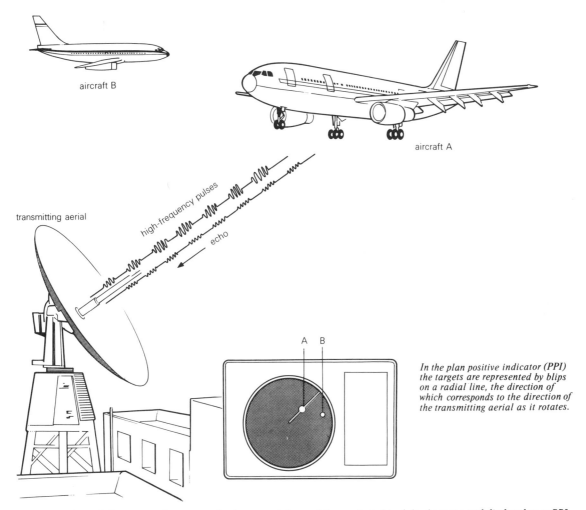

aircraft B

aircraft A

transmitting aerial

high-frequency pulses

echo

A   B

In the plan positive indicator (PPI) the targets are represented by blips on a radial line, the direction of which corresponds to the direction of the transmitting aerial as it rotates.

RADAR   *The high-frequency pulses sent out by the transmitting aerial are reflected back by the target and displayed on a PPI.*

position indicates the direction of the located object. Brightness indicates the strength of the reflected signal, i.e. strong for solid objects, weak for water. The distance from the center of the screen shows the delay between transmission and reception of the reflected signal, i.e. the distance away of the object. The screen continues to glow for a short time after the beam has passed so that a picture is built up with each successive rotation. Radar is now fitted to most aircraft and ships to provide a means of navigation in the dark, cloud, or fog.

Radcliffe, Ann (Ward)   (1764–1823) British novelist. Despite their technical clumsiness and lack of characterization, her gothic novels, such as *The Mysteries of Udolfo* (1794) and *The Italian* (1797), were important influences in the change of literary taste and the increasing interest in Romantic characters, description, etc.

Radcliffe-Brown, Alfred Reginald   (1881–1955) British anthropologist. A pioneer of social anthropology, Radcliffe-Brown held professorships at Chicago, Sydney, Cape Town, and Oxford Universities. His specific contribution to anthropology lies in his studies of *kinship and society, for which he did field work in Australia and the Andaman Islands.

Radek, Karl   (1885–?1939) Soviet politician and journalist. Radek participated in the Russian Revolutions of 1905 and 1917. In 1920 he became secretary of Comintern and served until 1924. Accused of being a Trotskyite, Radek was expelled from the Communist Party in 1927. After recanting in 1929, he wrote for the newspaper *Izvestia* and helped to draft the 1936 constitution. Accused of treason in 1937, he probably died in a Siberian labor camp.

radial velocity   The velocity of a star, etc., along the line of sight, i.e., toward or away from the earth. It is calculated from the Doppler shift of the lines of the star's spectrum (*see* Doppler effect).

radian (rad)   The *SI unit of plane angle equal to the angle subtended at the center of a circle by an arc equal in length to the radius of the circle.

radiation   The propagation of energy by means of beams of particles or waves. It includes all electromagnetic waves, beams of elementary particles, ions, etc., and sound waves.

radiation sickness   Illness caused by exposure to *ionizing radiation, either naturally occurring or from nuclear weapons, X-ray machines, etc. The radiation affects the cells of the body in various ways depending on its intensity. Short-term effects include nausea and diarrhea, while long-term effects include sterility, hemorrhage, loss of hair, and cancer. However, sufficiently intense radiation can kill cancer cells or prevent them from reproducing, hence its use in *radiotherapy.

Radić, Stjepan   (1871–1928) Croatian statesman. Founder of the Croatian Peasant Party (1904), Radić advocated a federated Yugoslavia with Croatian autonomy and opposed *Pašić's centralized Yugoslav Government. In 1925, however, he became minister of education but resigned a year later. He was assassinated in parliament.

radical   A group of atoms in a chemical compound that behaves as a unit in chemical reactions. For example, the methanol molecule (CH_3OH) can be considered as a methyl radical (CH_3.) and a hydroxyl radical (.OH). In this sense, radicals are often simply referred to as groups, a functional group being one responsible for the characteristic reactions of a class of compounds. Thus, the hydroxyl group is the functional group of alcohols. **Free radicals** are groups existing independently. Because they have unpaired electrons they are usually extremely reactive transient species. They can be produced by *pyrolysis or *photolysis and are important intermediates in many reactions, particularly photochemical, combustion, and polymerization reactions.

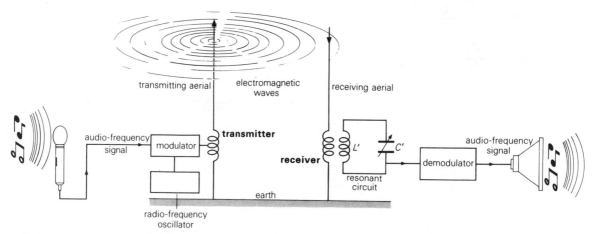

RADIO *The transmission and reception of sound broadcasts.*

Radiguet, Raymond (1903–23) French novelist. His precocious talent was recognized by several prominent literary and artistic figures, especially Jean Cocteau. His two novels were *Le Diable au corps* (1923), a story of adolescent passion and cruelty, and *Le Bal du Comte d'Orgel* (1924).

radio The transmission of sound or other information by radio-frequency (3 kilohertz to 300 gigahertz) electromagnetic waves. The use of radio waves for communication was pioneered by *Marconi in 1895, although their existence had been postulated by *Maxwell in 1873 and demonstrated by *Hertz in 1888.

A **radio transmitter** generates a radio-frequency electrical signal (carrier wave) in an oscillator and superimposes the sound signal on it by a *modulation process. The composite signal is then fed to an aerial, which transmits electromagnetic waves. Although the waves travel in straight lines, transmission beyond the horizon is made possible by the ionosphere, a layer of the upper atmosphere that reflects radio waves in the long and medium wavebands. Long-wave (30 to 300 kilohertz) and medium-wave (300 to 3000 kilohertz) radio is used for direct (ground-wave) transmission in amplitude-modulated (AM) sound broadcasting. Short-wave radio is used for AM sound broadcasting over longer distances using the ionosphere (sky waves) and for communication to ships and aircraft. VHF (very high frequency; 30 to 300 megahertz) is used for *stereophonic sound broadcasting in frequency modulated (FM) transmissions. Television uses mostly UHF (ultrahigh frequency). Neither VHF nor UHF are reflected by the ionosphere, but can be relayed by *communications satellites. All **radio receivers**, from the pocket transistor radio to the most sophisticated and sensitive systems, consist of an *aerial, which detects the signal and converts it to an electrical current; a resonant circuit, which selects the required frequency band; a demodulator to retrieve the audio-frequency signal from the modulated carrier wave; an amplification system; and one or more *loudspeakers to reproduce the sound.

radioactive tracer A radioactive *isotope used for following the course of a substance during a physical, biological, or chemical process. A nonradioactive isotope in the substance is replaced by a radioactive isotope of the same element, which can then be detected by observing its emitted radiation with, for example, a *Geiger counter. Substances containing such radioisotopes are called labeled compounds. Radioactive tracing is a sensitive technique used in medical, scientific, and industrial research.

radioactive waste Waste products from nuclear reactors, uranium-processing plants, etc., that have become radioactive. The disposal of these waste products, which include solids, liquids, and gases, constitutes a major problem as some materials have a very long mean life. At present solid waste is either stored in tanks under ground or placed in drums weighted with concrete and sunk in deep sea water. Liquid waste represents the most difficult problems owing to the possibility of leakage. Gaseous waste is usually released into the atmosphere in small quantities.

radioactivity The spontaneous emission of a particle by an atomic nucleus. The emitted particle may be an alpha particle (a helium nucleus consisting of two protons and two neutrons), in which case the process is known as *alpha decay; or it may be a beta particle (an *electron), when the process is known as *beta decay. Highly energetic X-rays (*see* gamma radiation) may also be emitted simultaneously. In both alpha and beta decay the nucleus changes into that of another element. A less common method of decay is the emission of a *positron, the antiparticle of the

electron, the process being similar to that of beta decay. Radioactive decay is a random process and its occurrence for a single nucleus can be neither predicted nor controlled. However, for a large number of nuclei the time taken for a certain fraction of nuclei to decay can be accurately predicted as either its *mean life or *half-life. These quantities vary from about 10^{-8} second to 10^{10} years depending on the isotope. The phenomenon was first discovered in 1898 by *Becquerel in uranium and elucidated by the *Curies, *Rutherford, and *Soddy.

radio astronomy The study of celestial objects by means of the radio waves they emit. This radio emission was first noticed by K. G. *Jansky in the US in 1932 and it now forms an important branch of *astronomy. *See* radio telescope.

radio beacon An automatic navigational beacon that broadcasts a coded radio signal. The angular position of the source of the signal can be determined by a vessel or aircraft carrying a radio direction finder or radio compass and can be identified by its code, usually given in Morse. Where two such radio beacons can be received, the exact position of the receiver can be determined by triangulation.

radiocarbon dating A method of estimating the age of a material, such as wood, that was once living. Atmospheric carbon dioxide contains a small proportion of the radioisotope carbon-14. As all living things absorb carbon from atmospheric carbon dioxide, either directly or indirectly, they too contain a constant proportion of carbon-14. However, once dead, the level of carbon-14 falls as a result of *beta decay. By measuring the radioactivity of a material, the concentration of carbon-14 and hence its age can be estimated. The method is accurate within stated limits for ages up to 4500 years. *See also* radiometric dating.

radiochemistry The branch of chemistry concerned with compounds containing radioactive *isotopes of elements. It includes chemical techniques for isotope separation, and the use of *radioactive tracers for investigating the mechanisms of chemical reactions.

radio galaxy A *radio source that lies beyond our Galaxy, is identified with an optical *galaxy, and the radio-power output of which greatly exceeds that of a normal galaxy. The size can be immense. A massive *black hole at the galaxy center has been postulated as a possible energy source.

radiography The technique of examining the internal structure of a solid body by passing *X-rays or *gamma radiation through it to produce an image on a photographic plate or fluorescent screen. Radiography is used in medicine for the diagnosis of disease (*see* radiology) and in industry to examine objects, etc., for structural defects.

radio interferometer. *See* radio telescope.

radioisotope (*or* radioactive isotope) An *isotope that is radioactive. Radioisotopes are used in the production of *nuclear energy, in *radiotherapy, as *radioactive tracers, and in *dating techniques. Some are naturally occurring (those with mass numbers in excess of 208) while others can be made radioactive by neutron bombardment.

Radiolaria An order of single-celled animals (*see* Protozoa) found chiefly in the sea, as a component of plankton. Radiolarians are typically spherical, 0.004 in (0.1 mm) to several millimeters in diameter, with a silicaceous skeleton of radiating spines from which long thin pseudopodia extend to capture food particles. The skeletal remains of dead radiolarians sink to the ocean floor to form a deposit called radiolarian ooze. Class: *Sarcodina*. □Protozoa.

radiology The branch of medicine concerned with the use of X-rays and other forms of radiation and radioactive substances in the diagnosis and treatment of disease. *Radiography is used to diagnose a wide range of disorders, including fractures, ulcers, and cancer: hollow organs are often visualized by injecting a fluid that is opaque to X-rays. A radiologist is a doctor specialized in the interpretation of X-ray photographs and films. Recent advances in radiology include the CAT-scan, the use of computer-aided tomography, in which X-ray "slices" of the body are recorded with an X-ray scanner and integrated by a computer to produce a cross-sectional image. *See also* radiotherapy.

radiometric dating A method of dating rocks, developed mainly in the 1950s, by observing the extent to which a radioactive (parent) element in a rock has decayed to form a stable daughter element. Since the half-life or rate of decay of the radioactive element chosen is known, the age of the rock can be calculated from the ratio of parent to daughter isotopes present. The most frequently used methods are *radiocarbon dating, *potassium-argon dating, and *rubidium-strontium dating. Methods based on uranium-lead and thorium-lead decays are also sometimes used.

radio source A celestial object that emits radio waves and can be detected by a *radio telescope. The sun and Jupiter are solar-system sources. Other radio sources within our Galaxy are pulsars, supernova remnants, interstellar hydrogen clouds, and the galactic center. Extragalactic sources include spiral galaxies, radio galaxies, and some quasars. The spatial distribution and intensity of the radio emission can be shown on a contour map.

radio telescope An instrument for detecting and measuring the radio emissions from celestial *radio sources. It consists of an antenna, or system of antennas, the radio-frequency signals of which are carried by wires or waveguides to one or more receivers. The receiver output signal is finally displayed on a graph, stored on magnetic tape, etc. The antenna may be a large metal parabolic or spherical dish, usually steerable, that brings radio waves from a radio source to a focus on a secondary antenna. Alternatively simple dipole antennas may be used. An antenna system may consist of two separate units the signals of which are fed to a common receiver. This radio interferometer has a very much greater resolving power than a single antenna.

radiotherapy The use of X-rays and other forms of radiation, either produced by machines or emitted by radioactive isotopes, for treating disease. The radiation may be directed at the target organ from a distance or radioactive needles, wires, pellets, etc., may be implanted in the body. Radiation is particularly destructive to rapidly dividing cells: it is therefore used in treating various forms of *cancer and certain other tumors as well as overactivity of the thyroid gland.

radish An annual or biennial herb, *Raphanus sativus*, widely grown for its edible fleshy hot-tasting root, which may be red, white, or purple. Spring varieties are quick-growing while winter varieties may be stored. The plant bears white flowers. Family: *Cruciferae.

radium (Ra) A metallic element, discovered in pitchblende in 1898 by Pierre and Marie Curie. It is a divalent alkaline-earth element, forming a number of simple salts, such as the chloride ($RaCl_2$). It decays to form the noble gas radon and is used in radiotherapy for the treatment of cancers. At no 88; at wt (226); mp 1293°F (700°C); bp 2086°F (1140°C).

radius. *See* arm.

Radom 51 26N 21 10E An industrial city in SE central Poland. Founded in 1340, it was held successively by Austria and Russia before returning to Poland in 1918. Industries include leather, glass, and chemicals. Population (1979 est): 188,000.

radon (Rn) The heaviest noble gas, produced by the decay of radium, thorium, and actinium. It is radioactive, the longest-lived isotope (^{222}Rn) having a half-life of 3.825 days. Like the other noble gases, Rn forms clathrates and fluorides. Increased radon levels have been noted in ground water shortly before earthquakes. At no 86; at wt (222); mp –96°F (–71°C); bp –79°F (–61.8°C).

Raeder, Erich (1876–1960) German admiral; commander in chief of the navy (1928–43). In contravention of the Treaty of Versailles, he rebuilt the German navy in the years before World War II but was dismissed after disagreeing with Hitler over strategy. He was sentenced to life imprisonment for war crimes but was released in 1955.

raffia (*or* raphia) A *palm tree of the genus *Raphia*, especially *R. peduncalata* (or *R. ruffia*), native to Madagascar and cultivated for its fiber. Its leaves, up to 65 ft (20 m) long, are composed of 80–100 leaflets from which the fiber is torn in thin strips and dried in the sun. Raffia is soft, strong,

pliable, and resistant to shrinking; it is woven into mats and baskets and used in horticulture, etc.

Raffles, Sir Thomas Stamford (1781–1826) British colonial administrator and oriental scholar, who acquired Singapore for the East India Company (1819). In 1805 he became assistant secretary to the governor of Penang and was lieutenant governor of Java (1811–16) while it was under British rule and then of Bengkulu (1818–23) in W Sumatra.

Rafflesia A genus of Malaysian parasitic herbs (12 species), the vegetative parts of which are reduced to fungus-like threads that extract food from the roots and stems of other plants. The monster plant (*R. arnoldii*) has the world's largest flower—up to 18 in (45 cm) across and weighing up to 22 lb (10 kg). It smells of rotten meat and attracts carrion flies, which act as pollinators. The genus was named for Sir Stamford *Raffles. Family: *Rafflesiaceae*.

raga (Sanskrit: color) In Indian music, a type of *scale used as the basis for improvisation. There are many different ragas, some of which are associated with particular moods, feelings, times of day, etc.

ragged robin A Eurasian perennial herb, *Lychnis flos-cuculi*. Growing to a height of 30 in (75 cm), it has rose-red flowers with five deeply divided ragged petals. It is common in damp places and has been introduced to North America. Family: *Caryophyllaceae*.

Raglan, FitzRoy James Henry Somerset, 1st Baron (1788–1855) British field marshal. After service in the Napoleonic Wars (in which he lost his sword arm at Waterloo), he became secretary to Wellington, whom he succeeded as master general of the ordnance in 1852. In 1854 he became commander in the *Crimean War and, in spite of success at *Inkerman, his strategy was much criticized (*see also* Balaclava, Battle of). The Raglan sleeve, extending to the neck without shoulder seams, is named for him.

RAGNARÖK *The gods struggle against the evil progeny of Loki at the end of the world. Thor (right) battles with the serpent Jörmungandr, Odin with the wolf Fenris, and Frey with the fire-giant Surtr. Bifrost, the rainbow bridge connecting Asgard and earth, is in the background.*

Ragnarök In Norse mythology, doomsday, when a catastrophic battle between the gods and the forces of evil will occur. It will be preceded by warning signals: three years of perpetual winter will be followed by three years of moral decline among men. After the defeat of the gods by the forces of evil, led by *Loki, everyone will be destroyed except for *Lif and Lifthrasir.

ragtime A precursor of *New Orleans style jazz. Ragtime developed from minstrel-band music, but many rags were published as piano compositions. Ragtime was characterized by syncopation in the melody against a regular marchlike accompaniment and was popular from the 1890s until around 1920. Famous rags include "Harlem Rag" (1895) and "Maple Leaf Rag" (1899), written by Scott *Joplin, the first ragtime composer to write down his music.

Ragusa (ancient name: Hybla Heraca) 36 56N 14 44E A town in Italy, in Sicily on the Irminio River. It has an 18th-century cathedral. Oil production and asphalt mining are the chief industrial activities. Population (1971): 59,509.

ragweed An annual plant, *Ambrosia*, that grows up to 12 ft (3.7 m) high and has green flowers atop thin clustered stems with large leaves. Found mainly in North America, the ragweed's pollen, especially that of the common ragweed (*Ambrosia elatior*), causes hay fever, an allergic reaction. Family: *Compositae*.

ragworm A marine *annelid worm, *Nereis cultrifera*, also called chainworm, of European coastal waters. 2–4 in (5-10 cm) long, ragworms swim by means of paddle-like structures occurring in pairs on each body segment. Most live in burrows in sand or mud or among stones, feeding on dead organisms and detritus using a pair of horny jaws inside a protrudable mouth tube. Class: *Polychaeta*.

ragwort A perennial or biennial herb, *Senecio jacobaea*, that grows up to 60 in (150 cm) high and has much-divided leaves and dense flat-topped heads of yellow flowers. It is found on dunes, waste places, and pastures of Eurasia and N Africa and has been introduced to New Zealand and North America. When eaten in large quantities it is poisonous to livestock. Family: *Compositae*.

rail A slender secretive ground-dwelling bird belonging to a widely distributed family (*Rallidae*; about 300 species), occurring mostly in swamps, marshes, and fresh waters. 4.3–18 in (11–45 cm) long, rails have short rounded wings, a short tail, and typically a dull gray or brown plumage, often barred for camouflage. They feed on plant material, invertebrates, and birds' eggs. Order: *Gruiformes* (cranes, rails, etc.). *See also* coot; corncrake; gallinule.

railroad A permanent track, consisting of parallel rails, on which □locomotives draw wagons or cars for transporting goods or passengers. Wooden rails have been in use in mines since the 14th century, but flanged wheels running on cast-iron rails were not introduced until 1789. Thereafter they were quite widely used in the mining and metallurgical industries, although cars were horse-drawn until the invention of the steam locomotive at the beginning of the 19th century. The first effective railroad in the world opened in England in 1825 and ran between Stockton and Darlington, using *Stephenson's *Locomotion* as the locomotive. The US railroad boom began in the 1830s, and systems grew rapidly before the Civil War. After the war, the system expanded greatly, symbolized by the completion of the transcontinental railroad in 1869.
Since World War II the growth of internal air services, the development of efficient road-haulage services, and the spread of private automobiles have led to the decline of the railroads in industrial countries, causing services to be reduced. However the introduction of high-speed trains has enabled them to survive. In the developing countries they still play an essential role in transporting goods and passengers over long distances.

rain A form of precipitation composed of liquid water drops ranging in size from about 0.02 to 0.20 in (0.5 to 5 mm) diameter. Minute droplets of water in clouds may coalesce to form larger drops; if these are sufficiently heavy they will fall as rain. The amount of rain, together with other forms of precipitation, that falls in a specific time is usually measured with a **rain gauge**. This is a cylindrical container with a funnel of standard diameter into which the rain falls. The water collected is periodically measured and recorded in millimeters or inches; some rain gauges are designed to record automatically.

rainbow An optical phenomenon consisting of an arc of light across the sky composed of the colors of the spectrum. It is caused by the refraction of sunlight through falling water drops; the larger the drops the more spectacular are the colors.

Raine, Kathleen (1908–) British poet. Her volumes of poetry, which include *Stone and Flower* (1943) and *The Lost Country* (1971), are noted for their visionary lyricism. She has also published several studies of William Blake, notably *Blake and Tradition* (1969).

Rainier, Mount A mountain in the US, the highest peak in Washington state and the Cascade Mountains. It is noted for its many glaciers. Height: 14,408 ft (4392 m).

Rainier III (1923–) Prince of Monaco (1949–). He repudiated the principle of the *divine right of kings in a new constitution (1962). In 1956 he married Grace *Kelly. Their three children are Prince Albert (1958–), Princess Caroline (1957–), and Princess Stephanie (1965–).

Rais, Gilles de (*or* G. de Retz; 1404–40) French marshal, who fought with *Joan of Arc. After her capture he retired to his estates in Brittany and dabbled in alchemy and witchcraft. In 1440 he was sentenced to death for the torture and murder of over 140 children. He was later associated with the story of Bluebeard, immortalized by Charles *Perrault.

Rajasthan A state in NW India, extending from the Thar Desert along Pakistan's border SE into forested hills. The economy depends primarily on grain and livestock farming, as well as cotton, sugar cane, and pulses. Coal, phosphates, gypsum, marble, mica, and salt are mined. Industries include textiles, cement, and glass. *History*: Rajasthan flourished in the Harappan period (3rd–2nd millenniums BC). Under Rajput princes (from the 7th century AD), it withstood Muslim invaders but succumbed to British ex-

pansion (19th century). Area: 132,095 sq mi (342,214 sq km). Population (1981): 34,102,912. Capital: Jaipur.

Rajkot 22 18N 70 53E A city in India, in Gujarat. A commercial and industrial center, it produces textiles and chemicals. Population (1971): 300,612.

Rajput A group of clans in N and central India, now numbering about 11 million people. They appeared in about the 5th century AD and are believed to have been descended from invading tribes from Central Asia, although they claim descent from more ancient Indian tribes. Because of their warfaring occupation they were at some time included within the Ksatriya (warrior) caste of Hindu society. The Rajput states fought vigorously against the Muslim invaders, maintaining their independence in Rajasthan. They acknowledged the overlordship of the Moguls in the 16th century, the Marathas in the 18th century, and the British in 1808. Rajput dynasties were responsible for building many fine temples.

Rákóczy II, Ferenc (1676–1735) Hungarian revolutionary. In 1703 Rákóczy led a peasant uprising against Austria and in 1704 he was elected Prince of Transylvania. After two serious defeats in 1708 and 1710, Hungary signed the Peace of Szatmár (1711) with Austria. Rákóczy rejected it and went abroad, dying in Turkey.

Raleigh 35 46N 78 39W The capital city capital of North Carolina. Named for Sir Walter Raleigh, its industries include the manufacture of computers and textiles. North Carolina State University (1887) and Shaw University (1865) are situated here. Population (1980): 149,771.

Raleigh, Sir Walter (1554–1618) British explorer and writer; half-brother of Humphrey *Gilbert. He became a favorite of Elizabeth I. He was unsuccessful in his attempts (1584–89) to found a colony in Virginia (now North Carolina) but brought back the potato and tobacco plant from America. In 1595–96 he led an expedition to South America, which he described in *The Discoverie of Guiana* (1596), and in 1596 took part in the sack of Cádiz. At James I's accession (1603) he stood trial for treason, but the death sentence was commuted to imprisonment; while in the Tower of London he wrote *The History of the World* (1614). He was released in 1616 to search for gold along the Orinoco but his mission was a failure and after his return his death sentence was invoked and he was executed.

rally 1. A competitive automobile racing event, in which drivers have to reach checkpoints by certain times. The routes are normally over public roads, but rallies often also include speed or other tests after the route has been completed. Major events, such as the Monte Carlo Rally (first held in 1911), require extensively modified cars. 2. A similar event for motorcycles, but usually with more emphasis on the social and touring aspects than the competitive.

Rama The seventh incarnation of *Vishnu, appearing as a hero in the epics the *Ramayana and *Mahabharata. In the *Upanishads and elsewhere he appears as a god. Since about the 15th century he has been widely worshiped as the supreme deity, epitomizing reason and virtue. He is usually represented holding a bow and arrow and attended by his wife.

Ramadan The ninth month of the Muslim year. It is a time of atonement, and every Muslim is required to observe a strict fast daily from dawn to dusk until the new moon of the next month is visible.

Ramakrishna (1836–86) Hindu saint and religious teacher. Son of an impoverished Brahmin family, he had little formal education, but he gathered a following throughout the world. He condemned greed, lust, and the caste system, teaching the essential unity and truth of all religions.

Raman, Sir Chandrasekhara Venkata (1888–1970) Indian physicist, who was professor at Calcutta University. He won the Nobel Prize in 1930 for his discovery that there is a change in the wavelength of light or ultraviolet radiation when scattered by certain molecules (**Raman effect**). This discovery was used to determine some of the finer details of molecular structure.

Ramanuja (11th century AD) Hindu philosopher and theologian, born in Kanchipuram (S India). He diverged sharply from the tradition in *Vedanta associated with *Sankara, insisting upon the value and reality of the physical world. In religion he provided an influential philosophical basis for devotional worship (*bhakti*), based upon his concept of a personal God epitomized by the god *Vishnu.

Ramapithecus A genus of fossil *hominids that lived during the late Miocene and early Pliocene. It is represented by fossil remains found in India in 1934. They were about the size of a gibbon, possibly walked erect, and may represent the earliest ancestors of modern man after the divergence of his evolutionary line from the apes.

Ramat Gan 32 04N 34 48E A city in central Israel, just E of Tel Aviv-Yafo. It has some manufacturing and is the seat of Bar-Ilan University. Population (1979 est): 120,400.

Ramayana (Sanskrit: romance of Rama) Hindu epic poem in seven books. Probably composed in its present form after the 4th century BC, it tells the story of *Rama and his devoted wife Sita, her abduction by the demon king Ravana, and Rama's struggle to recover her with the aid of *Hanuman. The *Ramayana* and *Mahabharata* are the two great classics of Sanskrit literature.

Rambert, Dame Marie (Cyvia Rabbam, later Miriam Rambach; 1888–1982) British ballet dancer and choreographer, born in Poland. She worked with Diaghilev's Ballets Russes in 1913 and was naturalized as a British citizen in 1918. As director of the Carmargo Society, which in 1935 became the Ballet Rambert, she trained and encouraged many young British dancers and choreographers.

Rambouillet 48 39N 1 50E A city in N France, in the Yvelines department. Its chateau (14th–18th centuries) is now the summer residence of French presidents. Population (1975): 20,056.

rambutan A Malaysian tree, *Nephelium lappaceum*, that grows 65 ft (20 m) high and produces edible plum-sized red or yellow spiny fruit. It is cultivated in moist tropical lowlands. Family: *Sapindaceae*.

Rameau, Jean Philippe (1683–1764) French composer. He held several posts as organist and wrote a *Traité de l'harmonie* (1722), a significant contribution to modern musical theory, before beginning to compose. His works include chamber, keyboard, and vocal music, as well as 24 operas, including the opera *Hippolyte et Aricie* (1733), and opera-ballets, including *Les Indes galantes* (1735) and *Castor et Pollux* (1737). There was great rivalry between his adherents and those of Lully and Pergolesi.

ramie A perennial plant, *Boehmeria nivea*, also called China grass, native to E Asia and cultivated, chiefly in China, for its stem fibers. Each plant produces several stalks, up to 7.9 ft (2.4 m) high, with clusters of greenish-white flowers in the leaf axils. Although strong and durable, ramie fiber is not widely used due to difficulties in extraction, spinning, and weaving. Family: *Urticaceae* (nettle family).

Ramillies, Battle of (May 23, 1706) The battle in the War of the *Spanish Succession in which British, Dutch, and Danish forces under Marlborough defeated the French 13 mi (21 km) N of Namur. The victory gave much of the Spanish Netherlands to the allies.

Ramón y Cajal, Santiago (1852–1934) Spanish histologist, who established the neuron (nerve cell) as the basic unit of the nervous system. Ramón improved staining techniques to distinguish the complex connections between neurons in the brain, spinal tissue, and the retina of the eye. He was awarded the 1906 Nobel Prize with Camillo *Golgi.

Ramsay, Sir William (1852–1916) Scottish chemist, whose work on the *noble gases earned him the 1904 Nobel Prize for Chemistry. His interest was kindled when *Rayleigh discovered that atmospheric nitrogen was slightly heavier than laboratory-prepared nitrogen. In 1894, Ramsay, working with Rayleigh, removed all known gases from some air and discovered a small residue, which they identified spectroscopically as a new element, naming it argon (inert). By fractionally distilling argon, Ramsay isolated neon, xenon, and krypton in 1898. In 1895 he had discovered the inert gas helium, being given off by the mineral cleveite.

Ramses (II) the Great King of Egypt (1304–1237 BC) of the 19th dynasty. He fortified the coast road to repel nomads and pirates. His more serious, though indecisive, warfare against the Hittites, whose success at Qadesh (c. 1300) unsettled Egypt's Palestinian subjects, ended in lasting peace around 1284. Ramses built, or enlarged, more temples than any other pharaoh and built the temple complex of *Abu Simbel. He is probably the pharaoh who oppressed the Israelites.

Ramses III King of Egypt (1198–1166 BC) of the 20th dynasty, famous for two victories against the invading Sea Peoples. The first recorded strike in history occurred during his reign, when workers building a necropolis protested against the government's failure to deliver grain rations.

Ram Singh (1816–85) Indian Sikh leader. He organized a new, severely puritanical, sect of Sikhs, the Kukas, and worked to oust the British from India. His men were brutally punished for their attacks on Muslims and Ram Singh died after a long exile in Burma.

Ramus, Petrus (Pierre de la Ramée; 1515–72) French humanist scholar. In *Aristotelicae Animadversiones* and *Dialecticae Institutiones* (both 1543), Ramus attacked *Aristotelianism mainly on the grounds that it falsified the logic of the human mind. An intellectual hero to Protestant Europe, Ramus was murdered in the *St Bartholomew's Day Massacre.

Rancagua 34 10S 70 45W A city in N central Chile. Industries are chiefly related to processing agricultural produce and copper from the El Teniente mine. Population (1976 est): 117,550.

Rance River A river in NW France, rising in Brittany and flowing generally E and N to the Gulf of St Malo. It powers the world's first successful tidal power station, opened in 1966. Length: 62 mi (100 km).

Rand, Ayn (1905–82) US author; born in Russia. She began her writing career as a screenwriter (1932–34; 1944–49). Her first book, *We, the Living*, was published in 1936 and the works that followed promoted her doctrine, Objectivism, which advocated self-interest and fulfillment in a capitalist world. Her works include *Anthem* (1938), *The Fountainhead* (1943), *Atlas Shrugged* (1957), *The Virtue of Selfishness* (1965), and *Philosophy: Who Needs It?* (1982).

Rand, The. See Witwatersrand.

Randolph, A(sa) Philip (1889–1979) US labor and civil-rights leader. He founded the *Messenger*, a radical black magazine, in 1917, and by 1925 was urging unionization of railroad porters. He organized the Brotherhood of Sleeping Car Porters in 1925 and served as its president until 1968. A threat to march on Washington with 50,000 blacks in 1941 resulted in equal rights for blacks in government and the defense industries. He was a vice-president of the *American Federation of Labor-Congress of Industrial Organizations (AFL-CIO) from 1957 and one of the directors of the 1963 March on Washington for jobs and freedom.

Randolph, Edward Jennings (1753–1813) US statesman. He was a member of the Continental Congress (1779–82) and governor of Virginia (1786–88). As leader of the Virginia delegation to the *Annapolis Convention, he was the author of the *Virginia Plan and wrote the final draft of the US Constitution, but did not sign it. He served as US attorney general (1789–94) and secretary of state (1794–95), retiring after being falsely accused of accepting French bribes. He was defense lawyer for Aaron *Burr in 1807.

RANGOON *A complex of pagodas and temples surround the Shwe Dagon Pagoda, one of the great Buddhist pilgrimage centers.*

Rangoon 16 47N 96 10E The capital of Burma, a port in the S on the Rangoon River. Industry has increased greatly since independence in 1948. Its university was founded in 1920. *History*: a settlement grew up in very early times around the Shwe Dagon Pagoda, which is the focal point of Burmese religious life. King Alaungpaya made it his capital in the 18th century. Twice captured by the British in the 19th century, it became the capital of all Burma in 1886. It was badly damaged in World War II during the Japanese occupation (1942–45). Population (1973): 1,586,422.

Ranjit Singh, Maharaja (1780–1839) Sikh ruler, known as the Lion of the Punjab. At the age of 20 he took control of Lahore and in 1802 seized Amritsar, the holy city of the Sikhs. With an enormous army based on the European model, he became master of a large part of the Punjab. In spite of uneasy relations with the British, he supported them against Afghanistan in 1838.

Rank, Otto (1884–1939) Austrian psychiatrist, noted for his theory that emotional disorders could stem from psychological trauma experienced during birth. Rank was a colleague of Sigmund *Freud and applied Freudian psychology to an analysis of many literary works, pointing especially to the *Oedipus complex as a commonly recurring theme.

Ranke, Leopold von (1795–1886) German historian. A professor at Berlin University from 1825 to 1871, von Ranke published work on German, French, Spanish, Italian, and English history. His *History of the Latin and Teutonic Nations (1494–1535)* (1824) demonstrated his abilities in source criticism and is generally regarded as the first critical historical work.

Ransom, John Crowe (1888–1974) US poet and critic. At Vanderbilt University he was a founder of the Fugitives, a group of agrarian poets. He founded the *Kenyon Review* (1939), a literary organ for the school of criticism that took its name from his book *The New Criticism* (1941). His formal ironic poetry is included in *Poems About God* (1919), *Chills and Fever* (1924), *Two Gentlemen in Bonds* (1926), *Selected Poems* (1945), and other volumes.

Ranunculaceae A family of herbaceous and woody plants (about 1300 species), found all over the world but most abundant in N temperate and Arctic regions. They are mainly bitter-tasting and sometimes poisonous. The family includes many garden flowers, such as *Anenome, *Aquilegia, *Clematis, and *Delphinium, as well as common weeds, e.g. *buttercup.

Rapallo 44 21N 9 13E A port and resort in NW Italy, in Liguria on the Gulf of Genoa. It was the scene of the signing of two treaties after World War I, the first between Italy and Yugoslavia (1920) and the second between the Soviet Union and Germany (1922). Olive oil, wine, and cement are manufactured here. Population (1971): 26,713.

Rapanui. *See* Easter Island.

rape (botany) An annual or biennial herb, *Brassica napus* var. *arvensis*, also called oilseed rape or coleseed, that grows to a height of 40 in (1 m) and has deeply divided lobed leaves and yellow flowers. It is widely cultivated for its seeds, contained in pods, which yield an edible oil; the residue is used as a cattle feed. Family: *Cruciferae.

rape (law) Sexual intercourse with a woman against her will or without her voluntary permission. The woman's accusation must be supported by other evidence; for example, there must be proof of penetration.

Raphael (Raffaello Sanzio; 1483–1520) Italian Renaissance painter and architect, born in Urbino, the son of a painter. He trained under *Perugino, in Perugia, where he painted *The Marriage of the Virgin* before moving to Florence in 1504. There, influenced by *Leonardo and *Michelangelo, he painted numerous Madonnas and also the portraits of Angelo and Maddalena Doni. Settling in Rome in 1508, he decorated the papal apartments in the Vatican with frescoes, which include the *School of Athens* and the *Disputa*. He painted his patron Pope Julius II and the *Sistine Madonna*. In 1514 he succeeded Bramante as architect of St Peter's but only a few of his architectural projects were realized, for example the Chigi chapel in Sta Maria del Popolo. In 1515 he designed tapestries for the Sistine Chapel. His last work, the *Transfiguration*, which was completed by Giulio Romano, anticipates *mannerism.

Rapp, George (Johann Georg R.; 1757–1847) US religious leader, born in Germany. He came to the US in 1803, seeking religious freedom for his sect, the Rappites, and a site upon which to establish a utopian community. They settled Harmony, Penn., in 1805, but, seeking land more suitable for their grape-growing and wine-making businesses, moved W to found Harmonie, Ind. By 1825 they had returned to Pennsylvania and established Economy, on the Ohio River. Rappite members practiced celibacy, which, with lack of new member recruitment, caused the sect to die out by the early 1900s.

Rarotonga 21 15S 159 45W A mountainous island in the SW Pacific Ocean, the administrative center of the *Cook Islands. Copra and citrus fruit are exported. Area: 26 sq mi (67 sq km). Population (1976): 9811. Chief town: Avarua.

Rashi (Solomon ben Isaac; 1040–1105) French rabbi. He established a school at Troyes that attracted pupils from many countries. His most cele-

brated works are his commentaries (in Hebrew) on the Bible and the Babylonian *Talmud, which are remarkable for their simplicity, conciseness, and scholarly accuracy.

Rashid. *See* Rosetta Stone.

Rasht (*or* Resht) 37 18N 49 38E A city in N Iran, near the Caspian Sea. It is an agricultural trading center and has a university (1977). Population (1976): 187,203.

Rasmussen, Knud Johan Victor (1879–1933) Danish explorer and ethnologist, who led a series of Arctic expeditions from Greenland to study Eskimo culture, which he believed to be akin to that of the North American Indians. In the longest recorded dog-sledge ride (1921–24) he reached the Bering Strait, describing the journey in *Across Arctic America* (1927).

raspberry A prickly woody perennial plant, *Rubus idaeus*, native to woods and heaths of Eurasia and North America. Up to 5 ft (1.5 m) high, it bears five-petaled white flowers, which produce red (or occasionally yellow) sweet fruits. There are many cultivated varieties, fruiting in summer or autumn. Upright canes grow from basal buds and bear fruit in their first autumn or second summer. The old canes, which die after fruiting, should be removed and the young canes pruned. Family: *Rosaceae.

Rasputin, Grigori Yefimovich (c. 1872–1916) Russian mystic, who was a favorite of Emperor *Nicholas II and *Alexandra. A Siberian peasant, Rasputin's apparent ability to ease the bleeding of the hemophiliac crown prince brought him considerable influence over the royal family and thus over the government: high offices were held by his hangers-on, who were invariably corrupt and incompetent. His unpopularity, aggravated by his debauchery, led to his murder by a group of nobles: his assassins attempted to poison him and when this inexplicably failed he was shot and thrown into the River Neva.

rat A *rodent belonging to the suborder *Myomorpha*, distributed worldwide. Typical rats belong to the Old World genus *Rattus* (137 species) and are among the most successful rodents. The black rat (*R. rattus*), originally Asian, has spread by traveling on ships to most regions of the world, living in human habitations and sewers. The brown rat (*R. norvegicus*), also called Norway rat, is larger, measuring 12–18 in (30–45 cm) including its tail (6–8 in [15–20 cm]), and tends to live outdoors in burrows. It has displaced the black rat in many places. Both species eat a wide variety of plant and animal materials, often causing serious damage to stored food, gnawing through pipes and cables, and transmitting such diseases as typhus and food poisoning. Rats are commonly bred for use as laboratory animals in scientific research. *See also* mouse.

RATEL *This animal uses its long claws to rip open bees' nests for honey. It may be led to a nest by a honeyguide, this bird then sharing the honey that the ratel extracts.*

ratel An omnivorous mammal, *Mellivora capensis*, also called honey badger, of Africa and S Asia. About 28 in (70 cm) long, gray above and black underneath, it lives in thick woods, eating almost anything from ants to young antelopes (especially honey). Family: *Mustelidae.

ratfish. *See* chimaera.

Rathenau, Walther (1867–1922) German industrialist and politician, who organized Germany's economy both during and after World War I. As minister of reconstruction (1921–22), he recommended the prompt payment of German reparations. Becoming foreign minister in 1922, he concluded the Treaty of Rapallo with the Soviet Union shortly before being assassinated. In *The New Economy* (1918) he expressed his belief in industrial self-government with worker participation.

Rathlin Island 55 17N 6 15W An island in Northern Ireland, off the N coast of Antrim in the North Channel. It was the refuge of Robert the Bruce (1306).

rationalism A philosophical movement stemming from 17th-century attempts to study the universe using reason, in the form of deductive and mathematical methods, rather than sense-experience. *Descartes, for example, tried to deduce what God's world is like from the axioms of divine existence and goodness. The scientific interests of the early rationalists made use of their religious views, but conflict between the new sciences and religion developed, and is reflected in the work of *Spinoza, *Arnauld, and *Leibniz. By the 19th century a compromise evolved, allocating science and religion to their separate spheres. Kant was called a rationalist in so far as he believed in the possibility of synthetic *a priori propositions. Recent intuitionists (*see* intuitionism) have been sympathetic to rationalism.

Ratisbon. *See* Regensburg.

ratite A bird characterized by a smooth breastbone that lacks a keel for the attachment of flight muscles. Ratites are flightless and usually large and swift-running and include the cassowary, emu, kiwi, ostrich, and rhea and the extinct moa.

rat kangaroo A *marsupial belonging to the subfamily *Potoroinae* (9 species), of Australia (including Tasmania). Two species are commonly known as boodies and two others as potoroos. Measuring 9–17 in (23–44 cm) excluding the tail (6–15 in [15–38 cm]), rat kangaroos are related to kangaroos and have a long narrow ratlike face. They have large canine teeth and long claws and forage at night for grubs and tubers. Family: *Macropodidae*.

rattan The stems of climbing *palms of the genus *Calamus* (375 species), native to Old World tropical regions. Up to 425 ft (130 m) long, the stems are stripped of leaves and used in furniture, matting, baskets, brooms, etc.

Rattigan, Sir Terence (1911–77) British dramatist. His highly successful plays include upper-class comedies (*French without Tears*, 1936), more ambitious studies of human relationships (*The Deep Blue Sea*, 1952), and studies of historical characters (*Ross*, 1960). During the late 1950s and 1960s his immaculately constructed plays became unfashionable but in the years immediately preceding his death they were again acclaimed.

rattlesnake A *pit viper belonging to either of two genera, *Sisturus* (2 species) or *Crotalus* (28 species), and characterized by having a rattle composed of loosely connected horny tail segments, which is vibrated to produce a warning sound. Rattlesnakes occur in both North and South America, usually in dry regions, and are 1–8 ft (0.3–2.5 m) long with dark diamond, hexagonal, or spotted markings on a pale background. They feed on rabbits, rodents, lizards, etc., and bear live young. *See also* diamondback; sidewinder.

Rauschenberg, Robert (1925–) US artist. A leading exponent of *pop art, he studied under Josef *Albers. In the early 1950s he produced collages and assemblages made from rusty nails, rags, Coca-Cola bottles, etc. His best-known works are probably those produced in the 1960s, when he adopted the silk-screen printing technique for transferring photographic images to canvases.

Rauwolfia A tropical genus of trees and shrubs (50 species). The dried roots of some species, including *R. serpentina* of India and *R. vomitoria* of Africa, contain alkaloids with sedative effects, now used in medicine to treat hypertension. Family: *Apocynaceae*.

Ravel, Maurice (1875–1937) French composer of the impressionist school. A pupil of Fauré, he repeatedly entered compositions for the Prix de Rome, his failures provoking strong critical protest. His works include, for piano, *Pavane pour une infante défunte* (1899), *Valses nobles et sentimentales* (1911), and *Le Tombeau de Couperin* (1914–17), which were all later orchestrated, the suite *Gaspard de la nuit* (1908), and two piano concertos (one for left hand alone); for orchestra, *La Valse* (1920), *Boléro* (1927), and the ballet *Daphnis and Chloe* (1909–12); the opera *L'Enfant et les sortilèges* (1920–25); many songs; and an orchestration (1922) of Mussorgski's *Pictures at an Exhibition*.

raven A large glossy black crow, *Corvus corax*, about 25 in (63 cm) long with bristling feathers at the throat, a massive bill, and a wedge-shaped tail.

It feeds on carrion, small animals, seeds, and fruits and often roosts in large colonies. Ravens occur in mountain and moorland regions of the N hemisphere where numbers are increasing again after being almost exterminated.

Ravenna 44 25N 12 12E A city and port in N Italy, in Emilia-Romagna, connected to the Adriatic Sea by canal. Ravenna is said to have been founded by the Sabines. It was the capital of the western Roman Empire (402–76 AD), of the Ostrogothic kings (476–526), and of the Byzantine exarchate (military governorship) from 584 to 751. It is noted for its ancient mosaics. Today Ravenna is a growing industrial center, based principally on oil and natural-gas refining. Population (1980 est): 139,662.

Ravi River A river in NW India and Pakistan, one of the five rivers of the Punjab. Rising in the Himalayas, it flows W and SW to join the Chenab River. Length: 450 mi (724 km).

Rawalpindi 33 40N 73 08E A city in N Pakistan, 9 mi (14 km) SW of the national capital, Islamabad. From 1959 until 1969 it acted as the interim capital while the new capital at Islamabad was being built. Rawalpindi is an important military, commercial, and trading center with varied industries, including oil refining, chemicals, and railroad engineering. Population (1972): 615,392.

Rawlings, Marjorie (Kinnan) (1896–1953) US author. At first a journalist (1918–28), she became a Florida orange farmer and devoted her spare time to writing. *South Moon Under* (1933) preceded *The Yearling* (1938), which brought her a Pulitzer Prize in 1939 and which became a classic motion picture in 1946. Other works include the novels *Golden Apples* (1935) and *The Sojourner* (1953); a short story collection, *When the Whippoorwill* (1940); and an autobiographical work, *Cross Creek Cookery* (1942).

Rawlinson, Sir Henry Creswicke (1810–95) British orientalist. As an army officer and later consul at Baghdad, Rawlinson tried for years (1835–46) to obtain a complete copy of the trilingual *cuneiform text carved (516 BC) by Darius I on the sheer rock face at Behistun (Iran). He eventually deciphered two of its three scripts: Old Persian (1847) and Babylonian (1857).

Rawsthorne, Alan (1905–71) British composer. He studied in Manchester and Berlin and gained attention with his *Symphonic Studies* (1938) at a festival in Warsaw. His works include three symphonies, various concertos, a ballet, chamber music, and some film music.

ray A predominantly marine *cartilaginous fish of the worldwide order *Batoidea* (or *Rajiformes*; about 350 species). Rays have a flattened head and body with greatly enlarged winglike pectoral fins; the tapering tail often bears sharp poison spines. The mouth and gill slits are ventral and a pair of openings (spiracles), located behind the dorsally situated eyes, are used to take in water for respiration. Rays are generally bottom-dwelling and move using their pectoral fins. They feed mainly on fish and invertebrates. Subclass: *Elasmobranchii*. □fish.

Ray, John (1627–1705) English naturalist, who originated basic principles of plant classification. After compiling a survey of English plants, Ray's botanical studies culminated in his *Historia plantarum* (3 vols, 1686–1704). This was followed by works on birds, fishes, quadrupeds, and insects. Ray made the important taxonomic distinction between monocotyledonous and dicotyledonous plants and established the species as the basic taxonomic unit. He emphasized the importance of internal anatomy as a taxonomic criterion.

Ray, Man (1890–) The pseudonym of a US artist and photographer, whose real name is unknown. He first achieved prominence as cofounder with *Duchamp of the New York *dada movement (1917) and for his ready-mades, notably his iron armed with nails and ironically called *The Gift* (1921). After moving to Paris (1921), where he was associated with *surrealism, he became highly successful as a portrait and fashion photographer.

Ray, Satyajit (1921–) Indian film director. He achieved an international reputation with *Pather Panchali* (1955), *The Unvanquished* (1956), and *The World of Apu* (1959), a trilogy of films about social change in modern India. His other films, all characterized by a humanistic understanding of both eastern and western values, include *Days and Nights in the Forest* (1970), *The Chess Players* (1977), and *The Home and the World* (1984).

Rayburn, Sam (Samuel Taliaferro R.; 1882–1961) US politician. A member of the US House of Representatives (1913–61) as a Democrat from Texas, he served as Speaker of the House (1940–47; 1949–53; 1955–61), the longest of any speaker. He was known for his support of

*New Deal legislation, knowledge of rules and procedures, and quiet, but effective, vote-mustering.

Rayleigh, John William Strutt, 3rd Baron (1842–1919) British physicist. His work on black-body radiation was upset by *Planck's discovery of the quantum theory but he did much valuable work in optics, hydrodynamics, and the theory of electrical units. He was awarded the 1904 Nobel Prize for his discovery of argon, in conjunction with Sir William *Ramsay.

rayon A textile fiber or fabric made from *cellulose. **Viscose rayon** is made by dissolving wood pulp in a mixture of sodium hydroxide and carbon disulfide. The fibers are reconstituted in an acid bath. **Acetate rayon** is made by mixing wood pulp with acetic anhydride, acetic acid, and sulfuric acid to form cellulose acetate, which is then dissolved in a solvent and forced through fine holes to form fibers as the solvent evaporates.

Razi ar- (*or* Rhazes; c. 865–c. 928 AD) Persian physician and philosopher. In his *Comprehensive Book*, he surveyed the medical knowledge of the Greeks, Syrians, and Arabs and he wrote works on alchemy, philosophy, and diseases, such as smallpox and measles.

Razin, Stenka (d. 1671) Cossack leader. From 1667 to 1669 Razin led a group of propertyless Cossacks in raids along the Volga River and the Caspian Sea. In 1670 Razin commanded a revolt against the tsar and was executed after his capture.

RAZORBILL *Formerly killed for its feathers and used for bait by fishermen, this bird is now a protected species. The largest of the auks, it often nests on cliff tops.*

razorbill A black-and-white *auk, *Alca torda*, that breeds around N Atlantic coasts and winters in the Mediterranean. 16 in (40 cm) long, it has a laterally compressed bill. The wings are used as paddles in diving to catch fish, shellfish, and worms.

razor shell A burrowing *bivalve mollusk of the family *Solenidae* (about 40 species), also called a jack-knife clam, of Atlantic and Pacific coasts. The common razor (*Ensis siliqua*), about 6 in (15 cm) long, has a narrow □shell with squared ends; its curved foot is used to burrow up to 12 in (30 cm) into sand.

reactance. *See* impedance.

Read, Sir Herbert (1893–1968) British poet and critic. The son of a Yorkshire farmer, he served as an infantry officer in World War I, and his war poetry constitutes a large proportion of his *Collected Poems* (1966). His art criticism, written from the basis of a personal philosophy of anarchism, promoted the work of Henry *Moore and many other artists of his generation. His literary criticism was chiefly concerned with the Romantic poets.

Reade, Charles (1814–84) British novelist. His best-known novel is the historical romance *The Cloister and the Hearth* (1861), set in Europe during the Reformation. His other novels are chiefly concerned with topical social issues.

Reading 51 28N 0 59W A city in S England, the administrative center of Berkshire on the River Thames. It has the remains of a 12th-century Benedictine abbey and a university (1892). An important railroad junction, Reading has light engineering and electronics works and is the headquarters of several international industries. Population (1981): 123,731.

Reading 40 20N 75 55W A city in E Pennsylvania. It grew as an iron and steel center, linked by canal and rail to nearby anthracite mines. Industries today include the manufacture of bricks, speciality steels, and textiles. Population (1980): 78,686.

ready-made An everyday manufactured object elevated to artistic status by the personal whim of the artist. The *dada painter Marcel *Duchamp produced the first ready-made, a bicycle wheel on a stool, in 1913; it was followed by his snow shovel (1915), and his notorious urinal (1917). The ready-made is also a feature of *surrealism and *pop art.

RONALD REAGAN *President whose conservative policies helped end a recession and who was overwhelmingly reelected in 1984.*

Reagan, Ronald (1911–) US statesman; 40th President of the United States (1981–). Beginning his professional career as an actor, Reagan appeared in more than 50 films and twice served as president of one of the most important film labor organizations, The Screen Actors' Guild (1947–52, 1959–60). Reagan became increasingly involved in politics during the early 1960s and although he was formerly a liberal Democrat, he joined the Republican Party in 1962. After serving two terms as governor of California (1966–74), he campaigned unsuccessfully for the Republican presidential nomination in 1976. Four years later, however, he gained the nomination and defeated incumbent President Jimmy *Carter. Reagan began his administration with a series of sweeping economic reforms designed to reduce the growth of federal social programs, but he was also committed to expanding the nation's defense capabilities. The Reagan foreign policy was characterized by a hard line toward the Soviet Union and active military intervention in Central America, the Caribbean, and the Middle East. Early in 1981 he survived an assassination attempt. In 1984 he was re-elected in a sweeping victory over Democrat Walter *Mondale.

realism **1.** The medieval philosophical theory that general terms (called universals) have a real existence, that is that there is some abstract entity that corresponds with the term. For example, blueness is not just one idea of the sum of all blue objects (called particulars), but a really existing entity. *Plato and *Aristotle were realists in believing that the universe contained universals in addition to particulars. The difference between them was that Plato thought universals, which he called Forms, merely could have corresponding particulars and were independent of them, while Aristotle thought that Forms must have particulars and could exist only as instantiated in things. *Aquinas and *Duns Scotus were leading realists. *Compare* nominalism. **2.** In modern philosophy, a stance opposed to *idealism. Realists, such as G. E. *Moore (*see also* common sense, philosophy of), assert that objects exist independently of being perceived. Mathematical realism implies that mathematical entities exist in this way as well and that mathematical truths are independent of our ability to prove them.

real tennis. *See* court tennis.

Réaumur, René-Antoine Ferchault de (1683–1757) French physicist, whose work on thermometers led him to devise the temperature scale that bears his name. On this scale water freezes at 0° and boils at 80°. He also carried out experiments on animals to show that digestion was a chemical process and not, as certain scientists believed, a mechanical one.

Rebellion of 1837 Canadian uprising against British rule and lack of French-Canadian autonomy. Led by Louis *Papineau and William *Mackenzie, the two-year rebellion, although unsuccessful, resulted in the Durham Report (1839) and the *Act of Union (1841). *See also* Durham, John George Lambton, 1st Earl of.

Reber, Grote (1911–) US astronomer, who, following *Jansky's discovery, built the first radio telescope (1937) and used it to discover a number of radio sources that had no visible counterparts. It was largely as a result of his published observations that several large radio telescopes were built after World War II.

recall A political device designed to enable voters dissatisfied with an elected official to replace him before the expiration of his term of office. The recall originated in Switzerland and has been operative in a number of US states since 1903. The usual procedure is the securing of a petition stating the charges against the official, the holding of an election to determine whether the official shall be removed, and the choice of a successor. Usually the official is allowed space on the ballot or petition in which to state his defense.

Recamier, Jeanne Françoise Julie Adelaide (1777–1849) French society hostess. She was married to a wealthy Parisian banker from 1792 to 1830. Her salon was attended by influential statesmen and politicians opposed to Napoleon. Her close friends included Mme de *Staël and *Chateaubriand.

recession A decline in the *trade cycle that, in a serious setback to the economy, becomes a transitory phase between *boom and *depression. In a recession, consumption demand falls off, investment (according to the *accelerator principle) suffers a decline, and business failures become more common.

recessive gene The *allele of a gene the function of which is hidden when the organism concerned is crossed with one carrying a different allele (called the dominant allele) for the same gene. *See* dominance.

Recife (*or* Pernambuco) 8 06S 34 53W A port in NE Brazil, the capital of Pernambuco state on the Atlantic Ocean. It is a major port; the chief exports are sugar and cotton. Industries include sugar refining and spirit distilling and it has two universities. Population (1980): 1,184,215.

Recklinghausen 51 37N 7 11E A city in NW West Germany, in North Rhine-Westphalia in the *Ruhr. Notable buildings include the 13th-century church (founded 1276) and the castle (1702). A port on the Rhine-Herne Canal, its manufactures include iron and steel, machinery, and textiles. Population (1980 est): 119,600.

Reconstruction (1865–77) The period after the *Civil War during which the defeated *Confederate states were brought back into the Union. Despite the intentions of President Abraham *Lincoln to offer the South a generous peace settlement and an honorable readmission to the Union, the Radical Republicans, led by Secretary of War Edwin *Stanton, insisted on severe measures after Lincoln's assassination in 1865. When President Andrew *Johnson announced his intention to adopt Lincoln's Reconstruction plans, intense opposition arose in Congress. Johnson immediately recognized the governments of Arkansas, Louisiana, Tennessee, and Virginia and had established provisional governments in the other seven Confederate states by early 1866. The Radical Republicans in Congress refused to acknowledge the president's action and overrode Johnson's veto to enact a law establishing five southern military districts subject to martial law. The conflict between the president and Congress led to Johnson's impeachment by the House of Representatives in 1868. However, he was acquitted in a trial before the Senate. Under Johnson's successor as president, Ulysses S. *Grant, the system of military districts was abolished and all of the southern states were readmitted to the Union, after accepting the 14th and 15th Amendments to the US Constitution, which guaranteed full citizenship and voting rights to former slaves. These Reconstruction state governments were controlled by Radical Republicans and their political allies, some of whom were actually transplanted northerners known as "carpetbaggers." The Reconstruction period formally ended with the withdrawal of federal troops from the South in 1877.

recorder (law). *See* judge.

recorder (music) A woodwind instrument of medieval origin, much used in music of the 17th and 18th centuries and revived in the 20th century. In contrast to the side-blown *flute, the recorder is end-blown, through a whistle mouthpiece mounted in a block (*or* fipple). The holes are covered with the fingers; the tone is quieter than that of the flute.

recording of sound A system for storing and reproducing sound. In music recording, the most common methods are tape recording, usually in *cassette form, and phonograph disks. The phonograph record is made by converting the sound into an electrical signal, which is normally temporarily stored on tape. This signal is amplified and used to control a cutter that produces a spiral undulating groove in a master disk. Plastic (vinyl) copies of this are mass-produced for sale. In a record-player, the stylus travels along the groove and reproduces the mechanical vibrations of the cutter. The *pick-up then converts these to an electrical signal, which is amplified and fed to a loudspeaker. Many electronic devices are used to ensure that the system will reproduce the original sound with a high fidelity, i.e. that sounds in the frequency range 80–12,000 hertz are reproduced without distortion. In **digital recording** the musical signal itself is not transmitted or recorded. Instead the signal is sampled, up to 30,000 times per second, and the characteristics of the sampled signal are represented by digits (as information is represented in a computer). The digits are then transmitted or recorded and reconstituted in the receiver or player. In this way the actual signal suffers no interference or distortion during transmission or in the recording process. The method is used when very high fidelity is required.

rectifier A device that allows electric current to flow in one direction only; it is generally used to convert alternating current to direct current. *Semiconductor diodes have now replaced thermionic valves (diodes) for lower voltage applications. For power supplies of several megawatts, mercury-arc rectifiers are used.

rectum. *See* intestine.

recycling The repeated use of the same resources. Recycling involves the manufacture of a complex product followed by breakdown of the spent product to release its constituents for reuse. This process—a feature of most natural *ecosystems—is becoming an economic necessity in industry in order to conserve scarce raw materials and reduce the quantities of waste products, which may cause pollution of the environment. Steel scrap, waste paper, and chemical solvents are often recycled.

red admiral A butterfly, *Vanessa atalanta*, found throughout Europe, Asia, and North America. The wings are black with red and white markings. Red admirals migrate to northern regions for the summer but do not survive the cold winters there; in warmer climates they hibernate. The caterpillars feed mainly on stinging nettles. Family: *Nymphalidae*.

red algae *Algae of the division *Rhodophyta* (about 3000 species), which are usually red or blue in color due to the presence of the pigments phycoerythrin (red) or phycocyanin (blue), which mask the green chlorophyll. They range from small unicellular or filamentous forms to branching or sheetlike *seaweeds, found mainly attached to other plants in deep warm seas or sometimes in rock pools. Reproduction is asexual or sexual.

Red Brigades (Italian name: Brigate Rosse) A group of Italian terrorists formed in 1969 and dedicated to the violent overthrow of capitalist society. They were responsible for the murder of the statesman Aldo Moro in 1978. Several of their leading members have been apprehended and sentenced to prison.

Red Cross, International An organization founded by the Geneva Convention of 1864 to provide care for the casualties of war. Inspired by Henri *Dunant, a Swiss philanthropist, its headquarters are in Geneva and its emblem, the red cross, represents the Swiss flag with its colors reversed. Muslim countries, however, have generally adopted the crescent as their emblem. The International Red Cross, which is staffed mainly by volunteers, has twice won the Nobel Peace Prize, in 1917 and 1944. National branches include the **American Red Cross**.

redcurrant A shrub of the genus *Ribes* (see currant), cultivated for its clusters of small acid-tasting red fruits, which may be made into jellies, jams, etc. Cultivated redcurrants have been derived from *R. rubrum* of Eurasia, *R. sativum* of W Europe, and *R. petraeum* of central and S Europe; they grow up to 7 ft (2 m) high. Whitecurrants are varieties that lack red pigment.

red deer A large reddish-brown deer, *Cervus elaphus*, of European and Asian woodlands. Over 48 in (120 cm) high at the shoulder, males have spreading branched antlers up to 50 in (125 cm) long; females are more lightly built. Stags and hinds live apart in spring and summer, coming together in the autumn for the rut, when mature males compete to gather a harem of hinds. As winter comes, stags and pregnant hinds separate. *See also* wapiti.

Redditch 52 19N 1 56W A city in the English Midlands, in Hereford and Worcester. It manufactures metal goods including fishing tackle and springs. Population (1981): 66,854.

Redford, Robert (1936–) US film actor. He costarred with Paul *Newman in *Butch Cassidy and the Sundance Kid* (1969) and *The Sting* (1973). His other films include *The Candidate* (1972) and *All the President's Men* (1976), as well as *Ordinary People* (1981), which he directed.

red fox A *fox, *Vulpes vulpes*, found throughout the N hemisphere. It is about 40 in (100 cm) long, including its bushy tail (20 in [50 cm]). There are a number of local races and the North American red fox and its gray-black variety, the silver fox, were once thought to be a separate species (*V. fulva*).

red giant A greatly distended cool but very luminous star, often variable in nature. It is one of the final evolutionary stages of a normal *star, attained when its central hydrogen has been converted to helium. Hydrogen burning in a shell surrounding the inert helium core causes a rapid expansion and cooling of the outer atmosphere of the star.

Redgrave, Sir Michael (1908–85) British Shakespearean actor, who has also performed in and directed modern plays. His films include *The Browning Version* (1951) and *The Go-Between* (1971). His daughter **Vanessa Redgrave** (1937–) has acted on stage and in a number of films including *Morgan* (1966), *Blow-Up* (1967), and *Julia* (1977), and is well known for her left-wing political activities. His daughter **Lynn Redgrave** (1944–) is also an actress.

red grouse A *grouse, *Lagopus lagopus scoticus*, found on moorlands of Great Britain and Ireland, where it is managed as a gamebird. 13–15 in (34–37 cm) long, it feeds chiefly on ling heather. The male is red-brown with red wattles above the eyes and the female is browner and heavily barred: both sexes have white underwing markings and white feathered feet.

Red Guards High-school and university students organized by Mao Tse-tung during the *Cultural Revolution (1966–68) to eliminate revisionism. The Red Guards destroyed property, humiliated foreign diplomats, and attacked those officials who opposed Mao's policies.

red-hot poker A plant of the African genus *Kniphofia*, especially *K. uvaria* and *K. rufa* (and their varieties), cultivated as garden plants. 18–47 in (45–120 cm) tall, they have long reedlike leaves and dense heads of tubular flowers, usually scarlet and/or yellow. Family: *Liliaceae*.

Redmond, John Edward (1856–1918) Irish politician. A member of parliament from 1881, in 1900 he reunited the pro- and anti-Parnellite factions under his leadership. In 1909 he allied his party with the Liberals to achieve *Home Rule. The rise of *Sinn Féin undermined the appeal of his moderate policies.

red mullet A fish, also called surmullet or goatfish, belonging to the family *Mullidae* (about 50 species), found usually in shallow warm seas. They have an elongated body, up to 10 in (25 cm) long, with two dorsal fins and two long flexible chin barbels. They feed on bottom-dwelling invertebrates and many species are valued food fish. Order: *Perciformes*.

Redon, Odilon (1840–1916) French symbolist painter and lithographer; a forerunner of *surrealism. Working exclusively in black and white in charcoal drawings, lithographs, and etchings until the 1890s, he created a fantasy world of plants with human heads, mythical figures, etc. From the 1890s he turned to oil painting and pastel, producing a number of flower paintings in powdery colors and paintings inspired by literary subjects.

Redouté, Pierre Joseph (1759–1841) French flower painter. He worked for all the French courts from Louis XV to Louis Philippe, painting his flowers, notably roses, chiefly in watercolors and after careful scientific study.

redox reactions. See oxidation and reduction.

redpoll A tiny finch, *Acanthis flammea*, about 5 in (12 cm) long with a brown streaked plumage, a red crown, and a black chin. The male has a red breast in summer. It breeds in the Arctic tundra and high mountains of Europe, migrating to central Europe and the N US in winter.

Red River (Vietnamese name: Song Hong) The chief river of N Vietnam, rising in S China and flowing SE to enter the Gulf of Tonkin via an extensive delta. Length: 310 mi (500 km).

Red River A river that flows from N Texas E into SW Oklahoma and forms the Texas-Oklahoma and Texas-Arkansas border before flowing S through Arkansas and SW through Louisiana, where it joins the Mississippi River above Baton Rouge. At its beginning it flows through red clay plains that color the water and gave the river its name. Lakes formed by

dams, such as Lake Texoma in S Oklahoma, were created for flood control. Length: 1018 mi (1639 km).

ODILON REDON *One of a set of six lithographs entitled* La Nuit.

Red River of the North (*or* Red River) A river in central North America, rising in W Minnesota and flowing N into Canada to empty into Lake Winnipeg. Although navigable, it is subject to severe floods that damage the farms of its fertile valley. Length: 621 mi (1000 km).

Red River Settlement A colony of immigrants led by Thomas Douglas, 5th Earl of Selkirk (1771–1820), settled in 1811 on the banks of the Red River in present-day Manitoba. In 1836 it was bought by the Hudson's Bay Company. In 1869 Louis *Riel led an uprising against the proposed transfer of the colony from the Company to Canada. The revolution was unsuccessful, and the transfer took place in 1870.

red salmon. See sockeye salmon.

Red Sea A long narrow arm of the Indian Ocean between Africa and Asia, extending some 1490 mi (2400 km) NNW beyond the Gulf of Aden and the Bab el-Mandeb. In the N, it is connected to the Mediterranean Sea by the Suez Canal, which has enormously increased shipping in the Red Sea. It is part of the *Great Rift Valley. Area: 169,076 sq mi (438,000 sq km).

redshank An Old World *sandpiper, *Tringa totanus*, that breeds in cool marshy regions of Eurasia. 12 in (30 cm) long, it has long reddish legs, a black-tipped red bill, and a brown-gray plumage with a white rump. It winters on mudflats of Africa and Asia, feeding on crustaceans, mollusks, and ragworms.

redshift An overall displacement toward larger wavelengths of the spectral lines of a celestial object. Its astronomical significance was suggested by Edwin *Hubble in 1929, when it was used as the basis of the theory that the universe is expanding (see expanding universe). A redshift usually arises from the *Doppler effect, that is from recession of a celestial object. It increases as the object's radial velocity increases and for an extragalactic body can be used as a measure of distance. A **gravitational redshift** occurs whenever radiation is emitted by a body: it is generally negligible except when the gravitational field is very strong.

red squirrel A tree *squirrel, *Sciurus vulgaris*, of Eurasia. About 8 in (20 cm) long with an 8-in (20-cm) tail, red squirrels have dark glossy red fur and tufted ears. They feed mainly on seeds and nuts but will eat buds and dried fungi in winter. They are less aggressive than the immigrant gray squirrels, which have displaced them in many areas.

redstart A small North American wood warbler of the genus *Setophago ruticilla* about 4.5–5.5 in (11–14 cm) long. The male redstart is black with a white belly and orange-patched wings and fanning tail. The female is olve-brown with a white belly and yellow-patched wings and tail. It is found in woodland and thickets from SE Alaska to S US. This species migrates to Central and South America for the winter.

reduction. *See* oxidation and reduction.

reductionism A 20th-century trend in philosophy prompted by skepticism. Reductionists argue that material objects are nothing but collections of sensations; other minds are nothing but the physical manifestations of their owners; statements about the past are nothing but aggregates of statements about the presently available evidence for them. Reduction of the meaning of a statement to statements of the evidence for it was popular among phenomenalists and logical positivists.

redwing A North American bird (*Agelaius phoeniceus*, about 7.5–9.5 in (19–24 cm) long, resembling a blackbird with red patches on the wings. The female is brownish, with heavy striping and a sharply pointed bill. Redwings breed mainly in swampy areas from E Canada to S US, migrating to Central America for the winter.

redwood A coniferous tree, *Sequoia sempervirens*, thought to be the tallest tree in the world and one of the longest lived: a specimen in California is over 364 ft (111 m) tall and some Californian trees are over 2000 years old. Also called coast redwood, it is native to the Pacific coast between Oregon and California and is an important timber tree in North America; in Europe it is planted mainly for ornament. It has brown-red fibrous bark, bladelike leaves, 0.6–0.8 in (1.5–2 cm) long, in two rows along the stems, and woody red-brown globular cones, about 0.8 in (2 cm) long. Family: *Taxodiaceae*. *See also* dawn redwood; sequoia.

Redwood National Park A national park in NW California, along the Pacific coast. Some of the world's tallest trees, more than 350 ft (110 m) tall, are here. The park was established in 1968 and expanded in 1978 to preserve a coastal species of redwood tree. Included in the park is 30 mi (48 km) of seashore. Area: 166 sq mi (429 sq km).

reed Any of several species of tall aquatic grasses, especially those of the genus *Phragmites* (2–3 species). The common reed (*P. communis*) has a creeping underground stem (rhizome) and grows worldwide along the margins of marshes, lakes, streams, and fens. 5–10 ft (1.5–3 m) tall, it has long flat leaves, 0.4–0.8 in (10–20 mm) wide, a stiff smooth stem, and clusters of purple-brown flowers. Dried reed stems have been used for arrows, basketry, pens, and in musical instruments.
The name is also given to similar but unrelated plants, such as the paper reed, *Cyperus papyrus* (see papyrus).

Reed, Sir Carol (1906–76) British film director. His best-known films include *The Fallen Idol* (1948) and *The Third Man* (1949) both with screenplays by Graham *Greene. His later, more commercial, films include *The Agony and the Ecstasy* (1965) and *Oliver!* (1968).

Reed, John (1887–1920) US journalist. He helped found the Communist Labor party in the US and was a personal friend of Lenin. *Ten Days that Shook the World* (1919) is an account of the 1917 Revolution in Russia, where he died.

Reed, Stanley Forman (1884–1980) US jurist; associate justice of the Supreme Court (1938–57). He served as general counsel to the Federal Farm Board (1929–32) and the Reconstruction Finance Corporation (1932–35), and as solicitor general (1935–38) before being appointed to the Supreme Court in 1938. Opposed to censorship and an advocate of civil rights, he was usually a part of the court's liberal faction.

Reed, Walter (1851–1902) US physician. After serving as an army surgeon, Reed was appointed to investigate yellow fever in Cuba, where C. J. *Finlay had suggested that the mosquito was the agent responsible for spreading the disease. Reed and his team subjected themselves to the bites of infected mosquitoes, one of the team dying as a result, but thereby proving that mosquitoes were responsible. Subsequent control of mosquito populations eliminated yellow fever from the region.

reedbuck An African antelope belonging to the genus *Redunca* (3 species). The common reedbuck (*R. arundinium*) grows to 35 in (90 cm) high at the shoulder and has a stiff gray coat and slender ridged horns and inhabits lush grassland. The bohor reedbuck (*R. redunca*) is smaller and lives in swampy regions, while the gregarious mountain reedbuck (*R. fulvorufula*) lives in hilly areas.

reed instruments Musical instruments in which a column of air is made to vibrate by a reed. The *clarinet family have a single (*or* beating) reed clamped to and vibrating against a slot in the mouthpiece. The *oboe and *bassoon use a double reed, the two halves bound together and forming the mouthpiece. The **reed organ** family contains such instruments as the *harmonium, *concertina, *accordion, and *harmonica, which have free reeds (sometimes made of some other substance, such as brass) that vibrate from side to side of the slot in which they are fixed.

reedling A Eurasian bird, *Panurus biarmicus*, about 6.3 in (16 cm) long, also called bearded tit. It lives in reedbeds, feeding on insects and seeds. The plumage is brown with pale underparts: the male has a gray head with a black moustache of feathers. Reedlings belong to the *babbler family.

reedmace A widely distributed perennial herbaceous plant, *Typha latifolia*, also called bulrush or cat's-tail, growing in reed swamps. It has an erect stem, 5–8.5 ft (1.5–2.5 m) high, bearing a terminal spike of male and female flowers, the latter developing into the cylindrical fruit, which tapers into the stem at its base. There are several other reedmaces of the genus *Typha* (see elephant grass). Family: *Typhaceae*.

reed warbler An acrobatic *warbler, *Acrocephalus scirpaeus*, about 5 in (12 cm) long with a reddish-brown plumage, pale underparts, and a pale eyestripe. It winters in SE Africa and breeds in European reedswamps, building a deep nest around the stems of several reeds and feeding on small marsh insects. It is frequently parasitized by cuckoos.

reef A ridge of rock lying just above or near the surface of the sea, built mainly of the skeletons of *coral or other sedentary marine organisms. **Barrier reefs** lie parallel to the coast with a deep lagoon between; **fringing reefs** are attached to the coast; bioherms are dome-shaped reefs; apron reefs are tabular masses; atolls are circular with a central lagoon. Reef formation was much more widespread in the geological past.

referendum and initiative Votes on specific legislation by the whole electorate. Referendums are votes on particular governmental questions and appear on the ballot during elections of public officials. Initiatives are proposals, drafted by a citizen or group of citizens, that by virtue of attaining a requisite number of signatures on a petition are put to the electorate for acceptance or rejection. Initiatives are used in about half of the states to decide matters of local government. *See also* plebiscite.

reflection The rebounding of a wave of light or other radiation when it strikes a surface. Reflected light obeys two laws: first, the normal (an imaginary line vertical to the surface at the point of impact), the incident ray, and the reflected rays all lie in the same plane; second, the angle of incidence (i.e. the angle between the incident ray and the normal) is equal to the angle of reflection. *See also* mirrors.

reflex An automatic and involuntary response by an organism to a change in the environment. An example is the rapid withdrawal of a finger in response to a pinprick, which occurs before the brain has had time to convey the necessary information to the muscles involved. *See also* conditioned reflex.

Reform Acts The legislation that reformed the British parliamentary system. The Reform Act of 1832 extended the franchise and gave parliamentary representation to new industrial towns, such as Birmingham and Manchester. However, it did not destroy the dominance over the electoral system by the landed classes. The 1867 Reform Act enfranchised many of the working class for the first time. It doubled the existing electorate to 2.4 million. The 1884 Reform Act increased the electorate to about five million. Adult male suffrage was achieved only in 1918 and women had to wait until 1928.

Reformation A religious movement in 16th-century Europe that began as an attempt to reform the *Roman Catholic Church and ended with the establishment of independent Protestant Churches (*see* Protestantism). The Reformation, which was preceded by such reform movements as those led by John *Wycliffe (the *Lollards) and Jan *Hus (the *Hussites), was caused by the inability of the Catholic Church to put its own, increasingly worldly, house in order; the critical examination of the Bible emphasized by the humanists (*see* humanism) and its translation into the vernaculars; the development of printing, which disseminated new ideas more widely and more quickly; and the growth of nationalism, which sought to weaken papal jurisdiction within the states of W Europe.
The Reformation began on October 31, 1517, when Martin *Luther nailed his 95 theses on the door of the castle church at Wittenburg. Luther's attack on the sale of *indulgences and, subsequently, on papal authority and the *sacraments (except baptism and the Eucharist) was condemned by the pope and the Holy Roman Emperor but gained the support of several German princes. The consequent conflict (*see* Charles V) was not resolved until 1555 (*see* Augsburg, Peace of).

In Switzerland, the Reformation was initiated by *Zwingli in Zurich in 1520, spreading to Basle, Berne, and also to Geneva, where it was led by John *Calvin. Calvinism was adopted in France, the Low Countries, England, Scotland, and subsequently in North America. In France, where Protestants were called Huguenots, the Reformation became involved in a political struggle for control of the crown, giving rise to the *Wars of Religion, and in the Low Countries it fired the *Revolt of the Netherlands against Spanish rule.

In England, Protestantism finally became the established *Church of England under Elizabeth I. Elsewhere in Europe Lutheranism was adopted by Sweden in 1527, by Denmark in 1546, and also became the established religions of Norway, Finland, and Iceland. *See also* Counter-Reformation.

Reformed Churches. *See* Protestantism.

Reform Judaism A religious movement attempting to adapt traditional Judaism to modern circumstances. It began in Germany in the early 19th century. The Liberal movement (founded 1903) instituted more radical reforms typical of US Reform Judaism. The World Union for Progressive Judaism, founded in London in 1926, is now based in Jerusalem. The reforms include abolition of many of the ritual laws, acceptance of modern biblical criticism, vernacular services, and full equality for women.

refraction The bending of a beam of radiation as it passes from one medium onto another. For a light ray the amount by which it is bent depends on the angle of the incident ray and on the refractive indices of the two media, the exact dependence being given by *Snell's law. Refraction is caused by the difference in the velocity of the radiation in the two media. The ratio of the velocity of light in the two media is known as the **refractive index**. If the first medium is a vacuum, the ratio is known as the absolute refractive index of the second medium. The refractive index of glass lies between 1.5 and 1.7, for diamond it is 2.1, and for water 1.33 (at 77°F [25°C]).

refractories Firebricks or other heat-resisting materials used for lining furnaces to retain the heat and protect the outer shell of the furnace. There are three types, characterized by their chemical interaction with the hot substances in the furnace: acid (e.g. silica); basic (e.g. dolomite); and neutral (e.g. carborundum).

refrigeration The process of lowering the temperature inside a closed insulated container. In the domestic refrigerator the method most commonly used is the vapor-compression cycle in which a liquid refrigerant, such as Freon (a compound of chlorine, fluorine, and carbon), is pumped through cooling coils formed into the ice-making compartment. In these coils the refrigerant evaporates, taking the latent heat required to make it into a gas from the surroundings (i.e. the inside of the ice compartment). It is then passed to an electrically driven compressor; after compression it condenses back to liquid, when the absorbed heat is given out (usually at the back of the refrigerator). This cycle is repeated over and over again until the required temperature (about 34–36°F [1–2°C] in the food chamber and 5°F (−15°C) in the deep-freeze compartment) is achieved. The compressor is then switched on and off by the thermostat. Other cycles (e.g. ammonia absorption) are also used, but in all of them the refrigerator functions as a heat engine in reverse: in order to transfer heat from the cold interior to the warmer surrounding air, work must be done. In the vapor-compression refrigerator this is supplied by the electricity that drives the compressor. *See also* cold storage; freezing.

Regency style An English decorative style fashionable from about 1800 to 1830 and influenced by the French *Empire style. Dark exotic woods and veneers, such as rosewood, were popular and were set off by ormolu mounts and grilles for doors. Leading designers produced rather heavy furniture purporting to derive from antique Greek, Roman, and Egyptian models. Concurrently there was a vogue for oriental motifs (*see* chinoiserie) and some magnificent lacquer was produced. Initially elegant, the style later became somewhat clumsy.

regeneration In biology, the regrowth and development of tissues or organs lost through injury, as a normal process (e.g. during molting), or by any other means. The ability to regenerate is present in all forms of life to some degree: it is particularly well developed in plants and simple animals. Thus, whole plants can regenerate from stem and leaf cuttings and simple animals, such as sponges and planarians, can develop from minute fragments. More complex animals, such as crustaceans, replace lost appendages, while lizards can grow new tails. In mammals regeneration is limited to wound healing and regrowth of peripheral nerve fibers.

Regensburg (English name: Ratisbon) 49 01N 12 07E A city in SE West Germany, in Bavaria at the confluence of the Danube and Regen rivers. Many medieval buildings survived the bombing of World War II, including the gothic cathedral (1275–1524). Its university was established

in 1962. It is a port and commercial and industrial center. *History*: originally a Celtic settlement, it became a Carolingian capital and a prosperous medieval trading center. From 1663 until 1806 the imperial diets (assemblies) were held here. Population (1980 est): 131,800.

Reger, Max (1873–1916) German composer, organist, and teacher. In Leipzig he was director of music at the university (1907–08) and professor of composition at the conservatoire. His vast output includes *Variations and Fugue on a Theme of Mozart* for orchestra and a *Fantasy and Fugue on BACH* for organ.

reggae A style of rock music combining West Indian rhythms and rhythm and blues. It became associated with the Jamaican cult of the Rastafarians and was popular in the US during the early 1970s.

Reggio di Calabria 38 06N 15 39E A seaport in Italy, in Calabria, on the Strait of Messina. It was founded by Greek colonists in the 8th century BC. Fruit, herbs, and oil are exported. Population (1980 est): 181,858.

Reggio nell'Emilia 44 42N 10 37E A city in Italy, in Emilia-Romagna. Dating from Roman times, it was ruled by the Este family (15th–18th centuries) and has a cathedral (rebuilt in the 13th century). The center of a rich agricultural area, its industries include agricultural engineering and meat canning. Population (1980 est): 130,159.

Regina 50 30N 104 38W A city in W Canada, the capital of Saskatchewan. Founded in 1882, it has expanded rapidly since 1945 as a center of agricultural industries, oil refining, and potash production. It houses the University of Regina (1917). Population (1976): 149,593.

Regiomontanus (Johannes Müller; 1436–76) German astronomer and mathematician, who introduced algebra and trigonometry to Germany. He produced a table of trigonometric functions that was printed by Johann Gutenberg and widely used by navigators. He was an ardent follower of *Ptolemy, producing a new translation of his *Almagest*. He also made observations of the sky and drew up a table of planetary motions.

Regnier, Henri François Joseph de (1864–1936) French poet. He published several early collections of Symbolist poetry written in *vers libre*, but in his later and better-known volumes, such as *Les Médailles d'argile* (1900), he reverted to classical forms. He also wrote fiction, mostly historical novels set in the 17th and 18th centuries.

Regulus, Marcus Attilus (died c. 251 BC) Roman general of the first *Punic War. In 256 he defeated the Carthaginian navy, invaded Africa, and overwhelmed the Carthaginians. Rejecting his peace terms, in 255 the Carthaginians utterly defeated Regulus, who was captured and sent to Rome to negotiate peace. Urging continued war, he returned to certain death in Carthage.

Rehnquist, William Hubbs (1924–) US lawyer and jurist; associate justice of the Supreme Court (1971–). After private law practice from 1953 he served as assistant attorney general in charge of the Department of Justice's Office of Legal Counsel (1969–71) before being appointed to the Supreme Court by President Richard M. *Nixon. He was an advocate of law and order and gained a reputation for being unsympathetic to issues favoring civil rights and labor.

Rehoboam King of Judah (c. 922–915 BC); the son of Solomon. His intransigent attitude to the northern tribes resulted in the secession of Israel under Jeroboam and the disintegration of Solomon's empire.

Reich, Wilhelm (1897–1957) US psychiatrist, born in Austria, noted for his controversial notion of a universal energy, which he called orgone, that is released during sexual intercourse. Failure to achieve regular release of this energy resulted, so he claimed, in both personal and social neuroses. Reich's "orgone box" was declared fraudulent and he was jailed for contempt of court in 1956. His works include *The Function of the Orgasm* (1948) and *Character Analysis* (1949).

Reichenberg. *See* Liberec.

Reichstag (Imperial Diet) The legislative assembly of the German Empire (1871–1918) and the Weimar Republic (1919–33). Its origins lay in the diet of the Holy Roman Empire. It was divided into an electoral college (*see* electors), a college of princes, and a college of cities. The decline of imperial control over the German states after the Thirty Years' War brought a corresponding decline in the power of the diet until its revival by Bismarck in 1867 as the representative assembly of the *North German Confederation, then of the German Empire, and finally of the Weimar Republic. In 1933 the Reichstag building was burned out; Nazi allegations of communist responsibility provided an excuse to ban opposition parties, and the Reichstag became a mere puppet under Hitler.

Reid, Thomas (1710–96) Scottish philosopher. He maintained that Hume, in his theory of ideas, had overlooked "common sense," which was to become the cornerstone of his own philosophy. In his *Enquiry into the*

Human Mind on the Principles of Common Sense (1764), he discussed "common sense," in linguistic and metaphysical, as well as mundane, contexts.

Reign of Terror (1793–94) The most violent period of the French Revolution. Dominated by *Robespierre, the governing Committee of Public Safety authorized severe measures against the Revolution's opponents. Over 250,000 suspects were arrested and about 1400 were summarily guillotined. Public reaction caused Robespierre's downfall and execution in July, 1794, thus ending the Terror.

Reims (*or* Rheims) 49 15N 4 02E A city in NE France, in the Marne department. An important Roman town, it was the scene of the coronations of most of the French kings. The magnificent gothic cathedral was badly damaged in World War I but it has gradually been restored. Its university was established in 1969. A center for the marketing of Champagne wines, it has varied manufacturing industries. Population (1975): 183,610.

reincarnation (*or* metempsychosis) The migration of the soul from one body at death and its re-entry into another (human or animal) body. Belief in reincarnation appears in many different cultures, partly because it offers an explanation for the perplexing differences between individuals' characters and destinies, these being ascribable to traces of previous characters and the rewards or punishments for actions in previous lives. The cycle of reincarnation (*samsara*) is fundamental to Hindu, Buddhist, and Jain conceptions of the world, all spiritual effort being directed toward release (*moksa*) from the cycle. *Plato and *Pythagoras also subscribed to reincarnation, but orthodox Christianity rejected it as contrary to belief in the resurrection of the body.

reindeer A large deer, *Rangifer tarandus*, of European and North American tundra (in America it is called a caribou). About 50 in (125 cm) high at the shoulder, reindeer have a gray-brown coat and spreading branched antlers—male antlers are larger with an extra forward point over the face. Reindeer feed mainly on lichens (reindeer moss) but also eat dwarf willow and other shrubs. The small summer groups gather into herds numbering several hundreds for their winter migration southward, at which time their coat fades to a dull white. □mammal.

reindeer moss A gray tufted *lichen, *Cladonia rangiferina*, that is very abundant in Arctic regions, especially Lapland. It has a stalked much-branched body, up to 3 in (8 cm) high, and covers immense areas of tundra, serving as the major food source for reindeer, moose, musk oxen, etc.

Reinhardt, Max (M. Goldmann; 1873–1943) Austrian theater director. His large-scale productions, involving massed crowds and spectacular lighting and scenery, included *Oedipus Rex* in Berlin in 1910 and *The Miracle* in London in 1911. He also directed more conventional theater productions, opera, and a film of *A Midsummer Night's Dream* (1935), and founded the Salzburg Festival in 1920. Fleeing Germany in 1938, he lived in the US.

relative aperture. *See* f-number.

relativistic mass The mass of a body that is moving at a velocity comparable to the *velocity of light. According to the theory of *relativity, if the velocity of the body is v then its mass is $m_0(1 - v^2/c^2)^{-1/2}$ where c is the velocity of light and m_0 the rest mass (the mass when stationary). The relativistic mass of an electron traveling at 99% of the velocity of light is seven times its rest mass.

relativity An important theory proposed by Albert *Einstein. The first part of the theory, published in 1905 and known as the special theory, applies only to motion in which there is no acceleration. The problem that Einstein set out to solve was concerned with the speed at which light travels relative to an observer.

Up to this time it was thought that light traveled through a stationary medium, called the ether, at a constant speed and that its speed relative to an observer could be calculated in the same way as the relative speed of any two moving objects. For example, if one car (A) traveling at 90 mph (145 kmph) on a highway overtakes another (B) traveling at 70 mph (113 kmph), the speed of the two cars relative to each other is 20 mph (32 kmph). In talking about relative speeds it is necessary to be precise about what a particular speed is relative to. Car A's speed relative to car B is 20 mph (32 kmph), but relative to the earth it is 90 mph (145 kmph). Relative to the sun it is about 24 million mph (39 million kmph). Because two American scientists, Michelson and Morley (*see* Michelson–Morley experiment), had shown that light traveled at the same speed whether measured in the direction of the earth's rotation or at right angles to this direction, Einstein suggested that the restriction about relative motion does not apply to light. It always has the same speed of 2.998×10^8 meters per second (186,000 miles per second), irrespective of the motion of the observer. The velocity of light, Einstein said, is absolute.

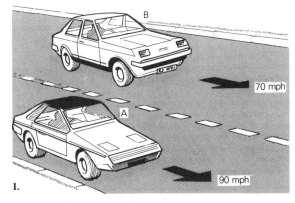

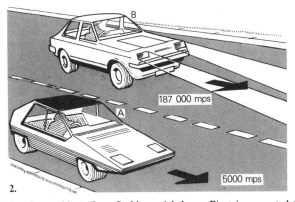

RELATIVITY   **1.** *Two cars, A and B, traveling along a highway. The speed of car A relative to the earth is 90 mph. The speed of car B relative to the earth is 70 mph. The speed of car A relative to car B is 90 – 70 = 20 mph.* **2.** *Car B is now stationary; its headlight beams are turned on as supercar A passes, traveling at 5000 miles per second. The speed of car B's headlight beam relative to car A is 187 000 miles per second (not 187 000 – 5000 miles per second). The velocity of light is absolute.*

This has far-reaching effects. In his special theory Einstein suggested that as bodies increase in speed they become shorter and heavier (see Lorentz, Hendrick). This effect is only noticeable as the speed of light is approached. Cars on the highway do get heavier and shorter but the effect is minute. On the other hand, an electron traveling at 99% of the speed of light becomes seven times heavier than its mass at rest. Einstein also showed that no body could actually travel at the speed of light itself. If it did it would be infinitely heavy and have zero length.

The increase in mass and decrease in length that a body undergoes when moving at high speeds led Einstein to the conclusion that mass (m) and energy (E) are two different aspects of the same thing; they are related by the simple equation $E = mc^2$, where c is the speed of light. The atom bomb and *nuclear energy both depend on this equation.

In the general theory of 1915, Einstein considered accelerated relative motion, especially as it is concerned with gravitation. In this theory, the gravitational force experienced by a body is treated as a property of space and time, which Einstein suggested was "curved" by the presence of the mass. The motion of the stars and planets is controlled by this curvature of space in the vicinity of matter. Light, too, is bent by the gravitational field of a massive body. The observed bending of light rays as they pass close to the sun and the shift of certain lines in the solar *spectrum have provided experimental verification of the theory.

relay, electric An electrical switching device in which one circuit is controlled by a separate circuit, often to avoid the danger of direct contact with high-voltage supplies or to reduce the length of high-current cable needed. Relays may involve mechanical movement and an electromagnetic connection between the two circuits or be controlled entirely by *solid-state electronic components.

relief sculpture A form of sculpture in which figures are attached to a background of stone, bronze, or wood, in contrast to free-standing sculpture seen in the round. There are four main types of relief: high relief, in which the figures project almost as much as free-standing sculptures; middle relief; bas-relief, in which the image is only very slightly raised and of which *Donatello developed a variation in the 15th century; and sunken or coelanaglyphic relief, also called *intaglio, particularly associated with ancient Egyptian sculpture.

reluctance (*or* magnetic resistance)   The ratio of the *magnetomotive force in a material to the total *magnetic flux induced by it. It is analogous to electrical *resistance.

remanence.   *See* ferromagnetism.

Remarque, Erich Maria   (1898–1970) German novelist. After being wounded in World War I, he worked as a journalist until the publication of his immediately successful *All Quiet on the Western Front* (1929), describing life in the trenches. His books banned by the Nazis, he lived in the US and Switzerland from 1932.

REMBRANDT   Self-Portrait Aged 63 *(1669), painted when the great artist was no longer popular.*

Rembrandt (Harmenszoon) van Rijn   (1606–69) Dutch painter and etcher, born in Leiden, the son of a miller. After studying briefly at Leiden University, he became the pupil of Jacob van Swanenburgh (c. 1571–1638) and later in Amsterdam of Pieter Lastman (1583–1633), who trained him in the Italian *baroque style and had a lasting influence on him, for example in encouraging him to paint historical and religious subjects. Settling permanently in Amsterdam (1631), he made his name as a portrait painter with *The Anatomy Lesson of Dr Tulp* (1632), a group portrait. It was followed by many other portraits, including those of his wife Saskia and culminating in the famous group portrait, *The Nightwatch* (1642). He also treated dramatic mythological and biblical subjects. Rembrandt was a popular teacher of painting and at the height of his success was an avid collector of art. He eventually had financial difficulties and became bankrupt, spending approximately the last 20 years of his life isolated from society. Many of his greatest works belong to this period, when he was no longer popular. He concentrated on depicting the inner life of his sitters and the biblical characters he painted. He also excelled as a landscapist and his etchings, which are among the finest ever produced, are remarkable for their freedom of handling.

Remington, Eliphalet   (1793–1863) US inventor and gun manufacturer. His innovations included a method of producing really straight gun barrels and the invention of a lathe for cutting gunstocks. In 1873 the business founded by Remington bought the patent rights of Christopher *Sholes' typewriter.

Remington, Frederic (Sackrider)   (1861–1909) US artist and writer. As a young man he lived and worked in the West. His paintings of the frontier West quickly established him as an illustrator for magazines and books in the 1880s and 1890s. He recorded events in words and pictures during the *Spanish American War (1898). After 1895 he also produced many bronze sculptures, including *The Bronco Buster* (1895), and several books, including *Crooked Trails* (1896), *John Ermine of the Yellowstone* (novel and stage play; 1902), and *The Way of an Indian* (1906).

Remonstrants   The Dutch adherents of Arminianism (*see* Arminius, Jacobus) who rejected the Calvinist doctrine of *predestination in a statement known as the Remonstrance (1610). Condemned by the Synod of Dort (1618–19), they suffered persecution until 1630. Their liberal theology influenced many subsequent Protestant thinkers, including *Locke and John *Wesley.

remora   A dark slender elongated fish, 12–36 in (30–90 cm) long, belonging to a family (*Echeneidae*; 8–10 species) found in warm marine waters. The dorsal fin is modified to form a flat oval sucking disk on its head by which it attaches itself to various marine animals (e.g. sharks and turtles) or ships to feed on scraps of food or the hosts' parasites. Order: *Perciformes.*

Remscheid   51 10N 7 11E A city in NW West Germany, in North Rhine-Westphalia on the Wupper River. An industrial center, it specializes in tool manufacture. It is the birthplace of Roentgen. Population (1980 est): 129,300.

Remus.   *See* Romulus and Remus.

Renaissance   (French: rebirth)   An intellectual and cultural movement that began in Italy in the 14th century, spread to N Europe, and flourished until the mid-16th century. Fundamental to the Renaissance were the revival of classical learning, art, and architecture and the concept of the dignity of man, which characterized *humanism. Both were advocated by the 14th-century poet and classical scholar *Petrarch. Other great writers of the Italian Renaissance were *Dante, *Boccaccio, *Machiavelli, and *Ariosto.

The first painter to mirror these new ideals was *Giotto. He was followed in the 15th century by *Masaccio, *Uccello, *Piero della Francesca, *Mantegna, and others, who helped place art on a scientific basis through their concern with the structure and proportions of the human body. They also introduced into painting the use of linear *perspective, the laws of which were developed by the architect *Brunelleschi. Humanism was reflected in the development of portrait painting and the emphasis upon human feelings in religious painting. The High Renaissance denotes the period between about 1500 and about 1520, when the artists *Leonardo da Vinci, *Raphael, and *Michelangelo were developing the harmony and balance associated with classical art to its highest form.

In sculpture the major figures were Nicola *Pisano, *Donatello, *Ghiberti, *Verrocchio, and Michelangelo. In building Brunelleschi was the first to revive the classical use of the *orders of architecture. Later architects, such as *Bramante, *Alberti, and *Palladio, also revived ancient temples and domed structures. *See also* Italian art.

In the 16th century the Renaissance spread to N Europe, where it manifested itself in the art of *Dürer, the scholarship of *Erasmus, the plays of *Shakespeare, and particularly in the courts of such rulers as Elizabeth I of England, where the ideal of Renaissance civilization was epitomized in the lifestyle of such courtiers as Sir Philip *Sidney.

Renan, (Joseph) Ernest   (1823–92) French philosopher and theologian. Renan's famous *Life of Jesus* (1863) undermined the supernatural aspects of Christ's life and the moral nature of his teachings. It was acclaimed by many romantics, including Oscar *Wilde.

Reni, Guido   (1575–1642) Italian painter, born in Bologna. He studied under the Flemish artist Denis Calvaert (c. 1575–1619) but was chiefly influenced by the *Caracci. In Rome (c. 1600–14) he established a studio and painted his masterpiece, the ceiling fresco of *Aurora.* Later, working mainly in Bologna, his highly idealized style became somewhat sentimental.

renin   An enzyme, secreted by the kidneys, that breaks down a liver protein to form the peptide angiotensin I. This is converted to angiotensin II, which constricts blood vessels—causing a rise in blood pressure—and increases the secretion of *aldosterone from the adrenal glands.

Rennes   48 06N 1 40W A city in NW France, in the Ille-et-Vilaine department. The capital of the old province of Brittany, it was badly damaged by fire in 1720 and most of its notable buildings, including the cathedral and university, were built after that date. The main commercial center of W France, Rennes is an important railroad junction and military headquarters and has textile, electrical, and pharmaceutical industries. Population (1975): 205,733.

rennet An extract, prepared from cows' stomachs, that contains the milk-coagulating enzyme rennin. It is used in the manufacture of cheese and junket.

Reno 39 32N 119 49W A city and resort in W Nevada, near the foot of the Sierra Nevada. Founded about 1860, it is known for its easily obtainable divorces and legalized gambling. The University of Nevada (1864) was moved here from Elko in 1886. Population (1980): 100,756.

Renoir, Pierre Auguste (1841–1919) French impressionist painter, born in Limoges. He trained as a decorator of porcelain before entering (1861) the studio of Charles Gleyre (1808–74) and meeting *Monet, with whom he frequently painted on the banks of the Seine. He exhibited at the first three impressionist exhibitions but largely abandoned impressionism after studying Renaissance art in Italy (1881–82). Increasingly crippled by arthritis, he spent his last years in the south of France, painting many sensuous nudes. His best-known works include *Les Parapluies* and *Le Moulin de la Galette*. His son **Jean Renoir** (1894–1978) was a film director whose films, *La Grande Illusion* (1937) and *La Règle du jeu* (1939), are personal and subtle reflections of prewar French society. During World War II he went to Hollywood but returned to Europe to make *The Golden Coach* (1953), *French Can-can* (1955), *Élena et les hommes* (1956), and other films.

Representatives, House of. *See* Congress.

repression In *psychoanalysis, the process of excluding unacceptable ideas from consciousness. Repressed wishes and thoughts continue to exist in the *unconscious mind and may give rise to symptoms. One of the goals of psychoanalytic treatment is to bring repressed material back into conscious awareness so that it can be coped with rationally. *See also* defense mechanism.

reproduction In biology, the generation of new individuals of the same species. In **asexual reproduction** individuals are derived from one parent and no special reproductive structures are involved. The simplest form is *fission, occurring mostly in unicellular organisms. Simple multicellular organisms, such as sponges and coelenterates, reproduce by budding: a new individual arises as an outgrowth (bud) from the parent. In fragmentation, the individual breaks into two or more parts, each capable of growth to form a new individual: this is seen in flatworms and some algae. Most animals and plants, however, reproduce by a process involving specialized reproductive cells (*see* gamete)—typically male and female—that fuse to produce a new individual with a different genetic makeup. This process, **sexual reproduction**, occurs in its simplest form in *conjugation. In more complex organisms the gametes are produced in special organs, e.g. the *carpel and *stamen in flowering plants and the *ovary and *testis in animals. The importance of sexual reproduction in nature is that it allows genetic variation in a population, which is therefore better able to adapt to the changing environment.

reptile A vertebrate animal belonging to the class *Reptilia* (about 6000 species), which includes *crocodiles, *turtles, *lizards, *snakes, and the *tuatara. Reptiles occur in terrestrial, freshwater, and marine habitats, chiefly in tropical regions. They have a covering of horny scales and are cold-blooded, i.e. their body temperature (and hence their activity) is determined by the environmental temperature. Fertilization of the egg by sperm takes place within the female, unlike fish and most amphibians. The egg is large and yolky, has special membranes that nourish the embryo, and a protective leathery or calcareous shell, i.e. features that enable it to be laid on land. In some lizards and snakes the eggs are retained inside the female and live young are born. Young reptiles resemble their parents and—unlike amphibians—do not undergo metamorphosis.
The primitive reptiles evolved from amphibians: their fossils are found in deposits of the Upper Carboniferous period, about 300 million years ago. During the following 240 million years, a variety of forms evolved, including the fishlike *ichthyosaurs, the flying *pterosaurs, and the mammal-like *therapsids, culminating in the giant *dinosaurs, which dominated the earth during the Cretaceous period (136–65 million years ago).

Republican Party One of the two major political parties in the US (*see also* Democratic Party). Although the name was used originally by Thomas *Jefferson's Republican-Democratic Party, founded in 1792, the modern Republican Party originated in 1854 as a coalition of former Whigs and Independent Democrats opposed to the extension of slavery to the new western states and territories. The first presidential candidate of the Republican Party was John C. *Fremont, who was defeated in the 1856 election. Four years later, with the nomination and election of Abraham *Lincoln, the Republicans began a long period of political ascendancy that lasted well into the 20th century. During the post-Civil War period, the Republican Party became increasingly identified with conservative business interests, and Republican presidents occupied the White House almost continually until the coming of the *Depression and the defeat of Herbert *Hoover in 1932. The Republican Party came to power again with the election of Dwight D. *Eisenhower in 1952, and later Republican presidents Richard *Nixon and Ronald *Reagan actively implemented the conservative policies of their party.

Republican River A river formed by the junction of the South Fork Republican River and the Arikaree River in SW Nebraska, which flows through S Nebraska and SW through Kansas where it meets the Kansas River at Junction City. Length: 422 mi (680 km).

requiem shark A *shark of the family *Carcharhinidae* (over 60 species), found worldwide mainly in warm and temperate oceans. 5–18 ft (1.5–5.5 m) long, they have two dorsal fins and are carnivorous, feeding on fish and various invertebrates. Some species are dangerous to man, for example the *tiger shark.

reservoirs Natural or artificial lakes in which water is trapped and stored for irrigation, to supply water for municipal needs, for hydroelectric power, or to control water flow. When artificially constructed they are made by placing dams across suitable land formations to create a lake. They may often combine several of the purposes above and are invaluable in areas in which rainfall is low or unpredictable. The water flowing into a reservoir must not contain too much sediment or the capacity of the reservoir will diminish.

Resht. *See* Rasht.

resins Adhesive nonflammable organic polymers, usually insoluble in water but soluble in organic solvents, such as alcohol. **Natural resins**, such as *rosin, *sandarac, and *shellac, are exuded by plants and insects. **Synthetic resins** are made by modifying natural polymers or by polymerization of petrochemicals. Thermosetting resins, those that harden on heating, include *epoxy, *urea-formaldehyde, and some *polyurethane resins. Thermoplastic resins, those that soften on heating, include *polyethylene, *polyvinyl chloride, *polypropylene, and cellulose acetates.

resistance The property of all materials, except superconductors (*see* superconductivity), that reduces the flow of electricity through them. It is defined by *Ohm's law as the ratio of the potential difference between the ends of a conductor to the current flowing through it. The resistance of a conductor depends on its dimensions, the material of which it is made, its temperature, and in some cases the extent to which it is illuminated. The unit of resistance is the *ohm. The reciprocal of the resistance in a direct current circuit is the conductance. Conductance is measured in *siemens (*see also* impedance).

Resnais, Alain (1922–) French film director. His films are characterized by experimental narrative techniques and a concern with the relationship between word and image. The scripts for his films *Hiroshima mon amour* (1959), *Last Year at Marienbad* (1961), and *Providence* (1977) were written by Marguerite Duras, Alain *Robbe-Grillet, and David Mercer respectively.

resolving power The ability of a *microscope to produce separate images of two neighboring points; the closer the two points, the greater the resolving power of the microscope. The resolving power may be increased by using shorter wavelength light (e.g. ultraviolet radiation) or by using very short wavelength electrons (as in the *electron microscope). Alternatively the refractive index of the medium between the specimen being examined and the objective lens may be increased. This is the basis of the *oil-immersion lens.

resonance (chemistry) The existence of a compound with a molecular structure that is intermediate between two or more conventional structures. For example, the polar molecule HCl, in which the hydrogen atom has some positive charge and the chlorine some negative charge, can be regarded as intermediate between two structures. One is the covalent molecule H–Cl and the other the ionic compound H^+Cl^-. The actual molecule is a **resonance hybrid** with contributions from the two forms, written H–Cl $\leftrightarrow$ H^+Cl^-.

resonance (physics) The sympathetic oscillation of a system in response to an external excitation. A wire under tension, for example, will not respond to an external vibration unless the vibration is at the natural frequency of oscillation of the wire, which depends on its length, tension, etc. It will then resonate at its natural frequency. Resonance also occurs in electrical, magnetic, and electromagnetic phenomena in which matter or energy is being changed periodically. A **resonant circuit** consists of a capacitance in parallel with an inductance. When the capacitor discharges through the inductor an induced emf is produced, which again charges the

REPTILE

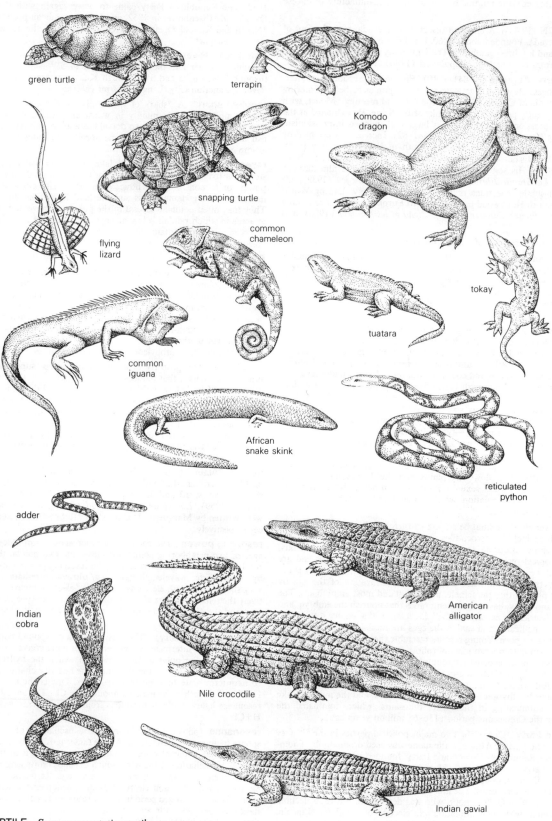

green turtle

terrapin

Komodo dragon

snapping turtle

flying lizard

common chameleon

common iguana

tuatara

tokay

African snake skink

reticulated python

adder

American alligator

Indian cobra

Nile crocodile

Indian gavial

REPTILE *Some representative reptiles.*

capacitor (in the opposite sense). The circuit will then continue to oscillate, provided that energy is supplied from an outside source, at a frequency determined by the values of the capacitor (which is usually a variable device) and the inductor. Such circuits, feeding an aerial, are used in *radio transmitters to generate radio-frequency oscillations and in receivers to detect incoming signals.

resonances Elementary particles with extremely short lifetimes (about 10^{-23} seconds). They are formed when colliding particles react together by the *strong interaction. Resonances are classified as either *mesons or *baryons (*see* particle physics).

Respighi, Ottorino (1879–1936) Italian composer. He became director of the Santa Cecilia in Rome (1923–25). He wrote several operas, the symphonic poems *The Fountains of Rome* (1917) and *The Pines of Rome* (1924), the orchestral suite *The Birds* (1927), based on themes by Rameau and others, and ballets, including *La Boutique fantasque* (1919), based on themes by Rossini.

respiration The process by which an organism takes up oxygen from its environment and discharges carbon dioxide into it. In man and most air-breathing animals the organs through which this takes place are the *lungs (aquatic animals use *gills; insects use *tracheae). Air is transported to and from the lungs by **breathing**, which involves movements of the muscular diaphragm and the rib cage. Oxygen-depleted blood is pumped from the *heart to the air sacs (alveoli) of the lungs, where it receives oxygen (from inhaled air) and releases carbon dioxide (which is exhaled). Oxygen in the blood is carried to the tissues and cells, where it oxidizes foodstuffs to produce energy, used for physiological processes, and carbon dioxide, which is transported in the blood to the lungs. This is called tissue, or cellular, respiration.

respirator A machine used to maintain breathing in patients whose respiratory muscles are paralyzed or not functioning for any other reason. The cabinet respirator (iron lung) encloses the patient in a sealed container from the neck down; by lowering the pressure in the cabinet the chest expands and draws air into the lungs. A positive-pressure respirator pumps air at regular intervals into the lungs through a tube placed in the windpipe; the air is exhaled naturally or removed by suction through the respirator.

Restoration (1660) The re-establishment of the monarchy in England following the fall of the *Protectorate. The Restoration of Charles II, whose father Charles I had been executed (1649) during the English Civil War, was engineered by General *Monck. In April, 1660, the Convention Parliament accepted Charles' Declaration of Breda, in which he promised religious toleration and an amnesty to all but 57 of those who had fought against the crown in the Civil War; it also arranged for the restoration of confiscated royalist lands and an income for Charles. The subsequent Cavalier Parliament (1661–79) enacted a religious settlement in the form of the anti-Nonconformist *Clarendon Code.

Restoration literature English literature written during the reigns of Charles II (1660–85) and James II (1685–88), following the Restoration of the monarchy in 1660 and the relaxation of restraints on literature imposed during the Puritan Interregnum. The period was especially distinguished by its drama, notably the witty comedies of manners of *Wycherley, *Etheridge, and *Congreve. In poetry, the period was characterized by the satires of *Dryden and the licentious verse of John Wilmot, Earl of *Rochester.

resurrection plant. *See* rose of Jericho.

retina The light-sensitive layer that forms the inner surface of the □eye. Light is focused by the lens onto the retina, which contains numerous interconnecting light-sensitive cells that send signals to the visual center of the brain via the optic nerve. These cells are of two kinds: the rods, which are sensitive to light and dark and are responsible for vision in dim light; and the cones, which are sensitive to color and visual detail. The greatest concentration of cones occurs at a small area at the back of the eye (the fovea), which is therefore the area of greatest visual acuity. *See also* detached retina.

retriever One of several breeds of large strongly built sporting dogs characterized by a "soft" mouth and good swimming ability. All are descended from the *Labrador retriever crossed with other breeds. The flat-coated retriever has a fine dense black or liver-colored coat while the curly-coated retriever has a coat of small tight curls, indicating possible poodle ancestry. The Chesapeake Bay retriever has a short thick coat and has been developed in the US. Height: 22–27 in (56–68 cm). *See also* golden retriever.

Retz, Jean François Paul de Gondi, Cardinal de (1613–79) French churchman, one of the leaders of the rebellion called the *Fronde (1648–53), which he used to further his own political ambitions at the expense of Cardinal *Mazarin. He was made a cardinal in 1652 but arrest-ed soon after. Exiled until 1662 he returned to France to become Abbot of Saint-Denis until his death. He is best known for his *Mémoires*, which recall his role in the Fronde.

Reuben, tribe of One of the 12 *tribes of Israel. It claimed descent from Reuben, the eldest son of Jacob and Leah. The territory allocated to Reuben's people was in the Transjordan, E of the Dead Sea.

Réunion A volcanic island and French overseas department in the W Indian Ocean, in the Mascarene Islands. It was settled in about 1642 by the French with their African and Indian slaves; increasing population has caused much emigration. Sugar, rum, and molasses are exported. Area: 970 sq mi (2512 sq km). Population (1978 est): 484,924. Capital: Saint-Denis.

Reuter, Paul Julius, Baron von (Israel Josephat; 1816–99) British founder of the first news agency. Born in Germany, he adopted the name of Reuter in 1844. He went to London in 1851 and opened a telegraph office from which he supplied newspapers with international news. He was made a German baron in 1871.

Reuther, Walter (1907–70) US labor leader. He was an organizer and president of Local 174, *United Automobile Workers (UAW) (1935–46) in Detroit, president of UAW (1946–70), president of the *Congress of Industrial Organizations (1952–55), and head of the AFL-CIO's Industrial Union Department from 1955, after the *American Federation of Labor and the CIO merged. He was known for his plan to produce airplanes in the automobile factories during World War II, for his organization of usually nonviolent strikes, and for union gains achieved through collective bargaining.

Reval. *See* Tallinn.

Revelation, Book of A prophetic book, the last in the New Testament, written perhaps about 90–95 AD by "John the Divine," who is often identified with the apostle John. It consists of seven highly symbolic visions that trace the fortunes of the Christian Church from its inception to the end of the world. The only example of apocalyptic literature in the New Testament, the book may have been written in reaction to the persecutions of the emperor Domitian.

reverberatory furnace A furnace designed for operations in which it is not desirable to mix the material being heated with the fuel. The flame is directed at the roof of the furnace and the heat radiated downward. This type of furnace is used in the smelting of copper and nickel ores.

PAUL REVERE *Warning other patriots of the coming of the British at the start of the American Revolution.*

Revere, Paul (1735–1818) American silversmith and patriot. Prominent in the colonial opposition to Britain, he became famous as the man who, on April 18, 1775, rode out to warn the people of Massachusetts that the British troops were on the march. On the following morning the first shots of the American Revolution were fired on the British at Lexington. Revere's ride is celebrated in a poem by Longfellow.

Revolt of the Netherlands The rebellion against Spanish rule in the Netherlands, inspired by political and economic grievances and resentment at the suppression of Protestantism. Revolt broke out in 1568 but only took fire in 1572, when the Dutch cause prospered in the strongly Protestant northern provinces under the leadership of *William the Silent. In 1576 the N was joined by the predominantly Roman Catholic provinces in the S but the union ended with the Spanish victory at Gembloux in 1578, when the S submitted once more to Spain. In the following year the seven northern provinces, by the Union of Utrecht, declared their independence from Spain. War continued, however, until the 12-year truce negotiated in 1609 by William's son and successor *Maurice of Nassau and was renewed in the Thirty Years' War (1618–48). By the Peace of Westphalia (1648) the independence of the United Provinces of the Netherlands was at last acknowledged.

Revolutionary and Napoleonic Wars (1792–1815) A series of European wars precipitated by the *French Revolution and *Napoleon's ambitions for the conquest of Europe. Revolutionary fervor within France and the hostile reaction of Austria and Prussia to the arrest of Louis XVI led to the outbreak of war. Initial French success prompted Britain, the Netherlands, and Spain to close ranks with Austria and Prussia in the first coalition (1793). Hard pressed, France was transformed into a nation at arms (*see* conscription) and its armies achieved a series of victories. In 1795 Prussia, the Netherlands, and Spain sued for peace and, following Napoleon's first Italian campaign (1796–97), Austria followed suit. French supremacy was thwarted only by British naval strength and Nelson's great victory of the *Nile (1798) brought Britain control of the Mediterranean. In 1798–99 the second coalition of Britain, the Ottoman Empire, Naples, Portugal, and Austria was formed but collapsed (1801) in the face of Napoleon's victories, especially at *Hohenlinden (1800), and the Revolutionary Wars ended with the uneasy Treaty of Amiens (1802) between Britain and France.

Napoleon's aggression, including his imposition of the *Continental System against Britain, led to the resumption of naval war between Britain and France. In 1805 Pitt the Younger negotiated a third coalition against Napoleon, by now emperor, and Nelson (although mortally wounded) won the naval victory at *Trafalgar. Napoleon now turned on the continental members of the coalition, defeating Austria and Russia at *Ulm and Austerlitz (1805), Prussia at *Jena and Auerstadt (1806), and Russia again at *Friedland (1807). With the failure of the Continental System and Wellington's victories in the *Peninsular War, Napoleon's dominance diminished. Following his disastrous Russian campaign (1812) the allies were able to defeat him at *Leipzig (1813) and then, following his return from exile, at *Waterloo (1815). The post-Napoleonic settlement of Europe was decided at the Congress of *Vienna.

Revolution of 1905 An insurrection in Russia, an expression of the widespread discontent that culminated in the *Russian Revolution of 1917. It began on January 22, 1905 (Bloody Sunday), when a group of striking workers marched peacefully on the Winter Palace in St Petersburg and were fired on by troops. The massacre precipitated nationwide strikes, uprisings, and mutinies (including the mutiny on the battleship *Potemkin*). By October Russia was gripped by a general strike, which with the establishment of the St Petersburg Soviet (workers' council), dominated by the *Mensheviks, including Trotsky, forced Emperor Nicholas II to promise constitutional government (*see* Duma). The Revolution was substantially crushed by the end of December.

Revolutions of 1848 A series of revolutions in continental Europe caused by economic distress and liberal agitation against the conservatism that characterized the post-Napoleonic era. The first revolution broke out in France, where the insurgents overthrew the July Monarchy of Louis Philippe, but a split in their ranks between moderates and socialists led to the suppression of the Left and the election of Louis Napoleon (later *Napoleon III) as president. In the Italian states the revolution had constitutional aims, in which it had some success in Piedmont, but also formed part of the movement against the Austrian presence in Italy (*see* Risorgimento). In the Austrian Empire revolts in Vienna secured the resignation of Metternich and the summoning of a constituent assembly. The revolution spread with short-lived success to Prague and Budapest before being suppressed by Schwarzenberg. In the German states the revolution began in Prussia, where Frederick William IV was forced to convene a constituent assembly. By December, however, the revolutions there and in other German states had been suppressed and in 1849 the Frankfurt Parliament, which had hoped to achieve a united Germany, was dissolved. The revolutions were all quelled but not without some concessions to liberal and nationalist movements, and 1848 is thus generally regarded as ending the post-1815 period of reaction that had been dominated by Metternich.

revolver A short-range *small arm having a revolving cylinder containing the rounds behind the barrel. In single-action types, pressing the trigger cocks the weapon and simultaneously rotates the cylinder; further pressure fires it. Double-action types perform these functions automatically but their stiffer mechanism impairs accuracy. Calibers range from .21 inches to .455 inches (5.3 millimeters to 11.5 millimeters). The first successful revolver was the *Colt, designed in 1835. *See also* pistol.

revue A theatrical entertainment consisting of a succession of songs, dances, and sketches of a topical and often satirical nature. Originating in France, revues attained great popularity in Britain and the US during the early 20th century with such spectacular productions as the *Ziegfeld Follies* (1907). As competition from the movies and television increased, revues

became more intimate in form. The success of *Beyond the Fringe* (1961) led to a succession of sophisticated satirical revues during the 1960s.

rex A breed of cat having a curly coat of very short fine hairs. Two breed types are recognized—the Cornish rex and the Devon rex, named for the English counties in which they originated. They have long slender bodies and may be of any color.

Reykjavik 64 10N 21 53W The capital of Iceland, an important fishing port, on Faxa Fjord in the SW. Founded by the Vikings in 874 AD, it became the seat of parliament (the Althing) in 1843 and capital of Iceland in 1918. Its university was founded in 1911. Most of the city's heating comes from natural hot springs. Population (1980 est): 83,766.

Reynaud, Paul (1878–1966) French politician, who was briefly prime minister before the German occupation of France in 1940. He was a forceful opponent of Nazism in the late 1930s and after the collapse of France was arrested by the Germans and held until 1945. After the war he again held ministerial posts and helped draft the constitution of the Fifth Republic (1959).

Reynolds, Sir Joshua (1723–92) British portrait painter. He studied in London (1740–43) under the portraitist Thomas Hudson (1701–79). In 1749 he traveled to Italy, staying for two years in Rome before returning to London. Using the techniques of the Old Masters in such paintings as *Sarah Siddons as the Tragic Muse*, Reynolds aimed to give portraits the prestige of historical paintings. In 1768 he became the first president of the Royal Academy, where he delivered the *Discourses*, which contain his artistic theories. His friends included Dr *Johnson and *Garrick, both of whom he painted.

Reynolds number (*Re*) In fluid dynamics, a dimensionless quantity associated with the flow of a fluid. $Re = \rho v l/\eta$, where ρ and η are the *density and *viscosity of the fluid moving with velocity v through a system characterized by a length l. If the Reynolds number of the fluid is less than about 1500, the flow is streamlined; above this number it becomes turbulent. Named for Osborne Reynolds (1842–1912).

Reza Shah Pahlavi (1878–1944) Shah of Iran (1925–41). After leading an army coup in 1921, he deposed Ahmad Shah Qajar (1898–1930) in 1925. As shah himself, Reza aimed at the modernization of Iran, following the example of *Atatürk in Turkey. In 1941 Britain and the Soviet Union, fearing German influence in Iran, invaded the country and forced Reza Shah to abdicate in favor of his son *Mohammed Reza Pahlavi. He died in exile in South Africa.

rhea A large flightless bird belonging to a family (*Rheidae*; 3 species) occurring in South America. 47 in (120 cm) tall, rheas have a brownish plumage and long legs with three toes. They live in flocks, feeding on leaves, roots, seeds, insects, and small vertebrates. The male builds the nest and incubates the eggs. Order: *Rheiformes*.

Rhea In Greek religion, a Titan, daughter of Uranus and Gaea. Her consort *Cronus swallowed her children, fearing that they would overthrow him. Rhea substituted a stone for one child, *Zeus, who eventually overthrew Cronus and forced him to disgorge the other children.

Rhee, Syngman (1875–1965) Korean statesman; president of South Korea (1948–60). He became leader of South Korea in 1945 during the US occupation and as its first president claimed his government's right to rule over all Korea. Popular unrest forced him to relinquish his post in 1960 and he went into exile.

Rheims. *See* Reims.

rhenium (Re) A dense (relative density 21.02) silvery-white transition metal with a very high melting point. The metal is very ductile and is used to alloy with tungsten. Alloys with molybdenum are superconducting. The metal is obtained as a by-product of molybdenum refining. At no 75; at wt 186.2; mp 3180°C; bp 5620°C.

rhesus factor (Rh factor) A blood protein present on the red cells in 83% of the population: the presence or absence of the Rh factor is the basis of the Rh *blood group system, people with the factor being described as Rh positive and those without as Rh negative. If a Rh-negative woman has a Rh-positive baby she may produce anti-Rh antibodies that will react against subsequent Rh-positive pregnancies. The affected baby's blood cells may be destroyed by these antibodies, leading to the severe anemia of hemolytic disease of the newborn. The incidence of this disease has been reduced by taking steps to prevent the formation of maternal anti-Rh antibodies soon after delivery of the first baby.

rhesus monkey A *macaque monkey, *Macaca mulatta*, of S Asia, widely used in medical research. In the wild, rhesus monkeys live in large colonies in forests or on hillsides, sometimes stealing fruit from orchards.

Rheticus (Georg Joachim von Lauchen; 1514–76) German mathematician, who was the first follower of *Copernicus. Rheticus wrote (1540) a summary of Copernicus' ideas and then persuaded him to publish the original book, *De Revolutionibus*, in which they were originally expressed. Rheticus was the first mathematician to regard the trigonometric functions in terms of angles rather than arcs of a circle.

rhetoric The art of using language for communicating information and for intellectual and emotional persuasion. Mastery of rhetoric by orators was considered essential training in ancient Greece and Rome. Influential textbooks were written by *Aristotle, *Quintilian, and *Cicero, and all classical literary criticism was based on rhetorical principles. Aristotle distinguished three modes of persuasion—logical, emotional, and ethical—and codified the rules for rhetorical composition under categories of invention, arrangement, and style. Together with logic and grammar, rhetoric formed the trivium, an essential part of the curriculum in medieval education, and its principles were adapted to medieval forms, such as sermons and legal documents. In the 20th century, the study of rhetoric forms part of the theoretical analysis of techniques of persuasion.

rheumatic fever A disease of children that occurs (rarely) after infection with a streptococcus bacterium. The symptoms develop 10–14 days after the original infection (which is usually of the throat) and include fever, aching joints, chorea (involuntary movements), and inflammation of the heart, which—in a few cases—may lead to chronic heart disease. Treatment is with bed rest, penicillin, aspirin, and sometimes steroids.

rheumatism Any condition involving pain in the joints. This may be caused by a simple strain or by rheumatoid *arthritis, *osteoarthritis, *gout, or *rheumatic fever.

Rheydt 51 10N 6 27E A city in NW West Germany, in North Rhine-Westphalia. Its Renaissance palace (1568–81) escaped the bombing of World War II. An industrial center, its main manufacture is textiles. Population (1971 est): 101,500.

Rhine, Joseph Banks (1895–) US psychologist, noted for his experiments in parapsychology, especially extrasensory perception (ESP). Using packs of specially designed cards in scientifically objective tests, Rhine produced statistical evidence to support the occurrence of ESP.

Rhine River (German name: Rhein; Dutch name; Rijn) A river in central and W Europe. Rising in SE Switzerland, it flows N into Lake Constance, continuing W along the Swiss-German border to Basle. It then flows generally N along the Franco-German border and into West Germany, turning NW past Bonn, Cologne, Düsseldorf, and Duisburg. It enters the Netherlands below Emmerich and splits into two major distributaries, the Lek and the Waal. The Lek continues W through Rotterdam and enters the North Sea at the Hook of Holland. The Waal joins the Meuse River and enters the North Sea by the Hollandsch Diep. The main tributaries are the Ruhr, Main, Moselle, and Neckar rivers. It is W Europe's main navigable waterway and passes through one of the most highly industrialized regions on the continent. Length: 820 mi (1320 km).

Rhine-Herne Canal A waterway in West Germany, in the *Ruhr. Completed in 1914, it forms part of the *Mitelland Canal and extends from Duisburg to Herne. Length: 24 mi (39 km).

Rhineland Palatinate (German name: Rheinland-Pfalz) A *Land* in W West Germany, bordering on France, Luxembourg, and Belgium. It includes the historic cities of Mainz, Speyer, Trier, and Worms. Over 75% of Germany's wine is produced in the river valleys of the Rhine, Moselle, and Nahe. Potatoes and grain are grown and livestock is important in the mountainous SW. Industries include chemicals, engineering, and shoe manufacture. Area: 7658 sq mi (19,838 sq km). Population (1980 est): 3,638,700. Capital: Mainz. *See also* Palatinate.

rhinoceros A large hoofed mammal belonging to the family *Rhinocerotidae* (5 species), of Asia and Africa. Rhinos have a massive virtually naked dark-skinned body with short thick legs, a short neck, and a large head. The Indian rhinoceros (*Rhinoceros unicornis*) has a single horn composed of solid fibrous *keratin; all other rhinos have two horns. Rhinos range in size from the large *white rhinoceros to the Sumatran rhinoceros (*Didermocerus sumatrensis*), which is up to 60 in (150 cm) high at the shoulder and weighs 1100–2200 lb (500–1000 kg). Rhinos are generally solitary, grazing or browsing on grass and leaves, and are fond of wallowing in muddy pools. All are now endangered species.

rhinoceros beetle A horned *scarab beetle, up to 6 in (150 mm) long (including the horn), so called because of the resemblance of its horn to that of a rhinoceros. The larvae of most rhinoceros beetles live in rotting wood, although some eat roots or burrow into the stems of palm trees. *Oryctes rhinoceros* is sometimes a serious pest in oriental coconut groves through its destruction of the leaf bases. *See also* Hercules beetle.

rhizome An underground plant stem producing aerial leaves and shoots. It may extend some distance below ground and can be fleshy (as in the iris) or wiry (as in couch grass). Rhizomes can function both as organs of vegetative reproduction and as overwintering structures. They usually grow horizontally; vertical rhizomes (e.g. of strawberry) are commonly called rootstocks.

Rhode Island A New England state, indented by Narragansett Bay. It is bounded on the N and E by Massachusetts, on the S by the Atlantic Ocean, and on the W by Connecticut. The smallest state, it is also the second most densely populated state. It is highly industrialized, the once important cotton industry having been replaced by modern technological industries, such as electronics and the manufacture of machine tools. It also has important naval installations. Agriculture is limited by the rocky terrain; it is famous for its poultry. *History*: purchasing land from the Narragansett Indians, Puritan Roger Williams established the first settlement at Providence after being banished from the Massachusetts Bay Colony in 1635. The new colony was known for its religious and political liberty. Settlers quickly established a prosperous shipping economy. Rhode Island, strongly opposing British interference in local shipping, was the first of the 13 original colonies to declare its independence. It was also the last to approve the US Constitution and did not become a state until 1790. Shipping declined after the American Revolution, but Rhode Island's plentiful water power resources combined with Samuel Slater's construction of the nation's first successful cotton textile mill (1790) facilitated the rapid growth of manufacturing. The burgeoning manufacturing industry attracted thousands of immigrants to the state. In the 20th century, however, the industry declined as a result of competition from the South. New industries emerged after World War II but unemployment has remained an ongoing problem. The expansion of such new high-technology industries as electronics has aided Rhode Island's economy. Area: 1214 sq mi (3144 sq km). Population (1980): 947,154. Capital: Providence.

Rhode Island Red A breed of domestic fowl developed from blackish-red Asiatic breeds kept on Rhode Island farms in the 19th century. It has a deep broad long body with a nearly horizontal back and a slightly curved beak. The plumage is red. It lays brown eggs and is used for both egg and meat production. Weight: 8.4 lb (3.8 kg) (cocks); 6.6 lb (3.0 kg) (hens).

Rhodes (Modern Greek name: Ródhos) A Greek island in the SE Aegean Sea, the largest of the Dodecanese group. It has a mountainous interior with fertile coastal strips, producing cereals, fruit, and wine. Tourism is an important source of revenue. *History*: colonized by Dorians before 1000 BC, Rhodes entered its period of greatest prosperity in the 3rd century BC. It suffered several earthquakes, one of which destroyed the *Colossus of Rhodes in 244 BC. It was occupied by the Knights *Hospitallers from 1282 until 1528, when it became part of the Ottoman Empire. Conquered by Italy in 1912, it was ceded to Greece in 1947. Area: 540 sq mi (1400 sq km). Population (1971); 32,092. Capital: Rhodes.

CECIL RHODES *At the spot, called World's View, in the Matopo Hills, Zimbabwe, where he was later buried.*

Rhodes, Cecil (John) (1853–1902) South African financier and statesman. Born in Britain, he went to Natal in 1870 and then to the Orange Free State to work in the Kimberley diamond mines. In 1888 his company, De Beers Consolidated Mines, bought up the Kimberley mines and in 1889 he gained a charter for the British South Africa Company to develop the territory that in 1895 was named Rhodesia in his honor. He became prime minister of Cape Colony in 1890 but was forced to resign in

1896. Rhodes endowed 170 Rhodes scholarships at Oxford University for students from the British Empire, the US, and Germany.

Rhodesia. *See* Zimbabwe.

Rhodesia and Nyasaland, Federation of (*or* Central African Federation) A former (1953–63) federation of the British colony of Southern Rhodesia (now Zimbabwe) and the British protectorates of Northern Rhodesia (now Zambia) and Nyasaland (now Malawi). It was opposed by Nyasaland nationalists on the grounds that it existed to further the economic interests of Southern Rhodesia, where most of the whites lived. Violent unrest in 1959 led to its dissolution. Zambia and Malawi became independent in 1964; Zimbabwe gained independence in 1980.

Rhodesian ridgeback A breed of hunting ☐dog originating in South Africa, characterized by a ridge of forward-growing hair along the back. The ridgeback is strongly built with a prominent muzzle and its short glossy coat is yellowish brown to reddish fawn. Height: 25–28 in (63–68 cm) (dogs); 24–26 in (61–66 cm) (bitches).

rhodium (Rh) A metal of the platinum group, discovered in 1803 by W. H. Wollaston (1766–1828). It is alloyed with platinum and palladium to form thermocouples and crucibles and is used in equipment for the production of glass fibers. It is a very hard highly reflective metal and is used to plate jewelry and optical instruments. At no 45; at wt 102.905; mp $3575 \pm 5°F$ (1966 $\pm 3°C$); bp $6747 \pm 212°F$ (3727 $\pm 100°C$).

Rhododendron A genus of small trees and shrubs (about 250 species), mainly of N temperate regions. They have leathery often evergreen leaves, large scaly winter buds, and terminal clusters of colorful fragrant bell- or funnel-shaped flowers. They occur in a variety of habitats and many, including *azaleas, are widely cultivated as ornamentals. Family: *Ericaceae*.

Rhône River A major river in W Europe. Rising in the Rhône Glacier in Switzerland, it flows through Lake Geneva to enter France, flowing generally SW between the Jura and the Alps. It merges with the Saône River at Lyon and flows S to enter the Gulf of Lions via la *Camargue. The Rhône-Saône Valley has historically been an important route and since 1976 the Rhône River has been canalized from Lyon to the Mediterranean Sea. This has provided improved navigation, hydroelectric power, and irrigation for agriculture and has encouraged industrial development along its length. Length 505 mi (812 km).

rhubarb A perennial plant, *Rheum rhaponticum*, possibly of Asian origin, widely cultivated for its juicy red or green leafstalks, up to 40 in (1 m) high, which are cooked in sugar. Later in the season, a central flower stalk may be produced bearing small greenish-white flowers. The leaves are poisonous. Family: *Polygonaceae*.

Rhum. *See* Rum.

rhyme Similarity in sound between two or more words, a device used in poetry to reinforce the metrical pattern of a poem. Usually the rhyme is between words occurring at the ends of lines, but internal rhymes, where the rhyme is between a word within a line and a word at the end of or within another line, are also used. The rhyme scheme of a poem is shown by assigning a single letter to each rhyme; thus the scheme of lines rhyming *house/cat/mouse/rat* would be noted *abab*. Masculine rhyme refers to words having the same vowel sounds in their final syllables (*night/delight*). Feminine rhyme refers to words having similar sounds in the last accented syllable and following syllables (*joviality/morality*). *See also* blank verse.

rhyolite A fine-grained or glassy acid igneous rock, mineralogically the volcanic equivalent of granite. It consists of alkali feldspars and quartz, with some ferromagnesian minerals; many rhyolites are porphyritic and display banding resulting from the flowing lava.

Rhys, Jean (1894–1979) British novelist. Born in Dominica, she wrote five books, including the novels *Voyage in the Dark* (1934) and *Good Morning, Midnight* (1939), about bohemian life in Paris and London. After living in seclusion for many years, she published a novel, *Wide Sargasso Sea* (1966), and two further collections of stories.

rhythm and blues A form of popular music of the 1940s and 1950s, resulting from the fusion of blues and jazz by black musicians. Rhythm and blues (often abbreviated to R and B) employed amplified instruments to produce powerful rhythms. One of the earliest rhythm and blues artists was Ray Brown (1926–81), who recorded "Good Rockin' Tonight" (1948). Other rhythm and blues musicians include Little Richard (1935–   ) and Lloyd Price (1932–   ). Rock musicians, such as John Mayall (1933–   ), have been influenced by rhythm and blues.

rhythm method. *See* contraception.

rib A curved bone, 12 pairs of which make up the rib cage, enclosing and protecting the heart and lungs. Each rib forms a joint with the vertebrae of the *spine, permitting movement of the rib cage during breathing. The

other ends of the upper seven ribs (the so-called true ribs) are fixed directly to the breastbone by means of a cartilage. Each of the next three pairs (the "false" ribs) is connected by the cartilage to the rib above it, and the two lowest ribs (the floating ribs) end in the muscles of the body wall.

Ribbentrop, Joachim von (1893–1946) German Nazi politician and diplomat. He joined the Nazi Party in 1932 and became Hitler's foreign-affairs adviser. From 1936 to 1938 he was ambassador to the UK and then became foreign minister. He secured the Nonaggression Pact with the Soviet Union in 1939 but thereafter his influence declined. He was arrested in 1945, found guilty of war crimes, and hanged.

ribbonfish An offshore marine fish, of the family *Trachipteridae*, that has a long ribbon-like body. Species include the *oarfish. Order: *Lampridiformes*.

ribbonworm A long flat wormlike animal, also called proboscis worm, belonging to the invertebrate phylum *Nemertina* (about 600 species). Ranging in length from 0.04 in to 1200 in (1 mm to 30 m), ribbonworms may be black, brown, or white but many are brightly patterned. Most live at the bottom of shallow seas, using a long sticky harpoon-like proboscis to capture annelid worms, mollusks, and crustaceans.

Ribeirão Prêto 21 09S 47 48W A city in S Brazil, in São Paulo state. It is the center of a coffee- and sugar-growing area. Population (1975 est): 258,741.

Ribera, José de (*or* Jusepe R.; 1591–1652) Spanish-born painter and etcher. He settled in Naples (1616), where he was known as Lo Spagnoletto (Little Spaniard). Influenced by the realism and dramatic lighting of *Caravaggio, he painted chiefly religious subjects and some everyday life scenes and portraits, the best examples of which are *The Martyrdom of St Bartholomew* and *Clubfooted Boy*. After 1630 he painted in richer colors and chose less gruesome subjects, probably as a result of his study of Venetian art and *Velázquez.

riboflavin. *See* vitamin B complex.

ribonucleic acid. *See* RNA.

ribose A simple sugar ($C_5H_{10}O_5$). Ribose and its derivative deoxyribose are important constituents of *RNA and *DNA respectively.

ribosome A granular particle present in enormous numbers in the cytoplasm of nearly all *cells, either free or bound to the surface of membranes within the cell. Ribosomes are composed of *RNA and protein and are the site of protein synthesis. During synthesis they often link together in a chain (polyribosome or polysome).

Ricardo, David (1772–1823) British political economist. Ricardo was the first economist to argue systematically from *a priori* assumptions. His main work, *Principles of Political Economy and Taxation* (1817), argued that exchange value is determined by the labor expended in production and put forward the theory of "comparative costs" as the determining factor in international exchange. As a member of parliament (1819–23), he contributed greatly to the free-trade movement.

Ricci, Matteo (1552–1610) Italian *Jesuit missionary and scholar. Working in China from 1583 until his death, he proselytized by methods that were later condemned by the Roman Catholic Church. He showed the converts European books, maps, and clocks and allowed them to retain some of their ancient religious traditions.

Ricci, Sebastiano (1659–1734) Venetian painter. Influenced by *Veronese, he worked in Bologna, Rome, Vienna, and London (1712–16), where he painted the *Resurrection* in the apse of Chelsea Hospital chapel. His nephew **Marco Ricci** (1676–1730), a landscape artist, occasionally collaborated with him after about 1707.

Riccio, David (*or* D. Rizzio; c. 1533–66) Italian secretary to *Mary, Queen of Scots. His close relationship with the queen aroused the jealousy of her husband, Lord *Darnley, and other nobles, who had him murdered.

Rice, Elmer (Elmer Leopold Reizenstein; 1892–1967) US dramatist. He became a lawyer in 1913, but did not practice his profession after his first play, *On Trial*, was produced on Broadway in 1914. *The Adding Machine* (1923) and *Street Scene* (1929; Pulitzer Prize) established his reputation as a major playwright. Other works include *Left Bank* (1931), *Counsellor-at-Law* (1931), *We, the People* (1933), *Judgment Day* (1934), *Between Two Worlds* (1934), *American Landscape* (1939), and *Dream Girl* (1945).

rice An annual cereal *grass, *Oryza sativa*, or its edible grain, probably native to India but widely cultivated throughout tropical, subtropical, and warm temperate regions. There are many varieties, growing up to 40 in (1 m) high and bearing spikes of flower clusters. Seedlings are generally transplanted to flooded paddy fields, although varieties of upland rice do not require flooding. The field is drained to enable mechanical harvesting.

Milling the grain removes either the outer husk alone, resulting in brown rice, or both the husk and the bran layer, resulting in vitamin-B-deficient white rice. Apart from being a major staple food, rice is used as a source of starch and for alcohol production.

Rich, Richard, 1st Baron (c. 1496–1567) English lawyer, who was the chief prosecutor in the trial of Sir Thomas More. He subsequently assisted in the dissolution of the monasteries, becoming a privy councillor (1540). As Lord Chancellor (1547–51) under Edward VI he helped oust the protector, *Somerset (1549).

Richard (I) the Lionheart (1157–1199) King of England (1189–99); a hero of medieval legend, he spent all but six months of his reign abroad. The third son of Henry II and *Eleanor of Aquitaine, he became Duke of Aquitaine in 1168 and of Poitiers in 1172. He joined the third Crusade in 1189 and conquered Messina and Cyprus before arriving in the Holy Land. His victory at Arsuf gained Joppa (1191). On his way home he was captured in Austria and was only released by Emperor Henry VI after payment of an enormous ransom (1194). He returned briefly to England but died campaigning in France.

RICHARD II *A portrait by an unknown artist of the English king, who ascended the throne at the age of ten.*

Richard II (1367–1400) King of England (1377–99). Succeeding his grandfather Edward III, as a minor, government was largely in the hands of his uncle *John of Gaunt. Richard provoked considerable baronial opposition by his autocratic rule, defense of the royal prerogative, and reliance upon favorites. Factional struggles culminated in the banishment in 1398 of Gaunt's son Henry Bolingbroke. He returned in 1399, while Richard was in Ireland, and seized the throne as Henry IV. Richard died shortly afterward in mysterious circumstances.

Richard III (1452–85) King of England (1483–85). He was the youngest brother of Edward IV, on whose death in 1483 he became protector for Edward V, a minor. After destroying the power of the Woodville faction, Richard imprisoned Edward and his brother, declared Edward illegitimate, and seized the throne. It was, and continues to be, alleged that Richard murdered the boys, who disappeared in August, 1483. As king, he made important administrative and financial reforms but faced considerable opposition from Henry Tudor (subsequently *Henry VII), by whom Richard was defeated and killed at Bosworth.

Richards, I(vor) A(rmstrong) (1893–1979) English literary critic, linguist, and poet. With C. K. *Ogden, Richards compiled *Basic English and wrote *The Meaning of Meaning* (1923). An emeritus professor of Harvard University, Richards' publications include *Principles of Literary Criticism* (1924), *Goodbye Earth and Other Poems* (1958), and *Tomorrow Morning Faustus!* (1962).

Richardson, Henry Hobson (1838–86) US architect. The first stylistically independent US architect, Richardson graduated from Harvard and studied architecture in Paris. He used a revived romanesque style in different types of buildings, ranging from wholesale stores to railroad stations. Some of his best work was done for Harvard in the 1870s.

Richardson, Sir Ralph (1902–83) British actor. He established his reputation as an actor of Shakespearean and other classical roles while working with the Old Vic Company during the 1930s and 1940s. He also acted in modern plays, such as David Storey's *Home* (1970) and Harold Pinter's *No Man's Land* (1976) and made many films.

Richardson, Samuel (1689–1761) British novelist. His pioneering novel *Pamela* (1740), written in the form of correspondence between the characters, evolved from a publisher's commission for a book of model letters for inexperienced writers. His acute psychological characterization was further developed in *Clarissa* (1748), and in *Sir Charles Grandison* (1753) he attempted to portray the ideal Christian gentleman.

Richelieu, Armand Jean du Plessis, Cardinal de (1585–1642) French statesman, who greatly increased the absolute authority of the crown and France's power in Europe. He rose to prominence as adviser to Louis XIII's mother *Marie de' Medici, entering the king's employ in 1624 and officially becoming his chief minister in 1629. He ruthlessly suppressed the *Huguenots and by means of an extensive secret service thwarted a series of aristocratic conspiracies against himself. He directed France with brilliance in the Thirty Years' War, although he did not live to see the dominance of Spain over Europe replaced by that of France. A patron of learning, he founded the French Academy and was himself a writer.

Richler, Mordecai (1931–) Canadian novelist. He settled in England during the 1950s. He explores the dilemmas of his Jewish protagonists in an exuberant and often bawdy style. His novels include *The Apprenticeship of Duddy Kravitz* (1959), *St Urbain's Horseman* (1971), and *Joshua Now and Then* (1981). *Home, Sweet Home* (1984) is a collection of essays about his native Canada.

Richmond 37 34N 77 27W A city and port, the capital of Virginia, on the James River. Richmond was the capital of the Confederate states during the Civil War. It is an important educational center and site of the University of Richmond (1882). The chief manufacture is tobacco. Population (1980): 219,214.

Richter, Hans (1843–1916) Hungarian conductor. In 1866 he became an assistant to Wagner, of whose works he became the leading interpreter. He also conducted the Hallé Orchestra in England and championed the works of Brahms.

Richter, Johann Paul Friedrich. *See* Jean Paul.

Richter, Sviatoslav (Teofilovitch) (1914–) Soviet pianist. The winner of the Stalin Prize in 1949, he is famous worldwide as a concert and recording artist. He is particularly noted for his performances of Beethoven, Schubert, Schumann, and Prokofiev.

Richter scale A scale of earthquake magnitude devised in 1935 by C. F. Richter in California and now in worldwide use. It is a logarithmic scale from 0 to 9, the largest earthquakes having the highest numbers. It is based on seismic recordings, taking into account distance from the epicenter. The strongest earthquake so far recorded had a Richter scale value of 8.6.

Richthofen, Manfred, Freiherr von (1892–1917) German air ace of World War I, who shot down 80 Allied aircraft before being killed himself in action. His nickname, the Red Baron, referred to the color of his plane.

Rickenbacker, Eddie (Edward Vernon R.; 1890–1973) US aviator. A race car driver, he became a pilot in *World War I, in which he won the Congressional Medal of Honor and was responsible for shooting down 26 German aircraft. After working in the automobile and aircraft industries from 1919, he became president of Eastern Airlines (1938–63), taking leave during *World War II to inspect Pacific air bases. His books include *Fighting the Flying Circus* (1919) about his World War I experiences and *Seven Came Through* (1943) about his 23-day survival on a life raft with 7 others after being shot down over the Pacific during World War II.

rickets A disease of children affecting the bones and caused by *vitamin D deficiency. Vitamin D is derived from the diet and can be made in the skin in the presence of sunlight; with a poor diet and/or inadequate sunshine the bones become soft and do not grow properly and the child may be knock-kneed, bowlegged, or pigeon-chested. The disease is readily treated with vitamin D preparations or foods rich in vitamin D.

rickettsia A minute organism belonging to a group of parasites that—like viruses—cannot reproduce outside the bodies of their hosts. They infect arthropods (especially ticks and mites) and can be transmitted to man, in whom they cause such diseases as *typhus and Rocky Mountain spotted fever. All species live within the cytoplasm or nuclei of living cells: they are similar in structure to bacteria and are regarded as intermediate between bacteria and viruses. The name derives from the principal genus (*Rickettsia*), which was named for H. T. Ricketts (1871–1910), a US pathologist who died of typhus while investigating the cause of the disease.

Rickey, Branch (Wesley) (1881–1965) US baseball manager and executive. He held management positions with the St Louis Browns (1913–16), St Louis Cardinals (1917–42; 1962–64), Brooklyn Dodgers (1942–50), and Pittsburgh Pirates (1950–62). He initiated the farm system (1919) and was instrumental in opening the major leagues to blacks, signing Jackie *Robinson for the Dodgers (1946). He was elected to the Baseball Hall of Fame (1967).

Rickover, Hyman (George) (1900–) US naval officer, born in Russia. A graduate of the Naval Academy (1922) and Columbia University (1929), he headed the Atomic Energy Commission's nuclear propulsion program (1947–82). Called "father of the nuclear submarine," he was instrumental in the development of the first nuclear-powered submarine, *U.S.S. Nautilus* (1954). In 1973 he attained the rank of admiral. An outspoken critic of the US education system, he wrote *Education and Freedom* (1959) and *American Education: A National Failure* (1963).

Ridgway, Matthew Bunker (1895–) US army officer; chief of staff (1953–55). A graduate of West Point (1917), during World War II he led the 82nd Airborne Divison, which played a large part in the invasions of Normandy and Sicily, and later the 18th Airborne Corps in Europe. Commander of the US Eighth Army (1950–51) and then of UN forces in Korea, succeeding Douglas *MacArthur, he was appointed NATO commander in Europe in 1952 before becoming chief of staff.

Riebeeck, Jan van (1619–77) Dutch colonial administrator, who founded Cape Town in 1652. He was sent to the Cape by the Dutch East India Company to establish a provisioning port for ships. He became secretary to the Council of India in 1665.

Riefensthal, Leni (1902–) German film director and photographer. During the 1930s she produced propaganda films for the Nazis, notably *Triumph of the Will* (1936) and *Olympische Spiele* (1936). Her books include two photographic studies of Sudanese tribes, *People of Kau* (1976) and *Last of the Nuba* (1976).

Riel, Louis (1844–85) Canadian rebel. Attempting to resist surveys that he believed would lead to the métis (offspring of Indian-white parents) being robbed of their land, Riel led a rebellion of métis and set up a provisional government at Winnipeg (1869–70). Defeated and outlawed, he later led a similar rebellion (1884–85) that ended in his execution.

Riemann, Georg Friedrich Bernhard (1826–66) German mathematician, who, like *Lobachevski and *Bolyai before him, produced a *non-Euclidean geometry. **Riemannian geometry** involves the development of a generalized space (Riemannian space) of any dimensions in which measurements may vary from point to point. It was used by Einstein in his general theory of *relativity.

Rienzo, Cola di (1313–54) Roman popular leader, who during the papacy's sojourn in Avignon gained the support of the people of Rome against the nobles. He was proclaimed tribune (1347) and attempted to restore Rome to its ancient greatness. He was driven out by the nobles and later killed in a popular uprising.

Riesman, David (1909–) US social scientist and lawyer. Riesman's published work includes *The Lonely Crowd: A Study of the Changing Amer-

ican Character (1950), *Individualism Reconsidered* (1954), and *The Perpetual Dream: Experiment and Reform in the American College* (1978). Riesman's insights into US society are as profound and disturbing as those of his friend Erich *Fromm.

Rif A *Berber people of N Morocco. Most of the 19 tribes speak the Rif dialect of the Berber language but a few speak Arabic. Many are light skinned and have blue or gray eyes. The Rif are Muslims and are renowned for their warrior tradition. They are cereal cultivators, herdsmen, and, along the coast, sardine fishers.

rifle A shoulder *small arm with a spiral groove inside its long barrel to make the projectile spin during its trajectory. Invented in the 15th century, rifles were widely used in America in the 18th century. In Europe the rifle superseded the *musket after the invention of the Minié system (by the French officer, Claude-Etienne Minié (1814–79) in 1849) based on an expanding lead bullet. This was made obsolete in 1865 by the introduction of breech-loaded metal cartridges. During the 1880s breech-loading rifles became capable of firing more than one cartridge without reloading. These were the immediate predecessors of the modern repeating rifle. *See also* Mauser rifle; Browning Automatic rifle.

riflebird A large *bird of paradise having a black plumage with iridescent throat patches and small ornamental plumes. The magnificent riflebird (*Craspedophora magnifica*) is about 12 in (30 cm) long with a slender curved bill, a glossy green crown, and a purplish throat. The male performs its courtship display on specially selected and fiercely defended perches.

rifleman A tiny brown passerine bird, *Acanthisitta chloris*, occurring in forested regions of New Zealand. It feeds by creeping up and down tree trunks picking out insects from bark, crevices, and epiphytic plants with its fine pointed bill. Family: *Xenicidae* (New Zealand wrens).

rift valley A steep-sided valley with a flat floor formed as a result of the valley floor subsiding between two roughly parallel faults. Volcanic activity often occurs along these faults. The most notable example of this feature is the vast *Great Rift Valley in Africa; others include the central lowlands of Scotland and the Rhône rift valley.

Riga 56 53N 24 08E A port in the W Soviet Union, the capital of the Latvian SSR, on the Gulf of Riga in the Baltic Sea. It is an industrial and cultural center, with shipbuilding, machine-building, and many manufacturing industries. It has many historic buildings, especially in the picturesque old town. *History*: the order of Livonian Knights was founded here in 1201, and in 1282 Riga became a member of the Hanseatic League. A major trading center, after the demise of the Livonian Knights it passed to Poland (1581), to Sweden (1621), and then to Russia (1710). It was the capital of independent Latvia (1918–40) and was occupied by the Germans (1941–44) in World War II. Population (1981 est): 850,000.

Rigel A remote yet very conspicuous blue supergiant, apparent magnitude 0.1 and about 900 light years distant, that is the brightest star in the constellation *Orion.

right ascension An angular distance, analogous to terrestrial longitude, that is used with **declination** to specify the position of an astronomical body on the *celestial sphere. It is measured eastward along the celestial equator from the vernal *equinox. Declination, analogous to terrestrial latitude, is the angular distance of the body N or S of the celestial equator.

Rights of Man and of the Citizen, Declaration of the (1789) The formal expression of the ideals of the *French Revolution. Comprising 17 articles, it was drafted by the National Assembly to preface the constitution of 1791. Incorporating *Enlightenment theories and both English and American precedents (*see* Bill of Rights), the Declaration asserted that "all men are born free and equal in rights," such as equality before the law, freedom of speech, and ownership of property. The Declaration was an inspiration to later revolutionary movements.

right whale A *whale of the family *Balaenidae* (5 species), so called because they were the right whales to catch (by whalers). Up to 60 ft (18 m) long and weighing over 20 tons, they are large-headed slow-moving plankton feeders with very long baleen plates and a double-jetted blowhole.

Rigi 47 04N 8 28E A mountain in N central Switzerland, between Lake Lucerne and Lake Zug. It is popular for the fine views from the summit. Height: 5906 ft (1800 m).

rigor mortis The stiffening of a body after death caused by chemical changes in the muscle tissue. The time at which rigor mortis appears depends on the external temperature and the circumstances of death. It usually passes away after about 24 hours.

Riis, Jacob August (1849–1914) US journalist and reformer; born in Denmark. After coming to the US in 1870, he was a reporter for the *New York Tribune* (1877–88) and the *New York Evening Sun* (1888–99). Reporting on crime, he exposed conditions in the slums of New York City and crusaded for improvements through his newspaper articles and books. His works include *How the Other Half Lives* (1890), *The Children of the Poor* (1892), and *Children of the Tenements* (1903). He founded (1888) a settlement house, named for him, in New York City.

Rijeka (Italian name: Fiume) 45 20N 14 27E The chief seaport in Yugoslavia, in Croatia on the Adriatic Sea. Made a free port in 1723, it was annexed by Hungary in 1779. In 1919, following claims by Italian *Irredentists and Yugoslavia, *D'Annunzio led a force to capture it for Italy. It again became a free port in 1920, reverted to Italy in 1924, finally coming to Yugoslavia in 1947 as reparation after World War II. It has a university (1973) and varied industries, including oil refineries and shipyards. Population (1971): 132,222.

Rijksmuseum A museum and art gallery in Amsterdam, housing the national collection of the Netherlands. It originated in 1808 as the Royal Museum and became the Rijksmuseum in 1817. Its highlights are its paintings of the Dutch school, notably the celebrated *Night Watch* by *Rembrandt.

Rijswijk, Treaty of (1697) The treaty that ended the War of the *Grand Alliance between France and England, Spain, Austria, and the Netherlands. Louis XIV of France surrendered most of the territories he had conquered (retaining Alsace), recognized William III as King of England, and granted trading concessions to the Dutch.

Riley, Bridget Louise (1931–) British painter. In the early 1960s she began her black and white all-over patterns of repeated wavy lines, squares, etc., which associate her with *Op art.

Riley, James Whitcomb (1849–1916) US poet. He was born in Indiana and wrote verses for the *Indianapolis Journal* (1877–85) under the name "Benj. F. Johnson, of Boone." Frequently in Hoosier dialect, these verses earned him the title of "Hoosier poet." His poetry collections include *The Old Swimmin' Hole and 'Leven More Poems* (1883), *Afterwhiles* (1887), *Green Fields and Running Brooks* (1892), and *Home Folks* (1900).

Rilke, Rainer Maria (1875–1926) Austrian poet, born in Prague (then in Bohemia). After an unhappy childhood and a brief marriage, he traveled widely in Europe and Russia, becoming in Paris a friend of Rodin, and finally settled in Switzerland. Paris is the setting for the meditative prose of *Die Aufzeichnungen des Malte Laurids Brigge* (1910). In his poetry, the mysticism of his early devotional *Das Stunden-Buch* (1905) develops into a pantheistic celebration of life in the *Duino Elegies* (1923) and the *Sonnets to Orpheus* (1923).

Rimbaud, Arthur (1854–91) French poet. After writing "Le Bateau Ivre" and other early precocious poems he was welcomed to Paris in 1871 by *Verlaine, with whom he formed a tempestuous relationship that eventually ended in a violent quarrel. His visionary theories about poetry were expressed in the prose poems of *Une Saison en enfer* (1873) and *Les Illuminations* (1886). At the age of 20 he renounced poetry and wandered in Europe and the Near East, eventually becoming a gun-runner in Ethiopia. He died in Marseilles.

Rimini (Latin name: Ariminium) 44 03N 12 24E A town and resort in Italy, in Emilia-Romagna on the N Adriatic coast. It has various Roman and medieval remains. There is a textile industry and flour mills; pasta is produced. Population (1980 est): 128,010.

Rimsky-Korsakov, Nikolai (1844–1908) Russian composer. Largely self-taught, he started his career as a naval officer and was appointed professor of composition at the St Petersburg conservatoire in 1871. He was a member of the group of nationalist composers known as the Mighty Five, the others being Balakirev, Borodin, César Cui (1835–1918), and Mussorgski. He wrote 15 operas, including *The Snow Maiden* (1880–81) and *The Golden Cockerel* (1906–07), such orchestral works as *Scheherazade* (1888), chamber music, and songs. He also reharmonized Mussorgski's *A Night on the Bare Mountain*.

rinderpest A contagious virus disease, also known as cattle plague, affecting cattle and certain wild animals in Asia and Africa. Symptoms arise three to nine days after infection and include loss of appetite, fever, mouth ulcers, dysentery, and emaciation. 90% of acute cases are fatal; in chronic cases, mortality is lower. Compulsory slaughter and vaccination are used to control outbreaks of the disease.

Rinehart, Mary Roberts (1876–1958) US writer. A prolific writer of mysteries from 1908, she served as a war correspondent during World War I and also wrote plays; the best-known was *Mr. Big* (1920), cowritten with Avery Hopwood. Her novels include *The Circular Staircase* (1908), *The Amazing Adventures of Letitia Carberry* (1911), *Kings, Queens, and Pawns*

(1915), *The Altar of Freedom* (1917), *The Amazing Interlude* (1917), *The Breaking Point* (1922), *The Romantics* (1929), *The Wall* (1938), *The Yellow Room* (1945), and *The Frightened Wife* (1953).

ringhals. *See* cobra.

ringlet A *satyrid butterfly characterized by brownish wings marked with small white rings. The larval food plants are mainly grasses. Chief genera: *Aphantopus, Cacnonympha, Erebia*.

ring ouzel A shy songbird, *Turdus torquatus*, which replaces the closely related blackbird in mountainous regions. The male is black with a broad white crescent around the throat; the female is dark brown with less distinct marking. They migrate to S Europe and the Atlas mountains for the winter. Family: *Turdidae* (thrushes).

ringworm A highly infectious disease of the skin, hair, and nails that is caused by various fungi: it is known medically as tinea. Ringworm is usually transmitted by direct contact. The affected area, commonly on the scalp, feet (athletes' foot), armpits, or groin, is usually inflamed, scaly, itchy, and typically ring-shaped (especially on the scalp). Serious infections are treated with the antibiotic griseofulvin.

Río Bravo. *See* Rio Grande.

Rio de Janeiro 22 53S 43 17W The chief port in Brazil, the capital of Rio de Janeiro state situated on the SW shore of Guanabara Bay. Discovered by the Portuguese in 1502, it was the capital of Brazil from 1763 until 1960. Many colonial buildings remain, notably the 17th-century Candelaria church. It is renowned for its spectacular setting backed by mountains, the most famous of which is the conical Sugar Loaf Mountain. Another famous landmark is the giant figure of Christ standing on the highest peak, Corcovado, which is 2264 ft (690 m) high. The city is the site of several universities, the Oswaldo Cruz Institute (specializing in experimental medicine), and the Brazilian Academy of Science. It is an important port and trading center and has a fine natural harbor; exports include coffee, sugar, and iron ore. The chief industries include shipbuilding, sugar refining, and railroad engineering. Population (1980): 5,093,232.

Río de la Plata. *See* Plata, Río de la.

Rio Grande (Spanish names: Río Bravo; Río Bravo del Norte) The fifth longest river of North America. Rising in the Rocky Mountains, in Colorado, it forms the entire border between Texas and Mexico before entering the Gulf of Mexico. Length: 1885 mi (2040 km).

Río Muni. *See* Equatorial Guinea, Republic of.

Ríotinto, Minas de (or Minas de Río Tinto) A mining center in SW Spain, in Andalusia near the source of the Río Tinto. Worked since Roman times, its copper mines are among the most valuable in the world.

Ripley, George (1802–80) US reformer, journalist, and critic. A Unitarian minister, he had drifted into transcendentalism by 1841 and resigned from the ministry. He edited *The Dial* (1840–44), a transcendentalist publication he founded, and established *Brook Farm (1841–47), where he served as president and edited the journal *Harbinger* (1945–49). When Brook Farm failed, he moved to New York City and by 1849 became literary critic for the *New York Tribune*, a position he held until his death. *See also* Transcendentalists; New England.

Risorgimento (Italian: resurgence) The nationalist movement in 19th-century Italy that achieved the country's independence and unification. Secret societies, such as the *Carbonari and *Mazzini's Young Italy, encouraged Italian patriotism after 1815, and abortive uprisings occurred in Naples and Sicily (1820) and the papal states, Modena, and Parma (1830–31). Piedmont's attempts in 1848–49 to oust the Austrians from Lombardy ended in defeat at Custozza (1848) and Novara (1849) and afterward *Garibaldi's Roman Republic was suppressed by the French. In 1859, however, the Piedmontese prime minister *Cavour freed Lombardy and in 1860 Garibaldi surrendered to Piedmont the conquests made in the S by his Expedition of the *Thousand. In the same year Tuscany, Modena, Parma, Bologna, and Romagna formed an independent alliance, all accepting entry into the kingdom of Italy under the House of Piedmont, proclaimed in 1861. Unification was completed by Italy's annexation of Venetia in 1866 and of the papal states in 1870.

Rittenhouse, David (1732–96) US astronomer, surveyor, and inventor. He designed and made precision instruments, mainly clocks and optical instruments and is credited with making the first US telescope. Also a surveyor, he helped to establish the *Mason-Dixon line in 1763. By 1769 he had built an observatory at his home and tracked the planets, especially Venus, and refined the transit telescope. He was treasurer of Pennsylvania (1777–89), taught astronomy at the University of Pennsylvania (1779–82), directed the US Mint (1791–96), and was president of the American Philosophical Society (1791–96).

river A large body of water, confined within a channel by banks, that flows into the sea, a lake, or another river. Its source may be a spring, a lake, a number of rivulets, or a glacier. Rivers are sometimes classified according to their development, a youthful river having a narrow V-shaped valley with many rapids and a mature river having a broad flood plain, meanders, and oxbow lakes. Rivers are important in the processes of erosion and the transportation and deposition of material; they are thus responsible for many of the landforms in those parts of the world of which they are a feature. Throughout history rivers have attracted settlement by man; broad river valleys were the site of some of the earliest great civilizations, such as in the Nile valley, and many of the world's major cities are located on rivers. As important communications routes, rivers often provided the point of entry to the surrounding land for explorers, traders, and settlers. Other uses of rivers include irrigation, hydroelectric power generation, and fishing. *See also* flood.

Rivera, Diego (1886–1957) Mexican mural painter. In Mexico in the 1920s, with *Orozco and *Siqueiros, he revived the old techniques of *fresco and *encaustic painting in murals for educational institutions. His social and political subject matter are evident in works for the Ministry of Education in Mexico City (1923–28). His mural for the Rockefeller Center was removed because it included a portrait of Lenin.

Rivers, Larry (1923–) US artist. He began painting in the abstract expressionist style in the 1940s and 1950s, but then began incorporating imagery, especially human figures, into his works. His imagery, which sometimes used everyday popular themes, anticipated pop art. He is known for such works as *Washington Crossing the Delaware* (1953), *Double Portrait of Birdie* (1955), and *Dutch Masters Series* (1963).

Riverside 33 59N 117 22W A city in S California, on the Santa Ana River. A long-established citrus town, the state's first navel orange tree was introduced here in 1873. It is the site of the citrus experiment station (1907) of the University of California. Population (1980): 170,876.

Riviera (French name: Rivière) The narrow Mediterranean coastal belt of France and Italy, extending roughly between Toulon (France) and La Spezia (Italy). Its climate, coastal scenery, and beaches have made it a long-standing cosmopolitan resort. Panoramic roads follow the coast; the famous two-tiered Corniche roads extend along the French Riviera (also known as the Côte d'Azur) between Nice and Menton.

Riyadh 24 39N 46 46E A city in Saudi Arabia, in the center of the Arabian Peninsula. Riyadh and Mecca are joint capitals of the kingdom. The discovery of oil in Saudi Arabia in the 1930s has turned Riyadh into a thriving modern city, the commercial and communications center of the country; it has two universities (1950 and 1957). Population (1974): 666,840.

Rizzio, David. *See* Riccio, David.

RNA (*or* ribonucleic acid) A nucleic acid that is important in the synthesis of proteins by living organisms. In some viruses RNA is the genetic material. Structurally, it is similar to *DNA but usually occurs as a single-stranded molecule with the sugar ribose and the base uracil replacing the deoxyribose and thymine of DNA. There are three main types of RNA (most of which occurs in the cell cytoplasm): ribosomal RNA, messenger (m) RNA, and transfer (t) RNA. The *genetic code in DNA contains the information necessary for protein synthesis. This code is transcribed into a strand of mRNA and carried to the ribosomes (small cytoplasmic particles), where it is translated into a particular polypeptide chain. The amino acids making up the protein are brought to their correct positions in the chain by tRNA.

roach One of several freshwater fish related to carp, especially *Rutilus rutilus*, a game fish found in N Europe. It has an elongated body, 6–8 in (15–45 cm) long, olive-green to gray-green above and silvery white below with reddish fins and red eyes. It lives in shoals, feeding on small animals and plants.

Roach, Hal (1892–) US film producer. His production company, founded in 1914, produced many of the films of Harold *Lloyd, *Laurel and Hardy, and other comedians of the silent cinema. His single serious film was *Of Mice and Men* (1939).

roan antelope A large African antelope, *Hippotragus equinus*. 51–59 in (130–150 cm) high at the shoulder, it is roan or reddish gray with a black-and-white face, long tufted ears, and an erect mane. The horns are shorter than those of the related *sable antelope. Roan antelopes live in herds of up to 25 in scrub and woodland.

Roanoke 37 15N 79 58W A city in Virginia, on the Roanoke River. Settled in 1740, it is an industrial center and railroad junction. Manufactures include textiles and chemicals. Population (1980): 100,427.

Robbe-Grillet, Alain (1922–) French novelist. He trained as an agronomist and statistician. He is a leading theorist and practitioner of the *nouveau roman. Instantanés* (1961) and *Pour un nouveau roman* (1963) contain a number of influential essays on the subject. As well as his novels, which include *Le Voyeur* (1955) and *La Jalousie* (1957), he has written several film scripts, notably the scenario for *L'Année dernière à Marienbad* (1961).

robber crab (*or* coconut crab) A *crab, *Birgus latro*, found on the shores of the SW Pacific and Indian Oceans. It has an extremely large body (about 40 in [1 m] from head to tail), ranging from violet to deep purple or brown in color. It lives in sand burrows during the day, emerging at night to feed on coconuts broken open by its two large pincers. Tribe: *Anomura*.

robber fly A predatory fly, also called assassin fly, belonging to a worldwide family (*Asilidae*; over 4000 species) of insect eaters. Robber flies have prominent eyes and strong bristly legs. Many species have a humped thorax and a long slender abdomen, but some (e.g. *Asilis crabroniformis*) resemble bees and wasps. Most larvae are herbivorous and live in the soil.

Robbins, Frederick Chapman (1916–) US microbiologist, who, working with John *Enders and Thomas Weller (1915–), first cultivated poliomyelitis virus outside living organisms, using cultures of living human tissue in nutrient solution. This technique enabled the development of the polio vaccine and the culture of other viruses. He shared the 1954 Nobel Prize.

Robbins, Jerome (1918–) US ballet dancer and choreographer. He choreographed the dances for many musicals, including *The King and I* (1951), *West Side Story* (1957), and *Fiddler on the Roof* (1964). He has been choreographer for the New York City Ballet since 1969.

Robert (I) the Bruce (1274–1329) King of the Scots (1306–29). After a long career of rebellion against the English crown Robert seized the Scottish throne in 1306. Although immediately forced into exile by Edward I of England, on the accession of Edward II he slowly recovered the kingdom, decisively defeating the English forces at Bannockburn (1314). A period of consolidation of his power followed, culminating in English recognition of Scottish independence in 1328.

Robert (II) the Pious (c. 970–1031) King of France (996–1031), who conquered Burgundy (1015) after years of warfare with a rival claimant. He gained his nickname for his encouragement of monasticism.

Robert II Curthose (c. 1054–1134) Duke of Normandy (1087–1134); the eldest son of William the Conqueror. He twice rebelled against his father (1077, 1083) and came into conflict with his brother William II Rufus. After fighting courageously in the first Crusade, he attempted to usurp the English throne from his youngest brother Henry I and following defeat at Tinchebrai was imprisoned (1106–34).

Robert II (1316–90) The first *Stuart King of the Scots (1371–90). He was three times regent of Scotland (jointly 1334–35; alone 1338–41 and 1346–57) while his father *David II was imprisoned or in exile. His own rule, as an old man, was of little consequence.

Robert the Wise (1278–1343) King of Naples (1309–43), a leader of the Italian *Guelfs (papal party) against the Ghibellines (imperial party). He was an outstanding administrator (hence his nickname) and patron of scientists and writers, including Petrarch and Boccaccio.

Robeson, Paul (1898–1976) US actor and singer. His best-known stage performances were in the title roles of *Othello* and Eugene O'Neill's *Emperor Jones*. He sang spirituals, made several films, and actively campaigned for black civil rights.

Robespierre, Maximilien François Marie Isidore de (1758–94) French revolutionary. A lawyer, Robespierre was elected to the States General in 1789, on the eve of the *French Revolution, and became one of the leaders of the radical *Jacobins. He gained a wide following in Paris and after the execution of Louis XVI was instrumental in the overthrow of the Girondins (1793). He subsequently wielded supreme power on the Committee of *Public Safety, instituting the *Reign of Terror. In 1794 the tide turned against him and his cult of the Supreme Being, and he was denounced in the Legislative Assembly, arrested, and guillotined.

robin A small North American songbird, *Turdus migratorius*, about 8.5–10.5 in (21.5–26.5 cm) long. The male is gray, with a brick-red breast, a blackish tail and head, and a yellow beak. The female's head and tail are not as dark. Common on farmland, in woodland, and in towns and gardens from Canada to S US, a robin defends its territory fiercely, using its warbling song as a signal to warn off intruders. Family: *Turdidae* (thrushes).

PAUL ROBESON

Robin Hood An English outlaw, probably legendary, who figures in a series of ballads dating from the 14th century. According to the *Lytell Geste of Robyn Hoode* (c. 1495) he killed the evil sheriff of Nottingham, was visited in his forest home by the king, and was subsequently employed in the royal household. His mistress Maid Marian and his association with Sherwood were later additions to the story.

Robinson, Edward Arlington (1869–1935) US poet. Troubled by poverty and alcoholism throughout his life, he established himself with a novel in verse, *Captain Craig* (1902), and confirmed his reputation with the poems in *The Town Down the River* (1910) and *The Man against the Sky* (1916). He wrote a large number of dramatic monologues and several long narrative poems, including *Amaranth* and *King Jasper* (1935). Some of his best verse appeared in an early volume, *The Children of Night* (revised 1897). He won three Pulitzer Prizes.

Robinson, Edward G. (Emanuel Goldenberg; 1893–1972) US film actor, born in Romania. He was cast as a gangster in *Little Caesar* (1930) and other films during the 1930s but he played more varied roles in later films, such as *Double Indemnity* (1943) and *The Outrage* (1964).

Robinson, Frank (1935–) US baseball player. An outfielder and first baseman, he played for the Cincinnati Reds (1956–65), the Baltimore Orioles (1966–72), the Los Angeles Dodgers (1972–73), and the California Angels (1973–74). He managed the Cleveland Indians (1974–77), the first black manager in major league baseball. He was elected to the Baseball Hall of Fame (1982).

Robinson, Jackie (Jack Roosevelt R.; 1919–72) US baseball player. A high school and college star in several sports, he played with the Negro National baseball league in 1945 and was then signed by Branch *Rickey to play with the National League's Brooklyn Dodgers, the first black ever signed by a major league team. At second base, he began to play for the Dodgers in 1947, winning many honors and compiling a career batting average of .311 before his retirement in 1957. He was elected to the Baseball Hall of Fame in 1962.

Robinson, Sir Robert (1886–1975) British chemist, who investigated the structure of the alkaloids *morphine (1925) and *strychnine (1946). The latter work enabled Robert *Woodward to synthesize strychnine eight years later. Robinson received the Nobel Prize in 1947.

Robinson, Sugar Ray (Walker Smith; 1920–) US boxer, who was world welterweight champion (1946–51) and five times middleweight champion (twice in 1951, 1955, 1957, 1958–60). He fought 202 professional bouts, of which he lost only 19.

Robinson-Patman Act (1936) US law that prohibited price discrimination. Enacted to clarify part of the *Clayton Anti-Trust Act of 1914, this law prevented large chain-type stores from offering merchandise at a low price that could not be matched by small independent retailers.

Rob Roy (Robert Macgregor; 1671–1734) Scottish outlaw, whose violent life was romanticized in Sir Walter Scott's novel *Rob Roy* (1818). He embarked on his career of banditry after losing his family fortunes in 1712. He was eventually arrested and sentenced to transportation but was pardoned in 1727.

Rochdale 53 38N 2 09W A city in N England, in Greater Manchester. Engineering and textiles (particularly cotton spinning) are the main industries. Population (1981): 92,704.

Rochester 43 12N 77 37W A city in New York, on Lake Ontario and the Genesee River. Founded in 1789, it is the site of the University of Rochester (1850) and the Rochester Institute of Technology (1829). Its industries include horticulture and the manufacture of photographic and optical equipment. Population (1980): 241,509.

Rochester 44 01N 92 27W A city in Minnesota. It is the site of the Mayo Clinic (1889) and the Mayo Medical Center. Manufactures include electronic and recording equipment. Population (1980): 54,287.

Rochester 51 24N 0 30E A city and port in SE England. It was a Roman stronghold and has a 12th-century castle and a Norman cathedral. Population (1981): 52,505.

Rochester, John Wilmot, 2nd Earl of (1647–80) British poet. A dissolute member of the court of Charles II, he wrote many short poems famous for their uninhibited bawdiness. His longer satirical poems include *A Satire against Mankind* and *Upon Nothing*. He is said to have repented of his past life just before his death.

rock (music) A style of popular music dating from the early 1950s, resulting from the fusion of rhythm and blues with country music. The term **rock and roll** was originally applied to such songs as "Rock Around the Clock" (1955) by Bill Haley (1925–81) and the Comets and "Heartbreak Hotel" (1956) by Elvis Presley, whose bands consisted of electric guitars, drums, and amplified vocalists. In the 1960s the term "rock" replaced "rock and roll." Such groups as the Beatles and Chicago expanded the traditional band to include string backing and other instruments, and began to explore the possibilities offered by studio recording techniques, synthesizers, etc. Rock increasingly split into subgroups, such as **acid rock**, based on drug experiences (Jimi Hendrix, the Jefferson Airplane), and **hard rock**, emphasizing a strong rhythmic beat (the Byrds, the Bee Gees), and **progressive rock**, which admitted long instrumental solos and more advanced harmonies. In the late 1970s **punk rock** (*or* new wave) returned to a basic and very aggressive style of performance with such groups as the Sex Pistols. *Compare* pop music.

rock (petrology) A solid mixture of *minerals forming part of the earth's crust. The minerals are usually consolidated to form a hard compact mass, but geologists include unconsolidated material, such as sand, as rock. Rocks are classified according to their formation (*see* igneous rock; metamorphic rock; sedimentary rock), their age (*see* stratigraphy), and their composition. Individual rock types are much more varied in chemical composition than minerals, and most consist of several different minerals. Some minerals in rocks can be seen with the naked eye, such as the quartz, orthoclase, and biotite in granite, whereas the minerals in clay can only be seen under an electron microscope. The principal minerals in rocks are the silicates (including silica), carbonates, and oxides. The essential minerals in a rock are those that determine its classification; accessory minerals are those that do not affect its classification. *Petrology is the study of rocks.

rock crystal. *See* quartz.

rock dove A cliff-nesting dove, *Columba livia*, of S Europe, Asia, and N Africa. 13 in (32 cm) long, it has a gray plumage with a green-and-purple neck patch, two black wing bars, and a white rump. A fast flier with excellent homing ability, it feeds on seeds, grain, shellfish, and seaweed.

Rockefeller, John Davison (1839–1937) US industrialist and financier. Beginning his career as a clerk and bookkeeper, Rockefeller became involved in the early development of the Pennsylvania petroleum industry and organized the Standard Oil Co. in 1867. As president of Standard Oil, Rockefeller methodically eliminated the competition of other firms and by the mid-1870s controlled virtually the entire American oil refining and distribution industry. In 1882 his organization became the Standard Oil Trust, but an adverse ruling by the Ohio Supreme Court forced its dissolution in 1899. Rockefeller subsequently established a holding company for his assets called the Standard Oil Co. of New Jersey, but this too was dissolved by an anti-trust ruling of the US Supreme Court in 1911. Having amassed a fortune estimated at more than $1 billion, Rockefeller devoted his later years to philanthropic work. In 1892 he established the endowment of the University of Chicago, and with his son **John Davison Rockefeller, Jr.** (1874–1960), he established the Rockefeller Institute for Medical Research (1901) and the Rockefeller Foundation (1913).

Rockefeller, Nelson Aldrich (1908–79) US politician; vice president of the United States (1974–77). A grand nephew of financier John D. *Rockefeller, he became one of the leaders of the liberal wing of the Republican Party, serving four terms as governor of New York (1958–73). Rockefeller unsuccessfully sought the Republican presidential nomination in 1960, 1964, and 1968. In 1974, following the resignation of Richard *Nixon, he finally gained a national office through his appointment as vice president by Gerald *Ford. Rockefeller retired from public life in 1977 to devote himself to philanthropic work.

rocket Any of several annual or biennial herbaceous plants of the genus *Sisymbrium*, having yellow flowers. London rocket (*S. irio*), up to 24 in (60 cm) high, is found on roadsides, walls, and in waste places in Europe, W Asia, North America, and N Africa. Its name results from its abundance after the Great Fire of London in 1666. The name is also given to plants of several other related genera. Family: *Cruciferae*.

rockets Vehicles or missiles powered by jet propulsion that carry their own fuel and oxidizer and can therefore travel both in space and in the atmosphere. Rockets have no lift surfaces (*see* aeronautics), obtaining both lift and thrust from their propulsive jets. Solid-fuel firework rockets were known to the Chinese in the 13th century and have been used sporadically in war ever since. However, the first liquid-fueled rocket to fly was designed by the American R. H. *Goddard in 1926. This achievement attracted little interest, except in Germany, where the *Peenemünde rocket research station was set up. It was here that Werner von *Braun produced the *V-2 rocket in World War II. Intercontinental *ballistic missiles (with nuclear warheads), developed by both the US and Soviet Union from this model, now form part of the armory of all the principal nations. These rockets, in turn, led to the space rockets that carried man to the moon.

Space rockets are built in stages, a high-thrust vehicle providing lift-off and acceleration into the thinner atmosphere, where this first stage is jettisoned and the second stage takes over. The world's biggest space rocket, the US Saturn V, is a three-stage rocket weighing 3000 tons fully laden. The first stage burns kerosene and the second and third stages burn liquid hydrogen. Liquid oxygen (lox) is the oxidizer for all stages. This rocket can carry a load of 45 tons into space.

Fuel economy is one of the most important factors in rocket design—the specific impulse of a rocket being its most significant characteristic. The specific impulse is the time in seconds to burn one kilogram of fuel while producing one newton of thrust. Typical values are 3400 s for a solid fuel, 4500 s for liquid hydrogen-lox, and over 10,000 s for an ion engine. In an ion-engine rocket an easily ionized substance, such as cesium, is heated to produce ions, which are accelerated by an electric field to produce thrust. These engines of the future could be powered by nuclear energy or solar energy to produce the necessary 50 kW of electricity for each newton of thrust.

Rockford 42 17N 89 06W A city in N central Illinois, on the W bank of the Rock River, NW of Chicago. Settled in 1834 at a shallow ford, it manufactures machinery, appliances, tools, paints, leather and food products, and furniture. Population (1980): 139,712.

Rockhampton 23 22S 150 32E A city and port in Australia, in central Queensland on the Fitzroy River. It is a commercial center for an extensive hinterland producing meat, gold, copper, and coal. Population (1980 est): 53,500.

Rockingham, Charles Watson-Wentworth, 2nd Marquess of (1730–82) British statesman; prime minister (1765–66, 1782). As leader of the so-called Rockingham Whigs, he supported the American colonies in their conflict with Britain. In 1765 he repealed the *Stamp Act and led the opposition to Lord North's government during the American Revolution.

rockrose A small spreading shrub, *Helianthemum chamaecistus*, up to 11.8 in (30 cm) high with bright-yellow five-petaled flowers; it is found in grassland and scrub of Europe and W Asia. Hybrids of this and similar species are cultivated as garden ornamentals, with many different colored varieties. Family: *Cistaceae*.

rock tripe A leafy *lichen of the genus *Umbilicaria*, found in Arctic and temperate regions. It is rich in carbohydrates and is edible when boiled. In Japan it is considered a delicacy, being eaten in salads or deep fried. Some species are also used as dyes.

Rockwell, Norman (1894–1978) US artist. Best known for his covers for *The Saturday Evening Post*, the first of which appeared on a 1916 issue, he painted pictures of small-town everyday life situations. His *Four Freedoms* mural (1943) is housed in Nassau Tavern in Princeton, NJ, and was used by the Office of War Information during World War II.

Rocky Mountain National Park A national park in N central Colorado, NW of Boulder, that straddles the Continental Divide. Established in 1915, it includes over 100 peaks of the Rockies; the highest point in the park is Long's Peak (14,255 ft; 4345 m). Glaciers and evidences of the glacial age are abundant, as is the wildlife. With the exception of a few roads and camping sites, the park is wilderness. Area: 410 sq mi (1062 sq km).

Rocky Mountains (*or* Rockies) The chief mountain system in North America. It extends roughly N–S for about 3000 mi (4800 km) between New Mexico and the Yukon (Canada), forming the *Continental Divide. It rises to 14,431 ft (4399 m) at Mount Elbert. Some geographers consider the Yukon and Alaska ranges as part of the system, making Mount Logan, at 19,850 ft (6050 m), the highest point.

rococo A style dominant in the fine arts and decorative arts of France between about 1700 and 1750. Developing in reaction to the *baroque pomp of the Louis XIV period, it was characterized by curved forms, slender proportions, asymmetry, pastel colors, and a general effect of intimacy, gaiety, and delicacy. The rococo style was particularly manifest in the interior decoration of Parisian townhouses and furniture, porcelain, and metalwork. Famous rococo artists include the painters *Fragonard, *Boucher, and *Watteau and the sculptor *Clodion. The style spread to Austria and Germany, where the leading exponent was the architect Balthazar *Neumann. England remained largely untouched by it, although some rococo features appear in the work of *Hogarth and *Gainsborough. The rococo was supplanted by *neoclassicism.

rodent A mammal belonging to the order *Rodentia* (over 1700 species). Rodents are distributed worldwide and occupy a wide range of terrestrial and semiaquatic habitats. They range in size from about 2.9 in (7.5 cm) (the smallest mice) to 51 in (130 cm) (the capybara). Rodents have distinctive teeth. The single pairs of chisel-like incisors in each jaw continue to grow throughout life, as they are worn away by gnawing. There are no second incisor or canine teeth, leaving a gap between the front teeth and cheek teeth. When the rodent is gnawing, the cheeks are drawn into the gap and the lower jaw is moved forward so that the upper and lower incisors can meet. This prevents the rodent from swallowing gnawed material and from wearing out its cheek teeth.

Rodents are important to man as agricultural pests, fur animals, and as experimental animals for scientific research. They are divided into three suborders: *Hystricomorpha* (porcupines, cavies, chinchillas, etc.; 180 species); *Sciuromorpha* (squirrels, beavers, marmots, chipmunks, etc.; 366 species); and *Myomorpha* (rats, mice, lemmings, voles, etc.; 1183 species).

rodeo A sport that grew out of ranching skills after the Civil War, now controlled by the Rodeo Cowboys Association, founded in 1945, and the Girl's Rodeo Association, founded in 1948. A rodeo, or contest, includes six main events: bronco riding with and without a saddle, bull riding, calf roping, steer wrestling, and team roping. Professional rodeo riders are not hired to take part, but live on prize money.

Roderic. *See* Rory O'Connor.

Rodgers, Richard Charles (1902–79) US composer of musical comedies. With the lyricist Lorenz Hart (1895–1943) he wrote such works as *The Girl Friend* (1926) and *Pal Joey* (1940). After Hart's death he collaborated with Oscar *Hammerstein II in *Oklahoma* (1943), *The King and I* (1951), and other musicals.

Rodin, Auguste (1840–1917) French sculptor. He produced his first major work, *The Age of Bronze* (1877), after visiting Italy (1875), where he was influenced by the work of *Michelangelo and *Donatello. Its controversial realism was a factor in the vicissitudes of his public commissions: *The Burghers of Calais* (1884–86), his nude monument of Victor Hugo, and his dressing-gowned Balzac were all initially rejected. Nevertheless, by 1900 Rodin had established an international reputation, his bronze portrait busts and his figures in marble, notably *The Kiss* (1886), being particularly admired. His most personal work, *The Gates of Hell*, which was originally a government commission of the 1880s, was left unfinished at his death. Many of its symbolic figures, for example *The Thinker*, became well-known independent sculptures.

Rodney, George Brydges, 1st Baron (1719–92) British admiral. He wrecked (1759–60) a French invasion fleet during the Seven Years' War and won victories (1780–82) against the powers that supported the American Revolution. His victory over the French off Dominica (1782) helped Britain to gain favorable terms in the concluding Peace of Versailles (1783).

rods and cones. *See* retina.

Roebling, John Augustus (1806–69) US engineer, who with his son **Washington Augustus Roebling** (1837–1926) designed the Brooklyn Bridge in New York, which was opened in 1883. They also designed major suspension bridges, including those over the Niagara River at the Niagara Falls and over the Ohio River between Cincinnati and Covington. John Roebling died after an accident while supervising the construction of the Brooklyn Bridge.

roe deer A small deer, *Capreolus capreolus*, of temperate Eurasian forests. About 27.5 in (70 cm) high at the shoulder, roe deer have a dark-brown winter coat, a red-brown summer coat, and a large white rump patch; males have small three-pointed antlers. They feed at night on leaves, shoots, and berries and live in pairs or small family groups.

roentgen A unit of dose of ionizing radiation equal to the dose that produces ions of one sign carrying a charge of 2.58×10^{-4} coulomb in air.

Roentgen, Wilhelm Konrad (1845–1923) German physicist, who discovered *X-rays while professor at the University of Würzburg, Bavaria. In 1895 Roentgen was investigating the *luminescence that cathode rays produce in certain substances and discovered that the luminescence persisted when the cathode rays themselves were blocked by cardboard. He correctly concluded that some other type of radiation was coming from the cathode-ray tube. He named the radiation X-rays and his discovery that the rays pass through matter quickly led to their use in medical diagnosis. In 1901, he received the first Nobel Prize for physics. The unit of X-ray dose (*see* roentgen) is named for him.

Roeselare (French name: Roulers)   50 57N 3 08E A city in W Belgium. An important German base in World War I, it suffered much damage. Industries include textiles (particularly linen) and carpets. Population (1981 est): 51,945.

Roger II (1095–1154) Norman King of Sicily (1130–54). He became Count of Sicily in 1105 and created a strong kingdom augmented by the acquisition of Calabria (1122), Apulia (1127), Capua (1136), and Naples (1140) on the Italian mainland. He also attacked the Byzantine Empire, pillaging the coastal cities of Dalmatia and Epirus. His court was a great intellectual center for both Christian and Muslim scholars.

Rogers, Carl R(ansom) (1902–) US psychologist, who developed client- (or patient-) centered psychotherapy upon which present day psychotherapy procedures are based. He believed that only through a personal doctor-patient relationship can a patient realize his potential to solve his own problems. Rogers taught at several universities, including the University of Rochester, the University of Chicago, and the University of Wisconsin. Among his works are *Counseling and Psychotherapy* (1942), *Client-Centered Therapy* (1951), *On Becoming a Person* (1961), *The Therapeutic Relationships with Schizophrenics* (1967), and *Carl Rogers on Personal Power* (1977).

Rogers, Ginger (Virginia McMath; 1911–) US actress and singer. During the 1930s she partnered Fred *Astaire in many popular film musicals, including *Top Hat* (1935), *Swing Time* (1936), and *Follow the Fleet* (1936). She was also a talented comedy actress.

Rogers, Will (William Penn Adair R.; 1879–1935) US entertainer. He had learned the intricacies of lasso roping as a boy in Oklahoma and, from 1904, performed in Wild West and vaudeville shows. His rope-twirling act was combined with casual, but often biting, humorous comments on life and the social scene. He wrote a column for *The New York Times* (1922–35) and several books as well as appearing in the movies *A Connecticut Yankee* (1931), *State Fair* (1933), and *David Harum* (1934). He was killed when a plane, piloted by Wiley Post (1900–35), went down in N Alaska.

Roget, Peter Mark (1779–1869) British physician and philologist. He was secretary of the Royal Society from 1827 to 1849. His well-known *Thesaurus of English Words and Phrases* (1852), a dictionary of synonyms, has been revised in numerous editions.

Röhm, Ernst (1887–1934) German soldier, who organized Hitler's *Brownshirts. Röhm's ambition to increase the power of the Brownshirts led to his execution without trial.

Rokitansky, Karl, Freiherr von (1804–78) Austrian pathologist, whose detailed anatomical studies of numerous autopsies helped establish the science of pathological anatomy. Rokitansky is noted particularly for describing the different kinds of pneumonia and a liver disease known as Rokitansky's disease.

Roland, Song of. See chanson de geste.

Rolfe, Frederick William (1860–1913) British novelist, also known by the pseudonym Baron Corvo. A Roman Catholic convert, who was not accepted as a candidate for the priesthood his frustration and delusions

were expressed in the fantasy *Hadrian the Seventh* (1904), which concerns a convert who becomes pope. His other works include *Stories Toto Told Me* (1898) and *The Desire and Pursuit of the Whole* (1934).

Rolland, Romain (1866–1944) French novelist, dramatist, and essayist. He was also a distinguished musicologist, and his best-known novel, *Jean Christophe* (1904–12), concerns a German composer. His philosophical idealism, much influenced by Tolstoy, was expressed in numerous volumes of essays and biographies. He won the Nobel Prize in 1915.

roller A short-legged bird belonging to a family (*Coraciidae*; 12 species) occurring in warm regions of the Old World. 10–15 in (25–40 cm) long, rollers are blue or violet and have a large head, a strong slightly hooked bill, and a long tail. They feed in flocks on ants, locusts, and lizards. Order: *Coraciiformes* (hornbills, kingfishers, etc.).

Rolling Stones, the A British rock group, formed in 1962. Their early hits included "The Last Time" and "Satisfaction." They became famous for their notorious behavior in public, made successful tours of the US, and recorded a number of albums, including *Beggar's Banquet* (1968). The original members of the group were Mick *Jagger, Keith Richard (1943–), Bill Wyman (1941–), Charlie Watts (1941–), and Brian Jones (1944–69).

Rollo (c. 860–c. 931) Viking leader, who founded the duchy of Normandy. Having invaded NW France, Rollo was given the territory around Rouen by treaty (911) with Charles (III) the Simple (879–929; reigned 898–923), thus becoming the first Duke of Normandy.

Rolls, Charles Stewart (1877–1910) British automobile manufacturer and aviator. A car dealer, in 1906 he went into partnership with Henry *Royce to found Rolls-Royce Ltd. Rolls was the first to fly nonstop across the English Channel and back (1910), dying shortly afterward in an aircrash.

Romains, Jules (Louis Farigoule; 1885–1972) French poet, novelist, and dramatist. He was a leading exponent of the philosophical theory of *unanimisme*, which emphasized collective as opposed to individual emotions and psychology. His best-known works are the satirical play *Knock* (1923) and the novel cycle *Les Hommes de bonne volonté* (1932–46).

Roman art and architecture The styles of art and architecture of the ancient Romans. Deriving principally from their Greek and Etruscan predecessors, Roman styles in the fine and applied arts have profoundly influenced western traditions. The Romans' main contribution to classical architecture was the formal and structural development of the □arch, *dome, and *vault and the introduction of new types of building, such as *thermae, *amphitheaters, and triumphal arches. Their advanced building techniques and use of concrete were unsurpassed until the 19th century. The Pantheon and the Colosseum (both in Rome) remain as fine examples of their monumental building techniques, while the ruins of Pompeii provide an insight into their domestic architecture and their skill in town planning. In the other arts their style was modeled on that of the Greeks, although their sculptures were less idealistic and more inclined to personal portraiture. Little painting has survived, but from the evidence of Pompeii and elsewhere *mosaics and murals seem to have been popular.

Roman Catholic Church The Christian Church of which the pope is the temporal leader (*see* papacy). After the split with the Eastern *Orthodox Churches (1054; *see* Filioque), Roman Catholicism was the unchallenged spiritual authority in W Europe; Church dignitaries possessed great political, as well as spiritual, power and *monasticism flourished. In the early 16th century the rising tide of *Protestantism demonstrated the need for urgent reforms within the Church. The Council of Trent (1545–63), convoked to discuss these reforms, has largely determined the present dogmatic, disciplinary, and liturgical character of Roman Catholicism (*see also* Counter-Reformation), although important reforms were initiated by the second *Vatican Council. In general, a higher reliance is placed by Roman Catholics upon tradition and authority, especially regarding interpretation of the Bible, than is the case in most Protestant Churches. The Church organization is to an advanced degree centralized and hierarchical (*see* cardinals, college of; Roman Curia), and the pope's decisions are reinforced by the doctrine of *infallibility promulgated in 1870. Other accepted doctrines include *transubstantiation and *purgatory. The number of the *sacraments has been fixed at seven since the 12th century. The cult of the Virgin Mary, which flourished in the middle ages, underwent a major revival in the 19th century, and the veneration and invocation of *saints are encouraged. Church furnishings, music, and vestments are more elaborate than in Protestant Churches. Until the mid-20th century Latin was the sole language of the Mass. Roman Catholicism has spread worldwide due to strenuous missionary efforts since the 16th century (*see* Jesuits) and is the largest Christian denomination. In a world becoming progressively more disinclined to accept religious authority, the Catholic Church has managed to maintain its strong following, largely as a result of firm direction from Rome. However, some modernization has already taken place (the use of the vernacular in the Mass, changes in monastic dress, etc.), although other controversial issues (abortion, contraception, divorce, married priests, etc.) remain to be resolved.

romance A term loosely applied to a medieval verse or prose narrative that dealt with nonhistorical material and first became popular in 12th-century France. Its central themes were courtly love, chivalry, and adventure, and it was distinguished from the earlier *chanson de geste by being less heroic and more sophisticated in tone. It was intended as entertainment rather than for any religious or political purpose. Romances are conventionally classified into three types according to subject matter: (1) the Matter of Britain—romances based on the *Arthurian legend, which was popular throughout Europe; (2) the Matter of Rome—romances about the Trojan War, Thebes, or Alexander the Great; and (3) the Matter of France—romances about Charlemagne and his knights. Among the most famous medieval romances are the five Arthurian romances of *Chrétien de Troyes; the *Parzival* (c. 1210) of Wolfram von Eschenbach; the *Tristan und Isolde* (c. 1210) of Gottfried von Strassburg; the anonymous Middle English *Gawain and the Green Knight* (c. 1400); and Sir Thomas Malory's *Morte d'Arthur* (c. 1470).

Romance languages Descendants of the *Italic language group, in particular of the spoken form of *Latin, called Vulgar Latin. The group consists of modern *French, *Italian, *Spanish, *Portuguese, *Romanian, *Catalan, the Rhaetian (see *Romansch) group of dialects, Sardinian, and the now extinct Dalmatian. As this list shows, many Romance languages are in fact regional dialects rather than national languages. They are classified as a group on the basis of a shared section of basic vocabulary, which originated in the influence of the language of the Roman conquerors of the Mediterranean area in which the languages of the group are clustered. Since 1500 their use has spread outside Europe to South America and Africa, with French, Spanish, and Portuguese colonization.

Roman comedy A dramatic genre that developed chiefly from Greek sources and flourished in the late 3rd and 2nd centuries BC. The first Latin version of a Greek comedy was written by Livius Andronicus (c. 284–c. 204 BC) in 240 BC. His successors included Naevius (c. 270–c. 201 BC) and *Plautus, whose plays, based on those of Greek *New Comedy writers, especially Menander and Philemon, were enlivened by colloquial language and topical and bawdy humor. The plays of *Ter-

ence and Caecilius Statius (c. 219–168 BC) were more sophisticated in their plots and characterization. At the Renaissance the plays of Plautus and Terence, the only representatives of Roman comedy to survive complete, were revived and became the basis of modern ideas of comedy.

Roman Curia (Latin: *Curia Romana*) The papal court, comprising the chief judicial and administrative bodies of the *Roman Catholic Church. Its powers are delegated by the pope, who takes responsibility for its acts. Extensively reformed in 1967 by Pope Paul VI, it consists of three tribunals, which are mainly concerned with judicial matters; five offices, including the Chancery, which issues papal bulls, and the offices of the Palatinate Secretaries, such as that of the Cardinal Secretary of State, which deals with political affairs; and nine Roman Congregations, which are permanent commissions of cardinals having specific tasks (regarding rites, missions, etc.).

Roman Empire The imperial period of ancient Roman history from 27 BC, when Octavian became emperor as *Augustus, until 476 AD. Under imperial government many of the political institutions of the *Roman Republic, notably the Senate, continued to function, although Augustus and his successors enjoyed supreme power as *princeps* (chief citizen). Augustus, who created an efficient administrative system for the Empire, fostered peace and prosperity, which continued, despite outbreaks of rebellion, under the paternalistic rule of the Flavian (69–96 AD; see Vespasian; Titus; Domitian) and Antonine (96–180; see Nerva; Trajan; Hadrian; Antoninus Pius; Marcus Aurelius) emperors. Trade and industry flourished throughout the Empire, new cities were founded, and frontiers, although little extended, were strengthened. Civil war, however, followed the death of *Commodus (193), with provincial armies nominating their own imperial candidates. Order was briefly restored by Lucius Septimus *Severus (reigned 193–211), who openly acknowledged his dependence on military might, increasing the powers of the *Praetorian Guard (imperial bodyguard). The 3rd century saw a rapid succession of army-nominated emperors, while Rome's frontiers were threatened by the aggression of the *Sasanians and the Goths. *Diocletian (reigned 284–305) countered these attacks with the reorganization of the Empire between East (see Eastern Roman Empire) and West (293). It was reunited (324) under *Constantine the Great, the first Christian emperor, who founded a new imperial capital at Constantinople (see Istanbul). His attempts to establish unity were, however, short lived: civil war and economic decline followed his death and the western Empire fell prey to barbarian invasions. The Visigoths sacked Rome in 410; Carthage was captured in 439 by the Vandals,

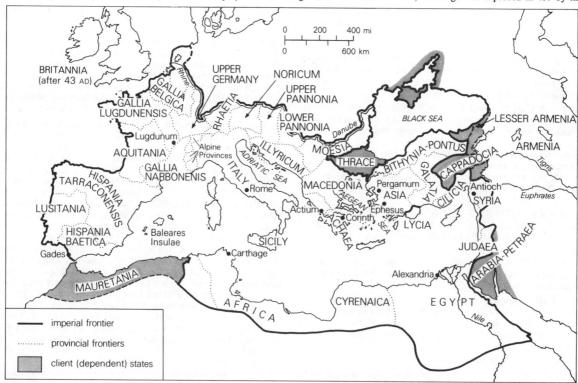

ROMAN EMPIRE *In 14 AD, at the death of Augustus, Roman rule or influence extended all the way around the Mediterranean.*

who in 455 also sacked Rome; in 476 the last Roman emperor of the West, *Romulus Augustulus, was deposed by the German king Odoacer. The Eastern Roman, or Byzantine, Empire survived until 1453.

romanesque art and architecture A style of art and architecture that flourished in Europe from the 11th century until the introduction of the *gothic in the mid-12th century. Its origins were mixed, being a combination of Carolingian, Roman, and Byzantine styles, and regional influences produced many variations between areas. Primarily an ecclesiastical art form, it was largely stimulated by the need for more churches, now possible on a large scale because of the arrival of relative peace after centuries of disturbance. The increasing complexity of Church ritual was reflected in the greater number of side chapels. The decline of building techniques since antiquity resulted in very solid buildings with thick walls, windows with semicircular arches, and simple stone vaulting. The other important branch of romanesque art was sculpture. It was primarily used to decorate churches, either with geometrical or plant and animal patterns on the fabric of the building, especially on the capitals, or statues of religious subjects inside the building. Many examples of romanesque art still survive, one of the most notable being Pisa Cathedral. *See also* Norman art and architecture. □arch.

Romania, Socialist Republic of A country in SE Europe, with an E coastline on the Black Sea. The Carpathian Mountains and the Transylvanian Alps in the center of the country separate the plains in the E and S from the Transylvanian plateau in the NW; the Danube River forms most of its S boundary. Most of the inhabitants are Romanians, who trace their ancestry back to the Latin settlers of the Roman province of Dacia. *Economy*: although there has been a pronounced shift in the balance of the economy toward industry since World War II, agriculture is still important, much of it organized in collectives and state farms. The main crops are corn, wheat, potatoes, sugar beet, and fruit. Livestock is also important and there is a growing wine industry. Minerals include oil and gas, salt, lignite, iron, and copper. Hydroelectricity is a valuable source of power, particularly since the opening of the Iron Gate facility on the Danube (shared with Yugoslavia) in 1972. Varied industries, all now nationalized although there has been a relaxation in central controls since 1978, include heavy industries such as mineral and metals, oil, motor vehicles, machinery, and chemicals, the products of which provide the main exports (mainly to communist countries). There is a considerable timber industry and tourism is of increasing importance to the economy. *History*: formed in 1861 from the principalities of *Moldavia and *Walachia, Romania gained independence from the Ottoman Empire in 1880 and in 1881 became a kingdom under Carol I. Romania joined (1916) the Allies in World War I and was occupied by the Germans. In 1918 it obtained Bessarabia, Bukovina, and Transylvania, which it was forced to relinquish to the Axis Powers in 1940. Shortly afterward Carol II abdicated in favor of his son Michael and Antonescu came to power. He gave Romanian military support to Germany until Soviet forces entered the country and Antonescu's government was overthrown (1944). After World War II a communist-dominated coalition was established (1945) and in 1947 Michael abdicated. Elections in 1948 resulted in a clear communist victory. Since the early 1960s Romania has become increasingly independent of the Soviet Union, especially in foreign affairs, condemning the Soviet invasions of Czechoslovakia and Afghanistan as well as establishing good relations with western countries and China. President: Nicolae Ceauçescu. Prime minister: Constantin Dascalescu. Official language: Romanian. Official currency: leu of 100 bani. Area: 91,699 sq mi (237,500 sq km). Population (1983 est): 22,649,000. Capital: Bucharest. Main port: Constanța.

Romanian A *Romance language, the main form of which is spoken in Romania and is known as Daco-Romanian. Other forms are Aromanian or Macedo-Romanian (Greece, Yugoslavia, Albania, and Bulgaria); Megleno-Romanian (N Greece); and Istro-Romanian (Istrian peninsula). Geographical proximity to the Slavonic languages has influenced Romanian's grammar, vocabulary, and phonology.

Roman law The body of laws compiled by the Romans, which forms the basis of the *civil law of many modern countries throughout the world. Although Roman law dates from the time of the kings (from c. 753 BC), the *Twelve Tables (450 BC) is regarded as the first major codification. Before about 150 BC these laws were elaborated as the *jus civile* (civil law), i.e. the law applicable exclusively to Roman citizens. With increasing territories, commercial interests, and foreign treaties, another system, the *jus gentium* (law of nations), was also applied by Roman courts. This system of international law derived from the philosophical concept of natural law (i.e. a law common to all men and to nature) and was used in cases involving provincial Roman subjects of different states and in suits between a foreigner or provincial and a Roman citizen. It gradually influenced the *jus*

civile, and the two systems came to have many identical features. As Roman law developed, by judicial interpretation, by edict, and by legislation, there arose a number of anomalies, until the Byzantine emperor *Justinian I sponsored legal reforms embodied in the definitive codification of Roman law, the *Corpus Juris Civilis* (Body of Civil Law) or Justinian Code, published between 529 and 565 AD. This consisted of four parts: (1) the *Codex Constitutionum*, a chronological collection of the ordinances (*constitutiones*) of the emperors, with all contradictions, anomalies, etc., eliminated; (2) the *Digest*, a collection of statements by jurists on points of law; (3) the *Institutes*, a textbook for law students explaining legal institutions; and (4) the *Novellae* or *Novels*, the new ordinances issued by Justinian after the publication of the *Codex*. Roman law, with local variations, continued in use throughout medieval Europe and after the fall of the Byzantine Empire. The impetus for its spread outside Europe in the 19th century was given by the most influential modern codification based on it, the *Code Napoléon*.

Roman literature. *See* Latin literature.

Romanovs The last ruling dynasty of Russia (1613–1917), noted for their absolutism and for transforming Russia into a large empire. The first Romanov tsar was *Michael, whose election ended the *Time of Troubles. His most famous successors were *Peter the Great, *Catherine the Great, *Alexander I, *Nicholas I, and *Alexander II. In March, 1917, during the Russian Revolution, Romanov rule ended with the abdication of *Nicholas II. He and his family were executed.

Roman religion The polytheistic religion of ancient Rome. The earliest cults worshiped local Italian deities of the fields, woods, springs, and hearth. As Rome grew to statehood its religion changed character: the gods of its Sabine and Etruscan neighbors (e.g. Quirinus and *Juno) were absorbed and *Mars, originally an agrarian spirit, became god of war. The state religion with its various priestly colleges (*see also* augury) centered on the temple of *Jupiter on the Capitoline hill (Rome). The influence of *Greek religion caused the identification of many Roman deities with Greek counterparts (Jupiter with *Zeus, *Vesta with *Hestia, etc.), but although their attributes changed their worship remained characteristically Roman. In 204 BC the orgiastic cult of *Cybele reached Rome, followed soon afterward by that of *Dionysus. The eastward expansion of Roman power brought contact with the esoteric cult of *Isis (*see also* mysteries) and *Mithraism. Emperor worship became an important part of official religion and a touchstone of loyalty. In the fringes of the Empire the Roman gods were often assimilated with local deities (e.g. at *Bath, England, Minerva was equated with the resident goddess Sulis and worshiped as Sulis Minerva). Official toleration of Christianity under *Constantine from 313 AD occasioned the gradual extinction of the old religion, despite attempts at revival (360–63) by *Julian the Apostate. *See also* ancestor worship; Feriae.

Roman Republic (510–27 BC) The period of ancient Roman history between the expulsion of *Tarquin the Proud and the proclamation as *Augustus of the first Roman emperor.

Republican government comprised two chief magistrates (later *consuls) elected annually, an increasing number of subordinate magistrates, the *Senate, and popular assemblies (*see* comitia). Power lay in the hands of the *patricians until the *plebeians, after two centuries of struggle, achieved access to all state offices.

Roman dominance over the rest of Italy was achieved by the early 3rd century: the tribes of Latium (the Latin League) were reduced by 338, victory against the Samnites of the S Apennines was attained by 290, and the Greek settlements in the S were conquered by 275. By the mid-2nd century Cisalpine *Gaul had been subdued and the *Punic Wars with Carthage brought control of the Mediterranean (146) and Rome's first overseas *provinces (Sicily, Sardinia, Spain, Africa). Concomitantly, dominance over Greece was achieved with the subjection of Illyria, Macedonia (*see* Macedonian Wars), and the Achaean League (*see* Achaea) and, following the acquisition of Pergamum in 133, control of much of Asia Minor. In the mid-1st century *Caesar completed the conquest of Transalpine Gaul.

The conquest of Italy was accompanied by the gradual extension of Roman citizenship (*see* civitas) and the construction of a network of roads, which brought Italy a degree of unity. The emergence, however, of a landowning elite who built up vast estates (*latifundia*) at the expense of small farmers resulted in serious unemployment. The attempts in the second half of the 2nd century of the *Gracchus brothers at agricultural reform, although partially successful, aggravated the conflict between the Optimates (the aristocratic party) and the Populares (the popular party). The Republic was further undermined by provincial unrest, which, together with the military ineptness of the Senate in the late 2nd century, brought a series of ambitious army commanders to the fore.

The first of these, *Marius, emerged as a champion of the people but the popular party lost a bloody power struggle to the aristocrat *Sulla, whose dictatorship (83–79) was marked by legislation to strengthen the Senate. This was revoked in 70 by *Pompey and *Crassus, who ten years later formed the so-called first *Triumvirate with Caesar. The death of Crassus (53) and Pompey's intrigues with Caesar's senatorial enemies brought civil war. Caesar's victory and subsequent short-lived dictatorship rang the knell of the Roman Republic, which was finally destroyed by Octavian's defeat of *Mark Antony and his assumption of absolute power as Augustus. *See also* Roman Empire.

Romans, Epistle of Paul to the A New Testament book written from Corinth by Paul in about 57 AD to the Christians at Rome. The first 11 chapters are a systematic explanation of Christian doctrine and explain the nature of the salvation provided by Christ. The remaining chapters are practical and explain how believers are expected to live in the Church and in society.

Romansch A *Romance language belonging to the Rhaetian group, spoken in N Italy and in the Rhine Valley in Switzerland. It is one of Switzerland's four national languages.

Romanticism A fundamental development in western art, literature, music, and their related fields of theory in the late 18th and early 19th centuries. Romanticism constituted a reaction against the unquestioned authority of reason and tradition (*see* classicism) and an affirmation of faith in man's innate powers of creativity. Its various manifestations included a passionate concern with the relationship between man and his natural environment and a new interest in the primitive and the irrational. In literature, English Romanticism is usually dated from the publication of *Lyrical Ballads* by Wordsworth and Coleridge in 1798 and is associated with the poetry of Keats, Shelley, and Byron and the novels of Walter Scott. Major German Romantic writers included the Schlegel brothers, Goethe, and Schiller, and in France, where the theories of Rousseau had anticipated many aspects of the movement, the important writers included Chateaubriand and Victor Hugo. The influence of Romanticism is seen in the works of such painters as Turner and Delacroix, and it was the dominant influence on musical composition from the time of Beethoven until the early 20th century.

Romany The language spoken by *gypsies. It is related to *Sanskrit and the *Indo-Aryan languages of N India but diverged from these about 1000 AD, when the gypsies began their nomadic way of life. Romany has been greatly influenced in vocabulary by the languages spoken in regions the gypsies have passed through, resulting in many different dialects. There is little written literature in Romany but a rich oral tradition.

ROME *Piazza Navona, built on the site of the Emperor Domitian's circus. In the center is Bernini's* Fountain of the Four Rivers *(1648-51). Borromini's imposing façade of S Agnese in Agone (1652) contrasts with the many cafés and restaurants.*

Rome (Italian name: Roma) 41 53N 12 33E The capital of Italy, on the Tiber River. It is mainly an administrative and cultural center and, with the *Vatican City within its boundaries, the focal point of the Roman Catholic Church. Known as the Eternal City, it is one of the world's greatest historical and art centers; tourism is an important source of revenue. The Italian film industry is centered here. Relics of classical times include the Forum, the *Pantheon, and the *Colosseum. There are many ancient churches the origins of which go back to the early Christian era; with the exception of Sta Maria Maggiore, the patriarchal basilicas (St Peter's in the Vatican City, S Giovanni in Laterano, S Lorenzo Fuori le Mura, and S Paolo Fuori le Muri) were built on the sites of martyrs' tombs. The Renaissance produced not only many outstanding buildings, such as St Peter's Basilica, but the paintings and sculpture of such artists as Michelangelo and Raphael. The 17th and 18th centuries brought more fine architecture, with squares, fountains, and façades designed by Borromini, Bernini, and others. The university was founded in 1303. *History*: according to legend Rome was founded on the Palatine Hill in 753 BC by Romulus, its first king, later spreading to six other hills E of the Tiber: the Aventine, Capitoline, Quirinal, Viminal, Esquiline, and Caelian. Seven kings were followed by the *Roman Republic, and the *Roman Empire was founded in the 1st century BC. As the Empire declined in the 5th century AD Rome, no longer its center, was sacked by Germanic tribes. From the time of Pope Gregory in the 6th century it regained importance, this time as an ecclesiastical power. In 800 Charlemagne was crowned emperor here. In succeeding centuries, it was sacked by Arabs and by Normans, and in the middle ages there was a continuing struggle between popes and emperors. It remained under papal control until 1871, when it became capital of the newly unified Italy. The popes however refused formally to relinquish their temporal power until the Lateran Treaty of 1929, when their jurisdiction was confined to the Vatican City. Mussolini's March on Rome in 1922 marked the beginning of his fascist rule; the city was occupied by the Allies in World War II. Population (1980 est): 2,916,414.

Rome, Treaties of (1957) Two treaties signed in Rome by the representatives of Belgium, France, Italy, Luxembourg, the Netherlands, and West Germany, which led to the establishment of the *European Economic Community and the *European Atomic Energy Community.

Rommel, Erwin (1891–1944) German general, known as the Desert Fox because of his victories in N Africa in World War II. In 1940 he became commander of the Seventh Panzer Division and, in 1941, of the Afrika Corps. In N Africa he was hailed as a liberator by the Arabs and gained the respect of the enemy but in 1943, after his defeat at Alamein (1942), he was recalled and became commander of the Channel defense. His involvement with the conspirators who attempted to assassinate Hitler in 1944 (*see* Stauffenberg, Claus, Graf von) led to his suicide, under pressure from Hitler, who wished to avoid a treason trial implicating his most popular general.

Romney, George (1734–1802) British portrait painter. Although his training was limited, he attracted a fashionable clientele and rivaled Reynolds when he moved to London in 1762. He is best known for his numerous portraits of Lady Emma *Hamilton, whom he met in 1781.

Romulus and Remus The legendary founders of Rome, the sons of Mars and Rhea Silvia, daughter of Numitor, King of Alba Longa. Amulius, who had deposed Numitor, threw the twin babies into the Tiber. They were washed ashore and suckled by a she-wolf and later adopted by a shepherd. They eventually founded Rome at the place where they had been rescued. Romulus built the city on the Palatine hill and became the first king.

Romulus Augustulus (b. ?461) The last Roman emperor in the West (475–76 AD). He was deposed by the German ruler *Odoacer.

Roncesvalles (French name: Roncevaux) 43 01N 1 19W A village in N Spain, in the Pyrenees. Nearby is the Pass of Roncesvalles, where Charlemagne's rearguard, under Roland, was ambushed by the Saracens (788 AD) on his retreat to France.

rondeau A short lyrical poem using an intricate verse form developed in 14th- and 15th-century France. Intended for singing, rondeaux were generally 10 or 13 lines long, used only two rhymes, and had an elaborate repetitive pattern of words and lines. Their subjects were the standard themes of the *courtly love tradition. The rondeau's virtuosity reached a peak in *Dufay's compositions.

rondo A musical form in which a recurring theme alternates with contrasting episodes. In its simplest form it consists of the pattern ABACADA, A being the rondo theme and B, C, and D the episodes. In this form it was much used in the 18th century; Mozart, Beethoven, Schubert, and others developed the rondo by combining it with *sonata form.

ronin A samurai (warrior) left masterless by the total defeat of his lord. In the 1860s, however, many patriotic samurai deliberately became *ronin* in order to engage in extremist political activities.

Ronsard, Pierre de (1524–85) French poet. He turned to literature after deafness interrupted his career at court and became a leading member of the *Pléiade. His *Odes* (1550) and *Amours* (1552) gained him the patronage of Charles IX. His later works include *La Françiade* (1572), an unfinished national epic, and *Sonnets pour Hélène* (1578), which contains his best-known love poems.

Roodepoort 26 10S 27 53E A city in South Africa, in the S Transvaal. A W suburb of Johannesburg, it has developed manufacturing industries and is an important residential area. Population (1980 est): 165,315.

rood screen (*or* chancel screen) The screen of wood or stone, often elaborately carved, that separated the chancel from the nave in a medieval church. The name derives from the cross (Old English: rood) that surmounted the screen.

rook A large blue-black Eurasian crow, *Corvus frugilegus*, about 18 in (45 cm) long and having a narrow gray bill with pale patches of bare skin at its base. It is highly gregarious, breeding in large colonies and forming well-developed communities. Rooks feed on earthworms, larvae, carrion, and grain, sometimes damaging newly sown crops.

Roon, Albrecht, Graf von (1803–79) Prussian general, who as war minister (1859–73) effected important military reforms. He introduced compulsory three-year service in the face of fierce opposition but his policies, which were supported by Bismarck, were vindicated by Prussian victory in the Austro-Prussian War (1866) and in the Franco-Prussian War (1870–71).

FRANKLIN D. ROOSEVELT

Roosevelt, Franklin Delano (1882–1945) US statesman; 32nd President of the United States (1933–45). Educated as a lawyer, Roosevelt began his political career as New York Democratic state senator (1911–13) and as assistant secretary of the Navy during the administration of Woodrow Wilson (1913–20). The unsuccessful Democratic vice-presidential nominee in 1920, he was stricken with poliomyelitis the following year. Despite his handicap, Roosevelt returned to public life and became one of the leaders of the Democratic Party with his election as governor of New York in 1928. After re-election in 1930, he received the 1932 Democratic presidential nomination and defeated the incumbent president, Herbert *Hoover.

Roosevelt came to office at a time of economic crisis brought on by the *Depression and immediately after his inauguration began to implement an ambitious program of fiscal and social reform that he called the *New Deal. The New Deal proved to be successful in stimulating employment, industry, and agriculture. Re-elected in 1936, Roosevelt unsuccessfully attempted to alter the judicial philosophy of the Supreme Court by adding new justices, but his attempt at "court packing" was unsuccessful.

With the outbreak of war in Europe in 1939, Roosevelt provided considerable military and economic support to Great Britain and the other allies. In 1940 he became the first American president to serve more than two terms, winning re-election against the Republican nominee, Wendell Willkie. After the Japanese bombing of Pearl Harbor in 1941, he led the country into war, being re-elected for a fourth term in the White House in 1944. His participitation in the *Teheran and *Yalta Conferences with Winston *Churchill and Joseph *Stalin helped to shape the strategic arrangement of the post-war world, but he died before the conclusion of the war. His wife, **(Anna) Eleanor Roosevelt** (1884–1962), was the niece of Theodore *Roosevelt, to whom Franklin himself was distantly related. She was a devoted advocate of human rights and educational causes and served as US ambassador to the United Nations (1945, 1949–52, 1961–62) and as chairperson of the UN Commission on Human Rights (1946–51).

Roosevelt, Theodore (1858–1919) US statesman; 26th President of the United States (1901–09). After spending time as a cattle rancher in North Dakota, Roosevelt entered politics, running unsuccessfully as the Republican candidate for mayor of New York City (1886) and later serving with distinction as US Civil Service Commissioner (1889–95). As assistant secretary of the Navy (1897–98) he helped to strengthen the nation's military preparedness and with the outbreak of the *Spanish-American War, he resigned from public office to found the 1st US Volunteer Cavalry, also known as the "Rough Riders." He gained national acclaim for his participation in the *Battle of San Juan Hill and after the war he was elected governor of New York. Roosevelt was elected vice president in 1900, and with the assassination of President William *McKinley the following year, he succeeded to the presidency himself.

As president, Roosevelt introduced the *Square Deal program for social reform and advocated an active foreign policy characterized by his famous dictum, "Talk softly and carry a big stick." He established US control over the construction of the *Panama Canal (1903) and made the US the dominant force in the Western Hemisphere. In 1905 he was awarded the Nobel Peace Prize for his arbitration of the Russo-Japanese War. Roosevelt was elected president in 1904, but chose not to run again in 1908. Becoming increasingly opposed to the policies of his successor, William H. *Taft, Roosevelt contended for the 1912 Republican nomination, and failing to gain it, he campaigned unsuccessfully for president as the candidate of his own Bull Moose Party.

root (algebra) **1.** One of the equal factors of a number. The square root is one of two equal factors; for example $\sqrt{9} = \pm 3$; the rth root of a number n is the number that when raised to the rth power gives n. **2.** The solution of an equation, i.e. the values of the variable that will satisfy the equation. *See* quadratic equation.

root (botany) The part of a □plant that provides anchorage and enables the uptake of water and nutrients from the soil. Roots contain vascular (conducting) tissue and just behind the tip is an area of root hairs, which increase the surface area for absorption. Some plants, such as the dandelion, have one main root with smaller branches—a tap root system; others, such as grasses, have a mass of similar-sized roots—a fibrous root system. Roots can act as food-storage organs, as in the carrot and turnip (tap roots); fibrous roots that become swollen with food are called tuberous roots, such as those of dahlias. Some roots grow in unusual positions, such as the aerial buttress roots of tropical trees, which act as supports.

Root, Elihu (1845–1937) US lawyer and statesman. A lawyer from 1867, he later became secretary of war (1899–1904) and secretary of state (1905–09). His achievements included reforms in the organization of the army, the improvement of relations with Latin America, and the Root-Takahira agreement with Japan (1908), committing the two nations to maintaining the status quo in the Pacific. A member of the Hague Tribunal (the Permanent Court of Arbitration), he received the Nobel Peace Prize in 1912.

root-mean-square value (*or* rms value) The square root of the arithmetic *average of the squares of a set of numbers; for example the rms of 2, 4, 5, 6 is $[(2^2 + 4^2 + 5^2 + 6^2)/4]^{1/2} = 4\frac{1}{2}$. The rms value is useful in continuous quantities, such as alternating electric current, in which the heating effect is proportional to the current squared. The rms value is therefore directly comparable to direct current.

ropes and cables Flexible lengths of material made from strands of natural *fibers (e.g. hemp, jute, sisal, manila), synthetic fibers (e.g. nylon, polypropylene), or wire. In natural-fiber ropes, the material is spun into yarn and then formed into strands, which are twisted around each other in an opposite direction to that of the yarn. For many purposes nylon and polypropylene ropes, made by a similar method, are replacing natural-fiber ropes. A hawser consists of three strands, a cable consists of three hawsers wound together, and a shroud-laid rope has a central strand with three or four strands wound around it. Wire ropes are made by a similar process: high-tensile steel wires are twisted together to form strands, which are then wound around each other to form the rope. In some cases the wires are preformed into helical strands to reduce internal stresses and are wound around a hemp core, which provides lubrication and flexibility.

Roquefort 43 59N 2 58E A village in SE France, in the Aveyron department. Roquefort is famous for the ewes' milk cheese named for it.

Roraima, Mount 5 14N 60 44W A mountain in South America, at the junction of the borders of Brazil, Guyana, and Venezuela. It is the highest peak in the Pacaraima Mountains. Height: 9219 ft (2810 m).

rorqual A small-headed fast-moving whalebone *whale of the family *Balaenopteridae* (6 species). The common rorqual (*Balaenoptera physalus*), also called fin whale or razorback, grows up to 80 ft (25 m) long; it has a dark back, shading to white underneath, and a small dorsal fin that shows when it is blowing. Common rorquals are found in all oceans. *See also* blue whale; humpback whale; sei whale.

Rorschach test A psychological test intended to measure aspects of personality. Devised by the Swiss psychiatrist Hermann Rorschach (1884–1922), it consists of ten inkblots in complex shapes. The way in which the subject describes these pictures gives the tester clues to his character. *See also* projection.

Rory O'Connor (*or* Roderic; ?1116–98) King of Connaught and last High King of Ireland. In 1171 he marched against *Dermot MacMurrough and his English allies but was defeated at Dublin. Later he was forced to recognize the overlordship of Henry II of England.

Rosa, Salvator (1615–73) Italian painter and etcher. Working in Naples, Rome (where he finally settled in 1649), and Florence (1640–49), he was also known as a poet, comic actor, and musician. His lasting reputation, however, rests on his wild and romantic landscapes.

Rosaceae A cosmopolitan family of trees, shrubs, and herbs (about 2000 species). Many are of economic value for their fruits, for example strawberries, raspberries, cherries, apricots, apples, and plums. Others are cultivated as ornamentals, including *Spiraea*, *Potentilla*, and roses.

Rosario 33 00S 60 40W The second largest city in Argentina, on the Río Paraná. It is an industrial and commercial center and the terminus of the pampas railroads. Industries include sugar refining and food processing. Its university was founded in 1968. Population (1975 est): 750,455.

rosary In the Roman Catholic Church, a religious devotion consisting of repeated prayers, particularly associated with the cult of the Virgin Mary. The recitation of a rosary is subdivided into 15 decades, each decade comprising an opening Paternoster, 10 Ave Marias, and a concluding Gloria. A subject of meditation, or Mystery, relating to the life of Christ or the Virgin is attached to each decade. By association the string of beads used to count the prayers is also called a rosary. The feast day established in 1716 in honor of the rosary is observed on Oct 7.

Roscelin (died c. 1125) French scholastic philosopher (*see* scholasticism). He was an early proponent of *nominalism, which he may even have originated. His philosophical belief that a being could have no parts led him to the Tritheist heresy, a deviant form of the doctrine of the Trinity. He was opposed by his famous pupil *Abelard.

Roscius, Quintus (d. 62 BC) Roman comic actor. He was praised by Cicero, and his name has been applied as an epithet to many outstanding actors of the modern theater.

Roscommon (Irish name: Ros Comáin) A county in the N Republic of Ireland, in Connacht. Predominantly low lying, it has many lakes and extensive bogs. Agriculture, especially cattle rearing, is the chief occupation. Area: 951 sq mi (2463 sq km). Population (1979): 54,189. County town: Roscommon.

rose A prickly shrub or climber of the genus *Rosa* (200–250 species), native to N temperate regions but widely cultivated. The leaves are compound, with leaflets arranged in pairs and small leafy stipules at the base of the leafstalk. The five-petaled flowers are usually white, yellow, pink, or red and the fruits are red, yellow, or black hips, rich in vitamin C, containing many seeds. Wild species include *dog rose and *sweet briar. Family: *Rosaceae*.

Modern hybrid roses—usually with double flowers—can be divided into several groups, the most important bedding varieties being the hybrid teas and floribundas. The former, derived from the tea rose (*R. odorata*), produce large shapely often fragrant blooms of good color. The floribundas bear clusters of flowers and are usually grown for their color effect rather than for the beauty of individual blooms. The climbers and ramblers are suitable for covering walls, fences, etc. Climbers produce thick basal stems infrequently; they include climbing forms of hybrid teas and floribundas as well as climbing species (such as *R. banksiae*). Ramblers, which produce many slender stems from the base each year, include the wichuraiana group of hybrids.

Rosebery, Archibald Philip Primrose, 5th Earl of (1847–1929) British statesman; Liberal prime minister (1894–95). He was foreign secretary (1886, 1892–94) under Gladstone, whom he replaced as prime minister. He resigned the Liberal leadership in 1896.

rosella A brighly colored *parakeet belonging to a genus (*Platycercus*; 7 species) occurring in Australia and New Zealand. 7 in (18 cm) long, rosellas have a long broad tail, which is usually blue or green edged with white,

black shoulders, and distinctive face and throat markings. They are largely ground-dwelling.

roselle An annual or perennial fibrous plant, *Hibiscus sabdariffa*, cultivated in tropical regions for its stem fibers, which are used for sacking and twine, and for its edible stalks, leaves, and flower parts. It grows up to 16 ft (5 m) high and bears solitary white or yellow flowers in the leaf axils. Family: *Malvaceae*.

rosemary An evergreen shrub, *Rosmarinus officinalis*, native to the Mediterranean region and W Asia. Up to 7 ft (2 m) high, it has bluish flowers and small needle-like aromatic leaves, up to 2 in (5 cm) long. It is widely cultivated for its oil, which is distilled from the flowering tops and used in toiletries; for its leaves, used as a culinary herb; and for ornament. Family: *Labiatae*.

Rosenberg, Julius (1918–53) US spy, who with his wife **Ethel Rosenberg** (1915–53) was executed for espionage activities. They were accused of gaining information about nuclear weapons from Ethel's brother and passing it on via a courier to the Russian vice consul in New York. Other members of the espionage ring were sentenced to long terms of imprisonment. The Rosenbergs proclaimed their innocence. The trial was extremely controversial, and many believed that the evidence was insufficient, the punishment too severe, and the verdict was influenced by Cold War hysteria.

rose of Jericho A perennial herb, *Anastatica hierochuntica*, also called resurrection plant, native to W Asia. During the dry season the leaves are shed and the branches curve inward so that the whole plant forms a wickerwork-like ball that is blown by the wind. When moistened, the plant regains its shape and produces tiny white flowers. Family: *Cruciferae*.

rose of Sharon. *See* Hibiscus; St John's wort.

Roses, Wars of the (1455–85) The civil wars between the Houses of *Lancaster (the red rose) and *York (the white rose) for possession of the English crown, which both claimed by right of descent from Edward III. The Lancastrian Henry VI's incompetent rule resulted in factional struggles led by the Lancastrian Beauforts and Richard Plantagenet, Duke of *York, and the Earl of *Warwick (the Kingmaker). Open warfare broke out in 1455. York was killed in 1460 and his son seized the crown in 1461, becoming Edward IV, and crushed the Lancastrians. In 1470–71 Henry VI was briefly restored by disaffected Yorkists but Edward returned after his victory at *Tewkesbury and ruled until 1483. He was succeeded by his brother Richard III, whose reign ended with his defeat by Henry (VII) at Bosworth (1485). The remaining Yorkists were finally overcome at Stoke in 1487.

Rosetta Stone An inscribed stone slab discovered (1799) at Rosetta (Arabic name: Rashid), near Alexandria (Egypt). It carries a decree (196 BC) of Ptolemy V Epiphanes (reigned 205–180) in two languages and three scripts: Egyptian *hieroglyphic and *demotic, and Greek. The repetition of Ptolemy's name in the different scripts gave Thomas *Young the clue to deciphering hieroglyphs; his work was continued by *Champollion.

rose window A decorative circular window in a medieval church. Rose windows, which were probably inspired by oriental models, had radiating tracery, usually glazed with *stained glass, and reached their apogee in 13th-century French *gothic architecture, although examples are known throughout W Europe.

rosewood An attractive hardwood, usually dark reddish and often rose-scented, derived from several tropical evergreen trees of the genus *Dalbergia* (family *Leguminosae*). These include Brazilian rosewood, or blackwood (*D. nigra*), used for veneers and cabinetwork; Honduras rosewood (*D. stevensoni*), used for musical instruments; and East Indian rosewood (*D. latifolia*), used mostly for small articles. Decreasing supplies have restricted their use.

Rosh Hashana (Hebrew: head of the year) The Jewish New Year festival, celebrated in Sept or Oct. Of biblical origin, it is regarded as a time of penitence and preparation for *Yom Kippur. A ram's horn (*shofar*) is blown in the synagogue.

Rosicrucianism An esoteric movement for spiritual renewal that originated in Protestant Germany in the early 17th century and spread across Europe. Its manifesto traces its source to a fictitious brotherhood founded by a certain Christian Rosenkreuz in 1484. The philosophical program propounded by its mainly anonymous adherents was a blend of theosophical and occult traditions, including *alchemy, *Hermeticism, and *Neoplatonism. *See also* freemasonry.

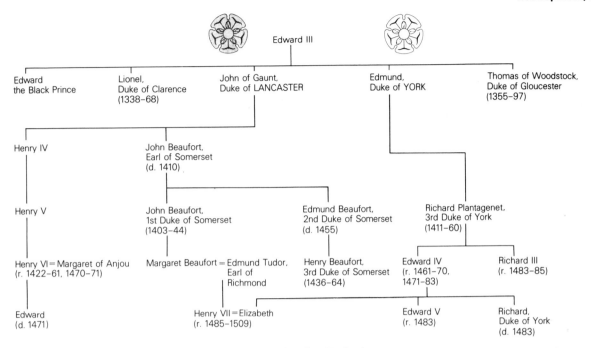

WARS OF THE ROSES   *The rival Houses of Lancaster and York in England.*

rosin (*or* colophony) A yellowish *resin obtained as a residue from the distillation of *turpentine. It is used in varnishes, soaps, soldering *flux, and to rub on violin bows.

Roskilde 55 39N 12 07E A seaport in Denmark, in Sœelland. It was the Danish capital until 1443, and most of Denmark's kings are buried in the 13th-century cathedral. A university was established in 1970. Its industries include tanning, meat canning, paper making, and agricultural engineering. Population (1974 est): 50,690.

Ross, Betsy (Elizabeth Griscom R.; 1752–1836) US patriot. After her husband John Ross's death in 1776, she continued to run his upholstery shop. According to popular legend, a committee headed by George *Washington commissioned her to fashion, from a rough drawing, the "Stars and Stripes," which was then designated the official flag of the US.

Ross, Sir James Clark (1800–62) British explorer. He accompanied (1819–27) Sir William *Parry on his Arctic expeditions and (1829–31) his uncle Sir John Ross (1777–1856), discovering the North Magnetic Pole (1831). He later (1839–43) explored the Antarctic, discovering the sea named for him.

Ross, Sir Ronald (1857–1932) British bacteriologist, who confirmed the theory of Sir Patrick Manson (1844–1922) that mosquitoes transmit malaria. While working in India, Ross discovered malaria parasites in the guts of *Anopheles* mosquitoes. Ross received the 1902 Nobel Prize for his work.

Ross Dependency An area in Antarctica claimed by New Zealand (since 1923), lying between longitudes 160°E and 150°W and including the Ross Sea and islands S of latitude 60°S. Area: about 160,000 sq mi (414,400 sq km).

Rosse, William Parsons, 3rd Earl of (1800–67) Irish astronomer, who constructed a large 72-inch (183 cm) reflecting telescope. In 1848 he used it to study one of the blurred objects listed by *Messier and named it the Crab Nebula, because of its shape. He also discovered the first spiral galaxy in 1845.

Rossellini, Roberto (1906–77) Italian film director. The neorealist style of *Rome, Open City* (1945), which included documentary film shot during the German occupation of Rome, greatly influenced postwar Italian cinema. His other films include *Paisà* (1946), also concerned with wartime Italy, *L'Amore* (1948), and *India* (1958), a documentary film. He subsequently worked mostly in television and the theater.

Rossetti, Dante Gabriel (Gabriel Charles Dante R.; 1828–82) British painter and poet. Rebelling against conventional instruction, in 1848 Rossetti joined with John Everett *Millais, William Holman *Hunt, and other artists to found the *Pre-Raphaelite Brotherhood. He founded the short-lived Pre-Raphaelite journal *The Germ* (1850–51), in which he began pub-

lishing his own verse. He later published several volumes of poetry and translations, including *Poems* (1870) and *Ballads and Sonnets* (1881). During his final years he lived virtually as a recluse, suffering from ill health. His sister **Christina Georgina Rossetti** (1830–74), a poet, was deeply influenced by the *Oxford Movement. *Goblin Market and Other Poems* (1862), her first published volume, gave literary expression to Pre-Raphaelite ideals and contains perhaps her best work.

Rossini, Gioacchino Antonio (1792–1868) Italian composer. His father was a trumpeter and his mother an opera singer. He studied at Bologna and wrote 36 highly successful operas, including *Tancredi* (1813), *The Italian Girl in Algiers* (1813), *The Barber of Seville* (1816), *La Cenerentola* (*Cinderella*) and *The Thieving Magpie* (both 1817), and *William Tell* (1829). At the age of 37 he gave up serious composition, although he did write a light-hearted *Petite Messe solennelle* (1863) and a number of little pieces, collectively entitled "Sins of My Old Age." He invented a number of recipes, including Tournedos Rossini.

Ross Island 77 40S 168 00E A volcanic island in the W Ross Sea, at the edge of the **Ross Ice Shelf**, a vast mass of permanent ice. Mount Erebus is situated here.

Ross Sea A large inlet of the S Pacific Ocean, in the Antarctic continent between Victoria Land and Byrd Land. Its S section is covered by the Ross Ice Shelf.

Rostand, Edmond (1868–1918) French dramatist. He gained international success with *Cyrano de Bergerac* (1897), a romantic comedy about a nobleman with an oversize nose. Sarah Bernhardt acted in many of his plays, notably *L'Aiglon* (1900).

Rostock 54 03N 12 07E A city and Baltic port in N East Germany, on the Warnow River. Once an important Hanseatic port, its fine medieval buildings have been restored following damage during World War II. Its university was established in 1419. The main industries are shipbuilding and fisheries. Population (1980 est): 230,280.

Rostov-na-Donu 47 15N 39 45E A port in the S Soviet Union, in the RSFSR on the Don River near its mouth on the Sea of Azov. It produces agricultural machinery and has ship-repairing, food-processing, and textile industries. Its importance owes much to its position on the route from the W to the Caucasus. Population (1981 est): 957,000.

Rostropovich, Mstislav (1927–   ) Soviet cellist. He left the Soviet Union in 1975. He is also a conductor, notably of opera, and as a pianist accompanies his wife the soprano Galina Vishnevskaya (1926–   ). Many composers, including Prokofiev, Britten, and Shostakovich, have written cello works for him.

Roth, Philip (1933–) US novelist. Middle-class Jewish themes predominated in his early works including *Goodbye, Columbus* (1959) and *Portnoy's Complaint* (1969), his most popular success. In later novels, such as *The Great American Novel* (1973), *My Life as a Man* (1974) *The Ghost Writer* (1979), *Zukerman Unbound* (1981), and *The Anatomy Lesson* (1983), the targets of his satire are more various.

Rothenburg ob der Tauber 49 23N 10 13E A town in S West Germany, in Bavaria. It is famed for its medieval town center, still enclosed in the town walls. Population (1970 est): 12,000.

Rotherham 53 26N 1 20W A town in N England, in South Yorkshire on the River Don. Rotherham has iron and steel, brassware, machinery, and glass industries and coal is mined locally. Population (1981): 81,988.

Rothko, Mark (Marcus Rothkovitch; 1903–70) Russian-born painter, who emigrated to the US in 1913. In the late 1940s, with Barnett Newman and Clyfford Still, he pioneered color-field painting (an abstract style using only color) on mural-size canvases covered with horizontal bands of hazy color.

Rothschild, Mayer Amschel (1744–1812) German merchant and banker, whose business in Frankfurt prospered during the Napoleonic Wars, making loans to the various combatants and trading in high-demand goods such as arms, wheat, and cotton. He was succeeded in Frankfurt by his son **Amschel Mayer Rothschild** (1773–1855). Four other sons established branches of the firm abroad. **Salomon Mayer Rothschild** (1774–1855) went to Vienna, **Nathan Mayer Rothschild** (1777–1836), to London, **Karl Mayer Rothschild** (1788–1855), to Naples, and **James Rothschild** (Jakob R.; 1792–1868), to Paris. In London, Nathan's son **Lionel Nathan Rothschild** (1808–79) was a member of parliament (1858–68, 1869–79) as was (1865–85) his grandson **Nathan Mayer, 1st Baron Rothschild** (1840–1915).

rotifer A tiny invertebrate animal belonging to the phylum *Rotifera* (about 2000 species), also called wheel animalcule, found mainly in fresh water. Rotifers vary in shape from spherical to wormlike and range between 0.004–0.02 in (0.1 and 0.5 mm) in length. Each has a ring of cilia (corona) around the mouth, beating in a wheel-like manner, for wafting food particles into the mouth and providing a means of locomotion in active species.

Rotterdam 51 55N 4 29E The chief port and second largest city in the Netherlands, in South Holland province on the New Meuse River. It became important during the 19th century, mainly with the opening of the 12 mi (35 km) long Nieuwe Waterweg (New Waterway) in 1872 linking it to the North Sea. During World War II the city center was destroyed; this has since been rebuilt with a subway system. Its notable buildings include the restored Groote Kerk (Great Church). The Erasmus University of Rotterdam was founded in 1973. The largest Atlantic port in Europe, Rotterdam handles considerable export trade from West Germany, including Ruhr coal. Its dockyards extend W along the Nieuwe Waterweg and include Europoort, on the North Sea. Begun in 1958, Europoort's huge facilities handle chiefly oil importing and refining. Rotterdam's industries include petroleum refining, shipbuilding, brewing, distilling, and engineering. Population (1981 est): 576,330.

Rottweiler A breed of working dog developed originally in Rottweil, Germany, as a guard dog and cattle drovers' dog. It is stockily built, having a broad round body, a strong neck, and a large head with a deep muzzle. The coarse short coat is black with tan markings. Height: 24.8–26.8 in (63–68 cm) (dogs); 22.8–24.8 in (58–63 cm) (bitches).

Rouault, Georges (Henri) (1871–1958) French artist. A major 20th-century religious artist, he was a largely independent figure, except for a brief and loose association with *fauvism. His favorite themes were clowns (sometimes modeled on himself or Christ) and prostitutes, expressing his sympathy with social outcasts. He was influenced by his early training as a stained-glass maker and was the favorite pupil of Gustave *Moreau. Until 1918 he worked chiefly in gouache and watercolor, using rich dark colors and heavy outlines. As a graphic artist his main achievement was his series of etchings (1916–27), entitled *Miserere* and *Guerre*.

Roubaix 50 42N 3 10E A city in N France, in the Nord department on the Roubaix Canal. Famous for its cloth since the 15th century, it is (together with Tourcoing) the center of the country's woolen industry. Population (1975): 109,797.

Roubillac, Louis François (*or* L. F. Roubiliac; 1695–1762) French sculptor. He fled (1727) for religious reasons to England, where his statue of Handel (1738) in London, secured his reputation. His portrait bust of Alexander Pope and full-length statue of Sir Isaac Newton are also outstanding. After a visit to Rome (1752) he executed the Nightingale and

Hargreaves monuments in Westminster Abbey, reflecting some of Bernini's dramatic power and skill in composition.

Rouen (Latin name: Rotomagus) 49 26N 1 05E A city and port in NW France, the capital of the Seine-Maritimes department on the Seine River. The ancient capital of Normandy, it was here that Joan of Arc was tried and burned in 1431. Many of its notable buildings, including the cathedral (13th–16th centuries), survived the damage of World War II. Its university was established in 1966. The main industries are textiles, petrochemicals, engineering, paper, and electronics. Population (1975): 118,332.

Rouget de l'Isle, Claude Joseph (1760–1836) French military engineer and composer. He composed the *Marseillaise in 1792 while stationed in Strasbourg at the outbreak of war between France and Austria. He was later imprisoned for a year for refusing to take the oath against the crown; he was reinstated in 1795 and published a volume of 50 *Chants français* in 1825.

Roulers. *See* Roeselare.

roulette A game of chance played in most casinos. Of obscure origins, it was developed in the Monte Carlo casino. The principle of the game is that a small white ball is thrown in a clockwise direction into a horizontal wheel spinning in a counterclockwise direction. The rim of the wheel is divided into numbered compartments. Players bet (against the bank) on the number of the compartment into which they predict the ball will come to rest. There are two main varieties of roulette: French roulette and American roulette. In the French game there are 37 numbered compartments on the wheel (0–36), and the color of the betting chips denotes their denomination. In the American game there are 38 compartments (00, 0–36), and each player has a distinctively colored set of chips. In both games bets are placed on green baize tables on which the numbers of the compartments are laid out in groups of three. In the French game a successful bet on a single number pays 35–1 (and the stake is returned), giving the bank an advantage of 2.7%. In the American game, the bank's advantage is increased to 5.4%. There are also three types of even-money bets that the player can make: red or black, even or odd numbers, and 1–18 or 19–36. The red or black bet arises because alternate numbers on the wheel are colored red and black. Between the extremes of even money odds and 35–1, the player can make virtually any odds he chooses by backing different groups of numbers.

rounders A nine-a-side bat-and-ball field game, which is probably the prototype of *baseball. The two teams take turns at batting and fielding and a match consists of two innings per team. The hard ball is delivered underarm to each batsman in turn until all are out. The batsmen try to score rounders by hitting it and running around the four bases without being caught or run out. The batsman's square and first base, first base and second base, and second base and third base are 39.5 ft (12 m) apart, but third and fourth base are only 28 ft (8.5 m) apart.

Roundheads The parliamentary party during the English *Civil War. The name referred originally to the short haircuts of the apprentices who demonstrated against the king at Westminster in 1640. It was later applied to all parliamentarians and referred to their drab appearance in contrast to the more flamboyant *Cavaliers.

Round Table Conference (1930–32) Three meetings held in London to discuss a form of government acceptable to India. The meetings were attended by representatives of the British Government and of India's major political parties and all its states. Mahatma *Gandhi, representing the *Indian National Congress, boycotted the first meeting. The result of the Conference was the *Government of India Act of 1935.

roundworm. *See* nematode.

Rousseau, Henri (1844–1910) French painter. Although known as Le Douanier (customs official) he was really a toll collector and as a painter was self-taught. From 1886 he exhibited at the Salon des Indépendants but his work, resembling folk art in technique (*see* primitivism), was ridiculed. After 1894, when he exhibited *War* (Louvre), followed by the *Sleeping Gypsy* (1897; New York), he received serious attention, particularly from *Picasso and the poet *Apollinaire. The childlike quality of his vision and the hallucinatory atmosphere in his portraits and jungle landscapes influenced a number of 20th-century painters, particularly several of the surrealists.

Rousseau, Jean Jacques (1712–78) French philosopher and writer. Through his acquaintance with *Diderot, Rousseau joined the *Encyclopedists. In the *Discourse on the Origin and Foundations of Inequality among Men* (1754) he argued that man's perfect nature is spoiled by corrupt society. *Émile* (1762), a novel on education, expanded his views on ideal unfallen human nature. Rousseau's political influence was significant and many of the ideas embodied in such works as *Du contrat social* (1762) were taken up by revolutionaries. His fine style and romantic outlook inspired Shelley, Byron, and Wordsworth. His continued belief in a somewhat emasculated Christianity was an effective counterbalance to the atheism of Voltaire and the rationalists.

Rousseau, (Pierre Étienne) Théodore (1812–67) French Romantic landscape painter and leader of the *Barbizon school. His melancholy scenes were influenced by *Constable and *Bonington but his practice of open-air painting anticipated *impressionism. After permanently settling in Barbizon in the 1840s he received official recognition of his work.

Roussel, Albert (1869–1937) French composer. Serving in the French navy until 1894, he sailed to Indochina in 1890. Eastern culture became one of his main sources of inspiration although his later works are predominantly neoclassical. His compositions include the ballet *The Spider's Banquet* (1912), the opera-ballet *Pâdmâvatî* (1914–18), four symphonies, a piano concerto, chamber music, and songs.

Roussel, Raymond (1877–1933) French writer and dramatist. His writings, constructed around elaborately contrived puzzles and linguistic games, include the prose works *Impressions d'Afrique* (1910) and *Locus Solus* (1914) and three plays the first productions of which caused scandals. He is regarded as a precursor of both surrealism and the *nouveau roman*.

Roux, Pierre Paul Emile (1853–1933) French bacteriologist, who, following the discovery of the Klebs-Loeffler (diphtheria) bacillus in 1884, showed that the disease symptoms were caused by a toxin released by the bacilli. Roux helped develop an antitoxin serum for diphtheria and—working with *Pasteur—discovered a vaccine for anthrax using attenuated bacilli. Roux was director of the Pasteur Institute (1904–33).

rove beetle A beetle belonging to the worldwide family *Staphylinidae* (about 27,000 species), having short wing cases covering the folded hindwings. Rove beetles range from 0.03–1.26 in (0.7 to 32 mm) in length although most are small. They are commonly found near dung and dead animal matter, preying upon the associated insects and mites. Some species, however, live in ant and termite nests. *See also* devil's coach horse.

rowan. *See* mountain ash.

rowing A sport using narrow light boats (*or* shells) propelled by two, four, or eight people and often steered by a coxswain, usually on a river or lake. The oarsmen sit in line in sliding seats, bracing their feet against stretchers. Each controls one oar set in a rowlock, the oars being arranged on alternate sides. **Sculling** is a form of rowing for one, two, or four people per boat, each person controlling two oars. The governing body is the Fédération internationale des Sociétés d'Aviron.

Rowley, Thomas (c. 1585–c. 1642) English dramatist and actor. He collaborated with many other Jacobean dramatists, notably with John Ford and Thomas Dekker on *The Witch of Edmonton* (1621) and with Thomas Middleton on *The Changeling* (1622). His own plays were mostly comedies.

Rowse, A(lfred) L(eslie) (1903–) British historian and literary critic. Rowse is best known for his books on the Tudor period, including *The Elizabethan Renaissance* (1971), and on Shakespeare, whose Dark Lady of the sonnets he controversially indentified as Emilia Lanier, daughter of a court musician.

Royal Academy An art society in London, England that holds annual summer exhibitions of contemporary British art, as well as exhibitions of modern artists and the old masters. Founded in 1768, it originally had an important teaching function.

Royal Air Force (RAF) A British armed service formed in 1918 by the amalgamation of the Royal Flying Corps (1912) with the Royal Naval Air Service (1914).

royal antelope The world's smallest antelope, *Neotragus pygmaeus*, of West African forests. 10–12 in (25–30 cm) high at the shoulder, it is red-brown with white underparts; males have short spiky horns. They are nocturnal and usually occur singly or in pairs.

Royal Ballet The leading British ballet company and school. Based at the Royal Opera House since 1946, it was known as the Sadler's Wells Ballet until 1956, when it was granted a royal charter. It was founded by Dame Ninette de Valois in 1931.

Royal Canadian Mounted Police (*or* Mounties) Canadian police force. Founded in 1873 as the North West Mounted Police to keep order in the Canadian west, it has become famous for the efficiency and discipline of its members, dressed in their distinctive scarlet tunics, blue breeches, and wide-brimmed hats.

royal fern. *See* Osmunda.

Royal Greenwich Observatory An observatory founded in 1675 by Charles II at Greenwich, London, in a building designed by Sir Christopher Wren. The meridian through Greenwich (0°) was internationally adopted as the prime meridian in 1884 and became the basis of Greenwich Mean Time.

royal jelly A thick white mixture of proteins, carbohydrates, minerals, and vitamins that is secreted by worker bees and fed to the larvae. Larvae destined to become queens are fed throughout their development on royal jelly. *See also* honeybee.

Royal Society The oldest and most important scientific society in the UK. It originated in 1645 with a group of thinkers, including Robert *Boyle and John Wilkins, who met to discuss the "new or experimental philosophy" popularized by Francis Bacon. It was incorporated by royal charter from Charles II in 1662. With the presidency from 1703–27 of Isaac *Newton, the Royal Society achieved great standing and financial security.

Royce, Sir (Frederick) Henry (1863–1933) British automobile manufacturer, who founded, with Charles *Rolls, Rolls-Royce Ltd (1906). In 1884 Royce opened an engineering business in Manchester and in 1904 began to build cars, which much impressed Rolls and led to the merger of their businesses.

Royce, Josiah (1855–1916) US philosopher. As an idealist, influenced by *Hegel, Royce believed that human thought was part of the cosmic order. Governing the natural order was a higher moral order, which it was man's duty to uphold. His numerous books include the *Spirit of Modern Philosophy* (1892).

RR Lyrae stars A class of short-period pulsating *variable stars that are very old giant stars found principally in globular *star clusters, all with about the same mean *luminosity.

Ruapehu, Mount 39 18S 175 36E An active volcano in New Zealand, the highest peak in North Island in Tongariro National Park. The last eruption was in 1945–46. Height: 9175 ft (2797 m).

Rub' al-Khali The S part of the Arabian Desert, mainly in Saudi Arabia. It is low lying and constitutes the largest continuous area of sand in the world. Area: about 308,815 sq mi (800,000 sq km).

rubber A synthetic or natural organic polymer that is elastic and tough. The name comes from its ability to erase pencil marks. **Natural rubber**, which consists mainly of polyisoprene—$(CH_2CH:C.CH_3:CH_2)_n$—is made from latex, a milky fluid collected from the trunk of the *rubber tree, which is specially cultivated for this purpose in Malaysia, Thailand, Indonesia, and other parts of SE Asia. The rubber is coagulated from latex (using acids) and pressed into sheets. *Vulcanization increases its durability.

Synthetic rubbers are made from petrochemicals (*see* oil). Styrene-butadiene rubber (SBR), now the commonest synthetic rubber, was introduced during World War II. It is made by the emulsion process, in which styrene and butadiene are mixed in soapy water containing a catalyst. Different proportions of ingredients and temperatures vary the properties. SBR is used in tires, often mixed with natural rubber to improve its resilience. Butyl rubber is made by *polymerization of isobutylene. It is used for inner tubes. Neoprene (polychloropene) is used for protective clothing and electrical insulation. Nitrile polyisoprene and the newer polyurethane and silicone rubbers are also used for specialist applications.

rubber plant A tree, *Ficus elastica*, native to India and Malaysia, where it grows to a height of 115 ft (35 m) in forests. Its latex is the source of Assam or India rubber. It is also a popular house plant, grown in pots or tubs for its oblong shiny leathery leaves. Family: *Moraceae*.

rubber tree A Brazilian tree, *Hevea brasiliensis*, also called Pará rubber, widely cultivated in humid tropical regions, especially SE Asia. Its milky latex is the chief source of natural *rubber, which is obtained by making sloping cuts in the trunk. Trees yield latex from about the sixth year and reach full height, about 65 ft (20 m), in eight years. *H. guianensis* and *H. pauciflora* are also sometimes cultivated for rubber. In 1876, some seeds of South American rubber trees were shipped to England. Seedlings were subsequently exported to Ceylon and SE Asia to form the basis of the rubber industry. Family: *Euphorbiaceae*.

rubella. *See* German measles.

Rubens, Peter Paul (1577–1640) Flemish painter, who was born in Seigen (Westphalia) but lived chiefly in Antwerp. The greatest of the *baroque artists and one of the finest European colorists, Rubens first worked for the Mantuan court in Italy (1600–08). Returning to Antwerp, he became court painter to the Archduke Albert and painted his first major works, *The Raising of the Cross* and *Descent from the Cross*. Many visits abroad, sometimes as a diplomatic envoy, and commissions followed, including a cycle for Marie de' Medici commemorating her marriage to Henry IV and the ceiling of the Banqueting House, Whitehall, for England's Charles I. Aided by a large workshop, he painted mythological, historical, and religious subjects but his most personal works are his portraits of his family, notably *Helena Fourment with a Fur Cloak* and such landscapes as *The Château de Steen*. His Antwerp house, now a museum, contains his fine art collection and furnishings.

RUBENS   Le Chapeau de Paille *(c. 1622-25), one of his noted portraits.*

Rubicon A stream in N central Italy flowing E into the Adriatic Sea, which formed the boundary between Italy and Cisalpine Gaul in the time of the Roman Republic. In 49 BC Julius Caesar, then provincial commander in Gaul, precipitated the civil war with Pompey by leading his army across the Rubicon into Italy. This action was tantamount to a declaration of war because it was forbidden for a general to lead an army outside the province in which he had been given command. Hence "crossing the Rubicon" has come to mean taking an irrevocable step.

rubidium (Rb) A highly electropositive alkali metal, discovered spectroscopically by R. W. Bunsen and G. R. Kirchhoff in 1861. The element is soft and silvery-white. It ignites spontaneously in air and reacts violently with water, liberating hydrogen and then setting fire to it. The isotope ^{87}Rb is radioactive with a half-life of 5×10^{11} years and is used in *rubidium-strontium dating. Rubidium forms ionic salts and four oxides (Rb$_2$O, Rb$_2$O$_2$, Rb$_2$O$_3$, RbO$_2$). At no 37; at wt 85.47; mp 38.89°C; bp 688°C.

rubidium-strontium dating A method of *radiometric dating, used mainly for rocks, fossils, etc. It utilizes the fact that naturally occurring rubidium contains about 28% of the radioactive isotope rubidium-87, which undergoes *beta decay to strontium-87 with a *half-life of 5×10^{11} years. Thus by measuring the ratio of rubidium-87 to strontium-87 in the sample, its age may be estimated. The method can date items several thousands of millions of years old.

Rubinstein, Anton (1829–94) Russian pianist and composer. He started performing abroad at the age of 12 and founded the St Petersburg conservatoire in 1862. His works include 20 operas, 6 symphonies, 5 piano concertos, 2 cello concertos, and numerous other piano pieces.

Rubinstein, Artur (1888–1982) Polish-born US pianist. He studied in Warsaw and Berlin and soon acquired a worldwide reputation, particularly as a performer of Chopin. He wrote two autobiographical volumes, *My Young Years* (1974) and *My Many Years* (1980).

Rublyov, Andrey (or A. Rublev; c. 1370–1430) A leading Russian icon painter. He sometimes collaborated with the Greek painter Theophanes and late in life became a monk. In his masterpiece *The Old Testament Trinity* (Tretyakov Gallery, Moscow) the influence of *Byzantine art is modified by a distinctive gracefulness.

Rubus A genus of prickly perennial herbs and shrubs (225 species), found worldwide, mainly in N temperate regions. Many species, including the *blackberry, *loganberry, and *raspberry, are grown for their juicy edible fruits (each fruit is a cluster of small berries). Family: *Rosaceae.

ruby A red transparent variety of *corundum, the color being due to traces of chromium. It is used as a gemstone and in lasers, watches, and other precision instruments. Many fine rubies come from Mogok in Upper Burma, where they occur in metamorphic limestones with other precious and semiprecious stones. Prior to the 14th century rubies were called carbuncles. Birthstone for July.

Ruda Śląska 51 10N 16 39E A city in SW Poland. The first coalmine in Poland was opened here (1751). Population (1979 est): 158,000.

Rudbeckia. *See* black-eyed Susan.

rudd A game fish, *Scardinius erythrophthalmus*, found among vegetation in fresh waters of Europe and W Asia. It has a stout body, 14–18 in (35–40 cm) long, colored golden- or olive-brown above and silvery white below, deep-red fins, and golden eyes.

Rudolf, Lake. *See* Turkana, Lake.

Rudolph (1858–89) Archduke of Austria. His liberal views brought him into conflict with his father Emperor Francis Joseph. He and his mistress Baroness Marie Vetsera were found dead at his hunting lodge of Mayerling, having apparently committed suicide.

Rudolph I (1218–91) The first *Habsburg Holy Roman Emperor (1273–91). His conquests in central Europe—Austria, Styria, Carinthia, and Carniola—formed the nucleus of future Habsburg territorial power.

Rudolph II (1552–1612) Holy Roman Emperor (1576–1612). A dilatory ruler, he was forced to relinquish his powers in Hungary (1608) and Bohemia (1611) to his brother *Matthias.

rue An evergreen shrub, *Ruta graveolens*, also known as herb of grace, native to S Europe. Growing up to 35 in (90 cm) high, it has fleshy blue-green leaves and terminal clusters of yellow flowers. The leaves yield a bitter oil, once used as a spice and in medicines. Family: *Rutaceae.

Rueil-Malmaison 48 52N 2 11E A city in France, a suburb of Paris in the Hauts-de-Seine department. Its chateau was once a favorite residence of Napoleon I and the Empress Josephine is buried here. Population (1975): 64,429.

ruff An Old World *sandpiper, *Philomachus pugnax*, that breeds in coastal wetlands of N Eurasia and winters on mudflats of South Africa and S Asia. The female (called a reeve) is 10 in (25 cm) long and has a gray-brown plumage; the larger male has a double crest and a multicolored collar in the breeding season.

Ruffin, Edmund (1794–1865) US agriculturalist, publisher, and slavery supporter. He worked with revitalization of soil through fertilization, the addition of calcium carbonate, and crop rotation and promoted his findings through his journal, *The Farmer's Register* (1833–42). At the outbreak of the Civil War he was chosen to fire the first shot on Fort Sumter (1861). He committed suicide after the war.

Rugby 52 23N 1 15W A city in the English Midlands, in Warwickshire. According to tradition, the game of rugby football originated here in 1823 at the famous school (1567), which was described in *Tom Brown's Schooldays*. Rugby's industries include engineering and cement. Population (1981): 59,564.

Rügen An East German island in the Baltic Sea, 1.5 mi (2.5 km) off Stralsund, to which it is connected by a road and rail causeway. Area: 358 sq mi (926 sq km). Population (1971 est): 86,216.

Ruggles, Carl (1876–1971) US composer. His works, although few, had considerable influence; they are generally dissonant and strident and include *Angels* (1939) for brass or strings and the orchestral works *Sun-Treader* (1932) and *Men and Mountains* (1924–36). He devoted the last years of his life to painting.

Ruhr River A river in West Germany, rising in the Sauerland and flowing NW and W past Essen to join the Rhine River at Duisburg. The Ruhr

Valley (German name: Ruhrgebiet) is the center of the German iron and steel industry. Length: 146 mi (235 km).

Ruisdael, Jacob van (?1628–82) The greatest of Dutch landscape painters. Born in Haarlem, he studied under his father and probably also under his uncle, the landscape painter **Salomon van Ruysdael** (c. 1600–70). His baroque compositions, regularly framed by fantastic trees, are noted for their dramatic contrasts of light and shade. *The Jewish Cemetery* (c. 1660) is a striking evocation of human mortality.

Ruiz, Juan (c. 1283–c. 1350) Spanish poet. Nothing is known of his life apart from the fact that he was Archpriest of Hita. His *Libro de buen amor* (1330) consists of a series of love stories interspersed with ironic didactic digressions.

rum A liquor distilled from molasses derived from sugar cane. Rum is colorless and is used in mixed drinks, especially punches, or with soda water, fruit juice, or soft drinks. Better-quality rums are aged in oak casks for several years. It is produced wherever sugar cane is grown, predominantly in the Caribbean region but also in the US.

Rumania. *See* Romania, Socialist Republic of.

Rumelia The Balkan possessions of the Ottoman Empire from the 14th to 19th centuries. The Congress of *Berlin (1878) divided Rumelia into the state of Bulgaria under Ottoman suzerainty, the autonomous province of Eastern Rumelia, and the provinces of Edirne, Salonica, and Monastir. Eastern Rumelia was annexed by Bulgaria in 1885 and Monastir and Salonica were ceded to Serbia and Greece respectively in 1913.

Rumford, Benjamin Thompson, Count (1753–1814) American-born scientist, who spied for the British in the American Revolution and was forced to flee to England in 1776. In England he carried out scientific research in ballistics and the theory of heat. Suspected of spying for the French, he left England in 1785 for Paris and then Bavaria, where he worked as an administrator for the elector, Karl Theodor (1724–99), who made him a count of the Holy Roman Empire in 1791. In 1975 he returned to England, where he helped to demolish the caloric theory and found the *Royal Institution (1799).

ruminant A hoofed mammal belonging to the suborder *Ruminantia* (about 175 species), which includes deer, cattle, antelopes, sheep, and goats. Ruminants eat grass, leaves, and other vegetation and are characterized by possession of a four-chambered stomach. The largest chamber (rumen) contains bacteria and protozoa, which ferment the stomach contents and enable the animal to digest and utilize its food efficiently. Ruminants regurgitate their food periodically to "chew the cud," which helps to break up the plant cell walls.

rummy games Various related card games, of which rummy is the basic form. Its object is to form melds (sets or sequences) composed of three or four cards of the same rank (such as four jacks) or sequences of three or more cards of the same suit (such as seven, eight, nine, and ten, of diamonds). In each turn a player takes a card from the pack and discards one. The first player to dispose of his cards wins, scoring points according to the cards left in his opponents' hands. In **gin rummy** (for two players) the object is to reach a certain score before one's opponent. No melds are laid down until a player's unmatched cards make a total of ten or less, when the player lays his whole hand down. It is a "gin" if he has no unmatched cards. **Canasta** itself has several variants but is usually a partnership game for four players. Two packs are used; the jokers and all the twos are "wild." The winners are the first to score 5000 by making melds and canastas (a meld of seven or more cards of the same value).

Rump Parliament. *See* Long Parliament.

Runcie, Robert Alexander Kennedy (1921–) British churchman; Archbishop of Canterbury (1980–).

Runcorn 53 20N 2 44W A city in NW England, on the Mersey River and Manchester Ship Canal. It has chemical and brewing industries. Population (1981): 64,106.

Rundstedt, (Karl Rudolf) Gerd von (1875–1953) German field marshal, who was recalled from retirement at the outbreak of World War II, becoming (1942) commander in chief in France. He held command in the battle of the Bulge (1944) and was a competent if uninspired general. He was captured in 1945 but his ill health secured his release.

Runeberg, Johan Ludvig (1804–77) Finnish poet of Swedish origin, who wrote in Swedish and whose style was influenced by his study of Finnish folk poetry. His major works include the epic poem *Kung Fjalar* (*King Fialar*; 1844), in which he attempted a synthesis of Christian and classical pagan ideals, and *Fänrik Ståls sägner* (*Tales of Ensign Stål*; 1848–60), a collection of patriotic ballads, one of which became the Finnish national anthem.

runic alphabet An alphabetical writing system used for Norse and certain other Germanic languages. It originated, probably as a modified version of the Etruscan or the Roman alphabet, in the 2nd or 3rd century AD, and went out of use gradually after the 14th century. The Gothic word *runa* means secret or mystery, and runes were always associated with magical powers. The runic alphabet, called the *futhark* from the names of the first six letters, consisted at first of 24 characters, extended in Old English to 28 and later 31.

runner bean A climbing plant, *Phaseolus coccineus*, also known as scarlet runner, native to South America and widely cultivated as a vegetable crop, especially in Britain. Growing up to 10 ft (3 m) high, it bears usually red five-petaled flowers, which give rise to edible bean pods, 8–24 in (20–60 cm) long, that are eaten cooked. Wild plants are perennial, but cultivated plants are treated as annuals. Family: *Leguminosae*.

Runnymede (*or* Runnimede) 51 26N 0 33W A meadow in SE England, on the S bank of the River Thames. The Magna Carta was granted here by King John (1215).

Runyon, Damon (1884–1946) US humorous writer. For his stories about New York characters, first collected in *Guys and Dolls* (1932) and notable for their lively slang, he drew on his long experience as a journalist and sports reporter. *Guys and Dolls* was made into extremely successful stage and screen productions.

Rupert, Prince (1619–82) Cavalry officer, who fought for the Royalists in the English Civil War; he was the son of Frederick the Winter King of the Palatinate and Elizabeth, daughter of James I of England. After Charles I's surrender he was banished from England. He returned at the Restoration (1660) and served as an admiral in the *Dutch Wars.

Rupert's Land (*or* Prince Rupert's Land) A region in N and W Canada around Hudson Bay. In 1670 it was granted by Charles II to the *Hudson's Bay Company, the first governor of which was Prince *Rupert. It is now an ecclesiastical province of the Anglican Church of Canada.

rupture. *See* hernia.

Rural Electrification Administration (REA) US agency, established in 1935, to expand the availability of electricity in rural areas. Part of President Franklin D. Roosevelt's *New Deal program, it implemented the extension of electric lines, considered unprofitable by privately-owned power companies, through government funding and labor.

Rurik (died c. 879) The semilegendary founder of the Rurik dynasty of Russian princes (862–1598). A Varangian chieftain, Rurik was allegedly Prince of Novgorod from 862. His descendants were grand princes of Kiev, Vladimir, and Muscovy.

Ruse (Russe *or* Roussé) 43 05N 25 59E A city in central N Bulgaria. It is the site of the Friendship Bridge (1954) over the Danube River into Romania and is Bulgaria's principal river port. Population (1979 est): 170,594.

Rush, Benjamin (1746–1813) US physician, educator, and patriot; signer of the Declaration of Independence. A medical doctor, he practiced in Philadelphia and taught chemistry at (now) the University of Pennsylvania. He was a delegate to the Second Continental Congress (1776) and surgeon general of the Continental Army (1777–78). He was vocal in his campaigns for the abolition of slavery and for prison reform, woman's rights, and opportunities for the poor. He fought a yellow-fever epidemic in Philadelphia in 1793 and was one of the first to link the disease with mosquitoes. A pioneer in the field of mental health, he wrote *Medical Inquiries and Observations upon the Diseases of the Mind* (1812).

rush A grasslike plant of the genus *Juncus* (over 300 species), found worldwide in damp temperate and cold regions. Rushes have tufts of slender rigid stalks, up to about 40 in (1 m) high, bearing long flat leaves and clusters of small green or brown flowers, which produce seed capsules. The leaves are used to make mats, baskets, etc. Family: *Juncaceae*.

The name is also applied to similar plants, including the *bulrush, *flowering rush, and *woodrush.

Rushdie, Salman (1947–) British novelist, born in India. His first novel *Grimus* (1975) was followed by the much acclaimed Booker prize-winner *Midnight's Children* (1981) and *Shame* (1983).

Rusk, (David) Dean (1909–) US statesman. After World War II he held posts in the State Department and in 1950 became assistant secretary of state for Far Eastern affairs, influencing US policy in the Korean War. As secretary of state (1961–69) successively under Presidents Kennedy and Johnson he defended US military involvement in Vietnam. In 1969 he became professor of international law at the University of Georgia.

Ruskin, John (1819–1900) British art and social critic. He began to write his first work of art criticism, *Modern Painters* (1843–60), to defend the paintings of J. M. W. Turner. In *The Stones of Venice* (1851–53) he promoted the gothic style in architecture. In *Unto This Last* (1862) and other volumes of social criticism he denounced materialism and laissez-faire economics from a moral and aesthetic perspective. His sonorous prose style is most fully developed in his unfinished autobiography, *Praeterita* (1885–89). During his last years he suffered recurrent attacks of insanity.

BERTRAND RUSSELL

Russell, Bertrand Arthur William, 3rd Earl (1872–1970) British philosopher, grandson of Lord John *Russell. His first major philosophical work, *Principia Mathematica* (1910–13), written with A. N. *Whitehead, presented pure mathematics as a development of *logic. On a smaller logical basis *Our Knowledge of the External World* (1914) attempted a new approach to traditional problems in epistemology. From his pupil *Wittgenstein, he also acquired a lasting interest in language.
His prolific writings on religion, politics, and morals always stimulated interest, often to his own detriment. He was imprisoned (1918) and deprived of a Cambridge University post for his outspoken pacifism. In 1940 a US court disqualified him from holding a professorship at New York University on account of his moral views. In 1961 he was again imprisoned for civil disobedience during the Campaign for Nuclear Disarmament. He was awarded the Nobel Prize for literature in 1950. He claimed that "longing for love, the search for knowledge, and unbearable pity for mankind" were the governing passions of his life.

Russell, John, 1st Earl (1792–1878) British statesman; Whig (Liberal) prime minister (1846–52, 1865–66); the grandfather of Bertrand Russell. Elected to parliament in 1813, he championed parliamentary reform in the 1820s. He was home secretary (1835–39), and secretary for war (1839–41). His first ministry was dominated by his foreign secretary Palmerston. Russell was himself foreign secretary (1852–53) and then colonial secretary (1855). He resigned as prime minister following defeat of a parliamentary reform bill.

Russell, Lillian (Helen Louise Leonard; 1861–1922) US entertainer and singer. She appeared in the light opera *The Great Mogul; or, the Snake Charmer* (1881) and from 1899–1904 with the burlesque team of Weber and Fields. *Barbara's Millions* (1906) and *Wildfire* (1908) were nonmusical comedies. Famous on the stage, she was equally renowned for her marriages and affairs, especially a 40-year relationship with Diamond Jim *Brady.

Russell's viper A common highly venomous viper, *Vipera russelli*, of SE Asia. Up to 5 ft (1.5 m) long, it is patterned with three rows of black-and-white ringed reddish spots. It is the cause of many snakebite deaths.

Russia. *See* Soviet Union.

Russian The main language of the Soviet Union, belonging to the East *Slavonic family. It is a highly inflected language with six cases and a notable feature is the frequency of clusters of consonants. It is written in the *Cyrillic alphabet. The standard form is based on the dialect of Moscow.

Russian literature Until the beginning of the 18th century Russian literature consisted chiefly of chronicles and religious works written in Old Slavonic. The outstanding early work is *The Song of Igor's Campaign* (c. 1187). The development of modern literature owed much to the political reforms of Peter the Great (reigned 1682–1725) and the artistic patronage of Catherine the Great (reigned 1762–96). Major writers of the 18th century included the poet and scholar M. V. Lomonosov (1711–65), the poet G. R. Derzhavin (1743–1816), and the fabulist I. A. Krylov (1768–1844). The first half of the 19th century was dominated by Pushkin and Lermontov and the second half, following the pioneering fiction of Gogol, by the novelists Tolstoy, Dostoievski, and Turgenev. They were followed by the dramatist and short-story writer Chekhov, whose detached compassion contrasted with the strong social commitment of Gorki. The political unrest of the early 20th century stimulated much artistic experimentation, but in the 1930s the Soviet authorities decreed that all literature must adhere to the official doctrine of *socialist realism. Writers whose works were banned in Russia include the poets Akhmatova, Mandelstan, and Tsvetaeva and the novelist Pasternak. The apparent liberalization of culture heralded by the publication of works by Solzhenitsyn, Yevtushenko, and Voznesenskii in the 1960s was short lived and in 1974 Solzhenitsyn joined the growing number of Russian writers living abroad.

Russian Orthodox Church An offshoot of the Greek Orthodox Church, dating from the baptism of the emperor Vladimir (later St Vladimir) in 988. Since 1328 the metropolitan see has been at Moscow. During the 15th century connections with the Greek parent Church were severed. In the 18th century the Church fell increasingly under state control. Since the 1917 Revolution it has been intermittently persecuted and at best regarded with suspicion and its activities restricted. *See also* Old Believers.

Russian Revolution (1917) The revolution between March and November (Old Style February and October), 1917, that overthrew the Russian monarchy and established the world's first communist state. It began with the February Revolution, when riots over shortage of bread and coal in Petrograd (formerly St Petersburg) led to the establishment of the Petrograd Soviet of Workers' and Soldiers' Deputies, dominated by *Mensheviks and Social Revolutionaries, and of a provisional government of *Duma deputies, which forced *Nicholas II to abdicate. The failure of the provisional government, under Prince *Lvov and then *Kerenski, to end Russia's participation in World War I and to deal with food shortages led to the demand of the *Bolsheviks under *Lenin for "All power to the Soviets." The Bolsheviks, who had gained a majority in the Soviet by September, staged the October (*or* Bolshevik) Revolution, seizing power and establishing the Soviet of People's Commissars. The new government came to terms with Germany in early 1918 but almost immediately faced opposition at home. In the subsequent civil war (1918–21) the Red Army was ultimately victorious against the anticommunist White Russians but with the loss of some 100,000 lives. In addition, some two million Russians emigrated.

Russian Soviet Federal Socialist Republic (*or* RSFSR) A constituent republic in the N Soviet Union. It is the largest, most heavily populated, and economically most important of the 15 Soviet republics, occupying some 76% of the total area of the Soviet Union, containing about 54% of its population, and producing 70% of its industrial and agricultural output. Its climate ranges from Arctic to subtropical and its geographical zones include tundra, forest, steppe, and rich agricultural soil. Over 80% of the population are Russians, the remainder consisting of 38 national minorities. The RSFSR contains outstanding mineral resources including iron ore, coal, oil, gold, platinum, copper, zinc, lead, and tin. The major industrial region is around Moscow. It produces ships, trucks, machine tools, electronic equipment, textiles, and chemicals. Because of the extensive forests, timber and related occupations are important. The main agricultural products are wheat, cotton, fruit and vegetables, tobacco, and sugar beet. The RSFSR was formed in 1917 and was joined with the Ukraine, Belorussia, and Transcaucasia in 1922 to constitute the Soviet Union. It consists of 6 territories, 49 regions, 16 Autonomous Soviet Socialist Republics, 5 autonomous regions, and 10 national areas. Area: 6,592,658 sq mi (17,074,984 sq km). Population (1981 est): 139,100,000. Capital: Moscow.

Russo-Finnish War (*or* Winter War; 1939–40) The war between the Soviet Union and Finland at the beginning of World War II. It was won by the Soviet Union, the aggressor, which gained part of the Karelian Isthmus.

Russo-Japanese War (1904–05) A confrontation arising from conflicting Japanese and Russian interests in Manchuria, where Russia controlled Port Arthur (now Lüda). In 1904 Japan attacked Port Arthur, which fell in January, 1905. In May a Japanese fleet under *Togo Heihachiro destroyed Russia's Baltic Fleet in the Tsushima Straits, forcing Russia's surrender. In the peace conference at Portsmouth, New Hampshire, over which Theodore Roosevelt presided, Japan gained the ascendancy in S Manchuria and Korea.

rust A reddish-brown solid consisting of hydrated iron oxide. Rusting is a special case of corrosion; the mechanism is complicated and still not fully understood but involves the setting up of a cell in which iron is the anode and a metal impurity the cathode. Both water and oxygen must be present for rust to form although the most serious damage, pitting, is always found in an oxygen-free portion of metal. Rust prevention usually involves protective coatings (paint, zinc plating, etc.) or alloying with chromium and other metals to produce stainless steels.

rust fungi Fungi, belonging to the order *Uredinales*, that are parasites of plants, forming spots, blotches, and pustules on the stems and foliage of their hosts. Several are important pests of cereal crops, including black rust (*Puccinia graminis*) of wheat. This forms red pustules on wheat leaves, releasing spores that infect barberry (*Berberis vulgaris*)—the secondary host—in which the life cycle continues. Control therefore involves eradication of barberry in wheat-growing areas as well as developing resistant strains of wheat. Other important wheat rusts include yellow rust (*P. striiformis*) and brown rust (*P. recondita*). Class: *Basidiomycetes*.

rutabaga A biennial herbaceous plant, *Brassica napobrassica*, growing to a height of 40 in (1 m), with deeply lobed leaves and yellow flowers. Also known as a swede, and closely related to the turnip, it is cultivated for its fleshy edible taproot, which is yellow or white; this is eaten as a vegetable and also fed to livestock. Family: *Cruciferae*.

Ruth A Gentile from Moab who was an ancestress of David. The Old Testament **Book of Ruth**, set in the time of the *Judges (c. 1000 BC), records the events by which Ruth came to marry Boaz, a Hebrew.

Ruth, Babe (George Herman R.; 1895–1948) US baseball player. He pitched for the Boston Red Sox (1914–19) and played outfield for the New York Yankees (1920–34) and Boston Braves (1935). Known as the "Sultan of Swat," he held the record for career home runs—714—until 1974. He was elected to the Baseball Hall of Fame in 1938, the year it was founded.

Ruthenia A region comprising the S slopes of the Carpathian Mountains, now part of the Ukrainian SSR (Soviet Union), which was part of Hungary until it was attached to Czechoslovakia in 1920. Following Hitler's seizure of Czechoslovakia in 1939, Ruthenia briefly proclaimed its independence, before being annexed by Hungary. After World War II it was ceded to the Soviet Union.

ruthenium (Ru) A hard metal of the platinum group, first separated in 1844 by K. K. Klaus (1796–1864). It is used to harden platinum and palladium for use in electrical contacts and is a versatile catalyst. The tetroxide (RuO_4), like that of osmium, is toxic. The element shows a wide range of *valence states. At no 44; at wt 101.07; mp 2310°C; bp 3900°C.

Rutherford, Ernest, 1st Baron (1871–1937) English physicist, born in New Zealand, who was a professor at Montreal (1898–1907), Manchester (1907–19), and Cambridge (1919–37). He made fundamental discoveries concerning the nature of *radioactivity, distinguishing between the three types of radiation, which he named alpha, beta, and gamma rays. Working with Hans *Geiger he discovered that alpha radiation consisted of positively charged helium atoms. In 1906, while bombarding gold foil with alpha particles, he deduced the existence of a heavy positively charged core in the atom, which he called the *nucleus. In 1908, Rutherford received the Nobel Prize for chemistry.

Rutherford, Dame Margaret (1892–1972) British actress. She was particularly successful in comedies, such as *Blithe Spirit* (1941). In her films, which included *Murder She Said* (1962) and *The VIPs* (1963), she specialized in the roles of elderly eccentrics.

rutherfordium. See kurchatovium.

rutile A brown to black form of natural titanium dioxide, TiO_2. It is found as an accessory mineral in igneous and metamorphic rocks, in veins, and as fibers in quartz, known as Venus' hair.

Rutledge, John (1739–1800) US political leader; chief justice of the Supreme Court (1795). He was a delegate to two continental congresses (1774–76; 1782–83), a signer of the US Constitution, and headed South Carolina, first as president (1776–78) and then as governor (1779–82). An associate justice of the US Supreme Court (1789–91), he was appointed chief justice in 1795 by George *Washington. He served for one month, failing to attain Senate confirmation due to his opposition to the recently-approved Jay's Treaty. (*See* Jay, John).

Rutledge, Wylie Blount, Jr. (1894–1949) US jurist; associate justice of the Supreme Court (1943–49). After teaching law at several universities, he was appointed to the US Court of Appeals in the District of Columbia

(1939–43). A liberal member of the Supreme Court, he was a vigorous supporter of civil rights.

Ruwenzori Mountains A mountain range in East Africa, on the Uganda-Zaïre border between Lakes Albert and Edward, rising to 16,795 ft (5119 m) at Mount Stanley.

Ruyter, Michiel Adriaanszoon de (1607–76) Dutch admiral, who served outstandingly in the *Dutch Wars (1652–54, 1665–67, 1672–78). In the battle of the Medway (1667) he destroyed most of the English fleet and his victories in 1672–73 saved the United Provinces from invasion. He was killed in action.

Rwanda, Republic of A small landlocked country in E central Africa. Lake Kivu forms most of its W boundary and the land is chiefly mountainous and rugged. The majority of the inhabitants are Bantu-speaking Hutu, the Nilotic Tutsi comprising less than 10% of the total. *Economy*: chiefly subsistence agriculture, including livestock. The main food crops are beans, cassava, and corn, and the principal cash crop is coffee, which, along with cassiterite, form the main exports. Methane gas has been found under Lake Kivu. Some small-scale industry is being developed including food processing and textiles. *History*: a Tutsi kingdom from the 16th century, the area (with present-day Burundi) came under German East Africa in 1890. From 1919, after World War I, it was administered by Belgium as the N part of Ruanda-Urundi, which was under League of Nations mandate and then a UN trust territory. In 1959 the Tutsi kingdom was overthrown by the Hutu, who in 1961 declared Rwanda a republic; independence was recognized by Belgium in 1962. There were further massacres of the Tutsi by the Hutu in 1964. In 1973 the government was overthrown in a bloodless coup and Major General Juvénal Habyalimana came to power. The first parliament under the new constitution was elected by popular vote in 1981; voting for the one-party list of candidates was mandatory. Rwandan refugees expelled from Uganda and living in border camps exacerbated tensions between the two countries as violence against Rwandans in Uganda escalated. Official languages: Kinyarwanda and French. Official currency: Rwanda franc of 100 centimes. Area: 10,166 sq mi (26,330 sq km). Population (1983 est): 5,644,000. Capital: Kigali.

Ryazan 54 37N 39 43E A city in the W central Soviet Union, in the RSFSR. Founded in 1095, it was the capital of a principality until annexed by Russia in 1521. Industries include oil refining, metalworking, and engineering. Population (1981 est): 470,000.

Rybinsk (name from 1946 until 1958: Shcherbakov) 58 01N 38 52E A port in the W central Soviet Union, in the RSFSR on the Volga River. It is situated below the **Rybinsk Reservoir**, an artificial lake of some 2000 sq mi (5200 sq km) created (1941) through the damming of the Volga at its confluence with the Suda and Sheksna rivers and forming the S stretch of the Volga–Baltic waterway. Rybinsk has a hydroelectric station and shipbuilding, engineering, and food-processing industries. Population (1981 est): 243,000.

Ryder Cup A biennial golf tournament between members of the US and British Professional Golfers' Associations, first played in 1927.

rye A cereal *grass, *Secale cereale*, native to W Asia but widely cultivated in cool temperate and upland regions. 3.5–7 ft (1–2 m) high, it bears a terminal spike, 4–6 in (10–15 cm) long, of numerous two- or three-flowered spikelets. The grain is milled to produce a dark-colored flour, which is used in making black bread or for livestock feed. Rye may be sown in autumn to provide winter grazing or as a green manure crop.

Rye House Plot (1683) A conspiracy to murder Charles II of England and his brother, the Duke of York (later James II), near Rye House, Hoddesdon, on their way to London from Newmarket. The plot failed but several conspirators, including Lord William Russell and Algernon Sidney, were tried and executed.

Rykov, Aleksei Ivanovich (1881–1938) Soviet politician. After the *Russian Revolution Rykov played a prominent part in the Soviet Government until 1930, when he was expelled from the Communist Party for opposing the brutality of collectivization. He was forced to recant in 1929 and perished in Stalin's purges.

Ryle, Gilbert (1900–76) British philosopher. He was Waynflete Professor of Metaphysical Philosophy at Oxford (1945–68) and editor of *Mind* (1947–71), exerting considerable influence as a writer and teacher. His philosophy centered around detailed analysis of mental concepts. *The Concept of Mind* (1949) maintained that *Descartes' idea of the human being consisting of mind and body ("the ghost in the machine") was misleading.

Ryle, Sir Martin (1918–84) British astronomer; professor at Cambridge University and astronomer royal (1972–84). A pioneer of radio telescopy, his most important work was the development of a technique for studying distant radio sources by using two radio telescopes placed a distance apart, thus increasing their effective aperture. In 1974 he shared the Nobel Prize for physics with Antony Hewish.

Ryukyu Islands A group of volcanic and coral islands in the W Pacific Ocean, extending almost 400 mi (660 km) from Kyushu to N Taiwan. An independent kingdom until the 14th century, the islands were dominated by the Chinese before becoming a part of Japan (1879). They were under US control (1945–72). The chief industries are agriculture and fishing. Area: 849 sq mi (2196 sq km). Population (1970): 945,111. Chief city: Naha (on Okinawa).

S

Saale River A river in West and East Germany, rising in NE Bavaria and flowing mainly N past Jena and Halle to join the Rhine River near Magdeburg. Length: 265 mi (426 km).

Saarbrücken (French name: Sarrebruck) 49 15N 6 58E A city in SW West Germany, the capital of Saarland on the Saar River near the French border. It was under French administration (1801–15, 1919–35, 1945–57). Some historic buildings, such as the gothic abbey church (1270–1330), survived World War II and it has a university (1948). Its industries include iron and steel and machinery manufacturing. Population (1980 est): 193,700.

Saarinen, Eero (1910–61) US architect, born in Finland. One of the most innovative of 20th-century architects, Saarinen emigrated (1923) to the US with his father, the architect Eliel Saarinen (1873–1950), and became his partner in 1938. His first independent design was the General Motors Technical Center in Warren, Michigan (1948–56). He designed two buildings for the Massachusetts Institute of Technology. His most famous building is the Trans World Airlines terminal at Kennedy Airport, New York (1956–62), which has reinforced concrete vaults spreading outward to suggest flight. Other works include the St Louis Arch (1964) and Dulles International Airport near Washington, DC, completed after his death.

Saarland A small *Land* in SW West Germany, bordering on France. The area has often passed between French and German control, but plebiscites held in 1935 and 1955 resulted in its union with Germany. Rich in coal, it has a large steel industry. Area: 992 sq mi (2569 sq km). Population (1980 est): 1,068,000. Capital: Saarbrücken.

Saar River (French name: Sarre) A river in W Europe, rising in the Vosges Mountains in NE France and flowing generally N into West Germany, then NW through Saarland to join the Moselle River above Trier. The Saar Valley is noted for its wines. Length: 149 mi (240 km).

Sabadell 41 33N 2 07E A city in NE Spain, in Catalonia. It has an important textile industry. Other industries include metallurgy and leather. Population (1970): 159,408.

Sabah (former name: North Borneo) A state in Malaysia, in NE *Borneo on the South China and Sulu Seas. Forested and mountainous, it rises to 13,533 ft (4125 m) at Mount Kinabalu, the highest peak in Malaysia and Borneo. It is largely undeveloped, but on the well-populated western coastal plain rice and rubber are grown. Since 1975 copper and oil resources have been exploited; timber, rubber, copra, and abaca are exported. *History*: until the European colonial period, most contact was with the Philippines. North Borneo was first colonized by the British in 1877, becoming a protectorate in 1882. In 1963 it joined Malaysia under its present name. Area: 29,388 sq mi (76,115 sq km). Population (1978 est): 981,544. Capital: Kota Kinabalu.

Sabatier, Paul (1854–1941) French chemist, who was professor at Toulouse University (1884–1941), where he discovered that nickel catalyzes hydrogenation reactions. Since nickel is relatively cheap, this enabled similar reactions to be performed on an industrial scale, e.g. in the production of margarine. He shared the 1912 Nobel Prize with F. A. V. Grignard, the discoverer of *Grignard reagents.

sabbath In Judaism, the seventh day of the week, ordained by God in the Pentateuch as a day of rest for the benefit of his people. It was reckoned from sunset on Friday to sunset on Saturday. The early Christian Church soon substituted Sunday as the Christian day of rest and worship because the resurrection of Jesus Christ took place on the first day of the (Jewish) week.

saber-toothed tiger An extinct *cat that lived 30 million years ago and became extinct in the Pleistocene epoch (1 million years ago). *Smilodon*, a Pleistocene form, was about the size of a tiger, with very long upper canine teeth used to pierce the thick hide of its prey. □fossil.

Sabin, Albert Bruce (1906–) US physician, born in Russia. A specialist in virology, he served on the medical school staff at the University of Cincinnati from 1939. Here, he researched crippling diseases of children and developed a live vaccine (1957) that, given orally, immunized against poliomyelitis (polio).

Sabine River A river that flows from NE Texas SE and then S along the Texas-Louisiana border through Sabine Lake and Sabine Pass into the Gulf

of Mexico. Its lower portion is part of the Gulf Intracoastal Waterway. Length: 360 mi (580 km).

Sabines The peoples of the scattered hilltop communities NE of ancient Rome. The legendary abduction of the Sabine women by Roman settlers, a favorite theme in the history of art, indicates the early interbreeding of Sabines with Romans. Sabine influence on Roman religion was especially strong. They became Roman citizens in 268 BC.

Sabin vaccine A vaccine that prevents poliomyelitis, developed by a US virologist, A. B. Sabin (1906–). It contains a weakened polio virus that stimulates the body's defense against polio without causing the disease. Sabin vaccine is given by mouth (often on a sugar lump) in three consecutive doses. *See also* Salk vaccine.

sable A carnivorous mammal, *Martes zibellina*, native to N Eurasia. It is less than 20 in (50 cm) long and has thicker legs and longer ears than other *martens. Its coat is thick, soft, and glossy and is valued as fur (Siberian sable).

sable antelope A large antelope, *Hippotragus niger*, of S African forests. About 4 ft 3 in (130 cm) high at the shoulder, it has backward-curving ringed horns up to 67 in (170 cm) long. The coat is black in males, lighter in females, with white on the face, rump, and belly.

Sable Island A sandy island in Canada, in the Atlantic Ocean off the coast of Nova Scotia. The scene of many shipwrecks, it is known as "the graveyard of the Atlantic."

Sacagawea (Sacajawea; Sahcargarweah; ?1787–?1812) US Shoshone Indian Guide. As a child she was sold by the *Mandan Indians, who had captured her, to Toussaint Charbonneau, a French-Canadian fur trapper. They married (1804) in North Dakota and that next year served as interpreters and guides to the *Lewis and Clark expedition to the Pacific coast. Sacagawea's contacts with the Shoshone ensured the expedition party's safe passage.

saccharin An organic compound ($C_7H_5NO_3S$) used as a sweetening agent in the food industry and as a sugar substitute by diabetics and others. It has about five hundred times the sweetening power of table sugar and passes through the body without being absorbed or changed.

Sacco-Vanzetti case The controversial trial of two US anarchists. Nicola Sacco and Bartolomeo Vanzetti were Italian-born immigrant workers convicted of murder on flimsy evidence. The verdict, which was reached largely because of their political activities and was influenced by current anti-alien and antiradical prejudice, aroused international protests. An investigative committee supported the sentence and Sacco and Vanzetti were executed in 1927, six years after being sentenced.

Sachs, Hans (1494–1576) German poet and folk dramatist, most famous of the *Meistersingers of Nuremberg. He wrote thousands of works, including lively farces still performed at annual festivals throughout Germany, verse tales, religious poetry, and other works in support of *Luther. He is the central character, portrayed as wise and philosophic, of Wagner's opera *The Mastersingers of Nuremberg* (1868).

Sachs, Nelly (Leonie) (1891–1970) German Jewish poet and dramatist. Helped by Selma *Lagerlöf, she escaped from Nazi Germany and settled in Sweden. Her best-known play is *Eli: Ein Mysterienspiel vom Leiden Israels* (1951). In 1966 she shared a Nobel Prize with Shmuel Yosef *Agnon.

sackbut. *See* trombone.

Sackville, Thomas, 1st Earl of Dorset (1536–1608) British poet and dramatist. He collaborated with Thomas Norton (1532–83) on *Gorbuduc* (1561), the first English play in blank verse, and planned and introduced *The Mirror for Magistrates* (1563), a collection of narrative poems based on the lives of eminent men.

sacrament In Christian theology, a ritual having a special significance as a visible sign of an inner grace in its participants. The *Roman Catholic Church and *Orthodox Churches accept seven sacraments: baptism, confirmation, penance, the *Eucharist, marriage, ordination, and extreme unction. Baptism and the Eucharist are the only commonly accepted sacraments among the Protestant Churches (*see* Protestantism).

Sacramento 38 32N 121 30W The capital city of California, on the Sacramento River. Founded in 1839, it grew after the discovery of gold at nearby Sutter's Mill in 1848. Linked by canal (1963) to San Francisco Bay, it is a deepwater port and serves an extensive agricultural area. Industries include food processing, aerospace, and printing. Population (1980): 275,741.

Sacramento, Battle of (1847) US-Mexican battle during the *Mexican War. US forces, under Colonel Alexander W. Doniphan, defeated Mexican troops N of Chihuahua, Mexico. Mexican casualties were high.

Sacramento River A river that flows from N central California through Shasta Lake to just below Sacramento where it joins the San Joaquin River and flows W through Suisun Bay to San Francisco Bay. The Central Valley Project on the river provides irrigation, hydroelectricity, water, and flood control for the river's valley. Length: 320 mi (515 km).

sacred ibis An African □ibis, *Threskiornis aethiopica*, that was revered in ancient Egypt. 30 in (75 cm) long, it is pure white except for dark ornamental plumes on its back, dark wing tips, and a black head and neck. It has a black bill and feeds in flocks along rivers, taking frogs and small aquatic animals.

Sadat, Anwar (1918–81) Egyptian statesman; president (1970–81). A colleague of *Nasser in the Free Officers movement, Sadat was twice vice president (1964–66, 1969–70) before becoming president on Nasser's death. He moved Egypt away from the Soviet Union and toward— the US, under the influence of which he negotiated a peace agreement with Israel in 1979 (□Carter, Jimmy). For this initiative and his courage in visiting Israel in the face of some Arab opposition he was awarded the 1978 Nobel Peace Prize jointly with Begin. He was assassinated (1981) by Islamic extremists while watching a military display in Egypt.

saddleback A very rare songbird, *Creadion carunculatus*, surviving only on small islands around New Zealand. It has a black plumage with a chestnut patch on its back and orange wattles at the base of the sharp pointed bill. Saddlebacks are weak fliers and feed in the undergrowth on larvae, insects, and fruits. Family: *Callaeidae* (wattlebirds).

Sadducees An ancient Jewish religious and political party. They formed a conservative and aristocratic group centering on the priesthood in Jerusalem. With the destruction of the temple the party ceased to exist, but many of its ideas surfaced later in medieval Jewish sects. *See also* Pharisees.

Sade, Donatien Alphonse François, Marquis de (1740–1814) French novelist. Most of his works of sexual fantasy and perversion, which include *Justine, La Philosophie dans le boudoir*, and *Les 120 Journées de Sodome*, were written in the 1780s and 1790s, during his many years of imprisonment for sexual offenses. During his last years he was confined to the mental asylum of Charenton. His moral nihilism has been seen as a stage in the development of *existentialism. The sexual perversion "sadism," in which sexual pleasure is derived from causing or observing pain, is named for him.

Sa'di (Mosleh al-Din S.; c. 1215–92) Persian poet, born in Shiraz, who studied in Baghdad and subsequently spent much of his life wandering in Asia Minor and Egypt, claiming also to have visited India and central Asia. He returned to Shiraz in 1256. His major works are *Bustan* (*The Orchard*; 1257), a didactic poem illustrating the Islamic virtues of justice, contentedness, and modesty, and *Galestan* (*The Rose Garden*; 1258), a collection of moralistic anecdotes. He also wrote a number of odes and popularized the *ghazal* form later used by *Hafiz.

Sadowa (Czech name: Sadorá) A village in W Czechoslovakia, in NE Bohemia. It was the scene of a battle in the Austro-Prussian War (1866) in which the Austrians were defeated by the Prussians.

Safavids The ruling dynasty of Persia from 1502 to 1706. It was founded by Esmail I (1486–1524) and named for his ancestor Safi od-Din (1252–1334), a Muslim saint. Esmail established Shiism (*see* Shiites) as the state religion. Among his descendants was *Abbas the Great (reigned 1588–1628). The Safavids were overthrown by *Nader Shah.

safflower An annual herbaceous plant, *Carthamus tinctorius*, native to Asia and Africa. 12–47 in (30–120 cm) tall, it has red, orange, yellow, or white flowers. It is cultivated in India, the Middle East, North America, and Australia for its seeds, which yield safflower oil, used in paints, varnishes, cooking oils, and margarines. A red dye can be obtained from the dried flowers. Family: *Compositae*.

saffron The dried orange-yellow stigmas of the saffron crocus (*C. sativa*), used for flavoring and coloring foods and liqueurs and formerly as a dye for fabrics. The crocus, which has purple flowers, is probably native to the Mediterranean region and SW Asia and has been cultivated since ancient times; today the main producing areas are France, Spain, and Italy. About 100,000 flowers are needed to produce 2 lb (1 kg) of saffron.

Safi (ancient name: Asfi) 32 20N 9 17W A port in Morocco, on the Atlantic coast. Its artificial harbor serves Marrakech, and exports include phosphates. Besides its important fishing industry, it manufactures pottery and has a chemical complex. Population (1973 est): 129,100.

Sagan, Carl (Edward) (1934–) US scientist and writer. Professor of astronomy and director of planetary studies at Cornell University (1968–), he worked on the Mariner (1962–73) and Viking (1975–76) space probes of Mars, Venus, and Mars and studied the aftermath of a hypothetical nuclear war (1983). His works include *The Cosmic Connection* (1973), *The Dragons of Eden* (1977; Pulitzer Prize, 1978), *Broca's Brain* (1979), and *Cosmos* (1980).

Sagan, Françoise (Françoise Quoirez; 1935–) French novelist. Her best-selling novels include *Bonjour Tristesse* (1954) and *Aimez-Vous Brahms?* (1959), which concern transitory love affairs between wealthy and cynical characters. She has also written several plays, including *Château en Suède* (1960) and *Zaphorie* (1973).

sagas Heroic prose narratives in Old Norse, the best of which were written down in Iceland in the 12th and 13th centuries (*see* Icelandic literature). Translations of French *romances, Latin histories, and saints' lives were part of the saga tradition but its characteristic subject matter was drawn from ancient Scandinavian oral traditions: fictionalized accounts of the deeds of Norwegian kings (e.g. Snorri *Sturluson's *Heimskringla*), heroic legends of the pagan past (e.g. *Volsungasaga*), and the "family" sagas that mirrored contemporary Icelandic society (e.g. *Egilssaga, Gíslasaga, Laxdaelasaga, Grettissaga*, and *Njálssaga*).

sage A perennial herb or shrub, *Salvia officinalis*, native to the Mediterranean region and widely cultivated for its leaves, which are used for flavoring foods. It grows 18–24 in (45–60 cm) high and has blue, pink, or white flowers. *See also* Salvia.

sage grouse A large □grouse, *Centrocercus urophasianus*, occurring in sagebrush deserts of western US. It is 30 in (75 cm) long and the male has ornamental wattles and a long slender tail, which is fanned out during its courtship display.

Sagittarius (Latin: Archer) A large constellation in the S sky, lying on the *zodiac between Capricornus and Scorpius. The brightest star is the 2nd-magnitude Kaus Australis. The constellation contains several notable *star clusters and emission *nebulae, including the **Lagoon nebula**. The center of the *Galaxy lies in the direction of Sagittarius.

sago A starchy food obtained from the sago *palms (*Metoxylon sagu* and *M. rumphii*), native to Indonesia and cultivated in Malaysia. The palms, up to 30 ft (9 m) high, take 15 years to mature and are harvested just before flowering. Their stems are swollen with a starchy pith, which is extracted, ground, and washed and used to make flour or pearl sago. The pithy stems of a *cycad, *Cycas circinalis*, also called sago palm, are used as a source of sago. The plant is native to tropical Asia and its attractive fernlike leaves are used for ornament.

saguaro A giant cactus, *Cereus* (or *Carnegiea*) *gigantea*, native to the S US and Mexico. It has a ribbed branched stem and is slow-growing, producing its white flowers from the age of 50–75 years; it may live for 200 years and reach a height of 40 ft (12 m).

Saguenay River A river in E Canada, in E Quebec flowing from Lac St Jean ESE into the St Lawrence estuary. Its upper reaches drop steeply, providing hydroelectric power, while the lower course flows between high cliffs, a popular tourist attraction. Length: 105 mi (170 km).

Sagunto (Latin name: Saguntum) 39 40N 0 17W A city in E Spain, in Valencia. It was captured by Hannibal in 219 BC, precipitating the second Punic War. There are many fine Roman remains including a theater and circus. It exports iron ore and citrus fruits. Population (1970): 47,026.

Sahara The largest desert in the world, covering most of N Africa. The terrain consists chiefly of a plateau with central mountains rising to 11,204 ft (3415 m) and some areas of sand dunes, such as the *Libyan Desert in the NE. The vegetation is sparse but sufficient in most parts for nomads to keep sheep and goats. Geological evidence shows that the Sahara was once well vegetated and that parts were formerly under the sea. There are large deposits of oil and gas in Algeria and Libya and phosphates in Morocco and Western Sahara. Rainfall is minimal and irregular, but there are numerous scattered oases watered from under ground that support small communities and are visited by nomads and travelers. Area: about 3,474,171 sq mi (9,000,000 sq km).

Sahel An area in West Africa, mainly in Mauritania, Mali, Niger, and Chad. It forms a band of savanna between the Sahara desert to the N and tropical vegetation to the S and is used as pasture. The desert is gradually encroaching on the area and from 1973 to 1974 and again in the 1980s it suffered a severe drought.

Saida. *See* Sidon.

saiga A small antelope, of Asian deserts and steppes. About 31 in (80 cm) high at the shoulder, saigas are slightly built with a pale woolly coat and a remarkable swollen snout with convoluted nasal tracts, thought to be an adaptation for warming inhaled air or to be related to their keen sense of smell. Males have straight ridged horns up to 12 in (30 cm) long. Saigas form large herds to migrate southward in winter. □mammal.

Saigon. *See* Ho Chi Minh City.

Saigo Takamori (1828–77) Japanese samurai famous for his tragic role in the Meiji restoration. He played a major part in the overthrow of the *Tokugawa regime (1868) but was opposed to radical modernization and the complete abolition of feudalism. When his supporters clashed with the government in 1877, he was torn between competing loyalties but committed himself to the rebellion and was eventually forced to commit hara-kiri.

sailfish A food and game fish, belonging to a genus (*Istiophorus*) related to marlins, that occurs in warm and temperate seas. Its slender body, deep blue above, silvery below, and up to 11 ft (3.4 m) long, has a long pointed snout, long pelvic fins, and a large sail-like dorsal fin. Sailfish feed mainly on other fish.

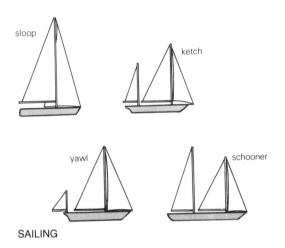

SAILING

sailing Cruising or racing in a boat fitted with one or more sails. Some smaller sailing boats are equipped with an outboard motor; larger boats have one or more inboard auxiliary engines, for use in calm weather and for navigating in and out of harbors. Craft used for recreation and sport range from dinghies of 7.5 ft (2.3 m) to oceangoing yachts of 75 ft (23 m) or more. All classes of boat can be used for racing but boats used primarily for racing have more complex sail plans requiring a relatively large crew, while the emphasis in a cruising boat is more on providing living accommodation. Racing, which became popular in the 19th century, is organized according to class of boat. Races are held either for yachts of the same design or for yachts of different designs competing with appropriate handicaps. Current Olympic classes (1980) are: Finn (15 ft [4.5 m]; single-handed), 470 (15 ft [4.7 m]; two-man), Flying Dutchman (20 ft [6.05 m]; two-man), Star (23 ft [6.91 m]; two-man), Soling (27 ft [8.16 m]; three-man), and Tornado (20 ft [6.1 m] catamaran; two-man).

Until the invention of nylon and Dacron, all sails were made of canvas. Modern sails, made of synthetic fabrics, are more durable, resist mildew (can be stored wet), and retain their shape better than canvas.

Many different types of rigging have been used for sailing vessels throughout history. Square sails, which are of little use except when a vessel is sailing away from the wind, were the type employed on square-riggers, a rig prevalent in Europe from the 14th to the 19th centuries. These were largely replaced by the quadrilateral sails of early schooner-rigged vessels. Called gaffsails because the upper part of the sail was supported by a gaff boom, these were succeeded by triangular sails, which are popular on yachts today. *Sloops, *ketches, *schooners, and *yawls now employ triangular sails. Gaff-rigged vessels have given way to marconi- or Bermuda-rigged sailing boats, i.e. those with triangular sails. Small boats—sailing dinghies, etc.—may have only one sail, usually a gunter-rigged triangular sail supported at the upper leading edge by a boom that fits onto the top of a stubby mast set well forward in the boat. This rig is a modern version of the traditional lateen rig, a native design from the Near East that also uses a triangular sail hung from a very long boom. In the late 19th century, yachtsmen enlarged jibs into foresails called genoas. They also developed lightweight triangular foresails, called spinnakers, which often have a cross section like a part of the surface of a sphere. *See also* ships.

Saimaa, Lake A lake in SE Finland. It is the primary lake in a system spread over most of S Finland. Area: about 680 sq mi (1760 sq km).

sainfoin A perennial herb, *Onobrychis viciifolia*, native to temperate regions of Eurasia and found on chalky soils. Up to 20 in (50 cm) tall, it has pale-pink flowers and has been cultivated as a forage plant. Family: *Leguminosae*.

saint In Christian belief, a person characterized by special holiness. In the early Church the term applied to all believers, and certain modern sects follow this practice in calling their adherents saints, for example the *Mormons. In the *Roman Catholic Church saints formally admitted to the calendar of saints by *canonization can be invoked as intercessors, although recently their numbers have been reduced in an effort to cut superstitious practices. *Protestantism rejects the invocation of saints, although the *Church of England's calendar recognizes a number of saints' days.

St Albans 51 46N 0 21W A city in SE England, in Hertfordshire. Across the River Ver stood the important Romano-British town of Verulamium, where the martyrdom of St Alban took place. The Benedictine abbey, founded in honor of the saint in 793 AD, was made a cathedral in 1877. St Albans' industries include printing, electrical equipment, and rubber goods. Population (1981): 50,888.

St Andrews 56 20N 2 48W A resort in E Scotland, on St Andrews Bay. An ancient ecclesiastical center, its university (1412) is the oldest in Scotland. The famous Royal and Ancient Golf Club was founded here in 1754. Population (1978 est): 13,300.

St Anthony's fire. *See* ergot.

St Augustine 29 54N 81 19W A city in Florida. The oldest city in the US, it was founded by the Spanish in 1565 and for most of the next two and a half centuries remained the most northerly outpost of the Spanish colonial empire. The Castillo de San Marcos (1672) stands as a reminder of Spanish rule. Tourism is the main source of revenue. Population (1980): 11,985.

St Bartholomew's Day Massacre The slaughter of *Huguenots that began on August 24, 1572, in Paris. The massacre was ordered by Charles IX of France under the influence of his mother, Catherine de' Medici. Some 3000 Huguenots died in Paris and many more were murdered in the provinces.

St Basil's Cathedral The cathedral of the Russian Orthodox Church in Moscow built between 1554 and 1560 for Ivan the Terrible. It is named for the Russian saint, who was buried there at the end of the 16th century.

St Bernard A breed of large working dog developed in Europe from Asian ancestors and employed as a rescue dog by the hospice of St Bernard in the Swiss Alps since the 17th century. It is massively built, having a large head with drooping ears. The coat may be either short or of medium length and is white marked with red-brown or brindle. Height: 25.5 in (65 cm) minimum.

St Bernard Passes Two mountain passes in the Alps, in central Europe. The **Great St Bernard Pass** on the Swiss-Italian border is one of the highest alpine passes at 8111 ft (2433 m). The hospice at its summit, founded (11th century) by St Bernard of Menthon, is famous for the St Bernard dogs that were formerly used to rescue snowbound travelers. The **Little St Bernard Pass** on the French-Italian border reaches 7177 ft (2187 m) and also has an 11th-century hospice.

St Catherines 43 10N 79 15W A city and port in E Canada, in S Ontario at the entrance to the *Welland Ship Canal. Founded in 1790, it is a fruit-farming and industrial center and houses Brock University (1962). Population (1976): 123,351.

St Clair, Lake A lake in E North America, on the US-Canadian border. It lies near Detroit, between Lakes Huron and Erie. Area: 460 sq mi (1190 sq km).

St-Cloud 46 22N 5 50E A city in France, a W suburb of Paris. Mainly residential, it is the site of the Sèvres porcelain factory. Population (1975): 28,350.

St Croix (*or* Santa Cruz) A West Indian island, the largest of the US Virgin Islands. The economy is based on tourism and agriculture. Area: 80 sq mi (207 sq km). Population (1980) 49,013. Chief town: Christiansted.

St Croix River A river that flows from Chiputneticook Lakes in E Maine–W New Brunswick, Canada, S forming the Maine–New Brunswick border to Passamaquoddy Bay on the Atlantic Ocean. Lumbering is important along the river. Length: 129 mi (208 km).

Saint-Cyr, École de French military academy founded in 1803 and established in 1808 at Saint-Cyr-l'École, near Versailles. Its buildings were destroyed in World War II and it is now at Coëtquidan, Brittany.

St Denis, Ruth (Ruth Dennis; 1877–1968) US dancer and choreographer. She began her career in vaudeville but by the early 1900s had become interested in ethnic, especially Oriental, dancing. From 1904 to 1913 she choreographed and performed *Radha*, *Egypta*, and *O-mika*. With her husband, dancer Ted Shawn (1891–1972), she founded the Denishawn school (1915), out of which came many of the dance innovations of the times.

St-Denis 20 52S 55 27E The capital of Réunion, on the W Indian Ocean. A port on the N of the island, its activities are mainly administrative, with some commerce. Population (1974): 103,512.

St-Denis 48 56N 2 21E A city in France, an industrial suburb of Paris in the Seine-St Denis department on the Seine River. Its gothic abbey contains the tombs of many French kings. Population (1975): 96,759.

Sainte-Beuve, Charles-Augustin (1804–69) French literary historian and critic. He first studied medicine, but abandoned it to write poetry. After writing the novel *Volupté* (1834), based in part on his love affair with Victor Hugo's wife, he devoted himself to criticism. His literary journalism helped to establish many young writers of the Romantic movement. His major critical works include *Critiques et portraits littéraires* (1836–39) and *Port-Royal* (1840–59), a study of Jansenism.

St Elias Mountains A mountain range in NW North America, running SE along the Alaska–Yukon (Canada) border. Many summits surpass 16,400 ft (5000 m) and it reaches 19,850 ft (6050 m) at Mount Logan, its highest point. The range also includes the world's largest nonpolar ice cap.

St Elmo's fire A small electrical discharge, with a luminous appearance, that is associated with stormy weather and seen around the extremities of tall objects, such as the tops of trees and mastheads.

St-Étienne 45 27N 4 22E A city in S central France, the capital of the Loire department. It has produced firearms since the 16th century and was the site of France's first steel mill (1815). More recent manufactures include aircraft engines, chemicals, and dyes. It has a famous school of mining engineering (1816) and a university. Population (1975): 221,775.

Saint-Exupéry, Antoine de (1900–44) French novelist and aviator. The themes of his novels, which include *Night Flight* (1931) and *Wind, Sand and Stars* (1939), derive from his experience as a pioneer of air-mail routes in N Africa and South America. He also wrote a fable for children, *The Little Prince* (1943), and an uncompleted philosophical book. He failed to return from a French air force mission.

St Gall (German name: Sankt Gallen) 47 25N 9 23E A city in NE Switzerland, S of Lake Constance. The Celtic missionary St Gall established a hermitage here (612 AD), later to become a Benedictine abbey. Monastic buildings remaining include the cathedral (1755–72) and the library, which contains a fine collection of manuscripts. Population (1973 est): 81,700.

Saint-Gaudens, Augustus (1848–1907) US sculptor; born in Ireland. He studied cameo cutting and sculpturing in the US, France, and Italy. From his studio in New Hampshire he sculpted bronze statues of American heroes, including Admiral David Farragut (1877), Abraham Lincoln (1887), and General William T. Sherman (1903), and worked with leading architects and artists. His "The Puritan" (Springfield, Mass., 1885), the draped figure on the Adams Memorial (Washington, D.C.; 1891), and Diana (Madison Square Garden, N.Y.C.; 1892), as well as commemorative medals and coins, are among his many other works.

St George's 12 04N 61 44W The capital of Grenada, on the SW coast. Founded by the French in the 17th century, it was capital of the British Windward Islands from 1885 to 1958. It is now a tourist resort as well as an important port. Population (1978 est): 110,394.

St George's Channel A channel between SE Ireland and Wales, linking the Irish Sea with the Atlantic Ocean. Length: about 100 mi (160 km). Maximum width: 90 mi (145 km).

St Gotthard Pass 46 34N 8 31E A pass in the Alps, in S Switzerland linking central Europe and Italy by road. The St Gotthard railroad tunnel (constructed 1872–80) below the pass is 9 mi (15 km) long and the second longest in the Alps. Height: 6935 ft (2114 m).

St Helena 15 58S 5 43W A mountainous island in the S Atlantic Ocean, a British dependent territory. Napoleon I was exiled here (1815–21). The economy declined when sailing ships stopped calling here following the opening of the Suez Canal (1869); it now depends on agriculture and UK subsidies. Area: 47 sq mi (122 sq km). Population (1976): 5147. Capital: Jamestown.

St Helens 53 28N 2 44W A city in NW England, in Merseyside. It has an important glass industry, besides brick and tile manufacturing, engineering, pharmaceutical production, brewing, and, nearby, coalmining. Population (1981): 98,769.

Saint John 45 16N 66 03W A city and port in E Canada, in New Brunswick at the mouth of the St John River. Originally a French fort (1631), it developed with the arrival of American Loyalists (1783) into the province's center of heavy industry and commerce. Population (1976): 85,956.

St John River A river in E North America. Rising in Maine, it flows NE to New Brunswick, Canada, and then SE to the Bay of Fundy, where high tides cause the river to reverse its course at the famous Reversing Falls. Length: 418 mi (673 km).

St John's 47 34N 52 41W A city in E Canada, the capital of Newfoundland. Settled in the 16th century, it is Canada's easternmost city, located beside a huge protected harbor. It was here in 1901 that Marconi received the first transatlantic radio message. St John's has two cathedrals (Roman Catholic and Anglican) and is the site of Memorial University (1925). Its industries include fishing, fish and food processing, shipbuilding, timber, and textiles. It is Newfoundland's distribution and commercial center. Population (1976): 88,576.

St John's 17 07N 61 51W The chief port of Antigua, on the NW coast. It handles the island's agricultural produce. Population (1975 est): 24,000.

St John's wort A perennial herb or shrub belonging to the genus *Hypericum* (400 species), found in temperate regions. They have yellow five-petaled flowers with many stamens and many species are cultivated for ornament, including *H. calycinum* (also known as rose of Sharon). The common European St John's wort (*H. perforatum*) reaches a height of 20 in (50 cm). Family: *Guttiferae*.

St Joseph 39 45N 94 51W A city in Missouri, on the Missouri River. Often referred to as St Joe, it is an important grain and livestock center, serving a large agricultural area. It was the home of the outlaw Jesse James. Population (1980): 76,691.

Saint-Just, Louis (Antoine Léon) de (1767–94) French politician, who supported *Robespierre in the French Revolution. His pamphlet, *Esprit de la révolution et de la constitution de France* (1791), calling for a new moral order, brought him to public notice. He was a member of the Committee of *Public Safety, supervising military affairs, and led the attack on the Austrians at Fleurus (1794). He was arrested and guillotined with Robespierre.

St Kitts-Nevis (or St Christopher-Nevis) Independent country in the West Indies, member of the Commonwealth of Nations. One of the Leeward Islands, it is located in the E Caribbean Sea. It formerly consisted of three islands, St Kitts, Nevis, and Anguilla, but the latter had its own constitution from 1976 and in 1980 was formally granted the status of a separate British dependency. The economy of St Kitts is primarily agricultural, sugar, molasses, cotton, and coconuts being the main products, but tourism is becoming increasingly important. Formerly a UK associated state, it achieved independence in 1983. A coalition government headed by Monsero Kennedy A. Simmonds was formed to lead the new nation. Area: 101 sq mi (262 sq km). Population (1983 est): 45,000. Capital: Basseterre, on St Kitts. *See also* Anguilla.

Saint Laurent, Louis Stephen (1882–1973) Canadian statesman; prime minister (1948–57). A French-Canadian, he was a lawyer and law professor (Laval University) from 1914. He served in various national positions from 1941, eventually becoming Liberal Party leader and prime minister in 1948. During his administration, Newfoundland was included in the Dominion of Canada (1949) and Canada became stronger internationally and more unified domestically.

Saint-Laurent, Yves (1936–) French fashion designer, who trained with *Dior and took over his fashion house (1957), opening his own in 1962. His creations for women have been predominantly influenced by male fashion and include black leather jackets edged with fur, thigh-length boots, safari jackets, and many trouser designs.

St Lawrence, Gulf of An arm of the Atlantic Ocean in E Canada, at the mouth of the St Lawrence River. Historically the gateway to Canada, it has always been an important fishing ground. Ice closes the gulf to navigation from early December until mid-April.

St Lawrence River A river in North America. Although the river proper is fairly short, it belongs to one of the world's greatest water systems, draining the *Great Lakes into the Atlantic Ocean. From Lake Ontario it flows NE along the Canadian-US border as a broad stream through the Thousand Islands, a major tourist district. Above Montreal it enters Canada and passes through rapids where hydroelectricity is produced. At Quebec it broadens into a long estuary that gradually merges with the Gulf of St Lawrence. The St Lawrence valley is an important agricultural and industrial belt as well as a rail, water, and road corridor. The river served as the original highway into Canada. The upper reaches of the river become unnavigable during winter months. Length: Lake Ontario to Quebec 298 mi (480 km); St Louis River headwaters to Anticosti Island 2110 mi (3395 km). *See also* St Lawrence Seaway.

St Lawrence Seaway A navigable waterway in North America through the St Lawrence River and the Great Lakes, completed in 1959. With a season of over eight months, it admits ships of up to 9000 tons, mainly carrying heavy nonperishables.

St-Lo 49 01N 1 05W A city in NW France, the capital of the Manche department. A market town famous for its horse breeding, it was virtually destroyed in *World War II. Population (1975): 25,037.

St Louis 38 40N 90 15W A city and port in Missouri, on the Mississippi River. It was a major center in the colonization of the West, outfitting such exploring parties as that of Lewis and Clark (1804–06), as well as pioneers using the Santa Fe, California, and Oregon Trails. It has four universities, including St Louis University (1818), which maintains a library built to house microfilms of Vatican Library treasures. The state's largest city, it is an important market, trading in livestock, wool, grain, and timber. Industries include aircraft, cars, chemicals, and iron and steel. Population (1980): 453,085.

St Louis 16 00N 16 27W A port in W Senegal, on an island in the Senegal River estuary. It was the capital of Senegal until replaced by Dakar (1958). Population (1976 est): 81,204.

St Lucia An island country in the West Indies, in the Windward Islands in the E Caribbean Sea. It is a mountainous island of volcanic origin. The population is mainly of African descent. *Economy*: mainly agricultural, the chief products are bananas and coconuts. Tourism is a growing industry and attempts are being made to develop the manufacturing sector. An oil-refining and transshipment complex was in the process of being built (S of Castries) at the time of the island's independence (1979). It is a member of CARICOM. *History*: it became internally self-governing in 1967 and attained full independence within the Commonwealth of Nations in February, 1979. Prime minister: John Compton. Official language: English. Official currency: East Caribbean dollar of 100 cents. Area: 238 sq mi (616 sq km). Population (1983 est): 119,000. Capital: Castries.

St-Malo 49 39N 2 00W A port and resort in NW France, in the Ille-et-Vilaine department on the English Channel. Many of its old buildings were destroyed during World War II, although its ramparts (12th–18th centuries) remain. A flourishing trading, fishing, and passenger port, it has shipbuilding and electrical industries. Population (1975): 46,270.

St Mark's Cathedral The cathedral church of Venice since 1807. It was built in the 9th century to house the relics of St Mark but rebuilt in the 11th century after a fire. Designed as a Greek cross surmounted by five domes, it is strongly influenced by *Byzantine art and is famous for its opulent mosaic and sculptural decoration both inside and out.

St Martin (Dutch name: Sint Maarten) 18 05N 63 05W A West Indian island in the Lesser Antilles, administratively divided between France and the Netherlands. The N part is a dependency of Guadeloupe, area 20 sq mi (52 sq km) with a population (1974) of 6191; the S is part of the Netherlands Antilles, area 13 sq mi (33 sq km) with a population (1979) of 11,379. Salt is the main export.

St Moritz (German name: Sankt Moritz) 46 30N 9 51E A resort in SE Switzerland, on St Moritz Lake. A renowned winter-sports center at a height of 5978 ft (1822 m), its famous Cresta Run (for bobsleds) dates from 1885. Population (1970): 5699.

St-Nazaire 47 17N 2 12W A major port in W France, in the Loire-Atlantique department on the Loire estuary. An important German submarine base in World War II, it was virtually destroyed by Allied bombing. Its main industries are shipbuilding, aircraft construction, chemicals, and oil refining. Population (1975): 69,769.

St Paul 45 00N 93 10W The capital city of Minnesota, on the Mississippi River. Adjacent to Minneapolis, the Twin Cities comprise the commercial and industrial center of an extensive grain and cattle area. St Paul's industries include oil refining, car assembly, and food processing. Population (1980): 270,230.

ST PAUL'S CATHEDRAL *Its dome is considered to be one of the most nearly perfect in the world.*

St Paul's Cathedral The cathedral of the diocese of London. Originally a Saxon and later a gothic structure, it burned down in the Great Fire of 1666, and Christopher *Wren was appointed to rebuild it. His design (1672–1717), combining *classicism and the *baroque style, features a traditional cruciform plan, a two-tiered portico, a great dome, and flanking towers.

St Peter's Basilica The Catholic basilica in the Vatican City, Rome. The original basilica, a huge gothic building, was pulled down by Pope Julius II in the early 16th century. Its replacement is the largest church in the world. Its general shape was determined by *Bramante, although it was designed together with its enormous dome by *Michelangelo. *Vignola continued the work and the nave and façade were added by *Maderna. *Bernini completed the building in the 17th century, adding the huge baldacchino and the colonnade to the piazza outside.

St Petersburg 27 45N 82 40W A city in Florida, on Tampa Bay. It is primarily a tourist resort. Population (1980): 236,893.

St Petersburg. *See* Leningrad.

St Pierre 14 44N 61 11W A small port in Martinique, at the foot of the volcano Mount Pelée. In 1902 an eruption destroyed the town leaving only one survivor. It is now the center of an area growing sugar cane.

St Pierre et Miquelon A French overseas department, consisting of two neighboring islands in the NW Atlantic Ocean S of Newfoundland. All that remained to France of its Canadian territories after 1763, they have traditionally been bases for fishing and smuggling. More recently tourism has been developed. Area: St Pierre 10 sq mi (26 sq km): Miquelon 83 sq mi (215 sq km). Population (1981 est): 6272.

St-Quentin 49 51N 3 17E A city in NE France, in the Aisne department on the Somme River. It was the scene of French defeats by Spain (1557) and by Prussia (1871) in the Franco-Prussian War and was almost completely destroyed in *World War I. It has textile, electrical, and metallurgical industries. Population (1975): 69,153.

Saint-Saëns, Camille (1835–1921) French composer, conductor, pianist, and organist. He began to perform and compose while still a child. He studied with Halévy and Gounod and held various organ posts, including nearly 20 years at the Madeleine. His piano pupils included Messager and Fauré, and he championed the music of Liszt, Berlioz, and Wagner. He wrote 12 operas, five symphonies (the third with organ; 1886), *The Carnival of the Animals* (published posthumously; 1922) for two pianos and orchestra, five piano, three violin, and two cello concertos, chamber music, and choral works.

Saint-Simon, Claude Henri de Rouvroy, Comte de (1760–1825) The founder of French socialism. Saint-Simon was educated by *D'Alembert. Having witnessed the horror and chaos of the French Revolution, Saint-Simon was concerned to reconstruct society and his writings have a positive and idealistic tone. In *Du système industriel* (1821) he declared his aim of achieving an industrial state in which poverty is eliminated and in which science replaces religion as the spiritual authority.

Saint-Simon, Louis de Rouvroy, Duc de (1675–1755) French memoir writer. He lived at the court of Louis XIV and although he exercised some influence during the regency of Philippe, Duc d'Orléans (1715–23), his ambitions at court were never realized. His *Mémoires*, covering the years 1694–1723, are enlivened by his prejudices, his sharp observation of detail, and his brilliant portraits. The definitive edition was not published until 1879–1923.

St Stephen's Crown The crown of Hungary, which was reputedly first used by Stephen I. It was originally a Byzantine circlet made between 1074 and 1077 and converted into an emperor's crown by Hungarians in the 12th century. It fell into the hands of the US army in 1945 but was returned in 1978.

St Thomas 18 22N 64 57W A West Indian island in the US Virgin Islands, in the Lesser Antilles. After 1680 it became a major Caribbean sugar producer and later, after 1764, the largest slave-trading port. Tourism is now of major importance. Area: 28 sq mi (83 sq km). Population (1980): 44,218. Capital: Charlotte Amalie.

St Vincent, Cape (Portuguese name: Cabo de São Vicente) 37 01N 8 59W A promontory in the extreme SW of Portugal, in the Algarve on the Atlantic Ocean. A number of naval battles have been fought off the cape; in 1797 the Spanish fleet was defeated by the British under Admiral Jervis during the Napoleonic Wars.

Saint Vincent, Gulf An inlet of the Indian Ocean, in S Australia E of Yorke Peninsula. It has an important salt industry on the E coast. Length: about 90 mi (145 km). Width: about 45 mi (73 km).

St Vincent and the Grenadines A country in the E Caribbean Sea, in the Windward Islands of the Lesser Antilles. It consists of the principal island of St Vincent together with its dependencies of the Grenadine islets. It became a British possession in 1763 and attained internal self-government in 1969. In 1979 it became fully independent. It is predominantly agricultural, the chief crops being arrowroot (of which it is the world's chief producer), sugar cane, and bananas. Prime minister: R. Milton Cato. Area: 150 sq mi (390 sq km). Population (1983 est): 128,000. Capital: Kingstown.

St Vitus's dance The old name for *chorea, so called because of the uncontrolled movements characteristic of the disease and because sufferers in the middle ages prayed for a cure at the shrine of St Vitus (the patron saint of dancers).

Saipan 15 12N 145 43E One of the Northern Mariana Islands, in the W Pacific Ocean. It was the administrative center of the UN Trust Territory of the Pacific Islands (1947–75). Area: 70 sq mi (180 sq km). Population (1970): 10,458. Chief town: Susupe.

saithe A food fish, *Pollachius* (or *Gadus*) *virens*, also called coalfish or coley, that is related to cod and lives in shoals in the North Atlantic. Its elongated body, up to about 48 in (120 cm) long, is greenish brown above and silvery white below.

Sakai 34 35N 135 28E A city in Japan, in S Honshu on the Yamato delta. Formerly an important port (15th–17th centuries), it is part of the Osaka-Kobe industrial complex. Population (1980): 810,000.

saké (*or* rice wine) An alcoholic drink made in Japan from steamed rice, to which a special yeast is added, and slowly fermented. It resembles a light sherry in taste and is served warm.

Sakhalin (Japanese name: Karafuto) An island in the Soviet Union, in the RSFSR off the SE coast between the Sea of Okhotsk and the Sea of Japan. It comprises two parallel mountain ranges on either side of a central valley and is heavily forested. Timber, coal- and iron-mining, and paper milling are important industrial activities, and there are oilfields in the NE that serve the Soviet Far East. Agriculture, principally the cultivation of vegetables and dairy farming, is pursued in the S. *History*: a Russo-Japanese condominium from 1855 until 1875, it then passed to Russia but in 1905 was again divided between the two countries. In 1945 the Soviet Union acquired the whole island and its Japanese population (some 400,000

souls) was expelled. Area: about 29,300 sq mi (76,000 sq km). Population (1970): 615,652.

ANDREI SAKHAROV

Sakharov, Andrei Dimitrievich (1921–) Soviet physicist. After working on the development of the Soviet hydrogen bomb during the 1940s and 1950s he spoke out against nuclear weapons in the 1960s and went on to argue the need for freedom of speech in the Soviet Union. He was awarded the Nobel Peace Prize in 1975. His exile to Gorkii in 1980 aroused international protest.

saki A South American monkey belonging to the genus *Pithecia* (3 species), found in forests. Sakis are 22–50 in (55–125 cm) long including the tail (10–22 in [25–55 cm]) and have a thick shaggy coat and hairy hood. Wholly arboreal, they feed on berries, honey, leaves, and small animals. Family: *Cebidae*.

Saki (H(ector) H(ugh) Munro; 1870–1916) British humorous short-story writer. Born in Burma, he worked as a foreign correspondent before settling in London in 1908. He published several volumes of humorous stories many of which were based on the outrageous activities of his fastidious and snobbish heroes Clovis and Reginald. He also wrote a novel, *The Unbearable Bassington* (1912). He was killed in action in World War I.

Sakkara. *See* Saqqarah.

Saladin (Arabic name: Salah ad-Din; ?1137–93) The leader of the Muslims against the Crusaders in Syria. Of Kurdish descent, he obtained control over the Muslim lands in Egypt, of which he became sultan in 1175, and Syria. He then captured the Kingdom of Jerusalem following his great victory over the Crusaders at the battle of Hattin (1187). The last years of his life were spent fighting the third *Crusade, during which he won his legendary reputation as a chivalrous warrior.

Salado, Río The name of several South American rivers, meaning salty river. **1.** A river in N Argentina, rising in the Andes and flowing SE to join the Río Paraná. Length: 1250 mi (2012 km). **2.** A river in W Argentina, rising near the Chilean border and flowing S to join the Río Colorado. Length: about 850 mi (1365 km).

Salam, Abdus (1926–) Pakistani physicist, who became professor of physics at Imperial College, London, in 1957. He is also director of the International Center for Theoretical Physics in Trieste. In 1979 he shared the Nobel Prize with the US physicists Sheldon Glashow (1932–) and Steven Weinberg (1933–) for their work on *weak interactions.

Salamanca 40 58N 5 40W A city in central Spain, in León. During the Peninsular War the battle of Salamanca was fought here on July 22, 1812, in which Wellington secured a decisive victory over the French. An intellectual center of Renaissance Europe, Salamanca remains an important cultural center with a university (founded 1218). Its many notable old buildings include two cathedrals and it has a fine Roman bridge. Population (1974 est): 139,818.

salamander A tailed *amphibian belonging to a widely distributed order (*Urodela* or *Caudata*; about 225 species). Salamanders have short legs and long bodies and move by bending the body from side to side to give as wide a movement as possible for their feet. They usually hide in damp places when not hunting small worms and insects. Their habits range from the wholly aquatic Japanese giant salamander (*Megalobatrachus japonicus*), 0.6 in (1.5 cm) long, to the American woodland salamanders (genus *Plethodon*) that live entirely on land. *See also* congo eel; hellbender; mudpuppy; olm; newt; siren.

Salamis A Greek island in the Aegean Sea. It was the scene of a Greek naval victory over the Persians in 480 BC. Area: 37 sq mi (95 sq km). Population (1971): 18,364. Chief town: Salamis.

sal ammoniac (*or* ammonium chloride; NH_4Cl) A white crystalline solid, used in batteries and as a pickling agent in zinc coating and tinning.

Salazar, António de Oliveira (1889–1970) Portuguese dictator. Salazar became prime minister in 1932 and ruled until suffering a stroke in 1968. His New State imposed his corporatist ideas on Portugal. It repressed political opposition and fought long colonial wars in Africa, which gravely impeded the country's economic development.

Salé 34 04N 6 50W A port in NW Morocco, on the Atlantic coast opposite Rabat. It was an important medieval port and during the 17th century was the base for the Sallee Rovers, a notorious group of Barbary pirates. Population (1971): 155,557.

Salem 11 38N 78 08E A city in India, in Tamil Nadu. A developing industrial center, it has large-scale textile manufacturing. Population (1971): 308,716.

Salem 42 31N 70 55W A city and port in NE Massachusetts NW of Boston. Settled in 1626, it became a center of practicing witchcraft. As fears grew, more were convicted of witchcraft, and, ultimately, 19 persons were hanged. In the early 1700s the witchcraft cases were annulled. Tourism is important to the city; the Salem Maritime National Historic Site and the House of Seven Gables from Nathaniel Hawthorne's novel are here. Industries include leather and chemicals. Population (1980): 28,220.

Salem 42 32N 70 53W The capital city of Oregon on the Willamette River. Founded in 1840, it is a food-processing center for a large agricultural area. Willamette University was established here in 1844. Population (1980): 89,161.

Salerno 40 40N 14 46E A port in Italy, in Campania on the Gulf of Salerno. Founded by the Romans in 197 BC, Salerno is best known for its medical school, which flourished here in the middle ages. It was the scene of heavy fighting during World War II, following major Allied troop landings here in 1943. Notable buildings include the 11th-century cathedral, where Gregory VII is buried. The chief industries are engineering, flour milling, textiles, and cement. Population (1980 est): 161,863.

Salford 53 30N 2 16W A city in NW England, near Manchester on the Manchester Ship Canal. The docks for Manchester are here. Salford has an important engineering industry and manufactures textiles, electrical equipment, chemicals, tires, and clothing. Population (1981): 98,024.

Salic Law The law of the Salian *Franks issued under Clovis in the early 6th century. Owing little to other contemporary law codes or to Roman law, it is concerned with both criminal and civil law. Its importance for later periods lies in its prohibition against women inheriting land. This canon was invoked in France in 1316 and 1321 to prevent a woman from succeeding to the throne and, in 1328, Edward III's claim to the French crown was rejected on the grounds that his claim was by female descent.

Salicornia. *See* glasswort.

salicylic acid An antiseptic compound (OHC_6H_4COOH) that causes the skin to peel. It is used to treat certain skin conditions, including psoriasis, eczema, warts, and corns. Aspirin (*see* aspirin) is a derivative.

Salieri, Antonio (1750–1825) Italian composer and conductor. He studied and worked in Vienna from 1766. His pupils included Beethoven, Schubert, and Liszt. Because of his rivalry with Mozart, he was fancifully credited with having poisoned him.

Salinger, J(erome) D(avid) (1919–) US novelist. After contributing stories to the *New Yorker* he achieved great popular success with his novel *The Catcher in the Rye* (1951). Later works include *Nine Stories* (1953), *Franny and Zooey* (1961), *Raise High the Roof Beam, Carpenters* (1963), and *Seymour, An Introduction* (1963).

Salisbury. *See* Harare.

Salisbury 51 05N 1 48W A city in S England, at the confluence of the Rivers Avon and Wylye. Its 13th-century cathedral has the highest spire in the country, 403 ft (123 m) high. Nearby is Old Sarum, the site of an Iron Age hill fort with extensive earthworks. Population (1981): 35,355.

Salisbury, Robert Cecil, 1st Earl of. *See* Burghley, William Cecil, Lord.

Salisbury, Robert Arthur Talbot Gascoyne-Cecil, 3rd Marquess of (1830–1903) British statesman; Conservative prime minister (1886–92, 1895–1900, 1900–02). Elected to parliament in 1853, he was twice secretary for India (1866–67, 1874–78) before becoming Disraeli's foreign secretary (1878). His policy as prime minister has been characterized as one of "splendid isolation." Although he negotiated the Mediterranean Agreements with Italy and Austria-Hungary in 1887, under Salisbury Britain had no formal ally until alliance was concluded with Japan in 1902.

Salisbury Plain An area of open chalk downs in S England, in Wiltshire. It contains many prehistoric remains, notably *Stonehenge. Extensively used as a military training ground, the first permanent camp was established at Tidworth (1902). Area: about 200 sq mi (518 sq km).

saliva The fluid secreted by three pairs of **salivary glands** around the mouth in response to the sight, smell, taste, or thought of food. Although saliva contains the enzyme *amylase, which aids the digestion of starch, its major role is to bind the food particles and to lubricate the mouth and gullet.

Salk, Jonas (Edward) (1914–) US scientist; microbiologist who developed the first poliomyelitis vaccine (1952). An inactive virus vaccine, it was tested (1953–54) and used in the mid and late 1950s to vaccinate large segments of the population against crippling polio before Albert *Sabin's oral live vaccine was developed.

sallow. *See* willow.

Sallust (Gaius Sallustius Crispus; c. 86–c. 34 BC) Roman politican and historian. Expelled from the Senate for alleged immorality, he supported Julius Caesar in the war against Pompey and became governor of Numidia. He was accused of corruption and extortion and retired from politics in about 44 BC. His best-known works are the monographs *Bellum Catilinae* and *Bellum Jugurthinum*, noted for their forceful dramatic style.

salmon One of several fish of the genera *Oncorhynchus* or *Salmo*, especially the Atlantic salmon (*S. salar*)—a valuable food and game fish. It has an elongated body, up to 60 in (150 cm) long, and two dorsal fins. Salmon live mainly in the sea, feeding on other fish, especially herrings. However, they migrate into fresh water to spawn, at which time they change from silvery-blue or green to become brownish or greenish with orange markings. The spawned fish (kelts) either die or return to the sea and spawn in successive years. On hatching the young fish are known as alevins, although when they start feeding they are called parr. At about two years the coat becomes silver and the fish (smolt) migrate to the sea to reach maturity. After about two to three years they return to their native spawning waters as grilse, guided upstream by their sense of smell. Salmon is eaten freshly cooked (and canned) or smoked (Scotch salmon being regarded as the best). Family: *Salmonidae*; order: *Salmoniformes*.

Salmonella A genus of rod-shaped bacteria that are parasites of animals and man and cause several diseases: *S. typhi* and *S. paratyphi* cause *typhoid fever in man while *S. typhimurium* is a common cause of *food poisoning. Other species infect other mammals and birds.

Salò, Republic of (1943–45) The fascist government established by *Mussolini after Italy's surrender in World War II. Mussolini, rescued from prison by German parachute troops, set up his government at Salò in German-controlled N Italy. Partisan opposition, Mussolini's death, and Germany's surrender caused its collapse.

Salome The daughter of Herodias by her first husband, Herod Philip. The Jewish historian Josephus identifies her with the unnamed girl in the Gospels who requested the head of *John the Baptist from her stepfather, *Herod Antipas, as a reward for her dancing.

Salon The annual exhibition held by the French Royal Academy, which was founded in 1648. Housed in the Salon d'Apollon, in the Louvre, it became a bulwark of conservative art in the 19th century. The **Salon des Refusés** (1863) was a special exhibition held at the instigation of Napoleon III to exhibit the enormous number of paintings rejected by the Salon jury that year. Its contributors included *Manet, *Pissarro, and *Whistler.

Salon des Indépendants   The annual exhibition of the Société des Artistes Indépendants in Paris. The Société was founded in 1884 to enable such avantgarde painters as *Cézanne and *Seurat to exhibit works that had been or would have been rejected by the French Royal Academy's *Salon. Unlike the Salon, the Salon des Indépendants had no jury.

Salonika.   *See* Thessaloníki.

salp.   *See* tunicate.

salsify   A biennial herb, *Tragopogon porrifolius*, native to the Mediterranean region, also called vegetable oyster or oyster plant. It is cultivated in temperate regions for its fleshy white root, supposed to taste like oysters when cooked. The plant has long narrow leaves and a head of purple flowers surrounded by stiff pointed green sepals. The leaves may be eaten in salads. Family: *Compositae.

salt   **1.** (sodium chloride; NaCl) The crystalline solid that is used for seasoning and preserving food and is present in sea water and halite, which are its chief sources (naturally occurring sodium chloride is often called rock salt). NaCl forms cubic crystals. It has an important function in the human body and is used in the manufacture of many chemicals, such as soap, fertilizer, and ceramics. **2.** Any similar compound formed, together with water, when an acid reacts with a base, for example the salt potassium sulfate is formed when sulfuric acid reacts with potassium hydroxide: $H_2SO_4 + 2KOH \rightarrow K_2SO_4 + 2H_2O$.

SALT   (Strategic Arms Limitation Talks).   *See* disarmament.

Salta   24 46S 65 28W A city in N Argentina. It is a commercial center on the Trans-Andean Railroad and trades with Bolivia and Chile. Population (1975 est): 176,216.

SALT Agreements   (1968–72) Strategic Arms Limitation Talks agreements reached between the US and the Soviet Union to control the nuclear arms race. Talks begun in 1968 resulted in the signing of agreements in 1972 that limited anti-ballistic missile and offensive strategic missile systems in both countries. SALT II, signed in 1979, further limited these weapons.

saltbush   A salt-tolerant herb or shrub, especially one belonging to either of the genera *Atriplex* or *Chenopodium*. They have inconspicuous flowers and are used as forage plants in dry salty regions of Australia and North America. Family: *Chenopodiaceae*.

Saltillo   25 30N 101 00W A city in NE Mexico. The focal point of road and rail routes, it is the commercial center for an agricultural region. Its university (1867) was refounded in 1957. Population (1978 est): 245,738.

Salt Lake City   40 45N 111 55W The capital city of Utah near Great Salt Lake. Founded in 1847 by the Mormons under the leadership of Brigham Young, it is the world headquarters of the Mormon Church. It has the Mormon tabernacle (1867) and the University of Utah (1850) is here. It is a commercial center for nearby mining operations and its industries include food processing, textiles, oil refining, and printing and publishing. Population (1980): 163,033.

Salto   31 27S 57 50W A port in NW Uruguay, on the Uruguay River. It is an important meat-packing center; other products include wine and soft drinks. Population (1975 est): 80,000.

saltpeter   (potassium nitrate *or* niter; KNO_3)   A white crystalline solid used as a fertilizer, a food preservative, and in *gunpowder and fireworks.

saltwort   An annual or perennial herb belonging to the widely distributed genus *Salsola* (50 species), found on seashores and salt marshes. They have fleshy spiked leaves and small flowers. The European saltwort (*S. kali*) grows up to 24 in (60 cm) tall. Family: *Chenopodiaceae*.

saluki   A breed of hunting dog dating back over 8000 years in Egypt and used by Arabs for hunting gazelle. It has a slender streamlined body with long legs, giving speed and agility, and a small head with a long narrow muzzle. The smooth soft coat can be white, brownish, reddish, or black, tan, and white. Height: 20–28 in (50–70 cm).

Salvador   (*or* Bahia)   12 58S 38 29W A port in NE Brazil, the capital of Bahia state on the Atlantic Ocean. It has a fine natural harbor; exports include cocoa, sugar, tobacco, and diamonds. The chief industries are food and tobacco processing. It is the seat of two universities. Population (1980): 1,496,276.

Salvador.   *See* El Salvador, Republic of.

SALVATION ARMY   *A band and chorus campaign in a small town in England.*

Salvation Army   The international Christian organization founded in 1865 in London by William *Booth. Run on strictly military lines and led by an official called a general, it exacts absolute obedience from its members, who wear a characteristic uniform on public occasions. Morality in practical Christian living is more esteemed than doctrinal niceties and the Army rejects the sacraments. It is famous for its social and missionary work, especially in disaster relief and in poor urban areas, where it runs shelters, soup kitchens, hostels, and counseling, particularly for alcohol and drug abuse.

Salvia   A genus of perennial herbs and shrubs (about 700 species), widely distributed in temperate and tropical regions. Many are cultivated for ornament, including the Brazilian scarlet sage (*S. splendens*) and the blue-flowered *S. patens*. Common *sage is the culinary herb. Family: *Labiatae*.

sal volatile   (*or* ammonium carbonate)   A mixture of ammonium salts, or their solution in alcohol, that is used in smelling salts. It smells of ammonia and is made by heating ammonium chloride (*or* sal ammoniac) with calcium sulfate.

Salween River   (Chinese name: Nu Jiang *or* Nu Chiang)   A river in SE China and E Burma, rising in Tibet and flowing E then S to an inlet of the Andaman Sea. Little of its length is navigable but it supplies hydroelectric power. Length: 1500 mi (2400 km).

Salyut   A continuing series of manned Soviet space stations first launched into earth orbit in 1971. Salyut 7, launched in 1982, should be operational for several years. Cosmonauts from E Europe are conveyed to and from the orbiting laboratory by Soyuz spacecraft. They remain on the space station for long periods, in weightless conditions, conducting a variety of experiments and observations. Their physical and psychological fitness is carefully monitored. Salyut stations are smaller than the US *Skylab space station.

Salzburg   47 54N 13 03E A city in central Austria, the capital of Salzburg. Its many fine buildings include the fortress of Hohensalzburg and the cathedral (1614–28). Salzburg University was refounded in 1962. Mozart was born here and a famous musical event, the Salzburg Festival, is held annually. Industries include textiles and leather. Population (1981): 138,317.

Salzgitter   52 02N 10 22E A city in NE West Germany, in Lower Saxony formed in 1942 from 29 separate towns. The area is rich in iron ore, which is used in the manufacture of steel products. Population (1980 est): 113,500.

samadhi   The state of perfect concentration attained in deep meditation. In Hinduism it is taken to be union with *Brahman or with a deity. In Buddhism it refers to transcending the distinction between subject and object. Its attainment is a precondition of spiritual liberation.

Samar   The third largest island in the Philippines, in the Visayan Islands linked by bridge to Leyte. Its frequent typhoons restrict agriculture; the chief products are rice, coconuts, and hemp. Copper and iron ore are mined. Area: 5181 sq mi (13,415 sq km). Population (1970): 1,019,358. Chief town: Catbalogan.

Samara.   *See* Kuibyshev.

Samaria   **1.** The central region of ancient Palestine, which became part of the northern kingdom of Israel in the 10th century BC. *See also* Samaritans. **2.** 32 17N 35 12E The capital from the 9th century until its destruction in about 721 BC of the kingdom of Israel. Occupied from the 4th millennium BC, the site was excavated in 1908–10, 1931–33, and 1935. Among the discoveries unearthed were a collection of 9th-century BC ivory carvings. The city was rebuilt in the 1st century AD under Herod the Great and renamed Sebaste (modern name: Sebastiyah, in Jordan).

Samaritans 1 A people of ancient Samaria (now in N Israel), with a religion closely akin to Judaism. Numerous in Roman and Byzantine times and much disliked by the Jews, they declined under Muslim rule. They now number only a few hundred. They have a conservative religious tradition and many distinctive beliefs and customs. **2** A telephone service for the suicidal and despairing started in 1953 by the Rev Chad Varah in London, England. It is now a worldwide organization with several branches in the US, mainly on the east coast (New York, Boston, Providence, etc.)

samarium (Sm) A *lanthanide element discovered spectroscopically by Lecoq de Boisbaudran in 1879. It occurs naturally, with other lanthanides, in monazite ($CePO_4$). The oxide (Sm_2O_3) is used in glasses that absorb infrared radiation and the element is used in lasers as a dopant in calcium fluoride. At no 62; at wt 150.4; mp 1970 $\pm$9°F (1077 $\pm$ 5°C); bp 3256°F (1791°C).

Samarkand 39 40N 66 57E A city in the S central Soviet Union, in the Uzbek SSR. The principal industrial activities are cotton and silk manufacturing, winemaking, and metalworking but its interest lies chiefly in its past. *History*: it was the chief junction of the ancient *Silk Road between China and the Mediterranean and, conquered by the Arabs in the 8th century, became the Abbasids' capital (9th–10th centuries) and a great Islamic center. In the 14th century it became the capital of Timur's mighty empire, coming later under the rule of the Uzbek people (16th–19th centuries). The city's remarkable historic buildings include Timur's mausoleum. Population (1981 est): 489,000.

Samarra' 34 13N 43 52E A city in central Iraq, N of Baghdad. It is a Shiite Muslim pilgrimage center with a 17th-century mosque and many ruins dating from the 9th century, when Samarra' was the capital of the Abbasid caliphs (Islamic leaders). Population (1970 est): 62,008.

samizdat (Russian: self-publication) The underground system of distribution within the Soviet Union of literature, the open publication of which is prohibited by the authorities. Literature circulated in this way, usually in the form of typewritten copies, includes work by such writers as *Solzhenitsyn and *Sakharov.

Samoa A chain of volcanic islands in the S central Pacific Ocean. Discovered by the Dutch in the 18th century, the islands were politically divided in 1900 between the US and Germany. **American Samoa**, comprising the E islands of the chain, is an unincorporated US territory consisting of the chief island of Tutuila and several smaller ones. Agriculture is the main occupation; canned tuna is an important export. Area: 76 sq mi (197 sq km). Population (1981 est): 33,000. Capital: Pago Pago. **Western Samoa** was a German protectorate until World War I and then under New Zealand control, becoming an independent state in 1962. It consists of the main islands of Savai'i and Upolu and several smaller islands and islets. Subsistence agriculture is the main occupation and exports, chiefly to New Zealand, are copra, bananas, and cocoa. Some industrial development has taken place in recent years. Head of state: HH Malietoa Tanumafili II. Official languages: Samoan and English. Official currency: Western Samoa dollar. Area: 1097 sq mi (2842 sq km). Population (1983): 160,000. Capital: Apia.

Sámos A Greek island in the SE Aegean Sea, lying close to the mainland of Turkey. Already one of the principal commercial centers of Greece by the 7th century BC, it achieved its greatest prosperity under the tyrant Polycrates in the 6th century. It is the birthplace of the mathematician and philosopher Pythagoras. Area: 190 sq mi (492 sq km). Population (1971): 32,671.

Samothrace (Modern Greek name: Samothráki) A Greek island in the N Aegean Sea. The statue of the Winged Victory (now in the Louvre) was discovered here in 1863. Area: 70 sq mi (181 sq km). Population (1971): 3012.

Samoyed (dog) A breed of dog developed in Siberia and used by the Samoyed tribesmen as a sledge dog. It is robustly built with husky-like features; the white or cream coat consists of a short soft undercoat and a long coarse outer coat. Height: 20–22 in (51–56 cm) (dogs; 18–20 in (46–51 cm) (bitches).

Samoyed (people) A group of Siberian peoples of the tundra and N forest region of the central Soviet Union. They were traditionally nomadic reindeer hunters and fishers, now mainly settled by Soviet collectivization as reindeer breeders. *Shamanism dominates their religious life. Of the five Samoyed languages, which, with the *Finno-Ugric languages, comprise the

*Uralic family, only Nenets (*or* Yurak) has a considerable number of speakers.

samphire A perennial herb, *Crithmum maritimum*, native to rocky coasts of S England. Up to 12 in (30 cm) high, it has small white or yellowish flowers, a succulent stem, and slender fleshy leaves, which may be used in salads or pickles. Family: *Umbelliferae.

The golden samphire (*Inula crithmoides*), also native to British coasts, grows to 32 in (80 cm) and has broader leaves and larger yellow flowers. Family: *Compositae. See also glasswort (marsh samphire).

Samsun 41 17N 36 22E A port in central N Turkey, on the Black Sea. It exports cereals, copper, and tobacco and has a university (1975). Population (1980): 198,749.

Samudra Gupta (died c. 380 AD) Emperor of India (c. 330–c. 380) of the *Gupta dynasty and grandson of *Chandra Gupta I. He strove to expand and consolidate his empire, making many conquests, and kings of neighboring dynasties paid him tribute.

Samuel In the Old Testament, the first of the Hebrew prophets and the last of the "judges," who led the Israelites before the establishment of the monarchy in Palestine. The two **Books of Samuel** appear to be compiled from various sources. They are the principal sources for the history of the Israelites in the 11th and 10th centuries BC and contain the biography of Samuel and the history of the reigns of *Saul and *David, both of whom Samuel anointed as the first two Kings of Israel.

Samuelson, Paul Anthony (1915–) US economist; Nobel Prize for economics (1970). A teacher at Massachusetts Institute of Technology (1940–), he modified and analyzed the theories of John Maynard *Keynes and used mathematics applied to economic problems in *Foundations of Economic Analysis* (1947). His textbook *Economics* (1st ed., 1948) is widely used.

samurai The provincial warriors (also known as *bushi*; see Bushido), who rose to power in Japan in the 11th century. The term originally referred to the armed retainers employed by court nobles from the late 8th century. The samurai mostly became the vassals of *daimyo* and after 1600, when they comprised about 6% of the population, they were generally forced to reside in their lord's castle town. The samurai class was sharply divided from other classes by its superior status and marked distinctions also existed within its own ranks. After the Meiji restoration (1868) the samurai lost their special position but ex-samurai became leaders in various areas of modern Japanese life.

San'a' 15 23N 44 14E The capital of North Yemen, in the center of the country. Until the formation of the state of Israel, there was a large Jewish ghetto in the city. Notable buildings include the Great Mosque, where there is a sacred Muslim shrine, and the Liberty Gate. A university was founded here in 1970 with Kuwaiti assistance. Population (1980): 277,817.

San Andreas Fault A notorious fracture in the earth's crust, 750 mi (1200 km) in length, running through California. In 1906 a horizontal displacement of about 20 ft (6 m) and a lateral displacement of only 3 ft (1 m) caused an earthquake that devastated San Francisco. These movements, constantly recorded by seismographs, are now interpreted as resulting from collision of tectonic plates, a rotating Pacific plate and an American plate.

San Antonio 29 25N 98 30W A city in S central Texas. Founded in 1718, it was the scene of the Mexican attack on the *Alamo (1836) during the Texan revolution. San Antonio has several military bases and is a commercial and industrial center for a large agricultural region. The Alamo and other historical places of interest make it a popular tourist center. The mild climate has attracted many retired people. Population (1980): 785,410.

San Bernardino 34 07N 117 18W A city in California. Situated in a fruit-growing area, it is the site of the annual National Orange Show but industrial developments in aerospace and steel are now the main economic activities. Population (1980): 118,057.

San Cristóbal 7 46N 72 15W A city in W Venezuela. It is the commercial center for an area producing maize, cassava, sugar cane, and coffee. Its university was founded in 1962. Population (1976 est): 241,000.

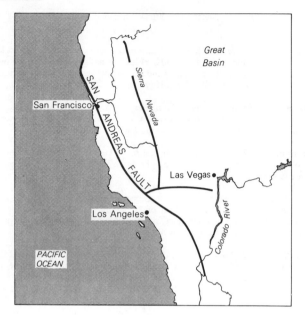

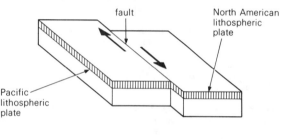

SAN ANDREAS FAULT   *An example of a tear fault in which the rocks are being displaced horizontally.*

sanctions   Penalties imposed for breaking a law, especially international law. First imposed by the *League of Nations on Italy following its invasion of Ethiopia, the most recent example of sanctions are those imposed by UN countries against Rhodesia (now *Zimbabwe), following its unilateral declaration of independence in 1965. These sanctions were broken by oil companies and others, which suggests that when there are economic pressures against imposing sanctions, they are difficult to enforce.

sanctuary   The holiest part of a church or temple, where the main altar stands. During the middle ages criminals could claim right of sanctuary, i.e. they took refuge in a church and were thus immune from prosecution for 40 days, during which time they could opt to accept a safe conduct out of the country.

sand   Unconsolidated grains of rock, varying in size from 0.002–0.08 in (0.06 to 2.00 mm) in diameter. Consolidated sands form *sandstones; grits are coarse sandstones with angular grains. Most sands consist principally of quartz, derived from the weathering of quartz-bearing rocks. Sand is used in glass and cement production, and as an abrasive.

Sand, George   (Aurore Dupin, Baronne Dudevant; 1804–76) French novelist. In 1831 she left her husband and went to Paris to write her first novel, *Indiana* (1832), a plea for women's right to independence, the first of an enormous number of successful novels. Among her many lovers were Alfred de Musset and Frédéric Chopin.

Sandage, Allan Rex   (1926–   ) US astronomer, who in 1961 discovered the first *quasar, which he originally named a "quasi-stellar radio object" since it emitted radio waves. Using the 200-inch (254 cm) reflecting telescope at Mt Palomar, California, he went on to discover a number of other quasars, including some that were not radio sources.

sandalwood   An evergreen tree belonging to the genus *Santalum* (about 25 species), native to SE Asia and the Pacific Islands. The true sandalwood (*S. album*) grows to a height of about 33 ft (10 m) and is partially parasitic on the roots of other trees. Its white wood is used to make boxes and furniture and, when distilled, yields sweet-scented sandalwood oil, used in perfumes, incense, candles, etc. Family: *Santalaceae*.

sandarac   The *resin of a N African conifer, *Tetraclinis articulata*, used in making varnishes.

Sandburg, Carl   (1878–1967) US poet and author. Sandburg first gained a national following with the publication of his *Chicago Poems* (1915). As a historian, he published the first volume of his Lincoln biography, *The Prairie Years*, in 1926 and as a collector of folksongs, he published *The American Songbag* in 1927. Among his later works, *The People, Yes* expressed his hope for an ideal society. In 1940 he won the Pulitzer Prize in history for the second volume of his Lincoln biography, *The War Years*, and in 1951, he won the Pulitzer prize in poetry for his *Complete Poems*.

sand dollar   A marine invertebrate animal, also called cake urchin, belonging to an order (*Clypeastroida*) of *echinoderms. Its round flat rigid body is covered with small spines and saclike organs (tube feet). Sand dollars live on the sea bed and sift minute food particles from the sand in which they burrow. Class: *Echinoidea*.

sand dune   The accumulation of wind-blown sand into a mound. Sand dunes are characteristic of desert areas where there is a plentiful sand supply and of coastal areas. They are unvegetated and two main forms occur in desert areas: the barchan, or crescent-shaped dune, and the seif, or longitudinal dune. In coastal areas dunes generally become "fixed" by vegetation.

sanderling   A bird, *Calidris alba*, that nests on Arctic coasts and winters on shores worldwide. 8 in (20 cm) long, it has a rust-colored upper plumage, changing to pale-brown in winter, and a long white wing stripe. It feeds on shrimps, sandhoppers, and mollusks with its straight slender bill. Family: *Scolopacidae* (sandpipers).

sand flea.   *See* sand hopper.

sandfly   A small fly belonging to the widely distributed genus *Phlebotomus*. Sandflies are among the worst pests of the tropics: the bloodsucking females can give a painful bite and several species are carriers of serious human diseases, including infections caused by the parasite *Leishmania* (*see* leishmanaisis).

The name has also been used for many bloodsucking *gnats and *midges of sandy places.

San Francisco Conference on International Organization   (1945)   Meeting of delegates of 51 nations in San Francisco, Calif, at the end of World War II, to form the United Nations. The UN charter, drafted at this conference in April, was signed in June.

sandgrouse   A bird belonging to a family (*Pteroclidae*; 16 species) occurring in warm arid regions of Europe and Africa. 9–16 in (22–40 cm) long, sandgrouse have camouflaging plumage, long pointed wings, short legs, feathered feet, and a very tough skin. They are gregarious and feed on plant material, flying long distances to water at dawn and dusk. Although resembling grouse, they belong to the order *Columbiformes* (pigeons).

sand hopper   A small terrestrial jumping *crustacean, also called beach hopper and sand or beach flea, belonging to the family *Talitridae*. Its body, 0.4–1 in (10–25 mm) long, is laterally flattened and lacks a carapace. During the day it is buried in sand but at night it emerges to feed on organic debris under stones or among seaweed. Order: *Amphipoda*.

Sandhurst   51 02N 0 34E A village in SE England. The Royal Military Academy (1799) for training officers is situated here. Population (1971): 6445.

San Diego   32 45N 117 10W A city in California, on San Diego Bay. It has a US naval base and large naval air service facilities. Employment is mainly dependent on the aircraft and aerospace industries. San Diego is also an important center of scientific research and is the site of the Scripps Institute of Oceanography (1903). Population (1980): 875,504.

sand lizard   A slender long-tailed European lizard, *Lacerta agilis*, occurring in sandy regions. Up to 8 in (20 cm) long, it is pale-brown or gray with whitish underparts and three rows of white-centered dark spots along its back. It feeds on insects and spiders. Family: *Lacertidae*.

sandpiper   A wading bird belonging to a family (*Scolopacidae*; 82 species) occurring chiefly in the N hemisphere, breeding in northerly latitudes and migrating south to winter. 5–24 in (12–60 cm) long, sandpipers typically have long legs, long wings, a mottled brown or gray plumage, which commonly changes color seasonally, and a long slender bill. They nest in marshy regions or on mud flats and feed on small invertebrates. Order: *Charadriiformes* (gulls, plovers, etc.).

sandstone   A sedimentary rock consisting of consolidated *sand, cemented mainly by calcareous, siliceous, or ferruginous minerals. They may be deposited by wind action in deserts or in shallow seas, estuaries and deltas, and along low-lying coasts by water. Sandstones vary in color from red to yellow to white according to the presence of other minerals (feldspar, mica, glauconite, iron oxides, etc.) in addition to the quartz.

Sandwich Islands. *See* Hawaii.

San Francisco 37 40N 122 25W A city in N California, situated on a peninsula between San Francisco Bay and the Pacific Ocean. A major seaport, San Francisco serves a large agricultural and mining area and is the financial and insurance center of the West Coast. Industries include food processing, shipbuilding, and petroleum refining. Among its many famous landmarks are the San Francisco–Oakland Bay Bridge (1936), the Golden Gate Bridge (1937), Chinatown, and the city's cable cars. A major cultural and educational center, it is the site of several universities and colleges. *History*: founded by the Spanish in 1776, it was still a village when captured by US troops (1846) during the Mexican War. It expanded rapidly following the discovery of gold in California (1848) and it was during this period that the first Chinese settled in the city. In 1906 there was a sudden violent movement in the massive San Andreas Fault, which extends along the Californian coast, and San Francisco was almost completely destroyed by an earthquake and three-day fire. Population (1980): 678,974.

Sanger, Frederick (1918–) British biochemist, who determined the order of *amino acids in the insulin molecule. This work, at Cambridge University, started in 1945 and took him eight years to complete. He was awarded Nobel Prizes in 1958 and 1980.

Sanger, Margaret (Higgins) (1883–1966) US reformer. She worked as a nurse in New York City's poorer sections and saw the deaths from self-induced abortions. She went to Europe in 1913 to learn more about contraception methods; upon her return to the US (1914) she published *Woman Rebel*, a magazine about birth control, a term she coined. Her clinic, the first for birth control guidance, opened in 1916 in New York City, and although it was raided and she was jailed many times, she persevered. She founded the National Birth Control League (later Planned Parenthood Federation of America; 1917) and the International Planned Parenthood Federation (1952).

sangha The Buddhist monastic order. Together with the *Buddha and *dharma, it forms the third of the *tri-ratna of Buddhism. An individual may become a monk temporarily or for life.

Sanhedrin The highest court of the Jews, which met in Jerusalem. Its development is unclear; in early New Testament times the Greeks allowed the establishment of a senate and later forms became known as the Sanhedrin. Its composition and its jurisdiction varied with its history. In New Testament times, the high priest was president and its functions were administrative, judicial, and religious.

sanicle A perennial herb belonging to the genus *Sanicula* (37 species), distributed worldwide except for Australia and New Guinea. The common European sanicle (*S. europaea*) grows to a height of 20 in (50 cm) and has several broad lobed leaves and clusters of small pinkish flowers. Family: *Umbelliferae*.

San Ildefonso (*or* La Granja) 40 53N 4 01W A town in central Spain. It has a magnificent royal palace built by Philip V of Spain (18th century); the palace chapel contains his tomb. Population (1970): 4164.

San Jacinto, Battle of (1836) US-Mexican clash that brought independence for Texas. American troops, under General Sam *Houston, defeated forces under Mexican General Antonio *Santa Anna near present-day Houston, Texas. Mexican casualties were high,and Santa Anna was taken prisoner.

San José 37 20N 121 55W A city in N California, on the S arm of San Francisco Bay. Founded in 1777, it was the first city in California and state capital (1849–51). Situated in the fertile Santa Clara Valley, it has many food-processing plants and wineries as well as aerospace and electronics industries. Population (1980): 636,550.

San José 9 50N 84 02W The capital of Costa Rica, situated in the center of the country in a high fertile valley. Founded in 1736, it became a center of the tobacco trade and later of coffee production. The University of Costa Rica was founded in 1843. Population (1981 est): 259,126.

San Juan 18 29N 66 08W The capital and main port of Puerto Rico, in the N. Founded by the Spanish in 1508, it was later attacked by the English and by the Dutch; in 1898 it was captured by the US navy. It has expanded considerably in the 20th century and is now also an industrial and tourist center. The chief exports are coffee, sugar, and tobacco. The Inter-American University of Puerto Rico was founded in 1912 and a campus of the University of Puerto Rico in 1950. Population (1980): 432,973.

San Juan 31 33S 68 31W A city in W Argentina. Severely damaged by an earthquake (1944), it is the commercial center of a wine-producing area. Population (1975 est): 112,582.

San Juan Hill, Battle of (1898) US-Spanish conflict at San Juan, Cuba, during the *Spanish-American War. As part of a land and sea operation, US troops, among them Theodore *Roosevelt and his Rough Rider unit, stormed the hills outside of Santiago, Cuba. Successful, US troops commanded the city and the Spanish admiral, Pascual Cervera, fled the harbor, resulting in destruction of his fleet.

Sankara (8th century AD) Hindu philosopher. Sankara left his native Kerala to become a wandering holy man. It was popularly believed that he was an incarnation of *Shiva. He wrote commentaries on the *Brahmasutras*, the *Bhagavadgita*, and the *Upanishads* and founded the Smarta Brahmin sect and several monasteries. He made major contributions to the *Vedanta philosophical tradition, believing that the physical world relates to the ultimate reality as a state of ignorance does to knowledge.

San Lorenzo, Treaty of. *See* Pinckney, Charles.

San Luis Potosí 22 10N 101 00W A city in NE Mexico. It is the industrial center for a rich agricultural and silver-mining area and has a fine baroque cathedral and a university (founded 1826). Population (1978 est): 315,228.

SAN MARINO *The first of three fortresses situated on the central limestone mass of Monte Titano.*

San Marino, Republic of A small independent republic, an enclave in Italian territory, situated on the slopes of the Apennines mountain range, SW of Rimini. *Economy*: farming, tourism, and the sale of postage stamps are the main sources of income. *History*: dating from the 4th century AD, it was an independent commune by the 12th century. In 1862, the newly established kingdom of Italy guaranteed San Marino's independence and a customs union. Executive power lies in the Congress of State and two regents elected by the Great and General Council. Official language: Italian. Official currency: both Italian and Vatican City currencies are in use. Area: 24 sq mi (61 sq km). Population (1981): 21,622. Capital: San Marino.

San Martín, José de (1778–1850) South American soldier and statesman; the national hero of Argentina. After participating in the struggle of Buenos Aires against the Spanish, he raised and trained an army in Argentina (1814–16), which he led heroically across the Andes, and, with Bernardo *O'Higgins, defeated the Spanish at Chacubuco (1817) and Maipo (1818), achieving the liberation of Chile. In 1821, after creating a Chilean navy, he entered Lima, proclaimed the independence of Peru, and became its "protector." He resigned in 1822, after differences with Bolívar, and retired to France.

San Miguel de Tucumán (*or* Tucumán) 26 47S 65 15W A city in NW Argentina, at the foot of the E Andes. It has a cathedral and a university (1914) and is an important sugar-refining center. Population (1975 est): 321,567.

San Pedro Sula 15 26N 88 01W A city in NW Honduras. It serves an agricultural area producing bananas and sugar cane and is the chief industrial center of the country. Population (1980 est): 342,800.

San Remo 43 48N 7 46E A port and resort in Italy, in Liguria near the French border. It has a 12th-century romanesque cathedral. There is a market in flowers and fruit. Population (1971): 62,210.

San Salvador 13 59N 89 18W The capital of El Salvador, situated in the center of the country. Founded by the Spanish in 1525, it was capital of the Central American Federation from 1831 until 1838, becoming capital of El

Salvador in 1839. It has suffered several severe earthquakes. Industries include textiles and food processing. The University of El Salvador was founded in 1841. Population (1980): 1,902,500.

San Salvador Island (former name: Watling Island) 24 00N 74 32W A West Indian island in the central Bahamas. It was Columbus' first sight of land (1492) in the New World. Area: 60 sq mi (156 sq km). Population (1970): 776.

sans-culottes (French: without knee breeches) The violent extremists of the French Revolution, so called because they wore trousers rather than the knee breeches of the aristocracy. The original sans-culottes were the Paris workers who stormed the Bastille and led the food riots in 1789. Later radical extremists, such as Marat and Danton, who used the Paris mobs to gain control, were also called sans-culottes.

San Sebastián 43 19N 1 59W A seaside resort in N Spain, in the Basque Provinces on the Bay of Biscay. It possesses a cathedral and its palace was formerly the summer residence of the Spanish royal family. The La Concha beaches attract many tourists. Population (1970): 165,829.

Sansevieria A genus of herbaceous perennial plants (60 species) native to tropical and S Africa and S Asia. They have a basal rosette of stiff swordlike leaves arising from thick creeping underground stems (rhizomes). *S. trifasciata* var. *laurentii* (mother-in-law's tongue) is a popular house plant with ornamental leaves, striped green and yellow, up to 35 in (90 cm) long. The leaves of several species (e.g. *S. zeylanica*) yield a fiber (bowstring hemp) used for ropes, mats, etc. Family: *Liliaceae*.

Sanskrit The classical literary language of the Hindu scriptures, belonging to the *Indo-Aryan family. From it the *Prakrits and modern N Indian languages developed. It was spoken in NW India from 1500 BC, became a scholarly language when the grammarian *Panini standardized it (5th century BC), and is still used as a sacred language. It is highly complex and is written in the *Devanagari script.

San Stefano, Treaty of (1878) The treaty that concluded the war between the Ottoman Empire and Russia (1877–78). The defeated Ottomans recognized the independence of Serbia, Romania, and Montenegro and the autonomy of Bosnia-Herzegovina and Bulgaria. At the Congress of *Berlin (1878), the other great powers, fearing that the Balkans would fall under the dominance of Russia, modified the treaty.

Santa Ana 14 00N 79 31W The second largest city in El Salvador. It is a major coffee center and has one of the largest coffee mills in the world. Population (1980): 203,713.

Santa Ana 33 43N 117 54W A city in SW California, SE of Los Angeles. Founded in 1869, it produces food goods; rubber, fiberglass, and electronic products; and aircraft. Population (1980): 204,023.

Santa Anna, Antonio López de (1794–1876) Mexican soldier and statesman; president (1833–36) and dictator (1839, 1841–45). After engineering *Iturbide's downfall in 1823, Santa Anna dominated Mexican politics for the next 20 years. He is best known for his defeat of Texan forces at the *Alamo (1836). Subsequently taken prisoner by the Americans, he was forced to retire but twice returned to power before being driven into exile (1845–74).

Santa Barbara 54 25N 119 42W A city on the SW coast of California. The University of California at Santa Barbara (1891) is here. The Santa Barbara Mission, founded in 1786, and the beaches are major tourist attractions. Off-shore oil drilling, aerospace research, electronics products, and fishing are important to the economy. Population (1980): 74,542.

Santa Clara 22 25N 79 58W A city in central Cuba. It is the commercial center for an agricultural area producing sugar and tobacco. Population (1981): 525,402.

Santa Claus. *See* Nicholas, St.

Santa Cruz 17 45S 63 14W A city in SE Bolivia. It is the commercial center for an area producing chiefly sugar cane, rice, and coffee. Industries include the manufacture of cigarettes and sugar refining. It is the site of a university (1880). Population (1976): 237,128.

Santa Cruz de Tenerife 28 28N 16 15W A city in the Canary Islands, in NE Tenerife. An uprising that began the Spanish Civil War took place here (1936). It is a major fueling station with an oil refinery. Population (1970): 151,361.

Santa Fe 35 41N 105 57W A city, resort, and the capital of New Mexico, on the Santa Fe River. Following Mexico's attainment of independence from Spain in 1821, Santa Fe developed a commercial route (the **Santa Fe Trail**) with the US. Population (1980): 48,953.

Santa Fé 31 38S 60 43W A port in E Argentina, the furthest point accessible to oceangoing vessels on the Río Paraná. Founded in 1573, it has a

cathedral (1685) and a university (1919) and is the center of a grain-growing and stock-rearing area. Population (1975 est): 244,655.

Santa Fe Trail A trail that began near Independence, Missouri, and led west through Raton Pass and along the Arkansas River (later, across the Cimarron Desert) to Santa Fe, New Mexico. Blazed in 1821 by William Becknell, the trail opened up a southern overland trade route through the central US. Its importance diminished in about 1880 with the coming of the railroad. Length: c. 800 mi (1300 km).

Santa Isabel. *See* Malabo.

Santa Marta 11 18N 74 10W A port in N Colombia, on the Caribbean Sea. The chief exports are bananas, coffee, and cocoa. Simón *Bolívar, leader of the South American independence movement, died here (1830). Population (1978 est): 144,200.

Santa Monica 34 01N 118 30W A resort city in SW California, W of Los Angeles, on Santa Monica Bay. Founded in 1875, the city has fine beaches and attracts tourists. Industries include aerospace and plastic components, aircraft, cosmetics, and laser systems. Population (1980): 88,314.

Santander 43 28N 3 48W A city and port in N Spain, in Old Castile on Cape Mayor. Part of the city was rebuilt after being burned in 1941. It possesses a gothic cathedral. Its industries include fishing and shipbuilding. Population (1974 est): 161,947.

Santayana, George (1863–1952) Spanish-born US philosopher and poet. He taught at Harvard (1889–1911) and eventually settled in Rome (1924). He believed that the mind was largely governed by physical and biological considerations and his philosophy, set out in *Realms of Being* (1927–40), consequently tended toward materialism. He wrote in an unusually witty and urbane style. His works include *The Sense of Beauty* (1896), *The Life of Reason* (1905–06), *Skepticism and Animal Faith* (1923), and *Dominations and Powers* (1951). His novel *The Last Puritan* (1935) was very popular.

Santiago (or Santiago de Chile) 33 35S 70 40W The capital of Chile, situated in the center of the country at the foot of the Andes. It was founded by the Spanish in 1541. About half of Chile's industry is centered here, including food processing, textiles, and metallurgy. There are three universities. Population (1976 est): 3,361,200.

Santiago de Compostela 42 52N 8 33W A city in NW Spain, in Galicia. Since the 9th century AD it has been a famous place of pilgrimage reputedly containing the tomb of St James, the patron saint of Spain. Its romanesque cathedral (1078–1211) was built on the site of the tomb. The university was founded in 1532. Population (1970): 70,893.

Santiago de Cuba 20 00N 75 49W A port in Cuba, on the Caribbean Sea. It was the scene of Fidel *Castro's July 26 revolt (1953). Exports include metal ores, sugar, coffee, and tobacco. It is the site of the University of Oriente (1947) and has a large cathedral. Population (1981): 563,455.

Santiago del Estero 27 48S 64 15W A city in N Argentina. It is a commercial center serving an agricultural area producing wheat, cotton, maize, and livestock. The chief industry is food processing. Population (1975 est): 105,127.

Santiago de los Caballeros 19 30N 70 42W A city in the N Dominican Republic. The commercial center for a fertile agricultural region, its industries include the manufacture of cigarettes, pharmaceuticals, and furniture. Population (1970): 155,000.

Santo Domingo 18 32N 69 50W The capital of the Dominican Republic, a port on the S coast. Founded by Bartolomeo Columbus in 1496, it became the capital of the first Spanish colony in the Americas. It was under French rule (1795–1809), and later under that of Haiti, becoming capital of the new Dominican Republic in 1844. During the rule of the dictator *Trujillo, it was known for a time (1936–61) as Ciudad Trujillo. It is the site of the first cathedral (1521) and the first university (1538) in the New World. A second university was established in 1966. Population (1970): 673,470.

Santorini. *See* Thera.

Santos 23 56S 46 22W A city in SE Brazil, in São Paulo state on the Atlantic Ocean. It is the leading coffee port of the world. Population (1980): 411,023.

São Luís 2 34S 44 16W A port in N Brazil, the capital of Maranhão state. The chief exports are babaçu palm products, cotton, sugar, and balsam. It is the site of the University of Maranhão (1966). Population (1975 est): 330,311.

Saône River A river in E France, rising in Lorraine and flowing mainly S to join the Rhône River at Lyons. It is linked by canal to the Moselle, Rhine, Loire, Seine, and Meuse rivers. Length: 298 mi (480 km).

São Paulo 23 33S 46 39W The largest city in Brazil, the capital of São Paulo state. Founded in 1554, it grew rapidly after 1880 with the development of coffee plantations. Coffee remains important but there has been considerable diversification of industry and it is now the fastest-growing city in Brazil, sometimes called the "Chicago of South America." Industries include food processing and the manufacture of textiles, electrical appliances, and chemicals. It has several universities, including the University of São Paulo (1934). It also contains the Butantan Institute, a scientific research establishment with a famous snake farm. Population (1980): 7,033,529.

São Tomé and Príncipe, Democratic Republic of A small island country off the coast of West Africa, in the Gulf of Guinea. An archipelago, it comprises the two main islands with coastal plains rising to volcanic mountains in their interiors, together with the islets of Pedras Tinhosas and Rolas. Most of the population is descended from African slaves and southern Europeans, with comparatively recent influxes from Mozambique and Angola. *Economy*: chiefly agricultural, the main crops being cocoa, copra (which is the main export), palm oil and kernels, and coffee. Rice is being developed and livestock is also important. *History*: discovered by the Portuguese in 1471, the islands came under Portuguese rule in 1522. They became an overseas province in 1951 and gained independence in 1975, forming a democratic republic. President: Dr Manuel Pinto da Costa. Official language: Portuguese. Official currency: dobra of 100 centavos. Area: 372 sq mi (964 sq km). Population (1983 est): 88,000. Capital and main port: São Tomé.

sap The fluid found in the vascular (conducting) system of plants. It consists of water and minerals, absorbed from the soil and transported through the plant in the *xylem, and sugars, made in the leaves and distributed in solution in the *phloem.

Sapir, Edward (1884–1939) US linguist and anthropologist, born in Germany. Much of his work was done on American-Indian languages and cultures. His book *Language* (1921) is notably lucid. He was interested in all aspects of communication and in the role played by language in determining the personality of the individual in relation to society. *See also* Whorf, Benjamin Lee.

sapodilla An evergreen tree, *Achras sapota*, native to Central America but cultivated elsewhere in the tropics. Up to 65 ft (20 m) tall, it produces edible brown rounded fruits, up to 4 in (20 cm) across, with a juicy pulp surrounding black seeds. It tastes of pears and brown sugar. Milky latex from the bark is a source of chicle gum, used in chewing gum. Family: *Sapotaceae*.

saponins Plant glycosides (sugar compounds) that form lathery emulsions in water. The saponins are extremely potent in destroying red blood cells. They are used as foam producers in fire extinguishers and as emulsifiers, *detergents, etc.

sappan A tree, *Caesalpinia sappan*, native to SE Asia. The wood (sappanwood) is used in making furniture and yields a red dye. An extract of the bark produces a black dye when mixed with iron salts. Family: *Leguminosae*.

Sapper (H(erman) C(yril) McNeile; 1888–1937) British novelist. After distinguished service in World War I he achieved literary success with his popular thriller *Bulldog Drummond* (1920), about an adventure-seeking ex-officer, and its sequels.

sapphire A transparent variety of *corundum that may be any color except red (*see* ruby) due to traces of iron and titanium. It is used as a gemstone and in record-player styluses. Sapphires occur in igneous and metamorphic rocks but most are obtained from detrital gravels. Many sapphires come from Sri Lanka, Kashmir, Burma, East Africa, the US, and Australia. Artificial sapphires are manufactured from ammonium alum. Birthstone for September.

Sappho (c. 612–c. 580 BC) Greek poet. She and her contemporary *Alcaeus pioneered the form of the brief subjective lyric. Her passionate poetry, which has survived in fragments, was written for her group of female admirers on the island of Lesbos (from which the term "lesbianism" is derived). She appears to have been married and had one child; according to a romantic and unreliable legend, she committed suicide by throwing herself from a rock off the coast of Epirus because of an unhappy love affair.

Sapporo 43 5N 141 21E A city in Japan, in SW Hokkaido. It is the island's main administrative and educational center; Hokkaido University was established here in 1918. It is also a ski resort famed for its annual festival of snow sculpture and was the site of the 1972 winter Olympics. Industries include flour and timber milling, printing, and machinery manufacture. Population (1980): 1,402,000.

saprophyte An organism that obtains its energy by feeding on dead or decaying tissue. Bacteria and fungi are important saprophytes, using enzymes to break down organic material and release nutrients into the soil, which can be used by plants (*see* decomposition).

Saqqarah A mortuary area near ancient *Memphis. The most famous monument here is the stone-built Step Pyramid, designed (c. 2630 BC) for Pharaoh *Djoser by his architect *Imhotep. It is architecturally the immediate forerunner of the Giza *pyramids. The bulls sacred to *Apis were buried in the Sarapeum.

Saracens Before Islam, the term used by the non-Arab peoples of the Middle East to refer to the Arabs. After the establishment of Islam, Saracen was usually synonymous with Muslim. The origin of the word is unknown.

Saragossa. *See* Zaragoza.

Sarajevo 43 52N 18 26E A city in W central Yugoslavia, the capital of Bosnia and Hercegovina. A center of resistance to Austrian domination, it was here that the heir apparent to the Dual Monarchy of Austria-Hungary, *Francis Ferdinand, was assassinated (June 28, 1914), precipitating World War I. It was the site of the 1984 Winter Olympics. Sarajevo has two cathedrals, several mosques, and a university (1946). A busy industrial center, its manufactures include carpets, pottery, sugar, and beer. Population (1971): 243,980.

Saransk 54 12N 45 10E A city in the W central Soviet Union, the capital of the Mordvinian ASSR in the RSFSR. It is an industrial center, producing machinery, electrical goods, and food. Population (1981 est): 280,000.

Sarasota 27 20N 82 34W A resort city in W central Florida, S of St Petersburg on the Gulf of Mexico. The winter headquarters of Ringling Barnum and Bailey Circus is here, as are several circus Museums. Tourism is important to the economy. Population (1980): 48,868.

Saratoga, Battles of (September 19 and October 7, 1777) Two battles fought near Saratoga, New York, which formed the turning point of the *American Revolution. The first saw the defeat of the British attempt to open a route to Albany. The second ended with the surrender of Gen Burgoyne to the Americans. The outcome of the battles helped persuade the French to recognize the US and give it decisive military support.

Saratoga Springs 27 17N 82 28W A resort city in E central New York, N of Albany. Skidmore College (1911) is here. The mineral springs drew visitors from the Mid-1800's on, making it the most popular US health resort. Saratoga Race Track has long attracted horse racing enthusiasts and tourists. Population (1980): 23,906.

Saratov 51 30N 45 55E A city in the W Soviet Union, in the RSFSR on the Volga River. Baku oil is transported from here and a natural-gas pipeline supplies Moscow. Other industrial activities include ship repairing and the manufacture of precision instruments. Population (1981 est): 873,000.

Sarawak A state in Malaysia, in NW *Borneo on the South China Sea. It has a mountainous forested interior with a swampy coastal plain, where rubber, pepper, sago, and rice are grown. Oil production is of prime importance; crude oil, petroleum products, timber, and pepper are the chief exports. *History*: it was given in 1841 by the sultan of Brunei to the Englishman James Brooke, who as "white rajah" tried to suppress piracy and headhunting. Although it became a British protectorate in 1888, it was ruled by the Brooke family until World War II, when it was occupied by the Japanese. Ceded to Britain in 1946, it joined Malaysia in 1963. Area: 48,250 sq mi (124,970 sq km). Population (1980): 1,294,753. Capital: Kuching.

Sarcodina A class of minute single-celled animals (*see* Protozoa) that form cellular extensions called pseudopodia for locomotion and feeding. Many forms, including *Ameba, are naked while others, for example the *Foraminifera and *Radiolaria, have a shell or skeleton. Sarcodines are chiefly free-living inhabitants of soils, fresh waters, and seas.

sarcoma. *See* cancer.

sarcophagus A stone or terracotta coffin, often elaborately decorated with ritual motifs. Sarcophagi evolved in ancient Egypt to protect mummies, and Minoan, Greek, Roman, and early Christian examples survive.

sardine A young *pilchard or any of several species of food fish of the family *Clupeidae*, especially members of the genera *Sardina*, *Sardinops*, and *Sardinella*. They are canned in oil, an industry centered on Portugal and Spain.

Sardinia (Italian name: Sardegna) The second largest island in the Mediterranean Sea, comprising an autonomous region of Italy. It is largely mountainous. Agriculture is important, especially on the fertile Campidano (a broad alluvial plain in the SW) where cereals, vines, and olives are cultivated. Sheep are raised on the hills. Its major industry is mineral production, especially lead, zinc, coal, fluorspar, and sea salt. Modern industries, especially petrochemicals, chemicals, and food processing, are being developed. Tourism is a growing source of revenue. *History*: first settled by the Phoenicians, it was ceded to Savoy by Austria (1720) in exchange for Sicily and formed the kingdom of Sardinia with Piedmont, which formed the basis of a unified Italy. Area: 9194 sq mi (23,813 sq km). Population (1980 est): 1,610,260. Capital: Cagliari.

Sardis 38 28N 28 02E The capital of ancient Lydia, 35 mi (56 km) NE of present-day Izmir (Turkey), famous for its coinage and craftwork. After Persia conquered Lydia, overthrowing Croesus about 550 BC, its strategic position made Sardis Asia Minor's political center until Hellenistic times.

sardonyx. See onyx.

Sardou, Victorien (1831–1908) French dramatist. His many successful comedies and historical dramas include *Les Pattes de mouche* (1860) and *Tosca* (1887), a melodrama on which Puccini's opera is based. Sarah Bernhardt acted in many of his plays.

Sargasso Sea An elliptical section of the N Atlantic Ocean, extending between latitudes 20°N and 35°N and longitudes 30°W and 70°W. Contained within a current system, it is still and warm. It takes its name from the floating brown seaweed of the genus *Sargassum*, found abundantly in it.

Sargent, John Singer (1856–1925) US portrait painter, born in Italy. Working in Paris, London, and the US, he achieved considerable success with his elegant portraits of such celebrities as Ellen Terry, R. L. Stevenson, Isabella Stewart Gardner, Madame Gautreau (Mme. X) and John D. Rockefeller. In watercolor, he produced remarkable landscape studies of World War I.

Sargon II (d. 705 BC) King of Assyria (722–705). Perhaps a usurper (Sargon means "legitimate king"), he deliberately named himself after the legendary *Sargon of Akkad. He was constantly occupied in warfare to maintain Assyrian power in Elam, Urartu, Babylonia, Syria, and Palestine, where he captured and depopulated Samaria. He was succeeded by *Sennacherib.

Sargon of Akkad The semilegendary Semitic ruler (c. 2334–c. 2279 BC) of territories extending from the Mediterranean to the Persian Gulf. According to tradition, he was brought up by a gardener, who retrieved his cradle adrift in the River Euphrates. After usurping kingly power, he founded *Akkad and established an empire that lasted more than a century.

Sark (French name: Sercq) 49 26N 2 22W The smallest of the four main Channel Islands, in the English Channel. It consists of Great Sark and Little Sark, connected by a narrow isthmus. It is governed by a hereditary seigneur or dame in a semifeudal system. Area: 2 sq mi (5 sq km). Population (1978 est): 600.

Sarnia 42 57N 82 24W A city and port in E Canada, in SW Ontario at the S end of Lake Huron. With the discovery of local oil (1858) and the completion of the oil pipeline from Alberta, it grew into a major refining and petrochemical center. Steel and salt are also important. Population (1981): 47,586.

Saronic Gulf (or Gulf of Aegina) An inlet of the W Aegean Sea between the Attic Peninsula (on which lie Athens and its port Piraeus) and the Peloponnese. It contains the island of Salamis.

saros The period of about 18 years (6585.3 days) at which *eclipses of the sun and moon repeat in the same order and with nearly the same time intervals.

Saroyan, William (1908–81) US dramatist and fiction writer. Beginning with *The Daring Young Man on the Flying Trapeze* (1934) he wrote a rapid succession of stories, novels, and autobiographical works. His best-known play is *The Time of Your Life* (1939). His other works include the play *My Heart's in the Highlands* (1939), a novel, *The Human Comedy* (1943); and the autobiographical *My Name Is Adam* (1940) and *Obituarias* (1979).

Sarraute, Nathalie (1902–) French novelist, born in Russia. She practiced as a lawyer until 1939. Her work includes *Tropismes* (1939), a collection of sketches analyzing human behavior in great psychological detail, *Le Planétarium* (1959), *Les Fruits d'or* (1963), and the autobiographical *Childhood* (1984). She is a leading exponent of the *nouveau roman*, and her essays are collected in *L'Ère du soupçon* (1956).

sarsaparilla An extract of the roots of several perennial climbing or trailing vines of the genus *Smilax*, especially *S. aristolochiaefolia*, cultivated in Central and South America. The roots are harvested and dried for use as a tonic and as flavoring for medicines and beverages. Family: *Smilacaceae*.

Sartre, Jean-Paul (1905–80) French philosopher, novelist, dramatist, and critic. After World War II, during which he was an active member of the resistance, he founded the journal *Les Temps modernes* and became a leading public exponent of *existentialism. His major works of philosophy include *Being and Nothingness* (1943) and *Critique de la raison dialectique* (1960). His novels include *Nausea* (1938) and the trilogy *The Roads to Freedom* (1945–49). Among his several plays are *The Flies* (1943), *In Camera* (1944), *The Respectable Prostitute* (1946), and *Lucifer and the Lord* (1951). He also wrote literary criticism and autobiographical works. In 1964 he refused the Nobel Prize. He had a close association with Simone de *Beauvoir, whom he met while a student. He was an adherent of Marxism and frequently supported left-wing political groups.

Sarum. See Salisbury.

Sasanians The dynasty that ruled Persia from 224 AD until overthrown by the Arabs about 636. *Ardashir I (reigned 224–41) founded the dynasty (named for his grandfather Sasan), overthrowing the Parthian empire (see Parthia) and seizing its capital *Ctesiphon. His most notable successors were *Shapur II (reigned 309–79), *Khosrau I (reigned 531–79), and *Khosrau II (reigned 590–628). The Sasanian empire, which at its greatest extent stretched from Syria to India, saw the establishment of Zoroastrianism as the state religion and a resurgence of art and architecture (see Persian art and architecture).

Sasebo 33 10N 129 42E A port in Japan, in W Kyushu on the East China Sea. It was a village until the late 19th century, when it became a naval base. Its main industries are shipbuilding and engineering. Population (1976 est): 254,313.

Saskatchewan A province of W Canada, on the Great Plains. The N is covered by forest, mostly noncommercial, with lakes and swamps. The S is open prairie, now chiefly comprising large highly mechanized farms, and is one of the world's most important wheatlands; the province normally produces about two thirds of Canada's wheat. There are highly developed marketing cooperatives, begun in the early 20th century. Saskatchewan is rich in minerals, including uranium, oil, natural gas, potash, zinc, and copper; associated industries are important. *History*: explored in the 17th and 18th centuries, Saskatchewan was first exploited for furs. Agricultural settlement began slowly (1870s) but sped up in the decade before 1914. The area became a province in 1905 and was the first part of North America to elect a socialist government (1944–64, 1971–82). Area: 220,181 sq mi (570,269 sq km). Population (1981): 968,313. Capital: Regina.

Saskatchewan River A river in W Canada, rising in two separate branches in the Rocky Mountains and flowing generally E through prairie grainlands to unite in central Saskatchewan. The river then continues to Lake Winnipeg. Length: 1205 mi (1940 km).

Saskatoon 52 10N 106 40W A city in W Canada, in central Saskatchewan. Founded in 1883, it is the distribution center of a vast grain area, with numerous agricultural industries. Other industries include potash, metals, clothing, and chemicals. Saskatoon houses the University of Saskatchewan (1907). Population (1981): 154,210.

sassafras A tree, *Sassafras albidum*, native to North America. Up to 65 ft (20 m) high, it bears clusters of yellow flowers and dark-blue berries. The aromatic roots are dried for use in medicines and also yield oil of sassafras, which is used in perfumes and as flavoring for beverages. Family: *Lauraceae*.

Sassari 40 43N 8 34E A city in Italy, near the N coast of Sardinia. It has a cathedral (12th–18th centuries) and a university (1562). It is the agricultural trading center of N Sardinia. Population (1980 est): 120,478.

Sassetta (Stefano di Giovanni; c. 1392–c. 1450) A leading painter of the Sienese school. Some of his work reflects his admiration of Florentine art, for example *Madonna of the Snow*, painted for Siena Cathedral (Contini Bonacossi collection, Florence); his later work, however, typifies the *international gothic style. He painted many altarpieces, for example a now dismembered altarpiece, originally painted for the church of S Francesco in Sansepolcro, notable for its scenes from the life of St Francis of Assisi.

Sassoon, Siegfried (1886–1967) British poet and writer. In 1917 his disgust with World War I led him to make a public refusal to serve. His antiwar poetry appeared in *The Old Huntsman* (1917) and *Counterattack* (1918), and he wrote several volumes of autobiographical war memoirs.

Satan. See Lucifer.

satanism Worship of the forces of evil. Formerly a synonym for atheism or certain heresies, the term now generally applies to beliefs and practices, such as the *black mass, that parody Christian equivalents. Evolving in this form in late-19th-century France, satanism is usually a blend of magic, religion, and bizarre sexual practices. Aleister Crowley (1875–1947) was a notorious modern exponent.

Planet & Satellite	diameter (km)	distance from primary (km)	year of discovery	Planet & Satellite	diameter (km)	distance from primary (km)	year of discovery
EARTH				SATURN			
Moon	3476	384 400	—	Janus	200	159 000	1966
				Mimas	400	186 000	1789
MARS				Enceladus	600	238 000	1789
Phobos	27	9380	1877	Tethys	1000	295 000	1684
Deimos	15	23 500	1877	Dione	800	377 000	1684
				Rhea	1500	527 000	1672
JUPITER				Titan	5800	1 222 000	1655
Adrastea	40?	128 000	1979	Hyperion	400	1 483 000	1848
Metis	40?	128 000	1979	Iapetus	1500	3 560 000	1671
Amalthea	150	181 000	1892	Phoebe	200	12 950 000	1898
Thebe	80?	221 000	1979	URANUS			
Io	3630	422 000	1610	Miranda	400	130 000	1948
Europa	3140	671 000	1610	Ariel	1400	192 000	1851
Ganymede	5260	1 070 000	1610	Umbriel	1000	267 000	1851
Callisto	4800	1 880 000	1610	Titania	1800	438 000	1787
Leda	10?	11 110 000	1974	Oberon	1600	586 000	1787
Himalia	180?	11 470 000	1904	NEPTUNE			
Lysithea	20?	11 710 000	1938	Triton	3800	355 000	1846
Elara	80?	11 740 000	1905	Nereid	300	5 562 000	1949
Ananke	20?	20 700 000	1951	PLUTO			
Carme	30?	22 350 000	1938	I	800?	20 000?	1978
Pasiphae	40?	23 300 000	1908				
Sinope	30?	23 700 000	1914				

PLANETARY SATELLITES

satellite 1. A celestial body orbiting a *planet. The planets of the solar system have 48 known satellites, ranging greatly in size. The small bodies comprising the rings of Saturn, Uranus, and Jupiter may also be regarded as satellites. Mercury and Venus have no satellites. The earth's satellite is the *moon. The two small heavily cratered Martian satellites, Phobos and Deimos, have been extensively studied by Mariner and Viking planetary probes. The largest and most studied of Jupiter's 16 satellites are Io, Europa, and the heavily cratered Ganymede and Callisto; Io and possibly Europa are volcanically active. Saturn has 21 satellites, the largest, Titan, having an atmosphere. Uranus has five satellites, four moderately sized, while Neptune has two, Triton and the much smaller Nereid, both moving in unusual orbits. Pluto, possibly once a satellite of Neptune, was found in 1978 to possess a satellite. 2. A spacecraft that is launched into orbit around the earth or enters an orbit around some other solar-system body. It may be a *communications satellite, retransmitting radio signals from one location on earth to another. Alternatively, its instruments may gather information from earth or from other celestial objects and transmit it, by radio signals, to ground-based receiving stations. This information is used, for example, in weather forecasting, navigation, scientific and astronomical research, and for military purposes. A further function, under investigation, is the conversion of solar power into microwaves that could be beamed to earth and used as an energy source.

Satie, Erik (1866–1925) French composer. He studied briefly at the Paris conservatoire and, aged 39, at the Schola Cantorum with Roussel and d'Indy. Satie was well known for his eccentricity and for the whimsical titles of his compositions. He influenced such composers as Milhaud and Poulenc by turning away from impressionism toward a clear-textured style that admitted humor. His works include the ballet *Parade* (1916), piano pieces, including *Trois Gymnopédies* (1888), *Pièces froides* (1897), and *Trois morceaux en forme de poire* (1903), and many songs.

satinwood A tree, *Chloroxylon swietenia*, native to S India and Sri Lanka. Its wood is valued in cabinetmaking for its lustrous golden-yellow fine-grained finish; it was used in particular by Thomas *Sheraton. The wood of certain West Indian species is also known as satinwood. Family: *Meliaceae*.

satire A literary or dramatic work that ridicules human or social pretensions. Among the earliest satirists were the Roman poets *Juvenal and *Horace. In European literature, satire became a dominant literary form during the late-17th and 18th centuries. Major writers included *Dryden, *Pope, and *Swift in England and *Voltaire in France. During the 19th century *Byron continued the tradition of verse satire, but prose fiction became the usual medium, as in the works of Samuel *Butler. In the 20th

century novelists have been the dominant practitioners, for example Evelyn *Waugh in England and Joseph *Heller in the US.

Sato Eisaku (1901–75) Japanese conservative statesman, under whose unusually long prime ministership (1964–72) Japan became an economic superpower. His most significant personal achievement was the reversion of Okinawa from US rule (1972). He shared the Nobel Peace Prize in 1974 for his opposition to nuclear weapons.

satsuma. *See* tangerine.

Saturn (astronomy) The second largest planet, orbiting the sun every 29.5 years at a mean distance of 886,165,000 mi (1427 million km). It is the most oblate planet (equatorial diameter 74,500 mi [120,000 km], polar diameter 67,000 mi [108,000 km]) and has the lowest mean density (0.7 g cm^{-3}). In a telescope dark and light yellowish cloud bands are visible, running parallel to the equator. The dominant feature, however, is **Saturn's rings**, lying in the equatorial plane and tilted at 27° to the orbital plane. The four rings differ in brightness but are all composed of small icy chunks. The overall diameter is about 169,500 mi (273,000 km) but the thickness is only a few kilometers. The outermost ring, A, and the brightest one, B, are separated by Cassini's division. Saturn also has 21 known *satellites. Saturn is made up primarily of hydrogen and helium, possibly with a central rocky core surrounded by liquid hydrogen. *See also* planetary probe.

Saturn (mythology) The Roman god of agriculture and father of the gods, identified with the Greek *Cronus. His consort was Ops, identified with the Greek *Rhea. Various aspects of the Saturnalia, his annual festival held in December, at which presents were exchanged and normal social rules relaxed, were taken over by the Christian festivals of Christmas and the New Year. His name survives in *Saturday*.

saturniid moth A moth belonging to the widely distributed mainly tropical family *Saturniidae* (about 800 species). They are usually large and characterized by a transparent eyespot near the center of each wing. Their silken cocoons can be a source of silk (*see* silkworm moth) and the larvae are typically green, feeding chiefly on tree foliage. *See also* cecropia moth; emperor moth; hercules moth.

satyagraha The Sanskrit expression referring to *Gandhi's policy of nonviolent resistance to British rule in India.

satyrid butterfly A butterfly of the worldwide family *Satyridae*. The wings are mainly brownish with a few or numerous eyespots. Their forelegs are rudimentary and the flight weak and fluttering. Satyrids hide when alarmed, folding the forewings inside the camouflaged hindwings. The striped pale-green or brown caterpillars feed on grasses.

Satyrs and Sileni In Greek mythology, male fertility spirits of the woods and fields, usually portrayed with goats' legs and pointed ears or horns. They were associated with *Dionysus and were typically drunk and lustful. *See also* Silenus.

sauce A thickened savory or sweet liquid accompanying a dish and enhancing its flavor. Many classic dishes are named for the sauce served with them (e.g. *spaghetti bolognese, poulet chasseur, sole bonne femme*). Sauces often require a liaison, which binds together the liquids and other ingredients, the commonest being a *roux* (a paste of melted butter and flour). Other liaisons are egg yolks and butter kneaded with flour (*beurre manié*). Flour-based sauces include béchamel (white sauce), mornay (cheese sauce), soubise (onion sauce), and parsley sauce. Hollandaise and béarnaise sauces are made with wine vinegar, spices, and egg yolks. Other well-known sauces are mint sauce (with lamb), apple sauce (with pork), cranberry sauce (with turkey), horseradish sauce (with beef), tartare sauce (with fish), and tomato sauce. Among sweet sauces are butterscotch sauce (made with corn syrup and sugar), chocolate sauce, and melba sauce (puréed raspberries and icing sugar).

Saud (1902–69) King of Saudi Arabia (1953–64). He continued the modernization programs begun by his father *Ibn Saud but was unable to deal competently with the financial complexities of Saudi's oil revenues. He was deposed and the throne passed to his brother *Faisal.

Saudi Arabia, Kingdom of A country in the Middle East comprising most of *Arabia, bordering on the Red Sea and the Persian Gulf. In the W a line of mountains runs close to the Red Sea, while the *Najd, the central plateau, slopes downward W–E. In the N and SE are large areas of desert. The population, densest in the SW, is mainly Arab Muslim, the majority being Sunnite with some Shiites in the E. About 27% are nomads. There are also many foreign workers, chiefly unskilled Yemenis and skilled Americans and Europeans. *Economy*: based on oil, discovered in 1936 in the Persian Gulf and exploited since 1938; some is refined locally. The country, a member of OPEC, is the world's greatest exporter of oil, the revenues being used to diversify the economy and provide education and health services. Recent industries include petrochemicals, fertilizers, and steel production; considerable mineral resources have also been discovered. Income is also derived from pilgrims visiting Mecca, Medina, and Jidda. Apart from land reclaimed by irrigation, only Asir (the sole part of the country in which there is sufficient rainfall for agriculture) and the oases are cultivated; livestock is kept on the extensive pasture land. Consumer and capital goods and foodstuffs (particularly cereals) are imported, mainly from Japan, the US, West Germany, and the UK. *History*: the establishment of Saudi Arabia (1932) under *Ibn Saud followed the 19th-century struggle by the Saud family to dominate the warring tribes of the peninsula and take overall control from Turkey. Asir was incorporated in 1934. Saudi Arabia became a founding member of the Arab League (1945). Under Ibn Saud's son, *Saud, conflict with Egypt developed, especially during the North Yemen civil war, in which Saudi Arabia supported the royalists and Egypt the republicans. Saud's brother, *Faisal Ibn Abdul Aziz, who replaced him (1964), restored relations with Egypt and also used the oil crisis of the early 1970s to increase Saudi holdings in oil operations. On Faisal's apparently motiveless assassination (1975) he was replaced as king by his brother, *Khalid Ibn Abdul Aziz. On Khalid's death (1982) his brother, Fahd Ibn Abdul Aziz, became king. Official language: Arabic. Official currency: rial of 100 nilalas. Area: 927,000 sq mi (2,400,000 sq km). Population (1983 est): 10,443,000. Capital: Riyadh. Chief port: Jidda.

Saul In the Old Testament, the first King of Israel, who reigned in the 11th century BC. Son of Kish, he was anointed king by *Samuel. He began his reign with a great victory over the Ammonites, followed by many battles against the Philistines. Following an act of disobedience during the Israelite destruction of the *Amalekites, Saul, according to the Old Testament, lost divine favor; his last years were marked by a growing enmity with *David. He committed suicide after being wounded and defeated by the Philistines.

Sault Ste Marie Canals (also Soo Canals) A series of canals in S Ontario, Canada, and NE Michigan. The canals bypass St Mary's Falls on the St Mary's River, between lakes Superior and Huron. There are two waterways on the US side and one waterway on the Canadian side, and a total of five locks. Begun in 1853, the approximately 1.5 mi (2.7 km) of canals are part of the Great Lakes waterway system.

Sault Ste Marie 46 32N 84 20W A city in E Canada, in NW Ontario on the St Mary's River opposite Sault Ste Marie, Mich. Its canal allows ships to bypass local rapids that provide hydroelectricity for steel and other heavy industry. Population (1981): 82,697.

Sault Ste Marie 46 29N 84 22W A city in Michigan, on the St Mary's River opposite Sault Ste Marie, Canada. It serves the traffic of the St Lawrence Seaway by way of the Soo locks, which attract large numbers of tourists to the city. Population (1980): 14,448.

Saumur 47 16N 0 05W A city in W France, in the Maine-et-Loire department on the Loire River. A former Huguenot stronghold, it is the site of a famous cavalry school (1768) and is renowned for its sparkling white wines. Population (1975): 34,191.

Saurischia An order of *dinosaurs that were dominant in the Jurassic period (about 195–130 million years ago). They had hip bones arranged like those of modern lizards (the name means "lizard hips") and were mostly bipedal carnivores, although some were large quadrupedal herbivores. *See also* Allosaurus; Apatosaurus; Ornitholestes; Tyrannosaurus.

saury A marine fish, also called skipper, belonging to the family *Scomberesocidae* (about 4 species). It has a long slim body, up to 20 in (50 cm) long, blue or olive above and golden or silvery below, with beaklike jaws and finlets behind the dorsal and anal fins. Sauries occur in large shoals in tropical and temperate surface waters, feeding on crustaceans and small fish. They are often seen leaping or skipping over the surface to escape predators. Order: *Atheriniformes*.

Saussure, Ferdinand de (1857–1913) Swiss linguist. His great influence on 20th-century linguistics is due to the posthumously published *Course in General Linguistics* (1916), compiled by his pupils from lecture notes. It offers an integrated picture of all aspects of language. De Saussure's distinction between *parole* (the utterance of the individual) and *langue* (the common language of a community) was of great importance to both sociolinguistics and structural linguistics (*see* linguistics). He also drew influential distinctions between diachronic (historical) and synchronic linguistics and between syntagmatic (collocational) and paradigmatic (organizational) relations in language.

Savage, Michael Joseph (1872–1940) New Zealand statesman; the first Labour prime minister of New Zealand (1935–40). His ministry, which included (Sir) William Nash, dealt successfully with the economic problems of the Depression.

Savai'i 13 44S 172 18W The largest island of Western Samoa. There was a volcanic eruption in 1905 and lava flows laid waste a large area. Copra, bananas, and cocoa are exported. Area: 662 sq mi (1174 sq km). Population (1976 est): 41,488. Chief town: Tuasivi.

SAVANNA *Flat-topped acacia trees rise above grassland in the Serengeti National Park (Tanzania).*

savanna (*or* savannah) The extensive tropical grasslands, bordering on the equatorial rain forests in both the N and S hemispheres. They cover extensive areas in N Australia, Africa, and South America (where they are known as the *llanos in Venezuela and Colombia and the campos in Brazil). The vegetation of savannas is dominated by tall grasses, such as elephant grass, interspersed with low often flat-topped trees and bushes. Grazed by herds of hooved animals, savannas are ideal cattle-rearing areas.

Savannah 32 04N 81 07W A city in Georgia, on the Savannah River. Established by James Oglethorpe in 1733, it was an important colonial port and settlement. The first Atlantic steamship crossing was from here to Liverpool, England, in 1819. A major tourist center and seaport, its industries include shipbuilding and chemicals. Population (1980): 141,634.

Savery, Thomas (c. 1650–1715) English engineer, who in 1698 constructed the first practical steam engine. Savery's engine, which was dangerous because it utilized high-pressure steam, was superseded by *Newcomen's engine.

savin A low-growing *juniper shrub, *Juniperus sabina*, native to mountainous regions of S and central Europe. It has scalelike leaves and blue-black berry-like cones, 0.16–0.24 in (4–6 mm) long. The shrub has a strong unpleasant smell and yields a poisonous oil used in medicine and veterinary work.

Savona 44 18N 8 28E A port in NW Italy, in Liguria on the Gulf of Genoa. It rivaled Genoa in the middle ages but was subjugated by the Genoese in 1528. It has a cathedral dating from the 16th century. Savona is an important center of the Italian iron and steel industry. Population (1971): 79,618.

Savonarola, Girolamo (1452–98) Italian religious reformer. Joining the Dominicans in 1474, he became a lecturer in the Convent of San Marco, Florence, and later its prior (1491). There he began a crusade against religious and political corruption, centering his attacks on the papacy and the Medici. His fervent preaching attracted a large following, and he became the virtual ruler of Florence when the Medici were expelled by the populace in 1494. Excommunicated by Alexander VI in 1497, he was imprisoned, hanged, and burned for heresy by his political rivals.

savory An herb belonging to the genus *Satureja*, of warm and temperate regions. Summer savory (*S. hortensis*) is an annual, native to central Europe and Asia. Both the dried leaves and the oil extract are used for flavoring foods. The perennial winter savory (*S. montana*) grows to a height of 16 in (40 cm), has small white flowers, and is also a culinary herb. Family: *Labiatae*.

Savoy An Alpine frontier region of SE France corresponding to the present-day departments of Savoie and Haute-Savoie. Strategically important for its mountain passes, the county of Savoy was founded in 1034 by Umberto Biancomano (Umberto I). He and his successors extended Savoyard territory, acquiring Piedmont in the 14th century. In 1416 *Amadeus the Peaceful became a duke and was subsequently elected antipope as Felix V. After acquiring Sardinia in 1720, Savoyard dukes took the title King of Sardinia, which in 1748 became the kingdom of Piedmont-Sardinia. Savoy (but not Sardinia) was annexed by France during the Revolutionary Wars but restored in 1815 and Piedmont-Sardinia became the leading spirit in the movement for Italian unification (*see* Risorgimento). Savoy became part of France in 1860 in return for Napoleon III's assistance against Austria but the House of Savoy ruled the newly formed kingdom of Italy (1861–1946).

sawfish A *ray fish of the family *Pristidae* that occurs mainly in salt and brackish waters of tropical and subtropical regions. Its sharklike body, up to 23 ft (7 m) long, bears a long bladelike snout edged with teeth and is used to forage along the bottom or to catch prey.

sawfly An insect belonging to the widely distributed suborder *Symphyta* and so named because the female possesses a needle-like tubular ovipositor, which is used as a saw or drill to insert eggs into foliage and timber. Adults are 0.20–2 in (5–50 mm) long and the larvae, resembling caterpillars, damage trees. Chief families: *Argidae, Siricidae, Cimbicidae, Diprionidae, Tenthredinidae*; order: *Hymenoptera.

Saxe, Maurice, Comte de (1696–1750) Marshal of France, the illegitimate son of Augustus the Strong of Poland. He fought in the French army, outstandingly in the War of the *Austrian Succession (1740–48), and wrote *Mes Rêveries* (1757) on warfare.

Saxe-Coburg-Gotha The ruling dynasty of a German duchy. The children of Duke Francis Frederick (1750–1806) included Victoria Mary Louisa (1786–1861), who married (1818) Edward, Duke of Kent (their daughter was Queen Victoria); and Leopold, who became *Leopold I of Belgium. Francis' son Ernest I (1806–44) was the father of Prince Albert, who married Queen Victoria in 1840. The UK royal house was called Saxe-Coburg-Gotha until 1917, when the name *Windsor was adopted.

saxhorn A valved wind instrument of the bugle type, patented by the Belgian Adolphe Sax (1814–94) in Paris in 1845. It is made in several sizes; the tenor saxhorn (*or* tenor horn) is used in the military and brass bands and occasionally in the orchestra, as in Mahler's seventh symphony.

saxifrage A perennial herb belonging to certain genera of the family *Saxifragaceae*, found in cold and temperate regions. The leaves may either form a basal rosette or occur in pairs along the stem and the flowers are white, yellow, purple, or red. Most are fairly small, although the European meadow saxifrage (*Saxifraga granulata*) may reach a height of 18 in (45 cm). *See also* London pride.

Saxo Grammaticus (c. 1150–c. 1206) Danish chronicler. Little is known of his life, except that he served as secretary to the Archbishop of Roskilde. He was the author of *Gesta Danorum*, a Latin history of the Danes, the first part of which is based on mythological and legendary material. It includes the legend of Balder and the story of Amleth, one of the sources for the plot of Shakespeare's *Hamlet*. The latter part of the chronicle contains more definitely historical material.

Saxons A Germanic people who, during the 5th century AD, expanded from their Baltic coastal homelands to other areas of N Germany, the coast of Gaul (France), and (with the *Angles and *Jutes) to Britain. Charlemagne eventually defeated the continental Saxons and converted them to Christianity, incorporating their lands into his empire after a long period of warfare (772–804 AD). *See also* Anglo-Saxons.

Saxony (German name: Sachsen) An ancient NW German duchy. Named for its original inhabitants, the *Saxons (who expanded to Britain in the 5th century), they were conquered by Charlemagne in the 8th century and subsequently became a duchy. In 919 AD Henry, Duke of Saxony, became German king and his son *Otto the Great, the first Saxon Holy Roman Emperor. In 1142 Saxony passed to *Henry the Lion but in 1180 the duchy was broken up, to be reformed in various territorial combinations in following centuries. In the 13th century Saxony became an electorate and in the 16th and 17th centuries a leading German Protestant state. In 1697 Elector Frederick Augustus I (1670–1733) became King of Poland and Saxony's subsequent involvement in Polish affairs kept it apart from German power struggles until the 19th century. Conquered by Napoleon in 1806, N Saxony was annexed by Prussia in 1815 and in 1866 joined the Prussian-dominated *North German Confederation. The remainder of Saxony joined the German Empire in 1871.

saxophone A woodwind instrument with a brass body, keys, and a single reed mouthpiece similar to that of a *clarinet. It was invented by the Belgian Adolphe Sax (1814–94) and patented in France in the 1840s. The most common sizes of saxophone are the soprano, alto, tenor, and baritone. They are most commonly used as solo instruments in jazz; they are sometimes used in classical music.

Sayan Mountains A mountain range in the central S Soviet Union, extending some 497 mi (800 km) E–W and rising to 11,453 ft (3491 m) in Munku Sardyk in the extreme SE. The Yenisei river and many of its tributaries rise here.

Sayers, Dorothy L(eigh) (1893–1957) British writer, educated at Oxford, who is best known for her series of detective novels, beginning with *Whose Body?* (1923), featuring the erudite detective Lord Peter Wimsey. She also wrote plays on Christian themes and a translation of Dante's *Divine Comedy*.

scabies A contagious skin infection caused by the *itch mite, which tunnels and breeds in the skin, causing intense itching. The burrows of the mites are seen between the fingers, on the side of the hands, in the armpits, and on the groin, nipples, and buttocks. Treatment is by application of benzylbenzoate cream, and clothing and bedding should be disinfested.

scabious An annual or perennial herb belonging to the genus *Scabiosa* (80–100 species), native to the Mediterranean region and temperate parts of Eurasia and Africa. The small scabious (*S. columbaria*) is widely distributed on chalky soils. 6–27.5 in (15–70 cm) high, it has a cluster of small bluish-lilac flowers borne on a long stalk. The field scabious, *S.* (or *Knautia*) *arvensis*, is very similar and may reach a height of 40 in (1 m). Family: *Dipsacaceae*.

Scafell Pike 54 28N 3 12W The highest peak in England, in Cumbria, in the Lake District. It is popular for walking and rock climbing. Height: 3210 ft (978 m).

scalar quantity A quantity that is represented by magnitude only. Unlike a *vector quantity, a scalar quantity has no direction. Examples include mass, time, and speed.

scale (music) An ascending or descending succession of notes, characterized by a fixed succession of intervals between the notes that constitute it. Many thousands of different scales exist; all the major musical traditions of the world are based upon them.

In western music there are three **diatonic scales**, which derive from the ancient Greek *modes: the major scale, the harmonic minor scale, and the melodic minor scale. The octave is divided into 12 notes (*see* temperament) and any of these scales may be constructed on any of these notes. The version of the scale produced is associated with a particular *tonality. The **chromatic scale** includes all 12 semitones of the octave. The **pentatonic scale**, consisting of only 5 notes, is common in Chinese and Scottish music.

scale (zoology) A platelike structure that generally forms part of a protective body covering in many vertebrate animals. Fish and certain reptiles have an overlapping series of bony scales, derived from the deep layers of the skin (dermis). The periodic growth of fish scales gives rise to annual rings, by which the age of the fish may be estimated. In reptiles the scales are periodically renewed and may be modified and enlarged as spines.

scale insect An insect belonging to the superfamily *Coccoidea* (about 4000 species), abundant in warm and tropical regions. Scale insects are usually small (on average 0.04–0.59 in [1–15 mm] long) and the females are often legless, wingless, and eyeless and covered by a waxy scale or mass of threads. They become encrusted on plants and suck the juices, often becoming serious pests. Other species are of value by producing *shellac, *cochineal, and various waxes. Suborder: *Homoptera*; order: *Hemiptera*.

Scaliger, Julius Caesar (1484–1558) Italian humanist scholar. He engaged in controversy with *Erasmus and wrote several commentaries on classical writers. Aristotle's theories of tragedy became known to the French 17th-century dramatists through his discussion of them in the *Poetice* (1561). His son **Joseph Justus Scaliger** (1540–1609), born in France, was an outstanding classical scholar and published many works of historical scholarship, notably the *Opus de emendatione tempore* (1583), a scientific study of chronology.

scallion Any *onion or related plant that produces small white-skinned mild-flavored bulbs, with a long neck and stiff leaves. Examples are spring onions and *shallots, used in salads. Leeks and chives may also be called scallions.

scallop A *bivalve mollusk belonging to the family *Pectinidae* (about 400 species), of warm and temperate seas. 0.8–8 in (2–20 cm) across, the valves of the shell are broad, flattened, and deeply fluted, and the animal swims by flapping them with a single powerful muscle. Scallops are important as seafood.

scaly-tailed squirrel An African arboreal *rodent belonging to the family *Anomaluridae* (9 species). They range in size from 3–18 in (8–45 cm) and most species have a gliding membrane like that of the *flying squirrel. Their name refers to the backward-pointing scales under the tail that grip the tree trunk when the squirrel is clinging to it.

Scandinavia Geographically, a peninsula in NW Europe, comprising Norway and Sweden. Culturally and historically, it also includes Denmark, Iceland, and the Faeroe Islands, and Finland, too, is often considered part of the region.

Scandinavian languages A subgroup of the *Germanic group of languages consisting of *Swedish, *Norwegian, *Danish, *Icelandic, and Faeroese. The first three are similar enough to be mutually intelligible, their separateness being imposed by their history and political boundaries. They all developed from a common Scandinavian ancestor, which originally used the *runic alphabet (*see also* Old Norse). This language spread with the Vikings to Iceland, the Faeroes, and to other Baltic and Atlantic islands.

scandium (Sc) The first transition metal, predicted by Mendeleyev and discovered in 1879 by L. F. Nilson (1840–99). It is trivalent, forming an oxide (Sc_2O_3), halides (for example ScF_3), and other compounds. It is light (relative density 2.989) and has a much higher melting point than aluminum, making it of interest as a possible spacecraft material. At no 21; at wt 44.956; mp 2809°F (1541°C); bp 5133°F (2831°C).

Scapa Flow A section of the Atlantic Ocean off the N coast of Scotland, in the Orkney Islands. Of naval importance during both World Wars, it was the main base of the British Grand Fleet during World War I. Following its surrender, the German fleet scuttled itself here (1919). Length: about 15 mi (24 km). Width: 8 mi (13 km).

scapegoat An animal, person, or object chosen as the symbolic bearer of the sins or misfortunes of an individual or group. At the ancient Jewish ritual of the Day of Atonement, a goat was chosen to bear the sins of the people and then driven off or thrown from a cliff. Similar rituals were practiced in ancient Greece and Rome and among many primitive peoples.

scapula. *See* shoulder.

scarab An ancient Egyptian seal or amulet made of stone or faience in the shape of a dung beetle. Associated with the sun's regenerative powers, scarabs were often buried with the dead.

scarab beetle A beetle belonging to the worldwide family *Scarabaeidae* (over 19,000 species). Scarabs show a great variety in size and form: the largest beetles—the *goliath and *hercules beetles—are scarabs, while other species have developed extraordinary horns (*see* rhinoceros beetle). In general the family can be divided into two main groups—the *dung beetles and *chafers. Certain dung-rolling beetles, especially *Scarabaeus sacer*, were the sacred scarabs of the ancient Egyptians.

Scarlatti, Domenico (1685–1757) Italian composer and noted harpsichordist and organist. After studying in Venice and holding court posts in Rome and Naples, he was engaged by Princess Maria Barbara of Portugal in Lisbon in 1720. When she married into the Spanish royal family in 1729 he moved with her to Madrid, where he stayed until his death. Besides some operas and church music, he wrote over 600 harpsichord sonatas, many of which were highly innovative and contributed to subsequent piano technique. His father **Alessandro Scarlatti** (1660–1725) was also a composer. He worked chiefly in Rome and Naples. He was maestro successively to Queen Christina of Sweden, to the Spanish viceroy, at Sta Maria Maggiore in Rome, and at the royal chapel in Naples. His works include over a hundred operas, 600 chamber cantatas, 200 masses, 12 chamber symphonies, and 14 oratorios.

scarlet fever A highly infectious disease of children caused by streptococcus bacteria. Since these bacteria are much less virulent now than formerly, the disease is much milder now than it was at the beginning of the century. After an incubation period of 2–4 days the child develops a sore throat, fever, and headache; 24–48 hours later a red rash spreads from the chest over the whole body. Before antibiotics scarlet fever killed many children or left them disabled with *rheumatic fever, kidney disease, or ear infections; it can now be rapidly cured with penicillin.

Scarron, Paul (1610–60) French poet, dramatist, and satirist. His writings are enlivened by a burlesque irreverent style. His best-known work is the picaresque novel *Le Roman comique* (1651–57). From the age of 30 he suffered from paralysis. Despite this handicap, in 1652 he married Françoise d'Aubigné, who later became, as Madame de Maintenon, the wife of Louis XIV.

scattering The deflection of waves or particles by the atoms or molecules of the medium through which they are passing or by other particles. The scattering of waves is due to either *reflection or *diffraction. For particles, the scattering is described as inelastic if the scattered particles gain or lose energy during the process. Otherwise it is elastic. An example of inelastic scattering is the *Raman effect.

SCAUP *A female on its nest. Scaups breed in groups on lake islands.*

scaup A *diving duck, *Aythya marila*, that breeds in northern latitudes and winters on more southerly coasts. 16–18 in (40–45 cm) long, it dives deeply to feed on mussels and small crabs. The male has green-black fore parts, a gray back, white flanks, and a brown rump and tail; females are dark brown with a white patch around the bill.

Schacht, Hjalmar (1877–1970) German financier and politician. As president of the Reichsbank (1923–30), he checked Germany's rampant inflation. He was reappointed by Hitler in 1933 but was dismissed in 1939. From 1934 to 1937 he served as minister of economics. He was acquitted at Nuremberg of war crimes.

Schechter Poultry Corporation v. United States (1935) US Supreme Court decision that declared the *New Deal's National Recovery Act invalid. Violations, by the Schechter Corp, of fair competition codes established in the act were at issue, and the Court ruled that those not involved in interstate commerce were not liable under the act.

Scheel, Walter (1919–) West German statesman; president (1974–79). He served in the Luftwaffe during World War II and was minister for economic cooperation (1961–66) and foreign minister (1969–74) before becoming president. In 1967 he became chairman of the Free Democrats.

Scheele, Carl Wilhelm (1742–86) Swedish chemist, who discovered a number of compounds and elements. His greatest work in this field was the discovery of oxygen (c. 1771), but as his results were not published until 1777 *Priestley is usually credited with the discovery. Scheele was also the first to isolate and prepare the gases hydrogen sulfide, hydrogen cyanide, and hydrogen fluoride.

scheelite A tungsten ore mineral, $CaWO_4$, occurring in veins and contact-metamorphic rocks. It is yellowish white or brown. *See also* wolframite.

Scheldt River (French name: Escaut; Flemish and Dutch name: Schelde) A river in W Europe. Rising in NE France, it flows generally NNE through W Belgium to Antwerp, then NW to the North Sea in the SW Netherlands. Canals connect it to the Somme, Seine, Sambre, Meuse, and Rhine rivers. Length: 270 mi (435 km).

Schelling, Friedrich (1775–1854) German philosopher. Schelling was first influenced by the writings of *Fichte and *Kant. Later, he became convinced that knowledge could not be confined to phenomena and argued that there was "a secret wonderful faculty which dwells in us all." His *System of Transcendental Idealism* (1800) contains his metaphysical philosophy, which, with his insistence that human consciousness is fulfilled by art, made him an important influence upon *Romanticism and in particular upon *Coleridge.

Schenectady 42 48N 73 57W A city in New York, on the Mohawk River. In 1886 the Thomas Edison Machine Works was moved here, later becoming the General Electric Company, which dominates the city today. Population (1980): 67,877.

Schenck v. United States (1919) US Supreme Court decision that introduced the *clear and present danger interpretation regarding the 1st Amendment. The Court ruled that Congress can prevent speech that presents a "clear and present danger that . . . will bring about . . . substantive evils." The case was brought against Charles Schenck of the Socialist Party for attempts to encourage military insubordination and to discourage military service.

Scheveningen. *See* Hague, The.

Schiaparelli, Elsa (1896–1973) Italian-born fashion designer, who opened fashion houses in Paris (late 1920s) and New York (1949). Her designs and use of color were flamboyant and daring; she is particularly associated with the padded shoulder and "shocking pink."

Schick test A skin test for the presence of antibodies to *diphtheria. Injection of small amounts of diphtheria toxin causes a localized inflammation of the skin in those who have not been vaccinated or have not had diphtheria. The test was devised in 1913 by an Austrian pediatrician, Bela Schick (1877–1967).

Schiedam 51 55N 4 25E A city in the W Netherlands, in South Holland province. It has famous gin distilleries. Population (1981 est): 74,233.

Schiele, Egon (1890–1918) Austrian expressionist painter. Influenced first by the French impressionists and by *Klimt, Schiele often painted portraits and nudes and was able to express both a disturbing anguished quality and eroticism through a distorted use of line. With *Kokoschka he was a leader of Austrian expressionism until his untimely death from influenza.

Schiller, (Johann Christoph) Friedrich (von) (1759–1805) German dramatist, poet, and writer. His first, anonymously published, play, *Die Räuber* (1781), typifies the *Sturm und Drang call for political freedom. His next important play and his first in blank verse was the tragedy *Don Carlos* (1787), set in the time of Philip II of Spain. With Goethe's friendly encouragement from 1794, Schiller turned from the historical and academic studies with which he had been involved and produced the brilliant dramas of the last decade of his life: the trilogy *Wallenstein* (1798–99), *Maria Stuart* (1800), based on the life of Mary, Queen of Scots, *Die Jungfrau von Orleans* (1801), concerned with Joan of Arc, and *Wilhelm Tell* (1804). His nondramatic works include poems, the important essay on aesthetics, *Über naïve und sentimentalische Dichtung* (1795–96), and a history of the Thirty Years' War (1793).

schipperke A breed of □dog originating in Flanders and used as a guard dog on barges. It has a stocky tailless body with short legs and a foxlike head with erect ears. The dense coat is usually black and thick around the neck, forming a mane. Height: 12–13 in (30.5–33 cm).

schist A coarse-grained *metamorphic rock with a pronounced banded structure, in which the minerals show parallel alignment at right angles to the direction of stress, leaving no trace of the original bedding. The minerals are segregated into alternate thin layers rich in mica and quartz/feldspar, and the rock readily splits along these schistosity planes. Schists are named according to the dominant minerals, e.g. mica-schist.

schistosomiasis (or bilharziasis) A widespread disease of the tropics caused by blood flukes of the genus *Schistosoma* (or *Bilharzia*). The disease is contracted by bathing in water contaminated by snails, which harbor the larvae of the parasite. The larvae penetrate the skin and—when mature—settle in the blood vessels of the intestine or bladder. Symptoms, caused by the release of eggs by adult flukes, include anemia, inflammation, and diarrhea and dysentery (from an intestinal infection), or cystitis and blood in the urine (from a bladder infection). The disease is treated by drugs that destroy the parasite.

schizophrenia A severe mental disorder characterized by disintegration of the processes of thinking, contact with reality, and emotional responsiveness. Delusions and *hallucinations are common, especially those that produce the feeling of a loss of personal identity. Schizophrenics often become withdrawn and apathetic. The condition tends to get worse (in about half of all cases) unless treatment is given. Modern treatment has improved the outlook: it consists of such drugs as *phenothiazines and vigorous psychological and social rehabilitation. Schizophrenia is largely caused by genetic factors, but environmental stress can trigger an episode of illness. *See also* paranoia; psychosis.

Schlegel, August Wilhelm von (1767–1845) German critic, poet, and translator. With his brother, he exerted a powerful influence on the early Romantics through critical works, such as *Über dramatische Kunst und Literatur* (3 vols, 1809–11), and translations, especially his superb rendering of Shakespeare. His brother (**Carl Wilhelm**) **Friedrich von Schlegel** (1772–1829) was a writer and critic. The chief influence on the Romantic movement, his literary and philosophical works appeared first in *Das Athenäum*, a periodical published by him and his brother. He later studied Sanskrit in Paris and published the first study in comparative philology (1808).

Schleiden, Matthias Jakob (1804–81) German botanist, who first formulated the theory that plants are composed of *cells (this was later extended to animals by Theodor *Schwann). Schleiden also recognized the importance of the cell nucleus, although he mistakenly believed that new cells budded from its surface.

Schlesinger, Arthur M(eier), Jr. (1917–) US historian and statesman. He taught at Harvard University (1946–61) and served as a special assistant to President John F. *Kennedy (1961–64). His works include *The Age of Jackson* (1945; Pulitzer Prize), *The Vital Center* (1949), *The Age of Roosevelt* (3 vols., 1957–60), *A Thousand Days* (1965; Pulitzer Prize), *The Imperial Presidency* (1973), and *Robert Kennedy and His Times* (1978).

Schleswig A breed of draft horse originating in the Danish duchy of Schleswig. It has a long body with relatively short legs, a powerful neck and a fairly large head. The coat is usually chestnut but sometimes bay or gray. Height: about 5 ft (1.60 m) (15⅓ hands).

Schleswig-Holstein A low-lying *Land* in NE West Germany bordering on the North Sea, the Baltic Sea, and Denmark. Grain and potatoes are grown and cattle reared; industries include shipbuilding and engineering. *History*: during the 19th century the **Schleswig-Holstein question** arose when Denmark and the Austrian-led German confederacy both laid claim to the two duchies of Schleswig and Holstein. War broke out in 1863 and the duchies were annexed to Prussia in 1866. In 1949 the *Land* of Schleswig-Holstein was formed. Area: 6059 sq mi (15,696 sq km). Population (1980 est): 2,605,200. Capital: Kiel.

Schlick, Moritz (1882–1936) German philosopher. Schlick was professor of philosophy of the inductive sciences at Vienna University (1922–36). The leader of the *Vienna Circle (*see also* logical positivism), he approached philosophy in a basically experimental way and concerned himself with problems of truth and verifiability. His published work includes the *General Theory of Knowledge* (1918) and *Problems of Ethics* (1930).

Schlieffen, Alfred, Graf von (1833–1913) German general, who, as chief of the general staff (1891–1905) devised the **Schlieffen Plan**, on which German strategy at the outbreak of World War I was unsuccessfully based. The plan provided for a concentration of German forces on the Western Front, which would rapidly defeat France in a flanking movement through the Low Countries, while a smaller army held off Russia in the east.

Schliemann, Heinrich (1822–90) German archeologist. After a successful business career, Schliemann retired (1863) to pursue his childhood ambition of discovering Homeric *Troy. Ignoring scholarly derision, he excavated Hissarlik on the Asia Minor coast of Turkey, finding ruins of nine consecutive cities. The second oldest (Troy II), which he wrongly identified with Homer's city, yielded a hoard that Schliemann romantically called "Priam's Treasure." His spectacular finds at *Mycenae (1874–76), Orchomenos in Boeotia (1880), and *Tiryns (1884–85) established him as the discoverer of *Mycenaean civilization.

HEINRICH SCHLIEMANN *A contemporary engraving showing his excavations at Hissarlik.*

Schlieren photography A method of observing differences of density in a transparent medium, such as air. Light from a spark is photographed as it passes through the medium; any differences in density present cause local variations in the refractive index, which show up as streaks (German word: *Schlieren*) in the photograph. The method is used for observing sound waves, shock waves, and flaws in glass.

Schmeling, Max (1905–) German boxer, the first European to win the world heavyweight title in the 20th century (1930). In 1936 he beat Joe *Louis but Louis took his revenge in two minutes in 1938.

Schmidt, Helmut (1918–) West German statesman; Social Democratic chancellor (1974–82). He worked in transport administration in Hamburg before entering Federal politics (1953). He became minister for domestic affairs in Hamburg (1961–65) and was then Federal minister of defense (1969–72) and for finance (1972–74) before becoming chancellor. He has written several books, mainly on foreign affairs. □Giscard d'Estaing, Valéry.

Schmidt telescope A *telescope developed by the Estonian instrument maker Bernard Voldemar Schmidt (1879–1935). It produces very sharp photographic images of celestial objects over a very wide angle of sky. The incoming light passes through a thin correcting plate, is reflected by a large short-focus spherical mirror, and focused on a curved photographic plate.

Schnabel, Artur (1882–1951) Austrian pianist, especially famous for his performances of Beethoven. He studied in Vienna and in Berlin, where he later taught until 1933, after which he lived mainly in Switzerland and the US. He also composed three symphonies and a piano concerto.

schnauzer A breed of dog originating in Germany and used as a guard dog. Strongly built with a docked tail, it has a characteristic square muzzle with long sidewhiskers. The wiry coat is black or light gray and brown. Two varieties have been bred from the standard schnauzer—the giant schnauzer for farm and police work and the miniature schnauzer as pet. Height: 13–14 in (33–35 cm) (miniature); 18–19 in (45–48 cm) (standard); 21–25.5 in (54–65 cm) (giant).

Schnitzler, Arthur (1862–1931) Austrian Jewish dramatist and novelist. A physician, he was especially interested in psychiatry and his works are notable for their psychological observation. They include the witty dramatic cycles *Anatol* (1893) and *Reigen* (1900; filmed as *La Ronde,* 1950) and his prose masterpiece, *Leutnant Gustl* (1901).

Schoenberg, Arnold (1874–1951) Austrian-born composer. He studied in Vienna with Alexander von Zemlinsky (1872–1942) and began his career by orchestrating theater music. In 1910 he became a teacher at the Vienna Academy; his students included Berg and Webern. Mahler became a champion of his music. In 1933 Schoenberg, as a Jew, was forced to leave Berlin; he became a US citizen in 1941 and was professor at the University of California (1936–44). His early compositions, in a late Romantic style, include two string quartets, *Verklärte Nacht* (for string sextet; 1899), and the symphonic poem *Pelleas und Melisande* (1902–03). His subsequent works were characterized by *atonality; they include the melodrama *Pierrot Lunaire* (for soprano and five instruments; 1912) in which the voice part is noted in *Sprechgesang* (German: speech song). Schoenberg subsequently developed the theory and technique of *serialism (1924), which he employed in most of his later works, including a violin concerto (1936), a

piano concerto (1942), and the unfinished opera *Moses und Aaron* (1932–51).

scholasticism The intellectual discipline comprising all the philosophical and theological activities pursued in the medieval universities (schools). As the international philosophy of Christendom it respected orthodoxy and was concerned with the philosophies of *Plato and *Aristotle as assimilated over centuries of Christian thought. For scholastics religion was predominant and in their method philosophy was the servant of theology. It was by theology that the selection of problems for study and the scope of scientific enquiry were to be decided. *Anselm was an early scholastic, and *Abelard perfected its method. After *Aquinas, *Aristotelianism became increasingly important until, in the Renaissance, it was virtually synonymous with scholasticism.

schooner A □sailing vessel with at least two masts, a shorter one set near the bow, a taller one at some distance behind it. Schooners, being quite fast and efficient when sailing off the wind, were widely used before the advent of steam and motor vessels in both coastal and long-distance commercial trade, especially fishing. Because they do not sail well into the wind, they are not a favored rig for racing yachts.

Schopenhauer, Arthur (1788–1860) German philosopher. Schopenhauer's main contribution to philosophy is contained in the emphasis that he placed upon the human will. The will was, he maintained, the means by which all other things were understood. *The World as Will and Idea* (1818) sets out his principal ideas and pessimistic conclusions. He was distrustful of rationalism and the scientific method and was instead concerned with intuitive cognition. He saw the ideal state of man as one of contemplative freedom, achieved through art.

Schrödinger, Erwin (1887–1961) Austrian physicist and one of the major contributors to *quantum theory. He shared the 1933 Nobel Prize with *Dirac for his development of the form of the quantum theory known as *wave mechanics. Although not Jewish, he was an ardent anti-Nazi and went to England when Hitler took Austria. He was professor at the School for Advanced Studies in Dublin, Ireland (1940–56), returning to Vienna after his retirement.

Schubert, Franz (Peter) (1797–1828) Austrian composer, who had a musical upbringing but little formal training, other than at the imperial choir school in Vienna. He made a precarious living as a composer and teacher, rarely leaving Vienna and achieving little recognition. He died from typhoid fever at the age of 31. Schubert's melodic genius is perhaps most evident in his 600 *Lieder*, which include such famous examples as "Erlkönig," "Death and the Maiden," and "The Trout." Some of his greatest songs are to be found in the song-cycles *Die Schöne Müllerin* (1823) and *Die Winterreise* (1827). His other works demonstrate his mastery of large-scale composition. They include nine symphonies (of which one is lost and the eighth is unfinished), string quartets, piano trios, an octet, two quintets, piano sonatas and pieces, and much choral music. He also wrote several operas, the only musical genre in which he had little success.

Schuman, Robert (1886–1963) French statesman. He held several ministerial posts from 1946 to 1956 and was briefly prime minister (1947–48). As foreign minister (1948–52), he proposed the **Schuman Plan** (1950) for European unity, which advocated the establishment (achieved in 1952) of the *European Coal and Steel Community. He was president of the EEC assembly (1958–60).

Schuman, William (Howard) (1910–) US composer. He taught at Sarah Lawrence College in New York (1935–45) and was president of the Juilliard School of Music (1945–61). His compositions include *The Undertow* (1945), a ballet, choral works, nine symphonies, an opera about baseball, entitled *The Mighty Casey* (1953), *Song of Orpheus* (for cello and orchestra; 1962), and a cantata, *A Free Song* (1943) which won a Pulitzer Prize.

Schumann, Elisabeth (1885–1952) German-born soprano. She settled in the US in 1938, becoming a citizen in 1944. She performed in operas, concerts, and recitals, excelling in the interpretation of Mozart and Richard Strauss.

Schumann, Robert (Alexander) (1810–56) German composer. He played and composed music from an early age and at Leipzig University devoted more time to it than to his law studies. Almost all his musical compositions up to 1840 were for the piano; he also wrote much as a critic, editing (1835–44) the journal *Die Neue Zeitschrift für Musik*, which he had founded. Gradual insanity in later life culminated in his attempt to drown himself and he died in an asylum. His compositions include four symphonies, the opera *Genoveva* (1847–50), songs, including the cycles *Dichterliebe* (1840) and *Frauenliebe und Leben* (1840), violin, piano, and cello concertos, and piano pieces, including the *Davidsbündlertänze* (1837) and *Kreisleriana* (1838).

His wife **Clara Schumann** (1819–96), whom he married in 1840, was the daughter of Friedrich Wieck (1788–1873), with whom he had studied the piano in Leipzig (1830–32). She was a famous pianist and became a great interpreter and editor of her husband's works. She was also a composer and a noted teacher.

Schuschnigg, Kurt von (1897–1977) Austrian statesman; chancellor (1934–38). He tried in vain to prevent the Nazi annexation (**Anschluss*) and was forced to resign after Hitler's invasion of the country. He was imprisoned by Hitler throughout World War II. After his release he taught in the US until 1967, when he returned to Austria.

Schütz, Heinrich (1585–1672) German composer. He sang in the choir of the royal chapel at Kassel and studied with Giovanni Gabrieli in Venice (1609–12). He was court kapellmeister in Dresden after 1615. He composed much sacred music, including Passions and *The Seven Words of Christ on the Cross* (c. 1645), as well as madrigals and the first German opera, *Dafne* (1627), which is now lost.

Schwann, Theodor (1810–82) German physiologist, who applied *Schleiden's cell theory to animals—an important conceptual advance in biology. Schwann pointed out that egg cells develop by successive divisions and he identified the Schwann cells that surround nerve fibers. He was the first person to isolate a digestive enzyme (pepsin) from animal tissue and he also coined the term metabolism for the chemical changes that take place in living tissues.

Schwarzenberg, Felix, Fürst zu (1800–52) Austrian statesman. He served in the diplomatic corps before becoming first minister during the Revolution of 1848. He restored order in the Habsburg Empire, issuing a new constitution (1849) that strengthened the absolute power of the emperor. He also frustrated Prussia's attempts to establish a Prussian-dominated union of German states.

Schwarzkopf, Elisabeth (1915–) German soprano. She studied and made her debut (1938) in Berlin and then sang in opera, concerts, and recitals in Vienna, London, Milan, and the US. She is especially noted for her interpretation of Mozart and Richard Strauss.

Schwarzwald. *See* Black Forest.

Schweitzer, Albert (1875–1965) Alsatian-born theologian, medical missionary, and organist. A theologian in the liberal Protestant tradition, Schweitzer wrote *The Quest of the Historical Jesus* (1906), emphasizing Christ's humanity. His writings on Bach and his recitals of Bach's organ music were highly acclaimed. From 1913 until his death, Schweitzer practiced as a doctor in the hospital he founded in Gabon at the jungle village of Lambaréné. His philosophy is best summarized in his ethic of "reverence for life." In 1952 he received the Nobel Peace Prize.

Schwerin 53 38N 11 25E A city in NW East Germany, on Lake Schwerin. Largely destroyed by fire in the 16th and 17th centuries the city was rebuilt with squares and wide streets. Schwerin has machinery and chemical industries. Population (1980 est): 119,961.

Schwitters, Kurt (1887–1958) German artist and poet, born in Hanover. Associated with the *dada art movement, he became famous for his poems of meaningless sounds and his invention of elaborate structures and collages of ticket stubs, broken glass, and other trash, which he salvaged from gutters and garbage cans and labeled *Merz* (trash) constructions. He worked in Britain from 1940 until his death.

sciatica Severe pain that starts in a buttock and spreads down the back of the leg. It is caused by pressure on the roots of the sciatic nerve—the longest nerve in the body. The commonest cause is pressure from a slipped disk in the backbone. Other kinds of injury to the back may also lead to sciatica. The pain usually disappears eventually: treatment is by bed rest and pain killers.

science fiction A literary genre in which scientific knowledge is used as a basis for imaginative fiction. The chief precursors of modern science fiction were Jules *Verne, who made use of speculative developments in engineering in such works as *Twenty Thousand Leagues Under the Sea* (1869) and *Propeller Island* (1895), and H. G. Wells, who dealt with time travel, space travel, and alien invasion in *The Time Machine* (1895), *The First Men in the Moon* (1901), and *The War of the Worlds* (1898). In the 20th century such magazines as *Amazing Stories* (founded 1926) and *Astounding Science Fiction* reflected a growing popular interest in the science fiction inspired by advances in the fields of rocketry, electronics, and computers. Notable works of science fiction have been written by such scientists as Fred Hoyle and Isaac Asimov. Among writers who have written imaginative accounts of the origin, evolution, and destiny of the human race are

Olaf Stapleton (1886–1950), author of *Last and First Men* (1931), and Arthur C. Clarke (1917–), author, with Stanley *Kubrick, of *2001: A Space Odyssey* (film, 1967; novel, 1968). Other leading writers of science fiction include Edgar Rice Burroughs, Robert Heinlein, Aldous Huxley, Brian Aldiss, Ray Bradbury, Kurt Vonnegut, Jr, and Anthony Burgess.

scientology The doctrine of the Church of Scientology, founded in 1954 in California by L(afayette) Ron(ald) Hubbard (1911–). Originally this doctrine was presented as a method of psychotherapy in Hubbard's *Dianetics: The Modern Science of Mental Health* (1950). It was later presented as a religious philosophy by which the member passes through many rigidly structured levels, increasing his IQ, creativity, etc., until he is finally "not on the body level" at all and has realized his full spiritual potential. While claiming to achieve man's spiritual liberation, its methods, particularly its practice of counseling ("auditing") to release adherents from past emotional bonds, have been widely criticized.

Scilly, Isles of (*or* Scillies) A group of British islands, consisting of about 140 islands and islets in the Atlantic Ocean, off the extreme SW coast of England. Only five are inhabited. Their mild climate has been exploited to produce early spring flowers for the UK market, their major source of income. Area: 6 sq mi (16 sq km). Population (1981): 2628. Chief town: Hugh Town.

scintillation counter An instrument that measures the number of radioactive atoms that decay in a certain time. The emitted radiation strikes a scintillation crystal causing it to emit a flash of light. The light then activates a *photomultiplier, producing a pulse of electrons, which are counted to enable the activity of the source to be calculated. A **scintillation spectrometer** is used to show the energy distribution of a source.

Scipio Aemilianus Africanus (c. 185–129 BC) Roman general, politician, and literary patron; the grandson by adoption of Scipio Africanus. After military successes in Greece and Spain, he blockaded and destroyed Carthage in 146 (*see* Punic Wars), becoming a national hero. After subduing Spain with the destruction of Numantia in 133, he lost popular support when he attacked the reforms of his murdered brother-in-law, Tiberius *Gracchus. Scipio died during the subsequent political upheaval.

Scipio Africanus (236–183 BC) Roman general of the second *Punic War. After defeating the Carthaginians in Spain, he won permission, despite *Fabius' opposition, to invade Africa. After crushing Hannibal at the battle of Zama in 202, he became a national hero, receiving the title Africanus. Subsequent pro-Greek policies provoked political hostility and he retired from public life. His son was the adoptive father of Scipio Aemilianus Africanus.

sclerosis Stiffening and hardening of the tissues. This is a feature of many diseases: it can affect the brain and spinal cord, causing *multiple sclerosis, and the walls of the arteries, causing *arteriosclerosis or *atherosclerosis.

Scone 56 25N 3 24W A parish in E central Scotland. It consists of the villages of New Scone and Old Scone, the Pictish and later Scottish capital where most Scottish kings were crowned. The coronation stone was taken from here by Edward I in 1296 and placed in Westminster Abbey.

Scopes Trial (1925) US court trial, also known as the "monkey trial," of John T. Scopes, a Tennessee high school teacher, who taught *Darwin's theory of evolution to his students. Testing a Tennessee law forbidding the teaching of anything but literal interpretation of the Bible, the case was prosecuted by William Jennings *Bryan and defended by Clarence *Darrow. Scopes was convicted of breaking the law, but the publicity from the case was instrumental in making it very difficult for similar laws to be passed.

scopolamine A drug with similar uses and actions to *atropine. It also has a depressant effect on the brain and is therefore used to prevent motion sickness and for sedation before surgery.

scops owl A small *owl of the mainly tropical genus *Otus*, also called screech owl because of its call. Scops owls are 8–12 in (20–30 cm) long and mostly arboreal, with camouflaging plumage resembling bark. They feed on insects, birds, and small mammals.

Scorpio (astrology). *See* zodiac.

scorpion An *arachnid of the order *Scorpionida* (about 800 species), found in warm dry regions. Scorpions are 0.51–7 in (13–175 mm) long; the second pair of appendages (pedipalps) form large pincers and the elongated abdomen curls upward and bears a poisonous sting, which can be fatal to man. They live under stones or in shallow burrows in soil during the day and prey at night, mainly on insects and spiders. Mating is preceded by a courtship dance and the female produces live young, which ride on her back for several days.

scorpion fish A carnivorous fish, often called rockfish or zebra fish, belonging to the family *Scorpaenidae*, found mainly on rocky beds of tropical and temperate coastal waters. It has a stout body, up to 40 in (1 m) long, a large spiny head, and strong fin spines, which can inflict painful wounds and may be venomous. Order: *Scorpaeniformes*.

scorpion fly An □insect of the order *Mecoptera* (400 species), so called because the males of many species curl the abdomen over the body, like a scorpion. 0.47–1 in (12–25 mm) long, scorpion flies have long legs and antennae and, typically, two similar pairs of net-veined wings. The larvae develop in soil, feeding—like the adults—on dead animals and plants.

Scorpius (Latin: Scorpion) A conspicuous constellation in the S sky, lying on the *zodiac between Sagittarius and Libra. The brightest star is *Antares. The constellation contains several notable open and globular *star clusters and the intense X-ray binary star **Scorpius X-1**.

Scotland A country occupying the N part of Great Britain and comprising a political division of the *United Kingdom. Most of the population lives in a narrow lowland belt, which runs E–W across the country and separates the lower hills of the S (including the Tweedsmuir and Cheviot Hills) from the higher mountains of the N (including the Grampian and Cairngorm Mountains). Ben Nevis in the W is the highest point in the British Isles at 4406 ft (1343 m). There are many islands off the N and W coasts, including the Hebrides and the Isle of Arran to the W and the Orkneys and Shetlands to the N. The principal rivers are the Clyde, which flows into the North Channel, and the Forth, Tay, and Spey, which flow into the North Sea. There are several lochs (lakes) in the northern mountains, including Loch Ness. *Economy*: the central belt of the country is highly industrialized, based originally on coal, still mined in the Lothian and Fife Regions. Other long-established industries include shipbuilding (on the Clyde) and steelmaking. Whisky, for which Scotland is internationally famous, is produced in Highland and Grampian Regions. The discovery of oil in the North Sea has led to a boom on the E coast of the country. Agriculture remains important and includes sheep farming in the upland areas (especially in the border hills, where there is a famous textile industry), dairying in the SW, and beef production in the E and NE lowlands. Fishing is a major source of revenue, especially on the E coast at such ports as Aberdeen. *History*: Scotland was never completely subdued by the Romans, but the barbaric northern tribes were kept N of *Hadrian's Wall and, for some 40 years, the more northerly *Antonine Wall. The diverse peoples (Picts, Scots, Britons, and Angles) of Scotland gradually united, helped by the spread of Christianity, and Kenneth I MacAlpine (died c. 858) is regarded as their first king. During the middle ages there was recurrent war between England and Scotland. In 1296 Edward I of England declared himself King of Scotland but after his death Robert the Bruce reasserted Scottish independence, which was recognized by England in 1328. In 1603 James VI of Scotland succeeded as James I to the throne of England but political union between the two countries was not established until 1707 (*see* Union, Acts of). Rapid industrialization in the 19th century encouraged considerable Irish immigration. Area: 30,405 sq mi (78,769 sq km). Population (1981): 5,116,000. Capital: Edinburgh.

Scots law Originally Scots law differed little from English law, but from the beginning of the 16th century there was a tendency to introduce elements of *Roman law, especially as embodied in the *civil law of France and the Netherlands. This resulted in marked differences from English law, which were retained after Scotland's union with England in 1707.

Scott, Paul (Mark) (1920–78) British novelist. He is best known for the "Raj Quartet," a series of novels dealing with the dramatic changes and conflicts of the final period of British rule in India. They are *The Jewel in the Crown* (1966), *The Day of the Scorpion* (1968), *The Towers of Silence* (1972), and *A Division of the Spoils* (1975). His last novel, *Staying On* (1977), was awarded Britain's prestigious Booker Fiction Prize.

Scott, Robert Falcon (1868–1912) British explorer and naval officer. He led two expeditions to the Antarctic, the first in the *Discovery* (1900–04) and the second (1910–12) in the *Terra Nova*. With a party of four he reached the South Pole by sledge on January 17, 1912, only to find that *Amundsen had preceded them. Delayed by illness and blizzards they perished only a few miles from safety. Their bodies and Scott's diaries were found in November.

Scott, Sir Walter (1771–1832) Scottish novelist. His early works included a collection of border ballads (1802–03) and the popular narrative poem *The Lay of the Last Minstrel* (1805). *Waverley* (1814) was the first of a series of hugely successful historical novels that included *Old Mortality* (1816) and *The Heart of Midlothian* (1818). His last years were spent in frantic literary activity to pay off his creditors after his bankruptcy in 1826.

Scott, Winfield (1786–1866) US Army officer. He served in the *War of 1812 and in various campaigns from the Indian wars in Florida to the *Aroostook border dispute in Canada. He was made general in chief of the Army (1841–61) and headed US forces during the *Mexican War, leading the troops in their long victorious trek to capture Mexico City, where he governed for almost a year (1847–48). He was the Whig nominee for president in 1852, but was defeated by Democrat Franklin *Pierce. He continued as head of the Army until 1861 and helped plan strategy at the beginning of the Civil War.

Scottish literature The literature of Scotland comprises a diversity of works in Scottish Gaelic, Lowland Scots (Lallans), English, and combinations of these. Literary Gaelic as practiced by the *bards continued in use up to the 18th century and drew upon the same traditions as *Irish literature (especially the Ulster cycle and the *Fenian cycle). In the Scottish (non-Gaelic) vernacular, the first important work is John *Barbour's 14th-century epic *The Bruce*. In the 15th and 16th centuries were produced the greatest works of early Scottish literature, the poetry of the *makaris* or Scottish Chaucerians. In the 17th century, by contrast, there was little outstanding literary production. *Burns' evocative use of the Lowlands dialect in the 18th century had a lasting effect on Scottish literature and national consciousness and influenced later poets. Many Scottish writers since the 17th century have written in English: the works of *Boswell, *Smollett, Sir Walter *Scott, *Carlyle, Robert Louis *Stevenson, and many others form an essential part of the literature of English.

Scottish National Party (SNP) A political party, founded in 1928, dedicated to the achievement of Scottish independence from the UK. The party achieved some popularity with the rise of nationalist sentiment in the 1960s and 1970s.

Scottish terrier A breed of dog, originally called Aberdeen terrier, used to chase foxes from their burrows. It is thickset with short legs, a short erect tail, and pricked ears. The long muzzle has characteristically long whiskers and the wiry coat can be black, brindle, gray, or yellow-brown. Height: 10–11.2 in (25–28 cm).

Scouting A movement founded by Britain's Robert *Baden Powell in 1908 to encourage boys to become enterprising members of society. Powell founded the Scout Association in Britain. The Boy Scouts of America was founded two years later. The Scouts' motto is *Be Prepared*. The Boy Scouts Association classifies its members into Cub Scouts (for boys aged 8–10), Scouts (11–17), and Explorers (15–20). There are 14 million Scouts throughout the world. The Girl Scouts of America was founded in 1912 by Juliette Low, who modeled the group on the British Girl Guides Association. Girls 6–8 are Brownies, 9–11 are Junior Girl Scouts, 12–14 are Cadettes and 15–17 are Senior Girl Scouts.

Scranton 41 25N 75 40W A city in Pennsylvania. It had a thriving anthracite industry and iron and steel operations until the 1950s. Since then it has shown great initiative in attracting many light industries to the city. It is the site of the University of Scranton (1888). Population (1980): 88,117.

screamer A marsh-dwelling bird belonging to a family (*Anhimidae*; 3 species) occurring in tropical and subtropical South America. 30 in (75 cm) long, screamers have dark plumage, a short hook-tipped bill, two paired wing spurs, and either a crest or a horny protuberance on the head. They feed on water plants and the skin contains air sacs that can produce crackling noises. Order: *Anseriformes* (ducks, geese, etc.).

scree. *See* talus.

screech owl. *See* scops owl.

screw pine A treelike plant of the genus *Pandanus* (about 150 species), native to the Old World tropics. The name derives from the spiral arrangement of the leaves, which leave scars in a corkscrew spiral when they fall. Stout aerial prop roots grow down from the stem into the ground: the part of the stem below these roots decays, so that the plant is supported entirely by the prop roots. The leaves, which are long and stiff with parallel sides, are used for matting and weaving. The flowers grow in large heads enclosed in leafy structures (spathes) and the fruits of some species are edible. Several species are grown as house plants. Family: *Pandanaceae*.

screwworm. *See* blowfly.

Scriabin, Alexander (1872–1915) Russian composer and pianist. His mature compositions were characterized by chords built on the interval of the fourth. His works include three symphonies—the third entitled *The Divine Poem* (1903)—a piano concerto (1894), ten piano sonatas, and *Prometheus* or *The Poem of Fire* (1909–10), intended to be accompanied by a sequence of colored lights projected onto a screen.

scribes (Hebrew: *sofrim*) Ancient Jewish biblical scholars. They preserved the textual tradition of the *Torah and cultivated its study and interpretation. In the Gospels they are frequently linked with the *Pharisees. In later Jewish usage the term applies to copyists of the Torah and other sacred texts.

Scriblerus club An English literary club founded in about 1713. Its members included *Pope, *Swift, *Gay, and John *Arbuthnot. In their collaborative *Memoirs of Martinus Scriblerus* (1741) they ridiculed literary pretentiousness.

scrofula Ulceration of a lymph node infected with *tuberculosis, seen most commonly in the neck. This form of tuberculosis is now uncommon in developed countries but is still seen in poorer countries. Treatment is with antibiotic drugs and surgery. It was formerly known as king's evil, as it was believed that the touch of the sovereign would cure it.

scrub Vegetation consisting mainly of short evergreen often aromatic shrubs, typically found in coastal regions with hot dry summers: the Mediterranean maquis and the Californian chaparral are examples. This type of vegetation is transitional between grasslands and forests. The shrubs are adapted to survive dry summers and usually flower and fruit in the spring.

scrub bird A rare Australian passerine bird belonging to a primitive family (*Atrichornithidae*; 2 species). Scrub birds are brown with long pointed tails and loud voices, and are poor fliers, feeding on insects and nesting on the ground. The noisy scrub bird (*Atrichornis clamosus*) is about 9 in (22 cm) long and occurs in SW Australia, where it was thought to be extinct until 1961. The smaller rufous scrub bird (*A. rufescens*) is found only in the wet forests of New South Wales.

Scullin, James Henry (1876–1953) Australian statesman; Labor prime minister (1929–1931). The problems of the Depression plagued his administration, his deflationary measures bringing electoral defeat in 1931.

sculpin. *See* bullhead.

SCULPTURE *A cast of one of the relief sculptures of Trajan's Column, depicting Trajan speaking to his soldiers inside a fortified camp. The Column, which was erected in the Roman forum in 113 AD., is 125 ft (38 m) high. Its spiral frieze depicts the emperor's campaigns in Dacia (modern Romania). The detail and crude realism of the many panels are typical of Roman sculpture.*

sculpture The art of shaping or modeling such materials as stone, wood, clay, and metal either in relief (*see* relief sculpture) or in the round. Stone, particularly marble, has been most popular with sculptors since it is the most durable material for outdoor sculptures. Wood is principally associated with *African art and medieval indoor sculptures (*see also* wood carving). Clay is most often employed in preliminary models for sculptures later cast in metal. Of all the metals, bronze has been most favored for casting, although in the 20th century aluminum, iron, and sheet metal have been increasingly used to fabricate sculptural concepts.
Most civilizations have left a legacy of sculpture, the earliest known work being Paleolithic representations of human and animal figures, believed to be of religious significance. More detailed figures, indicating the hierarchy of the social organization, appeared in Egypt in the 3rd millennium BC. The 5th and 4th centuries BC saw the rise of classical Greek sculpture with the work of *Praxiteles, *Phidias, and others. The Romans subsequently developed these classical themes, introducing more personalized portrait sculp-

ture. In India from the 2nd century BC, Japan from the 6th century AD, and China from the 7th century AD, sculpture was devoted primarily to representations of the Buddha and his life. In medieval Europe, sculpture became largely an embellishment of architecture, until the revival of classical ideals in the Italian Renaissance with the works of such major sculptors as *Donatello and *Michelangelo. The spread of Renaissance ideas throughout the rest of Europe led to the work of Jean *Goujon in France and Grinling *Gibbons in England, while baroque sculpture attained its finest expression in the virtuosity of *Bernini. The neoclassicism of the 18th century saw a new respect for ancient Greek models. Outstanding among the sculptors of 19th-century Romanticism was *Rodin. Although the figural tradition has been continued into the 20th century by such sculptors as Marino *Marini and Ernst *Barlach, semiabstract and abstract sculpture, influenced by African and other primitive carving, have become the principal forms of sculptural expression. Semiabstract sculptures include the innovative work of *Modigliani, *Epstein, and Henry *Moore, as well as the geometricized forms of Jacques *Lipchitz and the simplified shapes of Constantin *Brancusi. Abstract or nonrepresentative sculpture includes the organic forms of such sculptors as *Arp and the geometric constructions of Naum *Gabo (*see also* constructivism). Kinetic and environmental sculpture are also specifically 20th-century developments. Kinetic sculptures, i.e. sculptures that move either by motor, magnetism, or air currents, were pioneered by Gabo and Alexander *Calder (*see also* mobiles). Environmental sculpture is the recreation of an environment as in Claes *Oldenburg's work of the 1960s. The principal uses of sculpture have been architectural and commemorative, that is for memorial monuments and tombs.

scurvy A disease caused by deficiency of *vitamin C (which is present in most fresh fruits and vegetables). In the past scurvy was common among sailors on long voyages, but it is now rarely seen except in old debilitated people. The symptoms are weakness and aching joints and muscles, progressing to bleeding of the gums and—later—other organs. Scurvy can be readily treated by giving vitamin C or fresh fruit.

scurvy grass An annual, biennial, or perennial herb of the genus *Cochlearia* (about 25 species), occurring in temperate regions, especially near coasts. Up to 20 in (50 cm) tall, it has simple often heart-shaped leaves and the white or mauve flowers, each with four rounded petals, are borne in small clusters. Family: *Cruciferae*.

Scutari. *See* Shkodër (Albania); Üsküdar (Turkey).

Scylla and Charybdis In Greek mythology, two sea monsters on opposite sides of the Strait of Messina who menaced *Odysseus, the *Argonauts, and other legendary heroes. Scylla was a monster with six heads and a pack of baying hounds, while Charybdis was a raging whirlpool.

Scyphozoa. *See* jellyfish.

Scythians An Indo-European people who temporarily settled in Asia Minor before settling in what is now S Russia in the 6th century BC. The true Scythians, called Royal Scyths, established a kingdom N of the Black Sea and traded wheat for luxury goods with the Greek colonies there. Their skill as horsemen and archers halted Persian and Macedonian invasions but they remained a nomadic people until their disappearance from history during the Gothic onslaughts of the 3rd century AD. Objects recovered from their royal tombs demonstrate their metalworking skill and, especially in the animal designs that predominate as decorations, their artistry.

sea anemone A sedentary marine invertebrate animal belonging to a worldwide order (*Actiniaria*; over 1000 species) of *coelenterates. It has a soft columnar body (*see* polyp) of a few millimeters to about 5 ft (1.5 m) in diameter, with a mouth at the top surrounded by rings of tentacles, which—when expanded—give the animal a flower-like appearance. Sea anemones are usually blue, green, or yellow and are found attached to rocks and weeds or associated with other invertebrates. They feed mainly on fish and other animals. Class: *Anthozoa*.

sea bass A carnivorous fish, also called sea perch, of the family *Serranidae* (about 400 species), found mainly in coastal waters of tropical and temperate seas. Its elongated body ranges up to 12 ft (3.75 m) long and varies in color with the species. They may be active or sedentary and certain species are *hermaphrodite while others, such as *groupers, are able to change sex. Many are valued food and game fish. Order: *Perciformes*. *See also* bass.

Seaborg, Glenn Theodore (1912–) US physicist, who as professor at the University of California has led the search for *transuranic elements. Working with Edwin *McMillan, he produced plutonium in 1940 by bombarding neptunium with neutrons. Working with another group of researchers, Seaborg has prepared samples of all the transuranic elements with atomic numbers from 95 to 105 by similar methods. For this work he shared the Nobel Prize with McMillan in 1951.

sea bream A fish, also called porgy, belonging to a family (*Sparidae*; about 400 species) found mainly in shallow waters of tropical and subtropical seas. It has a deep laterally flattened body covered with large scales, a single long dorsal fin, and well-developed teeth. It lives in shoals and feeds by scraping algae and small animals off rocks.

sea butterfly A *gastropod mollusk belonging to the subclass *Opisthobranchia*, also called pteropod. Some sea butterflies (order *Thecosomata*) have a shell, are filter feeders, and swim by means of winglike appendages (parapodia). Others (order *Gymnosomata*) are naked, with only small parapodia, and prey on small animals.

sea cow. *See* dugong.

sea cucumber A marine invertebrate animal belonging to a worldwide class (*Holothuroidea*; 1100 species) of *echinoderms. Its cucumber-shaped body, 0.8–79 in (2–200 cm) long, is covered with leathery skin containing small calcareous plates or spicules. There is a mouth at one end surrounded by a ring of tentacles, which are used for feeding on detritus and plankton. It crawls sluggishly on the sea bottom or burrows in sand or mud. □oceans.

sea eagle An *eagle belonging to the widely distributed genus *Haliaeetus* (8 species). 28–48 in (70–120 cm) long, sea eagles have a wedge-shaped tail and are typically brown with white markings. The smaller species feed mostly on fish but the larger species eat carrion, large birds, and mammals.

sea fan A colonial *coral of the genus *Gorgonia*, in which the tiny cylindrical *polyps have a horny internal skeleton and grow upon one another to produce a fanlike structure. Sea fans are commonly yellow, pink, brown, or purple and occur mainly in shallow tropical waters.

sea-floor spreading A concept developed in the 1960s that provides a mechanism for *continental drift. Magma rises from the earth's mantle to the surface along midocean ridges (constructive plate margins; *see* plate tectonics), cools to form new oceanic crust, and displaces the older material sideways at an average rate of 1.5 in (4 cm) per year. Magnetic reversals recorded in the rocks in approximately symmetrical strips at each side of the midocean ridges provide strong evidence for sea-floor spreading.

sea gooseberry. *See* ctenophore.

seagull. *See* gull.

sea hare A marine *gastropod mollusk belonging to the family *Aplysiidae*. Growing up to 14 in (35 cm) long, sea hares are often green or yellow in color; they have a pair of tentacles (resembling a hare's ears) and a much-reduced shell. When disturbed, they eject a cloud of purple ink into the water. Subclass: *Opisthobranchia*.

sea holly 1. A perennial herb, *Eryngium maritimum*, found on sandy and pebbly European shores. Growing to a height of 12–24 in (30–60 cm), it has spiked holly-like leaves and bears clusters of purplish-blue flowers. Family: *Umbelliferae*. 2. *See* gulfweed.

sea horse One of several small bony-plated marine □fish of the family *Syngnathidae* (*see also* pipefish), especially the genus *Hippocampus*, that lives in shallow warm waters. They are 1.5–12 in (4–30 cm) long and the horselike head with its long tubular snout is set at an angle to the body. They use the prehensile tail to cling to seaweed and swim in a vertical position by undulating the dorsal fin. The males have a brood pouch in which the young are hatched. Order: *Gasterosteiformes*.

Sea Islands A chain of islands off the coasts of South Carolina, Georgia, and Florida. Production of long-stapled Sea Island cotton was important until infestation by the boll weevil in the 1920s. The islands are popular for vacations.

sea kale A bushy perennial herb, *Crambe maritima*, found on Atlantic coasts of Europe. Growing to a height of 16–24 in (40–60 cm), it has cabbage-like leaves and bears clusters of small white flowers. It may be cultivated for its tender young edible shoots. Family: *Cruciferae*.

seal (sigillography) A stone, metal, or wooden stamp and its impression in wax or lead used to authenticate documents. The engraved surface of a seal is usually rock crystal or other hard stone but bronze and gold are also used. The impression cut into the seal generally consists of a central device of a heraldic or personal motif, surrounded by a legend. Officials' seals are practical in design but other seals, such as desk seals and fob seals (worn as jewels), enable jewelers and goldsmiths to exhibit their skills. **Sigillography** is the study of seals.

seal (zoology) A carnivorous marine mammal belonging to the order *Pinnipedia* (32 species). Seals have a streamlined body with a smooth rounded head and an insulating layer of blubber under the sleek-coated skin. Both pairs of limbs flatten into flippers. They feed mainly on fish and breed on land or ice.

There are two main families: the *Otariidae* (eared seals; 13 species) including fur seals and *sealions, which have external ears and can turn their hind flippers forward for walking on land; and the *Phocidae* (true seals; 18 species), which lack external ears and have trailing hind flippers. The *walrus is the only member of its family, *Odobenidae*.

sea lavender A perennial or annual herb of the genus *Limonium* (about 300 species), found on coasts and salt marshes of W Asia, Europe, and North America. The common sea lavender (*L. vulgare*) has a basal rosette of slender leaves and a branched flower stem, 3.1–12 in (8–30 cm) high, bearing clusters of purple-blue flowers. Family: *Plumbaginaceae*.

sea lettuce A green *seaweed of the genus *Ulva*, found mainly between high and low tide levels on most rocky shores. It has broad flat translucent fronds, which resemble lettuce leaves, and grows in bunches up to about 12 in (30 cm) long. It is rich in iodine and vitamins and is sometimes used in salads and soups.

sea lily. *See* crinoid.

sealion A large *seal belonging to the family *Otariidae*. Californian sealions (*Zalophus californianus*) of the Californian coast are popular circus animals. They grow to 7 ft (2 m) and live in groups with a definite social hierarchy. Steller's sealion (*Eumetopias jubatus*) is the largest species, growing to over 10 ft (3 m).

Sealyham terrier A breed of □dog developed between 1850 and 1891 in Wales, for hunting foxes and badgers. It is sturdily built with short legs, drooping ears, and a short thin tail. White with darker markings, Sealyhams have a soft under coat and a wiry outer coat. Height: 11–12 in (27–30 cm).

sea mouse A marine *annelid worm belonging to a family (*Aphroditidae*) found in North Atlantic coastal waters. Sea mice grow up to 7 in (18 cm) long and 3 in (7 cm) wide with 15 pairs of scales buried in a dense covering of irridescent hairs. They are foraging carnivores and are generally found buried in fine sand or mud with only the hind end protruding. Class: *Polychaeta*.

sea otter A marine *otter, *Enhydra lutris*, of the N Pacific. 4 ft (1.2 m) long and weighing 77 lb (35 kg), it floats in colonies of up to 90 individuals. The cubs, well-furred and with open eyes and sharp teeth, are born in the sea. Sea otters feed on mollusks, crustaceans, and fish and can crack open shells using a pebble balanced on the chest. Once hunted for their valuable fur, they are now a protected species.

sea pen A fleshy colonial marine invertebrate animal belonging to an order (*Pennatulacea*; 300 species) of *coelenterates, especially one forming a feather-like colony (e.g. *Leioptilus*). A central stalklike individual—the primary *polyp—is anchored into mud or sand and secondary polyps branch from it. Class: *Anthozoa*.

Sea Peoples The seafaring tribes who colonized Asia Minor, the Aegean, and N Africa in the 13th and 12th centuries BC, destroying the *Hittite empire. About 1170 they were almost annihilated by Rameses III of Egypt and those that survived scattered—to Palestine, the Aegean, and perhaps to the W Mediterranean. They have been variously and uncertainly identified and may have been Achaeans, Etruscans, or Philistines.

sea perch. *See* sea bass.

Searle, Ronald William Fordham (1920–) British cartoonist. He worked for such journals as the *Sunday Express* and *Punch* but is best known for his cartoon creation of the outrageous schoolgirls of St Trinian's, who subsequently featured in four films.

sea robin. *See* gurnard.

sea sickness. *See* travel sickness.

sea slug A marine *gastropod mollusk of the order *Nudibranchia*. Sea slugs have exposed feathery gills, two pairs of tentacles, and no shell. They browse on sponges, sea anemones, and corals and are often brightly colored. Some sea slugs retain the stinging cells of their prey for their own defense.

sea snake A venomous fish-eating snake belonging to the family *Hydrophiidae* (50 species) occurring mainly in coastal waters of Australasia and SE Asia. Sea snakes are adapted to an underwater life by having a flattened body with an oarlike tail and valvelike closures in the nostrils. Most produce live young (rather than eggs).

sea spider A spider-like marine arthropod of the class *Pycnogonida* (or *Pantopoda*; over 600 species). Its short thin body, 0.12–20 in (3–500 mm) long, usually bears four pairs of walking legs and a long sucking proboscis. Sea spiders occur up to depths of 11,800 ft (3600 m), feeding on soft-bodied invertebrate animals. Fertilized eggs are carried by the males and many larvae are parasitic on polyps or mollusks.

sea squirt. *See* tunicate.

SEATO. *See* South East Asia Treaty Organization.

Seattle 47 35N 122 20W A city in Washington, between Puget Sound and Lake Washington. A port of entry to the Klondike, it became a boom town with the 1897 Alaska Gold Rush. Educational institutions include the University of Washington (1861) and Seattle University (1852). It is Alaska's main supply port. There are large timber mills and various forest-based industries. Other major industries include the manufacture of aircraft, shipbuilding, and ship repair. Population (1980): 493,846.

sea urchin A marine invertebrate animal, belonging to the class *Echinoidea*, with a typically spherical rigid body covered by long movable spines. Sea urchins live on shores and ocean floors and use a complex feeding apparatus—Aristotle's lantern—to masticate algae and other organic material scraped off rocks. Phylum: *Echinodermata* (*see* echinoderm).

sea water The water constituting the world's oceans and seas. It is usually saline, average salinity being about 15 g per lb (35 g per kg) of sea water. The principal dissolved salts are sodium chloride (2.8%), magnesium chloride (0.4%), and magnesium sulfate (0.2%). Where evaporation is high, salinity is increased, as in the Red Sea. Sea water is desalinated (*see* desalination) in some areas, e.g. Saudi Arabia, to obtain fresh water, although the process is costly. The properties of sea water, including its chemical composition, temperature, and movements (waves and tides) are studied in *oceanography.

seaweed Large multicellular red, brown, or green marine *algae that are generally found attached to the sea bed, rocks, or other solid structures by rootlike structures called holfasts. The plants have stemlike stalks and fronds, which may be flat and undivided, threadlike, or branched, sometimes with small air bladders for buoyancy. Seaweeds often occur in dense aggregations along shores but are also found to depths of about 650 ft (200 m). Many are of commercial importance as food (e.g. *carrageen, *laver, and *sea lettuce), as fertilizers, in chemical and pharmaceutical products, etc. *See also* kelp; wrack.

sebaceous glands. *See* skin.

Sebastian, St (3rd century AD) Roman martyr. According to tradition, he was an officer of the Praetorian Guards until his Christianity was discovered by Diocletian. His martyrdom at the hands of archers is a frequent subject of painting. Feast day: Jan 20. Emblem: an arrow.

Sebastiano del Piombo (S. Luciano; c. 1485–1547) Venetian painter. Although he was a pupil of Giovanni Bellini, his early works, notably *St John Chrysostom* (c. 1509; S Giovanni Crisostomo, Venice), were influenced by Giorgione. Moving to Rome in 1511, he painted decorations in the Farnesina with *Raphael, whose *Transfiguration* he directly challenged with his *Raising of Lazarus* (1517–19; National Gallery, London). He was also known as a portraitist; his sitters included Christopher Columbus and Pope Clement VII, who appointed him keeper of the papal seals (*piombi*) in 1531—hence his nickname.

Sebastopol. *See* Sevastopol.

second 1. (s) The *SI unit of time equal to the duration of 9,192,631,770 periods of the radiation corresponding to a specified transition of the cesium-133 atom. The unit was formerly defined by astronomical measurement. *See also* cesium clock; time measurement. **2.** A unit of angle equal to one-sixtieth of a minute.

secondary emission The ejection of electrons from the surface of a metal when it is bombarded with charged particles of sufficient energy. Secondary emission is best observed when the bombarding particles are themselves electrons, which are then known as primary electrons; the ejected electrons are called secondary electrons. In certain metals, as many as ten secondary electrons can be emitted by the impact of one primary electron. The effect is used in such devices as the electron multiplier.

secretary bird A long-legged terrestrial bird of prey, *Sagittarius serpentarius*, that lives in dry uplands of Africa. 48 in (120 cm) tall with a 80 in (200 cm) wingspan, it has a hawklike face and a gray plumage with a long pair of central tail feathers and a black crest of quills behind its head—hence its name. It feeds on snakes and lizards and is the only member of its family (*Sagittaridae*). Order: *Falconiformes* (falcons, hawks, etc.).

Secret Service, United States US division of the Department of the Treasury, charged with law enforcement. Established in 1865, it is responsible for protecting the president and the vice president, and also presidential candidates, the president-elect, and their families. It watches over the Treasury, detecting counterfeiting and guarding the buildings and vaults. Originally established by President Abraham Lincoln to combat counterfeiting, the Secret Service's duties increased through the years.

Securities and Exchange Commission (SEC) US government agency that helps to regulate the securities and financial markets. In the interest of protecting the public and investors, it is charged with keeping the investment public informed of malpractices and irregularities. The commission, consisting of 5 members appointed by the president, oversees the stock exchange and investment and holding companies and also serves as adviser to district courts in connection with reorganization proceedings for debtor corporations. It was created under the authority of the Securities Exchange Act of 1934.

Sedan 49 42N 4 57E A city in NE France, in the Ardennes department on the Meuse River. It was the site of a decisive defeat (1870) for the French in the Franco-Prussian War. Its industries include textiles, metallurgy, and food processing. Population (1975): 25,430.

Sedan, Battle of (September 1, 1870) The battle in the *Franco-Prussian War in which German forces, invading France, surrounded the army of Napoleon III and forced him to surrender with 100,000 men. The French defeat precipitated revolution in Paris (*see* Commune of Paris) and marked the end of the Second Empire.

sedan chair An enclosed single-seater chair carried on poles by two men, one in front and one behind. Sedans probably originated in Italy.

sedatives Drugs that relieve restlessness, anxiety, and tension. Most drugs that depress the activity of the nervous system have this effect (including barbiturates and narcotics), but the most widely used sedatives are the minor tranquilizers, for example *benzodiazepines, as they relieve anxiety without causing sleep and their use carries less risk of dependence. Sedatives are also useful in the treatment of muscular aches associated with tension and stress.

Seddon, Richard John (1845–1906) New Zealand statesman, born in England; prime minister (1893–1906). His government implemented labor-protection measures and introduced old-age pensions and women's suffrage.

sedge A perennial herbaceous grasslike plant of the genus *Carex* (about 2000 species), growing throughout the world, mainly in swampy places. Sedges have solid stems, triangular in cross section, with long narrow leaves and small male and female flowers usually grouped into separate clusters (spikes). The sand sedge (*C. arenaria*), found on the coasts of Europe and North America, has been used to bond sand dunes. Family: *Cyperaceae*.

Sedgemoor, Battle of (July 6, 1685) A battle in England SE of Bridgewater, in which the forces of James II of England defeated the rebellion of his nephew, the Duke of *Monmouth.

sedimentary rock One of the three major categories into which rocks are divided (*compare* igneous rock; metamorphic rock). Sedimentary rocks are deposited mainly under water, usually in approximately horizontal layers (beds). **Clastic sedimentary rocks** are formed from the erosion and deposition of pre-existing rocks and are classified according to the size of the particles. Arenaceous rocks have sand-grade particles and include the sandstones; argillaceous rocks have silt- or clay-grade particles and include siltstones and mudstones; rudaceous rocks, with gravel-grade and larger fragments, include the breccias, conglomerates, etc. Organically formed sedimentary rocks are derived from the remains of plants and animals, for example limestone and coal. Chemically formed sedimentary rocks result from natural chemical processes and include sedimentary iron ores. Many sedimentary rocks show complex internal structures, formed during or after deposition.

Sedum. *See* stonecrop.

Seebeck effect. *See* thermoelectric effects.

seed The reproductive structure formed after pollination and fertilization in higher plants. In flowering plants (angiosperms) the seed begins to develop after the *pollen nucleus has fused with the egg. In gymnosperms (conifers and related plants) the ovule begins dividing before pollination. All seeds contain an embryo and usually a food store, which is mobilized on germination. Angiosperm seeds are surrounded by a seed coat (testa) and contained within a *fruit; gymnosperm seeds are naked (*see* cone). The development of the "seed habit" has given the higher plants a marked advantage over the ferns, mosses, algae, and fungi. Water is not needed for fertilization, and therefore the plants can colonize arid habitats. In addition, seeds—unlike the spores of lower plants—can survive adverse conditions and may remain viable for many years before germinating.

seed fern A *gymnosperm plant belonging to the extinct order *Pteridospermales*, abundant during the Carboniferous and Permian periods (370–240 million years ago). Seed ferns had large fernlike fronds but—unlike ferns—produced seeds, in cuplike structures. They were probably the ancestors of plants that evolved into the angiosperms (flowering plants).

Seeger, Pete (1919–) US folksinger and songwriter, who, with Woody Guthrie, led the US folksong revival in the 1960s. He worked to collect folk songs before becoming a founder of the Weavers singing group. He wrote such songs as "Where Have All the Flowers Gone" and "Kisses Sweeter than Wine." He was also an active conservationist, particularly on the Hudson River.

Seferis, George (Georgios Seferiadis; 1900–71) Greek poet and diplomat. He was influenced by the French Symbolists and by T. S. *Eliot, whose poetry he translated into Greek. His lyrical poetry was published in a number of collections, including *Strophe* (1931) and *Poiimata* (1940). He won the Nobel Prize in 1963.

Seghers, Hercules Pieterzoon (c. 1589–c. 1638) Dutch landscape painter and etcher. His desolate and dramatically lit mountain landscapes influenced *Rembrandt, who owned some of Seghers' works. He is also known for his novel method of etching with colored paper and inks.

Segovia 40 57N 4 07W A city in central Spain, in Old Castile. It has a fine Roman aqueduct that still supplies the city with water, a 16th-century cathedral, and the restored alcázar (citadel). Industries include potteries and flour milling. Population (1970): 41,880.

Segovia, Andrés (1893–) Spanish guitarist. He has played all over the world, reviving the popularity of the guitar as a concert instrument and inspiring composers to write new works for it.

Segrè, Emilio (1905–) US physicist, born in Italy, who shared the 1959 Nobel Prize with Owen *Chamberlain for their discovery in 1955 of the antiproton (*see* antimatter). Segrè was also the first physicist to produce an artificial element, *technetium, by bombarding molybdenum with deuterium nuclei.

Seine River A river in N France. Rising on the Plateau de Langres, it flows mainly NW through Paris to the English Channel, S of Le Havre. It is the second longest river in France, linked by canal with the Somme, Scheldt, Meuse, Rhine, Saône, and Loire rivers. Length: 482 mi (776 km).

seismic belts (*or* seismic zones) The narrow distinct belts on the earth's surface that are subject to frequent earthquakes. They usually follow the line of plate boundaries (*see* plate tectonics), especially along midocean ridges, near young orogenic belts, along island arc systems, and along major *faults.

seismic wave An elastic shock wave emanating from the focus of an *earthquake or explosion. When seismic activity is recorded, several types of wave can be identified: longitudinal P (*primae*) waves and transverse S (*secundae*) waves are small rapid vibrations that come directly through the earth's interior. They form the first and second parts of the preliminary tremor of an earthquake. The main earthquake consists of large slow L (*longae*) waves traveling along the surface. This type of wave is limited to a narrow depth range and can also occur along deeper strata. Its components are Rayleigh waves (after R. J. S. Rayleigh), which are vertical vibrations in the plane of propagation, and Love waves (after A. E. H. Love; 1863–1940), which are horizontal and transverse. The study of seismic waves has provided much of our knowledge of the earth's interior.

seismology The branch of geophysics concerned with the study of *earthquakes: their origin, the waves they produce (*see* seismic wave), their effects, and their distribution. The instruments used are the **seismograph**, which records the magnitude of the oscillations during an earthquake, and the **seismometer**, which detects and records the motions of the earth in a particular direction (usually used in sets of three). In recent years considerable research has gone into the prediction and modification of earthquakes. The study of nuclear explosions has also concerned seismologists, since in many respects they resemble earthquakes. Seismological data has provided the bulk of our knowledge of the earth's interior. It is estimated that an average of 14,000 lives are lost annually through earthquakes.

sei whale A widely distributed *rorqual, *Balaenopteris borealis*, also called sardine whale. Up to 60 ft (18 m) long, it has a dark back, a white belly, and a large dorsal fin.

Sekhmet An Egyptian war goddess, consort of the creator-god Ptah and destroyer of the enemies of Ra. She was usually portrayed as a lioness or with a lion's head.

Sekondi-Takoradi 4 59N 1 43W A port in Ghana, on the Gulf of Guinea. Formerly two separate towns, Sekondi and Takoradi were linked in 1946. Bauxite is exported and industries include food processing. Population (1970): 254,543.

Selaginella A genus of mosslike *pteridophyte plants (about 700 species), also called spike mosses, found mainly in damp tropical forests. They are similar to the related *clubmosses but differ in having scales (ligules) at the bases of the leaves and two kinds of spore capsules (male and female). The prickly clubmoss (*S. selaginoides*) occurs in arctic and N temperate regions. Family: *Selaginellaceae*; class: *Lycopsida*.

Selangor A state in W Peninsular Malaysia, on the Strait of Malacca. It became a British protectorate in 1874. It is the economic center of Malaysia with industry concentrated in the Klang Valley, mainly between Kuala Lumpur and Port Klang; the chief products are tin and rubber. Area: 3167 sq mi (8202 sq km). Population (1980): 1,467,441. Capital: Shah Alam.

Selby 53 48N 1 04W A market city in N England, in North Yorkshire on the River Ouse. It has a famous 12th-century abbey church. Industries include beet-sugar refining, shipbuilding, paper, and chemicals, and development of the rich Selby coalfield is under way (the first mine went into production in 1983). Population (1981): 107,726.

Selective Service Acts US laws requiring military service registration. The Act of 1917 enabled the military to draft 500,000 men between 21 and 30 years old (extended in 1918 to ages 31–40) for the duration of World War I. The Act of 1940 required all men between 21 and 35 years of age to register (extended to age 45 in 1941). After World War II the draft declined and in 1948 another selective service act (later amended) was passed that required all men between 19 and 26 years, who had not previously served, to register and serve. The draft lasted until 1973. A new law in 1980 required registration of all 19- and 20-year-old males and thereafter, whenever a male reached his 18th birthday. Although no draft existed, the purpose was to facilitate mobilization of forces if necessary.

Selene The Greek moon-goddess, daughter of the Titan Hyperion and sister of Helios (the sun) and Eos (dawn). She became identified with the later Greek goddess *Artemis and with the Roman *Diana.

selenium (Se) A chemical element that is a member of the sulfur family and is obtained from sludges produced during electrolytic copper refining. It exists in several forms, including deep-red crystals, but the commonest allotrope is gray. The element has photovoltaic properties and is used in photocells, light meters, and in photocopying machines. It is a semiconductor and is widely used in rectifiers. The hydride (H_2Se) has a very noxious smell and, like other selenium compounds, is very toxic. At no 34; at wt 78.96; mp 423°F (217°C); bp 1266°F (685°C). *See also* selenium cell.

selenium cell A type of *photocell based on the *photovoltaic effect. It consists of a metal disk coated with selenium on top of which is placed a layer of gold or platinum sufficiently thin to transmit light. When light falls on the disk a small current is generated. They are used in exposure meters in cameras, etc.

Seleucids A Middle Eastern dynasty of the Hellenistic age (323–27 BC) founded by *Seleucus I Nicator, the Macedonian general who, after Alexander the Great's death, became governor and then ruler (312) of Babylonia. He extended his kingdom to the frontiers of India in the east and then into Syria in the west but his successors, in the face of Egyptian aggression and internal unrest provoked by the Seleucid promotion of Greek culture, failed to maintain his conquests. *Antiochus the Great (reigned 223–187) briefly restored Seleucid power in the east but could not prevent Rome's Mediterranean expansion. Under *Antiochus IV Epiphanes (175–163) the empire was further weakened by the revolt of the *Maccabees and although they were repressed by *Antiochus VII Sidetes (139–129) his failure to push back the Parthians anticipated the final disintegration of the Seleucid empire. In 64 BC Pompey annexed what was left of it to form the Roman province of Syria.

Seleucus I Nicator (c. 356–280 BC) Macedonian general, who founded the *Seleucid dynasty. After Alexander the Great's death (323) Seleucus became governor and then ruler (312) of Babylonia, taking the title of king in 305. He subsequently conquered Syria, which brought him into conflict with the Ptolemies of Egypt, Asia Minor, and Macedonia before being murdered by Ptolemy Ceraunus (d. 279 BC), the son of Ptolemy I Soter.

self-heal A perennial herb, *Prunella vulgaris*, common in grassland and on waste ground in temperate Eurasia, N Africa, North America, and Australia. 2–12 in (5–30 cm) high, it has tapering leaves and terminal clusters of small, usually violet, flowers. Extracts were formerly used to treat a variety of illnesses. Family: *Labiatae*.

Seljuqs A Turkish dynasty that ruled in E Islam from 1055. During the 10th century the Seljuqs (descended from Seljuq, chief of the Oguz tribes) led bands of migrating Turks into the Islamic world and in 1055 their head, *Toghril Beg, captured Baghdad. The dynasty was at its peak under Toghril Beg and his successors *Alp Arslan and *Malik-Shah, under whom the great vizier *Nizam al-Mulk administered the empire. After the death of Malik-Shah the empire disintegrated into rival kingdoms. His successors in Persia maintained a nominal suzerainty over the other kingdoms until defeated by invaders from central Asia in 1153. In Anatolia the Seljuqs of Rum ruled an important independent kingdom until coming under the domination of the Mongols in 1243.

Selkirk, Alexander (1676–1721) Scottish sailor. He joined the South Sea buccaneers and in 1704, after quarreling with his captain, was voluntarily left on one of the uninhabited Juan Fernández Islands. He was discovered in 1709 by a ship piloted by *Dampier. His experience inspired Defoe's *Robinson Crusoe* (1719).

Selkirk, Thomas Douglas, 5th Earl of (1771–1820) Canadian settler; born in Scotland. He founded a settlement on Prince Edward Island in Canada in 1803 for Scottish immigrants wishing to escape poverty. By 1810 he acquired land, through part ownership by the Hudson's Bay Company, and established the *Red River Settlement (1812), now Winnipeg, Manitoba.

Sellers, Peter (1925–80) British comic actor. He made his name in the 1950s in the radio comedy series *The Goon Show*. His many films include *I'm All Right, Jack* (1959), *The Millionairess* (1961), *Dr Strangelove* (1963), *What's New, Pussycat?* (1965), *The Pink Panther* series (1963–77), and *Being There* (1980).

Selznick, David O(liver) (1902–65) US film producer. In 1936 he formed his own production company and produced *A Star Is Born* (1937) and *Gone with the Wind* (1939) among other films. Many of his later films, including *Duel in the Sun* (1946) and *A Farewell to Arms* (1957), starred Jennifer Jones (1919–), his second wife.

semantics Broadly, the branch of philology concerned with the study of the relationship between words and meanings. The study of signs and their relationships to the things or concepts that they signify is also called semiotics or semiology and has application in mathematical logic and in the philosophy of language. Semantics as the study of meaning in individual words is part of *linguistics, but there are philosophical problems involved in trying to account for the relationship between words and the objects they refer to, particularly when a theory is extended to cover words that have no concrete referent (e.g. "honesty"). A distinction is often made between literal (or cognitive) meaning and associative meaning, and many linguists believe that the meaning of words can be broken into constituents by means of analyzes similar to those used by *Chomsky to derive the surface structure of sentences from their deep structure. Some linguistic philosophers, such as *Wittgenstein in his later period and J. L. *Austin, account for word meaning not in terms of logical structures but rather according to the speaker's intention in using a word or utterance. However, logical analysis is widely accepted in explaining the aspect of meaning that is a function of grammatical structure, i.e. sentence meaning is seen as a matter of internal relationships among the words, word particles, and phrases involved.

semaphore 1. A visual method of communication between ships at sea, used mainly by warships wishing to maintain radio silence, and consisting of a pattern of signaling by the use of two flags, held by a signalman, their relative positions symbolizing an alphabetical or numerical character. 2. A mechanical railroad signaling device, consisting of a steel arm the position of which is changed by a signalman or by the tripping of a release by a passing train.

Semarang 6 58S 110 29E A port in Indonesia, in central Java on the Java Sea. A commercial center with textile and shipbuilding industries, it exports sugar, rubber, coffee, kapok, and copra. The port is sometimes disrupted by the monsoon. Its university was established in 1960. Population (1971): 646,590.

Semele In Greek mythology, the daughter of *Cadmus, King of Thebes. She was killed by lightning when her lover Zeus appeared to her in his divine form but her unborn child, the god *Dionysus, was saved.

semen. *See* sperm; testis.

semiconductor A crystalline material in which the electrical conductivity increases with temperature and is between that of a conductor and an *insulator. The conductivity is also sensitive to minute quantities of impurities in the crystal lattice (▢energy band). Some (donor) impurities increase the number of negative charge carriers (electrons), creating what is known as an n-type semiconductor. Other (acceptor) impurities increase the number of positive charge carriers (holes), creating a p-type semiconductor. The introduction of these impurities is called doping. *Solid-state electronic components, such as diodes, *transistors, and *integrated circuits depend on the properties of junctions between p-type and n-type regions in the same piece of semiconductor crystal (p-n junctions). Metal oxide semiconductor (MOS) devices also use the properties of a thin layer

of insulating oxide on the semiconductor surface. The element silicon is now the most widely used semiconducting material. Others are germanium, now used only for special applications, and gallium arsenide, which is used in high-speed logic circuits and microwave equipment.

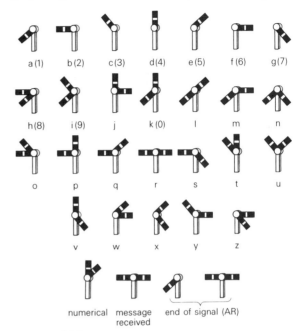

SEMAPHORE

semiconductor diode A *solid-state electronic device with two electrodes. It consists of a single p-n junction (*see* semiconductor). When the p-region is at a more positive voltage than the n-region (forward bias), the current flow increases exponentially as the voltage rises. In reverse bias, very little current flows until a sufficiently high reverse voltage has built up to cause breakdown; the current then increases sharply. The diode is, therefore, commonly used as a rectifier. The **Zener diode** is designed to break down at a specific reverse bias voltage, above which the voltage across it remains effectively constant. The higher the doping levels on both sides of the junction, the lower the breakdown voltage. It is used as a voltage regulator.

Semiconductor diodes, which have largely replaced thermionic diodes, are also used to generate microwaves by the *Gunn effect, to detect light in *photocells, and to emit light in low-voltage displays. The latter, called **light-emitting diodes** (LEDs), are widely used in calculators and digital watches. They emit radiation (light) when holes and electrons combine, the color of the light depending on the material of the crystal.

Seminole A group of North American Indians related to the *Creeks, who speak a Muskogean language. In the late 18th century they migrated from Georgia to Florida, where, in several wars, they resisted domination by the government. They developed a simple hunting and fishing culture suited to the conditions of the region.

Seminole War (1835–42) Second US-Seminole Indian conflict. Protesting US expansion, slave policies, and treaty injustices, the Seminoles, led by *Osceola and others, employed guerrilla-warfare tactics against the larger superior US forces. The long frustrating war ended victoriously for the government in 1842; most of the Seminole Indians were relocated to Indian Territory in the west. *See also* Seminole.

semiotics (*or* semiology) *See* semantics.

Semipalatinsk 50 26N 80 16E A city in the Soviet Union, in the NE Kazakh SSR on the Irtysh River. Its name means "seven palaces" and refers to the nearby remains of seven ancient stone structures. Meat packing, food processing, and metalworking are among its industrial activities, and it is an important communications center. Population (1981 est): 291,000.

semipermeable membrane A material that allows certain molecules in a fluid to pass through it but not others. It will usually permit solvent particles to pass but not the solute molecules. It thus creates *osmosis when placed in a suitable fluid. Examples of semipermeable membranes include cell walls and parchment.

Semiramis A legendary queen of Assyria, who, with her legendary husband Ninus, was the alleged builder of *Babylon and, after his death, ruler of a vast empire extending to India.

Semites A group of peoples, including the *Jews and *Arabs, said in the Bible to be descended from Shem, Noah's eldest son. The Babylonians, Assyrians, Canaanites, and Phoenicians were ancient Semitic peoples.

Semitic alphabets The earliest known truly alphabetic writing systems, developed among the Semitic peoples of the E Mediterranean around 2000 BC. From them all the major alphabets of today are derived: the south Semitic version gave rise to the modern Amharic script of Ethiopia; from North Semitic were derived Greek (and from Greek came the Roman, *Cyrillic, *runic, and other alphabets), Phoenician, and Aramaic (from which came the scripts of Hebrew, Arabic, and *Devanagari in India). The earliest records in North Semitic date from around 1300 BC and indicate that it was a purely consonantal system of 22 letters, generally written from left to right.

Semitic languages A subgroup of the *Hamito-Semitic language family spoken in a large area of N Africa, extending through Palestine to the SW corner of Asia. The Semitic languages originated in Mesopotamia in the 3rd millennium BC and are recorded in Sumerian *cuneiform inscriptions. There are three subgroups recognized by language scholars, although, in comparison to other language groups, these subdivisions are very similar to each other in structure and vocabulary. NW Semitic consisted of Ugaritic, Canaanite, and *Aramaic, all now extinct. From these are descended Phoenician and *Hebrew, the only living language of this subgroup. NE Semitic, the second subgroup, consisted of Assyrian and Babylonian, both now extinct. The third group, S Semitic, is that from which modern *Arabic and Maltese are descended, as well as Amharic (see Amhara) and Tigrinya, the language of Eritrea.

semolina Fine grains of durum wheat used in the manufacture of *pasta and also for making milk puddings.

Senanayake, D(on) S(tephen) (1884–1952) Ceylonese statesman; the first prime minister (1947–52) of Ceylon (now Sri Lanka). In 1919 he helped to found the Ceylon National Congress and campaigned for the introduction of legal and constitutional reforms by the British Government. His son **Dudley Senanayake** (1911–73) was prime minister (1952–53, 1960, 1965–70).

Senate In ancient Rome, the state council. During Republican times the Senate was largely composed of ex-magistrates and, although its role was primarily to advise the magistrates, it carried much weight, especially in foreign policy, finance, and religion. Under the Empire membership of the Senate became largely hereditary and its chief function was to ratify imperial decisions. *See also* curia.

Senate of the United States Upper chamber of the Congress. Its 100 members consist of two senators from each state who are elected by popular vote and serve six-year terms, staggered so that about one third of the Senate is elected every two years. A candidate for the Senate must be at least 30 years old, a US Citizen for nine years, and a resident of the state represented. The US vice-president is president of the Senate; the *president pro tempore is chosen by his colleagues and presides in the absence of the Senate president. The majority leader, elected by majority party members and assisted by the majority whip, directs and coordinates the daily routine of the Senate. Besides approving Congressional acts, the Senate is empowered to ratify treaties (by a two-thirds vote) and to approve or reject appointments made by the US president. It also hears impeachment trials, which are initiated by the *House of Representatives.

Sendai 38 16N 140 52E A city in Japan, in NE Honshu. It is the largest city of N Japan and an important commercial center. Tohoku University was established here in 1907. Population (1980): 665,000.

Seneca North American Iroquoian-speaking Indian tribe, part of the *Five Nations, found in central New York. Hunters, traders, and warriors, the men generally left the agricultural activities to the women. They sided with the British during the American Revolution. Descendants of the Seneca live in New York and Ontario, Canada.

Seneca Falls Convention (1848) US woman suffrage meeting at Seneca Falls, NY Led by Elizabeth Cady *Stanton and Lucretia Coffin *Mott, women began their movement for equal rights. Their Declaration of Sentiments, consisting of 11 resolutions, included the adoption of women's voting rights.

Seneca the Elder (Marcus Annaeus Seneca; c. 55 BC–c. 41 AD) Roman rhetorician, born at Córdoba (Spain). Parts of his work on oratory, ad-

dressed to his sons, have survived: the *Suasoriae* (a compendium of styles and themes of earlier rhetoricians) and the *Controversiae* (imaginary court cases). One of his sons, **Seneca the Younger** (Lucius Annaeus Seneca; c. 4 BC–65 AD), was an author and politician. His career at court, interrupted by exile (41–49 AD), culminated in his appointment as tutor and later chief minister to *Nero. Retiring in 64 AD as a millionaire, he was accused of treason and forced to commit suicide. 13 philosophical treatises and numerous essays disguised as letters advocate *Stoicism in a highly rhetorical style. His nine tragedies, which influenced the Elizabethan dramatists, also survive.

Seneca Lake A long, narrow lake in W central New York, one of the Finger Lakes. It is connected to the New York State Barge Canal system by the Seneca River on the N. Area: 67 sq mi (174 sq km).

Senefelder, Aloys (1771–1834) German playwright and engraver, born in Prague and famous for his invention (1798) of lithography (*see* printing) after accidentally discovering (1796) the possibilities of drawing with greasy chalk on wet stone.

Senegal, Republic of A country in West Africa, on the Atlantic Ocean. The Senegal River forms its N boundary and the Gambia River flows E–W through the country to the border of The Gambia, which forms an enclave within Senegalese territory. Senegal consists chiefly of level plains rising to a dissected plateau in the SE. The majority of the population are Wolof, Sere, and Tukolor. *Economy*: chiefly agricultural, the production of groundnuts being dominant. Other crops include millet, rice, and corn; livestock is important and fishing is being developed with foreign aid. Phosphates, iron ore, and offshore oil and natural gas have been found in significant quantities. Hydroelectricity is a valuable source of power. Industry, mainly concentrated on Dakar, includes cement, food processing, and textiles; tourism is expanding. The main exports are phosphates, groundnuts, and preserved fish. *History*: in the 14th and 15th centuries the area was part of the Mali empire. St Louis was founded in 1659 by the French, who extended their control in the mid-19th century over most of the region. The country achieved self-government in 1958 as a member of the French Community and in 1959–60 briefly formed the Federation of Mali with Sudan. Senegal became a separate independent republic in 1960, with Léopold Senghor as its first president. In 1966 all parties except the Senegalese Progressive Union (UPS) were made illegal but in 1976 the existence of up to three parties was permitted. In 1982 it formed the Senegambia Confederation with Gambia, with each country retaining its independence but having joint defense, foreign, and monetary policies. President: Abdou Diouff (1935–). Official language: French. Official currency: CFA (Communauté financière africaine) franc of 100 centimes. Area: 76,320 sq mi (197,722 sq km). Population (1983 est): 6,335,000. Capital and main port: Dakar.

Senegal River A river in West Africa. Rising in the Fouta Djallon highlands in N Guinea, it flows mainly NW to the Atlantic Ocean forming part of the Mauritania–Senegal border. Length: 1050 mi (1690 km).

Senghor, Léopold Sédar (1906–) Senegalese statesman; president (1960–80). Educated in France, he was Senegalese deputy to the French National Assembly (1946–58). He formed the Senegalese Progressive Union, which took Senegal to independence in 1960. He is also a poet, the author of *Chants d'ombres* (1945), *Ethiopiques* (1956), and *Nocturnes* (1961).

senna. See Cassia.

Sennacherib (d. 681 BC) King of Assyria (704–681); the son and successor of *Sargon II. After 16 years of leniency toward the constantly rebellious Babylonians he sacked the city of Babylon in 689. He also crushed an Egyptian-inspired revolt of Palestine led by *Hezekiah. A patron of art and learning, he restored *Nineveh. Murdered by one of his sons, probably incited by Babylonian rebels, he was succeeded by *Esarhaddon.

Sennar 13 31N 33 38E A city in the SE Sudan, on the Blue Nile River. It is the site of the Makwar Dam (completed 1925), a part of the *Gezira irrigation system. Population (1972 est): 10,000.

Sennett, Mack (Michael Sinott; 1884–1960) US film producer and director, born in Canada. In 1912 he joined the Keystone Company, for which he produced numerous short slapstick films featuring the *Keystone Kops and such comic actors as Charlie Chaplin and Harold Lloyd.

Sens 48 12N 3 18E A city in central France, in the Yonne department on the Yonne River. The site of one of the earliest gothic cathedrals in France, its manufactures include agricultural implements, leather products, and chemicals. Population (1975): 27,930.

sensitive plants. *See* Mimosa.

sentimental novel A type of fiction popular in 18th-century England and France in which scenes of emotional distress were intended to arouse the reader's pity and compassion. Examples include *Manon Lescaut* (1731) by the Abbé *Prévost and *Pamela* (1740) by Samuel *Richardson.

Seoul 37 30N 127 00E The capital of the Republic of (South) Korea, in the NW on the Han River near the coast. The capital of Korea since 1394, the city served as the center of Japanese-occupied Korea (1910–45). It suffered considerable damage in the Korean War (1950–53). It is a rapidly developing industrial as well as administrative and commercial center. Its 16 universities include the Seoul National University (1946). Population (1975): 6,889,470.

sepak takraw A three-a-side ball game similar to *badminton and *volleyball, played in SE Asia. The ball may be played with the feet and other parts of the body but not the hands.

separation of powers The division of governmental powers between legislature, executive, and judiciary. Such separation is most clearly seen in the institutions established by the US *constitution, in the drafting of which separation of powers was seen as the best way to safeguard liberty and the risk of ineffective government seemed preferable to governmental despotism. These institutions are the Congress (legislature), presidency (executive), and Supreme Court (judiciary). One branch is not permitted to encroach on the domain of another.

Sephardim (Hebrew *Sepharad*: Spain) Jews who went to Spain and Portugal in the *diaspora. When the Jews were expelled from Spain in 1492 they spread to many parts of the world, preserving their customs and their language, *Ladino. The term is now sometimes applied, especially in Israel, to all non-*Ashkenazim.

September Ninth month of the year. Derived from the Latin word *septus*, which means seven, it was the seventh month of the ancient Roman calendar. It has 30 days. The zodiac signs for September are Virgo and Libra; the flowers are morning glory and aster, and the birthstone is the sapphire. In the US, Labor Day is celebrated on the first Monday of the month.

septicemia. *See* blood poisoning.

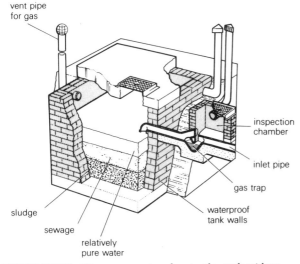

vent pipe for gas

inspection chamber

inlet pipe

gas trap

waterproof tank walls

sludge

sewage

relatively pure water

SEPTIC TANK *The sewage enters low in the tank without disturbing the contents. Purer water separates at the top and sludge forms at the bottom.*

septic tank A large tank of steel or concrete sunk in the ground to provide *sewage disposal for isolated buildings or small communities. Effluent flows into the tank, the settled sludge being decomposed to a certain extent by bacterial action.

Sept Îles 50 13N 66 22W A city and port in E Canada, in Quebec on the Gulf of St Lawrence. Founded in 1650, it developed with the construction of a railroad to large iron-ore mines in the interior (1950). Population (1976): 30,617.

Septuagint (Latin: seventy) A Greek translation of the *Old Testament and *Apocrypha made for the use of Greek-speaking Jews in Egypt and improved and completed in stages between the 3rd century BC and the 1st century AD. It derives its name and symbol (LXX) from the legend that 72 Jewish scholars completed the work in 72 days. Many Old Testament quotations in the New Testament are taken from it.

sequence An ordered set of numbers, generally denoted by a_1, $a_2, \ldots a_r, \ldots$, in which the rth term a_r can be expressed as a function of r. *See also* series.

sequoia Either of two Californian coniferous trees, the *redwood (*Sequoia sempervirens*), which is the world's tallest tree, or the giant sequoia, *Sequoiadendron giganteum* (formerly *Sequoia gigantea*). The giant sequoia forms natural forests in California's Sierra Nevada, where some trees are over 3000 years old, with a height of over 262 ft (80 m) and a girth of over 79 ft (24 m). In Europe it is grown as an ornamental. The red-brown bark is soft and fibrous and the shoots are densely covered with pointed scalelike leaves. The woody brown egg-shaped cones are 2–3.1 in (5–8 cm) long. Family: *Taxodiaceae*.

Sequoia National Park A national park in central California, SE of Fresno. In the Sierra Nevada, the park includes Mt Whitney (14,494 ft; 4418 m), the highest mountain in the contiguous United States. Established in 1890, the park protects the giant sequoia trees that grow on the slopes of the mountains. Area: 386,863 acres (156,563 hectares).

Serang. *See* Ceram.

seraphim. *See* cherubim and seraphim.

Serapis A god combining Greek and Egyptian elements, introduced into Egypt by *Ptolemy I in order to unite the worship of the two peoples. He was the lord of the universe and was identical with *Osiris, with characteristics borrowed from *Zeus and *Asclepius. The center of his cult was Alexandria.

Serbia (Serbo-Croat name: Srbija) A constituent republic of Yugoslavia, incorporating the autonomous regions of Vojvodina and Kosovo. It is chiefly mountainous, descending in the N to the basin of the Danube River. Agriculture is of major importance, especially stock raising and the growing of wheat, maize, and vines. It possesses important mineral deposits including copper (at Bor), antimony, coal, and chrome. *History*: first settled by the Serbs in the 7th century AD, it later came under Turkish control (1389–1804), finally regaining its independence in 1878. It played a major role in events leading up to World War I: in 1914 Austria accused Serbia of direct involvement in the assassination of Archduke Francis Ferdinand and subsequently declared war. Serbia suffered badly during the war, losing about 23% of the population. In 1918 it became part of the kingdom of Serbs, Croats, and Slovenes, later renamed Yugoslavia. Area: 49,528 sq mi (128,278 sq km). Population (1971): 8,446,591. Capital: Belgrade.

Serbo-Croat The language of the Serbs and Croats of Yugoslavia, where it is the most widely spoken language. Serbian and Croatian differ only marginally in terms of vocabulary and not at all in grammar but Serbian is written in *Cyrillic and Croatian in Latin script. The standard literary form is based on a central dialect known as Shtokavian. Written texts date from the 12th century.

serf An unfree peasant of the middle ages. Serfdom was characteristic of the manorial economic system (*see* manor). A serf was bound to the soil he tilled, paying his lord a fee and providing service in return for the use of his land. Serfs had their own homes, plots, and livestock and enjoyed customary rights that distinguished them from slaves (*see* slavery). While serfdom declined in W Europe in the late middle ages, it was strengthened in E Europe, where it was only abolished in the 19th century.

Sergius of Radonezh, St (1314–92) Russian monk, who founded the monastery of the Holy Trinity (now called Zagorsk) in the forest of Radonezh near Moscow. It became a famous spiritual and missionary center, helping to re-establish monasticism after the disruption caused by the invading Tatars. Feast day: Sept 25.

serialism (*or* twelve-tone music) A method of composing music using all 12 notes of the chromatic scale equally, invented by Arnold Schoenberg in the 1920s. Schoenberg sought an alternative to *chromaticism and *atonality by using a fixed sequence of 12 notes (called a **series** or tone row) as a source of melody and harmony. The series could be transposed so as to begin on any degree of the scale and could also be inverted and used in a retrograde form. In strict serialism no single note of the row could be repeated until the other 11 had occurred in melody or harmony; Schoenberg himself did not always follow this rule.

In place of traditional *harmony he developed chords built on fourths. Schoenberg's pupils (Webern, Berg, and others) adopted serialism, although sometimes in a modified form.

In **total serialism** musical elements, such as rhythmical figurations, degrees of volume, and types of tone color are classified in strict serial form. Such composers as Berio and Boulez have used this technique.

seriema A bird belonging to a family (*Cariamidae*; 2 species) occurring in dry grassland regions of South America. The crested seriema (*Cariama cristata*) is 24 in (60 cm) tall and has a brown plumage with pale underparts and a red bill and legs. Seriemas feed on insects, snails, reptiles, and berries. Order: *Gruiformes* (cranes, rails, etc.).

series The sum of the terms in a *sequence, written as $a_1 + a_2 + a_3 + \ldots a_r + \ldots$. The partial sum to the nth term is denoted by S_n. A series is convergent if S_n approaches a particular value as n increases and divergent if it increases without limit. A geometric series has the general form $a + an + an^2 + \ldots$, where a and n are constant. It is convergent if n is less than one, divergent if n is greater than or equal to one. A power series has the general form $a_0 + a_1x + a_2x^2 + a_3x^3 + \ldots$, where x is a *variable. *See also* arithmetic progression.

serin The smallest European *finch, *Serinus serinus*, closely related to the canary and having a sweet trilling song. Serins have a streaked olive-colored plumage with a bright-yellow rump and, in the male, a yellow head and breast. Although a southern species, its range extends to N Europe.

serotine bat An insect-eating *bat, *Eptesicus serotinus*, of Eurasia. It is about 5 in (12 cm) long including the tail and has a 14 in (35 cm) wingspan. Dark brown in color, it flies at early dusk and dawn. Family: *Vespertilionidae*.

serotonin (*or* 5-hydroxytryptamine) A compound, synthesized from the amino acid tryptophan, that occurs in certain nerve endings of the *hypothalamus (in the brain) and the autonomic nervous system. It is involved in the regulation of emotion; such drugs as LSD affect mood and behavior by altering serotonin levels in the brain.

serow A hoofed mammal, *Capricornis sumatraensis*, inhabiting wooded mountainous regions of S Asia. About 35 in (90 cm) high at the shoulder, serows have short wrinkled horns and a coarse black or reddish-gray coat with white patches on the face and legs. Serows and *gorals are sometimes called goat antelopes. Family: *Bovidae*.

serpentine A group of minerals consisting mainly of hydrous magnesium silicates, with a layered structure. They are usually green or white, and often streaked or mottled like a snake's skin. The two main varieties are chrysotile (fibrous, used in the manufacture of asbestos) and antigorite (platy). They occur in basic and ultrabasic igneous rocks from the breakdown of olivines and pyroxenes. **Serpentinite** is a rock consisting mainly of serpentine, formed by the hydrothermal alteration of ultramafic rocks; some are quarried for ornamental stone.

serpulid A small marine *annelid worm belonging to the family *Serpulidae*. Serpulids build limy tubes on stones and seaweed and extend a crown of tentacles to feed in the same way as the related *fanworms. Class: *Polychaeta*.

serum The fluid that remains after blood has been allowed to clot. It can be obtained by centrifuging clotted blood and is similar in composition to plasma, except that it lacks the factors, such as fibrinogen, that are involved in blood clotting.

serum sickness Illness resulting from an allergic reaction to injected serum or antiserum. It is seen most commonly following the injection of horse tetanus antitoxin. 6 to 12 days after the injection the patient develops fever, a rash, and painful joints. Treatment is with steroids.

serval A slender long-legged *cat, *Felis serval*, of the African bush. It is about 4 ft (1.25 m) long including the tail (1 ft; 30 cm) and has large ears and a spotted coat. Servals hunt birds and small mammals, such as hares and duikers, mainly at night.

Servetus, Michael (Spanish name: Miguel Serveto; 1511–53) Spanish theologian and physician, who discovered that the blood circulates to the lungs from the right chamber of the heart. Working chiefly in France, he published several treatises attacking the orthodox doctrine of the Trinity. These incurred the hostility of both Roman Catholics and Protestants and, while hiding from the Inquisition in Geneva, he was arrested by Calvin and burned as a heretic.

Service, Robert William (1874–1958) Canadian writer and poet; born in England. He emigrated to Canada in 1894 and then traveled in W Canada and the US. During World War I he worked as a correspondent and ambulance driver and was in the Canadian Army. After the war he lived in France, returning to Canada only during World War II. His poetry is collected in *Songs of a Sourdough* (also known as *The Spell of the Yukon*; 1907), *Rhymes of a Rolling Stone* (1912), and *Ballads of a Red Cross Man* (1917). His novels include *The Roughneck* (1923) and *The House of Fear* (1927). His two most popular poems are "The Shooting of Dan McGrew" and "Cremation of Sam McGee."

service tree A tree, *Sorbus domestica*, about 5 ft (15 m) high, native to S Europe, W Asia, and N Africa and commonly grown for ornament. Related to the *mountain ash, it has compound leaves of 11–21 leaflets and its small green fruits are used for making wine. The wild service tree (*S. torminalis*) has simple lobed leaves, while the bastard service tree is an ornamental hybrid between the mountain ash and the *whitebeam. Family: *Rosaceae*.

sesame An annual herb, *Sesamum indicum*, cultivated in Central and South America, the Middle East, and SE Asia. Several varieties are known, growing 20–98 in (50–250 cm) high and bearing small purplish flowers. The seeds are used in confectionery and as food flavoring. Oil extracted from the seeds is used as a cooking and salad oil and in margarines and other products; the residue (sesame cake) is used as cattle feed. Family: *Pedaliaceae*.

Sesostris I King of Egypt (c. 1971–1928 BC) of the 12th dynasty. He extended Egyptian rule into Nubia, exploiting its mineral resources. His ambitious building projects include a magnificent funerary complex at Lisht.

Sesostris II King of Egypt (c. 1897–1878 BC) of the 12th dynasty. He began the land-reclamation works in El *Faiyum continued by *Amenemhet III. Excavations at the town he founded, al-Lahun, have produced much valuable evidence about this period.

Sesostris III King of Egypt (1878–1843 BC) of the 12th dynasty. The sudden cessation of the construction of the nobles' extravagant tombs and an evident rise in middle-class prosperity indicate great changes in Egyptian society during his reign. Sesostris extended his control of Nubia as far south as Wadi Halfa.

Sesshu (Sesshu Toyo; 1420–1506) Japanese landscape painter. After a visit to China (c. 1467) he introduced into Japan the Chinese techniques of monochrome ink painting on long scrolls.

Sessions, Roger (1896–1985) US composer. A pupil of Ernest Bloch, he has held several teaching posts in the US. From 1925 to 1933 he lived mainly in Germany and Italy. His works include two operas, *The Trial of Lucullus* (1947) and *Montezuma* (1962), eight symphonies, a violin concerto, a piano concerto, and chamber music, including *When the Lilacs Last in the Dooryard Bloom'd*.

Set An Egyptian deity. Originally a sun and sky god, he was the murderer of his brother *Osiris and so came to represent all evil. He was killed by *Horus, son of Osiris. He is usually portrayed as a composite figure with various animal features.

Sète (former name: Cette) 43 25N 3 43E A major port in S France, in the Hérault department on the Gulf of Lions. Established in 1666, it developed as the terminus of the Canal du Midi and today has shipbuilding, oil-refining, metallurgical, and fishing industries. It is the birthplace of Paul Valéry. Population (1975): 40,179.

Seton, (Saint) Elizabeth Ann (1774–1821) US religious leader and teacher. A convert to Roman Catholicism (1805) after the death of her husband, she founded a Roman Catholic girls' school in Baltimore, Md., in 1809 and is credited with starting the US parochial school system. With a group of women from the school, she organized the Sisters of Charity (1812), the first American order of nuns, whose activities were mainly teaching and performing charitable works. She was canonized in 1975.

Seto-Naikai. *See* Inland Sea.

Seton, Ernest Thompson (1860–1940) US naturalist and writer, born in England. His experiences as a hunter in Canada were the foundation for his many books about animals, notably *Wild Animals I Have Known* (1898). He was actively concerned with conservation and was a founder of the Boy Scouts of America.

setter One of three breeds of sporting □dog with a lean deep-chested body and drooping ears. Setters are named for their habit of squatting flat ("setting") after finding game. The English setter has a long white silky coat flecked with darker markings. The heavier Gordon setter is black with chestnut markings, while the Irish, or red, setter has a flat silky chestnut coat. Height: 24–27 in (61–69 cm).

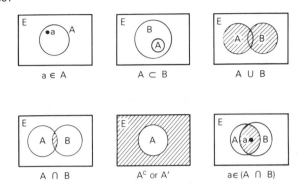

a ∈ A   A ⊂ B   A ∪ B

A ∩ B   Aᶜ or A′   a∈ (A ∩ B)

SET THEORY *Venn diagrams.*

set theory The study, founded by Georg *Cantor, of the logical and mathematical laws of sets. A set is a defined collection of objects or elements; for example the set of odd integers between 0 and 10 is {1, 3, 5, 7, 9}. The empty or null set, denoted by the symbol *0*, has no elements. All sets are contained in the universal set *E*. The relationships between sets can be illustrated in a Venn diagram, named for the British logician John Venn (1834–1923), or shown by symbols. *a ∈ A* means the element *a* is a member of the set *A*. *A ⊂ B* means set *A* is contained in set *B*. *A ∪ B* means the union of *A* and *B*. *A ∩ B* means the intersection of *A* and *B*, i.e. those elements in both. *Aᶜ* or *A′* is the complement of *A*, all elements in *E* but not in *A*.

Settlement, Act of (1701) The act that established the Hanoverian succession to the English throne. In the absence of heirs to William III or Anne, the crown was to pass to James I's granddaughter *Sophia, Electress of Hanover, or to her Protestant descendants. The act stipulated that the monarch must be a Protestant and that foreigners must not hold public office or enter parliament. Anne was succeeded by the first Hanoverian king, George I, in 1714.

Setúbal 38 31N 8 54W A port in SW Portugal, on the Bay of Setúbal. It is an important center for sardine fishing with associated fish-curing industries. Exports include oranges and muscatel wine and grapes. Population (1970): 64,531.

Seurat, Georges (1859–91) French painter, famous for developing neoimpressionism, popularly called *pointillism. Influenced by writings on aesthetics and the color theories of *Delacroix and the chemist Michel-Eugène Chevreul (1786–1889), he based his dots of pure color and static compositions on scientific study. Although he finished only seven paintings in this demanding style, for example the famous *Sunday Afternoon on the Island of the Grande Jatte* (1884–86; Art Institute of Chicago) and *Le Cirque* (1890–91; Louvre), his work was very influential, one disciple being Paul *Signac.

Sevastopol (English name: Sebastopol) 44 36N 33 31E A port in the Soviet Union, in the Crimean *oblast* (region) of the S Ukrainian SSR on the Black Sea. It is a popular seaside resort. *History:* founded in 1783, after Russia's annexation of the Crimea it became an important naval base and, later, a commercial port. It was besieged by the British and French during the Crimean War, falling after 11 months. Population (1981 est): 315,000.

Seven against Thebes In Greek legend, seven champions who fought against Eteocles, who had gained the throne of Thebes after the death of his father Oedipus and refused to relinquish it to his brother *Polyneices when his term as ruler had ended. The seven champions, led by Polyneices, attacked the seven gates of Thebes. Eteocles and Polyneices died at each other's hand. The story is the subject of a play by *Aeschylus. *See also* Antigone.

Seven Deadly Sins Pride, covetousness, lust, envy, gluttony, anger, and sloth. The traditional Christian list was already established by the 6th century and during the middle ages representations of the Seven Deadly Sins were a common feature of art and literature.

Seven Sleepers of Ephesus A legend of seven Christian soldiers who were entombed in a cave while hiding to escape religious persecution under the Emperor Decius in the 3rd century. They slept until the reign of Theodosius II (408–50), who, on hearing their miraculous experience, was converted to belief in the resurrection.

seventeenth parallel The latitude of 17°N and the line of demarcation between North and South Vietnam established by the *Geneva Conference (1954).

Seventh Day Adventists. *See* Adventists.

Seven Weeks' War. *See* Austro-Prussian War.

Seven Wonders of the World The supreme man-made structures of the ancient world. They were the *Pyramids of Egypt, the *Colossus of Rhodes, the *Hanging Gardens of Babylon, the *Mausoleum of Halicarnassus, the statue of *Zeus at Olympia, the temple of *Artemis at Ephesus, and the *Pharos of Alexandria. Only the Pyramids have survived.

Seven Years' War (1756–63) The war between Prussia, Britain, and Hanover on one side and France, Austria, Russia, and Spain on the other. The war had two main aspects: the rivalry between Austria and Prussia for domination of Germany and the struggle between France and Britain for overseas supremacy. The conflict in North America, known as the *French and Indian War, effectively ended French influence. The war was precipitated by Austria's desire to regain Silesia, lost to Frederick the Great of Prussia in the War of the *Austrian Succession, and began with Frederick's invasion of Saxony. Russia's defection (1762) to Prussia enabled Frederick ultimately to emerge victorious and Prussian ascendancy was confirmed by the Peace of Hubertusberg. Overseas, the British despite initial reverses won a series of spectacular victories in India (by *Clive) and Canada (by *Wolfe). By the Treaty of *Paris (1763) Britain was confirmed as the supreme world power.

Severini, Gino (1883–1966) Italian painter, born in Cortona. After training under *Balla, he moved to Paris (1906), where he became a pointillist. In 1910 he signed the futurist manifesto and thereafter his work combined *futurism and *cubism, especially in his nightclub scenes and his few military subjects. He later returned to painting more conventional landscapes and figure studies.

Severn River (Welsh name: Hafren) The longest river in the UK, rising in central Wales and flowing NE and E into England, then S to the Bristol Channel. It is linked by canal to the Thames and Trent Rivers and is spanned near its estuary by the **Severn Bridge**. Length: 220 mi (354 km).

Severus, Lucius Septimius (c. 145–211 AD) Roman emperor (193–211). Severus was governor of Upper Pannonia (S of the Danube) before being proclaimed emperor. He defeated his rival Pescennius Niger in 194 and embarked on a punitive campaign against Pescennius' supporters. He introduced administrative and military reforms at Rome before embarking on a campaign in Britain, where he died.

Severus Alexander (?208–35 AD) Roman emperor (222–35); the adopted son of his predecessor Elagabalus. Severus' mother, Julia Mamaea, murdered Elagabalus to secure Severus' accession. Severus' rule depended upon the army, which construed his attempt to prevent warfare on the German frontier as cowardice, and murdered him and his mother.

Sevier, John (1745–1815) US pioneer and soldier; first governor of Tennessee (1796–1801; 1803–09). He fought in *Lord Dunmore's War and in the *American Revolution where he distinguished himself at the battle of King's Mountain (1780) in Tennessee. He was part of an unsuccessful plan by settlers to establish the separate state of Franklin in 1784. A member of the US House of Representatives from North Carolina (1789–91), he was elected governor of the new state of Tennessee in 1796 and later served again in the US House of Representatives (1811–15).

Sévigné, Marie de Rabutin-Chantal, Marquise de (1626–96) French letter writer. In over 1500 letters, mostly written to her two children after the death of her husband in 1651, she described the social pleasures and intellectual diversions of Parisian society—and life at her country house in Brittany—in a style that became a model for letter writing throughout Europe.

Seville (Spanish name: Sevilla) 37 24N 5 59W A city and port in SW Spain, in Andalusia on the Guadalquivir River. Important during Roman times, it also thrived under the Moors (711–1248) as a cultural center and became a major port with a monopoly of trade with the West Indies in the 16th century. The painters Velázquez and Murillo were born here. There is a university (founded 1502) and one of the world's largest cathedrals (1401–1591). The Easter festival with its procession of floats bearing religious subjects is a notable event. It is an important industrial center, with textiles and engineering; exports include wine, fruit, and olive oil. Population (1974 est): 588,784.

Sèvres porcelain The finest French porcelain, first produced in 1738. Originally at Vincennes, the Sèvres factory moved to near *Versailles in 1756. It always enjoyed royal patronage and by 1759 Louis XV was proprietor. The early products were soft-paste porcelain but from 1768 hard-paste was made. Products were figures, vases, ornaments, and table services with blue, rose Pompadour, yellow, or green grounds richly gilded for royal taste. Now the national porcelain factory, it continues its fine output.

sewage disposal The collection, treatment, and eventual discharge of domestic sewage and industrial waste. Sewers, systems of underground piping, channel the effluent to a sewage-treatment plant. There it is screened to remove solid objects before passing to a primary sedimentation tank, where suspended solids settle out. The liquid then passes through aeration tanks, where the oxygen content is increased by blowing air through it, and a final sedimentation tank before being discharged into rivers, etc. The solids meanwhile enter a sludge digester, a tank in which bacterial action partially eats away the organic material. Following thickening and drying the solid residue is incinerated, spread on the land, or sold as fertilizer. In some coastal areas raw sewage is pumped into the sea untreated.

Seward, William H(enry) (1801–72) US statesman; secretary of state (1861–69). He was governor of New York (1838–41) and a member of the US Senate from 1848, until chosen by President Abraham *Lincoln to be his secretary of state, continuing through Andrew *Johnson's administration. He was an efficient administrator and helped to prevent European support of the Confederacy during the Civil War and to implement *Reconstruction. In 1867 he purchased Alaska from Russia; although ridiculed at the time, he was later vindicated. *See also* Alaska Purchase.

Sewell, Anna (1820–78) British children's writer. A childhood accident left her a semicripple for life. Her only book, *Black Beauty* (1877), is a protest against the cruel treatment of horses, told from the horse's point of view.

sewing machine A device for sewing together pieces of cloth or other materials. The familiar lockstitch machine was invented in the US and patented by Isaac Merrit Singer in 1851. In this machine, a needle with a thread passing through its eye penetrates the cloth from above, a loop being formed below the cloth either by passing a separate thread from a bobbin through the loop or by a rotary hook carrying the loop around a stationary bobbin. A toothed platform moves the material forward in preparation for the next stitch. Sewing machines are powered by hand, treadle, or electric motor and modern machines have facilities for hemming, buttonholing, etc.

sex chromosome A *chromosome that carries the genes for determining the sex of an individual. In humans there are two types of sex chromosomes, called X and Y. The body cells of normal males possess one X and one Y chromosome while those of normal females have two X chromosomes. Human sperm is therefore either "male" or "female" depending on whether it carries an X or a Y chromosome. The sex of the embryo is determined by which type of sperm fertilizes the female egg (which always carries an X chromosome). Abnormal numbers of sex chromosomes cause a range of disabilities, including physical abnormalities, mental retardation, and sterility.

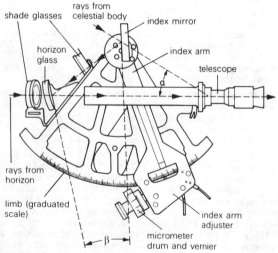

SEXTANT *Angle α measures the angle between horizon and reference arm; β is the angle between index mirror and horizon glass, marked by the angular movement of the index arm along the limb. α = 2β, therefore the graduations on the scale are marked twice the actual angular movement to give the correct altitude reading of the reference star.*

sex hormones Hormones that regulate the growth, development, and functioning of the reproductive organs and determine external sexual char-

acteristics. The major female sex hormones are the *estrogens, *progesterone, and *prolactin while the *androgens are the principal male ones. Their production is regulated by *gonadotrophins from the pituitary gland.

sextant An instrument used primarily in navigation for determining latitudes by measuring the angle subtended by some celestial body to the horizon. Thomas Godfrey of Philadelphia and John Hadley of London, working independently, discovered the sextant's principle in 1730. The graduated metal strip, shaped in an arc of the sixth part of a circle, gave the instrument its name. In use the movable index arm is slid along the scale until the image of the reference star as viewed in the half-silvered index mirror is aligned with the horizon. The reading on the scale then indicates the angle subtended.

sexton beetle. *See* burying beetle.

Seychelles, Republic of A country consisting of 87 widely scattered islands in the W Indian Ocean, NE of Madagascar. The main island is Mahé and others include Praslin, Silhouette, and La Digue; the islands of Aldabra, Farquhar, and Desroches were returned to the Seychelles in 1976. Most of the population is of mixed African and European descent. *Economy*: the chief products and exports are copra and cinnamon bark. Other occupations include fishing and some industry, including tobacco and brewing. Tourism is important and has expanded rapidly since the opening of a new airport (1971). *History*: the uninhabited islands became a French colony in the mid-18th century as a spice plantation. Captured by the British in 1794, they became a dependency of Mauritius from 1814 until 1903, when they became a British crown colony. In 1976 the country became an independent republic within the Commonwealth of Nations, with James Mancham as its first president. While attending the Commonwealth conference in London in 1977, he was overthrown and superseded as president by his prime minister, Albert René. An invasion by mercenaries in 1981, in which South Africa was implicated, attempted to overthrow the government. It was the third attempt by forces from outside the country to seize power. Official languages: English and French; the majority speak Creole. Official currency: Seychelles rupee of 100 cents. Area: 171 sq mi (444 sq km). Population (1983 est): 65,000. Capital and main port: Victoria.

Seyfert galaxy A class of galaxies with exceptionally bright central regions the majority of which are otherwise normal spiral galaxies. Radiation is emitted from the center at radio, infrared, visible, and, especially, X-ray wavelengths, the source of this energy being relatively small. This type of galaxy was first described by the US astronomer C. K. Seyfert (1911–60).

Seymour, Jane (c. 1509–37) The third wife (1536–37) of Henry VIII of England. She had been a lady in waiting to both his former wives, Catherine of Aragon and Anne Boleyn, and married Henry 11 days after Anne's execution. Jane was the mother of Edward VI, dying shortly after his birth.

Sfax 34 45N 10 43E The second largest city in Tunisia and a major port on the Gulf of Gabes. It developed as an early trade center and still fulfills that role today, exporting phosphates, olive oil, cotton and woolen goods, and sponges. Population (1976 est): 475,000.

Sforza An Italian family that ruled Milan from 1450 to 1499, 1512 to 1515, and 1522 to 1535. Originating in Romagna as the Attendoli, its name was changed to Sforza (Italian: force) by the condottiere **Muzio Attendoli** (1369–1424). His son **Francesco Sforza** obtained Milan by his marriage (1441) to Bianca Maria, the only child of Filippo Maria *Visconti. Francesco was succeeded by **Galeazzo Maria Sforza** (1444–76), a notable patron of the arts. Soon after his assassination his brother **Lodovico Sforza** (1452–1508), known as Lodovico il Moro (the Moor), seized power (1480) from Galeazzo's son **Gian Galeazzo Sforza** (1469–94). Lodovico made Milan one of the most powerful Italian states and was also an outstanding patron of artists, including Leonardo da Vinci. He was expelled from the duchy in 1499 by Louis XII of France. After a brief restoration (1512–15), the Sforza were again ousted by the French but in 1522 Lodovico's son **Francesco Maria Sforza** (1495–1535) was re-established by Emperor Charles V. With the failure of the line at Francesco's death, Milan passed to Charles.

's Gravenhage. *See* Hague, The.

Shaba (former name: Katanga) A province in SE Zaïre, bordering on Zambia. Economically and politically the most advanced of the provinces, it was directly involved in the civil war in Zaïre following decolonization by Belgium in 1960 (*see also* Zaïre). It is an extremely important mining area (especially of copper) centered on Kolwezi. Other minerals include cobalt and zinc. Area: 191,878 sq mi (496,964 sq km). Population (1976 est): 3,239,431. Capital: Lubumbashi.

Shache (So-ch'e or Yarkand)   38 27N 77 16E A city in NW China, in Xinjiang Uygur AR on a fertile oasis in the *Tarim Basin. It is an agricultural and trading center on the *Silk Road to Europe. Many handicrafts are produced.

Shackleton, Sir Ernest Henry   (1874–1922) British explorer. He accompanied *Scott's expedition of 1901–04 and on his own expedition in 1908–09 nearly reached the South Pole. In an expedition of 1914–16 his ship, the *Endurance*, was marooned but he and his men reached Elephant Island by sledge and boats. With five others he then journeyed 800 mi (1300 km) to find relief. He died on his fourth expedition.

shad   A food fish, belonging to a genus (*Alosa*) related to herrings, that occurs in the Atlantic, Mediterranean, and North Sea. It has one or a succession of black spots along each side and a notch in the upper jaw. They migrate in large shoals to spawn in fresh waters. The American shad (*A. sapidissima*) occurs from Canada to Florida and has been introduced along the Pacific coast. It reaches a length of 30 in (75 cm). The slightly smaller hickory shad (*A. mediocris*) is also found along the Atlantic coast. The allis shad (*A. alosa*), about 30 in (75 cm) long, and the smaller twaite shad (*A. fallax*) are European species.

shaddock   An evergreen tree, *Citrus grandis*, also called pomelo, native to SE Asia and cultivated in tropical regions of the Old and New Worlds. Growing 20–43 ft (6–13 m) high, it bears pale-yellow oval fruits, with coarse thick skins and bitter-tasting pulp, which are sometimes eaten or used to make liqueurs. Family: *Rutaceae. See also* Citrus.

shadoof   An ancient water-raising device still used, especially in Egypt and S India, for irrigation. It consists of a pole mounted on a pivot with a bucket at one end and a counterbalancing weight at the other.

Shadwell, Thomas   (c. 1642–92) British dramatist. His varied dramatic works included the comedies *Epsom Wells* (1672) and *The Virtuoso* (1676). He sustained a lengthy political and literary feud with *Dryden, who satirized him in *Absalom and Achitophel* (1681) and *MacFlecknoe* (1682). He succeeded Dryden as poet laureate in 1688.

Shaffer, Peter   (1926–) British dramatist. He established his reputation with the domestic drama *Five-Finger Exercise* (1958). His ambitious epic treatment of the Spanish conquest of Peru, *The Royal Hunt of the Sun* (1964), was later filmed and made into an opera. His later plays include *Equus* (1973) and *Amadeus* (1979).

Shaftesbury, Anthony Ashley Cooper, 1st Earl of   (1621–83) English statesman. In the 1650s he sat in Oliver Cromwell's parliaments before participating in the Restoration of Charles II (1660). Becoming chancellor of the exchequer (1661–72), lord chancellor (1672–73), he was a member of the political group called the *Cabal. Dismissed in 1673 he led the movement to exclude the Roman Catholic James, Duke of York (later James II), from the succession. Charged with treason in 1681, the case was dismissed but Shaftesbury fled to Amsterdam, where he died. He was satirized as the Achitophel in Dryden's *Absalom and Achitophel* (1681). His grandson **Anthony Ashley Cooper, 3rd Earl of Shaftesbury** (1671–1713) is best known for his collection of essays, *Characteristics of Men, Manners, Opinions, Times* (1711) on a variety of philosophical and other topics.

Anthony Ashley Cooper, 7th Earl of Shaftesbury (1801–85) was a reformer and philanthropist. He became a member of parliament from 1826 and obtained important reforms in industrial conditions and child labor laws.

shag   A small *cormorant, *Phalacrocorax aristotelis*, confined to rocky coasts and offshore islands of Europe and North Africa. It is 30 in (75 cm) long and has a glossy green-black plumage with a distinct crest in the breeding season. It feeds on fish.

Shah Jahan   (1592–1666) Emperor of India (1628–58) of the Mogul dynasty; the son of *Jahangir. His powerful reign was as ruthless as his means of attaining it; he put his nearest relatives to death in 1628. His passion for fine architecture produced such monuments as the *Taj Mahal and the Delhi Red Fort. He was deposed by his son *Aurangzeb.

Shahn, Ben   (1898–1969) Lithuanian-born US artist, who lived in New York from 1906. He is best known for his social realist and political paintings, notably the series (1931–32) on the Italian anarchists Nicola Sacco and Bartolomeo Vanzetti.

Shah of Iran.   *See* Mohammed Reza Pahlavi; Reza Shah Pahlavi.

Shaka   (c. 1787–1828) Zulu chief, who made the Zulu nation the strongest in S Africa and set the period of warfare called the *Mfecane in motion. Shaka claimed the Zulu chieftainship in about 1816, introduced military reforms, and ruthlessly expanded his possessions. He was stabbed to death by his half-brothers Dingane and Mhlangana.

Shakers   An austere sect originating in England as an offshoot of the *Quakers (1747). Led by Ann Lee (Mother Ann; d. 1784), in whose person they believed the Second Coming of Christ to be accomplished (*see* millenarianism), the Shakers founded a colony in New York and later other communities were established; eventually there were 18 in several states. They flourished until the 20th century. In the 1980s there was disagreement among the few remaining members concerning the disposal of the fortune amassed by the nearly extinct sect. Celibacy, faith healing, common ownership of property, prescribed modes of dress, separation from the world in self-regulating communities, and abstinence from tobacco and alcohol characterized their way of life. Known more formally as the Millennial Church, they received their popular name from their practice of violent trembling in religious ecstasies during their meetings.

WILLIAM   SHAKESPEARE *An engraving by Martin Droeshout, perhaps based on a portrait from life, which was printed in early editions of Shakespeare's works.*

Shakespeare, William   (1564–1616) English dramatist, universally recognized as the greatest English writer. The son of a tradesman who became high bailiff (mayor) of Stratford-upon-Avon in 1568, he was educated at the local grammar school and in 1582 married a local girl, Anne Hathaway, by whom he had three children. Soon afterward he went to London, where he became an actor in the leading theatrical company, the Lord Chamberlain's Men (called the King's Men after 1603). The historical tetralogy comprising the three parts of *Henry VI* and *Richard III* were his first plays (1589–92). His dramatic poems *Venus and Adonis* (1593) and *The Rape of Lucrece* (1594) were dedicated to his patron Henry Wriothesley, 3rd Earl of *Southampton. His *Sonnets* (1609), probably written at this time, betray nothing of his private life despite their themes of love and friendship. His early comedies (1593–95) were *Love's Labour's Lost*, *The Two Gentlemen of Verona*, and *The Taming of the Shrew*. These were followed (1595–1600) by *A Midsummer Night's Dream*, *The Merchant of Venice*, *Much Ado About Nothing*, *Twelfth Night*, and *As You Like It*. During this period he also wrote his first significant tragedy, *Romeo and Juliet*, as well as *Richard II* and *Julius Caesar*. In 1597 he bought New Place, a large house in Stratford, and later became a shareholder in the Globe Theater in London and bought other property in London and Stratford. The two parts of *Henry IV* were completed before *Hamlet*, *Othello*, *King Lear*, and *Macbeth*, his major tragedies, which were written between 1600 and 1606. His final experimental plays, including *The Winter's Tale* (c. 1610) and *The Tempest* (c. 1611), were written for the educated audience of the indoor theater at Blackfriars, which the King's Men had acquired in 1608. In about 1611 he retired to Stratford, where he died. The first collected edition of his works, known as the First Folio and containing 36 plays, was published in 1623. His other plays were: *The Comedy of Errors*, *Titus Andronicus*, *Henry V*, *Antony and Cleopatra*, *Coriolanus*, *Troi-*

lus and Cressida, Measure for Measure, All's Well That Ends Well, Timon of Athens, Pericles, Cymbeline, and (in collaboration with John *Fletcher) *Henry VIII* and *The Two Noble Kinsmen.*

Shakhty 47 43N 40 16E A city in the Soviet Union, in the W RSFSR. Situated in the E Donets Basin, it is a major coalmining center. Population (1981 est): 214,000.

shale A fine-grained *sedimentary rock that splits easily along the closely spaced bedding planes as a result of the alignment of the clay mineral particles parallel to the bedding planes. Shales may disintegrate in water but do not become plastic. They are softer and lighter than *slate.

shallot A hardy perennial herbaceous plant, *Allium ascalonium,* probably of Asiatic origin. Its small hollow cylindrical leaves are often used for dressing food and in salads. Its small angular bulbs occur in garlic-like clusters and are used for flavoring and pickling. Family: *Liliaceae.*

shamanism The religious beliefs and practices common in certain tribal societies of Asia, such as the *Samoyed. The term is also applied to North American Indian practices. The shaman is a tribal priest generally felt to be possessed by a spirit or deity and hence to have supernatural powers. He is liable to trances or ecstasies, may diagnose and cure disease, find lost or stolen goods, or foretell the future. He is usually a source of beneficial (white) magic, able to counteract the effects of evil men or spirits. As the intermediary between man and the spirit world, he may also act as the tribal ruler and judge. The office may be hereditary or there may be a long training period.

Shamir, Yitzhak (1915–) Israeli statesman; prime minister (1983–84); born in Poland. He came to Israel in 1935 and graduated from law school. A member, and eventually a leader, of the Freedom Fighters of Israel during World War II, he was forced to flee to France in 1946. Upon his return in 1948 he worked with the Freedom Fighters until the organization was dissolved (1948). He was in the secret intelligence service (Mossad) (1955–65) and was first elected to the Knesset in 1973. He became foreign minister in 1980, before succeeding Menahem *Begin as prime minister in 1983. His failure to stabilize Israel's inflationary economy led to an indecisive election in 1984, after which a coalition was formed between his Likud Party and the Labour Party, led by Shimon Peres (1923–). Peres agreed to be prime minister until September 1986, when Shamir will take over for two years.

shamrock Any of several plants bearing leaves with three leaflets, especially various *clovers, black *medick (*Medicago lupulina*), and *wood sorrel (*Oxalis acetosella*). St Patrick is said to have adopted the shamrock as a symbol of the Holy Trinity and it is worn on St Patrick's Day.

Shandong (*or* Shantung) A province in NE China, on the Yellow Sea, with central mountains. Densely populated, its fertile farmland produces chiefly wheat and cotton. From early times it has been an important trading area. Floods and famine in the 19th and 20th centuries have led to much emigration northward. Area: 59,189 sq mi (153,300 sq km). Population (1980 est): 72,310,000. Capital: Jinan.

Shandong Peninsula (*or* Shantung Peninsula) A hilly peninsula in E China. Together with the *Liaodong Peninsula opposite, it forms the mouth of the Gulf of Chihli.

Shanghai 31 13N 121 25E An administratively autonomous port in E China, on the Yangtze estuary. The largest city in China, it is its chief port and industrial city. Its many educational establishments include two universities. It grew rapidly after it was opened to foreign trade in 1842, coming under British, US, and French rule until World War II. Industries include steel, textiles, chemicals, shipbuilding, engineering, and publishing. Population (1970 est): 10,820,000.

Shankar, Ravi (1920–) Indian *sitar player, who has toured the US and Europe. He has popularized Indian music in the West, influencing the Beatles, performing with Yehudi Menuhin, and inspiring André Previn to write a sitar concerto.

Shannon, River The longest river in the Republic of Ireland. Rising in NW Co Cavan, it flows S to Limerick and then W into an estuary 70 mi (113 km) long, before entering the Atlantic Ocean. It powers Ireland's main hydroelectric plant. Length: 161 mi (260 km).

Shansi. *See* Shanxi.

Shantou (*or* Swatow) 23 23N 116 39E A port in SE China, in Guangdong province on the South China Sea. A village until the 19th century, it has developed greatly since 1949 and its varied industries include food processing and shipbuilding. Population (1953): 280,400.

Shantung. *See* Shandong.

Shantung Peninsula. *See* Shandong Peninsula.

Shanxi (Shan-hsi *or* Shansi) A province in NE China. It is mainly a high hilly plateau, prone to drought, although irrigation and reforestation projects are now under way. It is important for its coal and iron reserves and the industry they supply. Its relatively sparse Chinese population lives chiefly by keeping animals and growing cotton and cereals. It is famous for its traditional opera, metalwork, and pottery. *History*: a buffer zone between the settled Chinese and the nomadic tribes of the N and W in the middle ages, it became politically stable in about the 14th century. In the 18th and 19th centuries it was famous for its merchants and bankers. Opposition to foreigners was strong and the *Boxer rebellion broke out here (1900). Its industry was established by the warlord Yan Xi-shan (*or* Yen Hsi-shan; ruled 1911–49). Area: 60,656 sq mi (157,099 sq km). Population (1980 est): 24,470,000. Capital: Taiyuan.

Shapur II (309–79 AD) King of Persia (309–79) of the Sasanian dynasty; the posthumous son of his father and predecessor. During his long and successful wars to recover lost territory in Armenia and Mesopotamia from Rome, the emperor *Julian was killed and Christians, suspected as followers of Rome's official religion, were persecuted.

shares. *See* stocks and shares.

Shari River. *See* Chari River.

shari'ah. *See* Islamic law.

Sharjah. *See* United Arab Emirates.

shark A *cartilaginous fish belonging to the worldwide order *Selachii* (about 250 species). Ranging in size from the smallest *dogfish to the enormous *whale shark, they have a torpedo-shaped body with a muscular tail used in swimming, five to seven pairs of gill slits on the sides of the head, and numerous sharp teeth. They are chiefly marine and carnivorous, feeding on fish and invertebrates but in some cases, plankton, carrion, and other vertebrates. They produce live young or lay eggs. Subclass: *Elasmobranchii.*

Sharon, Plain of A coastal plain in Israel, extending 50 mi (80 km) between Haifa and Tel Aviv-Yafo. It is noted for the production of citrus fruit.

Sharpeville A black African town in South Africa, in the S Transvaal near Vereeniging. It was the scene of a riot on March 21, 1960, in which a crowd of African demonstrators were fired on by the police. Over 60 of the demonstrators were killed and many others wounded.

Sharpsburg, Battle of (1862) Name used by the Confederates for the Battle of *Antietam because it was fought at Sharpsburg, Md.

Shastri, Shri Lal Bahadur (1904–66) Indian statesman; prime minister (1964–66). As a young man he was imprisoned by the British while a member of Gandhi's noncooperation movement. He held four ministerial positions before becoming prime minister. His greatest achievement was in negotiating the ceasefire agreement with *Ayub Khan after the India-Pakistan war. He died the following day.

Shatt al-Arab A river in SE Iraq, formed by the confluence of the Tigris and Euphrates rivers. It enters the Persian Gulf via a delta in Kuwait, Iraq, and Iran, passing Basra and Abadan along its course. Length: 118 mi (190 km).

Shaw, Artie (Arthur Arshawsky; 1910–) US jazz clarinetist and band leader, who introduced strings into his swing band in 1935. His version of Cole Porter's "Begin the Beguine," recorded in 1938, was a great success. After 1955 he gave up his band to write and compose.

Shaw, George Bernard (1856–1950) Irish dramatist, critic, and man of letters, born in Dublin. He went to London in 1876 and after writing five unsuccessful novels, he became a music and drama critic, an active socialist, and one of the founding members of the Fabian Society. He soon made a reputation with his brilliant speeches and pamphlets supporting the Fabian cause. He popularized the works of Wagner (*The Perfect Wagnerite,* 1898) and Ibsen, (*The Quintessence of Ibsenism* 1891). Concerned with the moral and social issues of the times, he turned to writing drama. He wrote more than 40 plays, the first of which, *Widowers' Houses* (1892), an attack on slum landlords, was printed in *Plays Pleasant and Unpleasant* (1898), which included *The Philanderer, Mrs Warren's Profession* (on prostitution), and the "pleasant" comedies *Arms and the Man, You Never Can Tell, Candida,* and *The Man of Destiny.* With *Three Plays for Puritans* (published 1901), which comprised *The Devil's Disciple, Caesar and Cleopatra,* and *Captain Brassbound's Conversion,* Shaw achieved a certain popularity. The epic comedy of ideas, *Man and Superman* (1903), was based on the Don Juan legend and developed Shaw's ideas on the "life force" and social evolution; it was followed by *John Bull's Other Island* (1904) and *Major Barbara* (1905). His next plays were *The Doctor's Dilemma* (1906), *Getting Married* (1908), *Misalliance* (1910), and *Androcles and the Lion*

(1913). *Pygmalion* (1913) was an outstanding commercial success and became a perennial favorite (and the basis of the musical *My Fair Lady*, 1955). It was followed by *Heartbreak House* (1917) and the series of plays entitled *Back to Methuselah* (1921). The historical drama *St Joan* (1924), on Joan of Arc, is generally regarded as his greatest work. His late plays (from 1929 onward) include *The Apple Cart*, *The Village Wooing*, and *In Good King Charles's Golden Days*. In 1925 he was awarded the Nobel Prize. Among many important prose works are *The Intelligent Woman's Guide to Socialism and Capitalism* (1928) and *The Black Girl in Search of God* (1932).

Shaw, (Richard) Norman (1831–1912) British architect. In partnership with W. E. Nesfield (1835–88), he broke the hold of the *gothic revival on English architecture. Using a variety of styles, including gothic, Tudor, Queen Anne, and later *classicism, Shaw produced more comfortable buildings than those of his predecessors.

Shawinigan 46 33N 72 45W A city in E Canada, in Quebec on the St Maurice River near waterfalls 150 ft (46 m) high. Developed around 1900 to utilize their hydroelectric potential, Shawinigan is a center for pulp and paper, chemicals (especially calcium carbide), and other heavy industries. Population (1976): 24,921.

Shawnee North American Algonkian-speaking Indian tribe, found in the mid-Atlantic area, especially Pennsylvania, South Carolina, Kentucky, and Tennessee. By 1798 they had settled in Indiana and Ohio and resisted the westward advances of white settlers. Under *Tecumseh they fought and were defeated by the US forces at the Battle of *Tippecanoe (1811). Descendants of the Shawnee live on reservations in Oklahoma.

Shays' Rebellion (1786–87) Uprising in W Massachusetts by disgruntled farmers and debtors who were dispersed by federal troops. Protesting excess taxation, low farm prices, and unfair debtor laws, dissidents, organized and led by former soldier Daniel Shays, attempted to capture the arsenal at Springfield, raided border towns, and were finally dispersed at Petersham. A new state legislature, elected in 1787, brought about reform regarding taxes and the jailing of debtors; however, the matter of the issuance of paper currency and other demands of the dissidents were not met.

Shcherbakov. *See* Rybinsk.

shear stress A form of *stress in which the applied force acts tangentially to the surface of the body. Thus a shear stress applied to the top of a pack of cards would cause the cards to slide over each other.

shearwater One of a group of birds (about 15 species) of the oceanic family *Procellariidae*. 11–35 in (27–90 cm) long, shearwaters have a dark plumage (some species have white underparts), long narrow wings, and slender bills; they feed on fish from the sea surface. The great shearwater (*Puffinus gravis*) breeds in the South Atlantic, migrating to spend summer and autumn in the North Atlantic. The Manx shearwater (*P. puffinus*) breeds off British and Mediterranean coasts and winters in E South America and Australia. Order: Procellariiformes. *See also* petrel.

sheathbill A small compact scavenging bird belonging to a family (*Chionidae*; 2 species) occurring on coasts near Antarctica. Sheathbills are 16 in (40 cm) long and have a thick white plumage, shortish wings, and a horny sheath covering the nostrils at the base of the bill. Order: *Charadriiformes* (gulls, plovers, etc.).

Sheba In the Bible, a land corresponding to Sabaea in present-day Yemen (SW Arabia). It was known for its trade in spices and gold. Its most famous monarch was the Queen of Sheba who visited King Solomon in Jerusalem (I Kings 10.1–13). According to Ethiopian tradition, she bore him a son, the first King of Ethiopia.

Shechem. *See* Nablus.

sheep A hoofed *ruminant mammal belonging to the genus *Ovis* (7 species), native to mountainous regions of Eurasia and North America. Related to goats, sheep are generally 30–40 in (75–100 cm) tall at the shoulder and weigh 110–330 lb (50–150 kg). They have a compact body with slender legs and a short tail and the coat ranges from white to brown in color. Males (rams) have large spiraled horns; females (ewes) have smaller less curved horns. There are over 200 breeds of domestic sheep (*O. aries*), probably descended from the Asian red sheep (*O. orientalis*), which are reared worldwide for meat, wool, and milk (*see* livestock farming). They typically have a long woolly coat, unlike the coarser coat of wild sheep. Family: *Bovidae. See also* aoudad; argali; bighorn; mouflon.

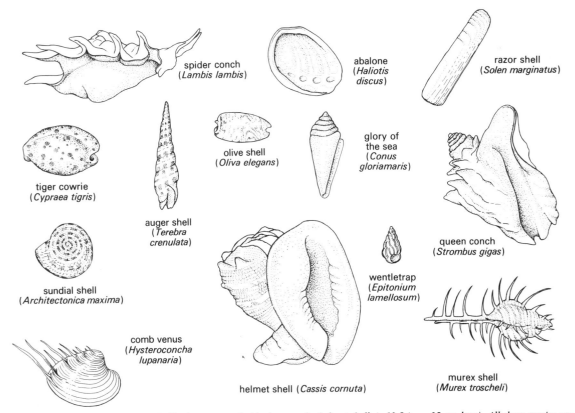

SHELLS *A selection of mollusk shells, drawn to scale (the largest, the helmet shell, is 13.5 in or 35 cm long). All these species are marine and several, including the glory of the sea, are collectors' items.*

sheepdog A dog used for handling sheep. Many breeds are used for this purpose, including the *collie, *German shepherd dog, *Old English sheepdog, and *Shetland sheepdog, as well as crossbred derivatives.

sheep ked A flat wingless fly, *Melophagus ovinus*, also called sheep tick, that is parasitic upon sheep. Both sexes are bloodsuckers and are attached to the fleece, often causing serious skin irritations. The larvae are retained within the body of the female until they reach maturity, when they are deposited on the ground. Family: *Hippoboscidae*.

Sheffield 52 23N 1 30W A city in N England, on the Don River. It is world famous for steel, produced here since the mid-18th century. Special and alloy steels are now more important than the traditional cutlery and tool-making trades. Sheffield also produces silverware, glass, and engineering products. There is a cathedral (partly 15th century) and a university (1905). Population (1981): 477,142.

Sheffield plate Articles that are made by fusing a silver coat onto copper. The process was discovered (c. 1742) by a Sheffield, England, cutler. Used as a substitute for solid silver, Sheffield-plated articles, usually tableware, followed contemporary silver designs and were of the highest quality. Sheffield plate became obsolete after the introduction of electroplating in the mid-19th century, but Sheffield-plated articles are now prized.

Shelburne, William Petty Fitzmaurice, 2nd of (1737–1805) British statesman; prime minister (1782–83). An advocate of conciliation toward the American colonies, his ministry negotiated the Treaty of Paris (1783), which ended the American Revolution.

shelduck A large *duck, *Tadorna tadorna*, found around coasts of W and central Eurasia. It is 25.5 in (65 cm) long and has black-and-white plumage with a green head, chestnut shoulders, and a red bill, which in the male has a red knob at the base. It feeds chiefly on mollusks and nests in disused rabbit burrows.

shellac A natural thermoplastic *resin made from the secretions of the lac insect, *Laccifer lacca*, which is parasitic on certain trees in India and Thailand. It was formerly used for molding records but has now been replaced by vinyl resins. Its solution in alcohol is used as a varnish and in lacquers. It is also used in sealing wax, printing inks, and electrical insulation.

Shelley, Percy Bysshe (1792–1822) British poet. Expelled from Oxford University for publishing a pamphlet defending atheism in 1811, he settled briefly in the Lake District. He wrote the revolutionary poem *Queen Mab* in 1813 and soon after left for the Continent, where he met Byron. From 1818 until his death he lived in Italy, where he wrote the verse dramas *The Cenci* (1819) and *Prometheus Unbound* (1818–19), the elegy *Adonais* (1821) prompted by the death of Keats, and much lyrical poetry. He was drowned in a sailing accident off the Italian coast. His wife **Mary Wollstonecraft Shelley** (1797–1851), British novelist, was the daughter of William *Godwin and Mary *Wollstonecraft. She eloped with Shelley in 1814 and married him in 1816. In addition to her best-known book, *Frankenstein: the Modern Prometheus* (1818), she edited Shelley's *Poetical Works* (1839).

Shelley, Percy Bysshe (1792–1822) British poet. Expelled from Oxford University for publishing a pamphlet defending atheism in 1811, he settled briefly in the Lake District. He wrote the revolutionary poem *Queen Mab* in 1813 and soon after left for the Continent, where he met Byron. From 1818 until his death he lived in Italy, where he wrote the verse dramas *The Cenci* (1819) and *Prometheus Unbound* (1818–19), the elegy *Adonais* (1821) prompted by the death of Keats, and much lyrical poetry. He was drowned in a sailing accident off the Italian coast. His wife **Mary Wollstonecraft Shelley** (1797–1851), British novelist, was the daughter of William *Godwin and Mary *Wollstonecraft. She eloped with Shelley in 1814 and married him in 1816. In addition to her best-known book, *Frankenstein: the Modern Prometheus* (1818), she edited Shelley's *Poetical Works* (1839).

shells The hard casings secreted by some animals to protect themselves or their eggs. The term usually refers to the shells of mollusks, which consist largely of calcium carbonate and come in a wide variety of shapes and sizes. They may be spiraled or flat, with one valve (in gastropods, such as snails) or two (in bivalves, such as mussels). A single valve of a giant clam may weigh up to 200 lb (90 kg). The pearly nautilus has a many chambered shell, which provides buoyancy, while the female paper nautilus (*Argonauta*) secretes a shell-like cradle to transport its eggs and young. The shells of marine mollusks, particularly gastropods, are prized by collectors. □p. 891.

Shenandoah National Park A national park in N Virginia, in the Blue Ridge Mountains. It preserves the spectacular scenery of the mountains and the valley of the Shenandoah River. Heavily forested, the park, established in 1935, includes many species of plants, wildlife, and birds. Area: 300 sq mi (777 sq km).

Shenandoah River A river in the E US, flowing mainly NE through Virginia to join the Potomac River as its main tributary. It was a major *Civil War battleground (*see also* Sheridan, Philip H.). The **Shenandoah National Park**, in the Blue Ridge section of the Appalachian Mountains, lies to the S of the river. Length: 55 mi (88 km).

Shensi. *See* Shenxi.

Shenxi (Shen-hsi *or* Shensi) A mountainous province in central China. In the Wei He (River) and Han River valleys wheat, millet, and cotton are grown. Coal, iron, and oil are also produced. *History*: the Wei He valley was the center of successive Chinese dynasties from 1122 BC. Its economy rested on an impressive irrigation system from about 300 BC until about 600 AD, when it began to deteriorate. From about 1860 until 1928 the N suffered from famines, epidemics, and civil wars. Following the *Long March, it was the communist base (1936–1949). Area: 75,598 sq mi (195,800 sq km). Population (1980 est): 28,070,000. Capital: Xi An.

Shenyang (former name: Mukden) 41 50N 123 26E A city in NE China, on the Hun River, the capital of Liaoning province and the site of its university. China's fourth largest city, it is a major industrial center. The **Mukden Incident** (1931), an explosion on the Japanese-controlled South Manchurian Railroad, was the pretext for the Japanese occupation of Manchuria (*see* Manchukuo). Population (1957 est): 2,411,000.

she oak. *See* Casuarina.

Shepard, Jr, Allan Bartlett (1923–) US astronaut, who on May 5, 1961, became the first American in space. His flight, which came 23 days after *Gagarin's flight, lasted 15 minutes and reached a height of 115 mi (185 km). He also commanded the Apollo 14 flight to the moon in 1971.

shepherd's purse An annual or biennial herb, *Caspella bursa-pastoris*, found growing as a weed throughout the world. It has a basal rosette of leaves and a branching leafy stem, 1.2–16 in (3–40 cm) high, bearing tiny white flowers that produce small purse-shaped fruits. Its ability to self-pollinate produces distinctive local populations. Family: *Cruciferae*.

sheradizing A process for galvanizing iron or steel (i.e. protecting the metal from corrosion by coating it with zinc) by placing it in a rotating drum with zinc dust and heating to about 500°F (260°C). At this temperature the iron and zinc amalgamate forming an internal layer of zinc-iron alloys and an external layer of pure zinc. Named for the British inventor Sherard Cowper-Coles (d. 1935).

Sheraton, Thomas (1751–1806) British furniture designer. Settling in London (c. 1790), he made his name with the designs in his *Cabinet-Maker and Upholsterer's Drawing Book* (1791–94). Influenced by *Adam and contemporary French styles, these designs were characterized by elegance, delicacy, straight lines, and inlaid decoration.

Sherbrooke 45 24N 71 54W A city in E Canada, in S Quebec. Founded in 1794, it is the farming, transportation, commercial, and cultural center of the *Eastern Townships. Its manufactures include textiles, machinery, paper, and dairy produce. Sherbrooke houses the French-speaking University of Sherbrooke (1954). Population (1981): 74,315.

Sheridan, Philip H(enry) (1831–88) US general. After graduation from West Point in 1853, Sheridan began his military career with service in the cavalry on the western frontier. At the outbreak of the *Civil War, he gained distinction as a Union infantry captain and was promoted to the rank of brigadier general in 1862. Appointed commander of the Army of the Shenandoah, he led a number of destructive raids into Confederate territory. His deployments in April, 1865 forced the Confederate army to evacuate Petersburg and helped lead to the surrender of General Robert E. *Lee at Appomattox. During the early *Reconstruction period, Sheridan served as the military governor of Louisiana and Texas and his harsh administration of those states brought him into conflict with President Andrew *Johnson. Transferred to Missouri, he supervised the resettlement of various Indian groups. Sheridan ended his active military career with service as US military observer in the *Franco-Prussian War (1870).

Sheridan, Richard Brinsley (1751–1816) Anglo-Irish dramatist. He wrote witty comedies of manners, of which the best known are *The Rivals* (1775), in which his most famous character, Mrs Malaprop, appears, and *School for Scandal* (1777). He was a manager of the Drury Lane Theatre and a Whig member of parliament from 1780 to 1812, during which time he was recognized as being one of the great parliamentary orators.

sheriff An official with administrative and judicial responsibilities in the US, England, and Scotland. Originating in 10th-century England, the sheriffs' powers were reduced by Henry II (reigned 1154–89) and became little more than ceremonial in the 16th century. US Sheriffs are elected and are the principal law enforcement officers in a county.

Sherman, William Tecumseh (1820–91) US general. An 1840 graduate of West Point, Sherman served in the *Mexican War, but resigned from the Army in 1855 to pursue a career in banking. He returned to the Army as a Union officer at the beginning of the Civil War and served at the first Battle of *Bull Run (1861) and at the Battle of *Shiloh (1862), where he was promoted to the rank of major general. Replacing General U. S. *Grant as commander of the West (1864), Sherman launched his invasion of Georgia, capturing and burning Atlanta and leading the famous "march to the sea." After the capture of Savannah, he continued the march northward through the Carolinas, eventually joining Grant's forces in Virginia in April, 1865. In 1869 he succeeded Grant as commanding general of the US Army, a post he held until his retirement in 1884. His brother **John Sherman** (1823–1900) was a politician who began his political career as a Republican congressman from Ohio (1855–61). After serving almost three terms in the US Senate (1861–77), he resigned to become secretary of the Treasury in the administration of Rutherford B. *Hayes (1877–81). Sherman returned to the Senate after Hayes' retirement and served as the chairman of the Finance Committee (1881–97). The *Sherman Anti-Trust Act was largely his work. He was later named secretary of State in the administration of President William *McKinley (1897–98).

Sherman Anti-Trust Act (1890)   US law that prohibited competition restraint abuses and monopolies. Named for Senator John *Sherman, the act prohibited business combinations in any way that violated fair competition practices between states and in international trade.

Sherman Silver Purchase Act (1890)   US law that required the federal government to purchase a substantial amount of US-produced silver with treasury notes redeemable in either gold or silver. Enacted to increase the amount of currency in circulation, it instead drained government gold reserves and precipitated the Panic of 1893, at which time the act was repealed. *See also* Free Silver.

Sherpa   A people of Nepal who speak a dialect of Tibetan. They are farmers, cattle breeders, and traders and also spin and weave woolen cloth. They often act as porters for Himalayan expeditions. With Edmund Hillary, the Sherpa *Tenzing Norgay reached the summit of Everest in 1953.

Sherrington, Sir Charles Scott (1857–1952)   British physiologist, whose work provided the basis for present-day understanding of the nervous system. Sherrington demonstrated that reflex actions in higher animals and man are integrated with the rest of the nervous system and do not occur as isolated activities. He proposed the terms neuron for a nerve cell and synapse for the point at which an impulse is transmitted between nerve cells. He shared a Nobel Prize (1932) with Lord *Adrian.

sherry   A fortified *wine, made around Jerez de la Frontera (whence its name) in S Spain; similar wine is now also made elsewhere. It is blended by the *solera* system: sherry is drawn off from several different casks to make a blend and those casks are then topped up with younger sherry, maintaining its future character. There are two basic types of sherry: fino is a pale dry wine on which the *flor* (flower or yeast) has developed fully; oloroso is a rich full-bodied wine on which the *flor* is little developed. Other types of sherry are related to these two, for example amontillado is a strong dark derivative of a fino and cream sherry is a heavily sweetened oloroso.

's Hertogenbosch (*or* Den Bosch)   51 41N 5 19E A city in the S central Netherlands, the capital of North Brabant province. It has a famous gothic cathedral (rebuilt 1419–1520). The painter Hieronymus Bosch was born here. Population (1981 est): 88,585.

Sherwood, Robert Emmet (1896–1955)   US playwright and writer. Between 1919 and 1928 he was an editor or drama critic for various magazines, including *Vanity Fair, Life,* and *Scribner's,* and the New York *Herald.* He later worked in Franklin D. Roosevelt's administration, in which he was director of the overseas Office of War Information (1941–44). His plays include *The Road to Rome* (1927), *Reunion in Vienna* (1931), *The Petrified Forest* (1934), *Idiot's Delight* (Pulitzer Prize, 1936), *Abe Lincoln in Illinois* (1938; Pulitzer Prize, 1939), and *There Shall Be No Night* (1948; Pulitzer Prize, 1949). A book about the Roosevelt administration, *Roosevelt and Hopkins* (1948) brought him his fourth Pulitzer Prize in 1949, and his movie, *The Best Years of Our Lives,* received an Academy Award (1946).

Sherwood Forest   An ancient forest in the Midlands of England, in Nottinghamshire. Once an extensive royal hunting ground, it is now much reduced; it is famous for its associations with Robin Hood.

Shetland Islands   A group of about 100 islands in the North Sea, off the N coast of Scotland. The largest islands include Mainland, Yell, and Unst. Agriculture, based on crofting, chiefly produces wool; Shetland ponies are also bred. Herring fishing, centered on Lerwick, is important. The few

industries include fish curing and knitting (especially in the Shetland and Fair Isle patterns). The islands are a base for North Sea oil exploitation. Area: 551 sq mi (1427 sq km). Population (1981): 26,716. Administrative center: Lerwick.

Shetland pony   Small British pony, native to the Shetland Islands. It has a sturdy compact body with short legs and a relatively large head. The mane and tail are profuse and the coat becomes thick in winter. Shetlands are now popular pets for children. Height: up to 3.4 ft (1.05 m) (10½ hands).

Shetland sheepdog (*or* Sheltie)   A breed of dog developed in the Shetland Islands for working sheep. Related to and resembling the *collie, it has a soft undercoat and a long outer coat and may be black, brown, or blue-gray, with white and tan markings. Height: 14 in (36 cm) (dogs); 14 in (35 cm) (bitches).

shield   An extensive rigid block of Precambrian rocks unaffected by later periods of mountain building. Shields are the oldest continental regions, frequently of igneous granite or metamorphic gneiss. The shields were once the site of Precambrian mountain belts, although the mountains have been completely eroded. The **Canadian** (*or* Laurentian) **Shield** is the largest, covering about 2 million square miles (5002 million sq km) of NE North America. The **Baltic Shield** (*or* Fennoscandia), reaching the surface in Finland and Sweden, is another well-known example.

shield bug   A *plant bug, also called stink bug, belonging to the families *Acanthosomidae, Cydnidae, Scutelleridae,* or *Pentatomidae.* Shield bugs have heavy shieldlike bodies, 0.20–2 in (5–50 mm) long, and are usually green or brown. They suck insect or plant juices, often becoming agricultural pests. Some species also foul plants with an evil-smelling secretion. □insect.

shield fern   A tufted *fern of the widely distributed genus *Polystichum* (about 135 species). It has a scaly stem and tapering branched fronds made up of toothed pointed leaflets. Small round clusters of spore capsules (sori) occur in rows on the undersides of the leaflets. The soft shield fern (*P. setiferum*) and the hard shield fern (*P. aculeatum*) are common species. Family: *Aspidiaceae.*

Shih-chia-chuang.   *See* Shijiazhuang.

Shih Huang Ti.   *See* Qin.

Shih tzu   A breed of small dog originating in Tibet. It has a long body with short legs, a short muzzle, and drooping ears. The long straight coat can be of various colors and the plumed tail is held over the back. Height: about 10 in (26 cm).

Shiites (*or* Shiah)   The general term applied to a number of different Muslim sects, the main body of which is dominant in Iran. The distinctive belief of the Shiites, which differentiates them from the other major Muslim group, the *Sunnites, is that *Ali, the fourth caliph, is the only legitimate successor of Mohammed. The leader of Islam, the *imam, must be a descendant of Ali and has exclusive authority in secular and religious matters. The Shiites differ among themselves as to the true line of imams after a certain stage. Some, known as "the twelvers," expect the return of the 12th imam (d. 9th century AD) at the end of time, while others recognize a different line from the seventh imam onward.

Shijiazhuang (*or* Shih-chia-chuang)   38 04N 114 28E A city in NE China, the capital of Hebei province and the site of its university. A communications center, its industries include coalmining, textiles, chemicals, and engineering. Population (1957 est): 598,000.

Shikoku   The smallest of the four main islands of Japan, separated from Honshu and Kyushu by the Inland Sea. Mountainous and forested, its population is concentrated on the coastal plains, with industry mainly in the N. Copper is mined at Besshi; other products are fish, rice, grain, tobacco, mulberry, and camphor. Area: 6857 sq mi (17,759 sq km). Population (1970): 3,904,014. Chief cities: Matsuyama and Takamatsu.

Shillong   25 34N 91 53E A city in India, the capital of Meghalaya. Rebuilt following its virtual destruction by an earthquake in 1897, Shillong is an important military base and agricultural trading center and has a university (1973). Population (1971): 87,659.

Shiloh   32 03N 35 18E A city of Samaria in ancient N Palestine, now in Jordan. Hannah brought her son Samuel to this important Israelite religious center to dedicate him to God in the temple where Eli was priest of the *Ark of the Covenant. Shiloh was the traditional sanctuary of the Ark until the Philistines destroyed the city and captured the Ark in the mid-11th century BC.

Shiloh, Battle of (1862)   Civil War battle in SW Tennessee; also known as the Battle of Pittsburg Landing. Having suffered extensive losses in the area, Confederate forces under General Albert Sidney Johnston (1803–62) surprised General Ulysses S. *Grant's troops, who were awaiting reinforcements. Although both sides claimed victory, the Union fared better, regaining all ground lost in the initial attack and forcing the retreat of the Confederates. Casualties were extremely high for both armies.

Shimonoseki 33 59N 130 58E A seaport in Japan, in SW Honshu, linked to *Kitakyushu by tunnels under the Shimonoseki Strait. The treaty ending the first Sino-Japanese War was signed here (1895). Industries include engineering, shipbuilding, chemicals, and fishing. Population (1980): 269,000.

shingles An infection caused by the *herpes zoster virus, which lodges in nerve cells in the spinal cord. Shingles affects adults who have had chickenpox as children. It usually starts with pain along the course of a sensory nerve, followed by a band of blisters around half of the body or face. The rash usually eventually disappears but the patient may be left with severe neuralgia.

Shinto The native religion of Japan. Shinto is primarily an attitude of nationalistic and aesthetic reverence toward— familiar places and traditions, rather than a set of religious beliefs. However, the central themes are the belief in numerous usually amoral *kamis* or nature spirits, together with ancestor worship and an ideal of military chivalry.

The two principal *kamis* are the sun-goddess (reputedly mother of the emperor) and her brother the storm-god. The conflict between them expresses the creative and destructive forces of nature. The scriptures of Shinto, the *Ko ji ki* and the *Nihon Shoki*, are both semimythological histories of Japan, written around 720 AD. The hereditary priesthood officiates at ceremonies of birth, marriage, and death, ensuring ritual purification. After World War II, Shinto was disestablished as the state religion.

ship money A tax raised by English monarchs in times of emergency for the defense of the coast. It gained notoriety under Charles I, who levied it indiscriminately between 1634 and 1639. It was pronounced illegal by the *Long Parliament.

ships Man's earliest sea voyages were probably made on rafts and in hollowed-out tree trunks. Larger and more stable vessels were certainly known to the ancient Egyptians, whose rock carvings and paintings depict ships that were made of planks and were propelled both by oars and sails. Other early mariners included the Chinese and the Phoenicians; the short broad 13th-century Phoenician merchant ships (known as round ships) were propelled by oars and a single square sail to catch the prevailing wind (see sailing). The Greeks developed biremes (with two banks of oars) and triremes (with three banks) as warships, especially strengthened for ramming enemy vessels. The Romans also relied on oars, but their larger grain ships, capable of carrying up to 300 tons of cargo, had a number of square sails. In the N the longships of the Vikings were double-ended and rose high out of the water to cope with the rough and windy North Sea; they still relied on oarsmen but the holes for the oars were fitted with shutters that could be closed when the ship was under sail. Developed in the 8th century AD, ships of this kind brought William the Conqueror to England. It was not until the 12th century and the stimulus of the Crusades that the art of using sails was sufficiently developed for oars to be dispensed with. Sailing into the wind was originally pioneered by the Chinese in their junks, but it was the Arabs who perfected the lateen sail, which made it a reliable means of propulsion for large ships. By the 14th century sailing ships were commonplace. The warships of the period had "castles" built at each end to house fighting men, and guns were usually carried on the forecastle. However, muzzle-loading cannons were too heavy to be mounted on the forecastle and by the end of the 15th century they were carried in gun ports low in the hull. During this period, too, the single-master with one large heavy sail gave way to the three-master with more manageable small sails and full rigging. During the next 300 years sailing ships developed in many ways, usually with the merchantmen following the innovations in hull design and rigging made by the designers of warships. Sailing ships reached their zenith in the 19th-century *clippers, which remained supreme until Newcomen's *steam engine revolutionized seafaring. The first steamer to cross the Atlantic (in April, 1827) was the Dutch *Curaçao*. For the next century the N Atlantic crossing continued to be a proving ground for great ships. The propeller completely replaced the paddle and the steam *turbine largely replaced the reciprocating engine. Passenger travel across the Atlantic has now been almost entirely captured by the airlines; modern shipbuilding concentrates on cargo vessels, especially oil *tankers.

Warships in the age of steam were largely modeled on the turbine-driven *battleship *Dreadnought* (1906), which together with the *cruiser, *destroyer, *frigate, and *submarine dominated naval warfare in World War I. By World War II the *aircraft carrier had evolved and with its long-range striking power became the supreme weapon of the war at sea. However, since the middle of the 20th century the importance of the surface warship

has diminished and the strength of navies is now calculated in terms of their nuclear-powered submarines armed with long-range missiles.

Since the innovation of steam, the main developments in ships have been the use of *nuclear energy, especially in submarines, and the invention of the *Hovercraft and the *hydrofoil to remove the hull from the water in order to reduce drag.

shipworm A *bivalve mollusk belonging to the family *Teredidae*, also called pileworm. The shell plates of a shipworm are small with sharp ridges used for boring into wooden structures. The resulting burrow is lined with a limy material, encasing the long body (up to 71 in [180 cm]). Shipworms can damage wooden ships, piers, etc.

Shiraz 29 38N 52 34E A city in S central Iran. It is a trading center for the surrounding region and is connected by road to the port of Bushire; Pahlavi University was established here in 1945. Population (1976): 416,408.

shire A district, with a central town, used by the Anglo-Saxons as a unit of local government. Many modern counties in the UK were originally shires.

Shiré Highlands An upland area in S Malawi, with an average height of about 3000 ft (900 m). Tea and tobacco are cultivated here.

Shire horse A breed of draft horse descended from the English warhorse and one of the world's largest horses. It is massively built with characteristic long white hair (called feathering) covering the lower parts of the legs. The coat is gray, bay, or black. Height: about 6 ft (1.73 m) (17 hands).

Shiva The third member of the Hindu trinity, the *Trimurti. He is known as the Destroyer, but also represents the principle of generation symbolized by the lingam or phallus. His female counterpart is Parvati, also known in her more ominous aspects as Kali and Durga. He is often portrayed in human form with four arms, a third eye in the center of the forehead, and sometimes wearing a necklace of skulls. His most famous depiction is as *Nataraja* (king of dancing), his dance symbolizing the cosmic rhythm of creation and destruction. The worship of Shiva is characterized by an asceticism that contrasts with the gentler worship of *Vishnu, the other major sect of modern Hinduism.

Shizuoka 34 59N 138 24E A port in Japan, in SE Honshu on an inlet of the Pacific Ocean. It is the center of Japan's chief tea-producing region. Its university was established in 1949. Population (1980): 458,000.

Shkodër (Italian name: Scutari) 42 03N 19 01E A city in NW Albania, on Lake Scutari. It has been ruled successively by many peoples, including the Turks. Local industries include food canning and the manufacture of cement and weapons. Population (1978 est): 62,500.

shock 1. A severe condition resulting from failure of the circulatory system, when the blood supply to the tissues is inadequate. The shock may be caused by failure of the heart to pump sufficiently strongly, for example after a heart attack; by loss of blood fluid, for example through *hemorrhage or *burns; or by widening of the blood vessels so that there is not enough blood to fill them, for example after injury or during a very severe infection. The patient is in a state of collapse (possibly unconscious)—pale, sweaty, and nauseated, with low blood pressure and a weak fast pulse. Shock due to hemorrhage is treated with blood transfusions while that due to infection is treated with antibiotics and also often with fluid transfusions. There is no adequate treatment for shock caused by a failing heart. 2. Injury resulting from electrocution. The extent of the injury depends on the current passing through the body, which is related to the voltage and the skin resistance. As skin resistance is greatly reduced when it is wet, mains voltage (240 V) can cause a lethal current (about 15 milliamps) to flow through the body if live terminals are touched with wet hands.

Shockley, William Bradfield (1910–) US physicist, born in England, who shared the 1956 Nobel Prize with John *Bardeen and Walter *Brattain for their discovery of the *transistor while working at the Bell Telephone laboratories in 1948. This discovery revolutionized the electronics and computer industries. He is also known for his controversial views concerning the relationship between race and intelligence.

shock wave A narrow region of a high pressure in a fluid, created when a fast-moving body passes through the fluid. The waves are propagated outward from the body and occur, for example, when an aircraft passes through the *sound barrier.

shoebill A large bird, *Balaeniceps rex*, occurring in papyrus swamps of E Africa. 47 in (120 cm) tall, it has pale-gray plumage, long legs, and a large head with a broad shoe-shaped bill used to probe for lungfish. It is the only member of its family (*Balaenicipitridae*). Order: *Ciconiiformes* (herons, storks, etc.).

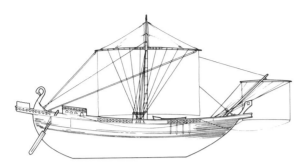

Roman merchantman (c. 100 AD) *The Romans' need to transport grain from N Africa to Europe encouraged the building of imposing ships up to 180 ft (55 m) long.*

Portuguese caravel (c. 1450) *Although it was only a little longer than a large rowing boat, the caravel took part in most of the 15th-century voyages of discovery. The lateen sail, derived from Arab examples, enabled it to sail against the prevailing winds.*

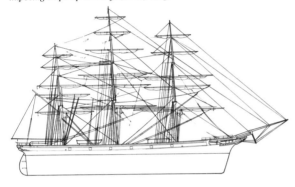

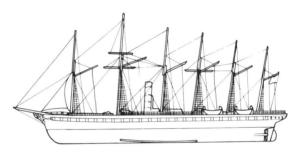

Cutty Sark (1869) *The 19th-century clippers were renowned for their speed and grace. The* Cutty Sark, *built to bring tea from China, was one of the fastest and most consistent sailing ships of its time. It is now permanently moored at Greenwich, England.*

Great Britain (1843) *The second steam ship designed by I. K. Brunel, the* Great Britain *was the first all-iron propeller-driven ship to cross the Atlantic, taking 15 days between Liverpool and New York. Wrecked off the Falkland Islands in 1937, it was returned to England in 1970 for restoration.*

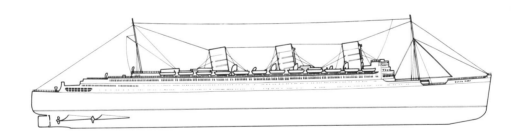

Queen Mary (1934) *In 1938 this British passenger liner captured the Blue Riband for the fastest Atlantic crossing with a time of 3 days 20 hours 42 minutes. In 1967 it was anchored off Long Beach, California, as a tourist attraction.*

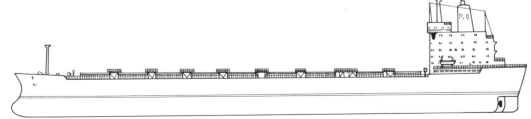

oil tanker (1968) *The largest vessels afloat today, some of these giant ships have a deadweight capacity of over 300 000 tons.*

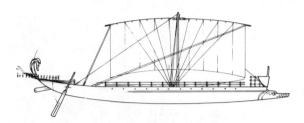

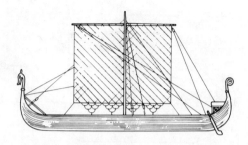

Greek bireme (c. 500 BC) *Propelled during an attack by its two ranks of oars, the bireme was strongly built around a keel to support the strain of the ram attached to its bows.*

Viking longship (c. 1000 AD) *The clinker-built, double-ended longship, propelled by oars and sail, was used mainly to transport fighting men.*

medieval nef (c. 1400) *This single-masted vessel had platforms (castles) for fighting men at either end and one on the mast (topcastle) from which missiles could be hurled.*

Victory (1778) *Nelson's flagship at the battle of Trafalgar (1805), the* Victory *carried 100 guns and a crew of 850. It is now preserved at Portsmouth, England.*

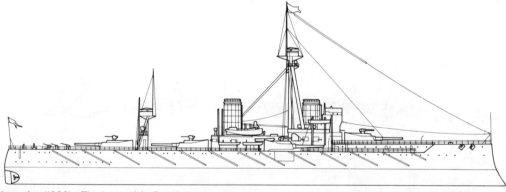

Dreadnought (1906) *The design of the British* Dreadnought *became the model for battleships in a period in which a country's naval strength was calculated in terms of how many battleships it possessed. The* Dreadnought *carried ten 12-inch guns, 27 smaller guns, and five underwater torpedo tubes.*

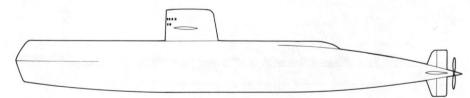

Nautilus (1954) *The first nuclear-powered warship, the US* Nautilus *heralded an era in which naval strength is calculated in terms of nuclear submarines. They are armed with torpedoes and long- and short-range missiles carrying nuclear warheads, all of which can be fired while the vessel is submerged.*

shofar A Jewish ceremonial trumpet used in the synagogue. It is made of a ram's horn, flattened and bent by a steaming process. Its use as a prelude to proclamations and to sound the alarm is recorded in the Old Testament.

shogi A board game for two players, a Japanese form of chess. Each player starts with 20 flat pieces distinguished by size and markings. As in chess the pieces have prescribed moves and the object is to checkmate the enemy king, but unlike chess captured pieces may be used in the game by the player who captures them.

shogun A military title held hereditarily by the heads of three families; they were successively the actual rulers of Japan, although the emperors retained formal sovereignty. The shogunate was secured for the Minamoto from the emperor in 1192 after *Minamoto Yoritomo's victory over the Taira league. From 1338 to 1573 the Ashikaga family held the title and in 1603 *Tokugawa Ieyasu, who claimed Minamoto ancestry, revived it. The last shogun was Tokugawa Keiki (1827–1913; ruled 1867–68).

Sholapur 17 43N 75 56E A city in India, in Maharashtra. It is a major cotton textile center. Population (1971): 398,361.

Sholes, Christopher Latham (1819–90) US inventor of the typewriter, which he patented, with two others, in 1868. After spending several years perfecting his inventory, he sold his patent to Eliphalet *Remington's company in 1873.

Sholokhov, Mikhail (1905–84) Soviet novelist. After service with the Red Army during the Civil War he returned to his native village in the Don Cossack region, the setting for his first major novel (1928–40), translated in two parts as *And Quiet Flows the Don* and *The Don Flows Home to the Sea*. His authorship of this novel has been questioned by Solzhenitsyn and others. He won the Nobel Prize in 1965.

shooting Discharging a weapon at a target or at game. The two main categories of **target shooting** for rifles are small bore (.22 caliber) at ranges of 27–219 yd (25–200 m), and full bore (7.62 caliber) at ranges of 200–1200 yd (183–1097 m); full-bore courses are fired from standing, sitting, kneeling, and prone (lying down) positions. Weapons for pistol shooting range from the .177 air pistol to the .45 pistol, with ranges between 10 and 50 yd (9–45 m). In **clay-pigeon shooting** (*or* trapshooting) clay disks are mechanically flung into the air and fired at with shotguns.

shop steward Part-time *labor-union officials, who represent the union members with whom they work. The function of the shop steward is to represent his fellow workers in negotiations with management and in talks with other labor-union officials.

shorthand Any form of writing designed to be written quickly, especially for the transcription of spoken language. Most forms of shorthand are based on the principle of recording only as many letters or sounds as are necessary for reasonably accurate reading back, generally in simplified characters that are fast to write. In the Pitman System, for example, the characters are based on segments of a circle or straight lines; vowels are indicated only where the writer thinks it necessary, by a system of dots in descending order; voicing of consonants is indicated by thickening of strokes (thus, *b* is represented by ₎ *p* by ₎). The most popular US system is that invented by John Robert Gregg (1867–1948). In these systems speeds of up to 300 words per minute can be achieved. **Speedwriting**, devised in the US in the 1920s, uses ordinary Roman alphabet characters, omitting all but the essential ones. **Stenotypy** is a form of machine shorthand using a limited keyboard; it is widely used for reporting court proceedings. The use of shorthand is of great antiquity; for example, Cicero's secretary Tiro had devised a Latin shorthand system in the 1st century BC.

Shoshoni A group of North American Indian tribes of the Great Basin region who spoke a language of the Uto-Aztecan family. They lived by gathering wild fruits and insects and trapping small game. Some acquired horses and moved onto the Plains to hunt buffalo and adopted much of the culture of this region. One such group was the *Comanche.

Shostakovich, Dmitri (1906–75) Russian composer. He was a pupil of Glazunov at the St Petersburg conservatory. His first symphony, written when he was 18, was very successful. Subsequent works, especially the operas *The Nose* (1927–28) and *Lady Macbeth of Mtsenk* (1930–32), brought allegations of formalism and decadence from the Soviet press. Shostakovich regained official favor with his fifth symphony (1937), subtitled "A Soviet artist's reply to just criticism." His compositions also include ten subsequent symphonies, including the wartime seventh symphony (*The Leningrad*; 1941), two concertos each for piano, violin, and cello, 15 string quartets, and much other music.

shotgun A smoothbore firearm with pump or automatic-repeating action. It may have one or two barrels and fires shot (small pellets) into a pattern covering a broad target. Guns with tapered barrels gain range but

reduce the pattern area. Shot is used against small game, while lead slugs and balls are used against deer.

shot put (*or* putting the shot) A field event in athletics, in which an iron or brass sphere is thrown as far as possible. It weighs 16 lb (7.26 kg) for men and 8.8 lb (4 kg) for women. It is thrown, or put, one-handed from in front of the shoulder and the putter must stay within a circle 7 ft (2.1 m) in diameter.

shoulder The part of the body to which the *arm is attached. The skeleton of the shoulder consists of the scapula (shoulder blade), which forms a ball-and-socket joint with the humerus, permitting free movement of the arm. It is also the site of attachment of muscles of the arm and back. It is braced by the clavicle.

SHOVELER DUCK *Distinguished from all other ducks by its large spatulate bill with fringed edges, seen in this male.*

shoveler duck A *duck, *Spatula clypeata*, found in the N hemisphere, having a large bill specialized for feeding on water plants and invertebrates on the surface of fresh water. 20 in (50 cm) long, it has a pale-blue wing flash; the male has a dark-green head, white breast, and chestnut underparts and the female is speckled brown.

showjumping Competitive jumping of horses, often against the clock, over a series of artificial obstacles of varying severity. Penalties are given for knocking down or refusing fences. Since World War II it has become a major international sport.

Shrapnel, Henry (1761–1842) British army officer, who invented the shrapnel shell. First used in 1804, the shell comprised a projectile that sprayed bullets when activated by a timing device.

Shreveport 32 30N 93 40W A city in Louisiana, on the Red River. It is the industrial center of a large oil and natural-gas region. Timber, cotton, and metal are also important products. Population (1980): 205,815.

shrew A small insectivorous mammal belonging to the family *Soricidae* (265 species), found all over the world except Australasia and the Polar regions. The dwarf shrew (*Suncus etruscus*) is the smallest mammal in the world, weighing only 0.07 oz (2 g) and measuring 2.8–3.1 in (7–8 cm). Shrews are very active: the common shrew (*Sorex araneus*) eats its own weight in food every 24 hours in order to meet its energy requirements. Order: *Insectivora*.

Shrewsbury 52 43N 2 45W A city in W central England, on the Severn River. It achieved importance as a gateway to Wales, and a castle was built in 1070 Shrewsbury is a market town for the surrounding agricultural area, with engineering and malting industries; market gardening is also important. Population (1981): 58,826.

shrike A fierce predatory songbird belonging to a family (*Laniidae*; 74 species) occurring in Eurasia, Africa, and North America and also called butcherbird. Shrikes range from 6–14 in (15 to 36 cm) in length and have soft black, gray, or brown plumage. They dive on insects and small vertebrates from the air, killing them with their hooked falcon-like bills, often impaling prey on thorns.

shrimp A *crustacean, usually 1.6–3.1 in (4–8 cm) long, belonging to a worldwide suborder (*Natantia*; about 2000 species) that occurs in fresh and salt water. Shrimps have a semitransparent body with long slender legs (the first pair pincer-like), a fanlike tail, and whiplike antennae, nearly as long as the body. Shrimps swim backward by rapid flexions of the abdomen and tail and they feed on small animals or plants. Many species, including the European *Crangon vulgaris*, are commercially important as food. Order: *Decapoda*.

shrimp plant A popular ornamental plant, *Beloperone guttata*, native to warm regions of the Americas. About 18 in (45 cm) high, it has inconspicuous white flowers enclosed by reddish-brown leaflike bracts, so that the whole flower cluster resembles a shrimp. Family: *Acanthaceae*.

Shropshire A county in the West Midlands of England, bordering on Wales. The Severn River separates the lowlands in the N and E from the uplands in the S and W. Area: 1348 sq mi (3490 sq km). Population (1981): 375,610. Administrative center: Shrewsbury.

Shroud of Turin A relic believed to be the linen cloth used to wrap Christ's body for burial. It bears impressions of a human body marked with wounds consonant with Christ's at the crucifixion. It has been kept in Turin since 1578, but there are gaps in its history prior to the 14th century. It has been subjected to a number of tests, some with surprising results, although none can be said to have confirmed or disproved its authenticity.

Shrove Tuesday The day before the beginning of Lent (*see* Ash Wednesday), so called from the "shriving" (i.e. confession and absolution) of the faithful that was customary before the Lenten season. In many countries carnivals are held, including New Orleans' famous Mardi Gras (Fat Tuesday) celebration.

shrub. *See* tree.

Shumen. *See* Kolarovgrad.

Shute, Nevil (Nevil Shute Norway; 1899–1960) British novelist. He combined novel writing with his professional career as an aeronautical engineer. He settled in Australia after World War II. His many popular novels include *A Town Like Alice* (1950) and *On the Beach* (1957), which concerns the destruction of mankind in an atomic war.

sial The earth's continental crust, which is composed of granitic rocks rich in silicon (Si) and aluminum (Al). It is less dense than the underlying layer of *sima and much thicker.

Sialkot 32 29N 74 35E A city in Pakistan. The shrine of the first Sikh guru, Nanak, is situated here. Industries include textiles, surgical instruments, and sporting goods. Population (1972): 203,779.

Siam. *See* Thailand.

Siam, Gulf of An arm of the South China Sea, about 310 mi (500 km) wide and 435 mi (700 km) long, bordering on Thailand, Kampuchea, and Vietnam.

siamang The largest of the *gibbons, *Hylobates syndactylus*, found in Malaya and Sumatra. Up to 35 in (90 cm) tall, with arms spanning 60 in (150 cm), siamangs have a large naked vocal sac on the throat, which expands to give volume to their cries.

Siamese cat A breed of short-haired cat, originating from SE Asia. The Siamese has a graceful slender body, a wedge-shaped head with slanted blue eyes and large pointed ears, and a long slim tapering tail. The fur on the body is cream-colored or off-white, shading into one of several colors (seal-brown, blue-gray, chocolate, lilac, tabby, or red) on the ears, mask, paws, and tail (the "points"). The seal-pointed and blue-pointed varieties are probably the most popular.

Siamese twins Identical twins who are fused together, usually at the head or along the trunk. They may have developed equally or unequally; in the latter case, one baby is fairly normal but is attached to a wasted remnant of a fetus. Siamese twins can sometimes be surgically separated, providing that vital organs are not involved in the point of union. The original Siamese twins, Chang and Eng (1811–74), were born in Siam; they were joined at the hip and remained fused, despite which they each married and fathered children.

Sian. *See* Xi An.

Sian incident. *See* Xi An incident.

Sibelius, Jean (Johan Julius Christian S.; 1865–1957) Finnish composer. He began to compose as a child and studied at the Helsinki conservatoire and in Berlin and Vienna. In 1897 the government made him a grant for ten years to enable him to compose full time. Many of his works have Finnish associations and many were inspired by the epic poem the *Kalevala*. His works include seven symphonies, the symphonic poems *Kullervo* (choral; 1892), *En Saga* (1892), *The Swan of Tuonela* (1893), *Finlandia* (1899–1900), and *Tapiola* (1925), a violin concerto, a string quartet entitled "Voces Intimae," and many songs.

Siberia A region in the Soviet Union, chiefly in the RSFSR. Corresponding to N Asia, it is bordered on the W by the Ural Mountains, on the N by the Arctic Ocean, on the E by the Pacific Ocean, and on the S by Mongolia and China; the Soviet Union excludes, for administrative purposes, parts of the extreme W, E, and S. Siberia comprises three geographical areas—the West Siberian Plain, the Central Siberian Plateau, and the Soviet Far East. It is notorious for its long harsh winters, during which the lowest temperatures anywhere in the world have been recorded. Its outstandingly rich mineral resources include coal, especially in the *Kuznetsk Basin, petroleum, diamonds, and gold. Forestry is also important and Siberia's many rivers (notably the Ob, Yenisei, and Lena) are harnessed for hydroelectric power. The Russian settlement of Siberia began in 1581 but was intermittent until the building (1891–1905) of the Trans-Siberian Railroad. Siberia has long been a place of exile for Russian criminals and political prisoners. Area: about 5,330,896 sq mi (13,807,037 sq km).

Siberian Husky. *See* Husky.

Sibiu 45 46N 24 09E A city in central Romania. An important center for Transylvania in the 15th century, it possesses the Brukenthal Museum, one of the oldest in Europe, and much medieval architecture. It is now a major industrial center, manufacturing machinery, textiles, and food products. Population (1979 est): 156,854.

Sibyl In Greek and Roman mythology, any of various divinely inspired prophetesses, the most famous of which was the Sibyl of Cumae, near Naples. Three books of these Sibylline prophecies were preserved in the Temple of Jupiter on the Capitoline hill at Rome and were consulted in national emergencies.

Sica, Vittorio De. *See* De Sica, Vittorio.

Sichuan (Ssu-ch'uan *or* Szechwan) A province in central China, on the Yangtze River, surrounded by mountains. The center is a plateau and the E a fertile plain. Warm and humid and China's most productive rice area, it is prosperous and densely populated, with several ethnic groups. Besides rice, produce includes corn, sugar cane, wheat, cotton, and forest products. The W is good grazing land, exporting pig bristles. Salt, gas, oil, coal, and other minerals are produced. Despite great difficulties with transport because of its mountainous surroundings, it has flourishing industries. It is also known for its crafts. *History*: it was among the first areas settled by the Chinese, important from the 3rd century BC, when China's oldest irrigation system was constructed here. A kingdom in the 3rd century AD, separatism often flourished because of the area's self-sufficiency and impenetrable position; it became the center of the Nationalist government during the Sino-Japanese War (1937–45). Economic development was stimulated at this time by migration from the coasts and has again speeded up since the 1950s. Area: about 220,000 sq mi (569,800 sq km). Population (1976 est): 80,000,000. Capital: Chengdu.

Sicilian Vespers (1282) The massacre of 2000 French residents of Palermo that began the Sicilian revolt, backed by Pedro III of Aragon (1236–85; reigned 1276–85), against the oppressive regime of the Angevin *Charles I. General war ensued between the Aragonese, Sicilians, and Italian Ghibellines on one side and the Angevins, French, and Italian Guelfs, supported by the papacy, on the other. Aragonese control was finally established in 1302 under Pedro's son Frederick II (1272–1337). *See also* Guelfs and Ghibellines.

Sicily The largest island in the Mediterranean Sea, which together with adjacent islands comprises an autonomous region of Italy. It is separated from the mainland by the Strait of Messina. Sicily is largely mountainous, rising to over 5,900 ft (1800 m) with its highest point at Mount Etna. Although most of the population is concentrated in urban centers, the region is underdeveloped and there is much poverty. The service sector is important, as is the mining industry, especially oil. The region's farmers produce citrus fruits, vegetables, wheat, rye, olives, and wine. Manufacturing industries include oil refining, petrochemicals, chemicals, pharmaceuticals, and food processing. *History*: settled by the Greeks in the 8th century BC, it was later occupied by the Carthaginians and between 241 and 211 BC it became a Roman province. It was conquered by the Arabs in the 9th century AD and in 1060 the Norman conquest of Sicily began. In 1266 Charles I became the first Angevin King of Sicily, which was conquered by Aragon in 1284 following the revolt called the *Sicilian Vespers. In 1734 Don Carlos of Bourbon became Charles IV (*see* Charles III of Spain) of Naples and Sicily, which formally became the Kingdom of the Two Sicilies in 1815 under *Ferdinand I. After conquest by Garibaldi (1860), Sicily was united with the rest of Italy. Since then Sicily's history has been one of trouble and discontent as a result of an ailing economy and the persistence of widespread poverty, which has not been helped by the island's social structure, the *Mafia, and other conservative forces on the island presenting an obstacle to reform. Area: 9927 sq mi (25,710 sq km). with adjacent islands. Population (1980 est): 5,024,316. Capital: Palermo.

Sickert, Walter Richard (1860–1942) British impressionist painter and etcher, born in Munich of Danish and Irish parentage. He studied under *Whistler and *Degas. His paintings of Venice and Dieppe (1895–1905) and scenes from the music hall and domestic life are distinguishable from French *impressionism chiefly by their somber colors.

sickle-cell disease A condition resulting from the production of an abnormal form of hemoglobin (the pigment of red blood cells). The disease is hereditary and affects only blacks. When the blood is deprived of oxygen the abnormal hemoglobin crystallizes and distorts the red cells into a sickle shape: these sickle cells are removed from the blood by the spleen, which leads to *anemia. Children affected with the severest form of the disease do not usually survive until adulthood; those less severely affected do survive and even tend to have some built-in resistance to malaria, which may partly explain the persistence of this harmful gene in the population.

sidereal period The time taken by a planet or satellite to return to the same point in its orbit, i.e. to complete one revolution, with reference to the background stars. It can be determined from the body's *synodic period.

sidewinder A small nocturnal *rattlesnake, *Crotalus cerastes*, occurring in deserts of the SW US and Mexico, that has a sideways looping method of locomotion enabling it to move quickly over loose sand. 18–30 in (45–75 cm) long, it is usually pale brown or gray with indistinct darker spotting and a hornlike scale above each eye.

Sidgwick, Henry (1838–1900) British moral philosopher. Sidgwick's major academic work, *The Methods of Ethics* (1874), was a comparative study of moral philosophy, which focused on *hedonism and *utilitarianism. As a university teacher, he worked for the abolition of religious tests at Cambridge and the admission of women students. He was the first president of the Society for Psychical Research (1882–85).

Sidi-Bel-Abbès 35 12N 0 42W A city in NW Algeria. An old Moorish town, it was the headquarters of the French Foreign Legion until 1962. It lies in a fertile area renowned for its wine. Population (1974 est): 151,148.

Sidmouth, Henry Addington, 1st Viscount. *See* Addington, Henry, 1st Viscount Sidmouth.

Sidney, Algernon (1622–83) English politician, who was beheaded for complicity in a plot against Charles II and the king's brother James, Duke of York. In exile after the Restoration of Charles in 1660, he returned in 1677 and became prominent in attempts to exclude the Roman Catholic James from the succession.

Sidney, Sir Philip (1554–86) English poet and courtier. A man of letters and man of action, he typified the Renaissance ideal of the complete gentleman. His works include the prose romance *Arcadia* (1580), the sequence of Petrarchan sonnets, *Astrophel and Stella* (1591), and an important work of critical theory, *The Defense of Poesy* (1595). A gifted linguist, he served as a diplomat in Europe and was killed while fighting the Spanish in the Netherlands.

Sidon (*or* Saida) 33 32N 35 22E A small seaport in S Lebanon. It was an important Phoenician city, several references are made to it in the Bible, and it was greatly damaged during the Crusades. It is now the terminus of an oil pipeline from Saudi Arabia.

Siegen 50 52N 8 02E A city in NW West Germany, in North Rhine-Westphalia. A former center for the mining of iron ore, its manufactures now include office equipment and computers. It is the birthplace of Rubens and has a university (1972). Population (1980 est): 112,500.

Siegfried A hero of Germanic legend, who also appears in early Scandinavian legend as Sigurd. The two best-known versions of his story are the Germanic *Nibelungenlied* and the Old Norse *Volsungasaga*. In the former, Siegfried wins *Brunhild for his brother-in-law Gunther, but a quarrel between Brunhild and Siegfried's wife Kriemhild leads to Siegfried's death by treachery. In the *Volsungasaga*, Sigurd is betrothed to Brynhild (the Old Norse version of her name) but is tricked (by a magic potion) into forgetting her and marries Gudrun. He then wins Brynhild for his brother-in-law Gunnar; later Brynhild incites Gunnar to kill him. Siegfried is the hero of the last two operas of *Wagner's *The Ring of the Nibelung*.

siemens (S) The *SI unit of conductance equal to the conductance between two points on a conductor when a potential difference of one volt between the points causes a current of one ampere to flow. Named for—Ernst Werner von *Siemens.

Siemens, Ernst Werner von (1816–92) German electrical engineer, who opened a telegraph factory in 1847 and, a year later, laid a government telegraph line from Berlin to Frankfurt. Together with his brother **Karl Siemens** (1829–1906), he established telegraph factories in a number of European cities. A third brother **Sir William Siemens** (Karl Wilhelm S.; 1823–83) moved to England in 1844. He invented the open-hearth method

of making steel in 1861, which was based on the principle of heat regeneration previously patented by a fourth brother **Friedrich Siemens** (1826–1904).

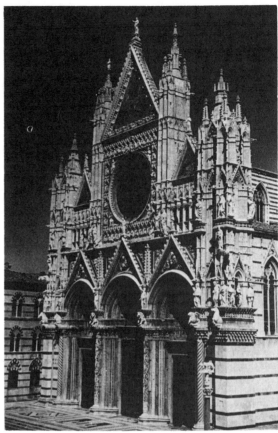

SIENA   *The cathedral.*

Siena 43 19N 11 19E A city in central Italy, in Tuscany. Founded by the Etruscans, it was an important commercial and artistic center in the middle ages. Its many fine buildings include a 13th-century gothic-romanesque cathedral, a university (1240), and several palaces, especially the Palazzo Pubblico (1297–1310) with its slender tower 328 ft (100 m) high. There are horse races through the main square of the city during the annual Palio festival. Tourism is Siena's main source of revenue. Population (1971): 65,347.

Sienkiewicz, Henryk (1846–1916) Polish novelist. His only novel generally known outside Poland is *Quo Vadis* (1896), a historical epic set in Rome under the emperor Nero; it has been the subject of many films. He also wrote a trilogy celebrating Poland's military struggles during the 17th century. He traveled extensively in Europe and the US and won the Nobel Prize in 1905.

Sierra Leone, Republic of A country in West Africa, on the Gulf of Guinea. Coastal plains, fringed by mangrove swamps, rise to higher land in the interior reaching heights of almost 6500 ft (2000 m). The majority of the population is African, the main groups being Mende and Temne. *Economy*: chiefly agricultural, organized mainly in smallholdings. The principal food crop is rice and cash crops include palm kernels, cocoa, coffee, and ginger. Livestock is important, particularly cattle in the N, and there has been considerable recent development in the fishing industry as well as in forestry. Minerals, including diamonds, iron ore, and bauxite, are the main exports and the country has important deposits of rutile, which are being exploited. *History*: in 1787 local chiefs ceded to Britain a piece of land along the coast for the settlement of slaves freed in the colonies. In 1896 the region became a British protectorate, gaining independence within the Commonwealth in 1961. In 1967 a military coup and countercoup took place and after further upheaval civilian rule was restored in 1968. In 1971 Sierra Leone became a republic. In 1977 one-party government (by the All-People's Congress) was introduced. President: Dr Siaka Stevens

(1905–). Official language: English; Krio is widely spoken. Official currency, since 1964: leone of 100 cents. Area: 27,925 sq mi (73,326 sq km). Population (1983 est): 3,705,000. Capital and main port: Freetown.

Sierra Madre   The chief mountain system of Mexico. It extends for about 1500 mi (2500 km) SE from the US border, reaching 18,697 ft (5699 m) at Citlaltépetl. It comprises the Sierra Madre Oriental (E), the Sierra Madre del Sur (S), and the Sierra Madre Occidental (W).

Sierra Maestra   A mountain range in Cuba. It extends along the extreme SE coast reaching 6476 ft (1974 m) at the Pico Turquino. Fidel *Castro established his guerrilla base here in the 1950s.

Sierra Morena   A mountain range in S Spain, extending about 249 mi (400 km) E–W between the Guadiana and Guadalquivir rivers.

Sierra Nevada   A mountain range in the US. It extends generally NW–SE through California, reaching 14,495 ft (4418 m) at Mount Whitney. It contains Yosemite National Park.

Sierra Nevada   A mountain range in S Spain. It rises to 11,421 ft (3481 m) at Mulhacén, the highest point in Spain.

Sieyès, Emmanuel Joseph   (1748–1836) French churchman, who was a leading figure in the *French Revolution. His pamphlet *Qu'est-ce que le tiers état?* (*What Is the Third Estate?*, 1789) greatly influenced the revolt of the Third Estate at the start of the Revolution. He voted for the execution of the king but withdrew from politics during the Jacobins' ascendancy. In 1799 he became a member of the *Directory and helped to bring about the coup that established Napoleon Bonaparte in power. His influence thereafter declined.

sifaka   A *prosimian primate belonging to the genus *Propithecus* (2 species), of Madagascar. About 20 in (50 cm) long, with a tail the same length, sifakas have long white fur with red or orange and black markings. They have long hind legs and are mainly arboreal, feeding on leaves, buds, fruit, and bark. Family: *Indriidae*.

Siger of Brabant   (c. 1240–c. 1284) French theologian. A teacher at Paris University, Siger was accused of heresy (1276) on account of his criticisms of Aristotle, in which he appeared to dissent from doctrines of immortality and the afterlife. *Aquinas wrote a treatise against him, but Dante placed him among the 12 sages.

Sigismund   (1368–1437) Holy Roman Emperor (1411–37; crowned 1433) and King of Hungary (1387–1437) and of Bohemia (1419–37). He conducted two unsuccessful crusades against the Turks (1396; 1428) and was largely responsible for the summoning of the Council of *Constance to heal the Great Schism. Implicated in the treacherous burning of John *Hus in 1415, he fought the *Hussites throughout the 1420s.

Sigismund (I) the Old   (1467–1548) King of Poland (1506–48). Sigismund gained control of E Prussia (1525) after defeating the *Teutonic Knights. He encouraged the development of the Renaissance in Poland.

Sigismund II Augustus   (1520–72) King of Poland (1548–72); the last of the Jagiellon dynasty. Sigismund's reign saw the Union of *Lublin (1569), which united Poland with Lithuania, and the expansion of the Polish Reformation.

Sigismund III Vasa   (1566–1632) King of Poland (1587–1632) and Sweden (1592–99). Sigismund was deposed from the Swedish throne by his uncle, later *Charles IX of Sweden, and failed in his subsequent attempts to regain the crown. Charles' son *Gustavus II Adolphus conquered Poland's Livonian territory (1621). Sigismund had some success against Russia, capturing and holding Moscow (1610–12).

Siglo de Oro   The Golden Age of Spanish literature that lasted from about 1550 to 1650. The literature of this period was characterized by patriotism and new attitudes of critical realism. Leading writers included the dramatist Lope de Vega, the novelist Cervantes, and the poet Luis de Góngora.

Signac, Paul   (1863–1935) French painter and art theorist associated with *pointillism. A disciple of *Seurat, he is known chiefly for his mosaic-like paintings of European harbors and his treatise *D'Eugène Delacroix au Néo-impressionisme* (1899).

Signorelli, Luca   (c. 1441–1523) Italian Renaissance painter, born in Cortona. Probably the pupil of *Piero della Francesca, he worked in Florence, Perugia, and in the Vatican, where he painted a fresco for the Sistine Chapel (c. 1481). He completed frescoes in Orvieto Cathedral begun by Fra *Angelico and painted his masterpiece, *The Last Judgment*, there (1499). His studies of muscular nudes were admired by and influential on Michelangelo.

signoria   (Italian: lordship)   A form of government in late medieval Italian city states following the collapse of communal government caused by

factional struggles. Control was given (sometimes voluntarily) to a *signore* (lord), who formed a more or less despotic government. *Signori* established dynasties, especially in N Italy (e.g. the *Visconti and *Este), which often gained reputations for good government and artistic patronage.

Sigurdsson.   *See* Sverrir.

Sihanouk, Norodim, Prince   (1923–) King (1941–70) of Cambodia (now Kampuchea). When the Japanese occupation ended in 1945, Sihanouk, after much opposition and factional strife, achieved Cambodia's independence from France (1953). Abdicating in 1955, he continued to dominate Cambodian politics as prime minister until 1970, when his regime was overthrown by a military coup and he went into exile in China. After the victory of the Khmer Rouge guerrillas (1975) he again became head of state but retired in 1976. He continues in exile his efforts to regain control of the Cambodian government.

sika   A deer, *Cervus nippon*, also called Japanese deer, native to S Asia, Japan, and Taiwan and introduced to New Zealand and Europe. Gray-brown in winter and chestnut with white spots in summer, its shoulder height is 27.5–40 in (70–100 cm). Stags have slender eight-pointed antlers about 32 in (80 cm) long.

Sikhism   The religion of some nine million Indians, mostly inhabiting the Punjab. Founded in the 15th century by the Guru *Nanak, Sikhism combines Hindu and Islamic ideas. The Hindu concepts of *karma and rebirth are accepted, but the caste system is rejected. Sikhs believe that god is the only reality and that spiritual release can be obtained by taming the ego through devotional singing, recitation of the divine name, meditation, and service. The guidance of the *guru is essential. The concept of Khalsa, a chosen race of warrior-saints, is central, as are the so-called five Ks: *kangha* (comb); *kacch* (shorts); *kirpan* (sword); *kara* (steel bracelet); and *kes* (uncut hair and beard). *See also* 'Adi Granth. The Sikhs came to world attention in 1984 with the occupation of their holy temple at Amritsar by Indian troops, which was followed a few months later by the assassination of Indian prime minister Indira Gandhi by her Sikh bodyguards. Violent reprisals against Sikhs took place throughout India.

Sikh Wars   1.   (1845–46) The war caused by the invasion of British India by the Sikhs from their territory in the Punjab. The Sikh defeat resulted in the loss of territory that included Kashmir. **2.** (1848–49) The war that developed from a Sikh revolt at Multan. Following the Sikh defeat, by Gough at Gujarat (February 22, 1849), the Punjab was annexed by the British.

Sikkim   A state in NE India, in the Himalayas E of Nepal. Low valleys rise to Mount Kangchenjunga, 8598 m (28,208 ft), providing a tremendous range in climate and vegetation. The world's biggest cardamom producer, Sikkim also grows mandarin oranges, grains, potatoes, pulses, and ginger. Copper is mined and the jungle exploited for timber. A variety of people, most of whom are Buddhists, inhabit Sikkim. *History*: ruled by a Buddhist dynasty, Sikkim passed under British and then Indian protection (1947). Following a plebiscite Sikkim became the 22nd state of India in 1975. Area: 2817 sq mi (7298 sq km). Population (1981 est): 315,682. Capital: Gangtok.

Sikorski, Władysław   (1881–1943) Polish general and statesman. Sikorski was prime minister (1922–23) and minister of military affairs (1924–25). After Poland's collapse in 1939, he became prime minister of the Polish government-in-exile in London. The circumstances of his death, in an airplane crash near Gibraltar, are the subject of a controversial play by Rolf *Hochhuth.

Sikorsky, Igor Ivan   (1889–1972) Russian-born US aeronautical engineer, who invented the helicopter. He began experimenting with helicopter designs in 1909 but his early models failed and he turned to the design and construction of aircraft, producing the S-1 biplane in 1910. In 1919 he moved to the US, returning to the problem of helicopters in the 1930s and completing the first successful model, the VS-300, in 1939.

silage   A cattle food produced from a fresh fodder crop, usually grass or a green cereal crop, that has been preserved by controlled bacterial fermentation. The crop is placed in an airtight structure (silo) and allowed to ferment; the organic acids produced "pickle" the crop and prevent further decay, resulting in highly digestible and nutritious food. Silage making is a rapid and versatile method of fodder conservation.

Silchester   (Latin: Calleva Atrebatum)   An ancient capital of the British tribe of Atrebates in S England. Rebuilt after the Roman conquest, Silchester was inhabited until the 6th century AD. The Roman town wall (c. 200 AD) is still visible.

Silenus In Greek mythology, an elderly *Satyr, companion of the god *Dionysus. He was famed for his wisdom and prophetic powers as well as his drunkenness. The Sileni were his fellow nature spirits.

Silesia A region of E central Europe now in Czechoslovakia and Poland. Because of its geographical position, mineral wealth, and industrial potential, Silesia has been disputed territory since the 17th century, when it was claimed by both Austria and Prussia. Its seizure by Frederick the Great of Prussia, which precipitated the War of the *Austrian Succession, was finally recognized by Austria in 1763, after the *Seven Years' War. After World War I it was divided between Czechoslovakia, Germany, and Poland and after World War II, between Czechoslovakia and Poland.

silhouette In art, a profile image or portrait in black on a white background or vice versa. Named for the French finance minister Étienne de Silhouette (1709–67), who made paper cut-outs of silhouettes, this type of portrait was very popular in the late 18th and early 19th centuries until it was supplanted by photography.

silica The mineral silicon dioxide, SiO_2, the most abundant of all minerals. There are three main forms of silica: *quartz, tridymite, and cristobalite, the last two occurring in acidic volcanic rocks. Cryptocrystalline silica is *chalcedony; amorphous silica is *opal. Creosite is a high-pressure variety, found near meteorite craters. Lechatelierite is a natural silica glass. Silica content is used to classify igneous rocks into acidic (over 65% silica), intermediate (52–66% silica), basic (45–52% silica), and ultrabasic (under 45% silica) varieties. Since these terms do not reflect pH value, another classification based on silica content is also frequently used; in this igneous rocks are classified as oversaturated (containing free silica), saturated (all silica combined with no unsaturated minerals, e.g. feldspathoids), or undersaturated (containing unsaturated minerals). *See also* silicate minerals.

silicate minerals A group of minerals that constitute about 90% of the earth's crust and one third of all minerals. They consist of silicates of calcium, magnesium, aluminum, or other metals, in varying degrees of complexity. They are classified according to their atomic structure; all are based on the tetrahedral unit SiO_4. *Feldspar and *quartz (which is chemically an oxide but resembles the silicates more closely in many properties and is usually included in this group) are the most common. *See also* amphiboles; clay; garnet; micas; olivine; pyroxene.

silicon (Si) The second most abundant element in the earth's crust, after oxygen. It is a major constituent of almost all rock-forming minerals (*see* silicate minerals). The element was discovered by J. J. Berzelius in 1824 and is extracted by reduction of the oxide (silica; SiO_2) with carbon in an electric furnace. Pure silicon is now of great importance in the electronics industry as a semiconductor. It is prepared by decomposition of trichlorosilane ($SiCl_3H$). Silicates have been important for centuries as the main constituents of pottery, glasses, and many building materials. Silicon carbide (*see* carborundum) is a widely used abrasive, refractory, and semiconductor. Organic silicon compounds are known as *silicones. At no 14; at wt 28.086; mp 2573°F (1410°C); bp 4275°F (2355°C).

silicon chip. *See* integrated circuit.

silicones Synthetic polymers consisting of chains of alternating silicon and oxygen atoms, with organic groups attached to the former. The chains can be cross-linked to varying degrees. Silicones include fluids, greases, rubbers, and resins. All have similar chemical properties: stability to heat, oxidation, many chemicals, and oils. The main applications are in adhesives, paints, elastomers, and waterproofing agents.

silicosis A lung disease caused by prolonged inhalation of silica dust: an occupational disease of stone cutters, quarry workers, etc. Silica causes more damage than an equivalent amount of coaldust: the air sacs of the lungs become thickened and scarred, causing breathlessness and coughing in the patients. There is no specific treatment and prevention by use of masks and other safety measures is essential. *See also* pneumoconiosis.

silk The thread produced by the caterpillar of the *silkworm moth and the fabric woven from it. The cocoons are unraveled and the filaments from several twisted together; processing this raw silk includes combining these strands, washing away the sticky sericin secretion, and sometimes adding metallic salts for weight. China, where silk production was first practiced, and Japan are the leading producers of pure silk; wild silk, produced by silkworms that feed on leaves other than mulberry or by uncultivated silkworms, includes a coarser brown Indian silk. Lustrous, elastic, absorbent, and very strong, silk remains a luxury fabric considerably superior to its synthetic imitations.

silk-cotton tree. *See* kapok.

Silk Road A trade route, 4000 mi (6400 km) long, that connected China with the Mediterranean. It was most used in antiquity, when silk was taken westward and wool and precious metals eastward, but was again traveled in the later middle ages, notably by Marco Polo.

silkworm A caterpillar that spins a silken cocoon, especially one that is suitable for commercial silk production. The commonest is the Chinese silkworm (*Bombyx mori*), which feeds on mulberry leaves. The pupae are killed by heat and the silken thread, up to 2,953 ft (900 m) long, is then unwound. 50,000 cocoons are needed to produce 2.2 lb (1 kg) of silk. The Japanese oak silkmoth (*Antherea yamanai*) and the Chinese species *A. pernyi* are also used. Some American moths, such as the *cecropia and *io, also produce silk.

silky oak One of two species of Australian trees. *Grevillea robusta*, found in forests of E Australia, grows to a height of 115 ft (35 m) and has fernlike leaves. It is widely cultivated in the tropics as an ornamental or shade tree. The northern silky oak (*Cardwellia sublimis*) is an important timber tree, its pinkish soft wood being used in furniture manufacturing and for building purposes.

silky terrier A breed of toy dog developed in Australia by crossing the Australian terrier with the Yorkshire terrier. Formerly called the Sydney silky, it has a compact body with short legs. The long fine glossy coat is blue and tan or gray-blue and tan. Height: 9–10 in (23–25 cm).

sill A horizontal or near-horizontal sheetlike mass of intrusive igneous rock, lying parallel to the layering of the rock into which it is intruded. Most sills consist of medium-grained hypabyssal rock, the commonest being dolerite. *Compare* dike.

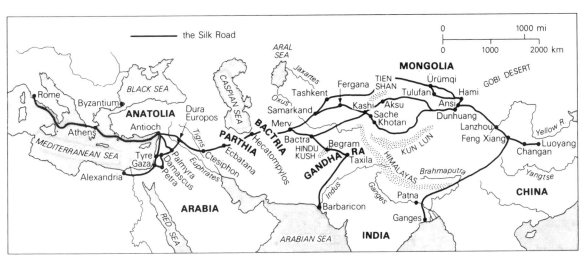

SILK ROAD *Between the 1st century BC and the 3rd century AD Chinese silks traveled westwards to the Mediterranean in exchange for precious metals.*

Sillitoe, Alan (1928–) British novelist. He won immediate success with his first novel, *Saturday Night and Sunday Morning* (1958), about the violent and alienated life of a Nottingham factory worker. This was followed by a book of short stories, *The Loneliness of the Long Distance Runner* (1959). His many later books include the semiautobiographical *Raw Material* (1972), and additional short stories, *The Second Chance* (1981).

Sills, Beverly (Belle Silverman; 1929–) US soprano. She sang with the Philadelphia Civic Opera in 1948 and with the San Francisco Opera Company (1953–55). Although she joined the New York City Opera in 1955, it was not until 1966 that she began to sing lead roles, including Cleopatra in *Julius Caesar*. She made her guest debut at La Scala in Milan, Italy (1969) and at the Metropolitan Opera House (1975). Meanwhile, she remained at the New York City Opera and became its managing director in 1980.

Silone, Ignazio (Secondo Tranquilli; 1900–78) Italian novelist. He helped found the Italian Communist Party in 1921, lived in exile in Switzerland from 1930 until after World War II, and then returned to Italy to lead the Democratic Socialist Party until 1950. He became disillusioned with communism, but his novels, especially *Fontamara* (1930) and *Bread and Wine* (1937), express his strong socialist concern for the peasants of S Italy.

silt A fine-grained sedimentary deposit, the rock particles of which range from 0.0008–0.002 in (0.002 to 0.06 mm) in diameter. Silts consist mainly of clay minerals, with iron oxides and hydroxides and silica. They collect in sheltered marine environments, such as estuaries, making dredging necessary if the estuary is to be navigable. Consolidated silts form siltstones.

Silurian period A geological period of the Lower Paleozoic era between the Ordovician and Devonian periods, lasting from about 445 to 415 million years ago. Conditions were mainly marine and the first true fish appeared. The first evidence of land plants also comes from Silurian rocks. The Caledonian period of mountain building reached its peak toward the end of the period.

Silvanus A Roman woodland god, sometimes identified with the Greek *Pan. He was usually portrayed as an old countryman. He was worshiped at sacred groves or trees.

silver (Ag) A metallic element, known since ancient times. It occurs in nature as the metal, as argentite (Ag_2S), and in lead, zinc, and copper ores. Pure silver has the highest electrical and thermal conductivity known and is used in some printed electrical circuits. In air, silver tarnishes forming a coating of the black sulfide (Ag_2S). Alloys of silver are used as solders and sterling silver (92.5% pure) is used for jewelry. Although not a reactive metal, silver forms many compounds including the oxide (Ag_2O), the nitrate ($AgNO_3$), and halides (for example AgCl, AgBr). Silver salts are of great importance in photography since they are light sensitive, and some 30% of the silver produced is used in this way. Silver iodide (AgI) has been used in attempts to seed clouds to induce rainfall. At no 47; at wt 107.868; mp 1765°F (962°C); bp 4017°F (2212°C).

Silver Age, Latin The period (18–c. 130 AD) succeeding the *Golden Age of *Latin literature. During this time rhetorical brilliance and ornamentation became prized for its own sake. Major writers include the satirist *Juvenal, the epigrammatist *Martial, the historians *Tacitus and *Suetonius, and the philosopher and dramatist *Seneca.

silverfish A widely distributed primitive wingless ☐insect, *Lepisma saccharina*, also called fish moth. One of the three-pronged *bristletails, it is covered with silvery scales and is common in buildings, especially kitchens, bakeries, and libraries, feeding on starchy materials, including books and fabrics. Family: *Lepismatidae*.

silver fox. *See* red fox.

silverplate Any object that is plated with silver rather than being solid silver. The first substitute for pure silver for tableware, etc., was the invention of *Sheffield plate in 1742. In 1840 the advent of *electroplating brought silverplated domestic articles to a much wider public. Many silverplated articles are marked EPNS (electroplated nickel silver)—nickel silver itself is an alloy of copper, nickel, and zinc and contains no silver; in this process a layer of silver is electroplated onto the nickel-silver base.

silverside A fish, also called sand smelt or whitebait, belonging to a family (*Atherinidae*) found in fresh and coastal waters of warm and temperate regions. Its small slim body, up to 28 in (70 cm) long, bears a silvery band along each side and two dorsal fins. Order: *Atheriniformes*.

sima The earth's oceanic crust, which is composed of basaltic rocks rich in silica (Si) and magnesium (Mg). It is denser than the *sial of the continental crust and is believed to continue beneath it.

Si-ma Qian (*or* Ssu-ma Ch'ien; c. 145–c. 85 BC) Chinese historian, astronomer, and calendar reformer. He succeeded his father as historian to the Han Emperor Wu, but he offended the emperor and was castrated and imprisoned. He later became palace secretary. His *Records of the Historian*, the first major Chinese historical work, included the entire documented history of China to that date.

GEORGES SIMENON

Simenon, Georges (1903–) Belgian novelist. The best known of his several hundred novels are his detective stories featuring the Parisian *commissaire de police*, Maigret, who first appeared in 1931. His other novels, written in a brisk colloquial style and with intuitive psychological perception, include *La Neige était sale* (1948) and the semiautobiographical *Pedigree* (1948).

Simeon, tribe of One of the 12 *tribes of Israel. It claimed descent from Simeon, the son of Jacob and Leah. The territory allocated to the tribe was S of that of Judah, W and SW of the Dead Sea. It was eventually assimilated into Judah.

Simeon Stylites, St (c. 390–459 AD) Syrian monk and hermit, who lived for over 35 years on a small platform on top of a tall pillar (Greek, *stylos*). His many imitators were known as stylites. Feast day: Jan 5.

Simferopol 44 57N 34 05E A city in the Soviet Union, the capital of the Crimean *oblast* (autonomous region) in the S Ukrainian SSR. It has food-processing, engineering, and consumer-goods industries. Population (1981 est): 314,000.

simile A figure of speech in which two things are compared in order to emphasize a particular feature or quality they share. A simile differs from a *metaphor in being an explicit comparison, usually using the words *as* or *like*, for example "He fought like a lion."

Simla 31 07N 77 09E A city in India, the capital of Himachal Pradesh situated in the foothills of the Himalayas. It was the summer capital of India (1865–1939). Population (1971): 55,326.

Simms, William Gilmore (1806–70) US novelist. He wrote many historical romances concerning life in the South, including *Guy Rivers* (1834) and *The Yemassee* (1835). He edited various Southern magazines, defended slavery, and suffered personal ruin in the Civil War.

Simnel, Lambert (c. 1475–1535) English impostor whom the Yorkists tried to pass off as Edward, Earl of Warwick (1475–99), a Yorkist claimant to the throne, in a plot to overthrow Henry VII. Simnel was captured in 1487 and subsequently worked in the king's kitchens.

Simon, St In the New Testament, one of the 12 Apostles. He is surnamed the Canaanite or Zelotes, which possibly means that he was one of the *Zealots. He preached in Egypt and joined St *Jude in Persia, where, according to one tradition, he was martyred by being cut in half with a saw. Feast day: Oct 28.

Simonov, Konstantin (1915–79) Soviet novelist, playwright, poet, and journalist. His writings, which focus chiefly on World War II, include the poem "Wait for Me" and the novels *Days and Nights* (1945), on the defense of Stalingrad, and *Victims and Heroes* (1959).

simple harmonic motion Any oscillation performed by a body about some reference point so that the restraining force is directly proportional to its displacement from that point. Examples of simple harmonic motion include a *pendulum swinging through a small angle and a vibrating string. The maximum displacement of the system is known as the amplitude and the time taken for one complete oscillation, the *period. The displacement, x, at a time t is simply represented by the equation $x = A\sin\omega t$, where A is the amplitude and ω the angular frequency, which is related to the period T by $\omega = 2\pi/T$. Thus a graph of the displacement x plotted against time t has the shape of a sine wave, i.e. it is sinusoidal.

Simplon Pass An alpine pass linking Brig in Switzerland with Iselle in Italy. It was built between 1800 and 1807 on Napoleon's orders and reaches a height of 6590 ft (2009 m). The **Simplon Tunnel** to the NE is, at 12 mi (20 km), the longest rail tunnel in the world. Built in 1890 by Alfred Brandt (1846–99), it was opened in 1906.

Simpson, George Gaylord (1902–) US paleontologist, noted for his contributions to knowledge of the early history of mammals and the intercontinental migration of species. Simpson studied mammalian fossil remains in both North and South America and, in *The Meaning of Evolution* (1949), discussed the philosophical implications of evolutionary theory.

Simpson Desert (*or* Arunta Desert) A desert of central Australia, mainly in Northern Territory. It consists of an arid region covered by parallel sand dunes, which extend to 100 mi (160 km) in length. Area: about 29,723 sq mi (77,000 sq km).

Sinai A desert peninsula in Egypt, bounded by Israel and the Gulf of Aqaba to the E and the Gulf of Suez and mainland Egypt to the W. Mount Sinai, 7497 ft (2285 m) high, is in the mountain range in the S. According to the Old Testament it was on this mountain that Moses received the tablets of the law from Jehovah (Exodus 24). The N half of the desert is plateau. The chief resources of the region are manganese and the oil deposits in the W, based on Sudr; agriculture is practiced on the Mediterranean coast. Sinai was occupied by Israel in the 1956 and again in the 1967 Arab-Israeli Wars and following the 1973 war Egyptian and Israeli lines were established on either side of a UN buffer zone. Under the 1979 Egyptian-Israeli agreement a large proportion of the area was returned to Egypt, with Israel withdrawal completed in 1982.

FRANK SINATRA *He is seen (left) in a comic scene with Bing Crosby (center) and Dean Martin.*

Sinatra, Frank (Francis Albert S.; 1915–) US singer and film actor, who recorded his first hit, "All or Nothing at All," in 1943. His nonsinging role in the film *From Here to Eternity* (1953), earned him an Oscar; he subsequently appeared in such films as *Guys and Dolls* (1955), *The Manchurian Candidate* (1962), and *The First Deadly Sin* (1980). He recorded such hits as "Strangers in the Night" (1966) and his concerts continue to be very popular.

Sinclair, Upton (1878–1968) US novelist. A committed socialist, he used the profits from *The Jungle* (1906), a novel of social protest, to establish a cooperative for left-wing writers and to finance several unsuccessful political campaigns. The best known of his many polemical novels are the 11-volume Lanny Budd series known as *World's End* (1940–53).

Sind A province in SE Pakistan, on the Arabian Sea. From the broad Indus lowland it extends E into the Thar Desert and W into rocky hills. Grains, other crops, and livestock are raised. Important industries include textiles, chemicals, and cement. *History*: Sind's history goes back 5000 years. Islam was introduced in 711–12 AD and British rule established in 1843. Area: 54,407 sq mi (140,914 sq km). Population (1972): 13,965,000. Capital: Karachi.

Singapore, Republic of A republic in SE Asia, off the S tip of Peninsular Malaysia, consisting of the island of Singapore and over 50 islets. The city of Singapore, located in the S, occupies a substantial part of the island's area. The majority of the diverse population is Chinese with minorities of Malays, Indians, and others. *Economy*: Singapore is the largest port in SE Asia and one of the largest in the world, its importance being as an entrepôt port on a major searoute. It is a major commercial center and in recent years industry has been expanded and diversified. The chief industries are oil refining (it has the third largest refining complex in the world), ship building and repairing, textiles, and electronics. The fishing industry is being developed, ornamental fish being an important export. The main exports are rubber, oil and oil products, machinery, and transport equipment. *History*: although a prosperous commercial center in the middle ages, the island was largely uninhabited in 1819 when Sir Stamford Raffles established a station of the British East India Company here. In 1824 it was ceded to Britain as part of the *Straits Settlements. During World War II it was occupied by the Japanese, the British defense forces having surrendered in 1942. It became a separate British colony in 1946 and gained its independence in 1959. It joined the Federation of Malaysia on its formation (1963) but broke away in 1965, following conflict with the predominantly Malay central government, and formed an independent republic. President: C. V. Devan Nair. Prime minister: Lee Kuan Yew (1922–). Official languages: Chinese, English, Malay, and Tamil. Official currency: Singapore dollar of 100 cents. Area: 232 sq mi (602 sq km). Population (1983): 2,503,000.

Singer, Isaac Bashevis (1904–) US novelist and short-story writer. Born into a rabbinical Jewish family in Poland, he emigrated to the US in 1935. His novels and collections of stories, written in Yiddish and frequently dramatizing traditional themes from Jewish life in Poland, include *Gimpel the Fool* (1957), *The Slave* (1960), *Shosha* (1978), *Old Love* (1979), and *The Collected Stories of Isaac Bashevis Singer* (1982).

Singer, Isaac Merrit (1811–75) US inventor, who in 1857 designed and built the first commercially successful domestic sewing machine. It was a great improvement on Elias *Howe's machine and incorporated a number of innovations, such as continuous stitching, that remain the basis of all modern sewing machines.

singing The use of the human voice as a musical instrument, involving the control of a column of air sent from the lungs through the larynx, where it activates the vocal cords, and the subsequent resonance of the sounds produced within the sinus and mouth cavities. Styles of singing vary enormously in an art that covers many traditional folk techniques as well as those cultivated in Europe for opera and art song. The greatest European school of singing was the lyrical *bel canto (Italian: fine singing) style taught by the Italians in the 17th and 18th centuries. In the 19th century singers developed more dramatic and declamatory techniques in order to be heard over the increasingly large orchestra. In the 20th century singers have made use of microphones to amplify the voice, particularly in pop music. *See also* alto; baritone; bass; contralto; countertenor; soprano; tenor.

Sing Sing. *See* Ossining.

Sinhalese The major ethnic group in Sri Lanka. They speak an *Indo-Aryan language that has been much influenced by *Pali and the Dravidian languages, particularly *Tamil. They are descended from migrants from Bengal who colonized Sri Lanka during the 5th century BC. An agricultural people, they base their social organization on caste and practice Theravada Buddhism.

sinkhole (*or* sink) A saucer-like hollow in the ground surface, typical of chalk and limestone areas. It may form through the solvent action on limestone of rain containing dissolved carbon dioxide; alternatively it may be due to a rock collapse. Sinkholes often act as channels down which water seeps into underground drainage systems.

Sinkiang Uigur. *See* Xinjiang Uygur Autonomous Region.

Sinn Féin (Irish: Ourselves) An Irish nationalist party organized by Arthur Griffith in 1905. In 1918, under Eamon *De Valera, it won a majority of the Irish seats in the British parliament and achieved the creation of the Irish Free State in 1922. Sinn Féin exists today as the political wing of the republican movement. *See also* Irish Republican Army.

Sino-Japanese Wars 1. (1894–95) The war between China and Japan resulting from rivalry in Korea. War was declared after the Japanese sank the *Kowshing*, which was transporting Chinese reinforcements to aid the Korean king in suppressing the Tonghak uprising. Japan inflicted a crushing defeat on China, which was forced to pay a large indemnity and cede Taiwan, the Pescadores, and the Liaodong peninsula. 2. (1937–45) The war between China and Japan brought about by Japanese expansion into China in the 1930s. The Japanese had established a puppet state in Manchuria (*see* Manchukuo) in 1932 but only after the negotiation of a Nationalist-Communist *United Front against Japan did full war break out. The Japanese took Shanghai and Nanchang in 1937 and Wuhan and Canton in 1938. Their position remained strong until the US entered World War II (1941) and gave China assistance. After Japan's surrender (1945) China regained Manchuria, Taiwan, and the Pescadores.

Sinop 42 02N 35 09E A port in central N Turkey, on the Black Sea. Ancient Sinope was the most important Greek colony on the Euxine (Black) Sea and flourished under Mithridates the Great, during whose reign fine buildings and a harbor were constructed. It became part of the Ottoman Empire in 1458. Population (1970): 15,096.

Sino-Tibetan languages A group of languages spoken in E Asia. It includes all the *Chinese dialects (which use the same alphabet but differ substantially in sound), the Tibeto-Burman languages (Tibetan, Burmese, and many related languages spoken in the valleys of the Himalayas), and probably the Tai languages, such as Siamese, Laotian, and Shan. The main characteristic that justifies this large grouping is the monosyllabic nature of the vocabulary of all these languages and their use of tonality to differentiate otherwise similar words. They are all isolating languages, that is they use word order, not inflection, to determine grammatical relations.

sintering The heating without melting of powdered substance, usually metal or plastic, so that it becomes a solid mass. *See also* powder metallurgy.

Sintra (former name: Cintra) 38 48N 9 22W A city in central Portugal. Its beauty has been celebrated by several literary figures, including Byron in his *Childe Harolde*. The many notable buildings include the royal palace (14th–15th centuries) in Moorish and gothic styles. It is a tourist and agricultural center. Population (1960): 20,321.

Sinŭiju 40 04N 124 25E A port in North Korea, on the Yalu River opposite Andong, China. Its industrial development began during the Japanese occupation (1910–45) and its principal industries include sawmilling and the manufacture of paper. Population (1967 est): 165,000.

sinus A hollow cavity, especially one in a bone. The term usually refers to the air sinuses of the head, which are cavities in the facial bones; all have connections to the nasal cavity and they are susceptible to infection (*see* sinusitis). The term is also used for a pus-filled channel leading from an infected organ or tissue to a surface (usually the skin).

sinusitis Inflammation of the sinuses—the spaces in the skull that are connected to the nose. They commonly become infected when a patient has a cold or similar infection, causing pain in the face and prolonging the original illness. Sinusitis can also be caused by an allergic reaction. If the inflammation persists the affected sinuses may need to be surgically drained or washed out.

Siouan languages A family of North American Indian languages including Dakota *Sioux, *Crow, and several others. Most are spoken by Plains tribes. Some experts classify the Siouan languages as a branch of a larger family called Macro-Siouan, which includes the Iroquoian and Caddoan languages.

Sioux A confederation of North American Plains Indian tribes, also known as the Dakota. They fought fiercely against white encroachments upon their territories and defeated General Custer at the battle of the *Little Bighorn (1876) under their leaders Sitting Bull and Crazy Horse. The last conflict with the whites resulted in the massacre of a group of Sioux at *Wounded Knee (1890).

Sioux City 42 30N 96 28W A city in Iowa, on the Missouri River. An agricultural trading center, it has a large livestock market and many food-processing plants. Population (1980): 82,003.

Sioux Falls 43 34N 96 42W A city in South Dakota, on the Big Sioux River. Founded in 1857, it has one of the country's largest sheep and cattle

markets and is an important wheat center. Manufactures include farm machinery and electrical components. Population (1980): 81,071.

Siqueiros, David Alfaro (1896–) Mexican painter, one of the leaders in the Mexican Revolution of 1910 and one of the founders of modern Mexican art. A committed socialist from the start of his career, Siqueiros is best known for his monumental murals that reflect his intimate knowledge of the Mexican people. His first major murals were painted in collaboration with *Rivera and *Orozco in the National Preparatory School, Mexico City; perhaps the most impressive is *The March of Humanity*, measuring 50,000 sq ft (4600 sq m), which Siqueiros painted while he was in prison for his political activities. Since the 1950s he has been internationally recognized as one of Mexico's greatest artists.

siren An eel-like *salamander belonging to a North American family (*Sirenidae*; 3 species). Sirens have no hind legs, very small forelegs, and permanent gills. They hunt for worms, snails, etc., in ponds and swamps. The largest species is the 24 in (60 cm) mud-colored great siren (*Siren lacertina*) and the smallest is the gray mud siren (*Pseudobranchus striatus*), about 8 in (20 cm) long.

Sirens In Greek mythology, female creatures, sometimes portrayed with birdlike features, who lured sailors to their island by their singing and then destroyed them. *Odysseus saved himself by tying himself to the mast of his ship and filling the ears of his crew with wax. The *Argonauts were protected by the superior singing of *Orpheus.

Sirius (*or* Dog Star) The brightest star in the sky, with an apparent magnitude of −1.47. It occurs in the constellation Canis Major and can be found by following the descending line of Orion's Belt. It is also one of the nearest stars, lying 8.7 light years away. It forms a visual *binary star with Sirius B, which was the first *white dwarf to be detected, in 1925.

sirocco (*or* scirocco) A southerly wind occurring in N Africa, Sicily, and S Italy. Hot and dry on the N African coast, it picks up moisture as it crosses the Mediterranean Sea bringing extensive cloud to S Italy.

SISAL *The fiber is obtained from the leaves of the plant, which are up to 6 ft (1.8 m) long. Mature plants produce flower stalks, up to 20 ft (6 m) high, bearing yellow flowers.*

sisal A perennial plant, *Agave sisalana*, native to central America and cultivated throughout the tropics for its fiber. The plant, the stem of which grows to a height of only 35 in (90 cm), matures three to five years after planting and yields fiber for seven to eight years. Sisal fiber is obtained by crushing the leaves to a pulp and then scraping the pulp from the fiber, which is washed and dried. It is used in shipping, general industry, and agriculture.

siskin A Eurasian *finch, *Carduelis spinus*, occurring in N forests and at high altitudes in the south. It is about 5 in (12 cm) long with a dark yellow-green plumage, paler streaked underparts, bright-yellow wingbars, and in the male a black chin and crown. Siskins feed on small seeds, particularly those extracted from alder cones.

Sisley, Alfred (1839–99) Impressionist painter, born in Paris of British parents. In 1862, he met *Monet and *Renoir and later exhibited with them. In the 1870s he produced some of his best landscapes, for example *Misty Morning* (Louvre), and three pictures of the *Floods at Port-Marly*. Unable to sell his works, he spent his last years in poverty.

Sistine Chapel The principal chapel of the Vatican, so called because it was built for Pope Sixtus V (1473) by Giovanni dei Dolci. It is the meeting place for the College of Cardinals but is chiefly famous for its Renaissance interior decoration, with murals by *Perugino, *Botticelli, and *Ghirlandaio and the roof and ceiling by *Michelangelo.

Sisyphus A legendary Greek king of Corinth. For various offenses he was condemned in the underworld eternally to roll a boulder to the top of a hill, from whence it always rolled down again.

sitar An Indian long-necked *lute with a resonating body made from a large gourd, seven metal strings stopped against movable arched frets, and a series of sympathetic strings. The distinctive pitch distortions of sitar music are achieved by pulling and easing the strings over the raised frets. □musical instruments.

sitatunga A spiral-horned antelope, *Tragelaphus spekei*, of central African swamplands, also called marshbuck or water kodoe. Long-legged and up to 48 in (120 cm) high at the shoulder, it is deep brown with white markings on the face, chest, and back. The female lacks horns. Sitatungas feed on shrubs and aquatic plants.

Sitka 57 05N 135 20W A port in Alaska, on Baranof Island. Founded in 1799, it was the capital of Russian America until 1867 and is the site of a Russian Orthodox cathedral (1848). It was an important US naval base during World War II. The main industries are fishing and timber. Population (1970): 3370.

SITTING BULL *Chief of the Sioux who led the victorious Indian forces against Custer at The Little Big Horn in 1876.*

Sitting Bull (c. 1834–93) Chief of the Northern Sioux Indians. Early in his career he acquiesced to the demands of the Army that his people be resettled on the North Platte River (1868), but when the terms of the treaty were violated, he led a confederation of Indian forces in active opposition to the Army. Following the massacre of General George A. *Custer and his troops at the Battle of the *Little Big Horn, Sitting Bull fled with his men into Canada. After an amnesty (1881), he settled on a Dakota reservation but was killed during further hostilities in the 1890s.

Sitwell, Edith (1887–1964) British poet and writer. A lighthearted aestheticism characterizes her early experimental poetry, especially *Façade* (1923), and *Gold Coast Customs* (1929). Her brother **Sir Osbert Sitwell** (1892–1969) wrote poems, short stories, and novels, notably *Before the Bombardment* (1926), but his best-known works are his nostalgic autobiographical memoirs. Both he and his sister gave encouragement to a number

of writers, artists, and musicians. The youngest brother **Sir Sacheverell Sitwell** (1897–) is best known as an art critic, especially of baroque art, and as a travel-book writer.

SI units (Système International d'Unités) An international system of units, based on the *m.k.s. system, used for all scientific purposes. It has seven base units (meter, kilogram, second, ampere, kelvin, candela, and mole) and two supplementary units (radian and steradian). All physical quantities are expressed in these units or in derived units consisting of combinations of these units, 17 of which have special names and agreed symbols. Decimal multiples of all units are expressed by a set of prefixes. Where possible a prefix representing 10 raised to a power that is a multiple of 3 is used.

Sivaji (1627–80) Emperor of India (1647–80), who founded the Maratha dynasty. Born and reared in Poona (later the Maratha capital), he raised a guerrilla force and soon took control of a large part of Maharashtra. A strong opponent of the Mogul Empire, he was crowned as independent king in 1647 and spread his dominion into S India, leaving a powerful legacy for his successors.

Sivas 39 44N 37 01E A city in central Turkey. It is a trading center for grain, wine, and minerals and has 13th-century Seljuq buildings and a university (1973). Population (1980): 172,864.

Six, Les Six French composers: Auric, Louis Durey (1888–1979), Honegger, Milhaud, Poulenc, and Germaine Tailleferre (1892–1983). These composers came briefly under the influence of Cocteau and Satie in the 1920s; their chief common feature was protest against lingering Romanticism and impressionism in French music. They each developed an individual style, however, and did not long remain a group.

Six Nations US Indian tribes of the Iroquois group, mainly in N New York and W Massachusetts and Connecticut. Originally five in number—the Mohawk, Cayuga, Oneida, Seneca, and Onondaga nations—they were joined by the Tuscarora nation in 1722.

Sixtus IV (Francesco della Rovere; 1414–84) Pope (1471–84), notorious for his nepotism, especially in his support of his nephew, the future *Julius II, and for political intrigue, especially against the Medici in Florence. A patron of arts and learning, he instigated the building of the Sistine Chapel and founded its choir.

Sixtus V (Felice Peretti; 1521–90) Pope (1585–90), who reformed papal administration and taxation. He issued a revised version of the Vulgate and was a notable patron of the arts, instigating the building of the Vatican Library and Lateran Palace.

Sjælland (English name: Zealand; German name: Seeland) The largest of the Danish islands, bounded by the Kattegat, the Sound, the Baltic Sea, and the Great Belt. Predominantly low lying and undulating, its fertile soil is important for both arable and dairy farming. Area: 2709 sq mi (7016 sq km). Population (1970): 2,129,846. Chief town: Copenhagen.

Skagerrak A channel in N Europe, lying between Denmark and Norway and connecting the Kattegat to the North Sea.

skaldic poetry Old Norse poetry originally recited by skalds (professional bards generally attached to a princely or noble retinue). In contrast to the heroic poetry of the Eddaic tradition (*see* Eddas), it was descriptive and occasional, characterized by elaborate alliteration, internal rhyming, convoluted word order, and highly allusive, often riddling phrases called "kennings." It apparently originated in 9th-century Norway, but its outstanding practitioners were Icelanders (*see* Icelandic literature).

Skalkottas, Nikos (1904–49) Greek composer. He was a pupil of Kurt Weill and Schoenberg. His works include two piano concertos, 36 Greek dances for orchestra, four string quartets, and a ballet suite *La Mer grecque* (1948).

skanda (Kumara *or* Karttikeya) In Hindu mythology, a battle god. In one account he is the son of *Shiva, born to defend the gods against the demons. He is represented with 6 heads and 12 arms and rides on a peacock.

Skanderbeg (George Kastrioti; c. 1404–68) Albanian national hero. Brought up in Islam as a hostage of the Turkish sultan, Skanderbeg led (1444–68) the Albanian resistance movement against Turkey. The use of guerrilla tactics aided by Albania's mountainous topography and a series of alliances with the great powers of Europe ensured his success but after his death the movement collapsed.

Skåne (*or* Scania) A peninsular area in S Sweden, on the Baltic Sea and the Sound. It is known as the "granary of Sweden," its fertile plains producing wheat, rye, barley, oats, potatoes, and sugar beet. Area: 4230 sq mi (10,957 sq km).

Skara Brae A late Neolithic village in Scotland, in Mainland, Orkney, dating to about 2000 BC. The houses were built of dry stone with stone slabs for furniture, all very well preserved. An artificial mound of refuse was heaped over the entire settlement, probably as protection against the weather.

skate A large *ray fish belonging to the family *Rajidae* (over 100 species), especially the genus *Raja*. 20–80 in (50–200 cm) long, skates have a diamond-shaped flattened body with spiny or thorny structures on the upper surface and often an extremely long snout. They lay eggs and some have weak *electric organs on the tail.

skateboarding The recreation and competitive sport of riding on a board about 2.3 ft (70 cm) long to which two pairs of roller-skate wheels are attached. The sport began in about 1960 in California and combines surfing, skiing, and roller-skating techniques. Speeds of up to 66 mph (107 km per hour) have been attained. The first world championships were staged in 1966.

skeleton The rigid supporting framework of an animal's body. In such animals as arthropods it lies outside the body (exoskeleton) and must be shed periodically during growth. Vertebrates, including man, have a skeleton (endoskeleton) of *bones and cartilage that is entirely within the body and grows with age. The human skeleton is made up of over 200 bones, which are connected to each other at *joints and held together by ligaments. The skeleton protects and supports the soft tissues of the body and provides a firm surface for the attachment of muscles and a system of levers that are essential for movement.

Skelton, John (c. 1460–1529) English poet. He was court poet to Henry VII and tutor to the future Henry VIII. His poems include *Speke Parot* (1521), *Colin Clout* (1522), and other satires, several of them attacks on Cardinal *Wolsey. Essentially medieval in form and theme, the most interesting of his poems are often written in short rhyming lines of doggerel verse, known as Skeltonics.

skepticism The philosophical tradition that absolute certainty or knowledge cannot be attained. It began perhaps with ancient Greek skepticism about the senses (*see* Pyrrhon). Sometimes the skeptic's claim was that any knowledge attained must go unrecognized; sometimes he systematically suspected certain subjects, such as reality, religious beliefs, or moral principles, on the grounds, for example, of the relativity or subjectivity of such beliefs.

skiing A recreational and competitive sport consisting of sliding over snow on a pair of specially shaped runners (skis) attached to the feet. Skis have been used in Scandinavia since the Stone Age, but skiing for pleasure did not develop until the late 19th century. It is divided into **Alpine** (or downhill) **skiing**, which includes the events of "downhill" (straightforward racing), slalom (a winding course through "gates"), and giant slalom (faster and less winding than slalom) and **Nordic skiing**, comprising cross-country (or *langlauf*) skiing, which involves self-propulsion and requires lighter equipment than Alpine skiing, and ski-jumping. Alpine and Nordic competitions are controlled by the International Ski Federation. There is also freestyle skiing (downhill skiing that is both balletic and gymnastic), skijoring (being towed on skis by a horse or vehicle), and ski-flying, which is *hang-gliding on skis. Recreational skiing has become a vast holiday industry, the most notable skiing areas of the world being the Rockies and the Alps.

Skikda (former name: Philippeville) 36 58N 6 51E A port in NE Algeria, on the Mediterranean Sea. Occupying the site of the Roman port of Rusicade, it has the remains of a Roman theater. It receives natural gas from the Sahara and exports iron ore. Population (1974 est): 127,968.

skimmer A black-and-white bird belonging to a family (*Rhynchopidae*; 3 species) occurring chiefly around western Atlantic coasts and African and Asian rivers. The skimmer fishes by flying close to the water, shearing the surface with the lower mandible and snapping the bill shut as soon as a fish is caught.

skin The tissue that covers the body. The outer layer (epidermis) consists of several layers of cells: the outermost layer contains dead cells made of keratin, which are constantly sloughed off and replaced by the deeper layers of continuously dividing cells. The inner layer of skin (dermis) contains *connective tissue with blood vessels, sensory nerve endings, *sweat glands, sebaceous glands (which secrete an oily substance, sebum, that protects the skin surface), and *hair follicles. The skin has several important functions. It protects the body from external injury and desiccation; it assists in regulating body temperature (e.g. by sweating); and it is sensitive to touch, temperature, and pain. The branch of medicine concerned with the diagnosis and treatment of skin disorders is called **dermatology**. Skin

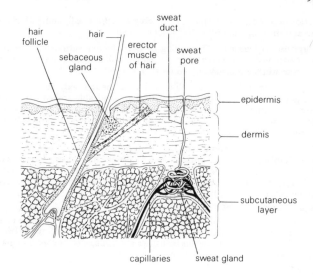

SKIN *A vertical section through the human skin shows its microscopical structure. The subcutaneous layer of fat cells provides insulation.*

grafting is one of the most important and successful *transplantation operations.

skink A lizard belonging to the family *Scincidae* (600 species), occurring throughout the tropics and in temperate North America. Skinks are well adapted for burrowing: up to 20 in (50 cm) long, they have cylindrical streamlined bodies with smooth scales, internal eardrums, a transparent covering over the eye, and often reduced limbs. Many skinks have an elongated tail and move with sideways undulations of the body. They feed on insects or plant material and many bear live young. □reptile.

Skinner, Burrhus Frederic (1904–) US psychologist and advocate of *behaviorism. Many of Skinner's experiments involved teaching animals (such as rats and pigeons) by reinforcing the desired action, when achieved, with rewards of food. He developed equipment, including the Skinner box, in order to standardize the teaching of simple actions to small animals and applied his principles to human educational aids. His novel *Walden Two* (1948) describes a utopian society based on his behaviorist principles. His other works include *The Behavior of Organisms* (1938), *Science and Human Behavior* (1953), and *Beyond Freedom and Dignity* (1971).

Skinner, Cornelia Otis (1901–79) US actress and writer. From a theatrical family, she first acted with her father Otis Skinner (1858–1942) in *Blood and Sand* (1921). After touring the US and Europe doing monologues she had written, she appeared in *Major Barbara* (1956) and *The Pleasure of His Company* (1958), which she coauthored. Her essays are collected in *Excuse It, Please* (1936), *Nuts in May* (1950), *The Ape in Me* (1959), and *Elegant Wits and Grand Horizontals* (1962). She also wrote *Our Hearts Were Young and Gay* (1942) with Emily Kimbrough, *Family Circle* (1948), and *Madame Sarah* (1967).

skipjack A *tuna fish, *Euthynnus pelamis*, also called ocean bonito, found in all warm seas. It has four to seven dark horizontal stripes along its belly and grows to about 28 in (70 cm) long.

skipper A butterfly belonging to the widely distributed family *Hesperiidae* (about 3000 species). The adults are small and have a stout body and head resembling a moth and a swift darting flight. The caterpillars feed on plants and pupate in cocoons made of silk and leaves.

Skopje (Turkish name: Usküb) 42 00N 21 28E A city in S Yugoslavia, the capital of Macedonia, on the Vardar River. It became the capital of Serbia in the 14th century and was occupied by the Turks (1392). It was burned down in 1689 to stop a cholera epidemic and almost completely destroyed by an earthquake in 1963. It has a university (1949) and varied industries, including cement, brick, glass, and steel. Population (1971): 312,980.

skua A large hook-billed seabird belonging to a family (*Stercorariidae*; 4 species), also called jaeger, breeding in Arctic and Antarctic regions and wintering in warmer latitudes. 20–23 in (52–58 cm) long, skuas are strong fliers and have a dark plumage with two long central tail feathers. They scavenge around seabird colonies, feeding on eggs, chicks, and food scraps. Order: *Charadriiformes* (gulls, plovers, etc.).

skull The skeleton of the head, made up of 22 bones of varying shapes and sizes. The cranium consists of eight flat platelike bones that surround and protect the brain. Some of these contribute to the formation of the facial skeleton. The remaining 14 bones, including the mandible (*see* jaw), form the face: the mandible is the only movable bone in the skull; the rest are connected by immovable joints called sutures. Numerous holes puncture the skull to allow blood vessels and nerves to pass to and from the brain. The largest of these is the foramen magnum at the base of the skull, through which the spinal cord passes.

skunk A black and white carnivorous mammal of the family *Mustelidae* that is known for its defensive habit of ejecting a foul-smelling fluid. The nine species are found in North, South, and Central America. The best known is the North American striped skunk (*Mephitis mephitis*), which inhabits woodland, feeding at night on insects, mice, and fruit.

skydiving (*or* freefalling) The sport of jumping from an airplane with a parachute and performing maneuvers before opening it. During this period of "free fall" the parachutist positions his body to glide or performs rolls, turns, or other stunts. In a team event divers pass a baton to each other or form a star pattern by joining hands. *See also* parachuting.

Skye The largest and most northerly island of the Inner Hebrides group, off the W coast of Scotland. The island's economy is based chiefly on crofting and tourism; sheep and cattle are also raised. Area: 670 sq mi (1735 sq km). Population (1971): 7372. Chief town: Portree.

Skye terrier A breed of dog originating on the Scottish island of Skye and used to flush foxes and badgers from cover. It has a long body, short legs, and a large head with erect or drooping ears. The soft undercoat is covered by a long straight outer coat which may reach the ground. Colors are gray, fawn, cream, or black. Height: 10 in (25 cm).

Skylab A US manned space station launched into earth orbit in May, 1973. Three groups of three US astronauts were conveyed to and from the orbiting laboratory by modified Apollo spacecraft (*see* Apollo moon program). They remained on board for a total of 513 man days during the period May, 1973, to February, 1974. In a weightless environment, they conducted a variety of experiments and observations (especially of the sun). Physical and psychological fitness were carefully monitored. Skylab's orbit eventually became unstable and it crashlanded in July, 1979, in Western Australia.

skylark A *lark, Alauda arvensis*, occurring in Eurasia and N Africa and noted for its sustained warbling flight song. It is about 7 in (17 cm) long and has a streaked brown plumage, a small crest and a white stripe above the eye. Skylarks were a delicacy in the 19th century and are still trapped in parts of Europe.

Skyros (Modern Greek name: Skíros) A Greek island in the central Aegean Sea, the largest of the Northern Sporades. Area: 79 sq mi (205 sq km). Population (1971): 2352.

skyscraper A multistory building. Skyscraper building was stimulated by the commercial need for space in cities where land was scarce and land rents high. The first skyscraper, the Equitable Life Assurance Society, was built in New York City in 1868. Architecturally it was made possible by the development of high-speed elevators in the 1850s, although it was only the introduction of a metal frame in Chicago in the 1880s that made further advances possible. The Empire State Building (1930–32) in New York was the tallest in the world until the completion in the 1970s, in the same city, of the World Trade Center, which is 1353 ft (412 m) high. In 1974 the Sears Tower in Chicago rose even higher, to 1454 ft (473 m), to become the world's tallest skyscraper.

Slade, Felix (1790–1868) British art collector, who bequeathed his collection of books, glass, and engravings to the British Museum. He also endowed professorships of art at the Universities of Oxford and Cambridge and at University College, London. The Slade School of Fine Art is named for him.

slander. *See* defamation.

Slánský, Rudolf (1901–52) Czechoslovak statesman, who was the victim of an antisemitic purge. Slánský was secretary general of the Communist Party in Czechoslovakia's postwar government. In 1951 he and nine other Jews were executed for espionage. He was posthumously absolved.

slate A fine-grained rock produced by the low-grade metamorphism of mudstone, siltstone, or other argillaceous sediments. Its perfect cleavage is due to the parallel alignment of platy crystals of mica and chlorite. Slate is used as a constructional material, formerly for roofs but now mainly for facing and ornamental purposes.

Slater, Samuel (1768–1835) US industrialist and inventor; born in England. He emigrated to the US in 1789 and, from memory, recreated the Arkwright spinning frame for an American textile manufacturer in Rhode Island and soon became an owner of the company. He also formed his own company for the manufacture of cotton thread, another firm that specialized in building textile plants (1798), and several other mills and factories throughout New England. *See also* Arkwright, Sir Richard.

slave-making ant An *ant, confined to the N hemisphere, that raids colonies of other ants to capture larvae and pupae, which develop into worker "slaves." Genera: *Harpagoxenus, Formica, Polyergus, Anergates*. *See also* Amazon ant.

Slave River A river in W Canada, flowing N from Lake Athabasca (Alberta) to Great Slave Lake (Mackenzie district); part of the *Mackenzie River system. Length: 258 mi (415 km).

slavery The condition in which human beings are owned by others as private property. Slavery was common throughout the world from earliest times. In ancient Greece and Rome, captives from conquered lands were the chief source of slaves. While most were forced to perform heavy labor, others, with special skills, were often well treated and sometimes freed. The condition of slaves in later Roman times worsened until the deteriorating economy led to the virtual disappearance of slaves and the emergence of *serfs in the Middle Ages. The slave trade again became a lucrative business in the 16th century, when European traders began to transport thousands of Africans to the Americas. By the early 19th century, English humanitarians, such as William *Wilberforce, attacked slavery on moral grounds and it was abolished in all British territories by 1834. In the US, the *Abolition Movement, headed by such leaders as William Lloyd *Garrison and Frederick *Douglass, campaigned against slavery in the South. The issue of slavery eventually became one of the central causes of the *Civil War. In 1863, President Abraham *Lincoln issued the *Emancipation Proclamation, which officially liberated all slaves in the southern states. The 13th Amendment to the Constitution, ratified in 1865, officially abolished the institution of slavery in the US.

Slavonic languages A subgroup of the *Indo-European language family. Slavonic languages are native to E Europe and NW Asia. They are often classified into three groups: South Slavonic (languages of Yugoslavia and Bulgaria, including *Serbo-Croat, Slovene, *Bulgarian, and Macedonian); West Slavonic (languages spoken in Czechoslovakia, Poland, and E Germany, including Czech, *Slovak, Sorbian, and Polish); and East Slavonic (Russian, Belorussian, and Ukrainian). The similarities and differences between languages of the three groups are not as clearcut as the geographical classification suggests. All the dialects can be related to each other historically and all developed from a common ancestor, Proto-Slavonic. Russian is a common language for most Slavs, many of whom learn it as a second language.

Slavs Peoples of E Europe and parts of W Asia. They may be divided into three groups: Eastern Slavs (including Russians, Ukrainians, and Belorussians); Western Slavs (including Poles, Czechs, Slovaks, and Sorbs or Wends); and Southern Slavs (including Serbs, Croats, Slovenes, Macedonians, and Bulgarians). The *Slavonic languages form a branch of the Indo-European family. Migrating from Asia these peoples settled this region during the second or third millennium BC. The present Slav nations began to emerge around the 5th and 6th centuries AD, when there was further westward movement.

sleep A naturally occurring state of unconsciousness. Orthodox sleep occurs in four stages, which vary in depth. The electrical activity of the brain continues but is more rhythmical than when awake and reacts less to outside stimuli. It is periodically interrupted by paradoxical sleep, in which the eyes move rapidly and the brain is more active, but the muscles are especially relaxed. Paradoxical sleep is particularly associated with *dreams. Sleep is biologically necessary and probably helps to control physical growth; individuals' needs vary widely between three and ten hours a night. Sleeplessness can be caused by changes of routine, *anxiety, and *depression, and by many drugs (*see also* insomnia). Disorders of sleep include *sleepwalking and night terrors (*see* nightmares).

sleeping sickness A disease caused by infection with a protozoan of the genus *Trypanosoma*, which is transmitted by the tsetse fly and occurs only in East, central, and West Africa: it is the African form of *trypanosomiasis. Initial symptoms are swelling of the lymph nodes and fever, which persists for several months. The brain is then infected, causing lethargy, weakness, and depression: without treatment the patient dies. The drugs pentamidine and suramin can be used to treat the early stages of the disease; arsenic-based compounds are needed when the brain is affected. Attempts to prevent the disease by eradicating the fly have not yet proved successful.

sleepwalking (*or* somnambulism) A disorder of *sleep in which the sleeper walks about and performs complex activities automatically and without regaining consciousness. It is quite common in children and not a sign of illness. In adults it can indicate immaturity or *neurosis.

sleepy sickness A highly infectious viral disease of the brain. Known medically as *encephalitis lethargica, it is marked by drowsiness leading eventually to coma. A worldwide epidemic of the disease occurred between 1917 and 1924.

Slidell, John (1793–1871) US politician and Confederate diplomat. He served in the US House of Representatives (1843–45), as US minister to Mexico (1845), and US senator (1853–61). At the outbreak of the Civil War, he left the Senate to become the Confederacy's minister to France. His passage aboard the British ship *Trent* ended in capture by the US Navy and imprisonment until early 1862. When he finally arrived in France, his quest for financial aid for and recognition of the Confederacy failed. *See also* Trent Affair.

slide rule A mathematical instrument for performing multiplication and division. It consists of a rule that slides along a groove in another rule. Both rules are marked with logarithmic scales so that products and quotients can be calculated by effectively adding and subtracting *logarithms in the form of lengths of rule. Slide rules have now been largely replaced by pocket *calculators.

Sligo (Irish name: Contae Shligigh) A county in the NW Republic of Ireland, in Connacht bordering on the Atlantic Ocean. Chiefly hilly, much of the land is devoted to pasture; cattle rearing and dairy farming are important. It possesses some coal, lead, and copper. Area: 693 sq mi (1795 sq km). Population (1979): 54,610. County town: Sligo.

Slim, William Joseph, 1st Viscount (1891–1970) British field marshal. In World War II he became commander of the 14th Army (the "forgotten army") in Burma (1943). After successful operations against the Japanese he became commander in chief of Allied land forces in SE Asia. In 1948 he became chief of the imperial general staff and was then governor general of Australia (1953–60).

slime molds Organisms belonging to the group *Myxomycophyta*, usually regarded as fungi (since they produce fruiting bodies) but having affinities with the protozoa. The so-called true slime molds (*Myxomycetes*) are found beneath logs and in other damp places. They consist of slimy sheets of protoplasm that engulf bacteria, wood particles, etc. The cellular slime molds (*Acrasiales*) are single-celled ameba-like organisms found in soil. The parasitic slime molds (*Plasmodiophorales*) live in the tissues of plants; the species *Plasmodiophora brassicae* causes *clubroot in cabbages.

slipper orchid A terrestrial *orchid of the tropical Asian genus *Paphiopedilum* (about 50 species) and the related genera *Cypripedium* and *Phragmipedilum*. They are characterized by their flowers, which have a pouched slipper-shaped lip and are usually borne singly or in clusters of two or three. *Paphiopedilum* flowers are usually a mixture of white, brown, and green, often with darker markings; the leaves may also be mottled or otherwise marked. Slipper orchids are popular greenhouse ornamentals.

slippery elm Either of two North American trees, *Fremontodendron californica* (family *Bombacaceae*) or *Ulmus fulva* (family *Ulmaceae*). Mucilage extracted from the bark has been used in poultices and to treat diarrhea, dysentery, and other conditions.

Sliven 42 40N 26 19E A city in E central Bulgaria. Its main industry is textiles, the first mill in Bulgaria having been opened here in 1834. Population (1979 est): 96,090.

Sloane, Sir Hans (1660–1753) British physician and naturalist, whose collection of books, manuscripts, pictures, etc., formed the nucleus of the *British Museum. He succeeded Sir Isaac Newton as president of the Royal Society (1727–41).

sloe. *See* blackthorn.

sloop A □sailing vessel with a single mast set approximately one third of the boat's length from the bows. Formerly used extensively in coastal fishing, sloops are now a favored rig for yacht racing, since they are the most efficient design for sailing toward the wind. Older sloops were gaff-rigged; more modern vessels are marconi-rigged or Bermuda-rigged. Sloops more than 60 ft (20 m) long are rare because of the number of crew required to handle the large sails. *See also* ketch; yawl.

SLIPPER ORCHID *The flower of a cultivated variety of* Paphiopedilum.

sloth A primitive arboreal *mammal belonging to the family *Bradypodidae* (7 species) of Central and South America, also called ai or unau. 20–25.5 in (50–65 cm) long sloths are slow-moving and hang upside down from branches, feeding on leaves and fruit. Their grayish-brown fur lies so that rain runs off easily and is often greenish from algae living there, which helps to camouflage them. They cannot walk on the ground. Order: *Edentata*.

sloth bear A shaggy black *bear, *Melursus ursinus*, of S India and Sri Lanka. 5 ft (1.5 m) long and weighing about 220 lb (100 kg), it feeds on bees or termites by tearing open nests with its long claws and sucking up the insects using its long snout.

Slovak A Western Slavonic language, closely related to *Czech, spoken in E Czechoslovakia, where it is an official language. It is written in the Latin alphabet. There are three distinct dialects.

Slovakia (Czech name: Slovensko) A mountainous area and former province of E Czechoslovakia. Lying mainly within the Carpathian Mountains, it descends SW to the plains of the Danube Valley. It is chiefly agricultural, producing cereals, wine, fruit, and tobacco. *History*: settled by Slavic Slovaks (6th–7th centuries AD), Slovakia was incorporated into Great *Moravia in the 9th century. Conquered by the Magyars in the 10th century, Slovakia was part of Hungary until 1918 when it became a province of the Czechoslovak Republic, remaining as such until 1949, except for a period of independence during World War II. Chief town: Bratislava.

Slovenia (Serbo-Croat name: Slovenija) A constituent republic of N Yugoslavia. It is mountainous and drained mainly by the Sava and Drava rivers. Agriculture includes livestock raising; potatoes, cereals, and vegetables are grown. The republic possesses important deposits of coal, mercury, and zinc. *History*: it was chiefly under Habsburg rule from the 14th century until 1918, when it was incorporated into the kingdom of Serbs, Croats, and Slovenes, later renamed Yugoslavia. Area: 7819 sq mi (20,251 sq km). Population (1978): 1,891,000. Capital: Ljubljana.

slowworm A legless lizard, *Anguis fragilis*, also called blindworm, occurring in heaths and open woodlands of Europe. It is about 12 in (30 cm) long, usually brown, gray, or reddish, and feeds on snails, slugs, and other soft-bodied invertebrates. Family: *Anguidae* (glass snakes and slowworms).

slug A *gastropod mollusk of the order *Stylommatophora*, widely distributed in moist terrestrial habitats. Slugs have slimy soft bodies with the shell vestigial or absent. They may reach 8 in (20 cm) in length, and can range in color from yellow through red-brown to black. Some are carnivorous or scavenging while others feed on soft plant tissues. Subclass: *Pulmonata*. Compare sea slug.

slump. *See* depression.

Sluter, Claus (c. 1345–1406) Dutch sculptor. Working in Dijon under the patronage of Philip the Bold, Duke of Burgundy, he produced his most famous works for the ducal mausoleum in the monastery of Champmol. These included the portal sculptures, the *Well of Moses*, and figures on the duke's tomb. Breaking away from the *international gothic style, Sluter developed a bold realism, which influenced many European sculptors and painters of the 15th century.

Sluys, Battle of (June 24, 1340) A naval battle in the *Hundred Years' War, off the coast of Flanders, in which the French fleet was destroyed by the skillful use of archers by *Edward III's army. The victory gave the English crucial strategic control over the English Channel.

smallage. *See* celery.

small arms Short-range low-weight *firearms, originally defined as capable of being handled by one individual, they included pistols, submachine guns, rifles, grenades, and shotguns. An artificial caliber ceiling of 0.60 in (1.5 cm) or, in some classification systems, 0.78 in (20 mm) has had to be abandoned with the introduction of small rocket antitank guided missiles.

smallpox A highly infectious virus disease marked by a skin rash that leaves permanent pitted scars. Smallpox is transmitted by direct contact; the initial symptoms of fever, prostration, severe headache, and backache are followed by the appearance of the rash on the face and limbs. Secondary infection with staphylococci is often fatal. There is no specific treatment and as recently as 1967 the disease caused two million deaths. After a worldwide vaccination program sponsored by the World Health Organization smallpox was officially declared to have been eradicated in 1979.

smell, sense of. *See* nose.

smelt A slender food fish of the genus *Osmerus* and family *Osmeridae*, occurring in coastal and estuarine waters of Europe and North America. It migrates to fresh water to spawn. The European smelt (*O. eperlanus*), up to about 12 in (30 cm) long, also called sparling, is greenish gray above and silvery below. It has a cucumber-like smell when eaten fresh. Order: *Salmoniformes*.

smelting The extraction of a metal from its ore by heating. The method used depends on the metal, the type of ore, and the melting points of both. The smelting takes place either in a *blast furnace (e.g. to extract iron) or a *reverberatory furnace (e.g. to extract copper).

Smetana, Bedřich (1824–84) Bohemian composer. He studied in Prague and took part in the revolution against Austria in 1848. In 1859 he left Sweden (where he had been conducting) and returned to Prague, joining a group of composers who were establishing a national opera. *The Brandenburgers in Bohemia* (1862–63) and *The Bartered Bride* (1863–66) were composed for it. In 1874 he became totally deaf but continued to compose, writing the four symphonic poems *Má Vlast* (1874–79) and a string quartet "From My Life" (1876). He died insane in an asylum.

smew A sawbilled *duck, *Mergus albellus*, that breeds in N Eurasia and winters south in the Mediterranean. It is 16–17 in (40–44 cm) long, has a short bill, and feeds on fish and crustaceans. Drakes are white with black markings; females are gray with a chestnut head and white throat and cheeks.

Smilax A genus of shrubs and vines (about 300 species), also called catbriers, native to warm temperate and tropical regions. Many have prickly stems and the white or yellowish-green flowers produce red or bluish-black berries. Family: *Smilacaceae*. *See also* sarsaparilla.

Smith, Adam (1723–90) Scottish moral philosopher and political economist. At Edinburgh University (1752–63), he lectured and wrote on moral philosophy. In 1776, he published *An Enquiry into the Nature and Causes of the Wealth of Nations*, an attack on *mercantilism that was to become the bible of the free-trade movement. He held that employment, trade, production, and distribution are as much a part of a nation's wealth as its money. An individual allowed to promote his own interests freely within the law often promotes the interests of society as a whole.

Smith, Alfred E (manuel) ("Al"; 1873–1944) US politician. A Tammany Hall Democrat, he served in the New York state legislature (1903–15) and as governor (1918–20; 1922–28), where he was known for his government reorganization and welfare programs. Thwarted in his quest for the Democratic presidential nomination in 1924, he became the first Roman Catholic nominee in 1928. His religion and opposition to Pro-

hibition, as well as the success of the previous Republican administration, led to his defeat by Herbert *Hoover.

Smith, Bessie (1894–1937) US jazz singer and songwriter, known as "Empress of the Blues," who began her career in traveling shows and carnivals. In the 1920s she made records with Louis Armstrong and Fletcher Henderson (1898–1952). Her popularity declined in the 1930s. She died in an automobile accident.

Smith, David (Roland) (1906–65) US sculptor. After studying art in New York City and Europe, he worked in an autombile factory and, during World War II, in a locomotive factory where he became interested in welding as art. His first series, *Agricola*, of sculptures were spaces outlined by wires and bent rods. His *Tank Totem* and *Sentinel* series of the 1950s used parts from cars or other pieces of machinery. In the 1960s, he turned to large, depersonalized geometrical shapes, welded together at various angles, in his *Zig* and *Cubi* series. He was killed in an automobile accident in 1965.

Smith, Ian (Douglas) (1919–) Prime minister (1964–79) of Rhodesia (now *Zimbabwe). An advocate of white supremacy, he demanded full independence for Southern Rhodesia in 1964 but opposed Britain's stipulation that black majority rule be prepared for. In 1965 he made a unilateral declaration of independence, which he maintained until 1976, when he agreed to the principle of black majority rule. He was a minister in the preindependence government (1979–80).

Smith, John (c. 1580–1631) English colonist. In 1606, he invested in the new Virginia Company, which was granted a charter to settle in North America. On arrival at what became Jamestown, Va, he explored and charted the region. In 1607 he was saved from death at the hands of Indians by *Pocahontas. He returned to England in 1609 and wrote valuable accounts of his experiences, including *Description of New England* (1616), *Map of Virginia* (1612), and *General Historie of Virginia* (1624).

Smith, Joseph (1805–44) US founder of the Church of Jesus Christ of Latter Day Saints (*Mormons). Smith announced in 1827 his discovery of the sacred *Book of Mormon*, which he claimed he had translated from two gold tablets written by a prophet named Mormon. His new church, founded in Fayette, NY (1830), grew rapidly but attracted considerable opposition because of its doctrines. Smith encouraged westward migration and the group established itself in Nauvoo, Ill, (1840), where they were welcomed at first. Smith became mayor. Rumors that the Mormons practiced polygamy spurred opposition. While in jail on charges of conspiracy, Smith was killed by an angry mob. The Mormons continued their migration westward to Utah under Brigham *Young.

Smith, Stevie (Florence Margaret S.; 1902–71) British poet. She published highly original and deceptively simple poetry, the characteristic tone of which was a blend of tenderness, toughness, and humor. The best known of her idiosyncratic novels is *Novel on Yellow Paper* (1936). Her *Collected Poems* (1975) were published posthumously.

Smithsonian Institution A research institution in Washington, DC. The Institution was founded in 1846 with a bequest from Englishman James Smithson (1765–1829) as "an establishment for the increase and diffusion of knowledge." It has carried out important scientific work and explorations throughout the world, and administers several important history, science, and art museums, including the National Air and Space Museum and the National Collection of Fine Arts.

smog A fog containing a high proportion of smoke (its name is abbreviated from smoke fog) occurring chiefly in urban and industrial areas. Occasionally it may be particularly dense, as it can be in cities like New York, Los Angeles, London, and Denver, where geography and certain weather conditions intensify its effects. Emissions from automobiles, and the burning of oil and coal are the chief pollutants. Legislation to require the burning of cleaner fuels, and the use of pollution control devices have reduced the incidence of severe smog.

smoke tree (*or* smoke bush) One of several species of trees and shrubs having a whitish cloudy appearance at some stage of the season. The American smoke tree (*Cotinus obovatus*) grows to a height of 30 ft (9 m) and has a smokelike mass of whitish flower heads, as does the Australian smoke bush (*Conospermum stoechadis*). *Rhus cotinus* is the common smoke bush native to the Mediterranean area and parts of Asia.

Smolensk 54 49N 32 04E A city in the Soviet Union, in the W RSFSR on the Dnepr River. It has engineering, textile, and consumer-goods industries and several educational institutions. *History*: dating to at least the 9th century, it was sacked by the Tatars (13th century) and was subsequently disputed between Lithuania (and later Poland) and Russia, falling finally to the latter in 1654. It is on the route of Napoleon's retreat from Moscow in 1812 and was badly damaged in World War II. Population (1981 est): 311,000.

Smollett, Tobias (George) (1721–71) British novelist. Born and educated in Scotland, he settled in London in 1744. His picaresque novels, lively in style and unsophisticated and rambling in structure, include *Roderick Random* (1748), *Peregrine Pickle* (1751), and *Humphry Clinker* (1771). He was also a prolific journalist and translator.

smooth snake A widespread Eurasian snake, *Coronella austriaca*, that has smooth glossy scales and is brown or reddish with a pale belly and dark spots along its back and tail. Up to 26 in (65 cm) long, it favors sandy heathlands and feeds on lizards, small snakes, and rodents. Family: *Colubridae*.

smuggling The illegal import or export of goods to evade payment of duties or official restrictions. Trading countries often impose bans, limitations, or taxes on certain goods, the evasion of which provides an incentive for smugglers. Smuggling has flourished from the time of the Greek city states until the present day. After World War II smuggling of guns, narcotics, gold, diamonds, and illegal immigrants became rife, particularly through international airlines and remote frontier towns. In recent years one of the primary concerns of world customs authorities, the function of which is to detect and prevent smuggling, has been the breaking of international narcotic smuggling networks.

smut A disease affecting flowering plants, particularly the cereals and grasses, caused by various *basidiomycete fungi of the genus *Ustilago*. Infection is not usually apparent until spore formation, when dark powdery masses of spores are released over the flower head. Stinking smuts, or bunts, are caused by fungi belonging to the related genus *Tilletia*. Both types of smut cause reduced yields of grain and are controlled by spraying crops with fungicide and by treating seed before sowing.

JAN SMUTS *On campaign in S Africa in 1914, at the outbreak of World War I.*

Smuts, Jan (Christiaan) (1870–1950) South African statesman and general; prime minister (1919–24, 1939–48). Educated in England, he returned to South Africa in 1895. He was a commando leader in the second *Boer War (1899–1902) but thereafter worked for reconciliation with Britain. He played an important part in the achievement of responsible government for the Transvaal (1906) and the Union of South Africa (1910). He was a member of Britain's imperial war cabinet in World War I and helped establish the League of Nations. He succeeded *Botha as prime minister in 1919 but was defeated in 1924. In 1939 he again became prime minister, advocating South Africa's entry into World War II. His desire to maintain South Africa's links with the British Commonwealth made him unpopular among Afrikaners.

Smyrna. *See* Izmir.

snail A *gastropod mollusk with a spirally coiled shell, including terrestrial, freshwater, and marine forms. The common garden snail (*Helix pomatia*) grows to about 1.2 in (3 cm) and is active at night, feeding on vegetation and sheltering by day in crevices. In dry weather, a temporary covering is secreted over the shell aperture to prevent desiccation. The giant African land snail (*Achatina fulica*) grows up to 5 in (12 cm) long.

snake A legless *reptile belonging to the suborder *Serpentes* (about 3000 species), occurring worldwide but especially common in the tropics. Snakes are long and slender: they range from 0.39–33 ft (0.12–10 m) in length and grow throughout their lives, periodically shedding the skin in one piece. They feed chiefly on other vertebrates and are adapted to swallowing prey whole, having flexible ligaments and joints allowing the two parts of the lower jaw to move apart during swallowing. Prey may be killed by constriction, by engulfing it alive, or by the injection of a potent neurotoxic or hemorrhagic venom by means of hollow or grooved fangs. The major families are the *Boidae* (pythons, boas, etc.), the *Colubridae* (typical snakes, e.g. the grass snake), the *Elapidae* (cobras, coral snakes, etc.), and the *Viperidae* (vipers, etc.). Order: *Squamata* (lizards and snakes).

snakebird. *See* darter.

snakefly An insect of the family *Raphidiidae* (about 80 species), so called because its small head and long slender thorax ("neck") resemble a snake about to strike. It is found in woodland areas of every continent except Australia and uses chewing mouthparts to feed on small insects. Eggs are laid beneath bark. Order: *Neuroptera*.

snake gourd An annual or perennial vine of the genus *Trichosanthes* (about 15 species), especially *T. anguina*, native to tropical SE Asia and Australia. It is widely cultivated for its long tapering green edible fruits, which often exceed 40 in (1 m) in length. Family: *Cucurbitaceae*.

snake-necked turtle A freshwater turtle belonging to the family *Chelyidae* (35 species), found in South America, Australia, and New Guinea. They have a long snakelike neck that is extended to catch prey and breathe air at the surface. It cannot be retracted into the shell but is tucked sideways into a fold of shoulder skin. A South American species, the matamata (*Chelys fimbriata*), has a jagged well-camouflaged shell, 12–16 in (30–40 cm) long, and a pointed head.

Snake River A river in the NW US. Rising in the Yellowstone National Park in Wyoming, it flows W through Idaho to join the Columbia River in Washington. Length: 1038 m (1670 km).

snakeroot Any of various plants the roots of which were formerly reputed to cure snakebites. Snakeroots include the *bistort and several North American species, such as the herbs *Cimicifuga racemosa*, *Aristolochia reticulata*, and *Eupatorium urticoefolium*.

snapdragon. *See* Antirrhinum.

snapper A carnivorous shoaling fish of the family *Lutjanidae* (about 250 species), found in tropical seas. It has an elongated body, usually 24–36 in (60–90 cm) long, a large mouth, and sharp teeth. Snappers are valuable food fish, especially the red snapper (*Lutjanus blackford*), although others may be poisonous.

snare drum (*or* side drum) A small drum with gut strings (snares) stretched across the lower skin. These make a rattling sound when the drum is played. It is used in the orchestra and in the military band.

sneeze A reflex violent expulsion of air through the mouth and nose caused by irritation of the lining of the nasal cavity. The irritation may be due to inflammation of the nasal passages, such as occurs with a cold and hay fever. Sneezing is the principal means by which colds and similar infections are spread, since it expels a cloud of droplets containing the infective microbes.

Snefru King of Egypt (c. 2600 BC); founder of the 4th dynasty traditionally noted for his kindliness, in contrast with his son *Khufu. He encouraged shipping to facilitate communications within Egypt and to import materials from abroad. Two pyramids at Dashur are attributed to him.

Snell's law When a ray of light passes from one medium to another the angle (r) between the refracted ray and a line normal to the interface between the media is related to the angle (i) of the incident ray, also taken to the normal, by the equation $\sin i / \sin r = n$, where n is the relative refractive index of the media (*see* refraction). It is named for the Dutch astronomer Willebrord Snell (1591–1626), who discovered it in 1621. It was not published until 1638, when Descartes announced it without crediting Snell.

snipe A *sandpiper belonging to a subfamily (*Scolopacine*; 10 species) occurring in wet areas of warm and temperate regions. Snipe have a long flexible bill used to probe for worms, and a barred and striped brown, black, and white plumage. The common snipe (*Gallinago gallinago*) is 12 in (30 cm) long and a popular gamebird.

snooker A game, deriving from *billiards, that arose among British officers in India (1875). It is played by two players or pairs of players on a billiards table. There are 22 balls: 1 white cue ball, 15 red balls (value 1 point each), and 6 colored balls—yellow (2 points), green (3), brown (4), blue (5), pink (6), black (7). The object is to pocket a red ball and a colored ball alternately, each time returning the colored ball to its prescribed spot on the table. The red balls are not replaced. When all the red balls have been sunk the colors are sunk in order of numerical value.

snoring Noisy breathing occurring during sleep, caused by vibration of the soft palate at the back of the mouth. Snoring generally occurs when sleeping on the back with the mouth open. It is most liable to occur when the nose is blocked (e.g. by a cold) and the person must breathe through the mouth.

snow A solid form of precipitation composed of ice crystals or snow-flakes. Ice crystals occur when temperatures are well below freezing point; with temperatures nearer to 0°C (32°F) snowflakes develop through the clustering together of crystals. Snow is usually measured with a graduated ruler, which is inserted into the flat surface of undrifted snow. Approximately 1 ft (0.3 m) of snow is equivalent to 1 in (25 mm) of rainfall.

Snow, C(harles) P(ercy), Baron (1905–80) British novelist and scientist. The moral problems of politics and power are a recurrent theme of his series of novels beginning with *Strangers and Brothers* (1940) and ending with *Last Things* (1970). His lecture *The Two Cultures and the Scientific Revolution* (1959) prompted a lively controversy with the critic F. R. *Leavis. He was married to the writer Pamela Hansford Johnson (1912–81).

snowball tree. *See* guelder rose.

snow bunting A short-billed *bunting, *Plectrophenax nivalis*, of Arctic snowfields, that visits Britain in winter. It is about 6 in (16 cm) long and has a brownish plumage with white underparts and black wingtips. In summer the male is white with an orange bill and black markings. It nests in rock crevices and feeds on seeds and insects.

Snowdon (Welsh name: Eryri) 53 04N 4 05W The highest mountain in Wales, in Gwynedd. The surrounding area, **Snowdonia**, is popular for walking, rock climbing, and mountaineering. Height: 3560 ft (1085 m).

Snowdon, Antony Armstrong-Jones, Earl of (1930–) British photographer. His work includes several television documentaries and photographic books, such as *Venice* (1972). His marriage (1960–78) to Britain's Princess Margaret ended in divorce.

snowdrop A small early spring-blooming herbaceous plant of the genus *Galanthus* (about 10 species) native to Europe and W Asia. They grow from bulbs to produce grasslike leaves and slender stems bearing solitary nodding white flowers, tipped with green or yellow. There are over 50 cultivated varieties, which are easily grown in gardens and survive for years without attention. *G. nivalis* is the common European snowdrop; *G. elwesi* is the giant snowdrop of SW Asia. Family: *Amaryllidaceae*.

snow goose An Arctic *goose, *Anser caerulescens*. It is 28–31 in (70–78 cm) long and is either pure white with black wingtips, pink legs, and a red bill or blue-gray with a white head. Snow geese winter in the southern US, Japan, and China.

snow leopard A big *cat, *Panthera* (or *Uncia*) *uncia*, also called ounce, found in the mountains of central Asia. It is 6.2 ft (1.9 m) long, with a thick ash-gray coat marked with dark rosettes. It hunts mountain goats, sheep, and marmots, catching its prey by stalking.

snow-on-the-mountain A hardy annual plant, *Euphorbia marginata*, native to North America and widely cultivated as a garden foliage plant. Up to 24 in (60 cm) high, it has pale-green pointed leaves, 1.2–3.1 in (3–8 cm) long, with white margins (sometimes the whole leaf is white). Family: *Euphorbiaceae*.

snowshoe hare A *hare, *Lepus americanus*, of N North America, also called varying hare. Up to 28 in (70 cm) long, it has a white winter coat and leaves tracks similar to snowshoes. Populations of snowshoe hares can vary greatly from year to year; similar fluctuations occur in the populations of lynxes—their chief predator.

Snowy Mountains A mountain range in Australia. It lies within the *Australian Alps, and contains Australia's highest mountain, Mount *Kos-

ciusko. The Snowy Mountains Hydroelectric Authority has diverted rivers and constructed dams and reservoirs for irrigation and hydroelectric purposes.

snowy owl A large *owl, *Nyctea scandiaca*, occurring chiefly in Arctic tundra regions. 20–26 in (52–65 cm) long, it has broad wings, a round head, and a snow-white plumage with black barring. It nests on open ground and feeds on lemmings, hares, and birds.

snuff A preparation of tobacco and other ingredients that is sniffed rather than smoked. The character of a particular variety of snuff depends on the coarseness of the tobacco used, the moisture content, and the added ingredients, such as lavender and menthol, which introduce flavor and scent to the mixture.

Spaniards discovered snuff-taking among the natives of the Americas in the 16th century. The habit was fashionable until the early 19th century, when it was largely replaced by the *cigar. Highly decorated snuffboxes were made as valuable items of jewelry.

Snyders, Frans (1579–1657) Flemish animal painter, born in Antwerp. He studied under Pieter *Brueghel the Younger. At first a still-life painter, he later specialized in hunting scenes, being employed in the workshop of *Rubens and by Archduke Albert.

Soane, Sir John (1753–1837) British architect, who developed *neo-classicism into a highly original style. His first major commission was the rebuilding of the Bank of England (1788–1833; now destroyed), the striking austerity of which was relieved only by simplified classical motifs.

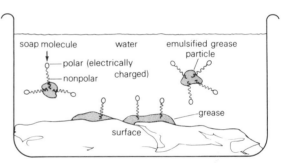

SOAPS *The action of soap in emulsifying grease. The nonpolar hydrocarbon end of the soap molecule attaches itself to the grease. The attraction of the polar end to water breaks up the grease and distributes it throughout the solution.*

soaps Salts of *fatty acids. Normal household soap (**hard soap**) is a mixture of sodium stearate, oleate, and palmitate. It is made by the *hydrolysis of *fats with caustic soda (sodium hydroxide), thus converting the glycerides of stearic, oleic, and palmitic acids into sodium salts and glycerol. **Soft soap** is made with potassium hydroxide instead of sodium hydroxide. Soaps have a cleansing action because they contain negative ions composed of a long hydrocarbon chain attached to a carboxyl group. The hydrocarbon chain has an affinity for grease and oil, and the carboxyl group has an affinity for water. Particles of grease or oil are therefore emulsified in soapy water. Insoluble salts of other metals with fatty acids are used as fillers and waterproofing agents and are also called soaps. *See also* detergents.

soapstone. *See* talc.

soapwort A perennial herb, *Saponaria officinalis*, native to Europe and temperate Asia and introduced to North America. The shoots grow to a height of 12–36 in (30–90 cm) and bear pink flowers. The leaves and roots contain a lathering agent (saponin), formerly used for washing clothes. Family: *Caryophyllaceae*.

Soares, Mario (1924–) Portuguese statesman; prime minister (1976–79; 1983–). He was a critic of *Salazar and lived in exile from 1970 to 1974, when he became foreign minister in the newly established military government. He became prime minister as leader of the Portuguese Socialist Party.

soccer. *See* football.

So-ch'e. *See* Shache.

Sochi 43 35N 39 46E A city in the SW Soviet Union, in the RSFSR on the Black Sea. It is a popular resort, where, since 1977, smoking has been forbidden. Population (1981 est): 295,000.

social contract An agreement under which people consent to surrender liberties in return for the guarantee of responsible government. Hobbes saw the contract as one in which citizens surrender the freedom inherent in a state of nature to an absolute sovereign; Locke, however, argued that the sovereign is limited by the obligation to preserve certain fundamental liberties; and Rousseau, the third of the chief theorists of the social contract, believed that governments require the support of the general will of the people.

social credit An economic theory that finds the cause of depression in the lack of purchasing power and advocates the payment of a regular dividend to every citizen. Formulated by C. H. Douglas (1879–1952), a British engineer and economist in Canada, it became the central platform of the Social Credit Party, formed in Canada in 1935. It maintained political power in Alberta and British Columbia until the early 1970s.

social Darwinism A group of theories suggesting that the principles governing the evolution of biological species by natural selection also govern the affairs of society and social evolution. Either relations in society are held to be determined by a "struggle for existence" between individuals and groups or history is interpreted as a series of conflicts in which only the "fittest" social systems thrive.

Social Democratic Party (SDP) A moderate British political party of the center, formed in 1981 by Labour Party dissidents.

socialism A concept that has various meanings, resulting in diverse political movements, but one that generally emphasizes the establishment of cooperation rather than competition among men. The word was first used in the early 19th century to describe the followers of Robert *Owen in England and François Fourier and *Saint-Simon in France. From the beginning two main senses of the word emerged. The first sense was in effect a continuation of liberalism, the emphasis being on reform of the social system to develop liberal values, such as political freedom, and the ending of class privileges. Socialism in the second sense was explicitly contrasted with a competitive individualist form of society; practical cooperation could not be achieved until a society based on private property was replaced by one based on social ownership and control. The resulting controversy between reformists and revolutionaries has been long and bitter.
In 1848 Marx and Engels laid down the principles of scientific socialism in *The Communist Manifesto* and *Marxism became the theoretical basis for most socialist thought. The British *Fabian Society (founded 1884) revived a variant of the first sense of the term, which later found political expression in the *Labour Party. It was the split in Russia, however, between the revolutionary *Bolsheviks and the reformist *Mensheviks that led to the decisive distinction between the terms *communism and socialism as they are now generally understood, socialists being those who seek change by peaceful reform and communists being those dedicated to change by revolution.

Socialist Party US political party formed by the merger of the Socialist Labor Party and the Social Democratic Party in 1901. The party repeatedly nominated presidential candidates, including Eugene V. *Debs (1900–12; 1920) and Norman M. *Thomas (1928–48), offering government ownership of all businesses necessary to public welfare as an alternative to capitalism.

socialist realism A theory of literary composition decreed by the Soviet authorities in Russia in 1932 to be the official literary doctrine to which all communist writers must adhere. It defined the purpose of literature as the promotion of socialism and resulted in the production of much literature that was little more than political propaganda. Mikhail *Sholokhov is the most notable of the few writers who have managed to transcend its restrictions.

Social Security Act (1935) US law that provided guaranteed benefits for retirement-aged workers (65 or over), based on income and worker and employer contributions. Part of President Franklin D. Roosevelt's *New Deal program, it was, in effect, a pension plan to provide for old age in a nuclear family society. Subsequent amendments provided for dependents of deceased workers, disabled and unemployed workers, and health insurance benefits. The Social Security Administration is the agency in charge of the program.

Society Islands An archipelago in French Polynesia. It consists of two island groups, the **Windward Islands** (including Tahiti and Moorea) and the **Leeward Islands** (including Raiatea and Huahine). The capital of French Polynesia, Papeete, is on Tahiti. Discovered in 1767, they are mountainous and the site of ruined Polynesian stone temples. Copra, vanil-

la, phosphates, and mother-of-pearl are produced. Area: 616 sq mi (1595 sq km). Population (1977 est): 117,703.

Society of Friends. *See* Quakers.

Society of Jesus. *See* Jesuits.

Socinus, Laelius (Italian name: Lelio Francesco Maria Sozini; 1525–62) Italian Protestant reformer. He traveled widely in N Europe, meeting other leading Protestant reformers. His anti-Trinitarian beliefs and his desire to reconcile Christianity with humanism deeply influenced his nephew **Faustus Socinus** (Fausto Paolo Sozini; 1539–1604). He settled in Poland in 1579, where he became leader of an anti-Trinitarian branch of the Reformed Church. Its doctrine, known as Socinanism, contributed to the development of Unitarian theology (*see* Unitarianism).

sociobiology The study of social behavior in animals and man. Sociobiologists believe that such aspects of behavior as aggression, male dominance, and the roles of the sexes have developed through evolution in the same way as structural features. The study was developed in the 1970s.

sociology The systematic study of the development, organization, functioning, and classification of human societies. Its growth was stimulated by the rapid industrial and social change in Europe in the early 19th century, Auguste *Comte (the first to use the term "sociology"), Emile *Durkheim, and Max *Weber being among the founding fathers of the discipline, which was established in several universities by the early 20th century. Precluded from experimental methods, the discipline has employed techniques of participant observation, the systematic comparison of different societies, and surveys of social conditions, attitudes, and behavior. Contemporary sociology is divided into several specialized subdisciplines including demography, political, educational, and urban sociology as well as sociological studies of deviance, religion, and culture.

sockeye salmon A *salmon, *Oncorhynchus nerka*, also called red salmon or blueback, that lives in the N Pacific and spawns in Canadian fresh waters.

Socotra A South Yemeni island in the Indian Ocean, off Somalia. It is generally barren, rising to 4931 ft (1503 m), but in some valleys such crops as dates are grown and livestock is raised. It came under British protection in 1886 but has belonged to South Yemen since 1967. Area: 1197 sq mi (3100 sq km). Chief town: Tamrida.

Socrates (c. 469–399 BC) Athenian philosopher. He wrote nothing himself but his disciples *Plato and *Xenophon stress his intellect, integrity, courage, humor, and sense of divine guidance. *Aristophanes caricatured him in *The Clouds* as an eccentric intellectual. Socrates diverted philosophy from the physical speculations of the *Presocratics toward *ethics. His insistence upon thorough critical analysis of ethical concepts also marked the beginning of *logic. The "Socratic method" of teaching was by eliciting answers from interlocutors to reveal inconsistencies in accepted opinions, a method particularly effective against the *Sophists. His resolute stance against tyranny, whether exercised by the mob or oligarchs, brought about his trial on charges of atheism and "corrupting the youth," and he was condemned to die by drinking hemlock. Plato's *Phaedo* is an eloquent account of his death.

Soddy, Frederick (1877–1956) British chemist, who worked under *Rutherford and *Ramsay and went on to win the 1921 Nobel Prize for his discovery of *isotopes. His scientific books included *The Interpretation of the Atom* (1932); he also wrote on economics, his main work being *Cartesian Economics* (1922).

Söderblom, Nathan (1866–1931) Swedish churchman; Archbishop of Uppsala (1914–31). A pioneer of the modern ecumenical movement, he made new contacts with Anglican and Eastern Orthodox Churches and was a chief initiator of conferences on "Faith and Order" (Uppsala, 1919) and "Life and Work" (Stockholm, 1925). He received the Nobel Peace Prize in 1930.

sodium (Na) A highly reactive alkali metal, long-recognized in compounds but first isolated as the element by Sir Humphry Davy in 1807 by electrolysis of the molten hydroxide (NaOH; caustic soda). It is now obtained commercially by electrolysis of common salt (NaCl). It occurs naturally in some silicate minerals (for example *feldspars; $NaAlSi_3O_8$), as well as in salt deposits and in the oceans. The metal is soft, bright, and less dense (relative density 0.97) than water, with which it reacts violently, liberating hydrogen. For safety, it has to be stored in mineral oil. It is used in organic chemistry as a reducing agent and in the production of *tetraethyl lead. Sodium forms a low-melting-point (−12.3°C) alloy with potassium, but liquid sodium itself is used as the coolant in fast-breeder nuclear reactors. It is a highly electropositive element, forming many ionic salts of great importance, such as the chloride (common salt; NaCl), the carbonate (soda ash;

Na_2CO_3), the bicarbonate (baking-soda; $NaHCO_3$), various phosphates, the nitrate ($NaNO_3$), and many others. *Soap is usually the sodium salt of fatty acids (e.g. sodium stearate). Sodium gives a strong yellow color to flames. At no 11; at wt 22.9898; mp 208.2°F (97.8°C); bp 1622.8°F (882.9°C).

sodium bicarbonate (sodium hydrogen carbonate *or* bicarbonate of soda; $NaHCO_3$)   The white soluble powder that is a constituent of *baking powder and is used to make fizzy drinks and as an antacid in medicine. It is made from *sodium carbonate by passing *carbon dioxide through a saturated solution.

sodium carbonate (Na_2CO_3)   A white soluble salt. The commercial form (**soda ash**) is a white anhydrous powder and is used in making glass, soap, paper, as well as other chemicals. **Washing soda**, its hydrated form ($Na_2CO_3.10H_2O$), is a white crystalline solid used as a domestic cleanser and water softener.

sodium hydroxide (*or* caustic soda; $NaOH$)   A white solid that is strongly alkaline in aqueous solution and is very corrosive to organic tissue. It is made by electrolysis of salt solution and is used in making rayon, paper, detergents, and other chemicals.

Sodom and Gomorrah   In the Old Testament, two cities of Palestine, known as the "cities of the plain," S of the Dead Sea in the area in which Lot, the nephew of Abraham, settled. According to Genesis (18, 19), they were destroyed by fire and brimstone from heaven because of the utter depravity of their inhabitants.

Sofia (Bulgarian name: Sofiya)   42 40N 23 18E The capital of Bulgaria, situated on a plateau in the W of the country. Industries include engineering, metals, textiles, and food processing. It contains some ancient churches, including that of St Sofia (6th–7th centuries), as well as two mosques. The university was founded in 1888. *History*: a Roman town (known as Serdica) from the 1st to the 4th centuries AD, it was destroyed by the Huns in 447. It came under the Byzantine Empire in the 6th century and was taken over by the Bulgars in the 9th century. Under Turkish rule from 1382, it was liberated by the Russians in 1878 and became the national capital (1879). Population (1979 est): 1,047,920.

soft-shelled turtle   A freshwater turtle belonging to the family *Trionychidae* (20–25 species), occurring in North America, Africa, and Asia. They have a flat almost circular shell covered by a leathery skin instead of horny plates, a long neck with a small head, and webbed feet. They are carnivorous and often lie buried in mud but can be fast-moving and aggressive. Chief genus: *Trionyx*.

software   The *programs written to set up a computer system for operation, as distinct from the physical equipment or hardware. Computer manufacturers generally supply machines complete with most of the basic software, which is regarded as an integral part of the computer. It includes the programs that convert high-level programming languages to low-level or assembly languages and programs that translate assembly language into the machine code, the code the machine itself can follow.

Sogne Fjord   The longest and deepest fjord in Norway, extending 127 mi (204 km) inland N of Bergen. It is flanked by spectacular mountain scenery. Depth: about 4000 ft (1220 m).

soil   The mixture of unconsolidated mineral particles, derived from weathered rock, and organic matter (humus), derived from the breakdown of plant tissue by living organisms, that covers much of the earth's land surface and provides a medium for plant growth. Soil formation (pedogenesis) depends on the nature of the parent material, the climate and topography of the region, the organisms present in the soil, and the time that has elapsed since pedogenesis began on a bare surface. Soils are characterized by their texture, which depends on particle sizes (*see* sand; silt; clay), and their structure, which depends on the way the particles are bound into aggregates (e.g. crumbs, granules, flakes, etc.). These are important factors in determining the fertility of the soil, particularly its moisture and air content, susceptibility to leaching (the removal of nutrients to deeper levels by percolating water), and ease of cultivation. Soils are also classified according to their profiles—the arrangement of the layers (horizons) between the ground surface and the bedrock. *See also* chernozem; loam; podzol.

Soissons   49 23N 3 20E A city in France, in the Aisne department on the Aisne River. Strategically situated on the NE approaches to Paris, it has been sacked many times. It has a fine 13th-century cathedral. Soissons is a market town and has metallurgical industries. Population (1975): 32,112.

Sokoto   13 02N 5 15E A city in NW Nigeria. It is a major trade center for livestock and agricultural products. The University of Sokoto was founded in 1975. Population (1971 est): 108,565.

sol.   *See* colloid.

Solanaceae   A family of herbaceous plants and shrubs (about 2000 species), widely distributed but chiefly tropical. Their flowers have five fused sepals and petals and are usually pollinated by insects. The family includes several commercially important species (e.g. the potato, tomato, pepper, and tobacco) and some ornamentals (e.g. *Petunia*); various other members are poisonous (e.g. the nightshades).

solar cell.   *See* solar power.

solar constant   The total amount of solar energy passing perpendicularly through unit area per unit time at a particular distance from the sun. It is about $1.36 kW m^{-2}$ at the earth's mean orbital distance.

solar flare   A sudden brightening, within minutes, of areas in the sun's atmosphere, resulting from an explosive release of energetic particles and radiation. Flares occur in regions of intense localized magnetic field, often above *sunspot groups, and take up to an hour to fade. Large flares affect radio transmission on earth and produce *auroras.

solar power   The use of the sun's energy to provide heating or to generate electricity. A vast amount of solar energy (about 3×10^{24} joules) falls on the earth every year. This energy can be converted into heat, the commonest method being by direct heating of water flowing through special panels on the roof of a building. The temperature rise produced is fairly small but it reduces the energy required from other sources for hot water and space heating. Higher temperatures, sufficient to form steam for electricity generation, are possible using mirrors to collect and focus the sun's rays. It is estimated that 7000 square meters of mirror is required to generate 1 megawatt of electricity by boiling water to drive a turbogenerator. Direct conversion of solar radiation into electrical energy is possible with **solar cells**. These devices consist of semiconductor junctions in silicon crystals that are sensitive to the *photovoltaic effect. The method is used mainly in small-scale specialized applications, for example powering remote monitoring equipment, spacecraft, marine beacons, etc. For this method to have widespread commercial applications the cost of solar cells would need to be reduced by a factor of about 10. Intense research to make economical use of solar energy is progressing in a number of countries.

SOLAR PROMINENCES   *A photograph of the solar eclipse on May 29, 1929, showing a solar prominence.*

solar prominences   Immense clouds of gas in the solar atmosphere, visible, usually only spectroscopically, as flamelike projections beyond the sun's limb. They show great diversity in structure. **Quiescent prominences** persist for possibly several months at high solar latitudes, reaching, typically, a height and length of 25,000 mi (40,000 km) and 125,000 mi (200,000 km). **Active prominences** are short lived in comparison and may alter their shape considerably in minutes.

solar system   A system comprising the *sun and the astronomical bodies gravitationally bound to the sun, that is the nine major *planets, their *satellites, and the immense numbers of *minor planets, *comets, and *meteoroids. Almost all the mass of the solar system (99.86%) resides in the sun. The planets orbit the sun in the same direction and, with the exception of Pluto, move in paths close to the earth's orbit (i.e. close to the *ecliptic) and the sun's equator. This and other information is taken as evidence of the common origin of the sun and planets, some 4600 million years ago,

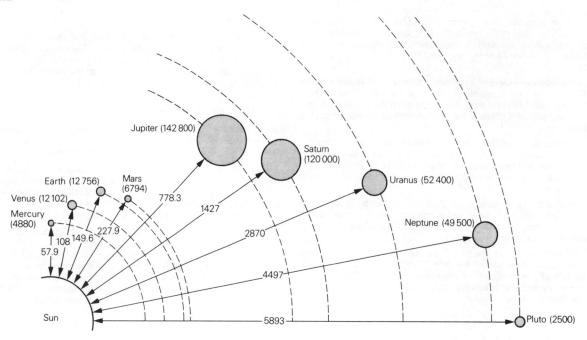

SOLAR SYSTEM *The planets with their equatorial diameters in kilometers (in brackets after the planet's name) and their distance from the sun in millions of kilometers (not to scale).*

following the contraction and subsequent flattening of a rotating cloud of interstellar gas and dust.

solar wind An almost radial outflow of charged particles discharged from the sun's corona into interplanetary space. The particles, mainly protons and electrons, are moving at speeds between 125–559 mi (200 and 900 km) per second in the vicinity of the earth's orbit and although low in density (about 8 per cubic centimeter) can still interact with the earth's *magnetosphere.

solder An *alloy that is melted to form a joint between other metals or, occasionally, nonmetals. The surfaces to be joined are heated by a soldering iron or by a flame, but are not melted. **Soft solder** is usually made of lead and tin and melts in the range 392–482°F (200–250°C). Because the solder itself is not very strong, it is not used for joints that have to stand up to stress or heat, but is used for making secure electrical connections. **Brazing,** also called **hard soldering,** uses a harder alloy with a higher melting temperature (1,563–1,654°F [850–900°C]), usually a *brass with 60% zinc and 40% copper. **Silver solder** originally contained silver and was used for jewelry. It has a slightly lower melting point (1,167–1,527°F [630–830°C]) than brass, and often contains antimony or other metals but no silver. Like brazing, its strength makes it useful in engineering applications. A flux of zinc chloride or a resin is applied to the hot surfaces before soldering to clean them and to enable the solder to flow. In some solders (resin-cored) the flux is contained inside the solder.

soldier beetle A slender soft-bodied beetle with hairy wing cases, belonging to a small but widely distributed family (*Cantharidae*; 3500 species). Brightly colored and 0.20–0.59 in (5–15 mm) long, the adults are attracted to flowers, particularly those of the parsley family (*Umbelliferae*), although most feed on small insects. The larvae are found in soil and moss.

sole An elongated *flatfish of the family *Soleidae* (over 100 species), found in temperate and tropical seas. The common European sole (*Solea solea*), also called Dover sole, is a valuable food fish and has a blotchy brown body, up to 20 in (50 cm) long, with a black spot on each pectoral fin. *See also* lemon sole.

solenodon A shrewlike insectivorous mammal belonging to the family *Solenodontidae* (2 species) found in Cuba and Haiti. Solenodons measure 11–12.5 in (28–32 cm) and have a long naked tail and a long snout with large upper incisor teeth. They feed chiefly on insects, using their long claws to tear open rotten wood. Order: *Insectivora*.

solenoid A coil of wire usually forming a long cylinder. When electric current flows through it a *magnetic field is created. This field can be used to move an iron rod placed on its axis. Solenoids are often used to operate

mechanical valves attached to the iron rod by switching on or off the current. In most cars a solenoid is used to operate the heavy-current switch that supplies energy to the starter motor.

solfeggio. *See* solmization.

Solferino, Battle of (June 24, 1859) An indecisive battle between Austria on one side and Sardinia-Piedmont and France on the other. As the Austrians withdrew, Solferino was technically a French victory but the French emperor Napoleon III, alarmed by unrest in Paris and the strength of the Austrians, made peace at Villafranca less than three weeks after the battle. The heavy casualties (about 30,000 dead) led an eyewitness, Henri *Dunant, to campaign for the establishment of the International *Red Cross.

solid state One of the four states of matter and that to which all substances, except helium, revert at sufficiently low temperatures. It is distinguished from the other states by being the only one in which matter retains its shape, as a result of the stronger intermolecular forces.

solid-state devices Electronic devices made with solid *semiconductor components. They have no moving parts and depend for their operation on the movement of charges within a crystalline solid. Solid-state devices are smaller, lighter, physically more robust, and more easily mass-produced than *thermionic valve equipment, which they have now superseded for most uses. *See also* semiconductor diode; thyristor; transistor.

solifluction A process of mass movement of soil and rock debris, associated with areas bordering on ice sheets in which *permafrost is a feature. During the summer season the top layer of soil thaws but as the ground below remains frozen the water is unable to drain away. The soil therefore becomes saturated and on slopes will flow downhill.

Solingen 51 10N 7 05E A city in NW West Germany, in North Rhine-Westphalia. Its reputation for blades and cutlery dates to the middle ages. It was severely damaged in World War II. Population (1980 est): 166,600.

solipsism The philosophical view that the human mind has no logical justification for believing in the existence of anything other than itself. It is thus an extreme form of *idealism in which the outside world exists only in the mind of the observer. Many philosophers have tried to refute the theory and some have concluded that it is irrefutable. Modern critics, including *Wittgenstein, regard it as incompatible with the existence of a language capable of expressing the view.

solmization A method of teaching sight-singing that eliminates learning to read music notation from the stave. The tonic sol-fa system derived from the hexachord invented by *Guido d'Arezzo. It was systematized in the 1840s by John *Curwen: the notes of the rising major scale are represented by the syllables doh, ray, me, fah, soh, lah, ti, and doh. The system can be applied in any key, and modulation to a different key simply involves shifting doh to another pitch. Vocal exercises on solmization syllables are known by the Italian word solfeggio.

Solo. See Surakarta.

Solomon In the Old Testament, the third King of Israel, son of *David and Bathsheba, who reigned in the 10th century BC. During his peaceful reign several foreign alliances were formed (notably with Phoenicia and Egypt), trade and commerce were expanded and the *Temple at Jerusalem as well as many palaces were built. To realize his schemes he had to impose heavy taxation and use compulsory labor, which resulted in the revolt of N Israel. He was famous for his wisdom, and much of the "wisdom" literature of the Old Testament, such as the Song of Solomon, Proverbs, and Ecclesiastes, is attributed to him.

Solomon Islands, State of A country in the Pacific Ocean, E of New Guinea. It consists of a 900 mi (1450 km) chain of numerous small islands, the largest of which are *Guadalcanal, Malaita, San Cristobal, New Georgia, Santa Isabel and Choiseul. *Bougainville, within the Solomon Islands archipelago, is part of Papua New Guinea. The larger islands are mainly forested and mountainous, with some active volcanoes. Most of the population are Melanesian, with Polynesian and Micronesian minorities. *Economy*: the chief product is copra, which, with timber, is the main export. Oil palms, forestry, and fishing are being developed. *History*: the islands were discovered by the Spanish in 1568. The four main islands became a British protectorate in 1893 and others were added in 1898–99. During World War II they were the scene of fighting between the Japanese and Allied forces. They achieved self-government in 1976 and became independent within the Commonwealth of Nations in 1978. Chief Minister: Solomon Mamaloni. Official language: English. Official currency: Australian dollar of 100 cents. Area: 11,500 sq mi (29,785 sq km). Population (1983 est): 256,000. Capital and main port: Honiara.

Solomon's seal A hardy perennial herbaceous plant of the genus *Polygonatum* (about 25 species), native to moist shady woods of the N hemisphere, especially *P. multiflorum*. Its arching stem, 12–31 in (30–80 cm) long, bears two rows of broad spindle-shaped leaves, 2–5 in (5–12 cm) long, in the axils of which grow clusters of 2–5 greenish-white tubular flowers followed by red berries. The plant has a fleshy white underground stem (rhizome) marked with prominent scars (hence, probably, the name). Family *Liliaceae*.

Solon (6th century BC) Athenian statesman, who laid the foundations of Athenian democracy. As archon (c. 594–593), Solon cancelled debts for which land or liberty was the security and introduced a new coinage and system of weights and measures. He also reformed the constitution, dividing the citizens into four classes, and issued a more lenient legal code.

Solothurn (French name: Soleure) 47 13N 7 32E A city in NW Switzerland. It has a cathedral (1762–73) and a former arsenal containing an excellent collection of armor and old weapons. Industries include watchmaking and precision instruments. Population (1970): 17,708.

Soloviov, Vladimir Sergevich (1853–1900) Russian philosopher, poet, and theologian. A friend of Dostoievski, Soloviov was influenced by *Hegel and the mysticism of Jacob *Boehme. He held that there was a female principle, which he called Sophia, the world-soul.

solstice Either of two points on the *ecliptic, midway between the *equinoxes, at which the sun reaches its greatest angular distance above or below the celestial equator (see celestial sphere). In the N hemisphere the sun's northernmost position occurs at the **summer solstice**, usually on June 21, when daylight hours are at a maximum. Its southernmost position occurs at the **winter solstice**, usually on December 21, when daylight hours are minimal.

Solti, Sir Georg (1912–) Hungarian-born, British conductor and pianist. He studied in Budapest with Kodály and Dohnányi and was conductor of Britain's Royal Opera (1961–71). He became conductor of the Chicago Symphony Orchestra in 1969.

solution A homogenous liquid mixture of two or more substances. Solutions, unlike *colloids, contain no identifiable particles of different substances. The components mix as single molecules, ions, or atoms. When a solid or gas is dissolved in a liquid, the liquid is known as the solvent and the dissolved material the solute. If the components are all liquid, the one in excess is the solvent. In a **solid solution**, molecules, atoms, or ions of one component occupy positions in the crystal structure of the other.

Solutrean A culture of the Upper *Paleolithic succeeding *Gravettian. Named for the site of Solutré near Mâcon (E France), it existed in W Europe from about 18000 to 15000 BC in the warmer climate that followed

the Wurm *glaciation. It is characterized by symmetrical pressure-flaked flint and other stone points of laurel- and willow-leaf (foliate) shape, which foreshadow the concern for aesthetic expression more fully realized in the subsequent *Magdalenian culture.

Solvay process An industrial process for the production of sodium carbonate from salt, limestone, and ammonia. Limestone is first heated strongly to produce calcium oxide and carbon dioxide: $CaCO_3 \rightarrow CaO + CO_2$. The carbon dioxide gas is passed through brine saturated with ammonia, precipitating sodium hydrogen carbonate ($NaHCO_3$). This, on mild heating, yields sodium carbonate and some carbon dioxide, which is recycled. The ammonia is also recovered from the supernatant liquor from the second step, by the action of lime produced in the first step. Named for E. Solvay (1833–1922).

Solway Firth An inlet of the Irish Sea between Dumfries and Galloway Region in SW Scotland and Cumbria in NW England. Length: about 35 mi (56 km).

Solzhenitsyn, Aleksandr (1918–) Russian novelist. After distinguished service in World War II, he was arrested and held in prison camps until his rehabilitation in 1956. The cultural liberalization heralded by the publication of *A Day in the Life of Ivan Denisovich* (1962), dealing with life in the Stalinist labor camps, was short lived and in 1974 he was forced to leave the Soviet Union and eventually settled in Vermont. His major works, published only in the West, include *The Cancer Ward* (1966), *The First Circle* (1968) and *The Gulag Archipelago* (1974–78). He won the Nobel Prize in 1970. His memoirs, *The Oak and the Calf*, appeared in 1980.

soma A plant of uncertain identity. In the Vedic religion of India its intoxicating or hallucinogenic juice was used in sacrifices, especially to *Indra. It is also personified as a god in a number of hymns in the *Rigveda*.

Somali An E African people occupying Somalia, Djibouti (where they are called Issas), Ethiopia, and NW Kenya. There are many tribes, which are divided into patrilineal clans headed by a chief chosen by the senior men. Among the nomadic herdsmen of the interior blood feud is common. Dwellers in towns and along the coast are traders and farmers. All are at least nominally Muslims. Their language belongs to the Cushitic branch of the *Hamito-Semitic family.

Somalia (official name: Somali Democratic Republic) A country in East Africa, occupying most of the Horn of Africa between the Gulf of Aden and the Indian Ocean. Coastal plains rise in the N to a plateau reaching heights of over 6000 ft (1800 m). Most of the inhabitants are nomadic *Somalis with minorities of Sab, Bantu, and others. *Economy*: chiefly agricultural, with livestock raising (including sheep, goats, cattle, and camels) being especially important. There is some crop growing in the S, including sugar, maize, sorghum, bananas, and other fruit. The limited mineral resources are being exploited and include tin, iron ore, gypsum, and uranium. Fishing is being encouraged, and industry concentrates mainly on leather and food processing. Communications are difficult; there are no railroads, but an extensive road-building program is being carried out with Chinese and other aid. The main exports are livestock, hides and skins, and fruit (especially bananas). *History*: colonized by Muslims from the 7th century AD, the region was occupied in the 19th century by the French, British, and Italians (see Somaliland). The former British and Italian territories gained independence in 1960 (while the French territory of the Afars and Issas became independent Djibouti in 1977). In 1969, after a military coup, a Supreme Revolutionary Council was established in Somalia under Gen Mohamed Siad Barré (1919–). The country has had serious territorial disputes with Ethiopia (see Ogaden), which has a considerable Somali population. In the early 1980s northern dissident expatriates, claiming neglect and political inequities on the part of the southern-based government, launched attacks from Ethiopia on southern Somalia. Official language: Somali; Arabic, Italian, and English are used extensively. Official religion: Islam. Official currency: Somali shilling of 100 centesimi. Area: 270,000 sq mi (700,000 sq km). Population (1983 est): 6,248,000. Capital and main port: Mogadishu.

Somaliland A region corresponding to present-day Somalia and Djibouti. Between the 7th and 12th centuries AD the coastal region was occupied by Muslim traders while the N was settled from the 10th century by nomadic Somalis. During the 19th century the region was divided between France, Britain, and Italy. Italian Somaliland was united with Ethiopia by Mussolini to form Italian East Africa (1935) and was acquired by Britain in World War II. British Somaliland became independent as Somalia in 1960 and the French territory, Afars and Issas, as Djibouti in 1977.

somatotrophin. See growth hormone.

Somerset A county of SW England, bordering on the Bristol Channel. It consists mainly of a flat plain enclosed by the Quantock Hills and Exmoor in the W, the Blackdown Hills in the S, and the Mendip Hills in the NE. It is predominantly agricultural; dairy farming is especially important. The few scattered industries include food processing and textiles. Tourism is an important source of revenue. Area: 1335 sq mi (3458 sq km). Population (1981): 424,988. Administrative center: Taunton.

Somerset, Edward Seymour, 1st Duke of (c. 1500–52) English statesman, who was ruler of England (1547–49) during the minority of Edward VI. Seymour's advancement was facilitated by the marriage of his sister Jane Seymour to Henry VIII, on whose death he became Protector of England and a duke. He defeated the Scots in 1547 and furthered the Protestant *Reformation with the first Book of Common Prayer (1549). He fell from power in 1549 and was subsequently executed.

Somme River A river in N France, rising in the Aisne department and flowing mainly W through Amiens and Abbeville to the English Channel. It was the scene of extensive fighting in *World War I (1916). Length: 152 mi (245 km).

Sommerfeld, Arnold Johannes Wilhelm (1868–1951) German physicist, who did his most important work on atomic structure while he was professor at Munich (1906–31). His modifications of the *Bohr atom included the introduction of elliptical orbits for the electrons and azimuthal and magnetic *quantum numbers. He also worked on *wave mechanics and the theory of electrons in metals.

sonar. *See* echo sounding.

sonata (Italian: sounded, as opposed to *cantata*, sung) A piece of music for one or more instruments. The name has been used of a variety of abstract musical forms, including baroque works for one or more instruments and continuo, the one-movement keyboard sonatas of Scarlatti, and the piano sonatas of Haydn and Mozart. **Sonata form**, the normal structure of the first movement of the classical sonata, was based on the exposition, development, and recapitulation of two contrasting themes. It was applied to the first movement of the *symphony and of *chamber music compositions as well as the sonata proper. Beethoven and his successors enlarged the formal boundaries of the sonata; Liszt evolved a single-movement form out of the three or four movements of the classical sonata. In the 20th century sonata form has been adapted in a variety of ways and new formal patterns have been evolved by such composers as Bartók, Hindemith, Stravinsky, and Tippett.

Sondheim, Stephen (Joshua) (1930–) US composer, who studied lyric writing with Oscar Hammerstein II and composition with Milton Babbitt. He wrote the lyrics for the musicals *West Side Story* (1957), *A Little Night Music* (1973), and *Sweeney Todd* (1979); *Side by Side by Sondheim* (1976), a successful revue in New York and London, contains many of his songs.

son et lumière (French: sound and light) A nighttime, open-air dramatization of the history of a building, town, etc., using theatrical lighting effects with a synchronized sound track of music and speech. It was developed in 1952 at the Château de Chambord, France, by the Château's curator, Paul Robert-Houdin.

song A short composition for one or more singers, with or without accompaniment. Song is usually regarded as the foundation of music and is certainly the oldest form of musical expression. Besides the folksong traditions of every race, solo song has been a significant part of established musical tradition. In western music the French chansons of the 15th century, the Italian *frottola, the lute songs of the Elizabethans, operatic *arias, German *Lieder* (as treated by Schubert, Schumann, and Wolf), and the French tradition of *mélodies* (as treated by Duparc and Fauré) are all of great importance. A **song cycle** is a group of songs intended to be performed in sequence: the texts are either thematically related, or are all by the same poet.

Song (*or* Sung) (960–1279) A Chinese dynasty that may be divided into the Northern and Southern Song periods. It was founded in N China by Zhao Guang Yin (*or* Chao K'uang Yin; 927–76), who reunited the war-torn country but, despite a strong administration, was never able to control the *Juchen. These tribes forced the Song south in 1127 and founded their own dynasty in the N. The Southern Song established a new capital at Hangzhou, where a great flourishing of Chinese poetry, painting, and pottery occurred. The Song were overthrown by the Mongols under Kublai Khan in 1279.

Song, T. V. (*or* T. V. Sung; 1894–1971) Chinese banker and politician. He was finance minister (1925–31) and foreign minister (1942–45) in the Chinese Nationalist Government. After 1949 he lived in the US. His elder sister **Song Qing-Ling** (*or* Sung Ch'ing-ling; 1892–1981) married *Sun Yat-sen (1914) and herself became a revolutionary leader and later a member of the Chinese Communist Party. His younger sister **Song Mei-ling** (*or*

Sung Mei-ling; 1897–) married *Chiang Kai-shek, fleeing with him to Taiwan in 1949.

songbird A *passerine bird belonging to the suborder *Oscines* (about 4000 species), in which the vocal organ (syrinx), at the junction of the trachea (windpipe) and bronchi, is highly developed. The flow of air vibrates the vocal membranes; muscles alter their tension and so produce the different notes. Bird song communicates the identity and whereabouts of an individual to other birds and also signals alarm and sexual intentions; it is especially important in birds that feed or migrate in flocks.

Songhai A West African people inhabiting the region of the Middle Niger River S of Timbuktu. Adopting the Islamic religion in the 11th century AD and influenced by Muslim traders from Africa, the Songhai became prosperous and cultured traders. Between about 1350 and 1600 their kings developed a vast commercial empire, based on the gold and salt trade, which extended from the West African coast to Lake Chad and absorbed the earlier empire of Mali. After the Moroccan invasion of 1591, the Songhai empire collapsed.

Songhua River (*or* Sungari R.) A river in NE China, rising in *Jilin province and flowing roughly NE to the Heilong (*or* Amur) River on the border with the Soviet Union. Length: over 800 mi (1300 km).

Song of Solomon An Old Testament book, also known as the Song of Songs or Canticles. It was traditionally ascribed to *Solomon but was probably written in the 2nd century BC. Written in extravagantly erotic language, it is a series of oriental love poems concerning a bridegroom and his bride, "the Shulamite." Both Jews and Christians interpreted the work allegorically as describing the relation between God and Israel or, for Christian commentators, between Christ and the Church.

song thrush A Eurasian thrush, *Turdus philomelos*, about 9 in (22 cm) long and having a brown back, pale breast streaked with brown, and orange underwings. Its song is loud and distinctive, each phrase being repeated several times. It feeds on invertebrates and smashes snails against a stone before eating them.

sonic boom. *See* sound barrier.

sonnet A poem of 14 lines originating in Italy in the 13th century and introduced into England in the 16th century by Sir Thomas *Wyatt. Its two principal variations are the Petrarchan sonnet, usually divided into an octet rhyming *abbaabba* and a sestet rhyming *cdecde*, and the Shakespearean sonnet, usually rhyming *abab cdcd efef gg*. Sonnets have been written by Milton, Wordsworth, and G. M. Hopkins and it remains one of the few traditional forms still employed by major 20th-century poets. *See also* rhymes.

Soochow. *See* Suzhou.

Sophia (1657–1704) Regent of Russia (1682–89) for her brother Ivan V (1666–96) and half-brother *Peter the Great. She was overthrown by Peter and forced to retire to a convent, where she died.

Sophia (1630–1714) Electress of Hanover (1658–1714), in whom the Act of *Settlement (1701) vested the English crown. Sophia, the wife of Elector Ernest Augustus (1629–98; ruled 1692–98), was the granddaughter of James I of England and the daughter of Frederick the Winter King, of the Palatinate. Her son succeeded to the British throne as George I.

Sophists The Greek sages of the 5th and early 4th centuries BC who were itinerant experts on various subjects including public speaking, grammar, ethics, literature, mathematics, and elementary physics. They were not a clearly defined school, but they did have certain interests in common. In philosophy they attacked the *Eleatics' account of reality and tried to explain the phenomenal world. Their educational program centered on the belief that virtue can be taught. From their opponent *Plato, they acquired a bad name as philosophical tricksters, more interested in money and prestige than in truth. In Roman times the term "sophist" came to mean simply a teacher of rhetoric.

Sophocles (c. 496–406 BC) Greek dramatist; with Aeschylus and Euripides, one of the three great Athenian tragic dramatists. He developed the more static drama of Aeschylus by introducing a third actor and reducing the role of the chorus. Of his 123 plays, 7 survive: *Ajax*, *Women of Trachis*, *Electra*, *Philoctetes*, and his three most famous plays dealing with Thebes, *Oedipus Rex*, *Oedipus at Colonus*, and *Antigone*. He led an active public life, being a friend of Pericles and holding several important civil and military administrative posts.

soprano (Italian: upper) The highest female singing voice. Range: middle C to the C above the treble stave. The **mezzo-soprano** voice lies between the soprano and the contralto. Range: A below middle C to F an octave and a sixth above.

Soranus of Ephesus (2nd century AD) Greek physician, whose works were a major influence on gynecology and obstetrics until the 17th century. He described contraception, abortion, and procedures during childbirth and also wrote about fractures and diseases.

Sorbonne One of the oldest parts of the university in Paris, France, founded by the theologian Robert de Sorbon (1201–74) in about 1257. The present site of the Sorbonne, off the Boulevard Saint-Michel, dates from 1627 and was the scene of the first confrontations between students and police in the riots of May, 1968.

Sorel, Georges (1847–1922) French social philosopher. As a political activist, Sorel believed that socialism could only come about through a general strike (*see* syndicalism). His theory of the "social myth," which held that the proletariat could be manipulated by propaganda, was, ironically, most successfully proved by the fascist dictators.

Sorghum A genus of annual or perennial *grasses (about 30 species), native to Africa, especially *S. vulgare*, of which there are several varieties, such as sweet sorghum, *durra, and *kaffir corn, widely cultivated as cereal crops. Usually growing up to 8 ft (2.5 m) high, they have rigid stalks, sometimes containing a sweet sap, long flat leaves, and terminal flower clusters bearing 800–3000 starch-rich seeds. The seeds are used as grain for making bread, etc., and as a source of edible oil, starch, and sugar. The stalks are used as fodder or sometimes for syrup manufacture.

Sorocaba 23 30S 47 32W A city in S Brazil, in São Paulo state on the Río Sorocaba. It is a major industrial center; manufactures include textiles, fertilizers, and wine. Population (1975 est): 208,287.

sorrel A perennial herb, *Rumex acetosa*, common throughout temperate Eurasia and North America. It grows to a height of 40 in (1 m) and bears numerous small red flowers. The tangy-tasting leaves are used as a culinary flavoring and in salads. Family: *Polygonaceae*. *See also* wood sorrel.

Sorrento 40 37N 14 23E A seaport in SW Italy, in Campania. A resort since Roman times, it is the birthplace of the poet Tasso. Oranges and lemons are grown. Population (1971): 15,040.

Sosigenes of Alexandria (1st century BC) Greek astronomer, about whom little is known except that, on his advice, Julius Caesar reformed the calendar and added an extra day every four years to produce the modern system of leap years. This system is known as the Julian *calendar.

Sosnowiec 50 16N 19 07E A town in S Poland. It is a metallurgical center; other industries include engineering, chemicals, and the manufacture of textiles. Population (1979 est): 241,000.

Sotho A large group of Bantu-speaking peoples of S Africa. The term applies in a general sense to the peoples of Botswana, Lesotho, and the Transvaal (South Africa) but, more specifically, to one of the four main divisions of these peoples, the Sotho of Lesotho. The other branches are the Tswana, Pedi, and Venda, each with many tribes. All live by combined agriculture and animal husbandry and have a broadly similar culture, now disintegrating under the impact of urbanization.

Soto The largest Japanese school of Zen Buddhism, founded in China in the 9th century AD and brought to Japan by *Dogen in 1227. Soto emphasizes meditation and morality. Adherents strive to live as what they hope to become, perfect Buddhas.

Soto, Hernando de (?1496–1542) Spanish explorer. After exploration in Central America, he set out in 1539 to conquer Florida. He landed with 600 men at Tampa Bay and journeyed circuitously through what became the S US in search of gold. In 1541 he crossed the Mississippi, the first white man to do so, but died on the return journey.

Soufflot, Jacques Germain (1713–80) French architect. After training in Italy (1731–38), Soufflot became the leading French exponent of *neoclassicism. Apart from the Hôtel Dieu in Lyons (1841–48), his most famous building is the Church of St Geneviève in Paris (begun in 1757), now called the *Panthéon.

Soult, Nicolas Jean de Dieu, Duc de Dalmatie (1769–1851) French general in the Revolutionary and Napoleonic Wars. A sergeant at the outbreak of the French Revolution, he rose to the rank of general in 1794 and later commanded in the Peninsular War. He became president of the council (1832–34, 1839–40, 1840–47) under Louis Philippe.

sound A disturbance propagated through a medium by longitudinal waves. Strictly the term applies only to those waves that are audible to the human ear, i.e. with frequencies between about 20 and 20,000 hertz, those with frequencies above 20,000 hertz being called ultrasound and those below 20 hertz infrasound. Sound is propagated by vibrations of molecules in the medium, producing fronts of compression and rarefaction. Sound waves are longitudinal as the molecules vibrate in the direction of propagation; the velocity of sound in air at 0°C is about 332 meters per second (760 mph

at 32°F). The three principal characteristics of a sound are its pitch (the frequency of the wave), loudness (the amplitude of the wave), and *timbre (the extent to which it contains harmonics of the fundamental frequency). However, there is a relationship between pitch and loudness (*see* sound intensity). *See also* acoustics.

Sound, the (Danish name: =O/resund; Norwegian name: Öresund) A sea channel in N Europe, between Denmark (Sjælland) and Sweden, linking the Kattegat and the Baltic Sea. Length: 70 mi (113 km). Narrowest point: 2.5 mi (4 km).

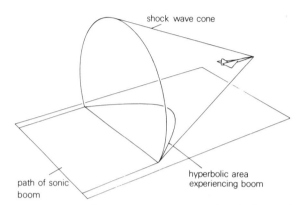

shock wave cone

path of sonic boom

hyperbolic area experiencing boom

SOUND BARRIER *As an aircraft passes through the sound barrier the sonic boom is heard along a hyperbolic area on the ground.*

sound barrier An obstacle experienced by subsonic *aircraft attempting to fly at or above the speed of sound. Drag increases sharply, lift falls off, and the aircraft becomes difficult to control (*see* aeronautics). At subsonic speeds the pressure waves created by the aircraft as it flies through the air are able to move ahead of the aircraft; at supersonic speeds they cannot escape in a forward direction as the source is moving faster than the pressure waves themselves. Thus shock waves build up on the aircraft's wings and fuselage, creating an apparent barrier to supersonic flight. The barrier was overcome for the first time by the US Bell X1 rocket aircraft in 1947. Since then many aircraft capable of supersonic flight have been built (including Concorde) by greater streamlining, sweptback wings, and more powerful engines. As these aircraft cross the sound barrier a **sonic boom** is heard. This is created by a shock-wave cone with the nose of the aircraft at its vertex. In level flight the intersection of this cone with the ground produces a hyperbola at all points along which the boom is heard.

sound intensity The rate at which sound energy is propagated through a unit area perpendicular to the direction of propagation. It is measured in watts per square meter. The intensities of two sound levels are compared by a unit called the *decibel. The intensity of sound is not the same as its loudness, the latter being the magnitude of the sensation produced by the human ear, which is dependent on the frequency of the sound.

Souphanouvong, Prince (1912–) Laotian statesman; president (1975–). In the civil war in Laos (1953–73) he led the revolutionary Pathet Lao and, on its conclusion, joined the coalition government established in 1974. In 1975, however, Pathet Lao forces seized complete control and Souphanouvong became president.

soursop An evergreen tree belonging to the tropical American genus *Annona*, especially *A. muricata*, widely cultivated in the Old World tropics. It grows to a height of 26 ft (8 m) and produces large oval spiny green fruit, the flesh of which can be eaten or used as an ingredient of soft drinks, ice cream, etc. Family: *Annonaceae*.

Sousa, John Philip (1854–1933) US composer and bandmaster. In 1880 he was appointed leader of the Marine Corps Band and in 1892 formed his own band, which toured the world. He wrote military marches including "The Stars and Stripes Forever," "The Washington Post," "Semper Fidelis," and "Liberty Bell" and invented the **sousaphone**, a tuba-like band instrument with a forward-facing bell.

souslik (*or* suslik) A nocturnal *ground squirrel belonging to the genus *Citellus* (34 species), of E Europe, Asia, and North America (where it is sometimes called a gopher). The European souslik (*C. citellus*) is yellowish brown with large eyes and small ears and lives in burrows in dry open country, feeding on seeds, nuts, and bulbs. *See also* chipmunk.

Sousse 35 50N 10 38E A port in central Tunisia, on the Mediterranean coast. It was founded by the Phoenicians as a port and trade center. Its industries include sardine fishing and canning and olive-oil manufacture. Population (1976 est): 255,000.

Soustelle, Jacques (Émile) (1912–) French anthropologist and politician. A member of the *Free French during World War II, he became secretary general of de Gaulle's Rassemblement du Peuple français in 1947. He was governor general of Algeria (1955–56) and subsequently opposed the policies of successive French governments toward Algeria, living in exile from 1961 to 1968. He then became director of the prestigious École pratique des hautes Études. His books include *Arts of Ancient Mexico* (1967).

South Africa, Republic of (Afrikaans name: Suid-Afrika) A country occupying the S tip of Africa. Narrow coastal plains rise to plateaus in the interior, with the Drakensberg mountains in the E reaching 10,822 ft (3299 m). The N is mainly desert. The Limpopo, Molopo, and Orange Rivers mark the N boundary. The Vaal, a tributary of the Orange, is another important river. The majority of the inhabitants are Africans (71%) with white, Coloured (an official category) and Asian (mostly Indian) minorities. *Economy*: although South Africa is highly industrialized, agriculture is still important, with cereals, fruit growing, and cotton, as well as livestock. Citrus fruit is particularly important and there is a considerable wine industry. Fishing is a valuable source of income and whaling continues although efforts at conservation have reduced its scale. Rich and varied mineral resources include gold, diamonds, chrome, platinum, uranium, coal, manganese, phosphates, and iron. South Africa leads the world in the production of gold, gem diamonds, antimony, and vanadium. Hydroelectricity is a valuable source of power. Well-developed and diverse industry includes metals, machinery, and chemicals, as well as light industry, such as food processing and textiles. Main exports include metals (especially gold), citrus fruits, sugar, wines, and textiles. *History*: originally inhabited by San (Bushmen) and Khoikhoi peoples. Bantu-speaking tribes moved southward to present-day South Africa between 1000 and 1500. The Portuguese under *Dias first sighted the Cape of Good Hope (1488) but made no permanent settlement there. The Dutch East India Company settlement (1652) at Table Bay (Cape Town) expanded into a colony that spread into the interior, meeting little resistance from the *Khoisan inhabitants. After Louis XIV revoked the Edict of Nantes (1685), Huguenot refugees augmented the white settlers. During the Napoleonic Wars Britain acquired the Cape Colony for strategic reasons, a possession confirmed in 1814. In the 1830s increasing numbers of Dutch farmers (or Boers, forebears of the modern Afrikaners) moved in vast numbers E and N to escape British rule (*see* Great Trek). Bloody warfare (primarily with the Zulus) ensued as the *Bantu peoples who were migrating southward clashed with the Boers. The Boers founded two independent republics, the Orange Free State and the Transvaal (*see* Sand River Convention), but their republic in Natal was soon annexed by the British (1843), who were also expanding the eastern boundaries of the Cape Colony (*see* Cape Frontier Wars). *Kruger's assertion of Boer independence led to war (1880–81), which broke out again between the Boers and the British after the discovery of gold (1886) in the Transvaal had led to hostility between the Boers and the immigrant golddiggers (*see* Boer Wars). The need for cooperation led the two former Boer republics and the two British colonies to combine in the Union of South Africa (1910). The Depression of the 1930s saw the emergence of both African and Afrikaner nationalism as unskilled laborers from both groups were forced into the cities to compete for jobs. In 1913 a segregation policy was instituted to safeguard South Africa as a white country; the creation of the bantustans or African homelands ensued, thus ensuring the forcible exclusion of Africans from the political and social life of the country. All of South Africa's "people of Colour" became subject to discriminatory laws, although Coloureds and Asians were granted somewhat broader privileges. In both World Wars South Africa, under J. C. *Smuts, enthusiastically supported Britain, but anti-British Afrikaner interests grew steadily stronger. In 1948 Smuts was ousted by the Afrikaner National Party and the even harsher segregationist policy known as apartheid or "separate development" became official. A program of Bantu self government, whereby 10 Bantustans, or black homelands, were to achieve independence was enacted. (In 1976 *Transkei became the first Bantu homeland to receive independence.) In 1961 because of disapproval on the part of the Commonwealth nations South Africa became a republic outside the Commonwealth. Since the 1950s the African movement against apartheid has intensified, leading to numerous clashes between blacks and the government in which many blacks have died. Under Prime Minister Pieter Botha the South African government moved to modify some of its apartheid laws and in 1983 revised its constitution for the first time. Despite severe censure from the world community, South Africa has remained dogged in its pursuit of a

political and social philosophy of white supremacy. It has also played an important role in the affairs of neighboring states, intervening in *Angola (1976), administering *Namibia despite a United Nations mandate declaring its independence, and supporting white minorities in *Zimbabwe and *Mozambique in opposition to efforts of the majorities in these countries to establish African rule. State president: Pieter W. Botha (1916–). Official languages: Afrikaans and English. Official currency, since 1959: rand of 100 cents. Area: 472,359 sq mi (1,221,042 sq km). Population (1983): 30,938,000. Capitals: Pretoria (administrative), Bloemfontein (judicial), Cape Town (legislative).

South African Wars. *See* Boer Wars.

South America The fourth largest continent, lying chiefly in the S of the W hemisphere between the Pacific and Atlantic Oceans. Roughly triangular in shape and tapering in the S, it is linked to the continent of North America by the Isthmus of Panama. An ancient shield occupies much of the NE part of the continent and forms the Brazilian and Guiana Highlands. These are separated by the vast basins of the Orinoco, Amazon, and Paraná–Paraguay river systems. In the extreme W, beyond a series of plains, rise the mountains and high plateaus of the *Andes, the world's longest mountain system. The Andes rise to their highest point at Mount *Aconcagua and contain Lake *Titicaca, the continent's largest lake. South America's climate varies considerably, largely because of its length, but much is tropical with vast areas of tropical rainforest (selva). The population consists chiefly of the indigenous Indians, Europeans (especially Spanish and Portuguese), and mestizos together with large numbers of Negroids. *History*: much archeological evidence remains of the flourishing kingdoms of South America (such as those of the *Incas and *Chibchas), which were vanquished by the Spanish conquistadors. The entire continent was divided—Portugal taking the NE portion (now Brazil) and Spain the remainder—during the 16th century. With the collapse of the Spanish Empire during the early 19th century, there followed struggles for independence under national leaders, who included *Bolívar and *San Martin. Large-scale European immigration (including German and Italian) occurred in the 19th century. During the 20th century the constituent nations have become increasingly industrialized and seen rapid rises in their populations. Area: 17,767,331 sq km (6,858,527 sq mi). Population (1971 est): 291,000,000.

South American languages The indigenous languages of South America, the Antilles, and parts of Central America, many of which are now extinct. Brought originally from North America by migrating Indians, the languages are extremely diverse in nature. The number of speakers is currently estimated at 11,200,000, the majority of whom are to be found in the central Andes. The classification of the 600 documented languages, based on lexical and syntactic similarities, presents no very clear picture. Although linguists agree that the languages probably shared a common source, there is no consensus on the relationships among the major and minor groupings.

Southampton 50 55N 1 25W A city in S England, an inlet of the English Channel. It is the UK's principal passenger port, used by the largest transatlantic liners. Southampton's industries include marine engineering, electrical equipment, and yachtbuilding. The University of Southampton was established in 1952. Population (1981): 204,406.

Southampton, Henry Wriothesley, 3rd Earl of (1573–1624) English courtier, famous as the patron of Shakespeare: *Venus and Adonis* (1593) and *The Rape of Lucrece* (1594) were dedicated to him. He was involved in the Earl of Essex's conspiracy against Elizabeth I (1600), persuading the players of the Globe Theatre to perform Shakespeare's *Richard III* (about the deposition of a king) to encourage revolt. His death sentence was commuted to life imprisonment and he was released by James I (1603).

South Australia A state of S central Australia, bordering on the Indian Ocean. It consists chiefly of low-lying plains with the *Great Victoria Desert in the W, rising in the NW to the Musgrave Ranges and in the SE to the Flinders Range. The only major river is the Murray. Lake Eyre is frequently only an immense salt flat. Intensive agriculture is restricted to the S. Its vineyards produce almost half of Australia's wine. Mineral resources include iron ore from the Middleback Ranges, low-grade coal at Leigh Creek, large natural gas fields in the N, and opals. Industry, concentrated in Adelaide, includes the manufacture of motor vehicles, textiles, and chemicals. Area: 380,070 sq mi (984,377 sq km). Population (1980 est): 1,299,100. Capital: Adelaide.

South Bend 41 40N 86 15W a city in Indiana on the St Joseph River. Industries include the manufacture of aircraft, motor-vehicle parts, and machinery. The University of Notre Dame is here. Population (1980): 109,727.

South Carolina A state in the SE, on the Atlantic coast. It is bounded on the S and E by the Atlantic Ocean, on the S and W by Georgia, and on the N by North Carolina. Lowlands make up two thirds of the state, rising to uplands (the Piedmont Plateau) culminating in the Blue Ridge Mountains in the extreme NW. Major rivers include the Savannah. Although the population is predominantly rural (55%) with blacks comprising 31% of the total, South Carolina is undergoing a transition from a basically agrarian economy to one dominated by industry. The large areas of woodland supply the furniture industries and the large textile and clothing industries are based on the region's cotton crop. Other leading manufactures include chemicals, machinery, and food products. South Carolina's beaches along the NW coast (the most famous being Myrtle Beach) and the popular Sea Islands (including Cumberland Island and Hilton Head) with wildlife sanctuaries and resort areas, are tourist attractions. Charleston, the capital, and a major US port of entry, is famous for the unique charm of its antebellum homes, flowering gardens, and picturesque winding streets. *History*: what was perhaps the first but short-lived white settlement in North America was founded by the Spanish in 1526 at an unknown site in present-day South Carolina. French Huguenots later attempted to colonize the area but were thwarted by the Spanish, whose missions dotted the SW coast from Florida to what is now Charleston. With the arrival of the English during the reign of Charles II (for whom Charleston was named), Carolina was settled as a proprietary colony (1670). Dissatisfaction with the despotic rule of the small group of proprietors resulted in revolt by the colonists, and in 1719 the Carolinas were made a royal colony with a royal governor. South Carolina was made a separate colony in 1729. White immigration was encouraged to offset the growing population of imported black slaves. Sectionalism began to emerge with the poor lowland farmers in the NW demanding political equality with the wealthy plantation lords in the S. The Stamp Act and the Townshend Acts transformed sentiments in South Carolina to favor revolution. After the American Revolution the invention of the cotton gin and the subsequent glut in the cotton market by growing cotton production in the W states precipitated a decline in prosperity. South Carolina's John Calhoun, defending the doctrine of states' rights, became the philosophical founding father of much of the political and intellectual basis of the Confederacy. South Carolina was the first state to secede from the Union and shots fired at Fort Sumter signaled the outbreak of the Civil War. Regarded as the birthplace of secession, South Carolina suffered severe, deliberate, and devastating reprisals at the hands of Union soldiers, culminating in the burning of Columbia. During Reconstruction, South Carolina also experienced great hardship and corruption, emerging as a state in which white political supremacy prevailed but whose agrarian economy had been virtually destroyed. In the 1920s Jim Crow laws were instituted. Hard hit by the Depression and a serious boll weevil infestation, the state rallied with state work programs provided by the New Deal. The political and legal position of the blacks, now a minority, underwent gradual improvement into the 1980s.

South Caucasian languages A group of languages, also known as the Kartvelian languages, spoken by the people of W Transcaucasia and adjacent regions. It includes *Georgian, Svan, Mingrelian, and Laz. Only Georgian possesses a literary tradition and is used for literary purposes by speakers of the other languages.

South China Sea (Chinese name: Nanhai) A section of the W Pacific Ocean, between SE Asia, Borneo, the Philippines, and Taiwan. A monsoon area, it is heavily fished.

South Dakota One of the Plains states in the N central part of the country. It is bordered by North Dakota on the N, by Iowa and Minnesota on the E, by Nebraska on the S, and by Montana and Wyoming on the W. The Missouri River separates the arid Badlands, the Black Hills, and the Great Plains in the W from the flat fertile prairie in the E, which forms the basis of South Dakota's predominantly agrarian economy. Livestock and livestock products are the chief source of revenue. Although it has the largest gold mine in the US, mineral extraction is minimal. *History*: Home of the nomadic Sioux and the sedentary Arikara, the area was partially explored (1742–43) by the French. It was part of the Louisiana Purchase (1803) and was explored by the Lewis and Clark expedition shortly thereafter. Early settlement was spurred by the fur trade and the subsequent development of farms, but it was Colonel George Custer's confirmation of the existence of gold in the Black Hills (1874) that lured hordes of prospectors. The Indians were gradually subdued, ending with the massacre at Wounded Knee (1890). The arrival of the railroads stimulated the development of ranching and farming and the years 1880 to 1890 saw a tripling of Dakota Territory's population. In 1889 the lines between North and South were drawn and both states entered the Union. From this time until after World War II, South Dakota was severely harmed by droughts and economic depressions. A new prosperity emerged after the war as a result

of the establishment of hydroelectric projects, control of the Missouri River, growth of industry and tourism, and mechanization of farms. Area: 77,047 sq mi (199,551 sq km). Population (1980): 690,178. Capital: Pierre.

South East Asia Treaty Organization (SEATO) An organization formed to protect SE Asia from possible communist aggression. It was analogous to the *North Atlantic Treaty Organization. The treaty was signed in Manila in 1954 by Australia, France, New Zealand, Pakistan, the Philippines, Thailand, the UK, and the US. Pakistan withdrew in 1973 and the organization was formally ended in 1977. *See also* Association of South East Asian Nations.

Southend-on-Sea 51 33N 0 43E A resort in SE England, on the lower Thames estuary. It is the nearest seaside resort to London and has the world's longest pleasure pier. Population (1981): 156,683.

Southern Alps The highest range of mountains in New Zealand. It extends SW–NE through South Island and contains many peaks over 10,000 ft (3000 m), including Mount *Cook. Glaciers, fed by the central snowfields, flank the mountains and include Tasman Glacier. It is an important winter-sports area.

Southern Christian Leadership Congress (SCLC) US civil-rights organization founded by Martin Luther *King, Jr. in 1957. Advocating a policy of nonviolence, he hoped to bring about equal rights in the South. It backed the successful desegregation of public facilities (1963) and the March on Washington (1963). After King's assassination (1968), it was led by Ralph *Abernathy and then Joseph Lowery, but its influence declined.

Southern Cross. See Crux.

Southern Rhodesia. *See* Zimbabwe, State of.

southernwood A perennial herb, *Artemisia abrotanum*, also called lad's love, native to S Europe and Asia and cultivated for its aromatic leaves, which can be used to make a beverage. Family: *Compositae*. *See also* wormwood.

Southey, Robert (1774–1843) British poet and writer. He was a close associate of *Wordsworth and *Coleridge and in 1803 settled in the Lake District. He became poet laureate in 1813. His poetry lacks originality and was overshadowed by the work of his greater contemporaries. He wrote several historical books, notably *The Life of Nelson* (1813).

South Georgia An island in the S Atlantic Ocean, a dependency of the Falkland Islands. King Edward Point is a base for members of the British Antarctic Survey. With the Falkland Islands, it was invaded by Argentina in April, 1982, but was recaptured by British forces the same month. Area: 1450 sq mi (3755 sq km).

South Holland (Dutch name: Zuid-Holland) A province in the W central Netherlands, on the North Sea. Its S part consists of several islands. It is densely populated and agriculture, especially cattle raising and flower bulbs, is the chief occupation. The extensive trading and shipping industry is centered on the port of Rotterdam. Tourism is also important. Area: 1287 sq mi (3333 sq km). Population (1981 est): 3,106,697. Capital: The Hague.

South Island The larger of the two principal islands of New Zealand, separated from North Island by Cook Strait. It is generally mountainous, rising over 11,483 ft (3500 m) in the *Southern Alps in the W, with coastal plains.

SOUTHLAND PLAIN

Southland Plain A low-lying area of New Zealand, on SE South Island bordering on the Pacific Ocean. Sheep rearing and dairying are important.

South Orkney Islands A group of islands within the British Antarctic Territory, in the S Atlantic Ocean. A dependency of the Falkland Islands until 1962, their major importance is as a whaling base. They are also claimed by Argentina.

South Ossetian autonomous region An autonomous region (*oblast*) in the W Soviet Union, in the Georgian SSR. Its inhabitants comprise chiefly Orthodox Christian Ossetians, a Caucasian people. Timber is produced and its many rivers are used to generate hydroelectric power. Livestock are raised in the higher regions. Area: 1500 sq mi (3900 sq km). Population (1981 est): 97,000. Capital: Tskhinvali.

Southport 53 39N 3 01W A city and resort in NW England, on the Irish Sea. Its annual flower show is famous and there is a well-known golf course at nearby Birkdale. Population (1981): 89,745.

South Sea Bubble (1720) The collapse of the British market in South Sea stocks that had far-reaching political repercussions. The South Sea Company was founded in 1711 to trade with Spanish America. A boom in South Sea stock was followed by collapse and the subsequent inquiry revealed corruption among ministers and even touched the king. The day was saved by Sir Robert *Walpole, who transferred the South Sea stocks to the Bank of England and the East India Company.

South Shetland Islands An uninhabited archipelago within the British Antarctic Territory, in the S Atlantic Ocean. Until 1962 they were a dependency of the British Falkland Islands.

South Shields 55 00N 1 25W A port in NE England, on the Tyne estuary. Industries include shipbuilding, marine engineering, petrochemicals, and paint manufacture. Population (1981): 87,203.

South West Africa. *See* Namibia.

Soutine, Chaim (1893–1943) Lithuanian-born painter, who emigrated to Paris in 1913. There influenced by *expressionism, he achieved recognition in the 1920s despite his reluctance to exhibit his work. Using thickly applied paint, intense color, and distorted and writhing forms, he was, together with *Chagall, the leading representative of French expressionism.

Sovetsk (name until 1945: Tilsit) 55 02N 21 50E A city of the Soviet Union, in the W RSFSR on the Nemen River. Founded by the Teutonic Knights in 1288, it was here that the Treaties of *Tilsit were signed (1807) between Napoleon and, respectively, Prussia (which held the town until 1945) and Russia. Industries include food processing and the manufacture of pulp. Population (1970): 38,000.

soviet A government council in the Soviet Union. Soviets originated as committees of workers' deputies in the *Revolution of 1905 and were again established in the *Russian Revolution of 1917, which established the *Soviet Union. The Supreme Soviet is in theory the supreme organ of government in the Soviet Union and soviets are also elected at the local, provincial, and republican levels. Candidates, one for each deputy, are selected by the Communist Party.

Soviet Far East. *See* Siberia.

Soviet Union (official name: Union of Soviet Socialist Republics) The world's largest country and its third most populous, covering N Eurasia and bordering on the Pacific and Arctic Oceans and the Baltic, Black, Caspian, and Aral Seas. It is officially a federal state comprising 15 constituent republics: the Armenian, Azerbaidzhan, Belorussian, Estonian, Georgian, Kazakh, Kirghiz, Latvian, Lithuanian, Moldavian, Russian Soviet Federal, Tadzhik, Turkmen, Ukrainian, and Uzbek Soviet Socialist Republics. Administrative subdivisions include 20 Autonomous Soviet Socialist Republics and, within some of these, 8 autonomous regions (Russian *oblast*, region). The area W of the River Yenisei consists of vast plains and depressions, dissected by the Ural Mountains, while the E consists mainly of mountains and plateaus. The mountain belt along the S border includes the Carpathian, Caucasus, Pamir, and Sayan Mountains, the Stanovoi Range, and the Tien Shan. The rivers mainly flow N to the Arctic Ocean. The population includes over a hundred national groups, for whom many of the country's subdivisions were established. The most numerous are the Russians, Ukrainians, Uzbeks, Belorussians, Tatars, and Kazakhs. Population is most dense W of the Urals, where most of the large industrial cities are situated. *Economy*: based on the system of state ownership, it is controlled through Gosplan (the State Planning Commission) and Gosbank (the State Bank). It has been directed since 1928 by a series of *five-year plans and the economy is now the largest and strongest after the US. Its main asset is the country's vast natural resources and the Soviet Union is the world's leading producer of oil, coal, iron ore, cement, and steel; manganese, gold, natural gas, and other minerals are also of major importance.

Industry was long concentrated after 1928 on the production of capital goods through metalworking, machine manufacture, and the chemical industry, and relatively few consumer goods were produced. During the 1960s and 1970s the latter have received slightly more emphasis. Agriculture, organized in a system of state and collective farms, is on a large scale and is highly mechanized but is not highly productive, hampered in many areas by the climate and by a shortage of resources. The Soviet Union is one of the world's greatest producers of cereals, although bad harvests (as in 1972 and 1975) have necessitated imports and hampered the economy. The 1976–80 five-year plan shifted resources to agriculture, and 1978 saw a record harvest. Fishing, forestry, and dependent industries are also important; the country is the world's greatest producer of timber. Largely self-sufficient, it trades little in comparison to its economic strength, although trade with noncommunist countries increased greatly during the 1970s. Fuels, metals, machinery, and timber are exported, while machinery, consumer goods, and occasionally grain are imported. *History*: the area has been populated for three to four millenniums, although little is known of its history until the 8th century AD, when European and Middle Eastern traders began its exploration. Control of the area between the Baltic and Black Seas was established by Scandinavian adventurers by 1000. Dominated by Kiev from the mid-10th to mid-11th centuries, these Varangian principalities submitted (after 1223) to the overrule of the Golden Horde. By the time of the Horde's collapse in the 14th century, Moscow, ruled by Rurik princes, had emerged as a powerful principality, becoming the capital of a united Russia under Ivan the Great in the 15th century. Contact with W Europe was established in the late 17th century by Peter the Great, who also established the Russian bureaucracy and educational system and built a new capital, St Petersburg (present-day Leningrad). By the 19th century Russian territories had been greatly extended but, although a force to be reckoned with in the world, Russia was industrially far behind the UK, Germany, and the US, its bureaucracy had grown unwieldy and oppressive, and its Romanov emperors (tsars) were opposed to any political change. Revolutionary activity began with the Dekabrists' conspiracy, uncovered in 1825, and, although serfdom was abolished in 1861, its abolition was achieved on terms unfavorable to the peasants and served to encourage revolutionaries, a group of whom assassinated Alexander II in 1881. Bloody Sunday (January 22, 1905), on which several hundred workers were killed during a demonstration in St Petersburg, was followed by great disorder (*see* Revolution of 1905). A parliament, the *Duma, was established in 1906, but political unrest continued and was aggravated during World War I by military defeat and food shortages. The February and October Revolutions (*see* Russian Revolution) were followed by a period of civil war (1918–22), after which communist control was complete. After Lenin's death (1924) Stalin had emerged as leader by 1928, having ousted Trotsky. Under Stalin, who replaced Lenin's New Economic Policy with five-year plans and collective farms, the Soviet Union (established 1922) became a major industrial power but a totalitarian state, with effective political opposition eliminated during the 1930s by purges. World War II established the Soviet Union as one of the two major world powers, a position maintained since then through military strength, aid to developing countries, and scientific research, especially into weaponry and space technology. Relations with the other superpower, the US, have improved after the *Cold War, with agreements on *disarmament, although the Soviet invasion of Afghanistan (1979) provoked US condemnation. Internal dissension is still viewed as a threat, as shown by the trials of human-rights activists. Dissension within the communist bloc (*see* Warsaw Pact) provokes a similar response from the Soviet Government, which intervened in the Hungarian Revolution (1956) and the Czechoslovakian liberalization program (1968) and which directed the suppression of the Solidarity labor movement in Poland in 1981. Strained relations with the US were marked by the US boycott of the 1980 Olympics in Moscow and the Soviet boycott of the 1984 Olympics in Los Angeles, but more importantly by the breakdown in 1983 of nuclear arms control talks. The Communist Party, with a membership of over 15,000,000, maintains total control of government. A new constitution became law in 1977 and elections are held, although in practice each constituency has only one candidate and political parties other than the Communist Party are illegal. The Soviet Union is a member of *COMECON. Chairman of the Presidium of the Supreme Soviet: Konstantin Chernenko. Official language: Russian. Official currency: rouble of 100 kopeks. Area: 8,647,675 sq mi (22,402,200 sq km). Population (1983): 272,308,000. Moscow.

Soweto 26 10S 28 02E A large urban area in South Africa, in the Transvaal forming a suburb of Johannesburg. It is inhabited solely by black Africans and comprises 36 townships, divided into tribal areas. In June, 1976, it was the scene of serious rioting by African students during which over a hundred people died. Population (1970): 558,798.

sow thistle An herb of the genus *Sonchus*, especially *S. oleraceus*, occurring widely as a weed in Europe, W Asia, and N Africa. Growing to a height of 8–59 in (20–150 cm), its oval leaves have prickly edges and it produces clusters of yellow flowers. Family: **Compositae*.

soybean An annual plant, *Glycine max*, widely cultivated for its seeds. The many commercial varieties grow to heights of 8–79 in (20–200 cm) and produce clusters of pods, each containing two or three seeds. The ripe seeds contain 35% protein. Soybean oil is extracted for use in making margarines, cooking oils, resins, and paints and for many other foods, chemicals, and textiles. The meal residue is an important protein food for livestock and a meat substitute for man. The beans are also eaten whole, ground into soy flour, and used to make soy sauce. Family: **Leguminosae*.

Soyinka, Wole (1934–) Nigerian dramatist and poet. He was educated in Nigeria and England. His works, characterized by a lively and often satirical style, include the play *The Lion and the Jewel* (1963) and the novels *The Interpreters* (1965), *The Man Died* (1973), and *Aké* (1982). He edited the literary journal *Black Orpheus* (1960–64) and was imprisoned during the Nigerian civil war (1967–69).

Soyuz. *See* Salyut.

Spa 50 29N 5 52E A town in SE Belgium. It is a tourist resort, renowned since the 14th century for its mineral springs. Population (1972): 9600.

Spaak, Paul Henri (1899–1972) Belgian statesman, the first socialist prime minister of Belgium (1938–39, 1947–50) and foreign minister (1936–38, 1939–46, 1954–57, 1961–65). He negotiated the Treaties of Rome, which established the EEC, and was president of the EEC assembly in 1949. From 1957 to 1961 he was secretary general of NATO.

spacecraft A vehicle designed to be launched into space and to function effectively for a considerable period in the hostile conditions of space. Due to the immense expense and the difficulties involved in prolonged space travel, most spacecraft are unmanned. Their instruments are powered by arrays of solar cells (*see* solar power), for craft out to about Mars' orbit, and can be controlled by ground stations. Their information is sent back to earth as radio transmissions. Unmanned craft include several thousand *satellites of diverse functions and numerous *planetary probes. In manned craft, such as the *Skylab and *Salyut orbiting space laboratories and the vehicles taking part in the *Apollo moon program, the weightless conditions require the careful monitoring of physiological and psychological reactions both during and after the flight.

space exploration The space age began with the launching of the Soviet satellite Sputnik 1 on October 4, 1957. The first manned flight, one earth orbit, was made by the Soviet cosmonaut Yuri *Gagarin on April 12, 1961. Man first flew round the moon in December, 1968, aboard the US Apollo 8 and first landed on the lunar surface in the lunar module of Apollo 11 in July, 1969 (*see* Apollo moon program). Although manned exploration of space has at present gone no further than the moon, unmanned *planetary probes have been sent to every planet as far as Saturn, reached by Pioneer 11 in September, 1979. If successful, Voyager 2 should approach Uranus in 1986 and Neptune in 1990. Most probes have made a close fly-by of targeted planets and the Mariner 9, Viking, and Pioneer Venus orbiters of Mars and Venus were able to make more extensive observations.

space shuttle A manned reusable US space transportation system developed by *NASA for operational use in the 1980s. It consists of a delta-wing Orbiter that has three powerful rocket engines, a large cargo bay in which satellites, etc., are carried into earth orbit, and passenger and crew space. It is launched by rocket propulsion. Although its two externally mounted rocket boosters can be recovered after they detach shortly after launch, the huge external propellant tank is discarded. The first two-day test flight of the Columbia shuttle, crewed by John Young and Robert Crippen, took place in April, 1981. It made an unpowered landing. Subsequent flights have been frequent, testing a large range of equipment and conducting scientific experiments.

space-time continuum A coordinate system that has four dimensions, three representing physical space and the fourth time. The four-dimensional space-time continuum is used in *relativity to define an event. For example, an event occurring on the sun would be observed at different times on earth and on Jupiter, as light from the sun takes some 35 minutes longer to reach Jupiter than to reach the earth. Thus the concept of simultaneity requires a four-dimensional coordinate system to define events without ambiguity.

spadefoot toad A nocturnal burrowing *toad belonging to a widely distributed family (*Pelobatidae*). Spadefoot toads survive in arid regions by digging themselves deep holes in sand or mud with a special horny structure on the foot. The European spadefoot (*Pelobates fuscus*) exudes a garlic-smelling secretion when harmed.

Spain, Kingdom of A country in SW Europe, occupying over four fifths of the Iberian Peninsula. The Balearic and Canary Islands are also part of Spain. It consists mainly of a high plateau, rising over 10,000 ft (3000 m) in the Pyrenees in the NE. *Economy*: traditionally agricultural, the industrial sector had begun to predominate by the early 1970s. After many years of economic stagnation, there was a remarkable improvement in the 1960s with the development of the motor-vehicle, machine-tool, shipbuilding, and chemical industries. Tourism, an important source of foreign currency, began to flourish again by late 1976. There is both livestock and crop farming and varied crops include wheat, barley, citrus fruit, and vegetables (especially potatoes, onions, sugar beet, and tomatoes). There is a thriving wine industry. Forestry is important, as well as fishing (sardines, tuna, and cod), and rich mineral resources include coal, lignite, anthracite, and iron ore. Hydroelectricity is a valuable source of power. However, the economy has not been unaffected by the worldwide recession of the mid-1970s. *History*: remains of Neanderthal man have been found at Gibraltar, Valencia, and Gerona, and Spain was subsequently inhabited by Iberians, Celts, Phoenicians, and Greeks. In the 3rd century BC the Carthaginians under Hamilcar Barca conquered most of the Iberian peninsula but were expelled by the Romans in the second *Punic War (218–201 BC). Christianity was introduced in the 1st century AD and by the 5th century the Romans had given way to German tribes, including the Vandals and then the Visigoths. The Visigothic kingdom collapsed (711) in the face of Muslim invaders, who dominated most of the central and S parts of the peninsula under a series of powerful dynasties (*see* Umayyads; Abbadids; Almoravids; Almohads). The Reconquest of Muslim Spain was pursued throughout the middle ages by the Christian kingdoms in the N and was completed in 1492 with the conquest of Granada by Ferdinand of Aragon and Isabella of Castile. The union of Spain, begun by the union of Aragon and Castile following the marriage of Ferdinand and Isabella, was now complete. The year 1492 also saw the expulsion from Spain of the Jews, who were followed after much persecution (1609) by the Muslims; the influence of both peoples on Spanish culture was enormous. The 16th century was Spain's golden age. Overseas exploration led to the formation of an empire in the New World, which brought great wealth to Spain. The country's prestige and power, as well as its possessions, in Europe were furthered by the Habsburg kings Charles I (who as *Charles V was also Holy Roman Emperor) and his son Philip II but the latter's reign witnessed the beginnings of decline. The *Revolt of the Netherlands against Spanish rule led to the secession (1581) of the northern Dutch provinces and in 1588 Spain suffered the humiliating defeat of the Armada by the English. Following the Thirty Years' War Spain lost to France its position as the leading European power (1659). The death in 1700 of the last Habsburg king (Charles II), without an heir, led to the War of the *Spanish Succession (1701–14). This confirmed the Bourbon succession and also deprived Spain of the Spanish Netherlands, Milan, Naples, Sardinia, and Sicily. In the second half of the 18th century Spain's decline was arrested by reform, especially under *Charles III, but in 1808 Napoleon established his brother Joseph Bonaparte on the Spanish throne. The Spanish resistance to their French conquerors contributed to the defeat of Napoleon (*see* Peninsular War) and in 1814 the Bourbon Ferdinand VII was restored. *Carlism and conflict between monarchists and republicans (the latter achieved short-lived victory in 1873–74) dominated the 19th century, during which Spain also lost its last American possessions. It was neutral in World War I, following which *Primo de Rivera established a military dictatorship that undermined the position of the monarchy. In 1931 Alfonso XIII abdicated and the Second Republic was established. The electoral victory of the Popular Front under Azaña in 1936 precipitated a military revolt led by General *Franco that became the *Spanish Civil War (1936–39). Franco's victory initiated over three decades of Nationalist dictatorship. Following Franco's death in 1975, the monarchy was restored and Prince Juan Carlos de Borbón became king and head of state. After widespread demonstrations and industrial conflict Carlos Arias Navarro was replaced as prime minister by Adolfo Suárez and the return to a more democratic form of government proceeded more rapidly. In 1978 provisional regional self-government was granted to Catalonia, Valencia, the Canary Islands, Aragon, Galicia, and the Basque provinces, although terrorist activities by Basque separatists continued. Spain's first Socialist government in nearly 50 years was elected in 1982 under Felipe González, who had campaigned on a moderate platform, moved discreetly to reform the armed forces, which contains many Franco Loyalists among its officers. Spain joined the North Atlantic Treaty Organization (NATO) in 1982. Official language: Spanish. Official religion: Roman Catholic. Official currency: peseta of 100 céntimos. Area: 194,883 sq mi (504,879 sq km). Population (1983 est): 38,234,000. Capital: Madrid. Main port: Barcelona.

Spalato. *See* Split.

Spallanzani, Lazzaro (1729–99) Italian physiologist, noted for his studies of microscopic life. Spallanzani demonstrated that microorganisms arose not by spontaneous generation but from spores present in the air. He also studied regeneration, digestion, and spermatozoa. He showed that contact by semen was necessary for development of the egg and he achieved the first successful artificial insemination of a dog.

Spandau 52 32N 13 13E A district in West Berlin, West Germany, at the confluence of the Havel and Spree Rivers. Nazi war criminals were imprisoned in the 16th-century fortress after 1946. It is West Berlin's main industrial district. Population (1972 est): 195,600.

spaniel One of several breeds of sporting dogs developed in Britain and thought to have originated in Spain. The English springer spaniel is typical, having a lean compact body, long muzzle, and long drooping ears. It is longer in the leg than the similar *cocker spaniel but has the same flat wavy weather-resistant coat. It is generally black and white or liver and white, while the smaller Welsh springer spaniel is always red and white.

The white Clumber spaniel, is the heaviest breed. The Irish water spaniel has a distinctive curly dark-brown coat and is a strong swimmer. Height: 20 in (51 cm) (English springer); 21–24 in (53–61 cm) (Irish water); 18–19 in (46–48 cm) (Welsh springer). *See also* King Charles spaniel.

Spanish A *Romance language spoken in Spain, Latin America, the Philippines, and elsewhere by about 145 million people. The standard form is based on the Castilian dialect, originally spoken in the Burgos region, and became the official language of Spain in the late 15th century.

Spanish-American War (1898) Conflict between the US and Spain, fought in Cuba and the Philippines over Spanish possessions in the Americas. Spurred by US interests in Spanish-controlled Cuba, Cuban nationalists' desire for independence, stories of Spanish atrocities, and, more immediately, the sinking of the US battleship *Maine* in Havana's harbor, the US demanded withdrawal of Spain from Cuba and planned to blockade all Spanish ports. Spain retaliated with a declaration of war. The few battles involved took place in Cuba and the Philippines. Admiral George *Dewey took Manila in the Philippines, and the Spanish fleet under Admiral Pascual Cervera was defeated while fleeing Santiago de Cuba's harbor. US forces, by scaling the hills surrounding Santiago with the aid of Teddy *Roosevelt and his Rough Riders, were able to take the city. The war was in effect ended, and peace negotiations began, resulting in independence for Cuba and cession of the Philippines, Puerto Rico, and Guam to the US. The US, in turn, paid Spain $20 million. The treaty, signed in Paris, signaled the end of Spanish possessions in the Americas. *See also* San Juan Hill, Battle of.

Spanish Civil War (1936–39) The civil war in Spain precipitated by a military revolt on July 18, 1936, led by the Nationalist Gen *Franco, against the Republican Government of *Azaña. By the end of 1936 the Nationalists had gained control of most of W and S Spain, while the Republicans held the urban areas of the E and N, including Madrid, Valencia, Barcelona, and Bilbao. During 1937 the Nationalists, with Italian and German help, failed in their attempt to take Madrid but captured Bilbao; in April occurred the indiscriminate bombing by German planes of the town of Guernica, an event commemorated in a famous painting by Picasso. In 1938, however, in spite of the assistance of the *International Brigade and, to a lesser extent, of the Soviet Union, the Republican front was broken and early in 1939 Barcelona, Valencia, and then Madrid fell to the victorious Nationalists. The Republican cause in the war, which claimed some 750,000 Spanish lives, rallied liberals throughout Europe and North America in the fight against fascism.

Spanish fly A golden-green European *blister beetle, *Lytta vesicatoria*, that is the chief source of cantharidin. This chemical can be extracted from its dried body—especially the wing cases—and was formerly used as a blistering agent and diuretic in medicine (it was also reputedly an aphrodisiac).

Spanish Guinea. *See* Equatorial Guinea, Republic of.

Spanish literature The earliest major work of Spanish literature is the heroic epic *Poema de mío Cid*, dating from the 12th century and written in the Castilian vernacular. Catalan poetry flourished during the 15th century, but after the union of Aragon and Castile in 1479, the Castilian language became dominant throughout Spain. Major writers of the *Siglo de Oro, which lasted from about 1550 to 1650, include *Cervantes and *Lope de Vega. After the death of *Calderon, little literature of major importance was produced until the regional novels of Juan Valera (1824–1905) and *Pérez Galdós appeared in the late 19th century. A dominant influence during the early 20th century was the philosopher and novelist Miguel de *Unamuno. The major poets were Ruben *Dario, who introduced modernist theories to Spain from his native Nicaragua, and *Garcia Lorca. Many writers went into exile during the Civil War, and most of the best literature

in Spanish in recent years has been produced in Latin America by such writers as *Borges, *Neruda, and *Paz.

SPANISH MOSS *This unusual plant grows on trees and resembles a lichen. Dried, it is used like horsehair.*

Spanish moss 1. An epiphytic plant, *Tillandsia usneoides* (or *Dendropogon usneoides*), also known as black moss, long moss, and vegetable horsehair, and found in warm regions of America. Its seeds are windblown to trees, where they germinate and grow downward in large silvery-gray beardlike masses, 20–25 ft (6–7.5 m) long. It is covered with hairlike scales, which absorb water from the air. When dried it can be used as packing material or upholstery. Family: *Bromeliaceae*. 2. A tropical lichen, *Usnea longissima*, which resembles *T. usneoides*.

Spanish Riding School (full name: Imperial Spanish Riding School of Vienna) A center for classical horsemanship in Vienna. Founded in the Habsburg imperial palace, probably in the late 16th century, it was moved to its present building, designed by *Fischer von Erlach, in about 1730. Here the purest *haute école* *dressage as taught in the 16th and 17th centuries is practiced. The white *Lipizzaner stallions used here have been bred from horses imported from Spain in the 16th century—hence the title "Spanish." □horse.

Spanish Sahara. *See* Western Sahara.

Spanish Succession, War of the (1701–14) The third of the European wars caused by Louis XIV's attempts to increase French power. The immediate cause of conflict was the dispute over the succession to the Spanish throne. Following the death of the childless Charles II, Louis proclaimed the succession of his grandson as Philip V. England felt menaced by the prospect of a union of French and Spanish dominions and by French commercial expansion. England, the Dutch Republic, and the Holy Roman Emperor formed an alliance against France in 1701 and were joined by most German states upon the outbreak of general hostilities (1702). Spain, Bavaria, Portugal, and Savoy supported France. The English won a series of brilliant victories under the Duke of *Marlborough but pressed for peace in 1712, when a Spanish-Austrian union threatened. The Treaties of *Utrecht (1713–14) concluded the war, which marked the end of French expansionism under Louis.

Spanish Town 17 59N 76 58W A town in SE Jamaica, on the Rio Cobre. Founded in 1525, it was the capital of Jamaica until 1871.

Spark, Muriel (1918–) British novelist. After several volumes of poetry and criticism, she achieved success with a series of witty satirical novels including *Memento Mori* (1959) and *The Prime of Miss Jean Brodie* (1961). Her later novels include *The Hot House by the East River* (1973), *The Abbess of Crewe* (1974), *The Takeover* (1976), *Territorial Rights* (1979), *Loitering With Intent* (1981), and *The Only Problem* (1984).

spark chamber A device that detects charged particles. It consists of a gas-filled chamber containing a number of thin parallel wires or plates separated by a few centimeters and held at a high voltage. An incoming particle causes a spark to jump from plate to plate across the chamber, enabling the progress of the particle to be photographed.

sparrow A small thick-billed member of the *weaverbird family. Sparrows range from 4–7 in (10–17 cm) in length and are generally brown and gray in color, often with black or bright yellow patches. They are mostly tropical Old World species but also occur in Eurasia and have been introduced to North America where the *house sparrow is a pest. Sparrows eat seeds, feeding on the ground and nesting in holes in banks and buildings. Many similar small birds, especially buntings and finches, are also called sparrows. Subfamily: *Passerinae*.

sparrowhawk A small woodland *hawk, *Accipiter nisus*, occurring in Eurasia and NW Africa. It has a long tail and short rounded wings and the male (11 in [27 cm] long) is gray with brown-barred white underparts; females (15 in [38 cm] long) are brown above. It hunts small birds.

Sparta 37 05N 22 25E In ancient Greece, the capital of Laconia on the Eurotas River in the S Peloponnese. Developing from Dorian settlements during the 10th century BC, Sparta controlled much of Laconia and Messenia by 700 BC. The indigenous peoples became *helot serfs or semi-independent half-citizens (*perioeci*) and were subject to the governing class of Spartiates. Two hereditary kings ruled, with a powerful body of magistrates (*ephors*) and a council of elders (*gerousia*); there was also a citizen assembly (*apella*). Sparta became an austere militaristic state, where weaker boys were abandoned at birth and those that survived were subjected from the age of seven to a rigid military training. Its military strength brought conflict in the 5th century with Athens, and Sparta's ultimate victory (404) in the consequent *Peloponnesian War brought it a short-lived supremacy in Greece: defeat by the Thebans at *Leuctra (371) marked the beginning of Spartan decline. The ancient city was destroyed by the Visigoths in 396 AD and the modern town S of its ruins dates from 1834. Population (1981): 15,915.

Spartacus Thracian gladiator, who led a revolt against Rome in 73 BC. After defeating the Romans in five separate engagements in Italy, he moved N to Cisalpine *Gaul. When his followers refused to disperse, Spartacus marched S again and was defeated by Marcus Licinius *Crassus (71). He and his followers were crucified.

Spartacus League A German socialist group, founded during World War I, that adopted the name of the leader of a slave revolt in ancient Rome, *Spartacus. Its leaders were Rosa *Luxemburg and Karl *Liebknecht, both of whom were murdered after an attempted rising in 1919. The German Communist Party grew out of the League.

Spartina A genus of *grasses (16 species), known as cordgrass, found on salt marshes and tidal flats of North America, Europe, and Africa. They have stiff erect stems, 0.98 in–10 ft (0.3–3 m) tall, long narrow grooved leaves, and yellowish flower spikes. Townsend's cord grass (*S. townsendii*), also called rice grass, a natural hybrid, has been used extensively to help reclaim coastal land.

Spassky, Boris (1937–) Soviet chess player. He was world champion from 1969 to 1972, when he lost the title to *Fischer at Reykjavík.

spastic. *See* cerebral palsy.

Speaker of the House Member of the US House of Representatives majority party who is elected by fellow members to preside over the House. His duties include selecting the leaders and members of certain committees and signing documents for the House as a whole. He is second in line, after the vice president, in succession to the presidency.

Spearman, Charles Edward (1863–1945) US psychologist, whose statistical studies of the results from various kinds of intelligence tests led him to postulate a factor of intelligence, G, that is common to all aspects of intelligence. His work led to the development of factorial analysis as an important statistical method.

spearmint An aromatic perennial herb, *Mentha spicata*, native to central and S Europe and widely cultivated as a culinary herb. It grows to a height of 12–36 in (30–90 cm) and has spikes of small lilac flowers. The oil extract from the leaves is used to flavor sweets, toothpastes, chewing gum, etc. Family: *Labiatae*.

Special Drawing Rights (SDRs) The rights of member countries of the *International Monetary Fund to draw on the fund to finance *balance-of-payments deficits. First instituted in 1970, SDRs (unlike normal drawings) do not have to be repaid and therefore form a permanent addition to the drawing country's reserves, functioning as an international reserve currency and supplementing its holdings of gold and convertible currencies. The value of SDRs is computed as a weighted average of 16 currencies. Their advantage over gold and other reserve currencies is that their supply can be

controlled and does not depend either on the discovery of mineral deposits or on the US balance of payments.

special education A wide range of facilities that aim to provide suitable education for children with physical or mental disabilities or for exceptionally gifted children. Although special education dates back to the 18th century, it was not until the mid-20th century that mentally and physically handicapped children ceased to be dealt with as a separate group and were regarded like other children as needing an education appropriate to age, aptitude, and ability. Special education is provided either within regular schools or in special schools.

species A unit of classification of animals and plants. Individuals of the same species usually resemble one another closely and can breed among themselves to produce fertile offspring that resemble the parents. Examples of species are the domestic cat, the dogrose, and the field mushroom.

Some species are subdivided into subspecies and varieties. Breeds of domestic animals and cultivated varieties of plants have been specially developed by man for economic or other purposes and are all derived from a few wild species. Those originating from the same species can interbreed, despite obvious differences in character. All breeds of domestic dog, for instance, belong to the same species—*Canis familiaris*—and types as diverse as the poodle, corgi, and greyhound can breed together.

specific gravity. *See* density.

specific heat capacity (*c*) The quantity of heat needed to raise a unit mass of substance by 1°C. It is measured in *SI units in joules per kelvin per kilogram. For gases, the specific heat capacity at constant pressure (c_p) exceeds that at constant volume (c_v) as heat is required to do work against the surroundings during the expansion. The ratio c_p/c_v (symbol: γ) is 1.66 for monatomic gases, 1.4 for diatomic gases, and about 1 for other gases.

spectacled bear The only South American *bear, *Tremarctos ornatus*, also called Andean bear. Up to 5 ft (1.5 m) long, it is brownish-black with white circles around the eyes and climbs trees to feed on leaves, nuts, and fruit.

spectacles Lenses worn in frames in front of the eyes to correct defective vision. Convex lenses bend parallel light rays inward; they are used by those unable to focus on close objects (*see* farsightedness). Concave lenses have the opposite effect and are used by those unable to focus on distant objects (*see* nearsightedness). *Astigmatism is treated by wearing lenses that produce a compensating distortion of the light rays. Bifocal spectacles have convex lenses consisting of upper and lower parts of different curvatures, for focusing on distant and near objects, respectively: they are worn for presbyopia. *See also* contact lenses.

spectral type. *See* Harvard classification system.

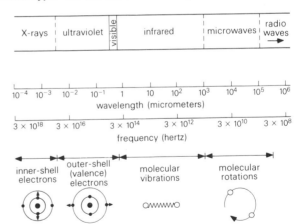

SPECTRUM *Energetic photons in the X-ray region of the spectrum alter the excitation of atomic inner-shell electrons. The ultraviolet and visible photons interact with the outer-shell electrons that participate in chemical reactions. Infrared photons alter the vibrational states of molecules and microwave photons effect molecular rotation.*

spectrum In general, the way in which a particular property of a system is distributed over its components. The visible spectrum, for example, is observed in a *rainbow, which shows the distribution of frequencies when sunlight is split up into its components by raindrops. The visible spectrum, however, is only a small part of the *electromagnetic spectrum, which ranges from X-rays to radio waves. **Spectroscopy** is concerned with observing and analyzing the emission and absorption of electromagnetic energy by atoms and molecules.

According to the *quantum theory, atoms and molecules can only emit or absorb energy in discrete amounts, called quanta. When an atom or molecule is heated, bombarded with electrons, etc., it absorbs energy (becomes excited); on falling back to its lower state it emits a photon (a quantum of radiation energy). The energy of this photon is equal to hf, where f is the frequency of the radiation and h is *Planck's constant. Each atom or molecule can only make specific energy transitions. This means that as well as the continuous *black-body radiation produced by thermal agitation, atoms can emit and absorb radiation at particular frequencies, which show up as colored lines in their spectrum. These **line spectra** can be used to identify particular elements. The spectrum formed by atoms or molecules that are emitting radiation is called an **emission spectrum**.

As atoms absorb energy at the same frequency as they emit it, if a substance lies in the path of radiation its atoms will absorb certain of the energy quanta in the radiation, producing dark lines in the spectrum. These dark lines are **absorption spectra**. For example, the sun's spectrum contains many dark lines (called Fraunhofer lines). These are caused by atoms of hydrogen, helium, etc., in the sun's atmosphere absorbing energy from the radiation produced in the center of the sun.

Spectroscopes (*or* spectrometers) are instruments for analyzing a spectrum. They usually consist of a collimator to collect the radiation from the source, a grating or prism to split it into its components and a telescope to view the refracted radiation. A means of recording the spectrum photographically is needed for ultraviolet and infrared radiation.

speedwell An annual or perennial herbaceous plant of the genus *Veronica* (about 200 species), up to 24 in (60 cm) high, occurring throughout temperate regions. The flowers, borne singly or in clusters in the axils of the simple toothed leaves, are usually blue, sometimes white or pinkish, with four unequal petals. The fruit is a flattened heart-shaped capsule. Two common species are *V. officinalis* and the germander speedwell (*V. chamaedrys*). Family: *Scrophulariaceae*.

Speedwriting. *See* shorthand.

Speke, John Hanning (1827–64) British explorer. He accompanied Richard *Burton on the expeditions (1855, 1857–58) to discover the source of the Nile. They discovered Lake Tanganyika and then Speke went on alone to discover Lake Victoria, which on a second visit in 1860, he established to be the source of the Nile.

speleology The study and exploration of *caves and underground water courses. This includes the survey of caves and the study of their formation, plant and animal life (past and present), and geology. Potholing—or descending through potholes into underground drainage passages in order to follow the course of underground streams—is an increasingly popular although relatively dangerous activity.

spelling The conventional representation of spoken words in an alphabetic writing system. The underlying principle of alphabetic writing is that there should be a consistent one-for-one relationship between speech sounds and written letters but this is rarely fully realized in practice. Inconsistencies arise because a change in pronunciation is not always matched by a corresponding spelling change. In English, for example, an extensive change in the value of vowels took place in the 15th century (*see* Great Vowel Shift), -*e* at the end of a word ceased to be pronounced, and the sound represented by -*gh*- (the sound of -*ch* in Scottish *loch*) dropped out or changed to /f/.

Spencer, Lady Diana *See* Charles, Prince.

Spencer, Herbert (1820–1903) British philosopher. As subeditor of the *Economist* (1843–53), Spencer was an influential exponent of *laissez-faire. His early book *Social Statics* (1851) was strongly tinged with an individualistic outlook, as was his multi-volume *System of Synthetic Philosophy* (1860–96), of which the most important volume was *First Principles* (1862). He believed that state intervention limited progress and he developed this idea fully in his popular *The Man versus the State* (1884). Spencer's other writings include works on psychology, ethics, and sociology. He supported Charles *Darwin's theory of evolution by natural selection, coining the phrase "survival of the fittest," and applied evolutionary ideas to social development.

Spencer Gulf An inlet of the Indian Ocean, in S Australia situated between Eyre Peninsula and Yorke Peninsula, with Port Augusta, Port Pirie, and Whyalla located on its shores. Length: about 200 mi (320 km). Width: about 75 mi (120 km).

Spender, Stephen (1909–) British poet and critic. A friend of W. H. Auden, he published left-wing poetry during the 1930s and was briefly a member of the Communist Party. His later poetry, included in *Collected Poems* (1955) and *The Generous Days* (1971), is more personal and lyrical. He has also published several volumes of criticism and an autobiography, *World within World* (1951).

Spengler, Oswald (1880–1936) German philosopher. Spengler's most famous work, *The Decline of the West* (1918), argued that nations and cultures have a natural lifespan and their rise is inevitably followed by their eclipse. His ideas appealed to the German fascists, as he emphasized the individual's duty of obedience to the state.

Spenser, Edmund (c. 1552–99) English poet. He dedicated *The Shepheardes Calendar* (1579), pastoral poems arranged by the months of the year, to Sir Philip Sidney, nephew of his patron the Earl of Leicester. In 1580 he was appointed secretary to the Lord Deputy of Ireland, where he became a prominent landowner. His major work, *The Faerie Queene*, a long moral allegory in nine-line "Spenserian" stanzas, was dedicated to Elizabeth I and published in six books in 1590 and 1596. His other works include the sonnet sequence *Amoretti* (1595) and the *Epithalamion* (1595), celebrating his second marriage.

Speranski, Mikhail Mikhailovich (1772–1839) Russian statesman, described by Napoleon as "the only clear head in Russia." Speranski, as Alexander I's chief adviser (1807–12), presented proposals for the reform of the administration and for the drafting of a new constitution. His unpopularity with colleagues led to his exile until 1816. In 1826 he began his greatest achievement, the codification of Russian law.

sperm (*or* spermatozoon) The reproductive cell of male animals, which is formed in the *testis and fertilizes an egg cell during sexual *reproduction. A sperm usually has a head region, containing the genetic material, and a tail, by means of which it swims to the egg. In man, sperms develop and mature in the testes, where the temperature is 3.5°F (2°C) below body temperature. At ejaculation they are mixed with secretions from various glands (including the *prostate gland) to form semen.

spermaceti A *wax obtained from the head cavity and from the oils of whales, dolphins, and porpoises. It is liquid at room temperature and is separated from the oil by chilling. Spermaceti is used in ointments, cosmetics, fine candles, and textile finishing.

spermatophyte Any plant that reproduces by means of *seeds rather than spores. Spermatophytes include the *gymnosperms (conifers, cycads, etc.) and the *angiosperms (flowering plants).

sperm whale A large toothed *whale, cathodon, also called cachalot. It is about 60 ft (18 m) long, gray-blue above and pale beneath, with tiny flippers and large tail flukes. The blowhole is near the tip of the snout and it can dive up to 0.6 mi (1 km) in search of octopus and squid, sometimes staying under water for over one hour. Family: *Physeteridae*.

Spey River A fast-flowing river in NE Scotland, flowing mainly NE through the Grampian Mountains to Spey Bay. It is known for its salmon fishing. Length: 107 mi (172 km).

Speyer (English name: Spires) 49 18N 8 26E A city in SW West Germany, in Rhineland-Palatinate on the Rhine River. The cathedral (1030) contains the tombs of eight emperors. An important diet (assembly) was held here in 1529 (*see* Protestantism). It is a port and industrial center. Population (1971 est): 42,800.

Sphagnum A widely distributed genus of mosses (over 300 species), called bog or peat moss, forming dense raised clumps in bogs and other waterlogged places. Green to dark red in color and up to 12 in (30 cm) high, the fine stems bear clusters of threadlike branches, densely clothed with tiny leaves, and globular spore capsules. The ability of the stems and leaves to retain water (up to 20 times the weight of the plant) is responsible for the outstanding ability of these mosses to drain very wet ground and form bogs. The dead remains of the plants accumulate to form *peat—an important fuel and ingredient of horticultural composts. Family: *Sphagnaceae*.

sphalerite (*or* zinc blende) The principal ore of zinc, a sulfide, usually brown or black in color. It frequently occurs with *galena in metasomatic deposits, and in hydrothermal veins and replacement deposits.

spherical coordinates. *See* coordinate systems.

SPHINX *The Great Sphinx at Giza is thought to be a portrait statue of King Khafre (c. 2550* BC*).*

sphinx A mythological creature with a lion's body and a human head, occurring in the art and legends of most ancient Near and Middle Eastern civilizations. The most famous representation is the Great Sphinx at Giza, Egypt, dating from the 3rd millennium BC. In Greek legend, the Sphinx was a female monster that preyed on travelers going to Thebes. She killed those who could not answer her riddle, which was finally solved by *Oedipus.

sphygmomanometer A device for measuring arterial *blood pressure. It consists of an inflatable arm cuff connected via a rubber tube to a column of mercury with a graduated scale or an aneroid device. The cuff is inflated until the pulse can no longer be detected (using a stethoscope) and then slowly deflated until first the systolic and then the diastolic pressure can be recorded as the pulse returns.

Spica A conspicuous blue star, apparent magnitude 0.97 and about 215 light years distant, that is the brightest star in the constellation Virgo. It is an eclipsing *binary star.

Spice Islands. *See* Moluccas.

spices. *See* herbs and spices.

spider An *arachnid belonging to the worldwide order *Araneae* (or *Araneida*; over 30,000 species). 0.04–3.5 in (1–90 mm) long, the body of a spider consists of a cephalothorax and abdomen separated by a narrow "waist." There are eight walking legs, up to eight eyes, and several pairs of spinnerets, which produce silk used for making webs, egg cocoons, etc. Spiders are predominantly terrestrial and prey mainly on insects, hunting them or trapping them in their webs. The victims are killed with poison-bearing fangs; in a few species the poison is harmful to man. The female is generally larger than the male, which she sometimes kills and eats after mating. She then deposits the eggs on or near the web, among leaves or twigs, etc., or carries them until they hatch. The young go through a series of molts to reach the adult stage. *See also* black widow; tarantula; water spider; wolf spider.

spider crab A marine *crab belonging to the widely distributed family *Maiidae*, especially one of the genus *Libinia*. It has a thick rounded body, with long spindly legs and generally moves slowly. Most spider crabs are scavengers, especially of dead animals.

spider mite A red or yellow *mite, 0.02 in (0.5 mm) long, also called red spider mite, belonging to the family *Tetranychidae*. It sucks plant juices from foliage and fruits and is a serious pest of orchard trees, crops, and house plants.

spider monkey A monkey belonging to the genus *Ateles* (4 species), of Central and South American forests. Spider monkeys have very long legs and are 35–60 in (88–150 cm) long including the prehensile tail 20–35 in (50–90 cm), which is capable of supporting their weight. They live in family groups in thick forest, feeding on seeds and leaves. Family: *Cebidae*.

spider plant A plant of the genus *Chlorophytum*, especially *C. elatum*, native to South Africa and widely grown as a house plant. It has narrow green and white striped leaves, 24–36 in (60–90 cm) long, and periodically produces a stem bearing small white flowers or young plantlets. Family: *Liliaceae*.

spider wasp A solitary *wasp belonging to a family (*Pompilidae*) of worldwide distribution. It preys chiefly on spiders, which are also paralyzed and stored in underground nests as food for the larvae. Spider wasps have dark slender bodies (0.2–3 in [5–75 mm] long), long legs, and usually smoky or amber-colored wings.

spiderwort. *See* Tradescantia.

spikenard A perennial Himalayan herb, *Nardostachys jatamansi*, growing to a height of 24 in (60 cm) and bearing tiny purple flower clusters. It is cultivated for an essential oil derived from its roots, which is used for perfumes and various medicines. Family: *Valerianaceae*.

Plowman's spikenard (*Inula conyza*) is a perennial herb of Europe and N Africa with yellow flowers and fragrant roots. Family: *Compositae.

Spillane, Mickey (Frank Morrison S.; 1918–) US detective-story writer. His numerous crime novels featuring the detective Mike Hammer, the popular success of which was due to the uninhibited description of sex and violence, include *I, the Jury* (1947) and *The Twisted Thing* (1966).

spin A property possessed by elementary particles as a result of which they possess a constant angular momentum that is independent of their motion. The spin is quantized and labeled by a spin *quantum number (symbol: s), which may be integral or half-integral.

spina bifida A defect, present at birth, in which the backbone fails to fuse properly, leaving the spinal cord and its coverings exposed. Commonly the child has paralyzed legs and disordered bladder and bowel function. The degree of the handicap varies: children who survive and are severely affected require crutches or wheelchairs and need special surgical procedures to help their bladder function. The intelligence of children with spina bifida is often normal, but the condition is frequently associated with *hydrocephalus. Spina bifida can be diagnosed during pregnancy (*see* amniocentesis).

spinach An annual herbaceous plant, *Spinacia oleracea*, native to Asia and widely cultivated as a vegetable. Its edible leaves are rich in iron and vitamins A and C and are boiled as a vegetable and used in salads, soups, soufflés, etc. Family: *Chenopodiaceae*.

spinal cord An elongated part of the central *nervous system, running downward from the base of the brain and consisting of a core of gray matter (nerve cell bodies) surrounded by white matter (nerve fibers). It is surrounded and protected by the spine and is enclosed in membranes (meninges). It gives off spinal nerves, usually in pairs, and ends in a bundle of nerves supplying the legs and lower part of the body. Through it run the nerve fibers between the brain and the body; injury can therefore cause paralysis and loss of sensation.

spindle tree A Eurasian tree or shrub, *Euonymus europaeus*, that grows to a height of about 20 ft (6 m). It produces small white flowers and pink and orange fleshy fruits, 0.4–0.6 in (10–15 mm) across, which yield a yellow food dye. The fine-grained wood has been used to make spindles and clothespins. The winged spindle tree (*E. alatus*) occurs in China. Family: *Celastraceae*. *See also* Euonymus.

spine In anatomy, the backbone, or vertebral column: a series of small bones (vertebrae) that runs up the center of the back. The spine encloses and protects the spinal cord, articulates with the skull, ribs, and pelvis, and provides attachment for muscles of the back. There are 26 vertebrae in the adult spine, which are subdivided as follows: 7 cervical, in the neck; 12 thoracic, in the chest region attached to the ribs; 5 lumbar, in the lower back; 5 sacral, attached to the hip bone (fused into a single bone—the sacrum); and 4 coccygeal (fused into a single bone—the coccyx). The vertebrae are connected by tough disks of cartilage (intervertebral disks), which absorb the shock produced by running and other movements.

spinel A group of oxide minerals, usually occurring as octahedral crystals. The spinel minerals form a compositional series between true spinel ($MgAl_2O_4$) and hercynite ($Fe^{2+}Al_2O_4$). Magnetite ($Fe^{2+}Fe_2^{3+}O_4$) is the most common and is an important iron ore. Chromite, a source of chromium, is $Fe^{2+}Cr_2O_4$. Spinels occur mostly in metamorphic rocks, especially limestones, and in basic and ultrabasic igneous rocks.

spinet A plucked keyboard instrument of the *harpsichord family that superseded the *virginals in the 17th century. It is wing shaped, the strings (one to each note) being at an angle of 45° to the keyboard.

Spingarn, Joel Elias (1875–1939) US educator and reformer. A professor at Columbia University (1909–11), he wrote *The New Criticism* (1911) and, later, *Creative Criticism* (1917). He served as an adviser (1919–32) at Harcourt, Brace, and Company, a publishing firm he cofounded. Long active in the *National Association for the Advancement of Colored People, he was its president (1930–39); its Spingarn Medal, an annual achievement award given to a black American, is named for him. He was also instrumental in the establishment of black officer training programs during World War I.

Spinifex A genus of *grasses (3 species), native to S and E Asia and Australia. They grow on sand dunes and form long underground stems (rhizomes), which stabilize the dunes. The heads of spiny one-flowered spikelets break off and are blown about by wind. The name is also used for other Australian grasses that form spiny hummocks, especially *Triodia hirsuta* and *T. irritans*, also called porcupine grass.

spinning The process of converting cleaned and straightened fibers into yarn by twisting overlapping fibers together; until the 18th century this was a household task. Yarn was made originally by drawing out a length of fiber from the mass and attaching it to a vertically hanging stick (spindle) that was weighted to help it spin around; as it spun, the fiber wound onto it. This process was mechanized first by the spinning wheel (in Europe not until the 14th century, although it was used in India long before). The 16th-century Saxony wheel was an improved version, which could be operated continuously. The inventions of James *Hargreaves, Richard *Arkwright, and Samuel *Crompton in the late 18th century industrialized the process. Modern spinning machines produce thousands of meters of yarn every hour. As applied to synthetic fibers, spinning is the extrusion of viscous solutions to form continuous filaments.

Spinoza, Benedict (or Baruch de S.; 1632–77) Dutch philosopher, theologian, and scientist of Jewish parentage. Influenced by the writings of *Descartes, *Hobbes, and *Bruno, Spinoza rejected the concepts of the personal nature of God and the immortality of the soul. The Jewish community of his native Amsterdam expelled him in 1656 on account of his unorthodoxy and his *Tractatus Theologico-Politicus* (1670) was furiously attacked by Christian scholars. The idea of God as the basis of all things (*Deus sive Natura*—God or Nature—in his phrase) was, however, central to his philosophy. For this reason he is often cited as the herald of modern *pantheism. He maintained that man's highest good is his "knowledge of the union existing between the mind and the whole of Nature." His major work, the *Ethica ordine geometrico demonstrata*, generally known as the *Ethics*, could only be published posthumously in 1677. Both *Schleiermacher and *Hegel were greatly influenced by his writings.

spiny lobster A *lobster, also called sea crayfish or crawfish, belonging to the mainly tropical family *Palinuridae*. Its carapace is covered with spines and it lacks pincers, but the antennae are strongly developed.

spiracle The external opening of a respiratory tubule (trachea) of insects and spiders. The term is also used for the paired gill openings of cartilaginous fishes, such as sharks, and for the respiratory openings of tadpoles and whales.

Spirea A genus of shrubs (about 100 species), widely distributed in N temperate regions. Many are cultivated as ornamentals, including the willow spirea (*S. salcifolia*), which grows to a height of 40–80 in (1–2 m) and bears dense clusters of small pink flowers. Other species and hybrids may have white or crimson flowers. Family: *Rosaceae.

Spires. *See* Speyer.

spirits Distilled liquor generally defined as having an alcohol content of at least 40%. Spirits are derived from fermented liquids, for example wine (giving brandy); fruit wines (giving fruit brandies, such as slivovitz from plums and *kirsch from cherries); cider (giving calvados or applejack); grain or potatoes (giving *whisky, *gin, *vodka, or *aquavit). These liquids are distilled, i.e. some of the water is removed by vaporization to increase the alcohol content of the remaining liquid.

spiritual A type of religious song developed by US plantation slaves, with texts adapted from the Bible. The spiritual was often extemporized, with a lead singer relating the story in stanzas and a chorus singing the refrain. Harmonized arrangements of spirituals have eliminated the improvisational quality. Famous spirituals include "Steal Away," "Go Down, Moses," and "Deep River."

spiritualism Any theory that emphasizes the direct intervention of spiritual and supernatural forces in the everyday world. The term can cover phenomena as disparate as *extrasensory perception, *telekinesis, and various states associated with religious ecstasy, such as glossolalia (speaking in tongues, or making unintelligible utterances). In western societies, spiritualism commonly means the practice of communicating with the spirits of the dead through a medium in seances or with a *ouija board. Organizations devoted to *psychical research have amassed considerable evidence for spiritualist phenomena, some occurring under rigidly controlled conditions to preclude fraud, although much of it is not the reproducible kind of evidence that scientists seek.

spirochete A bacterium belonging to the order *Spirochaetales*. Spirochetes are corkscrew-shaped, flexible, and up to 0.01 in (0.5 mm) long: they swim by means of bending and looping motions, achieved by contraction of a bundle of fibrils (the axial filament) within the cell. Some spirochetes cause diseases, including syphilis and yaws in man.

Spirogyra A genus of *green algae, also called mermaid's tresses or pond scum, in the form of threadlike strands of connected cells up to about 12 in (30 cm) long. Large masses may be found floating near the surface of quiet fresh waters. Reproduction is asexual (by fragmentation) or sexual (*see* conjugation).

spit A linear deposit of sand or pebbles extending from a coastline. It often occurs where the coastline changes direction sharply and is deposited by the movement of beach material by wave action.

Spitsbergen. *See* Svalbard.

spittlebug. *See* froghopper.

spitz One of a group of dog breeds originating in N Eurasia and having a thick coat, small pricked ears, and a brushlike tail carried over the back. The Finnish spitz, bred in Finland as a hunting and guard dog, has a reddish-brown or yellowish-red coat while the Lapland spitz is either white, brown and black, or blackish brown. *Husky breeds also show spitz characteristics. Height (Finnish spitz): 17 in (44 cm) (dogs); 15 in (39 cm) (bitches).

MARK SPITZ *The swimmer won seven gold medals at the 1972 Olympic Games in Munich. Here (center) he is seen with the silver and bronze medalists at the ceremony following his victory in the men's 200 meters butterfly event.*

Spitz, Mark (Andrew) (1950–) US swimmer, who won a record seven gold medals in the Munich Olympic Games (1972). In the period 1967–72 he won altogether nine Olympic golds and set 27 individual world records for freestyle and butterfly.

spleen A rubbery dark-red organ, about 5.5 in (14 cm) long, situated in the abdomen just beneath the lower border of the left side of the rib cage. The spleen assists in the body's defense mechanisms by producing antibodies in newborn babies and by absorbing and digesting bacteria in the bloodstream. It also removes worn-out and abnormal red blood cells and other particles from the circulation. The spleen becomes enlarged in some diseases, including liver disease and severe infections. The spleen can be removed in adults without any ill effects.

spleenwort A tufted *fern of the genus *Asplenium* (about 700 species), growing on walls and rocks throughout the world. The tapering branched fronds are about 2–12 in (5–30 cm) long, with triangular lobed leaflets bearing oval or spindle-shaped clusters of spore capsules. The name derives from the former use of some species to treat disorders of the spleen and liver. Family: *Aspleniaceae*. *See also* bird's nest fern.

Split (Italian name: Spalato)   43 31N 16 28N A port in W Yugoslavia, in Croatia on the Adriatic Sea. The vast 3rd-century AD Palace of Diocletian contains the present-day city center, including the cathedral, which was Diocletian's mausoleum. It has a university (1974) and diverse industries. Population (1971): 152,905.

Spock, Benjamin McLane   (1903–   ) US physician and pediatrician, whose books on child care and development have become best sellers, especially his *Common Sense Book of Baby and Child Care* (1946). He was a prominent opponent of US policy during the Vietnam War.

Spode porcelain   Fine tableware and other porcelain made in the Staffordshire, England, factory started by Josiah Spode I in 1770. Josiah Spode II introduced "Feldspar" porcelain and "Stone China" as well as using *creamware. The meticulous decoration used transfer printing and painted Japan patterns enhanced by careful gilding.

Spohr, Louis   (Ludwig S.; 1784–1859) German violinist and composer. His works include operas, oratorios, symphonies, violin concertos, a concerto for string quartet and orchestra, and a nonet for strings and wind.

Spokane   47 40N 117 25W A city in Washington. It is a trade and shipping center for a four-state area called the Inland Empire, which has mineral deposits and farms producing cattle, wheat, and fruit. Industries include timber and food processing. Population (1980): 171,300.

Spoleto   42 44N 12 44E A city in Italy, in Umbria. Dating from Etruscan times, it has Roman remains and a 12th-century cathedral. Its annual festival of music and drama was founded in 1958 by Gian Carlo *Menotti. There is a textile industry. Population (1971): 37,396.

sponge   An aquatic invertebrate animal belonging to the phylum *Porifera* (about 5000 species). Most sponges are marine, found attached to rocks or the sea bed, and measure up to several meters across: they may be treelike, cylindrical (*see* Venus's flower basket), or flat irregular masses. Sponges have an internal skeleton of lime, silica, or a fibrous protein (spongin). Bath sponges are spongin skeletons without the living animals. The simplest type of sponge has a vase-shaped body with a pore at the top and smaller pores in the sides. The inside is lined with flagellated collar cells, which maintain a flow of water in through the side pores and out at the top. Food particles in the water are extracted by the collar cells; other cells in the body wall digest food, secrete the skeleton, and produce eggs and sperm. Fertilized eggs are dispersed in the water current and the free-swimming larvae eventually settle and become new sponges. The animals can also reproduce asexually, by budding or fragmentation.

spontaneous generation (*or* abiogenesis)   The theory that living organisms arise from nonliving materials. It was widely upheld for many centuries, based on such observations as the appearance of tadpoles from mud and maggots in decaying meat. Belief in the spontaneous development of microorganisms continued until the 19th century, when Louis *Pasteur proved that, like higher organisms, they were capable of reproduction.

spoonbill   A long-legged wading bird belonging to a subfamily (*Plataleinae*; 6 species) occurring around estuaries and lakes in tropical and subtropical regions worldwide. 24–32 in (60–80 cm) long, spoonbills are usually entirely white, often with a naked head. They feed on fish and crustaceans picked up by sweeping the large spatulate bill from side to side in mud or shallow water. Family: *Threskiornithidae* (ibises and spoonbills); order: *Ciconiiformes* (herons, storks, etc.).

Spooner, William Archibald   (1844–1930) British clergyman and academic. Spooner became famous for his frequent transposition of the first letters of words, for example "a well-oiled bicycle" became "a well-boiled icicle." Such a transposition became known as a **Spoonerism**.

Sporades   Two groups of Greek islands in the Aegean Sea, the **Northern Sporades**, which include Skyros, and the **Southern Sporades**, which, with the exception of Sámos and Ikaría, constitute the *Dodecanese.

spore   The small, often single-celled, reproductive unit of plants, protozoa, and bacteria, which may serve either as a rapid means of propagation or as a dormant stage in the life cycle. Spores may be produced sexually or asexually, i.e. fusion of sex cells (gametes) may or may not occur before their formation. In plants exhibiting an *alternation of generations spores are formed by the sporophyte following meiosis and give rise to the gametophyte, which produces the sex cells. In some algae and fungi spores are produced following cell division (*see* mitosis) and thus give rise to an exact replica of the parent.

sporophyte. *See* alternation of generations.

Sporozoa   A phylum of microscopic single-celled animals (*see* Protozoa), all of which are parasites with complex life cycles involving asexual

and sexual forms of reproduction. They are often found in the intestinal tracts or blood of animals and form resistant spores or cysts, which can remain dormant until entering a suitable host. The phylum includes the malaria parasite (*see* Plasmodium).

sprat   A small food fish, *Clupea* (*Sprattus*) *sprattus*, also called brisling, that is similar and related to the herring. Up to 7 in (17 cm) long, it lives in shoals in the E Atlantic, N Mediterranean, and British coastal waters. The young are known as *whitebait.

spring   An emission of water from the ground. Springs occur where the water table intersects the surface or where a subsurface stream flowing over an impermeable rock stratum reaches the ground surface. Small outflows of water (seepages) may create a small localized marsh or bog. *See also* hot spring.

spring balance   A device for measuring weights. The simplest form consists of a helical spring fixed at its upper end; from the lower end the load is suspended, extending the spring in direct proportion to its weight (according to *Hooke's law).

springbok   A rare antelope, *Antidorcas marsupialis*, inhabiting arid regions of S Africa. About 32 in (80 cm) high at the shoulder, the springbok has a white face with a black line along each side of the muzzle, a fawn body with dark flank hairs, and a patch of white hairs on the rump, which can be flashed as an alarm signal. It is the national emblem of South Africa. □mammal.

Springfield   39 49N 89 39W The capital city of Illinois, on the Sangamon River. Abraham Lincoln lived here from 1837 until 1861 and is buried nearby; his home is preserved as a national historic site. Situated in an agricultural area, Springfield is an administrative, commercial, and medical center with varied industries. Population (1980): 99,637.

Springfield   42 07N 72 35W A city in S central Massachusetts, on the Connecticut River. The arsenal operating here from 1794 until 1966 developed the Springfield and Garand rifles. Industries include chemicals and plastic. Population (1980): 152,319.

Springfield   37 11N 93 19W A city in Missouri, in the Ozark Mountains. The commercial center for an agricultural region, its industries include railroad engineering and the manufacture of furniture and textiles. Population (1980): 133,116.

springhaas   A nocturnal kangaroo-like rodent, *Pedetes capensis*, inhabiting the grasslands of eastern and southern Africa. Also called the Cape jumping hare, it is about 14 in (35 cm) long with yellowish-brown fur and a long bushy black-tipped tail. The springhaas uses the long claws on its forelimbs for excavating burrows and digging up the roots and tubers on which it feeds.

Springs   26 15S 28 26E A city in South Africa, in the S Transvaal. Founded in 1885, it became the center of extensive goldfields and today is a mining and manufacturing center producing gold and uranium. Population (1980 est): 153,974.

springtail   An eyeless wingless □insect of the worldwide order *Collembola* (about 3500 species). 0.12–0.40 in (3–10 mm) long, it has a forked appendage on the abdomen, which is used for jumping. Springtails crawl about in moist soil and leaf litter or on water or snow and feed on decaying vegetable material, sometimes becoming minor pests of garden crops.

spring tide   A □tide of relatively large range that occurs near the times of full and new moon. Low tides are lower and high tides higher than normal, and flooding may occur if strong onshore winds coincide with high water. *Compare* neap tide.

sprinkler system   A safety system often installed in hotels, warehouses, factories, etc., for *fire prevention. It consists of a set of sprinkler valves connected to a water supply and an initiating alarm mechanism sensitive to heat or smoke. This may be a thin alloy bar in each sprinkler that bends at a low temperature or a sophisticated electronic sensor.

spruce   A coniferous □tree of the genus *Picea* (about 50 species), widely distributed in the N hemisphere. Its needles grow in spirals and leave peglike projections on the shoots when they fall. The woody cones, 2–6 in (5–15 cm) long, hang down from the branches. An important and widely grown timber tree is the Norway spruce (*Picea abies*), of which the timber is used for paper pulp, roofing, barrels, boxes, etc. This conifer can reach a height of 131 ft (40 m,) but young specimens are used as Christmas trees. Family: *Pinaceae*.

sprue   A disease of the lining of the small intestine in which food is not properly absorbed. It is common in the tropics, often affecting people who have moved from temperate regions. Symptoms include diarrhea, anemia, and weight loss, and patients are treated with antibiotics, vitamin preparations, and a special diet.

spurge An annual or perennial herb of the genus *Euphorbia*, especially the hardier temperate species, which have been used as purgatives. Many are weeds but some are cultivated as ornamentals, including the Cypress spurge (*E. cyparissias*). Family: *Euphorbiaceae*.

spurrey One of several annual or perennial herbs that are found on sandy soils and salt marshes, chiefly in N temperate regions. The corn spurrey (*Spergula arvensis*) grows to a height of 2.8–16 in (7–40 cm) and has long thin leaves and white flowers. The sand spurreys (genus *Spergularia*; about 20 species) are smaller and usually have pinkish flowers. Family: *Caryophyllaceae*.

Spurs, Battle of the (August 16, 1513) The battle in which Henry VIII of England defeated the French at Guinegate, near Thérouanne (N France). The battle was so called because of the speed of the French retreat. The English victory led to the capture of Tournai.

Sputnik A series of Soviet unmanned satellites, the first of which was the first spacecraft to be launched (October 4, 1957). It burned up in the atmosphere after 92 days. Sputnik 2, launched November 3, 1957, carried the first animal, the dog Laika, into space.

Squanto (?–1622) American Indian of the New England Pawtuxet tribe. Before the Pilgrims landed, he had lived in England and been enslaved in Spain; he became the friend of and interpreter for the Pilgrims in Plymouth, Mass, in 1620. He taught them how to live in their new land and made possible treaties of friendship with surrounding tribes.

Square Deal (1901–09) A program of economic and social reform introduced by President Theodore *Roosevelt to benefit the "plain man". In addition to its strict enforcement of anti-trust laws, it sponsored federal supervision of big business, including federal wage and hour standards, and established the Food and Drug Administration (1906) to regulate the quality of processed foods and pharmaceuticals.

square root. *See* root.

squash The fruit of certain plants, some of which grow on bushes, others on trailing or climbing vines, most prominently *Cucurbita pepo* or summer squash. It is probably native to the Americas and includes several varieties widely cultivated as vegetable crops. Squashes bear yellow or orange cup-shaped flowers and large elongated fleshy fruits, which have orange, green, or yellow skins and are eaten as cooked vegetables. Winter squashes, *C. maxima*, include hubbard and butternut. Zucchini are a variety of squash eaten when small and immature (up to 15 cm long). Family: *Cucurbitaceae*.

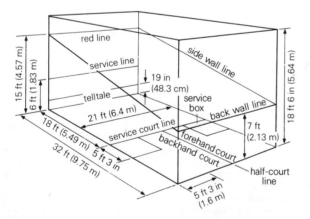

SQUASH RACKETS *The dimensions of the court.*

squash rackets A racket-and-ball game played in a four-walled court. It originated from an older English game (rackets), played at Harrow School, London, in the mid-19th century. Players hit a small ball of synthetic rubber with the object of making a shot that the opponent cannot return. (When the ball is played it must hit the front wall of the court and may hit any other wall.) The service each time goes to the winner of the previous point. The US version is a singles or doubles game, in which either side may score and the game goes to 15 points.

squid A *cephalopod mollusk of the order *Decapoda*. Surrounding the mouth, squids have ten arms bearing suckers; two arms are long retractile tentacles used for capturing prey. Their cylindrical tapering bodies have fins on either side and a reduced internal stiffening shell. Squids feed on fish and mollusks, using a siphon to produce a jet of water to dart forward. The giant squid (genus *Architeuthis*) can reach 65 ft (20 m) in length. □oceans.

squill A perennial herbaceous plant of the genus *Scilla* (100 species), native to temperate Europe and Asia. Growing from bulbs, they produce long narrow leaves and blue, white, or purple flowers borne in a cluster on a leafless stalk. Some species, including *S. nonscripta* and *S. sibirica* are cultivated as garden ornamentals. Family: *Liliaceae*.

squint (*or* strabismus) A condition in which both the eyes cannot focus on the same object at the same time. This may be caused by paralysis of one of the nerves moving the eye, in which case the squint is often temporary. Nonparalytic squints are often seen in children and may be corrected by special lenses, eye exercises, or surgery.

squirrel A *rodent belonging to the family *Sciuridae*, which includes *ground squirrels, *flying squirrels, and tree squirrels, distributed worldwide.

The gray squirrel (*Sciurus carolinensis*), native to North America but now found in most parts of the world, is a typical tree squirrel, being an agile climber with a long bushy balancing tail and grasping hands. Gray squirrels feed chiefly on nuts, berries, and buds and have become a pest of orchards and gardens. They do not hibernate, but store food for the winter. *See also* red squirrel.

squirrel monkey A long-tailed monkey, *Saimiri sciureus*, common in Amazonian forests. Squirrel monkeys are 24–32 in (60–80 cm) long including the tail 14–17 in (35–43 cm) and live in large troops, feeding on flowers, fruits, and small animals. They have tufted ears and white rings round their eyes with greenish fur and orange feet. Family: *Cebidae*.

squirting cucumber A perennial herb, *Ecballium elaterium*, native to the Mediterranean region. It has spreading hairy stems and leaves and its yellow flowers produce elastic-walled fruits that eject the seeds up to a distance of several meters when the fruit is ripe. Family: *Cucurbitaceae*.

Sri Lanka, Democratic Socialist Republic of (name until 1972: Ceylon) An island country in the Indian Ocean, to the E of the S tip of the Indian subcontinent, from which it is separated by the Gulf of Mannar and the Palk Strait. Broad coastal plains rise to a mountainous area in the S central part of the island. Sri Lanka is primarily a land of villages, with less than a quarter of the inhabitants living in urban centers. The population consists of two main groups: the Sinhalese, who are mainly Buddhists, and the Tamils, who are chiefly Hindus. *Economy*: predominantly agricultural, the chief activities are the processing and export of tea, rubber, and coconuts. The industrial sector has expanded considerably in recent years and the main products include cement, paper, ceramics, leather goods, chemicals, textiles, steel, and fertilizers. There is little mineral wealth, the most valuable deposits being graphite and gemstones. *History*: according to tradition an Indian prince, Vijaya, conquered the island in the 6th century AD and became the first King of the Sinhalese. In 1505 the Portuguese established settlements in the W and S, which passed to the Dutch in the mid-17th century and to the British in 1796. In 1802 the whole of the island was made a separate crown colony. Following World War II Ceylon became a dominion (1948) within the British Commonwealth and in 1972 Sri Lanka became a republic. Conflict between the Buddhist Sinhalese and Hindu Tamil communities has been a continuing problem and there was serious rioting in August, 1977. Following the general election of the same year, in which the United National Party (UNP) was victorious, the Tamil United Liberation Front (TULF) emerged for the first time as the main parliamentary opposition. The government of President Junius Richard Jayawardene was confirmed in the first election under the presidential system established in the 1978 constitution. Serious violence, the worst outbreaks between Sinhalese and Tamils since Sri Lanka's independence, preceded the election. Head of state: President Junius Richard Jayawardene. Prime minister: Ranasinghe Premadasa. Official language: Sinhala (Tamil and English are both recognized as national languages). Official currency: Sri Lanka rupee of 100 cents. Area: 25,332 sq mi (65,610 sq km). Population (1983): 15,647,000. Capital: Colombo.

Srinagar 34 08N 74 50E A city in India, the summer capital of Jammu and Kashmir on the Jhelum River. It has numerous museums, palaces, mosques, and a fortress, and is the site of the University of Jammu and Kashmir (1948). Industries include carpets, silver, silk, and leather. Population (1971): 403,612.

SS (German: Schutzstaffel, Defense Squad) The elite Nazi military corps, created in 1925 as Hitler's bodyguard and commanded by Heinrich Himmler from 1929. The SS, or Blackshirts, by the mid-1930s controlled the Nazis' security system, including the *Gestapo, *concentration camp guards, and the Waffen SS, an elite corps of combat troops in World War II. After the German defeat Himmler committed suicide and the activities of the SS were condemned at the Nuremburg trials (1946).

Ssu-ma Ch'ien. *See* Si-ma Qian.

St. Names beginning St are listed under Saint.

stabilizers (shipbuilding) Adjustable finlike devices, projecting from the hull of a vessel, that reduce the vessel's motion in a heavy sea. They are operated automatically by a heavy gyroscope and are often called gyrostabilizers.

stadholder (or stadtholder) The ruler of the United Provinces of the Netherlands. Originally a provincial governor responsible to the central government of the Netherlands' Burgundian and then Spanish rulers, following the *Revolt of the Netherlands in the 16th century the secessionist United Provinces elected *William the Silent as their stadholder. The office was traditionally held by the House of Orange until the fall of the republic in 1795.

Staël, Anne Louise Germaine Necker, Madame de (1766–1817) French writer, daughter of the financier *Necker. Her Paris salon became a center of liberal intellectual opposition to Napoleon, with whom she quarreled and consequently, after 1803, was forced to live in exile, mostly at her chateau on Lake Geneva. She traveled widely in Europe, studied with Schiller and Goethe in Weimar, and returned to Paris after the Bourbon restoration in 1814. Her most important literary work was *De l'Allemagne* (1810), which introduced German literature to France. She also wrote two novels featuring unconventional young heroines, *Delphine* (1802) and *Corinne* (1807).

Staffa 56 26N 6 21W An uninhabited island off the W coast of Scotland, in the Inner Hebrides. Composed largely of basalt columns, it is famous for its spectacular coast and caves, including *Fingal's Cave.

Stafford 52 48N 2 07W A market city in the English Midlands, the administrative center of Staffordshire. The ruined castle occupies the site of a Saxon fortress. Footwear, chemicals, and electrical goods are manufactured. Population (1981): 55,497.

Staffordshire A county in the Midlands of England. It consists mainly of gently undulating lowlands rising to moorlands in the N, with the River Trent flowing SE. Agriculture is important, especially dairy farming. Industries include the pottery industry, which became famous during the 18th century, especially through the work of Josiah *Wedgwood. Area: 1049 sq mi (2716 sq km). Population (1981): 1,012,320. Administrative center: Stafford.

Staffordshire bull terrier A breed of dog developed in England from a bulldog-terrier cross as a pit dog. It is stockily built with a broad deep head and a short smooth coat that is pure white; red, fawn, black, or blue; or any of these colors in combination with white. Height: 14–16 in (35–40 cm) (English); 17–19 in (43–48 cm) (American).

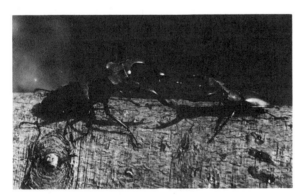

STAG BEETLE *Two males of the European species* Lucanus cervus *using their enormous mandibles to fight for a female.*

stag beetle A beetle belonging to a family (*Lucanidae*; about 900 species) occurring mostly in the tropical regions. The males have well-developed mandibles that in many species resemble antlers—sometimes equal to the length of the body (which is about 0.31–1.5 in [8–40 mm] long). They are used during combat with other males. Most stag beetles are black or brown, although tropical species are often more colorful. The scavenging larvae develop from eggs laid in rotten wood.

stagecoach A large four-wheeled carriage drawn by four or six horses and used for scheduled long-distance transport services from the mid 17th century until the advent of railroad travel. The journey was divided into stages; horses, kept at strategically sited stops, were changed after each stage. The coach usually had seats for six inside and poorer passengers rode

on the roof. After 1784 mails were carried by coach. In the US stagecoaches remained important auxiliaries to the developing railroad systems throughout the 19th century.

staghorn fern A *fern of the genus *Platycerium*, which grows upon other plants but is not a parasite. The fronds fork repeatedly into long pointed leaflets, resembling antlers, and the spore capsules are borne on their undersides. The fern, which is native to most warm regions, is cultivated as a pot plant. Family: *Polypodiaceae*.

staghound A *foxhound used for hunting wild deer. *See also* deerhound.

Stahl, Georg Ernst (1660–1734) German physician and chemist, who in about 1700 formulated the *phlogiston theory of combustion. Stahl had an alchemical disregard for quantitative measurement and consequently the phlogiston theory does not take changes of mass on combustion into account. Stahl's work in physiology was equally unscientific in modern terms, relying on a vitalist approach.

stained glass Colored glass panels formed of fragments of glass cut to shape according to a pictorial or abstract design and held together by "H" section lead strips. The earliest surviving stained-glass windows date from the 12th century AD, but this principle of embellishing buildings was known much earlier. The glass used was either colored throughout by the addition of metallic oxides (e.g. copper oxide (CuO) for ruby red) while molten or dipped into molten colored glass to obtain a fine film of color on both sides (flashed glass). From the 16th century painted glass displaced the more expensive colored glass. The 12th century saw considerable production of religious stained glass windows in N Europe. Much survives in France. Less exuberant colors and a classical restraint marked the post-Renaissance use of stained glass until leading designers exploited its decorative potential in the 19th century. Modern stained glass employs abstract patterns in secular as well as ecclesiastical surroundings.

stainless steel An alloy *steel containing up to 20% chromium and 10% nickel. It is corrosion resistant because the oxide that forms on the surface remains intact and protects the metal, unlike other steels in which it flakes off. Stainless steel is used in a wide variety of engineering applications where this property is important, as well as in kitchen utensils. It is more expensive to produce than ordinary carbon steel and more difficult to machine.

Stakhanovite A member of a Soviet labor movement that strove to increase industrial production. Named for Aleksei Grigorievich Stakhanov (1906–77), a coalminer who in 1935 reorganized his work gang to increase its daily production sevenfold, the movement failed because quality could not be maintained.

stalactites and stalagmites Deposits of calcium carbonate in limestone caves; stalactites are conical or cylindrical projections from the cave roof, while stalagmites grow upward from the floor and are generally more stumpy. They sometimes meet to form a continuous column. They are gradually formed from water containing calcium bicarbonate dripping from the roof. When the water evaporates a solid residue of calcium carbonate is left.

Stalin, Joseph (J. Dzhugashvili; 1879–1953) Soviet statesman. Born in Georgia, Stalin became a Marxist in the 1890s and was expelled from a theological college for his revolutionary activity (1899). In 1903 he joined the *Bolsheviks under Lenin and in the years preceding the Russian Revolution (1917) was repeatedly imprisoned and exiled. In 1921 he became commissar for nationalities and in 1922 general secretary of the Communist Party. After Lenin's death in 1924 Stalin struggled to eliminate his rivals, above all *Trotsky, and emerged as supreme dictator in 1929. He abandoned Lenin's *New Economic Policy, initiating a series of five-year plans to enforce, with great brutality, the collectivization of industry and agriculture. The 1930s saw the reign of terror, culminating in the great purge, in which Stalin sought to enhance his power by the removal of his real, or imagined, rivals. In World War II, Stalin became chairman of the Council of People's Commissars and, following Hitler's invasion of the Soviet Union (1941), reversed the German alliance of 1939. He attended Allied conferences at *Tehran (1943) and at *Yalta and Potsdam (1945), where his negotiating skills were noted by Roosevelt and Churchill. In the postwar years, when Stalin's autocracy intensified, he pursued a foreign policy of imperialism toward the communist countries of E Europe together with unremitting hostility toward the noncommunist world.

Stalinabad. *See* Dushanbe.

Stalingrad. *See* Volgograd.

STALIN

Stalingrad, Battle of (1942–43) A battle in World War II, in which the German 6th Army under *Paulus, having entered Stalingrad (now Volgograd), was forced to surrender to the Russians under *Zhukov. The Germans lost 200,000 men.

Stalinsk. *See* Novokuznetsk.

Stamboul. *See* Istanbul.

stamen The part of a flower that produces the *pollen (male gametes). It comprises an anther, a lobed structure consisting of four pollen sacs, borne on a stalk (filament). The pollen develops within the sacs, which split open to release it. In self-pollinated flowers, the stamens open inward, toward the pistil, but in cross-pollinated flowers they open outward. *See also* flower. ⯂plant.

Stamford 41 03N 73 32W A city in SW Connecticut, on Long Island Sound. Settled in 1641, it changed from a farming to an industrial center in the mid-1800s with the coming of the railroad. Industries include chemical, drug, electrical, and optical research as well as food processing, business machinery, and cosmetics. Population (1980): 102,453.

Stamford Bridge 53 59N 0 55W A village in N England, in Humberside on the Derwent River. Here King Harold defeated Tostig and King Harald of Norway in 1066, three weeks before his own defeat at Hastings by William the Conqueror.

Stamitz, Johann (Jan Stamic; 1717–57) Bohemian composer. He was director of the Mannheim court orchestra. His innovations in composition helped to establish *sonata form and he introduced the controlled crescendo into his symphonies.

stammering A disorder of the rhythm of speech, known medically as dysphemia. The normal flow of speech is interrupted by hesitations, repetitions of syllables, and sometimes by grimaces. Stammering is common in children, especially if speech is slow to develop, and does not indicate any illness. It is often made worse by anxiety and can become persistent; even then it usually improves with speech therapy.

Stamp Act (1765) The first British Act that imposed direct taxes on the American colonies, requiring that a stamp be affixed to all documents, newspapers, and dice. The revenue was to be used to finance the troops stationed in the colonies. Groups such as the Sons of Liberty organized to resist the act. Parliament was forced by colonial hostility to repeal the Act but asserted its right to impose laws on the colonies (Declaratory Act, 1766), thus aggravating the opposition that led to the *American Revolution.

standard deviation. *See* variance.

standardwing A *bird of paradise, *Semioptera wallacei*, discovered in 1858 in the Moluccan Islands. The male is about 10 in (25 cm) long and has two long white ribbon-like feathers at each shoulder, which are erected over the back during its courtship display.

Standish, Myles (c. 1584–1656) English colonist in America. He sailed to America on the *Mayflower*, becoming military leader of the first settlement in New England, at Plymouth.

Stanford, (Amasa) Leland (1824–93) US businessman and politician. He served as governor of California (1861–63), during which time he helped to organize the Central Pacific Railroad and served as its president (1861–93). Eventually, through merger and construction of railroads, he headed the Southern Pacific Company, the parent company of a transcontinental line. Stanford University at Palo Alto was founded by him (in memory of his son) as Leland Stanford Junior University in 1885.

Stanford, Sir Charles (Villiers) (1852–1924) Irish composer. Among his compositions are six operas, seven symphonies, concertos, chamber music, songs, and Anglican church music.

Stanhope, James, 1st Earl (1673–1721) British soldier and statesman; George I's chief minister (1717–21). He served in the War of the Spanish Succession (1701–14) and helped suppress the *Jacobite uprising (1715). His grandson **Charles, 3rd Earl Stanhope** (1753–1816) was a politician and scientist. Becoming a member of parliament in 1780, he urged parliamentary reform and supported the French Revolution. His inventions included two calculating machines and a microscope lens; he also experimented with electricity.

Stanislavsky, Konstantin (K. Alekseyev; 1863–1938) Russian actor and theater director. As director of the Moscow Art Theater, which he founded in 1898 with Nemirovich Danchenko (1859–1943), he developed an innovatory style of naturalistic production. His theories about acting, published in *My Life in Art* (1924) and *An Actor Prepares* (1926) and later developed in the US as "method" acting at the *Actors' Studio, emphasized the value of ensemble playing and of the actor's complete identification with the character he played.

Stanisław I Leszczyński (1677–1766) King of Poland (1704–09, 1733–35) and Duke of Lorraine (1735–66). Stanisław was placed on the throne by *Charles XII of Sweden, after whose defeat Stanisław was deposed. He regained the throne by election but lost the subsequent War of the Polish Succession and became Duke of Lorraine.

Stanisław II Poniatowski (1732–98) The last King of Poland (1764–95). Stanisław became a favorite of Catherine the Great of Russia, who secured his election to the throne and dominated his reign. In 1772 parts of Poland were annexed by Russia, Prussia, and Austria; in 1793 it was again partitioned (by Russia and Prussia). After the failure of *Kosciuszko's rebellion, and the third partition of Poland, Stanisław abdicated.

Stanisław, St (*or* Stanislaus; 1030–79) The patron saint of Poland. Of noble birth, he was elected Bishop of Cracow in 1072. He was implicated in a plot against Bolesław II and murdered in mysterious circumstances. Feast day: May 7.

Stanley 51 45S 57 56W The capital of the Falkland Islands, in NE East Falkland Island on the Atlantic Ocean. A whaling base, it exports wool, skin, tallow, and seal oil. It was the focal point of the Falklands War of 1982. Population (1980 est): 1000.

Stanley, Sir Henry Morton (1841–1904) British explorer and journalist. He went to the US in 1859, joined the *New York Herald*, and in 1871 was sent by James Gordon *Bennett to search for David ☐Livingstone in Africa. Having found him at Ujiji, the two men explored Lake Tanganyika together. On a second expedition (1874–77) Stanley followed the Congo River (now Zaïre River) to its mouth. By obtaining Belgian sponsorship for exploration in the Congo he was instrumental in securing Belgian sovereignty over the Congo Free State. His last African expedition (1886–89) relieved *Emin Paşa in the S Sudan.

Stanley Falls. *See* Boyoma Falls.

Stanley Pool. *See* Malebo Pool.

Stanleyville. *See* Kisangani.

Stanovoi Range A mountain range in the SE Soviet Union extending about 500 mi (800 km) E–W. It rises to 8143 ft (2482 m) and forms part of the watershed between the Arctic and Pacific Oceans.

Stanton, Edward McMasters (1814–69) US lawyer and statesman. From 1836 he practiced law in Ohio, Pennsylvania, and Washington, DC, before being appointed attorney general (1860–62). In 1862 he became secretary of war, a position he held through the Civil War and Reconstruction period under Presidents Abraham *Lincoln and Andrew *Johnson until 1868. A Radical Republican, he was often at odds with President Johnson, who ultimately tried, unsuccessfully, to force his resignation. He was appointed to the US Supreme Court in 1869, but died before he could take his seat.

Stanton, Elizabeth Cady (1815–1902) US reformer and pioneer in the women's rights movement. Frustrated in her attempts to obtain education open to males only, she married abolitionist Henry Brewster Stanton in 1840. Settling in Seneca Falls, NY, by 1846, she and Lucretia *Mott held the *Seneca Falls Convention (1848). She later worked closely with Susan B. *Anthony in advancing women's rights and served as president of the National Woman Suffrage Association (1869–90) and the *National American Woman Suffrage Association from 1890.

Staphylococcus A genus of spherical bacteria, some of which are disease-causing parasites of animals and man. *S. aureus* is responsible for boils and mastitis, *S. pyogenes* infects wounds, and certain strains cause acute food poisoning.

star A luminous ball of gas that is visible in the night sky. The sun is a typical star: stellar mass ranges from about 0.005 to 50 times the sun's mass. A star's mass determines its *luminosity, surface temperature, size, and other properties as well as its evolutionary path and lifetime: the higher the mass, the brighter, hotter, and larger the star and the shorter its life. During the course of their history stars evolve, a process called stellar evolution. Young stars, recently evolved from the *protostar stage, generate energy by the thermonuclear fusion of hydrogen to form helium. This continues for some 10^{10} years for stars of solar mass but for only a few million years for the most massive stars. When the hydrogen is exhausted, stars evolve into *red giants. Further thermonuclear reactions occur involving fusion of helium and possibly the heavier elements in more massive stars. A low-mass star finally evolves to a *white dwarf. More massive stars explode as *supernovae, the surviving cores possibly forming *neutron stars or *black holes depending on mass. Stars are not distributed uniformly throughout the *universe, but are grouped into enormous clusters, called *galaxies, as a result of gravitational forces. The sun forms part of the *Galaxy (written with a capital G), often known as the Milky Way system. The nearest galaxy to ours is some 16×10^5 light years away and the nearest star to the sun within the Galaxy is about 4 light years away.

star apple An evergreen tree, *Chrysophyllum cainito*, native to the West Indies and Central America. Growing to a height of 50 ft (15 m), it has purplish-white flowers and bears sweet-tasting smooth-skinned fruits that resemble apples, red to yellow in color with star-shaped cores. Family: *Sapotaceae*.

Stara Zagora 42 25N 25 37E A city in central Bulgaria. The city was rebuilt after its destruction by the Turks in the late 19th century and has grown much since World War II. Fruit, in particular, is grown in the surrounding area. Population (1979 est): 133,201.

starch A carbohydrate that is an important storage product of many plants. Chemically it consists of linked glucose units in the form of two polysaccharides, amylose and amylopectin, which are present in varying proportions. Starch occurs naturally as white powdery granules that are insoluble in cold water but form a gelatinous solution in hot water. Plants manufacture starch by photosynthesis and it is a major constituent of seeds, fruits, roots, and tubers and a major source of dietary energy for animals and man. It is also used in the paper and textile industries.

Star Chamber, Court of A court, originating in the king's council of medieval England, that met in the Star Chamber at Westminster Palace. It was concerned chiefly with breaches of the peace. Its misuse by Charles I to enforce his unpopular policies led to its abolition (1641).

star cluster A group of physically associated stars that shared a common origin. **Open** (*or* galactic) **clusters** are diffuse asymmetrical groupings of up to a few hundred stars and occur in the disk of our *Galaxy. **Globular clusters** are compact spherical groupings containing many thousands of very old stars and occur in the Galactic halo.

starfish A marine invertebrate animal, also called sea star, belonging to a worldwide class (*Asteroidea*; 1800 species) of *echinoderms. Its fleshy star-shaped body is covered with a spiny skin and has five or more radiating arms. Starfish occur on shores and ocean floors and move slowly, using saclike tube feet on the underside of the arms. They feed mainly on mollusks, crustaceans, and other invertebrates.

stargazer A fish belonging to either of the families *Uranoscopidae* (electric stargazers; about 25 species) or *Dactyloscopidae* (sand stargazers; about 24 species), found in tropical and temperate seas. Stargazers have a tapering body, up to 12 in (30 cm) long, a vertically slanting mouth, and

eyes on top of the head. They lie buried in sand awaiting prey. Order: *Perciformes*.

starling A noisy sharp-winged songbird, *Sturnus vulgaris*, having a black plumage speckled with iridescent purple, green, and white. It is a versatile bird, common on farmland, where it probes the soil for insects, and also in cities, where it is a scavenger. It is gregarious and commonly nests in flocks in buildings and trees, sometimes becoming a serious crop and environmental pest. Family: *Sturnidae*.

star-of-Bethlehem A spring-blooming perennial plant, *Ornithogalum umbellatum*, native to the Mediterranean and grown in gardens. Growing from a bulb, it has grasslike basal leaves and a slender stalk, up to 12 in (30 cm) tall, bearing clusters of star-shaped white flowers striped with green. Family: *Liliaceae*.

star of David (Hebrew *magen David*: shield of David) A six-pointed star or hexagram, composed of two equilateral triangles. Widely used from antiquity as an ornament or magical sign, it has been regarded since the 17th century as a Jewish symbol and was imposed on the Jews as a "badge of shame" by the Nazis. In 1897 it was officially adopted as an emblem of Zionism and it now appears on the flag of Israel.

Starr, Ringo (Richard Starkey; 1940–) British rock musician, former drummer of the *Beatles. After the Beatles disbanded, Starr acted in such films as *The Magic Christian* (1970). His solo albums include *Ringo* (1973), which temporarily reunited the group.

Star-Spangled Banner, The National anthem of the US. The words, written (1814) by Francis Scott *Key during the War of 1812, were set to the music *To Anacreon in Heaven* (1780) of John Stafford Smith. Long sung in the US, it was adopted as the national anthem in 1931.

Stassfurt 51 51N 11 35E A town in W East Germany, on the Bode River. The Stassfurt deposits consist of several strata, some 3600 ft (1100 m) thick, providing since 1861 a valuable source of sodium and potassium compounds, magnesium bromide, and rock salt.

State, Department of US cabinet-level agency that advises the president in the formulation and execution of foreign policy. Headed by the secretary of state, the department determines and analyzes US overseas interests, makes recommendations regarding policy, and represents the US in the UN, other international organizations, foreign countries, and negotiations for treaties and agreements. Established in 1789, the department includes the US Mission to the United Nations and the Foreign Service, which oversees US embassies and consulates throughout the world.

Staten Island An island in New York, one of the five boroughs of New York City. Largely residential, it is the least densely populated of the city's boroughs. Area: 57 sq mi (148 sq km). Population (1970): 295,443.

States General 1. In France, the assembly of representatives of the three estates—clergy, nobility, and the Third Estate or commons. First summoned by Philip the Fair in 1302, the States General did not meet after 1614 until summoned by Louis XVI in 1789 on the eve of the *French Revolution. The Third Estate declared itself a National Assembly, which replaced the States General. 2. In the Netherlands, the assembly of provincial representatives created by its Burgundian rulers in the 15th century. Following the *Revolt of the Netherlands against Spain, it became (1579) the chief organ of the United Provinces' central government.

states of matter Any of three distinct physical states: solid, liquid, and gas. A fourth state, *plasma, is often added. The different states are distinguished by the strength of the intermolecular forces compared to their random thermal motion. For example, in a solid the intermolecular forces are sufficiently strong to hold the molecules to an approximately fixed position, whereas in a gas the intermolecular forces have hardly any effect on the random movements of the atoms and molecules. Liquids represent an intermediate state.

states' rights The rights of the individual US states in relation to the power of the federal government. The issue arose in debates over the *constitution (1789), which established a strong federal government. Subsequent assertion of states' rights, especially that of secession from the Union, led eventually to the *Civil War.

static electricity The effects created by electrical charges at rest. Current electricity is an effect resulting from a flow of electrons; in static electricity electrons from one object are pulled onto another object, usually by rubbing them together, but they do not flow. The effect can be observed with many nonconducting materials, for example a comb passing through dry hair or a leather sole on a nylon carpet. A force exists between two charged bodies (*see* electric field), attractive if they have opposite charges, repulsive if the charges are similar; the magnitude of the force is given by *Coulomb's law. Static electricity can often cause problems (*see* lightning) but can be useful in electrostatic precipitators. *See also* electroscope; electrostatic generators.

statics. *See* mechanics.

Stations of the Cross A series of 14 pictures or images depicting the final events of the life of Christ, beginning at Pontius *Pilate's house, where he was condemned to death, and concluding at the sepulcher. They are usually arranged on the walls of a church and form the basis of a devotion in which prayers are recited as each station is visited in turn. The devotion was popularized in the middle ages by the Franciscans but derived from the early custom of pilgrims who followed the Way of the Cross in Jerusalem.

statistics The study of methods for collecting and analyzing quantitative data. The data measure certain characteristics of a group of people or objects, called the population; usually the whole population cannot be observed, often because it is too large, so data are collected from a representative sample of the population (*see* random sampling). The sample is analyzed and conclusions are inferred about the whole population, using *probability theory because the inferences cannot be certain. A population that has what is called a normal or Gaussian distribution (named for Karl *Gauss) varies randomly about a mean value. The standard deviation, the root-mean-square deviation from the mean value, is a measure of the spread in the population. The higher the standard deviation, the larger the sample size needed to be representative of the population. In binomial distributions the population consists of only two possible outcomes, as in tossing a coin, and in this case different statistical methods are used. In descriptive (*or* deductive) statistics data for a group are collected and analyzed without conclusions being drawn about a larger group.

Statue of Liberty A statue of a woman 152 ft (46 m) high holding a torch in her raised right hand, on Liberty Island in New York harbor. Designed by the French architect *Bartholdi, it was given to the Americans by the French in 1884 to commemorate the French and American Revolutions. Unveiled and dedicated in 1886, it has been a US national monument since 1924. In the 1980s it underwent a complete renovation. US national monument.

Staudinger, Hermann (1881–1965) German chemist, who was professor at Freiburg University. He won the 1953 Nobel Prize for his work on the molecular structure of polymers. Staudinger showed that polymer molecules consisted of chains of repeated units and not a random distribution of such units as was previously thought. His work was of great importance to the developing plastics industry.

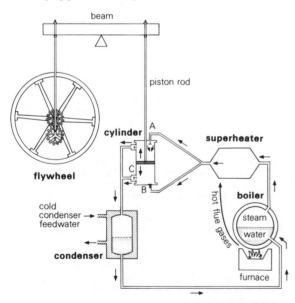

STEAM ENGINE *The principle of a double-action beam engine of the kind patented by James Watt. During the first half of the cycle, valve A opens, steam flows in and pushes the cyclinder down, and steam flows out to the condenser through valve C. During the second half of the cycle, B opens and the steam pushes the piston the other way.*

Stauffenberg, Claus, Graf von (1907–44) German army officer, who attempted to assassinate Hitler in 1944. Stauffenberg served in N Africa,

where he was badly wounded. He tried to eliminate Hitler by bombing his headquarters at Rastenburg. He and his fellow conspirators were executed.

Stavanger 61 32N 5 12E A seaport in SW Norway. Its 12th-century cathedral was built by Bishop Reinald from Winchester. Its industries include fish canning and shipbuilding. Stavanger is also the center of Norway's North Sea oil industry. Population (1981 est): 90,687.

Stavisky affair A French political scandal. In 1933 the fraudulent dealings of a financier Serge Alexandre Stavisky (c. 1866–1934) were revealed and shortly afterward he was found dead. Attempts by the government to hush up the affair encouraged rumors that Stavisky had been murdered to prevent him from exposing the involvement of public figures in his affairs. Consequent right-wing riots led to the replacement of the left-wing government with a broad-based coalition.

Stavropol 1. 45 03N 41 59E A city in the Soviet Union, in the SW RSFSR. The center of a fertile agricultural region, it has food-processing industries. It possesses several educational institutions. Population (1981 est): 271,000. **2.** *See* Togliatti.

steady-state theory A cosmological theory (*see* cosmology) proposed in 1948 by *Bondi, *Hoyle, and T. Gold (1920–) in which the universe is regarded as having always existed in a steady state. The *expansion of the universe is compensated by the continuous creation of new matter. On the present evidence this theory has largely been discredited in favor of the *big-bang theory.

steam engine A □heat engine in which heat from a furnace is used to raise steam, the expansion of which forces a piston to move up and down in a cylinder to provide mechanical energy. A primitive steam engine was invented in 1698 in England to pump water from mines. In 1711 *Newcomen improved on this design but still relied on cooling the cylinder with a jet of water after each stroke. *Watt's single-acting steam engine, patented in 1769, was the first to use a separate condenser. Watt went on to invent the double-acting engine, the crank and crosshead mechanism, and the governor. Thus by the end of the 18th century man had, for the first time, a reliable source of power that did not rely on muscles or the wind. It was largely this engine that created the *industrial revolution. In 1808 Richard *Trevithick made the first use of a steam engine to drive a carriage, but it was not until the end of the century that steam-driven automobiles were in use—and they were quickly replaced by automobiles using Otto's gasoline engine. The steam engine, however, was the supreme prime mover of *railroads throughout the world from 1829 (when *Stephenson built his first *locomotive) until World War II, when steam was largely replaced by electric and diesel-electric trains. From the beginning of the 19th century steam engines were also widely used in place of sails in *ships. Moreover, it was the steam engine that drove the first electricity generators for public supply. However, the more compact and efficient steam *turbine has now replaced the steam engine for this purpose.

steatite. *See* talc.

steel An *alloy of iron containing a small carefully controlled proportion of carbon, usually less than 1%. Carbon steels contain principally iron and carbon. Alloy steels have other metals added. Steel products form the basis of modern technology and steel production is therefore a key factor in the world economy. The uses of steel range from steel girders in bridges and buildings to kitchen utensils. For many engineering products the starting material is **mild steel**, a carbon steel with between 0.2% and 0.8% carbon and sometimes a little manganese or silicon. It can be further improved by *heat treatment. Alloy steels, such as *stainless steel, are usually more expensive to produce. They are used where special hardness, strength, or corrosion resistance are needed.

Steel is made by *smelting iron ore in a blast furnace to produce pig iron, which is added to melted down scrap iron before being further purified in an open-hearth furnace, *Bessemer converter, or *electric-arc furnace.

Steele, Sir Richard (1672–1729) British essayist and dramatist. Born in Dublin, he served in the English army from 1692 to 1705 and wrote a number of successful sentimental comedies, beginning with *The Funeral* (1701). He edited the *London Gazette* (1707–10), the official government journal. He is best remembered for his essays in *The Tatler* (1709–11) and the *Spectator* (1711–12), periodicals that he founded and on which he collaborated with Joseph *Addison.

Steen, Jan (c. 1626–79) Dutch painter. After training under Adriaen Van *Ostade and Jan van *Goyen, whose daughter he married, he worked in The Hague, Delft, and Haarlem, but principally in Leiden, where he kept a tavern. Although he painted some landscapes and biblical and mythological subjects, he is best known for his humorous and sometimes bawdy tavern and domestic scenes. Representative works are *The Feast of St Nich-

olas (Rijksmuseum, Amsterdam) and *The Morning Toilet* (Buckingham Palace).

steeplechase **1.** A form of horse race that grew out of *foxhunting, in which horses jump artificial hedges and ditches. The difficulty of the obstacles varies between courses and between countries. Hurdling is a less taxing version over lower lighter fences and shorter distances. The horses used are either trained for the purpose or turn to steeplechasing after their *flat-racing careers are over. Point-to-points are steeplechases for amateur riders, run by the local hunt clubs. **2.** A track event for men in athletics over a 1.85 mi (3000 m) course that includes 28 hurdles 3 ft (91 cm) high and seven water jumps 12 ft (3.66 m) across per lap.

Stefan-Boltzmann law The total energy emitted per unit time and per unit area by a *black body at an absolute temperature T is proportional to T^4. The constant of proportionality, known as Stefan's constant, is equal to 5.6697×10^{-8} W m^{-2}K^{-4}. The law is named for the Austrian physicist Joseph Stefan (1835–93), who first discovered it, and Ludwig *Boltzmann, who derived it thermodynamically.

Stefan Dušan (1308–55) King of Serbia (1331–55). Serbia's foremost medieval ruler, Stefan Dušan established Serbian supremacy in the Balkans by conquering Macedonia, Albania, and parts of Greece; in 1346 he was crowned Emperor of the Serbs and Greeks. He introduced a new legal code.

Stegodon A genus of long-legged extinct *elephants that lived in Asia and Africa between 12 and 1 million years ago. The first of the true elephants, it gave rise to the now extinct *mammoths and to the Indian and African elephants.

STEGOSAURUS *It was originally thought that the plates on the back of this dinosaur were erect and probably functioned as weapons. Recent theories, however, postulate a horizontal arrangement of plates, which acted as heat exchangers.*

Stegosaurus A dinosaur of the late Jurassic period (about 150–135 million years ago). 23 ft (7 m) long and weighing 1.75 tons, it had a double row of large triangular plates arranged in pairs along its back and two pairs of spikes at the end of its tail. *Stegosaurus* had a small head and fed on soft plants. Order: *Ornithischia*.

Steichen, Edward (1879–1973) US photographer; born in Luxembourg. From the early 1900s he was involved in photography, serving as head of the Army's Air Service photographic division during World War I and as head of Navy combat photography during World War II. His Gallery 291, run with Alfred Stieglitz, opened in 1905; from 1923 to 1938, his work was devoted to photographing the rich and famous. He directed photography (1947–62) at the Museum of Modern Art, where he assembled his well-known *Family of Man* exhibit (1955).

Stein, Sir (Marc) Aurel (1862–1943) British explorer and archeologist of Hungarian birth. Stein made expeditions to India, Persia, Turkistan, and the Far East, which resulted in many discoveries, including the Cave of the Thousand Buddhas near Dun-Huang (W China), with its paintings and documents. His books include *Ancient Khotan* (1907) and *Innermost Asia* (1928).

Stein, Gertrude (1874–1946) US writer. From 1903 she lived in Paris, where she presided over the American expatriate literary community, including Hemingway and Fitzgerald. Her experiments in prose, which include *Three Lives* (1909) and *Tender Buttons* (1914), were influenced by the cubist theories of Picasso, Braque, and other painters whom she helped. Her most accessible work is *The Autobiography of Alice B. Toklas* (1933).

Stein, Karl, Freiherr vom (1757–1831) Prussian statesman. He became first minister to Frederick William III in 1807, after serving as finance minister (1804–07), and introduced major administrative and economic reforms that helped Prussia to recover from its defeat by Napoleon. Dismissed in 1808, he then became adviser to Alexander I of Russia.

Steinbeck, John (1902–68) US novelist. First receiving national attention for his realistic novel *Tortilla Flats* (1935), Steinbeck later wrote *In Dubious Battle* (1936), *Of Mice and Men* (1937), and *The Grapes of Wrath* (1939). This latter work, for which he was awarded the Pulitzer prize in literature in 1940, has been widely acclaimed as an epic account of the lives of a group of migrant farm workers during the Depression and deals frankly with the difficult social and economic conditions of Steinbeck's native California. Among his later works were the novels *Cannery Row* (1945), *The Pearl* (1947), *East of Eden* (1952), *The Winter of Our Discontent* (1961), and an autobiographical work, *Travels with Charley* (1962). In recognition of his dedication to portraying the plight of the poor and disenfranchised elements of American society, Steinbeck was awarded the Nobel Prize for literature in 1962.

steinbok A small solitary African antelope, *Raphicerus campestris*, inhabiting long grass or thinly forested areas. Steinboks are about 20 in (50 cm) high at the shoulder with a reddish-brown coat; males have small horns.

Steiner, Rudolf (1861–1925) Austrian-born founder of *anthroposophy. Steiner rejected the oriental associations of *theosophy, with which he was originally associated, and aimed in his system to reintegrate man with the world of the spirit. He founded his first school in 1919 and his teachings are now propagated in over 70 Rudolf Steiner schools, which aim to develop the child's whole personality, not only his intellect.

Steinmetz, Charles Proteus (1865–1923) US electrical engineer, born in Germany, who developed the mathematical theory of *alternating current, introducing both real and imaginary components. This work greatly stimulated the development of devices running on alternating current. Steinmetz also discovered the law of *hysteresis and made some 200 inventions in electrical engineering, including a high-voltage generator.

Steinway, Henry (Engelhard) (Heinrich Steinweg; 1797–1871) German-born US piano maker. He emigrated to the US in 1849 and founded the piano firm of Steinway and Sons in New York, branches of which were opened in London (1875) and Hamburg (1880).

stela (*or* stele) A free-standing oblong slab, used in ancient Greece and the Near East as a grave or boundary marker. The Greek grave stelae were usually inscribed and ornamented with relief sculptures of the dead. The *Maya of Central America set up stelae with calendrical information.

stellar evolution. *See* star.

Stendhal (Henri Beyle; 1783–1842) French novelist. Between 1799 and 1813 he became acquainted with social life in Paris and also served with Napoleon's armies in Italy, Germany, Russia, and Austria. From 1814 to 1821 he lived in Italy and returned there as consul in 1830. His two major novels, *Le Rouge et le noir* (1830) and *La Chartreuse de Parme* (1839), are notable for their blend of romantic vigor with dispassionate and often ironical psychological analysis. He also wrote works of literary, artistic, and musical appreciation.

sten gun A 0.35 in (9 mm) submachine gun designed during World War II. Some four million of these simple weapons were produced. They were dangerously short and sometimes unreliable but some are still in use among terrorists.

Steno, Nicolaus (*or* Niels Stensen; 1638–86) Danish anatomist and geologist, who established that fossils were the petrified remains of ancient living organisms and that the layers (strata) of rocks represented stages in their deposition. Originally a physician—he discovered the duct of the parotid salivary gland, he later became a bishop.

Stentor A genus of tiny single-celled animals (*see* Protozoa) occurring in fresh water. Up to 0.08 in (2 mm) long, they are trumpet-shaped, with tracts of hairlike cilia over the body surface, and are often attached by a stalk to the substrate. They feed by wafting currents of water containing bacteria, algae, and protozoans into the funnel-shaped gullet entrance. Class: *Ciliata*.

Stephanotis A genus of evergreen climbing shrubs (5 species), also called Madagascar jasmine, native to Madagascar, and including some ornamental species. *S. floribunda* is a popular greenhouse plant with small fragrant white waxy flowers. Family: *Asclepiadaceae*.

Stephen (c. 1097–1154) King of England (1135–54); grandson of William the Conqueror. Stephen seized the throne from Henry I's daughter Matilda, who invaded England in 1139. The civil war that followed proved Stephen a brave soldier but revealed his lack of political sense. In 1152, after much of the country had been ravaged in factional fighting and the royal administration had broken down, Stephen recognized Matilda's son Henry (later Henry II) as heir to the throne.

Stephen I, St (?975–1038) The first King of Hungary (997–1038). Stephen was crowned on Christmas Day, 1000, allegedly with a crown sent by Pope *Sylvester II—the St *Stephen's Crown. Stephen's promotion of Christianity led to his canonization in 1083.

Stephen, St In the New Testament, the first Christian martyr. According to Acts 6, he was one of the seven deacons appointed by the Apostles to provide charity for the Greek-speaking widows in the Christian community. Also a preacher and miracle worker, he was accused of blasphemy and stoned to death by the Jews. Feast day: Dec 26.

Stephen Báthory (1533–86) King of Poland (1575–86). Stephen defeated *Ivan the Terrible of Muscovy in the *Livonian War but his plan to conquer Muscovy was cut short by his death.

Stephens, Alexander Hamilton (1812–83) US politician; Confederate vice president. He graduated from the University of Georgia (1832), taught school (1832–34), and became a lawyer (1834). He served in the US House of Representatives (1843–59) before being elected vice president of the Confederacy in 1861. After the Civil War he again served in the House of Representatives (1873–82) and as governor of Georgia (1882–83).

Stephenson, George (1781–1848) British engineer, who developed a greatly improved steam ☐locomotive. Stephenson became interested in locomotives in 1813. Two years later he built the *Blucher*, which could draw 30 tons of coal at 4 mph. He went on to construct a number of improved models, culminating in his most famous locomotive, the *Rocket*, built in 1829. It carried passengers at a speed of 36 mph on the new Liverpool–Manchester line and stimulated railroad development throughout Europe and in North America.

steppes The midlatitude grasslands of Eurasia extending in a broad belt from the Ukraine to SW Siberia. They correspond to the prairies of North America and consist chiefly of level, virtually treeless, plains.

steradian (sr) The *SI unit of solid angle equal to a solid angle that encloses a surface on a sphere equal to the square of its radius.

stere A metric unit of volume equal to one cubic meter.

stereochemistry. *See* isomers.

stereophonic sound Sound reproduction in which two signals are used to give a directional quality. It results in more realistic reproduction than a single signal system (monophonic sound) because the brain distinguishes the direction by assessing the difference between the sound in each ear. For recording, either two directional *microphones at right angles in one place or two separated microphones are needed. Playing back requires at least two *loudspeakers, one for each signal.

sterility Inability to produce offspring by sexual reproduction. Sterility, or infertility, in men may be caused by various conditions in which the sperms are deficient in numbers or defective in quality. It may also result from psychological problems causing *impotence. In women sterility may be due to disease of the womb, blockage of the Fallopian tubes leading from the ovaries to the womb, or failure of the ovaries to produce egg cells. Generalized illness can also affect fertility. Numerous methods of treatment are possible depending on the cause; if the underlying condition cannot be treated, the couple may consider *artificial insemination. Sterility can also be deliberately induced (*see* sterilization).

sterilization The surgical technique or any other means used to induce *sterility. Surgical sterilization may be performed for contraceptive purposes or when pregnancy would damage the health of the woman. For men, the operation—vasectomy—involves cutting and tying the duct (vas deferens) that conveys sperm from the testicle. In women the Fallopian tubes are clipped or tied (tubal ligation), which prevents the passage of the egg cells to the womb. This operation is now performed, using a fiberoptic laparoscope, through a minute incision in the abdominal wall. Neither operation affects sexual desire or the ability to satisfy it. Sterilization should be considered as irreversible. *See also* castration.

sterling 1. The currency of the UK. The pound sterling is named for the Norman *steorling*, a coin with a star (*steorra*) on one face. 2. Sterling silver is a silver alloy containing at least 92.5% silver.

Sterling Heights 44 02N 84 02W A city in SE Michigan, on the W shore of Lake Saint Clair, NE of Detroit. The city's economy centers

around the automobile industry. More recently, the aerospace industry has become important, and some missiles are manufactured. Population (1980): 108,999.

ISAAC STERN *He is shown (center) with Yehudi Menuhin and Leonard Bernstein (at the harpsichord), rehearsing Bach's double-violin concerto at Carnegie Hall, New York.*

Stern, Isaac (1920–) Russian-born US violinist. He was taken to the US as a young child and studied and made his debut in San Francisco. He is a world-famous soloist and has toured extensively.

Stern, Otto (1888–1969) US physicist who won the Nobel Prize for physics in 1943. Born in Germany, he did most of his work there on methods f studying the magnetic characteristics of atoms using molecular beams. The Stern-Gerlach experiment (with Walter Gerlach) established the validity of space quantization, a valuable piece of evidence in favor of the quantum theory. In opposition to Hitler he came to the US in 1933.

Sternberg, Josef von (J. Stern; 1894–1969) US film director, born in Austria. He directed films noted for their pictorial quality, the best known being a series starring Marlene *Dietrich, including *The Blue Angel* (1930), *Blonde Venus* (1932), *Shanghai Express* (1932), and *The Scarlet Empress* (1934). He wrote the scripts for most of his films and published an autobiography, *Fun in a Chinese Laundry* (1965).

Sterne, Laurence (1713–68) British novelist. Born in Ireland, he was educated at Cambridge and became a clergyman in England. After the publication of the first two volumes of *Tristram Shandy* (1759), an eccentric comic novel consisting largely of sentimental rhetoric and witty digressions, he was lionized by London society. His second novel, *A Sentimental Journey* (1768), was based on his travels on the Continent undertaken for health reasons. He also published several volumes of sermons.

sternum. *See* thorax.

steroids A class of organic chemical compounds with a basic structure of three six-membered carbon rings joined to a five-membered ring. Steroids and their hydroxy derivatives (**sterols**) fulfil many biological roles in plants and animals and include the *sex hormones, *corticosteroids, *bile acids, *vitamin D, and molting hormones in insects. *Cholesterol is an important precursor in the synthesis of many steroids.

stethoscope An instrument widely used by doctors to listen to sounds within the body (*see* auscultation). The first stethoscope was invented by R. T. H. *Laënnec. Modern instruments consist of two earpieces joined by two tubes to a head, which is placed on the body. The head usually has a diaphragm (for high-pitched sounds) and a bell (for low-pitched sounds). More sophisticated stethoscopes are fitted with electronic amplification devices.

Stettin. *See* Szczecin.

Steuben, Frederick William, Baron von (1730–94) US soldier; born in Prussia. He came to the US (1777) after serving in King Frederick II's Prussian army. By 1778 he was major general and was appointed inspector-general of George *Washington's army. He fought with distinction throughout the American Revolution and played a key role in molding the untrained American troops. He wrote *Regulations for the Order and Discipline of the Troops of the United States* (1780), a US Army manual. After the war he became an American citizen and settled in New York state.

Stevenage 51 55N 0 14W A city in SE England, in Hertfordshire. The first of the new towns (1946) to be developed after World War II, it is now an important industrial center manufacturing aircraft, electrical, and plastic goods. Population (1981): 74,365.

Stevens, John Paul (1920) US jurist; associate justice of the Supreme Court (1975–). He graduated from law school at Northwestern University (1947) and then served as a law clerk to Wiley B. *Rutledge, Jr., an associate justice of the Supreme Court. Appointed judge of the seventh circuit US Court of Appeals (1970–75), Stevens was chosen by President Gerald *Ford to replace William O. *Douglas on the Supreme Court. He basically held moderate views.

Stevens, Thaddeus (1792–1868) US politician. Against slavery and an advocate of public education, he served in the US House of Representatives (1848–53; 1858–68), first as a Whig and then as a Republican, where he chaired the powerful ways and means and appropriation committees. Always urging equality of men, he was in favor of, and attempted to legislate, strong Reconstruction policies after the Civil War. Opposed to the more lenient Reconstruction policies of President Andrew *Johnson, Stevens headed impeachment proceedings against the president.

Stevens, Wallace (1879–1955) US poet. He worked as an insurance executive and wrote most of his poetry after the age of 50. In many of his best-known poems, such as "The Man with the Blue Guitar," he explores the relationship between reality and imagination. His poems are collected in *Ideas of Order* (1936), *Notes Toward a Supreme Fiction* (1942), *Transport to Summer* (1947), *Collected Poems* (1954), which won a Pulitzer Prize, and *Opus Posthumus* (1957) and his essays in *The Necessary Angel* (1951).

Stevenson, Adlai E(wing) (1900–65) US politician. Trained as a lawyer, Stevenson spent much of his early career in private practice in Chicago (1927–41), but he served briefly during the Roosevelt administration as special counsel to the *Agricultural Adjustment Administration (1933–34). During World War II, he was appointed special assistant to the secretary of the Navy (1941–44), and after the war he was a member of the US delegation to the *United Nations (1945–47). In 1948, Stevenson was elected governor of Illinois and, during his four years in office, achieved reforms in civil service, police, and public education. In 1952 and 1956 he received the Democratic presidential nomination, but was defeated in both elections by the Republican candidate, Dwight D. *Eisenhower. Stevenson later served as US ambassador to the UN during the Kennedy and Johnson administrations (1961–65).

Stevenson, Robert Louis (1850–94) British novelist, In 1880 he married Fanny Osbourne, whom he had met in France and followed to her native California. Returning to his native Scotland, he published several books, which established his reputation and which remain among the best-known works of fiction in the language: the classic adventure tale *Treasure Island* (1883), *Kidnapped* (1886), set in Scotland after the 1745 Jacobite rebellion, and *The Strange Case of Dr Jekyll and Mr Hyde* (1886). Constantly troubled by respiratory disease, he returned to the US in 1887 and finally settled on the island of Samoa in 1890. His other works include the novel *The Master of Ballantrae* (1889) and the unfinished *Weir of Hermiston* (1896).

Stewart, Jackie (John Young S.; 1939–) British automobile-racing driver, who won a record number of Grand Prix victories and was world champion in 1969, 1971, and 1973. He retired in 1973.

Stewart, James (Maitland) (1908–) US film actor. He began his Hollywood career in 1935 and established himself as an incorruptible hero with a distinctive drawl in numerous films, including *Mr Smith Goes to Washington* (1939), *Destry Rides Again* (1939), *The Philadelphia Story* (1940), *The Glen Miller Story* (1953), *Shenandoah* (1965), and *Airport 77* (1977).

Stewart, Potter (1915–) US jurist; associate justice of the Supreme Court (1958–81). After filling various public positions in Ohio, he was appointed to the sixth circuit, US Court of Appeals (1954–58). He was appointed to the Supreme Court by President Dwight D. *Eisenhower and was considered a moderate who treated each case individually and who was often called upon to cast the deciding vote.

Stewart Island (Maori name: Rakiura) 47 00S 168 00E A volcanic island of New Zealand, separated from S South Island by Foreaux Strait. Area: 670 sq mi (1735 sq km).

Stewarts. *See* Stuarts.

stibnite An ore mineral of antimony, SbS_3. It is a lead-gray color with a metallic luster and often occurs as distinctive radiating crystals. It is found in low-temperature hydrothermal veins and in replacement deposits.

stick insect An □insect, also called walking stick, belonging to the family *Phasmidae*. Up to 12.6 in (320 mm) long, it has a twiglike body and long spindly legs and the wings are reduced or absent. Males are rare; the females live in trees or shrubs, producing eggs that drop to the ground and develop without fertilization (*see* parthenogenesis). Order *Phasmida*.

stickleback A fish of the family *Gasterosteidae* (about 12 species), found in both fresh and salt water in temperate regions of the N hemisphere. Up to 7 in (17 cm) long, sticklebacks have a row of spines along the back. The male builds a nest for the eggs and guards the young. Order: *Gasterosteiformes*.

Stieglitz, Alfred (1864–1946) US photographer. He is famous for his promotion of European and US modern art in the US and his technical innovations in and development of photography as an art form. His famous Photo-Secession gallery in New York (1905–17), known as 291, put on exhibitions of Matisse (1908), children's art (1912), and *Brancusi (1914). Among his most admired photographs are those of his wife, the painter Georgia *O'Keeffe, his studies of New York City, and a series on clouds.

Stiernhielm, Georg Olofson (1598–1672) Swedish poet and scholar, known as the father of Swedish poetry. Believing that Swedish was man's original language, he tried to purify it by excluding loan words. His greatest work is the didactic epic poem *Hercules* (c. 1647).

stigma The part of the pistil of a flower that is specialized to receive *pollen. In insect-pollinated flowers the stigma is sticky, whereas wind-pollinated flowers have large feathery stigmas.

stigmata (Greek: marks) Marks appearing on the body of a living person that resemble the five wounds (in the hands, feet, and side) that Christ received at the crucifixion. There have been more than 300 reported cases, typically involving devoutly religious persons. The stigmata are unknown before the 13th century, St *Francis of Assisi being the first saint to receive them. A number of natural explanations have been advanced, and the Roman Catholic Church takes a cautious view of the phenomenon, which does not constitute grounds for canonization.

Stijl, de (Dutch: the Style) A group of 20th-century Dutch artists and architects, who launched the art periodical *De Stijl* (1917–1928). Prominent members were the painters *Mondrian and Theo van Doesburg (1883–1931) and the architects J. J. P. Oud (1890–1963) and Gerrit Rietveld (1888–1964). The group adhered to the principles of Mondrian's neoplasticism, an abstract style that sought to establish a harmonious and universal means of expression applicable to all branches of art. This would be achieved by reducing form to horizontals and verticals and colors to the three *primary colors and black, white, and gray. In architecture and design neoplasticism was seen at its purest in Rietveld's Schröder house at Utrecht (1924) and in his furniture. Many of its principles were influential at the *Bauhaus.

Stilicho, Flavius (d. 408 AD) Roman general under *Theodosius I, who appointed him guardian of his son *Honorius. On Theodosius' death in 395, Honorius was proclaimed western emperor but Stilicho ruled in effect, ruthlessly removing opposition. He repulsed invasions by the Visigoths under Alaric and by the Ostrogoths but his political intrigues with Alaric and others eventually brought about his execution on Honorius' orders.

still-life A branch of painting concerned with the representation of inanimate objects. Although still-life was used in religious paintings and portraits, it did not appear as an art form until the 16th century and then only in the Netherlands. Particularly popular were still-lifes of objects symbolizing the transience of life—skulls, guttering candles, etc. Still-lifes of food and drink became the favorite subjects of such noted painters as *Zurbaran, *Chardin, *Cézanne, and *Braque, while specialists in flowerpieces have included Jan *Brueghel and Pierre *Redouté.

stilt A wading bird belonging to the family *Recurvirostridae* (avocets and stilts). 14–18 in (35–45 cm) long, stilts occur in warm wet regions, where they probe in mud for small aquatic animals. The common stilt (*Himantopus himantopus*) has black-and-white plumage, pink legs, and red eyes.

Stilwell, Joseph Warren (1883–1946) US general. Fluent in Chinese, Stilwell was an uncompromising military commander who became popularly known as "Vinegar Joe." He graduated from West Point in 1904. In

1941, Stilwell was appointed *Chiang Kai-shek's chief of staff and in the following year, after US entry into World War II, he was named chief of staff of Allied forces in China, India, and Burma. Later in the war, however, his personal differences with the British commander Lord Louis *Mountbatten and with Chiang resulted in his recall in 1944. After the surrender of Japan, Stilwell served as commander of the US 10th Army in the Pacific.

Stimson, Henry Lewis (1867–1950) US lawyer and statesman. After serving as US attorney (1906–09) in New York City, he was appointed secretary of war (1911–13) under William Howard *Taft. He was governor of the Philippines (1927–29) and then secretary of state (1929–33), during which time he formulated the Stimson Doctrine, a refusal to recognize the Japanese takeover of Manchuria. Again secretary of war (1940–45), under President Franklin D. Roosevelt, he directed US forces and policy during World War II.

stimulants A large group of drugs that stimulate activity of the nervous system. Caffeine (in tea and coffee) and nicotine (in cigarettes) are stimulants used widely to reduce feelings of tiredness and to improve concentration. *Hallucinogens, *amphetamine, and *cocaine are also stimulants. Stimulants may affect other parts of the body, particularly the heart.

stimulated emission. See laser.

stingray A round or diamond-shaped *ray fish belonging to a family (*Dasyatidae*; 89 species) found mainly in warm shallow ocean waters. Most species have a whiplike tail armed with one or more saw-edged venomous spines, which can inflict an intensely painful wound causing paralysis and occasionally death. Live young are born.

stink bug. See shield bug.

stinkhorn A fungus of the order *Phallales*, producing a phallus-shaped fruiting body. This consists of a stout whitish stalk arising from a basal egg-shaped structure and bearing a thimble-shaped cap containing spores. When the spores are ripe the cap produces a strong-smelling secretion that attracts flies, which disperse the spores. The common stinkhorn (*Phallus impudicus*) reaches a height of 4–8 in (10–20 cm). Class: *Basidiomycetes*.

stinkwood One of several species of trees with unpleasant-smelling timber, including *Gustavia augusta* of tropical America and the African species *Celtis kraussiana* and *Ocotea bullata* (black stinkwood). The wood can be used in furniture making.

Stirling, James (1692–1770) Scottish mathematician, best known for the widely used mathematical formula named for him. Stirling's formula gives the approximate value for the factorial of a large number. It was in fact first derived by Abraham de Moivre (1667–1754).

stitchwort A perennial herb belonging to the widely distributed genus *Stellaria* (85 species), having white starlike flowers. The greater stitchwort (*S. holostea*) is a common woodland and roadside plant of Europe, N Africa, and W Asia, growing to a height of 6–24 in (15–60 cm). Family: *Caryophyllaceae*.

STOCK-CAR RACING *The Permatex 300 event at Daytona Beach, Florida.*

stoat A small carnivorous mammal, *Mustela erminea*, of Europe, Asia, and North America. About 14 in (35 cm) long, with a long sinuous body,

flattish head, and short legs, it can be distinguished from a *weasel by its black-tipped tail. Stoats prey mainly on rabbits. *See also* ermine.

stock One of several herbaceous plants of the genus *Matthiola* that are cultivated as ornamentals. Many garden varieties, including ten-week stocks and Brompton stocks, are derived from the European biennial *M. incana*, which grows to a height of 12–24 in (30–60 cm) and has clusters of purple flowers. The night-scented stock (*M. bicornis*) has small lilac flowers that emit their fragrance at night. Family: *Cruciferae*.

stock-car racing A form of *automobile racing that originated in the US in the 1920s, when cars were modified for transporting illegally made whiskey, for which speed was all-important. Stock cars are specially built steel-bodied cars weighing around 4400 lb (2000 kg); they withstand frequent accidents. They are raced on oval tracks at speeds up to about 200 mph (320 km per hour).

stock exchange A market in which securities are bought and sold. The three largest stock exchanges are in New York City, London, and Tokyo. A stock exchange is an essential part of the capital market, providing capital for industry and a form of investment for savers.

Stockhausen, Karlheinz (1928–) German composer, a pupil of Messiaen and Milhaud. From 1953 he worked at the West German Radio Studio for electronic music in Cologne. His early works employed serialism but he later rejected traditional forms and techniques, developing a concept of music as a sequence of sound "events" in such works as *Gruppen* (for three orchestras; 1955–57), *Zyklus* (for solo percussionist; 1959), and *Kontra-Punkte* (for ten instruments; 1962). Later works, such as *Stimmung* (for six singers; 1968) and *Mantra* (for two pianos and percussion; 1970) were influenced by Indian mysticism and Stockhausen's "rediscovery" of tonality.

Stockholm 59 20N 18 95E The capital of Sweden, built on several islands between Lake Mälar and the Baltic Sea. It is the country's second largest port and its varied industries include shipbuilding, engineering, sugar refining, and brewing. The old town contains many buildings erected in the middle ages and in the 16th and 17th centuries, including the Royal Palace and Storkyrkan, Stockholm's cathedral. Its university was established in 1877. *History*: a settlement from very early times, it developed in the 13th century around a fortress erected to protect the entrance to the trading centers of Lake Mälar. It became the capital in 1436 and enjoyed great prestige and influence in the 17th century. Population (1978 est): 647,214.

Stockport 53 25N 2 10W A town in N England, in Greater Manchester on the River Mersey. Traditionally a textile town (particularly for cotton), Stockport also manufactures hats and caps, textile and electrical machinery, paper, plastics, and chemicals. Population (1981): 136,496.

Stockton 37 59N 121 20W A city and port in California, on the San Joaquin River. It can accommodate oceangoing vessels and is a distributing and processing center for the fertile San Joaquin Valley. Population (1980): 149,779.

Stockton-on-Tees 53 34N 1 19W A city in NE England, on the River Tees. The first passenger railroad was built from here to Darlington in 1825, and it was once an important port. Engineering and ship repairing are major industries. Population (1981): 154,585.

Stoicism The philosophical school founded about 300 BC in the Painted Porch (Greek: Stoa Poikile) at Athens by *Zeno of Citium. Stoics believed that God (identified with reason) was the basis of the universe, that human souls were sparks of the divine fire, and that the wise man lived "in harmony with nature." Knowledge of virtue was all-important. Stoicism was subsequently modified to stress the primacy of active virtue and duty. *Epictetus (55–135 AD) taught that all men were brothers. Stoicism appealed strongly to many prominent Romans, including Marcus *Brutus and *Marcus Aurelius, and its doctrines influenced many later thinkers.

Stoke-on-Trent 53 00N 2 10W A city in England, on the River Trent. Formed in 1910 by the amalgamation of five towns, the area is known as the Potteries and is the center of the British ceramic industry. There are also engineering, and tire and cable manufacturing industries. Population (1981): 252,351.

Stoker, Bram (Abraham S.; 1847–1912) Irish novelist. He worked as a civil servant (1867–77), wrote drama criticism, and became secretary and manager to the actor Henry *Irving in 1878. Stoker is chiefly remembered as the author of *Dracula* (1897), a horror story in the *Gothic novel tradition. *See also* Dracula, Count; vampires.

Stokes, Sir George Gabriel (1819–1903) British physicist and mathematician, who was professor of mathematics at Cambridge University. He discovered the law concerning the terminal velocity of a sphere falling through a viscous fluid (*see* Stokes' law). He also attempted to deduce a mathematical model of the luminiferous ether, the medium in which light was at that time thought to vibrate.

Stokes' law The resisting force acting on a sphere, radius r, moving through a fluid under gravity with velocity v is $6\pi r\eta v$, where η is the *viscosity of the fluid. The law is used in the determination of viscosity. Named for Sir George *Stokes.

Stokowski, Leopold (1882–1977) British-born US conductor. An ardent supporter of modern music, Stokowski also became well known for his orchestral transcriptions of Bach's organ music, as well as his flamboyant style. He conducted many of the leading US orchestras, including the Cincinnati Symphony Orchestra (1909–12) and the Philadelphia Orchestra (1912–38).

Stolypin, Petr Arkadievich (1863–1911) Russian statesman. Tsarist Russia's last gifted politician, Stolypin became prime minister in 1906. He promoted many reforms, outstandingly the land reforms that enabled many peasants to live an economically independent life. He became unpopular with both Right and Left owing to his disregard of the views of the Duma and his harsh treatment of revolutionaries; he was assassinated in Kiev.

stomach A muscular sac, just beneath the diaphragm, that opens from the esophagus (gullet) and leads to the duodenum (part of the small intestine). The stomach secretes gastric juice, containing hydrochloric acid and the enzyme *pepsin, which continue the digestion of food that started in the mouth. Release of acid is triggered by the *vagus nerve and by a hormone (gastrin) secreted by the stomach in response to the presence of food. The churning action of the stomach ensures constant mixing of the food and its secretions.

Stone Age The cultural phase during which man relied on stone, supplemented by wood, bone, or antler, as material for weapons and tools. It is the earliest phase in the system devised (1816) by Christian Thomsen (1788–1865) for classifying human technological progress (*compare* Bronze Age; Iron Age). The Stone Age is subdivided into: Old (*see* Paleolithic), Middle (*see* Mesolithic), and New (*see* Neolithic).

stone bass. *See* wreckfish.

stonechat A small *chat, *Saxicola torquata*, occurring in Eurasia and N Africa and feeding chiefly on insects and their larvae. Measuring about 5 in (12 cm) long, the male has a dark-brown head and back, chestnut underparts, and white rump; the female is a drabber brown. Stonechats favor dry heathland regions.

stonecrop An annual or perennial herb belonging to the genus *Sedum* (600 species), found chiefly in warm N temperate regions and also in Central and South America. They have small thick fleshy leaves and clusters of white, pink, or yellow flowers. Some are popular ornamentals, including autumn glory (*S. spectabile*), which grows to a height of 12–18 in (30–45 cm). Family: *Crassulaceae*.

stone curlew A ground-nesting bird belonging to a widely distributed family (*Burhinidae*; 9 species) characterized by thickened tarsal joints, also called thickknee. They are typically nocturnal, living in stony barren regions and feeding on beetles, worms, and other small animals. Order: *Charadriiformes* (gulls, plovers, etc.).

Stone, Edward Durell (1902–78) US architect. Noted for his functional, and later decorative style, he designed Washington, DC's John F. Kennedy Center for the Performing Arts (1972). Other well-known structures include New York's Museum of Modern Art (1939) and Huntington Hartford Museum (1962), New Delhi's US Embassy (1958), and the US pavilion at the Brussels World's Fair (1958).

stonefish A fish, belonging to the genus *Synanceja*, that occurs in shallow waters of the Indian and Pacific Oceans. It has a robust body, up to 14 in (35 cm) long, covered with wartlike lumps and fleshy flaps, a large head, and poisonous dorsal fins. It lies camouflaged and motionless among rocks or coral to await its prey. Family: *Synancejidae*.

stonefly An insect of the order *Plecoptera* (3000 species), 0.24–2.4 in (6–60 mm) long with long antennae and two pairs of membranous wings. The short-lived adults rarely feed and are found near fresh water. The aquatic *nymphs, which favor fast-flowing streams with stony bottoms, feed on plants, decaying organic material, or other insects.

Stone, Harlan Fiske (1872–1946) US lawyer and jurist; Supreme Court chief justice (1941–46). He was dean of Columbia Law School (1910–23) before being appointed US attorney general in 1924. The next year he was appointed to the Supreme Court. As an associate justice (1925–41) and chief justice, he was generally a conservative, but was strongly in favor of civil rights. He supported most of President Franklin D. Roosevelt's *New Deal programs.

Stonehenge A famous megalithic structure, the focus of a cluster of ceremonial sites on Salisbury Plain in Wiltshire, England. Scientific study and excavation over many years have revealed a complex history with three main phases of modification (c. 2500–1500 BC) contributing to the Stone-

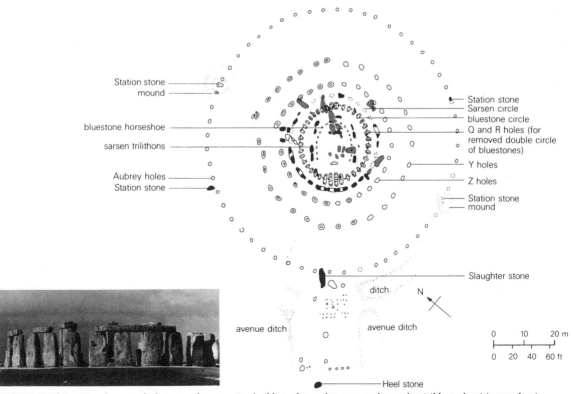

STONEHENGE   *The plan reveals features of consecutive building phases that may no longer be visible to the visitor to the site.*

henge seen today. Sarsens and bluestones, the latter brought from S Wales, are set upright in concentric circles and horseshoes the orientation of which suggests one purpose as being sun and moon observation. The alleged "Druid" connection is entirely spurious, dating only from the 18th century AD. *See also* megalith.

Stone, Lucy Blackwell (1818–93) US reformer and pioneer in the woman's rights movement. After graduating from Oberlin College (1847), she initiated a woman's rights convention in Worcester, Mass, in 1850. She, with the help of her husband, Henry Brown Blackwell, was responsible for organizing various woman's suffrage associations throughout New England and in New Jersey; and she was instrumental in the formation of the American Woman Suffrage Association, which later became part of the *National American Woman Suffrage Association in 1890. She and her husband established *Woman's Journal* in 1870.

stone pine A *pine tree, *Pinus pinea*, native to SW Europe and Asia but planted throughout Mediterranean regions since Roman times for its edible seeds. Up to 100 ft (30 m) high, it has spreading branches and an umbrella-shaped crown, needles grouped in pairs, and cones about 5 in (12.5 cm) long. The oily seeds are eaten raw or roasted or are used to flavor stews, etc.

stoneworts *Green algae of the class *Charophyceae*, many of which contain stony deposits of calcium carbonate. The plants have an erect stem-like axis with whorls of branches and rootlike threads (rhizoids), by which they are anchored to muddy bottoms of fresh or brackish waters.

Stoppard, Tom (1937–) British dramatist, born in Czechoslovakia. After working as a journalist, he achieved international success with his play *Rosencrantz and Guildenstern Are Dead* (1967), using characters from Shakespeare's *Hamlet*. In his later plays, such as *Jumpers* (1972), *Travesties* (1975), *Night and Day* (1978), and *The Real Thing* (1982), he explored philosophical and political ideas with wit and great verbal facility.

storax A tree or shrub belonging to the genus *Styrax* (130 species), occurring in warm and tropical regions. They have small white star-shaped flowers and several species are cultivated as ornamentals, including the Japanese snowbell (*S. japonicum*), which grows to a height of 30 ft (9 m), and *S. officinalis*, from which the vanilla-scented resin known as storax was formerly obtained. The storax used today in cough mixtures, pastilles, etc., is extracted from trees of the genus *Liquidambar*. The Sumatran species *S. benzoin* is a source of *benzoin. Family: *Styracaceae*.

Store Bælt. *See* Great Belt.

Storey, David (1933–) British novelist and dramatist. He was an art student and professional rugby player before achieving literary success with his novel *This Sporting Life* (1960). His later novels include *Pasmore* (1972) and *Saville* (1976), and his plays include *In Celebration* (1969), *Home* (1970), and *The Changing Room* (1971).

stork A large long-legged bird belonging to a widely distributed family (*Ciconiidae*; 17 species) occurring in warm and temperate regions. 24–60 in (60–150 cm) tall, storks have a long neck and a long heavy bill and are mostly white with black markings. They feed chiefly on fish, frogs, mollusks, and insects—caught in shallow waters or grasslands—and build a large nest platform of twigs in a tree or on a rooftop. Order: *Ciconiiformes* (herons, storks, flamingos). *See also* adjutant stork; marabou.

storksbill An herb belonging to the genus *Erodium* (about 90 species) occurring in Eurasia, Australia, and South America. The seeds have a long slender beaklike projection (hence the name) that is spirally twisted at maturity and unwinds when in contact with a damp surface to release the seeds. The common storksbill (*E. cicutarium*) grows to a height of 24 in (60 cm) and has purplish-pink flowers. Family: *Geraniaceae*.

Storm, (Hans) Theodor Woldsen (1817–1888) German writer. A lawyer, he spent most of his life in his native Schleswig, which inspired the chief themes of his works, in such novellas as *Immensee* (1849) and *Der Schimmelreiter* (1888).

storm petrel A small seabird belonging to a family (*Hydrobatidae*; 20 species) occurring in all oceans. 5–10 in (13–25 cm) long, storm petrels have dark-gray or brown plumage, often with paler underparts. Species of southern oceans have square tails, long legs, and short toes and feed by "walking" on the water with wings outstretched, picking up plankton. Northern species have longer wings and a forked or wedge-shaped tail and feed by swooping on fish. Order: *Procellariiformes* (petrels).

Story, Joseph (1779–1845) US jurist and scholar; associate justice of the Supreme Court (1811–45). He served in the US House of Representatives (1808–09). Appointed by President James *Madison to the Supreme Court, he was the youngest ever to serve and was instrumental in establishing federal supremacy (*Martin v. Hunter's Lessee*, 1816) and the illegality

of the slave trade (*Amistad Case). He wrote law commentaries that included *Bailments* (1832) and *Equity Jurisprudence* (1836).

Stoss, Veit (c. 1445–1533) German gothic sculptor and woodcarver. Working chiefly in Nuremberg but also in Poland, Hungary, and Bohemia, Stoss developed a style that combined Flemish realism with swirling draperies and expressive gestures and faces. His most important work is the altar of the *Life of the Virgin* for the Church of St Mary, Cracow.

Stourbridge 52 27N 2 09W A city in central England, on the River Stour. Dr Johnson attended the grammar school (founded 1552). There are glass-manufacturing and iron-working industries. Population (1981): 54,661.

stout. *See* beer and brewing.

HARRIET BEECHER STOWE *Writer whose best selling novel* Uncle Tom's Cabin, *a cry for an end to slavery, greatly angered the South.*

Stowe, Harriet Beecher (1811–96) US novelist. A school teacher, she was a member of a prominent Calvinist family and wrote frequently on religious themes. *Uncle Tom's Cabin*, published in serial form in 1851–52 and in book form in 1852, with its graphic descriptions of the harshness of slavery, had a significant effect on antislavery feeling. It was an international bestseller and greatly stimulated the *Abolition movement. She also published another antislavery novel, *Dred* (1856).

strabismus. *See* squint.

Strabo (c. 64 BC–c. 21 AD) Greek geographer, born at Amaseia (now Amasya, Turkey). His *Geography*, in 17 books, is an invaluable source of information about the ancient world. After a survey of previous geographers and a discussion of mathematical geography and maps, Strabo describes the Europe-Asia-Africa land mass clockwise around the Mediterranean, from Spain to N Africa. He marshals the evidence of other writers and his own observations into a comprehensive account, and is a master of historical and political geography, notably when describing the growth of the Roman Empire.

Strachey, (Giles) Lytton (1880–1932) British biographer and essayist. He was a leading member of the *Bloomsbury group. His irreverent attitude toward his subjects (Thomas Arnold, Florence Nightingale, Cardinal Manning, and others) in *Eminent Victorians* (1918) revolutionized the ponderous Victorian tradition of biography. His other biographical studies include *Queen Victoria* (1921) and *Elizabeth and Essex* (1928).

Stradivari, Antonio (?1644–1737) Italian violin maker. He was a pupil of Niccolò *Amati. From 1666 he and two of his sons made outstanding violins, violas, and cellos at their workshop in Cremona. Stradivari signed his instruments with the Latin form of his name, Stradivarius.

Strafford, Thomas Wentworth, 1st Earl of (1593–1641) English statesman, one of the chief administrators of Charles I's unpopular personal rule (1629–40). As Lord Deputy of Ireland (1633–39) his policy ruthlessly strengthened royal power and brought him enormous unpopularity that was intensified by his attempt to suppress the *Bishops' Wars (1639–40) in Scotland. He was impeached by the *Long Parliament and executed on the eve of the Civil War.

strain In physics, the deformation of a body when it is subjected to a *stress. **Longitudinal strain** is the extension per unit length when a body is stretched; **bulk strain** is the volume change per unit volume when a body is compressed; and **shear strain** is an angular measure of deformation. *See also* elasticity.

Straits Settlements A former British crown colony on the Strait of Malacca founded in 1867 and comprising the settlements of Penang, Singapore, Malacca, and Labuan. In 1946 Singapore became a separate crown colony, Labuan was incorporated in North Borneo, and Penang and Malacca joined the Malayan Union. In 1963 all became part of Malaysia. Singapore subsequently became independent.

Stralsund 54 18N 12 58E A city and port in N East Germany, on an inlet of the Baltic Sea. Founded in 1209, it became an important Hanseatic port. Industries include shipbuilding, fish processing, and the manufacture of machinery. Population (1973 est): 72,236.

strangeness A property of matter, expressed as a *quantum number (s), postulated to account for the unusually long lifetime of some *hadrons. In the quark model (*see* particle physics) strange hadrons contain the strange quark or its antiquark. Strangeness is conserved in *strong interactions and *electromagnetic interactions.

Strasbourg (German name: Strassburg) 48 35N 7 45E A city in NE France, the capital of the Bas-Rhin department on the Ill River. An important inland port, it trades in wine, iron ore, and potash; it has varied industries, including chemicals, oil refining, and textiles as well as the long-established printing and publishing industries. It is famous for its *pâté de foie gras*. Notable buildings include the cathedral (11th–15th centuries) and the university (1538). *History*: made a free imperial city in the 13th century, it was ceded to France in 1697. Captured by the Germans (1871), it was returned to France after World War I. Population (1975): 257,303.

Strategic Arms Limitation Talks (SALT). *See* disarmament.

Stratford 43 22N 81 00W A city in E Canada, in SW Ontario. Founded in 1831, it houses the Stratford Festival (1953), an important Shakespearean event. Stratford is also a center for light industry and dairying. Population (1981): 26,262.

Stratford-on-Avon 52 12N 1 41W A city in central England, on the River Avon. It is famous as the birthplace of William Shakespeare. The Royal Shakespeare Theatre (opened in 1932) is devoted mainly to Shakespeare's plays. Tourists visit Shakespeare's birthplace (now a museum), Holy Trinity Church (where he and his wife Anne Hathaway are buried), Anne Hathaway's cottage nearby, and many other buildings associated with the playwright. Population (1981): 20,858.

stratification The layering of sedimentary rocks in approximately horizontal beds, known as strata. (Certain volcanic deposits also show stratification.) The bed is the smallest division of stratified sedimentary rocks, being a single distinct sheetlike layer of sediment separated from overlying and underlying beds by a surface (the bedding plane), which marks a break in sedimentation. An unconformity is a surface representing a gap in the stratigraphic succession caused by changing conditions; it shows a period of erosion or nondeposition.

stratigraphy The branch of geology concerned with the formation, composition, sequence in time, and spatial correlation of the stratified rocks. **Lithostratigraphy** involves the lithological features and spatial relations of rock units. **Biostratigraphy** utilizes fossils in calibrating rock successions. **Chronostratigraphy** involves placing rock bodies in a time scale according to the time of their formation (*see* geological time scale).

stratocumulus cloud (Sc) A low type of *cloud composed of dark gray globular masses, often forming extensive sheets.

stratosphere. *See* atmosphere.

Stratton, Charles. *See* Tom Thumb.

stratus cloud A low type of *cloud generally forming below 7900 ft (2400 m), having a low base and a gray uniform appearance; it may actually occur at ground level as hill fog. Precipitation, if any, is usually no more than a fine drizzle.

Strauss, Richard (1864–1949) German composer and conductor. He studied in Munich and Berlin and conducted opera at Munich, Bayreuth, and Vienna. Strauss was much influenced by Wagner, whose use of *leitmotifs he adopted, both in opera and orchestral works. From 1887 to 1899 Strauss wrote a series of symphonic poems, including *Death and Transfiguration* (1889), *Till Eulenspiegels lustige Streiche* (1894–95), *Also sprach Zarathustra* (1895–96), *Don Quixote* (1897), and *Ein Heldenleben* (1898). He then turned to opera, writing 15 works, including *Salome* (1905), *Elektra* (1906–08), *Der Rosenkavalier* (1909–10), and *Ariadne auf Naxos* (1912). His compositions also include two concertos for horn, one for oboe and one for violin, many songs, and *Metamorphosen* for 23 solo strings (1944–45).

Strauss the Younger, Johann (1825–99) Austrian violinist, conductor, and composer. He led his own dance ensemble from the age of 18 and was conductor of the Vienna court balls (1863–70). He wrote a great many dance pieces, including such waltzes as "The Blue Danube," "Vienna Blood," and "Tales from the Vienna Woods," as well as polkas and marches. He also wrote 16 operettas, including *Die Fledermaus* (1874), *A Night in Venice* (1883), and *The Gipsy Baron* (1885).

His father **Johann Strauss the Elder** (1804–49) played in the orchestra of the popular composer Joseph Lanner (1801–43), before forming his own, with which he toured abroad. He was made conductor of the Vienna court balls in 1845, and composed 152 waltzes as well as quadrilles, marches (including the "Radetzky March"), galops, etc. Strauss and Lanner are credited with the creation of the Viennese waltz.

Stravinsky, Igor (1882–1971) Russian-born composer. He became a US citizen in 1945. His father was an opera singer and Stravinsky was a pupil of Rimsky-Korsakov in St Petersburg. He became famous with the series of ballet scores commissioned by Diaghilev for the Ballets Russes, including *The Firebird* (1910), *Petrushka* (1911), and *The Rite of Spring* (1913), which was extremely modern in its use of rhythm and dissonance; it provoked demonstrations at its premiere and had a strong influence on 20th-century music. Stravinsky subsequently developed a neoclassical style in which he attempted to revive baroque and classical composition in a modern form. His works in this style include a piano concerto (1924), the oratorio *Oedipus Rex* (1927), the ballet *Apollon Musagète* (1928), and the opera *The Rake's Progress* (1951). Toward the end of his life Stravinsky adopted *serialism in such works as *Canticum Sacrum* (1955).

strawberry A perennial herb belonging to the genus *Fragaria* (15 species), native to N temperate regions and widely cultivated for its edible □fruit. Most of the commercial varieties are hybrids derived from the European hautbois strawberry (*F. moschata*), the Chilean strawberry (*F. chiloensis*), and the North American scarlet strawberry (*F. virginiana*). The plants are low growing, with creeping stems and small clusters of usually white flowers. It is the flower base (receptacle) that develops into the red fleshy "fruit": the true fruits (achenes) appear as "seeds" embedded in its surface. Strawberries are consumed fresh or used for canning, freezing, and jam making. Family: *Rosaceae*.

strawberry tree. *See* Arbutus.

strawflower. *See* everlasting flower.

Strawson, Peter Frederick (1919–) British philosopher. He became professor of metaphysical philosophy at Oxford in 1968. Strawson's early philosophy centers around the relationship between logic and language. His later work in descriptive metaphysics revived the popularity of this field. His books include *The Bounds of Sense* (1966) and *Freedom and Restraint* (1974).

streamlining The process of shaping the contours of a body so that it presents the least resistance to motion through a fluid. The mathematical study of these contours is part of *aerodynamics and *hydrodynamics. Streamlining must take into account drag forces, which are always present in real fluids, and is important in the design of aircraft, especially for supersonic flight (*see* sound barrier). *See also* turbulence.

stream of consciousness A technique used by novelists in which the flow of impressions, thoughts, and feelings are recorded as they pass through a character's mind. The term was first used by William *James in *Principles of Psychology* (1890). The technique was used by James *Joyce in *Ulysses* (1922) and also by Virginia *Woolf and William *Faulkner.

Streicher, Julius (1885–1946) German Nazi journalist, who spread antisemitic propaganda. A collaborator in Hitler's Munich Putsch (1923), he was then editor of *Der Stürmer* (1923–45). He was hanged as a war criminal.

Streisand, Barbra (1942–) US singer and actress. She has performed on stage and in film musicals including *Funny Girl* (1968), for which she received an Academy Award, *Hello Dolly* (1969), *The Way We Were* (1973), *A Star is Borne* (1976), and *Yentl* (1983), which she wrote, produced, directed, and starred in. She has also acted in comedy films, such as *What's Up, Doc?* (1972).

Streptococcus A genus of spherical anaerobic bacteria many of which live as parasites in the respiratory and digestive systems of animals and man. *S. pyogenes* causes scarlet fever in man, *S. agalactiae* is responsible for bovine mastitis, and *S. lactis* produces lactic acid and causes souring of milk. *See also* pneumococcus.

streptomycin An *antibiotic, obtained from the bacterium *Streptomyces griseus*, that revolutionized the treatment of tuberculosis. It is usually administered (by injection) in combination with other antibiotics, such as isoniazid, as bacteria soon become resistant to it. In some patients it may cause serious side effects, resulting in deafness and disturbance of balance.

Stresemann, Gustav (1878–1929) German statesman; chancellor (1923) and foreign minister (1923–29) of the Weimar Republic. He brought about a rapprochement in Anglo-German and Franco-German relations after World War I, negotiating the *Locarno Pact and securing the admittance (1926) of Germany to the League of Nations. He shared the Nobel Peace Prize with Briand in 1926.

stress (physics) An effect that causes a deformation (or *strain) in a body, equal to the force causing the effect divided by the area over which it acts. **Tensile stress** tends to stretch a body; **bulk stress** tends to compress it; and **shear stress,** which acts tangentially, tends to twist it. *See also* elasticity.

stress (psychology) Any condition or circumstance that endangers the wellbeing of an individual and upsets his or her psychological equilibrium. Prolonged stress causes initial alarm, followed by attempts at coping; if these are not successful, then physical and mental symptoms appear. These symptoms are also known as stress and they vary from person to person. Stress can lead to *anxiety, *depression, and *psychosomatic disorders and it can trigger an episode of mental illness in vulnerable people.

strike A form of industrial action in which a group of employees, usually organized in a labor union (or unions), withdraws its labor in order to achieve its demands. A strike is the last resort in the process of *collective bargaining: it may prompt a settlement either because it proves that neither side is bluffing or because the costs involved (in terms of lost pay and profits) force a compromise. As future orders and job security may be jeopardized by a strike, which is contrary to the long-term interests of both sides, responsible unions only resort to the measure in extreme cases.

An authorized strike is one that is recognized by a labor union, whereas an unofficial (or wildcat) strike is a walkout organized by workers without official union backing. *See also* picketing; *compare* lockout.

AUGUST STRINDBERG

Strindberg, August (1849–1912) Swedish dramatist and writer, born in Stockholm. After 1883 he lived chiefly in Berlin and Paris. His unhappy childhood and three unsuccessful marriages gave rise to mental instability and a violent hatred of women. This is reflected in the plays *The Father* (1887) and *Miss Julie* (1888), the autobiographical prose work *Confessions of a Fool* (1912), and a study of mental illness entitled *Inferno* (1897). Returning to Sweden in 1898, Strindberg began work on a cycle of history plays and the dramatic religious trilogy *To Damascus* (1904). The other major works of this period are *The Dance of Death* (1900), on marital tensions, the symbolistic *Easter* (1901), and *A Dream Play* (1901), in which Strindberg abandoned the naturalism that had figured in his earlier plays. His late chamber plays, such as *The Ghost Sonata* (1907), combine irrational elements with realistic settings; they anticipated and were highly influential on many of the later innovations of 20th-century drama.

stringed instruments Musical instruments in which notes are produced by the vibration of stretched strings. The strings may be plucked, as in the guitar, lyre, harp, lute, balalaika, zither, banjo, and ukulele; bowed, as in the violin family and viol family; plucked mechanically, as in the harpsichord; struck mechanically, as in the clavichord and piano; or played with hammers, as in the dulcimer and cimbalom. *Compare* drums; percussion instruments; wind instruments.

stroboscope An instrument used to study periodic motion using a flashing light of known frequency. For example, if a disk revolving at 50 revolutions per second is illuminated by 50 hertz alternating-current mains lighting, it will appear to be stationary. This is because the eye, for any particular flash, sees the disk in exactly the same position as it was for the previous flash. Strobe lighting is used in discotheques to accentuate the music's beat, with which it flashes in time.

Stroheim, Erich von (Hans Erich Maria Stroheim von Nordenwall; 1885–1957) US film director and actor, born in Austria. His films as director include *Greed* (1923), *The Wedding March* (1927), and *Queen Kelly* (1928). As an actor, he specialized in the roles of villains and German officers, as in *La Grande Illusion* (1937). In *Sunset Boulevard* (1950) he played a director from Hollywood's past.

stroke (*or* apoplexy) Sudden loss of consciousness with weakness or paralysis of one side of the body, caused by interruption of the blood supply to the brain. This may be due to a blood clot in one of the arteries of the brain (*see* embolism; thrombosis) or to the rupture of a blood vessel in the brain (cerebral hemorrhage). The underlying causes include untreated atherosclerosis and hypertension (high blood pressure) and diseases affecting the valves of the heart. With careful nursing and physiotherapy to restore the function of paralyzed limbs many patients recover completely.

Stromboli An Italian island in the Tyrrhenian Sea, in the *Lipari Islands. Its active volcano produces a stream of lava.

strong interaction One of the four basic forces in the universe; it occurs between the class of elementary particles called hadrons (*see* particle physics). It is the strongest of the four (being 100 times stronger than the electromotive interaction) but is effective only over a very short range of about 10^{-15} meter. It is the force that holds the protons and neutrons together in the nucleus. *Compare* weak interaction.

strontium (Sr) A reactive *alkaline-earth metal, discovered by Sir Humphry Davy in 1808 and named for Strontian, a town in Scotland where the carbonate ($SrCO_3$) is found. It also occurs as the sulfate, celestine ($SrSO_4$). It is a highly reactive metal, being more electropositive than calcium and reacting vigorously with water to liberate hydrogen. It imparts a strong red color to flames and is used in fireworks. The isotope ^{90}Sr is produced in nuclear fallout. It emits high-energy beta-rays and has a half-life of 28 years; it consequently presents a serious health hazard as owing to its chemical similarity to calcium it can become incorporated into bone. At no 38; at wt 87.62; mp 1418°F (769°C); bp 2526°F (1384°C).

Strophanthus A genus of trees, shrubs, and vines (about 60 species), native to tropical regions of Africa and SE Asia. The petals of some species have long threadlike extensions. The bark and seeds yield the drug strophanthin, which resembles *digitalis and is used medicinally as a heart stimulant. Family: *Apocynaceae*.

structuralism An approach to the study of culture and society that seeks to uncover underlying patterns and structures and the basic elements from which such patterns are constructed. The leading figure of this school is the French social anthropologist Claude *Lévi-Strauss, whose work on kinship, art, myth, ritual, and religion has been concerned also with the elucidation of universal laws of human thought through the analysis of its underlying structure. This approach was stimulated by the structural school in *linguistics.

Struve, Otto (1897–1963) US astronomer, born in Russia, who discovered the existence of interstellar clouds and observed that they contain hydrogen and calcium. He also noticed that certain stars, including our own sun, rotate much more slowly than others and suggested that this is because they possess planetary systems.

strychnine An alkaloid poison derived from plants of the genus *Strychnos*. It acts on the central nervous system, causing convulsions and ultimately death. Strychnine has been used in "tonics" and is still used as a poison for pests (such as moles).

Stuarts (*or* Stewarts) The ruling dynasty of Scotland from 1371 to 1714 and of England from 1603 to 1714. The family originated in the 11th century in Brittany and in the 12th century entered Scottish royal service with the appointment of Walter (d. 1177) as steward to David I. The sixth steward, Walter (1293–1326), married (1315) Marjory, the daughter of Robert the Bruce, and their son became Robert II in 1371. The direct male line ended with the death of James V in 1542, when the throne passed to his daughter Mary, Queen of Scots, and following her abdication (1567) to her son James VI, who inherited the English crown (1603) as James I. He was succeeded by Charles I (executed 1649), Charles II, James II, Mary II (and her husband William III), and Anne (d. 1714). The crown then passed to the Hanoverians (*see* Settlement, Act of) but the Stuart claim was kept alive by *James Edward Stuart the Old Pretender, and his son, *Charles Edward Stuart the Young Pretender. The last royal Stuart was Henry Stuart, Cardinal York (d. 1807), the younger son of the Old Pretender.

Stuart, Gilbert (Charles) (1755–1828) US portrait painter. At 19, he went to London and studied (1777–82) with Benjamin *West. Returning to the US (1793), he set up his studio in Philadelphia, where he did his most famous works, three life portraits of President George Washington. At his studio in Washington, DC, (1803–05) he painted portraits of the famous, including Thomas Jefferson and James Madison.

Stuart, James Ewell Brown ("Jeb;" 1833–64) US Confederate general. He commanded cavalry troops at the Battles of *Bull Run; just before the second battle (1862), he accurately gathered information about the enemy by traveling completely around the Union troops over a period of three days. He fought bravely at *Fredericksburg and *Chancellorsville and continued his scouting work for the Confederate Army. He was fatally wounded at Yellow Tavern while defending Richmond.

Stubbs, George (1724–1806) British animal painter. Largely self-taught as an artist, Stubbs studied anatomy and his earliest works included illustrations for a midwifery textbook (1751) and *The Anatomy of the Horse* (1766), for which he made dissections. He is best known for his horse paintings, such as *Mares and Foals in a Landscape*, but he also painted portraits and farming scenes. His meticulous observation of nature reflects his maxim that nature is always superior to art.

stupa A Buddhist shrine in the form of a mound or dome with a central projection. An early example (c. 100 AD) at Sanchi in N central India is a solid brickwork mound surrounded by a carved stone railing. Some fine later stupas survive in Sri Lanka. When modified to become a reliquary the stupa evolved into the *pagoda.

sturgeon A *bony fish belonging to a family (*Acipenseridae*; about 24 species) found in N temperate fresh and salt waters. Sturgeons have a large sharklike body, up to 27.5 ft (8.4 m) long, with five longitudinal rows of sharp bony plates, a small ventral mouth, and four sensory barbels. They feed near the bottom on small animals and plants. Eggs are laid in fresh water and are commercially important as caviar. *See also* beluga. ☐fish.

Sturluson, Snorri (1178–1241) Icelandic poet, who was also the author of the *Prose Edda* (see Eddas). A leading Icelandic nobleman, Sturluson visited Norway (1218, 1237) and intrigued against King Haakon, who intended to invade Iceland. Haakon had Sturluson murdered in 1241. His work includes a life of St Olaf and the *Heimskringla* (1223–35), a series of sagas about the Norse kings.

Sturm und Drang (German: Storm and Stress) A German literary movement of the late 18th century that anticipated many aspects of Romanticism. Its influence is most notable in the drama, characterized by epic scale and the rejection of structural conventions. Goethe and Schiller were leading writers of this movement during their early careers.

Stuttgart 48 47N 9 12E A city in SW West Germany, the capital of Baden-Württemberg on the Neckar River. It became the capital of Württemberg in 1482. It was largely destroyed in World War II. One of West Germany's main industrial centers, its manufactures include electrical goods, cars, and metallurgical goods. It is also a center for banking, exhibitions, and publishing. It has a university (1967). Population (1980 est): 582,400.

Stuyvesant, Peter (c. 1610–72) Dutch colonial administrator; governor of New Netherland (1647–64). His unpopular autocratic rule, which denied religious and political freedom, ended when the British forcibly took over the colony, dividing it into New York and New Jersey.

stye A small abscess at the root of an eyelash. Styes, which commonly occur in crops, are usually treated with warm compresses to drain the pus.

stylops A minute insect of the order Strepsiptera (about 400 species), which is parasitic on bees and other insects, affecting their reproductive systems and secondary sexual characteristics. The grublike female lives permanently inside the host's body; the winged male, often less than 0.16 in (4 mm) long, leaves its host to find and fertilize a female. After hatching, the larvae complete their development in a larval host.

Styria (German name: Steiermark) A federal state in SE Austria, bordering on Yugoslavia. It possesses important mineral resources and the Erzberg is Austria's chief source of iron ore; other minerals include lignite and magnesite. Area: 6326 sq mi (16,384 sq km). Population (1981): 1,184,175. Capital: Graz.

Styron, William (Clark, Jr.) (1925–) US novelist. He wrote *Lie Down in Darkness* (1951), *The Long March* (1953), and *Set This House on Fire* (1960) before receiving a Pulitzer Prize (1968) for *The Confessions of Nat Turner* (1967), a fictional account as told by leader Nat *Turner of the 1831 slave uprising. He also wrote *Sophie's Choice* (1979; film, 1982) and *This Quiet Dust* (1982).

Styx In Greek mythology, the main river of Hades across which the souls of the dead were ferried by *Charon. It was sometimes personified as the daughter of Oceanus. After she helped Zeus in his war against the Titans, oaths sworn in her name were held to be inviolable.

Suárez (Gonzalez), Adolfo, Duke of (1932–) Spanish statesman; prime minister (1976–81). He was appointed by King Juan Carlos to guide Spain into democracy.

Suarez, Francisco de (1548–1617) Spanish Jesuit theologian. He is known for his synthesis of Thomist and Aristotelian philosophy. He developed the theological system of congruism, the reconciliation of grace and free will. In *De legibus* (1612), he expounded the principles of natural and divine law.

subconscious. *See* unconscious.

sublimation In chemistry, the evaporation of a solid without melting. For any substance the liquid phase only occurs within certain limits of temperature and pressure—if the pressure is low enough, heating a solid will result in sublimation. Substances that sublime at atmospheric pressure include carbon dioxide (dry ice) and iodine.

submachine gun A light short-range *small arm developed from the infantry light machine gun. Submachine guns became militarily popular after 1918, filling the gap between the pistol and the rifle, by offering greater fire-power than either. They are also more accurate than the pistol and smaller than the rifle. The first successful type was the *tommy gun, but now all major armies have their own designs. Almost all use 0.35 in (9 mm) ammunition, fire automatically, and depend on blowback action (i.e. use the expanding gas of the ammunition to activate the reloading mechanism).

submarine A warship designed for sustained operation under water. The earliest record of a submarine craft is that developed by Cornelis Drebbel (1572–1634) of Holland in 1620, demonstrated before England's James I in 1624 in the Thames estuary. A more practical model, the "Turtle," was invented by David Bushnell (1742–1824) of Connecticut in 1776, and saw limited use in the American Revolution. Submarines, called U-boats (German name: *Unterseeboot*, undersea boat), were first used extensively by the German navy in World War I. They became an important armament in World War II, when the German navy sank millions of tons of Allied ships, especially supply ships in convoy from the US to the UK and the Soviet Union. The US navy used submarines to advantage against the Japanese, when 63% of all Japanese merchant shipping exceeding 1000 tons of cargo weight was sunk and 276 war vessels of various kinds were destroyed. Modern submarines may be powered by nuclear reactors, which require no air for recharging batteries and, hence, can remain submerged for months at a time. These vessels also carry one or more guns mounted on deck, torpedoes for firing under water, and surface-to-air or surface-to-surface missiles that can be launched when the submarine is submerged.

Subotica 46 04N 19 41E A city in N central Yugoslavia, in Serbia near the Hungarian border. It has a large Hungarian minority and is an agricultural trading center. Its manufactures include metal goods, chemicals, and food products. Population (1971): 88,787.

subsidence The sinking of part of the earth's surface relative to the surrounding area. On a large scale it may result from crustal movements (e.g. rift valleys). On a small scale it may result from collapsed mining excavations, collapsed roofs of limestone caves, etc. Subsidence involves vertical movement and lacks the horizontal component of landslides, etc.

substitution reaction A type of chemical reaction in which one atom or group of atoms is displaced by another. An example is the reaction of methyl chloride (CH_3Cl) with hydroxide ions (OH^-) to give methanol (CH_3OH) and chloride ions (Cl^-). The hydroxide ion, in this case, is referred to as the substituent. *See also* addition reaction.

succession In ecology, the process of continual change that takes place in the composition of a *community of organisms occupying a particular habitat from the time of its initial colonization to the establishment of a stable *climax community. Succession is influenced by many factors, principally the nature of the habitat, climatic changes, and the effects of colonization on the habitat.

Suckling, Sir John (1609–42) English Cavalier poet and dramatist. Famous for his wit, generosity, and his taste for gambling, he was a loyal supporter of Charles I at the beginning of the Civil War. He was later discovered to be involved in a plot (1641) to free the imprisoned Earl of *Strafford and was forced to flee to Paris, where he committed suicide. He wrote four plays and many elegant short lyrics.

Sucre 19 00S 65 15W The capital of Bolivia, in the S at an altitude of 9153 ft (2790 m). It was founded by the Spanish in 1538 on the site of an Indian settlement. The center of the revolutionary movement against Spain, it became the capital in 1859. The seat of government was moved to La Paz in 1898. The St Francis Xavier University was established in 1624. Population (1976): 63,000.

Sucre, Antonio José de (1795–1830) South American revolutionary, born in Venezuela. The most able of *Bolívar's generals, Sucre defeated the Spaniards at the decisive battle of Ayacucho (1824) and established the republic of Bolivia. He was its president from 1826 to 1828, when he resigned after a rebellion. The capital city, Sucre, is named for him.

sucrose (cane sugar *or* beet sugar *or* saccharose) A carbohydrate consisting chemically of one molecule each of *glucose and *fructose linked together. It is commercially the most important of the *sugars, being used as a sweetener in foods and drinks. When heated to 160°C it forms barley sugar and at 200°C becomes caramel.

Sudan, Democratic Republic of the A large country in NE Africa, bordering on the Red Sea. It consists chiefly of a vast plateau rising to mountains in the S and W, reaching heights of over 10,000 ft (3000 m). The main rivers are the Blue Nile and White Nile, which join at Khartoum and provide the country's main source of water. About half the population are Arabs, and there are minorities of *Dinka, Nubians, and others. *Economy*: chiefly agricultural, the main cash crop and export being cotton; other crops include sorghum, sugar, and groundnuts, and production is being increased by means of irrigation schemes, such as the *Gezira irrigation scheme. Livestock rearing is also important. Forest products include gum arabic, of which the Sudan is the world's main producer. Mineral resources include iron ore, gold, and manganese. *History*: the NE was part of ancient *Nubia, which dominated Egypt (c. 730–670 BC). The region was Christianized in the 6th century and resisted invasion from the N until the 13th century, after which it was converted to Islam. In 1821 it was conquered by the Egyptians, against whom a revolt under the Mahdi (*see* Mahdi, al-) took place in 1881. In 1898 an Anglo-Egyptian force under Kitchener subdued his followers and in 1899 an Anglo-Egyptian condominium was established. In 1956 the Sudan became an independent republic. After a coup in 1958 it was ruled by a military government until 1964, when civilian rule was restored. Another coup in 1969 brought Colonel Jaafar al Nemery (1929–) to power. A revolt in the S against the domination of the N lasted from 1955 until 1973, when a new constitution gave the S a certain measure of self-government. In the 1980s al Nemery thwarted attempts, supported by Libya, to overthrow him. Official language: Arabic; English is widely spoken. Official currency: Sudanese pound of 100 piastres and 1000 millièmes. Area: 967,500 sq mi (2,500,000 sq km). Population (1980 est): 18,400,000. Capital: Khartoum. Main port: Port Sudan.

Sudbury 46 30N 81 01W A city in E Canada, in Ontario. Established in 1883, it is one of the world's greatest mining cities, especially for nickel and copper. A distribution and commercial center for NE Ontario, Sudbury has important timber and tool industries. It houses the bilingual Laurentian University (1960). Population (1976): 97,604.

Sudden Infant Death Syndrome (SIDS *or* crib death) Sudden death of an infant, up to one year old, from unknown causes, usually occurring while the infant is sleeping. A respiratory virus is suspected, and research has shown certain abnormalities in the central nervous system, adrenal glands, and pulmonary arteries.

Sudetenland A mountainous region on the W borders of Czechoslovakia. The Sudetenland, incorporated in Czechoslovakia in 1919, formed a defensible frontier with Germany, with which its predominantly German population wanted reunion. Nazi pressure resulted in the *Munich Agreement of 1938, which permitted German reoccupation of the area. After World War II Czechoslovakia regained the Sudetenland and expelled the Sudeten Germans.

Su Dong Po (*or* Su Tung-p'o; 1036–1101) Chinese poet, essayist, and painter, whose father Su Hsün (*or* Su Xun; 1009–66) and brother Su Tse-yu (*or* Su Ze-yu; 1039–1112) were also famous writers. An imperial official, he was imprisoned and exiled on several occasions for his satirical verses and criticisms of government policies. His poems introduced more varied meters and subjects into the traditional verse forms of his period.

Sue, Eugène (Joseph Marie S.; 1804–57) French novelist. He worked as a ship's doctor until 1829. He achieved popular success with his novels about the Parisian underworld, notably *Les Mystères de Paris* (1842–43). *Le Juif errant* (1844–45) expressed his socialist sympathies.

Suetonius (Gaius Suetonius Tranquillius; c. 69–c. 140 AD) Roman historian and biographer. He was a friend of Pliny the Younger and served as secretary to the emperor Hadrian. Of his many works only *Lives of the Twelve Caesars* and fragments of *Lives of Famous Men* survive. His work is especially informative about the private lives of his subjects.

Suez (Arabic name: As-Suways) 29 59N 32 33E A port in Egypt, on the Gulf of Suez near the mouth of the Suez Canal. An important refueling station, it was virtually deserted following the Arab-Israeli War of 1967 and its oil refineries were damaged. Since the reopening of the Suez Canal (1975), rebuilding has taken place. Population (1976): 194,000.

Suez Canal A canal in Egypt connecting the Mediterranean Sea and the Red Sea. Running between Port Said in the N and Suez in the S (via the Great and Little Bitter Lakes), it is 103 mi (165 km) long. It is of great importance to much of the world's shipping. It was designed by the French engineer Ferdinand de Lesseps and was opened in 1869. In 1888 it became a neutral zone, with Britain the guarantor of its status. In 1956, following the withdrawal of British troops, President Nasser nationalized the canal, provoking an Anglo-French attack on Egypt. However, they withdrew within a few days in the face of international censure. The canal was closed from 1967 to 1975 because of Arab-Israeli hostilities and was not opened to Israeli ships until April, 1979. The canal is being deepened to take the much larger oil tankers now in use.

Suffolk A county in E England, bordering on the North Sea. It consists of undulating lowlands. It is mainly agricultural, producing cereals and sugar beet, and is noted for its horse breeding. Industries are generally related to agriculture. Fishing is centered on Lowestoft. Area: 1467 sq mi (3800 sq km). Population (1981): 596,354. Administrative center: Ipswich.

suffragettes. *See* women's movement.

Sufism (Arabic *sufi*: wearer of a woolen cloak, mystic) A mystical movement arising within Islam in the 8th and 9th centuries AD. The goal of the Sufis was mystical union with God achieved by fervent worship. Later Sufism shows the influence of Neoplatonism and some devotional practices, such as rhythmical body movements, may derive from Hindu asceticism. Sufi thought has influenced leading Arabic and Persian poets. As it evolved, Sufism divided into different orders or brotherhoods, a number of which survive at present and have been introduced into the West. *See also* dervishes.

Sugar Act (*or* Revenue Act; 1764) British revenue-raising law imposed on the American colonists. A duty collected by British customs officers was put on each gallon of West Indian molasses traded for American lumber. The molasses, made into rum and traded for African slaves to be sold in the West Indies, was an integral part of the triangular trade carried on by America, the West Indies, and Africa. These early restrictions ultimately contributed to the start of the *American Revolution.

sugar beet A biennial herb derived from the European sea *beet (*Beta vulgaris*). Sugar beet is widely cultivated for the sucrose content of its large roots, which is over 20% by weight in modern commercial varieties. Sugar was first extracted from beet in the 18th century and the plant is now a major source of sugar, especially in Europe and the Soviet Union. Family: *Chenopodiaceae*.

sugar cane A perennial grass of the tropical genus *Saccharum* (5 species), especially *S. officinarum*, which is cultivated in tropical and subtropical regions for its sugar content. The clumps of stalks (canes), 10–26 ft (3–8 m) high, have lance-shaped leaves and may bear dense woolly clusters of female flowers. Usually, the canes are cut before flowering and crushed between rollers to extract the sugary liquid. This is concentrated and refined to produce sucrose crystals for table sugar, etc. The remaining liquor (molasses) is used for animal feedstuffs, industrial alcohol, etc., and is fermented to make rum. The fibrous residue (bagasse) is used as fuel and for paper making, cattle feed, etc.

sugars A class of sweet-tasting *carbohydrates, classified chemically as *monosaccharides or *disaccharides. The sugar widely used to sweeten food, drinks, and confectionery is the disaccharide *sucrose, some 70–80 million tons of which are produced annually. Half of this total is derived from the stems of sugar cane (11–15% sucrose) and half from the roots of sugar beet (17% sucrose).

Sugar manufacture is believed to have originated in India (Sanskrit *sarkara*, sand) around 3000 BC, the method traveling westward through Arab countries (*sukkar*), Greece (*sákharon*), Italy (*zucchero*), and France (*sucre*). It was taken to the New World by Christopher Columbus in 1493. Until the mid-18th century it was an expensive luxury, used primarily as a medicinal sedative.

Sucrose is extracted from raw sugar cane by pressure, the extract being crystallized by evaporation. It is extracted from beet by hot water. Raw cane sugar and beet sugar are further refined to produce the granulated, caster, icing, and cube sugars familiar to commerce. By-products from sugar processing include molasses and sugar-beet pulp, both of which are used in animal feedstuffs.

Suger of Saint-Denis (1081–1151) French abbot and statesman. Suger was educated at the Abbey of Saint-Denis, becoming abbot in 1122. He introduced reforms based on the example of St *Bernard of Clairvaux. As adviser to both Louis VI (1081–1137; reigned 1108–37) and Louis VII (c. 1121–80; reigned 1137–80), Suger wielded considerable political influence.

Suharto (1921–) Indonesian statesman and general; president (1968–). He gained prominence in the struggle for Indonesian independence from the Netherlands, becoming chief of the army staff in 1965. He came to power in the gradual overthrow (1965–68) of Sukarno.

suicide Intentional self-destruction. Condemned by Christianity, Judaism, and Islam, suicide is a criminal offense in some societies. In many traditional societies suicide, whether voluntary or an honorable obligation, is an accepted practice. Compulsory suicide may be performed out of loyalty to a dead master or spouse, derived from the once widespread custom of immolating wives and servants, or in the interest of the group as a whole, such as self-murder by elderly members of a community no longer able to provide for their own subsistence. In certain instances suicide might be offered to a privileged few as an alternative to execution, as among the Greeks (*see* Socrates), the Roman nobility, and the feudal Japanese aristocracy. With the breakdown of traditional practices, especially in industrial societies, the causes of suicide become less clear. Since Durkheim's classic statistical study *Suicide* (1897) sociologists have sought to relate the incidence of suicide to social pressures and the importance of social integration (*see* anomie). Psychologists have emphasized the importance of guilt, anxiety, and loneliness; they have also distinguished between attempted suicide (when death is intended but averted) and parasuicide (when self-injury but not death is intended). *See also* Samaritans.

Sukarnapura. *See* Jajapura.

Sukarno (1901–70) Indonesian statesman, the first president of Indonesia (1945–65). He helped to found the Indonesian Nationalist Party in 1927 and was Indonesia's leader during the Japanese occupation (1942–45). When Indonesia was declared independent he became president. In 1957 with popular and military support, he introduced so-called Guided Democracy. A military coup deposed him in 1965–66.

Sukhumi 43 01N 41 01E A port in the SW Soviet Union, the capital of the Abkhaz ASSR in the Georgian SSR on the Black Sea. It occupies the site of the ancient Greek colony of Dioscurias and is a popular resort. Population (1981 est): 114,000.

Sukkur 27 42N 68 54E A city in Pakistan, on the Indus River. Nearby is the major irrigation project, the Sukkur (or Lloyd) Barrage (1923–32). Industries include textiles and cement. Population (1972): 158,876.

Sulawesi (former name: Celebes) An island in Indonesia, off E Borneo. Irregularly shaped, it is mountainous and forested, with rich mineral deposits. It is Indonesia's chief producer of copra and nickel. Area, including adjacent islands: 72,986 sq mi (189,033 sq km). Population (1971): 8,535,164. Chief towns: Ujung Padang and Menado.

Suleiman (I) the Magnificent (?1494–1566) Ottoman sultan (1520–66), under whom the Ottoman Empire reached its peak. Suleiman captured Belgrade in 1521 and Rhodes in 1522. In 1526 he defeated the

Hungarians at *Mohács and annexed large parts of Hungary. In 1529 he besieged Vienna. In campaigns against Persia he made many conquests, including Baghdad (1534), and the Ottoman navy, under *Barbarossa and others, controlled the E Mediterranean. To the Turks Suleiman is known as the Lawgiver because of the many regulations issued during his reign.

sulfonamides (*or* sulfa drugs) A group of drugs derived from sulfanilamide, that prevent the growth of bacteria and were first used in 1936, to treat infections associated with childbirth. Sulfonamides are used to treat a wide variety of infections, particularly those of the urinary tract (e.g. sulfamethiazole) and the eye (e.g. sulfacetamide). Sulfonamides are also combined with trimethoprim (*see* co-trimoxazole), which improves their effectiveness. The sulfonamide sulfasalazine helps the treatment of ulcerative colitis and Crohn's disease. In some patients sulfonamides may cause severe allergic disorders.

sulfur (S) A yellow nonmetallic solid element, occurring in various crystalline and amorphous forms. Sulfur was known in ancient times as brimstone. It is found near volcanoes and in large deposits associated with oil trapped against salt domes, from which it is extracted commercially. Extraction is by the Frasch process, in which the sulfur is melted with superheated steam and pumped to the surface. Sulfur reacts readily with many elements to form sulfides, sulfates, and oxides. Common compounds include sodium sulfide (Na_2S), zinc sulfide (ZnS), the poisonous gas hydrogen sulfide (H_2S), copper sulfate ($CuSO_4$), and calcium sulfate ($CaSO_4$). The oxides SO_2 and SO_3 are acidic gases that dissolve in water to form sulfurous acid (H_2SO_3) and *sulfuric acid (H_2SO_4). At no 16; at wt 32.06; mp 236°F (113°C); bp 833°F (444.6°C).

sulfuric acid (H_2SO_4) A colorless oily liquid that has a great affinity for water and is used as a drying agent. Mixing with water must be carried out carefully because of the heat produced. H_2SO_4 is made by the contact process, in which sulfur dioxide is heated and passed through columns of platinized asbestos catalyst to produce sulfur trioxide (SO_3). The SO_3 is then dissolved in water to form H_2SO_4. Adding further SO_3 to H_2SO_4 produces fuming sulfuric acid (oleum; $H_2S_2O_7$), a fuming liquid that forms a crystalline solid on cooling.

Sulfuric acid is one of the most important industrial chemicals, being used in the manufacture of fertilizers, paints, rayon, explosives, and many other products, as well as in oil refining and car batteries.

sulky A two-wheeled vehicle drawn by a horse, consisting of a light springy frame bearing a single seat for the driver and supported on wheels like bicycle wheels. Used now in *harness racing, this type of cart was used in the 19th century by doctors and others needing to travel alone.

Sulla, Lucius Cornelius (c. 138–78 BC) Roman dictator, associated with the aristocratic party; an opponent of *Marius and *Cinna. Nicknamed Felix (Lucky), he enjoyed early success. Enraged because his command against *Mithridates was transferred to Marius, he stormed Rome (87), forcing Marius and Cinna to flee. Although outlawed when his rivals returned, he successfully concluded the campaign against Mithridates and in 83 invaded Italy and took Rome. Elected dictator, Sulla butchered his political opponents. After legislating to restore the Senate's constitutional powers, he retired into private life (79).

Sullivan, Sir Arthur (1842–1900) British composer. He is best known for his collaboration with the librettist W. S. *Gilbert in such comic operas as *The Pirates of Penzance* (1879), *The Mikado* (1885), and *The Yeomen of the Guard* (1888). He also composed the grand opera *Ivanhoe* (1891).

Sullivan, John Lawrence (1858–1918) US boxer, generally considered the first modern world heavyweight champion (1882–92). He lost his title to Jim Corbett (1866–1933) in the first championship fought under the Queensberry Rules (*see* boxing).

Sullivan, Louis Henry (1856–1924) US architect. Working principally in Chicago, Sullivan was one of the leading figures of the modern architectural movement. His work, begun in the classical style, was modified by *Art Nouveau and developed into a form of *functionalism, the basic tenet being "form follows function." He was among the first to design skyscrapers, such as the Wainwright building, St Louis (1890), the Transportation Building at the Columbian Exposition in Chicago (1893), and the Carson store, Chicago (1899), in both of which the structural framework is clearly visible.

Sully, Maximilien de Béthune, Duc de (1560–1641) French statesman; chief minister to *Henry IV. Sully's financial reforms were fundamental in restoring prosperity after the *Wars of Religion. He retired (1611) following Henry's assassination.

Sully-Prudhomme, René François Armand (1839–1907) French poet. His early verse was lyrical and subjective, but his involvement with the *Parnassians, who favored greater impersonality, led to his attempts in *La Justice* (1878) and other works to write epical philosophic verse. He won the Nobel Prize in 1901.

Sulu Archipelago An island group in the SW Philippines, between Borneo and Mindanao. The most important of its 400 volcanic and coral islands are Basilan and Jolo. Area: 1087 sq mi (2815 sq km). Population (1970): 425,617. Chief town: Jolo.

sumach (*or* sumac) A tree or shrub of the genus *Rhus* (250 species), native to warm temperate and subtropical regions. The leaves of the Sicilian sumach (*R. coraria*) yield a substance used in tanning and dyeing. Several species are cultivated as garden ornamentals: the stag's-horn sumach (*R. typhina*) of North America grows to a height of 23–39 ft (7–12 m) and has a crimson or orange autumn foliage. Some species are poisonous and irritate the skin on contact, particularly the American *poison ivy and poison sumach (*R. vernix*). Family: *Anacardiaceae*. See also lacquer tree.

Sumatra (*or* Sumatera) The second largest Indonesian island, separated from Peninsular Malaysia by the Strait of Malacca. The mountainous volcanic spine descends in the NE to swamps. Producing over 75% of the country's exports, it is Indonesia's chief rubber and oil producer and also possesses large natural gas deposits and other minerals. Crops include coffee, tea, and pepper. *History*: the Buddhist kingdom of Sri Vijaya (7th–13th centuries) was based in Palembang, spreading through Indonesia and the Malay Peninsula. During the 15th century the Islamic influence became dominant, resisting Dutch domination in the N until 1908. Since 1949 there has been considerable separatist activity directed against the Java-based government. Area: 202,311 sq mi (524,097 sq km). Population (1971): 20,812,682. Chief towns: Palembang and Medan.

Sumer The area in S Mesopotamia in which the earliest civilization evolved during the 4th millennium BC. The fertile natural environment encouraged settlements that grew into such cities as *Ur and *Eridu with all the prerequisites of civilized life: a writing system (*see* cuneiform), accumulation of wealth through trade, specialist organization of labor, and sophisticated crafts and architecture. Politically Sumer was a collection of independent city states, each with its own patron deity. Centralized control was temporarily asserted by neighboring *Akkad (c. 2300 BC) and after 2000 BC Sumer was gradually absorbed into *Babylonia.

summer cypress Either of two annual herbaceous plants, *Kochia scoparia* or *K. trichophylla*, native to temperate Eurasia and cultivated as ornamentals. They form compact bushes, 40–60 in (1–1.5 m) high, and the foliage assumes an attractive red-bronze color in autumn. Family: *Chenopodiaceae*.

Sumner, Charles (1811–74) US politician and reformer. Elected to represent Massachusetts in the US Senate in 1851, he fought against slavery, especially the *Fugitive Slave Law of 1850, and the *Kansas-Nebraska Act of 1854. Attacked by a southern congressman, angered over Sumner's antislavery stance, Sumner was incapacitated for three years (1856–59), but he kept his seat in the Senate. In 1861 he was appointed chairman of the Senate Foreign Relations Committee, a post he held until 1871. He advocated a strong Reconstruction policy and supported impeachment proceedings against President Andrew *Johnson.

Sumter, Fort A fort in Charleston, South Carolina, on an island at the mouth of the city's harbor on the Atlantic Ocean. Built 1829–60 on a manmade island, it defended the city and was the first place fired upon (1861) by the Confederates in the Civil War. The fort was taken by the Confederates in two days and was not reoccupied by Union troops until the Confederate evacuation of Charleston in 1865. It was made a national monument in 1948.

sun The nearest star, lying at an average distance of 92.9 million mi (149.6 million km) from earth at the center of the *solar system. It has a diameter of 864,500 mi (1,392,000 km), a mass of 1.99×10^{30} kg, and rotates on its axis in a mean period of 25.38 days (the period lengthening as solar latitude increases). It is a typical yellow (G2) main-sequence star and is composed primarily (99%) of hydrogen and helium in the approximate ratio 3:1 by mass.

In its hot central core, about 250,000 mi (400,000 km) in diameter, energy is generated by nuclear fusion reactions. This energy is transported to the sun's surface, from where it is radiated into space, mainly as heat and light. The surface, called the *photosphere, is the boundary between the opaque outer (convective) zone of the sun's interior and its transparent atmosphere. The atmosphere comprises the *chromosphere and the inner and outer *corona. The corona extends many millions of kilometers into interplanetary space. There are regions of intense localized magnetic fields on the sun, extending from the photosphere through the chromosphere to the

corona. A variety of phenomena occur in these active regions, including *sunspots, *solar prominences, and *solar flares. *See also* solar wind.

sun bear A *bear, *Helarctos malayanus*, of tropical forests of Asia, Sumatra, and Borneo. It is the smallest bear, (43–55 in [110–140 cm] long) and climbs well, hunting in tall trees for small vertebrates, fruit, and its favorite food, honey.

sunbird An arboreal bird belonging to a tropical family (*Nectariniidae*; 104 species) ranging from Africa to Australasia. Sunbirds are 3.5–6 in (9–15 cm) long and have a brilliant metallic plumage, slender down-curved bills, and long extensible tongues for feeding on nectar. Sunbirds are similar to New World hummingbirds but perch on flowers to feed rather than hovering in front of them.

sun bittern A Central American ground-dwelling bird, *Eurypyga helias*, that occurs in wet forests. 17 in (43 cm) long, it has a brown, yellow, black, and white spotted plumage and feeds on insects with its sharp bill. It is the only member of its family (*Eurypygidae*). Order: *Gruiformes* (cranes, rails, etc.).

Sunda Islands An Indonesian group of islands, the W part of the Malay Archipelago between the Indian Ocean and South China Sea. It consists of the **Greater Sunda Islands** including Sumatra, Java, Borneo, and Sulawesi and *Nusa Tenggara (formerly the Lesser Sunda Islands).

Sunday, Billy (William Ashley S.; 1862–1935) US revivalist and baseball player. He played professional baseball (1883–86), but then turned his attention to religion, becoming a Presbyterian in 1888. By 1903 he had become a minister and was soon well known for his fundamentalist revival meetings around the country.

Sunderland 54 55N 1 23W A port in NE England, at the mouth of the River Wear. Sunderland has exported coal from the Durham coalfield since the 14th century. Shipbuilding and ship repairing are important industries; there is also engineering, glass, pottery, chemicals, and paper manufacture. Population (1981): 196,152.

sundew A perennial or annual *carnivorous plant of the genus *Drosera* (about 100 species), of temperate and tropical regions. Sundews have a basal rosette of leaves covered with sticky reddish gland-tipped hairs, used to trap insects. The cup-shaped flowers are usually borne in a group on a stalk 2.4–14 in (6–35 cm) long and are white, red, or purple. The fruit is a capsule. Family: *Droseraceae*.

sundial An instrument that indicates the time by the direction or length of the shadow cast by an indicator (gnomon) mounted on a calibrated hour scale. Sundials may be fixed (mounted perpendicularly or horizontally) or portable (in which case they incorporate a device for direction finding) and come in a wide range of shapes. Known from ancient Egypt, Greece, and Rome, sundials reached the peak of their popularity between about 1500 and 1800, being used as a check on the accuracy of mechanical *clocks, which eventually superseded them.

Sundsvall 62 22N 17 20E A port in E Sweden, on the Gulf of Bothnia. It is icebound in winter. Industries include timber processing and timber and wood pulp are the main exports. Population (1978 est): 94,742.

sunfish An omnivorous fish of the family *Molidae*, especially *Mola mola*, found in all tropical and temperate seas. It has a disk-shaped laterally flattened body, up to 10 ft (3 m) long, with the tail fin reduced to a wavy frill attached to the triangular dorsal and anal fins. Order: *Tetraodontiformes*.

The name is also applied to several carnivorous freshwater food and game fish of the North American family *Centrarchidae*. They have deep laterally flattened bodies, 1–32 in (2.5–80 cm) long, and a single long dorsal fin. Order: *Perciformes*.

sunflower A herbaceous plant of the genus *Helianthus*, native to North and South America but widely cultivated for its showy flowers. A popular annual sunflower is the giant *H. annuus*, about 10 ft (3 m) high with rough hairy leaves and yellow flower heads, up to 14 in (35 cm) in diameter. It is cultivated both for ornament and for its seeds, from which oil is obtained. Perennial sunflowers include *H. salicifolius* and *H. decapetalus*. Family: *Compositae*.

Sung. *See* Song.

Sungari River. *See* Songhua River.

sunn An annual herb, *Crotalaria juncea*, cultivated in India for its stem fibers—called sunn hemp or sann hemp. It grows to a height of 7–10 ft (2–3 m) and produces small yellow flowers that give rise to seed pods, at which stage the crop is cut. The fibers, comparable in strength to true *hemp, are used for netting, canvas, yarns, and in certain paper products. Family: *Leguminosae*.

Sunnites (*or* Sunni; Arabic *sunna*: custom)   The name of the larger of the two main Muslim sects. In contrast to the *Shiite Muslims, the Sunnites accept the first three caliphs as Mohammed's legitimate successors. They are strictly orthodox in their obedience to the Koran and in the emphasis they place on following the deeds and utterances of the Prophet. They form the majority party in most Islamic countries except Iran.

Sunnyvale   37 23N 122 01W A city in W central California, SE of San Francisco. Settled in 1849, the aeronautic, aerospace, and electronic industries are important to the economy. Other industries include chemicals and food processing. Population (1980): 106,618.

sun spider   A large *arachnid (0.4–2 in [10–50 mm] long), also called sun scorpion, belonging to an order (*Solpugida* or *Solifugae*; 800 species) found in tropical and semitropical deserts. It has a hairy spider-like body, usually golden in color, and a large powerful pair of pincers. Sun spiders are voracious carnivores, the larger species even killing small vertebrates.

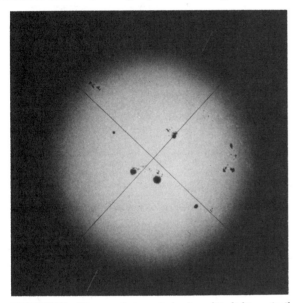

SUNSPOTS   *The sun photographed using white light on April 9, 1970.*

sunspots   Comparatively dark markings on the sun's *photosphere, typically a few thousand kilometers across with the central region being darkest and coolest. They tend to occur in groups. They are centers of intense localized magnetic fields, the majority forming and disappearing within two weeks. The number of sunspots seen in a year, and their mean solar latitude, varies in a cycle of about 11 years, known as the **sunspot cycle**.

sunstroke   A form of *heatstroke caused by overexposure to the sun. **Sunburn** is damage to the skin resulting from overexposure to the sun's rays. This may vary from slight reddening to large painful blisters: fair-skinned people are more susceptible to sunburn due to lack of the protective pigment melanin in the surface layers of the skin. The burn is treated with soothing creams.

Sun Yat-sen   (*or* Sun Zhong Shan; 1866–1925) Chinese revolutionary. He qualified as a doctor but abandoned a medical career to pursue his political interests. After an abortive attempt to overthrow the Qing dynasty in 1895, he lived in exile and, while in Britain, was briefly imprisoned in the Chinese legation (1896). After establishing various revolutionary groups in Europe, he founded the Alliance Society in Japan (1905). Following the 1911 Chinese Revolution he returned to China, became president of the new republic but resigned almost immediately in favor of *Yuan Shi Kai. In 1913 Sun led an unsuccessful revolt against Yuan's dictatorial government and again left China. He returned after Yuan's death (1916) and in 1923 became president of a government based at Canton. Coming under Soviet influence he reorganized the *Guomindang (Nationalist People's Party), cooperated with the communists, and elaborated his political thought, which was based on Three Principles of the People—nationalism, democracy, and social reform. He remains a hero of both the Nationalist and communist Chinese governments.

superconductivity   A phenomenon in which the electrical resistance of certain metals (e.g. tin, zinc, and aluminum) vanishes when they are cooled to within a few degrees of *absolute zero. The temperature at which superconductivity occurs is called the transition temperature and varies for different metals. If a loop of a superconducting metal is placed in a weak magnetic field and cooled to below its transition temperature, a current will flow through the loop even when the field is removed. Known as the Meissner effect, this phenomenon is used to produce superconducting magnets.

supercooling   The reduction in the temperature of a liquid below its freezing point without its solidification. The effect can only be achieved by slow and continuous cooling with pure liquids, since the presence of any solid matter would cause the liquid to solidify around it. A supercooled liquid is in a metastable state and any disturbance will cause solidification.

superego   In *psychoanalysis, the part of the mind that acts as a moral conscience. It was believed by *Freud to result from the incorporation of the parent's instructions into a child's mind. *See also* ego; id.

superfluid   A fluid that exhibits a very high thermal conductivity and virtually no friction at temperatures close to absolute zero. Such a fluid will flow up the sides and out of an open container. Liquid helium becomes a superfluid at 2.19 kelvins, called the lambda point.

supergiant   The largest and most luminous type of star, bright enough to be visible in nearby galaxies. They are very rare. *Rigel, *Betelgeuse, and *Antares are examples.

superheated steam   Dry steam that has been heated to a temperature above 212°F (100°C). It is widely used as a working medium for converting heat into mechanical energy, for which purpose it is more efficient than normal steam.

superheterodyne   A system widely used in radio receivers; the incoming radio-frequency signal is combined with a locally generated carrier wave to give an intermediate frequency between radio- and audio-frequency (*see* modulation). The intermediate frequency is easier to amplify than radio-frequency, giving less noisy reception and better tuning.

Superior, Lake   The largest of the Great Lakes in North America and one of the largest freshwater lakes in the world, situated between the US and Canada. Its surrounding areas have valuable mineral resources and the lake is important for shipping (especially iron ore and grain). Area: 31,800 sq mi (82,362 sq km).

supernova   A cataclysmic stellar explosion, seen as a sudden increase in a *star's brightness by a million times or more. It results from uncontrolled nuclear reactions in certain massive stars, late in their evolution. Most or all of the star's substance is blown off at high velocity, forming an expanding gas shell—the **supernova remnant**. If the star's core survives, it will most probably end up as a *neutron star or *black hole. *See also* Crab nebula.

superphosphates   Highly active phosphorus-containing fertilizers. Single superphosphate is made by reacting sulfuric acid with insoluble calcium phosphate rock to form calcium sulfate and soluble calcium hydrogen phosphate $Ca(H_2PO_4)_2$. Often the process is carried out under pressure. The product also contains sulfates of impurities present in the calcium phosphate. Triple superphosphate is more concentrated, since phosphoric acid is used instead of sulfuric, thereby creating fewer by-products.

Suppiluliumas I   King of the *Hittites (c. 1375–c. 1335 BC); founder of the Hittite empire. He subdued the Mitanni kingdom and conquered N Syria, displacing the Egyptians, then ruled by Akhenaton (*see also* Ankhesenamen). Suppiluliumas rebuilt the Hittite capital Hattusas (*see* Boğazköy).

supply and demand   Two concepts fundamental to economics. Supply is the amount of a commodity that producers are willing and able to sell, while demand is that amount that consumers wish to and are able to buy. These amounts vary with price: as the price rises, producers wish to sell more, while consumers wish to buy less, and vice versa as the price goes down. There is one price (the equilibrium price) at which producers wish to sell the same amount as consumers wish to buy (i.e. the market clears). The **market forces** of supply and demand in a free economy thus control the market price. However, they are almost completely suppressed in communist economies and in *mixed economies they may have only a restricted effect, depending on the extent to which government policy influences supply, demand, or price.

suprematism   An abstract Russian art movement founded (c. 1913) by the painter *Malevich. It was the first and one of the most austere geometrical styles of the 20th century. Although Malevich declared in 1919 that suprematism was over, it continued to be influential in the 1920s, particularly at the *Bauhaus (*see also* Kandinsky).

Supreme Court of the United States   The highest judicial body in the US, consisting of a chief justice and eight associate justices, each of whom is appointed by the president for life. The Supreme Court, as one of the three autonomous branches of the federal government, is empowered to review the constitutionality of federal and state legislation with regard to individual rights and court procedures. The Supreme Court itself was authorized by Article III of the US *Constitution, but its organization and procedures were first established by the Judiciary Act of 1789. The nine-member composition of the court has remained constant since 1869. Although the Supreme Court's function in the early history of the United States was unclear, it became an important force for expansion of federal power during the term of Chief Justice John *Marshall (see Marbury v. Madison, Dartmouth College v. Woodward, and McCulloch v. Maryland). In the years before the Civil War, the court upheld the institution of slavery (see Dred Scott v. Sanford) and at the end of the 19th century, it upheld the practice of racial segregation (see Plessy v. Ferguson), but beginning in the 1950s it reversed its earlier position and became a protector of the civil rights of minority groups (see Brown v. Board of Education) and of defendants in criminal proceedings (see Gideon v. Wainwright and Miranda v. Arizona). Many of the liberal rulings of the court under Chief Justice Earl *Warren were later restricted by the justices of the more conservative court headed by Chief Justice Warren *Burger. Throughout its entire history, the Supreme Court was composed of male justices, but in 1981 President Ronald Reagan broke that precedent by appointing Sandra Day *O'Connor to become the first woman justice on the Supreme Court.

Sur. *See* Tyre.

Surabaja 7 14S 112 45E A port in Indonesia, in E Java on the Mas estuary. It was bombed by the British in 1945 during the struggle for the Indonesian Republic. It is Indonesia's second largest city and chief naval base, with a naval college and university (1954). Its industries include shipbuilding, oil refining, and rubber processing. Population (1971): 1,556,285.

Surakarta (*or* Solo) 7 32S 110 50E A city in Indonesia, in central Java on the Solo River. A cultural center noted for its shadow plays, it is the site of a sultan's palace (1745). Batiks, musical instruments, and gold objects are produced. Population (1971): 414,285.

Surat 21 10N 72 54E A city in India, in Gujarat on the Tapti River. It was the Mogul Empire's chief port (16th–17th centuries). The first British trading post was established here (1612) and it was the headquarters of the East India Company until 1687. It has textile industries. Population (1971): 471,656.

surface tension A force occurring on the surface of a liquid that makes it behave as if the surface has an elastic skin. It is caused by forces between the molecules of the liquid: only those at the surface experience forces from below, whereas those in the interior are acted on by intermolecular forces from all sides. Surface tension causes a meniscus to form, liquids to rise up capillary tubes, paper to absorb water, and droplets and bubbles to form. It is defined as the force acting tangentially to the surface on one side of a line of unit length (newtons per meter) or as the work required to produce unit increase in surface area (joules per square meter).

surfactant A substance that lowers the surface tension of a liquid, thus allowing easier penetration and spreading. For this reason they are often known as **wetting agents**. Surfactants active in water are usually organic substances, for example *alcohols and *soaps, the molecules of which contain both a water-soluble and a water-repelling portion; it is the latter that forces the molecules to the surface. Surfactants are widely used in *detergents, emulsifiers, paints, adhesives, inks, etc.

surgeonfish A tropical marine fish, also called tang, belonging to the family *Acanthuridae* (about 100 species). Its deep laterally flattened body, up to about 20 in (50 cm) long, is often brightly colored, with a single long dorsal fin, and a sharp bladelike spine on each side of the tail. They feed mainly on algae. Order: *Perciformes*.

surgery The branch of medicine in which disorders and injuries are treated by operation, usually with the patient in a state of *anesthesia. Amputations and some elementary surgical operations have been performed since ancient times in Egypt, Greece, India, and China; the skills required were transmitted by Arab surgeons to Europe, where they were mostly practiced in monasteries. Blood-letting—regarded as an antidote for most ailments—was widely practiced.

The 19th century saw the foundation of modern surgery, with the introduction of anesthetics, *Lister's discovery of antisepsis, and a greater knowledge of anatomy and physiology. In the 20th century the advent of antibiotics has made surgery safe from infection, the use of blood transfusions, intravenous drips, and electrolyte control have overcome problems of shock, and better knowledge of anesthetics and relaxant drugs has made surgery a less hurried procedure. Moreover, specialization (e.g. gastrointes-

tinal surgery, neurosurgery, ophthalmological surgery) and great ingenuity in the design of surgical instruments have made surgery a safe and usually successful procedure.

Recent advances include techniques in *transplantation surgery, operations on the exposed heart, the use of extreme cold to destroy tissues (cryosurgery), the use of *lasers and *ultrasonics, and the development of microsurgery, in which surgeons operate through a special microscope using miniaturized instruments. *See also* plastic surgery.

Suriname, Republic of (name until 1948: Dutch Guiana) A country on the N coast of South America, on the Atlantic Ocean. Much of the land is covered by tropical forest, with coastal plains rising to higher land in the interior. The majority of the population is of Indian and mixed descent, with minorities of African descent, East Indians, and others. *Economy*: based primarily on bauxite, the chief industry is aluminum processing, and bauxite, alumina, and aluminum comprise the main exports. Its great agricultural potential remains relatively underdeveloped, the rice industry being the only fully developed sector. The vast forests are largely unexploited. Fishing is important, especially for shrimps. Hydroelectricity is a valuable source of power. *History*: sighted by Columbus in 1498, the first permanent settlement was established by the English in 1650. It was ceded to the Netherlands in 1667. During the Revolutionary and Napoleonic Wars it was again (1799–1802, 1804–16) under British rule. In 1949 it gained a certain measure of self-government, subsequently becoming an autonomous part of the Netherlands (1954) and then an independent republic (1975). At independence some 40,000 Surinamers emigrated to the Netherlands, to the detriment of Suriname's economy. Following a coup in 1980, the National Military Council took power with Dr Hendrick R. Chin A Sen as prime minister and later president. His government resigned in 1982. The National Military Council then announced a new administration and succeeded in maintaining power. Relations between Suriname and Netherlands were virtually suspended. Official language: Dutch; English, Hindustani, and Javanese are widely spoken and the local vernacular, Surinamese, is used as a lingua franca. Official currency: Suriname guilder of 100 cents. Area: 63,020 sq mi (163,265 sq km). Population (1983): 353,000. Capital and main port: Paramaribo.

Surratt, Mary Eugenia (1820–65) US co-conspirator in the assassination plot against President Abraham *Lincoln. She owned a boarding house in Washington, DC, where it is thought assassination plans, of which her son was a part, were discussed. Because of this association, she was tried and found guilty by a civil jury; she was hanged in 1865.

surrealism A European movement in art and literature of the 1920s and 1930s. Surrealism began as a literary movement, when its leader, the poet André *Breton, published the surrealist manifesto in Paris (1924). Unlike its predecessor, the *dada movement, surrealism was not anti-art. Instead it aimed, under the influence of *Freud, to embody in art and poetry the irrational forces of dreams and the subconscious mind. To achieve this, such new techniques as automatic drawing and writing were employed. These involved allowing the subconscious mind to guide the pencil or the thoughts to produce an unpremeditated design or poem. The leading surrealists were the poets *Aragon and *Eluard and the painters *Ernst, *Miró, *Dali, *Magritte, *Delvaux, and *Tanguy.

Surrey A county in SE England, bordering on Greater London. It is mainly low lying with the North Downs running E–W across the middle of the county. Although it has developed primarily as a residential and recreational area, agriculture is important in the S. Industry is mainly concentrated in the NE. Area: 639 sq mi (1655 sq km). Population (1981): 999,393. Administrative center: Kingston-upon-Thames.

Surtsey 63 18N 20 37W An island in the N Atlantic Ocean off S Iceland. It was formed by an underwater volcanic eruption (1963). Many scientific studies have been made here, especially of the colonization of flora and fauna.

surveying The measurement of distances, levels, angles, etc., on, above, or below the earth's surface. It is necessary for the delineation of property lines (**boundary surveying**) and for planning the construction of almost any building or structure. **Plane surveying** is suitable for smaller areas as it neglects the earth's curvature, whereas **geodetic surveying** does not. Topographic surveys locate natural features and elevations for map making, dam planning, etc.

Surya In Hindu mythology, the sun-god. He appears as a major deity in the *Vedas and remained prominent as patron of numerous Hindu royal dynasties. Like his Greek counterpart *Apollo, he is represented as a charioteer.

Susa (*or* Shushan) An ancient city in SW Iran. Occupied since the 4th millennium BC, it was a capital of *Elam, whose rulers made successful forays against *Ur and *Babylon during the 2nd millennium. Susa's heyday was as administrative capital of the *Achaemenian kings of Persia (521–331). It continued to be important under Seleucid, Parthian, and Sassanian rule.

Suslov, Mikhail (1902–82) Soviet politician. A Communist Party member from 1921, Suslov rose in the Party hierarchy during the 1930s and 1940s. He fought all deviation from Soviet policy, especially that of Yugoslavia in 1948. In 1964 he helped to oust *Khrushchev.

Susquehanna River A river in the E US. It rises in Otsego Lake in central New York State and flows mainly S through Pennsylvania before entering Chesapeake Bay. It caused serious flooding in 1972 to several cities, especially *Harrisburg. Length: 444 mi (715 km).

Sutherland, Graham Vivian (1903–80) British artist. After working primarily as an etcher and engraver he turned to painting in 1935, specializing in disturbing landscapes, usually magnifying insect and plant forms, and scenes of desolation. Also well known are his *Crucifixion* (1946), his tapestry for Coventry Cathedral, and his portraits, e.g. that of Somerset Maugham and his controversial portrait of Winston Churchill.

Sutherland, Joan (1926–) Australian operatic soprano. She established her reputation at Covent Garden in 1959 in the title role of Donizetti's *Lucia di Lammermoor*. She specializes in coloratura roles.

Sutlej River A river in India and Pakistan, the longest of the five rivers of the Punjab. Rising in SW Tibet, it flows mainly SW across the Punjab plain into Pakistan, where it joins the Chenab River. It is an important source of irrigation and hydroelectric power. Length: 850 mi (1368 km).

suttee An ancient Hindu custom of self-immolation of widows on their husbands' funeral pyres. It was officially abolished in India by the British in 1829.

Sutter, Johann Augustus (1803–80) US pioneer; born in Germany. He came to the US in 1834 and traveled westward, finally settling in California (1839). Here, he became a Mexican citizen and established Sutter's Fort. Gold, discovered on his land shortly before California became part of the US, precipitated the Gold Rush of 1848, and Sutter, unable legally to keep the squatters from his land, was financially ruined.

Sutton, Walter Stanborough (1877–1916) US geneticist, who linked observations of chromosome behavior during cell division with *Mendel's observations of inheritance of physical characteristics. Sutton postulated that chromosomes carried the units of inheritance (genes) and that their behavior during sex cell formation (meiosis) explained some of Mendel's findings.

Sutton Coldfield 52 34N 1 48W A city in England, in West Midlands, a mainly residential suburb of Birmingham. It contains Sutton Park, a large area of woodland, lakes, and heathland. Population (1981): 86,494.

SUTTON HOO *A large inlaid gold buckle found in the burial ship.*

Sutton Hoo The site of a Saxon ship burial near Woodbridge, in Suffolk (E England). Excavations in 1939 revealed the remnants of a 38-oar boat containing a magnificent treasure hoard: gilt bronze helmet, sword decorated with gold and garnets, royal scepter, silver dishes, drinking vessels, and jewelry. The mound is thought to be a cenotaph (as it contained no body) to King Raedwald (died c. 625 AD).

Suva 18 08S 178 25E The capital of Fiji, on the S coast of Viti Levu. Its industries include tourism and the production of coconut oil and soap. The University of the South Pacific was established here in 1968. Population (1979 est): 66,018.

Suvorov, Aleksandr Vasilievich, Count (1729–1800) Russian field marshal. Following outstanding victories against the French revolutionary armies in Italy (1799), the defeat of a Russian force at Zurich forced his withdrawal. The winter retreat, achieved against desperate odds, assured Suvorov's reputation as a brilliant tactician.

Suwanee River (*or* Swanee R.) A river in the SE US, flowing from the Okefenokee Swamp in SE Georgia across Florida to the Gulf of Mexico. It is the Swanee River of the well-known song by Stephen Foster. Length: 200 mi (400 km).

Suzhou (Su-chou *or* Soochow) 31 21N 120 40E A city in E China, in Jiangsu province on the Yangtze delta and the *Grand Canal. Famed for its many beautiful canals and gardens, it is a center of culture and handicrafts. Founded in about 484 BC, it prospered, especially between the 14th and 19th centuries, as a result of its silk industry. The chief industry is still textiles. Population (1957 est): 633,000.

Svalbard (*or* Spitsbergen) A Norwegian archipelago in the Arctic Ocean, the chief islands being Spitsbergen (formerly Vestspitsbergen), Edgeøya, Nordaustlandet, Barentsøya, and Prins Karls Forland. Following disputes over their sovereignty, they were granted to Norway in 1920. Mountainous and covered largely by icefields and glaciers their major importance is as a source of coal; other minerals include asbestos and copper. Area: 23,958 sq mi (62,050 sq km). Population (1976 est): 3495. Chief town: Longyearbyen.

Sverdlovsk (name until 1924: Ekaterinburg) 56 52N 60 35E A city in the Soviet Union, in the NW RSFSR. Nicholas II and his family were executed here in 1918. It is a major industrial and cultural center, with engineering, metallurgical, and chemical industries and many educational institutions. Population: (1981 est): 1,239,000.

Sverrir (*or* Sigurdsson; c. 1149–1202) King of Norway (1177–1202). He claimed the throne after being informed by his mother that he was the son of a former king, but did not defeat his predecessor, Magnus V (1156–84; reigned 1162–84), until 1184. His story is told in the Icelandic *Sverris Saga*.

Svevo, Italo (Ettore Schmitz; 1861–1928) Italian novelist. His first two novels, *A Life* (1892) and *As a Man Grows Older* (1898), were unsuccessful, but he was encouraged by James *Joyce, who taught him English in Trieste in 1907 and later publicized his work. His best-known novel is *Confessions of Zeno* (1923), a portrait of an introspective ineffectual hero.

Swabia (German name: Schwaben) A former region in SW Germany now divided between Germany, Switzerland, and France. Swabia became one of the leading German duchies in the middle ages, passing in 1079 to the *Hohenstaufen. When the dynasty died out in 1268 Swabia was divided among local noble families. A series of Swabian leagues culminated in that of 1488–1534, which foundered on religious differences during the Reformation. When Napoleon reconstructed European boundaries in 1807, Swabia was finally partitioned among neighboring states; its distinguishing dialect still survives.

Swahili (*or* Kiswahili) A Bantu language of East Africa and the lingua franca of Tanzania, Kenya, Zaïre, and Uganda. There are three main dialects but standard Swahili is based on the Zanzibari form known as Kiunguja. It has been much influenced by Arabic.

swallow A songbird belonging to a cosmopolitan family (*Hirundidae*; 78 species) of acrobatic fliers that catch insects on the wing. Swallows are 4–9 in (10–22 cm) long, with short necks, long pointed wings, short legs, and often forked tails. All temperate swallows migrate to hot climates for the winter. The barn swallow (*Hirundo rustica*) visits Europe and North America in summer and has a glossy blue-black upper plumage with a red forehead and throat, a blue breast band, and white underparts. *See also* martin.

swallowtail butterfly A *papilionid butterfly having long swallow-like tails on the hindwings. Many species are tropical and brightly colored, with the sexes often of different colors. The caterpillars feed on a variety of plants and possess scent organs behind the head, giving off a strong odor if the caterpillar is disturbed. □insect.

Swammerdam, Jan (1637–80) Dutch naturalist and microscopist, who first observed red blood cells. However, much of Swammerdam's work was concerned with collecting and studying insects, describing their anatomy and life histories, and classifying them into four groups, three of which are still embodied in modern classification systems. He discovered the Swammerdam valves in lymphatic vessels and established that muscles do not change in volume during contraction.

swamp An area of permanently water-saturated land, usually covered with such vegetation as reeds or mangroves. It is an intermediate stage between an entirely aquatic environment and a temporarily saturated marsh. Once drained, swamps produce fertile soils as a result of their high humus content.

swamp cypress A deciduous conifer, *Taxodium distichum*, also called bald cypress, native to swampy regions of the SE US and grown for its timber and as an ornamental. In waterlogged soils its roots produce domed "knees," which protrude above the water and probably help in respiration. Up to 150 ft (45 m) high, it has soft needles arranged in two rows and globular cones, 1 in (2.5 cm) across and brown when ripe. Family: *Taxodiaceae*.

swamp eel A slim eel-like bony fish of the order *Synbranchiformes*, unrelated to true eels and found in fresh and brackish tropical waters. 8–20 in (20–50 cm) long, they have no pectoral fins and the gills often have only one opening. Oxygen is sometimes absorbed through the throat or intestine. Swamp eels are used for food in Asia.

swan A large waterbird belonging to a genus (*Cygnus*; 7–8 species) occurring worldwide on fresh waters or sheltered coasts and estuaries. 40–63 in (100–160 cm) long, swans are usually white with black legs and have large feet, a long neck, and a powerful spatulate bill, which they use to feed on underwater plants. Immature swans have a mottled brown plumage until about two years old. *See also* black swan; mute swan; trumpeter. Family: *Anatidae* (ducks, geese, swans).

Swanscombe skull Fossil cranial remains of a *hominid, fragments of which were found at Swanscombe in Kent (England) in River Thames gravels (1935, 1936). It seems to be an early example of *Homo sapiens* dating from about 200,000 years ago. *See* Homo.

Swansea (Welsh name: Abertawe) 51 38N 3 57W A city and port in South Wales, on Swansea Bay. It is a major industrial center with tinplate manufacturing, chemicals, and oil refining. The main exports are coal and coke, steel rails, iron work, tinplate, and oil. Swansea University opened in 1920. Population (1981): 167,796.

swastika An ancient symbol of uncertain origin, generally held to signify prosperity and creativity. It is a cross, the four arms of which are deflected at right angles either clockwise or anticlockwise. It has been revered by Buddhists, Hindus, Celts, and North American Indians. The Nazis adopted the symbol, mistakenly believing it to be of pure Aryan origins.

Swatow. *See* Shantou.

Swazi A Bantu-speaking people who occupy Swaziland and adjacent areas of the E Transvaal (South Africa). They are an agricultural and pastoral people, traditionally ruled by a hereditary paramount chief together with his mother. Descent, inheritance, and group membership are patrilineal. Polygyny is practiced by senior men, the chief taking many wives who are dispersed in a number of royal villages throughout the territory. *Age-set organization was the basis of military service. Traditionally *ancestor worship, witchcraft, and magic were features of religious life.

Swaziland, Kingdom of A small country in SE Africa between South Africa and Mozambique. It consists of three distinct regions extending N–S: the Highveld in the W, the Middleveld in the center, and the Lowveld in the E (*see* veld). *Economy*: chiefly agricultural, the main food crop being maize. The chief cash crop is sugar; other crops include rice, citrus fruit, and cotton, and livestock raising is also important. Rich mineral resources include iron ore, asbestos, and coal, and hydroelectric plants provide irrigation as well as power. Exports include sugar, wood pulp, and asbestos. *History*: the *Swazi occupied the area in the late 18th century. It became a South African protectorate in 1894 and, in 1902, after the Boer War it came under British rule. It attained internal self-government in 1967 and became an independent kingdom within the British Commonwealth in 1968. In 1973, King Sobhuza II increased his personal power and, in the new constitution (1978), political parties were banned. With the death of Sobhuza II in 1982, a power struggle erupted within the royal family; Prince Bhekimpi Diamini emerged as head of state. Subsequently controversy arose over South Africa's offer to turn over two black homelands to Swaziland. Conservative elements in Swaziland backed South Africa and cooperated with counterinsurgency efforts against the African National Congress, a guerrilla force that sought the overthrow of the South African government. Official languages: Siswati and English. Official currency, since 1974: emalangeni of 100 lilangeni; South African currency is also legal tender. Area: 6705 sq mi (17,400 sq km). Population (1983 est): 632,000. Capital: Mbabane; Lomamba is the royal and projected legislative capital.

sweat (*or* perspiration) A watery fluid, consisting mainly of sodium chloride and urea in solution, that is secreted by the sweat glands in the skin. Sweating is a means of excreting nitrogenous waste products, but it is also, and more importantly, a means of temperature regulation. Evaporation of sweat from the skin surface has a cooling effect; therefore in hot weather, or when the individual feels hot through exercise, more sweat is produced. Sweating is also increased by nervousness and nausea; it is decreased by colds.

sweating sickness An illness that devastated Renaissance Europe in several epidemics. It was characterized by copious sweating, high fever,

pains in the extremities and over the heart, and breathlessness and was often fatal. It may have been a severe form of *influenza.

swede. *See* rutabaga.

Sweden, Kingdom of (Swedish name: Sverige) A country in N Europe occupying the E part of the Scandinavian peninsula. It borders on the Gulf of Bothnia and the Baltic Sea in the E and S and on the Kattegat and Skagerrak in the SW. Undulating land in the S rises to mountains in the N. There are numerous lakes and approximately half the country is forested. *Economy*: rich in mineral resources, notably iron ore, which forms the basis of the country's heavy industry (metalworking, steel, machinery, and chemicals) and is a major export. Other minerals include copper and zinc. 70% of power comes from hydroelectric sources. The large forests support important pulp and paper industries as well as shipbuilding. There is a thriving fishing industry. Agricultural activities are concentrated in the S, the principal crops being barley, wheat, oats, and potatoes, although there is some livestock raising in the N. *History*: the area was inhabited from early times by German tribes, the Swedes in the N and the Goths in the S, and its people participated in the exploits of the Vikings. Christianity was introduced in the 9th century but not established until the 12th century. Finland was acquired in the 13th century and the 14th century witnessed the Kalmar Union of Sweden with Denmark and Norway. Independence was achieved in 1523 under Gustavus I Vasa, during whose reign Lutheranism was introduced, and in the 17th century, under Gustavus Adolphus, Sweden emerged from the *Thirty Years' War as a major European power, a position undermined by the Great *Northern War (1700–21). In 1809, during the Napoleonic Wars, Finland was surrendered to Russia. In 1814 Norway was ceded to Sweden, the two countries remaining united until 1905, and in 1818, with the extinction of the *Vasa dynasty, a Frenchman, *Bernadotte, became Charles XIV John. Sweden remained neutral in both World Wars, and for four decades (1932–76) was governed by the Social Democrats, during which time a highly developed welfare state was developed. On the accession of Carl XVI Gustaf in 1975 a new constitution considerably reduced the power of the monarchy. In 1976 a center-right government led by Thorbjörn Fälldin came to power. This resigned in 1978 but Fälldin was returned as prime minister in 1979. The Social Democrats led by Olof Palme were returned to power in the 1982 elections. Official language: Swedish. Official currency: krona of 100 oere. Area: 158,830 sq mi (411,479 sq km). Population (1983 est): 8,331,000. Capital and main port: Stockholm.

Swedenborg, Emanuel (1688–1772) Swedish scientist, mystic, and philosopher. He did pioneering scientific work in such fields as magnetic theory and crystallography but later became more concerned to show by scientific and logical analysis that the universe was of spiritual origin. After 1743 his ideas became more mystically orientated in accordance with the visions that he claimed to have had. His work includes *Arcana Coelestia* (1756), *The New Jerusalem and Its Heavenly Doctrine* (1758), and *Divine Love and Wisdom* (1763). The sect calling itself the New Jerusalem Church was founded by his followers in London in 1787.

Swedish A language belonging to the *Scandinavian branch of the North *Germanic group. It is the official language of Sweden and is spoken by a minority of the population of Finland, where it is also officially recognized. The standard literary form is based mainly on the dialect of Stockholm known as Svea.

sweet briar A stiffly branched prickly fragrant *rose, *Rosa rubiginosa* (or *R. eglanteria*), also called eglantine. Found in scrub and chalk grassland across the N hemisphere, it grows to a height of 7 ft (2 m) and has bright-pink flowers.

sweet corn. *See* maize.

sweet gale A widely distributed shrub, *Myrica gale*, also called bog myrtle, that grows to a height of 24–100 in (60–250 cm) in bogs and wet heaths. It produces reddish-brown catkins and the leaves yield an aromatic resin used in medicines. Family: *Myricaceae*.

sweet gum A tree, *Liquidambar styraciflua*, native to E North America. Up to 150 ft (45 m) high, it has triangular-lobed leaves, small greenish flowers, and spiky fruits and yields a useful timber (satin walnut). The oriental sweet gum (*L. orientalis*), of SW Asia, is the chief source of *storax, a fragrant balsam. Family: *Hamamelidaceae*.

sweet pea An annual climbing herb, *Lathyrus odoratus*, native to Sicily and widely cultivated as a garden ornamental. The scented flower consists of a large petal (the standard) with two lateral wing petals and a front keel petal. Many color varieties have been developed, including shades of red, purple, blue, white, and yellow. The fruit is a hairy pod, about 2 in (5 cm) long. Family: *Leguminosae*.

sweet potato An annual herb, *Ipomoea batatas*, native to tropical America and widely cultivated for its starchy edible tubers (swollen roots), which are reddish-brown with white or orange flesh. The trailing stems bear pinkish flowers and, after a growing season of 4–5 months, the tubers are lifted and cooked like potatoes or yams. Family: *Convolvulaceae*.

sweetsop A small tree, *Annona squamosa*, also called sugar apple, native to tropical America and cultivated for its yellowish-green edible fruits. The yellow flesh is soft and sweet and makes a tasty dessert. Family: *Annonaceae*.

sweet william A usually biennial herb, *Dianthus barbatus*, native to S Europe and widely cultivated as a garden ornamental. Growing to a height of 12–27.5 in (30–70 cm), sweet williams produce dense flower heads, colored red or pink in the wild but of various shades and patterns in cultivated varieties. Family: *Caryophyllaceae*.

Sweyn I Forkbeard (d. 1014) King of Denmark (c. 986–1014). After conquering Norway in 1000, Sweyn's regular raids on SE England to avenge Ethelred's massacre of Danes in 1002 culminated in an invasion in the course of which he died. He was the father of *Canute II.

swift A bird belonging to a widely distributed family (*Apodidae*; 75 species). 3.5–9 in (9–23 cm) long, swifts have gray or brown plumage with white markings; a wide slightly curved bill, and forked tail. With scimitar-shaped wings and a high-speed flight that may reach nearly 70 mph (110 kph), they spend much of their time flying, capturing insects and even mating and sleeping on the wing. Order: *Apodiformes* (swifts, hummingbirds, etc.).

Swift, Jonathan (1667–1745) Anglo-Irish clergyman, poet, and satirist. Born in Dublin, he became an Anglican priest in 1695. In England he met Hester Johnson (1681–1728), the "Stella" of his letters recounting his life in London and later collected as *Journal to Stella* (1710–13). He was also close to Esther Vanhomrigh (1690–1723), whom he called "Vanessa" in his writings. While in England, he wrote the satire *A Tale of a Tub* (1704). He became the leading Tory political journalist and was appointed dean of St Patrick's, Dublin, in 1713. After the accession of George I in 1714, he returned to Dublin, where he wrote his satirical masterpiece, *Gulliver's Travels* (1726), the story of an imaginary voyage.

Swift and Company v. United States (1905) US Supreme Court decision that upheld the *Sherman Anti-Trust Act. Meat-packing companies, accused of creating a monopoly by price fixing and restraining sales, claimed exemption from anti-trust laws because these practices occurred within one state, not interstate. The Court ruled that the implications reached far outside the boundaries of one state, and, therefore, laws regulating interstate commerce applied.

swiftlet A small *swift belonging to a genus (*Collocalia*; 15–20 species) occurring in SE Asia and Australia. 3.5–6 in (9–15 cm) long, swiftlets use echolocation to navigate in the caves where they nest; their nests, made chiefly of saliva, are the main ingredient of bird's nest soup.

swift moth A moth belonging to the widely distributed family *Hepialidae* (about 300 species), also called ghost moth. The adults lack a proboscis and are unable to feed. The caterpillars feed under ground on roots and the pupae are soft-skinned and active, moving to the surface before the adults emerge.

swimming Moving through water by means of leg and arm strokes, popular for recreation and sport. Major competitive events, held in pools 55 yd (50 m) long, include freestyle races (the crawl—invented in Australia—is invariably used) over 100, 200, 400, 800, and 1500 m and the 4 × 100 m and 4 × 200 m relay; breaststroke, butterfly, and backstroke races over 100 and 200 m; and medley races over 200 and 400 m and 4 × 100 m relay. The most popular marathon swim is across the English Channel (first swum in 1875).

Swinburne, Algernon Charles (1837–1909) British poet. His poetry, especially in the first volume of *Poems and Ballads* (1866), is characterized by sensuous flowing rhythms and imagery. He supported republican movements in Europe and rebelled against conventional British morality. His alcoholism led to the collapse of his health, and from 1879 he was cared for by his friend, the critic Theodore Watts-Dunton (1832–1914).

Swindon 51 34N 1 47W A city in S England, in Wiltshire. It developed around the workshops of the former Great Western Railroad and has a railroad museum. Population (1981): 91,136.

swine fever An infectious virus disease of pigs also known as hog cholera. In young pigs the disease is usually acute, with fever, loss of appetite, lethargy, diarrhea, and distressed breathing, resulting in death. In older pigs the symptoms are less noticeable. Animals are treated with antibiotics to combat secondary infection.

swing A style of *jazz popular in the 1930s. The original jazz band was expanded to include the saxophone and additional cornets and trombones, making an average swing band of 15 players. Colorful orchestrations replaced the improvisational qualities of early jazz, and the swing bands of Benny Goodman, Duke Ellington, and Glenn Miller functioned chiefly as dance bands.

switch grass A perennial pasture *grass, *Panicum virgatum*, which is a major component of the North American prairie flora. It forms clumps, 40–80 in (1–2 m) tall, and is sometimes used to control erosion because of its penetrating underground stems.

Swithin, St (d. 862) English churchman. A counselor to Kings Egbert and Ethelwulf, he was appointed Bishop of Winchester in 852. His tomb in Winchester Cathedral has become a famous shrine and according to legend the weather conditions on his feast day, July 15, continue for 40 days.

Switzerland, Confederation of (French name: Suisse; German name: Schweiz; Italian name: Svizzera) A small landlocked country in central Europe. Undulating land in the N rises to the Jura Mountains in the W and the high peaks of the Alps in the S, reaching heights of over 14,500 ft (4500 m). The Rhine River and Lake Constance form most of the N and E boundaries, while in the S the Rhône River flows through Lake Geneva to the French border. The majority of the population is German, with large French and Italian minorities; there is a very small Romansch population. *Economy*: although lacking in mineral wealth, Switzerland owes much of its prosperity to its terrain and central European position. The latter has led to its development as a center for trade, banking, and insurance, while the magnificent scenery has long been a major tourist attraction. The fast-flowing rivers of the Alps provide abundant hydroelectric power and heavy industries, such as engineering and chemicals, have been developed as well as the smaller traditional industries (watches and clocks, precision instruments, and jewelry). Agricultural products include dairy goods, grains, and fruit and vegetables, and there is an important wine industry. The principal exports are machinery, watches, chemicals, and textiles. *History*: its Celtic inhabitants (the Helvetii) were conquered by the Romans in the 1st century BC and the region was overrun by German tribes in the 5th century AD, becoming part of the Holy Roman Empire in the 10th century. In 1291 Uri, Schwyz, and Nidwalden formed the Everlasting League, which is traditionally regarded as the origin of the Swiss Federation. By 1499 the Federation had achieved virtual independence of the Empire and in the 16th century became an important center of the Reformation, notably under Zwingli in Zürich. In 1648, at the conclusion of the Thirty Years' War, its independence was formally recognized by the European powers. The French conquered Switzerland in 1798, establishing the Helvetian Republic, but after Napoleon's fall (1815) the Congress of Vienna guaranteed Swiss neutrality. Religious conflict led to war between Protestant and Roman Catholic cantons and a modified constitution (1848) by which Switzerland became a unified federal state. It maintained its neutrality through both World Wars and has become the headquarters of many international organizations. Switzerland's postwar prosperity has been assisted by migrant workers (*see* migration, human) the repatriation of whom was rejected in a referendum in 1975. Another controversial issue was the enfranchisement of women, which was finally achieved in 1971. Switzerland is governed by a federal council composed of seven councillors, elected for four years, from whom a president and vice president are elected yearly. Official languages: French, German, Italian, and Romansch. Official currency: Swiss franc of 100 centimes (*or* Rappen). Area: 15,941 sq mi (41,288 sq km). Population (1980): 6,365,960. Capital: Bern.

sword A weapon consisting of a cutting or stabbing blade on a short handle, used in hand-to-hand fighting. Of uncertain origin, the sword evolved in the Bronze Age. The Roman soldier's principal weapon was a short, two-edged, iron-bladed sword (*gladius*). In the middle ages heavier and longer swords, some needing to be wielded with two hands, developed in response to heavier armor. The advent of gunpowder forced foot soldiers gradually to abandon swords, but cavalry units until the 20th century fought with long often curved blades. *See also* fencing.

swordfish A food and game fish, *Xiphias gladius*, related to tuna and found in all tropical and temperate seas. It has an elongated body, up to 15 ft (4.6 m) long, a triangular front dorsal fin, no pelvic fins, and an elongated swordlike snout used to slash at shoaling fish on which it feeds. It is the only member of its family (*Xiphiidae*).

swordtail A tropical freshwater fish of the genus *Xiphophorus*, especially *X. helleri*. It has an elongated body, up to 5 in (13 cm) long, and males have a long swordlike extension of the lower lobe of the tail fin. Swordtails are naturally green with a red strip on each side, but have been bred in many colors for aquaria. Family: *Poeciliidae*; order: *Atheriniformes*.

Sybaris 39 39N 16 20E A Greek settlement founded about 700 BC near present-day Terranova di Sibari in S Italy. Territorial expansion and a monopoly of Etruscan trade brought prosperity and Sybarites were famous for their luxurious lives (hence the word sybaritic, meaning pleasure seeking). In 510 and again in 457 Sybaris was destroyed by its neighbor Croton. Rebuilt a third time, its inhabitants were subsequently exiled by the Athenians.

sycamore A large *maple tree, *Acer pseudoplatanus*, native to central and S Europe and widely grown elsewhere. Up to 100 ft (30 m) tall, it has five-lobed leaves and produces clusters of winged □fruits. The wood is used for violin cases, carvings, and furniture.

SYDNEY *As seen from the northern approaches to the Sydney Harbour Bridge. Behind the bridge rise the tall blocks of the city center and on the left are the sail-like roofs of Sydney Opera House.*

Sydney 33 55S 151 10E The oldest and largest city in Australia, the capital of New South Wales, situated on *Port Jackson inlet. It is essentially a commercial, cultural, and financial center dependent on its port for its prosperity. The N site of Port Jackson is predominantly residential, industry being located to the S. The two shores are connected by Sydney Harbour Bridge (1932), the second largest single span bridge in the world. Industry is diverse and includes shipbuilding, chemicals, and the manufacture of consumer goods; Botany Bay is developing as the main industrial area. The chief exports are wheat and wool. A cultural center, Sydney possesses three universities, including Sydney University (1850), and the world-famous Sydney Opera House (opened 1973), designed by Jørn Utzon as the result of an international competition in 1955. There are abundant sports facilities, including many nearby beaches. *History*: a penal settlement (Sydney Cove) was established by Captain Arthur Phillip at Port Jackson (in 1788). Under the governorship of Lachlan Macquarie (1810–21), aided by a convict-architect, Francis Greenway, it developed into a thriving town and grew rapidly between 1850 and 1890. Area: 670 sq mi (1735 sq km). Population (1980 est): 3,231,000.

Sydney 46 10N 60 10W A city and port in SE Canada, in Nova Scotia on Cape Breton Island. Founded in 1785, it is located on a major coalfield and has an important steel industry. Population (1976): 30,645.

syenite A range of coarse-grained intrusive rocks (*see* igneous rocks) consisting mainly of alkali feldspar or feldspathoids, together with hornblende and biotite.

Syktyvkar 61 42N 50 45E A city in the NW Soviet Union, the capital of the Komi ASSR in the RSFSR. Founded in the 16th century, it became a place of exile for criminals and political prisoners. Notable industries are timber and paper and pulp manufacturing. Population (1981 est): 180,000.

syllabaries Writing systems in which each symbol represents a syllable in the language rather than a concept (*compare* ideographic writing systems). The only major language using a syllabary today is Japanese. However, the North *Semitic alphabet, from which all the world's major alphabets are derived, almost certainly developed out of a syllabary, in which the symbols came to represent speech sounds rather than concepts as in ideography.

syllogism A form of deductive argument, rules for the validity of which were developed by *Aristotle. Each syllogism must be composed of three propositions—two premises and a conclusion—and one of its forms may thus be schematically represented: "All As are Bs. All Cs are As. Therefore all Cs are Bs." Since the conclusion that all Cs are Bs "follows" from the premises, one cannot without self-contradiction assert the premises and deny the conclusion, and this is true of all forms of valid syllogism.

Sylvester II (Gerbert of Aurillac; c. 940–1003) Pope (999–1033), who was also a mathematician and astronomer. He attempted to reform abuses and organized the Churches of Poland and Hungary. His reputation as a scholar (his learning was popularly credited to have been acquired by magic) survived his pontificate.

symbiosis Any close relationship between individuals of two different species of organisms. The term can therefore include parasitism (*see* parasite), *commensalism, and *inquilinism but is often restricted to—and used synonymously with—**mutualism**, in which both partners (symbionts) benefit from the association. An example of such a symbiotic relationship is provided by a sea anemone (*Adamsia paliata*), which lives attached to the snail shell inhabited by the hermit crab (*Eupagurus prideauxii*). The anemone protects and camouflages the crab, from which it receives food and transport in return.

Symbolists A group of French poets in the late 19th century whose poetry, which they regarded as a means of transcending reality, was determined by their belief in the power of words and images to evoke responses in the subconscious mind. They included *Mallarmé, *Verlaine, and *Rimbaud, and acknowledged the influence of *Baudelaire. They were precursors of the Surrealist movement and had a profound influence on poets in Russia and many other countries.

Symons, Arthur (William) (1865–1945) British poet and critic. He coedited the literary journal *Savoy* (1896) with Aubrey Beardsley and published several volumes of lyrical poetry, the best of which he selected and published in *Poems* (2 vols, 1902). A disciple of Walter *Pater, his critical work included the influential study *The Symbolist Movement in Literature* (1899).

symphonic poem (*or* tone poem) A one-movement orchestral composition based on a literary, dramatic, or pictorial theme. The symphonic poem was invented by *Liszt, who composed a series of such works, the most famous of which is *Les Préludes* (1854), after Lamartine's poem *Méditations Poétiques*. Smetana, Richard Strauss, Tchaikovsky, Sibelius, Respighi, and Elgar, among others, composed notable works in this genre.

symphony An orchestral composition, usually in four movements. The classical symphony evolved in the mid-18th century and was perfected by Haydn and Mozart: the fast first movement was generally in *sonata form, the second was slow and expressive, the third a *minuet and trio, and the fourth fast. Beethoven extended the formal and emotional range of the symphony, introducing a chorus and soloists in the last movement of his ninth symphony. In the 19th century Schubert, Schumann, Mendelssohn, Brahms, Dvořák, and Tchaikovsky all wrote symphonies broadly in this tradition. In the hands of such composers as Bruckner and Mahler the symphony underwent further enlargement: Mahler's eighth symphony (1907) requires a thousand performers. Sibelius developed a concentrated approach to symphonic writing: his seventh symphony (1924) is in one movement. Nielsen, Shostakovich, Vaughan Williams, and others have all developed the symphony in differing ways.

synagogue A Jewish place of worship. The synagogue probably originated during the *Babylonian exile as a substitute for the Temple at Jerusalem. In antiquity it was a public meeting place, devoted mainly to the reading and exposition of the *Torah. It is now primarily a house of prayer, but often has a communal center attached. The principal piece of furniture is the cupboard (Ark) containing the Torah scrolls. A synagogue service requires a quorum (*minyan*) of ten adult males. US Reform Judaism prefers the term "temple."

synapse The meeting point between one nerve cell and another (*see* neuron). The nerve impulse, as it arrives at the end of one nerve process, causes a chemical neurotransmitter (e.g. *acetylcholine or noradrenaline) to be released. This reaches receptors on the opposite neuron and produces a new nerve impulse.

synchrocyclotron A type of *cyclotron in which the frequency of the accelerating electric field can be varied to compensate for the relativistic increase in the mass of the accelerated particles. This enables energies of up to 500 MeV to be obtained.

synchrotron A particle *accelerator, similar to the *cyclotron, in which protons or electrons are accelerated in a circular path by an alternating electric field. The frequency of the field is synchronized with the energy of the particles to counteract their relativistic increase in the mass. Proton energies of several hundred GeV have been attained in these devices. *See also* bevatron.

synchrotron radiation Electromagnetic radiation emitted in certain directions by a charged particle when the presence of a magnetic field confines its motion to a circle. The particle has to be moving at speeds comparable to that of light for a noticeable amount of radiation to be emitted. Therefore a high magnetic field is needed. Such fields are used in *synchrotrons, a type of particle *accelerator. The emission of radio-frequency radiation also occurs from interstellar gas clouds in radio galaxies and, by analogy, is also known as synchrotron radiation.

syncline A trough-shaped fold or downfold in folded rock strata, the strata dipping toward a central axis (*compare* anticline). The youngest rocks occur in the core unless very complex deformation has occurred. Where the strata dip inward from all directions the resulting feature is called a structural basin.

syndicalism A type of *socialism, advocated by *Sorel, under which the workers, not the state, would take over the productive resources of industry. Syndicalists were widely influential in Europe from the late 19th century until World War I. They worked through industrial action, rather than political or parliamentary means, to substitute for the state a federation of functional economic units (syndicats).

Synge, John Millington (1871–1909) Anglo-Irish dramatist. Most of his plays, the realism and poetic intensity of which contributed greatly to the *Irish Literary Renaissance, were inspired by his experience of life in an isolated Irish community, recorded in *The Aran Islands* (1907). His best-known play, *The Playboy of the Western World* (1907), caused riots at its first performance at the Abbey Theatre, Dublin.

synodic period The average time taken by a planet or satellite to return to the same point in its orbit, relative to the sun, as seen from earth. It is therefore the interval between *oppositions or between identical *phases.

synovitis Inflammation of the synovium—the membrane lining the joints. This usually results from mild injuries to joints, such as those affecting footballers early in the season, and causes pain and swelling.

syntax. See grammar.

synthesizer A device that can reproduce the sounds of conventional instruments electronically or produce a variety of artificial tones. Electronic oscillators produce a range of signals, which after amplification and appropriate filtering are converted to sound waves, of which some have the characteristic resonances of musical instruments, some are pure tones, and some are arbitrary combinations of sounds. Individual circuits can be plugged in and out by the player, enabling a wide range of sounds to be produced. The Moog synthesizer, invented by Robert Moog (1934–) in 1965, can play one note at a time and is controlled by a keyboard. More recent **polyphonic synthesizers** can be programed to produce any number of different tones simultaneously.

synthetism A style of painting developed by *Gauguin and Émile Bernard (1868–1941) in Brittany in 1888. The visual arts' counterpart to the Symbolist literary movement, synthetism sought to express an idea or emotion through formal correspondences of line and color. It was also known as cloisonnisme, since its use of rich unmodulated color contained within thick black contours resembled *cloisonné enamelwork, as well as Japanese prints. Synthetism greatly influenced the art of the *Nabis.

syphilis A venereal disease caused by the *spirochete bacterium *Treponema pallidum*, which in nearly all cases is transmitted during sexual intercourse. The effects of the disease occur in three stages. In primary syphilis chancres (hard ulcers) appear after about 25 days at the site of infection (usually the genitals). The chancre disappears after about eight weeks, but weeks or months later the rash of secondary syphilis occurs. Arthritis, meningitis, and hepatitis may also occur at this stage. Without treatment the tertiary stage of syphilis may appear up to 30 years later and give rise to a variety of symptoms, including large tumor-like masses (gummas) in many organs, heart disease, blindness, and madness and paralysis (general paralysis of the insane). The disease can be passed on to an unborn child by an infected mother (congenital syphilis). Syphilis can be treated with penicillin. The *Wasserman test is one of many blood tests available for diagnosing the disease.

Syracuse (Italian name: Siracusa) 37 04N 15 18E A seaport in Italy, in SE Sicily on the Ionian Sea. Founded by Greeks from Corinth in 734 BC, it became an important cultural center in the 5th century. The Greek poet Theocritus and the Greek mathematician and scientist Archimedes were born here. In 212 BC Syracuse fell to the Romans after a three-year siege. There are many ancient remains, including a Greek temple, a Roman amphitheater, and a fortress built by Dionysius I. Today Syracuse is a processing center for agricultural produce, with some light industry. Population (1977 est): 122,534.

Syracuse 43 03N 76 10W A city in N central New York. Founded in 1788, it had a thriving saltmaking industry until after the Civil War. In 1819 the Erie Canal was opened and the railroads followed, attracting many industries. Today its many manufactures include aircraft parts, typewriters, and chemicals. Syracuse University was established here in 1849. Population (1980): 170,105.

Syr Darya River (ancient name: Jaxartes) A river in the S central Soviet Union, rising in the Tian Shan and flowing mainly W to the Aral Sea. It is the longest river in Central Asia. Length: 1800 mi (2900 km).

Syria (official name: Syrian Arab Republic) A country in the Middle East, bordering on the Mediterranean Sea. In the W the Ghab depression (an extension of the *Great Rift Valley) runs N–S, separated from the coast by a mountain range. To the E of this is plateau of steppe and desert with some mountains. The main fertile areas, in which the population is concentrated, are the coastal strip and the basin of the Euphrates River (see Fertile Crescent). Nomads live in the center and E; ethnic minorities include Kurds (in the NE), Turks, Armenians, Assyrians, Circassians, and Jews. The population is predominantly Muslim (mainly Sunnites with some Shiites). *Economy*: largely agricultural; cotton and grain are the main crops and livestock are kept. Natural resources include oil, natural gas, phosphates, and salt. Industries, mainly developed since the 1940s, include food processing, oil refining, and the manufacture of textiles, clothing, cement, and chemicals. Syria has a planned socialist economy; much of its industry is nationalized, and land has been redistributed in favor of the peasants (1958, 1963, and 1966). *History*: before the 20th century Syria, together with Palestine, extended over the area that is now Lebanon, Israel, Jordan, W Iraq, and N Saudi Arabia. In ancient times the *Amorites settled here and later *Phoenicia flourished. It was frequently conquered; Islam was introduced by conquering Arabs (c. 640 AD). Under Turkish control from the 11th century, it was the site of battles with the Crusaders. From 1517 until World War I it was part of the Ottoman Empire. In 1920 it became part of a French mandate, from which Lebanon was separated in 1926. Demands for Syrian independence were finally satisfied in 1946. Since then Syria's history has been marked by economic growth, political instability with many coups, and militant participation in the Arab-Israeli Wars. It united briefly with Egypt in the United Arab Republic (1958–61) but withdrew because of Egyptian domination. In 1971 Syria, Libya, and Egypt united loosely in the Federation of Arab Republics but disagreement with Egypt developed over its attitude toward Israel. Syria intervened in the civil war in Lebanon (1975–76), at first as a mediator but then supporting the Christians. It remained in occupation of the eastern part of the country, from which after 1982 it aided Muslim factions opposed to the national government of Christian leader Amin Gemayel as well as to Israeli occupation forces in southern Lebanon. President: Lieutenant General Hafiz al-Assad (1928–). Prime minister: Abdel Raouf al-Kasm. Official language: Arabic. Official currency: Syrian pound of 100 piastres. Area: 72,772 sq mi (185,680 sq km). Population (1983 est): 9,739,000. Capital: Damascus.

Syriac A *Semitic language based on the dialect of *Aramaic spoken in Edessa (now Urfa, SE Turkey). It became an important literary and liturgical language in which many scriptures, biblical commentaries, hymns, etc., were written during the 3rd to the 7th centuries AD when Edessa was an important Christian center.

syringa. See lilac; mock orange.

syrinx The vocal organ of birds, located at the base of the windpipe. Air from the lungs vibrates membranes within a resonating chamber. Muscular tension alters pitch, and the two halves of the syrinx can produce different notes simultaneously.

Syros (Modern Greek name: Síros) A Greek island in the S Aegean Sea, in the Cyclades. The chief town, Hermopolis, is the capital of the Cyclades. Area: 33 sq mi (85 sq km). Population (1971): 18,642.

systole. See blood pressure; heart.

Szczecin (German name: Stettin) 53 25N 14 32E A city in the extreme NW of Poland, on the Oder River 40 mi (65 km) upstream from the Baltic Sea. It is a major port, the chief export being coal. Shipbuilding is the principal industry; others include engineering, chemicals, and the manufacture of textiles. *History*: it became a member of the Hanseatic League in 1360. Seized by the Swedes (1648) it passed to Prussia in 1720, remaining under German control until being ceded to Poland (1945). It suffered severe damage during World War II. Population (1979 est): 388,000.

Szechwan. See Sichuan.

Szeged 46 15N 20 09E A city in S Hungary, on the Tisza River. Replanned with concentric and radiating streets after a flood in 1879, it has a university (1872) and considerable industry. Population (1976 est): 171,851.

Székesfehérvár 47 11N 18 22E A city in W central Hungary. It was the capital of the Hungarian kingdom from the 10th until the 16th century. It was almost totally destroyed in World War II. Population (1980): 102,000.

Szell, George (1897–1970) Hungarian conductor. He studied in Vienna, conducted in various German opera houses, and came to the US in 1942. In 1946 he became permanent conductor of the Cleveland Orchestra, a post he held until his death.

Szent-Györgyi, Albert (von Nagyrapolt) (1893–   ) US biochemist, born in Hungary. He identified the role of ascorbic acid in living cells and later showed it to be *vitamin C. Szent-Györgyi determined certain organic compounds involved in the breakdown of carbohydrates by cells to produce energy—a prelude to *Krebs' major discoveries in this field. He also found that the proteins actin and myosin, working in conjunction with ATP, formed the basis of the contractile apparatus of muscles. Szent-Györgyi was awarded a Nobel Prize (1937).

Szilard, Leo (1898–1964) US physicist, born in Hungary, who in 1934, while working in England, conceived the idea of a self-sustaining nuclear chain reaction. Szilard emigrated to the US in 1937 and when he heard of *Hahn and *Meitner's work on the fission of uranium, recognized its significance in terms of nuclear weapons. He joined *Teller in persuading Einstein to write to Roosevelt to warn him of the possibility that Germany might make an atom bomb first. During World War II he actually worked on the atom bomb, but later regretted its development and pressed for the abolition of all nuclear weapons.

Szymanowski, Karol (1882–1937) Polish composer. He studied at the Warsaw conservatoire, where in 1926 he became director. The influences on his music include Chopin, Liszt, Scriabin, Debussy, and Polish folk music. His works include three symphonies, a *Symphonie Concertante* (for piano and orchestra; 1931–32) two violin concertos, the ballet *Harnasie* (1926), the opera *King Roger* (1920–24), and *Mythes* (for violin and piano; 1915).

T

Tabari, Muhammad ibn Jarir al- (838–923 AD) Arab historian. His works include an important commentary on the Koran and the *Annals*, a history of the world from the Creation to the year 915 AD.

tabasco A hot red pepper or sauce made from the entire fruits of a variety of the South American plant *Capsicum frutescens* and used to flavor soups, stews, curries, etc. Family: *Solanaceae*.

tabernacle **1.** The portable sanctuary or "tent of meeting" used by the Israelites in the wilderness (Exodus 25–31, 33, 35–40). **2.** The English name of the *sukkah*, a hut made of greenery, used by Jews during the autumn festival of Tabernacles (*sukkot*). For seven days it is customary to live, or at least eat, in the *sukkah*.

Table Bay 33 50S 18 25E An inlet of the Atlantic Ocean, on the coast of SW Africa. The Dutch settled here in 1652, founding Cape Town on the S shore. Length: about 6 mi (10 km).

table tennis (*or* Ping-Pong) An indoor game for two or four players. It is played on a table 9 ft (2.74 m) long and 5 ft (1.52 m) wide, divided across its width by a net 6 in (15.25 cm) high and along its length by a line separating right-hand from left-hand half courts for doubles play. The players hit a resilient small hollow plastic ball with a rubber-faced wooden bat. A point is scored when the opponent fails to return the ball after it has bounced once. Each player serves five consecutive points and the winner of a game is the first to reach 21 points with at least a two-point lead.

taboo A ritual prohibition relating to things that are considered either sacred, powerful, and dangerous (*see also* totemism) or unclean and polluting. The term is derived from Polynesian *tapu*, forbidden, and may apply to things, animals, plants, people, places, words and names, or actions. Customs of this kind are widespread in all societies, but actual practices vary greatly. Certain things may be taboo for all people in a society (as eating pork is for Jews). Other things are taboo for only certain categories of persons (*see* incest). Some things are taboo for particular people at particular times (e.g. in many societies menstruating women are subject to restrictions as to what they may touch).

Tabora 5 02S 32 50E A city in W central Tanzania. It was an important center for trade in ivory and slaves; today trade remains significant and includes groundnuts and sunflower seeds. Population (1978): 67,392.

Tabriz 38 05N 46 18E A city in NW Iran, close to the Soviet and Turkish borders. It has several times suffered earthquakes. The most notable buildings are the Blue Mosque (15th century) and the citadel, and Tabriz is famous for its carpets; it is connected by rail to Tehran and the Soviet Union and has an airport. Tabriz University was opened in 1949. Population (1976): 598,576.

tachometer An instrument for measuring the speed of rotation of a shaft, such as a revolution counter in a car. Centrifugal tachometers measure the force experienced by rotating masses. Others are electrical or magnetic, measuring electrical current or force generated by a small generator in the instrument.

tachyon A hypothetical particle that travels faster than the speed of light. Such a particle would have either an imaginary rest mass or an imaginary energy and no such particle has ever been detected.

Tacitus, Cornelius (c. 55–c. 120 AD) Roman historian. After holding various provincial administrative posts he established his reputation as a public orator in Rome and became consul in 97 AD; in 112–13 he was governor of Asia. In 98 he wrote two historical monographs, *Germania* and *Agricola*, the latter an account of his father-in-law's career. His major works, the *Histories* and the *Annals*, survey Roman history during the periods 69–96 AD and 14–68 AD and are noted for their terse and vivid style and acute understanding of the men and issues involved. Although claiming impartiality, Tacitus appears to concentrate on the evils of imperial government.

Tacna 18 00S 70 15W A city in S Peru. It was under Chilean occupation (1883–1929). It serves an agricultural area producing tobacco, cotton, and sugar cane. Population (1970 est): 33,821.

Tacoma 47 16N 122 30W A city in Washington, on Puget Sound. Founded in 1868, it grew as the terminus of the North Pacific Railroad (1873). The University of Puget Sound was established here in 1888. An important port, its main industry is timber; other industries include meat packing, railroad workshops, and foundries. Tacoma is the gateway to several national parks. Population (1980): 158,501.

tadpole The aquatic larva of frogs and toads. The newly hatched tadpole feeds on vegetation but later becomes carnivorous. The external gills of the young tadpole are gradually replaced by internal gills, and after about ten weeks the limbs start to appear, the tail degenerates, the lungs develop, and the circulatory system changes to enable the adult to lead a terrestrial life. Metamorphosis is complete after about three months, depending on the external temperature and available food.

tadpole shrimp A freshwater crustacean belonging to an order (*Notostraca*) that occurs in North America and the Arctic. Up to 1.2 in (30 mm) long, it has a shieldlike carapace, short antennae, 35–70 pairs of appendages, and two long tail filaments. Subclass: *Branchiopoda*.

Tadzhiks An Iranian people of Afghanistan and Soviet Turkistan. They are an agricultural people using irrigation to grow cereal crops and fruit trees. Trade has also been important traditionally because of their position on the caravan routes between China, India, and Persia. They speak a form of Persian and are Muslims.

Tadzhik Soviet Socialist Republic (*or* Tadzhikistan) A constituent republic in the S Soviet Union. Largely mountainous, it contains *Communism Peak. Some 53% of the population are *Tadzhiks. The economy is primarily agricultural, although there are growing mining, engineering, and other industries. Health resorts have grown up around its many mineral springs. Area: 55,240 sq mi (143,100 sq km). Population (1981 est): 3,400,000. Capital: Dushanbe.

Taegu 35 52N 128 36E A city in SE South Korea, the capital of North Kyongsang province. An old cultural center, it is the site of a university (1946). It has an important textile industry. Population (1975): 1,309,131.

Taejon 36 20N 127 26E A city in SE South Korea, capital of South Chungchong province. It is an agricultural and industrial center, with a university (1952). Some 70% of the city was destroyed during the Korean War (1950–53). Population (1975): 506,223.

Tafilalt (*or* Tafilelt) An oasis in SE Morocco, in the Sahara. It stretches for about 31 mi (50 km) along the Ziz River and includes the towns of Erfoud and Rissani.

Taft, William Howard (1857–1930) US statesman and jurist; 27th President of the US (1909–13). Taft first came to national prominence as US solicitor general during the administration of President Benjamin *Harrison (1890–92) and as a federal judge (1892–1900). After the *Spanish-American War, he served as governor of the Philippines (1901–04) and was named secretary of war in the cabinet of President Theodore *Roosevelt. With Roosevelt's decision not to seek re-election, Taft received the Republican nomination in 1908, and defeated the Democratic candidate, William Jennings *Bryan. As president, Taft supported vigorous enforcement of the *Sherman Anti-Trust Act, but his high tariff policies aroused considerable opposition within his own party. Although he was renominated in 1912, he was defeated in the general election by Woodrow *Wilson.

After a brief retirement from public life, Taft was appointed by President Warren G. *Harding in 1921 to become chief justice of the US Supreme Court and became the only individual in American history ever to hold both the presidency and the chief justiceship. Taft's tenure on the court was characterized by a conservative judicial philosophy, restricting the power of labor unions and overturning federal legislation against child labor. His son, **Robert Alphonso Taft** (1889–1953), served as US senator from Ohio (1938–53) and became one of the leaders of the Republican Party. Although he was an unsuccessful candiate for the Republican presidential nomination in 1940, 1944, 1948, and 1952, he secured the passage of several important legislative proposals, including the *Taft-Hartley Act of 1947.

Taft-Hartley Act (*or* Labor-Management Relations Act; 1947) US law, sponsored by Senator Robert A. Taft and Republican Fred A. Hartley, aimed at correcting union and employer abuses. It further amended the Wagner Act (1935) and reorganized and enlarged the *National Labor Relations Board. Closed shops were banned and union shops were allowed only by employee vote. It also required unions to limit political activity, reveal certain aspects of financial standing, and sign non-Communist affidavits. The government was granted permission to invoke an 80-day injunction in cases of strikes thought to endanger national safety.

Tagalog A people of Luzon and Mindanao islands in the Philippines who speak an *Austronesian language. Although less numerous than the speakers of the related language of Cebuano, they tend to dominate in the economic, professional, and political spheres. Tagalog is the basis of the national language and is spoken by the population of the capital, Manila. The rural Tagalog are mainly rice farmers.

Taganrog 47 14N 38 55E A port in the Soviet Union, in the SW RSFSR of the Gulf of Taganrog in the Sea of Azov. Its port serves the coalmines of the Donets Basin and industries include steel making. The playwright Chekhov was born here. Population (1981 est): 281,000.

Tagore, Rabindranath (1861–1941) Indian poet, philosopher, and teacher. Knighted in 1915, he resigned the honor in 1919 as a protest against the Amritsar massacre. He wrote poetry, drama, and fiction in the Bengali language and was also a celebrated artist and musician. In 1901 he founded a school near Calcutta, which later became an international university. He advocated cultural links between the East and the West and won the Nobel Prize for literature in 1913 after the publication in English of *Gitanjali* (1912), a volume of spiritual poetry.

Tagus River (Portuguese name: Tejo; Spanish name: Tajo) A river in SW Europe. Rising in E central Spain, it flows NW and then SW across the arid areas of Spain and Portugal to the Atlantic Ocean at Lisbon. Length: 626 mi (1007 km).

Tahiti The largest of the Society Islands in the S central Pacific Ocean, in French Polynesia. Mountainous and famous for its beauty, it was Gauguin's home for two years (1891–93). Settled by Polynesians in the 14th century, it was first visited by Europeans in 1767. It became French in 1842. Tourism is important, and copra, sugar cane, vanilla, and coffee are exported. Area: 388 sq mi (1005 sq km). Population (1977): 95,604. Chief town: Papeete.

tahr A wild goat belonging to the genus *Hemitragus* (3 species), inhabiting forested mountain slopes of S Asia. 24–40 in (60–100 cm) high at the shoulder, the large Himalayan tahr (*H. jemlahicus*) and the smaller Nilgiri tahr (*H. hylocrius*) have long coarse shaggy brownish hair; the Arabian tahr (*H. jayakari*) is slender and sandy-colored.

Tai Peoples of SE Asia and China who speak a group of related languages probably belonging to the *Sino-Tibetan family. They are traditionally rice cultivators dwelling in villages with elected headmen. The nuclear family is the basic social unit and women have high status. They are mainly Theravada Buddhists, the monks having considerable influence and authority. Major groupings are the Thai or Siamese, the Lao, Shan, and Lu. *See also* Austro-Asiatic languages.

Taibei. *See* Taipei.

T'ai-chung. *See* Taizhong.

taiga The coniferous forests, composed chiefly of spruces, pines, and firs, in the N hemisphere in subpolar latitudes. It extends from Norway across Sweden, Finland, and the Soviet Union (including Siberia), in Eurasia. The coniferous forests of North America, extending across Canada and Alaska, are also known as taiga.

Taika (Japanese: great change; 645–50 AD) The period associated with the first major upheaval in Japanese history. Influenced by the Tang dynasty of China, Japanese leaders introduced a Chinese-style system of government, including land nationalization and the establishment of a centralized bureaucracy. Their program was not completed, however, until the erection of a permanent capital at Nara in 710.

taille An income and property tax in France before the Revolution. Originally levied for royal expenses and paid in lieu of military service, the taille was a major source of grievance since clergy and nobility were exempt and commoners alone paid the tax. It was abolished in 1789.

tailorbird A S Asian *warbler belonging to the genus *Orthotomus* (9 species), named for its habit of sewing the edges of a large leaf together with plant fibers or gossamer to form a bag in which the nest is built.

Taimyr Peninsula (*or* Taymyr Peninsula) A promontory in the central N Soviet Union, between the Kara Sea and the Laptev Sea with Cape *Chelyuskin at its extremity.

Tainan 23 01N 120 14E A city in SW Taiwan, the island's third largest. It is the island's former capital (1683–1891). The National University was established in 1971. An agricultural and fish market, it has varied industries and handicrafts. Population (1970 est): 474,835.

Taine, Hippolyte Adolphe (1828–93) French writer and critic. In contrast to the prevailing *Romanticism, Taine was intensely logical and positivist in his approach. In works such as the *Philosophy of Art* (1865–69),

his analysis is conducted in scientific, mathematical, physiological, or environmental terms.

taipan A small-headed *cobra, *Oxyuranus scutellatus*, that occurs in NE Australia and New Guinea. Up to 11 ft (3.3 m) long, it has a ridged brown back and a yellow belly. The venom of the taipan contains a blood-clotting agent that is fatal within a few minutes.

Taipei (*or* Taibei) 25 00N 121 32E The capital of Taiwan, in the N of the island. Founded in the 18th century, it was under Japanese occupation (1895–1945) and became the seat of the Nationalist Government (*see* Guomindang) in 1949. It is an important industrial center, especially for textiles, food processing, and machinery. The National University was founded in 1928. Population (1979 est): 2,200,000.

Taiping Rebellion (1851–64) A peasant rebellion in China that seriously undermined the Qing dynasty. In 1851 a Hakka peasant, *Hong Xiu Quan, claiming he was the brother of Christ come to save his people from their Qing rulers, proclaimed himself "Heavenly King of the Taiping (Heavenly Peace) Kingdom." He soon won converts among the southern peasantry and anti-Qing secret societies. The rebels marched N, capturing Nanjing in 1853 and declaring it their Heavenly Capital. They then marched on Peking but imperial forces, and cold weather, drove them back. The rebellion, which devasted 17 provinces, was weakened by internal division and finally crushed. When Nanjing fell, Hong and his followers committed mass suicide.

Taira An important Japanese military clan of imperial descent. After gaining many vassals in the provinces, the Taira became involved in politics in the capital, Kyoto, in the 12th century and under the leadership of Taira Kiyomori (1118–81) came to dominate the imperial government. Shortly before Kiyomori's death, Taira power was challenged by the leaders of a rival clan, the Minamoto (*see* Minamoto Yoritomo), and destroyed in the Gempei War (1180–85).

Taiwan (Republic of China) An island off the SE coast of mainland China. Together with several nearby islands, including the Penghu Islands and the islands of *Jinmen and *Mazu, it comprises the Republic of China. Taiwan Island is largely mountainous, apart from narrow plains along the W coast, and two thirds of the land is under forest. The people are predominantly Chinese, but there is friction between the island Chinese, who make up the overwhelming majority of the population, and those who came from the mainland. *Economy*: in recent years the balance of the economy has shifted from agriculture to industry, a trend that began under the Japanese and has continued under the *Guomindang with US economic aid. Iron and steel are important and the large volume of exports also includes television and radio sets, plastic goods, chemicals, textiles, sugar, and vegetables. As well as coal, gold, and other minerals, small quantities of oil and natural gas have been found, although timber remains the main natural resource. Agriculture is still important, the chief crops being sugar cane, rice, and sweet potatoes. Fishing has increased in recent years, particularly since the introduction of fish farming. *History*: the island, named Formosa ("beautiful") by the Portuguese, who discovered it in 1590, was ceded by China to Japan in 1897. It surrendered to General *Chiang Kai-shek in 1945 and after the defeat of his Nationalist (Guomindang) Government by the Chinese communists he fled here in 1949. Following threats by the People's Republic of China the US undertook in 1955 to protect Taiwan from outside attacks. However, Taiwan's importance in international affairs has diminished, as the People's Republic has gained increasing recognition by the major powers: in 1971 it lost its seat at the UN to the People's Republic and in 1979 the US, on establishing diplomatic relations with mainland China, severed those with Taiwan. Chiang Kai-shek died in 1975 and power is now in the hands of his son General Jiang Jing Guo (Chiang Ching-kuo). Official language: Mandarin Chinese. Official currency: new Taiwan dollar of 100 cents. Area: 13,892 sq mi (35,981 sq km). Population (1981 est): 19,117,000. Capital: Taibei. Main port: Kaohsiung.

Taiyuan 37 50N 112 30E A city in NE China, the capital of Shanxi province. An ancient fortified city, it is a center of technology, coalmining, and heavy industry. Population (1957 est): 1,020,000.

Taizé A Protestant religious community based in Taizé, a village in the SE of France. Founded in 1940 by Roger Schutz (1915–), its members pursue a life of celibacy, obedience, and community of goods in the ways of traditional monasticism and it is also an ecumenical center for young people interested in furthering Christian unity.

Taj Mahal The mausoleum in Agra (N India) built (1631–53) for Mumtaz-i-Mahal, wife of the Mogul emperor *Shah Jahan, who is also buried here. Set in formal gardens, the Taj Mahal is built mainly of white marble, delicately carved and inlaid with precious stones. Its graceful and symmetrical design reflects Persian influence. *See also* Mogul architecture.

TAJ MAJAL *Over 20,000 workmen were employed in the building of the mausoleum (1631-53), which was constructed from pure white Makrana marble.*

Tajo River. *See* Tagus River.

takahe A rare flightless New Zealand bird, *Notornis mantelli*, thought to be extinct but rediscovered on South Island in 1948. 24 in (60 cm) tall, it has a bright blue-and-green plumage and a heavy red conical bill surmounted by a red frontal shield. Takahes feed on seeds. Family: *Rallidae* (rails).

Takao. *See* Gaoxiong.

Takoradi. *See* Sekondi-Takoradi.

Talaing. *See* Mon.

talapoin The smallest *guenon monkey, *Cercopithecus talapoin*, of central West Africa, also called pygmy guenon. With head and body only 12 in (30 cm) long, it has slightly webbed fingers and inhabits swampy forests. It has olive-green fur and conspicuously swollen genitals.

talc A white or pale-green mineral consisting of hydrated magnesium silicate, $Mg_3(Si_4O_{10})(OH)_2$, with a layered structure. It is soft (hardness 1 on *Mohs' scale) and greasy to the touch. Soapstone (steatite) is a rock consisting almost wholly of talc. Talc is formed by the hydrothermal alteration of basic and ultrabasic igneous rocks and by the low-grade thermal metamorphism of siliceous dolomites. Besides its use as talcum powder, it is also used as a mineral filler in many manufacturing processes, as a soft abrasive, and as a lubricant.

Talca 35 28S 71 40W A city in central Chile. The site of the declaration of Chile's independence (1815), it was rebuilt following an earthquake in 1928. Talca serves a rich wine-producing area and has a large match industry. Population (1976 est): 124,260.

Talcahuano 36 40S 73 10W A major port in S Chile, on Concepción Bay. It serves as an outlet for Concepción and is Chile's chief naval base. Population (1976 est): 197,287.

Ta-lien. *See* Lüda.

Taliesin (6th century AD) Welsh poet. He is mentioned in the 9th-century *Historia Britonum* of Nennius. The poems attributed to him in the manuscript *Book of Taliesin* (c. 1275) include odes eulogizing the Welsh king Urien Rheged and lamenting the death of his son Owain.

talipot palm A *palm tree, *Corypha umbraculifera*, cultivated in India, Sri Lanka, and Burma. Its trunk, up to 85.5 ft (26 m) high, bears fan-shaped leaves with a diameter of up to 16 ft (5 m). Trees may be 80 years old before flowering, after which they die. The pyramid-shaped flower cluster, more than 23 ft (7 m) tall, is the largest in the plant kingdom. The hard seeds are used for buttons and ornaments and the leaves for matting, fans, and thatching.

Tallahassee 30 26N 84 19W The capital city of Florida. It is the site of Florida State University (1857) and an agricultural and mechanical university (1887). A trade center for timber, cotton, and livestock, industries include metal and concrete. Population (1980): 81,548.

Talleyrand (Charles Maurice de Talleyrand-Périgord; 1754–1838) French politician and diplomat. He took holy orders in 1775 but was excommunicated by the pope for the part he played in the reform of the church during the *French Revolution. He was foreign minister from 1797 until 1807, when he quarreled with Napoleon, and again under the restored Louis XVIII. He represented France at the *Congress of Vienna and ended his career as ambassador to Great Britain (1830–34).

Tallien, Jean Lambert (1767–1820) French politician in the *French Revolution. He helped overthrow Robespierre in 1774 and under the *Directory was a member of the Council of Five Hundred. He subsequently served in Napoleon's Egyptian campaign.

Tallinn (German name: Reval) 59 22N 24 48E A port in the NW Soviet Union, the capital of the Estonian SSR on Tallinn Bay in the Gulf of Finland. Its varied industries include shipbuilding and it possesses many educational institutions and historic buildings. *History*: it occupies the site of an ancient settlement and was ruled by Denmark and then Sweden before being captured (1710) by Peter the Great. A member of the Hanseatic League, it was a prominent trading center in the middle ages. It was independent Estonia's capital (1918–40) and, following annexation by the Soviet Union, was occupied by the Germans in World War II. Population (1981 est): 442,000.

Talmud Two of the most important works of Jewish religious literature: the Babylonian and the Palestinian (or Jerusalem) Talmud. The Babylonian Talmud is more than three times as long as the Palestinian and enjoys greater authority. Both Talmuds have the same form: they are written in a mixture of Hebrew and Aramaic and are presented as a commentary (*gemara*) on the *Mishnah. They contain records of rabbinic discussions on a wide range of subjects but concentrating especially on *halakhah. The rabbis mentioned in the Talmuds are called *Amoraim* (as opposed to *Tannaim*, the rabbis of the Mishnah, and *Savoraim*, later rabbis thought to have edited the Babylonian Talmud). The Palestinian *Amoraim* flourished in the 3rd and 4th centuries AD; the Babylonian *Amoraim* continued to about 500.

talus (*or* scree) The accumulation of weathered debris at the foot of a cliff that has originated from erosion of the rock face above.

Tamale 9 26N 0 49W A city in N Ghana. It is an educational center and has a trade in cotton and groundnuts. Population (1970): 120,000.

tamandua An insect-eating mammal, *Tamandua tetradactyla*, of Central and South American forests, also called lesser *anteater. Almost 40 in (1 m) long including the long prehensile tail, it is pale in color and has a shorter snout than the giant anteater. It feeds on termites using its long sticky tongue. Family: *Myrmecophagidae*; order: *Edentata*.

tamarin A South American monkey found in open woodland and forests, closely related to *marmosets. Tamarins are 15.5–35 in (39–88 cm) long including the tail (8–16.5 in [20–42 cm]), have tusklike lower canine teeth, and feed on fruit, insects, eggs, etc. Chief genera: *Leontocebus* (21 species), *Leontideus* (3 species); family: *Callithricidae*.

tamarind An evergreen tree, *Tamarindus indica*, probably native to tropical Africa and cultivated in tropical regions for its fruit. It grows to a height of 80 ft (24 m) and bears clusters of yellow flowers. The fruit is a plump pod containing seeds and a bitter-sweet pulp, which is used in chutneys, curries, and medicines. Family: *Leguminosae*.

tamarisk A tree or shrub belonging to the genus *Tamarix* (90 species), native to W and S Europe, central Asia, and India. Tamarisks have small scalelike leaves and produce feathery clusters of small pink flowers. Their deep roots enable them to grow on arid salt flats and sand dunes and they have been widely planted to stabilize sand dunes. *T. mannifera* of the Middle East and central Asia exudes a sweet white edible substance (manna) when the stems are punctured by certain insects. The false tamarisks (genus *Myricaria*; 10 species), native to temperate Eurasia, are similar to the true tamarisks. Family: *Tamaricaceae*.

tamarou (*or* tamarau) A rare hoofed mammal, *Anoa mindorensis*, of lowland forests of the Philippines. A little larger than the closely related *anoa, it is similarly dark brown or black with short horns and it feeds at night on sugar cane and water plants.

Tamatave (*or* Toamasina) 18 10S 49 23E The chief port of Madagascar, on the Indian Ocean. It was destroyed by hurricane in 1927. Since rebuilt, it is the country's major commercial center and industries include rum distilling. Population (1978 est): 59,100.

Tambov 52 44N 41 28E A city in the Soviet Union, in the W RSFSR. It is an important engineering center. Population (1981 est): 277,000.

Tamerlane. *See* Timur.

Tamil A *Dravidian language of S India and Sri Lanka. It is the official language of the state of Tamil Nadu. There are a number of regional dialects as well as those associated with different caste groups, such as Brahmins and non-Brahmins. It is written in a script known as Vattelluttu and there are marked differences between the written and spoken forms. Tamil society is highly stratified into caste groups and based on descent in the male line. They are mainly Hindu, and devotional (*bhakti*) cults are prevalent.

Tamil Nadu (name until 1968: Madras) A state in SE India, at the tip of the peninsula. From the Western *Ghats it slopes E over lower plateaus and the Eastern Ghats to the Bay of Bengal. Important crops include rice, cotton, and coffee. One of India's more urbanized states, it produces cotton textiles, machinery, and electrical and leather goods. Tamil literature, music, and dance continue to thrive. *History*: flourishing Hindu dynasties extended Tamil influence into medieval SE Asia until Muslims conquered Tamil Nadu (1565). British power was established in the 17th century. The present state was formed in 1956. Area: 50,318 sq mi (130,357 sq km). Population (1981): 48,297,456. Capital: Madras.

Tammany Hall The Democratic Party organization in New York City, which became notorious for its political corruption. It maintained power by the use of bribes and patronage. Among its most notorious "bosses" was William M. *Tweed. Its power was largely curtailed by the reforming mayor *La Guardia and disintegrated during the administration (1966–73) of John V(liet) Lindsay.

Tammuz A Mesopotamian fertility god identified with the Greek *Adonis. Originally a pastoral god, he became an agricultural god of Assyria. The annual seasonal cycle was symbolized in the myth of his descent to the underworld, from whence he was recovered by the goddess *Ishtar.

Tampa 28 10N 82 20W A city and port in Florida, on Tampa Bay. It is a major resort and phosphate-mining center. Manufactures include cigars, cement, and fertilizers. Two universities are situated here. Population (1980): 271,523.

Tampere (Swedish name: Tammerfors) 61 32N 23 45E The second largest city in Finland. It has a 20th-century cathedral and a university (1925). It is the country's main industrial center, being well provided with hydroelectric power from the Tammerkoski Rapids. Its manufactures include railroad rolling stock, textiles, wood pulp, paper, and footwear. Population (1980): 166,228.

Tampico 22 18N 97 52W A port and winter resort in SE Mexico, on the Río Panuco. Oil refining is the chief industry. Population (1978 est): 239,970.

tam-tam. *See* gong.

Tamworth 52 39N 1 40W A city in central England. It is a market center with engineering, brick and tile manufacturing, and clothing industries. The castle was built in Saxon times. Population (1981): 64,315.

Tana, Lake (*or* Lake Tsana) 12 00N 37 20E A lake in NW Ethiopia. Its surface is 6004 ft (1830 m) above sea level and it is the source of the Blue Nile River. Area: about 1200 sq mi (3100 sq km).

tanager A brightly colored songbird belonging to a family (*Thraupidae*; 222 species) occurring in tropical and subtropical America. Tanagers are 4–8 in (10–20 cm) long, plumpish, with a short neck and a conical bill. They live mainly in forests and feed on fruit, nectar, and insects.

Tanagra figurines In Greek art, molded terracotta statuettes of about 300 BC found at Tanagra (Boeotia). These charming and technically excellent figures represent everyday subjects, usually women in quiet poses.

Tananarive. *See* Antananarivo.

Tancred (c. 1078–1112) Norman Crusader, prominent at the siege of Antioch and the conquest of Jerusalem (1099; *see* Crusades), who was regent of Antioch (1101–03, 1104–12) for Bohemond I. He is portrayed in *Tasso's *Gerusalemme liberata* (1575).

Taney, Roger Brooke (1777–1864) US lawyer; chief justice of the Supreme Court (1836–64). After serving in various state positions in Maryland, including attorney general (1827–31), he became US attorney general in 1831. His appointments as secretary of the treasury (1833) and associate justice on the Supreme Court (1835) were never confirmed by the Senate. In 1836 when President Andrew Jackson appointed him chief justice of the Supreme Court, a change in Senate membership allowed confirmation, and he succeeded John *Marshall. He presided over the court during the *Dred Scott v. Sanford* decision.

Tang (*or* T'ang; 618–906 AD) A Chinese dynasty that established an empire extending over much of central Asia and Korea. In Tang times foreign trade was encouraged and many Chinese scientific ideas, such as gunpowder, which was invented under the Tang for fireworks, spread to the West. Arts, especially poetry, flourished, Neo-Confucianism was revived, printing was invented (the world's first known book, the Buddhist *Diamond sutra*, was printed in 868), and paper money was used for the first time. In 751 Arab forces recaptured Turkestan and the Tang empire began to disintegrate. Disastrous revolts and invasions decimated the population and two great rebellions finally led to the collapse of the dynasty and the division of China into many kingdoms.

Tanga 5 07S 39 05E A port in Tanzania, in NE Zanzibar. It became an important port under German colonial rule but has since declined in importance. Population (1978): 103,409.

Tanganyika. *See* Tanzania, United Republic of.

Tanganyika, Lake A lake in E central Africa, in Zaïre, Burundi, Tanzania, and Zambia. Discovered for Europeans by Burton and Speke in 1858, it is drained intermittently to the W by the Lukuga River. Area: about 12,750 sq mi (33,000 sq km).

Tange Kenzo (1913–) Japanese architect. The most famous modern Japanese architect, Tange combines the influence of *Le Corbusier with traditional Japanese architecture. He has built many civic buildings in Japan, notably the Kurashiki city hall (1960). Other designs include the National Gymnasium (1961–64) for the 1964 Tokyo Olympics and St Mary's Cathedral (1962–64) in Tokyo. As a town planner he has produced programs for Tokyo (1960) and Skopje, Yugoslavia (1965).

tangent A straight line that touches a curve at only one point, known as the point of contact. A tangent plane is one that touches a curved surface at one point. *See also* trigonometry; calculus.

tangerine The fruit of a tree, *Citrus reticulata*, also called mandarin, native to SE Asia and cultivated in the S US and the Mediterranean region. The orange fruit, which peels easily and readily splits into segments, is usually eaten fresh. Many varieties have been developed, including the satsuma and clementine. The temple orange is a hybrid between the *orange and the tangerine.

Tangier (*or* Tangiers) 35 48N 5 45W A port in N Morocco, on a bay on the Strait of Gibraltar. An important Roman town, it was held successively by many powers until it was established as an international zone in 1923. During World War II it was under Spanish occupation (1940–45) and its international status was abolished on Moroccan independence (1956). It has a university (1971). Its industries include cigarette and textile manufacture, fishing, and market gardening, and it is also a tourist center. Population (1971): 187,874.

tango **1.** A Spanish flamenco dance. **2.** A ballroom dance in 2/4 time, first performed in a fast form in the 1880s in the poor quarters of Buenos Aires. In the 1920s it spread to the US and Europe, where it developed melancholic musical rhythms and a stylized elegance.

Tangshan 39 37N 118 05E A city in NE China, in Hebei province. A center of heavy industry, its coalmines were under British control until 1952. China's first railroad began here (1882). Population (1957 est): 800,000.

Tanguy, Yves (1900–55) French surrealist painter. Entirely self-taught, in 1927 he began to paint bizarre forms, partly organic and partly mechanical, which he situated in barren landscapes. He continued to explore this unique vision after emigrating to the US in 1939.

Tanizaki Jun-ichiro (1886–1965) Japanese novelist. His first short stories of the early 1900s were a brilliant success. Their sensuous and grotesque themes are reminscent of Edgar Allan Poe's work. In the 1930s, while updating *The Tale of Genji* by *Murasaki, he became strongly influenced by early Japanese literature. Such later novels as *The Makioka Sisters* (1943–48) show appreciation for the traditional Japanese way of life.

Tanjore. *See* Thanjavur.

tank An armor-plated military vehicle, self-propelled on caterpillar tracks and typically armed with a *gun (usually turret-mounted) and machine guns. Tanks are classified as main battle tanks (MBTs), for independent operation, and light tanks, for reconnaissance and other specialized uses. First used in World War I during the Somme offensive in France September, 1916, their true value became evident at Cambrai in November, 1917. In World War II the Germans initially achieved great success by using their Panzer divisions as an independent force rather than as infantry support or cavalry replacement. Tank battles across Europe and N Africa replaced the static trench warfare of World War I. They were also important in the Korean War but played a more limited role in the Vietnam War, where the jungle terrain hindered their effectiveness. In the Arab-Israeli War of 1973 guided missiles caused heavy Israeli tank losses. Modern tank development has concentrated on improving weapons, armor, and computer-aided navigation and fire control. *See also* armored car.

tanker A seagoing vessel equipped with a large cargo tank for transporting liquids, especially oil. The forerunner of the modern tanker, the *Gluckauf* (2307 tons) was built in 1885; modern **supertankers** with a carrying capacity of 75,000 tons were developed after World War II in response to the increased world demand for oil. Ultra-Large Crude Carriers (ULCCs) have deadweights of up to nearly half a million tons. Size is not always an advantage, however, as such vessels can only enter certain ports, cannot

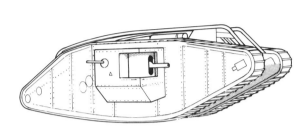

Mark IV British   *Tanks were first successfully used during World War I in the battle of Cambrai in November, 1917. They were designed to be able to cross trenches.*

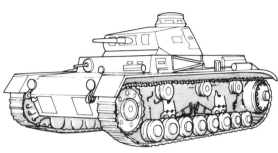

German Pz III   *At the beginning of World War II the German Panzer divisions were based on Pz III tanks, armed with a 50-mm gun and having a maximum speed of 30 mph (48 km per hour).*

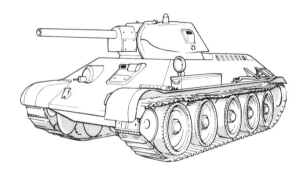

Soviet T-34   *The Nazi invasion of the Soviet Union (1941) met resistance from the T-34, then probably the best design in the world. It had a 76.2-mm gun and a top speed of 32 mph (51 km per hour).*

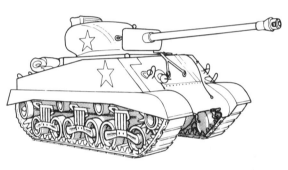

US M-4   *A US design used extensively in World War II was the M-4, known as the "General Sherman." Introduced in 1942, it had a 75-mm gun and a top speed of 24 mph (38 km per hour).*

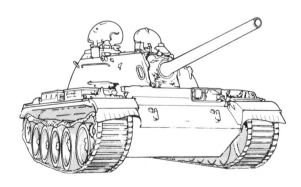

Soviet T-54   *This main battle tank, with its 100-mm gun, effective use of armor, and road speed of 34 mph (54 km per hour) was the most advanced tank in the world when it appeared in 1954.*

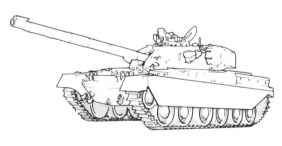

British Chieftain   *Introduced in 1966, this main battle tank is heavily armed with a high-velocity 120-mm gun and has a top speed of 25 mph (40 km per hour).*

negotiate the Suez Canal, and can cause ecological disasters if they are wrecked and spill their enormous cargoes into the sea.

Tannenburg, Battles of 1. (July 5, 1410) The battle in which Polish and Lithuanian troops defeated the *Teutonic Knights, whose drive into E Europe was thereby arrested. 2. (August 26–30, 1914) The battle early in World War I in which Germany defeated Russia, thus thwarting the Russian invasion of Prussia. Some 100,000 Russians were captured.

Tannhäuser (c. 1200–c. 1270) German poet. A Minnesinger several of whose lyrics survive, he traveled widely, serving in various courts. Wagner's opera is based on the legend of his seduction by Venus, his life of sensuality at her court, and his pilgrimage to seek papal forgiveness.

tannin (or tannic acid) One of a group of phenol derivatives present in the bark, leaves, fruits, and galls of many plants. Tannins are used as mordants for many dyes, in tanning leather, and in making ink.

tansy A perennial herb, *Tanacetum* (or *Chrysanthemum*) *vulgare*, native to temperate Eurasia. Growing to a height of 12–40 in (30–100 cm), it has flat-topped clusters of yellow flowers and was formerly cultivated for its aromatic leaves, used for cooking and medicinal purposes. Family: *Compositae.*

Tanta 30 48N 31 00E A city in Egypt, on the Nile Delta. It is noted for its fairs and Muslim festivals and is an important commercial center with cotton and tobacco industries. Population (1976): 285,000.

tantalum (Ta) A very hard gray dense metallic element, discovered in 1802 by A. K. Ekeberg (1767–1813). It is similar to niobium (Nb) and is difficult to separate from it. Tantalum occurs naturally in the ore columbite ($Fe(Nb,Ta)_2O_6$). It is resistant to chemical attack and is used in alloys, for example in surgical materials for implantation in the body and in incandescent filaments. The oxide (Ta_2O_5) is used in special glass, with high refractive index, for camera lenses. At no 73; at wt 180.948; mp 5430°F (2996°C); bp 10,007 ± 180°F (5425 ± 100°C).

Tantalus A legendary Greek king of Lydia, son of Zeus and Pluto and father of *Niobe and *Pelops. In Hades he was punished for certain offenses against the gods by being made to stand within reach of water and fruits that moved away whenever he tried to drink or eat.

Tantras A group of Sanskrit religious texts written in India in the 5th century AD. The contents are miscellaneous but they form the basis of esoteric systems of meditation in both Hinduism and Buddhism. In the **Tantric yoga** of Hinduism, two principles are postulated: Shiva and Shakti, male and female, mind and creative energy, situated in the head and at the base of the spine, respectively. The object of tantric practices is to arouse the female element, which can be focused in various centers of the body, and ultimately to unite it with the male principle. **Tantric Buddhism** involves an elaborate system of meditation by means of mudras (gestures), mantras (symbolic sounds; *see* Om), and mandalas (diagrams). The imagery of sexual union is the distinctive feature of both systems, which are unusual in emphasizing the fulfillment of bodily desires rather than the ascetic practices that are more typical of Hinduism and Buddhism.

Tanzania, United Republic of A country in East Africa, on the Indian Ocean. It consists of a mainland area (formerly the republic of Tanganyika) and the islands of *Zanzibar and *Pemba, as well as some smaller islands. On the mainland its boundaries are formed partly by Lakes Victoria, Tanganyika, and Malawi. The land rises from the coast through plateaus to mountains, especially in the N, with Mount Kilimanjaro at 19,520 ft (5950 m). The majority of the population is African, mainly of Bantu origin. *Economy*: chiefly agricultural, especially subsistence farming. In mainland Tanzania the chief crops are cotton, corn, and cassava. Sisal, once important, is now in decline and there are plans for diversification of crops as well as development in forestry and livestock. Zanzibar (with Pemba) is the world's largest producer of cloves, with coconuts as the second cash crop. Food crops include rice, bananas, and cassava. Minerals extracted in Tanzania include diamonds, gold, tin, and salt, and coal and iron have been found, as well as offshore gas. Hydroelectricity is a valuable source of power. The main exports are coffee, cloves, cotton, and diamonds. Tourism is important with Tanzania's many game parks and beaches. *History*: important prehistoric remains have been found by the *Leakey family. The area was visited by the Arabs in the middle ages and by the Portuguese in the 16th century. Tanganyika was occupied by the Germans in the 1880s, becoming a German protectorate in 1891. After World War I it was under British rule, first under League of Nations mandate and then as a UN trust territory. It gained independence in 1961 and in 1962 became a republic within the British Commonwealth with Dr Julius K. Nyerere as its first president. In 1964 Tanganyika and Zanzibar joined to form the United Republic of Tanganyika and Zanzibar, now known as Tanzania. In 1977 the official political parties of the two countries merged to form the Revolu-

tionary Party. In the Arusha Declaration (1967) Nyerere launched a policy of decentralization, which has involved the division of rural areas into cooperative communities (Ujamaas). Tanzania was instrumental in the overthrow in Uganda of *Amin. Relations with Zambia are close, particularly since the opening of the Chinese-built Tanzam Railway (1975). Nyerere's great socialist experiment, espousing social and economic self-reliance, appeared to be faltering in the wake of the acute economic hardships of the early 1980s. While his charismatic personality continued to anchor the political processes of the country, public dissatisfaction was increasingly evident. Official languages: Swahili and English. Official currency, since 1966: Tanzanian shilling of 100 cents. Area: 364,900 sq mi [945,087 sq km]. Population (1983 est): 20,524,000. Capital and main port: Dar es Salaam; Dodoma is the projected future capital.

Taoism Emerging in the 6th century BC, Taoism is one of the two great native Chinese religio-philosophical systems (the other is *Confucianism) and a major influence in the development of Chinese culture. The goal of Taoism as a philosophy, as expressed in the *Tao Te Ching* of *Lao-zi, the *Chuang Tzu*, and the *Lieh Tzu*, is profound, joyful, mystical, and practical harmony with the universe. In politics and livelihood, the Taoist seeks the effective path of least resistance and of inconspicuousness. All extreme positions revert to their opposites. All is in flux except Tao (the Way) itself. *Yin* (the feminine) balances *yang* (the masculine). Meditation, spontaneity, and simplicity are stressed. *Te* (virtue) and *Ch'i* (energy) represent the power of effortless action accessible to the Taoist. As a religion Taoism emphasizes the alchemical relations between macrocosm and microcosm, seeking a formula for immortality by breath control, diet, exercises, sexual continence, or chemical elixirs. A priesthood, a huge hierarchical pantheon of gods, and a multitude of sacred texts and rituals associated with various sects arose. Later monasticism developed. Since the Chinese Cultural Revolution (1966–68) religious Taoism survives mainly in Taiwan. Western interest has been aroused by philosophical Taoism, especially by the *I Ching*, an oracular work that claims to demonstrate purpose in chance events.

tape recorder A device for recording and playing back sound stored on magnetic tape. In recording, the sound is converted to an electrical signal by a *microphone and then amplified before being fed to an electromagnet in the recording head. The varying field of the magnet leaves a pattern of magnetization in the iron (or sometimes chromium) oxide coating of the tape as it passes through the machine. To play back, the magnetized tape induces a current in a coil as it passes the reproducing head. The coil current is then amplified and fed to loudspeakers. Tape recorders provide a compact and portable means of recording sounds of all kinds; the tapes are usually wound into *cassettes or cartridges, which can be purchased prerecorded with music, etc., or clean for recording upon.

tapestry A decorative or pictorial woven textile, used as wall hangings, furniture covers, etc. Tapestry weaving has been practiced since antiquity but it only flourished in Europe from the 14th century, the major centers of production being Arras, Tournai, and Brussels in Flanders, and Beauvais and the *Gobelins factory in France. Medieval tapestries, often of floral and leaf patterns, were used as portable draft screens; others showing religious scenes were made for churches. From the 16th century painters, notably *Raphael and *Boucher, were commissioned to design tapestries. In the 19th century machine-made tapestries were introduced.

tapeworm A parasitic hermaphrodite *flatworm of the class *Cestoda* (about 3000 species). Tapeworms range from 0.75 in–50 ft (20 mm to 15 m) in length and anchor themselves inside the intestine of their host by means of hooks and suckers on the head. They have no gut or sense organs, the body consisting of a chain of progressively large segments through which food is absorbed. The terminal segments—full of eggs—are regularly shed, passing out of the host's body to infect a secondary host, where larvae invade muscle tissue. Species infecting man include the beef tapeworm (*Taenia saginata*) and the pork tapeworm (*T. solium*).

tapioca. See cassava.

tapir A shy nocturnal hoofed mammal belonging to the genus *Tapirus* (4 species). The largest species is the black and white Malayan tapir (*T. indicus*), reaching about 40 in (1 m) at the shoulder and weighing up to 770 lb (350 kg). The remaining species of Central and South America are brown. All have a sparse covering of hairs and a large head with a short fleshy snout. Young tapirs are marked with white spots and stripes. Tapirs inhabit forests near water, feeding on leaves and shoots. Family: *Tapiridae*; order: *Perissodactyla.*

tar A thick black semisolid substance of organic origin, especially coaltar obtained when coal is heated to over 1834°F (1000°C) in the absence of air (2.2 lb [1 kg] of coal yielding about 1.8 oz [50 g] of tar). Tar can be used as it is, e.g. for the production of roofing felt, or can be distilled to produce a wide range of organic chemicals including benzene, naphthalene, and anthracene and their derivatives. The substance remaining is called pitch.

Tara 53 34N 6 35W A village in the Republic of Ireland, in Co Meath. The Hill of Tara was the ancient religious and political center of Ireland and here the early Irish Kings lived and were crowned. The original coronation stone is reputed to have been taken to Scone, Scotland.

Taranto 40 28N 17 15E A seaport in Italy, in Apulia on the Gulf of Taranto. Founded by the Greeks in the 8th century BC, it has an 11th-century cathedral. It is an important naval base, with shipyards. Its large iron and steel works were established in 1965. Population (1980 est): 248,611.

tarantula A large dark hairy spider (up to 3 in [75 mm] long) of the family *Theraphosidae*, found in tropical America. Many tarantulas live on trees or in burrows in the soil, feeding mainly at night on insects and occasionally frogs, toads, mice, and small birds. Their poisonous bite is painful but not fatal to man.

The name was originally given to a *wolf spider (*Lycosa tarentula*) of Taranto (Italy). In the middle ages it was believed that the poisonous effects of the bite of this spider could be eliminated by dancing (the dance came to be known as the tarantella).

Tarbell, Ida (Minerva) (1857–1944) US muckraking journalist and writer. An editor (1894–1906) of *McClure's Magazine*, she exposed unfair practices in the oil industry through articles that were consolidated in *A History of the Standard Oil Company* (1904). From 1906 she co-edited *American Magazine*, a publication she helped to establish. Other works included *Life of Abraham Lincoln* (1900), *The Tariff in Our Times* (1911), *The Business of Being a Woman* (1913), and *The Nationalizing of Business, 1878–1898* (1936).

Tarbes 43 14N 0 05E A city in SW France, the capital of the Hautes-Pyrénées department. A Huguenot stronghold (16th–17th centuries), it has a 13th-century cathedral and trades in horses and agricultural produce. Population (1975): 57,765.

Tardigrada A phylum of tiny invertebrate animals (about 350 species), known as water bears, sometimes regarded as a class of arthropods. About 0.04 in (1 mm) long, they are almost transparent, with four pairs of short legs ending in claws. Tardigrades are found in terrestrial, freshwater, and marine habitats, feeding on the sap of mosses and other plants.

tare One of several annual herbs of the genus *Vicia* (which also includes *vetches) that grow as weeds on cultivated land throughout the world. Tares have slender trailing stems, up to 24 in (60 cm) long, and branches with paired leaflets and terminal climbing tendrils. The tiny white or bluish flowers give rise to seed pods. Family: *Leguminosae.

targum (Aramaic: translation) An Aramaic translation of part of the Bible. There are several targumim, notably those of Onkelos (of the Torah) and Pseudo-Jonathan (of the Prophets). They were produced in Palestine and Babylonia in the Talmudic and gaonic periods, and include a great deal of *Midrash.

Tariff of 1828 (*or* Tariff of Abominations) US law that levied high taxes on wool, hemp, and other raw materials, as well as on finished goods. Passed for political reasons, parts of the bill were revised by the Tariff of 1832.

Tariff of 1832 US legislation that revised the Tariff of 1828. It removed a tariff on raw wool and flax imports and increased the duty on finished woolen goods. It was nullified in 1833.

tariffs A surcharge imposed by a government on imported goods. Several arguments are used to justify tariffs. The "infant industry" argument is that tariffs are needed to protect a domestic industry while it becomes established. Other arguments include the need to protect employment in domestic industries, the need to provide a counter to "dumping" (foreign industries selling goods at a lower price abroad than at home), and the benefit of the revenue that will accrue from tariffs. The secretariat of the *General Agreement on Tariffs and Trade serves as a center for negotiating tariff agreements. *See also* customs unions.

Tarim Basin A great depression in NW China, covering the area between the *Tian Shan in the N and the *Kunlun Mountains in the S. Drained by the Dalimu (*or* Tarim) River, it consists of the Takelamagan (*or* Takla Makan) Desert with the salt lake of *Lop Nor in the E, where nuclear tests have been held. Although there are oasis towns, the region is largely undeveloped. Area: about 350,000 sq mi (906,500 sq km).

Tarkington, (Newton) Booth (1869–1946) US novelist. His first novel, *The Gentleman from Indiana*, was published in 1899. Subsequent novels, *The Magnificent Ambersons* (1918) and *Alice Adams* (1921), were awarded Pulitzer Prizes, and he is well known for his classic teenage novels, *Penrod* (1914) and *Seventeen* (1916).

taro A perennial herbaceous plant, *Colocasia esculenta*, also known as eddo, dasheen, and elephant's ear, native to tropical Asia and widely cultivated in tropical and subtropical areas for its edible tubers. The tubers, which are large, starchy, and spherical, contain more protein than potatoes and are eaten cooked as vegetables or made into puddings or bread. Family: *Araceae*.

TAROT *The Wheel of Fortune, the 10th card of the Greater Arcana, from a pack of French tarot cards.*

tarot A pack of 78 cards used primarily in fortune telling, although they are also the forerunners of modern *playing cards, and games are still played with them. They originated in 14th-century Italy, although their symbolism probably draws on a far older tradition. The original pack is now known as the Greater Arcana; this consists of 22 cards (believed to correspond to the letters of the Hebrew alphabet), 21 numbered cards representing natural elements, vices, and virtues and a "Fool" (the original joker). During the 14th century these were combined with 56 number cards of the Asian kind then also beginning to be used. Now known as the Lesser Arcana, these 56 are in 4 suits: cups, swords, money, and clubs or rods, representing clergy, nobility, merchants, and peasants. Each suit consists of number cards from one to ten and four court cards: king, queen, knave, and knight.

tarpan A Eurasian wild horse, *Equus caballus*, that became extinct in the early 20th century. It was small and dun-colored with a long flowing mane. Attempts have been made to reconstitute the tarpan by crossing various modern breeds that are thought to be related to it.

Tarpeia In Roman legend, a Roman commander's daughter who offered to betray Rome to the attacking Sabines in return for what they wore on their left arms, meaning their golden bracelets. When the Sabines overran the citadel, they literally obeyed her wish by crushing her to death with their shields.

tarpon A marine game fish belonging to the family *Elopidae*. It has a slender body covered by large thick silvery scales. The Atlantic tarpon, *Tarpon* (or *Megalops*) *atlanticus*, reaches up to 7 ft (2 m) in length and occurs inshore in warm waters. Order: *Elopiformes*.

Tarquin the Proud (Tarquinius Superbus) The last King of Rome, who ruled, according to Roman tradition, from 534 to 510 BC. Tarquin is probably a historical figure but many myths evolved to account for the nickname Superbus; he was expelled from Rome and brought monarchy into permanent disrepute there.

tarragon A perennial herb, *Artemisia dracunculus*, native to central Asia and widely cultivated. It grows to a height of about 24 in (60 cm) and has slender leaves and flowers, which are often dried and used in salads, sauces, pickles, etc. It also yields an essential oil used in cooking and perfumery. Family: *Compositae*.

Tarragona (Latin name: Tarraco)   41 07N 1 15E A port in NE Spain, in Catalonia on the Mediterranean Sea. It was a major Roman port and has many Roman ruins, including an aqueduct; it also possesses a cathedral (12th–13th centuries). An agricultural center, it also has a petrochemicals industry. Population (1970): 78,238.

Tarrasa 41 38N 2 00E A city in NE Spain, in Catalonia. An important industrial center, it is famous for its woolen textiles; other industries include glass and fertilizers. Population (1974 est): 138,697.

tarsier A small nocturnal *prosimian primate belonging to the genus *Tarsius* (3 species), of Sumatra, Borneo, Celebes, and the Philippines. 9–17 in (22–43 cm) long including the naked tail (5–11 in [13–27 cm]), tarsiers have enormous eyes, large hairless ears, and gripping pads at the end of their digits. They are mainly arboreal, using both hands to seize small insects and lizards. Family: *Tarsiidae*. □mammal.

Tarsus 36 52N 34 52E A city in central S Turkey, near Adana. The first known settlement here was Neolithic; it was Assyrian for many centuries and an important town in the Roman and Byzantine Empires. St Paul was born here. Population (1970): 78,033.

tartan. *See* Highland dress.

tartaric acid (HOOC(CHOH)$_2$COOH) A white crystalline powder with an acid taste; it is a constituent of *baking powder.

Tartarus In Greek religion, the place of punishment and perpetual torment in the underworld. The *Titans were imprisoned there after their defeat by the gods.

Tartu (German and Swedish name: Dorpat)   58 20N 26 44E A city in the Soviet Union, in the SE Estonian SSR. Although an industrial center, it is best known for its university founded (1632) by Gustavus II Adolphus of Sweden, Tartu being held successively by Sweden, Poland, and Russia to which it was finally ceded in 1704. Population (1970): 90,459.

Tasaday A people of the rain forests of Mindanao in the Philippines having an extremely rudimentary culture based on food gathering using simple stone and wooden tools. They are cave dwellers who wear leaves for clothing and only became known to the outside world in 1971.

Tashkent 41 16N 69 13E A city in the S central Soviet Union, the capital of the Uzbek SSR. It is the oldest and largest city of central Asia, being a major communications, industrial, and cultural center. Textiles (based on cotton from the surrounding oasis), food- and tobacco-processing, and chemical industries are important. *History*: dating from at least the 1st century BC, it fell successively to the Arabs (7th century) and the Turks (12th century), becoming a great commercial center under Timur. It was captured by Russia in 1865. Tashkent was severely damaged by earthquake in 1966. Population (1981 est): 1,858,000.

Tasman, Abel Janszoon (c. 1603–c. 1659) Dutch navigator. Commissioned in 1642 by van *Dieman to explore the S Pacific, Tasman sighted present-day Tasmania (which he named Van Dieman's Land, after his patron), New Zealand, and in 1643 Tonga and Fiji. In 1644 he sailed along the N coast of Australia, thus proving it continuous.

Tasmania An island and the smallest state of Australia, separated from the SE corner of the mainland by Bass Strait. Discovered by Abel *Tasman in 1642, it was called Van Dieman's Land until 1856. It is the most mountainous of the Australian states and is dominated by the Central Plateau. Agriculture is important with mixed and dairy farming, sheep rearing, and the cultivation of apples and hops. More than 40% of the island is covered by forest and the export of wood chips to Japan is a significant industry. Large mineral deposits include tin, iron ore, zinc, lead, and copper; King Island, off the NW coast, is Australia's main producer of tungsten. Area: 26,383 sq mi (68,332 sq km). Population (1980 est): 422,900. Capital: Hobart.

Tasmanian devil A carnivorous marsupial, *Sarcophilus harrisi*, formerly found on the Australian mainland but now restricted to Tasmania. About 40 in (1 m) long, it is black with a large head and wide jaws containing doglike teeth. Strong and heavily built, it feeds on wallabies, birds, and lizards and fights ferociously when cornered. Family: *Dasyuridae* (dasyures).

Tasmanian wolf. *See* thylacine.

Tasman Sea A section of the SW Pacific Ocean, lying between SE Australia and Tasmania on the W and New Zealand on the E. Area: about 900,000 sq mi (2,300,000 sq km).

Tass. *See* news agency.

Tassili-n-Ajjer A sandstone massif in the central Sahara containing numerous caves decorated with rock paintings of people and animals (c. 8000–c. 100 BC). Depictions of hippopotamuses and vast herds of cattle indicate a far damper climate than at present.

Tasso, Torquato (1544–95) Italian poet. After studying law at Padua and publishing his epic *Rinaldo* (1562) he joined the court of the Este family at Ferrara, where he wrote the pastoral drama *Aminta* (1573) and his major work, the romantic epic *Gerusalemme liberata* (1575). For the rest of his life he suffered from mental instability but continued to write lyrics, religious poems, philosophical dialogues, and a tragedy, *Re Torrismondo* (1587).

taste. *See* tongue.

Tatar Autonomous Soviet Socialist Republic (*or* Tataria) An administrative division in the W central Soviet Union, in the RSFSR. The *Tatars, who comprise some 50% of the population, were conquered by Ivan the Terrible in the 16th century. The region became an autonomous republic in 1920. The region is the country's main producer of oil and natural gas and also has deposits of coal and other minerals. There are highly developed engineering, oil, and chemical industries, and the timber, textile, and food industries are now also expanding. Agricultural products include fodder crops and cereals. Area: 26,250 sq mi (68,000 sq km). Population (1981 est): 3,453,000. Capital: Kazan.

Tatars A people, mainly living in the Tatar ASSR of the Soviet Union, who belong to the NW division of the Turkic-speaking peoples. They traditionally lived by farming and herding. There are many Tatar dialects, one of which, Kazan Tatar, is a literary language that goes back to the 13th century. The Tatars are descended from peoples associated with the various states of the Mongol empire and the name was often used to refer to all the nomadic Turkic and Mongol peoples of the steppes. Their society was traditionally a stratified one divided into noble and commoner groups ruled by khans. They are mainly Muslim. *See also* Golden Horde.

Tate, Allen (1899–) US poet and critic. He was one of the founders of the Fugitives, a group of agrarian poets at Vanderbilt University. The Civil War is the main subject of his novel *The Fathers* (1938) and his best-known poem "Ode to the Confederate Dead" (1926). He published much criticism, including *On the Limits of Poetry* (1948), and his verse is collected in *Collected Poems* (1978).

Tate, Nahum (1652–1715) British poet. Born in Dublin, he is best remembered for his version of Shakespeare's *King Lear*, which omitted the Fool and ended happily with Cordelia marrying Edgar. He was coauthor of the second part of Dryden's *Absalom and Achitophel* (1681). He became Britain's poet laureate in 1692.

Tate Gallery An art gallery in London, England, housing paintings of the British school and modern foreign paintings and sculpture. It was built in 1897 with the financial support of Sir Henry Tate (1819–99), who had donated his collection of British paintings to the nation in 1890. Highlights are its Pre-Raphaelite works and the paintings by *Turner.

Tati, Jacques (J. Tatischeff; 1908–82) French film actor and director. He was a music-hall performer before he turned to films. He wrote, directed, and acted in a number of popular award-winning comedies, such as *Jour de Fête* (1947), *Monsieur Hulot's Holiday* (1952), *Mon Oncle* (1958), and *Playtime* (1968), the humor of which is achieved by imaginative visual gags and Tati's talent for pantomime.

Tatra Mountains Two mountain ranges in central E Europe: the **High Tatras** (Polish name: Tatry Wysokie; Czech name: Vysoké Tatry), which extend 56 mi (90 km) E–W along the Polish-Czech border and constitute the highest area of the *Carpathian Mountains, and, to the S, the **Low Tatras** (Czech name: Nizké Tatry), which run parallel for some 93 mi (150 km) and rise to 6703 ft (2043 m).

Tatum, Art(hur) (1910–56) US jazz pianist, who began playing as a child when he was already blind. A well-known soloist in the 1930s, he formed his own trio in 1943. His superb technique and advanced sense of harmony earned him a high reputation among both jazz and classical musicians.

Tatum, Edward Lawrie (1909–75) US geneticist, who (working with G. W. *Beadle on mutant strains of bread mold) provided evidence that specific genes determine the structure of specified enzymes. In 1946 Tatum and J. *Lederberg discovered the phenomenon of genetic recombination in certain bacteria. Tatum shared a Nobel Prize (1958) with Beadle and Lederberg.

tau particle An elementary particle with a very short lifetime (5×10^{-12} second) and a mass about 3500 times that of the *electron. It is classified as a lepton (*see* particle physics). It reacts by the *weak interaction.

Taupo, Lake (*or* Taupomoana) The largest lake in New Zealand. It lies on the volcanic plateau of central North Island and is drained by the Waikato River. Area: 238 sq mi (616 sq km).

Taurus (Latin: Bull) A large constellation in the N sky near Orion, lying on the *zodiac between Gemini and Aries. The brightest star is *Aldebaran. The constellation contains the *Hyades and *Pleiades star clusters and the *Crab nebula with its associated pulsar.

Taurus Mountains A mountain range in S Turkey. It extends 348 mi (560 km) parallel to the Mediterranean coast and rises to 12,251 ft (3734 m) at Ala Dağ, or to 12,848 ft (3916 m) at Erciyas Dağı if the Anti-Taurus range (an extension to the NE) is included.

tautology A statement that is always true and therefore gives no information. For example, "It is either raining or it is not raining."

tautomerism. *See* isomers.

Tawney, R(ichard) H(enry) (1880–1962) British economic historian. Influenced by the theories of Max *Weber, Tawney wrote on capitalism, his most famous book being *Religion and the Rise of Capitalism* (1926). A professor at London University (1931–49), he was a formative influence on the British Labour Party.

tawny owl A common *owl, *Strix aluco*, occurring in Europe and SE Asia. 15 in (38 cm) long, it has short rounded wings, dark-brown eyes, a mottled brown plumage, and lacks ear tufts.

taxation The means by which a government raises funds to finance its spending and, to some extent, by which it regulates the economy (*see* fiscal policy) or achieves its social and political aims (e.g. the equal distribution of wealth). Direct taxes are paid by individuals (e.g. *income tax, *capital-gains tax), or companies through corporation taxes directly to the tax authorities; indirect taxes are levied on goods and services (e.g. sales taxes). In most cases taxation is levied when funds change hands. Progressive taxation, in which those with higher incomes or greater wealth pay more in proportion than those with lower incomes or less wealth, is a means of achieving social or political objectives. *See also* customs and excise duties.

tax haven (*or* tax shelter) A country or area that has low taxes and can therefore offer advantages to foreign individuals or companies that pay high taxes in their own countries. Individuals have to take up residence in these countries, giving up their domiciliary rights in their own countries; companies can open offices and subsidiary companies in the haven countries, through which they can put part of their business.

taxi. *See* cab.

taxidermy The art of making lifelike zoological models of creatures by preserving their skins and mounting them on suitable dummies. Taxidermy dates from the 17th century but improved technology and the use of plastic body forms have resulted in greater degrees of realism.

Taxila The site of an *Achaemenian and Greek city near Rawalpindi (N Pakistan). Occupied from the 5th century BC, it was a famous center of learning. Excavations revealed a blend of Greek and Buddhist elements, typical of the *Gandhara culture. The *Huns destroyed Taxila in 460 AD.

taxis The movement of a living organism or cell in response to an external stimulus: the movement is either toward or away from the stimulus, i.e. a positive or negative taxis. Taxes are specified according to the type of stimulus. For example, **chemotaxis** is the response to a change in the concentration of a chemical. Many insects, for example, respond chemotactically to the scents emitted by the opposite sex. **Phototaxis** is the response to light: cockroaches are negatively phototactic. *Compare* tropism.

taxonomy The study of the classification and nomenclature of organisms. The principles of taxonomy were established in the 18th century by the work of *Linnaeus (*see also* binomial nomenclature). As far as possible, organisms are arranged into a hierarchy of groups (called taxa) based on degrees of relationship (*see* phylogeny). When knowledge of the evolution of a group is lacking taxonomy is based on structural and other similarities. The basic unit of classification is the *species. Related species are grouped into genera, which are arranged into orders and then classes. Related classes are regarded as belonging to the same *phylum. The two main methods used in determining taxonomic positions are classical taxonomy, which is based on morphological and biochemical data, and numerical taxonomy, in which mathematical and statistical methods are used to assess similarities and differences.

Tay River The longest river in Scotland, rising in the Grampian Mountains and flowing generally NE through Loch Tay before flowing SE to enter the North Sea through the Firth of Tay. Length: 120 mi (193 km).

Taylor, A(lan) J(ohn) P(ercivale) (1906–) British historian, who specializes in modern European political history. Among his many books is *The Origins of the Second World War* (1961).

Taylor, Brook (1685–1737) English mathematician, best known for the Taylor series in calculus. He also made contributions to the mathematics of perspective. Taylor, educated at Cambridge, was secretary of the Royal Society between 1714 and 1719.

Taylor, Elizabeth (1932–) US film actress, born in England. She began her career as a child star, notably in *National Velvet* (1944). Her other films include *Giant* (1956), *Butterfield 8* (1961), *Who's Afraid of Virginia Woolf?* (1966), in which she costarred with Richard *Burton, to whom she was twice married, and *The Blue Bird* (1976).

Taylor, Frederick Winslow (1856–1915) US engineer, who pioneered the techniques of scientific management. In 1881, while working for the Midvale Steel Company, he introduced time and motion study as a means of increasing efficiency, incurring considerable resentment from those affected by it. He later became a management consultant to many firms.

Taylor, Zachary (1784–1850) US general and statesman; 12th President of the US (1849–50). Beginning his military career in the *War of 1812, Taylor later participated in the *Black Hawk and *Seminole wars and served as commander of the Department of Florida (1838–40). During the *Mexican War, he gained national acclaim and his nickname "Old Rough and Ready" for his important victories at Monterrey and at the Battle of *Buena Vista. Receiving the presidential nomination of the Whig Party in 1848, Taylor defeated the Democratic candidate, Lewis Cass, in the general election. However, he served as president for less than two years, dying in office in 1850.

Tbilisi (Russian name: Tiflis) 41 43N 44 48E A city in the SW Soviet Union, the capital of the Georgian SSR on the Kura River. A major industrial center, engineering and the manufacture of textiles, wine, and food are the principal economic activities; Tbilisi also has a lively cultural life. *History*: founded in the mid-5th century, it fell successively to the Persians, Byzantines, Arabs, Mongols, Turks, and, finally, the Russians (1801). Its name was changed to the Georgian Tbilisi in 1936. Population (1981 est): 1,095,000.

Tchaikovsky, Peter Ilich (1840–93) Russian composer. He studied under Anton Rubinstein in St Petersburg and became professor at the Moscow conservatoire in 1866. After the success of his first piano concerto, Tchaikovsky was offered financial support from Nadezhda von Meck (1831–94), a wealthy widow, whom he never met. In 1877 Tchaikovsky made a disastrous marriage and began to suffer from depression, although many of his works were extremely successful. He died of cholera, from drinking unboiled water, in 1893. Among his compositions are six symphonies, including the *Pathétique* (1893), three piano concertos (one unfinished), a violin concerto, string quartets, the opera *Eugene Onegin* (1877–78), and the ballets *Swan Lake* (1876–77) and the *Nutcracker* (1891–92).

tea The dried leaves and shoots of the evergreen shrub or tree *Camellia sinensis*, which yield a beverage when infused with water. Native to parts of India and China, the tea plant has three major varieties—China, Assam, and Cambodia—and numerous hybrids, ranging from 9–60 ft (2.75 to 18 m) in height. The shoots and young leaves are picked by hand and left to wilt before being lightly rolled and dried. Before drying, the leaves may be allowed to ferment, producing either black tea or, if only partially fermented, oolong tea. Leaves that are not fermented produce green tea. The major tea exporters are India and Sri Lanka; most of China's production goes for home consumption. Tea is also produced in SE Asia and parts of Africa and South America. Tea is sold in the form of chopped leaves—loose or contained in small porous paper bags (tea bags)—or as a soluble powdered extract (instant tea). Its stimulating effect is due to the caffeine content (about 3.5%); flavor depends on the presence of volatile oils, and tannins are responsible for its color. Family: *Theaceae*.

Tea Act (1773) *See* Boston Tea Party.

tea ceremony. *See* cha-no-yu.

Teach, Edward (d. 1718) British pirate, nicknamed Blackbeard, who molested shipping in the Atlantic from his headquarters in N Carolina. In 1718 he was killed by a punitive force sent from Virginia.

teak A tropical □tree, *Tectonia grandis*, native to SE Asia and cultivated for its timber. Growing to a height of 150 ft (45 m) in its natural state, it has small white flowers and fleshy fruits. The aromatic golden-yellow heartwood becomes brown with darker mottling when seasoned and is very hard and durable, being used for furniture, door and window frames, construction purposes, etc. Burma is the major teak exporter. Family: *Verbenaceae*.

teal A small *dabbling duck, *Anas crecca*, of the N hemisphere, nesting on marshes and wintering on mudflats and estuaries. 14 in (35 cm) long, it feeds on water plants and aquatic invertebrates. Drakes are grey and have a chestnut head with a cream-edged green eye stripe and a white wing stripe; females are mottled brown and both sexes have a green-and-black wing patch.

Teapot Dome Scandal (1921–24) US political scandal during the administration of President Warren G. *Harding that involved the illegal leasing of government oil reserve lands. Secretary of the Interior Albert B. Fall leased Navy oil reserve lands at Elk Hills, Calif, and Teapot Dome, Wyo, to private businessmen Harry F. Sinclair and Edward Doheny, in exchange for payments totaling $409,000. Fall was prosecuted and convicted of bribery charges; Sinclair and Doheny were acquitted of conspiracy charges. The reputation of the entire Harding administration was clouded by the affair.

tear gas (*or* lachrymator) A substance, generally an atomized liquid rather than a gas, that is used to control crowds by causing acute eye irritation with temporary blindness and copious flow of tears. Side effects include lasting damage to the eyes and nasal and lung tissues and dermatitis. Chloroacetophenone (Mace) is the best-known example. *See also* chemical warfare.

Teasdale, Sara (1884–1933) US poet. Using simple, traditional lyric forms, she wrote the collections *Helen of Troy and Other Poems* (1911) and *Rivers to the Sea* (1915) before being awarded a Pulitzer Prize for *Love Songs* (1917). Other works include *Flame and Shadow* (1920), *Rainbow Gold* (1922), *Dark of the Moon* (1926), and *Strange Victory* (1933), which was published after her suicide.

teasel A biennial herb, *Dipsacus fullonum*, native to Europe, W Asia, and N Africa. The prickly stems grow to a height of 7 ft (2 m) and bear conical heads of blue, purple, or white flowers with stiff hooked bracts. Fuller's teasel (*D. fullonum sativus*) was formerly cultivated for its flower heads, which were used to tease fabrics and raise a nap. Family: *Dipsacaceae*.

technetium (Tc) A silvery-gray radioactive element that was the first to be produced artificially. It does not occur naturally on earth but has been observed spectroscopically in a number of stars, where it is being continuously formed by nuclear reactions. It is chemically similar to rhenium and the compound $KTcO_4$ is a remarkable corrosion inhibitor in steels. At no 43; at wt (99); mp 4045°F (2227°C); bp 8369°F (4627°C).

tectonics The study of the major structural features of the earth's crust and the processes by which they are constructed. Thus a feature described as tectonic is formed by deformational movements of the earth's crust or by volcanic action rather than by geomorphological processes. A tectonic map shows structural features, usually over large areas. The most modern interpretation of global tectonics is the theory of *plate tectonics.

Tecumseh (c. 1768–1813) American Shawnee Indian chief, who led an Indian confederacy against the advance of white settlement in the NW. After his tribe was surprised at the battle of Tippecanoe (1811) he swore eternal war on the settlers. The conviction among frontiersmen that the British in Canada were helping Tecumseh led to a demand among the so-called War Hawks in Congress for war with Britain, the *War of 1812, in which Tecumseh was killed.

Tees River A river in N England. Rising in the Pennines in Cumbria, it flows mainly E into the Teesmouth estuary at Middlesbrough to join the North Sea. Length: 70 mi (113 km).

teeth Hard structures in the mouth, embedded in the jaws, used for biting and chewing food. The human adult (permanent) dentition consists of 32 teeth, including incisors (8), canines (4), premolars (8), and molars (12). Young children have a milk (deciduous) dentition of 20 teeth (incisors, canines, and molars), which are replaced by the permanent teeth between the ages of 6 and 12. The third molar (wisdom tooth) on each side of both jaws does not normally appear until the age of about 20 (sometimes later). The crown of a tooth consists of very dense hard enamel (largely *apatite) overlying the yellow bonelike dentine, which is slightly spongy and very sensitive to touch, temperature, and pain. The pulp at the center contains blood vessels and nerve fibers. The principal disorders affecting teeth are *caries and *periodontal disease. *See also* dentistry.

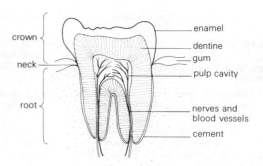

molar tooth *The root of the tooth is anchored into the socket by a bonelike substance, cement.*

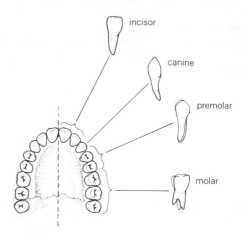

teeth in the adult upper jaw *The incisors and canines are used principally for biting; the premolars and molars are for grinding and chewing. The lower jaw contains the same number and type of teeth.*

TEETH

Tegucigalpa 14 20N 87 12W The capital of Honduras, situated in the center of the country in a high valley. Founded in 1579, it was an important center of gold and silver mining. It became the capital in 1824. The University of Honduras was founded in 1847. Population (1980 est): 472,700.

Tehran (*or* Teheran) 35 40N 51 26E The capital of Iran, in the N center of the country at the foot of the Elburz Mountains. Most of its buildings are modern, but the Gulistan Palace, which houses the Crown Jewels, is a notable older structure. Tehran is the commercial, industrial, administrative, and cultural center of the country, with six universities (oldest 1934). It became the capital in 1788 and has been greatly enlarged this century. Fierce rioting here preceded the overthrow (1979) of the Shah of Iran. Population (1976): 4,498,159.

Tehran Conference (1943) The conference in World War II attended by President Franklin D. Roosevelt (US), Stalin (Soviet Union), and Churchill (UK). Its chief purpose was to coordinate Allied strategy in W and E Europe.

Tehuantepec, Isthmus of An isthmus in S Mexico, between the Gulf of Campeche and the Gulf of Tehuantepec.

Teilhard de Chardin, Pierre (1881–1955) French Jesuit theologian and paleontologist. Teilhard de Chardin's philosophical books were suppressed by the Roman Catholic Church during his lifetime. He is best known for his creative synthesis of natural science and religion and his Christian metaphysical philosophy. In his books *The Phenomenon of Man* (1955) and *Le Milieu divin* (1957), he maintained that the universe and mankind are in constant evolution toward a perfect state.

Tejo River. *See* Tagus River.

tektites Small glassy objects, which have been found in certain parts of the earth, often strewn over immense areas. They are apparently composed of rapidly cooled molten material, probably terrestrial in origin and formed during the impact of giant meteorites.

Telanaipura. *See Jambi.*

Tel Aviv-Yafo 32 05N 34 46E A city in central Israel, on the Mediterranean coast. Most of the buildings in the city are modern structures, but some old streets have been restored. It is the largest city in Israel, and the country's commercial, industrial, and cultural center. Israel's stock exchange is here, and there are two universities (1953 and 1974). The city's port is at Ashdod, to the S. *History*: Tel Aviv was originally a suburb to the N of Jaffa (ancient name: Joppa; Arabic name: Yafa), founded in 1909 to relieve the overpopulation of the Jewish quarter of an otherwise Arab town. Following tension between Arabs and Jews, the two towns were separated in 1921, and, as Jewish immigration increased, Tel Aviv expanded rapidly becoming by 1936 the largest city in Palestine. Almost the entire Arab population fled Jaffa on its capture by Jewish forces in 1948, and the two cities were reunited in 1950 as Tel Aviv-Yafo. Population (1979 est): 336,300.

telecommunications The transfer of information by any electromagnetic means, such as wire or radio waves. It includes telephones, telegraphy, *radio, *televison, etc. Generally, a telecommunications system consists of a transmitter, a transmission channel, and a receiver. The input to the transmitter is usually coded in some way and then fed to a modulator, in which it is combined with a carrier signal (*see* modulation).
The transmission channel may be a wire, an optical fiber, or radio waves within a specified frequency range (the bandwidth). A single channel may carry several signals if a *multiplexer is used. The receiver demodulates the signal and decodes it, converting it into the desired form of output, which may be sound, an electrical signal to a computer, a teleprinter printout, etc. Distortion may occur in the transmission because the signal has taken two different paths (shadowing) or because the channel may not respond equally to all the frequencies being transmitted. Noise (spurious signals) may arise at any stage of the transmission and reception process.
The **telephone**, which was invented by Alexander Graham Bell in 1875, carries speech in the form of electrical signals along a wire. A carbon *microphone in the mouthpiece produces an electrical signal that passes through a network of exchanges and relays to the receiving earpiece, where it is converted back into sound by a small diaphragm *loudspeaker. Telephone connections are now normally made automatically, first going through a local exchange and then, for long-distance calls, through the trunk network. All the switching operations are activated by the caller and controlled and monitored electronically. Telephone connections exist to almost all parts of the world through undersea cables and *communications satellites. **Telegraphy** is the transmission of written or printed messages by electrical signals and was developed before the telephone, in 1837, by Samuel F. B. *Morse. Now telegrams and *Telex messages are carried along the same wires as telephone conversations, using different frequency ranges. Radiotelegraphy uses radio waves instead of a wire to carry the message. Like long-distance telephone links it may be relayed by communications satellites. Optical fibers transmitting beams of laser light have been developed and can carry considerably more information than an electric cable of the same thickness. *See also* teletext; viewdata.

telekinesis Apparent change in or movement of material objects, caused by mental effort alone. It is also called psychokinesis (PK). The claims of Uri Geller (1946–), an Israeli, to break metal objects merely by concentrating on them have received great publicity. Telekinesis has been evoked to explain levitation and certain *poltergeist manifestations.

Telemachus In Greek legend, the son of *Odysseus and *Penelope. He searched for his lost father and then helped him kill the suitors of Penelope. After Odysseus' death he married *Circe.

Telemann, Georg Philipp (1681–1767) German composer, born in Magdeburg. While studying law at Leipzig University he taught himself to play various instruments and to compose, obtaining a post in 1704 as organist at the New Church. He held other musical posts in various cities, including Frankfurt and Hamburg (1721). His output was very large and included operas, oratorios, church music, and much chamber music.

teleology The philosophical study of ends, goals, and the ultimate good. It has application in both ethics (*see* utilitarianism) and *metaphysics. Teleology was studied by *Kant who used it to provide a proof of the existence of God in terms of the purposiveness of the universe.

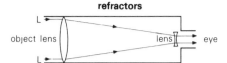

refractors

Galilean *The simplest practical form of refracting telescope was developed by Galileo in about 1609 from Lippershey's invention.*

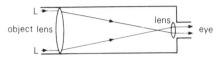

Keplerian *Kepler's arrangement produces an inverted image but was much used for astronomical observations in which the inversion did not matter.*

reflectors

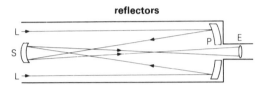

Gregorian *James Gregory proposed this design in 1663 but it has had little general application.*

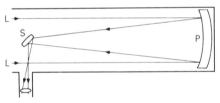

Newtonian *In Newton's 1671 design the secondary mirror is placed at an angle of 45° to the axis of the beam.*

Cassegrain *Widely used, this form was invented by the obscure French astronomer N. Cassegrain in 1672.*

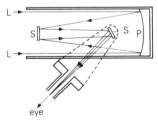

coudé (French: angled) *This arrangement is valuable in larger telescopes as it increases their focal length.*

L = *light rays*   P = *primary mirror*
E = *eyepiece*   S = *secondary mirror*

TELESCOPE

teleost Any *bony fish belonging to the infraclass *Teleostei* (over 20,000 species), which includes nearly all the important food and game fish and many aquarium fish. Teleosts have a symmetrically divided (homocercal) tail fin and an air-filled swim bladder, which is emptied or filled to regulate

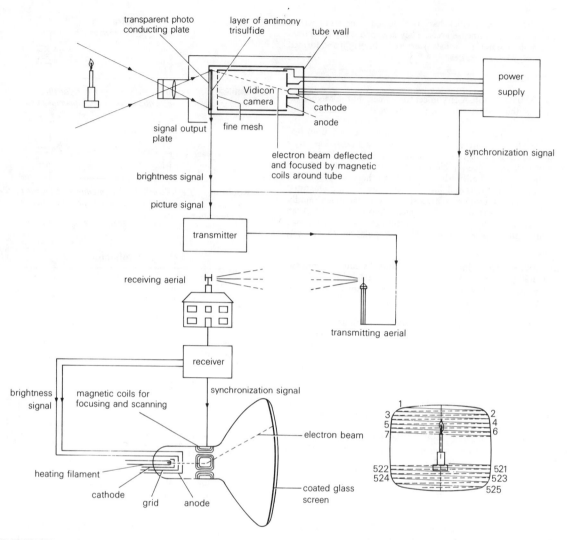

TELEVISION

buoyancy and give great maneuverability. They are solitary or shoaling fish and most lay eggs on rocks or plants, or freely in the water, although some bear live young. Males or sometimes the females may guard the young. Chief orders: *Clupeiformes* (*see* herring; anchovy), *Salmoniformes* (*see* salmon; trout; pike), *Cypriniformes* (*see* carp), *Gadiformes* (*see* cod; hake), *Perciformes* (*see* perch; mackerel), *Pleuronectiformes* (*see* flatfish); subclass: *Actinopterygii*.

telepathy. *See* extrasensory perception.

telephone. *See* telecommunications.

telephoto lens A camera lens that gives a bigger image than a normal lens without moving the camera closer to the subject or extending the camera. It consists of two groups of lenses. The front unit converges the light rays and the rear unit partially corrects this. The light reaching the film appears to converge from a point some distance in front of the camera. Telephoto lenses tend to result in a slightly flattened perspective in the final picture.

telescope An optical instrument that produces a magnified image of distant objects. It is used on land and as a major research tool in astronomy. The first **reflecting telescope** was produced by *Newton in 1668. In the reflecting telescope the light from an object is collected by a concave, usually paraboloid, mirror of long focal length. This primary mirror reflects the light into a secondary optical system, which in turn reflects it into a short-focus eyepiece. The eyepiece lenses produce a magnified image that can be viewed by eye, photographed, or otherwise analyzed. Depending on the secondary optics, reflectors are called **Gregorian**, **Newtonian**, **Cassegrain**, or **coudé telescopes**.

The **refracting telescope** was invented in 1608 by *Lippershey in Holland and developed by *Galileo as an astronomical instrument a year later. The light in the refracting telescope falls on a converging long-focus objective lens. The resulting image is then magnified by the short-focus eyepiece to produce the final image. An example is the **Keplerian telescope**, which was the first major improvement on Galileo's original design. Refractors are also used as terrestrial telescopes, usually containing an additional lens or a prism to cause the inverted image to be seen erect.

A telescope's light-gathering power depends on the area of the primary mirror or the objective lens. Since large mirrors are easier to fashion and mount than large lenses, the major astronomical telescopes are reflectors. In addition, unlike the objective in refractors, the reflector's mirror suffers no chromatic *aberration and its spherical aberration and coma are minimal. The world's largest optical telescope is the Soviet Academy of Sciences' 20 ft (6 m) reflector in the Northern Caucasus. *See also* Schmidt telescope; radio telescope.

Telesio, Bernardino (1509–88) Italian humanist. His philosophy was influenced by the ancient Greeks and was strongly empirical and opposed to *Aristotelianism. He founded a scientific society (1566) to propagate his approach and among those he influenced were *Campanella and Giordano *Bruno.

teletext An information service in which pages of text are transmitted together with normal television broadcasts for display on a modified domestic television set. The system utilizes two of the unused lines between picture frames. All the stored information, which may be weather reports, news flashes, sports results, etc., is sent out continuously in the blanking period of the television signals. The required pages are selected for display by keyboard, and the user may have to wait a few minutes for them to come up on the screen if the cycle is a long one containing a large number of transmissions.

television (TV) The broadcasting of pictures and sound by *radio waves or electric cable. Television was invented by John Logie Baird in 1926. At a TV studio or outside-broadcast unit, a television *camera converts the picture into an electrical signal. In the US the picture consists of 525 lines made by an electron beam scanning the screen of a *cathode-ray tube, 30 such pictures being formed every second. In most of Europe 625 lines and 25 frames per second are used. A brightness signal and a synchronization signal (to form the lines and frames of the picture) make up the picture signal, which is used to modulate (see modulation) a VHF or UHF carrier wave and is broadcast with the modulated sound carrier wave (which has a slightly different frequency). In color TV, a color signal has to be added to the picture signal.

The aerial of the TV receiver detects the broadcast radio waves and the picture and sound signals are separated within the receiver. The picture signal is demodulated, and the resulting current is used to control the electron beam in a cathode-ray tube so that the picture is reconstructed, the scanning being sufficiently fast to give the impression of a continuous moving picture.

In a **color television** camera light from the scene to be televised is filtered into three primary color components: red, green, and blue. Light of each color goes to a separate image tube. There are three systems in use for encoding color picture information for transmission: the US system, also used in Canada, Mexico, and Japan; the PAL (phase alteration line) system used in most W European countries; and SECAM (système électronique couleur avec mémoire), used in France, E Europe, and the Soviet Union. All of these combine color and intensity information with sound and synchronization in a similar way to black-and-white television. The color television receiver splits the signal into red, green, and blue components and applies these to three separate electron guns. The beam from each gun activates a set of phosphor dots of that color on the screen, thus reconstructing the red, green, and blue components of the picture.

Telex A telegraphy system using telephone lines to transmit printed messages from one terminal (the teleprinter) to another. The message is typed onto a keyboard transmitter, which converts the characters into a coded electrical signal for transmission. A printing receiver (combined with the transmitter) carries out the reverse process, typing out messages as they arrive. Telex messages are directed through the telephone lines by the subscribers' numbers, each subscriber also being identified by his call sign. The system is extensively used by commercial and other organizations, because it costs less than a telephone call and provides both parties with a written copy of the messages. To increase the speed of transmission most teleprinters are equipped with a paper-tape punch to prerecord messages.

Tell, William A Swiss national hero who is first mentioned in a 15th-century chronicle and who, in Schiller's play *Wilhelm Tell* (1804), embodies the Swiss struggle for independence from the Austrian Habsburgs. After refusing to do homage as required by Gessler, the Austrian governor, Tell was ordered to shoot an apple from his son's head with a crossbow at 80 paces. He passed this test and later killed Gessler.

Tell el-Amarna The site of Akhetaten, the capital founded (c. 1375 BC) by the heretic Egyptian pharaoh *Akhenaten. It was to have been the center of Akhenaten's new religion but was abandoned shortly after his death (c. 1360). Amarna is associated with a naturalistic art style and a diplomatic correspondence (the *Amarna Tablets) showing the decline of Egyptian prestige in W Asia.

Teller, Edward (1908–) US physicist, born in Hungary. After studying in Germany he left in 1933, going first to London and then to Washington, DC. He worked on the fission bomb during World War II and subsequently on the fusion bomb, making a significant contribution to its development. He is sometimes known as "the father of the H-bomb." Teller's unfavorable evidence in the Robert *Oppenheimer security-clearance hearing lost him some respect among scientists.

tellurium (Te) A silvery-white semiconductor of the sulfur group, discovered by Müller von Reichenstein in 1782. The hydride (H_2Te) is volatile and toxic, with a powerful smell of bad eggs. Bismuth telluride (BiTe) is used as an effective thermoelectric cooler. The metal is used in some special alloys and in some semiconducting devices. At no 52; at wt 127.60; mp 842 ± 0.5°F (449.5 ± 0.3°C); bp 1814 ± 5°F (989 ± 3°C).

Telstar. *See* communications satellite.

Telukbetung 5 28S 105 16E A port in Indonesia, in S Sumatra on the Sunda Strait. It was devastated by the eruption of *Krakatoa in 1883. Exports include rubber, coffee, and cinchona. Population (1971): 198,986.

Tema 5 41N 0 00E A port in Ghana, on the Atlantic coast. It has Africa's largest man-made harbor (opened 1962). Industries include oil refining, chemicals, and fishing. Population (1970 est): 58,800.

Tempe, Vale of (Modern Greek name: Témbi) A valley in N Greece, leading down to the Aegean Sea SE of Mount Olympus. In ancient times it was dedicated to the god Apollo.

Tempe 33 25N 111 56W A city in S central Arizona, on the Salt River, just SE of Phoenix. Arizona State University (1885) is here. Settled in 1871 as a mill, it is a popular retirement, health, and tourist resort because of its dry climate. Clothing, steel, and electronic products are manufactured. Population (1980): 106,743.

tempera A method of painting, using ground pigment and a water-soluble gelatinous base, usually egg yolk. It was a very common medium for murals and easel paintings until it was supplanted by oils during the 15th century. It has lately been revived by German and US artists for its strong pure colors.

temperament The method of tuning the notes of the scale to allow music in all *tonalities to sound in tune. The necessity arises because of the way scales are constructed in western music; systems of temperament sharpen or flatten certain notes in order to compensate for the slight discrepancy that arises in the interval between C and the C seven octaves higher. This interval should be (on the basis of seven octaves) $2^7 = 128$. However, in passing through the cycle of 12 keys, each using as its fundamental the fifth of its predecessor, the interval between Cs becomes $(3/2)^{12} = 129.75$. This difference, known as the comma of Pythagoras, can be compensated in several ways. From the 16th to the early 18th centuries the system of **meantone temperament** prevailed, in which the interval of a fifth was reduced to $^4\sqrt{5} = 1.495$; with this arrangement music written in tonalities with few sharps or flats sounded acceptably in tune. This was succeeded by **equal temperament**, in which the interval between each of 12 semitones of the octave is exactly equal, the advantages of this system were demonstrated by Bach in *The Well-Tempered Clavichord* (1722), a collection of keyboard preludes and fugues in all keys. This system prevails today.

temperance movement The promotion of abstinence from, or at least moderation in, the consumption of alcohol. The earliest organized temperance societies were the 19th century US groups, which by 1833 had 6000 local groups (see also Prohibition). The Ulster Temperance Society, founded in 1829, was the first European society. The movement then spread to Scandinavia, where societies were established in Norway (1836) and Sweden (1837).

temperature A physical quantity that is a measure of the average *kinetic energy of the constituent particles of a body. It determines the direction in which *heat flows when two bodies are in contact, the body with the higher temperature losing heat to that with the lower. The temperature of a body is measured in kelvins, degrees Celsius, or degrees Fahrenheit either by a *thermometer, if the temperature is below about 933°F (500°C), or, if above, by a *pyrometer.

Templars (Poor Knights of Christ and of the Temple of Solomon) A religious order of knighthood founded (c. 1120) in Jerusalem by a group of French knights. The Templars were, with the *Hospitallers, the most important military order of the *Crusades. Accused of heresy and immorality by Philip IV of France, who feared their power, the Templars were suppressed by the papacy in 1312 with great cruelty.

Temple, Shirley (1928–) US film actress. She featured as a child star in many films during the 1930s, including *Little Miss Marker* (1934), *Bright Eyes* (1934), *Heidi* (1937), and *Rebecca of Sunnybrook Farm* (1938). She won a special Academy Award in 1934. During the 1960s she went into politics and was appointed a delegate to the UN (1969). In 1974 she served as US Chief of Protocol. She was also US ambassador to Ghana in 1974 under her married name, Shirley Temple Black.

Temple of Jerusalem The ancient center of Jewish religious life. The first Temple was built by King Solomon (c. 950 BC) and destroyed by Nebuchadnezzar in 586 BC. The second Temple was built in the later 6th century BC, restored by the *Maccabees and later by Herod the Great, and destroyed by the Romans in 70 AD. The Temple was a place of pilgrimage and worship. It was a magnificent building, richly furnished and decorated, and set in a fortified enclosure. The worship, which included animal sacrifices, was directed by priests, assisted by *Levites, who also provided the music. An attempt was made to rebuild the Temple under the Roman emperor Julian (362 AD) but it was abandoned and the site is now a Muslim holy place. *See also* high priest; Holy of Holies; Wailing Wall.

temples In ancient Greece and Rome, the sanctuaries of the gods. The first Greek temples were built of timber or brick but by the 6th century BC stone and marble were being used. They were rectangular buildings surrounded by a colonnade, with an inner sanctum containing the altar and a sculpture of the deity to whom they were dedicated. The best known is the *Parthenon.

Roman temples were raised on pedestals and usually had solid walls and a deep central *portico. The Maison Carrée at Nîmes, France (1st century BC), and the domed *Pantheon in Rome are famous surviving examples.

Temuco 38 45S 72 40W A city in S Chile and the gateway to Chile's lake district. It serves an area producing chiefly cereals, apples, and timber. Population (1976 est): 150,560.

tench An elongated food and game fish, *Tinca tinca*, that is related to *carp and occurs in European fresh waters. Its slimy body, 7–18 in (18–45 cm) long, is greenish or blackish above with lighter undersides. It lives in quiet waters that are rich in vegetation, feeding on small animals and plants.

Ten Commandments The *covenant, also called the Decalogue, delivered by Jehovah to Moses on two stone tablets at Mount Sinai (Exodus 20.1–17; Deuteronomy 5.6–21). According to Exodus, Moses broke the original tablets when he descended from Mount Sinai and discovered the idolatry of the Israelites; they were replaced by two others, which were kept in the *Ark of the Covenant. Jews, Roman Catholics, and Protestants are not agreed as to the exact numbering of the commandments. The New Testament insists that unlike many other Old Testament laws they are binding on all mankind.

tendon A strong fibrous cord that joins a muscle to a bone. The tendon fibers merge with the muscle fibers and extend to the fibrous tissue lining the bone, serving to concentrate the pull of the muscle on a small part of the bone.

Tenerife 28 15N 16 35W A Spanish island in the Atlantic Ocean, the largest of the Canary Islands. Its Pico de Teide mountain is, at 12,172 ft (3710 m), the highest in Spain. Early fruit and vegetables, such as bananas and tomatoes, are produced and the island is popular for vacations. Area: 780 sq mi (2020 sq km). Population (1970): 473,971. Chief town: Santa Cruz de Tenerife.

Teng Hsiao-p'ing. *See* Deng Xiao Ping.

Teniers the Younger, David (1610–90) Flemish painter. Known chiefly for his peasant scenes, he also made historically valuable copies of the paintings in the collection of Archduke Leopold Wilhelm, whose court painter he became in Brussels in 1651. His father **David Teniers the Elder** (1582–1649) was a painter of religious subjects.

Ten Lost Tribes of Israel The Hebrew tribes that rebelled against *Solomon's successor, Rehoboam, and formed a separate kingdom. This kingdom, which they called Israel, lay to the N of the territory occupied by the two remaining tribes of *Judah and of *Benjamin, which together constituted the southern kingdom of Judah. In 722 BC the northern kingdom was conquered by the Assyrians, many of its inhabitants deported, and their ethnic identity lost.

Tennessee A S central state bordered by Kentucky and Virginia (N); North Carolina (E); Georgia, Alabama, and Mississippi (S); and the Mississippi River (W), beyond which lie Arkansas and Missouri. Geographically, the state can be divided into East, Middle, and West Tennessee. In the E there is an upland region of thickly wooded mountains and in Middle Tennessee, in the loop of the Tennessee River, an area of upland plateau and rolling hills gives way in the W to an area of lowland plains and swamps situated between the Tennessee and Mississippi Rivers. An agriculturally poor state, its major crops are tobacco, soybeans, and cotton. Beef and dairy products are also important. Manufacturing is being encouraged especially by the Tennessee Valley Authority (see Tennessee River) and the leading industries produce chemicals, food products, electrical and nonelectrical machinery, and textiles. The state is an important hardwood producer in the S. It is the US's largest producer of zinc and the extraction of stone is a major source of revenue. Memphis, on the Mississippi River, is the largest and commercially the most important city; the state capital of Nashville has long associations with country music. *History*: The area was first explored by the Spanish in the 16th century. Thinly settled before the American Revolution, it attracted easterners hungry for land after the war. North Carolina laid claims to the region and the unrecognized State of Franklin was organized before Tennessee became a territory (1790) and a state (1796). Although Tennessee joined the Confederacy in the Civil War, Union sentiment was strong in the non-slave holding eastern parts of the state. Because of its strategic importance on the border of the Union and on the Mississippi, many key Civil War battles were fought there. Industrial development began in the late 19th century. Martin Luther *King Jr was

assassinated in Memphis in 1968. Area: 42,244 sq mi (109,411 sq km). Population (1980): 4,590,750. Capital: Nashville.

Tennessee River A river in SE US. It follows a U-shaped course from E Tennessee, flowing through NE Alabama before returning across Tennessee to join the Ohio River as its main tributary at Paducah, Kentucky. **The Tennessee Valley Authority**, created in 1933, constructed a series of dams along the river to control floods and arrest soil erosion as well as to generate electricity. Length: 652 mi (1049 km).

Tennessee Walking Horse A breed of □horse developed in Tennessee and used by plantation owners for its characteristic running walk, which gives a smooth ride. It is solidly built with a thick neck and full mane and tail. The coat may be black, brown, bay, chestnut, or roan. Height: 15½–16 hands (1.57–1.63 m).

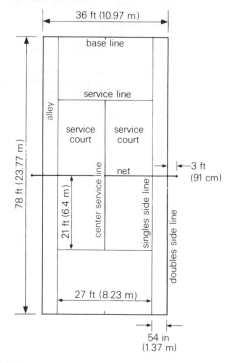

TENNIS *The dimensions of the court. For single games the posts holding the net are moved to inside the doubles sidelines. The net is 3 ft (91.4 cm) high at the center.*

tennis (*or* lawn tennis) A game for two or four players using rackets to hit a cloth-covered rubber ball on a grass or composition (hard) court. It originated in England in the mid-19th century and was highly popular by 1877, when the first Wimbledon championships were staged. A match lasts a maximum of five sets for men and three for women and the minimum number of games per set is six. A lead of two games is needed to win a set. However, if the score reaches six games each a tiebreaker is played. The scoring system derives from *real tennis and a minimum of four points is needed for a game: 15, 30, 40, and game; a lead of two points is also needed to win a game. A score of 40 on both sides is called "deuce"; the side that wins the next point then has the "advantage," which can either be clinched to win the game with a further point or nullified by the opposing side winning a point, in which case the score returns to deuce. Players take turns to serve for a game. A player is allowed two attempts to serve into the service court diagonally opposite, alternating courts between points. To win points players must return the ball over the net either before it bounces (volley) or after the first bounce, trying to position it so that their opponents cannot return it. The game is immensely popular at all levels of play, from beginners to professionals.

Tennis Court Oath (1789) The oath taken by the Third Estate of the *States-General of France at the start of the French Revolution. After declaring itself a National Assembly, the Third Estate was excluded from its meeting place at Versailles. Adjourning to a nearby tennis court, the Assembly defiantly swore not to disband until the French kingdom had a written constitution.

Tennyson, Alfred, Lord (1809–92) British poet. He published two volumes in 1830 and 1832, but he gained general acclaim only with his 1842 volume, which included "Morte d'Arthur." In 1850 he married, became Britain's poet laureate, and published *In Memoriam*, a sequence of elegiac lyrics mourning the death of his close friend Arthur Hallam (1811–33). Now established as the national poet of the Victorian age, he reinforced his popularity with *Idylls of the King* (1859) and other poems.

tenor A high adult male singing voice. The word comes from the Latin *tenere*, to hold; in Renaissance polyphonic music the tenor part held the melody on which the music was based. Range: C on the bass stave to C two octaves above.

tenrec An insect-eating mammal belonging to the family *Tenrecidae* (30 species), found only in Madagascar and the Comoro Islands. Tenrecs measure 2–16 in (5–40 cm), some with long tails and some tailless, and generally have a brownish coat of bristly hairs or spines. Most tenrecs live in burrows and are nocturnal, feeding mainly on small invertebrates with some plant material. They are prolific breeders, producing litters of over 20. Order: **Insectivora*.

tensile strength The ability of a material to withstand a "pulling" stress (**tensile stress**). It is usually measured by taking a bar of the material and stretching it to destruction. The ultimate tensile strength is the maximum load divided by the bar's cross-sectional area and is measured in newtons per square meter.

Tenure of Office Act (1867) US law that restricted presidential powers. Because President Andrew *Johnson wished to oust government officials who favored harsh Reconstruction policies, Congress passed a law that prohibited presidential removal of Senate-appointed officials without Senate approval. Johnson's defiance of the law in 1868 led to impeachment proceedings.

Tenzing Norgay (c. 1914–) Sherpa mountaineer, who, with Sir Edmund *Hillary, was the first man to reach the summit of Mount Everest (1953), after working as a porter in 19 Himalayan expeditions from 1935. He later became a director at the Himalayan Mountaineering Institute, Darjeeling.

Teotihuacán An ancient city in central Mexico. Between 300 and 650 AD Teotihuacán controlled a wide area. It was destroyed about 750. The pyramid temples of the sun, moon, and *Quezalcóatl are the most impressive remains.

tepee. *See* wigwam.

Teplice (*or* Teplice Šarnov) 50 40N 13 50E An industrial city and spa in Czechoslovakia, in N Bohemia. Industries include paper, glass, and potteries. Population (1970): 51,300.

tequila A Mexican alcoholic beverage made of the fermented juice of an agave plant, water, and, sometimes, sulfuric acid and yeast. The spirit is distilled twice in potstills then may be aged in casks. It is produced near the town of Tequila.

terbium (Tb) A *lanthanide element, discovered in 1843 by C. G. Mosander (1797–1858) and named for the village Ytterby in Sweden. It is obtained from monazite ($CePO_4$), and the brown oxide (Tb_2O_3) is used as a phosphor in color-television tubes. The metal is silvery-gray and can be cut with a knife. At no 65; at wt 158.92; mp 2473°F (1356°C); bp 5511°F (3041°C).

Terborch, Gerard (1617–81) Dutch painter. He visited England (1635), Rome (1640), and Westphalia, where he painted the Dutch and Spanish diplomats signing the *Peace of Münster* (1648; National Gallery, London). His portraits and his family and guardroom scenes are remarkable for their skilled rendering of expression and textures.

Terbrugghen, Hendrik (1588–1629) Dutch painter of the Utrecht school. After studying under the mannerist painter Abraham Bloemaert (1564–1651), he went to Italy in 1604, returning to Utrecht in 1614, where he specialized in religious and musical subjects in the style of *Caravaggio.

terebinth A small tree, *Pistacia terebinthus*, native to the Mediterranean region. It has small flowers producing purple fruit and was formerly an important source of turpentine. Family: *Pistaciaceae*.

Terence (Publius Terentius Afer; c. 185–c. 159 BC) Roman dramatist. Born in Carthage, he was taken to Rome as a slave by a senator who educated and later freed him. His six plays were all adapted from Greek New Comedy writers, especially Menander. He achieved popular success only with *The Eunuch* (161 BC), his style being more refined and sophisticated than that of his rival *Plautus. His work influenced several 17th- and 18th-century European writers.

Teresa, Mother (1910–) Yugoslav nun, who founded the Order of the Missionaries of Charity in Calcutta in 1948. Her nuns work throughout the world helping lepers, cripples, and the aged and dying. She received the first Pope John XXIII Peace Prize (1971) and the 1979 Nobel Peace Prize.

Teresa of Ávila, St (1515–82) Spanish Carmelite nun and mystic, who dedicated her life to reforming the Carmelite order. Of noble birth, she joined the Carmelites at Ávila in 1533 and in 1555 experienced a spiritual awakening followed by several visions. To restore the original Carmelite rule she founded the Convent of St Joseph in Ávila in 1562 and later other religious houses with the help of St *John of the Cross. The mystical side of her life is described in her books, notably *Life* (1562–65), *The Way of Perfection* (after 1565), and *The Interior Castle* (1577), which are regarded as classics of mysticism.

Teresina 5 09S 42 46W A city in NE Brazil, the capital of Piauí state on the Rio Parnaíba. It is a commercial center; exports include cattle, hides, cotton, rice, and manioc. Its university was founded in 1968. Population (1975 est): 290,268.

Terman, Lewis Madison (1877–1956) US psychologist, who published the first widely used intelligence test in the US. Developed at Stanford University, his Stanford–Binet test was scored on an *intelligence quotient (IQ) rating based on both chronological and mental ages. In 1921 Terman established a long-term study of gifted children and he also estimated the IQs of famous people, rating Goethe at 210 and Darwin at 165.

terminal velocity The maximum velocity attained by a body falling through a fluid. It occurs when the drag balances the gravitational force on the body: until the terminal velocity is reached the falling body accelerates; thereafter the velocity remains constant. According to *Stokes' law the terminal velocity of a sphere (radius r) falling through a fluid with a coefficient of viscosity η is $2\phi r^2 g/9\eta$, where ϕ is the difference between the body and fluid densities and g is the acceleration of free fall.

termite A social □insect, also called white ant (although unrelated to the ants), belonging to the mainly tropical order *Isoptera* (2000 species). Termite colonies nest in tunnels and galleries in wood, soil, or earth mounds (termitaria). There are three major castes: winged reproductives, workers, and soldiers. The reproductives swarm to found new colonies, a single pair (king and queen) producing huge numbers of offspring. The workers construct galleries, feed the colony, and care for the young, while the soldiers are concerned with defense. Termites eat cellulose and are very destructive when they invade houses and attack wood products.

tern A seabird belonging to a subfamily (*Sterninae*; 35–40 species) occurring around coasts and inland waters worldwide and often called sea swallow or noddy. 8–22 in (20–55 cm) long, terns have long wings, short legs, usually a forked tail, and their plumage is white, black-and-white, or almost totally black. They feed on fish and crustaceans and often migrate long distances (*see* Arctic tern). Family: *Laridae* (gulls and terns).

Terni 42 34N 12 39E A city in Italy, in Umbria on the Nera River. Industries include the manufacture of iron and steel, machinery, firearms, soap, and textiles. It is reputed to be the birthplace of Tacitus. Population (1980 est): 113,108.

terpenes Naturally occurring hydrocarbons found in the essential oils of plants. Typically they are volatile compounds with pleasant odors and are widely used in flavoring foods and in perfumes. Their molecules are made up of isoprene units (C_5H_8). *Rubber is an example of a polyterpene.

terracotta (Italian: baked earth) A fired clay, usually reddish in color, used to make sculpture, tiles, bricks, containers, etc. It is principally associated with sculpture. Terracotta figurines, often painted, were very common in ancient Greece and Rome, a famous Greek type being the *Tanagra figurines. The art was revived during the *Renaissance, when the *Della Robbia family in Florence specialized in enameled terracotta Madonnas. Later sculptors in terracotta include the Frenchman *Clodion.

terrapin A small edible turtle belonging to the family *Emydidae*, occurring chiefly in the New World. The diamondback terrapin (*Malaclemys terrapin*), which occurs in coastal waters and salt marshes of North America, has diamond-shaped patterns on its dark carapace and is yellow with black speckles underneath. It is one of several terrapins regarded as a table delicacy and often reared for this purpose. □reptile.

terrarium A transparent receptacle for land plants, used for propagation, decoration, or scientific study. The plants grow in a bottom layer usually consisting of sand or pebbles mixed with some charcoal and covered by topsoil.

Terre Adélie (*or* Adélie Land) The only French territory in Antarctica, in the French Southern and Antarctic Territories on the coast of the Indian

Ocean between longitudes 136°E and 142°E. It is the site of a French research station.

terrier One of about 20 breeds of □dog characterized by their small compact sturdy build and traditionally used for hunting vermin and rousing foxes and badgers from cover. The Scottish breeds, such as the *cairn terrier, *Scottish terrier, *Skye terrier, and *West Highland white terrier, tend to be smaller and longer haired than other terriers, which are descended from the ancient black-and-tan hunting terrier and other breeds.

territory In ecology, a defined area defended by an animal against intrusion by another animal, usually of the same species. Territories can either reduce competition for food or serve to protect mates and young from interference. They vary in size according to their function, the fitness of the defending animal, and the population density of the species.

Terry, Dame Ellen (Alice) (1847–1928) British actress. A member of a large and talented family of actors, from 1878 to 1898 she acted with Sir Henry *Irving, achieving particular success in the major Shakespearean roles. She later managed the Imperial Theatre, toured extensively, and gave lectures on Shakespeare. Her correspondence with G. B. *Shaw was published in 1931.

Tertiary period The first geological period of the Cenozoic era, following the Cretaceous period and preceding the Quaternary (which is sometimes considered a continuation of the Tertiary). It lasted from about 65 to 1.8 million years ago and contains the Paleocene, Eocene, Oligocene, Miocene, and Pliocene epochs, in ascending order. Most of the rocks of the period were laid down in shallow water. Modern invertebrates and mammals evolved and became increasingly abundant; the modern angiosperms became the dominant plants. The Alpine period of mountain formation extended through the period and reached its peak in the Miocene. The climate began to deteriorate in the Oligocene, finally leading to the Ice Age of the Pleistocene.

Tertullian (us), Quintus Septimius Florens (c. 160–225 AD) African Father of the Church, born in Carthage. Educated in law, he was converted to Christianity by 197 and became a leading Christian apologist. He strongly defended the Montanists (see Montanism), whom he joined in 213. His writings, which include *Apologeticum*, *Ad nationes*, and *De praescriptione haereticorum*, were the first major Christian works in Latin.

terza rima A verse form consisting of a series of three-line stanzas the second lines of which rhyme with the first and third lines of the preceding stanza (aba/cac/dcd/ede/ . . .). It originated in Italy and was used by *Dante in the *Divine Comedy*. It was introduced into England by Sir Thomas *Wyatt in the 16th century. *See also* rhyme.

tesla (T) The *SI unit of magnetic flux density equal to one weber per square meter. Named for Nikola *Tesla.

Tesla, Nikola (1856–1943) US electrical engineer, born in Croatia, who recognized the advantages of distributing electricity using alternating current, rather than direct current, and did much to make this feasible. He fought a long and bitter battle with Thomas *Edison over this principle. The unit of magnetic flux density (see tesla) is named for him.

Test Acts In England, the acts stipulating that public office holders must take Holy Communion in the Church of England (1673) and excluding all Roman Catholics except the Duke of York (later James II) from parliament (1678). They were not formally repealed until the mid-19th century.

testes The organ of male animals in which *sperm is produced. In men there is a pair of testes, or testicles, which produce both sperm and sex hormones (see androgen). Before birth the testicles descend into the scrotum—a sac of skin outside the abdominal cavity—since sperms require a temperature lower than that of the body to mature. The sperms complete their development in a convoluted tube (epididymis) outside the testis. At ejaculation the sperms pass through a duct (the vas deferens) to the urethra and out through the penis.

testosterone A steroid hormone—the most important of the *androgens. First isolated from bull testes in 1935, testosterone is now manufactured for medical uses, including the treatment of certain forms of sterility in men.

test-tube baby A baby produced by fertilizing the mother's egg cell with sperm from the father in a test tube: the fertilized egg is then implanted surgically into the mother's womb and allowed to come to term in the normal way. It is a means of overcoming sterility in a woman due to blocked Fallopian tubes or any similar defect. The technique was developed in Britain, and the first test-tube baby was born in 1978. Since that time test-tube babies have been born in many countries.

tetanus A serious disease caused by the bacterium *Clostridium tetani* entering wounds and producing a powerful toxin (poison) that irritates the

nerves supplying muscles. The organism is particularly prevalent in soil contaminated with animal droppings. After an incubation period of seven–ten days, stiffness, spasm, and rigidity of the muscles affects the jaw (hence the popular name—lockjaw) and spreads to other muscles. In severe cases the whole body is seized with spasms and the patient may die from asphyxia. The disease is treated with tetanus antitoxin and penicillin; it can be prevented by completing a full course of antitetanus immunization.

Teton Range A mountain range in W Idaho and E Wyoming, S of Yellowstone National Park. Grand Teton, the highest point, rises at 13,766 ft (4196 m). Much of the range, especially in the S, is included in Grand Teton National Park (1929).

tetra One of several small brightly colored freshwater fish of the family *Characidae* (see characin), found in South America and Africa and popular for aquaria. Well-known species include black tetra (*Gymnocorymbus ternetzi*), glowlight tetra (*Hemigrammus erythrozonus*), neon tetra (*Hyphessobrycon innesi*), and silver tetra (*Ctenobrycon spilurus*).

tetracyclines A group of *antibiotics derived from *Streptomyces* bacteria. Tetracyclines are active against a large number of different bacteria (i.e. they are broad-spectrum antibiotics) and are frequently the first choice of antibiotic for infections in which the causative organism has not been identified. Tetracyclines, which are taken by mouth, may cause the side effects of diarrhea, nausea, and discoloration of growing teeth and bones.

tetraethyl lead ($Pb(C_2H_5)_4$) A colorless poisonous oily liquid. It is made by treating lead-sodium alloys with chloroethane and is added to gasoline to prevent *knocking in internal-combustion engines.

Tetrazzini, Luisa (1871–1940) Italian coloratura soprano. Born in Florence, she attended the Liceo Musicale there with her sister Eva, making her debut as Inez in Meyerbeer's opera *L'Africaine* in 1895. She toured the US, Russia, Mexico, and Europe with great success.

Tetuán 35 34N 5 22W A city in N Morocco. Its port, on the Mediterranean coast, handles livestock and agricultural produce. The city produces textiles and light manufactured products. Population (1973 est): 137,080.

Tetzel, Johann (c. 1465–1519) German Dominican friar, a famous preacher of *indulgences. His attempt to sell indulgences, which had been authorized to raise funds for the renovation of St Peter's in Rome, provoked Luther's publication of the 95 theses and a famous debate between the two men.

Teutonic Knights (Knights of the Teutonic Order) A religious order of knighthood founded (c. 1190) at Acre. In 1211 they moved from Palestine to E Europe, where they campaigned against pagan peoples, notably the Prussians, whom they had conquered by the end of the 13th century. They colonized Prussia and established their headquarters at Marienburg in 1309. They also gained control over much of the E Baltic region, as well as parts of Germany. During the 15th century they were repeatedly defeated by the Poles, of whose king the order's grand master became a vassal. At the Reformation the order was dissolved except for one branch, which survived in Germany until its abolition by Napoleon (1809).

Texas The second largest state and the third most populous, situated in the SW and bordered by Oklahoma (N), Arkansas and Louisiana (E), the Gulf of Mexico and Mexico (S), and New Mexico (W). It consists of four main physical regions: the West Gulf Coastal Plain in the SE covering more than two fifths of the state; the Central Lowland; the Great Plains, which extend mainly W from the Central Lowland into New Mexico; and the Trans-Pecos or mountainous area in the W. The Rio Grande forms the border with Mexico and is the chief river. The chief producer of minerals since 1935, it leads the nation in the production of oil and natural gas; it is also a major producer of sulfur. Oil-related industries dominate the manufacturing sector, the most important being the chemical industry, especially along the Gulf Coast. There is also an important space center at Houston and Dallas is a major commercial and industrial center. Texas is a major agricultural region and has more farmed land than any other US state. It produces a variety of crops, especially cotton, sorghum grains, rice, and peanuts, and it is a leading livestock producer. *History*: Explored by the Spanish in the 16th century and colonized by them in the 17th as part of Mexico, it was entered in large numbers by US settlers, led by Stephen F. *Austin, after Mexico became independent in 1821. In 1836 the Texans set up a provisional government in opposition to the Mexican dictatorship of Antonio López de Santa Anna and following the heroic defense of the *Alamo, the revolutionary army under Sam Houston finally defeated Mexican forces in April of the same year. A republic was established and Texas remained independent for almost a decade until annexation by the US was agreed upon and Texas became a state. It was a supporter of the Confederate cause during the US Civil War. Sustained growth for the state began in

1901 when the famous Spindletop oil discovery was made. Oil and gas soon replaced livestock in importance, and the economy is now supported by a variety of high technology and defense industries. Changes in the course of the Rio Grande, which forms part of the border beween Texas and Mexico, has led to several border disputes between the US and Mexico and in 1970 the two countries agreed on plans to prevent any further substantial changes in the river's course. During the 1970s and 1980s, the flood of illegal Mexican immigrants into Texas strained the state's social services and relations with Mexico. Area: 267,338 sq mi (692,402 sq km). Population (1980): 14,228,383. Capital: Austin.

Texas Rangers US law enforcers. Begun by Stephen F. *Austin in 1823 to protect the frontier in Mexican Texas, it became an official law enforcement agency of Texas in 1836. They fought bravely in the *Mexican War, and by 1881 the Rangers had ended Indian hostilities in Texas. Since 1935 a part of the Texas Department of Public Safety, the Rangers work with other state law enforcement agencies.

Texas v. White (1869) US Supreme Court decision that affirmed the indissolubility of the US and the illegality of state secession. Government bonds, paid to Texas in 1850, came due in 1864. When the Civil War broke out, Texas seceded from the Union and sold the bonds to George White. After the war Texas, under reconstructive government, sued White for return of the bonds. The court ruled that states cannot secede from the Union and, therefore, the bonds had been sold illegally.

textiles Fabrics made from natural or synthetic *fibers. Textiles can either be made directly from these fibers, as in felt and bonded fabrics, or be woven or knitted from yarn spun from the fibers. Braiding, netting, and lace making are less common ways of producing textiles from yarn. The fibers used include animal fibers, such as *wool, hair, and *silk; vegetable fibers, such as *cotton, *flax, and *hemp; and synthetic fibers, such as rayon, nylon, and acrylic. Wool and hair were used in prehistoric times; *linen, derived from flax, was also an early discovery, which only began to decline in use when cotton textiles, mass produced by the new industrial machines, became available cheaply. The invention of synthetic fibers (such as rayon and nylon) and their combination with natural fibers has enormously increased the textile industry's range. *See also* spinning; weaving.

Tezcatlipoca The Aztec god of the night sky, identified with the constellation Ursa Major and associated with witchcraft and evil. He was a creator-god and had many different functions. He was usually portrayed with an obsidian mirror as a foot.

Thackeray, William Makepeace (1811–63) British novelist. He was educated at Cambridge University and became a professional journalist. After publishing several early novels in magazines under pseudonyms, he won fame and financial success with *Vanity Fair* (1847–48), which he followed with the semiautobiographical *The History of Pendennis* (1848–50) and the historical novel *Henry Esmond* (1852).

Thailand, Kingdom of (name until 1939: Siam) A country in SE Asia, on the Gulf of Thailand. Fertile plains and hills in the S rise to mountains in the N. The main river is the Chao Phraya and the Mekong forms part of the E boundary. Most of the population is Thai, with Chinese and Malay minorities. *Economy*: the chief food crop is rice, which is also the main export. Production is being increased by irrigation projects, such as the Chao Phraya Dam. Forests cover 60% of the land, producing especially teak and rubber in the N and yang in the S. Rich and varied mineral resources include tin, manganese, antimony, and zinc. Industry is based mainly on textiles and cement. Tourism is important. *History*: there are indications of human settlement from very early times, and by the 6th century AD the Thais had reached the area from the N. They conquered the Mons to the S and in succeeding centuries gained power and influence in the region, being involved in frequent struggles with the Burmese and Khmers. In the 19th century they lost some territory to the French and the British but remained independent. In 1932 the long-standing absolute monarchy was replaced by a constitutional monarchy, since when civil and military governments have alternated, accompanied by political upheavals and violence. The country was occupied by the Japanese in World War II. The army has controlled the country since a 1976 coup. In recent years it has developed closer links with its communist neighbors, although relations with Vietnam deteriorated to a state of war in 1980 over Thailand's accepting refugees from Vietnam. Head of state: King Bjumibol Adulyadej (1927–   ). Prime minister: Gen Prem Tinsulanonda. Official language: Thai. Official religion: Hinayana Buddhism. Official currency: baht of 100 satang. Area: 198,250 sq mi (514,000 sq km). Population (1984 est): 51,727,000. Capital and main port: Bangkok.

Thais (4th century BC) Greek courtesan, who accompanied *Alexander the Great's army during its invasion of Persia. According to tradition, she instigated the burning of the palace of Xerxes in Persepolis in 331 BC.

thalassemia A form of *anemia caused by an inherited abnormality of the hemoglobin molecule (the pigment of red blood cells). The disease is seen most commonly around the Mediterranean but can also affect any people of Mediterranean origin. Patients inheriting the abnormality from both parents suffer from the major form of the disease, which requires repeated blood transfusions; such patients rarely live to adulthood. Those inheriting the disease from one parent are often free of symptoms.

Thales (c. 624–547 BC) The first of the Greek speculative scientists, born at *Miletus. He used the data from Babylonian astronomers to predict the solar eclipse of May 28, 585 BC, advised on stellar navigation, and introduced Egyptian methods of land measurement into Greece. He held that all things derive from water and set the *Presocratics on their quest for the basic substance of the universe.

Thalia In Greek religion, one of the nine *Muses, the patron of comedy. She was the mother, by Apollo, of the *Corybantes.

thalidomide A sedative drug that was found to cause severe developmental defects in the fetus when taken during pregnancy. The most common thalidomide-induced abnormality is phocomelia, in which the feet and hands develop normally without corresponding growth of the bones of the arms and legs. Some 8000–10,000 afflicted children were born to mothers who took the drug, primarily in European countries, before the effects were discovered in 1961. The drug was never used clinically in the US.

thallium (Tl) A metallic element, discovered spectroscopically by Sir William Crookes in 1861 and named for the Greek *thallos*, a green shoot, because of its bright-green spectral line. The metal is soft and malleable and reacts easily to form numerous salts. The sulfate (Tl_2SO_4) is widely used as a rat poison as it is tasteless and odorless. It occurs naturally in sulfide ores of lead and zinc and in iron pyrites (FeS_2). At no 81; at wt 204.37; mp 578.8°F (303.5°C); bp 2657 ± 18°F (1457 ± 10°C).

Thallophyta In some plant classification systems, a subkingdom containing all those plants that lack true stems, leaves, and roots, i.e. the algae, fungi, and lichens. The plant body is a thallus and lacks the vascular (conducting) tissue of higher plants.

Thames River The longest river in England. Rising in the Cotswold Hills near Cirencester, it flows mainly ESE through Oxford, Reading, and London to enter the North Sea at the Nore. It is tidal as far as Teddington, and Tilbury can dock the largest oceangoing vessels. It is economically the most important river in the UK, with vast amounts of cargo passing through the Port of *London. Length: 210 mi (338 km).

Thanet, Isle of 51 22N 1 15E An island in SE England, separated from the Kent mainland by two channels of the Stour River. It contains the resorts of Ramsgate and Margate. Area: 42 sq mi (109 sq km).

Thanjavur (former name: Tanjore) 10 46N 79 09E A city in India, in Tamil Nadu. It has an 11th-century Hindu temple and a 16th-century raja's palace. Industries include textiles and jewelry. Population (1971): 140,547.

Thanksgiving Day A US national holiday, celebrated on the fourth Thursday in November. Thanksgiving Day was originally observed by the Pilgrim Fathers, who in 1621 celebrated their first harvest in North America. It became a national holiday in 1863. Americans traditionally eat roast turkey and pumpkin pie on Thanksgiving Day. It is also celebrated in Canada, on the second Monday in October.

Thant, U (1909–74) Burmese diplomat; secretary general of the UN (1962–72), elected after serving as acting secretary general following the death in office of his predecessor Dag Hammarskjöld. U Thant helped to resolve the US-Soviet crisis over the Soviet installation of missile bases in Cuba.

Thapsus, Battle of (46 BC) The battle in which Julius Caesar crushed *Pompey's supporters in North Africa. The battle was part of Caesar's campaign to retain control of Rome after defeating Pompey at Pharsalus.

Thar Desert (or Great Indian Desert) A large arid area lying along the central 500 mi (800 km) of the India-Pakistan border, mostly in India. Area: about 96,500 sq mi (250,000 sq km).

Tharpe, Twyla (1941–   ) US choreographer and dancer. She danced for the Paul Taylor Dance Company (1963–65) and began choreographing her own pieces for the group. By 1965 she had formed her own company. Her early works were performed on bare stages, outside or in gyms, without scenery and music, and with basic costumes. She based her movements on various dance styles, incuding jazz and tap, as well as ballet, and became known for her "pop" ballets. Her works include *Eight Jelly Rolls* (1971), *The Raggedy Dances* (1972), *Deuce Coupe* (1973), *Push Comes to Shove* (1976), and *Baker's Dozen* (1979).

Thásos A Greek island in the N Aegean Sea. Much archeological excavation has been done here and zinc is mined. Area: 154 sq mi (399 sq km). Population (1971): 13,316.

MARGARET THATCHER *After the Conservatives won the general election (1979) she became prime minister.*

Thatcher, Margaret (Hilda) (1925–) British stateswoman; Conservative prime minister (1979–). After working as a research chemist and then a barrister, she entered parliament in 1959 and was appointed minister of pensions and national insurance in 1961. In 1969 she became opposition spokesman on education and was secretary of state for education and science from 1970 to 1974. In 1975 she succeeded Edward Heath as Conservative leader and in 1979 became the first woman prime minister of the UK. After assuming office, she instituted cuts in government spending and faced a worsening economy. In 1982 she used Britain's military forces to retain control of the Falkland Islands. Her government continued following a landslide victory in 1983.

Theater of Cruelty A term derived from the theories of Antonin *Artaud, who believed that drama was essentially a ceremony the ritual function of which was to destroy the superficial restraints of civilized life and liberate repressed emotions from the subconscious. *Les Cenci* (1935), his chief experimental production, was a failure, but his theories influenced many later writers and directors, including Jean-Louis *Barrault, *Camus, and *Genet.

Theater of the Absurd A term ("the Absurd" being borrowed from the existentialist philosophy of Albert *Camus) popularized in the 1960s to describe certain plays in which the human condition is presented as absurd. It was applied to the plays of Eugene *Ionesco, Samuel *Beckett, Arthur *Adamov, and others, which were characterized by lack of logical form and which use comic effects in developing pessimistic philosophical themes. The influence of Alfred *Jarry and the surrealists is discernible in the works of some of these playwrights.

theaters and stages The design of buildings specifically for the staging of plays has been governed by the shifting religious and social significance of the drama and the type of illusion or effect intended by different sorts of play. Ancient Greek theaters adjoined such religious centers as *Athens, *Epidaurus, and *Delphi. The secularized theaters that were a feature of most Roman towns were particularly adapted to the production of *Roman comedy. Christian drama evolved from the liturgy but in late medieval Europe moved outside the churches as the craft guilds assumed responsibility for productions of *miracle plays. Renaissance court theaters mainly imitated Roman models, while the open-air Elizabethan theater represented a more popular tradition. During the 17th century elaboration of stage machinery (*see* masque), demands for illusionism, and the development of *opera and *ballet stimulated the spread of the proscenium arch stage design, which was virtually universal until the 20th century. The modern drama's tendency toward abstraction and evocation of mood, going hand-in-hand with nonrealistic scenery and stage lighting, have fostered renewed interest in theater-in-the-round (seats around a central acting arena) and the potential of the Elizabethan apron stage.

Thebes An ancient city in Upper Egypt and capital of all Egypt (c. 1570–c. 1085 BC). Thebes' power was linked with the supremacy of its god *Amon in the Egyptian pantheon. With its associated sites of *Karnak, *Luxor, and the *Valley of the Kings, Thebes testifies to the splendor of ancient Egyptian civilization.

Thebes 88 19N 23 19E A city in Boeotia, in central Greece. It was founded in Mycenaean times and its legendary history was a favorite theme in Greek drama. Predominant among its Boeotian neighbors, Thebes lost influence by supporting the Persians in 480 BC. Expedient alliances subsequently increased its power and Thebes briefly became the leading Greek state after defeating the Spartans at Leuctra (371). Opposition to Macedonian expansionism led to destruction (336). Although refounded, it never regained significance. Population (1971 est): 15,899.

thegn A person in Anglo-Saxon England who held land from his lord in return for service. The status of thegn (meaning one who serves) was hereditary. The king's thegns had military and administrative duties and also attended the *witan (king's council). Their importance declined in the early 11th century, and the thegns died out after the Norman conquest.

theism The belief in a personal God as creator and preserver of the universe, who reveals himself by supernatural means to his creatures. Apparently coined (1678) by *Cudworth as an opposite to *atheism, theism has been refined in meaning to exclude both *pantheism and *deism. It is central to Christian, Judaic, and Islamic thought.

Themis The Greek goddess of justice and wisdom, often portrayed carrying a pair of scales. She was a Titan, the daughter of Uranus and Gaea and the second wife of Zeus. As the wife of the Titan Iapetus, she was also the mother of *Prometheus.

Themistocles (c. 528–462 BC) Athenian statesman, who built Athens' naval power. Themistocles persuaded Athens to expand its navy (483) and to transfer its port from Phaleron to the more defensible Piraeus. These policies, and his leadership at the battle of *Salamis, saved Greece from Persia (480) (*see* Greek-Persian Wars). Themistocles argued successfully for the fortification of Athens, despite Spartan opposition, but his opponents caused him to be ostracized in about 471. Themistocles subsequently fled to Asia, where he died.

Thénard, Louis-Jacques (1777–1867) French chemist, who in 1808 was the first to isolate the element *boron in collaboration with *Gay-Lussac. He also discovered hydrogen peroxide in 1813 and produced a pigment known as Thénard's blue, which is stable at high temperatures and so can be used in porcelain.

Theocritus (c. 310–250 BC) Greek poet. Born in Sicily, he worked for part of his life on the island of Cos and at Alexandria. His surviving poems, the *Idylls*, include six poems cast in the dramatic form of dialogues or contests between countrymen. These poems on Sicilian rural life are unsurpassed examples of the pastoral, a form which Theocritus originated and which influenced many later works, such as Milton's *Lycidas*.

theodolite An instrument used in *surveying to measure horizontal and vertical angles. It consists of a telescope, with crosshairs in the eyepiece for focusing on the target, that can swivel on horizontal and vertical axes, which pass through two circular scales. It has a spirit level to indicate when the instrument is horizontal and is mounted on a tripod with adjustable legs.

Theodora (c. 500–48 AD) Byzantine empress (527–48); the wife of *Justinian I. Theodora was the daughter of a circus bearkeeper and had been an actress before she married Justinian in 525 and became one of the most influential women in the history of the Eastern Roman Empire. Justinian consulted her on all affairs of state and his reign achieved little of consequence after her death. She was noted for her early championship of the rights of women.

Theodorakis, Mikis (1925–) Greek composer, who led a revival of Greek folk music in the 1960s and has incorporated elements of it into his compositions, which include music for the film *Zorba the Greek* (1964). He has also been politically active in Greece.

Theodore I Lascaris (c. 1175–1222) The founder of the Byzantine empire at Nicaea after Constantinople fell to the Crusaders (1204). In 1214, following a period of warfare, Theodore and the Latins determined the borders between Constantinople and Nicaea.

Theodoric the Great (c. 445–526) King of the Ostrogoths (471–526), who ruled Italy (493–526). He defeated *Odoacer in 493 and established an Ostrogothic kingdom with its capital at Ravenna, ensuring peace by religious toleration and marriage alliances with the other barbarian kingdoms. However, territorial expansion brought conflict with the Frankish king *Clovis and his death left Italy leaderless and ripe for Byzantine annexation.

Theodosius (I) the Great (347–95 AD) Roman emperor in the East (379–94) and sole emperor (394–95). Theodosius allowed the Visigoths independence on Roman territory by a treaty in 382 and they undertook to supplement the Roman army. A devout and orthodox Christian, he imposed Christianity on the Empire in 391, closing pagan temples and forbidding sacrifices.

The Theater of Dionysus at Athens during the Hellenistic period. The chorus stood in the front semicircular area (orchestra). Behind them were musicians, while the speaking actors performed in front of the screen.

Medieval miracle and mystery plays were performed on large wagons in public places. Different wagons were used for different scenes.

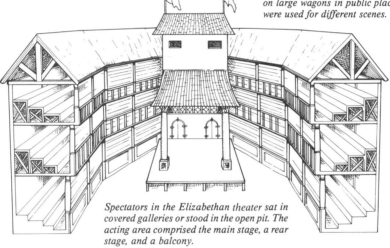

Spectators in the Elizabethan theater sat in covered galleries or stood in the open pit. The acting area comprised the main stage, a rear stage, and a balcony.

The proscenium arch allowed the audience to view a scene as if through a window. The depth and width of the stage made possible the use of elaborately realistic scenery and lighting.

The theater-in-the-round design recalls a primary feature of Elizabethan theater – close contact between actors and audience.

Theodosius II (401–50 AD) Eastern Roman emperor (408–50). He was strongly influenced by his sister, his wife, and a series of advisers. He sponsored the compilation of the **Theodosian Code** (438), a collection of laws that had been issued since 312.

theology Literally, the study of *God. Each of the higher religions has its own theology. Christian theology includes within its scope the nature of God, his relationship with the universe, his providence regarding man, and the teachings of the Church. Different traditions exist within the Roman Catholic, Orthodox, and Protestant communions, but typical subdivisions of theology are dogmatic, historical, and pastoral theology. Until the emergence of Renaissance *humanism, theology was accounted the highest science (see scholasticism) but in the 19th and 20th centuries its findings came under hostile scrutiny from physicists, philosophers, anthropologists, and others.

Theophilus (d. 842 AD) Byzantine emperor (829–42). He was a man of great learning and, despite frequent attacks by the Muslims, stimulated a resurgence of cultural activity. He was the last emperor to uphold *iconoclasm.

Theophrastus (c. 370–286 BC) Greek philosopher and scientist. He studied under *Plato and became *Aristotle's closest friend, succeeding him as head of the *Lyceum. He established botany as a science and lectured and wrote on a vast number of subjects.

theorbo A large double-necked *lute having two sets of strings. One set could be stopped against a fingerboard, the other plucked as open strings.

theosophy Speculation tending toward a mystical understanding of the divine. The term originated in *Neoplatonism but is now mainly applied to the blend of Hindu and Neoplatonic doctrines propounded by the Theosophical Society, which was founded by Helena *Blavatsky in 1875. Compare anthroposophy.

Thera (or Santoríni; Modern Greek name: Thíra) A Greek island in the Aegean Sea, the southernmost of the Cyclades group. The present island is the E side of a volcano the catastrophic explosion of which (c. 1450 BC) precipitated the decline of *Minoan civilization on Crete, 70 mi (110 km) to the S (see also Atlantis). In 1966 a well-preserved Minoan town was found on Thera itself. Area: 29 sq mi (75 sq km).

therapsid An extinct reptile belonging to the order *Therapsida*, which lived during the Permian and Triassic periods (280–200 million years ago). Therapsids were the ancestors of the mammals and had a number of mammal-like features: the limbs were positioned under the body to carry it well off the ground; the skull was deep with a fairly large braincase; and the teeth were specialized for different functions. There were both carnivorous and herbivorous forms.

Theravada The old conservative school of *Buddhism, also called Hinayana (Pali: lesser vehicle) by its detractors. Prevalent in Burma, Cambodia, Laos, Sri Lanka, and Thailand, it emphasizes the ideal of the arhat—one who, as a monk, achieves enlightenment by his own efforts. In Theravada, the *Buddha is revered but not the Bodhisattvas, and only the oldest works, the Pali canon, are considered orthodox.

Thérèse, St (Marie Françoise Thérèse Martin; 1873–97) French *Carmelite nun, known as the Little Flower of Jesus. She entered the Carmelite convent at Lisieux when only 15 and died there 9 years later of tuberculosis. Her fame rests on her spiritual autobiography, *Histoire d'une âme* (1898), showing that spiritual perfection could be attained through childlike humbleness and goodness. She was canonized in 1925. Feast day: Oct 3.

thermae Ancient Roman public baths. They reached their height of architectural sophistication under the Empire, being equipped with libraries and other amenities for relaxation. The best surviving examples include the baths of Titus (81 AD) and Caracalla (217).

thermal reactor A nuclear reactor (see nuclear energy) in which natural or enriched uranium is used with a moderator, in most cases to generate heat for a *power station. The moderator slows down the neutrons emitted during the fission of uranium-235, so that their velocities are comparable to the velocities of gas molecules ("thermal" velocities).

In a thermal reactor, fuel rods made of uranium metal or oxide are surrounded by a moderator (together forming the reactor core), the heat of the reaction being removed by a coolant. After leaving the core, the coolant passes to a heat exchanger in which steam is raised. The rate of reaction is controlled by a series of control rods, which can move in and out of the core: the rods contain a neutron-absorbing element, such as boron or cadmium.

The first nuclear reactor was built by *Fermi in 1942, using natural uranium, a graphite moderator, and a water coolant. British thermal reactors use a gas coolant (usually carbon dioxide) and later types use an enriched fuel. American designs use a liquid as both moderator and coolant. Using ordinary water in a pressurized-water reactor or a boiling-water reactor, enriched fuel is needed; using heavy water, natural uranium can be used. Compare fast reactor.

Thermidorian Reaction See French Revolution.

thermionic valve A device consisting of a sealed glass or metal tube, either evacuated or containing gas at low pressure, into which two or more electrodes are inserted. One heated electrode, the cathode, emits electrons, which are attracted to the positively charged anode, forming an electric current. This current flows in one direction only and can be controlled by the voltage applied at one or more other electrodes (called grids). The **diode valve** was invented in 1904 by Sir John Ambrose Fleming. It has two electrodes and functions as a simple *rectifier. The **triode valve** with one grid was invented in 1910 by Lee De Forest; it was the first to function as an amplifier. The weak signal fed to the grid produces a stronger signal in the anode circuit. Diode and triode valves made possible the development of radio transmitters and receivers, although now *semiconductor diodes and *transistors have largely replaced them. The gas-filled **thyratron** functions as a switch by using a positive grid voltage pulse to initiate a continuing discharge of electrons from the cathode to the anode. It is used in switching and counting circuits, but, like most thermionic valves, has been superseded by its semiconductor equivalent, the *thyristor.

thermistor A *semiconductor device with an electrical resistance that decreases sharply as temperature increases. It is used in temperature-control circuits and can be calibrated for use as a thermometer.

thermite A mixture of powdered aluminum and iron oxide. When ignited, aluminum oxide and iron are produced. The reaction is highly exothermic, yielding molten iron at a temperature of over 3636°F (2000°C). It is used in welding steel and in incendiary bombs.

thermocline A layer within the oceans between about 325 ft (100 m) and 650 ft (200 m) below the surface, in which there is a marked increase in temperature with depth. Above and for some distance below it, there is little vertical temperature gradient.

thermocouple A type of thermometer consisting of an electric circuit formed by two dissimilar metals joined at each end. One junction is exposed to the temperature to be measured, a voltage being generated between it and the other (reference) junction as a result of the temperature difference between them (see thermoelectric effects). The output is usually displayed on a *galvanometer. Copper-constantan junctions are used up to 933°F (500°C) and platinum-rhodium alloy up to 2735°F (1500°C). A **thermopile** consists of several thermocouples connected in series to increase the voltage output for a particular temperature difference.

thermodynamics The study of *heat and its relationship with other forms of energy. Thermodynamics is primarily a statistical subject, thermodynamic quantities, such as *temperature and *entropy, being dependent on the statistical behavior of the particles that comprise a system. There are three fundamental laws of thermodynamics. The first law states that the energy of a closed system remains constant during any process. This law is a restatement of the law of *conservation of mass and energy. The second law states that heat cannot flow from a cold body to a hot body without the expenditure of external work. Another way of stating this law is to say that the entropy of a closed system can never decrease. If the entropy change is zero then the process is said to be reversible. The third law states that as the thermodynamic temperature of a system aproaches *absolute zero, its entropy approaches zero.

Thermodynamics has proved most valuable in studying *heat engines and chemical reactions, but it also has wider implications in other statistical sciences. See heat death of the universe.

thermoelectric effects The effects of changes of temperature on electric circuits or devices. The **Seebeck effect**, named for Johann Seebeck (1770–1831), provides the basis for the *thermocouple; it occurs when a circuit has two junctions between dissimilar metals. If the junctions are maintained at different temperatures, a voltage is generated between them. The **Peltier effect**, named afer Jean Peltier (1785–1845), is the converse of this. One junction heats up and the other cools down when a steady current flows through such a circuit. In the **Thomson** (or Kelvin) **effect**, named for Lord *Kelvin, a temperature gradient along a single metal conductor causes a current to flow through it.

thermoluminescence *Luminescence caused by heating a substance and thus liberating electrons trapped in its crystal defects. The phenomenon is used as a dating technique, especially for pottery. The number of trapped electrons is assumed to be related to the quantity of *ionizing radiation to which the specimen has been exposed since firing (as the crystal defects are caused by ionizing radiation). Thus, by measuring the amount of light emitted on heating, an estimate of the age of the pottery can be made by assuming that the amount of ionizing radiation to which it has been exposed is related to its age.

thermometer An instrument used for measuring temperature. Thermometers make use of some property of a substance that varies uniformly with temperature, most commonly the expansion of a liquid, such as mercury or alcohol colored with dye. A clinical thermometer is a typical mercury-in-glass thermometer; it has a constriction in the stem above the bulb so that the mercury stays at its maximum reading until "shaken down". More accurate thermometers use the expansion of a gas, which is much greater than that of a liquid. Other thermometers include the resistance thermometer, which depends on the variation in the resistance of a wire (usually platinum); the bimetallic strip in which the unequal expansion of two metals welded together to form a strip causes a pointer to move round a dial; and the thermistor, in which the change in conductivity of a semiconductor is used as a measure of temperature. High temperatures are measured by a *pyrometer.

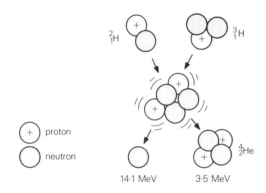

deuterium-tritium fusion reaction

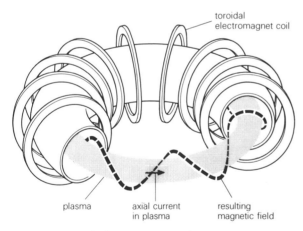

fusion reactor experiment

THERMONUCLEAR REACTOR *The combination of deuterium (^2_1H) and tritium (^3_1H) in a fusion reaction that forms helium. This is being attempted using a toroidal electromagnet to contain plasma consisting of deuterium and tritium nuclei.*

thermonuclear reactor A reactor in which a fusion reaction (*see* nuclear energy) takes place with the controlled release of energy. After over 30 years of research in several countries, it is now generally accepted that a working thermonuclear reactor is unlikely to be in commission before the next century.
A typical fusion reaction is the combination of deuterium and tritium to form helium ($^2_1H + ^3_1H = ^4_2He + n + 17.6 \, MeV$). To overcome the *electromagnetic interaction between nuclei a temperature of about 72 million °F (40 million °C) is needed. Containing the *plasma (as the high-temperature ionized gas is called) is the problem to be solved. In magnetic containment a high current passed through the plasma creates a *magnetic bottle that keeps the plasma away from the containing walls. To produce

useful energy at this temperature, the product of the plasma density and the containment time must exceed 10^{14} particle seconds per cm³. Russian toroidal Tokamak devices have so far only achieved a figure of 10^{12}; moreover the problems of magnetic instabilities have not yet been solved. Other possible devices include a pellet of fuel exposed to pulses from *laser beams. The virtually inexhaustible supply of thermonuclear fuel (hydrogen and its isotopes) makes the fusion reactor an extremely attractive goal.

thermopile. *See* thermocouple.

Thermopylae, Battle of (480 BC) The battle in which the Greeks under the Spartan king *Leonidas attempted for three days to hold the pass of Thermopylae in E central Greece against the Persians. After the main Greek force had retreated the Spartans and Thespians, surrounded and outnumbered, fought to the death. Their heroic stand inspired continued Greek resistance to Persia (*see* Greek-Persian Wars).

Theseus A legendary Greek hero, son of Aegeus, King of Athens, or of Poseidon. He freed the Athenians from their annual tribute to *Minos by killing the *Minotaur of Crete with the help of *Ariadne, who escaped with him. He extended the rule of Athens over various Attic communities and was the subject of many legends. He was father of *Hippolytus by Hippolyte, Queen of the Amazons, and he married *Phaedra, sister of Ariadne.

Thespiae An ancient city of Boeotia at the foot of Mount Helicon, the Muses' traditional home. *Praxiteles' famous Statue of Eros was at Thespiae. Thespians were the only Boeotians to resist the Persian invasion (*see* Greek-Persian Wars) and fought alongside the Spartans at *Thermopylae (480 BC). It retained its importance under the Romans.

Thespis (6th century BC) Semilegendary Greek poet. He won a prize for tragedy at Athens in about 534 BC. Traditionally held to be the inventor of tragedy, he was said to have introduced a single actor in dramatic performances that had hitherto been exclusively choral. He was also believed to have introduced the wearing of linen masks.

Thessalonians, Epistles of Paul to the Two New Testament books written by Paul to new converts in Thessalonica in about 51 AD. They are therefore among the earliest books of the New Testament. The first letter is filled with reminiscences, thanksgiving, and instruction but gives special prominence to the second coming of Christ. The second letter is a sequel, warning against the neglect of everyday duties caused by an overenthusiastic expectation of the second coming.

Thessaloníki (English name: Salonika) 40 38N 22 58E The second largest port in Greece, in Macedonia on the Gulf of Salonika. Founded in 315 BC as Thessalonica, it became the capital of Macedonia. It was captured by the Turks (1430) and remained in the Ottoman Empire until ceded to Greece (1913). During World War I it was a base for Allied operations. Notable Byzantine architecture includes the Panaghia Chalkeon (1028). Its university was founded in 1925. The port handles about one third of Greek exports, including chrome, manganese, and agricultural produce. Industries include the manufacture of textiles and food processing. Population (1981): 402,443.

Thessaly (Modern Greek name: Thessalía) A region of E central Greece, bordering on the Aegean Sea. In the 4th century BC it was briefly a strong and united state before falling to Philip of Macedon. Freed from Macedonian rule by Rome in 196 BC, it was incorporated in the Roman province of Macedonia in 148 BC. It subsequently formed part of the Byzantine Empire, falling to Turkey in the late 14th century AD. It was annexed by Greece in 1881.

Thetis In Greek mythology, one of the *nereids. She was courted by Zeus and Poseidon, but after hearing that she was fated to bear a son greater than its father they married her to the mortal Peleus, to whom she bore *Achilles.

thiamine. *See* vitamin B complex.

thiazine An organic compound that has a molecular structure containing a ring of four carbon atoms and two sulfur atoms. Thiazine derivatives are used in such drugs as tranquilizers, antihistamines, and antibiotics, as well as in various dyes.

thiazole (C_3H_3NS) An organic compound that has a molecular structure containing a ring of three carbon atoms, one sulfur atom, and one nitrogen atom. Thiazole derivatives occur in thiamine (vitamin B_1), penicillin, and in numerous synthetic drugs, dyes, and chemicals.

Thibaud, Jacques (1880–1953) French violinist. He studied at the Paris conservatoire and after a period playing at the Café Rouge in Paris he made his concert debut in 1898. In 1905 he formed a trio with Cortot and Casals. He was killed in an air crash.

thickhead An insectivorous songbird belonging to a family (*Pachycephalidae*; 35 species) occurring in mangrove swamps, scrub, and open forests in S Asia and Australasia. Thickheads are 6–7 in (15–18 cm) long and have large heavy heads and a loud whistling song. Male birds of the chief genus, *Pachycephalus*, are typically yellow and green with black, white, or brown markings.

Thiers, Louis Adolphe   (1797–1877) French statesman and historian; the first president of the Third Republic (1870–73). He served Louis Philippe in various ministerial posts and was a critic of Napoleon III, after whose fall during the Franco-Prussian War Thiers became president. He negotiated peace with Prussia and his economic policies facilitated France's economic recovery. He was responsible for the suppression of the Commune of Paris (1871). His publications include *Histoire de la Révolution française* (10 vols, 1823–27).

Thimphu (*or* Thimbu)   27 29N 89 40E The capital of Bhutan since 1962, situated in the foothills of the E Himalayas. Population (1969 est): 8000.

Thira. *See* Thera.

Third Reich   (1933–45) The Nazi regime in Germany. The name refers to the Nazi ambition to revive the medieval Holy Roman Empire (the first Reich) and the German Empire (the second Reich; 1871–1918). The Third Reich succeeded the Weimar Republic and ended with Germany's defeat in World War II.

third stream   A name for a type of music created by the fusion of jazz and classical music. The word was coined by the composer Gunther Schuller (1925–), who encouraged classically trained jazz musicians, such as Charlie Mingus and John Coltrane (1926–), and composers interested in jazz, such as Milton Babbitt, to work together.

Third World. *See* developing countries.

Thirteen Colonies   The 13 North American colonies that became the United States of America in 1776 (*see* American Revolution). They were Connecticut, Delaware, Georgia, Maryland, Massachusetts, New Hampshire, New Jersey, New York, North Carolina, Pennsylvania, Rhode Island, South Carolina, and Virginia.

thirty-eighth parallel   The latitude of 38°N that approximates to the border between North and South Korea. It was the line, agreed at the *Yalta Conference at the end of World War II, N of which Soviet troops accepted the Japanese surrender and S of which US troops did so. Hostility between the Soviet-dominated North Korea and the US-dominated South Korea led to the *Korean War, after which the thirty-eighth parallel was confirmed as the demarcation line.

Thirty-Nine Articles   (1563) The doctrine, together with the Book of *Common Prayer, of the *Church of England. The Articles do not represent a creed; rather they deal with specific points that were matters of controversy and give in broad terms the Anglican position with regard to these points, especially as distinguished from the Roman Catholic, Calvinist, or Anabaptist views. The clergy of the Church of England promise not to teach beliefs that contradict them. Other Anglican churches, such as the Protestant Episcopal Church in the US, have adopted many of the Articles.

Thirty Years' War   (1618–48) The conflict between rival dynastic and religious interests in the Holy Roman Empire that escalated into a major European war. It was caused by the revolt of Protestants in Bohemia against the Counter-Reformation policies of the imperial government at Prague. Although imperial forces defeated the Bohemians in 1620, the revolt spread, with the German Protestants under *Mansfeld receiving sporadic support from the English, Dutch, and Danes. With the Edict of Restitution (1629) Emperor Ferdinand II, helped by the armies of *Wallenstein and *Tilly, dispossessed many German Protestants, who were only saved by the intervention in 1630 of Sweden under *Gustavus II Adolphus. In 1635 France, hoping to contain the power of Spain and the Empire, entered the conflict. The war ended with the Peace of *Westphalia (1648), although the Franco-Spanish conflict continued until 1659 (*see* Pyrenees, Treaty of the). The war caused serious economic and demographic reverses in Germany.

Thisbe. *See* Pyramus and Thisbe.

thistle   A prickly-leaved herb belonging to one of several genera of the family *Compositae, especially *Carduus* (120 species), *Cirsium* (120 species), *Carlinus* (20 species), and *Onopordum* (20 species), distributed throughout the N hemisphere. Thistles characteristically have heads of small purple flowers and spiny stems. The perennial creeping thistle (*Cirsium arvense*) grows to a height of 40 in (1 m) and is a persistent weed, having spreading roots that give rise to new plants. *See also* globe thistle; sow thistle.

Thistlewood, Arthur. *See* Cato Street Conspiracy.

thixotropy   A property possessed by certain gels as a result of which they become liquid when stirred and return to a gel-like state when left to stand.

Thixotropic gels are used in nondrip paints as they prevent the various components from settling out during storage without affecting the fluid properties of the paint when applied. Certain types of quicksand are naturally thixotropic.

DYLAN THOMAS

Thomas, Dylan   (1914–53) Welsh poet. Born in Swansea, Wales, he moved to London after the publication of *18 Poems* in 1934 and worked for the BBC. *Deaths and Entrances* (1946) contains many of his best-known poems. In 1949 he returned to Wales, where he wrote his popular radio play *Under Milk Wood* (1954). Alcoholism precipitated his death, while on a US tour.

Thomas, Norman (Mattoon)   (1884–1968) US socialist leader, reformer, and author. He founded the National Civil Liberties Bureau in 1917 and joined the Socialist Party in 1918. His early pacifism and his concern for civil liberties led to leadership of the Socialist Party from 1926 and its nomination for president six times—from 1928 to 1948. He helped to found the National Civil Liberties Bureau (1917) and *The World Tomorrow* (1918) and worked as an editor on *The Nation* (1921–22). His works include *The Conscientious Objector in America* (1923), *Socialism of Our Time* (1929), *Human Exploitation* (1934), *Socialist's Faith* (1951), and *Socialism Reexamined* (1963).

Thomas, St   In the New Testament, one of the 12 Apostles. He is known as "Doubting Thomas" because he refused to believe in the resurrection until he had seen and touched Christ. Feast day: Dec 21.

Thomas à Kempis   (Thomas Hemmerken; c. 1380–1471) German spiritual writer and monk. He spent most of his life writing and teaching novices at the Augustinian convent of Agnietenberg near Zwolle (Netherlands). His fame rests on his devotional treatise, *The Imitation of Christ*, although his authorship has been doubted by some scholars.

Thomism. *See* Aquinas, St Thomas.

Thomson, Sir Joseph John   (1856–1940) British physicist, who discovered the *electron. Thomson studied *cathode rays, the nature of which was then unknown and in 1897 he succeeded in deflecting cathode rays by an electric field, thus showing that they consisted of negatively charged particles. He also measured the ratio of their charge to mass and, using the known figure for the minimum charge on an ion, deduced that electrons were about 2000 times lighter than the hydrogen atom. Thomson thought that atoms consist of electrons embedded in a positively charged sphere, a concept that was superseded by *Rutherford's model. For his discovery of the electron, Thomson was awarded the Nobel Prize in 1906.

His son **Sir George Paget Thomson** (1892–1975) was also a physicist, who discovered the effect of electron diffraction (1927). He shared the 1937 Nobel Prize with Clinton Davisson (1881–1958), who had independently discovered the same effect.

Thomson, Virgil   (1896–) US composer, music critic, and conductor. He studied composition with Nadia Boulanger in Paris. His compositions include two operas with libretti by Gertrude Stein: *Four Saints in Three Acts* (1928) and *The Mother of Us All* (1947). He has composed a variety of other vocal and instrumental music, including music for the film *Louisiana Story* (1948). His writings include *The Art of Judging Music* (1948) and *American Music Since 1910* (1971).

Thomson, William. *See* Kelvin, William Thomson, 1st Baron.

Thomson effect (*or* Kelvin effect). *See* thermoelectric effects.

Thonburi 13 43N 100 27E A city in central Thailand, part of Bangkok Metropolis on the Chao Phraya River. It is noted for the Wat Arun temple. Industries include rice and timber milling. Population (1970): 627,989.

Thor The Teutonic god of thunder, in some legends the son of *Odin. He presided over the home and controlled the weather and crops; he was also worshiped as a god of war. Armed with a magic hammer, similar to a boomerang, and a belt, which increased his strength, he battled frequently against giants and monsters. His name survives in *Thursday*. □Ragnarök.

thorax In mammals (including man), the region of the body between the *diaphragm and the neck, which contains the lungs and heart and their associated vessels. The skeleton of the thorax is formed by the breastbone at the front, the spine at the back, and the ribs at the sides. In arthropods the thorax is the part of the body between the head and abdomen.

HENRY DAVID THOREAU *Writer whose observations on life and his surroundings were recorded in* Walden.

Thoreau, Henry David (1817–62) US naturalist and writer. His early work appeared in the *Dial* and also included *A Week on the Concord and Merrimack Rivers* (1849). Thoreau is best known for his Walden experiment (1845–46) during which he lived as a recluse in the woods of Walden near his native Concord, Mass. He developed a great love and knowledge of animals, which was more intuitive than scientific. *Walden* was published in 1854. Influenced by *Emerson and *Hawthorne, Thoreau also wrote poems and essays, many about his beloved homeland. His best known essay, "Civil Disobedience," grew out of his opposition to the Mexican War. *See also* Transcendentalists, New England.

thorium (Th) A naturally occurring radioactive metal. It is possible that thorium-fueled nuclear reactors may be developed in the future, since it is more abundant than uranium and does not produce plutonium-239 in appreciable quantities (*see* uranium). Thorium oxide (ThO_2) has one of the highest known melting points (5972°F; 3300°C), which led to its use in gas mantles, as it glows white when heated. At no 90; at wt 232.038; mp 3185°F (1750°C); bp 6878°F (3800°C).

thorium series One of three naturally occurring series of radioactive decays. The thorium series is headed by thorium-232, which undergoes a series of alpha and beta decays ending with the stable isotope lead-208. *See also* actinium series; uranium series.

thorn apple An annual herb, *Datura stramonium*, also called jimsonweed, occurring in N temperate and subtropical regions. Growing to a height of 40 in (1 m), it has white trumpet-shaped flowers producing a fruit with a spiny capsule that splits to release the black seeds. All parts of the plant are very poisonous, containing the alkaloids hyoscyamine, hyoscine, and scopolamine. Family: *Solanaceae*.

thornbill A drab-colored Australian bird belonging to one of three genera, especially *Acanthiza*, and occurring in trees and thickets. The yellow-tailed thornbill (*A. chrysorrhoea*) builds a very long oval nest with several nest chambers, the upper being used to rear young and the lower providing accommodation for the male. Family: *Muscicapidae* (*see* flycatcher).

Thorndike, Dame Sybil (1882–1976) British actress. She acted many Shakespearean roles at the Old Vic between 1914 and 1918 and played the title role in the first production of G. B. Shaw's *St Joan* in 1924. She also acted in several films.

Thornhill, Sir James (1675–1734) English *baroque decorative painter. One of the first native-born English painters with any pretensions to an international reputation, Thornhill is best remembered for his decoration of the Painted Hall at Greenwich Hospital (1704), the interior of the dome of *St Paul's Cathedral (1707), and the hall at Blenheim Palace. He was the teacher and father-in-law of *Hogarth.

Thoroughbred A breed of □horse descended from three Arab stallions brought to England between 1689 and 1728. Thoroughbreds have a refined streamlined build and a sensitive temperament and are noted for speed and stamina, being used worldwide for racing and as bloodstock to improve other breeds. They may be any solid color. Height: 1.52–1.73 m (15–17 hands).

Thorpe, Jim (James Francis T.; 1888–1953) US athlete. Of Indian descent, he was an all-American football player (1911; 1912) while attending the Carlisle Indian School. He won gold medals for the decathlon and the pentathlon in the Olympic games (1912), but was forced to return the medals because he had played baseball semi-professionally. (They were returned to his descendants in 1973.) Named the greatest athlete of the first half of the 20th century, he played professional baseball (1913–19) and professional football (1915–26) and headed the American Professional Football Association in 1920.

Thorvaldsen, Bertel (*or* B. Thorwaldsen; 1768–1844) Danish sculptor. His highly successful career began in Rome, where he worked from 1797 until his return to Copenhagen in 1838. Reviving the tradition of ancient Greek sculpture in his mythological and religious statues, he became one of the leading figures in *neoclassicism. Many of his works are in the Thorvaldsen Museum, Copenhagen.

Thoth The Egyptian god of learning, the scribe and arbiter of the gods, usually portrayed with the head of an ibis. He was the inventor of writing, arithmetic, and geometry and the keeper of various magic formulae. *See also* Hermes Trismegistos.

Thousand, Expedition of the (1860) The expedition of about a thousand volunteers, led by Giuseppe *Garibaldi, which embarked from Genoa and, after landing in Sicily, overthrew the Kingdom of the Two Sicilies, enabling S Italy to be united with the N. *See also* Risorgimento.

Thousand Islands A group of about 1700 small islands and islets in North America, in the St Lawrence River. They are chiefly in Ontario (Canada) with a few in New York state and are a popular resort area.

Thrace The Balkan region bordered by the Black Sea, the Aegean, Macedonia, and the Danube River. From the 8th century BC Greek cities colonized the coasts, while the independent inland tribes were an easy target for invaders—the Persians in about 516 BC and then Philip II of Macedon in the mid-4th century. After Alexander the Great's death (323) it passed to his general Lysimachus (c. 355–c. 281 BC) and then to Macedonia before coming under the influence of Rome in 168 BC; it became a Roman province in 46 AD. Famous for its horses and horsemen, and for ecstatic religious rituals, Thrace was traditionally the birthplace of the mysteries and orgiastic rites associated with the worship of Dionysus. It is now divided between Turkey, Greece, and Bulgaria.

Thrale, Hester Lynch. See Piozzi, Hester Lynch.

threadfin A fish, also called threadfish, belonging to the family *Polynemidae* (about 24 species), that is found along warm seashores. It has a silvery elongated body, usually 12–24 in (30–60 cm) long, two dorsal fins, and four to seven long threadlike pectoral fin rays. Order: *Perciformes*.

threadworm. See pinworm.

Three Mile Island An island in the Susquehanna River in SE Pennsylvania, just S of Harrisburg. The nuclear power plant located here was the focus of attention in 1979 when one of its reactors experienced a breakdown in its emergency core cooling system. Although widespread dissemination of radioactive material never occurred, the incident precipitated far-reaching investigations of the proper design, maintenance, and operation of nuclear reactors.

Three Rivers. *See* Trois-Rivières.

Three Wise Men. *See* Magi.

thresher shark A *shark of the family *Alopiidae* (5 species), found usually in offshore waters of tropical and temperate seas. About 20 ft (6 m) long, it has a long scythelike extension of the upper tail lobe, which it uses to thrash the water while circling its prey (squid and schooling fish), forcing them into tighter groups, which it then attacks. □fish.

thrift A perennial herb, *Armeria maritima*, also called sea pink, native to mountains, salt marshes, and sandy coastal regions of N Europe. The flower stem, up to 12 in (30 cm) high, rises from a basal tuft of long narrow grasslike leaves and bears a cluster of rose-pink or white flowers. The Jersey thrift (*A. arenaria*) is taller with a denser tuft of broader leaves and grows on sand dunes in central and S Europe. Family: *Plumbaginaceae*.

thrips A minute insect, also called thunder fly, belonging to the order *Thysanoptera* (about 3000 species). Thrips have dark slender bodies, 0.01–0.2 in (0.5–5 mm) long, and usually two pairs of narrow fringed wings. Many species suck the juices of flowering plants, often causing serious damage and spreading plant diseases. Others eat fungi, decaying organic material, mites, and small insects. In some species there are no males and the larvae develop from unfertilized eggs (*see* parthenogenesis).

thrombosis The formation of a blood clot inside a blood vessel, which often obstructs the flow of blood. Thrombosis is more likely to occur if the blood vessel is damaged, if the blood flow is very slow, or if the blood is in a condition in which it is more likely to clot. The commonest site of thrombosis is in the veins of the legs. This is particularly likely to occur if a person is bedridden for a long time and it is often accompanied by inflammation of the vein (*see* phlebitis). The clot may become detached and carried to the lungs, causing pulmonary *embolism. The patient is treated with *anticoagulants.
Thrombosis can also occur in the arteries supplying the heart (coronary thrombosis), causing a heart attack (*see* myocardial infarction), or the brain, causing *stroke.

thrush (bird) A songbird belonging to a family (*Turdidae*; 300 species) found throughout the world but predominantly in Old World regions. Thrushes are slender billed, 5–12 in (13–30 cm) long, and usually brown—often with speckling or patches of red, yellow, or blue. They may be terrestrial or arboreal, feeding chiefly on insects and fruit and often having melodious songs. Northern species are migratory. *See also* blackbird; fieldfare; mistle thrush; redwing; ring ouzel; song thrush.

thrush (disease). *See* candidiasis.

Thucydides (c. 460–c. 400 BC) Greek historian. He served as an Athenian general in the Peloponnesian War but was banished in 424 BC for allowing the Spartan general Brasidas to capture the colony of Amphipolis. He remained in exile until 404 BC. His eight-volume *History of the Peloponnesian War*, written in a plain narrative style, is notable for its political, moral, and psychological analysis of the issues and leaders involved.

Thugs (Sanskrit word: *sthaga*, deceiver) A Hindu sect, members of which worked in small gangs, murdering (usually by strangulation), robbing, and burying travelers in India. They worshiped Kali, the Hindu goddess of death, and observed strict rules, employing a private language among themselves. They were suppressed in the 1830s.

Thuja. *See* arborvitae.

Thule **1.** A far northern land first described in the 4th century BC by *Pytheas. It is tentatively identified with Norway or Iceland. **2.** An Eskimo culture of the Arctic region, dating from between about 500 and 1300 AD.

thulium (Tm) The least abundant of the *lanthanide elements, discovered in 1879 by P. T. Cleve (1840–1905). It forms the oxide Tm_2O_3. Radioactive ^{169}Tm is used in portable X-ray generators. At no 69; at wt 168.934; mp 2816°F (1545°C); bp 3540°F (1947°C).

Thun (French name: Thoune) 46 46N 7 38E A city in central Switzerland, on Lake Thun. It is the center of the Bernese Oberland; industries include cheese production and watchmaking. Population (1970): 36,523.

Thunder Bay 48 20N 89 23W A city and port in E Canada, in Ontario on Lake Superior. Settled after 1800, it consists of Fort William and Port Arthur, which amalgamated in 1970. A major wheat-exporting port, Thunder Bay is also a transportation hub and mining center. Pulp and paper, timber, aircraft, buses, and shipbuilding are economically important. Lakehead University (1965) is situated here. Population (1981): 112,486.

thunderstorm A storm of rain, hail, or snow, accompanied by thunder and *lightning. A lightning flash is an electrical discharge causing sudden heating and expansion of air as the flash passes through the atmosphere, resulting in the sound of thunder. Although both occur simultaneously, thunder is heard later than lightning is seen, as light travels faster than sound. An approximate measure of distance from a storm is 1 mi (1.6 km) for every 5 seconds between flash and thunder.

Thurber, James (1894–1961) US humorous writer and cartoonist. An early and continuing contributor to the *New Yorker*, he satirized intellectual fashions and domestic habits with irony and sophistication. His essays and stories are collected in *The Thurber Carnival* (1945) and other volumes.

Thuringia A historic region of central Germany, N of Bavaria and W of Saxony. Dominated by the Thuringian forests and strategically positioned, Thuringia became a buffer state against invaders from the E. Frequently partitioned during the middle ages, it passed to the Wettin family in 1265. It is now part of East Germany.

Thurmond, (James) Strom (1902–) US politician; senator (1954–). A Democrat, he was governor of South Carolina (1947–51) and ran for president (1948) as the States' Rights Democrat (Dixiecrat) candidate. He switched to the Republican Party in 1964. He became president pro tempore of the Senate (1981) and chairman of the Judiciary Committee (1981) and was elected overwhelmingly to a 6th term in the Senate in 1984.

Thursday Island 10 37S 142 10E An Australian island in Torres Strait, off the N coast of Queensland. Pearl fishing is the main industry. Area: 1.5 sq mi (4 sq km). Chief town: Port Kennedy.

Thutmose I King of Egypt (c. 1512–c. 1504 BC) of the 18th dynasty. He conquered Nubia beyond the Fourth Nile Cataract and Syria as far as the Euphrates River. He enlarged and embellished the temple of Amon at *Karnak.

Thutmose II King of Egypt (c. 1525–c. 1512 BC) of the 18th dynasty, the son of *Thutmose I and the brother and husband of *Hatshepsut. He crushed a rebellion in Nubia before dying young.

Thutmose III (d. 1450 BC) King of Egypt (c. 1504–1450 BC) of the 18th dynasty, who ruled Egypt at its most powerful and prosperous. In his first year of independent rule, after the death of his half-sister *Hatshepsut (1468), he defeated Syrian rebels at Megiddo and in later campaigns advanced beyond the Euphrates River. He organized and supervised the country's complicated administration and was an outstanding athlete and big-game hunter. A patron of art and architecture, he collected foreign plants, birds, and beasts on campaign. His mummy is to be seen in Cairo.

Thutmose IV King of Egypt (1425–1417 BC) of the 18th dynasty. He cultivated the alliance of Babylonia and the Mitanni kingdom against the Hittites and built extensively at *Karnak.

thylacine The largest carnivorous *marsupial, *Thylacinus cynocephalus*, also called Tasmanian wolf or tiger. About 5 ft (1.5 m) long, it resembles a dog with dark stripes across its gray-brown back. Its teeth—adapted for eating meat—include pointed canines and shearing premolars. The dingo has exterminated thylacines on the Australian mainland, but a few may have survived in Tasmania. Family: *Dasyuridae*.

thyme A small shrub belonging to the genus *Thymus* (about 50 species), native to temperate Eurasia. Garden thyme (*T. vulgaris*) is cultivated for its fragrant leaves and small mauve flowers, which are dried and used as a culinary herb. An oil extract is used in perfumes and medicines. The common wild thyme (*T. drucei*) has a branching creeping stem up to 3 in (7.5 cm) long and clusters of rose-purple flowers. Family: *Labiatae*.

thymus An organ situated at the base of the neck, above the heart. The thymus is well developed at birth and grows until puberty, after which it shrinks and ceases to function. During infancy the thymus produces lymphocytes (a type of white blood cell) that form the *antibodies associated with allergic responses and the rejection of transplanted tissues and organs. *See also* immunity.

thyratron. *See* thermionic valve.

thyristor A solid-state electronic device, also called a semiconductor or silicon-controlled rectifier; it consists of four layers of *semiconductor forming three p-n junctions. It acts as a switch, blocking the current through two terminals until it has been turned on by a pulse applied to the third terminal. This pulse can be initiated by light or a temperature change. Thyristors are used in a wide range of power-switching and control-circuit applications. They can pass currents ranging from milliamperes to several hundred amperes and for many purposes have replaced the thyratron (*see* thermionic valve).

thyroid gland An *endocrine gland situated at the base of the neck, in front and on either side of the windpipe. It secretes two hormones, the most important of which is thyroxine, which controls the basal metabolism of the body; thyroxine secretion is regulated by thyroid-stimulating hormone, released from the *pituitary gland. Because thyroxine production requires iodine, deficiency of iodine causes the thyroid to enlarge in an attempt to produce adequate amounts of the hormone (*see* goiter). *See also* cretinism; hyperthyroidism; myxedema.

Tianjin (T'ien-ching *or* Tientsin) 39 08N 117 12E An administratively autonomous port in NE China, the third largest city in the country, on the *Grand Canal. A prosperous city for centuries, it was the scene of much friction between Chinese and Europeans in the late 19th century. It is the site of two universities. Industries include chemicals, machinery, and textiles. Population (1980 est): 7,390,000.

Tian Shan (*or* Tien Shan) A mountain system of central Asia. It extends about 1500 mi (2500 km) NE from the *Pamir Mountains in the Soviet Union, through NW China to the Mongolian border, reaching 24,406 ft (7439 m) at Pobeda Peak.

Tibaldi, Pellegrino (1527–96) Italian architect and painter, a leading exponent of *mannerism. Paintings by him survive in Rome and Bologna. In Spain (1587–96), at the invitation of Philip II, he oversaw the construction and decoration of the *Escorial.

Tiber River (Italian name: Tevere; Latin name: Tiberis) A river in central Italy, rising in the Apennines of Tuscany and flowing mainly S through Rome to the Tyrrhenian Sea near Ostia. Length: 252 mi (405 km).

Tiberias 32 48N 35 32E A city in N Israel, on the W shore of the Sea of Galilee. Founded by Herod Antipas in about AD 20 and named for the Roman Emperor Tiberius, it became the center of Jewry in Palestine after the Roman destruction of Jerusalem. It is now a resort. Population (1970 est): 23,900.

Tiberias, Sea of. *See* Galilee, Sea of.

Tiberius (42 BC–37 AD) Roman emperor (14–37 AD). Tiberius, who was *Livia Drusilla's son by her first husband, was recognized by her stepfather, Emperor Augustus, as his successor in 4 AD. As emperor his policies were unambitious though sound but he faced the Senate's hostility, family intrigue, and military rebellion. Tiberius' reign saw a series of treason prosecutions before his retirement to Capri in 26 AD, where he gained a reputation for depravity.

Tibesti Mountains A mountain range in N Africa, in the central Sahara. It lies chiefly in NW Chad but extends NE into Libya and rises to 11,204 ft (3415 m) at Emi Koussi, the highest peak in the Sahara.

Tibet (Chinese name: Xizang Autonomous Region) An administrative region in W China, bordering on India, Nepal, Bhutan, and Burma. It consists of a high plateau and is surrounded by mountains, including the Himalayas and the Kunlun Mountains. Most agriculture and the country's cities are in the river valleys, while nomads herd such animals as yaks on the plateau. The area is rich in minerals, not mined until the 1950s because of religious proscription. Tibet is famous for its Buddhist-inspired art and its handicrafts. *History*: Buddhism, introduced in the 7th century AD, has exerted a profound influence on Tibetan history. The lamas (priests) of *Tibetan Buddhism attained political power in the 13th century, when Kublai Khan gave the government of his conquests in E Tibet to the Saskya lama. Subsequent disunity was brought to an end in 1642, when the fifth *Dalai Lama became ruler of all Tibet. In 1720 the Chinese Qing dynasty established a control over Tibet that lasted until the Qing's overthrow in 1911. Independence was declared, but in 1950 Tibet again fell to the Chinese. An uprising in 1959 was brutally suppressed and the Dalai Lama, together with thousands of refugees, fled. Tibet was subsequently subjected to Chinese influence. Area: 471,660 sq mi (1,221,601 sq km). Population (1980 est): 1,830,000. Capital: Lhasa.

Tibetan Buddhism (*or* lamaism) A form of Mahayana Buddhism as practiced in Tibet and Mongolia. Introduced into Tibet in the 7th century AD, it is characterized by a complex symbolic literature and monastic discipline, with surviving features of *Bon shamanism. Buddhist elements are explored in their esoteric significance, hence the array of deities, *mandalas, etc. The *guru is of prime importance; some are held to be reincarnations of previous lamas. Until the Chinese invasion of Tibet in 1959, the *Dalai Lama was both temporal and spiritual head of the state. *See also* Panchen Lama.

tibia. *See* leg.

Tibullus, Albius (c. 55–c. 19 BC) Roman poet. He lived quietly on his estate near Rome and was a friend of Horace and Ovid. His elegiac poetry, noted for its smooth and rhythmical style, is mostly addressed to his patron, M. Valerius Messalla. Two books of his poems were published during his lifetime and were known as "Delia" and "Nemesis" after the pseudonyms of the women who were the subjects of the poems.

Ticino River A river in Switzerland and Italy. It flows mainly S from the Leopontine Alps to the Po River near Pavia in Italy. Length: 154 mi (248 km).

tick A parasitic *arachnid of the worldwide suborder *Metastigmata* (850 species), which sucks the blood of birds and mammals and may transmit such diseases as *typhus and relapsing fever. Its round unsegmented body, up to 1.2 in (30 mm) long, bears eight bristly legs and may be covered by a dorsal shield. After feeding for a certain time, the adults drop off the host and lay eggs on the ground. The larvae attach themselves to a suitable victim, feed, then drop off and molt into nymphs, which repeat the procedure. Order: *Acarina* (or *Acari*). *Compare* mite.

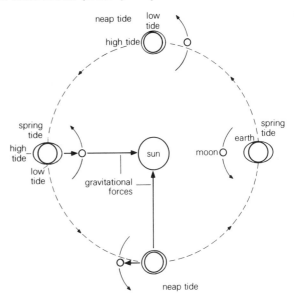

TIDES *The force of gravity between the earth and the moon pulls the waters of the seas towards the moon, creating high tides once a day. The second daily high tide occurs because the moon pulls the earth itself away from the water on the far side from the moon. Exceptionally high spring tides occur twice monthly when the gravitational force of the moon is in line with that of the sun. The lower neap tides occur when these two forces are at right angles.*

tides The regular rising and falling of seawater level resulting from the gravitational attraction between the earth, sun, and moon. Variations in their relative positions produce variations in tidal range (*see* spring tide; neap tide). Most parts of the world experience semidiurnal tides (occurring twice per tidal day—24 hours 5 minutes). Tidal currents are periodic horizontal flows of water resulting from the rise and fall of the tide. Near the coast they are usually perpendicular to it and reversing, but in the ocean they flow in a rotary manner around a series of nodal points; water level remains approximately constant at these points, tidal range increasing concentrically outward, and high water rotates about them.

Tieck, (Johann) Ludwig (1773–1853) German writer. Associated with *Novalis, the *Schlegels, and other Romantic writers centered in Jena, Tieck was highly versatile, writing romantic and realistic tales, novels, and plays, translating, and publishing a collection of medieval lyrics. His works include the romantic fairytale, *Der blonde Eckbert* (1797) and the satirical comedy, *Der gestiefette Kater* (1797).

Tientsin. *See* Tianjin.

Tiepolo, Giovanni Battista (1696–1770) Venetian *rococo painter, who was one of the greatest decorators of the 18th century. Influenced by *Veronese, his early somber style evolved into the exuberance of his first major frescoes, for the Archbishop's Palace at Udine (1725–29). These were followed by decorations for many N Italian palaces and churches. Abroad he decorated the Residenz Palace, Würzburg, built by the rococo architect *Neumann, with historical and allegorical subjects (1750–53), and the Royal Palace in Madrid (1762–66). One of his assistants and imitators was his son **Giovanni Domenico Tiepolo** (1727–1804), best known for his paintings of clowns and acrobats.

Tierra del Fuego An archipelago separated from the mainland of S South America by the Strait of Magellan. The W and S belong to Chile, the E to Argentina. Sheep farming and oil production are the principal economic activities. Chief towns: Punta Arenas (Chile); Ushuaia (Argentina).

Tiflis. *See* Tbilisi.

tiger A large *cat, *Panthera tigris*. Tigers are usually about 10 ft (3 m) long, but the race of Siberian tigers can reach 13 ft (4 m). Tigers evolved in Siberia and have spread south to most of Asia; they shed their coat seasonally and shelter from hot sun during the day. They hunt at night, stalking their prey (mainly antelope). A fully grown tiger will eat up to 55 lb (25 kg) of meat at one feeding.

tiger beetle A long-legged beetle, with pointed mandibles, belonging to a family (*Cicindelidae*; 2000 species) occurring mainly in the tropics and subtropics. Tiger beetles range from 0.24 to 2.75 in (6 to 70 mm) in length; although most are black or brown some are brilliantly colored. Both adults and larvae are predatory—the adults hunt for their prey while the larvae wait at the entrance to their burrows.

tigerfish Any fish that resembles a tiger, especially members of the genus *Hydrocynus*, family *Characidae* (*see* characin), found in fresh waters of Africa and South America. They have horizontally striped elongated bodies, reaching 40 in (1 m) in length, and feed voraciously on other fish. Tigerfish of the family *Theraponidae* (order *Perciformes*) occur in Indo-Pacific marine and fresh waters and include the three-striped tigerfish (*Therapon jarbua*), also called saltwater zebra fish.

tiger moth A moth belonging to the family *Arctiidae*, occurring in Eurasia, N Africa, and North America. The adults have a stout body and are brightly colored, often orange and black. The hairy larvae, commonly called woolly bears, incorporate their hairs into the cocoon and are seldom destructive, eating various wild plants.

tiger shark A large *requiem shark, *Galeocerdo cuvieri*, that lives mainly in tropical seas. It has a grayish-brown body, up to about 18 ft (5.5 m) long, patterned with vertical bars and a lighter underside. It is a voracious omnivore and eats virtually anything, including mammals, birds, fish, invertebrates, refuse, and man.

Tiglath-pileser I King of Assyria (c. 1120–1074 BC), who greatly extended Assyrian territory, reaching the Mediterranean coast in the W. He patronized art and architecture and collected one of the oldest surviving libraries.

Tiglath-pileser III King of Assyria (c. 745–727 BC). Probably a usurper, he restored Assyrian military power in Babylonia, Syria, and against Urartu in the N. He also improved the efficiency of Assyrian administration, appointing provincial governors.

tigon A sterile hybrid cat, resulting from the mating of a lion and a tiger, also called a liger. This can only happen in captivity, because lions and tigers naturally inhabit different continents.

Tigre. *See* Amhara.

Tigris River A river in SW Asia, rising in SE Turkey and flowing SE through Diyarbakir, along the Turkish-Syrian border, and into Iraq. 118 mi (190 km) from the Persian Gulf it joins the Euphrates River to form the Shatt al-Arab. Length: 1150 mi (1850 km).

Tihwa. *See* Ürümqi.

Tijuana 39 29N 117 10W A city in NW Mexico, on the US border. It is the main entry point to Mexico from California and is a popular tourist resort. Population (1978 est): 534,993.

Tikal An ancient *Maya city in N Guatemala. After about 300 AD it grew into the largest Maya ceremonial center, with imposing pyramid temples. It was mysteriously abandoned about 900.

Tilak, Bal Gangadhar (*or* Lokamanya; 1856–1920) Indian nationalist leader. Joining the *Indian National Congress (1885) he changed its policy to one of resistance to British rule, advocating Indian independence. He was the first leader to propose the adoption of Hindi as the national language.

Tilburg 51 34N 5 05E A city in the S Netherlands, in South Brabant province. A major industrial center, it produces textiles. Population (1981 est): 153,117.

Tilden, Samuel Jones (1814–86) US political leader, lawyer, and reformer. A member of the New York bar from 1841 and a successful businessman, he allied himself with the *barnburners and *Free-Soil Party in

the 1840s and then joined the Democratic Party. As New York state Democratic Committee chairman (1866–74), he was instrumental in breaking the Tweed ring (*see* Tweed, William Marcy). He was governor of New York (1874–76) and was the Democratic presidential nominee in 1876. He won the popular vote in the election, but the electoral college, in a contested vote, elected Rutherford B. *Hayes.

till (*or* boulder clay) The unstratified material that ranges from clay to angular stones and boulders, deposited by glaciers and ice sheets. Its form depends on the rock from which it originated. Large areas of N Europe are covered by till remaining from the Ice Age.

Tillich, Paul (Johannes) (1886–1965) US Protestant theologian of German birth. A Lutheran pastor and later a professor at several German universities, he moved to the US in 1933, when Hitler came to power. He lectured in New York and at Harvard and Chicago Universities. In *Systematic Theology* (3 vols, 1950–63) he attempted to demonstrate Christianity's relevance to contemporary life.

Tilly, Johan Tserclaes, Graf von (1559–1632) Bavarian general, who commanded the Catholic League in the *Thirty Years' War. He won the battle of the White Mountain (1620) and went on to gain control of NW Germany. He defeated the Swedes at Lutter (1626) and, in command of imperial forces, as well as the League's, razed Magdeburg (1631), gaining a reputation for brutality. He was killed in action after being defeated (1631) by the Swedes at Breitenfeld.

Tilsit. *See* Sovetsk.

Tilsit, Treaties of (1807) The two treaties that France signed at Tilsit (now Sovetsk, Soviet Union) with Russia and Prussia respectively after Napoleon's defeat of the Prussians at *Jena and Auerstädt and the Russians at *Friedland. Russia became an ally of France and Prussia, its territory considerably reduced, was occupied by French troops. Both Russia and Prussia joined the *Continental System of blockade against British trade.

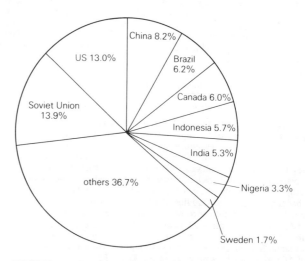

TIMBER *World production of timber, both hardwoods and softwoods.*

timber Sawed wood used for purposes other than fuel. Timber is divided into hardwoods (derived from broad-leaved trees) and softwoods (derived from conifers). The bulk of the world's softwoods are derived from the Soviet Union, Canada, the US, and Scandinavia. Hardwoods, which take longer to grow, are not confined to one specific climate zone. Uses for timber include furniture manufacture (usually hardwoods), building construction, and paper manufacture (largely softwoods).

timber wolf A large shaggy-coated *wolf of North America, also called the gray wolf. A Texas variety with a tawny coat is called the red wolf.

timbre A quality in the sound of a musical instrument, voice, etc., that distinguishes it from others. Thus a violin and a clarinet sound different even when they are playing the same note. The difference arises because each type of instrument produces different overtones in different strengths when a note is played. The production of overtones is controlled by the way the note is produced (plucking, blowing, etc.) and by the characteristics of the individual instrument.

Timbuktu (French name: Tombouctou) 16 49N 2 59W A town in E central Mali, on the Niger River. It was an important center on the trans-Saharan caravan route and an Islamic cultural center (1400–1600). It declined after its conquest by Morocco (1591). Population (1967 est): 9000.

time A concept that measures the duration of events and the periods that separate them. It is a fundamental parameter of all changes, measuring the rates at which they occur; it provides a scale of measurement enabling events that have occurred to be distinguished from those that are occurring and those that will occur. It appears, intuitively, to be flowing at a constant rate in one direction only, for all observers. However, according to Einstein's theory of *relativity this is not the case. The rate at which time passes (as measured by a clock) is not the same for observers in different frames of reference that are moving at a constant velocity with respect to each other. Thus, according to the *time-dilation effect, if two observers are moving at a constant velocity relative to each other it appears to each that the other's time processes are slowed down. This means that events that appear to be simultaneous to observers in the same frame of reference would not be simultaneous to observers in different frames of reference. In order to pinpoint an event in the universe, its position in a four-dimensional space-time continuum must be specified. This continuum consists of three space dimensions and one of time.
Historically, the measurement of time on earth has been based on astronomical observations—the time taken for the earth to revolve on its axis (the day) or for it to complete its orbit round the sun (the year). However, in modern science the basis of time measurement is the *second, which is defined in terms of the frequency of the radiation emitted in a specified transition of an isotope of cesium (*see* cesium clock).

time and motion study A study of a machine and its operator in a factory, measuring the time taken to complete each action and the sequence of the operator's movements. The study is then used to recommend methods of speeding up the operation and reducing the effort involved in order to utilize labor as economically as possible.

time dilation An effect predicted by Einstein's special theory of *relativity. If two observers, A and B, are moving at a velocity v relative to each other, it will appear to A that B's clock will show that *time is running more slowly; thus a time t measured on A's clock will be $t(1-v^2/c^2)^{1/2}$ on B's clock, where c is the velocity of light. The effect has been observed in some particles moving at high velocities, which appear to have an anomalously long lifetime.

Time of Troubles A period of political confusion in Russian history following the death of Boris *Godunov (1605). Godunov was succeeded by a Polish-supported pretender, the so-called False Dimitrii, who claimed to be the son (murdered in 1591, perhaps by Godunov) of Tsar Ivan the Terrible. The False Dimitrii was assassinated in 1606 by Muscovite nobles, who raised Vasilii Shuiski (1552–1612) to the throne. His rule was threatened by a second False Dimitrii, who established a rival court at Tushino in 1608. Shuiski was deposed and the second False Dimitrii was murdered in 1610, following a successful Polish invasion of Russia. A third False Dimitrii asserted his claim during 1611–12 but a successful rebellion against the Poles brought *Michael Romanov to the throne in 1613 and the end of the Time of Troubles.

Timişoara (Hungarian name: Temesvár) 45 45N 21 15E A city in W Romania, near the Yugoslav border. It is a commercial and cultural center with a university (1945) and has two cathedrals. Population (1979 est): 281,320.

Timor An Indonesian island, the largest of the *Nusa Tenggara group. Mountainous and dry, it is largely undeveloped. Crops include coffee, coconut, and sandalwood. *History*: in 1859 it was divided between Portugal and Holland. West (Dutch) Timor was included in independent Indonesia (1949). East Timor, scheduled for independence from Portugal in 1978, erupted in civil war in 1975 and was annexed by Indonesia (1976). Area: 11,883 sq mi (39,775 sq km). Chief cities: Kupang and Dili.

Timoshenko, Semyon Konstantinovich (1895–1970) Soviet marshal, who rebuilt the army after the initial defeats in the *Russo-Finnish War. He commanded at *Stalingrad in World War II but failed to stem a German advance (1942–43) and was reassigned to the staff.

timothy A perennial *grass, *Phleum pratense*, also called herd's grass or cat's tail, native to Europe. It forms large clumps, 20–40 in (0.5–1 m) tall, with swollen bulblike bases and dense cylindrical flower clusters. It is widely cultivated as a hay and pasture grass, especially as part of a mixture with other grasses.

Timothy, St In the New Testament, a disciple of *Paul, whom he accompanied on many missions. According to tradition he was martyred in Ephesus. Feast day: Feb 6.

The Epistles of Paul to Timothy, in the New Testament, consist of advice and directions concerning Timothy's personal conduct and public responsibilities. The second letter contains Paul's last known words before his martyrdom under Nero.

timpani (*or* kettledrums) Tuned percussion instruments consisting of a large copper bowl or "kettle" with parchment or plastic stretched across the top. The pitch can be altered by means either of metal keys around the circumference or a pedal mechanism. The sound also depends on the type of sticks used and where they strike the head; a glissando can be obtained by use of the pedals. □musical instruments.

Timur (*or* Tamerlane; c. 1336–1405) Mongol conqueror, a descendant of Genghis Khan. After winning control of Turkestan in central Asia, Timur left his capital Samarkand to conquer the world. Ruthlessly sweeping through Mongolia, Persia, Turkey, Russia, and India, leaving death and destruction behind him, he sought conquest rather than a permanent empire. Paradoxically, he spared and encouraged all kinds of artists.

tin (Sn) A silvery-white metal known to the ancients. Its principal ore is the oxide cassiterite (SnO_2), often found in alluvial concentrations. The element exists as at least two allotropes—the gray alpha-tin, and beta-tin, which is the common form above 13.2°C. At low temperature beta-tin slowly changes into alpha-tin causing **tin plague**. It is obtained by reduction with coal in a reverberatory furnace. In addition to the oxide, compounds include tin chloride ($SnCl_2$), which is used as a reducing agent and in the dyeing industry. The major use of tin is in *tinplate. It alloys with copper to form *bronzes and with niobium to give a superconducting composition, which is used in electromagnets. Some organic compounds of tin are toxic. At no 50; at wt 118.69; mp 160.69°F (231.89°C); bp 4122°F (2270°C).

tinamou A solitary ground-dwelling bird belonging to a family (*Tinamidae*; 50 species) occurring in Central and South America. 9–15 in (23–38 cm) long, tinamous are well camouflaged with a mottled gray or brown plumage. They have small wings and a very short tail and are poor fliers. They feed on seeds, fruit, and insects and are the only members of the order *Tinamiformes*.

Tinbergen, Jan (1903–) Dutch economist. Tinbergen was adviser to the League of Nations from 1936 to 1938. He was corecipient with Ragnar *Frisch of the first Nobel Prize for Economics (1969).

Tinbergen, Niko (laas) (1907–) Dutch zoologist and pioneer ethologist. Like Konrad *Lorenz, Tinbergen concentrated on studying the behavior of animals in their natural surroundings. Tinbergen, with Lorenz, was responsible for tracing the evolutionary development of social behavior patterns, such as courtship displays. His works include *The Herring Gull's World* (1953), *Social Behavior in Animals* (1953), and *Animal Behavior* (1965). Tinbergen shared a Nobel Prize (1973) with Lorenz and von *Frisch.

tineid moth A moth of the widespread family *Tineidae*. The adults are usually small with a golden or silvery sheen and frequently do not feed. The caterpillars feed on a variety of plant and animal matter; especially well known are those of the *clothes moth.

tinplate A mild *steel sheet coated with a very thin film of tin, usually deposited by *electrolysis. Tinplate combines the strength and rigidity of steel with the attractive appearance and corrosion resistance of tin. It began to be used in the 19th century for cans in which to preserve food, still its widest use, although it was used for decorative purposes in the 13th century.

Tintoretto (Jacopo Robusti; 1518–94) Venetian painter, whose nickname, meaning "little dyes," derived from his father's profession of silk dyeing. His three paintings of the *Miracles of St Mark* (1562–66) for the Confraternity of S Marco were followed by his series of the life of Christ (1564–87; Scuola di S Rocco) and his paintings for the Doge's Palace, including the enormous *Paradise*. He combines Michelangelo's figure style and Titian's rich color with dramatic movement and perspectives. As a portraitist, he was particularly adept at painting old men, for example *Bearded Man with Fur* (Kunsthistorisches Museum, Vienna).

Tippecanoe, Battle of (1811) US–Indian conflict in NW Indiana, on the Tippecanoe River near Lafayette. *Shawnee Indians led by *Tecumseh's brother, the Prophet, and US forces under Willian Henry *Harrison fought over US settlement on Indian lands in Indiana Territory. The victory for Harrison and his troops greatly enhanced Harrison's reputation. Losses were heavy for both sides.

Tipperary (Irish name: Contae Tiobraid Árann) A county in the S Republic of Ireland, in Munster. Mountainous in parts, it contains part of the Golden Vale (one of the most fertile areas in Ireland) in the SW. Predominantly agricultural, dairy farming is especially important. Industries are mainly related to processing agricultural produce. Area: 1643 sq mi (4255 sq km). Population (1971): 123,565. County town: Clonmel.

Tippett, Sir Michael (1905–) British composer. He has written four operas: *The Midsummer Marriage* (1947–52), *King Priam* (1958–61), *The Knot Garden* (1966–70), and *The Ice Break* (1977), acting as his own librettist. His other works include four symphonies, four string quartets, three piano sonatas, a concerto for double string orchestra (1939), the oratorio *A Child of Our Time* (1940), and the cantata *The Vision of St Augustine* (1965). In 1983 he was appointed president of the London College of Music.

Tipu Sahib (1749–99) Sultan of Mysore (1782–99); the son of *Hyder Ali. A good administrator in his own state, he was an opponent of British power in India and entered into a tentative alliance with the French. Defeated by *Cornwallis in 1792, he continued his opposition and was killed by the British while defending his capital Seringapatam.

Tirana (Albanian name: Tiranë) 41 20N 19 49E The capital of Albania, situated on a fertile plain in the center of the country. Founded in the 17th century by a Turkish general, it became the capital in 1920. There has been considerable industrial expansion since World War II. The university was founded in 1957. Population (1978 est): 198,000.

Tiresias In Greek legend, a blind Theban seer who lived for seven generations. For part of his life he had been transformed into a woman, after coming upon a pair of snakes and killing the female. *Oedipus learned from him of his own patricide and incest and *Odysseus consulted him in the underworld, where he retained his prophetic powers. According to one of various legends, he was struck blind by Hera after supporting Zeus' opinion in an argument, namely that love was more enjoyable for women than men. In compensation Zeus granted him longevity and the gift of prophecy.

Tirich Mir, Mount 36 18N 71 55E A mountain in NW Pakistan, the highest in the Hindu Kush. Height: 25,236 ft (7692 m).

TIROL *The winter sports resort of Seefeld, NW of Innsbruck.*

Tirol (*or* Tyrol) A mountainous federal state in W Austria, bordering on West Germany and Italy. It is alpine in character having an international reputation for winter sports, especially at Kitzbühel, and tourism is important throughout the year. The chief occupations are agriculture and forestry, with some mining and manufacturing industries. Area: 4883 sq mi (12,648 sq km). Population (1981): 586,297. Capital: Innsbruck.

Tirpitz, Alfred von (1849–1930) German admiral, who as secretary of state for the navy (1897–1916) rebuilt the German fleet to rival Britain's naval supremacy. His advocacy of intensive submarine warfare in World War I was opposed by the chancellor, Bethmann-Hollweg, and Tirpitz resigned.

Tirso de Molina (Gabriel Téllez; c. 1584–1648) Spanish dramatist, a literary disciple of Lope de *Vega, who wrote over 300 comedies and historical and religious plays. His tragedy *El Burlador de Sevilla* (1635) is the earliest recorded literary portrayal of *Don Juan.

Tirthankara In Jainism, one who has attained spiritual liberation from rebirth and serves as a guide for others. Every eon is said to produce 24 Tirthankaras, each associated with a particular symbol and color. *Mahavira is the last of the present series.

Tiruchirappalli (*or* Trichinopoly) 10 50N 78 43E A city in India, in Tamil Nadu on the Cauvery River. The city is dominated by the Rock of Trichinopoly with its fort and temple. An important railroad center, the city produces textiles. Population (1971): 307,400.

Tiryns A *Mycenaean citadel near Mycenae (S Greece). First excavated (1884–85) by *Schliemann, Tiryns was occupied from Neolithic times. The Bronze Age Mycenaean palace, first built in the early 14th century BC and sacked about 1200 BC, possessed frescoes showing *Minoan influence and massive defensive walls, much of which still stand.

Tissot, James Joseph Jacques (1836–1902) French painter and etcher. In Paris he was influenced by *Degas and Japanese prints but after settling in England in the 1870s he became known for his charming scenes of Victorian life, notably *The Ball on Shipboard* (Tate Gallery).

tissue In anatomy, a group of cells specialized to perform a particular function. The cells may be of the same type (e.g. the muscle cells of muscles) or of different types (as in connective tissue). Combinations of tissues make up organs. The study of tissues is *histology.

Tisza River (Slavonic and Romanian name: Tisa) A river in S central Europe. Rising in the Soviet Union, in the W Ukrainian SSR, it flows generally W and S across the Hungarian Plain to join the Danube River below Novi Sad in Yugoslavia. It is a source of irrigation and power, especially in NE Hungary. Length: 610 mi (980 km).

tit A small acrobatic songbird (also called titmouse) belonging to a family (*Paridae*; 65 species) occurring in North America, Eurasia, and Africa. Tits are versatile birds and frequent woodlands and gardens, feeding chiefly on insects. They are 2.8–8 in (7–20 cm) long. The best-known species is the tufted titmouse, about 6 in (15 cm) long, which is white underneath and gray above, topped by a prominent crest. *See also* blue tit; coal tit; crested tit; great tit; long-tailed tit.

Titanic A luxury British passenger ship that on April 14–15, 1912, struck an iceberg near Newfoundland on its maiden voyage and sank causing the loss of 1513 lives. Because of its special design it was thought to be unsinkable and carried enough lifeboats for only half the passengers. As a result of the disaster safety rules for ships at sea were drawn up by the International Convention for Safety of Life at Sea (1913) and the International Ice Patrol was established.

titanium (Ti) A relatively light strong transition metal discovered in 1791 by W. Gregor (1761–1817). It occurs in nature in the minerals rutile (TiO_2), ilmenite ($FeTiO_3$), sphene ($CaTiO_3$), and in some iron ores. Rutile and ilmenite beach sands are mined as a source of titanium. The dioxide (TiO_2) is widely used as a constituent of white paint as it has excellent opacity. The metal is as strong as steel but 45% lighter (relative density 4.54) and 60% heavier than aluminum but twice as strong. It is therefore used in alloys for missiles and high-speed aircraft. At no 22; at wt 47.90; mp 3023°F (1660°C; bp 5955°F (3287°C).

titanothere An extinct North American mammal, related to horses and rhinoceroses, that lived between 45 and 20 million years ago. Later Oligocene forms were 15 ft (4.5 m) long and 8 ft (2.8 m) high at the shoulder. They fed on soft vegetation and became extinct possibly because their simple teeth were unable to cope with a change in the vegetation.

Titans In Greek mythology, 12 primeval gods and goddesses, the children of Uranus (Heaven) and Gaea (Earth). They were Oceanus, Coeus, Crius, Hyperion, Iapetus, Cronus, Thea, Rhea, Themis, Mnemosyne, Phoebe, and Tethys. They were overthrown by Zeus and the Olympian deities.

tithes The tenth part of an income allotted to religious purposes. Originating in the offering of the "first fruits" as a divine sacrifice, tithes were decreed by Mosaic law, which demanded payment in kind from all agricultural produce. Christian ecclesiastical law also enjoined tithes to maintain churches and clergy. Gradually exemptions were made, money payments replaced payments in kind, and as organized religion declined the tithe laws were repealed. Tithes are still voluntarily paid by individual believers.

titi A small monkey belonging to the genus *Callicebus* (8 species), of the Amazonian jungle. Titis are 20–45 in (50–115 cm) long including the tail (10–22 in [25–55 cm]) and live in treetops in family groups. They have soft thick fur, often brightly colored. Family: *Cebidae*.

Titian (Tiziano Vecellio; c. 1488–1576) Venetian painter of the High Renaissance, born in Pieve di Cadore, in the Dolomites. His earliest influences were Giovanni Bellini, his teacher, and Giorgione, with whom he collaborated on frescoes for the façade of the German Exchange (1508). In his *Assumption of the Virgin* (Sta Maria dei Frari) his more monumental style links him with such Florentine painters as Raphael. His greatest works were for the Habsburgs, who patronized him from 1530 onward, were the equestrian portrait of Emperor Charles V at Mühlberg (1548; Prado) and *Philip II* (1550–51; Prado). He painted Pope Paul III twice, in Bologna (1543) and in Rome with his grandsons (1546). Both portraits are in Naples. His mythological works include *Bacchus and Ariadne* (National

Gallery, London). His last religious paintings, such as the *Pietà* (Accademia, Venice), seem to be inspired by a new emotional intensity.

Titicaca, Lake A lake in South America, between Peru and Bolivia, in the Andes. At an altitude of 12,497 ft (3809 m) it is the world's highest lake navigable to large vessels. It is fed by 25 rivers but possesses only one outlet, the Desaguadero River. Area: 3141 sq mi (8135 sq km). Depth: 1214 ft (370 m).

titmouse. *See* tit.

TITO *The Yugoslav leader (right) discusses strategy with Britain's Gen Alexander in Belgrade (February, 1945).*

Tito (Josip Broz; 1892–1980) Yugoslav statesman; president 1953–80. Tito was captured by the Russians in World War I and subsequently fought with the Red Army in the Russian civil war. He returned to Yugoslavia in 1920, joined the Communist Party, and was briefly imprisoned (1928–29); in 1937 he became secretary general of the Party. In World War II he led the partisans in resistance to the German occupation, becoming a marshal in 1943, when he also gained Allied recognition, previously given to the *Chetniks. He became Yugoslavia's postwar leader and introduced the policy of decentralization to workers' councils that distinguishes Yugoslav socialism. Following Yugoslavia's expulsion (1948) from the *Cominform, Tito successfully maintained his country's independence from Soviet interference, pursuing a foreign policy of nonalignment.

Titograd (name until 1948: Podgorica) 42 28N 19 17E A city in S central Yugoslavia, the capital of Montenegro. It was renamed in honor of Marshal Tito on being rebuilt following extensive damage during World War II. Its university was established in 1973. Population (1971): 54,509.

Titus (Flavius Vespasianus) (39–81 AD) Roman emperor (79–81). He fought with his father Vespasian in Judea and ended the Jewish revolt (70) by capturing Jerusalem. Proclaimed emperor after Vespasian's death, Titus proved a popular ruler; when Vesuvius erupted (79), he aided the victims generously. At his death he was called "darling of the human race" and deified.

Titus, St In the New Testament, a disciple and assistant of Paul. He organized the collection of alms for poor Christians in Judea and replaced Timothy as Paul's commissioner at Corinth. Feast day: Feb 6. In the **Epistle of Paul to Titus**, written between 60 and 64 AD, Paul tells Titus how to organize and superintend the new churches of Crete.

Tivoli 41 58N 12 48E A city in central Italy, in Lazio. A summer resort in Roman times, it possesses the remains of Hadrian's villa and the Renaissance Villa d'Este, with its terraced water gardens. Paper and wine are produced. Population (1971): 41,740.

Tiw. *See* Tyr.

Tjirebon (*or* Cheribon) 6 46S 108 33E A port in Indonesia, in N Java on the Java Sea. The **Tjirebon Agreement** of Indonesian independence was

signed here (1946) by the Dutch. It is an agricultural and manufacturing center. Population (1971): 178,529.

Tlaloc An Aztec rain god, equivalent in status with the sun and war god *Huitzilopochtli. He possessed both creative and destructive powers and children were ritually sacrificed to him.

Tlaxcala (*or* Tlaxcala de Xicohténcatl) 19 20N 98 12W A city in Mexico, on the central plateau. One of the oldest cities in Mexico, it is the site of the Church of San Francisco, which was founded by *Cortés (1521) and is the oldest in the Americas. Population (1970): 21,424.

Tlemcen (Latin name: Pomaria) 34 55N 1 20W A city in NW Algeria, near the Moroccan border. It became an important Islamic religious center in the middle ages, flourishing until the 16th century; many old buildings remain, notably the 12th-century Great Mosque. Industries include leatherwork and carpets; blankets and olive oil are exported. Population (1974 est): 115,054.

Tlingit A North American Indian people of the NW Pacific coast in SE Alaska. There were 14 tribes divided into independent matrilineal clans, each headed by a chief. They lived by salmon fishing and hunting, built wooden houses, and practiced the *potlatch at the death of a chief. Their language belongs to the *Na-Dené group.

TNT (trinitrotoluene; $C_6H_2(NO_2)_3CH_3$) A highly explosive pale yellow crystalline solid. It is prepared from toluene treated with concentrated sulfuric and nitric acids and is used in shells, bombs, etc., as well as in commercial blasting explosives.

toad A tail-less amphibian belonging to a widely distributed order (*Anura*; about 2600 species). Toads usually move on land by leaping, having long hind legs and short forelegs; they swim by means of partially webbed feet. They have a long sticky tongue, attached at the front of their mouth, that can extend very rapidly to capture flying insects. Some species use the throat as a resonating chamber to amplify their mating calls. *See also* clawed frog; midwife toad; natterjack; tree frog; spadefoot toad.

toadfish A bottom-dwelling carnivorous *bony fish of the order *Batachoidiformes* (about 45 species), found mainly in tropical and subtropical seas. It has a heavy brownish body, up to 12 in (30 cm) long, a broad flat head, and a wide mouth. It makes grunting or croaking sounds resembling a toad. *See also* midshipman.

toadflax An annual or perennial herb belonging to the genus *Linaria* (about 150 species), especially *L. vulgaris*, found in the Mediterranean area, temperate Eurasia, and North America. It grows to a height of 12–30 in (30–80 cm) and has an elongated terminal cluster of yellow snap-dragon-like flowers (*see* Antirrhinum). Purple toadflax (*L. purpurea*) is cultivated in gardens. Family: *Scrophulariaceae*.

toadstool. *See* mushroom.

tobacco A plant belonging to the genus *Nicotiana*, especially *N. tabacum* and *N. rustica*, which are cultivated for their leaves, used to make *cigarettes, *cigars, *snuff, etc. Commercial tobacco plants grow to a height of 3–10 ft (1–3 m) and bear pink, white, or greenish flowers. After harvesting, their large sticky leaves are slowly dried in the sun, hot air, or smoke for up to two months and then fermented for another four–six weeks. The main growing regions are the US, China, India, and the Soviet Union, with additional production in E Europe, South America, SE Asia, and S Africa.

Tobacco contains about 2–4% nicotine, which produces its stimulant and addictive properties. However, it is the tar content that is responsible for the diseases caused by smoking and chewing tobacco. Family: *Solanaceae*.

Tobago Island. See Trinidad and Tobago, Republic of.

Tobata. *See* Kitakyushu.

Tobey, Mark (1890–1976) US painter. He is known for paintings in which colored forms are overlaid by white brush strokes. He adopted this so-called "white writing" technique after he visited Japan and China (1934), where he was influenced by oriental calligraphy. His work in this style developed from representational treatments to more abstract paintings in his later years.

tobogganing The recreation and sport of sliding down snow or ice on a toboggan, a low platform on steel runners, of which there are two competitive types: the luge, for one or two riders lying almost flat on their backs, and the skeleton or Cresta (named for the Cresta Run at St Moritz, Switzerland), for one rider lying prone. Like *bobsledding, both were developed at St Moritz and other Swiss resorts in the late 19th century. In races competitors slide, one vehicle at a time, down a narrow icy chute some 1094 yd (1000 m) long with high banked turns, reaching speeds of over

80 mph (130 km per hour) and steering only by shifts of weight and by touching down with either foot.

Tobolsk 58 15N 68 12E A port in the central Soviet Union, in the RSFSR at the confluence of the Irtysh and Tobol Rivers. Founded by the Cossacks in 1587, it has shipbuilding, timbering, and food-processing industries. Population (1970): 49,260.

Tobruk A port in NE Libya, on the Mediterranean coast. During World War II it was the scene of heavy fighting and changed hands five times before being finally recaptured by the British in 1942. Population (1970 est): 28,000.

Toby jug An English pottery jug in the shape of a seated middle-aged man in 18th-century dress, holding a tankard and pipe. Toby jugs, first made in the 1760s, depict various characters, e.g. Squire Toby and Sailor Toby. Production of Toby jugs still continues.

Tocharian An extinct *Indo-European language of the Tarim Basin region of Chinese Turkistan. It is mainly known from Buddhist scriptures written between about 500 and 1000 AD in the N Indian Brahmi script. Its relationship to the other Indo-European languages is highly debatable.

Tocqueville, Alexis de (1805–59) French political scientist, historian, and politician. After visiting the US (1831–32) Tocqueville wrote *Démocratie en Amerique*, a study of US democracy that also dealt with the constitutions of France and Europe. Tocqueville argued that the French Revolution had not achieved a break with the past, since an egalitarian society required greater centralization and thus sacrificed liberty. Elected to the Chamber of Deputies in 1839, he became vice president of the Constituent Assembly and briefly minister of foreign affairs in 1849. After Louis Napoleon's coup d'état he retired to write *L'Ancien Régime et la révolution* (1856).

Todd, Alexander Robertus, Baron (1907–) British biochemist, who helped determine the molecular basis of genetics through his work on nucleic acids (DNA and RNA). In 1949 Todd synthesized ADP and *ATP, substances vital to energy utilization by living cells. He received a Nobel Prize (1957).

toga The outer garment worn by the ancient Romans, originally by both sexes and all classes but finally only by male patricians on formal occasions. It consisted of a semicircular piece of cloth draped intricately around the body; color and markings were prescribed according to status.

Toghril Beg (c. 990–1063) Sultan of Turkey (1055–63), who founded the Seljuq dynasty. His conquests in central Asia culminated in the conquest of Baghdad (1055). An uprising forced his expulsion in 1058 but by 1060 he had suppressed it.

Togliatti (name until 1964: Stavropol) 53 32N 49 24E A city in the W central Soviet Union, in the RSFSR on the Volga River. It was renamed in honor of the Italian communist leader Palmiro Togliatti. Industries include ship repairing, engineering, and food processing. Population (1981 est): 533,000.

Togliatti, Palmiro (1893–1964) Italian politician, the leader of the Italian Communist Party (1926–64). In exile from 1926 to 1944, after Mussolini's fall he became a minister (1944) and then vice premier (1945). He was the author of *Italian Road to Socialism* and his ideas greatly influenced communism in Italy and were also influential in the Soviet Union.

Togo, Republic of (French name: République Togolaise) A small narrow country in West Africa, on the Gulf of Guinea between Ghana and Benin. Coastal swamps rise to higher land in the interior. The majority of the population is African, mainly Ewe in the S. *Economy*: chiefly agricultural, food crops consist mainly of cassava, maize, and rice and cash crops include cocoa, coffee, and cotton. Forests produce not only timber but oil palms and dyewoods. There are rich deposits of phosphates, which, with cocoa and coffee, are the main export. Bauxite was found in the 1950s and there is some, as yet unexploited, limestone and iron ore. Industry is being developed, concentrating mainly on food processing, but there is also a large cement plant and a new oil refinery. *History*: settled by the Ewe in the 12th and 13th centuries, the area was raided for slaves from the 17th to 19th centuries. From 1884 to 1914 Togoland was a German protectorate and after World War I it was divided between France and the UK, first (1922) under League of Nations mandate and then (1946) as a UN trustee territory. The French territory became an autonomous republic within the French Union in 1956 and gained full independence in 1960. (The British part joined Ghana in 1957.) The president was killed in a coup in 1963 and a further coup in 1967 brought Lt Colonel (later General) Etienne Gnassingbe Eyadéma to power. Official language: French. Official currency: CFA (Communauté financière africaine) franc of 100 centimes. Area:

21,616 sq mi (56,000 sq km). Population (1983 est): 2,823,000. Capital and main port: Lomé.

Togo Heihachiro (1847–1934) Japanese admiral. His destruction of the Russian fleet in the battle of Tsushima Strait in May, 1905, ensured Japan's victory in the *Russo-Japanese War (1904–05).

Tojo Hideki (1884–1948) Japanese general, who was war minister (1940–44) and also prime minister (1941–44) during World War II. After Japan's defeat he was executed as a war criminal.

Tokaj (*or* Tokay) 48 08N 21 23E A small town in NE Hungary, at the confluence of the Bodrog and Tisza rivers. It has given its name to the famous wine produced in the area.

tokay. *See* gecko.

Tokelau Islands A group of three coral atolls in the SW Pacific Ocean, an overseas territory of New Zealand. Chief exports are copra and woven goods. Area: 4 sq mi (10 sq km). Population (1980 est): 1620.

Tokugawa The military family that controlled Japan from 1603 to 1867. *Tokugawa Ieyasu secured the title of *shogun (military overlord) from the emperor in 1603 and established his capital at Edo (Tokyo). Ieyasu's immediate successors were responsible for isolating Japan from the outside world, a policy that established domestic peace but ultimately led to political stagnation and technological backwardness. After Japan's reopening under western pressure in the 1850s the reluctance of the family to abandon its monopoly of power brought about the overthrow of the last shogun, Tokugawa Keiki (1827–1913; ruled 1867–68).

Tokugawa Ieyasu (1542–1616) Japanese *shogun (military overlord), who completed the re-establishment of central authority in feudal Japan. A vassal of both Oda Nobunaga and Hideyoshi, he steadily increased his domain and in 1600 was able to defeat his rivals in the decisive battle of Sekigahara. In 1603, having confiscated much enemy territory, he acquired from the emperor the title of shogun. He passed this to his son in 1605 but continued to supervise the *Tokugawa administration.

TOKYO *Ginza, one of the city's main shopping streets.*

Tokyo 35 40N 139 45E The capital of Japan, in E central *Honshu on Tokyo Bay (an inlet of the Pacific). Administratively joined to its port Yokohama and to the industrial center of Kawasaki, Greater Tokyo is the world's largest city. It has over 100 universities, including the University of Tokyo (1877). *History*: site of human settlements from very early times, the village of Edo was founded in the 12th century, growing in importance as a city by the 17th century. As Tokyo, it replaced Kyoto as imperial capital in 1868. It was badly damaged by an earthquake in 1923 and by bombing during World War II, since when its industrial growth has been spectacular. Industrial development has not been without problems, however, and Tokyo now suffers from serious atmospheric pollution as well as traffic congestion. Population (1980): 8,349,000.

Toledo 41 40N 83 35W A city in Ohio, at the mouth of the Maumee River on Lake Erie. The development of the coalfields and the discovery of oil and gas in the late 19th century stimulated its growth and today it is a major Great Lakes port, shipping oil, coal, and farm products. Industrial activities include shipbuilding and oil refining. Population (1980): 354,635.

Toledo 39 52N 4 02W A city in central Spain, in New Castile on the Tagus River. It was formerly the capital of Spain. It has a magnificent cathedral (13th–17th centuries). Famous for its swords and knives, it produces metalwork engraved in the Moorish tradition. Population (1970): 44,382.

Tolkien, J(ohn) R(onald) R(euel) (1892–1973) British scholar and writer. He was professor of Anglo-Saxon (1925–45) and of English language and literature (1945–49) at Oxford University. His trilogy *The Lord of the Rings* (1954–55), in which he created a richly detailed fantasy world, became an international bestseller. Related works include *The Hobbit* (1937) and *The Silmarillion* (1977). Previously unpublished works were issued after his death.

Toller, Ernst (1893–1939) German playwright and poet. After being wounded in World War I, he became committed to revolutionary politics and in 1919 was imprisoned for five years for his activities. His reputation was established soon after his release by experimental expressionist plays, such as *Die Wandlung* (1919) and *Masse Mensch* (1920). Driven into exile in 1932, he committed suicide in New York.

Tolpuddle Martyrs Six English union members from Tolpuddle, Dorset. They were unfairly charged with administering unlawful oaths and transported to Australia. They were pardoned in 1836. The Tolpuddle Martyrs are regarded as among the founders of English labor unionism.

Tolstoy, Leo (Nikolaevich), Count (1828–1910) Russian writer and moralist. After active service in the Crimean War, he traveled in Europe and then returned to his family estate of Yasnaya Polyana, where he devoted much energy to the education of his peasants. Following his marriage in 1862 he wrote two novels, *War and Peace* (1865–69), concerning the Napoleonic War, and *Anna Karenina* (1875–77), both acknowledged masterpieces of Russian literature. Around 1879 he underwent a spiritual crisis from which he emerged with a faith in an extreme form of Christian anarchism. He worked and dressed as a peasant, became a vegetarian, espoused total pacifism, repudiated his former literary works, and divided his property among the members of his family. His numerous moral tracts and stories gained him an international discipleship, but his family relationships suffered. He died at 82 of pneumonia a few days after secretly leaving his home in order to live in solitude. Tolstoy was one of the most prolific of writers, his literary work filling 45 volumes. His other works include the story "The Death of Ivan Ilyich" (1884–86) and the novel *Resurrection* (1899).

Toltecs An Indian people who dominated much of central Mexico between the 10th and 12th centuries AD. Their language, *Nahuatl, was also spoken by the Aztecs. A militaristic people, they sacked the city of *Teotihuacán (c. 750) and eventually fused the many small states of the area into an empire. They introduced the cult of *Quetzalcoatl and were accomplished temple builders. The *Aztecs destroyed their capital of *Tula in the mid-12th century.

Toluca (or Toluca de Lerdo) 19 20N 99 40W A city in central Mexico. The center of a stock-raising area, its industries include the processing of agricultural products. Population (1978 est): 222,885.

toluene ($C_6H_5CH_3$) A colorless flammable liquid obtained by catalytic reforming of *oil. It is used in aviation fuels, as a solvent, and to produce *phenol and *TNT.

tolu tree A tree, *Myroxylon balsamum*, native to South America. Growing to a height of over 65 ft (20 m), it has whitish flowers and yields a *balsam from its trunk, used in cough mixtures and perfumery. Family: *Leguminosae.

tomato An annual plant, *Lycopersicon esculentum*, native to South America and widely cultivated for its fleshy red □fruit. In warm temperate regions, tomatoes are grown in fields and are low branching and spreading plants; the hothouse tomatoes of cooler regions are often trained to grow a single erect fruiting stem. The clusters of yellow flowers produce rounded or pear-shaped fruits, 0.8–4 in (2–10 cm) in diameter, which are eaten fresh or canned and made into purée, pickles, etc. Family: *Solanaceae.

Tombouctou. See Timbuktu.

Tombstone 31 44N 110 04W A town in Arizona. Scene of a silver rush from 1877, it is famous for the gunfight (1881) that took place at the OK Corral between the Clanton gang and Wyatt Earp, his brother Virgil, and Doc Holliday. Population (1970): 1241.

tommy gun A light US .45 caliber submachine gun invented by General John Thompson (1860–1940) in 1918. Widely used between 1938 and 1945 in various models, especially the M1 and the M3 "blowbacks," some are still in use today.

Tomsk 56 30N 85 05E A port in the central Soviet Union, in the RSFSR on the Tom River. Industries include engineering and it has several educational institutions, including a university (1888). Population (1981 est): 439,000.

Tom Thumb (Charles Stratton; 1838–83) US midget, who was publicly exhibited by the circus impresario P. T. *Barnum. He grew to a height of only 40 in. In 1863 he married another midget, Lavinia Warren (1841–1919).

ton A short ton is a unit of weight equal to 2000 lb (907 kg). A long ton is equal to 2240 lb or 1016 kilograms. The metric ton (or **tonne**) is equal to 1000 kilograms.

tonality The presence of a tonal center or *key in a musical composition. Musical compositions from at least the early 17th century to about 1900 are in distinct keys. These are based on individual scales, in which certain notes (the tonic and dominant degrees) form tonal centers to which the music periodically returns. Once such a center has been established, the music can modulate into other keys and return to the home key (or underlying tonality). Music in which tonal centers are deliberately avoided exhibits *atonality; this is characteristic of some music written after 1900. See also serialism.

Tone, (Theobald) Wolfe (1763–98) Irish nationalist, who was inspired by the French Revolution to work for an independent Irish republic. In 1791 he founded the Society of United Irishmen and unsuccessfully sought French aid for a revolt against British rule. He was captured and sentenced to death, but committed suicide before the sentence could be carried out.

tone poem. *See* symphonic poem.

Tonga, Kingdom of (or Friendly Islands) A country in the SW Pacific Ocean, E of Fiji. It consists of 169 small islands (36 of them permanently inhabited); the E islands are low lying, while those to the W are hilly and volcanic. *Economy*: chiefly agricultural, the main products and exports are copra and bananas. Oil has been discovered recently, and tourism is becoming increasingly important. *History*: under King Taufa'ahau Tupou (George I; 1797–1893) in the 19th century, the civil war between rival dynasties was ended and the islands converted to Christianity. The country became a British protectorate in 1900, and in 1970 became an independent state within the British Commonwealth. Head of State: King Taufa'ahau Tupou IV (1918–   ). Official languages: Tongan and English. Official currency: pa'anga of 100 seniti. Area: 270 sq mi (700 sq km). Population: (1976) 90,128. Capital and main port: Nuku'alofa.

tongue A muscular organ situated in the floor of the mouth. The root of the tongue is attached by muscles to the U-shaped hyoid bone in the neck. The tongue is the main organ of taste: its surface is covered by minute projections (giving it a rough appearance) around which the taste buds are grouped, detecting sweet, sour, salt, and bitter tastes. It also manipulates food during chewing and swallowing and plays an important role in the articulation of speech. Furring of the tongue is a symptom of fever; a smooth and sore tongue is seen in some forms of anemia.

Tong Zhi (or T'ung-chih; 1856–75) The title of Cai-chun (or Tsai-ch'un), Chinese emperor (1862–75); the son of *Zi Xi, who acted as regent until he was 17. The Tong Zhi Restoration (his title means Union for Order) aimed to repair the upheaval of the *Taiping Rebellion but was thwarted by the corrupt court, which dominated the young emperor.

tonic sol-fa. *See* solmization.

tonka bean The seed of the tonka tree, *Coumarouna odorata*, native to N South America. Coumarin, a fragrant edible extract of the black almond-shaped seeds, has been used as a flavoring and in perfumes and snuff. Family: *Leguminosae.

Tonkin (or Tongking) A region in N Vietnam, long ruled from Hanoi. The Chinese, who had occupied it in 111 BC, were driven out in 939 AD, and from then until 1802 it was an independent state. Following the dissolution of the Vietnamese empire it became a French protectorate (1884). In 1949 it became part of independent Vietnam.

Tonkin, Gulf of (Chinese name: Beibu Gulf) An inlet of the South China Sea between China, N Vietnam, and Hainan Island.

Tonle Sap A lake in W central Kampuchea. For most of the year it is drained by the River Tonle Sap into the Mekong, but in the monsoon season the swollen Mekong reverses the flow, and the lake roughly quadruples in depth and area to about 3850 sq mi (10,000 sq km). There is carp fishing here.

tonsillitis Inflammation of the *tonsils due to infection of the upper respiratory tract. Symptoms include fever, a sore throat, and difficulty in swallowing. If the tonsils become chronically infected, causing recurrent sore throats, they can be surgically removed.

tonsils Patches of tissue situated on each side at the back of the mouth and below the tongue that produce lymphocytes: a type of white blood cell that protects the body against infection. Inflammation of the tonsils may be caused by a variety of infections (*see also* tonsillitis).

tontine A financial scheme to provide life *annuities to a group of subscribers; when a member dies his share is divided among the others until the last survivor enjoys the whole income. The idea of an Italian banker (Lorenzo Tonti) in 1653, it was popular in the 18th century.

Toowoomba 27 34S 151 54E A city in Australia, in SE Queensland. It is a commercial center for an agricultural region specializing in sheep and dairy farming. It is the site of the Perseverance Creek Water Supply Scheme. Population (1980 est): 72,800.

topaz A mineral consisting of a hydrous fluosilicate of aluminum, $Al_2SiO_4(OH,F)_2$. It occurs in acidic igneous rocks, in pegmatites and veins. It is usually colorless or yellow, and when cut and polished it is used as a gemstone. The finest specimens come mainly from the Urals, Brazil, and Ceylon. All yellow gemstones were formerly known as topaz. Birthstone for November.

tope A slender *requiem shark, *Galeorhinus galeus*, that is up to 7 ft (2 m) long with a dark-gray body and a white belly. It lives in shallow tropical and temperate seas and feeds on bottom-dwelling fish and invertebrates.

Topeka 39 02N 95 41W The capital city of Kansas, on the Kansas River. An agricultural trading and processing center, Topeka is famous as a center for psychiatric research and is the site of the Menninger Clinic. Population (1980): 115,266.

top minnow. *See* killifish.

topology The branch of *geometry concerned with the properties of an object that do not change under *homeomorphisms, i.e. when the object is bent, stretched, or shrunk but not torn or deformed so that several points on it are fused. The hole in a doughnut is such a property; for example if a rubber doughnut is distorted to the shape of a cup the hole is still there in the handle. Topology is often called rubber-sheet geometry because rubber objects can be suitably distorted. It was formerly called analysis situs. One application is in networks (e.g. an electricity-distribution network) in which the topological properties depend on the so-called Euler characteristic (named for Leonhard *Euler) $V - E + F$, where V is the number of vertices in the network, E the number of edges, and F the number of areas enclosed by the edges.

TORAH *Worshippers wearing prayer shawls and phylacteries (on their foreheads and left hands, as on left of illustration) surround the scrolls of the Toroh.*

Torah (Hebrew: instruction) The five books of Moses (Genesis, Exodus, Leviticus, Numbers, and Deuteronomy), which constitute the first of the three divisions of the Hebrew *Bible. In Judaism, the term is also applied more widely to the whole body of religious teachings, viewed as the revealed word of God and including both the written and the oral Torah. The reading of the Torah, from a manuscript scroll (*sepher Torah*), occupies a central place in *synagogue services.

Torgau 51 35N 12 58E A city and port in S East Germany, on the Elbe River. A league of Protestant princes was formed here in 1526. In 1760 a battle was fought nearby, in which the Austrians were defeated by Frederick II of Prussia. Population (1970 est): 20,000.

Tories Members of a British political group that became the *Conservative Party in the 1830s; Tory is still used synonymously with Conservative. It was applied in 1679 to a supporter, in opposition to the *Whigs, of the succession to the throne of the future James II. The Tories were later associated with the rebellious Jacobites and were excluded from politics until the 1780s, when they re-emerged under the leadership of William *Pitt the Younger. They represented the interests of the country gentry, merchants, and Anglicans. They became the Conservative Party under the leadership of Robert *Peel.

Torino. *See* Turin.

tormentil A perennial herb, *Potentilla erecta*, native to Europe, W Asia, and N Africa. Its slender stems, 4–12 in (10–30 cm) long, bear yellow flowers and grow from a woody rootstock, which has astringent properties. The trailing tormentil (*P. anglica*) has creeping flower stems up to 28 in (70 cm) long and larger flowers. Family: *Rosaceae*.

tornado A violently rotating column of air, small in diameter, characterized by a funnel-shaped cloud, which may reach ground surface. Wind speeds of up to 200 knots (100 m per second) have been experienced. Occurring over land, tornadoes cause large-scale destruction and are a considerable problem in the central US and Australia, where they frequently occur as groups.

Toronto 43 42N 79 25W A city and port in E Canada, the capital of Ontario on Lake Ontario. Canada's second largest city, it is very prosperous, housing a stock exchange and the headquarters of banks, insurance companies, and large corporations. With Canada's busiest airport, Toronto is also a water, road, and rail hub. Its diversified industries include heavy engineering, electrical, chemical, and wood products, foods, clothing, sporting goods, publishing, and films. With theaters, orchestras, museums, opera, ballet, three universities, and a cosmopolitan population, Toronto is the cultural center of English-speaking Canada. *History*: established as Upper Canada's capital and military center (1793), Toronto was burned by American troops (1813) and was the scene of the Mackenzie Rebellion (1837) against oligarchic government. It became an industrial and commercial center with the development of railroads (1850s). Population (1976): 633,318.

torpedo (armament) A self-propelled guided underwater missile carrying a high-explosive warhead. They can be launched by ships or aircraft but have been used most successfully by submarines. Designed in 1866 by British engineer Robert Whitehead, they were extremely effective against shipping in World Wars I and II. Modern torpedos are driven by steam turbines or by battery-powered electric motors and have sophisticated active or passive acoustic homing systems (active devices send out sounds and are guided by the echo from the target; passive devices are guided by sounds from the target).

torpedo (fish). *See* electric ray.

Torquemada, Tomás de (1420–98) Spanish Dominican friar and Grand Inquisitor. Confessor to Ferdinand and Isabella, he was appointed head of the Spanish *Inquisition in 1483. His sentences were extremely harsh and he was responsible for the expulsion of the Jews from Spain in 1492.

Torrance 33 50N 118 19W A city in SW California, SW of Los Angeles. Founded in 1912 by Jared L. Torrance, it was a planned industrial and residential city. Oil is drilled and refined here, and aircraft, missiles, metals, electronic parts, chemicals, and foodstuffs are produced. Population (1980): 131,497.

Torreón 25 34N 103 25W A city in NE Mexico. It is the center of La Laguna, a vast state-controlled agricultural cooperative producing cotton and wheat. Population (1978 est): 268,664.

Torres Strait A channel between New Guinea and Cape York Peninsula, N Australia, linking the Arafura Sea and Coral Sea. It was discovered (1606) by the Spanish navigator, Luis Vaez de Torres. Width: about 90 mi (145 km).

Torricelli, Evangelista (1608–47) Italian physicist, who succeeded *Galileo as professor of mathematics at Florence University. He discovered that the atmosphere exerts a pressure and demonstrated it by showing that it could support a column of mercury in a tube, thus inventing the mercury barometer (1643). He also created the first man-made vacuum in his simple barometer, the space above the mercury still being callid a Torricellean vacuum.

tort In law, a civil wrong that constitutes a breach of a duty established by law rather than by *contract. It is distinguished from a crime in that it affects the interests of the injured person rather than of the state. Thus in tort the offender may be sued for damages.

Tortelier, Paul (1914–) French cellist. He won first prize at the Paris conservatoire at the age of 16. After playing in orchestras in the US he began a career as a soloist, composer, and teacher. He has made many recordings and has written a book on cello playing.

tortoise A slow-moving herbivorous reptile belonging to the family *Testudinidae* (40 species), occurring in deserts, grassland, and forests of the Old and New Worlds, especially in Africa. Tortoises have a protective high-domed shell, tough scaly legs, and range in size from about 4 in to 5 ft (10 cm to 1.5 m) (*see* Galápagos giant tortoise). Tortoises lay eggs and have long lifespans, reputedly up to 150 years in some cases. The common Mediterranean tortoise (*Testudo graeca*) is a popular pet; in colder climates, it must hibernate during the winter. *Compare* turtle; terrapin.

tortoise beetle   A *leaf beetle with a carapace-like shield. Tortoise beetles are 0.35–0.47 in (9–12 mm) long and many tropical species are brilliantly colored (the South American species *Desmonota variolosa* is emerald green). The flat spiny larvae have a forked appendage at the rear end of the body to which they attach excrement for camouflage.

tortoiseshell butterfly   A *nymphalid butterfly whose wings are mainly orange with black markings. Tortoiseshells are found in Europe, Asia, and North America. The caterpillars feed mainly on nettles and willows. The adults hibernate. Chief genera: *Aglais, Nymphalis.*

Tortoiseshell cat   A breed of cat whose coat consists of distinct evenly spread patches of black, red, and cream. All Tortoiseshells are female (any males produced are sterile); they have compact bodies, short legs, and yellow or orange eyes. There are both long- and short-haired breeds.

Tortuga Island (French name: Île de la Tortue)   1 00S 90 55W A West Indian island, N of Haiti in the Greater Antilles. It was a haunt of buccaneers during the 17th century. Area: 70 sq mi (180 sq km).

Toruń (German name: Thorn)   53 01N 18 35E A city in N central Poland, on the Vistula River. Copernicus, the Polish astronomer, was born here (1473). Its university was founded in 1945. Industries include precision engineering and chemicals. Population (1979 est): 170,000.

Toscanini, Arturo (1867–1957) Italian conductor. He began his career as a cellist. He made his debut in Rio de Janeiro in 1886 in Verdi's *Aida* and subsequently conducted at La Scala, Milan, and at the Metropolitan Opera in New York. From 1937 until his death he conducted the NBC (National Broadcasting Company) Symphony Orchestra.

Tosks   One of the two divisions of the Albanian people living in the S of the country. *See also* Ghegs.

Tostig (d. 1066) Earl of Northumbria from 1055 until his exile in 1065 following a revolt against his misrule. He allied with Harold III Hardraade of Norway and invaded N England but was killed by his brother, Harold II, at Stamford Bridge.

totemism   In primitive societies, the common occurrence of a special relationship of ritual significance between certain animal and plant species or other natural phenomena and certain social groups or individuals. Features of this relationship are belief in descent from the totem species (which may include animal worship), a *taboo on killing or eating it except at special ritual feasts, and clan exogamy, but only among Australian aborigines do all these occur together. The Indians of the NW Pacific coast of America also practice totemism, as did the ancient Indo-European peoples.

totem pole   Among the Indians of the NW Pacific coast, a carved and painted pole used to commemorate important events, as a house post, or to mark or contain funerary remains. The carvings are largely of animals associated with particular families and their histories and legends.

Totila (d. 552 AD) King of the Ostrogoths (541–52), who temporarily recovered much of central and S Italy from the Eastern Roman Empire. He took Rome in 546, lost it to *Belisarius, and then recaptured it. He was finally defeated and killed by *Narses.

toucan   A noisy forest-dwelling bird belonging to a family (*Ramphastidae*; 37 species) occurring in tropical America. 10–24 in (25–60 cm) long, toucans have huge brightly colored bills and typically black plumage with a brightly colored breast. They feed on fruit. Order: *Piciformes* (woodpeckers, etc.).

touch-me-not   A European annual herbaceous plant, *Impatiens nolitangere*, 8–40 in (20–100 cm) high. It has narrow leaves and bright-yellow tubular flowers, each with a large lower lip and a long curled spur, borne on slender drooping stalks. The ripe fruits split open at the slightest touch to expel the seeds explosively. Family: *Balsaminaceae.*

touchstone   A black or gray flintlike stone, formerly used for testing the purity of gold and silver. The metal to be tested and one of known purity are both rubbed with the touchstone and compared. The color of the marks left indicates the impurities present. Treatment with nitric acid highlights the marks. The method is still sometimes used to test the purity of gold.

Toulon   43 07N 5 55E A port in SE France, in the Var department on the Mediterranean Sea. In 1942 most of the French fleet was scuttled here to prevent its capture by the Germans. Toulon is one of France's principal naval bases and has marine engineering, chemical, oil, and textile industries. Population (1975): 185,050.

Toulouse   43 33N 1 24E A city in S France, the capital of the Haute-Garonne department on the Garonne River. A major commercial and industrial center, it has aircraft, armaments, chemical, and textile industries. It is also an important agricultural trading center. Notable buildings include the basilica (11th–13th centuries), the gothic cathedral, and the university (1230). *History*: capital of the Visigoths and later of the kingdom of Aquitaine, it passed to France in 1271. It suffered badly during the campaign against the Albigenses. Population (1975): 383,176.

TOULOUSE-LAUTREC   *A lithograph of the popular singer Yvette Guilbert (1867-1944), one of a series of 16 studies for a poster (1894).*

Toulouse-Lautrec, Henri (Marie Raymond) de (1864–1901) French artist, born in Albi of aristocratic descent. Stunted in growth by a childhood accident, he settled in Paris, where he trained under two conservative artists in the early 1880s and led an unconventional life among the music halls and cafés of Montmartre. His comic but sympathetic studies of popular entertainers (for example Jane Avril and Aristide Bruant), circus life, and prostitutes in posters, lithographs, and paintings were influenced by *Degas and Japanese prints. Characteristic paintings are *At the Moulin Rouge* and *La Toilette.*

touraco.   *See* turaco.

Touraine   A former province of France. Once independent, later under Angevin control, and in 1641 incorporated into the French kingdom, Touraine was famous until the late 17th century for its Huguenot silk weavers. The region is noted for its royal chateaux.

Tourcoing   50 44N 3 10E A city in N France, in the Nord department. Together with its twin town, Roubaix, it forms the center of the French woolen industry. Population (1975): 102,543.

Tour de France   The main European professional cycling race. Founded in 1903, the road race, of some 20 stages, lasts three weeks or more and has a maximum length of approximately 2480 mi (4000 km). The race starts in a different town each year but always ends in Paris. The teams are commercially sponsored.

Touré, (Ahmed) Sékou (1922–84) Guinean statesman; president (1961–   ). Active in trade unionism in French West Africa, in 1956 Touré was elected to the French National Assembly. He opposed de Gaulle's plan of federalism in French West Africa and lost French support on independence (1958), when he became head of state and then president.

tourmaline A group of minerals composed of complex cyclosilicates containing boron. There are numerous varieties, some being used as gemstones and some for their piezoelectric and polarizing properties. Tourmalines are found in veins and pegmatites in granite rocks.

Tournai (Flemish name: Doornik) 50 36N 3 24E A city in W central Belgium, on the Scheldt River. It has a notable cathedral (11th–14th centuries). Industries include carpets, textiles, and leather. Population (1981 est): 69,718.

tournament In medieval Europe, a festival at which knights competed in various military tests of skill and courage. The best-known example was jousting, in which mounted knights charged each other with lances. Combatants were usually limited to members of noble families and weapons were usually blunt. Tournaments originated in France in the 11th century and had died out by the end of the 16th century. In modern times, the word refers to a military display and to competitions in various sports.

Tournefort, Joseph Pitton de (1656–1708) French botanist, who proposed a system of plant classification that used a single Latin name to distinguish a particular genus. This was later incorporated in the binomial system of nomenclature developed by *Linnaeus.

Tourneur, Cyril (c. 1575–1626) English dramatist. He published several poems, including the satire *The Transformed Metamorphosis* (1600), and is the presumed author of *The Atheist's Tragedy* (1611) and *The Revenger's Tragedy* (1607). The latter play has also been attributed to Thomas *Middleton. He died in Ireland after taking part in an expedition to Cádiz.

Tours 47 23N 0 42E A city in central France, the capital of the Indre-et-Loire department situated between the Loire and Cher rivers. Its prosperous silk industry declined following the revocation of the Edict of Nantes (1685) and the exodus of the Huguenot weavers. Notable buildings include the gothic cathedral, the archiepiscopal palace (17th–18th centuries), and the university (1970). Tours is a tourist center for the Loire Valley and has varied manufacturing industries. Population (1975): 145,441.

Toussaint-L'Ouverture, François Dominique (c. 1743–1803) Haitian slave, who led a slave rebellion in Haiti that achieved self-government under French protection. L'Ouverture became lieutenant governor of Haiti in 1794 and established a free society, expelling the Spanish and British landowners. He became govenor general in 1801 but the French, afraid of his power, forcibly retired him in 1802. He was then arrested for plotting a rebellion and imprisoned.

Tower of London A royal fortress on the N bank of the River Thames, to the E of the City of London. It was begun in the 11th century, with the White Tower (1078), and added to in subsequent centuries. It was a royal palace until the 17th century and a state prison, which held such famous prisoners as Lady Jane *Grey and Anne *Boleyn. It is now a barracks, armory, and museum, containing the British crown jewels and regalia.

Townes, Charles Hard (1915–) US physicist, who constructed the first *maser (1953). For this work he shared the 1964 Nobel Prize with Nikolai Bosov (1922–) and Aleksandr Prokhorov (1916–), two Soviet physicists, who independently worked out the theory of the maser.

town planning. *See* Urban Planning.

Townshend Acts (or American Import Duties Act; 1767) Four acts passed by Britain to assert its authority over the American colonies by imposing revenue duties on tea, paper, glass, and painters' colors. They were named for Charles Townshend (1725–67), chancellor of the exchequer (1766–67). The acts, the uses to which the resulting revenues were put, and their repressive enforcement provoked violent resentment that contributed to the outbreak of the *American Revolution.

Townsville 19 13S 146 48E A port in Australia, in NE Queensland on Cleveland Bay. It is the commercial center; industries include sugar processing, copper refining, and meat packing. Population (1980 est): 84,300.

toxemia The presence of bacterial toxins, such as those of diphtheria and tetanus, in the blood. However, the term is most often used to describe a condition affecting pregnant women, formerly thought to be due to toxins but is now known to be caused by *hypertension (raised blood pressure). Hypertension in pregnancy is often accompanied by protein in the urine and *edema (fluid in the tissues). In very severe cases the patient may develop fits.

toxicology. *See* poisons.

toxin A poison produced by a living organism. Many microorganisms, including bacteria and fungi, produce toxins. In diphtheria and tetanus the toxin is produced by the bacteria within the body of the infected person; in botulism the toxin is produced in contaminated food and ingested by the patient. Some toxins are useful: penicillin is a toxin, produced by fungi, that kills bacteria.

Toyama 36 42N 137 14E A city in Japan, in central Honshu on the Sea of Japan. It has been known since the 17th century for its pharmaceutical industry. Population (1980): 305,000.

Toynbee, Arnold (Joseph) (1889–1975) British historian. After holding several university posts, he was director of studies at the Royal Institute of International Affairs (1925–55). His major work, *A Study of History* (12 vols, 1934–61), structured according to the rise and fall of civilizations, embodies his theory of historical progress.

Trabzon (former name: Trebizond) 41 00N 39 43E A port in NE Turkey, on the Black Sea. It was the capital of the Comnenian empire (1204–1461) and has a university (1963). Population (1980): 108,403.

trace element A chemical element required by an organism for normal healthy growth but only in minute amounts. Higher plants, for instance, require traces of copper, zinc, etc. Many trace elements are constituents of vitamins and enzymes.

tracer bullet A bullet that when ignited by the propellant emits light or smoke. In flight, its path appears as a continuous streak enabling the gunner to correct his aim. Mixed with other types of bullets during loading, tracer bullets are used in aircraft and by ground troops both during combat and as an aid to maintaining direction during a night attack.

tracery In *gothic architecture, decorative stonework supporting the glass in windows. Molded stone bars were introduced as an ornamental element in 13th-century France and England. Designs were at first geometric but later became curvilinear (*see* Decorated; Flamboyant). In England the regular rectangular tracery of the *Perpendicular style enabled windows of enormous size to be built.

trachea **1.** The windpipe: a tube that conducts air from the larynx to the left and right bronchi, which continue to the *lungs. The trachea is lined by *mucous membrane and supported by hoops of cartilage in its wall. **2.** One of the air passages in insects, which lead directly to the tissues. Each trachea has an external opening (spiracle) that can be opened and closed.

trachoma An eye disease that occurs in dry poor parts of the world and is caused by a large virus-like organism of the genus *Chlamydia*. It is a severe form of *conjunctivitis in which the membrane lining the eyelids and covering the cornea becomes scarred and shrunken and the eyelids become deformed. Trachoma is the world's most common cause of blindness; it is treated with antibiotics.

tractor A self-propelled vehicle designed to provide high power and traction at relatively low speeds for use in agriculture, construction, etc. Tractors were developed from mobile versions of the steam engines used in the 19th century. The American Burger tractor of 1889 was the first to use an internal-combustion engine. The modern tractor is usually powered by a diesel engine and equipped with a cab that insulates the driver from weather and noise. A power take-off (PTO) and hydraulically operated fittings enable powerful and versatile implements to be operated by the tractor, including shovels, loaders, mowing machines, spreaders, and cultivators.

Tracy, Spencer (1900–67) US film actor. He began his film career in the 1930s by playing gangsters, but later costarred with Katherine *Hepburn in nine films, including *Woman of the Year* (1942), *Adam's Rib* (1949), *Pat and Mike* (1952), *Desk Set* (1956), and *Guess Who's Coming to Dinner* (1967). Other notable films include *The Old Man and the Sea* (1958), *Inherit the Wind* (1960), and *Judgement at Nuremberg* (1961).

Trade and Navigation Acts. *See* Navigation Acts.

trade cycle The repeated cycle of *boom, *recession, *depression, recovery, and boom in an economy. In the 19th century, the trade cycle displayed regularity and stability; in the 20th century, it has fluctuated more. The *Depression of the 1930s was a severe and protracted world slump followed, after World War II, by a period of boom, interrupted by only minor recessions, which persisted until a serious recession began in the 1970s. The causes of the cycle are uncertain, but it may result from the persistence of erratic shocks to the economy, such as wars, political increases in the prices of essential commodities (such as oil), etc. Governments have tried to temper the effects of the trade cycle by imposing government spending policies.

trademarks Distinctive emblems owned by a manufacturer or trader and applied to his goods to identify them as produced or sold by him. The owner of a trademark has the right to its exclusive use in connection with the goods associated with it. Any trademark can be protected against infringement by legal action and registered trademarks enjoy additional statutory protection.

Tradescantia A genus of flowering plants (about 60 species), native to North and Central America and popular as ornamentals. Varieties of the wandering jew (*T. fluminensis*) are popular house plants, having oval green leaves, tinged with pink or mauve or with silver stripes. Spiderworts, derived from *T. virginia*, have three-petaled blue, purple, red, or white flowers and grasslike leaves; they are attractive border plants. Family: *Commelinaceae*.

trade union. *See* labor union.

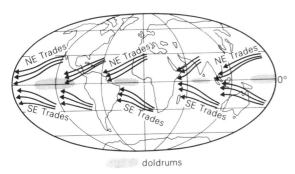

TRADE WINDS

trade winds (*or* tropical easterlies) The predominantly easterly winds that blow in the tropics. They blow generally from a NE direction in the N hemisphere and from a SE direction in the S hemisphere, converging toward the equator. They are noted for their constancy of direction and speed.

trading stamps Stamps given by a retailer to customers in proportion to the price of goods purchased. The customer can exchange these stamps (when he has collected enough of them) for merchandise. The retailer buys the stamps from a trading-stamp company and seeks to recover his cost from higher profits resulting from increased turnover.

Trafalgar, Battle of (October 21, 1805) The naval battle in the Napoleonic Wars in which the British under Nelson (in the *Victory*; □ships) defeated the French W of Cape Trafalgar, between Cádiz and Gibraltar (SW Spain). Nelson's skilful tactic of attacking enemy lines at right angles was an important element in the British success, which was tragically marred by Nelson's death. It ended the threat of a French invasion of Britain and established conclusively British naval supremacy.

tragacanth. *See* gums.

tragedy A form of drama recounting the fall (usually, the death) of a noble protagonist. The form evolved in ancient Greece from the *dithyramb, a choral song, and was fully developed in the plays of Aeschylus, Sophocles, and Euripides. Little tragic drama of worth was then written until the Elizabethan period of English literature, when Marlowe prepared the way for the tragedies of Shakespeare and his followers. In 17th-century France the neoclassical tragedies of Racine and Corneille were carefully based on principles derived from Aristotle's *Poetics* (*see* unities). During the 19th century the essential elements of tragedy were more apparent in the novel than in drama. Ibsen and Strindberg in Europe and Eugene O'Neill in the US contributed to the development of tragic drama, but few 20th-century dramatists have attempted to write tragedies in the classical or Elizabethan sense.

tragicomedy A genre of drama developed by European writers in the late 16th and early 17th centuries. Its combination of tragic and romantic elements was pioneered by the Italian dramatist *Guarini in *Il pastor fido* (c. 1583) and was further developed in France and by several Jacobean and Restoration dramatists in England. The term is often applied to any play containing both tragic and comic elements, such as those of Chekhov.

tragopan A short-tailed *pheasant belonging to a genus (*Tragopan*) occurring in wet forests of the Himalayas. Male tragopans have vivid plumage, including long crown feathers, and two erectile blue fleshy "horns" on the head; a fold of skin beneath the bill forms a large bib during display.

Trail of Tears The journey of the Indian tribes, forced to migrate (1829–43) to new homes in Oklahoma Territory. The long hard trip to the West produced severe hardships for the Indians; one of every four who started out died as a result of disease, famine, or abuse.

Trajan(us), Marcus Ulpius (53–117 AD) Roman emperor (98–117). Trajan's early military successes led to his adoption by *Nerva in 97 AD. After his arrival in Rome as emperor his virtues were praised by Pliny in the *Panegyric*. His domestic policies were munificent and humane: corn was freely distributed, taxes were lessened, and much public building was car-

ried out. He conducted two important wars: a successful Dacian campaign and a fruitless Parthian war. He died in Cilicia on his way back to Rome. □sculpture.

tranquilizers A group of drugs used to quiet aggressive, restless, or anxious patients. The major tranquilizers are powerful drugs used in the treatment of schizophrenia and other mental disorders. They include reserpine, the *phenothiazines, and the butyrophenones (e.g. haloperidol). Minor tranquilizers, which include the *benzodiazepines, are used for the treatment of neuroses and anxiety. Side effects of the major tranquilizers may be severe, and these drugs are usually prescribed only for serious psychological disorders.

Transcaucasia A region in the SE Soviet Union, in the Georgian, Azerbaidzhan, and Armenian SSRs. The Great *Caucasus range is in the N and the Little Caucasus, in the S. Its resources include oil and it is an important agricultural region. In 1918 Georgia, Azerbaidzhan, and Armenia formed the short-lived Transcaucasian Federative Republic, the basis of the Transcaucasian Soviet Federated Republic (1922–36).

transcendentalism A philosophy that emphasizes the modes of thought and apprehension beyond the world of experience. In the philosophy of *Kant, everything beyond man's limited experience is transcendental and essentially unknowable. Human intuitions about time and space and understanding of quality and quantity are vital for experience, but are transcendent in that they do not come from that experience. *See also* Transcendentalists.

Transcendentalists A group of mid-19th century US writers and philosophers united by their philosophic idealism and their trust in the moral value of intuition. Their beliefs derived from the philosophy of Kant, especially as interpreted by Carlyle and Coleridge. Leading members of the group included Ralph Waldo *Emerson, Henry David *Thoreau, Margaret Fuller, Bronson Alcott, and George Ripley. They advocated social, political, and religious reforms, and many of their writings were published in the periodical *The Dial* (1840–44).

transducer Any device that changes a signal or physical quantity into another form. *Microphones, *loudspeakers, and *thermocouples are examples. It is also usually the primary sensor in a measurement or sensing system.

transformer A device for converting alternating current from one voltage to another. The input is fed to a primary winding, a coil of wire around a soft iron core, creating an oscillating magnetic field in the core. This field induces a secondary current of the same frequency in the secondary winding wound on the same core. The ratio of primary to secondary voltage is equal to the ratio of the number of turns in the secondary coil to that in the primary. The device is widely used both in electronic circuits and in the transmission and distribution of electric power (*see* electricity supply).

transhumance A form of pastoral nomadism in which livestock are moved seasonally between mountain summer pastures and lower lying winter pastures, or between northern and southern or wet and dry season grazing areas.

transistor A *semiconductor device with three or more electrodes. Transistors form the basic elements of electronic *amplifiers and logic circuits, often combined with other components in *integrated circuits. They were first developed in 1948 by William *Shockley and his coworkers at the Bell Telephone Co and now replace *thermionic valves in most applications. The term transistor usually refers to the **bipolar junction transistor**, which consists of two junctions between p-type and n-type semiconductors forming either a p-n-p or n-p-n structure. Current is carried across these junctions by both negative and positive charge carriers (electrons and holes). The current between the emitter and the collector electrodes varies not only with the voltage drop across them, but also with the voltage or current level at the base (the third electrode). Depending on how it is connected into a circuit, the junction transistor can act as a voltage or current amplifier in much the same way as a triode valve. Transistors, however, work at a much lower voltage than valves, are more compact and robust, emit less heat, and are cheaper to make.

Originally, junction transistors were made by alloying the impurity metal onto the semiconductor crystal or by adding impurities as the crystal was being grown. Now the doping is diffused in as a gas, introduced by ion implantation, or, more commonly, achieved by a combined process of etching and diffusion, known as the planar process.

The **field effect transistor** (FET) is a unipolar device, in which current is carried by only one type of charge. There are two types: the junction FET (JFET) has a region of semiconductor of one doping type flanked by two highly doped layers of the opposite type. Current flows parallel to the junctions, between the so-called source and drain electrodes, through a

Germanium is a typical semiconductor. The four outer electrons in each of its atoms form covalent bonds with adjacent atoms. In the pure state it acts as an insulator as no electrons are available to carry current.

Arsenic atoms have five outer electrons. Germanium containing arsenic atoms as an impurity can carry current because the fifth electron is available as a carrier. This is an n-type semiconductor because current is carried by negative electrons.

Indium atoms have three outer electrons. Germanium doped with indium therefore has holes in its electronic structure. These can be filled by electrons from neighboring atoms, creating new holes; this has the effect of positive charge moving through the crystal in the opposite direction to electrons. This is p-type germanium.

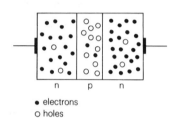

- electrons
○ holes

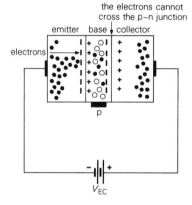

the electrons cannot cross the p–n junction

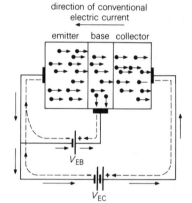

direction of conventional electric current

In the bipolar junction transistor a piece of p-type material is sandwiched between two n-type pieces, making an n-p-n structure (p-n-p transistors are also used).

In an n-p-n transistor, a negative voltage is applied to one end (the emitter) and a positive to the other (the collector). No current flows, however, because a potential barrier forms at the junction between the emitter and the central region (the base).

If the base region is positively biased, the free electrons in the emitter are attracted to the p-type base and current flows through the thin base to the collector. As the collector current depends on the amount of bias to the base, the device can be used as an amplifier.

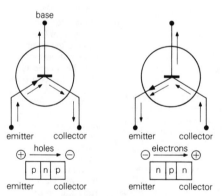

In the symbolic representation of a transistor, the direction of the arrow on the emitter indicates current direction and the type of transistor (n-p-n or p-n-p).

TRANSISTOR *The operation of the bipolar junction transistor.*

narrow channel between the highly doped regions (the gate); it is controlled by the electric field arising from the gate input voltage, which alters the width of the conducting channel. The JFET is used as a separate component in amplifiers and switches. In the insulated-gate FET (IGFET) the source and drain electrodes are highly doped regions in a substrate of the opposite type. The gate electrode is a conductor separated from the substrate by a thin insulating layer across the surface. The electric field caused by the gate voltage controls the source-drain current on the other side of the insulator. The IGFET is used mainly in metal-oxide semiconductor (MOS) integrated circuits. It is smaller than the equivalent bipolar junction transistor and uses less power.

transit instrument   A telescope theodolite, or similar device, that can be adjusted over a range of angular settings and is used to measure angular position. In astronomy, for instance, transit telescopes measure the vertical angles of stars or planets.

transition elements   A large group of metallic elements, including most of the commonly used metals, the inner electron shells of which are incomplete. The *lanthanides and the *actinides are sometimes included in this definition. The elements show considerable similarities to their horizontal neighbors in the *periodic table. In general, they are hard, brittle, high-melting, and excellent conductors of heat and electricity. Their chemistry is complicated; they have multiple valencies and tend to form colored compounds.

Transjordan.   *See* Jordan, Hashemite kingdom of.

Transkei, Republic of   A small country in South Africa, consisting of three separate areas. Most of the population is *Xhosa. *Economy*: chiefly subsistence agriculture, especially livestock, although such cash crops as tea, coffee, and flax are now being developed. Many adult males still work and live in South Africa. *History*: created in 1963, when South Africa granted self-government to the Xhosa nation, as the first of the Bantu Homelands, it became independent in 1976. All black Africans of Transkeian origin became its citizens, simultaneously losing their South African citizenship. Its independence is, however, recognized only by South Africa. In 1978, after constant disputes, especially over territorial rights, it broke off diplomatic relations with South Africa, in spite of continuing economic dependence on it. President: Paramount Chief Botha Jongilizwe Sigcau. Prime minister: Paramount Chief Kaiser Matanzima. Official currency: South African rand. Area: 16,675 sq mi (43,188 sq km). Population (1983 est): 2,775,000. Capital: Umtata.

translucence   One of the degrees of transparency used by geologists for classifying minerals.   A mineral is translucent if it transmits light but not sufficiently so to enable the outline of an object to be seen.

transmigration of souls.   *See* reincarnation.

transmutation   The conversion of one element into another. It was originally the (unfulfilled) aim of alchemists to bring about the transmutation of base metals into gold (*see* alchemy). Transmutations were achieved in the 20th century by bombarding elements with *alpha particles or *neutrons. An example is the production of oxygen-17 when nitrogen-14 is bombarded with alpha particles.

transpiration   The loss of water vapor from the surface of a plant, which occurs primarily through small pores (stomata) in the leaves but also (slowly) through the cuticle of the *epidermis. The rate of water loss is controlled by the opening and closing of the stomata, greater loss occurring during the day than at night.

transplantation   The surgical implantation of a tissue or organ derived either from another part of the body of the patient himself or from another individual (the donor). Skin grafting is an example of the former type of operation: it is used particularly to repair damage and disfigurement caused by burns and other injuries. Transplantation of donor organs is usually far less successful since the body's immune system reacts against and rejects the foreign tissue. These operations require careful matching of the donor's and recipient's tissues together with the use of drugs that suppress the recipient's immune responses (*see* immunosuppression). The first successful heart transplant operation was performed by Christiaan *Barnard in 1967, and since then many such operations have been performed in various countries, especially the US. Other organs that have been transplanted include the kidneys, lung, and liver, of which kidney transplants have been the most successful. Transplantation of bone marrow, heart valves, and pieces of bone have also been attempted.

transponder   In telecommunications, a combined transmitter and receiver that sends out a signal automatically on receiving a predetermined trigger signal.

transportation   In British law, the practice of sending a convicted criminal to some place outside Britain, usually to one of the colonies, to be kept in hard labor. Transportation was replaced by imprisonment at the end of the 18th century.

Transportation, Department of (DOT)   US cabinet-level agency that establishes the country's overall transportation policy, including that of highway planning and construction, urban mass transit, railroads, aviation, and the safety of waterways, ports, highways, and oil and gas pipelines. Established in 1966, it is headed by the secretary of transportation, who oversees the US Coast Guard (*see* Coast Guard), the Maritime Administration, the St Lawrence Seaway Development Corporation, and the various transportation administrations.

transsexualism.   *See* transvestism.

Trans-Siberian Railway   The world's longest railroad, running 5800 mi (9335 km) from Moscow to Vladivostok, known as Siberia's lifeline. Double track, largely electrified, has replaced the original single track line built between 1891 and 1905. The complete journey with nearly a hundred stops takes nine days.

transubstantiation   In Roman Catholic theology, the doctrine that the substance of the elements of bread and wine in the *Eucharist is changed at consecration into the substance of the body and blood of Christ. Only the accidents (i.e. the qualities apparent to the senses) of the bread and wine remain. *Compare* consubstantiation.

transuranic elements   Elements with higher atomic number than uranium. Apart from traces of neptunium and plutonium, none of these have ever been detected in nature, since no isotopes of sufficient *half-life exist; they have been created since 1940, usually in minute amounts, in nuclear reactions. At present, over a dozen are known. *See also* actinides.

Transvaal   The most northerly province in South Africa. Much of it is plateau with rolling country and high ridges, including the Witwatersrand. Heavily populated in the S, it is the most prosperous province and contains the country's main industrial area, centered on the Witwatersrand; iron, steel, and chemicals are produced. Mineral deposits include gold, diamonds, uranium, coal, chromite, and tin, and it has important deposits of platinum. It has a well-developed agriculture producing maize, wheat, peanuts, citrus fruit, cotton, and tobacco; sheep and cattle are raised. Forestry is also important. *History*: originally an Afrikaner republic, it fought in the *Boer Wars against Britain (1880–81, 1899–1902). It joined the Union of South Africa in 1910. Area: 109,621 sq mi (283,917 sq km). Population (1970): 8,717,530. Capital: Pretoria.

transvestism   The practice of wearing clothes appropriate to the opposite sex, usually for sexual pleasure. Many transvestites are heterosexual males and do not wish to change their sex. Psychotherapy and aversion therapy can provide effective treatment for those requiring it. **Transsexualism** is the settled belief that one's psychological gender is opposite to one's physical sex, and this can cause considerable suffering. Psychological treatments are usually unhelpful. Some transsexuals manage to pass successfully as members of the opposite sex; hormone therapy and plastic surgery on genitals and breasts can help this adjustment by effecting an apparent sex change.

Transylvania   A region of SE Europe, bounded by the Carpathian Mountains and the Transylvanian Alps, now in Romania. Transylvania retained its distinctive character under successive Roman, Magyar, and Hungarian rulers; during the 16th and 17th centuries, it was a self-governing princedom within the Ottoman Empire. Restored to Hungary, within the Holy Roman Empire, in 1687, Transylvania became part of Romania after World War I.

Transylvanian Alps (*or* Southern Carpathian Mountains; Romanian name: Carpaţii Meridionali)   A mountain range extending 227 mi (360 km) E–W across S central Romania and rising to 8343 ft (2543 m) at Mount Moldoveanu.

Trapani   38 02N 12 32E A seaport in Italy, in NW Sicily. A Carthaginian naval base, it was ceded to Rome after the first Punic War. Its industries include fishing, fish processing, salt production, and marbleworking. Population (1971): 69,771.

trap-door spider   A *spider, especially one of the family *Ctenizidae*, that constructs a silk-lined burrow in the ground covered by a tight-fitting silk-hinged door. Ctenizids are dull brown, with short stout legs. They occur in tropical and subtropical regions and only leave their burrows to hunt.

Trappists A Roman Catholic monastic order, officially known as the *Cistercians of the Strict Observance. It was founded in 1664 at the abbey of La Trappe in Normandy by D. A. J. le B. de Rancé (1626–1700). When the monks were expelled during the French Revolution, the order established houses in other countries; there are now monasteries in Britain, Ireland, North America, and elsewhere. The order is notable for its austerity, which includes the observance of strict silence, manual labor, and a simple vegetarian diet.

Trasimeno, Lake (or Lake Perugia) A lake in central Italy. It is drained via an artificial tunnel by the Tiber River. Area: 50 sq mi (129 sq km).

traveler's-tree A palmlike tree, *Ravenala madagascariensis*, native to Madagascar. It grows over 90 ft (27 m) tall and bears a crown of banana-like leaves, 48–72 in (120–180 cm) long, on long stalks 7–13 ft [2–4 m] long). Each leaf base, shaped like a huge cup, holds about 1 quart (one liter) of water, which can provide a drink for thirsty passers-by (hence the name). Family: *Strelitziaceae*.

Traven, B(en) (Berick Traven Torsvan; 1890–1969) US novelist. Despite much speculation, his identity remains uncertain. He was probably born in Chicago of German ancestry, worked in Germany in 1918–19, and lived in Mexico from the 1920s. His allegorical novels include *The Death Ship* (1926) and *The Treasure of the Sierra Madre* (1927).

Travis, William Barret (1809–36) US lawyer and soldier, instrumental in the fight for Texas independence. A practicing lawyer in Alabama, he moved to Texas in 1831. During the war for independence in Texas he died leading the volunteer troops at the *Alamo, having replaced an ill James *Bowie.

trawler A vessel equipped for catching fish by towing nets. Such vessels are often designed with cold storage facilities for the catch for extended voyages at sea.

treadmill A penal device used in 19th-century prisons. It consisted of a hollow cylinder with a series of steps. A prisoner treading on the steps would set the cylinder in motion, which could then be used for grinding corn, etc.

treason The violation by a citizen of his allegiance to the sovereign or the state. Treason consists of two elements: adherence to the enemy, and rendering him aid and comfort. A conviction may be obtained only if 1) there are two witnesses to testify against the accused or, 2) there is a confession in open court.

Treasury, Department of US cabinet-level agency that formulates and recommends economic, financial, tax, and fiscal policies, serves as a financial agent for the federal government, enforces the law, and manufactures coins and currency. Established in 1789, it is headed by the secretary of the treasury, who is a major policy adviser to the president and who oversees such divisions of the department as the US Customs Service, the Bureau of Printing and Engraving, the US Mint, and the Internal Revenue Service.

Treaty of Paris (1898) Treaty signed in Paris, France, that ended the *Spanish–American War. The US acquired the Philippines, Puerto Rico, and Guam; Cuba became independent.

treaty ports The five Chinese ports that were opened to British consuls and merchants in 1842 at the end of the first *Opium War. They were Canton, Amoy, Fuzhou, Ningbo, and Shanghai.

Trebizond. See Trabzon.

tree A tall perennial woody plant, usually with a single main stem (the trunk) and secondary stems (the branches) arising some distance above ground level. (Shrubs are smaller bushier woody perennials without a distinct trunk.) Most tree species are either *dicotyledons (angiosperms)— the broad-leaved trees—or *conifers (gymnosperms). These are the only trees that form true *wood and they are of economic importance as producers of hardwoods and softwoods, respectively. Other groups containing trees are the cycads (gymnosperms), monocotyledons (notably the *palms), and the ferns. Trees grow wherever the annual rainfall exceeds 30 in (76 cm) but a few have adapted to desert conditions. The conifers and tropical trees are mostly *evergreen plants, while broad-leaved trees growing in regions with marked seasonal changes in climate are typically deciduous.

The tallest existing tree on record is a Californian redwood, which has attained a height of 364 ft (111 m). The study of the ecology and classification of trees is called **dendrology**. *See also* forest.

treecreeper A small songbird belonging to a family (*Certhiidae*; 5 species) occurring in Europe and Asia and occasionally in North America. It has a brownish streaked plumage with pale silvery underparts, long claws, and a slender down-curved bill. The European treecreeper (*Certhia fami-*

liaris), 5 in (12.5 cm) long, occurs mainly in coniferous woods, where it creeps up tree trunks to probe for small beetles, spiders, woodlice, etc.

tree fern A tropical *fern belonging to the genus *Cyathea* (600 species), found mainly in moist mountainous regions. It has a trunklike stem, 10–80 ft (3–25 m) high, and a crown of large tapering branched fronds. Family: *Cyatheaceae*.

tree frog A small toad belonging to a widely distributed family (*Hylidae*; about 500 species). They have adapted to living in trees and have adhesive pads on their toes that enable them to cling to leaves and branches, leaping acrobatically to capture insects. Most species breed in water although some carry the developing eggs on their backs.

treehopper A winged insect, less than 1.5 in (13 mm) long, belonging to the mainly tropical family *Membracidae* (2600 species). An enlargement of the thorax extends over the body to form a "hood," which varies in color and shape to camouflage the insects against the background vegetation on which they live and feed. Suborder: *Homoptera*; order *Hemiptera*.

tree kangaroo A *wallaby of the genus *Dendrolagus* (9 species) of Australia and New Guinea. The black tree kangaroo (*D. ursinus*) is an agile climber that feeds at night on the ground and sleeps during the day in trees.

tree of heaven A tree, *Ailanthus altissima*, native to central Asia and planted elsewhere as an ornamental. Growing to a height of 100 ft (30 m), it has compound leaves, up to 40 in (1 m) long, composed of paired leaflets. Male and female flowers appear on separate trees, forming greenish-white clusters; the female flowers produce winged fruits. The trees are resistant to pollution and hence popular in urban areas. Family: *Simaroubaceae*.

tree shrew A primitive *prosimian primate belonging to the family *Tupaiidae* (18 species), found in Java, Borneo, Sumatra, the Philippines, and S Asia. The common tree shrew (*Tupaia glis*) is 12–18 in (30–45 cm) long including the tail (6–9 in [15–23 cm]) and has a slender pointed face. It darts among the branches, feeding chiefly on insects with some fruit and seeds.

tree snake Any of a number of slender tree-dwelling snakes that hunt birds, frogs, and lizards in tropical forests. The blunt-headed tree snake (*Imantodes cenchoa*) of Central and South America can stiffen most of its 24–36 in (60–90 cm) body length to reach another branch while supported by only a single coil of the tail. *See also* flying snake; vine snake.

trefoil One of several annual herbs of the genus *Trifolium* (which also includes the *clovers), characterized by leaves consisting of three leaflets. The hop trefoil (*T. campestre*), found on grassland and roadsides of Europe, W Asia, N Africa, and North America, grows to a height of 14 in (35 cm) and has compact globular heads of yellow flowers. The birdsfoot trefoils belong to the genus *Lotus* (about 70 species), of temperate Eurasia, Africa, and Australia. The leaves have five leaflets and the yellow or reddish flowers have a prominent keel resembling a lip. A common species is *L. corniculatus*, a perennial grassland herb growing to a height of 4–16 in (10–40 cm). Family: *Leguminosae*.

Trematoda. *See* fluke.

Trengganu A state in NE Peninsular Malaysia, on the South China Sea. Mountainous and forested inland, it is settled mainly along the coast, with fish, rice, rubber, and copra being the chief products. Area: 5002 sq mi (12,955 sq km). Population (1980): 542,280. Capital: Kuala Trengganu.

Trent, Council of (1545–63) The 19th general council of the Roman Catholic Church, an expression of the *Counter-Reformation, which was summoned by Pope Paul III to strengthen the Church in its confrontation with Protestantism. It was held in Trento (N Italy). There were three sessions (1545–47, 1551–52, 1562–63), which clarified doctrine and instituted reforms: the Council condemned Luther's doctrine of justification by faith alone and defined *transubstantiation. It also strengthened episcopal authority and issued decrees on clerical abuses and education.

Trent, River A river in central England. Flowing mainly NE from Staffordshire through Nottingham, it joins the Ouse River to form the Humber estuary. The Midlands' main river, it is linked to the Mersey by the Trent, Mersey, and Grand Union Canals. Length: 170 mi (270 km).

Trent Affair (1861) US–British incident during the Civil War that established policy regarding freedom of the seas. US naval officers aboard the *San Jacinto* seized two Confederate commissioners, traveling on the British ship *Trent* in waters off Havana, Cuba. The British government, angered at the violation of neutrality, demanded that the Confederates be released. More than a month later, the US government condemned the act and ordered the prisoners released.

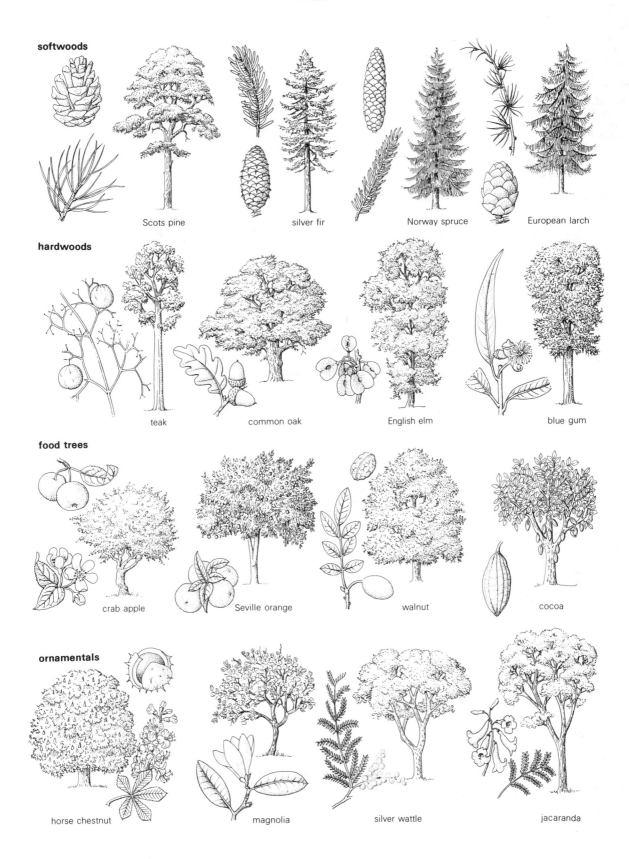

softwoods

Scots pine   silver fir   Norway spruce   European larch

hardwoods

teak   common oak   English elm   blue gum

food trees

crab apple   Seville orange   walnut   cocoa

ornamentals

horse chestnut   magnolia   silver wattle   jacaranda

Trentino-Alto Adige (Former name: Venetia Tridentina) An autonomous region in N Italy. Formerly part of Austria, it passed to Italy after World War I and has a large German-speaking population. It is a mountainous forested region, situated entirely within the Alps. The fertile valleys of the Adige River and its tributaries produce wine, fruit, and dairy products. Timber is an important industry. Numerous hydroelectric plants have encouraged the development of manufacturing industry. Tourism is an important source of revenue. Area: 5256 sq mi (13,613 sq km). Population (1980 est): 878,296. Capital: Trento.

Trento (German name: Trent) 46 04N 11 08E A city in N Italy, the capital of Trentino-Alto Adige on the Adige River. Dating from pre-Roman times, it has a romanesque cathedral (12th-century) and the 16th-century Church of Sta Maria Maggiore, where the Council of *Trent met. Its products include chemicals, electrical goods, and silk. Population (1971): 91,767.

Trenton 40 15N 74 43W The capital city of New Jersey. George Washington defeated the British here in 1776. Industries include the manufacture of pottery, cable, rope, and metal. Population (1980): 92,124.

trepang (or bêche-de-mer) The boiled, dried, and smoked body wall of certain *sea cucumbers, used to make soup in the East. It is produced mainly from animals of the genera *Holothuria, Stichopus,* and *Thelonota,* found on coral reefs of the SW Pacific.

trephine A surgical saw used to remove a circular section of the skull in order to release pressure caused by bleeding within the skull or to provide access to the brain. The use of trephines dates from ancient times.

Trevelyan, Sir George Otto (1838–1928) British statesman and historian, nephew and biographer of Lord Macaulay. He was a member of parliament from 1868 to 1897 and held various political posts.

Trèves. *See* Trier.

Trevino, Lee (1939–) US golfer, who was US Open champion (1968, 1971), British Open champion (1971, 1972), and US Professional Golfers Association champion (1974).

Treviso 45 40N 12 15E A city in Italy, in Veneto. Dating from Roman times, it has an 11th-century cathedral and other historic buildings, including several ancient palaces. Its manufactures include ceramics and agricultural machinery. Population (1971): 90,945.

Trevithick, Richard (1771–1833) British engineer, who developed high-pressure steam engines that were sufficiently light and powerful to be used in locomotives. He built the first steam-driven carriage to carry passengers (1801) and the first locomotive to run on smooth wheels on smooth rails (1804). He died penniless.

Trevor-Roper, Hugh Redwald, Baron Dacre (1914–) British historian. Trevor-Roper's many books, notable for their literary merit, include *Archbishop Laud* (1940) and *The Last Days of Hitler* (1947).

triangle A percussion instrument consisting of a steel rod bent into the shape of a triangle. The triangle was first used in late 18th-century orchestral works to provide a "Turkish" atmosphere. □musical instruments.

Triangle trade A trading system among the West Indies, American colonies, and Africa. The New England and Middle Atlantic colonies manufactured rum from West Indian molasses. The rum was brought to Africa and traded for slaves who were then taken to the West Indies and sold for molasses.

Trianon, Grand and Petit Two villas in the grounds of the Palace of Versailles, near Paris. The Grand Trianon was built in 1687 for Louis XIV by *Mansart and the Petit Trianon from 1762 to 1768 for Louis XV by Jacques Ange Gabriel (1698–1782).

Triassic period (or Trias) A period of geological time at the beginning of the Mesozoic era, lasting from about 240 to 200 million years ago. The rocks of the period, laid down mainly under continental conditions, so greatly resemble those of the preceding *Permian period that the two are often considered together as the Permo-Trias(sic). The dinosaurs, ichthyosaurs, and plesiosaurs appeared in the Triassic.

tribes of Israel In the Bible, the Hebrew people. The 12 tribes, descended from the sons of Jacob, were *Reuben, *Simeon, *Judah, *Issachar, *Zebulun, *Benjamin, *Dan, *Naphtali, *Gad, *Asher, Levi (*see* Levites), and *Ephraim and *Manasseh. These last two were counted as one, except in parts of the Bible where the tribal lists omit either Levi or Simeon. After the death of Solomon, ten of the tribes broke away from Benjamin and Judah to form the northern kingdom of Israel (*see* Ten Lost Tribes of Israel).

tribology The study of *friction and such allied topics as lubrication, abrasives, surface wear, etc. The effects of friction, such as triboluminescence and frictional electricity, are also studied.

tribune In ancient Rome, a plebeian magistrate appointed to protect *plebeians' rights. Instituted during the 5th-century political struggles between *patricians and plebeians, the tribunes, first two, later ten, in number, could veto legislative proposals of the Senate or popular assemblies and could themselves propose legislation without senatorial approval. This power, to obstruct and circumvent the Senate, considerably influenced Roman politics from the Gracchi's revolutionary times (*see* Gracchus, Tiberius Sempronius) to Augustus' assumption of tribunicial power in the late 1st century BC.

Triceratops A three-horned dinosaur of the late Cretaceous period (about 100–65 million years ago) and one of the last of the dinosaurs. 26 ft (8 m) long and weighing 8.5 tons, it had an enormous head with one horn on the snout and one (up to 40 in [1 m] long) over each eye. It also had a large bony neck frill and short limbs with hoofed feet and browsed on tough plants. Order: *Ornithischia.* □fossil.

Trichinopoly. *See* Tiruchirappalli.

Trier (French name: Trèves) 49 45N 6 39E A city in SW West Germany, in Rhineland-Palatinate on the Moselle River. Founded by the Emperor Augustus, it has important Roman remains including the amphitheater. The cathedral (11th–12th centuries) is built around the 4th-century basilica. It shares a university with Kaiserslautern (1970) and is the birthplace of Karl Marx. It is a wine-trading and industrial center. Population (1975 est): 100,338.

Trieste (Serbo-Croat name: Trst) 45 39N 13 47E A seaport in Italy, the capital of Friuli-Venezia Giulia, situated on the Gulf of Trieste at the head of the Adriatic Sea. An important transit port for central Europe, it has shipyards, oil refineries, and a steel industry. It has a 14th-century cathedral and a university (1938). *History*: an important Roman port in the 1st century AD, it passed to Austria in 1382. It expanded rapidly in the 19th century as an outlet for Austrian goods and in 1920 was ceded to Italy. Following World War II it became the capital of the Free Territory of Trieste, which was established by the UN (1947) following a dispute between Italy and Yugoslavia. In 1954 most of the N of the Territory (including Trieste) passed to Italy and the remainder to Yugoslavia. Population (1980 est): 257,697.

triggerfish A shallow-water fish, belonging to a family (*Balistidae*) related to *puffers, that occurs in tropical seas. Its deep laterally flattened body, up to 24 in (60 cm) long, is covered with large scales. The strong spine of the first dorsal fin is erected and locked into position by the second dorsal fin, forming a "trigger" that wedges the fish into crevices. It feeds on mollusks and crustaceans.

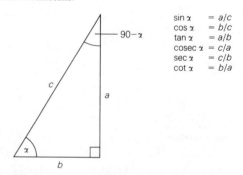

TRIGONOMETRY *Definitions of the trigonometric functions sine, cosine, and tangent and of their reciprocals cosecant, secant, and cotangent.*

trigonometry A branch of mathematics founded by Hipparchus in the mid-2nd century BC, concerned originally with the measurement of triangles. The ratios of the lengths of the sides of a right-angled triangle are used to define the sine, cosine, and tangent of one of the angles of the triangle. Trigonometry deals with the properties of these and related functions. Its study is essential to most branches of physics and mathematics, particularly those involving cyclic quantities.

Trilling, Lionel (1905–75) US literary critic. In *The Liberal Imagination* (1950), *Sincerity and Authenticity* (1974), and other works, he expressed a moral concern with all aspects of modern culture. His novel *The Middle of* *the Journey* (1947) is concerned with moral and political issues of the 1930s and 1940s.

trilobite An extinct marine *arthropod belonging to a subphylum (*Trilobita*; over 4000 species) that flourished between Cambrian and Permian times, i.e. 500–200 million years ago. Trilobite ☐fossils are abundant in rocks of this period. Its flattened oval body, 0.40–26.5 in (10–675 mm) long, was divided by two longitudinal furrows into three lobes. The head bore a pair of antennae and usually a pair of compound eyes and each segment of the thorax and tail region carried a pair of forked appendages. Many trilobites burrowed in sand or mud, preying on other animals or scavenging.

trimaran A modern sailing vessel with three parallel hulls, a larger central one and two smaller ones used as stabilizers or outriggers. Trimarans are usually rigged as sloops. It is modeled on the outrigger canoe, or **proa**, of the SW Pacific. *See also* catamaran.

Trimurti The Hindu triad of gods, *Brahma, *Vishnu, and *Shiva, representing the creative, sustaining, and destructive aspects of reality respectively, sometimes portrayed as one body with three heads.

Trinidad and Tobago, Republic of A country off the N coast of South America, consisting of the islands of Trinidad and Tobago. Both are hilly and wooded. Most of the population is of African and East Indian descent. *Economy:* oil and asphalt have replaced cocoa and sugar as the main source of the country's wealth and reserves of offshore gas have also been discovered. Other industrial developments include aluminum smelting, plastics, electronics, iron and steel, and petrochemicals. Tourism is a growing industry. It is a member of CARICOM. *History:* Trinidad was inhabited by Arawak and Carib Indians when it was discovered by Columbus in 1498. It was a Spanish colony from the 16th century until 1802, when it was ceded to Britain; it joined with Tobago in 1809. During World War II bases were leased to the US but most have since been given up. The country was a member of the short-lived Federation of the West Indies from 1958 to 1961 and became an independent state within the British Commonwealth in 1962. In 1970 there was considerable unrest, partly because of the black power movement. In 1976 it became a republic with the former governor general, Ellis Clarke, as its first president. Prime minister: George Chambers. Official language: English. Official currency: Trinidad and Tobago dollar of 100 cents. Area: 1980 sq mi (5128 sq km). Population (1983 est): 1,211,000. Capital and main port: Port-of-Spain.

Trinity, the A central doctrine of Christian theology, stating that God is one substance but with three distinct, coequal, and coeternal "persons," the Father, the Son, and the *Holy Spirit. The belief is based on a number of passages in the New Testament. It was given a first formal definition by the Council of *Nicaea (325), which asserted that the Son was "of the same essence (*homoousios*) as the Father." In the West, St Augustine and St Thomas Aquinas developed the doctrine. The Eastern Church rejects the so-called "double procession" of the Holy Spirit from the Father and the Son, which is accepted by the Western Church (*see* Filioque).

triode. *See* thermionic valve.

Triple Alliance (1882) An alliance between Germany, Austria-Hungary, and Italy, which with the opposing *Triple Entente shaped European diplomacy in the decades before World War I. At the outbreak of war (1914) Italy declared its neutrality, thus breaking the alliance.

Triple Alliance, War of the (*or* Paraguayan War; 1865–70) The war between Paraguay and a coalition of Argentina, Brazil, and Uruguay. Conflict was precipitated by the belligerent diplomacy of Paraguay's dictator, F. S. *López, toward— Argentina, which with Brazil and Uruguay invaded Paraguay. López refused to surrender and following the capture of Asunción in 1868 waged a guerrilla war in the N until taken prisoner in 1870. The war shattered the economy of Paraguay, which lost about half its population.

Triple Crown The three major races for three-year-old horses in the US: the Kentucky Derby, the Preakness Stakes, and the Belmont Stakes.

Triple Entente An informal combination of France, Russia, and Britain resulting from the Franco-Russian alliance (1893), the Franco-British *Entente Cordiale (1904), and the Anglo-Russian agreement (1907). It was formed in opposition to the *Triple Alliance.

triple jump (former name: hop, step, and jump) A field event for men in athletics, similar to the *long jump but executed as a continuous series of three jumps. The jumper lands first on the takeoff foot and then on the other, which becomes the takeoff foot for the final jump.

Tripoli (Arabic name: Tarabulus) 32 58N 13 12E The capital and main port of Libya, on the Mediterranean Sea. Originally founded as Oea by the Phoenicians, it has come under the rule of many different countries through

the ages. It became the capital of Libya on independence in 1951. Its notable buildings include a Spanish fortress and it has a university (1973). Exports include fruit and olive oil and it is a transshipment center. Population (1973): 281,497.

Tripoli (Arabic name: Tarabalus) 34 27N 35 50E A port in NW Lebanon, on the Mediterranean Sea. It was the capital of a Phoenician federation of three other cities (hence its name, from Greek *tripolis*). Iraqi oil is brought by pipeline to the refinery here. The city was heavily damaged in 1983 as a result of fighting between Syrian forces and the Palestine Liberation Organization during Lebanon's civil war. Population (1978 est): 175,000.

Tripolitania A region of N Africa, between Tunisia and Cyrenaica. Colonized in the 7th century BC by the Phoenicians, who founded three cities, including Tripoli, the coast was controlled by a succession of foreign powers, including Romans, Arabs, Ottoman Turks, and Italians, while the nomadic Berbers of the interior were generally unaffected by political changes. Since 1951 Tripolitania has been part of Libya.

Tripura A state in NE India, in tropical jungle and plains E of Bangladesh. Rice, jute, tea, and bamboo are produced. Local cottage industries are flourishing. *History:* the Moguls ended 1000 years of Hindu monarchy (18th century) before Britain won Tripura. In 1949 it entered the Indian Union. Area: 4044 sq mi (10,477 sq km). Population (1971): 1,556,342. Capital: Agartala.

tri-ratna (Sanskrit: three jewels) In Buddhism, the *Buddha, *Dharma, and *sangha, that is, the spiritual ideal, the truth regarding the means to its attainment, and the monastic order of those who strive toward it.

trireme. *See* ships.

Tristan The tragic hero of several medieval romances. After accidentally drinking a magic love potion, he becomes the lover of Iseult (Isolde), who is betrothed to his uncle, King Mark of Cornwall. He later renounces Iseult and goes to Brittany, where he marries the duke's daughter. Dying from a wound, he sends a ship to bring back Iseult to nurse him. By his wife's treachery, she arrives too late and dies of grief at his side. Of Celtic origin, the legend appeared in a French poem, written in about 1150 (now lost). Other 12th-century versions include one by an Anglo-Norman poet, Thomas, and *Gottfried von Strassburg's *Tristan und Isolde*, the source of Wagner's opera. In a 13th-century prose romance the story was incorporated into the *Arthurian legend.

Tristan da Cunha 37 15S 12 30W A group of four small islands in the S Atlantic Ocean, a dependency of St Helena. The only settlement, Edinburgh, which is on Tristan (the largest island), grew from a British garrison (established 1816). Situated on the main sailing route, it originally flourished but became isolated when steam replaced sail. In 1961 the inhabitants were evacuated to the UK to escape a volcanic eruption but most chose to return in 1963. The economy is based on crawfish canning and postage stamps. Area: about 40 sq mi (100 sq km). Population (1980): 323.

tritium (T *or* ³H) A radioactive isotope of hydrogen, the nucleus of which contains one *proton and two *neutrons. It does not occur naturally but is produced in nuclear reactors and is used as a radioactive tracer and in nuclear weapons. Tritium decays with a half-life of 12.3 years, emitting beta-rays.

Triton In Greek mythology, a sea deity, the son of Poseidon and Amphitrite. He is usually portrayed as human above the waist and as a dolphin below; he blows a shell in order to control the waves.

triton shell A *gastropod mollusk of the family *Cymatiidae* (about 100 species), occurring mainly in tropical seas. Triton trumpets (genus *Charonia*) grow to 16 in (40 cm) and have ribbed shells, often with prominent knobs. They are carnivorous, feeding on mollusks and echinoderms. Hairy tritons have a rough hairy shell.

triumvirate In Roman affairs, a board of three men officially appointed for special administrative duties. The so-called first Triumvirate (60 BC) of Caesar, Pompey, and Crassus was merely a private arrangement for mutual convenience. The triumvirate, or triple dictatorship, of Mark Antony, Lepidus, and Octavian was unique; appointed in 43 BC to maintain public order in Rome, they held office with absolute powers until Lepidus was ousted in 36 and power was divided between Mark Antony and Octavian.

Trivandrum 8 41N 76 57E A city in India, the capital of Kerala. A cultural, commercial, and communications center, it processes minerals and is the site of the University of Kerala (1937). Population (1971): 409,672.

Trnova. *See* Tŭrnovo.

Trobriand Islands A group of coral islands in the SW Pacific Ocean, in Papua New Guinea. The largest is Kiriwana (Trobriand). It produces yams, mother-of-pearl, and trepang (edible sea cucumber). The islands became famous through the studies of the anthropologist Bronisław Malinowski. Area: about 170 sq mi (440 sq km).

trogon An insectivorous bird belonging to a family (*Trogonidae*; 35 species) occurring in forested regions of Africa, Asia, and America. 9.5–18 in (24–46 cm) long, trogons have iridescent plumage, which in males is usually dark with a bright red or yellow belly. They have rounded wings, a short curved bill, and a long tail and are the sole family of the order *Trogoniformes*. *See also* quetzel.

Troilus In Greek mythology, a son of King Priam of Troy who was killed by Achilles. The story of his love for Cressida, who deserted him for the Greek Diomedes, first appeared in the *Roman de Troie* by the 12th-century French poet Benoît de Sainte-Maure.

Trois-Rivières 46 21N 72 34W A city and deepwater port in E Canada, in Quebec on the St Lawrence River. Founded in 1610, it is a transport and industrial center, producing a large proportion of the world's newsprint. Population (1981): 50,466.

Trojan Horse In Greek legend, a gigantic hollow wooden horse devised by Odysseus or by its builder, Epeius, in the *Trojan War. The Trojans hauled it inside their city, believing it to be a gift to Athena, and Greek warriors then emerged from it to open the gates to their army.

Trojan War In Greek legend, a ten years' war waged by the Greeks against *Troy after the abduction of *Helen, wife of King Menelaus of Sparta, by Paris, a Trojan prince. Its history, probably based on an actual war fought in the 12th century BC, is related in Homer's *Iliad*. The Greeks were led by *Agamemnon and their champions included *Achilles, *Diomedes, and *Odysseus. The chief Trojan warriors were *Hector and *Paris, sons of King Priam. Most of the action in the *Iliad* is concentrated in the final year of the war and culminates in the capture of Troy by the stratagem of the *Trojan Horse.

troll In Scandinavian folklore, originally a gigantic ogre-like creature imagined as guarding treasure, inhabiting a castle, and stalking through the forest only at night since they are destroyed or turned to stone if they see the sun. In later folklore, trolls were conceived as dwarflike cave- and mountain-dwellers who were skilled craftsmen.

Trollope, Anthony (1815–82) British novelist. He worked for the post office (1834–67). He established his reputation with a series of novels set in the imaginary county of Barsetshire with a cast of predominantly clerical characters. These books include *The Warden* (1855), *Barchester Towers* (1857), and *The Last Chronicle of Barset* (1867). A second series of novels, set against a political background, includes *Phineas Finn* (1869) and *The Eustace Diamonds* (1873).

trombone A brass musical instrument, consisting of a cylindrical tube, about 10 ft (3 m) long, turned back upon itself, a cup-shaped mouthpiece, and a flaring bell. By means of a slide that is used in seven positions and by varying lip pressure, seven different harmonic series can be produced, covering a chromatic range of almost three octaves above E below the bass stave in the tenor trombone. A bass instrument also exists. The trombone has been part of the symphony orchestra since the late 18th century and is frequently used in jazz. The old English name for the trombone was the **sackbut**.

Tromp, Maarten (Harpertszoon) (1598–1653) Dutch admiral. He defeated a numerically superior Spanish fleet at the battle of the Downs (1639). His encounter with the English (1652) began the first *Dutch War, during which he defeated the English off Dungeness (1652). He died in action. His son **Cornelis (Martenszoon) Tromp** (1629–91) was an admiral in the second and third *Dutch Wars and was briefly commander in chief of the Dutch fleet (1665), being replaced by de *Ruyter.

trompe l'oeil (French: fool the eye) A method of painting figures and objects to create the illusion that they are real rather than painted. The elaborate arches, vistas, doors, etc., painted on walls in Pompeii are an example of this visual illusion. It is also associated with Italian *baroque art.

Tromsø 69 42N 19 00E A seaport in N Norway, on an island just off the mainland. The largest town N of the Arctic Circle, its industries include fishing, sealing, and fish processing. Its university was established in 1968. Population (1981 est): 46,454.

Trondheim 63 36N 10 23E A city and seaport in W Norway on Trondheim Fjord. It has a famous cathedral (12th–14th centuries) where Norwegian sovereigns have been crowned since early times. The Technical University of Norway was established here in 1900 and the University of Trondheim in 1968. Its industries include shipbuilding and fishing; the

main exports are timber, wood pulp, fish, and metal goods. Population (1981 est): 134,976.

tropic bird A white seabird belonging to a family (*Phaethontidae*; 3 species) occurring in tropical and subtropical waters. Tropic birds have black eye and wing markings and are up to 20 in (50 cm) long excluding the long streamer-like tail feathers. Tropic birds spend most of their lives at sea. Order: *Pelecaniformes* (cormorants, pelicans, etc.).

tropics The area of the earth's surface lying roughly between the Tropic of Cancer on the 23°30′ N parallel of latitude and the Tropic of Capricorn on the 23°30′ S parallel.

tropism The growth of a plant or sedentary animal in response to a directional external stimulus: a growth movement toward the stimulus is a positive tropism; the opposite response is a negative tropism. Different forms of tropism are named according to the type of stimulus. For example, positive **hydrotropism** is growth toward water, observed in plant roots; negative **geotropism** is growth away from the pull of gravity, which occurs in plant stems.

troposphere. *See* atmosphere.

Trossachs, the 56 13N 4 23W A picturesque glen in central Scotland, in the Central Region between Loch Katrine and Loch Achray. It was popularized by Sir Walter Scott in his poem *The Lady of the Lake*.

Trotsky, Leon (Lev Bronstein; 1879–1940) Russian revolutionary and Marxist theorist. Trotsky became a Marxist in the 1890s and was imprisoned and exiled for participating in revolutionary activities. He lived in W Europe from 1902 until the Revolution of 1905. Again imprisoned and exiled, he escaped abroad (1907), where he remained until 1917. On the outbreak of the Russian Revolution, he returned to Russia and abandoned his previous *Menshevik loyalties to become a *Bolshevik. He played a major role in the October Revolution, which brought the Bolsheviks to power, and as war commissar during the civil war (1918–20) directed the Red Army to victory. Under Lenin, Trotsky was Russia's second most powerful man but lost to Stalin the power struggle that followed Lenin's death and was banished from the Soviet Union. He moved eventually to Mexico, where he was murdered, probably by a Soviet agent. *See also* Trotskyism.

Trotskyism The form of Marxism developed by Leon *Trotsky, who advocated world revolution in opposition to the view that socialism could be achieved in one country in isolation. Stalin sought to secure the Soviet Union against the counter-revolutionary forces of capitalism, primarily by military and economic means. Trotskyists believed that the revolution could only be maintained and capitalism defeated by developing the strength and solidarity of the working class throughout the world, since the main struggle was against the capitalist class and not between states. To this end Trotsky and his supporters founded the Fourth International in 1937, after what they saw as the degeneration of the Third International under the influence of Stalinism. Despite Trotsky's murder in 1940 and various subsequent internal splits, in 1979 the Fourth International had functioning sections in over 60 countries. These and other revolutionary groups with Trotskyist aims are regarded as dangerous and counter-revolutionary by the leaders of the Soviet Union and other communist states.

troubadours Provençal poets of the 12th to 14th centuries whose lyric poetry had a profound influence on both the subject matter and form of subsequent European verse. A number of the troubadours were of noble birth and were enthusiastically patronized by several European courts. Both poets and composers, the troubadours wrote songs introducing a new concept of love, later labeled *courtly love (although they were also noted for their satires and poems on political subjects). They developed several poetic genres and verse forms, including the *canso d'amor* (a love song in five or six stanzas), the *pastorela* (a narrative relating a meeting between a knight and a shepherdess), the *alba* (a song of lovers parting at dawn), the *tenso* or *partimen* (a debate on love), and the *sestina* (a poem of six stanzas with the same end-words repeated in each stanza according to a shifting pattern). The earliest troubadour was Guillaume, 9th Duc d'Aquitaine (1071–1127). Other famous troubadours were Marcabru (mid-12th century); Bertrand de Born, Vicomte de Hautefort (c. 1140–c. 1207); Arnaut Daniel (c. 1180), who was credited with inventing the *sestina* and was considered the greatest craftsman by Dante; and Bernard de Ventadour (late 12th century), in whose lyrics the conventions of courtly love were most clearly developed. *See also* trouvères.

Troubles, Council of. *See* Blood, Council of.

trout One of several predatory fish belonging to the family *Salmonidae*, especially the genus *Salmo*, that are native to the N hemisphere but introduced elsewhere as food and game fish. It has a stout body with a blunt head and varies in color from blackish to light olive with characteristic black or red spots or X-shaped markings. Trout occur mainly in fresh water but in some cases the young migrate to the sea to mature and return annually to streams to spawn. The common European brown trout (*S. trutta*), up to 55 in (140 cm) long, has a migratory variety called the sea trout. The North American rainbow trout (*S. gairdneri*), up to 27.5 in (70 cm) long, is distinguished by a broad purple band along its sides. Order: *Salmoniformes*.

trouvères Medieval poets of N France, especially Picardy, who were contemporary with, and influenced in subject matter and style by, the *troubadours. Notable trouvères include Conon de Béthune (d. 1224), Thibaud (IV) de Champagne, King of Navarre (d. 1253), *Adam de la Halle, and Rutebeuf (13th century).

Troy An ancient city in Asia Minor, near the Dardanelles. According to legend, when the Trojan prince *Paris abducted *Helen, her husband's brother, *Agamemnon, led a Greek force to recover her, captured Troy by the stratagem of the wooden horse after ten years' fighting, and destroyed it (traditional date: 1184 BC). □Schliemann's excavations (1870) identified Troy at Hissarlik. Excavations have revealed nine superimposed cities, the seventh of which (not the second, as Schliemann thought) was contemporary with the legendary siege and had met a violent end. *See also* Homer; Trojan War.

Troy 42 43N 73 40W A city in E central New York where the Mohawk River flows into the Hudson River, NE of Albany. Rensselaer Polytechnic Institute (1824) and Russell Sage College (1916) are here. Founded in 1789, the city became the starting point of the Erie Canal in 1825 and is now the beginning of the New York State Barge Canal. Industries include textiles and clothing, especially shirts; automotive supplies, steel, machinery, paper, and food processing. Population (1980): 56,638.

Troyes 48 18N 4 05E A city in NE France, the capital of the Aube department on the Seine River. The capital of the old province of Champagne, it has a cathedral (13th–16th centuries) and many fine churches. Manufactures include textiles, machinery, and food products. Population (1975): 75,500.

Trudeau, Pierre Elliott (1919–) Canadian statesman; Liberal prime minister (1968–79, 1980–). A French Canadian, he nevertheless opposed French separatism and in 1970 briefly introduced martial law to deal with separatist agitation in Quebec. In the same year his government recognized the People's Republic of China. Trudeau's dashing image was reinforced by his young wife, Margaret Trudeau, but the couple finally separated in 1977 after a series of much publicized estrangements. Defeated in 1979 by Joseph *Clark, he was re-elected in 1980. Trudeau retired from ofice in 1984, and his Liberal Party lost the subsequent general election.

Truffaut, François (1932–84) French film director. He wrote for the magazine *Cahiers du Cinéma* during the 1950s and was an influential member of the *New Wave. His films, noted for their visual charm and elegance, include *The 400 Blows* (1959), *Shoot the Pianist* (1960), *Jules et Jim* (1961), *L'Enfant sauvage* (1970), *Day for Night* (1973), *The Story of Adele H.* (1975), and *Love on the Run* (1978).

truffle A fungus belonging to the order *Tuberales*. Up to 4 in (10 cm) across, truffles are rounded, often with a rough pitted surface, and occur in chalky soils, usually in association with tree roots. Having a strong smell and taste, they are unearthed and eaten by squirrels, rabbits, etc., which disperse the spores in their feces. Several species are regarded as delicacies, including the black Périgord truffle (*Tuber melanosporum*) and the white Piedmont truffle (*T. magnatum*). They are collected in oak woods using trained pigs or dogs. The bluish-black English truffle (*T. aestivum*) is found mainly in beech woods. Class: *Ascomycetes*.

Trujillo 8 06S 79 00W A city in Peru, situated 8 mi (13 km) from its port, Salaverry, on the Pacific coast. Founded in 1535, it has many colonial buildings and a university (established in 1824 by Simón Bolívar). Trujillo is the commercial center for an area producing sugar cane and rice. Population (1972): 240,322.

Trujillo (Molina), Rafael (Leónidas) (1891–1961) Dominican dictator, who governed the Dominican Republic, directly or indirectly, from 1938 to 1961, aided by a powerful police force. His tyranny led to his assassination.

Truman, Harry S (1884–1972) US statesman; 33rd President of the United States (1945–53). After service in World War I, Truman studied law and began his political career as presiding judge of Jackson County, Mo (1926–34). Elected to the US Senate in 1934, Truman was chosen as the vice-presidential running mate of President Franklin *Roosevelt in 1944. After Roosevelt's death the following year, Truman succeeded to the presidency and inherited the responsibility of bringing World War II to an end.

HARRY S TRUMAN *President (1945-53) who ended World War II by ordering the atomic bomb dropped on Japanese cities.*

During his first year in office he authorized the atomic bombing of Hiroshima and Nagasaki to force Japan's surrender and played an important part in the *Potsdam Conference that determined the fate of the post-war world. Later in his administration, he introduced the **Truman Doctrine** to provide economic and military aid to countries threatened by interference from other states (1947) and the *Marshall Plan of post-war economic aid to Europe (1948). In 1948 he also ordered a massive airlift to prevent the Communist takeover of West Berlin. Winning reelection by his victory over the Republican candidate, Thomas E. *Dewey, in the 1948 elections, Truman began his second term in office by announcing his *Fair Deal program of domestic social reform. During his second term, however, Truman was increasingly preoccupied with foreign affairs. In 1949 he helped to establish the *North Atlantic Treaty Organization, and, beginning in 1950, he directed the American military participation in the *Korean War, which included a dramatic confrontation with General Douglas *MacArthur. Truman retired from public office at the end of his second term in 1953.

trumpet A brass □musical instrument. The modern trumpet consists of a cylindrical tube, 5 ft (1.5 m) long, turned back on itself, a cup-shaped mouthpiece, and a flaring bell. Three valves alter the effective length of the tube, allowing the notes of the harmonic series on six successive semitones to be played. With varying lip pressure the B flat trumpet has a chromatic range of two and a half octaves below E below middle C. The early trumpet (from the Renaissance to the early 19th century) could only produce the notes of its natural harmonic series. The upper notes of the series were known as the *clarino* (Italian: clarinet) register, much used for brilliant effects by such composers as Bach.

trumpet creeper A vine of the genus *Campsis*. The American trumpet creeper (*C. radicans*) is native to the S US and the Chinese trumpet creeper (*C. grandiflora*) is of Asian origin. Both produce trumpet-shaped orange flowers and are cultivated as ornamentals. Family: *Bignoniaceae*.

trumpeter A long-legged ground-dwelling bird belonging to a family (*Psophiidae*; 3 species) occurring in forests of N South America. 20 in (50 cm) long, trumpeters have a small head, soft dark plumage, and short bills, feeding on insects and berries. They travel in small flocks and have a loud trumpeting call. Order: *Gruiformes* (cranes, rails, etc.).

trunkfish A tropical fish, also called boxfish or cowfish, belonging to a family (*Ostraciidae*) related to *puffers, that occurs in the Atlantic and Pacific Oceans. Its body is often brightly colored and encased in a boxlike shell of fused bony plates with spaces for the fins, etc.

trust In law, a binding arrangement between two persons (or groups) in which one (the trustee, who may be an individual or a corporation) has control of property (the trust property), which he administers for the benefit of the other (the beneficiary). The trustee may himself be one of the beneficiaries. Trusts developed in the middle ages when certain parties, such as religious orders, had the use or benefit of property that they were not allowed to own.

trust territory A territory being prepared for self-government, for which the UN is responsible. There is now only one—Micronesia. The trust territories replaced the *mandates of the League of Nations.

Truth, Sojourner (Isabella Baumfree; ?1797–1883) US evangelist and reformer. A former slave (?1797–1827) in New York state, she took her symbolic name and traveled the country, preaching in favor of the emancipation of slaves and women's rights. She claimed to have had visions and heard voices instructing her in her work. She later was appointed by President Lincoln to aid freedmen.

trypanosomiasis Any infection caused by parasitic protozoa of the genus *Trypanosoma*. In Africa the parasite is transmitted by the tsetse fly and causes *sleeping sickness. In South America another species is transmitted by a bug and causes *Chagas' disease.

trypsin A digestive enzyme, secreted by the pancreas, that breaks down dietary proteins in the small intestine. It is secreted in an inactive form, which is converted to trypsin by the enzyme enterokinase in the intestine.

Ts'ao Chan. *See* Cao Chan.

tsar The title (derived from the Latin, Caesar) of the rulers of Russia from 1547 to 1721. It was first adopted by Ivan the Terrible and, though commonly used until 1917, was officially replaced with the title Emperor by Peter the Great.

Tsaritsyn. *See* Volgograd.

Tselinograd (name until 1961: Akmolinsk) 51 10N 71 28E A city in the Soviet Union, in the W Kazakh SSR. It produces agricultural machinery and is a railroad junction. Population (1981 est): 241,000.

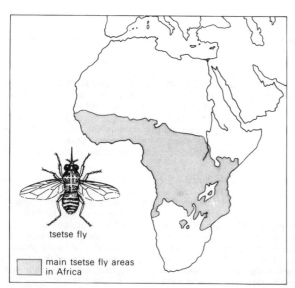

tsetse fly

main tsetse fly areas in Africa

TSETSE FLY *Several species of tsetse fly carry the parasites causing sleeping sickness in man and cattle. The tsetse areas in Africa correspond to the areas where sleeping sickness is endemic.*

tsetse fly A fly, 0.25–0.6 in (6–16 mm) long, belonging to a genus (*Glossina*; 22 species) restricted to tropical Africa. Both sexes bite and suck the blood of mammals, transmitting trypanosomes to man and domestic animals. Thus *G. palpalis* carries human sleeping sickness and *G. morsitans* transmits nagana in cattle. The larvae develop to maturity within the female before being deposited in the soil to pupate. Family: *Muscidae*.

Tshombe, Moise (Kapenda) (1919–69) Congolese statesman; prime minister (1964–65) of the Congo (now Zaïre). He led the secession of the copper-rich Katanga (now Shaba) province of the Congo in 1960, which for three years maintained its independence under Tshombe's presidency. On its collapse Tshombe fled to Spain but was recalled briefly to become the Congo's prime minister. Dismissed by President Kasavubu in 1965, he returned to Spain and died of a heart attack in Algeria.

Tsinan. *See* Jinan.

Tsinghai. *See* Qinghai.

Tsingtao. *See* Qingdao.

Tsiolkovski, Konstantin Eduardovich (1857–1935) Russian aeronautical engineer, who pioneered space and rocket research. Becoming deaf as a child he studied mathematics and physics. In 1892 he built the first wind tunnel in Russia, which he used for testing his designs of dirigibles. He then went on to investigate the use of rockets in space travel and anticipated many of the ideas that Robert *Goddard was later to develop, especially liquid-fueled rockets.

Tsushima A group of five Japanese islands, in the Korea Strait. During the Russo-Japanese War, Russia suffered a major naval defeat near here (1905). Fishing is the chief industry. Area: 269 sq mi (698 sq km). Population (1970): 59,000. Capital: Izuhara.

Tsvetaeva, Marina (1892–1941) Russian poet. Her highly original and emotionally powerful poetry was praised by Akhmatova, Pasternak, and other contemporaries. She opposed the Revolution and left Russia in 1922 to live in Prague, Berlin, and Paris. In 1939 she followed her husband back to Russia. He was shot, and she later committed suicide.

Tuamotu Archipelago A chain of about 80 coral atolls in the S Pacific Ocean, in French Polynesia. Rangiroa is the largest island and Fakarava, the most important economically. French nuclear tests were held here during the 1960s. Mother-of-pearl, phosphate, and copra are produced. Area: 332 sq mi (860 sq km). Population (1977): 8537. Administrative center: Apataki atoll.

tuatara A lizard-like reptile, *Sphenodon punctatus*, that is the only living representative of the primitive order *Rhynchocephalia*, which lived 200 million years ago. It is found only on islands off the North Island of New Zealand and has a brown-black to greenish body with a crest of spines running from head to tail; up to 27.5 in (70 cm) long, it may live 100 years. Tuataras live in burrows during the day and emerge at night to feed on spiders, insects, and birds' eggs. The clutch of 8–14 eggs is incubated for 13–14 months before hatching.

Tuatha Dé Danann (Old Irish: people of the goddess *Danu) In Old Irish mythology, a divine race, one of the several mythological groups believed to have invaded and settled in Ireland. According to the *Book of Invasions*, they came from the east in the mid-15th century BC and were learned in science and the arts of the Druids. Sometimes they are portrayed as mortal men but exceptionally strong, beautiful, learned, etc.

tuba A valved brass instrument with a conical bore and low pitch, derived originally from the *saxhorn. Various types of tuba exist under a variety of names; the instrument is used in the symphony orchestra as well as in the military band. The **Wagner tuba** is not a true tuba but a bass version of the *French horn.

tuber A swollen underground plant stem in which carbohydrates (often in the form of starch) are stored. Some tubers, for example potatoes and yams, are important human foods. Tuber-bearing plants may reproduce vegetatively from buds on the tuber, and tuber crops are usually grown from tubers rather than seed.

tuberculin A protein derived from tuberculosis bacilli that have been killed. In the Mantoux test tuberculin is injected into the skin to test whether a person has been in contact with tuberculosis. The appearance of an inflamed patch (a positive reaction) indicates previous exposure to the bacilli (and therefore some immunity) but not necessarily active infection.

tuberculosis An infectious disease caused by the bacillus *Mycobacterium tuberculosis* (which was first recognized by Robert *Koch in 1882). In pulmonary tuberculosis the bacillus is inhaled into the lungs, where it forms a primary tubercle that usually heals without trouble. Alternatively the disease may smolder for months without showing any symptoms: affected people can act as carriers without being aware that they are infected. Reactivation of the primary disease, or reinfection, may lead to active tuberculosis ("consumption"), characterized by a cough (often producing some blood), fever, lassitude, weight loss, and breathlessness. The infection may also spread to other organs. The TB bacillus can also enter the body through drinking infected cows' milk, setting up a primary tubercle in the abdominal lymph nodes. Improved environmental conditions, pasteurization of milk, X-ray screening, and *BCG vaccinations have all reduced the incidence of TB in developed countries. Treatment consists of rest, isolation, and such antibiotics as streptomycin, isoniazid (INH), and para-aminosalicylic acid (PAS).

tuberose A perennial summer-flowering garden plant, *Polianthes tuberosa*, native to SW North America. It has tuberous roots, long narrow bright-green leaves clustered at the base of the stem, and smaller clasping leaves along the stem. Its fragrant waxy-white flowers are arranged in pairs on a terminal spike and are used to manufacture perfume. Family: *Amaryllidaceae*.

tubifex A freshwater *annelid worm, also called bloodworm, belonging to the widely distributed family *Tubificidae*. Found along muddy rivers and estuaries, the most common species is the bright-red extremely active *Tubifex tubifex*, up to 3.34 in (85 mm) long. Class: *Oligochaeta*.

Tübingen 48 32N 9 04E A city in SW West Germany, in Baden-Württemberg on the Neckar River. The university (1477) is famed for its theological faculty established in the 19th century. Industries include publishing and textile manufacture. Population (1971 est): 67,800.

Tubman, Harriet (Araminta T.; c. 1820–1913) US abolitionist. An escaped (1849) slave herself, she aided other slaves in escaping to the North via the *Underground Railroad. In all, she is credited with guiding more than 300 slaves to freedom along a dangerous South-to-North route. During the Civil War she worked for the Union Army.

Tubman, William V(acanarat) S(hadrach) (1895–1971) Liberian statesman; president (1943–71). A lawyer and Methodist lay preacher, he was largely responsible for welding together into a modern nation state the peoples of diverse origins in Liberia and passed much social and political reform.

Tubuai Islands (*or* Austral Is) 23 23S 149 27W A group of seven islands in S French Polynesia, including Tubuai and Rurutu. Coffee, copra, and arrowroot are produced. Area: 67 sq mi (173 sq km). Population (1977): 5208.

tubular bells A tuned percussion instrument consisting of a row of metal tubes, graduated in length, hung on a frame and struck with a leather-covered hammer.

Tucson 32 15N 110 57W A city and health resort in Arizona. Its growth came with the arrival of the Southern Pacific Railroad (1880) and the discovery of silver at nearby Tombstone. Tucson is an industrial center for the surrounding agricultural and mining district and site of the University of Arizona (1885). Population (1980): 330,537.

Tucumán. *See* San Miguel de Tucumán.

Tudors The ruling dynasty of England from 1485 to 1603. Owen Tudor (c. 1400–61), a Welshman, entered the service of Henry V and married (1422) his widow Catherine of Valois (1401–37). Their eldest son Edmund, Earl of Richmond (c. 1430–56), married Margaret *Beaufort, the great-great-granddaughter of Edward III, and their son became the first Tudor monarch, Henry VII. Subsequent Tudor monarchs were Henry VIII, Edward VI, Mary I, and Elizabeth I.

tuff. *See* pyroclastic rock.

tufted titmouse. *See* tit.

Tu Fu. *See* Du Fu.

Tugela River A river in South Africa, flowing generally E from the Drakensberg Mountains, where it forms the **Tugela Falls**, 2810 ft (856 m) high, to the Indian Ocean. Length: about 312 mi (500 km).

tui A black *honeyeater, *Prosthemadera novaeseelandiae*, occurring in mountain forests of New Zealand. It is about 10.6 in (27 cm) long and has a white tufted throat. Once common, it has been extensively captured for its ability to mimic human speech and is now very rare.

Tula An ancient *Toltec city in central Mexico. Adopted as the Toltec capital around 980 AD, Tula was destroyed in 1168. Distinctive Toltec features here include a terraced pyramid, colonnaded buildings, and extensive use of militaristic motifs in relief sculptures.

Tula 54 11N 37 38E A city in the W central Soviet Union, in the RSFSR 105 mi (169 km) S of Moscow. An important ironworking center since the 17th century, it also has food-processing industries. Tolstoy lived at nearby Yasnaya Polyana. Population (1981 est): 521,000.

tulip A perennial herbaceous plant of the genus *Tulipa* (about 100 species), native to the Old World but widely cultivated for ornament. Growing from bulbs, most tulips have a solitary bell-shaped flower, with bluish-green leaves—ranging from long and narrow to oval and pointed—clustered at the base of the plant. There are nearly 4000 varieties of garden tulips,

which show enormous variation in color and type: the older varieties are descended from *T. gesneriana* and *T. suaveolens*; the newer ones often have *T. kaufmanniana*, *T. greigi*, or *T. fosteriana* as one of the parent species. The Netherlands, the Channel Islands, and Lincolnshire (England) are main commercial growing areas. Family: *Liliaceae*.

tulip tree A tree, *Liriodendron tulipifera*, native to E North America and widely planted for ornament. Reaching a height of 190 ft (58 m) in the wild, it has three-lobed blunt-ended leaves, which turn golden yellow in autumn. The flowers are large and tulip-like, greenish white or yellow, and produce papery cones containing winged fruits. The wood, known as white wood, is used for furniture, plywood, paper, and boxes. The Chinese tulip tree (*L. chinense*) is similar but smaller. Family: *Magnoliaceae*.

Tull, Jethro (1674–1741) English agriculturalist, best known for his invention in 1701 of the seed drill. The drill planted seeds in straight lines, thus facilitating weeding, and automatically covered them with soil to protect them from birds. He made many other innovations in agricultural methods.

Tulsa 36 07N 95 58W A city in Oklahoma, on the Arkansas River. Oil was discovered in 1901 and today over 800 oil companies have established plants here. It has also developed as a port since the opening of a waterway (1971) linking Tulsa to the Gulf of Mexico. Population (1980): 360,919.

Tulsidas (c. 1532–1623) Indian poet. He was a brahmin and lived at Benares. His best-known work is the *Ramcaritmanas* (c. 1574–77), a Hindi version of a Sanskrit epic that advocates devotion to *Rama as a means of salvation. It had a lasting influence throughout N India.

Tulufan Depression (Turpan Depression *or* Turfan Depression) A mountain basin in NW China. Known for its fruit, it was the center of an Indian-Persian civilization (3rd–4th centuries AD). Lowest point: 505 ft (154 m) below sea level.

tumor Any swelling in the body caused by the abnormal proliferation of cells. Tumors that do not spread to other parts of the body (i.e. are noncancerous) are described as benign. They are usually harmless but may become very large, exerting pressure on neighboring tissues: in such cases they are often surgically removed. Tumors that destroy the tissue in which they arise and spread to other parts of the body are described as malignant (*see* cancer).

tuna A carnivorous food and game fish, sometimes called tunny, belonging to a family (*Scombridae*) found in warm seas. Its elongated robust body is generally dark above and silvery below, with a keeled tail base and finlets behind the anal and dorsal fins. The large bluefin tuna (*Thunnus thynnus*) reaches 14 ft (4.3 m) in length. Large quantities of canned tuna are consumed throughout the world. Order: *Perciformes*. *See also* albacore; skipjack; yellowfin tuna. □oceans.

tundra The level, virtually treeless, areas in the N hemisphere (in Eurasia and North America) lying between the most northerly region in which trees grow and the polar regions of perpetual snow and ice. Winters are long and severe with brief summers in which temperatures remain below 50°F (10°C); *permafrost is a feature. Vegetation is able to grow in summer and includes mosses, lichens, dwarf shrubs, herbaceous perennials, and a few stunted trees, such as willows and birches. Through freeze-thaw processes on the ground a variety of patterns can form, such as stone polygons and soil circles.

T'ung-chih. See Tong Zhi.

tung oil (*or* wood oil) A pale-yellow oil obtained from the seeds of the tung tree (*Aleurites fordii*; family *Euphorbiaceae*), found in China. It polymerizes spontaneously (and on heating) to a hard gel and is used in paints and varnishes.

tungsten (*or* wolfram; W) A gray brittle metal with the highest melting point of any element. It was discovered in 1779 and is obtained from the ores wolframite ($FeWO_4$) and scheelite ($CaWO_4$) by reduction with hydrogen or carbon. It oxidizes readily when heated, forming the oxide WO_3. The metal is used extensively as filaments in electric light bulbs, as well as in television tubes, contact breakers, and X-ray tubes. It is also used in many hard alloys for high-speed cutting tools. Tungsten carbide (WC) is very hard and is used for tipping drill bits. At no 74; at wt 183.85; mp 6176 ± 36°F (3410 ± 20°C); bp 10,230°F (5660°C).

Tung-t'ing, Lake. *See* Dongting, Lake.

Tunguska River Three rivers in the Soviet Union, in Siberia comprising tributaries of the Yenisei River. These are the **Lower** (Nizhnyaya) **Tunguska**, 1670 mi (2690 km) long, the **Stony** (Podkammenaya) **Tunguska**, 960 mi (1550 km) long, and the **Upper** (Verkhnyaya) **Tunguska**, the lower course of the Angara River.

tunicate A small marine animal belonging to the subphylum *Urochordata* (or *Tunicata*; about 2000 species). Tunicates are cylindrical, spherical, or irregular in shape, ranging from several millimeters to over 12 in (30 cm) in size. They have a saclike cellulose tunic covering the body; water is drawn in through a siphon at the top and expelled through a second siphon. Food particles are filtered out and propelled along flagellated grooves to the mouth. Individuals are hermaphrodite and produce free-swimming tadpole-like larvae that show the major characteristics of all *Chordates. They subsequently undergo metamorphosis, losing their chordate features and becoming adults. The class *Larvacea* retain their larval characteristics throughout life. Sea squirts (class *Ascidacea*) live attached to rocks, etc., singly or in colonies, while the salps (class *Thaliacea*) float in the sea, sometimes as chains of several hundred individuals.

tuning fork A two-pronged metal fork that vibrates at a fixed frequency when struck. It is used by musicians to verify *pitch. Electrically maintained tuning forks, operated by an electromagnet, are also used in scientific experiments.

Tunis (Arabic name: Tunus) 36 48N 10 13E The capital of Tunisia, on the Gulf of Tunis. It was developed by the Arabs in the 7th century AD. It came under French rule in the late 19th century, and became the capital on independence in 1956. The Islamic university was founded in 1960. Industries include chemicals, lead smelting, and textiles. Population (1976 est): 944,000.

Tunisia, Republic of (Arabic name: al-Jumhuriyah at-Tunisiyah) A small country in N Africa, bordering on the Mediterranean Sea. Its narrow coastal zone, where over half the total population live, extends into desert in the S and rises to uplands in the N. The population is largely Arabic with a Berber minority. *Economy*: predominantly agricultural, the chief products include wheat, olive oil, citrus fruits, dates, and wine; livestock, including sheep, cattle, and goats, is also important. Mining is a major source of revenue and Tunisia is one of the world's largest producers of phosphates. Oil reserves were discovered in 1964 and exploitation began in 1972; iron ore and lead are also mined. Manufacturing industry is based largely on processing the local raw materials and includes oil refining, cement, and steel processing. Fine beaches and notable architecture contribute to Tunisia's popularity with tourists. *History*: first settled by the Phoenicians, it developed into the empire of Carthage and was later absorbed into the Roman Empire, becoming "the granary of Rome." Under the dynasty of the Berber Hafsids (1207–1574) it became powerful. During the 19th century Tunisia's strategic importance aroused European interest and in 1883 it became a French protectorate. It was the scene of fierce fighting in World War II and gained independence from France (1956) following the nationalist agitation of the postwar years. Habib Bourguiba was elected president in 1957 and reelected as life president in 1974. Official religion: Islam. Official language: Arabic; French is widely spoken. Official currency: Tunisian dinar of 1000 millimes. Area: 63,362 sq mi (164,150 sq km). Population (1983 est): 7,020,000. Capital: Tunis.

tunnel effect The passage of an electron or other particle through a potential barrier when, according to classical mechanics, it has insufficient energy to do so. It is explained by *wave mechanics on the basis that the electron is not completely localized in space, part of the energy of the associated wave being able to tunnel through the barrier. The effect has a negligible probability in large-scale systems, but a finite probability in microscopic systems. It is the basis of some radioactive decay processes and is made use of in the **tunnel diode**, a semiconductor device that has a negative resistance over part of its operating range.

tunnels Underground passages for roads, railroads, sewers, or aqueducts for power stations. Tunnels through rock are formed by first drilling holes for explosive, blasting out the rock, removing the debris, and then lining the inside of the tunnel. Tunneling through softer substances requires special techniques: a tunneling shield with a diameter slightly larger than that of the finished tunnel is forced into the ground by hydraulic piston jacks, the earth inside the shield is removed, and the tunnel is then lined, often with concrete sections. *See also* Channel tunnel; Simplon Pass; Mont Blanc.

Tunney, Gene (James Joseph) (1897–1978) US boxer. Although a natural light heavyweight, Tunney defeated heavyweight champion Jack Dempsey in 1926, retaining his title until his retirement from boxing in 1928. Tunney's most famous and controversial title defense came in his 1927 rematch against Dempsey. Known as the "Battle of the Long Count," this bout was highlighted by the referee's delay in beginning the count for a Tunney knockdown until Dempsey went to a neutral corner. Tunney recovered and went on to win the fight.

tunny. *See* tuna.

Tupac Amarú (José Gabriel Condorcanqui; ?1742–81) Peruvian revolutionary. A direct descendant of the last Inca emperor, he led an unsuccessful Indian revolt against Spanish rule in 1780 and was executed. The Tupamaros, the 20th-century South American urban guerrillas, derived their name from his.

Tupi A group of South American Indian peoples and languages including the *Guarani. They are mainly a tropical rainforest people who practice slash and burn agriculture. They also fish in the rivers and off the coast where their villages are located. In some areas, these were fortified against warfare. Cannibalism was common. Culture varied considerably from one region to another. Religion emphasized nature spirits and the "Grandfather Cult," associated with thunder, often led to migrations in search of a promised paradise.

Tupolev, Andrei Niklaievich (1888–1972) Soviet designer of the first supersonic passenger aircraft, the TU-144, tested in 1969. He also designed supersonic bombers, such as the TU-22, and swing-wing bombers. His TU-104, first produced in 1955, was one of the first passenger jet aircraft.

TURACO *The feathers of the white-cheeked turaco* (Tauraco leucotis), *like those of other members of its family, contain a pure-green pigment, turacoverdin (in most birds green is a combination of two pigments—melanin and yellow carotenoid).*

turaco (*or* touraco) A brightly colored arboreal bird belonging to a family (*Musophagidae*; 18 species) occurring in Africa. 13.7–27.5 in (35–70 cm) long, turacos have short rounded wings, a short down-curved bill, and are often crested. Most species have a greenish plumage. They feed on fruit and insects. Order: *Cuculiformes* (cuckoos and turacos).

turbine A device in which a moving fluid drives a wheel or motor, converting the kinetic energy of the fluid into mechanical energy. In its simplest form it is known as a **water wheel**, which has been in use since ancient times to drive mills, pumps, etc. The principle of the water wheel forms the basis of the hydraulic turbine, used in the generation of *hydroelectricity. The most widely used types are the Pelton wheel, patented in 1889 by Lester Allen Pelton (1829–1918), the radial Francis turbine, designed in 1849 by J. B. Francis (1815–92), and the Kaplan turbine, designed by Viktor Kaplan (1876–1937). The Pelton wheel, consisting of a ring of buckets or bucket-shaped vanes arranged around the periphery of a wheel, is known as an impulse turbine as it is only the impulse of the water that makes the wheel turn. The Francis turbine, with its outer ring of stationary guide vanes and inner ring of curved vanes on the surface of one side of the wheel, is a reaction turbine; part of the energy is derived from the impulse of the water and part from the reaction between the water and the blades.
The steam-driven turbine was invented in the 1st century AD by *Hero of Alexandria. However, the first practical turbine to be driven by steam was a reaction device with several rows of turbine wheels (enabling the energy of the expanding steam to be utilized in stages) invented in 1884 by Sir Charles *Parsons. An impulse turbine using several steam nozzles was invented by Carl de Laval (1845–1913) in the 1890s. Since the beginning of the 20th century steam turbines based on these designs have replaced the *steam engine as the prime mover in *power stations. *See also* gas turbine.

turbot A *flatfish, *Scophthalmus maximus*, that occurs off European shores down to 230 ft (70 m) and sometimes in brackish water. It has a broad circular body, up to 40 in (1 m) long, which is usually light- or gray-

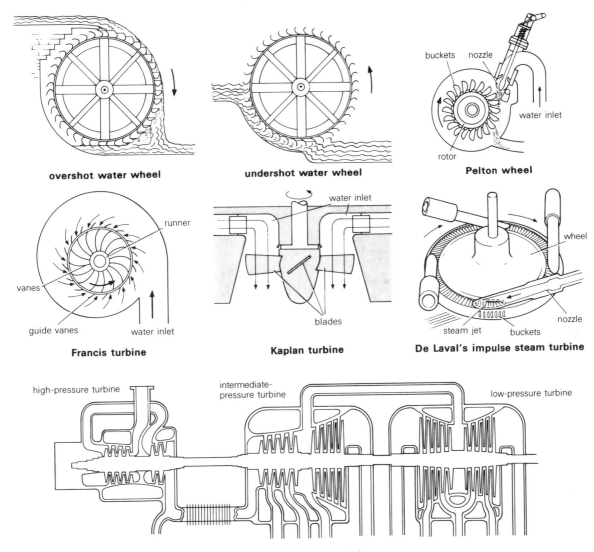

overshot water wheel   undershot water wheel   **Pelton wheel**
buckets   nozzle
water inlet
rotor

runner
vanes
guide vanes   water inlet
Francis turbine

water inlet
blades
Kaplan turbine

wheel
nozzle
steam jet   buckets
De Laval's impulse steam turbine

high-pressure turbine   intermediate-pressure turbine   low-pressure turbine

multistage steam turbine

TURBINE

brown on the upper (left) side and whitish underneath. It is a valuable food fish. Family: *Bothidae*.

turbulence Any random irregularity in the distribution of velocity or pressure in a fluid. Most flows of rivers and winds are turbulent and turbulence in the atmosphere affects aircraft. Turbulence also causes the laminar layers of flow around an irregular object, or a smooth object at high velocities, to be disturbed, creating a sharp increase in drag. It is to avoid turbulent flow that such objects as airfoils are streamlined (*see* streamlining; aerodynamics). In some cases turbulence is desirable; in the combustion chamber of a gasoline or diesel engine the designer seeks to create turbulence to improve mixing of the fuel and air to improve combustion.

Turenne, Henri de la Tour d'Auvergne, Vicomte de (1611–75) French marshal, who made his name in the *Thirty Years' War. At the outbreak (1649) of the rebellion against Mazarin (*see* Fronde) he supported the rebels, who were led by his rival *Condé, but in 1652, after transferring his loyalties to the crown, he received a royal command and by 1653 had brilliantly suppressed the revolt. In 1658, at the battle of the Dunes, he again defeated Condé, who now held a Spanish command. He subsequently fought in the War of *Devolution (1667–68) and the third *Dutch War (1672–75), dying in action at Sasbach. He was much admired by Napoleon.

Turfan Depression. *See* Tulufan Depression.

Turgenev, Ivan (1818–83) Russian novelist. His criticism of the Russian social system in his *Sportsman's Sketches* (1852) led indirectly to his

brief imprisonment and confinement to his family estate at Spasskoye. His later works, of which the best known are the novel *Fathers and Sons* (1862) and the long story *The Torrents of Spring* (1872), are noted for their analysis of intellectual and social trends. He also wrote poetry and plays, notably *A Month in the Country* (1870). A lifelong admirer of western society, he went into self-imposed exile in Baden Baden (1862–70) and Paris (1871–83), where he was befriended by many European writers.

Turgot, Anne Robert Jacques, Baron de l'Aulne (1727–81) French economist, who served under Louis XV and XVI. Educated at the Sorbonne, he was one of the *Physiocrats and an advocate of *laissez-faire. He became comptroller general in 1774. There was great opposition to his reforms, especially the Six Edicts, which included the abolition of forced labor, and he was dismissed in 1776.

Turin (Italian name: Torino) 45 04N 7 40E A city in NW Italy, the capital of Piedmont on the Po River. Dating from Roman times, it was associated with the House of Savoy during the middle ages. It was the first capital (1861–65) of united Italy. Turin has an ancient university (1404), a 15th-century cathedral, a 17th-century palace, and other notable buildings. It is a center of commerce and industry and is important for the production of motor vehicles. Other industries include engineering, publishing, and the manufacture of textiles, paper, and leather goods. Chocolate and wine are also produced. Population (1980 est): 1,143,263.

Turing machine A hypothetical computing machine used to determine whether a particular type of mathematical problem can be solved by a computation procedure (algorithm). It is postulated that the machine has an infinite tape that stores characters in a number of discrete locations. The machine goes through a set procedure of scanning and altering the characters, regarded as a series of active states. If the problem is soluble, the machine finally settles in a passive state, in which the tape contains the solution. The concept was developed in 1936 by Alan Mathison Turing (1912–54) and others and represented an important advance in the theory of computer logic.

Turkana, Lake (name until 1979: Lake Rudolph)   A lake in Kenya and Ethiopia. Fish and birds abound here and, since it has no outlet, it has become increasingly saline through evaporation. Significant fossil finds have been made here by Richard Leakey. Area: about 2473 sq mi (6405 sq km).

turkey   A large terrestrial bird belonging to a family (*Meleagrididae*; 2 species) native to North and Central American woodlands. Wild turkeys reach 50 in (130 cm) in length and have green-bronze plumage, a warty red neck, and a long fleshy bill ornament and throat wattle. They feed on seeds and insects. The common turkey (*Meleagra gallopavo*) was first domesticated by Mexican Indians and is now raised on large farms for meat. Order: *Galliformes* (pheasants, turkeys, etc.).

Turkey, Republic of   A country in the Middle East. The large Asian area, Anatolia, lies between the Mediterranean Sea and the Black Sea. The small European area, Thrace, is bordered by Greece and Bulgaria. Anatolia consists of a central plateau surrounded by mountains, the Pontic Mountains in the N and the *Taurus Mountains in the S. The plateau is semiarid and contains several shallow salt lakes. The high E range contains Mount *Ararat. The coastal areas are the most populous. Minority population groups include Kurds, Arabs, Greeks, Circassians, Georgians, Armenians, Lazes, and Jews; 98% of the population is Muslim. *Economy*: mainly agricultural. Wheat, barley, sugar beet, potatoes, and rice are grown in the interior, and cotton, tobacco, and citrus fruit are grown for export around the coast. Cattle, sheep, and goats are kept for skins, wool, and mohair, which are exported. Copper, chromium, borax, coal, bauxite, and oil are produced, although minerals are not greatly exploited. The main industries are steel, cement, textiles, and fertilizers. Machinery, chemicals, and metals are imported, chiefly from W Europe and the US. Turkey is an associate member of the EEC. Many Turks work in Europe, mainly West Germany, for long periods at a time. *History*: Anatolia, formerly known as *Asia Minor, was dominated by the *Seljuqs (1055–1243) and later became the core of the *Ottoman Empire (c. 1300–1922). Under Kemal *Atatürk, who ruled as a virtual dictator, the new Republic of Turkey (declared 1923) was rapidly westernized; religious orders were abolished and Islam was disestablished; polygamy was forbidden and women were enfranchised; the Arabic alphabet was replaced by the Roman; and relations with W Europe became closer. Economic problems were tackled by the establishment of new industries under state ownership. After the death of Kemal (1938) and World War II, in which Turkey was neutral until finally siding with the Allies in 1945, it became less stable politically, although more democratic. The Democratic Party, previously in opposition, came to power in 1950 but grew increasingly reactionary; unrest increased until a military coup took place in 1960. The army again intervened in 1971, when martial law was imposed (until 1973). Violence has continued with clashes between left- and right-wing students, and trouble also between Kurds and Turks and between Sunni and Shiite Muslims. Economic difficulties continued during the 1970s and early 1980s with rapid inflation, a large trade deficit, high unemployment, and a reduction in the amount of money sent home by Turks abroad. Relations with Greece have been a further problem; apart from rivalry over Cyprus, which almost resulted in war in 1974, when the island was invaded by Turkish troops, there has also been friction (1976) over Turkey's exploration for oil in the Aegean Sea. A military coup in 1980, led by Gen Kenan Evren (1913–   ), overthrew the government of Suleiman Demeril (1924–   ). Evren assumed the powers of head of state and a new constitution was introduced in 1982. Turgut Ozal (1927–   ) was returned as prime minister following elections held in 1983. Official language: Turkish; Kurdish and Arabic are also spoken. Official currency: Turkish lira of 100 kurus. Area: 330,883 sq mi (779,452 sq km). Population (1983): 49,155,000. Capital: Ankara.

Turkic languages   A group of languages of the *Altaic language family, related to *Mongolian and *Manchu-Tungus. Spoken by more than 66 million people, the languages are spread over a geographical area extending from Turkey to Siberia. Originally written in the Arabic script in the 9th century, the languages are now written in the *Cyrillic alphabet in the Soviet Union and in Latin script in Turkey. Phonological processes are characterized by vowel harmony and morphological processes by agglutination.

Turkish   A *Turkic language, spoken mainly in Turkey. Since 1929 it has been written in a modified Latin alphabet, replacing Arabic script. Its grammatical system is based on the use of suffixes.

Turkish cat   A breed of long-haired cat originating from Turkey. They have long sturdy bodies, chalk-white coats with auburn markings on the face and an auburn tail, and amber-colored eyes. Unusually for cats, they are fond of swimming.

Turkistan (*or* Turkestan)   A region of central Asia, now comprising the Xinjiang Uygur AR of the People's Republic of China and the Kazakh, Turkmen, Tadzhik, Kirghiz, and Uzbek SSRs of the Soviet Union. A historic route of travel, migration, and invasion between Asia and Europe, Turkistan has come under many different rulers. The W has been ruled by the Persians from the 6th century BC, Islam from the 7th century AD, and the Russians from the 18th century; the E was long disputed between Chinese dynasties and nomadic tribes.

Turkmen (*or* Turkoman)   A people of SW Asia speaking a language that is part of the *Turkic language group. The majority live as settled farmers in the Turkmen SSR, but groups in Iran, Afghanistan, E Turkey, N Syria, and N Iraq retain their traditional nomadic existence. Rug making is still an important craft. Their main social division is between those engaged in agriculture and the more prestigious livestock farming. They are Sunni Muslims.

Turkmen Soviet Socialist Republic (*or* Turkmenistan)   A constituent republic in the S Soviet Union. Some 90% of Turkmenistan comprises desert, including the *Kara Kum, and most of the population (66% of which comprises *Turkmen) are concentrated in oases. The principal occupation is agriculture, mainly cotton, wool, and Karakul pelts. Turkmenistan (founded in 1925) is rich in minerals, including oil and natural gas, and industry is being developed, especially chemicals, textiles, and food. Area: 186,400 sq mi (488,100 sq km). Population (1981 est): 2,900,000. Capital: Ashkhabad.

Turks and Caicos Islands   A British crown colony consisting of a series of over 30 islands in the Atlantic Ocean, to the SE of the Bahamas. The most important are Grand Turk, Grand Caicos, and Salt Cay. Most of the inhabitants are of African descent. *Economy*: mainly based on fishing, with exports of conchs, conch shells, crawfish, salt, and fishmeal. Tourism is being developed. *History*: the islands were discovered by the Spanish in 1512, but remained uninhabited until 1678, when a Bermudan salt-panning industry was set up. A dependency of Jamaica (1874–1959), they became a crown colony after the dissolution of the Federation of the West Indies in 1962, and gained internal self-government in 1976. Official language: English. Official currency: US dollar of 100 cents. Area: 192 sq mi (430 sq km). Population (1980): 7436. Capital: Grand Turk.

Turku (Swedish name: Åbo)   60 27N 22 15E A seaport and third largest city in Finland, on the Gulf of Bothnia. Capital of Finland until 1812, it has Finnish (1920) and Swedish (1917) universities. Its industries include shipbuilding, saw milling, and engineering. Population (1980): 163,680.

turmeric   A perennial herbaceous plant, *Curcuma longa*, native to S India and Indonesia and cultivated for its underground rhizomes. It has narrow leaves, 12–18 in (30–45 cm) long, and bears yellow flowers in dense heads, 4–7 in (10–18 cm) long. The rhizomes are boiled and dried in the sun for 5–7 days, then polished and usually sold in ground form. Turmeric is used as a spice in curries, etc., and as a yellow dye. Family: *Zingiberaceae*.

Turner, Frederick Jackson (1861–1932) US historian. A history professor at the University of Wisconsin (1891–1910) and Harvard University (1910–24), he developed the "frontier thesis" as a way of interpreting history. He maintained that Americans were the way they were because of their pioneering way of life for the previous 300 years. His theories, which greatly influenced the teaching of history through the 1930s, were outlined in many books, including *The Significance of History* (1891), *The Significance of the Frontier in American History* (1920), and *The Significance of Sections in American History* (1932; Pulitzer Prize, 1933).

Turner, Joseph Mallord William (1775–1851) British landscape and marine painter, born in London, the son of a barber. After studying at the Royal Academy schools and painting many topographical watercolors, he achieved success in the late 1790s with his first landscapes in oil. In 1809 he made the first of several continental tours, which were to provide him with such scenic subjects as the Alps, Venice, and Rome. While supervising the publication of his *Liber Studiorum* (1807–19), a series of engravings based on his works, his style evolved from the Dutch landscape tradition and the classicism of the landscapists *Poussin and *Claude Lorraine into a roman-

TURNER   Peace: Burial at Sea *(1842), oil painting showing the artist's fascination with light.*

tic vision of color, light, and weather anticipating French *impressionism. This vision becomes the real subject of such late paintings as *Rain, Steam, and Speed* (National Gallery, London) and *Interior at Petworth* (Tate Gallery). He bequeathed most of his works to the nation.

Turner, Nat (1800–31) US slave, who led the only substantial US slave revolt. Believing himself to be a divine instrument, he instigated the so-called **Southampton Insurrection,** an attempt by 75 slaves to capture a Virginia armory. More than 50 whites were killed before Turner and many of the rebels were captured and executed. Resulting uneasiness in the South led to repressive antislave legislation.

turnip A biennial plant, *Brassica rapa*, probably native to Asia and widely cultivated for its thick fleshy root, which is used as a vegetable. An erect branching stem, up to 40 in (1 m) high, grows out of the basal leaf rosette in the plant's second season and produces clusters of bright-yellow flowers. However, turnips are usually harvested in the first season. Family: *Cruciferae.*

turnstone A small *plover, *Arenaria interpres*, that breeds around Arctic coasts and migrates to the S hemisphere to winter. 8 in (20 cm) long, it has a black-and-brown upper plumage, becoming tortoiseshell in summer, and white underparts. Turnstones have short black bills used to turn over pebbles and shells in search of mollusks, small fish, and sandhoppers.

turpentine An oily liquid extracted from pine resin. Its main constituent is pinene ($C_{10}H_{16}$); it is used as a solvent for paints.

turpentine tree One of several trees yielding a viscous resin. The Australian turpentine tree (*Syncarpia glomuliferae*) grows to a height of about 150 ft (45 m) and has deeply furrowed bark. The timber, which is durable and resistant to fire and wood-boring *shipworms, is used to construct piers, ships, etc. The brush turpentine tree (*S. leptopetala*) is smaller. Family: *Myrtaceae.*

The tropical African tree *Copaifera mopane* (family *Leguminosae*) is also called turpentine tree.

Turpin, Dick (1706–39) British highwayman. He was hanged at York for murder and horse stealing. The story of his ride from London to York on his horse Black Bess, popularized in Harrison Ainsworth's novel *Rookwood* (1834), is probably based on a much older legend.

turquoise An opaque greenish-blue mineral used as a gem. It consists of a basic aluminum phosphate, traces of copper providing the color. Fine specimens have been found in Iran. Birthstone for December.

turtle An aquatic reptile belonging to the order *Chelonia, which also includes *tortoises and *terrapins. 4–80 in (10–200 cm) long, turtles have broad paddle-like flippers and a streamlined shell and occur in most seas, often migrating long distances to lay eggs on traditional nesting beaches.

They are graceful and swift swimmers but clumsy on land. Their diet consists of worms, snails, crustaceans, and fish. Some turtles live in fresh water. *See also* green turtle; leatherback turtle; snake-necked turtle; soft-shelled turtle.

turtle dove A small slender dove, *Streptopelia turtur*, occurring in S Europe and N Africa, visiting N Europe in the summer. 10 in (26 cm) long, it has a checkered red-brown back, gray wings, a pink breast, a black-and-white striped neck patch, and a long white-tipped tail. It feeds on seeds. Family: *Columbidae* (pigeons).

Tuscaloosa 33 13N 87 33W A city in W central Alabama, on the Black Warrior River, SW of Birmingham. The University of Alabama (1831) is here. Settled in 1809 as Tuscaloosa, an Indian word for "black warrior," it served as the state capital (1826–46). Industries include chemical, rubber, lumber, and cottonseed products, paper, and metal pipes. Population (1980): 75,211.

Tuscan order. *See* orders of architecture.

Tuscany (Italian name: Toscana) A region in N central Italy, consisting mainly of hills and mountains with coastal lowlands in the W. It is a predominantly agricultural region producing cereals, wines (Chianti), olives, and fruit. The major manufacturing industries are iron, steel, and shipbuilding. The most important mining region in Italy, it produces lignite, iron, mercury, salt, borax, and marble. Florence is an important tourist and cultural center. Area: 8876 sq mi (22,989 sq km). Population (1980 est): 3,602,684. Capital: Florence.

Tuscarora War (1711–13) Series of battles between US colonists and the Tuscarora Indians over continuing encroachment by the settlers upon Indian lands and the capturing and selling of young Indians as slaves. Militias from North Carolina, South Carolina, and Virginia finally defeated the Tuscarora, who had attacked the settlers; the Indians relocated to W Pennsylvania and joined the Iroquois League (*see* Iroquois).

Tusculum An ancient city of central Italy, near modern Frascati. A rival of *Rome before about 480 BC but later a staunch ally, Tusculum was granted Roman citizenship in 381 BC. In the 1st century BC Tusculum became a fashionable resort: *Lucullus, *Maecenas, and *Cicero owned villas nearby.

Tuskegee Institute A private coeducational nonsectarian university in Tuskegee, Alabama. It was founded (1881) as the Tuskegee Normal and Industrial Institute for training black teachers by Booker T. *Washington, who was its president until 1915. It became Tuskegee Institute in 1937 and by 1943 offered graduate studies. It contains an extensive library, with special concentration on information pertaining to blacks, and houses the George Washington *Carver Museum.

tusk shell A marine *mollusk of the class *Scaphopoda* (about 200 species), also called tooth shell. The common tusk shell (*Dentalium entale*) grows to 2 in (5 cm); its shell is tusk-shaped and open at both ends and it lives partly buried in sand. The mollusk has a digging foot and tentacles around the mouth for collecting microscopic plants and animals. It has no head or gills.

Tussaud, Marie (Marie Grosholtz; 1761–1850) French wax modeler, who went to London in 1802 and founded the famous waxworks museum there. She had previously worked as tutor to Louis XVI's sister and had been imprisoned during the French Revolution.

tussock moth A moth belonging to the family *Lymantriidae*, occurring in both the Old and New Worlds and including the vaporers, tussocks, and *gypsy moths. The caterpillars, cocoons, and adults are typically hairy, frequently causing skin irritation and swelling if handled. Some can be economic pests. Hairs of the caterpillar are arranged in tufts or tussocks.

Tutankhamen King of Egypt (c. 1361–1352 BC) of the 18th dynasty. Tutankhamen, perhaps Akhenaton's son, became king at the age of 11 after the brief reign of *Akhenaton's immediate successor. He abandoned Akhenaton's worship of the sun-god Aton, reinstating that of *Amon and transferring the capital once more to Thebes. His splendid and elaborate tomb, discovered by Howard *Carter in 1922, is the only Egyptian royal tomb to remain substantially intact to modern times. The beauty and craftsmanship of its contents have continued to fascinate the world. □Osiris.

Tutu, Desmond (Bishop) (1931–) South African clergyman; Nobel Peace Prize (1984). A member of the Anglican Church, he attended a teachers' college where he was strongly influenced by Bishop Trevor Huddleston, an outspoken opponent of apartheid. Tutu left teaching and was ordained a minister in 1960. By 1975 he became Anglican Dean of Johannesburg and, in 1978, General Secretary of the South African Council of

Churches, which has a membership of 12 million. He was the first black to achieve either position. He continued to express his opposition to apartheid and worked to eliminate segregation.

Tutuola, Amos (1920–) Nigerian writer. Drawing on Yoruba tribal myths and legends, he created vivid fantasies in which the real and the supernatural coexist. His works include *The Palm-Wine Drunkard* (1952) and the short-story collection *Feather Woman of the Jungle* (1962).

Tuva Autonomous Soviet Socialist Republic (*or* Tuvinian ASSR) An administrative division in the S Soviet Union, in the RSFSR. The region is mostly mountainous. Some 50% of the population comprise Tuvinians, a Turkic-speaking people, who are mainly herdsmen and cattle farmers. Industry is rapidly developing. Area: 65,800 sq mi (170,500 sq km). Population (1981 est): 269,000. Capital: Kizyl.

Tuvalu, State of (name until 1976: Ellice Islands) A small country in the SW Pacific Ocean. It consists of a group of nine islands, the main one being Funafuti. Most of the population is Polynesian. *Economy*: subsistence agriculture and fishing are the chief occupations. The main export is copra. *History*: formerly part of the Gilbert and Ellice Islands colony, it became a separate colony after a referendum in 1974 and gained independence in 1978. Tuvalu is a member of the Commonwealth of Nations. Prime minister: Dr Tomasi Puapua. Official language: Tuvalu. Official currency: Australian dollar of 100 cents. Area: 9.5 sq mi (24 sq km). Population (1983): 8000. Capital: Funafuti.

Tver. *See* Kalinin.

MARK TWAIN *Author whose best known works,* Tom Sawyer *and* Huckleberry Finn, *tell of boyhood on the Mississippi river.*

Twain, Mark (pen name of Samuel Langhorne Clemens; 1835–1910) US journalist and novelist. Early in his career, Mark Twain worked as a steamboat pilot on the Mississippi River and later settled in California, where he became a newspaper reporter. A skillful short story writer, he first gained a national reputation with "The Celebrated Jumping Frog of Calaveras County" (1865), a humorous tale of life in the Far West. Twain later served as a foreign correspondent, collecting his colorful travel experiences in *The Innocents Abroad* (1869). Returning to the US, he began to lecture widely.

His most famous novels, written after his retirement from journalism in 1871, portray characters drawn from his childhood in Missouri. They include *The Adventures of Tom Sawyer* (1872), *Life on the Mississippi* (1883), *The Adventures of Huckleberry Finn* (1884), and *The Tragedy of Pudd'nhead Wilson* (1894). In a completely different vein are his historical novels, *The Prince and the Pauper* (1882) and *A Connecticut Yankee in King Arthur's Court* (1889). Mark Twain's dry idiomatic wit had a lasting effect on the American literary scene. Late in life, however, suffering from the tragedies of the sudden deaths of his wife and daughter, Mark Twain became embittered and his last works, *What is Man?* (1906) and *The Mysterious Stranger* (1916) reflected his deep pessimism. His personal memoir, *Mark Twain's Autobiography*, was published in 1924.

twayblade The most common European orchid, *Listera ovata*, which grows in damp woods, meadows, etc. Up to 24 in (60 cm) high, it has a pair of rounded leaves situated about halfway down the stem. The flowering stalk, which is sticky with glands, carries a long narrow head of small greenish flowers.

tweed A woolen fabric, more closely woven than *cheviot. Hardwearing, often with a roughened surface texture, tweed is manufactured in various weave patterns, such as checks, stripes, flecks, and herringbones. Coats, skirts, and suits are made from famous traditional tweeds, such as Harris and Donegal cloth. It derives its name from "tweel" a Scottish word for *twill.

Tweed, William Marcy (1823–78) US politician. He entered politics as a Democrat in the 1850s and by 1861 he was considered head of *Tammany Hall, the Democratic organization that, at the time, controlled New York City's government. Called "Boss" Tweed, his "ring" members made inroads into all phases of city—and state—government. Corruption and plunder of taxpayers' money was rampant, and in 1873 Tweed, then a multimillionaire, was convicted of fraud. He jumped bail and fled to Spain (1875), but was arrested and returned to New York (1876), where he spent the rest of his life in jail.

Tweed River A river in SE Scotland and NE England. Flowing E from the Tweedsmuir Hills to the North Sea at Berwick, it forms part of the border between England and Scotland. Length: 97 mi (156 km).

Twelfth Day. *See* Epiphany.

Twelve Tables (450 BC) The earliest codification of *Roman law, in full known as the Law of the Twelve Tables (*Lex duodecim tabularum*). The laws were engraved on bronze tablets, which were permanently displayed in public. None of the original text survives, although fragments have been preserved in quotations. The tablets dealt with (1) proceedings preliminary to trial; (2) trial; (3) enforcing judgments; (4) rights of fathers; (5) inheritance; (6) ownership of property; (7) land law; (8) *trusts; (9) public law; (10) sacred law (burials etc.); (11 and 12) supplementary matters.

twelve-tone music. *See* serialism.

twill Any woven fabric with a diagonal rib, produced by varying the regular weave of plain cloth (*see* weaving); herringbone is a common variation. Twilled fabrics are much used for making suits and pants. *See also* tweed.

twins Two individuals born from the same pregnancy: 1 out of every 83 human pregnancies results in twins. Identical twins are produced when a fertilized egg splits in two and develops as two fetuses of the same sex; identical twins are very difficult to tell apart and they usually have a great emotional affinity for each other. More commonly, nonidentical (or fraternal) twins are produced when two eggs are fertilized at the same time; they may be of different sexes and are no more alike than other siblings. *See also* Siamese twins.

Tyche A Greek goddess personifying fortune, daughter of Oceanus or Zeus and Tethys. She is identical with the Roman *Fortuna.

Tyler, John (1790–1862) US statesman; 10th President of the United States (1841–45). A planter from Virginia, Tyler began his political career as a state legislator (1811–16), US congressman (1817–21), governor of Virginia (1825–27), and as US senator (1827–36). Initially a strong supporter of President Andrew *Jackson, Tyler split with him over the *Bank of the United States controversy and joined the Whig Party. In 1840 he received the Whig vice-presidential nomination, joining William Henry *Harrison in the successful campaign that became famous for its slogan, "Tippecanoe and Tyler Too." Harrison's sudden death only a month after taking office brought Tyler to the presidency. The most significant achievement of his single term in office was the annexation of Texas to the US in 1844. Tyler was not renominated by the Whig Party and retired to private life. At the outbreak of the *Civil War, he supported the cause of the Confederacy and was elected to the Confederate Congress, but died before it convened.

Tyler, Wat (d. 1381) English rebel, who led the Kentish peasants during the *Peasants' Revolt (1381). He was the peasants' most influential spokesman until his murder during negotiations with Richard II.

Tylor, Sir Edward Burnett (1832–1917) British anthropologist. The first professor of anthropology at Oxford (1896) and the foremost 19th-century British anthropologist, Tylor developed his interest in the subject when he visited Mexico with the US ethnologist Henry Chrysty. His *Primitive Culture: Researches into the Development of Mythology, Philosophy, Religion, Language, Art, and Custom* (1871) became the standard English-language work on anthropology.

Tyndale, William (c. 1494–1536) English biblical translator. His influential translation of the New Testament, begun at Cologne in 1525 and completed at Worms, was a major source of the later Authorized or King James Version. In 1520 he published a translation of the Pentateuch. Accused of heresy, he was taken by imperial officers at Antwerp in 1535 and strangled and burned at Vilvorde, Belgium.

Tyndall, John (1820–93) Irish physicist, who in 1869 discovered the scattering of light by microscopic particles, such as those in dust and colloids (**Tyndall effect**). He used this effect to explain the blue of the sky and was also the first to demonstrate that the air contains microorganisms, which helped to refute the theory of spontaneous generation of fungi, etc.

Tyne River A river in N England. Flowing E from the SW Cheviot Hills to the North Sea at Tynemouth, it passes through Newcastle, Gateshead, and Jarrow. Length: 30 mi (48 km).

Tyne and Wear A metropolitan county of NE England, created in 1974 from SE Northumberland and NE Durham. It comprises the districts of Newcastle-upon-Tyne, North Tyneside, Gateshead, South Tyneside, and Sunderland. It was the first major industrial region in Great Britain, developing long before the industrial revolution. Industries grew up along the Tyne River allied to the large coalfields. In the 19th century most of the region became industrialized; the development of the shipyards was especially important. During the Depression of the 1930s it suffered severely due to its dependence on heavy industry. The whole county is now designated a special development area. Area: 208 sq mi (540 sq km). Population (1981): 1,143,245. Administrative center: Newcastle upon Tyne.

Tynemouth 55 01N 1 24W A city in NE England, in Tyne and Wear at the mouth of the Tyne River. It includes the port of North Shields and is itself a resort. Population (1981): 60,022.

typesetting The process by which type is assembled for *printing. Until the 15th century, type was cut or engraved, a page at a time, in blocks of wood or metal; with **movable type**, invented by *Gutenberg, each character is cast on a separate piece of metal for assembling by hand and is reusable. This was the only method available until 1884 when the American Ottmar Mergenthaler (1854–99) invented the **Linotype** machine, on which the compositor operates a keyboard to assemble character matrices from a magazine; when a line is complete, molten *type metal is pumped into the matrices to form a solid line of type. The **Monotype** system, invented in 1885 by the American Tolbert Lanson (1844–1913), comprises separate keyboard and casting machines: as the compositor operates the keyboard, a punched paper tape is produced; when this is fed through the caster, the punched codes select characters in a matrix into which type metal is pumped to form individual pieces of type, which are accumulated, in the correct sequence, in a tray. Since the 1950s **phototypesetting** (photosetting *or* filmsetting) machines have revolutionized printing. Instead of casting type from hot metal, they create images of characters on photographic paper or film, which is then used for *platemaking. The compositor operates a keyboard to produce a punched paper tape or magnetic tape, which then drives the phototypesetter. Some machines flash light through an actual negative image of each character onto the paper or film; others build up its shape with tiny dots of light from a *cathode-ray tube controlled by a computer memory. The latter kind can set 20,000 or more characters per second.

typewriter A hand-operated machine for producing printed symbols. The first machine was invented in the US in 1867 but the commercial success of the typewriter began in 1874 with the machines produced by the arms manufacturers Remington and Sons. With minor modifications this design, with the paper held in a moving platen, remained the basis of the typewriter until the advent of electric golf-ball machines, with a stationary platen, in the early 1960s. These golf balls consist of spheres carrying the

type in circles around their surface—they are easily replaced to provide additional typefaces (e.g. italic) or symbols (e.g. mathematical). More sophisticated machines are now available providing, in conjunction with a microcomputer, proportional spacing, justification, and word processing.

typhoid fever An infectious disease of the digestive tract caused by the bacterium *Salmonella typhi*. This disease (and paratyphoid fever) are usually contracted by drinking infected water and occur predominantly in places without a clean water supply. The symptoms, which begin 10–14 days after ingesting the bacterium, include fever, headache, cough, loss of appetite, and constipation; a characteristic red rash may appear. If untreated, the patient may develop bowel hemorrhage or perforations. Treatment is by administration of fluids and the antibiotic chloramphenicol. A vaccine provides temporary immunity.

Typhon In Greek mythology, a monster with a hundred heads, the son of Tartarus and Gaea. He was conquered by Zeus and buried under a volcano, usually identified as Mount Etna. His monstrous children included the *Chimera, the *Hydra, and *Cerberus.

typhoon A tropical cyclone or *hurricane with winds above force 12 on the *Beaufort scale occurring in the China Sea and the W Pacific Ocean. The name is derived from a Chinese word meaning great wind.

typhus An infection caused by certain bacteria-like microorganisms (*see* rickettsia), which are transmitted to man by lice, fleas, mites, or ticks. There are many different forms of typhus, caused by different species of rickettsiae, but they share the symptoms of fever, headache, pains in muscles and joints, delirium, and a rash. These symptoms may be very mild throughout the disease. Treatment is with tetracycline antibiotics or chloramphenicol. Epidemic (or classical) typhus is carried by lice and was formerly very prevalent in overcrowded unhygienic conditions, with a high mortality rate. A vaccine against it is now available.

typography 1. The art of *printing from movable type. 2. The aspect of printing concerned with the design and composition of printing type. Early typefaces, which imitated handwriting, belonged to three main groups: gothic (or black-letter), used by N European printers such as *Gutenberg and *Caxton; roman, introduced at Venice about 1470; and *italic, also Venetian, first used in 1501 (*see* incunabula). Holland dominated type-founding for most of the 16th and 17th centuries but England produced two outstanding typographers in the 18th century: William Caslon (1692–1766) and John Baskerville (1706–75). Between 1800 and 1850 the so-called modern-face type designs predominated; they differed from the preceding old-face designs by their pronouncedly upright appearance and horizontal serifs (short finishing strokes on the ends of the main lines of letters). Sanserif (i.e. without serifs) typefaces originated in early 19th-century designs but only came into their own in the 1920s and 1930s through the work of the German *Bauhaus typographers. In England, William *Morris revitalized book design at the end of the 19th century, producing several handsome typefaces for his Kelmscott Press. Influential 20th-century typographers include the Dutchman Jan van Krimpen, the Englishmen Eric Gill and Stanley Morison, and the American F. W. Goudy.

Tyr (*or*, in Old English, Tiw) In Teutonic mythology, the god of war; with *Odin and *Thor, he is one of the three main Germanic gods. His name is linguistically related to *Zeus* (although Latin writers, beginning with Tacitus, identified him with Mars) and survives in *Tuesday*.

Tyrannosaurus A huge bipedal dinosaur that lived in North America during the late Cretaceous period (about 100–65 million years ago). This animal was 50 ft (15 m) long, stood 20 ft (6.5 m) tall, and weighed up to 10 tons. It had a massive body with a short thick neck supporting a large head, large muscular hind limbs with clawed feet, and tiny fore legs. It was a carnivore with long dagger-like teeth but was probably quite rare and fed infrequently. Order: *Saurischia*.

tyrant In antiquity, a ruler who obtained absolute power without election or right of succession. In the Greek city states tyrants were often leading members of oligarchies who obtained popular support. Generally they ruled benevolently, conforming to established institutions, and were often significant patrons of the arts. Famous tyrants include *Aristagoras of Miletus, *Agathocles and *Dionysius I of Syracuse, *Phalaris of Agrigento, *Pisistratus of Athens, and *Polycrates of Samos.

tyrant flycatcher A passerine bird belonging to the New World family *Tyrannidae* (365 species), ranging from 3.5–10.6 in (9–27 cm) in length, often with a long tail, and generally gray, brown, or olive-colored with paler underparts. They are typically arboreal and dart out from a perch to seize flying insects. Tyrant flycatchers are very aggressive and will attack large birds that enter their breeding territories. *Compare* flycatcher.

Tyre (modern name: Sur) 33 12N 35 11E A port in SW Lebanon, on the Mediterranean Sea. It was important to the Phoenicians for several centuries and was taken by Alexander the Great after a seven-month siege in 322 BC and by the Romans in 68 BC. The city was long held by the Crusaders but fell to Muslim forces in 1291. Population (1978 est): 14,000.

Tyrol. *See* Tirol.

Tyrone A county of W Northern Ireland, bordering on the Republic of Ireland. It is predominantly hilly descending in the E to Lough Neagh. Agriculture is important with cattle and sheep farming and the production of barley, potatoes, flax, and turnips. Small-scale manufacturing is carried out in the larger towns. Area: 1260 sq mi (3263 sq km). Population (1971): 139,073. County town: Omagh.

Tyumen 57 11N 65 29E A port in the central Soviet Union, in the RSFSR on the Tura River. It serves as a transport center for the oil and natural gas that are mined nearby. Population (1981 est): 378,000.

Tzu-ch'eng. *See* Zibo.

Tz'u-hsi. *See* Zi Xi.

Tzu-po. *See* Zibo.

U

Ubangi-Shari. *See* Central African Republic.

Uccello, Paolo (P. di Dono; 1397–1475) Florentine painter and craftsman. He trained in the *Ghiberti workshop. From 1425 to 1431 he worked in St Mark's, Venice, as master mosaicist. His frescoes for Sta Maria Novella, Florence, include the famous *Flood*, which shows his preoccupation with perspective and foreshortening. In the three paintings of the battle of San Romano, commissioned by the Medici, he combines a geometric structure with the rich decoration of the *international gothic style.

Udaipur 24 36N 73 47E A city in India, in Rajasthan. Formerly the capital of Udaipur (*or* Mewar) princely state, its lake contains an island with a marble palace. Udaipur has chemical, asbestos, and zinc-smelting industries and a university (1962). Population (1971): 161,278.

Udall, Nicholas (1505–56) English dramatist. He was headmaster of Eton College and later of Westminster School. *Ralph Roister Doister* (c. 1553), influenced by classical Roman drama and probably written for his pupils, was the first full-length English comedy.

Udine 46 04N 13 14E A city in NE Italy, in Friuli-Venezia Giulia. It was partially damaged in an earthquake in 1976. There are textile and leather industries. Population (1980 est): 102,408.

Udmurt Autonomous Soviet Socialist Republic (*or* Udmurtia) An administrative division in the W central Soviet Union, in the RSFSR. The Udmurts, comprising about 50% of the population, speak a Finno-Ugric language. The region has rich oil, shale, timber, and peat resources and manufactures locomotives, machine tools, and other engineering products. Cereals, flax, and some vegetables are grown. Area: 16,250 sq mi (42,100 sq km). Population (1981 est): 1,516,000. Capital: Izhevsk.

Ufa 54 45N 55 58E A city in the W central Soviet Union, the capital of the Bashkir ASSR in the RSFSR. Situated in the Ural Mountains, it has oil refineries and a large chemical industry; its university was founded in 1957. Population (1981 est): 1,009,000.

Uffizi An art gallery in Florence, containing the art treasures of the Medici. Built by *Vasari in the 16th century to house government offices, the Uffizi was opened as a museum in 1765. The major part of its collection comprises Italian Renaissance paintings, although it also includes sculpture and Flemish, Dutch, German, and French paintings.

UFOs. *See* unidentified flying objects.

Uganda, Republic of A landlocked country in East Africa. It consists chiefly of a high plateau rising to mountains, including the Ruwenzori Mountains in the W and Mount Elgon in the E, and a considerable proportion of the total area is occupied by lakes, notably Lake Victoria. The majority of the population is African, especially *Ganda, with dwindling minorities of Europeans and Asians. *Economy*: chiefly agricultural, the main food crops being maize, millet, yams, and other tropical plants. Cash crops include coffee (the main export), tea, tobacco, and cotton; livestock is also important. There has been an increase in forestry production, almost

all hardwood. Uganda's freshwater fishing industry is one of the largest in the world, and fish farming is being developed. The chief mineral resource is copper, much of which is exported to Japan. Hydroelectricity is a valuable source of power and there is some industry, including food processing, textiles, and cement. *History*: the area was dominated by the kingdom of *Buganda from the 18th to the late 19th centuries, becoming a British protectorate in 1894. It became an independent state within the British Commonwealth in 1962 and the following year a republic was established with *Obote as prime minister. In 1971 the government was overthrown in a military coup that brought General Idi *Amin to power. His repressive regime was overthrown in April, 1979, by Ugandan exiles aided by Tanzanian troops. The subsequent provisional government was headed by Yusuf Lule (1912–85) until June, 1979. A military coup in 1980 overthrew his successor, Godfrey Binaisa (1920–), and Obote was re-elected president. Battling for control of the government by opposition groups, which included several of the former political heads (who denied contact with Amin), followed Obote's assumption of the presidency. A gradual restoration of stability and repair of the devastations inflicted by the Amin regime were apparent as the new government maintained control in the early 1980s. Official language: English; Swahili is widely spoken and the most important local language is Luganda. Official currency, since 1967: Ugandan shilling of 100 cents. Area: 91,343 sq mi (236,860 sq km). Population (1983 est): 13,819,000. Capital: Kampala.

Ugarit An ancient town on the Syrian coast (now Ras Shamra). Repeatedly destroyed and rebuilt from Neolithic times, Ugarit became a great international port between 1500 BC and its ultimate destruction about 1200. Pottery, carvings, and diplomatic correspondence recovered here bear witness to strong Mycenaean, Hittite, and Egyptian links. There were temples to *Baal and his father Dagon, and a set of religious texts, written in a type of alphabetic *cuneiform unique to Ugarit, throw light on religious cults in ancient *Canaan.

ugli A hybrid cross between a *grapefruit and a *tangerine. The fruit resembles a small grapefruit with brownish-yellow warty skin and orange-colored flesh. It is grown in the West Indies.

Uhland, (Johann) Ludwig (1787–1862) German poet. A lawyer, he was also an active democrat. He collected folk songs, wrote historical dramas, and is noted for his popular ballads.

Ujjain 23 11N 75 50E A city in India, in Madhya Pradesh. An ancient city, it lay on the first meridian of Hindu geographers and was the capital of the Avanti kingdom (6th–4th centuries BC). One of the seven sacred Hindu cities, it is the scene of the 12-yearly bathing festival (Kumbh Mela). It is an agricultural trading center with textile industries and has a university, founded in 1957. Population (1971): 203,278.

Ujung Padang (Makassar *or* Macassar) 5 09S 119 08E A port in central Indonesia, in SW Sulawesi. Already a flourishing port when the Portuguese

PAOLO UCCELLO *Detail from* A Hunt in a Forest *(c. 1460)*.

arrived in the 16th century, its exports now include coffee, copra, resins, and vegetable oils. There is some manufacturing industry. Its university was established in 1956. Population (1971): 434,766.

ukiyo-e (Japanese: pictures of the floating world)   A Japanese art style concerned with the depiction of everyday life. It was popular among the middle classes in the 17th and 18th centuries. Favorite subjects included prostitutes, women engaged in domestic tasks, actors, etc. Ukiyo-e began as a style of painting but it is most closely associated with Japanese color woodblock prints. The first ukiyo-e printmaker was probably Hishikawa Moronobu (c. 1618–94). The art culminated in the landscapes of *Hokusai and *Hiroshige, which were highly influential on *impressionism, *postimpressionism, and the *Nabis in 19th-century France.

Ukrainian Soviet Socialist Republic (*or* Ukraine)   A constituent republic in the SW Soviet Union. It is a very fertile wooded region and is second only to the RSFSR as the economically most important Soviet republic. Some 96% of the population comprises Slavs, mostly Ukrainians. There are major coalfields and iron-ore mines (including the *Donets Basin), resulting in the development of a large ferrous metallurgical industry. The machine-building, chemical, consumer-goods, and food industries are also important. The region possesses some of the most fertile land in the Soviet Union and crops grown include wheat (comprising nine tenths of Soviet exports), sugar beet, cotton, and tobacco. *History*: it was dominated by the Khazars from the 7th to the 9th centuries and then by the Rurik princes of Kiev. In the 13th century the Golden Horde overran the region, which subsequently came under the rule of Lithuania and, in the 16th century, Poland. In the 17th century many Ukrainians fled the harsh Polish government, becoming *Cossaks. Polish domination was followed by Russian rule. After a national and cultural revival in the late 19th century the Ukraine declared independence in 1918 but subsequently submitted to Soviet armies, becoming (1922) one of the original constituent republics of the Soviet Union. The Ukraine has a separate seat in the UN. Area: 231,990 sq mi (603,700 sq km). Population (1981 est): 50,135,000. Capital: Kiev.

ukulele   A small guitar, patented in Hawaii in 1917. The fingerboard of a ukulele is fretted; the four gut or nylon strings are strummed with fingers or a small plectrum. Originally used to play chordal accompaniments to folksongs, the ukulele became popular in US jazz.

Ulan Bator (*or* Ulaanbaatar; former name: Urga)   47 54N 106 52E The capital of the Mongolian People's Republic, situated on a plateau in the N of the country. Built around a monastery, in the 17th century it developed as a center of trade between China and Japan. It became the capital when Outer Mongolia declared its independence in 1911. It is Mongolia's main center of industry. The Mongolian State University was founded in 1942. Population (1978 est): 400,000.

Ulanova, Galina (1910–)   Russian ballet dancer. From 1928 she danced with the Leningrad Kirov Ballet, where she excelled in classical ballets, such as *Swan Lake* and *Giselle*, and from 1944 with the Moscow Bolshoi Ballet, for which she made several films. She retired from the stage in 1962.

Ulan Ude   51 55N 107 40E A city in the SE Soviet Union, in the Buryat ASSR, in the RSFSR on the Selenga River. It is a transport center and has boatbuilding, ship-repairing, and machinery-manufacturing industries. Population (1981 est): 310,000.

Ulbricht, Walter (1893–1973)   East German statesman. A fervent Stalinist, Ulbricht rose rapidly in the Communist Party ranks. He lived in the Soviet Union during the Nazi period and after World War II was the leading architect of the German Democratic Republic. He was general secretary of the Socialist Unity Party from 1950 and in 1960 became chairman of the newly established council of state. In 1961 he erected the Berlin Wall.

ulcer   An inflamed eroded area of skin or mucous membrane. There are many forms of ulcer, one of the most prevalent being *peptic ulcers, which affect the stomach and duodenum. Ulcers may also occur in the mouth— small irritating aphthous ulcers affect many people—and in the intestine in inflammatory bowel disease (*see* colitis). Varicose ulcers may develop in the skin, particularly around the ankles, of patients with chronic *varicose veins.

Uleåborg. *See* Oulu.

Ulm   48 24N 10 00E An industrial city and port in SW West Germany, in Baden-Württemberg on the Danube River. Its gothic cathedral (1377) escaped the damage of World War II. Napoleon defeated the Austrian army here in 1805 and it is the birthplace of Einstein. Population (1970 est): 93,800.

Ulm, Battle of (September 25–October 20, 1805)   A battle in which Napoleon with 210,000 men defeated 72,000 Austrians in Bavaria. The Austrians were taken by surprise in the rear and capitulated. Napoleon thus prevented a union between Austrian and Russian forces.

ulna. *See* arm.

Ulster   A province in the Republic of Ireland and former kingdom of N Ireland. The land passed to the English crown in 1461 and during the 17th century most was confiscated and given to English and Scottish settlers (*see* Plantation of Ireland). It was partitioned in 1921 to form the six counties of Northern Ireland and the Ulster province of the Republic of Ireland, consisting of the counties of Cavan, Donegal, and Monaghan. Area: 3094 sq mi (8013 sq km). Population (1979): 226,037.

ultramicroscope   A type of microscope, invented by *Zsigmondy in 1902, used to study colloidal particles in a liquid medium. A beam of light illuminates the particles from the side, the scattered light enabling the movements of the particles to be observed as flashes against a dark background (dark-field illumination).

Ultramontanism (Latin: beyond the mountains, i.e. within Italy)   A tendency within the Roman Catholic Church that supports the centralized power of the pope and the *Roman Curia as against nationalist movements, such as *Gallicanism, or greater independence at the diocesan level. The high point of Ultramontanism was the promulgation of papal *infallibility (1870). The Second *Vatican Council encouraged a devolution of authority.

ultrasonics   The study of *sound waves the frequencies of which are too high to be audible to the normal human ear, i.e. above about 20,000 hertz. Such waves are known as ultrasound and may be produced by *magnetostriction or by applying a rapidly alternating voltage across a *piezoelectric crystal. Ultrasound now has a number of applications, for example utilizing its rapid vibrations to destroy bacteria in milk, break up large molecules, and clean surfaces.

ultraviolet radiation   *Electromagnetic radiation the frequency of which lies between that of the violet end of the visible spectrum and *X-rays, i.e. between about 380 and 5 nanometers. Ultraviolet radiation is produced during arc discharges and by gas-discharge tubes (e.g. the mercury-vapor lamp). It is also produced in large quantities by the sun, although the radiation below 200 nm is absorbed by the *ozone layer of the atmosphere.

Ulyanovsk (name until 1924: Simbirsk)   54 19N 48 22E A port in the W central Soviet Union, in the RSFSR on the Volga River. Industries include food processing, vodka distilling, and motor-vehicle manufacture. It was renamed in honor of Lenin (originally V. I. Ulyanov), who was born here. Population (1981 est): 485,000.

Ulysses. *See* Odysseus.

Umar. *See* Omar.

Umayyads (*or* Omayyads)   The first dynasty of *caliphs, which ruled Islam from 661 to 750 AD. Their capital was Damascus. After reluctantly accepting Islam, the family obtained some of the leading positions in the state and one of them, *Mu'awiyah, became caliph (661) on the death of his rival *Ali. The dynasty reached its peak with *'Abd al-Malik (reigned 685–705). The Umayyads were overthrown by a rebellion of discontented Arabs and pious Muslims and were replaced by the *Abbasids, a rival family. In Muslim Spain, an Umayyad, *'Abd ar-Rahman, seized power in 756 and established a dynasty that ruled until 1030.

Umbelliferae   A widely distributed family of plants (2850 species), most abundant in N temperate regions. Most species are herbaceous, with much-divided leaves and umbrella-shaped heads (umbels) of tiny flowers, each usually with five petals and five sepals. A few species have dome-shaped flower heads. The fruits are ridged, splitting into two parts when ripe. The family includes vegetables, such as the carrot, celery, and parsnip, and many culinary herbs and spices, such as angelica, caraway, chervil, coriander, dill, fennel, and parsley.

Umberto I (1844–1900)   King of Italy (1878–1900). He commanded with distinction in the war against the Austrians (1866). As king he led Italy into the *Triple Alliance with Germany and Austria (1882) and encouraged Italian colonialism in Africa. Defeat by the Ethiopians at Adowa (1896) and economic difficulties led to unrest at home and the imposition of martial law in 1898. Two unsuccessful attempts on Umberto's life were followed by his assassination at Monza.

Umberto II (1904–83)   The last King of Italy (1946), following the abdication of his father Victor Emmanuel III. He himself was forced to abdicate after a referendum approved the establishment of republican government and he retired to Portugal as the Count of Sarre.

umbilical cord The structure, about 50 cm long, that connects a fetus to the *placenta in the uterus. It contains three blood vessels (two arteries and one vein) that convey blood to and from the placenta. At birth the umbilical cord is tied off and cut; the part connected to the baby subsequently degenerates, leaving a scar on the abdomen (see navel).

umbrella bird A fruit-eating songbird of the genus *Cephalopterus* of tropical American forests. Male birds have a large umbrella-shaped crest that is raised over the head during display. They also have fleshy wattles hanging from the chest—ranging from the short naked red wattle of the bare-necked umbrella bird (*C. glabriollis*) to the feather-covered pendulous wattle of the ornate umbrella bird (*C. ornatus*). Family: *Cotingidae* (90 species).

umbrella tree A small North American tree, *Magnolia tripetala*, up to 40 ft (12 m) high, that has umbrella-like clusters of large leaves (16 in [40 cm] long) at the ends of the branches. The large flowers are creamy white with a strong scent and the fruits are scarlet; the tree is grown as an ornamental in temperate regions. Family: *Magnoliaceae*.

Umbria A landlocked mountainous region in central Italy. Its agriculture produces cereals, vines, and olives. Hydroelectricity powers modern industries producing iron, steel, chemicals, engineering, and food products. The Umbrian school of painting, which included Perugino and Raphael, was established here during the Renaissance. Area: 3265 sq mi (8456 sq km). Population (1980 est): 810,713. Capital: Perugia.

Umtali. See Mutare.

Umtata 31 35S 28 47E The capital of the Transkei, in S Africa. It has an Anglican cathedral. Population (1976): 24,805.

Un-American Activities Committee, House (HUAC) US House of Representatives committee established in 1935 to investigate subversive organizations in the US. Headed by Representative Martin Dies, the committee investigated Nazism, Fascism, and Communism in the US, as well as those liberals, many of them involved in *New Deal programs, thought to have Communist connections. It was responsible for the blacklisting of Hollywood writers and directors alleged to be communists and for the investigations in 1948 of government officials, especially Alger Hiss. The *Internal Security Act of 1950 originated from these committee hearings. Before being abolished (1975) its name had been changed to the Internal Security Committee (1969).

Unamuno y Jugo, Miguel de (1864–1936) Spanish writer and philosopher, of Basque parentage. Unamuno's chief philosophical work, *The Tragic Sense of Life* (1913), reflects the influence of *Kant, *Hegel, and *Kierkegaard. This work and his novels are concerned with the themes of faith, free will, the immortality of the soul, and the struggle for moral integrity.

uncertainty principle. See Heisenberg uncertainty principle.

Uncle Sam A personification of the people or government of the US, usually portrayed as a lean figure with white hair and whiskers, wearing a tall hat, swallow-tail coat, and striped trousers. The name is associated with a certain meat inspector, Samuel Wilson (1766–1854), who confused the initials of the United States with those of his own nickname.

unconscious In *psychoanalysis, the part of the mind that includes ideas and impulses of which the individual is unaware and which cannot readily be brought back into awareness. (It is distinguished from the **subconscious**, which comprises ideas and impulses that can readily be recalled to consciousness.) The unconscious mental processes are unacceptable to the conscious mind and are kept unconscious by the process of *repression. Psychoanalytic *psychotherapy attempts to bring these processes back into consciousness by overcoming the resistances to them.

Underground Railroad A pre-Civil War secret organized system that helped escaped slaves in the South reach freedom in the North. Because the Fugitive Slave laws of 1793 and 1850 made it legal for owners to recapture slaves, sympathetic northerners set up a loose network of safe hiding places called stations, usually in the homes of supporters, for slaves making their way north as far as Canada. The slaves were led by conductors, the most famous of whom was Harriet *Tubman.

underground railroads Apart from short sections of tunnel on mainline railroads, the world's first urban underground railroad (1863) was built in London using the cut and cover method (cutting a trench from above and filling in over the railroad). The first "tube" railroad (1890), cut by boring through the earth, was also in England and used electric trains. Other major cities to have an underground railroad include New York (subway), Paris (*métro*), Moscow, Tokyo, Buenos Aires, Madrid, and Hong Kong.

underwing moth A moth whose brightly colored hindwings are hidden by the camouflaged forewings when at rest. When disturbed the moth flies off flashing its bright colors, which startles and confuses predators. Underwings belong to several families and are found in Europe, Asia, and North America.

underwriting. See insurance; Lloyd's.

Undset, Sigrid (1882–1949) Norwegian novelist, best known for *Kristin Lavransdatter* (1920–22), a trilogy of historical novels set in 14th-century Norway. She wrote a number of other novels, most of them dealing with themes that reflect her conversion to Roman Catholicism in 1924. She also wrote essays and lives of the Norwegian saints.

undulant fever. See brucellosis.

unemployment The total number of people unable to find work at a given time. A certain amount of **frictional unemployment**, i.e. unemployment due to people changing jobs, etc., is inevitable. **Structural unemployment** is due to people having the wrong skills, living in different areas from vacancies, etc. The proportion of the workforce unemployed also increases with a downturn in the *trade cycle (this is **demand-deficient unemployment**); it hit an all-time high in the *Depression of the 1930s reaching over eight million in the US. While it is accepted that even with "full" employment up to about 3% of the workforce may be out of work (as a result of frictional and structural unemployment) considerable controversy remains as to the extent of structural unemployment as compared to demand-deficient unemployment. Monetarists (see monetarism) believe that, provided the *money supply is adequate, unemployment is largely due to structural problems and they advocate such measures as mobility allowances and retraining schemes. They claim that attempts to boost the economy by *deficit financing, as advocated by *Keynesianism, will not help the problem and will merely fuel *inflation.

UNESCO. See United Nations Educational, Scientific and Cultural Organization.

Ungaretti, Giuseppe (1888–1970) Italian poet. He was born in Egypt and studied in Paris, where he met *Apollinaire, *Valéry, and other avant-garde writers and artists. His poetry, beginning with the war poems of *Il porto sepolto* (1916) and *L'allegria* (1919), was highly experimental, dispensing with rhyme and other conventions. The difficult language and symbolism of a later volume, *Sentimento del tempo* (1933), led a critic to describe Ungaretti's verse as *ermetico* (obscure), a term that was soon applied to the style of *Montale and *Quasimodo as well, the three being the leading practitioners of *La poesia ermetica*. Ungaretti's later volumes include *La terra promessa* (1950) and *Morte delle stagioni* (1967).

Ungava A region in E Canada, in N Quebec E of Hudson Bay. A rocky plateau with many lakes, it is rich in minerals (especially iron ore) but sparsely populated. Area: 351,780 sq mi (911,110 sq km).

ungulate A hoofed mammal. The term is not used in modern scientific classifications, the hoofed mammals being grouped into the orders *Perissodactyla* (horses, tapirs, and rhinoceroses) and *Artiodactyla*, which includes pigs, camels, deer, cattle, etc.

uniat churches Various churches of Eastern Orthodox Christianity that are in full communion with the Roman Catholic Church. Although completely Catholic in faith and doctrine, they retain their own traditional liturgies and canon law. Generally they differ from Rome in giving communion under both kinds, practicing baptism by immersion, and allowing marriage of the clergy.

UNICEF. See United Nations International Children's Emergency Fund.

unicorn A mythical animal described by classical writers as living in India and resembling a white horse, but with one long straight horn on its forehead. In the middle ages it was symbolically associated with chastity or virginity (and thus could be captured only by a virgin) and also with Christ's love of mankind. Its horn was supposed to reveal the presence of poison in food or drink. In heraldry it figured in the arms of Scotland and was combined with the lion in the arms of the British crown after the accession of James I.

unidentified flying objects (UFOs) Objects reported to have been seen in the sky (usually at night) that have not been identified as aircraft, satellites, balloons, or known astronomical bodies. Often described as saucer shaped (and known as "flying saucers"), they have been taken by some observers to be spacecraft from extraterrestrial sources—a view for which there is little credible evidence. They have, however, provided a source of considerable speculation and excitement among those who believe that they have witnessed an event that has passed unnoticed by the rest of mankind.

UNICORN *A representation of a unicorn from a 15th-century tapestry in the Musée Cluny, Paris.*

Unification Church A religious sect founded in South Korea in 1954 by a millionaire Korean businessman, Sun Myung Moon (1920–). In the early 1960s it was introduced into the US as a right-wing Christian Youth Crusade and is now also active in other countries. The ideology of the cult is summarized in Moon's book, *Divine Principle*, which he claims was revealed to him by Christ in 1936. Moon is presented as the Second Messiah, the head of a family of perfect children (i.e. his followers, the Moonies), who will succeed in redeeming mankind from Satan. Absolute obedience is demanded of members, who spend most of their waking hours earning money for the organization by selling such items as artificial flowers in the streets. The large tax-exempt sums realized in this way have enabled Moon to build an extensive property and business empire in the US, where he has lived since 1972, but he was sentenced to prison for tax evasion in 1984.

unified field theory A theory that encompasses the four fundamental interactions—*strong, *weak, *electromagnetic, and *gravitational—in terms of a single field, analogous to the electromagnetic or gravitational fields. Einstein failed after many attempts to unify gravitation and electromagnetism and it may be that no simple unification is possible.

uniformitarianism The generally accepted theory that all geological changes have occurred through gradual processes operating over a long period and continuing today, although not necessarily at the same rate or intensity. *Compare* catastrophism.

Union, Acts of **1.** The acts (1536–43) uniting England and Wales. They imposed English law and administration on Wales and made English the language of officialdom. **2.** The act (1707) uniting England and Scotland to form Great Britain. **3.** The act (1800) that united Great Britain and Ireland to form (1801) the United Kingdom. After the establishment of the Irish Free State (1921; *see* Home Rule), the act united Britain with Northern Ireland.

Union, Act of (1841) Act that began self-government in Canada by uniting Upper and Lower Canada. Proposed by Britain's governor-general, Lord *Durham, and fashioned by Lord Russell, the act provided equal representation for British and French Canadians.

Union of Soviet Socialist Republics. *See* Soviet Union.

Unitarians A group of Christians who reject the doctrine of the Trinity and the divinity of Christ, believing instead in the single personality of God and regarding Christ as a religious teacher. They have no formal creeds but stress reason and conscience as the bases of religion and view human nature as essentially good; they therefore also reject orthodox Christian teaching on original sin and atonement. Modern Unitarian thought dates from the Reformation, but congregations were first formed in Britain and the US in the 18th century. These are now associated in the General Assembly of Unitarian and Free Christian Churches.

unitary symmetry A method of classifying *hadrons. It is found that by plotting *isotopic spin against hypercharge (the sum of *strangeness and *baryon number) on a graph for particular values of *spin and *parity, a symmetric pattern of hadrons is obtained. In this way families of hadrons can be constructed. The theory was used to predict the existence and properties of the omega-minus particle, which were later confirmed.

United Arab Emirates (UAE; former name: Trucial States) A federation of seven sheikdoms in the Middle East, in *Arabia on the S coast of the Persian Gulf and the Gulf of Oman, comprising Abu Dhabi, Ajman, Dubai, Fujairah, Ras al-Khaimah, Sharjah, and Umm al-Qaiwain. Abu Dhabi occupies 87% of the total area and Abu Dhabi and Dubai each have about one third of the population, which is mainly Arab and Sunnite Muslim. The terrain is flat sandy desert, below 656 ft (200 m) except for a slight rise to the NE. *Economy*: fishing and pearls are still important, but the oil of Abu Dhabi and Dubai, both underground and offshore, is the chief product and export: it has made Abu Dhabi one of the richest per capita political units in the world. *History*: the sheikdoms signed several common treaties with Britain from 1820; that of 1892 made them protectorates—the Trucial States—and British troops were stationed there until independence. The federation was formed in 1971 (Ras al-Khaimah not joining until 1972) and is a member of OPEC. President: Sheik Zayed bin Sultan al-Nahayan of Abu Dhabi. Prime minister: Sheik Rashid bin Said al-Maktoum. Official language: Arabic. Official currency: UAE dirham of 10 dinars and 1000 fils. Area: 32,290 sq mi (83,650 sq km). Population (1983): 1,374,000. Provisional capital: Abu Dhabi. Chief port: Dubai.

United Arab Republic (UAR) The state created by the union of Egypt and Syria in 1958. Joined by North Yemen in the same year, it collapsed in 1961, when Syria withdrew, but Egypt retained the name until 1971.

United Australia Party (UAP) A political party, comprising the Nationalist Party and ex-members of the *Labor Party, that governed Australia (sometimes in coalition with the Country Party) from 1931 to 1941. It was dissolved in 1944 to be succeeded by the *Liberal Party.

United Empire Loyalists Those Americans who remained loyal to England in the American Revolution and were forced after the colonists' victory in 1783 to migrate to Canada.

United Fronts In China, two periods of cooperation between the Chinese Communist Party and its opponent, the *Guomindang. The first United Front (1924–27) was brought about, under Soviet influence, to defeat the *warlords and dissolved as relations between the two parties declined into civil war. The second United Front (1937–45) was formed following the *Xi An incident, which forced *Chiang Kai-shek to abandon civil war with the communists for an alliance against the Japanese invasion (*see* Sino-Japanese Wars).

United Irishmen, Society of An Irish secret society established in Belfast in 1791 by Wolfe *Tone to press for an independent Irish republic. Hopes of French aid in the 1790s were frustrated but in 1798 the United Irishmen rose in Ulster and Wexford, being suppressed with some difficulty.

United Kingdom (UK) A country in N Europe, consisting of *England, *Scotland, *Wales, and the province of Northern Ireland (*see* Ireland). The United Kingdom of Great Britain and Ireland, formed in 1801, became the United Kingdom of Great Britain and Northern Ireland in 1922, following the creation of the Irish Free State. Head of state: Queen Elizabeth II. Prime minister: Margaret Thatcher. Languages: English, with Gaelic and Welsh minority languages. Area: 94,214 sq mi (244,014 sq km). Population (1981 est): 55,670,000. Capital: London.

United Nations (UN) An organization established to maintain international peace and to foster international cooperation in the resolution of economic, social, cultural, and humanitarian problems. The UN was founded on October 24, 1945 (United Nations Day), when the major powers ratified a charter that had been drawn up earlier in the year in San Francisco. There were 51 founder members, including the US, which thus abandoned the isolationist stance it had taken to the UN's predecessor, the *League of Nations. Most of the countries of the world are now members of the UN, the chief exceptions being North and South Korea, Switzerland, and *Taiwan, which lost its seat to the People's Republic of *China in 1971.
The headquarters of the UN are in New York City. The organization's main deliberative organ is the **General Assembly**, which meets for three months every year. Each member state has one equal vote in the Assembly, which can only adopt recommendations: as a body of independent sovereign states, it cannot impose its will upon members. The **Security Council** bears the chief responsibility for maintaining international peace. Its permanent members are China, France, the Soviet Union, the UK, and the US; a further ten members are elected by the General Assembly for two-year terms. Decisions, except on procedure, must be agreed by nine members, including all the permanent members (the so-called veto privilege). In

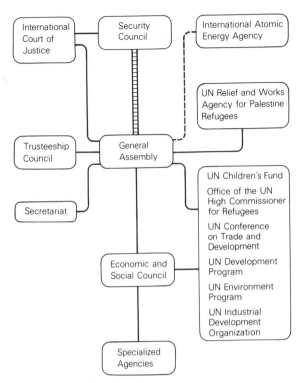

UNITED NATIONS *The structure of the organization.*

the event of a breach of international peace the Council may commit military forces to an attempt to re-establish peace, as for example during the *Korean War. The **Economic and Social Council** (ECOSOC) coordinates the economic and social work of the UN and has regional commissions in Europe, Asia and the Pacific, Latin America, Africa, and Western Asia. The **Trusteeship Council** is responsible for the one remaining *trust territory (Micronesia). The principal judicial organ of the UN is the *International Court of Justice. The **Secretariat**, headed by the secretary general (currently Javier Pérez de Cuellar), is responsible for administration.

Other UN bodies are the **United Nations Development Program** (UNDP), which fosters the economic growth of the *developing countries; its headquarters are in New York; the **United Nations Conference on Trade and Development** (UNCTAD), which encourages international trade, especially for the purpose of accelerating the economic development of developing countries; its headquarters are in Geneva; the **United Nations Industrial Development Organization** (UNIDO), which promotes industrial development in the developing countries; its headquarters are in Vienna; the **United Nations Environment Program** (UNEP), which is concerned with international cooperation in the protection of the environment; its headquarters are in Nairobi; the Office of the *United Nations High Commissioner for Refugees; the *United Nations International Children's Emergency Fund; and the *United Nations Relief and Works Agency for Palestine Refugees in the Near East. There are in addition a number of specialized agencies, each charged with a specific function. These include the *Food and Agriculture Organization, *International Civil Aviation Organization, *International Labor Organisation, *International Monetary Fund, *International Telecommunication Union, *United Nations Educational, Scientific and Cultural Organization, *International Bank for Reconstruction and Development, *World Health Organization, and the *World Meteorological Organization.

United Nations Educational, Scientific and Cultural Organization (UNESCO) A specialized agency of the *United Nations established in 1945 to promote international cooperation in education, science, and culture. It collects and distributes information, provides operational assistance (e.g. funds for teacher training) to *developing countries, and sponsors research. Its headquarters are in Paris.

United Nations High Commissioner for Refugees, Office of the (UNHCR) A *United Nations body established in 1950 to provide international protection for refugees. It seeks permanent solutions to their problems through voluntary repatriation, resettlement in other countries, or

integration into the country of present residence. The UNHCR has recently been concerned with refugees from Chile, Cyprus, Angola, and Vietnam. Its headquarters are in Geneva. It won the Nobel Peace Prize in 1981.

United Nations International Children's Emergency Fund (UNICEF) A *United Nations body established in 1946 to carry out postwar relief work in Europe. It is now chiefly concerned with providing health care, education, and improved nutrition to *developing countries. Most of UNICEF's funds come from voluntary government contributions. Its headquarters are in Geneva. It won the Nobel Peace Prize in 1965.

United Nations Relief and Works Agency for Palestine Refugees in the Near East (UNRWA) A *United Nations body founded in 1950 to provide relief, health, education, and welfare services for Palestinian refugees in the Middle East (*see* Palestine). Its permanent headquarters are in Beirut (Lebanon).

United Provinces of the Netherlands The northern provinces of the Netherlands, which united (1579) during the *Revolt of the Netherlands against Spain and formed (1581) a self-governing independent federation. The so-called Dutch Republic survived until conquered by the French (1795) during the Revolutionary Wars.

United States of America (USA) A country in North America, the fourth largest country in the world. The USA is a federal republic comprising 50 states, including two separated from the others: Alaska, in the extreme NW of the continent, and Hawaii, in the central Pacific Ocean. The US borders on Canada in the N and Mexico in the S. The Pacific mountain system and the Rocky Mountains, the watershed of the country, extend N–S in the W with an arid area between, while the Appalachian Mountains extend N–S in the E. In the center lie vast plains. The population is of mixed ethnic stock, the majority being of European descent; other groups include blacks, Chinese, Japanese, and American Indians (the majority of whom live on reservations). *Economy*: the US is the world's greatest industrial producer, with a highly diversified economy. Its large resources of minerals and fuels make it the leading producer of natural gas, lead, copper, aluminum, and sulfur and of electrical and nuclear energy. It is almost self-sufficient in raw materials, although as its mineral resources are depleted it is having to increase its imports, notably of petroleum. The chief manufactures are steel, motor vehicles, chemicals, electronic equipment, and consumer goods. Although only 4% of the workforce are employed in agriculture, 15% of all exports are agricultural products. Farming is highly mechanized, with efficient control of disease and pests. Cereals, cotton, and tobacco are the main crops. Main exports include motor vehicles, aircraft, machinery, grain, and chemicals, while main imports include petroleum and petroleum products, chemicals, metals, machinery, cars, and newsprint. *History*: extensively explored following its discovery by Columbus in 1492, America was settled from 1565, chiefly by the Spanish, French, and British. The British colonies, in the E, had the greatest religious and economic freedom and were therefore the most attractive and successful. However, during the 18th century conflict developed between local colonial assemblies and their British governors, particularly over taxation. The colonists' confidence in themselves was strengthened by their success against the French in the *French and Indian Wars (1754–1763) and the 13 colonies finally won independence in the *American Revolution (1775–83). The US rapidly expanded W from this time acquiring vast territories with the Louisiana Purchase (1803). Through the *Mexican War (1846–48) California and other western lands were added. The discovery of gold in California (1848) further encouraged settlement in the W. By 1820 conflict was developing between the cotton-growing states of the South (where African slaves had worked since the late 17th century) and the commercial North (where the industrial revolution was under way and slavery was opposed). As the new states of the West aligned themselves with the North, the South felt increasingly threatened. This led to the *Civil War (1861–65), which ended in victory for the North and the abolition of slavery. It was followed by a period of rapid industrial and economic expansion, while territorial expansion continued with the purchase of Alaska (1867), the annexation of Hawaii (1898), and the *Spanish-American War (1898), in which the US acquired the Philippines, Puerto Rico, Guam, and a measure of control over Cuba.

Intervention in Colombia led to the construction of the Panama Canal (opened 1914). Economic and territorial expansion made the US a world power, a status confirmed by its role in World War I, which it entered reluctantly (1917) because of its policy of isolationism. The 1920s saw another industrial and commercial boom, which ended in the *Depression that followed the Crash of 1929. The US was also reluctant to enter World War II but was forced to do so by the Japanese bombing of Pearl Harbor in Hawaii (Dec. 7, 1941). US troops and weapons played a major part in defeating the Axis Powers in Europe and its development and use of the atom bomb ended the war against Japan. The key US role in the establishment of the United Nations (1945) involved it inextricably in international affairs, in which it has since played a leading role. Postwar fear of Soviet expansion resulted in the Marshall Plan (1947), designed to render Europe less susceptible to communism by bolstering it economically, in involvement in the *Cold War, and in the harassment of supposed communists at home (*see also* McCarthy, Joseph R.). Fear of the spread of communism led also to military involvement in Korea (1950–53), Cuba (1961–62), and Vietnam (1961–75) and in the use of foreign aid to maintain the status quo in developing countries. After 1963 relations with the Soviet Union improved, with strategic arms limitation discussed (*see* disarmament), and diplomatic relations were established with China in 1979. Interventionist policy continued, however, with the role of the CIA in foreign affairs criticized and investigated (1975–76) following the government's loss of credibility resulting from the *Watergate affair (1972–74). US support of Israel, the linchpin of its Middle East policy, embroiled the US further in the war in Lebanon. In Central America the US supported an unpopular conservative government in El Salvador and aided enemies of the leftist Sandinista regime in Nicaragua in the early 1980s. In the Caribbean US troops invaded (1983) the tiny island of Grenada to help overthrow the governing Marxist regime. Nuclear arms control talks with the Soviet Union broke down as the US deployed missiles in Western Europe in response to the threat of increasing Soviet missile development. Domestic problems since World War II have included the difficulties of effecting racial integration, with race riots in the mid and late 1960s followed by extensive opposition to the *Vietnam War. The postwar economic boom was followed by decline in the early 1970s, with continuing inflation. Depletion and pollution of natural resources is making such measures as energy saving a necessary part of the economy. With its increasing dependence on petroleum imports the country suffered through the drying up of supplies from Iran (1978–79) and rises in world petroleum prices. Relationships with Iran were further strained when Iranian students took 52 US diplomats hostage in the American Embassy, Tehran, in 1979, only releasing them in January, 1981, soon after Reagan's inauguration. In the early 1980s the country experienced the worst recession since the Great Depression, marked by high unemployment, soaring inflation, record trade deficits, and enormous budget deficits. By the end of Reagan's first term reduced spending on social programs and tax cuts resulted in economic revival, but the country's huge deficit evoked increasing concern. President: Ronald Reagan. Official language: English. Official currency: US dollar of 100 cents. Area: 3,614,343 sq mi (9,363,123 sq km). Population (1983): 234,193,000. Capital: Washington, DC.

United States Air Force Academy   A four-year higher-education institution that trains men and women to be officers in the *Air Force. Located in Colorado Springs, Colo, it was established in 1958. Graduates receive a

bachelor of science degree and a commission as a second lieutenant in the Air Force.

United States Military Academy   A four-year higher-education institution that trains men and women to be officers in the US *Army. Located at West Point, NY, it was established in 1802 for men only; women have been admitted since 1976. Graduates receive a bachelor of science degree and a commission as a second lieutenant in the Army.

United States Naval Academy   A four-year higher-education institution that trains men and women to be officers in the US *Navy or *Marine Corps. Located in Annapolis, Md, it was established in 1845 as the Naval School for men only; women have been admitted since 1976. Graduates receive a bachelor of science degree and a commission as a second lieutenant in the Navy.

United States v. E. C. Knight Company (1895)   US Supreme Court decision that defined the *Sherman Anti-Trust Act and confirmed the law's intent of applying only to interstate trade. The American Sugar Refining Company had created a sugar market monopoly by buying and consolidating four other competitors. The court ruled that the antitrust law did not apply in this case, which concerned the processing of a product, not the marketing of it. Furthermore, the processing took place in one state; thus, interstate conditions required in the law did not exist.

unities   Three principles concerning the representation in drama of action, time, and space. According to the interpretation of Aristotle's *Poetics* by 16th- and 17th-century neoclassical critics, a play must represent a single action occurring in a single setting during the course of a single day. The unities were strictly observed in much 17th-century French drama, notably in the tragedies of *Racine and *Corneille, but were largely ignored in England.

Universal Decimal Classification (*or* Brussels Classification)   A system of library classification developed in 1895 at the International Institute of Bibliography in Brussels. It extends the division of the *Dewey Decimal Classification, on which it is based, by using various symbols of notation as well as Arabic numerals.

universe   The sum of all potentially knowable objects—the earth, sun, and other solar-system bodies, the stars and other members of our *Galaxy, countless millions of other *galaxies, and the matter between these objects. The universe is thought to be 10–20 thousand million years old and is at present expanding (*see* big-bang theory; cosmology). Its unimaginable vastness in both space (about 10^{10} light years across) and time (about 10^{10} years old) has only been accepted in this century. The possibility of life elsewhere in the universe is fairly high (i.e. there is a high probability that there are millions of stars with similar planetary systems and conditions to those of the solar system), but because distances are so enormous there is very little chance of ascertaining the existence of life elsewhere.

UR   *The "Standard" of Ur (c. 2500* BC; *British Museum, London). It consists of a hollow box, the sides of which depict a king's campaign, decorated with lapis lazuli, shell, and red limestone. The side shown depicts animals being taken to be killed for the victory banquet.*

universities Independent degree-awarding institutions of higher education. They evolved in Europe in the middle ages from the *studia generalia*, schools open to scholars from all parts of Europe, and by the end of the 14th century consisted of lawful communities of teachers and scholars, recognized by civil or ecclesiastical authorities. Among the earliest were those founded at Bologna (1088), Paris (c. 1150), Prague (1348), Vienna (1365), and Heidelberg (1386). The first universities in England were established at Oxford and Cambridge in the 12th century. In the US the first universities evolved from institutions established prior to the American Revolution, such as *Harvard (1636), *Yale (1701) and *Princeton (1746). Following industrialization during the 19th century, many new universities were established, a process that continued into the 20th century, especially after World War II. Increasing emphasis was placed upon the development of technical studies. Two year community (junior) colleges developed, offering liberal arts and vocational training.

Upanishads About 200 prose and verse treatises on metaphysical philosophy, produced as commentaries on the *Vedas* and dating from around 400 BC. They deal with the nature of *Brahman and the soul and are reputedly divinely inspired. Many different, sometimes contradictory, views are represented.

upas An evergreen tropical tree, *Antiaris toxicana*, native to SE Asia. Up to 100 ft (30 m) high, it has a crown of short spreading branches and long simple leaves; the flowers give rise to fleshy red pear-shaped fruits. The milky latex is a source of arrow poison. Family: *Moraceae*.

Updike, John (Hoyer) (1932–) US novelist and short-story writer. Until 1959 he worked for the *New Yorker* magazine. In novels, such as *Rabbit, Run* (1960), *Couples* (1968) *Rabbit Redux* (1970), *Bech: A Book* (1971), *Marry Me* (1976), *Bech Is Back* (1982), and *The Witches of Eastwick* (1984), he has explored the moral confusions of contemporary US society. He has moved beyond the suburban scene of much of his writing in *The Coup* (1979), a novel set in an emergent African country. His novel *Rabbit is Rich* (1981) won a Pulitzer Prize (1982).

Upolu The most populous island in Western Samoa. It is fertile and copra, cacao, bananas, and rubber are produced. Area: 430 sq mi (1114 sq km). Population (1976): 109,765. Chief town: Apia.

Upper Canada A former province (1791–1841) in SE Canada, corresponding to the S half of modern Ontario province. Including the area west of the Ottawa River and north of the Great Lakes, it became Canada West in 1841 and part of Ontario in 1867.

Upper Volta, Republic of. *See* Burkina Faso.

Uppsala 59 55N 17 38E A city in E central Sweden. It is a historic and cultural center, with a famous library, a gothic cathedral, and Sweden's oldest university (1477), where *Linnaeus taught. Population (1978 est): 146,192.

Ur An ancient city of *Sumer (S Iraq). Mentioned in Genesis as *Abraham's homeland, its site remained unidentified until 1854. Sir Leonard *Woolley's excavations (1922–34) made famous the spectacularly rich royal burials of about 2500 BC and seemed to provide historical evidence for *Noah's flood. The leading city in Sumer when it was sacked by barbarians about 2000 BC, Ur was superseded by *Babylon. Ur remained a center for the worship of the moon god Nanna until changes in the course of the Euphrates forced its remaining inhabitants away (5th century BC).

uremia The accumulation of *urea in the blood due to kidney failure. Kidney failure can occur suddenly due to shock, obstruction of both ureters, injury, or acute kidney disease or it may arise slowly due to *nephritis or other diseases. In acute kidney failure the kidneys will often recover after *dialysis with a kidney machine. In chronic conditions, requiring long-term dialysis, a kidney transplant (if available) is preferred.

Ural River A river in the central Soviet Union, rising in the S Ural Mountains, and flowing mainly S to the Caspian Sea near Guryev. Length: 1575 mi (2534 km).

Uralic languages A major language family comprising two related groups of languages, the *Finno-Ugric and the Samoyedic (*see* Samoyed). Originating from a common source over 10,000 years ago in an area N of the Ural Mountains, the two branches of the Uralic language family have developed into multiple forms covering an extensive geographical area in Europe, Scandinavia, and Asia.

Ural Mountains A mountain range in the NW central Soviet Union. It extends 1243 mi (2000 km) N–S from the Kara Sea to the steppes NE of the Caspian Sea and traditionally divides Europe from Asia. The highest point is Mount Narodnaya, in the N, at 6214 ft (1894 m). Most industrial metals are obtained here, as well as some precious stones, such as emerald

and amethyst, and the S part is an important industrial area, including the towns of Sverdlovsk and Magnitogorsk.

Urania In Greek mythology, one of the nine *Muses, the patron of astronomy. She was often portrayed with a globe and compass.

uranium (U) The radioactive metallic element used as a fuel for nuclear reactors (*see* nuclear energy). Uranium is a silvery-white metal, almost as hard as steel and very dense (relative density 18.95). Before the development of nuclear power, one of its major uses was in making yellow glass. Uranium has the highest atomic number of the naturally occurring elements. It was first isolated in 1841 by E. Péligot (1811–90), although it had been identified before this in pitchblende. It is also found in the ores uranite, carnotite, and monazite; it is mined primarily in Canada, Australia, S Africa, and the Soviet Union. Natural uranium contains three isotopes: ^{238}U (99.283%), ^{235}U (0.711%), and ^{234}U (0.006%). ^{238}U has a half-life of 4.51×10^9 years and is useful in dating rocks, as well as in fuel for fast reactors. The most important isotope in the nuclear industry is ^{235}U, which is used in *thermal reactors. Some reactors use metallic fuel, others uranium dioxide (UO_2). Other oxides include U_3O_8 and UO_3. The volatile gas uranium hexafluoride (UF_6) is used to separate uranium isotopes by gaseous diffusion. At no 94; at wt 238.029; mp 2072°F (1132°C); bp 6911°F (3818°C).

uranium series One of three naturally occurring series of radioactive decays. The uranium series is headed by uranium-238, which undergoes a series of alpha and beta decays ending with the stable isotope lead-206. *See also* actinium series; thorium series.

Uranus (astronomy) A giant planet, orbiting the sun every 84 years (between Saturn and Neptune) at a mean distance of about 1.8 billion mi (2.9 billion km). Its axis of rotation is close to its orbital plane. It is somewhat larger (32,540 mi [52,400 km] in diameter) than Neptune and exhibits a similar greenish featureless disk in a telescope. In its equatorial plane lie five *satellites and a system of about nine narrow rings (similar to, but less visible than, Saturn's rings), discovered in 1977. Composed predominantly of hydrogen and helium, with cloud layers of methane and possibly ammonia, its atmospheric and interior structure are thought to be almost identical to those of Neptune. Uranus was discovered telescopically in 1781 by Sir William Herschel.

Uranus (Greek mythology) The personification of Heaven. He was the son of Gaea (Earth), and his children by her included the *Titans and the *Cyclops. He was castrated by his son Cronus and his genitals were thrown into the sea, which gave birth to *Aphrodite.

Urartu (biblical name: Ararat) A kingdom flourishing between about 850 and 650 BC in E Turkey. The inhabitants, of *Hurrian stock, made their capital at Van (ancient Tushpa). Their metalwork was famous, examples even reaching Etruscan Italy. Urartu was frequently at war with neighboring Assyria.

Urban II (Odo of Lagery; c. 1042–99) Pope (1088–99). Until 1094 his rule was challenged by Guibert of Ravenna (d. 1100), the antipope set up by Emperor Henry IV. A Cluniac monk, he was made a cardinal by *Gregory VII, whose reform policies he continued. Councils at Melfi (1089) and at Piacenza and Clermont (1095) condemned simony, lay investiture, and clerical marriage. At Clermont he also proclaimed the first *Crusade. He was beatified in 1881. Feast day: July 29 or 30.

Urban VI (Bartolommeo Prignano; c. 1318–89) Pope (1378–89). His anti-French policies and dictatorial behavior inspired the French cardinals to declare his election void and to elect an antipope, thereby beginning the *Great Schism.

Urban VIII (Maffeo Barberini; 1568–1644) Pope (1623–44) during the *Thirty Years' War, in which he supported Richelieu against the Habsburgs. A great scholar, Urban supported new religious orders and reforms, including the revision of the Missal and new canonization procedures. He promulgated several measures against heresy and condemned the writings of Galileo and Jansen.

urban planning The designing of town and city areas with a view to providing adequate public facilities, healthy and pleasant surroundings, and good communications. Among the first urban planners were the Romans, who evolved a characteristic grid plan for many of their towns. Interest in the subject revived during the *Renaissance but it only became of major importance during the 19th-century urban expansion, when the need for an assured supply of housing and services became urgent. As a branch of the social sciences urban planning has become highly sophisticated in the 20th century, now having to deal not only with unprecedented concentrations of people but also with large quantities of traffic.

Urbino 43 43N 12 38E A city in Italy, in Marche. The birthplace of Raphael, Urbino possesses a 15th-century ducal palace and a university (1506). Its manufactures include textiles and majolica. Population (1971): 16,296.

Urdu An *Indo-Aryan language of N India and Pakistan, where it is an official language. Like *Hindi it arose from *Hindustani, but since it was used largely by Muslims in this region, while Hindi has been progressively influenced by *Sanskrit, the two now differ considerably. It is written in a modified Arabic script.

urea (or carbamide) A white crystalline compound ($CO(NH_2)_2$) derived from ammonia and carbon dioxide. It is widely used as a nitrogen fertilizer, a feed supplement for ruminant animals, and in the plastics and pharmaceutical industries. Urea is the excretory product of nitrogen metabolism in mammals and is present in *urine.

urea-formaldehyde resins Synthetic thermosetting resins that are made by the condensation in aqueous solution of urea and formaldehyde with an ammonia catalyst. Cellulose filler is added to the colorless syrupy solution produced and a molding powder forms when it dries. This powder can be colored with pigment and used to make cups, bathroom fittings, electrical fittings, etc.

urethane A white crystalline solid, $CO(NH_2)(OC_2H_5)$, made by heating ethanol with urea nitrate. It is soluble in water and alcohol and is used to manufacture *polyurethane foam.

Urey, Harold Clayton (1893–1981) US physicist, who received the Nobel Prize in 1934 for his discovery of deuterium. He also did valuable work on the separation of isotopes, which was useful in the manufacture of the hydrogen bomb. In postwar years, as professor at Chicago University (1945–52) and then at the University of California, he turned to geophysics.

Urfa (ancient name: Edessa) 37 08N 38 45E A city in S Turkey, near the Syrian border. It was the birthplace of Abraham. It has changed hands frequently, being occupied by Crusaders from 1098 to 1637. Population (1980): 147,488.

Urfé, Honoré d' (1568–1625) French novelist. His major work was the prose romance, *L'Astrée* (1607–27), which is set in his native Lyonnais in the 5th century and combines elements of pastoral and adventure; it is considered to be the first French novel. He also wrote the pastoral dramas *Sireine* and *Sylvanire* (1627).

Urga. See Ulan Bator.

uric acid A compound ($C_5H_4N_4O_3$) formed during the nitrogen metabolism of animals and the chief nitrogenous excretory product of reptiles and birds. In man, raised levels of uric acid in the blood are associated with gout.

urine The fluid that is formed by the kidneys and contains the waste products of metabolism and surplus water and salts. In man the kidneys normally produce 1–1.6 qt (0.9–1.5 l) of urine per day, containing some 1.75–2.5 oz (50–70 g) of solids—mostly urea, creatine, uric acid, and inorganic salts. The composition of urine depends on the type of animal and the need to conserve body water.

Uris, Leon Marcus (1924–) US writer. His best-known work is *Exodus* (1958), about the founding of present-day Israel; it was made into a successful movie in 1961. His works, usually incorporating history with fiction, include *Battle Cry* (1953), *Armageddon* (1964), *Topaz* (1967), *QB VII* (1970) and *Trinity* (1976). He wrote the scripts for those of his works that were made into films.

Urmia, Lake A shallow lake in NW Iran, the largest in the country, lying 4265 ft (1300 m) above sea level. It has no outlet and consequently is salty and varies in size. Average area: 1930 sq mi (5000 sq km).

Urnfield A group of Bronze Age cultures originating in central Europe. Urnfield peoples characteristically cremated their dead and buried the ashes in cemeteries of pottery urns. Their culture spread to most of Europe before being displaced by Iron Age *Hallstatt or Roman influence. Urnfields are commonly associated with groups who later became identifiable as the *Celts.

Ursa Major (Latin: great bear) A large conspicuous constellation in the N sky. The brightest stars, all of 2nd magnitude, are Alioth, Alcaid, and Dubhe. The seven brightest stars form the Big Dipper.

Ursa Minor (Latin: little bear) A constellation in the N sky that contains the N celestial pole. The brightest star is *Polaris, the present pole star.

Ursula, St A legendary British martyr. According to tradition, she and 11,000 virgins were murdered by the Huns at Cologne while returning from a pilgrimage to Rome in the 3rd or 5th century. She is first mentioned in the 10th century. She has given her name to numerous religious establishments, including the *Ursulines. Feast day: Oct 21.

Ursulines A Roman Catholic religious order for women, named for its patron St *Ursula, founded in Brescia in 1535 by St Angela Merici (1474–1540). It is devoted to educational work and is the oldest teaching order of women.

urticaria (or hives) An acute or chronic allergic disorder in which itching white raised patches surrounded by red areas appear on the skin: they resemble nettle stings (hence the alternative name—nettle rash). Acute urticaria usually arises from allergy to food or drugs and usually disappears quickly if the cause is removed. Chronic urticaria occurs in young people and its cause is not certain. Urticaria is treated with *antihistamines.

Uruguay, Oriental Republic of A country in the SE of South America, on the Atlantic Ocean and the Río de la Plata, bounded by Argentina and Brazil. Coastal plains rise to higher ground, especially in the N. The Uruguay River forms its W boundary and the other main river is the Negro. Most of the population is of Spanish and Italian descent. *Economy*: the traditional livestock industry was badly affected by the 1974 EEC ban on meat imports, although new markets have subsequently been found. The cultivation of the principal crops (wheat, corn, sorghum) has been intensified and the fishing industry has been expanded with government assistance. The principal industries include food processing, hides and leather, textiles, construction, metallurgy, and rubber. Hydroelectricity is a valuable source of power. *History*: explored by the Spanish in the 16th century, its early history was one of rivalry between Spanish and Portuguese settlements. In the 18th century Spain established its control of Uruguay, which in 1776 became part of the viceroyalty of the Río de la Plata. Under the leadership of Artigas, Uruguay joined Argentina in the movement for independence against Spain but was subsequently fought over by Argentina and Brazil. In 1828, with British help, Uruguay achieved independence, since when politics have been dominated by two parties, the Colorados (liberals) and the Blancos (conservatives). The late 19th century saw the beginning of considerable immigration from Europe, which was encouraged by the establishment in the first decades of the 20th century of what is regarded as Latin America's first welfare state. Uruguay is renowned for its literature and art. In the late 1960s there was considerable unrest caused partly by the Tupamaro urban guerrillas (see Tupac Amarú). In 1972 they were crushed by the army, which subsequently imposed repressive measures that led to international protests against violations of human rights. In 1982 a limited form of democracy was introduced with the approval of the organization of three political parties. An election was held in 1984. However, dissent was still repressed, and the economy continued unstable. The military president General Gregorio Alvarez Armelino resigned in 1985 in favor of a democratically-elected president, Sr Julio Sanguinetti. Uruguay is a member of the OAS and LAFTA. Official language: Spanish. Official currency: new Uruguayan peso of 100 centésimos. Area: 72,172 sq mi (186,926 sq km). Population (1983 est): 2,954,000. Capital and main port: Montevideo.

Uruguay River (Portuguese name: Rio Uruguai; Spanish name: Río Uruguay) A river in South America. Rising in S Brazil, it flows generally SW forming the Argentina–Brazil and Argentina–Uruguay borders before joining the Rio Paraná to form the Río de la Plata. Length: about 1000 mi (1600 km).

Uruk (biblical name: Erech; modern name: Warka) An ancient city in S Mesopotamia. The site testifies to the beginnings of Sumerian civilization in the 4th millennium BC; significant finds include pictographic writing and pottery made on a wheel. In the 3rd millennium, Uruk was a center for the worship of the god *Anu. *Gilgamesh was one of its rulers. Supplanted by *Ur (c. 2100), Uruk nevertheless remained inhabited until the early Christian era.

Ürümqi (or Urumchi; former name: Tihwa) 43 43N 87 38E A city in NW China, the capital of Xinjiang Uygur AR, and the site of its university. Industries include iron and steel and machine building. Population (1957 est): 275,000.

ushabti A figurine of faience, wood, or stone placed in an ancient Egyptian tomb to serve the deceased in the afterlife. Called "answerers," they carried inscriptions asserting their readiness to answer the gods' summons to work.

Ushant (French name: Ouessant) 48 28N 5 05W A French island off the W coast of Brittany. Two naval battles (1778 and 1794) between the British and the French were fought off its coast. Area: about 6 sq mi (16 sq km).

Usküb. See Skopje.

Üsküdar (former name: Scutarı)   41 02N 29 02E A town in NW Turkey, a suburb of Istanbul on the opposite side of the Bosporus. The British military base here during the Crimean War included the hospital in which Florence Nightingale worked.

Uspallata   32 43S 69 24W A pass through the Andes, in S South America at the foot of Mount Aconcagua, linking Santiago (Chile) with Mendoza (Argentina). The statue *Christ of the Andes* was erected here in 1904. Height: 12,600 ft (3840 m).

USSR.   *See* Soviet Union.

Ussuri River   A river in E Asia, rising in the extreme E Soviet Union and forming part of the border with China as it flows N to the Amur River at Khabarovsk. Border fighting between Soviet and Chinese forces has occurred here (1964, 1972). Length: about 500 mi (800 km).

PETER USTINOV   *As an unsavory legionnaire in the comedy film* The Last Remake of Beau Geste *(1977).*

Ustinov, Peter (Alexander)   (1921–   ) British actor, director, and dramatist of Russian descent. In the theater he acted mostly in his own plays, which include *The Love of Four Colonels* (1951) and *Romanoff and Juliet* (1956); his many films include *Death on the Nile* (1978). He has written novels and an autobiography; he is also well known as an impersonator and television personality.

Ust-Kamenogorsk   49 58N 82 36E A port in the Soviet Union, in the E Kazakh SSR on the Irtysh River. It is the center of a zinc-, copper-, and lead-mining region. Population (1981 est): 286,000.

Ustyurt Plateau (*or* Ust Urt Plateau)   A desert upland in the SW Soviet Union, lying between the Caspian and Aral Seas in the Kazakh and Uzbek SSRs at an average height of about 656 ft (200 m). Area: about 200,000 77,204 sq mi (sq km).

Usumbura.   *See* Bujumbura.

usury   In medieval canon law, the charging of interest for the loan of money. Although Christians were debarred from being moneylenders, the profession was permitted to Jews by the fourth Lateran Council (1215). Since Jews were allowed by the Pentateuch to lend money at interest to strangers, and were excluded from many alternative occupations, they comprised the majority of moneylenders. By the late middle ages, however, with growing demand for credit to meet the needs of trade, many Christians, notably at Cahors and in Lombardy, ignored canonical prohibition and became moneylenders and usury came to mean the charging of extortionate interest.

Utagawa Kuniyoshi   (Igusa Magosaburo; 1797–1861) Japanese painter and printmaker of the *ukiyo-e movement. He is known for his warrior and landscape prints.

Utah   One of the mountain states, bordered by Nevada (W), Idaho and Wyoming (N,NE), Colorado (E), and Arizona (S). The Wasatch Range of the Rocky Mountains divides the state into two arid regions: the Great Basin, which includes the Great Salt Lake, and the Great Salt Lake Desert in the W and the Colorado Plateau in the E. The raising of livestock is the principal agricultural activity but further growth in this sector is limited by the lack of irrigation and by soil erosion. Manufacturing is increasing in importance, especially food products, fabricated steel, spacecraft and, more recently, electronics equipment. There are significant deposits of copper, oil, natural gas, and uranium. Scenic attractions, such as Bryce Canyon and Zion National Park, make it a popular tourist area. *History*: the area was inhabited from c.9000 BC. Europeans (Spanish missionaries) first entered the area in 1776 and the region was held by the Spanish until ceded to the US by Mexico in 1848. The persecuted Mormons, who had emigrated from New York, began major settlements here in 1847, thereby dispossessing the Ute Indians, and their religion continues to exert a dominating influence over the life of the state. After conflict between the Mormons and the federal government over the issue of polygamy was resolved, Utah was finally admitted to the Union in 1896. Area: 84,916 sq mi (219,931 sq km). Population (1980): 1,461,037. Capital: Salt Lake City.

Utamaro.   *See* Kitagawa Utamaro.

uterus   The part of a woman's reproductive tract in which the fetus develops. The uterus is a hollow muscular organ, about 3 in (7.5 cm) long in the absence of pregnancy. It is connected by the vagina to the outside and to the ovaries by the Fallopian tubes. In a nonpregnant woman the lining of the uterus is shed at monthly intervals (*see* menstruation). During *childbirth the uterus, which is greatly enlarged (about 12 in [30 cm] long), undergoes strong contractions to expel the baby. *See also* cervix.

Utica   43 06N 75 15W A city in New York, on the Mohawk River. F. W. Woolworth opened his first store here in 1879. There is an annual Utica Eisteddfod, sponsored by its many Welsh inhabitants. Industries include dairy farming and textiles. Population (1980): 75,435.

utilitarianism   An ethical doctrine holding that the best action is the one that will result in the greatest happiness and least pain for the greatest number of people. Utilitarianism flourished in Britain from the mid-18th century to the mid-19th century. *Hume, *Bentham, and James *Mill propounded it and John Stuart Mill defended it. It influenced all thought in politics and morals and was the most widespread British contribution to such thought. Both *intuitionism and *idealism have developed critiques of the doctrine, based on its inherent unfairness, the difficulty of assessing consequences, and the belief that some acts are intrinsically good or intrinsically bad, regardless of outcome.

utopianism   A program of total social and political reform with the object of establishing a perfect society. The term derives from the imaginary state depicted in Thomas *More's *Utopia* (1516). Utopian schemes have sometimes found practical expression in social experiment, such as Robert *Owen's communities. Others, such as *Utopia* itself, are literary satires attacking existing institutions by comparing them unfavorably with imaginary ideals. Utopianism advocates a communistic organization of society, but the concomitant authoritarianism reveals that no way has been found of reconciling individual freedom and happiness with social justice.

Utrecht   52 06N 5 07E A city in the central Netherlands, the capital of Utrecht province. The Union of Utrecht (1579) united the northern provinces of the Netherlands against Spain. The Treaties of *Utrecht (1713–14) were concluded here. Its notable buildings include the gothic cathedral (14th century) and its famous university (founded 1636). An important railroad center, its industries include textiles, chemicals, and metallurgy. An annual trade fair is held here. Population (1981 est): 236,211.

Utrecht, Treaties of   (1713–14) A series of treaties between France and, respectively, Britain, the Netherlands, Prussia, Portugal, and Savoy that concluded the War of the *Spanish Succession. Further treaties arranged settlements with Spain and the Holy Roman Empire. The effect of the treaties was to end Louis XIV's attempts at European expansion.

Utrillo, Maurice   (1883–1955) French painter, the illegitimate son of Suzanne Valadon (1867–1938), an artist's model who later became an artist. For almost his entire life, he suffered from alcoholism and drug addiction. He specialized in painting often deserted street scenes, notably of Montmartre, which are distinguished by their near-monochrome colors and precise drawing. These were often based on picture-postcards and after 1916 became somewhat repetitive.

Uttar Pradesh   A state in N India, stretching from highlands N across the Ganges plain into the Himalayas. The most populous state, it produces grains, pulses, and sugar cane. Forestry is important but there is little industry. *History*: the center of N Indian culture, Uttar Pradesh was also the core of the Mogul Empire. It was the center of the Indian Mutiny (1857–59) against British rule and of Indian nationalism. Area: 113,643 sq mi (294,413 sq km). Population (1981): 110,858,019. Capital: Lucknow.

uvula. *See* palate.

Uzbek Soviet Socialist Republic (*or* Uzbekistan) A constituent republic in the S Soviet Union. The NW comprises desert but fertile land is found in the SE. The Uzbeks, who are Turkic-speaking Sunnite Muslims, make up two thirds of the population. Uzbekistan is rich in mineral deposits, including oil, coal, and copper, and has more than 20 hydroelectric plants and 3 natural gas pipelines in operation. Industries include mining, chemicals, textiles, and paper. The region is the chief cotton-growing area in the Soviet Union and the third most important in the world. Rice is also produced. *History*: the region was invaded by the Persians under Darius I, the Macedonians under Alexander the Great, and then by the Arabs (8th century AD) and the Mongols (13th century). In the 16th century the Uzbeks became the dominant people in the region, which was annexed by Russia in the 19th century. The Uzbek SSR was formed in 1924. Area: 173,546 sq mi (449,600 sq km). Population (1981 est): 16,158,000. Capital: Tashkent.

V

V-1 A German World War II unguided missile, also called a flying bomb. It carried about 2000 pounds (900 kg) of high explosive. Some 8000 missiles were launched against London between June 1944 and March 1945, killing over 5500 civilians. The "V" stands for the German *Vergeltungswaffe*, retaliation weapon.

V-2 A German World War II *ballistic missile powered by a rocket engine using alcohol and liquid oxygen as fuel. It carried about 2000 pounds (900 kg) of high explosive. Some 4000 were used against Britain and the Low Countries in 1944 and 1945. It became the basis for both US and Soviet postwar rocket design.

Vaal River A river in South Africa, rising in the SE Transvaal. It flows generally W and SW, to join the Orange River and forms part of the Orange Free State–Transvaal border. The **Vaal Dam**, near Vereeniging, supplies water to the mines of the Witwatersrand. Length: 750 mi (1210 km).

Vaasa (Swedish name: Vasa) 63 06N 21 36E A seaport in W Finland, on the Gulf of Bothnia. Founded in 1606, it was rebuilt nearer the sea following a fire in 1852. Its industries include ship repairing, textiles, and food processing. Population (1980): 53,758.

vaccination (*or* inoculation) The introduction of inactivated or dead disease-causing microorganisms (vaccine) into the body to stimulate the formation of *antibodies to these agents without producing the disease (*see also* immunity). The first vaccination (against smallpox) was performed by Edward *Jenner in 1798. Vaccination is now routinely used to prevent such life-threatening infections as poliomyelitis, diphtheria, tetanus, and tuberculosis. It is also used to protect visitors to areas where such infections as yellow fever, cholera, and typhoid fever are endemic. Vaccines are usually given by injection but some can be administered through skin scratches and some are taken by mouth. Vaccination against German measles (rubella) may be given to nonpregnant women of child-bearing age to prevent the malformations in the fetus that this disease can cause. The use of the whooping cough vaccine is controversial as in very rare cases it has caused brain damage.

vacuum A region of space that contains no matter. In practice, a perfect vacuum is impossible to obtain and any region in which the pressure of the gas is less than about one millimeter of mercury may be considered a vacuum. In technical work a soft (*or* low) vacuum goes down to a pressure of 10^{-4} mmHg, a hard (*or* high) vacuum is between 10^{-4} and 10^{-9} mmHg, and an ultrahigh vacuum is below 10^{-9} mmHg. Vacuum technology is used in making cathode-ray tubes, light bulbs, etc., and is used in certain forms of food preservation. **Vacuum gauges** include the *McLeod gauge and *Pirani gauge.

vacuum flask. *See* Dewar flask.

Vadodara. *See* Baroda.

Vaduz 47 08N 9 32E The capital of the principality of Liechtenstein. It is a tourist center and its castle (restored 1905–16) is the residence of the ruling prince. Population (1980): 4606.

vagina The part of the reproductive tract of women and other female mammals into which the *penis is inserted during sexual intercourse. It connects the uterus to the exterior and is readily distensible to allow for childbirth.

vagus nerve An important nerve that connects the brain with the throat, larynx, heart, lungs, stomach, and gut. Surgical cutting of a branch of the vagus nerve (**vagotomy**) is sometimes carried out to reduce the secretion of acid by the stomach in the treatment of a peptic ulcer.

Valdemar I (*or* Waldemar; 1131–82) King of Denmark (1157–82). His defeat of rival claimants to the throne ended a prolonged civil war in Denmark. His campaigns against the Wends (1159–69), assisted by his minister *Absalon, ended in victory with the seizure of Rügen. He subsequently repressed internal unrest.

Valdemar II (*or* Waldemar; 1170–1241) King of Denmark (1202–41); the son of Valdemar I. Before becoming king he conquered Holstein and Hamburg (1200–01) and later conducted successful campaigns in the E Baltic region. In 1219 he conquered Estonia but from 1223 to 1225 was imprisoned by a German vassal. At home he introduced military and legal reforms, issuing a revised legal code, the Law of Jutland (1241).

Valdemar IV Atterdag (*or* Waldemar; c. 1320–75) King of Denmark (1340–75). He was brought up at the court of Emperor Louis IV, Denmark being in the hands of foreign princes. Recognized as king in 1340, his reunification of Danish territories was completed by the recovery of Skåne from Sweden in 1360. His conquest of Gotland in the Baltic (1361) brought opposition from the Hanseatic League, which defeated Valdemar (1368) and forced him to accept the unfavorable Treaty of Stralsund (1370). His daughter *Margaret became Queen of Denmark, Norway, and Sweden.

Valdivia 39 46S 73 15W A port in S Chile, on the Río Valdivia near the Pacific coast. It was badly damaged by earthquake (1960). Industries include tanning, shipbuilding, and sugar refining. It contains the Southern University of Chile (1954). Population (1976 est): 103,600.

valence (*or* valency) The combining power of an atom, ion, or radical. It is equal to the number of hydrogen atoms that the atom, ion, or radical can combine with or replace in forming compounds, i.e. it is the number of single covalent or electrovalent bonds (*see* chemical bonds) that an atom, etc., can make. Many elements have more than one valence, for example phosphorus has valences of three and five. A **valence electron** is an electron in the outer shell of an atom that participates in forming chemical (valence) bonds. *See also* energy band.

Valence 44 56N 4 54E A city in SE France, the capital of the Drôme department on the Rhône River. It has a cathedral (11th–12th centuries) and is a commercial center for agricultural produce. Population (1975): 70,307.

Valencia 39 29N 0 24W The third largest city in Spain, on the Guadalaviar estuary. In 1021 it became the capital of the Moorish kingdom of Valencia. El Cid, the legendary Spanish hero, took the city from the Moors and held it from 1094 until his death in 1099. Its many notable buildings include the cathedral (1262–1482); the university was founded in 1500. The center of a productive agricultural area, Valencia has an important trade in oranges, rice, and silk. Population (1976 est): 713,026.

Valencia 10 14N 67 59W The third largest city in Venezuela. It is the focus of the country's most productive agricultural area and is a major industrial center. The University of Carabobo was founded here in 1852. Population (1976 est): 439,000.

Valencia A former kingdom in E Spain, corresponding approximately to the present-day province of Valencia. It was taken from the Moors by El Cid during the 11th century and came under the rule of Aragon in 1238.

Valenciennes 50 22N 3 32E A city in N France, in the Nord department. It has metallurgical and textile industries and an oil refinery. Its once famous lace industry is being revived. Population (1975): 43,202.

Valens (d. 378 AD) Eastern Roman emperor (364–78). Valens owed his accession to his brother *Valentinian, emperor in the West. During Valens' reign the Visigoths crossed the Danube and killed Valens at the battle of *Adrianople.

valentine A greeting card sent anonymously on February 14 as a declaration of affection. In ancient Rome boys drew girls' names from a love urn on February 15 and the early Christian Church transferred this popular pagan custom to St Valentine's feast day rather than abolish it. Paper valentines date from the 16th century.

Valentine, St (died c. 269) Roman priest and martyr, known as the patron of lovers. The customs practiced on his feast day (Feb 14) have no connection with his life (*see* valentine).

Valentinian I (d. 375 AD) Western Roman emperor (364–75). Valentinian became emperor by the acclamation of the army at Nicaea and shortly afterward made his brother *Valens emperor in the East. Reputedly of cruel disposition, he fought campaigns in the north of the Empire, restoring the Rhine frontier and Hadrian's Wall.

Valentino, Rudolf (Rodolpho Gugliemi di Valentina d'Antonguolla; 1895–1926) US film actor, born in Italy. He held various laboring jobs between arriving in the US in 1913 and going to Hollywood in 1918. His performances in *Four Horsemen of the Apocalypse* (1921), *The Sheik* (1921), *Blood and Sand* (1922), *Son of the Sheik* (1926), and othe romantic dramas of the early silent cinema established him as the leading cinema idol of the 1920s.

RUDOLF VALENTINO *In one of his most popular films* Blood and Sand *(1922).*

Valera, Eamon De. *See* De Valera, Eamon.

valerian A perennial or (rarely) annual herb of either of the genera *Valeriana* (200 species) or *Centranthus* (12 species), native to the N hemisphere. Up to about 40 in (1 m) high, the plants usually have lobed leaves and small fragrant pink, red, or white five-lobed funnel-shaped flowers clustered into terminal heads. The root of the common valerian (*V. officinalis*), of Eurasia, has sedative properties. Family: *Valerianaceae*.

Valéry, Paul (1871–1945) French poet, essayist, and critic. After publishing some early Symbolist verse he devoted himself for many years to abstract metaphysical study. *Cahiers* (29 vols, 1957–60) is a record of his daily speculations from 1894 until his death. His later poetry in *La Jeune Parque* (1917) and *Charmes* (1922) combines sensuous lyricism with intellectual force. He published many collections of essays on literary, scientific, and political topics.

Valhalla In Teutonic mythology, one of the three homes of *Odin, imagined as an enormous hall the rafters of which are spears and the walls shields. Half of the warriors who die in battle are brought by the *Valkyries to Valhalla, where they spend their days in battle and their nights in feasting and listening to songs of their heroic exploits.

Valium. *See* benzodiazepines.

Valkyries In Teutonic mythology, beautiful maidens, between 3 and 27 in number, who are the personal attendants of *Odin. They wear helmets and armor, carry spears and, led by *Freyja, ride on horseback over battlefields in order to find and carry away the slain warriors whom Odin has chosen to live with him in *Valhalla.

Valla, Lorenzo (1405–57) Italian Renaissance humanist. He was a violent opponent of *scholasticism and an able scholar. In his *De voluptate* (*On Pleasure*; 1431), he argued that the pleasures of the senses were the greatest good. Valla's iconoclastic views had a considerable influence upon later Renaissance thought.

Valladolid 41 39N 4 45W A city in central Spain, in Old Castile. It was formerly the capital of Castile and León (14th–15th centuries). It has a 16th-century cathedral and contains Cervantes' house; its university was founded in 1346. Christopher Columbus died here (1506). An industrial center, its industries include brewing and textiles. Population (1974 est): 275,012.

Valle d'Aosta An autonomous region in NW Italy, consisting of the upper basin of the Dora Baltea River. Created in 1945, it has a large French-speaking population. Industry is replacing agriculture as the main activity and there are valuable hydroelectric resources. Tourism is important. Area: 1260 sq mi (3262 sq km). Population (1980 est): 114,469. Capital: Aosta.

Valletta 35 54N 14 32E The capital of Malta, a port on the N coast with one of the finest harbors in the world. Founded in 1566 by the Knights of St John, its main buildings include the 16th-century St John's Co-Cathedral and the University of Malta (1769). Formerly an important British naval base, its dockyards have been converted to commercial use and it is now an important transit center for Mediterranean shipping. Population (1980): 14,073.

valley An elongated depression in the earth's surface. It is usually occupied by a river or stream at its base and terminates on joining another river, a lake, or the ocean. Valleys have various origins but the common **V-shaped valley** is formed as the result of erosion by a river. Those that originated through glacial erosion are **U-shaped valleys**, with steep sides and broad floors, often occupied by deep lakes (*see* fjord). *See also* rift valley.

Valley Forge The site, 22 mi (35 km) NW of Philadelphia, of the headquarters of General *George Washington's forces in the winter of 1777–78 during the *American Revolution. Despite a severe lack of food and warm clothing, Washington's men remained loyal to the cause of American independence and emerged ready for an offensive against the British forces in the spring of 1778. Their fighting capacity was greatly improved by the training they received from Baron Friedrich Wilhelm Von *Steuben, a former Prussian officer, who became inspector general of the Continental Army.

Valley of Ten Thousand Smokes A volcanic area in S Alaska. Its name derives from the many fissures spouting smoke, gas, and steam.

Valley of the Kings The cemetery of the Egyptian pharaohs from about 1580 to about 1085 BC, W of the Nile, near *Thebes. Tombs were tunneled in the limestone cliffs while mortuary temples were built in the valley below. All the tombs were robbed, except that of *Tutankhamen.

Valois The royal dynasty of France from 1328 to 1589, succeeding the *Capetians. The *Hundred Years' War (1337–1453) nearly destroyed Valois power, which was saved by *Charles VII (reigned 1422–61). He and his son *Louis XI vigorously extended royal authority. Their successors, *Charles VIII and *Louis XII, waged disastrous wars in Italy, where they opposed the *Habsburgs. The last Valois were the victims of rival religious factions at court (*see* Wars of Religion) and were succeeded by the *Bourbons.

Valois, Dame Ninette de. *See* de Valois, Dame Ninette.

Valona. *See* Vlora.

Valparaíso 33 05S 71 40W The second largest city in Chile, on the Pacific Ocean. Founded by the Spanish (1536), it has suffered several earthquakes. Notable surviving buildings include the cathedral. It is the site of two universities (1926 and 1928). Valparaíso is a major port, handling most Chilean imports, and is an important industrial and commercial center. Manufactures include chemicals, textiles, and vegetable oils. Population (1976 est): 248,440.

value-added tax (VAT) An indirect tax on goods calculated by adding a percentage to the value of a product as it increases at each stage of production; the whole cost of the tax is eventually passed on to the consumer.

vampire In folklore, a soulless or "undead" corpse that rises from its coffin at night, sometimes taking the form of a vampire bat, and sucks the blood of living victims (who are thus also transformed into vampires). The vampire cannot lie at rest but must continually find new victims. It attacks only at night and is repelled by crucifixes, garlic, and the light of day. The body of a vampire can be destroyed by being beheaded, burned, having a stake driven through its heart, or by exposure to sunlight. Although appearing in many cultures, the vampire legend is particularly associated with E European folklore and was popularized by Bram Stoker's *Dracula* (1897), the source of many modern vampire films.

VAMPIRE BAT *Its chisel-like incisor teeth are used to cut the flesh of the victims to cause a flow of blood.*

vampire bat A bat of the family *Desmodontidae* (3 species), of Central and South America. The most common species is *Desmodus rotundus*, 3–3.5 in (7.5–9 cm) long. Vampire bats feed on the blood of mammals or birds. They make a small incision in the skin with their sharp incisor teeth and lap up the blood of their sleeping victim with a grooved tongue. Vampire bats are too small to cause serious blood loss to their host; they do, however, transmit dangerous diseases, including rabies.

Van, Lake A lake in SW Turkey. It has no outlet and is therefore salty; sodium carbonate is extracted by evaporation, and the lake is fished for darekh. Area: 1443 sq mi (3738 sq km).

vanadium (V) A transition metal, named for the Norse goddess Vanadis. The metal is isolated by reduction of the trichloride (VCl₃) with magnesium or of the pentoxide (V₂O₅) with calcium. It is an important additive to rust-resistant *steels and high-speed tool steels. The pentoxide is a useful catalyst in the oil industry. Complex vanadate ions (for example $VO_{3/4}^{-}$) exist in solution. At no 23; at wt 50.942; mp 1890 ± 10°C; bp 3380°C.

Van Allen, James Alfred (1914–) US physicist, who during World War II developed a proximity fuse for anti-aircraft shells. After the war he used rockets for research into the upper atmosphere, being especially interested in cosmic rays. In 1958, while professor of physics at Iowa University, he used the results of the Explorer satellites to deduce the existence of belts of charged particles (*see* Van Allen radiation belts) above the earth.

Van Allen radiation belts Two regions of charged particles in the earth's *magnetosphere. The toroidal inner belt lies 620–3,105 mi (1000–5000 km) above the equator and contains protons and electrons captured from the *solar wind or derived from cosmic-ray interactions. The outer belt lies 9,315–15,525 mi (15,000–25,000 km) above the equator, curving down toward the earth's magnetic poles, and contains mainly electrons from the solar wind. The belts were discovered in 1958 by James *Van Allen on his analysis of observations by early Explorer satellites.

Vanbrugh, Sir John (1664–1726) English architect and dramatist. England's most successful *baroque architect, his most impressive buildings were Castle Howard (1699–1726), Blenheim Palace (begun 1705), and Seton Delaval (begun 1720). Highly imaginative and extravagant in his designs and costs, Vanbrugh rarely finished buildings. His plays include *The Provoked Wife* (1690–92) and *The Relapse* (1697).

Van Buren, Martin (1782–1862) US statesman; 8th President of the US (1837–41). After serving as a New York state senator (1812–20) and US senator (1821–28) Van Buren was elected governor of New York in 1828. Since he had helped to establish the *Democratic Party and was a strong supporter of President Andrew *Jackson, Van Buren resigned the governorship after only three months in office to accept appointment as secretary of state. During Jackson's second term, Van Buren served as vice president and was Jackson's personal choice to succeed him as the Democratic presidential nominee in 1836. Victorious in the general election, Van Buren began his administration during the Panic of 1837, the country's first great economic depression, which was caused largely by a wave of land speculation in the West. His conservative fiscal policies and his refusal to provide government aid to prop up the economy led to his defeat in the 1840 election.

Vance, Cyrus (1917–) US statesman; secretary of state (1977–80). He represented President Johnson in Cyprus (1967) and Korea (1968) and was US negotiator at the Paris peace talks on Vietnam (1968–69). He resigned as secretary of state in opposition to President Carter's attempt to rescue the US hostages held in Tehran (Iran).

Vancouver 49 13N 123 06W A city and port in W Canada, in British Columbia on Burrard Inlet and the Fraser River delta. Established in 1862 on a beautiful site at the S end of the Coast Mountains, it has developed a rich tourist industry. Vancouver is Canada's largest Pacific port and railhead. With a large airport, it is a center for international trade and warehousing. It is the commercial and industrial center of British Columbia, important especially for its timber, paper, and associated industries. Other industries include food processing, ship repairing, and fishing. Vancouver has two universities and a thriving cultural life. Population (1976): 410,118.

Vancouver, George (c. 1758–98) British navigator. He served his apprenticeship under Capt *Cook and in 1791 set out on a long voyage in the Pacific. He visited Australia and then proceeded NW, charting the W coast of America and circumnavigating the island named for him.

Vancouver Island A Canadian island off the Pacific coast of British Columbia. Its E coastal plain rises to glaciers and forested mountains. The economy depends on timber, mining, fishing, and tourism; it is also a popular retirement area. Area: 12,408 sq mi (32,137 sq km). Population (1971 est): 380,000. Chief town: Victoria.

Vandals A Germanic tribe that during the first four centuries AD migrated southward from Scandinavia and the S Baltic coast through Europe to Spain and Africa. There, in 429, they established a kingdom under Genseric and in 455 sacked Rome. The devastation they caused gave rise to the term vandalism. In 534, however, their kingdom was destroyed by the Byzantine general *Belisarius.

Van de Graaff generator A type of *electrostatic generator, invented by the US physicist Robert Jemison Van de Graaff (1901–67), that produces static potentials of millions of volts. Charge from an external source is fed onto a continuously moving belt, which transfers it to the inside of a large hollow conducting sphere. The charge moves to the outer surface of the sphere, leaving the inside neutral and able to collect more charge. This type of generator can be used to provide a high-voltage source for the Van de Graaff *accelerator.

Vanderbilt, Cornelius (1794–1877) US financier. Establishing a small ferry service in New York harbor at the age of 16, Vanderbilt gradually expanded his maritime interests to include regular schooner service in Long Island Sound and steamboat service on the Hudson River. At the time of the California *Gold Rush (1848–49), Vanderbilt eagerly sought to transport would-be miners to the gold fields, and he negotiated with the Nicaraguan government to obtain transit rights that made his New York-to-San Francisco sea and land route shorter than the routes of any of his competitors. In 1855 he also established transatlantic service. By the time of the Civil War, Vanderbilt had become increasingly interested in railroad investments, and after selling off his various shipping lines, he purchased several railroads that he combined into the New York Central R. R. Late in life, he endowed Vanderbilt University in Nashville, Tennessee (1873).

Van der Post, Laurens (1906–) South African novelist. His travel books include *Venture to the Interior* (1952) and *The Lost World of the Kalahari* (1958). His novels, often imbued with deep feeling for the African landscape, include *The Hunter and the Whale* (1967) and *A Story Like the Wind* (1972).

Van der Waals, Johannes Diderik (1837–1923) Dutch physicist, who was professor at Amsterdam University (1877–1907). He was awarded the 1910 Nobel Prize for his work on the intermolecular forces (Van der Waals' forces) and his equation of state (*see* Van der Waals' equation), which takes these forces into account.

Van der Waals' equation A modification of the ideal gas equation, $pV = RT$, where p is the pressure exerted by a gas with volume V and absolute temperature T. R is the *gas constant. Van der Waals adjusted V to $(V - b)$ to take account of the volume occupied by the gas molecules. He also assumed that forces of attraction exist between the gas molecules and therefore adjusted the pressure term to $(p - a/V^2)$. Both a and b are constant for a particular gas. The intermolecular forces are known as **Van der Waals' forces** and are caused by molecules inducing electric *dipole moments in neighboring molecules.

van de Velde A family of 17th-century Dutch painters. **Willem van de Velde the Elder** (1611–93) and his eldest son **Willem van de Velde the Younger** (1633–1707) were both marine artists, who lived in England after 1672 in the service of Charles II. His younger son **Adriaen van de Velde** (1636–72) was a landscape painter, who was often employed by such artists as *Ruisdael and *Hobbema to paint the figures in their landscapes. **Esaias van de Velde** (c. 1591–1630), the landscape painter, was probably the brother of Willem van de Velde the Elder. He is best known as the teacher of the landscape painter Jan van *Goyen and for such works as *Winter Scene*, which herald the realistic landscapes of the later 17th-century Dutch school.

van de Velde, Henry (1863–1957) Belgian *Art Nouveau architect and interior designer. A painter until about 1890, he took up design under the influence of William *Morris and the *Arts and Crafts movement. In 1901, after working in Paris and Berlin, he settled in Weimar, where he directed (1901–14) its School of Arts and Crafts, later part of the *Bauhaus.

Van Dieman's Land. *See* Tasmania.

van Dieman, Anthony. *See* Dieman, Anthony van.

Van Dyck, Sir Anthony (*or* Vandyke; 1599–1641) Flemish *baroque painter, born in Antwerp. Early in his career, he was assistant to *Rubens, who greatly influenced his work. After working in England for James I, he visited Italy (1621–27). In 1632 he returned to England as painter to □Charles I. Although he painted many religious and mythological subjects, such as *Cupid and Psyche*, his reputation rests largely on his portraits of the English court. Many of these are in Britain's Royal Art Collection. *Charles I on Horseback*, and *Thomas Killigrew and Lord Croft* demonstrate the elegance and grandeur of his style. He had a profound influence on the development of British portraiture.

Vänern, Lake The largest lake in Sweden. It drains into the Kattegat via the Göta River, a major source of hydroelectric power. Area: 2141 sq mi (5546 sq km).

Vane the Elder, Sir Henry (1589–1655) English politician. He represented Charles I in negotiations with parliament (1640) but fought against the king in the English Civil War. His son **Sir Henry Vane the Younger** (1613–62), a staunch Puritan, emigrated to New England in 1635 but returned to England in 1637 and was prominent in the opposition to the king. A member of the state council during the Commonwealth (1649–53) he then retired (1653), participated in the overthrow of Richard Cromwell (1659), and was executed after the Restoration.

van Eyck, Jan (c. 1390–1441) Flemish painter, who also served as diplomatic envoy of Philip the Good, Duke of Burgundy. The controversial *Adoration of the Lamb* altarpiece (Cathedral of S Bavon, Ghent) was probably begun by his elder brother **Hubert van Eyck** (d. 1426) and completed by Jan after Hubert's death. Jan is noted for his realistic portraits, particularly *The Arnolfini Marriage* and *Man in a Red Turban*. He certainly perfected and possibly invented the Flemish technique of oil painting, in which the pigment is mixed with oil and turpentine and applied in thin glazes.

Van Gogh, Vincent (1853–90) Dutch postimpressionist painter, born at Zundert, the son of a pastor. He worked as an art dealer, a teacher in England, and a missionary among coalminers before taking up painting in about 1880. His early works were chiefly drawings of peasants. After a limited training in The Hague and in Antwerp, where he studied the works of *Rubens and Japanese prints, he moved to Paris (1886). Here he briefly adopted the style of *impressionism and later of *pointillism. In Arles in 1888 he painted his best-known works—orchards, sunflowers, and the local postman and his family—but only one painting was sold during his lifetime. The visit of his friend *Gauguin ended in a quarrel during which Van Gogh cut off part of his own left ear. In 1889 he entered a mental asylum at Saint-Rémy. The ominous *Wheatfield with Crows* was painted shortly before his suicide, in Auvers. His letters to his brother (Theo) contain the best account of his life and work. *See* expressionism.

Vanilla A genus of climbing *orchids (about 90 species), native to tropical Asia and America. They have long fleshy stems attached to trees by aerial roots and produce large white and yellow flowers. Several species are cultivated commercially for the flavoring agent vanilla, the most important being *V. planifolia*. The fruit—a pod—contains an oily pulp and minute seeds and reaches a length of 8 in (20 cm). The aroma of vanilla is due to vanillin, a volatile oil resulting from curing and fermentation of the pods.

Van't Hoff, Jacobus Henricus (1852–1911) Dutch chemist, who pioneered the field of stereoisomerism, showing that the bonds of a carbon atom are arranged in a tetrahedron. This enabled him to explain *optical activity in terms of molecular structure. He also contributed to chemical thermodynamics and to the theory of solutions, for which he won the 1901 Nobel Prize. He was professor at Amsterdam University from 1878 to 1896, when he moved to the Academy of Sciences in Berlin.

Vanua Levu A volcanic island in the S Pacific Ocean, the second largest in Fiji. Sugar, copra, and gold are exported. Area: 2137 sq mi (5535 sq km). Chief town: Lambasa.

Vanuatu (formerly New Hebrides; French: Nouvelles-Hebrides) republic in the SW Pacific Ocean, consisting of 12 main islands and 60 smaller islets comprising a chain about 500 mi (800 km) long. The largest of the islands, most of which are heavily forested and volcanic, are Espiritu Santo and Malikula. Discovered by the Portuguese (1606), they were jointly administered as a condominium by France and the UK (1906–80). In 1978 they became partially self-governing as a preliminary to their independence as the Republic of Vanuatu in 1980. Copra, cocoa, coffee, and beef are exported. Industries include tourism, fishing, and mining of manganese. The population is primarily Melanesian. Area: about 5700 sq mi (14,760 sq km). Population (1983 est): 127,000. Capital: Vila, on Efate.

vapor pressure The pressure of the vapor given off by a liquid or solid. The vapor pressure increases with temperature; when it equals the external pressure, the liquid boils. If the liquid or solid is in an enclosed space the number of molecules leaving it eventually reaches an equilibrium with the number of molecules returning to it. At this point the vapor is saturated and the pressure is the **saturated vapor pressure**.

Varanasi (*or* Benares) 25 20N 82 00E A city in India, in Uttar Pradesh on the Ganges River. A major place of pilgrimage for Hindus, Jains, Sikhs, and Buddhists, it has 3 mi (5 km) of ghats (steps), from which thousands of Hindus bathe in the sacred river. There are also burning ghats, from which the ashes of the cremated are scattered over the water. The city contains 1500 temples and two universities. Industries include engineering and brassware. Population (1971): 583,856.

Varèse, Edgard (1883–1965) French composer. He settled in the US in 1915. Pursuing his concept of music as "organized sound," he composed music characterized by dissonance, the use of unpitched sounds, and complex rhythms. His works include *Ionisation* (for 41 percussion instruments and two sirens; 1931), *Density 21.5* (for solo flute; 1935), and *Déserts* (for wind instruments and tape; 1949–54).

Vargas, Getúlio (1883–1954) Brazilian statesman; president (1934–45, 1951–54). He came to power in the revolution of 1930, which he led after losing the presidential election. In 1937 he announced the fascist New State, modeled on that of Portugal. He was overthrown in 1945 and re-elected in 1950 but, threatened with a military coup, he committed suicide.

variable A mathematical symbol for a quantity that can take any value from a set of values called the range. A variable that can take any value between two given values is called continuous; otherwise it is discrete. A quantity that can only take one value is called a constant.

variable stars Stars the brightness of which varies with time, the variations being regular, irregular, or a mixture of the two. In regular variables the brightness completes a cycle of changes in a period ranging from hours to years. The brightness variation can be up to several *magnitudes. The three major groups are: eclipsing *binary stars, which include *Algol variables; cataclysmic variables, such as *novae; and pulsating stars, which periodically brighten and fade as their surface layers expand and contract and which include *Cepheid variables, *RR Lyrae stars, and Mira stars (*see* Mira Ceti).

variance In a set of numbers, usually measurements, the quantity obtained by summing the squares of the differences between each number and the average value of the set and then dividing by the number of members of the set. Variance and, more often, its square root, called the **standard deviation**, are used to estimate scatter or random error in experimental results.

varicose veins Swollen tortuous veins in the legs caused by malfunctioning of the valves in the veins, which obstructs blood flow. Varicose veins tend to run in families and are commoner in older and fat people, women, and those who are constantly standing. They may produce a dull ache and later may be the cause of thrombosis or infection. To avoid these complications and for cosmetic reasons the veins are often injected with a substance that makes them shrivel up or they may be surgically removed.

Varna 43 12N 27 57E A city and port in E Bulgaria, on the Black Sea. Founded in the 6th century BC, it finally passed to Bulgaria in 1878. Processed foods and livestock are exported and it has engineering and boatbuilding industries. Population (1979 est): 286,382.

Varna, Battle of (November 10, 1444) The battle in which the Hungarians were decisively defeated by the Turks. It enabled the Turks to expand further into the Balkans and ultimately to capture Constantinople (1453).

varnish A resinous solution in oil or alcohol that dries to form a hard transparent coating on wood, metal, etc. The *resins may be natural, synthetic, or mixed. The natural resins used include *shellac, copal, dammar, and congo. *Polyurethane is a particularly durable and chemical-resistant synthetic resin used for protecting wood and metal in harsh environments. Polyesters and alkyds are also used, for example for coating paper containers or as a protective finish for ink.

varnish tree. *See* lacquer tree.

Varro, Marcus Terentius (116–27 BC) Roman scholar and poet. After a varied public career he was appointed public librarian by Julius Caesar in 47 BC. He wrote scholarly works on many subjects as well as satires and other poems. Only a 3-volume work, *On Agriculture*, and parts of a 25-volume work, *On the Latin Language*, survive.

varve dating A technique used in geology and archeology to give the age of a sediment and to provide information about the climate during which it was formed. Varves are layers of claylike sediment deposited from a melting glacier into a lake. Each varve represents a single year's deposition; a thick varve indicates that the sediment was deposited during a hot summer (since the glacier would melt more quickly and therefore deposit more material). Varves are particularly well developed in Scandinavia and in some regions their formation has continued from the Pleistocene Ice Age to the present: by counting the varves the absolute age of a particular sediment can be calculated.

Vasa The ruling dynasty of Sweden (1523–1818) and of Poland (1587–1668) founded by *Gustavus I Vasa. John III (1537–92; reigned 1568–92) married into the Polish royal house and his son Sigismund III (1566–1632) became King of both Poland (1587) and Sweden (1592). Sigismund was deposed (1599) in Sweden, where he was succeeded by his uncle *Charles IX, and the Vasa split into two competing lines. The best-known Vasa monarchs in Sweden were *Gustavus II Adolphus and *Christina.

Vasarely, Victor (1908–) Hungarian-born painter. After training in Budapest, he moved to Paris (1930), where his abstract paintings of geometric forms were initially influenced by *constructivism. By the 1950s and 1960s he was painting dazzling patterns that appear to move; these works are regarded as leading examples of *Op art.

Vasari, Giorgio (1511–74) Italian painter, architect, and writer. In Florence, under Medici patronage, he painted fresco cycles in the Palazzo Vecchio and built the *Uffizi, both works showing his respect for *mannerism. However he is best known for his *Lives of the Most Eminent Italian Architects, Painters, and Sculptors*, tracing the history of Renaissance art from Giotto to Michelangelo. First published in 1550, it is still popular and useful today, despite some inaccuracies.

vasectomy. *See* sterilization.

Västerås 59 36N 16 32E A city in central Sweden, on Lake Mälar. An important city in medieval times, it has a 12th-century castle and a gothic cathedral. It is a major center of the electrical industry. Population (1978 est): 117,487.

VAT. *See* value-added tax.

Vatican City, State of the A small independent state within the city of Rome, the seat of government of the Roman Catholic Church. St Peter's Square, St Peter's Basilica, the Vatican Palace, and Papal Gardens are within its area, and it includes 12 buildings outside its boundary, notably several churches and the pope's summer palace at Castel Gandolfo. It has its own army, police, diplomatic service, coinage, postal facilities, and radio station (Radio Vaticano, which provides an all-day service in 31 languages giving information on the Church). *History*: it came into being in 1929, when Pius XI signed the *Lateran Treaty with Mussolini, thereby ending a dispute between church and state dating from the incorporation of the *papal states into newly unified Italy in 1870. The state is governed by a commission appointed by the pope. Supreme pontiff: John Paul II. Official language: Italian. Area: 109 acres (44 hectares). Population (1976 est): 726.

Vatican Councils The 20th and 21st ecumenical councils of the Roman Catholic Church, held at Rome. **1.** (1869–70) The council that was convoked by *Pius IX to deal with a variety of topics but was overshadowed by the question of papal authority and resulted in the promulgation of the doctrine of papal *infallibility. The council was suspended because of the Franco-Prussian War. **2.** (1962–65) The council that was convoked by *John XXIII and continued by *Paul VI. Its main purpose, in Pope John's words, was *aggiornamento*, a bringing-up-to-date of the Church. It promulgated no dogmas but instead initiated fundamental changes, including reform of the liturgy and commitment to the *ecumenical movement and to greater collegiality in Church government. It established an atmosphere in which progressive critics could freely express their views.

Vatnajökull An icefield in SE Iceland. Several peaks protrude above the ice level rising to 6952 ft (2119 m) at Öræfajökull, the highest point on the island. Area: 3139 sq mi (8133 sq km).

Vauban, Sébastien Le Prestre de (1633–1707) French military engineer, who revolutionized siege warfare. Appointed engineer to Louis XIV of France in 1655, he directed sieges at Gravelines (1658), Maastricht (1673), and Luxembourg (1684).

vaudeville A type of popular entertainment featuring a variety of performers including singers, dancers, comedians, magicians, jugglers, and acrobats. It developed from entertainments given in taverns and from the music halls of 19th-century England. Vaudeville declined in the 1920s and 1930s with the rise of the rival attractions of motion pictures and the radio. Celebrated vaudeville performers, many of whom later became film and television performers, include W. C. *Fields, Will Rogers (1879–1935), Bob *Hope, George Burns (1896–), Gracie Allen (1906–64), Jack Benny (1894–1974), Jimmy Durante (1893–1980), and Fanny Brice (1891–1951).

Vaughan, Henry (c. 1622–95) English poet. After producing two volumes of secular verse, he turned to Metaphysical poetry, expressing a mystical religious awareness in vivid colloquial language. His best-known volumes are *Silex Scintillans* (1650; enlarged 1655) and *The Mount of Olives* (1652), a book of prose meditations.

Vaughan Williams, Ralph (1872–1958) British composer. He had lessons from Ravel. Influenced by English folksong and Tudor music, he developed a modal style that found its first full expression in *Fantasia on a Theme by Tallis* (for string orchestra; 1910). His works include nine symphonies of which the first, *A Sea Symphony* (1903–09), is choral. He also wrote the ballet *Job* (1931) and the opera *The Pilgrim's Progress* (1951).

vault An arched roof usually in brick or stone and first developed in ancient Egypt. The simplest and oldest type is the barrel or tunnel vault, a single continuous arch, which originally had to be supported by very thick walls. A more complicated type is the groin vault of the Roman and medieval periods, using a series of mutually supporting interlocking arches, which could span greater distances. The rib vault, consisting of a skeleton of diagonal ribs to support the interlocking arches, was developed by gothic builders. Its decorative counterpart is the fan vault with its multiplication of radiating ribs, a principal feature of the *Perpendicular style. With the invention of reinforced concrete, vaulting has advanced enormously, allowing huge distances to be covered without much support.

Vavilov, Nikolai Ivanovich (1887–1943) Soviet plant geneticist. He traveled widely, amassing a vast collection of plant varieties, particularly varieties of wheat. His researches into the origins of cultivated plants led him to propose 12 world centers of plant origin. Although a leading administrator of Soviet science, Vavilov's views brought him into conflict with *Lysenko and Stalinist ideology. He was arrested and imprisoned in 1940.

Veblen, Thorstein Bunde (1857–1929) US economist. He coined the term "conspicuous consumption" to define his theory that people make purchases for status, not for practical application of the product or service. The higher the cost of an article, the more exclusive it becomes. As the exclusive filters down to the lower classes, the upper class adopts new exclusive articles that filter down, continuing the cycle. He described this concept in *The Theory of The Leisure Class* (1899) and *Theory of Business Enterprise* (1904).

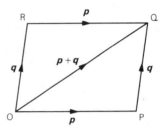

VECTORS *The two vectors OP (**p**) and PQ (**q**) add to give the resultant vector OQ (**p + q**). OR = PQ = **q**; OP = RQ = **p**. OQP is a vector triangle and ORQP is a parallelogram of vectors.*

vector (mathematics) A quantity that has both magnitude and direction. Examples of vectors include velocity, force, magnetic flux density, etc. A vector needs three numbers (called components) to be defined, each number representing its magnitude in one of three mutually perpendicular directions. Two vectors are added by adding the corresponding components and may be multiplied to give either a *scalar quantity or another vector.

vector (medicine) An organism capable of transmitting a disease-causing organism (pathogen) from one organism to another. Transmission may be accidental, for example the housefly carries bacteria picked up from its food, or the vector may play a significant role in the life cycle of the pathogen, for example the malarial parasite spends part of its life cycle in the mosquito, which transmits it to man.

Vedanta The various philosophical schools of Hinduism, which derive from the commentaries on the *Vedas*, especially the *Upanishads, the *Brahmasutras*, and the *Bhagavadgita*. The schools differ in their views on the nature of *Brahman and the individual soul, but have in common the belief in reincarnation, the truth of the *Vedas*, the law of *karma, and the need for spiritual release. Believing Brahman to be the cause of the world, they condemn Buddhism and Jainism.

Vedas (Sanskrit: divine knowledge) The basic Hindu scriptures, written in archaic Sanskrit (Vedic) around 1500 BC. It comprises hymns, invocations, mantras, spells, and rituals, mostly concerning the sacrificial worship of gods representing various natural forces. The canon comprises four main collections: the *Rigveda*, the *Samaveda*, the *Yajurveda*, and the *Atharvaveda*. The *Brahmanas*, the *Aranyakas*, and the *Upanishads*, which are later commentaries, may also be considered canonical. These scriptures are widely revered among Hindus.

veduta (Italian: view) A painting, drawing, or print of a view of a town or city. Examples of vedute are *Piranesi's engravings of Rome and *Canaletto's paintings of Venice. The **capriccio** is a specialized form of veduta consisting of various architectural elements combined to produce an imaginary setting. A famous capriccio is the etching of *St Paul's Cathedral in London with the Grand Canal of Venice* by William Marlow (1740–1813).

Vega A conspicuous white star, apparent magnitude 0.03 and 26.5 light years distant, that is the brightest star in the constellation Lyra.

Vega (Carpio), Lope Félix de (1562–1635) Spanish poet and dramatist. After serving with the Spanish Armada (1588) he became secretary to the Duke of Alba in Toledo, and settled in Madrid in 1610. His numerous love affairs continued after his ordination as priest in 1614, but his later years were saddened by the deaths of his wife, children, and mistresses. Most of his numerous plays, such as *Fuenteovejuna* (1612–14) and *El caballero de Olmeda* (1615–26), were based on Spanish history.

vegetarianism The practice of abstaining from eating animal flesh for ethical, religious, or nutritional reasons. Some vegetarians will not eat any animal products, including milk, cheese, eggs, etc., and are called **vegans**. Vegetarianism occurs in many religious traditions, including Buddhism, Jainism, and Hinduism, and it was advocated by *Pythagoras, *Plato, and many other thinkers.

vein (physiology) A thin-walled blood vessel that carries oxygen-depleted blood from the tissues to the *heart. Most of the smaller veins have valves to prevent backflow of blood. Damage to these valves leads to dilation of the veins (*see* varicose veins). The veins opening directly into the heart are the superior and inferior vena cavae and the pulmonary veins from the lungs, which are unique in carrying oxygenated blood.

Velázquez, Diego Rodriguez de Silva (1599–1660) Spanish painter, born in Seville. He trained under Francisco de *Herrera the Elder and Francisco Pacheco (1564–1654), his father-in-law, although he was most strongly influenced by *Titian. Initially he specialized in painting religious subjects and scenes from everyday life with still-lifes, before becoming (1623) court painter to Philip IV (1605–65; reigned 1621–65) and thereafter painting chiefly portraits of the royal family and the chief minister Olivares. Other works include his famous *Pope Innocent X* and the *Rokeby Venus*, painted during his second visit to Italy (1649–51). *Las Meninas* (c. 1656) is typical of the informality of his later court portraits.

veld (*or* veldt) A tract of open grassland on the plateau of S Africa. It includes the Highveld (over 4900 ft [1500 m]), Middleveld (4900–2,950 ft [1500–900 m]), and Lowveld (below 2,950 ft [900 m]).

velocity The rate of change of a body's position in a given direction. The speed of a body is not in a specified direction. Velocity is thus a *vector quantity and speed is a scalar quantity. **Angular velocity** is the rate of change of a body's motion about an axis. It is measured in radians per second.

velocity of light (*c*) The speed with which all *electromagnetic radiation travels through a vacuum, equal to $2.997,925 \times 10^8$ meters per second. It is one of the *fundamental constants and, according to the special theory of *relativity, is independent of the speed of the observer and cannot be exceeded by any material body.

velocity ratio. *See* mechanical advantage.

Venda, Republic of The smallest country in mainland Africa, within South African territory. Most of the population is Venda. *Economy*: chiefly agricultural, the main crop being maize; the timber industry is also developed. *History*: it was the third *Bantu Homeland to be granted full independence from South Africa (1979), but this is not recognized elsewhere in the world. President: Chief Patrick Mphephu (1925–). Official currency: South African rand. Area: 2861 sq mi (7410 sq km). Population (1980 est): 513,890. Capital: Thokoyandou.

Vendée A department in W France, in Pays de la Loire region. A series of peasant-royalist insurrections, the **Wars of the Vendée**, took place here (1793–1832). The first rebellion, catalyzed by the Republican government's introduction of conscription, was also fueled by loyalty to the Roman Catholic Church. After initial success the rebels were decisively defeated at Savenay (December, 1793). Subsequent abortive uprisings (1796, 1815, and 1832) failed to attract popular support. Area: 2709 sq mi (7016 sq km). Population (1975): 461,928. Capital: La Roche-sur-Yon.

Vendôme, Louis Joseph, Duc de (1654–1712) French marshal under Louis XIV. He fought in the Wars of the *Grand Alliance (1689–97) and of the Spanish Succession (1701–14). He was victorious at Luzzara (1702) and Cassano (1705) but was defeated by Marlborough at Oudenaarde (1708) and was then recalled. From 1710 until his death he campaigned successfully in Spain.

Venera probes A series of Soviet *planetary probes to Venus, first launched in 1961. Veneras 4 to 8 sent capsules into the hostile atmosphere, those of 7 and 8 surviving to reach the surface (1970, 1972). The Lander sections of Veneras 9 and 10 (1975), 11 and 12 (1978), and 13 and 14

(1982) all successfully reached the surface, relaying photographs back to earth via the Orbiter sections. Veneras 15 and 16 were launched in 1983.

venereal disease A disease spread predominantly by sexual intercourse, the most important of which are *syphilis and *gonorrhea.

Venetia A region of NE Italy between the Po River, the Alps, and the Adriatic Sea. The mainland territory of the Republic of Venice until 1797, Venetia then came under Austrian control and in 1815 formed part of the new kingdom of Lombardy-Venetia. Venetia was incorporated into the kingdom of Italy in 1866 and after World War I formed the "Three Venices"—Venezia Tridentina, Venezia Euganea, and Venezia Giulia. Most of the latter was lost to Yugoslavia after World War II and Italian Venetia was divided into the regions of Friuli-Venezia Giulia, Veneto, and Trentino-Alto-Adige.

Venezuela, Republic of A country on the N coast of South America bounded by the Caribbean Sea (N), Guyana (E), Brazil (S), and Colombia (SW and W). The plains of the Orinoco basin in the N rise to the Guiana Highlands in the SE, and in the NW the N end of the Andean chain reaches heights of over 16,000 ft (5000 m). Also in the NW is Lake Maracaibo. Most of the population is of mixed European and Indian descent. *Economy*: based chiefly on oil, first discovered in 1917 and of which Venezuela is now one of the world's largest producers and exporters. The industry was nationalized in 1976. Efforts are being made to diversify the economy, including plans to use the country's vast iron-ore deposits to increase steel production. Another major project is the construction of the world's largest aluminum smelter, which will be able to utilize the recent discovery of bauxite. Venezuela is also rich in diamonds, gold, zinc, copper, lead, silver, phosphates, manganese, and titanium. The agricultural sector remains relatively underdeveloped, although a large share of the oil revenues has been spent in attempts to develop this area. Crop growing in the N includes coffee, cocoa, sugar, corn, and rice, while further S stock raising is the principal agricultural activity. The vast forests remain largely unexploited. *History*: sighted by Columbus in 1498, it was visited in 1499 by Vespucci, who named it Venezuela ("Little Venice") on seeing Indian villages built on stilts over Lake Maracaibo. Spanish settlement began in 1520 and Venezuela remained under Spanish rule until liberated by Bolívar in 1821. It then formed part of Colombia until 1830. Independent Venezuela was ruled by a succession of dictators, notably *Guzmán Blanco and *Gómez, until the post-World War II period, which has witnessed the development of more democratic and stable governments, made possible in part by oil revenues. In the early 1980s oil revenues declined sharply, foreign debt increased, and an economic crisis ensued. Venezuela is a member of the OAS, LAFTA, and OPEC. President: Dr Jaime Lusinchi. Official language: Spanish. Official currency: bolívar of 100 céntimos. Area: 352,143 sq mi (912,050 sq km). Population (1983 est): 17,993,000. Capital: Caracas. Main port: Maracaibo.

VENICE *St. Mark's Square flooded with rainwater. Venice in Peril, an international organization, raises money to help save the threatened city.*

Venice (Italian name: Venezia) 45 26N 12 20E A city in NE Italy, the capital of Veneto. It is a seaport built on over 100 islands in the Lagoon of Venice (an inlet of the Gulf of Venice at the head of the Adriatic Sea). Venice is a center of commerce and tourism and its manufactures include glassware, textiles, and lace. The rise of the industrial suburbs of Mestre and Marghera on the mainland, however, has led to the economic decline of the old city. The Grand Canal and about 170 smaller canals provide waterways for the city transport, which includes water buses (*vaporetti*) and gondolas. Famous bridges include the Rialto Bridge and the *Bridge of Sighs. Situated at the center of Venice is the famous St Mark's Square (Piazza San Marco) overlooked by *St Mark's Cathedral, the 15th-century

Clock Tower, the Campanile, and the Doge's Palace. An outstanding collection of Venetian paintings, including works by Bellini, Mantegna, Canaletto, and Titian, is housed in the Accademia. The fashionable seaside resort, the Lido, is situated 2 mi (3 km) to the SE, on the outer edge of the lagoon. *History*: originally settled by refugees fleeing the barbarian invasions on the mainland (5th century AD onward), Venice was united under the first *doge in 697. Strategically positioned between Europe and the East, it became an independent republic and a great commercial and maritime power, defeating its greatest rival Genoa in 1380. Its decline began in the 16th century following the discovery of the Cape route to India. Venice is currently endangered by floods, pollution, and subsidence. Population (1980 est): 352,453.

Venizélos, Eleuthérios (1864–1936) Greek statesman; prime minister (1910–15, 1917–20, 1924, 1928–32, 1933). During the *Balkan Wars (1912–13), Venizélos expanded Greek territory by acquiring the Aegean islands and Crete. In 1917 he succeeded in drawing Greece into World War I on the side of the Allies. His unsuccessful attempt to instigate a revolt in Crete led to his exile in 1935.

Venn diagram. *See* set theory.

ventricle. *See* brain; heart.

Ventris, Michael (1922–56) British architect and scholar, famous for his decipherment of *Linear B. First inspired by hearing Sir Arthur *Evans lecture in 1936, Ventris studied tablets from *Knossos and *Pylos. In 1952 he realized that their language was a form of Greek. After his death in an automobile accident, his results were consolidated by his collaborator, John Chadwick.

Venturi tube A device consisting of an open-ended tube with a central constriction, used to measure the rate of flow of a fluid, which can be calculated from the pressure difference between the center and the ends. It is extensively used to measure the airspeed of aircraft. Invented by G. B. Venturi (1746–1822).

Venus (goddess) A Roman goddess originally of gardens and fertility who became identified with the Greek *Aphrodite as goddess of love. This identification followed the introduction into Rome of the cult of Aphrodite of Eryx in Sicily and was further established by the Julian family, whose members included the emperors from Augustus to Nero and who claimed descent from *Aeneas, son of Aphrodite. Having no myths of her own, she assumed those of Aphrodite.

Venus (planet) The second planet in order from the sun, orbiting the sun every 225 days at an average distance of 67 million mi (108 million km). It is 7,515 mi (12,102 km) in diameter and has an extremely long period of axial rotation (243 days). It can be one of the most brilliant objects in the sky, reaching a *magnitude of –4.4, and like the moon exhibits *phases. Its surface is totally obscured by dense swirling yellowish clouds of sulfuric acid droplets and sulfur particles. The atmosphere is primarily (98%) carbon dioxide. *Planetary probes have shown that the surface temperature is a hostile 879°F (470°C) and the surface atmospheric pressure is about 90 times that of earth. The surface has now been carefully mapped and photographed by the Pioneer Venus Orbiter and the *Venera probes.

Venus flytrap A *carnivorous plant, *Dionaea muscipula*, native to the eastern US. The upper part of each leaf is hinged at the midrib and an alighting insect triggers the leaf to snap shut, with its spined margins interlocking, thus trapping the prey. A cluster of five-petaled white flowers is borne on a long stalk. Family: *Droseraceae*.

Venus's flower basket A *sponge of the genus *Euplectella*, found in parts of the Pacific and Indian Oceans. They form enclosed cylindrical colonies, up to 12 in (30 cm) long, with a delicate skeletal lattice of silica.

Venus's girdle A marine invertebrate animal, *Cestum veneris*, belonging to an order (*Cestida*) of *ctenophores. Its transparent ribbon-like body is about 2 in (5 cm) wide and 40 in (1 m) or more long. It occurs in the Mediterranean Sea and Atlantic Ocean and swims with an undulating motion.

Veracruz (*or* Veracruz Llave) 19 11N 96 10W A major port in E Mexico, on the Gulf of Mexico. Industries include iron and steel processing, shipbuilding, and sugar refining; the chief exports are coffee, chicle, and tobacco. It contains the Regional Technical Institute of Veracruz (1957). Population (1978 est): 295,297.

Verbena A genus of herbaceous plants or dwarf shrubs (about 250 species), chiefly native to North and South America. The leaves are simple, often with narrow lobes, and the funnel-shaped flowers have five spreading often two-lipped lobes and form dense elongated or flat-topped clusters. Several species are grown as ornamentals, especially *V.* × *hybrida* from South America. Lemon verbena (*Lippia citriodora*) is a related shrub from tropical America, the lemon-scented leaves of which yield an oil used in perfumery. Family: *Verbenaceae. See also* vervain.

Vercelli 45 19N 8 26E A city in NW Italy, in Piedmont. An ancient Ligurian and later a Roman city, it has an outstanding library of manuscripts (notably the *Codex Vercellensis*, an early English manuscript dating from the late 10th century, which contains the texts of several poems and other literature). Vercelli lies at the center of Europe's main rice-producing area. Population (1971): 56,494.

Vercingetorix (d. 46 BC) Gallic chieftain, who led the revolt of the tribes of Gaul against Julius Caesar in 52. After early successes Vercingetorix was besieged at Alesia and his capture ended Gallic resistance to Rome. He was subsequently executed.

Verde, Cape (French name: Cap Vert) 14 43N 17 33W The westernmost point of Africa, in Senegal, consisting of a promontory extending into the Atlantic Ocean.

Verdi, Giuseppe (1813–1901) Italian composer of operas. He studied privately in Milan before beginning a career as a composer. He had an early success with *Nabucco* (1842) but his first mature work was *Rigoletto* (1851); this was quickly followed in 1853 with *La Traviata* and *Il Trovatore*. In 1869 he was commissioned to write an opera for the opening of the Suez Canal; the result was *Aida* (1871). His last works were the *Requiem* (in memory of Alessandro Manzoni; 1874) and the operas *Otello* (1887) and *Falstaff* (1893), with librettos, based on Shakespeare's plays, by Arrigo *Boito.

verdigris A green copper acetate used as a paint pigment. The term is also applied to the green coating, consisting of copper sulfate or carbonate, that forms on copper roofs, etc.

Verdun 49 10N 5 24E A city in NE France, in the Meuse department on the Meuse River. Strategically positioned on the E approach to the Paris Basin, Verdun has long been an important fortress. It was the scene of a major battle in 1916 (*see* World War I). It has brewing, textile, and metallurgical industries. Population (1975): 26,927.

Vereeniging 26 41S 27 56E A city in South Africa, in the S Transvaal, on the Vaal River. Founded in 1892, it was the site for negotiations to end the second Boer War (1902). It is an important coalmining center with iron and steel industries. Population (1980 est): 149,410.

Verhaeren, Émile (1844–96) The chief Belgian poet associated with Symbolism (*see* Symbolists). Beginning with the realistic verse of *Les Flamandes* (1883), he published many volumes of poetry the themes of which included his patriotism, his socialism, and his love for his wife. He was also a distinguished art critic.

Verlaine, Paul (1844–96) French poet. His early poetry, notably *Fêtes galantes* (1869), reflects his association with the *Parnassians. His tempestuous relationship with *Rimbaud, who influenced his more experimental *Romances sans paroles* (1874), resulted in the break-up of his marriage, and in 1873 he was imprisoned for shooting and wounding Rimbaud. His later poetry concerned the conflicts inherent in his attempts to lead a reformed life. After the publication of *Les Poètes maudits* (1884), which included studies of Corbière, Mallarmé, Rimbaud, and "Pauvre Lelian" (Verlaine's anagram for himself) among others, Verlaine was the acknowledged leader of the Symbolist poets.

Vermeer, Jan (1632–75) Dutch painter, who spent his entire life in Delft and whose importance was only established in the 19th century after centuries of obscurity. Despite his everyday subject matter, favorite themes being women reading or writing letters and playing musical instruments, his works are remarkable for their motionless figures, technical finish; and skillful use of light. His best-known paintings include *The Milkmaid, The Lacemaker*, and *Allegory of Painting*, showing himself at work.

vermiculite A *clay mineral with the property of expanding up to 22 times its original thickness on heating, when the water molecules between the silicate layers are driven off. In this form it is light and water-absorbent, and is used as a heat- or sound-insulating material, packaging material, fire extinguisher, and a growing medium for plants. Vermiculite results from the hydrothermal alteration of biotite and the intrusion of acid magma into basic rock.

vermilion Red mercuric sulfide (HgS). It sublimes readily on heating and occurs naturally as the mineral cinnabar. It is used as a pigment, often mixed with red lead and ferric oxide.

Vermont A state in the NE US, in New England bordered by New York (W), Quebec, Canada (N), New Hampshire (E), and Massachusetts (S). The extensively forested Green Mountains run N–S through the center of the state, with the lowlands of the Champlain Valley in the NW and the

Connecticut Valley in the E. Small manufacturing industries and tourism are the main sectors of the economy and a variety of goods are produced, particularly wood and paper products. Mining is important, especially the extraction of stone, asbestos, sand, and gravel. The state's farmers produce dairy products, hay, potatoes, and corn. Vermont is famous for its maple syrup. *History*: settled by the British in 1724, it declared its independence in 1777 and joined the Union in 1791, the first state admitted after the signing of the Constitution. It has maintained a staunch independence from federal intervention in state affairs. Area: 9609 sq mi (24,887 sq km). Population (1980): 511,456. Capital: Montpelier.

JAN VERMEER The Music Lesson (c. 1660). *The woman, whose face can be seen in the mirror, stands to play the virginals. The instrument on the floor is a bass viol.*

vermouth   An alcoholic drink made from white wine distilled with herbs. The best-known vermouths are French and Italian and are drunk as aperitifs either neat, with soda or tonic water, or with *gin.

Verne, Jules   (1828–1905) French writer. He studied law in Paris but chose to follow a literary career. Verne's *Voyages extraordinaires*, beginning with *Five Weeks in a Balloon* (1863), introduced such scientific and technological marvels as the submarine, space travel, and television. They included *Journey to the Center of the Earth* (1864), *From the Earth to the Moon* (1865), and *Twenty Thousand Leagues Under the Sea* (1873). One of the precursors of *science fiction, Verne wrote over 100 adventure stories, including *Around the World in Eighty Days* (1873).

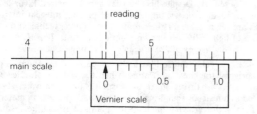

VERNIER SCALE *An auxiliary scale used to measure accurately to two places of decimals.*

Vernier scale   A device for measuring subdivisions of a scale, such as those on a pair of calipers. The auxiliary Vernier scale is divided so that ten of its subdivisions correspond to nine of those on the main scale. If the reading falls between two main-scale divisions, say between 4.6 and 4.7, the zero mark on the Vernier scale is slid along so that its zero is lined up with the reading. By noting the division on the Vernier scale that is exactly in line with a main-scale division, the second decimal place of the measurement is obtained. If the fourth Vernier division is in line with a main-scale division, the reading would be 4.64. Named for Pierre Vernier (1580–1637).

Verona   45 26N 11 00E A city in N Italy, in Veneto on the Adige River. Strategically situated at the junction of major routes between Italy and N Europe, its history dates from Roman times. It possesses a Roman amphitheater, a 12th-century cathedral, and the medieval Castelvecchio. A popular tourist center, its manufactures include textiles, paper, furniture, and leather goods. Population (1980 est): 268,178.

Veronese, Paolo   (P. Caliari; 1528–88) Italian painter of the Venetian school, born in Verona. After training for his father's trade of stonecutter, he studied under minor artists but was chiefly influenced by *Titian. In 1553 he settled in Venice, where he worked on decorations in the Ducal Palace and S Sebastiano. In the Villa Barbaro at Maser, designed by *Palladio, he painted illusionistic landscapes, mythological scenes, and portraits. His religious works, for example *Marriage at Cana*, were often pretexts for depicting contemporary banquets in impressive architectural settings and were sometimes the cause of controversy. Thus the *Last Supper* was condemned by the Inquisition for its irreverence; Veronese thereupon retitled the painting *Feast in the House of Levi*.

Veronica.   *See* speedwell.

Verrocchio, Andrea del   (Andrea del Cione; c. 1435–88) Florentine Renaissance sculptor, painter, and goldsmith, who ran a large and influential workshop. His only known painting is the *Baptism of Christ*, in which his famous pupil *Leonardo da Vinci reputedly assisted. As a sculptor Verrocchio enjoyed great success, his major works being *Doubting Thomas* (c. 1481) *David*, and the equestrian monument of Bartolommeo Colleoni in the Campo SS Giovanni e Paolo, Venice.

verruca.   *See* wart.

Versailles   48 48N 2 08E A city in N central France, in the Yvelines department. Versailles is chiefly famed for its baroque palace, the residence of the French kings from 1678 to 1769. It was built for Louis XIV between 1676 and 1708 on the site of a hunting lodge; the design includes architecture by J. H. Mansart (1646–1708), interior decoration by *Le Brun, and formal gardens by *Le Nôtre. In addition to the Grand Château, there are two smaller chateaus: the Grand Trianon and the Petit Trianon (a favorite residence of Marie Antoinette). Historic events enacted at the palace include Britain's recognition of American independence (1783), the crowning (1871) of William I as German emperor, and the signing of the Treaty of *Versailles (1919). Population (1975): 97,133.

Versailles, Treaty of   (1919) The treaty, signed at the *Paris Peace Conference after World War I, between the Allied and Associated Powers and defeated Germany. Versailles declared Germany guilty of causing the war, imposed heavy reparations payments, and limited the German army and navy to nominal strength. Territorial provisions included the return of Alsace and Lorraine to France, the cession of parts of Germany to Poland, and the Allied occupation of the Rhineland. Further, most of Germany's colonies were to become *mandates of the *League of Nations, which was established by the treaty. The US refused to ratify the treaty and did not make peace with Germany until 1921.

vertebra.   *See* spine.

Vertebrata   (*or* Craniata) A subphylum of animals that includes the fish, amphibians, reptiles, birds, and mammals. They are characterized by a backbone consisting of interlocking vertebrae, which forms the main support for the body and protects the nerve cord (spinal cord). The skeleton may be of cartilage or bone and includes two pairs of fin or limb elements that articulate with girdles attached to the backbone. The brain is large and housed in a protective skull. Their highly versatile skeleton has enabled vertebrates to develop many specializations and adaptations for a wide variety of lifestyles in water, on land, and in the air. Phylum: *Chordata*.

vervain   A slender erect branching perennial herb, *Verbena officinalis*, found on waste ground throughout Eurasia and N Africa. 12–30 in (30–75 cm) high, it has deeply lobed leaves and narrow spikes of tiny pinkish flowers. The fruit splits into four nutlets. Cultivated forms of *Verbena* may also be called vervain.

vervet.   *See* grass monkey.

Verwoerd, Hendrik Frensch   (1901–66) South African statesman; prime minister (1958–66). Verwoerd's commitment to *apartheid sparked demonstrations among blacks, including one at *Sharpeville during which the police fired on the crowd. He took South Africa out of the Commonwealth in 1960. He was assassinated in parliament in Cape Town.

Vesalius, Andreas (1514–64) Flemish anatomist, whose major work, *The Seven Books on the Structure of the Human Body* (1543), contained some of the first accurate descriptions of human anatomy together with illustrations of his dissections. Vesalius' observations challenged the prevailing theories of the Greek physician *Galen, opening up a new era of scientific investigation.

Vespasian (9–79 AD) Roman emperor (69–79). He was acclaimed emperor by the army in Egypt (July, 69) but he was not recognized at Rome until the death in December of his rival Vitellius (15–69). Vespasian's decisive policies brought an end to civil war and he increased taxes and reformed the army. He was deified after his death.

Vespucci, Amerigo (1454–1512) Italian navigator, after whom America is named. In 1499 he explored the NE coast of South America, discovering the mouths of the Amazon, and in 1501, under Portuguese auspices, he explored the E coast as far as Rió de La Plata, which he discovered.

Vesta (goddess) The Roman goddess of the hearth, identified with the Greek *Hestia. She was worshiped in private households, and her annual festival, the Vestalia, was held in June. The **Vestal Virgins**, her priestesses, tended the eternal fire at her shrine in Rome. They served for periods of 30 years under strict vows of chastity.

Vesta (astronomy) The third largest *asteroid, 334 mi (538 km) in diameter, and the only one occasionally visible with the naked eye. Its orbit lies between those of Mars and Jupiter.

Vestmannaeyjar (*or* Westman Islands) A group of rocky islands off the S coast of Iceland. In 1963 the volcanic island of Surtsey emerged from the ocean and the volcano, Helgafell, erupted in 1974 destroying part of the chief settlement of Vestmannaeyjar on the island of Heimaey.

Vesuvius 40 49N 14 26E A volcano in S central Italy, in Campania region near Naples. It was presumed to be extinct until it erupted in 79 AD engulfing the towns of *Herculaneum and *Pompeii; the last eruption was in 1944. Wine is made from the grapes grown on its exceptionally fertile slopes. Average height: 4003 ft (1220 m).

vetch A climbing or trailing annual or perennial herb of the genus *Vicia* (about 150 species), native to N temperate regions and South America. The leaves comprise several pairs of leaflets, often modified into tendrils, and the blue, purple, yellow, or white flowers are borne either in long spikes or singly in the leaf axils. Some species are grown as fodder crops or for green manure. Family: *Leguminosae.

Veterans' Administration (VA) US federal agency that administers a system of benefits for veterans and their dependents, including military service-related death or disability compensation, pensions for non-service-related disabilities or deaths, medical programs, home loans, and education, rehabilitation, and burial benefits. Established in 1930, it consolidated existing separate veterans' benefits organizations; it is headed by the administrator of veterans' affairs who is appointed by the president.

veterinary science The scientific discipline concerned with animal health and welfare. Some of the earliest descriptions of animal diseases were made by *Aristotle and, by the middle ages, veterinary practice was an established trade. Control and eradication of livestock diseases have enabled improved productivity and the introduction of modern intensive farming methods. The care of domestic pets utilizes many of the diagnostic and surgical techniques of human medicine.

vetiver A perennial *grass, *Vetiveria zizanioides*, also known as khus-khus, native to tropical Asia and introduced to South Africa. Its thick fragrant roots contain an oil used in perfumes.

Viareggio 43 52N 10 15E A city and resort in Italy, in Tuscany on the Ligurian Sea. Shelley was cremated in Viareggio and Puccini is buried here. Population (1971): 55,737.

Viborg 56 28N 9 25E A city in N central Denmark, in Jutland. It has a 12th-century cathedral and its industries include iron founding, distilling, and the manufacture of textiles and machinery. Population (1974 est): 37,645.

vibraphone A type of *xylophone in which a characteristic vibrato effect is produced by electrically operated fans installed at the upper ends of the resonator tubes. □musical instruments.

Vibrio A genus of freshwater and marine bacteria. They are rod-shaped, either straight or curved, and swim by means of whiplike flagella at one end of the cell. *V. cholerae* causes *cholera in man and other types may cause gastroenteritis.

Viburnum A genus of shrubs and small trees (about 200 species), mostly native to N temperate regions. They have rounded heads of small funnel-shaped white or pink flowers, each with five spreading white lobes. Many

species and varieties are grown as garden shrubs and pot plants, including the snowball tree (*see* guelder rose) and *laurustinus. Family: *Caprifoliaceae*. See also wayfaring tree.

Vicente, Gil (c. 1465–1536) Portuguese dramatist. He wrote court entertainments, plays based on religious and chivalric stories, and comedies satirizing the clergy and nobility, including *Comedia de Rubena* (1521) and *Auto da Mofina Mendes* (1534). He wrote in both Portuguese and Spanish, and has been identified with a goldsmith of the same name. His plays were published by his son and daughter in 1562.

Vicenza 45 33N 11 33E A city in NE Italy, in Veneto. It was the home of the 16th-century architect Andrea Palladio and many of his finest works are sited here. Vicenza has iron, steel, and textile industries. Population (1980 est): 116,781.

Vice President of the United States Second-ranking executive branch officer. Elected by the voters on the same ticket as the president, the vice president holds office for 4 years and succeeds to the presidency in case of death, disability, resignation, or impeachment of the president. He presides over the Senate, but only votes (not being a member of the Senate) in cases of a tie vote. He attends cabinet meetings and is, by law, a member of the National Security Council and the Board of Regents of the Smithsonian Institution.

Vichy 46 07N 3 25E A spa in central France, in the Allier department on the Allier River. From 1940 until 1944, during World War II, it was the seat of the French government of Marshal Pétain. Its waters, which were known to the Romans, are bottled and exported worldwide. Population (1975): 32,251.

Vicksburg 32 21N 90 51W A city in Mississippi, on the Mississippi River. During the Civil War it was the site of the Vicksburg campaign, a 47-day siege in 1863 in which General Grant successfully gained control of the Mississippi River after the city fell and thereby split the Confederacy. Vicksburg is an important distribution center for cotton, timber, and livestock. Population (1980): 25,434.

Vico, Giambattista (*or* Giovanni Battista Vico; 1668–1744) Italian historical philosopher. Vico was one of the first philosophers to attempt a critical philosophy of history. He rejected Descartes' negative attitude to the study of history and argued that philosophers had underrated "the study of the world of nations, which since men made it, men should come to know." Language, ritual, and myth were, he maintained, essential clues to an understanding to the past. His ideas were particularly influential in the later 18th century.

Victor Emmanuel II (1820–78) King of Italy (1861–78). He succeeded to the throne of Sardinia-Piedmont in 1849, following the abdication of his father Charles Albert. His appointment (1852) of *Cavour as prime minister was crucial to the achievement of Italian unification (*see* Risorgimento). Victor Emmanuel fought at Magenta and Solferino against the Austrians, freeing Lombardy, and coordinated with *Garibaldi in the campaign that freed S Italy. After becoming King of Italy he completed its unification by the acquisition of Venetia (1866) and of Rome (1870), which he made the Italian capital.

Victor Emmanuel III (1869–1947) King of Italy (1900–46) following the assassination of his father Umberto I. He acquiesced in Mussolini's seizure of power (1922) and after Mussolini's fall (1943) relinquished his powers to his son Umberto II. He formally abdicated in 1946, shortly before Italy became a republic.

Victoria A state of SE Australia, bordering on the Tasman Sea, Bass Strait, and the Indian Ocean. It consists of central uplands, an extension of the *Great Dividing Range, descending to plains in the N and S. Agriculture is diverse with fruit and vineyards in the Murray Basin and wheat and sheep farming to the SW. Gippsland is a noted dairying area; 50% of the country's cattle are now concentrated in S Victoria. Brown coal is mined in Central Gippsland and gas and oil are piped from fields in the Bass Strait. Industry, concentrated on Melbourne, includes engineering, oil refining, and the manufacture of cars and textiles. Area: 87,884 sq mi (227,600 sq km). Population (1980 est): 3,887,000. Capital: Melbourne.

Victoria 22 16N 114 13E The capital of Hong Kong, situated on the N of the island. The University of Hong Kong was established here in 1911. Population (1961): 633,138.

Victoria 48 26N 123 20W A city and port in W Canada, the capital of British Columbia on S Vancouver Island. Founded in 1843, it is a commercial and distribution center. Victoria's mild climate attracts tourists and retired people. It has some industry, but the provincial government and federal dockyards are the main employers. Victoria University (1963) is situated here. Population (1976): 62,551.

VICTORIA *The queen is photographed at a country estate in 1891, reviewing state papers and attended by her Indian servant.*

Victoria (1819–1901) Queen of the United Kingdom (1837–1901), whose sense of duty and strict moral code came to symbolize the ethos of the mid- and late-19th-century, a period that came to be known as the Victorian Age. The granddaughter of George III, Victoria succeeded her uncle William IV. In 1840 she married her cousin Prince *Albert of Saxe-Coburg-Gotha, who exerted considerable, and generally beneficial, influence over her. They had nine children, including Victoria, who became Empress of Germany as the wife of Frederick III, and Edward, later Edward VII; Arthur; Leopold. Albert's death in 1861 was a severe blow to Victoria and she resolved thereafter to act exactly as he would have wished.

She had an exalted view of the monarch's role in government, failing to appreciate the limitations of constitutional monarchy. Her close friendship with *Disraeli, who made her Empress of India (1876), contrasted with her strained relations with his rival *Gladstone. In the last years of her reign, especially after her Golden Jubilee (1887), she enjoyed enormous popularity and greatly enhanced the prestige of the crown.

Victoria, Lake (*or* Victoria Nyanza) The largest lake in Africa, in Uganda, Tanzania, and Kenya. The second largest freshwater lake in the world (after Lake Superior), it was discovered for Europeans in 1858 by Speke in his search for the source of the River Nile, of which Lake Victoria is the chief reservoir. The level was raised by the construction of the *Owen Falls Dam. There is fishing here and the main ports are Jinja, Kisumu, Mwanza, and Bukoba. Area: 26,826 sq mi (69,485 sq km).

Victoria, Tomás Luis de (c. 1548–1611) Spanish composer. He studied in Rome and in 1571 succeeded Palestrina as maestro di cappella at the Roman Seminary. In about 1582 he returned to Spain as chaplain to the dowager Empress Maria, the sister of *Philip II. He composed many motets and more than 20 masses in the polyphonic style.

Victoria and Albert Museum A London museum founded in 1853 to house and collect examples of applied arts of all periods and cultures. It was given its present name in 1899.

Victoria Falls 17 55S 25 52E A waterfall in the Zambezi River on the border of Zimbabwe and Zambia. The river flows over an abrupt rock edge 1 mi (1.6 km) wide, dropping as much as 420 ft (128 m), and then through a narrow gorge known as the **Boiling Pot**. A major tourist attraction, the falls also provide hydroelectric power.

Victoria Island A Canadian island in the Arctic Ocean, in Franklin district. The third largest island in Canada, its lowlands rise to high cliffs in the NW. The scanty population is clustered in a few settlements. Area: 212,199 sq km (81,930 sq mi).

vicuna A hoofed mammal, *Vicugna vicugna*, of high ORAndean plateaus. Resembling a small camel, the vicuna is 30 in (75 cm) at the shoulder and has a tawny-brown coat with a white bib and underparts. Hardy and aggressively territorial, they have never been domesticated but their wool is highly valued and wild herds are rounded up for shearing. Family: *Camelidae* (camels, etc.).

Vidal, Gore (1925–) US novelist and essayist. His moral concern with contemporary society is expressed with wit and elegance in both his essays and his novels, which range from historical studies, such as *Burr* (1974),

1876 (1976), and *Lincoln* (1984), to satires, such as *Myra Breckinridge* (1968) and essays, in *The Second American Revolution* (1982).

Vidal de la Blache, Paul (1845–1918) French geographer. A professor at the Sorbonne, Paris (1898–1918), Vidal was the most eminent French human geographer of his day. His work includes *États et nations de l'Europe* (1889) and *Principes de géographie humaine* (1922). He was the founding editor of *Annales de géographie* in 1891.

videogames Electronic games played by one or two people, in which the players have to control objects or figures moving over a screen (a television can be used) to intercept another moving object. Such games as table tennis and squash are easily adapted.

video recording The storage of a *television program on magnetic tape. Because the demodulated video (vision) signal can have frequencies in the megahertz range, a video tape cannot be used like a sound tape in which the highest frequencies will be less than 20 kilohertz. It would not be practical to run the tape one thousand times faster than a sound tape; instead the signal is recorded diagonally on the tape (each diagonal line representing one line of the picture) and the tape is run slowly over a drum on which the recording and reading heads rotate at high speeds. Such devices are available for use with domestic television sets. Video disks are disks for the storage of television pictures from which the optically stored signal can be retrieved by a laser system.

Vienna (German name: Wien) 48 12N 16 20E The capital of Austria, in the NE at the foot of the Vienna Woods (Wienerwald) on the Danube River. With its musical and theatrical life, its museums, and parks, it is a popular tourist attraction. Trade and industry, however, form the basis of the economy, the major industrial products being machinery, textiles, chemicals, and furniture. Most of the chief buildings lie on or within the Ringstrasse, the boulevard built in 1857 to replace the old city ramparts. These include the Cathedral of St Stephen (begun about 1135); the Hofburg (the former imperial palace); the Rathaus (1873–83); the parliament buildings (1883); the Opera House and Burgtheater; and the university (1365). *History*: seat of the Habsburgs (1278–1918) and residence of the Holy Roman Emperor (1558–1806), Vienna became an important political and cultural center in the 18th and 19th centuries, having associations with many composers, including Haydn, Mozart, Beethoven, Schubert, and the Strauss family. At the end of World War I it became the capital of the small republic of Austria. It suffered considerable damage during World War II and was jointly occupied by the Allied Powers (1945–55). Population (1976 est): 592,800.

Vienna, Congress of (1814–15) A conference of European powers that met following the fall of Napoleon. The chief countries represented were Austria (by *Metternich), Britain (by *Castlereagh and Wellington), Russia, Prussia, France (by *Talleyrand), and the papacy. Its Final Act created a kingdom of the Netherlands, a German confederation of 39 states, Lombardy-Venetia subject to Austria, and the *Congress Kingdom of Poland. Legitimate monarchs were restored in Spain, Naples, Piedmont, Tuscany, and Modena, and Louis XVIII was confirmed as King of France.

Vienna Circle The group of scientific philosophers who developed the doctrine of *logical positivism (*or* logical empiricism). Founded by *Schlick in 1924, the Vienna Circle flourished until 1939. Philosophers and scientists cooperated to analyze and clarify both philosophical and scientific concepts and to set up criteria of meaningfulness for propositions other than the truths of logic. Members included *Carnap, *Gödel, and Otto Neurath (1882–1945). They did not consciously set out radically to revise traditional views about philosophy, but they had this effect, notably in America and Britain. *See also* Ayer, Sir Alfred (Jules).

Vienne River A river in W central France, flowing mainly NNW from the Correze department to the Loire River. Length: 220 mi (354 km).

Vientiane 18 06N 102 30E The capital of Laos, a port on the Mekong River on the border with Thailand (formerly Siam). Founded in the 13th century, it came under Siamese control in the 18th century and was destroyed (1828) following a revolt against Siamese rule. It became capital of the French protectorate of Laos in the late 19th century. The Université Sisavangvong was founded here in 1958. Population (1973): 176,637.

Vierwaldstättersee. *See* Lucerne, Lake.

Viet Cong Communist guerrillas who fought the government of South Vietnam during the *Vietnam War (1954–75). Dedicated to the union of North and South, in 1960 they established a political organization, the National Liberation Front, which amalgamated the various groups committed to the overthrow of the South Vietnamese Government.

Viet Minh The Vietnam League for Independence, formed in 1941 by *Ho Chi Minh to overthrow French rule and to create an independent

Vietnamese republic. Officially a multiparty movement, the Viet Minh was dominated by the communists and opposed by many nationalist leaders. Following the refusal of the French to recognize Vietnamese independence after World War II, the Viet Minh played a prominent role in the *Indochina war against France (1946–54).

Vietnam, Socialist Republic of A country in SE Asia, occupying the E part of the Indochina peninsula on the South China Sea. It is bordered by China (N), the South China Sea (E and S), and by Cambodia and Laos (W). Fertile coastal lowlands rise to forested plateaus and mountains, the most populated areas being around the Mekong delta in the S and the Red River delta in the N. The inhabitants are mainly Vietnamese, with minorities of Chinese and others. *Economy*: seriously affected by the wars of recent decades, some progress has been made since 1975. Agriculture remains the most important sector and there have been further moves toward greater collectivization of the land. Irrigation schemes have helped to increase production although self-sufficiency in the staple food, rice, has not yet been achieved. Other important crops include sugar cane, tea, maize, coffee, and rubber. Teak and bamboo are the chief forest products and fishing is also important. Industrial developments, including steel, have been concentrated mainly in the N, based on the coal, tin, zinc, and other metals to be found there, but recent discoveries of offshore oil SE of Ho Chi Minh City open up the possibility of industral expansion in the S. The principal exports are coal, rubber, wood, tea, spices, and coffee. *History*: the northern kingdom of Nam Viet was conquered in 111 BC by the Chinese. In 939 AD it broke free and resisted further Chinese invasions until the 15th century, when it was again briefly occupied. Its southward expansion culminated in the establishment (1802) of a united Vietnamese empire, which incorporated the three historic regions of Annam, Cochinchina, and Tonkin. The subsequent French conquest resulted in the institution of protectorates over Cochinchina, Tonkin, and Annam, which were joined with Cambodia (and later Laos) to form (1887) the Union of *Indochina. Vietnam was occupied by the Japanese in World War II, during which Ho Chi Minh formed the Viet Minh league to fight for independence. France's refusal in 1945 to recognize his government led to war (1946–54) after which, following defeat at Dien Bien Phu, the French withdrew. The Geneva Conference (1954) divided Vietnam along the seventeenth parallel into communist North Vietnam and noncommunist South Vietnam, between which civil war ensued. In 1961 the US extended assistance to the South and remained involved in the conflict until 1973 (*see* Vietnam War). The civil war continued until 1975, when the North emerged victorious, proclaiming (1976) the reunited Socialist Republic of Vietnam. Since then attempts at reconstruction have been hindered by further political developments. A deterioration of Sino-Vietnamese relations led to the withdrawal of all Chinese aid in 1978, and following Vietnam's invasion of Kampuchea (December, 1978–January, 1979) many other nations suspended aid leading to an increased reliance on the Soviet Union. The Chinese invasion of Vietnam (February–March, 1979) led to a massive increase in the number of Chinese refugees attempting to leave Vietnam by small craft across the South China Sea. Many of these refugees, known as the Boat People, died by drowning or from disease, and the reluctance of some countries to provide new homes for the survivors led to the holding of an international conference in Geneva to deal with the Boat People's dilemma (1979). The fifth congress of the Vietnamese Communist Party (1982) attempted to rejuvenate Vietnam's aged leadership by dismissals and promotions. Economic dependence on the Soviet Union and economic crises have continued in the early 1980s with severe shortages of goods and services, a huge trade deficit, and an unstable market. Malnutrition remains widespread. Hanoi announced a withdrawal of occupation troops from Cambodia, but reportedly sent in replacement troops. By 1983 the limited private enterprise that had been permitted in Vietnam for two years was again severely restricted. Prime minister: Pham Van Dong (1906–   ). Official language: Vietnamese. Offical currency: dong of 100 hao. Area: 329,466 127,180 sq mi (sq km). Population (1983): 57,036,000. Capital: Hanoi. Main port: Haiphong.

Vietnam War (1954–75) The war between South Vietnamese communist insurgents, supported by North Vietnam, and the government forces of South Vietnam, aided from 1961 by the US. It resulted in communist victory and the union (1976) of North and South Vietnam. From 1954 guerrilla warfare was waged against South Vietnam by the communist *Viet Cong, who were reinforced by North Vietnamese troops in 1959. In 1961 the US, seeking to halt the spread of communism in SE Asia, dispatched troops (numbering 550,000 by 1969) in support of the beleaguered South; in 1965 US air raids on the North had begun. US participation was lessened after peace negotiations were initiated in 1969, but the war again took fire following the US–South Vietnamese invasion of Cambodia in 1970. A massive communist offensive in 1972, together with the strength of domestic oppo-

sition to US involvement in the war, prompted the US to reopen negotiations for peace. These led to the Paris Agreement (January, 1973) and the withdrawal of US troops. By 1975 the North had emerged victorious. About 900,000 Viet Cong and North Vietnamese, 50,000 Americans, and some 400,000 South Vietnamese died in the war. *See also* Indochina.

viewdata An information storage and retrieval system in which pages of text are transmitted as coded signals along telephone wires and displayed on a domestic television receiver. The user has direct access to a central computer store via a keyboard, and there is therefore no delay in response, unlike the alternative *teletext system.

Vignola, Giacomo da (1507–73) Roman mannerist architect (*see* mannerism). Vignola was the leading architect of his day in Rome, carrying on the building of *St Peter's Basilica after the death of *Michelangelo. Among his other works were the Palazzo Farnese (1564) in Piacenza and the influential church of Il Gesù, Rome (begun 1568). He was also the author of a popular architectural treatise.

Vigny, Alfred de (1797–1863) French poet, novelist, and dramatist. He associated with many Romantic writers while serving as an army officer from 1814 to 1827. His fiction includes the historical novel *Cinq-Mars* (1826) and his plays include *Chatterton* (1835), his masterpiece, and several adaptions from Shakespeare. His poetry, especially in *Les Destinées* (1867), expresses through impersonal symbolic techniques his philosophy of stoical pessimism.

Vigo 42 15N 8 44W A port and naval base in NW Spain, in Galicia on the Atlantic coast. In 1702 an English-Dutch fleet sank a Spanish treasure fleet here. Population (1974 est): 197,144.

Viipuri. *See* Vyborg.

Vijayanagar A Hindu empire established from the town of that name in S India during the first half of the 14th century. It enjoyed a reputation for trade, opulence, and cultural and artistic distinction. Its Muslim neighbors, with whom it had always had uneasy relations, defeated Vijayanagar at the battle of Talikota in 1565 and totally destroyed the city.

Vijayawada (former name: Bezwada) 16 34N 80 40E A city in India, in Andhra Pradesh on the Krishna River. Industries include engineering and rice milling. Population (1971): 317,258.

Viking probes Two identical US spacecraft that went into orbit around Mars in 1976. The Lander sections landed on the surface in July and September and performed various experiments, including tests for possible microorganisms; none were found. The Orbiter sections took extensive measurements and photographs of Mars' surface and two satellites.

Vikings Scandinavian sea warriors active from the late 8th to the mid-11th centuries. They established important settlements in the British Isles (especially at York and Dublin), where an Anglo-Danish dynasty was founded (1016) by *Canute, and in Normandy. Swedish Vikings raided, and then settled, in the E Baltic, established the Russian Kievan state, and traded with Constantinople, where they provided the imperial guard. They also established settlements in *Vinland and Greenland. Viking literature (the sagas) and art are noted for their dynamic vitality.

villa A country house in Italy or the South of France. Villas date back to Roman times, when they were used as vacation retreats or as farmhouses. The Emperor Hadrian's Villa at Tivoli (123 AD) was built on a palatial scale with extensive parks. During the Renaissance the villa with its substantial estate was revived, particularly in Venetia in N Italy, where *Palladio designed them to combine farming and pleasure purposes. Gardens with grottoes, fountains, and sculptures became an integral part of such Renaissance villas as the Villa d'Este (1550) at Tivoli, built by Pirro Ligorio (c. 1500–83).

Villa, Pancho (Francesco V.; 1878–1923) Mexican revolutionary. An outlaw, Villa supported successive revolts against Mexican governments and came to dominate the north with an irregular army. In 1916 he raided Texas and New Mexico and a US force was sent into Mexico to capture him. It failed to do so but, after an agreement with the Mexican Government in 1920, he disbanded his army. He was later assassinated.

Villa-Lobos, Heitor (1887–1959) Brazilian composer. He toured Brazil collecting folksongs and in 1945 founded the Brazilian Academy of Music. His music is characterized by native rhythms and exotic tone colors. His vast output includes 12 symphonies, *Bachianas Brasileiras* (1930–45), a series of pieces inspired by Bach, concertos for cello, guitar, and harp, 15 string quartets, guitar music, *Rudepoema* (1921–26) for piano, and the ballet *Uirapurú* (1917).

Villanovan The earliest Iron Age culture of N Italy, named for the site of Villanova near Bologna. Emerging in the 9th century BC Villanovan culture is characterized by sophisticated metalworking, using local mineral resources. The dead were cremated and their bronze or pottery urns were often shaped like wattle and daub huts. Villanovan settlements preceded most of the important towns of the *Etruscans.

Villars, Claude Louis Hector, Duc de   (1653–1734) French marshal under Louis XIV. He fought in the third *Dutch War (1672–78) but his greatest achievements came in the War of *Spanish Succession (1701–14). He rallied France's flagging fortunes after Marlborough's victory at *Blenheim (1704) and imposed devastating losses on the allies at *Malplaquet (1709). He last saw active service when well into his 80s in the War of the *Polish Succession (1733–38).

Villehardouin, Geoffroi de   (c. 1150–c. 1213) French medieval chronicler. A participant in the fourth Crusade and witness of the fall of Constantinople (1204), Villehardouin wrote the best source description of these events in his *Conquête de Constantinople*. However, his bias toward the Latins possibly distorts the account.

villein   The unfree peasant of medieval Europe, holding land from the lord of the *manor in return for labor. Villeins were the most numerous class in England from the 11th to late 14th centuries, when many villeins acquired written titles to their holdings following the *Peasants' Revolt.

Villiers de l'Isle-Adam, Philippe Auguste, Comte de   (1838–89) French poet, novelist, and dramatist. He was the impoverished descendant of an ancient aristocratic family. His best-known works are *Contes cruels* (1883) and the symbolist drama *Axël* (1886).

Villon, François   (1431–?1463) French poet. He studied at the University of Paris but thereafter led a life of vagrancy and crime. He was condemned to be hanged in 1463 but was banished from Paris instead, and nothing is known of him after that date. Only about 3000 lines of his work survive. The ballades and other poems in his *Lais* and *Grand Testament* are characterized by compassion, irony, and a fascination with death and decay. Among the best known of his poems are the *Ballade des dames du temps jadis* and his epitaph, the *Ballade des pendus*.

Vilnius   (Polish name: Wilno)   54 40N 25 19E A city in the W Soviet Union, the capital of the Lithuanian SSR on the Neris River. A commercial, industrial, and educational center, it is a railroad junction and has a wide range of manufacturing industries and a university founded (1579) by Stephen Báthory. *History*: it dates back to the 14th century, when it became Gediminas' capital but declined following Lithuania's union with Poland. It was ceded to Russia in 1795. After World War I it was given to newly independent Lithuania but was seized by Poland in 1922. Restored to Lithuania in 1940, it then became part of the Soviet Union. The Germans occupied Vilnius in World War II, when its large Jewish population was virtually exterminated. Population (1981 est): 503,000.

Vimy.   *See* World War I.

Viña del Mar   33 02S 71 35W A seaside resort in W central Chile, a suburb of Valparaíso on the Pacific Ocean. Its attractions include a casino, beaches, hotels, and a racecourse. Population (1976 est): 250,670.

Vincent de Paul, St   (c. 1580–1660) French priest, known for his work among the poor and sick. Captured by Barbary pirates on his way to Marseilles (1605), he escaped and in 1625 founded the Congregation of the Mission Priests (*see* Lazarists). In 1633 he founded the Daughters of Charity. Feast day: July 19.

Vincent of Beauvais   (c. 1190–1264) French Dominican friar, scholar, and encyclopedist. His greatest achievement was a Latin encyclopedia, the *Speculum maius*, which he compiled from the whole range of knowledge available to him. In three parts, it dealt with natural history, theological doctrine, and history.

vine   Any climbing or trailing plant that requires a support for upward growth. The term is often restricted to the *grape vine (*Vitis vinifera*) and other plants of the genus *Vitis*, which climb by means of tendrils.

vinegar   A dilute solution of *acetic acid, produced from soured wine, beer (malt vinegar), or other dilute alcoholic liquids. It is used in salad dressings, preserving, and other foods.

vinegar eel   A *nematode worm, *Anguillula* (or *Turbatrix*) *aceti*, that lives in fermenting vinegar. It feeds on the microorganisms that convert alcohol to acetic acid in the formation of vinegar.

vine snake   One of several species of slender venomous tree-dwelling snakes belonging to the family *Colubridae*. The South American green vine snake (*Oxybelis fulgidus*), up to 48 in (120 cm) long, moves swiftly through trees, where it is well camouflaged, preying on small lizards, which it paralyzes before eating.

Vinland   The Viking name for the area of NE America, probably Newfoundland, explored and briefly settled by *Leif Ericsson (c. 1000). It is

possible that the area was visited a decade earlier by Bjarni Herjolfsson. Ericsson's achievement is celebrated in an important saga.

Vinnitsa   49 11N 28 30E A city in the Soviet Union, in the central Ukrainian SSR. Originally Polish, it was ceded to Russia in 1793. It is the center of a sugar-beet region and food processing is the principal industrial activity. Population (1981 est): 332,000.

Vinson, Frederick Moore   (1890–1953) US political leader and jurist; Supreme Court chief justice (1946–53). A Democrat from Kentucky, he served in the US House of Representatives (1924–29; 1931–38). He sat on the US Court of Appeals (1938–42), directed the war mobilization office (1943–45), and was secretary of the Treasury (1945–46), before being appointed chief justice by President Harry S Truman. He supported civil rights and believed in broad powers for the federal government.

Vinson Massif   78 02S 22 00W The highest peak in Antarctica, in the Ellsworth Mountains in Ellsworth Land. It was discovered in 1935. Height: 16,864 ft (5140 m).

vinyl resins.   *See* polyvinyl chloride; polyvinyl acetate.

viol   A bowed stringed instrument, common from the 15th until the early 18th centuries, when it was eclipsed by the *violin. Viols differ from violins in that they have six strings, tuned mainly in fourths, a shallower bridge, gut frets on the fingerboard, sloping shoulders, and flatter backs. They are held between the knees when played and the bow is held in an underhand grip. A consort of viols comprises treble, alto, tenor, and bass instruments; there is also a **violine** pitched an octave lower than the bass. The bass viol acquired the name **viola da gamba** from the Italian *gamba*, leg.

viola   A □musical instrument of the *violin family. It is similar to the violin, although larger in size, having thicker strings and a heavier bow. It has a range of over four octaves from the C below middle C; its strings are tuned C, G, D, A. It is a member of the orchestra and the string quartet.

violet   A perennial herb of the genus *Viola*, up to 16 in (40 cm) tall, whose solitary flowers, usually blue, purple, or white, have two upright petals, two horizontally spreading ones, and a lower central one with guidelines for pollinating insects seeking nectar. The toothed leaves are oval or heart-shaped, often in a basal rosette, and the seeds are released explosively from a three-valved capsule. The sweet-scented garden violets are derived from the Eurasian sweet violet (*V. odorata*). The dog violet (*V. canina*) is another common species, and the genus also includes the *pansies. Family: *Violaceae*.

violin   A bowed string instrument, the soprano member of the family that includes the viola, cello, and double bass. It has four strings tuned in fifths (G, D, A, E), an arched bridge, and a smooth fingerboard. It has a range of over four octaves from the G below middle C. Early violins used gut strings; modern strings are steel or gut-covered steel. The violin is played with a bow strung with horsehair; the strings can also be plucked. The design of the violin was perfected by the Amati, Guarneri, and Stradivari families in Italy between the mid-16th and early 18th centuries. It is widely used as a solo concerto instrument, in the orchestra, in the string quartet, and in folk music. □musical instruments.

Viollet-le-Duc, Eugène Emmanuel   (1814–79) French architect and author. He began his career as a restorer of medieval buildings, working on the Ste Chapelle and *Notre-Dame in Paris. Viollet was the champion of both the revived gothic style and contemporary developments in architecture, his *Dictionnaire raisonée de l'architecture française* (1854–68) and later books indicating the similarities he saw between gothic and contemporary industrial methods of construction.

violoncello.   *See* cello.

viper   A venomous snake, belonging to the family *Viperidae* (150 species), that has long erectile fangs, which are folded back when not in use. 10 in–10 ft (0.3–3 m) long, vipers feed on small animals, which are injected with venom and then trailed until they die. Most give birth to live young. Old World vipers (subfamily *Viperinae*) are stout-bodied and broad-headed and mostly ground-dwelling, although some are burrowers and some arboreal. New World vipers (subfamily *Crotalinae*) are known as *pit vipers.

Virchow, Rudolf   (1821–1902) German pathologist and statesman. He originated the concept that disease arises in the individual cells of a tissue and—with publication of his *Cellular Pathology* (1858)—founded the science of cellular pathology. Virchow held public office, supervising improvements in standards of public health, and he also helped develop the science of anthropology in Germany.

Virgil   (Publius Vergilius Maro; 70–19 BC) Roman poet. He was born into a farming family near Mantua in N Italy. He completed his education in Rome, where he became a friend of Horace and *Maecenas. Reacting against the troubled political background of civil war, he described in his *Eclogues* (42–37 BC) an idealized pastoral landscape. His more practical vision of Italy in the *Georgics* (36–29 BC) is informed by his passionate interest in agriculture. During his final years he worked on the *Aeneid*, a national epic in 12 books describing the wanderings of Aeneas, the founding of Rome, and extolling the Julian dynasty and Augustus, who claimed descent from Aeneas. He died of fever after returning from a voyage to Greece. The supreme poet of imperial Rome, Virgil became the object of superstitious reverence to later generations. The *Aeneid* was used for divination and its author was imagined to be a magician with supernatural power. In the middle ages, Virgil was treated almost as a Christian prophet because of a passage in the fourth *Eclogue* that seems to predict the birth of Christ.

VIRGINALS

virginals A keyboard instrument of the 16th and 17th centuries, the earliest and simplest form of the *harpsichord. Often made in the form of a box, which could be set on the table, the strings (one to each note) run parallel to the keyboard.

Virginia A state on the mid-Atlantic coast bordered by Kentucky and West Virginia (W and NW), Maryland (N), the Atlantic Ocean (E), and North Carolina and Tennessee (S and SW). The low-lying coastal plain is separated from the forested Appalachian Mountains in the W by a region of rolling upland. Manufacturing is very important and the principal industries are chemicals and tobacco processing. Fishing and mining (especially of coal) are also significant sectors of the economy. Numerous historic sites and monuments, beaches, mountains, springs, and national parks are the basis for a thriving tourist industry. The state's farmers produce tobacco, hay, corn, apples, and peaches. Timber, especially for shipbuilding, has long been important. *History*: one of the 13 original colonies, it was named for Elizabeth I of England, the Virgin Queen. A period of expansion followed the establishment of the first permanent English settlement in the New World by the Virginia Company (1607) and demands for self-government grew. It provided many of the leaders for the American Revolution, becoming a state in 1788. Four of the first five US presidents came from Virginia and during the Civil War, Richmond was the capital of the Confederacy. Area: 105,716 40,817 sq mi (sq km). Population (1980): 5,346,279. Capital: Richmond.

Virginia Beach 36 51N 75 58W A resort city in SE Virginia, on the Atlantic Ocean, E of Portsmouth and Norfolk. The first English colonists, later settlers of Jamestown, landed here in 1607. It is an independent city that was merged with Princess Anne County in 1963. Its 38 miles (61 kilometers) of coastline attract tourists to the many resorts, the basis of the economy. There are several military bases nearby. Population (1980): 262,199.

Virginia creeper A climbing shrub, also called woodbine, of the genus *Parthenocissus*, especially *P. tricuspidata* of SE Asia and *P. quinquefolia* of North America. It clings by means of branched tendrils with suckers and is often grown as an ornamental for its attractive red autumn foliage. The compound leaves have five pointed oval toothed leaflets and the tiny clustered flowers have five petals. Family: *Vitaceae*.

Virginia Plan (1787) A plan of central government presented by the Virginia delegation at the *Constitutional Convention. It called for a bicameral legislature; the upper-house members were to be elected by lower-house members, who had been elected by popular vote. The number of each state's representatives in both houses was to be based on the state's population and wealth. The president and Supreme Court members were to be chosen by the legislature. Although it was felt that this plan was advantageous to the larger states, it was adopted in part, after modification by the *Connecticut Compromise.

Virgin Islands A West Indian group of approximately one hundred small islands and cays in the Lesser Antilles, administratively divided between the US and the UK. **The Virgin Islands of the United States** consist of three main islands, the largest being *St Croix, and about 50 smaller ones. They were purchased from Denmark in 1917 for their strategic importance. Tourism is the principal industry; other industries include rum distilling and textiles. Area: 133 sq mi (344 sq km). Population (1980): 95,591. Capital: Charlotte Amalie. **The British Virgin Islands** consist of about 40 islands, the largest being Tortola. They became a British crown colony following the defederation of the Leeward Islands colony in 1956. Tourism is replacing agriculture as the colony's chief source of wealth. Area: 59 sq mi (153 sq km). Population (1980): 12,034. Capital: Road Town.

Virgo (Latin: Virgin) A large equatorial constellation that lies on the *zodiac between Libra and Leo. The brightest star is *Spica. The constellation contains the **Virgo cluster** of galaxies, which contains over 2500 members, the majority of which are spiral galaxies.

virtual particle A short-lived particle that is used in quantum mechanics to represent the interaction between stable particles. For example, in classical physics two electrically charged particles are represented as interacting by the overlapping of the two fields that surround them; in quantum mechanics this interaction would be represented by the exchange of virtual photons between them. The *strong interaction is represented by the exchange of virtual pions, the *weak interaction by the exchange of intermediate vector bosons, and the *gravitational interaction by the exchange of virtual gravitons.

virus A minute noncellular particle that can reproduce only in living cells. Viruses consist of a core of nucleic acid (either *DNA or *RNA), surrounded by a protein coat (capsule) and, in some types, a lipid-containing envelope. Some bacterial viruses have tails (*see* bacteriophage). They may be spherical, ellipsoid, rod-shaped, or polyhedral, with sizes in the range 20–450 nanometers (nm; *see* SI units), although some tailed forms may reach 800 nm. Viruses alternate between an inert virion stage and an infective stage, in which the capsule binds to the host cell and the viral nucleic acid (containing its genes) enters the cell and directs the components of the host cell to assemble replica viruses. These are finally liberated, often with damage to or death of the host cell.

Viruses are responsible for a wide range of diseases in plants and animals, including influenza, measles, rabies, and smallpox. They can also cause the formation of tumors.

Visby 57 37N 18 20E A port and resort in SE Sweden, on the W coast of Gotland Island. It was an early member of the Hanseatic League and a major commercial center in the middle ages. Its industries include sugar refining and metal working. Population (1970): 19,596.

viscacha A gregarious South American *rodent, *Lagostomus maximus*, related to *chinchillas. Over 20 in (50 cm) in length, viscachas live in warrens of 12-15 burrows often with piles of earth outside. They are nocturnal and feed on grasses, roots, and seeds. Family: *Chinchillidae*.

Visconti An Italian family that established (1310) lordship over Milan under **Matteo I Visconti** (1250–1322) and then, in spite of papal opposition, gained control over many Lombard cities. Skillful marriage alliances both within Italy and outside expanded their influence. By 1400, under **Gian Galeazzo Visconti** (1351–1402), the family's most brilliant representative, they controlled most of N Italy, centered on Milan and Pavia. Temporary reverses under his son **Giovanni Maria Visconti** (1388–1412) were arrested but the death of his brother **Filippo Maria Visconti** (1392–1447) without heirs led to the establishment of *Sforza control over the duchy.

Visconti, Luchino (1906–76) Italian film director. Born into a noble family, he became a committed Marxist. His late films especially are characterized by elaborate and formal visual composition. They include *The Leopard* (1963), *The Damned* (1970), and *Death in Venice* (1971). He also directed many opera and drama productions.

viscosity A measure of the degree to which a fluid resists a deforming force. Viscosity is defined by Newton's law of viscosity: if two layers of a fluid, area A and distance x apart, flow with a relative velocity v, there is a force between them equal to $\eta Av/x$. η is called the coefficient of viscosity. Viscosity is measured in newton seconds per square meter. The **kinematic viscosity** is the coefficient of viscosity divided by the density of the fluid.

Vishakhapatnam 17 42N 83 24E A city in India, in Andhra Pradesh on the Bay of Bengal. An important port, India's first steamer was launched here in 1948. Industries include shipbuilding and oil refining. Population (1971): 352,504.

VISHNU *The god is portrayed reclining on Sesha, the king of the nagas. From the south face of the 6th-century temple of Vishnu at Deogarh (India).*

Vishnu The second member of the Hindu trinity, the *Trimurti. He is known as the Preserver, complementing *Brahma the Creator and *Shiva the Destroyer, and is married to *Lakshmi. He has ten avatars or manifestations, the most famous of which are *Rama and *Krishna. He is often portrayed as lying asleep on a seven-headed snake in the intervals between his appearances in successive universes. His devotees are the Vaishnavas, a sect founded by the scholar and philosopher Chaitanya (1486–c. 1534 AD), who stressed devotion to the god regardless of *caste.

Visigoths A branch of the *Goths. Forced by the *Huns across the Danube (376 AD), they destroyed a Roman army at *Adrianople (378) and established themselves in the Balkans, expanding southward and, under *Alaric I, sacking Rome in 410. Moving into France and Spain, they ruled first as Roman subjects and then independently. Their rule in France was destroyed by the *Franks (507) and in Spain by the Muslims (711).

Vislinsky Zaliv. *See* Vistula Lagoon.

Vistula Lagoon (German name: Frisches Haff; Polish name: Wiślany Zalew; Russian name: Vislinsky Zaliv) An inlet of the Baltic Sea on the coast of Poland and the Soviet Union, almost totally enclosed by a narrow spit of land. Area: 330 sq mi (855 sq km).

Vistula River (Polish name: Wisła) The longest river of Poland, rising in the S of the country, in the Carpathian Mountains, and flowing generally N and NW through Warsaw and Toruń, then NE to enter the Baltic Sea via an extensive delta region near Gdańsk. It provides an important economic link in the transportation system of eastern Europe. Length: 1090 km (677 mi).

vitalism The theory that living organisms contain a vital force that distinguishes them from nonliving things. It was proposed by the French philosopher Henri *Bergson, who believed that a vital force (*élan vital*)—a form of energy—controlled the form, development, and activities of organisms.

vitamin An organic compound, other than a protein, fat or carbohydrate, that is required in small amounts by living organisms for normal growth and maintenance of life. For animals vitamins must be supplied in the diet, although some group B vitamins may be produced by microorganisms present in the digestive tract. Vitamins function as *coenzymes in many metabolic reactions; they are involved in the formation and maintenance of membranes, in the absorption and metabolism of calcium and phosphorus, and in many other essential processes. Many can now be synthesized commercially but some are easily destroyed by light or heat, e.g. in storage or cooking. Vitamins A, D, E, and K are classifed as fat-soluble; group B vitamins and vitamin C are water-soluble.

vitamin A (*or* retinol) A fat-soluble vitamin and an essential constituent of the visual pigments of the eyes. It also functions in the maintenance of healthy mucous membranes. Vitamin A deficiency leads to dryness of membranes lining the mouth and respiratory tract, blindness, and defective growth. Sources include liver, fish-liver oils, and egg yolk, while precursors of vitamin A, such as beta-carotene, occur in green plants and vegetables (e.g. carrots).

vitamin B complex A group of water-soluble vitamins that are all constituents of *coenzymes involved in metabolic reactions. Thiamine (B_1) is important in carbohydrate metabolism: it occurs in cereal grains, beans, peas, and pork. Deficiency leads to *beriberi. Riboflavin (B_2) is involved in carbohydrate and amino acid metabolism and sources include yeast, liver, milk, and green leafy plants. Nicotinamide (nicotinic acid *or* niacin) can be synthesized from the amino acid tryptophan; liver is a rich source of the vitamin and milk and eggs of tryptophan. Vitamin B_6 (pyridoxine) is essential for amino acid metabolism and is widely distributed in yeast, liver, milk, beans, and cereal grains. Also common in many foods are pantothenic acid, a constituent of coenzyme A; biotin, which is synthesized by intestinal bacteria; and choline, a precursor of *acetylcholine (which transmits nervous impulses). Folic acid and vitamin B_{12} (cyanocobalamin) can be synthesized by intestinal bacteria: deficiency of either causes megaloblastic or pernicious *anemia. Liver is a good source of vitamin B_{12}.

vitamin C (*or* ascorbic acid) A water-soluble compound that is required for several metabolic processes, especially for the maintenance of healthy connective tissue. It cannot be synthesized by man and certain animals, in whom it must form part of the diet. Fruit and vegetables, especially citrus fruits, are good sources. Deficiency of vitamin C leads to *scurvy. Claims that large doses of the vitamin prevent colds have not been scientifically accepted.

vitamin D A fat-soluble vitamin consisting of several related compounds (sterols), principally cholecalciferol (D_3) and ergocalciferol (D_2). Vitamin D is important in calcium and phosphorus metabolism, especially in the absorption of calcium from the gut and the deposition and resorption of bone minerals. Vitamin D_3 is produced by the action of sunlight on skin, which normally meets all the body's requirements. Fish and fish-liver oils are the main natural sources, while vitamin D_2 is added to margarine. Deficiency in infants causes *rickets.

vitamin E A vitamin consisting of a group of related compounds that function as biological antioxidants, inhibiting the oxidation of unsaturated fatty acids. The most potent form of vitamin E is alpha-tocopherol, found in green leafy plants, cereal grains, and eggs. Deficiency (which is rare) may lead to anemia.

vitamin K A vitamin consisting of a group of quinone-based compounds that are necessary for the formation of prothrombin, important in blood clotting. Vitamin K occurs in vegetables, cereals, and egg yolk and can be synthesized by intestinal bacteria. Deficiency is rare.

Vitebsk 55 10N 30 14E A port in the W Soviet Union, in the Belorussian SSR on the Western Dvina River. It serves as the transport center of an agricultural region; industries include food processing. Population (1981 est): 310,000.

Viterbo 42 24N 12 06E A city in Italy, in Lazio. A favorite papal residence in the 13th century, it has a 12th-century gothic cathedral. Its manufactures include pottery, furniture, and textiles. Population (1971): 58,618.

Viti Levu The largest Fijian island, in the S Pacific Ocean. Mount Victoria, the highest mountain in Fiji, rises to 4341 ft (1302 m). Sugar, pineapples, cotton, and rice are produced and gold is mined. Area: 4010 sq mi (10,386 sq km). Chief settlement: Suva.

Vitória 20 19S 40 21W A port in E Brazil, the capital of Espírito Santo state. It serves the coffee-growing and mining areas of the state of Minas Gerais. Its university was founded in 1961. Population (1975 est): 163,877.

Vitoria 42 51N 2 40W A city in N Spain, in the Basque Provinces. During the Peninsular War Wellington defeated the French under Joseph Bonaparte here (1813). A manufacturing and commercial center, it has a trade in cereals and wine. Population (1974 est): 169,410.

Vitruvius (Marcus Vitruvius Pollio; 1st century BC) Roman architect and military engineer, famous as the author of the only complete architectural treatise to survive from antiquity. In the ten books of *De architectura* he describes all the main aspects of Roman architecture—public and domestic buildings, temples, the *orders of architecture, interior decoration, town planning, engineering, etc. Rediscovered in Renaissance Italy, it strongly influenced such architects as *Alberti and *Palladio.

Vittorini, Elio (1908–66) Italian novelist. He was an outspoken critic of fascism and was imprisoned in 1943 following the publication of his novel

Conversation in Sicily (1941). Released after the German occupation of Italy, he joined the resistance. He translated the works of many US writers and in postwar Italy had great influence as a literary critic.

Vittorino da Feltre (V. Ramboldini; 1378–1446) Italian Renaissance humanist and educationalist. At his school in Mantua Vittorino educated the children of both the aristocracy and the poor. He developed a broad curriculum, including classics, gymnastics, drawing, and science.

Vivaldi, Antonio (1678–1741) Italian composer and violinist. He was ordained priest in 1703 and taught music at the Ospedale della Pietà in Venice, for whose orchestra many of his works were written. Toward the end of his life he toured Europe and died in poverty in Vienna. Besides operas and sacred music, Vivaldi wrote over 450 concertos for a wide range of solo instruments, including a set of four violin concertos entitled *The Four Seasons*, which are musical illustrations of four sonnets by the composer.

Vivekananda, Swami (1862–1902) Hindu philosopher. Born in Bengal, he studied western thought and science, which he realized was required to improve conditions in India. He dedicated himself to social reforms and to amalgamating western scientific materialism with eastern spirituality. He founded the Vedanta movement in the west, where, as the best-known disciple of *Ramakrishna, he was well received and where his teaching has had a continuing influence.

Viverridae A family of mammals of the order *Carnivora. The 82 species include the genets, civets, linsangs, and mongooses. Viverrids typically have a long body and tail and short legs.

Vivés, Juan Luis (1492–1540) Spanish humanist and writer. He visited England (1523, 1527–28) but lived mainly at Bruges. His *De anima et vita* (1538) is a psychological work of some depth. He also wrote a treatise on educational theory, *De disciplinis* (1531).

viviparity A reproductive process in animals in which the embryo develops within the maternal body, from which it obtains continuous nourishment. Viviparity occurs in most mammals—the embryos being nourished through the placenta—and in some snakes, lizards, and sharks. In **ovoviviparity** the embryo develops within the mother but is surrounded by egg membranes and derives its food from the yolk. It occurs in certain snakes and fish. It should be distinguished from **oviparity**, occurring in birds and many other animals, in which fertilized eggs are laid or spawned by the mother.

vivisection The use of live animals for experiments. Many animals, especially rats, mice, rabbits, guinea pigs, and monkeys, are used worldwide to determine the effects of drugs, cosmetics, food additives, and other chemicals on living organisms, often as an indication of their likely effects on man. They are also used in medical and biological research and for many standard biological tests and assays. In many countries vivisection is controlled by legislation. Alternatives to live animals include the use of test-tube (*in vitro*) techniques, tissue cultures, and computer-based mathematical models.

Vlaardingen 51 55N 4 20E A major port in the SW Netherlands, in South Holland province on the Nieuwe Waterweg (New Waterway). It has the largest shipyard in Holland; other industries include herring fishing. Population (1981 est): 79,100.

Vladimir 56 08N 40 25E A city in the W central Soviet Union, in the RSFSR 115 mi (185 km) NE of Moscow. It is a rail junction and a manufacturing and tourist center. Its fine medieval buildings include the Cathedral of St Dimitrii (1197). *History*: founded in the early 12th century, it was the capital (c. 1157–1238) of the grand duchy of Vladimir. It was then virtually destroyed by the Tatars and in 1364 passed under the rule of Moscow. Population (1981 est): 307,000.

Vladimir I, St (c. 965–1015) Prince of Novgorod (970–80) and Grand Prince of Kiev (980–1015). In about 987 Vladimir became a Christian and introduced the Byzantine rite to Kiev and Novgorod.

Vladivostok 43 09N 131 53E A port of the SE Soviet Union, in the RSFSR on the Sea of Japan. It is the terminus of the Trans-Siberian Railway and a major Soviet naval base, also supporting fishing and whaling fleets. Ice breakers are employed to keep its harbor open in winter. Industries include shipbuilding and food processing. Population (1981 est): 565,000.

Vlaminck, Maurice de (1876-1958) French painter. A self-taught artist, he worked with *Derain from 1899 and from 1901 was strongly influenced by *Van Gogh. He became a leading exponent of *fauvism, painted under the influence of *Cézanne from 1908, but returned after 1915 to a style expressing his aggressive temperament in numerous stormy landscapes, which hold a minor place in 20th-century *expressionism.

Vlissingen. *See* Flushing.

Vlora (*or* Vlorë; Italian name: Valona) 40 29N 19 29E An important seaport in SW Albania, on the Adriatic Sea. After centuries of foreign domination, the independence of Albania was proclaimed here on November 28, 1912. Industries include fishing and an olive-oil refinery. Population (1978 est): 58,400.

Vltava River A river in Czechoslovakia, rising in the Forest of Bohemia and flowing mainly SE then N to join the Elbe River near Melnik. It is an important source of hydroelectric power. Length: 270 mi (434 km).

vocal cords. *See* larynx.

vodka A *liquor distilled from potatoes, rye, barley, or malt, usually in E Europe. Being colorless and without a distinctive flavor, vodka is used in many mixed drinks, such as Screwdriver (vodka and orange juice) and Bloody Mary (vodka and tomato juice).

voiceprint A graphic record of the sounds produced during speech. The record shows the range of frequencies and harmonics produced and can be used to identify any individual voice. Although there are certain standards in articulation, which are recorded on the voiceprint, individual timbre and harmonics are produced by the shape and flexibility of the larynx and the oral cavity, which are as distinctive as faces or fingerprints. Voiceprints are used in phonetics and in forensic science.

Vojvodina An autonomous province of NE Yugoslavia, in the republic of Serbia. Predominantly low lying and fertile, it is one of the chief agricultural areas of Yugoslavia, producing cereals, fruit, and vegetables. Area: 8683 sq mi (22,489 sq km). Population (1971): 1,935,115. Capital: Novi Sad.

volcanoes Vents or fissures in the earth's surface, either on land or under the sea, through which magma rises from the earth's interior and erupts lava, gases, and pyroclastic material. Many volcanoes have cones consisting of ash, pyroclastic deposits, and lava. Basaltic lava tends to produce gently sloping cones, the lava flowing over a wide area, whereas the more viscous acid lava produces a steeper-sided cone. Volcanic cones are often topped by craters, created by volcanic explosions, and craters of over 0.6 mi (1 km) in diameter (calderas) sometimes occur through the collapse or explosive removal of the top of a volcano. Volcanoes may be active, quiescent (dormant), or extinct. The world's highest volcano (extinct) is Aconcagua (22,831 ft [6959 m]) in the Andes. Volcanoes frequently occur along plate boundaries (*see* plate tectonics).

Volcano Islands A group of three small volcanic Japanese islands in the W Pacific Ocean. Claimed in 1891, they were under US administration (1951–68). Sulfur and sugar are produced. Area: about 11 sq mi (28 sq km).

vole A small short-tailed *rodent belonging to the subfamily *Microtinae* (which also includes lemmings). Voles are found in Europe, Asia, and North America and range in size from 28–14 in (7–35 cm). They have blunt noses and their cheek teeth grow continuously. The common field voles (genus *Microtus*; 42 species) live under surface vegetation of meadowland, eating nearly their own weight in seeds, roots, and leaves every 24 hours. Family: *Cricetidae*.

Volga River A river in the W Soviet Union, the longest river in Europe. Rising in the Valdai Range, it flows mainly E and S through Volgograd to the Caspian Sea. It drains most of the W Soviet Union and its many large reservoirs provide important irrigation and hydroelectric power. The Moscow–Volga Canal, the Volga–Don Canal, and the Mariinsk Canal system form navigable waterways from the capital to the White Sea, the Baltic Sea, the Caspian Sea, the Black Sea, and the Sea of Azov. Length: 2293 mi (3690 km).

Volgograd (name until 1925: Tsaritsyn; name from 1925 until 1961: Stalingrad) 48 45N 44 30E A city in the Soviet Union, in the SW RSFSR on the Volga River. It has been rapidly redeveloped since its virtual destruction in World War II (*see* Stalingrad, Battle of) and it is now a major industrial city, having steel plants and factories manufacturing especially machinery, footwear, and food. Population (1981 est): 948,000.

volleyball A six-a-side court game invented in the US in 1895, in which an inflated ball is hit with the hands or arms. After the service each team is allowed to hit the ball three times before it crosses the net. A rally ends when the ball touches the ground or is not returned correctly. Only the serving side can score; if the receiving side wins a rally, it serves next. Players rotate on the court so that each has an opportunity of serving. A game goes to 15 points and a 2-point lead is required to win. It is an Olympic Games sport for both men and women.

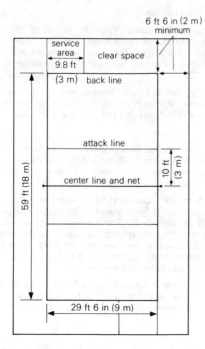

VOLLEYBALL *The dimensions of the court. The height of the ceiling is a minimum of 23 ft (7 m). The top of the center of the net is 8 ft (2.43 m) above the floor for men or 7 ft 4 in (2.24 m) for women.*

Volstead Act (1919) A US law that prohibited the production, sale, and transportation of alcoholic beverages. Written by US Representative Andrew J. Volstead (1860–1947), it gave power to the government to enforce the provisions of the 18th Amendment. *See also* Prohibition.

volt (V) The *SI unit of potential, potential difference, or electromotive force equal to the potential difference between two points on a conductor carrying a steady current of one ampere when the power dissipated is one watt. Named for— Alessandro *Volta.

Volta, Alessandro Giuseppe Antonio Anastasio, Count (1745–1827) Italian physicist, who invented the electrophorus (1775), a device used to accumulate electric charge and the forerunner of the modern capacitor. His greatest invention, the Voltaic pile or cell, was the first practical battery and led to a number of important discoveries in electricity. He was professor of physics at Pavia University (1779–1815) and was made a count by Napoleon in 1801. The unit of potential difference is named for him.

Volta River A river in West Africa. Its headstreams, the Black Volta and White Volta Rivers, join in N central Ghana to form the Volta River, which then flows S to enter the Bight of Benin. The Akosombo Dam, completed in 1965 as part of the Volta River scheme, provides Ghana's hydroelectric-power requirements and powers its important aluminum smelter. Length: 300 mi (480 km).

Voltaire (François-Marie Arouet; 1694–1778) French man of letters, philosopher, scientist, and moralist, whose versatile work epitomizes the age of Enlightenment. He conducted a lifelong campaign against injustice and intolerance. For offending the Duc de Rohan, he was briefly imprisoned in the Bastille (1717) and then went into exile in England (1726–29). After the publication of his *Lettres philosophiques* (1734), which advocated political and religious toleration, he fled to Cirey in Champagne, where he lived with his mistress, Madame de Châtelet. He subsequently lived in Germany (1750–53) having earlier been on friendly terms with Frederick the Great through their correspondence, and in Switzerland (from 1754), chiefly at Ferney near Geneva. His voluminous writings cover history, science, philosophy, and verse drama (for which he was most popular among his contemporaries), and include the satirical and philosophical fable *Candide* (1759), *Traité de la tolérance* (1763), the *Dictionnaire philosophique* (1764), and histories of Peter the Great and Louis XV.

Volta Redonda 22 31S 44 05W A city in S Brazil, in Rio de Janeiro state on the Rio Paraíba. It has the largest steelworks in South America. Population (1975 est): 147,261.

voltmeter A device for measuring voltage. A voltmeter should draw as little current as possible from the circuit and therefore requires a high input impedance. In the direct-current moving-coil voltmeter the magnetic force on a coil in a magnetic field is used to deflect a needle, the high impedance being provided by a high resistance in series with the coil. *Cathode-ray oscilloscopes and digital voltmeters, used for both direct and alternating current, have high internal impedances.

Volturno River A river in S central Italy, flowing SE and SW to the Tyrrhenian Sea. In 1860 it was the scene of a battle in which Garibaldi defeated the Neapolitans during the wars for Italian unity (*see* Risorgimento). It was the German line of defense during World War II. Length: 109 mi (175 km).

Volunteers in Service to America (VISTA) US federal agency, part of the independent agency ACTION, that provides Americans with opportunities to work, on a full-time volunteer basis, to improve the lives of the economically disadvantaged in the US. Volunteers serve for 1 year and live and work among the poor in urban or rural areas, or on Indian reservations, sharing skills and experiences. In order to qualify for service, a volunteer must be a resident of the US or one of its territories. The VISTA program was founded in 1964.

Volvox A genus of freshwater single-celled organisms that live in hollow spherical colonies of 500–50,000 individuals, which are linked together by fine strands of cytoplasm; the center of the sphere contains a gelatinous mass. New colonies are formed asexually by division of certain cells or by sexual reproduction, in which the fertilized eggs become dormant cysts that subsequently form new colonies. *Volvox* is regarded by some authorities as an alga (it contains the green pigment chlorophyll) and by others as a protozoan of the class *Flagellata*. □Protozoa.

Von Braun, Wernher (1912–77) US rocket engineer, born in Germany. Beginning his research into the design of rocket engines in 1932, he was director of the German Rocket Test Center at Peenemünde during World War II. It was here that the *V-2 rocket was finally perfected, being launched on London in 1944. After the war Von Braun was taken to the US where he worked on space rockets, including the Saturn launch vehicles (*see* rockets).

Vondel, Joost van den (1587–1679) Dutch dramatist and poet. His works, which adhere to classical models, reflect his deep involvement in contemporary political and religious disputes and his gradual change from Calvinist to Catholic views. His masterpieces, *Lucifer* (1654), *Adam in Ballingschap* (1664), and *Jephtha* (1659), treat biblical themes.

Vonnegut, Kurt (1922–) US novelist. His novels and stories are noted for their satirical use of science-fiction techniques. *Slaughterhouse Five* (1969) is based on his experience as a prisoner of war during the fire-bombing of Dresden in 1945. His other works include *Cat's Cradle* (1963), *Breakfast of Champions* (1973), *Slapstick* (1976), *Jailbird* (1979), *Palm Sunday* (1981), and *Deadeye Dick* (1982).

voodoo Magical and animistic cults of West African origin, practiced by blacks in Haiti and elsewhere in the Caribbean and in parts of South America. Trances induced by spirit possession are central to voodoo ritual. Other elements in the nocturnal rites are animal sacrifice, drum beating, dancing, and debased elements of Roman Catholic liturgy.

Voronezh 51 40N 39 13E A city in the Soviet Union, in the W RSFSR. It is at the center of an agricultural region and food processing is an important economic activity. Its educational institutions include a university that was transferred here from Tartu in 1918. Population (1981 est): 809,000.

Voroshilov, Kliment Yefremovich (1881–1969) Soviet marshal and statesman. Voroshilov was a Red Army commander in the civil war (1918–20) and then commissar for defense (1925–40). He lost his command of the NW armies in 1941 for failing to raise the German siege of Leningrad. He was president of the Soviet Union from 1953 to 1960.

Voroshilovgrad (name until 1935: Lugansk) 48 35N 39 20E A city in the Soviet Union, in the E Ukrainian SSR. In the coal-producing Donets Basin, it manufactures mining machinery and has iron and steel and chemical industries. Population (1981 est): 474,000.

Vorster, Balthazar Johannes (1915–83) South African statesman; prime minister (1966–78) and briefly president (1978). A lawyer, Vorster became minister of justice and police in 1960 and was known for his extreme right-wing views and strict enforcement of racial policies. Becoming prime minister after Verwoerd's assassination, he attempted to improve South Africa's relations with black Africa. He retired during investigations of financial irregularities in his term as prime minister.

vortex The circular motion of a fluid about a vertical axis. Examples include whirlpools, hurricanes, and cyclones. A vortex may be formed in a fluid at a point just behind a blunt obstacle past which it is flowing. The direction of rotation of a naturally occurring vortex is often determined by the direction in which the *Coriolis force is acting.

Vorticella A genus of microscopic aquatic single-celled animals found in dense clusters or singly. 0.002–0.6 in (0.05–0.15 mm) long, they are bell-shaped and attached to the substrate by a long coiled contractile stalk. Cilia around the mouth of the "bell" create currents that carry food particles into the mouth. □Protozoa.

vorticism A British art movement inaugurated in 1913 by the writer and painter Wyndham *Lewis. Influenced by *cubism and *futurism, it called for an art expressing the advanced technology and pace of modern life. Its journal, *Blast*, included contributions from Ezra *Pound and T. S. *Eliot. The sculptors *Gaudier-Brzeska and *Epstein were also associated with the movement.

Vosges A range of mountains in NE France. It extends roughly N–S to the W of the Rhine River between Basle and Karlsruhe, rising to 4672 ft (1423 m) at Ballon de Guebwiller, close to the source of the Moselle River.

vote The expression of a choice or opinion, by ballot by voice, especially for the purpose of electing members to representative assemblies. In the US all persons over the age of 18 may vote in local, state, and national elections.

Voyager probes Two US *planetary probes launched in 1977 toward the outer planets. Voyager 1 approached Jupiter in 1979 before being accelerated toward Saturn, which it reached in 1980. Voyager 2 flew past Jupiter en route for Uranus (1986) and Neptune (1990).

Voznesenskii, Andrei (1933–) Soviet poet. He has traveled in the US and Europe and is, with *Yevtushenko, the best-known contemporary Soviet poet. His poems are noted for their lively originality and inventiveness. His translated poetry includes *Selected Poems* (1964) and *Antiworlds* (1967).

VTOL aircraft. *See* aircraft.

Vuillard, (Jean) Édouard (1868–1940) French artist. He was a member of the *Nabis in Paris and his work was influenced chiefly by Japanese prints. His intimate domestic scenes in paintings and lithographs featured large expanses of patterned wallpapers and textiles and became labeled intimist (*see* intimism). After 1900 he concentrated on society portraiture but also produced murals for public buildings.

Vulcan The Roman god of fire. Originally associated with purely destructive manifestations, such as volcanoes, he became patron of smiths and metalworkers after his identification with the Greek *Hephaestus, whose myths he assumed.

Vulcanite (*or* Ebonite) A hard black insulating material made by heating rubber with sulfur (which makes up about 30% of the product).

vulcanization A process in which sticky natural rubber is made into a harder useful material by heating it with sulfur. Rubber consists of polymer chains with frequent double bonds; the vulcanization process involves the formation of sulfur bridges (–S–S–) between the chains. An inert filler, such as carbon black, is incorporated at the same time.

Vulgate The Latin translation of the Bible made by St Jerome in the 4th century AD. It is the oldest surviving translation of the whole Bible and differs from earlier Latin versions in translating the *Old Testament direct from Hebrew rather than from Greek. It was adopted by the Council of Trent (1546) as the official version of the Roman Catholic Church and is the basis of later English versions, such as the *Douai Bible.

vulture A large carrion-eating bird belonging to the order *Falconiformes*. 24–40 in (60–100 cm) long with a wingspan of up to 105 in (270 cm), vultures have a fleshy naked head, a large crop, and a graceful soaring flight. New World vultures (family *Cathartidae*; 6 species) have a slender hooked bill, large feet, and are voiceless. *See also* condor.
Old World vultures (subfamily *Aegypiinae*; 20 species) are widely distributed in open temperate and tropical regions except Australia. They have heavy chopping bills, strong grasping feet, and a feathered ruff at the base of the neck. Family: *Accipitridae* (hawks and eagles). *See also* griffon vulture; lammergeier.

Vyborg (Finnish name: Viipuri; Swedish name: Viborg)   60 45N 28 41E A port in the Soviet Union, in the NW RSFSR on Vyborg Bay in the Gulf of Finland 70 mi (113 km) NW of Leningrad. It supports a fishing fleet, and shipbuilding and lumbering are important industries. *History*: founded (1293) by the Swedes as a fortress, it was taken by Peter the Great in 1710 but belonged to Finland from 1918 to 1940. It passed finally to the Soviet Union in 1944. Population (1970): 65,000.

Vyshinskii, Andrei Yanuareevich (1883–1954) Soviet diplomat and lawyer. Vyshinskii was a professor of law and chief prosecutor in Stalin's purge trials (1934–38). He became foreign minister in 1949 and remained in office until Stalin's death when he was demoted to deputy foreign minister and permanent delegate to the UN.

W

Wabash River A river of the E central US, flowing from W Ohio through Indiana to join the Ohio River. Length: 764 km (475 mi).

Wace (c. 1180–c. 1175) Anglo-Norman poet. His major works are the *Roman de Rou* (1160–74), concerning the history of Normandy, and the *Roman de Brut* (1155), which was dedicated to Eleanor of Aquitaine and contained much new material relating to the *Arthurian legend.

Waco 31 55N 97 08W A city in E central Texas, on the Brazos River, SE of Fort Worth. Baylor University (1845) is here. Settled in 1849 and named after the Waco Indians, it is a distribution center for the area's agricultural products. Cotton is important, and textiles, clothing, furniture, glass, tires, and aircraft components are manufactured. Population (1980): 101,261.

Wade–Davis Bill (1864) US law, vetoed by President Abraham Lincoln, that established procedures for *Reconstruction. Drafted by senators Benjamin F. Wade and Henry W. Davis, it stated that the government of a seceded state could not be reorganized until a majority of white males pledged allegiance to the US.

Wade–Giles system. *See* Chinese.

wadi A normally dry valley in a desert or semidesert area. It will occasionally contain water following the infrequent violent downpours of rain that occur in these areas.

Wad Medani 14 24N 33 30E A city in the E central Sudan, on the Blue Nile River. Its recent growth has been due to its central position in the *Gezira irrigation scheme. Population (1973): 106,776.

RICHARD WAGNER *A contemporary caricature of Richard Wagner, emphasizing the composer's shortness.*

Wagner, (Wilhelm) Richard (1813–83) German composer. He studied at the Thomasschule in Leipzig. His early attempts at composition were unsuccessful but productions of his operas *Rienzi* (1842) and *The Flying Dutchman* (1843) led to his appointment as conductor at the Dresden opera house. In 1845 his opera *Tannhäuser* was successfully performed there but in 1848, after the failure of the May uprising, Wagner fled to Zürich, where he began the composition of the operatic cycle *Der Ring des Nibelungen*, an epic treatment of German mythology. Wagner developed the use of composition with *leitmotifs in order to achieve an integration of music and drama in opera, having as an ideal that of the *Gesamtkunstwerk* (German: complete work of art). During the composition of the *Ring*, he fell in love with Mathilde Wesendonck (1828–1902), who inspired the opera *Tristan und Isolde*. Wagner continued to face financial difficulties until, in 1864, King Ludwig II of Bavaria befriended him, financing the first performance of *Tristan* in 1865. Shortly afterward Wagner eloped with

Cosima von Bülow (1837–1930), Liszt's daughter, whom he married in 1870. In 1868 he produced his comic opera *Die Meistersinger von Nürnberg* and continued work on the *Ring*, raising money to build a theater in Bayreuth for the first performance of the cycle (1876). His last opera, *Parsifal*, was produced in Bayreuth in 1882. Wagner was also a prolific writer on music, the theory of music drama (*see* opera), art, and other subjects. His son **Siegfried Wagner** (1869–1930) and grandson **Wieland Wagner** (1917–66) directed annual productions of Wagner's music dramas at Bayreuth after his death.

Wagner von Jauregg, Julius (1857–1940) Austrian psychiatrist who, as professor of psychiatry and neurology at Vienna University, successfully treated patients suffering from progressive syphilitic brain disease by means of a controlled malarial infection. His work led to the introduction of fever therapy for various mental disorders and he was awarded the 1927 Nobel Prize.

Wagram, Battle of (July 5–6, 1809) The battle in which Napoleon won a major victory over the Austrians. Fought NE of Vienna, it forced Austria to concede general defeat to the French. Wagram witnessed the largest concentration of field artillery in recorded history.

wagtail A slender fine-billed songbird noted for its constantly bobbing tail. The pied wagtail (*Motacilla alba*) is black, gray, and white, about 7 in (18 cm) long, and commonly occurs near houses. The larger gray wagtail (*M. cinerea*) lives near streams, catching flying insects. In summer the male has a bright-yellow breast, black throat, and bluish upper parts. The yellow wagtail (*M. flava*) visits Britain in the summer. Family: *Motacillidae* (wagtails and pipits).

Wahhabiyah A Muslim sect founded by Muhammad ibn Abd al-Wahhab (1691–1787). It stresses the need for a Muslim state based on strict adherence to the literal authority of the *Koran and *Hadith. It is responsible for the creation of the kingdom of Saudi Arabia.

Waikato River The longest river in New Zealand, in North Island. Rising in Mount Ruapehu, it flows generally NW through Lake Taupo to enter the Tasman Sea near Auckland. It is an important source of hydroelectric power. Length: 220 mi (350 km).

Wailing Wall Part of the western wall of the *Temple of Jerusalem; it is the only part of the wall that formerly surrounded the Temple still standing. Since late Roman times Jews have gathered here to pray and to mourn over the Temple's destruction.

Wairarapa Plain A low-lying sedimentary area in New Zealand, on SE North Island. Sheep and dairy farming are important. Area: about 320 sq mi (830 sq km).

Waitangi, Treaty of (1840) A treaty between the British government and 46 Maori chiefs in New Zealand, which gave the Maori full rights and confirmed their possession of their lands. Its infringement by settlers led to the *Maori Wars.

Waite, Morrison Remick (1816–88) US lawyer and jurist; chief justice of the Supreme Court (1874–88). A successful lawyer, he worked behind the scenes in Ohio politics and represented the US in the *Alabama* claims case (1871) in Geneva, Switzerland. He was appointed chief justice by President Ulysses S. *Grant and worked to define and clarify post-Civil War legislation. He held that the due process clause of the 14th Amendment was instrumental in defining states' rights in the Granger cases (1876) and further defined the states' role in segregation in the *Civil Rights cases.

Wajda, Andrzej (1926–) Polish film director. He established his international reputation with *A Generation* (1954), *Kanal* (1957), and *Ashes and Diamonds* (1958), a trilogy of films concerning Poland during and after World War II. In later films, such as *Landscape after Battle* (1970) and *The Wedding* (1972), he continued to explore social and political themes.

Wakamatsu. *See* Kitakyushu.

Wakashan languages A group of *North American Indian languages of the NW Pacific coast, including *Nootka and *Kwakiutl.

Wakefield 53 42N 1 29W A city in N England, on the Calder River. In a battle (1460) during the Wars of the Roses, Richard, Duke of York, was defeated and killed by the Lancastrians. The chief industries are wool textiles, chemicals, machine tools, and coalmining. Population (1981): 60,540.

Wake Island   19 18N 166 36E A coral atoll in the central Pacific Ocean, a US air base. It was taken by the Japanese following the Pearl Harbor attack (December 7, 1941). Area: 3 sq mi (8 sq km).

Waksman, Selman Abraham   (1888–1973) US microbiologist, born in Russia. Waksman coined the term antibiotic for naturally occurring antibacterial substances. His search for these among soil microorganisms led to the discovery of actinomycin (1940) and *streptomycin (1943), the first effective agent for the treatment of tuberculosis. Waksman was awarded a Nobel Prize (1952).

Walachia (*or* Wallachia)   A principality in SE Europe between the lower Danube River in the E and the Transylvanian Alps in the N and NE. Founded in 1290, it was a Hungarian fief until 1330. In the late 14th century it came under Turkish domination, which lasted until the 19th century. In 1859 Walachia united with *Moldavia to form Romania, the independence of which was recognized in 1878.

Walafrid Strabo   (c. 808–49 AD) German scholar and poet. He became Abbot of Reichenau in 838. His fame rests on such poems as *Visio Wetteni*, which in describing the hereafter anticipates Dante's *Divine Comedy*, and a handbook on liturgical and archeological subjects, which is of great historical interest.

Wałbrzych (German name: Waldenburg)   50 48N 16 19E An industrial city in SW Poland, in the Sudeten Mountains. It is a coalmining center and has engineering and chemical industries. Population (1976 est): 128,700.

Walburga, St   (*or* St Walpurgis; c. 710–79 AD) English nun and missionary to Germany; the sister of the English missionary St Willibald (700–86), Bishop of Eichstätt. She worked with St *Boniface in Germany, where she became abbess of Heidenheim, an important cultural center. It is not certain why *Walpurgisnacht* (May 1), the traditional German witches' sabbath, is associated with her name. Feast day: Feb 25.

Waldemar.   *See* Valdemar.

Waldenburg.   *See* Wałbrzych.

Waldenses (*or* Vaudois)   A Christian group founded in the 12th century by Peter Waldes (d. 1217), a wealthy merchant of Lyons, who apparently gave his wealth to the poor and formed a community known as "the poor men of Lyons." The first settlements were in the French Alps, but religious persecution, which continued sporadically to the 18th century, scattered the Waldenses to Italy, Bohemia, Germany, Spain, and eventually North America. They were supported at the Reformation by other Protestant groups. They reject many Roman doctrines (e.g. transubstantiation, purgatory, celibacy of the clergy); at present they number about 20,000.

KURT WALDHEIM   *The former UN secretary general (center) with the Greek-Cypriot president of Cyprus, Kyprianou (right) and Denktash, president of the Turkish Federated State of Cyprus.*

Waldheim, Kurt   (1918–) Austrian diplomat; secretary general of the UN (1972–81). He served in Paris and Canada before becoming Austria's permanent representative to the UN (1964–68, 1970–71); he was Austria's minister of foreign affairs (1968–70).

Wales (Welsh name: Cymru)   A principality in the W of Great Britain, a political division of the *United Kingdom. It is bordered by England to the E, the Irish Sea to the N, St George's Channel to the W, and the Bristol Channel to the S. Much of the country is covered by hills and mountains, including the Brecon Beacons to the S, the Cambrian Mountains in central Wales, and the mountains of Snowdonia in the NW. The Isle of Anglesey lies off the NW coast. The principal rivers are the Usk, Rhymney, Taff, Neath, Towry, and Dovey. Central Wales is sparsely populated, most of the population living in the valleys and coastal plains of the S and along the coastal strip in the N. *Economy*: the valleys and coastal plain in the S are highly industrialized, based on the extensive coal fields. Steelmaking has long been associated with these coalfields, and Wales accounts for about half the UK's production of steel sheet and almost all its production of tinplate. Light industry has also been encouraged by the government. Milford Haven, in the far SW, is famous for its deepwater port, used for the importing of oil, which has given rise to oil refining and associated petrochemical industries. Towns on the coast of North Wales derive an important revenue from tourism. *History*: the Celtic inhabitants of Wales were little affected by the Roman occupation and were christianized in the 3rd century AD. King *Offa of Mercia built a great dike (8th century) stretching from sea to sea, providing a frontier behind which the Welsh kingdoms were contained. Edward I of England defeated *Llywelyn ap Gruffud (d. 1282) and established English supremacy in Wales. Owen *Glendower's revolt in the early 14th century was also crushed and English rule was formalized with the Acts of *Union (1536–43). In common with England, Wales adopted Protestantism in the 16th century. The early 19th century was characterized by rural overpopulation and near famine, which was alleviated by industrialization in the S and NE, and Wales also suffered during the Depression of the 1930s. Politically, Welsh nationalism has been a powerful force. Area: 8016 sq mi (20,767 sq km). Population (1981): 2,790,000. Capital: Cardiff.

Walesa, Lech   (1943–) Polish labor leader, who was awarded the Nobel Peace Prize (1983). An electrician, fired (1976) for protesting against working conditions at the Lenin Shipyard in Gdansk, he worked underground in the labor movement and eventually founded Solidarity (1980), a national federation uniting individual unions. A general strike that same year forced the Polish Communist government to grant workers the right to organize. Solidarity was outlawed in 1981, and Walesa was imprisoned until 1982.

Waley, Arthur   (1889–1966) British translator and poet. His translations of Chinese and Japanese poetry influenced many western poets, notably Ezra Pound. He also translated novels and plays and wrote several studies of oriental literature and art.

walking (*or* race walking)   In athletics, a form of racing in which a particular gait is used; the advancing foot must touch the ground before the other leaves it. Races are held on a track or on roads.

wallaby   A herbivorous marsupial belonging to the *kangaroo family (*Macropodidae*). Wallabies are smaller than kangaroos. Hare wallabies (genus *Lagorchestes*; 3 species) are the smallest, measuring up to 35 in (90 cm) in length. Rock wallabies (genus *Petrogale*; 6 species) have a squarish tail and rough-soled feet for negotiating rocky ground. Scrub wallabies (genus *Protemnodon*; about 11 species) inhabit brush or open forest, browsing on leaves and grass.

Wallace, Alfred Russel   (1823–1913) British naturalist, who formulated a theory of evolution by natural selection independently of Charles *Darwin. Wallace spent eight years (1854–62) assembling evidence in the Malay Archipelago, sending his conclusions to Darwin in England. Their findings were presented to the Linnaean Society in 1858. Wallace found that Australian species were more primitive, in evolutionary terms, than those of Asia, and that this reflected the stage at which the two continents had become separated. He proposed an imaginary line (Wallace's line) dividing the fauna of the two regions.

Wallace, Edgar   (1875–1932) British novelist. The illegitimate son of an actress, he was the prolific and enormously successful author of over 170 popular novels and detective stories. He died in Hollywood, where he was a scriptwriter.

Wallace, George Corley   (1919–) US politician; governor of Alabama (1963–67; 1971–79; 1983–). He served in various state positions until 1962 when he was elected governor for the first time. In 1963 he became prominent nationally when he defied a court order to integrate the University of Alabama; he eventually complied when the National Guard was called out. Not eligible to run for a second consecutive term as governor, he campaigned for his wife **Lurleen Burns Wallace** (1926–68) who became governor in 1967. He campaigned for the Democratic presidential nomination three times (1964, 1972, 1976) and once ran for president on the American Independent Party ticket (1968). In an assassination attempt in the 1972 campaign he was shot and left partially paralyzed. A defiant segregationist during the 1960s into the 1970s, he accepted integration and received considerable support from blacks in his successful 1982 gubernatorial campaign.

Wallace, Henry Agard   (1888–1965) US statesman and agriculturalist; vice president (1941–45). He edited *Wallace's Farmer* (1924–29) and *Iowa Homestead* (1929–33) and experimented with hybrid corn. He served as secretary of agriculture (1933–40) during which time he was responsible for implementing the *Agricultural Adjustment Act. As vice president during President Franklin D. *Roosevelt's third term, he worked to better Latin American and Asian relations with the US. He was secretary of commerce (1945–46) and ran for president in 1948 on the Progressive Party ticket.

Wallace, Lew(is)   (1827–1905) US soldier, diplomat, and author. He served in the *Mexican War (1846–47), as a Union general in the *Civil War, as governor of New Mexico (1878–81), and minister to Turkey (1881–85). He wrote the bestseller *Ben Hur* (1880).

Wallachia.   *See* Walachia.

wallaroo   An Australian *kangaroo, *Macropus robustus*. Smaller than red or gray kangaroos, wallaroos are heavy-set and have long thick dark-gray fur. They are found mainly in Queensland and New South Wales.

wallcreeper   A Eurasian songbird, *Tichodroma muraria*, about 7 in (17 cm) long with a gray plumage and broad black wings patched with red. It climbs rock faces, clinging with its sharp claws and square tail and probing crevices for insects with its long curved bill. Family: *Sittidae* (nuthatches).

Wallenstein, Albrecht Wenzel von   (1583–1634) Bohemian-born general, who commanded the imperial forces (1625–30, 1632–34) in the *Thirty Years' War. He raised an army of 24,000 men for the emperor Ferdinand I, with which he won a series of victories, acquiring considerable territories for himself. His growing independence led Ferdinand to dismiss him in 1630 but he was recalled to deal with the Swedish threat in 1632. He subsequently betrayed Ferdinand and was murdered by a group of British officers.

Waller, (Thomas) Fats   (1904–1943) US jazz musician and songwriter. Waller played the piano in cabarets and accompanied such singers as Bessie Smith. In the 1930s he organized small bands and recorded many of his own compositions, including "Honeysuckle Rose" and "Ain't Misbehavin'."

wallflower   An annual or perennial herb of either of the genera *Cheiranthus* (about 10 species), native to Eurasia and North America, or *Erysimum* (about 80 species), native to Eurasia. Wallflowers have narrow leaves and four-petaled flowers, usually orange, yellow, red, or brown. Many varieties of *C. cheiri* are cultivated as garden ornamentals. The Siberian wallflower (*E. × marshallii*) has brilliant orange or yellow flowers. Family: *Cruciferae*.

Wallis and Futuna   A French overseas territory in the SW Pacific Ocean comprising two small groups of islands. Formerly a French protectorate, its status was changed following a referendum (1959). The chief of the **Wallis Islands** is Uvéa, while the **Futuna Islands** (or Îles de Horne) consist of Futuna and Alofi. Copra and timber are produced. Area: 106 sq mi (275 sq km). Population (1976): 9192. Capital: Matautu, on Uvéa.

Walloons   The French-speaking inhabitants of Belgium, who live mainly in the S and E of the country. They are descended from the northernmost group of *Franks who adopted the Romance speech. *Compare* Flemings.

Wall Street   The center of the financial district in New York City, in which the New York Stock Exchange is situated. Wall Street, often known as the Street, is synonymous with the stock exchange.

walnut   A □tree of the genus *Juglans* (about 17 species), especially the Eurasian species *J. regia*, which produces the best quality nuts. Up to 100 ft (30 m) tall, it has gray deeply furrowed bark and its leaves comprise seven oblong leaflets grouped in opposite pairs. Separate male and female catkins occur on the same tree, and the plum-sized green fruits each contain a kernel enclosed in a wrinkled pale-brown shell. The kernels are eaten as dessert nuts or used in baking and confectionery, and the whole fruits may be eaten pickled. The timber of this species and of the American black walnut (*J. nigra*) is valued for furniture. Family: *Juglandaceae*.

WALL STREET   *The Depression of the early 1930s was triggered by the collapse of the New York Stock Exchange in 1929. During the severe winter of 1931, free coal was distributed to the poor in New York.*

Walpole, Sir Hugh (Seymour)   (1884–1941) British novelist. Born in New Zealand, he worked as a teacher before becoming a full-time writer. His many novels inclue *The Dark Forest* (1916), set in Russia, *The Cathedral* (1922), and a four-volume family saga, *The Herries Chronicle* (1930–33).

Walpole, Sir Robert, 1st Earl of Orford   (1676–1745) British statesman, regarded as the first prime minister (1721–42). He became a Whig member of parliament in 1700. After his effective handling of the *South Sea Bubble he became (1721) first lord of the treasury and chancellor of the exchequer. He maintained his position by adroit patronage and skillful management of the House of Commons but his government was weakened by legislative failures and by his unpopular foreign policy. Conflict with Spain led to the War of *Jenkins' Ear and Walpole was forced to resign.

His fourth son **Horace Walpole, 4th Earl of Orford** (1717–97) was a writer. He published memoirs, antiquarian works, and one of the most popular of gothic novels, *The Castle of Otranto* (1765).

walrus   A large *seal, *Odobenus rosmarus*, of coastal Arctic waters. Males are up to 12 ft (3.7 m) long and weigh about 3100 lb (1400 kg). Walruses have tusks—elongated upper canine teeth up to 40 in (1 m) long—used in digging for mollusks on the sea bed and for fighting and display. They have an inflatable bag of skin on each side of the neck, used for buoyancy when sleeping in the sea. Family: *Odobenidae*. □mammal.

Walsall   52 35N 1 58W An industrial city in central England, in West Midlands near Birmingham. Industries include coalmining, engineering, machine tools, aircraft components, electronics, leather goods, hardware, and chemicals. Population (1981): 178,900.

Walter, Bruno   (B. W. Schlesinger; 1876–1962) German conductor. He became director of the Vienna Court Opera (1901–12) and went to the US after the outbreak of World War II. There he was associated with the Metropolitan Opera and the New York Philharmonic Orchestra. He was famous as an interpreter of Mahler and conducted the first performance of *Das Lied von der Erde* in 1911.

Waltham   42 23N 71 14W A city in E Massachusetts, on the north bank of the Charles River, west of Boston. Brandeis University (1947) is here. The first US paper mill was started in Waltham in 1788, and the first power loom for the manufacture of cotton textiles was introduced by Francis Cabot Lowell in 1813. Long known as a watchmaking center, Waltham now houses many electronics and precision-instrument industries. Population (1980): 58,200.

Walther von der Vogelweide (c. 1170–c. 1230) German poet. After studying under the court poet of Vienna, he earned a precarious living as a Minnesinger at various courts until he was granted a fief by the Emperor Frederick II. His finest works are love poems and poems inspired by his loyalty to the Holy Roman Empire.

Walton, Ernest Thomas Sinton (1903–   ) Irish physicist, who shared the 1951 Nobel Prize with Sir John *Cockcroft for their invention in 1929 of the first particle accelerator.

Walton, Izaak (1593–1683) English writer. His best-known work is *The Compleat Angler* (1653), a relaxed and entertaining treatise on fishing. He also wrote short biographies of John Donne (1640), George Herbert (1670), and other churchmen.

Walton, Sir William (Turner) (1902–83) British composer. He first became well known through *Façade* (1922), a setting of poems by Edith Sitwell for reciter and instrumental group. Later works include two symphonies (1932–35, 1960), the opera *Troilus and Cressida* (1954), concertos for viola (1929), violin (1939), and cello (1957), the oratorio *Belshazzar's Feast* (1931), and music for Laurence Olivier's films of Shakespeare's *Hamlet, Henry V*, and *Richard III*.

waltz A ballroom dance in 3/4 time in which couples revolve round the room with gliding steps. It originated in Austria and Germany in the late 18th century from a popular folk dance, the *Ländler*. Although many considered it indecorous, it quickly spread to France and reached England in about 1812. Its variations include the skipping French waltz in 6/8 time, the slow Boston waltz, and the galloping Viennese waltz, for which the Strauss family composed their most famous music.

Walvis Bay A port on the Atlantic coast of Namibia, comprising an exclave of Cape Province, South Africa. Annexed to the Cape Colony in 1884, it has been administered as part of South West Africa (now Namibia) since 1922. It is a major port, handling most Namibian imports, and has important fishing industries. Area: 434 sq mi (1124 sq km). Population (1961): 16,490.

wampum Strings, belts, or ornaments of shell-beads, made by Indians of the NE regions of the US and used by them originally as a record of a treaty or agreement and later, after contact with Europeans, as a form of money.

wandering Jew. *See* Tradescantia.

Wandering Jew In legend, a Jew who rebuked Christ as he was carrying the cross to Calvary and told him to go faster; he was condemned to wander the earth until Christ's second coming. The story is of an early date, a version being given by the English chronicler Matthew Paris (d. 1259); however, its popularity dates from 1602, when a pamphlet was published containing the story of a bishop of Schleswig who had met a certain Ahasuerus, who claimed to be the Wandering Jew.

Wang. *See* Koryŏ.

Wang An Shi (or Wang An-shih; 1021–86) Chinese statesman and writer. As a leading minister (1069–76) during the Song dynasty, he introduced wide-ranging economic reforms (including a fund to make loans to farmers), known as the New Policies. Conservative opposition led to his retirement from office, after which he devoted his energies to scholarship and poetry.

Wang Jing Wei (or Wang Ching-wei; 1883–1944) Chinese revolutionary, who attempted unsuccessfully to assassinate the Qing prime minister (1910). Wang later became a rival of *Chiang Kai-shek for the leadership of the *Guomindang (Nationalist People's Party) and in 1927, in opposition to Chiang, he established a short-lived government at Wuhan. Reconciled with Chiang in 1932, Wang subsequently became prime minister of a Japanese puppet government in Nanjing and died in disgrace.

Wankel engine A four-stroke rotary *internal-combustion engine. It consists of a triangular-shaped rotating piston, with outward curved sides and rounded corners. This rotates in an oval-shaped chamber, slightly narrowed in the middle, which has inlet and exhaust ports and a spark plug. The piston has an inner toothed annulus, which rotates about a central stationary gear, the whole piston being connected via gears to an output shaft. The fuel is drawn in, compressed, and ignited in the chamber spaces provided by the pistons as it rotates. The small number of moving parts and the lack of vibration are the chief advantages of this type of engine, but gas leakage around the seals between the piston ends and the cylinder has been the principal problem. It is, however, used in some cars. It was invented by the German engineer Felix Wankel.

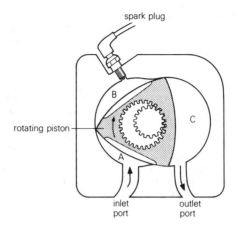

WANKEL ENGINE *The rotary piston draws the fuel mixture through the inlet port into chamber A. At the same time the gas drawn into chamber B in the previous third of a cycle is compressed and ignited to drive the piston around. Meanwhile, the gas in chamber C is discharged through the outlet port.*

wapentake Any of the medieval administrative subdivisions into which the parts of England settled by the Danes (see Danelaw) were divided. They corresponded to the *hundreds found in the rest of England. Derived from the Old Norse words for *weapon* and *take*, the term probably refers to the Scandinavian custom of brandishing weapons in an assembly as a gesture of assent.

wapiti A large *red deer of North America, sometimes regarded as a separate species (*Cervus canadensis*). Males may exceed 5 ft (1.5 m) at the shoulder and have antlers up to 4 ft (1.2 m) high.

waratah A many-branched Australian shrub, *Telopea speciosissima*: the floral emblem of New South Wales. Up to 7 ft (2 m) tall, it has leathery sometimes toothed leaves and crimson or scarlet flowers borne in large round terminal heads surrounded by ribbon-like red bracts. The fruit is a leathery capsule containing winged seeds. Family: *Proteaceae*.

Warbeck, Perkin (c. 1474–99) Flemish-born impostor, the focus of a Yorkist plot against Henry VII of England. Pretending to be the Duke of York (presumed murdered with his brother Edward V in 1483) he landed in Cornwall in 1497 but he and his 6000 followers fled in the face of Henry's troops. He was later hanged.

warble fly A parasitic fly belonging to the family *Oestridae*, widespread in Europe and North America. *Hypoderma boris* and *H. lineatum* attack cattle: eggs are laid on the legs and the larvae burrow into the tissue, coming to lie beneath the hide of the back. There they produce swellings (warbles), each pierced with a hole for breathing. When mature the larvae leave the warble and pupate in the ground. *See also* gad fly.

warbler A small active songbird belonging to a family (*Sylviidae*; 400 species) widely distributed in Old World regions and belonging to a subfamily (*Parulidae*; 109 species) widely distributed in New World regions. The Old World warblers, ranging from 3.5–10 in (9–25 cm) in length, have slender bills, soft thick plumage, and feed on insects and berries. They are usually drab brown or olive in color and many have beautiful songs. Among the New World warblers sizes vary, with many about 5.5 in (14 cm) in length, with plumage similar to Old World varieties. *See* blackcap; chiffchaff; reed warbler; whitethroat.

war crimes Acts contrary to rules of *international law governing the conduct of war, mainly contained in the Hague Convention (1907) and the Geneva Convention (1949). Persons suspected of war crimes may be tried and punished by the state that obtains custody of them. The *Nuremberg Trials established the most important principle regarding war crimes, that "the fact that the defendant acted pursuant to the order of his government or of a superior shall not free him from responsibility . . . ."

Ward, Artemus (Charles Farrar Browne; 1834–67) US humorous writer. While working as a journalist for the Cleveland *Plain Dealer*, he wrote comic letters, the supposed author of which was an itinerant showman, Artemus Ward. He gained national fame as a lecturer using this pseudonym. His writings include *Artemus Ward: His Book* (1862), *Artemus Ward: His Travels* (1865), and *Artemus Ward in London* (1867).

Ward, Barbara, Baroness Jackson (1914–81) British economist and conservationist. She has written several books on ecology and political economy, including *Spaceship Earth* (1966) and, with US bacteriologist René Dubos, *Only One Earth* (1972).

Ward, Sir Joseph George (1856–1930) New Zealand statesman; Liberal (1906–12) and United Party (1928–30) prime minister. He entered parliament in 1887, advocated greater unity within the British Empire in foreign affairs, and led the Liberals in the coalition government (1915–19) before becoming leader of the Liberal Party's successor, the United Party.

war games Simulations in miniature of military maneuvers and combat, using models and rules that enable authentic situations to be reproduced on the playing table. They originated in German states in the late 18th century and were developed by the Prussian army for training purposes during the 19th century. By World War I the military staffs of many countries were using them to assist in the preparation of plans and the training of commanders. War gaming is now a popular pastime.

War Hawks Members of the *Democratic-Republicans in favor of nationalism and Western expansion of the US. Led by Henry *Clay and John C. *Calhoun, they advocated and helped to precipitate the *War of 1812.

Warhol, Andy (Andrew Warhola; 1926–) US *pop artist and film producer. Originally a commercial artist, he achieved notoriety in the early 1960s with paintings of soup cans and portraits of film stars, notably Marilyn Monroe, made with the *silk-screen printing technique. His erotic, lengthy, and controversial films include *Sleep* (1963) and *The Chelsea Girls* (1966).

warlords Local despots who seized control of China following the death of the first president of Republican China, *Yuan Shi Kai, in 1916. These local tyrants, with their own private armies, attempted to increase their personal power by engaging in civil war, which was only ended by Chiang Kai-shek's Northern Expedition against them in 1926. They continued to exert power in China until Liberation (1949).

warm-bloodedness. *See* homoiothermy.

Warm Springs 32 53N 84 42W A village in Georgia. Its water, popular as a health cure since the 19th century, was used by Franklin D. Roosevelt after his attack of poliomyelitis and he subsequently established a foundation (1927) to help other victims of the disease. He died here in 1945.

War of 1812 (1812–14) The war declared on Great Britain by the US in response to Britain's impressment of sailors from American ships, its blockade on US shipping during the Napoleonic Wars, and its assistance to Indians harassing the NW settlements (*see* Tecumseh). Despite the opposition of New England merchants who feared the severe economic consequences of the war, the *War Hawks in Congress and President James *Madison authorized the beginning of hostilities against the British in Canada and on the high seas. The US forces proved to be weaker than expected, although impressive victories were won in 1813 by Commodore Oliver *Perry on Lake Erie and by General William H. *Harrison at the Battle of the Thames in Canada. In 1814 the British invaded Maryland and briefly occupied Washington, setting fire to the White House and the Capitol. In the meantime, General Andrew *Jackson soundly defeated the British at the Battle of Horseshoe Bend in Alabama. Negotiations to end the war began in Ghent, Belgium, and successfully concluded with a truce in December 1814. Before the news of the truce reached the US, however, General Andrew *Jackson defeated the British once more at the Battle of *New Orleans.

Warren 42 28N 83 01W A city in SE Michigan, N of Detroit. Originally called Hickory Township and then Aba, it became Warren shortly after 1838. It is the home of General Motors Technical Center, and automobile manufacturing and automobile technology are the major economic activities. Electrical components, tools and dies, and steel are also produced. Population (1980): 161,134.

Warren, Earl (1891–1974) US politician and jurist. After a long and distinguished legal career as district attorney of Alameda County, Calif (1925–39) and state attorney general (1939–43), Warren entered politics, serving almost three terms as governor of California (1943–53). As the unsuccessful Republican vice-presidential nominee in 1948, Warren became one of the national leaders of the party and in 1953 he was nominated by President Dwight *Eisenhower to become chief justice of the US *Supreme Court.

Warren's tenure on the court was marked by a series of landmark decisions that dramatically affected government enforcement of *civil rights. Among the Warren Court's most important decisions were those in the cases of *Brown v. Board of Education* (1954), in which it ruled that racial segregation in the public schools was unconstitutional; *Engel v. Vitale* (1962), in which it ruled that compulsory prayer in the public schools was a violation of the separation between church and state; *Reynolds v. Sims*, in which it ruled that legislative districts must be drawn to ensure proportional representation; and **Miranda v. Arizona* (1966), in which it ruled that suspects in criminal investigations must be advised of their constitutional rights at the time of their arrest. Following the assassination of President John F. *Kennedy, Warren was appointed to head a presidential commission (*see* Warren Commission) to investigate the crime. Warren retired from the Supreme Court in 1969.

Warren, Robert Penn (1905–) US poet and writer. Part of the Fugitive group of poets at Vanderbilt University under John Crowe *Ransome, he wrote primarily about the South. He taught at the University of Minnesota (1942–50) and at Yale University (1950–56; 1961–73). His best-known epic poem is *Brother to Dragons* (1953) and his poetry is collected in *Promises* (1957; Pulitzer Prize, 1958), *Selected Poems: 1923–1975* (1977), *Now and Then: Poems 1976–1978* (1978; Pulitzer Prize, 1979), and *Being Here* (1980). His novel *All the King's Men* (1946) paralleled the life of Huey *Long, and won a Pulitzer Prize for literature in 1947; the film version earned him an Academy Award in 1949. Other novels included *At Heaven's Gate* (1943), *World Enough and Time* (1950), and *A Place to Come to* (1977).

Warren Commission (1963–64) US committee, under the chairmanship of Supreme Court Chief Justice Earl *Warren, designated to investigate all aspects of President John F. *Kennedy's assassination. Although the conclusions of the commission found that a conspiracy or group was not involved in the assassination, controversy still surrounds the incident and different groups continue investigations.

Warrington 53 24N 2 37W A city in NW England, on the River Mersey and the Manchester Ship Canal. There are engineering, iron-founding, brewing, tanning, chemical, and detergent-manufacturing industries. Population (1981): 135,568.

Warrumbungle Range A mountain range of Australia. It lies in N New South Wales, reaching 4028 ft (1228 m) at Mount Exmouth, and contains the Breadknife, a rock 300 ft (90 m) high but only 5 ft (1.5 m) wide.

Warsaw (Polish name: Warszawa) 52 15N 21 00W The capital of Poland, in the E on the Vistula River. Settlements in the early middle ages had developed into a city by the end of the 15th century and it became the capital in 1611. Thereafter it suffered a decline but it rose to power again in the 18th century. It was occupied by Russia in 1794 and later by France and Prussia. It played an important role in the Polish struggles for independence in the 19th century and, after German occupation in World War I, became the capital again when independence was achieved (1918). During the German occupation of the city in World War II, a ghetto was established (1940) for 400,000 Jews and in February, 1943, the survivors (about 100,000) staged an uprising, after which they were put to death. By the end of the occupation Warsaw was almost completely in ruins. After the war much of the old town was faithfully reconstructed. It has expanded in recent years and is now an important industrial and communications center. The University of Warsaw was founded in 1818 and the Technical University in 1826. Population (1979 est): 1,572,000.

Warsaw Pact (or Warsaw Treaty Organization) A military treaty signed in 1955 by the Soviet Union, Albania (until 1968), Bulgaria, Czechoslovakia, East Germany, Hungary, Poland, and Romania. It was formed as a communist counterpart to NATO. The Soviet army marshal is the head of the Pact's forces and its headquarters are in Moscow.

warships. *See* ships; aircraft carrier; battleship; corvette; cruiser; destroyer; destroyer escort; frigate; submarine.

Wars of Religion (1562–98) French civil wars arising out of the struggle of the Huguenots (French Protestants) for religious liberty and the rivalry between Protestants and Roman Catholic nobles for control of the crown. The main parties were the Catholic *Guise family and successive Huguenot leaders, the Dukes of *Condé, Gaspard de *Coligny, and Henry of Navarre. The wars, comprising eight distinct conflicts, were exacerbated by the weakness of the monarchy under Charles IX and Henry III, who were dominated by their mother *Catherine de' Medici. The wars ended in the victory of Henry of Navarre, who after becoming a Catholic ascended the throne as *Henry IV. In 1598 he issued the Edict of *Nantes, which gave the Huguenots religious freedom.

wart (or verruca) A small leathery growth on the skin, caused by viruses. Warts are commonest in children and usually appear on the hands and on the soles of the feet. They appear suddenly and may disappear without treatment. Persistent warts can be treated by cauterization, freezing, or with drugs (such as podophylline), but no treatment is entirely satisfactory.

warthog A wild pig, *Phocochoerus aethiopicus*, of tropical African woodland. Short-legged, with a large head, bulging eyes, and long curved tusks, warthogs grow to about 30 in (75 cm) high at the shoulder. They are gray-brown with sparse body hair except on the shoulders and along the spine and they feed during the day on roots, grass, etc., often sheltering in disused aardvark burrows.

wart snake A thick-bodied fish-eating aquatic snake belonging to the family *Acrochordidae* (2 species), having valves that close the mouth and nostrils when under water. The brown Javan wart snake (*Acrochordus javanicus*), also known as the elephant's-trunk snake, is 4 ft (1.2 m) long and occurs in rivers and coastal waters of Australia and SE Asia; it is killed for its skin.

Warwick 41 43N 71 28W A resort city in E central Rhode Island on Narragansett Bay, S of Providence. Founded in 1642 it became a cotton milling center. Now chiefly a residential community, its beaches and boating facilities attract many visitors. Population (1980): 87,123.

Warwick, Richard Neville, Earl of (1428–71) English statesman, known as the Kingmaker. He was the most prominent English magnate during the Wars of the *Roses. A supporter of the Yorkist cause from 1453, he was responsible for the seizure of the crown in 1461 by Edward, Duke of York (Edward IV). In 1470, losing influence at court, he changed sides and briefly restored Henry VI to the throne. In 1471 the Lancastrians were routed, and Warwick was killed.

Warwickshire A county in the Midlands of England. It consists mainly of undulating countryside, drained to the SW by the River Avon. It is predominantly agricultural, dairy farming being especially important. Area: 765 sq mi (1981 sq km). Population (1981): 473,620. Administrative center: Warwick.

Wash, the A shallow inlet of the North Sea, in E England between Lincolnshire and Norfolk, into which the Rivers Witham, Welland, Nene, and Great Ouse flow. Length: about 30 km (19 mi). Width: 15 mi (24 km).

Washington One of the NW Pacific states, bordered by the Pacific Ocean (W), British Columbia (N), Idaho (E), and Oregon (S). Mountains ring the state, including the Mount St Helens volcano that erupted violently in 1980, and the Columbia Basin covers much of the central area, cut by the Columbia and Snake Rivers. The lowland around the Puget Sound in the W is highly populated, urbanized, and industrialized, while the E is predominantly rural and sparsely populated. The state's major manufacturing industry is the construction of aircraft. Washington is also a leader in nuclear research and timber production, although in 1983 construction of two of five projected nuclear power plants was halted, terminating the most costly public works project ever undertaken. Attempts to diversify the economy have led to a concentration on the growing tourist industry attracted by numerous spectacular national parks, and there is significant mineral extraction, especially of gold, silver, and uranium. Fishing is important as are foreign trade. Seattle is a major shipping center for trade with the Orient and gateway to Alaska and center of the spacecraft industry. In agriculture, wheat, potatoes, and fruit (especially apples) are grown and dairy farming is important. *History*: the British Hudson Bay Company dominated the area until the 1840s. In 1846 the boundary between Washington and Canada was agreed upon and the state (1889) was named for George Washington. Washington was the site of numerous labor disputes during the early 20th century; during and after World War II it enjoyed great prosperity as a center of the defense industry. Area: 68,192 sq mi (176,616 sq km). Population (1980): 4,130,163. Capital: Olympia.

Washington, DC 38 55N 77 00W The capital of the US, in the E of the country on the Potomac River. Coextensive with the District of Columbia, it is the legislative, judicial, and administrative center of the federal government. It is non-industrial and most of its inhabitants are government employees. Its many notable landmarks include the Washington Monument, the Lincoln Memorial, the Capitol, the □White House, the *Pentagon, the National Gallery of Art, the Hirshhorn Museum, the Phillips Gallery of Art, the Freer Gallery of Art, the Corcoran Gallery of Art, the Library of Congress, the Folger Shakespeare Library, the John F. Kennedy Center for the Performing Arts, the Washington Convention Center, the Smithsonian Institution, the Arlington National Cemetery, the Vietnam Veterans Memorial, Washington National Cathedral, and the National Shrine of the Immaculate Conception. There are five universities and most of the nation's cultural organizations have their headquarters here. *History*: its location as the nation's capital was chosen by George Washington and approved by Congress in 1790. Planned by the French engineer Pierre L'Enfant (1754–1825), its first constructions date from 1793. Almost all of the early government buildings were destroyed during the War of 1812 when

British troops occupied the city in the summer of 1814 and burned all public buildings except the post office. New construction began as soon as the war ended (1815). During the Civil War Confederats forces often threatened the capital but never reached it. In the 20th century the city has grown substantially as the federal government has expanded. Population (1980): 637,651.

BOOKER T. WASHINGTON *Educator who founded Tuskegee Institute and who advocated education for blacks as the doorway to equality.*

Washington, Booker Taliaferro (1856–1915) US educator. Son of a slave, Washington worked as a laborer at various jobs before beginning studies at the Hampton Institute in Virginia, a segregated vocational school where he later taught. In 1881, Washington was hired by the Alabama legislature to establish a technical school for black students at Tuskegee and in later years, this school, the *Tuskegee Institute, became one of the foremost institutions of its kind in the country. Washington served as director of the school until his death. He also became one of the most influential US black leaders. Traveling throughout the country on the lecture circuit, Washington supported the cause of *civil rights through education rather than political agitation. Among his most widely-read published works are *The Future of the American Negro* (1899), *Sowing and Reaping* (1900), *Frederick Douglass* (1907), and his autobiography, *Up From Slavery* (1901).

GEORGE WASHINGTON

Washington, George (1732–99) US general and statesman; 1st President of the United States (1789–97). Born to a wealthy Virginia family and trained as a surveyor, Washington began his career by establishing territorial boundaries in western Virginia. During the *French and Indian Wars he served as a lieutenant colonel in the British army, playing an important role in the capture of Fort Duquesne (1758). In 1759, Washington married Martha Custis and was elected to the Virginia House of Burgesses. He later became a strong supporter of the cause of American independence and was chosen to be a member of the 1st and 2nd *Continental Congresses (1774–76).

At the outbreak of the *American Revolution, he was named commander in chief of the Continental Army. His early victories at the Battles of Trenton and Princeton (1776) were followed by defeat at the Battle of *Brandywine (1777) and the cold and hunger of the winter at *Valley Forge (1777–78), but he was able to maintain the morale of the American forces, eventually accepting the surrender of British general Charles *Cornwallis at Yorktown (1781). After briefly retiring to private life, Washington served as a delegate to the *Annapolis Convention (1786) and presided over the *Constitutional Convention in Philadelphia (1787).

With the ratification of the US Constitution and the first national elections, Washington took office as the first President of the United States in New York City in 1789. During his two terms in office, he was able to place the federal government on a sound footing, adopting the fiscal policies of Alexander *Hamilton, suppressing the *Whiskey Rebellion (1794), and supporting the ratification of *Jay's Treaty (1795). He left office in 1797, urging future US leaders to avoid foreign entanglements. Washington's important contributions to the early history of the US earned him the familiar title "Father of His Country."

Washington Armament Conference (1921–22) A meeting of Britain, France, Japan, Italy, and the US in Washington, DC, to discuss arms limitations. The treaties that resulted from the conference set naval limitations for the countries involved.

Washington's Farewell Address (1796) The retirement from public office speech, published in the press, of President George *Washington. Because he was not seeking a third term as president, Washington advised the Federalists on the upcoming election and warned in the address against the nation dividing or becoming entangled in international politics, for there were too many important domestic issues that needed attention.

wasp A stinging insect, 0.25–1.5 in (6–40 mm) long, belonging to the order *Hymenoptera. The social wasps (family *Vespidae*) form colonies that consist of a queen, males, and workers. The nests are built under ground, in bushes, or in hollow trees. The adults feed on nectar, ripe fruit, insects, etc.; the larvae are usually fed on insects and insect larvae. Fertilized eggs produce queens or workers and unfertilized eggs produce the males. New colonies are established by young fertilized queens—the only individuals to survive the winter. Certain parasitic wasps lay their eggs in the nests of other wasps. Solitary wasps (family *Sphecidae*) lay their eggs in individual nests that are stocked with food and sealed by the parent. *See also* digger wasp; gall wasp; hornet; potter wasp; spider wasp.

Wasserman, August von (1866–1925) German bacteriologist, who invented the Wasserman test for detecting *syphilis, based on the complement-fixation studies of *Bordet. Wasserman made many other contributions to immunology, including a test for tuberculosis and an antitoxin against diphtheria.

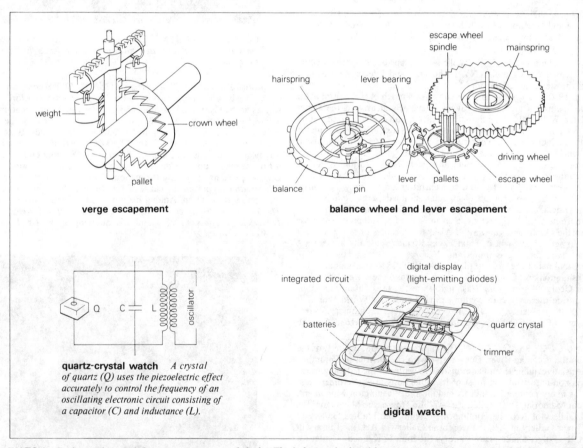

WATCH *Early watches used the verge escapement of clocks. The balance wheel and lever escapement dominated watch design until the quartz crystal and digital watch emerged in the 20th century.*

watch A timepiece small enough to be worn by a person. Watches, as small clocks, first came into use at the beginning of the 16th century with the invention by Peter Henlein (1480–1542) of the mainspring as the energy store in place of the earlier falling weight. Based on a verge escapement, watches were then bulky devices, often cylindrical, worn on the girdle. The invention of the balance spring in 1675 converted the watch from a highly decorated ornament into a more functional article that could be concealed in the pocket. By the 18th century pocket watches had attained a high degree of accuracy. At the beginning of the 20th century wrist watches were introduced and with World War I their advantages to men in uniform made them overwhelmingly popular. Between the wars wrist watches became smaller and cheaper or boasted such features as rust and shock resistance, luminous dials, or self-winding mechanisms. In the early 1950s the first electromagnetic watches were developed (powered by tiny batteries), but it was not until the late 1960s that the first electronic watch appeared. This used the piezoelectric oscillations of a quartz crystal as the time source and an electronic circuit to reduce the frequency to that required to drive the hands. In the 1970s quartz watches were developed without moving parts: this is the solid-state digital watch in which the dial and hands are replaced by a digital display. This can be made so small that some digital wrist watches incorporate several additional functions (e.g. date, stopwatch, alarm, reminder) as well as a tiny calculator.

water (H_2O) A colorless odorless tasteless liquid consisting of eight parts of oxygen to two parts of hydrogen by weight. Water covers 72% of the earth's surface and is found in all living matter, in minerals, and as a small but important constituent of the atmosphere. The solid form of water (ice) is less dense (916.8 kg/m^3) than the liquid at 0°C (999.84 kg/m^3), which is why ice floats and frozen water pipes burst. The maximum density (999.97 kg/m^3) occurs at 3.98°C, unlike most liquids in which the maximum density occurs at the melting point. The molecules of water are polar, i.e. they have a positive electric charge at one end and a negative at the other. This makes it an excellent solvent.

Water supplies: an adequate supply of clean water is a prerequisite of all communities. Rain is the prime source, although in arid areas *desalination of *sea water may be necessary. Rain water for distribution is collected in reservoirs, which may also be fed by rivers, streams, etc. The stored water is purified by filtration, usually through a deep bed of sand. Most of the impurities are trapped in the top 2–2.4 in (5–6 cm), which are periodically replaced. In fast filtration processes the addition of a coagulant (e.g. aluminum sulfate) is used to cause most particle impurities to fall to the bottom. The water then passes through several tanks of coarse sand. Disinfectants, usually chlorine, are added to kill microorganisms. Sufficient chlorine is added to leave about 0.2 mg/liter of uncombined chlorine after 30 minutes. In superchlorination larger quantities are added, followed by subsequent dechlorination with sulfur dioxide. *See also* fluoridation.

water beetle A beetle of the family *Dytiscidae* (*see* diving beetle)—the so-called true water beetles. The name is also used loosely for any aquatic beetle, including the *whirligig beetles (family *Cyrinidae*); the water scavenging water beetles (family *Hydrophilidae*), which resemble diving beetles but feed on algae or decaying organic matter; and the crawling water beetles (family *Haliplidae*), which crawl and feed on algae.

water boatman A *water bug belonging to the cosmopolitan family *Corixidae* (over 300 species). It has a flattened boat-shaped body with fringed oarlike hind legs and feeds on plant debris and algae, scooped up by the spoon-shaped front legs. It is normally attached to bottom vegetation of fresh and brackish waters, rising only to replenish its air store.

waterbuck A large African antelope, *Kobus ellipsiprymnus*. About 50 in (130 cm) high at the shoulder, waterbucks have a long wiry brown coat with a white rump patch and long spreading horns. Small groups spend the night in riverside cover and graze on the plains during the day.

water buffalo A large buffalo, *Bubalus bubalis*, also called Asiatic buffalo or carabao, found wild in swampy land of SE Asia and widely domesticated throughout Asia. Up to 6 ft (180 cm) at the shoulder and heavily built, water buffaloes are gray-black with long backward-curving horns and can be dangerous. Domestic breeds are more docile and have shorter horns: they are used for milk and as draft animals.

water bug An insect of the suborder *Heteroptera* (*see* Hemiptera) that lives in or on fresh or brackish water. True water bugs include the *backswimmer, *giant water bug, *water boatman, and *water scorpion. The surface water bugs include the *pond skater, water cricket (*Vellidae*), and water measurer (*Hydrometridae*).

Waterbury 41 33N 73 03W A city in Connecticut. It was the nation's largest producer of brass products in the 19th century. Other manufactures include watches, clocks, and electronic parts. Population (1980): 103,266.

water chestnut An annual aquatic plant of the genus *Trapa*, especially the Eurasian species *T. natans*, which has a rosette of diamond-shaped toothed floating leaves, feathery submerged leaves, and small white flowers. The hard spiny dark-gray fruit, up to 2 in (5 cm) across, contains edible seeds that are eaten raw, roasted, boiled, or in porridge. Family: *Trapaceae*. The Chinese water chestnut is the tuber of an E Asian sedge, *Eleocharis tuberosa*: it is cooked and eaten in various Chinese dishes. Family: *Cyperaceae*.

watercolor A painting medium consisting of pigments bound with gum, which are diluted with water before being applied to a surface of white or tinted paper. Its special characteristics are its transparency and its white accents, which are created by leaving parts of the paper unpainted. Water-

color made opaque by the addition of white pigment and more glue is known as gouache or poster paint. Practiced since ancient times, watercolor painting in postmedieval Europe was chiefly of a monochrome variety until the late 18th century, when it was developed to perfection by a series of British landscape artists, notably *Turner and *Blake. The 19th century's outstanding water colorists include *Horner, *Sargent, *Delacroix, and *Daumier.

watercress Either of two perennial herbs, *Nasturtium officinale* or *N. microphyllum* $\times$ *officinale*, native to Eurasia and widely cultivated for the peppery young shoots, which are used in salads. Watercress grows submerged or floating in streams or on mud; it has compound leaves, with roundish or oval leaflets, and bears clusters of four-petaled white flowers. Family: *Cruciferae*.

waterfall A steep fall of water along the course of a river or stream. It may be produced by the river crossing a band of hard rock; where the rock strata are horizontal the fall is likely to be steep. Falls also occur at the edges of plateaus or where faulting has taken place. The waterfall will continually retreat upstream through erosion. Large waterfalls and series of falls are also known as **cataracts**. The energy of a waterfall can be harnessed to provide hydroelectric power.

water flea A small freshwater *crustacean of the suborder *Cladocera* (about 430 species). Its compact body, usually 0.04–0.12 in (1–3 mm) long, is covered, behind the head, by a laterally flattened transparent carapace, which encloses 4–6 pairs of appendages. It swims by means of two large forked antennae. Common genera: *Daphnia*, *Leptodora*; subclass: *Branchiopoda*.

Waterford (Irish name: Port Lairge) 52 15N 7 06W A city and port in the SE Republic of Ireland, the county town of Co Waterford. It has Protestant and Roman Catholic cathedrals. It is an important trading and distribution center; industries include light engineering, paper making, and glass making, for which it is famous. Population (1979): 87,278.

Waterford (Irish name: Contae Port Lairge) A county in the S Republic of Ireland, in Munster bordering on the Atlantic Ocean. Chiefly hilly, it is drained by the Rivers Blackwater and Suir. Agriculture is the main occupation with dairy farming and cattle rearing. The traditional glass-making industry is of note. Area: 710 sq mi (1838 sq km). Population (1971): 77,315. County town: Waterford.

water gas A mixture of equal amounts of hydrogen and carbon monoxide made by passing steam over red hot coke: $H_2O + C \geq H_2 + CO$. The mixture is a useful fuel gas but the reaction producing it is endothermic and heat must be supplied to the coke. One way of doing this is to make water gas in conjunction with an exothermic reaction—that between air and carbon: $O_2 + 4N_2 + 2C \geq 2CO + 4N_2$. The mixture of carbon monoxide and nitrogen is called **producer gas**. Although it has a lower calorific value than water gas the products are hot as a result of the high temperature of the reaction. The heating value of water gas can be improved by passing it through petroleum while hot, thus cracking liquid hydrocarbons to gaseous ones, which escape with the water gas. The process, known as carbureting, can almost double the calorific value. Water gas, however, is not as effective a fuel gas as *natural gas and its use is mainly as a raw material for chemical-manufacturing processes, such as the *Haber process.

Watergate A building complex in Washington, DC, that gave its name to a political scandal leading to the resignation of the Republican president Richard M. Nixon. Amid growing suspicion of corruption among presidential officials, the *Washington Post* exposed their involvement during the 1972 presidential election in a burglary of the headquarters of the Democratic Party at the Watergate, and in subsequent arrangements (the "cover-up") to buy off the convicted burglars. Amid the resignation and prosecution of top White House staff, who alleged that Nixon had connived in Watergate, he resigned under the threat of impeachment (1974). He was pardoned by President Gerald Ford.

water glass (*or* sodium silicate) A mixture of silicates with the general chemical formula $x\mathrm{Na_2O}.y\mathrm{SiO_2}$, forming a clear viscous solution in water. It is made by fusing *sodium carbonate and sand (*silica) in an electric furnace and is used in making silica gel, detergents, and textiles.

Waterhouse, Alfred (1830–1905) British architect of the *gothic revival. His early work was done in Manchester and included the Assize Court (1859) and the Town Hall (1868). Therafter he came to London, where he built the romanesque Natural History Museum (1881), and the gothic redbrick St Paul's School (1885) and the City and Guilds College (1879).

water hyacinth An aquatic plant of the genus *Eichhornia* (about 5 species), native to tropical America. They have slender creeping rhizomes, rosettes of stalked leaves, and clusters of flowers in the leaf axils. Some species float in shallow water; others are rooted in muddy stream banks and lake edges. *E. crassipes* is the most widely distributed species; it is used as an ornamental plant in pools and aquariums and has become a troublesome weed in the S US, Australia, and Africa. Family: *Pontederiaceae.*

water lily An annual or perennial freshwater plant of the family *Nymphaeaceae* (75 species), native to temperate and tropical regions. Water lilies have round wax-coated leaves floating on the water surface and borne on long central stalks arising from creeping stems buried in the mud below. The large showy flowers, whose stalks may rise above the water surface, are cup-shaped, with several whorls of oval pointed petals, usually white, yellow, pink, red, blue, or purple in color. Most cultivated water lilies are hybrids and varieties derived from species of *Nymphaea. See also* lotus.

Waterloo 43 27N 80 30W A city in E Canada, in SW Ontario on the N side of *Kitchener. Founded by Mennonites (1806), it houses several insurance companies and two universities and is a musical center. Its varied industries include distilling, brewing, furniture, and farm machinery. Population (1981): 49,428.

Waterloo, Battle of (June 18, 1815) The battle in which *Napoleon Bonaparte was finally defeated by British, Dutch, Belgian, and German forces commanded by Wellington and the Prussians under von Blücher. Napoleon caught Wellington 3 mi (5 km) S of Waterloo (Belgium) in isolation from the Prussians and attempted to smash his army by a direct offensive. The British lines held the French columns until the Prussians arrived. A concerted charge brought victory and four days later Napoleon's second, and final, abdication.

water louse A freshwater crustacean of the genus *Asellus,* related to the *woodlouse. It is found on submerged plants or the bottom of weedy streams and ponds. Order: *Isopoda.*

watermark A distinctive mark produced in *paper during manufacture by making it slightly thinner in some places than in others. In handmade paper, the watermark is formed by the wires in the bottom of the mold. In machine-made paper the mark is put in by a roller that has the mark in a raised form on its surface.

watermelon The fruit of an annual climbing plant, *Citrullus vulgaris,* native to Africa but widely cultivated. The plant has hairy deeply lobed leaves and the yellow flowers produce large oval fruits, up to 10 in (25 cm) across, with a shiny dark-green rind and red, yellow, or white flesh, which is juicy and sweet-flavored. The seeds are also edible. Family: *Cucurbitaceae. See also* melon.

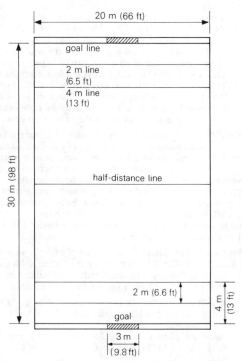

WATER POLO *The dimensions of the pool for international play. The water must be 2 m deep in international competition.*

water milfoil A submerged or floating perennial freshwater aquatic plant of the worldwide genus *Myriophyllum* (about 45 species). It has whorls of finely divided feathery leaves and the green, white, or red flowers are borne in aerial spikes. A few species are grown in aquaria. Family: *Haloragaceae.*

water moccasin A heavy-bodied venomous *pit viper *Agkistrodon piscivorus,* occurring in marshes of the S US and also called cottonmouth because it shows the white inside of its mouth when threatened. Up to 5 ft (1.5 m) long, it is brown with dark bands and hunts fish, turtles, and waterbirds.

water polo A ball game played seven-a-side (with four substitutes), usually in a swimming pool. It originated in England in the 1870s, with players riding floating barrels to resemble horses and hitting the ball with paddles; in the modern game players swim. The object is to score goals with an inflated ball that is passed between players by throwing. Except for the goalkeepers, players may not walk, jump, punch the ball, or touch it with both hands together. It is a men's sport in the Olympic Games.

water rat A large aquatic *rodent belonging to the subfamily *Hydromyinae* (13 species) found in Australia, New Guinea, and the Philippines. The Australian water rat (*Hydromys chrysogaster*) is about 14 in (35 cm) long and has otter-like fur and a white-tipped tail. Family: *Muridae.*

*Water voles and *muskrats, are also known as water rats.

water scorpion A *water bug of the worldwide family *Nepidae* (about 200 species). Its scorpion-like "tail" is actually a breathing tube (siphon), which protrudes from the water while the insect hangs upside down from aquatic vegetation or the surface film of water. Water scorpions prey on small arthropods, tadpoles, and small fish.

watershed (*or* divide) The dividing line, usually a ridge, between the *catchment areas of two separate river systems. The term is also used for the entire catchment area of the drainage basin. *See also* continental divide.

water shrew A long-snouted Eurasian aquatic *shrew, *Neomys fodiens.* About 4 in (10 cm) from nose to tail, water shrews feed chiefly on aquatic invertebrates but also take small fish and frogs, aided by their venomous saliva. Their hair-fringed toes assist in swimming.

water skiing Planing on water on wooden skis (or a single ski for slalom competitions), often with fins attached for stability. It originated in the 1920s. The skier is towed by a rope usually 75 ft (23 m) long attached to a powerboat traveling at a minimum of about 15 mph (25 km per hour). Competitions are held for jumping, slalom (through a course of buoys), and trick riding. Barefoot water skiing is also practiced, requiring speeds of 35–40 mph (55–65 km per hour).

water snake. *See* grass snake.

water spider A European freshwater *spider, *Argyronecta aquatica,* that lives under water in a bell-shaped structure constructed from silk and plant material and filled with bubbles of air brought down in its body hairs. It feeds inside on small animals taken from the water surface. The male (0.6 in [15 mm] long) is—usually—larger than the female (0.4 in [10 mm] long).

waterspout A funnel-shaped cloud extending from the base of a cumulonimbus cloud to the surface of the sea. It is a small-scale intense low-pressure system, the equivalent of a *tornado on land, characterized by intense rotating winds, which create violent agitation of the water surface and lift drops up into the cloud.

water strider. *See* pond skater.

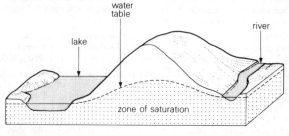

WATER TABLE

water table The upper level of the water that has percolated into the ground and become trapped within pores, cracks, and fissures in permeable rocks. The level of the water table varies with the topography and local rainfall. *See also* artesian well.

Waterton Lakes National Park A national park (1895) in SW Alberta, Canada, in the eastern Rocky Mountains, adjoining Glacier National Park in northern Montana. With Glacier National Park it forms Waterton-Glacier International Peace Park (1932) and is connected to it by highway and the Continental Divide, which runs through the park. The highest point is Mt Blakiston (9600 ft; 2926 m). Area: 203 sq mi (526 sq km).

water vole A large *vole, *Arvicola terristris*, of Europe and Asia. 6–8 in (15–20 cm) long, they are heavily built with a short tail and light-brown to black fur. Water voles burrow into river banks and feed on aquatic vegetation often during the daytime.

water wheel. *See* turbine.

Watford 51 40N 0 25W A city in SE England. It has paper-making, printing, engineering, and electronics industries. Population (1981): 74,356.

Watling Island. *See* San Salvador Island.

Watling Street The Roman road that traversed Britain from its commercial center, London, via St Albans to the strategically sited Roman town near Wroxeter, with a branch to the legionary fortress at Chester.

Watson, James Dewey (1928–) US geneticist, who (with Francis *Crick) proposed a model for the molecular structure of *DNA (1953). Following this fundamental breakthrough, Watson investigated the *genetic code and the way in which it is "read" by the cell. His *Molecular Biology of the Gene* (1965) has become an influential text, and *The Double Helix* (1968) gave a popular account of his work on DNA. He received a Nobel Prize (1962) with Crick and Maurice *Wilkins.

Watson, John Broadus (1878–1958) US psychologist and founder of the US school of psychology known as *behaviorism. Watson declared that speculations about animal behavior should be based entirely on observations made under laboratory conditions. In *Psychology from the Standpoint of the Behaviorist* (1919), Watson applied his principles to human behavior, which he regarded in terms of conditioned responses, excluding the possible contributions of reasoning and original thought. One of his most notable followers was B. F. *Skinner.

Watson-Watt, Sir Robert Alexander (1892–1973) Scottish physicist, who during the 1920s and 1930s pioneered the development of *radar. In 1935 the British Government, realizing the strategic importance of the invention, set up a research team working under Watson-Watt, who had put it into operation by World War II.

watt (W) The *SI unit of power equal to one joule per second. In electrical terms it is the energy per second expended by a current of one ampere flowing between points on a conductor between which there is a potential difference of one volt. Named for James *Watt.

Watt, James (1736–1819) British engineer, whose contributions to the development of the □steam engine made him one of the most important figures of the *industrial revolution. In 1764 while repairing a model of a *Newcomen engine he realized that the machine could be made more efficient if the steam was condensed in a separate chamber. Watt's steam engine, completed in 1769, soon replaced the Newcomen engine, especially after Watt had introduced a double-acting model. In 1774 he began to manufacture steam engines and by 1800 some 500 stationary Watt engines were in use for a variety of purposes. He later invented the centrifugal governor. Watt devised the unit "horsepower" and the metric unit of power is named for him.

Watteau, (Jean) Antoine (1684–1721) French rococo painter. Settling in Paris (1702), he trained under a painter of theatrical scenery and under the curator of the Luxembourg Palace, where he studied the works of *Rubens. Despite his early death from tuberculosis, he achieved fame both in Paris and London (which he visited in 1719) with his charming *fêtes galantes* (scenes of gallantry) and paintings of comedians. His best-known works are *L'Embarquement pour l'île de Cythère* and the portrait of the clown *Gilles* (both Louvre).

wattle Any of various Australian □trees and shrubs, especially those of the genus *Acacia, the stems and branches of which are used for fencing and were formerly employed in the wattle and daub construction of houses. The commonest are the black wattle (*A. binervata*), the golden or green wattle (*A. pycnantha*), and the silver wattle (*A. dealbata*), which has silvery fernlike leaves and fluffy globular heads of tiny yellow flowers and is used by florists under the name of mimosa. Wattles are used as shade trees, ornamentals, and livestock fodder.

wattmeter An instrument for measuring electrical power. The most common type has two conducting coils connected in series, one fixed and one movable. The magnetic forces between them produce a deflection of the movable coil proportional to the square of the current, which is in turn proportional to the power.

Waugh, Evelyn (Arthur St John) (1903–66) British novelist. With *Decline and Fall* (1928) and other novels, including *Vile Bodies* (1930), *A Handful of Dust* (1934), and *The Loved One* (1948), he established his reputation as the most brilliant social satirist of his generation. After his conversion to Roman Catholicism in 1930, religious themes played an increasing part in his novels, especially in *Brideshead Revisited* (1945). Later novels include his war trilogy—*Men at Arms* (1952), *Officers and Gentlemen* (1955), and *Unconditional Surrender* (1961)—and the semiautobiographical *The Ordeal of Gilbert Pinfold* (1957). His elder brother **Alec (Raban) Waugh** (1898–1981), was a novelist and travel writer. Many of his later novels, such as *Island in the Sun* (1956), deal with life in tropical countries. Evelyn's son **Auberon Waugh** (1939–) is a novelist and journalist.

wave Any periodic change in a property of a system that is propagated through a medium (or through space). Waves are classified according to the curve produced when their magnitude is plotted against time on a graph. If the wave is shaped like a sine curve, it is known as a sine (or sinusoidal) wave. Examples of sine waves include electromagnetic waves and sound waves. A wave is characterized by three parameters: amplitude, the maximum displacement of the wave; *wavelength; and *frequency. The wave may propagate energy, in which case it is known as a traveling wave, or it may not, when it is known as a standing or stationary wave. For traveling waves the displacement may be either perpendicular to the direction of the propagation of the wave (a transverse wave) or in the direction of propagation (a longitudinal wave). Waves on water and electromagnetic waves are transverse, while sound waves are longitudinal.

waveguide A hollow conductor for transmitting microwaves over short distances. The electromagnetic radiation is guided along the tube, being reflected from the internal walls. The waveguide is usually filled with air but occasionally some other *dielectric is used.

wavelength The distance between successive peaks (or troughs) of a wave. It is equal to the velocity of the wave divided by its frequency. For electromagnetic radiation it is the most commonly used parameter for specifying the part of the *electromagnetic spectrum to which the radiation belongs.

Wavell, Archibald Percival, 1st Earl (1883–1950) British field marshal. After service in World War I he became *Allenby's chief of staff in Palestine. In World War II, as commander in chief in the Middle East, he defeated the Italians in N and East Africa. After the failure of his offensive against Rommel in June, 1941, he was transferred to SE Asia, where he was again replaced after failing to halt the Japanese advance. He was viceroy of India from 1943 to 1947.

wave mechanics A branch of *quantum theory in which elementary particles are treated as *de Broglie waves. Systems of particles are described by a wave equation, known as the *Schrödinger equation. The solutions of this equation give the allowed values of the energy of each particle (eigenvalues) and the associated wave functions (eigenfunctions); the wave functions provide a measure of the probability that each particle will appear at different points in space. The theory, first proposed by de Broglie, was developed by Erwin Schrödinger.

wave number The inverse of *wavelength, i.e. the number of cycles executed by a wave in a unit length.

wave power The use of the energy of wave motion in the sea to generate electricity. Wave-power generators of various types have been developed, the best known being the "nodding-duck" type, which consists of a string of floats that bob up and down in the waves. The bobbing motion turns a generator. However only a fraction of this would become electricity. One of the disadvantages of wave power is that it is variable and unpredictable although, like *wind power, its peak output is likely to coincide with peak demand. Another is that since it is sited off the coast it may be obstructive to shipping and difficult to maintain. In addition, the design and construction of generators and transmission lines to work at sea presents a formidable engineering problem.

wax A smooth substance of low melting point 104°–176°F (40–80°C) obtained from plants (e.g. *carnauba wax) or animals (e.g. *beeswax, *lanolin) or made synthetically. They consist of esters of higher fatty acids than are found in fats, usually with monohydric alcohols. Mineral waxes also exist, the most common being paraffin wax, which is a mixture of the higher hydrocarbons obtained from the distillation of petroleum. Waxes are used in making polishes, candles, moldings, etc., and in modeling.

waxbill A bird of the *weaverfinch family having a stout waxy-red conical bill. Most waxbills inhabit open grassy regions of Africa. They are

3–6 in (7.5–15 cm) long and typically gray or brown with red, yellow, or brown markings and fine barring on the wings. Many waxbills rear the nestlings of the *whydahs, which lay their eggs in waxbills' nests.

wax moth A moth whose caterpillars live in the nests of bees and wasps, where they eat refuse, honeycomb, and young host insects. Some are cannibalistic. The bee moth (*Galleria Mellonella*) is the best-known species, having spread to many parts of the world. Chief genera: *Galleria*, *Achroea*.

waxplant An evergreen climbing plant, *Hoya carnosa*, native to China and Australia. It produces clusters of large fragrant waxy white flowers with pink centers and is cultivated as an ornamental. Other cultivated species include *H. bella*, a dwarf shrub with crimson- or violet-centered waxy white flowers. Family: *Asclepiadaceae*.

waxwing A broad-billed fruit-eating songbird, *Bombycilla garrulus*, occurring in N coniferous forests and birch woods, sometimes migrating south in hard winters. It has a soft plumage, liver-colored above with a reddish crest, a yellow-banded tail, and a black throat and eyestripe. The red tips of the flight feathers resemble sealing wax. Family: *Bombycillidae* (9 species).

wayfaring tree A deciduous shrub, *Viburnum lantana*, growing in woodlands and hedges over much of Europe. Up to 20 ft (6 m) tall, it has oval to heart-shaped toothed leaves and flat-topped clusters of small creamy-white funnel-shaped flowers. The oval fruits ripen from red to black. Family: *Caprifoliaceae*.

Wayland (or Weland) In Teutonic mythology, a skilled smith. He was captured and lamed by a Swedish king, Nidudr, who kept him on an island, where he was forced to practice his metalworking for the king. Wayland secretly murdered the king's sons, made ornaments of their skulls, eyes, and teeth, raped the king's daughter, and then revealed all to Nidudr before escaping.

Wayne, Anthony ("Mad Anthony") (1745–96) American Revolutionary War officer and Indian fighter. Wayne was a surveyor and farmer who was briefly active in politics before being commissioned a colonel and assisting Benedict *Arnold in his retreat from Quebec. He held a variety of increasingly responsible commands during the *American Revolution. He was with *Washington in New Jersey and shared the privations of the winter at Valley Forge (1777–78); in 1779 he took Stony Point, NY. Wayne was sent south in 1781 and was trapped by Cornwallis' superior force at Green Spring, Va, but succeeded in escaping with his command intact. He then served under General *Greene in Georgia before retiring to farming and business interests. Recalled by Washington in 1792 (as a major general) to command the Army of the West against the Indians, he was victorious at the Battle of Fallen Timbers (1794), securing a treaty that made possible the settlement of Ohio and Indiana. He built Ft Wayne, Ind., and died in Pennsylvania in 1796 while taking possession of abandoned British forts.

JOHN WAYNE *He is seen here (with Richard Widmark, right) as Davy Crockett, hero of* The Alamo *(1960), which he also directed and produced.*

Wayne, John (Marion Michael Morrison; 1907–79) US film actor. Following his success in *Stagecoach* (1939) he played the tough hero of numerous classic westerns including *Red River* (1948), *She Wore a Yellow Ribbon* (1949), *Rio Bravo* (1959), and *True Grit* (1969). He played similar roles in many war films, from *The Sands of Iwo Jima* (1945) to *The Green*

Berets (1968). He was awarded a special Academy Award shortly before his death from cancer.

Waziristan A mountainous area in Pakistan, bordering on Afghanistan. The Waziris, a *Pathan tribe who inhabit the area, are noted for their warlike behavior.

weak interaction One of the four fundamental interactions between elementary particles (*see* particle physics), the others being the *strong, *electromagnetic, and *gravitational interactions. The weak interaction is about 10^{10} times weaker than the electromagnetic interaction. It is believed to be generated by the exchange of *virtual particles known as *intermediate vector bosons.

weasel A small carnivorous mammal, *Mustela nivalis*, of Europe, Asia, and N Africa, recently introduced into New Zealand. Growing to about 10 in (25 cm) long, it is long-bodied and short-legged, bright red-brown above with white underparts. Weasels feed on rats, mice, and voles, hunting along hedgerows and ditches and entering burrows. They swim well but do not climb. Family: *Mustelidae*.

weather. *See* meteorology.

weathering The physical and chemical disintegration of the rocks of the earth's crust on exposure to the atmosphere. Most rocks were formed under conditions in which temperatures and pressures were higher than those to which they are now exposed; weathering is largely a response to lower temperatures and pressures and the effects of air and water.

WEAVERBIRD *Communal nests of the sociable weaver, seen from below. The birds, which are found in SW Africa, build individual nests close together then cover them with a common roof.*

weaverbird A small songbird belonging to a mainly tropical Old World family (*Ploceidae*; 132 species) noted for its nest-building activities. Most species build domed nests with long entrance tunnels, often elaborately woven with loops and knots to form a durable structure. Some species build huge communal nests—the nest of the sociable weaver (*Philetairus socius*) reaches about 7 ft (2 m) across and houses 20–30 pairs of birds. Weavers are seed eaters with stout conical bills and variously colored plumage. *See also* sparrow; quelea.

weaverfinch A small finchlike seed-eating songbird belonging to a family (*Estrildidae*; 108 species) occurring in tropical regions of Africa, SE Asia, and Australasia. Weaverfinches have large conical bills and are usually brightly colored. *See* avadavat; grassfinch; mannikin; waxbill; zebra finch.

weaving The process of interlacing two or more *yarns at right angles to produce a fabric. The equipment used is called a loom, which is first set up with a series of longitudinal threads (warp). In plain weave, alternate warp threads are raised and lowered by means of wires or cords (heddles) to allow the crosswire threads (weft), wound onto a bobbin (shuttle), to pass between them. Different kinds of weave, such as *twill and herringbone, are made by altering the pattern of interlacing. Hand looms have been in use all over the world since ancient times. Power looms, in which the shuttle is moved across the warp automatically, were invented by Edmund *Cartwright in 1786, since when many improvements have been made to increase the speed of travel of the shuttle and to enable more complicated designs to be woven.

Webb, Sidney (James), Baron Passfield (1859–1947) British economist and socialist. He helped to organize the *Fabian Society in 1884 and was one of the founders of the London School of Economics (1895). He initiated many educational reforms and, after entering parliament in 1922, held several important government posts. His wife **Beatrice (Potter) Webb** (1858–1943), collaborated with him on a number of books. Their work and writings had a lasting influence on the development of social policies within and outside the Labour Party.

weber (Wb) The *SI unit of magnetic flux equal to the flux linking a circuit of one turn that produces an electromotive force of one volt when reduced uniformly to zero in one second. Named for Wilhelm Weber (1804–91).

Weber, Carl Maria von (1786–1826) German composer, a pupil of Michael Haydn (1737–1806) and Abbé Vogler (1749–1814). His most successful opera, *Der Freischütz* (1821), based on a German fairy story, was the first opera in the German Romantic tradition. The operas *Euryanthe* (1823) and *Oberon* (1826) were less successful. Weber also composed a large number of orchestral works and much piano music.

Weber, Ernst Heinrich (1795–1878) German physiologist, who became professor at Leipzig University in 1818. He is remembered for his discovery that the experience of differences in the intensity of human sensations (pressure, temperature, light, sound) depends on percentage differences in the stimuli rather than absolute differences. This is called the Weber-Fechner Law because Weber's discovery was popularized by Gustav Fechner (1801–87). His brother **Wilhelm Eduard Weber** (1804–91) was professor of physics at Göttingen University. He worked with *Gauss on magnetism and introduced a logical system of electrical units. The SI unit of magnetic flux is named for him.

Weber, Max (1864–1920) German sociologist, who was one of the founding fathers of modern *sociology. His best-known work, *The Protestant Ethic and the Spirit of Capitalism* (1904), relates the emergence of a particular type of economic system to the effects of religious values. In attempting to explain why capitalism developed first in Europe, he produced extensive studies in comparative sociology. His *Methodology of the Social Sciences* (1904) remains a major text, as does his account of social and economic organization, *Wirtschaft und Gesellschaft* (1922). Bureaucracy and secularization are also recurrent themes. He was politically active during the last years of his life and served on the committee that drafted the constitution of the *Weimar Republic.

Webern, Anton von (1883–1945) Austrian composer. He studied with Schoenberg and earned his living as a conductor and teacher. Webern adopted the theory of *serialism, as defined by Schoenberg in 1924. His compositions, which are characterized by great brevity, extreme dynamic contrast, and dissonant counterpoint, include Concerto for Nine Solo Instruments (1934) and a string quartet (1938). His music has greatly influenced Boulez, Stravinsky, and many other composers.

webspinner A brownish soft-bodied insect, 0.16–0.28 in (4–7 mm) long, belonging to the mainly tropical order *Embioptera* (150 species). Biting jaws are used by the wingless females to feed on dead plant material; the males, which are mostly winged, are carnivores. Webspinners live in communities and make silken webs and tunnels under stones or in soil. The young are cared for by the females.

Webster, Daniel (1782–1852) US statesman and orator. Webster graduated from Dartmouth College in 1801 and was admitted to the bar in 1805. Opposing Jefferson's policies and the War of 1812, he was elected to the House of Representatives in 1812. In 1816 he moved to Boston and gained fame as a brilliant lawyer and orator. He was elected to the House again in 1822 and the Senate in 1827. In his noted reply to Hayne (1830) he defended the Union against states' rights and urged "Liberty *and* Union, now and forever, one and inseparable!" Webster became secretary of state under Harrison and Tyler and was responsible for the Webster-Ashburton Treaty. He left the cabinet (1843), rejoined the Senate (1845), and opposed the acquisition of Texas and war with Mexico. He defended Henry Clay's Compromise of 1850 despite the unpopular Fugitive Slave Act. He was secretary of state again (1850) under Fillmore and died in 1852, having been instrumental in holding the Union together and advancing the ideal of a strong federal government.

Webster, John (c. 1580–c. 1625) English dramatist. Little is known of his life. He collaborated with Thomas Dekker and other dramatists. His own major plays are *The White Devil* (1612) and *The Duchess of Malfi* (c. 1613). Despite their typically Jacobean preoccupation with lust and violence, the plays are distinguished by their poetic intensity and psychological insight.

Webster, Noah (1758–1843) US lexicographer and author of numerous books on English. His *American Dictionary of the English Language* (1828) took over 20 years to compile and was the most influential of all American dictionaries. Webster also did much to standardize American spelling.

Webster-Ashburton Treaty A treaty negotiated in 1842 by Daniel Webster (US) and Lord Ashburton (Britain), which settled the disputed northeastern boundary between Maine and New Brunswick, Canada.

Weddell Sea A large inlet of the S Atlantic Ocean in Antarctica, between the Antarctic Peninsula and Coats Land. Its S section is covered by the Ronne and Filchner Ice Shelves. It is named for the British explorer and seal hunter James Weddell (1787–1834).

Wedekind, Frank (1864–1918) German dramatist. A vivid personality, he was also an actor, singer, poet, and essayist. His tragedy *Frühlings Erwachen* (1891), produced by *Reinhardt (1905), caused a scandal by criticizing the bourgeois attitude to sex. Berg's opera *Lulu* (1937) is based on his plays *Erdgeist* (1895) and *Die Büchse der Pandora* (1904).

Wedgwood, Josiah (1730–95) British potter and industrialist. Trained under his brother Thomas, he was a partner of Thomas Whieldon (1719–95) from 1754 until 1759, when he opened his own factory in Staffordshire (England). In 1769 he opened a new factory where he also built a village for his workmen, displaying his interest in social welfare. Employing leading designers and artists, Wedgwood popularized the neoclassical taste in pottery and was a leading exporter to the Continent.

weed Any plant growing where it is not wanted, especially in areas cultivated or tended by man. Weeds are most important in agriculture, competing with crop plants for space, light, and nutrients, reducing yields, and contaminating the crop. The major weeds of temperate regions include docks, thistles, nettles, shepherd's purse, groundsel, dandelions, couch grass, and wild oats. Some, such as ragwort, may be toxic to grazing livestock. Weeds may also damage paths and buildings and choke waterways.

Weed control has traditionally relied on repeated soil cultivation and crop rotation; modern methods involve use of selective and nonselective *herbicides and, in a few cases, *biological control.

weever A slender carnivorous fish of the genus *Trachinus*, found in sandy bottoms of European coastal waters. Up to 1.8 in (4.6 cm) long, it has an upward slanting mouth, eyes near the top of its head, and venomous spines on the gill covers and first dorsal fin, which can inflict painful wounds. Family: *Trachinidae*; order: *Perciformes*.

weevil A beetle, also called a snout beetle, belonging to the largest family (*Curculionidae*; about 60,000 species) in the animal kingdom. Most weevils are small (less than 0.25 in [6 mm]) and their mouthparts are at the tip of a beaklike rostrum, which can sometimes exceed the body length. Many species are serious pests of gardens, crops, and stored grains and cereals, e.g. the *boll weevil, the grain weevil (*Sitophilus granarius*), and the rice weevil (*S. oryzae*). The larvae are particularly destructive, burrowing or boring into all parts of the plant but especially into wood, fruit, and seeds. *See also* curculio.

Wegener, Alfred Lothar (1880–1930) German geologist, who (in 1912) proposed the theory of *continental drift to account for his observations of the movements of land masses. Wegener also demonstrated how bombardment by meteors could have caused lunar craters. He died while on his fourth expedition to Greenland.

Weigela A genus of E Asian flowering shrubs (12 species), including several ornamentals, often called Japanese honeysuckles. Up to 13 ft (4 m) high, they have simple leaves and small clusters of funnel-shaped white to red flowers, about 1.3 in (3.5 cm) long, with four or five spreading lobes. The fruit is a long narrow seed pod. Family: *Caprifoliaceae*.

weight. *See* mass and weight.

weightlessness The condition in which a body possesses no weight. Such a body still possesses mass but its weight (*see* mass and weight) can become negligible when the gravitational field is extremely weak, as for example in space. It can also be produced artificially by creating a force that is equal and opposite to gravity. The physiological effects of weightlessness are important in long space flights and are countered by pressure suits, exercise routines, and correct control of cabin pressure, temperature, and humidity.

weight lifting A sport in which men and women compete to lift weighted barbells. In the most common form of competition the contestants make three attempts in each of two styles, the snatch and the clean and jerk. The weights, of their own choice, can be increased but not reduced. Power lifting requires different styles, the squat, dead lift, and bench press.

Weil, Simone (1909–43) French mystic and philospher. An active socialist in the 1930s, she worked briefly in a car factory to gain insight into working-class problems and served in a nonmilitary capacity on the Republican side in the Spanish Civil War. She also taught philosophy at secondary schools until 1938. After a mystical experience she became a convinced Roman Catholic, although she refused baptism. During World War II she worked for the Free French Resistance in London. Her writings on spiritual and social themes, published posthumously, include *Waiting for God* (1951) and *The Need for Roots* (1952).

Weill, Kurt (1900–50) German composer. He studied under Busoni in Berlin. His collaboration with Bertolt *Brecht began with the opera *The Rise and Fall of the City of Mahagonny* (1927), a satirical portrayal of American life. Their most famous work was *The Threepenny Opera* (1928), a modernistic version of *The Beggar's Opera* (*see* Gay, John). The rise of Nazism forced Weill to leave Germany; he settled in the US in 1935 and wrote successfully for Broadway musicals. His wife, the singer Lotte *Lenya, frequently performed in his works.

Weimar 50 59N 11 15E A city in SW East Germany, on the Ilm River near Erfurt. Weimar has associations with Goethe, Schiller, and Liszt and was the cultural center of Germany in the late 18th and early 19th centuries. It was the capital of the grand duchy of Saxe-Weimar-Eisenach (1815–1918). In 1919 the German National Assembly met in the city and drew up the constitution of the new *Weimar Republic. Population (1973 est): 63,285.

Weimaraner (*or* Weimeraner) A breed of dog developed by the nobility of Weimar, Germany, for hunting and retrieving game. It is a lithe dog with drooping ears and a short slender tail. The short sleek coat is silvergray or mouse-gray. Height: 24–27 in (61–69 cm) (dogs); 22–25 in (56–64 cm) (bitches).

Weimar Republic The government of Germany from 1919 to 1933. Named for the town in which the new German constitution was formulated, the republic faced constant political and economic crises and was finally overthrown by Hitler.

Weismann, August Friedrich Leopold (1834–1914) German biologist, who (in 1883) proposed that heredity was based upon the transfer, from generation to generation, of a substance—germ plasm—with a definite molecular constitution. Weismann also predicted that germ plasm must undergo a special nuclear division to produce gametes for the next generation. Weismann's ideas have since been generally accepted and he is regarded as one of the founders of modern genetics.

Weiss, Peter (1916–82) German dramatist and novelist. After leaving Nazi Germany, he settled in Sweden (1939). His plays include the highly successful *Marat/Sade* (short title; 1964), set in a lunatic asylum, and *The Investigation* (1965), recreating the Auschwitz trials.

Weissmuller, Johnny (1904–84) US swimmer, who won five Olympic gold medals (three in 1924 and two in 1928) and set 24 world records. He was the first man to swim 325 ft (100 m) in less than a minute (1922). He later became the first Tarzan of sound films (1932–48) and had a successful television series.

Weizmann, Chaim (Azriel) (1874–1952) Israeli statesman; the first president of Israel (1949–52). Born in Russia, he settled in England in 1904 and worked as a chemist. A leader of the English Zionist movement, his discovery (1916) of a manufacturing process for the production of acetone, which contributed to the British war effort, facilitated the Zionist negotiations with the British Government that led to the *Balfour Declaration (1917). His moderate policies as president (1920–31, 1935–46) of the World Zionist Movement brought the hostility of Zionist extremists but he played an important part in the establishment of Israel in 1948.

Weld, Theodore Dwight (1803–95) US abolitionist. Influenced by revivalist preacher Charles G. Finney, he became an evangelist and preached both temperance and the abolition of slavery. He joined the American Anti-Slavery Society and married abolitionist Angelina Grimké. He wrote anti-slavery tracts, including *American Slavery As It Is* (1839), which influenced Harriet Beecher *Stowe's *Uncle Tom's Cabin*. A moderate, Weld led an anti-slavery lobby in Washington before retiring to school teaching.

welding A method of joining metals by melting the two parts together, pressing them together, or both (*see also* soldering). In forge welding, which is used to make steel chains, the two parts are heated and then hammered together. Electrical methods use an electric current passed through two metal surfaces in close contact. The temperature rises at the interface because of the high electrical resistance and welds the surfaces

together. In spot welding, point contact electrodes press the metal surfaces together. In seam welding, the electrodes are in the form of rollers. Both these methods are used in mass production. Gas welding uses an oxy-acetylene flame to heat the metal and a rod of metallic filler material. Molten filler material runs between the two heated edges and solidifies to form the joint. Another method, similar to gas welding, is electric-arc welding. The filler rod forms one electrode and the metal itself another. Current passes by arcing or sparking across the gap between them, melting the rod and the metal edges. Arc welding is generally used for thicker pieces of metal and higher temperatures than gas welding and for small delicate jobs *lasers have been used. A great deal of skill is required to produce a strong reliable weld. The results are often examined by X-rays or other means in, for example, pressure vessels, where reliability is crucial.

Welensky, Sir Roy (1907–) Rhodesian statesman; prime minister of the Federation of *Rhodesia and Nyasaland (1956–63). A professional boxer, he was chairman (1953–63) of the Railway Workers Union in Northern Rhodesia. Welensky was largely responsible for the creation of the Federation but his aim to establish a harmonious multiracial society was unfulfilled.

welfare state A state that provides a minimum level of wellbeing for all its members, especially the most vulnerable: the young, the old, the unemployed, and the sick. The UK and the Scandinavian countries are the most advanced in providing these services.

Welkom 27 59S 26 44E A town in South Africa, in N central Orange Free State. It was founded in 1947 and rapidly developed after the discovery of gold. Population (1980 est): 176,608.

Welland Ship Canal A canal in S central Canada, in S Ontario bypassing Niagara Falls. Part of the St Lawrence Seaway, it links Lake Erie to Lake Ontario and has a total lift of 326 ft (99 m). Length: 28 mi (45 km).

Weller, Thomas Huckle (1915–) US bacteriologist and virologist. Weller received his medical degree from Harvard Medical School, where he worked with Dr John Frederick Enders on *in vitro* (test tube) virus cultivation. After service in the Army Medical Corps (1942–46), Weller returned to work with Enders and Dr Frederick C. Robbins on the tissue culture method whereby the virus for poliomyelitis was developed *in vitro* in nonnerve tissue. For this work, which made possible the development of the polio vaccine, Weller, Enders, and Robbins shared the Nobel Prize for physiology or medicine in 1954.

Welles, (George) Orson (1915–) US film actor and director. After establishing his reputation as a theater and radio producer he went to Hollywood in 1940. His first film, *Citizen Kane* (1941), became one of the most famous of all time. His other films include *The Magnificent Ambersons* (1942), *Macbeth* (1948), *The Trial* (1962), and *Chimes at Midnight* (1966). As a film actor he is best remembered for the title part in *The Third Man* (1949).

Wellesley, Richard Colley, Marquess. *See* Wellington, Arthur Wellesley, Duke of.

Wellesz, Egon (1885–1974) Austrian composer and musicologist. He studied in Vienna under Schoenberg and his complex compositions employed *serialism.

Wellington 41 17S 174 47E The capital of New Zealand, a port in S North Island on Cook Strait. It became the seat of central government in 1865 and is now the commercial and communications center of New Zealand. Notable buildings include the Government Building (1876), one of the world's largest wooden buildings, and Victoria University (1897). A major manufacturing center, it has engineering, food-processing, and textile industries; the chief exports are wool, meat, dairy products, and fruit. Population (1977 est): 139,700.

Wellington, Arthur Wellesley, 1st Duke of (1769–1852) British general and statesman, known as the Iron Duke; prime minister (1828–30). In 1787 he entered the army and in 1799 went to India. In the Napoleonic Wars he was responsible for victory (1814) against the French in the *Peninsular War, for which he was made a duke. He commanded British, German, and Dutch forces at Waterloo (1815), where he and the Prussian general *Blücher finally defeated Napoleon. He represented Britain at the Congresses of *Aix-la-Chapelle (1818) and Verona (1822). As prime minister he came to support *Catholic emancipation. Wellington's opposition to parliamentary reform remained firm and brought about his resignation under pressure. He was commander in chief of the British army from 1827 to 1828 and again from 1842 to 1852.

Wellingtonia. *See* sequoia.

HENRY WELLS *Wells, Fargo, and Company ran a perilous mail and stage coach service across the US.*

Wells, Henry (1805–78) US businessman, who with **William Fargo** (1818–81) and others founded Wells, Fargo and Company (1852). An express business, it carried mail to and from the newly developed West. It also controlled banks and later ran a stagecoach service.

Wells, H(erbert) G(eorge) (1866–1946) British novelist. After working as a shopkeeper's apprentice and a teacher, he studied biology with T. H. Huxley. He won literary success with *The Time Machine* (1895) and other science-fiction novels and increased his popularity with a series of comic social novels. A member of the Fabian Society, he engaged in frequent controversy with G. B. Shaw and others concerning social and political issues. He wrote distinguished theoretical works, including *The Outline of History* (1920) and *The Shape of Things to Come* (1933).

wels A large nocturnal predatory *catfish, *Silurus glanis*, also called waller, found in fresh waters of Europe and W Asia. Up to 15 ft (4.5 m) long, it has three pairs of barbels, a long anal fin, and is usually mottled olive-green to blue-black with a paler belly.

Wels 48 10N 14 02E A city in N central Austria, in Upper Austria. It has a castle in which Emperor Maximilian I died. Industries include agricultural machinery, textiles, and food processing. Population (1981): 51,033.

Welsh literature The most important literature written in the Welsh language is poetry belonging to the early and medieval periods prior to the anglicization that began in the 16th century. Much of the poetry of the *Cynfeirdd*, or early poets of the 6th century, is anonymous. The works of the period are preserved in the "Four Ancient Books of Wales," manuscripts dating from the 12th, 13th, and 14th centuries. The *Gogynfeirdd*, or medieval poets, belong to the Norman period (up to the loss of independence in 1282). These poets were *bards, who held important offices in the courts of Welsh princes; Cynddelw (12th century) is regarded as the greatest of them. The 14th century was dominated by Wales' greatest poet, *Dafydd ap Gwilym, who introduced techniques and a sensuous richness of metaphor that influenced all subsequent Welsh poetry. The first record of an *eisteddfod dates from the 15th century, although it is believed that such bardic contests must date from a much earlier period. The 16th century marks the beginning of a decline in the use of Welsh, although the language has recently been revived and continues to be used as a literary medium.

Welsh pony One of two breeds of pony originating in Wales. The Welsh Mountain pony, used for riding, has a compact muscular body with short strong legs and a profuse mane and tail. It has been used to develop the larger Welsh riding pony, which is a popular children's mount. Both may be any solid color. Height: Mountain pony: up to 4 ft (1.22 m) (12 hands); riding pony: up to 4.5 ft (1.37 m) (13½ hands).

Welsh poppy A perennial herbaceous plant, *Mecanopsis cambrica*, up to 15 in (38 cm) tall and found in damp regions of W Europe. It has fernlike deeply lobed leaves and bears solitary yellow flowers, up to 3 in (7.5 cm) across. Cultivated ornamental forms may have either single or double orange or yellow flowers.

Welty, Eudora (1909–) US author. Acclaimed author of short stories and novels, Welty received six O. Henry awards and the Pulitzer Prize in 1973 for *The Optimist's Daughter* (1972). Other works include *Delta Wedding* (1946), *The Golden Apples* (1949), *The Ponder Heart* (1954), *The*

Shoe Bird (1964), and *Losing Battles* (1970). Her autobiography, *One Writer's Beginnings*, appeared in 1984.

welwitschia An unusual *gymnosperm plant, *Welwitschia mirabilis*, confined to the deserts of SW Africa. The very short stem bears two strap-shaped waxy leaves, which grow continuously and are up to 40 in (1 m) long. The long taproot absorbs water from the desert subsoil, and small conelike flowers produce winged seeds, which are dispersed by the wind. Individual plants may live for more than a hundred years. Order: *Gnetales*.

Wenceslas (1361–1419) King of Bohemia (1363–1402, 1404–19) and German king and Holy Roman Emperor (1376–1400). An extremely weak king, in Bohemia he was twice imprisoned by rebellious nobles (1393–94, 1402) and briefly deposed. In Germany, princes deposed him in 1400 but he retained the title of king until his death.

Wenceslas, St (d. 929 AD) Duke of Bohemia (?924–29), famous for his piety. Wenceslas' unpopular submission to the German king Henry the Fowler gave rise to a conspiracy of nobles, who incited Wenceslas' brother to assassinate him. He became Bohemia's patron saint.

Wenchow. *See* Wenzhou.

wentletrap A *gastropod mollusk of the worldwide family *Epitoniidae* (about 200 species), often found in association with sea anemones and corals. 0.8–4 in (2–10 cm) long, wentletraps have □shells with long spires, usually white but sometimes tinged with brown (that of the precious wentletrap (*Epitonium scalare*) has long been prized by collectors). They can produce a purple substance used as a dye.

Wentworth, Thomas. *See* Strafford, Thomas Wentworth, 1st Earl of.

Wenzhou (Wen-chou *or* Wenchow) 28 02N 120 40E A port in SE China, in Zhejiang province on the Ou Jiang (River). It is the site of many historic buildings. A trading center, it has processed food, paper, and handicraft industries. Population (1953): 201,600.

WEREWOLF *Reports of werewolves were particularly common in 16th-century France. The illustration claims to be an exact representation of one.*

werewolf In folklore, a man who becomes a wolf by night and preys on humans. Some werewolves, who have no power over their condition because it is hereditary or the result of a spell or another werewolf's bite, only change form during a full moon, a transformation known as lycanthropy. Belief in werewolves is worldwide and of ancient origin. In countries where wolves are rare, some men are believed to turn into other fierce animals.

Werfel, Franz (1890–1945) Austrian Jewish poet, dramatist, and novelist. A leading expressionist, his pacifism and desire for human brotherhood are reflected in his poetry and plays, including *Der Spiegelmensch* (1920). His later novels include *The Song of Bernadette* (1941).

Wergeland, Henrik Arnold (1808–45) Norwegian poet, known as the "uncrowned king" of Norway because of his involvement in nationalist politics. He is best known for his lyric poetry and for an epic on the Creation, entitled *Skabelsen, Mennesket, og Messias* (*Creation, Humanity, and Messiah*; 1830).

wergild The sum payable as compensation in Anglo–Saxon England to the family of a slain man by his assassin or the latter's kin. The amount was regulated by law according to the status and nationality of the victim and varied in different regions.

Weser River A river in N West Germany. It flows NW from Münden, through Bremen, to the North Sea at Bremerhaven. The Mitelland Canal connects it to the Rhine and Elbe rivers. Length: 296 mi (477 km).

Wesley, John (1703–91) British religious leader, founder of *Methodism. As a student at Oxford and later, Wesley was one of a group nicknamed "Methodists," who sought to live disciplined religious lives. His younger brother **Charles Wesley** (1707–88) was also a member. The brothers, both ordained, sailed to Georgia as missionaries in 1735, but returned disillusioned in 1738. In the same year both experienced a spiritual awakening while attending meetings of the *Moravians as a result of which they toured the country preaching a message of repentance, faith, and love. Anglican opposition forced them out of the churches into open-air meetings; they were also obliged to organize societies for their many working-class converts. They did not intend to form a new denomination, the Wesleyan Methodist Church being organized only after their death. John was a tireless writer and administrator, while Charles was the author of many well-known hymns.

Wessex The kingdom of the West *Saxons, under which Anglo-Saxon England was united in the 9th century. Wessex centered on the upper Thames basin and from the late 6th century expanded southwestward. Its expansion northward was frustrated by the power of Mercia, which was supreme until Egbert, King of Wessex (802–39), destroyed Mercian ascendancy in 825 and made possible the subsequent union of England under the leadership of the Wessex king, Alfred the Great.

West, Benjamin (1738–1820) US painter. After achieving acclaim as a portraitist in New York, he visited Italy (1760–63), where he was influenced by *neoclassicism, before settling permanently in England. There, patronized by George III and exhibiting at the Royal Academy of which he became president in 1792, he made his name as a history painter, particularly with his controversially realistic *Death of General Wolfe*.

West, Mae (1892–1980) US actress. Her unashamedly sensual performances in vaudeville, the theater, and films established her as an international sex symbol during the 1930s, although she is perhaps best known for her comic talent. Her early stage successes included *Sex* (1926) and *Diamond Lil* (1928). Her films, many of which she wrote, include *She Done Him Wrong* (1933), *I'm No Angel* (1933), and *My Little Chickadee* (1939).

West, Nathaniel (Nathan Weinstein; 1903–40) US novelist. The best known of his four short novels are *Miss Lonely-hearts* (1933), about an advice columnist, and *The Day of the Locust* (1939), a satire of the grotesque world of Hollywood, where he worked as a scriptwriter. He was killed in an automobile accident.

West, Dame Rebecca (Cicely Isabel Fairfield, 1892–1983) British novelist and journalist. She was the author of several novels, including *The Thinking Reed* (1936) and *The Birds Fall Down* (1966). Among a number of books of political journalism are *The Meaning of Treason* (1949) and *A Train of Powder* (1955), which includes her reports on the Nuremberg trials.

West Atlantic languages A subgroup of the *Niger-Congo family, spoken in Guinea and Senegal. It includes the languages Wolof and *Fulani, and, despite being a small group, is found over a wide area since the speakers of West Atlantic languages are mainly nomadic.

West Bank A territory in the Middle East, on the W bank of the Jordan River. It comprises the hills of Judea and Samaria (which Israel considers to be of crucial strategic importance with regard to the security of its coastal settlements) and part of the city of *Jerusalem. Formerly part of *Palestine, it was left in Arab hands after partition (1948), became part of Jordan following the ceasefire of 1949, and was occupied by Israeli forces in 1967. Israel has since been under pressure from the Arabs, especially the *Palestine Liberation Organization, to withdraw from the territory and allow an autonomous Palestinian state to be set up. In the Camp David agreement (1978) proposals were put forward for future negotiations leading to the setting up of a self-governing authority in the West Bank. Area: about 2320 sq mi (6000 sq km).

West Bengal A state in NE India, stretching along the Bangladeshi W border from the Ganges delta N into the Himalayan foothills. Rice, jute, tea, and other crops are farmed. Fishing, forestry, and mining are also important, as well as industry (especially engineering, steel, chemicals, and motor cars). Bengali culture remains very strong. Area: 33,911 sq mi (87,853 sq km). Population (1981): 54,485,560. Capital: Calcutta. *See also* Bengal.

West Bromwich 52 31N 1 59W An industrial city in central England, in the West Midlands. Metal goods (kitchen utensils, springs, nails, scales) are manufactured, as well as chemicals and paint. Population (1981): 154,930.

westerlies The chief winds blowing between 30° and 70° latitude. Their name derives from the prevailing wind direction; in the N hemisphere winds blow mainly from the SW and in the S hemisphere, from the NW.

Western Australia The largest state of Australia, bordering on the Indian Ocean, Timor Sea, and Great Australian Bight. It is mainly an arid undulating plateau with the Great Sandy Desert, the Gibson Desert, and the Great Victoria Desert in the interior. In the SW is the Darling Range, a scarp behind the city of Perth (where most of the population is concentrated). In the N the broken edge of the plateau is marked by the Kimberleys. Agricultural activities include dairy farming, lumbering, and the cultivation of citrus fruits, wheat, and wine grapes in the extreme SW. Western Australia is rich in mineral resources; bauxite in the Darling Range, nickel in the S central part, oil near Barrow Island off the NW coast, and gold in the SW around Kalgoorlie. Probably the most important discoveries have been the huge deposits of ferrous minerals in the NW. Industry is located chiefly around Perth and includes the manufacture of iron and steel, chemicals, textiles, and oil refining. Area: 975,920 sq mi (2,527 sq km). Population (1980 est): 1,265,000. Capital: Perth.

Western European Union An organization formed in 1955 by the UK, Belgium, France, Italy, Luxembourg, the Netherlands, and West Germany to coordinate defense policy and equipment and to cooperate in political and other spheres. It succeeded the *European Defense Community and collaborates closely with the *North Atlantic Treaty Organization.

westerns A US genre of popular novels and films set in the American West during that region's development in the 19th century. Its rigid conventions of plot and character invested the struggles of pioneers and the battles between lawmen and outlaws with mythical significance. Notable writers include Owen Wister (1860–1938), the prolific Zane Grey (1872–1939), and Louis L'Amour (1908–). The first film western was *The Great Train Robbery* (1903). Other notable films include *Stagecoach* (1939), *Red River* (1948), and *High Noon* (1952); directors who have specialized in this genre include John Ford (1895–1973) and Howard Hawks (1896–1978).

Western Sahara (name until 1975: Spanish Sahara) A territory in NW Africa, bordering on the Atlantic Ocean, Mauritania, and Morocco. It consists chiefly of desert and has phosphate deposits (the chief export) SE of El Aaiún. *History*: in 1884 Spain claimed a protectorate over the S coastal zone of Río de Oro and in 1958 Spanish Sahara became a province of Spain with its capital at El Aaiún. In 1976 Spain withdrew from the province and it was partitioned between Mauritania and Morocco. Since then the Polisario Front, an organization engaged in guerrilla activities to establish Western Sahara as the independent Saharan Arab Democratic Republic, has been supported by Algeria. Mauritania withdrew from the S part of Western Sahara in 1979 and it came under Moroccan occupation with active opposition from the Polisario Front and Algeria. Area: 102,680 sq mi (266,000 sq km). Population (1970): 76,425.

West Germany. *See* Germany.

West Highland white terrier A breed of dog thought to have originated in Argyll, Scotland. Known affectionately as the westie, it is compact and alert-looking with short legs and a long double-layered pure white coat. Height: about 11 in (28 cm).

West Indies An archipelago extending in a curved chain for over 1500 mi (2400 km) from the Florida peninsula in North America to the coast of Venezuela enclosing the Caribbean Sea. It is often subdivided into the *Greater Antilles, the *Lesser Antilles, and the *Bahamas. The islands are chiefly of volcanic origin but some, including the Bahamas and Antigua, are composed largely of coral. Hurricanes occur frequently, often causing serious damage. The West Indian people are of mixed origin but the descendants of African slaves form the largest group. The original Arawak and Carib Indians have virtually disappeared, although some Caribs remain on Dominica. *Economy*: sugar-cane cultivation has been of importance throughout the West Indies since the beginning of colonization. Many islands also grow a major subsidiary crop, such as tobacco, bananas, spices, or coffee. The few mineral deposits include asphalt from Trinidad's unique Pitch Lake and bauxite from Hispaniola and Jamaica. *History*: Columbus discovered the archipelago in 1492 and named it in the belief that he had found the west route to India. The Spanish, who were the first Europeans to settle, introduced the cultivation of sugar and imported African slaves to work the plantations. The slave trade was maintained until its abolition during the 19th century. In 1958 the Federation of the West Indies was created, comprising Antigua, Dominica, Grenada, Jamaica, Montserrat, St Kitts with Nevis and Anguilla, St Lucia, St Vincent, and Trinidad and Tobago. The federal parliament was situated at Port-of-Spain, Trinidad, but following the withdrawal of Jamaica and then Trinidad and Tobago the Federation was dissolved in 1962. However, further attempts were made at regional economic integration by what became the *Caribbean Community. In 1967 the noncolonial status of associated state was adopted by Antigua, Dominica, Grenada, St Kitts-Nevis-Anguilla, St Lucia, and by St Vincent in 1969. Grenada became independent in 1974, Dominica in 1978, St Lucia and St Vincent in 1979, and St Kitts-Nevis in 1983. Area: over 91,000 sq mi (235,000 sq km).

Westinghouse, George (1846–1914) US mechanical engineer, inventor, and manufacturer. After training in his father's machine shop and serving in the Civil War, Westinghouse settled in Pittsburgh and invented (1869) the air brake for railroad cars, which made high-speed railroad travel safe. On the basis of this success, he organized the Westinghouse Air Brake Company and developed railroad switching and signaling systems. He developed a safe system for transporting natural gas, and a system for using alternating current for electrical power. To promote the latter he formed Westinghouse Electric Company, which grew to be a leading manufacturer of electrical equipment.

West Irian (Indonesian name: Irian Jaya) A province in E Indonesia comprising W *New Guinea. Mountainous and densely forested with coastal swamps, it is largely undeveloped although it possesses important mineral resources including oil, nickel, and copper. Formerly under Dutch rule, it was transferred to Indonesia in 1963. Area: 161,000 sq mi (416,990 sq km). Population (1980): 1,173,875. Capital: Jajapura.

West Jersey Name given to the western part of the New Jersey colony under the Quintipartite Deed of 1676. The colony had been settled by the Swedes and the Dutch before the English took control and divided it into the two proprietorships. West Jersey was granted to Lord John Berkeley, who sold out to Edward Byllinge, who in turn sold most of West Jersey to a Quaker group. In 1702, East and West Jersey were combined into the Province of New Jersey.

Westmeath (Irish name: Contae Na Hiarmhidhe) A county in the central Republic of Ireland, in Leinster. Predominantly low lying with areas of bog, much of the land is under pasture. Agriculture consists chiefly of cattle fattening and dairy farming. Area: 681 sq mi (1764 sq km). Population (1979): 59,885. County town: Millingar.

Westminster Abbey A historic abbey church in the city of Westminster in greater London, England. The present building was begun in 1245 and since William I, every English monarch (with two exceptions—Edward V and Edward VIII) has been crowned in Westminster Abbey and many are buried there. The Coronation Chair, first used in 1307, stands here upon the Stone of Scone, captured by Edward I from the Scots in 1296. Other notable features include Poets' Corner, where Chaucer, Spenser, Dryden, Tennyson, Dickens, Browning, Kipling, and many others are buried or have memorials.

Weston-super-Mare 51 21N 2 59W A resort in SW England, on the Bristol Channel. Originally a fishing village, it developed as a resort in the 19th century. Population (1981): 57,980.

Westphalia A region of NW Germany, approximating to present-day Nordrhein-Westfalen. By the 12th century Westphalia comprised many small principalities and in the 18th century came largely under Prussian control. During the period 1807–13 Prussian Westphalian territories became the kingdom of Westphalia, which Napoleon placed under the rule of his brother Jérôme Bonaparte. The Congress of Vienna (1815) dissolved the kingdom and restored most of Westphalia to Prussia.

WESTMINSTER ABBEY

Westphalia, Peace of (1648) The agreements, negotiated in Osnabrück and Münster (Westphalia), that ended the *Thirty Years' War. The peace marked the end of the supremacy in Europe of the Holy Roman Empire and the emergence of France (which gained the bishoprics of Metz, Toul, and Verdun and also Alsace) as a dominant power (*see also* Pyrenees, Treaty of). It recognized the sovereignity of the German states, the Swiss Confederation, and the Netherlands, previously subject to the Empire, and granted W Pomerania to Sweden. Lutherans, Calvinists, and Roman Catholics were given equal rights.

West Point 41 23N 73 58W A military reservation in New York state. It is the site of the *United States Military Academy (1802).

West Virginia A state in the E central US, bordered by Kentucky and Ohio (W and NW), Pennsylvania and Maryland (NE), and Virginia (E and S). It consists of a ridge and valley region (the Great Appalachian Valley) in the E and the rugged Appalachian Plateau, which constitutes the remaining two thirds of the state. Most of the larger cities lie on the Ohio River in the W. Although predominantly a rural state, manufacturing and mining (the state is the foremost US producer of bituminous coal) are important. The principal manufactures are chemicals, primary metals, and stone and clay products. The state's farmers concentrate on livestock products. A growing tourist industry is based upon the state's spectacular scenery and varied recreational facilities. *History*: first inhabited by the Mound Builders, the area was sparsely populated when European traders and explorers penetrated it in the late 1600s. German and Scots-Irish settlers fought for land with the Indians and the French. After the Revolution, the area became part of Virginia; it refused to secede with the state, and became West Virginia on joining the Union as a separate state in 1863. Area: 24,181 sq mi (62,628 sq km). Population (1980): 1,949,644. Capital: Charleston.

wet rot The decay that affects timber with a relatively high moisture content, caused by the cellar fungus (*Coniophora cerebella*) and characterized by the formation of a dark surface mass. Treatment is by drying affected timbers, and wet rot is prevented by the application of tar-based preservatives, such as creosote. *Compare* dry rot.

Wexford (Irish name: Loch Garman) 52 20N 6 27W A port in the Republic of Ireland, the county town of Co Wexford on the River Slaney estuary. Industries include the manufacture of agricultural machinery and food processing. Population (1971): 11,849.

Wexford (Irish name: Contae Loch Garman) A county in the SE Republic of Ireland, in Leinster bordering on the Irish Sea. It was the first Irish county to be colonized from England (1169). Consisting chiefly of lowlands, it rises to mountains in the W. Cattle rearing is the main agricultural occupation. Area: 908 sq mi (2352 sq km). Population (1979): 96,421. County town: Wexford.

Weyden, Rogier van der (c. 1400–64) Flemish painter of portraits and religious altarpieces. Almost nothing is known of his early life, but he was probably the pupil of the Master of *Flémalle, whose influence is evident in *The Deposition*. From 1436 until his death he was city painter of Brussels and frequently worked for the Burgundian court. In 1450 he visited Italy and paintings from this period, for example the *Entombment*, show Italian influences. His work became widely known in Europe during his lifetime.

whale A large marine mammal belonging to the order *Cetacea*. Whales have no hind limbs; their forelimbs are flippers and their tails are horizontally flattened to form a pair of flukes. They breath through a blowhole on top of the head, which is closed when they are submerged. Whales are virtually hairless and insulated by a thick layer of blubber under the skin. They bear their young and suckle them at sea.

There are two suborders. The whalebone whales (*Mysticetae*; 12 species)—including the *rorquals, *blue whale, and *right whales—are large and slow-moving and feed on krill, which they filter from the water using a sieve of whalebone (*see* baleen) plates. They have a double blowhole. Toothed whales (*Odontocetae*; 80 species)—including the *dolphins, *narwhal, and *sperm whale—are smaller and more agile. They feed on fish and squid and are often gregarious, communicating by underwater sounds. *See also* whaling.

whalebone. *See* baleen.

whale shark A gigantic but harmless *shark, *Rhincodon typus*, that has a gray or brown spotted body with pale undersides, ridges along its sides, and a terminal mouth. Up to 60 ft (18 m) long, it swims slowly, mainly in tropical waters, and feeds near the surface on small fish, invertebrates, and plankton. Family: *Rhincodontidae*.

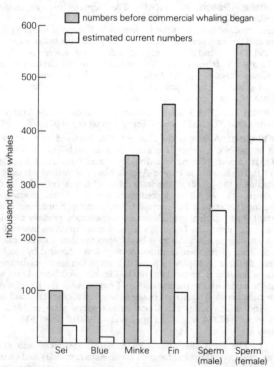

WHALING   *Effects of whaling on populations of various whale species.*

whaling The hunting and slaughter of whales for their carcasses. Traditionally, whales were hunted offshore and processed on land, but modern commercial whaling fleets comprise a mother factory ship for processing the carcasses at sea and a fleet of small hunter vessels equipped with harpoon guns and winches. The carcasses are a source of meat, fats, oils, and other chemicals used in many industries. Whaling has depleted whale populations to the point that some species, such as the blue whale and bowhead whale, are in danger of extinction. Many conservationists are campaigning

for a complete ban on whaling, especially since substitutes for most whale products are available. Catch quotas for whaling nations, principally the Soviet Union and Japan, are set annually by the International Whaling Commission.

whangee A hard white-skinned tropical *bamboo of the genus *Phyllostachys*, from SE Asia, the stems of which are used as canes or walking sticks. The woody jointed stems arise from a creeping underground stem; whorls of slender shoots with narrow leaves are produced from each joint.

Wharton, Edith (Newbold) (1862–1937) US novelist. Her novels about New York society, such as *The House of Mirth* (1905) and *The Age of Innocence* (1920), which won a Pulitzer Prize, were influenced by her friend Henry *James. From 1907 she lived in Paris, and France during World War I was the subject of *The Marne* (1918) and *Son at the Front* (1923). Her short fiction was printed in *Collected Short Stories* (2 vols, 1968). Her later work includes *Hudson River Bracketed* (1929), *The Gods Arrive* (1932) and her autobiography, *A Backward Glance* (1934). *Ethan Frome* (1911), a short tragic novel set in New England, remains her best-known work.

wheat A cereal *grass belonging to the genus *Triticum*, native to W Asia but widely cultivated in subtropical and temperate regions. With the exception of einkorn (*T. monococcum*), most commercial wheats are hybrids with the genus *Aegilops*. Many different varieties have been developed; winter wheats, sown in autumn, are hardier than spring wheats. The stems, up to 40 in (1 m) high, each bear a cylindrical head of up to a hundred flower clusters, grouped in vertical rows and sometimes bearing bristles (awns) up to 4 in (10 cm) long. The grain of bread wheat (*T. aestivum*) is milled to produce flour for bread, cakes, biscuits, etc. Hard or durum wheat (*T. durum*) is used to make pasta and semolina. Surplus grain, bran, etc., is fed to livestock. Wheat is also a commercial source of alcohol, dextrose, gluten, malt, and starch.

wheatear A migratory songbird, *Oenanthe oenanthe*, that winters in tropical Africa and Eurasia, and breeds in N tundra regions, nesting in holes in the ground. It is about 8 in (15 cm) long and in summer the male has a blue-gray back, white rump, and a black mask and wings. In winter, males resemble females, having a brown mask, back, and wings. Family: *Turdidae* (thrushes).

Wheatstone, Sir Charles (1802–75) British physicist. He was the first to patent the electrical telegraph and recognized the value of the network used to measure resistances now called the *Wheatstone bridge (invented by Samuel Hunter Christie; 1784–1865).

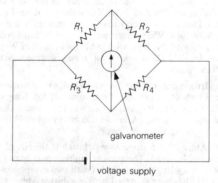

WHEATSTONE BRIDGE

Wheatstone bridge An arrangement of four resistances used to measure the value of one of the resistances when the other three are known. The resistances are arranged to form a square with a voltage applied across two opposite junctions and a galvanometer connected across the other two opposite junctions. When the galvanometer indicates that no current is flowing the bridge is balanced and $R_1/R_2 = R_3/R_4$.

wheel animalcule. *See* rotifer.

Wheeler, Sir (Robert Eric) Mortimer (1890–1976) British archeologist. Wheeler's skill in excavating, recording, and interpreting archeological strata was renowned. He excavated Romano-British sites (e.g. *Maiden Castle) and was influential as director of the Archaeological Survey of India (1944–48).

wheel of life. *See* Bhavachakra.

whelk A *gastropod mollusk of the family *Buccinidae* (over 400 species), of warm and cold seas. 1.6–4.7 in (4–12 cm) long, whelks feed on mollusks and worms. The common northern whelk (*Buccinum undatum*), 2 in (5 cm) long, has a drab yellow-brown shell and edible flesh. Tropical species are more colorful.

whidah. *See* whydah.

Whigs Members of a British political group that became the *Liberal Party after about 1868. The Whigs dominated politics in the first half of the 18th century, forming rival aristocratic groups. When in the late 18th century the Tories re-emerged, the Whigs formed a more united group under Charles James *Fox. Identifying with industrialist, Nonconformist, and reforming interests, they became the Liberal Party under *Gladstone.

whimbrel A *curlew, *Numenius phaeopus*, that breeds on Arctic tundra and winters in Africa, South America, and S Asia. 16 in (40 cm) long, it has a streaked brown plumage and a dark crown with a pale central stripe. It feeds on insects, spiders, worms, and snails.

whinchat A migratory *chat, *Saxicola rubetra*, common on open farmland. It winters in Africa and breeds in Eurasia, nesting in rough vegetation and feeding on flies and moths. The male has a streaked brown plumage, pale chestnut breast, white wingbars, and a white eyestripe; the female is duller.

whipbird A shy songbird belonging to the Australian genus *Psophodes* (2 species). They are about 10 in (25 cm) long with a dark-green plumage, and feed on insects among scrub and undergrowth. The eastern whipbird (*P. olivaceus*) has a long whistling call ended by a whipcrack sound. Family: *Muscicapidae*.

whippet A breed of dog developed in England during the 19th century from terrier and greyhound stock and used for coursing and racing. It has a slender streamlined build with a smooth whiplike tail and long tapering muzzle. The fine short coat can be any mixture of colors. Height: 18 in (46 cm) (dogs); 17 in (43 cm) (bitches).

whippoorwill A North American *nightjar, *Caprimulgus vociferus*, named for its distinctive call. About 9.4 in (24 cm) long, it has a mottled brown plumage; the male has a white collar and tail markings. It lives in woodland and feeds on insects.

whip scorpion A nocturnal *arachnid, sometimes called vinegarroon, belonging to a suborder (*Uropygi*; about 75 species) found in tropical and subtropical regions. Up to 5 in (13 cm) long, it has large spiny pincers and a whiplike tail and it secretes acetic acid for defense. Order: *Pedipalpi*.

whip snake A slender arboreal snake belonging to the genus *Zamenis* (5 species). The common European speckled gray whip snake (*Z. gemonensis*) reaches a length of 6 ft (1.8 m) and feeds on other snakes and lizards. The pencil-thin green whip snakes (genus *Dryophis*; 8 species) occur in tropical Asia and Australasia and grow to a length of 40 in (1 m). Family: *Colubridae*.

whirligig A dark shiny *water beetle belonging to the widely distributed family *Gyrinidae* (about 700 species). It spins around on the surface of still or slow-moving fresh water, feeding on insects or other small animals that have fallen in. The aquatic larvae prey on mayfly or dragonfly nymphs. If disturbed, whirligig beetles dive from the surface and exude a foul-smelling milky liquid.

whirlpool A violent circular eddy in the sea or a large river, caused by opposing currents or winds or where a strong current is impeded by some obstacle. Large-scale whirlpools are rare. *See also* Maelstrom.

whirlwind A small revolving column of air, which whirls around a low-pressure center produced by local heating and convectional uprising. It may pick up small pieces of debris and dust and in desert areas may cause *sandstorms.

whiskey A *liquor distilled from malted grain. The word comes from the Gaelic *uisgebeatha*, water of life. The milled grain is mixed with water to form a mash, which must be converted to sugar before fermentation; the resulting alcoholic liquid is distilled and then aged in the cask for at least three years (generally for much longer). Whiskey is classified according to where it is produced, e.g. Scotch whisky (distilled from barley and spelled without an e), Irish whiskey, or, as in the US, by type. Most US whiskey is either rye or bourbon (named for the county in Kentucky where it was first produced).

Whiskey Rebellion (1794) An uprising in protest against a federal excise tax on whiskey. Farmers in W Pennsylvania usually made whiskey from excess grain and traded it. They gathered in armed groups and terrorized some federal officials, but the rebellion was easily ended when George Washington, on the advice of Secretary of State Alexander Hamilton, called out the federal militia. All the participants who were tried were acquitted or pardoned, but the incident served as a demonstration of federal strength.

whist A card game for two pairs of partners; it originated in the 17th century and was popularized by *Hoyle. A pack of 52 cards is dealt out, the last card determining the trump suit. The object of the game is to win the highest number of tricks by playing the highest card of a suit (the cards ranking from ace high) or by trumping (one may also discard a nontrump when one cannot follow suit). The winner of a trick leads the next card. Each trick over the first six (the "book") scores a point to the partners; five or (in long whist) ten points make a game and two out of three games win the rubber. There are a number of variations. *See also* bridge.

Whistler, James (Abbott) McNeill (1834–1903) US painter and etcher. After briefly attending West Point, from which he was dismissed, he settled in Paris (1855), where he was particularly influenced by oriental art, especially Japanese prints. Moving to England (1859), he specialized in portraits and landscapes dominated by one or two colors, the best known being a portrait of his mother, *Arrangement in Gray and Black* (1872) and *Old Battersea Bridge* (1872–73). In 1877 *Ruskin described one of Whistler's works as "flinging a pot of paint in the public's face" and was sued for libel (1878); although Whistler won the case his legal costs ruined him. Whistler was also famous as a wit and as the author of *The Gentle Art of Making Enemies* (1890).

whistling duck A long-legged long-necked *duck belonging to a tribe (*Dendrocygnini*; 8 species), also called tree duck, ranging throughout tropical regions. They have a distinctive whistling cry. The fulvous tree duck (*Dendrocygnus bicolor*) is 22 in (55 cm) long and has a red-brown plumage with cream stripes on the flanks.

Whitby, Synod of (663 AD) A council convened at Whitby (England) by King Oswy of Northumbria to decide whether to adopt Roman or Celtic Church usages in Britain. The major source of controversy was the dating of Easter. The Roman view triumphed, with the result that the English Church was brought into line with the Continent.

White, Byron Raymond (1917–) US jurist; associate justice of the Supreme Court (1972–). He gained his nickname of "Whizzer White" while an outstanding student and football player at the University of Colorado. He played professional football (1938–39) before leaving for England as a Rhodes scholar in 1939. With the outbreak of World War II, White returned to the US and attended Yale Law School while again playing football (1940–41). When the US entered the war, he joined the Navy and served in the South Pacific. In 1946 he received his law degree from Yale; from 1947–61 he practiced corporate law with a Denver firm. In 1961 he was named deputy US attorney general, and in 1962 he became President Kennedy's first appointee to the Supreme Court.

White, Edward Douglass (1845–1921) US jurist; associate (1894–1910) and chief justice (1910–21) of the US Supreme Court. He served in the Confederate Army and was admitted to the bar in 1868. White was a Louisiana state senator in 1874, a Louisiana supreme court judge (1879–80), and was elected to the US Senate in 1890. In 1894, White was appointed to the Supreme Court by President Grover Cleveland; he served as an associate justice until 1910, when President William Taft appointed him chief justice, a post he held until his death. A moderate, he is particularly known for his "rule of reason" interpretation of anti-trust laws and his support of an 8-hour work day for railroad workers.

White, E(lwyn) B(rooks) (1899–) US poet, essayist, and author. After graduating from Cornell University, he was variously a reporter for the Seattle *Times*, a ship's messboy, an advertising copywriter in New York City, and a staff writer for the *New Yorker* (1926–38) with his column "Talk of the Town." In 1937 he moved to a farm in Maine and had a monthly column (1938–43) "One Man's Meat" in *Harper's* magazine. Among his many works are *The Lady Is Cold* (1929), a collection of poems; *Is Sex Necessary* (1929), satire written with James Thurber; *Quo Vadimus?* (1939), *The Wild Flag* (1946), *The Second Tree From the Corner* (1954), *The Points of My Compass* (1962), and *Essays of E. B. White* (1977), all collections of essays; and his children's stories *Stuart Little* (1945), *Charlotte's Web* (1952), and *Trumpet of the Swan* (1970). He is also noted for his best-selling revision of William Strunk Jr's *The Elements of Style* (1959). Among his many awards are the Laura Ingalls Wilder Medal for contributions to children's literature (1970) and a special Pulitzer Prize recognizing the full body of his work (1978).

White, Patrick (1912–) Australian novelist. Born in England and educated at Cambridge University, he settled in Australia after World War II and explored the national consciousness in his epic novels *The Tree of Man* (1955) and *Voss* (1957). His other works include *Riders in the Chariot* (1961), *The Solid Mandala* (1966), *The Eye of the Storm* (1974), *The*

Vivisector (1970), *A Fringe of Leaves* (1976), *The Twyborn Affair* (1980), and *Flaws in the Glass* (1982). He won the Nobel Prize in 1973.

White, T(erence) H(anbury) (1906–64) British novelist. He lived for long periods as a recluse in Ireland and in the Channel Isles. His books include a retelling of the Arthurian legend, *The Once and Future King* (1958), and several works of social history.

white ant. *See* termite.

whitebait The young of *herrings, *sprats, and sometimes *silversides. They are highly valued as food.

whitebeam A tree, *Sorbus aria*, up to 50 ft (15 m) tall and found mainly in S and central Europe. The young leaves are covered with fine white down, which persists on the under surface. The creamy-white five-petaled flowers are borne in branched clusters and produce red berries. Swedish whitebeam (*S.* × *intermedia*), a hybrid between whitebeam and *mountain ash, is often planted in parks. Family: *Rosaceae*.

white dwarf A very small faint low-mass star (less than 1.44 solar masses) that has undergone *gravitational collapse following exhaustion of its nuclear fuel. Electrons are stripped from the constituent atoms, and it is the pressure exerted by these densely packed electrons that eventually halts the star's contraction. The density is then 10^7–10^{11} kg m^{-3}. As they cool, their colors change from white (for the brightest) through yellow and red until they become cold black objects.

white-eye A small long-tailed songbird belonging to a family (*Zosteropidae*; 85 species) occurring in Old World tropical regions. White-eyes are less than 6 in (15 cm) long, typically yellow-green with white underparts, and have characteristic white rings around the eyes. They are arboreal and have brush-tipped tongues for feeding on nectar; they also eat insects and sweet fruits, sometimes damaging cultivated fruit crops.

Whitefield, George (1714–70) British Methodist preacher. Ordained an Anglican minister, he was not allowed to preach in Anglican churches, where his evangelism was considered extreme. An associate of the Wesleys at Oxford, Whitefield began open-air preaching in England in 1739 and in 1740, during one of his seven visits to America, he became associated with the *Great Awakening in New England. His preaching was strongly Calvinist, in contrast to the Wesleys' Arminianism.

whitefish A slender fish, belonging to a genus (*Coregonus*) related to trout, that occurs mainly in deep northern lakes and rivers of Europe, Asia, and North America. It has a small mouth, minute teeth, and a covering of large silvery scales. Whitefish feed on insects and other small animals and most are food and game fish.

white fly A small winged insect of the mainly tropical family *Aleyrodidae*. 0.08–0.12 in (2–3 mm) long, it is covered with a mealy white powder and resembles a minute moth. White flies suck plant juices and exude honeydew on which a sooty black mold grows, often damaging crops. The larvae go through a sedentary stage, in which they are scalelike and covered with a cottony wax. Suborder: *Homoptera*; order *Hemiptera*.

Whitehead, A(lfred) N(orth) (1861–1947) British philosopher and mathematician. Whitehead's first major work, the *Principia Mathematica* (1910–13), was written in collaboration with Bertrand *Russell. In later books, such as the *Principles of Natural Knowledge* (1919) and *The Concept of Nature* (1920), he explored the relationships that exist between concepts and sense perception. Thereafter, his philosophy became more metaphysical.

Whitehorse 60 40N 135 08W A city in NW Canada, the capital of the *Yukon. Founded in 1900, at the time of the Klondike gold rush, it is now a center for distribution, administration, and tourism. Population (1976): 13,311.

White House The official residence of the president of the US. In Washington, DC, on Pennsylvania Avenue, the building was designed by James Hoban (*c*. 1762–1831) in 1792. It was burned (1814) by the British during the *War of 1812 but was subsequently restored under Hoban's supervision, being painted white to hide the smoke stains (its name, however, had been adopted earlier). It was partly rebuilt (1949–52).

White Mountains A mountain range in N central New Hampshire and W central Maine, part of the Appalachian Mountains. The highest point is Mt Washington (6288 ft; 1917 m) in the Presidential Range in E New Hampshire. Franconia Notch is typical of the many glacier-carved passes here. The Androscoggin, Saco, and Pemigewasset rivers rise in the White Mountains. The area has long been popular with summer and winter vacationers.

white rhinoceros The largest species of *rhinoceros, *Diceros simus*, of South Africa. It is grayish brown and has a broad square upper lip. Up to

7 ft (2 m) high at the shoulder and weighing up to 3.5 tons, white rhinos are now very rare.

WHITE HOUSE *The colonnaded north portico was added in the 1820s.*

White Russia. *See* Belorussian SSR.

White Russians The Russians who fought against the Soviet Red Army in the civil war (1917–21) that followed the *Russian Revolution. The name derives from that of the royalist opponents to the French Revolution, called Whites because they adopted the white flag of the Bourbon dynasty.

White Sea (Russian name: Beloye More) A gulf of the Arctic Ocean in the NW Soviet Union, to the S and E of the Kola Peninsula. It gives access to Archangel and the fishing port and aluminum works of Kandalaksha and is connected by inland waterways to the Gulf of Finland.

white shark A dangerous man-eating *mackerel shark, *Carcharodon carcharias*, that occurs singly or in groups, mainly in tropical and temperate seas. Its heavy body, up to 36 ft (11 m) long, is gray-brown to slate-blue with light-gray undersides and it feeds voraciously on fish, turtles, seals, etc.

whitethroat An Old World *warbler, *Sylvia communis*, that breeds in N Eurasia and winters in central Africa. It is about 5.5 in (14 cm) long including its long slender tail. The male is russet brown with a grayish head and white throat and performs a tumbling courtship display in flight. The female is a duller brown.

white whale A small Arctic toothed *whale, *Delphinapterus leucas*, also called beluga. Young white whales are blue-gray, but change to white as they mature. About 15 ft (4.5 m) long, with a rounded head and large flukes and flippers, they feed mainly on fish. Family: *Monodontidae*.

whiting A marine food and game fish belonging to the genus *Gadus* (or *Merlangius*) related to cod, especially *M. merlangus* found in shallow European waters, down to 650 ft (200 m). It has a slender body, up to 27.5 in (70 cm) long, which is olive, sandy, or bluish above and silvery white below, a black blotch on each pectoral fin, and three dorsal and two anal fins.

Whitlam, (Edward) Gough (1916–) Australian statesman; Labor prime minister (1972–75). He became Labor leader in 1967. As prime minister he ended conscription, relaxed rules on non-white immigration, and tried to lessen US influence in Australia. In 1975, during a budget crisis, Whitlam was dismissed by the governor, an unprecedented step in the history of Australian politics. Whitlam resigned the Labor leadership in 1977.

Whitman, Walt (1819–92) US poet. As a young man he worked as a printer, teacher, journalist, and property speculator and contributed unoriginal poems to various magazines. He expressed his democratic idealism and passionate love of life in the revolutionary free-verse poems of *Leaves of Grass* (1855), which was revised and enlarged in nine editions during his lifetime. Its publication marked the beginning of his career as a poet, helping to earn him the distinction of being one of the principal 19th century American poets. During the Civil War he nursed wounded soldiers, and subsequently suffered from illness himself. His later works include the prose *Democratic Vistas* (1871).

WALT WHITMAN *Poet who described America and its spirit in his works, the best known of which are collected in* Leaves of Grass.

Whitney, Eli (1765–1825) American inventor, best known for his invention of the cotton gin, a machine that separated cotton fiber from the seeds. The device, patented in 1793, greatly stimulated cotton growing in the southern states. Whitney subsequently turned to firearms manufacture, into which he introduced the concept of interchangeable parts.

Whitney, Mount A mountain in Sequoia National Park in W central California in the Sierra Nevada. It is the highest point in the contiguous United States, rising to 14,494 ft (4418 m). First measured in 1864 by Josiah Dwight Whitney, it was not scaled until 1873. Owens Valley is on the east side of the mountain, and the valley of the Kern River on the west.

Whittier, John Greenleaf (1807–92) US poet. An active Quaker and humanitarian, he championed the antislavery cause in both his journalism and his early poetry. His later and better-known poetry includes "Maude Miller" (1854), "The Barefoot Boy" (1855), "Barbara Frietchie" (1863), and *Snowbound* (1866).

Whittington, Dick (Richard W.; d. 1423) English merchant, who was three times Lord Mayor of London (1397–98, 1406–07, 1419–20). He traded with, and made loans to, both Henry IV and Henry V. The legend of Whittington and his cat dates from the early 17th century.

WHO. *See* World Health Organization.

whooping cough (pertussis) A respiratory infection of children caused by the bacterium *Bordetella pertussis*. After an incubation period of 7–14 days, the child develops a cough, a nasal discharge, and low fever, followed a week or two later by paroxysms of coughing accompanied by a characteristic whooping sound. The disease may persist for months and it may be complicated by pneumonia or convulsions. A vaccine is now available.

whooping crane A rare bird, *Grus americana*, that breeds in the marshlands of NW Canada and winters in the swamps of SE Texas: 60 in (150 cm) tall with a wingspan of 7 ft (210 cm), it has a white plumage with black-tipped wings, black legs, and a bare red face and has a loud whooping call. Captive breeding programs may prevent its extinction. Family: *Gruidae* (cranes).

Whorf, Benjamin Lee (1897–1941) US linguist, who studied American Indian and other languages as a hobby. In *Language, Thought, and Reality* (1956) he argued that human conceptual systems are dependent upon individual languages and that comparison of different languages reveals that different peoples analyze the world in very different ways. This controversial form of linguistic relativism was also argued by *Sapir and has been influential in psycholinguistics (*see* linguistics).

whortleberry. *See* bilberry.

whydah (*or* whidah) A small *weaverbird belonging to the genus *Vidua* (11 species), also called widowbird and occurring in open grassy regions of Africa. The males have long ornamental tail feathers used in the courtship display and the females lay their eggs in the nests of closely related *waxbills, which rear their young. The young whydals closely resemble the offspring of their host species although the adults are very different in appearance.

Whymper, Edward (1840–1911) British mountaineer, explorer, artist, and author. He led the first ascent of the Matterhorn (1865), in which four members of the team died on the descent. He also visited Greenland, the Andes, and Canada on explorations.

Wichita 37 43N 97 20W A city in Kansas, on the Arkansas River. Founded in 1864, it had developed into an important agricultural trading center by the late 19th century. Today Wichita is the state's largest city and the principal commercial and industrial center of S Kansas with railroad workshops, oil refineries, and an aircraft industry. It is the site of two universities, including Wichita State University (1895). Population (1980): 279,272.

Wicklow (Irish name: Contae Chill Mhantáin) A county in the E Republic of Ireland, in Leinster bordering on the Irish Sea. Fertile lowlands rise to the central Wicklow Mountains. Agriculture is the chief occupation; along the coast are several resorts, notably Bray. Area: 782 sq mi (2025 sq km). Population (1971): 66,295. County town: Wicklow.

Widor, Charles Marie (1844–1937) French organist and composer. He was organist of Saint-Sulpice in Paris for over 60 years. His compositions include eight symphonies for the organ, concertos, chamber music, and choral music.

Wieland, Christoph Martin (1733–1813) German novelist and poet. His first distinguished work is the romance *Agathon* (1766–67), while his translations of Shakespeare later influenced the *Sturm und Drang* movement. The verse epic *Oberon* (1780) introduced exotic Middle Eastern matter into European literature.

Wien. *See* Vienna.

Wiener, Norbert (1894–1964) US mathematician. During World War II he worked on the problem of aiming an anti-aircraft gun by computing such factors as the speed and direction of the aircraft, wind speed, etc. He thus developed an interest in the mathematics of information and communication, which he called *cybernetics. After the war Wiener, refusing to do any more military research, spent the rest of his life writing about the social problems resulting from automation.

Wiesbaden 50 05N 8 15E A spa city in SW West Germany, the capital of Hesse on the Rhine River. Its hot saline springs have made it a popular resort since Roman times. A center of the wine industry, its manufactures include chemicals and plastics. Population (1980 est): 273,700.

Wigan 53 33N 2 38W A city in NW England, in Greater Manchester. It is an industrial and market town in a coalmining area, made famous by George Orwell's *Road to Wigan Pier*. Population (1981): 79,535.

wigeon A fast-flying *duck, *Anas penelope*, that breeds on tundra and moorland of N Eurasia and winters on mudflats, estuaries, and lakes as far south as Africa and S Asia. 18 in (45 cm) long, it has a pale-gray black-tipped bill; males have a chestnut head with a yellowish crown and gray back, while females are brown with a white belly and white shoulders.

Wight, Isle of (Latin name: Vectis) 50 40N 1 15W An island and county in S England, separated from the mainland by the Solent and Spithead. It consists chiefly of undulating chalk downs. Tourism is important, especially in the coastal resorts; yachting is an added attraction. Other occupations include agriculture and shipbuilding. Area: 147 sq mi (380 sq km). Population (1981): 118,192. Administrative center: Newport.

WIGEON *Drakes, seen here preening and sleeping, have a high whistling note. Females make a lower purring noise.*

Wigner, Eugene Paul (1902–) US physicist, born in Hungary, who worked out the theory of neutron absorption by nuclei and discovered that solids change their size under radiation (Wigner effect). Wigner helped *Szilard and *Teller persuade *Einstein to warn Roosevelt of the dangers of an atomic bomb being made by the Germans, and he worked with Fermi on the first atomic pile. He won a share of the 1963 Nobel Prize for his work on nuclear physics.

wigwam **1.** Strictly, a square dome-roofed hut made of saplings covered with bark or rush matting used by some North American Indian peoples. **2.** (*or* tepee) A conical tent made of a framework of poles tied together at the top and covered with decorated buffalo skins, used by the Plains tribes.

Wilberforce, William (1759–1833) British philanthropist, who played a major part in the antislavery movement. As a member of parliament (1780–1825) he led the parliamentary campaign to abolish the slave trade (achieved in 1807) and then to emancipate existing slaves (achieved a month after his death). He was a founder of the Society for the Abolition of the Slave Trade (1787) and of the Antislavery Society (1823).

wildcat A *cat, *Felis sylvestris*, of Europe and W Asia. About 30 in (75 cm) long, it has a bushy rounded tail and thick striped coat. Wildcats inhabit dense woodland and breed once a year, in a den in a hollow log or tree. They may interbreed with domestic cats.

Wilde, Oscar (Fingal O'Flahertie Wills W.; 1854–1900) British dramatist and poet, born in Dublin. He dazzled London literary society with his charm and wit and became a leading figure of the *Aesthetic movement. His works include *Poems* (1881), a novel, *The Picture of Dorian Gray* (1891), and a series of brilliant social comedies: *Lady Windermere's Fan* (1892), *A Woman of No Importance* (1893), *An Ideal Husband* (1895), and *The Importance of Being Earnest* (1895). Socially and financially ruined by a trial in 1895 arising from his homosexual relationship with Lord Alfred Douglas (1870–1945), he was imprisoned for two years and lived in exile in France from 1897. While in prison he wrote a long letter on his relationship with Douglas, passages of which were published as *De profundis* (1905). In exile he produced his last and best-known poem, *The Ballad of Reading Gaol* (1898).

wildebeest. *See* gnu.

Wilder, Billy (Samuel W.; 1906–) US film director, born in Austria. He went to Hollywood in 1934. His films are characterized by his acerbic humor and his unconventional choice of subject matter. They include *The Lost Weekend* (1945), *Sunset Boulevard* (1950), and *Some Like It Hot* (1959).

Wilder, Laura Ingalls (1867–1957) US author. At the age of 65, Wilder began her series of children's stories at the urging of her daughter. Based on her early life as a pioneer, the series includes *Little House In the Big Woods* (1932), *Little House on the Prairie* (1935), and *Little Town on the Prairie* (1941), among others. In 1954 the American Library Association estab-

lished its Laura Ingalls Wilder Award for lasting contributions to children's literature. Wilder's stories formed the basis for a successful television series.

Wilder, Thornton (1897–1975) US novelist and dramatist. His best-known plays are *Our Town* (1938) and *The Skin of Our Teeth* (1942), and his novels include *The Bridge of San Luis Rey* (1927). He was a skilled literary craftsman who enjoyed great popular success.

Wilderness, Battle of the (May 5–6, 1864) Civil War battle. General Ulysses S. *Grant, newly appointed as commander of the Union forces, joined General George C. Meade's Army of the Potomac (with more than 100,000 men) in Virginia. General Robert E. *Lee's Confederate Army of Northern Virginia (with just over 60,000 men) held the forested area on the south bank of the Rapidan River. The two-day battle was bloody and indecisive; although the Union forces lost at least twice as many men (about 18,000) as Lee, the Confederates had fewer reserves to draw upon. This battle opened two months of warfare and led to Grant's siege of Petersburg and Richmond.

Wilderness Road A trail that led settlers from SW Virginia W through the Appalachian Mountains and the Cumberland Gap to Louisville, Kentucky. Branches led to Boonesboro on the Kentucky River and Nashville, Tennessee. Blazed by Daniel Boone in 1775 from an old Indian route, the overland trail opened up lands further W; it was the main road westward until the early 1800s when the National Road was built further north. It is now part of the Dixie Highway.

wildfowl Waterbirds, usually ones that are shot for sport, especially ducks and geese but sometimes also coots, rails, and grebes.

Wilhelmina (1880–1962) Queen of the Netherlands (1890–1948), who encouraged Dutch resistance to the German occupation in World War II, making radio broadcasts from London throughout the war. She abdicated in favor of her daughter Juliana.

Wilhelmshaven 53 32N 8 07E A seaport in NW West Germany, in Lower Saxony on the North Sea. It was founded in 1869 as the main Prussian (later German) naval base. Now also a popular resort and an oil port, its manufactures include machinery and electrical goods. Population (1976 est): 102,539.

Wilkes, John (1725–97) British journalist and politician. In 1757 he became a member of parliament and in 1762 founded the weekly *North Briton*, in which he attacked George III's ministers and accused the government of lying. Wilkes was arrested for libel. In 1764 while in Paris he was expelled from the House of Commons and outlawed. In 1768 he returned to England and was twice elected to parliament and twice expelled. After serving as lord mayor of London (1774) he was re-elected to parliament and at last permitted to take his seat (1774–90).

Wilkie, Sir David (1785–1841) Scottish painter, acclaimed for his scenes of everyday life in the Dutch 17th-century tradition. He became painter to William IV in 1830.

Wilkins, Maurice Hugh Frederick (1916–) New Zealand physicist, who worked in California on the atom bomb during World War II. After the war, uneasy about nuclear weapons, he turned to life sciences and developed a method of using X-ray diffraction, which assisted James *Watson and Francis *Crick in determining the structure of DNA. These three scientists were awarded the 1962 Nobel Prize for this work.

Wilkins, Roy (1901–81) US civil rights leader. A graduate of the University of Minnesota, he was a journalist for the Kansas City (Mo) *Call*, a black weekly, before joining the National Association for the Advancement of Colored People in 1931 as assistant executive secretary. He edited *Crisis*, the official organ of the NAACP, from 1934 to 1949. He was named administrator of internal affairs in 1950, and he led the organization as executive secretary (1955) and executive director (1964) until his retirement in 1977. Wilkins urged economic and civil rights in a moderate fashion and was instrumental in preparing the legal challenge that led to school desegregation in 1954.

Wilkinson, James (1757–1825) US army officer. Wilkinson served in the Revolutionary War and became a brigadier general in 1777, but was forced to resign after taking part in an effort to replace George Washington as commander in chief. Wilkinson moved to Kentucky and entered into an agreement with the Spanish governor of Louisiana to help Spain gain control of the Kentucky region in exchange for money and trade concessions for himself. While still in Spain's pay, he served under General Anthony *Wayne in the Indian wars in Ohio and became commander in chief of the army after Wayne's death (1796). Wilkinson officiated at the transfer of Louisiana to the US in 1803 and was governor of the territory (1805–06). He was accused of conspiring with Aaron *Burr to form a separate republic under Burr in the southwest (including Louisiana), and testified for the prosecution at Burr's trial. Both Burr and Wilkinson (who was also tried) were acquitted. Wilkinson served as a major general in the War of 1812, and was tried for negligence in the campaign against Montreal. He was acquitted. Honorably discharged from the army in 1815, he died in Mexico in 1825.

will In law, the written declaration of a person's intentions in relation to the disposal of his property after his death. By its own nature, a will is ambulatory and revocable during his lifetime. Two witnesses are required to authenticate the will. Dependents of the deceased inadequately provided for may challenge the will, the provisions of which are carried out by one or more executors.

Willemstad 12 12N 68 56W The capital and main port of the *Netherlands Antilles, on the SE coast of Curaçao. It is an important free port and a refining center for Venezuelan oil. Population (1974 est): 234,374.

William (I) the Bad (1120–66) Norman King of Sicily (1154–66). In 1155 he reconquered Apulia from the Byzantines and in 1156 (the Concordat of Benevento) gained papal acknowledgement of his possessions. His attempts to reduce the power of the barons incited a revolt, which he was able to suppress. An outstanding patron of learning, he welcomed many Muslim scholars to his court.

William (I) the Conqueror (c. 1028–1087) Duke of Normandy (1035–87) and the first Norman King of England (1066–87). He claimed to have been named by Edward the Confessor as heir to the English throne. When Harold II succeeded Edward, William invaded England, defeated and killed his rival at the battle of Hastings, and became king. The *Norman conquest of England was completed by 1072, aided by the establishment of *feudalism, under which his followers were granted land in return for pledges of service and loyalty. As king, William was noted for his efficient, if harsh, rule. His administration relied upon Norman and other foreign personnel, especially *Lanfranc, Archbishop of Canterbury. In 1085 William initiated the compilation of *Domesday Book.

William (I) the Lion (1143–1214) King of the Scots (1165–1214). After his capture in a revolt against *Henry II of England in 1174, he became a vassal of the English throne. On Henry's death in 1189 he regained independence for his kingdom in return for a payment to Richard I.

William (I) the Silent (1533–84) The leader of the *Revolt of the Netherlands against Spanish rule. He was the son of the Count of Nassau and in 1544 became Prince of Orange. Appointed to the Council of State in 1555, he became governor of Holland, Zeeland, and Utrecht in 1559. He opposed the autocracy of the Spanish Government and its persecution of Protestants (he himself became a Protestant in 1573), withdrawing with Egmont and Horn from the Council of State in 1563. When open revolt broke out in 1568, William soon emerged as its leader and in 1576 succeeded in uniting the Roman Catholic provinces in the south with the Protestant north. This union was short lived, however, and in 1579 the northern provinces declared their independence of Spain, with William as their first stadholder (chief magistrate). He was assassinated by a Spanish agent.

William I (1772–1843) King of the Netherlands (1815–40). Following Napoleon's conquest of the Netherlands (1795), he lived in exile until Napoleon's defeat (1813), becoming King of the United Netherlands, which included Belgium and Luxembourg. He fostered the Netherlands' economic recovery but antagonized the Belgians, who achieved independence (1831) by revolt. William abdicated in favor of his son William II.

William I (1797–1888) King of Prussia (1861–88) and German emperor (1871–88). His advocacy of using arms against the Revolution of 1848 brought him the nickname Prince of Grapeshot and he was forced into exile (1848–49). He became regent for his brother Frederick William IV in 1858. His reign was dominated by *Bismarck, who achieved German unification under Prussian leadership in 1871, when William was proclaimed German emperor.

William II Rufus (c. 1056–1100) King of England (1087–1100), succeeding his father William the Conqueror. His harsh rule aroused baronial and ecclesiastical opposition, notably from *Anselm, Archbishop of Canterbury. He made several attempts to recover Normandy from his elder brother Robert (d. 1134) and was killed by an arrow while hunting in the New Forest. He may have been assassinated by order of his younger brother, who became Henry I.

William (II) the Good (1154–89) The last Norman King of Sicily (1166–89). He ruled in person from 1171, engaging in intermittent war against the Byzantine Empire until final defeat near Constantinople in 1185. In 1177 he married Joan (1165–99), the daughter of Henry II of England.

William II (1792–1849) King of the Netherlands (1840–49), following the abdication of his father William I. His authorization of a liberal constitution (1848) prevented the spread of the *Revolutions of 1848 to the Netherlands.

William II (1859–1941) German emperor (1888–1918); grandson of Britain's Queen Victoria. After securing □Bismarck's resignation as chancellor, William encouraged policies that were regarded abroad as warmongering. The German navy was built up, friendly overtures were made to Turkey and to the Transvaal, and Germany interfered against France in the Morocco crises (1905, 1911). William supported Austria-Hungary's ultimatum to Serbia and then tried in vain to prevent the conflict from escalating into a world war. Following Germany's defeat, he was forced to abdicate.

William III (1650–1702) King of England (1689–1702) and Stadholder (chief magistrate) of the United Provinces (1672–1702), known as William of Orange. Grandson of Charles I of England and son of William II, Prince of Orange (1626–50), in 1677 he married James II of England's daughter Mary. In 1688 he was invited by the opposition to his father-in-law to invade England and in 1689 was proclaimed joint sovereign with his wife, Mary II (see Glorious Revolution). William defeated the former king at the *Boyne in Ireland in 1690. On the Continent he was successful in the War of the *Grand Alliance (1689–97) against Louis XIV of France, leaving a strong army that, under the Duke of Marlborough, was to crush France after his death.

William IV (1765–1837) King of England and Hanover (1830–37), known as the Sailor King or Silly Billy. He served in the Royal Navy from 1778 to 1790. He had ten illegitimate children by the Irish actress Dorothea Jordan before marrying (1818) Adelaide of Saxe-Meiningen (1792–1849). Their two daughters died in infancy and William was succeeded in England by his niece Victoria and in Hanover by his brother Ernest Augustus (1771–1851).

William and Mary style An English derivative (1689–1702) of the *Louis XIV style of furniture. The Huguenot artisans patronized by William III were trained in France and their tastes and techniques predominated. The cabriole leg was a typical innovation replacing the preceding twist turned legs. Rich gilding was common and some important furniture was made of cast silver. Cabinet furniture was finely veneered with *marquetry or lacquered and gilded.

William of Ockham (c. 1285–1349) English scholastic philosopher (see scholasticism). A pupil of *Duns Scotus and later his rival, Ockham is best known for his revival of *nominalism. He systematized the theories on the meaning of universals and linked them with logical principles. See also Ockham's Razor.

William of Orange. See William III (King of England).

William of Tyre (c. 1130–85) French historian and churchman, born in the Latin kingdom of Jerusalem. He became chancellor of the kingdom in 1174 and Archbishop of Tyre in 1175. His only extant work is *Historia rerum in partibus transmarinis gestarum*, a history of medieval Palestine and a valuable source of information on the early Crusades.

Williams, Roger (c. 1604–83) English colonizer, who founded the colony of Rhode Island. A Puritan, Williams settled in Boston in 1631 but was banished in 1635 because he disagreed with the theocratic government of Massachusetts, advocating the separation of church and state. He founded a new settlement (1636) at Providence, Rhode Island, the patent of which allowed full religious freedom. There he established the first Baptist Church in America.

Williams, Tennessee (1911–83) US dramatist. *The Glass Menagerie* (1945), his first major success, was partly autobiographical and introduced his recurrent themes of family tensions and sexual frustration, which were treated with increasing violence in *A Streetcar Named Desire* (1947) and *Cat on a Hot Tin Roof* (1955), both set in the South. After recovering from a mental and physical breakdown, he continued to write plays, including *Vieux Carré* (1978).

Williams, William Carlos (1883–1963) US poet. The influences of *Imagism and of Ezra *Pound, whom he met while studying medicine at the University of Pennsylvania, are apparent in his early poetry, and he continued to develop a style noted for its clarity, directness, and use of natural speech rhythms. His volumes of poetry include *Collected Poems* (1934) and *Pictures from Brueghel* (1963), which won a Pulitzer Prize. *Paterson* (5 vols, 1946–58) is an ambitious epic poem employing various experimental techniques.

Williamsburg 37 17N 76 43W A city in Virginia. Once the state capital (1699–1779), many of its colonial buildings have been renovated or completely rebuilt, attracting many tourists to the city. One of the country's oldest colleges, the College of William and Mary (1693), is also situated here. Population (1970): 9069.

will-o'-the-wisp. *See* ignis fatuus.

willow A tree or shrub of the genus *Salix* (about 300 species), native to temperate and arctic regions. Most willows have long narrow leaves (an exception is the Eurasian goat willow (*S. caprea*), also called sallow and pussy willow, which has oval pointed leaves). Male and female catkins are borne on separate trees and open before the leaves; the seeds have long silky hairs. Willows are common in wet places and along stream banks and some are grown as ornamentals, especially the weeping willow (*S. babylonica*), with its slender drooping branches, and the bay willow (*S. pentandra*). Cricket bats are made from the wood of the cricket bat willow (*S. alba* var. *coerulea*). Family: *Salicaceae*. See also osier.

willowherb A perennial herb of either of the genera *Epilobium* (160 species) or *Chamaenerion* (about 8 species), of temperate and arctic regions. Rosebay willowherb, or fireweed (*E. angustifolium*), 12–48 in (30–120 cm) high, is a common and fast-growing weed on waste ground in woodland clearings and gardens, etc. It has showy spikes of purple flowers and white fluffy seeds. Family: *Onagraceae*.

willow pattern A *chinoiserie pattern attributed to Thomas Minton (*see* Minton ware) and introduced about 1780. It was extensively used on 19th-century English ceramics. The elements are a willow tree, pagoda, figures on a river bridge, and two flying birds in an elaborate border.

Willow South A city in S Alaska situated about 70 mi (113 km) NW of Anchorage. In 1976 it was chosen as the site of the new state capital, planned to replace Juneau in the 1980s.

Wills (Moody), Helen (1905–) US tennis player, who won the singles title at Wimbledon a record eight times between 1927 and 1938. She also won between 1923 and 1938 the US singles title seven times and the French title four times.

Wilmington 39 46N 75 31W A city in North Carolina, on the Cape Fear River. The first armed resistance against the Stamp Act occurred here in November, 1765. The state's chief seaport, Wilmington is also a resort and has varied manufactures. Population (1970): 46,169.

Wilmot Proviso (1846) Proposed constitutional amendment. Following the Mexican War, an appropriations bill was introduced to provide funds for territorial negotiations in the settlement of the US–Mexican boundary. David Wilmot (Democrat, Pa) proposed an amendment, called the Wilmot Proviso, which provided that "neither slavery nor involuntary servitude shall ever exist in any part of said territory." The bill, which provoked bitter controversy and exacerbated North–South differences, passed in the House of Representatives twice (1846, 1847) but did not pass in the Senate. The new Republican Party later adopted the proviso as part of its platform.

Wilson, Sir Angus (1913–) British novelist. His satirical novels and collections of short stories include *Hemlock and After* (1952), *Anglo-Saxon Attitudes* (1956), *No Laughing Matter* (1967), *As If By Magic* (1973), and *Setting the World on Fire* (1980). He has also published several works of criticism.

Wilson, Charles Thomson Rees (1869–1959) British physicist, who won the 1927 Nobel Prize for his invention of the Wilson *cloud chamber. During the 1890s Wilson was experimenting on cloud formation and supersaturated air. He discovered that moisture condensed in the presence of ions and, when X-rays and radioactivity were discovered, applied his discoveries to invent the cloud chamber for detecting ionizing radiation. It was perfected in 1911.

Wilson, Edmund (1895–1972) US critic and essayist. He gave valuable encouragement to young writers in his journalism from the 1920s to the 1940s. His books include *Axel's Castle* (1931), a study of symbolist writers, *To the Finland Station* (1940), on the origins of the Russian Revolution, *The Scrolls from the Dead Sea* (1955), *The American Earthquake* (1958), and *Patriotic Gore* (1962).

Wilson, Edmund Beecher (1856–1939) US biologist, who proposed that sex is determined by the presence or absence of certain chromosomes. Wilson's research and his *Cell in Development and Inheritance* (1896) were a major influence in genetics.

Wilson, (James) Harold, Baron (1916–) British statesman; Labour prime minister (1964–70, 1974–76). An economist, after World War II he became a member of parliament (1945) and president of the Board of Trade in 1947, resigning in 1951 over cuts in social-services expenditure. As Labour leader after 1963 he achieved electoral victory in 1964, but lost the 1970 election. His second ministry saw the renegotiation of the UK's terms of membership to the EEC, which was confirmed by a referendum in 1975.

In 1976 Wilson unexpectedly resigned. His publications include *The Labour Government* (1964–70) and *The Governance of Britain* (1976). He was made a life peer in 1983.

Wilson, Richard (1714–82) British landscape painter. He worked as a portraitist in London before visiting Italy (1750–c. 1757), where he gave up portraiture for landscape painting. After his return to England, he continued to paint Italian scenes as well as English country houses and their parks and scenes of the Welsh mountains. In their feeling for atmosphere and light these paintings established him as the first great British landscapist.

WOODROW WILSON *President whose Fourteen Points were incorporated into the Treaty of Versailles, ending World War I.*

Wilson, (Thomas) Woodrow (1856–1924) US statesman; 28th President of the United States (1913–21). A nationally recognized scholar of political economics, Wilson was a professor (1890–1902) and president (1902–10) of Princeton University, before beginning his political career. In 1910 he was elected governor of New Jersey as the Democratic Reform candidate and during his two-year term in that office, he succeeded in reorganizing the state government. Wilson received the Democratic presidential nomination in 1912, and because of a bitter split in the Republican Party between the supporters of President William H. *Taft and former President Theodore *Roosevelt, Wilson won the election with a plurality of the popular vote.

True to his progressive ideals, Wilson introduced several reform proposals during his first term. These included the enactment of the Underwood Tarriff (1913), which lowered the duties on imported goods; the Federal Reserve Act (1913), which established the *Federal Reserve System; the *Federal Trade Commission Act (1914); and the *Clayton Anti-Trust Act (1914), which extended and strengthened many of the provisions of the earlier *Sherman Anti-Trust Act. Although Wilson pledged to maintain American neutrality after the outbreak of World War I in 1914 in Europe and was re-elected in 1916 with the slogan "he kept us out of war," he was forced to change his policy in the spring of 1917. With the resumption of unrestricted German submarine warfare in the Atlantic, the US officially entered the war. Shortly before the 1918 armistice, Wilson proposed his *Fourteen Points, which he hoped could serve as the basis for the rebuilding of the post-war world. One of the most important of these proposals was the establishment of a *League of Nations, an idea incorporated into the Treaty of *Versailles (1919). Despite Wilson's personal campaign for the League of Nations in the US, conservative opponents in the Senate prevented the entry of the US into that international body. Wilson suffered a stroke while touring the country to gain support for the League of Nations and retired from public life in 1921.

Wiltshire A county of S England. It consists of a rolling chalk plateau, which includes the Marlborough Downs and Salisbury Plain, bordered by lowlands in the NW and SE. It is predominantly agricultural; the chief crops are wheat, oats, and barley, and pig and sheep farming are important.

There are many remaining features of prehistoric times, notably the Neolithic *Stonehenge and *Avebury. Area: 1344 sq mi (3481 sq km). Population (1981): 518,167. Administrative center: Trowbridge.

Winchester 51 04N 1 19W A city in S England, the administrative center of Hampshire. As capital of Saxon Wessex and residence of the Saxon kings, it rivaled the supremacy of London. The cathedral, built in the 11th century on earlier Saxon foundations, is the longest in England and contains many royal tombs. Winchester College (1382), is England's oldest private secondary school. Population (1981): 30,642.

Winckelmann, Johann Joachim (1717–68) German art historian, who worked mainly in Rome. His promotion of the critical study of Greek and Roman art was encouraged by contemporary discoveries at *Pompeii and *Herculaneum. His *History of Ancient Art* (1764), which exalted Greek art of the 5th and 4th centuries BC and denigrated Roman art in comparison, pioneered modern art historiography.

wind The horizontal movement of air over the earth's surface and one of the basic elements of weather. Thermal differences throughout the world produce variations in air pressure and air will flow generally from high-pressure to low-pressure areas. A wind is classified according to the direction from which it blows, i.e. a wind blowing from the S is a southerly wind. Its speed is usually measured in knots or in meters per second, actual velocities being measured by an anemometer, and it may be classified according to the *Beaufort scale. The major wind systems in the world include the trade winds and *westerlies. ▢trade winds; ▢meteorology.

Wind Cave National Park A national park in SW South Dakota, in the S Black Hills, SW of Rapid City. The main feature of the park, established in 1903, is Wind Cave, a limestone cave with a small natural opening, through which a wind blows in and out. The maze of chambers and hallways within the cave are lined with honeycomb-patterned boxwork and frosted deposits of calcite crystals. The park is also a game preserve and is home to prairie dogs, bison, and other wildlife. Area: 44 sq mi (114 sq km).

Windhoek 22 34S 17 06E The capital of Namibia. It is the center of the world's karakul (Persian lamb) skin industry; other industries include meat canning and bone-meal production. Population (1960): 36,051.

wind instruments Musical instruments in which notes are produced by a vibrating column of air. *Brass instruments are activated by lip pressure; *reed instruments employ double or single reed mouthpieces; the *flute is side blown; the *recorder has a mouthpiece and fipple (whistle hole); *organ pipes have air blown into them by mechanically activated bellows. *Compare* drums; percussion instruments; stringed instruments.

windmills Machines that enable useful work to be obtained from wind power. The principle is that the energy of the wind turns a set of vanes or sails mounted on a horizontal shaft, the rotation of which is transmitted by gearing to working machinery. Windmills had appeared by 1150 in NE Europe and were used for grinding corn, pumping water, and powering light industry, until they were superseded by steam engines in the 19th century. Two common designs were the Dutch mill, in which only the sails and the conical roof moved to catch the wind, and the German post mill, in which the whole millhouse with sails attached rotated around a central supporting pole. The modern metal windmill with multiple-bladed sails is found all over the world in rural areas, pumping water or powering small electric generators. The use of windmills for electricity generation on a large scale has long been considered and is now technically feasible (*see* wind power).

windpipe. *See* trachea.

wind power The use of wind energy to generate electricity. Because of the world shortage of conventional energy resources, wind-power generators, like other *alternative energy sources, have now become more attractive economically. Some advantages of wind power are that it is free from pollution, uses no fuel, and the times of peak output are likely to coincide with peak demand (i.e. cold windy days). Among the disadvantages are that it must be supplemented by other means, ideally including electricity storage, since it is not sufficiently predictable. It takes up a great deal of space and the best sites are on open ground rather than in the cities, where most power is needed.

There are several different designs of wind-power generators: some with a horizontal axis and blades like the familiar *windmill; some with specially shaped blades rotating on a vertical axis. Larger generators, producing about 1–45 megawatts, are being considered for supplying electricity by some utility companies. Smaller units may be useful for supplying one or two houses in a local community.

Windsor 42 18N 83 00W A city and port in E Canada, in SW Ontario on the Detroit River opposite *Detroit. Settled in the 18th century by French colonists, it is a transportation and manufacturing center, producing motor vehicles, foods, pharmaceuticals, machinery, and metals. Windsor is the center of a rich farming district. The University of Windsor (1963) is situated here. Population (1981): 192,083.

Windsor, House of The name of Britain's royal family from 1917, when it replaced that of House of Saxe-Coburg-Gotha, of which Prince *Albert had been a member. In 1960 Elizabeth II declared that those of her descendants in the male line who were not princes or princesses would take the surname Mountbatten-Windsor, Mountbatten being Prince *Philip's surname.

Windsor Castle A royal residence in Windsor, begun by William the Conqueror. Many additions were made, notably the keep by Henry III, St George's Chapel by Edward IV, and the Albert Memorial Chapel (so called by Queen Victoria) by Henry VII. Many British rulers are buried in these chapels. In the 16th and 17th centuries it began to be altered from a fortress to a palace with substantial rebuilding being carried into the 19th century.

wind tunnel A device for testing the flow of air around an object, for example an airfoil or aircraft, with a view to studying the lift, drag, streamlining, onset of *turbulence, etc. It consists of a duct with an electrically driven fan, usually with water-cooling systems to maintain the air at the correct temperature. *See also* aerodynamics; aeronautics.

Windward Islands (Spanish name: Islas de Barlovento) A West Indian group of islands forming part of the S Lesser Antilles. They comprise the islands of Martinique, St Lucia, St Vincent, the N Grenadines, and Grenada.

Champagne   Bordeaux   Burgundy   Alsatian white

WINE *The major French wine-producing regions and some standard bottle shapes.*

wine An alcoholic drink made from fermented grape juice. The grapes are first crushed, traditionally by treading, now generally by machine. This process brings the yeast on the grapeskins, visible as the "bloom," into contact with the sugar in the juice, which it then converts into ethanol (ethyl alcohol). Depending upon whether the fermentation is stopped when all, part, or only a little of the sugar has been converted, the resulting wine is dry, medium, or sweet. Table wines contain about 9–13% alcohol.

Fortified wines (e.g. *port, *sherry), to which a liquor is added at some stage in production, contain about 16–23% alcohol. The bubbles in sparkling wines are caused by a secondary fermentation in the bottle (*see also* champagne).

Wines may be red, white, or rosé. Red wines are made from whole grapes; for white wines the grapeskins are removed at an early stage in production. True rosé wines are made from the grenache grape, from which the skins are removed before the juice is deeply stained by them. Favored varieties of wine grapes include Pinot, Cabernet, Hermitage, Riesling, and Sylvaner. The variety of grape, the soil of the vineyard, and the local climate govern a wine's quality. The appellation "vintage" is now used by wine producers under strictly regulated conditions to designate a wine of a particular year that shows outstanding quality.

French wines are famous for their quality and diversity, espcially those produced in Burgundy and the chateaux of the Bordeaux area (the red varieties of which are called clarets). Germany produces fine white wines (hocks). Italian wines are very diverse, including red Lambrusco, red or white Chianti, red Valpolicella, and sweet Marsala. Spain and other European countries produce notable wines. In the US, where the first vinyards date from the 18th century, the best commercial wines are produced in California and New York. Local traditions of wine making are also well established in South Africa, Australia, Chile, and several other countries.

Wingate, Orde Charles (1903–44) British soldier, who organized the *Chindits in Burma in World War II. A Zionist, he organized Jewish guerrillas in Palestine (1936–39). In World War II, after taking Addis Ababa from the Italians (1941), he organized the Chindits to disrupt communications behind the Japanese lines in Burma. He was killed in an aircrash.

Winnipeg 49 53N 97 10W A city in W Canada, capital of Manitoba at the junction of the Assiniboine and Red Rivers. Established as a fur-trading post (1806), it expanded with the growth of farming and the arrival of the railroad (1881) from E Canada. It is the distribution, wholesaling, financial, and manufacturing center of the Canadian prairies and a major transportation junction. Winnipeg is the site of the University of Manitoba and the Royal Winnipeg Ballet. Population (1981): 564,473.

Winnipeg, Lake A lake in W Canada, in S Manitoba. Emptying via the Nebon Rivers into Hudson Bay, it drains much of the Canadian prairies. It is exploited for tourism, fishing, and shipping. Area: 9465 sq mi (24,514 sq km).

Winnipesaukee, Lake A lake in E central New Hampshire, in the White Mountain foothills. The largest lake (25 mi long, 12 mi wide; 40 km long; 19 km wide) in New Hampshire, it is a popular resort area. A western outlet, the Winnipesaukee River, flows SW into the Merrimack River at Franklin. Area: 71 sq mi (184 sq km).

Winston Salem 36 05N 80 18W A city and port in North Carolina. A major tobacco-growing and manufacturing center, other products include textiles and furniture. Population (1980): 131,885.

winter aconite An early-flowering perennial herb of the genus *Eranthis* (7 species), native to temperate Europe, especially *E. hyemalis*, which is often grown in gardens. The flowers are cup-shaped, with six golden-yellow petals surrounded by larger leaflike structures, and appear before the leaves. Family: *Ranunculaceae*.

wintergreen An evergreen creeping perennial herb or small shrub of the family *Pyrolaceae* (about 35 species), found in N temperate and arctic regions. The leaves are simple and the flowers are borne singly or in a terminal spike. They are white or pale-pink with five petals and the fruit is a capsule. Oil of wintergreen comes from the leaves of the winterberry (*Gaultheria procumbens*), a North American shrub, whereas the common wintergreen (*Pyrola minor*) is a herb of Eurasia and North America. Also in the family are the North American pipsissewas (genus *Chimaphila*), woodland herbs with leathery leaves and fragrant flowers.

Winterhalter, Franz Xavier (1806–73) German painter and lithographer, famous for his portraits of European royalty. His sitters included King Louis Philippe and Napoleon III of France as well as Queen Victoria and her family.

Winterthur 47 30N 8 45E A city in N Switzerland. It is an industrial center with heavy engineering and cotton textiles. Population (1980 est): 86,758.

Winter War. *See* Russo-Finnish War.

Winthrop, John (1588–1649) English colonizer; the first governor of the *Massachusetts Bay Company (1629–33, 1637–39, 1642–43, 1646–48). Leaving England in 1630, he helped to found the colony at Boston. He led the colony as governor and deputy governor for two decades. His *History of New England from 1630 to 1649* is an important chronicle of the colony's development. His son **John Winthrop** (1606–76) was an American colonial governor. Educated at Trinity College, Dublin, he followed his father to the Massachusetts Colony. In 1633, he settled Ipswich, Mass. He returned to London in 1634, but was commissioned to return to Massachusetts and begin a new settlement on the Connecticut River, called Saybrook, named after his patrons. In 1657 he became governor of the Connecticut colony, a position he held until his death. In 1662 he secured a charter from Charles II, which united the colonies of Connecticut and New Haven. He was an enthusiastic amateur chemist, physician, astronomer, and economist, the first American to become a member of the British Royal Society.

wirehaired pointing griffon A breed of hunting dog developed in France during the late 19th century. It is strongly built with a short tail and a longish square muzzle. The harsh bristly coat is a mixture of gray, white, and brown. Height: 21–23 in (54–59 cm) (dogs); 19–21 in (49–54 cm) (bitches).

wireworm. *See* click beetle.

Wisconsin A state in the N central US, situated between the Mississippi River in the W, Lake Michigan in the E, and Lake Superior in the N. It is bordered by Iowa and Minnesota (SW and W), Lake Superior (N), Michigan (NE), Lake Michigan (E), and Illinois (S). The Central Lowlands, which cover the lower two thirds of the state, give way in the N to the Superior Upland, which is part of the Canadian Shield and contains many forests and lakes. Manufacturing is the state's major economic activity and its industrial belt in the SE links Milwaukee to the Chicago area. The state has 14 ports on the Great Lakes. Leading products include metal goods, lumber, machinery, paper products, and electrical and transport equipment. The state is famous for its dairy products and livestock; it is among the highest producers of hay, alfalfa, and corn and food processing is a major industry. Tourism is growing, attracted by numerous state parks and forests and developing recreational facilities. *History*: the first European fur traders, explorers, and missionaries entered the area in the 1630s, followed by major tribal shifting among Indian peoples driven westward. The French lost their control of the area to the British at the end of the *French and Indian Wars (1763). Ceded to the US by the British in 1783, large-scale immigration in the 1820s led to its organization as a territory (1836) and it became a state in 1848. During and after the Civil War the area was enormously productive in industry and agriculture. World War II shipbuilding increased the state's prosperity, and the state remains a great industrial center. Area: 56,154 sq mi (145,438 sq km). Population (1980): 4,705,335. Capital: Madison.

Wisdom of Solomon Book of the *Apocrypha, an important example of Jewish "wisdom literature," which also includes the books of Proverbs, Job, Ecclesiastes, and Ecclesiasticus. It was originally written in Greek, probably by a Hellenized Jew of Alexandria in the 2nd century BC. In encouraging a search for wisdom, it describes its benefits, praises its divine source, which is God, and traces how wisdom has helped the Jews and confounded their enemies.

Wise, Isaac Mayer (1819–1900) US rabbi, born in Bohemia. Wise had congregations in Albany, NY, and Cincinnati, Ohio, where the changes he urged led to his becoming a leader of Reformed Judaism in the US. He founded the Union of American Hebrew Congregations (1873), the Hebrew Union College (1875), of which he was president for 25 years, and the Central Conference of American Rabbis (1889).

Wise, Stephen Samuel (1874–1949) US rabbi, born in Hungary. Wise received his doctorate from Columbia University in 1901 and founded the Free Synagogue in New York City in 1907. An ardent Zionist, he founded the American and the World Jewish Conferences, and the Jewish Institute of Religion, which later united with the Hebrew Union College. Wise was involved in political struggles for better government and social legislation.

wisent. *See* bison.

Wiślany Zalew. *See* Vistula Lagoon.

Wismar 53 54N 11 23E A town and Baltic port in NW East Germany. Once a Hanseatic port, it passed to Sweden under the Peace of *Westphalia (1648). Although pledged to Mecklenburg-Schwerin in 1803, Sweden did not renounce all rights to the city until 1903. Its industries include shipbuilding, fishing, and sugar refining. Population (1973 est): 56,762.

Wissler, Clark (1870–1947) US anthropologist. Professor of anthropology at Yale University (1924–40), Wissler was famous for his research on the geographical and regional aspects of race and culture. His best-known book is *The American Indian* (1917).

Wister, Owen (1860–1938) US novelist. A graduate of Harvard (1882), he studied music in Paris before returning to Harvard for a law degree. He spent his summers in Wyoming and made the West the topic of most of his fiction: the collections *Red Men and White* (1896), *Lin McLean* (1898), and *The Jimmyjohn Boss and Other Stories* (1900). His best-known work, a novel entitled *The Virginian* (1902), became a bestseller with a play, three films, and a television series based on it. The title character, strong and taciturn, became a model for the Western hero. Wister also wrote biographies of Ulysses S. Grant, George Washington, and Theodore Roosevelt.

Wisteria A genus of twining usually woody vines (10 species), native to E Asia and North America and grown as ornamentals, especially *W. floribunda* from Japan, which may reach a height of 100 ft (30 m). The compound leaves have paired pointed leaflets and the flowers, usually purple, are borne in large hanging clusters, up to 35 in (90 cm) long. Family: *Leguminosae*.

witan A body of 30 to 40 high-ranking laymen and ecclesiastics, which advised Anglo-Saxon kings on such major policy matters as foreign policy and taxation. It met only at the king's will and had no fixed procedure. As a court, it decided on cases affecting the king and other important persons.

witchcraft The supposed manipulation of natural events by persons using supernatural means to harmful ends. In Europe the biblical injunction "Thou shalt not suffer a witch to live" (Exodus 22.18) sanctioned widespread persecution. Social and religious upheavals in the 16th and 17th centuries brought an upsurge in witch hunts; the famous outbreak at Salem, Massachusetts (1692), is a case of witch hysteria. Witches were accused of worshiping the devil at nocturnal orgies (sabbaths), of keeping evil spirits (familiars), and of killing livestock, wrecking crops, and causing barrenness, impotence, and fits. Many traditional African communities hold witchcraft accountable for a similar range of inexplicable misfortunes. It is countered by witch-doctors who identify witches and suggest means of neutralizing their malign psychic powers.

witch hazel A shrub or small tree of the genus *Hamamelis* (6 species), native to E Asia and North America, especially the American *H. virginiana*, which is the source of witch-hazel lotion used in pharmacy. This and several other species are often grown as ornamentals, having small clusters of attractive yellow flowers, each with four strap-shaped petals. The fruit is a woody capsule surrounded by a yellow cuplike calyx. Family: *Hamamelidaceae*.

witchweed A parasitic herb of the genus *Striga* (about 10 species), native to the Old World tropics. Up to 30 in (75 cm) tall, it has rough narrow sometimes scalelike leaves and solitary blue, purple, red, yellow, or white two-lipped flowers. The roots derive nutrients from the roots of other plants, including many crops. Family: *Scrophulariaceae*.

Witte, Sergei Yulievich (1849–1915) Russian statesman. As finance minister (1892–1903) Witte initiated the Russian industrial revolution, making capital available to industry and obtaining foreign loans. He greatly encouraged railroad construction. As prime minister (1905–06), he was instrumental in founding the *Duma following the Revolution of 1905.

Wittelsbach The ruling dynasty of Bavaria and the Rhine Palatinate. Wittelsbachs ruled these German states from the late 12th century until deposed in 1918 in a republican coup.

Wittenberg 53 00N 11 41E A city in central East Germany, on the *Elbe River. The Reformation began here on October 31, 1517, when Martin Luther nailed his 95 theses to the door of All Saints Church. The town is an important industrial center. Population (1973 est): 45,700.

Wittgenstein, Ludwig (1889–1951) Austrian philosopher. After studying engineering in Vienna he turned to philosophy, studying under Bertrand *Russell at Cambridge (1912–13), where he eventually succeeded G. E. *Moore as professor. His two major works are the *Tractatus Logico-philosophicus* (1921) and the posthumously published *Philosophical Investigations* (1953). Wittgenstein's abiding preoccupation was with language, particularly with the problems that language's relationship to things pose for the philosopher. In his earlier work he developed the "picture theory" of language—words represent things by established conventions—but later he developed the more sophisticated "game" or "toolkit" models, in which actual usage is more important than set convention. This approach to language as a predominantly social phenomenon has been enormously influential among English-speaking philosophers.

Witwatersrand (*or* the Rand) A ridge of hills in NE South Africa. It extends about 100 mi (160 km) chiefly W of Johannesburg, forming the watershed between the Limpopo and Orange river systems. It has been worked for gold since the 1880s and now produces about one third of the world's gold output.

woad A branching perennial or biennial herb, *Isatis tinctoria*, native to central and S Europe. Formerly cultivated for the blue dye extracted from its crushed leaves, it is now rare. Up to 48 in (120 cm) tall, it has narrow leaves and terminal branching clusters of tiny four-petaled yellow flowers. Family: *Cruciferae*.

Wodehouse, Sir P(elham) G(renville) (1881–1975) US humorous writer, born in Britain. After 1909 he lived mostly abroad and became a US citizen in 1955. In his many comic novels featuring Bertie Wooster and his manservant Jeeves, including *The Inimitable Jeeves* (1923) and *The Code of the Woosters* (1938), he portrayed an English upper-class society fixed forever in the 1920s.

Woden. See Odin.

Wöhler, Friedrich (1800–82) German chemist, who, while professor of chemistry at Göttingen University, synthesized urea from ammonium cyanate (1828). This was the first organic compound to have been derived from an inorganic compound, providing evidence against the theory that organic compounds contained a "vital force" absent in inorganic compounds. He also succeeded in isolating the elements aluminum, beryllium, and titanium.

wolf A wild *dog, *Canis lupus*, of Eurasia and North America. Wolves are 55–75 in (140–190 cm) long including the tail (12–22 in [30–55 cm]). They live in packs of 5–30 animals—which patrol their own territories—and feed mainly on mice, fish, and carrion but also attack deer. Mating is often for life and both parents may share in rearing the pups.

Wolves in colder climate are generally larger and shaggier and form bigger packs. There is an almost white N Siberian race, while the Indian pale-footed wolf is small and gray. *See also* timber wolf. □mammal.

Wolf, Hugo (1860–1903) Austrian composer. He studied briefly at the Vienna conservatoire and earned his living as a teacher, conductor, and critic. He died insane in an asylum. He wrote 300 *Lieder* (many of which were settings of poems by Goethe and Mörike), the opera *Der Corregidor* (1895), and an *Italian Serenade* for string quartet.

Wolfe, James (1727–59) British soldier. After the outbreak of the Seven Years' War he was sent to Canada. He excelled, under *Amherst, in the capture of Louisburg from the French (1758) and in the following year he besieged *Montcalm in Quebec. His forces scaled the undefended Heights of Abraham from the St Lawrence and a pitched battle ensued in which both commanders were killed. The British victory established their supremacy in Canada.

Wolfe, Thomas (1900–38) US novelist. After abandoning his studies at Harvard University, where he had hoped to become a playwright, Wolfe taught literature at New York University (1924–30) before receiving national attention with the publication of his massive first novel, *Look Homeward, Angel* (1929). His later novels, based for the most part on autobiographical material and set in his native North Carolina, include *Of Time and the River* (1935), *The Web and the Rock* (1939), and *You Can't Go Home Again* (1940). The final two works were published posthumously.

Wolf-Ferrari, Ermanno (1876–1948) Italian composer of German-Italian parentage. He spent most of his life in Venice, composing such operas as *The School for Fathers* (1906) and *Susanna's Secret* (1909).

wolf fish A slender marine fish, *Anarhichas lupus*, also called catfish, found in the N Atlantic and North Sea, down to 1000 ft (300 m). It has a blue-green or greenish body up to 47 in (120 cm) long, with dark vertical bars, a long blunt head, doglike teeth, long dorsal and anal fins, and no pelvic fins. It feeds on bottom-dwelling hard-shelled animals. Family: *Anarhichadidae*; order: *Perciformes*.

Wölfflin, Heinrich (1864–1945) Swiss art historian. A pupil of Jakob Burckhardt (1818–97), Wölfflin wrote chiefly on baroque and classical art. He was the principal exponent of the formal school of art historians, which analyzes style by changes of form in art.

wolfhound. *See* borzoi; Irish wolfhound.

wolfram. *See* tungsten.

wolframite The principal ore of tungsten, consisting of ferrous tungstate, (Fe,Mn)WO$_4$. It is brown, black, gray, or reddish in color and is found particularly in quartz veins associated with granitic rocks. *See also* scheelite.

Wolfram von Eschenbach (c. 1170–c. 1220) German poet. A knight, he served at several courts. His great romance, *Parzifal* (c. 1212), is the first German work to use the story of the Holy Grail and is the basis of

Wagner's opera. Allegorizing man's spiritual development, it tells how the innocent fool becomes the wise keeper of the Grail.

wolfsbane. *See* aconite.

Wolfsburg 52 27N 10 49E A city in NE West Germany, in Lower Saxony on the Mittelland Canal. Founded in 1938, it grew around the Volkswagen car factory. Population (1980 est): 126,800.

wolf spider A *spider, also called hunting spider, belonging to a widespread family (*Lycosidae*; over 175 species). Wolf spiders, up to 1 in (25 mm) long, are dark brown with long stout legs and live on or in the ground, often in specially constructed tubes. They are usually active at night, hunting prey rather than trapping it in webs. The female carries the eggs and young.

Wollstonecraft, Mary (1759–97) British writer. She was a member of a group of political radicals that included Tom Paine and her husband, the social philosopher William *Godwin. Her best-known work is *A Vindication of the Rights of Women* (1792), which argued for equal opportunities for all in education. She died in giving birth to her daughter, who became Mary *Shelley.

Wolsey, Thomas, Cardinal (c. 1475–1530) English churchman and statesman; Lord Chancellor (1515–29) under Henry VIII. He entered Henry's service in 1509 and became Archbishop of York and (1515) a cardinal. He used his position to amass a huge personal fortune that did much on the eve of the Reformation to bring the Church into disrepute. Wolsey's attempts to raise taxes to pay for his foreign policy encountered violent opposition. He fell from power after failing to persuade the pope to permit Henry to divorce Catherine of Aragon and died on his way to face trial in London.

Wolverhampton 52 36N 2 08W A city in central England. Metalworking and engineering are the principal industries. Traditionally known for locks and keys, it also produces bicycles, tools, hardware, and chemicals. Population (1981): 252,447.

wolverine A carnivorous mammal, *Gulo gulo*, also called glutton, inhabiting northern evergreen forests of Europe, Asia, and America. It is heavily built, about 40 in (1 m) long and weighing about 55 lb (25 kg), and hunts alone, typically ambushing lemmings and rabbits (although it can overcome an old or unfit deer). Family: *Mustelidae*.

Woman's Christian Temperance Union (WCTU) Organization founded in 1874 in Cleveland, Ohio, to work for the abolition of liquor traffic. Now an international organization with over 300,000 members, the WCTU is fighting liquor and narcotics as well as concerning itself with civil and philanthropic works. It publishes the *Union Signal* and the *Young Crusader* and sponsors the Youth Temperance Council (ages 13–29) and the Loyal Temperance Legion (ages 6–12).

womb. *See* uterus.

wombat A bearlike *marsupial belonging to the family *Phascolomidae* (2–3 species), of Australia (including Tasmania). The coarse-haired wombat (*Phascolomis ursinus*) is about 40 in (1 m) long and has short powerful legs with strong claws, which it uses for tunneling underground. It feeds on grass, roots, and tree bark.

Women's Liberation Movement The movement for female equality, which underwent a resurgence in the 1960s and now embraces many different political and social goals. Among the rights feminists demand are: equal pay for equal work, equal educational and job opportunities, the right of the individual to control her own reproductive choices (contraceptives and abortion), the end to segregated clubs or professional organizations, affordable child care, and the passage of the ERA (Equal Rights Amendment). Additionally, adherents believe that attitudes and social customs must be changed if women are to be "liberated." The portrayal of women in the media, a double standard of sexual behavior, and views of women as primarily childbearers or housekeepers, are some of the areas where change is mandated, feminists believe. One of the leading advocates of women's liberation is NOW (*National Organization for Women), founded in 1966 by Betty *Friedan. This and many other organizations continue to work toward the goals of women's liberation.

Women's Rights Movement The movement for women's rights was originally concerned with the issue of female suffrage. In the US, the *Seneca Falls Convention in 1848, organized by Elizabeth Cady *Stanton and Lucretia *Mott, began the movement. In 1869 the *National Woman Suffrage Association, led by Susan B. *Anthony and Stanton, and the *National American Woman Suffrage Association, led by Lucy *Stone, were established. The two groups merged in 1890, but it was not until the passage of the 16th Amendment in 1920 that women gained the right to vote. The movement faded for a time, but has worked in recent decades for equal

pay, educational and employment opportunities, liberal abortion laws, child care, and the ERA (*Equal Rights Amendment). While the women's rights and the *women's liberation movements share many of the same goals, both are general designations that include different activities undertaken by different groups at various times and places.

Wŏnsan 39 20N 127 25E A port in SE North Korea, on the Sea of Japan. Badly damaged during the Korean War (1950–53), its industries have since been rebuilt and include oil refining, shipbuilding, railroad engineering, and chemicals. Population (1967 est): 215,000.

Wood, Grant (1891–1942) US artist. Wood studied at the Art Institute of Chicago, served with the army in World War I, and studied in Paris in 1923. In 1927 he went to Germany and was influenced both by the "new realism" and by German and Flemish artists of the 15th and 16th centuries. His best subjects were the simple, sturdy, rural folk of his native Iowa, and his most famous work, "American Gothic" (1930), depicts such a couple. His style, known as American regionalism, gives great attention to realism and detail, but with satiric overtones. Other works include "Daughters of Revolution" (1932) and "Parson Weems' Fable" (1939).

wood The hard tissue of the stems and branches of trees and shrubs, beneath the bark, consisting of *xylem cells strengthened with deposits of lignin. The newest xylem—sapwood—is essential for transport of water and nutrients up the tree. As the xylem ages lignin is deposited within the cells, which eventually die. The central part of the trunk—heartwood—consists of dead xylem, which is darker than sapwood due to deposits of tannins and resins. Conifers are referred to as softwoods because the xylem is porous; broad-leaved (angiosperm) trees, which are called hardwoods, contain more fibers and are therefore stronger (*see* timber). □plant.

woodbine. *See* honeysuckle; Virginia creeper.

wood carving The art of carving sculptures or architectural and furniture decoration in wood. It has been practiced universally since ancient times. *African art principally consists of wood carving. In Europe some of the finest decorative wood carving was achieved in medieval churches. In the 20th century sculptors, such as *Brancusi and Henry *Moore, have exploited the special characteristics of wood—its vertical graining and organic nature—in the trend toward retaining the inherent characteristics of materials in finished sculptures.

woodchat A small *shrike, *Lanius senator*, occurring in wooded Mediterranean regions. The male has dark wings, back, and tail patches, white underparts, a chestnut neck and cap, and a broad black band across the forehead; the female is duller.

woodchuck. *See* marmot.

woodcock Two species of gamebird, *Scolopax rusticola*, occurring in fresh-water marshes and dense damp woodland and generally active at night. They have long bills and feed on worms and insect larvae. Males perform a slow display flight (called roding) during courtship. The American woodcock (*Philohela minor*) is brownish red underneath with a "dead-leaf" pattern above. About 11 in (28 cm) long, it is very stocky with almost no neck. The Eurasian woodcock has a stocky body, 13 in (34 cm) long, and a russet plumage with a dark-barred head and underparts and a white-tipped tail. Family: *Scolopacidae* (sandpipers, snipe).

woodcreeper An arboreal passerine bird belonging to a family (*Dendrocolaptidae*; 48 species) ranging through Central and South America. Woodcreepers are typically 8–12 in (20–30 cm) long and have stout bills, powerful feet with long claws, and an olive-brown plumage with pale stripes on the head and underparts. The tail is stiff, providing support when it climbs spirally up trees, prising off bark and probing in crevices for insects and spiders.

woodcut A relief *printing technique. The design is drawn on the surface of a block of wood, all the undrawn parts being cut away to produce the white areas of the print. The design is then transferred to paper by pressing the inked block onto the paper. The woodcut was used in China (c. 5th century AD) for textile design but its history in Europe dates from the 14th century and is closely connected with the early printed book. Its special qualities—cheapness, boldness, and simplicity—made it particularly suitable for popular book illustration. Leading 16th-century German artists, such as *Dürer and *Holbein, used the medium to supreme effect. Although subsequently used for book illustration, it was only revived as an art form in the late 19th century by *Gauguin and *Munch.

wood engraving A technique of printing images, refined in the 18th century by Thomas Bewick and used extensively during the 19th century for reproductive engraving. The surface of the woodblock is cut away to leave raised areas which, when treated with ink, will appear dark when printed, in contrast to the white line of the incised areas. Boxwood is used for its fine grain, the block being cut transversely. Wood engraving produces a more subtle effect than *woodcut.

woodlouse   A terrestrial crustacean of the suborder *Oniscoidea*, found in damp shady places under stones, logs, etc. Woodlice have a body covering of armor-like plates: they can breathe air (through specially modified gills) but require damp surroundings to avoid desiccation. A common species is the pill bug or woodlouse (*Armadillidium vulgare*), about 0.66 in (17 mm) long, which rolls into a ball when disturbed. It has spread from Europe to occur in leaf litter in wooded areas all over the world. Common genera: *Oniscus, Porcellio*; order: *Isopoda.

WOODPECKER   *The European green woodpecker* (Picus viridis) *bringing food to its young, which are housed in a tree hole.*

woodpecker   A bird belonging to a family (*Picidae*; about 220 species) occurring worldwide except Madagascar, Australia, and New Zealand. 3.5–22 in (9–57 cm) long, woodpeckers have multicolored plumage, often barred or spotted. Most are exclusively arboreal, chiseling through bark with their long straight bills in search of insects, which are extracted with a long sticky protrusible tongue. Their short strong feet with large claws and the stiff wedge-shaped tail are adaptations for climbing. *See also* ivory-billed woodpecker; wryneck.

wood pigeon   A large Eurasian *pigeon, *Columba palumbus*, which is a serious pest on farmland, eating grain and other crops. 16 in (40 cm) long, it has a predominantly gray plumage with a black-tipped tail, brownish back and wings, white wing patches, and a green, purple, and white neck patch.

woodrush   A grasslike perennial plant of the genus *Luzula* (about 80 species), occurring chiefly in cold N temperate regions. The Eurasian great woodrush (*L. sylvatica*) has leaves up to 12 in (30 cm) long and 0.8 in (2 cm) wide, which are fringed with colorless hairs. Family: *Juncaceae* (rush family).

wood sorrel   A herbaceous plant of the genus *Oxalis* (about 800 species), of temperate and tropical regions, especially *O. acetosella*, of Europe. This species has compound three-part leaves (made up of heart-shaped leaflets) and solitary white five-petaled flowers. Many species are ornamentals and some, including the vegetable oca (*O. tuberosa*), have edible tubers. Family: *Oxalidaceae.

Woodville, Elizabeth   (c. 1437–92) The wife from 1464 of Edward IV of England. Royal patronage of her family caused dissensions among Edward's Yorkist supporters and on his death (1483) the power of the Woodvilles was undermined by the Duke of Gloucester, who deposed Elizabeth's son Edward V and became Richard III. Elizabeth was retired to a convent.

Woodward, Robert Burns   (1917–   ) US chemist, who, while working at Harvard, won the 1965 Nobel Prize for his syntheses of a number of organic compounds. His first success was his synthesis of quinine in 1944. He then went on to synthesize strychnine, cortisone, cholesterol, and chlorophyll as well as an antibiotic.

woodwasp   A *sawfly belonging to the families *Xiphydriidae* (Europe and North America), *Sytexidae* (North America), or *Orussidae* (worldwide). *Xiphydriidae* larvae bore into deciduous trees, such as alder, birch, and maple. *Sytexidae* are restricted to the incense cedar tree. *Orussidae* larvae are external parasites on wood-dwelling beetle larvae. *See also* horntail.

woodwind instruments   Blown musical instruments in which a column of air is made to vibrate either by blowing across a mouth hole, as in the flute, or by making a single or a double reed vibrate, as in the oboe, bassoon, clarinet, and saxophone. The length of the vibrating column is varied by opening and closing holes, either with the finger or by means of keys.

woodworm   A wood-boring beetle of the genus *Anobium*, especially the furniture beetle (*A. punctatum*), 0.20 in (5 mm) long, which damages furniture and old buildings. The larvae bore into wood and emerge when adult, leaving large numbers of holes. In time, the wood is reduced to dust. Family: *Anobiidae.

wool   Fibers obtained from the coats or fleeces of domestic sheep. Elastic, resilient, and absorbent, it is also an excellent insulator because of its bulk, the result of its curliness (crimp). The fleeces of different breeds vary widely. *Merino wool is the best in quality; it is short, fine, soft, and the most crimpy. It now comes chiefly from Australia, South Africa, South America, and the US. Since World War II synthetic fibers have been mixed with wool.

Woolf, (Adeline) Virginia   (*born* Stephen; 1882–1941) British novelist. A central figure of the *Bloomsbury group, she developed an impressionistic style in which she attempted to express the essential fluidity of existence. Her novels include *Mrs Dalloway* (1925), *To the Lighthouse* (1927), and *The Waves* (1931). She also wrote biographies and criticism, including a series of essays entitled *The Common Reader* (1925–32). She committed suicide by drowning after the recurrence of a mental illness. Her husband **Leonard (Sidney) Woolf** (1880–1969), whom she married in 1912 and with whom she founded the Hogarth Press in 1917, was literary editor of the *Nation* (1923–30) and wrote five volumes of autobiography (1960–69).

Woollcott, Alexander Humphreys   (1887–1943) US journalist and critic. He worked as drama critic for *The New York Times* before serving on the army newspaper *Stars and Stripes* during World War I. He returned as drama critic for the *Times* until 1922, then reviewed for the *Herald* (1922–25) and the *World* (1925–28). Known for his acid wit and theater gossip, he had a successful radio program, "The Town Crier." Among his collected writings are *Shouts and Murmurs* (1922), *Enchanted Isles* (1924), *While Rome Burns* (1934), and *Long, Long Ago* (1943). Woollcott had some acting roles and performed in *The Man Who Came to Dinner* as a character George S. Kaufman and Moss Hart modeled on Woollcott himself.

Woolley, Sir Leonard   (1880–1960) British archeologist. He worked at *Carchemish and *Tell el-Amarna but is famous chiefly for his brilliant excavations at *Ur (1922–34), his popular accounts of which stimulated widespread interest in the archeology of the biblical lands.

woolly bear.   See tiger moth.

woolly monkey   A large long-tailed monkey belonging to the genus *Lagothrix* (3 species), of South America. The smoky woolly monkey (*L. cana*) has short pale hair and dark head, arms, legs, and tail. Males may grow to 48 in (120 cm) long including the tail 24–27.5 in (60–70 cm). They have strong teeth and jaws and feed on fruit, leaves and unripe nuts. Family: *Cebidae.

woolly rhinoceros   A rhinoceros belonging to the extinct genus *Coelodonta*, which inhabited Eurasia and North Africa during the Pleistocene epoch (2.5 million to 10,000 years ago). Well-preserved specimens found in ice and oil deposits show that it was a large shaggy-coated animal with two horns, the front one very long and sharp.

woolly spider monkey   A rare monkey, *Brachyteles arachnoides*, of SE Brazil. It has long legs, short woolly fur, and a prehensile tail and is thought to be arboreal and vegetarian. Family: *Cebidae.

Woolworth, F(rank) W(infield)   (1852–1919) US businessman, who created a chain of over a thousand shops across the US selling low-priced goods. The first was opened in 1879 in Utica, New York. He also opened stores in many other countries. The Woolworth Building in New York City, which he commissioned, was the world's tallest building (1913–30).

Worcester   42 17N 71 48W   A city in Massachusetts on the Blackstone River. Settled in 1673, textile manufacturing began in 1789 and the country's first corduroy cloth was produced here. The Free-Soil Party, which opposed the extension of slavery, developed from a meeting held here in

1848. A cultural and educational center, it is the site of Clark University (1887) and several other colleges and universities. Manufactures include precision instruments and chemicals. Population (1980): 161,799.

Worcester 52 11N 2 13W A city in W central England, on the Severn River. The cathedral, begun in 1084, is mainly 14th-century. At the battle of Worcester (1651) Charles II was defeated by Cromwell. Worcester is famous for its porcelain. Population (1981): 74,247.

WILLIAM WORDSWORTH *A profile of Wordsworth drawn in 1807.*

Wordsworth, William (1770–1850) British poet. He became an enthusiastic republican during a visit to Revolutionary France (1791–92). In 1795 he met S. T. *Coleridge, with whom he collaborated on *Lyrical Ballads* (1798), a seminal work of the Romantic movement. In 1799 he settled in the Lake District of England, where, cared for devotedly by his wife Mary and his sister Dorothy, he wrote what is usually considered his masterpiece, a verse autobiography entitled *The Prelude* (completed 1805; published 1850). In this and other poems he described his feelings of mystical union with nature.

work The product of a force and the distance through which it causes a body to move in the direction of the force. Work, like energy, is measured in *joules.

work hardening The strengthening of metal by hammering or rolling it without heating. Metal consists of small crystals (grains). Softness or ductility is caused by irregularities (dislocations) in the grains that are able to move and change the crystal shape under stress. Movement of dislocations is blocked at the boundaries between grains. Continued working makes the dislocations collect at the grain boundaries, thus making the metal harder. *See also* heat treatment.

workhouses Institutions set up in the 17th century in Europe, primarily Britain, to provide employment and shelter for paupers. An 1834 British law made it necessary for anyone seeking assistance to enter a workhouse, which because of their inhuman rules and severe discipline soon became dreaded places.

Works Progress Administration (WPA) A federal agency created in 1935 as part of President Franklin D. Roosevelt's *New Deal program. It was renamed the Works Projects Administration in 1939. Its purpose was to provide employment during the *Depression, and during the years 1935–43 it employed 8.5 million people at a cost of nearly $11 billion. The WPA sponsored a construction program that built roads, buildings, bridges, and airports, and an arts program that employed artists, musicians, sculptors, and writers, as well as the National Youth Administration, which found part-time work for young people. The agency was disbanded in 1943 in the wake of the increased prosperity that accompanied World War II.

World Bank. *See* International Bank for Reconstruction and Development.

World Council of Churches An organization of more than 200 Protestant and Orthodox churches. One of the principal results of the *ecumenical movement of the first half of the 20th century, it was founded at Amsterdam in 1948, with headquarters at Geneva. Its membership includes almost all major Christian Churches except the Roman Catholic, which sends observers and cooperates closely with it.

World Cup An international soccer competition first held in 1930 and thereafter every four years, except during World War II. It is organized by the *Fédération internationale de Football association.

World Federation of Trade Unions An international association of national federations of labor unions, founded in 1945. A number of western labor-union federations withdrew in 1949 to establish the *International Confederation of Free Trade Unions.

World Health Organization (WHO) A specialized agency of the *United Nations established in 1948 to facilitate "the attainment by all peoples of the highest possible level of health." WHO supports programs to eradicate diseases (in 1979 WHO was able to report that smallpox had ceased to exist), carries out and finances epidemiological research, trains health workers, strengthens national health services, and has established international health regulations; it also provides aid in emergencies and disasters. Its headquarters are in Geneva.

World Meteorological Organization (WMO) A specialized agency of the *United Nations established in 1951 with the aim of standardizing international meteorological observations and improving the exchange of weather information. Its chief activities are the World Weather Watch program, which coordinates facilities and services provided by member states, and a research and development program that aims to extend knowledge of the natural and human-induced variability of climate. Its headquarters are in Geneva.

WORLD WAR I *The Eastern Front.*

World War I (1914–18) The Great War between the *Allied Powers, including the UK, with countries of the British Empire, France, Russia, Belgium, Japan, Serbia, Italy (from May, 1915), Portugal (from March, 1916), Romania (from August, 1916), the US (from April, 1917), and Greece (from July, 1917) on one side, and the *Central Powers, including

Germany, Austria-Hungary, Turkey (from November, 1914), and Bulgaria (from October, 1915) on the other. Its causes included fear of the German Empire's European and colonial ambitions since its defeat of France in the Franco-Prussian War (1870–71). Tensions among European powers were expressed by the formation of the *Triple Alliance of Germany and Austria-Hungary (1879) and Italy (1882) and of the *Triple Entente between France and Russia (1893) and France and the UK (1904; see Entente Cordiale). Rivalries surfaced in the crises in Morocco in 1905–06 and 1911 and in Bosnia in 1909; the immediate cause of the war lay in the conflict of interests between Russia and Austria-Hungary in the Balkans. On June 28, 1914, the heir to the Austro-Hungarian throne, Archduke Francis Ferdinand, was assassinated at Sarajevo in Bosnia by a Serbian nationalist and on July 28 Austria-Hungary, with German support, declared war on Serbia. On July 29 Russia mobilized its forces in support of Serbia; on August 1 Germany declared war on Russia and on August 3, upon France. Germany's invasion of Belgium brought the UK into the war at midnight on August 4. The main theaters of war were the Western and Eastern Fronts, the Middle East, Italy, and the German colonies in Africa and the Pacific.

Western Front: German strategy at the start of the war was based on the *Schlieffen plan, which envisaged a rapid flanking movement through the Low Countries. The German forces under von Moltke advanced rapidly through Belgium until they were forced by the British Expeditionary Force (BEF) and the French under Joffre, at the first battle of the Marne (Sept 5–9), to retreat across the River Aisne. Germany's effort to reach the Channel was thwarted at the first battle of Ypres (Oct 12–Nov 11) and the combatants settled, on either side of a line from Ostend to Switzerland, to the futile trench warfare for which World War I is notorious. The year 1915 saw a series of inconclusive battles with huge loss of life—at Neuve-

Chapelle (March), again at Ypres (April–May), where the Germans used poison gas for the first time, and at Loos (Sept). On February 21, 1916, the Germans launched a crippling attack on the French at Verdun but on July 1 Haig, who had succeeded Sir John French as commander of the BEF, opened the crucial battle of the Somme, during which *tanks were used (by the British) for the first time and where the Allies lost some 600,000 men and the Germans, about 650,000. In early 1917 the Germans under Ludendorff withdrew behind the *Hindenburg line; in April Haig took Vimy Ridge (with the loss of 132,000 men); but the French campaign in Champagne was disastrous and in mid-May General R. G. Nivelle (1856–1924) was replaced by Pétain. With the US (incensed by German *submarine warfare) now participating, on July 31 Britain launched the third battle of Ypres and by November 6 had taken Passchendaele. In the spring of 1918 Germany thrust a bulge in the Allied line, which Foch was able to wipe out at the second battle of the Marne. Ludendorff was forced back to the Hindenburg line, which in September was broken between Saint Quentin and Cambrai. By October Germany was suing for peace.

Eastern Front: in August, 1914, the Russians advanced into E Prussia but were defeated at *Tannenburg. When late in 1914 Turkey attacked Russia in the Caucasus Mountains, the Allies launched the **Gallipoli campaign**, at first a naval (Feb-March) and then a military operation fought mainly by Australian and New Zealand forces (see ANZAC). It failed to break through the Dardanelles and by January, 1916, the Allies had withdrawn. Germany's offensive on the Eastern Front in the summer of 1915 forced Russia back and after the Central Powers had overcome Poland, most of Lithuania, and Serbia the Allies landed at Salonika; the ensuing **Macedonian campaign** continued without progress until Bulgaria at last capitulated in September, 1918. The failure of the Allies to relieve Russia led to its collapse following the outbreak of the Russian Revolution (March, 1917).

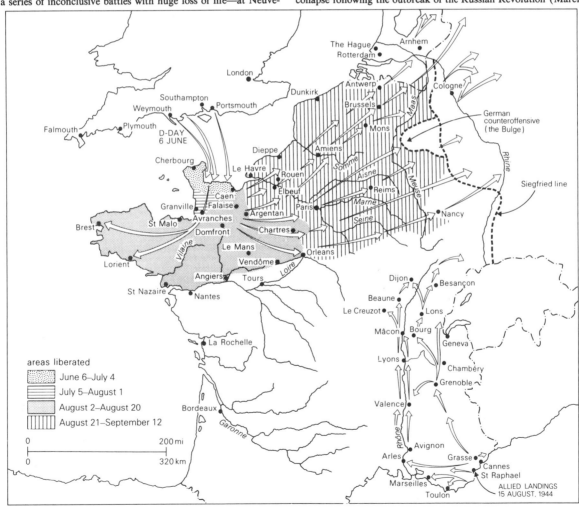

WORLD WAR II   *The development of the Western Front after the Allied D-Day invasion of Normandy.*

Middle East: the **Mesopotamian campaign**, intended to protect oil installations, was launched with the landing of an Indian force at Abadan on November 6, 1914. Early advances were halted when the Allies failed to take Baghdad (November, 1915) and in April, 1916, they lost Kut al-Amara to the Turks. In February, 1917, it was retaken and, in March, Baghdad fell. Meanwhile the Allies had invaded Palestine and, aided by the Arab revolt, Allenby took Jerusalem in December, 1917; his victory at Megiddo (September, 1918) and capture of Damascus and Aleppo finally crushed the Turks.

Italy: the Italian front was maintained along the River Isonzo through 11 battles until 1917, when the Italians were forced by Austria-Hungary to retreat from Caporetto (Oct-Nov) in an overwhelming defeat. In October, 1918, however, Austria-Hungary was defeated at Vittorio-Veneto and in November finally capitulated.

War at sea and in the air: at **sea** the superior British navy was dominant until shaken by the battle of *Jutland in May, 1916. Although defeated off Coronel in November, 1914, victory in December off the Falkland Islands enabled Britain, with Australia, New Zealand, and Japan, to take the German colonies in Africa and the Pacific by September, 1916. The real threat to the Allies at sea came from the German U-boats, which sunk some 6000 ships, including the *Lusitania*, in the course of the war. At their most active in 1917, their effectiveness was reduced following the introduction of the convoy system. World War I was the first war in which **aircraft** were used: in 1915 the German Zeppelins began to attack British cities and in 1917 German aircraft were also introduced. Some air combat took place on the Western and Eastern Fronts and toward the end of the war the Allies were bombing German cities.

Conclusion: with the defeat of the Turks and Bulgarians in September, 1918, and of Germany on the Western Front and Austria-Hungary in Italy in October, revolt broke out in Germany. On November 9 the German emperor, William II, fled and on November 11 Germany signed the armistice. On January 18, 1919, the Allies met at the *Paris Peace Conference to determine the peace settlement, which was signed by Germany (the Treaty of Versailles) on June 28. The Allies lost some 5 million lives (of which 3 million were French and Russian) in the war and the Central Powers, some 3.5 million (of which 3 million were German and Austro-Hungarian). A further 21 million combatants were wounded.

World War II (1939–45) The war between the Allied Powers, including the UK and countries of the Commonwealth, France (until June 1940; thereafter the Free French), the Soviet Union (from June, 1941), the US (from December, 1941), and China (from December, 1941) on one side, and the *Axis Powers, including Germany, Italy (from June, 1940), and Japan (from December, 1941) on the other. The war was caused by the failure of the *Paris Peace Conference to provide for the maintenance of international security after World War I and by the territorial ambitions of Nazi Germany under Adolf Hitler. In March, 1938, Germany annexed Austria (*see* Anschluss) and in September, following the *Munich Agreement, the *Sudetenland. In March, 1939, Hitler occupied the rest of Czechoslovakia and Britain and France guaranteed to support Poland—Hitler's next objective—against German aggression. On May 23 Hitler came to an agreement with Mussolini's Italy, which in April had conquered Albania. Hitler's and Stalin's nonaggression pact followed on August 23 and Britain, France, and Poland made an agreement of mutual assistance on Aug 25. On September 1 Germany invaded Poland and two days later Britain and France declared war.

Western Europe (1939–41): by September 27 Poland had succumbed to the German *Blitzkreig. The Soviet invasion of Finland (*see* Russo-Finnish War) brought Finnish capitulation by March, 1940, and in April Germany invaded Denmark and Norway. The Allied failure in Scandinavia led to Neville Chamberlain's resignation and on May 10, the day that Germany invaded Belgium and the Netherlands, Churchill became Britain's prime minister. The German advance across the Meuse River to the coast outflanked the *Maginot line and separated the main French force from the French First Army, the Belgian army, and the British Expeditionary Force; on May 26 an Allied evacuation from the Continent was ordered. Between May 29 and June 4, some 338,226 Allied troops were rescued from Dunkirk by the British navy and a fleet of small private boats. On June 22 Pétain signed the French armistice with Germany, following which French resistance to the Axis Powers was directed by de Gaulle from London, where he organized the *Free French (*see also* Maquis).

Britain now faced an imminent German invasion. In August and September, 1940, the German *Luftwaffe attacked SE England and then London in a series of daytime raids. In October German bombing was carried out at night and extended to other British cities in the following months. The Luftwaffe failed to cripple the RAF or to terrorize the British people and

by the end of October the so-called battle of Britain had been won by the RAF. The RAF lost 915 aircraft in the conflict and the Luftwaffe some 1733.

Africa and the Middle East (1940–43): in September, 1940, Italy advanced from Libya into Egypt but the Italians were forced to retreat by British troops. By February 6, 1941, the Allies had captured 113,000 Italian soldiers but their success was undermined by the arrival in N Africa of Rommel and the German Afrika Corps. In March the British force was weakened by the dispatch of troops to aid Greece against an imminent German invasion (Yugoslavia and Greece were to fall in April and Crete in May) and Rommel was able to force an Allied retreat to the Egyptian border.

In November the Allies launched an offensive against Rommel but by January, 1942, had again been forced to withdraw, taking up a defensive position at El-Alamein, inside the Egyptian frontier. In the decisive battle of Alamein (Oct 23–Nov 4) Britain's Montgomery defeated Rommel, forcing his retreat along the N African coast. On November 8 an Anglo-US force under Eisenhower landed on the coast of French N Africa. The French under Darlan surrendered and the Allies advanced through Tunisia to make contact (April 7, 1943) with Montgomery's Eighth Army, which was moving N from Alamein. On May 7 the Allies took Bizerte and Tunis and on May 13 the Axis forces surrendered; some 248,000 German and Italian troops were captured.

In **East Africa**, the British had taken Addis Ababa from the Italians in April, 1941, and were in control of Ethiopia, as well as British Somaliland (captured by Italy in August, 1940), by May. In the **Middle East**, in April Britain occupied Iraq, by June Lebanon and Syria were in Allied hands, and in August the Allies gained control of Iran.

Italy (1943–45): on July 10, 1943, the Allies landed in Sicily. On July 25 Mussolini fell and on Sept 3 the Italian armistice was signed and the Allies landed on the Italian mainland. The Germans held back the Allies at the Ortona-Garigliano line until an Allied offensive, launched on May 12, 1944, succeeded in breaking through to Rome (June 4). In the following months the Allied forces made their way northward; Bologna and then Milan were taken in April, 1945, and on May 2, shortly before the final German collapse, Trieste fell.

Eastern Front (1941–45): Germany, with Finland, Hungary, and Romania, invaded the Soviet Union on June 22, 1941. The Axis forces took the Crimea and the Ukraine in the S, besieged Leningrad in the N, and by November were in sight of Moscow. The Soviets staged an effective counterattack in the winter of 1941–42 but Germany retaliated in June with a new offensive and by August the famous battle of *Stalingrad had begun. This heroic Soviet victory resulted in a decimated German Sixth Army and the capture (January, 1943) of its commander Paulus. The Germans launched a new offensive in July but were gradually forced back until expelled from Soviet soil in August, 1944. On August 23 the Soviet Union secured a Romanian armistice and on Sept 19, a Finnish armistice. Also in September Bulgaria declared war on Germany and the Germans evacuated Greece. On October 5 Belgrade fell following collaboration between the Red Army and Tito's Partisans. In October Soviet troops invaded Germany and in January, 1945, launched a final offensive, taking Poland, Austria, and Hungary and entering Czechoslovakia. Berlin fell on May 2, shortly after Hitler's suicide.

Western Front (1944–45): on June 6, 1944, D-Day, the Allied invasion of Normandy began under the supreme command of Eisenhower. Allied bombers had prepared the way with an operation of strategic bombing in place of the relatively ineffective (although destructive of life) bombing of German cities that had reached its peak early in 1944. By July 2 one million US and British troops had landed in Normandy. The British took Caen and US troops, after capturing St Lô (July), invaded Brittany. The Canadians took Falaise on August 17, shortly after US and French troops had landed in the South of France from the Mediterranean. On August 25 Paris fell to the Allies, who now pursued Montgomery's plan for advancing into the Ruhr from Belgium and the Zuider Zee.

At the battle of Arnhem in September airborne troops were dropped to secure bridges but were withdrawn after ground forces were delayed in breaking through the German defense. In December the Germans launched a counteroffensive (the battle of the Bulge), driving a bulge, or salient, into Allied lines in the Ardennes region of S Belgium. US troops forced the Germans to retreat in January, 1945, and the final Allied offensive was launched. The Rhine was crossed, with air support, in March and by April 1 the Ruhr was encircled. On May 4, two days after the fall of Berlin to Soviet troops, German forces surrendered in NW Germany, Holland, and Denmark at Lüneburg Heath. On May 7 the Germans signed a general surrender at Reims, which was ratified two days later in Berlin.

War at sea: The battle for control of the sea routes, known as the **battle of the Atlantic**, was fought from December, 1939, when the German *Graf*

Spee inflicted considerable damage on HMS *Exeter* in the battle of the Río de la Plata in the S Atlantic. In November, 1940, a successful naval air attack was launched on Taranto and in March, 1941, at Cape Matapan the British Mediterranean fleet thwarted an Italian attempt to prevent the transfer of British troops from Egypt to Greece. In May occurred the famous sinking of the *Hood* by the *Bismarck* and, three days later, of the *Bismarck* by the *Dorsetshire*. However, as in World War I, the major threat to Allied naval supremacy in western waters was posed by the German U-boats. These reached their height of effectiveness early in 1943 but by the summer, partly owing to the introduction of Allied escort carriers, 37 U-boats had been sunk and the battle of the Atlantic was over.

Asia (1941–45): the Japanese attack on US military installations at Pearl Harbor, Hawaii, on December 7, 1941, initiated a truly "world" war. The US immediately declared war on Japan and the other Axis powers. On December 10 Germany and Italy declared war on the US and the second *Sino-Japanese War now became part of the wider conflict.

Japan invaded Malaya on December 8 and captured Hong Kong (Dec 25), Manila (January 3, 1942), and Singapore (Feb 15) together with 90,000 British and Commonwealth troops. The Dutch East Indies (Sumatra, Java, and parts of New Guinea) fell on March 10— and the Philippines and Burma in May. The Japanese seemed within reach of India and Australia when the US naval and air victories of the *Coral Sea (May 4–8), *Midway Island (June 4–6), and *Guadalcanal (August) halted Japan's eastward expansion. In October, 1944, the Japanese fleet was decisively defeated at *Leyte Gulf and the Allied conquest of Manila (February, 1945), the Philippines (June), and Borneo (May–June) followed. Burma was reconquered between January and May, 1945. Japanese resistance was finally ended by the atomic bombing on August 6 and 9 respectively of Hiroshima and Nagasaki, and Japan formally surrendered on August 14.

Conclusion: in May, 1945, with the fall of Berlin and the German collapse in Italy and on the Western Front, the war in Europe was over. The postwar settlement was decided upon at the *Potsdam Conference, held near ruined Berlin, in July and August (*see also* Tehran Conference; Yalta Conference).

In the course of the war Germany lost some 3.5 million combatants and 780,000 civilians In contrast the Soviet Union lost 11 million combatants and 7 million civilians; the Japanese 1.3 million and 672,000 respectively; the US, 292,131 and 6000 and the UK 264,443 and 92,673. In addition some 5.7 million Jews died in Nazi *concentration camps; of these 3.2 millions were Poles.

World's Columbia Exposition   (May 5–October 30, 1893) International-al exposition, or world's fair, held in Chicago to celebrate the 400th anniversary of Christopher Columbus' discovery of America. Covering 666 acres (270 hectares) in Jackson Park, on the shores of Lake Michigan, the fair boasted 150 buildings known as the "White City" because of their white plaster facades. Their style influenced American architecture greatly in the following century. Total attendance was 27 million people; the fair cost $31 million and showed a profit of $1.85 million. It was the first exposition to incude a separate "midway," or amusement area.

worm   A soft-bodied elongated invertebrate. The term is applied to members of several different groups, especially *earthworms and various parasitic species, and sometimes the larvae of insects. *See also* annelidworm; beardworm; flatworm; nematode; ribbon worm.

worm lizard.   *See* amphisbaena.

Worms   49 38N 8 23E A city in SW West Germany, in Rhineland-Palatinate on the Rhine River. Heavily bombed during World War II, it has an 11th-century cathedral and a romanesque-gothic synagogue (1034). It is an industrial center and is famed for its local wine, *Liebfraumilch*. *History*: in the 5th century AD it was the capital of the kingdom of Burgundy. Among the imperial diets (assemblies) held here was that of 1521 at which Luther refused to recant. It was annexed by France in 1797 and passed to Hesse-Darmstadt in 1815. Population (1971 est): 76,900.

wormwood   An aromatic herb or shrub of the worldwide genus *Artemisia* (about 200 species), especially *A. absinthium*, which is found chiefly in grasslands of the N hemisphere and is the source of *absinthe. Up to 31 in (80 cm) high, it has deeply divided leaves and small yellow flowers grouped into long loose spikes. Family: *Compositae.

Worthing   50 48N 0 23W A resort in S England, on the West Sussex coast. Nearby on the South Downs is the neolithic site of Cissbury Ring. Population (1981): 91,668.

Wotan.   *See* Odin.

Wouk, Herman   (1915–   ) US novelist. He wrote radio scripts before starting his first novel while in the US Navy during World War II. Among his works are *Aurora Dawn* (1947), *The City Boy* (1948), *The Caine Muti-*

ny (1951), for which he won the Pulitzer Prize, *Marjorie Morningstar* (1955), *Youngblood Hawke* (1962), *The Winds of War* (1971), and *War and Remembrance* (1978). Several of Wouk's works have been adapted as movies or television miniseries.

Wounded Knee   The site in SW South Dakota of the last confrontation (December 29, 1890) between the Indians and US troops. Fearing that the anti-white Ghost Dance cult (the popularity of which was in part a response to the wretchedness of life on reservations) would cause an uprising among the discontented Sioux, troops killed more than 200 men, women, and children at Wounded Knee creek. In 1973 some 200 members of the American Indian Movement occupied the village of Wounded Knee in protest against government Indian policies. After a 69-day siege, in which two Indians were killed, they were forced to surrender.

woundwort   An annual or perennial herb of the widely distributed genus *Stachys* (about 200 species). It has square stems and lance-shaped or heart-shaped toothed leaves. Whorls of two-lipped tubular flowers, yellowish-white, pink, deep-red, or purple, are borne in the leaf axils and the fruit is a small nutlet. Family: *Labiatae.

Wouwerman, Philips   (1619–68) Dutch painter, born in Haarlem. Influenced by the Dutch painter Bamboccio (Pieter van Laer; c. 1592–1642), he specialized in camp and battle scenes, particularly studies of horses. Some of his prolific output is attributed to his brothers **Pieter Wouwerman** (1623–82) and **Jan Wouwerman** (1629–66).

wrack   A large brown *seaweed of the order *Fucales*, found almost worldwide on rocky shores and particularly prominent in colder regions. Leathery straplike branching fronds arise from a circular rootlike anchor (holdfast), often bearing numerous air bladders to aid flotation. Examples are bladderwrack (*Fucus vesiculosus*) and serrated wrack (*F. serratus*).

Wrangel, Ferdinand Petrovich, Baron von   (1794–1870) Russian explorer. He led a Russian naval expedition to the Arctic (1820–24). Both the Wrangell Mountains and Wrangel Island are named for him. As governor of Russian territories in Alaska (1829–35), he opposed its sale to the US.

Wrangel, Peter Nikolaievich, Baron   (1878–1928) Russian general. A divisional commander in World War I, following the Russian Revolution he joined the White armies against the Bolsheviks, distinguishing himself at Tsaritsyn (now Volgograd; 1919). Succeeding *Denikin as commander, he lost Sevastopol and was forced to evacuate his armies from the Crimea (1920).

Wrangel Island   (Russian name: Ostrov Vrangelya)   A Soviet island in the Arctic Ocean, between the East Siberian Sea and the Chukchi Sea. Since 1926 there has been a small Chukchi and Eskimo population. Area: about 2818 sq mi (7300 sq km).

wrasse   A fish of the family *Labridae* (300 species) found near rocks or coral reefs in shallow tropical and temperate seas. It has a slender often brilliantly colored body, 2–79 in (5–200 cm) long, long dorsal and anal fins, and thick lips. They are known for their elaborate courtship and nesting behavior and many species can change their sex and coloring. They feed on marine invertebrates and the external parasites of other fish. Order: *Perciformes. See also* hogfish.

wreckfish   A carnivorous fish, *Polyprion americanus*, also called stone bass, found in Mediterranean and Atlantic offshore waters, often associated with floating wreckage and seaweed. It has a deep heavy body, up to 7 ft (2 m) long, dark brown above and yellowish below, a large head, and a jutting lower jaw. Family: *Serranidae*; order: *Perciformes*.

wren   A small brown bird belonging to a family (*Troglodytidae*; 63 species) found in North and South America. Wrens are 3.5–9 in (9–22 cm) long with sharp slender bills and short cocked tails. The only Eurasian species, *Troglodytes troglodytes*, is about 4 in (10 cm) long and has a reddish-brown plumage with barring on the wings and tail. It lives mainly in undergrowth, feeding on small insects and spiders.

The name is also given to small songbirds of the families *Maluridae* (Australian wrens, e.g. the *emu wren) and *Xenicidae* (New Zealand wrens, e.g. the rifleman).

Wren, Sir Christopher   (1632–1723) English architect and scientist. He was a founder member of Britain's Royal Society and later its president (1680–82). His first architectural designs were for Pembroke College chapel, Cambridge (1663), and the Sheldonian Theater, Oxford (1664). A short trip to Paris (1665–66) led him to adopt his typically baroque style. Within days of the Fire of London in 1666, Wren produced a new plan for the whole city, incorporating spacious avenues and piazzas. The plan was rejected but Wren was commissioned to rebuild 51 city churches and some 36 company halls. Basing many of his designs for the churches on *Vitruvius' Roman basilica, Wren showed enormous ingenuity in fitting his buildings into the old irregular sites. His design for St Paul's Cathedral was accepted, after many modifications, in 1675. His later buildings include the Greenwich Hospital (begun in 1694) and additions to Hampton Court (1698).

Wren, P(ercival) C(hristopher) (1885–1941) British novelist. He spent his early life wandering the world, working mostly as a soldier. The best known of his many popular adventure novels are those concerning the French Foreign Legion, especially *Beau Geste* (1924).

wren babbler An insect-eating bird belonging to one of several genera of the family *Timaliidae* (*see* babbler), occurring chiefly in S Asia. 4–6 in (10–15 cm) long, wren babblers have a shortish upturned tail and short straight bill. They usually live on the ground, feeding in small flocks beneath bushes and forest undergrowth.

wrestling A form of unarmed combat, one of the most ancient sports, in which two people attempt to throw and hold each other down. It first became an Olympic sport in 704 BC. Modern wrestling became an organized sport in the 18th century. There are two main international styles. **Graeco-Roman wrestling** is the most popular style on the European continent; holds on the body below the waist and the use of legs to hold or trip are not allowed. They are, however, allowed in **freestyle wrestling** (which developed from the Anglo-American **catch-as-catch-can** form). In both styles a wrestler wins a match by securing a fall (throwing his opponent onto his back and pinning both shoulders to the mat for one second) or by accumulating the most points according to a complex scoring system. If neither wrestler achieves a fall or is disqualified the bout lasts for three three-minute rounds. There are ten weight categories. **Sambo wrestling** is the third recognized international style, originating from styles found in the Soviet Union. **Sumo** is the highly popular Japanese style in which the wrestlers, usually weighing around 285 lb (130 kg), attempt to force each other out of the ring. The international governing body is the Fédération internationale des Luttes amateurs. *See also* judo.

Wright, Frank Lloyd (1869–1959) US architect of international fame, whose style was among the most individual of the modern movement. A pupil of Louis *Sullivan from 1888 to 1893, he first demonstrated his originality in a series of Chicago houses between 1900 and 1909, the most famous being the Robie house (1909). These long low spacious designs have proved very influential. Later buildings include Falling Water in Bear Run, Pa. (1936), the Johnson Wax factory at Racine, Wisconsin (1936–39), Taliesin West (1938), his winter home in the Arizona desert, where he established an architectural community, and the Guggenheim Museum (1959). □architecture.

Wright, Orville (1871–1948) US aviator, who with his brother **Wilbur Wright** (1867–1912) made the first powered and controlled flights on December 17, 1903. They took place near Kitty Hawk, North Carolina, and in the second, lasting about a minute, the aircraft covered a distance of 820 ft (250 meters). The flight failed to interest either the US public or the government but the brothers continued to make improvements to their machine, eventually succeeding in staying airborne for an hour. In 1908 Wilbur Wright shipped the aircraft to France, where it was enthusiastically received, and in 1909 Orville secured a US army contract. □aircraft.

Wright, Richard (1908–60) US novelist and critic. He was born into a poor family. His works include *Native Son* (1940), a seminal novel of social protest, the autobiographical *Black Boy* (1945) and its sequel *American Hunger* (1977), *The Outsider* (1953), *Black Power* (1954), and *White Man, Listen!* (1957). From 1946 he lived in Paris.

writing systems The recording of human communication using signs or symbols to represent spoken words or concepts. The earliest known writing systems were all originally *pictographic; if they survived at all they developed into *ideographic systems (*see also* Chinese). True alphabetic writing developed around the E Mediterranean about 2000 BC (*see* Semitic alphabets). An intermediate stage is the use of *syllabaries.

Wrocław (German name: Breslau) 51 05N 17 00E A city in SW Poland, on the Oder River. Founded during the 10th century, it developed as an important center on the amber trade route between the Roman Empire and the Baltic Sea. During World War II it suffered severe damage under siege from the Soviet armies (1945). Old buildings that have been reconstructed include the 13th-century cathedral. Its university was founded in 1945. It is now an important industrial and communications center; industries include electronics, engineering, and food processing. Population (1979): 608,000.

wrought iron An almost pure form of iron, often with less than 0.1% carbon. It was originally produced by a laborious process of repeatedly hammering and folding hot *pig iron to squeeze out the impurities. The *puddling process has now superseded hand working.

wrybill A New Zealand *plover, *Anarhynchus frontalis*. 6 in (15 cm) long, it has a gray plumage with white underparts and a black breast band. The bill, which is curved to the right, is used to probe for insects under stones and in muddy shallow water.

wryneck A small *woodpecker belonging to a subfamily (*Jynginae*; 2 species) occurring in Eurasia. 6 in (16 cm) long, wrynecks have a gray-brown mottled plumage and a small bill. They do not drill holes but feed mostly on ants and pupae and nest in empty holes.

Wuchow. *See* Wuzhou.

Wuhan 30 35N 114 19E A port in E central China, the capital of Hubei province at the confluence of the Yangtze and Han Rivers. Formed by the amalgamation (1950) of the ancient cities of Hankou (or Hankow), Hanyang, and Wuchang, it is the commercial and industrial center of central China. The university was established in 1913. It was a center of both the Taiping Rebellion (1851–64) and 1911 revolution. Its chief industry is iron and steel. Population (1957 est): 2,146,000.

Wu Hou (625–705 AD) A Chinese empress of the Tang dynasty. Following the death of her husband, the emperor, she ruled through two puppet emperors until 690 when she seized the throne and the imperial title. Although a capable ruler, she was forced to relinquish the throne shortly before her death.

Wu-hsi. *See* Wuxi.

Wu-hsing. *See* Wuxing.

Wundt, Wilhelm (1832–1920) German physiologist and pioneer of modern experimental psychology. His *Principles of Physiological Psychology* (2 vols, 1873–74) was one of the first scientific approaches to the study of the conscious mind. Wundt also wrote works on human physiology and perception.

Wuppertal 51 05N 7 10E A city in NW West Germany, in North Rhine-Westphalia in the *Ruhr. It was formed in 1929 from six towns, including Elberfeld, and was heavily bombed in World War II. It is a textile-producing center. Population (1980 est): 393,800.

Württemberg A former kingdom in W Europe. It became a duchy in 1495 and a kingdom in 1806. Divided into two West German *Länder* following World War II, these became part of the *Land* of *Baden-Württemberg (1952).

Würzburg 49 48N 9 57E A city in S West Germany, in Bavaria on the Main River. The former episcopal residence (1720–44), containing frescoes by Tiepolo, was damaged in the bombing of World War II but later restored, as was the cathedral (1034). Roentgen taught at the university (founded 1582). A wine-producing center, its manufactures include machine tools and chemicals. Population (1980 est): 127,900.

Wuxi (*or* Wu-hsi) 31 35N 120 19E A city in E China, in Jiangsu province on the *Grand Canal. A major grain market since the 7th century AD, it is also an industrial center. Population (1957 est): 613,000.

Wuzhou (Wu-chou *or* Wuchow) 23 30N 111 21E A city in S China, in Guangxi Zhuang AR. An old garrison town, it is now a commercial center. Industries include silk textiles, chemicals, and engineering. Population (1953): 110,800.

Wyatt, Sir Thomas (1503–42) English poet. A member of the court of Henry VIII, he served on various foreign diplomatic missions. He was one of those responsible for introducing Italian verse forms and meters, notably the Petrarchan sonnet, into English poetry. 96 of his poems, were included in the influential collection known as *Tottel's Miscellany* (1557).

Wycliffe, John (c. 1329–84) English religious reformer. Wycliffe spent most of his life at Oxford, first as a student and then as lecturer in philosophy. Although initially protected by friends at court, he made increasingly radical criticisms of the Church, resulting in his enforced retirement to Lutterworth and his condemnation as a heretic. He attacked the doctrine of transubstantiation and emphasized the importance of the Bible, of which he supervised the first English translation from the Latin. Wycliffe's adherents, the *Lollards, were forerunners of English Protestantism.

Wye River A river in E Wales and W England. Flowing mainly SE from Plynlimmon through Builth Wells and Monmouth, it joins the Severn River near Chepstow. It is noted for its beautiful scenery and has valuable salmon fisheries. Length: 130 mi (210 km).

Wyeth, Andrew (Newell) (1917–) US painter; the son and pupil of artist/illustrator N(ewell) C(onvers) Wyeth (1882–1945). One of the best-known 20th century American artists, his most famous work is *Christina's World* (1948). Wyeth's realistic style is spare and somber, as he uses watercolor and tempera to record scenes of everyday life in rural America with meticulous detail. His son **Andrew Wyeth** (1946–) is a well-known painter with many of the artistic characteristics of his father.

Wylie, Philip Gordon (1902–71) US author. His works include *Heavy Laden* (1928) and *Opus 21* (1949), as well as some science fiction and the essays *A Generation of Vipers* (1942) and *Essay on Morals* (1947). He combined an interest in Jungian psychology with a critical view of such aspects of American society as women's influence over men ("momism"), religion, attitudes toward sex, conservation, and ecology.

Wyoming One of the mountain states in the NW US, bordered by Idaho (W), Montana (N), South Dakota and Nebraska (E), and Colorado and Utah (S and SW). The topography is one of forested mountains (the state is crossed diagonally from the NW by the Rocky Mountains) and grassy plains. Its economy is based on natural resources, especially oil; other important minerals are natural gas, uranium, coal, trona, bentonite clay, and iron ore. Livestock, principally cattle, production dominates farming. There is very little manufacturing; the main activities are oil refining, food processing, printing and publishing. Tourism is significant with visitors attracted by the superb scenery of Grand Teton and Yellowstone national parks. *History*: part of the territory acquired from France by the Louisiana Purchase (1803), the area became a major crossing in the expansion westward; the arrival of the Union Pacific Railroad (1867–69) brought settlement in the S and the area became a state in 1890. Agrarian development has been encouraged by liberal legislation and progressive conservation policies. Area: 97,914 sq mi (253,596 sq km). Population (1980): 470,816. Capital: Cheyenne.

Wyss, Johann Rudolph (1782–1830) Swiss writer. A professor of philosophy, he collected and published Swiss folk tales and folklore. He also completed his father's manuscript of the successful novel *The Swiss Family Robinson* (1812–27) and wrote the Swiss national anthem.

Wyszyński, Stefan, Cardinal (1901–81) Polish Roman Catholic churchman. Ordained in 1924, he became Bishop of Lublin in 1946, and Archbishop of Gniezno and Warsaw and Primate of Poland in 1949. He was imprisoned in 1953 for condemning communist opposition to the Church. On release (1956) he enjoyed considerable pastoral liberty, serving as president of the Second Vatican Council in 1962.

X

Xanthus A city of ancient Lycia in Asia Minor famous for its heroic resistance to the Persians about 540 BC and to Brutus' Roman forces in about 43 BC.

Xenakis, Yannis (1922–) Greek composer, who studied engineering and architecture before turning to music. He developed a method of composition based on mathematical studies of probability. His compositions include *Duel* (for 54 instruments and 2 conductors; 1959).

xenon (Xe) A noble gas, present in the atmosphere and discovered in 1898 by Sir William Ramsay and M. W. Travers (1872–1961), in the residue of distilled liquid air. The first noble gas compounds were discovered by N. Bartlett (1932–), by reacting xenon with dioxygenyl platinum hexafluoride ($O+_2PtF^{-6}$) to form $Xe+PtF^{-6}$, which is a white solid. Several compounds are now known. Xenon is used in special lamps and the radioactive isotope ^{133}Xe is produced in nuclear reactors. It is a "poison," i.e. a neutron absorber, and is a crucial factor in the control of the chain reaction (*see* nuclear energy), building up to a constant level during steady operation and decaying with a half-life of a few days on shutdown. At no 54; at wt 131.3; mp –170°F (–111.9°C); bp –161°F (–107°C).

Xenophanes (6th century BC) Greek poet. Born in Ionia, he traveled extensively in the Mediterranean countries and lived mostly in Sicily and S Italy. Only a few fragments survive of a philosophical poem on nature and of some elegies. He was a monotheist, rejecting Homeric mythology and traditional Greek religious beliefs.

Xenophon (c. 430–c. 354 BC) Greek historian and soldier. He was born in Athens and, although he had little talent for philosophy, made the acquaintance of Socrates and became his devoted disciple. In 410 he joined a group of Greek mercenaries serving under the Persian prince Cyrus, who was leading an expedition against his brother, Artaxerxes II, King of Persia. Cyrus was killed in battle, the Asiatic army fled, and the force of 10,000 Greeks was left isolated. Xenophon as commander successfully led the mercenaries in a heroic retreat through the hostile Persian Empire to the Black Sea, a feat that formed the subject of his best-known work, the *Anabasis*. He later served in the Spartan army under King Aegesilaus. He wrote numerous other works, including *Memorabilia*, *Apology*, and *Symposium*, which deal with Socrates.

Xenopus. *See* clawed frog.

Xerography. *See* photocopying machine.

xerophyte A plant that lives in a hot dry climate, such as a desert, and is adapted for conserving water. Cacti, for example, often have spiny leaves (to prevent water loss) and green succulent stems (in which water is stored). A **xeromorph** is a plant that shows some of the features of xerophytes but may not live in desert areas.

Xerxes I (d. 465 BC) King of Persia (486–465). Having brutally repressed revolts in Egypt, he invaded Greece (*see* Greek-Persian Wars) with huge forces (480), at first successfully. However, defeat at *Salamis (480), *Plataea and Mycale (479), and the consequent revolt of the Asiatic Greeks forced him to withdraw. This tyrannous ruler and compulsive builder was assassinated in a court intrigue.

Xhosa A Bantu people of the *Transkei (South Africa). They are primarily cultivators, with some cattle. Today many Xhosa are migrant laborers in other areas of South Africa. Their language employs click sounds borrowed from the *Khoisan languages.

Xia Gui (*or* Hsia Knei; c. 1180–c. 1230) Chinese landscape painter, who worked for the Song emperors. His lyrical and mystical interpretations of landscape, in which human figures are dwarfed by mist-swathed mountains and dramatically poised trees, influenced later Chinese and Japanese artists.

Xiamen (Hsia-men *or* Amoy) 24 26N 118 07E A city in SE China on the island of Xiamen, in Fujian province, situated on Taiwan Strait. It is linked to the mainland by a causeway. The university was established in 1921. Industries include shipbuilding, engineering, fishing, and food processing. *History*: Xiamen has traded intermittently with Europeans since 1544. After its capture by the British during the Opium War (1841) it became a major tea-exporting port, through which many Chinese emigrants passed. Population (1953): 224,300.

Xi An (Hsi-an *or* Sian) 34 16N 108 54E A city in central China, the capital of Shenxi province on the Wei Ho (River). It contains many Tang pagodas and a noted museum. An important industrial center, its industries include steel, chemicals, textiles, and electronics. *History*: as a Tang capital (618–906 AD) it attracted many Buddhist, Muslim, and Christian missionaries. After 1935 it was a Guomindang (Nationalist) base (*see* Xi An incident). Population (1957 est): 1,310,000.

Xiangtan (*or* Hsiang-t'an) 27 55N 112 47E A port in SE China, in Hunan province on the Xiang Jiang (River; *or* Hsiang Chiang). The commercial center of an agricultural area, its products include textiles, iron and steel, and pig bristles. Population (1953): 183,600.

Xi An incident (1936) The kidnapping of Chiang Kai-shek by his mutinous army in Manchuria. Chiang was captured by two young marshals, who demanded an end to fighting between Chinese Nationalists (Guomindang) and communists in the face of the Japanese invasion. Chiang was released when the communists announced that they would cooperate with the Guomindang in opposing Japan (*see* United Fronts).

Xi Jiang (*or* Hsi Chiang) The most important river in S China, rising in Yunnan province and flowing E to form the densely populated Canton delta and the *Zhu Jiang. Most of its length is navigable by large ships. Length: about 1200 mi (1900 km).

Xingu River A river in central Brazil, rising on the Mato Grosso plateau and flowing generally N to enter the Amazon delta. Length: 1200 mi (1932 km).

Xining (*or* Hsi-ning) 36 35N 101 55E A city in N central China, the capital of Qinghai province. Formerly on the W Chinese border, it was strategically important. Industries include chemicals, metals, wool, and leather. Population (1957 est): 300,000.

Xinjiang Uygur Autonomous Region (*or* Sinkiang Uigur AR) An administrative region in NW China, the largest, covering one sixth of the country. It borders on the Soviet Union, Mongolia, Kashmir, and Tibet. Very dry with extreme temperatures, it consists of mountains in the center with the Junggar Pendi in the N and the mainly desert Tarim Basin in the S. The Muslim Uigurs and the Chinese are the largest ethnic groups. Nomads in the N herd livestock, and wheat, cotton, and fruit are grown in oases and valleys. Oil and minerals are produced. *History*: from 206 BC to 1756 AD, Chinese rule alternated with rule by Uigurs, Tibetans, and Mongols, and rebellions against Chinese government continued until 1949. It has recently been greatly developed by the central government. The scene of border clashes with the Soviet Union in 1969, it has great strategic importance. Area: 635,829 sq mi (1,646,799 sq km). Population (1980 est): 12,560,000. Capital: Ürümqi.

Xiong Nu (*or* Hsiung-nu) Turkish and Mongol tribes on the N and NW borders of China, which threatened Chinese security from about 500 BC. They depended on herding animals for their livelihood and, skilled horseback warriors, conducted raids in times of hardship to plunder the settled Chinese farming communities. The Chinese attempted to control the Xiong Nu by building the frontier walls that eventually became the Great Wall of China, marrying their daughters to Xiong Nu leaders, and trading with them.

Xochimilco 19 08N 99 09W A town in central Mexico, on Lake Xochimilco. It is famous for its chinamoas (floating gardens), which originated as soil covered rafts on which fruit and vegetables were grown and have since become islands.

X-ray diffraction The *diffraction of *X-rays when they strike a crystal. The angle through which the X-rays are diffracted depends on the spacing between the different planes in the crystal in a manner given by *Bragg's law. The technique is used in studying crystal structure.

X-rays Electromagnetic radiation lying between ultraviolet radiation and gamma rays in the *electromagnetic spectrum. X-rays may have wavelengths between 10^{-9} meter and 10^{-11} meter, the shorter wavelengths being known as hard X-rays and the longer wavelengths as soft X-rays. Discovered by Wilhelm *Roentgen (and formerly called Roentgen rays) in 1895, they are produced when heavy metal atoms (usually tungsten) are struck by sufficiently energetic electrons, as in an **X-ray tube**. The electrons in an X-ray tube are produced by a heated cathode in an evacuated tube and accelerated to the heavy-metal anode by an electric field. The collisions knock inner electrons from the atoms, X-rays being emitted when the vacancy is filled by outer electrons. X-rays cause ionization in gases and penetrate matter. X-rays have many uses including the examination of internal organs and structures in medical diagnosis, the killing of cancer cells in *radiotherapy, investigating structures for flaws, and in *X-ray diffraction by crystals in order to study their structure.

Xuan Cang (*or* Hsuan-tsang; 602–64 AD) Chinese Buddhist monk. He traveled alone to India and after studying there for about 10 years returned with Buddhist texts, 75 of which he translated. He also left a record of his travels, of great historical value.

xylem A plant tissue specialized for the transport of water and salts. The main cells are tubelike, with their walls strengthened by deposits of *lignin in a spinal arrangement, which aids upward movement of materials by capillary action. In trees and shrubs the lignin deposits eventually block the tubes completely: this tissue forms *wood, and new secondary xylem is produced to transport water.

xylene (*or* dimethyl benzene; $C_6H_4(CH_3)_2$) A colorless toxic flammable liquid consisting of a mixture of three isomers. It is obtained by fractional distillation of petroleum and is used as an aviation fuel and as a solvent.

xylophone A pitched percussion instrument, consisting of a frame on which wooden bars in the pattern of a keyboard are fixed, each with a tubular metal resonator beneath it. It is played with two sticks. Orchestral xylophones usually have a compass of three octaves. *See also* vibraphone.

XYZ Affair (c. 1796–1800) A controversy between the US and France. France expressed its dissatisfaction with the US-British accord of 1794 (Jay's Treaty) by interfering with American shipping. President *Washington's emissary, Charles Pinckney, was insulted by the French in 1796 but returned to France the next year, together with John Marshall and Eldridge Gerry, at President John *Adams' request. After many delays by French officials, the Americans were approached by three unofficial agents (the so-called X, Y, and Z of President Adams' later report to Congress), who volunteered to arrange negotiations in return for a bribe of $250,000 to French foreign minister Talleyrand, loans, and other US concessions. The Americans refused, the proceedings were made public, and outraged Americans threatened war. However, Adams appointed another three-man commission, which arranged the Treaty of Mortefontaine (Convention of 1800) with France.

Y

Yahweh The conjectural pronunciation of one of the Hebrew names of God. The name YHWH (the Tetragrammaton or "four-letter" name) occurs very frequently in the Bible; out of reverence it was traditionally not pronounced, but replaced by *Adonai* (Lord) or *Hashem* (the Name), except by the *high priest when he entered the *Holy of Holies. "Jehovah" represents another attempt to pronounce this name.

yak A shaggy-coated wild ox, *Bos grunniens*, inhabiting mountain pastures of central Asia. Yaks have long been domesticated for draft purposes and milk; their dung is used as fuel. Wild yaks, up to 7 ft (2 m) high at the shoulder with long upward-curving horns, are larger than domestic yaks and are always black; they live in large herds, feeding on coarse grasses, and are expert climbers.

Yakut Autonomous Soviet Socialist Republic (*or* Yakutia) An administrative division in the E Soviet Union, in the RSFSR. The Yakuts, a Mongoloid people, are traditionally nomadic herdsmen but have become sedentary. In NE Siberia, Yakutia (an autonomous republic since 1922) is one of the world's coldest inhabited regions, and agriculture is only possible in the S. Mining for diamonds, gold, tin, and coal is the main occupation, and trapping and breeding of sable, squirrel, and silver fox are also important. Area: 1,197,760 sq mi (3,103,000 sq km). Population (1981 est): 883,000. Capital: Yakutsk.

Yale University One of the oldest universities in the US (founded 1701), situated at New Haven, Connecticut. It is named for Elihu Yale (1648–1721), who donated his books to the college.

Yalow, Rosalyn S(ussman) (1921–) US medical physicist who won the Nobel Prize in medicine (1977). Her research with Dr Solomon A. Berson led to their development of the radioimmunoassay (RIA) test, which measures minute concentrations of biologically active substances (such as hormones, enzymes, and proteins) in the blood or other body fluids.

Yalta 44 30N 34 09E A port in the Soviet Union, in the S Ukrainian SSR on the Black Sea. It is the Crimea's largest seaside resort and was the site of the Allied *Yalta Conference in 1945. Population (1970): 62,170.

Yalta Conference (1945) The conference toward the end of World War II attended by Franklin D. Roosevelt (US), Stalin (Soviet Union), and Churchill (UK). They agreed upon the postwar occupation of Germany by the US, Soviet Union, UK, and France and decided that German surrender must be unconditional.

yam A twining herbaceous plant of the genus *Dioscorea*, cultivated in wet tropical regions for its tubers, which are eaten like potatoes. Yams have long slender climbing stems, bearing entire or lobed leaves, and unisexual flowers in long clusters. Tubers can reach a length of 8.5 ft (2.6 m) and a weight of 100 lb (45 kg); species commonly cultivated are *D. alata* (white yam), *D. rotundata* (white guinea yam), *D. batatas* (Chinese yam), and *D. cayenensis* (yellow yam). Family: *Dioscoreaceae*.

Yamagata Aritomo (1838–1922) Japanese soldier and statesman. As commander of the Imperial Guard, he created a modern conscript army and while home minister (1885–89) he shaped Japan's modern local government. He twice served as prime minister (1890–91, 1898–1900) and played an important role in Japan's victories over China (1894–95) and Russia (1904–05).

Yamani, Ahmed Zaki, Sheik (1930–) Saudi Arabian politician. As minister of petroleum and mineral resources (1962–), Yamani exerts worldwide economic influence.

Yamasee War (1715–16) A war between British settlers and the Yamasee Indians living in South Carolina and Georgia. The Yamasee were driven southward and eventually absorbed by the Seminoles of Florida.

Yamato The ruling dynasty of Japan under which the country was united in the 4th century AD. All subsequent Japanese emperors have claimed descent from the Yamato, under whom Buddhism was introduced in the 6th century.

Yang, Chen Ning (1922–) US physicist, born in China, who shared the 1957 Nobel Prize with his countryman Tsung-Dao *Lee for their theoretical work suggesting that parity would not be conserved in the *weak interaction. Their hypothesis was quickly confirmed by observations of beta decay.

Yangtze River (Chinese name: Chang Jiang *or* Ch'ang Chiang) The longest river in China and the third longest in the world. Rising in a remote mountain range on the borders of Tibet and Qinghai province, it flows roughly E to enter the East China Sea via an extensive delta. A Chinese survey (late 1970s), which finally established the true source of the river, estimated its total power potential to be 230,000 MW (greater than that of all the rivers in the US). The Yangtze is one of China's main transport routes and its densely populated basin is China's most productive agricultural region. Length: 3964 mi (6380 km).

SHEIK YAMANI

Yantai (Yentai *or* Chefoo) 37 30N 121 22E A port in E China, on the Shandong Peninsula. Following the Chefoo Convention, signed in 1876 by Britain and China, many foreign traders lived here. The chief industries are fishing and food processing. Population (1953): 116,000.

Yaoundé (*or* Yaunde) 3 51N 11 31E The capital of Cameroon. Founded under the German protectorate of Kamerun in 1888, it was capital of Cameroun from 1922 until independence in 1960 (except during World War II). The Federal University of Cameroon was founded in 1962. Population (1976): 313,706.

yard A basic unit of length in the English system originally defined as the distance between two gold plugs on a bronze bar. In 1959 this definition was replaced, and the yard is now defined as exactly 0.9144 meter (*see* metric system).

Yarkand. *See* Shache.

Yaroslavl 57 34N 39 52E A city in the Soviet Union, in the W RSFSR on the Volga River. It has been a textile center since the 18th century. Population (1981 est): 608,000.

yarrow A perennial herb, *Achillea millefolium*, also called milfoil, native to pastures of Europe and W Asia. Up to 18 in (45 cm) high, it has feathery strongly scented leaves and small white daisy-like flowers borne in flat-topped clusters. Family: *Compositae*.

Yawata. *See* Kitakyushu.

yawl A □sailing vessel with two masts, a tall one set approximately one third of the boat's length from the bows and a very short one just behind the rudder post. Yawls, like ketches, are a favored rig for yachts, for the split rig reduces the area of each sail, making handling easier. Yawls do not sail as well toward the wind as sloops do. *See also* ketch; sloop.

yaws A chronic tropical disease caused by a *spirochete bacterium, *Treponema pertenue*. It occurs mostly among poor children and is spread by skin contact. After an incubation period of three to four weeks a growth appears on the thighs or buttocks; later, multiple growths that look like squashed raspberries appear all over the skin. Bones may also be affected and if not treated the disease can be very disfiguring. Treatment with penicillin is highly effective.

Yazd (*or* Yezd) 31 55N 54 22E A city in central Iran. It has several mosques, some built in the 11th century, and produces silk fabrics. Population (1976): 135,978.

year The time taken by the earth to complete one revolution around the sun. This is equal to the period of the sun's apparent motion around the *ecliptic. The **tropical year**, of 365.2422 days, is the interval between two successive passages of the sun through the vernal *equinox. The **sidereal year**, of 365.2564 days, refers to successive passages of the sun through a point relative to the background stars. These periods differ because of the *precession of the equinoxes. *See also* calendar.

yeast A single-celled fungus that is capable of fermenting carbohydrates and that reproduces asexually by budding new cells from its surface. Typical yeasts belong to the family *Saccharomycetaceae*. Strains of *Saccharomyces cerevisiae*, the cells of which are 0.0001–0.0078 in (0.004–0.02 mm) in diameter, are widely used to cause *fermentation in baking, brewing, and the manufacture of wines and spirits. Yeast extracts are used as a food for their high vitamin B content. Class: *Ascomycetes*.

W. B. YEATS

Yeats, William Butler (1865–1939) Irish poet and dramatist. In London in the 1890s he helped found the Rhymers' Club, pursued his lifelong interest in the occult, and published several volumes of symbolist verse. His best-known poems, many of which appeared in *The Tower* (1928) and *The Winding Stair* (1929), included tragic meditations on personal and political themes. Among them are "Easter, 1916," "The Second Coming," and "Sailing to Byzantium." He was an admirer of Maud Gonne (1866–1953), Irish actress and nationalist, and with Lady *Gregory in 1904 he founded the Abbey Theatre, Dublin, for which he wrote many plays. He was a senator of the Irish Free State (1922–28) and won the Nobel Prize in 1923. His brother **Jack Butler Yeats** (1831–1957) was a noted Irish painter, born in London. After a childhood in Ireland he returned to London to study, but his paintings were essentially Irish, depicting life in bars, music halls, and racetracks in dark colors, often shot with bright explosions of color applied with a palette knife.

Yellow-Dog Contract A contract between employer and employee, usually as a condition of employment, in which the employee agrees not to join a union or assist a union by joining in a strike. The name was applied by labor unionists who claimed only a "yellow dog," or coward, would allow such coercion. The contracts were declared unenforceable in 1932 by the Norris-LaGuardia Act.

yellow fever An acute viral infection transmitted by female mosquitoes of the genus *Aëdes*, which occur in areas of tropical rain forest. After an incubation period of 3–14 days the patient develops a fever with aching muscles. In severe cases the virus affects the liver causing jaundice (hence the name), the kidneys, and the heart; death may result from liver or heart failure. There is no specific treatment but two kinds of vaccine are available for prevention.

yellowfin tuna A large tuna fish, *Thunnus albacares*, distinguished by yellow fins and a golden stripe along its sides. It is found worldwide and is a valued food and game fish.

yellow-green algae *Algae of the division *Chrysophyta* (about 6000 species), which are yellow-green to brown in color depending on the proportion of green chlorophyll masked by the pigments fucoxanthin or diadinoxanthin. Most are unicellular or colonial and they form a major constituent of plankton (*see also* diatoms). Most reproduce asexually by spores.

yellowhammer A Eurasian *bunting, *Emberiza citrinella*, that occurs on farmland and roadsides, where it feeds on grain and seeds. It is about 6 in (16 cm) long and has a distinctive yellow plumage. The male has a bright-yellow head and underparts, chestnut rump, and a brown-streaked back; females are less colorful.

Yellowknife 62 30N 114 29W A city in N Canada, the capital of the Northwest Territories. Founded in 1935, it is the commercial and administrative center of the territory, with an airport and gold mines. Population (1981): 9483.

Yellow River (Chinese name: Huang He *or* Huang Ho) A river in China, rising in the W and flowing roughly E to enter the Gulf of Chihli via a fertile delta. Its summer floods have resulted in frequent disasters and changes of course. Its diversion as a measure against the Japanese invasion (1938) resulted in the death of 900,000 people. Length: about 2700 mi (4350 km).

Yellow Sea (Chinese name: Huang Hai) A large shallow inlet of the W Pacific Ocean, bordered by China and Korea. It is so called because of the yellowish silt deposited by the Chinese rivers. It is rich in fish.

Yellowstone National Park The largest US national park, chiefly in NW Wyoming but extending into S Montana and E Idaho. Established in 1872, it consists mainly of forested volcanic plateaus. Its many active geysers include Old Faithful, which erupts regularly at approximately hourly intervals. Area: 3458 sq mi (8956 sq km).

Yellowstone River A river, rising in NW Wyoming and flowing N through the *Yellowstone National Park then E to join the Missouri River in North Dakota. Length: 671 mi (1080 km).

yellowwood An evergreen coniferous tree or shrub of the genus *Podocarpus* (over 100 species), mostly of warm temperate and tropical regions of the S hemisphere. The hard leathery leaves are strap-shaped and the green berry-like fruits are borne on fleshy stalks. Yellowwoods are important timber trees; the light elastic nonresinous wood is used for building, furniture, carving, and ships. A few species are grown in the S US; others are popular as houseplants. Family: *Podocarpaceae*.

Yemen, People's Democratic Republic of (*or* South Yemen; name until 1970: People's Republic of Southern Yemen) A country in the Middle East, in S *Arabia bordering on the Gulf of Aden and the Arabian Sea. It includes the islands of Kamaran in the Red Sea, *Perim Island, *Socotra, and the *Kuria Maria Islands. Mountains dissected by wadis—chiefly Wadi Hadhramaut—rise from the narrow coastal plain; the N and E are desert. The mainly Arab population is largely Sunnite Muslim. There are nomadic tribes in the N. *Economy*: mainly agricultural, although little land is cultivated. Cotton is the main crop, others include cereals, coffee, tobacco, fruit, and vegetables. Sardine fishing is important; mineral deposits are not yet exploited. Industry consists chiefly of an oil refinery and a little light industry in Aden. The economy suffered badly from the closure of the Suez Canal (1967–75). Refined oil, cotton, fish products, hides, and incense are exported and food, textiles, and crude oil are imported. Aid is received mainly from China and the Soviet Union. *History*: ruled by the imams (priest-kings) of Yemen, the area (excluding Aden) was nominally part of the Ottoman Empire from the 16th century to 1918. Aden was captured from the Turks in 1839 and occupied by the British East India Company. The British made protectorate treaties with other local rulers (1886–1914) to safeguard Aden and its trade routes; these 24 sultanates, emirates, and sheikdoms were called the Aden Protectorate (1937). In 1963 Aden and ten others formed the Federation of South Arabia. This collapsed in 1967, when anti-British nationalist groups in Aden took control (although the British had already agreed to withdraw), and South Yemen then became independent. Its history has been marked chiefly by border disputes with Oman (until 1976) and with North Yemen, despite an agreement to unite North and South Yemen (1972). In 1983 diplomatic progress toward unification advanced. Yemen established diplomatic relations with Oman for the first time in a decade. Relations with the UK and Saudi Arabia also improved. Head of state: President Ali Nasser Mohammed. Official currency: South Yemen dinar of 1000 fils. Official language: Arabic. Area: about 130,066 sq mi (336,870 sq km). Population (1983 est): 2,086,000. Capital: Aden.

Yemen Arab Republic (or North Yemen) A country in the Middle East in SW *Arabia, bordering on the Red Sea. It consists of a narrow dry W coastal plain, central mountains (the wettest and most fertile in Arabia), and E desert. There are no rivers but many wadis, oases, and springs. The Arab population is Muslim, either Sunnite or Zaidi, the Jews having emigrated after 1918. *Economy*: mainly agricultural; cotton, coffee, cereals, vegetables, fruit, and the narcotic qat are the chief crops and livestock are kept. Industry includes textile, soft-drink, and cigarette factories; salt is mined and handicrafts are important. Machinery, oil, and textiles are imported. North Yemen receives money from Yemeni workers abroad (over one sixth of the population works in Saudi Arabia) and relies on foreign aid (chiefly from the US, the World Bank, and other Arab countries). *History*: rule by a Muslim imam (priest-king) originated in the 9th century and lasted until 1962, although from 1520 until 1918 the area was nominally part of the Ottoman Empire. North Yemen's boundaries were fixed in 1934 by treaty with Saudi Arabia and the UK, although clashes with the British over the control of Aden continued. It joined the Arab League (1945) and the UN (1947) and was loosely allied with Egypt and Syria (1958–61) in the United Arab Republic. Internal disorders, during which the imam was assassinated (1948), culminated in civil war (1962–70), which ended with the recognition of a republican regime. Another coup took place in 1974 and successive heads of state were assassinated in 1977 and 1978. Relations with South Yemen have been strained. Although moves were made toward uniting the two Yemens following the border clashes of 1967–72, continual conflict and distrust between the two countries have prevented union. Allegations of South Yemeni involvement in the 1978 assassination were followed by increased border fighting. President: Lieutenant Colonel Ali Abdullah Saleh (1942–). Official currency: riyal of 100 rial. Area: 73,300 sq mi (195,000 sq km). Population (1983 est.): 5,744,000. Capital: San'a. Chief port: Hodeida.

Yenisei River A river in the central Soviet Union, rising in the Sayan Mountains and flowing N to **Yenisei Bay** on the Kara Sea. There is a hydroelectric power station at Krasnoyarsk. Length: about 2485 mi (4000 km).

Yentai. See Yantai.

Yerevan (Russian name: Erivan) 40 10N 44 31E A city in the SW Soviet Union, the capital of the Armenian SSR. A commercial center, it has chemical, textile, and food-processing industries. *History*: it occupies the site of an ancient fortress, the city itself dating from at least the 7th century AD. Long disputed by Persia and Turkey, it was ceded to Russia in 1828. Population (1981 est): 1,050,000.

Yerwa. See Maiduguri.

Yesenin, Sergei Aleksandrovich (1895–1925) Russian poet. He emerged from a peasant background into Moscow literary society during a period of hectic revolutionary activity. He traveled in the US and Europe, was briefly married to the US dancer Isadora Duncan, suffered from alcoholism and drug addiction, and finally committed suicide. His volumes include *Confessions of a Hooligan* (1924).

Yeti. See Abominable Snowman.

Yevtushenko, Yevgenii (1933–) Soviet poet. His implicit criticism of the Soviet authorities in such poems as *Babi Yar* (1961) gained him wide popularity among both Soviet and western readers. He has given many poetry readings in Europe and the US.

yew A coniferous tree or shrub of the genus *Taxus* (10 species), native to the N hemisphere. Yews have dark-green leathery bladelike leaves, 0.04–0.16 in (1–4 cm) long and arranged in two rows along the stems, and the male and female flowers grow on separate trees. The female flowers produce bright-red cup-shaped berry-like fruits, each containing a single seed. The berries are sweet-tasting and attractive to birds, but the seeds and leaves are poisonous. The most widespread species is the common yew (*T. baccata*), of Europe, SW Asia, and N Africa; it grows to a height of 80 ft (25 m) but cultivated forms—grown for shelter, ornament, and topiary work—are often smaller. Family: *Taxaceae*.

Yezd. See Yazd.

Yezidis The name of a Kurd tribe of Iraq and their tribal religion. The sect, the center of which is in Mosul, is a synthetic religion that combines Islamic, Christian, Judaic, and other ancient elements.

Yezo. See Hokkaido.

Yggdrasill In Norse mythology, an evergreen ash tree embracing the whole universe. Its three roots join the underworld, the land of giants, and the home of the gods (Asgard). Demons threaten its existence; the serpent Nidhögg constantly chews at one of its roots, while four stags eat its buds. However, it is preserved by the *Norns (the Fates), who water it from one of the three fountains at its base. The maypole and the Christmas tree are possibly symbolic derivatives of Yggdrasill.

Yibin (or I-pin) 28 50N 104 35E A port in S central China, in Sichuan province at the confluence of the Yangtze and Min Rivers. A commercial center, salt is mined here and chemicals and paper are manufactured. Population (1953): 177,500.

Yichang (or I-ch'ang) 30 43N 111 22E A port in E central China, in Hubei province on the Yangtze River. An old commercial center, it marked the limit of the Japanese advance during the Sino-Japanese War (1937–45). Population (1953 est): 50,000–100,000.

Yiddish A language used by *Ashkenazim (East European) Jews and based on a dialect of High German. It emerged during the 9th century and has absorbed many Slavonic and other influences. It is written in the *Hebrew alphabet. Yiddish literature flourished in the 19th and early 20th centuries, but after the *holocaust it has yielded its place as the principal literary language of the Jews to Hebrew.

yield point The point at which a body becomes permanently deformed when subjected to a sufficiently large stress. Below the yield point the body is elastic, above the yield point it becomes plastic. *See also* elasticity; plasticity.

YIN AND YANG *The symbols are interlocked and each contains a tiny portion of the other.*

yin and yang Contrasting but complementary principles at the root of traditional Chinese cosmology. Yin is the negative feminine mode, associated with the earth, darkness, and passivity. Yang is the positive dynamic principle of masculine energy associated with heaven and light. The principles antedate *Confucius and are particularly important in *Taoism, serving, for example, to explain the cycle of the seasons.

ylang-ylang A slender evergreen tropical Asian tree, *Cananga odorata*, also called perfume tree. It has pointed oval leaves, up to 8 in (20 cm) long, and bears drooping clusters of fragrant stalked greenish-yellow flowers throughout the year. An oil distilled from the flowers is used in perfumery, cosmetics, and soaps. Family: *Annonaceae*.

YMCA. See Young Men's Christian Association.

yoga The principles and practice of self-training that permeates all Indian philosophical traditions. Traces of it exist from the *Indus Valley civilization before the Aryan invasion (1500 BC). The methods used are generally austere and ascetic and include physical control and meditative techniques. Physical control is stressed in Hindu yoga; in the Buddhist practice contemplative methods predominate; in Jainism asceticism is emphasized. Usually the aim is a state of release and liberation from the material world. The yoga so fashionable in the West frequently takes the form of hatha-yoga, which involves physical exercises to bring peace and insight.

yogurt. See dairy products.

Yokohama 35 28N 139 28E A port and second largest city of Japan, in SE Honshu on Tokyo Bay. Together with Tokyo it forms Japan's greatest urban and industrial area and handles 30% of foreign trade. Its industries include shipbuilding, oil refining, chemicals, steel, and textiles. Its two universities were both established in 1949. *History*: It grew rapidly after 1859 as a second port for Tokyo, with which it was linked by Japan's first railroad (1872). It was almost destroyed by the 1923 earthquake and badly bombed during World War II. Population (1980): 2,774,000.

Yokosuka 35 18N 139 39E A port in Japan, in SE Honshu on Tokyo Bay. William Adams (d. 1620), the first Englishman to visit Japan (1600), is buried here. It has a major naval base and its chief industry is shipbuilding. Population (1981 est): 421,000.

Yom Kippur (Hebrew: Day of Atonement)   A Jewish holy day, falling nine days after *Rosh Hashanah. It is a day of penitence and cleansing from sin and is marked by 24 hours' total fast. *See also* Holy of Holies.

Yong Le (*or* Yung-lo; 1360–1424)   The title of Ch'eng-tsu, Chinese emperor (1402–24), after usurping the throne. He was a vigorous builder and expander of the *Ming dynasty, dispatching fleets to SE Asia and personally leading military expeditions. He transferred the capital to Peking from Nanjing.

Yonkers   40 56N 73 54W   A city in S New York state on the Hudson River. Industries include elevators, carpets, chemicals, and clothing. Population (1980): 195,351.

York (Latin name: Eboracum)   53 58N 1 05W   A city in N England, on the River Ouse. It was the principal Roman garrison in Britain and was long regarded as the northern capital. The cathedral, seat of the Archbishop of York, was begun in 1154 and dominates the city. The medieval walls and four city gateways remain. Industries include chocolate manufacturing, sugar, glass, and railroad engineering. York is a major tourist center as well as an important market town and educational center. Population (1981): 99,787.

York   A ruling dynasty of England descended from Edmund, Duke of York (1342–1402), the fourth son of Edward III. Richard Plantaganet, Duke of *York, led the Yorkist opposition to Henry VI's Lancastrian government in the Wars of the □Roses (1455–85), in which the Yorkist emblem was the white rose. His son Edward IV, established the royal dynasty. After the brief rule of his son Edward V and the overthrow of Richard III (1485) the crown passed to Henry VII, the first *Tudor monarch, who married Edward IV's daughter Elizabeth.

York, Archbishop of   The second of the two archbishops of England and head of the northern province of the Church of England. York became an archiepiscopal see in 735 AD. Controversy between Canterbury and York regarding primacy was settled by Pope Innocent II (1352–62), with precedence given to the Archbishop of *Canterbury.

York, Richard Plantagenet, 3rd Duke of   (1411–60)   English magnate, who was descended from the third son of Edward III. His claim to the throne against Henry VI (who was descended from Edward III's fourth son) resulted in the outbreak of the Wars of the *Roses in 1455. He was killed in a skirmish at Wakefield. His sons became Edward IV (1461) and Richard III (1483).

York mystery plays   A cycle of 48 plays originating in the 14th century and performed by the trade guilds of York, England, on the feast of Corpus Christi. The most extensive cycle of medieval plays in England, the York cycle covered the whole of history from a Christian viewpoint, from the creation of the angels to the last judgment, concentrating on the fall of man and his redemption by Christ. They were all performed in chronological order in the course of one day. The series of 14 plays devoted to Christ's Passion were revised into alliterative verse at one stage and are notable for their sometimes disturbing realism.

Yorkshire   A former county in NE England, bordering on the North Sea. From the late middle ages onward it was an important center of the wool industry.

Yorkshire terrier   A breed of toy □dog developed from several terrier breeds in N England during the 19th century. It is small and compact with a very long straight coat that trails on the ground. This is black at birth but matures to steel-blue with tan on the head and chest. Height: 8–9 in (20–23 cm).

Yorktown   37 14N 76 32W   A village in Virginia on the York River. The last important battle of the American Revolution was fought here in 1781.

Yorktown Campaign   (1781)   The final decisive action of the American Revolution. In 1781, *Washington and French General Rochambeau moved their troops south to Virginia, where Britain's Cornwallis had entrenched his troops in the peninsular town of Yorktown, at the mouth of the York River. Washington had ordered the Marquis de *Lafayette to block Cornwallis by land, and the Chesapeake Bay was occupied by the French admiral De Grass, who successfully repulsed British ships. Washington and Rochambeau joined Lafayette and opened the battle on October 6; on Oct 19, 1781, Cornwallis surrendered.

Yosemite National Park   A national park in central California. The scenic Yosemite Valley, which lies within the park, contains the world's three largest monoliths of exposed granite. There are also many lakes, rivers, and waterfalls including the Yosemite Falls, which are the highest in North America with a drop in two segments of 2425 ft (739 m). Area: 1182 sq mi (3061 sq km).

Yoshkar-Ola   56 38N 47 52E   A city in the W central Soviet Union, the capital of the Mari ASSR. Founded in 1578, it has manufacturing and food-processing industries. Population (1981 est): 213,000.

Young, Andrew   (1932–   )   US politician and diplomat. As a Congregational Church minister in the Southern Christian Leadership Conference, Young was an associate of the civil-rights leader Martin Luther *King. A Democrat in the House of Representatives (1973–77), Young was US Ambassador to the UN from 1977 until 1979, when he resigned following criticism of his meeting, in contradiction of official US policy, with a representative of the Palestine Liberation Organization. He was elected mayor of Atlanta, Ga, in 1981.

BRIGHAM YOUNG   *Religious leader who succeeded Joseph Smith as head of the Mormons and who led them to Utah.*

Young, Brigham   (1801–77)   US religious leader. After being converted to the *Mormon faith by Joseph *Smith in 1832, Young quickly became one of the leading members of the church. He served briefly as head of the Mormon Mission in England and became the successor to Joseph Smith after the latter's violent death at the hands of an angry mob in Carthage, Ill, in 1844. Two years later, Young led Mormon settlers on a mass migration westward to establish the colony of Deseret in the Valley of the Great Salt Lake (1846–47). In addition to being president of the Mormon Church, he also served as governor of the Utah Territory (1850–57), but was removed from that post by federal authorities because of government objections to the observance of polygamy among the Mormons. Young himself had 19 wives and 56 children. Retaining his leadership of the church until his death, Young established the administrative organization still used by the Mormon church in its activities throughout the world.

Young, Denton Tru   ("Cy") (1867–1955)   US baseball pitcher. Active from 1890 to 1911, he set the record for most games won (511). He was elected to the Baseball Hall of Fame in 1937, and annual awards for baseball's best pitcher are named in his honor.

Young, Whitney M., Jr   (1921–71)   US social worker, educator, and civil rights leader. After military service in World War II, he worked with the National Urban League (1947–54), became dean of the Graduate School of Social Work at Atlanta University (1954), and joined the Urban League again in 1961 as executive director. He urged the improvement of black employment opportunities through job-training programs and favored cooperation rather than militant confrontation. Young wrote *To Be Equal* (1964).

Young Ireland An Irish nationalist movement formed by young Protestant radicals in the 1840s. Its uprising in 1848 under William Smith *O'Brien was a humiliating failure.

Young Italy A movement, founded by Giuseppe *Mazzini in 1831, that sought to establish a united republican Italy. After the failure of Mazzini's invasion of Savoy and other uprisings in the 1830s and 1840s its influence declined. *See also* Risorgimento.

Young Men's Christian Association (YMCA) A Christian organization for young men and, since 1971, for young women, founded in 1844 by George Williams (1821–1905), in England. Its aim is to encourage Christian morality and qualities of leadership. The World Alliance of YMCAs, formed in 1855 in Geneva, consists of 20 million members in 84 countries.

Young's modulus. *See* elastic modulus.

Youngstown 41 05N 80 40W A city in E Ohio. It is a center of an extensive iron and steel industry and produces aluminum, office furniture, and aircraft. Youngstown State University was established here in 1908. Population (1980): 115,436.

Youngstown Sheet and Tube Company v. Sawyer (1952) US Supreme Court decision that held that the principle of separation of powers had been violated by President Harry Truman's order to his secretary of commerce Charles Sawyer to seize and operate steel mills during a strike. Truman had feared the strike's impact on the Korean War effort.

Young Turks A Turkish revolutionary group. In 1908 the Young Turks, officially named the Committee of Union and Progress, led the revolution that resulted in Sultan *Abdülhamid's abdication. Under *Enver Pasha and Talaat Pasha (1872–1921), they were the dominant force in Turkish politics until 1918.

Young Women's Christian Association (YWCA) A Christian organization for women (to which men may now also belong). Founded in 1855 in England to promote unity among Christians and understanding between those of different faiths. It provides social welfare, education, and recreational facilities, as well as accommodation in hostels. It is a member of the world movement of the YWCA, formed in 1894 and having branches in over 80 countries.

Ypsilanti A Greek family prominent in Balkan revolts against the Ottoman Empire. **Alexander Ypsilanti** (c. 1725–c. 1807), governor of Walachia (1774–82, 1796–97) and of Moldavia (1786–88), was executed for allegedly conspiring against the sultan. His son **Constantine Ypsilanti** (1760–1816), governor of Walachia (1802–06, 1807), participated in a Serbian revolt against the Turks. His elder son **Alexander Ypsilanti** (1792–1828) led an uprising in Moldavia and proclaimed Greek independence (1821). Defeated, he fled to Austria, where he was imprisoned (1821–27). Alexander's brother **Demetrios Ypsilanti** (1793–1832) played a prominent part in the War of *Greek Independence.

Ysselmeer. *See* IJsselmeer.

ytterbium (Yb) A *lanthanide element, named, like yttrium, erbium, and terbium, after the village of Ytterby in Sweden. It forms trivalent compounds, including the oxide (Yb_2O_3) and trihalides (for example $YbCl_3$). At no 70; at wt 173.04; mp 819°C; bp 1194°C.

yttrium (Y) A *lanthanide element, discovered in 1794 by J. Gadolin (1760–1852). It is widely used as the oxide (Y_2O_3) to make red television-tube phosphors. At no 39; at wt 88.906; mp 1522 ± 8°C; bp 3338°C.

Yuan (1279–1368) A Mongol dynasty that ruled China after overthrowing the *Song dynasty. The first and strongest Mongol ruler was *Kublai Khan, who held the empire together by military force. Later, revolts broke out and the Mongols were eventually driven out of their capital, Peking, following 27 years of fighting.

Yuan Shi Kai (*or* Yüan Shih-k'ai; 1859–1916) Chinese general, who became president of the new Chinese republic in 1912 after the downfall of the *Qing dynasty. His attempts to rule dictatorially and to found a new dynasty brought about civil war with the followers of *Sun Yat-sen. Yuan died suddenly, leaving China in chaos.

Yucatán A peninsula of Central America, chiefly in SE Mexico but extending into Belize and Guatemala, separating the Gulf of Mexico from the Caribbean Sea. It was a center of the civilization of the □Maya; many relics remain, notably at Uxmal and Chichén Itzá. Area: about 70,00 sq mi (181,300 sq km).

Yucca A genus of succulent plants (about 40 species), native to S North America and varying in height from small shrubs to 50-ft (15-m)-high trees. Most are stemless and have a rosette of stiff sword-shaped leaves crowded on a stout trunk. The waxy white bell-shaped flowers are borne in a dense terminal cluster and are pollinated by female yucca moths (genus *Pronuba*) when they lay their eggs inside the flowers. Several species are cultivated as ornamentals, including Adam's needle (*Y. filamentosa*) and Spanish dagger (*Y. gloriosa*). Family: *Agavaceae*. *See also* Joshua tree.

Yugoslavia, Socialist Federal Republic of (Serbo-Croat name: Jugoslavija) A country in SE Europe, bounded by the Adriatic Sea (W), Italy, Austria, and Hungary (NW and NE), Rumania and Bulgaria (E), and Greece and Albania (S). The fertile plains of the Danube-Sava basin in the NE rise to mountains in the S and W, reaching heights of almost 10,000 ft (3000 m). The Serbs and the Croats make up the majority of the population, with minorities of Slovenes, Macedonians, Albanians, and others. In the early 1980s political tension between the minorities resulted in violence and repression. *Economy*: agriculture, mainly organized in cooperatives, is important although the numbers employed in this sector have decreased dramatically in recent years. Mechanization has improved agricultural output and the country is now self-sufficient in chemical fertilizers. Livestock is especially important and the principal crops are wheat, corn, sugar beet, sunflowers, and potatoes. There is a thriving wine industry and forestry and fishing are important sources of revenue. Rich mineral resources include coal, iron ore, copper, and lead, and some oil is produced. Over half the country's power comes from hydroelectric sources. Development of heavy and light industry has been rapid since World War II and there is a growing tourist industry. Exports include meat, machinery, nonferrous metals, timber, textiles, and ships. *History*: Yugoslavia was so named in 1927 but was formed in 1918 as the kingdom of the Serbs, Croats, and Slovenes by the federation of Serbia, Montenegro, Croatia, Slovenia, and Bosnia-Herzegovina. Alexander I assumed absolute power in 1929 and was assassinated by Croatian nationalists in 1934. In World War II Yugoslavia was occupied by the Germans and Peter II fled to London. Internal resistance to the Germans became divided between the *Chetniks and the Partisans, the latter gaining Allied support in 1943. After the war the Partisans' leader *Tito became head of a communist government. In 1948 relations with the Soviet Union were broken off and, although they became closer again after the death of Stalin, Yugoslavia has preserved a policy of nonalignment in foreign affairs and a decentralized form of socialism that aims to give more direct power to the workers. The early 1980s witnessed severe economic crises, high unemployment, and political repression. In 1982 Milka Planinc became the first female premier of Yugoslavia. Tito's policies, formerly upheld, are increasingly criticized. The Soviet Union has become Yugoslavia's principal trading partner. Official languages: all national languages, with Serbo-Croat serving as the lingua franca. Official currency: dinar of 100 para. Area: 98,725 sq mi (255,804 sq km). Population (1983 est.): 22,826,000. Capital: Belgrade. Main port: Rijeka.

Yukawa, Hideki (1907–81) Japanese physicist, who, while working at Kyoto University, postulated (1935) that the *strong interaction could be accounted for by the exchange of *virtual particles. He calculated the mass of the particle involved, but at that time no such particle was known. *Anderson's discovery of the muon was thought to have confirmed Yukawa's prediction. But in fact the confirmation did not come until 1947, when Cecil *Powell discovered the pion. Yukawa was awarded a Nobel Prize in 1949 for his work.

Yukon A territory of NW Canada, on the Beaufort Sea. Mostly high mountains and plateaus of the Cordillera, it is covered by tundra in the N. Poor soils and low precipitation produce only sparse vegetation, except in S valleys. The population is concentrated on the central plateau, where silver, lead, zinc, copper, and asbestos are mined. There is some lumbering, and tourism is expanding rapidly. The Yukon is a frontier region that was first opened up by the *Klondike gold rush (1897–99) and military projects (since 1939). Area: 205,345 sq mi (531,844 sq km). Population (1978 est): 21,700. Capital: Whitehorse.

Yukon River A river in NW North America. Rising in NW Canada on the border between the Yukon and British Columbia, it flows N through Alaska, then SW into the Bering Sea. Its great potential as a source of hydroelectricity has yet to be fully exploited. Length: 1979 mi (3185 km).

Yunnan A mountainous province in S China, bordering on Burma, Laos, and North Vietnam. The ethnically varied population includes aboriginal groups in the mountains. It is China's greatest tin-producing area and rice and timber are grown. *History*: part of China since the 13th century, it was for long rebellious and little developed. It became industrialized during the Sino-Japanese War (1937–45), when many industries moved here from the coast. Area: 168,400 sq mi (436,200 sq km). Population (1980 est): 31,350,000. Capital: Kunming.

YWCA. *See* Young Women's Christian Association.

Z

Zaandam 52 27N 4 49E A port in the W Netherlands, in North Holland province. Peter the Great of Russia studied shipbuilding here in 1697. It is a center of the timber trade; industries include paper and paint manufacture. Population (1971): 65,981.

Zabaleta, Nicanor (1907–) Spanish harpist. He studied in Paris with Marcel Tournier (1879–1951). He has commissioned many new works for the harp as well as reviving forgotten compositions.

Zabrze (German name: Hindenburg) 50 18N 18 47E A city in SW Poland. It is a coalmining center; industries include steel processing, engineering, and chemicals. Population (1976 est): 204,000.

Zacynthus (or Zante; Modern Greek name: Zákinthos) A Greek island in the SE Ionian Sea, the southernmost of the Ionian Islands. Most of the island is fertile and currants are the main product. Area: 157 sq mi (406 sq km). Population (1971): 30,187.

Zadar (Italian name: Zara) 44 07N 15 14E A port in W Yugoslavia, in Croatia on the Adriatic Sea. It has a natural deepwater harbor and was the most heavily fortified Adriatic town until the late 19th century. There are many old churches and a Roman forum. Local industries produce maraschino liqueur, cigarettes, rope, and glass. Population (1970 est): 43,000.

Zadkine, Ossip (1890–1967) French sculptor of Russian birth. He settled in Paris (1909), where he developed a cubist style in his monumental figure sculptures. His best-known work is the war memorial in Rotterdam, entitled *The Destroyed City* (1954).

Zagazig (or az-Zaqazig) 30 36N 31 30E A city in N Egypt, on the Nile Delta. The ruins of the ancient city of *Bubastis are nearby. It has a major trade in cotton and cereals. Population (1975 est): 200,800.

Zaghlul, Saad (1857–1927) Egyptian nationalist politician; prime minister (1924). In 1918 he helped to found the nationalist Wafd party. He was arrested by the British but after the granting of limited independence in 1922 he became prime minister. He was forced by the British to resign shortly afterward but was active behind the scenes until his death.

Zagorsk (name until 1930: Sergiyev) 56 20N 38 10E A city in the Soviet Union, in the W RSFSR 45 mi (72 km) NE of Moscow. It grew around the famous Trinity-St Sergius monastery (1337–40), the buildings within which, notably the Trinity Cathedral (1422–23) and the Cathedral of the Assumption (1559–85), may still be seen. Population (1977 est): 101,000.

Zagreb 45 48N 15 58E The second largest city of Yugoslavia and capital of Croatia on the Sava River. A cultural center of the Croats since the 16th century, it possesses a university (1669) and a gothic cathedral. Industries include textiles, machinery, and paper manufacture. Population (1971): 566,224.

Zagros Mountains A mountain system in W Iran, extending 1000 mi (1600 km) NW–SE between the Soviet border and the Strait of Hormuz. It consists of many parallel ranges and rises to 15,784 ft (4811 m) in the N at Sabalan.

Zaïre, Republic of (name from 1960 until 1971: Congo) A large country in central equatorial Africa, with a short coastline on the Atlantic Ocean, bounded by Central African Republic, Sudan, Uganda, Rwanda, Burundi, Tanzania, Zambia, Angola, and Congo. The central part of the country is dominated by a vast plateau, rising to the Ruwenzori Mountains in the SE. It is drained by the Zaïre River and its many tributaries and fringed along its E border by a chain of lakes, including Lake Tanganyika, comprising part of the *Great Rift Valley. Most of the population is African, the largest groups being Luba, Mongo, and Kongo. *Economy*: efforts are being made to increase agricultural production, which has fallen in recent years through droughts and political unrest. The chief cash crops are coffee, cotton, palm oil, and rubber; corn, rice, and cassava are grown extensively as the staple food crops. Zaïre has rich and varied mineral resources, principally copper (the chief export) from the Shaba mines, and is the world's chief producer of industrial diamonds and cobalt. Other minerals include manganese, zinc, and uranium and oil has been found offshore (exploited since 1975). Hydroelectricity is a valuable source of power and Zaïre is estimated to have about 50% of Africa's total potential hydroelectric capacity. The rivers, especially the Zaïre River, are also important for transport. *History*: when the Portuguese penetrated the region in the late 15th century it was dominated by the kingdom of the Kongo. In the late 19th century it was explored by David *Livingstone and, under Belgian auspices, by H. M. Stanley. Leopold II of the Belgians established personal rule over the Congo Free State, which was recognized by the European powers at the Conference of Berlin (1884–85). In 1908 it was annexed by Belgium, becoming the colony of the Belgian Congo. Independence was obtained in 1960 with Kasavubu as president and Patrice Lumumba as prime minister of the newly named Republic of the Congo. The almost immediate secession of Katanga province under Tshombe resulted in civil war in which the UN intervened (an international force remained in the country until 1964). In 1965 Mobutu Sese Seko seized power and in 1971 the Congo was renamed Zaïre. In 1977 and again in 1978 an invasion force entered *Shaba (formerly Katanga) province from Angola, in unsuccessful attempts to topple Mobutu, and on the second occasion the massacre of Europeans in Kolwezi brought French and Belgian forces to Zaïre. In 1978 a constitution was ratified making Zaïre a one-party nation; in 1982 a group challenging Mobutu's government on charges of financial corruption was imprisoned for founding a new political party. The early 1980s witnessed a major slump in Zaïre's economy, border disputes, and a continuation of political repression. Official language: French. Official currency, since 1967: zaïre of 100 makuta. Area: 2,345,409 895,348 sq mi (sq km). Population (1983 est): 31,250,000. Capital: Kinshasa. Main port: Matadi.

Zaïre River (former name: Congo R.) The second longest river in Africa. Its true source is disputed, one headstream being the *Lualaba River and the other the Chambezi River (later the Luvua River), which rises in a high plateau between Lakes Malawi and Tanganyika. Below the confluence of the two headstreams it flows N, being known as the Lualaba until the Boyoma Falls, where it becomes the Zaïre River. It flows generally W then SW, through Malebo Pool, to enter the Atlantic Ocean via a delta at Boma. The Zaïre River is an important potential source of hydroelectric power with the construction of dams in the 1970s. Length: 3000 mi (4820 km).

zaltys A green snake that was a symbol of wealth and fertility in the Baltic region in ancient times. Households often kept a zaltys and it was believed that misfortune would befall anyone who killed one.

Zambezi River A river in S Africa. Rising in NW Zambia, it flows generally S through E Angola before re-entering Zambia and curving E along the Caprivi Strip frontier of Namibia. It then forms the Zambian–Zimbabwe border, the *Victoria Falls and Kariba Dam (see Kariba, Lake) being located along this course, before flowing SE through Mozambique to enter the Indian Ocean via an extensive delta. It has the fourth largest drainage area in Africa with an area of about 520,000 sq mi (1,347,000 sq km). Length: 1700 mi (2740 km).

Zambia, Republic of (name until 1974: Northern Rhodesia) A landlocked country in S central Africa bordered by Zaïre, Tanzania, Malawi, Mozambique, Zimbabwe, South West Africa/Namibia, and Angola. It consists chiefly of low undulating plateaus and is drained along its southern border by the Zambezi River; other main rivers are the Kafue and Luangwa. The swampy Lake Bangweulu lies in the N. The population is virtually all African, largely Bantu, with small minorities of Europeans, Asians, and Chinese. *Economy*: the mining sector is responsible for producing most of Zambia's wealth from the rich mineral resources. Copper accounts for about 96% of the total mineral production and comes mainly from the *Copperbelt. Lead and zinc from Kabwe are also important, some coal is mined, and there are extensive iron-ore deposits, as yet unexploited. Agriculture is a major occupation; the chief subsistence crop is corn. Cash crops include tobacco, groundnuts, cotton, and sugar but commercial agriculture declined during the 1970s. Livestock and forestry are also important. Communications, which were hampered by the closure of the Rhodesian border (1973) and by unrest in Mozambique, were aided by the opening (1975) of the Chinese-built Tanzam Railway to Dar es Salaam (Tanzania). *History*: the area had already been occupied by Bantu peoples when it was raided by Arab slave traders in the 18th century. In the 19th century British missionaries, notably David *Livingstone, paved the way for Cecil *Rhodes, who incorporated the region into a territory named Rhodesia in his honor and administered by the British South Africa Company. Constituted as Northern Rhodesia in 1911, it became a British protectorate in 1924. It formed part of the Federation of Rhodesia and Nyasaland (1953–63), obtaining internal self-government and, shortly afterward, full independence within the British Commonwealth as the Republic of Zambia (1964). Kenneth *Kaunda, in 1982 elected to his fifth term of office, has been president since independence. In 1972 a new constitution led to one-party (the United

National Independence Party) rule. Zambia supports the Zimbabwe nationalist movement, providing a base for Nkomo's arm of the Patriotic Front, and its border with Rhodesia (now Zimbabwe) was closed from 1973 until 1980. Economic crises of the early 1980s resulted in the presentation of a harsh budget and currency devaluation. Official language: English. Official currency, since 1968: kwacha of 100 ngwee. Area: 290,586 sq mi (752,262 sq km). Population (1983 est): 6,346,000. Capital: Lusaka.

Zamboanga 6 55N 122 05E A port in the S Philippines, in SW Mindanao. A resort, it is noted for its picturesque setting and tropical flowers and has a 17th-century Spanish fort. Brass and bronzeware are produced and it exports copra, hardwoods, and hemp. Population (1975): 261,978.

Zamoyski A prominent Polish family, which became powerful under **Jan Zamoyski** (1542–1605), who was adviser to Sigismund II Augustus (*see* Jagiellons) and to *Stephen Báthory. **Andrzej Zamoyski** (1716–92) worked for parliamentary reform and the abolition of serfdom, freeing his own serfs. Andrzej's son **Stanisław Zamoyski** (1775–1856) played an important role in the November Insurrection against Russian dominance, as did Stanisław's son **Andrzej Zamoyski** (1800–74), who also participated in the January Insurrection, for which he was exiled (*see* Congress Kingdom of Poland).

Zamyatin, Yevgenii Ivanovich (1884–1937) Russian novelist. His works include vivid satirical studies of life in provincial Russia and England, where he worked during World War I. He was severely criticized after the European publication of his novel *We* (1924), a bleak prophecy of a totalitarian future, and from 1931 he lived in Paris.

Zante. *See* Zacynthus.

Zanzibar An island in Tanzania, off the NE coast of the mainland. It came under Arab influence early on in its history and was, together with *Pemba, a sultanate from 1856 to 1964. It was under British rule from 1890 until it became independent within the British Commonwealth in 1963. In 1964 the Sultan was exiled and Zanzibar united with Tanganyika to form Tanzania. It exports mainly cloves and copra. Area: 640 sq mi (1658 sq km). Population (1976 est): 431,000. Chief town: Zanzibar.

Zao Zhan. *See* Cao Chan.

Zapata, Emiliano (?1877–1919) Mexican revolutionary, who championed the cause of agrarian reform against Porfirio *Díaz and succeeding governments. By late 1911 he controlled the state of Morelos, where he carried out land reforms, chasing out the estate owners and dividing their land among the peasants. In 1919 he was tricked into an ambush and assassinated.

Zaporozhye (name until 1921: Aleksandrovsk) 47 50N 35 10E A city in the SW Soviet Union, in the Ukrainian SSR on the Dnepr River. A large hydroelectric station, built here in the years 1927–32, was destroyed in World War II but subsequently rebuilt. There is an important iron and steel industry and a variety of engineering activities. Population (1977 est): 760,000.

Zapotecs An American Indian people of the Oaxaca valleys (S Mexico). Their traditional culture, emerging about 300 AD, developed into one of the classic Mesoamerican Indian civilizations. Monte Alban, their chief city, declined under pressure from the *Mixtecs (c. 900–50).

Zara. *See* Zadar.

Zaragoza (English name: Saragossa) 41 39N 0 54W A city in NE Spain, in Aragon on the Ebro River. During the Peninsular War it heroically resisted a French siege until about 50,000 of its defenders had died (1808–09). It has two cathedrals and a university (founded 1533). An industrial center, it produces paper and wine. Population (1974 est): 547,317.

Zarathustra. *See* Zoroaster.

Zaria 11 01N 7 44E A city in Nigeria. Founded in the 16th century, it became the capital of the emirate of Zaria. It has textile, cosmetics, and cigarette industries. Nearby is the Ahmadu Bello University (1962). Population (1975 est): 224,000.

Zátopek, Emil (1922–) Czech long-distance runner. In 1948 he won his first Olympic gold medal, for the 10,000 meters. At the Helsinki Olympics (1952) he won gold medals for the 5000 meters, 10,000 meters, and the marathon.

Zealand. *See* Sjælland.

Zealots A Jewish political party of the 1st century AD. They were bitterly opposed to Roman rule in Judea, and played a leading part in the revolt of 66 AD. Their last stronghold, *Masada, fell in 73. After the war their

influence in Judea was minimal but they may have been responsible for the further revolts in Egypt, Libya, and Cyprus in 115 AD.

EMILIANO ZAPATA *This photograph shows the machismo associated with the Mexican revolutionary.*

Zeami Motokiyo (1363–c. 1443) Japanese playwright, son of the dramatist Kanami Kiyotsugu (1333–84). He achieved fame first as an actor but later became a leading theorist of No drama, his best-known treatise being *Kadensho*. He wrote over 150 plays.

zebra An African wild horse having characteristic black and white stripes covering part or all of the body. There are three races of the plains zebra (*Equus burchelli*), distinguished by the extent and nature of their stripes. The mountain zebra (*E. zebra*) has very bold stripes and a dewlap on the throat, while Grévy's zebra (*E. grevyi*) is the largest species, standing over 5 ft (1.5 m) at the shoulder with narrow stripes.

zebra finch An Australian *grassfinch, *Taeniopyga castanotis*, occurring in large flocks in the interior grasslands. It has a red bill and the males are gray above with white underparts, reddish flanks, red-brown ear patches, and black-and-white barred throat, breast, and tail. Zebra finches are popular cagebirds and have been selectively bred to produce a white form with the black-and-white barring.

zebra fish A tropical freshwater fish, *Brachydanio rerio*, also called zebra danio, found in E India and popular in aquaria. It has a shiny blue body, up to 1.8 in (4.5 cm) long, with four longitudinal yellowish gold stripes along its sides. *See also* scorpion fish; tigerfish.

zebra wood Any of several tropical trees that yield hard striped timber, used in furniture, especially *Connarus guianensis*, of Guyana. It has compound leaves with paired oval leaflets and clusters of five-petaled flowers. Family: *Connaraceae*.

zebu The domestic *cattle of Asia and Africa, *Bos indicus*, also called Brahmin (*or* Brahman). Larger and leaner than western cattle, zebus have a distinctive hump over the shoulders, a large dewlap under the throat, and long horns. They are generally gray or red, but a number of other color varieties exist. Zebus are no longer found in the wild state and have been exported to many hot countries to confer their qualities of heat tolerance and insect resistance in crosses with beef breeds.

Zebulun, tribe of One of the 12 *tribes of Israel. It claimed descent from Zebulun, the son of Jacob and Leah. Its people lived to the W and SW of the Sea of Galilee.

Zechariah An Old Testament prophet of Judah, who delivered his prophecies about 520 BC. **The Book of Zechariah** relates a series of eight visions calculated to inspire the people to rebuild the Temple at Jerusalem. The book also deals with questions concerning fasting and predicts the coming of a kingly messiah and the end of the Diaspora.

Zedekiah The last king of Judah (597–586 BC). Having rebelled against *Nebuchadnezzar, Zedekiah was forced to witness his sons' execution and was then blinded and removed to *Babylon. The prophet Jeremiah, an eyewitness, vividly describes these events.

Zeeland A province in the SW Netherlands, on the Scheldt delta. It consists mainly of islands, including Walcheren. Severe flooding in 1953 necessitated the Delta Plan, under which several major dams have been constructed and dikes strengthened. The important mussel and oyster fisheries of the Oosterschelde estuary have been preserved. Agricultural produce includes wheat, sugar beet, fruit, and dairy products. Area: 1060 sq mi (2746 sq km). Population (1976 est): 335,624. Capital: Middelburg.

Zeeman, Pieter (1865–1943) Dutch physicist, who, while working at Leiden University, discovered (1886) the splitting of the spectral lines of a substance when placed in a magnetic field (**Zeeman effect**). It is caused by changes in the energy levels of the electrons of the emitting atoms as a result of interaction between the magnetic moment of the orbit and the external field. For this discovery he shared the 1902 Nobel Prize with Hendrik *Lorentz, who had predicted the existence of such an effect.

Zeffirelli, G. Franco (1923–) Italian director and stage designer. Having started as an actor under the direction of *Visconti, he went on to direct film versions of *The Taming of the Shrew* (1966) and *Romeo and Juliet* (1968). He has worked on numerous operas in England, New York, and in Italy. His many stage productions include *Othello* (1961) and *Hamlet* (1964) and he made a film version of *La Traviata* (1983).

Zeiss, Carl (1816–88) German industrialist and manufacturer of optical instruments. Zeiss opened his first workshop in Jena (1846) and later employed Ernst Abbe (1840–1905) to advise him on theoretical advances in optics.

Zen Buddhism (Japanese *Zen*, meditation) In China and Japan, a Buddhist school emphasizing the transmission of enlightenment from master to disciple without reliance on the scriptures. It derives from the teaching of *Bodhidharma, who came to China in 520 AD. The two major sects, *Soto and Rinzai, stress meditation and the use of logical paradoxes (*koans*) respectively, in order to confound the rational mind so that transcendental wisdom can arise and the disciple can realize his own Buddha-nature. Much of Japanese and Chinese art, music, and literature, as well as calligraphy, the tea ceremony (*see* cha-no-yu), the martial arts, etc., express the spontaneous Zen attitude to life. Recently Zen has gained followers in the West, where its opposition to rationalism has popular appeal.

Zener diode. *See* semiconductor diode.

Zenger, John Peter (1697–1746) German-born American printer. He immigrated to New York City in 1710 and was apprenticed to the colony's official printer, William Bradford, until 1719. In 1726 he established his own printing shop and became the publisher and printer of the *New York Weekly Journal*, which sharply criticized the incompetent governor, Colonel William Crosby. Zenger was imprisoned for 9 months in 1734–35 on the charge of seditious libel and was finally brought to trial with noted Philadelphia attorney Andrew Hamilton defending him. Hamilton took a new approach by arguing that Zenger had published truth, not libel, and Zenger was acquitted. The trial set a precedent for the establishment of freedom of the press in America.

zenith The point in the sky lying directly above an observer and 90° from all points on his horizon. The (unobservable) point diametrically opposite the zenith is the nadir. □celestial sphere.

Zenobia (3rd century AD) The wife of Odaenathus of Palmyra, whom she may have murdered (267) and whom she succeeded as regent for their son. Zenobia occupied Syria, Egypt, and much of Asia Minor before *Aurelian defeated and captured her in 272. She enjoyed a reputation for beauty and intelligence.

Zeno of Citium (c. 335–262 BC) Greek philosopher, who was born in Cyprus of Phoenician stock, came to Athens in 313 BC, and attended lectures at *Plato's Academy. He was influenced by various philosophical

schools, including the *Cynics, before evolving his own doctrine of *Stoicism.

Zeno of Elea (born c. 490 BC) Greek philosopher. Zeno's paradoxes, supporting *Parmenides' doctrines that reality is indivisible and reason is at variance with the senses, are the first dialectic arguments, eliciting contradictory conclusions from an opponent's hypotheses. These paradoxes include: Achilles and the tortoise—if space is infinitely divisible, once Achilles has given the tortoise a start he cannot overtake it, for whenever he arrives where the tortoise was it has already moved on; the flying arrow—if space is divisible into finite parts, a moving arrow at each moment of its flight is opposite a particular piece of ground and therefore stationary.

zeolites A group of complex silicate minerals containing loosely held water. They are divided into three groups: fibrous (natrolite, mesolite, scolecite), platy (heulandite, stilbite), and equant (harmatome, chabazite). Most occur in cavities in basic volcanic rocks. They are usually colorless or white and are relatively soft. Because of their property of base exchange they were used as water softeners before the introduction of artificial substitutes. They are also used as molecular sieves in the petroleum industry and as drying agents.

Zephaniah (late 7th century BC) An Old Testament prophet of Judah. **The Book of Zephaniah** records his condemnation of those who continued as idolaters despite the reforms carried out by Josiah (d. 608 BC) and predicts universal judgment from which few will escape.

Zeppelins. *See* airships.

Zermatt 46 01N 7 45E A village in S Switzerland, at the foot of the Matterhorn. A popular resort, it is also a famous mountaineering and winter-sports center, at a height of 5315 ft (1620 m). Population (1970): 3101.

Zernicke, Frits (1888–1966) Dutch physicist, who was awarded the 1953 Nobel Prize for his invention of the phase-contrast microscope (1934). This invention enabled the parts of a cell to be seen without staining.

Zetkin, Clara (1857–1933) German communist and feminist leader. Zetkin founded the International Socialist Women's Congress in 1907 and joined the German Communist Party in 1919. She was a leader of the pro-Soviet wing of the Party and spent much time in the Soviet Union.

Zetland. *See* Shetland Islands.

Zeus The Greek sky and weather god, the supreme deity, identified with the Roman *Jupiter. He was the son of Cronus and Rhea, and brother of Poseidon and Hades. His defeat of Cronus and the *Titans represents the triumph of the Olympian deities over their predecessors. His offspring included *Athena, *Apollo, and *Dionysus and from his many love affairs, which excited the jealousy of his wife, *Hera, were produced numerous other divine and semidivine children. He was usually portrayed as a bearded man, with thunderbolts and the eagle as his attributes.

Zeus, statue of The chryselephantine statue designed by the Greek sculptor *Phidias in about 430 BC for the temple of Zeus at Olympia. One of the *Seven Wonders of the World, it was 40 ft (12 m) high and covered with jewels and gold. It was destroyed in the 5th century AD.

Zeuxis (late 5th century BC) Greek painter, born at Heracleia (S Italy). Zeuxis improved the contemporary use of perspective, shading, and mixed colors. His *trompe l'oeil* effect, it is said, induced birds to peck at grapes painted by him. He specialized in mythological subjects.

Zhangjiakou (or Chang-chia-k'ou; Mongolian name: Kalgan) 40 51N 114 59E A city in NE China, in Hebei province near the *Great Wall. It was historically important for defense against and trade with the Mongols and is the site of two forts (1429, 1613). Industries include textiles and machinery. Population (1953): 229,300.

Zhao Guang Yin. *See* Song.

Zhdanov (name until 1948: Mariupol) 47 05N 37 34E A port in the Soviet Union, in the SE Ukrainian SSR on an estuary leading to the Sea of Azov. A railroad (1882) connects it with the Donets Basin and it exports coal. It has a variety of industries and supports a fishing fleet. Population (1977 est): 467,000.

Zhejiang (Che-chiang or Chekiang) A mountainous province in E China, on the East China Sea. Densely populated, it has been a cultural center since the Southern *Song dynasty was centered here (12th–13th centuries). It is a highly productive agricultural area and silk and fishing are important. Area: 39,780 sq mi (102,000 sq km). Population (1976 est): 35,000,000. Capital: Hangzhou.

Zheng Cheng Gong (or Cheng Ch'eng-kung; 1624–62) Chinese pirate also known as Koxinga, who controlled most of the Fujian coast from his base in Amoy. He led the Ming resistance to the new Qing rulers and attempted to recapture Nanjing. This failed but he seized Formosa (now Taiwan) from the Dutch in 1661, which became the last Ming stronghold.

Zheng He (or Cheng Ho; died c. 1433) A Chinese eunuch of the Ming dynasty, who in 1405 built a fleet and set out on a famous mission to Indochina. Further expeditions to Indochina and the Middle East re-established trade links that had been severed on the collapse of Yuan rule in 1368.

Zhengzhou (or Cheng-chou) 34 35N 113 38E A city in E China, the capital of Henan province. An old administrative center, it has many industries developed since 1949. Population (1957 est): 766,000.

Zhitomir 50 18N 28 40E A city in the Soviet Union, in the central Ukrainian SSR. Dating from at least the 13th century, it was subsequently held by Lithuania and then Poland before being restored to Russia in 1793. A communications center, it processes the produce of the surrounding agricultural region. Population (1977 est): 229,000.

Zhivkov, Todor (1911–) Bulgarian statesman, noted, as head of state (1954–), for encouraging friendly relations with other Balkan countries. A partisan leader in World War II, Zhivkov led the communist overthrow of the monarchy in 1944. He became first secretary of the Bulgarian Communist Party in 1954 and was prime minister (1962–71) before becoming president (1971).

Zhou (?1027–221 BC) The earliest Chinese dynasty of which there is accurate knowledge. The dynasty was founded in the area now called Shenxi after the Zhou ruler, Wu Wang, had annihilated the armies of the preceding Shang dynasty and set up a system of government under feudal rulers. These undermined Zhou authority in the so-called Warring States period (481–221), after which the *Qin emerged to unite China. Under the Zhou human sacrifice was abolished and the Chinese idea of *ancestor worship came into being. The late Zhou was also the great period of Chinese philosophy, when Taoist and Confucian thought (see Taoism; Confucianism) first emerged.

Zhuangzi (or Chuang-tzu; c. 369–286 BC) Chinese philosopher. He is known only through the book to which he gave his name, a work of Taoist philosophy containing allegories, anecdotes, and satires on Confucius. The book, which greatly influenced the development of Chinese Buddhism, advocated spiritual harmony with Tao, the essential principle of the universe, through liberation from all worldly circumstances.

Zhu De (or Chu Teh; 1886–1976) Chinese marshal. He joined the Chinese Communist Party while a student in Germany and after his return helped organize the Nanchang communist uprising against the *Guomindang (Nationalists; 1927). He joined Mao Tse-tung in 1928 and became commander of the Fourth Red Army (later the People's Liberation Army), a post he retained until 1954. He served with Mao throughout the period leading to the establishment of the People's Republic of *China (1949), during which his kindness to his troops became legendary.

Zhu Jiang (or Chu Chiang; English name: Pearl River) A river in S China, formed by the confluence of the *Xi Jiang and Bei (or Pei) River near Canton and flowing into an estuary that is used by oceangoing ships. Length: 110 mi (177 km).

Zhukov, Georgi Konstantinovich (1896–1974) Soviet marshal. An armored-warfare expert, he became chief of the army general staff (1941). He planned or commanded almost every major Soviet military operation in World War II, including the Soviet occupation force in Germany. Under Khrushchev he became defense minister and then a member of the presidium of the Communist Party.

Zia ul-Haq, Gen Mohammad (1924–) Pakistani statesman; president (1978–). In 1976 he was appointed chief of the army staff and in the following year led the coup that overthrew *Bhutto, becoming chief martial law administrator (1977). In 1979 Zia refused worldwide appeals to commute Bhutto's sentence of death for conspiracy to murder.

Ziaur Rahman (1936–81) Bangladesh statesman and army officer; president (1977–81). He fought in the war against Pakistan in 1971 and became chief of staff of the armed forces in 1975. He became chief martial law administrator in 1976, during the period of political instability that followed *Mujibur Rahman's assassination (1975), and president but was himself assassinated during an unsuccessful insurrection.

Zibo (or Tzu-po) 36 32N 117 47E A city in E China, in Shandong province, formed by the amalgamation of Zi-cheng (or Tzu-ch'eng) and Boshan (or Po-shan). It has coalmining, chemical, electrical, and machine-building industries. Population (1957 est): 806,000.

Ziegfeld, Florenz (1867–1932) US theatrical producer. His lavish revues were modeled on the *Folies-Bergère. The Ziegfeld Follies, billed as "An American Institution," appeared annually from 1907 until his death.

Using the slogan "Glorifying the American Girl," he created such hits as Sally (1920), Show Boat (1927), and Bitter Sweet (1929). He also launched Will Rogers, W. C. Fields, Eddie Cantor, and others on their careers.

Ziegler, Karl (1898–1973) German chemist, who shared the 1963 Nobel Prize with Giulio Natta (1903–) for their work on plastics and polymers. Ziegler showed that certain organometallic compounds (**Ziegler catalysts**) would catalyze the *polymerization of ethylene giving unbranched polymers that were tougher and had a higher melting point than those previously obtainable.

ziggurat An ancient Mesopotamian brick-built temple tower. Ziggurats were constructed of rectangular terraces of diminishing size, generally with a shrine for the god on top. They existed in every major Sumerian, Babylonian, and Assyrian center, the one at Babylon being the probable original of the Tower of *Babel.

Zimbabwe, State of (name until 1979: Rhodesia) A landlocked country in SE Africa. It is bounded by Zambia, Mozambique, South Africa and Botswana, and geographically in the N by the Zambezi River and in the S by the Limpopo River. Much of the land consists of plateau, generally over 3300 ft (1000 m), with extensive areas of savanna. The majority of the population is Bantu, with small minorities of Europeans, Asians, and others. Economy: agriculture is important, but the imposing of economic sanctions (1965–79) has changed its emphasis. The production of tobacco has declined and a diversification to cotton and cattle has taken place; other cash crops include sugar, tea, and citrus fruit. The chief subsistence crops are corn, millet, and groundnuts. Forestry and fishing are important with fish farming on Lake Kariba. Zimbabwe has rich mineral resources including copper, asbestos, gold, chrome, and nickel, but it has no oil reserves. Industry is expanding and includes food processing, metal processing, engineering, and textiles. The main exports are tobacco, nickel, copper, asbestos, and sugar. History: ruins at *Great Zimbabwe attest the existence of a medieval Bantu civilization in the region. In 1837 its Mashona inhabitants were conquered by the Matabele and later in the 19th century it was explored by European missionaries, notably David *Livingstone. In 1889 Cecil *Rhodes obtained a charter for the British South Africa Company, which conquered the Matabele and their territory, named Rhodesia (1895) in Rhodes' honor. In 1911 it was divided into Northern Rhodesia (now *Zambia) and Southern Rhodesia, the latter becoming a self-governing British colony in 1922. In 1953 the two parts of Rhodesia were reunited in the Federation of *Rhodesia and Nyasaland, and after its dissolution in 1963 the whites demanded independence for Southern Rhodesia (Rhodesia from 1964). The UK's refusal to permit independence without a guarantee of majority rule within a specific period led the Rhodesian prime minister Ian *Smith to issue a unilateral declaration of independence (UDI) in 1965. Both the UK and the UN imposed economic sanctions on Rhodesia but these and further talks in 1966 and 1968 proved fruitless. In 1970 Rhodesia declared itself a republic. In 1974 the Rhodesian government opened negotiations with the leaders of the Zimbabwe African People's Union (ZAPU) and the Zimbabwe African National Union (ZANU), which had pursued guerrilla activities since the 1960s. Smith failed to negotiate an agreement with the black nationalists, who remained seriously divided under the nominal umbrella of the African National Council (ANC). In 1978, following the intervention of the US secretary of state Henry Kissinger (1976) and the UK (1977), agreement was reached between Smith and the ANC on a transitional government leading to black majority rule. However, the failure of the subsequent government under Muzorewa to obtain the support of the Patriotic Front led to agreement at the 1979 Commonwealth Conference to hold an all-party conference in an attempt to achieve internal unity. Following the conference, held in London (1979–80), Britain's Lord *Soames was appointed governor to oversee the disarming of guerrillas, the holding of elections (which brought Robert *Mugabe, leader of ZANU (PF), to power), and the granting of independence to Zimbabwe as a member of the Commonwealth (1980). Mugabe formed an uneasy coalition government with Joshua Nkomo, head of the Zimbabwe African People's Union, which was shattered in 1982 when Nkomo, thought to be planning a coup, was dismissed from the cabinet. Mugabe supported an increasingly socialist plan of government and sought one-party rule. Economic problems including inflation, fuel shortages, and severe drought plagued Zimbabwe in the early 1980s. Armed violence increased as did rumors of political repression. Large numbers of whites left Zimbabwe. Despite a policy of hostility to South Africa, Zimbabwe retained a preferential trade agreement that made South Africa its principal trading partner. President: Canaan Banana. Official language: English; the most important African languages are Ndebele and Shona. Official currency, since 1970: Rhodesian dollar of 100 cents. Area: 150,820 sq mi (390,622 sq km). Population (1983 est): 8,376,000. Capital: Harare.

zinc (Zn) A bluish-white metal known in antiquity in India and the Middle East and rediscovered in Europe in 1846 by A. S. Marggraf (1709–82). It occurs in nature principally in the ores calamine ($ZnCO_3$), zincite (ZnO), and zinc blende (ZuS). It is extracted by reduction of the oxide (ZnO) with carbon. The metal is more electropositive than iron and is widely used to make *galvanized steel. Zinc forms a number of useful low-melting alloys, including *brass and type metal, and is also used to make castings. The sulfide (ZnS) is a phosphor and is used in making television screens and fluorescent tubes. Zinc oxide (ZnO) is widely used as a paint pigment and in medicines, batteries, cosmetics, plastics, and other products. Trace amounts of zinc are also important for growth in animals, including human beings. At no 30; at wt 65.37; mp 788°F (419.58°C); bp 1666°F (907°C).

zinc blende. See sphalerite.

zincite A minor ore of zinc, consisting of zinc oxide. It is often found in association with *sphalerite and probably results from the alteration of sphalerite. It usually contains some manganese.

zinc yellow A greenish yellow pigment, usually made by reaction of zinc oxide, potassium dichromate, and sulfuric acid. It is light fast, inhibits rusting, and is resistant to sulfides.

Zinjanthropus. See Australopithecus.

Zinnia A genus of herbs and shrubs (about 15 species), mostly native to North America. They have stiff hairy stems, oval to heart-shaped leaves, and daisy-like flower heads with yellow or brownish central disk florets and variously colored ray florets. Cultivated zinnias are hybrids derived from the Mexican species Z. elegans. They have double flowers, about 4.3 in (11 cm) across, and most are half-hardy annuals. Family: *Compositae.

Zinoviev, Grigori Yevseevich (1883–1936) Soviet politician. Zinoviev became a member of the politburo (1918) and chairman of the Comintern (1919) but was expelled from the Communist Party in 1927. In 1935 he was accused of complicity in the murder of *Kirov and was executed.

Zinzendorf, Nikolaus Ludwig, Graf von (1700–60) German nobleman and churchman, who re-formed the *Moravian Brethren by settling Hussite refugees from Moravia on his estate in Saxony. Exiled from Saxony (1736–47), he became a bishop of the Moravian Church in 1737, spreading its beliefs in England, America, and elsewhere.

Zion (or Sion) A stronghold (II Samuel 5.6–7) on the SE hill of Jerusalem, captured by David, who made it the center of his capital (Jerusalem). Another name for Jerusalem, it is also described throughout the Old Testament as the place in which God dwells and reigns. In the New Testament and in later Christian writings, it symbolizes heaven.

Zionism A Jewish nationalist movement. It emerged during the 19th century on a tide of European nationalism, and was formally established (against considerable Jewish opposition) at the First Zionist Congress (Basle, 1897). The Congress defined its political aim as the establishment of a Jewish national home in Palestine; the World Zionist Organization was set up, with Theodor *Herzl as its first president. Jewish immigration into Palestine (aliyah) was encouraged, especially through the Jewish National Fund (founded 1901) and the Jewish Agency for Palestine (1929). Among other breakaway groups, the Territorialists sought a land outside Palestine, and the Revisionists opposed collectivism and collaboration with the British. Since the establishment of *Israel in 1948 the Zionist movement has continued to foster aliyah and support for and interest in Israel. See also Ahad Ha'am; Balfour Declaration.

Zion National Park A national park in SW Utah. The main feature of the park is Zion Canyon, an 8 mi (13 km) long, one-half mi (0.8 km) deep gorge, carved by the Virgin River. Its sandstone walls exhibit many different shades of red and other colors. Sentinel Mountain rises to 7157 ft (2182 m). Discovered in 1858, the canyon was given its name by Mormon settlers in 1861; a national park was established in 1919 and added to in 1956. Area: 230 sq mi (595 sq km).

zircon A mineral consisting of zirconium silicate, found as an accessory mineral in intermediate and acid igneous rocks. It is usually colorless or yellowish. Gem varieties include hyacinth (red) and jargoon (colorless or smoky gray). It is the chief ore of zirconium and is used as a refractory material.

zirconium (Zr) A gray high-melting-point transition metal, isolated by J. J. Berzelius in 1824. It occurs in nature as zircon (zirconium silicate; $ZrSiO_4$), which is used as a gemstone. The dioxide (zirconia; ZrO_2) has a high melting point (2715°C) and is used as a refractory and crucible material. The metal is used in cladding fuel elements in nuclear reactors. At no 40; at wt 91.22; mp 3365°F (1852°C); bp 7910°F (4377°C).

zither A plucked stringed instrument of ancient origin, consisting of a flat resonating box fitted with 30 to 40 strings, approximately 5 of which lie across a fretted fingerboard for playing the melody. The rest are used for playing accompanying chords. It is particularly popular in Bavaria and the Tyrol.

Zi Xi (or Tz'u-hsi; 1835–1908) Chinese empress. The daughter of a middle-class Manchu family, she became an imperial concubine. She was made empress on the birth of her son *Tong Zhi, becoming his regent and, after his death, regent for her young nephew *Guang Xu. She thus wielded enormous power over state affairs, her reactionary policies being largely responsible for the fall of imperial China.

Žižka, Jan, Count (c. 1370–1424) Bohemian military leader, who was head of the *Hussite military community at Tabar. He was victorious against the Holy Roman Emperor Sigismund, using armored farm wagons and tactics that anticipated modern tank warfare.

Zlatoust 55 10N 59 38E A city in the Soviet Union, in the W RSFSR. It has been the largest metallurgical center in the Urals since the 18th century. Population (1977 est): 195,000.

ZODIAC *The signs of the zodiac from* De astrorum scientia *by Leopold of Austria (Augsburg, 1489).*

zodiac A zone of the heavens extending about 8° on either side of the *ecliptic. Within it lies the apparent annual path of the sun, as seen from the earth, and the orbits of the moon, and major planets, apart from Pluto. The 12 constellations in the zodiac are known as "signs" or "houses" to astrologers, who believe them capable of stamping their individual dispositions upon those born under their influence (see astrology). The 12 signs and their astrologically effective dates (different from their astronomical periods on account of *precession) are: Aries, the Ram Mar 21–Apr 19; Taurus, the Bull Apr 20–May 20; Gemini, the Twins May 21–June 21; Cancer, the Crab June 22–July 22; Leo, the Lion July 23–Aug 22; Virgo, the Virgin Aug 23–Sept 22; Libra, the Scales Sept 23–Oct 23; Scorpio, the Scorpion Oct 24–Nov 21; Sagittarius, the Archer Nov 22–Dec 21; Capricornus, the Goat Dec 22–Jan 19; Aquarius, the Water-carrier Jan 20–Feb 18; and Pisces, the Fish Feb 19–Mar 20.

zodiacal light A faint glow that is visible in the western sky just after sunset and the eastern sky just before sunrise, especially in the tropics. It can be seen along the direction of the *ecliptic, tapering upward from the horizon to an altitude of perhaps 20°. It is sunlight reflected from interplanetary dust particles.

Zog I (1895–1961) King of Albania (1928–39). Zog was proclaimed king after serving as prime minister (1922–24) and president (1925–28).

He let Albania fall under Italian economic domination and when Mussolini invaded Albania (1939), he fled into exile.

Zohar (Hebrew: splendor) The classical text of the *kabbalah. Written in Aramaic, it purports to be a mystical commentary on the *Torah and a collection of theosophical discussions dating from the time of the *Mishnah. It was actually written about 1280 by the Spanish kabbalist Moses de Leon, although it contains some later additions.

Zola, Émile (1840–1902) French novelist. He went to Paris in 1858 and lived in poverty, working as a journalist and as a clerk in a publishing firm until the success of his first major novel, *Thérèse Raquin* (1867). He then dedicated himself to a literary career, conceiving the plan for the series of 20 novels entitled *Les Rougon-Macquart* (1871–93), which concern a family during the Second Empire (1852–70). Despite the pseudoscientific theory of Naturalism that first motivated his fiction, his talent for detailed realism produced powerful exposés of social problems. *L'Assommoir* (1877) describes the effects of drink on the disintegration of a working-class family. *Nana* (1880), concerning a girl from the slums, *Germinal* (1885), about a mining community, and *La Terre* (1887), concerning the life of peasants, are among his outstanding novels. He fled to England after defending *Dreyfus in an open letter, *J'accuse* (1898), but was welcomed back as a hero after Dreyfus had been cleared of the charges against him.

Zollverein A customs union of 18 German states formed under Prussian dominance in 1834. By 1867 all German states except Hamburg and Bremen had joined. This commercial union helped pave the way for German unification under Prussian leadership (1871).

Zomba 15 23S 35 19E A city in Malawi, in the Shire Highlands. It was the capital of Malawi until 1975 and has the University of Malawi (1964). It is the center of a tobacco-growing and dairy-farming area. Population (1977): 15,705.

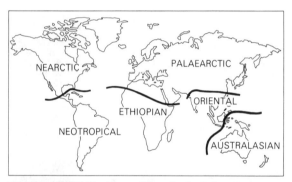

ZOOGEOGRAPHY *The world can be divided into six regions according to the distribution of its animals. Since some animals are less fixed in their habitats than others and may be found in more than one region, the divisions between the regions are somewhat arbitrary. For example, Wallace's line, separating the Oriental and Australasian regions, has been modified since Wallace proposed it.*

zoogeography The study of the geographical distribution of animals. It is based mainly on the work of A. R. *Wallace (with later modifications), who divided the world into a number of zoogeographical regions, each with a distinctive fauna. The present-day distribution of animals reflects both their evolutionary history and the movements of the land masses in past geological ages (*see* continental drift). Thus the concentration of marsupials in the Australasian region is explained by the fact that the separation of Australia from the Asian mainland coincided with the evolutionary radiation of this group. The Australian marsupials therefore avoided competing with the more efficient placental mammals, which subsequently evolved on the mainland.

zoological gardens Places in which wild animals are housed in captivity for scientific study or display. Private zoos were maintained by many rulers in the past, probably including King Solomon and Emperor Charlemagne. Zoos have contributed to knowledge of animals and in many cases have helped save endangered species through establishing breeding colonies. Among the world's outstanding zoos are those in San Diego, the Bronx (N.Y.), Chicago, Philadelphia, London, Berlin, Tokyo, Amsterdam, Sydney, and Paris.

zoology The branch of *biological sciences specializing in the scientific study of animals. This includes their classification, anatomy, physiology,

ecology, behavior, evolution, etc. The importance of animals as food producers, pests, etc., in relation to man makes many aspects of zoology economically significant. *See also* entomology; ichthyology; ornithology.

zorilla An African carnivorous mammal, *Ictonyx striatus*, also called striped weasel. It is 20–27.5 in (50–70 cm) long including the tail 8–12 in (20–30 cm) with distinct longitudinal black and white stripes. It hunts at night, preying on small reptiles and birds. When attacked, it ejects a vile-smelling fluid from anal glands. Family: *Mustelidae.*

Zorn, Anders (Leonard) (1860–1920) Swedish artist, best known as an etcher. Traveling in Europe and the US until 1896, he then returned to his native Mora in Sweden. He is noted for his impressionist landscapes and scenes of peasant girls bathing. He also produced portraits and some sculpture.

Zoroaster (*or* Zarathustra; c. 628–c. 551 BC) Iranian prophet, founder of *Zoroastrianism. Probably born near Tehran, he is believed to have been a priest in the ancient polytheistic religion when he received a vision of *Ahura Mazda, who exhorted him to preach a new faith based on his worship. Zoroaster introduced reforms, abolishing orgiastic rituals, although animal sacrifice and the ancient fire cult continued to be practiced. The teachings attributed to him are preserved in the Gathas (hymns) in the *Avesta.

Zoroastrianism The pre-Islamic dualistic religion of Persia founded by *Zoroaster, surviving there in some areas and in India among the Parsees (*see* Parseeism). It recognizes two principles, good and evil, as personified by *Ahura Mazda and *Ahriman. Life is the struggle between these forces. The dualism is not equal, for good will eventually outweigh evil and Ahura Mazda will triumph, resurrecting the dead and creating a paradise on earth, presaged by the return of Zoroaster. Man's irreversible free choice of good or evil renders him responsible for his fate after death in heaven or hell. Procreation and life are extolled, but death defiles—hence the custom of exposing corpses to be devoured by vultures.

Zorrilla y Moral, José (1817–93) Spanish poet and dramatist. In *Cantos del trovador* (1840–41), *Granada* (1852), and other volumes of poetry he evoked the history and legends of Spain. His best-known play is *Don Juan Tenorio* (1844), a version of the *Don Juan story with a happy ending.

Zoser. *See* Djoser.

Zouaves Members of a French infantry corps, originally recruited from the Algerian Zwawa tribe following the French conquest of Algeria (1830). The Algerians were replaced after 1840 with French soldiers. The Zouaves' colorful uniforms, with their baggy red trousers, inspired other armies to form similarly dressed units.

Zsigmondy, Richard Adolph (1865–1929) Austrian chemist, whose interest in colloids led him to use the Tyndall effect to devise the *ultramicroscope (1902). In 1908 he was appointed professor at Göttingen University and was awarded the Nobel Prize for Chemistry in 1925.

Zuccarelli, Francesco (1702–88) Italian painter. He worked chiefly in Venice (after 1732) and in England (1752–62, 1765–71). A founding member of Britain's Royal Academy, he specialized in picturesque landscapes.

Zuccari Two Italian painters, born at Sant' Angelo in Vado. Both leading figures in Roman *mannerism, **Taddeo Zuccari** (1529–66) is known for his frescoes, while his brother and pupil **Federico Zuccari** (c. 1540–1609) was also an art theorist. Federico painted Elizabeth I in England (1575) and decorated the dome of the Duomo, Florence, and the high altar in the *Escorial.

zucchini. *See* squash.

Zugspitze 47 25N 11 00E The highest mountain in West Germany, in the S on the Austrian border. Height: 9721 ft (2963 m).

Zuider Zee A former inlet of the SE North Sea, within the Netherlands. The N part, the *Waddenzee, is separated from the S part (now the *IJsselmeer) by a huge dam (completed 1932).

Zululand An area of South Africa, in NE Natal. The home of the *Zulu people, it became a powerful state during the 1820s under their king *Shaka. Following conflict with the Boers the Zulus, under *Cetshwayo, were defeated by the British (1879) and Zululand was incorporated into Natal in 1897. It comprises part of the *Bantu Homeland of KwaZulu.

Zulus A Bantu people of Natal (South Africa). They are traditionally cattle herders and cattle are still a prestige possession. Polygyny is practiced by important men. In the 19th century under *Shaka, the Zulus conquered an extensive empire until eventually defeated in wars with the Europeans. Their highly efficient military organization was based on the age-set system; warriors could not marry until they attained a certain grade. *Ancestor worship and witchcraft were prominent in their religious beliefs and the king had important ritual functions. Today, many Zulus are migrant laborers.

Zurbarán, Francisco de (1598–1664) Spanish painter. Working chiefly in Seville, where he was appointed the city painter, and for religious orders, he specialized in scenes from the lives of the saints, in the manner of *Caravaggio, portraits, and still-lifes. In Madrid (1634) he painted historical and mythological subjects for the Buen Retiro Palace and settled there permanently in 1658. The paintings of the last few years of his life are characterized by a sentimental piety and lack the austere realism of his greatest works.

Zürich 47 23N 8 33E The largest city in Switzerland, on Lake Zürich. It is the commercial and industrial center of Switzerland; heavy engineering and machine production are the chief industries; banking and insurance are of international importance. Zürich's Alpine setting has contributed to the rise of its tourist industry. It has a notable romanesque cathedral, a university (1833), and the Federal Institute of Technology (1854). *History*: the Romans occupied the site in the 1st century BC. During the middle ages it became the most important Swiss town and joined the Swiss confederation in 1351. A leading center of the Reformation under Ulrich Zwingli, Zürich became a refuge for those persecuted in the Counter-Reformation. Population (1976 est): 389,600.

Zweig, Arnold (1887–1968) East German Jewish novelist. After exile in Palestine, he returned to Germany in 1948. His pacifism and social criticism are reflected in such novels as *The Case of Sergeant Grischa* (1927).

Zweig, Stefan (1881–1942) Austrian Jewish writer. After studying in Austria, France, and Germany, he settled in Salzburg. Exiled in 1934, he later committed suicide with his wife in Brazil. His interest in Freud is reflected in acute historical and biographical analyses of a number of great European writers. *The Tide of Fortune* (1927) deals with European culture in crisis. He also produced poetry, novels, stories, and translations.

Zwickau 50 42N 12 25E A city in S East Germany, on the Zwickauer Mulde River. The birthplace of Robert Schumann, it has fine medieval and Renaissance buildings. Its industries include coalmining and the manufacture of automobiles, chemicals, and machinery. Population (1977 est): 122,640.

Zwingli, Ulrich (1484–1531) Swiss Protestant reformer. A Roman Catholic priest and a chaplain to Swiss mercenaries, he became people's vicar at the Grossmünster in Zürich in 1518. There he emerged as a reformer, welcoming the writings of *Luther and preaching the doctrine of salvation by faith. He opposed his bishop, supported by the civil authorities, and by 1525 had established a reformed church. He separated from Luther over the theology of the Eucharist, regarding Luther's views as a persistence of Roman doctrine. Zwingli was killed during fighting between Roman Catholic and Protestant cantons.

zwitterion An *ion that has both positive and negative charges on the same group of atoms. Zwitterions can be formed under suitable conditions from molecules that have both basic and acidic groups attached. *Amino acids, for instance, can form zwitterions by transfer of a proton from the carboxyl group to the amino group.

Zwolle 52 31N 6 06E A city in the central Netherlands, the capital of Overijssel province. Thomas à Kempis lived at a nearby monastery. A trading center, its industries include chemicals and shipbuilding. Population (1977 est): 78,585.

Zworykin, Vladimir Kosma (1889–) US physicist, born in Russia, who went to the US in 1919 and eventually became a vice president of the Radio Corporation of America. Working with cathode-ray tubes, he invented the form of television camera called the iconoscope (1938) and a year later produced the first *electron microscope.

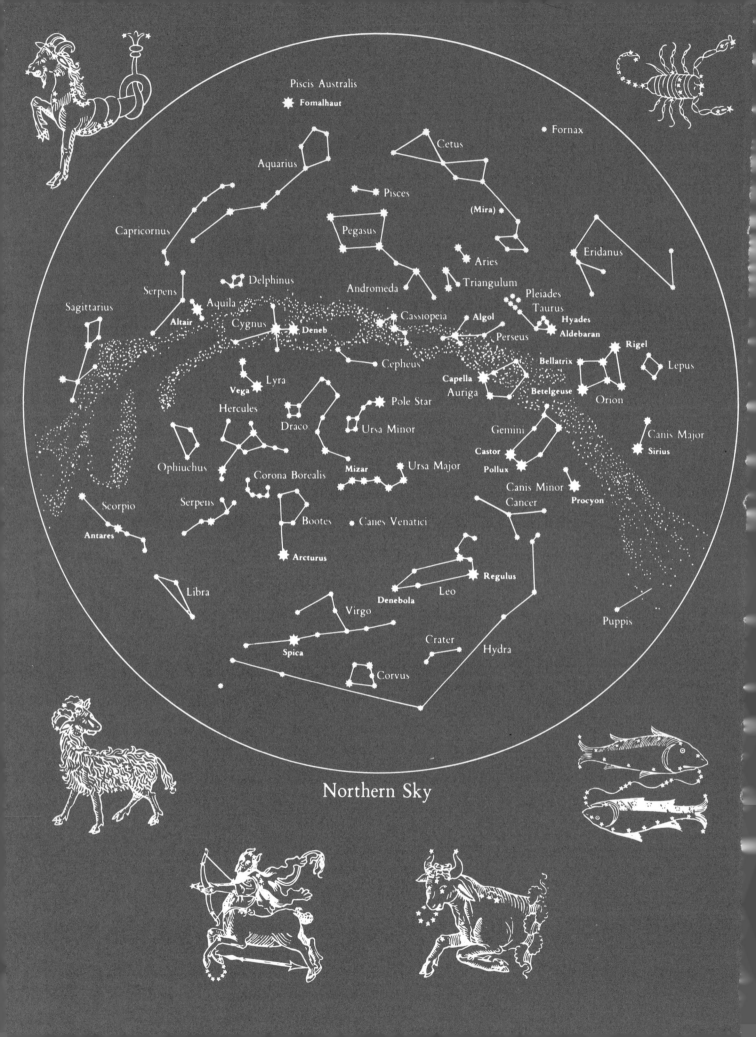

Piscis Australis
★ Fomalhaut

Fornax

Cetus

Aquarius
Pisces

(Mira)

Pegasus
Aries

Capricornus
Eridanus

Triangulum

Delphinus
Andromeda
Pleiades

Serpens
Taurus

Aquila
Cassiopeia
Hyades

Sagittarius
Algol
Aldebaran

Altair
Cygnus
Perseus
Rigel

Deneb
Bellatrix

Cepheus
Capella

Vega
Lyra
Auriga
Betelgeuse

Pole Star
Lepus

Hercules
Orion

Draco
Gemini
Canis Major

Ursa Minor

Ophiuchus
Castor
Sirius

Mizar
Ursa Major
Pollux

Scorpio
Corona Borealis
Canis Minor

Serpens
Cancer
Procyon

Antares
Canes Venatici
Bootes

Libra
Regulus

Arcturus
Leo

Denebola

Virgo

Spica
Crater
Hydra

Corvus
Puppis

Northern Sky